Whitaker's Almanack

1994

J. WHITAKER & SONS LTD

12 DYOTT STREET · LONDON WCIA IDF

J. WHITAKER AND SONS LTD
12 Dyott Street, London WCIA IDF

Whitaker's Almanack published annually since 1868
© 126th edition J. Whitaker and Sons Ltd 1993

Standard edition (1280 pages)
Cloth covers
0 85021 238 3

Leather binding
0 85021 239 1

Designed by Douglas Martin
Jacket design by Carroll Associates
Typeset by Clowes Computer Composition
Printed and bound in Great Britain by
Clays Ltd, part of St Ives PLC, Bungay, Suffolk

Contents

CONTENTS CONTINUED

Preface

TO THE 126TH ANNUAL VOLUME 1994

The last edition of Whitaker's Almanack broke with tradition, introducing the first change of size and layout in 125 years. The many letters we received from readers in response to the changes were almost universally positive, welcoming the improved legibility and clarity of the pages. It was a very gratifying response for all involved in introducing the new format, and we were grateful also for the comments and suggestions that helped us in refining aspects of the design for this edition.

Resisting the temptation to rest on our laurels after last year, a number of new items and revisions are included in the 126th edition of Whitaker. A new article about intellectual property describes the operation of copyright, patents, trade marks and design registration in the United Kingdom. The funding of the royal family, heatedly debated in the past year, is the subject of a revised and expanded article on royal finances. Also the subject of debate was the General Synod's vote in favour of ordaining women as priests; events leading to the vote and subsequent developments are summarized at the beginning of the Church of England section. Summaries of the Calcutt report on press self-regulation and the various discussion documents about the future of the BBC are included in the Media section, and the recommendations of the Royal Commission on Criminal Justice are included with White Papers, etc.

The replacement of the community charge by the council tax has occasioned a rewrite and expansion of the information about local government. The Countries of the World section has expanded with the inclusion of new entries for all the former Soviet and former Yugoslav republics, the separated Czech and Slovak republics and the newly independent Eritrea.

As ever, we wish to thank the many organizations and individuals who have provided us with information for this edition and whose assistance has been invaluable.

12 DYOTT STREET
LONDON WC1A 1DF
TEL 071-836 8911

HILARY MARSDEN
Editor

OCTOBER 1993

The Year 1994

CHRONOLOGICAL CYCLES AND ERAS

Dominical Letter	B
Epact	17
Golden Number (Lunar Cycle)	XIX
Julian Day, 1 January (from noon)	2,449,354
Julian Period	6707
Roman Indiction	2
Solar Cycle	15

	Beginning
Japanese year Heisei 6	1 January
Regnal year 43	6 February
Chinese year of the Dog	10 February
Indian (Saka) year 1916	22 March
Hindu new year	11 April
Sikh new year	13 April
Muslim year AH 1415	10 June
Jewish year AM 5755	6 September
Roman year 2747 AUC	

RELIGIOUS CALENDARS

Epiphany	6 January
Makara Sankranti	14 January
Birthday of Guru Gobind Singh Ji	19 January
Ramadan, first day	12 February
Sarasvati-puja	15 February
Ash Wednesday	16 February
Shivaratri	10 March
Holi	26 March
Passover, first day	27 March
Good Friday	1 April
Easter Day (Western churches)	3 April
Easter Day (Greek Orthodox)	3 April
Baisakhi Mela	13 April
Ramanavami	20 April
Rogation Sunday	8 May
Ascension Day	12 May
Feast of Weeks, first day	16 May
Pentecost (Whit Sunday)	22 May
Idu-l-kabir	c. 22 May
Trinity Sunday	29 May
Corpus Christi	2 June
Martyrdom of Guru Arjan Dev Ji	13 June
Raksha-bandhan	21 August
Janmashtami	29 August
Ganesh Chaturthi, first day	9 September
Yom Kippur (Day of Atonement)	15 September
Feast of Tabernacles, first day	20 September
Navaratri festival, first day	5 October
Durga-puja	11 October
Dasara	13 October
Diwali (Hindu) begins	1 November
Diwali (Sikh)	3 November
Diwali Day (Hindu), last day	4 November
Birthday of Guru Nanak Dev Ji	18 November
First Sunday in Advent	27 November
Chanucah, first day	28 November
Martyrdom of Guru Teg Bahadur Ji	7 December
Christmas Day	25 December

CIVIL CALENDAR

Accession of Queen Elizabeth II	6 February
Duke of York's birthday	19 February
St David's Day	1 March
Prince Edward's birthday	10 March
Commonwealth Day	14 March
St Patrick's Day	17 March
Birthday of Queen Elizabeth II	21 April
St George's Day	23 April
Coronation of Queen Elizabeth II	2 June
Duke of Edinburgh's birthday	10 June
The Queen's Official Birthday	11 June
Princess of Wales' birthday	1 July
Queen Elizabeth the Queen Mother's birthday	4 August
Princess Royal's birthday	15 August
Princess Margaret's birthday	21 August
Lord Mayor's Day	12 November
Remembrance Sunday	13 November
Prince of Wales' birthday	14 November
Wedding Day of Queen Elizabeth II	20 November
St Andrew's Day	30 November

LEGAL CALENDAR

LAW TERMS

Hilary Term	11 January to 30 March
Easter Term	12 April to 27 May
Trinity Term	7 June to 30 July
Michaelmas Term	1 October to 21 December

QUARTER DAYS

England, Wales and Northern Ireland

Lady	25 March
Midsummer	24 June
Michaelmas	29 September
Christmas	25 December

TERM DAYS

Scotland

Candlemas	28 February
Whitsunday	28 May
Lammas	28 August
Martinmas	28 November
Removal Terms	28 May, 28 November

1994

JANUARY

Sunday		2	9	16	23	30
Monday		3	10	17	24	31
Tuesday		4	11	18	25	
Wednesday		5	12	19	26	
Thursday		6	13	20	27	
Friday		7	14	21	28	
Saturday	1	8	15	22	29	

FEBRUARY

Sunday		6	13	20	27
Monday		7	14	21	28
Tuesday	1	8	15	22	
Wednesday	2	9	16	23	
Thursday	3	10	17	24	
Friday	4	11	18	25	
Saturday	5	12	19	26	

MARCH

Sunday		6	13	20	27
Monday		7	14	21	28
Tuesday	1	8	15	22	29
Wednesday	2	9	16	23	30
Thursday	3	10	17	24	31
Friday	4	11	18	25	
Saturday	5	12	19	26	

APRIL

Sunday		3	10	17	24
Monday		4	11	18	25
Tuesday		5	12	19	26
Wednesday		6	13	20	27
Thursday		7	14	21	28
Friday	1	8	15	22	29
Saturday	2	9	16	23	30

MAY

Sunday	1	8	15	22	29
Monday	2	9	16	23	30
Tuesday	3	10	17	24	31
Wednesday	4	11	18	25	
Thursday	5	12	19	26	
Friday	6	13	20	27	
Saturday	7	14	21	28	

JUNE

Sunday		5	12	19	26
Monday		6	13	20	27
Tuesday		7	14	21	28
Wednesday	1	8	15	22	29
Thursday	2	9	16	23	30
Friday	3	10	17	24	
Saturday	4	11	18	25	

JULY

Sunday		3	10	17	24	31
Monday		4	11	18	25	
Tuesday		5	12	19	26	
Wednesday		6	13	20	27	
Thursday		7	14	21	28	
Friday	1	8	15	22	29	
Saturday	2	9	16	23	30	

AUGUST

Sunday		7	14	21	28
Monday	1	8	15	22	29
Tuesday	2	9	16	23	30
Wednesday	3	10	17	24	31
Thursday	4	11	18	25	
Friday	5	12	19	26	
Saturday	6	13	20	27	

SEPTEMBER

Sunday		4	11	18	25
Monday		5	12	19	26
Tuesday		6	13	20	27
Wednesday		7	14	21	28
Thursday	1	8	15	22	29
Friday	2	9	16	23	30
Saturday	3	10	17	24	

OCTOBER

Sunday		2	9	16	23	30
Monday		3	10	17	24	31
Tuesday		4	11	18	25	
Wednesday		5	12	19	26	
Thursday		6	13	20	27	
Friday		7	14	21	28	
Saturday	1	8	15	22	29	

NOVEMBER

Sunday		6	13	20	27
Monday		7	14	21	28
Tuesday	1	8	15	22	29
Wednesday	2	9	16	23	30
Thursday	3	10	17	24	
Friday	4	11	18	25	
Saturday	5	12	19	26	

DECEMBER

Sunday		4	11	18	25
Monday		5	12	19	26
Tuesday		6	13	20	27
Wednesday		7	14	21	28
Thursday	1	8	15	22	29
Friday	2	9	16	23	30
Saturday	3	10	17	24	31

PUBLIC HOLIDAYS

	England and Wales	Scotland	Northern Ireland
New Year	3 January	3, 4 January	3 January
St Patrick's Day	—	—	17 March
*Good Friday	1 April	1 April	1 April
Easter Monday	4 April	—	4 April
May Day	2 May	30 May	2 May
Spring	30 May	2 May	30 May
Battle of Boyne	—	—	12 July
Summer	29 August	1 August	29 August
*Christmas	26, 27 December	26, 27 December	26, 27 December

* In England, Wales, and Northern Ireland, Christmas Day and Good Friday are common law holidays.
  In the Channel Islands, Liberation Day (9 May) is a bank and public holiday.

1995

JANUARY

Sunday	1	8	15	22	29
Monday	2	9	16	23	30
Tuesday	3	10	17	24	31
Wednesday	4	11	18	25
Thursday	5	12	19	26
Friday	6	13	20	27
Saturday	7	14	21	28

FEBRUARY

Sunday		5	12	19	26
Monday		6	13	20	27
Tuesday		7	14	21	28
Wednesday	1	8	15	22
Thursday	2	9	16	23
Friday	3	10	17	24
Saturday	4	11	18	25

MARCH

Sunday		5	12	19	26
Monday		6	13	20	27
Tuesday		7	14	21	28
Wednesday	1	8	15	22	29
Thursday	2	9	16	23	30
Friday	3	10	17	24	31
Saturday	4	11	18	25

APRIL

Sunday	2	9	16	23	30
Monday	3	10	17	24
Tuesday	4	11	18	25
Wednesday	5	12	19	26
Thursday	6	13	20	27
Friday	7	14	21	28
Saturday	1	8	15	22	29

MAY

Sunday		7	14	21	28
Monday	1	8	15	22	29
Tuesday	2	9	16	23	30
Wednesday	3	10	17	24	31
Thursday	4	11	18	25
Friday	5	12	19	26
Saturday	6	13	20	27

JUNE

Sunday		4	11	18	25
Monday		5	12	19	26
Tuesday		6	13	20	27
Wednesday		7	14	21	28
Thursday	1	8	15	22	29
Friday	2	9	16	23	30
Saturday	3	10	17	24

JULY

Sunday	2	9	16	23	30
Monday	3	10	17	24	31
Tuesday	4	11	18	25
Wednesday	5	12	19	26
Thursday	6	13	20	27
Friday	7	14	21	28
Saturday	1	8	15	22	29

AUGUST

Sunday		6	13	20	27
Monday		7	14	21	28
Tuesday	1	8	15	22	29
Wednesday	2	9	16	23	30
Thursday	3	10	17	24	31
Friday	4	11	18	25
Saturday	5	12	19	26

SEPTEMBER

Sunday		3	10	17	24
Monday		4	11	18	25
Tuesday		5	12	19	26
Wednesday		6	13	20	27
Thursday		7	14	21	28
Friday	1	8	15	22	29
Saturday	2	9	16	23	30

OCTOBER

Sunday	1	8	15	22	29
Monday	2	9	16	23	30
Tuesday	3	10	17	24	31
Wednesday	4	11	18	25
Thursday	5	12	19	26
Friday	6	13	20	27
Saturday	7	14	21	28

NOVEMBER

Sunday		5	12	19	26
Monday		6	13	20	27
Tuesday		7	14	21	28
Wednesday	1	8	15	22	29
Thursday	2	9	16	23	30
Friday	3	10	17	24
Saturday	4	11	18	25

DECEMBER

Sunday		3	10	17	24	31
Monday		4	11	18	25
Tuesday		5	12	19	26
Wednesday		6	13	20	27
Thursday		7	14	21	28
Friday	1	8	15	22	29
Saturday	2	9	16	23	30

PUBLIC HOLIDAYS

	England and Wales	*Scotland*	*Northern Ireland*
New Year	2 January	2, 3 January	2 January
St Patrick's Day	—	—	17 March
*Good Friday	14 April	14 April	14 April
Easter Monday	17 April	—	17 April
May Day	†	29 May	†
Spring	29 May	1 May	29 May
Battle of Boyne	—	—	12 July
Summer	28 August	7 August	28 August
*Christmas	25, 26 December	25, 26 December	25, 26 December

† In 1993 it was proposed that the May Day bank holiday in England, Wales and Northern Ireland should be abolished and replaced by an autumn bank holiday from 1995. No further details were available at the time of going to press.

FORTHCOMING EVENTS 1994

This is the UN International Year for the Family, the EC Year of Food and Nutrition, and the Arts Council Year for Drama, based in the city of Manchester.
The European City of Culture 1994 is Copenhagen.
* Provisional dates

6–16 January	London International Boat Show Earls Court, London
10–13 March	Cruft's Dog Show National Exhibition Centre, Birmingham
17 March–10 April	Ideal Home Exhibition Earls Court, London
20–22 March	London International Book Fair Olympia, London
7–13 April	International Antiques Fair National Exhibition Centre, Birmingham
29 April–21 May	Mayfest 1994 Glasgow
29 April–8 October	Pitlochry Festival Theatre season Pitlochry, Tayside
May–September	Chichester Festival Theatre season, West Sussex
11–15 May	Royal Windsor Horse Show Home Park, Windsor
26–27 May	Chelsea Flower Show Royal Hospital, Chelsea
27 May–12 June	Bath International Festival Bath
28 May–25 August	Glyndebourne Festival Opera season Glyndebourne, Lewes, East Sussex
June–August	Royal Academy Summer Exhibition Piccadilly, London
10–26 June	Aldeburgh Festival of Music and Arts, Suffolk
11 June	Trooping the Colour Horse Guards Parade, London
*13–31 July	Buxton Festival Derbyshire
4–7 July	The Royal Show Stoneleigh Park, Kenilworth, Warks
*15–23 July	Welsh Proms 1994 St David's Hall, Cardiff
15 July– 10 September	Promenade Concerts season Royal Albert Hall, London
19–30 July	Royal Tournament Earls Court, London
30 July–6 August	Royal National Eisteddfod of Wales Neath, West Glamorgan
*5–27 August	Edinburgh Military Tattoo Edinburgh Castle
12 August	Battle of Flowers Jersey
14 August– 3 September	Edinburgh International Festival
21–26 August	Three Choirs Festival Hereford
2 September– *6 November	Blackpool Illuminations
3 September	Braemar Royal Highland Gathering Braemar, Aberdeenshire
*16–24 September	Southampton International Boat Show Western Esplanade, Southampton
22–30 October	British International Motor Show National Exhibition Centre, Birmingham
6 November	London to Brighton Veteran Car Run
*7–22 November	London International Film Festival
12 November	Lord Mayor's Procession and Show City of London
17–27 November	Huddersfield Contemporary Music Festival
27–31 November	Royal Smithfield Show and Agricultural Machinery Exhibition, Earls Court, London

SPORTS EVENTS

15 January	Rugby Union: France v. Ireland Parc des Princes, Paris Wales v. Scotland Cardiff Arms Park
5 February	Rugby Union: Ireland v. Wales Lansdowne Road, Dublin Scotland v. England Murrayfield, Edinburgh
19 February	Rugby Union: Wales v. France Cardiff Arms Park England v. Ireland Twickenham, London
5 March	Rugby Union: Ireland v. Scotland Lansdowne Road, Dublin France v. England Parc des Princes, Paris
19 March	Rugby Union: Scotland v. France Murrayfield, Edinburgh England v. Wales Twickenham, London
26 March	University Boat Race Putney to Mortlake, London
16 April–2 May	Snooker: World Professional Championships Crucible Theatre, Sheffield
17 April	Athletics: London Marathon
30 April	Rugby League: Challenge Cup final Wembley Stadium, London
5–8 May	Badminton Horse Trials Badminton, Avon
7 May	Rugby Union: Pilkington Cup final Twickenham, London
14 May	Football: FA Cup final Wembley Stadium, London
15 May	Welsh FA Cup final Cardiff Arms Park
*19 May	Cricket: One-day International England v. New Zealand Edgbaston, Birmingham
*21 May	Cricket: One-day International England v. New Zealand Lord's, London
21 May	Football: Scottish FA Cup final Hampden Park, Glasgow
29 May–11 June	Cycling: Open Tour of Britain (formerly Milk Race)
30 May–4 June	Golf: British Amateur Championship Nairn

30 May–10 June	International TT Motorcycle Races
	Isle of Man
*2–6 June	Cricket: 1st Test Match
	England v. New Zealand
	Trent Bridge, Nottingham
*16–20 June	Cricket: 2nd Test Match
	England v. New Zealand
	Lord's, London
20 June–3 July	Lawn Tennis Championships
	Wimbledon, London
29 June–3 July	Henley Royal Regatta
	Henley-on-Thames
*30 June–5 July	Cricket: 3rd Test Match
	England v. New Zealand
	Old Trafford, Manchester
*9 July	Cricket: Benson & Hedges Cup final
	Lord's, London
*9–23 July	Shooting: NRA Imperial Meetings
	Bisley Camp, Woking, Surrey
*10 July	British Formula 1 Grand Prix
	Silverstone, Northants
14–17 July	Golf: Open Championship
	Turnberry, Ayrshire
*21–25 July	Cricket: 1st Test Match
	England v. South Africa
	Lord's, London
30 July–6 August	Yachting: Cowes Week
	Isle of Wight
*4–8 August	Cricket: 2nd Test Match
	England v. South Africa
	Headingley, Leeds
*18–22 August	Cricket: 3rd Test Match
	England v. South Africa
	The Oval, London
*25 August	Cricket: One-day International
	England v. South Africa
	Edgbaston, Birmingham
*27 August	Cricket: One-day International
	England v. South Africa
	Old Trafford, Manchester
1–4 September	Eventing: Burghley Horse Trials
	Burghley, Lincs
*3 September	Cricket: NatWest Trophy final
	Lord's, London
*4–10 October	Horse of the Year Show
	Wembley Arena, London

HORSE-RACING

17 March	Cheltenham Gold Cup
	Cheltenham
26 March	Lincoln Handicap
	Doncaster
9 April	Grand National
	Aintree
28 April	One Thousand Guineas
	Newmarket
30 April	Two Thousand Guineas
	Newmarket
1 June	The Derby
	Epsom
2 June	Coronation Cup
	Epsom
4 June	The Oaks
	Epsom
14–17 June	Royal Ascot
23 July	King George VI and Queen
	Elizabeth Diamond Stakes
	Ascot

10 September	St Leger
	Doncaster
1 October	Cambridgeshire Handicap
	Newmarket
15 October	Cesarewitch
	Newmarket

The horse-racing fixtures are the copyright of The Jockey Club.

CENTENARIES OF 1994

1494

20 April	Johannes Agricola, German Protestant reformer, born
4 May	Christopher Columbus landed in Jamaica

1594

2 February	Giovanni Palestrina, Italian composer, born
31 May	Jacopo Tintoretto, Venetian artist, died
22 November	Sir Martin Frobisher, navigator and explorer, died
5 December	Gerardus Mercator, Flemish mathematician and geographer, died

1694

27 July	Bank of England established by charter
21 November	François-Marie Voltaire, French philosopher, born
22 November	John Tillotson, Archbishop of Canterbury, died
28 December	Queen Mary II died

1794

16 January	Edward Gibbon, writer and historian, died
5 April	Georges Jacques Danton, French Revolutionary leader, executed
8 May	Antoine Lavoisier, French chemist, executed
1 June	Battle of the Glorious First of June
28 July	Maximilien Robespierre, French Revolutionary leader, executed

1894

1 January	Manchester Ship Canal opened to traffic
10 February	Harold Macmillan, 1st Earl of Stockton, Prime Minister 1957–63, born
21 February	Andres Segovia, Spanish classical guitarist, born
10 April	Ben Nicholson, artist, born
17 April NS	Nikita Krushchev, Soviet leader, born
23 June	King Edward VIII, later Duke of Windsor, born
30 June	Tower Bridge, London, opened
26 July	Aldous Huxley, author, born
1 August	Start of Sino-Japanese War
13 September	J. B. Priestley, author, born
14 October	e. e. cummings, American poet, born
20 November	Anton Rubinstein, Russian pianist and composer, died
24 November	Herbert Sutcliffe, cricketer, born
3 December	Robert Louis Stevenson, poet and author, died
7 December	Ferdinand de Lesseps, French diplomatist and maker of the Suez Canal, died
8 December	James Thurber, American humorist, born
20 December	Sir Robert Menzies, Australian Prime Minister 1939–41 and 1949–66, born
29 December	Christina Rossetti, poet and hymn writer, died
30 December	Amelia Bloomer, women's rights campaigner, died

CENTENARIES OF 1995

1695

21 November	Henry Purcell, composer, died

1795

3 January	Josiah Wedgwood, potter, died
19 May	James Boswell, biographer of Dr Johnson, died
13 June	Thomas Arnold, headmaster of Rugby, born
31 October	John Keats, poet, born
4 December	Thomas Carlyle, essayist and historian, born

1895

1 January	J. Edgar Hoover, American head of the FBI for nearly fifty years, born
24 January	Lord Randolph Churchill, politician, died
1 February	John Ford, American film director, born
10 March	Charles Frederick Worth, costumier, died
25 April	Sir Stanley Rous, founder member of the Football Association, born
29 April	Sir Malcolm Sargent, conductor, born
6 May	Rudolf Valentino, film actor, born
15 May	Joseph Whitaker, publisher, founder and first editor of *Whitaker's Almanack*, died
24 June	Jack Dempsey, American boxer, born
10 July	Carl Orff, German composer, born
12 July	Oscar Hammerstein, American librettist, born
	Kirsten Flagstad, Norwegian opera singer, born
26 July	Robert Graves, poet and novelist, born
5 August	Friedrich Engels, German socialist, died
29 August	Founding of Northern Rugby Football Union (known since 1922 as the Rugby Football League) at the George Hotel, Huddersfield
28 September	Louis Pasteur, French chemist, died
4 October	Buster Keaton, American film comedian, born
8 October	Juan Peron, Argentine soldier and politician, born
15 October	First British Motor Show, at Tunbridge Wells
25 October	Sir Charles Halle, pianist and conductor, died
16 November	Paul Hindemith, German composer, born
27 November	Alexandre Dumas (younger), French novelist, playwright and essayist, died
14 December	King George VI born
	Paul Éluard, French poet, born
29 December	Jameson Raid in Transvaal, South Africa
30 December	L. P. Hartley, novelist, born

Astronomy

The following pages give astronomical data for each month of the year 1994. There are four pages of data for each month. All data are given for 0h Greenwich Mean Time (GMT), i.e. at the midnight at the beginning of the day named. This applies also to data for the months when British Summer Time is in operation (for dates, *see* below).

The astronomical data are given in a form suitable for observation with the naked eye or with a small telescope. These data do not attempt to replace the *Astronomical Almanac* for professional astronomers.

A fuller explanation of how to use the astronomical data is given on pages 71–3.

CALENDAR FOR EACH MONTH

The calendar for each month shows dates of religious, civil and legal significance for the year 1994.

The days in bold type are the principal holy days and the festivals and greater holy days of the Church of England as set out in the calendar of the *Alternative Service Book 1980*. Observance of certain festivals and greater holy days is transferred if the day falls on a principal holy day. The calendar shows the date on which holy days and festivals are to be observed in 1994.

The days in small capitals are dates of significance in the calendars of non-Anglican denominations and non-Christian religions.

The days in italic type are dates of civil and legal significance. The royal anniversaries shown in italic type are the days on which the Union flag is to be flown.

The rest of the calendar comprises days of general interest and the dates of birth or death of well-known people.

Fuller explanations of the various calendars can be found under Time Measurement and Calendars (pages 81–9).

The Zodiacal signs through which the Sun is passing during each month are illustrated. The date of transition from one sign to the next, to the nearest hour, is also given.

The longest day of the year, measured from sunrise to sunset, is at the summer solstice. For the remainder of this century the longest day in the United Kingdom will fall each year on 21 June. *See also* page 81.

The shortest day of the year is at the winter solstice. For the remainder of this century the shortest day in the United Kingdom will fall on 21 December in 1996, 1997, 2000, and on 22 December in 1994, 1995, 1998, 1999. *See also* page 81.

The equinox is the point at which day and night are of equal length all over the world. *See also* page 81.

In popular parlance, the seasons in the northern hemisphere comprise the following months:

Spring	March April May
Summer	June July August
Autumn	September October November
Winter	December January February

BRITISH SUMMER TIME

British Summer Time is the legal time for general purposes during the period in which it is in operation. During this period, clocks are kept one hour ahead of Greenwich Mean Time. The hour of changeover is 01h Greenwich Mean Time. The duration of Summer Time in 1994 is:

March 27 01h GMT to October 23 01h GMT

SEASONS

The seasons are defined astronomically as follows:

Spring	from the vernal equinox to the summer solstice
Summer	from the summer solstice to the autumnal equinox
Autumn	from the autumnal equinox to the winter solstice
Winter	from the winter solstice to the vernal equinox

The seasons in 1994 are:

Northern hemisphere

Vernal equinox	March 20d 20h GMT
Summer solstice	June 21d 15h GMT
Autumnal equinox	September 23d 06h GMT
Winter solstice	December 22d 02h GMT

Southern hemisphere

Autumnal equinox	March 20d 20h GMT
Winter solstice	June 21d 15h GMT
Vernal equinox	September 23d 06h GMT
Summer solstice	December 22d 02h GMT

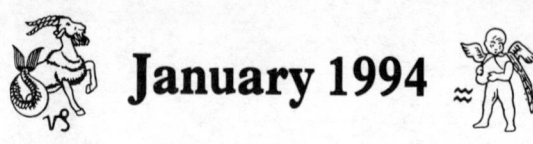

January 1994

FIRST MONTH, 31 DAYS. *Janus*, god of the portal, facing two ways, past and future

Sun's Longitude 300° ≈ 20ᵈ07ʰ

1	Saturday	**The Naming of Jesus.** E. M. Forster *b.* 1879	*week 52 day 1*
2	Sunday	**2nd S. after Christmas.** Isaac Asimov *b.* 1920	*week 1 day 2*
3	Monday	*Bank Holiday in the UK.* Lord Haw Haw *exec.* 1946	3
4	Tuesday	*Bank Holiday in Scotland.* Jacob Grimm *b.* 1785	4
5	Wednesday	Edward the Confessor *d.* 1066	5
6	Thursday	**The Epiphany.** Gustave Doré *b.* 1833	6
7	Friday	Francis Poulenc *b.* 1899. Trevor Howard *d.* 1988	7
8	Saturday	Giotto (Ambrogio di Bondone) *d.* 1337	8
9	Sunday	**1st S. after Epiphany.** Sir Robert Mayer *d.* 1985	*week 2 day 9*
10	Monday	Penny post introduced 1840. Sinclair Lewis *d.* 1951	10
11	Tuesday	*Hilary Law Sittings begin.* William James *b.* 1842	11
12	Wednesday	Herman Goering *b.* 1893. Dame Agatha Christie *d.* 1976	12
13	Thursday	Stephen Foster *d.* 1864	13
14	Friday	Albert Schweitzer *b.* 1875. Lewis Carroll *d.* 1898	14
15	Saturday	Martin Luther King *b.* 1929	15
16	Sunday	**2nd S. after Epiphany.** Start of Prohibition (USA) 1920	*week 3 day 16*
17	Monday	Rutherford B. Hayes *d.* 1893. Clyde Walcott *b.* 1926	17
18	Tuesday	William of Prussia proclaimed first German Emperor 1871	18
19	Wednesday	Sir Henry Bessemer *b.* 1813	19
20	Thursday	Sir Roy Welensky *b.* 1907. Edmund Blunden *d.* 1974	20
21	Friday	Lenin *d.* 1924. Jack Nicklaus *b.* 1940	21
22	Saturday	Francis Bacon *b.* 1561. Queen Victoria *d.* 1901	22
23	Sunday	**3rd S. after Epiphany.** Vietnam War Treaty 1973	*week 4 day 23*
24	Monday	William Congreve *b.* 1670. Edward Jenner *d.* 1823	24
25	Tuesday	**Conversion of St Paul.** Robert Burns *b.* 1759	25
26	Wednesday	Proclamation of Republic of India 1950	26
27	Thursday	Mozart *b.* 1756. Verdi *d.* 1901	27
28	Friday	Henry VII *b.* 1457. Henry VIII *d.* 1547	28
29	Saturday	Frederick Delius *b.* 1862. H. E. Bates *d.* 1974	29
30	Sunday	**9th S. before Easter.** Stanley Holloway *d.* 1982	*week 5 day 30*
31	Monday	Guy Fawkes *exec.* 1606. Anna Pavlova *b.* 1885	31

ASTRONOMICAL PHENOMENA

d	h	
1	12	Mars in conjunction with Mercury. Mars 0°.8 N.
2	06	Earth at perihelion (147 million km)
3	20	Mercury in superior conjunction
6	05	Mars in conjunction with Venus. Mars 0°.3 S.
6	21	Jupiter in conjunction with Moon. Jupiter 3° N.
11	08	Neptune in conjunction with Sun
11	16	Mars in conjunction with Moon. Mars 5° S.
11	21	Venus in conjunction with Moon. Venus 5° S.
12	10	Mercury in conjunction with Moon. Mercury 6° S.
12	17	Uranus in conjunction with Sun
14	19	Saturn in conjunction with Moon. Saturn 6° S.
17	02	Venus in superior conjunction

CONSTELLATIONS

The following constellations are near the meridian at

	d	h		d	h
December	1	24	January	16	21
December	16	23	February	1	20
January	1	22	February	15	19

Draco (below the Pole), Ursa Minor (below the Pole), Camelopardus, Perseus, Auriga, Taurus, Orion, Eridanus and Lepus

MINIMA OF ALGOL

d	h	d	h	d	h
2	04.6	13	15.9	25	03.2
5	01.4	16	12.7	28	00.0
7	22.2	19	09.5	30	20.8
10	19.1	22	06.3		

THE MOON

Phases, Apsides and Node	d	h	m
☾ Last Quarter	5	00	01
● New Moon	11	23	10
☽ First Quarter	19	20	27
○ Full Moon	27	13	23
Perigee (370,142 km)	6	01	16
Apogee (404,362 km)	19	05	15
Perigee (367,408 km)	31	03	43

Mean longitude of ascending node on January 1, 241°

THE SUN

s.d. 16′.3

Day	Right Ascension	Dec. —	Equation of time	Rise 52°	Rise 56°	Transit	Set 52°	Set 56°	Sidereal time	Transit of First Point of Aries
	h m s	° ′	m s	h m	h m	h m	h m	h m	h m s	h m s
1	18 44 59	23 02	− 3 18	8 08	8 31	12 04	15 59	15 36	6 41 40	17 15 30
2	18 49 23	22 57	− 3 46	8 08	8 31	12 04	16 00	15 37	6 45 37	17 11 34
3	18 53 48	22 52	− 4 14	8 08	8 31	12 04	16 01	15 38	6 49 34	17 07 38
4	18 58 12	22 46	− 4 42	8 08	8 30	12 05	16 02	15 40	6 53 30	17 03 42
5	19 02 36	22 40	− 5 09	8 07	8 30	12 05	16 04	15 41	6 57 27	16 59 46
6	19 06 59	22 33	− 5 36	8 07	8 29	12 06	16 05	15 43	7 01 23	16 55 50
7	19 11 22	22 26	− 6 02	8 07	8 29	12 06	16 06	15 44	7 05 20	16 51 54
8	19 15 44	22 18	− 6 28	8 06	8 28	12 07	16 08	15 46	7 09 16	16 47 58
9	19 20 06	22 10	− 6 53	8 06	8 27	12 07	16 09	15 47	7 13 13	16 44 02
10	19 24 28	22 01	− 7 18	8 05	8 26	12 08	16 10	15 49	7 17 09	16 40 06
11	19 28 49	21 52	− 7 43	8 04	8 26	12 08	16 12	15 51	7 21 06	16 36 10
12	19 33 09	21 43	− 8 06	8 04	8 25	12 08	16 13	15 52	7 25 03	16 32 14
13	19 37 29	21 33	− 8 30	8 03	8 24	12 09	16 15	15 54	7 28 59	16 28 19
14	19 41 48	21 23	− 8 52	8 02	8 23	12 09	16 16	15 56	7 32 56	16 24 23
15	19 46 06	21 12	− 9 14	8 01	8 22	12 09	16 18	15 58	7 36 52	16 20 27
16	19 50 24	21 01	− 9 35	8 01	8 20	12 10	16 19	16 00	7 40 49	16 16 31
17	19 54 41	20 50	− 9 56	8 00	8 19	12 10	16 21	16 02	7 44 45	16 12 35
18	19 58 57	20 38	−10 15	7 59	8 18	12 10	16 23	16 03	7 48 42	16 08 39
19	20 03 13	20 25	−10 35	7 58	8 17	12 11	16 24	16 05	7 52 38	16 04 43
20	20 07 28	20 13	−10 53	7 56	8 15	12 11	16 26	16 07	7 56 35	16 00 47
21	20 11 42	20 00	−11 10	7 55	8 14	12 11	16 28	16 09	8 00 32	15 56 51
22	20 15 55	19 46	−11 27	7 54	8 12	12 12	16 29	16 11	8 04 28	15 52 55
23	20 20 08	19 33	−11 43	7 53	8 11	12 12	16 31	16 13	8 08 25	15 48 59
24	20 24 20	19 19	−11 58	7 52	8 09	12 12	16 33	16 16	8 12 21	15 45 04
25	20 28 31	19 04	−12 13	7 50	8 08	12 12	16 35	16 18	8 16 18	15 41 08
26	20 32 41	18 49	−12 26	7 49	8 06	12 13	16 37	16 20	8 20 14	15 37 12
27	20 36 50	18 34	−12 39	7 48	8 04	12 13	16 38	16 22	8 24 11	15 33 16
28	20 40 59	18 19	−12 51	7 46	8 03	12 13	16 40	16 24	8 28 07	15 29 20
29	20 45 06	18 03	−13 02	7 45	8 01	12 13	16 42	16 26	8 32 04	15 25 24
30	20 49 13	17 47	−13 13	7 43	7 59	12 13	16 44	16 28	8 36 01	15 21 28
31	20 53 19	17 30	−13 22	7 42	7 57	12 13	16 46	16 30	8 39 57	15 17 32

DURATION OF TWILIGHT (in minutes)

Latitude	52°	56°	52°	56°	52°	56°	52°	56°
	1 January		11 January		21 January		31 January	
Civil	41	47	40	45	38	43	37	41
Nautical	84	96	82	93	80	90	78	87
Astronomical	125	141	123	138	120	134	117	130

THE NIGHT SKY

Mercury passes through superior conjunction on the 3rd and remains too close to the Sun for observation for most of January. However, for the last three or four days of the month it should be possible to detect Mercury low above the SW horizon at the end of evening civil twilight: its magnitude is −0.9.

Venus is at superior conjunction on the 17th and is unsuitably placed for observation throughout the month.

Mars passed through conjunction towards the end of last month and remains too close to the Sun for observation throughout January.

Jupiter, magnitude −1.9, is a bright object, visible for several hours in the SE sky before sunrise. Jupiter is in Libra.

The Moon, just after Last Quarter, will be seen in the vicinity of the planet on the mornings of the 6th and 7th.

Saturn is an evening object in the SW sky, magnitude +0.9. It is only seen at a low altitude and by the end of January it is a difficult object to detect, being very low on the horizon by the time that the twilight has faded sufficiently for it to be seen. Saturn is in the constellation of Aquarius. The thin crescent Moon passes 6° north of Saturn on the evening of the 14th.

THE MOON

Day	RA h m	Dec. °	Hor. par. ′	Semi-diam. ′	Sun's co-long. °	PA of Bright Limb °	Phase %	Age d	Rise 52° h m	Rise 56° h m	Transit h m	Set 52° h m	Set 56° h m
1	9 17	+10.6	58.3	15.9	132	114	89	18.6	20 44	20 39	2 40	9 39	9 46
2	10 09	+ 5.9	58.6	16.0	144	115	82	19.6	22 03	22 02	3 31	10 02	10 05
3	11 01	+ 0.8	58.9	16.0	156	115	72	20.6	23 21	23 25	4 21	10 25	10 23
4	11 54	− 4.3	59.1	16.1	168	115	61	21.6	—	—	5 11	10 47	10 42
5	12 47	− 9.2	59.2	16.1	180	113	50	22.6	0 41	0 49	6 02	11 13	11 03
6	13 42	−13.6	59.2	16.1	193	110	39	23.6	2 00	2 13	6 56	11 42	11 27
7	14 39	−17.3	59.2	16.1	205	107	28	24.6	3 18	3 36	7 51	12 17	11 58
8	15 37	−19.9	59.1	16.1	217	103	18	25.6	4 33	4 54	8 48	13 01	12 39
9	16 37	−21.3	58.8	16.0	229	99	11	26.6	5 39	6 02	9 47	13 54	13 31
10	17 37	−21.4	58.5	15.9	241	97	5	27.6	6 35	6 57	10 45	14 57	14 35
11	18 36	−20.1	58.0	15.8	253	100	1	28.6	7 20	7 40	11 41	16 07	15 48
12	19 32	−17.8	57.5	15.7	266	177	0	0.0	7 56	8 12	12 34	17 19	17 05
13	20 26	−14.5	56.9	15.5	278	237	1	1.0	8 24	8 36	13 23	18 32	18 21
14	21 17	−10.6	56.2	15.3	290	242	5	2.0	8 48	8 56	14 10	19 43	19 37
15	22 05	− 6.3	55.6	15.2	302	243	10	3.0	9 09	9 13	14 55	20 52	20 49
16	22 51	− 1.9	55.1	15.0	314	243	17	4.0	9 28	9 28	15 38	21 59	22 01
17	23 37	+ 2.5	54.6	14.9	327	244	24	5.0	9 47	9 44	16 20	23 05	23 11
18	0 21	+ 6.8	54.4	14.8	339	245	33	6.0	10 06	9 59	17 02	—	—
19	1 07	+10.8	54.2	14.8	351	247	42	7.0	10 28	10 17	17 45	0 10	0 20
20	1 53	+14.3	54.3	14.8	3	250	52	8.0	10 52	10 38	18 30	1 15	1 29
21	2 41	+17.3	54.5	14.9	15	253	61	9.0	11 21	11 04	19 17	2 19	2 36
22	3 31	+19.6	54.9	15.0	27	256	70	10.0	11 57	11 36	20 06	3 22	3 42
23	4 23	+21.0	55.4	15.1	39	260	78	11.0	12 41	12 19	20 58	4 21	4 43
24	5 17	+21.4	56.1	15.3	52	264	86	12.0	13 35	13 13	21 51	5 15	5 37
25	6 12	+20.7	56.8	15.5	64	267	92	13.0	14 39	14 19	22 45	6 01	6 22
26	7 08	+18.9	57.6	15.7	76	267	97	14.0	15 50	15 33	23 38	6 41	6 58
27	8 03	+16.0	58.2	15.9	88	251	99	15.0	17 06	16 54	—	7 14	7 27
28	8 59	+12.1	58.8	16.0	100	146	100	16.0	18 26	18 18	0 32	7 42	7 51
29	9 53	+ 7.5	59.3	16.2	112	124	97	17.0	19 46	19 43	1 24	8 07	8 12
30	10 47	+ 2.4	59.6	16.2	124	120	92	18.0	21 07	21 09	2 16	8 30	8 31
31	11 41	− 2.8	59.7	16.3	137	118	85	19.0	22 28	22 35	3 07	8 54	8 50

MERCURY

Day	RA h m	Dec. °	Diam. "	Phase %	Transit h m	5° high 52° h m	5° high 56° h m
1	18 38	−24.8	5	100	11 58	9 11	9 53
3	18 52	−24.7	5	100	12 04	14 53	14 12
5	19 06	−24.5	5	100	12 11	15 02	14 21
7	19 21	−24.1	5	100	12 17	15 12	14 32
9	19 35	−23.7	5	100	12 23	15 22	14 45
11	19 49	−23.2	5	99	12 30	15 33	14 58
13	20 03	−22.6	5	98	12 36	15 45	15 12
15	20 18	−21.8	5	98	12 42	15 58	15 27
17	20 32	−21.0	5	96	12 49	16 11	15 42
19	20 46	−20.1	5	95	12 55	16 25	15 58
21	20 59	−19.0	5	93	13 00	16 39	16 14
23	21 13	−17.9	5	91	13 06	16 52	16 30
25	21 26	−16.7	6	87	13 11	17 06	16 45
27	21 39	−15.4	6	83	13 16	17 19	17 00
29	21 50	−14.1	6	78	13 19	17 31	17 14
31	22 02	−12.7	6	72	13 22	17 42	17 27

VENUS

Day	RA h m	Dec. °	Diam. "	Phase %	Transit h m	5° high 52° h m	5° high 56° h m
1	18 28	−23.6	10	100	11 47	14 45	14 08
6	18 56	−23.4	10	100	11 55	14 56	14 19
11	19 23	−22.8	10	100	12 03	15 09	14 34
16	19 50	−21.9	10	100	12 10	15 23	14 52
21	20 17	−20.8	10	100	12 17	15 40	15 11
26	20 43	−19.4	10	100	12 23	15 57	15 31
31	21 08	−17.8	10	100	12 29	16 15	15 52

MARS

Day	RA h m	Dec. °	Diam. "	Phase %	Transit h m	5° high 52° h m	5° high 56° h m
1	18 40	−24.0	4	100	11 58	9 03	9 42
6	18 56	−23.7	4	100	11 55	8 57	9 35
11	19 13	−23.3	4	100	11 52	8 51	9 27
16	19 30	−22.8	4	100	11 48	8 43	9 17
21	19 46	−22.2	4	100	11 45	8 35	9 07
26	20 03	−21.5	4	100	11 42	8 25	8 56
31	20 19	−20.7	4	100	11 39	8 15	8 44

SUNRISE AND SUNSET

	London		Bristol		Birmingham		Manchester		Newcastle		Glasgow		Belfast	
	0°05′	51°30′	2°35′	51°28′	1°55′	52°28′	2°15′	53°28′	1°37′	54°59′	4°14′	55°52′	5°56′	54°35′
	h m	h m	h m	h m	h m	h m	h m	h m	h m	h m	h m	h m	h m	h m
1	8 06	16 02	8 16	16 12	8 18	16 04	8 25	16 00	8 31	15 49	8 47	15 54	8 46	16 09
2	8 06	16 03	8 16	16 13	8 18	16 05	8 25	16 01	8 31	15 50	8 47	15 55	8 46	16 10
3	8 06	16 04	8 16	16 14	8 18	16 07	8 25	16 03	8 31	15 51	8 47	15 56	8 46	16 11
4	8 06	16 05	8 15	16 15	8 18	16 08	8 24	16 04	8 30	15 53	8 46	15 58	8 45	16 12
5	8 05	16 06	8 15	16 17	8 17	16 09	8 24	16 05	8 30	15 54	8 46	15 59	8 45	16 14
6	8 05	16 08	8 15	16 18	8 17	16 10	8 24	16 06	8 30	15 55	8 45	16 00	8 44	16 15
7	8 05	16 09	8 14	16 19	8 17	16 12	8 23	16 08	8 29	15 57	8 45	16 02	8 44	16 16
8	8 04	16 10	8 14	16 20	8 16	16 13	8 23	16 09	8 28	15 58	8 44	16 03	8 43	16 18
9	8 04	16 12	8 13	16 22	8 16	16 14	8 22	16 11	8 28	16 00	8 43	16 05	8 43	16 19
10	8 03	16 13	8 13	16 23	8 15	16 16	8 21	16 12	8 27	16 01	8 43	16 07	8 42	16 21
11	8 02	16 14	8 12	16 25	8 14	16 17	8 21	16 14	8 26	16 03	8 42	16 08	8 41	16 22
12	8 02	16 16	8 12	16 26	8 14	16 19	8 20	16 15	8 25	16 05	8 41	16 10	8 40	16 24
13	8 01	16 17	8 11	16 28	8 13	16 20	8 19	16 17	8 24	16 06	8 40	16 12	8 39	16 26
14	8 00	16 19	8 10	16 29	8 12	16 22	8 18	16 18	8 23	16 08	8 39	16 14	8 39	16 27
15	8 00	16 20	8 09	16 31	8 11	16 23	8 17	16 20	8 22	16 10	8 38	16 15	8 38	16 29
16	7 59	16 22	8 09	16 32	8 10	16 25	8 16	16 22	8 21	16 12	8 37	16 17	8 36	16 31
17	7 58	16 24	8 08	16 34	8 09	16 27	8 15	16 23	8 20	16 13	8 35	16 19	8 35	16 33
18	7 57	16 25	8 07	16 35	8 08	16 28	8 14	16 25	8 19	16 15	8 34	16 21	8 34	16 35
19	7 56	16 27	8 06	16 37	8 07	16 30	8 13	16 27	8 18	16 17	8 33	16 23	8 33	16 36
20	7 55	16 28	8 05	16 39	8 06	16 32	8 12	16 29	8 16	16 19	8 31	16 25	8 32	16 38
21	7 54	16 30	8 04	16 40	8 05	16 34	8 11	16 31	8 15	16 21	8 30	16 27	8 30	16 40
22	7 53	16 32	8 02	16 42	8 04	16 35	8 09	16 32	8 14	16 23	8 29	16 29	8 29	16 42
23	7 51	16 34	8 01	16 44	8 03	16 37	8 08	16 34	8 12	16 25	8 27	16 31	8 28	16 44
24	7 50	16 35	8 00	16 45	8 01	16 39	8 07	16 36	8 11	16 27	8 26	16 33	8 26	16 46
25	7 49	16 37	7 59	16 47	8 00	16 41	8 05	16 38	8 09	16 29	8 24	16 35	8 25	16 48
26	7 48	16 39	7 57	16 49	7 59	16 42	8 04	16 40	8 08	16 31	8 22	16 37	8 23	16 50
27	7 46	16 40	7 56	16 51	7 57	16 44	8 02	16 42	8 06	16 33	8 21	16 39	8 22	16 52
28	7 45	16 42	7 55	16 52	7 56	16 46	8 01	16 44	8 05	16 35	8 19	16 41	8 20	16 54
29	7 43	16 44	7 53	16 54	7 54	16 48	7 59	16 46	8 03	16 37	8 17	16 44	8 19	16 56
30	7 42	16 46	7 52	16 56	7 53	16 50	7 58	16 47	8 01	16 39	8 15	16 46	8 17	16 58
31	7 41	16 48	7 50	16 58	7 51	16 52	7 56	16 49	7 59	16 41	8 14	16 48	8 15	17 00

JUPITER

Day	RA	Dec.	Transit	5° high	
				52°	56°
	h m	° ′	h m	h m	h m
1	14 30.9	−13 40	7 48	3 37	3 54
11	14 36.6	−14 05	7 14	3 06	3 24
21	14 41.4	−14 26	6 40	2 34	2 52
31	14 45.3	−14 42	6 04	2 00	2 19

Diameters – equatorial 35″ polar 33″

SATURN

Day	RA	Dec.	Transit	5° high	
				52°	56°
	h m	° ′	h m	h m	h m
1	21 58.9	−13 51	15 15	19 25	19 08
11	22 02.7	−13 30	14 39	18 51	18 35
21	22 06.9	−13 07	14 04	18 19	18 03
31	22 11.3	−12 43	13 29	17 46	17 31

Diameters – equatorial 16″ polar 14″
Rings – major axis 36″ minor axis 7″

URANUS

Day	RA	Dec.	Transit	10° high	
				52°	56°
	h m	° ′	h m	h m	h m
1	19 33.6	−22 09	12 50	10 33	11 30
11	19 36.1	−22 04	12 13	9 55	10 51
21	19 38.6	−21 58	11 36	9 17	10 12
31	19 41.1	−21 52	10 59	8 39	9 33

Diameter 4″

NEPTUNE

Day	RA	Dec.	Transit	10° high	
				52°	56°
	h m	° ′	h m	h m	h m
1	19 28.1	−21 16	12 44	10 18	11 07
11	19 29.7	−21 13	12 07	9 39	10 28
21	19 31.3	−21 10	11 29	9 01	9 50
31	19 32.9	−21 06	10 51	8 23	9 11

Diameter 2″

February 1994

SECOND MONTH, 28 DAYS. *Februa*, Roman festival of Purification

Sun's Longitude 330° ⊀ 18ᵈ21ʰ

1	*Tuesday*	Sir Stanley Matthews *b.* 1915	*week 5 day* 32
2	*Wednesday*	**Presentation of Christ.** Fritz Kreisler *b.* 1875	33
3	*Thursday*	Beau Nash *d.* 1762. Walter Bagehot *b.* 1826	34
4	*Friday*	End of sweet rationing 1953	35
5	*Saturday*	Sir John Pritchard *b.* 1921	36
6	*Sunday*	**8th S. before Easter.** *Queen's Accession 1952*	*week 6 day* 37
7	*Monday*	Sir Thomas More *b.* 1478. Mrs Ann Radcliffe *d.* 1823	38
8	*Tuesday*	Mary, Queen of Scots *exec.* 1587	39
9	*Wednesday*	Alban Berg *b.* 1885. Jim Laker *b.* 1922	40
10	*Thursday*	*Chinese Year of the Dog.* Samuel Plimsoll *b.* 1824	41
11	*Friday*	Lateran Treaty signed 1929. Mary Quant *b.* 1934	42
12	*Saturday*	RAMADAN begins. Abraham Lincoln *b.* 1809	43
13	*Sunday*	**7th S. before Easter.** Massacre of Glencoe 1692	*week 7 day* 44
14	*Monday*	St Valentine's Day. Francesco Cavalli *b.* 1602	45
15	*Tuesday*	Shrove Tuesday. Sir Ernest Shackleton *b.* 1874	46
16	*Wednesday*	**Ash Wednesday.** Angela Carter *d.* 1992	47
17	*Thursday*	Molière *d.* 1673. Heinrich Heine *d.* 1856	48
18	*Friday*	Queen Mary *b.* 1516. Michelangelo Buonarroti *d.* 1564	49
19	*Saturday*	*Duke of York b. 1960.* Cdr. Robert Peary *d.* 1920	50
20	*Sunday*	**1st S. in Lent.** Dame Marie Rambert *b.* 1888	*week 8 day* 51
21	*Monday*	Andres Segovia *b.* 1894. W. H. Auden *b.* 1907	52
22	*Tuesday*	1st Baron Baden-Powell *b.* 1857	53
23	*Wednesday*	George Watts *b.* 1817. Sir Adrian Boult *d.* 1983	54
24	*Thursday*	Wilhelm Grimm *b.* 1786. Joseph Rowntree *d.* 1925	55
25	*Friday*	Pierre Renoir *b.* 1841. Tennessee Williams *d.* 1983	56
26	*Saturday*	Victor Hugo *b.* 1802. Sir Harry Lauder *d.* 1950	57
27	*Sunday*	**2nd S. in Lent.** Lawrence Durrell *b.* 1912	*week 9 day* 58
28	*Monday*	Relief of Ladysmith 1900	59

ASTRONOMICAL PHENOMENA

d	h	
1	18	Saturn in conjunction with Mercury. Saturn 1° S.
3	07	Jupiter in conjunction with Moon. Jupiter 3° N.
4	21	Mercury at greatest elongation E.18°
9	16	Mars in conjunction with Moon. Mars 6° S.
11	03	Venus in conjunction with Moon. Venus 6° S.
11	09	Saturn in conjunction with Moon. Saturn 6° S.
11	21	Mercury in conjunction with Moon. Mercury 2° S.
14	03	Saturn in conjunction with Venus. Saturn 0°.05 N.
16	17	Venus in conjunction with Mercury. Venus 5° S.
19	08	Saturn in conjunction with Mercury. Saturn 5° S.
20	08	Mercury in inferior conjunction
21	17	Saturn in conjunction with Sun
28	01	Mars in conjunction with Mercury. Mars 4° S.

CONSTELLATIONS

The following constellations are near the meridian at

	d	h		d	h
January	1	24	February	15	21
January	16	23	March	1	20
February	1	22	March	16	19

Draco (below the Pole), Camelopardus, Auriga, Taurus, Gemini, Orion, Canis Minor, Monoceros, Lepus, Canis Major and Puppis

MINIMA OF ALGOL

d	h	d	h	d	h
2	17.6	14	04.9	22	19.4
5	14.4	17	01.7	25	16.2
8	11.3	19	22.6	28	13.0
11	08.1				

THE MOON

Phases, Apsides and Node	d	h	m
☾ Last Quarter	3	08	06
● New Moon	10	14	30
☽ First Quarter	18	17	47
○ Full Moon	26	01	15
Apogee (404,980 km)	16	01	35
Perigee (361,845 km)	27	22	08

Mean longitude of ascending node on February 1, 239°

THE SUN

s.d. 16′.2

Day	Right Ascension	Dec. −	Equation of time	Rise 52°	Rise 56°	Transit	Set 52°	Set 56°	Sidereal time	Transit of First Point of Aries
	h m s	° ′	m s	h m	h m	h m	h m	h m	h m s	h m s
1	20 57 25	17 13	−13 31	7 40	7 55	12 14	16 47	16 33	8 43 54	15 13 36
2	21 01 29	16 56	−13 39	7 39	7 53	12 14	16 49	16 35	8 47 50	15 09 40
3	21 05 33	16 39	−13 46	7 37	7 52	12 14	16 51	16 37	8 51 47	15 05 44
4	21 09 36	16 21	−13 53	7 36	7 50	12 14	16 53	16 39	8 55 43	15 01 49
5	21 13 38	16 03	−13 58	7 34	7 48	12 14	16 55	16 41	8 59 40	14 57 53
6	21 17 39	15 45	−14 03	7 32	7 45	12 14	16 57	16 43	9 03 36	14 53 57
7	21 21 40	15 27	−14 07	7 30	7 43	12 14	16 59	16 46	9 07 33	14 50 01
8	21 25 40	15 08	−14 10	7 29	7 41	12 14	17 00	16 48	9 11 30	14 46 05
9	21 29 39	14 49	−14 13	7 27	7 39	12 14	17 02	16 50	9 15 26	14 42 09
10	21 33 37	14 29	−14 14	7 25	7 37	12 14	17 04	16 52	9 19 23	14 38 13
11	21 37 34	14 10	−14 15	7 23	7 35	12 14	17 06	16 54	9 23 19	14 34 17
12	21 41 31	13 50	−14 15	7 21	7 33	12 14	17 08	16 57	9 27 16	14 30 21
13	21 45 27	13 30	−14 15	7 19	7 30	12 14	17 10	16 59	9 31 12	14 26 25
14	21 49 22	13 10	−14 13	7 18	7 28	12 14	17 12	17 01	9 35 09	14 22 29
15	21 53 16	12 50	−14 11	7 16	7 26	12 14	17 14	17 03	9 39 05	14 18 34
16	21 57 10	12 29	−14 08	7 14	7 24	12 14	17 15	17 05	9 43 02	14 14 38
17	22 01 03	12 08	−14 05	7 12	7 21	12 14	17 17	17 08	9 46 59	14 10 42
18	22 04 55	11 47	−14 00	7 10	7 19	12 14	17 19	17 10	9 50 55	14 06 46
19	22 08 47	11 26	−13 55	7 08	7 17	12 14	17 21	17 12	9 54 52	14 02 50
20	22 12 38	11 05	−13 49	7 06	7 14	12 14	17 23	17 14	9 58 48	13 58 54
21	22 16 28	10 43	−13 43	7 04	7 12	12 14	17 25	17 16	10 02 45	13 54 58
22	22 20 17	10 21	−13 36	7 01	7 09	12 14	17 26	17 19	10 06 41	13 51 02
23	22 24 06	9 59	−13 28	6 59	7 07	12 13	17 28	17 21	10 10 38	13 47 06
24	22 27 54	9 37	−13 20	6 57	7 05	12 13	17 30	17 23	10 14 34	13 43 10
25	22 31 42	9 15	−13 11	6 55	7 02	12 13	17 32	17 25	10 18 31	13 39 14
26	22 35 29	8 53	−13 01	6 53	7 00	12 13	17 34	17 27	10 22 28	13 35 19
27	22 39 15	8 31	−12 51	6 51	6 57	12 13	17 36	17 29	10 26 24	13 31 23
28	22 43 01	8 08	−12 40	6 49	6 55	12 13	17 37	17 31	10 30 21	13 27 27

DURATION OF TWILIGHT (in minutes)

Latitude	52°	56°	52°	56°	52°	56°	52°	56°
	1 February		11 February		21 February		28 February	
Civil	37	41	35	39	34	38	34	38
Nautical	77	86	75	83	74	81	73	81
Astronomical	117	130	114	126	113	125	112	124

THE NIGHT SKY

Mercury, being at greatest eastern elongation (18°) on the 4th, is visible as an evening object, magnitude −0.8 to +2.0, for the first half of the month. It may be seen low above the WSW horizon around the time of end of evening civil twilight. If conditions are very good on the evening of the 11th it may be possible to see the thin sliver of the New Moon, just over one day old, about 3° to the right of Mercury, just before setting in the west. On the evening of the 1st Mercury passes only 1° north of Saturn, though this event is unlikely to be detected without optical aid.

Venus is too close to the Sun for observation at first. However, during the last ten days of the month it is visible in the evenings for a short while after sunset, though only about 5° above the WSW horizon. The magnitude of Venus is −3.9.

Mars remains too close to the Sun for observation.

Jupiter, magnitude −2.1, is a brilliant object in the SE sky in the mornings. On the morning of the 3rd, the Moon, at Last Quarter, will be seen passing 3° south of the planet. On the last day of the month Jupiter reaches its first stationary point and will then commence its retrograde motion.

Saturn has come to the end of its evening apparition and will not be seen again until April.

Zodiacal Light. The evening cone may be observed in the western sky after the end of twilight from the beginning of the month until the 11th and again after the 26th. This faint phenomenon is only visible in good conditions, in the absence of both moonlight and artificial lighting.

THE MOON

Day	RA h m	Dec. °	Hor. par. ′	Semi-diam. ′	Sun's co-long. °	PA of Bright Limb °	Phase %	Age d	Rise 52° h m	Rise 56° h m	Transit h m	Set 52° h m	Set 56° h m
1	12 35	− 7.9	59.6	16.2	149	115	76	20.0	23 48	—	3 59	9 19	9 10
2	13 30	−12.5	59.4	16.2	161	113	65	21.0	—	0 00	4 52	9 47	9 34
3	14 26	−16.3	59.2	16.1	173	109	54	22.0	1 07	1 23	5 47	10 20	10 03
4	15 24	−19.2	58.8	16.0	185	104	43	23.0	2 22	2 42	6 43	11 00	10 40
5	16 22	−20.9	58.4	15.9	197	100	32	24.0	3 30	3 52	7 40	11 49	11 27
6	17 21	−21.3	58.0	15.8	210	95	22	25.0	4 28	4 51	8 37	12 48	12 25
7	18 19	−20.5	57.6	15.7	222	91	14	26.0	5 16	5 37	9 32	13 53	13 33
8	19 15	−18.6	57.1	15.6	234	89	7	27.0	5 55	6 12	10 25	15 03	14 47
9	20 09	−15.7	56.6	15.4	246	90	3	28.0	6 26	6 39	11 16	16 14	16 02
10	21 00	−12.0	56.1	15.3	258	108	1	29.0	6 51	7 01	12 03	17 25	17 17
11	21 49	− 7.9	55.6	15.2	270	203	0	0.4	7 13	7 19	12 49	18 35	18 31
12	22 36	− 3.6	55.2	15.0	283	232	2	1.4	7 33	7 35	13 32	19 43	19 43
13	23 21	+ 0.9	54.8	14.9	295	238	6	2.4	7 53	7 51	14 15	20 49	20 53
14	0 07	+ 5.2	54.4	14.8	307	241	11	3.4	8 12	8 07	14 57	21 55	22 03
15	0 52	+ 9.3	54.2	14.8	319	244	18	4.4	8 33	8 24	15 40	23 00	23 12
16	1 38	+13.0	54.1	14.8	331	247	25	5.4	8 56	8 43	16 24	—	—
17	2 25	+16.1	54.2	14.8	344	251	34	6.4	9 23	9 07	17 10	0 04	0 20
18	3 14	+18.6	54.5	14.8	356	255	43	7.4	9 55	9 36	17 57	1 07	1 25
19	4 04	+20.3	54.9	14.9	8	259	53	8.4	10 35	10 13	18 47	2 07	2 28
20	4 56	+21.1	55.4	15.1	20	263	62	9.4	11 23	11 01	19 38	3 02	3 24
21	5 50	+20.9	56.2	15.3	32	268	72	10.4	12 20	12 00	20 31	3 51	4 12
22	6 45	+19.6	57.0	15.5	44	272	80	11.4	13 27	13 09	21 24	4 33	4 52
23	7 40	+17.2	57.9	15.8	57	275	88	12.4	14 40	14 26	22 17	5 09	5 24
24	8 35	+13.8	58.7	16.0	69	276	94	13.4	15 58	15 48	23 10	5 40	5 51
25	9 30	+ 9.5	59.5	16.2	81	270	98	14.4	17 19	17 14	—	6 07	6 14
26	10 25	+ 4.5	60.1	16.4	93	210	100	15.4	18 42	18 41	0 03	6 32	6 34
27	11 21	− 0.7	60.5	16.5	105	132	99	16.4	20 05	20 10	0 56	6 56	6 54
28	12 16	− 6.0	60.6	16.5	117	121	94	17.4	21 29	21 38	1 50	7 22	7 15

MERCURY

Day	RA h m	Dec. °	Diam. ″	Phase %	Transit h m	5° high 52° h m	5° high 56° h m
1	22 07	−12.1	6	69	13 23	17 48	17 33
3	22 16	−10.7	7	61	13 24	17 56	17 43
5	22 24	− 9.5	7	53	13 24	18 02	17 51
7	22 29	− 8.4	8	43	13 21	18 05	17 55
9	22 33	− 7.4	8	34	13 16	18 04	17 55
11	22 34	− 6.7	9	24	13 08	18 00	17 51
13	22 32	− 6.3	9	16	12 58	17 51	17 42
15	22 28	− 6.3	10	9	12 45	17 38	17 29
17	22 22	− 6.5	10	4	12 31	17 21	17 12
19	22 14	− 7.0	10	1	12 15	17 02	16 53
21	22 06	− 7.7	11	1	11 59	7 15	7 25
23	21 58	− 8.6	11	3	11 43	7 04	7 15
25	21 50	− 9.5	11	6	11 28	6 54	7 06
27	21 44	−10.3	10	10	11 15	6 46	6 58
29	21 40	−11.1	10	15	11 03	6 38	6 52
31	21 38	−11.8	10	20	10 54	6 32	6 47

VENUS

Day	RA h m	Dec. °	Diam. ″	Phase %	Transit h m	5° high 52° h m	5° high 56° h m
1	21 13	−17.4	10	100	12 30	16 18	15 56
6	21 38	−15.6	10	100	12 35	16 36	16 17
11	22 03	−13.5	10	100	12 40	16 54	16 38
16	22 27	−11.3	10	99	12 44	17 12	16 58
21	22 50	− 9.0	10	99	12 48	17 29	17 18
26	23 14	− 6.5	10	99	12 51	17 46	17 38
31	23 37	− 4.0	10	98	12 55	18 03	17 57

MARS

Day	RA h m	Dec. °	Diam. ″	Phase %	Transit h m	5° high 52° h m	5° high 56° h m
1	20 22	−20.5	4	100	11 38	8 13	8 42
6	20 38	−19.6	4	100	11 34	8 03	8 29
11	20 54	−18.5	4	100	11 31	7 52	8 16
16	21 10	−17.4	4	99	11 27	7 40	8 02
21	21 26	−16.3	4	99	11 23	7 28	7 48
26	21 41	−15.0	4	99	11 18	7 15	7 34
31	21 56	−13.7	4	99	11 14	7 03	7 19

SUNRISE AND SUNSET

	London		Bristol		Birmingham		Manchester		Newcastle		Glasgow		Belfast	
	0°05′	51°30′	2°35′	51°28′	1°55′	52°28′	2°15′	53°28′	1°37′	54°59′	4°14′	55°52′	5°56′	54°35′
	h m	h m	h m	h m	h m	h m	h m	h m	h m	h m	h m	h m	h m	h m
1	7 39	16 49	7 49	17 00	7 50	16 54	7 54	16 51	7 58	16 43	8 12	16 50	8 13	17 02
2	7 38	16 51	7 47	17 01	7 48	16 55	7 53	16 53	7 56	16 45	8 10	16 52	8 12	17 04
3	7 36	16 53	7 46	17 03	7 46	16 57	7 51	16 55	7 54	16 47	8 08	16 54	8 10	17 06
4	7 34	16 55	7 44	17 05	7 45	16 59	7 49	16 57	7 52	16 49	8 06	16 57	8 08	17 08
5	7 33	16 57	7 43	17 07	7 43	17 01	7 48	16 59	7 50	16 51	8 04	16 59	8 06	17 10
6	7 31	16 59	7 41	17 09	7 41	17 03	7 46	17 01	7 48	16 54	8 02	17 01	8 04	17 12
7	7 29	17 00	7 39	17 10	7 39	17 05	7 44	17 03	7 46	16 56	8 00	17 03	8 02	17 14
8	7 28	17 02	7 37	17 12	7 38	17 07	7 42	17 05	7 44	16 58	7 58	17 05	8 00	17 16
9	7 26	17 04	7 36	17 14	7 36	17 09	7 40	17 07	7 42	17 00	7 56	17 07	7 58	17 18
10	7 24	17 06	7 34	17 16	7 34	17 11	7 38	17 09	7 40	17 02	7 54	17 10	7 56	17 21
11	7 22	17 08	7 32	17 18	7 32	17 13	7 36	17 11	7 38	17 04	7 51	17 12	7 54	17 23
12	7 20	17 10	7 30	17 20	7 30	17 14	7 34	17 13	7 36	17 06	7 49	17 14	7 52	17 25
13	7 19	17 11	7 28	17 21	7 28	17 16	7 32	17 15	7 34	17 08	7 47	17 16	7 50	17 27
14	7 17	17 13	7 27	17 23	7 26	17 18	7 30	17 17	7 32	17 10	7 45	17 18	7 48	17 29
15	7 15	17 15	7 25	17 25	7 24	17 20	7 28	17 19	7 30	17 13	7 42	17 21	7 46	17 31
16	7 13	17 17	7 23	17 27	7 22	17 22	7 26	17 21	7 27	17 15	7 40	17 23	7 44	17 33
17	7 11	17 19	7 21	17 29	7 20	17 24	7 24	17 23	7 25	17 17	7 38	17 25	7 41	17 35
18	7 09	17 20	7 19	17 31	7 18	17 26	7 22	17 25	7 23	17 19	7 36	17 27	7 39	17 37
19	7 07	17 22	7 17	17 32	7 16	17 28	7 20	17 27	7 21	17 21	7 33	17 29	7 37	17 39
20	7 05	17 24	7 15	17 34	7 14	17 30	7 18	17 29	7 18	17 23	7 31	17 31	7 35	17 41
21	7 03	17 26	7 13	17 36	7 12	17 31	7 15	17 31	7 16	17 25	7 28	17 34	7 32	17 43
22	7 01	17 28	7 11	17 38	7 10	17 33	7 13	17 33	7 14	17 27	7 26	17 36	7 30	17 45
23	6 59	17 29	7 09	17 40	7 08	17 35	7 11	17 35	7 11	17 29	7 24	17 38	7 28	17 47
24	6 57	17 31	7 07	17 41	7 06	17 37	7 09	17 37	7 09	17 31	7 21	17 40	7 26	17 49
25	6 55	17 33	7 05	17 43	7 04	17 39	7 07	17 39	7 07	17 33	7 19	17 42	7 23	17 51
26	6 53	17 35	7 02	17 45	7 01	17 41	7 04	17 40	7 04	17 35	7 16	17 44	7 21	17 53
27	6 50	17 37	7 00	17 47	6 59	17 43	7 02	17 42	7 02	17 37	7 14	17 46	7 19	17 55
28	6 48	17 38	6 58	17 48	6 57	17 44	7 00	17 44	7 00	17 40	7 11	17 49	7 16	17 57

JUPITER

Day	RA	Dec.	Transit	5° high	
				52°	56°
	h m	° ′	h m	h m	h m
1	14 45.7	−14 44	6 01	1 57	2 15
11	14 48.4	−14 54	5 24	1 21	1 40
21	14 50.0	−14 59	4 46	0 44	1 03
31	14 50.3	−14 59	4 08	0 05	0 24

Diameters – equatorial 38″ polar 36″

SATURN

Day	RA	Dec.	Transit	5° high	
				52°	56°
	h m	° ′	h m	h m	h m
1	22 11.7	−12 40	13 26	17 43	17 27
11	22 16.3	−12 15	12 51	17 11	16 56
21	22 21.0	−11 49	12 16	16 39	16 24
31	22 25.6	−11 24	11 42	16 06	15 52

Diameters – equatorial 15″ polar 14″
Rings – major axis 35″ minor axis 6″

URANUS

Day	RA	Dec.	Transit	10° high	
				52°	56°
	h m	° ′	h m	h m	h m
1	19 41.3	−21 52	10 56	8 35	9 29
11	19 43.7	−21 46	10 19	7 57	8 51
21	19 45.9	−21 41	9 42	7 19	8 12
31	19 47.9	−21 36	9 04	6 41	7 33

Diameter 4″

NEPTUNE

Day	RA	Dec.	Transit	10° high	
				52°	56°
	h m	° ′	h m	h m	h m
1	19 33.1	−21 06	10 47	8 19	9 07
11	19 34.5	−21 03	10 10	7 41	8 28
21	19 35.9	−21 00	9 32	7 02	7 49
31	19 37.1	−20 57	8 54	6 23	7 10

Diameter 2″

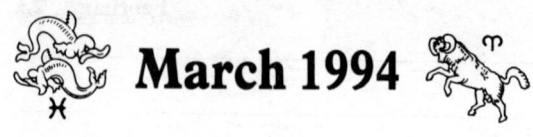

March 1994

THIRD MONTH, 31 DAYS. *Mars*, Roman god of battle

Sun's Longitude 0° ♈ 20ᵈ 20ʰ

1	*Tuesday*	St David's Day. David Niven *b.* 1910	*week* 9 *day* 60
2	*Wednesday*	Cardinal Archbishop of Westminster *b.* 1923	61
3	*Thursday*	William Macready *b.* 1793. Sir Henry Wood *b.* 1869	62
4	*Friday*	Patrick Moore *b.* 1923. Jim Clark *b.* 1936	63
5	*Saturday*	Henry II *b.* 1133. Josef Stalin *d.* 1953	64
6	*Sunday*	**3rd S. in Lent.** Cyrano de Bergerac *b.* 1619	*week* 10 *day* 65
7	*Monday*	First patent of Bell telephone 1876	66
8	*Tuesday*	Kenneth Grahame *b.* 1859. Hector Berlioz *d.* 1869	67
9	*Wednesday*	Amerigo Vespucci *b.* 1451. Yuri Gagarin *b.* 1934	68
10	*Thursday*	*Prince Edward b. 1964.* Owen Brannigan *b.* 1908	69
11	*Friday*	Sir Malcolm Campbell *b.* 1885	70
12	*Saturday*	Cesare Borgia *d.* 1507. Thomas Arne *b.* 1710	71
13	*Sunday*	**4th S. in Lent.** Mothering Sunday	*week* 11 *day* 72
14	*Monday*	Commonwealth Day. Maxim Gorky *b.* 1868	73
15	*Tuesday*	Julius Caesar *assass.* 44 BC	74
16	*Wednesday*	Aubrey Beardsley *d.* 1898	75
17	*Thursday*	St Patrick's Day. *Bank Holiday in Northern Ireland*	76
18	*Friday*	Nikolai Rimsky-Korsakov *b.* 1844	77
19	*Saturday*	**St Joseph of Nazareth.** Dr David Livingstone *b.* 1813	78
20	*Sunday*	**5th S. in Lent.** Dame Vera Lynn *b.* 1917	*week* 12 *day* 79
21	*Monday*	Sharpeville Massacre, South Africa 1960	80
22	*Tuesday*	Sir Anthony van Dyck *b.* 1599	81
23	*Wednesday*	Princess Eugenie of York *b.* 1990	82
24	*Thursday*	Union of English and Scottish crowns 1603	83
25	*Friday*	**The Annunciation.** Treaty of Rome 1957	84
26	*Saturday*	A. E. Housman *b.* 1859. Sir Noël Coward *d.* 1973	85
27	*Sunday*	**Palm Sunday.** PASSOVER begins	*week* 13 *day* 86
28	*Monday*	Dame Flora Robson *b.* 1902	87
29	*Tuesday*	John Major *b.* 1943. Joyce Cary *d.* 1957	88
30	*Wednesday*	*Hilary Law Sittings end.* Paul Verlaine *b.* 1844	89
31	*Thursday*	**Maundy Thursday.** René Descartes *b.* 1596	90

ASTRONOMICAL PHENOMENA

d	h	
2	15	Jupiter in conjunction with Moon. Jupiter 2° N.
10	01	Mercury in conjunction with Moon. Mercury 4° S.
10	18	Mars in conjunction with Moon. Mars 6° S.
10	23	Saturn in conjunction with Moon. Saturn 6° S.
13	12	Venus in conjunction with Moon. Venus 5° S.
14	05	Saturn in conjunction with Mars. Saturn 0°.3 S.
19	02	Mercury at greatest elongation W.28°
20	20	Equinox
24	10	Saturn in conjunction with Mercury. Saturn 0°.2 N.
29	22	Jupiter in conjunction with Moon. Jupiter 2° N.

CONSTELLATIONS

The following are near the meridian at

	d	h		d	h
February	1	24	March	16	21
February	15	23	April	1	20
March	1	22	April	15	19

Cepheus (below the Pole), Camelopardus, Lynx, Gemini, Cancer, Leo, Canis Minor, Hydra, Monoceros, Canis Major and Puppis

MINIMA OF ALGOL

d	h	d	h	d	h
3	09.8	14	21.1	23	11.6
6	06.7	17	18.0	26	08.4
9	03.5	20	14.8	29	05.2
12	00.3				

THE MOON

Phases, Apsides and Node	d	h	m
☾ Last Quarter	4	16	53
● New Moon	12	07	05
☽ First Quarter	20	12	14
○ Full Moon	27	11	10
Apogee (405,892 km)	15	17	12
Perigee (357,959 km)	28	06	13

Mean longitude of ascending node on March 1, 238°

THE SUN

s.d. 16′.1

Day	Right Ascension	Dec.	Equation of time	Rise 52°	Rise 56°	Transit	Set 52°	Set 56°	Sidereal time	Transit of First Point of Aries
	h m s	° ′	m s	h m	h m	h m	h m	h m	h m s	h m s
1	22 46 46	−7 45	−12 29	6 46	6 52	12 12	17 39	17 34	10 34 17	13 23 31
2	22 50 31	−7 23	−12 17	6 44	6 50	12 12	17 41	17 36	10 38 14	13 19 35
3	22 54 15	−7 00	−12 05	6 42	6 47	12 12	17 43	17 38	10 42 10	13 15 39
4	22 57 59	−6 37	−11 52	6 40	6 45	12 12	17 45	17 40	10 46 07	13 11 43
5	23 01 43	−6 14	−11 39	6 38	6 42	12 12	17 46	17 42	10 50 03	13 07 47
6	23 05 26	−5 50	−11 26	6 35	6 40	12 11	17 48	17 44	10 54 00	13 03 51
7	23 09 08	−5 27	−11 12	6 33	6 37	12 11	17 50	17 46	10 57 56	12 59 55
8	23 12 50	−5 04	−10 57	6 31	6 34	12 11	17 52	17 48	11 01 53	12 55 59
9	23 16 32	−4 40	−10 43	6 29	6 32	12 11	17 53	17 50	11 05 50	12 52 04
10	23 20 14	−4 17	−10 28	6 26	6 29	12 10	17 55	17 53	11 09 46	12 48 08
11	23 23 55	−3 53	−10 12	6 24	6 27	12 10	17 57	17 55	11 13 43	12 44 12
12	23 27 36	−3 30	− 9 57	6 22	6 24	12 10	17 59	17 57	11 17 39	12 40 16
13	23 31 16	−3 06	− 9 41	6 20	6 21	12 10	18 01	17 59	11 21 36	12 36 20
14	23 34 57	−2 42	− 9 24	6 17	6 19	12 09	18 02	18 01	11 25 32	12 32 24
15	23 38 37	−2 19	− 9 08	6 15	6 16	12 09	18 04	18 03	11 29 29	12 28 28
16	23 42 16	−1 55	− 8 51	6 13	6 14	12 09	18 06	18 05	11 33 25	12 24 32
17	23 45 56	−1 31	− 8 34	6 10	6 11	12 08	18 07	18 07	11 37 22	12 20 36
18	23 49 35	−1 08	− 8 17	6 08	6 08	12 08	18 09	18 09	11 41 19	12 16 40
19	23 53 14	−0 44	− 7 59	6 06	6 06	12 08	18 11	18 11	11 45 15	12 12 45
20	23 56 53	−0 20	− 7 42	6 03	6 03	12 08	18 13	18 13	11 49 12	12 08 49
21	0 00 32	+0 03	− 7 24	6 01	6 00	12 07	18 14	18 15	11 53 08	12 04 53
22	0 04 11	+0 27	− 7 06	5 59	5 58	12 07	18 16	18 17	11 57 05	12 00 57
23	0 07 49	+0 51	− 6 48	5 56	5 55	12 07	18 18	18 19	12 01 01	11 57 01
24	0 11 28	+1 14	− 6 30	5 54	5 53	12 06	18 20	18 21	12 04 58	11 53 05
25	0 15 06	+1 38	− 6 12	5 52	5 50	12 06	18 21	18 23	12 08 54	11 49 09
26	0 18 44	+2 02	− 5 53	5 50	5 47	12 06	18 23	18 25	12 12 51	11 45 13
27	0 22 23	+2 25	− 5 35	5 47	5 45	12 05	18 25	18 27	12 16 48	11 41 17
28	0 26 01	+2 49	− 5 17	5 45	5 42	12 05	18 26	18 30	12 20 44	11 37 21
29	0 29 39	+3 12	− 4 58	5 43	5 39	12 05	18 28	18 32	12 24 41	11 33 25
30	0 33 17	+3 35	− 4 40	5 40	5 37	12 05	18 30	18 34	12 28 37	11 29 30
31	0 36 56	+3 59	− 4 22	5 38	5 34	12 04	18 32	18 36	12 32 34	11 25 34

DURATION OF TWILIGHT (in minutes)

Latitude	52°	56°	52°	56°	52°	56°	52°	56°
	1 March		11 March		21 March		31 March	
Civil	34	38	34	37	34	37	34	38
Nautical	73	81	73	80	74	82	76	84
Astronomical	112	124	113	125	116	129	120	136

THE NIGHT SKY

Mercury is unsuitably placed for observation throughout the month.

Venus, magnitude −3.9, is visible as an evening object, low in the western sky after sunset. On the evening of the 13th, the thin crescent Moon is near the planet.

Mars is still too close to the Sun for observation.

Jupiter, magnitude −2.3, is a brilliant morning object in the constellation of Libra. Jupiter is now visible from the early evening onwards as it moves towards opposition in April. On the night of the 2nd to 3rd and again on the 29th to 30th the gibbous Moon will be seen passing about 3° south of the planet. The four Galilean satellites are readily observable with a small telescope, or a good pair of binoculars provided that they are held rigidly. Times of eclipses and shadow transits of these satellites are given on page 70.

Saturn remains too close to the Sun for observation throughout the month.

Zodiacal Light. The evening cone may be observed stretching up from the western horizon, along the ecliptic, after the end of twilight, from the beginning of the month until the 13th and again after the 27th.

THE MOON

Day	RA	Dec.	Hor. par.	Semi- diam.	Sun's co- long.	PA of Bright Limb	Phase	Age	Rise 52°	Rise 56°	Transit	Set 52°	Set 56°
	h　m	°	′	′	°	°	%	d	h　m	h　m	h　m	h　m	h　m
1	13 13	−10.9	60.5	16.5	129	116	88	18.4	22 51	23 05	2 45	7 50	7 39
2	14 11	−15.1	60.1	16.4	142	111	79	19.4	—	—	3 41	8 22	8 07
3	15 10	−18.3	59.6	16.2	154	106	69	20.4	0 10	0 28	4 38	9 01	8 42
4	16 09	−20.3	59.0	16.1	166	101	58	21.4	1 21	1 43	5 36	9 48	9 27
5	17 08	−21.1	58.3	15.9	178	95	47	22.4	2 23	2 45	6 33	10 44	10 22
6	18 06	−20.6	57.6	15.7	190	90	36	23.4	3 14	3 35	7 29	11 47	11 26
7	19 02	−18.9	57.0	15.5	202	86	26	24.4	3 55	4 13	8 22	12 54	12 37
8	19 56	−16.3	56.5	15.4	215	83	18	25.4	4 28	4 42	9 12	14 04	13 50
9	20 47	−12.9	55.9	15.2	227	81	11	26.4	4 55	5 06	10 00	15 14	15 04
10	21 35	− 9.0	55.5	15.1	239	81	5	27.4	5 18	5 25	10 45	16 22	16 17
11	22 22	− 4.8	55.1	15.0	251	87	2	28.4	5 39	5 42	11 29	17 30	17 29
12	23 08	− 0.5	54.7	14.9	263	122	0	29.4	5 58	5 58	12 12	18 37	18 39
13	23 53	+ 3.8	54.4	14.8	276	219	1	0.7	6 18	6 14	12 54	19 43	19 49
14	0 39	+ 8.0	54.2	14.8	288	237	3	1.7	6 38	6 30	13 37	20 48	20 58
15	1 24	+11.7	54.1	14.7	300	244	7	2.7	7 00	6 49	14 20	21 52	22 06
16	2 11	+15.0	54.0	14.7	312	248	12	3.7	7 26	7 11	15 05	22 55	23 12
17	2 59	+17.7	54.1	14.7	324	253	19	4.7	7 56	7 39	15 52	23 55	—
18	3 49	+19.7	54.4	14.8	337	258	27	5.7	8 33	8 12	16 40	—	0 15
19	4 39	+20.7	54.8	14.9	349	263	36	6.7	9 16	8 55	17 29	0 51	1 13
20	5 32	+20.9	55.3	15.1	1	267	45	7.7	10 09	9 48	18 20	1 42	2 03
21	6 25	+20.0	56.0	15.3	13	272	55	8.7	11 09	10 50	19 11	2 26	2 45
22	7 18	+18.1	56.9	15.5	25	276	65	9.7	12 17	12 01	20 03	3 03	3 20
23	8 12	+15.2	57.8	15.7	38	280	75	10.7	13 31	13 19	20 55	3 36	3 49
24	9 06	+11.3	58.8	16.0	50	282	84	11.7	14 49	14 41	21 47	4 04	4 13
25	10 01	+ 6.7	59.7	16.3	62	283	91	12.7	16 10	16 07	22 40	4 30	4 35
26	10 56	+ 1.6	60.5	16.5	74	280	97	13.7	17 33	17 35	23 34	4 55	4 55
27	11 51	− 3.7	61.0	16.6	86	261	100	14.7	18 58	19 05	—	5 20	5 16
28	12 49	− 8.8	61.2	16.7	98	136	99	15.7	20 24	20 36	0 29	5 48	5 39
29	13 48	−13.4	61.2	16.7	110	116	96	16.7	21 47	22 04	1 27	6 19	6 06
30	14 48	−17.1	60.8	16.6	123	108	91	17.7	23 05	23 25	2 26	6 57	6 40
31	15 50	−19.6	60.2	16.4	135	102	83	18.7	—	—	3 26	7 43	7 22

MERCURY

Day	RA	Dec.	Diam.	Phase	Transit	5° high 52°	5° high 56°
	h　m	°	″	%	h　m	h　m	h　m
1	21 40	−11.1	10	15	11 03	6 38	6 52
3	21 38	−11.8	10	20	10 54	6 32	6 47
5	21 38	−12.3	9	25	10 46	6 27	6 42
7	21 39	−12.7	9	30	10 40	6 23	6 39
9	21 41	−12.9	9	35	10 35	6 19	6 35
11	21 46	−13.0	8	39	10 31	6 16	6 32
13	21 51	−13.0	8	43	10 29	6 14	6 29
15	21 57	−12.9	8	47	10 27	6 11	6 27
17	22 04	−12.6	8	50	10 27	6 09	6 24
19	22 12	−12.2	7	54	10 27	6 06	6 21
21	22 20	−11.8	7	57	10 27	6 04	6 18
23	22 29	−11.2	7	60	10 28	6 01	6 15
25	22 38	−10.5	7	62	10 30	5 59	6 12
27	22 48	− 9.8	7	65	10 32	5 56	6 08
29	22 58	− 8.9	6	67	10 34	5 54	6 05
31	23 09	− 7.9	6	69	10 37	5 51	6 01

VENUS

Day	RA	Dec.	Diam.	Phase	Transit	5° high 52°	5° high 56°
	h　m	°	″	%	h　m	h　m	h　m
1	23 27	− 5.0	10	98	12 53	17 57	17 49
6	23 50	− 2.5	10	98	12 57	18 13	18 08
11	0 13	+ 0.1	10	98	13 00	18 29	18 27
16	0 36	+ 2.6	10	97	13 02	18 46	18 45
21	0 58	+ 5.2	10	97	13 05	19 02	19 03
26	1 21	+ 7.7	10	96	13 09	19 18	19 21
31	1 44	+10.1	10	95	13 12	19 33	19 39

MARS

Day	RA	Dec.	Diam.	Phase	Transit	5° high 52°	5° high 56°
1	21 50	−14.3	4	99	11 16	7 08	7 25
6	22 06	−12.9	4	99	11 11	6 55	7 11
11	22 21	−11.5	4	99	11 06	6 42	6 56
16	22 35	−10.1	4	99	11 02	6 29	6 41
21	22 50	− 8.6	4	99	10 57	6 15	6 26
26	23 05	− 7.1	4	98	10 52	6 02	6 11
31	23 19	− 5.6	4	98	10 46	5 48	5 56

SUNRISE AND SUNSET

	London		Bristol		Birmingham		Manchester		Newcastle		Glasgow		Belfast	
	0°05'	51°30'	2°35'	51°28'	1°55'	52°28'	2°15'	53°28'	1°37'	54°59'	4°14'	55°52'	5°56'	54°35'
	h m	h m	h m	h m	h m	h m	h m	h m	h m	h m	h m	h m	h m	h m
1	6 46	17 40	6 56	17 50	6 55	17 46	6 57	17 46	6 57	17 42	7 09	17 51	7 14	17 59
2	6 44	17 42	6 54	17 52	6 53	17 48	6 55	17 48	6 55	17 44	7 06	17 53	7 11	18 01
3	6 42	17 44	6 52	17 54	6 50	17 50	6 53	17 50	6 52	17 46	7 04	17 55	7 09	18 03
4	6 40	17 45	6 50	17 55	6 48	17 52	6 51	17 52	6 50	17 48	7 01	17 57	7 07	18 05
5	6 37	17 47	6 47	17 57	6 46	17 54	6 48	17 54	6 47	17 50	6 59	17 59	7 04	18 07
6	6 35	17 49	6 45	17 59	6 44	17 55	6 46	17 56	6 45	17 52	6 56	18 01	7 02	18 09
7	6 33	17 51	6 43	18 01	6 41	17 57	6 43	17 58	6 42	17 54	6 54	18 03	6 59	18 11
8	6 31	17 52	6 41	18 02	6 39	17 59	6 41	18 00	6 40	17 56	6 51	18 05	6 57	18 13
9	6 29	17 54	6 39	18 04	6 37	18 01	6 39	18 01	6 37	17 58	6 49	18 08	6 54	18 15
10	6 26	17 56	6 36	18 06	6 34	18 03	6 36	18 03	6 35	18 00	6 46	18 10	6 52	18 17
11	6 24	17 58	6 34	18 08	6 32	18 04	6 34	18 05	6 32	18 02	6 43	18 12	6 49	18 19
12	6 22	17 59	6 32	18 09	6 30	18 06	6 32	18 07	6 30	18 04	6 41	18 14	6 47	18 21
13	6 20	18 01	6 30	18 11	6 27	18 08	6 29	18 09	6 27	18 06	6 38	18 16	6 44	18 23
14	6 17	18 03	6 27	18 13	6 25	18 10	6 27	18 11	6 25	18 08	6 36	18 18	6 42	18 25
15	6 15	18 04	6 25	18 14	6 23	18 12	6 24	18 13	6 22	18 10	6 33	18 20	6 39	18 27
16	6 13	18 06	6 23	18 16	6 20	18 13	6 22	18 14	6 20	18 12	6 30	18 22	6 37	18 29
17	6 11	18 08	6 21	18 18	6 18	18 15	6 20	18 16	6 17	18 14	6 28	18 24	6 34	18 31
18	6 08	18 10	6 18	18 20	6 16	18 17	6 17	18 18	6 15	18 16	6 25	18 26	6 32	18 33
19	6 06	18 11	6 16	18 21	6 13	18 19	6 15	18 20	6 12	18 18	6 23	18 28	6 29	18 35
20	6 04	18 13	6 14	18 23	6 11	18 20	6 12	18 22	6 10	18 20	6 20	18 30	6 27	18 37
21	6 02	18 15	6 12	18 25	6 09	18 22	6 10	18 24	6 07	18 21	6 17	18 32	6 24	18 39
22	5 59	18 16	6 09	18 26	6 06	18 24	6 07	18 26	6 05	18 23	6 15	18 34	6 22	18 41
23	5 57	18 18	6 07	18 28	6 04	18 26	6 05	18 27	6 02	18 25	6 12	18 36	6 19	18 43
24	5 55	18 20	6 05	18 30	6 02	18 27	6 03	18 29	5 59	18 27	6 09	18 38	6 17	18 44
25	5 52	18 21	6 02	18 31	5 59	18 29	6 00	18 31	5 57	18 29	6 07	18 40	6 14	18 46
26	5 50	18 23	6 00	18 33	5 57	18 31	5 58	18 33	5 54	18 31	6 04	18 42	6 12	18 48
27	5 48	18 25	5 58	18 35	5 55	18 33	5 55	18 35	5 52	18 33	6 02	18 44	6 09	18 50
28	5 46	18 26	5 56	18 36	5 52	18 34	5 53	18 37	5 49	18 35	5 59	18 46	6 07	18 52
29	5 43	18 28	5 53	18 38	5 50	18 36	5 50	18 38	5 47	18 37	5 56	18 48	6 04	18 54
30	5 41	18 30	5 51	18 40	5 48	18 38	5 48	18 40	5 44	18 39	5 54	18 50	6 02	18 56
31	5 39	18 31	5 49	18 41	5 45	18 40	5 46	18 42	5 42	18 41	5 51	18 52	5 59	18 58

JUPITER

Day	RA	Dec.	Transit	5° high	
				52°	56°
	h m	° ′	h m	h m	h m
1	14 50.4	−14 59	4 15	0 13	0 32
11	14 49.7	−14 55	3 35	23 29	23 47
21	14 47.9	−14 45	2 54	22 46	23 04
31	14 44.9	−14 30	2 12	22 02	22 20

Diameters – equatorial 42″ polar 39″

SATURN

Day	RA	Dec.	Transit	5° high	
				52°	56°
	h m	° ′	h m	h m	h m
1	22 24.7	−11 29	11 49	7 25	7 39
11	22 29.2	−11 03	11 14	6 47	7 01
21	22 33.7	−10 38	10 39	6 10	6 23
31	22 37.9	−10 14	10 04	5 33	5 45

Diameters – equatorial 15″ polar 14″
Rings – major axis 35″ minor axis 5″

URANUS

Day	RA	Dec.	Transit	10° high	
				52°	56°
	h m	° ′	h m	h m	h m
1	19 47.5	−21 37	9 12	6 49	7 41
11	19 49.4	−21 33	8 34	6 10	7 02
21	19 50.9	−21 29	7 57	5 32	6 23
31	19 52.1	−21 26	7 18	4 53	5 44

Diameter 4″

NEPTUNE

Day	RA	Dec.	Transit	10° high	
				52°	56°
	h m	° ′	h m	h m	h m
1	19 36.9	−20 57	9 01	6 31	7 18
11	19 38.0	−20 55	8 23	5 52	6 39
21	19 38.9	−20 52	7 45	5 14	6 00
31	19 39.6	−20 51	7 06	4 35	5 21

Diameter 2″

April 1994

FOURTH MONTH, 30 DAYS. *Aperire*, to open; Earth opens to receive seed

Sun's Longitude 30° ♉ 20ᵈ 08ʰ

1	Friday	**Good Friday.** *Public Holiday in the UK*	*week* 13 *day* 91
2	Saturday	**Easter Eve.** Sergei Rachmaninoff b. 1873	92
3	Sunday	**Easter Day.** Brahms d. 1897	*week* 14 *day* 93
4	Monday	*Bank Holiday in England, Wales and Northern Ireland*	94
5	Tuesday	Sir Joseph Lister b. 1827. Chiang Kai-shek d. 1975	95
6	Wednesday	Cdr. Peary reaches North Pole 1909	96
7	Thursday	William Godwin d. 1836	97
8	Friday	El Greco d. 1614. Mary Pickford b. 1893	98
9	Saturday	National Gallery opened 1838	99
10	Sunday	**1st S. after Easter.** Evelyn Waugh d. 1966	*week* 15 *day* 100
11	Monday	Abdication of Napoleon 1814	101
12	Tuesday	*Easter Law Sittings begin*	102
13	Wednesday	Lord North b. 1732. Thomas Jefferson b. 1743	103
14	Thursday	Simone de Beauvoir d. 1986	104
15	Friday	Joe Davis b. 1901. Sinking of the Titanic 1912	105
16	Saturday	Culloden 1746. Sir Charles Chaplin b. 1889	106
17	Sunday	**2nd S. after Easter.** Benjamin Franklin d. 1790	*week* 16 *day* 107
18	Monday	Irish Free State becomes Republic of Ireland 1949	108
19	Tuesday	David Ricardo b. 1772. Lord Byron d. 1824	109
20	Wednesday	Napoleon III b. 1808. Bram Stoker d. 1912	110
21	Thursday	Queen Elizabeth II b. 1926	111
22	Friday	Henry Fielding b. 1707. Sir Henry Royce d. 1933	112
23	Saturday	St George's Day. Dame Ngaio Marsh b. 1899	113
24	Sunday	**3rd S. after Easter.** Sir Stafford Cripps b. 1889	*week* 17 *day* 114
25	Monday	**St Mark.** ANZAC landings at Gallipoli 1915	115
26	Tuesday	David Hume b. 1711. Eugene Delacroix b. 1798	116
27	Wednesday	Samuel Morse b. 1791. William Macready d. 1873	117
28	Thursday	Mutiny on the Bounty 1789	118
29	Friday	Duke Ellington b. 1899. Glen Byam Shaw d. 1986	119
30	Saturday	George Headley b. 1909. George Balanchine d. 1983	120

ASTRONOMICAL PHENOMENA

d	h	
4	21	Mars in conjunction with Mercury. Mars 1° N.
7	10	Saturn in conjunction with Moon. Saturn 6° S.
8	21	Mars in conjunction with Moon. Mars 5° S.
9	04	Mercury in conjunction with Moon. Mercury 6° S.
12	23	Venus in conjunction with Moon. Venus 1° S.
26	04	Jupiter in conjunction with Moon. Jupiter 3° N.
30	09	Jupiter at opposition
30	10	Mercury in superior conjunction

CONSTELLATIONS

The following constellations are near the meridian at

	d	h
March	1	24
March	16	23
April	1	22
April	15	21
May	1	20
May	16	19

Cepheus (below the Pole), Cassiopeia (below the Pole), Ursa Major, Leo Minor, Leo, Sextans, Hydra and Crater

MINIMA OF ALGOL

d	h	d	h	d	h
1	02.1	12	13.3	24	00.6
3	22.9	15	10.2	26	21.4
6	19.7	18	07.0	29	18.2
9	16.5	21	03.8		

THE MOON

Phases, Apsides and Node	d	h	m
☾ Last Quarter	3	02	55
● New Moon	11	00	17
☽ First Quarter	19	02	34
○ Full Moon	25	19	45
Apogee (406,468 km)	11	23	49
Perigee (356,929 km)	25	17	17

Mean longitude of ascending node on April 1, 236°

THE SUN
s.d. 16′.0

Day	Right Ascension	Dec. +	Equation of time	Rise 52°	Rise 56°	Transit	Set 52°	Set 56°	Sidereal time	Transit of First Point of Aries
	h m s	° ′	m s	h m	h m	h m	h m	h m	h m s	h m s
1	0 40 34	4 22	− 4 04	5 36	5 31	12 04	18 33	18 38	12 36 30	11 21 38
2	0 44 13	4 45	− 3 46	5 33	5 29	12 04	18 35	18 40	12 40 27	11 17 42
3	0 47 52	5 08	− 3 28	5 31	5 26	12 03	18 37	18 42	12 44 23	11 13 46
4	0 51 31	5 31	− 3 11	5 29	5 24	12 03	18 38	18 44	12 48 20	11 09 50
5	0 55 10	5 54	− 2 53	5 26	5 21	12 03	18 40	18 46	12 52 16	11 05 54
6	0 58 49	6 17	− 2 36	5 24	5 18	12 02	18 42	18 48	12 56 13	11 01 58
7	1 02 29	6 39	− 2 19	5 22	5 16	12 02	18 44	18 50	13 00 10	10 58 02
8	1 06 08	7 02	− 2 02	5 20	5 13	12 02	18 45	18 52	13 04 06	10 54 06
9	1 09 48	7 24	− 1 46	5 17	5 11	12 02	18 47	18 54	13 08 03	10 50 10
10	1 13 28	7 47	− 1 29	5 15	5 08	12 01	18 49	18 56	13 11 59	10 46 15
11	1 17 09	8 09	− 1 13	5 13	5 05	12 01	18 50	18 58	13 15 56	10 42 19
12	1 20 50	8 31	− 0 57	5 11	5 03	12 01	18 52	19 00	13 19 52	10 38 23
13	1 24 31	8 53	− 0 42	5 08	5 00	12 01	18 54	19 02	13 23 49	10 34 27
14	1 28 12	9 15	− 0 27	5 06	4 58	12 00	18 56	19 04	13 27 45	10 30 31
15	1 31 54	9 36	− 0 12	5 04	4 55	12 00	18 57	19 06	13 31 42	10 26 35
16	1 35 36	9 58	+ 0 03	5 02	4 53	12 00	18 59	19 08	13 35 39	10 22 39
17	1 39 18	10 19	+ 0 17	5 00	4 50	12 00	19 01	19 10	13 39 35	10 18 43
18	1 43 01	10 40	+ 0 31	4 58	4 48	11 59	19 02	19 12	13 43 32	10 14 47
19	1 46 44	11 01	+ 0 44	4 55	4 45	11 59	19 04	19 14	13 47 28	10 10 51
20	1 50 28	11 22	+ 0 57	4 53	4 43	11 59	19 06	19 16	13 51 25	10 06 56
21	1 54 11	11 42	+ 1 10	4 51	4 40	11 59	19 07	19 18	13 55 21	10 03 00
22	1 57 56	12 03	+ 1 22	4 49	4 38	11 59	19 09	19 20	13 59 18	9 59 04
23	2 01 40	12 23	+ 1 34	4 47	4 36	11 58	19 11	19 23	14 03 14	9 55 08
24	2 05 26	12 43	+ 1 45	4 45	4 33	11 58	19 13	19 25	14 07 11	9 51 12
25	2 09 11	13 03	+ 1 56	4 43	4 31	11 58	19 14	19 27	14 11 08	9 47 16
26	2 12 57	13 22	+ 2 07	4 41	4 28	11 58	19 16	19 29	14 15 04	9 43 20
27	2 16 44	13 41	+ 2 17	4 39	4 26	11 58	19 18	19 31	14 19 01	9 39 24
28	2 20 31	14 00	+ 2 26	4 37	4 24	11 57	19 19	19 33	14 22 57	9 35 28
29	2 24 19	14 19	+ 2 35	4 35	4 21	11 57	19 21	19 35	14 26 54	9 31 32
30	2 28 07	14 38	+ 2 44	4 33	4 19	11 57	19 23	19 37	14 30 50	9 27 36

DURATION OF TWILIGHT (in minutes)

Latitude	52°	56°	52°	56°	52°	56°	52°	56°
	1 April		11 April		21 April		30 April	
Civil	34	38	35	40	37	42	39	44
Nautical	76	85	79	90	84	96	89	105
Astronomical	121	137	128	148	138	167	152	200

THE NIGHT SKY

Mercury is not suitably placed for observation in April, passing through superior conjunction on the 30th.

Venus, magnitude − 3.9, continues to be visible for a short time in the evenings, low in the western sky after sunset. On the evening of the 12th the thin crescent Moon, less than two days old, will be seen approaching Venus.

Mars continues to remain too close to the Sun for observation.

Jupiter reaches opposition on the last day of the month and therefore is visible throughout the hours of darkness. Jupiter is in Libra and a magnificent object in the night sky, magnitude − 2.5. The Full Moon passes 3° south of the planet in the early hours of the 26th.

Saturn is still too close to the Sun for observation during the first half of the month. Later, it gradually becomes visible as a difficult morning object, low in the SE sky before the morning twilight inhibits observation. Its magnitude is + 1.0. Saturn is in the constellation of Aquarius.

THE MOON

Day	RA	Dec.	Hor. par.	Semi- diam.	Sun's co- long.	PA of Bright Limb	Phase	Age	Rise 52°	Rise 56°	Transit	Set 52°	Set 56°
	h m	°	′	′	°	°	%	d	h m	h m	h m	h m	h m
1	16 51	−20.8	59.4	16.2	147	96	73	19.7	0 13	0 34	4 25	8 37	8 15
2	17 51	−20.6	58.5	15.9	159	90	62	20.7	1 09	1 30	5 23	9 39	9 19
3	18 49	−19.2	57.7	15.7	171	85	51	21.7	1 54	2 13	6 18	10 47	10 29
4	19 43	−16.8	56.9	15.5	184	81	41	22.7	2 30	2 45	7 09	11 56	11 42
5	20 35	−13.6	56.2	15.3	196	78	31	23.7	2 59	3 10	7 58	13 06	12 55
6	21 24	− 9.8	55.5	15.1	208	75	22	24.7	3 23	3 31	8 44	14 14	14 08
7	22 11	− 5.7	55.0	15.0	220	74	14	25.7	3 44	3 49	9 27	15 22	15 19
8	22 57	− 1.5	54.6	14.9	232	75	8	26.7	4 04	4 05	10 10	16 28	16 29
9	23 42	+ 2.8	54.3	14.8	245	77	4	27.7	4 24	4 21	10 52	17 33	17 38
10	0 27	+ 6.9	54.1	14.7	257	85	1	28.7	4 44	4 37	11 35	18 38	18 47
11	1 12	+10.7	54.0	14.7	269	155	0	29.7	5 05	4 55	12 18	19 43	19 55
12	1 59	+14.2	53.9	14.7	281	240	1	1.0	5 30	5 17	13 03	20 46	21 02
13	2 46	+17.0	54.0	14.7	293	250	4	2.0	5 59	5 42	13 48	21 47	22 06
14	3 36	+19.1	54.1	14.8	306	257	8	3.0	6 33	6 14	14 36	22 44	23 05
15	4 26	+20.4	54.4	14.8	318	262	14	4.0	7 14	6 53	15 25	23 36	23 58
16	5 17	+20.8	54.8	14.9	330	267	21	5.0	8 03	7 42	16 14	—	—
17	6 09	+20.2	55.3	15.1	342	272	29	6.0	9 00	8 40	17 04	0 22	0 42
18	7 02	+18.6	55.9	15.2	355	277	39	7.0	10 03	9 46	17 54	1 01	1 19
19	7 54	+16.1	56.7	15.4	7	281	49	8.0	11 12	10 59	18 44	1 34	1 49
20	8 46	+12.7	57.6	15.7	19	284	60	9.0	12 26	12 16	19 35	2 03	2 14
21	9 39	+ 8.5	58.5	15.9	31	287	70	10.0	13 43	13 38	20 25	2 29	2 36
22	10 32	+ 3.7	59.4	16.2	43	288	80	11.0	15 02	15 02	21 17	2 54	2 56
23	11 26	− 1.4	60.3	16.4	55	288	88	12.0	16 25	16 29	22 11	3 18	3 16
24	12 22	− 6.5	60.9	16.6	68	286	95	13.0	17 49	17 59	23 07	3 44	3 38
25	13 20	−11.4	61.3	16.7	80	279	99	14.0	19 15	19 29	—	4 14	4 03
26	14 21	−15.6	61.4	16.7	92	139	100	15.0	20 37	20 56	0 06	4 48	4 33
27	15 23	−18.6	61.2	16.7	104	105	98	16.0	21 53	22 14	1 07	5 31	5 12
28	16 27	−20.4	60.6	16.5	116	97	93	17.0	22 57	23 18	2 09	6 23	6 02
29	17 29	−20.7	59.8	16.3	129	90	86	18.0	23 48	—	3 10	7 25	7 03
30	18 30	−19.6	58.9	16.0	141	85	77	19.0	—	0 08	4 08	8 33	8 13

MERCURY

Day	RA	Dec.	Diam.	Phase	Transit	5° high 52°	5° high 56°
	h m	°	″	%	h m	h m	h m
1	23 14	− 7.4	6	71	10 38	5 50	5 59
3	23 25	− 6.4	6	73	10 41	5 47	5 55
5	23 26	− 5.2	6	75	10 45	5 44	5 52
7	23 48	− 4.0	6	77	10 49	5 41	5 47
9	0 00	− 2.7	6	80	10 53	5 38	5 43
11	0 12	− 1.3	6	82	10 57	5 35	5 39
13	0 24	+ 0.1	5	84	11 02	5 32	5 35
15	0 37	+ 1.6	5	87	11 07	5 29	5 31
17	0 50	+ 3.2	5	89	11 12	5 27	5 27
19	1 04	+ 4.8	5	91	11 18	5 24	5 23
21	1 18	+ 6.4	5	94	11 24	5 22	5 20
23	1 32	+ 8.1	5	95	11 31	5 20	5 16
25	1 47	+ 9.9	5	97	11 38	5 18	5 13
27	2 03	+11.6	5	99	11 46	5 16	5 10
29	2 18	+13.3	5	100	11 54	5 15	5 07
31	2 35	+15.0	5	100	12 02	18 52	19 02

VENUS

Day	RA	Dec.	Diam.	Phase	Transit	5° high 52°	5° high 56°
	h m	°	″	%	h m	h m	h m
1	1 49	+10.6	10	95	13 13	19 37	19 42
6	2 12	+12.9	11	94	13 16	19 52	20 00
11	2 36	+15.1	11	94	13 20	20 08	20 18
16	3 00	+17.1	11	93	13 25	20 24	20 35
21	3 24	+18.9	11	92	13 30	20 39	20 52
26	3 49	+20.6	11	91	13 35	20 54	21 09
31	4 15	+22.0	11	90	13 41	21 08	21 25

MARS

Day	RA	Dec.	Diam.	Phase	Transit	5° high 52°	5° high 56°
1	23 22	− 5.3	4	98	10 45	5 45	5 53
6	23 37	− 3.7	4	98	10 40	5 32	5 38
11	23 51	− 2.1	4	98	10 35	5 18	5 23
16	0 05	− 0.6	4	98	10 29	5 05	5 08
21	0 19	+ 1.0	4	97	10 24	4 51	4 53
26	0 34	+ 2.5	4	97	10 18	4 38	4 39
31	0 48	+ 4.1	4	97	10 13	4 24	4 24

SUNRISE AND SUNSET

	London		Bristol		Birmingham		Manchester		Newcastle		Glasgow		Belfast	
	0°05′	51°30′	2°35′	51°28′	1°55′	52°28′	2°15′	53°28′	1°37′	54°59′	4°14′	55°52′	5°56′	54°35′
	h m	h m	h m	h m	h m	h m	h m	h m	h m	h m	h m	h m	h m	h m
1	5 36	18 33	5 46	18 43	5 43	18 41	5 43	18 44	5 39	18 43	5 48	18 54	5 57	19 00
2	5 34	18 35	5 44	18 45	5 41	18 43	5 41	18 46	5 37	18 45	5 46	18 56	5 54	19 02
3	5 32	18 36	5 42	18 46	5 38	18 45	5 38	18 47	5 34	18 47	5 43	18 59	5 52	19 04
4	5 30	18 38	5 40	18 48	5 36	18 47	5 36	18 49	5 31	18 49	5 41	19 01	5 49	19 06
5	5 27	18 40	5 37	18 50	5 34	18 48	5 34	18 51	5 29	18 51	5 38	19 03	5 47	19 07
6	5 25	18 41	5 35	18 51	5 31	18 50	5 31	18 53	5 26	18 53	5 35	19 05	5 44	19 09
7	5 23	18 43	5 33	18 53	5 29	18 52	5 29	18 55	5 24	18 55	5 33	19 07	5 42	19 11
8	5 21	18 45	5 31	18 55	5 27	18 54	5 26	18 57	5 21	18 57	5 30	19 09	5 39	19 13
9	5 18	18 47	5 29	18 56	5 24	18 55	5 24	18 58	5 19	18 59	5 28	19 11	5 37	19 15
10	5 16	18 48	5 26	18 58	5 22	18 57	5 22	19 00	5 16	19 00	5 25	19 13	5 34	19 17
11	5 14	18 50	5 24	19 00	5 20	18 59	5 19	19 02	5 14	19 02	5 23	19 15	5 32	19 19
12	5 12	18 52	5 22	19 01	5 18	19 01	5 17	19 04	5 11	19 04	5 20	19 17	5 30	19 21
13	5 10	18 53	5 20	19 03	5 15	19 02	5 15	19 06	5 09	19 06	5 18	19 19	5 27	19 23
14	5 08	18 55	5 18	19 05	5 13	19 04	5 12	19 07	5 07	19 08	5 15	19 21	5 25	19 25
15	5 05	18 57	5 15	19 06	5 11	19 06	5 10	19 09	5 04	19 10	5 13	19 23	5 22	19 27
16	5 03	18 58	5 13	19 08	5 09	19 08	5 08	19 11	5 02	19 12	5 10	19 25	5 20	19 28
17	5 01	19 00	5 11	19 10	5 06	19 09	5 05	19 13	4 59	19 14	5 08	19 27	5 18	19 30
18	4 59	19 02	5 09	19 11	5 04	19 11	5 03	19 15	4 57	19 16	5 05	19 29	5 15	19 32
19	4 57	19 03	5 07	19 13	5 02	19 13	5 01	19 17	4 55	19 18	5 03	19 31	5 13	19 34
20	4 55	19 05	5 05	19 15	5 00	19 15	4 59	19 18	4 52	19 20	5 00	19 33	5 10	19 36
21	4 53	19 07	5 03	19 16	4 58	19 16	4 56	19 20	4 50	19 22	4 58	19 35	5 08	19 38
22	4 51	19 08	5 01	19 18	4 56	19 18	4 54	19 22	4 47	19 24	4 55	19 37	5 06	19 40
23	4 49	19 10	4 59	19 20	4 53	19 20	4 52	19 24	4 45	19 26	4 53	19 39	5 04	19 42
24	4 47	19 12	4 57	19 21	4 51	19 22	4 50	19 26	4 43	19 28	4 50	19 41	5 01	19 44
25	4 45	19 13	4 55	19 23	4 49	19 23	4 48	19 27	4 41	19 30	4 48	19 43	4 59	19 46
26	4 43	19 15	4 53	19 25	4 47	19 25	4 46	19 29	4 38	19 32	4 46	19 45	4 57	19 48
27	4 41	19 17	4 51	19 26	4 45	19 27	4 43	19 31	4 36	19 34	4 43	19 47	4 55	19 49
28	4 39	19 18	4 49	19 28	4 43	19 28	4 41	19 33	4 34	19 35	4 41	19 49	4 52	19 51
29	4 37	19 20	4 47	19 30	4 41	19 30	4 39	19 35	4 32	19 37	4 39	19 51	4 50	19 53
30	4 35	19 21	4 45	19 31	4 39	19 32	4 37	19 36	4 29	19 39	4 36	19 53	4 48	19 55

JUPITER

Day	RA	Dec.	Transit	5° high	
				52°	56°
	h m	° ′	h m	h m	h m
1	14 44.6	−14 28	2 08	21 58	22 16
11	14 40.6	−14 09	1 24	21 12	21 30
21	14 36.0	−13 47	0 41	20 26	20 43
31	14 31.0	−13 24	23 52	19 40	19 56

Diameters – equatorial 44″ polar 41″

SATURN

Day	RA	Dec.	Transit	5° high	
				52°	56°
	h m	° ′	h m	h m	h m
1	22 38.4	−10 12	10 00	5 29	5 42
11	22 42.3	− 9 50	9 25	4 51	5 04
21	22 46.0	− 9 30	8 49	4 14	4 26
31	22 49.2	− 9 12	8 13	3 36	3 48

Diameters – equatorial 16″ polar 14″
Rings – major axis 36″ minor axis 4″

URANUS

Day	RA	Dec.	Transit	10° high	
				52°	56°
	h m	° ′	h m	h m	h m
1	19 52.2	−21 26	7 15	4 50	5 40
11	19 53.1	−21 24	6 36	4 11	5 01
21	19 53.7	−21 22	5 57	3 32	4 22
31	19 53.8	−21 22	5 18	2 53	3 43

Diameter 4″

NEPTUNE

Day	RA	Dec.	Transit	10° high	
				52°	56°
	h m	° ′	h m	h m	h m
1	19 39.7	−20 51	7 02	4 31	5 17
11	19 40.1	−20 49	6 23	3 52	4 38
21	19 40.3	−20 49	5 44	3 13	3 59
31	19 40.3	−20 49	5 05	2 33	3 19

Diameter 2″

May 1994

FIFTH MONTH, 31 DAYS. *Maia*, goddess of growth and increase

Sun's Longitude 60° II 21^{d}07^h

1	*Sunday*	**4th S. after Easter.** Great Exhibition opened 1851	*week* 18 *day* 121
2	*Monday*	**SS Philip and James.** *Bank Holiday in the UK*	122
3	*Tuesday*	Festival of Britain opened 1951	123
4	*Wednesday*	Start of the General Strike 1926	124
5	*Thursday*	Field Marshal Earl Wavell *b.* 1883	125
6	*Friday*	First four-minute mile run 1954	126
7	*Saturday*	Robert Browning *b.* 1812. Kitty Godfree *b.* 1896	127
8	*Sunday*	**5th S. After Easter.** Friedrich von Hayek *b.* 1899	*week* 19 *day* 128
9	*Monday*	Joseph Gay-Lussac *d.* 1850. Glenda Jackson *b.* 1936	129
10	*Tuesday*	Fred Astaire *b.* 1899. Sir Henry Stanley *d.* 1904	130
11	*Wednesday*	Spencer Perceval *assass.* 1812	131
12	*Thursday*	**Ascension Day.** Collapse of General Strike 1926	132
13	*Friday*	John Nash *d.* 1835. Sir Frank Brangwyn *b.* 1867	133
14	*Saturday*	**St Matthias.** Eric Morecombe *b.* 1926	134
15	*Sunday*	**S. after Ascension Day.** James Mason *b.* 1909	*week* 20 *day* 135
16	*Monday*	FEAST OF WEEKS begins. John Sell Cotman *b.* 1782	136
17	*Tuesday*	Summer Time Act came into force 1916	137
18	*Wednesday*	Pope John Paul II *b.* 1920	138
19	*Thursday*	Anne Boleyn *exec.* 1536. John Betjeman *d.* 1984	139
20	*Friday*	First Chelsea Flower Show 1913	140
21	*Saturday*	Albrecht Dürer *b.* 1471. Henry VI *killed* 1471	141
22	*Sunday*	**Pentecost (Whit Sunday).** Laurence Olivier *b.* 1907	*week* 21 *day* 142
23	*Monday*	Coalition Ministry dissolved 1945	143
24	*Tuesday*	British Legion founded 1921	144
25	*Wednesday*	Pedro Caldéron de la Barca *d.* 1681	145
26	*Thursday*	Last public hanging in England 1868	146
27	*Friday*	*Easter Law Sittings end.* Isadora Duncan *b.* 1878	147
28	*Saturday*	George I *b.* 1660. Earl Russell *d.* 1878	148
29	*Sunday*	**Trinity Sunday.** Mt Everest conquered 1953	*week* 22 *day* 149
30	*Monday*	*Bank Holiday in the UK.* Alfred Austin *b.* 1835	150
31	*Tuesday*	Jutland 1916. Sir Angus Wilson *d.* 1991	151

ASTRONOMICAL PHENOMENA

d	h	
4	21	Saturn in conjunction with Moon. Saturn 6° S.
8	00	Mars in conjunction with Moon. Mars 4° S.
10		Annular eclipse of Sun (*see* page 66)
11	22	Mercury in conjunction with Moon. Mercury 3° N.
13	07	Venus in conjunction with Moon. Venus 4° N.
17	20	Pluto at opposition
23	09	Jupiter in conjunction with Moon. Jupiter 3° N.
25		Partial eclipse of Moon (*see* page 66)
30	07	Mercury at greatest elongation E. 23°

CONSTELLATIONS

The following constellations are near the meridian at

	d	h		d	h
April	1	24	May	16	21
April	15	23	June	1	20
May	1	22	June	15	19

Cepheus (below the Pole), Cassiopeia (below the Pole), Ursa Minor, Ursa Major, Canes Venatici, Coma Berenices, Bootes, Leo, Virgo, Crater, Corvus and Hydra

MINIMA OF ALGOL

Algol is inconveniently situated for observation during May.

THE MOON

Phases, Apsides and Node		d	h	m
☽ Last Quarter		2	14	32
● New Moon		10	17	07
☾ First Quarter		18	12	50
○ Full Moon		25	03	39
Apogee (406,423 km)		9	02	18
Perigee (358,816 km)		24	02	55

Mean longitude of ascending node on May 1, 235°

THE SUN

s.d. 15′.8

Day	Right Ascension	Dec. +	Equation of time	Rise 52°	Rise 56°	Transit	Set 52°	Set 56°	Sidereal time	Transit of First Point of Aries
	h m s	° ′	m s	h m	h m	h m	h m	h m	h m s	h m s
1	2 31 56	14 56	+2 51	4 31	4 17	11 57	19 24	19 39	14 34 47	9 23 41
2	2 35 45	15 14	+2 59	4 29	4 15	11 57	19 26	19 41	14 38 43	9 19 45
3	2 39 35	15 32	+3 05	4 27	4 12	11 57	19 28	19 43	14 42 40	9 15 49
4	2 43 25	15 50	+3 12	4 25	4 10	11 57	19 29	19 45	14 46 37	9 11 53
5	2 47 16	16 07	+3 17	4 23	4 08	11 57	19 31	19 47	14 50 33	9 07 57
6	2 51 07	16 24	+3 22	4 22	4 06	11 57	19 33	19 49	14 54 30	9 04 01
7	2 54 59	16 41	+3 27	4 20	4 04	11 57	19 34	19 51	14 58 26	9 00 05
8	2 58 52	16 58	+3 31	4 18	4 02	11 56	19 36	19 53	15 02 23	8 56 09
9	3 02 45	17 14	+3 34	4 16	3 59	11 56	19 38	19 55	15 06 19	8 52 13
10	3 06 39	17 30	+3 37	4 15	3 57	11 56	19 39	19 57	15 10 16	8 48 17
11	3 10 34	17 46	+3 39	4 13	3 55	11 56	19 41	19 59	15 14 12	8 44 21
12	3 14 29	18 01	+3 40	4 11	3 53	11 56	19 42	20 00	15 18 09	8 40 26
13	3 18 24	18 16	+3 41	4 10	3 52	11 56	19 44	20 02	15 22 06	8 36 30
14	3 22 20	18 31	+3 42	4 08	3 50	11 56	19 45	20 04	15 26 02	8 32 34
15	3 26 17	18 45	+3 42	4 07	3 48	11 56	19 47	20 06	15 29 59	8 28 38
16	3 30 14	19 00	+3 41	4 05	3 46	11 56	19 49	20 08	15 33 55	8 24 42
17	3 34 12	19 13	+3 40	4 04	3 44	11 56	19 50	20 10	15 37 52	8 20 46
18	3 38 10	19 27	+3 38	4 02	3 42	11 56	19 52	20 12	15 41 48	8 16 50
19	3 42 09	19 40	+3 36	4 01	3 41	11 56	19 53	20 13	15 45 45	8 12 54
20	3 46 08	19 53	+3 33	3 59	3 39	11 56	19 54	20 15	15 49 41	8 08 58
21	3 50 08	20 05	+3 30	3 58	3 37	11 57	19 56	20 17	15 53 38	8 05 02
22	3 54 09	20 18	+3 26	3 57	3 36	11 57	19 57	20 19	15 57 35	8 01 06
23	3 58 10	20 29	+3 22	3 56	3 34	11 57	19 59	20 20	16 01 31	7 57 11
24	4 02 11	20 41	+3 17	3 54	3 33	11 57	20 00	20 22	16 05 28	7 53 15
25	4 06 13	20 52	+3 11	3 53	3 31	11 57	20 01	20 24	16 09 24	7 49 19
26	4 10 15	21 03	+3 05	3 52	3 30	11 57	20 03	20 25	16 13 21	7 45 23
27	4 14 18	21 13	+2 59	3 51	3 28	11 57	20 04	20 27	16 17 17	7 41 27
28	4 18 22	21 23	+2 52	3 50	3 27	11 57	20 05	20 28	16 21 14	7 37 31
29	4 22 26	21 33	+2 45	3 49	3 26	11 57	20 06	20 30	16 25 10	7 33 35
30	4 26 30	21 42	+2 37	3 48	3 25	11 57	20 08	20 31	16 29 07	7 29 39
31	4 30 35	21 51	+2 29	3 47	3 23	11 58	20 09	20 33	16 33 04	7 25 43

DURATION OF TWILIGHT (in minutes)

Latitude	52°	56°	52°	56°	52°	56°	52°	56°
	1 May		11 May		21 May		31 May	
Civil	39	45	41	49	44	53	46	57
Nautical	90	106	97	121	106	143	116	TAN
Astronomical	154	209	179	TAN	TAN	TAN	TAN	TAN

THE NIGHT SKY

Mercury is at greatest eastern elongation (23°) on the 30th and thus is visible in the evenings, magnitude −1.1 to +0.6, after the first ten days of the month. It may be detected low above the WNW horizon around the time of end of evening civil twilight. This evening apparition is the most favourable one of the year for observers in the northern hemisphere. Mercury will be passing about 8° north of Aldebaran on the 14th to 16th.

Venus is a brilliant object, magnitude −3.9, visible in the western sky for nearly two hours after sunset. The New Moon will be seen near the planet on the 12th to 13th. Venus passes 6° north of Aldebaran on the 5th.

Mars is unsuitably placed for observation.

Jupiter, magnitude −2.4, is only just past opposition and therefore continues to be visible throughout the hours of darkness. The Moon, near Full, is close to Jupiter on the 23rd.

Saturn, magnitude +1.0, is a morning object, visible in the SE sky for a while before dawn, though never at any great altitude. The thin crescent Moon will be seen near Saturn on the mornings of the 4th and 5th.

Eclipse. A partial eclipse of the Moon occurs on the 25th, visible from the British Isles (*see* page 66 for details).

THE MOON

Day	RA	Dec.	Hor. par.	Semi- diam.	Sun's co- long.	PA of Bright Limb	Phase	Age	Rise 52°	Rise 56°	Transit	Set 52°	Set 56°
	h m	°	′	′	°	°	%	d	h m	h m	h m	h m	h m
1	19 27	−17.5	57.9	15.8	153	80	67	20.0	0 29	0 45	5 03	9 44	9 28
2	20 21	−14.4	57.0	15.5	165	76	56	21.0	1 01	1 14	5 54	10 55	10 43
3	21 11	−10.7	56.2	15.3	177	73	46	22.0	1 27	1 36	6 41	12 05	11 57
4	21 59	− 6.7	55.5	15.1	189	71	36	23.0	1 50	1 55	7 26	13 13	13 09
5	22 46	− 2.4	54.9	15.0	202	70	27	24.0	2 10	2 12	8 09	14 20	14 20
6	23 31	+ 1.8	54.5	14.8	214	70	19	25.0	2 29	2 28	8 51	15 25	15 29
7	0 16	+ 6.0	54.2	14.8	226	71	12	26.0	2 49	2 44	9 34	16 30	16 37
8	1 01	+ 9.9	54.0	14.7	238	73	7	27.0	3 10	3 02	10 16	17 34	17 46
9	1 47	+13.4	54.0	14.7	251	76	3	28.0	3 34	3 22	11 00	18 38	18 53
10	2 34	+16.3	54.0	14.7	263	80	0	29.0	4 01	3 46	11 46	19 40	19 58
11	3 23	+18.6	54.1	14.7	275	254	0	0.3	4 34	4 15	12 33	20 39	20 59
12	4 13	+20.1	54.3	14.8	287	264	2	1.3	5 13	4 53	13 22	21 33	21 54
13	5 05	+20.7	54.6	14.9	300	269	5	2.3	6 00	5 38	14 11	22 21	22 41
14	5 57	+20.4	55.0	15.3	312	274	10	3.3	6 54	6 34	15 01	23 01	23 20
15	6 49	+19.0	55.5	15.1	324	278	16	4.3	7 55	7 37	15 51	23 36	23 52
16	7 41	+16.7	56.0	15.3	336	283	25	5.3	9 02	8 47	16 40	—	—
17	8 32	+13.6	56.7	15.4	349	286	34	6.3	10 12	10 01	17 29	0 06	0 18
18	9 24	+ 9.7	57.4	15.6	1	289	44	7.3	11 25	11 19	18 18	0 32	0 40
19	10 15	+ 5.3	58.2	15.9	13	290	55	8.3	12 41	12 39	19 07	0 56	1 00
20	11 07	+ 0.4	59.0	16.1	25	291	66	9.3	13 59	14 02	19 58	1 20	1 20
21	12 00	− 4.6	59.8	16.3	37	291	77	10.3	15 20	15 27	20 51	1 44	1 40
22	12 56	− 9.4	60.5	16.5	50	289	86	11.3	16 43	16 55	21 47	2 10	2 02
23	13 54	−13.8	60.9	16.6	62	287	93	12.3	18 06	18 23	22 46	2 41	2 28
24	14 55	−17.4	61.1	16.6	74	284	98	13.3	19 26	19 46	23 48	3 19	3 02
25	15 58	−19.8	61.0	16.6	86	300	100	14.3	20 37	20 58	—	4 06	3 46
26	17 02	−20.7	60.6	16.5	98	86	99	15.3	21 36	21 57	0 50	5 04	4 42
27	18 04	−20.2	59.9	16.3	110	83	95	16.3	22 23	22 41	1 52	6 10	5 50
28	19 05	−18.4	59.1	16.1	123	79	89	17.3	23 00	23 14	2 50	7 23	7 05
29	20 01	−15.6	58.1	15.8	135	75	81	18.3	23 29	23 40	3 44	8 37	8 23
30	20 55	−12.0	57.2	15.6	147	72	72	19.3	23 54	—	4 35	9 50	9 40
31	21 45	− 8.0	56.3	15.3	159	69	62	20.3	—	0 00	5 22	11 00	10 55

MERCURY

Day	RA	Dec.	Diam.	Phase	Transit	5° high 52°	5° high 56°
	h m	°	″	%	h m	h m	h m
1	2 35	+15.0	5	100	12 02	18 52	19 02
3	2 51	+16.6	5	99	12 11	19 10	19 22
5	3 08	+18.2	5	98	12 20	19 28	19 41
7	3 25	+19.6	5	95	12 29	19 45	20 00
9	3 43	+20.9	5	91	12 39	20 02	20 18
11	3 59	+22.1	6	87	12 48	20 18	20 35
13	4 16	+23.1	6	81	12 56	20 32	20 51
15	4 32	+23.9	6	76	13 04	20 45	21 04
17	4 48	+24.6	6	70	13 12	20 56	21 16
19	5 02	+25.0	6	65	13 18	21 05	21 26
21	5 16	+25.4	7	59	13 24	21 13	21 34
23	5 29	+25.6	7	54	13 29	21 18	21 40
25	5 41	+25.6	7	49	13 33	21 22	21 43
27	5 52	+25.6	8	44	13 35	21 24	21 45
29	6 02	+25.4	8	40	13 37	21 24	21 45
31	6 10	+25.2	8	35	13 37	21 22	21 43

VENUS

Day	RA	Dec.	Diam.	Phase	Transit	5° high 52°	5° high 56°
	h m	°	″	%	h m	h m	h m
1	4 15	+22.0	11	90	13 41	21 08	21 25
6	4 41	+23.1	11	89	13 47	21 21	21 39
11	5 07	+24.0	12	88	13 53	21 33	21 52
16	5 33	+24.6	12	87	14 00	21 43	22 03
21	6 00	+24.9	12	85	14 07	21 52	22 12
26	6 26	+25.0	12	84	14 14	21 58	22 19
31	6 52	+24.7	13	82	14 20	22 02	22 22

MARS

Day	RA	Dec.	Diam.	Phase	Transit	5° high 52°	5° high 56°
1	0 48	+ 4.1	4	97	10 13	4 24	4 24
6	1 02	+ 5.6	4	97	10 07	4 11	4 10
11	1 16	+ 7.1	4	97	10 01	3 58	3 55
16	1 30	+ 8.5	4	96	9 56	3 45	3 41
21	1 44	+ 9.9	4	96	9 50	3 32	3 27
26	1 59	+11.3	4	96	9 45	3 20	3 14
31	2 13	+12.6	4	96	9 40	3 07	3 00

SUNRISE AND SUNSET

	London		Bristol		Birmingham		Manchester		Newcastle		Glasgow		Belfast	
	0°05′	51°30′	2°35′	51°28′	1°55′	52°28′	2°15′	53°28′	1°37′	54°59′	4°14′	55°52′	5°56′	54°35′
	h m	h m	h m	h m	h m	h m	h m	h m	h m	h m	h m	h m	h m	h m
1	4 33	19 23	4 43	19 33	4 37	19 34	4 35	19 38	4 27	19 41	4 34	19 55	4 46	19 57
2	4 31	19 25	4 41	19 35	4 35	19 35	4 33	19 40	4 25	19 43	4 32	19 57	4 44	19 59
3	4 29	19 26	4 39	19 36	4 33	19 37	4 31	19 42	4 23	19 45	4 30	19 59	4 42	20 01
4	4 27	19 28	4 37	19 38	4 31	19 39	4 29	19 44	4 21	19 47	4 28	20 01	4 40	20 03
5	4 25	19 30	4 36	19 40	4 29	19 40	4 27	19 45	4 19	19 49	4 25	20 03	4 38	20 05
6	4 24	19 31	4 34	19 41	4 28	19 42	4 25	19 47	4 17	19 51	4 23	20 05	4 36	20 06
7	4 22	19 33	4 32	19 43	4 26	19 44	4 23	19 49	4 15	19 53	4 21	20 07	4 33	20 08
8	4 20	19 34	4 30	19 44	4 24	19 45	4 21	19 51	4 13	19 55	4 19	20 09	4 32	20 10
9	4 19	19 36	4 29	19 46	4 22	19 47	4 20	19 52	4 11	19 56	4 17	20 11	4 30	20 12
10	4 17	19 38	4 27	19 47	4 20	19 49	4 18	19 54	4 09	19 58	4 15	20 13	4 28	20 14
11	4 15	19 39	4 25	19 49	4 19	19 50	4 16	19 56	4 07	20 00	4 13	20 15	4 26	20 16
12	4 14	19 41	4 24	19 51	4 17	19 52	4 14	19 58	4 05	20 02	4 11	20 17	4 24	20 17
13	4 12	19 42	4 22	19 52	4 15	19 54	4 13	19 59	4 03	20 04	4 09	20 19	4 22	20 19
14	4 11	19 44	4 21	19 54	4 14	19 55	4 11	20 01	4 01	20 06	4 07	20 21	4 20	20 21
15	4 09	19 45	4 19	19 55	4 12	19 57	4 09	20 03	3 59	20 07	4 05	20 22	4 19	20 23
16	4 08	19 47	4 18	19 57	4 11	19 58	4 08	20 04	3 58	20 09	4 04	20 24	4 17	20 24
17	4 06	19 48	4 16	19 58	4 09	20 00	4 06	20 06	3 56	20 11	4 02	20 26	4 15	20 26
18	4 05	19 50	4 15	20 00	4 08	20 01	4 04	20 07	3 54	20 13	4 00	20 28	4 14	20 28
19	4 03	19 51	4 13	20 01	4 06	20 03	4 03	20 09	3 53	20 14	3 58	20 30	4 12	20 29
20	4 02	19 53	4 12	20 02	4 05	20 04	4 01	20 11	3 51	20 16	3 57	20 31	4 10	20 31
21	4 01	19 54	4 11	20 04	4 04	20 06	4 00	20 12	3 50	20 18	3 55	20 33	4 09	20 33
22	3 59	19 55	4 10	20 05	4 02	20 07	3 59	20 14	3 48	20 19	3 53	20 35	4 07	20 34
23	3 58	19 57	4 08	20 07	4 01	20 09	3 57	20 15	3 47	20 21	3 52	20 37	4 06	20 36
24	3 57	19 58	4 07	20 08	4 00	20 10	3 56	20 17	3 45	20 22	3 50	20 38	4 05	20 37
25	3 56	19 59	4 06	20 09	3 58	20 11	3 55	20 18	3 44	20 24	3 49	20 40	4 03	20 39
26	3 55	20 01	4 05	20 10	3 57	20 13	3 53	20 19	3 42	20 25	3 47	20 41	4 02	20 40
27	3 54	20 02	4 04	20 12	3 56	20 14	3 52	20 21	3 41	20 27	3 46	20 43	4 01	20 42
28	3 53	20 03	4 03	20 13	3 55	20 15	3 51	20 22	3 40	20 28	3 45	20 44	4 00	20 43
29	3 52	20 04	4 02	20 14	3 54	20 17	3 50	20 23	3 39	20 30	3 44	20 46	3 58	20 45
30	3 51	20 05	4 01	20 15	3 53	20 18	3 49	20 25	3 38	20 31	3 42	20 47	3 57	20 46
31	3 50	20 07	4 00	20 16	3 52	20 19	3 48	20 26	3 36	20 32	3 41	20 49	3 56	20 47

JUPITER

Day	RA	Dec.	Transit	5° high	
				52°	56°
	h m	° ′	h m	h m	h m
1	14 31.0	−13 24	23 52	4 08	3 52
11	14 26.1	−13 01	23 08	3 27	3 11
21	14 21.5	−12 39	22 24	2 45	2 29
31	14 17.6	−12 22	21 41	2 04	1 48

Diameters – equatorial 44″ polar 42″

SATURN

Day	RA	Dec.	Transit	5° high	
				52°	56°
	h m	° ′	h m	h m	h m
1	22 49.2	− 9 12	8 13	3 36	3 48
11	22 52.0	− 8 58	7 37	2 58	3 10
21	22 54.3	− 8 46	7 00	2 20	2 31
31	22 56.0	− 8 38	6 22	1 42	1 53

Diameters – equatorial 17″ polar 15″
Rings – major axis 38″ minor axis 3″

URANUS

Day	RA	Dec.	Transit	10° high	
				52°	56°
	h m	° ′	h m	h m	h m
1	19 53.8	−21 22	2 53	2 53	3 43
11	19 53.7	−21 23	4 39	2 13	3 03
21	19 53.1	−21 25	3 59	1 34	2 24
31	19 52.3	−21 27	3 19	0 54	1 45

Diameter 4″

NEPTUNE

Day	RA	Dec.	Transit	10° high	
				52°	56°
	h m	° ′	h m	h m	h m
1	19 40.3	−20 49	5 05	2 33	3 19
11	19 40.1	−20 49	4 25	1 54	2 40
21	19 39.6	−20 50	3 45	1 14	2 00
31	19 39.0	−20 52	3 05	0 34	1 21

Diameter 2″

June 1994

SIXTH MONTH, 30 DAYS. *Junius*, Roman *gens* (family)

Sun's Longitude 90° ♋ 21ᵈ 15ʰ

1	*Wednesday*	John Masefield *b.* 1878. Sir Hugh Walpole *d.* 1941	*week 22 day* 152
2	*Thursday*	**Corpus Christi.** *Coronation Day 1953*	153
3	*Friday*	Jefferson Davis *b.* 1808. Samuel Plimsoll *d.* 1898	154
4	*Saturday*	Giovanni Casanova de Seingalt *d.* 1798	155
5	*Sunday*	**2nd S. after Pentecost.** Adam Smith *b.* 1723	*week 23 day* 156
6	*Monday*	Pierre Corneille *b.* 1606. Carl Jung *d.* 1961	157
7	*Tuesday*	*Trinity Law Sittings begin.* Paul Gauguin *b.* 1848	158
8	*Wednesday*	John Smeaton *b.* 1724. Thomas Paine *d.* 1809	159
9	*Thursday*	George Stephenson *b.* 1781. Angus McBean *d.* 1990	160
10	*Friday*	MUSLIM NEW YEAR (1415). *Duke of Edinburgh b. 1921*	161
11	*Saturday*	**St Barnabas.** Queen's Official Birthday	162
12	*Sunday*	**3rd S. after Pentecost.** Leon Goossens *b.* 1897	*week 24 day* 163
13	*Monday*	W. B. Yeats *b.* 1865. Sir Henry Segrave *b.* 1930	164
14	*Tuesday*	Harriet Beecher Stowe *b.* 1811	165
15	*Wednesday*	Magna Carta sealed 1215. Watt Tyler *exec.* 1381	166
16	*Thursday*	Field Marshal Earl Alexander of Tunis *d.* 1969	167
17	*Friday*	Edward I *b.* 1239. Joseph Addison *d.* 1719	168
18	*Saturday*	Waterloo 1815. Samuel Butler *d.* 1902	169
19	*Sunday*	**4th S. after Pentecost.** Blaise Pascal *b.* 1623	*week 25 day* 170
20	*Monday*	Errol Flynn *b.* 1909. Sir Charles Groves *d.* 1992	171
21	*Tuesday*	Prince William of Wales *b.* 1982	172
22	*Wednesday*	Rider Haggard *b.* 1856. Judy Garland *d.* 1969	173
23	*Thursday*	Edward VIII *b.* 1894. Sir Leonard Hutton *b.* 1916	174
24	*Friday*	**St John the Baptist.** John Hampden *d.* 1643	175
25	*Saturday*	Earl Mountbatten of Burma *b.* 1900	176
26	*Sunday*	**5th S. after Pentecost.** Gilbert White *d.* 1793	*week 26 day* 177
27	*Monday*	Harriet Martineau *d.* 1876. Helen Keller *b.* 1880	178
28	*Tuesday*	Treaty of Versailles signed 1919	179
29	*Wednesday*	**St Peter.** Trades unions legalized 1871	180
30	*Thursday*	William Barents *d.* 1597. Tower Bridge opened 1894	181

ASTRONOMICAL PHENOMENA

d	h	
1	07	Saturn in conjunction with Moon. Saturn 6° S.
6	03	Mars in conjunction with Moon. Mars 2° S.
10	23	Mercury in conjunction with Moon. Mercury 3° N.
12	10	Venus in conjunction with Moon. Venus 7° N.
19	15	Jupiter in conjunction with Moon. Jupiter 3° N.
21	15	Solstice
25	10	Mercury in inferior conjunction
28	16	Saturn in conjunction with Moon. Saturn 6° S.

CONSTELLATIONS

The following constellations are near the meridian at

	d	h
May	1	24
May	16	23
June	1	22
June	15	21
July	1	20
July	16	19

Cassiopeia (below the Pole), Ursa Minor, Draco, Ursa Major, Canes Venatici, Bootes, Corona, Serpens, Virgo and Libra

MINIMA OF ALGOL

Algol is inconveniently situated for observation during June.

THE MOON

Phases, Apsides and Node	d	h	m
☾ Last Quarter	1	04	02
● New Moon	9	08	26
☽ First Quarter	16	19	57
○ Full Moon	23	11	33
☾ Last Quarter	30	19	31
Apogee (405,693 km)	5	12	38
Perigee (362,954 km)	21	06	43

Mean longitude of ascending node on June 1, 233°

THE SUN

s.d. 15′.8

Day	Right Ascension	Dec. +	Equation of time	Rise 52°	Rise 56°	Transit	Set 52°	Set 56°	Sidereal time	Transit of First Point of Aries
	h m s	° ′	m s	h m	h m	h m	h m	h m	h m s	h m s
1	4 34 40	21 59	+2 20	3 46	3 22	11 58	20 10	20 34	16 37 00	7 21 47
2	4 38 46	22 08	+2 11	3 45	3 21	11 58	20 11	20 35	16 40 57	7 17 51
3	4 42 52	22 15	+2 01	3 45	3 20	11 58	20 12	20 37	16 44 53	7 13 56
4	4 46 58	22 23	+1 51	3 44	3 19	11 58	20 13	20 38	16 48 50	7 10 00
5	4 51 05	22 30	+1 41	3 43	3 18	11 58	20 14	20 39	16 52 46	7 06 04
6	4 55 12	22 36	+1 31	3 43	3 18	11 59	20 15	20 40	16 56 43	7 02 08
7	4 59 20	22 42	+1 20	3 42	3 17	11 59	20 16	20 41	17 00 39	6 58 12
8	5 03 28	22 48	+1 08	3 42	3 16	11 59	20 17	20 42	17 04 36	6 54 16
9	5 07 36	22 54	+0 57	3 41	3 16	11 59	20 18	20 43	17 08 33	6 50 20
10	5 11 44	22 58	+0 45	3 41	3 15	11 59	20 18	20 44	17 12 29	6 46 24
11	5 15 53	23 03	+0 33	3 40	3 14	12 00	20 19	20 45	17 16 26	6 42 28
12	5 20 02	23 07	+0 21	3 40	3 14	12 00	20 20	20 46	17 20 22	6 38 32
13	5 24 11	23 11	+0 08	3 40	3 14	12 00	20 20	20 47	17 24 19	6 34 36
14	5 28 20	23 14	−0 04	3 40	3 13	12 00	20 21	20 47	17 28 15	6 30 40
15	5 32 29	23 17	−0 17	3 39	3 13	12 00	20 22	20 48	17 32 12	6 26 45
16	5 36 38	23 20	−0 30	3 39	3 13	12 01	20 22	20 49	17 36 08	6 22 49
17	5 40 48	23 22	−0 43	3 39	3 13	12 01	20 23	20 49	17 40 05	6 18 53
18	5 44 57	23 24	−0 56	3 39	3 13	12 01	20 23	20 49	17 44 02	6 14 57
19	5 49 07	23 25	−1 09	3 39	3 13	12 01	20 23	20 50	17 47 58	6 11 01
20	5 53 16	23 26	−1 22	3 39	3 13	12 01	20 24	20 50	17 51 55	6 07 05
21	5 57 26	23 26	−1 35	3 40	3 13	12 02	20 24	20 50	17 55 51	6 03 09
22	6 01 36	23 26	−1 48	3 40	3 13	12 02	20 24	20 51	17 59 48	5 59 13
23	6 05 45	23 26	−2 01	3 40	3 14	12 02	20 24	20 51	18 03 44	5 55 17
24	6 09 54	23 25	−2 14	3 40	3 14	12 02	20 24	20 51	18 07 41	5 51 21
25	6 14 04	23 24	−2 26	3 41	3 14	12 03	20 24	20 51	18 11 37	5 47 25
26	6 18 13	23 22	−2 39	3 41	3 15	12 03	20 24	20 51	18 15 34	5 43 30
27	6 22 22	23 20	−2 52	3 42	3 15	12 03	20 24	20 50	18 19 31	5 39 34
28	6 26 31	23 18	−3 04	3 42	3 16	12 03	20 24	20 50	18 23 27	5 35 38
29	6 30 40	23 15	−3 16	3 43	3 17	12 03	20 24	20 50	18 27 24	5 31 42
30	6 34 48	23 12	−3 28	3 43	3 17	12 04	20 23	20 49	18 31 20	5 27 46

DURATION OF TWILIGHT (in minutes)

Latitude	52°	56°	52°	56°	52°	56°	52°	56°
	1 June		11 June		21 June		30 June	
Civil	47	58	48	61	49	63	49	62
Nautical	117	TAN	125	TAN	128	TAN	125	TAN
Astronomical	TAN	TAN	TAN	TAN	TAN	TAN	TAN	TAN

THE NIGHT SKY

Mercury may possibly be detected, magnitude +1, low above the WNW horizon, around the time of end of evening civil twilight, for the first week of the month. For the remainder of June it is unsuitably placed for observation, inferior conjunction occurring on the 25th.

Venus, magnitude −4.0, is visible in the western sky in the evenings. Although it is continuing to increase its eastern elongation from the Sun, the period available for observation actually decreases slightly during the month because it is moving southwards in declination and also because the Sun is setting about a quarter of an hour later at the end of the month than it is at the beginning. The three-day-old Moon will be seen near Venus on the 11th to 12th.

Mars, magnitude +1.2, is very gradually emerging from the long morning twilight. It will not be an easy object to detect, low above the eastern horizon before the sky gets too bright.

Jupiter is a brilliant evening object in Virgo, magnitude −2.3. By the end of the month it will be too low in the southwest for observation after midnight. It is slowing down in its retrograde path and is virtually stationary by the end of the month. The gibbous Moon is near the planet on the 19th.

Saturn is a morning object, in Aquarius, reaching its first stationary point on the 23rd. It is gradually becoming visible for longer each night and by the end of June should be visible low above the ESE horizon shortly before midnight. Its magnitude is +0.9. On the morning of the 1st the Moon, near Last Quarter, passes 6° north of the planet. The Moon is again in the vicinity of Saturn on the mornings of the 28th and 29th.

THE MOON

Day	RA	Dec.	Hor. par.	Semi-diam.	Sun's co-long.	PA of Bright Limb	Phase	Age	Rise 52°	Rise 56°	Transit	Set 52°	Set 56°
	h m	°	′	′	°	°	%	d	h m	h m	h m	h m	h m
1	22 32	− 3.7	55.6	15.1	171	68	52	21.3	0 15	0 18	6 06	12 08	12 07
2	23 18	+ 0.6	55.0	15.0	184	68	42	22.3	0 35	0 35	6 49	13 15	13 17
3	0 03	+ 4.9	54.5	14.8	196	68	33	23.3	0 55	0 51	7 32	14 20	14 26
4	0 49	+ 8.8	54.2	14.8	208	69	24	24.3	1 16	1 08	8 14	15 25	15 35
5	1 35	+12.5	54.1	14.7	220	71	16	25.3	1 38	1 27	8 58	16 29	16 42
6	2 22	+15.6	54.1	14.7	233	73	10	26.3	2 04	1 50	9 43	17 32	17 49
7	3 10	+18.1	54.2	14.8	245	75	5	27.3	2 35	2 17	10 29	18 32	18 52
8	4 00	+19.8	54.4	14.8	257	76	2	28.3	3 12	2 52	11 18	19 28	19 49
9	4 52	+20.7	54.7	14.9	269	59	0	29.3	3 56	3 35	12 07	20 18	20 40
10	5 44	+20.6	55.1	15.0	282	289	0	0.6	4 48	4 27	12 58	21 02	21 22
11	6 36	+19.5	55.5	15.1	294	284	3	1.6	5 48	5 29	13 48	21 39	21 56
12	7 29	+17.4	55.9	15.2	306	286	7	2.6	6 53	6 37	14 38	22 10	22 24
13	8 21	+14.5	56.4	15.4	318	289	13	3.6	8 03	7 51	15 27	22 38	22 47
14	9 12	+10.8	57.0	15.5	331	291	21	4.6	9 15	9 07	16 15	23 02	23 07
15	10 03	+ 6.5	57.6	15.7	343	293	30	5.6	10 29	10 25	17 04	23 25	23 26
16	10 53	+ 1.8	58.2	15.9	355	293	41	6.6	11 44	11 45	17 53	23 48	23 45
17	11 45	− 3.1	58.8	16.0	7	293	52	7.6	13 02	13 07	18 43	—	—
18	12 38	− 7.9	59.4	16.2	19	292	63	8.6	14 21	14 31	19 36	0 13	0 06
19	13 34	−12.3	59.9	16.3	32	290	74	9.6	15 42	15 56	20 32	0 40	0 29
20	14 32	−16.1	60.2	16.4	44	287	84	10.6	17 01	17 19	21 30	1 14	0 58
21	15 32	−18.9	60.4	16.5	56	284	91	11.6	18 15	18 36	22 31	1 55	1 36
22	16 35	−20.5	60.3	16.4	68	282	97	12.6	19 20	19 41	23 33	2 46	2 24
23	17 38	−20.6	60.1	16.4	80	295	100	13.6	20 13	20 33	—	3 47	3 26
24	18 39	−19.4	59.5	16.2	93	58	100	14.6	20 55	21 12	0 33	4 58	4 38
25	19 38	−17.0	58.8	16.0	105	68	97	15.6	21 28	21 41	1 30	6 12	5 56
26	20 34	−13.6	58.0	15.8	117	68	92	16.6	21 56	22 04	2 23	7 27	7 16
27	21 26	− 9.6	57.2	15.6	129	67	85	17.6	22 19	22 24	3 13	8 41	8 33
28	22 16	− 5.3	56.4	15.4	141	66	77	18.6	22 40	22 41	4 00	9 52	9 48
29	23 03	− 0.9	55.6	15.2	154	65	68	19.6	23 00	22 58	4 44	11 00	11 01
30	23 49	+ 3.4	55.0	15.0	166	66	58	20.6	23 21	23 15	5 28	12 07	12 12

MERCURY

Day	RA	Dec.	Diam.	Phase	Transit	5° high 52°	5° high 56°
	h m	°	″	%	h m	h m	h m
1	6 14	+25.0	8	33	13 37	21 21	21 41
3	6 21	+24.6	9	29	13 36	21 17	21 36
5	6 27	+24.2	9	25	13 33	21 11	21 30
7	6 31	+23.7	10	22	13 29	21 04	21 22
9	6 34	+23.2	10	18	13 24	20 55	21 13
11	6 36	+22.7	11	14	13 18	20 45	21 02
13	6 36	+22.2	11	11	13 10	20 33	20 50
15	6 35	+21.6	11	8	13 01	20 21	20 37
17	6 33	+21.1	12	6	12 50	20 07	20 22
19	6 30	+20.6	12	4	12 39	19 53	20 08
21	6 26	+20.1	12	2	12 27	19 38	19 52
23	6 21	+19.7	12	1	12 14	19 23	19 37
25	6 16	+19.3	12	1	12 02	19 08	19 22
27	6 11	+19.0	12	1	11 49	4 43	4 30
29	6 07	+18.8	12	2	11 37	4 32	4 19
31	6 03	+18.7	11	4	11 25	4 21	4 08

VENUS

Day	RA	Dec.	Diam.	Phase	Transit	5° high 52°	5° high 56°
	h m	°	″	%	h m	h m	h m
1	6 58	+24.6	13	82	14 21	22 03	22 23
6	7 24	+24.0	13	81	14 28	22 05	22 24
11	7 49	+23.1	13	79	14 33	22 04	22 22
16	8 14	+21.9	14	78	14 38	22 02	22 18
21	8 38	+20.5	14	76	14 43	21 58	22 13
26	9 02	+18.9	15	74	14 47	21 52	22 05
31	9 25	+17.1	15	73	14 50	21 45	21 56

MARS

Day	RA	Dec.	Diam.	Phase	Transit	5° high 52°	5° high 56°
1	2 16	+12.8	4	96	9 38	3 05	2 58
6	2 30	+14.1	4	95	9 33	2 53	2 45
11	2 45	+15.2	4	95	9 28	2 41	2 32
16	2 59	+16.4	5	95	9 23	2 30	2 19
21	3 14	+17.4	5	95	9 17	2 19	2 08
26	3 28	+18.4	5	94	9 12	2 09	1 56
31	3 43	+19.3	5	94	9 07	1 58	1 45

SUNRISE AND SUNSET

	London		Bristol		Birmingham		Manchester		Newcastle		Glasgow		Belfast	
	0°05′	51°30′	2°35′	51°28′	1°55′	52°28′	2°15′	53°28′	1°37′	54°59′	4°14′	55°52′	5°56′	54°35′
	h m	h m	h m	h m	h m	h m	h m	h m	h m	h m	h m	h m	h m	h m
1	3 49	20 08	3 59	20 18	3 51	20 20	3 47	20 27	3 35	20 34	3 40	20 50	3 55	20 49
2	3 48	20 09	3 58	20 19	3 51	20 21	3 46	20 28	3 34	20 35	3 39	20 51	3 54	20 50
3	3 48	20 10	3 58	20 20	3 50	20 22	3 45	20 29	3 34	20 36	3 38	20 53	3 53	20 51
4	3 47	20 11	3 57	20 21	3 49	20 23	3 45	20 30	3 33	20 37	3 37	20 54	3 52	20 52
5	3 46	20 12	3 56	20 22	3 48	20 24	3 44	20 32	3 32	20 39	3 36	20 55	3 52	20 53
6	3 46	20 13	3 56	20 23	3 48	20 25	3 43	20 33	3 31	20 40	3 35	20 56	3 51	20 54
7	3 45	20 14	3 55	20 23	3 47	20 26	3 43	20 33	3 30	20 41	3 35	20 57	3 50	20 55
8	3 45	20 14	3 55	20 24	3 47	20 27	3 42	20 34	3 30	20 42	3 34	20 58	3 50	20 56
9	3 44	20 15	3 54	20 25	3 46	20 28	3 42	20 35	3 29	20 43	3 33	20 59	3 49	20 57
10	3 44	20 16	3 54	20 26	3 46	20 29	3 41	20 36	3 29	20 43	3 33	21 00	3 49	20 58
11	3 43	20 17	3 54	20 27	3 45	20 29	3 41	20 37	3 28	20 44	3 32	21 01	3 48	20 59
12	3 43	20 17	3 53	20 27	3 45	20 30	3 40	20 38	3 28	20 45	3 32	21 02	3 48	21 00
13	3 43	20 18	3 53	20 28	3 45	20 31	3 40	20 38	3 27	20 46	3 32	21 03	3 48	21 00
14	3 43	20 19	3 53	20 28	3 45	20 31	3 40	20 39	3 27	20 46	3 31	21 03	3 47	21 01
15	3 43	20 19	3 53	20 29	3 44	20 32	3 40	20 39	3 27	20 47	3 31	21 04	3 47	21 01
16	3 42	20 20	3 53	20 29	3 44	20 32	3 40	20 40	3 27	20 48	3 31	21 04	3 47	21 02
17	3 42	20 20	3 53	20 30	3 44	20 33	3 39	20 40	3 27	20 48	3 31	21 05	3 47	21 02
18	3 42	20 20	3 53	20 30	3 44	20 33	3 39	20 41	3 27	20 48	3 31	21 05	3 47	21 03
19	3 43	20 21	3 53	20 31	3 44	20 34	3 39	20 41	3 27	20 49	3 31	21 06	3 47	21 03
20	3 43	20 21	3 53	20 31	3 44	20 34	3 40	20 41	3 27	20 49	3 31	21 06	3 47	21 04
21	3 43	20 21	3 53	20 31	3 45	20 34	3 40	20 42	3 27	20 49	3 31	21 06	3 47	21 04
22	3 43	20 21	3 53	20 31	3 45	20 34	3 40	20 42	3 27	20 49	3 31	21 06	3 47	21 04
23	3 43	20 22	3 53	20 31	3 45	20 34	3 40	20 42	3 27	20 50	3 31	21 07	3 48	21 04
24	3 44	20 22	3 54	20 31	3 45	20 35	3 41	20 42	3 28	20 50	3 32	21 07	3 48	21 04
25	3 44	20 22	3 54	20 31	3 46	20 35	3 41	20 42	3 28	20 50	3 32	21 07	3 48	21 04
26	3 44	20 22	3 55	20 31	3 46	20 34	3 41	20 42	3 29	20 50	3 33	21 06	3 49	21 04
27	3 45	20 22	3 55	20 31	3 47	20 34	3 42	20 42	3 29	20 49	3 33	21 06	3 49	21 04
28	3 45	20 21	3 56	20 31	3 47	20 34	3 42	20 42	3 30	20 49	3 34	21 06	3 50	21 04
29	3 46	20 21	3 56	20 31	3 48	20 34	3 43	20 41	3 30	20 49	3 34	21 06	3 50	21 03
30	3 47	20 21	3 57	20 31	3 48	20 34	3 44	20 41	3 31	20 49	3 35	21 05	3 51	21 03

JUPITER

Day	RA	Dec.	Transit	5° high	
				52°	56°
	h m	° ′	h m	h m	h m
1	14 17.2	−12 20	21 36	1 59	1 44
11	14 14.3	−12 07	20 54	1 18	1 04
21	14 12.0	−12 00	20 13	0 38	0 23
31	14 11.6	−11 59	19 33	23 54	23 39

Diameters – equatorial 42″ polar 39″

SATURN

Day	RA	Dec.	Transit	5° high	
				52°	56°
	h m	° ′	h m	h m	h m
1	22 56.2	− 8 37	6 18	1 38	1 49
11	22 57.3	− 8 33	5 40	0 59	1 10
21	22 57.8	− 8 32	5 01	0 20	0 31
31	22 57.7	− 8 35	4 22	23 37	23 48

Diameters – equatorial 17″ polar 16″
Rings – major axis 40″ minor axis 3″

URANUS

Day	RA	Dec.	Transit	10° high	
				52°	56°
	h m	° ′	h m	h m	h m
1	19 52.2	−21 28	3 15	0 50	1 41
11	19 51.1	−21 31	2 34	0 10	1 01
21	19 49.7	−21 35	1 54	23 26	0 22
31	19 48.2	−21 39	1 13	22 46	23 38

Diameter 4″

NEPTUNE

Day	RA	Dec.	Transit	10° high	
				52°	56°
	h m	° ′	h m	h m	h m
1	19 38.9	−20 52	3 01	0 30	1 17
11	19 38.1	−20 54	2 21	23 47	0 37
21	19 37.1	−20 56	1 41	23 07	23 54
31	19 36.0	−20 59	1 01	22 27	23 14

Diameter 2″

July 1994

SEVENTH MONTH, 31 DAYS. *Julius* Caesar, formerly *Quintilis*, fifth month of Roman pre-Julian calendar

Sun's Longitude 120° ♌ 23ᵈ02ʰ

1	*Friday*	*Princess of Wales b. 1961.* Boyne 1690	*week 26 day 182*
2	*Saturday*	Sir Tyrone Guthrie *b.* 1900. Ernest Hemingway *d.* 1961	183
3	*Sunday*	**St Thomas. 6th S. after Pentecost**	*week 27 day 184*
4	*Monday*	Independence Day, USA. Louis Armstrong *b.* 1900	185
5	*Tuesday*	National Health Service started 1948	186
6	*Wednesday*	Beatrix Potter *b.* 1866. Otto Klemperer *d.* 1973	187
7	*Thursday*	Gustave Mahler *b.* 1860. Sir Arthur Conan Doyle *d.* 1930	188
8	*Friday*	Edward, the Black Prince *d.* 1376	189
9	*Saturday*	Ottorino Respighi *b.* 1879. Edward Heath *b.* 1916	190
10	*Sunday*	**7th S. after Pentecost.** John Calvin *b.* 1509	*week 28 day 191*
11	*Monday*	Robert the Bruce *b.* 1274. Oudenarde 1708	192
12	*Tuesday*	*Bank Holiday in Northern Ireland*	193
13	*Wednesday*	Jean-Paul Marat *assass.* 1793	194
14	*Thursday*	Fête Nationale, France. Emmeline Pankhurst *b.* 1858	195
15	*Friday*	St Swithin's Day. Inigo Jones *b.* 1573	196
16	*Saturday*	Mary Baker Eddy *b.* 1821. Miles Copeland *b.* 1913	197
17	*Sunday*	**8th S. after Pentecost.** Hardy Amies *b.* 1909	*week 29 day 198*
18	*Monday*	Dr W. G. Grace *b.* 1848. Sir Stanley Rous *d.* 1986	199
19	*Tuesday*	*Mary Rose* sank 1545. Edgar Degas *b.* 1834	200
20	*Wednesday*	Sir Edmund Hillary *b.* 1919	201
21	*Thursday*	Tate Gallery opened 1897. First men on the moon 1969	202
22	*Friday*	**St Mary Magdalen.** Revd William Spooner *b.* 1844	203
23	*Saturday*	Gen. Ulysses Grant *d.* 1885	204
24	*Sunday*	**9th S. after Pentecost.** Peter Sellers *d.* 1980	*week 30 day 205*
25	*Monday*	**St James.** S. T. Coleridge *d.* 1834	206
26	*Tuesday*	George Borrow *d.* 1881. Aldous Huxley *b.* 1894	207
27	*Wednesday*	Bank of England established 1694	208
28	*Thursday*	J. S. Bach *d.* 1750. Gerard Manley Hopkins *b.* 1844	209
29	*Friday*	Defeat of Spanish Armada 1588. Robert Schumann *d.* 1856	210
30	*Saturday*	*Trinity Law Sittings end.* William Penn *d.* 1718	211
31	*Sunday*	**10th S. after Pentecost.** St Ignatius Loyola *d.* 1556	*week 31 day 212*

ASTRONOMICAL PHENOMENA

d	h	
5	05	Mars in conjunction with Moon. Mars 0°.3 N.
5	19	Earth at aphelion (152 million km)
7	13	Mercury in conjunction with Moon. Mercury 1° S.
12	07	Venus in conjunction with Moon. Venus 6° N.
14	16	Neptune at opposition
16	21	Jupiter in conjunction with Moon. Jupiter 2° N.
17	04	Uranus at opposition
17	14	Mercury at greatest elongation W. 21°
25	23	Saturn in conjunction with Moon. Saturn 6° S.

CONSTELLATIONS

The following constellations are near the meridian at

	d	h
June	1	24
June	15	23
July	1	22
July	16	21
August	1	20
August	16	19

Ursa Minor, Draco, Corona, Hercules, Lyra, Serpens, Ophiuchus, Libra, Scorpius and Sagittarius

MINIMA OF ALGOL

d	h	d	h	d	h
1	20.2	13	07.4	24	18.6
4	17.0	16	04.2	27	15.5
7	13.8	19	01.0	30	12.3
10	10.6	21	21.8		

THE MOON

Phases, Apsides and Node	d	h	m
● New Moon	8	21	37
☽ First Quarter	16	01	12
○ Full Moon	22	20	16
☾ Last Quarter	30	12	40
Apogee (404,677 km)	3	04	40
Perigee (367,865 km)	18	17	31
Apogee (404,086 km)	30	22	56

Mean longitude of ascending node on July 1, 232°

THE SUN

s.d. 15′.8

Day	Right Ascension	Dec. +	Equation of time	Rise 52°	Rise 56°	Transit	Set 52°	Set 56°	Sidereal time	Transit of First Point of Aries
	h m s	° ′	m s	h m	h m	h m	h m	h m	h m s	h m s
1	6 38 57	23 08	−3 40	3 44	3 18	12 04	20 23	20 49	18 35 17	5 23 50
2	6 43 05	23 04	−3 52	3 45	3 19	12 04	20 23	20 49	18 39 13	5 19 54
3	6 47 13	23 00	−4 03	3 46	3 20	12 04	20 22	20 48	18 43 10	5 15 58
4	6 51 21	22 55	−4 14	3 46	3 21	12 04	20 22	20 47	18 47 06	5 12 02
5	6 55 28	22 50	−4 25	3 47	3 22	12 05	20 21	20 47	18 51 03	5 08 06
6	6 59 35	22 44	−4 35	3 48	3 23	12 05	20 21	20 46	18 55 00	5 04 10
7	7 03 42	22 38	−4 45	3 49	3 24	12 05	20 20	20 45	18 58 56	5 00 15
8	7 07 48	22 31	−4 55	3 50	3 25	12 05	20 20	20 44	19 02 53	4 56 19
9	7 11 54	22 25	−5 05	3 51	3 26	12 05	20 19	20 43	19 06 49	4 52 23
10	7 15 59	22 17	−5 14	3 52	3 27	12 05	20 18	20 42	19 10 46	4 48 27
11	7 20 05	22 10	−5 22	3 53	3 29	12 05	20 17	20 41	19 14 42	4 44 31
12	7 24 09	22 02	−5 30	3 54	3 30	12 06	20 16	20 40	19 18 39	4 40 35
13	7 28 13	21 53	−5 38	3 55	3 31	12 06	20 16	20 39	19 22 35	4 36 39
14	7 32 17	21 45	−5 45	3 56	3 33	12 06	20 15	20 38	19 26 32	4 32 43
15	7 36 20	21 36	−5 52	3 58	3 34	12 06	20 14	20 36	19 30 29	4 28 47
16	7 40 23	21 26	−5 58	3 59	3 36	12 06	20 13	20 35	19 34 25	4 24 51
17	7 44 25	21 16	−6 03	4 00	3 37	12 06	20 11	20 34	19 38 22	4 20 55
18	7 48 27	21 06	−6 09	4 01	3 39	12 06	20 10	20 32	19 42 18	4 17 00
19	7 52 28	20 56	−6 13	4 03	3 40	12 06	20 09	20 31	19 46 15	4 13 04
20	7 56 28	20 45	−6 17	4 04	3 42	12 06	20 08	20 29	19 50 11	4 09 08
21	8 00 28	20 33	−6 20	4 05	3 44	12 06	20 07	20 28	19 54 08	4 05 12
22	8 04 28	20 22	−6 23	4 07	3 45	12 06	20 05	20 26	19 58 05	4 01 16
23	8 08 27	20 10	−6 26	4 08	3 47	12 06	20 04	20 25	20 02 01	3 57 20
24	8 12 25	19 58	−6 27	4 09	3 49	12 06	20 03	20 23	20 05 58	3 53 24
25	8 16 22	19 45	−6 28	4 11	3 51	12 06	20 01	20 21	20 09 54	3 49 28
26	8 20 19	19 32	−6 29	4 12	3 52	12 06	20 00	20 19	20 13 51	3 45 32
27	8 24 16	19 19	−6 29	4 14	3 54	12 06	19 58	20 18	20 17 47	3 41 36
28	8 28 12	19 05	−6 28	4 15	3 56	12 06	19 57	20 16	20 21 44	3 37 40
29	8 32 07	18 51	−6 27	4 17	3 58	12 06	19 55	20 14	20 25 40	3 33 44
30	8 36 02	18 37	−6 25	4 18	4 00	12 06	19 54	20 12	20 29 37	3 29 49
31	8 39 56	18 23	−6 22	4 20	4 01	12 06	19 52	20 10	20 33 34	3 25 53

DURATION OF TWILIGHT (in minutes)

Latitude	52°	56°	52°	56°	52°	56°	52°	56°
	1 July		11 July		21 July		31 July	
Civil	48	61	46	58	44	53	41	49
Nautical	124	TAN	116	TAN	107	144	98	122
Astronomical	TAN	TAN	TAN	TAN	TAN	TAN	180	TAN

THE NIGHT SKY

Mercury, although reaching greatest western elongation (21°) on the 17th, will be a very difficult object to observe from the British Isles because of the long duration of twilight. It may be possible to detect it low above the ENE horizon at the time of beginning of morning civil twilight, within a day or so of the 21st.

Venus, magnitude −4.1, continues to be visible as a brilliant object low in the western sky after sunset. The crescent Moon is near the planet on the evenings of the 11th and 12th. On the evening of the 10th, Venus will be seen passing 1° north of Regulus, though closest approach occurs before sunset.

Mars is visible as a morning object, magnitude +1.2. Mars is in Taurus, passing between the Hyades and the Pleiades early in the month. On the morning of the 5th the old crescent Moon will be seen approaching Mars.

Jupiter, magnitude −2.1, continues to be visible as a brilliant evening object. It reaches its second stationary point on the 2nd, resuming its direct motion. On the evening of the 16th the Moon, at First Quarter, passes 3° south of the planet.

Saturn, magnitude +0.8, continues to be visible as a morning object in Aquarius. The gibbous Moon is near Saturn on the morning of the 26th.

Uranus is at opposition on the 17th, in Sagittarius. Uranus is barely visible to the naked eye since its magnitude is +5.6, but it is readily located with small optical aid.

Neptune is at opposition on the 14th, also in Sagittarius. It is not visible to the naked eye since its magnitude is +7.9.

THE MOON

Day	RA	Dec.	Hor. par.	Semi-diam.	Sun's co-long.	PA of Bright Limb	Phase	Age	Rise 52°	Rise 56°	Transit	Set 52°	Set 56°
	h m	°	′	′	°	°	%	d	h m	h m	h m	h m	h m
1	0 35	+ 7.5	54.6	14.9	178	67	48	21.6	23 43	23 33	6 10	13 12	13 21
2	1 21	+11.3	54.3	14.8	190	69	39	22.6	—	23 54	6 54	14 17	14 29
3	2 08	+14.6	54.2	14.8	203	71	30	23.6	0 07	—	7 38	15 20	15 36
4	2 56	+17.3	54.2	14.8	215	74	22	24.6	0 36	0 19	8 24	16 22	16 40
5	3 45	+19.3	54.4	14.8	227	77	14	25.6	1 10	0 51	9 12	17 20	17 40
6	4 36	+20.5	54.7	14.9	239	79	8	26.6	1 51	1 30	10 01	18 13	18 34
7	5 28	+20.7	55.1	15.0	252	81	4	27.6	2 41	2 19	10 52	19 00	19 20
8	6 21	+19.9	55.6	15.2	264	74	1	28.6	3 38	3 18	11 43	19 40	19 57
9	7 15	+18.1	56.1	15.3	276	352	0	0.1	4 42	4 25	12 33	20 13	20 28
10	8 07	+15.4	56.6	15.4	288	302	1	1.1	5 51	5 38	13 24	20 42	20 53
11	8 59	+11.8	57.1	15.6	301	297	5	2.1	7 04	6 54	14 13	21 08	21 15
12	9 51	+ 7.6	57.6	15.7	313	296	11	3.1	8 18	8 13	15 02	21 32	21 35
13	10 42	+ 3.0	58.1	15.8	325	296	18	4.1	9 34	9 33	15 51	21 55	21 54
14	11 34	− 1.8	58.5	15.9	337	295	28	5.1	10 50	10 54	16 41	22 19	22 13
15	12 26	− 6.6	58.9	16.0	349	294	38	6.1	12 08	12 16	17 32	22 45	22 35
16	13 20	−11.1	59.2	16.1	2	292	50	7.1	13 26	13 39	18 25	23 15	23 01
17	14 16	−15.0	59.4	16.2	14	289	61	8.1	14 44	15 01	19 21	23 52	23 34
18	15 14	−18.1	59.6	16.2	26	285	72	9.1	15 58	16 18	20 19	—	—
19	16 14	−20.0	59.6	16.2	38	281	82	10.1	17 05	17 27	21 19	0 37	0 17
20	17 15	−20.7	59.5	16.2	51	277	90	11.1	18 02	18 23	22 18	1 32	1 11
21	18 16	−20.0	59.2	16.1	63	276	96	12.1	18 49	19 07	23 16	2 37	2 17
22	19 16	−18.1	58.8	16.0	75	283	99	13.1	19 26	19 41	—	3 49	3 32
23	20 12	−15.1	58.2	15.9	87	10	100	14.1	19 56	20 07	0 11	5 04	4 50
24	21 06	−11.4	57.6	15.7	99	55	98	15.1	20 22	20 28	1 02	6 18	6 09
25	21 57	− 7.2	56.9	15.5	112	60	94	16.1	20 44	20 47	1 51	7 31	7 26
26	22 46	− 2.7	56.2	15.3	124	62	89	17.1	21 05	21 04	2 37	8 42	8 41
27	23 33	+ 1.7	55.5	15.1	136	63	82	18.1	21 26	21 21	3 22	9 50	9 53
28	0 20	+ 6.0	55.0	15.0	148	65	73	19.1	21 47	21 39	4 05	10 57	11 04
29	1 06	+ 9.9	54.6	14.9	160	67	64	20.1	22 11	21 59	4 49	12 02	12 13
30	1 53	+13.4	54.3	14.8	173	69	55	21.1	22 38	22 23	5 33	13 07	13 21
31	2 40	+16.3	54.3	14.8	185	72	46	22.1	23 09	22 51	6 18	14 09	14 26

MERCURY

Day	RA	Dec.	Diam.	Phase	Transit	5° high 52°	5° high 56°
	h m	°	″	%	h m	h m	h m
1	6 03	+18.7	11	4	11 25	4 21	4 08
3	6 00	+18.7	11	6	11 14	4 10	3 57
5	5 58	+18.8	11	9	11 05	4 00	3 47
7	5 58	+19.0	10	12	10 57	3 50	3 37
9	5 58	+19.2	10	16	10 50	3 42	3 29
11	6 01	+19.5	9	20	10 45	3 35	3 21
13	6 04	+19.9	9	25	10 41	3 29	3 15
15	6 10	+20.3	8	30	10 39	3 24	3 09
17	6 17	+20.7	8	36	10 38	3 21	3 06
19	6 25	+21.1	8	41	10 39	3 19	3 03
21	6 35	+21.4	7	48	10 41	3 19	3 03
23	6 46	+21.7	7	54	10 45	3 20	3 04
25	6 58	+21.9	6	61	10 50	3 24	3 07
27	7 12	+22.0	6	68	10 56	3 29	3 12
29	7 27	+22.0	6	75	11 03	3 36	3 20
31	7 43	+21.8	6	81	11 11	3 46	3 29

VENUS

Day	RA	Dec.	Diam.	Phase	Transit	5° high 52°	5° high 56°
	h m	°	″	%	h m	h m	h m
1	9 25	+17.1	15	73	14 50	21 45	21 56
6	9 48	+15.1	16	71	14 53	21 37	21 46
11	10 09	+13.0	16	69	14 55	21 27	21 34
16	10 30	+10.7	17	67	14 56	21 17	21 22
21	10 51	+ 8.4	17	65	14 57	21 05	21 09
26	11 11	+ 6.0	18	63	14 57	20 53	20 55
31	11 31	+ 3.5	19	61	14 57	20 41	20 40

MARS

Day	RA	Dec.	Diam.	Phase	Transit	5° high 52°	5° high 56°
1	3 43	+19.3	5	94	9 07	1 58	1 45
6	3 58	+20.1	5	94	9 02	1 49	1 34
11	4 12	+20.8	5	94	8 57	1 39	1 24
16	4 27	+21.5	5	94	8 52	1 30	1 14
21	4 42	+22.0	5	93	8 47	1 22	1 05
26	4 57	+22.5	5	93	8 42	1 14	0 57
31	5 11	+22.9	5	93	8 37	1 07	0 49

SUNRISE AND SUNSET

	London		Bristol		Birmingham		Manchester		Newcastle		Glasgow		Belfast	
	0°05′	51°30′	2°35′	51°28′	1°55′	52°28′	2°15′	53°28′	1°37′	54°59′	4°14′	55°52′	5°56′	54°35′
	h m	h m	h m	h m	h m	h m	h m	h m	h m	h m	h m	h m	h m	h m
1	3 47	20 21	3 57	20 30	3 49	20 33	3 44	20 41	3 32	20 48	3 36	21 05	3 52	21 03
2	3 48	20 20	3 58	20 30	3 50	20 33	3 45	20 40	3 33	20 48	3 37	21 04	3 53	21 02
3	3 49	20 20	3 59	20 30	3 51	20 33	3 46	20 40	3 34	20 47	3 38	21 04	3 53	21 02
4	3 49	20 20	4 00	20 29	3 51	20 32	3 47	20 39	3 34	20 47	3 39	21 03	3 54	21 01
5	3 50	20 19	4 00	20 29	3 52	20 32	3 48	20 39	3 35	20 46	3 40	21 03	3 55	21 01
6	3 51	20 18	4 01	20 28	3 53	20 31	3 49	20 38	3 36	20 45	3 41	21 02	3 56	21 00
7	3 52	20 18	4 02	20 28	3 54	20 30	3 50	20 38	3 37	20 45	3 42	21 01	3 57	20 59
8	3 53	20 17	4 03	20 27	3 55	20 30	3 51	20 37	3 39	20 44	3 43	21 00	3 58	20 58
9	3 54	20 17	4 04	20 26	3 56	20 29	3 52	20 36	3 40	20 43	3 44	20 59	4 00	20 58
10	3 55	20 16	4 05	20 26	3 57	20 28	3 53	20 35	3 41	20 42	3 45	20 58	4 01	20 57
11	3 56	20 15	4 06	20 25	3 58	20 27	3 54	20 34	3 42	20 41	3 47	20 57	4 02	20 56
12	3 57	20 14	4 07	20 24	3 59	20 27	3 55	20 33	3 43	20 40	3 48	20 56	4 03	20 55
13	3 58	20 13	4 08	20 23	4 00	20 26	3 56	20 32	3 45	20 39	3 49	20 55	4 04	20 54
14	3 59	20 12	4 09	20 22	4 02	20 25	3 57	20 31	3 46	20 38	3 51	20 54	4 06	20 53
15	4 00	20 11	4 11	20 21	4 03	20 24	3 59	20 30	3 47	20 37	3 52	20 53	4 07	20 51
16	4 02	20 10	4 12	20 20	4 04	20 23	4 00	20 29	3 49	20 35	3 54	20 51	4 08	20 50
17	4 03	20 09	4 13	20 19	4 05	20 21	4 01	20 28	3 50	20 34	3 55	20 50	4 10	20 49
18	4 04	20 08	4 14	20 18	4 07	20 20	4 03	20 27	3 52	20 33	3 57	20 48	4 11	20 48
19	4 05	20 07	4 15	20 17	4 08	20 19	4 04	20 25	3 53	20 31	3 58	20 47	4 13	20 46
20	4 07	20 06	4 17	20 16	4 09	20 18	4 06	20 24	3 55	20 30	4 00	20 46	4 14	20 45
21	4 08	20 05	4 18	20 15	4 11	20 17	4 07	20 23	3 56	20 28	4 02	20 44	4 16	20 43
22	4 09	20 03	4 19	20 13	4 12	20 15	4 08	20 21	3 58	20 27	4 03	20 42	4 17	20 42
23	4 11	20 02	4 21	20 12	4 13	20 14	4 10	20 20	3 59	20 25	4 05	20 41	4 19	20 40
24	4 12	20 01	4 22	20 11	4 15	20 12	4 11	20 18	4 01	20 24	4 07	20 39	4 20	20 39
25	4 13	19 59	4 23	20 09	4 16	20 11	4 13	20 17	4 03	20 22	4 08	20 37	4 22	20 37
26	4 15	19 58	4 25	20 08	4 18	20 10	4 14	20 15	4 04	20 20	4 10	20 36	4 24	20 36
27	4 16	19 57	4 26	20 06	4 19	20 08	4 16	20 14	4 06	20 19	4 12	20 34	4 25	20 34
28	4 18	19 55	4 28	20 05	4 21	20 06	4 18	20 12	4 08	20 17	4 14	20 32	4 27	20 32
29	4 19	19 54	4 29	20 03	4 22	20 05	4 19	20 11	4 09	20 15	4 15	20 30	4 29	20 30
30	4 21	19 52	4 31	20 02	4 24	20 03	4 21	20 09	4 11	20 13	4 17	20 28	4 30	20 29
31	4 22	19 50	4 32	20 00	4 25	20 02	4 22	20 07	4 13	20 11	4 19	20 26	4 32	20 27

JUPITER

Day	RA	Dec.	Transit	5° high	
				52°	56°
	h m	° ′	h m	h m	h m
1	14 11.6	−11 59	19 33	23 54	23 39
11	14 12.0	−12 04	18 54	23 15	23 00
21	14 13.5	−12 15	18 17	22 36	22 21
31	14 16.1	−12 31	17 40	21 57	21 42

Diameters – equatorial 38″ polar 36″

SATURN

Day	RA	Dec.	Transit	5° high	
				52°	56°
	h m	° ′	h m	h m	h m
1	22 57.7	− 8 35	4 22	23 37	23 48
11	22 57.0	− 8 42	3 42	22 58	23 09
21	22 55.7	− 8 53	3 01	22 18	22 29
31	22 53.8	− 9 06	2 20	21 38	21 50

Diameters – equatorial 18″ polar 17″
Rings – major axis 42″ minor axis 4″

URANUS

Day	RA	Dec.	Transit	10° high	
				52°	56°
	h m	° ′	h m	h m	h m
1	19 48.2	−21 39	1 13	3 35	2 43
11	19 46.5	−21 43	0 32	2 54	2 01
21	19 44.8	−21 47	23 47	2 12	1 19
31	19 43.2	−21 52	23 06	1 30	0 36

Diameter 4″

NEPTUNE

Day	RA	Dec.	Transit	10° high	
				52°	56°
	h m	° ′	h m	h m	h m
1	19 36.0	−20 59	1 01	3 30	2 43
11	19 34.9	−21 01	0 20	2 50	2 02
21	19 33.8	−21 04	23 36	2 09	1 21
31	19 32.6	−21 06	22 55	1 28	0 40

Diameter 2″

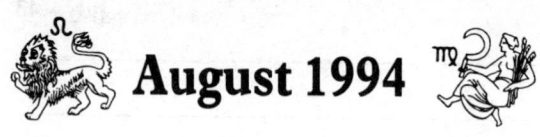

August 1994

EIGHTH MONTH, 31 DAYS. Julius Caesar *Augustus*, formerly *Sextilis*, sixth month of Roman pre-Julian calendar

Sun's Longitude 150° ♍ 23ᵈ09ʰ

1	Monday	Bank Holiday in Scotland. Herman Melville *b.* 1819	*week 31 day* 213
2	Tuesday	Sir Arthur Bliss *b.* 1891, Enrico Caruso *d.* 1921	214
3	Wednesday	Sir Roger Casement *exec.* 1916. Colette *d.* 1954	215
4	Thursday	Queen Elizabeth the Queen Mother *b.* 1900	216
5	Friday	Guy de Maupassant *b.* 1850. Richard Burton *d.* 1984	217
6	Saturday	**The Transfiguration.** Sir Alexander Fleming *b.* 1881	218
7	Sunday	**11th S. after Pentecost.** Sidney Buller *d.* 1970	*week 32 day* 219
8	Monday	Princess Beatrice of York *b.* 1988	220
9	Tuesday	Singapore became independent 1965	221
10	Wednesday	Charles Keene *b.* 1823. James Whistler *b.* 1834	222
11	Thursday	Sir Angus Wilson *b.* 1913. Andrew Carnegie *d.* 1919	223
12	Friday	Thomas Bewick *b.* 1753. Ian Fleming *d.* 1964	224
13	Saturday	John Logie Baird *b.* 1888. Jules Massenet *d.* 1912	225
14	Sunday	**12th S. after Pentecost.** Leonard Woolf *d.* 1969	*week 33 day* 226
15	Monday	*Princess Royal b. 1950.* James Keir Hardie *b.* 1856	227
16	Tuesday	Robert van Bunsen *d.* 1899. Georgette Heyer *b.* 1902	228
17	Wednesday	Wilfrid Scawen Blunt *b.* 1840	229
18	Thursday	Godfrey Evans *b.* 1920. Sir Frederick Ashton *d.* 1988	230
19	Friday	Sir Henry Wood *d.* 1944. Bill Clinton *b.* 1946	231
20	Saturday	Raymond Poincaré *b.* 1860. Rajiv Gandhi *b.* 1944	232
21	Sunday	**13th S. after Pentecost.** *Princess Margaret b. 1930*	*week 34 day* 233
22	Monday	Richard III *d.* 1485. Henri Cartier-Bresson *b.* 1908	234
23	Tuesday	1st Duke of Buckingham *assass.* 1628	235
24	Wednesday	**St Bartholomew.** Eruption of Mt Vesuvius AD 79	236
25	Thursday	Leonard Bernstein *b.* 1918. Liberation of Paris 1944	237
26	Friday	Prince Albert *b.* 1819. Sir Francis Chichester *d.* 1972	238
27	Saturday	Earl Mountbatten of Burma *assass.* 1979	239
28	Sunday	**14th S. after Pentecost.** Goethe *b.* 1749	*week 35 day* 240
29	Monday	*Bank Holiday in England, Wales and Northern Ireland*	241
30	Tuesday	Mary Wollstonecraft Shelley *b.* 1797	242
31	Wednesday	Théophile Gautier *b.* 1811. John Ford *d.* 1973	243

Astronomical Phenomena

d	h	
3	05	Mars in conjunction with Moon. Mars 3° N.
6	20	Mercury in conjunction with Moon. Mercury 6° N.
10	21	Venus in conjunction with Moon. Venus 3° N.
13	01	Mercury in superior conjunction
13	06	Jupiter in conjunction with Moon. Jupiter 2° N.
22	05	Saturn in conjunction with Moon. Saturn 6° S.
24	23	Venus at greatest elongation E. 46°

Constellations

The following constellations are near the meridian at

	d	h
July	1	24
July	16	23
August	1	22
August	16	21
September	1	20
September	15	19

Draco, Hercules, Lyra, Cygnus, Sagitta, Ophiuchus, Serpens, Aquila and Sagittarius

Minima of Algol

d	h	d	h	d	h
2	09.1	13	20.3	25	07.5
5	05.9	16	17.1	28	04.4
8	02.7	19	13.9	31	01.2
10	23.5	22	10.7		

The Moon

Phases, Apsides and Node	d	h	m
● New Moon	7	08	45
☽ First Quarter	14	05	57
○ Full Moon	21	06	47
☾ Last Quarter	29	06	41
Perigee (369,464 km)	12	23	10
Apogee (404,343 km)	27	17	52

Mean longitude of ascending node on August 1, 230°

THE SUN

s.d. 15′.8

Day	Right Ascension	Dec. +	Equation of time	Rise 52°	Rise 56°	Transit	Set 52°	Set 56°	Sidereal time	Transit of First Point of Aries
	h m s	° ′	m s	h m	h m	h m	h m	h m	h m s	h m s
1	8 43 50	18 08	− 6 19	4 21	4 03	12 06	19 50	20 08	20 37 30	3 21 57
2	8 47 42	17 53	− 6 16	4 23	4 05	12 06	19 49	20 06	20 41 27	3 18 01
3	8 51 35	17 37	− 6 12	4 24	4 07	12 06	19 47	20 04	20 45 23	3 14 05
4	8 55 27	17 22	− 6 07	4 26	4 09	12 06	19 45	20 02	20 49 20	3 10 09
5	8 59 18	17 06	− 6 02	4 27	4 11	12 06	19 43	20 00	20 53 16	3 06 13
6	9 03 08	16 49	− 5 56	4 29	4 13	12 06	19 42	19 58	20 57 13	3 02 17
7	9 06 58	16 33	− 5 49	4 31	4 15	12 06	19 40	19 56	21 01 09	2 58 21
8	9 10 48	16 16	− 5 42	4 32	4 17	12 06	19 38	19 53	21 05 06	2 54 25
9	9 14 37	15 59	− 5 34	4 34	4 19	12 05	19 36	19 51	21 09 03	2 50 29
10	9 18 25	15 42	− 5 26	4 35	4 20	12 05	19 34	19 49	21 12 59	2 46 34
11	9 22 12	15 24	− 5 17	4 37	4 22	12 05	19 32	19 47	21 16 56	2 42 38
12	9 25 59	15 06	− 5 07	4 39	4 24	12 05	19 30	19 44	21 20 52	2 38 42
13	9 29 46	14 48	− 4 57	4 40	4 26	12 05	19 28	19 42	21 24 49	2 34 46
14	9 33 32	14 30	− 4 47	4 42	4 28	12 05	19 26	19 40	21 28 45	2 30 50
15	9 37 17	14 11	− 4 35	4 43	4 30	12 04	19 24	19 37	21 32 42	2 26 54
16	9 41 02	13 53	− 4 24	4 45	4 32	12 04	19 22	19 35	21 36 38	2 22 58
17	9 44 46	13 34	− 4 11	4 47	4 34	12 04	19 20	19 33	21 40 35	2 19 02
18	9 48 30	13 15	− 3 58	4 48	4 36	12 04	19 18	19 30	21 44 31	2 15 06
19	9 52 13	12 55	− 3 45	4 50	4 38	12 04	19 16	19 28	21 48 28	2 11 10
20	9 55 56	12 36	− 3 31	4 52	4 40	12 03	19 14	19 25	21 52 25	2 07 15
21	9 59 38	12 16	− 3 17	4 53	4 42	12 03	19 12	19 23	21 56 21	2 03 19
22	10 03 20	11 56	− 3 02	4 55	4 44	12 03	19 10	19 21	22 00 18	1 59 23
23	10 07 01	11 36	− 2 47	4 56	4 46	12 03	19 08	19 18	22 04 14	1 55 27
24	10 10 42	11 15	− 2 31	4 58	4 48	12 02	19 06	19 16	22 08 11	1 51 31
25	10 14 22	10 55	− 2 15	5 00	4 50	12 02	19 03	19 13	22 12 07	1 47 35
26	10 18 02	10 34	− 1 58	5 01	4 52	12 02	19 01	19 11	22 16 04	1 43 39
27	10 21 42	10 13	− 1 41	5 03	4 54	12 02	18 59	19 08	22 20 00	1 39 43
28	10 25 21	9 52	− 1 24	5 05	4 56	12 01	18 57	19 05	22 23 57	1 35 47
29	10 29 00	9 31	− 1 06	5 06	4 58	12 01	18 55	19 03	22 27 54	1 31 51
30	10 32 38	9 10	− 0 48	5 08	5 00	12 01	18 52	19 00	22 31 50	1 27 55
31	10 36 17	8 48	− 0 30	5 10	5 02	12 00	18 50	18 58	22 35 47	1 24 00

DURATION OF TWILIGHT (in minutes)

Latitude	52°	56°	52°	56°	52°	56°	52°	56°
	1 August		11 August		21 August		31 August	
Civil	41	48	39	45	37	42	35	40
Nautical	97	120	89	106	83	96	79	89
Astronomical	177	TAN	153	205	138	166	127	147

THE NIGHT SKY

Mercury is unsuitably placed for observation, superior conjunction occurring on the 13th.

Venus is visible low in the western sky after sunset, magnitude − 4.6. Although greatest eastern elongation (46°) occurs on the 24th, Venus is only visible for a short time after sunset. The thin crescent Moon will be seen passing 3° south of Venus on the evening of the 10th. On the evening of the last day of the month Venus passes 0°.7 south of Spica, though this event is only likely to be seen with optical aid, as the two objects are less than 10° above the WSW horizon at sunset.

Mars, magnitude + 1.2, is visible in the SE sky in the mornings. During the month Mars moves from Taurus into Gemini. On the morning of the 3rd the old crescent Moon will be seen approaching the planet.

Jupiter is a brilliant object in the SW sky in the evenings, magnitude − 1.9. Early in the month Jupiter passes from Virgo into Libra. The crescent Moon will be seen near the planet on the evenings of the 12th and 13th.

Saturn, magnitude + 0.6, is approaching opposition and is therefore visible throughout the hours of darkness. On the morning of the 22nd the gibbous Moon passes 6° north of the planet.

Meteors. The maximum of the famous Perseid meteor shower occurs on the night of the 12th to 13th. As the crescent Moon sets in the early evening, there will be no interference by moonlight. The parent comet of this shower (Comet Swift-Tuttle) returned to perihelion in the autumn of 1992 and its next return is expected in 2126.

THE MOON

Day	RA h m	Dec. °	Hor. par. ′	Semi-diam. ′	Sun's co-long. °	PA of Bright Limb °	Phase %	Age d	Rise 52° h m	Rise 56° h m	Transit h m	Set 52° h m	Set 56° h m
1	3 29	+18.6	54.4	14.8	197	76	36	23.1	23 47	23 27	7 05	15 08	15 28
2	4 19	+20.0	54.6	14.9	209	80	27	24.1	—	—	7 53	16 03	16 24
3	5 11	+20.6	55.0	15.0	221	83	19	25.1	0 33	0 12	8 43	16 53	17 13
4	6 04	+20.2	55.5	15.1	234	87	12	26.1	1 26	1 06	9 34	17 36	17 54
5	6 57	+18.7	56.1	15.3	246	88	6	27.1	2 28	2 10	10 25	18 12	18 28
6	7 50	+16.4	56.8	15.5	258	86	2	28.1	3 36	3 21	11 16	18 44	18 56
7	8 43	+13.1	57.4	15.6	270	58	0	29.1	4 48	4 37	12 07	19 12	19 20
8	9 36	+ 9.0	58.0	15.8	283	321	1	0.6	6 03	5 56	12 57	19 37	19 41
9	10 28	+ 4.5	58.5	15.9	295	304	3	1.6	7 19	7 17	13 47	20 01	20 01
10	11 21	− 0.4	58.9	16.0	307	299	9	2.6	8 37	8 39	14 37	20 25	20 21
11	12 14	− 5.3	59.1	16.1	319	297	16	3.6	9 56	10 02	15 29	20 51	20 43
12	13 08	− 9.9	59.3	16.2	332	294	25	4.6	11 15	11 26	16 22	21 20	21 08
13	14 03	−14.0	59.3	16.2	344	290	36	5.6	12 32	12 48	17 17	21 54	21 38
14	15 01	−17.2	59.3	16.2	356	286	47	6.6	13 47	14 06	18 14	22 36	22 17
15	16 00	−19.4	59.2	16.1	8	282	59	7.6	14 55	15 16	19 12	23 27	23 06
16	17 00	−20.4	59.0	16.1	21	277	70	8.6	15 55	16 16	20 10	—	—
17	17 59	−20.1	58.7	16.0	33	272	79	9.6	16 44	17 03	21 07	0 27	0 06
18	18 58	−18.7	58.3	15.9	45	269	88	10.6	17 24	17 40	22 01	1 34	1 15
19	19 54	−16.1	57.9	15.8	57	268	94	11.6	17 56	18 09	22 53	2 46	2 31
20	20 48	−12.7	57.4	15.6	69	272	98	12.6	18 24	18 32	23 43	3 59	3 48
21	21 40	− 8.7	56.9	15.5	81	306	100	13.6	18 47	18 52	—	5 12	5 05
22	22 29	− 4.4	56.3	15.3	94	40	99	14.6	19 09	19 10	0 30	6 23	6 20
23	23 17	− 0.0	55.8	15.2	106	56	97	15.6	19 30	19 27	1 15	7 33	7 34
24	0 04	+ 4.3	55.2	15.1	118	61	92	16.6	19 52	19 45	1 59	8 41	8 46
25	0 50	+ 8.4	54.8	14.9	130	64	86	17.6	20 15	20 05	2 43	9 47	9 56
26	1 37	+12.0	54.5	14.8	142	67	79	18.6	20 40	20 27	3 27	10 52	11 04
27	2 25	+15.2	54.3	14.8	155	71	71	19.6	21 10	20 53	4 12	11 55	12 10
28	3 13	+17.6	54.2	14.8	167	75	62	20.6	21 45	21 26	4 58	12 55	13 14
29	4 02	+19.4	54.4	14.8	179	79	53	21.6	22 26	22 06	5 46	13 52	14 12
30	4 53	+20.2	54.7	14.9	191	83	43	22.6	23 16	22 55	6 34	14 43	15 04
31	5 45	+20.2	55.1	15.0	203	87	34	23.6	—	23 54	7 24	15 28	15 48

MERCURY

Day	RA h m	Dec. °	Diam. ″	Phase %	Transit h m	5° high 52° h m	5° high 56° h m
1	7 51	+21.6	6	84	11 15	3 51	3 35
3	8 07	+21.2	5	89	11 24	4 03	3 47
5	8 25	+20.5	5	93	11 34	4 16	4 01
7	8 42	+19.7	5	96	11 43	4 30	4 16
9	8 59	+18.8	5	98	11 52	4 45	4 32
11	9 16	+17.7	5	99	12 01	19 00	19 11
13	9 32	+16.5	5	100	12 09	19 01	19 11
15	9 48	+15.2	5	100	12 17	19 01	19 10
17	10 03	+13.8	5	99	12 24	19 01	19 09
19	10 18	+12.4	5	98	12 31	19 00	19 06
21	10 32	+10.9	5	96	12 37	18 58	19 04
23	10 46	+ 9.4	5	95	12 43	18 56	19 00
25	10 59	+ 7.8	5	94	12 48	18 54	18 56
27	11 12	+ 6.3	5	92	12 53	18 50	18 52
29	11 24	+ 4.8	5	90	12 58	18 47	18 47
31	11 36	+ 3.3	5	89	13 01	18 43	18 42

VENUS

Day	RA h m	Dec. °	Diam. ″	Phase %	Transit h m	5° high 52° h m	5° high 56° h m
1	11 35	+ 3.0	19	60	14 57	20 38	20 37
6	11 54	+ 0.6	20	58	14 56	20 24	20 21
11	12 12	− 1.9	21	56	14 55	20 10	20 05
16	12 30	− 4.4	22	53	14 53	19 56	19 48
21	12 48	− 6.8	23	51	14 51	19 40	19 31
26	13 05	− 9.2	25	48	14 49	19 25	19 13
31	13 22	−11.4	26	45	14 46	19 08	18 54

MARS

Day	RA h m	Dec. °	Diam. ″	Phase %	Transit h m	5° high 52° h m	5° high 56° h m
1	5 14	+23.0	5	93	8 36	1 05	0 47
6	5 29	+23.3	5	92	8 31	0 58	0 40
11	5 43	+23.5	5	92	8 26	0 52	0 33
16	5 58	+23.6	5	92	8 21	0 45	0 27
21	6 12	+23.7	5	92	8 15	0 40	0 21
26	6 26	+23.6	5	91	8 10	0 34	0 16
31	6 40	+23.5	5	91	8 04	0 29	0 11

SUNRISE AND SUNSET

	London		Bristol		Birmingham		Manchester		Newcastle		Glasgow		Belfast	
	0°05′	51°30′	2°35′	51°28′	1°55′	52°28′	2°15′	53°28′	1°37′	54°59′	4°14′	55°52′	5°56′	54°35′
	h m	h m	h m	h m	h m	h m	h m	h m	h m	h m	h m	h m	h m	h m
1	4 24	19 49	4 34	19 59	4 27	20 00	4 24	20 05	4 15	20 10	4 21	20 24	4 34	20 25
2	4 25	19 47	4 35	19 57	4 29	19 58	4 26	20 04	4 16	20 08	4 23	20 22	4 36	20 23
3	4 27	19 45	4 37	19 55	4 30	19 56	4 27	20 02	4 18	20 06	4 25	20 20	4 37	20 21
4	4 28	19 44	4 38	19 54	4 32	19 55	4 29	20 00	4 20	20 04	4 26	20 18	4 39	20 19
5	4 30	19 42	4 40	19 52	4 33	19 53	4 31	19 58	4 22	20 02	4 28	20 16	4 41	20 17
6	4 31	19 40	4 41	19 50	4 35	19 51	4 32	19 56	4 24	20 00	4 30	20 14	4 43	20 15
7	4 33	19 38	4 43	19 48	4 37	19 49	4 34	19 54	4 26	19 58	4 32	20 12	4 44	20 13
8	4 34	19 37	4 44	19 47	4 38	19 47	4 36	19 52	4 27	19 56	4 34	20 10	4 46	20 11
9	4 36	19 35	4 46	19 45	4 40	19 45	4 38	19 50	4 29	19 53	4 36	20 07	4 48	20 09
10	4 37	19 33	4 47	19 43	4 41	19 43	4 39	19 48	4 31	19 51	4 38	20 05	4 50	20 07
11	4 39	19 31	4 49	19 41	4 43	19 41	4 41	19 46	4 33	19 49	4 40	20 03	4 52	20 05
12	4 40	19 29	4 51	19 39	4 45	19 40	4 43	19 44	4 35	19 47	4 42	20 01	4 54	20 03
13	4 42	19 27	4 52	19 37	4 46	19 38	4 44	19 42	4 37	19 45	4 44	19 58	4 55	20 01
14	4 44	19 25	4 54	19 35	4 48	19 35	4 46	19 40	4 38	19 43	4 46	19 56	4 57	19 58
15	4 45	19 23	4 55	19 33	4 50	19 33	4 48	19 38	4 40	19 40	4 48	19 54	4 59	19 56
16	4 47	19 21	4 57	19 31	4 51	19 31	4 50	19 36	4 42	19 38	4 50	19 51	5 01	19 54
17	4 48	19 19	4 59	19 29	4 53	19 29	4 51	19 34	4 44	19 36	4 52	19 49	5 03	19 52
18	4 50	19 17	5 00	19 27	4 55	19 27	4 53	19 31	4 46	19 33	4 54	19 47	5 05	19 49
19	4 52	19 15	5 02	19 25	4 56	19 25	4 55	19 29	4 48	19 31	4 55	19 44	5 06	19 47
20	4 53	19 13	5 03	19 23	4 58	19 23	4 57	19 27	4 50	19 29	4 57	19 42	5 08	19 45
21	4 55	19 11	5 05	19 21	5 00	19 21	4 58	19 25	4 52	19 26	4 59	19 39	5 10	19 43
22	4 56	19 09	5 06	19 19	5 01	19 19	5 00	19 22	4 53	19 24	5 01	19 37	5 12	19 40
23	4 58	19 07	5 08	19 17	5 03	19 16	5 02	19 20	4 55	19 22	5 03	19 35	5 14	19 38
24	5 00	19 05	5 10	19 15	5 05	19 14	5 04	19 18	4 57	19 19	5 05	19 32	5 15	19 35
25	5 01	19 03	5 11	19 13	5 06	19 12	5 05	19 16	4 59	19 17	5 07	19 30	5 17	19 33
26	5 03	19 00	5 13	19 10	5 08	19 10	5 07	19 13	5 01	19 14	5 09	19 27	5 19	19 31
27	5 04	18 58	5 14	19 08	5 10	19 08	5 09	19 11	5 03	19 12	5 11	19 25	5 21	19 28
28	5 06	18 56	5 16	19 06	5 11	19 05	5 11	19 09	5 05	19 10	5 13	19 22	5 23	19 26
29	5 08	18 54	5 18	19 04	5 13	19 03	5 12	19 06	5 07	19 07	5 15	19 20	5 25	19 23
30	5 09	18 52	5 19	19 02	5 15	19 01	5 14	19 04	5 08	19 05	5 17	19 17	5 27	19 21
31	5 11	18 50	5 21	18 59	5 16	18 59	5 16	19 02	5 10	19 02	5 19	19 14	5 28	19 19

JUPITER

Day	RA	Dec.	Transit	5° high	
				52°	56°
	h m	° ′	h m	h m	h m
1	14 16.5	−12 33	17 36	21 54	21 38
11	14 20.2	−12 54	17 01	21 16	21 00
21	14 24.8	−13 19	16 26	20 39	20 22
31	14 30.2	−13 48	15 52	20 02	19 45

Diameters – equatorial 35″ polar 33″

SATURN

Day	RA	Dec.	Transit	5° high	
				52°	56°
	h m	° ′	h m	h m	h m
1	22 53.6	− 9 07	2 16	21 34	21 46
11	22 51.3	− 9 23	1 34	20 54	21 06
21	22 48.7	− 9 40	0 52	20 14	20 26
31	22 45.9	− 9 58	0 10	19 33	19 46

Diameters – equatorial 19″ polar 17″
Rings – major axis 43″ minor axis 5″

URANUS

Day	RA	Dec.	Transit	10° high	
				52°	56°
	h m	° ′	h m	h m	h m
1	19 43.0	−21 52	23 02	1 26	0 32
11	19 41.4	−21 56	22 21	0 44	23 46
21	19 40.0	−21 59	21 40	0 03	23 04
31	19 38.8	−22 02	21 00	23 18	22 22

Diameter 4″

NEPTUNE

Day	RA	Dec.	Transit	10° high	
				52°	56°
	h m	° ′	h m	h m	h m
1	19 32.5	−21 07	22 51	1 24	0 36
11	19 31.5	−21 09	22 11	0 43	23 50
21	19 30.6	−21 11	21 31	0 02	23 09
31	19 29.8	−21 13	20 51	23 18	22 29

Diameter 2″

September 1994

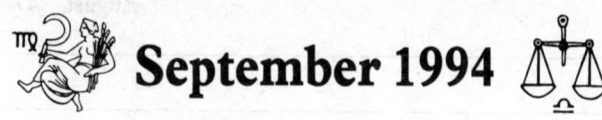

NINTH MONTH, 30 DAYS. *Septem* (seven), seventh month of Roman pre-Julian calendar

Sun's Longitude 180° ♎ 23ᵈ06ʰ

1	*Thursday*	Edward Alleyn *b*. 1566. James Corbett *b*. 1866	*week 35 day* 244
2	*Friday*	Baron de Coubertin *d*. 1937. Laura Riding *d*. 1991	245
3	*Saturday*	Start of Second World War 1939	246
4	*Sunday*	**15th S. after Pentecost.** Albert Schweitzer *d*. 1965	*week 36 day* 247
5	*Monday*	Jesse James *b*. 1847. Sir Douglas Bader *d*. 1982	248
6	*Tuesday*	JEWISH NEW YEAR (5755). Marquis de La Fayette *b*. 1757	249
7	*Wednesday*	Elizabeth I *b*. 1533. Catherine Parr *d*. 1548	250
8	*Thursday*	**Blessed Virgin Mary.** Richard I *b*. 1157	251
9	*Friday*	Henri de Toulouse-Lautrec *d*. 1901	252
10	*Saturday*	Treaty of St Germain signed 1919	253
11	*Sunday*	**16th S. after Pentecost.** David Ricardo *d*. 1823	*week 37 day* 254
12	*Monday*	Cleopatra's Needle erected, London, 1878	255
13	*Tuesday*	J. B. Priestly *b*. 1894. John Smith *b*. 1938	256
14	*Wednesday*	Duke of Wellington *d*. 1852. Sir Peter Scott *b*. 1909	257
15	*Thursday*	YOM KIPPUR. Prince Henry of Wales *b*. 1984	258
16	*Friday*	Henry V *b*. 1387. Fire of Moscow 1812	259
17	*Saturday*	Sir Frederick Ashton *b*. 1904. Stirling Moss *b*. 1929	260
18	*Sunday*	**17th S. after Pentecost.** Dr Samuel Johnson *b*. 1709	*week 38 day* 261
19	*Monday*	Poitiers 1356. Sir James Dewar *b*. 1842	262
20	*Tuesday*	FEAST OF TABERNACLES begins	263
21	*Wednesday*	**St Matthew.** Gustav Holst *b*. 1874	264
22	*Thursday*	Zutphen 1586. Michael Faraday *b*. 1791	265
23	*Friday*	Baroness Orczy *b*. 1865. Sigmund Freud *d*. 1939	266
24	*Saturday*	Horace Walpole *b*. 1717. Scott Fitzgerald *b*. 1896	267
25	*Sunday*	**18th S. after Pentecost.** Samuel Butler *d*. 1680	*week 39 day* 268
26	*Monday*	Sir Barnes Wallis *b*. 1887. Béla Bartok *d*. 1945	269
27	*Tuesday*	George Cruikshank *b*. 1792. Dame Gracia Fields *d*. 1979	270
28	*Wednesday*	Georges Clemenceau *b*. 1841. Miles Davis *d*. 1991	271
29	*Thursday*	**St Michael and all Angels.** Mrs Gaskell *b*. 1810	272
30	*Friday*	Lord Raglan *b* 1788. Rudolf Diesel *d*. 1913	273

ASTRONOMICAL PHENOMENA

d	h	
1	02	Mars in conjunction with Moon. Mars 4° N.
1	17	Saturn at opposition
7	07	Mercury in conjunction with Moon. Mercury 3° N.
9	02	Venus in conjunction with Moon. Venus 2° S.
9	19	Jupiter in conjunction with Moon. Jupiter 1° N.
18	08	Saturn in conjunction with Moon. Saturn 6° S.
23	06	Equinox
26	16	Mercury at greatest elongation E. 26°
28	22	Venus at greatest brilliancy
29	20	Mars in conjunction with Moon. Mars 6° N.
29	22	Jupiter in conjunction with Venus. Jupiter 7° N.

CONSTELLATIONS

The following constellations are near the meridian at

	d	h		d	h
August	1	24	September	15	21
August	16	23	October	1	20
September	1	22	October	16	19

Draco, Cepheus, Lyra, Cygnus, Vulpecula, Sagitta, Delphinus, Equuleus, Aquila, Aquarius and Capricornus

MINIMA OF ALGOL

d	h	d	h	d	h
2	22.0	14	09.2	22	23.6
5	18.8	17	06.0	25	20.5
8	15.6	20	02.8	28	17.3
11	12.4				

THE MOON

Phases, Apsides and Node	d	h	m
● New Moon	5	18	33
☽ First Quarter	12	11	34
○ Full Moon	19	20	01
☾ Last Quarter	28	00	23
Perigee (365,148 km)	8	14	23
Apogee (405,245 km)	24	12	03

Mean longitude of ascending node on September 1, 228°

THE SUN

s.d. 15′.9

Day	Right Ascension	Dec.	Equation of time	Rise 52°	Rise 56°	Transit	Set 52°	Set 56°	Sidereal time	Transit of First Point of Aries
	h m s	° ′	m s	h m	h m	h m	h m	h m	h m s	h m s
1	10 39 55	+8 27	−0 11	5 11	5 04	12 00	18 48	18 55	22 39 43	1 20 04
2	10 43 32	+8 05	+0 08	5 13	5 06	12 00	18 46	18 53	22 43 40	1 16 08
3	10 47 10	+7 43	+0 27	5 14	5 07	11 59	18 43	18 50	22 47 36	1 12 12
4	10 50 47	+7 21	+0 46	5 16	5 09	11 59	18 41	18 47	22 51 33	1 08 16
5	10 54 24	+6 59	+1 06	5 18	5 11	11 59	18 39	18 45	22 55 29	1 04 20
6	10 58 00	+6 36	+1 26	5 19	5 13	11 58	18 36	18 42	22 59 26	1 00 24
7	11 01 37	+6 14	+1 46	5 21	5 15	11 58	18 34	18 40	23 03 23	0 56 28
8	11 05 13	+5 52	+2 06	5 23	5 17	11 58	18 32	18 37	23 07 19	0 52 32
9	11 08 49	+5 29	+2 27	5 24	5 19	11 57	18 29	18 34	23 11 16	0 48 36
10	11 12 25	+5 06	+2 48	5 26	5 21	11 57	18 27	18 32	23 15 12	0 44 40
11	11 16 00	+4 44	+3 08	5 27	5 23	11 57	18 25	18 29	23 19 09	0 40 45
12	11 19 36	+4 21	+3 29	5 29	5 25	11 56	18 23	18 26	23 23 05	0 36 49
13	11 23 11	+3 58	+3 51	5 31	5 27	11 56	18 20	18 24	23 27 02	0 32 53
14	11 26 47	+3 35	+4 12	5 32	5 29	11 56	18 18	18 21	23 30 58	0 28 57
15	11 30 22	+3 12	+4 33	5 34	5 31	11 55	18 16	18 18	23 34 55	0 25 01
16	11 33 57	+2 49	+4 55	5 36	5 33	11 55	18 13	18 16	23 38 52	0 21 05
17	11 37 32	+2 26	+5 16	5 37	5 35	11 55	18 11	18 13	23 42 48	0 17 09
18	11 41 07	+2 03	+5 38	5 39	5 37	11 54	18 08	18 10	23 46 45	0 13 13
19	11 44 42	+1 39	+5 59	5 40	5 39	11 54	18 06	18 08	23 50 41	0 09 17
20	11 48 17	+1 16	+6 20	5 42	5 41	11 53	18 04	18 05	23 54 38	0 05 21
21	11 51 53	+0 53	+6 42	5 44	5 43	11 53	18 01	18 02	23 58 34	0 01 25 / 23 57 30
22	11 55 28	+0 30	+7 03	5 45	5 45	11 53	17 59	18 00	0 02 31	23 53 34
23	11 59 03	+0 06	+7 24	5 47	5 46	11 52	17 57	17 57	0 06 27	23 49 38
24	12 02 39	−0 17	+7 45	5 49	5 48	11 52	17 54	17 55	0 10 24	23 45 42
25	12 06 14	−0 41	+8 06	5 50	5 50	11 52	17 52	17 52	0 14 20	23 41 46
26	12 09 50	−1 04	+8 27	5 52	5 52	11 51	17 50	17 49	0 18 17	23 37 50
27	12 13 26	−1 27	+8 48	5 54	5 54	11 51	17 47	17 47	0 22 14	23 33 54
28	12 17 02	−1 51	+9 08	5 55	5 56	11 51	17 45	17 44	0 26 10	23 29 58
29	12 20 39	−2 14	+9 28	5 57	5 58	11 50	17 43	17 41	0 30 07	23 26 02
30	12 24 15	−2 37	+9 48	5 59	6 00	11 50	17 40	17 39	0 34 03	23 22 06

DURATION OF TWILIGHT (in minutes)

Latitude	52°	56°	52°	56°	52°	56°	52°	56°
	1 September		11 September		21 September		30 September	
Civil	35	39	34	38	34	37	34	37
Nautical	79	89	76	84	74	82	73	80
Astronomical	127	146	120	135	115	129	113	126

THE NIGHT SKY

Mercury, despite reaching greatest eastern elongation (26°) on the 26th, is unsuitably placed for observation.

Venus is a magnificent object in the SW sky in the early evenings for a very short time after sunset, its magnitude being −4.6. The crescent Moon will be seen in the vicinity of Venus on the evenings of the 8th and 9th. Venus is gradually drawing closer to the Sun and is unlikely to be seen after the first fortnight in September.

Mars continues to be visible as a morning object in Gemini, magnitude +1.1. During the second part of September it will be seen passing south of the Heavenly Twins, Castor and Pollux. By the end of the month it should be visible low above the ENE horizon by midnight. The reddish tint of Mars should assist in its identification. On the morning of the 1st and again on the mornings of the 29th and 30th the old Moon will be seen near the planet.

Jupiter, magnitude −1.8, is a bright evening object in the SW sky but is now coming to the end of its evening apparition and before the end of September it will be lost to view in the evening twilight. The crescent Moon passes 2° south of the planet on the evening of the 9th.

Saturn reaches opposition on the first day of the month and is therefore visible throughout the hours of darkness. Its magnitude is +0.5. On the morning of the 18th the Moon, near Full, will be seen passing 6° north of the planet.

Zodiacal Light. The morning cone may be seen stretching up from the eastern horizon along the ecliptic before the beginning of morning twilight, from the 4th until the 17th.

THE MOON

Day	RA h m	Dec. °	Hor. par. ′	Semi-diam. ′	Sun's co-long. °	PA of Bright Limb °	Phase %	Age d	Rise 52° h m	Rise 56° h m	Transit h m	Set 52° h m	Set 56° h m
1	6 37	+19.2	55.7	15.2	216	91	25	24.6	0 13	—	8 14	16 08	16 25
2	7 30	+17.2	56.4	15.4	228	95	17	25.6	1 17	1 01	9 05	16 41	16 55
3	8 23	+14.3	57.2	15.6	240	97	10	26.6	2 27	2 14	9 56	17 11	17 21
4	9 16	+10.6	58.0	15.8	252	96	4	27.6	3 41	3 32	10 46	17 38	17 44
5	10 09	+ 6.2	58.7	16.0	265	85	1	28.6	4 58	4 53	11 37	18 03	18 05
6	11 02	+ 1.4	59.4	16.2	277	348	0	0.2	6 17	6 17	12 29	18 28	18 26
7	11 56	− 3.6	59.8	16.3	289	306	2	1.2	7 37	7 41	13 22	18 54	18 48
8	12 52	− 8.4	60.0	16.4	301	297	7	2.2	8 58	9 07	14 16	19 23	19 12
9	13 48	−12.8	60.0	16.4	314	292	14	3.2	10 18	10 32	15 11	19 56	19 42
10	14 47	−16.3	59.9	16.3	326	287	23	4.2	11 36	11 53	16 09	20 37	20 18
11	15 46	−18.8	59.6	16.2	338	282	33	5.2	12 47	13 07	17 07	21 25	21 05
12	16 46	−20.1	59.1	16.1	350	277	45	6.2	13 49	14 10	18 05	22 22	22 01
13	17 46	−20.1	58.7	16.0	2	272	56	7.2	14 41	15 01	19 02	23 27	23 07
14	18 44	−18.9	58.2	15.8	15	267	67	8.2	15 23	15 40	19 57	—	—
15	19 40	−16.6	57.6	15.7	27	263	77	9.2	15 58	16 11	20 48	0 36	0 20
16	20 34	−13.5	57.1	15.6	39	261	85	10.2	16 26	16 36	21 38	1 47	1 35
17	21 25	− 9.8	56.6	15.4	51	260	92	11.2	16 51	16 57	22 25	2 59	2 50
18	22 14	− 5.7	56.1	15.3	63	261	96	12.2	17 13	17 16	23 10	4 09	4 05
19	23 02	− 1.4	55.7	15.2	76	272	99	13.2	17 35	17 33	23 55	5 18	5 18
20	23 49	+ 2.9	55.2	15.0	88	3	100	14.2	17 56	17 51	—	6 26	6 30
21	0 36	+ 7.0	54.8	14.9	100	55	99	15.2	18 19	18 10	0 38	7 33	7 40
22	1 23	+10.8	54.5	14.8	112	64	96	16.2	18 43	18 31	1 23	8 38	8 49
23	2 10	+14.1	54.3	14.8	124	69	91	17.2	19 11	18 56	2 07	9 42	9 56
24	2 58	+16.8	54.1	14.7	136	74	85	18.2	19 44	19 26	2 53	10 43	11 01
25	3 47	+18.7	54.1	14.7	149	78	77	19.2	20 23	20 03	3 39	11 41	12 00
26	4 37	+19.8	54.3	14.8	161	83	69	20.2	21 09	20 48	4 27	12 34	12 54
27	5 28	+20.1	54.6	14.9	173	87	60	21.2	22 02	21 42	5 16	13 21	13 41
28	6 19	+19.4	55.1	15.0	185	92	50	22.2	23 01	22 44	6 05	14 02	14 20
29	7 10	+17.9	55.7	15.2	197	96	40	23.2	—	23 53	6 54	14 38	14 53
30	8 02	+15.4	56.5	15.4	210	100	31	24.2	0 07	—	7 44	15 08	15 20

MERCURY

Day	RA h m	Dec. °	Diam. ″	Phase %	Transit h m	5° high 52° h m	5° high 56° h m
1	11 42	+ 2.5	5	88	13 03	18 41	18 39
3	11 53	+ 1.0	5	86	13 07	18 37	18 34
5	12 05	− 0.5	5	84	13 10	18 32	18 28
7	12 15	− 1.9	5	82	13 13	18 28	18 22
9	12 26	− 3.3	6	81	13 15	18 23	18 16
11	12 36	− 4.7	6	79	13 18	18 18	18 10
13	12 46	− 6.1	6	77	13 20	18 12	18 03
15	12 56	− 7.4	6	75	13 21	18 07	17 56
17	13 05	− 8.6	6	73	13 23	18 01	17 50
19	13 14	− 9.8	6	70	13 24	17 55	17 43
21	13 23	−11.0	6	68	13 24	17 49	17 35
23	13 31	−12.1	6	65	13 25	17 43	17 28
25	13 39	−13.1	7	62	13 24	17 37	17 21
27	13 46	−14.0	7	59	13 24	17 31	17 13
29	13 53	−14.8	7	55	13 22	17 24	17 06
31	13 59	−15.5	7	51	13 20	17 18	16 58

VENUS

Day	RA h m	Dec. °	Diam. ″	Phase %	Transit h m	5° high 52° h m	5° high 56° h m
1	13 25	−11.9	27	45	14 45	19 05	18 50
6	13 41	−14.0	28	42	14 41	18 48	18 30
11	13 56	−16.0	30	39	14 37	18 30	18 10
16	14 11	−17.9	33	35	14 31	18 12	17 49
21	14 23	−19.6	35	32	14 24	17 53	17 26
26	14 35	−21.0	38	28	14 15	17 33	17 03
31	14 44	−22.3	41	24	14 04	17 12	16 39

MARS

Day	RA h m	Dec. °	Diam. ″	Phase %	Transit h m	5° high 52° h m	5° high 56° h m
1	6 43	+23.5	5	91	8 03	0 28	0 10
6	6 56	+23.3	5	91	7 57	0 23	0 05
11	7 10	+23.1	5	91	7 50	0 19	0 01
16	7 23	+22.7	6	90	7 44	0 14	23 56
21	7 36	+22.4	6	90	7 37	0 10	23 52
26	7 48	+22.0	6	90	7 30	0 05	23 48
31	8 01	+21.5	6	90	7 22	0 00	23 44

SUNRISE AND SUNSET

	London		Bristol		Birmingham		Manchester		Newcastle		Glasgow		Belfast	
	0°05′	51°30′	2°35′	51°28′	1°55′	52°28′	2°15′	53°28′	1°37′	54°59′	4°14′	55°52′	5°56′	54°35′
	h m	h m	h m	h m	h m	h m	h m	h m	h m	h m	h m	h m	h m	h m
1	5 12	18 47	5 22	18 57	5 18	18 56	5 18	18 59	5 12	19 00	5 21	19 12	5 30	19 16
2	5 14	18 45	5 24	18 55	5 20	18 54	5 19	18 57	5 14	18 57	5 23	19 09	5 32	19 14
3	5 16	18 43	5 26	18 53	5 21	18 52	5 21	18 55	5 16	18 55	5 25	19 07	5 34	19 11
4	5 17	18 41	5 27	18 51	5 23	18 49	5 23	18 52	5 18	18 52	5 27	19 04	5 36	19 09
5	5 19	18 38	5 29	18 48	5 25	18 47	5 25	18 50	5 20	18 50	5 29	19 01	5 38	19 06
6	5 20	18 36	5 30	18 46	5 26	18 45	5 26	18 47	5 21	18 47	5 30	18 59	5 39	19 04
7	5 22	18 34	5 32	18 44	5 28	18 42	5 28	18 45	5 23	18 45	5 32	18 56	5 41	19 01
8	5 23	18 32	5 34	18 42	5 30	18 40	5 30	18 43	5 25	18 42	5 34	18 54	5 43	18 59
9	5 25	18 29	5 35	18 39	5 31	18 38	5 31	18 40	5 27	18 39	5 36	18 51	5 45	18 56
10	5 27	18 27	5 37	18 37	5 33	18 35	5 33	18 38	5 29	18 37	5 38	18 48	5 47	18 54
11	5 28	18 25	5 38	18 35	5 35	18 33	5 35	18 35	5 31	18 34	5 40	18 46	5 48	18 51
12	5 30	18 22	5 40	18 32	5 36	18 31	5 37	18 33	5 33	18 32	5 42	18 43	5 50	18 49
13	5 31	18 20	5 42	18 30	5 38	18 28	5 38	18 30	5 35	18 29	5 44	18 41	5 52	18 46
14	5 33	18 18	5 43	18 28	5 40	18 26	5 40	18 28	5 36	18 27	5 46	18 38	5 54	18 44
15	5 35	18 16	5 45	18 25	5 41	18 23	5 42	18 25	5 38	18 24	5 48	18 35	5 56	18 41
16	5 36	18 13	5 46	18 23	5 43	18 21	5 44	18 22	5 40	18 22	5 50	18 33	5 58	18 38
17	5 38	18 11	5 48	18 21	5 45	18 19	5 45	18 21	5 42	18 19	5 52	18 30	5 59	18 36
18	5 39	18 09	5 49	18 19	5 46	18 16	5 47	18 18	5 44	18 16	5 54	18 27	6 01	18 33
19	5 41	18 06	5 51	18 16	5 48	18 14	5 49	18 16	5 46	18 14	5 56	18 25	6 03	18 31
20	5 43	18 04	5 53	18 14	5 50	18 12	5 51	18 13	5 48	18 11	5 58	18 22	6 05	18 28
21	5 44	18 02	5 54	18 12	5 51	18 09	5 52	18 11	5 49	18 09	6 00	18 19	6 07	18 26
22	5 46	17 59	5 56	18 09	5 53	18 07	5 54	18 08	5 51	18 06	6 02	18 17	6 09	18 23
23	5 47	17 57	5 57	18 07	5 55	18 04	5 56	18 06	5 53	18 04	6 03	18 14	6 10	18 21
24	5 49	17 55	5 59	18 05	5 56	18 02	5 58	18 03	5 55	18 01	6 05	18 11	6 12	18 18
25	5 51	17 52	6 01	18 02	5 58	18 00	5 59	18 01	5 57	17 58	6 07	18 09	6 14	18 16
26	5 52	17 50	6 02	18 00	6 00	17 57	6 01	17 59	5 59	17 56	6 09	18 06	6 16	18 13
27	5 54	17 48	6 04	17 58	6 01	17 55	6 03	17 56	6 01	17 53	6 11	18 04	6 18	18 11
28	5 55	17 46	6 06	17 56	6 03	17 53	6 05	17 54	6 03	17 51	6 13	18 01	6 20	18 08
29	5 57	17 43	6 07	17 53	6 05	17 50	6 06	17 51	6 04	17 48	6 15	17 58	6 22	18 06
30	5 59	17 41	6 09	17 51	6 06	17 48	6 08	17 49	6 06	17 46	6 17	17 56	6 23	18 03

JUPITER

Day	RA	Dec.	Transit	5° high	
				52°	56°
	h m	° ′	h m	h m	h m
1	14 30.8	−13 51	15 49	19 58	19 41
11	14 37.1	−14 23	15 16	19 22	19 04
21	14 44.0	−14 57	14 43	18 46	18 27
31	14 51.5	−15 32	14 12	18 10	17 51

Diameters – equatorial 33″ polar 31″

SATURN

Day	RA	Dec.	Transit	5° high	
				52°	56°
	h m	° ′	h m	h m	h m
1	22 45.6	−10 00	0 06	4 38	4 26
11	22 42.8	−10 18	23 20	3 55	3 42
21	22 40.1	−10 34	22 38	3 11	2 58
31	22 37.6	−10 48	21 56	2 28	2 14

Diameters – equatorial 19″ polar 17″
Rings – major axis 43″ minor axis 5″

URANUS

Day	RA	Dec.	Transit	10° high	
				52°	56°
	h m	° ′	h m	h m	h m
1	19 38.7	−22 02	20 56	23 14	22 18
11	19 37.9	−22 04	20 15	22 33	21 38
21	19 37.3	−22 05	19 36	21 53	20 57
31	19 37.1	−22 05	18 56	21 14	20 18

Diameter 4″

NEPTUNE

Day	RA	Dec.	Transit	10° high	
				52°	56°
	h m	° ′	h m	h m	h m
1	19 29.7	−21 14	20 47	23 14	22 25
11	19 29.1	−21 15	20 07	22 34	21 44
21	19 28.8	−21 16	19 27	21 54	21 05
31	19 28.6	−21 17	18 48	21 14	20 25

Diameter 2″

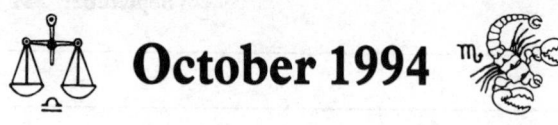

October 1994

TENTH MONTH, 31 DAYS. *Octo* (eight), eighth month of Roman pre-Julian calendar

Sun's Longitude 210° ♏ 23ᵈ 16ʰ

1	*Saturday*	*Michaelmas Law Sittings begin.* Henry III *b.* 1207	*week* 39 *day* 274
2	*Sunday*	**19th S. after Pentecost.** Richard III *b.* 1452	*week* 40 *day* 275
3	*Monday*	Reunification of Germany 1990	276
4	*Tuesday*	Max Planck *d.* 1947. *Sputnik I* launched 1957	277
5	*Wednesday*	Jacques Offenbach *d.* 1880. *R101* disaster 1930	278
6	*Thursday*	Jenny Lind *b.* 1820. Thor Heyerdahl *b.* 1914	279
7	*Friday*	Archbishop Laud *b.* 1573. Edgar Allen Poe *d.* 1849	280
8	*Saturday*	Kathleen Ferrier *d.* 1953. Clement Attlee *d.* 1967	281
9	*Sunday*	**20th S. after Pentecost.** John Lennon *b.* 1940	*week* 41 *day* 282
10	*Monday*	Jean Watteau *b.* 1684. Harold Pinter *b.* 1930	283
11	*Tuesday*	Camperdown 1797. James Joule *d.* 1889	284
12	*Wednesday*	Edward VI *b.* 1537. Vaughan Williams *b.* 1872	285
13	*Thursday*	Anatole France *d.* 1924. Lady Thatcher *b.* 1925	286
14	*Friday*	Dame Edith Evans *d.* 1976. Bing Crosby *d.* 1977	287
15	*Saturday*	First British Motor Show 1895	288
16	*Sunday*	**21st S. after Pentecost.** Oscar Wilde *b.* 1854	*week* 42 *day* 289
17	*Monday*	Saratoga 1777. Frederic Chopin *d.* 1849	290
18	*Tuesday*	**St Luke.** Canaletto *b.* 1697. Charles Gounod *d.* 1893	291
19	*Wednesday*	Charles I *b.* 1600. Jacqueline du Pré *d.* 1987	292
20	*Thursday*	Viscount Palmerston *b.* 1784. Bud Flanagan *d.* 1968	293
21	*Friday*	Alfred Nobel *b.* 1833. Aberfan disaster 1966	294
22	*Saturday*	Thomas Sheraton *d.* 1806. Paul Cézanne *d.* 1906	295
23	*Sunday*	**9th S. before Christmas.** Robert Bridges *b.* 1844	*week* 43 *day* 296
24	*Monday*	George Cadbury *d.* 1922. UN formally established 1945	297
25	*Tuesday*	Agincourt 1415. Georges Bizet *b.* 1838	298
26	*Wednesday*	Domenico Scarlatti *b.* 1685. William Hogarth *d.* 1764	299
27	*Thursday*	Theodore Roosevelt *b.* 1858	300
28	*Friday*	**SS Simon and Jude.** Statue of Liberty unveiled 1886	301
29	*Saturday*	Republic of Turkey proclaimed 1923	302
30	*Sunday*	**8th S. before Christmas.** George II *b.* 1683	*week* 44 *day* 303
31	*Monday*	Hallowmass Eve. Chiang Kai-shek *b.* 1887	304

ASTRONOMICAL PHENOMENA

d	h	
6	19	Mercury in conjunction with Moon. Mercury 3° S.
7	12	Jupiter in conjunction with Moon. Jupiter 0°.7 N.
7	13	Venus in conjunction with Moon. Venus 7° S.
15	04	Jupiter in conjunction with Venus. Jupiter 8° N.
15	11	Saturn in conjunction with Moon. Saturn 6° S.
21	05	Mercury in inferior conjunction
28	09	Mars in conjunction with Moon. Mars 7° N.

CONSTELLATIONS

The following constellations are near the meridian at

	d	h
September	1	24
September	15	23
October	1	22
October	16	21
November	1	20
November	15	19

Ursa Major (below the Pole), Cepheus, Cassiopeia, Cygnus, Lacerta, Andromeda, Pegasus, Capricornus, Aquarius and Piscis Austrinus

MINIMA OF ALGOL

d	h	d	h	d	h
1	14.1	13	01.3	24	12.6
4	10.9	18	18.9	27	09.4
7	07.7	21	15.8	30	06.2
10	04.5				

THE MOON

Phases, Apsides and Node	d	h	m
● New Moon	5	03	55
☽ First Quarter	11	19	17
○ Full Moon	19	12	18
☾ Last Quarter	27	16	44
Perigee (360,244 km)	6	14	06
Apogee (406,098 km)	22	01	52

Mean longitude of ascending node on October 1, 227°

THE SUN

s.d. 16′.1

Day	Right Ascension	Dec.	Equation of time	Rise 52°	Rise 56°	Transit	Set 52°	Set 56°	Sidereal time	Transit of First Point of Aries
	h m s	° ′	m s	h m	h m	h m	h m	h m	h m s	h m s
1	12 27 52	3 01	+10 07	6 00	6 02	11 50	17 38	17 36	0 38 00	23 18 11
2	12 31 30	3 24	+10 27	6 02	6 04	11 49	17 36	17 33	0 41 56	23 14 15
3	12 35 07	3 47	+10 46	6 04	6 06	11 49	17 34	17 31	0 45 53	23 10 19
4	12 38 45	4 10	+11 04	6 05	6 08	11 49	17 31	17 28	0 49 49	23 06 23
5	12 42 23	4 34	+11 23	6 07	6 10	11 48	17 29	17 26	0 53 46	23 02 27
6	12 46 02	4 57	+11 41	6 09	6 12	11 48	17 27	17 23	0 57 43	22 58 31
7	12 49 41	5 20	+11 58	6 10	6 14	11 48	17 24	17 20	1 01 39	22 54 35
8	12 53 20	5 43	+12 15	6 12	6 16	11 48	17 22	17 18	1 05 36	22 50 39
9	12 57 00	6 05	+12 32	6 14	6 18	11 47	17 20	17 15	1 09 32	22 46 43
10	13 00 40	6 28	+12 48	6 16	6 20	11 47	17 18	17 13	1 13 29	22 42 47
11	13 04 21	6 51	+13 04	6 17	6 22	11 47	17 15	17 10	1 17 25	22 38 51
12	13 08 02	7 14	+13 20	6 19	6 24	11 47	17 13	17 08	1 21 22	22 34 56
13	13 11 44	7 36	+13 35	6 21	6 27	11 46	17 11	17 05	1 25 18	22 31 00
14	13 15 26	7 59	+13 49	6 22	6 29	11 46	17 09	17 03	1 29 15	22 27 04
15	13 19 08	8 21	+14 03	6 24	6 31	11 46	17 07	17 00	1 33 12	22 23 08
16	13 22 52	8 43	+14 17	6 26	6 33	11 46	17 04	16 58	1 37 08	22 19 12
17	13 26 35	9 05	+14 29	6 28	6 35	11 45	17 02	16 55	1 41 05	22 15 16
18	13 30 20	9 27	+14 42	6 29	6 37	11 45	17 00	16 53	1 45 01	22 11 20
19	13 34 04	9 49	+14 53	6 31	6 39	11 45	16 58	16 50	1 48 58	22 07 24
20	13 37 50	10 11	+15 04	6 33	6 41	11 45	16 56	16 48	1 52 54	22 03 28
21	13 41 36	10 32	+15 15	6 35	6 43	11 45	16 54	16 45	1 56 51	21 59 32
22	13 45 23	10 53	+15 25	6 36	6 45	11 45	16 52	16 43	2 00 47	21 55 36
23	13 49 10	11 15	+15 34	6 38	6 47	11 44	16 50	16 41	2 04 44	21 51 41
24	13 52 58	11 36	+15 42	6 40	6 49	11 44	16 48	16 38	2 08 41	21 47 45
25	13 56 47	11 56	+15 50	6 42	6 51	11 44	16 46	16 36	2 12 37	21 43 49
26	14 00 37	12 17	+15 57	6 44	6 54	11 44	16 44	16 34	2 16 34	21 39 53
27	14 04 27	12 38	+16 03	6 45	6 56	11 44	16 42	16 31	2 20 30	21 35 57
28	14 08 18	12 58	+16 09	6 47	6 58	11 44	16 40	16 29	2 24 27	21 32 01
29	14 12 10	13 18	+16 13	6 49	7 00	11 44	16 38	16 27	2 28 23	21 28 05
30	14 16 03	13 38	+16 17	6 51	7 02	11 44	16 36	16 24	2 32 20	21 24 09
31	14 19 56	13 58	+16 20	6 53	7 04	11 44	16 34	16 22	2 36 16	21 20 13

DURATION OF TWILIGHT (in minutes)

Latitude	52°	56°	52°	56°	52°	56°	52°	56°
	1 October		11 October		21 October		31 October	
Civil	34	37	34	37	34	38	36	40
Nautical	73	80	73	80	74	81	75	83
Astronomical	113	125	112	124	113	124	114	126

THE NIGHT SKY

Mercury is unsuitably placed for observation at first, passing through inferior conjunction on the 21st. However, for the last few days of the month it becomes visible as a morning object low in the eastern sky, around the time of beginning of morning civil twilight. By the last day of the month its magnitude has brightened to +0.3.

Venus is unsuitably placed for observation. Although it is still almost 40° from the Sun at the beginning of the month, its declination of −23° completely nullifies this apparently favourable elongation, as seen from the latitudes of the British Isles.

Mars, magnitude +0.9, is a morning object in Cancer. Mars is visible in the SE sky during the early hours, crossing the meridian around daybreak. The Moon, at Last Quarter, will be seen approaching the planet on the morning of the 28th.

Jupiter is unsuitably placed for observation.

Saturn, magnitude +0.6, is an evening object in Aquarius. On the morning of the 15th the gibbous Moon will be seen in the vicinity of the planet. The rings of Saturn present a beautiful spectacle to the observer, even with only a small telescope, though they are now noticeably thinner than they were a few years ago, as the Earth passes through the ring plane next year.

THE MOON

Day	RA	Dec.	Hor. par.	Semi-diam.	Sun's co-long.	PA of Bright Limb	Phase	Age	Rise 52°	Rise 56°	Transit	Set 52°	Set 56°
	h m	°	′	′	°	°	%	d	h m	h m	h m	h m	h m
1	8 54	+12.0	57.4	15.6	222	102	22	25.2	1 18	1 07	8 34	15 36	15 44
2	9 47	+ 8.0	58.3	15.9	234	104	13	26.2	2 32	2 25	9 24	16 02	16 06
3	10 40	+ 3.4	59.2	16.1	246	104	7	27.2	3 49	3 47	10 15	16 27	16 27
4	11 34	− 1.5	59.9	16.3	258	100	2	28.2	5 09	5 11	11 07	16 53	16 49
5	12 29	− 6.5	60.5	16.5	271	60	0	29.2	6 31	6 38	12 02	17 21	17 13
6	13 27	−11.1	60.8	16.6	283	301	1	0.8	7 54	8 06	12 59	17 54	17 41
7	14 26	−15.0	60.8	16.6	295	290	5	1.8	9 16	9 32	13 58	18 33	18 16
8	15 27	−18.0	60.6	16.5	307	283	11	2.8	10 32	10 51	14 58	19 20	19 00
9	16 29	−19.7	60.1	16.4	319	227	20	3.8	11 40	12 01	15 58	20 16	19 55
10	17 31	−20.0	59.5	16.2	332	272	30	4.8	12 37	12 57	16 57	21 19	21 00
11	18 30	−19.1	58.8	16.0	344	266	41	5.8	13 23	13 40	17 53	22 28	22 11
12	19 27	−17.1	58.0	15.8	356	262	52	6.8	14 00	14 14	18 46	23 39	23 26
13	20 22	−14.2	57.3	15.6	8	258	63	7.8	14 30	14 40	19 35	—	—
14	21 13	−10.6	56.7	15.4	20	255	73	8.8	14 55	15 02	20 23	0 50	0 41
15	22 03	− 6.6	56.1	15.3	33	254	81	9.8	15 18	15 22	21 08	2 00	1 55
16	22 50	− 2.4	55.5	15.1	45	253	89	10.8	15 40	15 39	21 52	3 09	3 07
17	23 37	+ 1.8	55.1	15.0	57	254	94	11.8	16 01	15 57	22 36	4 16	4 18
18	0 23	+ 6.0	54.7	14.9	69	257	98	12.8	16 23	16 16	23 19	5 22	5 28
19	1 09	+ 9.8	54.4	14.8	81	269	100	13.8	16 47	16 36	—	6 28	6 37
20	1 56	+13.2	54.2	14.8	93	57	100	14.8	17 14	17 00	0 04	7 32	7 45
21	2 44	+16.0	54.1	14.7	106	72	98	15.8	17 45	17 28	0 49	8 34	8 50
22	3 33	+18.2	54.0	14.7	118	78	95	16.8	18 21	18 03	1 35	9 33	9 52
23	4 23	+19.5	54.0	14.7	130	83	90	17.8	19 05	18 44	2 23	10 27	10 47
24	5 13	+20.0	54.2	14.8	142	88	83	18.8	19 54	19 35	3 10	11 16	11 36
25	6 04	+19.6	54.5	14.9	154	93	75	19.8	20 51	20 32	3 59	11 59	12 17
26	6 54	+18.3	55.0	15.0	166	97	67	20.8	21 53	21 37	4 47	12 36	12 52
27	7 45	+16.2	55.6	15.1	179	101	57	21.8	22 59	22 47	5 35	13 07	13 21
28	8 36	+13.2	56.3	15.3	191	104	47	22.8	—	—	6 24	13 36	13 45
29	9 26	+ 9.5	57.2	15.6	203	107	37	23.8	0 10	0 01	7 12	14 01	14 07
30	10 17	+ 5.3	58.1	15.8	215	108	27	24.8	1 23	1 19	8 01	14 26	14 28
31	11 10	+ 0.6	59.1	16.1	227	109	17	25.8	2 40	2 40	8 52	14 51	14 49

MERCURY

Day	RA	Dec.	Diam.	Phase	Transit	5° high 52°	5° high 56°
	h m	°	″	%	h m	h m	h m
1	13 59	−15.5	7	51	13 20	17 18	16 58
3	14 04	−16.1	8	47	13 17	17 11	16 50
5	14 08	−16.6	8	42	13 13	17 04	16 43
7	14 11	−16.9	8	36	13 07	16 57	16 35
9	14 12	−17.0	9	30	13 00	16 49	16 28
11	14 11	−16.8	9	24	12 51	16 42	16 21
13	14 09	−16.4	9	18	12 40	16 34	16 14
15	14 04	−15.7	10	11	12 28	16 27	16 08
17	13 58	−14.7	10	6	12 13	16 19	16 02
19	13 50	−13.4	10	2	11 57	7 44	8 00
21	13 42	−11.9	10	0	11 41	7 19	7 33
23	13 33	−10.4	10	1	11 25	6 54	7 07
25	13 26	− 9.0	10	5	11 11	6 32	6 43
27	13 22	− 7.8	9	12	10 59	6 13	6 24
29	13 19	− 7.0	9	20	10 49	6 00	6 09
31	13 20	− 6.6	8	30	10 42	5 50	5 59

VENUS

Day	RA	Dec.	Diam.	Phase	Transit	5° high 52°	5° high 56°
	h m	°	″	%	h m	h m	h m
1	14 44	−22.3	41	24	14 04	17 12	16 39
6	14 50	−23.2	45	19	13 51	16 51	16 15
11	14 53	−23.8	49	15	13 34	16 30	15 52
16	14 53	−23.9	52	10	13 13	16 08	15 30
21	14 49	−23.5	56	6	12 49	15 48	15 11
26	14 41	−22.6	59	3	12 21	15 29	14 55
31	14 31	−21.1	61	1	11 52	15 12	14 42

MARS

Day	RA	Dec.	Diam.	Phase	Transit	5° high 52°	5° high 56°
1	8 01	+21.5	6	90	7 22	0 00	23 44
6	8 13	+21.0	6	90	7 15	23 55	23 40
11	8 24	+20.5	6	89	7 07	23 50	23 35
16	8 36	+19.9	6	89	6 58	23 45	23 31
21	8 47	+19.3	7	89	6 49	23 39	23 26
26	8 57	+18.7	7	89	6 40	23 33	23 21
31	9 07	+18.1	7	89	6 31	23 27	23 15

SUNRISE AND SUNSET

	London		Bristol		Birmingham		Manchester		Newcastle		Glasgow		Belfast	
	0°05′	51°30′	2°35′	51°28′	1°55′	52°28′	2°15′	53°28′	1°37′	54°59′	4°14′	55°52′	5°56′	54°35′
	h m	h m	h m	h m	h m	h m	h m	h m	h m	h m	h m	h m	h m	h m
1	6 00	17 39	6 10	17 49	6 08	17 46	6 10	17 46	6 08	17 43	6 19	17 53	6 25	18 01
2	6 02	17 36	6 12	17 46	6 10	17 43	6 12	17 44	6 10	17 41	6 21	17 50	6 27	17 58
3	6 04	17 34	6 14	17 44	6 12	17 41	6 14	17 42	6 12	17 38	6 23	17 48	6 29	17 56
4	6 05	17 32	6 15	17 42	6 13	17 39	6 15	17 39	6 14	17 35	6 25	17 45	6 31	17 53
5	6 07	17 30	6 17	17 40	6 15	17 36	6 17	17 37	6 16	17 33	6 27	17 43	6 33	17 51
6	6 09	17 27	6 19	17 37	6 17	17 34	6 19	17 34	6 18	17 30	6 29	17 40	6 35	17 48
7	6 10	17 25	6 20	17 35	6 18	17 32	6 21	17 32	6 20	17 28	6 31	17 37	6 37	17 46
8	6 12	17 23	6 22	17 33	6 20	17 29	6 23	17 30	6 22	17 25	6 33	17 35	6 39	17 43
9	6 14	17 21	6 24	17 31	6 22	17 27	6 24	17 27	6 24	17 23	6 35	17 32	6 40	17 41
10	6 15	17 19	6 25	17 29	6 24	17 25	6 26	17 25	6 26	17 21	6 37	17 30	6 42	17 38
11	6 17	17 16	6 27	17 26	6 25	17 23	6 28	17 23	6 27	17 18	6 39	17 27	6 44	17 36
12	6 19	17 14	6 29	17 24	6 27	17 20	6 30	17 20	6 29	17 16	6 41	17 25	6 46	17 33
13	6 20	17 12	6 30	17 22	6 29	17 18	6 32	17 18	6 31	17 13	6 43	17 22	6 48	17 31
14	6 22	17 10	6 32	17 20	6 31	17 16	6 34	17 16	6 33	17 11	6 45	17 20	6 50	17 29
15	6 24	17 08	6 34	17 18	6 33	17 14	6 35	17 13	6 35	17 08	6 47	17 17	6 52	17 26
16	6 25	17 06	6 35	17 16	6 34	17 11	6 37	17 11	6 37	17 06	6 49	17 15	6 54	17 24
17	6 27	17 03	6 37	17 14	6 36	17 09	6 39	17 09	6 39	17 04	6 51	17 12	6 56	17 22
18	6 29	17 01	6 39	17 11	6 38	17 07	6 41	17 07	6 41	17 01	6 53	17 10	6 58	17 19
19	6 31	16 59	6 41	17 09	6 40	17 05	6 43	17 04	6 43	16 59	6 56	17 07	7 00	17 17
20	6 32	16 57	6 42	17 07	6 41	17 03	6 45	17 02	6 45	16 56	6 58	17 05	7 02	17 15
21	6 34	16 55	6 44	17 05	6 43	17 01	6 47	17 00	6 47	16 54	7 00	17 03	7 04	17 12
22	6 36	16 53	6 46	17 03	6 45	16 59	6 48	16 58	6 49	16 52	7 02	17 00	7 06	17 10
23	6 38	16 51	6 47	17 01	6 47	16 56	6 50	16 56	6 51	16 50	7 04	16 58	7 08	17 08
24	6 39	16 49	6 49	16 59	6 49	16 54	6 52	16 53	6 53	16 47	7 06	16 55	7 10	17 05
25	6 41	16 47	6 51	16 57	6 50	16 52	6 54	16 51	6 55	16 45	7 08	16 53	7 12	17 03
26	6 43	16 45	6 53	16 55	6 52	16 50	6 56	16 49	6 57	16 43	7 10	16 51	7 14	17 01
27	6 45	16 43	6 54	16 53	6 54	16 48	6 58	16 47	7 01	16 41	7 12	16 49	7 16	16 59
28	6 46	16 41	6 56	16 51	6 56	16 46	7 00	16 45	7 01	16 38	7 14	16 46	7 18	16 57
29	6 48	16 39	6 58	16 49	6 58	16 44	7 02	16 43	7 03	16 36	7 16	16 44	7 20	16 55
30	6 50	16 38	7 00	16 48	7 00	16 42	7 04	16 41	7 05	16 34	7 19	16 42	7 22	16 52
31	6 52	16 36	7 01	16 46	7 01	16 40	7 06	16 39	7 07	16 32	7 21	16 40	7 24	16 50

JUPITER

Day	RA	Dec.	Transit	5° high	
				52°	56°
	h m	° ′	h m	h m	h m
1	14 51.5	−15 32	14 12	18 10	17 51
11	14 59.4	−16 08	13 40	17 35	17 15
21	15 07.8	−16 43	13 09	17 00	16 39
31	15 16.4	−17 19	12 39	16 25	16 03

Diameters – equatorial 31″ polar 29″

SATURN

Day	RA	Dec.	Transit	5° high	
				52°	56°
	h m	° ′	h m	h m	h m
1	22 37.6	−10 48	21 56	2 28	2 14
11	22 35.6	−10 59	21 15	1 45	1 32
21	22 34.1	−11 07	20 34	1 04	0 50
31	22 33.1	−11 12	19 54	0 23	0 09

Diameters – equatorial 18″ polar 17″
Rings – major axis 42″ minor axis 6″

URANUS

Day	RA	Dec.	Transit	10° high	
				52°	56°
	h m	° ′	h m	h m	h m
1	19 37.1	−22 05	18 56	21 14	20 18
11	19 37.2	−22 05	18 17	20 35	19 39
21	19 37.7	−22 03	17 38	19 56	19 01
31	19 38.6	−22 01	17 00	19 18	18 23

Diameter 4″

NEPTUNE

Day	RA	Dec.	Transit	10° high	
				52°	56°
	h m	° ′	h m	h m	h m
1	19 28.6	−21 17	18 48	21 14	20 25
11	19 28.7	−21 17	18 08	20 35	19 46
21	19 29.0	−21 17	17 29	19 56	19 07
31	19 29.6	−21 16	16 51	19 17	18 28

Diameter 2″

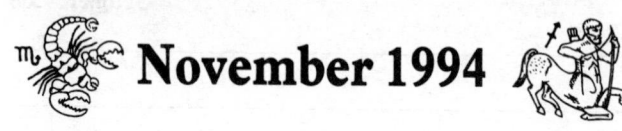

November 1994

ELEVENTH MONTH, 30 DAYS. *Novem* (nine), ninth month of Roman pre-Julian calendar

Sun's Longitude 240° ♐ 22ᵈ 13ʰ

1	*Tuesday*	**All Saints.** First premium bonds sold 1956	*week 44 day* 305
2	*Wednesday*	All Souls. Marie Antoinette *b.* 1755	306
3	*Thursday*	First dog in space 1957	307
4	*Friday*	Felix Mendelssohn *d.* 1847. Gabriel Fauré *d.* 1924	308
5	*Saturday*	Gunpowder Plot 1605. Robert Maxwell *d.* 1991	309
6	*Sunday*	**7th S. before Christmas.** Kate Greenaway *d.* 1901	*week 45 day* 310
7	*Monday*	October Revolution in Russia 1917 NS	311
8	*Tuesday*	César Franck *d.* 1890. Munich Putsch 1923	312
9	*Wednesday*	Edward VII *b.* 1841. Neville Chamberlain *d.* 1940	313
10	*Thursday*	Sir Jacob Epstein *b.* 1880. Sir Gordon Richards *d.* 1986	314
11	*Friday*	Armistice Day. Sören Kierkegaard *d.* 1855	315
12	*Saturday*	Mrs Gaskell *d.* 1865. Baroness Orczy *d.* 1947	316
13	*Sunday*	**6th S. before Christmas.** Archbishop Carey *b.* 1935	*week 46 day* 317
14	*Monday*	*Prince of Wales b. 1948.* Harold Larwood *b.* 1904	318
15	*Tuesday*	Brazil declared a Republic 1889	319
16	*Wednesday*	Paul Hindemith *b.* 1895. Clark Gable *d.* 1960	320
17	*Thursday*	Relief of Lucknow 1857. Eric Gill *d.* 1940	321
18	*Friday*	Sir David Wilkie *b.* 1785. Francis Thompson *d.* 1907	322
19	*Saturday*	Franz Schubert *d.* 1828. Sir Basil Spence *d.* 1976	323
20	*Sunday*	**5th S. before Christmas.** *Queen's Wedding Day* 1947	*week 47 day* 324
21	*Monday*	Natalia Makarova *b.* 1940. Edward Bawden *d.* 1989	325
22	*Tuesday*	George Eliot *b.* 1819. President Kennedy *assass.* 1963	326
23	*Wednesday*	Diane Quick *b.* 1946. Roald Dahl *d.* 1990	327
24	*Thursday*	Laurence Sterne *b.* 1713. Erskine Childers *exec.* 1922	328
25	*Friday*	Harley Granville-Barker *b.* 1877. Sir Anton Dolin *d.* 1983	329
26	*Saturday*	William Cowper *b.* 1731. John McAdam *d.* 1836	330
27	*Sunday*	**1st S. in Advent.** Anders Celsius *b.* 1701	*week 48 day* 331
28	*Monday*	CHANUCAH begins. Founding of Royal Society 1660	332
29	*Tuesday*	Claudio Monteverdi *d.* 1643. Louisa M. Alcott *b.* 1832	333
30	*Wednesday*	**St Andrew.** Cardinal Wolsey *d.* 1530. Mark Twain *b.* 1835	334

ASTRONOMICAL PHENOMENA

d	h	
2	07	Mercury in conjunction with Moon. Mercury 4° N.
2	23	Venus in inferior conjunction
3	12	Venus in conjunction with Moon. Venus 5° S.
3		Total eclipse of Sun (*see* page 66)
4	08	Jupiter in conjunction with Moon. Jupiter 0°.1 N.
6	01	Mercury at greatest elongation W. 19°
11	16	Saturn in conjunction with Moon. Saturn 6° S.
13	18	Venus in conjunction with Mercury. Venus 5° S.
17	20	Jupiter in conjunction with Sun
20	13	Pluto in conjunction with Sun
25	15	Mars in conjunction with Moon. Mars 7° N.
28	17	Jupiter in conjunction with Mercury. Jupiter 0°.4 N.
30	13	Venus in conjunction with Moon. Venus 2° N.

CONSTELLATIONS

The following constellations are near the meridian at

	d	h		d	h
October	1	24	November	15	21
October	16	23	December	1	20
November	1	22	December	16	19

Ursa Major (below the Pole), Cepheus, Cassiopeia, Andromeda, Pegasus, Pisces, Aquarius and Cetus

MINIMA OF ALGOL

d	h	d	h	d	h
2	03.0	13	14.3	25	01.5
4	23.8	19	07.9	27	22.3
7	20.6	22	04.7	30	19.2
10	17.5				

THE MOON

Phases, Apsides and Node	d	h	m
● New Moon	3	13	36
☽ First Quarter	10	06	14
○ Full Moon	18	06	57
☾ Last Quarter	26	07	04

	d	h	m
Perigee (357,240 km)	3	23	39
Apogee (406,347 km)	18	05	08

Mean longitude of ascending node on November 1, 225°

THE SUN
s.d. 16′.2

Day	Right Ascension	Dec. −	Equation of time	Rise 52°	Rise 56°	Transit	Set 52°	Set 56°	Sidereal time	Transit of First Point of Aries
	h m s	° ′	m s	h m	h m	h m	h m	h m	h m s	h m s
1	14 23 50	14 17	+16 23	6 54	7 06	11 44	16 32	16 20	2 40 13	21 16 17
2	14 27 45	14 36	+16 24	6 56	7 08	11 44	16 30	16 18	2 44 09	21 12 21
3	14 31 41	14 55	+16 25	6 58	7 11	11 44	16 29	16 16	2 48 06	21 08 26
4	14 35 38	15 14	+16 25	7 00	7 13	11 44	16 27	16 14	2 52 03	21 04 30
5	14 39 35	15 32	+16 24	7 02	7 15	11 44	16 25	16 12	2 55 59	21 00 34
6	14 43 34	15 51	+16 22	7 03	7 17	11 44	16 23	16 10	2 59 56	20 56 38
7	14 47 33	16 09	+16 20	7 05	7 19	11 44	16 22	16 07	3 03 52	20 52 42
8	14 51 33	16 26	+16 16	7 07	7 21	11 44	16 20	16 06	3 07 49	20 48 46
9	14 55 33	16 44	+16 12	7 09	7 23	11 44	16 18	16 04	3 11 45	20 44 50
10	14 59 35	17 01	+16 07	7 11	7 26	11 44	16 17	16 02	3 15 42	20 40 54
11	15 03 37	17 18	+16 01	7 12	7 28	11 44	16 15	16 00	3 19 38	20 36 58
12	15 07 41	17 34	+15 54	7 14	7 30	11 44	16 14	15 58	3 23 35	20 33 02
13	15 11 45	17 50	+15 47	7 16	7 32	11 44	16 12	15 56	3 27 32	20 29 06
14	15 15 50	18 06	+15 39	7 18	7 34	11 44	16 11	15 54	3 31 28	20 25 11
15	15 19 55	18 22	+15 29	7 19	7 36	11 45	16 09	15 53	3 35 25	20 21 15
16	15 24 02	18 37	+15 19	7 21	7 38	11 45	16 08	15 51	3 39 21	20 17 19
17	15 28 09	18 52	+15 09	7 23	7 40	11 45	16 07	15 49	3 43 18	20 13 23
18	15 32 18	19 07	+14 57	7 25	7 42	11 45	16 05	15 48	3 47 14	20 09 27
19	15 36 27	19 21	+14 44	7 26	7 44	11 45	16 04	15 46	3 51 11	20 05 31
20	15 40 36	19 35	+14 31	7 28	7 46	11 46	16 03	15 45	3 55 07	20 01 35
21	15 44 47	19 49	+14 17	7 30	7 48	11 46	16 02	15 43	3 59 04	19 57 39
22	15 48 59	20 02	+14 02	7 31	7 50	11 46	16 00	15 42	4 03 01	19 53 43
23	15 53 11	20 15	+13 46	7 33	7 52	11 46	15 59	15 40	4 06 57	19 49 47
24	15 57 24	20 27	+13 29	7 35	7 54	11 47	15 58	15 39	4 10 54	19 45 51
25	16 01 38	20 39	+13 12	7 36	7 56	11 47	15 57	15 38	4 14 50	19 41 56
26	16 05 53	20 51	+12 54	7 38	7 58	11 47	15 56	15 36	4 18 47	19 38 00
27	16 10 08	21 02	+12 35	7 39	7 59	11 48	15 55	15 35	4 22 43	19 34 04
28	16 14 25	21 13	+12 15	7 41	8 01	11 48	15 55	15 34	4 26 40	19 30 08
29	16 18 42	21 24	+11 55	7 42	8 03	11 48	15 54	15 33	4 30 36	19 26 12
30	16 22 59	21 34	+11 34	7 44	8 05	11 49	15 53	15 32	4 34 33	19 22 16

DURATION OF TWILIGHT (in minutes)

Latitude	52°	56°	52°	56°	52°	56°	52°	56°
	1 November		11 November		21 November		30 November	
Civil	36	40	37	41	38	43	39	45
Nautical	75	84	78	87	80	90	82	93
Astronomical	115	127	117	130	120	134	123	137

THE NIGHT SKY

Mercury is at greatest western elongation (19°) on the 6th. Thus it is a morning object at first, visible low above the eastern horizon around the time of beginning of morning civil twilight. During its period of visibility its magnitude brightens from +0.1 to −0.8. On the morning of the 2nd it may be possible to glimpse the old crescent Moon, only 1.2 days before New, below and to the right of the planet. Do not confuse Mercury with Venus when the two planets are near each other on the 13th to 14th, Mercury passing north of Venus. Mercury passes 4° north of Spica on the 3rd.

Venus is unsuitably placed for observation at first, inferior conjunction occurring on the 2nd. However, after the first ten days of the month Venus becomes visible low above the SE horizon before dawn, magnitude −4.6. The old crescent Moon will be seen approaching Venus on the morning of the 30th.

Mars brightens during the month, its magnitude changing from +0.7 to +0.3. Early in the month it moves from Cancer into Leo. The Moon, near Last Quarter, will be seen in the vicinity of the planet on the mornings of the 25th and 26th.

Jupiter is in conjunction with the Sun on the 17th and therefore unsuitably placed for observation.

Saturn, magnitude +0.8, is still an evening object in Aquarius, though no longer visible after midnight. It resumes its direct motion after reaching its second stationary point on the 9th. The Moon, near First Quarter, will be seen passing 6° north of the planet on the early evening of the 11th.

THE MOON

Day	RA h m	Dec. °	Hor. par. ′	Semi-diam. ′	Sun's co-long. °	PA of Bright Limb °	Phase %	Age d	Rise 52° h m	Rise 56° h m	Transit h m	Set 52° h m	Set 56° h m
1	12 04	− 4.3	60.0	16.3	239	109	10	26.8	3 59	4 04	9 44	15 17	15 11
2	13 00	− 9.1	60.7	16.5	252	107	4	27.8	5 22	5 31	10 40	15 48	15 37
3	13 59	−13.4	61.2	16.7	264	102	1	28.8	6 45	6 59	11 38	16 24	16 09
4	15 00	−16.8	61.4	16.7	276	284	0	0.4	8 06	8 24	12 40	17 07	16 49
5	16 04	−19.1	61.2	16.7	288	277	3	1.4	9 21	9 41	13 42	18 01	17 41
6	17 08	−20.0	60.7	16.5	300	271	9	2.4	10 25	10 46	14 44	19 04	18 44
7	18 10	−19.5	60.0	16.4	313	265	17	3.4	11 18	11 36	15 43	20 14	19 56
8	19 10	−17.7	59.2	16.1	325	261	26	4.4	11 59	12 15	16 39	21 27	21 12
9	20 07	−15.0	58.2	15.9	337	256	37	5.4	12 32	12 44	17 32	22 40	22 29
10	21 00	−11.5	57.4	15.6	349	253	47	6.4	13 00	13 08	18 20	23 51	23 44
11	21 51	− 7.5	56.5	15.4	1	251	58	7.4	13 24	13 28	19 06	—	—
12	22 39	− 3.4	55.8	15.2	14	250	68	8.4	13 45	13 46	19 51	1 00	0 57
13	23 26	+ 0.9	55.2	15.1	26	249	77	9.4	14 07	14 04	20 34	2 08	2 09
14	0 12	+ 5.0	54.8	14.9	38	250	84	10.4	14 28	14 22	21 18	3 14	3 19
15	0 58	+ 8.9	54.4	14.8	50	251	91	11.4	14 51	14 41	22 01	4 19	4 27
16	1 44	+12.4	54.2	14.8	62	252	95	12.4	15 17	15 04	22 46	5 23	5 35
17	2 32	+15.3	54.0	14.7	74	253	99	13.4	15 46	15 30	23 32	6 26	6 41
18	3 20	+17.7	54.0	14.7	86	243	100	14.4	16 21	16 03	—	7 26	7 44
19	4 10	+19.2	54.0	14.7	99	92	100	15.4	17 02	16 42	0 19	8 22	8 42
20	5 00	+20.0	54.1	14.7	111	92	97	16.4	17 50	17 30	1 07	9 13	9 34
21	5 51	+19.8	54.3	14.8	123	95	94	17.4	18 44	18 25	1 55	9 58	10 17
22	6 41	+18.8	54.6	14.9	135	99	88	18.4	19 44	19 27	2 44	10 37	10 54
23	7 32	+16.8	55.0	15.0	147	103	81	19.4	20 48	20 35	3 32	11 10	11 24
24	8 22	+14.1	55.5	15.1	159	106	73	20.4	21 55	21 46	4 19	11 38	11 49
25	9 11	+10.7	56.2	15.3	171	109	63	21.4	23 06	23 00	5 06	12 04	12 11
26	10 01	+ 6.7	56.9	15.5	184	111	53	22.4	—	—	5 53	12 28	12 32
27	10 51	+ 2.3	57.8	15.7	196	112	43	23.4	0 18	0 16	6 41	12 52	12 51
28	11 42	− 2.3	58.7	16.0	208	112	32	24.4	1 33	1 36	7 31	13 16	13 12
29	12 36	− 7.0	59.6	16.2	220	111	22	25.4	2 51	2 58	8 23	13 43	13 35
30	13 32	−11.5	60.4	16.5	232	110	13	26.4	4 12	4 23	9 18	14 15	14 03

MERCURY

Day	RA h m	Dec. °	Diam. ″	Phase %	Transit h m	5° high 52° h m	5° high 56° h m
1	13 21	− 6.6	8	35	10 40	5 48	5 57
3	13 25	− 6.7	7	45	10 36	5 45	5 54
5	13 31	− 7.2	7	54	10 35	5 46	5 56
7	13 38	− 7.8	7	62	10 35	5 50	6 00
9	13 47	− 8.7	6	69	10 36	5 56	6 07
11	13 57	− 9.7	6	75	10 38	6 03	6 16
13	14 08	−10.8	6	80	10 41	6 12	6 26
15	14 19	−11.9	6	84	10 44	6 22	6 37
17	14 30	−13.0	5	87	10 48	6 33	6 49
19	14 42	−14.2	5	90	10 52	6 44	7 02
21	14 54	−15.3	5	92	10 56	6 56	7 15
23	15 06	−16.4	5	94	11 00	7 07	7 28
25	15 19	−17.4	5	95	11 05	7 19	7 42
27	15 31	−18.4	5	96	11 10	7 31	7 55
29	15 44	−19.4	5	97	11 14	7 43	8 09
31	15 57	−20.3	5	98	11 19	7 55	8 23

VENUS

Day	RA h m	Dec. °	Diam. ″	Phase %	Transit h m	5° high 52° h m	5° high 56° h m
1	14 29	−20.8	61	1	11 45	8 23	8 52
6	14 18	−18.8	62	1	11 15	7 39	8 03
11	14 09	−16.7	60	3	10 47	6 56	7 17
16	14 03	−14.9	57	6	10 21	6 18	6 36
21	14 00	−13.3	54	10	10 00	5 47	6 03
26	14 02	−12.3	50	14	9 42	5 22	5 37
31	14 07	−11.7	46	19	9 27	5 04	5 19

MARS

Day	RA h m	Dec. °	Diam. ″	Phase %	Transit h m	5° high 52° h m	5° high 56° h m
1	9 09	+18.0	7	89	6 29	23 26	23 14
6	9 19	+17.4	7	89	6 19	23 19	23 08
11	9 28	+16.8	7	89	6 08	23 12	23 01
16	9 37	+16.3	8	89	5 57	23 04	22 53
21	9 45	+15.8	8	89	5 45	22 55	22 45
26	9 52	+15.3	8	90	5 33	22 45	22 36
31	9 59	+14.8	9	90	5 20	22 34	22 25

SUNRISE AND SUNSET

	London		Bristol		Birmingham		Manchester		Newcastle		Glasgow		Belfast	
	0°05′	51°30′	2°35′	51°28′	1°55′	52°28′	2°15′	53°28′	1°37′	54°59′	4°14′	55°52′	5°56′	54°35′
	h m	h m	h m	h m	h m	h m	h m	h m	h m	h m	h m	h m	h m	h m
1	6 53	16 34	7 03	16 44	7 03	16 39	7 07	16 37	7 10	16 30	7 23	16 37	7 26	16 48
2	6 55	16 32	7 05	16 42	7 05	16 37	7 09	16 35	7 12	16 28	7 25	16 35	7 28	16 46
3	6 57	16 30	7 07	16 40	7 07	16 35	7 11	16 33	7 14	16 26	7 27	16 33	7 30	16 44
4	6 59	16 29	7 09	16 39	7 09	16 33	7 13	16 31	7 16	16 24	7 29	16 31	7 32	16 42
5	7 00	16 27	7 10	16 37	7 11	16 31	7 15	16 29	7 18	16 22	7 31	16 29	7 34	16 40
6	7 02	16 25	7 12	16 35	7 12	16 29	7 17	16 28	7 20	16 20	7 33	16 27	7 36	16 38
7	7 04	16 23	7 14	16 34	7 14	16 28	7 19	16 26	7 22	16 18	7 36	16 25	7 38	16 37
8	7 06	16 22	7 16	16 32	7 16	16 26	7 21	16 24	7 24	16 16	7 38	16 23	7 40	16 35
9	7 07	16 20	7 17	16 30	7 18	16 24	7 23	16 22	7 26	16 14	7 40	16 21	7 42	16 33
10	7 09	16 19	7 19	16 29	7 20	16 23	7 25	16 21	7 28	16 12	7 42	16 19	7 44	16 31
11	7 11	16 17	7 21	16 27	7 22	16 21	7 27	16 19	7 30	16 10	7 44	16 17	7 46	16 29
12	7 13	16 16	7 23	16 26	7 23	16 20	7 28	16 17	7 32	16 09	7 46	16 15	7 48	16 28
13	7 14	16 14	7 24	16 24	7 25	16 18	7 30	16 16	7 34	16 07	7 48	16 14	7 49	16 26
14	7 16	16 13	7 26	16 23	7 27	16 17	7 32	16 14	7 36	16 05	7 50	16 12	7 51	16 24
15	7 18	16 11	7 28	16 22	7 29	16 15	7 34	16 13	7 38	16 04	7 52	16 10	7 53	16 23
16	7 20	16 10	7 29	16 20	7 31	16 14	7 36	16 11	7 40	16 02	7 54	16 08	7 55	16 21
17	7 21	16 09	7 31	16 19	7 32	16 12	7 38	16 10	7 42	16 00	7 56	16 07	7 57	16 20
18	7 23	16 07	7 33	16 18	7 34	16 11	7 40	16 08	7 44	15 59	7 58	16 05	7 59	16 18
19	7 25	16 06	7 35	16 16	7 36	16 10	7 41	16 07	7 46	15 57	8 00	16 04	8 01	16 17
20	7 26	16 05	7 36	16 15	7 38	16 08	7 43	16 06	7 48	15 56	8 02	16 02	8 03	16 15
21	7 28	16 04	7 38	16 14	7 39	16 07	7 45	16 04	7 49	15 55	8 04	16 01	8 05	16 14
22	7 30	16 03	7 39	16 13	7 41	16 06	7 47	16 02	7 51	15 53	8 06	15 59	8 07	16 13
23	7 31	16 02	7 41	16 12	7 43	16 05	7 48	16 02	7 53	15 52	8 08	15 58	8 08	16 11
24	7 33	16 01	7 43	16 11	7 44	16 04	7 50	16 01	7 55	15 51	8 10	15 57	8 10	16 10
25	7 34	16 00	7 44	16 10	7 46	16 03	7 52	16 00	7 57	15 50	8 12	15 55	8 12	16 09
26	7 36	15 59	7 46	16 09	7 47	16 02	7 53	15 59	7 59	15 48	8 14	15 54	8 14	16 08
27	7 37	15 58	7 47	16 08	7 49	16 01	7 55	15 58	8 00	15 47	8 16	15 53	8 15	16 07
28	7 39	15 57	7 49	16 07	7 51	16 00	7 57	15 57	8 02	15 46	8 17	15 52	8 17	16 06
29	7 40	15 56	7 50	16 07	7 52	15 59	7 58	15 56	8 04	15 45	8 19	15 51	8 19	16 05
30	7 42	15 56	7 52	16 06	7 54	15 59	8 00	15 55	8 05	15 44	8 21	15 50	8 20	16 04

JUPITER

Day	RA	Dec.	Transit	5° high	
				52°	56°
	h m	° ′	h m	h m	h m
1	15 17.3	−17 22	12 36	8 49	9 11
11	15 26.2	−17 56	12 05	8 23	8 46
21	15 35.2	−18 29	11 35	7 56	8 20
31	15 44.3	−19 00	11 04	7 30	7 55

Diameters – equatorial 31″ polar 29″

SATURN

Day	RA	Dec.	Transit	5° high	
				52°	56°
	h m	° ′	h m	h m	h m
1	22 33.0	−11 12	19 50	0 19	0 05
11	22 32.8	−11 12	19 10	23 36	23 22
21	22 33.2	−11 08	18 31	22 57	22 43
31	22 34.2	−11 00	17 53	22 20	22 06

Diameters – equatorial 18″ polar 16″
Rings – major axis 40″ minor axis 6″

URANUS

Day	RA	Dec.	Transit	10° high	
				52°	56°
	h m	° ′	h m	h m	h m
1	19 38.7	−22 01	16 56	19 14	18 19
11	19 39.9	−21 58	16 18	18 37	17 42
21	19 41.5	−21 54	15 40	18 00	17 06
31	19 43.3	−21 49	15 02	17 23	16 30

Diameter 4″

NEPTUNE

Day	RA	Dec.	Transit	10° high	
				52°	56°
	h m	° ′	h m	h m	h m
1	19 29.6	−21 16	16 47	19 14	18 24
11	19 30.4	−21 14	16 08	18 35	17 46
21	19 31.4	−21 12	15 30	17 57	17 09
31	19 32.6	−21 10	14 52	17 20	16 31

Diameter 2″

December 1994

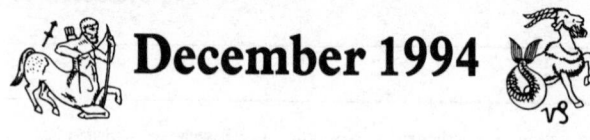

TWELFTH MONTH, 31 DAYS. *Decem* (ten), tenth month of Roman pre-Julian calendar

Sun's Longitude 270° ♑ 22ᵈ02ʰ

1	*Thursday*	Edmund Campion *exec.*1581. Queen Alexandra *b.* 1844	*week 48 day* 335
2	*Friday*	Napoleon Bonaparte crowned Emperor 1804	336
3	*Saturday*	Lord Leighton *b.* 1830. Mary Baker Eddy *d.* 1910	337
4	*Sunday*	**2nd S. in Advent.** Thomas Carlyle *b.* 1795	*week 49 day* 338
5	*Monday*	Walt Disney *b.* 1901. Claude Monet *d.* 1926	339
6	*Tuesday*	Warren Hastings *b.* 1732. Anthony Trollope *d.* 1882	340
7	*Wednesday*	Pearl Harbor 1941. Gordon Pirie *d.* 1991	341
8	*Thursday*	Jean Sibelius *b.* 1865. John Lennon *d.* 1980	342
9	*Friday*	John Milton *b.* 1608. R. A. Butler *b.* 1902	343
10	*Saturday*	Alfred Nobel *d.* 1896. Nobel Prizes first awarded 1901	344
11	*Sunday*	**3rd S. in Advent.** Colley Cibber *d.* 1757	*week 50 day* 345
12	*Monday*	Edvard Munch *b.* 1863. Douglas Fairbanks *d.* 1939	346
13	*Tuesday*	Abel Tasman discovered New Zealand 1642	347
14	*Wednesday*	C. P. E. Bach *d.* 1788. Andrei Sakharov *d.* 1989	348
15	*Thursday*	Harold Abrahams *b.* 1899. Grigori Rasputin *assass.* 1916	349
16	*Friday*	Jane Austen *b.* 1775. Somerset Maugham *d.* 1965	350
17	*Saturday*	Sir Herbert Beerbohm Tree *b.* 1853	351
18	*Sunday*	**4th S. in Advent.** Charles Wesley *b.* 1707	*week 51 day* 352
19	*Monday*	Leonid Brezhnev *b.* 1906. Stella Gibbons *d.* 1989	353
20	*Tuesday*	Sir Robert Menzies *b.* 1894. Bill Brandt *d.* 1983	354
21	*Wednesday*	*Michaelmas Law Sittings end.* Scott Fitzgerald *d.* 1940	355
22	*Thursday*	J. Arthur Rank *b.* 1888. Samuel Beckett *d.* 1989	356
23	*Friday*	Thomas Malthus *d.* 1834. Théophile Gautier *d.* 1872	357
24	*Saturday*	Christmas Eve. James Joule *b.* 1886	358
25	*Sunday*	**Christmas Day.** Sir Charles Chaplin *d.* 1977	*week 52 day* 359
26	*Monday*	**St Stephen.** Boxing Day. *Bank Holiday in the UK*	360
27	*Tuesday*	**St John the Evangelist.** *Bank Holiday in the UK*	361
28	*Wednesday*	**Holy Innocents.** Sir Arthur Eddington *b.* 1882	362
29	*Thursday*	Jameson Raid 1895. Harold Macmillan *d.* 1986	363
30	*Friday*	Rudyard Kipling *b.* 1865. Richard Rodgers *d.* 1979	364
31	*Saturday*	Peter May *b.* 1929. Sir Malcolm Campbell *d.* 1948	365

ASTRONOMICAL PHENOMENA

d	h	
2	05	Jupiter in conjunction with Moon. Jupiter 0°.5 S.
2	13	Mercury in conjunction with Moon. Mercury 2° S.
9	00	Saturn in conjunction with Moon. Saturn 6° S.
9	11	Venus at greatest brilliancy
14	03	Mercury in superior conjunction
22	02	Solstice
23	10	Mars in conjunction with Moon. Mars 8° N.
29	04	Venus in conjunction with Moon. Venus 3° N.
30	01	Jupiter in conjunction with Moon. Jupiter 1° S.

CONSTELLATIONS

The following constellations are near the meridian at

	d	h		d	h
November	1	24	December	16	21
November	15	23	January	1	20
December	1	22	January	16	19

Ursa Major (below the Pole), Ursa Minor (below the Pole), Cassiopeia, Andromeda, Perseus, Triangulum, Aries, Taurus, Cetus and Eridanus

MINIMA OF ALGOL

d	h	d	h	d	h
3	16.0	12	06.4	23	17.7
6	12.8	15	03.3	26	14.5
9	09.6	20	20.9	29	11.3

THE MOON

Phases, Apsides and Node	d	h	m
● New Moon	2	23	54
☽ First Quarter	9	21	06
○ Full Moon	18	02	17
☾ Last Quarter	25	19	06
● New Moon	32	10	56

Perigee (357,264 km)	2	12	19
Apogee (406,019 km)	15	07	47
Perigee (360,488 km)	30	23	04

Mean longitude of ascending node on December 1, 223°

THE SUN

s.d. 16′.3

Day	Right Ascension	Dec. −	Equation of time	Rise 52°	Rise 56°	Transit	Set 52°	Set 56°	Sidereal time	Transit of First Point of Aries
	h m s	° ′	m s	h m	h m	h m	h m	h m	h m s	h m s
1	16 27 18	21 44	+11 12	7 45	8 06	11 49	15 52	15 31	4 38 30	19 18 20
2	16 31 37	21 53	+10 49	7 47	8 08	11 49	15 52	15 30	4 42 26	19 14 24
3	16 35 56	22 02	+10 26	7 48	8 10	11 50	15 51	15 30	4 46 23	19 10 28
4	16 40 17	22 10	+10 03	7 49	8 11	11 50	15 51	15 29	4 50 19	19 06 32
5	16 44 38	22 18	+ 9 38	7 51	8 13	11 51	15 50	15 28	4 54 16	19 02 36
6	16 48 59	22 26	+ 9 13	7 52	8 14	11 51	15 50	15 27	4 58 12	18 58 41
7	16 53 21	22 33	+ 8 48	7 53	8 16	11 51	15 49	15 27	5 02 09	18 54 45
8	16 57 43	22 40	+ 8 22	7 54	8 17	11 52	15 49	15 26	5 06 06	18 50 49
9	17 02 06	22 46	+ 7 56	7 56	8 18	11 52	15 49	15 26	5 10 02	18 46 53
10	17 06 30	22 52	+ 7 29	7 57	8 20	11 53	15 49	15 26	5 13 59	18 42 57
11	17 10 53	22 57	+ 7 02	7 58	8 21	11 53	15 48	15 25	5 17 55	18 39 01
12	17 15 18	23 02	+ 6 34	7 59	8 22	11 54	15 48	15 25	5 21 52	18 35 05
13	17 19 42	23 07	+ 6 06	8 00	8 23	11 54	15 48	15 25	5 25 48	18 31 09
14	17 24 07	23 11	+ 5 38	8 01	8 24	11 55	15 48	15 25	5 29 45	18 27 13
15	17 28 32	23 14	+ 5 09	8 02	8 25	11 55	15 49	15 25	5 33 41	18 23 17
16	17 32 57	23 18	+ 4 41	8 02	8 26	11 56	15 49	15 25	5 37 38	18 19 21
17	17 37 23	23 20	+ 4 12	8 03	8 27	11 56	15 49	15 25	5 41 35	18 15 26
18	17 41 49	23 22	+ 3 42	8 04	8 28	11 57	15 49	15 25	5 45 31	18 11 30
19	17 46 15	23 24	+ 3 13	8 05	8 28	11 57	15 49	15 26	5 49 28	18 07 34
20	17 50 41	23 25	+ 2 43	8 05	8 29	11 58	15 50	15 26	5 53 24	18 03 38
21	17 55 07	23 26	+ 2 14	8 06	8 30	11 58	15 50	15 26	5 57 21	17 59 42
22	17 59 33	23 26	+ 1 44	8 06	8 30	11 59	15 51	15 27	6 01 17	17 55 46
23	18 04 00	23 26	+ 1 14	8 07	8 31	11 59	15 51	15 28	6 05 14	17 51 50
24	18 08 26	23 25	+ 0 44	8 07	8 31	12 00	15 52	15 28	6 09 10	17 47 54
25	18 12 53	23 24	+ 0 14	8 07	8 31	12 00	15 53	15 29	6 13 07	17 43 58
26	18 17 19	23 23	− 0 15	8 08	8 31	12 01	15 53	15 30	6 17 04	17 40 02
27	18 21 45	23 21	− 0 45	8 08	8 32	12 01	15 54	15 31	6 21 00	17 36 06
28	18 26 11	23 18	− 1 15	8 08	8 32	12 01	15 55	15 31	6 24 57	17 32 11
29	18 30 37	23 15	− 1 44	8 08	8 32	12 02	15 56	15 32	6 28 53	17 28 15
30	18 35 03	23 12	− 2 13	8 08	8 32	12 02	15 57	15 33	6 32 50	17 24 19
31	18 39 29	23 08	− 2 42	8 08	8 32	12 03	15 58	15 35	6 36 46	17 20 23

DURATION OF TWILIGHT (in minutes)

Latitude	52°	56°	52°	56°	52°	56°	52°	56°
	1 December		11 December		21 December		31 December	
Civil	40	45	41	47	41	47	41	47
Nautical	82	93	84	96	85	97	84	96
Astronomical	123	138	125	141	126	142	125	141

THE NIGHT SKY

Mercury is unsuitably placed for observation, superior conjunction occurring on the 14th.

Venus is a brilliant object, attaining its greatest brilliancy (magnitude −4.6) on the 9th. It completely dominates the SE sky for several hours before sunrise. On the morning of the 29th, the waning crescent Moon will be seen 4°–5° below the planet and observers who enjoy detecting Venus in daylight can use the Moon as a guide on that morning, just after sunrise. Observers with telescopes will notice that the phase of Venus increases noticeably during the month.

Mars is now visible from the late evening onwards, its magnitude brightening from +0.3 to −0.3 during the month. Mars is now in Leo and around the 8th will be seen passing 2° north of Regulus. It should be noted that Mars is a whole magnitude brighter than Regulus. On the morning of the 23rd the gibbous Moon will be seen approaching Mars, closest approach occurring after sunrise.

Jupiter is too close to the Sun for observation for the first ten days of the month but then emerges from the morning twilight to become visible low in the SE sky for a while before dawn. Its magnitude is −1.8.

Saturn, magnitude +1.0, continues to be visible as an evening object in the SW sky, in Aquarius. The Moon, near First Quarter, will be seen near the planet on the evening of the 8th.

Meteors. The maximum of the well-known Geminid meteor shower occurs during the early hours of the 14th. Bright moonlight will be a considerable hindrance to observation until shortly after 04h.

THE MOON

Day	RA	Dec.	Hor. par.	Semi-diam.	Sun's co-long.	PA of Bright Limb	Phase	Age	Rise 52°	Rise 56°	Transit	Set 52°	Set 56°
	h m	°	′	′	°	°	%	d	h m	h m	h m	h m	h m
1	14 31	−15.3	61.0	16.6	245	108	6	27.4	5 34	5 49	10 17	14 54	14 37
2	15 33	−18.2	61.3	16.7	257	108	2	28.4	6 53	7 12	11 19	15 42	15 22
3	16 38	−19.8	61.3	16.7	269	189	0	0.0	8 04	8 25	12 23	16 41	16 20
4	17 42	−19.9	61.0	16.6	281	258	2	1.0	9 04	9 24	13 25	17 49	17 30
5	18 45	−18.7	60.4	16.5	293	257	6	2.0	9 53	10 10	14 25	19 04	18 47
6	19 45	−16.2	59.5	16.2	306	254	13	3.0	10 31	10 45	15 21	20 20	20 07
7	20 42	−12.9	58.6	16.0	318	251	21	4.0	11 02	11 12	16 13	21 35	21 26
8	21 35	− 8.9	57.6	15.7	330	249	31	5.0	11 28	11 34	17 02	22 47	22 42
9	22 25	− 4.7	56.7	15.5	342	248	41	6.0	11 51	11 53	17 48	23 56	23 56
10	23 13	− 0.4	55.9	15.2	354	247	51	7.0	12 12	12 11	18 32	—	—
11	0 00	+ 3.9	55.2	15.0	6	247	61	8.0	12 34	12 29	19 16	1 04	1 07
12	0 46	+ 7.8	54.7	14.9	19	248	70	9.0	12 56	12 48	19 59	2 10	2 17
13	1 32	+11.5	54.3	14.8	31	250	79	10.0	13 21	13 09	20 44	3 14	3 25
14	2 19	+14.6	54.1	14.7	43	252	86	11.0	13 49	13 34	21 29	4 18	4 32
15	3 07	+17.1	54.0	14.7	55	254	92	12.0	14 21	14 04	22 16	5 19	5 36
16	3 57	+18.9	54.0	14.7	67	255	96	13.0	15 00	14 41	23 03	6 17	6 36
17	4 47	+19.9	54.1	14.8	79	251	99	14.0	15 45	15 25	23 52	7 10	7 30
18	5 38	+20.0	54.3	14.8	91	195	100	15.0	16 38	16 18	—	7 57	8 17
19	6 29	+19.2	54.6	14.9	103	115	99	16.0	17 36	17 19	0 41	8 38	8 56
20	7 20	+17.5	54.9	15.0	116	110	96	17.0	18 40	18 25	1 29	9 13	9 29
21	8 10	+14.9	55.3	15.1	128	110	92	18.0	19 46	19 35	2 17	9 43	9 56
22	9 00	+11.7	55.8	15.2	140	112	86	19.0	20 55	20 48	3 04	10 10	10 19
23	9 49	+ 7.9	56.4	15.4	152	113	78	20.0	22 06	22 02	3 51	10 34	10 39
24	10 38	+ 3.6	57.0	15.5	164	114	69	21.0	23 18	23 19	4 38	10 57	10 58
25	11 28	− 0.9	57.6	15.7	176	114	59	22.0	—	—	5 25	11 20	11 18
26	12 19	− 5.4	58.4	15.9	188	113	48	23.0	0 33	0 37	6 15	11 45	11 39
27	13 12	− 9.8	59.1	16.1	201	112	37	24.0	1 49	1 58	7 06	12 14	12 03
28	14 08	−13.8	59.8	16.3	213	109	26	25.0	3 07	3 21	8 01	12 47	12 33
29	15 07	−17.0	60.3	16.4	225	106	17	26.0	4 25	4 42	9 00	13 29	13 10
30	16 09	−19.2	60.7	16.5	237	103	9	27.0	5 39	5 59	10 01	14 20	14 00
31	17 12	−20.0	60.8	16.6	249	103	3	28.0	6 45	7 05	11 03	15 23	15 02

MERCURY

Day	RA	Dec.	Diam.	Phase	Transit	5° high 52°	5° high 56°
	h m	°	″	%	h m	h m	h m
1	15 57	−20.3	5	98	11 19	7 55	8 23
3	16 10	−21.1	5	99	11 25	8 06	8 37
5	16 23	−21.9	5	99	11 30	8 18	8 50
7	16 36	−22.6	5	99	11 35	8 29	9 03
9	16 49	−23.2	5	100	11 41	8 40	9 16
11	17 03	−23.8	5	100	11 46	8 50	9 29
13	17 17	−24.2	5	100	11 52	9 00	9 41
15	17 30	−24.6	5	100	11 58	9 10	9 52
17	17 44	−24.9	5	100	12 04	14 50	14 06
19	17 58	−25.1	5	100	12 10	14 54	14 10
21	18 12	−25.2	5	99	12 16	14 59	14 15
23	18 26	−25.2	5	99	12 23	15 06	14 21
25	18 40	−25.1	5	98	12 29	15 13	14 29
27	18 55	−24.9	5	98	12 35	15 22	14 39
29	19 09	−24.6	5	97	12 41	15 31	14 50
31	19 23	−24.3	5	96	12 48	15 41	15 02

VENUS

Day	RA	Dec.	Diam.	Phase	Transit	5° high 52°	5° high 56°
	h m	°	″	%	h m	h m	h m
1	14 07	−11.7	46	19	9 27	5 04	5 19
6	14 15	−11.6	42	24	9 16	4 52	5 06
11	14 25	−11.8	39	28	9 07	4 44	4 59
16	14 38	−12.4	36	32	9 00	4 41	4 56
21	14 52	−13.1	34	36	8 55	4 40	4 57
26	15 08	−14.0	31	39	8 51	4 43	5 00
31	15 26	−15.0	29	42	8 49	4 47	5 06

MARS

Day	RA	Dec.	Diam.	Phase	Transit	5° high 52°	5° high 56°
1	9 59	+14.8	9	90	5 20	22 34	22 25
6	10 05	+14.4	9	90	5 07	22 23	22 14
11	10 11	+14.1	9	91	4 52	22 10	22 02
16	10 15	+13.9	10	92	4 37	21 56	21 48
21	10 19	+13.7	10	92	4 21	21 40	21 32
26	10 22	+13.7	11	93	4 04	21 23	21 15
31	10 23	+13.7	11	94	3 46	21 05	20 57

OCCULTATIONS 1994

...ses during 1994, two of the Sun and ...mbral eclipses are not mentioned in ...ifficult to observe).

...of the Sun on May 10 is visible as a ...e eastern Pacific including Hawaii, ...h and Central America and the ...of Colombia and Venezuela, the ...ic Ocean, the Arctic Ocean, Green-...urope (including the British Isles), ...t Africa. The eclipse begins at 14h ...m. The track of the annular phase ...rom lower California to Nova Scotia ...th Atlantic to Morocco. The annular ...and ends at 19h 02m. The maximum ...hase is 6m 14s.

...rtial eclipse begins at 17h 36m and ...m. At Edinburgh the partial eclipse ...nds at 19h 25m. As seen from the ...tely half of the Sun is obscured at

...the Moon on May 25 is visible from ...British Isles), the Atlantic Ocean, ...land, southern Greenland, Antarc-...ot the extreme north-west) and the ...se begins at 02h 37m and ends at ...e British Isles, except the extreme ...nd Wales, and also for Ireland, the ...e the eclipse ends.

...e Sun on November 3 is visible as a ...astern South Pacific Ocean, Central ...Atlantic Ocean, part of Antarctica, ...agascar. The path of totality crosses ...Bolivia, Paraguay, and southern ...s at 11h 05m and ends at 16h 13m. ...12h 02m and ends at 15h 16m. The ...23s.

...s of occultations are made by both ...astronomers. Such observations are ...urate positions of the Moon; this is ...g the difference between ephemeris

...ns made by amateurs are obtained ...ch which is compared with a time-...he observation. Thus an accuracy ...second is obtainable, though the ...tion may amount to one-third or

...ncludes most of the occultations ...conditions in the British Isles. No ...ess the star is at least 10° above the ...iciently far below the horizon to ...with the naked eye or with a small ...nit is reduced from 10° to 2° for ...r than magnitude 2.0 and such ...ted in daylight.

...s (i) whether a disappearance (D) ...oe observed; and (ii) whether it is ...ght limb (B). The column headed ...agation of the Moon from the Sun, ...increases from 0° at New Moon ...on to 360° (or 0°) at New Moon ...angles (P), reckoned from the

north point in the direction north, east, south, west, are given for Greenwich (lat. 51° 30', long. 0°) and Edinburgh (lat. 56° 00', long. 3° 12' west).

The coefficients *a* and *b* are the variations in the GMT for each degree of longitude (positive to the west) and latitude (positive to the north) respectively; they enable approximate times (to within about 1m generally) to be found for any point in the British Isles. If the point of observation is $\Delta\lambda$ degrees west and $\Delta\phi$ degrees north, the approximate time is found by adding $a.\Delta\lambda + b.\Delta\phi$ to the given GMT.

Example: the reappearance of ZC668 on October 23 at Liverpool, found from both Greenwich and Edinburgh.

	Greenwich	Edinburgh
	°	°
Longitude	0.0	+3.2
Long. of Liverpool	+3.0	+3.0
$\Delta\lambda$	+3.0	−0.2
Latitude	+51.5	+56.0
Lat. of Liverpool	+53.4	+53.4
$\Delta\phi$	+1.9	−2.6
	h m	h m
GMT	3 32.8	3 23.8
$a.\Delta\lambda$	−4.8	+0.3
$b.\Delta\phi$	−1.5	+2.9
	3 26.5	3 27.0

If the occultation is given for one station but not the other, the reason for the suppression is given by the following code:
N = star not occulted
A = star's altitude less than 10° (2° for bright stars and planets)
S = Sun not sufficiently below the horizon
G = occultation is of very short duration
In some cases the coefficients *a* and *b* are not given; this is because the occultation is so short that prediction for other places by means of these coefficients would not be reliable.

SUNRISE AND SUNSET

	London		Bristol		Birmingham		Manchester		Newcastle		Glasgow		Belfast	
	0°05'	51°30'	2°35'	51°28'	1°55'	52°28'	2°15'	53°28'	1°37'	54°59'	4°14'	55°52'	5°56'	54°35'
	h m	h m	h m	h m	h m	h m	h m	h m	h m	h m	h m	h m	h m	h m
1	7 43	15 55	7 53	16 05	7 55	15 58	8 01	15 54	8 07	15 44	8 23	15 49	8 22	16 03
2	7 45	15 54	7 54	16 05	7 57	15 57	8 03	15 53	8 09	15 43	8 24	15 48	8 24	16 02
3	7 46	15 54	7 56	16 04	7 58	15 57	8 04	15 53	8 10	15 42	8 26	15 47	8 25	16 02
4	7 47	15 53	7 57	16 04	7 59	15 56	8 06	15 52	8 12	15 41	8 27	15 47	8 27	16 01
5	7 49	15 53	7 58	16 03	8 01	15 56	8 07	15 52	8 13	15 41	8 29	15 46	8 28	16 00
6	7 50	15 53	8 00	16 03	8 02	15 55	8 08	15 51	8 14	15 40	8 30	15 45	8 29	16 00
7	7 51	15 52	8 01	16 02	8 03	15 55	8 10	15 51	8 16	15 40	8 32	15 45	8 31	15 59
8	7 52	15 52	8 02	16 02	8 04	15 54	8 11	15 50	8 17	15 39	8 33	15 44	8 32	15 59
9	7 53	15 52	8 03	16 02	8 06	15 54	8 12	15 50	8 18	15 39	8 34	15 44	8 33	15 59
10	7 55	15 51	8 04	16 02	8 07	15 54	8 13	15 50	8 20	15 39	8 36	15 43	8 35	15 58
11	7 56	15 51	8 05	16 01	8 08	15 54	8 14	15 50	8 21	15 38	8 37	15 43	8 36	15 58
12	7 57	15 51	8 06	16 01	8 09	15 54	8 16	15 50	8 22	15 38	8 38	15 43	8 37	15 58
13	7 57	15 51	8 07	16 01	8 10	15 54	8 17	15 50	8 23	15 38	8 39	15 43	8 38	15 58
14	7 58	15 51	8 08	16 01	8 11	15 54	8 18	15 50	8 24	15 38	8 40	15 43	8 39	15 58
15	7 59	15 51	8 09	16 02	8 12	15 54	8 18	15 50	8 25	15 38	8 41	15 43	8 40	15 58
16	8 00	15 52	8 10	16 02	8 12	15 54	8 19	15 50	8 26	15 38	8 42	15 43	8 41	15 58
17	8 01	15 52	8 11	16 02	8 13	15 54	8 20	15 50	8 27	15 38	8 43	15 43	8 41	15 58
18	8 02	15 52	8 11	16 02	8 14	15 54	8 21	15 50	8 27	15 39	8 44	15 43	8 42	15 58
19	8 02	15 52	8 12	16 03	8 15	15 55	8 22	15 50	8 28	15 39	8 44	15 44	8 43	15 59
20	8 03	15 53	8 13	16 03	8 15	15 55	8 22	15 51	8 29	15 39	8 45	15 44	8 44	15 59
21	8 03	15 53	8 13	16 03	8 16	15 56	8 23	15 51	8 29	15 40	8 46	15 44	8 44	15 59
22	8 04	15 54	8 14	16 04	8 16	15 56	8 23	15 52	8 30	15 40	8 46	15 45	8 45	16 00
23	8 04	15 54	8 14	16 04	8 17	15 57	8 24	15 52	8 30	15 41	8 47	15 45	8 45	16 00
24	8 05	15 55	8 15	16 05	8 17	15 57	8 24	15 53	8 31	15 41	8 47	15 46	8 45	16 01
25	8 05	15 56	8 15	16 06	8 18	15 58	8 24	15 54	8 31	15 42	8 47	15 47	8 46	16 02
26	8 05	15 56	8 15	16 06	8 18	15 59	8 25	15 54	8 31	15 43	8 47	15 47	8 46	16 03
27	8 06	15 57	8 16	16 07	8 18	15 59	8 25	15 55	8 31	15 44	8 48	15 48	8 46	16 03
28	8 06	15 58	8 16	16 08	8 18	16 00	8 25	15 56	8 32	15 44	8 48	15 49	8 46	16 04
29	8 06	15 59	8 16	16 09	8 18	16 01	8 25	15 57	8 32	15 45	8 48	15 50	8 46	16 05
30	8 06	16 00	8 16	16 10	8 18	16 02	8 25	15 58	8 32	15 46	8 48	15 51	8 46	16 06
31	8 06	16 01	8 16	16 11	8 18	16 03	8 25	15 59	8 31	15 48	8 48	15 52	8 46	16 07

JUPITER

Day	RA	Dec.	Transit	5° high	
				52°	56°
	h m	° '	h m	h m	h m
1	15 44.3	−19 00	11 04	7 30	7 55
11	15 53.4	−19 28	10 34	7 03	7 29
21	16 02.2	−19 54	10 04	6 36	7 03
31	16 10.8	−20 18	9 33	6 08	6 36

Diameters – equatorial 31″ polar 29″

SATURN

Day	RA	Dec.	Transit	5° high	
				52°	56°
	h m	° '	h m	h m	h m
1	22 34.2	−11 00	17 53	22 20	22 06
11	22 35.9	−10 49	17 15	21 43	21 30
21	22 38.2	−10 34	16 38	21 08	20 55
31	22 41.0	−10 16	16 02	20 33	20 20

Diameters – equatorial 17″ polar 15″
Rings – major axis 38″ minor axis 5″

URANUS

Day	RA	Dec.	Transit	10° high	
				52°	56°
	h m	° '	h m	h m	h m
1	19 43.3	−21 49	15 02	17 23	16 30
11	19 45.3	−21 44	14 25	16 47	15 54
21	19 47.5	−21 39	13 48	16 11	15 19
31	19 49.9	−21 33	13 11	15 35	14 44

Diameter 4″

NEPTUNE

Day	RA	Dec.	Transit	10° high	
				52°	56°
	h m	° '	h m	h m	h m
1	19 32.6	−21 10	14 52	17 20	16 31
11	19 33.9	−21 07	14 14	16 42	15 54
21	19 35.4	−21 04	13 36	16 05	15 17
31	19 36.9	−21 01	12 58	15 28	14 40

Diameter 2″

RISING AND SETTING TIMES

TABLE 1. SEMI-DIURNAL ARCS (HOUR ANGLES AT RISING/SETTING)

Dec.	0°	10°	20°	30°	40°	45°	50°	52°	54°	56°	58°	60°	Dec.
	h m	h m	h m	h m	h m	h m	h m	h m	h m	h m	h m	h m	
0°	6 00	6 00	6 00	6 00	6 00	6 00	6 00	6 00	6 00	6 00	6 00	6 00	0°
1°	6 00	6 01	6 01	6 02	6 03	6 04	6 05	6 05	6 06	6 06	6 06	6 07	1°
2°	6 00	6 01	6 03	6 05	6 07	6 08	6 10	6 10	6 11	6 12	6 13	6 14	2°
3°	6 00	6 02	6 04	6 07	6 10	6 12	6 14	6 15	6 17	6 18	6 19	6 21	3°
4°	6 00	6 03	6 06	6 09	6 13	6 16	6 19	6 21	6 22	6 24	6 26	6 28	4°
5°	6 00	6 04	6 07	6 12	6 17	6 20	6 24	6 26	6 28	6 30	6 32	6 35	5°
6°	6 00	6 04	6 09	6 14	6 20	6 24	6 29	6 31	6 33	6 36	6 39	6 42	6°
7°	6 00	6 05	6 10	6 16	6 24	6 28	6 34	6 36	6 39	6 42	6 45	6 49	7°
8°	6 00	6 06	6 12	6 19	6 27	6 32	6 39	6 41	6 45	6 48	6 52	6 56	8°
9°	6 00	6 06	6 13	6 21	6 31	6 36	6 44	6 47	6 50	6 54	6 59	7 04	9°
10°	6 00	6 07	6 15	6 23	6 34	6 41	6 49	6 52	6 56	7 01	7 06	7 11	10°
11°	6 00	6 08	6 16	6 26	6 38	6 45	6 54	6 58	7 02	7 07	7 12	7 19	11°
12°	6 00	6 09	6 18	6 28	6 41	6 49	6 59	7 03	7 08	7 13	7 20	7 26	12°
13°	6 00	6 09	6 19	6 31	6 45	6 53	7 04	7 09	7 14	7 20	7 27	7 34	13°
14°	6 00	6 10	6 21	6 33	6 48	6 58	7 09	7 14	7 20	7 27	7 34	7 42	14°
15°	6 00	6 11	6 22	6 36	6 52	7 02	7 14	7 20	7 27	7 34	7 42	7 51	15°
16°	6 00	6 12	6 24	6 38	6 56	7 07	7 20	7 26	7 33	7 41	7 49	7 59	16°
17°	6 00	6 12	6 26	6 41	6 59	7 11	7 25	7 32	7 40	7 48	7 57	8 08	17°
18°	6 00	6 13	6 27	6 43	7 03	7 16	7 31	7 38	7 46	7 55	8 05	8 17	18°
19°	6 00	6 14	6 29	6 46	7 07	7 21	7 37	7 45	7 53	8 03	8 14	8 26	19°
20°	6 00	6 15	6 30	6 49	7 11	7 25	7 43	7 51	8 00	8 11	8 22	8 36	20°
21°	6 00	6 16	6 32	6 51	7 15	7 30	7 49	7 58	8 08	8 19	8 32	8 47	21°
22°	6 00	6 16	6 34	6 54	7 19	7 35	7 55	8 05	8 15	8 27	8 41	8 58	22°
23°	6 00	6 17	6 36	6 57	7 23	7 40	8 02	8 12	8 23	8 36	8 51	9 09	23°
24°	6 00	6 18	6 37	7 00	7 28	7 46	8 08	8 19	8 31	8 45	9 02	9 22	24°
25°	6 00	6 19	6 39	7 02	7 32	7 51	8 15	8 27	8 40	8 55	9 13	9 35	25°
26°	6 00	6 20	6 41	7 05	7 37	7 57	8 22	8 35	8 49	9 05	9 25	9 51	26°
27°	6 00	6 21	6 43	7 08	7 41	8 03	8 30	8 43	8 58	9 16	9 39	10 08	27°
28°	6 00	6 22	6 45	7 12	7 46	8 08	8 37	8 52	9 08	9 28	9 53	10 28	28°
29°	6 00	6 22	6 47	7 15	7 51	8 15	8 45	9 01	9 19	9 41	10 10	10 55	29°
30°	6 00	6 23	6 49	7 18	7 56	8 21	8 54	9 11	9 30	9 55	10 30	12 00	30°
35°	6 00	6 28	6 59	7 35	8 24	8 58	9 46	10 15	10 58	12 00	12 00	12 00	35°
40°	6 00	6 34	7 11	7 56	8 59	9 48	12 00	12 00	12 00	12 00	12 00	12 00	40°
45°	6 00	6 41	7 25	8 21	9 48	12 00	12 00	12 00	12 00	12 00	12 00	12 00	45°
50°	6 00	6 49	7 43	8 54	12 00	12 00	12 00	12 00	12 00	12 00	12 00	12 00	50°
55°	6 00	6 58	8 05	9 42	12 00	12 00	12 00	12 00	12 00	12 00	12 00	12 00	55°
60°	6 00	7 11	8 36	12 00	12 00	12 00	12 00	12 00	12 00	12 00	12 00	12 00	60°
65°	6 00	7 29	9 25	12 00	12 00	12 00	12 00	12 00	12 00	12 00	12 00	12 00	65°
70°	6 00	7 56	12 00	12 00	12 00	12 00	12 00	12 00	12 00	12 00	12 00	12 00	70°
75°	6 00	8 45	12 00	12 00	12 00	12 00	12 00	12 00	12 00	12 00	12 00	12 00	75°
80°	6 00	12 00	12 00	12 00	12 00	12 00	12 00	12 00	12 00	12 00	12 00	12 00	80°

TABLE 2. CORRECTION FOR REFRACTION AND SEMI-DIAMETER

	m	m	m	m	m	m	m	m	m	m	m	
0°	3	3	4	4	4	5	5	5	6	6	6	7	0°
10°	3	3	4	4	4	5	5	6	6	6	7	7	10°
20°	4	4	4	4	5	5	6	7	7	8	8	9	20°
25°	4	4	4	4	5	6	7	8	8	9	11	13	25°
30°	4	4	4	5	6	7	8	9	11	14	21	—	30°

NB: Regarding Table 1. If latitude and declination are of the same sign, take out the respondent directly. If they are of opposite signs, subtract the respondent from 12h.

Examples:

Lat.	Dec.	Semi-diurnal arc
+52°	+20°	7h 51m
+52°	−20°	4h 09m

SUNRISE AND SUNSET

The local mean time of sunrise or sunset may be found by obtaining the hour angle from Table 1 and applying it to the time of transit. The hour angle is negative for sunrise and positive for sunset. A small correction to the hour angle, which always has the effect of increasing it numerically, is necessary to allow for the Sun's semi-diameter (16′) and for refraction (34′); it is obtained from Table 2. The resulting local mean time may be converted into the standard time of the country by taking the difference between the longitude of the standard meridian of the country and that of the place, adding it to the local mean time if the place is west of the standard meridian, and subtracting it if the place is east.

Example – Required the New Zealand Mean Time (12h fast on GMT) of sunset on May 23 at Auckland, latitude 36° 50′ S. (or minus), longitude 11h 39m E. Taking the declination as +20°.6 (page 33), we find

		h m
Tabular entry for 30° Lat. and Dec. 20°, opposite signs		+ 5 11
Proportional part for 6° 50′ of Lat.		− 15
Proportional part for 0°.6 of Dec.		− 2
Correction (Table 2)		+ 4
Hour angle		4 58
Sun transits (page 33)		11 57
Longitudinal correction		+ 21
New Zealand Mean Time		17 16

MOONRISE AND MOONSET

It is possible to calculate the times of moonrise and moonset using Table 1, though the method is more complicated because the apparent motion of the Moon is much more rapid and also more variable than that of the Sun.

The parallax of the Moon, about 57′, is near to the sum of the semi-diameter and refraction but has the opposite effect on these times. It is thus convenient to neglect all three quantities in the method outlined below.

TABLE 3. LONGITUDE CORRECTION

A h \ X	40m	45m	50m	55m	60m	65m	70m
	m	m	m	m	m	m	m
1	2	2	2	2	3	3	3
2	3	4	4	5	5	5	6
3	5	6	6	7	8	8	9
4	7	8	8	9	10	11	12
5	8	9	10	11	13	14	15
6	10	11	13	14	15	16	18
7	12	13	15	16	18	19	20
8	13	15	17	18	20	22	23
9	15	17	19	21	23	24	26
10	17	19	21	23	25	27	29
11	18	21	23	25	28	30	32
12	20	23	25	28	30	33	35
13	22	24	27	30	33	35	38
14	23	26	29	32	35	38	41
15	25	28	31	34	38	41	44
16	27	30	33	37	40	43	47
17	28	32	35	39	43	46	50
18	30	34	38	41	45	49	53
19	32	36	40	44	48	51	55
20	33	38	42	46	50	54	58
21	35	39	44	48	53	57	61
22	37	41	46	50	55	60	64
23	38	43	48	53	58	62	67
24	40	45	50	55	60	65	70

Notation

φ = l

λ = l

T_{-1} =

T_0 =

T_1 =

δ_0 =

δ_R =

δ_S =

h_0 =

h_R =

h_S =

t_R =

t_S =

Meth

1. W
   de
   po
2. F

3. D

4. F

5.

E
V
T

ECLIPSES A

ECLIPSES

There will be thr one of the Moon this section as the

1. An annular partial eclipse fr northern Siberia, extreme northern West Indies, the land, Iceland, we and north-west ar 12m and ends at 2 crosses North Ame and then crosses th phase begins at 15h duration of the ann

At Greenwich th ends (at sunset) at begins at 17h 31m British Isles, appro maximum.

2. A partial eclip Europe (including Africa, Madagascar tica, the Americas a Pacific Ocean. The 04h 23m. For most south-west of Engla Moon will have set b

3. A total eclipse partial eclipse from and South America, southern Africa, and southern Peru, sout Brazil. The eclipse b The total phase begin maximum duration is

LUNAR OCCULTATI

Observations of the t amateur and professic later analysed to yield one method of determi time and universal tim

Many of the observ with the use of a stop- signal immediately aft of about one-fifth of observer's personal eq one-half of a second.

The list on page 6 visible under favourab occultation is included horizon and the Sun permit the star to be se telescope. The altitude stars and planets brig occultations are also pre

The column Phase sh or reappearance (R) is at the dark limb (D) or 'El. of Moon' gives the e in degrees. The elonga to 180° at Full Moon an again. Times and posi

LUNAR OCCULTATIONS 1994

Date		ZC No.	Mag.	Phase	El. of Moon	GREENWICH				EDINBURGH			
						UT	a	b	P	UT	a	b	P
					°	h m	m	m	°	h m	m	m	°
January	2	1495	5.9	R.D.	232					1 12.9			220
	15	3326	6.4	D.D.	46	18 47.5	−0.8	−1.5	87	18 39.6	−0.7	−1.0	71
	16	3455	6.4	D.D.	57	19 21.6	−0.7	−0.7	65	19 17.2	−0.6	−0.3	49
	16	3453	4.9	D.D.	57	19 27.0	−0.5	0.8	27	19 32.4			3
	17	29	7.2	D.D.	69	21 27.7	−0.4	−0.6	57	21 24.6	−0.4	−0.2	42
	21	497	6.5	D.D.	113	22 39.0	−0.7	−3.6	135	22 22.9	−0.9	−2.4	118
	22	628	4.8	D.D.	123	21 22.6	−1.6	1.1	51	21 25.2	−1.4	2.4	32
	24	915	4.7	D.D.	146	N				19 42.0			153
February	17	455	6.1	D.D.	81	21 23.4	−0.8	−1.1	75	21 16.8	−0.8	−0.8	63
	20	873	7.9	D.D.	115	23 7.8	0.0	−3.8	156	22 51.9	−0.4	−2.9	143
	21	892	6.6	D.D.	116	2 3.1	−0.2	−0.9	60	1 58.1	−0.3	−0.9	54
	21	894	4.6	D.D.	117	2 31.8	−0.1	−0.8	55	2 27.7	−0.2	−0.8	49
	21	1006	6.9	D.D.	125	18 30.0	−1.4	0.4	106	18 29.2	−1.1	1.0	92
	22	1038	6.8	D.D.	128	1 9.4	−0.4	−1.8	106	1 0.2	−0.5	−1.7	101
	22	1141	5.6	D.D.	137	19 23.1	−1.3	0.0	117	19 20.7	−1.1	0.6	103
	23	1281	6.4	D.D.	152	22 57.4	−1.3	−0.9	110	22 49.9	−1.3	−0.5	102
March	18	691	6.6	D.D.	73	22 52.2	0.4	−2.4	131	22 42.6	0.1	−2.3	123
	22	1212	7.1	D.D.	117	19 22.9			170	S			
	22	1234	6.1	D.D.	120	23 46.9	−1.1	−0.9	68	23 39.5	−1.2	−0.8	62
April	16	913	5.2	D.D.	64	21 45.2	−0.3	−1.3	75	21 38.3	−0.5	−1.2	69
	21	1543	6.6	D.D.	127	24 5.6	−0.7	−1.7	110	23 56.0	−0.7	−1.6	107
	22	1639	7.0	D.D.	138	20 22.3	−0.8	−1.2	151	S			
	22	1655	6.7	D.D.	140	23 27.3	−1.0	−1.4	117	23 18.3	−1.0	−1.2	114
	23	1670	5.1	D.D.	141	2 33.0	−0.2	−2.3	161	2 22.2	−0.3	−2.1	155
	28	2376	4.6	R.D.	212	2 31.7	−1.5	−0.1	266	2 26.9	−1.3	0.0	270
May	18	1495	5.9	D.D.	96	23 32.4	−0.3	−1.5	88	23 24.3	−0.4	−1.6	85
	19	1605	6.2	D.D.	108	22 55.6	−1.1	−0.9	60	22 48.1	−1.2	−0.8	55
	20	1723	7.1	D.D.	121	21 54.8	−1.1	−1.4	124	21 45.7	−1.0	−1.2	121
	21	1845	6.5	D.D.	135	22 34.5			186	22 21.9			179
	28	2791	5.4	R.D.	220	1 25.7	−1.4	0.9	251	1 25.6	−1.2	0.9	255
June	1	3320	5.3	R.D.	269	1 59.2	−0.6	2.1	225	2 6.7	−0.5	2.0	230
	18	1930	5.6	D.D.	117	20 49.5	−1.5	−0.6	93	S			
	21	2217	5.5	D.D.	146	0 24.5	−0.7	−0.1	38	0 23.0			25
	21	2376	4.6	D.D.	159	22 24.1	−1.4	−0.1	105	22 19.9	−1.2	0.1	102
July	18	2307	4.1	D.D.	127	20 34.2	−1.6	0.2	69	S			
	18	2310	4.6	D.D.	127	20 52.7	−1.4	−0.5	108	S			
	20	2633	4.0	D.D.	155	22 25.9	−1.5	−0.2	102	22 20.9	−1.3	0.0	97
	20	2638	5.4	D.D.	155	23 26.1	−1.0	0.4	39	23 25.0	−0.8	0.5	29
August	13	2119	6.7	D.D.	85	20 20.1	−1.0	−1.5	111	A			
	14	2267	5.1	D.D.	99	21 34.9	−0.9	−1.3	94	21 26.4	−0.9	−1.2	88
	24	105	4.6	R.D.	223	22 20.0	−0.9	1.1	296	22 21.9	−0.9	1.0	308
	31	895	5.9	R.D.	291	4 0.2	−1.4	−0.7	319	N			
October	10	2642	7.1	D.D.	77	18 21.1	−1.9	−1.8	136	18 9.8	−1.5	−1.0	125
	13	3093	4.5	D.D.	116	22 39.3	−0.4	0.4	32	22 41.6	−0.1	1.1	12
	17	3494	4.6	D.D.	153	3 13.3	−0.3	−1.2	78	3 7.5	−0.3	−0.9	64
	23	668	3.6	R.D.	219	3 32.8	−1.6	−0.8	273	3 23.8	−1.4	−1.1	287
	28	1318	5.7	R.D.	276	5 1.8	−1.0	−2.1	336	4 46.3			357
November	11	3320	5.3	D.D.	111	23 56.1	−0.7	−3.6	124	23 41.8	−0.6	−2.2	103
	12	3444	6.5	D.D.	122	23 23.3	−0.6	0.5	32	23 26.4	−0.3	1.6	11
	13	6	6.9	D.D.	131	19 44.9	−1.9	0.2	98	19 42.0	−1.4	0.8	85
	14	103	6.1	D.D.	141	17 26.0	−0.7	1.9	71	17 32.7	−0.5	2.0	64
	14	105	4.6	D.D.	142	18 8.4	−0.2	3.0	14	18 23.3			357
December	8	3259	7.4	D.D.	76	17 32.8	−1.3	0.5	55	17 32.2	−1.0	0.7	44
	12	209	7.2	D.D.	123	20 6.4	−1.6	0.5	74	20 5.2	−1.2	1.0	60
	21	1332	5.7	R.D.	223	21 5.1	−0.3	−0.4	329	A			

MEAN PLACES OF STARS 1994.5

Name	Mag.	RA	Dec.	Spectrum
		h m	° '	
α And *Alpheratz*	2.1	0 08.1	+29 04	A0p
β Cassiopeiae *Caph*	2.3	0 08.9	+59 07	F5
γ Pegasi *Algenib*	2.8	0 13.0	+15 09	B2
β Mensae	2.9	0 25.5	−77 17	G0
α Phoenicis	2.4	0 26.0	−42 20	K0
α Cassiopeiae *Schedar*	2.2	0 40.2	+56 30	K0
β Ceti *Diphda*	2.0	0 43.3	−18 01	K0
γ Cassiopeiae*	Var.	0 56.4	+60 41	B0p
β Andromedae *Mirach*	2.1	1 09.4	+35 35	M0
δ Cassiopeiae	2.7	1 25.5	+60 12	A5
α Eridani *Achernar*	0.5	1 37.5	−57 16	B5
β Arietis *Sheratan*	2.6	1 54.3	+20 47	A5
γ Andromedae *Almak*	2.3	2 03.6	+42 18	K0
α Arietis *Hamal*	2.0	2 06.9	+23 26	K2
α Ursae Minoris *Polaris*	2.0	2 25.9	+89 14	F8
β Persei *Algol**	Var.	3 07.8	+40 56	B8
α Persei *Mirfak*	1.8	3 23.9	+49 51	F5
η Tauri *Alcyone*	2.9	3 47.2	+24 05	B5p
α Tauri *Aldebaran*	0.9	4 35.6	+16 30	K5
β Orionis *Rigel*	0.1	5 14.3	− 8 12	B8p
α Aurigae *Capella*	0.1	5 16.3	+46 00	G0
γ Orionis *Bellatrix*	1.6	5 24.8	+ 6 21	B2
β Tauri *Elnath*	1.7	5 25.9	+28 36	B8
δ Orionis	2.2	5 31.7	− 0 18	B0
α Leporis	2.6	5 32.5	−17 50	F0
ε Orionis	1.7	5 35.9	− 1 12	B0
ζ Orionis	1.8	5 40.5	− 1 57	B0
κ Orionis	2.1	5 47.5	− 9 40	B0
α Orionis *Betelgeuse**	Var.	5 54.9	+ 7 24	M0
β Aurigae *Menkalinan*	1.9	5 59.1	+44 57	A0p
β CMa *Mirzam*	2.0	6 22.5	−17 57	B1
α Carinae *Canopus*	−0.7	6 23.8	−52 42	F0
γ Geminorum *Alhena*	1.9	6 37.4	+16 24	A0
α Canis Majoris *Sirius*	−1.5	6 44.9	−16 43	A0
ε Canis Majoris	1.5	6 58.4	−28 58	B1
δ Canis Majoris	1.9	7 08.2	−26 23	F8p
α Geminorum *Castor*	1.6	7 34.2	+31 54	A0
α CMi *Procyon*	0.4	7 39.0	+ 5 14	F5
β Geminorum *Pollux*	1.1	7 45.0	+28 02	K0
ζ Puppis	2.3	8 03.4	−39 59	Od
γ Velorum	1.8	8 09.4	−47 19	Oap
ε Carinae	1.9	8 22.4	−59 30	K0
δ Velorum	2.0	8 44.6	−54 41	A0
λ Velorum *Suhail*	2.2	9 07.8	−43 25	K5
β Carinae	1.7	9 13.1	−69 42	A0
ι Carinae	2.2	9 16.9	−59 15	F0
κ Velorum	2.6	9 21.9	−54 59	B3
α Hydrae *Alphard*	2.0	9 27.3	− 8 38	K2
α Leonis *Regulus*	1.3	10 08.1	+12 00	B8
γ Leonis *Algeiba*	1.9	10 19.7	+19 52	K0
β Ursae Majoris *Merak*	2.4	11 01.5	+56 25	A0
α Ursae Majoris *Dubhe*	1.8	11 03.4	+61 47	K0
δ Leonis	2.6	11 13.8	+20 33	A3
β Leonis *Denebola*	2.1	11 48.8	+14 36	A2
γ Ursae Majoris *Phecda*	2.4	11 53.5	+53 44	A0
γ Corvi	2.6	12 15.5	−17 31	B8
α Crucis	1.0	12 26.3	−63 04	B1
γ Crucis	1.6	12 30.9	−57 05	M3
γ Centauri	2.2	12 41.2	−48 56	A0
γ Virginis	2.7	12 41.4	− 1 25	F0
β Crucis	1.3	12 47.4	−59 40	B1
ε Ursae Majoris *Alioth*	1.8	12 53.8	+55 59	A0p
α Canum Venaticorum	2.9	12 55.8	+38 21	A0p
ζ Ursae Majoris *Mizar*	2.1	13 23.7	+54 57	A2p
α Virginis *Spica*	1.0	13 24.9	−11 08	B2
ε Centauri	2.6	13 39.5	−53 26	B1
η Ursae Majoris *Alkaid*	1.9	13 47.3	+49 20	B3
β Centauri *Hadar*	0.6	14 03.4	−60 21	B1
θ Centauri	2.1	14 06.4	−36 21	K0
α Bootis *Arcturus*	0.0	14 15.4	+19 12	K0
α Centauri *Rigil Kent*	0.1	14 39.2	−60 49	G0
ε Bootis	2.4	14 44.7	+27 06	K0
β UMi *Kochab*	2.1	14 50.7	+74 11	K5
α CrB *Alphecca*	2.2	15 34.5	+26 44	A0
β Trianguli Australis	3.0	15 54.7	−63 25	F0
δ Scorpii	2.3	16 00.0	−22 36	B0
β Scorpii	2.6	16 05.1	−19 47	B1
γ Ursae Minoris	3.1	15 20.7	+71 51	A2
α Scorpii *Antares*	1.0	16 29.1	−26 25	M0
α Trianguli Australis	1.9	16 48.1	−69 01	K2
ε Scorpii	2.3	16 49.8	−34 17	K0
α Herculis†	Var.	17 14.4	+14 24	M3
λ Scorpii	1.6	17 33.2	−37 06	B2
α Ophiuchi *Rasalhague*	2.1	17 34.7	+12 34	A5
θ Scorpii	1.9	17 36.9	−43 00	F0
κ Scorpii	2.4	17 42.1	−39 02	B2
γ Draconis	2.2	17 56.5	+51 29	K5
ε Sgr *Kaus Australis*	1.9	18 23.8	−34 23	A0
α Lyrae *Vega*	0.0	18 36.8	+38 47	A0
σ Sagittarii	2.0	18 54.9	−26 18	B3
β Cygni *Albireo*	3.1	19 30.5	+27 57	K0
α Aquilae *Altair*	0.8	19 50.5	+ 8 51	A5
α Capricorni	3.8	20 17.7	−12 34	G5
γ Cygni	2.2	20 22.0	+40 14	F8p
α Pavonis	1.9	20 25.2	−56 45	B3
α Cygni *Deneb*	1.3	20 41.2	+45 16	A2p
α Cephei *Alderamin*	2.4	21 18.4	+62 34	A5
ε Pegasi	2.4	21 43.9	+ 9 51	K0
δ Capricorni	2.9	21 46.7	−16 09	A5
α Gruis	1.7	22 07.9	−46 59	B5
δ Cephei†	3.7	22 29.0	+58 23	†
β Gruis	2.1	22 42.3	−46 55	M3
α PsA *Fomalhaut*	1.2	22 57.3	−29 39	A3
β Pegasi *Scheat*	2.4	23 03.5	+28 03	M0
α Pegasi *Markab*	2.5	23 04.5	+15 11	A0

*γ Cassiopeiae, 1993 mag. 2.5. β Persei, mag. 2.1 to 3.4.
α Orionis, mag. 0.1 to 1.2.
†α Herculis, mag. 3.1 to 3.9. δ Cephei, mag. 3.7 to 4.4,
Spectrum F5 to G0.

The positions of heavenly bodies on the celestial sphere are defined by two co-ordinates, right ascension and declination, which are analogous to longitude and latitude on the surface of the Earth. If we imagine the plane of the terrestrial equator extended indefinitely, it will cut the celestial sphere in a great circle known as the celestial equator. Similarly the plane of the Earth's orbit, when extended, cuts in the great circle called the ecliptic. The two intersections of these circles are known as the First Point of Aries and the First Point of Libra. If from any star a perpendicular be drawn to the celestial equator, the length of this perpendicular is the star's declination. The arc, measured eastwards along the equator from the First Point of Aries to the foot of this perpendicular, is the right ascension. An alternative definition of right ascension is that it is the angle at the celestial pole (where the Earth's axis, if prolonged, would meet the sphere) between the great circles to the First Point of Aries and to the star.

The plane of the Earth's equator has a slow movement, so that our reference system for right ascension and declination is not fixed. The consequent alteration in these quantities from year to year is called precession. In right ascension it is an increase of about 3s a year for equatorial stars, and larger or smaller changes in either direction for stars near the poles, depending on the right ascension of the star. In declination it varies between $+20''$ and $-20''$ according to the right ascension of the star.

A star or other body crosses the meridian when the sidereal time is equal to its right ascension. The altitude is then a maximum, and may be deduced by remembering that the altitude of the elevated pole is numerically equal to the latitude, while that of the equator at its intersection with the meridian is equal to the co-latitude, or complement of the latitude.

Thus in London (lat. 51° 30′) the meridian altitude of Sirius is found as follows:

	° ′
Altitude of equator	38 30
Declination south	16 43
Difference	21 47

The altitude of Capella (Dec. $+45° 59'$) at lower transit is:

	° ′
Altitude of pole	51 30
Polar distance of star	44 00
Difference	7 30

The brightness of a heavenly body is denoted by its magnitude. Omitting the exceptionally bright stars Sirius and Canopus, the twenty brightest stars are of the first magnitude, while the faintest stars visible to the naked eye are of the sixth magnitude. The magnitude scale is a precise one, as a difference of five magnitudes represents a ratio of 100 to 1 in brightness. Typical second magnitude stars are Polaris and the stars in the belt of Orion. The scale is most easily fixed in memory by comparing the stars with Norton's *Star Atlas* (*see* page 71). The stars Sirius and Canopus and the planets Venus and Jupiter are so bright that their magnitudes are expressed by negative numbers. A small telescope will show stars down to the ninth or tenth magnitude, while stars fainter than the twentieth magnitude may be photographed by long exposures with the largest telescopes.

MEAN AND SIDEREAL TIME

Acceleration				Retardation			
h	m s	m s	s	h	m s	m s	s
1	0 10	0 00	0	1	0 10	0 00	0
2	0 20	3 02	1	2	0 20	3 03	1
3	0 30	9 07	2	3	0 29	9 09	2
4	0 39	15 13	3	4	0 39	15 15	3
5	0 49	21 18	4	5	0 49	21 21	4
6	0 59	27 23	5	6	0 59	27 28	5
7	1 09	33 28	6	7	1 09	33 34	6
8	1 19	39 34	7	8	1 19	39 40	7
9	1 29	45 39	8	9	1 28	45 46	8
10	1 39	51 44	9	10	1 38	51 53	9
11	1 48	57 49	10	11	1 48	57 59	10
12	1 58	60 00		12	1 58	60 00	
13	2 08			13	2 08		
14	2 18			14	2 18		
15	2 28			15	2 27		
16	2 38			16	2 37		
17	2 48			17	2 47		
18	2 57			18	2 57		
19	3 07			19	3 07		
20	3 17			20	3 17		
21	3 27			21	3 26		
22	3 37			22	3 36		
23	3 47			23	3 46		
24	3 57			24	3 56		

The length of a sidereal day in mean time is 23h 56m 04s.09. Hence 1h MT = 1h + 9s.86 ST and 1h ST = 1h − 9s.83 MT.

To convert an interval of mean time to the corresponding interval of sidereal time, enter the acceleration table with the given mean time (taking the hours and the minutes and seconds separately) and add the acceleration obtained to the given mean time. To convert an interval of sidereal time to the corresponding interval of mean time, take out the retardation for the given sidereal time and subtract.

The columns for the minutes and seconds of the argument are in the form known as critical tables. To use these tables, find in the appropriate left-hand column the two entries between which the given number of minutes and seconds lies; the quantity in the right-hand column between these two entries is the required acceleration or retardation. Thus the acceleration for 11m 26s (which lies between the entries 9m 07s and 15m 13s) is 2s. If the given number of minutes and seconds is a tabular entry, the required acceleration or retardation is the entry in the right-hand column above the given tabular entry, e.g. the retardation for 45m 46s is 7s.

Example – Convert 14h 27m 35s from ST to MT

	h m s
Given ST	14 27 35
Retardation for 14h	2 18
Retardation for 27m 35s	5
Corresponding MT	14 25 12

For further explanation, *see* pages 73–4.

ECLIPSES AND SHADOW TRANSITS OF JUPITER'S SATELLITES 1994

GMT d h m	Sat.	Phen.
JANUARY		
3 05 50	I	Ec.D.
3 06 19	II	Sh.E.
4 05 13	I	Sh.E.
10 04 17	III	Ec.D.
10 06 32	II	Sh.I.
10 06 33	III	Ec.R.
10 07 43	I	Ec.D.
11 04 57	I	Sh.I.
11 07 06	I	Sh.E.
18 06 50	I	Sh.I.
19 03 39	II	Ec.D.
19 04 04	I	Ec.D.
19 06 02	II	Ec.R.
20 03 28	I	Sh.E.
26 05 57	I	Ec.D.
26 06 15	II	Ec.D.
27 03 12	I	Sh.I.
27 05 22	I	Sh.E.
28 03 13	II	Sh.E.
28 04 17	III	Sh.E.
FEBRUARY		
3 05 06	I	Sh.I.
3 07 15	I	Sh.E.
4 03 26	II	Sh.I.
4 05 46	II	Sh.E.
4 06 03	III	Sh.I.
10 06 59	I	Sh.I.
11 04 11	I	Ec.D.
11 05 59	II	Sh.I.
12 03 37	I	Sh.E.
13 03 07	II	Ec.R.
15 02 17	III	Ec.R.
18 06 03	I	Ec.D.
19 03 21	I	Sh.I.
19 05 30	I	Sh.E.
20 03 20	II	Ec.D.
20 05 43	II	Ec.R.
22 04 01	III	Ec.D.
22 06 13	III	Ec.R.
26 05 14	I	Sh.I.
27 02 24	I	Ec.D.
27 05 56	II	Ec.D.
28 01 52	I	Sh.E.
MARCH		
1 02 40	II	Sh.E.
6 04 17	I	Ec.D.
7 01 36	I	Sh.I.
7 03 45	I	Sh.E.
8 02 53	II	Sh.I.
8 05 13	II	Sh.E.
12 01 51	III	Sh.I.
12 04 00	III	Sh.E.
13 06 10	I	Ec.D.
14 03 29	I	Sh.I.
14 05 39	I	Sh.E.
15 00 39	I	Ec.D.
15 05 26	II	Sh.I.
16 00 07	I	Sh.E.
17 00 24	II	Ec.D.

GMT d h m	Sat.	Phen.
19 05 49	III	Sh.I.
21 05 23	I	Sh.I.
22 02 32	I	Ec.D.
22 23 51	I	Sh.I.
23 02 01	I	Sh.E.
24 03 00	II	Ec.D.
25 23 36	II	Sh.E.
29 04 25	I	Ec.D.
29 23 49	III	Ec.D.
30 01 45	I	Sh.I.
30 01 58	III	Ec.R.
30 03 55	I	Sh.E.
30 22 53	I	Ec.D.
31 05 35	II	Ec.D.
APRIL		
1 23 49	II	Sh.I.
2 02 10	II	Sh.E.
6 03 38	I	Sh.I.
6 03 46	III	Ec.D.
7 00 47	I	Ec.D.
7 22 07	I	Sh.I.
8 00 17	I	Sh.E.
9 02 23	II	Sh.I.
9 04 44	II	Sh.E.
14 02 40	I	Ec.D.
15 00 00	I	Sh.I.
15 02 11	I	Sh.E.
16 04 57	II	Sh.I.
16 21 41	III	Sh.I.
16 23 48	III	Sh.E.
18 00 04	II	Ec.D.
21 04 34	I	Ec.D.
22 01 54	I	Sh.I.
22 04 04	I	Sh.E.
22 23 02	I	Ec.D.
23 22 33	I	Sh.E.
24 01 40	III	Sh.I.
24 03 46	III	Sh.E.
25 02 40	II	Ec.D.
26 20 49	II	Sh.I.
26 23 10	II	Sh.E.
29 03 48	I	Sh.I.
30 00 56	I	Ec.D.
30 03 06	I	Ec.R.
30 22 17	I	Sh.I.
MAY		
1 00 27	I	Sh.E.
1 21 35	I	Ec.R.
3 23 23	II	Sh.I.
4 01 45	II	Sh.E.
4 21 46	III	Ec.R.
5 20 54	II	Ec.R.
8 00 11	I	Sh.I.
8 02 21	I	Sh.E.
8 23 29	I	Ec.R.
9 20 50	I	Sh.E.
11 01 58	II	Sh.I.
12 01 44	III	Ec.R.
12 23 30	II	Ec.R.
15 02 05	I	Sh.I.
16 01 23	I	Ec.R.

GMT d h m	Sat.	Phen.
16 20 34	I	Sh.I.
16 22 44	I	Sh.E.
20 02 05	II	Ec.R.
23 22 28	I	Sh.I.
24 00 38	I	Sh.E.
24 21 46	I	Ec.R.
28 22 49	II	Sh.E.
29 21 33	III	Sh.I.
29 23 36	III	Sh.E.
31 00 23	I	Sh.I.
31 23 41	I	Ec.R.
JUNE		
1 21 01	I	Sh.E.
4 23 04	II	Sh.I.
5 01 25	II	Sh.E.
6 01 31	III	Sh.I.
8 22 55	I	Sh.E.
13 23 08	II	Ec.R.
15 22 40	I	Sh.I.
16 00 49	I	Sh.E.

GMT d h m	Sat.	Phen.
16 21 36	III	Ec.R.
16 21 59	I	Ec.R.
23 23 31	III	Ec.D.
23 23 54	I	Ec.R.
24 21 13	I	Sh.E.
29 22 33	II	Sh.E.
JULY		
1 23 07	I	Sh.E.
6 22 48	II	Sh.I.
8 22 53	I	Sh.I.
9 22 13	I	Ec.R.
11 21 26	III	Sh.I.
15 22 46	II	Ec.R.
17 21 25	I	Sh.E.
24 21 11	I	Sh.I.
29 21 30	III	Ec.R.
AUGUST		
16 20 00	II	Ec.D.
17 20 47	I	Ec.R.

Jupiter's satellites transit across the disk from east to west, and pass behind the disk from west to east. The shadows that they cast also transit across the disk. With the exception at times of Satellite IV, the satellites also pass through the shadow of the planet, i.e. they are eclipsed. Just before opposition the satellite disappears in the shadow to the west of the planet and reappears from occultation on the east limb. Immediately after opposition the satellite is occulted at the west limb and reappears from eclipse to the east of the planet. At times approximately two to four months before and after opposition, both phases of eclipses of Satellite III may be seen. When Satellite IV is eclipsed, both phases may be seen.

The times given refer to the centre of the satellite. As the satellite is of considerable size, the immersion and emersion phases are not instantaneous. Even when the satellite enters or leaves the shadow along a radius of the shadow, the phase can last for several minutes. With satellite IV, grazing phenomena can occur so that the light from the satellite may fade and brighten again without a complete eclipse taking place.

The list of phenomena gives most of the eclipses and shadow transits visible in the British Isles under favourable conditions.

Ec.	= Eclipse	R.	= Reappearance
Sh.	= Shadow transit	I.	= Ingress
D.	= Disappearance	E.	= Egress

EXPLANATION OF ASTRONOMICAL DATA

Positions of the heavenly bodies are given only to the degree of accuracy required by amateur astronomers for setting telescopes, or for plotting on celestial globes or star atlases. Where intermediate positions are required, linear interpolation may be employed.

Definitions of the terms used cannot be given here. They must be sought in astronomical literature and textbooks. Probably the best source for the amateur is Norton's *Star Atlas and Reference Handbook* (Longman, 18th edition, 1989; £18.99), which contains an introduction to observational astronomy, and a series of star maps for showing stars visible to the naked eye. Certain more extended ephemerides are available in the British Astronomical Association Handbook, an annual popular among amateur astronomers. (Secretary: Burlington House, Piccadilly, London, W1V 9AG)

A special feature has been made of the times when the various heavenly bodies are visible in the British Isles. Since two columns, calculated for latitudes 52° and 56°, are devoted to risings and settings, the range 50° to 58° can be covered by interpolation and extrapolation. The times given in these columns are Greenwich Mean Times for the meridian of Greenwich. An observer west of this meridian must add his/her longitude (in time) and vice versa.

In accordance with the usual convention in astronomy, + and − indicate respectively north and south latitudes or declinations.

All data are, unless otherwise stated, for 0h Greenwich Mean Time (GMT), i.e. at the midnight at the beginning of the day named.

PAGE ONE OF EACH MONTH

The calendar for each month is explained on page 15.

Under the heading Astronomical Phenomena will be found particulars of the more important conjunctions of the Sun, Moon and planets with each other, and also the dates of other astronomical phenomena of special interest.

The Constellations listed each month are those that are near the meridian at the beginning of the month at 22h local mean time. Allowance must be made for British Summer Time if necessary. The fact that any star crosses the meridian 4m earlier each night or 2h earlier each month may be used, in conjunction with the lists given each month, to find what constellations are favourably placed at any moment. The table preceding the list of constellations may be extended indefinitely at the rate just quoted.

Times of Minima of Algol are approximate times of the middle of the period of diminished light.

The principal phases of the Moon are the GMTs when the difference between the longitude of the Moon and that of the Sun is 0°, 90°, 180° or 270°. The times of perigee and apogee are those when the Moon is nearest to, and farthest from, the Earth, respectively. The nodes or points of intersection of the Moon's orbit and the ecliptic make a complete retrograde circuit of the ecliptic in about 19 years. From a knowledge of the longitude of the ascending node and the inclination, whose value does not vary much from 5°, the path of the Moon among the stars may be plotted on a celestial globe or star atlas.

PAGE TWO OF EACH MONTH

The Sun's semi-diameter, in arc, is given once a month.

The right ascension and declination (Dec.) is that of the true Sun. The right ascension of the mean Sun is obtained by applying the equation of time, with the sign given, to the right ascension of the true Sun, or, more easily, by applying

12h to the column Sidereal Time. The direction in which the equation of time has to be applied in different problems is a frequent source of confusion and error. Apparent Solar Time is equal to the Mean Solar Time plus the Equation of Time. For example at noon on August 8 the Equation of Time is −5m 38s and thus at 12h Mean Time on that day the Apparent Time is 12h − 5m 38s = 11h 54m 22s.

The Greenwich Sidereal Time at 0h and the Transit of the First Point of Aries (which is really the mean time when the sidereal time is 0h) are used for converting mean time to sidereal time and vice versa.

The GMT of transit of the Sun at Greenwich may also be taken as the local mean time (LMT) of transit in any longitude. It is independent of latitude. The GMT of transit in any longitude is obtained by adding the longitude to the time given if west, and vice versa.

LIGHTING-UP TIME

The legal importance of Sunrise and Sunset is that the Road Vehicles Lighting Regulations 1989 (SI 1989 No. 1796) make the use of front and rear position lamps on vehicles compulsory during the period between sunset and sunrise. Headlamps on vehicles are required to be used during the hours of darkness on unlit roads or whenever visibility is seriously reduced. The hours of darkness are defined in these regulations as the period between half an hour after sunset and half an hour before sunrise.

In all laws and regulations 'sunset' refers to the local sunset, i.e. the time at which the Sun sets at the place in question. This common-sense interpretation has been upheld by legal tribunals. Thus the necessity for providing for different latitudes and longitudes, as already described, is evident.

SUNRISE AND SUNSET

The times of Sunrise and Sunset are those when the Sun's upper limb, as affected by refraction, is on the true horizon of an observer at sea-level. Assuming the mean refraction to be 34′, and the Sun's semi-diameter to be 16′, the time given is that when the true zenith distance of the Sun's centre is 90° + 34′ + 16′ or 90° 50′, or, in other words, when the depression of the Sun's centre below the true horizon is 50′. The upper limb is then 34′ below the true horizon, but is brought there by refraction. It is true, of course, that an observer on a ship might see the Sun for a minute or so longer, because of the dip of the horizon, while another viewing the sunset over hills or mountains would record an earlier time. Nevertheless, the moment when the true zenith distance of the Sun's centre is 90° 50′ is a precise time dependent only on the latitude and longitude of the place, and independent of its altitude above sea-level, the contour of its horizon, the vagaries of refraction or the small seasonal change in the Sun's semi-diameter; this moment is suitable in every way as a definition of sunset (or sunrise) for all statutory purposes. (For further information, *see* footnote.)

SUNRISE, SUNSET AND MOONRISE, MOONSET

The tables have been constructed for the meridian of Greenwich, and for latitudes 52° and 56°. They give Greenwich Mean Time (GMT) throughout the year. To obtain the GMT of the phenomenon as seen from any other latitude and longitude in the British Isles, first interpolate or extrapolate for latitude by the usual rules of proportion. To the time thus found, the longitude (expressed in time) is to be added if west (as it usually is in Great Britain) or subtracted if east. If the longitude is expressed in degrees and minutes of arc, it must be converted to time at the rate of 1° = 4m and 15′ = 1m.

A method of calculating rise and set times for other places in the world is given on pages 64 and 65.

TWILIGHT

Light reaches us before sunrise and continues to reach us for some time after sunset. The interval between darkness and sunrise or sunset and darkness is called twilight. Astronomically speaking, twilight is considered to begin or end when the Sun's centre is 18° below the horizon, as no light from the Sun can then reach the observer. As thus defined, twilight may last several hours; in high latitudes at the summer solstice the depression of 18° is not reached, and twilight lasts from sunset to sunrise.

The need for some sub-division of twilight is met by dividing the gathering darkness into four steps.

(1) *Sunrise or Sunset,* defined as above.

(2) *Civil twilight,* which begins or ends when the Sun's centre is 6° below the horizon. This marks the time when operations requiring daylight may commence or must cease. In England it varies from about 30 to 60 minutes after sunset and the same interval before sunrise.

(3) *Nautical twilight,* which begins or ends when the Sun's centre is 12° below the horizon. This marks the time when it is, to all intents and purposes, completely dark.

(4) *Astronomical twilight,* which begins or ends when the Sun's centre is 18° below the horizon. This marks theoretical perfect darkness. It is of little practical importance, especially if nautical twilight is tabulated.

To assist observers the durations of civil, nautical and astronomical twilights are given at intervals of ten days. The beginning of a particular twilight is found by subtracting the duration from the time of sunrise, while the end is found by adding the duration to the time of sunset. Thus the beginning of astronomical twilight in latitude 52°, on the Greenwich meridian, on March 11 is found as 06h 24m − 113m = 04h 31m and similarly the end of civil twilight as 17h 57m + 34m = 18h 31m.

The letters TAN (twilight all night) are printed when twilight lasts all night.

Under the heading The Night Sky will be found notes describing the position and visibility of all the planets and also of other phenomena.

PAGE THREE OF EACH MONTH

The Moon moves so rapidly among the stars that its position is given only to the degree of accuracy that permits linear interpolation. The right ascension (RA) and declination (Dec.) are geocentric, i.e. for an imaginary observer at the centre of the Earth. To an observer on the surface of the Earth the position is always different, as the altitude is always less on account of parallax, which may reach 1°.

The lunar terminator is the line separating the bright from the dark part of the Moon's disk. Apart from irregularities of the lunar surface, the terminator is elliptical, because it is a circle seen in projection. It becomes the full circle forming the limb, or edge, of the Moon at New and Full Moon. The selenographic longitude of the terminator is measured from the mean centre of the visible disk, which may differ from the visible centre by as much as 8°, because of libration.

Instead of the longitude of the terminator the Sun's selenographic co-longitude (Sun's co-long.) is tabulated. It is numerically equal to the selenographic longitude of the morning terminator, measured eastwards from the mean centre of the disk. Thus its value is approximately 270° at New Moon, 360° at First Quarter, 90° at Full Moon and 180° at Last Quarter.

The Position Angle (PA) of the Bright Limb is the position angle of the midpoint of the illuminated limb, measured eastwards from the north point on the disk. The column Phase shows the percentage of the area of the Moon's disk illuminated; this is also the illuminated percentage of the diameter at right angles to the line of cusps. The terminator is a semi-ellipse whose major axis is the line of cusps, and whose semi-minor axis is determined by the tabulated percentage; from New Moon to Full Moon the east limb is dark, and vice versa.

The times given as moonrise and moonset are those when the upper limb of the Moon is on the horizon of an observer at sea-level. The Sun's horizontal parallax (Hor. par.) is about 9″, and is negligible when considering sunrise and sunset, but that of the Moon averages about 57′. Hence the computed time represents the moment when the true zenith distance of the Moon is 90° 50′ (as for the Sun) minus the horizontal parallax. The time required for the Sun or Moon to rise or set is about four minutes (except in high latitudes). *See also* page 65 and footnote on page 71.)

The GMT of transit of the Moon over the meridian of Greenwich is given; these times are independent of latitude, but must be corrected for longitude. For places in the British Isles it suffices to add the longitude if west, and vice versa. For more remote places a further correction is necessary because of the rapid movement of the Moon relative to the stars. The entire correction is conveniently determined by first finding the west longitude λ of the place. If the place is in west longitude, λ is the ordinary west longitude; if the place is in east longitude λ is the complement to 24h (or 360°) of the longitude and will be greater than 12h (or 180°). The correction then consists of two positive portions, namely λ and the fraction $\lambda/24$ (or $\lambda°/360$) multiplied by the difference between consecutive transits. Thus for Sydney, New South Wales, the longitude is 10h 05m east, so $\lambda = 13$h 55m and the fraction $\lambda/24$ is 0.58. The transit on the local date 1994 January 4 is found as follows:

		d	h	m
GMT of transit at Greenwich	Jan.	3	04	21
λ			13	55
0.58 × (5h 11m − 4h 21m)				29
GMT of transit at Sydney		3	18	25
Corr. to NSW Standard Time			10	00
Local standard time of transit		4	04	25

As is evident, for any given place the quantities λ and the correction to local standard time may be combined permanently, being here 23h 55m.

Positions of Mercury are given for every second day, and those of Venus and Mars for every fifth day; they may be interpolated linearly. The diameter (Diam.) is given in seconds of arc. The phase is the illuminated percentage of the disk. In the case of the inner planets this approaches 100 at superior conjunction and 0 at inferior conjunction. When the phase is less than 50 the planet is crescent-shaped or horned; for greater phases it is gibbous. In the case of the exterior planet Mars, the phase approaches 100 at conjunction and opposition, and is a minimum at the quadratures.

Since the planets cannot be seen when on the horizon, the actual times of rising and setting are not given; instead, the time when the planet has an apparent altitude of 5° has been tabulated. If the time of transit is between 00h and 12h the time refers to an altitude of 5° above the eastern horizon; if between 12h and 24h, to the western horizon. The phenomenon tabulated is the one that occurs between sunset and sunrise. The times given may be interpolated for latitude and corrected for longitude as in the case of the Sun and Moon.

The GMT at which the planet transits the Greenwich meridian is also given. The times of transit are to be corrected to local meridians in the usual way, as already described.

PAGE FOUR OF EACH MONTH

The GMTs of sunrise and sunset for seven towns, whose adopted positions in longitude (W.) and latitude (N.) are given immediately below the name, may be used not only for these phenomena, but also for lighting-up times, which, under the Road Vehicles Lighting Regulations 1989, are from sunset to sunrise throughout the year. (*See* page 71 for a fuller explanation.)

The particulars for the four outer planets resemble those for the planets on Page Three of each month, except that, under Uranus and Neptune, times when the planet is 10° high instead of 5° high are given; this is because of the inferior brightness of these planets. The diameters given for the rings of Saturn are those of the major axis (in the plane of the planet's equator) and the minor axis respectively. The former has a small seasonal change due to the slightly varying distance of the Earth from Saturn, but the latter varies from zero when the Earth passes through the ring plane every 15 years to its maximum opening half-way between these periods. The rings were open at their widest extent in 1988.

TIME

From the earliest ages, the natural division of time into recurring periods of day and night has provided the practical time-scale for the everyday activities of the human race. Indeed, if any alternative means of time measurement is adopted, it must be capable of adjustment so as to remain in general agreement with the natural time-scale defined by the diurnal rotation of the Earth on its axis. Ideally the rotation should be measured against a fixed frame of reference; in practice it must be measured against the background provided by the celestial bodies. If the Sun is chosen as the reference point, we obtain Apparent Solar Time, which is the time indicated by a sundial. It is not a uniform time but is subject to variations which amount to as much as a quarter of an hour in each direction. Such wide variations cannot be tolerated in a practical time-scale, and this has led to the concept of Mean Solar Time in which all the days are exactly the same length and equal to the average length of the Apparent Solar Day.

The positions of the stars in the sky are specified in relation to a fictitious reference point in the sky known as the First Point of Aries (or the Vernal Equinox). It is therefore convenient to adopt this same reference point when considering the rotation of the Earth against the background of the stars. The time-scale so obtained is known as Apparent Sidereal Time.

GREENWICH MEAN TIME

The daily rotation of the Earth on its axis causes the Sun and the other heavenly bodies to appear to cross the sky from east to west. It is convenient to represent this relative motion as if the Sun really performed a daily circuit around a fixed Earth. Noon in Apparent Solar Time may then be defined as the time at which the Sun transits across the observer's meridian. In Mean Solar Time, noon is similarly defined by the meridian transit of a fictitious Mean Sun moving uniformly in the sky with the same average speed as the true Sun. Mean Solar Time observed on the meridian of the transit circle telescope of the Old Royal Observatory at Greenwich is called Greenwich Mean Time (GMT). The mean solar day is divided into 24 hours and, for astronomical and other scientific purposes, these are numbered 0 to 23, commencing at midnight. Civil time is usually reckoned in two periods of 12 hours, designated a.m. (*ante meridiem*, i.e. before noon) and p.m. (*post meridiem*, i.e. after noon).

UNIVERSAL TIME

Before 1925 January 1, GMT was reckoned in 24 hours commencing at noon; since that date it has been reckoned from midnight. In view of the risk of confusion in the use of the designation GMT before and after 1925, the International Astronomical Union recommended in 1928 that astronomers should employ the term Universal Time (UT) or Weltzeit (WZ) to denote GMT measured from Greenwich Mean Midnight.

In precision work it is necessary to take account of small variations in Universal Time. These arise from small irregularities in the rotation of the Earth. Observed astronomical time is designated UT0. Observed time corrected for the effects of the motion of the poles (giving rise to a 'wandering' in longitude) is designated UT1. There is also a seasonal fluctuation in the rate of rotation of the Earth arising from meteorological causes, often called the annual fluctuation. UT1 corrected for this effect is designated UT2 and provides a time-scale free from short-period fluctuations. It is still subject to small secular and irregular changes.

APPARENT SOLAR TIME

As has been mentioned above, the time shown by a sundial is called Apparent Solar Time. It differs from Mean Solar Time by an amount known as the Equation of Time, which is the total effect of two causes which make the length of the apparent solar day non-uniform. One cause of variation is that the orbit of the Earth is not a circle, but an ellipse, having the Sun at one focus. As a consequence, the angular speed of the Earth in its orbit is not constant; it is greatest at the beginning of January when the Earth is nearest the Sun.

The other cause is due to the obliquity of the ecliptic; the plane of the equator (which is at right angles to the axis of rotation of the Earth) does not coincide with the ecliptic (the plane defined by the apparent annual motion of the Sun around the celestial sphere) but is inclined to it at an angle of 23° 26'. As a result, the apparent solar day is shorter than average at the equinoxes and longer at the solstices. From the combined effects of the components due to obliquity and eccentricity, the equation of time reaches its maximum values in February (-14 minutes) and early November ($+16$ minutes). It has a zero value on four dates during the year, and it is only on these dates (approximately April 15, June 14, September 1, and December 25) that a sundial shows Mean Solar Time.

SIDEREAL TIME

A sidereal day is the duration of a complete rotation of the Earth with reference to the First Point of Aries. The term sidereal (or 'star') time is perhaps a little misleading since the time-scale so defined is not exactly the same as that which would be defined by successive transits of a selected star, as there is a small progressive motion between the stars and the First Point of Aries due to the precession of the Earth's axis. This makes the length of the sidereal day shorter than the true period of rotation by 0.008 seconds. Superimposed on this steady precessional motion are small oscillations called nutation, giving rise to fluctuations in apparent sidereal time amounting to as much as 1.2 seconds. It is therefore customary to employ Mean Sidereal Time, from which these fluctuations have been removed. The conversion of GMT to Greenwich sidereal time (GST) may be performed by adding the value of the GST at 0h on the day in question (Page Two of each month) to the GMT converted to sidereal time using the table on page 69.

Example – To find the GST at August 8d 02h 41m 11s GMT

	h	m	s
GST at 0h	21	05	06
GMT	2	41	11
Acceleration for 2h			20
Acceleration for 41m 11s			7
Sum = GST =	23	46	44

If the observer is not on the Greenwich meridian then his/her longitude, measured positively westwards from Greenwich, must be subtracted from the GST to obtain Local Sidereal Time (LST). Thus, in the above example, an observer 5h east of Greenwich, or 19h west, would find the LST as 4h 46m 44s.

Ephemeris Time

In the study of the motions of the Sun, Moon and planets, observations taken over an extended period are used in the preparation of tables giving the apparent position of the body each day. A table of this sort is known as an ephemeris, and may be used in the comparison of current observations with tabulated positions. A detailed examination of the observations made over the past 300 years shows that the Sun, Moon and planets appear to depart from their predicted positions by amounts proportional to their mean motions. The only satisfactory explanation is that the time-scale to which the observations were referred was not as uniform as had been supposed. Since the time-scale was based on the rotation of the Earth, it follows that this rotation is subject to irregularities. The fact that the discrepancies between the observed and ephemeris positions were proportional to the mean motions of the bodies made it possible to secure agreement by substituting a revised time-scale and recomputing the ephemeris positions. The time-scale which brings the ephemeris into agreement with the observations is known as Ephemeris Time (ET).

The second of ET is defined in terms of the annual motion of the Earth in its orbit around the Sun (1/31556925.9747 of the tropical year for 1900 January 0d 12h ET). The precise determination of ET from astronomical observations is a lengthy process, as the accuracy with which a single observation of the Sun can be made is far less than that obtainable in, for instance, a comparison between clocks. It is therefore necessary to average the observations over an extended period. Largely on account of its faster motion, the position of the Moon may be observed with greater accuracy, and a close approximation to Ephemeris Time may be obtained by comparing observations of the Moon with its ephemeris position. Even in this case, however, the requisite standard of accuracy can only be achieved by averaging over a number of years.

In 1976 the International Astronomical Union adopted a new dynamical time-scale for general use whose scale unit is the SI second (see under Atomic Time). ET is now of little more than historical interest.

Atomic Time

The fundamental standards of time and frequency must be defined in terms of a periodic motion adequately uniform, enduring and measurable. Progress has made it possible to use natural standards, such as atomic or molecular oscillations. Continuous oscillations are generated in an electrical circuit, the frequency of which is then compared or brought into coincidence with the frequency characteristic of the absorption or emission by the atoms or molecules when they change between two selected energy levels. The National Physical Laboratory routinely uses clocks of high stability produced by locking a quartz oscillator to the frequency defined by a caesium atomic beam.

International Atomic Time (TAI), established through international collaboration, is formed by combining the readings of many caesium clocks and was set close to the astronomically-based Universal Time (UT) near the beginning of 1958. It was formally recognized in 1971 and since 1988 January 1 has been maintained by the International Bureau of Weights and Measures (BIPM). The second markers are generated according to the SI definition of the second adopted in 1967 at the 13th General Conference of Weights and Measures: 'The second is the duration of 9 192 631 770 periods of the radiation corresponding to the transition between the two hyperfine levels of the ground state of the caesium-133 atom.'

Civil time in almost all countries is now based on Coordinated Universal Time (UTC), which differs from TAI by an integer number of seconds (determined from studies of the rate of rotation of the Earth) so that UTC does not depart from UT by more than 0.9s. UTC was designed to make both atomic time and UT accessible with accuracies appropriate for most users.

Radio Time-Signals

UTC is made generally available through time-signals and standard frequency broadcasts such as MSF in the UK, CHU in Canada and WWV and WWVH in the USA. These are based on national time-scales that are maintained in close agreement with UTC and provide traceability to the national time-scale and to UTC. The markers of seconds in the UTC scale coincide with those of TAI.

As the rate of rotation of the Earth is variable, the time-signals are adjusted by the introduction of a leap second when necessary in order that UTC shall not depart from UT by more than 0.9s. For convenience, leap seconds are introduced when necessary on the last second of the third, sixth, ninth or twelfth month, but preferably on December 31 and/or June 30. In the case of a positive leap second, 23h 59m 60s is followed one second later by 0h 0m 0s of the first day of the month. In the case of a negative leap second, 23h 59m 58s is followed one second later by 0h 0m 0s of the first day of the month. Notices concerning the insertion of leap seconds in UTC are issued by the International Earth Rotation Service at the Observatoire de Paris.

To disseminate the national time-scale in the UK, special signals are broadcast on behalf of the National Physical Laboratory from the BT (British Telecom) radio station at Rugby. The signals are controlled from a caesium beam atomic frequency standard and consist of a standard frequency carrier of 60 kHz (MSF) which switches off for half a second to denote the passing of one minute, and for a tenth of a second to denote the passing of one second. Also transmitted are two binary coded decimal (BCD) time codes giving time of day and calendar information. Summer and winter time changes are encoded on instruction from the British Government. Other broadcast signals in the UK include the BBC six pips signal, the BT Speaking Clock and a coded time-signal on the BBC 198 kHz Droitwich transmitter, which is used for timing in the electricity supply industry. From 1972 January 1 the six pips on the BBC have consisted of five short pips from second 55 to second 59 followed by one lengthened pip, the start of which indicates the exact minute. From 1990 February 5 these signals have been controlled by the BBC with respect to the broadcast MSF signal and are thus traceable to the National Physical Laboratory. Formerly they were generated by the Royal Greenwich Observatory. The BT Speaking Clock is connected to the National Physical Laboratory caesium beam atomic frequency standard at the Rugby radio station.

Accurate timing may also be obtained from the signals of

international navigation systems, such as the ground-based Loran-C or Omega, or satellite-based Global Positioning System (GPS) of the USA or the Russian GLONASS system.

STANDARD TIME

In the year 1880 it was enacted by statute that the word 'time', when it occurred in any legal document relating to Great Britain, was to be interpreted, unless otherwise specifically stated, as the mean time of the Greenwich meridian. Summer time is the legal time during the period in which its use is ordained.

Since the year 1883 the system of standard time by zones has been gradually accepted, and now throughout the world a standard time which differs from that of Greenwich by an integral number of hours, either fast or slow, is used. (For time zones of countries of the world, *see* Index.)

Variations from the standard time of some countries occur during part of the year; they are decided annually and are usually referred to as Summer Time or Daylight Saving Time.

The large territories of the United States and Canada are divided into zones approximately 7.5° on either side of central meridians.

At the 180th meridian the time can be either 12 hours fast on Greenwich Mean Time or 12 hours slow, and a change of date occurs. The internationally-recognized date or calendar line is a modification of the 180th meridian, drawn so as to include islands of any one group on the same side of the line, or for political reasons. The line is indicated by joining up the following co-ordinates:

Lat.	Long.	Lat.	Long.
60° S.	180°	48° N.	180°
51° S.	180°	53° N.	170° E.
45° S.	172.5° W.	65.5° N.	169° W.
15° S.	172.5° W.	75° N.	180°
5° S.	180°		

BRITISH SUMMER TIME

In 1916 an Act ordained that during a defined period of that year the legal time for general purposes in Great Britain should be one hour in advance of Greenwich Mean Time. The Summer Time Acts 1922 to 1925 defined the period during which Summer Time was to be in force, stabilizing practice until the Second World War.

During the war the duration of Summer Time was extended and in the years 1941-5 and in 1947 Double Summer Time (two hours in advance of Greenwich Mean Time) was in force. After the war, Summer Time was extended in each year from 1948-52 and 1961-4 by Order in Council.

Between 1968 October 27 and 1971 October 31 clocks were kept one hour ahead of Greenwich Mean Time throughout the year. This was known as British Standard Time, although Greenwich Mean Time remained the standard time of Great Britain.

The most recent legislation is the Summer Time Act 1972, which enacted that 'the period of summer time for the purposes of this Act is the period beginning at two o'clock, Greenwich mean time, in the morning of the day after the third Saturday in March or, if that day is Easter Day, the day after the second Saturday in March, and ending at two o'clock, Greenwich mean time, in the morning of the day after the fourth Saturday in October.'

The duration of Summer Time can be varied by Order in Council and in recent years alterations have been made to bring the operation of Summer Time in Britain closer to similar provisions in other countries of the European Community. The latest Order in Council is the Summer Time Order 1992, stipulating that the duration of Summer Time in 1994 will be from March 27 to October 23. As in recent years, the hour of changeover will be 01h Greenwich Mean Time.

The duration of Summer Time in the following years was:

1990 March 25-October 28
1991 March 31-October 27
1992 March 29-October 25
1993 March 28-October 24
1994 March 27-October 23

MEAN REFRACTION

Alt.	Ref.		Alt.	Ref.		Alt.	Ref.	
° ′	′		° ′	′		° ′	′	
1 20		21	3 12		13	7 54		6
1 30		20	3 34		12	9 27		5
1 41		19	4 00		11	11 39		4
1 52		18	4 30		10	15 00		3
2 05		17	5 06		9	20 42		2
2 19		16	5 50		8	32 20		1
2 35		15	6 44		7	62 17		0
2 52		14	7 54			90 00		
3 12								

The refraction table is in the form of a critical table (*see* page 69)

ASTRONOMICAL CONSTANTS

Solar Parallax	8″.794
Astronomical unit	149597870 km
Precession for the year 1994	50″.289
Precession in Right Ascension	3s.075
Precession in Declination	20″.044
Constant of Nutation	9″.202
Constant of Aberration	20″.496
Mean Obliquity of Ecliptic (1994)	23° 26′ 24″
Moon's Equatorial Hor. Parallax	57′ 02″.70
Velocity of light in vacuo per second	299792.5 km
Solar motion per second	20.0 km
Equatorial radius of the Earth	6378.140 km
Polar radius of the Earth	6356.755 km
North Galactic Pole (IAU standard)	
RA 12h 49m (1950.0). Dec. 27°.4 N.	
Solar Apex	RA 18h 06m Dec. +30°
Length of Year (in mean solar days)	
Tropical	365.24220
Sidereal	365.25636
Anomalistic	365.25964
(perihelion to perihelion)	
Eclipse	346.6200

Length of Month (mean values)	d	h	m	s
New Moon to New	29	12	44	02.9
Sidereal	27	07	43	11.5
Anomalistic	27	13	18	33.2
(perigee to perigee)				

ELEMENTS OF THE SOLAR SYSTEM

Orb	Mean distance from Sun (Earth=1)	km 10⁶	Sidereal period y	d	Synodic period days	Incl. of orbit to ecliptic °	′	Diameter km	Mass (Earth=1)	Period of rotation on axis d	h	m
Sun	—	—	—		—		—	1,392,000	332,948	25	09	
Mercury	0.39	58		88	116	7	00	4,880	0.055	59		
Venus	0.72	108		225	584	3	24	12,100	0.815	243		
Earth	1.00	150	1	0	—		—	12,756eq	1.00		23	56
Mars	1.52	228	1	322	780	1	51	6,790	0.107		24	37
Jupiter	5.20	778	11	315	399	1	18	142,800eq / 134,200p	318		9 / 9	50 / 56
Saturn	9.54	1427	29	167	378	2	29	120,000eq / 108,000p	95		10 / 10	14 / 38
Uranus	19.19	2870	84	6	370	0	46	52,000	14.6		16–28	
Neptune	30.07	4497	164	288	367	1	46	48,400	17.2		18–20	
Pluto	39.46	5950	247	255	367	17	09	2,445	0.01	6	09	

eq equatorial, *p* polar

THE SATELLITES

Name	Star mag.	Mean distance from primary km	Sidereal period of revolution d		Name	Star mag.	Mean distance from primary km	Sidereal period of revolution d
EARTH					SATURN			
Moon	—	384,400	27.322		Hyperion	14	1,481,000	21.278
					Iapetus	11	3,561,000	79.331
MARS					Phoebe	16	12,952,000	550.3
Phobos	12	9,400	0.319					
Deimos	13	23,500	1.262		URANUS			
					Cordelia	—	49,800	0.330
JUPITER					Ophelia	—	53,800	0.372
XVI Metis	17	128,000	0.295		Bianca	—	59,200	0.433
XV Adrastea	19	129,000	0.298		Juliet	—	61,800	0.464
V Amalthea	14	181,000	0.498		Desdemona	—	62,700	0.474
XIV Thebe	15	222,000	0.675		Rosalind	—	64,400	0.493
I Io	5	422,000	1.769		Portia	—	66,100	0.513
II Europa	5	671,000	3.551		Cressida	—	69,900	0.558
III Ganymede	5	1,070,000	7.155		Belinda	—	75,300	0.622
IV Callisto	6	1,880,000	16.689		Puck	—	86,000	0.762
XIII Leda	20	11,090,000	239		Miranda	17	129,000	1.414
VI Himalia	15	11,480,000	251		Ariel	14	191,000	2.520
X Lysithea	18	11,720,000	259		Umbriel	15	266,000	4.144
VII Elara	17	11,740,000	260		Titania	14	436,000	8.706
XII Ananke	19	21,200,000	631		Oberon	14	583,000	13.463
XI Carme	18	22,600,000	692					
VIII Pasiphae	18	23,500,000	735		NEPTUNE			
IX Sinope	18	23,700,000	758		Naiad	—	48,000	0.30
					Thalassa	—	50,000	0.31
SATURN					Despina	—	52,000	0.33
Pan	—	134,000	0.575		Galatea	—	62,000	0.43
Atlas	18	138,000	0.602		Larissa	—	74,000	0.55
Prometheus	16	139,000	0.613		Proteus	—	118,000	1.12
Pandora	16	142,000	0.629		Triton	14	355,000	5.877
Epimetheus	15	151,000	0.694		Nereid	19	5,510,000	360.21
Janus	14	151,000	0.695					
Mimas	13	186,000	0.942		PLUTO			
Enceladus	12	238,000	1.370		Charon	17	19,600	6.387
Tethys	10	295,000	1.888					
Telesto	19	295,000	1.888					
Calypso	18	295,000	1.888					
Dione	10	377,000	2.737					
Helene	18	377,000	2.737					
Rhea	10	527,000	4.518					
Titan	8	1,222,000	15.945					

THE EARTH

The shape of the Earth is that of an oblate spheroid or solid of revolution whose meridian sections are ellipses not differing much from circles, whilst the sections at right angles are circles. The length of the equatorial axis is about 12,756 kilometres, and that of the polar axis is 12,714 kilometres. The mean density of the Earth is 5.5 times that of water, although that of the surface layer is less. The Earth and Moon revolve about their common centre of gravity in a lunar month; this centre in turn revolves round the Sun in a plane known as the ecliptic, that passes through the Sun's centre. The Earth's equator is inclined to this plane at an angle of 23.4°. This tilt is the cause of the seasons. In mid-latitudes, and when the Sun is high above the Equator, not only does the high noon altitude make the days longer, but the Sun's rays fall more directly on the Earth's surface; these effects combine to produce summer. In equatorial regions the noon altitude is large throughout the year, and there is little variation in the length of the day. In higher latitudes the noon altitude is lower, and the days in summer are appreciably longer than those in winter.

The average velocity of the Earth in its orbit is 30 kilometres a second. It makes a complete rotation on its axis in about 23h 56m of mean time, which is the sidereal day. Because of its annual revolution round the Sun, the rotation with respect to the Sun, or the solar day, is more than this by about four minutes (see page 73). The extremity of the axis of rotation, or the North Pole of the Earth, is not rigidly fixed, but wanders over an area roughly 20 metres in diameter.

TERRESTRIAL MAGNETISM

A magnetic compass points along the horizontal component of a magnetic line of force. These directions converge on the 'magnetic dip-poles', the places where a freely suspended magnetized needle would become vertical. Not only do the positions of these poles change with time, but their exact locations are ill-defined, particularly so in the case of the north dip-pole where the lines of force on the north side of it, instead of converging radially, tend to bunch into a channel. Although it is therefore unrealistic to attempt to specify the locations of the dip-poles exactly, the present adopted positions are 78°.2 N., 103°.7 W. and 64°.8 S., 138°.8 E. The two magnetic dip-poles are thus not antipodal, the line joining them passing the centre of the Earth at a distance of about 1,200 kilometres. The distances of the magnetic dip-poles from the north and south geographical poles are about 1,400 and 2,700 kilometres respectively.

There is also a 'magnetic equator', at all points of which the vertical component of the Earth's magnetic field is zero and a magnetized needle remains horizontal. This line runs between 2° and 10° north of the geographical equator in the eastern hemisphere, turns sharply south off the West African coast, and crosses South America through Brazil, Bolivia and Peru; it recrosses the geographical equator in mid-Pacific.

Reference has already been made to secular changes in the Earth's field. The following table indicates the changes in magnetic declination (or variation of the compass). Similar, though much smaller, changes have occurred in 'dip' or magnetic inclination. Secular changes differ throughout the world. Although the London observations strongly suggest a cycle with a period of several hundred years, an exact repetition is unlikely.

London		Greenwich	
1580	11° 15′ E.	1850	22° 24′ W.
1622	5° 56′ E.	1900	16° 29′ W.
1665	1° 22′ W.	1925	13° 10′ W.
1730	13° 00′ W.	1950	9° 07′ W.
1773	21° 09′ W.	1975	6° 39′ W.

In order that up-to-date information on the variation of the compass may be available, many governments publish magnetic charts on which there are lines (isogonic lines) passing through all places at which specified values of declination will be found at the date of the chart.

In the British Isles, isogonic lines now run approximately north-east to south-west. Though there are considerable local deviations due to geological causes, a rough value of magnetic declination may be obtained by assuming that at 50° N. on the meridian of Greenwich, the value in 1994 is 3° 33′ west and allowing an increase of 12′ for each degree of latitude northwards and one of 22′ for each degree of longitude westwards. For example, at 53° N., 5° W., declination will be about 3° 33′ + 36′ + 110′, i.e. 5° 59′ west. The average annual change at the present time is about 8′ decrease.

The number of magnetic observatories is about 200, widely scattered over the globe. There are three in Great Britain run by the British Geological Survey: at Hartland, North Devon; at Eskdalemuir, Dumfriesshire; and at Lerwick, Shetland Islands. The following are some recent annual mean values of the magnetic elements for Hartland.

Year	Declination West		Dip or inclination		Horizontal force	Vertical force
	°	′	°	′	oersted	oersted
1955	10	30	66	49	0.1859	0.4340
1960	9	59	66	44	0.1871	0.4350
1965	9	30	66	34	0.1887	0.4354
1970	9	06	66	26	0.1903	0.4364
1975	8	32	66	17	0.1921	0.4373
1980	7	44	66	10	0.1933	0.4377
1985	6	56	66	08	0.1938	0.4380
1990	6	15	66	10	0.1939	0.4388
1992	6	00	66	09	0.1941	0.4392

The normal world-wide terrestrial magnetic field corresponds approximately to that of a very strong small bar magnet near the centre of the Earth but with appreciable smooth spatial departures. The origin and slow secular change of the normal field are not fully understood but are generally ascribed to electric currents associated with fluid motions in the Earth's core. Superimposed on the normal field are local and regional anomalies whose magnitudes may in places exceed that of the normal field; these are due to the influence of mineral deposits in the Earth's crust. A small proportion of the field is of external origin, mostly associated with electric currents in the ionosphere. The configuration of the external field and the ionization of the atmosphere depend on the incident particle and radiation flux from the Sun. There are, therefore, short-term and non-periodic as well as diurnal, 27-day, seasonal and 11-year periodic changes in the magnetic field, dependent upon the position of the Sun and the degree of solar activity.

MAGNETIC STORMS

Occasionally, sometimes with great suddenness, the Earth's magnetic field is subject for several hours to marked disturbance. During a very large storm in March 1989 the declination at Lerwick changed by almost 8° in less than an hour. In many instances, such disturbances are accompanied by widespread displays of aurorae, marked changes in the incidence of cosmic rays, an increase in the reception of 'noise' from the Sun at radio frequencies together with rapid changes in the ionosphere and induced electric currents within the Earth which adversely affect radio and telegraphic communications. The disturbances are caused by changes in the stream of neutral and ionized particles which emanates from the Sun and through which the Earth is continuously passing. Some of these changes are associated with visible eruptions on the Sun, usually in the region of sun-spots. There is a marked tendency for disturbances to recur after intervals of about 27 days, the apparent period of rotation of the Sun on its axis, which is consistent with the sources being located on particular areas of the Sun.

ARTIFICIAL SATELLITES

To consider the orbit of an artificial satellite, it is best to imagine that one is looking at the Earth from a distant point in space. The Earth would then be seen to be rotating about its axis inside the orbit described by the rapidly revolving satellite. The inclination of a satellite orbit to the Earth's equator (which generally remains almost constant throughout the satellite's lifetime) gives at once the maximum range of latitudes over which the satellite passes. Thus a satellite whose orbit has an inclination of 53° will pass overhead all latitudes between 53° S. and 53° N., but would never be seen in the zenith of any place nearer the poles than these latitudes. If we consider a particular place on the earth, whose latitude is less than the inclination of the satellite's orbit, then the Earth's rotation carries this place first under the northbound part of the orbit and then under the southbound portion of the orbit, these two occurrences being always less than 12 hours apart for satellites moving in direct orbits (i.e. to the east). (For satellites in retrograde orbits, the words 'northbound' and 'southbound' should be interchanged in the preceding statement.) As the value of the latitude of the observer increases and approaches the value of the inclination of the orbit, so this interval gets shorter until (when the latitude is equal to the inclination) only one overhead passage occurs each day.

OBSERVATION OF SATELLITES

The regression of the orbit around the Earth causes alternate periods of visibility and invisibility, though this is of little concern to the radio or radar observer. To the visual observer the following cycle of events normally occurs (though the cycle may start in any position): invisibility, morning observations before dawn, invisibility, evening observations after dusk, invisibility, morning observations before dawn, and so on. With reasonably high satellites and for observers in high latitudes around the summer solstice, the evening observations follow the morning observations without inter-

ruption as sunlight passing over the polar regions can still illuminate satellites which are passing over temperate latitudes at local midnight. At the moment all satellites rely on sunlight to make them visible, though a satellite with a flashing light has been suggested for a future launching. The observer must be in darkness or twilight in order to make any useful observations and the durations of twilight and the sunrise, sunset times given on Page Two of each month will be a useful guide.

Some of the satellites are visible to the naked eye and much interest has been aroused by the spectacle of a bright satellite disappearing into the Earth's shadow. The event is even more fascinating telescopically as the disappearance occurs gradually as the satellite traverses the Earth's penumbral shadow, and during the last few seconds before the eclipse is complete the satellite may change colour (in suitable atmospheric conditions) from yellow to red. This is because the last rays of sunlight are refracted through the denser layers of our atmosphere before striking the satellite.

Some satellites rotate about one or more axes so that a periodic variation in brightness is observed. This was particularly noticeable in several of the Soviet satellites.

Satellite research has provided some interesting results. Among them may be mentioned a revised value of the Earth's oblateness, 1/298.2, and the discovery of the Van Allen radiation belts.

LAUNCHINGS

Apart from their names, e.g. Cosmos 6 Rocket, the satellites are also classified according to their date of launch. Thus 1961 α refers to the first satellite launching of 1961. A number following the Greek letter indicated the relative brightness of the satellites put in orbit. From the beginning of 1963 the Greek letters were replaced by numbers and the numbers by roman letters e.g. 1963–01A. For all satellites successfully injected into orbit the table gives the designation and names of the main objects (in the order A, B, C . . . etc.), the launch date and some initial orbital data. These are the inclination to the equator (i), the nodal period of revolution (P), the eccentricity (e), and the perigee height.

Although most of the satellites launched are injected into orbits less than 1,000 km high there are an increasing number of satellites in geostationary orbits, i.e. where the orbital inclination is zero, the eccentricity close to zero, and the period of revolution is 1436.1 minutes. Thus the satellite is permanently situated over the equator at one selected longitude at a mean height of 35,786 km. Already this geostationary band is crowded; for example, the television satellite Astra 1A (1988–109B) has been placed only 0°.2 away from the communication satellite Arabsat 1A (1985–15A).

ARTIFICIAL SATELLITE LAUNCHES 1992

Desig- nation	Satellite	Launch date	i	P	e	Perigee height
			°	m		km
1992–						
21	Telecom 2B, Inmarsat 2F-4	April 15	0.1	1436.0	0.000	35777
22	Progress-M 12, rocket	April 19	51.6	90.5	0.003	279
23	USA 81, rocket	April 25				
24	Resurs-F14, rocket	April 29	82.1	89.2	0.000	231
25	Cosmos 2185, rocket	April 29	70.0	89.4	0.005	211
26	STS 49, Intelsat 6F-3	May 7	28.3	91.4	0.001	344
27	Palapa 7, rocket	May 14	0.2	1436.1	0.000	35777

Desig-nation	Satellite	Launch date	i	P	e	Perigee height
			°	m		km
1992–						
28	SROSS-C, rocket	May 20	46.0	91.2	0.013	250
29	Cosmos 2186, rocket	May 28	62.8	89.8	0.013	182
30	Cosmos 2187–2194, rocket	June 3	74.0	114.7	0.005	1402
31	EUVE	June 7	30.2	92.4	0.018	282
32	Intelsat K	June 10	2.7	1100.5	0.195	22065
33	Resurs F-15. rocket, engine	June 23	82.3	89.1	0.000	226
34	STS 50	June 25	28.5	90.4	0.000	300
35	Progress M-13, rocket	June 30	51.6	90.9	0.002	309
36	Cosmos 2195, rocket	July 1	82.9	104.8	0.004	958
37	DSCS 3B-02, IABS-02	July 2				
38	SAMPEX	July 3	81.7	96.8	0.013	515
39	Navstar 2A-05, rocket	July 7	55.0	717.9	0.008	19960
40	Cosmos 2196, launcher rocket, launcher, rocket	July 8	62.9	717.1	0.737	590
41	Insat 2A, Eutelsat 2 F-4	July 9	0.2	1438.4	0.007	35537
42	Cosmos 2197–2202, rocket	July 13	82.6	114.0	0.001	1397
43	Gorizont 26, launcher	July 14	1.5	1435.7	0.000	35762
44	Geotail, rocket	July 24	28.6	12346.6	0.963	185
45	Cosmos 2203, rocket	July 24	62.8	89.5	0.009	190
46	Soyuz TM15, rocket	July 27	51.6	88.3	0.001	190
47	Cosmos 2204–2206	July 30	64.8	675.8	0.000	19121
48	Cosmos 2207, rocket, engine	July 30	82.3	90.5	0.009	237
49	STS 46, Eureca 1	July 31	28.5	88.9	0.001	228
50	Molniya 1–84, launcher rocket, launcher, rocket	August 6	62.8	717.7	0.736	632
51	China 35, rocket	August 9	63.1	89.7	0.013	172
52	Topex/Poseidon, Uribyol 1, S80/T	August 10	66.1	112.1	0.001	1317
53	Cosmos 2208, rocket	August 12	74.0	100.9	0.001	788
54	Optus B1, rocket	August 13	0.3	1436.0	0.003	35675
55	Progress M-14, rocket	August 15	51.6	90.9	0.005	288
56	Resurs-F 16, rocket, Pion 5, Pion 6, engine	August 19	82.6	89.1	0.001	221
57	Satcom C4, rocket	August 31	0.1	1430.2	0.005	35470
58	Navstar 2A-06, rocket	September 9	54.8	722.9	0.012	19980
59	Cosmos 2209, launcher	September 10	1.3	1435.9	0.001	35764
60	Hispasat 1A, Satcom 3C	September 10	0.0	1436.2	0.000	35783
61	STS 47	September 12	57.0	90.6	0.001	299
62	Cosmos 2210, rocket	September 22	67.2	89.8	0.013	175
63	Mars Observer	September 25	(interplanetary space probe)			
64	Freja, China 38, rocket	October 6	63.0	109.0	0.077	596
65	Foton 5, rocket, engine	October 8	62.8	90.3	0.010	220
66	DFS 3, rocket	October 12	0.0	1436.0	0.000	35778
67	Molniya 3–42, launcher rocket, launcher, rocket	October 14	62.8	717.7	0.742	477
68	Cosmos 2211–2216, rocket	October 20	82.6	114.0	0.001	1400
69	Cosmos 2217, launcher rocket, launcher, rocket	October 21	62.9	717.8	0.737	599
70	STS 52, Lageos 2, CTA, IRIS, LAS	October 22	28.5	88.5	0.001	206
71	Progress M-15, rocket	October 27	51.6	90.4	0.004	269
72	Galaxy 7	October 28	0.1	1436.0	0.002	35715
73	Cosmos 2218, rocket	October 29	82.9	105.0	0.003	968
74	Ekran 20, launcher	October 30	1.6	1428.2	0.001	35575
75	Resurs-500, rocket, engine	November 15	82.6	89.5	0.009	187
76	Cosmos 2219, rocket	November 17	71.0	102.0	0.000	849
77	Cosmos 2220, rocket	November 20	67.1	89.6	0.013	167
78	MST 1	November 21	96.7	92.4	0.008	331
79	Navstar 2A-07, rocket	November 23	54.8	714.7	0.007	19926
80	Cosmos 2221, rocket	November 24	82.5	97.8	0.002	636

Desig-nation	Satellite	Launch date	i	P	e	Perigee height
1992–			°	m		km
81	Cosmos 2222, launcher rocket, launcher, rocket	November 25	62.9	708.1	0.735	591
82	Gorizont 27, launcher	November 27	1.5	1468.9	0.002	36358
83	USA 86	November 28				
84	Superbird A1	December 1	0.1	1436.0	0.001	35759
85	Molniya 3–43, launcher rocket, launcher, rocket	December 2	62.8	717.4	0.744	413
86	STS 53, DoD-1	December 2	57.0	92.0	0.001	369
87	Cosmos 2223, rocket	December 9	64.7	89.0	0.007	178
88	Cosmos 2224, launcher	December 17	2.3	1443.3	0.001	35882
89	Navstar 2A-08	December 18	54.7	717.9	0.001	20039
90	Optus B2	December 21	28.1	96.9	0.059	208
91	Cosmos 2225, rocket	December 22	64.9	89.7	0.007	214
92	Cosmos 2226, rocket	December 22	73.6	116.1	0.003	1478
93	Cosmos 2227, rocket	December 25	71.0	102.0	0.000	849
94	Cosmos 2228, rocket	December 25	82.5	97.8	0.003	633
95	Cosmos 2229, rocket	December 29	62.8	90.4	0.012	218
1993–						
01	Cosmos 2230	January 1	82.9	98.5	0.002	971
02	Molniya 1-85	January 13	62.8	735.5	0.741	608
03	STS 54, TDRS 6	January 13	28.5	90.4	0.001	296
04	Cosmos 2231	January 19	67.2	89.6	0.014	166
05	Soyuz TM-16	January 24	51.6	88.5	0.002	189
06	Cosmos 2232	January 26	62.8	709.6	0.736	591
07	USA 88	February 3	34.8	356.4	0.607	174
08	Cosmos 2233	February 9	82.9	104.8	0.004	956
09	OXP-1, SCD 1	February 9	25.0	99.8	0.005	721
10	Cosmos 2234–2236	February 17	64.9	670.0	0.001	18972
11	Astro D	February 20	31.1	96.3	0.008	532
12	Progress M-16	February 21	51.6	88.6	0.004	186
13	Raduga 29	March 25	1.4	1454.0	0.004	35980
14	START 1	March 25	75.8	101.5	0.020	684
15	UHF-F1	March 25	27.3	192.9	0.404	219
16	Cosmos 2237	March 26	71.0	102.0	0.000	850
17	USA 90	March 30	34.8	356.7	0.606	188
18	Cosmos 2238	March 30	65.0	92.8	0.001	404
19	Progress M-17	March 31	51.6	90.1	0.005	249
20	Cosmos 2239	April 1	82.9	104.8	0.002	970
21	Cosmos 2240	April 2	62.8	89.5	0.009	187
22	Cosmos 2241	April 6	62.9	706.0	0.733	631
23	STS 56	April 8	57.0	90.3	0.001	288
24	Cosmos 2242	April 19	82.5	97.8	0.002	635
25	Molniya 3-44	April 21	62.9	735.3	0.741	606

Time Measurement and Calendars

MEASUREMENTS OF TIME

Measurements of time are based on the time taken by the earth to rotate on its axis (day); by the moon to revolve round the earth (month); and by the earth to revolve round the sun (year). From these, which are not commensurable, certain average or mean intervals have been adopted for ordinary use.

THE DAY

The day begins at midnight and is divided into 24 hours of 60 minutes, each of 60 seconds. The hours are counted from midnight up to 12 noon (when the sun crosses the meridian), and these hours are designated a.m. (*ante meridiem*); and again from noon up to 12 midnight, which hours are designated p.m. (*post meridiem*), except when the 24-hour reckoning is employed. The 24-hour reckoning ignores a.m. and p.m., and the hours are numbered 0 to 23 from midnight.

Colloquially the 24 hours are divided into day and night, day being the time while the sun is above the horizon (including the four stages of twilight defined on page 72). Day is subdivided further into morning, the early part of daytime, ending at noon; afternoon, from noon to about 6 p.m.; and evening, which may be said to extend from 6 p.m. until midnight. Night, the dark period between day and day, begins at the close of astronomical twilight (*see* page 72) and extends beyond midnight to sunrise the next day.

The names of the days are derived from Old English translations or adaptations of the Roman titles.

Sunday	Sun	Sol
Monday	Moon	Luna
Tuesday	Tiw/Tyr (god of war)	Mars
Wednesday	Woden/Odin	Mercury
Thursday	Thor	Jupiter
Friday	Frigga/Freyja	
	(goddess of love)	Venus
Saturday	Saeternes	Saturn

THE WEEK

The week is a period of seven days.

THE MONTH

The month in the ordinary calendar is approximately the twelfth part of a year, but the lengths of the different months vary from 28 (or 29) days to 31.

THE YEAR

The equinoctial or tropical year is the time that the earth takes to revolve round the sun from equinox to equinox, i.e. 365.24219 mean solar days, or 365 days 5 hours 48 minutes and 45 seconds.

The calendar year usually consists of 365 days, but a year containing 366 days is called bissextile (*see* Roman Calendar) or leap year, one day being added to the month of February, so that a date 'leaps over' a day of the week.

A year is a leap year if the date of the year is divisible by four without remainder, unless it is the last year of the century. The last year of a century is a leap year only if its number is divisible by 400 without remainder, e.g. the years 1800 and 1900 had only 365 days but the year 2000 will have 366 days.

THE SOLSTICE

A solstice is the point in the tropical year at which the sun attains its greatest distance, north or south, from the Equator. In the northern hemisphere the furthest point north of the Equator marks the summer solstice and the furthest point south the winter solstice.

The date of the solstice varies according to locality. For example, if the summer solstice falls on 21 June late in the day by Greenwich time, that day will be the longest of the year at Greenwich though it may be by only a second, but it will fall on 22 June, local date, in Japan, and so 22 June will be the longest day there. The date of the solstice is also affected by the length of the tropical year, which is 365 days 6 hours less about 11 minutes 15 seconds. If a solstice happens late on 21 June in one year, it will be nearly six hours later in the next (unless the next year is a leap year), i.e. early on 22 June, and that will be the longest day.

This delay of the solstice does not continue because the extra day in leap year brings it back a day in the calendar. However, because of the 11 minutes 15 seconds mentioned above, the additional day in leap year brings the solstice back too far by 45 minutes, and the time of the solstice in the calendar is earlier, in a four-year pattern, as the century progresses. The last year of a century is in most cases not a leap year, and the omission of the extra day puts the date of the solstice later by about six hours too much. Compensation for this is made by the fourth centennial year being a leap year. The solstice has become earlier in date throughout this century and, because the year 2000 is a leap year, the solstice will get earlier still throughout the 21st century.

Similar considerations apply to the day of the winter solstice, the shortest day of the year. The difference due to locality also prevails in the same sense as for the longest day.

At Greenwich the sun sets at its earliest by the clock about ten days before the shortest day. The daily change in the time of sunset is due in the first place to the sun's movement southwards at this time of the year, which diminishes the interval between the sun's transit and its setting. However, the daily decrease of the Equation of Time causes the time of apparent noon to be continuously later day by day. This in a measure counteracts the first effect. The rates of the change of these two quantities are not equal, nor are they uniform, but are such that their combination causes the date of earliest sunset to be 12 or 13 December at Greenwich. In more southerly latitudes the effect of the movement of the sun is less, and the change in the time of sunset depends on that of the Equation of Time to a greater degree, and the date of earliest sunset is earlier than it is at Greenwich. For example, on the Equator it is about 1 November.

THE EQUINOX

The equinox is the point at which the sun crosses the Equator and day and night are of equal length all over the world. This occurs in March and September.

DOG DAYS

The days about the heliacal rising of the Dog Star, noted from ancient times as the hottest period of the year in the northern hemisphere, are called the Dog Days. Their incidence has been variously calculated as depending on the Greater or Lesser Dog Star (Sirius or Procyon) and their duration has been reckoned as from 30 to 54 days. A generally accepted period is from 3 July to 15 August.

CHRISTIAN CALENDAR

In the Christian chronological system the years are distinguished by cardinal numbers before or after the birth of Christ, the period being denoted by the letters BC (Before Christ) or, more rarely, AC (*Ante Christum*), and AD (*Anno Domini* – In the Year of Our Lord). The correlative dates of the epoch are the fourth year of the 194th Olympiad, the 753rd year from the foundation of Rome, AM 3761 (Jewish chronology), and the 4714th year of the Julian period.

The system was introduced into Italy in the sixth century. Though first used in France in the seventh century, it was not universally established there until about the eighth century. It has been said that the system was introduced into England by St Augustine (AD 596), but it was probably not generally used until some centuries later. It was ordered to be used by the Bishops at the Council of Chelsea (AD 816). The actual date of the birth of Christ is somewhat uncertain.

THE JULIAN CALENDAR

In the Julian calendar all the centennial years were leap years, and for this reason towards the close of the sixteenth century there was a difference of ten days between the tropical and calendar years; the equinox fell on 11 March of the calendar, whereas at the time of the Council of Nicaea (AD 325), it had fallen on 21 March. In 1582 Pope Gregory ordained that 5 October should be called 15 October and that of the end-century years only the fourth should be a leap year (*see* page 81).

THE GREGORIAN CALENDAR

The Gregorian calendar was adopted by Italy, France, Spain and Portugal in 1582, by Prussia, the Roman Catholic German states, Switzerland, Holland and Flanders on 1 January 1583, by Poland in 1586, Hungary in 1587, the Protestant German and Netherland states and Denmark in 1700, and by Great Britain and Dominions (including the North American colonies) in 1752, by the omission of eleven days (3 September being reckoned as 14 September). Sweden omitted the leap day in 1700 but observed leap days in 1704 and 1708, and reverted to the Julian calendar by having two leap days in 1712; the Gregorian calendar was adopted in 1753 by the omission of eleven days (18 February being reckoned as 1 March). Japan adopted the calendar in 1872, China in 1912, Bulgaria in 1915, Turkey and Soviet Russia in 1918, Yugoslavia and Romania in 1919, and Greece in February 1923.

In the same year that the change was made in England from the Julian to the Gregorian calendar, the beginning of the new year was also changed from 25 March to 1 January (*see* page 86).

THE ORTHODOX CHURCHES

Some Orthodox Churches still use the Julian reckoning, but the majority of Greek Orthodox Churches and the Romanian Orthodox Church have adopted a modified 'New Calendar', observing the Gregorian calendar for fixed feasts and the Julian for movable feasts.

The Orthodox Church year begins on 1 September. There are four fast periods, and in addition to Pascha (Easter), twelve great feasts, as well as numerous commemorations of the saints of the Old and New Testaments throughout the year.

THE DOMINICAL LETTER

The Dominical Letter is one of the letters A–G which are used to denote the Sundays in successive years. If the first day of the year is a Sunday the letter is A; if the second, B; the third, C; and so on. Leap year requires two letters, the first for 1 January to 29 February, the second for 1 March to 31 December (*see* page 84).

EPIPHANY

The feast of the Epiphany, commemorating the manifestation of Christ, later became associated with the offering of gifts by the Magi. The day was of exceptional importance from the time of the Council of Nicaea (AD 325), as the primate of Alexandria was charged at every Epiphany feast with the announcement in a letter to the churches of the date of the forthcoming Easter. The day was of considerable importance in Britain as it influenced dates, ecclesiastical and lay, e.g. Plough Monday, when work was resumed in the fields, falls upon the Monday in the first full week after Epiphany.

LENT

The Teutonic word *Lent*, which denotes the fast preceding Easter, originally meant no more than the spring season; but from Anglo-Saxon times at least it has been used as the equivalent of the more significant Latin term Quadragesima, meaning the 'forty days' or, more literally, the fortieth day. Ash Wednesday is the first day of Lent, which ends at midnight before Easter Day.

PALM SUNDAY

Palm Sunday, the Sunday before Easter and the beginning of Holy Week, commemorates the triumphal entry of Christ into Jerusalem and is celebrated in Britain (when palm is not available) by branches of willow gathered for use in the decoration of churches on that day.

MAUNDY THURSDAY

Maundy Thursday is the day before Good Friday, the name itself being a corruption of *dies mandati* (day of the mandate) when Christ washed the feet of the disciples and gave them the mandate to love one another.

EASTER DAY

Easter Day is the first Sunday after the full moon which happens upon, or next after, the 21st day of March; if the full moon happens upon a Sunday, Easter Day is the Sunday after.

This definition is contained in an Act of Parliament (24 Geo. II c. 23) and explanation is given in the preamble to the Act that the day of full moon depends on certain tables that have been prepared. These are the tables whose essential points are given in the early pages of the Book of Common Prayer. The moon referred to is not the real moon of the heavens, but a hypothetical moon on whose 'full' the date of Easter depends, and the lunations of this 'calendar' moon consist of twenty-nine and thirty days alternately, with certain necessary modifications to make the date of its full agree as nearly as possible with that of the real moon, which is known as the Paschal Full Moon. As at present ordained, Easter falls on one of 35 days (22 March to 25 April).

A FIXED EASTER

On 15 June 1928 the House of Commons agreed to a motion for the third reading of a bill proposing that Easter Day shall, in the calendar year next but one after the commencement of the Act and in all subsequent years, be the first Sunday after the second Saturday in April. Easter would thus fall between 9 and 15 April (inclusive), that is, on the second or third Sunday in April. A clause in the Bill provided that before it shall come into operation, regard shall be had to any opinion expressed officially by the various Christian churches. Efforts by the World Council of Churches to secure a unanimous choice of date for Easter by its member churches have so far been unsuccessful.

ROGATION DAYS

Rogation Days are the Monday, Tuesday and Wednesday preceding Ascension Day and in the fifth century were ordered by the Church to be observed as public fasts with solemn processions and supplications. The processions were discontinued as religious observances at the Reformation, but survive in the ceremony known as 'Beating the Parish Bounds'. Rogation Sunday is the Sunday before Ascension Day.

EMBER DAYS

The Ember Days at the four seasons are the Wednesday,

Friday and Saturday (*a*) before the third Sunday in Advent, (*b*) before the second Sunday in Lent, and (*c*) before the Sundays nearest to the festivals of St Peter and of St Michael and All Angels.

TRINITY SUNDAY

Trinity Sunday is eight weeks after Easter Day, on the Sunday following Pentecost (Whit Sunday). Subsequent Sundays are reckoned in the Book of Common Prayer calendar of the Church of England as 'after Trinity'.

Thomas Becket (1118–70) was consecrated Archbishop of Canterbury on the Sunday after Whit Sunday and his first act was to ordain that the day of his consecration should be held as a new festival in honour of the Holy Trinity. The observance thus originated spread from Canterbury throughout the whole of Christendom.

MOVABLE FEASTS TO THE YEAR 2026

Year	Ash Wednesday	Easter	Ascension	Pentecost (Whit Sunday)	Sundays after Pentecost	Advent Sunday
1994	16 February	3 April	12 May	22 May	21	27 November
1995	1 March	16 April	25 May	4 June	20	3 December
1996	21 February	7 April	16 May	26 May	21	1 December
1997	12 February	30 March	8 May	18 May	22	30 November
1998	25 February	12 April	21 May	31 May	20	29 November
1999	17 February	4 April	13 May	23 May	21	28 November
2000	8 March	23 April	1 June	11 June	19	3 December
2001	28 February	15 April	24 May	3 June	20	2 December
2002	13 February	31 March	9 May	19 May	22	1 December
2003	5 March	20 April	29 May	8 June	19	30 November
2004	25 February	11 April	20 May	30 May	20	28 November
2005	9 February	27 March	5 May	15 May	22	27 November
2006	1 March	16 April	25 May	4 June	20	3 December
2007	21 February	8 April	17 May	27 May	21	2 December
2008	6 February	23 March	1 May	11 May	23	30 November
2009	25 February	12 April	21 May	31 May	20	29 November
2010	17 February	4 April	13 May	23 May	21	28 November
2011	9 March	24 April	2 June	12 June	18	27 November
2012	22 February	8 April	17 May	27 May	21	2 December
2013	13 February	31 March	9 May	19 May	22	1 December
2014	5 March	20 April	29 May	8 June	19	30 November
2015	18 February	5 April	14 May	24 May	21	29 November
2016	10 February	27 March	5 May	15 May	22	27 November
2017	1 March	16 April	25 May	4 June	20	3 December
2018	14 February	1 April	10 May	20 May	22	2 December
2019	6 March	21 April	30 May	9 June	19	1 December
2020	26 February	12 April	21 May	31 May	20	29 November
2021	17 February	4 April	13 May	23 May	21	28 November
2022	2 March	17 April	26 May	5 June	19	27 November
2023	22 February	9 April	18 May	28 May	21	3 December
2024	14 February	31 March	9 May	19 May	22	1 December
2025	5 March	20 April	29 May	8 June	19	30 November
2026	18 February	5 April	14 May	24 May	21	29 November

NOTES

Ash Wednesday (first day in Lent) can fall at earliest on 4 February and at latest on 10 March

Mothering Sunday (fourth Sunday in Lent) can fall at earliest on 29 February and at latest on 4 April

Easter Day can fall at earliest on 22 March and at latest on 25 April

Ascension Day is forty days after Easter Day and can fall at earliest on 30 April and at latest on 3 June

Pentecost (Whit Sunday) is seven weeks after Easter and can fall at earliest on 10 May and at latest on 13 June

Trinity Sunday is the Sunday after Whit Sunday

Corpus Christi falls on the Thursday after Trinity Sunday

Sundays after Pentecost – there are not less than 18 and not more than 23

Advent Sunday is the Sunday nearest to 30 November

EASTER DAYS AND DOMINICAL LETTERS 1500 TO 2030

	1500–1599	1600–1699	1700–1799	1800–1899	1900–1999	2000–2030
March						
d 22	1573	1668	1761	1818		
e 23	1505/16	1600	1788	1845/56	1913	2008
f 24		1611/95	1706/99		1940	
g 25	1543/54	1627/38/49	1722/33/44	1883/94	1951	
A 26	1559/70/81/92	1654/65/76	1749/58/69/80	1815/26/37	1967/78/89	
b 27	1502/13/24/97	1608/87/92	1785/96	1842/53/64	1910/21/32	2005/16
c 28	1529/35/40	1619/24/30	1703/14/25	1869/75/80	1937/48	2027
d 29	1551/62	1635/46/57	1719/30/41/52	1807/12/91	1959/64/70	
e 30	1567/78/89	1651/62/73/84	1746/55/66/77	1823/34	1902/75/86/97	
f 31	1510/21/32/83/94	1605/16/78/89	1700/71/82/93	1839/50/61/72	1907/18/29/91	2002/13/24
April						
g 1	1526/37/48	1621/32	1711/16	1804/66/77/88	1923/34/45/56	2018/29
A 2	1553/64	1643/48	1727/38/52(NS)	1809/20/93/99	1961/72	
b 3	1575/80/86	1659/70/81	1743/63/68/74	1825/31/36	1904/83/88/94	
c 4	1507/18/91	1602/13/75/86/97	1708/79/90	1847/58	1915/20/26/99	2010/21
d 5	1523/34/45/56	1607/18/29/40	1702/13/24/95	1801/63/74/85/96	1931/42/53	2015/26
e 6	1539/50/61/72	1634/45/56	1729/35/40/60	1806/17/28/90	1947/58/69/80	
f 7	1504/77/88	1667/72	1751/65/76	1822/33/44	1901/12/85/96	
g 8	1509/15/20/99	1604/10/83/94	1705/87/92/98	1849/55/60	1917/28	2007/12
A 9	1531/42	1615/26/37/99	1710/21/32	1871/82	1939/44/50	2023
b 10	1547/58/69	1631/42/53/64	1726/37/48/57	1803/14/87/98	1955/66/77	
c 11	1501/12/63/74/85/96	1658/69/80	1762/73/84	1819/30/41/52	1909/71/82/93	2004
d 12	1506/17/28	1601/12/91/96	1789	1846/57/68	1903/14/25/36/98	2009/20
e 13	1533/44	1623/28	1707/18	1800/73/79/84	1941/52	
f 14	1555/60/66	1639/50/61	1723/34/45/54	1805/11/16/95	1963/68/74	
g 15	1571/82/93	1655/66/77/88	1750/59/70/81	1827/38	1900/06/79/90	2001
A 16	1503/14/25/36/87/98	1609/20/82/93	1704/75/86/97	1843/54/65/76	1911/22/33/95	2006/17/28
b 17	1530/41/52	1625/36	1715/20	1808/70/81/92	1927/38/49/60	2022
c 18	1557/68	1647/52	1731/42/56	1802/13/24/97	1954/65/76	
d 19	1500/79/84/90	1663/74/85	1747/67/72/78	1829/35/40	1908/81/87/92	
e 20	1511/22/95	1606/17/79/90	1701/12/83/94	1851/62	1919/24/30	2003/14/25
f 21	1527/38/49	1622/33/44	1717/28	1867/78/89	1935/46/57	2019/30
g 22	1565/76	1660	1739/53/64	1810/21/32	1962/73/84	
A 23	1508	1671		1848	1905/16	2000
b 24	1519	1603/14/98	1709/91	1859		2011
c 25	1546	1641	1736	1886	1943	

HINDU CALENDAR

The Hindu calendar is a lunar calendar of twelve months, each containing 29 days, 12 hours. Each month is divided into a light fortnight (Shukla or Shuddha) and a dark fortnight (Krishna or Vadya) based on the waxing and waning of the moon. In most parts of India the month starts with the light fortnight, i.e. the day after the new moon, although in some regions it begins with the dark fortnight, i.e. the day after the full moon.

The new year begins in the month of Chaitra (March/April) and ends in the month of Phalgun (March). The twelve months, Chaitra, Vaishakh, Jyeshtha, Ashadh, Shravan, Bhadrapad, Ashvin, Kartik, Margashirsh, Paush, Magh and Phalgun, have Sanskrit names derived from twelve asterisms (constellations). There are regional variations to the names of the months but the Sanskrit names are understood throughout India.

Whenever the difference between the Hindu year of 360 lunar days (354 days 8 hours solar time) and the 365 days 6 hours of the solar year reaches the length of one Hindu lunar month (29 days 12 hours), a 'leap' month is added to the Hindu calendar.

The leap month may be added at any point in the Hindu year. The name given to the month varies according to when it occurs but is taken from the month immediately following it. Leap months occur in 1993–4 (Bhadrapad), 1996–7 (Ashadh) and 1999–2000 (Jyeshtha).

The days of the week are called Raviwar (Sunday), Somawar (Monday), Mangalwar (Tuesday), Budhawar (Wednesday), Guruwar (Thursday), Shukrawar (Friday) and Shaniwar (Saturday). The names are derived from the Sanskrit names of the Sun, the Moon and five planets, Mars, Mercury, Jupiter, Venus and Saturn.

Most fasts and festivals are based on the lunar calendar but a few are determined by the apparent movement of the Sun, e.g. Sankranti, which is celebrated on 14/15 January to mark the start of the Sun's apparent journey northwards and a change of season.

Festivals celebrated throughout India are Chaitra (the New Year), Raksha-bandhan (the renewal of the kinship bond between brothers and sisters), Navaratri (a nine-night festival dedicated to the goddess Parvati), Dasara (the victory of Rama over the demon army), Diwali (a festival of lights), Makara Sankranti, Shivaratri (dedicated to Shiva), and Holi (a spring festival).

Regional festivals are Durga-puja (dedicated to the goddess Durga (Parvati)), Sarasvati-puja (dedicated to the goddess

Sarasvati), Ganesh Chaturthi (worship of Ganesh on the fourth day (Chaturthi) of the light half of Bhadrapad), Ramanavami (the birth festival of the god Rama) and Janmashtami (the birth festival of the god Krishna).

The main festivals celebrated in Britain are Navaratri, Dasara, Durga-puja, Diwali, Holi, Sarasvati-puja, Ganesh Chaturthi, Raksha-bandhan, Ramanavami and Janmashtami.

The dates of the main festivals in 1994 are given on page 9.

JEWISH CALENDAR

The story of the Flood in the Book of Genesis relates that the Flood began on the 17th day of the second month, that after the end of 150 days the waters were abated, and that on the 17th day of the seventh month the Ark rested on Mount Ararat. This indicates the use of a calendar of some kind and that the writers recognized thirty days as the length of a lunation. However, after the diaspora, Jewish communities were left in considerable doubt as to the times of fasts and festivals. This led to the formation of the Jewish calendar as used today. It is said that this was done in AD 358 by Rabbi Hillel II, a descendant of Gamaliel, though some assert that it did not happen until much later.

The calendar is luni-solar, and is based on the lengths of the lunation and of the tropical year as found by Hipparchus (c.120 BC), which differ little from those adopted at the present day. The year AM 5754 (1993–4) is the 16th year of the 303rd Metonic (Minor or Lunar) cycle of 19 years and the 14th year of the 206th Solar (or Major) cycle of 28 years since the Era of the Creation. Jews hold that the Creation occurred at the time of the autumnal equinox in the year known in the Christian calendar as 3760 BC (954 of the Julian period). The epoch or starting point of Jewish chronology corresponds to 7 October 3761 BC. At the beginning of each solar cycle, the Tekufah of Nisan (the vernal equinox) returns to the same day and to the same hour.

The hour is divided into 1080 minims, and the month between one new moon and the next is reckoned as 29 days, 12 hours, 793 minims. The normal calendar year, called a Common Regular year, consists of 12 months of 30 days and 29 days alternately. Since twelve months such as these comprise only 354 days, in order that each of them shall not diverge greatly from an average place in the solar year, a thirteenth month is occasionally added after the fifth month of the civil year (which commences on the first day of the month Tishri), or as the penultimate month of the ecclesiastical year (which commences on the first day of month Nisan). The years when this happens are called Embolismic or leap years.

Of the 19 years that form a Metonic cycle, seven are leap years; they occur at places in the cycle indicated by the numbers 3, 6, 8, 11, 14, 17 and 19, these places being chosen so that the accumulated excesses of the solar years should be as small as possible.

A Jewish year is of one of the following six types:

Minimal Common	353 days
Regular Common	354 days
Full Common	355 days
Minimal Leap	383 days
Regular Leap	384 days
Full Leap	385 days.

The Regular year has alternate months of 30 and 29 days. In a Full year, whether common or leap, Marcheshvan, the second month of the civil year, has 30 days instead of 29; in

Minimal years Kislev, the third month, has 29 instead of 30. The additional month in leap years is called Adar I and precedes the month called Adar in Common years. Adar II is called Ve-Adar, in leap years, and the usual Adar festivals are kept in Ve-Adar. Adar I and Adar II always have 30 days, but neither this, nor the other variations mentioned, is allowed to change the number of days in the other months which still follow the alternation of the normal twelve.

These are the main features of the Jewish calendar, which must be considered permanent because as a Jewish law it cannot be altered except by a great Sanhedrin.

The Jewish day begins between sunset and nightfall. The time used is that of the meridian of Jerusalem, which is 2h 21m in advance of Greenwich Mean Time. Rules for the beginning of sabbaths and festivals were laid down for the latitude of London in the eighteenth century and hours for nightfall are now fixed annually by the Chief Rabbi.

JEWISH CALENDAR 5754–5

AM 5754 (754) is a Full Common year of 12 months, 51 sabbaths and 355 days. AM 5755 (755) is a Regular Leap year of 13 months, 55 sabbaths and 384 days.

Jewish Month	AM 5754	AM 5755
Tishri 1	16 September 1993	6 September 1994
Marcheshvan 1	16 October	6 October
Kislev 1	15 November	4 November
Tebet 1	15 December	4 December
Shebat 1	13 January 1994	2 January 1995
*Adar 1	12 February	1 February
Ve-Adar 1		3 March
Nisan 1	13 March	1 April
Iyar 1	12 April	1 May
Sivan 1	11 May	30 May
Tammuz 1	10 June	29 June
Ab 1	9 July	28 July
Elul 1	8 August	27 August

*Known as Adar Rishon in leap years.

JEWISH FASTS AND FESTIVALS
For dates of principal festivals in 1994, *see* page 9

Tishri 1–2	Rosh Hashanah (New Year)
Tishri 3	*Fast of Gedaliah
Tishri 10	Yom Kippur (Day of Atonement)
Tishri 15–21	Succoth (Feast of Tabernacles)
Tishri 21	Hoshana Rabba
Tishri 22	Shemini Atseret (Solemn Assembly)
Tishri 23	Simchat Torah (Rejoicing of the Law)
Kislev 25	Chanukah (Dedication of the Temple) begins
Tebet 10	Fast of Tebet
†Adar 13	§Fast of Esther
†Adar 14	Purim
†Adar 15	Shushan Purim
Nisan 15–22	Pesach (Passover)
Sivan 6–7	Shavuot (Feast of Weeks)
Tammuz 17	*Fast of Tammuz
Ab 9	*Fast of Ab

*If these dates fall on the sabbath the fast is kept on the following day
†Ve-Adar in leap years
§This fast is observed on Adar 11 (or Ve-Adar 11 in leap years) if Adar 13 falls on a sabbath

THE MUSLIM CALENDAR

The Muslim era is dated from the *Hijrah*, or flight of the Prophet Muhammad from Mecca to Medina, the corresponding date of which in the Julian calendar is 16 July AD 622. Hijrah years (AH) are used principally in Iran, Turkey, Egypt, Malaysia, various Arab states and certain parts of India. The dating system was adopted about AD 639, commencing with the first day of the month Muharram. Muharram precedes the month in which the Hijrah took place and was recognized as the beginning of the year because it followed the month of pilgrimage.

The calendar is a lunar calendar and consists of twelve months containing an alternate sequence of 30 and 29 days, with the intercalation of one day at the end of the twelfth month at stated intervals in each cycle of 30 years. The object of the intercalation is to reconcile the date of the first day of the month with the date of the actual new moon.

Some adherents still take the date of the evening of the first physical sighting of the crescent of the New Moon as that of the first of the month. For this reason, the beginning of a new month and the date of religious festivals can vary by a few days from the published calendars.

In each cycle of 30 years, 19 years are common and contain 354 days, and 11 years are intercalary (leap years) of 355 days, the latter being called *kabishah*. The mean length of the Hijrah years is 354 days 8 hours 48 minutes and the period of mean lunation is 29 days 12 hours 44 minutes.

To ascertain if a year is common or kabishah, divide it by 30: the quotient gives the number of completed cycles and the remainder shows the place of the year in the current cycle. If the remainder is 2, 5, 7, 10, 13, 16, 18, 21, 24, 26 or 29, the year is kabishah and consists of 355 days.

MUSLIM CALENDAR 1414–15

Hijrah year 1414 AH (remainder 4) is a common year; 1415 AH (remainder 5) is a kabishah year.

Month (length)	1414 AH	1415 AH
Muharram (30)	21 June 1993	10 June 1994
Safar (29)	21 July	10 July
Rabi' I (30)	19 August	8 August
Rabi' II (29)	18 September	7 September
Jumada I (30)	17 October	7 October
Jumada II (29)	16 November	5 November
Rajab (30)	15 December	4 December
Shaabân (29)	14 January 1994	3 January 1995
Ramadân (30)	12 February	1 February
Shawwâl (29)	14 March	3 March
Dhû'l-Qa'da (30)	12 April	1 April
Dhû'l-Hijjah (29 or 30)	12 May	1 May

MUSLIM FESTIVALS

Ramadan is a month of fasting for all Muslims because it is the month in which the revelation of the *Qur'an* (Koran) began. During Ramadan Muslims abstain from food, drink and sexual pleasure from dawn until after sunset throughout the month.

The two major festivals are *Idu-l-fitr* and *Idu-l-adha*. Idu-l-fitr marks the end of the Ramadan fast and is celebrated on the day after the sighting of the new moon of the following month. Idu-l-adha, the festival of sacrifice (also known as the great festival), celebrates the submission of the Prophet Ibrahim (Abraham) to Allah. Idu-l-adha falls on the tenth day of Dhul-Hijjah, coinciding with the day when those on *hajj* (pilgrimage to Mecca) sacrifice animals.

Other days accorded special recognition are:

Muharram 1	New Year's Day
Muharram 10	Ashura (the day Prophet Nuh left the Ark and Prophet Musa was saved from Pharaoh (Sunni), the death of the Prophet's grandson Husain (Shi'ite))
Rabi'u-l-Awwal (Rabi I) 12	Mawlidu-n-Nabiyy (birthday of the Prophet Muhammad)
Rajab 27	Laylatu-l-Isra wa l-Miraj (Night of the Journey and Ascension)
Ramadan Odd-numbered nights in the last 10 of the month	Laylatu-l-Qadr (Night of Power)
Dhu'l-Hijjah 10	Idu-l-adha (Festival of Sacrifice)

THE SIKH CALENDAR

The Sikh calendar is a lunar calendar of 365 days divided into 12 months. The length of the months varies between 29 and 32 days.

There are no prescribed feast days and no fasting periods. The main celebrations are Baisakhi Mela (the new year and the anniversary of the founding of the Khalsa), Diwali Mela (festival of light), Hola Mohalla Mela (a spring festival held in the Punjab), and the Gurpurbs (anniversaries associated with the ten Gurus).

The dates of the major celebrations in 1994 are given on page 9.

CIVIL AND LEGAL CALENDAR

THE HISTORICAL YEAR

Before the year 1752, two calendar systems were in use in England. The civil or legal year began on 25 March, while the historical year began on 1 January. Thus the civil or legal date 24 March 1658, was the same day as the historical date 24 March 1659; and a date in that portion of the year is written as 24 March 165⅝, the lower figure showing the historical year.

THE NEW YEAR

In England in the seventh century, and as late as the thirteenth, the year was reckoned from Christmas Day, but in the twelfth century the Anglican Church began the year with the feast of the Annunciation of the Blessed Virgin (Lady Day) on 25 March and this practice was adopted generally in the fourteenth century. The civil or legal year in the British Dominions (exclusive of Scotland) began with 'Lady Day' until 1751. But in and since 1752 the civil year has begun with 1 January. Certain dividends are still paid by the Bank of England on dates based on Old Style. New Year's Day in Scotland was changed from 25 March to 1 January in 1600.

On the continent of Europe, 1 January was adopted as the first day of the year by Venice in 1522, Germany in 1544, Spain, Portugal, and the Roman Catholic Netherlands in 1556, Prussia, Denmark and Sweden in 1559, France in 1564, Lorraine in 1579, the Protestant Netherlands in 1583, Russia in 1725, and Tuscany in 1751.

REGNAL YEARS

The regnal years are the years of a sovereign's reign, and each begins on the anniversary of his or her accession, e.g. regnal year 43 of the present Queen begins on 6 February 1994.

The system was used for dating Acts of Parliament until 1962. The Summer Time Act 1925, for example, is quoted as 15 and 16 Geo. V c. 64, because it became law in the parliamentary session which extended over part of both of these regnal years. Acts of a parliamentary session during which a sovereign died were usually given two year numbers, the regnal year of the deceased sovereign and the regnal year of his or her successor. Acts passed in 1952 were dated 16 Geo. VI and 1 Elizabeth II. Since 1962, Acts of Parliament have been dated by the calendar year.

QUARTER AND TERM DAYS

Holy days and saints days were the normal factors in early times for setting the dates of future and recurrent appointments. The quarter days in England and Wales are the feast of the Nativity (25 December), the feast of the Annunciation (25 March), the feast of St John the Baptist (24 June) and the feast of St Michael and All Angels (29 September).

The term days in Scotland are Candlemas (the feast of the Purification), Whitsunday, Lammas (Loaf Mass), and Martinmas (St Martin's Day). These fell on 2 February, 15 May, 1 August and 11 November respectively. However, by the Term and Quarter Days (Scotland) Act 1990, the dates of the term days were changed to 28 February (Candlemas), 28 May (Whitsunday), 28 August (Lammas) and 28 November (Martinmas).

RED-LETTER DAYS

Red-letter days were originally the holy days and saints days indicated in early ecclesiastical calendars by letters printed in red ink. The days to be distinguished in this way were approved at the Council of Nicaea in AD 325.

These days still have a legal significance, as judges of the Queen's Bench Division wear scarlet robes on red-letter days falling during the law sittings. The days designated as red-letter days for this purpose are:

Holy and saints days
Conversion of St Paul, the Purification, Ash Wednesday, the Annunciation, the Ascension, the feasts of St Mark, SS Philip and James, St Matthias, St Barnabas, St Peter, St Thomas, St James, St Luke, SS Simon and Jude, All Saints, St Andrew.

Civil calendar
The anniversary of The Queen's accession, The Queen's birthday, The Queen's official birthday, The Queen's coronation, the birthday of the Duke of Edinburgh, the birthday of Queen Elizabeth the Queen Mother, the birthday of the Prince of Wales, St David's Day and Lord Mayor's Day.

PUBLIC HOLIDAYS

Public holidays are divided into two categories, common law, and statutory. Common law holidays are holidays 'by habit and custom'; in England, Wales and Northern Ireland these are Good Friday and Christmas Day.

Statutory public holidays, known as bank holidays, were first established by the Bank Holidays Act 1871. They were, literally, days on which the banks (and other public institutions) were closed and financial obligations due on that day were payable the following day. The legislation currently governing public holidays in the United Kingdom is the Banking and Financial Dealings Act 1971. It stipulates which days are to be public holidays in England, Wales, Scotland and Northern Ireland.

Certain holidays (indicated by * below) are granted annually by royal proclamation, either throughout the United Kingdom or in any place in the United Kingdom. The public holidays are:

England and Wales
*New Year's Day
Easter Monday
*The first Monday in May
The last Monday in May
The last Monday in August
26 December, if it is not a Sunday
27 December when 25 or 26 December is a Sunday

Scotland
New Year's Day, or if it is a Sunday, 2 January
2 January, or if it is a Sunday, 3 January
Good Friday
The first Monday in May
*The last Monday in May
The first Monday in August
Christmas Day, or if it is a Sunday, 26 December
*Boxing Day – if Christmas Day falls on a Sunday, 26 December is given in lieu and an alternative day is given for Boxing Day

Northern Ireland
*New Year's Day
17 March, or if it is a Sunday, 18 March
Easter Monday
*The first Monday in May
The last Monday in May
*12 July, or if it is a Sunday, 13 July
The last Monday in August
26 December, if it is not a Sunday
27 December if 25 or 26 December is a Sunday

For dates of public holidays in 1994 and 1995, *see* pages 10–11.

CHRONOLOGICAL CYCLES AND ERAS

SOLAR (OR MAJOR) CYCLE

The solar cycle is a period of twenty-eight years, in any corresponding year of which the days of the week recur on the same day of the month.

METONIC (LUNAR, OR MINOR) CYCLE

In the year 432 BC, Meton, an Athenian astronomer, found that 235 lunations are very nearly, though not exactly, equal in duration to 19 solar years, and, hence, after 19 years the phases of the Moon recur on the same days of the month (nearly). The dates of full moon in a cycle of 19 years were inscribed in figures of gold on public monuments in Athens, and the number showing the position of a year in the cycle is called the golden number of that year.

JULIAN PERIOD

The Julian period was proposed by Joseph Scaliger in 1582. The period is 7980 Julian years, and its first year coincides with the year 4713 BC. The figure of 7980 is the product of the number of years in the solar cycle, the Metonic cycle and the cycle of the Roman indiction (28 × 19 × 15).

ROMAN INDICTION

The Roman indiction is a period of fifteen years, instituted for fiscal purposes about AD 300.

EPACT

The epact is the age of the calendar Moon, diminished by one day, on 1 January, in the ecclesiastical lunar calendar.

CHINESE CALENDAR

A lunar calendar was the sole calendar in use in China until 1911, when the government adopted the new (Gregorian) calendar for official and most business activities. The Chinese tend to follow both calendars, the lunar calendar playing an important part in personal life, e.g. birth celebrations, festivals, marriages; and in rural villages the lunar calendar dictates the cycle of activities, denoting the change of weather and farming activities.

The lunar calendar is used in Hong Kong, Singapore, Malaysia, Tibet and elsewhere in south-east Asia. The calendar has a cycle of 60 years. The new year begins at the first new moon after the sun enters the sign of Aquarius, i.e. the new year falls between 21 January and 19 February in the Gregorian calendar.

Each year in the Chinese calendar is associated with one of 12 animals: the rat, the ox, the tiger, the rabbit, the dragon, the snake, the horse, the goat or sheep, the monkey, the chicken or rooster, the dog, and the pig.

The date of the Chinese new year and the astrological sign for the years 1994–2000 are:

1994	10 February	Dog
1995	31 January	Pig
1996	19 February	Rat
1997	7 February	Ox
1998	28 January	Tiger
1999	16 February	Rabbit
2000	5 February	Dragon

COPTIC CALENDAR

In the Coptic calendar, which is used by part of the population of Egypt and Ethiopia, the year is made up of 12 months of 30 days each, followed, in general, by five complementary days. Every fourth year is an intercalary or leap year and in these years there are six complementary days. The intercalary year of the Coptic calendar immediately precedes the leap year of the Julian calendar. The era is that of Diocletian or the Martyrs, the origin of which is fixed at 29 August AD 284 (Julian date).

INDIAN ERAS

In addition to the Muslim reckoning there are six eras used in India. The principal astronomical system was the Kaliyuga era, which appears to have been adopted in the fourth century AD. It began on 18 February 3102 BC. The chronological system of northern India, known as the Vikrama Samvat era, prevalent in western India, began on 23 February 57 BC. The year AD 1994 is, therefore, the year 2051 of the Vikrama era.

The Saka era of southern India dating from 3 March AD 78, was declared the uniform national calendar of the Republic of India with effect from 22 March 1957, to be used concurrently with the Gregorian calendar. As revised, the year of the new Saka era begins at the spring equinox, with five successive months of 31 days and seven of 30 days in ordinary years, and six months of each length in leap years. The year AD 1994 is 1916 of the revised Saka era.

The Saptarshi era dates from the moment when the Saptarshi, or saints, were translated and became the stars of the Great Bear in 3076 BC.

The Buddhists reckoned from the death of Buddha in 543 BC (the actual date being 487 BC); and the epoch of the Jains was the death of Vardhamana, the founder of their faith, in 527 BC.

JAPANESE CALENDAR

The Japanese calendar is essentially the same as the Gregorian calendar, the years, months and weeks being of the same length and beginning on the same days as those of the Gregorian calendar. The numeration of the years is different, for Japanese chronology is based on a system of epochs or periods, each of which begins at the accession of an Emperor or other important occurrence. The method is not unlike the former British system of regnal years, but differs from it in that each year of a period closes on 31 December. The Japanese chronology begins about AD 650 and the three latest epochs are defined by the reigns of Emperors, whose actual names are not necessarily used:

Epoch
Taishō 1 August 1912 to 25 December 1926
Shōwa 26 December 1926 to 7 January 1989
Heisei 8 January 1989

Hence the year Heisei 5 begins on 1 January 1994.

The months are not named. They are known as First Month, Second Month, etc., First Month being the equivalent to January. The days of the week are Nichiyōbi (Sun-day), Getsuyōbi (Moon-day), Kayōbi (Fire-day), Suiyōbi (Water-day), Mokuyōbi (Wood-day), Kinyōbi (Metal-day), Doyōbi (Earth-day).

THE MASONIC YEAR

Two dates are quoted in warrants, dispensations, etc., issued by the United Grand Lodge of England, those for the current year being expressed as *Anno Domini* 1994 – *Anno Lucis* 5994. This *Anno Lucis* (year of light) is based on the Book of Genesis 1:3, the 4000 year difference being derived, in modified form, from *Ussher's Notation*, published in 1654, which places the Creation of the World in 4004 BC.

OLYMPIADS

Ancient Greek chronology was reckoned in Olympiads, cycles of four years corresponding with the periodic Olympic Games held on the plain of Olympia in Elis once every four years, the intervening years being the first, second, etc., of the Olympiad which received the name of the victor at the Games. The first recorded Olympiad is that of Choroebus, 776 BC.

ZOROASTRIAN CALENDAR

Zoroastrians, followers of the Iranian prophet Zarathushtra (known to the Greeks as Zoroaster) are mostly to be found in Iran and in India, where they are known as Parsis.

The Zoroastrian era dates from the coronation of the last Zoroastrian Sasanian king in AD 631. The Zoroastrian calendar is divided into twelve months, each comprising 30 days, followed by five holy days of the Gathas at the end of each year to make the year consist of 365 days.

In order to synchronize the calendar with the solar year of 365 days, an extra month was intercalated once every 120 years. However, this intercalation ceased in the twelfth century and the New Year, which had fallen in the spring, slipped back until it now falls in August. Because intercalation ceased at different times in Iran and India, there was one month's difference between the calendar followed in Iran (Kadmi calendar) and by the Parsis (Shenshai calendar).

In 1906 a group of Zoroastrians decided to bring the calendar back in line with the seasons again and restore the New Year to 21 March each year (Fasli calendar).

The Shenshai calendar (New Year in August) is mainly used by Parsis. The Fasli calendar (New Year, 21 March) is mainly used by Zoroastrians living in Iran, in the Indian subcontinent, or away from Iran.

THE ROMAN CALENDAR

Roman historians adopted as an epoch the foundation of Rome, which is believed to have happened in the year 753 BC. The ordinal number of the years in Roman reckoning is followed by the letters AUC (*ab urbe condita*), so that the year 1994 is 2747 AUC (MMDCCXLVII). The calendar that we know has developed from one established by Romulus, who is said to have used a year of 304 days divided into ten months, beginning with March. To this Numa added January and February, making the year consist of 12 months of 30 and 29 days alternately, with an additional day so that the total was 355. It is also said that Numa ordered an intercalary month of 22 or 23 days in alternate years, making 90 days in eight years, to be inserted after 23 February.

However, there is some doubt as to the origination and the details of the intercalation in the Roman calendar. It is certain that some scheme of this kind was inaugurated and not fully carried out, for in the year 46 BC Julius Caesar, who was then Pontifex Maximus, found that the calendar had been allowed to fall into some confusion. He therefore sought the help of the Egyptian astronomer Sosigenes, which led to the construction and adoption (45 BC) of the Julian calendar, and, by a slight alteration, to the Gregorian calendar now in use. The year 46 BC was made to consist of 445 days and is called the Year of Confusion.

In the Roman (Julian) calendar the days of the month were counted backwards from three fixed points, or days, and an intervening day was said to be so many days before the next coming point, the first and last being counted. These three points were the Kalends, the Nones, and the Ides. Their positions in the months and the method of counting from them will be seen in the table below. The year containing 366 days was called *bissextillis annus*, as it had a doubled sixth day (*bissextus dies*) before the March Kalends on 24 February – *ante diem sextum Kalendas Martias*, or a.d. VI Kal. Mart.

Present days of the month	March, May, July, October have thirty-one days	January, August, December have thirty-one days	April, June, September, November have thirty days	February has twenty-eight days, and in leap year twenty-nine
1	Kalendis	Kalendis	Kalendis	Kalendis
2	VI ⎤	IV ⎤ ante	IV ⎤ ante	IV ⎤ ante
3	V ⎥ ante	III ⎦ Nonas	III ⎦ Nonas	III ⎦ Nonas
4	IV ⎥ Nonas	pridie Nonas	pridie Nonas	pridie Nonas
5	III ⎦	Nonis	Nonis	Nonis
6	pridie Nonas	VIII ⎤	VIII ⎤	VIII ⎤
7	Nonis	VII ⎥	VII ⎥	VII ⎥
8	VIII ⎤	VI ⎥ ante	VI ⎥ ante	VI ⎥ ante
9	VII ⎥	V ⎦ Idus	V ⎦ Idus	V ⎦ Idus
10	VI ⎥ ante	IV ⎥	IV ⎥	IV ⎥
11	V ⎦ Idus	III ⎦	III ⎦	III ⎦
12	IV ⎤	pridie Idus	pridie Idus	pridie Idus
13	III ⎦	Idibus	Idibus	Idibus
14	pridie Idus	XIX	XVIII ⎤	XVI ⎤
15	Idibus	XVIII	XVII	XV
16	XVII ⎤	XVII	XVI	XIV
17	XVI	XVI	XV	XIII
18	XV	XV	XIV	XII
19	XIV	XIV	XIII	XI
20	XIII	XIII	XII ⎤	X ⎤ ante Kalendas
21	XII	XII ⎤ ante Kalendas	XI ⎥ ante Kalendas	IX ⎦ Martias
22	XI ⎥ ante Kalendas	XI ⎥ (of the month	X ⎥ (of the month	VIII
23	X ⎥ (of the month	X ⎥ following)	IX ⎥ following)	VII
24	IX ⎥ following)	IX	VIII	*VI
25	VIII	VIII	VII	V
26	VII	VII	VI	IV
27	VI	VI	V	III ⎦
28	V	V	IV	pridie Kalendas Martias
29	IV	IV	III ⎦	
30	III ⎦	III ⎦	pridie Kalendas (Maias, Quinctilis, Octobris, Decembris)	* (repeated in leap year)
31	pridie Kalendas (Aprilis, Iunias, Sextilis, Novembris)	pridie Kalendas (Februarias, Septembris, Ianuarias)		

Calendar for Any Year 1770–2030

To select the correct calendar for any year between 1770 and 2030,
consult the index below
* leap year

Year		Year		Year		Year		Year		Year		Year		Year	
1770	C	1803	M	1836	L*	1869	K	1902	G	1935	E	1968	D*	2001	C
1771	E	1804	B*	1837	A	1870	M	1903	I	1936	H*	1969	G	2002	E
1772	H*	1805	E	1838	C	1871	A	1904	L*	1937	K	1970	I	2003	G
1773	K	1806	G	1839	E	1872	D*	1905	A	1938	M	1971	K	2004	J*
1774	M	1807	I	1840	H*	1873	G	1906	C	1939	A	1972	N*	2005	M
1775	A	1808	L*	1841	K	1874	I	1907	E	1940	D*	1973	C	2006	A
1776	D*	1809	A	1842	M	1875	K	1908	H*	1941	G	1974	E	2007	C
1777	G	1810	C	1843	A	1876	N*	1909	K	1942	I	1975	G	2008	F*
1778	I	1811	E	1844	D*	1877	C	1910	M	1943	K	1976	J*	2009	I
1779	K	1812	H*	1845	G	1878	E	1911	A	1944	N*	1977	M	2010	K
1780	N*	1813	K	1846	I	1879	G	1912	D*	1945	C	1978	A	2011	M
1781	C	1814	M	1847	K	1880	J*	1913	G	1946	E	1979	C	2012	B*
1782	E	1815	A	1848	N*	1881	M	1914	I	1947	G	1980	F*	2013	E
1783	G	1816	D*	1849	C	1882	A	1915	K	1948	J*	1981	I	2014	G
1784	J*	1817	G	1850	E	1883	C	1916	N*	1949	M	1982	K	2015	I
1785	M	1818	I	1851	G	1884	F*	1917	C	1950	A	1983	M	2016	L*
1786	A	1819	K	1852	J*	1885	I	1918	E	1951	C	1984	B*	2017	A
1787	C	1820	N*	1853	M	1886	K	1919	G	1952	F*	1985	E	2018	C
1788	F*	1821	C	1854	A	1887	M	1920	J*	1953	I	1986	G	2019	E
1789	I	1822	E	1855	C	1888	B*	1921	M	1954	K	1987	I	2020	H*
1790	K	1823	G	1856	F*	1889	E	1922	A	1955	M	1988	L*	2021	K
1791	M	1824	J*	1857	I	1890	G	1923	C	1956	B*	1989	A	2022	M
1792	B*	1825	M	1858	K	1891	I	1924	F*	1957	E	1990	C	2023	A
1793	E	1826	A	1859	M	1892	L*	1925	I	1958	G	1991	E	2024	D*
1794	G	1827	C	1860	B*	1893	A	1926	K	1959	I	1992	H*	2025	G
1795	I	1828	F*	1861	E	1894	C	1927	M	1960	L*	1993	K	2026	I
1796	L*	1829	I	1862	G	1895	E	1928	B*	1961	A	1994	M	2027	K
1797	A	1830	K	1863	I	1896	H*	1929	E	1962	C	1995	A	2028	N*
1798	C	1831	M	1864	L*	1897	K	1930	G	1963	E	1996	D*	2029	C
1799	E	1832	B*	1865	A	1898	M	1931	I	1964	H*	1997	G	2030	E
1800	G	1833	E	1866	C	1899	A	1932	L*	1965	K	1998	I		
1801	I	1834	G	1867	E	1900	C	1933	A	1966	M	1999	K		
1802	K	1835	I	1868	H*	1901	E	1934	C	1967	A	2000	N*		

A

January
Sun.	1	8	15	22	29
Mon.	2	9	16	23	30
Tue.	3	10	17	24	31
Wed.	4	11	18	25	
Thur.	5	12	19	26	
Fri.	6	13	20	27	
Sat.	7	14	21	28	

February
Sun.	5	12	19	26
Mon.	6	13	20	27
Tue.	7	14	21	28
Wed.	1	8	15	22
Thur.	2	9	16	23
Fri.	3	10	17	24
Sat.	4	11	18	25

March
Sun.	5	12	19	26	
Mon.	6	13	20	27	
Tue.	7	14	21	28	
Wed.	1	8	15	22	29
Thur.	2	9	16	23	30
Fri.	3	10	17	24	31
Sat.	4	11	18	25	

April
Sun.	2	9	16	23	30
Mon.	3	10	17	24	
Tue.	4	11	18	25	
Wed.	5	12	19	26	
Thur.	6	13	20	27	
Fri.	7	14	21	28	
Sat.	1	8	15	22	29

May
Sun.	7	14	21	28	
Mon.	1	8	15	22	29
Tue.	2	9	16	23	30
Wed.	3	10	17	24	31
Thur.	4	11	18	25	
Fri.	5	12	19	26	
Sat.	6	13	20	27	

June
Sun.	4	11	18	25	
Mon.	5	12	19	26	
Tue.	6	13	20	27	
Wed.	7	14	21	28	
Thur.	1	8	15	22	29
Fri.	2	9	16	23	30
Sat.	3	10	17	24	

July
Sun.	2	9	16	23	30
Mon.	3	10	17	24	31
Tue.	4	11	18	25	
Wed.	5	12	19	26	
Thur.	6	13	20	27	
Fri.	7	14	21	28	
Sat.	1	8	15	22	29

August
Sun.	6	13	20	27	
Mon.	7	14	21	28	
Tue.	1	8	15	22	29
Wed.	2	9	16	23	30
Thur.	3	10	17	24	31
Fri.	4	11	18	25	
Sat.	5	12	19	26	

September
Sun.	3	10	17	24
Mon.	4	11	18	25
Tue.	5	12	19	26
Wed.	6	13	20	27
Thur.	7	14	21	28
Fri.	1	8	15	22	29
Sat.	2	9	16	23	30

October
Sun.	1	8	15	22	29
Mon.	2	9	16	23	30
Tue.	3	10	17	24	31
Wed.	4	11	18	25	
Thur.	5	12	19	26	
Fri.	6	13	20	27	
Sat.	7	14	21	28	

November
Sun.	5	12	19	26	
Mon.	6	13	20	27	
Tue.	7	14	21	28	
Wed.	1	8	15	22	29
Thur.	2	9	16	23	30
Fri.	3	10	17	24	
Sat.	4	11	18	25	

December
Sun.	3	10	17	24	31
Mon.	4	11	18	25	
Tue.	5	12	19	26	
Wed.	6	13	20	27	
Thur.	7	14	21	28	
Fri.	1	8	15	22	29
Sat.	2	9	16	23	30

EASTER DAYS

March 26	1815, 1826, 1837, 1967, 1978, 1989
April 2	1809, 1893, 1899, 1961
April 9	1871, 1882, 1939, 1950, 2023
April 16	1775, 1786, 1797, 1843, 1854, 1865, 1911, 1922, 1933, 1995, 2006, 2017
April 23	1905

B (LEAP YEAR)

January
Sun.	1	8	15	22	29
Mon.	2	9	16	23	30
Tue.	3	10	17	24	31
Wed.	4	11	18	25	
Thur.	5	12	19	26	
Fri.	6	13	20	27	
Sat.	7	14	21	28	

February
Sun.	5	12	19	26	
Mon.	6	13	20	27	
Tue.	7	14	21	28	
Wed.	1	8	15	22	29
Thur.	2	9	16	23	
Fri.	3	10	17	24	
Sat.	4	11	18	25	

March
Sun.	4	11	18	25	
Mon.	5	12	19	26	
Tue.	6	13	20	27	
Wed.	7	14	21	28	
Thur.	1	8	15	22	29
Fri.	2	9	16	23	30
Sat.	3	10	17	24	31

April
Sun.	1	8	15	22	29
Mon.	2	9	16	23	30
Tue.	3	10	17	24	
Wed.	4	11	18	25	
Thur.	5	12	19	26	
Fri.	6	13	20	27	
Sat.	7	14	21	28	

May
Sun.	6	13	20	27	
Mon.	7	14	21	28	
Tue.	1	8	15	22	29
Wed.	2	9	16	23	30
Thur.	3	10	17	24	31
Fri.	4	11	18	25	
Sat.	5	12	19	26	

June
Sun.	3	10	17	24	
Mon.	4	11	18	25	
Tue.	5	12	19	26	
Wed.	6	13	20	27	
Thur.	7	14	21	28	
Fri.	1	8	15	22	29
Sat.	2	9	16	23	30

July
Sun.	1	8	15	22	29
Mon.	2	9	16	23	30
Tue.	3	10	17	24	31
Wed.	4	11	18	25	
Thur.	5	12	19	26	
Fri.	6	13	20	27	
Sat.	7	14	21	28	

August
Sun.	5	12	19	26	
Mon.	6	13	20	27	
Tue.	7	14	21	28	
Wed.	1	8	15	22	29
Thur.	2	9	16	23	30
Fri.	3	10	17	24	31
Sat.	4	11	18	25	

September
Sun.	2	9	16	23	30
Mon.	3	10	17	24	
Tue.	4	11	18	25	
Wed.	5	12	19	26	
Thur.	6	13	20	27	
Fri.	7	14	21	28	
Sat.	1	8	15	22	29

October
Sun.	7	14	21	28	
Mon.	1	8	15	22	29
Tue.	2	9	16	23	30
Wed.	3	10	17	24	31
Thur.	4	11	18	25	
Fri.	5	12	19	26	
Sat.	6	13	20	27	

November
Sun.	4	11	18	25	
Mon.	5	12	19	26	
Tue.	6	13	20	27	
Wed.	7	14	21	28	
Thur.	1	8	15	22	29
Fri.	2	9	16	23	30
Sat.	3	10	17	24	

December
Sun.	2	9	16	23	30
Mon.	3	10	17	24	31
Tue.	4	11	18	25	
Wed.	5	12	19	26	
Thur.	6	13	20	27	
Fri.	7	14	21	28	
Sat.	1	8	15	22	29

EASTER DAYS

April 1	1804, 1888, 1956
April 8	1792, 1860, 1928, 2012
April 22	1832, 1984

C

	January	February	March
Sun.	7 14 21 28	4 11 18 25	4 11 18 25
Mon.	1 8 15 22 29	5 12 19 26	5 12 19 26
Tue.	2 9 16 23 30	6 13 20 27	6 13 20 27
Wed.	3 10 17 24 31	7 14 21 28	7 14 21 28
Thur.	4 11 18 25	1 8 15 22	1 8 15 22 29
Fri.	5 12 19 26	2 9 16 23	2 9 16 23 30
Sat.	6 13 20 27	3 10 17 24	3 10 17 24 31

	April	May	June
Sun.	1 8 15 22 29	6 13 20 27	3 10 17 24
Mon.	2 9 16 23 30	7 14 21 28	4 11 18 25
Tue.	3 10 17 24	1 8 15 22 29	5 12 19 26
Wed.	4 11 18 25	2 9 16 23 30	6 13 20 27
Thur.	5 12 19 26	3 10 17 24 31	7 14 21 28
Fri.	6 13 20 27	4 11 18 25	1 8 15 22 29
Sat.	7 14 21 28	5 12 19 26	2 9 16 23 30

	July	August	September
Sun.	1 8 15 22 29	5 12 19 26	2 9 16 23 30
Mon.	2 9 16 23 30	6 13 20 27	3 10 17 24
Tue.	3 10 17 24 31	7 14 21 28	4 11 18 25
Wed.	4 11 18 25	1 8 15 22 29	5 12 19 26
Thur.	5 12 19 26	2 9 16 23 30	6 13 20 27
Fri.	6 13 20 27	3 10 17 24 31	7 14 21 28
Sat.	7 14 21 28	4 11 18 25	1 8 15 22 29

	October	November	December
Sun.	7 14 21 28	4 11 18 25	2 9 16 23 30
Mon.	1 8 15 22 29	5 12 19 26	3 10 17 24 31
Tue.	2 9 16 23 30	6 13 20 27	4 11 18 25
Wed.	3 10 17 24 31	7 14 21 28	5 12 19 26
Thur.	4 11 18 25	1 8 15 22 29	6 13 20 27
Fri.	5 12 19 26	2 9 16 23 30	7 14 21 28
Sat.	6 13 20 27	3 10 17 24	1 8 15 22 29

EASTER DAYS

March 25	1883, 1894, 1951
April 1	1866, 1877, 1923, 1934, 1945, 2018, 2029
April 8	1787, 1798, 1849, 1855, 1917, 2007
April 15	1770, 1781, 1827, 1838, 1900, 1906, 1979, 1990, 2001
April 22	1810, 1821, 1962, 1973

E

	January	February	March
Sun.	6 13 20 27	3 10 17 24	3 10 17 24 31
Mon.	7 14 21 28	4 11 18 25	4 11 18 25
Tue.	1 8 15 22 29	5 12 19 26	5 12 19 26
Wed.	2 9 16 23 30	6 13 20 27	6 13 20 27
Thur.	3 10 17 24 31	7 14 21 28	7 14 21 28
Fri.	4 11 18 25	1 8 15 22	1 8 15 22 29
Sat.	5 12 19 26	2 9 16 23	2 9 16 23 30

	April	May	June
Sun.	7 14 21 28	5 12 19 26	2 9 16 23 30
Mon.	1 8 15 22 29	6 13 20 27	3 10 17 24
Tue.	2 9 16 23 30	7 14 21 28	4 11 18 25
Wed.	3 10 17 24	1 8 15 22 29	5 12 19 26
Thur.	4 11 18 25	2 9 16 23 30	6 13 20 27
Fri.	5 12 19 26	3 10 17 24 31	7 14 21 28
Sat.	6 13 20 27	4 11 18 25	1 8 15 22 29

	July	August	September
Sun.	7 14 21 28	4 11 18 25	1 8 15 22 29
Mon.	1 8 15 22 29	5 12 19 26	2 9 16 23 30
Tue.	2 9 16 23 30	6 13 20 27	3 10 17 24
Wed.	3 10 17 24 31	7 14 21 28	4 11 18 25
Thur.	4 11 18 25	1 8 15 22 29	5 12 19 26
Fri.	5 12 19 26	2 9 16 23 30	6 13 20 27
Sat.	6 13 20 27	3 10 17 24 31	7 14 21 28

	October	November	December
Sun.	6 13 20 27	3 10 17 24	1 8 15 22 29
Mon.	7 14 21 28	4 11 18 25	2 9 16 23 30
Tue.	1 8 15 22 29	5 12 19 26	3 10 17 24 31
Wed.	2 9 16 23 30	6 13 20 27	4 11 18 25
Thur.	3 10 17 24 31	7 14 21 28	5 12 19 26
Fri.	4 11 18 25	1 8 15 22 29	6 13 20 27
Sat.	5 12 19 26	2 9 16 23 30	7 14 21 28

EASTER DAYS

March 24	1799
March 31	1771, 1782, 1793, 1839, 1850, 1861, 1907
	1918, 1929, 1991, 2002, 2013
April 7	1822, 1833, 1901, 1985
April 14	1805, 1811, 1895, 1963, 1974
April 21	1867, 1878, 1889, 1935, 1946, 1957, 2019, 2030

D (LEAP YEAR)

	January	February	March
Sun.	7 14 21 28	4 11 18 25	3 10 17 24 31
Mon.	1 8 15 22 29	5 12 19 26	4 11 18 25
Tue.	2 9 16 23 30	6 13 20 27	5 12 19 26
Wed.	3 10 17 24 31	7 14 21 28	6 13 20 27
Thur.	4 11 18 25	1 8 15 22 29	7 14 21 28
Fri.	5 12 19 26	2 9 16 23	1 8 15 22 29
Sat.	6 13 20 27	3 10 17 24	2 9 16 23 30

	April	May	June
Sun.	7 14 21 28	5 12 19 26	2 9 16 23 30
Mon.	1 8 15 22 29	6 13 20 27	3 10 17 24
Tue.	2 9 16 23 30	7 14 21 28	4 11 18 25
Wed.	3 10 17 24	1 8 15 22 29	5 12 19 26
Thur.	4 11 18 25	2 9 16 23 30	6 13 20 27
Fri.	5 12 19 26	3 10 17 24 31	7 14 21 28
Sat.	6 13 20 27	4 11 18 25	1 8 15 22 29

	July	August	September
Sun.	7 14 21 28	4 11 18 25	1 8 15 22 29
Mon.	1 8 15 22 29	5 12 19 26	2 9 16 23 30
Tue.	2 9 16 23 30	6 13 20 27	3 10 17 24
Wed.	3 10 17 24 31	7 14 21 28	4 11 18 25
Thur.	4 11 18 25	1 8 15 22 29	5 12 19 26
Fri.	5 12 19 26	2 9 16 23 30	6 13 20 27
Sat.	6 13 20 27	3 10 17 24 31	7 14 21 28

	October	November	December
Sun.	6 13 20 27	3 10 17 24	1 8 15 22 29
Mon.	7 14 21 28	4 11 18 25	2 9 16 23 30
Tue.	1 8 15 22 29	5 12 19 26	3 10 17 24 31
Wed.	2 9 16 23 30	6 13 20 27	4 11 18 25
Thur.	3 10 17 24 31	7 14 21 28	5 12 19 26
Fri.	4 11 18 25	1 8 15 22 29	6 13 20 27
Sat.	5 12 19 26	2 9 16 23 30	7 14 21 28

EASTER DAYS

March 24	1940
March 31	1872, 2024
April 7	1776, 1844, 1912, 1996
April 14	1816, 1968

F (LEAP YEAR)

	January	February	March
Sun.	6 13 20 27	3 10 17 24	2 9 16 23 30
Mon.	7 14 21 28	4 11 18 25	3 10 17 24 31
Tue.	1 8 15 22 29	5 12 19 26	4 11 18 25
Wed.	2 9 16 23 30	6 13 20 27	5 12 19 26
Thur.	3 10 17 24 31	7 14 21 28	6 13 20 27
Fri.	4 11 18 25	1 8 15 22 29	7 14 21 28
Sat.	5 12 19 26	2 9 16 23	1 8 15 22 29

	April	May	June
Sun.	6 13 20 27	4 11 18 25	1 8 15 22 29
Mon.	7 14 21 28	5 12 19 26	2 9 16 23 30
Tue.	1 8 15 22 29	6 13 20 27	3 10 17 24
Wed.	2 9 16 23 30	7 14 21 28	4 11 18 25
Thur.	3 10 17 24	1 8 15 22 29	5 12 19 26
Fri.	4 11 18 25	2 9 16 23 30	6 13 20 27
Sat.	5 12 19 26	3 10 17 24 31	7 14 21 28

	July	August	September
Sun.	6 13 20 27	3 10 17 24 31	7 14 21 28
Mon.	7 14 21 28	4 11 18 25	1 8 15 22 29
Tue.	1 8 15 22 29	5 12 19 26	2 9 16 23 30
Wed.	2 9 16 23 30	6 13 20 27	3 10 17 24
Thur.	3 10 17 24 31	7 14 21 28	4 11 18 25
Fri.	4 11 18 25	1 8 15 22 29	5 12 19 26
Sat.	5 12 19 26	2 9 16 23 30	6 13 20 27

	October	November	December
Sun.	5 12 19 26	2 9 16 23 30	7 14 21 28
Mon.	6 13 20 27	3 10 17 24	1 8 15 22 29
Tue.	7 14 21 28	4 11 18 25	2 9 16 23 30
Wed.	1 8 15 22 29	5 12 19 26	3 10 17 24 31
Thur.	2 9 16 23 30	6 13 20 27	4 11 18 25
Fri.	3 10 17 24 31	7 14 21 28	5 12 19 26
Sat.	4 11 18 25	1 8 15 22 29	6 13 20 27

EASTER DAYS

March 23	1788, 1856, 2008
April 6	1828, 1980
April 13	1884, 1952
April 20	1924

G

	January	*February*	*March*
Sun.	5 12 19 26	2 9 16 23	2 9 16 23 30
Mon.	6 13 20 27	3 10 17 24	3 10 17 24 31
Tue.	7 14 21 28	4 11 18 25	4 11 18 25
Wed.	1 8 15 22 29	5 12 19 26	5 12 19 26
Thur.	2 9 16 23 30	6 13 20 27	6 13 20 27
Fri.	3 10 17 24 31	7 14 21 28	7 14 21 28
Sat.	4 11 18 25	1 8 15 22	1 8 15 22 29

	April	*May*	*June*
Sun.	6 13 20 27	4 11 18 25	1 8 15 22 29
Mon.	7 14 21 28	5 12 19 26	2 9 16 23 30
Tue.	1 8 15 22 29	6 13 20 27	3 10 17 24
Wed.	2 9 16 23 30	7 14 21 28	4 11 18 25
Thur.	3 10 17 24	1 8 15 22 29	5 12 19 26
Fri.	4 11 18 25	2 9 16 23 30	6 13 20 27
Sat.	5 12 19 26	3 10 17 24 31	7 14 21 28

	July	*August*	*September*
Sun.	6 13 20 27	3 10 17 24 31	7 14 21 28
Mon.	7 14 21 28	4 11 18 25	1 8 15 22 29
Tue.	1 8 15 22 29	5 12 19 26	2 9 16 23 30
Wed.	2 9 16 23 30	6 13 20 27	3 10 17 24
Thur.	3 10 17 24 31	7 14 21 28	4 11 18 25
Fri.	4 11 18 25	1 8 15 22 29	5 12 19 26
Sat.	5 12 19 26	2 9 16 23 30	6 13 20 27

	October	*November*	*December*
Sun.	5 12 19 26	2 9 16 23 30	7 14 21 28
Mon.	6 13 20 27	3 10 17 24	1 8 15 22 29
Tue.	7 14 21 28	4 11 18 25	2 9 16 23 30
Wed.	1 8 15 22 29	5 12 19 26	3 10 17 24 31
Thur.	2 9 16 23 30	6 13 20 27	4 11 18 25
Fri.	3 10 17 24 31	7 14 21 28	5 12 19 26
Sat.	4 11 18 25	1 8 15 22 29	6 13 20 27

EASTER DAYS

March 23	1845, 1913
March 30	1777, 1823, 1834, 1902, 1975, 1986, 1997
April 6	1806, 1817, 1890, 1947, 1958, 1969
April 13	1800, 1873, 1879, 1941
April 20	1783, 1794, 1851, 1862, 1919, 1930, 2003, 2014, 2025

I

	January	*February*	*March*
Sun.	4 11 18 25	1 8 15 22	1 8 15 22 29
Mon.	5 12 19 26	2 9 16 23	2 9 16 23 30
Tue.	6 13 20 27	3 10 17 24	3 10 17 24 31
Wed.	7 14 21 28	4 11 18 25	4 11 18 25
Thur.	1 8 15 22 29	5 12 19 26	5 12 19 26
Fri.	2 9 16 23 30	6 13 20 27	6 13 20 27
Sat.	3 10 17 24 31	7 14 21 28	7 14 21 28

	April	*May*	*June*
Sun.	5 12 19 26	3 10 17 24 31	7 14 21 28
Mon.	6 13 20 27	4 11 18 25	1 8 15 22 29
Tue.	7 14 21 28	5 12 19 26	2 9 16 23 30
Wed.	1 8 15 22 29	6 13 20 27	3 10 17 24
Thur.	2 9 16 23 30	7 14 21 28	4 11 18 25
Fri.	3 10 17 24	1 8 15 22 29	5 12 19 26
Sat.	4 11 18 25	2 9 16 23 30	6 13 20 27

	July	*August*	*September*
Sun.	5 12 19 26	2 9 16 23 30	6 13 20 27
Mon.	6 13 20 27	3 10 17 24 31	7 14 21 28
Tue.	7 14 21 28	4 11 18 25	1 8 15 22 29
Wed.	1 8 15 22 29	5 12 19 26	2 9 16 23 30
Thur.	2 9 16 23 30	6 13 20 27	3 10 17 24
Fri.	3 10 17 24 31	7 14 21 28	4 11 18 25
Sat.	4 11 18 25	1 8 15 22 29	5 12 19 26

	October	*November*	*December*
Sun.	4 11 18 25	1 8 15 22 29	6 13 20 27
Mon.	5 12 19 26	2 9 16 23 30	7 14 21 28
Tue.	6 13 20 27	3 10 17 24	1 8 15 22 29
Wed.	7 14 21 28	4 11 18 25	2 9 16 23 30
Thur.	1 8 15 22 29	5 12 19 26	3 10 17 24 31
Fri.	2 9 16 23 30	6 13 20 27	4 11 18 25
Sat.	3 10 17 24 31	7 14 21 28	5 12 19 26

EASTER DAYS

March 22	1818
March 29	1807, 1891, 1959, 1970
April 5	1795, 1801, 1863, 1874, 1885, 1931, 1942, 1953, 2015, 2026
April 12	1789, 1846, 1857, 1903, 1914, 1925, 1998, 2009
April 19	1778, 1829, 1835, 1981, 1987

H (LEAP YEAR)

	January	*February*	*March*
Sun.	5 12 19 26	2 9 16 23	1 8 15 22 29
Mon.	6 13 20 27	3 10 17 24	2 9 16 23 30
Tue.	7 14 21 28	4 11 18 25	3 10 17 24 31
Wed.	1 8 15 22 29	5 12 19 26	4 11 18 25
Thur.	2 9 16 23 30	6 13 20 27	5 12 19 26
Fri.	3 10 17 24 31	7 14 21 28	6 13 20 27
Sat.	4 11 18 25	1 8 15 22 29	7 14 21 28

	April	*May*	*June*
Sun.	5 12 19 26	3 10 17 24 31	7 14 21 28
Mon.	6 13 20 27	4 11 18 25	1 8 15 22 29
Tue.	7 14 21 28	5 12 19 26	2 9 16 23 30
Wed.	1 8 15 22 29	6 13 20 27	3 10 17 24
Thur.	2 9 16 23 30	7 14 21 28	4 11 18 25
Fri.	3 10 17 24	1 8 15 22 29	5 12 19 26
Sat.	4 11 18 25	2 9 16 23 30	6 13 20 27

	July	*August*	*September*
Sun.	5 12 19 26	2 9 16 23 30	6 13 20 27
Mon.	6 13 20 27	3 10 17 24 31	7 14 21 28
Tue.	7 14 21 28	4 11 18 25	1 8 15 22 29
Wed.	1 8 15 22 29	5 12 19 26	2 9 16 23 30
Thur.	2 9 16 23 30	6 13 20 27	3 10 17 24
Fri.	3 10 17 24 31	7 14 21 28	4 11 18 25
Sat.	4 11 18 25	1 8 15 22 29	5 12 19 26

	October	*November*	*December*
Sun.	4 11 18 25	1 8 15 22 29	6 13 20 27
Mon.	5 12 19 26	2 9 16 23 30	7 14 21 28
Tue.	6 13 20 27	3 10 17 24	1 8 15 22 29
Wed.	7 14 21 28	4 11 18 25	2 9 16 23 30
Thur.	1 8 15 22 29	5 12 19 26	3 10 17 24 31
Fri.	2 9 16 23 30	6 13 20 27	4 11 18 25
Sat.	3 10 17 24 31	7 14 21 28	5 12 19 26

EASTER DAYS

March 29	1812, 1964
April 5	1896
April 12	1868, 1936, 2020
April 19	1772, 1840, 1908, 1992

J (LEAP YEAR)

	January	*February*	*March*
Sun.	4 11 18 25	1 8 15 22 29	7 14 21 28
Mon.	5 12 19 26	2 9 16 23	1 8 15 22 29
Tue.	6 13 20 27	3 10 17 24	2 9 16 23 30
Wed.	7 14 21 28	4 11 18 25	3 10 17 24 31
Thur.	1 8 15 22 29	5 12 19 26	4 11 18 25
Fri.	2 9 16 23 30	6 13 20 27	5 12 19 26
Sat.	3 10 17 24 31	7 14 21 28	6 13 20 27

	April	*May*	*June*
Sun.	4 11 18 25	2 9 16 23 30	6 13 20 27
Mon.	5 12 19 26	3 10 17 24 31	7 14 21 28
Tue.	6 13 20 27	4 11 18 25	1 8 15 22 29
Wed.	7 14 21 28	5 12 19 26	2 9 16 23 30
Thur.	1 8 15 22 29	6 13 20 27	3 10 17 24
Fri.	2 9 16 23 30	7 14 21 28	4 11 18 25
Sat.	3 10 17 24	1 8 15 22 29	5 12 19 26

	July	*August*	*September*
Sun.	4 11 18 25	1 8 15 22 29	5 12 19 26
Mon.	5 12 19 26	2 9 16 23 30	6 13 20 27
Tue.	6 13 20 27	3 10 17 24 31	7 14 21 28
Wed.	7 14 21 28	4 11 18 25	1 8 15 22 29
Thur.	1 8 15 22 29	5 12 19 26	2 9 16 23 30
Fri.	2 9 16 23 30	6 13 20 27	3 10 17 24
Sat.	3 10 17 24 31	7 14 21 28	4 11 18 25

	October	*November*	*December*
Sun.	3 10 17 24 31	7 14 21 28	5 12 19 26
Mon.	4 11 18 25	1 8 15 22 29	6 13 20 27
Tue.	5 12 19 26	2 9 16 23 30	7 14 21 28
Wed.	6 13 20 27	3 10 17 24	1 8 15 22 29
Thur.	7 14 21 28	4 11 18 25	2 9 16 23 30
Fri.	1 8 15 22 29	5 12 19 26	3 10 17 24 31
Sat.	2 9 16 23 30	6 13 20 27	4 11 18 25

EASTER DAYS

March 28	1880, 1948
April 4	1920
April 11	1784, 1852, 2004
April 18	1824, 1976

K

	January	February	March
Sun.	3 10 17 24 31	7 14 21 28	7 14 21 28
Mon.	4 11 18 25	1 8 15 22	1 8 15 22 29
Tue.	5 12 19 26	2 9 16 23	2 9 16 23 30
Wed.	6 13 20 27	3 10 17 24	3 10 17 24 31
Thur.	7 14 21 28	4 11 18 25	4 11 18 25
Fri.	1 8 15 22 29	5 12 19 26	5 12 19 26
Sat.	2 9 16 23 30	6 13 20 27	6 13 20 27

	April	May	June
Sun.	4 11 18 25	2 9 16 23 30	6 13 20 27
Mon.	5 12 19 26	3 10 17 24 31	7 14 21 28
Tue.	6 13 20 27	4 11 18 25	1 8 15 22 29
Wed.	7 14 21 28	5 12 19 26	2 9 16 23 30
Thur.	1 8 15 22 29	6 13 20 27	3 10 17 24
Fri.	2 9 16 23 30	7 14 21 28	4 11 18 25
Sat.	3 10 17 24	1 8 15 22 29	5 12 19 26

	July	August	September
Sun.	4 11 18 25	1 8 15 22 29	5 12 19 26
Mon.	5 12 19 26	2 9 16 23 30	6 13 20 27
Tue.	6 13 20 27	3 10 17 24 31	7 14 21 28
Wed.	7 14 21 28	4 11 18 25	1 8 15 22 29
Thur.	1 8 15 22 29	5 12 19 26	2 9 16 23 30
Fri.	2 9 16 23 30	6 13 20 27	3 10 17 24
Sat.	3 10 17 24 31	7 14 21 28	4 11 18 25

	October	November	December
Sun.	3 10 17 24 31	7 14 21 28	5 12 19 26
Mon.	4 11 18 25	1 8 15 22 29	6 13 20 27
Tue.	5 12 19 26	2 9 16 23 30	7 14 21 28
Wed.	6 13 20 27	3 10 17 24	1 8 15 22 29
Thur.	7 14 21 28	4 11 18 25	2 9 16 23 30
Fri.	1 8 15 22 29	5 12 19 26	3 10 17 24 31
Sat.	2 9 16 23 30	6 13 20 27	4 11 18 25

EASTER DAYS

March 28 — 1869, 1875, 1937, 2027
April 4 — 1779, 1790, 1847, 1858, 1915, 1926, 1999 2010, 2021
April 11 — 1773, 1819, 1830, 1841, 1909, 1971, 1982, 1993
April 18 — 1802, 1813, 1897, 1954, 1965
April 25 — 1886, 1943

M

	January	February	March
Sun.	2 9 16 23 30	6 13 20 27	6 13 20 27
Mon.	3 10 17 24 31	7 14 21 28	7 14 21 28
Tue.	4 11 18 25	1 8 15 22	1 8 15 22 29
Wed.	5 12 19 26	2 9 16 23	2 9 16 23 30
Thur.	6 13 20 27	3 10 17 24	3 10 17 24 31
Fri.	7 14 21 28	4 11 18 25	4 11 18 25
Sat.	1 8 15 22 29	5 12 19 26	5 12 19 26

	April	May	June
Sun.	3 10 17 24	1 8 15 22 29	5 12 19 26
Mon.	4 11 18 25	2 9 16 23 30	6 13 20 27
Tue.	5 12 19 26	3 10 17 24 31	7 14 21 28
Wed.	6 13 20 27	4 11 18 25	1 8 15 22 29
Thur.	7 14 21 28	5 12 19 26	2 9 16 23 30
Fri.	1 8 15 22 29	6 13 20 27	3 10 17 24
Sat.	2 9 16 23 30	7 14 21 28	4 11 18 25

	July	August	September
Sun.	3 10 17 24 31	7 14 21 28	4 11 18 25
Mon.	4 11 18 25	1 8 15 22 29	5 12 19 26
Tue.	5 12 19 26	2 9 16 23 30	6 13 20 27
Wed.	6 13 20 27	3 10 17 24 31	7 14 21 28
Thur.	7 14 21 28	4 11 18 25	1 8 15 22 29
Fri.	1 8 15 22 29	5 12 19 26	2 9 16 23 30
Sat.	2 9 16 23 30	6 13 20 27	3 10 17 24

	October	November	December
Sun.	2 9 16 23 30	6 13 20 27	4 11 18 25
Mon.	3 10 17 24 31	7 14 21 28	5 12 19 26
Tue.	4 11 18 25	1 8 15 22 29	6 13 20 27
Wed.	5 12 19 26	2 9 16 23 30	7 14 21 28
Thur.	6 13 20 27	3 10 17 24	1 8 15 22 29
Fri.	7 14 21 28	4 11 18 25	2 9 16 23 30
Sat.	1 8 15 22 29	5 12 19 26	3 10 17 24 31

EASTER DAYS

March 27 — 1785, 1842, 1853, 1910, 1921, 2005
April 3 — 1774, 1825, 1831, 1983, 1994
April 10 — 1803, 1814, 1887, 1898, 1955, 1966, 1977
April 17 — 1870, 1881, 1927, 1938, 1949, 2022
April 24 — 1791, 1859, 2011

L (LEAP YEAR)

	January	February	March
Sun.	3 10 17 24 31	7 14 21 28	6 13 20 27
Mon.	4 11 18 25	1 8 15 22 29	7 14 21 28
Tue.	5 12 19 26	2 9 16 23	1 8 15 22 29
Wed.	6 13 20 27	3 10 17 24	2 9 16 23 30
Thur.	7 14 21 28	4 11 18 25	3 10 17 24 31
Fri.	1 8 15 22 29	5 12 19 26	4 11 18 25
Sat.	2 9 16 23 30	6 13 20 27	5 12 19 26

	April	May	June
Sun.	3 10 17 24	1 8 15 22 29	5 12 19 26
Mon.	4 11 18 25	2 9 16 23 30	6 13 20 27
Tue.	5 12 19 26	3 10 17 24 31	7 14 21 28
Wed.	6 13 20 27	4 11 18 25	1 8 15 22 29
Thur.	7 14 21 28	5 12 19 26	2 9 16 23 30
Fri.	1 8 15 22 29	6 13 20 27	3 10 17 24
Sat.	2 9 16 23 30	7 14 21 28	4 11 18 25

	July	August	September
Sun.	3 10 17 24 31	7 14 21 28	4 11 18 25
Mon.	4 11 18 25	1 8 15 22 29	5 12 19 26
Tue.	5 12 19 26	2 9 16 23 30	6 13 20 27
Wed.	6 13 20 27	3 10 17 24 31	7 14 21 28
Thur.	7 14 21 28	4 11 18 25	1 8 15 22 29
Fri.	1 8 15 22 29	5 12 19 26	2 9 16 23 30
Sat.	2 9 16 23 30	6 13 20 27	3 10 17 24

	October	November	December
Sun.	2 9 16 23 30	6 13 20 27	4 11 18 25
Mon.	3 10 17 24 31	7 14 21 28	5 12 19 26
Tue.	4 11 18 25	1 8 15 22 29	6 13 20 27
Wed.	5 12 19 26	2 9 16 23 30	7 14 21 28
Thur.	6 13 20 27	3 10 17 24	1 8 15 22 29
Fri.	7 14 21 28	4 11 18 25	2 9 16 23 30
Sat.	1 8 15 22 29	5 12 19 26	3 10 17 24 31

EASTER DAYS

March 27 — 1796, 1864, 1932, 2016
April 3 — 1836, 1904, 1988
April 17 — 1808, 1892, 1960

N (LEAP YEAR)

	January	February	March
Sun.	2 9 16 23 30	6 13 20 27	5 12 19 26
Mon.	3 10 17 24 31	7 14 21 28	6 13 20 27
Tue.	4 11 18 25	1 8 15 22 29	7 14 21 28
Wed.	5 12 19 26	2 9 16 23	1 8 15 22 29
Thur.	6 13 20 27	3 10 17 24	2 9 16 23 30
Fri.	7 14 21 28	4 11 18 25	3 10 17 24 31
Sat.	1 8 15 22 29	5 12 19 26	4 11 18 25

	April	May	June
Sun.	2 9 16 23 30	7 14 21 28	4 11 18 25
Mon.	3 10 17 24	1 8 15 22 29	5 12 19 26
Tue.	4 11 18 25	2 9 16 23 30	6 13 20 27
Wed.	5 12 19 26	3 10 17 24 31	7 14 21 28
Thur.	6 13 20 27	4 11 18 25	1 8 15 22 29
Fri.	7 14 21 28	5 12 19 26	2 9 16 23 30
Sat.	1 8 15 22 29	6 13 20 27	3 10 17 24

	July	August	September
Sun.	2 9 16 23 30	6 13 20 27	3 10 17 24
Mon.	3 10 17 24 31	7 14 21 28	4 11 18 25
Tue.	4 11 18 25	1 8 15 22 29	5 12 19 26
Wed.	5 12 19 26	2 9 16 23 30	6 13 20 27
Thur.	6 13 20 27	3 10 17 24 31	7 14 21 28
Fri.	7 14 21 28	4 11 18 25	1 8 15 22 29
Sat.	1 8 15 22 29	5 12 19 26	2 9 16 23 30

	October	November	December
Sun.	1 8 15 22 29	5 12 19 26	3 10 17 24 31
Mon.	2 9 16 23 30	6 13 20 27	4 11 18 25
Tue.	3 10 17 24 31	7 14 21 28	5 12 19 26
Wed.	4 11 18 25	1 8 15 22 29	6 13 20 27
Thur.	5 12 19 26	2 9 16 23 30	7 14 21 28
Fri.	6 13 20 27	3 10 17 24	1 8 15 22 29
Sat.	7 14 21 28	4 11 18 25	2 9 16 23 30

EASTER DAYS

March 26 — 1780
April 2 — 1820, 1972
April 9 — 1944
April 16 — 1876, 2028
April 23 — 1848, 1916, 2000

GEOLOGICAL TIME

The earth is thought to have come into existence approximately 4,600 million years ago, but for nearly half this time, the Archean era, it was uninhabited. Life is generally believed to have emerged in the succeeding Proterozoic era. The Archean and the Proterozoic eras are often together referred to as the Precambrian.

Although primitive forms of life, e.g. algae and bacteria, existed during the Proterozoic era, it is not until the strata of Palaeozoic rocks is reached that abundant fossilized remains appear, initially of small shellfish, followed by plants, primitive fishes and, in the Devonian period (c.400 million BC), land-living plants and amphibia.

Since the Precambrian, there have been three great geological eras:

PALAEOZOIC ('ancient life')
c.570–c.250 million BC

Cambrian - Mainly sandstones, slate and shales; limestones in Scotland. Shelled fossils and invertebrates, e.g. trilobites and brachiopods appear
Ordovician - Mainly shales and mudstones, e.g. in north Wales; limestones in Scotland
Silurian - Shales, mudstones and some limestones, found mostly in Wales and southern Scotland
Devonian - Old red sandstone, shale, limestone and slate, e.g. in south Wales and the West Country. 'The age of fishes' - proliferation of fish fossils. First traces of land-living life
Carboniferous - Coal-bearing rocks, millstone grit, limestone and shale
Permian - Marls, sandstones and clays, named after the area of Russia where these strata are widespread. First large-scale appearance of reptile fossils

There were two great phases of mountain building in the Palaeozoic era: the Caledonian, characterized in Britain by NE–SW lines of hills and valleys; and the later Hercyian, widespread in west Germany and adjacent areas, and in Britain exemplified in E.–W. lines of hills and valleys.

The end of the Palaeozoic era was marked by the extensive glaciations of the Permian period in the southern continents and the decline of amphibians. It was succeeded by an era of warm conditions.

MESOZOIC ('middle forms of life')
c.250–c.65 million BC

Triassic - Mostly sandstone, e.g. in the West Midlands
Jurassic - Mainly limestones and clays, typically displayed in the Jura mountains, and in England in a NE–SW belt from Lincolnshire and the Wash to the Severn and the Dorset coast
Cretaceous - Mainly chalk, clay and sands, e.g. in Kent and Sussex

Giant reptiles were dominant during the Mesozoic era, but it was at this time that marsupial mammals first appeared, as well as *Archaeopteryx lithographica*, the earliest known species of bird. Coniferous trees and flowering plants also developed during the era and, with the birds and the mammals, were the main species to survive into the Caenozoic (or Cenozoic) era. The giant reptiles became extinct.

CAENOZOIC ('recent life')
from c.65 million BC

Eocene - The emergence of new forms of life, i.e. existing species

Oligocene - Fossils of a few still existing species
Miocene - Fossil remains show a balance of existing and extinct species
Pliocene - Fossil remains show a majority of still existing species
Pleistocene - The majority of remains are those of still existing species
Holocene - The present, post-glacial period. Existing species only, except for a few exterminated by man

In the last 25 million years, from the Miocene through the Pliocene periods, the Alpine-Himalayan and the circum-Pacific phases of mountain building reached their climax. During the Pleistocene period ice sheets repeatedly locked up masses of water as land ice; its weight depressed the land, but the locking-up of the water lowered the sea-level by 100–200 metres. The glaciations and interglacials of the Ice Age are extremely difficult to date and classify, but recent scientific opinion considers the Pleistocene period to have begun approximately 1.7 million years ago. The last glacial retreat, merging into the Holocene period, was 10,000 years ago.

HUMAN DEVELOPMENT

Any consideration of the history of mankind must start with the fact that all members of the human race belong to one species of animal, i.e. *Homo sapiens*, the definition of a species being in biological terms that all its members can interbreed. As a species of mammal it is possible to group man with other similar types, known as the primates. Amongst these is found a sub-group, the apes, which includes, in addition to man, the chimpanzees, gorillas, orang-utans and gibbons. All lack a tail, have shoulder blades at the back, and a Y-shaped chewing pattern on the surface of their molars, as well as showing the more general primate characteristics of four incisors, a thumb which is able to touch the fingers of the same hand, and finger and toe nails instead of claws. All the factors available to scientific study suggest that human beings have chimpanzees and gorillas as their nearest relatives in the animal world. However, there remains the possibility that there once lived creatures, now extinct, which were closer to modern man than the chimpanzees and gorillas, and which shared with modern man the characteristics of having flat faces (i.e. the absence of a pronounced muzzle), being bipedal, and possessing large brains.

There are two broad groups of extinct apes recognized by specialists. First the ramapithecines, the remains of which, mainly jaw fragments, have been found in east Africa, Asia, and Turkey. They lived about 14 to 8 million years ago, and from the evidence of their teeth it seems they chewed more in the manner of modern man than the other presently living apes. The second group, the australopithecines, have left much more numerous remains amongst which sub-groups may be detected, although the geographic spread is limited to south and east Africa. Living between 5 and 1.5 million years ago, they were closer relatives of modern man to the extent that they walked upright, did not have an extensive muzzle, and had similar types of pre-molars. The first australopithecine remains were recognized at Taung in South Africa in 1924, and subsequent discoveries include those at the famous site of Olduvai Gorge in Tanzania. Perhaps the most impressive discovery was made at Hadar in Ethiopia in 1974 when about half a skeleton, known as 'Lucy', was found.

Also in east Africa, between 2 million and 1.5 million years ago, lived a hominid group which not only walked upright, had a flat face, and a large brain case, but also made simple pebble and flake stone tools. On present evidence these habilines seem to have been the first people to make tools, however crude. This facility is related to the larger brain size and human beings are the only animals to make implements to be used in other processes. These early pebble tool users, because of their distinctive characteristics, have been grouped as a separate sub-species, now extinct, of the genus *Homo*, and are known as *Homo habilis*.

The use of fire, again a human characteristic, is associated with another group of extinct hominids whose remains, about a million years old, are found in south and east Africa, China, Indonesia, north Africa and Europe. No doubt the mastery of the techniques of making fire helped the colonization of the colder northern areas and in this respect the site of Vertesszollos in Hungary is of particular importance. *Homo erectus* is the name given to this group of fossils and it now includes a number of famous individual discoveries from earlier decades, for example, Solo Man, Heidelberg Man, and especially Peking Man who lived at the cave site at Choukoutien which has yielded evidence of fire and burnt bone.

The well-known group, Neanderthal Man, or *Homo sapiens neandertalensis*, is an extinct form of modern man who lived between about 100,000 and 40,000 years ago, thus spanning the last Ice Age. Indeed, its ability to adapt to the cold climate on the edge of the ice sheets is one of its characteristic features, the remains being found only in Europe, Asia and the Middle East. Complete neanderthal skeletons were found during excavations at Tabun in Israel, together with evidence of tool-making and the use of fire. Distinguished by very large brains, it seems that neanderthal man was the first to develop recognizable social customs, especially deliberate burial rites. Why the neanderthalers became extinct is not clear, but it may be connected with the climatic changes at the end of the Ice Ages, which would have seriously affected their food supplies; possibly they became too specialized for their own good.

The Swanscombe skull is the only known human fossil remains found in England. Some specialists see Swanscombe Man (or, more probably, woman) as a neanderthaler. Others group these remains together with the Steinheim skull from Germany, seeing both as a separate sub-species. Unfortunately there is too little evidence as yet on which to form a final judgement.

Modern Man, *Homo sapiens sapiens*, the surviving sub-species of *Homo sapiens*, had evolved to our present physical condition and had colonized much of the world by about 30,000 years ago. There are many previously distinguished individual specimens, for example Cromagnon Man, which may now be grouped together as *Homo sapiens sapiens*. It was modern man who spread to the American continent by crossing the landbridge between Siberia and Alaska and thence moved south through North America and into South America. Equally it is modern man who over the last 30,000 years has been responsible for the major developments in technology, art and civilization generally.

One of the problems for those studying fossil man is the lack in many cases of sufficient quantities of fossil bone for analysis. It is important that theories should be tested against evidence, and not the evidence made to fit the theory. The celebrated Piltdown hoax is perhaps the best-known example of 'fossils' being forged to fit what was seen in some quarters as the correct theory of man's evolution.

CULTURAL DEVELOPMENT

The Eurocentric bias of early archaeologists meant that the search for a starting point for the development and transmission of cultural ideas, especially by migration, trade and warfare, concentrated unduly on Europe and the Near East. The Three Age system, whereby pre-history was divided into a Stone Age, a Bronze Age, and an Iron Age, was devised by Christian Thomsen, curator of the National Museum of Denmark in the early nineteenth century, to facilitate the classification of the museum's collections. The descriptive adjectives referred to the materials from which the implements and weapons were made, and came to be regarded as the dominant features of the societies to which they related. The refinement of the Three Age system once dominated archaeological thought and still remains a generally accepted concept in the popular mind. However, it is now seen by archaeologists as an inadequate model for human development.

Common sense alone suggests that there were no complete breaks between one so-called Age and another, any more than contemporaries would have regarded 1485 as a complete break between medieval and modern English history. Nor can the Three Age system be applied universally. In some areas it is necessary to insert a Copper Age, while in Africa south of the Sahara there would seem to be no Bronze Age at all; in Australia, Old Stone Age societies survived, while in South America, New Stone Age communities existed into modern times. The civilizations in other parts of the world clearly invalidate a Eurocentric theory of human development.

The concept of the 'Neolithic revolution', associated with the domestication of plants and animals, was a development of particular importance in the human cultural pattern. It reflected change from the primitive hunter/gatherer economies to a more settled agricultural way of life and therefore, so the argument goes, made possible the development of urban civilization. However, it can no longer be argued that this 'revolution' took place only in one area from which all development stemmed. Though it appears that the cultivation of wheat and barley was first undertaken, together with the domestication of cattle and goats/sheep in the Fertile Crescent, there is evidence that rice was first deliberately planted and pigs domesticated in south-east Asia, maize first cultivated in Central America, and llamas first domesticated in South America. It has been recognized increasingly in recent years that cultural changes can take place independently of each other in different parts of the world at different rates and different times. There is no need for a general diffusionist theory.

Although scholars will continue to study the particular societies which interest them, it may be possible to obtain a reliable chronological framework, in absolute terms of years, against which the cultural development of any particular area may be set. The development and refinement of radio-carbon dating and other scientific methods of producing absolute chronologies is enabling the cross-referencing of societies to be undertaken. As the techniques of dating become more rigorous in application and the number of scientifically obtained dates increases, the attainment of an absolute chronology for prehistoric societies throughout the world comes closer to being achieved.

Tidal Tables

CONSTANTS

The constant tidal difference may be used in conjunction with the time of high water at a standard port shown in the predictions data (pages 98–109) to find the time of high water at any of the ports or places listed below.

EXAMPLE

Required times of high water at Stranraer at 1 *January* 1994
Appropriate time of high water at *Greenock*

Morning tide 1 *January*	0232 hrs	
Tidal difference	− 0020 hrs	
High water at *Stranraer*	0212 hrs	

The columns headed 'Springs' and 'Neaps' show the height, in metres, of the tide above datum for mean high water springs and mean high water neaps respectively.

* data very approximate
† data for first high water springs only
H. Harbour

Port		Diff. h m	Springs m	Neaps m
Aberdeen	Leith	− 1 19	4.3	3.4
Aberdovey	Liverpool	− 3 01	5.0	3.5
Aberystwyth	Liverpool	− 3 31	5.0	3.5
Aldeburgh	London	− 3 05	2.8	2.7
Alloa	Leith	+ 0 49	5.6	4.2
Amlwch	Liverpool	− 0 35	7.2	5.7
Anstruther Easter	Leith	− 0 22	5.5	4.4
Antwerp (Prosperpolder)	London	+ 0 50	5.8	4.8
Appledore	Avonmouth	− 1 16	7.5	5.2
Arbroath	Leith	− 0 33	5.0	4.1
Ardrossan	Greenock	− 0 15	3.2	2.7
*Arundel	London	− 2 04	3.2	2.1
Avonmouth	Avonmouth	0 00	13.2	9.8
Ayr	Greenock	− 0 25	3.0	2.6
Baie de Lampaul	London	+ 2 30	7.4	5.8
Ballycotton	Avonmouth	− 1 47	4.2	3.2
Banff	Leith	− 2 44	3.5	2.8
Bantry	Liverpool	+ 5 55	3.3	2.4
Bardsey Island	Liverpool	− 3 20	4.4	3.2
Barmouth	Liverpool	− 2 58	5.0	3.5
Barnstaple	Avonmouth	− 1 01	4.1	1.4
Barrow (Docks)	Liverpool	0 00	9.3	7.1
Barry	Avonmouth	− 0 22	11.4	8.5
Belfast	London	− 2 47	3.5	3.0
Berwick	Leith	− 0 03	4.7	3.8
Bideford	Avonmouth	− 1 16	5.9	3.6
Blackpool	Liverpool	− 0 10	8.9	7.0
Blacktoft	Hull	+ 0 31	5.7	3.9
Blakeney	Hull	+ 0 46	3.4	2.0
Blyth	Leith	+ 0 51	5.0	3.9
Boscastle	Avonmouth	− 1 21	7.3	5.6
Boulogne	London	− 2 44	8.9	7.2
Bovisand Pier	London	+ 3 55	5.3	4.3
Bowling	Greenock	+ 0 15	4.0	3.4
Braye (Alderney)	London	+ 5 33	6.3	4.7
Brest	London	+ 2 28	7.5	5.9
Bridgwater	Avonmouth	− 0 22	4.6	1.7
Bridlington	Leith	+ 2 04	6.1	4.7
Bridport (W. Bay)	London	+ 4 37	4.1	3.0
Brighton	London	− 2 51	6.6	5.0
Buckie	Leith	− 2 56	4.1	3.2
Bude Haven	Avonmouth	− 1 34	7.7	5.8
Bull Sand Fort	Hull	− 0 44	6.9	5.5
Burntisland	Leith	0 00	5.6	4.5
Calais	London	− 2 04	7.1	5.9
Campbeltown	Greenock	+ 0 07	2.9	2.6
Cape Cornwall	Avonmouth	− 2 31	6.0	4.3
Cardiff (Penarth)	Avonmouth	− 0 15	12.2	9.2
Cardigan Port	Liverpool	− 3 38	4.7	3.4
Carmarthen	Avonmouth	− 0 49	2.6	0.4
Cayeux	London	− 2 55	10.2	7.9
Chatham	London	− 1 08	6.0	4.9
Chepstow	Avonmouth	+ 0 20	No data	
Cherbourg	London	− 6 00	6.4	5.0
Chester	Liverpool	+ 1 05	4.0	2.0
Chichester H.	London	− 2 40	4.9	4.0
†Christchurch H.	London	− 5 08	1.8	1.4
Cobh	Liverpool	− 5 55	4.2	3.2
Coulport	Greenock	− 0 05	3.4	2.9
Coverack	Avonmouth	− 2 02	5.3	4.2
Cowes	London	− 2 38	4.2	3.5
Cromarty	Leith	− 2 56	4.3	3.4
Cromer	Hull	+ 0 15	5.2	4.1
Dartmouth	London	+ 4 25	4.9	3.8
Deal	London	− 2 37	6.1	5.0
Dieppe	London	− 3 03	9.3	7.2
Dingle H.	Liverpool	+ 5 34	3.9	2.8
Donegal H.	Liverpool	− 5 24	3.9	3.0
Douglas (IOM)	Liverpool	− 0 04	6.9	5.4
Dover	London	− 2 52	6.7	5.3
Duclair	London	− 1 48	7.5	6.3
Duddon Bar	Liverpool	+ 0 03	8.5	6.6
Dunbar	Leith	− 0 07	5.2	4.2
Dundalk (Sldr's Pt)	Liverpool	+ 0 21	5.1	4.2
Dundee	Leith	+ 0 11	5.4	4.3
Dungeness	London	− 3 04	7.7	5.9
Dunkirk	London	− 1 54	5.8	4.8
Eastbourne	London	− 2 51	7.4	5.5
East Loch Tarbert	Greenock	+ 0 05	3.4	2.9
Exmouth Dock	London	+ 4 55	4.0	2.8
Eyemouth	Leith	− 0 20	4.7	3.7
Falmouth	London	+ 3 35	5.3	4.2
Ferryside	Avonmouth	− 0 59	6.7	4.5
Filey Bay	Leith	+ 1 51	5.8	4.9
Fishguard	Liverpool	− 4 01	4.8	3.4
Folkestone	London	− 3 04	7.1	5.7
Formby	Liverpool	− 0 12	9.0	7.3
Fowey	London	+ 3 53	5.4	4.3
Fraserburgh	Leith	− 2 29	3.7	2.9
†Freshwater Bay	London	− 4 48	2.6	2.3
Galway	Liverpool	− 6 08	5.1	3.9
Glasgow	Greenock	+ 0 26	4.7	4.1
Goole	Hull	+ 1 00	5.7	3.7
Gorleston	London	− 5 00	2.4	2.0
Granton	Leith	0 00	5.6	4.5
Granville	London	+ 4 32	13.0	9.8
Grimsby	Hull	− 0 27	7.0	5.6
Hartlepool	Leith	+ 0 57	5.4	4.2
Harwich	London	− 2 06	4.0	3.4
Hastings	London	− 2 57	7.5	5.8
Haverfordwest	Liverpool	− 4 51	2.2	0.3

Port	Diff. h m	Springs m	Neaps m
Hestan Islet	Liverpool +0 25	8.3	6.3
Holyhead	Liverpool −0 50	5.6	4.4
Hook of Holland	London −0 01	2.1	1.7
†Hurst Point	London −3 53	2.7	2.3
Ijmuiden	London +1 03	2.0	1.6
Ilfracombe	Avonmouth −1 12	9.2	6.9
Inveraray	Greenock +0 11	3.3	3.0
Invergordon	Leith −2 48	4.4	3.5
Ipswich	London −1 46	4.2	3.4
Itchenor	London −2 38	4.8	3.8
Kinsale	Liverpool −6 07	4.0	3.2
Kirkcudbright	Liverpool +0 15	7.5	5.9
Kirkwall	Leith −4 15	2.9	2.2
Knights Town	Liverpool +5 32	3.6	2.8
Lamlash	Greenock −0 26	3.2	2.7
Le Havre	London −3 55	7.9	6.6
Lerwick	Leith −3 48	2.2	1.6
Limerick Dock	Liverpool −4 27	6.1	4.6
Littlehampton	London −2 39	5.9	4.5
Lizard Point	Avonmouth −2 17	5.3	4.2
Llanddwyn Island	Liverpool −1 55	4.9	3.9
Llanelli	Avonmouth −0 57	7.8	5.8
Loch Moidart	Greenock +5 58	4.8	3.5
Londonderry	London −5 37	2.7	2.1
Looe	London +3 55	5.4	4.2
Lossiemouth	Leith −3 01	4.1	3.2
Lowestoft	London −4 25	2.4	2.1
Lulworth Cove	London +4 59	2.3	1.5
Lundy Island	Avonmouth −1 24	8.0	5.9
Lyme Regis	London +4 55	4.3	3.1
†Lymington	London −3 48	3.0	2.6
Margate	London −1 53	4.8	3.9
Maryport	Liverpool +0 24	8.6	6.6
Menai Bridge	Liverpool −0 30	7.3	5.8
Mevagissey	London +3 53	5.4	4.3
Middlesbrough	Leith +1 08	5.6	4.5
Milford Haven	Liverpool −5 08	7.0	5.2
Minehead	Avonmouth −0 40	10.6	7.9
Montrose	Leith −0 19	4.8	3.9
Morecambe	Liverpool +0 07	9.5	7.4
Mostyn Quay	Liverpool +0 17	8.5	6.7
Newburgh	Leith +0 48	4.1	3.0
Newcastle upon Tyne	Leith +0 53	5.3	4.1
Newhaven	London −2 46	6.7	5.1
Newlyn	Avonmouth −2 25	5.6	4.4
Newport (Gwent)	Avonmouth −0 15	12.1	8.8
Newquay	Avonmouth −1 59	7.0	5.3
New Quay, Cardigan Bay	Liverpool −3 31	4.9	3.4
North Shields	Leith +0 50	5.0	3.9
North Sunderland	Leith +0 04	4.8	3.7
N. Woolwich	London −0 20	7.0	5.9
Oban	Greenock +5 43	4.0	2.9
Old Lynn Road	Hull +0 07	7.3	5.8
Orfordness	London −2 50	2.8	2.7
Ostend	London −1 32	5.1	4.2
Padstow	Avonmouth −1 46	7.3	5.6
Peel (IOM)	Liverpool −0 02	5.3	4.2
Peterhead	Leith −1 59	3.8	3.1
Plymouth	London +4 05	5.5	4.4
†Poole (Entrance)	London −5 18	2.0	1.6
Porlock Bay	Avonmouth −0 50	10.2	7.6
Porthcawl	Avonmouth −0 54	9.9	7.5
Portmadoc	Liverpool −2 46	5.1	3.4
Portland	London +5 09	2.1	1.4
Portpatrick	Liverpool +0 22	3.8	3.0
Portsmouth	London −2 38	4.7	3.8
Port Talbot	Avonmouth −0 54	9.6	7.3
Preston	Liverpool +0 10	5.3	3.3
Pwllheli	Liverpool −3 08	5.0	3.4
Ramsey (IOM)	Liverpool +0 10	7.6	5.9
Ramsgate	London −2 32	4.9	3.8
*Rosslare H.	Liverpool −5 24	1.9	1.4
Rosyth	Leith +0 09	5.8	4.7
Ryde	London −2 38	4.5	3.7
St Helier	London +4 48	11.1	8.1
St Ives	Avonmouth −1 56	6.6	4.9
St Malo	London +4 27	12.2	9.2
St Peter Port	London +4 54	9.3	7.0
Salcombe	London +4 10	5.3	4.1
Saltash	London +4 10	5.6	4.5
Scarborough	Leith +1 33	5.7	4.6
Scheveningen	London +1 02	2.1	1.6
Scrabster	Leith −6 06	5.0	4.0
Seaham	Leith +0 54	5.2	4.1
Selsey Bill	London −2 43	5.3	4.4
Sennen Cove	Avonmouth −2 31	6.1	4.8
Sharpness Dock	Avonmouth +0 42	9.3	5.6
Sheerness	London −1 19	5.7	4.8
Shoreham	London −2 44	6.3	4.9
Silloth	Liverpool +0 35	9.2	7.1
Southampton (1st high water)	London −2 54	4.5	3.7
Southend	London −1 23	5.7	4.8
Southwold	London −3 50	2.5	2.2
Stirling	Leith +1 15	2.9	1.6
Stonehaven	Leith −1 09	4.5	3.6
Stornoway	Liverpool −4 16	4.8	3.7
Stranraer	Greenock −0 20	3.0	2.5
Stromness	Leith −5 26	3.6	2.7
Sunderland	Leith +0 49	5.2	4.2
†Swanage	London −5 28	2.0	1.6
Swansea	Avonmouth −0 51	9.5	7.2
Tarn Point	Liverpool +0 05	8.3	6.4
Tay River (Bar)	Leith −0 19	5.2	4.2
Tees River (Entrance)	Leith +1 09	5.5	4.3
Teignmouth	London +4 37	4.8	3.6
Tenby	Avonmouth −1 06	8.4	6.3
Tilbury	London −0 49	6.4	5.4
Tobermory	Liverpool −5 11	4.4	3.3
Torquay	London +4 40	4.9	3.7
†Totland Bay	London −4 08	2.7	2.3
Troon	Greenock −0 25	3.2	2.7
Truro	London +3 43	3.5	2.4
Walton-on-Naze	London −2 10	4.2	3.4
Waterford	Liverpool −4 58	4.6	3.5
Weston-s.-Mare	Avonmouth −0 25	12.0	8.8
*Wexford H.	Liverpool −5 04	1.7	1.4
Whitby	Leith +1 23	5.6	4.3
Whitehaven	Liverpool +0 10	8.0	6.3
Wick	Leith −3 26	3.5	2.8
Wisbech Cut	Hull +0 03	7.0	5.1
Workington	Liverpool +0 21	8.2	6.4
Worthing	London −2 39	6.2	4.7
†Yarmouth (IOW)	London −3 43	3.1	2.5
Youghal	Liverpool −5 50	4.0	3.1

98   Tidal Predictions

JANUARY 1994   *High water*   GMT

		LONDON BRIDGE				AVONMOUTH				LIVERPOOL				HULL (*Albert Dock*)			
		*Datum of predictions 3.20 m below				*Datum of predictions 6.50 m below				*Datum of predictions 4.93 m below				*Datum of predictions 3.90 m below			
		hr	ht m	hr	ht m	hr	ht m	hr	ht m	hr	ht m	hr	ht m	hr	ht m	hr	ht m
1	Saturday	03 45	7.2	16 10	7.3	09 12	13.4	21 37	13.0	00 59	9.2	13 17	9.4	08 20	7.3	20 28	7.5
2	Sunday	04 23	7.1	16 51	7.2	09 53	13.2	22 18	12.7	01 41	9.1	13 58	9.3	09 01	7.3	21 09	7.4
3	Monday	05 02	6.9	17 33	6.9	10 36	12.8	23 02	12.2	02 25	8.9	14 43	9.1	09 44	7.1	21 53	7.3
4	Tuesday	05 43	6.7	18 21	6.6	11 21	12.2	23 48	11.6	03 14	8.7	15 34	8.8	10 31	6.8	22 42	7.0
5	Wednesday	06 32	6.5	19 17	6.4		—	12 13	11.6	04 07	8.4	16 31	8.5	11 26	6.6	23 41	6.8
6	Thursday	07 33	6.3	20 26	6.3	00 46	11.0	13 17	11.1	05 12	8.1	17 40	8.2	—	—	12 34	6.4
7	Friday	08 49	6.3	21 41	6.4	01 56	10.7	14 33	11.0	06 27	8.0	18 59	8.1	00 54	6.6	13 52	6.4
8	Saturday	10 09	6.4	22 54	6.5	03 15	10.9	15 49	11.2	07 41	8.1	20 13	8.3	02 16	6.6	15 08	6.5
9	Sunday	11 25	6.5	—		04 28	11.4	17 02	11.7	08 47	8.5	21 18	8.6	03 37	6.7	16 14	6.8
10	Monday	00 01	6.6	12 31	6.7	05 34	12.1	18 05	12.3	09 45	8.9	22 14	8.9	04 45	6.9	17 09	7.1
11	Tuesday	00 57	6.7	13 24	6.8	06 32	12.7	18 58	12.7	10 35	9.3	23 04	9.1	05 40	7.1	17 54	7.3
12	Wednesday	01 47	6.8	14 12	7.0	07 19	13.2	19 43	13.0	11 22	9.5	23 47	9.2	06 27	7.2	18 36	7.5
13	Thursday	02 29	7.0	14 54	7.2	08 02	13.4	20 24	13.1	—	—	12 03	9.6	07 10	7.2	19 14	7.6
14	Friday	03 08	7.1	15 34	7.3	08 41	13.4	21 01	13.1	00 27	9.2	12 42	9.6	07 48	7.1	19 50	7.7
15	Saturday	03 46	7.2	16 12	7.3	09 18	13.2	21 34	12.8	01 03	9.1	13 19	9.4	08 24	7.1	20 27	7.6
16	Sunday	04 21	7.1	16 48	7.1	09 51	12.8	22 05	12.3	01 38	8.9	13 54	9.1	08 58	6.9	21 01	7.5
17	Monday	04 55	6.9	17 23	6.8	10 22	12.2	22 34	11.7	02 12	8.6	14 29	8.8	09 32	6.7	21 36	7.2
18	Tuesday	05 29	6.6	18 01	6.5	10 53	11.5	23 03	11.1	02 47	8.2	15 07	8.4	10 05	6.5	22 14	6.9
19	Wednesday	06 07	6.4	18 42	6.2	11 26	10.8	23 37	10.4	03 27	7.8	15 49	7.9	10 43	6.2	22 57	6.5
20	Thursday	06 53	6.0	19 31	5.9		—	12 05	10.1	04 13	7.4	16 41	7.5	11 30	5.9	23 52	6.0
21	Friday	07 48	5.7	20 30	5.7	00 23	9.8	13 04	9.5	05 13	7.1	17 49	7.2	—	—	12 36	5.7
22	Saturday	08 54	5.5	21 32	5.6	01 36	9.4	14 28	9.5	06 31	7.0	19 06	7.2	01 11	5.8	13 56	5.7
23	Sunday	10 00	5.5	22 37	5.8	03 05	9.7	15 49	10.0	07 48	7.3	20 18	7.5	02 30	5.8	15 09	5.9
24	Monday	11 08	5.7	23 42	6.1	04 18	10.6	16 53	10.9	08 49	7.8	21 12	8.0	03 40	6.0	16 10	6.3
25	Tuesday	—	—	12 11	6.1	05 16	11.6	17 47	11.8	09 36	8.3	21 59	8.5	04 36	6.4	16 57	6.6
26	Wednesday	00 38	6.5	13 03	6.6	06 06	12.4	18 36	12.5	10 20	8.8	22 41	8.9	05 23	6.7	17 40	7.0
27	Thursday	01 26	6.8	13 48	7.0	06 53	13.0	19 21	13.0	11 01	9.2	23 22	9.3	06 05	7.0	18 18	7.3
28	Friday	02 09	7.2	14 32	7.4	07 36	13.5	20 03	13.4	11 42	9.6	—	—	06 44	7.3	18 56	7.6
29	Saturday	02 50	7.4	15 14	7.6	08 19	13.8	20 44	13.7	00 03	9.5	12 21	9.8	07 24	7.6	19 32	7.9
30	Sunday	03 29	7.5	15 53	7.6	08 59	14.0	21 23	13.7	00 43	9.6	13 02	9.9	08 03	7.7	20 11	8.0
31	Monday	04 07	7.4	16 34	7.4	09 40	13.9	22 03	13.4	01 26	9.6	13 42	9.8	08 42	7.6	20 51	7.9

FEBRUARY 1994   *High water*   GMT

		LONDON BRIDGE				AVONMOUTH				LIVERPOOL				HULL (*Albert Dock*)			
1	Tuesday	04 45	7.2	17 16	7.1	10 19	13.4	22 42	12.8	02 08	9.4	14 26	9.5	09 23	7.4	21 34	7.7
2	Wednesday	05 27	7.0	18 01	6.7	11 02	12.7	23 24	12.0	02 51	9.0	15 12	9.1	10 08	7.1	22 22	7.3
3	Thursday	06 12	6.7	18 52	6.4	11 48	11.8	—		03 42	8.6	16 06	8.5	10 59	6.7	23 19	6.9
4	Friday	07 10	6.4	19 55	6.3	00 15	11.1	12 46	11.0	04 42	8.1	17 15	8.0	—	—	12 02	6.4
5	Saturday	08 23	6.2	21 08	6.2	01 24	10.5	14 02	10.4	05 58	7.8	18 41	7.7	00 32	6.4	13 22	6.2
6	Sunday	09 45	6.2	22 27	6.3	02 48	10.4	15 29	10.5	07 23	7.8	20 05	7.8	02 04	6.3	14 48	6.3
7	Monday	11 09	6.3	23 43	6.5	04 12	10.9	16 50	11.2	08 37	8.2	21 14	8.2	03 34	6.4	16 00	6.6
8	Tuesday	—	—	12 18	6.6	05 23	11.8	17 55	12.0	09 36	8.7	22 07	8.6	04 42	6.6	16 56	6.9
9	Wednesday	00 43	6.7	13 13	6.9	06 19	12.6	18 46	12.6	10 26	9.1	22 52	9.0	05 33	6.8	17 40	7.2
10	Thursday	01 33	6.9	13 59	7.1	07 05	13.1	19 28	13.0	11 08	9.4	23 32	9.1	06 15	7.0	18 19	7.4
11	Friday	02 13	7.0	14 39	7.2	07 45	13.3	20 04	13.1	11 46	9.5	—	—	06 51	7.1	18 54	7.6
12	Saturday	02 50	7.1	15 15	7.3	08 20	13.4	20 37	13.2	00 07	9.2	12 21	9.5	07 25	7.2	19 28	7.7
13	Sunday	03 24	7.2	15 48	7.2	08 53	13.3	21 06	13.1	00 39	9.1	12 53	9.4	07 57	7.2	20 02	7.7
14	Monday	03 55	7.1	16 19	7.1	09 23	13.1	21 34	12.8	01 10	9.0	13 24	9.2	08 27	7.1	20 34	7.6
15	Tuesday	04 26	7.0	16 49	6.9	09 50	12.6	22 00	12.2	01 40	8.8	13 57	8.9	08 56	7.0	21 06	7.3
16	Wednesday	04 57	6.8	17 22	6.7	10 17	11.9	22 26	11.6	02 09	8.5	14 29	8.6	09 27	6.8	21 40	7.0
17	Thursday	05 32	6.6	17 58	6.4	10 45	11.1	22 53	10.8	02 42	8.2	15 04	8.1	10 00	6.5	22 18	6.5
18	Friday	06 11	6.2	18 38	6.1	11 14	10.3	23 27	10.1	03 19	7.7	15 46	7.6	10 38	6.1	23 02	6.1
19	Saturday	06 56	5.9	19 26	5.8	11 55	9.7	—		04 09	7.3	16 47	7.1	11 27	5.8	—	—
20	Sunday	07 52	5.5	20 27	5.5	00 22	9.6	13 11	9.2	05 23	7.0	18 11	6.9	00 06	5.7	12 51	5.5
21	Monday	09 05	5.4	21 43	5.5	01 59	9.4	15 01	9.5	06 55	7.0	19 38	7.2	01 45	5.6	14 24	5.7
22	Tuesday	10 26	5.6	23 04	5.8	03 37	10.2	16 19	10.6	08 12	7.5	20 44	7.8	03 05	5.9	15 33	6.1
23	Wednesday	11 42	6.0	—		04 46	11.4	17 20	11.7	09 08	8.2	21 35	8.4	04 10	6.3	16 29	6.5
24	Thursday	00 10	6.3	12 39	6.6	05 42	12.4	18 12	12.7	09 55	8.8	22 20	9.0	05 00	6.7	17 13	7.0
25	Friday	01 02	6.8	13 27	7.1	06 32	13.2	19 00	13.4	10 38	9.3	23 01	9.4	05 42	7.1	17 54	7.4
26	Saturday	01 45	7.3	14 11	7.5	07 17	13.8	19 43	13.8	11 20	9.8	23 43	9.8	06 23	7.5	18 32	7.8
27	Sunday	02 27	7.5	14 53	7.7	08 00	14.2	20 24	14.1	—	—	12 01	10.1	07 01	7.8	19 11	8.1
28	Monday	03 07	7.7	15 34	7.7	08 41	14.4	21 04	14.1	00 24	9.9	12 43	10.1	07 41	7.9	19 50	8.2

JANUARY 1994   *continued*

		GREENOCK				LEITH				DUN LAOGHAIRE				NOTES:
		*Datum of predictions 1.62 m below				*Datum of predictions 2.90 m below				†Datum of predictions 0.20 m above				*Difference of height in metres from Ordnance datum (Newlyn)
		hr	ht m	hr	ht m	hr	ht m	hr	ht m	hr	ht m	hr	ht m	†Difference of height in metres from Ordnance datum (Dublin)
1	Saturday	02 32	3.2	14 33	3.8	04 35	5.5	16 49	5.5	01 13	3.9	13 33	4.2	hr hour
2	Sunday	03 13	3.2	15 14	3.8	05 17	5.4	17 31	5.4	01 59	3.9	14 19	4.1	m metres
3	Monday	03 55	3.2	15 55	3.7	06 04	5.3	18 18	5.3	02 51	3.8	15 11	4.1	
4	Tuesday	04 39	3.2	16 40	3.6	06 53	5.1	19 10	5.2	03 47	3.7	16 08	4.0	
5	Wednesday	05 29	3.1	17 30	3.4	07 49	5.0	20 10	5.0	04 50	3.7	17 15	3.9	
6	Thursday	06 26	3.0	18 29	3.3	08 54	4.9	21 20	4.9	06 00	3.6	18 28	3.9	
7	Friday	07 40	2.9	19 46	3.1	10 03	4.8	22 36	4.9	07 10	3.7	19 40	3.9	
8	Saturday	09 12	3.0	21 25	3.1	11 13	4.9	23 49	5.0	08 14	3.8	20 43	4.0	
9	Sunday	10 20	3.2	22 37	3.2	----	---	12 18	5.1	09 13	4.0	21 42	4.0	
10	Monday	11 13	3.4	23 34	3.3	00 53	5.2	13 14	5.3	10 05	4.2	22 34	4.1	
11	Tuesday	12 01	3.6	----	---	01 48	5.4	14 03	5.5	10 52	4.3	23 21	4.1	
12	Wednesday	00 26	3.3	12 46	3.7	02 34	5.5	14 48	5.6	11 35	4.3	----	---	
13	Thursday	01 14	3.4	13 28	3.8	03 18	5.5	15 32	5.6	00 05	4.1	12 13	4.4	
14	Friday	01 55	3.4	14 06	3.8	04 00	5.5	16 12	5.6	00 43	4.0	12 51	4.3	
15	Saturday	02 32	3.4	14 42	3.8	04 39	5.4	16 52	5.5	01 19	3.9	13 29	4.2	
16	Sunday	03 07	3.4	15 17	3.8	05 17	5.2	17 31	5.3	01 57	3.8	14 08	4.1	
17	Monday	03 43	3.4	15 53	3.7	05 55	5.0	18 09	5.1	02 38	3.7	14 52	3.9	
18	Tuesday	04 20	3.4	16 31	3.5	06 36	4.8	18 51	4.9	03 22	3.5	15 41	3.7	
19	Wednesday	04 59	3.3	17 12	3.3	07 19	4.6	19 36	4.7	04 15	3.4	16 37	3.5	
20	Thursday	05 43	3.2	17 58	3.1	08 07	4.5	20 28	4.5	05 17	3.3	17 41	3.4	
21	Friday	06 32	3.1	18 51	2.9	09 02	4.4	21 26	4.4	06 28	3.3	18 52	3.3	
22	Saturday	07 30	3.0	19 58	2.8	10 03	4.3	22 35	4.3	07 35	3.3	19 58	3.4	
23	Sunday	08 42	3.0	21 28	2.8	11 13	4.4	23 48	4.5	08 35	3.4	20 52	3.4	
24	Monday	09 59	3.1	22 43	2.9	----	---	12 22	4.7	09 23	3.6	21 40	3.6	
25	Tuesday	10 53	3.3	23 33	3.0	00 50	4.7	13 15	5.0	10 04	3.7	22 19	3.7	
26	Wednesday	11 36	3.4	----	---	01 36	5.0	13 59	5.2	10 40	3.9	22 56	3.8	
27	Thursday	00 17	3.1	12 17	3.5	02 19	5.3	14 38	5.4	11 14	4.0	23 32	3.9	
28	Friday	00 59	3.2	12 57	3.6	02 58	5.5	15 15	5.6	11 50	4.2	----	---	
29	Saturday	01 40	3.2	13 38	3.8	03 36	5.6	15 51	5.7	00 10	4.0	12 28	4.3	
30	Sunday	02 19	3.3	14 19	3.8	04 15	5.7	16 31	5.8	00 51	4.1	13 11	4.3	
31	Monday	02 56	3.3	14 59	3.9	04 57	5.6	17 13	5.7	01 36	4.1	13 57	4.3	

FEBRUARY 1994   *continued*

		GREENOCK				LEITH				DUN LAOGHAIRE			
1	Tuesday	03 34	3.3	15 39	3.8	05 42	5.5	17 58	5.6	02 22	4.0	14 47	4.2
2	Wednesday	04 14	3.3	16 21	3.7	06 30	5.3	18 50	5.3	03 15	3.9	15 44	4.1
3	Thursday	04 57	3.2	17 08	3.5	07 22	5.0	19 49	5.0	04 16	3.7	16 53	3.9
4	Friday	05 47	3.1	18 00	3.2	08 24	4.8	21 01	4.8	05 28	3.7	18 10	3.8
5	Saturday	06 50	2.9	19 06	3.0	09 36	4.7	22 24	4.7	06 45	3.6	19 25	3.7
6	Sunday	08 49	2.9	21 22	2.9	10 55	4.7	23 44	4.8	07 56	3.7	20 35	3.8
7	Monday	10 08	3.1	22 36	3.0	----	---	12 08	4.9	09 01	3.9	21 37	3.9
8	Tuesday	11 02	3.4	23 31	3.1	00 50	5.0	13 08	5.1	09 56	4.1	22 30	4.0
9	Wednesday	11 50	3.5	----	---	01 42	5.2	13 56	5.3	10 43	4.2	23 13	4.0
10	Thursday	00 18	3.2	12 34	3.6	02 26	5.4	14 38	5.5	11 22	4.3	23 49	4.0
11	Friday	01 02	3.3	13 14	3.7	03 04	5.4	15 18	5.6	11 56	4.3	----	---
12	Saturday	01 39	3.3	13 50	3.7	03 39	5.4	15 53	5.5	00 20	3.9	12 28	4.2
13	Sunday	02 11	3.3	14 22	3.7	04 12	5.4	16 26	5.5	00 50	3.9	13 01	4.2
14	Monday	02 42	3.4	14 54	3.7	04 46	5.3	17 00	5.4	01 20	3.8	13 37	4.1
15	Tuesday	03 13	3.4	15 26	3.6	05 20	5.1	17 35	5.2	01 57	3.7	14 15	3.9
16	Wednesday	03 45	3.4	16 00	3.5	05 56	4.9	18 12	5.0	02 36	3.6	15 00	3.7
17	Thursday	04 21	3.3	16 37	3.3	06 36	4.7	18 54	4.7	03 22	3.5	15 51	3.5
18	Friday	05 01	3.2	17 20	3.1	07 19	4.5	19 41	4.5	04 16	3.3	16 51	3.4
19	Saturday	05 47	3.0	18 12	2.8	08 10	4.3	20 37	4.3	05 25	3.2	18 04	3.3
20	Sunday	06 43	2.9	19 15	2.7	09 11	4.2	21 46	4.2	06 46	3.2	19 20	3.3
21	Monday	07 51	2.8	20 40	2.7	10 21	4.3	23 04	4.3	07 58	3.3	20 24	3.4
22	Tuesday	09 11	2.9	22 17	2.8	11 41	4.5	----	---	08 51	3.4	21 15	3.5
23	Wednesday	10 20	3.1	23 11	3.0	00 18	4.6	12 44	4.8	09 36	3.6	21 56	3.7
24	Thursday	11 09	3.3	23 56	3.1	01 10	5.0	13 32	5.2	10 13	3.9	22 33	3.9
25	Friday	11 53	3.5	----	---	01 53	5.3	14 13	5.5	10 51	4.1	23 10	4.0
26	Saturday	00 38	3.2	12 37	3.6	02 33	5.6	14 51	5.8	11 28	4.3	23 48	4.1
27	Sunday	01 19	3.3	13 20	3.7	03 12	5.8	15 29	5.9	----	---	12 07	4.4
28	Monday	01 58	3.3	14 02	3.8	03 53	5.8	16 10	6.0	00 27	4.2	12 50	4.5

MARCH 1994   *High water*   GMT

		London Bridge			Avonmouth			Liverpool			Hull (Albert Dock)		
		*Datum of predictions 3.20 m below			*Datum of predictions 6.50 m below			*Datum of predictions 4.93 m below			*Datum of predictions 3.90 m below		
		hr	ht m	hr	ht m	hr	ht m	hr	ht m	hr	ht m	hr	ht m
1	Tuesday	03 46	7.7	16 14	7.5	09 20	14.2	21 43	13.8	01 06	9.9	13 24	10.0	08 20	7.9	20 33	8.1
2	Wednesday	04 27	7.5	16 57	7.2	10 01	13.7	22 21	13.1	01 47	9.6	14 08	9.7	09 02	7.6	21 18	7.8
3	Thursday	05 11	7.2	17 40	6.8	10 42	12.8	23 03	12.1	02 30	9.2	14 53	9.1	09 46	7.2	22 07	7.3
4	Friday	05 58	6.8	18 29	6.5	11 26	11.7	23 51	11.1	03 19	8.7	15 48	8.4	10 35	6.8	23 04	6.7
5	Saturday	06 55	6.5	19 27	6.2	—	—	12 22	10.7	04 19	8.1	16 57	7.8	11 37	6.3	—	—
6	Sunday	08 04	6.2	20 37	6.1	00 58	10.4	13 39	10.1	05 36	7.6	18 27	7.4	00 19	6.2	12 54	6.1
7	Monday	09 24	6.1	21 57	6.1	02 26	10.1	15 11	10.2	07 04	7.6	19 55	7.6	02 00	6.0	14 27	6.1
8	Tuesday	10 49	6.3	23 20	6.3	03 54	10.7	16 35	11.0	08 22	8.0	21 03	8.1	03 29	6.1	15 43	6.4
9	Wednesday	—	—	12 00	6.7	05 06	11.7	17 37	11.9	09 21	8.5	21 52	8.5	04 31	6.4	16 36	6.8
10	Thursday	00 22	6.7	12 55	7.0	05 59	12.5	18 25	12.6	10 07	8.9	22 34	8.8	05 17	6.7	17 20	7.1
11	Friday	01 12	6.9	13 40	7.2	06 43	13.0	19 04	12.9	10 47	9.2	23 09	9.0	05 55	6.9	17 56	7.3
12	Saturday	01 52	7.1	14 18	7.2	07 21	13.2	19 39	13.0	11 22	9.4	23 42	9.1	06 29	7.0	18 30	7.5
13	Sunday	02 27	7.1	14 50	7.2	07 55	13.2	20 09	13.1	11 56	9.4	—	—	07 00	7.2	19 04	7.6
14	Monday	03 00	7.1	15 21	7.1	08 24	13.2	20 37	13.1	00 11	9.1	12 27	9.3	07 28	7.3	19 36	7.6
15	Tuesday	03 28	7.1	15 48	7.1	08 52	13.1	21 04	12.9	00 41	9.1	12 56	9.2	07 57	7.2	20 07	7.5
16	Wednesday	03 56	7.0	16 16	7.0	09 20	12.7	21 29	12.5	01 09	8.9	13 26	9.0	08 26	7.1	20 40	7.2
17	Thursday	04 27	6.9	16 47	6.8	09 47	12.1	21 56	11.9	01 37	8.7	13 57	8.6	08 55	6.9	21 12	6.9
18	Friday	05 02	6.7	17 20	6.6	10 14	11.3	22 24	11.2	02 08	8.4	14 30	8.2	09 25	6.6	21 47	6.5
19	Saturday	05 39	6.5	17 57	6.4	10 42	10.6	22 55	10.5	02 43	8.0	15 10	7.8	09 58	6.2	22 28	6.1
20	Sunday	06 21	6.1	18 41	6.1	11 19	10.0	23 42	10.0	03 28	7.6	16 04	7.3	10 42	5.9	23 24	5.8
21	Monday	07 12	5.8	19 34	5.7	—	—	12 23	9.5	04 33	7.2	17 25	7.0	11 48	5.6	—	—
22	Tuesday	08 19	5.6	20 51	5.5	01 04	9.6	14 09	9.5	06 04	7.1	18 56	7.2	00 58	5.6	13 36	5.6
23	Wednesday	09 46	5.7	22 23	5.7	02 52	10.1	15 41	10.5	07 28	7.5	20 08	7.8	02 28	5.8	14 54	6.0
24	Thursday	11 08	6.1	23 37	6.3	04 11	11.3	16 48	11.7	08 33	8.1	21 04	8.4	03 36	6.3	15 53	6.5
25	Friday	—	—	12 11	6.7	05 11	12.4	17 44	12.7	09 25	8.8	21 52	9.1	04 31	6.7	16 42	7.0
26	Saturday	00 32	6.8	13 02	7.2	06 05	13.3	18 33	13.5	10 12	9.4	22 35	9.6	05 16	7.2	17 26	7.4
27	Sunday	01 19	7.2	13 47	7.5	06 53	13.9	19 18	14.0	10 55	9.9	23 19	9.9	05 58	7.6	18 06	7.9
28	Monday	02 02	7.5	14 29	7.7	07 38	14.3	20 02	14.2	11 39	10.1	—	—	06 37	7.8	18 49	8.1
29	Tuesday	02 43	7.7	15 11	7.7	08 20	14.4	20 42	14.2	00 01	10.1	12 22	10.2	07 17	8.0	19 32	8.2
30	Wednesday	03 25	7.7	15 53	7.5	09 01	14.2	21 22	13.9	00 45	10.0	13 06	10.0	07 59	7.9	20 17	8.0
31	Thursday	04 10	7.6	16 37	7.3	09 43	13.6	22 03	13.2	01 27	9.7	13 51	9.6	08 41	7.7	21 04	7.7

APRIL 1994   *High water*   GMT

		London Bridge			Avonmouth			Liverpool			Hull (Albert Dock)		
1	Friday	04 57	7.3	17 22	6.9	10 25	12.7	22 46	12.2	02 12	9.3	14 39	9.0	09 26	7.3	21 56	7.1
2	Saturday	05 47	6.9	18 11	6.5	11 11	11.6	23 35	11.2	03 01	8.8	15 34	8.3	10 17	6.8	22 55	6.5
3	Sunday	06 43	6.6	19 04	6.2	—	—	12 06	10.6	04 02	8.2	16 42	7.7	11 16	6.4	—	—
4	Monday	07 45	6.3	20 08	6.0	00 40	10.4	13 18	10.0	05 15	7.7	18 08	7.4	00 11	6.0	12 27	6.1
5	Tuesday	08 58	6.1	21 24	6.0	02 02	10.2	14 45	10.1	06 39	7.6	19 31	7.5	01 48	5.8	13 56	6.1
6	Wednesday	10 23	6.2	22 51	6.2	03 26	10.6	16 07	10.8	07 55	7.9	20 37	7.9	03 09	6.0	15 15	6.3
7	Thursday	11 34	6.6	23 56	6.6	04 36	11.5	17 07	11.7	08 54	8.3	21 27	8.3	04 08	6.3	16 10	6.6
8	Friday	—	—	12 29	7.0	05 31	12.2	17 55	12.3	09 41	8.7	22 06	8.6	04 53	6.5	16 53	6.9
9	Saturday	00 46	6.9	13 13	7.2	06 15	12.6	18 34	12.6	10 20	8.9	22 41	8.9	05 30	6.7	17 31	7.1
10	Sunday	01 27	7.0	13 51	7.2	06 51	12.8	19 08	12.7	10 55	9.1	23 13	9.0	06 02	7.0	18 05	7.3
11	Monday	02 02	7.0	14 23	7.1	07 25	12.8	19 39	12.9	11 27	9.2	23 43	9.1	06 32	7.1	18 39	7.4
12	Tuesday	02 32	7.0	14 51	7.0	07 55	12.8	20 06	12.9	11 58	9.1	—	—	07 00	7.2	19 11	7.4
13	Wednesday	03 00	7.0	15 17	7.0	08 24	12.8	20 34	12.9	00 12	9.1	12 29	9.1	07 28	7.2	19 43	7.3
14	Thursday	03 29	6.9	15 46	7.0	08 52	12.6	21 02	12.6	00 41	9.0	13 00	8.9	07 57	7.1	20 17	7.0
15	Friday	04 02	6.9	16 17	6.9	09 22	12.1	21 32	12.1	01 12	8.8	13 31	8.6	08 27	6.9	20 51	6.7
16	Saturday	04 37	6.8	16 52	6.8	09 51	11.5	22 03	11.5	01 42	8.6	14 06	8.3	08 59	6.6	21 26	6.4
17	Sunday	05 15	6.6	17 29	6.5	10 25	10.9	22 38	10.9	02 19	8.3	14 47	8.0	09 33	6.3	22 08	6.2
18	Monday	05 57	6.4	18 10	6.2	11 04	10.3	23 26	10.4	03 04	7.9	15 41	7.6	10 17	6.1	23 03	5.9
19	Tuesday	06 46	6.1	19 02	5.9	—	—	12 04	9.9	04 04	7.6	16 52	7.3	11 17	5.8	—	—
20	Wednesday	07 49	5.9	20 12	5.7	00 37	10.1	13 31	9.9	05 23	7.4	18 15	7.4	00 19	5.8	12 44	5.8
21	Thursday	09 11	5.9	21 42	5.8	02 10	10.4	15 01	10.6	06 45	7.7	19 28	7.7	01 49	5.9	14 09	6.0
22	Friday	10 33	6.3	22 59	6.3	03 32	11.3	16 11	11.6	07 54	8.2	20 29	8.5	02 58	6.3	15 13	6.5
23	Saturday	11 39	6.8	—	—	04 38	12.3	17 11	12.6	08 51	8.8	21 21	9.1	03 57	6.8	16 08	7.0
24	Sunday	00 00	6.7	12 34	7.2	05 34	13.1	18 05	13.3	09 42	9.4	22 09	9.5	04 46	7.2	16 57	7.4
25	Monday	00 52	7.1	13 21	7.4	06 26	13.7	18 53	13.8	10 30	9.8	22 55	9.9	05 31	7.5	17 44	7.7
26	Tuesday	01 37	7.3	14 06	7.4	07 14	14.0	19 39	14.0	11 18	10.0	23 40	10.0	06 15	7.7	18 30	8.0
27	Wednesday	02 22	7.5	14 50	7.5	08 00	14.1	20 23	14.1	—	—	12 04	10.0	06 57	7.8	19 17	8.0
28	Thursday	03 08	7.6	15 35	7.4	08 44	13.9	21 05	13.8	00 25	9.9	12 50	9.8	07 41	7.8	20 06	7.8
29	Friday	03 56	7.6	16 20	7.3	09 27	13.4	21 49	13.1	01 10	9.7	13 37	9.4	08 24	7.6	20 55	7.4
30	Saturday	04 45	7.4	17 06	7.0	10 12	12.6	22 34	12.3	01 58	9.3	14 26	8.9	09 11	7.3	21 47	6.9

MARCH 1994 *continued*

		GREENOCK *Datum of predictions 1.62 m below*				LEITH *Datum of predictions 2.90 m below*				DUN LAOGHAIRE †Datum of predictions 0.20 m above			
		hr	ht m	hr	ht m	hr	ht m	hr	ht m	hr	ht m	hr	ht m
1	Tuesday	02 35	3.4	14 43	3.8	04 35	5.8	16 53	5.9	01 09	4.2	13 36	4.4
2	Wednesday	03 11	3.4	15 23	3.8	05 20	5.6	17 41	5.7	01 57	4.1	14 26	4.3
3	Thursday	03 49	3.4	16 05	3.6	06 08	5.3	18 33	5.4	02 48	4.0	15 25	4.1
4	Friday	04 30	3.3	16 50	3.4	07 00	5.0	19 35	5.0	03 48	3.8	16 37	3.8
5	Saturday	05 19	3.1	17 42	3.1	08 02	4.7	20 48	4.7	05 02	3.7	17 55	3.7
6	Sunday	06 19	2.9	18 50	2.8	09 15	4.6	22 12	4.6	06 22	3.6	19 14	3.6
7	Monday	08 26	2.8	21 21	2.8	10 36	4.6	23 34	4.7	07 38	3.7	20 29	3.7
8	Tuesday	09 52	3.0	22 27	2.9	11 55	4.8	——	—	08 48	3.8	21 32	3.8
9	Wednesday	10 45	3.3	23 16	3.1	00 40	4.9	12 56	5.0	09 45	4.0	22 20	3.8
10	Thursday	11 31	3.4	——	—	01 29	5.1	13 42	5.2	10 30	4.1	22 58	3.9
11	Friday	00 00	3.2	12 14	3.5	02 09	5.3	14 21	5.4	11 05	4.1	23 29	3.9
12	Saturday	00 40	3.2	12 53	3.5	02 42	5.3	14 56	5.4	11 36	4.1	23 55	3.9
13	Sunday	01 14	3.2	13 28	3.5	03 15	5.3	15 29	5.5	——	—	12 05	4.1
14	Monday	01 44	3.3	13 59	3.5	03 44	5.3	16 01	5.4	00 20	3.9	12 35	4.1
15	Tuesday	02 13	3.3	14 29	3.4	04 17	5.3	16 34	5.3	00 50	3.9	13 08	4.0
16	Wednesday	02 41	3.4	14 59	3.4	04 49	5.1	17 07	5.2	01 23	3.8	13 45	3.9
17	Thursday	03 12	3.4	15 32	3.3	05 24	5.0	17 42	5.0	02 01	3.7	14 28	3.7
18	Friday	03 46	3.3	16 09	3.1	06 01	4.8	18 22	4.8	02 45	3.6	15 16	3.5
19	Saturday	04 23	3.2	16 50	2.9	06 40	4.6	19 05	4.5	03 37	3.4	16 14	3.4
20	Sunday	05 07	3.0	17 41	2.7	07 28	4.4	20 00	4.3	04 40	3.2	17 22	3.2
21	Monday	06 01	2.8	18 45	2.6	08 27	4.3	21 06	4.2	05 55	3.2	18 40	3.2
22	Tuesday	07 08	2.8	20 06	2.6	09 37	4.2	22 24	4.3	07 14	3.2	19 49	3.3
23	Wednesday	08 28	2.8	21 40	2.7	10 56	4.4	23 40	4.6	08 14	3.4	20 43	3.5
24	Thursday	09 42	3.0	22 40	2.9	——	—	12 05	4.8	09 03	3.6	21 28	3.7
25	Friday	10 38	3.2	23 27	3.1	00 37	5.0	12 58	5.2	09 46	3.9	22 07	3.9
26	Saturday	11 26	3.4	——	—	01 24	5.4	13 42	5.5	10 26	4.1	22 47	4.1
27	Sunday	00 10	3.2	12 13	3.5	02 06	5.6	14 23	5.8	11 05	4.3	23 25	4.2
28	Monday	00 53	3.3	12 59	3.6	02 47	5.8	15 05	6.0	11 48	4.5	——	—
29	Tuesday	01 33	3.4	13 44	3.7	03 29	5.9	15 50	6.0	00 06	4.3	12 33	4.5
30	Wednesday	02 12	3.4	14 27	3.7	04 14	5.8	16 36	5.9	00 48	4.3	13 19	4.4
31	Thursday	02 49	3.5	15 09	3.6	04 59	5.6	17 27	5.7	01 36	4.2	14 14	4.3

NOTES:
*Difference of height in metres from Ordnance datum (Newlyn)
†Difference of height in metres from Ordnance datum (Dublin)
hr hour
m metres

APRIL 1994 *continued*

		GREENOCK				LEITH				DUN LAOGHAIRE			
1	Friday	03 28	3.5	15 52	3.5	05 48	5.3	18 22	5.3	02 26	4.1	15 14	4.0
2	Saturday	04 10	3.3	16 39	3.2	06 41	5.0	19 24	4.9	03 27	3.9	16 24	3.8
3	Sunday	04 58	3.1	17 34	2.9	07 43	4.7	20 34	4.6	04 40	3.7	17 41	3.6
4	Monday	05 59	2.9	18 50	2.7	08 55	4.5	21 53	4.5	06 00	3.6	19 00	3.5
5	Tuesday	07 47	2.8	20 57	2.7	10 12	4.5	23 10	4.6	07 16	3.7	20 14	3.6
6	Wednesday	09 23	3.0	22 02	2.9	11 28	4.7	——	—	08 28	3.8	21 15	3.7
7	Thursday	10 19	3.2	22 50	3.0	00 15	4.8	12 29	4.9	09 24	3.9	22 00	3.7
8	Friday	11 05	3.3	23 31	3.1	01 04	5.0	13 17	5.0	10 07	3.9	22 36	3.8
9	Saturday	11 47	3.3	——	—	01 43	5.1	13 56	5.2	10 44	4.0	23 03	3.8
10	Sunday	00 09	3.1	12 27	3.3	02 17	5.2	14 31	5.3	11 13	4.0	23 28	3.8
11	Monday	00 43	3.1	13 02	3.2	02 48	5.2	15 04	5.3	11 41	3.9	23 55	3.9
12	Tuesday	01 14	3.2	13 33	3.2	03 18	5.3	15 36	5.3	——	—	12 12	3.9
13	Wednesday	01 43	3.2	14 03	3.1	03 50	5.2	16 08	5.2	00 24	3.9	12 44	3.9
14	Thursday	02 11	3.3	14 34	3.1	04 22	5.1	16 43	5.1	00 58	3.8	13 20	3.8
15	Friday	02 42	3.3	15 08	3.1	04 57	5.0	17 19	5.0	01 36	3.8	14 04	3.7
16	Saturday	03 16	3.3	15 45	3.0	05 33	4.8	17 58	4.8	02 19	3.6	14 51	3.5
17	Sunday	03 52	3.2	16 28	2.8	06 12	4.7	18 41	4.6	03 09	3.5	15 47	3.4
18	Monday	04 33	3.0	17 19	2.7	06 57	4.5	19 34	4.4	04 05	3.3	16 50	3.3
19	Tuesday	05 24	2.9	18 22	2.6	07 53	4.4	20 35	4.4	05 12	3.2	18 00	3.3
20	Wednesday	06 30	2.8	19 37	2.6	09 01	4.3	21 47	4.6	06 26	3.3	19 09	3.4
21	Thursday	07 48	2.8	20 58	2.7	10 14	4.5	23 00	4.7	07 33	3.4	20 07	3.5
22	Friday	09 04	3.0	22 04	2.8	11 24	4.8	——	—	08 26	3.6	20 56	3.7
23	Saturday	10 06	3.2	22 55	3.0	00 02	5.0	12 22	5.1	09 16	3.9	21 42	3.9
24	Sunday	10 58	3.3	23 41	3.1	00 53	5.4	13 11	5.5	10 01	4.1	22 23	4.1
25	Monday	11 47	3.4	——	—	01 39	5.6	13 57	5.8	10 47	4.3	23 05	4.2
26	Tuesday	00 26	3.3	12 37	3.5	02 23	5.8	14 44	5.9	11 32	4.4	23 48	4.3
27	Wednesday	01 10	3.4	13 25	3.6	03 08	5.8	15 33	6.0	——	—	12 19	4.4
28	Thursday	01 51	3.5	14 12	3.6	03 54	5.8	16 22	5.8	00 33	4.3	13 09	4.4
29	Friday	02 32	3.5	14 57	3.5	04 42	5.6	17 14	5.6	01 19	4.3	14 02	4.2
30	Saturday	03 12	3.5	15 42	3.3	05 31	5.3	18 11	5.3	02 11	4.2	15 02	4.0

MAY 1994 *High water* GMT

		London Bridge *Datum of predictions 3.20 m below*				Avonmouth *Datum of predictions 6.50 m below*				Liverpool *Datum of predictions 4.93 m below*				Hull (*Albert Dock*) *Datum of predictions 3.90 m below*			
		hr	ht m	hr	ht m	hr	ht m	hr	ht m	hr	ht m	hr	ht m	hr	ht m	hr	ht m
1	Sunday	05 36	7.1	17 54	6.7	10 59	11.6	23 23	11.4	02 47	8.9	15 19	8.3	10 00	6.9	22 45	6.4
2	Monday	06 28	6.7	18 43	6.4	11 51	10.8	—	—	03 43	8.4	16 23	7.8	10 53	6.6	23 52	6.0
3	Tuesday	07 24	6.4	19 40	6.1	00 20	10.7	12 53	10.2	04 48	7.9	17 36	7.5	11 56	6.3	—	—
4	Wednesday	08 27	6.2	20 46	5.9	01 29	10.3	14 06	10.1	06 01	7.7	18 52	7.5	01 15	5.8	13 11	6.1
5	Thursday	09 42	6.2	22 07	6.0	02 45	10.5	15 23	10.5	07 14	7.8	19 58	7.7	02 33	5.8	14 31	6.2
6	Friday	10 59	6.4	23 20	6.3	03 56	11.0	16 26	11.1	08 15	8.0	20 50	8.1	03 33	6.0	15 34	6.4
7	Saturday	11 56	6.7	—	—	04 52	11.6	17 17	11.7	09 05	8.3	21 32	8.4	04 19	6.3	16 22	6.6
8	Sunday	00 14	6.6	12 42	6.9	05 38	12.0	17 59	12.1	09 46	8.6	22 09	8.6	04 59	6.6	17 03	6.8
9	Monday	00 56	6.7	13 20	6.9	06 19	12.2	18 34	12.3	10 24	8.7	22 42	8.8	05 33	6.8	17 40	7.0
10	Tuesday	01 33	6.8	13 52	6.9	06 54	12.3	19 08	12.5	10 59	8.9	23 15	8.9	06 04	6.9	18 15	7.1
11	Wednesday	02 04	6.8	14 22	6.9	07 26	12.4	19 39	12.6	11 32	8.9	23 47	9.0	06 33	7.0	18 49	7.1
12	Thursday	02 34	6.8	14 51	6.9	07 59	12.5	20 10	12.7	—	—	12 05	8.9	07 03	7.1	19 24	7.0
13	Friday	03 07	6.9	15 22	6.9	08 30	12.4	20 42	12.6	00 18	9.0	12 39	8.8	07 35	7.0	19 59	6.9
14	Saturday	03 42	6.9	15 57	6.9	09 04	12.2	21 16	12.3	00 52	8.9	13 13	8.7	08 07	6.9	20 34	6.7
15	Sunday	04 20	6.9	16 33	6.8	09 39	11.8	21 51	11.9	01 26	8.7	13 51	8.5	08 42	6.7	21 13	6.5
16	Monday	04 59	6.8	17 09	6.7	10 17	11.4	22 31	11.5	02 05	8.5	14 33	8.2	09 19	6.5	21 57	6.4
17	Tuesday	05 40	6.7	17 50	6.4	10 59	10.9	23 19	11.0	02 50	8.3	15 24	7.9	10 04	6.3	22 48	6.2
18	Wednesday	06 28	6.4	18 39	6.2	11 54	10.6	—	—	03 45	8.0	16 27	7.8	10 57	6.1	23 51	6.1
19	Thursday	07 27	6.2	19 42	6.0	00 20	10.8	13 03	10.5	04 52	7.9	17 39	7.8	—	—	12 06	6.1
20	Friday	08 40	6.2	21 04	6.1	01 36	10.9	14 21	10.8	06 05	8.0	18 50	8.0	01 07	6.2	13 25	6.2
21	Saturday	09 59	6.4	22 21	6.3	02 54	11.3	15 34	11.4	07 16	8.3	19 55	8.5	02 20	6.4	14 34	6.5
22	Sunday	11 08	6.7	23 29	6.7	04 03	12.0	16 39	12.2	08 18	8.7	20 53	8.9	03 22	6.7	15 36	6.9
23	Monday	—	—	12 07	7.0	05 04	12.7	17 37	12.9	09 15	9.2	21 45	9.3	04 18	7.0	16 34	7.3
24	Tuesday	00 27	6.9	13 00	7.1	06 02	13.1	18 30	13.3	10 09	9.5	22 34	9.6	05 09	7.3	17 27	7.5
25	Wednesday	01 19	7.0	13 48	7.1	06 54	13.4	19 19	13.6	10 59	9.7	23 23	9.8	05 56	7.5	18 19	7.7
26	Thursday	02 08	7.2	14 33	7.2	07 43	13.6	20 07	13.7	11 49	9.7	—	—	06 41	7.6	19 08	7.6
27	Friday	02 56	7.4	15 19	7.2	08 31	13.5	20 52	13.6	00 10	9.8	12 38	9.6	07 25	7.6	19 57	7.5
28	Saturday	03 45	7.5	16 04	7.2	09 16	13.2	21 37	13.1	00 57	9.7	13 24	9.3	08 10	7.5	20 47	7.2
29	Sunday	04 33	7.4	16 49	7.1	10 01	12.6	22 21	12.5	01 44	9.4	14 12	8.9	08 55	7.4	21 34	6.9
30	Monday	05 20	7.2	17 34	6.8	10 45	11.9	23 06	11.7	02 30	9.0	15 01	8.4	09 40	7.1	22 25	6.5
31	Tuesday	06 08	6.9	18 19	6.5	11 30	11.1	23 55	11.1	03 19	8.6	15 53	8.0	10 28	6.8	23 19	6.1

JUNE 1994 *High water* GMT

		London Bridge				Avonmouth				Liverpool				Hull (*Albert Dock*)			
1	Wednesday	06 57	6.6	19 07	6.2	—	—	12 18	10.6	04 14	8.2	16 51	7.6	11 20	6.5	—	—
2	Thursday	07 51	6.3	20 05	6.0	00 49	10.6	13 15	10.2	05 13	7.8	17 57	7.4	00 20	5.9	12 22	6.2
3	Friday	08 54	6.1	21 12	5.9	01 52	10.3	14 23	10.1	06 21	7.7	19 06	7.5	01 34	5.8	13 32	6.1
4	Saturday	10 06	6.1	22 30	6.0	03 01	10.4	15 32	10.4	07 26	7.7	20 05	7.7	02 42	5.8	14 45	6.1
5	Sunday	11 13	6.3	23 34	6.2	04 04	10.8	16 29	10.9	08 23	7.9	20 54	8.0	03 37	6.0	15 44	6.3
6	Monday	—	—	12 04	6.5	04 57	11.2	17 19	11.5	09 11	8.2	21 36	8.3	04 22	6.3	16 34	6.5
7	Tuesday	00 22	6.4	12 46	6.6	05 42	11.6	18 01	11.9	09 55	8.4	22 14	8.6	05 02	6.6	17 16	6.6
8	Wednesday	01 02	6.5	13 21	6.7	06 25	11.9	18 40	12.2	10 33	8.6	22 51	8.8	05 37	6.7	17 54	6.8
9	Thursday	01 37	6.6	13 55	6.8	07 03	12.1	19 15	12.4	11 09	8.7	23 26	8.9	06 11	6.9	18 30	6.8
10	Friday	02 13	6.7	14 30	6.9	07 39	12.3	19 52	12.6	11 46	8.8	—	—	06 43	7.0	19 07	6.9
11	Saturday	02 50	6.8	15 07	6.9	08 14	12.4	20 28	12.7	00 01	9.0	12 22	8.9	07 17	7.0	19 43	6.9
12	Sunday	03 29	6.9	15 43	6.9	08 52	12.4	21 05	12.7	00 36	9.0	12 59	8.8	07 52	7.0	20 21	6.9
13	Monday	04 07	7.0	16 20	6.9	09 30	12.3	21 44	12.6	01 14	9.0	13 38	8.7	08 30	6.9	21 02	6.8
14	Tuesday	04 47	7.0	16 57	6.8	10 10	12.0	22 25	12.1	01 54	8.8	14 20	8.6	09 09	6.8	21 44	6.7
15	Wednesday	05 27	6.8	17 36	6.6	10 52	11.6	23 10	11.8	02 37	8.7	15 08	8.4	09 51	6.7	22 31	6.5
16	Thursday	06 12	6.6	18 21	6.4	11 40	11.2	—	—	03 27	8.5	16 02	8.2	10 39	6.6	23 24	6.4
17	Friday	07 04	6.4	19 17	6.3	00 02	11.4	12 36	10.9	04 24	8.3	17 05	8.1	11 37	6.5	—	—
18	Saturday	08 11	6.3	20 29	6.2	01 05	11.2	13 46	10.9	05 30	8.2	18 15	8.1	00 29	6.3	12 47	6.4
19	Sunday	09 25	6.4	21 49	6.4	02 19	11.2	15 01	11.2	06 42	8.3	19 24	8.3	01 42	6.4	14 00	6.6
20	Monday	10 38	6.6	23 02	6.5	03 32	11.6	16 10	11.7	07 51	8.5	20 29	8.7	02 51	6.6	15 12	6.8
21	Tuesday	11 44	6.7	—	—	04 39	12.0	17 14	12.3	08 56	8.8	21 27	9.0	03 56	6.8	16 19	7.0
22	Wednesday	00 08	6.7	12 42	6.8	05 44	12.5	18 13	12.8	09 55	9.1	22 20	9.4	04 52	7.1	17 20	7.2
23	Thursday	01 06	6.8	13 34	6.8	06 41	12.9	19 07	13.2	10 48	9.3	23 11	9.6	05 42	7.3	18 12	7.4
24	Friday	01 58	6.9	14 22	6.9	07 34	13.1	19 55	13.5	11 39	9.4	23 58	9.7	06 29	7.5	19 01	7.4
25	Saturday	02 46	7.2	15 07	7.1	08 20	13.2	20 40	13.5	—	—	12 25	9.4	07 12	7.6	19 48	7.3
26	Sunday	03 32	7.4	15 49	7.2	09 04	13.1	21 23	13.2	00 43	9.7	13 10	9.2	07 55	7.6	20 33	7.2
27	Monday	04 17	7.4	16 31	7.2	09 44	12.8	22 04	12.8	01 27	9.5	13 52	8.9	08 37	7.5	21 15	6.9
28	Tuesday	04 59	7.3	17 11	7.1	10 24	12.2	22 43	12.2	02 09	9.2	14 34	8.6	09 18	7.3	21 57	6.6
29	Wednesday	05 42	7.0	17 51	6.7	11 00	11.6	23 21	11.5	02 51	8.8	15 17	8.2	10 00	7.1	22 39	6.3
30	Thursday	06 24	6.6	18 34	6.4	11 38	10.9	—	—	03 35	8.4	16 03	7.8	10 43	6.7	23 24	6.1

MAY 1994   *continued*

	GREENOCK				LEITH				DUN LAOGHAIRE				NOTES:
	*Datum of predictions 1.62 m below				*Datum of predictions 2.90 m below				†Datum of predictions 0.20 m above				*Difference of height in metres from Ordnance datum (Newlyn)
	hr	m	hr	m	hr	m	hr	m	hr	m	hr	m	†Difference of height in metres from Ordnance datum (Dublin)
1 Sunday	03 55	3.4	16 32	3.1	06 26	5.1	19 10	4.9	03 09	4.0	16 08	3.7	hr hour
2 Monday	04 43	3.2	17 28	2.9	07 26	4.8	20 13	4.7	04 15	3.8	17 19	3.5	m metres
3 Tuesday	05 42	3.0	18 35	2.8	08 31	4.6	21 20	4.5	05 29	3.7	18 32	3.4	
4 Wednesday	07 00	2.9	20 00	2.7	09 39	4.5	22 31	4.5	06 43	3.6	19 42	3.5	
5 Thursday	08 38	2.9	21 17	2.8	10 48	4.6	23 34	4.7	07 52	3.6	20 40	3.5	
6 Friday	09 43	3.0	22 10	2.9	11 51	4.7	—	—	08 49	3.7	21 27	3.6	
7 Saturday	10 32	3.1	22 54	3.0	00 27	4.8	12 43	4.8	09 36	3.7	22 04	3.7	
8 Sunday	11 16	3.1	23 34	3.0	01 11	4.9	13 26	5.0	10 14	3.8	22 34	3.7	
9 Monday	11 56	3.1	—	—	01 48	5.0	14 03	5.1	10 48	3.8	23 03	3.8	
10 Tuesday	00 11	3.1	12 33	3.0	02 20	5.1	14 38	5.1	11 20	3.8	23 34	3.9	
11 Wednesday	00 44	3.1	13 06	3.0	02 54	5.2	15 12	5.2	11 52	3.8	—	—	
12 Thursday	01 15	3.2	13 38	2.9	03 26	5.2	15 47	5.1	00 05	3.9	12 26	3.8	
13 Friday	01 45	3.3	14 11	3.0	04 01	5.1	16 22	5.1	00 38	3.9	13 02	3.7	
14 Saturday	02 17	3.3	14 48	2.9	04 36	5.0	16 59	5.0	01 16	3.8	13 44	3.7	
15 Sunday	02 53	3.3	15 27	2.9	05 11	4.9	17 38	4.9	01 59	3.7	14 29	3.6	
16 Monday	03 30	3.3	16 11	2.8	05 51	4.8	18 22	4.8	02 45	3.6	15 21	3.5	
17 Tuesday	04 10	3.1	17 02	2.7	06 36	4.7	19 11	4.7	03 37	3.5	16 18	3.4	
18 Wednesday	04 57	3.0	18 01	2.7	07 28	4.6	20 10	4.6	04 36	3.4	17 21	3.4	
19 Thursday	05 57	2.9	19 07	2.6	08 30	4.6	21 15	4.6	05 40	3.4	18 26	3.4	
20 Friday	07 09	2.9	20 17	2.7	09 37	4.6	22 24	4.8	06 48	3.5	19 30	3.5	
21 Saturday	08 27	3.0	21 27	2.8	10 45	4.8	23 28	5.0	07 51	3.7	20 25	3.7	
22 Sunday	09 35	3.1	22 25	2.9	11 49	5.1	—	—	08 48	3.9	21 16	3.9	
23 Monday	10 33	3.2	23 16	3.1	00 25	5.3	12 46	5.4	09 40	4.1	22 04	4.1	
24 Tuesday	11 26	3.3	—	—	01 14	5.5	13 38	5.6	10 30	4.2	22 51	4.2	
25 Wednesday	00 04	3.2	12 18	3.4	02 02	5.6	14 28	5.8	11 20	4.3	23 35	4.3	
26 Thursday	00 51	3.4	13 10	3.4	02 49	5.7	15 19	5.8	—	—	12 09	4.3	
27 Friday	01 36	3.5	14 00	3.4	03 37	5.7	16 10	5.7	00 21	4.4	12 59	4.3	
28 Saturday	02 18	3.6	14 47	3.4	04 26	5.6	17 02	5.5	01 08	4.3	13 51	4.1	
29 Sunday	02 59	3.6	15 34	3.3	05 17	5.4	17 54	5.3	01 57	4.2	14 45	3.9	
30 Monday	03 42	3.5	16 21	3.2	06 09	5.2	18 47	5.0	02 50	4.1	15 44	3.7	
31 Tuesday	04 28	3.4	17 11	3.0	07 04	5.0	19 43	4.8	03 47	3.9	16 44	3.5	

JUNE 1994   *continued*

	GREENOCK				LEITH				DUN LAOGHAIRE			
1 Wednesday	05 19	3.2	18 05	2.9	08 00	4.8	20 40	4.6	04 50	3.7	17 48	3.4
2 Thursday	06 18	3.0	19 01	2.8	08 58	4.6	21 40	4.5	05 57	3.6	18 52	3.4
3 Friday	07 27	2.9	20 04	2.8	09 58	4.5	22 41	4.5	07 04	3.5	19 52	3.4
4 Saturday	08 48	2.9	21 13	2.8	11 02	4.5	23 41	4.6	08 05	3.5	20 43	3.5
5 Sunday	09 53	2.9	22 11	2.9	—	—	12 01	4.6	08 58	3.5	21 27	3.6
6 Monday	10 42	2.9	22 58	3.0	00 32	4.7	12 51	4.7	09 43	3.6	22 05	3.7
7 Tuesday	11 26	2.9	23 39	3.0	01 15	4.9	13 35	4.9	10 23	3.6	22 41	3.8
8 Wednesday	12 05	2.9	—	—	01 55	5.0	14 14	5.0	10 58	3.6	23 14	3.8
9 Thursday	00 16	3.1	12 42	2.9	02 31	5.1	14 51	5.1	11 35	3.7	23 48	3.9
10 Friday	00 49	3.2	13 17	2.9	03 06	5.2	15 27	5.1	—	—	12 09	3.7
11 Saturday	01 22	3.3	13 54	2.9	03 43	5.2	16 03	5.1	00 21	3.9	12 45	3.7
12 Sunday	01 57	3.3	14 32	2.9	04 18	5.2	16 41	5.1	00 58	3.9	13 24	3.7
13 Monday	02 34	3.4	15 13	2.9	04 55	5.1	17 19	5.1	01 38	3.9	14 08	3.7
14 Tuesday	03 12	3.4	15 56	2.9	05 33	5.0	18 02	5.0	02 22	3.8	14 55	3.6
15 Wednesday	03 52	3.3	16 43	2.9	06 16	5.0	18 50	4.9	03 09	3.8	15 47	3.6
16 Thursday	04 37	3.2	17 35	2.8	07 05	4.9	19 43	4.8	04 02	3.7	16 44	3.5
17 Friday	05 29	3.1	18 33	2.8	08 02	4.8	20 45	4.8	05 01	3.7	17 48	3.5
18 Saturday	06 31	3.0	19 37	2.7	09 05	4.8	21 51	4.8	06 10	3.7	18 53	3.6
19 Sunday	07 47	3.0	20 51	2.8	10 15	4.9	22 57	4.9	07 20	3.7	19 58	3.7
20 Monday	09 07	3.0	22 00	2.9	11 26	5.0	23 59	5.1	08 25	3.9	20 55	3.9
21 Tuesday	10 14	3.1	22 58	3.1	—	—	12 29	5.2	09 24	4.0	21 49	4.0
22 Wednesday	11 12	3.2	23 49	3.3	00 56	5.3	13 26	5.4	10 19	4.1	22 38	4.2
23 Thursday	12 07	3.3	—	—	01 48	5.5	14 19	5.5	11 11	4.2	23 25	4.3
24 Friday	00 37	3.4	13 01	3.3	02 35	5.6	15 08	5.7	—	—	12 00	4.2
25 Saturday	01 23	3.5	13 51	3.3	03 25	5.7	15 57	5.6	00 10	4.4	12 48	4.1
26 Sunday	02 06	3.6	14 37	3.3	04 12	5.6	16 45	5.5	00 54	4.4	13 36	4.0
27 Monday	02 46	3.7	15 20	3.3	05 00	5.5	17 31	5.3	01 38	4.3	14 21	3.9
28 Tuesday	03 26	3.6	16 01	3.3	05 48	5.3	18 19	5.1	02 23	4.1	15 08	3.7
29 Wednesday	04 07	3.5	16 44	3.2	06 34	5.1	19 05	4.8	03 11	4.0	15 58	3.6
30 Thursday	04 50	3.3	17 28	3.1	07 22	4.9	19 53	4.6	04 04	3.8	16 53	3.4

JULY 1994   *High water*   GMT

	LONDON BRIDGE *Datum of predictions 3.20 m below*				AVONMOUTH *Datum of predictions 6.50 m below*				LIVERPOOL *Datum of predictions 4.93 m below*				HULL (*Albert Dock*) *Datum of predictions 3.90 m below*			
	hr	ht m	hr	ht m	hr	ht m	hr	ht m	hr	ht m	hr	ht m	hr	ht m	hr	ht m
1 Friday	07 10	6.3	19 23	6.1	00 02	10.8	12 19	10.4	04 24	8.0	16 57	7.5	11 34	6.4	——	—
2 Saturday	08 05	6.0	20 22	5.9	00 51	10.3	13 14	10.0	05 22	7.6	18 01	7.3	00 19	5.8	12 36	6.1
3 Sunday	09 05	5.9	21 28	5.8	01 55	9.9	14 24	9.9	06 28	7.4	19 12	7.4	01 25	5.7	13 48	5.9
4 Monday	10 10	5.9	22 37	5.8	03 06	10.0	15 36	10.2	07 37	7.5	20 13	7.6	02 37	5.8	14 59	6.0
5 Tuesday	11 13	6.0	23 40	6.0	04 12	10.5	16 38	10.9	08 37	7.8	21 05	8.0	03 40	6.1	16 03	6.1
6 Wednesday	——	—	12 07	6.2	05 09	11.1	17 30	11.5	09 27	8.1	21 49	8.4	04 31	6.3	16 53	6.4
7 Thursday	00 29	6.2	12 50	6.4	05 56	11.6	18 15	12.1	10 10	8.4	22 30	8.7	05 11	6.6	17 35	6.6
8 Friday	01 12	6.4	13 33	6.7	06 41	12.0	18 57	12.5	10 49	8.7	23 08	9.0	05 49	6.8	18 13	6.8
9 Saturday	01 54	6.7	14 12	6.9	07 22	12.4	19 36	12.8	11 27	8.9	23 44	9.2	06 25	7.0	18 50	6.9
10 Sunday	02 34	6.9	14 53	7.0	08 02	12.6	20 16	13.0	——	—	12 05	9.0	07 00	7.2	19 28	7.1
11 Monday	03 14	7.1	15 31	7.1	08 41	12.8	20 55	13.2	00 22	9.3	12 45	9.1	07 36	7.3	20 06	7.2
12 Tuesday	03 53	7.2	16 06	7.1	09 19	12.9	21 34	13.1	01 00	9.3	13 24	9.1	08 14	7.3	20 45	7.2
13 Wednesday	04 31	7.2	16 42	7.0	09 58	12.7	22 14	12.8	01 40	9.3	14 05	9.0	08 52	7.3	21 26	7.1
14 Thursday	05 11	7.0	17 20	6.8	10 38	12.3	22 56	12.4	02 20	9.1	14 49	8.8	09 33	7.1	22 08	6.9
15 Friday	05 53	6.7	18 01	6.6	11 20	11.8	23 41	11.8	03 05	8.9	15 38	8.5	10 18	7.0	22 57	6.7
16 Saturday	06 41	6.5	18 53	6.4	——	—	12 09	11.2	03 57	8.6	16 34	8.2	11 11	6.7	23 56	6.4
17 Sunday	07 41	6.3	20 01	6.3	00 36	11.3	13 12	10.8	05 01	8.3	17 44	8.0	——	—	12 18	6.5
18 Monday	08 54	6.3	21 22	6.3	01 48	10.9	14 31	10.8	06 15	8.1	19 00	8.1	01 10	6.3	13 36	6.4
19 Tuesday	10 10	6.4	22 42	6.4	03 06	11.0	15 47	11.2	07 34	8.1	20 12	8.4	02 27	6.4	15 01	6.5
20 Wednesday	11 23	6.5	23 57	6.6	04 22	11.4	17 00	11.8	08 46	8.4	21 15	8.8	03 40	6.6	16 17	6.8
21 Thursday	——	—	12 28	6.7	05 33	12.0	18 04	12.5	09 48	8.8	22 12	9.2	04 41	6.9	17 17	7.0
22 Friday	00 57	6.7	13 23	6.8	06 33	12.5	18 57	13.1	10 41	9.1	23 01	9.5	05 31	7.2	18 08	7.2
23 Saturday	01 49	6.9	14 09	6.9	07 24	12.9	19 43	13.4	11 27	9.3	23 44	9.7	06 15	7.4	18 51	7.3
24 Sunday	02 36	7.1	14 51	7.1	08 07	13.2	20 26	13.5	——	—	12 10	9.3	06 56	7.6	19 32	7.3
25 Monday	03 18	7.3	15 31	7.2	08 47	13.2	21 04	13.4	00 27	9.7	12 49	9.2	07 35	7.7	20 10	7.2
26 Tuesday	03 57	7.3	16 09	7.2	09 23	13.0	21 40	13.1	01 04	9.6	13 27	9.0	08 13	7.7	20 48	7.1
27 Wednesday	04 35	7.2	16 44	7.0	09 56	12.6	22 14	12.5	01 42	9.3	14 02	8.8	08 51	7.5	21 23	6.9
28 Thursday	05 11	7.0	17 19	6.8	10 26	12.0	22 45	11.8	02 18	9.0	14 37	8.4	09 29	7.2	21 58	6.6
29 Friday	05 47	6.7	17 56	6.5	10 56	11.3	23 17	11.0	02 56	8.6	15 15	8.0	10 07	6.9	22 36	6.3
30 Saturday	06 27	6.4	18 39	6.2	11 28	10.6	23 54	10.3	03 36	8.1	16 00	7.6	10 49	6.4	23 20	6.0
31 Sunday	07 13	6.1	19 33	5.9	——	—	12 09	10.0	04 27	7.6	16 57	7.3	11 42	6.0	——	—

AUGUST 1994   *High water*   GMT

	LONDON BRIDGE				AVONMOUTH				LIVERPOOL				HULL (*Albert Dock*)			
1 Monday	08 09	5.8	20 36	5.6	00 46	9.6	13 12	9.5	05 30	7.2	18 11	7.1	00 20	5.7	12 56	5.7
2 Tuesday	09 11	5.7	21 42	5.5	02 03	9.4	14 41	9.6	06 49	7.1	19 31	7.3	01 36	5.7	14 14	5.7
3 Wednesday	10 16	5.7	22 52	5.7	03 29	9.8	16 00	10.3	08 04	7.4	20 34	7.7	02 52	5.8	15 30	5.9
4 Thursday	11 25	5.9	23 57	5.9	04 36	10.6	17 00	11.3	09 01	7.8	21 25	8.2	03 56	6.2	16 28	6.2
5 Friday	——	—	12 22	6.2	05 31	11.5	17 51	12.1	09 48	8.3	22 07	8.7	04 45	6.5	17 14	6.5
6 Saturday	00 48	6.3	13 09	6.6	06 19	12.2	18 36	12.7	10 28	8.7	22 47	9.1	05 26	6.8	17 54	6.8
7 Sunday	01 33	6.7	13 52	7.0	07 03	12.7	19 18	13.1	11 08	9.1	23 25	9.4	06 04	7.1	18 32	7.1
8 Monday	02 13	7.1	14 32	7.2	07 43	13.1	19 59	13.5	11 46	9.3	——	—	06 40	7.4	19 08	7.4
9 Tuesday	02 54	7.4	15 10	7.4	08 24	13.4	20 38	13.7	00 03	9.6	12 25	9.5	07 15	7.6	19 45	7.5
10 Wednesday	03 34	7.5	15 46	7.4	09 02	13.5	21 18	13.7	00 42	9.7	13 04	9.5	07 53	7.7	20 23	7.5
11 Thursday	04 12	7.4	16 24	7.3	09 40	13.3	21 57	13.4	01 21	9.7	13 44	9.3	08 31	7.7	21 04	7.4
12 Friday	04 51	7.1	17 02	7.0	10 19	12.8	22 36	12.7	02 01	9.5	14 26	9.1	09 13	7.5	21 44	7.2
13 Saturday	05 33	6.8	17 44	6.8	10 59	12.1	23 20	12.0	02 44	9.1	15 12	8.7	09 58	7.2	22 32	6.8
14 Sunday	06 18	6.5	18 35	6.5	11 45	11.3	——	—	03 35	8.7	16 09	8.3	10 50	6.8	23 28	6.5
15 Monday	07 16	6.2	19 42	6.3	00 12	11.1	12 46	10.7	04 38	8.2	17 20	7.9	11 58	6.4	——	—
16 Tuesday	08 26	6.1	21 03	6.2	01 22	10.5	14 07	10.4	05 58	7.8	18 43	7.9	00 43	6.2	13 26	6.2
17 Wednesday	09 45	6.2	22 27	6.3	02 48	10.4	15 33	10.8	07 26	7.8	20 02	8.2	02 10	6.3	15 02	6.3
18 Thursday	11 05	6.4	23 44	6.6	04 14	11.0	16 50	11.7	08 42	8.2	21 07	8.7	03 27	6.5	16 15	6.6
19 Friday	——	—	12 14	6.7	05 26	11.8	17 54	12.6	09 41	8.6	22 00	9.1	04 29	6.9	17 11	6.9
20 Saturday	00 46	6.9	13 09	6.9	06 23	12.6	18 44	13.2	10 30	9.0	22 47	9.5	05 17	7.2	17 56	7.1
21 Sunday	01 37	7.1	13 54	7.0	07 08	13.0	19 26	13.4	11 12	9.2	23 27	9.7	05 58	7.5	18 36	7.2
22 Monday	02 20	7.2	14 33	7.1	07 48	13.2	20 04	13.5	11 50	9.3	——	—	06 36	7.6	19 11	7.3
23 Tuesday	02 58	7.3	15 10	7.2	08 23	13.3	20 40	13.5	00 04	9.7	12 25	9.3	07 12	7.7	19 45	7.3
24 Wednesday	03 34	7.3	15 43	7.2	08 55	13.2	21 12	13.2	00 39	9.6	12 57	9.1	07 48	7.7	20 17	7.2
25 Thursday	04 06	7.1	16 14	7.1	09 25	12.9	21 41	12.7	01 12	9.4	13 28	8.9	08 23	7.6	20 49	7.0
26 Friday	04 37	6.9	16 45	6.9	09 53	12.3	22 10	12.0	01 44	9.0	13 59	8.6	08 58	7.3	21 20	6.8
27 Saturday	05 09	6.7	17 20	6.7	10 18	11.6	22 36	11.2	02 18	8.7	14 33	8.3	09 32	6.9	21 53	6.5
28 Sunday	05 44	6.5	18 00	6.4	10 45	10.9	23 06	10.4	02 54	8.2	15 11	7.8	10 10	6.4	22 29	6.1
29 Monday	06 24	6.2	18 45	6.0	11 17	10.1	23 44	9.6	03 36	7.7	16 00	7.4	10 53	5.9	23 17	5.8
30 Tuesday	07 12	5.8	19 41	5.6	——	—	12 06	9.5	04 35	7.2	17 11	7.0	11 58	5.6	——	—
31 Wednesday	08 12	5.5	20 50	5.4	00 51	9.1	13 36	9.2	05 57	6.9	18 41	7.1	00 37	5.5	13 34	5.4

JULY 1994   *continued*

		GREENOCK				LEITH				DUN LAOGHAIRE				NOTES:
		*Datum of predictions 1.62 m below				*Datum of predictions 2.90 m below				†Datum of predictions 0.20 m above				*Difference of height in metres from Ordnance datum (Newlyn)
		hr	ht m	hr	ht m	hr	ht m	hr	ht m	hr	ht m	hr	ht m	†Difference of height in metres from Ordnance datum (Dublin)
1	Friday	05 37	3.1	18 14	3.0	08 13	4.7	20 45	4.5	05 02	3.6	17 51	3.4	hr hour
2	Saturday	06 29	3.0	19 03	2.9	09 06	4.5	21 41	4.4	06 08	3.4	18 53	3.3	m metres
3	Sunday	07 29	2.8	20 01	2.8	10 05	4.4	22 42	4.4	07 16	3.4	19 54	3.4	
4	Monday	08 49	2.7	21 14	2.8	11 10	4.4	23 45	4.5	08 18	3.4	20 48	3.5	
5	Tuesday	10 07	2.8	22 20	2.9	———	—	12 13	4.5	09 13	3.4	21 36	3.6	
6	Wednesday	11 00	2.8	23 09	3.1	00 41	4.7	13 05	4.7	10 00	3.5	22 17	3.7	
7	Thursday	11 44	2.9	23 50	3.1	01 28	4.9	13 49	4.9	10 41	3.5	22 54	3.8	
8	Friday	12 24	2.9	———	—	02 09	5.1	14 28	5.1	11 17	3.6	23 28	3.9	
9	Saturday	00 26	3.2	13 03	2.9	02 47	5.2	15 06	5.2	11 50	3.7	———	—	
10	Sunday	01 02	3.3	13 40	3.0	03 23	5.3	15 43	5.3	00 02	3.9	12 26	3.8	
11	Monday	01 39	3.4	14 18	3.0	04 00	5.4	16 19	5.3	00 37	4.0	13 02	3.8	
12	Tuesday	02 17	3.5	14 57	3.0	04 35	5.4	16 59	5.3	01 13	4.1	13 43	3.8	
13	Wednesday	02 56	3.5	15 38	3.1	05 14	5.4	17 41	5.3	01 55	4.1	14 28	3.8	
14	Thursday	03 35	3.5	16 20	3.0	05 56	5.3	18 27	5.2	02 41	4.0	15 16	3.8	
15	Friday	04 17	3.4	17 06	3.0	06 43	5.2	19 18	5.0	03 33	4.0	16 11	3.7	
16	Saturday	05 04	3.3	17 57	2.9	07 36	5.0	20 16	4.9	04 30	3.9	17 12	3.6	
17	Sunday	05 59	3.1	18 56	2.8	08 41	4.9	21 22	4.8	05 40	3.8	18 24	3.6	
18	Monday	07 07	3.0	20 16	2.8	09 54	4.8	22 34	4.8	06 56	3.7	19 34	3.7	
19	Tuesday	08 45	2.9	21 44	2.9	11 11	4.9	23 42	5.0	08 08	3.8	20 38	3.9	
20	Wednesday	10 07	3.0	22 46	3.1	———	—	12 22	5.1	09 13	3.9	21 36	4.0	
21	Thursday	11 09	3.1	23 39	3.3	00 44	5.2	13 21	5.3	10 12	4.0	22 29	4.2	
22	Friday	12 03	3.2	———	—	01 38	5.4	14 11	5.5	11 04	4.1	23 15	4.3	
23	Saturday	00 27	3.5	12 54	3.3	02 26	5.6	14 56	5.6	11 52	4.1	23 59	4.4	
24	Sunday	01 12	3.6	13 41	3.3	03 12	5.7	15 40	5.6	———	—	12 34	4.0	
25	Monday	01 53	3.7	14 21	3.3	03 56	5.7	16 22	5.5	00 37	4.4	13 12	4.0	
26	Tuesday	02 30	3.7	14 58	3.3	04 38	5.6	17 04	5.3	01 15	4.3	13 50	3.9	
27	Wednesday	03 06	3.7	15 33	3.3	05 20	5.4	17 44	5.1	01 52	4.2	14 26	3.8	
28	Thurday	03 41	3.6	16 10	3.3	06 01	5.2	18 25	4.9	02 34	4.0	15 09	3.6	
29	Friday	04 18	3.4	16 48	3.3	06 41	5.0	19 07	4.7	03 18	3.8	15 55	3.5	
30	Saturday	04 58	3.2	17 30	3.2	07 26	4.7	19 53	4.5	04 09	3.6	16 51	3.4	
31	Sunday	05 43	3.0	18 16	3.0	08 16	4.5	20 45	4.4	05 11	3.4	17 55	3.3	

AUGUST 1994   *continued*

		GREENOCK				LEITH				DUN LAOGHAIRE			
1	Monday	06 36	2.8	19 08	2.9	09 12	4.3	21 44	4.3	06 25	3.3	19 06	3.3
2	Tuesday	07 41	2.7	20 11	2.9	10 17	4.3	22 50	4.4	07 40	3.3	20 11	3.4
3	Wednesday	09 20	2.7	21 33	2.9	11 31	4.4	———	—	08 43	3.3	21 06	3.5
4	Thursday	10 38	2.8	22 37	3.1	00 02	4.6	12 34	4.6	09 35	3.4	21 53	3.6
5	Friday	11 25	3.0	23 23	3.2	00 58	4.8	13 22	4.9	10 19	3.5	22 31	3.8
6	Saturday	12 06	3.0	———	—	01 43	5.1	14 03	5.2	10 54	3.6	23 03	3.9
7	Sunday	00 01	3.3	12 45	3.1	02 23	5.3	14 42	5.4	11 28	3.8	23 36	4.0
8	Monday	00 41	3.4	13 23	3.1	03 01	5.5	15 19	5.5	———	—	12 00	3.9
9	Tuesday	01 20	3.5	14 00	3.2	03 36	5.6	15 57	5.6	00 10	4.2	12 37	4.0
10	Wednesday	01 59	3.6	14 37	3.2	04 12	5.7	16 36	5.6	00 48	4.2	13 16	4.0
11	Thursday	02 38	3.7	15 15	3.3	04 52	5.7	17 19	5.5	01 30	4.3	13 59	4.0
12	Friday	03 17	3.7	15 54	3.2	05 35	5.6	18 05	5.4	02 16	4.2	14 48	4.0
13	Saturday	03 58	3.6	16 35	3.2	06 23	5.4	18 54	5.2	03 08	4.1	15 43	3.9
14	Sunday	04 42	3.4	17 23	3.1	07 18	5.1	19 52	4.9	04 07	3.9	16 46	3.8
15	Monday	05 33	3.1	18 20	2.9	08 24	4.9	20 59	4.8	05 19	3.8	18 00	3.7
16	Tuesday	06 38	2.9	19 47	2.9	09 43	4.7	22 15	4.8	06 43	3.7	19 14	3.7
17	Wednesday	08 44	2.8	21 34	3.0	11 06	4.8	23 31	4.9	07 59	3.7	20 24	3.9
18	Thursday	10 11	3.0	22 36	3.2	———	—	12 18	5.0	09 09	3.8	21 26	4.0
19	Friday	11 07	3.1	23 26	3.4	00 36	5.2	13 15	5.3	10 09	3.9	22 19	4.2
20	Saturday	11 56	3.2	———	—	01 29	5.4	14 02	5.4	10 58	4.0	23 03	4.3
21	Sunday	00 12	3.6	12 42	3.3	02 14	5.6	14 42	5.5	11 39	4.0	23 42	4.3
22	Monday	00 56	3.6	13 22	3.3	02 55	5.7	15 20	5.5	———	—	12 13	4.0
23	Tuesday	01 35	3.7	13 58	3.4	03 34	5.7	15 57	5.5	00 14	4.3	12 44	3.9
24	Wednesday	02 09	3.7	14 29	3.4	04 11	5.6	16 32	5.4	00 47	4.2	13 13	3.9
25	Thursday	02 41	3.6	15 01	3.4	04 48	5.4	17 09	5.2	01 20	4.1	13 47	3.9
26	Friday	03 13	3.6	15 34	3.4	05 24	5.3	17 45	5.0	01 58	4.0	14 25	3.8
27	Saturday	03 46	3.4	16 09	3.4	06 02	5.0	18 25	4.8	02 40	3.8	15 09	3.7
28	Sunday	04 22	3.3	16 48	3.3	06 44	4.8	19 08	4.6	03 29	3.6	16 01	3.5
29	Monday	05 04	3.1	17 33	3.1	07 31	4.5	19 57	4.5	04 26	3.4	17 02	3.4
30	Tuesday	05 55	2.8	18 25	3.0	08 26	4.3	20 55	4.3	05 37	3.3	18 18	3.3
31	Wednesday	07 00	2.7	19 27	2.9	09 30	4.2	22 01	4.3	07 02	3.2	19 33	3.3

SEPTEMBER 1994   *High water*   GMT

		London Bridge				Avonmouth				Liverpool				Hull (Albert Dock)			
		*Datum of predictions 3.20 m below				*Datum of predictions 6.50 m below				*Datum of predictions 4.93 m below				*Datum of predictions 3.90 m below			
		hr	ht m	hr	ht m	hr	ht m	hr	ht m	hr	ht m	hr	ht m	hr	ht m	hr	ht m
1	Thursday	09 25	5.5	22 07	5.5	02 41	9.3	15 19	9.9	07 26	7.1	19 59	7.5	02 06	5.6	14 54	5.7
2	Friday	10 44	5.7	23 22	5.9	04 03	10.2	16 29	11.0	08 32	7.7	20 54	8.1	03 18	6.0	15 58	6.1
3	Saturday	11 51	6.1	——	—	05 03	11.4	17 23	12.1	09 19	8.3	21 39	8.7	04 14	6.4	16 48	6.5
4	Sunday	00 19	6.4	12 42	6.6	05 52	12.4	18 11	13.0	10 02	8.8	22 20	9.2	04 57	6.9	17 28	6.9
5	Monday	01 06	6.9	13 26	7.1	06 39	13.0	18 56	13.5	10 42	9.3	22 59	9.6	05 37	7.3	18 06	7.3
6	Tuesday	01 49	7.3	14 06	7.4	07 21	13.5	19 38	13.9	11 22	9.6	23 39	9.9	06 15	7.6	18 43	7.6
7	Wednesday	02 30	7.5	14 46	7.6	08 02	13.8	20 19	14.1	——	—	12 01	9.8	06 51	7.8	19 21	7.8
8	Thursday	03 10	7.6	15 24	7.6	08 41	13.9	20 58	14.1	00 18	10.0	12 41	9.8	07 31	8.0	19 59	7.8
9	Friday	03 49	7.5	16 03	7.5	09 20	13.7	21 37	13.7	00 59	10.0	13 23	9.7	08 10	7.9	20 40	7.6
10	Saturday	04 30	7.2	16 45	7.2	09 58	13.1	22 18	12.9	01 41	9.7	14 05	9.3	08 54	7.7	21 22	7.3
11	Sunday	05 13	6.8	17 30	6.9	10 41	12.3	23 02	11.9	02 26	9.2	14 53	8.9	09 41	7.3	22 10	6.9
12	Monday	06 00	6.5	18 24	6.5	11 27	11.4	23 55	11.0	03 18	8.6	15 49	8.3	10 36	6.7	23 06	6.5
13	Tuesday	06 56	6.2	19 30	6.3	——	—	12 29	10.6	04 23	8.0	17 02	7.9	11 45	6.2	——	—
14	Wednesday	08 04	6.0	20 47	6.2	01 07	10.3	13 52	10.3	05 49	7.6	18 28	7.8	00 20	6.2	13 26	6.0
15	Thursday	09 21	6.1	22 10	6.3	02 34	10.2	15 20	10.7	07 19	7.7	19 49	8.1	01 52	6.2	14 59	6.2
16	Friday	10 44	6.3	23 27	6.7	04 03	10.9	16 38	11.7	08 32	8.1	20 53	8.7	03 13	6.5	16 07	6.5
17	Saturday	11 54	6.7	——	—	05 11	11.9	17 37	12.6	09 28	8.6	21 43	9.1	04 12	6.8	16 57	6.8
18	Sunday	00 28	7.0	12 49	7.0	06 04	12.6	18 25	13.2	10 12	9.0	22 26	9.4	04 59	7.2	17 38	7.0
19	Monday	01 17	7.3	13 33	7.2	06 47	13.0	19 04	13.4	10 51	9.2	23 04	9.6	05 38	7.4	18 13	7.1
20	Tuesday	01 58	7.3	14 12	7.2	07 24	13.2	19 39	13.4	11 25	9.3	23 39	9.6	06 13	7.6	18 44	7.2
21	Wednesday	02 34	7.3	14 46	7.2	07 56	13.2	20 11	13.3	11 57	9.3	——	—	06 49	7.7	19 17	7.3
22	Thursday	03 07	7.2	15 15	7.2	08 26	13.1	20 42	13.2	00 11	9.5	12 27	9.2	07 22	7.6	19 46	7.3
23	Friday	03 36	7.0	15 45	7.1	08 54	12.9	21 11	12.8	00 42	9.3	12 56	9.0	07 56	7.5	20 16	7.1
24	Saturday	04 03	6.9	16 14	6.9	09 19	12.5	21 37	12.1	01 13	9.0	13 26	8.8	08 28	7.2	20 45	6.9
25	Sunday	04 33	6.8	16 48	6.7	09 46	11.9	22 04	11.4	01 44	8.7	13 57	8.5	09 02	6.8	21 15	6.6
26	Monday	05 06	6.6	17 26	6.5	10 12	11.1	22 31	10.5	02 18	8.3	14 32	8.1	09 36	6.4	21 47	6.3
27	Tuesday	05 43	6.3	18 08	6.2	10 42	10.4	23 04	9.8	02 57	7.8	15 15	7.6	10 15	6.0	22 28	5.9
28	Wednesday	06 25	6.0	18 57	5.8	11 24	9.8	23 59	9.3	03 50	7.3	16 17	7.2	11 09	5.6	23 30	5.6
29	Thursday	07 17	5.6	19 59	5.6	——	—	12 37	9.4	05 06	7.0	17 46	7.1	——	—	12 43	5.4
30	Friday	08 27	5.4	21 22	5.6	01 42	9.2	14 28	9.7	06 38	7.1	19 12	7.5	01 17	5.6	14 11	5.6

OCTOBER 1994   *High water*   GMT

		London Bridge				Avonmouth				Liverpool				Hull (Albert Dock)			
1	Saturday	09 59	5.6	22 42	5.9	03 20	10.0	15 50	10.9	07 51	7.6	20 15	8.1	02 34	5.9	15 19	6.1
2	Sunday	11 13	6.1	23 46	6.5	04 26	11.3	16 49	12.1	08 46	8.3	21 04	8.7	03 34	6.4	16 12	6.6
3	Monday	——	—	12 08	6.6	05 21	12.4	17 41	13.0	09 31	8.9	21 49	9.3	04 24	6.9	16 57	7.0
4	Tuesday	00 38	7.0	12 56	7.1	06 09	13.2	18 29	13.7	10 13	9.4	22 31	9.8	05 06	7.3	17 38	7.4
5	Wednesday	01 23	7.4	13 38	7.5	06 56	13.7	19 14	14.1	10 55	9.8	23 13	10.1	05 47	7.7	18 18	7.7
6	Thursday	02 05	7.6	14 19	7.7	07 38	14.0	19 56	14.3	11 37	10.0	23 56	10.2	06 27	7.9	18 56	7.9
7	Friday	02 46	7.6	15 01	7.8	08 20	14.1	20 38	14.2	——	—	12 18	10.0	07 10	8.1	19 36	7.9
8	Saturday	03 28	7.5	15 45	7.7	09 01	13.9	21 20	13.7	00 39	10.1	13 02	9.9	07 53	8.0	20 17	7.7
9	Sunday	04 10	7.3	16 31	7.4	09 41	13.3	22 03	13.0	01 24	9.7	13 47	9.5	08 40	7.7	21 02	7.4
10	Monday	04 57	6.9	17 20	7.0	10 25	12.5	22 50	12.0	02 12	9.2	14 36	9.0	09 29	7.2	21 50	7.0
11	Tuesday	05 46	6.6	18 17	6.7	11 14	11.5	23 44	11.0	03 05	8.6	15 34	8.5	10 26	6.7	22 46	6.6
12	Wednesday	06 39	6.2	19 19	6.4	——	—	12 16	10.7	04 12	7.9	16 44	8.0	11 37	6.2	23 55	6.3
13	Thursday	07 42	6.1	20 27	6.2	00 51	10.3	13 34	10.4	05 33	7.6	18 07	7.9	——	—	13 17	6.0
14	Friday	08 53	6.0	21 46	6.3	02 14	10.2	14 58	10.8	06 59	7.7	19 24	8.1	01 25	6.2	14 41	6.1
15	Saturday	10 16	6.2	23 04	6.6	03 37	10.8	16 12	11.6	08 09	8.0	20 27	8.5	02 47	6.4	15 46	6.4
16	Sunday	11 29	6.6	——	—	04 45	11.7	17 10	12.4	09 04	8.5	21 18	8.9	03 47	6.7	16 35	6.7
17	Monday	00 04	7.0	12 24	7.0	05 37	12.4	17 58	13.0	09 46	8.8	22 00	9.2	04 35	7.0	17 14	6.9
18	Tuesday	00 52	7.2	13 09	7.1	06 19	12.8	18 37	13.0	10 24	9.0	22 37	9.3	05 14	7.2	17 48	7.0
19	Wednesday	01 34	7.3	13 47	7.2	06 56	12.9	19 12	13.0	10 58	9.2	23 11	9.3	05 51	7.4	18 19	7.2
20	Thursday	02 08	7.2	14 19	7.1	07 26	12.9	19 45	13.0	11 29	9.2	23 43	9.3	06 25	7.4	18 49	7.3
21	Friday	02 39	7.1	14 49	7.1	07 56	13.0	20 14	12.9	11 58	9.2	——	—	06 58	7.4	19 17	7.2
22	Saturday	03 05	7.0	15 17	7.0	08 24	12.9	20 42	12.6	00 15	9.2	12 28	9.1	07 32	7.3	19 46	7.1
23	Sunday	03 32	6.9	15 48	6.9	08 52	12.6	21 11	12.2	00 46	9.0	12 59	8.9	08 04	7.0	20 14	7.0
24	Monday	04 03	6.8	16 23	6.8	09 20	12.1	21 40	11.6	01 17	8.7	13 30	8.7	08 37	6.8	20 45	6.7
25	Tuesday	04 37	6.7	17 01	6.6	09 50	11.5	22 11	10.9	01 52	8.4	14 04	8.3	09 12	6.4	21 18	6.4
26	Wednesday	05 13	6.5	17 42	6.4	10 22	10.9	22 46	10.3	02 30	8.0	14 46	8.0	09 51	6.1	21 57	6.1
27	Thursday	05 53	6.2	18 27	6.1	11 04	10.3	23 37	9.8	03 19	7.6	15 41	7.6	10 41	5.8	22 50	5.8
28	Friday	06 41	5.9	19 24	5.9	——	—	12 06	9.9	04 26	7.3	16 55	7.4	11 51	5.7	——	—
29	Saturday	07 42	5.7	20 39	5.8	00 56	9.6	13 36	9.8	05 47	7.3	18 18	7.6	00 12	5.7	13 22	5.8
30	Sunday	09 08	5.7	22 02	6.1	02 30	10.1	15 04	10.8	07 03	7.7	19 28	8.1	01 43	5.9	14 34	6.1
31	Monday	10 30	6.1	23 11	6.5	03 44	11.1	16 11	11.9	08 05	8.3	20 25	8.7	02 49	6.3	15 33	6.6

SEPTEMBER 1994 *continued*

NOTES:
*Difference of height in metres from Ordnance datum (Newlyn)
†Difference of height in metres from Ordnance datum (Dublin)
hr hour
m metres

		GREENOCK				LEITH				DUN LAOGHAIRE			
		*Datum of predictions 1.62 m below				*Datum of predictions 2.90 m below				†Datum of predictions 0.20 m above			
		hr	ht m	hr	ht m	hr	ht m	hr	ht m	hr	ht m	hr	ht m
1	Thursday	08 26	2.7	20 42	2.9	10 45	4.3	23 17	4.5	08 12	3.3	20 33	3.4
2	Friday	10 12	2.8	21 58	3.1	11 58	4.6	—	—	09 08	3.4	21 22	3.6
3	Saturday	11 00	3.0	22 50	3.3	00 23	4.8	12 51	4.9	09 52	3.5	22 00	3.8
4	Sunday	11 41	3.1	23 33	3.4	01 12	5.2	13 35	5.3	10 27	3.7	22 34	3.9
5	Monday	12 19	3.2	—	—	01 53	5.5	14 14	5.5	11 00	3.9	23 07	4.1
6	Tuesday	00 15	3.5	12 58	3.3	02 31	5.7	14 54	5.7	11 34	4.0	23 45	4.3
7	Wednesday	00 58	3.6	13 36	3.3	03 09	5.9	15 32	5.8	—	—	12 10	4.1
8	Thursday	01 39	3.7	14 13	3.4	03 47	6.0	16 12	5.8	00 24	4.4	12 51	4.2
9	Friday	02 20	3.8	14 50	3.4	04 31	5.9	16 56	5.7	01 06	4.4	13 34	4.2
10	Saturday	03 00	3.7	15 28	3.4	05 16	5.8	17 42	5.5	01 55	4.3	14 22	4.1
11	Sunday	03 40	3.6	16 09	3.4	06 06	5.5	18 33	5.2	02 50	4.2	15 18	4.0
12	Monday	04 24	3.4	16 55	3.2	07 04	5.1	19 32	5.0	03 53	3.9	16 24	3.9
13	Tuesday	05 15	3.1	17 53	3.0	08 14	4.8	20 42	4.8	05 11	3.7	17 41	3.8
14	Wednesday	06 23	2.8	19 27	2.9	09 36	4.7	22 01	4.7	06 35	3.6	18 57	3.8
15	Thursday	08 51	2.8	21 19	3.1	10 57	4.8	23 19	4.9	07 55	3.6	20 09	3.9
16	Friday	10 04	3.0	22 19	3.3	—	—	12 08	5.0	09 06	3.7	21 13	4.0
17	Saturday	10 55	3.2	23 08	3.5	00 23	5.1	13 03	5.2	10 03	3.9	22 05	4.1
18	Sunday	11 39	3.3	23 52	3.6	01 14	5.4	13 46	5.4	10 47	3.9	22 47	4.2
19	Monday	12 19	3.4	—	—	01 57	5.5	14 23	5.5	11 21	3.9	23 20	4.2
20	Tuesday	00 34	3.6	12 56	3.4	02 34	5.6	14 56	5.5	11 49	3.9	23 49	4.2
21	Wednesday	01 11	3.6	13 28	3.4	03 09	5.6	15 29	5.5	—	—	12 13	3.9
22	Thursday	01 44	3.5	13 58	3.4	03 44	5.5	16 03	5.4	00 19	4.1	12 41	4.0
23	Friday	02 14	3.5	14 28	3.5	04 18	5.4	16 35	5.3	00 51	4.1	13 12	3.9
24	Saturday	02 45	3.5	14 59	3.5	04 53	5.3	17 10	5.1	01 27	4.0	13 51	3.9
25	Sunday	03 17	3.4	15 33	3.5	05 30	5.1	17 48	4.9	02 08	3.8	14 34	3.8
26	Monday	03 52	3.2	16 10	3.4	06 09	4.8	18 29	4.7	02 57	3.6	15 23	3.6
27	Tuesday	04 32	3.1	16 53	3.2	06 54	4.6	19 17	4.5	03 51	3.4	16 21	3.4
28	Wednesday	05 22	2.9	17 45	3.1	07 48	4.4	20 11	4.4	04 58	3.3	17 31	3.3
29	Thursday	06 28	2.7	18 48	3.0	08 49	4.3	21 18	4.4	06 21	3.2	18 48	3.3
30	Friday	07 48	2.7	20 00	3.0	10 01	4.4	22 31	4.5	07 34	3.3	19 51	3.4

OCTOBER 1994 *continued*

		GREENOCK				LEITH				DUN LAOGHAIRE			
1	Saturday	09 28	2.8	21 16	3.1	11 16	4.6	23 41	4.8	08 31	3.4	20 42	3.6
2	Sunday	10 26	3.0	22 15	3.3	—	—	12 16	5.0	09 16	3.6	21 23	3.8
3	Monday	11 09	3.2	23 03	3.5	00 34	5.2	13 04	5.4	09 54	3.8	22 01	4.0
4	Tuesday	11 49	3.3	23 48	3.6	01 19	5.5	13 46	5.7	10 30	4.0	22 40	4.2
5	Wednesday	12 29	3.4	—	—	02 00	5.8	14 26	5.9	11 07	4.2	23 20	4.4
6	Thursday	00 33	3.7	13 09	3.5	02 42	6.0	15 08	6.0	11 46	4.3	—	—
7	Friday	01 19	3.7	13 49	3.6	03 25	6.1	15 50	5.9	00 03	4.5	12 28	4.4
8	Saturday	02 02	3.8	14 27	3.6	04 11	6.0	16 35	5.8	00 50	4.5	13 13	4.4
9	Sunday	02 44	3.7	15 07	3.6	05 00	5.8	17 23	5.6	01 41	4.4	14 04	4.3
10	Monday	03 26	3.6	15 48	3.5	05 54	5.5	18 15	5.3	02 38	4.1	15 01	4.1
11	Tuesday	04 12	3.4	16 36	3.4	06 54	5.1	19 17	5.0	03 46	3.9	16 07	4.0
12	Wednesday	05 05	3.1	17 35	3.2	08 03	4.9	20 27	4.8	05 02	3.7	17 21	3.8
13	Thursday	06 21	2.9	19 04	3.1	09 20	4.7	21 41	4.8	06 24	3.6	18 38	3.8
14	Friday	08 30	2.9	20 50	3.1	10 38	4.8	22 56	4.9	07 45	3.6	19 49	3.9
15	Saturday	09 41	3.0	21 53	3.3	11 45	5.0	23 59	5.1	08 52	3.7	20 52	4.0
16	Sunday	10 30	3.2	22 42	3.5	—	—	12 39	5.2	09 45	3.8	21 43	4.0
17	Monday	11 12	3.3	23 27	3.5	00 51	5.3	13 22	5.3	10 24	3.9	22 23	4.1
18	Tuesday	11 50	3.4	—	—	01 34	5.4	13 59	5.4	10 56	3.9	22 54	4.1
19	Wednesday	00 07	3.5	12 25	3.4	02 11	5.4	14 31	5.4	11 21	3.9	23 22	4.0
20	Thursday	00 45	3.4	12 57	3.4	02 45	5.5	15 02	5.4	11 45	4.0	23 53	4.0
21	Friday	01 18	3.4	13 27	3.5	03 19	5.4	15 34	5.4	—	—	12 14	4.0
22	Saturday	01 48	3.4	13 57	3.5	03 51	5.4	16 07	5.3	00 26	4.0	12 47	4.0
23	Sunday	02 19	3.3	14 29	3.6	04 26	5.3	16 42	5.2	01 01	3.9	13 24	3.9
24	Monday	02 51	3.3	15 02	3.6	05 03	5.1	17 19	5.0	01 43	3.8	14 06	3.8
25	Tuesday	03 28	3.2	15 39	3.5	05 42	4.9	17 56	4.9	02 29	3.6	14 54	3.7
26	Wednesday	04 08	3.1	16 20	3.4	06 26	4.7	18 41	4.7	03 22	3.5	15 48	3.5
27	Thursday	04 56	2.9	17 08	3.2	07 15	4.6	19 36	4.5	04 24	3.3	16 48	3.4
28	Friday	05 59	2.8	18 08	3.1	08 14	4.5	20 38	4.5	05 34	3.3	17 57	3.4
29	Saturday	07 13	2.8	19 18	3.0	09 22	4.5	21 47	4.6	06 46	3.3	19 02	3.4
30	Sunday	08 35	2.8	20 33	3.1	10 34	4.7	22 56	4.9	07 47	3.4	19 58	3.6
31	Monday	09 44	3.0	21 39	3.3	11 37	5.0	23 56	5.2	08 36	3.6	20 47	3.8

NOVEMBER 1994 *High water* GMT

	London Bridge *Datum of predictions 3.20 m below*				Avonmouth *Datum of predictions 6.50 m below*				Liverpool *Datum of predictions 4.93 m below*				Hull (*Albert Dock*) *Datum of predictions 3.90 m below*			
	hr	ht m	hr	ht m	hr	ht m	hr	ht m	hr	ht m	hr	ht m	hr	ht m	hr	ht m
1 Tuesday	11 33	6.6	—	—	04 45	12.2	17 09	12.9	08 57	8.9	21 17	9.3	03 44	6.8	16 24	7.0
2 Wednesday	00 07	7.0	12 25	7.1	05 38	13.1	18 01	13.6	09 45	9.4	22 03	9.7	04 35	7.3	17 10	7.4
3 Thursday	00 56	7.3	13 13	7.4	06 29	13.7	18 50	14.0	10 30	9.8	22 49	10.0	05 21	7.6	17 52	7.7
4 Friday	01 41	7.4	13 58	7.6	07 15	14.0	19 36	14.2	11 15	10.1	23 36	10.1	06 08	7.9	18 34	7.9
5 Saturday	02 25	7.5	14 43	7.7	08 00	14.1	20 21	14.1	—	—	12 00	10.1	06 54	8.0	19 17	7.9
6 Sunday	03 08	7.5	15 31	7.7	08 44	14.0	21 06	13.7	00 24	10.0	12 45	9.9	07 41	7.9	20 02	7.8
7 Monday	03 55	7.3	16 20	7.5	09 29	13.5	21 53	13.0	01 10	9.7	13 33	9.6	08 30	7.6	20 47	7.5
8 Tuesday	04 42	7.1	17 11	7.3	10 15	12.7	22 39	12.1	02 01	9.2	14 23	9.2	09 20	7.2	21 34	7.2
9 Wednesday	05 32	6.8	18 04	6.9	11 04	11.9	23 31	11.3	02 54	8.6	15 18	8.7	10 15	6.7	22 26	6.8
10 Thursday	06 22	6.5	19 00	6.6	—	—	12 01	11.1	03 55	8.1	16 21	8.3	11 20	6.2	23 27	6.5
11 Friday	07 17	6.2	20 01	6.3	00 30	11.6	13 05	10.7	05 05	7.7	17 32	8.0	—	—	12 43	6.0
12 Saturday	08 20	6.1	21 11	6.2	01 39	10.3	14 20	10.7	06 22	7.6	18 46	8.0	00 40	6.3	14 06	6.0
13 Sunday	09 36	6.1	22 28	6.4	02 56	10.6	15 33	11.1	07 33	7.8	19 52	8.2	02 04	6.3	15 11	6.2
14 Monday	10 55	6.3	23 33	6.7	04 05	11.1	16 35	11.7	08 30	8.2	20 46	8.5	03 12	6.5	16 03	6.4
15 Tuesday	11 54	6.7	—	—	05 02	11.7	17 24	12.2	09 17	8.5	21 31	8.7	04 05	6.7	16 45	6.6
16 Wednesday	00 24	7.0	12 41	6.9	05 47	12.2	18 06	12.4	09 56	8.7	22 10	8.9	04 49	6.9	17 20	6.8
17 Thursday	01 04	7.1	13 20	7.0	06 25	12.4	18 44	12.5	10 31	8.9	22 45	9.0	05 27	7.0	17 52	7.0
18 Friday	01 41	7.0	13 54	7.0	06 58	12.6	19 18	12.6	11 04	9.1	23 19	9.1	06 04	7.1	18 23	7.1
19 Saturday	02 11	7.0	14 25	7.0	07 31	12.7	19 50	12.6	11 34	9.1	23 51	9.0	06 39	7.1	18 53	7.2
20 Sunday	02 40	7.0	14 56	7.0	08 00	12.7	20 20	12.5	—	—	12 07	9.1	07 11	7.1	19 21	7.1
21 Monday	03 10	6.9	15 29	6.9	08 30	12.6	20 51	12.3	00 25	8.9	12 38	9.0	07 45	7.0	19 52	7.0
22 Tuesday	03 43	6.9	16 06	6.9	09 02	12.4	21 25	11.9	00 57	8.8	13 12	8.8	08 19	6.8	20 26	6.9
23 Wednesday	04 17	6.8	16 42	6.8	09 36	12.0	21 58	11.5	01 34	8.5	13 47	8.6	08 55	6.6	21 01	6.7
24 Thursday	04 54	6.6	17 22	6.6	10 12	11.5	22 38	11.0	02 12	8.3	14 27	8.3	09 36	6.4	21 40	6.5
25 Friday	05 32	6.4	18 05	6.4	10 55	11.0	23 24	10.5	02 57	8.0	15 17	8.1	10 22	6.2	22 28	6.2
26 Saturday	06 14	6.2	18 56	6.2	11 47	10.7	—	—	03 53	7.7	16 17	7.9	11 17	6.0	23 30	6.1
27 Sunday	07 09	6.0	20 02	6.1	00 23	10.2	12 56	10.5	05 01	7.6	17 27	7.9	—	—	12 27	6.0
28 Monday	08 23	5.9	21 21	6.2	01 41	10.3	14 17	10.9	06 15	7.8	18 41	8.2	00 46	6.1	13 45	6.2
29 Tuesday	09 46	6.1	22 34	6.5	03 01	10.9	15 30	11.6	07 24	8.2	19 48	8.6	02 02	6.4	14 51	6.5
30 Wednesday	10 58	6.5	23 37	6.9	04 08	11.8	16 35	12.4	08 23	8.8	20 47	9.0	03 08	6.7	15 51	6.9

DECEMBER 1994 *High water* GMT

	London Bridge				Avonmouth				Liverpool				Hull (*Albert Dock*)			
1 Thursday	11 58	6.9	—	—	05 09	12.7	17 34	13.1	09 18	9.2	21 41	9.5	04 07	7.1	16 45	7.3
2 Friday	00 32	7.2	12 52	7.1	06 05	13.3	18 29	13.6	10 09	9.6	22 33	9.7	05 03	7.5	17 33	7.5
3 Saturday	01 23	7.2	13 42	7.3	06 56	13.8	19 21	13.8	10 58	9.9	23 22	9.9	05 55	7.7	18 19	7.7
4 Sunday	02 09	7.2	14 32	7.5	07 45	14.0	20 09	13.9	11 46	10.0	—	—	06 44	7.8	19 03	7.8
5 Monday	02 56	7.3	15 19	7.6	08 31	14.0	20 56	13.7	00 11	9.8	12 34	10.0	07 34	7.7	19 48	7.8
6 Tuesday	03 42	7.3	16 09	7.6	09 18	13.7	21 41	13.2	01 00	9.6	13 20	9.8	08 21	7.5	20 31	7.7
7 Wednesday	04 28	7.3	16 58	7.4	10 03	13.1	22 26	12.5	01 48	9.2	14 08	9.4	09 09	7.2	21 16	7.5
8 Thursday	05 15	7.0	17 47	7.1	10 49	12.4	23 11	11.6	02 37	8.8	14 57	9.0	09 58	6.8	22 04	7.2
9 Friday	06 00	6.7	18 36	6.8	11 37	11.6	23 59	11.0	03 28	8.3	15 49	8.5	10 50	6.4	22 55	6.8
10 Saturday	06 49	6.4	19 28	6.4	—	—	12 29	11.0	04 24	7.9	16 48	8.1	11 49	6.1	23 52	6.5
11 Sunday	07 42	6.1	20 29	6.2	00 53	10.5	13 29	10.6	05 29	7.6	17 54	7.8	—	—	13 03	5.9
12 Monday	08 47	6.0	21 39	6.1	01 59	10.2	14 38	10.5	06 41	7.5	19 03	7.8	01 03	6.2	14 17	5.9
13 Tuesday	10 04	6.0	22 52	6.3	03 12	10.4	15 47	10.8	07 47	7.7	20 06	7.9	02 20	6.2	15 19	6.1
14 Wednesday	11 18	6.2	23 49	6.5	04 17	10.8	16 45	11.2	08 42	8.0	20 58	8.2	03 27	6.3	16 10	6.3
15 Thursday	—	—	12 10	6.6	05 09	11.4	17 34	11.7	09 27	8.3	21 43	8.4	04 19	6.5	16 52	6.6
16 Friday	00 35	6.7	12 53	6.6	05 54	11.9	18 18	12.0	10 06	8.6	22 23	8.7	05 04	6.6	17 28	6.8
17 Saturday	01 13	6.8	13 30	6.7	06 33	12.2	18 56	12.2	10 41	8.9	22 59	8.8	05 45	6.8	18 02	7.0
18 Sunday	01 47	6.9	14 04	6.8	07 08	12.5	19 31	12.4	11 16	9.0	23 33	8.9	06 20	6.9	18 33	7.1
19 Monday	02 19	6.9	14 39	6.9	07 42	12.6	20 04	12.5	11 49	9.1	—	—	06 54	7.0	19 04	7.2
20 Tuesday	02 54	7.0	15 15	7.0	08 16	12.7	20 38	12.5	00 08	8.9	12 22	9.1	07 28	7.0	19 36	7.2
21 Wednesday	03 29	7.0	15 52	7.0	08 49	12.8	21 13	12.4	00 43	8.9	12 57	9.1	08 03	7.0	20 11	7.2
22 Thursday	04 04	6.9	16 30	7.0	09 26	12.6	21 50	12.2	01 19	8.8	13 33	8.9	08 41	7.0	20 48	7.1
23 Friday	04 40	6.8	17 06	6.9	10 04	12.3	22 28	11.8	01 57	8.6	14 12	8.8	09 20	6.8	21 26	6.9
24 Saturday	05 15	6.7	17 47	6.7	10 43	11.9	23 09	11.3	02 39	8.4	14 54	8.6	10 01	6.6	22 10	6.7
25 Sunday	05 54	6.5	18 32	6.4	11 28	11.4	23 56	10.9	03 27	8.2	15 46	8.4	10 49	6.5	23 00	6.6
26 Monday	06 41	6.3	19 30	6.2	—	—	12 23	11.1	04 23	8.0	16 47	8.2	11 45	6.3	—	—
27 Tuesday	07 45	6.1	20 43	6.2	01 00	10.6	13 34	10.9	05 32	8.0	17 58	8.2	00 02	6.4	12 57	6.3
28 Wednesday	09 07	6.1	21 59	6.4	02 19	10.7	14 54	11.2	06 46	8.1	19 14	8.3	01 18	6.4	14 13	6.4
29 Thursday	10 26	6.4	23 11	6.7	03 34	11.3	16 07	11.8	07 55	8.4	20 25	8.6	02 34	6.6	15 23	6.7
30 Friday	11 37	6.7	—	—	04 43	12.1	17 14	12.4	08 58	8.9	21 25	9.0	03 47	6.9	16 25	7.0
31 Saturday	00 14	6.9	12 39	6.9	05 47	12.8	18 15	13.0	09 55	9.3	22 21	9.4	04 52	7.2	17 19	7.3

NOVEMBER 1994   *continued*

		GREENOCK				LEITH				DUN LAOGHAIRE			
		*Datum of predictions 1.62 m below				*Datum of predictions 2.90 m below				†Datum of predictions 0.20 m above			
		hr	ht m	hr	ht m	hr	ht m	hr	ht m	hr	ht m	hr	ht m
1	Tuesday	10 34	3.2	22 33	3.5	—	—	12 30	5.4	09 22	3.8	21 32	4.1
2	Wednesday	11 19	3.4	23 22	3.6	00 47	5.5	13 17	5.7	10 03	4.1	22 16	4.3
3	Thursday	12 02	3.5	—	—	01 34	5.8	14 00	5.9	10 44	4.3	23 01	4.4
4	Friday	00 11	3.7	12 45	3.6	02 20	6.0	14 44	6.0	11 27	4.4	23 48	4.5
5	Saturday	00 59	3.7	13 28	3.7	03 06	6.1	15 29	6.0	—	—	12 12	4.5
6	Sunday	01 46	3.7	14 09	3.8	03 56	6.0	16 17	5.8	00 37	4.5	12 58	4.5
7	Monday	02 31	3.7	14 51	3.8	04 46	5.8	17 06	5.6	01 31	4.3	13 50	4.4
8	Tuesday	03 17	3.6	15 34	3.7	05 41	5.5	17 59	5.4	02 28	4.1	14 45	4.2
9	Wednesday	04 04	3.4	16 21	3.6	06 41	5.2	19 00	5.1	03 34	3.9	15 48	4.1
10	Thursday	04 59	3.2	17 18	3.4	07 46	4.9	20 06	4.9	04 47	3.6	16 57	3.9
11	Friday	06 07	3.0	18 29	3.2	08 54	4.8	21 13	4.8	06 03	3.5	18 08	3.8
12	Saturday	07 32	3.0	20 01	3.2	10 03	4.7	22 21	4.8	07 17	3.5	19 18	3.8
13	Sunday	08 57	3.0	21 16	3.3	11 09	4.8	23 26	4.9	08 22	3.6	20 21	3.8
14	Monday	09 53	3.2	22 11	3.3	—	—	12 05	5.0	09 13	3.7	21 12	3.9
15	Tuesday	10 37	3.3	22 57	3.4	00 20	5.0	12 51	5.1	19 54	3.8	21 54	3.9
16	Wednesday	11 17	3.4	23 40	3.4	01 07	5.2	13 32	5.2	10 27	3.9	22 29	3.9
17	Thursday	11 54	3.4	—	—	01 46	5.2	14 07	5.3	10 54	3.9	23 00	3.9
18	Friday	00 18	3.3	12 29	3.5	02 23	5.3	14 40	5.3	11 24	4.0	23 34	3.9
19	Saturday	00 54	3.3	13 00	3.5	02 56	5.3	15 12	5.4	11 55	4.0	—	—
20	Sunday	01 25	3.2	13 31	3.6	03 30	5.3	15 46	5.3	00 06	3.9	12 27	4.0
21	Monday	01 57	3.2	14 03	3.6	04 05	5.2	16 19	5.2	00 43	3.8	13 02	4.0
22	Tuesday	02 31	3.2	14 38	3.6	04 42	5.1	16 56	5.1	01 23	3.7	13 44	3.9
23	Wednesday	03 08	3.2	15 15	3.6	05 20	5.0	17 33	5.0	02 06	3.6	14 28	3.8
24	Thursday	03 49	3.1	15 55	3.5	06 02	4.9	18 15	4.9	02 55	3.5	15 16	3.6
25	Friday	04 35	3.0	16 38	3.4	06 49	4.8	19 04	4.8	03 50	3.4	16 09	3.5
26	Saturday	05 30	2.9	17 30	3.2	07 43	4.7	20 02	4.7	04 50	3.4	17 09	3.5
27	Sunday	06 35	2.9	18 33	3.2	08 45	4.7	21 06	4.7	05 55	3.4	18 14	3.6
28	Monday	07 46	2.9	19 46	3.2	09 53	4.8	22 14	4.9	07 00	3.5	19 17	3.7
29	Tuesday	08 59	3.0	21 01	3.3	10 59	5.0	23 20	5.1	07 59	3.7	20 15	3.9
30	Wednesday	10 00	3.2	22 04	3.4	11 58	5.3	—	—	08 51	3.9	21 09	4.1

NOTES:

*Difference of height in metres from Ordnance datum (Newlyn)

†Difference of height in metres from Ordnance datum (Dublin)

hr hour

m metres

DECEMBER 1994   *continued*

		GREENOCK				LEITH				DUN LAOGHAIRE			
1	Thursday	10 52	3.3	22 59	3.5	00 19	5.4	12 50	5.5	09 39	4.1	22 00	4.3
2	Friday	11 40	3.5	23 52	3.6	01 12	5.7	13 39	5.7	10 26	4.3	22 50	4.4
3	Saturday	12 26	3.6	—	—	02 03	5.9	14 26	5.9	11 11	4.4	23 38	4.4
4	Sunday	00 44	3.6	13 12	3.8	02 52	6.0	15 12	5.9	11 58	4.5	—	—
5	Monday	01 35	3.6	13 56	3.9	03 43	6.0	16 01	5.9	00 28	4.4	12 45	4.5
6	Tuesday	02 23	3.6	14 39	3.9	04 34	5.8	16 52	5.7	01 20	4.3	13 34	4.5
7	Wednesday	03 09	3.6	15 22	3.9	05 27	5.6	17 44	5.5	02 15	4.1	14 26	4.3
8	Thursday	03 55	3.5	16 07	3.8	06 22	5.3	18 39	5.3	03 12	3.8	15 22	4.1
9	Friday	04 44	3.3	16 56	3.6	07 18	5.0	19 36	5.0	04 15	3.6	16 22	3.9
10	Saturday	05 36	3.2	17 51	3.4	08 16	4.8	20 35	4.9	05 22	3.5	17 28	3.8
11	Sunday	06 33	3.1	18 54	3.3	09 16	4.7	21 37	4.7	06 31	3.5	18 36	3.7
12	Monday	07 38	3.0	20 14	3.1	10 19	4.6	22 41	4.7	07 35	3.5	19 40	3.7
13	Tuesday	08 53	3.1	21 30	3.1	11 21	4.7	23 42	4.8	08 31	3.6	20 36	3.7
14	Wednesday	09 56	3.2	22 27	3.2	—	—	12 16	4.9	09 17	3.7	21 23	3.7
15	Thursday	10 44	3.3	23 14	3.2	00 37	4.9	13 04	5.0	09 56	3.8	22 04	3.8
16	Friday	11 26	3.4	23 56	3.2	01 22	5.0	13 43	5.1	10 31	3.9	22 41	3.8
17	Saturday	12 04	3.5	—	—	02 02	5.1	14 20	5.2	11 05	4.0	23 17	3.8
18	Sunday	00 35	3.2	12 38	3.5	02 38	5.2	14 54	5.3	11 38	4.0	23 50	3.8
19	Monday	01 10	3.2	13 10	3.6	03 12	5.3	15 29	5.3	—	—	12 12	4.0
20	Tuesday	01 42	3.2	13 43	3.6	03 47	5.3	16 03	5.3	00 24	3.8	12 44	4.0
21	Wednesday	02 16	3.2	14 18	3.7	04 22	5.2	16 38	5.3	01 01	3.8	13 20	4.0
22	Thursday	02 53	3.2	14 56	3.7	05 00	5.2	17 13	5.2	01 41	3.7	14 01	3.9
23	Friday	03 32	3.2	15 34	3.6	05 40	5.1	17 52	5.1	02 25	3.7	14 45	3.8
24	Saturday	04 14	3.1	16 15	3.5	06 23	5.0	18 36	5.0	03 15	3.6	15 36	3.7
25	Sunday	05 00	3.0	17 00	3.4	07 14	4.9	19 28	4.9	04 09	3.5	16 32	3.7
26	Monday	05 54	3.0	17 53	3.3	08 10	4.8	20 27	4.9	05 11	3.5	17 34	3.7
27	Tuesday	06 56	2.9	18 55	3.2	09 13	4.8	21 36	4.9	06 18	3.5	18 43	3.8
28	Wednesday	08 11	2.9	20 18	3.2	10 22	4.9	22 49	5.0	07 25	3.7	19 51	3.9
29	Thursday	09 29	3.1	21 39	3.2	11 30	5.1	23 59	5.2	08 26	3.9	20 51	4.0
30	Friday	10 31	3.3	22 44	3.3	—	—	12 29	5.3	09 22	4.1	21 47	4.2
31	Sat day	11 24	3.5	23 41	3.4	01 00	5.5	13 22	5.5	10 12	4.3	22 41	4.3

World Geographical Statistics

THE EARTH

The shape of the Earth is that of an oblate spheroid or solid of revolution whose meridian sections are ellipses, whilst the sections at right angles are circles.

DIMENSIONS

Equatorial diameter = 12,756.28 km (7,926.38 miles)
Polar diameter = 12,713.50 km (7,899.80 miles)
Equatorial circumference = 40,075.01 km (24,901.45 miles)
Polar circumference = 40,008.00 km (24,859.82 miles)

The equatorial circumference is divided into 360 degrees of longitude, which is measured in degrees, minutes and seconds east or west of the Greenwich meridian (0°) to 180° (the meridian 180° E. coinciding with 180° W.). This was internationally ratified in 1884.

Distance north and south of the Equator is measured in degrees, minutes and seconds of latitude. The Equator is 0°, the North Pole is 90° N. and the South Pole is 90° S. The Tropics lie at 23° 26' N. (Tropic of Cancer) and 23° 26' S. (Tropic of Capricorn). The Arctic Circle lies at 66° 34' N. and the Antarctic Circle at 66° 34' S. (NB The Tropics and the Arctic and Antarctic circles are of variable latitude due to the mean obliquity of the Ecliptic; the values given are for 1994.5.)

AREA, ETC.

The surface area of the Earth is 510,069,120 km² (196,938,800 miles²), of which the water area is 70.92 per cent and the land area is 29.08 per cent.

The velocity of a given point of the Earth's surface at the Equator exceeds 1,000 miles an hour (24,901.45 miles in 24 hours, viz 1,037.56 mph); the Earth's velocity in its orbit round the Sun averages 66,629 mph (584,081,400 miles in 365.256363 days). The Earth is distant from the Sun 92,955,900 miles, on average.

Source: Royal Greenwich Observatory

OCEAN AREAS

	Area km²	miles²
Pacific	166,240,000	64,186,300
Atlantic	86,550,000	33,420,000
Indian	73,427,000	28,350,500
Arctic	13,223,700	5,105,700

GREATEST OCEAN DEPTHS

Greatest depth location	Depth metres	feet
Mariana Trench (Pacific)	10,916	35,839
Puerto Rico Trench (Atlantic)	8,605	28,232
Java Trench (Indian)	7,125	23,376
Eurasian Basin (Arctic)	5,450	17,880

SEA AREAS

	Area km²	miles²
South China	2,974,600	1,148,500
Caribbean	2,515,900	971,400
Mediterranean	2,509,900	969,100
Bering	2,226,100	873,000
Gulf of Mexico	1,507,600	582,100
Okhotsk	1,392,000	537,500
Japan	1,015,000	391,100
Hudson Bay	730,100	281,900
East China	664,600	256,600
Andaman	564,880	218,100
Black Sea	507,900	196,100
Red Sea	453,000	174,900
North Sea	427,100	164,900
Baltic Sea	382,000	147,500
Yellow Sea	294,000	113,500
Persian Gulf	230,000	88,800

THE CONTINENTS

There are six geographic continents, though America is often divided politically into North and Central America, and South America.

AFRICA is surrounded by sea except for the narrow isthmus of Suez in the north-east, through which is cut the Suez Canal. The Equator passes through the middle of the continent. Its extreme longitudes are 17° 20' W. at Cape Verde, Senegal, and 51° 24' E. at Ras Hafun, Somalia. The extreme latitudes are 37° 20' N. at Cape Blanc, Tunisia, and 34° 50' S. at Cape Agulhas, South Africa, about 4,400 miles apart.

NORTH AMERICA, including Mexico, is surrounded by ocean except in the south, where the isthmian states of CENTRAL AMERICA link North America with South America. Its extreme longitudes are 168° 5' W. at Cape Prince of Wales, Alaska, and 55° 40' W. at Cape Charles, Newfoundland. The extreme continental latitudes are Point Barrow, Alaska (71°22' N.) and 14°22' N. at Ocós in the south of Mexico. The West Indies, about 65,000 square miles in area, extend from about 27° N. to 10° N. latitude.

SOUTH AMERICA lies mostly in the southern hemisphere; the Equator passes through the north of the continent. It is surrounded by ocean except where it is joined to Central America in the north by the narrow isthmus through which is cut the Panama Canal. Its extreme longitudes are 34° 47' W. at Cape Branco in Brazil and 81° 20' W. at Punta Pariña, Peru. The extreme latitudes are 12° 25' N. at Punta Gallinas, Colombia, and 55° 59' S. at Cape Horn, Chile.

ANTARCTICA lies almost entirely within the Antarctic Circle (66° 34' S.) and is the largest of the world's glaciated areas. The continent has an area of about 5.5 million square miles, 99 per cent of which is permanently ice-covered. The ice amounts to some 7.2 million cubic miles and represents more than 90 per cent of the world's fresh water. The environment is too hostile for unsupported human habitation. *See also* Countries of the World.

ASIA is the largest continent and occupies almost a third of the world's land surface. The extreme longitudes are about 26° E. on the west coast of Asia Minor and 169° 40′ W. at Mys Dežneva (East Cape), Russia, a distance of about 6,000 miles. Its extreme northern latitude is 77° 45′ N. at Cape Čeljuskin, Russia, and it extends over 5,000 miles south to about 1° 15′ N. of the Equator. The islands of Japan, the Philippines and Indonesia ring the continent to the east and south-east.

AUSTRALIA is the smallest of the continents and lies in the southern hemisphere. It is entirely surrounded by ocean. Its extreme longitudes are 113° 9′ E. at Steep Point and 153° 38′ E. at Cape Byron. The extreme latitudes are 10° 40′ S. at Cape York and 39° S. at South East Point.

EUROPE, including European Russia, is the smallest continent in the northern hemisphere. Its extreme latitudes are 71° 11′ N. at North Cape in Norway, and 36° 23′ N. at Cape Matapan in southern Greece, a distance of about 2,400 miles. Its breadth from Cape da Roca in Portugal (9° 30′ W.) in the west to the Urals in the east is about 3,300 miles. The division between Europe and Asia is generally regarded as being the Ural Mountains and, in the south, the valley of the Manych, which stretches from the Caspian Sea to the mouth of the Don.

	Area km²	miles²
Asia	43,998,000	16,988,000
*America	41,918,000	16,185,000
Africa	29,800,000	11,506,000
Antarctica	c.13,600,000	c.5,500,000
†Europe	9,699,000	3,745,000
Australia	7,618,493	2,941,526

*North and Central America has an area of 24,255,000 km² (9,365,000 miles²)

†Includes 5,571,000 km² (2,151,000 miles²) of CIS territory west of the Ural Mountains

GLACIATED AREAS

It is estimated that 15,600,000 km² (6,020,000 miles²) or 10.51 per cent of the world's land surface is permanently covered with ice.

	Area km²	miles²
South Polar regions	13,597,000	5,250,000
North Polar regions (incl. Greenland or Kalaallit Nunaat)	1,965,000	758,500
Alaska-Canada	58,800	22,700
Asia	37,800	14,600
South America	11,900	4,600
Europe	10,700	4,128
New Zealand	984	380
Africa	238	92

PENINSULAS

	Area km²	miles²
Arabian	3,250,000	1,250,000
Southern Indian	2,072,000	800,000
Alaskan	1,500,000	580,000
Labradorian	1,300,000	500,000
Scandinavian	800,300	309,000
Iberian	584,000	225,500

LARGEST ISLANDS

Island (and Ocean)	Area km²	miles²
Greenland (Arctic)	2,175,500	840,000
New Guinea (Pacific)	792,500	306,000
Borneo (Pacific)	725,450	280,100
Madagascar (Indian)	587,040	226,658
Baffin Island (Arctic)	507,528	195,928
Sumatra (Indian)	427,350	165,000
Honshu (Pacific)	227,413	87,805
*Great Britain (Atlantic)	218,040	84,186
Victoria Island (Arctic)	217,290	83,895
Ellesmere Island (Arctic)	196,235	75,767
Sulawesi (Celebes) (Indian)	178,700	69,000
South Island, NZ (Pacific)	151,010	58,305
Java (Indian)	126,650	48,900
Cuba (Atlantic)	114,525	44,218
North Island, NZ (Pacific)	114,050	44,035
Newfoundland (Atlantic)	108,855	42,030
Luzon (Pacific)	105,880	40,880
Iceland (Atlantic)	103,000	39,770
Mindanao (Pacific)	95,247	36,775
Ireland (Atlantic)	82,462	31,839

*Mainland only

LARGEST DESERTS

	Area (approx.) km²	miles²
The Sahara (N. Africa)	8,400,000	3,250,000
Australian Desert	1,550,000	600,000
Arabian Desert	1,300,000	500,000
*The Gobi (Mongolia/China)	1,170,000	450,000
Kalahari Desert (Botswana/ Namibia/S. Africa)	520,000	200,000
Sonoran Desert (USA/Mexico)	310,000	120,000
Namib Desert (Namibia)	310,000	120,000
†Kara Kum (Turkmenistan)	270,000	105,000
Thar Desert (India/Pakistan)	260,000	100,000
Somali Desert (Somalia)	260,000	100,000
Atacama Desert (Chile)	180,000	70,000
†Kyzyl Kum (Kazakhstan/ Uzbekistan)	180,000	70,000
Dasht-e Lut (Iran)	52,000	20,000
Mojave Desert (USA)	35,000	13,500
Desierto de Sechura (Peru)	26,000	10,000

*Including the Takla Makan – 320,000 km² (125,000 miles²)

†Together known as the Turkestan Desert

DEEPEST DEPRESSIONS

	Maximum depth below sea level	
	metres	feet
Dead Sea (Jordan/Israel)	395	1,296
Turfan Depression (Sinkiang, China)	153	505
Qattara Depression (Egypt)	132	436
Mangyshlak peninsula (Kazakhstan)	131	433
Danakil Depression (Ethiopia)	116	383
Death Valley (California, USA)	86	282
Salton Sink (California, USA)	71	235
W. of Ustyurt plateau (Kazakhstan)	70	230
Prikaspiyskaya Nizmennost' (Russia/ Kazakhstan)	67	220
Lake Sarykamysh (Uzbekistan/ Turkmenistan)	45	148
El Faiyûm (Egypt)	44	147
Valdies peninsula, Lago Enriquillo (Dominican Republic)	40	131

The world's largest exposed depression is the Prikaspiyskaya Nizmennost' covering the hinterland of the northern third of the Caspian Sea, which is itself 28 m (92 ft) below sea level

Western Antarctica and Central Greenland largely comprise crypto-depressions under ice burdens. The Antarctic Wilkes subglacial basin has a bedrock 2,341 m (7,680 ft) below sea-level. In Greenland (lat. 73° N., long. 39° W.) the bedrock is 365 m (1,197 ft) below sea-level

LONGEST MOUNTAIN RANGES

Range (location)	Length	
	km	miles
Cordillera de Los Andes (W. South America)	7,200	4,500
Rocky Mountains (W. North America)	4,800	3,000
Himalaya-Karakoram-Hindu Kush (S. Central Asia)	3,800	2,400
Great Dividing Range (E. Australia)	3,600	2,250
Trans-Antarctic Mts (Antarctica)	3,500	2,200
Atlantic Coast Range (E. Brazil)	3,000	1,900
West Sumatran-Javan Range (Indonesia)	2,900	1,800
Aleutian Range (Alaska and NW Pacific)	2,650	1,650
Tien Shan (S. Central Asia)	2,250	1,400
Central New Guinea Range (Irian Jaya/ Papua New Guinea)	2,000	1,250

HIGHEST MOUNTAINS

The world's 8,000-metre mountains (with six subsidiary peaks) are all in the 3,800 km (2,400 mile) long Himalaya-Karakoram-Hindu Kush range of south central Asia.

Mountain	Height	
	metres	feet
Mt Everest*	8,848	29,028
K2	8,607	28,238
Kangchenjunga	8,597	28,208
Lhotse	8,511	27,923
Makalu I	8,481	27,824
Lhotse Shar	8,383	27,504
Dhaulagiri I	8,167	26,795
Manaslu I (Kutang I)	8,156	26,760
Cho Oyu	8,153	26,750
Nanga Parbat (Diamir)	8,125	26,660
Annapurna I	8,091	26,546
Gasherbrum I (Hidden Peak)	8,068	26,470
Broad Peak I	8,046	26,400
Shisha Pangma (Gosainthan)	8,046	26,398
Gasherbrum II	8,034	26,360
Annapurna East	8,010	26,280
Makalu South-East	8,010	26,280
Broad Peak Central	8,000	26,246

*Named after Sir George Everest (1790–1866), Surveyor-General of India 1830–43, in 1863. He pronounced his name Eve-rest

The culminating summits in the other major mountain ranges are:

Mountain (range or country)	Height	
	metres	feet
Pik Pobeda (Tien Shan)	7,439	24,406
Cerro Aconcagua (Cordillera de Los Andes)	6,960	22,834
Mt McKinley, S. Peak (Alaska Range)	6,194	20,320
Kilimanjaro (Tanzania)	5,894	19,340
Hkakabo Razi (Myanmar)	5,881	19,296
Citlaltépetl (Orizaba) (Sierra Madre Oriental, Mexico)	5,699	18,700
El'brus, W. Peak (Caucasus)	5,663	18,481
Vinson Massif (E. Antarctica)	4,897	16,067
Puncak Jaya (Central New Guinea Range)	4,884	16,023
Mt Blanc (Alps)	4,807	15,771
Klyuchevskaya Sopka (Kamchatka peninsula, Russia)	4,750	15,584
Ras Dashan (Ethiopian Highlands)	4,620	15,158
Zard Kûh (Zagros Mts, Iran)	4,547	14,921
Mt Kirkpatrick (Trans Antarctic)	4,529	14,860
Mt Belukha (Altai Mts, Russia/ Kazakhstan)	4,505	14,783
Mt Elbert (Rocky Mountains)	4,400	14,433
Mt Rainier (Cascade Range, N. America)	4,392	14,410
Nevado de Colima (Sierra Madre Occidental, Mexico)	4,268	14,003
Jebel Toubkal (Atlas Mts, N. Africa)	4,165	13,665
Kinabalu (Crocker Range, Borneo)	4,101	13,455
Kerinci (West Sumatran-Javan Range, Indonesia)	3,800	12,467
Jabal an Nabī Shu'ayb (N. Tihāmat, Yemen)	3,760	12,336
Teotepec (Sierra Madre del Sur, Mexico)	3,703	12,149
Thaban Ntlenyana (Drakensberg, South Africa)	3,482	11,425
Pico de Bandeira (Atlantic Coast Range)	2,890	9,482
Shishaldin (Aleutian Range)	2,861	9,387
Kosciusko (Great Dividing Range)	2,228	7,310

HIGHEST VOLCANOES

Volcano (last major eruption) and location	Height metres	feet
Guallatiri (1993), Andes, Chile	6,060	19,882
Lascar (1991), Andes, Chile	5,990	19,652
Cotopaxi (1975), Andes, Ecuador	5,897	19,347
Tupungatito (1986), Andes, Chile	5,640	18,504
Nevado del Ruiz, Colombia (1985, 1992)	5,400	17,716
Sangay (1988), Andes, Ecuador	5,230	17,159
Guagua Pichincha (1988), Andes, Ecuador	4,784	15,696
Purace (1977), Colombia	4,756	15,601
Klyuchevskaya Sopka (1991), Kamchatka peninsula, Russia	4,750	15,584
Nevado de Colima (1991), Mexico	4,268	14,003
Galeras (1991), Colombia	4,266	13,996
Mauna Loa (1987), Hawaii Is.	4,170	13,680
Cameroon (1982), Cameroon	4,070	13,354
Acatenango (1972), Guatemala	3,960	12,992
Fuego (1991), Guatemala	3,835	12,582
Kerinci (1987), Sumatra, Indonesia	3,800	12,467
Erebus (1991), Ross Island, Antarctica	3,794	12,450
Tacana (1988), Guatemala	3,780	12,400
Santiaguito (1902, 1991), Guatemala	3,768	12,362
Rindjani (1966), Lombok, Indonesia	3,726	12,224
Semeru (1991), Java, Indonesia	3,675	12,060
Nyirgongo (1977), Zaïre	3,475	11,400
Koryakskaya (1957), Kamchatka, Russia	3,456	11,339
Irazú (1992), Costa Rica	3,432	11,260
Slamet (1988), Java, Indonesia	3,428	11,247
Spurr (1953), Alaska, USA	3,374	11,069
Mt Etna (1169, 1669, 1992), Sicily, Italy	3,369	11,053
Raung, Java, Indonesia (1991)	3,322	10,932
Shiveluch (1964), Kamchatka, Russia	3,283	10,771
Agung (1964), Bali, Indonesia	3,142	10,308
Llaima (1990), Chile	3,128	10,239
Redoubt (1991), Alaska, USA	3,108	10,197
Tjareme (1938), Java, Indonesia	3,078	10,098
Iliamna (1978), Alaska, USA	3,076	10,092
On-Taka (1991), Japan	3,063	10,049
Nyamuragira (1991), Zaire	3,056	10,028

OTHER NOTABLE VOLCANOES

	Height metres	feet
Tambora (1815), Sumbawa, Indonesia	2,850	9,353
Mt St Helens (1980, 1986), Washington State, USA	2,530	8,300
Pinatubo (1991), Philippines	1,758	5,770
Hekla (1981), Iceland	1,491	4,892
Mt Pelée (1902), Martinique	1,397	4,583
Mt Unzen (1991), Kyushu, Japan	1,360	4,462
Vesuvius (AD 79, 1944), Italy	1,280	4,198
Kilauea (1988), Hawaii, USA	1,242	4,077
Stromboli (1992), Lipari Is., Italy	926	3,038
Krakatau (1883), Sunda Strait, Indonesia	804	2,640
Santorini (Thíra) (1628 BC), Aegean Sea, Greece	566	1,857
Vulcano (Monte Aria), Lipari Is., Italy	499	1,637

	Height metres	feet
Tristan da Cunha (1961), South Atlantic	243	800
Surtsey (1963–7), off Iceland	173	568

LARGEST LAKES

The areas of some of these lakes are subject to seasonal variation.

	Area km²	miles²	Length km	miles
Caspian Sea – Iran/ Azerbaijan/Russia/ Turkmenistan/ Kazakhstan	371,000	143,000	1,171	728
Superior – Canada/USA	82,100	31,700	563	350
Victoria – Uganda/ Tanzania/Kenya	69,500	26,828	362	225
Huron – Canada/USA	59,570	23,000	331	206
Michigan – USA	57,750	22,300	494	307
Aral Sea – Kazakhstan/ Uzbekistan	40,400	15,600	331	235
Tanganyika – Zaïre/ Tanzania/Zambia/ Burundi	32,900	12,700	675	420
*Baykal (Baikal) – Russia	31,500	12,162	635	395
Great Bear – Canada	31,328	12,096	309	192
Malawi – Tanzania/ Malawi/Mozambique	28,880	11,150	580	360
Great Slave – Canada	28,570	11,031	480	298
Erie – Canada/USA	25,670	9,910	388	241
Winnipeg – Canada	24,390	9,417	428	266
Ontario – Canada/USA	19,550	7,550	310	193
Balkhash – Kazakhstan	18,427	7,115	605	376
Ladozhskoye (Ladoga) – Russia	17,700	6,835	200	124

UNITED KINGDOM (BY COUNTRY)

	Area km²	miles²	Length km	miles
Lough Neagh – Northern Ireland	381.73	147.39	28.90	18.00
Loch Lomond – Scotland	71.12	27.46	36.44	22.64
Windermere – England	14.74	5.69	16.90	10.50
Lake Vyrnwy – Wales (artificial)	4.53	1.75	7.56	4.70
Llyn Tegid (Bala) – Wales (natural)	4.38	1.69	5.80	3.65

*World's deepest lake (1,940 m/6,365 ft)

LONGEST RIVERS

River (source and outflow)	Length km	miles
Nile (Bahr-el-Nil) (R. Luvironza, Burundi – E. Mediterranean Sea)	6,670	4,145
Amazon (Amazonas) (Lago Villafro, Peru – S. Atlantic Ocean)	6,648	4,007
Mississippi-Missouri (R. Red Rock, Montana – Gulf of Mexico)	5,970	3,710

River (source and outflow)	Length km	miles
Yenisey-Angara (W. Mongolia – Kara Sea)	5,540	3,442
Yangtze-Kiang (*Chang Jiang*) (Kunlun Mts, W. China – Yellow Sea)	5,530	3,436
Ob'-Irtysh (W. Mongolia – Kara Sea)	5,410	3,362
Huang He (*Yellow River*) (Bayan Har Shan range, central China – Yellow Sea)	4,830	3,000
Zaire (*Congo*) (R. Lualaba, Zaire-Zambia – S. Atlantic Ocean)	4,700	2,920
Amur-Argun (R. Argun, Khingan Mts, N. China – Sea of Okhotsk)	4,670	2,903
Lena-Kirenga (R. Kirenga, W. of Lake Baykal – Arctic Ocean)	4,345	2,700
Mackenzie-Peace (Tatlatui Lake, British Columbia – Beaufort Sea)	4,240	2,635
Mekong (Lants'ang, Tibet – South China Sea)	4,184	2,600
Niger (Loma Mts, Guinea – Gulf of Guinea, E. Atlantic Ocean)	4,184	2,600
Rió de la Plata-Paraná (R. Paranáiba, central Brazil – S. Atlantic Ocean)	4,000	2,485
Murray-Darling (SE Queensland – Lake Alexandrina, S. Australia)	3,750	2,330
Volga (Valdai plateau – Caspian Sea)	3,690	2,293
Zambezi (NW Zambia – S. Indian Ocean)	3,540	2,200

OTHER NOTABLE RIVERS

St Lawrence (Minnesota, USA – Gulf of St Lawrence)	3,130	1,945
Ganges-Brahmaputra (R. Matsang, SW Tibet – Bay of Bengal)	2,900	1,800
Indus (R. Sengge, SW Tibet – N. Arabian Sea)	2,880	1,790
Danube (*Donau*) (Black Forest, SW Germany – Black Sea)	2,850	1,770
Tigris-Euphrates (R. Murat, E. Turkey – Persian Gulf)	2,740	1,700
Irrawaddy (R. Mali Hka, N. Burma – Andaman Sea)	2,090	1,300
Don (SE of Novomoskovsk – Sea of Azov)	1,969	1,224

BRITISH ISLES

Shannon (Co. Cavan, Rep. of Ireland – Atlantic Ocean)	386	240
Severn (Powys, Wales – Bristol Channel)	354	220
Thames (Gloucestershire, England – North Sea)	346	215
Tay (Perthshire, Scotland – North Sea)	188	117
Clyde (Lanarkshire, Scotland – Firth of Clyde)	158	98½
Tweed (Peeblesshire, Scotland – North Sea)	155	96½
Bann (Upper and Lower) (Co. Down, N. Ireland – Atlantic Ocean)	122	76

GREATEST WATERFALLS – BY HEIGHT

Waterfall (river and location)	Total drop metres	feet	Greatest single leap metres	feet
Angel (Carrao, Venezuela)	979	3,212	807	2,648
Tugela (Tugela, S. Africa)	947	3,110	410	1,350

Waterfall (river and location)	Total drop metres	feet	Greatest single leap metres	feet
Utigård (Jostedal Glacier, Norway)	800	2,625	600	1,970
Mongefossen (Monge, Norway)	774	2,540	—	—
Yosemite (Yosemite Creek, USA)	739	2,425	435	1,430
Østre Mardøla Foss (Mardals, Norway)	656	2,154	296	974
Tyssestrengane (Tysso, Norway)	646	2,120	289	948
Cuquenán (Arabopó, Venezuela)	610	2,000	—	—
Sutherland (Arthur, NZ)	580	1,904	248	815
*Kjellfossen (Naeröfjord, Norway)	561	1,841	149	490

BRITISH ISLES (BY COUNTRY)

	Total drop metres	feet	Greatest single leap metres	feet
Eas a' Chuàl Aluinn (Glas Bheinn, Sutherland, Scotland)	200	658		
Powerscourt Falls (Dargle, Co. Wicklow, Rep. of Ireland)	106	350		
Pistyll-y-Llyn (Powys/ Dyfed border, Wales)	c.73	230– 240		(cascades)
Pistyll Rhyadr (Clwyd/ Powys border, Wales)	71.5	235		(single leap)
Caldron Snout (R. Tees, Cumbria/Durham, England)	60	200		(cascades)

*Volume often so low the fall atomizes into a 'bridal veil'

GREATEST WATERFALLS – BY VOLUME

Waterfall (river and location)	Mean annual flow m³/sec	galls/sec
Boyoma (R. Lualaba, Zaïre)	c.17,000	c.3,750,000
*Guairá (Alto Paraná, Brazil/ Paraguay)	13,300	2,930,000
Khône (Mekong, Laos)	11,500	2,530,000
Niagara (Horseshoe) (R. Niagara/Lake Erie–Lake Ontario)	3,000	670,000
Paulo Afonso (R. São Francisco, Brazil)	2,750	605,000
Urubupunga (Alto Paraná, Brazil)	2,800	625,000
Cataratas del Iguazú (R. Iguaçu, Brazil/ Argentina)	1,725	380,000
Patos-Maribando (Rio Grande, Brazil)	1,500	330,000
Victoria (*Mosi-oa-tunya*) (R. Zambezi, Zambia/ Zimbabwe)	1,000	220,000
Churchill (R. Churchill, Canada)	975	215,000
Kaieteur (R. Potaro, Guyana)	660	145,000

*Peak flow 50,000 m³/sec, 11,000,000 galls/sec

TALLEST INHABITED BUILDINGS

Building and city	Height metres	feet
Sears Tower, Chicago[1]	443	1,454
World Trade Center, New York[2]	417	1,368
Empire State Building, New York[3]	381	1,250
Bank of China, Hong Kong	368	1,209
Amoco Building, Chicago	346	1,136
John Hancock Center, Chicago	343	1,127
C. & S. Plaza, Atlanta	320	1,050
Chrysler Building, New York	319	1,046
Central Plaza, Hong Kong	313	1,028
First Interstate World Center, Los Angeles	310	1,017
Texas Commerce Tower, Houston	305	1,002
State University, Moscow[4]	302	994

[1] With TV antennae 475.18 m/1,559 ft
[2] With TV antennae, 521.2 m/1,710 ft; second tower, 415 m/1,362 ft
[3] With TV tower (added 1950–1), 430.9 m/1,414 ft
[4] Including spire

TALLEST STRUCTURES

Structure and location	Height metres	feet
*Warszawa Radio Mast, Konstantynow, Poland	646	2,120
KTHI-TV Mast, Fargo, North Dakota	629	2,063
CN Tower, Metro Centre, Toronto, Canada	555	1,822

*Collapsed during renovation, August 1991

LONGEST BRIDGES – BY SPAN

Bridge and location	Length metres	feet
SUSPENSION SPANS		
Humber Estuary, Humberside, England	1,410	4,626
Verrazano Narrows, Brooklyn–Staten I, USA	1,298	4,260
Golden Gate, San Francisco Bay, USA	1,280	4,200
Mackinac Straits, Michigan, USA	1,158	3,800
Bosporus, Istanbul, Turkey	1,074	3,524
George Washington, Hudson River, New York City, USA	1,067	3,500
Ponte 25 Abril (Tagus), Lisbon, Portugal	1,013	3,323
Firth of Forth (road), nr Edinburgh, Scotland	1,006	3,300
Severn River, Severn Estuary, England	988	3,240

The Akashi-Kaikyo road bridge (1988–98) will have a main span of 1,990 m/6,528 ft

CANTILEVER SPANS

| Pont de Québec (rail-road), St Lawrence, Canada | 548.6 | 1,800 |

Bridge and location	Length metres	feet
Ravenswood, W. Virginia, USA	525.1	1,723
Firth of Forth (rail), nr. Edinburgh, Scotland	521.2	1,710
Minato, Osaka, Japan	510.0	1,673
Commodore Barry, Chester, Pennsylvania, USA	494.3	1,622
Greater New Orleans, Louisiana, USA	480.0	1,575
Howrah (rail-road), Calcutta, India	457.2	1,500
STEEL ARCH SPANS		
New River Gorge, Fayetteville, W. Virginia, USA	518.2	1,700
Bayonne (Kill van Kull), Bayonne, NJ– Staten I, USA	503.5	1,652
Sydney Harbour, Sydney, Australia	502.9	1,650

The 'floating' bridging at Evergreen, Seattle, Washington State, USA, is 3,839 m/12,596 ft long
The longest stretch of bridgings of any kind are those between Mandeville and Jefferson, Louisiana, USA; the Lake Pontchartrain Causeway II 38.422 km/23.87 miles and Causeway I 38.352 km/23.83 miles

LONGEST VEHICULAR TUNNELS

Tunnel and location	Length km	miles
*Seikan (rail), Tsugaru Channel, Japan	53.90	33.49
Moscow metro, Belyaevo–Medved Kovo, Moscow, Russia	30.70	19.07
Northern line tube, East Finchley– Morden, London	27.84	17.30
Oshimizu, Honshū, Japan	22.17	13.78
Simplon II (rail), Brigue, Switzerland– Iselle, Italy	19.82	12.31
Simplon I (rail), Brigue, Switzerland– Iselle, Italy	19.80	12.30
Shin-Kanmon (rail), Kanmon Strait, Japan	18.68	11.61
Great Appennine (rail), Vernio, Italy	18.49	11.49
St Gotthard (road), Göschenen– Airolo, Switzerland	16.32	10.14
Rokko (rail), Ōsaka–Kōbe, Japan	16.09	10.00

*Sub-aqueous

The twin rail Eurotunnel under the English Channel between Cheriton, Kent and Sargette, near Calais, is due to open for freight in December 1993 and for passengers in mid 1994. The tunnels are 49.94 km/31.03 miles in length. Holing through was achieved on 30 October 1990
The longest non-vehicular tunnelling in the world is the Delaware Aqueduct in New York State, USA, constructed in 1937–44 to a length of 168.9 km/105 miles

BRITISH RAIL TUNNELS

	miles	yards
Severn, Bristol – Newport	4	484
Totley, Manchester – Sheffield	3	950
Standedge, Manchester – Huddersfield	3	66
Sodbury, Swindon – Bristol	2	924
Disley, Stockport – Sheffield	2	346
Ffestiniog, Llandudno – Blaenau Ffestiniog	2	338
Bramhope, Leeds – Harrogate	2	241
Cowburn, Manchester – Sheffield	2	182

LONGEST SHIP CANALS

Canal (opening date)	Length km	miles	Min. depth metres	feet
White Sea-Baltic (formerly Stalin) (1933) Canalized river; canal 51.5 km/32 miles	227	141.00	5.0	16.5
*Suez (1869) Links Red and Mediterranean Seas	162	100.60	12.9	42.3
V. I. Lenin Volga-Don (1952) Links Black and Caspian Seas	100	62.20	n/a	n/a
Kiel (or North Sea) (1895) Links North and Baltic Seas	98	60.90	13.7	45.0
*Houston (1940) Links inland city with sea	91	56.70	10.4	34.0
Alphonse XIII (1926) Gives Seville access to sea	85	53.00	7.6	25.0
Panama (1914) Links Pacific Ocean and Caribbean Sea; lake chain, 78.9 km/49 miles dug	82	50.71	12.5	41.0
Manchester Ship (1894) Links city with Irish Channel	64	39.70	8.5	28.0
Welland (1931) Circumvents Niagara Falls and Rapids	45	28.00	8.8	29.0
Brussels (Rupel Sea) (1922) Renders Brussels an inland port	32	19.80	6.4	21.0

*Has no locks

The first section of China's Grand Canal, running 1,780 km/1,107 miles from Beijing to Hangchou, was opened AD 610 but in undredged parts is today only 1.8 m/6 ft deep

The longest boat canal in the world is the Volga-Baltic canal from Astrakhan to St Petersburg with 2,300 route km/1,850 miles

The Seven Wonders of the World

I. THE PYRAMIDS OF EGYPT

The pyramids are found from Gizeh, near Cairo, to a southern limit 60 miles distant. The oldest is that of Zoser, at Saqqara, built c.2650 BC. The Great Pyramid of Cheops (built c.2580 BC) covers more than 13.12 acres and was originally 481 ft in height and 756 × 756 ft at the base.

II. THE HANGING GARDENS OF BABYLON

These adjoined Nebuchadnezzar's palace, 60 miles south of Baghdad. The terraced gardens, ranging from 75 ft to 300 ft above ground level, were watered from storage tanks on the highest terrace.

III. THE TOMB OF MAUSOLUS

Built at Halicarnassus, in Asia Minor, by the widowed Queen Artemisia about 350 BC. The memorial originated the term mausoleum.

IV. THE TEMPLE OF ARTEMIS AT EPHESUS

Ionic temple erected about 350 BC in honour of the goddess and burned by the Goths in AD 262.

V. THE COLOSSUS OF RHODES

A bronze statue of Apollo, set up about 280 BC. According to legend it stood at the harbour entrance of the seaport of Rhodes.

VI. THE STATUE OF ZEUS

Located at Olympia in the plain of Elis, and constructed of marble inlaid with ivory and gold by the sculptor Phidias, about 430 BC.

VII. THE PHAROS OF ALEXANDRIA

A marble watch tower and lighthouse on the island of Pharos in the harbour of Alexandria, built c.270 BC.

Distances from London by Air

The list of the distances in statute miles from London, Heathrow, to various cities (airport) abroad has been supplied by the publishers of *IATA/IAL Air Distances Manual*, Southall, Middx.

To	Miles
Abidjan	3,197
Abu Dhabi	3,425
Addis Ababa	3,675
Adelaide	1,011
Aden	3,670
Algiers	1,035
Amman	2,287
Amsterdam	230
Ankara	1,770
Athens	1,500
Atlanta	4,198
Auckland	11,404
Baghdad	2,551
Bahrain	3,163
Baku	2,485
Bangkok	5,928
Barbados	4,193
Barcelona	712
Basle	447
Beijing/Peking	5,063
Beirut	2,161
Belfast	325
Belgrade	1,056
Berlin (Tegel)	588
Bermuda	3,428
Berne	476
Bogota	5,262
Bombay	4,478
Boston	3,255
Brasilia	5,452
Bratislava	817
Brisbane	10,273
Brussels	217
Bucharest	1,307
Budapest	923
Buenos Aires	6,915
Cairo	2,194
Calcutta	4,958
Calgary	4,357
Canberra	10,563
Cape Town	6,011
Caracas	4,639
Casablanca	1,300
Chicago (O'Hare)	3,941
Cologne	331
Colombo	5,411
Copenhagen	608
Dakar	2,706
Dallas (Fort Worth)	4,736
Dallas (Lovefield)	4,732
Damascus	2,223
Dar-es-Salaam	4,662
Darwin	8,613
Delhi	4,180

To	Miles
Denver	4,668
Detroit	3,754
Dhahran	3,143
Dhaka	4,976
Doha	3,253
Dubai	3,414
Dublin	279
Durban	5,937
Düsseldorf	310
Entebbe	4,033
Frankfurt	406
Freetown	3,046
Geneva	468
Gibraltar	1,084
Gothenburg (Landvetter)	664
Hamburg	463
Harare	5,156
Havana	4,647
Helsinki (Vantaa)	1,147
Hobart	10,826
Ho Chi Minh City	6,345
Hong Kong	5,990
Honolulu	7,220
Houston (Intercontinental)	4,821
Houston (William P. Hobby)	4,837
Islamabad	3,767
Istanbul	1,560
Jakarta	7,295
Jeddah	2,947
Johannesburg	5,634
Kabul	3,558
Karachi	3,935
Kathmandu	4,570
Khartoum	3,071
Kiev (Borispol)	1,357
Kiev (Julyany)	1,337
Kingston, Jamaica	4,668
Kuala Lumpur	6,557
Kuwait	2,903
Lagos	3,107
Larnaca	2,036
Lima	6,303
Lisbon	972
Lomé	3,129
Los Angeles	5,439
Madras	5,113
Madrid	773
Malta	1,305
Manila	6,685
Marseilles	614
Mauritius	6,075
Melbourne (Essendon)	10,504
Melbourne (Tullamarine)	10,499
Mexico City	5,529
Miami	4,414
Milan	609
Minsk	1,176
Montego Bay	4,687
Montevideo	6,841
Montreal (Mirabel)	3,241

To	Miles
Moscow (Sheremetievo)	1,557
Munich (Franz Josef Strauss)	584
Muscat	3,621
Nairobi	4,248
Naples	1,011
Nassau	4,333
New York (J. F. Kennedy)	3,440
Nice	645
Oporto	806
Oslo (Fornebu)	722
Ottawa	3,321
Palma, Majorca	836
Paris (Charles de Gaulle)	215
Paris (Le Bourget)	215
Paris (Orly)	227
Perth, Australia	9,008
Port of Spain	4,404
Prague	649
Pretoria	5,602
Reykjavik	1,167
Rhodes	1,743
Rio de Janeiro	5,745
Riyadh	3,067
Rome (Fiumicino)	895
St John's, Newfoundland	2,308
St Petersburg	1,314
Salzburg	651
San Francisco	5,351
Sao Paulo	5,892
Sarajevo	1,017
Seoul	5,507
Shanghai	5,725
Shannon	369
Singapore	6,756
Sofia	1,266
Stockholm (Arlanda)	908
Suva	10,119
Sydney	10,568
Tangier	1,120
Tehran	2,741
Tel Aviv	2,227
Tokyo (Narita)	5,956
Toronto	3,544
Tripoli	1,468
Tunis	1,137
Turin (Caselle)	570
Ulan Bator	4,340
Valencia	826
Vancouver	4,707
Venice (Tessera)	715
Vienna (Schwechat)	790
Vladivostok	5,298
Warsaw	912
Washington	3,665
Wellington	11,692
Yangon/Rangoon	5,582
Yokohama (Aomori)	5,637
Yokohama (Kanagawa)	5,938
Zagreb	848
Zürich	490

The United Kingdom

The United Kingdom comprises Great Britain (England, Wales and Scotland) and Northern Ireland. The Isle of Man and the Channel Islands are Crown dependencies with their own legislative systems, and not a part of the United Kingdom.

AREA AS AT 31 MARCH 1981

	Land miles^2	km^2	*Inland water miles^2	km^2	Total miles^2	km^2
United Kingdom	93,027	240,939	1,242	3,218	94,269	244,157
England	50,085	129,720	293	758	50,377	130,478
Wales	7,968	20,636	50	130	8,018	20,766
Scotland	29,767	77,097	653	1,692	30,420	78,789
†Northern Ireland	5,215	13,506	246	638	5,461	14,144
Isle of Man	—	—	—	—	221	572
Channel Islands	—	—	—	—	75	194

*Excluding tidal water
†Excluding certain tidal waters that are parts of statutory areas in Northern Ireland

POPULATION

The first official census of population in England, Wales and Scotland was taken in 1801 and a census has been taken every ten years since, except in 1941 when there was no census because of war. The last official census in the United Kingdom was taken on 21 April 1991 and the next is due in April 2001.

The first official census of population in Ireland was taken in 1841. However, all figures given below refer only to the area which is now Northern Ireland. Figures for Northern Ireland in 1921 and 1931 are estimates based on the censuses taken in 1926 and 1937 respectively.

Estimates of the population of England before 1801, calculated from the number of baptisms, burials and marriages, are:

1570 4,160,221	1670 5,773,646
1600 4,811,718	1700 6,045,008
1630 5,600,517	1750 6,517,035

	United Kingdom			England and Wales			Scotland			Northern Ireland		
Thousands	Total	Male	Female	Total	Male	Female	Total	Male	Female	Total	Male	Female
CENSUS RESULTS 1801–1991												
1801	—	—	—	8,893	4,255	4,638	1,608	739	869	—	—	—
1811	13,368	6,368	7,000	10,165	4,874	5,291	1,806	826	980	—	—	—
1821	15,472	7,498	7,974	12,000	5,850	6,150	2,092	983	1,109	—	—	—
1831	17,835	8,647	9,188	13,897	6,771	7,126	2,364	1,114	1,250	—	—	—
1841	20,183	9,819	10,364	15,914	7,778	8,137	2,620	1,242	1,378	1,649	800	849
1851	22,259	10,855	11,404	17,928	8,781	9,146	2,889	1,376	1,513	1,443	698	745
1861	24,525	11,894	12,631	20,066	9,776	10,290	3,062	1,450	1,612	1,396	668	728
1871	27,431	13,309	14,122	22,712	11,059	11,653	3,360	1,603	1,757	1,359	647	712
1881	31,015	15,060	15,955	25,974	12,640	13,335	3,736	1,799	1,936	1,305	621	684
1891	34,264	16,593	17,671	29,003	14,060	14,942	4,026	1,943	2,083	1,236	590	646
1901	38,237	18,492	19,745	32,528	15,729	16,799	4,472	2,174	2,298	1,237	590	647
1911	42,082	20,357	21,725	36,070	17,446	18,625	4,761	2,309	2,452	1,251	603	648
1921	44,027	21,033	22,994	37,887	18,075	19,811	4,882	2,348	2,535	1,258	610	648
1931	46,038	22,060	23,978	39,952	19,133	20,819	4,843	2,326	2,517	1,243	601	642
1951	50,225	24,118	26,107	43,758	21,016	22,742	5,096	2,434	2,662	1,371	668	703
1961	52,709	25,481	27,228	46,105	22,304	23,801	5,179	2,483	2,697	1,425	694	731
1971	55,515	26,952	28,562	48,750	23,683	25,067	5,229	2,515	2,714	1,536	755	781
1981	55,848	27,104	28,742	49,155	23,873	25,281	5,131	2,466	2,664	*1,533	750	783
1991	56,467	27,344	29,123	49,890	24,182	25,707	4,999	2,392	2,606	1,578	769	809
†RESIDENT POPULATION: PROJECTIONS (MID-YEAR)												
1991	57,561	28,099	29,463	50,903	24,865	26,038	5,068	2,452	2,615	1,590	781	809
2001	59,174	29,069	30,105	52,526	25,819	26,708	5,026	2,449	2,577	1,622	802	820
2011	60,033	29,630	30,403	53,510	26,423	27,087	4,900	2,400	2,500	1,623	806	816
2021	60,743	30,049	30,694	54,411	26,927	27,484	4,727	2,322	2,405	1,605	800	805
2031	61,068	30,213	30,855	54,977	27,208	27,769	4,524	2,224	2,300	1,567	782	785

* figures include 44,500 non-enumerated persons   † projections are 1989 based

Source: HMSO – *Annual Abstract 1993*; OPCS – Census reports

ISLANDS: Census Results 1901–91

	Isle of Man			Jersey			*Guernsey		
	Total	Male	Female	Total	Male	Female	Total	Male	Female
1901	54,752	25,496	29,256	52,576	23,940	28,636	40,446	19,652	20,794
1911	52,016	23,937	28,079	51,898	24,014	27,884	41,858	20,661	21,197
1921	60,284	27,329	32,955	49,701	22,438	27,263	38,315	18,246	20,069
1931	49,308	22,443	26,865	50,462	23,424	27,038	40,643	19,659	20,984
1951	55,123	25,749	29,464	57,296	27,282	30,014	43,652	21,221	22,431
1961	48,151	22,060	26,091	57,200	27,200	30,000	45,068	21,671	23,397
1971	56,289	26,461	29,828	72,532	35,423	37,109	51,458	24,792	26,666
1981	64,679	30,901	33,778	77,000	37,000	40,000	53,313	25,701	27,612
1991	69,788	33,693	36,095	84,082	40,862	43,220	58,867	28,297	30,570

* Population of Guernsey, Herm, Jethou and Lithou. Figures for 1901–71 record all persons present on census night; census figures for 1981 and 1991 record all persons resident in the islands on census night.

Source: 1991 Census

RESIDENT POPULATION

MID-YEAR ESTIMATE

	1981	1991p
United Kingdom	56,352,000	57,649,000
England	46,820,000	48,069,000
Wales	2,814,000	2,886,000
Scotland	5,180,000	5,100,000
Northern Ireland	1,538,000	1,594,000

p provisional
Source: HMSO - *Annual Abstract of Statistics 1993*

BY AGE AND SEX 1991p

Males	*Under 16*	*Over 65*
United Kingdom	6,023,000	3,650,000
England	4,983,000	3,072,000
Wales	304,000	199,000
Scotland	525,000	299,000
Northern Ireland	211,000	80,000

Females	*Under 16*	*Over 60*
United Kingdom	5,708,000	6,934,000
England	4,720,000	5,789,000
Wales	287,000	375,000
Scotland	499,000	611,000
Northern Ireland	201,000	159,000

p provisional
Source: HMSO - *Population Trends 72*

BY ETHNIC GROUP (1991 CENSUS (GREAT BRITAIN))

Ethnic group	*Estimated population*	*Percentage*
Caribbean	500,000	16.6
African	212,000	7
Other black	178,000	5.9
Indian	840,000	27.9
Pakistani	477,000	15.8
Bangladeshi	163,000	5.4
Chinese	157,000	5.2
Other Asian	198,000	6.6
Other	290,000	9.6
Total ethnic minority groups	3,015,000	100
White	51,874,000	—
All ethnic groups	54,889,000	—

Source: HMSO - *Population Trends 72*

AVERAGE DENSITY

	Persons per hectare	
	1981	1991
England	3.55	3.61
Wales	1.34	1.36
Scotland	0.66	0.65
Northern Ireland	1.12	1.11

Sources: OPCS – Census reports

IMMIGRATION 1991

Acceptances for settlement in the UK by nationality

Region	*Number of persons*
Europe: total	5,530
European Community	1,420
Other Western Europe	3,000
Eastern Europe	1,110
Americas: total	7,220
USA	3,910
Canada	680
Africa: total	9,580
Asia: total	24,900
Indian sub-continent	14,290
Middle East	2,900
Australasia: total	2,440
Other	2,780
Stateless	1,430
Total	53,900
Foreign	22,850
Commonwealth	31,060
Old Commonwealth	3,120
New Commonwealth	27,930

Source: HMSO - *Annual Abstract of Statistics 1993*

LIVE BIRTHS AND BIRTH RATES 1991

	Live births	Birth rate*
United Kingdom	793,000	13.8
England and Wales	699,000	13.7
Scotland	67,000	13.1
Northern Ireland	26,000	16.5

*Live births per 1,000 population
Source: HMSO - *Annual Abstract of Statistics 1993*

LEGAL ABORTIONS 1991 (England and Wales)

Age group	Number†
Under 16	3,080
16–19	30,750
20–34	113,600
35–44	17,730
45 and over	400
Age not stated	20
Total	165,500

† provisional
Source: HMSO – Population Trends 72

BIRTHS OUTSIDE MARRIAGE (UK)

Age group	1981	1991
Under 20	30,000	50,000
20–24	33,000	87,000
25–29	16,000	58,000
Over 30	13,000	41,000
Total	91,000	236,000

Source: HMSO – Annual Abstract of Statistics 1993

MARRIAGE AND DIVORCE 1990

	Marriages	Divorces*
United Kingdom	375,410	—
England and Wales	331,150	153,386
Scotland	34,672	12,272
Northern Ireland	9,588	2,591

*Decrees absolute granted (in Northern Ireland, divorce petitions filed)
Source: HMSO – Annual Abstract of Statistics 1993

DEATHS AND DEATH RATES 1991

Males	Deaths	Death rate*
United Kingdom	314,427p	11.2p
England and Wales	277,582	—
Scotland	29,312	—
Northern Ireland	7,533p	—
Females		
United Kingdom	331,754p	10.6p
England and Wales	292,462	—
Scotland	31,729	—
Northern Ireland	7,563p	—

* Deaths per 1,000 population
p provisional
Source: HMSO – Annual Abstract of Statistics 1993

INFANT MORTALITY 1991

Deaths of infants under 1 year of age per 1,000 live births

	Number
United Kingdom	7.4p
England and Wales	7.4
Scotland	7.1
Northern Ireland	7.4p

p provisional
Source: HMSO – Annual Abstract of Statistics 1993

EXPECTATION OF LIFE   LIFE TABLES 1988–90 (INTERIM FIGURES)

Age	England and Wales		Scotland		Northern Ireland	
	Male	Female	Male	Female	Male	Female
0	73.0	78.5	70.8	76.6	71.3	77.2
5	68.8	74.2	66.6	72.2	67.1	72.9
10	63.9	69.2	61.6	67.2	62.2	67.9
15	58.9	64.3	56.7	62.3	57.2	63.0
20	54.1	59.4	51.9	57.4	52.5	58.1
25	49.3	54.4	47.2	52.5	47.8	53.2
30	44.5	49.5	42.4	47.6	43.0	48.3
35	39.7	44.6	37.7	42.7	38.3	43.4
40	35.0	39.8	33.0	38.0	33.6	38.6
45	30.3	35.1	28.4	33.2	29.0	33.8
50	25.8	30.5	24.0	28.7	24.5	29.2
55	21.5	26.0	19.9	24.3	20.2	24.9
60	17.5	21.7	16.2	20.2	16.4	20.7
65	14.0	17.8	12.9	16.5	13.0	16.9
70	11.0	14.2	10.2	13.2	10.2	13.4
75	8.4	11.0	7.8	10.2	7.8	10.2
80	6.4	8.2	5.9	7.6	5.7	7.4
85	4.9	5.9	4.4	5.4	4.1	5.1

Source: HMSO – Annual Abstract of Statistics 1993

DEATHS ANALYSED BY CAUSE 1991

	England & Wales	Scotland	N. Ireland†
TOTAL DEATHS	570,044	61,041	15,096
DEATHS FROM NATURAL CAUSES	549,706	58,509	14,377
Infections and parasitic diseases	2,406	310	44
Intestinal infectious diseases	169	14	1
Tuberculosis of respiratory system	334	46	6
Other tuberculosis, including late effects	240	38	2
Whooping cough	—	—	—
Meningococcal infection	170	10	6
Measles	1	1	—
Malaria	11	1	—
Syphilis	15	2	—
Neoplasms	145,355	15,031	3,551
Malignant neoplasm of stomach	8,427	833	233
Malignant neoplasm of trachea, bronchus and lung	34,190	4,209	787
Malignant neoplasm of breast	13,869	1,282	342
Malignant neoplasm of uterus	3,163	294	66
Leukaemia	3,687	268	83
Benign and unspecified neoplasms	1,337	112	38
Endocrine, nutritional and metabolic diseases and immunity disorders	10,538	776	68
Diabetes mellitus	8,087	530	41
Nutritional deficiencies	109	6	1
Other metabolic and immunity disorders	1,664	197	23
Diseases of blood and blood-forming organs	2,446	170	31
Anaemias	1,110	68	18
Mental disorders	13,500	1,110	68
Diseases of nervous system and sense organs	11,889	947	168
Meningitis	233	26	10
Diseases of the circulatory system	261,834	29,166	6,983
Rheumatic heart disease	2,193	180	56
Hypertensive disease	3,340	316	67
Ischaemic heart disease	150,090	16,866	4,223
Diseases of pulmonary circulation and other forms of heart disease	18,820	2,234	627
Cerebrovascular disease	68,669	7,968	1,711
Diseases of the respiratory system	63,273	7,068	2,494
Influenza	248	28	5
Pneumonia	28,504	3,785	1,684
Bronchitis, emphysema	6,773	378	150
Asthma	1,884	161	47
Diseases of the digestive system	18,508	2,059	395
Ulcer of stomach and duodenum	4,304	368	98
Appendicitis	108	10	2
Hernia of abdominal cavity and other intestinal obstruction	1,967	176	45
Chronic liver disease and cirrhosis	3,102	476	60
Diseases of the genito-urinary system	6,964	805	272
Nephritis, nephrotic syndrome and nephrosis	3,234	541	183
Hyperplasia of prostate	413	12	8
Complications of pregnancy, childbirth, etc.	45	9	1
Abortion	6	—	—
Diseases of the skin and subcutaneous tissue	930	82	36
Diseases of the musculo-skeletal system	5,417	270	54
Congenital anomalies	1,643	193	90
Certain conditions originating in the perinatal period	250	213	82
Birth trauma, hypoxia, birth asphyxia and other respiratory conditions	78	105	31
Signs, symptoms and ill-defined conditions	5,208	300	40
Sudden infant death syndrome	912	90	15
DEATHS FROM INJURY AND POISONING	17,286	2,532	719
All accidents	11,049	1,734	492
Motor vehicle accidents	4,470	513	195
Suicide and self-inflicted injury	3,893	525	129
All other external causes	2,344	273	98

† provisional
Source: HMSO - *Annual Abstract of Statistics 1993*

The National Flag

The national flag of the United Kingdom is the Union Flag, generally known as the Union Jack. (The name 'Union Jack' derives from the use of the Union Flag on the jack-staff of naval vessels.)

The Union Flag is a combination of the cross of St George, patron saint of England, the cross of St Andrew, patron saint of Scotland, and a cross similar to that of St Patrick, patron saint of Ireland.

Cross of St George: cross Gules in a field Argent (red cross on a white ground).

Cross of St Andrew: saltire Argent in a field Azure (white diagonal cross on a blue ground).

Cross of St Patrick: saltire Gules in a field Argent (red diagonal cross on a white ground).

The Union Flag was first introduced in 1606 after the union of the kingdoms of England and Scotland under one sovereign. The cross of St Patrick was added in 1801 after the union of Great Britain and Ireland.

DAYS FOR FLYING FLAGS

The correct orientation of the Union Flag when flying is with the broader diagonal band of white uppermost in the hoist (i.e. near the pole) and the narrower diagonal band of white uppermost in the fly (i.e. farthest from the pole).

It is the practice to fly the Union Flag daily on some Customs Houses. In all other cases, flags are flown on government buildings by command of The Queen.

Days for hoisting the Union Flag are notified to the Department of the Environment by The Queen's command and communicated by the department to the other government departments. On the days appointed, the Union Flag is flown on all government buildings in London and elsewhere in the United Kingdom from 8 a.m. to sunset.

The Queen's Accession	6 February
Birthday of The Duke of York	19 February
St David's Day (in Wales only)	1 March
Birthday of The Prince Edward	10 March
Commonwealth Day (1994)	14 March
Birthday of The Queen	21 April
St George's Day (in England only)	23 April
Where a building has two or more flagstaffs, the Cross of St George may be flown in addition to the Union Flag, but not in a superior position	
Coronation Day	2 June
Birthday of The Duke of Edinburgh	10 June
The Queen's Official Birthday (1994)	11 June
Birthday of The Princess of Wales	1 July
Birthday of Queen Elizabeth the Queen Mother	4 August
Birthday of The Princess Royal	15 August
Birthday of The Princess Margaret	21 August
Remembrance Sunday (1994)	13 November
Birthday of The Prince of Wales	14 November

The Queen's Wedding Day	20 November
St Andrew's Day (in Scotland only)	30 November
The occasion of the opening and closing of Parliament by The Queen, whether or not Her Majesty performs the ceremony in person (on government buildings in the Greater London area only)	

FLAGS AT HALF-MAST

Flags are flown at half-mast on the following occasions:

(a) From the announcement of the death up to the funeral of the Sovereign, except on Proclamation Day, when flags are hoisted right up from 11 a.m. to sunset

(b) The funerals of members of the Royal Family, subject to special commands from The Queen in each case

(c) The funerals of foreign rulers, subject to special commands from The Queen in each case

(d) The funerals of Prime Ministers and ex-Prime Ministers of the United Kingdom

(e) Other occasions by special command of The Queen

On occasions when days for flying flags coincide with days for flying flags at half-mast, the following rules are observed. Flags are flown:

(a) although a member of the Royal Family, or a near relative of the Royal Family, may be lying dead, unless special commands be received from The Queen to the contrary

(b) although it may be the day of the funeral of a foreign ruler

If the body of a very distinguished subject is lying at a government office, the flag may fly at half-mast on that office until the body has left (provided it is a day on which the flag would fly) and then the flag is to be hoisted right up. On all other government buildings the flag will fly as usual.

THE ROYAL STANDARD

The Royal Standard is hoisted only when The Queen is actually present in the building, and never when Her Majesty is passing in procession.

The Royal Family

THE SOVEREIGN

ELIZABETH II, by the Grace of God, of the United Kingdom of Great Britain and Northern Ireland and of her other Realms and Territories Queen, Head of the Commonwealth, Defender of the Faith

Her Majesty Elizabeth Alexandra Mary of Windsor, elder daughter of King George VI and of HM Queen Elizabeth the Queen Mother
Born 21 April 1926, at 17 Bruton Street, London WI
Ascended the throne 6 February 1952
Crowned 2 June 1953, at Westminster Abbey
Married 20 November 1947, in Westminster Abbey, HRH The Duke of Edinburgh
Official residences: Buckingham Palace, London SW1; Windsor Castle, Berks; Palace of Holyroodhouse, Edinburgh
Private residences: Sandringham, Norfolk; Balmoral Castle, Aberdeenshire
Office: Buckingham Palace, London SW1A 1AA. Tel: 071-930 4832

HUSBAND OF HM THE QUEEN

HRH THE PRINCE PHILIP, DUKE OF EDINBURGH, KG, KT, OM, GBE, AC, QSO, PC, Ranger of Windsor Park
Born 10 June 1921, son of Prince and Princess Andrew of Greece and Denmark (*see* page 135), naturalized a British subject 1947, created Duke of Edinburgh, Earl of Merioneth and Baron Greenwich 1947

CHILDREN OF HM THE QUEEN

HRH THE PRINCE OF WALES (Prince Charles Philip Arthur George), KG, KT, GCB and Great Master of the Order of the Bath, AK, QSO, PC, ADC(P)
Born 14 November 1948, created Prince of Wales and Earl of Chester 1958, succeeded as Duke of Cornwall, Duke of Rothesay, Earl of Carrick and Baron Renfrew, Lord of the Isles and Prince and Great Steward of Scotland 1952
Married 29 July 1981 Lady Diana Frances Spencer, now HRH The Princess of Wales (*born* 1 July 1961, youngest daughter of the 8th Earl Spencer and the Hon. Mrs Shand Kydd), *separated* 1992
Issue:
(1)   HRH Prince William of Wales (Prince William Arthur Philip Louis), *born* 21 June 1982
(2)   HRH Prince Henry of Wales (Prince Henry Charles Albert David), *born* 15 September 1984
Residences of the Prince of Wales: St James's Palace, London SW1; Highgrove, Doughton, Tetbury, Glos.
Residence of the Princess of Wales: Kensington Palace, London W8 4PU
Office: St James's Palace, London SW1A 1BS. Tel: 071-930 4832

HRH THE PRINCESS ROYAL (Princess Anne Elizabeth Alice Louise), GCVO
Born 15 August 1950, declared The Princess Royal 1987

Married (1) 14 November 1973 Captain Mark Anthony Peter Phillips, CVO (*born* 22 September 1948); marriage dissolved 1992; (2) 12 December 1992 Commander Timothy James Hamilton Laurence, MVO (*born* 1 March 1955)
Issue:
(1)   Peter Mark Andrew Phillips, *born* 15 November 1977
(2)   Zara Anne Elizabeth Phillips, *born* 15 May 1981
Residence: Gatcombe Park, Minchinhampton, Glos.
Office: Buckingham Palace, London SW1A 1AA. Tel: 071-930 4832

HRH THE DUKE OF YORK (Prince Andrew Albert Christian Edward), CVO, ADC(P)
Born 19 February 1960, created Duke of York, Earl of Inverness and Baron Killyleagh 1986
Married 23 July 1986 Sarah Margaret Ferguson, now HRH The Duchess of York (*born* 15 October 1959, younger daughter of Major Ronald Ferguson and Mrs Hector Barrantes), *separated* 1992
Issue:
(1)   HRH Princess Beatrice of York (Princess Beatrice Elizabeth Mary), *born* 8 August 1988
(2)   HRH Princess Eugenie of York (Princess Eugenie Victoria Helena), *born* 23 March 1990
Residences: Buckingham Palace, London SW1; Sunninghill Park, Ascot, Berks.
Office: Buckingham Palace, London SW1 1AA. Tel: 071-930 4832

HRH THE PRINCE EDWARD (Prince Edward Antony Richard Louis), CVO
Born 10 March 1964
Residence and Office: Buckingham Palace, London SW1A 1AA. Tel: 071-930 4832

SISTER OF HM THE QUEEN

HRH THE PRINCESS MARGARET, COUNTESS OF SNOWDON (Princess Margaret Rose), CI, GCVO, Royal Victorian Chain, Dame Grand Cross of the Order of St John of Jerusalem
Born 21 August 1930, younger daughter of King George VI and HM Queen Elizabeth the Queen Mother
Married 6 May 1960 Antony Charles Robert Armstrong-Jones, GCVO (*born* 7 March 1930, created Earl of Snowdon 1961, Constable of Caernarvon Castle); marriage dissolved 1978
Issue:
(1)   David Albert Charles, Viscount Linley, *born* 3 November 1961
(2)   Lady Sarah Armstrong-Jones (Sarah Frances Elizabeth), *born* 1 May 1964
Residence and Office: Kensington Palace, London W8 4PU. Tel: 071-930 3141

MOTHER OF HM THE QUEEN

HM QUEEN ELIZABETH THE QUEEN MOTHER (Elizabeth Angela Marguerite), Lady of the Garter, Lady of the Thistle, CI, GMVO, GBE, Dame Grand Cross of the Order of St John, Royal Victorian Chain, Lord Warden and

Admiral of the Cinque Ports and Constable of Dover Castle
Born 4 August 1900, youngest daughter of the 14th Earl of
Strathmore and Kinghorne
Married 26 April 1923 (as Lady Elizabeth Bowes-Lyon)
Prince Albert, Duke of York, afterwards King George VI
(*see* page 134)
Residences: Clarence House, St James's Palace, London SW1;
Royal Lodge, Windsor Great Park, Berks; Castle of Mey,
Caithness
Office: Clarence House, St James's Palace, London SW1A
1BA. Tel: 071-930 3141

AUNT OF HM THE QUEEN

HRH PRINCESS ALICE, DUCHESS OF GLOUCESTER
(Alice Christabel), GCB, CI, GCVO, GBE, Grand Cordon of
Al Kamal
Born 25 December 1901, third daughter of the 7th Duke of
Buccleuch and Queensberry
Married 6 November 1935 (as Lady Alice Montagu-
Douglas-Scott) Prince Henry, Duke of Gloucester, third son
of King George V (*see* page 134)

COUSINS OF HM THE QUEEN

HRH THE DUKE OF GLOUCESTER (Prince Richard
Alexander Walter George), GCVO, Grand Prior of the Order
of St John of Jerusalem
Born 26 August 1944
Married 8 July 1972 Birgitte Eva van Deurs, now HRH The
Duchess of Gloucester, GCVO (*born* 20 June 1946, daughter
of Asger Henriksen and Vivian van Deurs)
Issue:
(1) Earl of Ulster (Alexander Patrick Gregers Richard),
     born 24 October 1974
(2) Lady Davina Windsor (Davina Elizabeth Alice
     Benedikte), *born* 19 November 1977
(3) Lady Rose Windsor (Rose Victoria Birgitte Louise),
     born 1 March 1980
Residences: Kensington Palace, London W8 4PU; Barnwell
Manor, Peterborough, Northants. PE8 5PJ
Office: Kensington Palace, London W8 4PU. Tel: 071-937
6374

HRH THE DUKE OF KENT (Prince Edward George
Nicholas Paul Patrick), KG, GCMG, GCVO, ADC(P)
Born 9 October 1935
Married 8 June 1961 Katharine Lucy Mary Worsley, now
HRH The Duchess of Kent, GCVO (*born* 22 February 1933,
daughter of Sir William Worsley, Bt.)
Issue:
(1) Earl of St Andrews (George Philip Nicholas), *born* 26
     June 1962, *married* 9 January 1988 Sylvana Tomaselli,
     and has issue, Edward Edmund Maximilian George,
     Baron Downpatrick, *born* 2 December 1988; Lady
     Marina Charlotte Alexandra Katharine Windsor, *born*
     30 September 1992
(2) Lady Helen Taylor (Helen Marina Lucy), *born* 28
     April 1964, *married* 18 July 1992 Timothy Verner
     Taylor
(3) Lord Nicholas Windsor (Nicholas Charles Edward
     Jonathan), *born* 25 July 1970
Residences: York House, St James's Palace, London SW1 1BQ;
Crocker End House, Nettlebed, Oxon.
Office: York House, St James's Palace, London SW1A 1BQ.
Tel: 071-930 4872

HRH PRINCESS ALEXANDRA, THE HON. LADY OGILVY
(Princess Alexandra Helen Elizabeth Olga Christabel), GCVO
Born 25 December 1936
Married 24 April 1963 The Hon. Sir Angus Ogilvy, KCVO
(*born* 14 September 1928, second son of 12th Earl of Airlie)
Issue:
(1) James Robert Bruce Ogilvy, *born* 29 February 1964,
     married 30 July 1988 Julia Rawlinson
(2) Marina Victoria Alexandra, Mrs Mowatt, *born* 31 July
     1966, *married* 2 February 1990 Paul Mowatt, and has
     issue, Zenouska Mowatt, *born* 26 May 1990; a son,
     born 4 June 1993
Residence: Thatched House Lodge, Richmond Park, Surrey
Office: 22 Friary Court, St James's Palace, London SW1A 1BJ.
Tel: 071-930 1860

HRH PRINCE MICHAEL OF KENT (Prince Michael
George Charles Franklin), KCVO
Born 4 July 1942
Married 30 June 1978 Baroness Marie-Christine Agnes
Hedwig Ida von Reibnitz, now HRH Princess Michael of
Kent (*born* 15 January 1945, daughter of Baron Gunther von
Reibnitz)
Issue:
(1) Lord Frederick Windsor (Frederick Michael George
     David Louis), *born* 6 April 1979
(2) Lady Gabriella Windsor (Gabriella Marina Alexandra
     Ophelia), *born* 23 April 1981
Residences: Kensington Palace, London W8 4PU; Nether
Lypiatt Manor, Stroud, Glos.
Office: Kensington Palace, London W8 4PU. Tel: 071-938
3519

ORDER OF SUCCESSION

1   HRH The Prince of Wales
2   HRH Prince William of Wales
3   HRH Prince Henry of Wales
4   HRH The Duke of York
5   HRH Princess Beatrice of York
6   HRH Princess Eugenie of York
7   HRH The Prince Edward
8   HRH The Princess Royal
9   Peter Phillips
10 Zara Phillips
11 HRH The Princess Margaret, Countess of Snowdon
12 Viscount Linley
13 Lady Sarah Armstrong-Jones
14 HRH The Duke of Gloucester
15 Earl of Ulster
16 Lady Davina Windsor
17 Lady Rose Windsor
18 HRH The Duke of Kent
19 Baron Downpatrick
20 Lady Marina Charlotte Windsor
21 Lord Nicholas Windsor
22 Lady Helen Taylor
23 Lord Frederick Windsor
24 Lady Gabriella Windsor
25 HRH Princess Alexandra, the Hon. Lady Ogilvy
26 James Ogilvy
27 Marina, Mrs Paul Mowatt

The Earl of St Andrews and HRH Prince Michael of Kent
lost the right of succession to the throne under the Act of
Settlement 1701, through marriage to a Roman Catholic.
However, their children and descendants remain in
succession, provided that they are in communion with the
Church of England

Royal Households

THE QUEEN'S HOUSEHOLD

Lord Chamberlain, The Earl of Airlie, KT, GCVO, PC
Lord Steward, The Viscount Ridley, KG, TD
Master of the Horse, The Lord Somerleyton
Treasurer of the Household, G. Knight, MP
Comptroller of the Household, D. Lightbown, MP
Vice-Chamberlain, S. Chapman, MP

Gold Stick, Maj.-Gen. Lord Michael Fitzalan-Howard, GCVO, CB, CBE, MC; Gen. Sir Desmond Fitzpatrick, GCB, DSO, MBE, MC
Vice-Adm. of the United Kingdom, Adm. Sir Anthony Morton, GBE, KCB
Rear-Adm. of the United Kingdom, Adm. Sir James Eberle, GCB
First and Principal Naval Aide-de-Camp, Adm. Sir Benjamin Bathurst, GCB
Flag Aide de Camp, Adm. Sir John Kerr, KCB
Aides-de-Camp-General, Gen. Sir Peter Inge, GCB; Gen. Sir Michael Wilkes, KCB, CBE; Gen. Sir Charles Guthrie, KCB, LVO, OBE
Air Aides-de-Camp, Air Chief Marshal Sir Michael Graydon, GCB, CBE; Air Chief Marshal Sir Andrew Wilson, KCB, AFC

Mistress of the Robes, The Duchess of Grafton, GCVO
Ladies of the Bedchamber, The Countess of Airlie, CVO; The Lady Farnham
Extra Ladies of the Bedchamber, The Marchioness of Abergavenny, DCVO; The Dowager Countess of Cromer, CVO
Women of the Bedchamber, Hon. Mary Morrison, DCVO; Lady Susan Hussey, DCVO; Mrs John Dugdale, DCVO; The Lady Elton
Extra Women of the Bedchamber, Mrs John Woodroffe, CVO; Lady Rose Baring, DCVO; Mrs Michael Wall, DCVO; Lady Abel Smith, DCVO; Mrs Robert de Pass
Equerries, Lt.-Col. B. A. Stewart-Wilson, CVO; Capt. J. Patrick; Capt. P. Hopkins (temp.)
Extra Equerries, Vice-Adm. Sir Peter Ashmore, KCB, KCVO, DSC; Lt.-Col. The Lord Charteris of Amisfield, GCB, GCVO, OBE, QSO, PC; Maj.-Gen. Sir Simon Cooper, KCVO; Air Cdre the Hon. T. Elworthy, CBE; The Rt Hon. Sir Robert Fellowes, KCB, KCVO; Sir Edward Ford, KCB, KCVO, ERD; Rear-Adm. Sir John Garnier, KCVO, CBE; Rear-Adm. Sir Paul Greening, GCVO; Brig. Sir Geoffrey Hardy-Roberts, KCVO, CB, CBE; The Rt. Hon. Sir William Heseltine, GCB, GCVO, AC, QSO; Rear-Adm. Sir Hugh Janion, KCVO; Lt.-Col. Sir John Johnston, GCVO, MC; Lt.-Col. A. Mather, OBE; Sir Peter Miles, KCVO; Lt.-Col. Sir John Miller, GCVO, DSO, MC; Air Cdre Sir Dennis Mitchell, KBE, CVO, DFC, AFC; The Lord Moore of Wolvercote, GCB, GCVO, CMG, QSO; Lt.-Gen. Sir John Richards, KCB; Lt.-Col. W. H. M. Ross, OBE; Air Vice-Marshal Sir John Severne, KCVO, OBE, AFC; Gp Capt P. Townsend, CVO, DSO, DFC; Rear-Adm. Sir Richard Trowbridge, KCVO; Lt.-Col. G. West, CVO; Air Cdre Sir Archie Winskill, KCVO, CBE, DFC, AE; Rear-Adm. R. Woodard

THE PRIVATE SECRETARY'S OFFICE
Buckingham Palace, London SW1A 1AA

Private Secretary to The Queen, The Rt Hon. Sir Robert Fellowes, KCB, KCVO

Deputy Private Secretary, Sir Kenneth Scott, KCVO, CMG
Assistant Private Secretary, R. B. Janvrin, LVO
Press Secretary, C. V. Anson, LVO
Deputy Press Secretary, G. Crawford
Assistant Press Secretary, Miss P. Russell-Smith
Chief Clerk, Mrs G. S. Coulson, MVO
Secretary to the Private Secretary, Mrs J. Bean, LVO
Clerks, Miss A. Freeman; Mrs A. Galletly; Miss H. Spiller; Miss H. Staveley; Mrs E. Walsh Waring; Miss P. Brown; Miss M. Edwards; Mrs N. Miller; Mrs P. Penfold; Miss N. Thompson
Press Office, Miss K. McGrigor, MVO; Mrs G. Middleburgh; Mrs R. Murdo-Smith, LVO; Miss C. Sillars
Lady-in-Waiting's Office, Mrs D. Phillips; Mrs J. Vince

THE QUEEN'S ARCHIVES
Round Tower, Windsor Castle, Berks

Keeper of The Queen's Archives, The Rt Hon. Sir Robert Fellowes, KCB, KCVO
Assistant Keeper, O. Everett, CVO
Registrar, Lady de Bellaigue, MVO
Assistant Registrar, Miss P. Clark
Curator of the Photographic Collection, Miss F. Dimond, LVO

THE PRIVY PURSE AND TREASURER'S OFFICE
Buckingham Palace, London SW1A 1AA

Keeper of the Privy Purse and Treasurer to The Queen, Maj. Sir Shane Blewitt, KCVO
Deputy Keeper of the Privy Purse and Deputy Treasurer, J. Parsons, LVO
Chief Accountant and Paymaster, D. Walker, LVO
Personnel Officer, Miss P. Lloyd
Assistant Chief Accountant and Paymaster, Miss R. Ward
Assistant Personnel Officer, Mrs C. Jones
Clerks, Mrs C. Auton, MVO; I. Biss; Mrs N. Broad; J. Curr; Miss N. Mooney; Miss C. Robinson; Miss G. Wickham, MVO; Miss P. Green
Land Agent, Sandringham, J. Major
Resident Factor, Balmoral, M. Leslie, LVO

FINANCE AND PROPERTY SERVICES

Director of Finance and Property Services, M. Peat
Deputy Director, Property Services, J. H. Tiltman
Superintending Architect, S. Dhargalkar
Senior Architect, Miss H. Bell
Property Administrator, Miss M. Green
Deputy Property Administrator, M. Bourke
Fire Precautions and Health and Safety Manager, G. Griffiths, MVO
Maintenance Manager, Buckingham Palace, R. Brown
Maintenance Manager, St James's and Kensington Palaces, R. Mole.
Assistant Maintenance Managers, M. Harmer; A. Ryan
Assistant Property Administrator, Mrs H. Dunlop
Management Auditor, I. McGregor
Assistant Management Auditor, Mrs D. Mowbray
Information Systems Manager, I. Hardy
Clerks, Mrs. J. Hillyer; Mrs C. Sharma; Mrs J. Thomas; Miss R. Wickenden

WINDSOR CASTLE

Maintenance Manager, E. Norton
Deputy Maintenance Manager, P. Godwin
Administrative Assistant, Mrs C. Crook

ROYAL ALMONRY

High Almoner, The Rt. Revd the Lord Bishop of St Albans
Hereditary Grand Almoner, The Marquess of Exeter
Sub-Almoner, Revd W. Booth
Secretary, P. Wright, CVO
Assistant Secretary, C. Williams, RVM

THE LORD CHAMBERLAIN'S OFFICE
Buckingham Palace, London SW1A 1AA

Comptroller, Lt.-Col. M. Ross, OBE
Assistant Comptroller, Lt.-Col. A. Mather, OBE
Secretary, P. D. Hartley, MVO
Assistant Secretary, J. Spencer, MVO
State Invitations Assistant, vacant
Clerks, Miss L. Connor; Miss L. Dove; Mrs S. Scott; Miss
   A. Utting
Permanent Lords-in-Waiting, Lt.-Col. The Lord Charteris of
   Amisfield, GCB, GCVO, OBE, QSO, PC; The Lord Moore of
   Wolvercote, GCB, GCVO, CMG, QSO
Lords-in-Waiting, The Viscount Boyne; The Lord Camoys;
   The Viscount Long, CBE; The Viscount Astor; The
   Viscount St Davids; The Viscount Goschen
Baroness-in-Waiting, The Baroness Trumpington
Gentlemen Ushers, C. Greig, CVO, CBE; Gp Capt J. Slessor;
   Maj. N. Chamberlayne-Macdonald, LVO, OBE; Air
   Marshal Sir Roy Austen-Smith, KBE, CB, DFC; Vice-Adm.
   Sir David Loram, KCB, LVO; Capt. M. Barrow, DSO, RN;
   Capt. M. Fulford-Dobson, RN; Lt.-Gen. Sir Richard
   Vickers, KCB, LVO, OBE; Air Vice-Marshal B. Newton, CB,
   OBE; Col. M. Havergal, OBE
Extra Gentlemen Ushers, Maj. T. Harvey, CVO, DSO;
   Maj.-Gen. Sir Cyril Colquhoun, KCVO, CB, OBE; Lt.-Col.
   Sir John Hugo, KCVO, OBE; Vice-Adm. Sir Ronald
   Brockman, KCB, CSI, CIE, CVO, CBE; Air Marshal Sir
   Maurice Heath, KBE, CB, CVO; Sir James Scholtens, KCVO;
   Sir Patrick O'Dea, KCVO; Brig.-Gen. S. Cooper, CVO, OBE,
   CD; Adm. Sir David Williams, GCB; H. Davis, CVO, CM;
   Maj.-Gen. R. Reid, CVO, MC, CD; Lt.-Cdr. J. Holdsworth,
   CVO, OBE, RN; Col. G. Leigh, CVO, CBE; Lt.-Cdr. Sir
   Russell Wood, KCVO, VRD; Air Chief Marshal Sir Neville
   Stack, KCB, CVO, CBE, AFC; Maj.-Gen. Sir Desmond Rice,
   KCVO, CBE; Lt.-Col. Sir Julian Paget, Bt., CVO; S. W. F.
   Martin, CVO
Gentleman Usher to the Sword of State, Gen. Sir Edward
   Burgess, KCB, OBE
Gentleman Usher of the Black Rod, Adm. Sir Richard
   Thomas, KCB, OBE
Serjeants-at-Arms, D. Walker, LVO; Maj. B. Eastwood, MVO,
   MBE; P. Hartley, MVO

Marshal of the Diplomatic Corps, Vice-Adm. Sir James
   Weatherall, KBE
Vice-Marshal, A. St J. H. Figgis, CMG

Constable and Governor of Windsor Castle, Gen. Sir Patrick
   Palmer, KBE
Keeper of the Jewel House, Tower of London, Maj.-Gen.
   C. Tyler, CB
Master of The Queen's Music, Malcolm Williamson, CBE, AO
Poet Laureate, Ted Hughes, OBE
Bargemaster, R. Crouch
Warden of the Swans, Prof. C. Perrins, CVO
Marker of the Swans, D. Barber
Superintendent of the State Apartments, St James's Palace,
   vacant

ECCLESIASTICAL HOUSEHOLD
THE COLLEGE OF CHAPLAINS
Clerk of the Closet, Rt. Revd Bishop of Chelmsford

Deputy Clerk of the Closet, Revd W. Booth
Chaplains to The Queen, Revd A. H. H. Harbottle, LVO;
   Ven. D. N. Griffiths, RD; Revd Canon A. Glendining,
   LVO; Revd Canon J. V. Bean; Revd K. Huxley; Ven.
   P. Ashford; Revd Canon D. C. Gray, TD; Ven. D. Scott;
   Revd Canon E. James; Revd Canon J. Hester; Revd
   S. Pedley; Revd D. Tonge; Revd Canon N. M. Ramm;
   Revd Canon M. A. Moxon; Revd Canon
   R. T. W. McDermid; Revd Canon G. Murphy, LVO;
   Revd Canon R. H. C. Lewis; Revd D. J. Burgess; Revd
   E. R. Ayerst; Revd R. S. Clarke; Revd Canon C. J. Hill;
   Revd Canon K. Pound; Revd J. Haslam; Revd Canon
   G. Hall; Revd Canon A. C. Hill; Revd J. C. Priestley;
   Revd Canon J. O. Colling; Revd Canon G. Jones; Revd
   Canon D. G. Palmer; Revd Canon D. H. Wheaton; Revd
   Canon P. Boulton; Revd Canon R. A. Bowden; Revd
   Canon E. Buchanan; Revd Canon S. Goodridge; Revd
   J. Robson; Revd Canon J. Stanley
Extra Chaplains, Revd Canon J. S. D. Mansel, KCVO, FSA;
   Preb. S. A. Williams, CVO; Ven. E. J. G. Ward, LVO; Revd
   J. R. W. Stott; Revd Canon A. D. Caesar, CVO

CHAPELS ROYAL
Dean of the Chapels Royal, The Bishop of London
Sub-Dean of Chapels Royal, Revd W. Booth
Priests in Ordinary, Revd G. Watkins; Revd H. Mead; Revd
   S. E. Young
Organist, Choirmaster and Composer, R. J. Popplewell, MVO,
   FRCO, FRCM
Domestic Chaplain, Buckingham Palace, Revd W. Booth
Domestic Chaplain, Windsor Castle, The Dean of Windsor
Domestic Chaplain, Sandringham, Revd Canon G. R. Hall
Chaplain, Royal Chapel, Windsor Great Park, Revd Canon
   M. Moxon
Chaplain, Hampton Court Palace, Revd Canon M. Moore
Chaplain, Tower of London, Revd Canon
   J. G. M. W. Murphy, LVO
Organist and Choirmaster, Hampton Court Palace, Gordon
   Reynolds, LVO

MEDICAL HOUSEHOLD
Head of the Medical Household and Physician to The Queen,
   R. Thompson, DM, FRCP
Physician, R. W. Davey, MB, BS
Serjeant Surgeon, B. T. Jackson, MS, FRCS
Surgeon Oculist, P. Holmes Sellors, LVO, BM, B.ch., FRCS
Surgeon Gynaecologist, M. E. Setchell, FRCS, FRCOG
Surgeon Dentist, N. A. Sturridge, CVO, LDS, BDS, DDS
Orthopaedic Surgeon, R. H. Vickers, MA, BM, B.ch., FRCS
Physician to the Household, J. Cunningham, DM, FRCP
Surgeon to the Household, A. A. M. Lewis, MB, FRCS
Surgeon Oculist to the Household, T. J. ffytche, FRCS
Apothecary to The Queen and to the Household,
   N. R. Southward, LVO, MB, B.chir.
Apothecary to the Household at Windsor, J. H. D. Briscoe,
   MB, B.Chir., D.obst.
Apothecary to the Household at Sandringham,
   I. K. Campbell, MB, BS, FRCGP
Coroner of The Queen's Household, J. Burton, CBE, MB, BS

CENTRAL CHANCERY OF THE ORDERS OF
KNIGHTHOOD
St James's Palace, London SW1

Secretary, Lt.-Col. A. Mather, OBE
Assistant Secretary, Miss R. Wells, MVO
Clerks, J. Bagwell Purefoy; Miss F. Bean; Mrs T. Isaac; Miss
   S. Koller, MVO; J. McGurk, MVO; D. Pogson; Miss
   A Weatherall

THE HONOURABLE CORPS OF GENTLEMEN-AT-ARMS
St James's Palace, London SW1

Captain, The Lord Hesketh
Lieutenant, Lt.-Col. Sir James Scott, Bt.
Standard Bearer, Maj. Sir Fergus Matheson of Matheson, Bt.
Clerk of the Cheque and Adjutant, Col. T. Hall
Harbinger, Brig. A. N. Breitmeyer

Gentlemen of the Corps

Colonels, Sir Piers Bengough, KCVO, OBE; Hon. N. Crossley, TD; T. Wilson; D. Fanshawe, OBE; J. Baker; R. ffrench Blake; Sir William Mahon, Bt.
Lieutenant-Colonels, R. Mayfield, DSO; B. Lockhart; Hon. P. H. Lewis; R. Macfarlane; Hon. G. B. Norrie; J. H. Fisher, OBE; R. Ker, MC; P. Chamberlin
Majors, J. A. J. Nunn; Sir Philip Duncombe, Bt.; I. B. Ramsden, MBE; M. J. Drummond-Brady; A. Arkwright; G. M. B. Colenso-Jones; T. Gooch, MBE; J. B. B. Cockcroft; C. J. H. Gurney; J. R. E. Nelson; P. D. Johnson
Captain, The Lord Monteagle of Brandon

THE QUEEN'S BODY GUARD OF THE YEOMEN OF THE GUARD
St James's Palace, London SW1

Captain, The Earl of Strathmore and Kinghorne
Lieutenant, Col. A. B. Pemberton, CVO, MBE
Clerk of the Cheque and Adjutant, Col. G. W. Tufnell
Ensign, Lt.-Col. S. Longsdon
Exons, Maj. C. Marriott; Maj. C. Enderby

MASTER OF THE HOUSEHOLD'S
DEPARTMENT

BOARD OF GREEN CLOTH
Buckingham Palace, London SW1A 1AA

Master of the Household, Maj.-Gen. Sir Simon Cooper, KCVO
Deputy Master of the Household, Lt.-Col. B. A. Stewart-Wilson, CVO
Assistants to the Master of the Household, M. T. Parker, MVO; P. Jackson
Chief Clerk, M. C. W. N. Jephson, MVO
Chief Housekeeper, Miss H. Colebrook
Deputy to Assistant F, M. Bovaird
Senior Clerk G, S. Stacey
Clerks, Miss S. Bell; Miss S. Derry, LVO; Miss S. Fergus, MVO; Miss S. Hargreaves; Miss E. Henderson
Flower Arranger, Mrs P. Pentney
Palace Steward, A. Jarred, RVM
Royal Chef, L. Mann, RVM
Superintendent, Windsor Castle, Maj. B. Eastwood, MVO, MBE
Superintendent, The Palace of Holyroodhouse, Lt.-Col. D. Anderson

ROYAL MEWS DEPARTMENT
Buckingham Palace, London SW1W 0QH

Crown Equerry, Lt.-Col. S. Gilbart-Denham
Veterinary Surgeon, P. Scott Dunn, LVO, MRCVS
Superintendent Royal Mews, Buckingham Palace, Maj. A. Smith, MBE
Comptroller of Stores, Maj. L. Marsham, MVO
Chief Clerk, P. Almond, MVO
Deputy Chief Clerk, A. Marshall
Assistant Chief Clerk, Mrs J. Clark

THE ROYAL COLLECTION TRUST
St James's Palace, London SW1

Director of Royal Collection and Surveyor of The Queen's Works of Art, Sir Geoffrey de Bellaigue, KCVO, FBA, FSA
Deputy Director (Finance), J. Parsons, LVO
Surveyor of The Queen's Pictures, C. Lloyd
Surveyor Emeritus of The Queen's Pictures, Sir Oliver Millar, GCVO, FBA, FSA
Librarian, The Royal Library, Windsor Castle, O. Everett, CVO
Deputy Surveyor of The Queen's Works of Art, H. Roberts, FSA
Librarian Emeritus, Sir Robin Mackworth-Young, GCVO, FSA
Director of Media Affairs, R. Arbiter
Curator of the Print Room, The Hon. Mrs Roberts, MVO
Administrator and Assistant to The Surveyors (Military), D. Rankin-Hunt, MVO, TD
Assistant to The Surveyor of The Queen's Pictures, C. Noble, MVO
Secretary to the Director, Miss C. Paybody
Exhibitions Assistant (Pictures), Hon. C. Neville
Senior Picture Restorer, Miss V. Pemberton-Pigott, MVO
Chief Restorer, Old Master Drawings, M. Warnes, MVO
Senior Furniture Restorer, E. Fancourt, RVM
Armourer, J. Jackson, RVM
Chief Binder, R. Day, MVO, RVM
Deputy Curator of the Print Room, Mrs H. Ryan, MVO
Assistant Curator (Exhibitions), Miss T.-M. Morton
Bibliographer, Miss B. Wright, MVO
Superintendent Royal Collection Hampton Court Palace, J. Cowell, MVO
Computer Systems Manager, S. Patterson
Financial Controller, Mrs G. Johnson
Accountant, Miss M. O'Connell

ROYAL COLLECTION ENTERPRISES LTD

Managing Director, M. E. K. Hewlett
Secretary to the Managing Director, Mrs C. Murphy, MVO
Finance Director, Mrs G. Johnson
Retail Manager, S. R. Spencer
Administrator Public Enterprises, Buckingham Palace, Miss J. Grist
Administrator Public Enterprises, Windsor Castle, Mrs A. Laing
Assistant Administrator Public Enterprises, Windsor Castle, Mrs H. Tarrant
Head of Photographic Services, Miss G. Campling
Merchandise Consultant, Mrs K. Munro

ASCOT OFFICE
St James's Palace, London SW1
Tel 071-930 9882

Her Majesty's Representative at Ascot, Col. Sir Piers Bengough, KCVO, OBE
Secretary, Miss L. Thompson-Royds

THE QUEEN'S HOUSEHOLD IN
SCOTLAND

Hereditary Lord High Constable, The Earl of Erroll
Hereditary Master of the Household, The Duke of Argyll
Lord Lyon King of Arms, Sir Malcolm Innes of Edingight, KCVO, WS

Hereditary Bearer of the Royal Banner of Scotland, The Earl of Dundee
Hereditary Bearer of the Scottish National Flag, The Earl of Lauderdale
Hereditary Keepers:
  Palace of Holyroodhouse, The Duke of Hamilton and Brandon
  Falkland Palace, M. Crichton-Stuart
  Stirling Castle, The Earl of Mar and Kellie
  Dunstaffnage Castle, The Duke of Argyll
  Dunconnel Castle, Sir Fitzroy Maclean, Bt., CBE
Hereditary Carver, Sir Ralph Anstruther, GCVO, MC
Keeper of Dumbarton Castle, Brig. A. S. Pearson, CB, DSO, OBE, MC, TD
Governor of Edinburgh Castle, Maj.-Gen. M. Scott, CBE, DSO
Historiographer, vacant
Botanist, Prof. D. Henderson, CBE, FRSE
Painter and Limner, D. A. Donaldson, RSA, RP
Sculptor in Ordinary, Prof. Sir Eduardo Paolozzi, CBE, RA
Astronomer, vacant
Heralds and Pursuivants, see page 287.

ECCLESIASTICAL HOUSEHOLD
Dean of the Chapel Royal, Very Revd W. J. Morris, DD, LL.D
Dean of the Order of the Thistle, The Very Revd G. I. Macmillan
Chaplains in Ordinary, Very Revd W. J. Morris, DD, LL.D.; Revd J. McLeod; Very Revd G. I. Macmillan; Revd M. D. Craig; Revd W. B. R. Macmillan, LL.D, DD.; Revd J. L. Weatherhead; Revd A. S. Todd, DD; Revd C. Robertson; Revd J. A. Simpson; Revd N. W. Drummond
Extra Chaplains, Very Revd R. W. V. Selby Wright, CVO, TD, DD, FRSE, FSAScot.; Very Revd W. R. Sanderson, DD; Very Revd R. L. Small, CBE, DD; Revd T. J. T. Nicol, MVO, MBE, MC, TD; Very Revd Prof. J. McIntyre, CVO, DD, FRSE; Revd C. Forrester-Paton; Revd H. W. M. Cant; Very Revd R. A. S. Barbour, KCVO, MC, DD; Revd K. MacVicar, MBE, DFC, TD; Very Revd W. B. Johnston, DD; Revd A. J. C. Macfarlane; Revd M. I. Levison
Domestic Chaplain, Balmoral, Revd J. A. K. Angus, LVO, TD

MEDICAL HOUSEHOLD
Physicians in Scotland, P. Brunt, MD, FRCP; A. L. Muir, MD, FRCP
Surgeons in Scotland, I. B. Macleod, MB, ch.B., FRCS; J. Engeset, ch.M., FRCS
Apothecary to the Household at Balmoral, D. J. A. Glass, MB, ch.B.
Apothecary to the Household at the Palace of Holyroodhouse, Dr J. Cormack, MD, FRCGP.

THE QUEEN'S BODY GUARD FOR SCOTLAND

ROYAL COMPANY OF ARCHERS
Archers' Hall, Edinburgh

Captain-General and Gold Stick for Scotland, Col. the Lord Clydesmuir, KT, CB, MBE, TD
Captains, Maj. the Lord Home of the Hirsel, KT; The Duke of Buccleuch and Queensberry, KT; Sir Hew Hamilton-Dalrymple, Bt., KCVO; Maj. the Earl of Wemyss and March, KT
Lieutenants, The Earl of Airlie, KT, GCVO; Capt. Sir Iain Tennant, KT; Capt. N. E. F. Dalrymple-Hamilton, CVO, MBE, DSC, RN; The Marquess of Lothian, KCVO
Ensigns, Cdre Sir John Clerk of Penicuik, Bt., CBE, VRD; The Earl of Elgin and Kincardine, KT; Col. G. R. Simpson, DSO, LVO, TD; Maj. Sir David Butter, KCVO, MC

Brigadiers, The Earl of Minto, OBE; Maj.-Gen. Sir John Swinton, KCVO, OBE; Gen. Sir Michael Gow, GCB; The Hon. Lord Elliott, MC; Maj. the Hon. Sir Lachlan Maclean, Bt.; The Rt. Hon. Lord Younger of Prestwick, KCVO, TD; Capt. G. Burnet, LVO; The Duke of Montrose; Lt.-Gen. Sir Norman Arthur, KCB; The Hon. Sir William Macpherson of Cluny, TD; Sir David Nickson, KBE; Maj. the Lord Glenarthur; Earl of Dalkeith
Adjutant, Maj. the Hon. Sir Lachlan Maclean, Bt.
Surgeon, Dr P. A. P. Mackenzie, TD
Chaplain, Very Revd R. Selby Wright, CVO, TD, DD, FRSE
President of the Council and Silver Stick for Scotland, Maj. Sir Hew Hamilton-Dalrymple, Bt., KCVO
Vice-President, Capt. Sir Iain Tennant, KT
Secretary, Col. H. F. O. Bewsher, LVO, OBE
Treasurer, J. Martin Haldane

HOUSEHOLD OF THE PRINCE PHILIP, DUKE OF EDINBURGH

Treasurer, Sir Brian McGrath, KCVO
Private Secretary, Brig. M. G. Hunt-Davis, CBE
Equerry, Wg Cdr. C. H. Moran
Extra Equerries, J. B. V. Orr, CVO; Sir Richard Davies, KCVO, CBE; Lord Buxton of Alsa; Brig. C. Robertson, CVO
Temporary Equerries, Maj. I. Grant, RM; Capt. G. Inglis-Jones; Capt. E. Bearcroft
Chief Clerk and Accountant, V. G. Jewell, MVO

HOUSEHOLD OF QUEEN ELIZABETH THE QUEEN MOTHER

Lord Chamberlain, The Earl of Crawford and Balcarres, PC
Private Secretary, Comptroller and Equerry, Capt. Sir Alastair Aird, KCVO
Assistant Private Secretary and Equerry, Maj. R. Seymour, CVO
Treasurer and Equerry, Maj. Sir Ralph Anstruther, Bt., GCVO, MC
Equerry, Capt. the Hon. E. Dawson-Damer (*temp.*)
Extra Equerries, Maj. Sir John Griffin, KCVO; The Lord Sinclair, CVO; Maj. W. Richardson, LVO; Maj. D. McMicking, LVO; Capt. A. Windham, LVO
Apothecary to the Household, Dr N. Southward, LVO, MB, B.chir.
Surgeon-Apothecary to the Household (Royal Lodge, Windsor), Dr J. Briscoe, D.obst.
Mistress of the Robes, vacant
Ladies of the Bedchamber, The Dowager Viscountess Hambleden, GCVO; The Lady Grimthorpe, CVO
Women of the Bedchamber, Dame Frances Campbell-Preston, DCVO; Lady Angela Oswald, LVO; The Hon. Mrs Rhodes; Mrs Michael Gordon-Lennox
Extra Women of the Bedchamber, Lady Victoria Wemyss, CVO; Lady Jean Rankin, DCVO; Miss Jane Walker-Okeover; Lady Margaret Colville; Lady Elizabeth Basset, DCVO
Clerk Comptroller, M. Blanch, CVO
Clerk Accountant, J. P. Kyle, LVO
Information Officer, Mrs R. Murphy, LVO
Clerks, Miss F. Fletcher, MVO; Mrs W. Stevens

HOUSEHOLD OF THE PRINCE AND PRINCESS OF WALES

Private Secretary and Treasurer to The Prince of Wales, Cdr.
R. J. Aylard, RN
Private Secretary to the Princess of Wales, P. Jephson
Deputy Private Secretary to The Prince of Wales, S. Lamport.
Assistant Private Secretaries to The Prince of Wales,
H. Merrill; Miss B. Harley
Press Secretary to the Prince of Wales, A. Percival
Assistant Press Secretary to the Prince of Wales, Miss
A. Henney
Press Secretary to the Princess of Wales, G. Crawford
Equerry to The Prince of Wales, Cdr. R. Fraser
Equerry to The Princess of Wales, Capt. E. Musto, RM
Extra Equerries to The Prince of Wales, The Hon. Edward
Adeane, CVO; Maj.-Gen. Sir Christopher Airy, KCVO, CBE;
Sqn. Ldr. Sir David Checketts, KCVO; Sir David Landale,
KCVO; Sir John Riddle, Bt., CVO; G. J. Ward, CBE; Col.
J. Q. Winter, LVO
Ladies-in-Waiting, Miss Anne Beckwith-Smith, LVO;
Viscountess Campden; Mrs Max Pike; Miss Alexandra
Loyd; Mrs James Lonsdale
Extra Lady-in-Waiting, Lady Sarah McCorquodale
Secretary to the Duchy of Cornwall and Keeper of the Records,
J. N. C. James, CBE

HOUSEHOLD OF THE DUKE AND DUCHESS OF YORK

*Private Secretary, Treasurer and Extra Equerry to the Duke
and Duchess of York*, Capt. N. Blair, RN
*Comptroller and Assistant Private Secretary to the Duke and
Duchess of York*, Mrs Jonathan Mathias
Equerry to The Duke of York, Capt. R. Maitland-Titterton
Extra Equerry, Maj. G. W. McLean

HOUSEHOLD OF THE PRINCE EDWARD

Private Secretary, Lt.-Col. S. G. O'Dwyer
Assistant Private Secretary, Mrs R. Warburton, MVO

HOUSEHOLD OF THE PRINCESS ROYAL

Private Secretary, Lt.-Col. P. Gibbs, LVO
Assistant Private Secretary, The Hon. Mrs Louloudis
Ladies-in-Waiting, Mrs Richard Carew Pole, LVO; Mrs
Andrew Feilden, LVO; The Hon. Mrs Legge-Bourke, LVO;
Mrs William Nunneley; Mrs Timothy Holderness-
Roddam; Mrs Charles Ritchie; Mrs David Bowes Lyon
Extra Ladies-in-Waiting, Miss Victoria Legge-Bourke, LVO;
Mrs Malcolm Innes, LVO; The Countess of Lichfield

HOUSEHOLD OF THE PRINCESS MARGARET, COUNTESS OF SNOWDON

Private Secretary and Comptroller, The Lord Napier and
Ettrick, KCVO
Lady-in-Waiting, The Hon. Mrs Whitehead, LVO

Extra Ladies-in-Waiting, Lady Elizabeth Cavendish, LVO;
Lady Aird, LVO; Mrs Robin Benson, LVO, OBE; Lady Juliet
Townsend, LVO; Mrs Jane Stevens, LVO; The Hon. Mrs
Wills, LVO; The Lady Glenconner, LVO; The Countess
Alexander of Tunis, LVO; Mrs Charles Vyvyan

HOUSEHOLD OF THE DUKE AND DUCHESS OF GLOUCESTER

Private Secretary, Comptroller and Equerry, Maj.
N. M. L. Barne
Assistant Private Secretary to The Duchess of Gloucester, Miss
Suzanne Marland
Extra Equerry, Lt.-Col. Sir Simon Bland, KCVO
Ladies-in-Waiting, Mrs Michael Wigley, CVO; Mrs Euan
McCorquodale, LVO; Mrs Howard Page
Extra Lady-in-Waiting, Miss Jennifer Thomson
Temporary Lady-in-Waiting, The Lady Camoys

HOUSEHOLD OF PRINCESS ALICE, DUCHESS OF GLOUCESTER

Private Secretary, Comptroller and Equerry, Maj.
N. M. L. Barne
Extra Equerry, Lt.-Col. Sir Simon Bland, KCVO
Ladies-in-Waiting, Dame Jean Maxwell-Scott, DCVO; Mrs
Michael Harvey
Extra Ladies-in-Waiting, Miss Diana Harrison; The Hon.
Jane Walsh, LVO; Miss Jane Egerton-Warburton, LVO

HOUSEHOLD OF THE DUKE AND DUCHESS OF KENT

Private Secretary, Cdr. R. M. Walker
Extra Equerries, Lt.-Cdr. Sir Richard Buckley, KCVO; Cdr.
R. M. Walker
Temporary Equerry, Capt. A. Tetley
Ladies-in-Waiting, Mrs Fiona Henderson, CVO; Mrs David
Napier, LVO; Mrs Colin Marsh, LVO; Mrs Peter Wilmot-
Sitwell, LVO; Mrs Julian Tomkins; Mrs Peter Troughton

HOUSEHOLD OF PRINCE AND PRINCESS MICHAEL OF KENT

Personal Secretary, Miss E. Moore-Searson
Equerry, Lt.-Col. Sir Christopher Thompson, Bt.
Ladies-in-Waiting, The Hon. Mrs Sanders; Miss Anne
Frost; Lady Thompson
Extra Lady-in-Waiting, Mrs J. Fellowes

HOUSEHOLD OF PRINCESS ALEXANDRA, THE HON. LADY OGILVY

Comptroller and Private Secretary, Rear-Adm. Sir John
Garnier, KCVO, CBE
Extra Equerry, Maj. Sir Peter Clarke, KCVO
Lady-in-Waiting, Lady Mary Mumford, CVO
Extra Ladies-in-Waiting, Mrs Peter Afia; Lady Mary
Colman; Lady Nicholas Gordon Lennox; The Hon. Lady
Rowley; Dame Mona Mitchell, DCVO

Royal Finances

FUNDING

THE CIVIL LIST

The Civil List dates back to the late 17th century, when it was used by the Sovereign to pay the salaries of judges, ambassadors and other government offices as well as the expenses of the royal household. In 1760 on the accession of George III it was decided that the Civil List would be provided by Parliament in return for the King surrendering the hereditary revenues of the Crown. Each sovereign since then has agreed to continue the arrangement.

The Civil List paid to The Queen is charged on the Consolidated Fund. Until 1972, the amount of money allocated annually under the Civil List was set for the duration of a reign. The system was then altered to a fixed annual payment for ten years but from 1975 high inflation made an annual review necessary. The system of payments reverted to the practice of a fixed annual payment for ten years from 1 January 1991.

The Civil List Acts provide for other members of the royal family to receive parliamentary annuities from government funds to meet the expenses of carrying out their official duties. Since 1975 The Queen has reimbursed the Treasury for the annuities paid to the Duke of Gloucester, the Duke of Kent and Princess Alexandra. In November 1992 it was announced that from 1 April 1993 The Queen will reimburse all the annuities except those paid to Queen Elizabeth the Queen Mother and the Duke of Edinburgh.

The Prince of Wales does not receive a parliamentary annuity. He derives his income from the revenues of the Duchy of Cornwall and these monies meet the official and private expenses of the Prince of Wales and his family.

The annual payments for the years 1991–2000 are:

The Queen	£7,900,000
Queen Elizabeth the Queen Mother	643,000
The Duke of Edinburgh	359,000
*The Duke of York	249,000
*The Prince Edward	96,000
*The Princess Royal	228,000
*The Princess Margaret, Countess of Snowdon	219,000
*Princess Alice, Duchess of Gloucester	87,000
*The Duke of Gloucester	175,000
*The Duke of Kent	236,000
*Princess Alexandra	225,000
	10,237,000
*Refunded to the Treasury	1,515,000
Total	8,722,000

GRANT-IN-AID

Grant-in-aid is voted annually by Parliament to pay for the upkeep of the royal palaces which are used as royal residences or for official or ceremonial purposes.

THE PRIVY PURSE

The funds received by the Privy Purse pay for official expenses incurred by The Queen as head of state and for some of The Queen's private expenditure. The revenues of the Duchy of Lancaster are the principal source of income for the Privy Purse. The revenues of the Duchy were retained by George III in 1760 when the hereditary revenues were surrendered in exchange for the Civil List.

PERSONAL INCOME

The Queen's personal income derives mostly from investments, and is used to meet private expenditure.

DEPARTMENTAL VOTES

Other items of expenditure connected with the official duties of the royal family which fall on votes of government departments include:

The Royal Yacht; The Queen's Flight (Ministry of Defence)
Marshal of the Diplomatic Corps; overseas visits at the request of government departments (Foreign and Commonwealth Office)
Royal palaces (Department of National Heritage)
The Royal Train (Department of Transport)
Central Chancery of the Orders of Knighthood (HM Treasury)

TAXATION

The Sovereign is not legally liable to pay income tax, capital gains tax or inheritance tax. After income tax was reintroduced in 1842 some income tax was paid voluntarily by the Sovereign but over a long period these payments were phased out. In November 1992 the Prime Minister announced that The Queen had offered to pay tax on a voluntary basis from 6 April 1993, and that the Prince of Wales also wished to pay tax on a voluntary basis on his income from the Duchy of Cornwall. (He is already taxed in all other respects.)

The provisions for The Queen and the Prince of Wales to pay tax were set out in a Memorandum of Understanding on Royal Taxation presented to Parliament on 11 February 1993. The main provisions are that The Queen will pay income tax and capital gains tax in respect of her private income and assets, and on the proportion of the income and capital gains of the Privy Purse used for private purposes. Inheritance tax will be paid on The Queen's assets, except for those which pass to the next Sovereign, whether automatically or by gift or bequest. The Prince of Wales will pay income tax on income from the Duchy of Cornwall used for private purposes.

The Prince of Wales has confirmed that he intends to pay tax on the same basis following his accession to the throne.

Other members of the royal family are subject to tax as for any taxpayer.

Military Ranks and Titles

THE QUEEN

Lord High Admiral of the United Kingdom

Colonel-in-Chief
The Life Guards; The Blues and Royals (Royal Horse Guards and 1st Dragoons); The Royal Scots Dragoon Guards (Carabiniers and Greys); The Queen's Royal Lancers; Royal Tank Regiment; Corps of Royal Engineers; Grenadier Guards; Coldstream Guards; Scots Guards; Irish Guards; Welsh Guards; The Royal Welch Fusiliers; The Queen's Lancashire Regiment; The Argyll and Sutherland Highlanders (Princess Louise's); The Royal Green Jackets; Adjutant-General's Corps; The Governor-General's Horse Guards (of Canada); The King's Own Calgary Regiment; Canadian Forces Military Engineers Branch; Royal 22e Regiment (of Canada); Governor-General's Foot Guards (of Canada); The Canadian Grenadier Guards; Le Regiment de la Chaudiere (of Canada); 2nd Bn Royal New Brunswick Regiment (North Shore); The 48th Highlanders of Canada; The Argyll and Sutherland Highlanders of Canada (Princess Louise's); The Calgary Highlanders; Royal Australian Engineers; Royal Australian Infantry Corps; Royal Australian Army Ordnance Corps; Royal Australian Army Nursing Corps; The Corps of Royal New Zealand Engineers; Royal New Zealand Infantry Regiment; Royal New Zealand Army Ordnance Corps; Royal Malta Artillery; The Malawi Rifles

Captain-General
Royal Regiment of Artillery; The Honourable Artillery Company; Combined Cadet Force; Royal Regiment of Canadian Artillery; Royal Regiment of Australian Artillery; Royal Regiment of New Zealand Artillery; Royal New Zealand Armoured Corps

Patron
Royal Army Chaplains' Department

Air Commodore-in-Chief
Royal Auxiliary Air Force; Royal Air Force Regiment; Royal Observer Corps; Air Reserve (of Canada); Royal Australian Air Force Reserve

Commandant-in-Chief
Royal Air Force College, Cranwell

Hon. Air Commodore
RAF Marham

HM QUEEN ELIZABETH THE QUEEN MOTHER

Colonel-in-Chief
1st The Queen's Dragoon Guards; The Queen's Royal Hussars (The Queen's Own and Royal Irish); 9th/12th Royal Lancers (Prince of Wales's); The King's Regiment; The Royal Anglian Regiment; The Light Infantry; The Black Watch (Royal Highland Regiment); Royal Army Medical Corps; The Black Watch (Royal Highland Regiment) of Canada; The Toronto Scottish Regiment; Canadian Forces Medical Services; Royal Australian Army Medical Corps; Royal New Zealand Army Medical Corps

Hon. Colonel
The Royal Yeomanry; The London Scottish; Inns of Court and City Yeomanry

Commandant-in-Chief
Women's Royal Naval Service; Women's Royal Air Force; RAF Central Flying School

HRH THE PRINCE PHILIP, DUKE OF EDINBURGH

Admiral of the Fleet
Field Marshal
Marshal of the Royal Air Force

Admiral of the Fleet, Royal Australian Navy
Field Marshal, Australian Military Forces
Marshal of the Royal Australian Air Force

Admiral of the Fleet, Royal New Zealand Navy
Field Marshal, New Zealand Army
Marshal of the Royal New Zealand Air Force

Captain-General, Royal Marines

Admiral
Royal Canadian Sea Cadets

Colonel-in-Chief
The Duke of Edinburgh's Royal Regiment (Berkshire and Wiltshire); Queen's Own Highlanders (Seaforth and Camerons); Corps of Royal Electrical and Mechanical Engineers; Intelligence Corps; Army Cadet Force; The Royal Canadian Regiment; The Royal Hamilton Light Infantry (Wentworth Regiment) (of Canada); The Cameron Highlanders of Ottawa; The Queen's Own Cameron Highlanders of Canada; The Seaforth Highlanders of Canada; The Royal Canadian Army Cadets; The Royal Australian Corps of Electrical and Mechanical Engineers; The Australian Cadet Corps; The Royal New Zealand Corps of Electrical and Mechanical Engineers

Deputy Colonel-in-Chief
The Queen's Royal Hussars (The Queen's Own and Royal Irish)

Colonel
Grenadier Guards

Hon. Colonel
Edinburgh and Heriot-Watt Universities Officers' Training Corps; The Trinidad and Tobago Regiment

Air Commodore-in-Chief
Air Training Corps; Royal Canadian Air Cadets

Hon. Air Commodore
RAF Kinloss

HRH THE PRINCE OF WALES

Captain, Royal Navy
Group Captain, Royal Air Force

Colonel-in-Chief
The Royal Dragoon Guards; The Cheshire Regiment; The Royal Regiment of Wales (24th/41st Foot); The

Gordon Highlanders; The Parachute Regiment; 2nd King Edward VII's Own Gurkha Rifles (The Sirmoor Rifles); Army Air Corps; The Royal Canadian Dragoons; Lord Strathcona's Horse (Royal Canadians); Royal Regiment of Canada; Royal Winnipeg Rifles; Royal Australian Armoured Corps; 2nd Bn The Royal Pacific Islands Regiment

Colonel
Welsh Guards

Air Commodore-in-Chief
Royal New Zealand Air Force

Hon. Air Commodore
RAF Brawdy; RAF Valley

HRH THE PRINCESS OF WALES

Colonel-in-Chief
The Light Dragoons; The Princess of Wales's Royal Regiment (Queen's and Royal Hampshires); The Princess of Wales's Own Regiment (of Canada); The West Nova Scotia Regiment (of Canada); The Royal Australian Survey Corps

Hon. Air Commodore
RAF Wittering

HRH THE DUKE OF YORK

Lieutenant-Commander, Royal Navy

Admiral
Sea Cadet Corps

Colonel-in-Chief
The Staffordshire Regiment (The Prince of Wales's); The Royal Irish Regiment (27th (Inniskilling), 83rd, 87th and The Ulster Defence Regiment); Canadian Airborne Regiment

HRH THE PRINCESS ROYAL

Chief Commandant
Women's Royal Naval Service

Colonel-in-Chief
The King's Royal Hussars; Royal Corps of Signals; The Royal Scots (The Royal Regiment); The Worcestershire and Sherwood Foresters Regiment (29th/45th Foot); The Royal Logistic Corps; 8th Canadian Hussars (Princess Louise's); Canadian Forces Communications and Electronics Branch; The Grey and Simcoe Foresters; The Royal Regina Rifle Regiment; Royal Newfoundland Regiment; Royal Australian Corps of Signals; Royal New Zealand Corps of Signals; Royal New Zealand Nursing Corps

Hon. Colonel
London University Officers' Training Corps

Hon. Air Commodore
RAF Lyneham

Commandant-in-Chief
Women's Transport Service (FANY)

HRH THE PRINCESS MARGARET, COUNTESS OF SNOWDON

Colonel-in-Chief
The Royal Highland Fusiliers (Princess Margaret's Own Glasgow and Ayrshire Regiment); Queen Alexandra's Royal Army Nursing Corps; The Highland Fusiliers of Canada; The Princess Louise Fusiliers; The Bermuda Regiment

Deputy Colonel-in-Chief
The Royal Anglian Regiment

Hon. Air Commodore
RAF Coningsby

HRH PRINCESS ALICE, DUCHESS OF GLOUCESTER

Air Chief Marshal

Colonel-in-Chief
The King's Own Scottish Borderers; Royal Australian Corps of Transport; Royal New Zealand Corps of Transport

Deputy Colonel-in-Chief
The King's Royal Hussars; The Royal Anglian Regiment

Air Chief Commandant
Women's Royal Air Force

HRH THE DUKE OF GLOUCESTER

Colonel-in-Chief
The Gloucestershire Regiment

Deputy Colonel-in-Chief
The Royal Logistic Corps

Hon. Colonel
Royal Monmouthshire Royal Engineers (Militia)

Hon. Air Commodore
RAF Odiham

HRH THE DUCHESS OF GLOUCESTER

Colonel-in-Chief
Royal Australian Army Educational Corps; Royal New Zealand Educational Corps

Deputy Colonel-in-Chief
Adjutant-General's Corps

HRH THE DUKE OF KENT

Field Marshal
Hon. Air Vice-Marshal

Colonel-in-Chief
The Royal Regiment of Fusiliers; The Devonshire and Dorset Regiment; The Lorne Scots Regiment (Peel, Dufferin and Hamilton Regiment)

Colonel
Scots Guards

Hon. Air Commodore
RAF Leuchars

HRH THE DUCHESS OF KENT

Hon. Major-General

Colonel-in-Chief
The Prince of Wales's Own Regiment of Yorkshire

Deputy Colonel-in-Chief
The Royal Dragoon Guards; Adjutant-General's Corps;
The Royal Logistic Corps

HRH PRINCE MICHAEL OF KENT

Major (retd), The Royal Hussars (Prince of Wales's Own)

Hon. Auxiliary Commodore
Royal Naval Auxiliary Service

HRH PRINCESS ALEXANDRA, THE HON. LADY OGILVY

Patron
Queen Alexandra's Royal Naval Nursing Service

Colonel-in-Chief
The King's Own Royal Border Regiment; The Queen's
Own Rifles of Canada; The Canadian Scottish Regiment
(Princess Mary's)

Deputy Colonel-in-Chief
The Queen's Royal Lancers; The Light Infantry

Deputy Hon. Colonel
The Royal Yeomanry

Patron and Air Chief Commandant
Princess Mary's Royal Air Force Nursing Service

The Royal Arms

ENGLAND

1st and 4th quarters (representing England) – Gules, three
lions passant guardant in pale Or
2nd quarter (representing Scotland) – Or, a lion rampant
within a double tressure flory counterflory Gules
3rd quarter (representing Ireland) – Azure, a harp Or,
stringed Argent
The whole shield is encircled with the Garter

SCOTLAND

The Royal Arms shown with the Lion of Scotland in the 1st
and 4th quarters, and the Lions of England in the 2nd
quarter
The whole shield is encircled with the Thistle

SUPPORTERS (ENGLAND)

Dexter (right) – a lion rampant guardant Or, imperially
crowned (shown in Scotland on the sinister)
Sinister (left) – a unicorn Argent, armed, crined, and
unguled Or, gorged with a coronet composed of crosses
patées and fleurs-de-lis, a chain affixed, passing between
the forelegs, and reflexed over the back (shown in
Scotland on the dexter and imperially crowned)

CRESTS

England – the Royal Crown Proper thereon a lion statant
guardant Or imperially crowned also Proper
Scotland – upon an imperial crown Proper a lion sejant
affrontée Gules imperially crowned Or, holding in the
dexter paw a sword and in the sinister a sceptre erect, also
Proper
Ireland – a tower triple-towered of the First, from the portal
a hart springing Argent, attired and hooved Or

BADGES

England – the red and white rose united, slipped and leaved
proper
Scotland – a thistle, slipped and leaved proper
Ireland – a shamrock leaf slipped vert; also a harp or,
stringed argent
United Kingdom – the rose of England, the thistle of
Scotland, and the shamrock of Ireland engrafted on the
same stem proper, and an escutcheon charged as the
Union Flag (all ensigned with the Royal Crown)
Wales – upon a mount vert a dragon passant, wings elevated
gules

The House of Windsor

King George V assumed by royal proclamation (17 June 1917) for his House and family, as well as for all descendants in the male line of Queen Victoria who are subjects of these realms, the name of Windsor.

KING GEORGE V (George Frederick Ernest Albert), second son of King Edward VII, *born* 3 June 1865; *married* 6 July 1893 HSH Princess Victoria Mary Augusta Louise Olga Pauline Claudine Agnes of Teck (Queen Mary, *born* 26 May 1867; *died* 24 March 1953); *succeeded* to the throne 6 May 1910; *died* 20 January 1936. *Issue:*

1. HRH PRINCE EDWARD Albert Christian George Andrew Patrick David, *born* 23 June 1894, *succeeded* to the throne as King Edward VIII, 20 January 1936; *abdicated* 11 December 1936; created *Duke of Windsor*, 1936; *married* 3 June 1937, Mrs Wallis Warfield (Her Grace The Duchess of Windsor, *born* 19 June 1896; *died* 24 April 1986), *died* 28 May 1972

2. HRH PRINCE ALBERT Frederick Arthur George, *born* 14 December 1895, *created* Duke of York 1920; *married* 26 April 1923, Lady Elizabeth Bowes-Lyon, youngest daughter of the 14th Earl of Strathmore and Kinghorne (HM Queen Elizabeth the Queen Mother, *see* page 123–4), *succeeded* to the throne as King George VI, 11 December 1936; *died* 6 Feburary 1952, having had issue (*see* page 123)

3. HRH PRINCESS (Victoria Alexandra Alice) MARY (*Princess Royal*), *born* 25 April 1897, *married* 28 February 1922, Viscount Lascelles, later the 6th Earl of Harewood (1882–1947), *died* 28 March 1965. *Issue:*

(1) George Henry Hubert Lascelles, 7th Earl of Harewood, KBE, *born* 7 February 1923; *married* (1) 29 September 1949, Maria (Marion) Stein (marriage dissolved 1967); *issue*, (a) David Henry George, Viscount Lascelles, *born* 21 October 1950; (b) James

Edward, *born* 5 October 1953; (c) (Robert) Jeremy Hugh, *born* 14 February 1955; (2) 31 July 1967, Mrs Patricia Tuckwell; *issue*, (d) Mark Hubert, *born* 5 July 1964

(2) Gerald David Lascelles, *born* 21 August 1924, *married* (1) 15 July 1952, Miss Angela Dowding (marriage dissolved 1978); *issue*, (a) Henry Ulick, *born* 19 May 1953; (2) 17 November 1978, Mrs Elizabeth Colvin; *issue*, (b) Martin David, *born* 9 February 1962

4. HRH PRINCE HENRY William Frederick Albert, *born* 31 March 1900, *created* Duke of Gloucester, Earl of Ulster and Baron Culloden 1928, *married* 6 November 1935, Lady Alice Christabel Montagu-Douglas-Scott, daughter of the 7th Duke of Buccleuch (HRH Princess Alice, Duchess of Gloucester, *see* page 124); *died* 10 June 1974. *Issue:*

(1) HRH Prince William Henry Andrew Frederick, *born* 18 December 1941; *accidentally killed* 28 August 1972
(2) HRH Prince Richard Alexander Walter George (HRH The Duke of Gloucester), *see* page 124

5. HRH PRINCE GEORGE Edward Alexander Edmund, *born* 20 December 1902, *created* Duke of Kent, Earl of St Andrews and Baron Downpatrick 1934, *married* 29 November 1934, HRH Princess Marina of Greece and Denmark (*born* 30 November os, 1906; *died* 27 August 1968); *killed on active service*, 25 August 1942. *Issue:*

(1) HRH Prince Edward George Nicholas Paul Patrick (HRH The Duke of Kent), *see* page 124
(2) HRH Princess Alexandra Helen Elizabeth Olga Christabel (HRH Princess Alexandra, the Hon. Lady Ogilvy), *see* page 124
(3) HRH Prince Michael George Charles Franklin (HRH Prince Michael of Kent), *see* page 124

6. HRH PRINCE JOHN Charles Francis, *born* 12 July 1905; *died* 18 January 1919

Descendants of Queen Victoria

QUEEN VICTORIA (Alexandrina Victoria), *born* 24 May 1819; *succeeded* to the throne 20 June 1837; *married* 10 February 1840 (Francis) Albert Augustus Charles Emmanuel, Duke of Saxony, Prince of Saxe-Coburg and Gotha (HRH Albert, Prince Consort, *born* 26 August 1819, *died* 14 December 1861); *died* 22 January 1901. *Issue:*

1. HRH PRINCESS VICTORIA Adelaide Mary Louisa (Princess Royal) (1840–1901), *m.* 1858, Frederic (1831–88), Emperor of Germany March–June 1888. *Issue:*
(1) HIM Wilhelm II (1859–1941), Emperor of Germany 1888–1918, *m.* (1) 1881 Princess Augusta Victoria of Schleswig-Holstein-Sonderburg-Augustenburg (1858–1921); (2) 1922 Princess Hermine of Reuss (1887–1947). *Issue:*
(a) Prince Wilhelm (1882–1951), *Crown Prince* 1888–1918, *m.* 1905 Duchess Cecilie of Mecklenburg-Schwerin; *issue:* Prince Wilhelm (1906–40); Prince Ludwig Ferdinand (b. 1907), *m.* 1938 Grand Duchess Kira (*see* page 135); Prince Hubertus (1909–50); Prince Friedrich Georg (1911–66); Princess Alexandrine Irene (1915–); Princess Cecilie (1917–75)
(b) Prince Eitel-Friedrich (1883–1942), *m.* 1906 Duchess Sophie of Oldenburg (marriage dissolved 1926)
(c) Prince Adalbert (1884–1948), *m.* 1914 Duchess Adelheid of Saxe-Meiningen; *issue:* Princess Victoria Marina (1917–81); Prince Wilhelm Victor (1919–89)
(d) Prince August Wilhelm (1887–1949), *m.* 1908 Princess Alexandra of Schleswig-Holstein-Sonderburg-Glücksburg (marriage dissolved 1920); *issue:* Prince Alexander (1912–85)
(e) Prince Oskar (1888–1958), *m.* 1914 Countess von Ruppin; *issue:* Prince Oskar (1915–39); Prince Burchard (1917–); Princess Herzeleide (1918–89); Prince Wilhelm (b. 1922)

(f) Prince Joachim (1890–1920), *m.* 1916 Princess Marie of Anhalt; *issue:* Prince Karl (1916–75)
(g) Princess Viktoria Luise (1892–1980), *m.* 1913 Ernst, Duke of Brunswick 1913–18 (1887–1953); *issue:* Prince Ernst (1914–87); Prince Georg (b. 1915), *m.* 1946 Princess Sophie of Greece (*see* page 135) and has issue (two sons, one daughter); Princess Frederika (1917–81), *m.* 1938 Paul I, King of the Hellenes (*see* page 135); Prince Christian (1919–81); Prince Welf Heinrich (b. 1923)
(2) Princess Charlotte (1860–1919), *m.* 1878 Bernhard, Duke of Saxe-Meiningen 1914 (1851–1914). *Issue:* Princess Feodora (1879–1945), *m.* 1898 Prince Heinrich XXX of Reuss
(3) Prince Heinrich (1862–1929), *m.* 1888 Princess Irene of Hesse (*see* page 135). *Issue:*
(a) Prince Waldemar (1889–1945), *m.* Princess Calixsta of Lippe
(b) Prince Sigismund (1896–1978), *m.* Princess Charlotte of Saxe-Altenburg; *issue:* Princess Barbe (b. 1920); Prince Alfred (b. 1924)
(c) Prince Heinrich (1900–4)
(4) Prince Sigismund (1864–6)
(5) Princess Victoria (1866–1929), *m.* (1) 1890, Prince Adolf of Schaumburg-Lippe (1859–1916); (2) 1927 Alexander Zubkov
(6) Prince Joachim Waldemar (1868–79)
(7) Princess Sophie (1870–1932), *m.* 1889 Constantine I (1868–1923), King of the Hellenes 1913–17, 1920–3. *Issue:*
(a) George II (1890–1947), King of the Hellenes 1923–4 and 1935–47, *m.* 1921 Princess Elisabeth of Roumania (marriage dissolved 1935), (*see* page 135)
(b) Alexander I (1893–1920), King of the Hellenes 1917–20, *m.*

1919 Aspasia Manos; *issue:* Princess Alexandra (1921–93), *m.* 1944 King Petar II of Yugoslavia (*see below*)
(*c*) Princess Helena (1896–1982), *m.* 1921 King Carol of Roumania (*see below*), (marriage dissolved 1928)
(*d*) Paul I (1901–64), King of the Hellenes 1947–64, *m.* 1938 Princess Frederika of Brunswick (*see page 134*); *issue:* King Constantine II (*b.* 1940), *m.* 1964 Princess Anne-Marie of Denmark (*see page 136*), and has issue (three sons, two daughters); Princess Sophie (*b.* 1938), *m.* 1962 Juan Carlos I of Spain (*see page 136*); Princess Irene (*b.* 1942)
(*e*) Princess Irene (1904–74), *m.* 1939 4th Duke of Aosta; *issue:* Prince Amedeo (*b.* 1943)
(*f*) Princess Katherine (Lady Katherine Brandram) (*b.* 1913), *m.* 1947 Major R. C. A. Brandram, MC, TD; *issue:* R. Paul G. A. Brandram (*b.* 1948)
(8) Princess Margarethe (1872–1954), *m.* 1893 Prince Friedrich Karl of Hesse (1868–1940). *Issue:*
(*a*) Prince Friedrich Wilhelm (1893–1916)
(*b*) Prince Maximilian (1894–1914)
(*c*) Prince Philipp (1896–1980), *m.* 1925 Princess Mafalda of Italy; *issue:* Prince Moritz (*b.* 1926); Prince Heinrich (*b.* 1927); Prince Otto (*b.* 1937); Princess Elisabeth (*b.* 1940)
(*d*) Prince Wolfgang (*b.* 1896), *m.* (1) 1924 Princess Marie Alexandra of Baden; (2) 1948 Ottilie Möller
(*e*) Prince Richard (1901–)
(*f*) Prince Christoph (1901–43), *m.* 1930 Princess Sophie of Greece (*see below*) and has issue (two sons, three daughters)

2. HRH PRINCE ALBERT EDWARD (HM KING EDWARD VII), *b.* 9 November 1841, *m.* 1863 HRH Princess Alexandra of Denmark (1844–1925), *succeeded* to the throne 22 January 1901, *d.* 6 May 1910. *Issue:*
(1) Albert Victor, Duke of Clarence and Avondale (1864–92)
(2) George (HM KING GEORGE V) (*see page 134*)
(3) Louise (1867–1931) Princess Royal 1905–31, *m.* 1889 1st Duke of Fife (1849–1912). *Issue:*
(*a*) Princess Alexandra, Duchess of Fife (1891–1959), *m.* 1913 Prince Arthur of Connaught (*see page 136*)
(*b*) Princess Maud (1893–1945), *m.* 1923 11th Earl of Southesk (1893–1992); *issue:* The Duke of Fife (*b.* 1929)
(4) Victoria (1868–1935)
(5) Maud (1869–1938), *m.* 1896 Prince Charles of Denmark (1872–1957), later King Haakon VII of Norway 1905–57. *Issue:*
(*a*) Olav V, King of Norway 1957–91 (1903–91), *m.* 1929 Princess Märtha of Sweden (1901–54); *issue:* Princess Ragnhild (*b.* 1930); Princess Astrid (*b.* 1932); Harald V, King of Norway (*b.* 1937)
(6) Alexander (6–7 April 1871)

3. HRH PRINCESS ALICE Maud Mary (1843–78), *m.* 1862 Prince Louis (1837–92), Grand Duke of Hesse 1877–92. *Issue:*
(1) Victoria (1863–1950), *m.* 1884 Admiral of the Fleet Prince Louis of Battenberg (1854–1921), *cr.* 1st Marquess of Milford Haven 1917. *Issue:*
(*a*) Alice (1885–1969), *m.* 1903 Prince Andrew of Greece (1882–1944); *issue:* Princess Margarita (1905–81) *m.* 1931 Prince Gottfried of Hohenlohe-Langenburg (*see below*); Princess Theodora (1906–69), *m.* Prince Berthold of Baden (1906–63) and has issue (2 sons, one daughter); Princess Cecilie (1911–37), *m.* George, Grand Duke of Hesse (*see below*); Princess Sophie (*b.* 1914), *m.* (1) 1930 Prince Christoph of Hesse (*see above*); (2) 1946 Prince Georg of Hanover (*see page 134*); Prince Philip, Duke of Edinburgh (*b.* 1921) (*see page 123*)
(*b*) Louise (1889–1965), *m.* 1923 Gustaf VI Adolf (1882–1973), King of Sweden 1950–73
(*c*) George, 2nd Marquess of Milford Haven (1892–1938), *m.* 1916 Countess Nadejda, daughter of Grand Duke Michael of Russia; *issue:* Lady Tatiana (1917–88); David Michael, 3rd Marquess (1919–70)
(*d*) Louis, 1st Earl Mountbatten of Burma (1900–79), *m.* 1922 Edwina Ashley, daughter of Lord Mount Temple; *issue:* Patricia, Countess Mountbatten of Burma (*b.* 1924), Pamela (*b.* 1929)
(2) Elizabeth (1864–1918), *m.* 1884 Grand Duke Sergius of Russia (1857–1905)
(3) Irene (1866–1953), *m.* 1888 Prince Heinrich of Prussia (*see page 134*)
(4) Ernst Ludwig (1868–1937), Grand Duke of Hesse 1892–1918, *m.* (1) 1894 Princess Victoria Melita of Saxe-Coburg (*see below*), (marriage dissolved 1901); (2) 1905 Princess Eleonore of Solms-Hohensolmslich. *Issue:*
(*a*) Princess Elizabeth (1895–1903)

(*b*) George, Grand Duke of Hesse (1906–37), *m.* Princess Cecilie of Greece (*see above*), and had issue, 2 sons, accidentally killed with parents 1937
(*c*) Ludwig, Grand Duke of Hesse (1908–68), *m.* 1937 Margaret, daughter of 1st Lord Geddes
(5) Frederick William (1870–3)
(6) Alix (Tsaritsa of Russia) (1872–1918), *m.* 1894 Nicholas II (1868–1918) Tsar of All the Russias 1894–1917, assassinated 16 July 1918. *Issue:*
(*a*) Grand Duchess Olga (1895–1918)
(*b*) Grand Duchess Tatiana (1897–1918)
(*c*) Grand Duchess Marie (1899–1918)
(*d*) Grand Duchess Anastasia (1901–18)
(*e*) Alexis, Tsarevich of Russia (1904–18)
(7) Marie (1874–8)

4. HRH PRINCE ALFRED Ernest Albert, Duke of Edinburgh, *Admiral of the Fleet* (1844–1900), *m.* 1874 Grand Duchess Marie Alexandrovna of Russia (1853–1920); succeeded as Duke of Saxe-Coburg and Gotha 22 August 1893. *Issue:*
(1) Alfred (Prince of Saxe-Coburg) (1874–99)
(2) Marie (1875–1938), *m.* 1893 Ferdinand (1865–1927), King of Roumania 1914–27. *Issue:*
(*a*) Carol II (1893–1953), King of Roumania 1930–40, *m.* (2) 1921 Princess Helena of Greece (*see above*), (marriage dissolved 1928); *issue:* Michael (*b.* 1921), King of Roumania 1927–30, 1940–7, *m.* 1948 Princess Anne of Bourbon-Parma, and has issue (five daughters)
(*b*) Elisabeth (1894–1956), *m.* 1921 George II, King of the Hellenes (*see page 134*)
(*c*) Marie (1900–61), *m.* 1922 Alexander (1888–1934), King of Yugoslavia 1921–34; *issue:* Petar II (1923–70), King of Yugoslavia 1934–45, *m.* 1944 Princess Alexandra of Greece (*see above*) and has issue (one son); Prince Tomislav (*b.* 1928), *m.* (1) 1957 Princess Margarita of Baden (daughter of Princess Theodora of Greece and Prince Berthold of Baden, *see above*); (2) 1982 Linda Bonney; and has issue (three sons, one daughter); Prince Andrej (1929–90), *m.* (1) Princess Christina of Hesse (daughter of Prince Christoph of Hesse and Princess Sophie of Greece, *see above*); (2) 1963 Princess Kira-Melita of Leiningen (*see below*); and has issue (three sons, one daughter)
(*d*) Prince Nicolas (1903–)
(*e*) Princess Ileana (1909–91), *m.* (1) 1931 Archduke Anton of Austria; (2) 1954 Dr Stefan Issarescu; *issue:* Archduke Stefan (*b.* 1932); Archduchess Maria Ileana (1933–59); Archduchess Alexandra (*b.* 1935); Archduke Dominic (*b.* 1937); Archduchess Maria Magdalena (*b.* 1939); Archduchess Elisabeth (*b.* 1942)
(*f*) Prince Mircea (1913–16)
(3) Victoria Melita (1876–1936), *m.* (1) 1894 Grand Duke Ernst of Hesse (*see above*) (marriage dissolved 1901); (2) 1905 the Grand Duke Kirill of Russia (1876–1938). *Issue:*
(*a*) Marie Kirillovna (1907–51), *m.* 1925 Prince Friedrich Karl of Leiningen; *issue:* Prince Emich (*b.* 1926); Prince Karl (*b.* 1928); Princess Kira-Melita (*b.* 1930), *m.* Prince Andrej of Yugoslavia (*see above*); Princess Margarita (*b.* 1932); Princess Mechtilde (*b.* 1936); Prince Friedrich (*b.* 1938)
(*b*) Kira Kirillovna (1909–67), *m.* 1938 Prince Ludwig of Prussia (*see page 134*); *issue:* Prince Friedrich Wilhelm (*b.* 1939); Prince Michael (*b.* 1940); Princess Marie (*b.* 1942); Princess Kira (*b.* 1943); Prince Louis Ferdinand (1944–77); Prince Christian (*b.* 1946); Princess Xenia (*b.* 1949)
(*c*) Vladimir Kirillovich (1917–92), *m.* 1948 Princess Leonida Bagration-Mukhransky; *issue:* Grand Duchess Maria (*b.* 1953), *m.* and has issue
(4) Alexandra (1878–1942), *m.* 1896 Ernst, Prince of Hohenlohe Langenburg. *Issue:*
(*a*) Gottfried (1897–1960), *m.* 1931 Princess Margarita of Greece (*see above*); *issue:* Prince Kraft (*b.* 1935), Princess Beatrix (*b.* 1936), Prince George (*b.* 1938), Prince Ruprecht and Prince Albrecht (*b.* 1944)
(*b*) Maria (1899–1967), *m.* 1916 Prince Frederick of Schleswig-Holstein-Sonderburg-Glücksburg; *issue:* Prince Peter (1922–80); Princess Marie (*b.* 1927)
(*c*) Princess Alexandra (1901–63)
(*d*) Princess Irma (1902–)
(5) Princess Beatrice (1884–1966), *m.* 1909 Alfonso of Orleans, Infante of Spain. *Issue:*
(*a*) Prince Alvaro (*b.* 1910), *m.* 1937 Carla Parodi-Delfino; *issue:* Princess Gerarda (*b.* 1939); Prince Alonso (1941–75); Princess Beatriz (*b.* 1943); Prince Alvaro (*b.* 1947)

(b) Prince Alonso (1912–36)
(c) Prince Ataulfo (1913–)

5. HRH PRINCESS HELENA Augusta Victoria (1846–1923), m. 1866
Prince Christian of Schleswig-Holstein-Sonderburg-Augustenburg
(1831–1917). Issue:
   (1) Prince Christian Victor (1867–1900)
   (2) Prince Albert (1869–1931), Duke of Schleswig-Holstein
   1921–31
   (3) Princess Helena (1870–1948)
   (4) Princess Marie Louise (1872–1956), m. 1891 Prince Aribert of
   Anhalt (marriage dissolved 1900)
   (5) Prince Harold (12–20 May 1876)

6. HRH PRINCESS LOUISE Caroline Alberta (1848–1939), m. 1871 the
Marquess of Lorne, afterwards 9th Duke of Argyll (1845–1914);
without issue

7. HRH PRINCE ARTHUR William Patrick Albert, Duke of
Connaught, Field Marshal (1850–1942), m. 1879 Princess Louisa of
Prussia (1860–1917). Issue:
   (1) Margaret (1882–1920), m. 1905 Crown Prince Gustaf Adolf
   (1882–1973), afterwards King of Sweden 1950–73. Issue:
     (a) Gustaf Adolf, Duke of Västerbotten (1906–47), m. 1932
     Princess Sibylla of Saxe-Coburg-Gotha (see below); issue: Princess
     Margaretha (b. 1934); Princess Birgitta (b. 1937); Princess
     Désirée (b. 1938); Princess Christina (b. 1943); Carl XVI Gustaf,
     King of Sweden (b. 1946)
     (b) Count Sigvard Bernadotte (b. 1907); m., issue: Count Michael
     (b. 1944)
     (c) Princess Ingrid (Queen Mother of Denmark) (b. 1910), m.
     1935 Frederick IX (1899–72), King of Denmark 1947–72; issue:
     Margrethe II, Queen of Denmark (b. 1940); Princess Benedikte
     (b. 1944); Princess Anne-Marie (b. 1946), m. 1964 Constantine II
     of Greece (see page 135)
     (d) Prince Bertil, Duke of Halland (b. 1912), m. 1976 Mrs Lilian
     Craig
     (e) Count Carl Bernadotte (b. 1916), m. (1) 1946 Mrs Kerstin
     Johnson; (2) 1988 Countess Gunnila Busler
   (2) Arthur (1883–1938), m. 1913 HH the Duchess of Fife (see page
   135). Issue:
     Alastair Arthur, Duke of Connaught (1914–43)

(3) (Victoria) Patricia (1886–1974), m. 1919 Adm. Hon. Sir
Alexander Ramsay. Issue:
   Alexander Ramsay of Mar (b. 1919), m. 1956 Hon. Flora Fraser
   (Lady Saltoun)

8. HRH PRINCE LEOPOLD George Duncan Albert, Duke of Albany
(1853–84), m. 1882 Princess Helena of Waldeck (1861–1922). Issue:
   (1) Alice (1883–1981), m. 1904 Prince Alexander of Teck (1874–
   1957), cr. 1st Earl of Athlone 1917. Issue:
     (a) Lady May (b. 1906), m. 1931 Sir Henry Abel-Smith, KCMG,
     KCVO, DSO; issue: Anne (b. 1932); Richard (b. 1933); Elizabeth (b.
     1936)
     (b) Rupert, Viscount Trematon (1907–28)
     (c) Prince Maurice (March–September 1910)
   (2) Charles Edward (1884–1954), Duke of Albany 1884 until title
   suspended 1917, Duke of Saxe-Coburg-Gotha 1900–18, m. 1905
   Princess Victoria Adelheid of Schleswig-Holstein-Sonderburg-
   Glücksburg. Issue:
     (a) Prince Johann (1906–72), and has issue
     (b) Princess Sibylla (1908–72) m. 1932 Prince Gustav Adolf of
     Sweden (see above)
     (c) Prince Dietmar (1909–)
     (d) Princess Caroline (1912–83)
     (e) Prince Friedrich (b. 1918)

9. HRH PRINCESS BEATRICE Mary Victoria Feodore (1857–1944), m.
1885 Prince Henry of Battenberg (1858–96). Issue:
   (1) Alexander, 1st Marquess of Carisbrooke (1886–1960), m. 1917
   Lady Irene Denison. Issue:
     Lady Iris Mountbatten (1920–82)
   (2) Victoria Eugénie (1887–1969), m. 1906 Alfonso XIII (1886–
   1941) King of Spain 1886–1931. Issue:
     (a) Prince Alfonso (1907–38)
     (b) Prince Jaime (1908–75)
     (c) Princess Beatrice (b. 1909)
     (d) Princess Maria (b. 1911)
     (e) Prince Juan (1913–93) Count of Barcelona, and has issue:
     Princess Maria (b. 1936); Juan Carlos I, King of Spain (b. 1938),
     m. 1962 Princess Sophie of Greece (see page 135) and has issue
     (1 son, 2 daughters); Princess Margarita (b. 1939)
     (f) Prince Gonzale (1914–34)
   (3) Major Lord Leopold Mountbatten (1889–1922)
   (4) Maurice (1891–1914), died of wounds received in action

---

English Kings and Queens 927 TO 1603

HOUSES OF CERDIC AND DENMARK

Reign

927–939 ÆTHELSTAN
Second son of Edward the Elder, by Ecgwynn, and
grandson of Alfred
Acceded to Wessex and Mercia c.924, established
direct rule over Northumbria 927, effectively creating
the Kingdom of England
Reigned 15 years

939–946 EDMUND I
Born 921, fourth son of Edward the Elder, by Eadgifu
Married (1) Ælfgifu (2) Æthelflæd
Killed aged 25, *reigned* 6 years

946–955 EADRED
Fifth son of Edward the Elder, by Eadgifu
Reigned 9 years

955–959 EADWIG
Born before 943, son of Edmund and Ælfgifu
Married Ælfgifu
Reigned 3 years

959–975 EDGAR I
Born 943, son of Edmund and Ælfgifu
Married (1) Aethelflæd (2) Wulfthryth (3) Ælfthryth
Died aged 32, *reigned* 15 years

975–978 EDWARD I (the Martyr)
Born c.962, son of Edgar and Æthelflæd
Assassinated aged c.16, *reigned* 2 years

978–1016 ÆTHELRED (the Unready)
Born c.968/969, son of Edgar and Ælfthryth
Married (1) Ælfgifu (2) Emma, daughter of Richard I,
count of Normandy
1013–14 dispossessed of kingdom by Swegn
Forkbeard (king of Denmark 987–1014)
Died aged c.47, *reigned* 38 years

1016 EDMUND II (Ironside)
Born before 993, son of Æthelred and Ælfgifu
Married Ealdgyth
Died aged over 23, *reigned* 7 months (April–
November)

1016–1035 CNUT (Canute)
Born c.995, son of Swegn Forkbeard, king of
Denmark, and Gunhild
Married (1) Ælfgifu (2) Emma, widow of Æthelred the
Unready
Gained submission of West Saxons 1015,
Northumbrians 1016, Mercia 1016, king of all
England after Edmund's death
King of Denmark 1019–35, king of Norway 1028–35
Died aged c.40, *reigned* 19 years

1035–1040   HAROLD I (Harefoot)
*Born c.*1016/17, son of Cnut and Ælfgifu
Married Ælfgifu
1035 recognized as regent for himself and his brother
Harthacnut; 1037 recognized as king
Died aged *c.*23, *reigned* 4 years

1040–1042   HARTHACNUT
*Born c.*1018, son of Cnut and Emma
Titular king of Denmark from 1028
Acknowledged king of England 1035–7 with Harold I
as regent; effective king after Harold's death
Died aged *c.*24, *reigned* 2 years

1042–1066   EDWARD II (the Confessor)
Born between 1002 and 1005, son of Æthelred the
Unready and Emma
Married Eadgyth, daughter of Godwine, earl of Wessex
Died aged over 60, *reigned* 23 years

1066   HAROLD II (Godwinesson)
*Born c.*1020, son of Godwine, earl of Wessex, and
Gytha
Married (1) Eadgyth (2) Ealdgyth
Killed in battle aged *c.*46, *reigned* 10 months (January–
October)

THE HOUSE OF NORMANDY

1066–1087   WILLIAM I (the Conqueror)
Born 1027/8, son of Robert I, duke of Normandy;
obtained the Crown by conquest
Married Matilda, daughter of Baldwin, count of
Flanders
Died aged *c.*60, *reigned* 20 years

1087–1100   WILLIAM II (Rufus)
Born between 1056 and 1060, third son of William I;
succeeded his father in 1060 only
Killed aged *c.*40, *reigned* 12 years

1100–1135   HENRY I (Beauclerk)
Born 1068, fourth son of William I
Married (1) Edith or Matilda, daughter of Malcolm III
of Scotland (2) Adela, daughter of Godfrey, count of
Louvain
Died aged 67, *reigned* 35 years

1135–1154   STEPHEN
Born not later than 1100, third son of Adela, daughter
of William I, and Stephen, count of Blois
Married Matilda, daughter of Eustace, count of
Boulogne
1141 (February–November) held captive by adherents
of Matilda, daughter of Henry I, who contested the
crown until 1153
Died aged over 53, *reigned* 18 years

THE HOUSE OF ANJOU (PLANTAGENETS)

1154–1189   HENRY II (Curtmantle)
Born 1133, son of Matilda, daughter of Henry I, and
Geoffrey, count of Anjou
Married Eleanor, daughter of William, duke of
Aquitaine, and divorced queen of Louis VII of France
Died aged 56, *reigned* 34 years

1189–1199   RICHARD I (Coeur de Lion)
Born 1157, third son of Henry II
Married Berengaria, daughter of Sancho VI, king of
Navarre
Died aged 42, *reigned* 9 years

1199–1216   JOHN (Lackland)
Born 1167, fifth son of Henry II
Married (1) Isabella or Avisa, daughter of William, earl
of Gloucester (divorced) (2) Isabella, daughter of
Aymer, count of Angoulême
Died aged 48, *reigned* 17 years

1216–1272   HENRY III
Born 1207, son of John and Isabella of Angoulême

Married Eleanor, daughter of Raymond, count of
Provence
Died aged 65, *reigned* 56 years

1272–1307   EDWARD I (Longshanks)
Born 1239, eldest son of Henry III
Married (1) Eleanor, daughter of Ferdinand III, king
of Castile (2) Margaret, daughter of Philip III of
France
Died aged 68, *reigned* 34 years

1307–1327   EDWARD II
Born 1284, eldest surviving son of Edward I and
Eleanor
Married Isabella, daughter of Philip IV of France
Deposed January 1327, *killed* September 1327 aged 43,
reigned 19 years

1327–1377   EDWARD III
Born 1312, eldest son of Edward II
Married Philippa, daughter of William, count of
Hainault
Died aged 64, *reigned* 50 years

1377–1399   RICHARD II
Born 1367, son of Edward (the Black Prince), eldest
son of Edward III
Married (1) Anne, daughter of Emperor Charles IV
(2) Isabelle, daughter of Charles VI of France
Deposed September 1399, *killed* February 1400 aged
33, *reigned* 22 years

THE HOUSE OF LANCASTER

1399–1413   HENRY IV
Born 1366, son of John of Gaunt, fourth son of Edward
III, and Blanche, daughter of Henry, duke of
Lancaster
Married (1) Mary, daughter of Humphrey, earl of
Hereford (2) Joan, daughter of Charles, king of
Navarre, and widow of John, duke of Brittany
Died aged *c.*47, *reigned* 13 years

1413–1422   HENRY V
Born 1387, eldest surviving son of Henry IV and Mary
Married Catherine, daughter of Charles VI of France
Died aged 34, *reigned* 9 years

1422–1471   HENRY VI
Born 1421, son of Henry V
Married Margaret, daughter of René, duke of Anjou
and count of Provence
Deposed March 1461, *restored* October 1470
Deposed April 1471, *killed* May 1471 aged 49, *reigned*
39 years

THE HOUSE OF YORK

1461–1483   EDWARD IV
Born 1442, eldest son of Richard of York, who was the
grandson of Edmund, fifth son of Edward III, and the
son of Anne, great-granddaughter of Lionel, third son
of Edward III
Married Elizabeth Woodville, daughter of Richard,
Lord Rivers, and widow of Sir John Grey
Acceded March 1461, *deposed* October 1470, *restored*
April 1471
Died aged 40, *reigned* 21 years

1483   EDWARD V
Born 1470, eldest son of Edward IV
Deposed June 1483, *died* probably July–September
1483, aged 12, *reigned* 2 months (April–June)

1483–1485   RICHARD III
Born 1452, fourth son of Richard of York and brother
of Edward IV
Married Anne Neville, daughter of Richard, earl of
Warwick, and widow of Edward, Prince of Wales, son
of Henry VI
Killed in battle aged 32, *reigned* 2 years

THE HOUSE OF TUDOR

1485–1509	HENRY VII *Born* 1457, son of Margaret Beaufort, great-granddaughter of John of Gaunt, fourth son of Edward III, and Edmund Tudor, earl of Richmond *Married* Elizabeth, daughter of Edward IV *Died* aged 52, *reigned* 23 years
1509–1547	HENRY VIII *Born* 1491, second son of Henry VII *Married* (1) Catherine, daughter of Ferdinand II, king of Aragon, and widow of his elder brother Arthur (divorced) (2) Anne, daughter of Sir Thomas Boleyn (executed) (3) Jane, daughter of Sir John Seymour (died in childbirth) (4) Anne, daughter of John, duke of Cleves (divorced) (5) Catherine Howard, niece of the Duke of Norfolk (executed) (6) Catherine, daughter of Sir Thomas Parr and widow of Lord Latimer *Died* aged 55, *reigned* 37 years
1547–1553	EDWARD VI *Born* 1537, son of Henry VIII and Jane Seymour *Died* aged 15, *reigned* 6 years
1553	JANE *Born* 1537, daughter of Frances, daughter of Mary Tudor, the younger sister of Henry VIII, and Henry Grey, duke of Suffolk *Married* Lord Guildford Dudley, son of the Duke of Northumberland *Deposed* July 1553, *executed* February 1554 aged 16, *reigned* 14 days
1553–1558	MARY I *Born* 1516, daughter of Henry VIII and Catherine of Aragon *Married* Philip II of Spain *Died* aged 42, *reigned* 5 years
1558–1603	ELIZABETH I *Born* 1533, daughter of Henry VIII and Anne Boleyn *Died* aged 69, *reigned* 44 years

British Kings and Queens SINCE 1603

THE HOUSE OF STUART

1603–1625	JAMES I (VI OF SCOTLAND) *Born* 1566, son of Mary, queen of Scots and granddaughter of Margaret Tudor, elder daughter of Henry VII, and Henry Stewart, Lord Darnley *Married* Anne, daughter of Frederick II of Denmark *Died* aged 58, *reigned* 22 years (*see also* page 140)
1625–1649	CHARLES I *Born* 1600, second son of James I *Married* Henrietta Maria, daughter of Henry VI of France *Executed* 1649 aged 48, *reigned* 23 years
	COMMONWEALTH DECLARED 19 May 1649 1649–53 Government by a council of state 1653–8 Oliver Cromwell, *Lord Protector* 1658–9 Richard Cromwell, *Lord Protector*
1660–1685	CHARLES II *Born* 1630, eldest son of Charles I *Married* Catherine, daughter of John IV of Portugal *Died* aged 54, *reigned* 24 years
1685–1688	JAMES II (VII of Scotland) *Born* 1633, second son of Charles I *Married* (1) Lady Anne Hyde, daughter of Edward, earl of Clarendon (2) Mary, daughter of Alphonso, duke of Modena Reign ended with flight from kingdom December 1688 *Died* 1701 aged 67, *reigned* 3 years
	INTERREGNUM 11 December 1688 to 12 February 1689
1689–1702	WILLIAM III *Born* 1650, son of William II, prince of Orange, and Mary Stuart, daughter of Charles I *Married* Mary, elder daughter of James II *Died* aged 51, *reigned* 13 years
and 1689–1694	MARY II *Born* 1662, elder daughter of James II and Anne *Died* aged 32, *reigned* 5 years
1702–1714	ANNE *Born* 1665, younger daughter of James II and Anne *Married* Prince George of Denmark, son of Frederick III of Denmark *Died* aged 49, *reigned* 12 years

THE HOUSE OF HANOVER

1714–1727	GEORGE I (Elector of Hanover) *Born* 1660, son of Sophia (daughter of Frederick, elector palatine, and Elizabeth Stuart, daughter of James I) and Ernest Augustus, elector of Hanover *Married* Sophia Dorothea, daughter of George William, duke of Lüneburg-Celle *Died* aged 67, *reigned* 12 years
1727–1760	GEORGE II *Born* 1683, son of George I *Married* Caroline, daughter of John Frederick, margrave of Brandenburg-Anspach *Died* aged 76, *reigned* 33 years
1760–1820	GEORGE III *Born* 1738, son of Frederick, eldest son of George II *Married* Charlotte, daughter of Charles Louis, duke of Mecklenburg-Strelitz *Died* aged 81, *reigned* 59 years
	REGENCY 1811–20 Prince of Wales regent owing to the insanity of George III
1820–1830	GEORGE IV *Born* 1762, eldest son of George III *Married* Caroline, daughter of Charles, duke of Brunswick-Wolfenbüttel *Died* aged 67, *reigned* 10 years
1830–1837	WILLIAM IV *Born* 1765, third son of George III *Married* Adelaide, daughter of George, duke of Saxe-Meiningen *Died* aged 71, *reigned* 7 years
1837–1901	VICTORIA *Born* 1819, daughter of Edward, fourth son of George III *Married* Prince Albert of Saxe-Coburg and Gotha *Died* aged 81, *reigned* 63 years

THE HOUSE OF SAXE-COBURG AND GOTHA

1901–1910   EDWARD VII
Born 1841, eldest son of Victoria and Albert
Married Alexandra, daughter of Christian IX of
Denmark
Died aged 68, reigned 9 years

THE HOUSE OF WINDSOR

1910–1936   GEORGE V
Born 1865, second son of Edward VII
Married Victoria Mary, daughter of Francis, duke of
Teck
Died aged 70, reigned 25 years

1936   EDWARD VIII
Born 1894, eldest son of George V
Married (1937) Mrs Wallis Warfield
Abdicated 1936, died 1972 aged 77, reigned 10 months
(20 January to 11 December)

1936–1952   GEORGE VI
Born 1895, second son of George V
Married Lady Elizabeth Bowes-Lyon, daughter of 14th
Earl of Strathmore and Kinghorne (see also pages
123–4)
Died aged 56, reigned 15 years

1952–   ELIZABETH II
Born 1926, elder daughter of George VI
Married Philip, son of Prince Andrew of Greece (see
also page 123)
WHOM GOD PRESERVE

Kings and Queens of Scots 1016 TO 1603

Reign
1016–1034   MALCOLM II
Born c.954, son of Kenneth II
Acceded to Alba 1005, secured Lothian c.1016,
obtained Strathclyde for his grandson Duncan c.1016,
thus forming the Kingdom of Scotland
Died aged c.80, reigned 18 years

1034–1040   DUNCAN I
Son of Bethoc, daughter of Malcolm II, and Crinan
Married a cousin of Siward, earl of Northumbria
Reigned 5 years

1040–1057   MACBETH
Born c.1005, son of a daughter of Malcolm II and
Finlaec, mormaer of Moray
Married Gruoch, granddaughter of Kenneth III
Died aged c.52, reigned 17 years

1057–1058   LULACH
Born c.1032, son of Gillacomgan, mormaer of Moray,
and Gruoch (and stepson of Macbeth)
Died aged c.26, reigned 7 months (August–March)

1058–1093   MALCOLM III (Canmore)
Born c.1031, elder son of Duncan I
Married (1) Ingibiorg (2) Margaret (St Margaret),
granddaughter of Edmund II of England
Killed in battle aged c.62, reigned 35 years

1093–1097   DONALD III BÁN
Born c.1033, second son of Duncan I
Deposed May 1094, restored November 1094, deposed
October 1097, reigned 3 years

1094   DUNCAN II
Born c.1060, elder son of Malcolm III and Ingibiorg
Married Octreda of Dunbar
Killed aged c.34, reigned 6 months (May–November)

1097–1107   EDGAR
Born c.1074, second son of Malcolm III and Margaret
Died aged c.32, reigned 9 years

1107–1124   ALEXANDER I (The Fierce)
Born c.1077, fifth son of Malcolm III and Margaret
Married Sybilla, illegitimate daughter of Henry I of
England
Died aged c.47, reigned 17 years

1124–1153   DAVID I (The Saint)
Born c.1085, sixth son of Malcolm III and Margaret
Married Matilda, daughter of Waltheof, earl of
Huntingdon
Died aged c.68, reigned 29 years

1153–1165   MALCOLM IV (The Maiden)
Born c.1141, son of Henry, earl of Huntingdon, second
son of David I
Died aged c.24, reigned 12 years

1165–1214   WILLIAM I (The Lion)
Born c.1142, brother of Malcolm IV
Married Ermengarde, daughter of Richard, viscount of
Beaumont
Died aged c.72, reigned 49 years

1214–1249   ALEXANDER II
Born 1198, son of William I
Married (1) Joan, daughter of John, king of England
(2) Marie, daughter of Ingelram de Coucy
Died aged 50, reigned 34 years

1249–1286   ALEXANDER III
Born 1241, son of Alexander II and Marie
Married (1) Margaret, daughter of Henry III of
England (2) Yolande, daughter of the Count of Dreux
Killed accidentally aged 44, reigned 36 years

1286–1290   MARGARET (The Maid of Norway)
Born 1283, daughter of Margaret (daughter of
Alexander III) and Eric II of Norway
Died aged 7, reigned 4 years

FIRST INTERREGNUM 1290–2
Throne disputed by 13 competitors. Crown awarded to
John Balliol by adjudication of Edward I of England

THE HOUSE OF BALLIOL

1292–1296   JOHN (Balliol)
Born c.1250, son of Dervorguilla, great-great-
granddaughter of David I, and John de Balliol
Married Isabella, daughter of John, earl of Surrey
Abdicated 1296, died 1313 aged c.63, reigned 3 years

SECOND INTERREGNUM 1296–1306
Edward I of England declared John Balliol to have
forfeited the throne for contumacy in 1296 and took
the government of Scotland into his own hands

THE HOUSE OF BRUCE

1306–1329   ROBERT I (Bruce)
Born 1274, son of Robert Bruce and Marjorie, countess
of Carrick, and great-grandson of the second daughter

of David, earl of Huntingdon, brother of William I
Married (1) Isabella, daughter of Donald, earl of Mar
(2) Elizabeth, daughter of Richard, earl of Ulster
Died aged 54, *reigned* 23 years

1329–1371   DAVID II
Born 1324, son of Robert I and Elizabeth
Married (1) Joanna, daughter of Edward II of England
(2) Margaret Drummond, widow of Sir John Logie
(divorced)
Died aged 46, *reigned* 41 years

1332 Edward Balliol, son of John Balliol, crowned
King of Scots September, expelled December
1333–6 Edward Balliol restored as King of Scots

THE HOUSE OF STEWART

1371–1390   ROBERT II (Stewart)
Born 1316, son of Marjorie, daughter of Robert I, and
Walter, High Steward of Scotland
Married (1) Elizabeth, daughter of Sir Robert Mure of
Rowallan (2) Euphemia, daughter of Hugh, earl of
Ross
Died aged 74, *reigned* 19 years

1390–1406   ROBERT III
*Born c.*1337, son of Robert II and Elizabeth
Married Annabella, daughter of Sir John Drummond of
Stobhall
Died aged *c.*69, *reigned* 16 years

1406–1437   JAMES I
Born 1394, son of Robert III
Married Joan Beaufort, daughter of John, earl of
Somerset
Assassinated aged 42, *reigned* 30 years

1437–1460   JAMES II
Born 1430, son of James I
Married Mary, daughter of Arnold, duke of Gueldres
Killed accidentally aged 29, *reigned* 23 years

1460–1488   JAMES III
Born 1452, son of James II
Married Margaret, daughter of Christian I of Denmark
Assassinated aged 36, *reigned* 27 years

1488–1513   JAMES IV
Born 1473, son of James III
Married Margaret Tudor, daughter of Henry VII of
England
Killed in battle aged 40, *reigned* 25 years

1513–1542   JAMES V
Born 1512, son of James IV
Married (1) Madeleine, daughter of Francis I of France
(2) Mary of Lorraine, daughter of the Duc de Guise
Died aged 30, *reigned* 29 years

1542–1567   MARY
Born 1542, daughter of James V and Mary
Married (1) the Dauphin, afterwards Francis II of
France (2) Henry Stewart, Lord Darnley (3) James
Hepburn, earl of Bothwell
Abdicated 1567, prisoner in England from 1568,
executed 1587, *reigned* 24 years

1567–1625   JAMES VI (and I of England)
Born 1566, son of Mary, queen of Scots, and Henry,
Lord Darnley
Acceded 1567 to the Scottish throne, *reigned* 58 years
Succeeded 1603 to the English throne, so joining the
English and Scottish crowns in one person. The two
kingdoms remained distinct until 1707 when the
parliaments of the kingdoms became conjoined
For British Kings and Queens since 1603, *see* pages
138–9

Welsh Sovereigns and Princes

Wales was ruled by sovereign princes from the earliest times until the
death of Llywelyn in 1282. The first English Prince of Wales was the
son of Edward I, who was born in Caernarvon town on 25 April 1284.
According to a discredited legend, he was presented to the Welsh
chieftains as their prince, in fulfilment of a promise that they should
have a prince 'could not speak a word of English' and should be
native born. This son, who afterwards became Edward II, was created
'Prince of Wales and Earl of Chester' at the Lincoln Parliament on 7
February 1301.

The title Prince of Wales is borne after individual conferment and is
not inherited at birth, though some Princes have been declared and
styled Prince of Wales but never formally so created (s.). The title was
conferred on Prince Charles by The Queen on 26 July 1958. He was
invested at Caernarvon on 1 July 1969.

INDEPENDENT PRINCES AD 844 TO 1282

844–878	Rhodri the Great
878–916	Anarawd, son of Rhodri
916–950	Hywel Dda, the Good
950–979	Iago ab Idwal (or Ieuaf)
979–985	Hywel ab Ieuaf, the Bad
985–986	Cadwallon, his brother
986–999	Maredudd ab Owain ap Hywel Dda
999–1008	Cynan ap Hywel ab Ieuaf
1018–1023	Llywelyn ap Seisyll
1023–1039	Iago ab Idwal ap Meurig
1039–1063	Gruffydd ap Llywelyn ap Seisyll
1063–1075	Bleddyn ap Cynfyn
1075–1081	Trahaern ap Caradog
1081–1137	Gruffydd ap Cynan ab Iago
1137–1170	Owain Gwynedd

1170–1194	Dafydd ab Owain Gwynedd
1194–1240	Llywelyn Fawr, the Great
1240–1246	Dafydd ap Llywelyn
1246–1282	Llywelyn ap Gruffydd ap Llywelyn

ENGLISH PRINCES SINCE 1301

1301	Edward (Edward II)
1343	Edward the Black Prince, s. of Edward III
1376	Richard (Richard II), s. of the Black Prince
1399	Henry of Monmouth (Henry V)
1454	Edward of Westminster, son of Henry VI
1471	Edward of Westminster (Edward V)
1483	Edward, son of Richard III (d. 1484)
1489	Arthur Tudor, son of Henry VII
1504	Henry Tudor (Henry VIII)
1610	Henry Stuart, son of James I (d. 1612)
1616	Charles Stuart (Charles I)
c.1638 (s.)	Charles (Charles II)
1688 (s.)	James Francis Edward (The Old Pretender) (d. 1766)
1714	George Augustus (George II)
1729	Frederick Lewis, s. of George II (d. 1751)
1751	George William Frederick (George III)
1762	George Augustus Frederick (George IV)
1841	Albert Edward (Edward VII)
1901	George (George V)
1910	Edward (Edward VIII)
1958	Charles Philip Arthur George

The Peerage

and Members of the House of Lords

The rules which govern the creation and succession of peerages are extremely complicated. There are, technically, five separate peerages, the Peerage of England, of Scotland, of Ireland, of Great Britain, and of the United Kingdom. The Peerage of Great Britain dates from 1707 when an Act of Union combined the two Kingdoms of England and Scotland and separate peerages were discontinued. The Peerage of the United Kingdom dates from 1801 when Great Britain and Ireland were combined under an Act of Union. Some Scottish peers have received additional peerages of Great Britain or of the United Kingdom since 1707, and some Irish peers additional peerages of the United Kingdom since 1801.

The Peerage of Ireland was not entirely discontinued from 1801 but holders of Irish peerages, whether pre-dating or created subsequent to the Union of 1801, are not entitled to sit in the House of Lords if they have no additional English, Scottish, Great Britain or United Kingdom peerage. However, they are eligible for election to the House of Commons and to vote in Parliamentary elections, which other peers are not. An Irish peer holding a peerage of a lower grade which enables him to sit in the House of Lords is introduced there by the title which enables him to sit, though for all other purposes he is known by his higher title.

In the Peerage of Scotland there is no rank of Baron; the equivalent rank is Lord of Parliament, abbreviated to 'Lord' (the female equivalent is 'Lady'). All peers of England, Scotland, Great Britain or the United Kingdom who are 21 years or over, and of British, Irish or Commonwealth nationality are entitled to sit in the House of Lords.

No fees for dignities have been payable since 1937. The House of Lords surrendered the ancient right of peers to be tried for treason or felony by their peers in 1948.

HEREDITARY WOMEN PEERS

Most hereditary peerages pass on death to the nearest male heir, but there are exceptions, and several are held by women (*see* pages 149 and 161).

A woman peer in her own right retains her title after marriage, and if her husband's rank is the superior she is designated by the two titles jointly, the inferior one last. Her hereditary claim still holds good in spite of any marriage whether higher or lower. No rank held by a woman can confer any title or even precedence upon her husband but the rank of a hereditary woman peer in her own right is inherited by her eldest son (or perhaps daughter).

Since the Peerage Act 1963 hereditary women peers in their own right have been entitled to sit in the House of Lords, subject to the same qualifications as men.

LIFE PEERS

Since 1876 non-hereditary or life peerages have been conferred on certain eminent judges to enable the judicial functions of the House of Lords to be carried out. These Lords are known as Lords of Appeal or law lords and, to date, such appointments have all been male.

Since 1958 life peerages have been conferred upon distinguished men and women from all walks of life, giving them seats in the House of Lords in the degree of Baron or Baroness. They are addressed in the same way as hereditary Lords and Barons, and their children have similar courtesy titles.

PEERAGES EXTINCT SINCE THE LAST EDITION

EARLDOMS: Amherst (*cr.* 1826)

LIFE PEERAGES: Ewart-Biggs (*cr.* 1981); Hatch of Lusby (*cr.* 1978); Franks (*cr.* 1962); Ashby (*cr.* 1973); Airey of Abingdon (*cr.* 1979); Leatherland (*cr.* 1964); Willis (*cr.* 1963); Edmund-Davies (*cr.* 1974); Lloyd of Hampstead (*cr.* 1965); Bernstein (*cr.* 1969), Pennock (*cr.* 1982); Ridley of Liddesdale (*cr.* 1992); Underhill (*cr.* 1979); Bacon (*cr.* 1970); Zuckerman (*cr.* 1971); Elworthy (*cr.* 1972); Ross of Newport (*cr.* 1987), Gormley (*cr.* 1982); Strauss (*cr.* 1979); Winstanley (*cr.* 1975); Craigton (*cr.* 1959); Kadoorie (*cr.* 1981)

DISCLAIMER OF PEERAGES

The Peerage Act 1963 enables peers to disclaim their peerages for life. Peers alive in 1963 could disclaim within twelve months after the passing of the Act (31 July 1963); a person subsequently succeeding to a peerage may disclaim within twelve months (one month if an MP) after the date of succession, or of reaching 21, if later. The disclaimer is irrevocable but does not affect the descent of the peerage after the disclaimant's death, and children of a disclaimed peer may, if they wish, retain their precedence and any courtesy titles and styles borne as children of a peer. The disclaimer permits the disclaimant to sit in the House of Commons if elected as an MP.

EARLS: Durham (1970); Home (1963); Sandwich (1964)
VISCOUNTS: Hailsham (1963); Stansgate (1963)
BARONS: Altrincham (1963); Archibald (1975); Merthyr (1977); Reith (1972); Sanderson of Ayot (1971); Silkin (1972)

PEERS WHO ARE MINORS (i.e. under 21 years of age)

EARLS: Craven (*b.* 1989)
BARONS: Gretton (*b.* 1975)

CONTRACTIONS AND SYMBOLS

s. Scottish title
I. Irish title
* The peer holds also an Imperial title, specified after the name by Engl., Brit. or UK
° there is no 'of' in the title
b. born
s. succeeded
m. married
w. widower or widow
M. minor
† *heir* not ascertained at time of going to press

Hereditary Peers

ROYAL DUKES

Style, His Royal Highness The Duke of —
Style of address (formal) May it please your Royal Highness; *(informal)* Sir

Created	Title, order of succession, name, etc.	Heir
1947	*Edinburgh* (1st), The Prince Philip, Duke of Edinburgh, *(see* page 123)	The Prince of Wales
1337	*Cornwall,* Charles, Prince of Wales, *s.* 1952 *(see* page 123)	†
1398	*Rothesay,* Charles, Prince of Wales, *s.* 1952 *(see* page 123)	†
1986	*York* (1st), The Prince Andrew, Duke of York *(see* p. 123)	None
1928	*Gloucester* (2nd), Prince Richard, Duke of Gloucester, *s.* 1974 *(see* page 124)	Earl of Ulster *(see* page 124)
1934	*Kent* (2nd), Prince Edward, Duke of Kent, *s.* 1942 *(see* page 124)	Earl of St Andrews *(see* page 124)

† The title is not hereditary but is held by the Sovereign's eldest son from the moment of his birth or the Sovereign's accession

DUKES

Coronet, Eight strawberry leaves
Style, His Grace the Duke of —
Wife's style, Her Grace the Duchess of —
Eldest son's style, Takes his father's second title as a courtesy title
Younger sons' style, 'Lord' before forename and family name
Daughters' style, 'Lady' before forename and family name
For forms of address, *see* page 220

Created	Title, order of succession, name, etc.	Eldest son or heir
1868 I.*	*Abercorn* (5th), James Hamilton (6th *Brit. Marq.,* 1790, and 14th *Scott. Earl,* 1606, both *Abercorn*), *b.* 1934, *s.* 1979, *m.*	Marquess of Hamilton, *b.* 1969.
1701 S.*	*Argyll,* Ian Campbell (12th *Scottish* and 5th *UK* Duke, 1892, both *Argyll*), *b.* 1937, *s.* 1973, *m.*	Marquess of Lorne, *b.* 1968.
1703 S.	*Atholl* (10th), George Iain Murray, *b.* 1931, *s.* 1957.	John *M., b.* 1929.
1682	*Beaufort* (11th), David Robert Somerset, *b.* 1928, *s.* 1984, *m.*	Marquess of Worcester, *b.* 1952.
1694	*Bedford* (13th), John Robert Russell, *b.* 1917, *s.* 1953, *m.*	Marquess of Tavistock, *b.* 1940.
1663 S.*	*Buccleuch* (9th) & *Queensberry* (11th) (1684), Walter Francis John Montagu Douglas Scott, KT, VRD (8th *Engl. Earl, Doncaster,* 1662), *b.* 1923, *s.* 1973, *m.*	Earl of Dalkeith, *b.* 1954.
1694	*Devonshire* (11th), Andrew Robert Buxton Cavendish, MC, PC, *b.* 1920, *s.* 1950, *m.*	Marquess of Hartington, *b.* 1944.
1900	*Fife* (3rd), James George Alexander Bannerman Carnegie (12th *Scott. Earl, Southesk,* 1633, *s.* 1992), *b.* 1929, *s.* 1959. *(see* page 135).	Earl of Southesk, *b.* 1961.
1675	*Grafton* (11th), Hugh Denis Charles FitzRoy, KG, *b.* 1919, *s.* 1970, *m.*	Earl of Euston, *b.* 1947.
1643 S.*	*Hamilton* (15th) & *Brandon* (12th) *(Brit.* 1711), Angus Alan Douglas Douglas-Hamilton *(Premier Peer of Scotland), b.* 1938, *s.* 1973, *m.*	Marquess of Douglas and Clydesdale, *b.* 1978.
1766 I.*	*Leinster* (8th), Gerald FitzGerald *(Premier Duke and Marquess of Ireland;* 8th *Brit. Visct., Leinster,* 1747), *b.* 1914, *s.* 1976, *m.*	Marquess of Kildare, *b.* 1948.
1719	*Manchester* (12th), Angus Charles Drogo Montagu, *b.* 1938, *s.* 1985, *m.*	Viscount Mandeville, *b.* 1962.
1702	*Marlborough* (11th), John George Vanderbilt Henry Spencer-Churchill, *b.* 1926, *s.* 1972, *m.*	Marquess of Blandford, *b.* 1955.
1707 S.*	*Montrose* (8th), James Graham (6th *Brit. Earl, Graham,* 1722), *b.* 1935, *s.* 1992, *m.*	Marquess of Graham, *b.* 1973.
1483	*Norfolk* (17th), Miles Francis Stapleton Fitzalan-Howard, KG, GCVO, CB, CBE, MC *(Premier Duke;* 12th *Eng. Baron Beaumont,* 1309, *s.* 1971; 4th *UK Baron Howard of Glossop,* 1869, *s.* 1972), *b.* 1915, *s.* 1975, *m. Earl Marshal.*	Earl of Arundel and Surrey, *b.* 1956.
1766	*Northumberland* (11th), Henry Alan Walter Richard Percy, *b.* 1953, *s.* 1988.	Lord Ralph G.A.P., *b.* 1956.
1675	*Richmond* (10th) & *Gordon* (5th) *(UK* 1876), Charles Henry Gordon Lennox (10th *Scott.* Duke, *Lennox,* 1675), *b.* 1929, *s.* 1989, *m.*	Earl of March and Kinrara, *b.* 1955.

Created	*Title, order of succession, name, etc.*	*Eldest son or heir*
1707 S.*	*Roxburghe* (10th), Guy David Innes-Ker (5th *UK Earl, Innes,* 1837), *b.* 1954, *s.* 1974, *m.* (*Premier Baronet of Scotland*).	Marquess of Bowmont and Cessford, *b.* 1981.
1703	*Rutland* (10th), Charles John Robert Manners, CBE, *b.* 1919, *s.* 1940, *m.*	Marquess of Granby, *b.* 1959.
1684	*St Albans* (14th), Murray de Vere Beauclerk, *b.* 1939, *s.* 1988, *m.*	Earl of Burford, *b.* 1965.
1547	*Somerset* (19th), John Michael Edward Seymour, *b.* 1952, *s.* 1984, *m.*	Lord Seymour, *b.* 1982.
1833	*Sutherland* (6th), John Sutherland Egerton, TD (5th *UK Earl, Ellesmere,* 1846, *s.* 1944), *b.* 1915, *s.* 1963, *m.*	Francis R. E., *b.* 1940.
1814	*Wellington* (8th), Arthur Valerian Wellesley, KG, LVO, OBE, MC (9th *Irish Earl, Mornington,* 1760), *b.* 1915, *s.* 1972, *m.*	Marquess of Douro, *b.* 1945.
1874	*Westminster* (6th), Gerald Cavendish Grosvenor, *b.* 1951, *s.* 1979, *m.*	Earl Grosvenor, *b.* 1991.

MARQUESSES

Coronet, Four strawberry leaves alternating with four silver balls
Style, The Most Hon. the Marquess (of) __. In Scotland the spelling 'Marquis' is preferred for pre-Union creations
Wife's style, The Most Hon. the Marchioness (of) __
Eldest son's style, Takes his father's second title as a courtesy title
Younger sons' style, 'Lord' before forename and family name
Daughters' style, 'Lady' before forename and family name
For forms of address, *see* page 220

Created	*Title, order of succession, name, etc.*	*Eldest son or heir*
1916	*Aberdeen and Temair* (6th), Alastair Ninian John Gordon (12th *Scott. Earl, Aberdeen,* 1682), *b.* 1920, *s.* 1984, *m.*	Earl of Haddo, *b.* 1955.
1876	*Abergavenny* (5th), John Henry Guy Nevill, KG, OBE, *b.* 1914, *s.* 1954, *m.*	Christopher G. C. N., *b.* 1955.
1821	*Ailesbury* (8th), Michael Sidney Cedric Brudenell-Bruce, *b.* 1926, *s.* 1974	Earl of Cardigan, *b.* 1952.
1831	*Ailsa* (7th), Archibald David Kennedy, OBE, (19th *Scott. Earl, Cassillis,* 1509), *b.* 1925, *s.* 1957, *m.*	Earl of Cassillis, *b.* 1956.
1815	*Anglesey* (7th), George Charles Henry Victor Paget, *b.* 1922, *s.* 1947, *m.*	Earl of Uxbridge, *b.* 1950.
1789	*Bath* (7th), Alexander George Thynn, *b.* 1932, *s.* 1992, *m.*	Viscount Weymouth, *b.* 1974.
1826	*Bristol* (7th), (Frederick William) John Augustus Hervey, *b.* 1954, *s.* 1985.	Lord F. W. C. Nicholas W. H., *b.* 1961.
1796	*Bute* (7th), John Colum Crichton-Stuart (12th *Scott. Earl, Dumfries,* 1633), *b.* 1958, *s.* 1993, *m.*	Earl of Dumfries, *b.* 1989.
1812	°*Camden* (6th), David George Edward Henry Pratt, *b.* 1930, *s.* 1983.	Earl of Brecknock, *b.* 1965.
1815	*Cholmondeley* (7th), David George Philip Cholmondeley (11th *Irish Viscount, Cholmondeley,* 1661), *b.* 1960, *s.* 1990. *Lord Great Chamberlain.*	Charles G. C., *b.* 1959.
1816 I.*	°*Conyngham* (7th), Frederick William Henry Francis Conyngham (7th *UK Baron, Minster, UK* 1821), *b.* 1924, *s.* 1974, *m.*	Earl of Mount Charles, *b.* 1951.
1791 I.*	*Donegall* (7th), Dermot Richard Claud Chichester, LVO (7th *Brit. Baron, Fisherwick,* 1790, 6th *Brit. Baron, Templemore,* 1831), *b.* 1916, *s.* to Marquessate, 1975: to Templemore Barony, 1953, *m.*	Earl of Belfast, *b.* 1952.
1789 I.*	*Downshire* (8th), (Arthur) Robin Ian Hill (8th *Brit. Earl, Hillsborough,* 1772), *b.* 1929, *s.* 1989, *m.*	Earl of Hillsborough, *b.* 1959.
1801 I.*	*Ely* (8th) Charles John Tottenham (8th *UK Baron, Loftus,* 1801), *b.* 1913, *s.* 1969, *m.*	Viscount Loftus, *b.* 1943.
1801	*Exeter* (8th), (William) Michael Anthony Cecil, *b.* 1935, *s.* 1988, *m.*	Lord Burghley, *b.* 1970.
1800 I.*	*Headfort* (6th), Thomas Geoffrey Charles Michael Taylour (4th *UK Baron, Kenlis,* 1831), *b.* 1932, *s.* 1960, *m.*	Earl of Bective, *b.* 1959.
1793	*Hertford* (8th), Hugh Edward Conway Seymour (9th *Irish Baron, Conway,* 1712), *b.* 1930, *s.* 1940, *m.*	Earl of Yarmouth, *b.* 1958.
1599 S.*	*Huntly* (13th), Granville Charles Gomer Gordon (*Premier Marquess of Scotland*) (5th *UK Baron, Meldrum,* 1815), *b.* 1944, *s.* 1987, *m.*	Earl of Aboyne, *b.* 1973.
1784	*Lansdowne* (8th), George John Charles Mercer Nairne Petty-Fitzmaurice, PC (8th *Irish Earl, Kerry,* 1723), *b.* 1912, *s.* 1944, *w.*	Earl of Shelburne, *b.* 1941.
1902	*Linlithgow* (4th), Adrian John Charles Hope (10th *Scott. Earl, Hopetoun,* 1703), *b.* 1946, *s.* 1987, *m.*	Earl of Hopetoun, *b.* 1969.
1816 I.*	*Londonderry* (9th), Alexander Charles Robert Vane-Tempest-Stewart (6th *UK Earl, Vane,* 1823), *b.* 1937, *s.* 1955, *m.*	Viscount Castlereagh, *b.* 1972.
1701 S.*	*Lothian* (12th), Peter Francis Walter Kerr, KCVO (6th *UK Baron, Kerr,* 1821), *b.* 1922, *s.* 1940, *m.*	Earl of Ancram, MP, *b.* 1945.

Created	Title, order of succession, name, etc.	Eldest son or heir
1917	*Milford Haven* (4th), George Ivar Louis Mountbatten, *b.* 1961, *s.* 1970, *m.*	Earl of Medina, *b.* 1991.
1838	*Normanby* (4th), Oswald Constantine John Phipps, KG, CBE (8th *Irish Baron, Mulgrave,* 1767), *b.* 1912, *s.* 1932, *m.*	Earl of Mulgrave, *b.* 1954.
1812	*Northampton* (7th), Spencer Douglas David Compton, *b.* 1946, *s.* 1978, *m.*	Earl Compton, *b.* 1973.
1825 I.*	*Ormonde* (7th), James Hubert Theobald Charles Butler, MBE (7th *UK Baron, Ormonde,* 1821), *b.* 1899, *s.* 1971, *w.*	None to Marquessate. To Earldoms of Ormonde and Ossory, Viscount Mountgarret, *b.* 1936 (*see* p. 151).
1682 S.	*Queensberry* (12th), David Harrington Angus Douglas, *b.* 1929, *s.* 1954.	Viscount Drumlanrig, *b.* 1967.
1926	*Reading* (4th), Simon Charles Henry Rufus Isaacs, *b.* 1942, *s.* 1980, *m.*	Viscount Erleigh, *b.* 1986.
1789	*Salisbury* (6th), Robert Edward Peter Cecil, *b.* 1916, *s.* 1972, *m.*	Viscount Cranborne, *b.* 1946 (*see also* Baron Cecil, page 154).
1800 I.*	*Sligo* (11th), Jeremy Ulick Browne (11th *UK Baron, Monteagle,* 1806), *b.* 1939, *s.* 1991, *m.*	Sebastian U. *B.*, *b.* 1964.
1787	°*Townshend* (7th), George John Patrick Dominic Townshend, *b.* 1916, *s.* 1921, *w.*	Viscount Raynham, *b.* 1945.
1694 S.*	*Tweeddale* (13th), Edward Douglas John Hay (4th *UK Baron, Tweeddale,* 1881), *b.* 1947, *s.* 1979.	Lord Charles D. M. *H.*, *b.* 1947.
1789 I.*	*Waterford* (8th), John Hubert de la Poer Beresford (8th *Brit. Baron, Tyrone,* 1786), *b.* 1933, *s.* 1934, *m.*	Earl of Tyrone, *b.* 1958.
1551	*Winchester* (18th), Nigel George Paulet (*Premier Marquess of England*), *b.* 1941, *s.* 1968, *m.*	Earl of Wiltshire, *b.* 1969.
1892	*Zetland* (4th), Lawrence Mark Dundas (6th *UK Earl of Zetland,* 1838, 7th *Brit. Baron Dundas,* 1794), *b.* 1937, *s.* 1989, *m.*	Earl of Ronaldshay, *b.* 1965.

EARLS

Coronet, Eight silver balls on stalks alternating with eight gold strawberry leaves
Style, The Right Hon. the Earl (of) __
Wife's style, The Right Hon. the Countess (of) __
Eldest son's style, Takes his father's second title as a courtesy title
Younger sons' style, 'The Hon.' before forename and family name
Daughters' style, 'Lady' before forename and family name
For forms of address, *see* page 220

Created	Title, order of succession, name, etc.	Eldest son or heir
1639 S.	*Airlie* (13th), David George Coke Patrick Ogilvy, KT, GCVO, PC, *b.* 1926, *s.* 1968, *m. Lord Chamberlain.*	Lord Ogilvy, *b.* 1958.
1696	*Albemarle* (10th), Rufus Arnold Alexis Keppel, *b.* 1965, *s.* 1979.	Crispian W. J. *K.*, *b.* 1948.
1952	°*Alexander of Tunis* (2nd), Shane William Desmond Alexander, *b.* 1935, *s.* 1969, *m.*	Hon. Brian J. *A.*, *b.* 1939.
1662 S.	*Annandale and Hartfell* (11th), Patrick Andrew Wentworth Hope Johnstone, *b.* 1941, *claim established* 1985, *m.*	Lord Johnstone, *b.* 1971.
1789 I.	°*Annesley* (10th), Patrick Annesley, *b.* 1924, *s.* 1979, *m.*	Hon. Philip H.*A.*, *b.* 1927.
1785 I.	*Antrim* (9th), Alexander Randal Mark McDonnell, *b.* 1935, *s.* 1977, *m.* (*Viscount Dunluce.*)	Hon. Randal A. St J. *M.*, *b.* 1967.
1762 I.*	*Arran* (9th), Arthur Desmond Colquhoun Gore (5th *UK Baron Sudley,* 1884), *b.* 1938, *s.* 1983, *m.*	Paul A. *G.*, CMG, CVO, *b.* 1921.
1955	°*Attlee* (3rd), John Richard Attlee, *b.* 1956, *s.* 1991, *m.*	None.
1714	*Aylesford* (11th), Charles Ian Finch-Knightley, *b.* 1918, *s.* 1958, *m.*	Lord Guernsey, *b.* 1947.
1937	°*Baldwin of Bewdley* (4th), Edward Alfred Alexander Baldwin, *b.* 1938, *s.* 1976, *m.*	Viscount Corvedale, *b.* 1973.
1922	*Balfour* (4th), Gerald Arthur James Balfour, *b.* 1925, *s.* 1968, *m.*	Eustace A. G. *B.*, *b.* 1921.
1772	°*Bathurst* (8th), Henry Allen John Bathurst, *b.* 1927, *s.* 1943, *m.*	Lord Apsley, *b.* 1961.
1919	°*Beatty* (3rd), David Beatty, *b.* 1946, *s.* 1972, *m.*	Viscount Borodale, *b.* 1973.
1797 I.	*Belmore* (8th), John Armar Lowry-Corry, *b.* 1951, *s.* 1960, *m.*	Viscount Corry, *b.* 1985.
1739 I.*	*Bessborough,* Frederick Edward Neuflize Ponsonby (10th *Irish* and 2nd *UK Earl,* 1937, both *Bessborough*), *b.* 1913, *s.* 1956, *m.*	To Irish Earldom and UK Barony only, Arthur M. L. *P.*, *b.* 1912.
1815	*Bradford* (7th), Richard Thomas Orlando Bridgeman, *b.* 1947, *s.* 1981, *m.*	Viscount Newport, *b.* 1980.
1677 S.	*Breadalbane and Holland* (10th), John Romer Boreland Campbell, *b.* 1919, *s.* 1959.	None.
1469 S.*	*Buchan* (17th), Malcolm Harry Erskine, (8th *UK Baron Erskine* 1806), *b.* 1930, *s.* 1984, *m.*	Lord Cardross, *b.* 1960.

Created	*Title, order of succession, name, etc.*	*Eldest son or heir*
1746	*Buckinghamshire* (10th), (George) Miles Hobart-Hampden, *b.* 1944, *s.* 1983, *m.*	Sir John Hobart, Bt., *b.* 1945.
1800	°*Cadogan* (7th), William Gerald Charles Cadogan, MC, *b.* 1914, *s.* 1933, *m.*	Viscount Chelsea, *b.* 1937.
1878	°*Cairns* (6th), Simon Dallas Cairns, CBE, *b.* 1939, *s.* 1989, *m.*	Viscount Garmoyle, *b.* 1965.
1455 S.	*Caithness* (20th), Malcolm Ian Sinclair, PC, *b.* 1948, *s.* 1965, *m.*	Lord Berriedale, *b.* 1981.
1800 I.	*Caledon* (7th), Nicholas James Alexander, *b.* 1955, *s.* 1980, *m.*	Viscount Alexander, *b.* 1990.
1661	*Carlisle* (12th), Charles James Ruthven Howard, MC (12th *Scott. Baron, Ruthven of Freeland*, 1651), *b.* 1923, *s.* 1963, *m.*	Viscount Morpeth, *b.* 1949.
1793	*Carnarvon* (7th), Henry George Reginald Molyneux Herbert, KCVO, KBE, *b.* 1924, *s.* 1987, *m.*	Lord Porchester, *b.* 1956.
1748 I.*	*Carrick* (10th), David James Theobald Somerset Butler (4th *UK Baron, Butler*, 1912), *b.* 1953, *s.* 1992, *m.*	Viscount Ikerrin, *b.* 1975.
1800 I.	°*Castle Stewart* (8th), Arthur Patrick Avondale Stuart, *b.* 1928, *s.* 1961, *m.*	Viscount Stuart, *b.* 1953.
1814	°*Cathcart* (6th), Alan Cathcart, CB, DSO, MC (15th *Scott. Baron, Cathcart*, 1447), *b.* 1919, *s.* 1927, *m.*	Lord Greenock, *b.* 1952.
1647 I.	*Cavan* (13th), Roger Cavan Lambart, *b.* 1944, *s.* 1988.	Arthur O. R. *L.*, *b.* 1909.
1827	°*Cawdor* (7th), Colin Robert Vaughan Campbell, *b.* 1962, *s.* 1993.	Hon. Frederick W. *C.*, *b.* 1965.
1801	*Chichester* (9th), John Nicholas Pelham, *b.* 1944, *s.* 1944, *m.*	Richard A. H. *P.*, *b.* 1952.
1803 I.*	*Clancarty* (8th), William Francis Brinsley Le Poer Trench (7th *UK Visct. Clancarty*, 1823), *b.* 1911, *s.* 1975, *m.*	Nicholas P. R. *Le P. T.*, *b.* 1952.
1776 I.*	*Clanwilliam* (7th), John Herbert Meade (5th *UK Baron Clanwilliam*, 1828), *b.* 1919, *s.* 1989, *m.*	Lord Gillford, *b.* 1960.
1776	*Clarendon* (7th), George Frederick Laurence Hyde Villiers, *b.* 1933, *s.* 1955, *m.*	Lord Hyde, *b.* 1976.
1620 I.*	*Cork* (13th) & *Orrery* (13th)(I. 1660), Patrick Reginald Boyle (9th *Brit. Baron, Boyle of Marston*, 1711), *b.* 1910, *s.* 1967, *m.*	Hon. John W. *B.*, DSC, *b.* 1916.
1850	*Cottenham* (8th), Kenelm Charles Everard Digby Pepys, *b.* 1948, *s.* 1968, *m.*	Viscount Crowhurst, *b.* 1983.
1762 I.*	*Courtown* (9th), James Patrick Montagu Burgoyne Winthrop Stopford (8th *Brit. Baron, Saltersford*, 1796), *b.* 1954, *s.* 1975, *m.*	Viscount Stopford, *b.* 1988.
1697	*Coventry* (11th), George William Coventry, *b.* 1934, *s.* 1940, *m.*	Viscount Deerhurst, *b.* 1957.
1857	°*Cowley* (7th), Garret Graham Wellesley, *b.* 1934, *s.* 1975, *m.*	Viscount Dangan, *b.* 1965.
1892	*Cranbrook* (5th), Gathorne Gathorne-Hardy, *b.* 1933, *s.* 1978, *m.*	Lord Medway, *b.* 1968.
1801	*Craven* (9th), Benjamin Robert Joseph Craven, *b.* 1989, *s.* 1990, *M.*	Rupert J. E. *C.*, *b.* 1926.
1398 S.*	*Crawford* (29th) & *Balcarres* (12th) (S. 1651), Robert Alexander Lindsay, PC (*Premier Earl on Union Roll*, 5th *UK Baron, Wigan*, 1826, and *Baron Balniel* (Life Peer)), *b.* 1927, *s.* 1975, *m.*	Lord Balniel, *b.* 1958.
1861	*Cromartie* (5th), John Ruaridh Blunt Grant Mackenzie, *b.* 1948, *s.* 1989, *m.*	Viscount Tarbat, *b.* 1987.
1901	*Cromer* (4th), Evelyn Rowland Esmond Baring, *b.* 1946, *s.* 1991, *m.*	Hon. Vivian J. R. *B.*, *b.* 1950.
1633 S.*	*Dalhousie* (16th), Simon Ramsay, KT, GCVO, GBE, MC (4th *UK Baron, Ramsay*, 1875), *b.* 1914, *s.* 1950, *m.*	Lord Ramsay, *b.* 1948.
1725 I.*	*Darnley* (11th), Adam Ivo Stuart Bligh (20th *Engl. Baron, Clifton of Leighton Bromswold*, 1608), *b.* 1941, *s.* 1980, *m.*	Lord Clifton of Rathmore, *b.* 1968.
1711	*Dartmouth* (9th), Gerald Humphry Legge, *b.* 1924, *s.* 1962, *m.*	Viscount Lewisham, *b.* 1949.
1761	°*De La Warr* (11th), William Herbrand Sackville, *b.* 1948, *s.* 1988, *m.*	Lord Buckhurst, *b.* 1979.
1622	*Denbigh* (11th) & *Desmond* (10th) (I. 1622), William Rudolph Michael Feilding, *b.* 1943, *s.* 1966, *m.*	Viscount Feilding, *b.* 1970.
1485	*Derby* (18th), Edward John Stanley, MC, *b.* 1918, *s.* 1948, *w.*	Edward R. W. *S.*, *b.* 1962.
1553	*Devon* (17th), Charles Christopher Courtenay, *b.* 1916, *s.* 1935, *m.*	Lord Courtenay, *b.* 1942.
1800 I.*	*Donoughmore* (8th), Richard Michael John Hely-Hutchinson (8th *UK Visct., Hutchinson*, 1821), *b.* 1927, *s.* 1981, *m.*	Viscount Suirdale, *b.* 1952.
1661 I.*	*Drogheda* (12th), Henry Dermot Ponsonby Moore (3rd *UK Baron, Moore*, 1954), *b.* 1937, *s.* 1989, *m.*	Viscount Moore, *b.* 1983.
1837	*Ducie* (7th), David Leslie Moreton, *b.* 1951, *s.* 1991, *m.*	Lord Moreton, *b.* 1981.
1860	*Dudley* (4th), William Humble David Ward, *b.* 1920, *s.* 1969, *m.*	Viscount Ednam, *b.* 1947.
1660 S.*	*Dundee* (12th), Alexander Henry Scrymgeour (2nd *UK Baron, Glassary*, 1954), *b.* 1949, *s.* 1983, *m.*	Lord Scrymgeour, *b.* 1982.
1669 S.	*Dundonald* (15th), Iain Alexander Douglas Blair Cochrane, *b.* 1961, *s.* 1986, *m.*	Lord Cochrane, *b.* 1991.
1686 S.	*Dunmore* (11th), Kenneth Randolph Murray, *b.* 1913, *s.* 1981, *w.*	Viscount Fincastle, *b.* 1946.
1822 I.	*Dunraven and Mount-Earl* (7th), Thady Windham Thomas Wyndham-Quin, *b.* 1939, *s.* 1965, *m.*	None.
1833	*Durham.* Disclaimed for life 1970. (*Antony Claud Frederick Lambton, b.* 1922, *s.* 1970, *m.*)	Hon. Edward R. *L.*, *b.* 1961.
1837	*Effingham* (6th), Mowbray Henry Gordon Howard (16th *Engl. Baron, Howard of Effingham*, 1554), *b.* 1905, *s.* 1946, *m.*	Lt.-Cdr. David P. M. A. *H.*, *b.* 1939.

Created	Title, order of succession, name, etc.	Eldest son or heir
1507 s.*	Eglinton (18th) & *Winton* (9th) (1600), Archibald George Montgomerie (6th *UK Earl, Winton*, 1859), *b*. 1939, *s*. 1966, *m*.	Lord Montgomerie, *b*. 1966.
1733 I.*	Egmont (11th), Frederick George Moore Perceval (9th *Brit. Baron, Lovel & Holland*, 1762), *b*. 1914, *s*. 1932, *m*.	Viscount Perceval, *b*. 1934.
1821	Eldon (5th), John Joseph Nicholas Scott, *b*. 1937, *s*. 1976, *m*.	Viscount Encombe, *b*. 1962.
1633 s.*	Elgin (11th), & *Kincardine* (15th) (s. 1647), Andrew Douglas Alexander Thomas Bruce (4th *UK Baron, Elgin*, 1849), KT, *b*. 1924, *s*. 1968, *m*.	Lord Bruce, *b*. 1961.
1789 I.*	Enniskillen (7th), Andrew John Galbraith Cole (5th *UK Baron, Grinstead*, 1815) *b*. 1942, *s*. 1989, *m*.	Arthur G. *C*., *b*. 1920.
1789 I.*	Erne (6th), Henry George Victor John Crichton (3rd *UK Baron, Fermanagh*, 1876), *b*. 1937, *s*. 1940, *m*.	Viscount Crichton, *b*. 1971.
1452 s.	Erroll (24th), Merlin Sereld Victor Gilbert Hay, *b*. 1948, *s*. 1978, *m*. Hereditary Lord High Constable and Knight Marischal of Scotland.	Lord Hay, *b*. 1984.
1661	Essex (10th), Robert Edward de Vere Capell, *b*. 1920, *s*. 1981, *m*.	Viscount Malden, *b*. 1944.
1711	°Ferrers (13th), Robert Washington Shirley, PC, *b*. 1929, *s*. 1954, *m*.	Viscount Tamworth, *b*. 1952.
1789	°Fortescue (8th), Charles Hugh Richard Fortescue, *b*. 1951, *s*. 1993, *m*.	Hon. Martin D. *F*., *b*. 1924.
1841	Gainsborough (5th), Anthony Gerard Edward Noel, *b*. 1923, *s*. 1927, *m*.	Viscount Campden, *b*. 1950.
1623 s.*	Galloway (13th), Randolph Keith Reginald Stewart (6th *Brit. Baron, Stewart of Garlies*, 1796), *b*. 1928, *s*. 1978, *m*.	Andrew C. *S*., *b*. 1949.
1703 s.*	Glasgow (10th), Patrick Robin Archibald Boyle (4th *UK Baron, Fairlie*, 1897), *b*. 1939, *s*. 1984, *m*.	Viscount of Kelburn, *b*. 1978.
1806 I.*	Gosford (7th), Charles David Nicholas Alexander John Sparrow Acheson (5th *UK Baron, Worlingham*, 1835), *b*. 1942, *s*. 1966, *m*.	Hon. Patrick B. V. M. *A*., *b*. 1915.
1945	Gowrie (2nd), Alexander Patric Greysteil Hore-Ruthven, PC (3rd *UK Baron, Ruthven of Gowrie*, 1919), *b*. 1939, *s*. 1955, *m*.	Viscount Ruthven of Canberra, *b*. 1964.
1684 I.*	Granard (10th), Peter Arthur Edward Hastings Forbes, (5th *UK Baron, Granard*, 1806), *b*. 1957, *s*. 1992, *m*.	Viscount Forbes.
1833	°Granville (5th), Granville James Leveson-Gower, MC, *b*. 1918, *s*. 1953, *m*.	Lord Leveson, *b*. 1959.
1806	°Grey (6th), Richard Fleming George Charles Grey, *b*. 1939, *s*. 1963, *m*.	Philip K. *G*., *b*. 1940.
1752	Guilford (9th), Edward Francis North, *b*. 1933, *s*. 1949, *w*.	Lord North, *b*. 1971.
1619 s.	Haddington (13th), John George Baillie-Hamilton, *b*. 1941, *s*. 1986, *m*.	Lord Binning, *b*. 1985.
1919	°Haig (2nd), George Alexander Eugene Douglas Haig, OBE, *b*. 1918, *s*. 1928, *m*.	Viscount Dawick, *b*. 1961.
1944	Halifax (3rd), Charles Edward Peter Neil Wood (5th *UK Viscount, Halifax*, 1866), *b*. 1944, *s*. 1980, *m*.	Lord Irwin, *b*. 1977.
1898	Halsbury (3rd), John Anthony Hardinge Giffard, FRS, FEng., *b*. 1908, *s*. 1943, *w*.	Adam E. *G*., *b*. 1934.
1754	Hardwicke (10th), Joseph Philip Sebastian Yorke, *b*. 1971, *s*. 1974.	Richard C. J. *Y*., *b*. 1916.
1812	Harewood (7th), George Henry Hubert Lascelles, KBE, *b*. 1923, *s*. 1947, *m*. (See also page 134).	Viscount Lascelles, *b*. 1950.
1742	Harrington (11th), William Henry Leicester Stanhope (8th *Brit. Viscount, Stanhope of Mahon*, 1717), *b*. 1922, *s*. 1929, *m*.	Viscount Petersham, *b*. 1945.
1809	Harrowby (7th), Dudley Danvers Granville Coutts Ryder, TD, *b*. 1922, *s*. 1987, *m*.	Viscount Sandon, *b*. 1951.
1605 s.	Home. Disclaimed for life 1963. (*see* Lord Home of the Hirsel, page 164.)	Hon. David A. C. *D.-H*., *b*. 1943.
1821	°Howe (7th), Frederick Richard Penn Curzon, *b*. 1951, *s*. 1984, *m*.	Charles M. P. *C*., *b*. 1967.
1529	Huntingdon (16th), William Edward Robin Hood Hastings Bass, *b*. 1948, *s*. 1990, *m*.	Hon. Simon A. R. H. *H. B*., *b*. 1950.
1885	Iddesleigh (4th), Stafford Henry Northcote, *b*. 1932, *s*. 1970, *m*.	Viscount St Cyres, *b*. 1957.
1756	Ilchester (9th), Maurice Vivian de Touffreville Fox-Strangways, *b*. 1920, *s*. 1970, *m*.	Hon. Raymond G. *F.-S*., *b*. 1921.
1929	Inchcape (3rd), Kenneth James William Mackay, *b*. 1917, *s*. 1939, *m*.	Viscount Glenapp, *b*. 1943.
1919	Iveagh (4th), Arthur Edward Rory Guinness, *b*. 1969, *s*. 1992.	Hon. Rory M. B. *G*., *b*. 1974.
1925	°Jellicoe (2nd), George Patrick John Rushworth Jellicoe, KBE, DSO, MC, PC, *b*. 1918, *s*. 1935, *m*.	Viscount Brocas, *b*. 1950.
1697	Jersey (9th), George Francis Child-Villiers (12th *Irish Visct., Grandison*, 1620), *b*. 1910, *s*. 1923, *m*.	Viscount Villiers, *b*. 1948.
1822 I.	Kilmorey (6th), Richard Francis Needham, MP, *b*. 1942, *s*. 1977, *m*.	Viscount Newry and Morne, *b*. 1966.
1866	Kimberley (4th), John Wodehouse, *b*. 1924, *s*. 1941, *m*.	Lord Wodehouse, *b*. 1951.
1768 I.	Kingston (11th), Barclay Robert Edwin King-Tenison, *b*. 1943, *s*. 1948, *m*.	Viscount Kingsborough, *b*. 1969.
1633 s.*	Kinnoull (15th), Arthur William George Patrick Hay (9th *Brit. Baron, Hay of Pedwardine*, 1711), *b*. 1935, *s*. 1938, *m*.	Viscount Dupplin, *b*. 1962.
1677 s.*	Kintore (13th), Michael Canning William John Keith (3rd *UK Viscount, Stonehaven*, 1938), *b*. 1939, *s*. 1989, *m*.	Lord Inverurie, *b*. 1976.
1914	°Kitchener of Khartoum (3rd), Henry Herbert Kitchener, TD, *b*. 1919, *s*. 1937.	None.
1756 I.	Lanesborough (9th), Denis Anthony Brian Butler, TD, *b*. 1918, *s*. 1950.	Maj. Henry A. B. C. *B*., *b*. 1909.

Created	Title, order of succession, name, etc.	Eldest son or heir
1624 S.	Lauderdale (17th), Patrick Francis Maitland, b. 1911, s. 1968, m.	Viscount Maitland, b. 1937.
1837	Leicester (6th), Anthony Louis Lovel Coke, b. 1909, s. 1976, m.	Viscount Coke, b. 1936.
1641 S.	Leven (14th) & Melville (13th) (S. 1690), Alexander Robert Leslie Melville, b. 1924, s. 1947, m.	Lord Balgonie, b. 1954.
1831	Lichfield (5th), Thomas Patrick John Anson, b. 1939, s. 1960.	Viscount Anson, b. 1978.
1803 I.*	Limerick (6th), Patrick Edmund Pery, KBE (6th UK Baron, Foxford, 1815), b. 1930, s. 1967, m.	Viscount Glentworth, b. 1963.
1572	Lincoln (18th), Edward Horace Fiennes-Clinton, b. 1913, s. 1988, m.	Hon. Edward G. F.-C., b. 1943.
1633 S.	Lindsay (16th), James Randolph Lindsay-Bethune, b. 1955, s. 1989, m.	Viscount Garnock, b. 1990.
1626	Lindsey (14th) and Abingdon (9th) (1682), Richard Henry Rupert Bertie, b. 1931, s. 1963, m.	Lord Norreys, b. 1958.
1776 I.	Lisburne (8th), John David Malet Vaughan, b. 1918, s. 1965, m.	Viscount Vaughan, b. 1945.
1822 I.*	Listowel (5th), William Francis Hare, GCMG, PC, (3rd UK Baron, Hare, 1869), b. 1906, s. 1931, m.	Viscount Ennismore, b. 1964.
1905	Liverpool (5th), Edward Peter Bertram Savile Foljambe, b. 1944, s. 1969, m.	Viscount Hawkesbury, b. 1972.
1945	°Lloyd George of Dwyfor (3rd), Owen Lloyd George, b. 1924, s. 1968, m.	Viscount Gwynedd, b. 1951.
1785 I.*	Longford (7th), Francis Aungier Pakenham, KG, PC (6th UK Baron, Silchester, 1821; 1st UK Baron, Pakenham, 1945), b. 1905, s. 1961, m.	Thomas F. D. P., b. 1933.
1807	Lonsdale (7th), James Hugh William Lowther, b. 1922, s. 1953, m.	Viscount Lowther, b. 1949.
1838	Lovelace (5th), Peter Axel William Locke King (12th Brit. Baron, King, 1725), b. 1951, s. 1964, m.	None.
1795 I.*	Lucan (7th), Richard John Bingham (3rd UK Baron, Bingham, 1934), b. 1934, s. 1964, m.	Lord Bingham, b. 1967.
1880	Lytton (5th), John Peter Michael Scawen Lytton (18th Engl. Baron, Wentworth, 1529), b. 1950, s. 1985, m.	Viscount Knebworth, b. 1989.
1721	Macclesfield (9th), Richard Timothy George Mansfield Parker, b. 1943, s. 1992, m.	Hon. David J. G. P., b. 1945.
1800	Malmesbury (6th), William James Harris, TD, b. 1907, s. 1950, m.	Viscount FitzHarris, b. 1946.
1776 & 1792	Mansfield and Mansfield (8th), William David Mungo James Murray (14th Scott. Visct., Stormont, 1621), b. 1930, s. 1971, m.	Viscount Stormont, b. 1956.
1565 S.	Mar (13th) & Kellie (15th) (S. 1616), John Francis Hervey Erskine, b. 1921, s. 1955, m.	Lord Erskine, b. 1949.
1785 I.	Mayo (10th), Terence Patrick Bourke, b. 1929, s. 1962, m.	Lord Naas, b. 1953.
1627 I.*	Meath (14th), Anthony Windham Normand Brabazon (5th UK Baron, Chaworth, 1831), b. 1910, s. 1949, m.	Lord Ardee, b. 1941.
1766 I.	Mexborough (8th), John Christopher George Savile, b. 1931, s. 1980, m.	Viscount Pollington, b. 1959.
1813	Minto (6th), Gilbert Edward George Lariston Elliot-Murray-Kynynmound, OBE, b. 1928, s. 1975, m.	Viscount Melgund, b. 1953.
1562 S.*	Moray (20th) Douglas John Moray Stuart (12th Brit. Baron, Stuart of Castle Stuart, 1796), b. 1928, s. 1974, m.	Lord Doune, b. 1966.
1815	Morley (6th), John St Aubyn Parker, b. 1923, s. 1962, m.	Viscount Boringdon, b. 1956.
1458 S.	Morton (22nd), John Charles Sholto Douglas, b. 1927, s. 1976, m.	Lord Aberdour, b. 1952.
1789	Mount Edgcumbe (8th), Robert Charles Edgcumbe, b. 1939, s. 1982, m.	Piers V. E., b. 1946.
1831	Munster (7th), Anthony Charles FitzClarence, b. 1926, s. 1983, m.	None.
1805	°Nelson (9th), Peter John Horatio Nelson, b. 1941, s. 1981, m.	Viscount Merton, b. 1971.
1660 S.	Newburgh (12th), Prince Filippo Giambattista Camillo Francesco Aldo Maria Rospigliosi, b. 1942, s. 1986, m.	Princess Benedetta F. M. R., b. 1974.
1827 I.	Norbury (6th), Noel Terence Graham-Toler, b. 1939, s. 1955, m.	Viscount Glandine, b. 1967.
1806 I.*	Normanton (6th), Shaun James Christian Welbore Ellis Agar (9th Brit. Baron, Mendip, 1791, 4th UK Baron, Somerton, 1873), b. 1945, s. 1967, m.	Viscount Somerton, b. 1982.
1647 S.	Northesk (13th), Robert Andrew Carnegie, b. 1926, s. 1975, m.	Lord Rosehill, b. 1954.
1801	Onslow (7th), Michael William Coplestone Dillon Onslow, b. 1938, s. 1971, m.	Viscount Cranley, b. 1967.
1696 S.	Orkney (8th), Cecil O'Bryen Fitz-Maurice, b. 1919, s. 1951, m.	O. Peter St John, b. 1938.
1925	Oxford and Asquith (2nd), Julian Edward George Asquith, KCMG, b. 1916, s. 1928, m.	Viscount Asquith, OBE, b. 1952.
1929	°Peel (3rd), William James Robert Peel (4th UK Viscount Peel, 1895), b. 1947, s. 1969, m.	Viscount Clanfield, b. 1976.
1551	Pembroke (17th) & Montgomery (14th) (1605), Henry George Charles Alexander Herbert, b. 1939, s. 1969.	Lord Herbert, b. 1978.
1605 S.	Perth (17th), John David Drummond, PC, b. 1907, s. 1951, m.	Viscount Strathallan, b. 1935.
1905	Plymouth (3rd), Other Robert Ivor Windsor-Clive (15th Engl. Baron, Windsor, 1529), b. 1923, s. 1943, m.	Viscount Windsor, b. 1951.
1785 I.	Portarlington (7th), George Lionel Yuill Seymour Dawson-Damer, b. 1938, s. 1959, m.	Viscount Carlow, b. 1965.

Created	Title, order of succession, name, etc.	Eldest son or heir
1689	*Portland* (11th), Count Henry Noel Bentinck, *b.* 1919, *s.* 1990, *m.*	Viscount Woodstock, *b.* 1953.
1743	*Portsmouth* (10th), Quentin Gerard Carew Wallop, *b.* 1954, *s.* 1984, *m.*	Viscount Lymington, *b.* 1981.
1804	*Powis* (8th), John George Herbert (9th *Irish Baron, Clive*, 1762), *b.* 1952, *s.* 1993, *m.*	Viscount Clive, *b.* 1979.
1765	*Radnor* (8th), Jacob Pleydell-Bouverie, *b.* 1927, *s.* 1968, *m.*	Viscount Folkestone, *b.* 1955.
1831 I.*	*Ranfurly* (7th), Gerald Françoys Needham Knox (8th *UK Baron, Ranfurly*, 1826), *b.* 1929, *s.* 1988, *m.*	Viscount Northland, *b.* 1957.
1771 I.	*Roden* (9th), Robert William Jocelyn, *b.* 1909, *s.* 1956, *w.*	Viscount Jocelyn, *b.* 1938.
1801	*Romney* (7th), Michael Henry Marsham, *b.* 1910, *s.* 1975, *m.*	Julian C. *M.*, *b.* 1948.
1703 S.*	*Rosebery* (7th), Neil Archibald Primrose (3rd *UK Earl, Midlothian*, 1911), *b.* 1929, *s.* 1974, *m.*	Lord Dalmeny, *b.* 1967.
1806 I.	*Rosse* (7th), William Brendan Parsons, *b.* 1936, *s.* 1979, *m.*	Lord Oxmantown, *b.* 1969.
1801	*Rosslyn* (7th), Peter St Clair-Erskine, *b.* 1958, *s.* 1977, *m.*	Lord Loughborough, *b.* 1986.
1457 S.	*Rothes* (21st), Ian Lionel Malcolm Leslie, *b.* 1932, *s.* 1975, *m.*	Lord Leslie, *b.* 1958.
1861	°*Russell* (5th), Conrad Sebastian Robert Russell, *b.* 1937, *s.* 1987, *m.*	Viscount Amberley, *b.* 1968.
1915	°*St Aldwyn* (3rd), Michael Henry Hicks Beach, *b.* 1950, *s.* 1992, *m.*	Hon. David S. *H. B.*, *b.* 1955.
1815	*St Germans* (10th), Peregrine Nicholas Eliot, *b.* 1941, *s.* 1988.	Lord Eliot, *b.* 1966.
1660	*Sandwich.* Disclaimed for life 1964. ((*Alexander*) *Victor* (*Edward Paulet*) *Montagu*, *b.* 1906, *s.* 1962.)	John E. H. *M.*, *b.* 1943.
1690	*Scarbrough* (12th), Richard Aldred Lumley (13th *Irish Visct., Lumley*, 1628), *b.* 1932, *s.* 1969, *m.*	Viscount Lumley, *b.* 1973.
1701 S.	*Seafield* (13th), Ian Derek Francis Ogilvie-Grant, *b.* 1939, *s.* 1969, *m.*	Viscount Reidhaven, *b.* 1963.
1882	*Selborne* (4th), John Roundell Palmer, KBE, FRS, *b.* 1940, *s.* 1971, *m.*	Viscount Wolmer, *b.* 1971.
1646 S.	*Selkirk* (10th), (George) Nigel Douglas-Hamilton, KT, GCMG, GBE, AFC, AE, PC, QC, *b.* 1906, *s.* 1940, *m.*	The Master of Selkirk, *b.* 1939.
1672	*Shaftesbury* (10th), Anthony Ashley-Cooper, *b.* 1938, *s.* 1961, *m.*	Lord Ashley, *b.* 1977.
1756 I.*	*Shannon* (9th), Richard Bentinck Boyle (8th *Brit. Baron Carleton*, 1786), *b.* 1924, *s.* 1963.	Viscount Boyle, *b.* 1960.
1442	*Shrewsbury & Waterford* (22nd) (I. 1446), Charles Henry John Benedict Crofton Chetwynd Chetwynd-Talbot (*Premier Earl of England and Ireland; Earl Talbot*, 1784), *b.* 1952, *s.* 1980, *m.*	Viscount Ingestre, *b.* 1978.
1961	*Snowdon* (1st), Antony Charles Robert Armstrong-Jones, GCVO, *b.* 1930, *m.* (*see also* page 123).	Viscount Linley, *b.* 1961 (*see also* page 123).
1880	°*Sondes* (5th), Henry George Herbert Milles-Lade, *b.* 1940, *s.* 1970.	None.
1765	°*Spencer* (9th), Charles Edward Maurice Spencer, *b.* 1964, *s.* 1992, *m.*	G. C. Robert M. *S.*, *b.* 1932.
1703 S.*	*Stair* (13th), John Aymer Dalrymple, KCVO, MBE (6th *UK Baron, Oxenfoord*, 1841), *b.* 1906, *s.* 1961, *m.*	Viscount Dalrymple, *b.* 1961.
1984	*Stockton* (2nd), Alexander Daniel Alan Macmillan, *b.* 1943, *s.* 1986.	Viscount Macmillan of Ovenden, *b.* 1974.
1821	*Stradbroke* (6th), Robert Keith Rous, *b.* 1937, *s.* 1983, *m.*	Viscount Dunwich, *b.* 1961.
1847	*Strafford* (8th), Thomas Edmund Byng, *b.* 1936, *s.* 1984, *m.*	Viscount Enfield, *b.* 1964.
1606 S.*	*Strathmore & Kinghorne* (18th), Michael Fergus Bowes Lyon (16th *Scottish Earl, Strathmore*, 1677, & 18th *Kinghorne*, 1606; 5th *UK Earl, Strathmore & Kinghorne*, 1937), *b.* 1957, *s.* 1987, *m.*	Lord Glamis, *b.* 1986.
1603	*Suffolk* (21st) & *Berkshire* (14th) (1626), Michael John James George Robert Howard, *b.* 1935, *s.* 1941, *m.*	Viscount Andover, *b.* 1974.
1955	*Swinton* (2nd), David Yarburgh Cunliffe-Lister, *b.* 1937, *s.* 1972, *m.*	Hon. Nicholas J. *C.-L.*, *b.* 1939.
1714	*Tankerville* (10th), Peter Grey Bennet, *b.* 1956, *s.* 1980.	Revd the Hon. George A. G. *B.*, *b.* 1925.
1822	°*Temple of Stowe* (8th), (Walter) Grenville Algernon Temple-Gore-Langton, *b.* 1924, *s.* 1988, *m.*	Lord Langton, *b.* 1955.
1815	*Verulam* (7th), John Duncan Grimston (11th *Irish Visct., Grimston*, 1719; 16th *Scott. Baron, Forrester of Corstorphine*, 1633), *b.* 1951, *s.* 1973, *m.*	Viscount Grimston, *b.* 1978.
1729	°*Waldegrave* (12th), Geoffrey Noel Waldegrave, KG, GCVO, TD, *b.* 1905, *s.* 1936, *m.*	Viscount Chewton, *b.* 1940.
1759	*Warwick* & °*Brooke* (8th) (*Brit.* 1746), David Robin Francis Guy Greville (8th *Earl Brooke* and 8th *Earl of Warwick*), *b.* 1934, *s.* 1984.	Lord Brooke, *b.* 1957.
1633 S.*	*Wemyss* (12th) & *March* (8th) (s. 1697), Francis David Charteris, KT (5th *UK Baron, Wemyss*, 1821), *b.* 1912, *s.* 1937, *w.*	Lord Neidpath, *b.* 1948.
1621 I.	*Westmeath* (13th), William Anthony Nugent, *b.* 1928, *s.* 1971, *m.*	Hon. Sean C. W. *N.*, *b.* 1965.
1624	*Westmorland* (15th), David Anthony Thomas Fane, GCVO, *b.* 1924, *s.* 1948, *m.*	Lord Burghersh, *b.* 1951.
1876	*Wharncliffe* (5th), Richard Alan Montagu Stuart Wortley, *b.* 1953, *s.* 1987, *m.*	Viscount Carlton, *b.* 1980.
1801	*Wilton* (7th), Seymour William Arthur John Egerton, *b.* 1921, *s.* 1927, *m.*	Baron Ebury, *b.* 1934 (*see page* 155).
1628	*Winchilsea* (16th) & *Nottingham* (11th) (1675), Christopher Denys Stormont Finch Hatton, *b.* 1936, *s.* 1950, *m.*	Viscount Maidstone, *b.* 1967.

Created	Title, order of succession, name, etc.	Eldest son or heir
1766 I.	°*Winterton* (8th), (Donald) David Turnour, *b.* 1943, *s.* 1991, *m.*	Robert C. *T.*, *b.* 1950.
1956	*Woolton* (3rd), Simon Frederick Marquis, *b.* 1958, *s.* 1969, *m.*	None.
1837	*Yarborough* (8th), Charles John Pelham, *b.* 1963, *s.* 1991, *m.*	Lord Worsley, *b.* 1990.

COUNTESSES IN THEIR OWN RIGHT

Style, The Right Hon. the Countess (of) —
Husband, Untitled
Children's style, As for children of an Earl
For forms of address, *see* page 220

Created	Title, order of succession, name, etc.	Eldest son or heir
1643 S.	*Dysart* (11th in line), Rosamund Agnes Greaves, *b.* 1914, *s.* 1975.	Lady Katherine *Grant of Rothiemurchus*, *b.* 1918.
1633 S.	*Loudoun* (13th in line), Barbara Huddleston Abney-Hastings, *b.* 1919, *s.* 1960, *m.*	Lord Mauchline, *b.* 1942.
c.1115 S.	*Mar* (31st in line), Margaret of Mar (*Premier Earldom of Scotland*), *b.* 1940, *s.* 1975, *m.*	Mistress of Mar, *b.* 1963.
1947	°*Mountbatten of Burma* (2nd in line), Patricia Edwina Victoria Knatchbull, CBE, *b.* 1924, *s.* 1979, *m.*	Lord Romsey, *b.* 1947 (*see also* page 153).
c.1235 S.	*Sutherland* (24th in line), Elizabeth Millicent Sutherland, *b.* 1921, *s.* 1963, *m.*	Lord Strathnaver, *b.* 1947.

VISCOUNTS

Coronet, Sixteen silver balls
Style, The Right Hon. the Viscount —
Wife's style, The Right Hon. the Viscountess —
Children's style, 'The Hon.' before forename and family name
In Scotland, the heir apparent to a Viscount may be styled 'The Master of — (title of peer)'
For forms of address, *see* page 220

Created	Title, order of succession, name, etc.	Eldest son or heir
1945	*Addison* (4th), William Matthew Wand Addison, *b.* 1945, *s.* 1992, *m.*	Hon. Paul W. *A.*, *b.* 1973.
1946	*Alanbrooke* (3rd), Alan Victor Harold Brooke, *b.* 1932, *s.* 1972.	None.
1919	*Allenby* (3rd), Lt.-Col. Michael Jaffray Hynman Allenby, *b.* 1931, *s.* 1984, *m.*	Hon. Henry J. H. *A.*, *b.* 1968.
1911	*Allendale* (3rd), Wentworth Hubert Charles Beaumont, *b.* 1922, *s.* 1956, *m.*	Hon. Wentworth P. I. *B.*, *b.* 1948.
1642 S.	*of Arbuthnott* (16th), John Campbell Arbuthnott, CBE, DSC, *b.* 1924, *s.* 1966, *m.*	Master of Arbuthnott, *b.* 1950.
1751 I.	*Ashbrook* (10th), Desmond Llowarch Edward Flower, KCVO, MBE, *b.* 1905. *s.* 1936, *m.*	Hon. Michael L. W. *F.*, *b.* 1935.
1917	*Astor* (4th), William Waldorf Astor, *b.* 1951, *s.* 1966, *m.*	Hon. William W. *A.*, *b.* 1979.
1781 I.	*Bangor* (8th), William Maxwell David Ward, *b.* 1948, *s.* 1993, *m.*	Hon. Edward N. *W.*, *b.* 1953.
1925	*Bearsted* (4th), Peter Montefiore Samuel, MC, TD, *b.* 1911, *s.* 1986, *m.*	Hon. Nicholas A. *S.*, *b.* 1950.
1963	*Blakenham* (2nd), Michael John Hare, *b.* 1938, *s.* 1982, *m.*	Hon. Caspar J. *H.*, *b.* 1972.
1935	*Bledisloe* (3rd), Christopher Hiley Ludlow Bathurst, QC, *b.* 1934, *s.* 1979.	Hon. Rupert E. L. *B.*, *b.* 1964.
1712	*Bolingbroke* (7th) & *St John* (8th) (1716), Kenneth Oliver Musgrave St John, *b.* 1927, *s.* 1974.	Hon. Henry F. *St J.*, *b.* 1957.
1960	*Boyd of Merton* (2nd), Simon Donald Rupert Neville Lennox-Boyd, *b.* 1939, *s.* 1983, *m.*	Hon. Benjamin A. *L.-B.*, *b.* 1964.
1717 I.*	*Boyne* (10th), Gustavus Michael George Hamilton-Russell (4th *UK Baron*, Brancepeth, 1866), *b.* 1931, *s.* 1942, *m.*	Hon. Gustavus M. S. *H.-R.*, *b.* 1965.
1929	*Brentford* (4th), Crispin William Joynson-Hicks, *b.* 1933, *s.* 1983, *m.*	Hon. Paul W. *J.-H.*, *b.* 1971.
1929	*Bridgeman* (3rd), Robin John Orlando Bridgeman, *b.* 1930, *s.* 1982, *m.*	Hon. William O. C. *B.*, *b.* 1968.

Created	Title, order of succession, name, etc.	Eldest son or heir
1868	*Bridport* (4th), Alexander Nelson Hood (7th *Duke of Brontë in Sicily*, 1799, *and* 6th *Irish Baron Bridport*, 1794), *b.* 1948, *s.* 1969, *m.*	Hon. Peregrine A. N. *H.*, *b.* 1974.
1952	*Brookeborough* (3rd), Alan Henry Brooke, *b.* 1952, *s.* 1987, *m.*	Hon. Christopher A. *B.*, *b.* 1954.
1933	*Buckmaster* (3rd), Martin Stanley Buckmaster, OBE, *b.* 1921, *s.* 1974.	Hon. Colin J. *B.*, *b.* 1923.
1939	*Caldecote* (2nd), Robert Andrew Inskip, KBE, DSC, FEng., *b.* 1917, *s.* 1947, *m.*	Hon. Piers J. H. *I.*, *b.* 1947.
1941	*Camrose* (2nd), (John) Seymour Berry, TD, *b.* 1909, *s.* 1954, *m.*	Baron Hartwell, MBE, TD, *b.* 1911 (*see* page 164).
1954	*Chandos* (3rd), Thomas Orlando Lyttelton, *b.* 1953, *s.* 1980, *m.*	Hon. Oliver A. *L.*, *b.* 1986.
1665 I.	*Charlemont* (14th), John Day Caulfeild (18th *Irish Baron, Caulfeild of Charlemont*, 1620), *b.* 1934, *s.* 1985, *m.*	Hon. John D. *C.*, *b.* 1966.
1921	*Chelmsford* (3rd), Frederic Jan Thesiger, *b.* 1931, *s.* 1970, *m.*	Hon. Frederic C. P. *T.*, *b.* 1962.
1717 I.	*Chetwynd* (10th), Adam Richard John Casson Chetwynd, *b.* 1935, *s.* 1965, *m.*	Hon. Adam D. *C.*, *b.* 1969.
1911	*Chilston* (4th), Alastair George Akers-Douglas, *b.* 1946, *s.* 1982, *m.*	Hon. Oliver I. *A.-D.*, *b.* 1973.
1902	*Churchill* (3rd), Victor George Spencer (5th *UK Baron Churchill*, 1815), *b.* 1934, *s.* 1973.	None to Viscountcy. To Barony, Richard H. R. *S.*, *b.* 1926.
1718	*Cobham* (11th), John William Leonard Lyttelton (8th *Irish Baron, Westcote*, 1776), *b.* 1943, *s.* 1977, *m.*	Hon. Christopher C. *L.*, *b.* 1947.
1902	*Colville of Culross* (4th), John Mark Alexander Colville, QC (13th *Scott. Baron, Colville of Culross*, 1604), *b.* 1933, *s.* 1945, *m.*	Master of Colville, *b.* 1959.
1826	*Combermere* (5th), Michael Wellington Stapleton-Cotton, *b.* 1929, *s.* 1969, *m.*	Hon. Thomas R. W. *S.-C.*, *b.* 1969.
1917	*Cowdray* (3rd), Weetman John Churchill Pearson, TD (3rd *UK Baron, Cowdray*, 1910), *b.* 1910, *s.* 1933, *m.*	Hon. Michael O. W. *P.*, *b.* 1944.
1927	*Craigavon* (3rd), Janric Fraser Craig, *b.* 1944, *s.* 1974.	None.
1886	*Cross* (3rd), Assheton Henry Cross, *b.* 1920, *s.* 1932.	None.
1943	*Daventry* (3rd), Francis Humphrey Maurice FitzRoy Newdegate, *b.* 1921, *s.* 1986, *m.*	Hon. James E. *F.N.*, *b.* 1960.
1937	*Davidson* (2nd), John Andrew Davidson, *b.* 1928, *s.* 1970, *m.*	Hon. Malcolm W. M. *D.*, *b.* 1934.
1956	*De L'Isle* (2nd), Philip John Algernon Sidney, MBE, (7th *Baron De L'Isle and Dudley*, 1835), *b.* 1945, *s.* 1991, *m.*	Hon. Philip W. E. *S.*, *b.* 1985.
1776 I.	*De Vesci* (7th), Thomas Eustace Vesey (8th *Irish Baron, Knapton*, 1750), *b.* 1955, *s.* 1983, *m.*	Hon. Oliver I. *V.*, *b.* 1991.
1917	*Devonport* (3rd), Terence Kearley, *b.* 1944, *s.* 1973.	Chester D. H. *K.*, *b.* 1932.
1964	*Dilhorne* (2nd), John Mervyn Manningham-Buller, *b.* 1932, *s.* 1980, *m.*	Hon. James E.*M.-B.*, *b.* 1956.
1622 I.	*Dillon* (22nd), Henry Benedict Charles Dillon, *b.* 1973, *s.* 1982.	Hon. Richard A. L. *D.*, *b.* 1948.
1785 I.	*Doneraile* (10th), Richard Allen St Leger, *b.* 1946, *s.* 1983, *m.*	Hon. Nathaniel W. R. St J. *St L.*, *b.* 1971.
1680 I.*	*Downe* (11th), John Christian George Dawnay (4th *UK Baron, Dawnay*, 1897), *b.* 1935, *s.* 1965, *m.*	Hon. Richard H. *D.*, *b.* 1967.
1959	*Dunrossil* (2nd), John William Morrison, CMG, *b.* 1926, *s.* 1961, *m.*	Hon. Andrew W. R. *M.*, *b.* 1953.
1964	*Eccles* (1st), David McAdam Eccles, CH, KCVO, PC, *b.* 1904, *m.*	Hon. John D. *E.*, CBE, *b.* 1931.
1897	*Esher* (4th), Lionel Gordon Baliol Brett, CBE, *b.* 1913. *s.* 1963, *m.*	Hon. Christopher L. B. *B.*, *b.* 1936.
1816	*Exmouth* (10th), Paul Edward Pellew, *b.* 1940, *s.* 1970, *m.*	Hon. Edward F. *P.*, *b.* 1978.
1620 S.	*Falkland* (15th), Lucius Edward William Plantagenet Cary (*Premier Scottish Viscount on the Roll*), *b.* 1935, *s.* 1984, *m.*	Master of Falkland, *b.* 1963.
1720	*Falmouth* (9th), George Hugh Boscawen (26th *Eng. Baron, Le Despencer*, 1264), *b.* 1919, *s.* 1962, *m.*	Hon. Evelyn A. H. *B.*, *b.* 1955.
1918	*Furness* (2nd), William Anthony Furness, *b.* 1929, *s.* 1940.	None.
1720 I.*	*Gage* (7th), George John St Clere Gage, (6th *Brit. Baron, Gage*, 1790), *b.* 1932, *s.* 1982.	Hon. H. Nicolas *G.*, *b.* 1934.
1727 I.	*Galway* (12th), George Rupert Monckton-Arundell, *b.* 1922, *s.* 1980, *m.*	Hon. J. Philip *M.*, *b.* 1952.
1478 I.*	*Gormanston* (17th), Jenico Nicholas Dudley Preston (*Premier Viscount of Ireland*; 5th *UK Baron, Gormanston*, 1868), *b.* 1939, *s.* 1940, *w.*	Hon. Jenico F. T. *P.*, *b.* 1974.
1816 I.	*Gort* (8th), Colin Leopold Prendergast Vereker, *b.* 1916, *s.* 1975, *m.*	Hon. Foley R.S.P.*V.*, *b.* 1951.
1900	*Goschen* (4th), Giles John Harry Goschen, *b.* 1965, *s.* 1977, *m.*	None.
1849	*Gough* (5th), Shane Hugh Maryon Gough, *b.* 1941, *s.* 1951.	None.
1937	*Greenwood* (2nd), David Henry Hamar Greenwood, *b.* 1914, *s.* 1948.	Hon. Michael G. H. *G.*, *b.* 1923.
1929	*Hailsham.* Disclaimed for life 1963. (*see* Lord Hailsham of St Marylebone, page 164.)	Hon. Douglas M. *Hogg*, QC, MP, *b.* 1945.
1891	*Hambleden* (4th), William Herbert Smith, *b.* 1930, *s.* 1948, *m.*	Hon. William H. B. *S.*, *b.* 1955.
1884	*Hampden* (6th), Anthony David Brand, *b.* 1937, *s.* 1975.	Hon. Francis A. *B.*, *b.* 1970.
1936	*Hanworth* (2nd), David Bertram Pollock, *b.* 1916, *s.* 1936, *m.*	Hon. David S. G. *P.*, *b.* 1946.
1791 I.	*Harberton* (10th), Thomas de Vautort Pomeroy, *b.* 1910, *s.* 1980, *m.*	Hon. Robert W. *P.*, *b.* 1916.
1846	*Hardinge* (6th), Charles Henry Nicholas Hardinge, *b.* 1956, *s.* 1984, *m.*	Hon. Andrew H. *H.*, *b.* 1960.

Created	Title, order of succession, name, etc.	Eldest son or heir
1791 I.	Hawarden (9th), (Robert) Connan Wyndham Leslie Maude, b. 1961, s. 1991.	Hon. Thomas P. C. M., b. 1964.
1960	Head (2nd), Richard Antony Head, b. 1937, s. 1983, m.	Hon. Henry J. H., b. 1980.
1550	Hereford (18th), Robert Milo Leicester Devereux (Premier Viscount of England), b. 1932, s. 1952.	Hon. Charles R. de B. D., b. 1975.
1842	Hill (8th), Antony Rowland Clegg-Hill, b. 1931, s. 1974.	Peter D. R. C. C.-H., b. 1945.
1796	Hood (7th), Alexander Lambert Hood (7th Irish Baron, Hood, 1782), b. 1914, s. 1981, m.	Hon. Henry L. A. H., b. 1958.
1956	Ingleby (2nd), Martin Raymond Peake, b. 1926, s. 1966, m.	None.
1945	Kemsley (2nd), (Geoffrey) Lionel Berry, b. 1909, s. 1968, m.	Richard G. B., b. 1951.
1911	Knollys (3rd), David Francis Dudley Knollys, b. 1931, s. 1966, m.	Hon. Patrick N. M. K., b. 1962.
1895	Knutsford (6th), Michael Holland-Hibbert, b. 1926, s. 1986, m.	Hon. Henry T. H.-H., b. 1959.
1945	Lambert (3rd), Michael John Lambert, b. 1912, s. 1989, m.	None.
1954	Leathers (2nd), Frederick Alan Leathers, b. 1908, s. 1965, m.	Hon. Christopher G. L., b. 1941.
1922	Leverhulme (3rd), Philip William Bryce Lever, KG, TD, b. 1915, s. 1949, w.	None.
1781 I.	Lifford (9th), (Edward) James Wingfield Hewitt, b. 1949, s. 1987, m.	Hon. James T. W. H., b. 1979.
1921	Long (4th), Richard Gerard Long, CBE, b. 1929, s. 1967, m.	Hon. James R. L., b. 1960.
1957	Mackintosh of Halifax (3rd), (John) Clive Mackintosh, b. 1958, s. 1980, m.	Hon. Thomas H. G. M., b. 1985.
1955	Malvern (3rd), Ashley Kevin Godfrey Huggins, b. 1949, s. 1978.	Hon. M. James H., b. 1928.
1945	Marchwood (3rd), David George Staveley Penny, b. 1936, s. 1979, m.	Hon. Peter G. W. P., b. 1965.
1942	Margesson (2nd), Francis Vere Hampden Margesson, b. 1922, s. 1965, m.	Capt. Hon. Richard F. D. M., b. 1960.
1660 I.*	Massereene (14th) & Ferrard (7th) (1797), John David Clotworthy Whyte-Melville Foster Skeffington (7th UK Baron, Oriel, 1821), b. 1940, s. 1993, m.	Hon. Charles S., b. 1973.
1802	Melville (9th), Robert David Ross Dundas, b. 1937, s. 1971, m.	Hon. Robert H. K. D., b. 1984.
1916	Mersey (4th), Richard Maurice Clive Bigham, b. 1934, s. 1979, m.	Hon. Edward J. H. B., b. 1966.
1717 I.*	Midleton (12th), Alan Henry Brodrick (9th Brit. Baron, Brodrick of Peper Harow, 1796), b. 1949, s. 1988, m.	Hon. Ashley R. B., b. 1980.
1962	Mills (3rd), Christopher Philip Roger Mills, b. 1956, s. 1988, m.	None.
1716 I.	Molesworth (11th), Richard Gosset Molesworth, b. 1907, s. 1961, w.	Hon. Robert B. K. M., b. 1959.
1801 I.*	Monck (7th), Charles Stanley Monck (4th UK Baron, Monck, 1866), b. 1953, s. 1982.	Hon. George S. M., b. 1957.
1957	Monckton of Brenchley (2nd), Gilbert Walter Riversdale Monckton, CB, OBE, MC, b. 1915, s. 1965, m.	Hon Christopher W. M., b. 1952.
1935	Monsell (2nd), Henry Bolton Graham Eyres Monsell, b. 1905, s. 1969.	None.
1946	Montgomery of Alamein (2nd), David Bernard Montgomery, CBE, b. 1928, s. 1976, m.	Hon. Henry D. M., b. 1954.
1550 I.*	Mountgarret (17th), Richard Henry Piers Butler (4th UK Baron, Mountgarret, 1911), b. 1936, s. 1966, m.	Hon. Piers J. R. B., b. 1961.
1952	Norwich (2nd), John Julius Cooper, CVO, b. 1929, s. 1954, m.	Hon. Jason C. D. B. C., b. 1959.
1651 S.	of Oxfuird (13th), George Hubbard Makgill, b. 1934, s. 1986, m.	Master of Oxfuird, b. 1969.
1873	Portman, (9th), Edward Henry Berkeley Portman, b. 1934, s. 1967, m.	Hon. Christopher E. B. P., b. 1958.
1743 I.*	Powerscourt (10th), Mervyn Niall Wingfield (4th UK Baron, Powerscourt, 1885), b. 1935, s. 1973, m.	Hon. Mervyn A. W., b. 1963.
1900	Ridley (4th), Matthew White Ridley, KG, TD, b. 1925, s. 1964, m. Lord Steward.	Hon. Matthew W. R., b. 1958.
1960	Rochdale (2nd), St John Durival Kemp, b. 1938, s. 1993, m.	Hon. Jonathan H. D. K., b. 1961.
1919	Rothermere (3rd), Vere Harold Esmond Harmsworth, b. 1925, s. 1978, w.	Hon. H. Jonathan E. V. H., b. 1967.
1937	Runciman of Doxford (3rd), Walter Garrison Runciman, CBE, FBA (4th UK Baron, Runciman, 1933), b. 1934, s. 1989, m.	Hon. David W. R., b. 1967.
1918	St Davids (3rd), Colwyn Jestyn John Philipps (20th Engl. Baron Strange of Knokin, 1299, 8th Engl. Baron Hungerford, 1426, and De Moleyns, 1445), b. 1939, s. 1991, m.	Hon. Rhodri C. P., b. 1966.
1801	St Vincent (7th), Ronald George James Jervis, b. 1905, s. 1940, m.	Hon. Edward R. J. J., b. 1951.
1937	Samuel (3rd), David Herbert Samuel, PH.D., b. 1922, s. 1978, m.	Hon. Dan J. S., b. 1925.
1911	Scarsdale (3rd), Francis John Nathaniel Curzon (7th Brit. Baron, Scarsdale, 1761), b. 1924, s. 1977, m.	Hon. Peter G. N. C., b. 1949.
1905	Selby (4th), Michael Guy John Gully, b. 1942, s. 1959, m.	Hon. Edward T. W. G., b. 1967.
1805	Sidmouth (7th), John Tonge Anthony Pellew Addington, b. 1914, s. 1976, w.	Hon. Jeremy F. A., b. 1947.
1940	Simon (2nd), John Gilbert Simon, CMG, b. 1902, s. 1954, m.	Hon. Jan D. S., b. 1940.
1960	Slim (2nd), John Douglas Slim, OBE, b. 1927, s. 1970, m.	Hon. Mark W. R. S., b. 1960.
1954	Soulbury (2nd), James Herwald Ramsbotham, b. 1915, s. 1971, w.	Hon. Sir Peter E. R., GCMG, GCVO, b. 1919.
1776 I.	Southwell (7th), Pyers Anthony Joseph Southwell, b. 1930, s. 1960, m.	Hon. Richard A. P. S., b. 1956.
1942	Stansgate. Disclaimed for life 1963. (Rt. Hon. Anthony Neil Wedgwood Benn, MP, b. 1925, s. 1960, m.)	Stephen M. W. B., b. 1951.

Created	Title, order of succession, name, etc.	Eldest son or heir
1959	*Stuart of Findhorn* (2nd), David Randolph Moray Stuart, *b.* 1924, *s.* 1971, *m.*	Hon. J. Dominic S., *b.* 1948.
1957	*Tenby* (3rd), William Lloyd George, *b.* 1927, *s.* 1983, *m.*	Hon. Timothy H. G. L. G., *b.* 1962.
1952	*Thurso* (2nd), Robin Macdonald Sinclair, *b.* 1922, *s.* 1970, *m.*	Hon. John A. S., *b.* 1953.
1983	*Tonypandy* (1st), (Thomas) George Thomas, PC, *b.* 1909.	None.
1721	*Torrington* (11th), Timothy Howard St George Byng, *b.* 1943, *s.* 1961, *m.*	John L. B., MC, *b.* 1919.
1936	*Trenchard* (3rd), Hugh Trenchard, *b.* 1951, *s.* 1987, *m.*	Hon. Alexander T. T., *b.* 1978.
1921	*Ullswater* (2nd), Nicholas James Christopher Lowther, *b.* 1942, *s.* 1949, *m.*	Hon. Benjamin J. L., *b.* 1975.
1621 I.	*Valentia* (15th), Richard John Dighton Annesley, *b.* 1929, *s.* 1983, *m.*	Hon. Francis W. D. A., *b.* 1959.
1964	*Watkinson* (1st), Harold Arthur Watkinson, CH, PC, *b.* 1910, *m.*	None.
1952	*Waverley* (3rd), John Desmond Forbes Anderson, *b.* 1949, *s.* 1990.	None.
1938	*Weir* (3rd), William Kenneth James Weir, *b.* 1933, *s.* 1975, *m.*	Hon. James W. H. W., *b.* 1965.
1983	*Whitelaw* (1st), William Stephen Ian Whitelaw, KT, CH, MC, PC, *b.* 1918, *m.*	None.
1918	*Wimborne* (3rd), Ivor Fox-Strangways Guest (4th *UK Baron, Wimborne,* 1880), *b.* 1939, *s.* 1967, *m.*	Hon. Ivor M.V.G., *b.* 1968.
1923	*Younger of Leckie* (3rd), Edward George Younger, OBE, TD, *b.* 1906, *s.* 1946, *w.*	Baron Younger of Prestwick, KCVO, TD, PC, *b.* 1931 (*see* page 166).

BARONS/LORDS

Coronet, Six silver balls
Style, The Right Hon. the Lord __. In the Peerage of Scotland there is no rank of Baron; the equivalent rank is Lord of Parliament (*see* page 141) and Scottish peers should always be styled 'Lord', never 'Baron'
Wife's style, The Right Hon. the Lady __
Children's style, 'The Hon.' before forename and family name
In Scotland, the heir apparent to a Lord may be styled 'The Master of __ (title of peer)'
For forms of address, *see* page 220

Created	Title, order of succession, name, etc.	Eldest son or heir
1911	*Aberconway* (3rd), Charles Melville McLaren, *b.* 1913, *s.* 1953, *m.*	Hon. H. Charles M., *b.* 1948.
1873	*Aberdare* (4th), Morys George Lyndhurst Bruce, KBE, PC, *b.* 1919, *s.* 1957, *m.*	Hon. Alastair J. L. B., *b.* 1947.
1835	*Abinger* (8th), James Richard Scarlett, *b.* 1914, *s.* 1943, *m.*	Hon. James H. S., *b.* 1959.
1869	*Acton* (4th), Richard Gerald Lyon-Dalberg-Acton, *b.* 1941, *s.* 1989, *m.*	Hon. John C. F. H. L.-D.-A., *b.* 1966.
1887	*Addington* (6th), Dominic Bryce Hubbard, *b.* 1963, *s.* 1982.	Hon. Michael W. L. H., *b.* 1965.
1955	*Adrian* (2nd), Richard Hume Adrian, FRS, *b.* 1927, *s.* 1977, *m.*	None.
1907	*Airedale* (4th), Oliver James Vandeleur Kitson, *b.* 1915, *s.* 1958.	None.
1896	*Aldenham* (6th), and *Hunsdon of Hunsdon* (4th) (1923), Vicary Tyser Gibbs, *b.* 1948, *s.* 1986, *m.*	Hon. Humphrey W. F. G., *b.* 1989.
1962	*Aldington* (1st), Toby Austin Richard William Low, KCMG, CBE, DSO, TD, PC, *b.* 1914, *m.*	Hon Charles H. S. L., *b.* 1948.
1945	*Altrincham*. Disclaimed for life 1963. (*John Edward Poynder Grigg, b.* 1924, *s.* 1955, *m.*)	†
1929	*Alvingham* (2nd), Maj.-Gen. Robert Guy Eardley Yerburgh, CBE, *b.* 1926, *s.* 1955, *m.*	Capt. Hon. Robert R. G. Y., *b.* 1956.
1892	*Amherst of Hackney* (4th), William Hugh Amherst Cecil, *b.* 1940, *s.* 1980, *m.*	Hon. H. William A. C., *b.* 1968.
1881	*Ampthill* (4th), Geoffrey Denis Erskine Russell, CBE, *b.* 1921, *s.* 1973.	Hon. David W. E. R., *b.* 1947.
1947	*Amwell* (3rd), Keith Norman Montague, *b.* 1943, *s.* 1990, *m.*	Hon. Ian K. M., *b.* 1973.
1863	*Annaly* (6th), Luke Richard White, *b.* 1954, *s.* 1990, *m.*	Hon. Luke H. W., *b.* 1990.
1949	*Archibald*. Disclaimed for life 1975. (*George Christopher Archibald, b.* 1926, *s.* 1975, *m.*)	None.
1885	*Ashbourne* (4th), Edward Barry Greynville Gibson, *b.* 1933, *s.* 1983, *m.*	Hon. Edward C. d'O. G., *b.* 1967.
1835	*Ashburton* (7th), John Francis Harcourt Baring, KCVO, *b.* 1928, *s.* 1991, *m.*	Hon. Mark F. R. B., *b.* 1958.
1892	*Ashcombe* (4th), Henry Edward Cubitt, *b.* 1924, *s.* 1962, *m.*	Mark E. C., *b.* 1964.
1911	*Ashton of Hyde* (3rd), Thomas John Ashton, TD, *b.* 1926, *s.* 1983, *m.*	Hon. Thomas H. A., *b.* 1958.
1800 I.	*Ashtown* (7th), Nigel Clive Crosby Trench, KCMG, *b.* 1916, *s.* 1990, *m.*	Hon. Roderick N. G. T., *b.* 1944.
1956	*Astor of Hever* (3rd), John Jacob Astor, *b.* 1946, *s.* 1984, *m.*	Hon. Charles G. J. A., *b.* 1990.
1789 I.*	*Auckland* (9th), Ian George Eden (9th *Brit. Baron, Auckland,* 1793), *b.* 1926, *s.* 1957, *m.*	Hon. Robert I. B. E., *b.* 1962.

Created	Title, order of succession, name, etc.	Eldest son or heir
1313	*Audley* (25th), Richard Michael Thomas Souter, *b.* 1914, *s.* 1973, *m.*	Three co-heiresses.
1900	*Avebury* (4th), Eric Reginald Lubbock, *b.* 1928, *s.* 1971, *m.*	Hon. Lyulph A. J. *L.*, *b.* 1954.
1718 I.	*Aylmer* (13th), Michael Anthony Aylmer, *b.* 1923, *s.* 1982, *m.*	Hon. A. Julian *A.*, *b.* 1951.
1929	*Baden-Powell* (3rd), Robert Crause Baden-Powell, *b.* 1936, *s.* 1962, *m.*	Hon. David M. *B.-P.,* *b.* 1940.
1780	*Bagot* (9th), Heneage Charles Bagot, *b.* 1914, *s.* 1979, *m.*	Hon. C. H. Shaun *B.*, *b.* 1944.
1953	*Baillieu* (3rd), James William Latham Baillieu, *b.* 1950, *s.* 1973, *m.*	Hon. Robert L. *B.*, *b.* 1979.
1607 S.	*Balfour of Burleigh* (8th), Robert Bruce, *b.* 1927, *s.* 1967, *m.*	Hon. Victoria B., *b.* 1973.
1945	*Balfour of Inchrye* (2nd), Ian Balfour, *b.* 1924, *s.* 1988, *m.*	None.
1924	*Banbury of Southam* (3rd), Charles William Banbury, *b.* 1953, *s.* 1981.	None.
1698	*Barnard* (11th), Harry John Neville Vane, TD, *b.* 1923, *s.* 1964, *m.*	Hon. Henry F. C. *V.*, *b.* 1959.
1887	*Basing* (5th), Neil Lutley Sclater-Booth, *b.* 1939, *s.* 1983, *m.*	Hon. Stuart W. *S.-B.*, *b.* 1969.
1917	*Beaverbrook* (3rd), Maxwell William Humphrey Aitken, *b.* 1951, *s.* 1985, *m.*	Hon. Maxwell F. *A,* *b.* 1977.
1647 S.	*Belhaven and Stenton* (13th), Robert Anthony Carmichael Hamilton, *b.* 1927, *s.* 1961, *m.*	Master of Belhaven, *b.* 1953.
1848 I.	*Bellew* (7th), James Bryan Bellew, *b.* 1920, *s.* 1981, *m.*	Hon. Bryan E. *B.*, *b.* 1943.
1856	*Belper* (4th), (Alexander) Ronald George Strutt, *b.* 1912, *s.* 1956.	Hon. Richard H. *S.*, *b.* 1941.
1938	*Belstead* (2nd), John Julian Ganzoni, PC, *b.* 1932, *s.* 1958.	None.
1421	*Berkeley* (18th), Anthony Fitzhardinge Gueterbock, OBE, *b.* 1939, *s.* 1992, *m.*	Hon. Thomas F. *G.*, *b.* 1969.
1922	*Bethell* (4th), Nicholas William Bethell, MEP, *b.* 1938, *s.* 1967, *m.*	Hon. James N. *B.*, *b.* 1967.
1938	*Bicester* (3rd), Angus Edward Vivian Smith, *b.* 1932, *s.* 1968.	Hugh C. V. *S.*, *b.* 1934.
1903	*Biddulph* (5th), (Anthony) Nicholas Colin Maitland Biddulph, *b.* 1959, *s.* 1988, *m.*	Hon. William I. R. *M.B.*, *b.* 1963.
1938	*Birdwood* (3rd), Mark William Ogilvie Birdwood, *b.* 1938, *s.* 1962, *m.*	None.
1958	*Birkett* (2nd), Michael Birkett, *b.* 1929, *s.* 1962, *m.*	Hon. Thomas *B.*, *b.* 1982.
1907	*Blyth* (4th), Anthony Audley Rupert Blyth, *b.* 1931, *s.* 1977, *m.*	Hon. Riley A. J. *B.*, *b.* 1955.
1797	*Bolton* (7th), Richard William Algar Orde-Powlett, *b.* 1929, *s.* 1963, *m.*	Hon. Harry A. N. *O.-P.,* *b.* 1954.
1452 S.	*Borthwick* (23rd), John Henry Stuart Borthwick, TD, *b.* 1905, *claim succeeded* 1986, *w.*	Master of Borthwick, *b.* 1940.
1922	*Borwick* (4th), James Hugh Myles Borwick, MC, *b.* 1917, *s.* 1961, *m.*	Hon. George S. *B.*, *b.* 1922.
1761	*Boston* (10th), Timothy George Frank Boteler Irby, *b.* 1939, *s.* 1978, *m.*	Hon. George W. E. B. *I.*, *b.* 1971.
1942	*Brabazon of Tara* (3rd), Ivon Anthony Moore-Brabazon, *b.* 1946, *s.* 1974, *m.*	Hon. Benjamin R. *M.-B.*, *b.* 1983.
1880	*Brabourne* (7th), John Ulick Knatchbull, CBE, *b.* 1924, *s.* 1943, *m.*	Lord Romsey, *b.* 1947 (*see* page 149).
1925	*Bradbury* (2nd), John Bradbury, *b.* 1914, *s.* 1950, *m.*	Hon. John *B.*, *b.* 1940.
1962	*Brain* (2nd), Christopher Langdon Brain, *b.* 1926, *s.* 1966, *m.*	Hon. Michael C. *B.*, DM, *b.* 1928.
1938	*Brassey of Apethorpe* (3rd), David Henry Brassey, *b.* 1932, *s.* 1967, *m.*	Hon. Edward *B.*, *b.* 1964.
1788	*Braybrooke* (10th), Robin Henry Charles Neville, *b.* 1932, *s.* 1990, *m.*	George *N.*, *b.* 1943.
1957	*Bridges* (2nd), Thomas Edward Bridges, GCMG, *b.* 1927, *s.* 1969, *m.*	Hon. Mark T. *B.*, *b.* 1954.
1945	*Broadbridge* (3rd), Peter Hewett Broadbridge, *b.* 1938, *s.* 1972, *m.*	Martin H. *B.*, *b.* 1929.
1933	*Brocket* (3rd), Charles Ronald George Nall-Cain, *b.* 1952, *s.* 1967, *m.*	Hon. Alexander C. C. *N.-C.*, *b.* 1984.
1860	*Brougham and Vaux* (5th), Michael John Brougham, *b.* 1938, *s.* 1967.	Hon. Charles W. *B.*, *b.* 1971.
1945	*Broughshane* (2nd), Patrick Owen Alexander Davison, *b.* 1903, *s.* 1953, *m.*	Hon. W. Kensington *D.*, DSO, DFC, *b.* 1914.
1776	*Brownlow* (7th), Edward John Peregrine Cust, *b.* 1936, *s.* 1978, *m.*	Hon. Peregrine E. Q. *C.*, *b.* 1974.
1942	*Bruntisfield* (2nd), John Robert Warrender, OBE, MC, TD, *b.* 1921, *s.* 1993, *m.*	Hon. Michael J. V. *W.*, *b.* 1949.
1950	*Burden* (2nd), Philip William Burden, *b.* 1916, *s.* 1970, *m.*	Hon. Andrew P. *B.*, *b.* 1959.
1529	*Burgh* (7th), Alexander Peter Willoughby Leith, *b.* 1935, *s.* 1959, *m.*	Hon. A. Gregory D. *L.*, *b.* 1958.
1903	*Burnham* (6th), Hugh John Frederick Lawson, *b.* 1931, *s.* 1993, *m.*	Hon. Harry F. A. *L.*, *b.* 1968.
1897	*Burton* (3rd), Michael Evan Victor Baillie, *b.* 1924, *s.* 1962, *m.*	Hon. Evan M. R. *B.*, *b.* 1949.
1643	*Byron* (13th), Robert James Byron, *b.* 1950, *s.* 1989, *m.*	Hon. Charles R. G. *B.*, *b.* 1990.
1937	*Cadman* (3rd), John Anthony Cadman, *b.* 1938, *s.* 1966, *m.*	Hon. Nicholas A. J. *C.*, *b.* 1977.
1796	*Calthorpe* (10th), Peter Waldo Somerset Gough-Calthorpe, *b.* 1927, *s.* 1945, *m.*	None.
1945	*Calverley* (3rd), Charles Rodney Muff, *b.* 1946, *s.* 1971, *m.*	Hon. Jonathan E. *M.*, *b.* 1975.
1383	*Camoys* (7th), (Ralph) Thomas Campion George Sherman Stonor, *b.* 1940, *s.* 1976, *m.*	Hon. R. William R. T. *S.*, *b.* 1974.
1715 I.	*Carbery* (11th), Peter Ralfe Harrington Evans-Freke, *b.* 1920, *s.* 1970, *m.*	Hon. Michael P. *E.-F.*, *b.* 1942.
1834 I.*	*Carew* (6th), William Francis Conolly-Carew, CBE (6th *UK. Baron, Carew,* 1838), *b.* 1905, *s.* 1927, *w.*	Hon. Patrick T. *C.-C.*, *b.* 1938.
1916	*Carnock* (4th), David Henry Arthur Nicolson, *b.* 1920, *s.* 1982.	Nigel *N.*, MBE, *b.* 1917.
1796 I.*	*Carrington* (6th), Peter Alexander Rupert Carington, KG, GCMG, CH, MC, PC (6th *Brit. Baron, Carrington,* 1797), *b.* 1919, *s.* 1938, *m.*	Hon. Rupert F. J. *C.*, *b.* 1948.
1812 I.	*Castlemaine* (8th), Roland Thomas John Handcock, MBE, *b.* 1943, *s.* 1973, *m.*	Hon. Ronan M. E. *H*., *b.* 1989.

Created	Title, order of succession, name, etc.	Eldest son or heir
1936	*Catto* (2nd), Stephen Gordon Catto, *b.* 1923, *s.* 1959, *m.*	Hon. Innes G. *C.*, *b.* 1950.
1918	*Cawley* (3rd), Frederick Lee Cawley, *b.* 1913, *s.* 1954, *m.*	Hon. John F. *C.*, *b.* 1946.
1603	*Cecil*, a subsidiary title of the Marquess of Salisbury. His heir Viscount Cranborne was given a Writ in Acceleration in this title to enable him to sit in the House of Lords whilst his father is still alive (*see also* page 144)	
1937	*Chatfield* (2nd), Ernle David Lewis Chatfield, *b.* 1917, *s.* 1967, *m.*	None.
1858	*Chesham* (6th), Nicholas Charles Cavendish, *b.* 1941, *s.* 1989, *m.*	Hon. Charles G. C. *C.*, *b.* 1974.
1945	*Chetwode* (2nd), Philip Chetwode, *b.* 1937, *s.* 1950, *m.*	Hon. Roger *C.*, *b.* 1968.
1945	*Chorley* (2nd), Roger Richard Edward Chorley, *b.* 1930, *s.* 1978, *m.*	Hon. Nicholas R. D. *C.*, *b.* 1966.
1858	*Churston* (5th), John Francis Yarde-Buller, *b.* 1934, *s.* 1991, *m.*	Hon. Benjamin F. A. *Y.-B.*, *b.* 1974.
1946	*Citrine* (2nd), Norman Arthur Citrine, *b.* 1914, *s.* 1983, *m.*	Hon. Ronald E. *C.*, *b.* 1919.
1800 I.	*Clanmorris* (8th), Simon John Ward Bingham, *b.* 1937, *s.* 1988, *m.*	Robert D. de B. *B.*, *b.* 1942.
1672	*Clifford of Chudleigh* (14th), Thomas Hugh Clifford, *b.* 1948, *s.* 1988, *m.*	Hon. Alexander T. H. *C.*, *b.* 1985.
1299	*Clinton* (22nd), Gerard Nevile Mark Fane Trefusis, *b.* 1934, *title called out of abeyance* 1965, *m.*	Hon. Charles P. R. F. *T.*, *b.* 1962.
1955	*Clitheroe* (2nd), Ralph John Assheton, *b.* 1929, *s.* 1984, *m.*	Hon. Ralph C. *A.*, *b.* 1962.
1919	*Clwyd* (3rd), (John) Anthony Roberts, *b.* 1935, *s.* 1987, *m.*	Hon. J. Murray *R.*, *b.* 1971.
1948	*Clydesmuir* (2nd), Ronald John Bilsland Colville, KT, CB, MBE, TD, *b.* 1917, *s.* 1954, *m.*	Hon. David R. *C.*, *b.* 1949.
1960	*Cobbold* (2nd), David Antony Fromanteel Lytton Cobbold, *b.* 1937, *s.* 1987, *m.*	Hon. Henry F. L. *C.*, *b.* 1962.
1919	*Cochrane of Cults* (4th), (Ralph Henry) Vere Cochrane, *b.* 1926, *s.* 1990, *m.*	Hon. Thomas H. V. *C.*, *b.* 1957.
1954	*Coleraine* (2nd), (James) Martin (Bonar) Law, *b.* 1931, *s.* 1980, *m.*	Hon. James P. B. *L.*, *b.* 1975.
1873	*Coleridge* (5th), William Duke Coleridge, *b.* 1937, *s.* 1984, *m.*	Hon. James D. *C.*, *b.* 1967.
1946	*Colgrain* (3rd), David Colin Campbell, *b.* 1920, *s.* 1973, *m.*	Hon. Alastair C. L. *C.*, *b.* 1951.
1917	*Colwyn* (3rd), (Ian) Anthony Hamilton-Smith, CBE, *b.* 1942, *s.* 1966, *m.*	Hon. Craig P. *H.-S.*, *b.* 1968.
1956	*Colyton* (1st), Henry Lennox d'Aubigné Hopkinson, CMG, PC, *b.* 1902, *m.*	Alisdair J. M. *H.*, *b.* 1958.
1841	*Congleton* (8th), Christopher Patrick Parnell, *b.* 1930, *s.* 1967, *m.*	Hon. John P. C. *P.*, *b.* 1959.
1927	*Cornwallis* (3rd), Fiennes Neil Wykeham Cornwallis, OBE, *b.* 1921, *s.* 1982, *m.*	Hon. F. W. Jeremy *C.*, *b.* 1946.
1874	*Cottesloe* (4th), John Walgrave Halford Fremantle, GBE, TD, *b.* 1900, *s.* 1956, *m.*	Cdr. Hon. John T. *F.*, *b.* 1927.
1929	*Craigmyle* (3rd), Thomas Donald Mackay Shaw, *b.* 1923, *s.* 1944, *m.*	Hon. Thomas C. *S.*, *b.* 1960.
1899	*Cranworth* (3rd), Philip Bertram Gurdon, *b.* 1940, *s.* 1964, *m.*	Hon. Sacha W. R. *G.*, *b.* 1970.
1959	*Crathorne* (2nd), Charles James Dugdale, *b.* 1939, *s.* 1977, *m.*	Hon. Thomas A. J. *D.*, *b.* 1977.
1892	*Crawshaw* (4th), William Michael Clifton Brooks, *b.* 1933, *s.* 1946.	Hon. David G. *B.*, *b.* 1934.
1940	*Croft* (2nd), Michael Henry Glendower Page Croft, *b.* 1916, *s.* 1947, *w.*	Hon. Bernard W. H. P. *C.*, *b.* 1949.
1797 I.	*Crofton* (7th), Guy Patrick Gilbert Crofton, *b.* 1951, *s.* 1989, *m.*	Hon. E. Harry P. *C.*, *b.* 1988.
1375	*Cromwell* (7th), Godfrey John Bewicke-Copley, *b.* 1960, *s.* 1982, *m.*	Hon. Thomas D. *B.-C.*, *b.* 1964.
1947	*Crook* (2nd), Douglas Edwin Crook, *b.* 1926, *s* 1989, *m.*	Hon. Robert D. E. *C.*, *b.* 1955.
1920	*Cullen of Ashbourne* (2nd), Charles Borlase Marsham Cokayne, MBE, *b.* 1912, *s.* 1932, *m.*	Hon. Edmund W. M. *C.*, *b.* 1916.
1914	*Cunliffe* (3rd), Roger Cunliffe, *b.* 1932, *s.* 1963, *m.*	Hon. Henry *C.*, *b.* 1962.
1927	*Daresbury* (3rd), Edward Gilbert Greenall, *b.* 1928, *s.* 1990, *m.*	Hon. Peter G. *G.*, *b.* 1953.
1924	*Darling* (2nd), Robert Charles Henry Darling, *b.* 1919, *s.* 1936, *m.*	Hon. R. Julian H. *D.*, *b.* 1944.
1946	*Darwen* (3rd), Roger Michael Davies, *b.* 1938, *s.* 1988, *m.*	Hon. Paul *D.*, *b.* 1962.
1923	*Daryngton* (2nd), Jocelyn Arthur Pike Pease, *b.* 1908, *s.* 1949.	None.
1932	*Davies* (3rd), David Davies, *b.* 1940, *s.* 1944, *m.*	Hon. David D. *D.*, *b.* 1975.
1812 I.	*Decies* (7th), Marcus Hugh Tristram de la Poer Beresford, *b.* 1948, *s.* 1992, *m.*	Hon. Robert M. D. *de la P. B.*, *b.* 1988.
1299	*de Clifford* (27th), John Edward Southwell Russell, *b.* 1928, *s.* 1982, *m.*	Hon. William S. *R.*, *b.* 1930.
1851	*De Freyne* (7th), Francis Arthur John French, *b.* 1927, *s.* 1935, *m.*	Hon. Fulke C. A. J. *F.*, *b.* 1957.
1821	*Delamere* (5th), Hugh George Cholmondeley, *b.* 1934, *s.* 1979, *m.*	Hon. Thomas P. G. *C.*, *b.* 1968.
1838	*de Mauley* (6th), Gerald John Ponsonby, *b.* 1921, *s.* 1962, *m.*	Col. Hon. Thomas M. *P.*, TD, *b.* 1930.
1937	*Denham* (2nd), Bertram Stanley Mitford Bowyer, KBE, PC, *b.* 1927, *s.* 1948, *m.*	Hon. Richard G. G. *B.*, *b.* 1959.
1834	*Denman* (5th), Charles Spencer Denman, CBE, MC, TD, *b.* 1916, *s.* 1971, *w.*	Hon. Richard T. S. *D.*, *b.* 1946.
1885	*Deramore* (6th), Richard Arthur de Yarburgh-Bateson, *b.* 1911, *s.* 1964, *m.*	None.
1887	*De Ramsey* (4th), John Ailwyn Fellowes, *b.* 1942, *s.* 1993, *m.*	Hon. Freddie J. *F.*, *b.* 1978.
1264	*de Ros* (28th), Peter Trevor Maxwell, *b.* 1958, *s.* 1983, *m.* (*Premier Baron of England*).	Hon. Finbar J. *M.,*, *b.* 1988.
1881	*Derwent* (5th), Robin Evelyn Leo Vanden-Bempde-Johnstone, LVO, *b.* 1930, *s.* 1986, *m.*	Hon. Francis P. H. *V.-B.-J.*, *b.* 1965.
1831	*de Saumarez* (7th), Eric Douglas Saumarez, *b.* 1956, *s.* 1991, *m.*	Hon. Victor T. *S.*, *b.* 1956.
1910	*de Villiers* (3rd), Arthur Percy de Villiers, *b.* 1911, *s.* 1934.	Hon. Alexander C. *de V.*, *b.* 1940.

Created	Title, order of succession, name, etc.	Eldest son or heir
1930	Dickinson (2nd), Richard Clavering Hyett Dickinson, b. 1926, s. 1943, m.	Hon. Martin H. D., b. 1961.
1620 I. ⎫ 1765* ⎭	Digby (12th), Edward Henry Kenelm Digby (6th Brit. Baron, Digby), b. 1924, s. 1964, m.	Hon. Henry N. K. D., b. 1954.
1615	Dormer (16th), Joseph Spencer Philip Dormer, b. 1914, s. 1975.	Geoffrey H. D., b. 1920.
1943	Dowding (3rd), Piers Hugh Tremenheere Dowding, b. 1948, s. 1992.	Hon. Mark D. J. D., b. 1949.
1800 I.	Dufferin and Clandeboye. Heir had not established claim at time of going to press.	Sir John Blackwood, Bt., b. 1944.
1929	Dulverton (3rd), (Gilbert) Michael Hamilton Wills, b. 1944, s. 1992, m.	Hon. Robert A. H. W., b. 1983.
1800 I.	Dunalley (7th), Henry Francis Cornelius Prittie, b. 1948, s. 1992, m.	Hon. Joel H. P., b. 1981.
1324 I.	Dunboyne (28th), Patrick Theobald Tower Butler, VRD, b. 1917, s. 1945, m.	Hon. John F. B., b. 1951.
1802	Dunleath (5th), Michael Henry Mulholland, b. 1915, s. 1993, w.	Hon. Brian H. M., b. 1950.
1439 I.	Dunsany (19th), Randal Arthur Henry Plunkett (20th Irish Baron Killeen, 1449), b. 1906, s. 1957, m.	Hon. Edward J. C. P., b. 1939.
1780	Dynevor (9th), Richard Charles Uryan Rhys, b. 1935, s. 1962.	Hon. Hugo G. U. R., b. 1966.
1857	Ebury (6th), Francis Egerton Grosvenor, b. 1934, s. 1957, m.	Hon. Julian F. M. G., b. 1959.
1963	Egremont (2nd), & Leconfield (7th) (1859), John Max Henry Scawen Wyndham, b. 1948, s. 1972, m.	Hon. George R. V. W., b. 1983.
1643	Elibank (14th), Alan D'Ardis Erskine-Murray, b. 1923, s. 1973, m.	Master of Elibank, b. 1964.
1802	Ellenborough (8th), Richard Edward Cecil Law, b. 1926, s. 1945, w.	Maj. Hon. Rupert E. H. L., b. 1955.
1509 S.*	Elphinstone (18th), James Alexander Elphinstone (4th UK Baron Elphinstone, 1885), b. 1953, s. 1975, m.	Master of Elphinstone, b. 1980.
1934	Elton (2nd), Rodney Elton, TD, b. 1930, s. 1973, m.	Hon. Edward P. E., b. 1966.
1964	Erroll of Hale (1st), Frederick James Erroll, TD, PC, b. 1914, m.	None.
1964	Erskine of Rerrick (2nd), Iain Maxwell Erskine, b. 1926, s. 1980.	None.
1627 S.	Fairfax of Cameron (14th), Nicholas John Albert Fairfax, b. 1956, s. 1964, m.	Hon. Edward N. T. F., b. 1984.
1961	Fairhaven (3rd), Ailwyn Henry George Broughton, b. 1936, s. 1973, m.	Hon. James H. A. B., b. 1963.
1916	Faringdon (3rd), Charles Michael Henderson, b. 1937, s. 1977, m.	Hon. James H. H., b. 1961.
1756 I.	Farnham (12th), Barry Owen Somerset Maxwell, b. 1931, s. 1957, m.	Hon. Simon K. M., b. 1933.
1856 I.	Fermoy (6th), Patrick Maurice Burke Roche, b. 1967, s. 1984.	Hon. E. Hugh B. R., b. 1972.
1826	Feversham (6th), Charles Antony Peter Duncombe, b. 1945, s. 1963, m.	Hon. Jasper O. S. D., b. 1968.
1798 I.	ffrench (8th), Robuck John Peter Charles Mario ffrench, b. 1956, s. 1986, m.	Hon. John C. M. J. F. ff., b. 1928.
1909	Fisher (3rd), John Vavasseur Fisher, DSC, b. 1921, s. 1955, m.	Hon. Patrick V. F., b. 1953.
1295	Fitzwalter (21st), (Fitzwalter) Brook Plumptre, b. 1914, title called out of abeyance, 1953, m.	Hon. Julian B. P., b. 1952.
1776	Foley (8th), Adrian Gerald Foley, b. 1923, s. 1927, m.	Hon. Thomas H. F., b. 1961.
1445 S.	Forbes (22nd), Nigel Ivan Forbes, KBE (Premier Baron of Scotland), b. 1918, s. 1953, m.	Master of Forbes, b. 1946.
1821	Forester (8th), (George Cecil) Brooke Weld-Forester, b. 1938, s. 1977, m.	Hon. C. R. George W.-F., b. 1975.
1922	Forres (4th), Alastair Stephen Grant Williamson, b. 1946, s. 1978, m.	Hon. George A. M. W., b. 1972.
1917	Forteviot (4th), John James Evelyn Dewar, b. 1938, s. 1993, m.	Hon. Alexander J. E. D., b. 1971.
1951	Freyberg (3rd), Valerian Bernard Freyberg, b. 1970, s. 1993.	None.
1917	Gainford (3rd), Joseph Edward Pease, b. 1921, s. 1971, m.	Hon. George P., b. 1926.
1818 I.	Garvagh (5th), (Alexander Leopold Ivor) George Canning, b. 1920, s. 1956, m.	Hon. Spencer G. S. de R. C., b. 1953.
1942	Geddes (3rd), Euan Michael Ross Geddes, b. 1937, s. 1975, m.	Hon. James G. N. G., b. 1969.
1876	Gerard (5th), Anthony Robert Hugo Gerard, b. 1949, s. 1992, m.	Hon. Rupert B. C. G., b. 1981.
1824	Gifford (6th), Anthony Maurice Gifford, QC, b. 1940, s. 1961, m.	Hon. Thomas A. G., b. 1967.
1917	Gisborough (3rd), Thomas Richard John Long Chaloner, b. 1927, s. 1951, m.	Hon. T. Peregrine L. C., b. 1961.
1960	Gladwyn (1st), (Hubert Miles) Gladwyn Jebb, GCMG, GCVO, CB, b. 1900, w.	Hon. Miles A. G. J., b. 1930.
1899	Glanusk (4th), David Russell Bailey, b. 1917, s. 1948, m.	Hon. Christopher R. B., b. 1942.
1918	Glenarthur (4th), Simon Mark Arthur, b. 1944, s. 1976, m.	Hon. Edward A. A., b. 1973.
1911	Glenconner (3rd), Colin Christopher Paget Tennant, b. 1926, s. 1983, m.	Hon. Charles E. P. T., b. 1957.
1964	Glendevon (1st), John Adrian Hope, PC, b. 1912, m.	Hon. Julian J. S. H., b. 1950.
1922	Glendyne (3rd), Robert Nivison, b. 1926, s. 1967, m.	Hon. John N., b. 1960.
1939	Glentoran (2nd), Daniel Stewart Thomas Bingham Dixon, KBE, PC (NI), b. 1912, s. 1950, w.	Hon. Thomas R. V. D., CBE, b. 1935.
1909	Gorell (4th), Timothy John Radcliffe Barnes, b. 1927, s. 1963, m.	Hon. Ronald A. H. B., b. 1931.
1953	Grantchester (2nd), Kenneth Bent Suenson-Taylor, CBE, QC, b. 1921, s. 1976, m.	Hon. Christopher J. S-. T., b. 1951.
1782	Grantley (7th), John Richard Brinsley Norton, MC, b. 1923, s. 1954, m.	Hon. Richard W. B. N., b. 1956.
1794 I.	Graves (8th), Peter George Wellesley Graves, b. 1911, s. 1963, w.	Evelyn P. G., b. 1926.
1445 S.	Gray (22nd), Angus Diarmid Ian Campbell-Gray, b. 1931, s. 1946, w.	Master of Gray, b. 1964.

Created	Title, order of succession, name, etc.	Eldest son or heir
1950	*Greenhill* (3rd), Malcolm Greenhill, *b.* 1924, *s.* 1989.	None.
1927	*Greenway* (4th), Ambrose Charles Drexel Greenway, *b.* 1941, *s.* 1975, *m.*	Hon. Mervyn S. K. *G.*, *b.* 1942.
1902	*Grenfell* (3rd), Julian Pascoe Francis St Leger Grenfell, *b.* 1935, *s.* 1976, *m.*	Francis P. J. *G.*, *b.* 1938.
1944	*Gretton* (4th), John Lysander Gretton, *b.* 1975, *s.* 1989, *M.*	None.
1397	*Grey of Codnor* (5th), Charles Legh Shuldham Cornwall-Legh, CBE, AE, *b.* 1903, *title called out of abeyance* 1989, *m.*	Hon. Richard H. *C.-L.*, *b.* 1936.
1955	*Gridley* (2nd), Arnold Hudson Gridley, *b.* 1906, *s.* 1965, *m.*	Hon. Richard D. A. *G.*, *b.* 1956.
1964	*Grimston of Westbury* (2nd), Robert Walter Sigismund Grimston, *b.* 1925, *s.* 1979, *m.*	Hon. Robert J. S. *G.*, *b.* 1951.
1886	*Grimthorpe* (4th), Christopher John Beckett, OBE, *b.* 1915, *s.* 1963, *m.*	Hon. Edward J. *B.*, *b.* 1954.
1945	*Hacking* (3rd), Douglas David Hacking, *b.* 1938, *s.* 1971, *m.*	Hon. Douglas F. *H.*, *b.* 1968.
1950	*Haden-Guest* (4th), Peter Haden Haden-Guest, *b.* 1913, *s.* 1987, *m.*	Hon. Christopher *H.-G.*, *b.* 1948.
1886	*Hamilton of Dalzell* (4th), James Leslie Hamilton, *b.* 1938, *s.* 1990, *m.*	Hon. Gavin G. *H.*, *b.* 1968.
1874	*Hampton* (6th), Richard Humphrey Russell Pakington, *b.* 1925, *s.* 1974, *m.*	Hon. John H. A. *P.*, *b.* 1964.
1939	*Hankey* (2nd), Robert Maurice Alers Hankey, KCMG, KCVO, *b.* 1905, *s.* 1963, *m.*	Hon. Donald R. A. *H.*, *b.* 1938.
1958	*Harding of Petherton* (2nd), John Charles Harding, *b.* 1928, *s.* 1989, *m.*	Hon. William A. J. *H.*, *b.* 1969.
1910	*Hardinge of Penshurst* (3rd), George Edward Charles Hardinge, *b.* 1921, *s.* 1960, *m.*	Hon. Julian A. *H.*, *b.* 1945.
1876	*Harlech* (6th), Francis David Ormsby-Gore, *b.* 1954, *s.* 1985, *m.*	Hon. Jasset D. C. *O.-G.*, *b.* 1986.
1939	*Harmsworth* (3rd), Thomas Harold Raymond Harmsworth, *b.* 1939, *s.* 1990, *m.*	Hon. Dominic M. E. *H.*, *b.* 1973.
1815	*Harris* (6th), George Robert John Harris, *b.* 1920, *s.* 1984.	Derek M. *H.*, *b.* 1916.
1954	*Harvey of Tasburgh* (2nd), Peter Charles Oliver Harvey, *b.* 1921, *s.* 1968, *m.*	Charles J. G. *H.*, *b.* 1951.
1295	*Hastings* (22nd), Edward Delaval Henry Astley, *b.* 1912, *s.* 1956, *m.*	Hon. Delaval T. H. *A.*, *b.* 1960.
1835	*Hatherton* (8th), Edward Charles Littleton, *b.* 1950, *s.* 1985, *m.*	Hon. Thomas E. *L.*, *b.* 1977.
1776	*Hawke* (11th), Edward George Hawke, *b.* 1950, *s.* 1992.	None.
1927	*Hayter* (3rd), George Charles Hayter Chubb, KCVO, CBE, *b.* 1911, *s.* 1967, *m.*	Hon. G. William M. *C.*, *b.* 1943.
1945	*Hazlerigg* (2nd), Arthur Grey Hazlerigg, MC, TD, *b.* 1910, *s.* 1949, *w.*	Hon. Arthur G. *H.*, *b.* 1951.
1797 I.	*Headley* (7th), Charles Rowland Allanson-Winn, *b.* 1902, *s.* 1969, *w.*	Hon. Owain G. *A.-W.*, *b.* 1906.
1943	*Hemingford* (3rd), (Dennis) Nicholas Herbert, *b.* 1934, *s.* 1982, *m.*	Hon. Christopher D. C. *H.*, *b.* 1973.
1906	*Hemphill* (5th), Peter Patrick Fitzroy Martyn Martyn-Hemphill, *b.* 1928, *s.* 1957, *m.*	Hon. Charles A. M. *M.-H.*, *b.* 1954.
1799 I.*	*Henley* (8th), Oliver Michael Robert Eden (6th *UK Baron, Northington*, 1885), *b.* 1953, *s.* 1977, *m.*	Hon. John W. O. *E.*, *b.* 1988.
1800 I.*	*Henniker* (8th), John Patrick Edward Chandos Henniker-Major, KCMG, CVO, MC (4th *UK Baron, Hartismere*, 1866), *b.* 1916, *s.* 1980, *m.*	Hon. Mark I. P. C. *H.-M.*, *b.* 1947.
1886	*Herschell* (3rd), Rognvald Richard Farrer Herschell, *b.* 1923, *s.* 1929, *m.*	None.
1935	*Hesketh* (3rd), Thomas Alexander Fermor-Hesketh, PC, *b.* 1950, *s.* 1955, *m.*	Hon. Frederick H. *F.-H.*, *b.*1988.
1828	*Heytesbury* (6th), Francis William Holmes à Court, *b.* 1931, *s.* 1971, *m.*	Hon. James W. *H. à C.*, *b.* 1967.
1886	*Hindlip* (5th), Henry Richard Allsopp, *b.* 1912, *s.* 1966, *m.*	Hon. Charles H. *A.*, *b.* 1940.
1950	*Hives* (2nd), John Warwick Hives, CBE, *b.* 1913, *s.* 1965, *m.*	Matthew P. *H.*, *b.* 1971.
1912	*Hollenden* (3rd), Gordon Hope Hope-Morley, *b.* 1914, *s.* 1977, *m.*	Hon. Ian H. *H.-M.*, *b.* 1946.
1897	*HolmPatrick* (4th), Hans James David Hamilton, *b.* 1955, *s.* 1991, *m.*	Hon. Ion H. J. *H.*, *b.* 1956.
1933	*Horder* (2nd), Thomas Mervyn Horder, *b.* 1910, *s.* 1955.	None.
1797 I.	*Hotham* (8th), Henry Durand Hotham, *b.* 1940, *s.* 1967, *m.*	Hon. William B. *H.*, *b.* 1972.
1881	*Hothfield* (6th), Anthony Charles Sackville Tufton, *b.* 1939, *s.* 1991, *m.*	Hon. William S. *T.*, *b.* 1977.
1597	*Howard de Walden* (9th), John Osmael Scott-Ellis, TD (5th *UK Baron, Seaford*, 1826), *b.* 1912, *s.* 1946, *m.*	To Barony of Howard de Walden, four co-heiresses. To Barony of Seaford, Colin H. F. *Ellis*, *b.* 1946.
1930	*Howard of Penrith* (2nd), Francis Philip Howard, *b.* 1905, *s.* 1939, *m.*	Hon. Philip E. *H.*, *b.* 1945.
1960	*Howick of Glendale* (2nd), Charles Evelyn Baring, *b.* 1937, *s.* 1973, *m.*	Hon. David E. C. *B.*, *b.* 1975.
1796 I.	*Huntingfield* (6th), Gerard Charles Arcedeckne Vanneck, *b.* 1915, *s.* 1969, *m.*	Hon. Joshua C. *V.*, *b.* 1954.
1866	*Hylton* (5th), Raymond Hervey Jolliffe, *b.* 1932, *s.* 1967, *m.*	Hon. William H. M. *J.*, *b.* 1967.
1933	*Iliffe* (2nd), Edward Langton Iliffe, *b.* 1908, *s.* 1960, *m.*	Robert P. R. *I.*, *b.* 1944.
1543 I.	*Inchiquin* (18th), Conor Myles John O'Brien, *b.* 1943, *s.* 1982.	Murrough R. *O'B.*, *b.* 1910.
1962	*Inchyra* (2nd), Robert Charles Reneke Hoyer Millar, *b.* 1935, *s.* 1989, *m.*	Hon. C. James C. H. *M.*, *b.* 1962.
1964	*Inglewood* (2nd), (William) Richard Fletcher-Vane, MEP, *b.* 1951, *s.* 1989, *m.*	Hon. Henry W. F. *F.-V.*, *b.* 1990.
1919	*Inverforth* (4th), Andrew Peter Weir, *b.* 1966, *s.* 1982.	Hon. John V. *W.*, *b.* 1935.
1941	*Ironside* (2nd), Edmund Oslac Ironside, *b.* 1924, *s.* 1959, *m.*	Hon. Charles E. G. *I.*, *b.* 1956.

Created	Title, order of succession, name, etc.	Eldest son or heir
1952	*Jeffreys* (3rd), Christopher Henry Mark Jeffreys, *b.* 1957, *s.* 1986, *m.*	Hon. Arthur M. H. *J.*, *b.* 1989.
1906	*Joicey* (5th), James Michael Joicey, *b.* 1953, *s.* 1993, *m.*	Hon. William J. *J.*, *b.* 1990.
1937	*Kenilworth* (4th), (John) Randle Siddeley, *b.* 1954, *s.* 1981, *m.*	Hon. William R. J. *S.*, *b.* 1992.
1935	*Kennet* (2nd), Wayland Hilton Young, *b.* 1923, *s.* 1960, *m.*	Hon. W. A. Thoby *Y.*, *b.* 1957.
1776 I.*	*Kensington* (8th), Hugh Ivor Edwardes (5th *UK Baron, Kensington,* 1886), *b.* 1933, *s.* 1981, *m.*	Hon. W. Owen A. *E.*, *b.* 1964.
1951	*Kenswood* (2nd), John Michael Howard Whitfield, *b.* 1930, *s.* 1963, *m.*	Hon. Michael C. *W.*, *b.* 1955.
1788	*Kenyon* (6th), Lloyd Tyrell-Kenyon, *b.* 1947, *s.* 1993, *m.*	Hon. Lloyd N. *T.-K.*, *b.* 1972.
1947	*Kershaw* (4th), Edward John Kershaw, *b.* 1936, *s.* 1962, *m.*	Hon. John C. E. *K.*, *b.* 1971.
1943	*Keyes* (2nd), Roger George Bowlby Keyes, *b.* 1919, *s.* 1945, *m.*	Hon. Charles W. P. *K.*, *b.* 1951.
1909	*Kilbracken* (3rd), John Raymond Godley, DSC, *b.* 1920, *s.* 1950.	Hon. Christopher J. *G.*, *b.* 1945.
1900	*Killanin* (3rd), Michael Morris, MBE, TD, *b.* 1914, *s.* 1927, *m.*	Hon. G. Redmond F. *M.*, *b.* 1947.
1943	*Killearn* (2nd), Graham Curtis Lampson, *b.* 1919, *s.* 1964, *m.*	Hon. Victor M. G. A. *L.*, *b.* 1941.
1789 I.	*Kilmaine* (7th), John David Henry Browne, *b.* 1948, *s.* 1978, *m.*	Hon. John F. S. *B.*, *b.* 1983.
1831	*Kilmarnock* (7th), Alastair Ivor Gilbert Boyd, *b.* 1927, *s.* 1975, *m.*	Hon. Robin J. *B.*, *b.* 1941.
1941	*Kindersley* (3rd), Robert Hugh Molesworth Kindersley, *b.* 1929, *s.* 1976, *m.*	Hon. Rupert J. M. *K.*, *b.* 1955.
1223 I.	*Kingsale* (35th), John de Courcy (*Premier Baron of Ireland*), *b.* 1941, *s.* 1969.	Nevinson R. *de C.*, *b.* 1920.
1682 S.*	*Kinnaird* (13th), Graham Charles Kinnaird (5th *UK Baron, Kinnaird,* 1860), *b.* 1912, *s.* 1972, *m.*	None.
1902	*Kinross* (5th), Christopher Patrick Balfour, *b.* 1949, *s.* 1985, *m.*	Hon. Alan I. *B.*, *b.* 1978.
1951	*Kirkwood* (3rd), David Harvie Kirkwood, PH.D., *b.* 1931, *s.* 1970, *m.*	Hon. James S. *K.*, *b.* 1937.
1800 I.	*Langford* (9th), Geoffrey Alexander Rowley-Conwy, OBE, *b.* 1912, *s.* 1953, *m.*	Hon. Owain G. *R.-C.*, *b.* 1958.
1942	*Latham* (2nd), Dominic Charles Latham, *b.* 1954, *s.* 1970.	Anthony M. *L.*, *b.* 1954.
1431	*Latymer* (8th), Hugo Nevill Money-Coutts, *b.* 1926, *s.* 1987, *m.*	Hon. Crispin J. A. N. *M.-C.*, *b.* 1955.
1869	*Lawrence* (5th), David John Downer Lawrence, *b.* 1937, *s.* 1968.	None.
1947	*Layton* (3rd), Geoffrey Michael Layton, *b.* 1947, *s.* 1989, *m.*	Hon. David *L.*, MBE, *b.* 1914.
1839	*Leigh* (5th), John Piers Leigh, *b.* 1935, *s.* 1979, *m.*	Hon. Christopher D. P. *L.*, *b.* 1960.
1962	*Leighton of St Mellons* (2nd), (John) Leighton Seager, *b.* 1922, *s.* 1963, *m.*	Hon. Robert W. H. L. *S.*, *b.* 1955.
1797	*Lilford* (7th), George Vernon Powys, *b.* 1931, *s.* 1949, *m.*	Hon. Mark V. *P.*, *b.* 1975.
1945	*Lindsay of Birker* (2nd), Michael Francis Morris Lindsay, *b.* 1909, *s.* 1952, *m.*	Hon. James F. *L.*, *b.* 1945.
1758 I.	*Lisle* (7th), John Nicholas Horace Lysaght, *b.* 1903, *s.* 1919, *m.*	Patrick J. *L.*, *b.* 1931.
1850	*Londesborough* (9th), Richard John Denison, *b.* 1959, *s.* 1968, *m.*	Hon. James F. *D.*, *b.* 1990.
1541 I.	*Louth* (16th), Otway Michael James Oliver Plunkett, *b.* 1929, *s.* 1950, *m.*	Hon. Jonathan O. *P.*, *b.* 1952.
1458 S.*	*Lovat* (15th), Simon Christopher Joseph Fraser, DSO, MC, TD (4th *UK Baron, Lovat,* 1837), *b.* 1911, *s.* 1933, *m.*	Master of Lovat *b.* 1939.
1946	*Lucas of Chilworth* (2nd), Michael William George Lucas, *b.* 1926, *s.* 1967, *m.*	Hon. Simon W. *L.*, *b.* 1957.
1663	*Lucas* (11th) & *Dingwall* (8th) (*Scottish Lordship* 1609), Ralph Matthew Palmer, *b.* 1951, *s.* 1991, *m.*	Hon. Lewis E. *P.*, *b.* 1987
1929	*Luke* (2nd), Ian St John Lawson-Johnston, KCVO, TD, *b.* 1905, *s.* 1943, *m.*	Hon. Arthur C. St J. *L.-J.*, *b.* 1933.
1914	*Lyell* (3rd), Charles Lyell, *b.* 1939, *s.* 1943.	None.
1859	*Lyveden* (6th), Ronald Cecil Vernon, *b.* 1915, *s.* 1973, *m.*	Hon. Jack L. *V.*, *b.* 1938.
1959	*MacAndrew* (3rd), Christopher Anthony Colin MacAndrew, *b.* 1945, *s.* 1989, *m.*	Hon. Oliver C. J. *M.*, *b.* 1983.
1776 I.	*Macdonald* (8th), Godfrey James Macdonald of Macdonald, *b.* 1947, *s.* 1970, *m.*	Hon. Godfrey E. H. T. *M.*, *b.* 1982.
1949	*Macdonald of Gwaenysgor* (2nd), Gordon Ramsay Macdonald, *b.* 1915, *s.* 1966, *m.*	None.
1937	*McGowan* (3rd), Harry Duncan Cory McGowan, *b.* 1938, *s.* 1966, *m.*	Hon. Harry J. C. *M.*, *b.* 1971.
1922	*Maclay* (3rd), Joseph Paton Maclay, *b.* 1942, *s.* 1969, *m.*	Hon. Joseph P. *M.*, *b.* 1977.
1955	*McNair* (3rd), Duncan James McNair, *b.* 1947, *s.* 1989, *m.*	Hon. Thomas J. *M.*, *b.* 1990.
1951	*Macpherson of Drumochter* (2nd), (James) Gordon Macpherson, *b.* 1924, *s.* 1965, *m.*	Hon. James A. *M.*, *b.* 1979.
1937	*Mancroft* (3rd), Benjamin Lloyd Stormont Mancroft, *b.* 1957, *s.* 1987, *m.*	None.
1807	*Manners* (5th), John Robert Cecil Manners, *b.* 1923, *s.* 1972, *m.*	Hon. John H. R. *M.*, *b.* 1956.
1922	*Manton* (3rd), Joseph Rupert Eric Robert Watson, *b.* 1924, *s.* 1968, *m.*	Capt. Hon. Miles R. M. *W.*, *b.* 1958.
1908	*Marchamley* (3rd), John William Tattersall Whiteley, *b.* 1922, *s.* 1949, *m.*	Hon. William F. *W.*, *b.* 1968.
1964	*Margadale* (1st), John Granville Morrison, TD, *b.* 1906, *w.*	Hon. James I. *M.*, TD, *b.* 1930.
1961	*Marks of Broughton* (2nd), Michael Marks, *b.* 1920, *s.* 1964.	Hon. Simon R. *M.*, *b.* 1950.
1964	*Martonmere* (2nd), John Stephen Robinson, *b.* 1963, *s.* 1989.	David A. *R.*, *b.* 1965.
1776 I.	*Massy* (9th), Hugh Hamon John Somerset Massy, *b.* 1921, *s.* 1958, *m.*	Hon. David H. S. *M.*, *b.* 1947.
1935	*May* (3rd), Michael St John May, *b.* 1931, *s.* 1950, *m.*	Hon. Jasper B. St J. *M.*, *b.* 1965.
1928	*Melchett* (4th), Peter Robert Henry Mond, *b.* 1948, *s.* 1973.	None.

Created	Title, order of succession, name, etc.	Eldest son or heir
1925	Merrivale (3rd), Jack Henry Edmond Duke, b. 1917, s. 1951, m.	Hon. Derek J. P. D., b. 1948.
1911	Merthyr. Disclaimed for life 1977. (Trevor Oswin Lewis, Bt., CBE, b. 1935, s. 1977, m.)	David T. L., b. 1977.
1919	Meston (3rd), James Meston, b. 1950, s. 1984, m.	Hon. Thomas J. D. M., b. 1977.
1838	Methuen (6th), Anthony John Methuen, b. 1925, s. 1975.	Hon. Robert A. H. M., b. 1931.
1711	Middleton (12th), (Digby) Michael Godfrey John Willoughby, MC, b. 1921, s. 1970, m.	Hon. Michael C. J. W., b. 1948.
1939	Milford (2nd), Wogan Philipps, b. 1902, s. 1962, m.	Hon. Hugo J. L. P., b. 1929.
1933	Milne (2nd), George Douglass Milne, TD, b. 1909, s. 1948, m.	Hon. George A. M., b. 1941.
1951	Milner of Leeds (2nd), Arthur James Michael Milner, AE, b. 1923, s. 1967, m.	Hon. Richard J. M., b. 1959.
1947	Milverton (2nd), Revd Fraser Arthur Richard Richards, b. 1930, s. 1978, m.	Hon. Michael H. R., b. 1936.
1873	Moncreiff (5th), Harry Robert Wellwood Moncreiff, b. 1915, s. 1942, w.	Hon. Rhoderick H. W. M., b. 1954.
1884	Monk Bretton (3rd), John Charles Dodson, b. 1924, s. 1933, m.	Hon. Christopher M. D., b. 1958.
1885	Monkswell (5th), Gerard Collier, b. 1947, s. 1984, m.	Hon. James A. C., b. 1977.
1728	Monson (11th), John Monson, b. 1932, s. 1958, m.	Hon. Nicholas J. M., b. 1955.
1885	Montagu of Beaulieu (3rd), Edward John Barrington Douglas-Scott-Montagu, b. 1926, s. 1929, m.	Hon. Ralph D.-S.-M., b. 1961.
1839	Monteagle of Brandon (6th), Gerald Spring Rice, b. 1926, s. 1946, m.	Hon. Charles J. S. R., b. 1953.
1943	Moran (2nd), (Richard) John (McMoran) Wilson, KCMG, b. 1924, s. 1977, m.	Hon. James M. W., b. 1952.
1918	Morris (3rd), Michael David Morris, b. 1937, s. 1975, m.	Hon. Thomas A. S. M., b. 1982.
1950	Morris of Kenwood (2nd), Philip Geoffrey Morris, b. 1928, s. 1954, m.	Hon. Jonathan D. M., b. 1968.
1945	Morrison (2nd), Dennis Morrison, b. 1914, s. 1953.	None.
1831	Mostyn (5th), Roger Edward Lloyd Lloyd-Mostyn, MC, b. 1920, s. 1965, m.	Hon. Llewellyn R. L. L.-M., b. 1948.
1933	Mottistone (4th), David Peter Seely, CBE, b. 1920, s. 1966, m.	Hon. Peter J. P. S., b. 1949.
1945	Mountevans (3rd), Edward Patrick Broke Evans, b. 1943, s. 1974, m.	Hon. Jeffrey de C. R. E., b. 1948.
1283	Mowbray (26th), Segrave (27th) (1283), & Stourton (23rd) (1448), Charles Edward Stourton, CBE, b. 1923, s. 1965, m.	Hon. Edward W. S. S., b. 1953.
1932	Moyne (3rd), Jonathan Bryan Guinness, b. 1930, s. 1992, m.	Hon. Jasper J. R. G., b. 1954.
1929	Moynihan, the 3rd Baron died November 1991. His trustees recognized Daniel Antony Patrick Berkeley Moynihan, (b. January 1991) as the financial heir of the 3rd Baron but the succession to the title is not settled.	
1781 I.	Muskerry (9th), Robert Fitzmaurice Deane, b. 1948, s. 1988, m.	Hon. Jonathan F. D., b. 1986.
1627 S.	Napier (14th) & Ettrick (5th) (UK 1872), Francis Nigel Napier, KCVO, b. 1930, s. 1954, m.	Master of Napier, b. 1962.
1868	Napier of Magdala (6th), Robert Alan Napier, b. 1940, s. 1987, m.	Hon. James R. N., b. 1966.
1940	Nathan (2nd), Roger Carol Michael Nathan, b. 1922, s. 1963, m.	Hon. Rupert H. B. N., b. 1957.
1960	Nelson of Stafford (2nd), Henry George Nelson, FEng., b. 1917, s. 1962, m.	Hon. Henry R. G. N., b. 1943.
1959	Netherthorpe (3rd), James Frederick Turner, b. 1964, s. 1982, m.	Hon. Patrick A. T., b. 1971.
1946	Newall (2nd), Francis Storer Eaton Newall, b. 1930, s. 1963, m.	Hon. Richard H. E. N., b. 1961.
1776 I.	Newborough (7th), Robert Charles Michael Vaughan Wynn, DSC, b. 1917, s. 1965, m.	Hon. Robert V. W., b. 1949.
1892	Newton (5th), Richard Thomas Legh, b. 1950, s. 1992, m.	Hon. Piers R. L., b. 1979.
1930	Noel-Buxton (3rd), Martin Connal Noel-Buxton, b. 1940, s. 1980, m.	Hon. Charles C. N.-B., b. 1975.
1957	Norrie (2nd), (George) Willoughby Moke Norrie, b. 1936, s. 1977, m.	Hon. Mark W. J. N., b. 1972.
1884	Northbourne (5th), Christopher George Walter James, b. 1926, s. 1982, m.	Hon. Charles W. H. J., b. 1960.
1866	Northbrook (6th), Francis Thomas Baring, b. 1954, s. 1990, m.	None.
1878	Norton (7th), John Arden Adderley, OBE, b. 1915, s. 1961, m.	Hon. James N. A. A., b. 1947.
1906	Nunburnholme (4th), Ben Charles Wilson, b. 1928, s. 1974.	Hon. Charles T. W., b. 1935.
1950	Ogmore (2nd), Gwilym Rees Rees-Williams, b. 1931, s. 1976, m.	Hon. Morgan R.-W., b. 1937.
1870	O'Hagan (4th), Charles Towneley Strachey, MEP, b. 1945, s. 1961, m.	Hon. Richard T. S., b. 1950.
1868	O'Neill (4th), Raymond Arthur Clanaboy O'Neill, TD, b. 1933, s. 1944, m.	Hon. Shane S. C. O'N., b. 1965.
1836 I.*	Oranmore and Browne (4th), Dominick Geoffrey Edward Browne (2nd UK Baron Mereworth, 1926), b. 1901, s. 1927, m.	Hon. Dominick G. T. B., b. 1929.
1933	Palmer (4th), Adrian Bailie Nottage Palmer, b. 1951, s. 1990, m.	Hon. Hugo B. R. P., b. 1980.
1914	Parmoor (4th), (Frederick Alfred) Milo Cripps, b. 1929, s. 1977.	M. Anthony L. C., CBE, DSO, TD, QC, b. 1913.
1937	Pender (3rd), John Willoughby Denison-Pender, b. 1933, s. 1965, m.	Hon. Henry J. R. D.-P., b. 1968.
1866	Penrhyn (6th), Malcolm Frank Douglas-Pennant, DSO, MBE, b. 1908, s. 1967, m.	Hon. Nigel D.-P., b. 1909.
1603	Petre (18th), John Patrick Lionel Petre, b. 1942, s. 1989, m.	Hon. Dominic W. P., b. 1966.
1918	Phillimore (4th), Claud Stephen Phillimore, b. 1911, s. 1990, m.	Hon. Francis S. P., b. 1944.
1945	Piercy (3rd), James William Piercy, b. 1946, s. 1981.	Hon. Mark E. P. P., b. 1953.

Created	Title, order of succession, name, etc.	Eldest son or heir
1827	Plunket (8th), Robin Rathmore Plunket, b. 1925, s. 1975, m.	Hon. Shaun A. F. S. P., b. 1931.
1831	Poltimore (7th), Mark Coplestone Bampfylde, b. 1957, s. 1978, m.	Hon. Henry A. W. B., b. 1985.
1690 s.	Polwarth (10th), Henry Alexander Hepburne-Scott, TD, b. 1916, s. 1944, m.	Master of Polwarth, b. 1947.
1930	Ponsonby of Shulbrede (4th), Frederick Matthew Thomas Ponsonby, b. 1958, s. 1990.	None.
1958	Poole (2nd), David Charles Poole, b. 1945, s. 1993, m.	Hon. Oliver J. P., b. 1972.
1852	Raglan (5th), FitzRoy John Somerset, b. 1927, s. 1964.	Hon. Geoffrey S., b. 1932.
1932	Rankeillour (4th), Peter St Thomas More Henry Hope, b. 1935, s. 1967.	Michael R. H., b. 1940.
1953	Rathcavan (2nd), Phelim Robert Hugh O'Neill, PC (NI), b. 1909, s. 1982, m.	Hon. Hugh D. T. O'N., b. 1939.
1916	Rathcreedan (3rd), Christopher John Norton, b. 1949, s. 1990, m.	Hon. Adam G. N., b. 1952.
1868 I.	Rathdonnell (5th), Thomas Benjamin McClintock–Bunbury, b. 1938, s. 1959, m.	Hon. William L. M.-B., b. 1966.
1911	Ravensdale (3rd), Nicholas Mosley, MC, b. 1923, s. 1966, m.	Hon. Shaun N. M., b. 1949.
1821	Ravensworth (8th), Arthur Waller Liddell, b. 1924, s. 1950, m.	Hon. Thomas A. H. L., b. 1954.
1821	Rayleigh (6th), John Gerald Strutt, b. 1960, s. 1988, m.	Hon. John F. S., b. 1993.
1937	Rea (3rd), John Nicolas Rea, MD, b. 1928, s. 1981, m.	Hon. Matthew J. R., b. 1956.
1628 s.	Reay (14th), Hugh William Mackay, b. 1937, s. 1963, m.	Master of Reay, b. 1965.
1902	Redesdale (6th), Rupert Bertram Mitford, b. 1967, s. 1991.	None.
1940	Reith. Disclaimed for life 1972. (Christopher John Reith, b. 1928, s. 1971, m.)	Hon. James H. J. R., b. 1971.
1928	Remnant (3rd), James Wogan Remnant, CVO, b. 1930, s. 1967, m.	Hon. Philip J. R., b. 1954.
1806 I.	Rendlesham (8th), Charles Anthony Hugh Thellusson, b. 1915, s. 1943, w.	Hon. Charles W. B. T., b. 1954.
1933	Rennell (3rd), (John Adrian) Tremayne Rodd, b. 1935, s. 1978, m.	Hon. James R. D. T. R., b. 1978.
1964	Renwick (2nd), Harry Andrew Renwick, b. 1935, s. 1973, m.	Hon. Robert J. R., b. 1966.
1885	Revelstoke (4th), Rupert Baring, b. 1911, s. 1934.	Hon. John B., b. 1934.
1905	Ritchie of Dundee (5th), (Harold) Malcolm Ritchie, b. 1919, s. 1978, m.	Hon. C. Rupert R. R., b. 1958.
1935	Riverdale (2nd), Robert Arthur Balfour, b. 1901, s. 1957, m.	Hon. Mark R. B., b. 1927.
1961	Robertson of Oakridge (2nd), William Ronald Robertson, b. 1930, s. 1974, m.	Hon. William B. E. R., b. 1975.
1938	Roborough (3rd), Henry Massey Lopes, b. 1940, s. 1992, m.	Hon. Massey J. H. L., b. 1969.
1931	Rochester (2nd), Foster Charles Lowry Lamb, b. 1916, s. 1955, m.	Hon. David C. L., b. 1944.
1934	Rockley (3rd), James Hugh Cecil, b. 1934, s. 1976, m.	Hon. Anthony R. C., b. 1961.
1782	Rodney (10th), George Brydges Rodney, b. 1953, s. 1992.	Hon. Michael C. R., b. 1926.
1651 s.*	Rollo (13th), Eric John Stapylton Rollo (4th UK Baron, Dunning, 1869), b. 1915, s. 1947, m.	Master of Rollo, b. 1943.
1959	Rootes (3rd), Nicholas Geoffrey Rootes, b. 1951, s. 1992, m.	William B. R., b. 1944.
1796 I.*	Rossmore (7th), William Warner Westenra (6th UK Baron, Rossmore, 1838), b. 1931, s. 1958, m.	Hon. Benedict W. W., b. 1983.
1939	Rotherwick (2nd), (Herbert) Robin Cayzer, b. 1912, s. 1958, w.	Hon. H. Robin C., b. 1954.
1885	Rothschild (4th), (Nathaniel Charles) Jacob Rothschild, b. 1936, s. 1990, m.	Hon. Nathaniel P. V. J. R., b. 1971.
1911	Rowallan (4th), John Polson Cameron Corbett, b. 1947, s. 1993, m.	Hon. Jason W. P. C. C., b. 1972.
1947	Rugby (3rd), Robert Charles Maffey, b. 1951, s. 1990, m.	Hon. Timothy J. H. M., b. 1975.
1919	Russell of Liverpool (3rd), Simon Gordon Jared Russell, b. 1952, s. 1981, m.	Hon. Edward C. S. R., b. 1985.
1876	Sackville (6th), Lionel Bertrand Sackville-West, b. 1913, s. 1965, m.	Hugh R. I. S.-W., MC, b. 1919.
1964	St Helens (2nd), Richard Francis Hughes-Young, b. 1945, s. 1980, m.	Hon. Henry T. H.-Y., b. 1986.
1559	St John of Bletso (21st), Anthony Tudor St John, b. 1957, s. 1978.	Edmund O. St J., b. 1927.
1887	St Levan (4th), John Francis Arthur St Aubyn, DSC, b. 1919, s. 1978, m.	Hon. O. Piers St A., MC, b. 1920.
1885	St Oswald (5th), Derek Edward Anthony Winn, b. 1919, s. 1984, m.	Hon. Charles R. A. W., b. 1959.
1960	Sanderson of Ayot. Disclaimed for life 1971. (Alan Lindsay Sanderson, b. 1931, s. 1971, m.)	Hon. Michael S., b. 1959.
1945	Sandford (2nd), Revd John Cyril Edmondson, DSC, b. 1920, s. 1959, m.	Hon. James J. M. E., b. 1949.
1871	Sandhurst (5th), (John Edward) Terence Mansfield, DFC, b. 1920, s. 1964, m.	Hon. Guy R. J. M., b. 1949.
1802	Sandys (7th), Richard Michael Oliver Hill, b. 1931, s. 1961, m.	Marcus T. H., b. 1931.
1888	Savile (3rd), George Halifax Lumley-Savile, b. 1919, s. 1931.	Hon. Henry L. T. L.-S., b. 1923.
1447	Saye and Sele (21st), Nathaniel Thomas Allen Fiennes, b. 1920, s. 1968, m.	Hon. Richard I. F., b. 1959.
1932	Selsdon (3rd), Malcolm McEacharn Mitchell-Thomson, b. 1937, s. 1963, m.	Hon. Callum M. M. M.-T., b. 1969.
1916	Shaughnessy (3rd), William Graham Shaughnessy, b. 1922, s. 1938, m.	Hon. Michael J. S., b. 1946.
1946	Shepherd (2nd), Malcolm Newton Shepherd, PC, b. 1918, s. 1954, m.	Hon. Graeme G. S., b. 1949.
1964	Sherfield (1st), Roger Mellor Makins, GCB, GCMG, FRS, b. 1904, w.	Hon. Christopher J. M., b. 1942.

Created	Title, order of succession, name, etc.	Eldest son or heir
1902	*Shuttleworth* (5th), Charles Geoffrey Nicholas Kay-Shuttleworth, *b.* 1948, *s.* 1975, *m.*	Hon. Thomas E. *K.-S.*, *b.* 1976.
1950	*Silkin.* Disclaimed for life 1972. (*Arthur Silkin, b.* 1916, *s.* 1972, *m.*)	Hon. Christopher L. *S.*, *b.* 1947.
1963	*Silsoe* (2nd), David Malcolm Trustram Eve, QC, *b.* 1930, *s.* 1976, *m.*	Hon. Simon R. T. *E.*, *b.* 1966.
1947	*Simon of Wythenshawe* (2nd), Roger Simon, *b.* 1913, *s.* 1960, *m.*	Hon. Matthew *S.*, *b.* 1955.
1449 S.	*Sinclair* (17th), Charles Murray Kennedy St Clair, CVO, *b.* 1914, *s.* 1957, *m.*	Master of Sinclair, *b.* 1968.
1957	*Sinclair of Cleeve* (3rd), John Lawrence Robert Sinclair, *b.* 1953, *s.* 1985.	None.
1919	*Sinha* (4th), Susanta Prasanna Sinha, *b.* 1953, *s.* 1989, *m.*	Hon. A. K. *S.*, *b.* 1930.
1828	*Skelmersdale* (7th), Roger Bootle-Wilbraham, *b.* 1945, *s.* 1973, *m.*	Hon. Andrew *B.-W.*, *b.* 1977.
1916	*Somerleyton* (3rd), Savile William Francis Crossley, *b.* 1928, *s.* 1959, *m.* Master of the Horse.	Hon. Hugh F. S. *C.*, *b.* 1971.
1784	*Somers* (8th), John Patrick Somers Cocks, *b.* 1907, *s.* 1953, *m.*	Philip S. *S. C.*, *b.* 1948.
1780	*Southampton* (6th), Charles James FitzRoy, *b.* 1928, *s.* 1989, *m.*	Hon. Edward C. *F.*, *b.* 1955.
1959	*Spens* (3rd), Patrick Michael Rex Spens, *b.* 1942, *s.* 1984, *m.*	Hon. Patrick N. G. *S.*, *b.* 1968.
1640	*Stafford* (15th), Francis Melfort William Fitzherbert, *b.* 1954, *s.* 1986, *m.*	Hon. Benjamin J. B. *F.*, *b.* 1983.
1938	*Stamp* (4th), Trevor Charles Bosworth Stamp, MD, FRCP, *b.* 1935, *s.* 1987, *m.*	Hon. Nicholas C. T. *S.*, *b.* 1978.
1839	*Stanley of Alderley* (8th) & *Sheffield* (8th) (1738 I.), Thomas Henry Oliver Stanley (7th *UK Baron Eddisbury*, 1848), *b.* 1927, *s.* 1971, *m.*	Hon. Richard O. *S.*, *b.* 1956.
1318	*Strabolgi* (11th), David Montague de Burgh Kenworthy, *b.* 1914, *s.* 1953, *m.*	Andrew D. W. *K.*, *b.* 1967.
1954	*Strang* (2nd), Colin Strang, *b.* 1922, *s.* 1978, *m.*	None.
1955	*Strathalmond* (3rd), William Roberton Fraser, *b.* 1947, *s.* 1976, *m.*	Hon. William G. *F.*, *b.* 1976.
1936	*Strathcarron* (2nd), David William Anthony Blyth Macpherson, *b.* 1924, *s.* 1937, *m.*	Hon. Ian D. P. *M.*, *b.* 1949.
1955	*Strathclyde* (2nd), Thomas Galloway Dunlop du Roy de Blicquy Galbraith, *b.* 1960, *s.* 1985, *m.*	Hon. Charles W. du R. de B. *G.*, *b.* 1962.
1900	*Strathcona and Mount Royal* (4th), Donald Euan Palmer Howard, *b.* 1923, *s.* 1959, *m.*	Hon. D. Alexander S. *H.*, *b.* 1961.
1836	*Stratheden* & *Campbell* (1841) (6th), Donald Campbell, *b.* 1934, *s.* 1987, *m.*	Hon. David A. *C.*, *b.* 1963.
1884	*Strathspey* (6th), James Patrick Trevor Grant of Grant, *b.* 1943, *s.* 1991, *m.*	Hon. Michael P. *F. G.*, *b.* 1953.
1838	*Sudeley* (7th), Merlin Charles Sainthill Hanbury-Tracy, *b.* 1939, *s.* 1941.	D. Andrew J. *H-T.*, *b.* 1928.
1786	*Suffield* (11th), Anthony Philip Harbord-Hamond, MC, *b.* 1922, *s.* 1951, *m.*	Hon. Charles A. A. *H.-H.*, *b.* 1953.
1893	*Swansea* (4th), John Hussey Hamilton Vivian, *b.* 1925, *s.* 1934, *m.*	Hon. Richard A. H. *V.*, *b.* 1957.
1907	*Swaythling* (4th), David Charles Samuel Montagu, *b.* 1928, *s.* 1990, *m.*	Hon. Charles E. S. *M.*, *b.* 1954.
1919	*Swinfen* (3rd), Roger Mynors Swinfen Eady, *b.* 1938, *s.* 1977, *m.*	Hon. Charles R. P. S. *E.*, *b.* 1971.
1935	*Sysonby* (3rd), John Frederick Ponsonby, *b.* 1945, *s.* 1956.	None.
1831 I.	*Talbot of Malahide* (10th), Reginald John Richard Arundell, *b.* 1931, *s.* 1987, *w.*	Hon. Richard J. T. *A.*, *b.* 1957.
1946	*Tedder* (2nd), John Michael Tedder, SC.D., PH.D., D.SC., *b.* 1926, *s.* 1967, *m.*	Hon. Robin J. *T.*, *b.* 1955.
1884	*Tennyson* (5th), Mark Aubrey Tennyson, DSC, *b.* 1920, *s.* 1991, *m.*	Lt.-Cdr. James A. *T.*, DSC, *b.* 1913.
1918	*Terrington* (4th), (James Allen) David Woodhouse, *b.* 1915, *s.* 1961, *m.*	Hon. C. Montague *W.*, DSO, OBE, *b.* 1917.
1940	*Teviot* (2nd), Charles John Kerr, *b.* 1934, *s.* 1968, *m.*	Hon. Charles R. *K.*, *b.* 1971.
1616	*Teynham* (20th), John Christopher Ingham Roper-Curzon, *b.* 1928, *s.* 1972, *m.*	Hon. David J. H. I. *R.-C.*, *b.* 1965.
1964	*Thomson of Fleet* (2nd), Kenneth Roy Thomson, *b.* 1923, *s.* 1976, *m.*	Hon. David K. R. *T.*, *b.* 1957.
1792	*Thurlow* (8th), Francis Edward Hovell-Thurlow-Cumming-Bruce, KCMG, *b.* 1912, *s.* 1971, *w.*	Hon. Roualeyn R. *H.-T.-C.-B.*, *b.* 1952.
1876	*Tollemache* (5th), Timothy John Edward Tollemache, *b.* 1939, *s.* 1975, *m.*	Hon. Edward J. H. *T.*, *b.* 1976.
1564 S.	*Torphichen* (15th), James Andrew Douglas Sandilands, *b.* 1946, *s.* 1975, *m.*	Douglas R. A. *S.*, *b.* 1926.
1947	*Trefgarne* (2nd), David Garro Trefgarne, PC, *b.* 1941, *s.* 1960, *m.*	Hon. George G. *T.*, *b.* 1970.
1921	*Trevethin* (4th), *and Oaksey* (2nd), John Geoffrey Tristram Lawrence, OBE (2nd *UK Baron, Oaksey*, 1947), *b.* 1929, *s.* 1971, *m.*	Hon. Patrick J. T. *L.*, *b.* 1960.
1880	*Trevor* (4th), Charles Edwin Hill-Trevor, *b.* 1928, *s.* 1950, *m.*	Hon. Marke C. *H.-T.*, *b.* 1970.
1461 I.	*Trimlestown* (20th), Anthony Edward Barnewall, *b.* 1928, *s.* 1990, *m.*	Hon. Raymond C. *B.*, *b.* 1930.
1940	*Tryon* (3rd), Anthony George Merrik Tryon, *b.* 1940, *s.* 1976, *m.*	Hon. Charles G. B. *T.*, *b.* 1976.
1935	*Tweedsmuir* (2nd), John Norman Stuart Buchan, CBE, CD, *b.* 1911, *s.* 1940, *m.*	Hon. William *B.*, *b.* 1916.
1523	*Vaux of Harrowden* (10th), John Hugh Philip Gilbey, *b.* 1915, *s.* 1977, *m.*	Hon. Anthony W. *G.*, *b.* 1940.
1800 I.	*Ventry* (8th), Andrew Wesley Daubeny de Moleyns, *b.* 1943, *s.* 1987, *m.*	Hon. Francis W. *D. de M.*, *b.* 1965.
1762	*Vernon* (10th), John Lawrance Vernon, *b.* 1923, *s.* 1963, *m.*	Col. William R. D. *Vernon-Harcourt*, OBE, *b.* 1909.
1922	*Vestey* (3rd), Samuel George Armstrong Vestey, *b.* 1941, *s.* 1954, *m.*	Hon. William G. *V.*, *b.* 1983.
1841	*Vivian* (6th), Nicholas Crespigny Laurence Vivian, *b.* 1935, *s.* 1991, *m.*	Hon. Charles H. C. *V.*, *b.* 1966.

Created	*Title, order of succession, name, etc.*	*Eldest son or heir*
1934	*Wakehurst* (3rd), (John) Christopher Loder, *b.* 1925, *s.* 1970, *m.*	Hon. Timothy W. *L.*, *b.* 1958.
1723	*Walpole* (10th), Robert Horatio Walpole (*8th Brit. Baron Walpole of Wolterton*, 1756), *b.* 1938, *s.* 1989, *m.*	Hon. Jonathan R. H. *W.*, *b.* 1967.
1780	*Walsingham* (9th), John de Grey, MC, *b.* 1925, *s.* 1965, *m.*	Hon. Robert *de G.*, *b.* 1969.
1936	*Wardington* (2nd), Christopher Henry Beaumont Pease, *b.* 1924, *s.* 1950, *m.*	Hon. William S. *P.*, *b.* 1925.
1792 I.	*Waterpark* (7th), Frederick Caryll Philip Cavendish, *b.* 1926, *s.* 1948, *m.*	Hon. Roderick A. *C.*, *b.* 1959.
1942	*Wedgwood* (4th), Piers Anthony Weymouth Wedgwood, *b.* 1954, *s.* 1970, *m.*	John *W.*, CBE, MD, *b.* 1919.
1861	*Westbury* (5th), David Alan Bethell, MC, *b.* 1922, *s.* 1961, *m.*	Hon. Richard N. *B.*, MBE, *b.* 1950.
1944	*Westwood* (3rd), (William) Gavin Westwood, *b.* 1944, *s.* 1991, *m.*	Hon. William F. *W.*, *b.* 1972.
1935	*Wigram* (2nd), (George) Neville (Clive) Wigram, MC, *b.* 1915, *s.* 1960, *w.*	Maj. Hon. Andrew F. C. *W.*, MVO, *b.* 1949.
1491	*Willoughby de Broke* (21st), Leopold David Verney, *b.* 1938, *s.* 1986, *m.*	Hon. Rupert G. *V.*, *b.* 1966.
1946	*Wilson* (2nd), Patrick Maitland Wilson, *b.* 1915, *s.* 1964, *w.*	None.
1937	*Windlesham* (3rd), David James George Hennessy, CVO, PC, *b.* 1932, *s.* 1962, *w.*	Hon. James R. *H.*, *b.* 1968.
1951	*Wise* (2nd), John Clayton Wise, *b.* 1923, *s.* 1968, *m.*	Hon. Christopher J. C. *W.*, PH.D., *b.* 1949.
1869	*Wolverton* (7th), Christopher Richard Glyn, *b.* 1938, *s.* 1988, *m.*	Hon. Andrew J. *G.*, *b.* 1943.
1928	*Wraxall* (2nd), George Richard Lawley Gibbs, *b.* 1928, *s.* 1931.	Hon. Sir Eustace H. B. *G.*, KCVO, CMG, *b.* 1929.
1915	*Wrenbury* (3rd), John Burton Buckley, *b.* 1927, *s.* 1940, *m.*	Hon. William E. *B.*, *b.* 1966.
1838	*Wrottesley* (6th), Clifton Hugh Lancelot de Verdon Wrottesley, *b.* 1968, *s.* 1977.	Hon. Stephen J. *W.*, *b.* 1955.
1919	*Wyfold* (3rd), Hermon Robert Fleming Hermon-Hodge, *b.* 1915, *s.* 1942.	None.
1829	*Wynford* (8th), Robert Samuel Best, MBE, *b.* 1917, *s.* 1943, *m.*	Hon. John P. *B.*, *b.* 1950.
1308	*Zouche* (18th), James Assheton Frankland, *b.* 1943, *s.* 1965, *m.*	Hon. William T. A. *F.*, *b.* 1984.

BARONESSES/LADIES IN THEIR OWN RIGHT

Style, The Right Hon. the Lady ___, or The Right Hon. the Baroness ___, according to her preference. Either style may be used, except in the case of Scottish titles (indicated by s.), which are not baronies (*see* page 141) and whose holders are always addressed as Lady

Husband, Untitled

Children's style, As for children of a Baron

For forms of address, *see* page 220.

Created	*Title, order of succession, name, etc.*	*Eldest son or heir*
1455	*Berners*, in abeyance between two co-heiresses, daughters of the late Baroness Berners, died 1992.	
1529	*Braye* (8th in line), Mary Penelope Aubrey–Fletcher, *b.* 1941, *s.* 1985, *m.*	Two co-heiresses.
1321	*Dacre* (27th in line), Rachel Leila Douglas-Home, *b.* 1929, *title called out of abeyance*, 1970, *w.*	Hon. James T. A. *D.-H.*, *b.* 1952.
1332	*Darcy de Knayth* (18th in line), Davina Marcia Ingrams, *b.* 1938, *s.* 1943, *w.*	Hon. Caspar D. *I.*, *b.* 1962.
1439	*Dudley* (14th in line), Barbara Amy Felicity Hamilton, *b.* 1907, *s.* 1972, *m.*	Hon. Jim A. H. *Wallace*, *b.* 1930.
1490 S.	*Herries of Terregles* (14th in line), Anne Elizabeth Fitzalan-Howard, *b.* 1938, *s.* 1975, *m.*	Lady Mary *Mumford*, CVO, *b.* 1940.
1602 S.	*Kinloss* (12th in line), Beatrice Mary Grenville Freeman-Grenville, *b.* 1922, *s.* 1944, *m.*	Master of Kinloss, *b.* 1953.
1681 S.	*Nairne* (12th in line), Katherine Evelyn Constance Bigham (*Katherine, Viscountess Mersey*), *b.* 1912, *s.* 1944, *w.*	The Viscount Mersey, *b.* 1934 (*see* page 151).
1445 S.	*Saltoun* (20th in line), Flora Marjory Fraser, *b.* 1930, *s.* 1979, *m.*	Hon. Katharine I. M. *I. F.*, *b.* 1957.
1489 S.	*Sempill* (20th in line), Ann Moira Sempill, *b.* 1920, *s.* 1965, *w.*	Master of Sempill, *b.* 1949.
1628	*Strange* (16th in line), (Jean) Cherry Drummond of Megginch, *b.* 1928, *title called out of abeyance*, 1986, *m.*	Hon. Adam H. *D. of M.*, *b.* 1953.
1544-5	*Wharton* (11th in line), Myrtle Olive Felix Robertson, *b.* 1934, *title called out of abeyance*, 1990, *m.*	Hon. Myles C. D. *R.*, *b.* 1964.
1313	*Willoughby de Eresby* (27th in line), (Nancy) Jane Marie Heathcote-Drummond-Willoughby, *b.* 1934, *s.* 1983.	Two co-heiresses.

Life Peers

Between 1 September 1992 and 31 August 1993, the conferment of 16 life peerages was announced, three under the Appellate Jurisdiction Act 1876 and 13 under the Life Peerages Act 1958:

New Lords of Appeal in Ordinary: (announced 10 September 1992) the Rt. Hon. Sir Harry Woolf; (22 July 1993) *the Rt. Hon. Sir Anthony Lloyd; *the Rt. Hon. Sir Michael Nolan

New Year Honours (31 December 1992): the Rt. Hon. Shirley Williams

The Queen's Birthday Honours (12 June 1993): Sir Richard Attenborough, CBE; Sir Ralf Dahrendorf, KBE; the Rt. Hon. Robert (Robin) Leigh-Pemberton; Sir Yehudi Menuhin, OM, KBE

'Working' Peers (13 August 1993): *Miss Brenda Dean; *Mrs Joyce Gould; *Mrs Doreen Miller, MBE; *the Rt. Hon. Sir Paul Dean; *Simon Haskel; *Anthony Lester, QC; *Robert Dixon Smith; *Sir Christopher Tugendhat

*No title gazetted at time of going to press

CREATED UNDER THE APPELLATE JURISDICTION ACT 1876 (AS AMENDED)

BARONS

Created

1986   *Ackner*, Desmond James Conrad Ackner, PC, b. 1920, m.

1981   *Brandon of Oakbrook*, Henry Vivian Brandon, MC, PC, b. 1920, m.

1980   *Bridge of Harwich*, Nigel Cyprian Bridge, PC, b. 1917, m.

1982   *Brightman*, John Anson Brightman, PC, b. 1911, m.

1991   *Browne-Wilkinson*, Nicolas Christopher Henry Browne-Wilkinson, PC, b. 1930, m. Lord of Appeal in Ordinary.

1957   *Denning*, Alfred Thompson Denning, PC, b. 1899, w.

1986   *Goff of Chieveley*, Robert Lionel Archibald Goff, PC, b. 1926, m. Lord of Appeal in Ordinary.

1985   *Griffiths*, (William) Hugh Griffiths, MC, PC, b. 1923, m.

1987   *Jauncey of Tullichettle*, Charles Eliot Jauncey, PC, b. 1925, m. Lord of Appeal in Ordinary.

1977   *Keith of Kinkel*, Henry Shanks Keith, PC, b. 1922, m. Lord of Appeal in Ordinary.

1979   *Lane*, Geoffrey Dawson Lane, AFC, PC, b. 1918, m.

1992   *Mustill*, Michael John Mustill, PC, b. 1931, m. Lord of Appeal in Ordinary.

1986   *Oliver of Aylmerton*, Peter Raymond Oliver, PC, b. 1921, m.

1980   *Roskill*, Eustace Wentworth Roskill, PC, b. 1911, m.

1977   *Scarman*, Leslie George Scarman, OBE, PC, b. 1911, m.

1992   *Slynn of Hadley*, Gordon Slynn, PC, b. 1930, m. Lord of Appeal in Ordinary.

1982   *Templeman*, Sydney William Templeman, MBE, PC, b. 1920, w. Lord of Appeal in Ordinary.

1964   *Wilberforce*, Richard Orme Wilberforce, CMG, OBE, PC, b. 1907, m.

1992   *Woolf*, Harry Kenneth Woolf, PC, b. 1933, m. Lord of Appeal in Ordinary.

CREATED UNDER THE LIFE PEERAGES ACT 1958

BARONS

Created

1974   *Alexander of Potterhill*, William Picken Alexander, Ph.D., b. 1905, m.

1988   *Alexander of Weedon*, Robert Scott Alexander, QC, b. 1936, m.

1976   *Allen of Abbeydale*, Philip Allen, GCB, b. 1912, m.

1961   *Alport*, Cuthbert James McCall Alport, TD, PC, b. 1912, w.

1992   *Amery of Lustleigh*, Julian Amery, PC, b. 1919, w.

1965   *Annan*, Noel Gilroy Annan, OBE, b. 1916, m.

1992   *Archer of Sandwell*, Peter Kingsley Archer, PC, QC, b. 1926, m.

1992   *Archer of Weston-super-Mare*, Jeffrey Howard Archer, b. 1940, m.

1970   *Ardwick*, John Cowburn Beavan, b. 1910, m.

1988   *Armstrong of Ilminster*, Robert Temple Armstrong, GCB, CVO, b. 1927, m.

1992   *Ashley of Stoke*, Jack Ashley, CH, PC, b. 1922, m.

1993   *Attenborough*, Richard Samuel Attenborough, CBE, b. 1923, m.

1967   *Aylestone*, Herbert William Bowden, CH, CBE, PC, b. 1905, m.

1982   *Bancroft*, Ian Powell Bancroft, GCB, b. 1922, m.

1974   *Banks*, Desmond Anderson Harvie Banks, CBE, b. 1918, m.

1974   *Barber*, Anthony Perrinott Lysberg Barber, TD, PC, b. 1920, m.

1992   *Barber of Tewkesbury*, Derek Coates Barber, b. 1918, m.

1983   *Barnett*, Joel Barnett, PC, b. 1923, m.

1982   *Bauer*, Prof. Peter Thomas Bauer, D.SC., b. 1915.

1967   *Beaumont of Whitley*, Revd Timothy Wentworth Beaumont, b. 1928, m.

1979   *Bellwin*, Irwin Norman Bellow, b. 1923, m.

1981   *Beloff*, Max Beloff, b. 1913, m.

1981   *Benson*, Henry Alexander Benson, GBE, b. 1909, m.

1971   *Blake*, Robert Norman William Blake, FBA, b. 1916, m.

1983   *Blanch*, Rt. Revd Stuart Yarworth Blanch, PC, b. 1918, m.

1978   *Blease*, William John Blease, b. 1914, m.

1980   *Boardman*, Thomas Gray Boardman, MC, TD, b. 1919, m.

1986   *Bonham-Carter*, Mark Raymond Bonham Carter, b. 1922, m.

1976   *Boston of Faversham*, Terence George Boston, QC, b. 1930, m.

1984   *Bottomley*, Arthur George Bottomley, OBE, PC, b. 1907, m.

1972   *Boyd-Carpenter*, John Archibald Boyd-Carpenter, PC, b. 1908, m.

1992   *Braine of Wheatley*, Bernard Richard Braine, PC, b. 1914, w.

1987   *Bramall*, Edwin Noel Westby Bramall, KG, GCB, OBE, MC, Field Marshal, b. 1923, m.

1976   *Briggs*, Asa Briggs, b. 1921, m.

Created

1974 *Greenhill of Harrow,* Denis Arthur Greenhill, GCMG, OBE, *b.* 1913, *m.*

1975 *Gregson,* John Gregson, *b.* 1924.

1968 *Grey of Naunton,* Ralph Francis Alnwick Grey, GCMG, GCVO, OBE, *b.* 1910, *m.*

1991 *Griffiths of Fforestfach,* Brian Griffiths, *b.* 1941, *m.*

1983 *Grimond,* Joseph Grimond, TD, PC, *b.* 1913, *m.*

1970 *Hailsham of St Marylebone,* Quintin McGarel Hogg, KG, CH, PC, *b.* 1907, *m.*

1983 *Hanson,* James Edward Hanson, *b.* 1922, *m.*

1974 *Harmar-Nicholls,* Harmar Harmar-Nicholls, *b.* 1912, *m.*

1974 *Harris of Greenwich,* John Henry Harris, *b.* 1930, *m.*

1979 *Harris of High Cross,* Ralph Harris, *b.* 1924, *m.*

1968 *Hartwell,* (William) Michael Berry, MBE, TD, *b.* 1911, *w.*

1971 *Harvey of Prestbury,* Arthur Vere Harvey, CBE, *b.* 1906, *m.*

1974 *Harvington,* Robert Grant Grant-Ferris, AE, PC, *b.* 1907, *m.*

1990 *Haslam,* Robert Haslam, *b.* 1923, *m.*

1992 *Hayhoe,* Bernard John (Barney) Hayhoe, PC, *b.* 1925, *m.*

1992 *Healey,* Denis Winston Healey, CH, MBE, PC, *b.* 1917, *m.*

1984 *Henderson of Brompton,* Peter Gordon Henderson, KCB, *b.* 1922, *m.*

1979 *Hill-Norton,* Peter John Hill-Norton, GCB, *Admiral of the Fleet, b.* 1915, *m.*

1967 *Hirshfield,* Desmond Barel Hirshfield, *b.* 1913, *m.*

1979 *Holderness,* Richard Frederick Wood, PC, *b.* 1920, *m.*

1991 *Hollick,* Clive Richard Hollick, *b.* 1945, *m.*

1990 *Holme of Cheltenham,* Richard Gordon Holme, CBE, *b.* 1936, *m.*

1974 *Home of the Hirsel,* Alexander Frederick Douglas-Home, KT, PC, *b.* 1903, *w.*

1979 *Hooson,* (Hugh) Emlyn Hooson, QC, *b.* 1925, *m.*

1974 *Houghton of Sowerby,* (Arthur Leslie Noel) Douglas Houghton, CH, PC, *b.* 1898, *m.*

1992 *Howe of Aberavon,* (Richard Edward) Geoffrey Howe, PC, QC, *b.* 1926, *m.*

1992 *Howell,* Denis Herbert Howell, PC, *b.* 1923, *m.*

1978 *Howie of Troon,* William Howie, *b.* 1924, *m.*

1961 *Hughes,* William Hughes, CBE, PC, *b.* 1911, *m.*

1966 *Hunt,* (Henry Cecil) John Hunt, KG, CBE, DSO, *b.* 1910, *m.*

1980 *Hunt of Tanworth,* John Joseph Benedict Hunt, GCB, *b.* 1919, *m.*

1978 *Hunter of Newington,* Robert Brockie Hunter, MBE, FRCP, *b.* 1915, *m.*

1978 *Hutchinson of Lullington,* Jeremy Nicolas Hutchinson, QC, *b.* 1915, *m.*

1982 *Ingrow,* John Aked Taylor, OBE, TD, *b.* 1917, *m.*

1987 *Irvine of Lairg,* Alexander Andrew Mackay Irvine, QC, *b.* 1940, *m.*

1968 *Jacques,* John Henry Jacques, *b.* 1905, *m.*

1988 *Jakobovits,* Immanuel Jakobovits, *b.* 1921, *m.*

1987 *Jay,* Douglas Patrick Thomas Jay, PC, *b.* 1907, *m.*

1987 *Jenkin of Roding,* (Charles) Patrick (Fleeming) Jenkin, PC, *b.* 1926, *m.*

1987 *Jenkins of Hillhead,* Roy Harris Jenkins, PC, *b.* 1920, *m.*

1981 *Jenkins of Putney,* Hugh Gater Jenkins, *b.* 1908, *w.*

1981 *John-Mackie,* John John-Mackie, *b.* 1909, *m.*

1987 *Johnston of Rockport,* Charles Collier Johnston, TD, *b.* 1915, *m.*

Created

1987 *Joseph,* Keith Sinjohn Joseph, CH, PC, *b.* 1918, *m.*

1991 *Judd,* Frank Ashcroft Judd, *b.* 1935, *m.*

1976 *Kagan,* Joseph Kagan, *b.* 1915, *m.*

1980 *Keith of Castleacre,* Kenneth Alexander Keith, *b.* 1916, *m.*

1985 *Kimball,* Marcus Richard Kimball, *b.* 1928, *m.*

1983 *King of Wartnaby,* John Leonard King, *b.* 1918, *m.*

1993 *Kingsdown,* Robert (Robin) Leigh-Pemberton, PC, *b.* 1927, *m.*

1965 *Kings Norton,* Harold Roxbee Cox, ph.D., FEng., *b.* 1902, *m.*

1975 *Kirkhill,* John Farquharson Smith, *b.* 1930, *m.*

1974 *Kissin,* Harry Kissin, *b.* 1912, *m.*

1987 *Knights,* Philip Douglas Knights, CBE, QPM, *b.* 1920, *m.*

1991 *Laing of Dunphail,* Hector Laing, *b.* 1923, *m.*

1990 *Lane of Horsell,* Peter Stewart Lane, *b.* 1925, *w.*

1992 *Lawson of Blaby,* Nigel Lawson, PC, *b.* 1932, *m.*

1979 *Lever of Manchester,* Harold Lever, PC, *b.* 1914, *m.*

1982 *Lewin,* Terence Thornton Lewin, KG, GCB, LVO, DSC, *Admiral of the Fleet, b.* 1920, *m.*

1989 *Lewis of Newnham,* Jack Lewis, FRS, *b.* 1928, *m.*

1974 *Lovell-Davis,* Peter Lovell Lovell-Davis, *b.* 1924, *m.*

1979 *Lowry,* Robert Lynd Erskine Lowry, PC, PC(NI), *b.* 1919, *w. Lord of Appeal in Ordinary.*

1984 *McAlpine of West Green,* (Robert) Alistair McAlpine, *b.* 1942, *m.*

1988 *Macaulay of Bragar,* Donald Macaulay, QC, *b.* 1933.

1975 *McCarthy,* William Edward John McCarthy, *b.* 1925, *m.*

1976 *McCluskey,* John Herbert McCluskey, *b.* 1929, *m.*

1989 *McColl of Dulwich,* Ian McColl, FRCS, FRCSE, *b.* 1933, *m.*

1966 *McFadzean,* William Hunter McFadzean, KT, *b.* 1903, *m.*

1991 *Macfarlane of Bearsden,* Norman Somerville Macfarlane, *b.* 1926, *m.*

1978 *McGregor of Durris,* Oliver Ross McGregor, *b.* 1921, *m.*

1982 *McIntosh of Haringey,* Andrew Robert McIntosh, *b.* 1933, *m.*

1991 *Mackay of Ardbrecknish,* John Jackson Mackay, *b.* 1938, *m.*

1979 *Mackay of Clashfern,* James Peter Hymers Mackay, PC, *b.* 1927, *m. Lord High Chancellor.*

1988 *Mackenzie-Stuart,* Alexander John Mackenzie Stuart, , *b.* 1924, *m.*

1974 *Mackie of Benshie,* George Yull Mackie, CBE, DSO, DFC, *b.* 1919, *m.*

1982 *MacLehose of Beoch,* (Crawford) Murray MacLehose, KT, GBE, KCMG, KCVO, *b.* 1917, *m.*

1967 *Mais,* Alan Raymond Mais, GBE, TD, ERD, FEng., *b.* 1911, *m.*

1991 *Marlesford,* Mark Shuldham Schreiber, *b.* 1931, *m.*

1981 *Marsh,* Richard William Marsh, PC, *b.* 1928, *m.*

1985 *Marshall of Goring,* Walter Charles Marshall, CBE, FRS, *b.* 1932, *m.*

1987 *Mason of Barnsley,* Roy Mason, PC, *b.* 1924, *m.*

1980 *Matthews,* Victor Collin Matthews, *b.* 1919, *m.*

1983 *Maude of Stratford-upon-Avon,* Angus Edmund Upton Maude, TD, PC, *b.* 1912, *m.*

1981 *Mayhew,* Christopher Paget Mayhew, *b.* 1915, *m.*

1985 *Mellish,* Robert Joseph Mellish, PC, *b.* 1913, *m.*

1993 *Menuhin,* Yehudi Menuhin, OM, KBE, *b.* 1916, *m.*

1992 *Merlyn-Rees,* Merlyn Merlyn-Rees, PC, *b.* 1920, *m.*

1978 *Mishcon,* Victor Mishcon, *b.* 1915, *m.*

1981 *Molloy,* William John Molloy, *b.* 1918.

Created

1992   *Moore of Lower Marsh,* John Edward Michael Moore, PC, *b.* 1937, *m.*

1986   *Moore of Wolvercote,* Philip Brian Cecil Moore, GCB, GCVO, CMG, PC, *b.* 1921, *m.*

1990   *Morris of Castle Morris,* Brian Robert Morris, D.Phil., *b.* 1930, *m.*

1985   *Morton of Shuna,* Hugh Drennan Baird Morton, *b.* 1930, *m.*

1971   *Moyola,* James Dawson Chichester-Clark, PC (NI), *b.* 1923, *m.*

1984   *Mulley,* Frederick William Mulley, PC, *b.* 1918, *m.*

1985   *Murray of Epping Forest,* Lionel Murray, OBE, PC, *b.* 1922, *m.*

1964   *Murray of Newhaven,* Keith Anderson Hope Murray, KCB, Ph.D., *b.* 1903.

1979   *Murton of Lindisfarne,* (Henry) Oscar Murton, OBE, TD, PC, *b.* 1914, *m.*

1975   *Northfield,* (William) Donald Chapman, *b.* 1923.

1966   *Nugent of Guildford,* (George) Richard (Hodges) Nugent, PC, *b.* 1907, *m.*

1973   *O'Brien of Lothbury,* Leslie Kenneth O'Brien, GBE, PC, *b.* 1908, *m.*

1976   *Oram,* Albert Edward Oram, *b.* 1913, *m.*

1971   *Orr-Ewing,* (Charles) Ian Orr-Ewing, OBE, *b.* 1912, *m.*

1992   *Owen,* David Anthony Llewellyn Owen, PC, *b.* 1938, *m.*

1991   *Palumbo,* Peter Garth Palumbo, *b.* 1935, *m.*

1992   *Parkinson,* Cecil Edward Parkinson, PC, *b.* 1931, *m.*

1975   *Parry,* Gordon Samuel David Parry, *b.* 1925, *m.*

1990   *Pearson of Rannoch,* Malcolm Everard MacLaren Pearson, *b.* 1942, *m.*

1979   *Perry of Walton,* Walter Laing Macdonald Perry, OBE, FRS, FRSE, *b.* 1921, *m.*

1987   *Peston,* Maurice Harry Peston, *b.* 1931, *m.*

1983   *Peyton of Yeovil,* John Wynne William Peyton, PC, *b.* 1919, *m.*

1975   *Pitt of Hampstead,* David Thomas Pitt, *b.* 1913, *m.*

1992   *Plant of Highfield,* Prof. Raymond Plant, Ph.D., *b.* 1945, *m.*

1959   *Plowden,* Edwin Noel Plowden, GBE, KCB, *b.* 1907, *m.*

1987   *Plumb,* (Charles) Henry Plumb, MEP, *b.* 1925, *m.*

1981   *Plummer of St Marylebone,* (Arthur) Desmond (Herne) Plummer, TD, *b.* 1914, *m.*

1973   *Porritt,* Arthur Espie Porritt, GCMG, GCVO, CBE, *b.* 1900, *m.*

1990   *Porter of Luddenham,* George Porter, OM, FRS, *b.* 1920, *m.*

1992   *Prentice,* Reginald Ernest Prentice, PC, *b.* 1923, *m.*

1987   *Prior,* James Michael Leathes Prior, PC, *b.* 1927, *m.*

1975   *Pritchard,* Derek Wilbraham Pritchard, *b.* 1910, *m.*

1982   *Prys-Davies,* Gwilym Prys Prys-Davies, *b.* 1923, *m.*

1987   *Pym,* Francis Leslie Pym, MC, PC, *b.* 1922, *m.*

1982   *Quinton,* Anthony Meredith Quinton, *b.* 1925, *m.*

1978   *Rawlinson of Ewell,* Peter Anthony Grayson Rawlinson, PC, QC, *b.* 1919, *m.*

1976   *Rayne,* Max Rayne, *b.* 1918, *m.*

1983   *Rayner,* Derek George Rayner, *b.* 1926.

1987   *Rees,* Peter Wynford Innes Rees, PC, QC, *b.* 1926, *m.*

1988   *Rees-Mogg,* William Rees-Mogg, *b.* 1928, *m.*

1970   *Reigate,* John Kenyon Vaughan-Morgan, PC, *b.* 1905, *m.*

1991   *Renfrew of Kaimsthorn,* (Andrew) Colin Renfrew, FBA, *b.* 1937, *m.*

1979   *Renton,* David Lockhart-Mure Renton, KBE, TD, PC, QC, *b.* 1908, *w.*

Created

1990   *Richard,* Ivor Seward Richard, PC, QC, *b.* 1932, *m.*

1979   *Richardson,* John Samuel Richardson, LVO, MD, FRCP, *b.* 1910, *w.*

1983   *Richardson of Duntisbourne,* Gordon William Humphreys Richardson, KG, MBE, TD, PC, *b.* 1915, *m.*

1987   *Rippon of Hexham,* (Aubrey) Geoffrey (Frederick) Rippon, PC, QC, *b.* 1924, *m.*

1992   *Rix,* Brian Norman Roger Rix, CBE, *b.* 1924, *m.*

1961   *Robens of Woldingham,* Alfred Robens, PC, *b.* 1910, *m.*

1992   *Rodger of Earlsferry,* Alan Ferguson Rodger, PC, QC, FBA, *b.* 1944, *Lord Advocate.*

1992   *Rodgers of Quarry Bank,* William Thomas Rodgers, PC, *b.* 1928, *m.*

1977   *Roll of Ipsden,* Eric Roll, KCMG, CB, *b.* 1907, *m.*

1991   *Runcie,* Rt Revd Robert Alexander Kennedy Runcie, MC, PC, Royal Victoria Chain, *b.* 1921, *m.*

1975   *Ryder of Eaton Hastings,* Sydney Thomas Franklin (Don) Ryder, *b.* 1916, *m.*

1962   *Sainsbury,* Alan John Sainsbury, *b.* 1902, *w.*

1989   *Sainsbury of Preston Candover,* John Davan Sainsbury, KG, *b.* 1927, *m.*

1987   *St John of Fawsley,* Norman Antony Francis St John-Stevas, PC, *b.* 1929.

1985   *Sanderson of Bowden,* Charles Russell Sanderson, *b.* 1933, *m.*

1979   *Scanlon,* Hugh Parr Scanlon, *b.* 1913, *m.*

1976   *Schon,* Frank Schon, *b.* 1912, *m.*

1978   *Sefton of Garston,* William Henry Sefton, *b.* 1915, *m.*

1958   *Shackleton,* Edward Arthur Alexander Shackleton, KG, OBE, PC, *b.* 1911, *m.*

1989   *Sharp of Grimsdyke,* Eric Sharp, CBE, *b.* 1916, *m.*

1959   *Shawcross,* Hartley William Shawcross, GBE, PC, QC, *b.* 1902, *w.*

1980   *Sieff of Brimpton,* Marcus Joseph Sieff, OBE, *b.* 1913, *m.*

1971   *Simon of Glaisdale,* Jocelyn Edward Salis Simon, PC, *b.* 1911, *m.*

1991   *Skidelsky,* Robert Jacob Alexander Skidelsky, D.Phil., *b.* 1939, *m.*

1978   *Smith,* Rodney Smith, KBE, FRCS, *b.* 1914, *m.*

1965   *Soper,* Revd Donald Oliver Soper, Ph.D., *b.* 1903, *m.*

1990   *Soulsby of Swaffham Prior,* Ernest Jackson Lawson Soulsby, Ph.D., *b.* 1926, *m.*

1983   *Stallard,* Albert William Stallard, *b.* 1921, *m.*

1991   *Sterling of Plaistow,* Jeffrey Maurice Sterling, CBE, *b.* 1934, *m.*

1987   *Stevens of Ludgate,* David Robert Stevens, *b.* 1936, *m.*

1992   *Stewartby,* (Bernard Harold) Ian (Halley) Stewart, RD, PC, FBA, FRSE, *b.* 1935, *m.*

1981   *Stodart of Leaston,* James Anthony Stodart, PC, *b.* 1916, *m.*

1983   *Stoddart of Swindon,* David Leonard Stoddart, *b.* 1926, *m.*

1969   *Stokes,* Donald Gresham Stokes, TD, FEng., *b.* 1914, *m.*

1971   *Tanlaw,* Simon Brooke Mackay, *b.* 1934, *m.*

1978   *Taylor of Blackburn,* Thomas Taylor, CBE, *b.* 1929, *m.*

1992   *Taylor of Gosforth,* Peter Murray Taylor, PC, *b.* 1930, *m.*, *Lord Chief Justice of England.*

1968   *Taylor of Gryfe,* Thomas Johnston Taylor, *b.* 1912, *m.*

1982   *Taylor of Hadfield,* Francis Taylor, *b.* 1905, *m.*

1992   *Tebbit,* Norman Beresford Tebbit, CH, PC, *b.* 1931, *m.*

Created
1971   *Seear*, (Beatrice) Nancy Seear, PC, *b.* 1913.
1967   *Serota*, Beatrice Serota, DBE, *b.* 1919, *m.*
1973   *Sharples*, Pamela Sharples, *b.* 1923, *m.*
1974   *Stedman*, Phyllis Stedman, OBE, *b.* 1916, *w.*
1992   *Thatcher*, Margaret Hilda Thatcher, OM, PC, *b.* 1925, *m.*
1980   *Trumpington*, Jean Alys Barker, *b.* 1922, *w.*
1985   *Turner of Camden*, Muriel Winifred Turner, *b.* 1927, *m.*

Created
1974   *Vickers*, Joan Helen Vickers, DBE, *b.* 1907.
1985   *Warnock*, Helen Mary Warnock, DBE, *b.* 1924, *m.*
1970   *White*, Eirene Lloyd White, *b.* 1909, *w.*
1993   *Williams of Crosby*, Shirley Vivien Teresa Brittain Williams, PC, *b.* 1930, *m.*
1971   *Young*, Janet Mary Young, PC, *b.* 1926, *m.*

Lords Spiritual

The Lords Spiritual are the Archbishops of Canterbury and York and 24 diocesan bishops of the Church of England. The Bishops of London, Durham and Winchester always have seats in the House of Lords; the other 21 seats are filled by the remaining diocesan bishops in order of seniority. The Bishop of Sodor and Man and the Bishop of Gibraltar are not eligible to sit in the House of Lords.

ARCHBISHOPS

Style, The Most Revd and Right Hon. the Lord Archbishop of __
Addressed as Archbishop *or*, Your Grace

Introduced to House of Lords
1991   *Canterbury* (103rd), George Leonard Carey, PC, PH.D., *b.* 1935, *m. Consecrated Bishop of Bath and Wells* 1987, *trans.* 1991.
1973   *York* (95th), John Stapylton Habgood, PC, PH.D., *b.* 1927, *m. Consecrated Bishop of Durham* 1973, *trans.* 1983.

BISHOPS

Style, The Right Revd the Lord Bishop of __
Addressed as My Lord
elected = date of election as diocesan bishop

Introduced to House of Lords
1990   *London* (131st), David Michael Hope, PC, *b.* 1940, *cons.* 1985, *elected* 1985, *trans.* 1991.
1984   *Durham* (92nd), David Edward Jenkins, *b.* 1925, *m.*, *cons.* 1984, *elected* 1984.
1982   *Winchester* (95th), Colin Clement Walter James, *b.* 1926, *m.*, *cons.* 1973, *elected* 1977, *trans.* 1985.
1979   *Chichester* (102nd), Eric Waldram Kemp, DD, *b.* 1915, *m.*, *cons.* 1974, *elected* 1974.
1980   *Liverpool* (6th), David Stuart Sheppard, *b.* 1929, *m.*, *cons.* 1969, *elected* 1975.
1984   *Ripon* (11th), David Nigel de Lorentz Young, *b.* 1931, *m.*, *cons.* 1977, *elected* 1977.
1985   *Chelmsford* (7th), John Waine, *b.* 1930, *m.*, *cons.* 1975, *elected* 1978, *trans.* 1986.
1985   *Sheffield* (5th), David Ramsay Lunn, *b.* 1930, *cons.* 1980, *elected* 1980.
1985   *St Albans* (8th), John Bernard Taylor, *b.* 1929, *m.*, *cons.* 1980, *elected* 1980.

1985   *Newcastle* (10th), Andrew Alexander Kenny Graham, *b.* 1929, *cons.* 1977, *elected* 1981.
1986   *Salisbury* (76th), John Austin Baker, *b.* 1928, *m.*, *cons.* 1982, *elected* 1982.
1987   *Worcester* (111th), Philip Harold Ernest Goodrich, *b.* 1929, *m.*, *cons.* 1973, *elected* 1982.
1987   *Chester* (39th), Michael Alfred Baughen, *b.* 1930, *m.*, *cons.* 1982, *elected* 1982.
1988   *Guildford* (7th), Michael Edgar Adie, *b.* 1929, *m.*, *cons.* 1983, *elected* 1983.
1988   *Southwark* (7th), Robert Kerr Williamson, *b.* 1932, *m.*, *cons.* 1984, *elected* 1984, *trans.* 1991.
1989   *Lichfield* (97th), Keith Norman Sutton, *b.* 1934, *m.*, *cons.* 1978, *elected* 1984.
1989   *Peterborough* (36th), William John Westwood, *b.* 1925, *m.*, *cons.* 1975, *elected* 1984.
1989   *Portsmouth* (7th), Timothy John Bavin, *b.* 1935, *cons.* 1974, *elected* 1985.
1989   *Exeter* (69th), (Geoffrey) Hewlett Thompson, *b.* 1929, *m.*, *cons.* 1974, *elected* 1985.
1990   *Bristol* (54th), Barry Rogerson, *b.* 1936, *m.*, *cons.* 1979, *elected* 1985.
1991   *Coventry* (7th), Simon Barrington-Ward, *b.* 1930, *m.*, *cons.* 1985, *elected* 1985.
1991   *Norwich* (70th), Peter John Nott, *b.* 1933, *m.*, *cons.* 1977, *elected* 1985.
1991   *St Edmundsbury and Ipswich* (8th), John Dennis, *b.* 1931, *m.*, *cons.* 1979, *elected* 1986.
1993   *Lincoln* (70th), Robert Maynard Hardy, *b.* 1936, *m.*, *cons.* 1980, *elected* 1986.

Bishops awaiting seats, in order of seniority
Oxford (41st), Richard Douglas Harries, *b.* 1936, *m.*, *cons.* 1987, *elected* 1987.
Birmingham (7th), Mark Santer, *b.* 1936, *m.*, *cons.* 1981, *elected* 1987.
Derby (5th), Peter Spencer Dawes, *b.* 1928, *m.*, *cons.* 1988, *elected* 1988.
Southwell (9th), Patrick Burnet Harris, *b.* 1934, *m.*, *cons.* 1973, *elected* 1988.
Rochester (105th), (Anthony) Michael (Arnold) Turnbull, *b.* 1935, *m.*, *cons.* 1988, *elected* 1988.
Blackburn (7th), Alan David Chesters, *b.* 1937, *m.*, *cons.* 1989, *elected* 1989.
Carlisle (65th), Ian Harland, *b.* 1932, *m.*, *cons.* 1985, *elected* 1989.
Truro (13th), Michael Thomas Ball, *b.* 1932, *cons.* 1980, *elected* 1990.
Ely (67th), Stephen Whitefield Sykes, *b.* 1939, *m.*, *cons.* 1990, *elected* 1990.

Hereford (103rd), John Keith Oliver, *b.* 1935, *m.*, *cons.* 1990, *elected* 1990.
Leicester (5th), Thomas Frederick Butler, *b.* 1940, *m.*, *cons.* 1985, *elected* 1991.
Bath and Wells (77th), James Lawton Thompson, *b.* 1936, *m.*, *cons.* 1978, *elected* 1991.
Wakefield (11th), Nigel Simeon McCulloch, *b.* 1942, *m.*, *cons.* 1986, *elected* 1992.

Bradford (8th), David James Smith, *b.* 1935, *m.*, *cons.* 1987, *elected* 1992.
Manchester (10th), Christopher John Mayfield, *b.* 1935, *m.*, *cons.* 1985, *elected* 1993.
Gloucester (39th), David Edward Bentley, *b.* 1935, *m.*, *cons.* 1986, *elected* 1993.

Prime Ministers since 1782

Over the centuries there has been some variation in the determination of the dates of appointment of Prime Ministers. Where possible, the date given is that on which a new Prime Minister kissed the Sovereign's hands and accepted the commission to form a ministry. However, until the middle of the 19th century the dating of a commission or transfer of seals could be the date of taking office. Where the composition of the Government changed, e.g. became a coalition, but the Prime Minister remained the same, the date of the change of government is given.

The Marquess of Rockingham, *Whig*, 27 March 1782
The Earl of Shelburne, *Whig*, 4 July 1782
The Duke of Portland, *Coalition*, 2 April 1783
William Pitt, *Tory*, 19 December 1783
Henry Addington, *Tory*, 17 March 1801
William Pitt, *Tory*, 10 May 1804
The Lord Grenville, *Whig*, 11 February 1806
The Duke of Portland, *Tory*, 31 March 1807
Spencer Perceval, *Tory*, 4 October 1809
The Earl of Liverpool, *Tory*, 8 June 1812
George Canning, *Tory*, 10 April 1827
Viscount Goderich, *Tory*, 31 August 1827
The Duke of Wellington, *Tory*, 22 January 1828
The Earl Grey, *Whig*, 22 November 1830
The Viscount Melbourne, *Whig*, 16 July 1834
The Duke of Wellington, *Tory*, 17 November 1834
Sir Robert Peel, *Tory*, 10 December 1834
The Viscount Melbourne, *Whig*, 18 April 1835
Sir Robert Peel, *Tory*, 30 August 1841
Lord John Russell (subsequently the Earl Russell), *Whig*, 30 June 1846
The Earl of Derby, *Tory*, 23 February 1852
The Earl of Aberdeen, *Peelite*, 19 December 1852
The Viscount Palmerston, *Liberal*, 6 February 1855
The Earl of Derby, *Conservative*, 20 February 1858
The Viscount Palmerston, *Liberal*, 12 June 1859
The Earl Russell, *Liberal*, 29 October 1865

The Earl of Derby, *Conservative*, 28 June 1866
Benjamin Disraeli, *Conservative*, 27 February 1868
William Gladstone, *Liberal*, 3 December 1868
Benjamin Disraeli, *Conservative*, 20 February 1874
William Gladstone, *Liberal*, 23 April 1880
The Marquess of Salisbury, *Conservative*, 23 June 1885
William Gladstone, *Liberal*, 1 February 1886
The Marquess of Salisbury, *Conservative*, 25 July 1886
William Gladstone, *Liberal*, 15 August 1892
The Earl of Rosebery, *Liberal*, 5 March 1894
The Marquess of Salisbury, *Conservative*, 25 June 1895
Arthur Balfour, *Conservative*, 12 July 1902
Sir Henry Campbell-Bannerman, *Liberal*, 5 December 1905
Herbert Asquith, *Liberal*, 7 April 1908
Herbert Asquith, *Coalition*, 25 May 1915
David Lloyd-George, *Coalition*, 7 December 1916
Andrew Bonar Law, *Conservative*, 23 October 1922
Stanley Baldwin, *Conservative*, 22 May 1923
Ramsay MacDonald, *Labour*, 22 January 1924
Stanley Baldwin, *Conservative*, 4 November 1924
Ramsay MacDonald, *Labour*, 5 June 1929
Ramsay MacDonald, *Coalition*, 24 August 1931
Stanley Baldwin, *Coalition*, 7 June 1935
Neville Chamberlain, *Coalition*, 28 May 1937
Winston Churchill, *Coalition*, 10 May 1940
Winston Churchill, *Conservative*, 23 May 1945
Clement Attlee, *Labour*, 26 July 1945
Sir Winston Churchill, *Conservative*, 26 October 1951
Sir Anthony Eden, *Conservative*, 6 April 1955
Harold Macmillan, *Conservative*, 10 January 1957
Sir Alec Douglas-Home, *Conservative*, 19 October 1963
Harold Wilson, *Labour*, 16 October 1964
Edward Heath, *Conservative*, 19 June 1970
Harold Wilson, *Labour*, 4 March 1974
James Callaghan, *Labour*, 5 April 1976
Margaret Thatcher, *Conservative*, 4 May 1979
John Major, *Conservative*, 28 November 1990

COURTESY TITLES

From this list it will be seen that, for example, the Marquess of Blandford is heir to the Dukedom of Marlborough, and Viscount Amberley to the Earldom of Russell. Titles of second heirs are also given, and the courtesy title of the father of a second heir is indicated by *; e.g., Earl of Burlington, eldest son of *Marquess of Hartington For forms of address, *see* page 220.

MARQUESSES

Blandford – *Marlborough, D.*
Bowmont and Cessford – *Roxburghe, D.*
Douglas and Clydesdale – *Hamilton, D.*
*Douro – *Wellington, D.*
*Graham – *Montrose, D.*
Granby – *Rutland, D.*
Hamilton – *Abercorn, D.*
*Hartington – *Devonshire, D.*
*Kildare – *Leinster, D.*
Lorne – *Argyll, D.*
*Tavistock – *Bedford, D.*
*Worcester – *Beaufort, D.*

EARLS

*Aboyne – *Huntly, M.*
Altamont – *Sligo, M.*
Ancram – *Lothian, M.*
Arundel and Surrey – *Norfolk, D.*
*Bective – *Headfort, M.*
*Belfast – *Donegall, M.*
*Brecknock – *Camden, M.*
Burford – *St Albans, D.*
Burlington – **Hartington, M.*
*Cardigan – *Ailesbury, M.*
Cassillis – *Ailsa, M.*
Compton – *Northampton, M.*
*Dalkeith – *Buccleuch, D.*
*Dumfries – *Bute, M.*
*Euston – *Grafton, D.*
Glamorgan – **Worcester, M.*
Grosvenor – *Westminster, D.*
*Haddo – *Aberdeen and Temair, M.*
Hillsborough – *Downshire, M.*
Hopetoun – *Linlithgow, M.*
March and Kinrara – *Richmond, D.*
*Mount Charles – *Conyngham, M.*
Mornington – **Douro, M.*
Mulgrave – *Normanby, M.*
Offaly – **Kildare, M.*
Ronaldshay – *Zetland, M.*
*St Andrews – *Kent, D.*
*Shelburne – *Lansdowne, M.*
*Southesk – *Fife, D.*

Sunderland – **Blandford, M.*
*Tyrone – *Waterford, M.*
Ulster – *Gloucester, D.*
*Uxbridge – *Anglesey, M.*
Wiltshire – *Winchester, M.*
Yarmouth – *Hertford, M.*

VISCOUNTS

Amberley – *Russell, E.*
Andover – *Suffolk and Berkshire, E.*
Anson – *Lichfield, E.*
Asquith – *Oxford & Asquith, E.*
Boringdon – *Morley, E.*
Borodale – *Beatty, E.*
Boyle – *Shannon, E.*
Brocas – *Jellicoe, E.*
Calne and Calstone – **Shelburne, E.*
Campden – *Gainsborough, E.*
Carlow – *Portarlington, E.*
Carlton – *Wharncliffe, E.*
Castlereagh – *Londonderry, M.*
Chelsea – *Cadogan, E.*
Chewton – *Waldegrave, E.*
Chichester – **Belfast, E.*
Clanfield – *Peel, E.*
Clive – *Powis, E.*
Coke – *Leicester, E.*
Corry – *Belmore, E.*
Corvedale – *Baldwin of Bewdley, E.*
Cranborne – *Salisbury, M.*
Cranley – *Onslow, E.*
Crichton – *Erne, E.*
Crowhurst – *Cottenham, E.*
Dalrymple – *Stair, E.*
Dangan – *Cowley, E.*
Dawick – *Haig, E.*
Deerhurst – *Coventry, E.*
Drumlanrig – *Queensberry, M.*
Dunwich – *Stradbroke, E.*
Dupplin – *Kinnoull, E.*
Ebrington – *Fortescue, E.*
Ednam – *Dudley, E.*
Emlyn – *Cawdor, E.*
Encombe – *Eldon, E.*
Ennismore – *Listowel, E.*
Enfield – *Strafford, E.*
Erleigh – *Reading, M.*
Feilding – *Denbigh, E.*
Fincastle – *Dunmore, E.*

FitzHarris – *Malmesbury, E.*
Folkestone – *Radnor, E.*
Forbes – *Granard, E.*
Garmoyle – *Cairns, E.*
Garnock – *Lindsay, E.*
Glandine – *Norbury, E.*
Glenapp – *Inchcape, E.*
Glentworth – *Limerick, E.*
Grimstone – *Verulam, E.*
Gwynedd – *Lloyd George of Dwyfor, E.*
Hawkesbury – *Liverpool, E.*
Ikerrin – *Carrick, E.*
Ingestre – *Shrewsbury, E.*
Ipswich – **Euston, E.*
Jocelyn – *Roden, E.*
Kelburn – *Glasgow, E.*
Kingsborough – *Kingston, E.*
Knebworth – *Lytton, E.*
Lascelles – *Harewood, E.*
Lewisham – *Dartmouth, E.*
Linley – *Snowdon, E.*
Loftus – *Ely, M.*
Lowther – *Lonsdale, E.*
Lumley – *Scarbrough, E.*
Lymington – *Portsmouth, E.*
Macmillan of Ovenden – *Stockton, E.*
Maidstone – *Winchilsea and Nottingham, E.*
Maitland – *Lauderdale, E.*
Malden – *Essex, E.*
Mandeville – *Manchester, D.*
Medina – *Milford Haven, M.*
Melgund – *Minto, E.*
Merton – *Nelson, E.*
Moore – *Drogheda, E.*
Morpeth – *Carlisle, E.*
Mount Stuart – **Dumfries, E.*
Newport – *Bradford, E.*
Newry and Mourne – *Kilmorey, E.*
Northland – *Ranfurly, E.*
Parker – *Macclesfield, E.*
Perceval – *Egmont, E.*
Petersham – *Harrington, E.*
Pollington – *Mexborough, E.*
Raynham – *Townshend, M.*
Reidhaven – *Seafield, E.*
Ruthven of Canberra – *Gowrie, E.*
St Cyres – *Iddesleigh, E.*
Sandon – *Harrowby, E.*
Savernake – **Cardigan, E.*

Slane – **Mount Charles, E.*
Somerton – *Normanton, E.*
Stopford – *Courtown, E.*
Stormont – *Mansfield, E.*
Strathallan – *Perth, E.*
Stuart – *Castle Stewart, E.*
Suirdale – *Donoughmore, E.*
Tamworth – *Ferrers, E.*
Tarbat – *Cromartie, E.*
Vaughan – *Lisburne, E.*
Villiers – *Jersey, E.*
Weymouth – *Bath, M.*
Windsor – *Plymouth, E.*
Wolmer – *Selborne, E.*
Woodstock – *Portland, E.*

BARONS (LORD –)

Aberdour – *Morton, E.*
Apsley – *Bathurst, E.*
Ardee – *Meath, E.*
Ashley – *Shaftesbury, E.*
Balgonie – *Leven & Melville, E.*
Balniel – *Crawford and Balcarres, E.*
Berriedale – *Caithness, E.*
Bingham – *Lucan, E.*
Binning – *Haddington, E.*
Brooke – *Warwick, E.*
Bruce – *Elgin, E.*
Buckhurst – *De La Warr, E.*
Burghersh – *Westmorland, E.*
Burghley – *Exeter, M.*
Cardross – *Buchan, E.*
Carnegie – **Southesk, E.*
Clifton of Rathmore – *Darnley, E.*
Cochrane – *Dundonald, E.*
Courtenay – *Devon, E.*
Dalmeny – *Rosebery, E.*
Doune – *Moray, E.*
Downpatrick – **St Andrews, E.*
Eliot – *St Germans, E.*
Erskine – *Mar & Kellie, E.*
Eskdail – **Dalkeith, E.*
Fintrie – **Graham, M.*
Formartine – **Haddo, E.*
Gillford – *Clanwilliam, E.*
Glamis – *Strathmore, E.*
Greenock – *Cathcart, E.*
Guernsey – *Aylesford, E.*
Hay – *Erroll, E.*
Herbert – *Pembroke, E.*
Howland – **Tavistock, M.*
Hyde – *Clarendon, E.*

Inverurie – *Kintore, E.*
Irwin – *Halifax, E.*
Johnstone – *Annandale and Hartfell, E.*
Kenlis – **Bective, E.*
Langton – *Temple of Stowe, E.*
La Poer – **Tyrone, E.*
Leslie – *Rothes, E.*
Leveson – *Granville, E.*
Loughborough – *Rosslyn, E.*

Maltravers – **Arundel and Surrey, E.*
Mauchline – *Loudoun, C.*
Medway – *Cranbrook, E.*
Montgomerie – *Eglinton and Winton, E.*
Moreton – *Ducie, E.*
Naas – *Mayo, E.*
Neidpath – *Wemyss & March, E.*
Norreys – *Lindsey & Abingdon, E.*

North – *Guilford, E.*
Ogilvy – *Airlie, E.*
Oxmantown – *Rosse, E.*
Paget de Beaudesert – **Uxbridge, E.*
Porchester – *Carnarvon, E.*
Ramsay – *Dalhousie, E.*
Romsey – *Mountbatten of Burma, C.*
Rosehill – *Northesk, E.*
Scrymgeour – *Dundee, E.*

Seymour – *Somerset, D.*
Strathnaver – *Sutherland, C.*
Wodehouse – *Kimberley, E.*
Worsley – *Yarborough, E.*

PEERS' SURNAMES WHICH DIFFER FROM THEIR TITLES

The following symbols indicate the rank of the peer holding each title:
C. Countess
D. Duke
E. Earl
M. Marquess
V. Viscount
* Life Peer

Where no designation is given, the title is that of an hereditary Baron or Baroness

Abney-Hastings – *Loudoun, C.*
Acheson – *Gosford, E.*
Adderley – *Norton*
Addington – *Sidmouth, V.*
Agar – *Normanton, E.*
Aitken – *Beaverbrook*
Akers-Douglas – *Chilston, V.*
Alexander – *A. of Potterhill**
Alexander – *A. of Tunis, E.*
Alexander – *A. of Weedon**
Alexander – *A. of Caledon, E.*
Allen – *A. of Abbeydale**
Allen – *Croham**
Allanson-Winn – *Headley*
Allsopp – *Hindlip*
Amery – *A. of Lustleigh**
Anderson – *Waverley, V.*
Annesley – *Valentia, V.*
Anson – *Lichfield, E.*
Archer – *A. of Sandwell**
Archer – *A. of Weston-super-Mare**
Armstrong – *A. of Ilminster**
Armstrong-Jones – *Snowdon, E.*
Arthur – *Glenarthur*
Arundell – *Talbot of Malahide*
Ashley – *A. of Stoke**
Ashley-Cooper – *Shaftesbury, E.*
Ashton – *A. of Hyde*
Asquith – *Oxford & Asquith, E.*

Assheton – *Clitheroe*
Astley – *Hastings*
Astor – *A. of Hever*
Atkins – *Colnbrook**
Aubrey-Fletcher – *Braye*
Bailey – *Glanusk*
Baillie – *Burton*
Baillie Hamilton – *Haddington, E.*
Baldwin – *B. of Bewdley, E.*
Balfour – *B. of Inchrye*
Balfour – *Kinross*
Balfour – *Riverdale*
Bampfylde – *Poltimore*
Banbury – *B. of Southam*
Barber – *B. of Tewkesbury**
Baring – *Ashburton*
Baring – *Cromer, E.*
Baring – *Howick of Glendale*
Baring – *Northbrook*
Baring – *Revelstoke*
Barker – *Trumpington**
Barnes – *Gorell*
Barnewall – *Trimlestown*
Bathurst – *Bledisloe, V.*
Beauclerk – *St Albans, D.*
Beaumont – *Allendale, V.*
Beaumont – *B. of Whitley**
Beavan – *Ardwick**
Beckett – *Grimthorpe*
Bellow – *Bellwin**
Benn – *Stansgate, V.*
Bennet – *Tankerville, E.*
Bentinck – *Portland, E.*
Beresford – *Decies*
Beresford – *Waterford, M.*
Berry – *Camrose, V.*
Berry – *Hartwell**
Berry – *Kemsley, V.*
Bertie – *Lindsey, E.*
Best – *Wynford*
Bethell – *Westbury*
Bewicke-Copley – *Cromwell*
Bigham – *Mersey, V.*
Bigham – *Nairne*
Bingham – *Clanmorris*
Bingham – *Lucan, E.*
Blackwood – *Dufferin & Clandeboye*
Bligh – *Darnley, E.*

Bootle-Wilbraham – *Skelmersdale*
Boscawen – *Falmouth, V.*
Boston – *Boston of Faversham**
Bourke – *Mayo, E.*
Bowden – *Aylestone**
Bowes Lyon – *Strathmore, E.*
Bowyer – *Denham*
Boyd – *Kilmarnock*
Boyle – *Cork & Orrery, E.*
Boyle – *Glasgow, E.*
Boyle – *Shannon, E.*
Brabazon – *Meath, E.*
Braine – *B. of Wheatley**
Brand – *Hampden, V.*
Brandon – *B. of Oakbrook**
Brassey – *B. of Apethorpe*
Brett – *Esher, V.*
Bridge – *B. of Harwich**
Bridgeman – *Bradford, E.*
Brodrick – *Midleton, V.*
Brooke – *Alanbrooke, V.*
Brooke – *Brookeborough, V.*
Brooke – *B. of Ystradfellte**
Brooks – *B. of Tremorfa**
Brooks – *Crawshaw*
Brougham – *Brougham and Vaux*
Broughton – *Fairhaven*
Browne – *Kilmaine*
Browne – *Oranmore and Browne*
Browne – *Sligo, M.*
Bruce – *Aberdare*
Bruce – *Balfour of Burleigh*
Bruce – *B. of Donington**
Bruce – *Elgin and Kincardine, E.*
Brudenell-Bruce – *Ailesbury, M.*
Buchan – *Tweedsmuir*
Buckley – *Wrenbury*
Butler – *Carrick, E.*
Butler – *Dunboyne*
Butler – *Lanesborough, E.*
Butler – *Mountgarret, V.*
Butler – *Ormonde, M.*
Buxton – *B. of Alsa**
Byng – *Strafford, E.*
Byng – *Torrington, V.*

Callaghan – *C. of Cardiff**
Cameron – *C. of Lochbroom**
Campbell – *Argyll, D.*
Campbell – *Breadalbane and Holland, E.*
Campbell – *C. of Alloway**
Campbell – *C. of Croy**
Campbell – *C. of Eskan**
Campbell – *Cawdor, E.*
Campbell – *Colgrain*
Campbell – *Stratheden and Campbell*
Campbell-Gray – *Gray*
Canning – *Garvagh*
Capell – *Essex, E.*
Carington – *Carrington*
Carlisle – *C. of Bucklow**
Carmichael – *C. of Kelvingrove**
Carnegie – *Fife, D.*
Carnegie – *Northesk, E.*
Carr – *B. of Hadley**
Cary – *Falkland, V.*
Castle – *C. of Blackburn**
Caulfeild – *Charlemont, V.*
Cavendish – *C. of Furness**
Cavendish – *Chesham*
Cavendish – *Devonshire, D.*
Cavendish – *Waterpark*
Cayzer – *Rotherwick*
Cecil – *Amherst of Hackney*
Cecil – *Exeter, M.*
Cecil – *Rockley*
Cecil – *Salisbury, M.*
Chalker – *C. of Wallasey**
Chaloner – *Gisborough*
Chapman – *Northfield**
Charteris – *C. of Amisfield**
Charteris – *Wemyss and March, E.*
Cheshire – *Ryder of Warsaw**
Chetwynd-Talbot – *Shrewsbury, E.*
Chichester – *Donegall, M.*
Chichester-Clark – *Moyola**
Child-Villiers – *Jersey, E.*
Cholmondeley – *Delamere*
Chubb – *Hayter*
Clark – *C. of Kempston**
Clegg-Hill – *Hill, V.*

Clifford – *Clifford of Chudleigh*
Cochrane – *C. of Cults*
Cochrane – *Dundonald, E.*
Cocks – *C. of Hartcliffe*
Cocks – *Somers*
Cokayne – *Cullen of Ashbourne*
Coke – *Leicester, E.*
Cole – *Enniskillen, E.*
Collier – *Monkswell*
Colville – *Clydesmuir*
Colville – *C. of Culross, V.*
Compton – *Northampton, M.*
Conolly-Carew – *Carew*
Constantine – *C. of Stanmore**
Cooke – *C. of Islandreagh**
Cooper – *Norwich, V.*
Corbett – *Rowallan*
Courtenay – *Devon, E.*
Cox – *Kings Norton**
Craig – *C. of Radley**
Craig – *Craigavon, V.*
Crichton – *Erne, E.*
Crichton-Stuart – *Bute, M.*
Cripps – *Parmoor*
Crossley – *Somerleyton*
Cubitt – *Ashcombe*
Cunliffe-Lister – *Masham of Ilton**
Cunliffe-Lister – *Swinton, E.*
Curzon – *Howe, E.*
Curzon – *Scarsdale, V.*
Cust – *Brownlow*
Dalrymple – *Stair, E.*
Daubeny de Moleyns – *Ventry*
Davies – *Darwen*
Davis – *Clinton-Davis**
Davison – *Broughshane*
Dawnay – *Downe, V.*
Dawson-Damer – *Portarlington, E.*
Dean – *D. of Beswick**
Deane – *Muskerry*
de Courcy – *Kingsale*
de Grey – *Walsingham*
Delacourt-Smith – *Delacourt Smith of Alteryn**
Denison – *Londesborough*
Denison-Pender – *Pender*
Denton – *D. of Wakefield**
Devereux – *Hereford, V.*
Dewar – *Forteviot*
De Yarburgh-Bateson – *Deramore*
Dixon – *Glentoran*
Dodson – *Monk Bretton*
Donaldson – *D. of Kingsbridge**
Donaldson – *D. of Lymington**
Dormand – *D. of Easington**
Douglas – *Morton, E.*

Douglas – *Queensberry, M.*
Douglas-Hamilton – *Hamilton, D.*
Douglas-Hamilton – *Selkirk, E.*
Douglas-Home – *Dacre*
Douglas-Home – *Home of the Hirsel**
Douglas-Pennant – *Penrhyn*
Douglas-Scott-Montagu – *Montagu of Beaulieu*
Drummond – *Perth, E.*
Drummond of Megginch – *Strange*
Dugdale – *Crathorne*
Duke – *Merrivale*
Duncombe – *Feversham*
Dundas – *Melville, V.*
Dundas – *Zetland, M.*
Eady – *Swinfen*
Eccles – *E. of Moulton**
Eden – *Auckland*
Eden – *E. of Winton**
Eden – *Henley*
Edgcumbe – *Mount Edgcumbe, E.*
Edmondson – *Sandford*
Edwardes – *Kensington*
Edwards – *Chelmer**
Edwards – *Crickhowell**
Egerton – *Sutherland, D.*
Egerton – *Wilton, E.*
Eliot – *St Germans, E.*
Elliot – *E. of Harwood**
Elliot-Murray-Kynynmound – *Minto, E.*
Elliott – *E. of Morpeth**
Erroll – *E. of Hale*
Erskine – *Buchan, E.*
Erskine – *E. of Rerrick*
Erskine – *Mar & Kellie, E.*
Erskine-Murray – *Elibank*
Evans – *Mountevans*
Evans-Freke – *Carbery*
Eve – *Silsoe*
Ewing – *E. of Kirkford**
Eyres Monsell – *Monsell, V.*
Fairfax – *F. of Cameron*
Fane – *Westmorland, E.*
Feilding – *Denbigh, E.*
Fellowes – *De Ramsey*
Fermor-Hesketh – *Hesketh*
Fiennes – *Saye & Sele*
Fiennes-Clinton – *Lincoln, E.*
Finch Hatton – *Winchilsea, E.*
Finch-Knightley – *Aylesford, E.*
Fisher – *F. of Rednal**
Fitzalan-Howard – *Herries of Terregles*
Fitzalan-Howard – *Norfolk, D.*
FitzClarence – *Munster, E.*
FitzGerald – *Leinster, D.*
Fitzherbert – *Stafford*
Fitz-Maurice – *Orkney, E.*

FitzRoy – *Grafton, D.*
FitzRoy – *Southampton*
FitzRoy Newdegate – *Daventry, V.*
Fletcher-Vane – *Inglewood*
Flower – *Ashbrook, V.*
Foljambe – *Liverpool, E.*
Forbes – *Granard, E.*
Fox-Strangways – *Ilchester, E.*
Frankland – *Zouche*
Fraser – *F. of Carmyllie**
Fraser – *F. of Kilmorack**
Fraser – *Lovat*
Fraser – *Saltoun*
Fraser – *Strathalmond*
Freeman-Grenville – *Kinloss*
Fremantle – *Cottesloe*
French – *De Freyne*
Galbraith – *Strathclyde*
Ganzoni – *Belstead*
Gardner – *G. of Parkes**
Gathorne-Hardy – *Cranbrook, E.*
Gibbs – *Aldenham*
Gibbs – *Wraxall*
Gibson – *Ashbourne*
Giffard – *Halsbury, E.*
Gilbey – *Vaux of Harrowden*
Gilmour – *G. of Craigmillar**
Glyn – *Wolverton*
Godley – *Kilbracken*
Goff – *G. of Chieveley**
Gordon – *Aberdeen, M.*
Gordon – *Huntly, M.*
Gordon Lennox – *Richmond, D.*
Gore – *Arran, E.*
Gough-Calthorpe – *Calthorpe*
Graham – *G. of Edmonton**
Graham – *Montrose, D.*
Graham-Toler – *Norbury, E.*
Grant of Grant – *Strathspey*
Grant-Ferris – *Harvington**
Granville – *G. of Eye**
Gray – *G. of Contin**
Greaves – *Dysart, C.*
Greenall – *Daresbury*
Greene – *G. of Harrow Weald**
Greenhill – *G. of Harrow**
Greville – *Warwick, E.*
Grey – *G. of Naunton**
Griffiths – *G. of Fforestfach**
Grigg – *Altrincham*
Grimston – *G. of Westbury*
Grimston – *Verulam, E.*
Grosvenor – *Ebury*
Grosvenor – *Westminster, D.*
Gueterbock – *Berkeley*
Guest – *Wimborne, V.*
Guinness – *Iveagh, E.*
Guinness – *Moyne*

Gully – *Selby, V.*
Gurdon – *Cranworth*
Gwynne Jones – *Chalfont**
Hamilton – *Abercorn, D.*
Hamilton – *Belhaven and Stenton*
Hamilton – *Dudley*
Hamilton – *H. of Dalzell*
Hamilton – *Holm Patrick*
Hamilton-Russell – *Boyne, V.*
Hamilton-Smith – *Colwyn*
Hanbury-Tracy – *Sudeley*
Handcock – *Castlemaine*
Harbord-Hamond – *Suffield*
Harding – *H. of Petherton*
Hardinge – *H. of Penshurst*
Hare – *Blakenham, V.*
Hare – *Listowel, E.*
Harmsworth – *Rothermere, V.*
Harris – *H. of Greenwich**
Harris – *H. of High Cross**
Harris – *Malmesbury, E.*
Harvey – *H. of Prestbury**
Harvey – *H. of Tasburgh*
Hastings Bass – *Huntingdon, E.*
Hay – *Erroll, E.*
Hay – *Kinnoull, E.*
Hay – *Tweeddale, M.*
Heathcote-Drummond-Willoughby – *Willoughby de Eresby*
Hely-Hutchinson – *Donoughmore, E.*
Henderson – *Faringdon*
Henderson – *H. of Brompton**
Hennessy – *Windlesham*
Henniker-Major – *Henniker*
Hepburne-Scott – *Polwarth*
Herbert – *Carnarvon, E.*
Herbert – *Hemingford*
Herbert – *Pembroke, E.*
Herbert – *Powis, E.*
Hermon-Hodge – *Wyfold*
Hervey – *Bristol, M.*
Hewitt – *Lifford, V.*
Hicks Beach – *St Aldwyn, E.*
Hill – *Downshire, M.*
Hill – *Sandys*
Hill-Trevor – *Trevor*
Hilton – *H. of Eggardon**
Hobart-Hampden – *Buckinghamshire, E.*
Hogg – *Hailsham of St Marylebone**
Holland-Hibbert – *Knutsford, V.*
Hollis – *H. of Heigham**
Holme – *H. of Cheltenham**
Holmes à Court – *Heytesbury*
Hood – *Bridport, V.*
Hope – *Glendevon*

Hope – *Linlithgow, M.*
Hope – *Rankeillour*
Hope Johnstone –
  Annandale and Hartfell,
  E.
Hope-Morley – *Hollenden*
Hopkinson – *Colyton*
Hore Ruthven – *Gowrie, E.*
Houghton – *H. of Sowerby**
Hovell-Thurlow-Cumming-
  Bruce – *Thurlow*
Howard – *Carlisle, E.*
Howard – *Effingham, E.*
Howard – *H. of Penrith*
Howard – *Strathcona*
Howard – *Suffolk and*
  Berkshire, E.
Howe – *H. of Aberavon**
Howells – *Geraint**
Howie – *H. of Troon**
Hubbard – *Addington*
Huggins – *Malvern, V.*
Hughes – *Cledwyn of*
  Penrhos*
Hughes-Young – *St Helens*
Hunt – *H. of Tanworth**
Hunter – *H. of Newington**
Hutchinson – *H. of*
  Lullington*
Ingrams – *Darcy de Knayth*
Innes-Ker – *Roxburghe, D.*
Inskip – *Caldecote, V.*
Irby – *Boston*
Irvine – *I. of Lairg**
Isaacs – *Reading, M.*
James – *J. of Holland Park**
James – *Northbourne*
Jauncey – *J. of Tullichettle**
Jay – *J. of Paddington**
Jebb – *Gladwyn*
Jenkin – *J. of Roding**
Jenkins – *J. of Hillhead**
Jenkins – *J. of Putney**
Jervis – *St Vincent, V.*
Jocelyn – *Roden, E.*
Johnston – *J. of Rockport**
Jolliffe – *Hylton*
Joynson-Hicks – *Brentford,*
  V.
Kay-Shuttleworth –
  Shuttleworth
Kearley – *Devonport, V.*
Keith – *K. of Castleacre**
Keith – *K. of Kinkel**
Keith – *Kintore, E.*
Kemp – *Rochdale, V.*
Kennedy – *Ailsa, M.*
Kenworthy – *Strabolgi*
Keppel – *Albemarle, E.*
Kerr – *Lothian, M.*
Kerr – *Teviot*
King – *Lovelace, E.*
King – *K. of Wartnaby**
King-Tenison – *Kingston,*
  E.
Kitchener – *K. of*
  Khartoum, E.
Kitson – *Airedale*
Knatchbull – *Brabourne*

Knatchbull – *Mountbatten*
  of Burma, C.
Knox – *Ranfurly, E.*
Laing – *L. of Dunphail**
Lamb – *Rochester*
Lambart – *Cavan, E.*
Lambton – *Durham, E.*
Lampson – *Killearn*
Lane – *L. of Horsell**
Lascelles – *Harewood, E.*
Law – *Coleraine*
Law – *Ellenborough*
Lawrence – *Trevethin and*
  Oaksey
Lawson – *Burnham*
Lawson – *L. of Blaby**
Lawson-Johnston –
  Luke
Legge – *Dartmouth, E.*
Legh – *Grey of Codnor*
Legh – *Newton*
Leigh-Pemberton –
  Kingsdown*
Leith – *Burgh*
Lennox-Boyd – *Boyd of*
  Merton, V.
Le Poer Trench –
  Clancarty, E.
Leslie – *Rothes, E.*
Leslie Melville – *Leven and*
  Melville, E.
Lever – *Leverhulme, V.*
Lever – *L. of Manchester**
Leveson-Gower –
  Granville, E.
Lewis – *L. of Newnham**
Lewis – *Merthyr*
Liddell – *Ravensworth*
Lindesay-Bethune –
  Lindsay, E.
Lindsay – *Crawford, E.*
Lindsay – *L. of Birker*
Littleton – *Hatherton*
Llewelyn-Davies –
  Llewelyn-Davies of
  Hastoe*
Lloyd George – *Lloyd*
  George of Dwyfor, E.
Lloyd George – *Tenby, V.*
Lloyd-Mostyn – *Mostyn*
Loder – *Wakehurst*
Lopes – *Roborough*
Low – *Aldington*
Lowry-Corry – *Belmore, E.*
Lowther – *Lonsdale, E.*
Lowther – *Ullswater, V.*
Lubbock – *Avebury*
Lucas – *L. of Chilworth*
Lumley – *Scarbrough, E.*
Lumley-Savile – *Savile*
Lyon-Dalberg-Acton –
  Acton
Lysaght – *Lisle*
Lyttelton – *Chandos, V.*
Lyttelton – *Cobham, V.*
Lytton Cobbold – *Cobbold*
McAlpine – *M. of West*
  Green*
Macaulay – *M. of Bragar**

McClintock-Bunbury –
  Rathdonnell
McColl – *M. of Dulwich**
Macdonald – *M. of*
  Gwaenysgor
Macdonald of Macdonald –
  Macdonald
McDonnell – *Antrim, E.*
Macfarlane – *M. of*
  Bearsden*
McFarlane – *M. of*
  Llandaff*
McGregor – *M. of Durris**
McIntosh – *M. of Haringey**
Mackay – *Inchcape, E.*
Mackay – *M. of*
  Ardbrecknish*
Mackay – *M. of Clashfern**
Mackay – *Reay*
Mackay – *Tanlaw**
Mackenzie – *Cromartie, E.*
Mackie – *John-Mackie**
Mackie – *M. of Benshie**
Mackintosh – *M. of*
  Halifax, V.
McLaren – *Aberconway*
MacLehose – *M. of Beoch**
Macleod – *M. of Borve**
Macmillan – *Stockton, E.*
Macpherson – *M. of*
  Drumochter
Macpherson – *Strathcarron*
Maffey – *Rugby*
Maitland – *Lauderdale, E.*
Makgill – *Oxfuird, V.*
Makins – *Sherfield*
Manners – *Rutland, D.*
Manningham-Buller –
  Dilhorne, V.
Mansfield – *Sandhurst*
Marks – *M. of Broughton*
Marquis – *Woolton, E.*
Marshall – *M. of Goring**
Marsham – *Romney, E.*
Martyn-Hemphill –
  Hemphill
Mason – *M. of Barnsley**
Maude – *Hawarden, V.*
Maude – *M. of Stratford-*
  upon-Avon*
Maxwell – *de Ros*
Maxwell – *Farnham*
Meade – *Clanwilliam, E.*
Mercer Nairne Petty-
  Fitzmaurice –
  Lansdowne, M.
Millar – *Inchyra*
Milles-Lade – *Sondes, E.*
Milner – *M. of Leeds*
Mitchell-Thomson –
  Selsdon
Mitford – *Redesdale*
Monckton – *M. of*
  Brenchley, V.
Monckton-Arundell –
  Galway, V.
Mond – *Melchett*
Money-Coutts – *Latymer*
Montagu – *Manchester, D.*

Montagu – *Sandwich, E.*
Montagu – *Swaythling*
Montagu Douglas Scott –
  Buccleuch, D.
Montagu Stuart Wortley –
  Wharncliffe, E.
Montague – *Amwell*
Montgomerie – *Eglinton, E.*
Montgomery – *M. of*
  Alamein, V.
Moore – *Drogheda, E.*
Moore – *M. of Lower*
  Marsh*
Moore – *M. of Wolvercote**
Moore-Brabazon –
  Brabazon of Tara
Moreton – *Ducie, E.*
Morris – *Killanin*
Morris – *M. of Castle*
  Morris*
Morris – *M. of Kenwood*
Morrison – *Dunrossil, V.*
Morrison – *Margadale*
Morton – *M. of Shuna**
Mosley – *Ravensdale*
Mountbatten – *Milford*
  Haven, M.
Muff – *Calverley*
Mulholland – *Dunleath*
Murray – *Atholl, D.*
Murray – *Dunmore, E.*
Murray – *Mansfield and*
  Mansfield, E.
Murray – *M. of Epping*
  Forest*
Murray – *M. of Newhaven**
Murton – *M. of Lindisfarne**
Nall-Cain – *Brocket*
Napier – *Napier and Ettrick*
Napier – *N. of Magdala*
Needham – *Kilmorey, E.*
Nelson – *N. of Stafford*
Nevill – *Abergavenny, M.*
Neville – *Braybrooke*
Nicolson – *Carnock*
Nivison – *Glendyne*
Noel – *Gainsborough, E.*
North – *Guilford, E.*
Northcote – *Iddesleigh, E.*
Norton – *Grantley*
Norton – *Rathcreedan*
Nugent – *N. of Guildford**
Nugent – *Westmeath, E.*
O'Brien – *Inchiquin*
O'Brien – *O'Brien of*
  Lothbury*
Ogilvie-Grant – *Seafield, E.*
Ogilvy – *Airlie, E.*
Oliver – *O. of Aylmerton**
O'Neill – *Rathcavan*
Orde-Powlett – *Bolton*
Ormsby-Gore – *Harlech*
Page – *Whaddon**
Paget – *Anglesey, M.*
Pakenham – *Longford, E.*
Pakington – *Hampton*
Palmer – *Lucas & Dingwall*
Palmer – *Selborne, E.*
Park – *P. of Monmouth**

Orders of Chivalry

THE MOST NOBLE ORDER OF THE GARTER (1348)

KG

Ribbon, Blue
Motto, Honi soit qui mal y pense
  (*Shame on him who thinks evil of it*)
The number of Knights Companions is limited to 24

SOVEREIGN OF THE ORDER
The Queen

LADY OF THE GARTER
HM Queen Elizabeth the Queen
  Mother, 1936

ROYAL KNIGHTS
HRH The Duke of Edinburgh, 1947
HRH The Prince of Wales, 1958
HRH The Duke of Kent, 1985

EXTRA KNIGHTS COMPANIONS AND LADIES
HRH Princess Juliana of the
  Netherlands, 1958
HRH The Grand Duke of
  Luxembourg, 1972
HM The Queen of Denmark, 1979
HM The King of Sweden, 1983
HM The King of Spain, 1988
HM The Queen of the Netherlands,
  1989

KNIGHTS AND LADY COMPANIONS
Sir Cennydd Traherne, 1970
The Earl Waldegrave, 1971
The Earl of Longford, 1971
The Lord Shackleton, 1974
The Marquess of Abergavenny, 1974
The Lord Wilson of Rievaulx, 1976
The Duke of Grafton, 1976
The Lord Hunt, 1979
The Duke of Norfolk, 1983
The Lord Lewin, 1983
The Lord Richardson of
  Duntisbourne, 1983
The Marquess of Normanby, 1985
The Lord Carrington, 1985
The Lord Callaghan of Cardiff, 1987
The Viscount Leverhulme, 1988
The Lord Hailsham of St Marylebone,
  1988
Lavinia, Duchess of Norfolk, 1990
The Duke of Wellington, 1990
Field Marshal Lord Bramall, 1990
Sir Edward Heath, 1992
The Viscount Ridley, 1992

The Lord Sainsbury of Preston
  Candover, 1992

Prelate, The Bishop of Winchester
Chancellor, The Marquess of
  Abergavenny, KG, OBE
Register, The Dean of Windsor
Garter King of Arms, C. M. J. F. Swan,
  CVO, Ph.D., FSA
Gentleman Usher of the Black Rod,
  Adm. Sir Richard Thomas, KCB,
  OBE
Secretary, D. H. B. Chesshyre, LVO

THE MOST ANCIENT AND MOST NOBLE ORDER OF THE THISTLE (REVIVED 1687)

KT

Ribbon, Green
Motto, Nemo me impune lacessit (*No
  one provokes me with impunity*)
The number of Knights is limited to
16

SOVEREIGN OF THE ORDER
The Queen

LADY OF THE THISTLE
HM Queen Elizabeth the Queen
  Mother, 1937

ROYAL KNIGHTS
HRH The Duke of Edinburgh, 1952
HRH The Prince of Wales, Duke of
  Rothesay, 1977

KNIGHTS
The Lord Home of the Hirsel, 1962
The Earl of Wemyss and March, 1966
The Earl of Dalhousie, 1971
The Lord Clydesmuir, 1972
Sir Donald Cameron of Lochiel, 1973
The Earl of Selkirk, 1976
The Lord McFadzean, 1976
The Hon. Lord Cameron, 1978
The Duke of Buccleuch and
  Queensberry, 1978
The Earl of Elgin and Kincardine,
  1981
The Lord Thomson of Monifieth, 1981
The Lord MacLehose of Beoch, 1983
The Earl of Airlie, 1985
Capt. Sir Iain Tennant, 1986
The Viscount Whitelaw, 1990

Chancellor, The Duke of Buccleuch
  and Queensberry

Dean, The Very Revd G. I. Macmillan
Secretary and Lord Lyon King of Arms,
  Sir Malcolm Innes of Edingight,
  KCVO, WS
Usher of the Green Rod, Rear- Admiral
  D.A. Dunbar-Nasmith, CB, DSC

THE MOST HONOURABLE ORDER OF THE BATH (1725)

GCB *Military*   GCB *Civil*

GCB, Knight (or Dame) Grand Cross
KCB, Knight Commander
DCB, Dame Commander
CB, Companion

Ribbon, Crimson
Motto, Tria juncta in uno (*Three joined
  in one*)
Remodelled 1815, and enlarged many
times since. The Order is divided into
civil and military divisions. Women
became eligible for the Order from 1
January 1971

THE SOVEREIGN

GREAT MASTER AND FIRST OR
PRINCIPAL KNIGHT GRAND CROSS
HRH The Prince of Wales, KG, KT,
  GCB

Dean of the Order, The Dean of
  Westminster
Bath King of Arms, Air Chief Marshal
  Sir David Evans, GCB, CBE
Registrar and Secretary, Rear-Adm. D.
  E. Macey, CB
Genealogist, C. M. J. F. Swan, CVO,
  Ph.D., FSA
Gentleman Usher of the Scarlet Rod, Air
  Vice-Marshal Sir Richard Peirse,
  KCVO, CB
Deputy Secretary, The Secretary of the
  Central Chancery of the Orders of
  Knighthood
Chancery, Central Chancery of the
  Orders of Knighthood, St James's
  Palace, London SW1A 1BH

THE ORDER OF MERIT (1902)

OM *Military*   OM *Civil*

OM

Ribbon, Blue and crimson

This Order is designed as a special distinction for eminent men and women without conferring a knighthood upon them. The Order is limited in numbers to 24, with the addition of foreign honorary members. Membership is of two kinds, military and civil, the badge of the former having crossed swords, and the latter oak leaves

THE SOVEREIGN

HRH THE DUKE OF EDINBURGH, 1968

Dorothy Hodgkin, 1965
Dame Veronica Wedgwood, 1969
Sir Isaiah Berlin, 1971
Sir George Edwards, 1971
Sir Alan Hodgkin, 1973
The Lord Todd, 1977
Revd Prof. Owen Chadwick, KBE, 1983
Sir Andrew Huxley, 1983
Sir Michael Tippett, 1983
Frederick Sanger, 1986
Air Commodore Sir Frank Whittle, 1986
The Lord Menuhin, 1987
Prof. Sir Ernst Gombrich, 1988
Dr Max Perutz, 1988
Dame Cicely Saunders, 1989
The Lord Porter of Luddenham, 1989
Rt. Hon. Baroness Thatcher, 1990
Dame Joan Sutherland, 1991
Prof. Francis Crick, 1991
Dame Ninette de Valois, 1992
Sir Michael Atiyah, 1992
Honorary Member, Mother Teresa, 1983

Secretary and Registrar, Sir Edward Ford, KCB, KCVO, ERD
Chancery, Central Chancery of the Orders of Knighthood, St James's Palace, London SW1A 1BH

THE MOST EXALTED ORDER OF THE STAR OF INDIA (1861)

GCSI, Knight Grand Commander
KCSI, Knight Commander
CSI, Companion

Ribbon, Light blue, with white edges
Motto, Heaven's Light our Guide

THE SOVEREIGN

Registrar, The Secretary of the Central Chancery of the Orders of Knighthood
No conferments have been made since 1947

THE MOST DISTINGUISHED ORDER OF ST MICHAEL AND ST GEORGE (1818)

GCMG   KCMG

GCMG, Knight (or Dame) Grand Cross
KCMG, Knight Commander
DCMG, Dame Commander
CMG, Companion

Ribbon, Saxon blue, with scarlet centre
Motto, Auspicium melioris aevi (*Token of a better age*)

THE SOVEREIGN

GRAND MASTER
HRH The Duke of Kent, KG, GCMG, GCVO, ADC
Prelate, The Rt. Revd the Bishop of Coventry
Chancellor, The Lord Carrington, KG, GCMG, CH, MC, PC
Secretary, Sir David Gillmore, KCMG
Registrar, Sir John Graham, Bt., GCMG
King of Arms, Sir Oliver Wright, GCMG, GCVO, DSC
Gentleman Usher of the Blue Rod, Sir John Margetson, KCMG
Dean, The Dean of St Paul's
Deputy Secretary, The Secretary of the Central Chancery of the Orders of Knighthood
Chancery, Central Chancery of the Orders of Knighthood, St James's Palace, London SW1A 1BH

THE MOST EMINENT ORDER OF THE INDIAN EMPIRE (1868)

GCIE, Knight Grand Commander
KCIE, Knight Commander
CIE, Companion

Ribbon, Imperial purple
Motto, Imperatricis auspiciis (*Under the auspices of the Empress*)

THE SOVEREIGN

Registrar, The Secretary of the Central Chancery of the Orders of Knighthood

No conferments have been made since 1947

THE IMPERIAL ORDER OF THE CROWN OF INDIA (1877)
FOR LADIES

CI

Badge, the royal cipher in jewels within an oval, surmounted by an heraldic crown and attached to a bow of light blue watered ribbon, edged white
The honour does not confer any rank or title upon the recipient
No conferments have been made since 1947

HM The Queen, 1947
HM Queen Elizabeth the Queen Mother, 1931
HRH The Princess Margaret, Countess of Snowdon, 1947
HRH The Princess Alice, Duchess of Gloucester, 1937
HH Maharani of Travancore, 1929

THE ROYAL VICTORIAN ORDER (1896)

GCVO   KCVO

GCVO, Knight or Dame Grand Cross
KCVO, Knight Commander
DCVO, Dame Commander
CVO, Commander
LVO, Lieutenant
MVO, Member

Ribbon, Blue, with red and white edges
Motto, Victoria

THE SOVEREIGN
GRAND MASTER
HM Queen Elizabeth the Queen Mother
Chancellor, The Lord Chamberlain
Secretary, The Keeper of the Privy Purse
Registrar, The Secretary of the Central Chancery of the Orders of Knighthood
Chaplain, The Revd J. Robson
Hon. Genealogist, D. H. B. Chesshyre, LVO

THE MOST EXCELLENT ORDER OF THE BRITISH EMPIRE (1917)

GBE   KBE

The Order was divided into military and civil divisions in December 1918

GBE, Knight or Dame Grand Cross
KBE, Knight Commander
DBE, Dame Commander
CBE, Commander
OBE, Officer
MBE, Member

Ribbon, Rose pink edged with pearl grey with vertical pearl stripe in centre (military division); without vertical pearl stripe (civil division)
Motto, For God and the Empire

THE SOVEREIGN

GRAND MASTER
HRH The Prince Philip, Duke of Edinburgh, KG, KT, OM, GBE, PC, FRS
Prelate, The Bishop of London
King of Arms, Admiral Sir Anthony Morton, GBE, KCB
Registrar, The Secretary of the Central Chancery of the Orders of Knighthood
Secretary, Sir Robin Butler, GCB, CVO
Dean, The Dean of St Paul's
Gentleman Usher of the Purple Rod, Sir Robin Gillett, Bt., GBE, RD
Chancery, Central Chancery of the Orders of Knighthood, St James's Palace, London SW1A 1BH

ORDER OF THE COMPANIONS OF HONOUR (1917)

CH

Ribbon, Carmine, with gold edges
This Order consists of one class only and carries with it no title. The number of awards is limited to 65 (excluding honorary members)

Anthony, Rt. Hon. John, 1981
Ashley of Stoke, The Lord, 1975
Aylestone, The Lord, 1975
Baker, Rt. Hon. Kenneth, 1992
Brenner, Sydney, 1986
Brooke, Rt. Hon. Peter, 1992
Carrington, The Lord, 1983

Casson, Sir Hugh, 1984
Cledwyn of Penrhos, The Lord, 1976
de Valois, Dame Ninette, 1981
Eccles, The Viscount, 1984
Fraser, Rt. Hon. Malcolm, 1977
Freud, Lucian, 1983
Gielgud, Sir John, 1977
Glenamara, The Lord, 1976
Goodman, The Lord, 1972
Gorton, Rt. Hon. Sir John, 1971
Hailsham of St Marylebone, The Lord, 1974
Hawking, Prof. Stephen, 1989
Healey, The Lord, 1979
Houghton of Sowerby, The Lord, 1967
Jones, James, 1977
Joseph, The Lord, 1986
King, Rt. Hon. Tom, 1992
Lange, Rt. Hon. David, 1989
Needham, Joseph, 1992
Pasmore, Victor, 1980
Perutz, Prof. Max, 1975
Popper, Prof. Sir Karl, 1982
Powell, Anthony, 1987
Powell, Sir Philip, 1984
Pritchett, Sir Victor, 1992
Runciman, Hon. Sir Steven, 1984
Rylands, George, 1987
Sanger, Frederick, 1981
Sisson, Charles, 1993
Smith, Arnold Cantwell, 1975
Somare, Rt. Hon. Sir Michael, 1978
Talboys, Rt. Hon. Sir Brian, 1981
Tebbit, The Lord, 1987
Thorneycroft, The Lord, 1979
Tippett, Sir Michael, 1979
Trudeau, Rt. Hon. Pierre, 1984
Watkinson, The Viscount, 1962
Whitelaw, The Viscount, 1974
Widdowson, Dr Elsie, 1993
Honorary Members, Lee Kuan Yew, 1970; Dr Joseph Luns, 1971

Secretary and Registrar, The Secretary of the Central Chancery of the Orders of Knighthood

THE DISTINGUISHED SERVICE ORDER (1886)

DSO

Ribbon, Red, with blue edges
Bestowed in recognition of especial services in action of commissioned officers in the Navy, Army and Royal Air Force and (since 1942) Mercantile Marine. The members are Companions only. A Bar may be awarded for any additional act of service

THE IMPERIAL SERVICE ORDER (1902)

ISO

Ribbon, Crimson, with blue centre
Appointment as Companion of this Order is open to members of the Civil Services whose eligibility is determined by the grade they hold. The Order consists of The Sovereign and Companions to a number not exceeding 1,900, of whom 1,300 may belong to the Home Civil Services and 600 to Overseas Civil Services. The Prime Minister announced in March 1991 that no further recommendations for appointments to the Order will be made.

Secretary, Sir Robin Butler, GCB, CVO
Registrar, The Secretary of the Central Chancery of the Orders of Knighthood, St James's Palace, London SW1A 1BH

THE ROYAL VICTORIAN CHAIN (1902)

It confers no precedence on its holders

HM THE QUEEN
HM Queen Elizabeth the Queen Mother, 1937
HRH Princess Juliana of the Netherlands, 1950
HM The King of Thailand, 1960
HIH The Crown Prince of Ethiopia, 1965
HM The King of Jordan, 1966
HM King Zahir Shah of Afghanistan, 1971
HM The Queen of Denmark, 1974
HM The King of Nepal, 1975
HM The King of Sweden, 1975
The Lord Coggan, 1980
HM The Queen of the Netherlands, 1982
General Antonio Eanes, 1985
HM The King of Spain, 1986
HM The King of Saudi Arabia, 1987
HRH The Princess Margaret, Countess of Snowdon, 1990
The Lord Runcie, 1991
The Lord Charteris of Amisfield, 1992
HE François Mitterrand, 1992
HE Richard von Weizsäcker, 1992

Baronetage and Knightage

BARONETS

Style, 'Sir' before forename and surname, followed by 'Bt.'
Wife's style, 'Lady' followed by surname
For forms of address, *see* page 220

There are five different creations of Baronetcies: Baronets of England (creations dating from 1611); Baronets of Ireland (creations dating from 1619); Baronets of Scotland or Nova Scotia (creations dating from 1625); Baronets of Great Britain (creations after the Act of Union 1707 which combined the kingdoms of England and Scotland); and Baronets of the United Kingdom (creations after the union of Great Britain and Ireland in 1801).

Badge of Ulster   *Badge of Baronets of Nova Scotia*

Badge of Baronets of the United Kingdom

The patent of creation limits the destination of a baronetcy, usually to male descendants of the first baronet, although special remainders allow the baronetcy to pass, if the male issue of sons fail, to the male issue of daughters of the first baronet. In the case of baronetcies of Scotland or Nova Scotia, a special remainder of 'heirs male and of tailzie' allows the baronetcy to descend to heirs general, including women. There are four existing Scottish baronets with such a remainder, one of whom, the holder of the Dunbar of Hempriggs creation, is a Baronetess.

The Official Roll of Baronets is kept at the Home Office by the Registrar of the Baronetage. Anyone who considers that he is entitled to be entered on the Roll may petition the Crown through the Home Secretary. Every person succeeding to a Baronetcy must exhibit proofs of succession to the Home Secretary. A person whose name is not entered on the Official Roll will not be addressed or mentioned by the title of Baronet in any official document, nor will he be accorded precedence as a Baronet.

BARONETCIES EXTINCT SINCE THE LAST EDITION
Bowman (*cr.* 1961); Moore (*cr.* 1923)

Registrar of the Baronetage, R. M. Morris
Assistant Registrar, Mrs F. G. Bright
Office, Home Office, Queen Anne's Gate, London SWIH 9AT. Tel: 071-273 3498

KNIGHTS

Style, 'Sir' before forename and surname, followed by appropriate post-nominal initials if a Knight Grand Cross, Knight Grand Commander or Knight Commander
Wife's style, 'Lady' followed by surname
For forms of address, *see* page 220

The prefix 'Sir' is not used by knights who are clerics of the Church of England, who do not receive the accolade. Their wives are entitled to precedence as the wife of a knight but not to the style of 'Lady'.

ORDERS OF KNIGHTHOOD

Knight Grand Cross, Knight Grand Commander, and Knight Commander are the higher classes of the Orders of Chivalry (*see* pages 174–6). Honorary knighthoods of these Orders may be conferred on men who are citizens of countries of which The Queen is not head of state. As a rule, the prefix 'Sir' is not used by honorary knights.

KNIGHTS BACHELOR

The Knights Bachelor do not constitute a Royal Order, but comprise the surviving representation of the ancient State Orders of Knighthood. The Register of Knights Bachelor, instituted by James I in the 17th century, lapsed, and in 1908 a voluntary association under the title of The Society of Knights (now The Imperial Society of Knights Bachelor by royal command) was formed with the primary objects of continuing the various registers dating from 1257 and obtaining the uniform registration of every created Knight Bachelor. In 1926 a design for a badge to be worn by Knights Bachelor was approved and adopted; in 1974 a neck badge and miniature were added.

Knight Principal, Col. Sir Colin Cole, KCB, KCVO, TD
Chairman of Council, Sir David Napley
Prelate, Rt. Revd and Rt. Hon. The Bishop of London
Hon. Registrar, Sir Kenneth Newman, GBE, QPM
Hon. Treasurer, The Lord Lane of Horsell
Clerk to the Council, R. M. Esden
Office, 21 Old Buildings, Lincoln's Inn, London WC2A 3UJ

LIST OF BARONETS AND KNIGHTS
Revised to 31 August 1993

Peers are not included in this list

† Not registered on the Official Roll of the Baronetage at the time of going to press
( ) The date of creation of the baronetcy is given in parenthesis
I Baronet of Ireland
NS Baronet of Nova Scotia
S Baronet of Scotland

If a baronet or knight has a double barrelled or hyphenated surname, he is listed under the final element of the name

A full entry in italic type indicates that the recipient of a knighthood died during the year in which the honour was conferred. The name is included for purposes of record

Abal, Sir Tei, Kt., CBE

Abbott, Sir Albert Francis, Kt., CBE

Abdy, Sir Valentine Robert Duff, Bt. (1850)

Abel, Sir Seselo (Cecil) Charles Geoffrey, Kt., OBE

Abeles, Sir (Emil Herbert) Peter, Kt.

Abell, Sir Anthony Foster, KCMG

Abercromby, Sir Ian George, Bt. (s. 1636)

Abraham, Sir Edward Penley, Kt., CBE, FRS

Acheson, Prof. Sir (Ernest) Donald, KBE

Ackers, Sir James George, Kt.

Ackroyd, Sir John Robert Whyte, Bt. (1956)

Acland, Sir Antony Arthur, GCMG, GCVO

Acland, Maj. Sir (Christopher) Guy (Dyke), Bt., MVO (1890)

Acland, Sir John Dyke, Bt. (1644)

Acland, Maj.-Gen. Sir John Hugh Bevil, KCB, CBE

Acton, Sir Harold Mario Mitchell, Kt., CBE

Adam, Sir Christopher Eric Forbes, Bt. (1917)

Adams, Sir Philip George Doyne, KCMG

Adams, Sir William James, KCMG

Adamson, Sir (William Owen) Campbell, Kt.

Adrien, Hon. Sir Maurice Latour-, Kt.

Adye, Sir John Anthony, KCMG

Agnew, Sir Crispin Hamlyn, Bt. (s. 1629)

†Agnew, Maj. Sir George Keith, Bt., TD (1895)

Agnew, Sir (William) Godfrey, KCVO, CB

Ah-Chuen, Sir Moi Lin Jean Etienne, Kt.

Aiken, Air Chief Marshal Sir John Alexander Carlisle, KCB

Ainsworth, Sir (Thomas) David, Bt. (1916)

Aird, Capt. Sir Alastair Sturgis, KCVO

Aird, Sir (George) John, Bt. (1901)

Airey, Sir Lawrence, KCB

Airy, Maj.-Gen. Sir Christopher John, KCVO, CBE

Aisher, Sir Owen Arthur, Kt.

Aitchison, Sir Charles Walter de Lancey, Bt. (1938)

Aitken, Sir Robert Stevenson, Kt., MD, D.Phil.

Akehurst, Gen. Sir John Bryan, KCB, CBE

Albert, Sir Alexis François, Kt., CMG, VRD

Albu, Sir George, Bt. (1912)

Alcock, Air Chief Marshal Sir (Robert James) Michael, KBE, CB

Aldous, Hon. Sir William, Kt.

Alexander, Sir Alexander Sandor, Kt.

Alexander, Sir Charles Gundry, Bt. (1945)

Alexander, Sir Claud Hagart-, Bt. (1886)

Alexander, Sir Douglas, Bt. (1921)

Alexander, Sir (John) Lindsay, Kt.

Alexander, Prof. Sir Kenneth John Wilson, Kt.

Alexander, Sir Michael O'Donal Bjarne, GCMG

Alexander, Sir Norman Stanley, Kt., CBE

†Alexander, Sir Patrick Desmond William Cable-, Bt. (1809)

Allan, Sir Anthony James Allan Havelock-, Bt. (1858)

Allard, Sir Gordon Laidlaw, Kt.

Allen, Rear-Adm. Sir David, KCVO, CBE

Allen, Prof. Sir Geoffrey, Kt., ph.D., FRS

Allen, Hon. Sir Peter Austin Philip Jermyn, Kt.

Allen, Sir Richard Hugh Sedley, KCMG

Allen, Sir William Guilford, Kt.

Allen, Sir (William) Kenneth (Gwynne), Kt.

Alleyne, Sir George Allanmoore Ogarren, Kt.

Alleyne, Revd Sir John Olpherts Campbell, Bt. (1769)

Alliance, Sir David, Kt., CBE

Allinson, Sir (Walter) Leonard, KCVO, CMG

Alliott, Hon. Sir John Downes, Kt.

Alment, Sir (Edward) Anthony John, Kt.

Althaus, Sir Nigel Frederick, Kt.

Ambo, Rt. Revd George, KBE

Amies, Sir (Edwin) Hardy, KCVO

Amis, Sir Kingsley William, Kt., CBE

Amory, Sir Ian Heathcoat, Bt. (1874)

Anderson, Prof. Sir (James) Norman (Dalrymple), Kt., OBE, QC, FBA

Anderson, Maj.-Gen. Sir John Evelyn, KBE

Anderson, Sir John Muir, Kt., CMG

Anderson, Hon. Sir Kevin Victor, Kt.

Anderson, Vice-Adm. Sir Neil Dudley, KBE, CB

Anderson, Prof. Sir (William) Ferguson, Kt., OBE

Anderton, Sir (Cyril) James, Kt., CBE, QPM

Andrew, Sir Robert John, KCB

Andrews, Sir Derek Henry, KCB, CBE

Andrews, Hon. Sir Dormer George, Kt.

Angus, Sir Michael Richardson, Kt.

Annesley, Sir Hugh Norman, Kt., QPM

Ansell, Col. Sir Michael Picton, Kt., CBE, DSO

Anson, Vice-Adm. Sir Edward Rosebery, KCB

Anson, Sir John, KCB

Anson, Rear-Adm. Sir Peter, Bt., CB (1831)

Anstey, Brig. Sir John, Kt., CBE, TD

Anstruther, Maj. Sir Ralph Hugo, Bt. GCVO, MC (s. 1694)

Antico, Sir Tristan Venus, Kt.

Antrobus, Sir Philip Coutts, Bt. (1815)

Appleyard, Sir Raymond Kenelm, KBE

Arbuthnot, Sir Keith Robert Charles, Bt. (1823)

Arbuthnot, Sir William Reierson, Bt. (1964)

Archdale, Capt. Sir Edward Folmer, Bt., DSC, RN (1928)

Archer, Gen. Sir (Arthur) John, KCB, OBE

Arculus, Sir Ronald, KCMG, KCVO

Armitage, Air Chief Marshal Sir Michael John, KCB, CBE

Armstrong, Sir Andrew Clarence Francis, Bt., CMG (1841)

Armstrong, Sir Thomas Henry Wait, Kt., D.Mus.

Armytage, Sir John Martin, Bt. (1738)

Arnold, Rt. Hon. Sir John Lewis, Kt.

Arnold, Sir Malcolm Henry, Kt., CBE

Arnold, Sir Thomas Richard, Kt., MP

Arnott, Sir Alexander John Maxwell, Bt. (1896)

Arnott, Prof. Sir (William) Melville, Kt., TD, MD

Arrindell, Sir Clement Athelston, GCMG, GCVO, QC

Arthur, Lt.-Gen. Sir (John) Norman Stewart, KCB

Arthur, Sir Stephen John, Bt. (1841)

Ash, Prof. Sir Eric Albert, Kt., CBE, FRS, FEng.

Ashburnham, Sir Denny Reginald, Bt. (1661)

Ashe, Sir Derick Rosslyn, KCMG

Ashley, Sir Bernard Albert, Kt.

Ashmore, Admiral of the Fleet Sir Edward Beckwith, GCB, DSC

Ashmore, Vice-Adm. Sir Peter William Beckwith, KCB, KCVO, DSC

Ashworth, Sir Herbert, Kt.

Aske, Revd Sir Conan, Bt. (1922)

Askew, Sir Bryan, Kt.

Asscher, Prof. (Adolf) William, Kt., MD, FRCP

Astley, Sir Francis Jacob Dugdale, Bt. (1821)

Aston, Sir Harold George, Kt., CBE

Aston, Hon. Sir William John, KCMG

Astor, Hon. Sir John Jacob, Kt., MBE

Astwood, Hon. Sir James Rufus, Kt.

Astwood, Lt.-Col. Sir Jeffrey Carlton, Kt., CBE, ED

Atcherley, Sir Harold Winter, Kt.

Atiyah, Sir Michael Francis, Kt., OM, ph.D., FRS

Atkinson, Air Marshal Sir David William, KBE

Atkinson, Sir Frederick John, KCB

Atkinson, Sir John Alexander, KCB, DFC

Atkinson, Sir Robert, Kt., DSC, FEng.

Attenborough, Sir David Frederick, Kt., CVO, CBE, FRS

Atwell, Sir John William, Kt., CBE, FRSE, FEng.

Atwill, Sir (Milton) John (Napier), Kt.

Audland, Sir Christopher John, KCMG

Audley, Sir George Bernard, Kt.
Auld, *Hon.* Sir Robin Ernest, Kt.
Austin, Sir Michael Trescawen, Bt. (1894)
Austin, *Vice-Adm.* Sir Peter Murray, KCB
Austin, *Air Marshal* Sir Roger Mark, KCB, AFC
†Aykroyd, Sir James Alexander Frederic, Bt. (1929)
Aykroyd, Sir William Miles, Bt., MC (1920)
Aylmer, Sir Richard John, Bt. (I. 1622)
Bacha, Sir Bhinod, Kt., CMG
Backhouse, Sir Jonathan Roger, Bt. (1901)
Bacon, Sir Nicholas Hickman Ponsonby, Bt. *Premier Baronet of England* (1611 and 1627)
Bacon, Sir Sidney Charles, Kt., CB, FEng.
Baddeley, Sir John Wolsey Beresford, Bt. (1922)
Baddiley, *Prof.* Sir James, Kt., ph.D., D.SC., FRS, FRSE
Badenoch, Sir John, Kt., DM, FRCP
Badger, Sir Geoffrey Malcolm, Kt.
Bagge, Sir (John) Jeremy Picton, Bt. (1867)
Bagnall, *Field Marshal* Sir Nigel Thomas, GCB, CVO, MC
Bailey, Sir Alan Marshall, KCB
Bailey, Sir Brian Harry, Kt., OBE
Bailey, Sir Derrick Thomas Louis, Bt., DFC (1919)
Bailey, *Prof.* Sir Harold Walter, Kt., D.Phil., FBA
Bailey, Sir John Bilsland, KCB
Bailey, Sir Richard John, Kt., CBE
Bailey, Sir Stanley Ernest, Kt., CBE, QPM
Baillie, Sir Gawaine George Hope, Bt. (1823)
Baines, *Prof.* Sir George Grenfell-, Kt., OBE
Baird, Sir David Charles, Bt. (1809)
Baird, *Lt.-Gen.* Sir James Parlane, KBE, MD
Baird, Sir James Richard Gardiner, Bt., MC (s. 1695)
Baird, *Vice-Adm.* Sir Thomas Henry Eustace, KCB
Bairsto, *Air Marshal* Sir Peter Edward, KBE, CB
Baker, Sir (Allan) Ivor, Kt., CBE
Baker, Sir Robert George Humphrey Sherston-, Bt. (1796)
Baker, *Hon.* Sir (Thomas) Scott (Gillespie), Kt.
Balchin, Sir Robert George Alexander, Kt.
Balcombe, *Rt. Hon.* Sir (Alfred) John, Kt.
Balderstone, Sir James Schofield, Kt.
Baldwin, Sir Peter Robert, KCB
Balfour, *Gen.* Sir (Robert George) Victor FitzGeorge-, KCB, CBE, DSO, MC

Ball, *Air Marshal* Sir Alfred Henry Wynne, KCB, DSO, DFC
Ball, Sir Charles Irwin, Bt. (1911)
Ball, Sir Christopher John Elinger, Kt.
Ball, *Prof.* Sir Robert James, Kt., ph.D.
Balmer, Sir Joseph Reginald, Kt.
Bamford, Sir Anthony Paul, Kt.
Banham, Sir John Michael Middlecott, Kt.
Bannerman, Sir David Gordon, Bt., OBE (S. 1682)
Bannister, Sir Roger Gilbert, Kt., CBE, DM, FRCP
Barber, *Hon.* Sir (Edward Hamilton) Esler, Kt.
Barber, Sir William Francis, Bt., TD (1960)
Barbour, *Very Revd* Sir Robert Alexander Stewart, KCVO, MC
Barclay, Sir Colville Herbert Sanford, Bt. (s. 1668)
Barclay, Sir Peter Maurice, Kt., CBE
Barclay, Sir Roderick Edward, GCVO, KCMG
Barder, Sir Brian Leon, KCMG
Barker, Sir Alwyn Bowman, Kt., CMG
Barker, Sir Colin, Kt.
Barker, Sir Harry Heaton, Kt., KBE
Barlow, Sir Christopher Hilaro, Bt. (1803)
Barlow, Sir (George) William, Kt., FEng.
Barlow, Sir John Kemp, Bt. (1907)
Barlow, Sir Thomas Erasmus, Bt., DSC (1902)
Barnard, Sir (Arthur) Thomas, Kt., CB, OBE
Barnard, *Capt.* Sir George Edward, Kt.
Barnard, Sir Joseph Brian, Kt.
Barnes, Sir James George, Kt., MBE
Barnes, Sir Kenneth, KCB
Barnett, Sir Oliver Charles, Kt., CBE, QC
Barnewall, Sir Reginald Robert, Bt. (I. 1623)
Baron, Sir Thomas, Kt., CBE
Barraclough, *Air Chief Marshal* Sir John, KCB, CBE, DFC, AFC
Barraclough, Sir Kenneth James Priestley, Kt., CBE, TD
Barran, Sir David Haven, Kt.
Barran, Sir John Napoleon Ruthven, Bt. (1895)
Barratt, Sir Lawrence Arthur, Kt.
Barratt, Sir Richard Stanley, Kt., CBE, QPM
Barrett, *Lt.-Gen.* Sir David William Scott-, KBE, MC
Barrett, *Lt.-Col.* Sir Dennis Charles Titchener, Kt., TD
Barrett, Sir Stephen Jeremy, KCMG
Barrington, Sir Alexander (Fitzwilliam Croker), Bt. (1831)
Barrington, Sir Nicholas John, KCMG, CVO
Barron, Sir Donald James, Kt.
Barrow, *Capt.* Sir Richard John Uniacke, Bt. (1835)

Barrowclough, Sir Anthony Richard, Kt., QC
Barry, Sir (Lawrence) Edward (Anthony Tress), Bt. (1899)
Barry, Sir (Philip) Stuart Milner-, KCVO, CB, OBE
Bartlett, Sir John Hardington, Bt. (1913)
Barton, *Prof.* Sir Derek Harold Richard, Kt., FRS, FRSE
Barttelot, *Lt.-Col.* Sir Brian Walter de Stopham, Bt., OBE (1875)
Barwick, *Rt. Hon.* Sir Garfield Edward John, GCMG
Batchelor, Sir Ivor Ralph Campbell, Kt., CBE
Bate, Sir David Lindsay, KBE
Bate, Sir (Walter) Edwin, Kt., OBE
Bateman, Sir Cecil Joseph, KBE
Bateman, Sir Geoffrey Hirst, Kt., FRCS
Bateman, Sir Ralph Melton, KBE
Bates, *Prof.* Sir David Robert, Kt., D.SC., FRS
Bates, Sir Geoffrey Voltelin, Bt., MC (1880)
Bates, Sir John David, Kt., CBE, VRD
Bates, Sir (John) Dawson, Bt., MC (1937)
Batho, Sir Peter Ghislain, Bt. (1928)
Bathurst, *Adm.* Sir (David) Benjamin, GCB
Bathurst, Sir Frederick Peter Methuen Hervey-, Bt. (1818)
Bathurst, Sir Maurice Edward, Kt., CMG, CBE, QC
Batten, Sir John Charles, KCVO
Battersby, *Prof.* Sir Alan Rushton, Kt., FRS
Battishill, Sir Anthony Michael William, KCB
Batty, Sir William Bradshaw, Kt., TD
Baxendell, Sir Peter Brian, Kt., CBE, FEng.
Bayliss, *Prof.* Sir Noel Stanley, Kt., CBE
Bayliss, Sir Richard Ian Samuel, KCVO, MD, FRCP
Bayly, *Vice-Adm.* Sir Patrick Uniacke, KBE, CB, DSC
Bayne, Sir Nicholas Peter, KCMG
Baynes, Sir John Christopher Malcolm, Bt. (1801)
Bazley, Sir Thomas Stafford, Bt. (1869)
Beach, *Gen.* Sir (William Gerald) Hugh, GBE, KCB, MC
Beale, *Lt.-Gen.* Sir Peter John, KBE, FRCP
Beament, Sir James William Longman, Kt., SC.D., FRS
Beattie, *Hon.* Sir Alexander Craig, Kt.
Beattie, *Hon.* Sir David Stuart, GCMG, GCVO
Beauchamp, Sir Christopher Radstock Proctor-, Bt. (1745)
Beaumont, Sir George (Howland Francis), Bt. (1661)
Beaumont, Sir Richard Ashton, KCMG, OBE

Beavis, *Air Chief Marshal* Sir Michael Gordon, KCB, CBE, AFC

Becher, Sir William Fane Wrixon, Bt., MC (1831)

Beck, Sir Edgar Charles, Kt., CBE, FEng.

Beck, Sir Edgar Philip, Kt.

Beckett, *Capt.* Sir (Martyn) Gervase, Bt., MC (1921)

Beckett, Sir Terence Norman, KBE, FEng.

Bedingfeld, *Capt.* Sir Edmund George Felix Paston-, Bt. (1661)

Beecham, Sir John Stratford Roland, Bt. (1914)

Beeley, Sir Harold, KCMG, CBE

Beetham, *Marshal of the Royal Air Force* Sir Michael James, GCB, CBE, DFC, AFC

Beevor, Sir Thomas Agnew, Bt. (1784)

Begg, Sir Neil Colquhoun, KBE

Begg, *Admiral of the Fleet* Sir Varyl Cargill, GCB, DSO, DSC

Beit, Sir Alfred Lane, Bt. (1924)

Beith, Sir John Greville Stanley, KCMG

Belch, Sir Alexander Ross, Kt., CBE, FRSE

Beldam, *Rt. Hon.* Sir (Alexander) Roy (Asplan), Kt.

Belich, Sir James, Kt.

Bell, Sir Gawain Westray, KCMG, CBE

Bell, Sir (George) Raymond, KCMG, CB

Bell, Sir John Lowthian, Bt. (1885)

Bell, *Hon.* Sir Rodger, Kt.

Bell, Sir Timothy John Leigh, Kt.

Bell, Sir (William) Ewart, KCB

Bell, Sir William Hollin Dayrell Morrison-, Bt. (1905)

Bellew, Sir Henry Charles Gratton-, Bt. (1838)

Bellinger, Sir Robert Ian, GBE

Bellingham, Sir Noel Peter Roger, Bt. (1796)

Bengough, *Col.* Sir Piers, KCVO, OBE

Benn, Sir (James) Jonathan, Bt. (1914)

Bennett, Sir Charles Moihi Te Arawaka, Kt., DSO

Bennett, *Air Vice-Marshal* Sir Erik Peter, KBE, CB

Bennett, *Rt. Hon.* Sir Frederic Mackarness, Kt.

Bennett, Sir Hubert, Kt.

Bennett, Sir John Mokonuiarangi, Kt.

Bennett, *Gen.* Sir Phillip Harvey, KBE, DSO

Bennett, Sir Reginald Frederick Brittain, Kt., VRD

Bennett, Sir Ronald Wilfrid Murdoch, Bt. (1929)

Benson, Sir Christopher John, Kt.

Benson, Sir (William) Jeffrey, Kt.

Bentley, Sir William, KCMG

Beresford, Sir (Alexander) Paul, Kt., MP

Berger, *Vice-Adm.* Sir Peter Egerton Capel, KCB, MVO, DSC

Berghuser, *Hon.* Sir Eric, Kt., MBE

Berlin, Sir Isaiah, Kt., OM, CBE

Bernard, Sir Dallas Edmund, Bt. (1954)

Berney, Sir Julian Reedham Stuart, Bt. (1620)

Berrill, Sir Kenneth Ernest, GBE, KCB

Berriman, Sir David, Kt.

Berry, *Prof.* Sir Colin Leonard, Kt., FRCpath.

Berthon, *Vice-Adm.* Sir Stephen Ferrier, KCB

Berthoud, Sir Martin Seymour, KCVO, CMG

Best, Sir Richard Radford, KCVO, CBE

Bethune, Sir Alexander Maitland Sharp, Bt. (s. 1683)

Bethune, *Hon.* Sir (Walter) Angus, Kt.

Bevan, Sir Martyn Evan Evans, Bt. (1958)

Bevan, Sir Timothy Hugh, Kt.

Beverley, *Lt.-Gen.* Sir Henry York La Roche, KCB, OBE, RM

Beynon, *Prof.* Sir (William John) Granville, Kt., CBE, Ph.D., D.Sc., FRS

Bibby, Sir Derek James, Bt., MC (1959)

Bickersteth, *Rt. Revd* John Monier, KCVO

Biddulph, Sir Ian D'Olier, Bt. (1664)

Bide, Sir Austin Ernest, Kt.

Bidwell, Sir Hugh Charles Philip, GBE

Biggam, Sir Robin Adair, Kt.

Biggs, *Vice-Adm.* Sir Geoffrey William Roger, KCB

Biggs, Sir Norman Paris, Kt.

Billière, *Gen.* Sir Peter Edgar de la Cour de la, KCB, KBE, DSO, MC

Bing, Sir Rudolf Franz Josef, KBE

Bingham, *Hon.* Sir Eardley Max, Kt., QC

Bingham, *Rt. Hon.* Sir Thomas Henry, Kt.

Birch, Sir John Allan, KCVO, CMG

Birch, Sir Roger, Kt., CBE, QPM

Bird, Sir Richard Geoffrey Chapman, Bt. (1922)

Birkin, Sir John Christian William, Bt. (1905)

Birkin, Sir (John) Derek, Kt., TD

Birkmyre, Sir Archibald, Bt. (1921)

Birley, Sir Derek Sydney, Kt.

Birrell, Sir James Drake, Kt.

Birtwistle, Sir Harrison, Kt.

Bishop, Sir Frederick Arthur, Kt., CB, CVO

Bishop, Sir George Sidney, Kt., CB, OBE

Bishop, Sir Michael David, Kt., CBE

Bisson, *Rt Hon.* Sir Gordon Ellis, Kt.

Black, *Prof.* Sir Douglas Andrew Kilgour, Kt., MD, FRCP

Black, Sir James Whyte, Kt., FRCP, FRS

Black, *Adm.* Sir (John) Jeremy, GCB, DSO, MBE

Black, Sir Robert Brown, GCMG, OBE

Black, Sir Robert David, Bt. (1922)

Blacker, *Lt.-Gen.* Sir (Anthony Stephen) Jeremy, KCB, CBE

Blacker, *Gen.* Sir Cecil Hugh, GCB, OBE, MC

Blackett, Sir George William, Bt. (1673)

Blacklock, *Surgeon Capt. Prof.* Sir Norman James, KCVO, OBE

Blackman, Sir Frank Milton, KCVO, OBE

Blackwell, Sir Basil Davenport, Kt., FEng.

Blackwood, Sir John Francis, Bt. (1814)

Blair, Sir Alastair Campbell, KCVO, TD, WS

Blair, *Lt.-Gen.* Sir Chandos, KCVO, OBE, MC

Blair, Sir Edward Thomas Hunter, Bt. (1786)

Blake, Sir Alfred Lapthorn, KCVO, MC

Blake, Sir Francis Michael, Bt. (1907)

Blake, Sir (Thomas) Richard (Valentine), Bt. (1. 1622)

Blaker, Sir John, Bt. (1919)

Blaker, *Rt. Hon.* Sir Peter Allan Renshaw, KCMG

Blakiston, Sir Ferguson Arthur James, Bt. (1763)

Bland, Sir (Francis) Christopher (Buchan), Kt.

Bland, Sir Henry Armand, Kt., CBE

Bland, *Lt.-Col.* Sir Simon Claud Michael, KCVO

Blelloch, Sir John Nial Henderson, KCB

Blennerhassett, Sir (Marmaduke) Adrian Francis William, Bt. (1809)

Blewitt, *Maj.* Sir Shane Gabriel Basil, KCVO

Blofield, *Hon.* Sir John Christopher Calthorpe, Kt.

Blois, Sir Charles Nicholas Gervase, Bt. (1686)

Blomefield, Sir Thomas Charles Peregrine, Bt. (1807)

Bloomfield, Sir Kenneth Percy, KCB

Blosse, *Capt.* Sir Richard Hely Lynch-, Bt. (1622)

Blount, Sir Walter Edward Alpin, Bt., DSC (1642)

Blunden, Sir George, Kt.

†Blunden, Sir Philip Overington, Bt. (1. 1766)

Blunt, Sir David Richard Reginald Harvey, Bt. (1720)

Blyth, Sir James, Kt.

Boardman, *Prof.* Sir John, Kt., FSA, FBA

Boardman, Sir Kenneth Ormrod, Kt.

Bodilly, *Hon.* Sir Jocelyn, Kt., VRD

Bodmer, Sir Walter Fred, Kt., Ph.D., FRS

Body, Sir Richard Bernard Frank Stewart, Kt., MP

Boevey, Sir Thomas Michael Blake Crawley-, Bt. (1784)

Bogarde, Sir Dirk (Derek Niven van den Bogaerde), Kt.

Boileau, Sir Guy (Francis), Bt. (1838)

Boles, Sir Jeremy John Fortescue, Bt. (1922)

Boles, Sir John Dennis, Kt., MBE

Bolland, Sir Edwin, KCMG

Bollers, *Hon.* Sir Harold Brodie Smith, Kt.

Bolton, Sir Frederic Bernard, Kt., MC

Bona, Sir Kina, KBE

Bonallack, Sir Richard Frank, Kt., CBE

Bond, Sir Kenneth Raymond Boyden, Kt.

Bondi, *Prof.* Sir Hermann, KCB, FRS

Bonham, *Maj.* Sir Antony Lionel Thomas, Bt. (1852)

Bonsall, Sir Arthur Wilfred, KCMG, CBE

Bonsor, Sir Nicholas Cosmo, Bt., MP (1925)

Boolell, Sir Satcam, Kt.

Boon, Sir Peter Coleman, Kt.

Boord, Sir Nicolas John Charles, Bt. (1896)

Boorman, *Lt.-Gen.* Sir Derek, KCB

Booth, Sir Angus Josslyn Gore-, Bt. (I. 1760)

Booth, Sir Christopher Charles, Kt., MD, FRCP

Booth, Sir Douglas Allen, Bt. (1916)

Booth, Sir Gordon, KCMG, CVO

Booth, Sir Robert Camm, Kt., CBE, TD

Boothby, Sir Brooke Charles, Bt. (1660)

Boreel, Sir Francis David, Bt. (1645)

Boreham, Sir (Arthur) John, KCB

Boreham, *Hon.* Sir Leslie Kenneth Edward, Kt.

Bornu, The Waziri of, KCMG, CBE

Borrie, Sir Gordon Johnson, Kt., QC

Borthwick, Sir John Thomas, Bt. MBE (1908)

Bossom, *Hon.* Sir Clive, Bt. (1953)

Boswall, Sir (Thomas) Alford Houstoun-, Bt. (1836)

Boswell, *Lt.-Gen.* Sir Alexander Crawford Simpson, KCB, CBE

Bosworth, Sir Neville Bruce Alfred, Kt., CBE

Bottomley, Sir James Reginald Alfred, KCMG

Boughey, Sir John George Fletcher, Bt. (1798)

Boulton, Sir Clifford John, KCB

Boulton, Sir (Harold Hugh) Christian, Bt. (1905)

Boulton, Sir William Whytehead, Bt., CBE, TD (1944)

Bourn, Sir John Bryant, KCB

Bourne, Sir (John) Wilfrid, KCB

Bovell, *Hon.* Sir (William) Stewart, Kt.

Bowater, Sir Euan David Vansittart, Bt. (1939)

Bowater, Sir (John) Vansittart, Bt. (1914)

Bowden, Sir Frank, Bt. (1915)

Bowen, Sir Geoffrey Fraser, Kt.

Bowen, Sir Mark Edward Mortimer, Bt. (1921)

Bowen, *Hon.* Sir Nigel Hubert, KBE

†Bowlby, Sir Richard Peregrine Longstaff, Bt. (1923)

Bowman, Sir Jeffery Haverstock, Kt.

Bowman, Sir John Paget, Bt. (1884)

Bowmar, Sir Charles Erskine, Kt.

Bowness, Sir Alan, Kt., CBE

Bowness, Sir Peter Spencer, Kt., CBE

Boxer, *Air Vice-Marshal* Sir Alan Hunter Cachemaille, KCVO, CB, DSO, DFC

Boyce, Sir Robert Charles Leslie, Bt. (1952)

Boyd, Sir Alexander Walter, Bt. (1916)

Boyd, Sir John Dixon Iklé, KCMG

Boyd, Sir (John) Francis, Kt.

Boyd, *Prof.* Sir Robert Lewis Fullarton, Kt., CBE, D.SC., FRS

Boyes, Sir Brian Gerald Barratt-, KBE

Boyle, Sir Stephen Gurney, Bt. (1904)

Boyne, Sir Henry Brian, Kt., CBE

Boynton, Sir John Keyworth, Kt., MC

Boyson, *Rt. Hon.* Sir Rhodes, Kt., MP

Brabham, Sir John Arthur, Kt., OBE

Bradbeer, Sir John Derek Richardson, Kt., OBE, TD

Bradbury, *Surgeon Vice-Adm.* Sir Eric Blackburn, KBE, CB

Bradford, Sir Edward Alexander Slade, Bt. (1902)

Bradley, Sir Burton Gyrth Burton-, Kt., OBE

Bradman, Sir Donald George, Kt.

Bradshaw, Sir Kenneth Anthony, KCB

Bradshaw, *Lt.-Gen.* Sir Richard Phillip, KBE

Brain, Sir (Henry) Norman, KBE, CMG

Braithwaite, Sir (Joseph) Franklin Madders, Kt.

Braithwaite, Sir Rodric Quentin, KCMG

Bramall, Sir (Ernest) Ashley, Kt.

Bramley, *Prof.* Sir Paul Anthony, Kt.

Branch, Sir William Allan Patrick, Kt.

Brancker, Sir (John Eustace) Theodore, Kt., QC

Branigan, Sir Patrick Francis, Kt., QC

Bray, Sir Theodor Charles, Kt., CBE

Braynen, Sir Alvin Rudolph, Kt.

Bremridge, Sir John Henry, KBE

Brennan, *Hon.* Sir (Francis) Gerard, KBE

Brett, Sir Charles Edward Bainbridge, Kt., CBE

Brickwood, Sir Basil Greame, Bt. (1927)

Bridges, *Hon.* Sir Phillip Rodney, Kt., CMG

Brierley, Sir Ronald Alfred, Kt.

Bright, Sir Keith, Kt.

Brinckman, Sir Theodore George Roderick, Bt. (1831)

Brisco, Sir Donald Gilfrid, Bt. (1782)

†Briscoe, Sir John James, Bt. (1910)

Brise, Sir John Archibald Ruggles-, Bt., CB, OBE, TD (1935)

Bristow, *Hon.* Sir Peter Henry Rowley, Kt.

Brittan, *Rt. Hon.* Sir Leon, Kt., QC

Brittan, Sir Samuel, Kt.

Britton, Sir Edward Louis, Kt., CBE

Broackes, Sir Nigel, Kt.

†Broadbent, Sir Andrew George, Bt. (1893)

Broadhurst, *Air Chief Marshal* Sir Harry, GCB, KBE, DSO, DFC, AFC

Brocklebank, Sir Aubrey Thomas, Bt. (1885)

Brockman, *Vice-Adm.* Sir Ronald Vernon, KCB, CSI, CIE, CVO, CBE

Brockman, *Hon.* Sir Thomas Charles Drake-, Kt., DFC

Brodie, Sir Benjamin David Ross, Bt. (1834)

Brogan, *Lt.-Gen.* Sir Mervyn Francis, KBE, CB

Bromhead, Sir John Desmond Gonville, Bt. (1806)

Bromley, Sir Rupert Charles, Bt. (1757)

Bromley, Sir Thomas Eardley, KCMG

Brook, Sir Robin, Kt., CMG, OBE

†Brooke, Sir Alistair Weston, Bt. (1919)

Brooke, Sir Francis George Windham, Bt. (1903)

Brooke, *Hon.* Sir Henry, Kt.

Brooke, Sir Richard Neville, Bt. (1662)

Brookes, Sir Wilfred Deakin, Kt., CBE, DSO

Brooksbank, Sir (Edward) Nicholas, Bt. (1919)

Broom, *Air Marshal* Sir Ivor Gordon, KCB, CBE, DSO, DFC, AFC

Broomfield, Sir Nigel Hugh Robert Allen, KCMG

Broughton, *Air Marshal* Sir Charles, KBE, CB

†Broughton, Sir David Delves, Bt. (1661)

Broun, Sir Lionel John Law, Bt. (s. 1686)

Brown, Sir Allen Stanley, Kt., CBE

Brown, Sir (Arthur James) Stephen, KBE

Brown, *Adm.* Sir Brian Thomas, KCB, CBE

Brown, *Lt.-Col.* Sir Charles Frederick Richmond, Bt. (1863)

Brown, Sir (Cyril) Maxwell Palmer, KCB, CMG

Brown, Sir David, Kt.

Brown, *Vice-Adm.* Sir David Worthington, KCB

Brown, Sir Derrick Holden-, Kt.

Brown, Sir Douglas Denison, Kt.

Brown, *Hon.* Sir Douglas Dunlop, Kt.

Brown, *Prof.* Sir (Ernest) Henry Phelps, Kt., MBE, FBA

Brown, Sir (Frederick Herbert) Stanley, Kt., CBE, FEng.

Brown, *Prof.* Sir (George) Malcolm, Kt., FRS

Brown, Sir George Noel, Kt.

Brown, Sir John Douglas Keith, Kt.

Brown, Sir John Gilbert Newton, Kt., CBE

Brown, Sir Mervyn, KCMG, OBE

Brown, *Hon.* Sir Ralph Kilner, Kt., OBE, TD

Brown, Sir Robert Crichton-, KCMG, CBE, TD

Brown, *Rt. Hon.* Sir Simon Denis, Kt.

Brown, *Rt. Hon.* Sir Stephen, Kt.

Brown, Sir Thomas, Kt.

Brown, Sir William Brian Piggott-, Bt. (1903)

Browne, *Rt. Hon.* Sir Patrick Reginald Evelyn, Kt., OBE, TD

Brownrigg, Sir Nicholas (Gawen), Bt. (1816)

Bruce, Sir (Francis) Michael Ian, Bt. (s. 1628)

Bruce, Sir Hervey James Hugh, Bt. (1804)

Bruce, *Rt. Hon.* Sir (James) Roualeyn Hovell-Thurlow-Cumming-, Kt.

Brunner, Sir John Henry Kilian, Bt. (1895)

Brunton, Sir (Edward Francis) Lauder, Bt. (1908)

Brunton, Sir Gordon Charles, Kt.

Bryan, Sir Arthur, Kt.

Bryan, Sir Paul Elmore Oliver, Kt., DSO, MC

Bryce, *Hon.* Sir (William) Gordon, Kt., CBE

Bryson, *Adm.* Sir Lindsay Sutherland, KCB, FEng.

Buchan, Sir John, Kt., CMG

Buchanan, Sir Andrew George, Bt. (1878)

Buchanan, Sir Charles Alexander James Leith-, Bt. (1775)

Buchanan, *Prof.* Sir Colin Douglas, Kt., CBE

Buchanan, *Vice-Adm.* Sir Peter William, KBE

Buchanan, Sir Robert Wilson (Robin), Kt.

Buchanan, Sir (Ranald) Dennis, Kt., MBE

Buck, Sir (Philip) Antony (Fyson), Kt., QC

Buckley, *Rt. Hon.* Sir Denys Burton, Kt., MBE

Buckley, Sir John William, Kt.

Buckley, *Lt.-Cdr.* Sir (Peter) Richard, KCVO

Buckley, *Hon.* Sir Roger John, Kt.

Bulkeley, Sir Richard Thomas Williams-, Bt. (1661)

Bull, Sir Simeon George, Bt. (1922)

Bull, Sir Walter Edward Avenon, KCVO

Bullard, Sir Julian Leonard, GCMG

Bullus, Sir Eric Edward, Kt.

Bulmer, Sir William Peter, Kt.

Bultin, Sir Bato, Kt., MBE

Bunbury, Sir Michael William, Bt. (1681)

Bunbury, Sir (Richard David) Michael Richardson-, Bt. (I. 1787)

Bunch, Sir Austin Wyeth, Kt., CBE

Bunting, Sir (Edward) John, KBE

Bunyard, Sir Robert Sidney, Kt., CBE, QPM

Burbidge, Sir Herbert Dudley, Bt. (1916)

Burbury, *Hon.* Sir Stanley Charles, KCMG, KCVO, KBE

Burdett, Sir Savile Aylmer, Bt. (1665)

Burgen, Sir Arnold Stanley Vincent, Kt., FRS

Burgess, *Gen.* Sir Edward Arthur, KCB, OBE

Burgh, Sir John Charles, KCMG, CB

Burke, Sir James Stanley Gilbert, Bt. (I. 1797)

Burke, Sir (Thomas) Kerry, Kt.

Burley, Sir Victor George, Kt., CBE

Burman, Sir (John) Charles, Kt.

Burnet, Sir James William Alexander (Sir Alastair Burnet), Kt.

Burnett, *Air Chief Marshal* Sir Brian Kenyon, GCB, DFC, AFC

Burnett, Sir David Humphery, Bt., MBE, TD (1913)

Burnett, Sir John Harrison, Kt.

Burnett, Sir Walter John, Kt.

Burney, Sir Cecil Denniston, Bt. (1921)

Burns, Sir Terence, Kt.

Burns, *Maj.-Gen.* Sir (Walter Arthur) George, GCVO, CB, DSO, OBE, MC

Burrell, Sir John Raymond, Bt. (1774)

Burrenchobay, Sir Dayendranath, KBE, CMG, CVO

Burrows, Sir Bernard Alexander Brocas, GCMG

Burston, Sir Samuel Gerald Wood, Kt., OBE

Burt, *Hon.* Sir Francis Theodore Page, KCMG

Burton, Sir Carlisle Archibald, Kt., OBE

Burton, Sir George Vernon Kennedy, Kt., CBE

Burton, *Air Marshal* Sir Harry, KCB, CBE, DSO

Burton, Sir Michael St Edmund, KCVO, CMG

Busby, Sir Matthew, Kt., CBE

Bush, *Adm.* Sir John Fitzroy Duyland, GCB, DSC

Butler, *Rt. Hon.* Sir Adam Courtauld, Kt.

Butler, Sir Clifford Charles, Kt., PH.D., FRS

Butler, Sir (Frederick) (Edward) Robin, GCB, CVO

Butler, Sir Michael Dacres, GCMG

Butler, Sir (Reginald) Michael (Thomas), Bt. (1922)

Butler, *Hon.* Sir Richard Clive, Kt.

Butler, *Col.* Sir Thomas Pierce, Bt., CVO, DSO, OBE (1628)

Butt, Sir (Alfred) Kenneth Dudley, Bt. (1929)

Butter, *Maj.* Sir David Henry, KCVO, MC

Butterworth, Sir (George) Neville, Kt.

Buxton, *Hon.* Sir Richard Joseph, Kt.

Buxton, Sir Thomas Fowell Victor, Bt. (1840)

Buzzard, Sir Anthony Farquhar, Bt. (1929)

Byatt, Sir Hugh Campbell, KCVO, CMG

Byers, Sir Maurice Hearne, Kt., CBE, QC

Byford, Sir Lawrence, Kt., CBE, QPM

Byrne, Sir Clarence Askew, Kt., OBE, DSC

Cable, Sir James Eric, KCVO, CMG

Cadbury, Sir (George) Adrian (Hayhurst), Kt.

Cadell, *Vice-Adm.* Sir John Frederick, KBE

Cadogan, *Prof.* Sir John Ivan George, Kt., CBE, FRS, FRSE

Cadwallader, Sir John, Kt.

Cahn, Sir Albert Jonas, Bt. (1934)

Cain, Sir Edward Thomas, Kt., CBE

Cain, Sir Henry Edney Conrad, Kt.

Caine, Sir Michael Harris, Kt.

Caines, Sir John, KCB

Cairncross, Sir Alexander Kirkland, KCMG

Calcutt, Sir David Charles, Kt., QC

Calderwood, Sir Robert, Kt.

Caldwell, *Surgeon Vice-Adm.* Sir (Eric) Dick, KBE, CB

Callaghan, Sir Allan Robert, Kt., CMG

Callaghan, Sir Bede Bertrand, Kt., CBE

Callard, Sir Eric John, Kt., FEng.

Callaway, *Prof.* Sir Frank Adams, Kt., CMG, OBE

Calley, Sir Henry Algernon, Kt., DSO, DFC

Callinan, Sir Bernard James, Kt., CBE, DSO, MC

Calne, *Prof.* Sir Roy Yorke, Kt., FRS

Calthorpe, Sir Euan Hamilton Anstruther-Gough-, Bt. (1929)

Cameron of Lochiel, Sir Donald Hamish, KT, CVO, TD

Cameron, Sir (Eustace) John, Kt., CBE

Cameron, *Hon.* Sir John, KT, DSC, QC (Lord Cameron)

Cameron, Sir John Watson, Kt., OBE

Campbell, Sir Alan Hugh, GCMG

Campbell, Sir Colin Moffat, Bt., MC (s. 1668)

†Campbell, Sir Lachlan Philip Kemeys, Bt. (1815)

Campbell, Sir Ian Tofts, Kt., CBE, VRD

Campbell, Sir Ilay Mark, Bt. (1808)

Campbell, Sir Matthew, KBE, CB, FRSE

Campbell, Sir Niall Alexander Hamilton, Bt. (1831)

Campbell, Sir Robin Auchinbreck, Bt. (s. 1628)

Campbell, Sir Thomas Cockburn-, Bt. (1821)

Campbell, *Hon.* Sir Walter Benjamin, Kt.

Campbell, *Hon.* Sir William Anthony, Kt.

Campion, Sir Harry, Kt., CB, CBE

†Carden, Sir Christopher Robert, Bt. (1887)

Carden, Sir John Craven, Bt. (I. 1787)

Carew, Sir Rivers Verain, Bt. (1661)

Carey, Sir Peter Willoughby, GCB

Carlill, *Vice-Adm.* Sir Stephen Hope, KBE, CB, DSO

Carlisle, Sir John Michael, Kt.

Carmichael, Sir David Peter William Gibson-Craig-, Bt. (s. 1702 and 1831)

Carmichael, Sir John, KBE
Carnac, *Revd Canon* Sir (Thomas) Nicholas Rivett-, Bt. (1836)
Carnegie, *Lt.-Gen.* Sir Robin Macdonald, KCB, OBE
Carnegie, Sir Roderick Howard, Kt.
Carnwath, Sir Andrew Hunter, KCVO
Caro, Sir Anthony Alfred, Kt., CBE
Carpenter, *Very Revd* Edward Frederick, KCVO
Carpenter, *Lt.-Gen.* the Hon. Sir Thomas Patrick John Boyd-, KBE
Carr, Sir (Albert) Raymond (Maillard), Kt.
Carr, *Air Marshal* Sir John Darcy Baker-, KBE, CB, AFC
Carrick, *Hon.* Sir John Leslie, KCMG
Carsberg, *Prof.* Sir Bryan Victor, Kt.
Carswell, *Hon.* Sir Robert Douglas, Kt.
Carter, Sir Charles Frederick, Kt., FBA
Carter, Sir Derrick Hunton, Kt., TD
Carter, Sir John, Kt., QC
Carter, Sir John Alexander, Kt.
Carter, Sir Philip David, Kt., CBE
Carter, Sir Richard Henry Alwyn, Kt.
Carter, Sir William Oscar, Kt.
Cartland, Sir George Barrington, Kt., CMG
Cartledge, Sir Bryan George, KCMG
Cary, Sir Roger Hugh, Bt. (1955)
Casey, *Rt. Hon.* Sir Maurice Eugene, Kt.
Cash, Sir Gerald Christopher, GCMG, GCVO, OBE
Cass, Sir Geoffrey Arthur, Kt.
Cass, Sir John Patrick, Kt., OBE
Cassel, Sir Harold Felix, Bt., TD, QC (1920)
Cassels, *Field Marshal* Sir (Archibald) James Halkett, GCB, KBE, DSO
Cassels, Sir John Seton, Kt., CB
Cassels, *Adm.* Sir Simon Alastair Cassillis, KCB, CBE
Cassidi, *Adm.* Sir (Arthur) Desmond, GCB
Casson, Sir Hugh Maxwell, CH, KCVO, PPRA, FRIBA
Cater, Sir Jack, KBE
Cater, Sir John Robert, Kt.
Catford, Sir (John) Robin, KCVO, CBE
Catherwood, Sir (Henry) Frederick (Ross), Kt., MEP
Catling, Sir Richard Charles, Kt., CMG, OBE
Cato, *Hon.* Sir Arnott Samuel, KCMG
Caughey, Sir Thomas Harcourt Clarke, KBE
Caulfield, *Hon.* Sir Bernard, Kt.
Cave, Sir Charles Edward Coleridge, Bt. (1896)
Cave, Sir (Charles) Philip Haddon-, KBE, CMG
Cave, Sir Robert Cave-Browne-, Bt. (1641)
Cawley, Sir Charles Mills, Kt., CBE, Ph.D.
Cayley, Sir Digby William David, Bt. (1661)

Cayzer, Sir James Arthur, Bt. (1904)
Cazalet, *Hon.* Sir Edward Stephen, Kt.
Cazalet, Sir Peter Grenville, Kt.
Cecil, *Rear-Adm.* Sir (Oswald) Nigel Amherst, KBE, CB
Chacksfield, *Air Vice-Marshal* Sir Bernard Albert, KBE, CB
Chadwick, *Revd Prof.* Henry, KBE
Chadwick, *Hon.* Sir John Murray, Kt., ED
Chadwick, Sir Joshua Kenneth Burton, Bt. (1935)
Chadwick, *Revd Prof.* (William) Owen, OM, KBE, FBA
Chan, *Rt. Hon.* Sir Julius, KBE
Chance, Sir (George) Jeremy ffolliott, Bt. (1900)
Chandler, Sir Colin Michael, Kt.
Chandler, Sir Geoffrey, Kt., CBE
Chaney, *Hon.* Sir Frederick Charles, KBE, AFC
Chaplin, Sir Malcolm Hilbery, Kt., CBE
Chapman, Sir David Robert Macgowan, Bt. (1958)
Chapman, Sir George Alan, Kt.
Chapple, *Field Marshal* Sir John Lyon, GCB, CBE
Charles, Sir Joseph Quentin, Kt.
Charnley, Sir (William) John, Kt., CB, FEng.
Chatfield, Sir John Freeman, Kt., CBE
Chaytor, Sir George Reginald, Bt. (1831)
Checketts, *Sqn. Ldr.* Sir David John, KCVO
Checkland, Sir Michael, Kt.
Cheetham, Sir Nicolas John Alexander, KCMG
Chessells, Sir Arthur David (Tim), Kt.
Chesterman, Sir (Dudley) Ross, Kt., Ph.D.
Chesterton, Sir Oliver Sidney, Kt., MC
Chetwood, Sir Clifford Jack, Kt.
Chetwynd, Sir Arthur Ralph Talbot, Bt. (1795)
Cheung, Sir Oswald Victor, Kt., CBE
Cheyne, Sir Joseph Lister Watson, Bt., OBE (1908)
Chichester, Sir (Edward) John, Bt. (1641)
Child, Sir (Coles John) Jeremy, Bt. (1919)
Chilton, *Brig.* Sir Frederick Oliver, Kt., CBE, DSO
Chilwell, *Hon.* Sir Muir Fitzherbert, Kt.
Chinn, Sir Trevor Edwin, Kt., CVO
Chipperfield, Sir Geoffrey Howes, KCB
Chitty, Sir Thomas Willes, Bt. (1924)
Cholmeley, Sir Montague John, Bt. (1806)
Christie, Sir George William Langham, Kt.
Christie, *Hon.* Sir Vernon Howard Colville, Kt.
Christie, Sir William, Kt., MBE
Christison, *Gen.* Sir (Alexander Frank) Philip, Bt., GBE, CB, DSO, MC (1871)

Christopherson, Sir Derman Guy, Kt., OBE, D.Phil., FRS, FEng.
Chung, Sir Sze-yuen, GBE, FEng.
Clapham, Sir Michael John Sinclair, KBE
Clark, Sir Colin Douglas, Bt. (1917)
Clark, Sir Francis Drake, Bt. (1886)
Clark, Sir John Allen, Kt.
Clark, *Prof.* Sir John Grahame Douglas, Kt., CBE
Clark, Sir John Stewart-, Bt., MEP (1918)
Clark, Sir Robert Anthony, Kt., DSC
Clark, Sir Robin Chichester-, Kt.
Clark, Sir Terence Joseph, KBE, CMG, CVO
Clark, Sir Thomas Edwin, Kt.
Clarke, *Hon.* Sir Anthony Peter, Kt.
Clarke, Sir (Charles Mansfield) Tobias, Bt. (1831)
Clarke, *Prof.* Sir Cyril Astley, KBE, MD, SC.D., FRS, FRCP
Clarke, Sir Ellis Emmanuel Innocent, GCMG
Clarke, Sir (Henry) Ashley, GCMG, GCVO
Clarke, Sir Jonathan Dennis, Kt.
Clarke, *Maj.* Sir Peter Cecil, KCVO
Clarke, Sir Robert Cyril, Kt.
Clarke, Sir Rupert William John, Bt., MBE (1882)
Clay, Sir Richard Henry, Bt. (1841)
Clayton, Sir David Robert, Bt., (1732)
Clayton, Sir Robert James, Kt., CBE, FEng.
Cleaver, Sir Anthony Brian, Kt.
Clegg, Sir Walter, Kt.
Cleminson, Sir James Arnold Stacey, KBE, MC
Clerk, Sir John Dutton, Bt., CBE, VRD (s. 1679)
Clerke, Sir John Edward Longueville, Bt. (1660)
Clifford, Sir Roger Joseph, Bt. (1887)
Clothier, Sir Cecil Montacute, KCB, QC
Clucas, Sir Kenneth Henry, KCB
Clutterbuck, *Vice-Adm.* Sir David Granville, KBE, CB
Coates, Sir Ernest William, Kt., CMG
Coates, Sir Frederick Gregory Lindsay, Bt. (1921)
Coats, Sir Alastair Francis Stuart, Bt. (1905)
Coats, Sir William David, Kt.
Cobban, Sir James Macdonald, Kt., CBE, TD
Cochrane, Sir (Henry) Marc (Sursock), Bt. (1903)
Cockburn, Sir John Elliot, Bt. (s. 1671)
Cockburn, Sir Robert, KBE, CB, Ph.D., FEng.
Cockcroft, Sir Wilfred Halliday, Kt., D.Phil.
Cockerell, Sir Christopher Sydney, Kt., CBE, FRS
Cockram, Sir John, Kt.
Cockshaw, Sir Alan, Kt., FEng.
Codrington, Sir Simon Francis Bethell, Bt. (1876)

Codrington, Sir William Alexander, Bt. (1721)

Coghill, Sir Egerton James Nevill Tobias, Bt. (1778)

Cohen, Sir Edward, Kt.

Cohen, Sir Ivor Harold, Kt., CBE, TD

Cohen, Sir Stephen Harry Waley-, Bt. (1961)

Coldstream, Sir George Phillips, KCB, KCVO, QC

Cole, Sir (Alexander) Colin, KCB, KCVO, TD

Cole, Sir David Lee, KCMG, MC

Cole, Sir (Robert) William, Kt.

Coles, Sir (Arthur) John, KCMG

Colfox, Sir (William) John, Bt. (1939)

Collett, Sir Christopher, GBE

Collett, Sir Ian Seymour, Bt. (1934)

Collins, Sir Arthur James Robert, KCVO

Collins, Sir John Alexander, Kt.

Collyear, Sir John Gowen, Kt., FEng.

Colman, *Hon.* Sir Anthony David, Kt.

Colman, Sir Michael Jeremiah, Bt. (1907)

Colquhoun, *Maj.-Gen.* Sir Cyril Harry, KCVO, CB, OBE

Colquhoun of Luss, Sir Ivar Iain, Bt. (1786)

Colt, Sir Edward William Dutton Bt. (1694)

Colthurst, Sir Richard La Touche, Bt. (1744)

Combs, Sir Willis Ide, KCVO, CMG

Compston, *Vice-Adm.* Sir Peter Maxwell, KCB

Compton, Sir Edmund Gerald, GCB, KBE

Comyn, *Hon.* Sir James, Kt.

Conant, Sir John Ernest Michael, Bt. (1954)

Connell, *Hon.* Sir Michael Bryan, Kt.

Conran, Sir Terence Orby, Kt.

Cons, *Hon.* Sir Derek, Kt.

Constable, Sir Robert Frederick Strickland-, Bt. (1641)

Cook, *Prof.* Sir Alan Hugh, Kt.

Cook, Sir Christopher Wymondham Rayner Herbert, Bt. (1886)

Cooke, Sir Charles Fletcher-, Kt., QC

Cooke, *Lt.-Col.* Sir David William Perceval, Bt. (1661)

Cooke, Sir Howard Felix Hanlan, GCMG, ON, CD

Cooke, *Rt. Hon.* Sir Robin Brunskill, KBE

Cooksey, Sir David James Scott, Kt.

Cooley, Sir Alan Sydenham, Kt., CBE

Coop, Sir Maurice Fletcher, Kt.

Cooper, *Rt. Hon.* Sir Frank, GCB, CMG

Cooper, Sir (Frederick Howard) Michael Craig-, Kt., CBE, TD

Cooper, *Gen.* Sir George Leslie Conroy, GCB, MC

Cooper, Sir Louis Jacques Blom-, Kt., QC

Cooper, Sir Patrick Graham Astley, Bt. (1821)

Cooper, Sir Richard Powell, Bt. (1905)

Cooper, *Maj.-Gen.* Sir Simon Christie, KCVO

Cooper, Sir William Daniel Charles, Bt. (1863)

Coote, Sir Christopher John, Bt., *Premier Baronet of Ireland* (I. 1621)

Copas, *Most Revd* Virgil, KBE, DD

Cope, *Rt. Hon.* Sir John Ambrose, Kt., MP

Copisarow, Sir Alcon Charles, Kt.

Corbet, Sir John Vincent, Bt., MBE (1808)

Corby, Sir (Frederick) Brian, Kt.

Corfield, *Rt. Hon.* Sir Frederick Vernon, Kt., QC

Corfield, Sir Kenneth George, Kt.

Corley, Sir Kenneth Sholl Ferrand, Kt.

Cormack, Sir Magnus Cameron, KBE

Corness, Sir Colin Ross, Kt.

Cornford, Sir (Edward) Clifford, KCB, FEng.

Cornforth, Sir John Warcup, Kt., CBE, D.Phil., FRS

Corry, Sir William James, Bt. (1885)

Cortazzi, Sir (Henry Arthur) Hugh, GCMG

Cory, Sir (Clinton Charles) Donald, Bt. (1919)

Costar, Sir Norman Edgar, KCMG

Cotter, *Lt.-Col.* Sir Delaval James Alfred, Bt., DSO (I. 1763)

Cotterell, Sir John Henry Geers, Bt. (1805)

Cotton, Sir John Richard, KCMG, OBE

Cotton, *Hon.* Sir Robert Carrington, KCMG

Cottrell, Sir Alan Howard, Kt., Ph.D., FRS, FEng.

Cotts, Sir (Robert) Crichton Mitchell, Bt. (1921)

Coulson, Sir John Eltringham, KCMG

Couper, Sir (Robert) Nicholas (Oliver), Bt. (1841)

Court, *Hon.* Sir Charles Walter Michael, KCMG, OBE

Coutts, Sir David Burdett Money-, KCVO

Couzens, Sir Kenneth Edward, KCB

Covacevich, Sir (Anthony) Thomas, Kt., DFC

Coward, *Vice-Adm.* Sir John Francis, KCB, DSO

Cowdrey, Sir (Michael) Colin, Kt., CBE

Cowen, *Rt. Hon. Prof.* Sir Zelman, GCMG, GCVO, QC

Cowie, Sir Thomas (Tom), Kt., OBE

Cowperthwaite, Sir John James, KBE, CMG

Cox, *Prof.* Sir David Roxbee, Kt., FRS

Cox, Sir (Ernest) Gordon, KBE, TD, D.SC., FRS

Cox, Sir Geoffrey Sandford, Kt., CBE

Cox, Sir (George) Trenchard, Kt., CBE, FSA

Cox, *Vice-Adm.* Sir John Michael Holland, KCB

Cox, Sir Mencea Ethereal, Kt.

Cradock, *Rt. Hon.* Sir Percy, GCMG

Craig, Sir (Albert) James (Macqueen), GCMG

Cramer, *Hon.* Sir John Oscar, Kt.

Crane, Sir James William Donald, Kt., CBE

Craufurd, Sir Robert James, Bt. (1781)

Craven, *Air Marshal* Sir Robert Edward, KBE, CB, DFC

Crawford, *Prof.* Sir Frederick William, Kt., FEng.

Crawford, *Hon.* Sir George Hunter, Kt.

Crawford, Sir (Robert) Stewart, GCMG, CVO

Crawford, *Vice-Adm.* Sir William Godfrey, KBE, CB, DSC

Crawshay, *Col.* Sir William Robert, Kt., DSO, ERD, TD

Creagh, *Maj.-Gen.* Sir (Kilner) Rupert Brazier-, KBE, CB, DSO

Cresswell, *Hon.* Sir Peter John, Kt.

Crichton, Sir Andrew James Maitland-Makgill-, Kt.

Crill, Sir Peter Leslie, Kt., CBE

Cripps, Sir Cyril Humphrey, Kt.

Crisp, Sir (John) Peter, Bt. (1913)

Critchett, Sir Ian (George Lorraine), Bt. (1908)

Croft, Sir Owen Glendower, Bt. (1671)

Croft, Sir Thomas Stephen Hutton, Bt. (1818)

†Crofton, Sir Hugh Denis, Bt. (1801)

Crofton, *Prof.* Sir John Wenman, Kt.

Crofton, Sir Malby Sturges, Bt. (1838)

Croker, Sir Walter Russell, KBE

Crookenden, *Lt.-Gen.* Sir Napier, KCB, DSO, OBE

Cross, Sir Barry Albert, Kt., CBE, FRS

Cross, *Air Chief Marshal* Sir Kenneth Brian Boyd, KCB, CBE, DSO, DFC

Crossland, *Prof.* Sir Bernard, Kt., CBE, FEng.

Crossland, Sir Leonard, Kt.

Crossley, Sir Nicholas John, Bt. (1909)

Crouch, Sir David Lance, Kt.

Cruthers, Sir James Winter, Kt.

Cubbon, Sir Brian Crossland, GCB

Cubitt, Sir Hugh Guy, Kt., CBE

Cuckney, Sir John Graham, Kt.

Cullen, Sir (Edward) John, Kt., F.Eng.

Cumming, Sir William Gordon Gordon-, Bt. (1804)

Cuninghame, Sir John Christopher Foggo Montgomery-, Bt. (NS 1672)

†Cuninghame, Sir William Henry Fairlie-, Bt. (S. 1630)

Cunliffe, Sir David Ellis, Bt. (1759)

Cunningham, Sir Charles Craik, GCB, KBE, CVO

Cunningham, *Lt.-Gen.* Sir Hugh Patrick, KBE

Cunynghame, Sir Andrew David Francis, Bt. (S. 1702)

Curle, Sir John Noel Ormiston, KCVO, CMG

Curran, Sir Samuel Crowe, Kt., D.SC., Ph.D., FRS, FRSE, FEng.

Currie, *Prof.* Sir Alastair Robert, Kt., FRCP, FRCPE, FRSE

†Currie, Sir Donald Scott, Bt. (1847)

Currie, Sir Neil Smith, Kt., CBE

Curtis, Sir Barry John, Kt.

Curtis, Sir (Edward) Leo, Kt.

Curtis, *Hon.* Sir Richard Herbert, Kt.

Curtis, Sir William Peter, Bt. (1802)

Curtiss, *Air Marshal* Sir John Bagot, KCB, KBE

Curwen, Sir Christopher Keith, KCMG

Cuthbertson, Sir Harold Alexander, Kt.

Cutler, Sir (Arthur) Roden, VC, KCMG, KCVO, CBE

Cutler, Sir Charles Benjamin, KBE, ED

Cutler, Sir Horace Walter, Kt., OBE

Dacie, *Prof.* Sir John Vivian, Kt., MD, FRS

Dalais, Sir Adrien Pierre, Kt.

Dale, Sir William Leonard, KCMG

Dalrymple, *Maj.* Sir Hew Fleetwood Hamilton-, Bt., KCVO (S. 1697)

Dalton, Sir Alan Nugent Goring, Kt., CBE

Dalton, *Vice-Adm.* Sir Geoffrey Thomas James Oliver, KCB

Daly, *Lt.-Gen.* Sir Thomas Joseph, KBE, CB, DSO

Dalyell, Sir Tam, Bt., MP (NS 1685)

Daniel, Sir Goronwy Hopkin, KCVO, CB, D.Phil.

Daniell, Sir Peter Averell, Kt., TD

Danks, Sir Alan John, KBE

Darby, Sir Peter Howard, Kt., CBE, QFSM

Darell, Sir Jeffrey Lionel, Bt., MC (1795)

Dargie, Sir William Alexander, Kt., CBE

Dark, Sir Anthony Michael Beaumont-, Kt.

Darling, Sir Clifford, Kt.

Darling, Sir James Ralph, Kt., CMG, OBE

Darling, *Gen.* Sir Kenneth Thomas, GBE, KCB, DSO

Darlington, *Rear-Adm.* Sir Charles Roy, KBE

Darvall, Sir (Charles) Roger, Kt., CBE

Dashwood, Sir Francis John Vernon Hereward, Bt., *Premier Baronet of Great Britain* (1707)

Dashwood, Sir Richard James, Bt. (1684)

Daunt, Sir Timothy Lewis Achilles, KCMG

David, Sir Jean Marc, Kt., CBE, QC

Davidson, Sir Robert James, Kt., FEng.

Davie, Sir Antony Francis Ferguson-, Bt. (1847)

Davies, *Air Marshal* Sir Alan Cyril, KCB, CBE

Davies, *Hon.* Sir (Alfred William) Michael, Kt.

Davies, Sir Alun Talfan, Kt., QC

Davies, Sir David Henry, Kt.

Davies, *Hon.* Sir (David Herbert) Mervyn, Kt., MC, TD

Davies, *Vice-Adm.* Sir Lancelot Richard Bell, KBE

Davies, Sir Oswald, Kt., CBE

Davies, Sir Peter Maxwell, Kt., CBE

Davies, Sir Richard Harries, KCVO, CBE

Davies, Sir Victor Caddy, Kt., OBE

Davis, Sir Charles Sigmund, Kt., CB

Davis, Sir Colin Rex, Kt., CBE

Davis, *Hon.* Sir (Dermot) Renn, Kt., OBE

Davis, Sir (Ernest) Howard, Kt., CMG, OBE

Davis, Sir John Gilbert, Bt. (1946)

Davis, Sir Maurice Herbert, Kt., OBE

Davis, Sir Rupert Charles Hart-, Kt.

Davis, *Hon.* Sir Thomas Robert Alexander Harries, KBE

Davis, Sir (William) Allan, GBE

Davison, *Rt. Hon.* Sir Ronald Keith, GBE, CMG

Dawbarn, Sir Simon Yelverton, KCVO, CMG

Dawson, Sir Anthony Michael, KCVO, MD, FRCP

Dawson, *Hon.* Sir Daryl Michael, KBE, CB

Dawson, Sir Hugh Michael Trevor, Bt. (1920)

Dawson, *Air Chief Marshal* Sir Walter Lloyd, KCB, CBE, DSO

Dawtry, Sir Alan (Graham), Kt., CBE, TD

Day, Sir Derek Malcolm, KCMG

Day, Sir (Judson) Graham, Kt.

Day, Sir Michael John, Kt., OBE

Day, Sir Robin, Kt.

Deakin, Sir (Frederick) William (Dampier), Kt., DSO

Dean, *Rt. Hon.* Sir (Arthur) Paul, Kt.

Dean, Sir Patrick Henry, GCMG

Deane, *Hon.* Sir William Patrick, KBE

Dearing, Sir Ronald Ernest, Kt., CB

de Bellaigue, Sir Geoffrey, KCVO

Debenham, Sir Gilbert Ridley, Bt. (1931)

de Deney, Sir Geoffrey Ivor, KCVO

Deer, Sir (Arthur) Frederick, Kt., CMG

de Hoghton, Sir (Richard) Bernard (Cuthbert), Bt. (1611)

De la Bère, Sir Cameron, Bt. (1953)

de la Mare, Sir Arthur James, KCMG, KCVO

Delamere, Sir Monita Eru, KBE

de la Rue, Sir Andrew George Ilay, Bt. (1898)

Dellow, Sir John Albert, Kt., CBE

de Lotbinière, *Lt.-Col.* Sir Edmond Joly, Kt.

Delve, Sir Frederick William, Kt., CBE

de Montmorency, Sir Arnold Geoffroy, Bt. (I. 1631)

Denholm, Sir John Ferguson (Ian), Kt., CBE

Denman, Sir (George) Roy, KCB, CMG

Denny, Sir Alistair Maurice Archibald, Bt. (1913)

Denny, Sir Anthony Coningham de Waltham, Bt. (I. 1782)

Dent, Sir John, Kt., CBE, FEng.

Dent, Sir Robin John, KCVO

Denton, *Prof.* Sir Eric James, Kt., CBE, FRS

Derbyshire, Sir Andrew George, Kt.

Derham, Sir Peter John, Kt.

de Trafford, Sir Dermot Humphrey, Bt. (1841)

Deverell, Sir Colville Montgomery, GBE, KCMG, CVO

Devesi, Sir Baddeley, GCMG, GCVO

De Ville, Sir Harold Godfrey Oscar, Kt., CBE

Devitt, Sir Thomas Gordon, Bt. (1916)

de Waal, Sir (Constant Henrik) Henry, KCB, QC

Dewey, Sir Anthony Hugh, Bt. (1917)

Dewhurst, *Prof.* Sir (Christopher) John, Kt.

d'Eyncourt, Sir Mark Gervais Tennyson-, Bt. (1930)

Dhenin, *Air Marshal* Sir Geoffrey Howard, KBE, AFC, GM, MD

Dhrangadhra, HH the Maharaja Raj Saheb of, KCIE

Dibela, *Hon.* Sir Kingsford, GCMG

Dick, Sir John Alexander, Kt., MC, QC

Dickenson, Sir Aubrey Fiennes Trotman-, Kt.

Dickinson, Sir Harold Herbert, Kt.

Dickinson, Sir Samuel Benson, Kt.

Dilbertson, Sir Geoffrey, Kt., CBE

Dilke, Sir John Fisher Wentworth, Bt. (1862)

Dill, Sir Nicholas Bayard, Kt., CBE

Dillon, *Rt. Hon.* Sir (George) Brian (Hugh), Kt.

Dillon, Sir John Vincent, Kt., CMG

Dillon, Sir Max, Kt.

Diver, *Hon.* Sir Leslie Charles, Kt.

Dixon, Sir Jonathan Mark, Bt. (1919)

Djanogly, Sir Harry Ari Simon, Kt., CBE

Dobbs, *Capt.* Sir Richard Arthur Frederick, KCVO

Dobson, *Vice-Adm.* Sir David Stuart, KBE

Dobson, Sir Denis William, KCB, OBE, QC

Dobson, *Gen.* Sir Patrick John Howard-, GCB

Dobson, Sir Richard Portway, Kt.

Dodds, Sir Ralph Jordan, Bt. (1964)

Dodson, Sir Derek Sherborne Lindsell, KCMG, MC

Dodsworth, Sir John Christopher Smith-, Bt. (1784)

Doll, *Prof.* Sir (William) Richard (Shaboe), Kt., OBE, FRS, DM, MD, D.SC.

Dollery, Sir Colin Terence, Kt.

Donald, Sir Alan Ewen, KCMG

Donald, *Air Marshal* Sir John George, KBE

Donne, *Hon.* Sir Gaven John, KBE

Donne, Sir John Christopher, Kt.

Dookun, Sir Dewoonarain, Kt.

Dorey, Sir Graham Martyn, Kt.

Dorman, *Lt.-Col.* Sir Charles Geoffrey, Bt., MC (1923)

Dorman, Sir Maurice Henry, GCMG, GCVO

Dougherty, *Maj.-Gen.* Sir Ivan Noel, Kt., CBE, DSO, ED

Doughty, Sir William Roland, Kt.

Douglas, Sir (Edward) Sholto, Kt.

Douglas, Sir Robert McCallum, Kt., OBE

Douglas, *Hon.* Sir Roger Owen, Kt.

Douglas, *Rt. Hon.* Sir William Randolph, KCMG

Dover, *Prof.* Sir Kenneth James, Kt., D.Litt., FBA, FRSE

Down, Sir Alastair Frederick, Kt., OBE, MC, TD

Downes, Sir Edward Thomas, Kt., CBE

Downey, Sir Gordon Stanley, KCB

Downs, Sir Diarmuid, Kt., CBE, FEng.

Downward, Sir William Atkinson, Kt.

Dowson, Sir Philip Manning, Kt., CBE, ARA

Doyle, Sir Reginald Derek Henry, Kt., CBE

D'Oyly, Sir Nigel Hadley Miller, Bt. (1663)

Drake, Sir (Arthur) Eric (Courtney), Kt., CBE

Drake, *Hon.* Sir (Frederick) Maurice, Kt., DFC

Drew, Sir Arthur Charles Walter, KCB

Dreyer, *Adm.* Sir Desmond Parry, GCB, CBE, DSC

Drinkwater, Sir John Muir, Kt., QC

Driver, Sir Antony Victor, Kt.

Driver, Sir Eric William, Kt.

Drury, Sir (Victor William) Michael, Kt., OBE

Dryden, Sir John Stephen Gyles, Bt. (1733 and 1795)

du Cann, *Rt. Hon.* Sir Edward Dillon Lott, KBE

Duckmanton, Sir Talbot Sydney, Kt., CBE

Duckworth, *Maj.* Sir Richard Dyce, Bt. (1909)

du Cros, Sir Claude Philip Arthur Mallet, Bt. (1916)

Duff, *Rt. Hon.* Sir (Arthur) Antony, GCMG, CVO, DSO, DSC

Duffell, *Lt.-Gen.* Sir Peter Royson, KCB, CBE, MC

Duffus, *Hon.* Sir William Algernon Holwell, Kt.

Duffy, Sir (Albert) (Edward) Patrick, Kt., PH.D.

Dugdale, Sir William Stratford, Bt., MC (1936)

Dunbar, Sir Archibald Ranulph, Bt. (S. 1700)

Dunbar, Sir David Hope-, Bt. (S. 1664)

Dunbar, Sir Drummond Cospatrick Ninian, Bt., MC (S. 1698)

Dunbar, Sir Jean Ivor, Bt. (S. 1694)

Dunbar of Hempriggs, Dame Maureen Daisy Helen (Lady Dunbar of Hempriggs), Btss. (S. 1706)

Duncan, Sir James Blair, Kt.

Duncombe, Sir Philip Digby Pauncefort-, Bt. (1859)

Dundas, Sir Hugh Spencer Lisle, Kt., CBE, DSO, DFC

Dunham, Sir Kingsley Charles, Kt., PH.D., FRS, FRSE, FEng.

Dunlop, Sir Thomas, Bt. (1916)

Dunlop, Sir William Norman Gough, Kt.

Dunn, *Air Marshal* Sir Eric Clive, KBE, CB, BEM

Dunn, *Lt.-Col.* Sir (Francis) Vivian, KCVO, OBE

Dunn, *Air Marshal* Sir Patrick Hunter, KBE, CB, DFC

Dunn, *Rt. Hon.* Sir Robin Horace Walford, Kt., MC

Dunnett, Sir (Ludovic) James, GCB, CMG

Dunning, Sir Simon William Patrick, Bt. (1930)

Dunphie, *Maj.-Gen.* Sir Charles Anderson Lane, Kt., CB, CBE, DSO

Dunstan, *Lt.-Gen.* Sir Donald Beaumont, KBE, CB

†Duntze, Sir Daniel Evans, Bt. (1774)

Dupre, Sir Tumun, Kt., MBE

Dupree, Sir Peter, Bt. (1921)

Durand, Sir Edward Alan Christopher David Percy, Bt. (1892)

Durant, Sir (Robert) Anthony (Bevis), Kt., MP

Durham, Sir Kenneth, Kt.

Durie, Sir Alexander Charles, Kt., CBE

Durkin, *Air Marshal* Sir Herbert, KBE, CB

Durrant, Sir William Henry Estridge, Bt. (1784)

Duthie, *Prof.* Sir Herbert Livingston, Kt.

Duthie, Sir Robert Grieve (Robin), Kt., CBE

Duval, Sir (Charles) Gaetan, Kt.

Duxbury, *Air Marshal* Sir (John) Barry, KCB, CBE

Dyer, *Prof.* Sir (Henry) Peter (Francis) Swinnerton-, Bt., KBE, FRS (1678)

Dyke, Sir David William Hart, Bt. (1677)

Dyson, *Hon.* Sir John Anthony, Kt.

Earle, Sir (Hardman) George (Algernon), Bt. (1869)

East, Sir (Lewis) Ronald, Kt., CBE

Easton, Sir Robert William Simpson, Kt., CBE

Eastwood, Sir John Bealby, Kt.

Eaton, *Adm.* Sir Kenneth John, KCB

Eberle, *Adm.* Sir James Henry Fuller, GCB

Ebrahim, Sir (Mahomed) Currimbhoy, Bt. (1910)

Eburne, Sir Sidney Alfred William, Kt., MC

Eccles, Sir John Carew, Kt., D.Phil., FRS

Echlin, Sir Norman David Fenton, Bt. (I. 1721)

Eckersley, Sir Donald Payze, Kt., OBE

†Edge, Sir William, Bt. (1937)

Edmenson, Sir Walter Alexander, Kt., CBE

Edmonstone, Sir Archibald Bruce Charles, Bt. (1774)

Edwards, Sir Michael Owen, Kt.

Edwards, Sir Christopher John Churchill, Bt. (1866)

Edwards, Sir George Robert, Kt., OM, CBE, FRS, FEng.

Edwards, Sir (John) Clive (Leighton), Bt. (1921)

Edwards, Sir Llewellyn Roy, Kt.

Edwards, *Prof.* Sir Samuel Frederick, Kt., FRS

Egan, Sir John Leopold, Kt.

Egerton, Sir John Alfred Roy, Kt.

Egerton, Sir (Philip) John (Caledon) Grey-, Bt. (1617)

Egerton, Sir Seymour John Louis, GCVO

Egerton, Sir Stephen Loftus, KCMG

Eggleston, *Hon.* Sir Richard Moulton, Kt.

Eichelbaum, *Rt. Hon.* Sir Thomas, GBE

Eliott of Stobs, Sir Charles Joseph Alexander, Bt. (s. 1666)

Ellerton, Sir Geoffrey James, Kt., CMG, MBE

Elliot, Sir Gerald Henry, Kt.

Elliott, Sir Clive Christopher Hugh, Bt. (1917)

Elliott, Sir Randal Forbes, KBE

Elliott, *Prof.* Sir Roger James, Kt., FRS

Elliott, Sir Ronald Stuart, Kt.

Ellis, Sir John Rogers, Kt., MBE, MD, FRCP

Ellis, Sir Ronald, Kt., FEng.

Ellison, *Col.* Sir Ralph Harry Carr-, Kt., TD

Elphinstone, Sir John, Bt. (s. 1701)

Elphinstone, Sir (Maurice) Douglas (Warburton), Bt., TD (1816)

Elton, Sir Arnold, Kt., CBE

Elton, Sir Charles Abraham Grierson, Bt. (1717)

Elton, *Prof.* Sir Geoffrey Rudolph, Kt., FBA

Elwood, Sir Brian George Conway, Kt., CBE

Elworthy, Sir Peter Herbert, Kt.

Elyan, Sir (Isadore) Victor, Kt.

Emery, *Rt. Hon.* Sir Peter Frank Hannibal, Kt., MP

Empson, *Adm.* Sir (Leslie) Derek, GBE, KCB

Emson, *Air Marshal* Sir Reginald Herbert, KBE, CB, AFC

Engineer, Sir Noshirwan Phirozshah, Kt.

Engle, Sir George Lawrence Jose, KCB, QC

English, Sir Cyril Rupert, Kt.

English, Sir David, Kt.

English, Sir Terence Alexander Hawthorne, KBE, FRCS

Entwistle, Sir (John Nuttall) Maxwell, Kt.

Epstein, *Prof.* Sir (Michael) Anthony, Kt., CBE, FRS

Ereaut, Sir (Herbert) Frank Cobbold, Kt.

Errington, *Col.* Sir Geoffrey Frederick, Bt. (1963)

Errington, Sir Lancelot, KCB

Erskine, Sir (Thomas) David, Bt. (1821)

Esmonde, Sir Thomas Francis Grattan, Bt. (I. 1629)

Espie, Sir Frank Fletcher, Kt., OBE

Esplen, Sir John Graham, Bt. (1921)

Eustace, Sir Joseph Lambert, GCMG, GCVO

Evans, Sir Anthony Adney, Bt. (1920)

Evans, *Rt. Hon.* Sir Anthony Howell Meurig, Kt., RD

Evans, *Air Chief Marshal* Sir David George, GCB, CBE

Evans, *Air Chief Marshal* Sir David Parry-, GCB, CBE

Evans, Sir Francis Loring Gwynne-, Bt. (1913)

Evans, *Hon.* Sir Haydn Tudor, Kt.

Evans, Sir Richard Mark, KCMG, KCVO

Evans, Sir (Robert) Charles, Kt.

Evans, Sir (William) Vincent (John), GCMG, MBE, QC

Eveleigh, *Rt. Hon.* Sir Edward Walter, Kt., ERD

Everard, *Maj.-Gen.* Sir Christopher Earle Welby-, KBE, CB

Everard, Sir Robin Charles, Bt. (1911)

Everson, Sir Frederick Charles, KCMG

Every, Sir Henry John Michael, Bt. (1641)

Ewans, Sir Martin Kenneth, KCMG

Ewart, Sir (William) Ivan (Cecil), Bt., DSC (1887)

Ewbank, *Hon.* Sir Anthony Bruce, Kt.

Ewin, Sir (David) Ernest Thomas Floyd, Kt., OBE, MVO

Ewing, *Vice-Adm.* Sir (Robert) Alastair, KBE, CB, DSC

Ewing, Sir Ronald Archibald Orr-, Bt. (1886)

Eyre, Sir Graham Newman, Kt., QC

Eyre, *Maj.-Gen.* Sir James Ainsworth Campden Gabriel, KCVO, CBE

Eyre, Sir Reginald Edwin, Kt.

Faber, Sir Richard Stanley, KCVO, CMG

Fadahunsi, Sir Joseph Odeleye, KCMG

Fagge, Sir John William Frederick, Bt. (1660)

Fairbairn, *Hon.* Sir David Eric, KBE, DFC

Fairbairn, Sir (James) Brooke, Bt. (1869)

Fairbairn, Sir Nicholas Hardwick, Kt., QC, MP

Fairclough, Sir John Whitaker, Kt., FEng.

Fairgrieve, Sir (Thomas) Russell, Kt., CBE, TD

Fairhall, *Hon.* Sir Allen, KBE

Fairweather, Sir Patrick Stanislaus, KCMG

Falconer, *Hon.* Sir Douglas William, Kt., MBE

Falk, Sir Roger Salis, Kt., OBE

Falkiner, Sir Edmond Charles, Bt. (I. 1778)

Falkner, Sir (Donald) Keith, Kt.

Fall, Sir Brian James Proetel, KCMG

Falle, Sir Samuel, KCMG, KCVO, DSC

Fareed, Sir Djamil Sheik, Kt.

Farmer, Sir (Lovedin) George Thomas, Kt.

Farndale, *Gen.* Sir Martin Baker, KCB

Farquhar, Sir Michael Fitzroy Henry, Bt. (1796)

Farquharson, *Rt. Hon.* Sir Donald Henry, Kt.

Farquharson, Sir James Robbie, KBE

Farr, Sir John Arnold, Kt.

Farrer, Sir Charles Matthew, KCVO

Farrington, Sir Henry Francis Colden, Bt. (1818)

Fat, Sir (Maxime) Edouard (Lim Man) Lim, Kt.

Faulkner, Sir Eric Odin, Kt., MBE

Faulkner, Sir (James) Dennis (Compton), Kt., CBE, VRD

Fawcus, Sir (Robert) Peter, KBE, CMG

Fawkes, Sir Randol Francis, Kt.

Fay, Sir (Humphrey) Michael Gerard, Kt.

Fayrer, Sir John Lang Macpherson, Bt. (1896)

Fearn, Sir (Patrick) Robin, KCMG

Feilden, Sir Bernard Melchior, Kt., CBE

Feilden, Sir Henry Wemyss, Bt., (1846)

Feldman, Sir Basil Samuel, Kt.

Fell, Sir Anthony, Kt.

Fellowes, *Rt. Hon.* Sir Robert, KCB, KCVO

Fenn, Sir Nicholas Maxted, KCMG

Fennell, *Hon.* Sir (John) Desmond Augustine, Kt., OBE

Fennessy, Sir Edward, Kt., CBE

†Ferguson, Sir Ian Edward Johnson-, Bt. (1906)

Fergusson of Kilkerran, Sir Charles, Bt. (s. 1703)

Fergusson, Sir Ewan Alastair John, GCMG, GCVO

Fergusson, Sir James Herbert Hamilton Colyer-, Bt. (1866)

Feroze, Sir Rustam Moolan, Kt., FRCS

Ferris, *Hon.* Sir Francis Mursell, Kt., TD

ffolkes, Sir Robert Francis Alexander, Bt, OBE (1774)

Field, Sir Malcolm David, Kt.

Fielding, Sir Colin Cunningham, Kt., CB

Fielding, Sir Leslie, KCMG

Fiennes, Sir John Saye Wingfield Twisleton-Wykeham-, KCB, QC

Fiennes, Sir Maurice Alberic Twisleton-Wykeham-, Kt.

Fiennes, Sir Ranulph Twisleton-Wykeham-, Bt., OBE (1916)

Figg, Sir Leonard Clifford William, KCMG

Figgess, Sir John George, KBE, CMG

Figures, Sir Colin Frederick, KCMG, OBE

Fingland, Sir Stanley James Gunn, KCMG

Finlay, Sir David Ronald James Bell, Bt. (1964)

Finley, Sir Peter Hamilton, Kt., OBE, DFC

Firth, *Prof.* Sir Raymond William, Kt., Ph.D., FBA

Fish, Sir Hugh, Kt., CBE

Fisher, Sir George Read, Kt., CMG

Fisher, *Hon.* Sir Henry Arthur Pears, Kt.

Fisher, Sir Nigel Thomas Loveridge, Kt., MC

Fison, Sir (Richard) Guy, Bt., DSC (1905)

Fitch, *Adm.* Sir Richard George Alison, KCB

†Fitzgerald, *Revd* (Sir) Daniel Patrick, Bt. (1903)

FitzGerald, Sir George Peter Maurice, Bt., MC (*The Knight of Kerry*) (1880)

FitzHerbert, Sir Richard Ranulph, Bt. (1784)

Fitzpatrick, *Gen.* Sir (Geoffrey Richard) Desmond, GCB, DSO, MBE, MC

Fitzpatrick, *Air Marshal* Sir John Bernard, KBE, CB

Flanagan, Sir James Bernard, Kt., CBE

Flavelle, Sir (Joseph) David Ellsworth, Bt. (1917)

Fleming, *Instructor Rear-Adm.* Sir John, KBE, DSC

Fletcher, Sir Henry Egerton Aubrey-, Bt. (1782)

Fletcher, Sir James Muir Cameron, Kt.

Fletcher, Sir Leslie, Kt., DSC

Fletcher, *Air Chief Marshal* Sir Peter Carteret, KCB, OBE, DFC, AFC

Floissac, *Hon.* Sir Vincent Frederick, Kt., CMG, OBE, QC

Floyd, Sir Giles Henry Charles, Bt. (1816)

Foley, Sir (Thomas John) Noel, Kt., CBE

Follett, *Prof.* Sir Brian Keith, Kt., FRS

Foot, Sir Geoffrey James, Kt.

Foots, Sir James William, Kt.

Forbes, *Hon.* Sir Alastair Granville, Kt.

Forbes, *Maj.* Sir Hamish Stewart, Bt., MBE, MC (1823)

†Forbes of Craigievar, Sir John Alexander Cumnock Forbes-Sempill, Bt. (s. 1630)

Forbes, *Vice-Adm.* Sir John Morrison, KCB

Forbes, *Hon.* Sir Thayne John, Kt.

†Forbes of Pitsligo, Sir William Daniel Stuart-, Bt. (s. 1626)

Ford, Sir Andrew Russell, Bt. (1929)

Ford, Sir David Robert, KBE, LVO, OBE

Ford, *Maj.* Sir Edward William Spencer, KCB, KCVO

Ford, *Air Marshal* Sir Geoffrey Harold, KBE, CB, FEng.

Ford, *Prof.* Sir Hugh, Kt., FRS, FEng.

†Ford, Sir James Anson St Clair-, Bt. (1793)

Ford, Sir John Archibald, KCMG, MC

Ford, Sir Richard Brinsley, Kt., CBE

Ford, *Gen.* Sir Robert Cyril, GCB, CBE

Foreman, Sir Philip Frank, Kt., CBE, FEng.

Forman, Sir John Denis, Kt., OBE

Forrest, *Prof.* Sir (Andrew) Patrick (McEwen), Kt.

Forrest, *Rear-Adm.* Sir Ronald Stephen, KCVO

Forster, Sir Archibald William, Kt., FEng.

Forster, Sir Oliver Grantham, KCMG, MVO

Forwood, Sir Dudley Richard, Bt. (1895)

Foster, *Prof.* Sir Christopher David, Kt.

Foster, Sir John Gregory, Bt. (1930)

Foster, Sir Norman Robert, Kt.

Foster, Sir Robert Sidney, GCMG, KCVO

Foulis, Sir Ian Primrose Liston-, Bt. (s. 1634)

Foulkes, Sir Nigel Gordon, Kt.

Fowden, Sir Leslie, Kt., FRS

Fowke, Sir David Frederick Gustavus, Bt. (1814)

Fowler, Sir (Edward) Michael Coulson, Kt.

Fowler, *Rt. Hon.* Sir (Peter) Norman, Kt., MP

Fox, Sir (Henry) Murray, GBE

Fox, Sir (John) Marcus, Kt., MBE, MP

Fox, *Rt. Hon.* Sir Michael John, Kt.

Fox, Sir Paul Leonard, Kt., CBE

Frame, Sir Alistair Gilchrist, Kt., FEng.

France, Sir Arnold William, GCB

France, Sir Christopher Walter, KCB

Francis, Sir Horace William Alexander, Kt., CBE, FEng.

Frank, Sir Douglas George Horace, Kt., QC

Frank, Sir (Frederick) Charles, Kt., OBE, FRS

Frank, Sir Robert Andrew, Bt. (1920)

Frankel, Sir Otto Herzberg, Kt., D.SC., FRS

Franklin, Sir Eric Alexander, Kt., CBE

Franklin, Sir Michael David Milroy, KCB, CMG

Franks, Sir Arthur Temple, KCMG

Fraser, Sir Angus McKay, KCB, TD

Fraser, Sir Charles Annand, KCVO

Fraser, *Gen.* Sir David William, GCB, OBE

Fraser, *Air Marshal Revd* Sir (Henry) Paterson, KBE, CB, AFC

Fraser, Sir Ian, Kt., DSO, OBE

Fraser, Sir Ian James, Kt., CBE, MC

Fraser, Sir (James) Campbell, Kt.

Fraser, *Prof.* Sir James David, Bt. (1943)

Fraser, Sir William Kerr, GCB

Frederick, Sir Charles Boscawen, Bt. (1723)

Freeland, Sir John Redvers, KCMG

Freeman, Sir James Robin, Bt. (1945)

Freeman, Sir Ralph, Kt., CVO, CBE, FEng.

Freer, *Air Chief Marshal* Sir Robert William George, GBE, KCB

Freeth, *Hon.* Sir Gordon, KBE

French, *Hon.* Sir Christopher James Saunders, Kt.

Fretwell, Sir (Major) John (Emsley), GCMG

Freud, Sir Clement Raphael, Kt.

Froggatt, Sir Leslie Trevor, Kt.

Froggatt, Sir Peter, Kt.

Frossard, Sir Charles Keith, KBE

Frost, Sir David Paradine, Kt., OBE

Frost, *Hon.* Sir (Thomas) Sydney, Kt.

Fry, *Hon.* Sir William Gordon, Kt.

Fryberg, Sir Abraham, Kt., MBE

Fuchs, Sir Vivian Ernest, Kt., PH.D.

Fuller, *Hon.* Sir John Bryan Munro, Kt.

Fuller, Sir John William Fleetwood, Bt. (1910)

Fung, *Hon.* Sir Kenneth Ping-Fan, Kt., CBE

Furness, Sir Stephen Roberts, Bt. (1913)

Gadsden, Sir Peter Drury Haggerston, GBE, FEng.

Gage, Sir Berkeley Everard Foley, KCMG

Gairy, *Rt. Hon.* Sir Eric Matthew, Kt.

Gaius, *Rt. Revd* Saimon, KBE

Gallwey, Sir Philip Frankland Payne-, Bt. (1812)

Gamble, Sir David Hugh Norman, Bt. (1897)

Ganilau, *Ratu* Sir Penaia Kanatabatu, GCMG, KCVO, KBE, DSO

Gardiner, Sir George Arthur, Kt., MP

Gardner, Sir Douglas Bruce Bruce-, Bt. (1945)

Gardner, Sir Edward Lucas, Kt., QC

Garland, *Hon.* Sir Patrick Neville, Kt.

Garland, *Hon.* Sir Ransley Victor, KBE

Garlick, Sir John, KCB

Garner, Sir Anthony Stuart, Kt.

Garnier, *Rear-Adm.* Sir John, KCVO, CBE, LVO

Garrett, *Hon.* Sir Raymond William, Kt., AFC

Garrioch, Sir (William) Henry, Kt.

Garrod, *Lt.-Gen.* Sir (John) Martin Carruthers, KCB, OBE

Garthwaite, Sir William Francis Cuthbert, Bt., DSC (1919)

Gaskell, Sir Richard Kennedy Harvey, Kt.

Gatehouse, *Hon.* Sir Robert Alexander, Kt.

Geddes, Sir (Anthony) Reay (Mackay), KBE

George, Sir Arthur Thomas, Kt.

Gerken, *Vice-Adm.* Sir Robert William Frank, KCB, CBE

Gery, Sir Robert Lucian Wade-, KCMG, KCVO

Gethin, Sir Richard Joseph St Lawrence, Bt. (I. 1665)

Ghurburrun, Sir Rabindrah, Kt.

Gibb, Sir Francis Ross (Frank), Kt., CBE, FEng.

Gibbings, Sir Peter Walter, Kt.

Gibbon, *Gen.* Sir John Houghton, GCB, OBE

Gibbons, Sir (John) David, KBE

Gibbons, Sir William Edward Doran, Bt. (1752)

Gibbs, *Hon.* Sir Eustace Hubert Beilby, KCVO, CMG

Gibbs, *Rt. Hon.* Sir Harry Talbot, GCMG, KBE

Gibbs, *Field Marshal* Sir Roland Christopher, GCB, CBE, DSO, MC

Gibson, Sir Alexander Drummond, Kt., CBE

Gibson, Sir Christopher Herbert, Bt. (1931)

Gibson, *Revd* Sir David, Bt. (1926)

Gibson, *Vice-Adm.* Sir Donald Cameron Ernest Forbes, KCB, DSC

Gibson, *Rt. Hon.* Sir Peter Leslie, Kt.

Gibson, *Rt. Hon.* Sir Ralph Brian, Kt.

Giddings, *Air Marshal* Sir (Kenneth Charles) Michael, KCB, OBE, DFC, AFC

Gielgud, Sir (Arthur) John, Kt., CH

Giffard, Sir (Charles) Sydney (Rycroft), KCMG

Gilbert, *Air Chief Marshal* Sir Joseph Alfred, KCB, CBE

†Gilbey, Sir Walter Gavin, Bt. (1893)

Giles, *Rear-Adm.* Sir Morgan Charles Morgan-, Kt., DSO, OBE, GM

Gill, Sir Anthony Keith, Kt., F.Eng.

Gillett, Sir Robin Danvers Penrose, Bt., GBE, RD (1959)

Gillmore, Sir David Howe, KCMG

Gilmour, *Col.* Sir Allan Macdonald, KCVO, OBE, MC

Gilmour, Sir John Edward, Bt., DSO, TD (1897)

Gina, Sir Lloyd Maepeza, KBE

Gingell, *Air Chief Marshal* Sir John, GBE, KCB, KCVO

Girolami, Sir Paul, Kt.

Gladstone, Sir (Erskine) William, Bt. (1846)

Glasspole, Sir Florizel Augustus, GCMG, GCVO

Glen, Sir Alexander Richard, KBE, DSC

Glenn, Sir (Joseph Robert) Archibald, Kt., OBE

Glidewell, *Rt. Hon.* Sir Iain Derek Laing, Kt.

Glock, Sir William Frederick, Kt., CBE

Glover, *Gen.* Sir James Malcolm, KCB, MBE

Glover, Sir Victor Joseph Patrick, Kt.

Glyn, Sir Alan, Kt., ERD

Glyn, Sir Anthony Geoffrey Leo Simon, Bt. (1927)

Glyn, Sir Richard Lindsay, Bt. (1759 and 1800)

Goad, Sir (Edward) Colin (Viner), KCMG

Godber, Sir George Edward, GCB, DM

Goff, Sir Robert (William) Davis-, Bt. (1905)

Gohel, Sir Jayvantsinhji Kayaji, Kt., CBE

Gold, Sir Arthur Abraham, Kt., CBE

Gold, Sir Joseph, Kt.

Goldberg, *Prof.* Sir Abraham, Kt., MD, DSC, FRCP

Golding, Sir John Simon Rawson, Kt., OBE

Goldman, Sir Samuel, KCB

Goldsmith, Sir James Michael, Kt.

Gombrich, *Prof.* Sir Ernst Hans Josef, Kt., OM, CBE, Ph.D., FBA, FSA

Gooch, Sir (Richard) John Sherlock, Bt. (1746)

Gooch, Sir Trevor Sherlock (Sir Peter), Bt. (1866)

Goodall, Sir (Arthur) David Saunders, GCMG

Goodenough, Sir Richard Edmund, Bt. (1943)

Goodhart, Sir Philip Carter, Kt.

Goodhart, Sir Robert Anthony Gordon, Bt. (1911)

Goodhart, Sir William Howard, Kt., QC

Goodhew, Sir Victor Henry, Kt.

Goodison, Sir Alan Clowes, KCMG

Goodison, Sir Nicholas Proctor, Kt.

Goodson, Sir Mark Weston Lassam, Bt. (1922)

Goodwin, Sir Matthew Dean, Kt., CBE

Goody, *Most Revd* Launcelot John, KBE

Goold, Sir George Leonard, Bt. (1801)

Gordon, Sir Alexander John, Kt., CBE

Gordon, Sir Andrew Cosmo Lewis Duff-, Bt. (1813)

Gordon, Sir Charles Addison Somerville Snowden, KCB

Gordon, Sir Keith Lyndell, Kt., CMG

Gordon, Sir (Lionel) Eldred (Peter) Smith-, Bt. (1838)

Gordon, Sir Robert James, Bt. (s. 1706)

Gordon, Sir Sidney Samuel, Kt., CBE

Gordon Lennox, Lord Nicholas Charles, KCMG, KCVO

Gore, Sir Richard Ralph St George, Bt. (I. 1622)

Goring, Sir William Burton Nigel, Bt. (1627)

Gorton, *Rt. Hon.* Sir John Grey, GCMG, CH

Goschen, Sir Edward Christian, Bt., DSO (1916)

Gosling, Sir (Frederick) Donald, Kt.

Goswell, Sir Brian Lawrence, Kt.

Goulding, Sir (Ernest) Irvine, Kt.

Goulding, Sir (William) Lingard Walter, Bt. (1904)

Gourlay, *Gen.* Sir (Basil) Ian (Spencer), KCB, OBE, MC, RM

Gourlay, Sir Simon Alexander, Kt.

Govan, Sir Lawrence Herbert, Kt.

Gow, *Gen.* Sir (James) Michael, GCB

Gow, Sir Leonard Maxwell Harper, Kt., MBE

Gowans, Sir James Learmonth, Kt., CBE, FRCP, FRS

Gowans, *Hon.* Sir (Urban) Gregory, Kt.

Graaff, Sir de Villiers, Bt., MBE (1911)

Grabham, Sir Anthony Henry, Kt.

Graham, Sir Alexander Michael, GBE

Graham, Sir Charles Spencer Richard, Bt. (1783)

Graham, Sir James Bellingham, Bt. (1662)

Graham, Sir James Thompson, Kt., CMG

Graham, Sir John Alexander Noble, Bt., GCMG (1906)

Graham, Sir John Moodie, Bt. (1964)

Graham, Sir (John) Patrick, Kt.

Graham, Sir Norman William, Kt., CB

Graham, Sir Peter, KCB, QC

Graham, Sir Peter Alfred, Kt., OBE

Graham, *Lt.-Gen.* Sir Peter Walter, KCB, CBE

†Graham, Sir Ralph Stuart, Bt. (1629)

Graham, *Hon.* Sir Samuel Horatio, Kt., CMG, OBE

Grandy, *Marshal of the Royal Air Force* Sir John, GCB, GCVO, KBE, DSO

Grant, Sir Archibald, Bt. (s. 1705)

Grant, Sir Clifford, Kt.

Grant, Sir (John) Anthony, Kt., MP

Grant, Sir (Matthew) Alistair, Kt.

Grant, Sir Patrick Alexander Benedict, Bt. (s. 1688)

Gray, Sir John Archibald Browne, Kt., SC.D., FRS

Gray, *Vice-Adm.* Sir John Michael Dudgeon, KBE, CB

Gray, *Lt.-Gen.* Sir Michael Stuart, KCB, OBE

Gray, Sir William Hume, Bt. (1917)

Gray, Sir William Stevenson, Kt.

Graydon, *Air Chief Marshal* Sir Michael James, GCB, CBE

Grayson, Sir Jeremy Brian Vincent Harrington, Bt. (1922)

Green, Sir Allan David, KCB, QC

Green, Sir (Edward) Stephen (Lycett), Bt., CBE (1886)

Green, *Hon.* Sir Guy Stephen Montague, KBE

Green, Sir Kenneth, Kt.

Green, Sir Owen Whitley, Kt.

Green, Sir Peter James Frederick, Kt.

Greenaway, Sir Derek Burdick, Bt., CBE (1933)

Greenborough, Sir John, KBE

Greenbury, Sir Richard, Kt.

Greene, Sir (John) Brian Massy-, Kt.

Greengross, Sir Alan David, Kt.

Greening, *Rear-Adm.* Sir Paul Woollven, GCVO

Greenwell, Sir Edward Bernard, Bt. (1906)

Gregson, Sir Peter Lewis, KCB

Grenside, Sir John Peter, Kt., CBE

Grey, Sir Anthony Dysart, Bt. (1814)

Grey, Sir Roger de, KCVO, PRA

Grierson, Sir Michael John Bewes, Bt. (s. 1685)

Grierson, Sir Ronald Hugh, Kt.

Grieve, *Prof.* Sir Robert, Kt.

Griffin, *Adm.* Sir Anthony Templer Frederick Griffith, GCB

Griffin, *Maj.* Sir (Arthur) John (Stewart), KBE

Griffin, Sir (Charles) David, Kt., CBE

Griffiths, Sir Eldon Wylie, Kt.

Griffiths, Sir (Ernest) Roy, Kt.

Griffiths, Sir John Norton-, Bt. (1922)

Grimwade, Sir Andrew Sheppard, Kt., CBE

Grindrod, *Most Revd* John Basil Rowland, KBE

Grinstead, Sir Stanley Gordon, Kt.

Grose, *Vice-Adm.* Sir Alan, KBE

Grotrian, Sir Philip Christian Brent, Bt. (1934)

Grove, Sir Charles Gerald, Bt. (1874)
Grove, Sir Edmund Frank, KCVO
Grugeon, Sir John Drury, Kt.
Grylls, Sir (William) Michael (John), Kt., MP
Guinness, Sir Alec, Kt., CBE
Guinness, Sir Howard Christian Sheldon, Kt., VRD
Guinness, Sir Kenelm Ernest Lee, Bt. (1867)
Guise, Sir John Grant, Bt. (1783)
Gujadhur, Sir Radhamohun, Kt., CMG
Gull, Sir Rupert William Cameron, Bt. (1872)
Gunn, *Prof.* Sir John Currie, Kt., CBE
Gunn, Sir William Archer, KBE, CMG
†Gunning, Sir Charles Theodore, Bt. (1778)
Gunston, Sir John Wellesley, Bt. (1938)
Guthrie, *Gen.* Sir Charles Ronald Llewelyn, KCB, LVO, OBE
Guthrie, Sir Malcolm Connop, Bt. (1936)
Guy, *Gen.* Sir Roland Kelvin, GCB, CBE, DSO
Habakkuk, Sir John Hrothgar, Kt., FBA
Hackett, *Gen.* Sir John Winthrop, GCB, CBE, DSO, MC
Hadlee, Sir Richard John, Kt., MBE
Hadley, Sir Leonard Albert, Kt.
Hadow, Sir Gordon, Kt., CMG, OBE
Hadow, Sir (Reginald) Michael, KCMG
Hague, *Prof.* Sir Douglas Chalmers, Kt., CBE
Halberg, Sir Murray Gordon, Kt., MBE
Hale, *Prof.* Sir John Rigby, Kt.
Hall, Sir Arnold Alexander, Kt., FRS, FEng.
Hall, Sir Basil Brodribb, KCB, MC, TD
Hall, *Air Marshal* Sir Donald Percy, KCB, CBE, AFC
Hall, Sir Douglas Basil, Bt., KCMG (s. 1687)
Hall, Sir Ernest, Kt., OBE
Hall, Sir (Frederick) John (Frank), Bt. (1923)
Hall, Sir John, Kt.
Hall, Sir John Bernard, Bt. (1919)
Hall, Sir Peter Edward, KBE, CMG
Hall, Sir Peter Reginald Frederick, Kt., CBE
Hall, Sir Robert de Zouche, KCMG
Hall, *Brig.* Sir William Henry, KBE, DSO, ED
Halliday, *Vice-Adm.* Sir Roy William, KBE, DSC
Hallinan, Sir (Adrian) Lincoln, Kt.
Halpern, Sir Ralph Mark, Kt.
Halsey, *Revd* Sir John Walter Brooke, Bt. (1920)
Halstead, Sir Ronald, Kt., CBE
Ham, Sir David Kenneth Rowe-, GBE
Hambling, Sir (Herbert) Hugh, Bt. (1924)
Hamburger, Sir Sidney Cyril, Kt., CBE
Hamer, *Hon.* Sir Rupert James, KCMG, ED

Hamill, Sir Patrick, Kt., QPM
Hamilton, Sir Edward Sydney, Bt. (1776 and 1819)
Hamilton, Sir James Arnot, KCB, MBE, FEng.
Hamilton, *Adm.* Sir John Graham, GBE, CB
Hamilton, Sir Malcolm William Bruce Stirling-, Bt. (s. 1673)
Hamilton, Sir Michael Aubrey, Kt.
Hamilton, Sir (Robert Charles) Richard Caradoc, Bt. (s. 1646)
Hammett, *Hon.* Sir Clifford James, Kt.
Hammick, Sir Stephen George, Bt. (1834)
Hampshire, Sir Stuart Newton, Kt., FBA
Hanbury, Sir John Capel, Kt., CBE
Hancock, Sir David John Stowell, KCB
Hancock, *Air Marshal* Sir Valston Eldridge, KBE, CB, DFC
Hand, *Most Revd* Geoffrey David, KBE
Handley, Sir David John Davenport-, Kt., OBE
Hanham, Sir Michael William, Bt., DFC (1667)
Hanley, Sir Michael Bowen, KCB
Hanmer, Sir John Wyndham Edward, Bt. (1774)
Hannam, Sir John Gordon, Kt., MP
Hannay, Sir David Hugh Alexander, KCMG
Hanson, Sir Anthony Leslie Oswald, Bt. (1887)
Hanson, Sir (Charles) John, Bt. (1918)
Hardcastle, Sir Alan John, Kt.
Harders, Sir Clarence Waldemar, Kt., OBE
Hardie, Sir Charles Edgar Mathewes, Kt., CBE
Hardie, Sir Douglas Fleming, Kt., CBE
Harding, Sir Christopher George Francis, Kt.
Harding, Sir George William, KCMG, CVO
Harding, *Marshal of the Royal Air Force* Sir Peter Robin, GCB
Harding, Sir Roy Pollard, Kt., CBE
Hardinge, Sir Robert Arnold, Bt. (1801)
Hardman, Sir Henry, KCB
Hardy, Sir David William, Kt.
Hardy, Sir James Gilbert, Kt., OBE
Hardy, Sir Rupert John, Bt. (1876)
†Hare, Sir Philip Leigh, Bt. (1818)
Harford, Sir James Dundas, KBE, CMG
Harford, Sir (John) Timothy, Bt. (1934)
Hargroves, *Brig.* Sir Robert Louis, Kt., CBE
Harington, *Gen.* Sir Charles Henry Pepys, GCB, CBE, DSO, MC
Harington, Sir Nicholas John, Bt. (1611)
Harland, *Air Marshal* Sir Reginald Edward Wynyard, KBE, CB
Harman, *Gen.* Sir Jack Wentworth, GCB, OBE, MC

Harman, *Hon.* Sir Jeremiah LeRoy, Kt.
Harmer, Sir Frederic Evelyn, Kt., CMG
Harmsworth, Sir Hildebrand Harold, Bt. (1922)
Harpham, Sir William, KBE, CMG
Harris, *Prof.* Sir Alan James, Kt., CBE, FEng.
Harris, Sir Anthony Kyrle Travers, Bt. (1953)
Harris, *Prof.* Sir Charles Herbert Stuart-, Kt., CBE, MD
Harris, *Prof.* Sir Henry, Kt., FRCP, FRCPath., FRS
Harris, *Lt.-Gen.* Sir Ian Cecil, KBE, CB, DSO
Harris, Sir Jack Wolfred Ashford, Bt. (1932)
Harris, *Air Marshal* Sir John Hulme, KCB, CBE
Harris, Sir Philip Charles, Kt.
Harris, Sir Ronald Montague Joseph, KCVO, CB
Harris, Sir William Gordon, KBE, CB, FEng.
Harrison, *Prof.* Sir Donald Frederick Norris, Kt., FRCS
Harrison, Sir Ernest Thomas, Kt., OBE
Harrison, Sir Francis Alexander Lyle, Kt., MBE, QC
Harrison, *Surgeon Vice-Adm.* Sir John Albert Bews, KBE
Harrison, *Hon.* Sir (John) Richard, Kt., ED
Harrison, *Hon.* Sir Michael Guy Vicat, Kt.
Harrison, Sir Michael James Harwood, Bt. (1961)
Harrison, *Prof.* Sir Richard John, Kt., FRS
Harrison, Sir (Robert) Colin, Bt. (1922)
Harrop, Sir Peter John, KCB
Hartley, *Air Marshal* Sir Christopher Harold, KCB, CBE, DFC, AFC
Hartley, Sir Frank, Kt., CBE, Ph.D.
Hartopp, Sir John Edmund Cradock-, Bt. (1796)
Hartwell, Sir Brodrick William Charles Elwin, Bt. (1805)
Harvey, Sir Charles Richard Musgrave, Bt. (1933)
Haskard, Sir Cosmo Dugal Patrick Thomas, KCMG, MBE
Haslam, *Hon.* Sir Alec Leslie, Kt.
Haslam, *Rear-Adm.* Sir David William, KBE, CB
Hassan, Sir Joshua Abraham, GBE, KCMG, LVO, QC
Hassett, *Gen.* Sir Francis George, KBE, CB, DSO, MVO
Hastings, Sir Stephen Lewis Edmonstone, Kt., MC
Hatty, *Hon.* Sir Cyril James, Kt.
Haughton, Sir James, Kt., CBE, QPM
Havelock, Sir Wilfrid Bowen, Kt.
Hawkins, Sir Arthur Ernest, Kt.

†Hawkins, Sir Howard Caesar, Bt. (1778)

Hawkins, Sir Paul Lancelot, Kt., TD

Hawley, Sir Donald Frederick, KCMG, MBE

†Hawley, Sir Henry Nicholas, Bt. (1795)

Haworth, Sir Philip, Bt. (1911)

Hawthorne, *Prof.* Sir William Rede, Kt., CBE, SC.D., FRS, FEng.

Hay, Sir David Osborne, Kt., CBE, DSO

Hay, Sir David Russell, Kt., CBE, FRCP, MD

Hay, Sir Hamish Grenfell, Kt.

Hay, Sir James Brian Dalrymple-, Bt. (1798)

†Hay, Sir John Erroll Audley, Bt. (s. 1663)

†Hay, Sir Ronald Frederick Hamilton, Bt. (s. 1703)

Haydon, Sir Walter Robert, KCMG

Hayes, Sir Brian David, GCB

Hayes, Sir Claude James, KCMG

Hayes, *Vice-Adm.* Sir John Osier Chattock, KCB, OBE

Hayr, *Air Marshal* Sir Kenneth William, KCB, KBE, AFC

Hayter, Sir William Goodenough, KCMG

Hayward, Sir Anthony William Byrd, Kt.

Hayward, Sir Jack Arnold, Kt., OBE

Hayward, Sir Richard Arthur, Kt., CBE

Haywood, Sir Harold, KCVO, OBE

Head, Sir Francis David Somerville, Bt. (1838)

Healey, Sir Charles Edward Chadwyck-, Bt. (1919)

Heap, Sir Desmond, Kt.

Heath, *Rt. Hon.* Sir Edward Richard George, KG, MBE, MP

Heath, Sir Mark Evelyn, KCVO, CMG

Heath, *Air Marshal* Sir Maurice Lionel, KBE, CB, CVO

Heathcote, *Brig.* Sir Gilbert Simon, Bt., CBE (1733)

Heathcote, Sir Michael Perryman, Bt. (1733)

Heatley, Sir Peter, Kt., CBE

Heaton, Sir Yvo Robert Henniker-, Bt. (1912)

Heiser, Sir Terence Michael, GCB

Hele, Sir Ivor Thomas Henry, Kt., CBE

Hellaby, Sir (Frederick Reed) Alan, Kt.

Henderson, Sir Denys Hartley, Kt.

Henderson, Sir (John) Nicholas, GCMG, KCVO

Henderson, Sir William MacGregor, Kt., D.SC., FRS

Henley, Sir Douglas Owen, KCB

Henley, *Rear-Adm.* Sir Joseph Charles Cameron, KCVO, CB

Hennessy, Sir James Patrick Ivan, KBE, CMG

Hennessy, Sir John Wyndham Pope-, Kt., CBE, FBA, FSA

†Henniker, Sir Adrian Chandos, Bt. (1813)

Henry, Sir Denis Aynsley, Kt., OBE, QC

Henry, *Rt. Hon.* Denis Robert Maurice, Kt.

Henry, *Hon.* Sir Geoffrey Arama, KBE

Henry, Sir James Holmes, Bt., CMG, MC, TD, QC (1923)

Henry, *Hon.* Sir Trevor Ernest, Kt.

Hepburn, Sir John Alastair Trant Kidd Buchan-, Bt. (1815)

Herbecq, Sir John Edward, KCB

Herbert, *Adm.* Sir Peter Geoffrey Marshall, KCB, OBE

Hermon, Sir John Charles, Kt., OBE, QPM

Heron, Sir Conrad Frederick, KCB, OBE

Herries, Sir Michael Alexander Robert Young-, Kt., OBE, MC

Hervey, Sir Roger Blaise Ramsay, KCVO, CMG

Heseltine, *Rt. Hon.* Sir William Frederick Payne, GCB, GCVO

Hetherington, Sir Arthur Ford, Kt., DSC, FEng.

Hetherington, Sir Thomas Chalmers, KCB, CBE, TD, QC

Heward, *Air Chief Marshal* Sir Anthony Wilkinson, KCB, OBE, DFC, AFC

Hewetson, Sir Christopher Raynor, Kt., TD

Hewett, Sir Peter John Smithson, Bt., MM (1813)

Hewitt, Sir (Cyrus) Lenox (Simson), Kt., OBE

Hewitt, Sir Nicholas Charles Joseph, Bt. (1921)

†Heygate, Sir Richard John Gage, Bt. (1831)

Heyman, Sir Horace William, Kt.

Heywood, Sir Peter, Bt. (1838)

Hezlet, *Vice-Adm.* Sir Arthur Richard, KBE, CB, DSO, DSC

Hibbert, Sir Jack, KCB

Hibbert, Sir Reginald Alfred, GCMG

Hickey, Sir Justin, Kt.

Hickman, Sir (Richard) Glenn, Bt. (1903)

Hidden, *Hon.* Sir Anthony Brian, Kt.

Hielscher, Sir Leo Arthur, Kt.

Higgins, Sir Christopher Thomas, Kt.

Higgins, *Rt. Hon.* John Patrick Basil (Eoin), Kt.

Higgins, *Rt. Hon.* Sir Terence Langley, KBE, MP

Higginson, Sir Gordon Robert, Kt., PH.D., FEng.

Higgs, Sir (John) Michael (Clifford), Kt.

Hildyard, Sir David Henry Thoroton, KCMG, DFC

Hill, Sir Alexander Rodger Erskine-, Bt. (1945)

Hill, Sir Arthur Alfred, Kt., CBE

Hill, Sir Brian John, Kt.

Hill, Sir James Frederick, Bt. (1917)

Hill, Sir John McGregor, Kt., PH.D., FEng.

Hill, Sir John Maxwell, Kt., CBE, DFC

†Hill, Sir John Rowley, Bt. (I. 1779)

Hill, *Vice-Adm.* Sir Robert Charles Finch, KBE

Hillary, Sir Edmund, KBE

Hillhouse, Sir (Robert) Russell, KCB

Hills, Sir Graham John, Kt.

Hilton, *Col.* Sir Peter, KCVO, MC

Himsworth, Sir Harold Percival, KCB, MD, FRS

Hine, *Air Chief Marshal* Sir Patrick Bardon, GCB, GBE

Hines, Sir Colin Joseph, Kt., OBE

Hinsley, *Prof.* Sir Francis Harry, Kt., OBE, FBA

Hirsch, *Prof.* Sir Peter Bernhard, Kt., PH.D., FRS

Hirst, *Rt. Hon.* Sir David Cozens-Hardy, Kt.

Hirst, Sir Michael William, Kt.

Hoare, Sir Peter Richard David, Bt. (1786)

Hoare, Sir Timothy Edward Charles, Bt. (I. 1784)

Hobart, Sir John Vere, Bt. (1914)

Hobday, Sir Gordon Ivan, Kt.

Hobhouse, Sir Charles John Spinney, Bt. (1812)

Hobhouse, *Rt. Hon.* Sir John Stewart, Kt.

Hockaday, Sir Arthur Patrick, KCB, CMG

Hockley, *Gen.* Sir Anthony Heritage Farrar-, GBE, KCB, DSO, MC

Hodge, Sir John Rowland, Bt., MBE (1921)

Hodge, Sir Julian Stephen Alfred, Kt.

Hodges, *Air Chief Marshal* Sir Lewis MacDonald, KCB, CBE, DSO, DFC

Hodgkin, *Prof.* Sir Alan Lloyd, OM, KBE, FRS, SC.D.

Hodgkin, Sir Gordon Howard Eliot, Kt., CBE

Hodgkinson, *Air Chief Marshal* Sir (William) Derek, KCB, CBE, DFC, AFC

Hodgson, Sir Maurice Arthur Eric, Kt., FEng.

Hodgson, *Hon.* Sir (Walter) Derek (Thornley), Kt.

Hodson, Sir Michael Robin Adderley, Bt. (I. 1789)

Hoffenberg, *Prof.* Sir Raymond, KBE

Hoffman, *Rt. Hon.* Sir Leonard Hubert, Kt.

Hogg, *Maj.* Sir Arthur Ramsay, Bt., MBE (1846)

Hogg, Sir Christopher Anthony, Kt.

Hogg, Sir Edward William Lindsay-, Bt. (1905)

Hogg, *Vice-Adm.* Sir Ian Leslie Trower, KCB, DSC

Hogg, Sir John Nicholson, Kt., TD

Holcroft, Sir Peter George Culcheth, Bt. (1921)

Holden, Sir David Charles Beresford, KBE, CB, ERD

Holden, Sir Edward, Bt. (1893)

Holden, Sir John David, Bt. (1919)

Holder, Sir John Henry, Bt. (1898)

Holder, *Air Marshal* Sir Paul Davie, KBE, CB, DSO, DFC, ph.D.

Holderness, Sir Richard William, Bt. (1920)

Holdsworth, Sir (George) Trevor, Kt.

Holland, *Hon.* Sir Christopher John, Kt.

Holland, Sir Clifton Vaughan, Kt.

Holland, Sir Geoffrey, KCB

Holland, Sir Guy (Hope), Bt. (1917)

Holland, Sir Kenneth Lawrence, Kt., CBE, QFSM

Holland, Sir Philip Welsby, Kt.

Holliday, *Prof.* Sir Frederick George Thomas, Kt., CBE, FRSE

Hollings, *Hon.* Sir (Alfred) Kenneth, Kt., MC

Hollis, *Hon.* Sir Anthony Barnard, Kt.

Hollom, Sir Jasper Quintus, KBE

Holloway, *Hon.* Sir Barry Blyth, KBE

Holm, Sir Carl Henry, Kt., OBE

Holmes, *Prof.* Sir Frank Wakefield, Kt.

Holmes, Sir Maurice Andrew, Kt.

Holmes, Sir Peter Fenwick, Kt., MC

Holroyd, *Air Marshal* Sir Frank Martyn, KBE, CB

Holt, *Prof.* Sir James Clarke, Kt.

Home, Sir William Dundas, Bt. (s. 1671)

Honeycombe, *Prof.* Sir Robert William Kerr, Kt., FRS, FEng.

Honywood, Sir Filmer Courtenay William, Bt. (1660)

Hood, Sir Alexander William Fuller-Acland-, Bt. (1806)

Hood, Sir Harold Joseph, Bt., TD (1922)

Hookway, Sir Harry Thurston, Kt.

Hoole, Sir Arthur Hugh, Kt.

Hooper, Sir Leonard James, KCMG, CBE

Hope, Sir (Charles) Peter, KCMG, TD

Hope, Sir John Carl Alexander, Bt. (s. 1628)

Hope, Sir Robert Holms-Kerr, Bt. (1932)

Hopkin, Sir David Armand, Kt.

Hopkin, Sir (William Aylsham) Bryan, Kt., CBE

Hopkins, Sir Anthony Philip, Kt., CBE

Hopkins, Sir James Sidney Rawdon Scott-, Kt., MEP

Hordern, Sir Michael Murray, Kt., CBE

Hordern, *Rt. Hon.* Sir Peter Maudslay, Kt., MP

Horlick, *Vice-Adm.* Sir Edwin John, KBE, FEng.

Horlick, Sir John James Macdonald, Bt. (1914)

Hornby, Sir Derek Peter, Kt.

Hornby, Sir Simon Michael, Kt.

Horne, Sir Alan Gray Antony, Bt. (1929)

Horsfall, Sir John Musgrave, Bt., MC, TD (1909)

Horsley, *Air Marshal* Sir (Beresford) Peter (Torrington), KCB, CBE, MVO, AFC

Hort, Sir James Fenton, Bt. (1767)

Hoskyns, Sir Benedict Leigh, Bt. (1676)

Hoskyns, Sir John Austin Hungerford Leigh, Kt.

Hotung, Sir Joseph Edward, Kt.

Houghton, Sir John Theodore, Kt., CBE, FRS

†Houldsworth, Sir Richard Thomas Reginald, Bt. (1887)

Hounsfield, Sir Godfrey Newbold, Kt., CBE

House, *Lt.-Gen.* Sir David George, GCB, KCVO, CBE, MC

Houssemayne du Boulay, Sir Roger William, KCVO, CMG

Howard, Sir (Hamilton) Edward de Coucey, Bt., GBE (1955)

Howard, *Prof.* Sir Michael Eliot, Kt., CBE, MC

Howard, *Maj.-Gen.* Lord Michael Fitzalan-, GCVO, CB, CBE, MC

Howell, Sir Ralph Frederic, Kt., MP

Howells, Sir Eric Waldo Benjamin, Kt., CBE

Howard, Sir Walter Stewart, Kt., MBE

Howie, Sir James William, Kt., MD

Howlett, *Gen.* Sir Geoffrey Hugh Whitby, KBE, MC

Hoyle, *Prof.* Sir Fred, Kt., FRS

Hoyos, *Hon.* Sir Fabriciano Alexander, Kt.

Huckle, Sir (Henry) George, Kt., OBE

Huddie, Sir David Patrick, Kt., FEng.

Hudleston, *Air Chief Marshal* Sir Edmund Cuthbert, GCB, CBE

Hudson, Sir Havelock Henry Trevor, Kt.

Hudson, *Lt.-Gen.* Sir Peter, KCB, CBE

Huggins, *Hon.* Sir Alan Armstrong, Kt.

Hugh-Jones, Sir Wynn Normington, Kt., MVO

Hughes, Sir David Collingwood, Bt. (1773)

Hughes, *Prof.* Sir Edward Stuart Reginald, Kt., CBE

Hughes, Sir Jack William, Kt.

Hughes, *Air Marshal* Sir (Sidney Weetman) Rochford, KCB, CBE, AFC

Hughes, Sir Trevor Denby Lloyd-, Kt.

Hughes, Sir Trevor Poulton, KCB

Hugo, *Lt.-Col.* Sir John Mandeville, KCVO, OBE

Hull, *Prof.* Sir David, Kt.

Hulse, Sir (Hamilton) Westrow, Bt. (1739)

Hulton, Sir Geoffrey Alan, Bt. (1905)

Hume, Sir Alan Blyth, Kt., CB

Humphreys, Sir Olliver William, Kt., CBE

Humphreys, Sir (Raymond Evelyn) Myles, Kt.

Hunn, Sir Jack Kent, Kt., CMG

Hunt, Sir David Wathen Stather, KCMG, OBE

Hunt, Sir John Leonard, Kt., MP

Hunt, *Adm.* Sir Nicholas John Streynsham, GCB, LVO

Hunt, Sir Rex Masterman, Kt., CMG

Hunt, Sir Robert Frederick, Kt., CBE, FEng.

Hunter, *Hon.* Sir Alexander Albert, KBE

Hunter, Sir Ian Bruce Hope, Kt., MBE

Hurrell, Sir Anthony Gerald, KCVO, CMG

Hutchinson, *Hon.* Sir Ross, Kt., DFC

Hutchison, *Lt.-Cdr.* Sir (George) Ian Clark, Kt., RN

Hutchison, *Hon.* Sir Michael, Kt.

Hutchison, Sir Peter, Bt., CBE (1939)

Hutchison, Sir Peter Craft, Bt. (1956)

Hutton, *Rt. Hon.* Sir (James) Brian Edward, Kt.

Huxley, *Prof.* Sir Andrew Fielding, Kt., OM, FRS

Huxtable, *Gen.* Sir Charles Richard, KCB, CBE

Hyatali, *Hon.* Sir Isaac Emanuel, Kt.

Hyslop, Sir Robert John (Robin) Maxwell-, Kt.

Ibbs, Sir (John) Robin, KBE

Ihaka, *Ven.* Sir Kingi Matutaera, Kt., MBE

Imbert, Sir Peter Michael, Kt., QPM

Imray, Sir Colin Henry, KBE, CMG

Inch, Sir John Ritchie, Kt., CVO, CBE

Inge, *Gen.* Sir Peter Anthony, GCB

Ingham, Sir Bernard, Kt.

Ingilby, Sir Thomas Colvin William, Bt. (1866)

Inglis, Sir Brian Scott, Kt.

Inglis of Glencorse, Sir Roderick John, Bt. (s. 1703)

Ingram, Sir James Herbert Charles, Bt. (1893)

Inkin, Sir Geoffrey David, Kt., OBE

†Innes, Sir David Charles Kenneth Gordon, Bt. (NS 1686)

Innes of Edingight, Sir Malcolm Rognvald, KCVO

Innes, Sir Peter Alexander Berowald, Bt. (s. 1628)

Inniss, *Hon.* Sir Clifford de Lisle, Kt.

Irish, Sir Ronald Arthur, Kt., OBE

Irvine, *Dr* Sir Robin Orlando Hamilton, Kt.

Irving, Sir Charles Graham, Kt.

Isaacs, Sir Kendal George Lamon, KCMG, CBE, QC

Isham, Sir Ian Vere Gyles, Bt. (1627)

Jack, *Hon.* Sir Alieu Sulayman, Kt.

Jack, Sir David, Kt., CBE, FRS, FRSE

Jack, Sir David Emmanuel, GCMG, MBE

Jackson, *Air Chief Marshal* Sir Brendan James, GCB

Jackson, Sir (John) Edward, KCMG

Jackson, *Hon.* Sir Lawrence Walter, KCMG

Jackson, Sir Michael Roland, Bt. (1902)

Jackson, Sir Nicholas Fane St George, Bt. (1913)

Jackson, Sir Robert, Bt. (1815)

Jackson, *Gen.* Sir William Godfrey Fothergill, GBE, KCB, MC

Jackson, Sir William Thomas, Bt. (1869)

Jacob, Sir Isaac Hai, Kt., QC

Jacob, *Hon.* Sir Robert Raphael Hayim (Robin), Kt.

Jacobi, *Dr* Sir James Edward, Kt., OBE

Jacobs, Sir David Anthony, Kt.

Jacobs, *Hon.* Sir Kenneth Sydney, KBE

Jacobs, Sir Piers, KBE

Jacobs, Sir Wilfred Ebenezer, GCMG, GCVO, OBE, QC

Jacomb, Sir Martin Wakefield, Kt.

Jaffray, Sir William Otho, Bt. (1892)

Jakeway, Sir (Francis) Derek, KCMG, OBE

James, Sir Cynlais Morgan, KCMG

James, Sir Gerard Bowes Kingston, Bt. (1823)

James, Sir Robert Vidal Rhodes, Kt.

James, Sir Stanislaus Anthony, GCMG, OBE

Jamieson, *Air Marshal* Sir David Ewan, KBE, CB

Janion, *Rear-Adm.* Sir Hugh Penderel, KCVO

Jansen, Sir Ross Malcolm, KBE

Jardine, Sir Andrew Colin Douglas, Bt. (1916)

Jardine, *Maj.* Sir (Andrew) Rupert (John) Buchanan-, Bt., MC (1885)

Jardine of Applegirth, Sir Alexander Maule, Bt. (s. 1672)

Jarratt, Sir Alexander Anthony, Kt., CB

Jarrett, Sir Clifford George, KBE, CB

Jawara, *Hon.* Sir Dawda Kairaba, Kt.

Jay, Sir Antony Rupert, Kt., CVO

Jeewoolall, Sir Ramesh, Kt.

Jefferson, Sir George Rowland, Kt., CBE, FEng.

Jefferson, Sir Mervyn Stewart Dunnington-, Bt. (1958)

Jeffries, *Hon.* Sir John Francis, Kt.

Jehangir, Sir Hirji, Bt. (1908)

Jejeebhoy, Sir Rustom, Bt. (1857)

Jellicoe, Sir Geoffrey Alan, Kt., CBE, FRIBA

Jenkins, Sir Brian Garton, GBE

Jenkins, Sir Michael Romilly Heald, KCMG

Jenkins, Sir Owain Trevor, Kt.

Jenkinson, Sir John Banks, Bt. (1661)

Jenks, Sir Richard Atherley, Bt. (1932)

Jennings, Sir Albert Victor, Kt.

Jennings, Sir Raymond Winter, Kt., QC

Jennings, *Prof.* Sir Robert Yewdall, Kt., QC

Jephcott, Sir (John) Anthony, Bt. (1962)

Jessel, Sir Charles John, Bt. (1883)

Jewkes, Sir Gordon Wesley, KCMG

Joel, *Hon.* Sir Asher Alexander, KBE

John, Sir Rupert Godfrey, Kt.

†Johnson, Sir Allen Antony Wynn, Bt. (1818)

Johnson, *Rt. Hon.* Sir David Powell Croom-, Kt., DSC, VRD

Johnson, *Gen.* Sir Garry Dene, KCB, OBE, MC

Johnson, Sir John Rodney, KCMG

Johnson, Sir Peter Colpoys Paley, Bt. (1755)

Johnson, *Hon.* Sir Robert Lionel, Kt.

Johnson, Sir Ronald Ernest Charles, Kt., CB

Johnston, Sir Alexander, GCB, KBE

Johnston, Sir (David) Russell, Kt., MP

Johnston, Sir John Baines, GCMG, KCVO

Johnston, *Lt.-Col.* Sir John Frederick Dame, GCVO, MC

Johnston, *Lt.-Gen.* Sir Maurice Robert, KCB, OBE

Johnston, Sir Thomas Alexander, Bt. (s. 1626)

Johnstone, Sir Frederic Allan George, Bt. (s. 1700)

Johnstone, Sir (John) Raymond, Kt., CBE

Jolliffe, Sir Anthony Stuart, GBE

Jones, *Gen.* Sir (Charles) Edward Webb, KCB, CBE

Jones, Sir Christopher Lawrence-, Bt. (1831)

Jones, Sir David Akers-, KBE, CMG

Jones, *Air Marshal* Sir Edward Gordon, KCB, CBE, DSO, DFC

Jones, Sir (Edward) Martin Furnival, Kt., CBE

Jones, Sir Ewart Ray Herbert, Kt., D.Sc., Ph.D., FRS

Jones, Sir Francis Avery, Kt., CBE, FRCP

Jones, Sir Gordon Pearce, Kt.

Jones, Sir Harry Ernest, Kt., CBE

Jones, Sir James Duncan, KCB

Jones, Sir (John) Derek Alun-, Kt.

Jones, Sir John Henry Harvey-, Kt., MBE

Jones, Sir (John) Kenneth (Trevor), Kt., CBE, QC

Jones, Sir John Lewis, KCB, CMG

Jones, Sir John Prichard-, Bt. (1910)

Jones, Sir Keith Stephen, Kt.

Jones, *Hon.* Sir Kenneth George Illtyd, Kt.

Jones, *Air Marshal* Sir Laurence Alfred, KCB, CB, AFC

Jones, Sir (Owen) Trevor, Kt.

Jones, Sir (Peter) Hugh (Jefferd) Lloyd-, Kt.

Jones, Sir Richard Anthony Lloyd, KCB

Jones, Sir Robert Edward, Kt.

Jones, Sir Simon Warley Frederick Benton, Bt. (1919)

Jones, Sir (Thomas) Philip, Kt., CB

Jones, Sir (William) Emrys, Kt.

Jones, *Hon.* Sir William Lloyd Mars-, Kt., MBE

Jordan, *Air Marshal* Sir Richard Bowen, KCB, DFC

Joughin, Sir Michael, Kt., CBE

Jowitt, *Hon.* Sir Edwin Frank, Kt.

Judge, *Hon.* Sir Igor, Kt.

Jugnauth, *Rt. Hon.* Sir Anerood, KCMG, QC

Jungius, *Vice-Adm.* Sir James George, KBE

Junor, Sir John Donald Brown, Kt.

Jupp, *Hon.* Sir Kenneth Graham, Kt., MC

Kaberry, *Hon.* Sir Christopher Donald, Bt. (1960)

Kadoorie, Sir Horace, CBE

Kalo, Sir Kwamala, Kt., MBE

Kan Yuet-Keung, Sir, GBE

Kapi, *Hon.* Sir Mari, Kt., CBE

Katsina, The Emir of, KBE, CMG

Katz, Sir Bernard, Kt., FRS

Kavali, Sir Thomas, Kt., OBE

Kawharu, *Prof.* Sir Ian Hugh, Kt.

Kay, *Prof.* Sir Andrew Watt, Kt.

Kay, *Hon.* Sir John William, Kt.

Kaye, Sir David Alexander Gordon, Bt. (1923)

Kaye, Sir Emmanuel, Kt., CBE

Kaye, Sir John Phillip Lister Lister-, Bt. (1812)

Keane, Sir Richard Michael, Bt. (1801)

Keatinge, Sir Edgar Mayne, Kt., CBE

Keeble, Sir (Herbert Ben) Curtis, GCMG

Keith, *Prof.* Sir James, KBE

Kellett, Sir Brian Smith, Kt.

Kellett, Sir Stanley Charles, Bt. (1801)

Kelly, *Rt. Hon.* Sir (John William) Basil, Kt.

Kelly, Sir William Theodore, Kt., OBE

Kemball, *Air Marshal* Sir (Richard) John, KCB, CBE

Kemp, Sir (Edward) Peter, KCB

Kendrew, Sir John Cowdery, Kt., CBE, SC.D., FRS

Kenilorea, *Rt. Hon.* Sir Peter, KBE

Kennard, *Lt.-Col.* Sir George Arnold Ford, Bt. (1891)

Kennaway, Sir John Lawrence, Bt. (1791)

Kennedy, Sir Clyde David Allen, Kt.

Kennedy, Sir Francis, KCMG, CBE

Kennedy, *Hon.* Sir Ian Alexander, Kt.

†Kennedy, Sir Michael Edward, Bt., (1836)

Kennedy, *Rt. Hon.* Sir Paul Joseph Morrow, Kt.

Kennedy, *Air Chief Marshal* Sir Thomas Lawrie, GCB, AFC

Kennedy-Good, Sir John, KBE

Kenny, Sir Anthony John Patrick, Kt., D.Phil., D.Litt., FBA

Kenny, *Gen.* Sir Brian Leslie Graham, GCB, CBE

Kent, Sir Harold Simcox, GCB, QC

Kenyon, Sir George Henry, Kt.

Kermode, Sir (John) Frank, Kt., FBA

Kermode, Sir Ronald Graham Quale, KBE

Kerr, *Hon.* Sir Brian Francis, Kt.

Kerr, *Adm.* Sir John Beverley, GCB

Kerr, Sir John Olav, KCMG

Kerr, *Rt. Hon.* Sir Michael Robert Emanuel, Kt.

Kerruish, Sir (Henry) Charles, Kt., OBE

Kerry, Sir Michael James, KCB, QC

Kershaw, Sir (John) Anthony, Kt., MC

Keswick, Sir John Chippendale Lindley, Kt.

Kidd, Sir Robert Hill, KBE, CB

Kidu, *Hon.* Sir Buri (William), Kt.

Kikau, *Ratu* Sir Jone Latianara, KBE

Kiki, *Hon.* Sir (Albert) Maori, KBE

Kilfedder, Sir James Alexander, Kt., MP

Killen, *Hon.* Denis James, KCMG

Killick, Sir John Edward, GCMG

Kilpatrick, *Prof.* Sir Robert, Kt., CBE

Kimber, Sir Charles Dixon, Bt. (1904)

Kinahan, Sir Robert George Caldwell, Kt., ERD

King, Sir Albert, Kt., OBE

King, *Gen.* Sir Frank Douglas, GCB, MBE

King, Sir John Christopher, Bt. (1888)

King, *Vice-Adm.* Sir Norman Ross Dutton, KBE

King, Sir Richard Brian Meredith, KCB, MC

King, Sir Wayne Alexander, Bt. (1815)

Kingman, *Prof.* Sir John Frank Charles, Kt., FRS

Kingsland, Sir Richard, Kt., CBE, DFC

Kingsley, Sir Patrick Graham Toler, KCVO

Kinloch, Sir David, Bt. (s. 1686)

†Kinloch, Sir David Oliphant, Bt. (1873)

Kipalan, Sir Albert, Kt.

Kirby, *Hon.* Sir Richard Clarence, Kt.

Kirkpatrick, Sir Ivone Elliott, Bt. (s. 1685)

Kirkwood, *Hon.* Sir Andrew Tristram Hammett, Kt.

Kirwan, Sir (Archibald) Laurence Patrick, KCMG, TD

Kitcatt, Sir Peter Julian, Kt., CB

Kitson, *Gen.* Sir Frank Edward, GBE, KCB, MC

Kitson, Sir Timothy Peter Geoffrey, Kt.

Kitto, *Rt. Hon.* Sir Frank Walters, KBE

Kleinwort, Sir Kenneth Drake, Bt. (1909)

Klug, Sir Aaron, Kt.

Knight, Sir Allan Walton, Kt., CMG

Knight, Sir Arthur William, Kt.

Knight, Sir Harold Murray, KBE, DSC

Knight, *Air Chief Marshal* Sir Michael William Patrick, KCB, AFC

Knill, Sir John Kenelm Stuart, Bt. (1893)

Knott, Sir John Laurence, Kt., CBE

Knowles, Sir Charles Francis, Bt. (1765)

Knowles, Sir Leonard Joseph, Kt., CBE

Knowles, Sir Richard Marchant, Kt.

Knox, Sir Bryce Muir, KCVO, MC, TD

Knox, Sir David Laidlaw, Kt., MP

Knox, *Hon.* Sir John Leonard, Kt.

Knox, *Hon.* Sir William Edward, Kt.

Koraea, Sir Thomas, Kt.

Kornberg, *Prof.* Sir Hans Leo, Kt., D.SC., SC.D., Ph.D., FRS

Korowi, Sir Wiwa, GCMG

Krusin, Sir Stanley Marks, Kt., CB

Kulukundis, Sir Elias George (Eddie), Kt., OBE

Kurongku, *Most. Revd* Peter, KBE

Labouchere, Sir George Peter, GBE, KCMG

Lacon, Sir Edmund Vere, Bt. (1818)

Lacy, Sir Hugh Maurice Pierce, Bt. (1921)

Lacy, Sir John Trend, Kt., CBE

Lagesen, *Air Marshal* Sir Philip Jacobus, KCB, DFC, AFC

Laidlaw, Sir Christophor Charles Fraser, Kt.

Laing, Sir (John) Maurice, Kt.

Laing, Sir (William) Kirby, Kt., FEng.

Lake, Sir (Atwell) Graham, Bt. (1711)

Laker, Sir Frederick Alfred, Kt.

Lakin, Sir Michael, Bt. (1909)

Laking, Sir George Robert, KCMG

Lamb, Sir Albert (Larry), Kt.

Lamb, Sir Albert Thomas, KBE, CMG, DFC

Lambert, Sir Anthony Edward, KCMG

Lambert, Sir Edward Thomas, KBE, CVO

Lambert, Sir John Henry, KCVO, CMG

†Lambert, Sir Peter John Biddulph, Bt. (1711)

Lampl, Sir Frank William, Kt.

Landale, Sir David William Neil, KCVO

Landau, Sir Dennis Marcus, Kt.

Lane, Sir David William Stennis Stuart, Kt.

Lang, *Lt.-Gen.* Sir Derek Boileau, KCB, DSO, MC

Langham, Sir James Michael, Bt. (1660)

Langley, *Maj.-Gen.* Sir Henry Desmond Allen, KCVO, MBE

Langrishe, Sir Hercules Ralph Hume, Bt. (I. 1777)

Lapsley, *Air Marshal* Sir John Hugh, KBE, CB, DFC, AFC

Lapun, *Hon.* Sir Paul, Kt.

Larcom, Sir (Charles) Christopher Royde, Bt. (1868)

Large, Sir Peter, Kt., CBE

Larmour, Sir Edward Noel, KCMG

Lasdun, Sir Denys Louis, Kt., CBE, FRIBA

Latey, *Rt. Hon.* Sir John Brinsmead, Kt., MBE

Latham, *Hon.* Sir David Nicholas Ramsey, Kt.

Latham, Sir Michael Anthony, Kt.

Latham, Sir Richard Thomas Paul, Bt. (1919)

Latimer, Sir (Courtenay) Robert, Kt., CBE

Latimer, Sir Graham Stanley, KBE

Laucke, *Hon.* Sir Condor Louis, KCMG

Lauder, Sir Piers Robert Dick-, Bt. (s. 1690)

Laughton, Sir Anthony Seymour, Kt.

Laurantus, Sir Nicholas, Kt., MBE

Laurence, Sir Peter Harold, KCMG, MC

Laurie, Sir Robert Bayley Emilius, Bt. (1834)

Lauti, *Rt. Hon.* Sir Toaripi, GCMG

Lavan, *Hon.* Sir John Martin, Kt.

Law, *Adm.* Sir Horace Rochfort, GCB, OBE, DSC

Lawes, Sir (John) Michael Bennet, Bt. (1882)

Lawler, Sir Peter James, Kt., OBE

Lawrence, Sir David Roland Walter, Bt. (1906)

Lawrence, Sir Guy Kempton, Kt., DSO, OBE, DFC

Lawrence, Sir Ivan John, Kt., QC, MP

Lawrence, Sir John Patrick Grosvenor, Kt., CBE

Lawrence, Sir John Waldemar, Bt., OBE (1858)

Lawrence, Sir William Fettiplace, Bt. (1867)

Laws, *Hon.* Sir John Grant McKenzie, Kt.

Lawson, Sir Christopher Donald, Kt.

Lawson, *Col.* Sir John Charles Arthur Digby, Bt., DSO, MC (1900)

Lawson, Sir John Philip Howard-, Bt. (1841)

Lawson, *Hon.* Sir Neil, Kt.

Lawson, *Gen.* Sir Richard George, KCB, DSO, OBE

Lawton, *Prof.* Sir Frank Ewart, Kt.

Lawton, *Rt. Hon.* Sir Frederick Horace, Kt.

Layard, *Vice-Adm.* Sir Michael Henry Gordon, KCB, CBE

Layden, Sir John (Jack), Kt.

Layfield, Sir Frank Henry Burland Willoughby, Kt., QC

Lazarus, Sir Peter Esmond, KCB

Lea, *Vice-Adm.* Sir John Stuart Crosbie, KBE

Lea, Sir Thomas William, Bt. (1892)

Leach, *Admiral of the Fleet* Sir Henry Conyers, GCB

Leach, Sir Ronald George, GBE

Leahy, Sir Daniel Joseph, Kt.

Leahy, Sir John Henry Gladstone, KCMG

Learmont, *Gen.* Sir John Hartley, KCB, CBE

Leask, *Lt.-Gen.* Sir Henry Lowther Ewart Clark, KCB, DSO, OBE

Leather, Sir Edwin Hartley Cameron, KCMG, KCVO

Leaver, Sir Christopher, GBE

Le Bailly, *Vice-Adm.* Sir Louis Edward Stewart Holland, KBE, CB

Le Cheminant, *Air Chief Marshal* Sir Peter de Lacey, GBE, KCB, DFC

Lechmere, Sir Berwick Hungerford, Bt. (1818)

Ledger, Sir Frank, (Joseph Francis), Kt.

Ledwidge, Sir (William) Bernard (John), KCMG

Lee, Sir Arthur James, KBE, MC

Lee, *Air Chief Marshal* Sir David John Pryer, GBE, CB
Lee, Sir (Henry) Desmond (Pritchard), Kt.
Lee, *Brig.* Sir Leonard Henry, Kt., CBE
Lee, Sir Quo-wei, Kt., CBE
Lee, *Col.* Sir William Allison, Kt., OBE, TD
Leeds, Sir Christopher Anthony, Bt. (1812)
Lees, Sir David Bryan, Kt.
Lees, Sir Thomas Edward, Bt. (1897)
Lees, Sir Thomas Harcourt Ivor, Bt. (1804)
Lees, Sir (William) Antony Clare, Bt. (1937)
Leese, Sir John Henry Vernon, Bt. (1908)
Le Fanu, *Maj.* Sir (George) Victor (Sheridan), KCVO
le Fleming, Sir Quintin John, Bt. (1705)
Legard, Sir Charles Thomas, Bt. (1660)
Legg, Sir Thomas Stuart, KCB, QC
Leggatt, *Rt. Hon.* Sir Andrew Peter, Kt.
Leggatt, Sir Hugh Frank John, Kt.
Leggett, Sir Clarence Arthur Campbell, Kt., MBE
Leigh, Sir Geoffrey Norman, Kt.
Leigh, Sir Neville Egerton, KCVO
†Leigh, Sir Richard Henry, Bt. (1918)
Leighton, Sir Michael John Bryan, Bt. (1693)
Leitch, Sir George, KCB, OBE
Leith, Sir Andrew George Forbes-, Bt. (1923)
Le Marchant, Sir Francis Arthur, Bt. (1841)
Le Masurier, Sir Robert Hugh, Kt., DSC
Lemon, Sir (Richard) Dawnay, Kt., CBE
Leng, *Gen.* Sir Peter John Hall, KCB, MBE, MC
Lennard, *Revd* Sir Hugh Dacre Barrett-, Bt. (1801)
Leon, Sir John Ronald, Bt. (1911)
Leonard, *Rt. Revd and Rt. Hon.* Graham Douglas, KCVO
Leonard, *Hon.* Sir (Hamilton) John, Kt.
Lepping, Sir George Geria Dennis, GCMG, MBE
Le Quesne, Sir (Charles) Martin, KCMG
Le Quesne, Sir (John) Godfray, Kt., QC
Leslie, Sir Colin Alan Bettridge, Kt.
Leslie, Sir John Norman Ide, Bt. (1876)
†Leslie, Sir (Percy) Theodore, Bt. (s. 1625)
Leslie, Sir Peter Evelyn, Kt.
Lethbridge, Sir Thomas Periam Hector Noel, Bt. (1804)
Leuchars, Sir William Douglas, KBE

Leupena, Sir Tupua, GCMG, MBE
Levene, Sir Peter Keith, KBE
Lever, Sir (Tresham) Christopher Arthur Lindsay, Bt. (1911)
Levey, Sir Michael Vincent, Kt., MVO
Levine, Sir Montague Bernard, Kt.
Levinge, Sir Richard George Robin, Bt. (I. 1704)
Levy, Sir Ewart Maurice, Bt. (1913)
Lewando, Sir Jan Alfred, Kt., CBE
Lewinton, Sir Christopher, Kt.
Lewis, *Adm.* Sir Andrew Mackenzie, KCB
Lewis, Sir Kenneth, Kt.
Lewthwaite, Sir William Anthony, Bt. (1927)
Ley, Sir Francis Douglas, Bt., MBE, TD (1905)
Leyland, Sir Philip Vyvyan Naylor-, Bt. (1895)
Lickiss, Sir Michael Gillam, Kt.
Lickley, Sir Robert Lang, Kt., CBE, FEng.
Lidbury, Sir John Towersey, Kt.
Lidderdale, Sir David William Shuckburgh, KCB
Liggins, *Prof.* Sir Graham Collingwood, Kt., CBE, FRS
Lighthill, Sir (Michael) James, Kt., FRS
†Lighton, Sir Thomas Hamilton, Bt. (I. 1791)
Lim, Sir Han-Hoe, Kt., CBE
Linacre, Sir (John) Gordon (Seymour), Kt., CBE, AFC, DFM
Lincoln, Sir Anthony Handley, KCMG, CVO
Lindley, Sir Arnold Lewis George, Kt., FEng.
Lindop, Sir Norman, Kt.
Lindsay, Sir James Harvey Kincaid Stewart, Kt.
Lindsay, *Hon.* Sir John Edmund Frederic, Kt.
Lindsay, Sir Ronald Alexander, Bt. (1962)
Lintott, Sir Henry John Bevis, KCMG
Lipworth, Sir (Maurice) Sydney, Kt.
Lithgow, Sir William James, Bt. (1925)
Little, *Most Revd* Thomas Francis, KBE
Littler, Sir (James) Geoffrey, KCB
Livesay, *Adm.* Sir Michael Howard, KCB
Llewellyn, Sir Henry Morton, Bt., CBE (1922)
Llewellyn, *Lt.-Col.* Sir Michael Rowland Godfrey, Bt. (1959)
Llewelyn, Sir John Michael Dillwyn-Venables-, Bt. (1890)
Lloyd, *Rt. Hon.* Sir Anthony John Leslie, Kt.
Lloyd, Sir Ian Stewart, Kt.
Lloyd, Sir (John) Peter (Daniel), Kt.
Lloyd, Sir Nicholas Markley, Kt.
Lloyd, Sir Richard Ernest Butler, Bt. (1960)
Loader, Sir Leslie Thomas, Kt., CBE
Loane, *Most Revd* Marcus Lawrence, KBE

Lobo, Sir Rogerio Hyndman, Kt., CBE
Lock, *Cdr.* Sir (John) Duncan, Kt.
Lockhart, Sir Simon John Edward Francis Sinclair-, Bt. (s. 1636)
Loder, Sir Giles Rolls, Bt. (1887)
Lodge, Sir Thomas, Kt.
Logan, Sir Donald Arthur, KCMG
Logan, Sir Raymond Douglas, Kt.
Lokoloko, Sir Tore, GCMG, GCVO, OBE
Lombe, *Hon.* Sir Edward Christopher Evans-, Kt.
Longden, Sir Gilbert James Morley, Kt., MBE
Longland, Sir John Laurence, Kt.
Longley, Sir Norman, Kt., CBE
Loram, *Vice-Adm.* Sir David Anning, KCB, MVO
Lorimer, Sir (Thomas) Desmond, Kt.
Lousada, Sir Anthony Baruh, Kt.
Love, Sir Makere Rangiatea Ralph, Kt.
Lovell, Sir (Alfred Charles) Bernard, Kt., OBE, FRS
Lovelock, Sir Douglas Arthur, KCB
Loveridge, Sir John Henry, Kt., CBE
Loveridge, Sir John Warren, Kt.
Lovill, Sir John Roger, Kt., CBE
Low, Sir Alan Roberts, Kt.
Low, Sir James Richard Morrison-, Bt. (1908)
Lowe, *Air Chief Marshal* Sir Douglas Charles, GCB, DFC, AFC
Lowe, Sir Thomas William Gordon, Bt. (1918)
Lowry, Sir John Patrick, Kt., CBE
Lowson, Sir Ian Patrick, Bt. (1951)
Lowther, *Maj.* Sir Charles Douglas, Bt. (1824)
Loyd, Sir Francis Alfred, KCMG, OBE
Loyd, Sir Julian St John, KCVO
Lu, Sir Tseng Chi, Kt.
Lucas, Sir Cyril Edward, Kt., CMG, FRS
Lucas, Sir Thomas Edward, Bt. (1887)
Luce, *Rt Hon.* Sir Richard Napier, Kt.
Luckhoo, Sir Lionel Alfred, KCMG, CBE, QC
Lucy, Sir Edmund John William Hugh Cameron-Ramsay-Fairfax-, Bt. (1836)
Luddington, Sir Donald Collin Cumyn, KBE, CMG, CVO
Lumsden, Sir David James, Kt.
Lus, *Hon.* Sir Pita, Kt., OBE
Lush, *Hon.* Sir George Hermann, Kt.
Lushington, Sir John Richard Castleman, Bt. (1791)
Luttrell, *Col.* Sir Geoffrey Walter Fownes, KCVO, MC
Luyt, Sir Richard Edmonds, GCMG, KCVO, DCM
Lyell, *Rt. Hon.* Sir Nicholas Walter, Kt., QC, MP
Lygo, *Adm.* Sir Raymond Derek, KCB
Lyle, Sir Gavin Archibald, Bt. (1929)
Lyons, Sir Edward Houghton, Kt.
Lyons, Sir James Reginald, Kt.
Lyons, Sir John, Kt.
McAdam, Sir Ian William James, Kt., OBE

Macadam, Sir Peter, Kt.
McAlpine, Sir William Hepburn, Bt. (1918)
†Macara, Sir Hugh Kenneth, Bt. (1911)
Macartney, Sir John Barrington, Bt. (I. 1799)
McAvoy, Sir (Francis) Joseph, Kt., CBE
McCaffrey, Sir Thomas Daniel, Kt.
McCall, Sir (Charles) Patrick Home, Kt., MBE, TD
McCallum, Sir Donald Murdo, Kt., CBE, FEng.
McCamley, Sir Graham Edward, Kt., MBE
McCarthy, Rt. Hon. Sir Thaddeus Pearcey, KBE
McClellan, Col. Sir Herbert Gerard Thomas, Kt., CBE, TD
McClintock, Sir Eric Paul, Kt.
McColl, Sir Colin Hugh Verel, KCMG
McCollum, Hon. Sir William, Kt.
McConnell, Sir Robert Shean, Bt. (1900)
McCowan, Rt. Hon. Sir Anthony James Denys, Kt.
McCowan, Sir Hew Cargill, Bt. (1934)
McCrea, Prof. Sir William Hunter, Kt., FRS
McCrindle, Sir Robert Arthur, Kt.
McCullough, Hon. Sir (Iain) Charles (Robert), Kt.
McCusker, Sir James Alexander, Kt.
MacDermott, Rt. Hon. Sir John Clarke, Kt.
McDermott, Sir (Lawrence) Emmet, KBE
MacDonald, Gen. Sir Arthur Leslie, KBE, CB
McDonald, Air Chief Marshal Sir Arthur William Baynes, KCB, AFC
McDonald, Sir Duncan, Kt., CBE, FEng.
Macdonald of Sleat, Sir Ian Godfrey Bosville, Bt. (S. 1625)
Macdonald, Sir Kenneth Carmichael, KCB
Macdonald, Vice-Adm. Sir Roderick Douglas, KBE
McDonald, Sir Tom, Kt., OBE
McDonald, Hon. Sir William John Farquhar, Kt.
MacDougall, Sir (George) Donald (Alastair), Kt., CBE, FBA
McDowell, Sir Eric Wallalce, Kt., CBE
McDowell, Sir Henry McLorinan, KBE
Mace, Lt.-Gen. Sir John Airth, KBE, CB
McEwen, Sir John Roderick Hugh, Bt. (1953)
McFarland, Sir John Talbot, Bt. (1914)
Macfarlane, Sir (David) Neil, Kt.
Macfarlane, Sir George Gray, Kt., CB, FEng.
McFarlane, Sir Ian, Kt.
Macfarlane, Sir James Wright, Kt.
McGeoch, Vice-Adm. Sir Ian Lachlan Mackay, KCB, DSO, DSC
McGrath, Sir Brian Henry, KCVO
Macgregor, Sir Edwin Robert, Bt. (1828)

MacGregor of MacGregor, Sir Gregor, Bt. (1795)
McGregor, Sir Ian Alexander, Kt., CBE, FRS
MacGregor, Sir Ian Kinloch, Kt.
McGrigor, Capt. Sir Charles Edward, Bt. (1831)
McIntosh, Vice-Adm. Sir Ian Stewart, KBE, CB, DSO, DSC
McIntosh, Sir Ronald Robert Duncan, KCB
McIntyre, Sir Donald Conroy, Kt., CBE
McIntyre, Sir Meredith Alister, Kt.
McKaig, Adm. Sir (John) Rae, KCB, CBE
Mackay, Sir (George Patrick) Gordon, Kt., CBE
McKay, Sir John Andrew, Kt., CBE
Mackechnie, Sir Alistair John, Kt.
McKee, Maj. Sir (William) Cecil, Kt., ERD
McKellen, Sir Ian Murray, Kt., CBE
McKenzie, Sir Alexander, KBE
Mackenzie, Sir Alexander Alwyne Henry Charles Brinton Muir-, Bt. (1805)
Mackenzie, Vice-Adm. Sir Hugh Stirling, KCB, DSO, DSC
†Mackenzie, Sir (James William) Guy, Bt. (1890)
Mackenzie, Lt.-Gen. Sir Jeremy John George, KCB, OBE
†Mackenzie, Sir Peter Douglas, Bt. (S. 1673)
†Mackenzie, Sir Roderick McQuhae, Bt. (S. 1703)
McKenzie, Sir Roy Allan, KBE
Mackeson, Sir Rupert Henry, Bt. (1954)
Mackie, Sir Maitland, Kt., CBE
MacKinlay, Sir Bruce, Kt., CBE
McKinnon, Sir James, Kt.
McKinnon, Hon. Sir Stuart Neil, Kt.
McKissock, Sir Wylie, Kt., OBE, FRCS
Macklin, Sir Bruce Roy, Kt., OBE
Mackworth, Cdr. Sir David Arthur Geoffrey, Bt. (1776)
McLaren, Sir Robin John Taylor, KCMG
MacLaurin, Sir Ian Charter, Kt.
Maclean, Sir Donald Og Grant, Kt.
Maclean, Sir Fitzroy Hew, Bt., CBE (1957)
McLean, Sir Francis Charles, Kt., CBE
MacLean, Vice-Adm. Sir Hector Charles Donald, KBE, CB, DSC
Maclean, Sir Lachlan Hector Charles, Bt. (NS 1631)
Maclean, Sir Robert Alexander, KBE
McLennan, Sir Ian Munro, KCMG, KBE
McLeod, Sir Charles Henry, Bt. (1925)
McLeod, Sir Ian George, Kt.
†MacLeod, Hon. Sir John Maxwell Norman, Bt. (1924)
McLintock, Sir Michael William, Bt. (1934)

Maclure, Sir John Robert Spencer, Bt. (1898)
McMahon, Sir Brian Patrick, Bt. (1817)
McMahon, Sir Christopher William, Kt.
Macmillan, Sir (Alexander McGregor) Graham, Kt.
MacMillan, Lt.-Gen. Sir John Richard Alexander, KCB, CBE
McMullin, Rt. Hon. Sir Duncan Wallace, Kt.
Macnab, Brig. Sir Geoffrey Alex Colin, KCMG, CB
Macnaghten, Sir Patrick Alexander, Bt. (1836)
McNamara, Air Chief Marshal Sir Neville Patrick, KBE
Macnaughton, Prof. Sir Malcolm Campbell, Kt.
McNee, Sir David Blackstock, Kt., QPM
McNeice, Sir (Thomas) Percy (Fergus), Kt., CMG, OBE
MacPhail, Sir Bruce Dugald, Kt.
MacPherson, Sir Keith Duncan, Kt.
Macpherson, Sir Ronald Thomas Steward (Tommy), CBE, MC, TD
Macpherson of Cluny, Hon. Sir William Alan, Kt., TD
McQuarrie, Sir Albert, Kt.
MacRae, Sir (Alastair) Christopher (Donald Summerhayes), KCMG
Macrae, Col. Sir Robert Andrew Scarth, KCVO, MBE
Macready, Sir Nevil John Wilfrid, Bt. (1923)
McShine, Hon. Sir Arthur Hugh, Kt.
Mactaggart, Sir John Auld, Bt. (1938)
Macwhinnie, Sir Gordon Menzies, Kt., OBE
McWilliams, Sir Francis, GBE, FEng.
Madden, Adm. Sir Charles Edward, Bt., GCB (1919)
Maddocks, Sir Kenneth Phipson, KCMG, KCVO
Madigan, Sir Russel Tullie, Kt., OBE
Magnus, Sir Laurence Henry Philip, Bt. (1917)
Maguire, Air Marshal Sir Harold John, KCB, DSO, OBE
Mahon, Sir (John) Denis, Kt., CBE
Mahon, Sir William Walter, Bt. (1819)
Maiden, Sir Colin James, Kt., D.Phil.
Main, Sir Peter Tester, Kt., ERD
Maini, Sir Amar Nath, Kt., CBE
Maino, Sir Charles, KBE
Mais, Hon. Sir (Robert) Hugh, Kt.
Maitland, Sir Donald James Dundas, GCMG, OBE
Maitland, Sir Richard John, Bt. (1818)
Makins, Sir Paul Vivian, Bt. (1903)
Malcolm, Sir David Peter Michael, Bt. (S. 1665)
Malet, Sir Harry Douglas St Lo, Bt. (1791)
Mallaby, Sir Christopher Leslie George, GCVO, KCMG

Mallinson, Sir William John, Bt. (1935)

Malone, *Hon.* Sir Denis Eustace Gilbert, Kt.

Mamo, Sir Anthony Joseph, Kt., OBE

Manchester, Sir William Maxwell, KBE

Mander, Sir Charles Marcus, Bt. (1911)

Manduell, Sir John, Kt., CBE

Mann, *Rt. Hon.* Sir Michael, Kt.

Mann, *Rt. Revd* Michael Ashley, KCVO

Mann, Sir Rupert Edward, Bt. (1905)

Mansel, *Revd Canon* James Seymour Denis, KCVO

Mansel, Sir Philip, Bt. (1622)

Mansfield, *Vice-Adm.* Sir (Edward) Gerard (Napier), KBE, CVO

Mansfield, *Prof.* Sir Peter, Kt., FRS

Mansfield, Sir Philip (Robert Aked), KCMG

Mantell, *Hon.* Sir Charles Barrie Knight, Kt.

Manzie, Sir (Andrew) Gordon, KCB

Mara, *Rt. Hon.* Ratu Sir Kamisese Kapaiwai Tuimacilai, GCMG, KBE

Margetson, Sir John William Denys, KCMG

Marjoribanks, Sir James Alexander Milne, KCMG

Mark, Sir Robert, GBE

Markham, Sir Charles John, Bt. (1911)

Marking, Sir Henry Ernest, KCVO, CBE, MC

Marling, Sir Charles William Somerset, Bt. (1882)

Marr, Sir Leslie Lynn, Bt. (1919)

Marriner, Sir Neville, Kt., CBE

Marriott, Sir Hugh Cavendish Smith-, Bt. (1774)

Marsden, Sir Nigel John Denton, Bt. (1924)

Marshall, Sir Arthur Gregory George, Kt., OBE

Marshall, Sir Colin Marsh, Kt.

Marshall, Sir Denis Alfred, Kt.

Marshall, *Prof.* Sir (Oshley) Roy, Kt., CBE

Marshall, Sir Peter Harold Reginald, KCMG

Marshall, Sir Robert Braithwaite, KCB, MBE

Marshall, Sir (Robert) Michael, Kt., MP

Martell, *Vice-Adm.* Sir Hugh Colenso, KBE, CB

Martin, *Vice-Adm.* Sir John Edward Ludgate, KCB, DSC

Martin, *Prof.* Sir (John) Leslie, Kt., Ph.D.

Martin, *Col.* Sir (Robert) Andrew (St George), KCVO, OBE

Martin, Sir (Robert) Bruce, Kt., QC

Marychurch, Sir Peter Harvey, KCMG

Masefield, Sir Peter Gordon, Kt.

Mason, *Hon.* Sir Anthony Frank, KBE

Mason, Sir (Basil) John, Kt., CB, D.SC., FRS

Mason, *Prof.* Sir David Kean, Kt., CBE

Mason, Sir Frederick Cecil, KCVO, CMG

Mason, Sir Gordon Charles, Kt., OBE

Mason, Sir John Charles Moir, KCMG

Mason, *Prof.* Sir Ronald, KCB, FRS

Matane, Sir Paulias Nguna, Kt., CMG, OBE

Mather, Sir (David) Carol (Macdonell), Kt., MC

Mather, Sir William Loris, Kt., CVO, OBE, MC, TD

Mathers, Sir Robert William, Kt.

Matheson, Sir (James Adam) Louis, KBE, CMG, F.Eng.

†Matheson of Matheson, Sir Fergus John, Bt. (1882)

Matthews, Sir Peter Alec, Kt.

Matthews, Sir Peter Jack, Kt., CVO, OBE, QPM

Matthews, Sir Stanley, Kt., CBE

Maud, The Hon. Sir Humphrey John Hamilton, KCMG

†Maxwell, Sir Michael Eustace George, Bt. (s. 1681)

Maxwell, Sir Nigel Mellor Heron-, Bt. (s. 1683)

Maxwell, Sir Robert Hugh, KBE

May, *Hon.* Sir Anthony Tristram Kenneth, Kt.

May, *Rt. Hon.* Sir John Douglas, Kt.

May, Sir Kenneth Spencer, Kt., CBE

Mayhew, *Rt. Hon.* Sir Patrick Barnabas Burke, Kt., QC, MP

Maynard, *Hon.* Sir Clement Travelyan, Kt.

Maynard, *Air Chief Marshal* Sir Nigel Martin, KCB, CBE, DFC, AFC

Medlycott, Sir Mervyn Tregonwell, Bt. (1808)

Megarry, *Rt. Hon.* Sir Robert Edgar, Kt., FBA

Megaw, *Rt. Hon.* Sir John, Kt., CBE, TD

Meinertzhagen, Sir Peter, Kt., CMG

Melhuish, Sir Michael Ramsay, KBE, CMG

Mellon, Sir James, KCMG

Melville, Sir Harry Work, KCB, Ph.D., D.SC., FRS

Melville, Sir Leslie Galfreid, KBE

Melville, Sir Ronald Henry, KCB

Mensforth, Sir Eric, Kt., CBE, F.Eng.

Menter, Sir James Woodham, Kt., Ph.D., SC.D., FRS

Menteth, Sir James Wallace Stuart-, Bt. (1838)

Menzies, Sir Peter Thomson, Kt.

Messervy, Sir (Roney) Godfrey (Collumbell), Kt.

Meyer, Sir Anthony John Charles, Bt. (1910)

Meyjes, Sir Richard Anthony, Kt.

Meyrick, Sir David John Charlton, Bt. (1880)

Meyrick, Sir George Christopher Cadafael Tapps-Gervis-, Bt. (1791)

Miakwe, *Hon.* Sir Akepa, KBE

Michael, Sir Peter Colin, Kt., CBE

Middleton, Sir George Humphrey, KCMG

†Middleton, Sir Lawrence Monck, Bt. (1662)

Middleton, Sir Peter Edward, GCB

Miers, Sir (Henry) David Alastair Capel, KBE, CMG

Milbank, Sir Anthony Frederick, Bt. (1882)

Milburn, Sir Anthony Rupert, Bt. (1905)

Miles, Sir Peter Tremayne, KCVO

Miles, Sir William Napier Maurice, Bt. (1859)

Millais, Sir Geoffrey Richard Everett, Bt. (1885)

Millar, Sir Oliver Nicholas, GCVO, FBA

Millar, Sir Ronald Graeme, Kt.

Millard, Sir Guy Elwin, KCMG, CVO

Miller, Sir Donald John, Kt., FRSE, F.Eng.

Miller, Sir Douglas Sinclair, KCVO, CBE

Miller, Sir Hilary Duppa (Hal), Kt.

Miller, Sir (Ian) Douglas, Kt.

Miller, Sir John Holmes, Bt. (1705)

Miller, *Lt.-Col.* Sir John Mansel, GCVO, DSO, MC

Miller, Sir (Oswald) Bernard, Kt.

Miller, Sir Peter North, Kt.

Miller, Sir Ronald Andrew Baird, Kt., CBE

Miller, Sir Stephen James Hamilton, KCVO, MD, FRCS

Miller of Glenlee, Sir Stephen William Macdonald, Bt. (1788)

Millett, *Hon.* Sir Peter Julian, Kt.

Millichip, Sir Frederick Albert (Bert), Kt.

Milling, *Air Marshal* Sir Denis Crowley-, KCB, CBE, DSO, DFC

Mills, *Vice-Adm.* Sir Charles Piercy, KCB, CBE, DSC

Mills, Sir Frank, KCVO, CMG

Mills, Sir John Lewis Ernest Watts, Kt., CBE

Mills, Sir Peter Frederick Leighton, Bt. (1921)

Milman, *Lt.-Col.* Sir Derek, Bt. (1800)

Milne, Sir John Drummond, Kt.

Milner, Sir (George Edward) Mordaunt, Bt. (1717)

Milnes Coates, Sir Anthony Robert, Bt. (1911)

Miskin, *Hon.* Sir James William, Kt., QC

Mitchell, *Air Cdre* Sir (Arthur) Dennis, KBE, CVO, DFC, AFC

Mitchell, Sir David Bower, Kt., MP

Mitchell, Sir Derek Jack, KCB, CVO

Mitchell, *Prof.* Sir (Edgar) William John, Kt., CBE, FRS

Mitchell, *Hon.* Sir Stephen George, Kt.

Moate, Sir Roger Denis, Kt., MP

Mobbs, Sir (Gerald) Nigel, Kt.

Moberly, Sir John Campbell, KBE, CMG

Moberly, Sir Patrick Hamilton, KCMG

Moffat, *Lt.-Gen.* Sir (William) Cameron, KBE

Mogg, *Gen.* Sir (Herbert) John, GCB, CBE, DSO

Moir, Sir Ernest Ian Royds, Bt. (1916)

Moller, *Hon.* Sir Lester Francis, Kt.

†Molony, Sir Thomas Desmond, Bt. (1925)

Monro, Sir Hector Seymour Peter, Kt., MP

Montgomery, Sir (Basil Henry) David, Bt. (1801)

Montgomery, Sir (William) Fergus, Kt., MP

Mookerjee, Sir Birendra Nath, Kt.

Moollan, Sir Abdool Hamid Adam, Kt.

Moollan, *Hon.* Sir Cassam (Ismael), Kt.

Moon, Sir Peter Wilfred Giles Graham-, Bt. (1855)

†Moon, Sir Roger, Bt. (1887)

Moore, Sir Francis Thomas, Kt.

Moore, Sir Henry Roderick, Kt., CBE

Moore, *Hon.* Sir John Cochrane, Kt.

Moore, *Maj.-Gen.* Sir (John) Jeremy, KCB, OBE, MC

Moore, Sir John Michael, KCVO, CB, DSC

Moore, *Prof.* Sir Norman Winfrid, Bt. (1919)

Moore, Sir Patrick William Eisdell, Kt., OBE

Moore, Sir William Roger Clotworthy, Bt., TD (1932)

Moores, Sir John, Kt., CBE

Mootham, Sir Orby Howell, Kt.

Morauta, Sir Mekere, Kt.

Mordaunt, Sir Richard Nigel Charles, Bt. (1611)

Moreton, Sir John Oscar, KCMG, KCVO, MC

Morgan, *Maj.-Gen.* Sir David John Hughes-, Bt., CB, CBE (1925)

Morgan, Sir Ernest Dunstan, KBE

Morgan, Sir John Albert Leigh, KCMG

Morland, *Hon.* Sir Michael, Kt.

Morland, Sir Robert Kenelm, Kt.

Morpeth, Sir Douglas Spottiswoode, Kt., TD

Morris, *Air Marshal* Sir Arnold Alec, KBE, CB, FEng.

Morris, Sir (James) Richard (Samuel), Kt., CBE, FEng.

Morris, Sir Robert Byng, Bt. (1806)

Morrison, *Hon.* Sir Charles Andrew, Kt.

Morrison, Sir Howard Leslie, Kt., OBE

Morrison, *Rt. Hon.* Sir Peter Hugh, Kt.

Morritt, *Hon.* Sir (Robert) Andrew, Kt., CVO

Morrow, Sir Ian Thomas, Kt.

Morse, Sir Christopher Jeremy, KCMG

Morton, *Adm.* Sir Anthony Storrs, GBE, KCB

Morton, Sir (Robert) Alastair (Newton), Kt.

Morton, Sir William David, Kt., CBE

Moseley, Sir George Walker, KCB

Moser, *Prof.* Sir Claus Adolf, KCB, CBE, FBA

†Moss, Sir David John Edwards-, Bt. (1868)

Mostyn, *Gen.* Sir (Joseph) David Frederick, KCB, CBE

†Mostyn, Sir William Basil John, Bt. (1670)

Mott, Sir John Harmer, Bt. (1930)

Mott, Sir Nevill Francis, Kt., FRS

Mount, Sir James William Spencer, Kt., CBE, BEM

†Mount, Sir (William Robert) Ferdinand, Bt. (1921)

Mountain, Sir Denis Mortimer, Bt. (1922)

Mowbray, Sir John, Kt.

Mowbray, Sir John Robert, Bt. (1880)

Moynihan, Sir Noel Henry, Kt.

Muir, Sir John Harling, Bt. (1892)

Muir, Sir Laurence Macdonald, Kt.

Muirhead, Sir David Francis, KCMG, CVO

Mulcahy, Sir Geoffrey John, Kt.

Mullens, *Lt.-Gen.* Sir Anthony Richard Guy, KCB, OBE

Mummery, *Hon.* Sir John Frank, Kt.

Munn, Sir James, Kt., OBE

Munro, Sir Alan Gordon, KCMG

Munro, Sir Alasdair Thomas Ian, Bt. (1825)

Munro, Sir Ian Talbot, Bt. (s. 1634)

Munro, *Hon.* Sir Robert Lindsay, Kt., CBE

Munro, Sir Sydney Douglas Gun-, GCMG, MBE

Murley, Sir Reginald Sydney, KBE, TD, FRCS

Murphy, Sir Leslie Frederick, Kt.

Murray, *Rt. Hon.* Sir Donald Bruce, Kt.

Murray, Sir Donald Frederick, KCVO, CMG

Murray, Sir James, KCMG

Murray, Sir John Antony Jerningham, Kt., CBE

Murray, *Prof.* Sir Kenneth, Kt., FRCPath., FRS, FRSE

Murray, Sir Nigel Andrew Digby, Bt. (s. 1628)

Murray, Sir Patrick Ian Keith, Bt. (s. 1673)

†Murray, Sir Rowland William Patrick, Bt. (s. 1630)

Murrie, Sir William Stuart, GCB, KBE

Mursell, Sir Peter, Kt., MBE

Musgrave, Sir Christopher Patrick Charles, Bt. (1611)

Musgrave, Sir Richard James, Bt. (I. 1782)

Musson, *Gen.* Sir Geoffrey Randolph Dixon, GCB, CBE, DSO

Myers, Sir Kenneth Ben, Kt., MBE

Myers, Sir Philip Alan, Kt., QPM

Myers, *Prof.* Sir Rupert Horace, KBE

Mynors, Sir Richard Baskerville, Bt. (1964)

Nabarro, Sir John David Nunes, Kt., MD, FRCP

Naipaul, Sir Vidiadhar Surajprasad, Kt.

Nairn, Sir Michael, Bt. (1904)

Nairn, Sir Robert Arnold Spencer-, Bt. (1933)

Nairne, *Rt. Hon.* Sir Patrick Dalmahoy, GCB, MC

Nalder, *Hon.* Sir Crawford David, Kt.

Nall, Sir Michael Joseph, Bt., RN (1954)

Napier, Sir John Archibald Lennox, Bt. (s. 1627)

Napier, Sir Oliver John, Kt.

Napier, Sir Robin Surtees, Bt. (1867)

Napley, Sir David, Kt.

Neal, Sir Eric James, Kt., CVO

Neal, Sir Leonard Francis, Kt., CBE

Neale, Sir Alan Derrett, KCB, MBE

Neale, Sir Gerrard Anthony, Kt.

Neave, Sir Paul Arundell, Bt. (1795)

Nedd, *Hon.* Sir Robert Archibald, Kt.

Neill, *Rt. Hon.* Sir Brian Thomas, Kt.

Neill, Sir Francis Patrick, Kt., QC

Neill, *Rt. Hon.* Sir Ivan, Kt., PC(NI)

Nelson, *Maj.-Gen.* Sir (Eustace) John (Blois), KCVO, CB, DSO, OBE, MC

†Nelson, Sir Jamie Charles Vernon Hope, Bt. (1912)

Nelson, *Air Marshal* Sir (Sidney) Richard (Carlyle), KCB, OBE, MD

Nepean, *Lt.-Col.* Sir Evan Yorke, Bt. (1802)

Ness, *Air Marshal* Sir Charles Ernest, KCB, CBE

Neubert, Sir Michael John, Kt., MP

Nevile, *Capt.* Sir Henry Nicholas, KCVO

Neville, Sir Richard Lionel John Baines, Bt. (1927)

New, *Maj.-Gen.* Sir Laurence Anthony Wallis, Kt., CB, CBE

Newbold, Sir Charles Demorée, KBE, CMG, QC

Newington, Sir Michael John, KCMG

Newman, Sir Francis Hugh Cecil, Bt. (1912)

Newman, Sir Geoffrey Robert, Bt. (1836)

Newman, Sir Jack, Kt., CBE

Newman, Sir Kenneth Leslie, GBE, QPM

Newman, *Vice-Adm.* Sir Roy Thomas, KCB

Newman, *Col.* Sir Stuart Richard, Kt., CBE, TD

Newns, Sir (Alfred) Foley (Francis Polden), KCMG, CVO

Newsam, Sir Peter Anthony, Kt.

Newton, Sir (Charles) Wilfred, Kt., CBE

Newton, Sir (Harry) Michael (Rex), Bt. (1900)

Newton, Sir Kenneth Garnar, Bt., OBE, TD (1924)

Newton, Sir (Leslie) Gordon, Kt.

Ngata, Sir Henare Kohere, KBE

Niall, Sir Horace Lionel Richard, Kt., CBE

Nichol, Sir Duncan Kirkbride, Kt., CBE

Nicholas, Sir David, Kt., CBE

Nicholas, Sir Herbert Richard, Kt.,
  OBE
Nicholas, Sir John William, KCVO, CMG
Nicholls, *Rt. Hon.* Sir Donald James,
  Kt.
Nicholls, *Air Marshal* Sir John
  Moreton, KCB, CBE, DFC, AFC
Nicholson, Sir Bryan Hubert, Kt.
†Nicholson, Sir Charles Christian, Bt.
  (1912)
Nicholson, *Hon.* Sir David Eric, Kt.
Nicholson, *Hon.* Sir Michael, Kt.
Nicholson, Sir Paul Douglas, Kt.
Nicholson, Sir Robin Buchanan, Kt.,
  ph.D., FRS
Nickson, Sir David Wigley, KBE
Nicoll, Sir William, KCMG
Nicolson, Sir David Lancaster, Kt,
  FEng.
Nield, Sir Basil Edward, Kt., CBE, QC
Nield, Sir William Alan, GCMG, KCB
Nightingale, Sir Charles Manners
  Gamaliel, Bt. (1628)
Nightingale, Sir John Cyprian, Kt.,
  CBE, BEM, QPM
Nimmo, *Hon.* Sir John Angus, Kt.,
  CBE
Nixon, Sir Edwin Ronald, Kt., CBE
Nixon, *Revd* Sir Kenneth Michael
  John Basil, Bt. (1906)
Noad, Sir Kenneth Beeson, Kt., MD
Noble, Sir David Brunel, Bt. (1902)
Noble, Sir Iain Andrew, Bt., OBE
  (1923)
Noble, Sir (Thomas Alexander)
  Fraser, Kt., MBE
Nolan, *Rt. Hon.* Sir Michael Patrick,
  Kt.
Nombri, Sir Joseph Karl, Kt., ISO, BEM
Norman, Sir Arthur Gordon, KBE, DFC
Norman, Sir Mark Annesley, Bt.
  (1915)
Norman, Sir Robert Henry, Kt., OBE
Norman, Sir Robert Wentworth, Kt.
Normanton, Sir Tom, Kt., TD
Norris, *Air Chief Marshal* Sir
  Christopher Neil Foxley-, GCB, DSO,
  OBE
Norris, Sir Eric George, KCMG
North, Sir Thomas Lindsay, Kt.
North, Sir (William) Jonathan
  (Frederick), Bt. (1920)
Norton, *Vice-Adm.* *Hon.* Sir Nicholas
  John Hill-, KCB
Norwood, Sir Walter Neville, Kt.
Nossal, Sir Gustav Joseph Victor, Kt.,
  CBE
Nott, *Rt. Hon.* Sir John William
  Frederic, KCB
Nourse, *Rt. Hon.* Sir Martin Charles,
  Kt.
Nugent, Sir John Edwin Lavallin, Bt.
  (I. 1795)
Nugent, *Maj.* Sir Peter Walter James,
  Bt. (1831)
Nugent, Sir Robin George Colborne,
  Bt. (1806)
Nursaw, Sir James, KCB, QC

Nuttall, Sir Nicholas Keith Lillington,
  Bt. (1922)
Nutting, *Rt. Hon.* Sir (Harold)
  Anthony, Bt. (1903)
Oakeley, Sir John Digby Atholl, Bt.
  (1790)
Oakes, Sir Christopher, Bt. (1939)
Oakshott, *Hon.* Sir Anthony Hendrie,
  Bt. (1959)
Oates, Sir Thomas, Kt., CMG, OBE
Oatley, Sir Charles William, Kt., OBE,
  FRS, FEng.
Obolensky, *Prof.* Sir Dimitri, Kt.
O'Brien, Sir Frederick William
  Fitzgerald, Kt.
O'Brien, Sir Richard, Kt., DSO, MC
O'Brien, Sir Timothy John, Bt. (1849)
O'Brien, *Adm.* Sir William Donough,
  KCB, DSC
O'Connell, Sir Maurice James Donagh
  MacCarthy, Bt. (1869)
O'Connor, *Rt. Hon.* Sir Patrick
  McCarthy, Kt.
O'Dea, Sir Patrick Jerad, KCVO
Odell, Sir Stanley John, Kt.
Ogden, Sir (Edward) Michael, Kt., QC
Ogilvie, Sir Alec Drummond, Kt.
Ogilvy, *Hon.* Sir Angus James Bruce,
  KCVO
†Ogilvy, Sir Francis Gilbert Arthur, Bt.
  (S. 1626)
Ognall, *Hon.* Sir Harry Henry, Kt.
Ohlson, Sir Brian Eric Christopher,
  Bt. (1920)
Okeover, *Capt.* Sir Peter Ralph
  Leopold Walker-, Bt. (1886)
Olewale, *Hon.* Sir Niwia Ebia, Kt.
Oliphant, Sir Mark (Marcus Laurence
  Elwin), KBE, FRS
Oliver, Sir (Frederick) Ernest, Kt.,
  CBE, TD
O'Loghlen, Sir Colman Michael, Bt.
  (1838)
Olver, Sir Stephen John Linley, KBE,
  CMG
O'Neil, *Hon.* Sir Desmond Henry, Kt.
Ongley, *Hon.* Sir Joseph Augustine,
  Kt.
Onslow, *Rt. Hon.* Sir Cranley Gordon
  Douglas, KCMG, MP
Onslow, Sir John Roger Wilmot, Bt.
  (1797)
Oppenheim, Sir Alexander, Kt., OBE,
  D.SC., FRSE
Oppenheim, Sir Duncan Morris, Kt.
Oppenheimer, Sir Michael Bernard
  Grenville, Bt. (1921)
Oppenheimer, Sir Philip Jack, Kt.
Opperman, *Hon.* Sir Hubert
  Ferdinand, Kt., OBE
Orde, Sir John Alexander Campbell-,
  Bt. (1790)
O'Regan, *Hon.* Sir John Barry, Kt.
Orlebar, Sir Michael Keith Orlebar
  Simpson-, KCMG
Ormond, Sir John Davies Wilder, Kt.,
  BEM
Orr, Sir David Alexander, Kt., MC
Orr, Sir John Henry, Kt., OBE, QPM

Osborn, Sir John Holbrook, Kt.
Osborn, Sir Richard Henry Danvers,
  Bt. (1662)
Osborne, Sir Peter George, Bt.
  (I. 1629)
Osifelo, Sir Frederick Aubarua, Kt.,
  MBE
Osman, Sir (Abdool) Raman
  Mahomed, GCMG, CBE
Osmond, Sir Douglas, Kt., CBE
Osmond, Sir (Stanley) Paul, Kt., CB
Oswald, *Admiral of the Fleet* Sir (John)
  Julian Robertson, GCB
Otton, Sir Geoffrey John, KCB
Otton, *Hon.* Sir Philip Howard, Kt.
Oulton, Sir Antony Derek Maxwell,
  GCB, QC
Outram, Sir Alan James, Bt. (1858)
Overall, Sir John Wallace, Kt., CBE, MC
Owen, Sir Geoffrey, Kt.
Owen, Sir Hugh Bernard Pilkington,
  Bt. (1813)
Owen, Sir Hugo Dudley Cunliffe-, Bt.
  (1920)
Owen, *Hon.* Sir John Arthur Dalziel,
  Kt.
Owo, The Olowo of, Kt.
Oxburgh, *Prof.* Sir Ernest Ronald,
  KBE, Ph.D., FRS
Oxford, Sir Kenneth Gordon, Kt.,
  CBE, QPM
Packard, *Lt.-Gen.* Sir (Charles)
  Douglas, KBE, CB, DSO
Padmore, Sir Thomas, GCB
Page, Sir Alexander Warren, Kt., MBE
Page, Sir (Arthur) John, Kt.
Page, Sir Frederick William, Kt., CBE,
  FEng.
Page, Sir John Joseph Joffre, Kt., OBE
Paget, Sir Julian Tolver, Bt., CVO
  (1871)
Paget, Sir Richard Herbert, Bt. (1886)
Pain, *Lt.-Gen.* Sir (Horace) Rollo
  (Squarey), KCB, MC
Pain, *Hon.* Sir Peter Richard, Kt.
Palin, *Air Chief Marshal* Sir Roger
  Hewlett, KCB, OBE
Palliser, *Rt. Hon.* Sir (Arthur)
  Michael, GCMG
Palmar, Sir Derek James, Kt.
Palmer, Sir (Charles) Mark, Bt. (1886)
Palmer, *Gen.* Sir (Charles) Patrick
  (Ralph), KBE
Palmer, Sir Geoffrey Christopher
  John, Bt. (1660)
Palmer, *Rt. Hon.* Sir Geoffrey
  Winston Russell, KCMG
Palmer, Sir John Chance, Kt.
Palmer, Sir John Edward Somerset,
  Bt. (1791)
Palmer, *Maj.-Gen.* Sir (Joseph)
  Michael, KCVO
Palmer, Sir Reginald Oswald, GCMG,
  MBE
Pantlin, Sir Dick Hurst, Kt., CBE
Paolozzi, Sir Eduardo Luigi, Kt., CBE,
  RA
Pararajasingam, Sir Sangarapillai, Kt.
Parbo, Sir Arvi Hillar, Kt.

Parish, Sir David Elmer Woodbine, Kt., CBE
Park, *Hon.* Sir Hugh Eames, Kt.
Parker, Sir (Arthur) Douglas Dodds-, Kt.
Parker, Sir Eric Wilson, Kt.
Parker, *Hon.* Sir Jonathan Frederic, Kt.
Parker, Sir Peter, KBE, LVO
Parker, Sir Richard (William) Hyde, Bt. (1681)
Parker, *Rt. Hon.* Sir Roger Jocelyn, Kt.
Parker, *Vice-Adm.* Sir (Wilfred) John, KBE, CB, DSC
Parker, Sir William Peter Brian, Bt. (1844)
Parkes, Sir Edward Walter, Kt., FEng.
Parkinson, Sir Nicholas Fancourt, Kt.
Parsons, Sir Anthony Derrick, GCMG, MVO, MC
Parsons, Sir (John) Michael, Kt.
Parsons, Sir Richard Edmund (Clement Fownes), KCMG
Partridge, Sir Michael John Anthony, KCB
Pascoe, *Gen.* Sir Robert Alan, KCB, MBE
Pasley, Sir John Malcolm Sabine, Bt. (1794)
Paterson, Sir Dennis Craig, Kt.
Paterson, Sir George Mutlow, Kt., OBE, QC
Paterson, Sir John Valentine Jardine, Kt.
Paton, Sir (Thomas) Angus (Lyall), Kt., CMG, FRS, FEng.
Paton, *Prof.* Sir William Drummond Macdonald, Kt., CBE, DM, FRS, FRCP
Pattie, *Rt. Hon.* Sir Geoffrey Edwin, Kt., MP
Pattinson, *Hon.* Sir Baden, KBE
Pattinson, Sir (William) Derek, Kt.
Paul, Sir John Warburton, GCMG, OBE, MC
Paul, *Air Marshal* Sir Ronald Ian Stuart-, KBE
Payne, Sir Norman John, Kt., CBE, FEng.
Peach, Sir Leonard Harry, Kt.
Peacock, *Prof.* Sir Alan Turner, Kt., DSC
Pearce, Sir Austin William, Kt., CBE, ph.D., FEng.
Pearce, Sir (Daniel Norton) Idris, Kt., CBE, TD
Pearce, Sir Eric Herbert, Kt., OBE
Peard, *Rear-Adm.* Sir Kenyon Harry Terrell, KBE
Pearman, *Hon.* Sir James Eugene, Kt., CBE
Pearson, Sir Francis Nicholas Fraser, Bt. (1964)
Pearson, *Gen.* Sir Thomas Cecil Hook, KCB, CBE, DSO
Peart, *Prof.* Sir William Stanley, Kt., MD, FRS
Pease, Sir (Alfred) Vincent, Bt. (1882)
Pease, Sir Richard Thorn, Bt. (1920)

Peat, Sir Gerrard Charles, KCVO
Peat, Sir Henry, KCVO, DFC
Peck, Sir Edward Heywood, GCMG
Peck, Sir John Howard, KCMG
Pedder, *Vice-Adm.* Sir Arthur Reid, KBE, CB
Pedder, *Air Marshal* Sir Ian Maurice, KCB, OBE, DFC
Peek, Sir Francis Henry Grenville, Bt. (1874)
Peek, *Vice-Adm.* Sir Richard Innes, KBE, CB, DSC
Peel, Sir John Harold, KCVO
Peel, Sir (William) John, Kt.
Peierls, Sir Rudolf Ernst, Kt., CBE, D.SC., D.Phil., FRS
Peirse, Sir Henry Grant de la Poer Beresford-, Bt. (1814)
Peirse, *Air Vice-Marshal* Sir Richard Charles Fairfax, KCVO, CB
Pelgen, Sir Harry Friedrich, Kt., MBE
†Pelly, Sir Richard John, Bt. (1840)
Pemberton, Sir Francis Wingate William, Kt., CBE
Percival, Sir Anthony Edward, Kt., CB
Percival, *Rt. Hon.* Sir (Walter) Ian, Kt., QC
Pereira, Sir (Herbert) Charles, Kt., D.SC., FRS
Perkins, *Surgeon Vice-Adm.* Sir Derek Duncombe Steele-, KCB, KCVO
Perring, Sir Ralph Edgar, Bt. (1963)
Perris, Sir David (Arthur), Kt., MBE
Perry, Sir David Howard, KCB
Perry, Sir (David) Norman, Kt., MBE
Pestell, Sir John Richard, KCVO
Peterkin, Sir Neville, Kt.
Peters, *Prof.* Sir David Keith, Kt., FRCP
Petersen, Sir Jeffrey Charles, KCMG
Petersen, Sir Johannes Bjelke-, KCMG
Petit, Sir Dinshaw Manockjee, Bt. (1890)
Peto, Sir Henry George Morton, Bt. (1855)
Peto, Sir Michael Henry Basil, Bt. (1927)
Petrie, Sir Peter Charles, Bt., CMG (1918)
Pettigrew, Sir Russell Hilton, Kt.
Pettit, Sir Daniel Eric Arthur, Kt.
Philips, *Prof.* Sir Cyril Henry, Kt.
Phillips, *Prof.* Sir David Chilton, KBE, ph.D., FRS
Phillips, Sir Fred Albert, Kt., CVO
Phillips, Sir Henry Ellis Isidore, Kt., CMG, MBE
Phillips, Sir Horace, KCMG
Phillips, *Hon.* Sir Nicholas Addison, Kt.
Phillips, Sir Peter John, Kt., OBE
Phillips, Sir Robin Francis, Bt. (1912)
Pickering, Sir Edward Davies, Kt.
Pickthorn, Sir Charles William Richards, Bt. (1959)
Pidgeon, Sir John Allan Stewart, Kt.
Piers, Sir Charles Robert Fitzmaurice, Bt. (I. 1661)
Pigot, Sir George Hugh, Bt. (1764)

Pigott, Sir Berkeley Henry Sebastian, Bt. (1808)
Pike, Sir Michael Edmund, KCVO, CMG
Pike, Sir Philip Ernest Housden, Kt., QC
Pilcher, Sir (Charlie) Dennis, Kt., CBE
Pilditch, Sir Richard Edward, Bt. (1929)
Pile, Sir Frederick Devereux, Bt., MC (1900)
Pile, Sir William Dennis, GCB, MBE
Pilkington, Sir Antony Richard, Kt.
Pilkington, Sir Lionel Alexander Bethune, (Sir Alastair), Kt., FRS
Pilkington, Sir Thomas Henry Milborne-Swinnerton-, Bt. (s. 1635)
Pill, *Hon.* Sir Malcolm Thomas, Kt.
Pillar, *Adm.* Sir William Thomas, GBE, KCB
Pindling, *Rt. Hon.* Sir Lynden Oscar, KCMG
Pinker, Sir George Douglas, KCVO
Pinsent, Sir Christopher Roy, Bt. (1938)
Pippard, *Prof.* Sir (Alfred) Brian, Kt., FRS
Pirie, *Gp Capt* Sir Gordon Hamish, Kt., CVO, CBE
Pitblado, Sir David Bruce, KCB, CVO
Pitcher, Sir Desmond Henry, Kt.
Pitoi, Sir Sere, Kt., CBE
Pitt, Sir Harry Raymond, Kt., ph.D., FRS
Pitts, Sir Cyril Alfred, Kt.
Pixley, Sir Neville Drake, Kt., MBE, VRD
Plastow, Sir David Arnold Stuart, Kt.
†Platt, Sir (Frank) Lindsey, Bt. (1958)
Platt, *Prof.* Hon. Sir Peter, Bt. (1959)
Playfair, Sir Edward Wilder, KCB
Pliatzky, Sir Leo, KCB
Plowman, *Hon.* Sir John Robin, Kt., CBE
Plumb, *Prof.* Sir John Harold, Kt.
Pohai, Sir Timothy, Kt., MBE
†Pole, Sir (John) Richard (Walter Reginald) Carew, Bt. (1628)
Pole, Sir Peter Van Notten, Bt. (1791)
Pollen, Sir John Michael Hungerford, Bt. (1795)
Pollock, Sir George Frederick, Bt. (1866)
Pollock, Sir Giles Hampden Montagu-, Bt. (1872)
Pollock, *Admiral of the Fleet* Sir Michael Patrick, GCB, MVO, DSC
Pollock, Sir William Horace Montagu-, KCMG
Ponsonby, Sir Ashley Charles Gibbs, Bt., KCVO, MC (1956)
Pontin, Sir Frederick William, Kt.
Poore, Sir Herbert Edward, Bt. (1795)
Pope, *Vice-Adm.* Sir (John) Ernle, KCB
Pope, Sir Joseph Albert, Kt., D.SC., ph.D.
Popper, *Prof.* Sir Karl Raimund, Kt., CH, Ph.D., FRS
Popplewell, *Hon.* Sir Oliver Bury, Kt.
Portal, Sir Jonathan Francis, Bt. (1901)

Porter, Sir John Simon Horsbrugh-, Bt. (1902)

Porter, Sir Leslie, Kt.

Porter, *Air Marshal* Sir (Melvin) Kenneth (Drowley), KCB, CBE

Porter, *Hon.* Sir Murray Victor, Kt.

Porter, *Rt. Hon.* Sir Robert Wilson, Kt., PC(NI), QC

Posnett, Sir Richard Neil, KBE, CMG

Potter, Sir (Joseph) Raymond (Lynden), Kt.

Potter, *Hon.* Sir Mark Howard, Kt.

Potter, *Maj.-Gen.* Sir (Wilfrid) John, KBE, CB

Potter, Sir (William) Ian, Kt.

Potts, *Hon.* Sir Francis Humphrey, Kt.

Pound, Sir John David, Bt. (1905)

Pountain, Sir Eric John, Kt.

Powell, Sir (Arnold Joseph) Philip, Kt., CH, OBE, RA, FRIBA

Powell, Sir Charles David, KCMG

Powell, Sir Nicholas Folliott Douglas, Bt. (1897)

Powell, Sir Richard Royle, GCB, KBE, CMG

Power, Sir Alastair John Cecil, Bt. (1924)

Powles, Sir Guy Richardson, KBE, CMG, ED

Poynton, Sir (Arthur) Hilton, GCMG

Prendergast, Sir John Vincent, KBE, CMG, GM

Prendergast, Sir (Walter) Kieran, KCVO, CMG

Prentice, *Hon.* Sir William Thomas, Kt., MBE

Prescott, Sir Mark, Bt. (1938)

Preston, Sir Kenneth Huson, Kt.

Preston, Sir Peter Sansome, KCB

Preston, Sir Ronald Douglas Hildebrand, Bt. (1815)

Prevost, Sir Christopher Gerald, Bt. (1805)

Price, Sir Charles Keith Napier Rugge-, Bt. (1804)

Price, Sir David Ernest Campbell, Kt.

Price, Sir Francis Caradoc Rose, Bt. (1815)

Price, Sir Frank Leslie, Kt.

Price, Sir (James) Robert, KBE

Price, Sir Leslie Victor, Kt., OBE

Price, Sir Norman Charles, KCB

Price, Sir Robert John Green-, Bt. (1874)

Prickett, *Air Chief Marshal* Sir Thomas Other, KCB, DSO, DFC

Prideaux, Sir Humphrey Povah Treverbian, Kt., OBE

†Primrose, Sir John Ure, Bt. (1903)

Pringle, *Air Marshal* Sir Charles Norman Seton, KBE, FEng.

Pringle, *Hon.* Sir John, Kt.

Pringle, *Lt.-Gen.* Sir Steuart (Robert), Bt., KCB, RM (S. 1683)

Pritchard, Sir Neil, KCMG

Pritchett, Sir Victor Sawdon, Kt., CH, CBE

Proby, Sir Peter, Bt. (1952)

Proud, Sir John Seymour, Kt.

Prout, Sir Christopher James, Kt., TD, QC, MEP

Pryke, Sir David Dudley, Bt. (1926)

Pugh, Sir Idwal Vaughan, KCB

Pugsley, *Prof.* Sir Alfred Grenvile, Kt., OBE, D.SC., FRS, FEng.

Pullen, Sir William Reginald James, KCVO

Pullinger, Sir (Francis) Alan, Kt., CBE

Pumphrey, Sir (John) Laurence, KCMG

Purchas, *Rt. Hon.* Sir Francis Brooks, Kt.

Purves, Sir William, Kt., CBE, DSO

Purvis, *Vice-Adm.* Sir Neville, KCB

Quennell, Sir Peter, Kt., CBE

Quicke, Sir John Godolphin, Kt., CBE

Quigley, Sir (William) George (Henry), Kt., CB, Ph.D.

Quilliam, *Hon.* Sir (James) Peter, Kt.

Quilter, Sir Anthony Raymond Leopold Cuthbert, Bt. (1897)

Quinlan, Sir Michael Edward, GCB

Quinton, Sir James Grand, Kt.

Quirk, *Prof.* Sir (Charles)Randolph, Kt., CBE, FBA

Rabukawaqa, Sir Josua Rasilau, KBE, MVO

Radcliffe, Sir Sebastian Everard, Bt. (1813)

Radford, Sir Ronald Walter, KCB, MBE

Radzinowicz, *Prof.* Sir Leon, Kt., LL D

Rae, *Hon.* Sir Wallace Alexander Ramsay, Kt.

Raeburn, Sir Michael Edward Norman, Bt. (1923)

Raeburn, *Maj.-Gen.* Sir (William) Digby (Manifold), KCVO, CB, DSO, MBE

Raffray, Sir Piat Joseph Raymond Andre, Kt.

Raikes, *Vice-Adm.* Sir Iwan Geoffrey, KCB, CBE, DSC

Raison, *Rt. Hon.* Sir Timothy Hugh Francis, Kt.

Ralli, Sir Godfrey Victor, Bt., TD (1912)

Ramdanee, Sir Mookteswar Baboolall Kailash, Kt.

Ramphal, Sir Shridath Surendranath, GCMG

Ramphul, Sir Baalkhristna, Kt.

Ramphul, Sir Indurduth, Kt.

Rampton, Sir Jack Leslie, KCB

Ramsay, Sir Alexander William Burnett, Bt. (1806)

Ramsay, Sir Allan John (Hepple), KBE, CMG

Ramsay, Sir Thomas Meek, Kt., CMG

Ramsbotham, *Gen.* Sir David John, GCB, CBE

Ramsbotham, *Hon.* Sir Peter Edward, GCMG, GCVO

Ramsden, Sir John Charles Josslyn, Bt. (1689)

Ramsey, Sir Alfred Ernest, Kt.

Randle, *Prof.* Sir Philip John, Kt.

Ranger, Sir Douglas, Kt., FRCS

Rank, Sir Benjamin Keith, Kt., CMG

Rankin, Sir Alick Michael, Kt., CBE

Rankin, Sir Ian Niall, Bt. (1898)

Rasch, *Maj.* Sir Richard Guy Carne, Bt. (1903)

Rashleigh, Sir Richard Harry, Bt. (1831)

Rattee, *Hon.* Sir Donald Keith, Kt.

Rault, Sir Louis Joseph Maurice, Kt.

Rawlins, *Surgeon Vice-Adm.* Sir John Stuart Pepys, KBE

Rawlinson, Sir Anthony Henry John, Bt. (1891)

Read, *Air Marshal* Sir Charles Frederick, KBE, CB, DFC, AFC

Read, *Gen.* Sir (John) Antony (Jervis), GCB, CBE, DSO, MC

Read, Sir John Emms, Kt.

Reade, Sir Clyde Nixon, Bt. (1661)

Reay, *Lt.-Gen.* Sir (Hubert) Alan John, KBE

Redgrave, *Maj.-Gen.* Sir Roy Michael Frederick, KBE, MC

Redmayne, Sir Nicholas, Bt. (1964)

Redmond, Sir James, Kt., FEng.

Redwood, Sir Peter Boverton, Bt. (1911)

Reece, Sir Charles Hugh, Kt.

Reece, Sir James Gordon, Kt.

Reed, *Hon.* Sir Nigel Vernon, Kt., CBE

Rees, Sir (Charles William) Stanley, Kt., TD

Rees, Sir David Allan, Kt., Ph.D., D.SC., FRS

Rees, *Prof.* Sir Martin John, Kt., FRS

Reeve, Sir Anthony, KCMG

Reeve, Sir (Charles) Trevor, Kt.

Reeves, *Most Revd* Paul Alfred, GCMG, GCVO

Reffell, *Adm.* Sir Derek Roy, KCB

Refshauge, *Maj-Gen.* Sir William Dudley, Kt., CBE

Reid, Sir Alexander James, Bt. (1897)

Reid, *Hon.* Sir George Oswald, Kt., QC

Reid, Sir (Harold) Martin (Smith), KBE, CMG

Reid, Sir Hugh, Bt. (1922)

Reid, Sir John James Andrew, KCMG, CB, TD

Reid, Sir Norman Robert, Kt.

Reid, Sir Robert Basil, Kt., CBE

Reid, Sir Robert Paul, Kt.

Reiher, Sir Frederick Bernard Carl, KBE, CMG

Reilly, Sir (D'Arcy) Patrick, GCMG, OBE

Reilly, *Lt.-Gen.* Sir Jeremy Calcott, KCB, DSO

Renals, Sir Stanley, Bt. (1895)

Rendell, Sir William, Kt.

Rennie, Sir John Shaw, GCMG, OBE

Renouf, Sir Clement William Bailey, Kt.

Renouf, Sir Francis Henry, Kt.

Renshaw, Sir (Charles) Maurice Bine, Bt. (1903)

Renwick, Sir Richard Eustace, Bt. (1921)

Renwick, Sir Robin William, KCMG

Reporter, Sir Shapoor Ardeshirji, KBE

Reynolds, Sir David James, Bt. (1923)
Reynolds, Sir Peter William John, Kt., CBE
Rhodes, Sir Basil Edward, Kt., CBE, TD
Rhodes, Sir John Christopher Douglas, Bt. (1919)
Rhodes, Sir Peregrine Alexander, KCMG
Rice, *Maj.-Gen.* Sir Desmond Hind Garrett, KCVO, CBE
Richards, Sir (Francis) Brooks, KCMG, DSC
Richards, *Lt.-Gen.* Sir John Charles Chisholm, KCB, KCVO, RM
Richards, Sir Rex Edward, Kt., D.SC., FRS
Richardson, Sir Anthony Lewis, Bt. (1924)
Richardson, *Gen.* Sir Charles Leslie, GCB, CBE, DSO
Richardson, *Rt. Hon.* Sir Ivor Lloyd Morgan, Kt.
Richardson, Sir (John) Eric, Kt., CBE
Richardson, Sir Michael John de Rougemont, Kt.
Richardson, *Lt.-Gen.* Sir Robert Francis, KCB, CVO, CBE
Richardson, Sir Simon Alaisdair Stewart-, Bt. (s. 1630)
Riches, Sir Derek Martin Hurry, KCMG
Riches, *Gen.* Sir Ian Hurry, KCB, DSO
Richmond, Sir Alan James, Kt.
Richmond, *Rt. Hon.* Sir Clifford Parris, KBE
Richmond, Sir John Frederick, Bt. (1929)
Richmond, *Prof.* Sir Mark Henry, Kt., FRS
Rickett, Sir Denis Hubert Fletcher, KCMG, CB
Rickett, Sir Raymond Mildmay Wilson, Kt., CBE, Ph.D.
Ricketts, Sir Robert Cornwallis Gerald St Leger, Bt. (1828)
Riddell, Sir John Charles Buchanan, Bt., CVO (s. 1628)
Ridley, Sir Adam (Nicholas), Kt.
Ridley, Sir Sidney, Kt.
Ridsdale, Sir Julian Errington, Kt., CBE
Rigby, *Lt.-Col.* Sir (Hugh) John (Macbeth), Bt. (1929)
Riley, Sir Ralph, Kt., FRS
Ring, Sir Lindsay Roberts, GBE
Ringadoo, *Hon.* Sir Veerasamy, GCMG
Ripley, Sir Hugh, Bt. (1880)
Risk, Sir Thomas Neilson, Kt.
Risson, *Maj.-Gen.* Sir Robert Joseph Henry, Kt., CB, CBE, DSO, ED
Rix, *Hon.* Sir Bernard Anthony, Kt.
Rix, Sir John, Kt., MBE, FEng.
Roberts, Sir Bryan Clieve, KCMG, QC
Roberts, *Hon.* Sir Denys Tudor Emil, KBE, QC
Roberts, Sir (Edward Fergus) Sidney, Kt., CBE
Roberts, Sir Frank Kenyon, GCMG, GCVO

Roberts, Sir Geoffrey Newland, Kt., CBE, AFC
Roberts, *Brig.* Sir Geoffrey Paul Hardy-, KCVO, CB, CBE
Roberts, Sir Gilbert Howland Rookehurst, Bt. (1809)
Roberts, Sir Gordon James, Kt., CBE
Roberts, *Rt. Hon.* Sir (Ieuan) Wyn Pritchard, Kt., MP
Roberts, Sir Samuel, Bt. (1919)
Roberts, Sir Stephen James Leake, Kt.
Roberts, Sir William James Denby, Bt. (1909)
Robertson, Sir Lewis, Kt., CBE, FRSE
Robertson, *Prof.* Sir Rutherford Ness, Kt., CMG
Robins, Sir Ralph Harry, Kt., FEng.
Robinson, Sir Albert Edward Phineas, Kt.
†Robinson, Sir Christopher Philipse, Bt. (1854)
Robinson, Sir John James Michael Laud, Bt. (1660)
Robinson, *Rt. Hon.* Sir Kenneth, Kt.
Robinson, Sir Niall Bryan Lynch-, Bt., DSC (1920)
Robinson, Sir Wilfred Henry Frederick, Bt. (1908)
Robotham, *Hon.* Sir Lascelles Lister, Kt.
Robson, *Prof.* Sir James Gordon, Kt., CBE
Robson, Sir John Adam, KCMG
Roch, *Rt. Hon.* Sir John Ormond, Kt.
Roche, Sir David O'Grady, Bt. (1838)
Rodgers, Sir (John Fairlie) Tobias, Bt. (1964)
Rodrigues, Sir Alberto Maria, Kt., CBE, ED
Roe, *Air Chief Marshal* Sir Rex David, GCB, AFC
Rogers, Sir Frank Jarvis, Kt.
Rogers, *Air Chief Marshal* Sir John Robson, KCB, CBE
Rogers, Sir Philip James, Kt., CBE
Rogers, Sir Richard George, Kt., RA
Roll, *Revd* Sir James William Cecil, Bt. (1921)
Rooke, Sir Denis Eric, Kt., CBE, FRS, FEng.
Roper, *Hon.* Sir Clinton Marcus, Kt.
Ropner, Sir John Bruce Woollacott, Bt. (1952)
Ropner, Sir Robert Douglas, Bt. (1904)
Roscoe, Sir Robert Bell, KBE
Rose, *Rt. Hon.* Sir Christopher Dudley Roger, Kt.
Rose, Sir Clive Martin, GCMG
Rose, Sir David Lancaster, Bt. (1874)
Rose, Sir Julian Day, Bt. (1872 and 1909)
Rosier, *Air Chief Marshal* Sir Frederick Ernest, GCB, CBE, DSO
Ross, Sir Alexander, Kt.
Ross, Sir Archibald David Manisty, KCMG
Ross, Sir (James) Keith, Bt., RD, FRCS (1960)

Rosser, Sir Melvyn Wynne, Kt.
Rossi, Sir Hugh Alexis Louis, Kt.
Roth, *Prof.* Sir Martin, Kt., MD, FRCP
Rothnie, Sir Alan Keir, KCVO, CMG
Rothschild, Sir Evelyn Robert Adrian de, Kt.
Rougier, *Hon.* Sir Richard George, Kt.
Rous, Sir Anthony Gerald Roderick, KCMG, OBE
Rous, *Lt.-Gen.* the Hon. Sir William Edward, KCB, OBE
Row, *Hon.* Sir John Alfred, Kt.
Rowe, Sir Jeremy, Kt., CBE
Rowell, Sir John Joseph, Kt., CBE
Rowland, *Air Marshal* Sir James Anthony, KBE, DFC, AFC
Rowlands, *Air Marshal* Sir John Samuel, GC, KBE
Rowley, Sir Charles Robert, Bt. (1836)
Rowley, Sir Joshua Francis, Bt. (1786)
Rowling, *Rt. Hon.* Sir Wallace Edward, KCMG
Roxburgh, *Vice-Adm.* Sir John Charles Young, KCB, CBE, DSO, DSC
Royden, Sir Christopher John, Bt. (1905)
Rumbold, Sir Henry John Sebastian, Bt. (1779)
Rumbold, Sir (Horace) Algernon (Fraser), KCMG, CIE
Rumbold, Sir Jack Seddon, Kt.
Runchorelal, Sir (Udayan) Chinubhai Madhowlal, Bt. (1913)
Runciman, *Hon.* Sir James Cochran Stevenson (Sir Steven Runciman), Kt., CH
Rusby, *Vice-Adm.* Sir Cameron, KCB, MVO
Russell, Sir Archibald Edward, Kt., CBE, FRS, FEng.
Russell, Sir Charles Ian, Bt. (1916)
Russell, *Hon.* Sir David Sturrock West-, Kt.
Russell, Sir George, Kt., CBE
Russell, Sir George Michael, Bt. (1812)
Russell, Sir (Robert) Mark, KCMG
Russell, Sir Spencer Thomas, Kt.
Russell, *Rt. Hon.* Sir (Thomas) Patrick, Kt.
Rutter, Sir Frank William Eden, KBE
Rutter, *Prof.* Sir Michael Llewellyn, Kt., CBE, MD, FRS
Ryan, Sir Derek Gerald, Bt. (1919)
Rycroft, Sir Richard Newton, Bt. (1784)
Ryrie, Sir William Sinclair, KCB
Sachs, *Hon.* Sir Michael Alexander Geddes, Kt.
Sainsbury, Sir Robert James, Kt.
St Aubyn, Sir (John) Arscott Molesworth-, Bt. (1689)
St George, Sir George Bligh, Bt. (I. 1766)
St Johnston, Sir Kerry, Kt.
Sainty, Sir John Christopher, KCB
Sakzewski, Sir Albert, Kt.
Salt, Sir Patrick MacDonnell, Bt. (1869)

Salt, Sir (Thomas) Michael John, Bt. (1899)
Sampson, Sir Colin, Kt., CBE, QPM
Samuel, Sir Jon Michael Glen, Bt. (1898)
Samuelson, Sir (Bernard) Michael (Francis), Bt. (1884)
Sandberg, Sir Michael Graham Ruddock, Kt., CBE
Sanders, Sir John Reynolds Mayhew-, Kt.
Sanders, Sir Robert Tait, KBE, CMG
Sanderson, Sir Frank Linton, Bt. (1920)
Sandilands, Sir Francis Edwin Prescott, Kt., CBE
Sarei, Sir Alexis Holyweek, Kt., CBE
Sarell, Sir Roderick Francis Gisbert, KCMG, KCVO
Sargant, Sir (Henry) Edmund, Kt.
Saunders, Hon. Sir John Anthony Holt, Kt., CBE, DSO, MC
Saunders, Sir Owen Alfred, Kt., D.SC., FRS, FEng.
Saunders, Sir Peter, Kt.
Sauzier, Sir (André) Guy, Kt., CBE, ED
Savage, Sir Ernest Walter, Kt.
Savile, Sir James Wilson Vincent, Kt., OBE
Saville, Rt. Hon. Sir Mark Oliver, Kt.
Say, Rt. Revd Richard David, KCVO
Schiemann, Hon. Sir Konrad Hermann Theodor, Kt.
Schneider, Rt. Hon. Sir Lancelot Raymond Adams-, KCMG
Scholey, Sir David Gerald, Kt., CBE
Scholey, Sir Robert, Kt., CBE, FEng.
Scholtens, Sir James Henry, KCVO
Schubert, Sir Sydney, Kt.
Schuster, Sir (Felix) James Moncrieff, Bt., OBE (1906)
Scipio, Sir Hudson Rupert, Kt.
Scoon, Sir Paul, GCMG, GCVO, OBE
Scopes, Sir Leonard Arthur, KCVO, CMG, OBE
Scott, Sir Anthony Percy, Bt. (1913)
Scott, Sir (Charles) Peter, KBE, CMG
Scott, Sir David Aubrey, GCMG
†Scott, Sir Dominic James Maxwell, Bt. (1642)
Scott, Sir Ian Dixon, KCMG, KCVO, CIE
Scott, Sir James Walter, Bt. (1962)
Scott, Sir Kenneth Bertram Adam, KCVO, CMG
Scott, Sir Michael, KCVO, CMG
Scott, Sir Oliver Christopher Anderson, Bt. (1909)
Scott, Prof. Sir Philip John, KBE
Scott, Rt. Hon. Sir Richard Rashleigh Folliott, Kt.
Scott, Sir Walter John, Bt. (1907)
Scott, Rear-Adm. Sir (William) David (Stewart), KBE, CB
Scowen, Sir Eric Frank, Kt., MD, D.SC., LL D., FRCP, FRCS
Scrivenor, Sir Thomas Vaisey, Kt., CMG
Seale, Sir John Henry, Bt. (1838)
Seaman, Sir Keith Douglas, KCVO, OBE

†Sebright, Sir Peter Giles Vivian, Bt. (1626)
Seccombe, Sir (William) Vernon Stephen, Kt.
Secombe, Sir Harry Donald, Kt., CBE
Seconde, Sir Reginald Louis, KCMG, CVO
Sedley, Hon. Sir Stephen John, Kt.
Seely, Sir Nigel Edward, Bt. (1896)
Seeto, Sir Ling James, Kt., MBE
Seeyave, Sir Rene Sow Choung, Kt., CBE
Seligman, Sir Peter Wendel, Kt., CBE
Sells, Sir David Perronet, Kt.
Senior, Sir Edward Walters, Kt., CMG
Sergeant, Sir Patrick, Kt.
Series, Sir (Joseph Michel) Emile, Kt., CBE
Serpell, Sir David Radford, KCB, CMG, OBE
Seton, Sir Iain Bruce, Bt. (s. 1663)
Seton, Sir Robert James, Bt. (s. 1683)
Severne, Air Vice-Marshal Sir John de Milt, KCVO, OBE, AFC
Sewell, Sir (John) Allan, Kt., ISO
Seymour, Cdr. Sir Michael Culme-, Bt., RN (1809)
Shakerley, Sir Geoffrey Adam, Bt. (1838)
Shakespeare, Sir William Geoffrey, Bt. (1942)
Shapland, Sir William Arthur, Kt.
Sharp, Sir Adrian, Bt. (1922)
Sharp, Sir George, Kt., OBE
Sharp, Sir Kenneth Johnston, Kt., TD
Sharp, Sir Milton Reginald, Bt. (1920)
Sharp, Sir Richard Lyall, KCVO, CB
Sharp, Sir (William Harold) Angus, KBE, QPM
Sharpe, Hon. Sir John Henry, Kt., CBE
Sharpe, Sir Reginald Taaffe, Kt., QC
Shattock, Sir Gordon, Kt.
Shaw, Sir Brian Piers, Kt.
Shaw, Sir (Charles) Barry, Kt., CB, QC
Shaw, Sir (George) Neville Bowan-, Kt.
Shaw, Sir (John) Giles (Dunkerley), Kt., MP
Shaw, Sir John Michael Robert Best-, Bt. (1665)
Shaw, Sir Michael Norman, Kt.
Shaw, Sir Robert, Bt. (1821)
Shaw, Sir Roy, Kt.
Shaw, Sir Run Run, Kt., CBE
Sheehy, Sir Patrick, Kt.
Sheen, Hon. Sir Barry Cross, Kt.
Sheffield, Sir Reginald Adrian Berkeley, Bt. (1755)
Shehadie, Sir Nicholas Michael, Kt., OBE
Sheil, Hon. Sir John, Kt.
Sheldon, Hon. Sir (John) Gervase (Kensington), Kt.
Shelley, Sir John Richard, Bt. (1611)
Shelton, Sir William Jeremy Masefield, Kt.
Shepheard, Sir Peter Faulkner, Kt., CBE
Shepherd, Sir Peter Malcolm, Kt., CBE

Sheppard, Sir Allen John George, Kt.
Shepperd, Sir Alfred Joseph, Kt.
Sherlock, Sir Philip Manderson, KBE
Sherman, Sir Alfred, Kt.
Sherman, Sir Louis, Kt., OBE
Shields, Sir Neil Stanley, Kt., MC
Shields, Prof. Sir Robert, Kt., MD
Shiffner, Sir Henry David, Bt. (1818)
Shillington, Sir (Robert Edward) Graham, Kt., CBE
Shock, Sir Maurice, Kt.
Short, Brig. Sir Noel Edward Vivian, Kt., MBE, MC
Shuckburgh, Sir (Charles Arthur) Evelyn, GCMG, CB
Shuckburgh, Sir Rupert Charles Gerald, Bt. (1660)
Siaguru, Sir Anthony Michael, KBE
Sich, Sir Rupert Leigh, Kt., CB
Siddall, Sir Norman, Kt., CBE, FEng.
Sidey, Air Marshal Sir Ernest Shaw, KBE, CB, MD
Sie, Sir Banja Tejan-, GCMG
Simeon, Sir John Edmund Barrington, Bt. (1815)
Simmons, Air Marshal Sir Michael George, KCB, AFC
Simmons, Sir Stanley Clifford, Kt., FRCS, FRCOG
Simonet, Sir Louis Marcel Pierre, Kt., CBE
Simpson, Hon. Sir Alfred Henry, Kt.
Simpson, Sir Joseph Trevor, KBE
Simpson, Sir William James, Kt.
Sinclair, Sir Clive Marles, Kt.
Sinclair, Sir George Evelyn, Kt., CMG, OBE
Sinclair, Sir Ian McTaggart, KCMG, QC
Sinclair, Air Vice-Marshal Sir Laurence Frank, GC, KCB, CBE, DSO
Sinclair, Sir Patrick Robert Richard, Bt. (s. 1704)
Sinclair, Sir Ronald Ormiston, KBE
Singer, Hon. Sir Jan Peter, Kt.
Singh, Hon. Sir Vijay Raghubir, Kt.
Singhania, Sir Padampat, Kt.
Sinnamon, Sir Hercules, Kt., OBE
Sitwell, Sir (Sacheverell) Reresby, Bt. (1808)
Skeet, Sir Trevor Herbert Harry, Kt., MP
Skeggs, Sir Clifford George, Kt.
Skingsley, Air Chief Marshal Sir Anthony Gerald, GBE, KCB
Skinner, Sir (Thomas) Keith (Hewitt), Bt. (1912)
Skipwith, Sir Patrick Alexander d'Estoteville, Bt. (1622)
Skyrme, Sir (William) Thomas (Charles), KCVO, CB, CBE, TD
Slack, Sir William Willatt, KCVO, FRCS
Slade, Sir Benjamin Julian Alfred, Bt. (1831)
Slade, Rt. Hon. Sir Christopher John, Kt.
Slaney, Prof. Sir Geoffrey, KBE
Slater, Adm. Sir John (Jock) Cunningham Kirkwood, GCB, LVO
Sleight, Sir Richard, Bt. (1920)

Stephenson, Sir Henry Upton, Bt. (1936)

Stephenson, *Rt. Hon.* Sir John Frederick Eustace, Kt.

Sternberg, Sir Sigmund, Kt.

Stevens, Sir Laurence Houghton, Kt., CBE

Stevenson, *Vice-Adm.* Sir (Hugh) David, KBE

Stevenson, Sir Simpson, Kt.

Stewart, Sir Alan, KBE

Stewart, Sir Alan d'Arcy, Bt. (I. 1623)

Stewart, Sir David James Henderson-, Bt. (1957)

Stewart, Sir Edward Jackson, Kt.

Stewart, *Prof.* Sir Frederick Henry, Kt., ph.D., FRS, FRSE

Stewart, Sir Houston Mark Shaw-, Bt., MC, TD (S. 1667)

Stewart, Sir Hugh Charlie Godfray, Bt. (1803)

Stewart, Sir James Douglas, Kt.

Stewart, Sir (John) Simon (Watson), Bt. (1920)

Stewart, Sir Michael Norman Francis, KCMG, OBE

Stewart, Sir Robertson Huntly, Kt., CBE

Stewart, Sir Robin Alastair, Bt. (1960)

Stewart, Sir Ronald Compton, Bt. (1937)

Steyn, *Rt. Hon.* Sir Johan Van Zyl, Kt.

Stibbon, *Gen.* Sir John James, KCB, OBE

Stirling, Sir Alexander John Dickson, KBE, CMG

Stockdale, Sir Arthur Noel, Kt.

Stockdale, Sir Thomas Minshull, Bt. (1960)

Stocker, *Rt. Hon.* Sir John Dexter, Kt., MC, TD

Stoddart, *Wg Cdr.* Sir Kenneth Maxwell, KCVO, AE

Stoker, *Prof.* Sir Michael George Parke, Kt., CBE, FRCP, FRS, FRSE

Stokes, Sir John Heydon Romaine, Kt.

Stones, Sir William Frederick, Kt., OBE

Stonhouse, Sir Philip Allan, Bt. (1628)

Stonor, *Air Marshal* Sir Thomas Henry, KCB

Storey, *Hon.* Sir Richard, Bt. (1960)

Stormonth Darling, Sir James Carlisle, Kt., CBE, MC, TD

Stott, Sir Adrian George Ellingham, Bt. (1920)

Stow, Sir Christopher Philipson-, Bt., DFC (1907)

Stow, Sir John Montague, GCMG, KCVO

Stowe, Sir Kenneth Ronald, GCB, CVO

Stracey, Sir John Simon, Bt. (1818)

Strachey, Sir Charles, Bt. (1801)

Straker, Sir Michael Ian Bowstead, Kt., CBE

Strawson, *Prof.* Sir Peter Frederick, Kt., FBA

Street, *Hon.* Sir Laurence Whistler, KCMG

Streeton, Sir Terence George, KBE, CMG

Stringer, Sir Donald Edgar, Kt., CBE

Strong, Sir Roy Colin, Kt., ph.D., FSA

Stronge, Sir James Anselan Maxwell, Bt. (1803)

Stroud, *Prof.* Sir (Charles) Eric, Kt., FRCP

Strutt, Sir Nigel Edward, Kt., TD

Stuart, Sir James Keith, Kt.

Stuart, Sir Kenneth Lamonte, Kt.

†Stuart, Sir Phillip Luttrell, Bt. (1660)

Stubblefield, Sir (Cyril) James, Kt., D.SC., FRS

Stubbs, Sir James Wilfrid, KCVO, TD

Stucley, *Lt.* Sir Hugh George Coplestone Bampfylde, Bt. (1859)

Studd, Sir Edward Fairfax, Bt. (1929)

Studd, Sir Peter Malden, GBE, KCVO

Studholme, Sir Henry William, Bt. (1956)

Style, *Lt.-Cdr.* Sir Godfrey William, Kt., CBE, DSC, RN

†Style, Sir William Frederick, Bt. (1627)

Suffield, Sir (Henry John) Lester, Kt.

Sugden, Sir Arthur, Kt.

Sullivan, Sir Desmond John, Kt.

Sullivan, Sir Richard Arthur, Bt. (1804)

Summerfield, *Hon.* Sir John Crampton, Kt., CBE

Summers, Sir Felix Roland Brattan, Bt. (1952)

Sunderland, *Prof.* Sir Sydney, Kt., CMG

Sutherland, *Prof.* Sir James Runcieman, Kt., FBA

Sutherland, Sir John Brewer, Bt. (1921)

Sutherland, Sir Maurice, Kt.

Sutherland, Sir William George MacKenzie, Kt.

Suttie, Sir (George) Philip Grant-, Bt. (s. 1702)

Sutton, Sir Frederick Walter, Kt., OBE

Sutton, *Air Marshal* Sir John Matthias Dobson, KCB

Sutton, Sir Richard Lexington, Bt. (1772)

Swaffield, Sir James Chesebrough, Kt., CBE, RD

Swallow, Sir William, Kt.

Swan, Sir John William David, KBE

Swann, Sir Michael Christopher, Bt., TD (1906)

Swanwick, Sir Graham Russell, Kt., MBE

Swartz, *Hon.* Sir Reginald William Colin, KBE, ED

Sweetnam, Sir (David) Rodney, KCVO, CBE, FRCS

Swinburn, *Lt.-Gen.* Sir Richard Hull, KCB

Swinson, Sir John Henry Alan, Kt., OBE

Swinton, *Maj.-Gen.* Sir John, KCVO, OBE

Swire, Sir Adrian Christopher, Kt.

Swire, Sir John Anthony, Kt., CBE

Swiss, Sir Rodney Geoffrey, Kt., OBE

Swynnerton, Sir Roger John Massy, Kt., CMG, OBE, MC

Sykes, Sir Francis John Badcock, Bt. (1781)

Sykes, Sir John Charles Anthony le Gallais, Bt. (1921)

Sykes, *Prof.* Sir (Malcolm) Keith, Kt.

Sykes, Sir Tatton Christopher Mark, Bt. (1783)

Symington, *Prof.* Sir Thomas, Kt., MD, FRSE

Symons, *Vice-Adm.* Sir Patrick Jeremy, KBE

Synge, Sir Robert Carson, Bt. (1801)

Tait, *Adm.* Sir (Allan) Gordon, KCB, DSC

Tait, Sir James Sharp, Kt., D.SC., LL D., ph.D.

Tait, Sir Peter, KBE

Talbot, *Vice-Adm.* Sir (Arthur Allison) FitzRoy, KBE, CB, DSO

Talbot, *Hon.* Sir Hilary Gwynne, Kt.

Talboys, *Rt. Hon.* Sir Brian Edward, CH, KCB

Tancred, Sir Henry Lawson-, Bt. (1662)

Tangaroa, *Hon.* Sir Tangoroa, Kt., MBE

Tange, Sir Arthur Harold, Kt., CBE

Tapsell, Sir Peter Hannay Bailey, Kt., MP

Tate, *Lt.-Col.* Sir Henry, Bt. (1898)

Taukala, Sir David Dawea, Kt., MBE

Tavaiqia, *Ratu* Sir Josaia, KBE

Tavare, Sir John, Kt., CBE

Taylor, *Lt.-Gen.* Sir Allan Macnab, KBE, MC

Taylor, Sir (Arthur) Godfrey, Kt.

Taylor, Sir Cyril Julian Hebden, Kt.

Taylor, Sir Edward Macmillan (Teddy), Kt., MP

Taylor, Sir George, Kt., D.SC., FRS, FRSE

Taylor, Sir Henry Milton, Kt.

Taylor, Sir James, Kt., MBE, D.SC

Taylor, Sir John Lang, KCMG

Taylor, Sir Nicholas Richard Stuart, Bt. (1917)

Taylor, *Prof.* Sir William, Kt., CBE

Tebbit, Sir Donald Claude, GCMG

Te Heuheu, Sir Hepi Hoani, KBE

Telford, Sir Robert, Kt., CBE, FEng.

Temple, Sir Ernest Sanderson, Kt., MBE, QC

Temple, Sir John Meredith, Kt.

Temple, Sir Rawden John Afamado, Kt., CBE, QC

Temple, *Maj.* Sir Richard Anthony Purbeck, Bt., MC (1876)

Templeton, Sir John Marks, Kt.

Tennant, *Capt.* Sir Iain Mark, KT

Tennant, Sir Anthony John, Kt.

Tennant, Sir Peter Frank Dalrymple, Kt., CMG, OBE

Teo, Sir Fiatau Penitala, GCMG, GCVO, ISO, MBE

Terry, Sir George Walter Roberts, Kt., CBE, QPM

Terry, Sir John Elliott, Kt.

Terry, Sir Michael Edward Stanley Imbert-, Bt. (1917)
Terry, *Air Chief Marshal* Sir Peter David George, GCB, AFC
Tetley, Sir Herbert, KBE, CB
Tett, Sir Hugh Charles, Kt.
Thatcher, Sir Denis, Bt., MBE, TD (1990)
Thiess, Sir Leslie Charles, Kt., CBE
Thomas, Sir Derek Morison David, KCMG
Thomas, Sir Frederick William, Kt.
Thomas, Sir (Godfrey) Michael (David), Bt. (1694)
Thomas, Sir Jeremy Cashel, KCMG
Thomas, Sir (John) Alan, Kt.
Thomas, Sir John Maldwyn, Kt.
Thomas, *Prof.* Sir John Meurig, Kt., FRS
Thomas, Sir Keith Vivian, Kt.
Thomas, Sir Robert Evan, Kt.
Thomas, *Hon.* Sir Swinton Barclay, Kt.
Thomas, Sir William James Cooper, Bt., TD (1919)
Thomas, Sir (William) Michael (Marsh), Bt. (1918)
Thomas, *Adm.* Sir (William) Richard Scott, KCB, OBE
Thompson, Sir Christopher Peile, Bt. (1890)
Thompson, Sir Donald, Kt., MP
Thompson, Sir Edward Hugh Dudley, Kt., MBE, TD
Thompson, Sir Gilbert Williamson, Kt., OBE
Thompson, *Surgeon Vice-Adm.* Sir Godfrey James Milton-, KBE
Thompson, *Vice-Adm.* Sir Hugh Leslie Owen, KBE, FEng.
Thompson, Sir (Humphrey) Simon Meysey-, Bt. (1874)
Thompson, *Hon.* Sir John, Kt.
Thompson, *Prof.* Sir Michael Warwick, Kt., D.SC
Thompson, Sir Paul Anthony, Bt. (1963)
Thompson, Sir Peter Anthony, Kt.
Thompson, Sir Richard Hilton Marler, Bt. (1963)
Thompson, Sir (Thomas) Lionel Tennyson, Bt. (1806)
Thomson, Sir Adam, Kt., CBE
Thomson, *Air Chief Marshal* Sir (Charles) John, KCB, CBE, AFC
Thomson, Sir Evan Rees Whitaker, Kt.
Thomson, Sir (Frederick Douglas) David, Bt. (1929)
Thomson, Sir John, KBE, TD
Thomson, Sir John Adam, GCMG
Thomson, Sir John (Ian) Sutherland, KBE, CMG
Thomson, Sir Mark Wilfrid Home, Bt. (1925)
Thomson, Sir Thomas James, Kt., CBE, FRCP
Thorn, Sir John Samuel, Kt., OBE

Thorne, *Maj.-Gen.* Sir David Calthrop, KBE
Thorne, Sir Neil Gordon, Kt., OBE, TD
Thorne, Sir Peter Francis, KCVO, CBE
Thornton, Sir (George) Malcolm, Kt., MP
Thornton, *Lt.-Gen.* Sir Leonard Whitmore, KCB, CBE
Thornton, Sir Peter Eustace, KCB
Thorold, Sir Anthony Henry, Bt., OBE, DSC (1642)
Thorpe, *Hon.* Sir Mathew Alexander, Kt.
Thouron, Sir John Rupert Hunt, KBE
†Throckmorton, Sir Anthony John Benedict, Bt. (1642)
Thwaites, Sir Bryan, Kt., PH.D.
Thwin, Sir U, Kt.
Tibbits, *Capt.* Sir David Stanley, Kt., DSC
Tickell, Sir Crispin Charles Cervantes, GCMG, KCVO
Tidbury, Sir Charles Henderson, Kt.
Tikaram, Sir Moti, KBE
Tilney, Sir John Dudley Robert Tarleton, Kt., TD
Tims, Sir Michael David, KCVO
Tippet, *Vice-Adm.* Sir Anthony Sanders, KCB
Tippett, Sir Michael Kemp, Kt., OM, CH, CBE
Tirvengadum, Sir Harry Krishnan, Kt.
Titman, Sir John Edward Powis, KCVO
Tizard, Sir John Peter Mills, Kt.
Tod, *Air Marshal* Sir John Hunter Hunter-, KBE, CB
Todd, Sir Ian Pelham, KBE, FRCS
Todd, *Hon.* Sir (Reginald Stephen) Garfield, Kt.
Tollemache, Sir Lyonel Humphry John, Bt. (1793)
Tololo, Sir Alkan, KBE
Tomkins, Sir Alfred George, Kt., CBE
Tomkins, Sir Edward Emile, GCMG, CVO
Tomkys, Sir (William) Roger, KCMG
Tomlinson, *Prof.* Sir Bernard Evans, Kt., CBE
Tomlinson, Sir (Frank) Stanley, KCMG
Tooley, Sir John, Kt.
Tooth, Sir (Hugh) John Lucas-, Bt. (1920)
ToRobert, Sir Henry Thomas, KBE
Tory, Sir Geofroy William, KCMG
Touche, Sir Anthony George, Bt. (1920)
Touche, Sir Rodney Gordon, Bt. (1962)
Tovey, Sir Brian John Maynard, KCMG
ToVue, Sir Ronald, Kt., OBE
Townsend, *Rear-Adm.* Sir Leslie William, KCVO, CBE
Townsing, Sir Kenneth Joseph, Kt., CMG
Traherne, Sir Cennydd George, KG, TD
Traill, Sir Alan Towers, GBE
Trant, *Gen.* Sir Richard Brooking, KCB

Travers, Sir Thomas à'Beckett, Kt.
Treacher, *Adm.* Sir John Devereux, KCB
Trehane, Sir (Walter) Richard, Kt.
Trelawny, Sir John Barry Salusbury-, Bt. (1628)
Trench, Sir Nigel Clive Cosby, KCMG
Trench, Sir Peter Edward, Kt., CBE, TD
Trescowthick, Sir Donald Henry, KBE
Trethowan, *Prof.* Sir William Henry, Kt., CBE, FRCP
Trevelyan, Sir George Lowthian, Bt. (1874)
Trevelyan, Sir Norman Irving, Bt. (1662)
Trewby, *Vice-Adm.* Sir (George Francis) Allan, KCB, FEng.
Trippier, Sir David Austin, Kt., RD
Tritton, Sir Anthony John Ernest, Bt. (1905)
†Trollope, Sir Anthony Simon, Bt. (1642)
Trotter, Sir Ronald Ramsay, Kt.
Troubridge, Sir Thomas Richard, Bt. (1799)
Troup, *Vice-Adm.* Sir (John) Anthony (Rose), KCB, DSC
Trowbridge, *Rear-Adm.* Sir Richard John, KCVO
Truscott, Sir George James Irving, Bt. (1909)
Tuck, Sir Bruce Adolph Reginald, Bt. (1910)
Tucker, *Hon.* Sir Richard Howard, Kt.
Tuckey, *Hon.* Sir Simon Lane, Kt.
Tudor, *Hon.* Sir James Cameron, KCMG
Tugendhat, Sir Christopher Samuel, Kt.
Tuita, Sir Mariano Kelesimalefo, Kt., OBE
Tuite, Sir Christopher Hugh, Bt., PH.D. (1622)
Tuivaga, Sir Timoci Uluiburotu, Kt.
Tuke, Sir Anthony Favill, Kt.
Tupper, Sir Charles Hibbert, Bt. (1888)
Turbott, Sir Ian Graham, Kt., CMG, CVO
Turing, Sir John Dermot, Bt. (S. 1638)
Turnbull, Sir Richard Gordon, GCMG
Turner, Sir Colin William Carstairs, Kt., CBE, DFC
Turner, *Hon.* Sir Michael John, Kt.
Tuti, *Revd* Dudley, KBE
Tuzo, *Gen.* Sir Harry Craufurd, GCB, OBE, MC
Twiss, *Adm.* Sir Frank Roddam, KCB, KCVO, DSC
Tyree, Sir (Alfred) William, Kt., OBE
Tyrrell, Sir Murray Louis, KCVO, CBE
Tyrwhitt, Sir Reginald Thomas Newman, Bt. (1919)
Udoma, *Hon.* Sir (Egbert) Udo, Kt.
Unsworth, *Hon.* Sir Edgar Ignatius Godfrey, Kt., CMG
Unwin, Sir (James) Brian, KCB
Ure, Sir John Burns, KCMG, LVO

Urquhart, Sir Brian Edward, KCMG, MBE

Urwick, Sir Alan Bedford, KCVO, CMG

Usher, Sir Leonard Gray, KBE

Usher, Sir Robert Edward, Bt. (1899)

Ustinov, Sir Peter Alexander, Kt., CBE

Utting, Sir William Benjamin, Kt., CB

Vallat, Sir Francis Aimé, GBE, KCMG, QC

Vallings, *Vice-Adm.* Sir George Montague Francis, KCB

Vanderfelt, Sir Robin Victor, KBE

van der Post, Sir Laurens Jan, Kt., CBE

Vane, Sir John Robert, Kt., D.Phil., D.SC., FRS

Vanneck, *Air Cdre* Hon. Sir Peter Beckford Rutgers, GBE, CB, AFC

van Straubenzee, Sir William Radcliffe, Kt., MBE

Vasquez, Sir Alfred Joseph, Kt., CBE, QC

Vaughan, Sir (George) Edgar, KBE

Vaughan, Sir Gerard Folliott, Kt., MP, FRCP

Vavasour, *Cdr.* Sir Geoffrey William, Bt., DSC, RN (1828)

Veale, Sir Alan John Ralph, Kt., FEng.

Verco, Sir Walter John George, KCVO

†Verney, Sir John Sebastian, Bt. (1946)

Verney, *Hon.* Sir Lawrence John, Kt., TD

Verney, Sir Ralph Bruce, Bt., KBE (1818)

Vernon, Sir James, Kt., CBE

Vernon, Sir Nigel John Douglas, Bt. (1914)

Vesey, Sir (Nathaniel) Henry (Peniston), Kt., CBE

Vestey, Sir (John) Derek, Bt. (1921)

Vial, Sir Kenneth Harold, Kt., CBE

Vick, Sir (Francis) Arthur, Kt., OBE, Ph.D.

Vickers, *Lt.-Gen.* Sir Richard Maurice Hilton, KCB, MVO, OBE

Victoria, Sir (Joseph Aloysius) Donatus, Kt., CBE

Vincent, *Field Marshal* Sir Richard Frederick, GBE, KCB, DSO

Vincent, Sir William Percy Maxwell, Bt. (1936)

Vinelott, *Hon.* Sir John Evelyn, Kt.

Vines, Sir William Joshua, Kt., CMG

Vyvyan, Sir John Stanley, Bt. (1645)

Waddell, Sir Alexander Nicol Anton, KCMG, DSC

Waddell, Sir James Henderson, Kt., CB

Wade, *Prof.* Sir Henry William Rawson, Kt., QC, FBA

Wade, *Air Chief Marshal* Sir Ruthven Lowry, KCB, DFC

Wagner, Sir Anthony Richard, KCB, KCVO

Waite, *Rt. Hon.* Sir John Douglas, Kt.

Wake, Sir Hereward, Bt., MC (1621)

Wakefield, Sir (Edward) Humphry (Tyrell), Bt. (1962)

Wakefield, Sir Norman Edward, Kt.

Wakefield, Sir Peter George Arthur, KBE, CMG

Wakeford, *Air Marshal* Sir Richard Gordon, KCB, OBE, MVO, AFC

Wakeley, Sir John Cecil Nicholson, Bt., FRCS (1952)

†Wakeman, Sir Edward Offley Bertram, Bt. (1828)

Walker, *Revd* Alan Edgar, Kt., OBE

Walker, Sir Allan Grierson, Kt., QC

Walker, *Gen.* Sir Antony Kenneth Frederick, KCB

Walker, Sir Baldwin Patrick, Bt. (1856)

Walker, Sir (Charles) Michael, GCMG

Walker, Sir Colin John Shedlock, Kt., OBE

Walker, Sir David Alan, Kt.

Walker, Sir Gervas George, Kt.

Walker, *Rt. Hon.* Sir Harold, Kt., MP

Walker, Sir Harold Berners, KCMG

Walker, *Maj.* Sir Hugh Ronald, Bt. (1906)

Walker, Sir James Graham, Kt., MBE

Walker, Sir James Heron, Bt. (1868)

Walker, *Air Marshal* Sir John Robert, KCB, CBE, AFC

Walker, Sir Michael Leolin Forestier-, Bt. (1835)

Walker, Sir Patrick Jeremy, KCB

Walker, *Gen.* Sir Walter Colyear, KCB, CBE, DSO

Wall, *Dr Hon.* Sir Gerard Aloysius, Kt.

Wall, *Hon.* Sir Nicholas Peter Rathbone, Kt.

Wall, Sir Patrick Henry Bligh, Kt., MC, VRD

Wall, Sir Robert William, Kt., OBE

Wallace, Sir Ian James, Kt., CBE

Waller, *Hon.* Sir (George) Mark, Kt.

Waller, *Rt. Hon.* Sir George Stanley, Kt., OBE

Waller, Sir (John) Keith, Kt., CBE

Waller, Sir John Stainer, Bt. (1815)

Waller, Sir Robert William, Bt. (1. 1780)

Walley, Sir John, KBE, CB

Wallis, Sir Peter Gordon, KCVO

Walsh, Sir Alan, Kt., D.SC., FRS

Walsh, *Prof.* Sir John Patrick, KBE

†Walsham, Sir Timothy John, Bt. (1831)

Walter, Sir Harold Edward, Kt.

Walters, *Prof.* Sir Alan Arthur, Kt.

Walters, Sir Dennis Murray, Kt., MBE

Walters, Sir Frederick Donald, Kt.

Walters, Sir Peter Ingram, Kt.

Walters, Sir Roger Talbot, KBE, FRIBA

Walton, Sir John Robert, Kt.

Wan, Sir Wamp, Kt., MBE

Wanstall, *Hon.* Sir Charles Gray, Kt.

Ward, *Hon.* Sir Alan Hylton, Kt.

Ward, Sir Arthur Hugh, KBE

Ward, Sir Joseph James Laffey, Bt. (1911)

Ward, *Maj.-Gen.* Sir Philip John Newling, KCVO, CBE

Wardale, Sir Geoffrey Charles, KCB

Wardlaw, Sir Henry (John), Bt. (S. 1631)

Wardle, Sir Thomas Edward Jewell, Kt.

Waring, Sir (Alfred) Holburt, Bt. (1935)

Warmington, *Lt.-Cdr.* Sir Marshall George Clitheroe, Bt., RN (1908)

Warner, Sir (Edward Courtenay) Henry, Bt. (1910)

Warner, Sir Edward Redston, KCMG, OBE

Warner, Sir Frederick Archibald, GCVO, KCMG

Warner, *Prof.* Sir Frederick Edward, Kt., FRS, FEng.

Warner, *Hon.* Sir Jean-Pierre Frank Eugene, Kt.

Warnock, Sir Geoffrey James, Kt.

Warren, Sir Brian Charles Pennefather, Bt. (1784)

Warren, Sir Frederick Miles, KBE

Warren, Sir (Harold) Brian (Seymour), Kt.

Wass, Sir Douglas William Gretton, GCB

Waterhouse, *Hon.* Sir Ronald Gough, Kt.

Waterlow, Sir Christopher Rupert, Bt. (1873)

Waterlow, Sir (James) Gerard, Bt. (1930)

Waters, *Gen.* Sir (Charles) John, KCB, CBE

Wates, Sir Christopher Stephen, Kt.

Watkins, *Rt. Hon.* Sir Tasker, VC, GBE

Watson, Sir Bruce Dunstan, Kt.

Watson, Sir Duncan Amos, Kt., CBE

Watson, Sir (James) Andrew, Bt. (1866)

Watson, Sir John Forbes Inglefield-, Bt. (1895)

Watson, Sir Michael Milne-, Bt., CBE (1937)

Watson, Sir (Noel) Duncan, KCMG

Watson, *Vice-Adm.* Sir Philip Alexander, KBE, MVO

Watt, *Surgeon Vice-Adm.* Sir James, KBE, FRCS

Watt, Sir James Harvie-, Bt. (1945)

Watts, Sir Arthur Desmond, KCMG

Watts, *Lt.-Gen.* Sir John Peter Barry Condliffe, KBE, CB, MC

Wauchope, Sir Roger (Hamilton) Don-, Bt. (S. 1667)

Way, Sir Richard George Kitchener, KCB, CBE

Weatherall, *Prof.* Sir David John, Kt., FRS

Weatherall, *Vice-Adm.* Sir James Lamb, KBE

Weatherstone, Sir Dennis, KBE

Weaver, Sir Tobias Rushton, Kt., CB

Webb, *Lt.-Gen.* Sir Richard James Holden, KBE, CB

Webb, Sir Thomas Langley, Kt.

Webber, Sir Andrew Lloyd, Kt.

Webster, *Very Revd* Alan Brunskill, KCVO

Webster, *Vice-Adm.* Sir John Morrison, KCB

Webster, *Hon.* Sir Peter Edlin, Kt.

Wedderburn, Sir Andrew John Alexander Ogilvy-, Bt. (1803)

Wedgwood, Sir (Hugo) Martin, Bt. (1942)

Weinberg, Sir Mark Aubrey, Kt.

Weir, Sir Michael Scott, KCMG

Weir, Sir Roderick Bignell, Kt.

Welby, Sir (Richard) Bruno Gregory, Bt. (1801)

Welch, Sir John Reader, Bt. (1957)

Weldon, Sir Anthony William, Bt. (1. 1723)

Wellings, Sir Jack Alfred, Kt., CBE

Wells, Sir Charles Maltby, Bt., TD (1944)

Wells, Sir John Julius, Kt.

Westbrook, Sir Neil Gowanloch, Kt., CBE

Westerman, Sir (Wilfred) Alan, Kt., CBE

Weston, Sir Michael Charles Swift, KCMG, CVO

Weston, Sir (Philip) John, KCMG

Wheeler, Sir Frederick Henry, Kt., CBE

Wheeler, Sir Harry Anthony, Kt., OBE

Wheeler, *Air Chief Marshal* Sir (Henry) Neil (George), GCB, CBE, DSO, DFC, AFC

Wheeler, *Rt. Hon.* Sir John Daniel, Kt., MP

Wheeler, Sir John Hieron, Bt. (1920)

Wheeler, *Hon.* Sir Kenneth Henry, Kt.

Wheeler, *Lt.-Gen.* Sir Roger Neil, KCB, CBE

Wheler, Sir Edward Woodford, Bt. (1660)

Whishaw, Sir Charles Percival Law, Kt.

Whitaker, *Maj.* Sir James Herbert Ingham, Bt. (1936)

White, Sir Christopher Robert Meadows, Bt. (1937)

White, *Hon.* Sir Christopher Stuart Stuart-, Kt.

White, Sir David Harry, Kt.

White, Sir Frederick William George, KBE, Ph.D., FRS

White, Sir George Stanley James, Bt. (1904)

White, Sir Harold Leslie, Kt., CBE

White, *Wg Cdr.* Sir Henry Arthur Dalrymple-, Bt., DFC (1926)

White, *Adm.* Sir Hugo Moresby, KCB, CBE

White, *Hon.* Sir John Charles, Kt., MBE

White, Sir John Woolmer, Bt. (1922)

White, Sir Lynton Stuart, Kt., MBE, TD

White, *Adm.* Sir Peter, GBE

White, Sir Thomas Astley Woollaston, Bt. (1802)

Whitehead, Sir John Stainton, GCMG, CVO

Whitehead, Sir Rowland John Rathbone, Bt. (1889)

Whiteley, Sir Hugo Baldwin Huntington-, Bt. (1918)

Whiteley, *Gen.* Sir Peter John Frederick, GCB, OBE, RM

Whitfield, Sir William, Kt., CBE

Whitford, *Hon.* Sir John Norman Keates, Kt.

Whitley, *Air Marshal* Sir John René, KBE, CB, DSO, AFC

Whitmore, Sir Clive Anthony, GCB, CVO

Whitmore, Sir John Henry Douglas, Bt. (1954)

Whitteridge, Sir Gordon Coligny, KCMG, OBE

Whittle, *Air Cdre* Sir Frank, OM, KBE, CB, FRS, FEng.

Whittome, Sir Leslie Alan, Kt.

Wickerson, Sir John Michael, Kt.

Wicks, Sir James Albert, Kt.

Wicks, Sir Nigel Leonard, KCB, CVO, CBE

Wigan, Sir Alan Lewis, Bt. (1898)

Wiggin, Sir Alfred William (Jerry), Kt., TD, MP

†Wiggin, Sir Charles Rupert John, Bt. (1892)

Wigglesworth, Sir Vincent Brian, Kt., CBE, MD, FRS

Wigram, *Revd Canon* Sir Clifford Woolmore, Bt. (1805)

Wilbraham, Sir Richard Baker, Bt. (1776)

Wilford, Sir (Kenneth) Michael, GCMG

Wilkes, *Gen.* Sir Michael John, KCB, CBE

Wilkins, Sir Graham John, Kt.

Wilkins, *Lt.-Gen.* Sir Michael Compton Lockwood, KCB, OBE

Wilkinson, Sir (David) Graham (Brook) Bt. (1941)

Wilkinson, *Prof.* Sir Denys Haigh, Kt., FRS

Wilkinson, *Prof.* Sir Geoffrey, Kt., FRS

Wilkinson, Sir Peter Allix, KCMG, DSO, OBE

Wilkinson, Sir Philip William, Kt.

Wilkinson, Sir William Henry Nairn, Kt.

Willatt, Sir (Robert) Hugh, Kt.

Willcocks, Sir David Valentine, Kt., CBE, MC

Williams, Sir Alastair Edgcumbe James Dudley-, Bt. (1964)

Williams, Sir Alwyn, Kt., Ph.D., FRS

Williams, Sir Arthur Dennis Pitt, Kt.

Williams, Sir (Arthur) Gareth Ludovic Emrys Rhys, Bt. (1918)

Williams, *Prof.* Sir Bruce Rodda, KBE

Williams, *Adm.* Sir David, GCB

Williams, *Prof.* Sir David Glyndwr Tudor, Kt.

Williams, Sir David Innes, Kt.

Williams, *Hon.* Sir Denys Ambrose, KCMG

Williams, Sir Donald Mark, Bt. (1866)

Williams, Sir Edgar Trevor, Kt., CB, CBE, DSO

Williams, *Prof.* Sir (Edward) Dillwyn, Kt., FRCP

Williams, *Hon.* Sir Edward Stratten, KCMG, KBE

Williams, Sir Francis John Watkin, Bt., QC (1798)

Williams, Sir Henry Sydney, Kt., OBE

Williams, Sir (John) Leslie, Kt., CBE

Williams, Sir John Robert, KCMG

Williams, Sir Leonard, KBE, CB

Williams, Sir Osmond, Bt., MC (1909)

Williams, Sir Peter Watkin, Kt.

Williams, *Prof.* Sir Robert Evan Owen, Kt., MD, FRCP

Williams, Sir (Robert) Philip Nathaniel, Bt. (1915)

Williams, Sir Robin Philip, Bt. (1953)

Williams, Sir (William) Maxwell (Harries), Kt.

Williamson, *Marshal of the Royal Air Force* Sir Keith Alec, GCB, AFC

Williamson, Sir (Nicholas Frederick) Hedworth, Bt. (1642)

Willink, Sir Charles William, Bt. (1957)

Willis, *Hon.* Sir Eric Archibald, KBE, CMG

Willis, *Vice-Adm.* Sir (Guido) James, KBE

Willis, *Air Marshal* Sir John Frederick, KCB, CBE

Willison, *Lt.-Gen.* Sir David John, KCB, OBE, MC

Willison, Sir John Alexander, Kt., OBE

Wills, Sir David Seton, Bt. (1904)

Wills, Sir (Hugh) David Hamilton, Kt., CBE, TD

Wills, Sir John Vernon, Bt., TD (1923)

Wilmot, Sir Henry Robert, Bt. (1759)

Wilmot, *Cdr.* Sir John Assheton Eardley-, Bt., MVO, DSC, RN (1821)

Wilsey, *Gen.* Sir John Finlay Willasey, KCB, CBE

Wilson, Sir Alan Herries, Kt., FRS

Wilson, *Lt.-Gen.* Sir (Alexander) James, KBE, MC

Wilson, Sir Anthony, Kt.

Wilson, *Vice-Adm.* Sir Barry Nigel, KCB

Wilson, Sir Charles Haynes, Kt.

Wilson, Sir David, Bt. (1920)

Wilson, Sir David Mackenzie, Kt.

Wilson, Sir Geoffrey Masterman, KCB, CMG

Wilson, Sir James William Douglas, Bt. (1906)

Wilson, Sir John Foster, Kt., CBE

Wilson, Sir John Gardiner, Kt., CBE

Wilson, *Brig.* Sir Mathew John Anthony, Bt., OBE, MC (1874)

Wilson, *Hon.* Sir Nicholas Allan Roy, Kt.

Wilson, Sir Patrick Michael Ernest David McNair-, Kt., MP

Wilson, Sir Reginald Holmes, Kt.

Wilson, Sir Robert, Kt., CBE

Wilson, Sir Robert Donald, Kt.

Wilson, *Rt. Revd* Roger Plumpton, KCVO, DD

Wilson, Sir Roland, KBE

Wilson, *Air Chief Marshal* Sir (Ronald) Andrew (Fellowes), KCB, AFC

Wilson, *Hon.* Sir Ronald Darling, KBE, CMG

Wilton, Sir (Arthur) John, KCMG, KCVO, MC

Wiltshire, Sir Frederick Munro, Kt., CBE

Windeyer, Sir Brian Wellingham, Kt.

Wingate, *Capt.* Sir Miles Buckley, KCVO

Winnington, Sir Francis Salwey William, Bt. (1755)

Winskill, *Air Cdre* Sir Archibald Little, KCVO, CBE, DFC

Winterbottom, Sir Walter, Kt., CBE

Wiseman, Sir John William, Bt. (1628)

Wolfson, Sir Brian Gordon, Kt.

Wolseley, Sir Charles Garnet Richard Mark, Bt. (1628)

†Wolseley, Sir James Douglas, Bt. (I. 1745)

Wolstenholme, Sir Gordon Ethelbert Ward, Kt., OBE

Wombwell, Sir George Philip Frederick, Bt. (1778)

Womersley, Sir Peter John Walter, Bt. (1945)

Woo, Sir Leo Joseph, Kt.

Wood, Sir Alan Marshall Muir, Kt., FRS, FEng.

Wood, Sir Anthony John Page, Bt. (1837)

Wood, Sir David Basil Hill-, Bt. (1921)

Wood, Sir Frederick Ambrose Stuart, Kt.

Wood, Sir Henry Peart, Kt., CBE

Wood, *Prof.* Sir John Crossley, Kt., CBE

Wood, *Hon.* Sir John Kember, Kt., MC

Wood, Sir Martin Francis, Kt., OBE

Wood, Sir Russell Dillon, KCVO, VRD

Wood, Sir William Alan, KCVO, CB

Woodcock, Sir John, Kt., CBE, QPM

Woodfield, Sir Philip John, KCB, CBE

Woodhead, *Vice-Adm.* Sir (Anthony) Peter, KCB

Woodhouse, *Rt. Hon.* Sir (Arthur) Owen, KBE, DSC

Wooding, Sir Norman Samuel, Kt., CBE

Woodroffe, *Most Revd* George Cuthbert Manning, KBE

Woodroofe, Sir Ernest George, Kt., Ph.D.

Woodruff, *Prof.* Sir Michael Francis Addison, Kt., D.SC., FRS, FRCS

Woods, Sir Colin Philip Joseph, KCVO, CBE

Woods, *Rt. Revd* Robert Wilmer, KCMG, KCVO

Woodward, *Hon.* Sir (Albert) Edward, Kt., OBE

Woodward, *Adm.* Sir John Forster, GBE, KCB

Woolf, Sir John, Kt.

Woollaston, Sir (Mountford) Tosswill, Kt.

Wordie, Sir John Stewart, Kt., CBE, VRD

Worsley, *Gen.* Sir Richard Edward, GCB, OBE

Worsley, Sir (William) Marcus (John), Bt. (1838)

Worsthorne, Sir Peregrine Gerard, Kt.

Wraight, Sir John Richard, KBE, CMG

Wratten, *Air Marshal* Sir William John, KBE, CB, AFC

Wraxall, Sir Charles Frederick Lascelles, Bt. (1813)

Wrey, Sir George Richard Bourchier, Bt. (1628)

Wrigglesworth, Sir Ian William, Kt.

Wright, Sir Allan Frederick, KBE

Wright, Sir Denis Arthur Hepworth, GCMG

Wright, Sir Edward Maitland, Kt., D.Phil., LL D., D.SC., FRSE

Wright, *Hon.* Sir (John) Michael, Kt.

Wright, Sir (John) Oliver, GCMG, GCVO, DSC

Wright, Sir Patrick Richard Henry, GCMG

Wright, Sir Paul Hervé Giraud, KCMG, OBE

Wright, Sir Peter Robert, Kt., CBE

Wright, Sir Richard Michael Cory-, Bt. (1903)

Wrightson, Sir Charles Mark Garmondsway, Bt. (1900)

Wykeham, *Air Marshal* Sir Peter Guy, KCB, DSO, OBE, DFC, AFC

Wylie, Sir Campbell, Kt., ED, QC

Wynn, Sir David Watkin Williams-, Bt. (1688)

Yacoub, *Prof.* Sir Magdi Habib, Kt., FRCS

Yang, *Hon.* Ti Liang, Kt.

Yapp, Sir Stanley Graham, Kt.

Yarranton, Sir Peter George, Kt.

Yarrow, Sir Eric Grant, Bt., MBE (1916)

Yeend, Sir Geoffrey John, Kt., CBE

Yellowlees, Sir Henry, KCB

Yocklunn, Sir John (Soong Chung), KCVO

Yoo Foo, Sir (François) Henri, Kt.

Youens, Sir Peter William, Kt., CMG, OBE

Young, Sir Brian Walter Mark, Kt.

Young, *Lt.-Gen.* Sir David Tod, KBE, CB, DFC

Young, *Rt. Hon.* Sir George Samuel Knatchbull, Bt., MP (1813)

Young, *Hon.* Sir Harold William, KCMG

Young, Sir John Kenyon Roe, Bt. (1821)

Young, *Hon.* Sir John McIntosh, KCMG

Young, Sir Leslie Clarence, Kt., CBE

Young, Sir Norman Smith, Kt.

Young, Sir Richard Dilworth, Kt.

Young, Sir Robert Christopher Mackworth-, GCVO

Young, Sir Roger William, Kt.

Young, Sir Stephen Stewart Templeton, Bt. (1945)

Young, Sir William Neil, Bt. (1769)

Younger, *Maj.-Gen.* Sir John William, Bt., CBE (1911)

Zeeman, *Prof.* Sir (Erik) Christopher, Kt., FRS

Zeidler, Sir David Ronald, Kt., CBE

Zoleveke, Sir Gideon Pitabose, KBE

Zunz, Sir Gerhard Jacob (Jack), Kt., FEng.

Zurenuo, *Rt. Revd* Zurewe Kamong, Kt., OBE

The Military Knights of Windsor

The Military Knights of Windsor take part in all ceremonies of the Noble Order of the Garter and attend Sunday morning service in St George's Chapel, Windsor Castle, as representatives of the Knights of the Garter. The Knights receive a small stipend in addition to their army pensions and quarters in Windsor Castle.

The Knights of Windsor were originally founded in 1348 after the wars in France to assist English knights, who, having been prisoners in the hands of the French, had become impoverished by the payments of heavy ransoms. When Edward III founded the Order of the Garter later the same year, he incorporated the Knights of Windsor and the College of St George into its foundation and raised the number of Knights to 26 to correspond with the number of the Knights of the Garter. Known later as the Alms Knights or Poor Knights of Windsor, their establishment was reduced under the will of King Henry VIII to 13 and Statutes were drawn up by Queen Elizabeth I.

In 1833 King William IV changed their designation to The Military Knights and granted them their present uniform which consists of a scarlet tail-coat with white cross sword-belt, crimson sash and cocked hat with plume. The badges are the Shield of St George and the Star of the Order of the Garter.

Governor, Maj.-Gen. Peter Downward, CB, DSO, DFC
Military Knights, Brig. A. L. Atkinson, OBE; Brig.
J. F. Lindner, OBE, MC; Maj. W. L. Thompson, MVO, MBE, DCM; Maj. L. W. Dickerson; Maj. J. C. Cowley, DCM; Lt.-Col. N. L. West; Maj. G. R. Mitchell; MBE, BEM; Lt.-Col. R. L. C. Tamplin; Maj. P. H. Bolton, MBE; Lt.-Col. H. R. Rogers, MBE; Brig. T. W. Hackworth, OBE; Maj. R. J. Moore
Supernumerary, Brig. A. C. Tyler, CBE, MC

The Order of St John

THE MOST VENERABLE ORDER OF THE HOSPITAL OF ST JOHN OF JERUSALEM (1888)

GCStJ, Bailiff/Dame Grand Cross
KStJ, Knight of Justice/Grace
DStJ, Dame of Justice/Grace
ChStJ, Chaplain
CStJ, Commander
OStJ, Officer
SBStJ, Serving Brother
SSStJ, Serving Sister
EsqStJ, Esquire

Mottoes, Pro Fide *and* Pro Utilitate Hominum

The Order of St John, founded in the early 12th century in Jerusalem, was a religious order with a particular duty to care for the sick. In Britain the Order was dissolved by Henry VIII in 1540 but the British branch was revived in the early 19th century. The branch was not accepted by the Grand Magistracy of the Order in Rome but its search for a role in the tradition of the Hospitallers led to the founding of the St

John Ambulance Association in 1877 and later the St John Ambulance Brigade; in 1887 the St John Ophthalmic Hospital was founded in Jerusalem. A royal charter was granted in 1888 establishing the British Order of St John as a British Order of Chivalry with the Sovereign as its head.

Admission to the Order is conferred in recognition of service, usually in St John Ambulance. Membership does not confer any rank, style, title or precedence on a recipient.

SOVEREIGN HEAD OF THE ORDER
HM The Queen

GRAND PRIOR
HRH The Duke of Gloucester, GCVO
Lord Prior, The Lord Vestey
Prelate, The Rt. Revd M. A. Mann, KCVO
Chancellor, Prof. A. R. Mellows, TD
Bailiff of Egle, The Lord Remnant
Headquarters, St John's Gate, Clerkenwell, London ECIM 4DA

Dames Grand Cross and Dames Commanders

Style, 'Dame' before forename and surname, followed by appropriate post-nominal initials. Where such an award is made to a lady already in enjoyment of a higher title, the appropriate initials follow her name
Husband, Untitled
For forms of address, *see* page 220

Dame Grand Cross and Dames Commander are the higher classes for women of the Order of the Bath, the Order of St Michael and St George, the Royal Victorian Order, and the Order of the British Empire. Dames Grand Cross rank after the wives of Baronets and before the wives of Knights Grand Cross. Dames Commanders rank after the wives of Knights Grand Cross and before the wives of Knights Commanders

Honorary Dame Commanders may be conferred on women who are citizens of countries of which The Queen is not head of state

---

LIST OF DAMES   *Revised to 31 August 1993*

Women peers in their own right and life peers are not included in this list
If a dame has a double barrelled or hyphenated surname, she is listed under the final element of the name

HM Queen Elizabeth the Queen Mother, KG, KT, CI, GMVO
HRH The Princess Royal, GCVO
HRH The Princess Margaret, Countess of Snowdon, CI, GCVO
HRH The Duchess of Gloucester, GCVO
HRH Princess Alice, Duchess of Gloucester, GCB, CI, GCVO, GBE
HRH The Duchess of Kent, GCVO
HRH Princess Alexandra of Kent, GCVO
Abaijah, Dame Josephine, DBE
Abel Smith, Lady, DCVO
Abergavenny, The Marchioness of, DCVO
Albemarle, The Countess of, DBE
Anderson, *Brig.* Hon. Dame Mary Mackenzie (Mrs Pihl), DBE
Anglesey, The Marchioness of, DBE
Arden, Dame Mary Howarth (Mrs Mance), DBE
Baker, Dame Janet Abbott (Mrs Shelley), DBE
Ballin, Dame Reubina Ann, DBE
Baring, Lady Rose Gwendolen Louisa, DCVO
Barnes, Dame (Alice) Josephine (Mary Taylor), DBE, FRCP, FRCS
Barrow, Dame Jocelyn Anita (Mrs Downer), DBE
Barrow, Dame (Ruth) Nita, GCMG
Basset, Lady Elizabeth, DCVO
Beaurepaire, Dame Beryl Edith, DBE
Berry, Dame Alice Miriam, DBE
Blaize, Dame Venetia Ursula, DBE
Blaxland, Dame Helen Frances, DBE
Booth, *Hon.* Dame Margaret Myfanwy Wood, DBE
Bottomley, Dame Bessie Ellen, DBE
Bowman, Dame (Mary) Elaine Kellett-, *Hon.*, MP
Boyd, Dame Vivienne Myra, DBE
Bracewell, *Hon.* Dame Joyanne Winifred (Mrs Copeland), DBE

Brazill, Dame Josephine (Sister Mary Philippa), DBE
Breen, Dame Marie Freda, DBE
Bridges, Dame Mary Patricia, DBE
Brown, Dame Beryl Paston, DBE
Brown, Dame Gillian Gerda, DCVO, CMG
Browne, Lady Moyra Blanche Madeleine, DBE
Bryans, Dame Anne Margaret, DBE
Bryce, Dame Isabel Graham, DBE
Burnside, Dame Edith, DBE
Buttfield, Dame Nancy Eileen, DBE
Bynoe, Dame Hilda Louisa, DBE
Cartland, Dame Barbara Hamilton, DBE
Cartwright, Dame Mary Lucy, DBE, SC.D., D.Phil., FRS
Cartwright, Dame Silvia Rose, DBE
Casey, Dame Stella Katherine, DBE
Cayford, Dame Florence Evelyn, DBE
Charles, Dame (Mary) Eugenia, DBE
Chesterton, Dame Elizabeth Ursula, DBE
Clay, Dame Marie Mildred, DBE
Clayton, Dame Barbara Evelyn (Mrs Klyne), DBE
Cleland, Dame Rachel, DBE
Clode, Dame (Emma) Frances (Heather), DBE
Coles, Dame Mabel Irene, DBE
Cookson, Dame Catherine Ann, DBE
Cooper, Dame Whina, DBE
Corsar, The Hon. Dame Mary Drummond, DBE
Coulshed, Dame (Mary) Frances, DBE, TD
Cozens, *Brig.* Dame (Florence) Barbara, DBE, RRC
Crowe, Dame Sylvia, DBE
Daws, Dame Joyce Margaretta, DBE
Dell, Dame Miriam Patricia, DBE
Dench, Dame Judith Olivia (Mrs Williams), DBE
de Valois, Dame Ninette, OM, CH, DBE
Digby, Lady, DBE
Donaldson, Dame (Dorothy) Mary (Lady Donaldson of Lymington), GBE
Doyle, *Air Comdt.* Dame Jean Lena Annette Conan (Lady Bromet), DBE

Drake, *Brig.* Dame Jean Elizabeth Rivett-, DBE
Dugdale, Kathryn Edith Helen (Mrs John Dugdale), DCVO
Durack, Dame Mary (Mrs H. C. Miller), DBE
Ebsworth, *Hon.* Dame Ann Marian, DBE
Emerton, Dame Audrey Caroline, DBE
Evison, Dame Helen June Patricia, DBE
Fenner, Dame Peggy Edith, DBE, MP
Fitton, Dame Doris Alice (Mrs Mason), DBE
Fookes, Dame Janet Evelyn, DBE, MP
Fraser, Dame Dorothy Rita, DBE
Friend, Dame Phyllis Muriel, DBE
Frost, Dame Phyllis Irene, DBE
Fry, Dame Margaret Louise, DBE
Gallagher, Dame Monica Josephine, DBE
Gardiner, Dame Helen Louisa, DBE, MVO
Gibbs, Dame Molly Peel, DBE
Giles, *Air Comdt.* Dame Pauline (Mrs Parsons), DBE, RRC
Golding, Dame (Cecilie) Monica, DBE
Goodman, Dame Barbara, DBE
Gordon, Dame Minita Elmira, GCMG, GCVO
Gow, Dame Jane Elizabeth, DBE
Grafton, The Duchess of, GCVO
Green, Dame Mary Georgina, DBE
Grey, Dame Beryl Elizabeth (Mrs Svenson), DBE
Guilfoyle, Dame Margaret Georgina Constance, DBE
Guthardt, *Revd Dr* Dame Phyllis Myra, DBE
Haig, Dame Mary Alison Glen-, DBE
Hall, Dame Catherine Mary, DBE
Hambleden, Patricia, Viscountess, GCVO
Hammond, Dame Joan Hood, DBE
Harris, Dame (Muriel) Diana Reader-, DBE
Heilbron, *Hon.* Dame Rose, DBE
Henderson, Dame Louise Etiennette Sidonie, DBE
Henrison, Dame Anne Elizabeth Rosina, DBE

Chiefs of Clans and Names in Scotland

Only chiefs of whole Names or Clans are included, except certain special instances (marked *) who, though not chiefs of a whole name, were or are for some reason (e.g. the Macdonald forfeiture) independent. Under decision (*Campbell-Gray*, 1950) that a bearer of a 'double or triple-barrelled' surname cannot be held chief of a part of such, several others cannot be included in the list at present.

THE ROYAL HOUSE: HM The Queen

AGNEW: Sir Crispin Agnew of Lochnaw, Bt., 6 Palmerston Road, Edinburgh

ANSTRUTHER: Sir Ralph Anstruther of that Ilk, Bt., KCVO, MC, Balcaskie, Pittenweem, Fife

ARBUTHNOTT: The Viscount of Arbuthnott, CBE, DSC, Arbuthnott House, Laurencekirk, Kincardineshire

BARCLAY: Peter C. Barclay of that Ilk, 28A Gordon Place, London W8 4JE

BORTHWICK: The Lord Borthwick, TD, Crookston, Heriot, Midlothian

BOYD: The Lord Kilmarnock, 194 Regent's Park Road, London NWI 8XP

BOYLE: The Earl of Glasgow, Kelburn, Fairlie, Ayrshire

BRODIE: Ninian Brodie of Brodie, Brodie Castle, Forres, Morayshire

BRUCE: The Earl of Elgin and Kincardine, KT, Broomhall, Dunfermline, Fife

BUCHAN: David S. Buchan of Auchmacoy, Auchmacoy, Ellon, Aberdeenshire

BURNETT: J. C. A. Burnett of Leys, Crathes Castle, Banchory, Kincardineshire

CAMERON: Sir Donald Cameron of Lochiel, KT, CVO, TD, Achnacarry, Spean Bridge, Inverness-shire

CAMPBELL: The Duke of Argyll, Inveraray, Argyll

CARMICHAEL: Richard J. Carmichael of Carmichael, Carmichael, Thankerton, Biggar, Lanarkshire

CARNEGIE: The Duke of Fife, Elsick House, Stonehaven, Kincardineshire

CATHCART: Maj.-Gen. The Earl Cathcart, CB, DSO, MC, 2 Pembroke Gardens, London W8

CHARTERIS: The Earl of Wemyss and March, KT, Gosford House, Longniddry, East Lothian

CLAN CHATTAN: M. K. Mackintosh of Clan Chattan, Maxwell Park, Gwelo, Zimbabwe

CHISHOLM: Alastair Chisholm of Chisholm (*The Chisholm*), Silver Willows, Beck Row, Bury St Edmunds

COCHRANE: The Earl of Dundonald, Lochnell Castle, Ledaig, Argyllshire

COLQUHOUN: Sir Ivar Colquhoun of Luss, Bt., Camstraddan, Luss, Dunbartonshire

CRANSTOUN: David A. S. Cranstoun of that Ilk, Corehouse, Lanark

CRICHTON: vacant

DARROCH: Capt. Duncan Darroch of Gourock, The Red House, Branksome Park Road, Camberley, Surrey

DEWAR: Kenneth M. J. Dewar of that Ilk and Vogrie, The Dower House, Grayshott, Nr. Hindhead, Surrey

DRUMMOND: The Earl of Perth, PC, Stobhall, Perth

DUNBAR: Sir Jean Dunbar of Mochrum, Bt., 45–55 39th Street, Long Island City, New York, USA

DUNDAS: David D. Dundas of Dundas, 8 Derna Road, Kenwyn 7700, South Africa

DURIE: Raymond V. D. Durie of Durie, Court House, Pewsey, Wilts.

ELIOTT: Mrs Margaret Eliott of Redheugh, Redheugh, Newcastleton, Roxburghshire

ERSKINE: The Earl of Mar and Kellie, Claremont House, Alloa

FARQUHARSON: Capt. A. A. C. Farquharson of Invercauld, MC, Invercauld, Braemar, Aberdeenshire

FERGUSSON: Sir Charles Fergusson of Kilkerran, Bt., Kilkerran, Maybole, Ayrshire

FORBES: The Lord Forbes, KBE, Balforbes, Alford, Aberdeenshire

FORSYTH: Alistair Forsyth of that Ilk, Ethie Castle, by Arbroath, Angus

FRASER: The Lady Saltoun, Cairnbulg Castle, Fraserburgh, Aberdeenshire

*FRASER (OF LOVAT): The Lord Lovat, DSO, MC, TD, Balblair House, Beauly, Inverness-shire

GAYRE: Lt.-Col. Robert Gayre of Gayre and Nigg, 1–3 Gloucester Lane, Edinburgh

GORDON: The Marquess of Huntly, Aboyne Castle, Aberdeenshire

GRAHAM: The Duke of Montrose, Buchanan Auld House, Drymen, Stirlingshire

GRANT: The Lord Strathspey, The House of Lords, London SWIA OPW

GRIERSON: Sir Michael Grierson of Lag, Bt., 40C Palace Road, London

HAIG: The Earl Haig, OBE, Bemersyde, Melrose, Roxburghshire

HALDANE: Alexander N. C. Haldane of Gleneagles, Auchterarder, Perthshire

HANNAY: Ramsey W. R. Hannay of Kirkdale and of that Ilk, Cardoness House, Gatehouse-of-Fleet, Kirkcudbrightshire

HAY: The Earl of Erroll, Wolverton Farm, Wolverton, Basingstoke, Hants.

HENDERSON: John W. P. Henderson of Fordell, 7 Owen Street, Toowoomba, Queensland, Australia

HUNTER: Neil A. Hunter of Hunterston, Tour d'Escas, Carretera d'Escas, La Massana, Andorra

IRVINE OF DRUM: David C. Irvine of Drum, 29 Forest Road, Hoylake, Wirral, Merseyside

JARDINE: Sir Alexander Jardine of Applegirth, Bt., Ash House, Thwaites, Millom, Cumbria

JOHNSTONE: The Earl of Annandale and Hartfell, Raehills, Lockerbie, Dumfriesshire

KEITH: The Earl of Kintore, The Stables, Keith Hall, Inverurie, Aberdeenshire

KENNEDY: The Marquess of Ailsa, OBE, Blanefield, Kirkoswald, Ayrshire

KERR: The Marquess of Lothian, KCVO, Monteviot, Ancrum, Roxburghshire

KINCAID: Mrs Heather V. Kincaid of Kincaid, 4 Watling Street, Leintwardine, Craven Arms, Shropshire

LAMONT: Peter N. Lamont of that Ilk, St Patrick's College, Manly, NSW 2095, Australia

LEASK: Madam Leask of Leask, 1 Vincent Road, Sheringham, Norfolk

LENNOX: Edward J. H. Lennox of that Ilk, Pools Farm, Downton on the Rock, Ludlow, Shropshire

LESLIE: The Earl of Rothes, Tanglewood, West Tytherley, Salisbury, Wilts.

LINDSAY: The Earl of Crawford and Balcarres, PC, Balcarres, Colinsburgh, Fife

LOCKHART: Angus H. Lockhart of the Lee, Newholme, Dunsyre, Lanark

LUMSDEN: Gillem Lumsden of that Ilk and Blanerne, Kinderslegh, Bois Avenue, Chesham Bois, Amersham, Bucks

MacALESTER: William St J. S. McAlester of Loup and Kennox, 2 Avon Road East, Christchurch, Dorset

McBAIN: J. H. McBain of McBain, 7025, North Finger Rock Place, Tucson, Arizona, USA

MALCOLM (MacCALLUM): Robin N. L. Malcolm of Poltalloch, Duntrune Castle, Lochgilphead, Argyll

MACDONALD: The Lord Macdonald (*The Macdonald of Macdonald*), Kinloch Lodge, Sleat, Isle of Skye

*MACDONALD OF CLANRANALD: Ranald A. Macdonald of Clanranald, Wester Lix Cottage, Killin, Perthshire

*MACDONALD OF SLEAT (CLAN HUSTEAN): Sir Ian Bosville Macdonald of Sleat, Bt., Thorpe Hall, Rudston, Driffield, N. Humberside

*MACDONELL OF GLENGARRY: Air Cdre Aeneas R. MacDonell of Glengarry, CB, DFC, Elonbank, Castle Street, Fortrose, Ross-shire

MacDOUGALL: vacant

MACDOWALL: Fergus D. H. Macdowall of Garthland, 16 Tower Road, Nepean, Ontario, Canada

MacGREGOR: Sir Gregor MacGregor of MacGregor, Bt., Bannatyne, Newtyle, Angus

MacINTYRE: James W. MacIntyre of Glenoe, 15301 Pine Orchard Drive, Apartment 3H, Silver Spring, Maryland, USA

MACKAY: The Lord Reay, House of Lords, London SW1

MACKENZIE: The Earl of Cromartie, Castle Leod, Strathpeffer, Ross-shire

MACKINNON: Madam Anne Mackinnon of Mackinnon, 16 Purleigh Road, Bridgwater, Somerset

MACKINTOSH: The Mackintosh of Mackintosh, OBE, Moy Hall, Inverness

MacLACHLAN: Madam Marjorie MacLachlan of MacLachlan, Castle Lachlan, Argyll

MacLAREN: Donald MacLaren of MacLaren and Achleskine, Achleskine, Kirkton, Balquidder, Lochearnhead

MACLEAN: The Hon. Sir Lachlan Maclean of Duart, Bt., Duart Castle, Mull

MacLENNAN: vacant

MacLEOD: J. MacLeod of MacLeod, Dunvegan Castle, Isle of Skye

MacMILLAN: George MacMillan of MacMillan, Finlaystone, Langbank, Renfrewshire

MACNAB: J. C. Macnab of Macnab (*The Macnab*), West Kilmany House, Cupar, Fife

MACNAGHTEN: Sir Patrick Macnaghten of Macnaghten and Dundarave, Bt., Dundarave, Bushmills, Co. Antrim

MACNEACAIL: Iain Macneacail of Macneacail and Scorrybreac, 12 Fox Street, Ballina, NSW, Australia

MacNEIL OF BARRA: Ian R. Macneil of Barra (*The Macneil of Barra*), Kisimul Castle, Barra

MACPHERSON: The Hon. Sir William Macpherson of Cluny, TD, Newtown Castle, Blairgowrie, Perthshire

MacTHOMAS: Andrew P. C. MacThomas of Finegand, c/o The Clan MacThomas Society, 19 Warriston Avenue, Edinburgh

MAITLAND: The Earl of Lauderdale, 12 St Vincent Street, Edinburgh

MAKGILL: The Viscount of Oxfuird, Hill House, St Mary Bourne, Andover, Hants.

MAR: The Countess of Mar, St Michael's Farm, Great Witley, Worcs.

MARJORIBANKS: Andrew Marjoribanks of that Ilk

MATHESON: Maj. Sir Fergus Matheson of Matheson, Bt., Hedenham, Old Rectory, Bungay, Suffolk NR35 2LD

MENZIES: David R. Menzies of Menzies, 20 Nardina Crescent, Dalkeith, Western Australia

MOFFAT: Madam Moffat of that Ilk, St Jasual, Bullocks Farm Lane, Wheeler End Common, High Wycombe, Bucks.

MONCREIFFE: vacant

MONTGOMERIE: The Earl of Eglinton and Winton, The Dutch House, West Green, Hartley Wintney, Hants.

MORRISON: Dr Iain M. Morrison of Ruchdi, Magnolia Cottage, The Street, Walberton, Sussex

MUNRO: Patrick G. Munro of Foulis, TD, Foulis Castle, Ross

MURRAY: The Duke of Atholl, Blair Castle, Blair Atholl, Perthshire

NICOLSON: The Lord Carnock, 90 Whitehall Court, London SW1

OGILVY: The Earl of Airlie, KT, GCVO, PC, Cortachy Castle, Kirriemuir, Angus

RAMSAY: The Earl of Dalhousie, KT, GCVO, GBE, MC, Brechin Castle, Angus

RATTRAY: James S. Rattray of Rattray, Craighall, Rattray, Perthshire

ROBERTSON: Alexander G. H. Robertson of Struan (*Struan-Robertson*), The Breach Farm, Goudhurst Road, Cranbrook, Kent

ROLLO: The Lord Rollo, Pitcairns, Dunning, Perthshire

ROSE: Miss Elizabeth Rose of Kilravock, Kilravock Castle, Croy, Inverness

ROSS: David C. Ross of that Ilk, The Old Schoolhouse, Fettercairn, Kincardineshire

RUTHVEN: The Earl of Gowrie, PC, Castlemartin, Kilcullen, Co. Kildare, Republic of Ireland

SCOTT: The Duke of Buccleuch and Queensberry, KT, VRD, Bowhill, Selkirk

SCRYMGEOUR: The Earl of Dundee, Birkhill, Cupar, Fife

SEMPILL: The Lady Sempill, Druminnor Castle, Rhynie, Aberdeenshire

SHAW: John Shaw of Tordarroch, Newhall, Balblair, By Conon Bridge, Ross-shire

SINCLAIR: The Earl of Caithness, Churchill, Chipping Norton, Oxford OX7 5UX

STIRLING: Fraser J. Stirling of Cader, 17 Park Row, Farnham, Surrey

SUTHERLAND: The Countess of Sutherland, House of Tongue, Brora, Sutherland

SWINTON: John Swinton of that Ilk, 123 Superior Avenue SW, Calgary, Alberta, Canada

URQUHART: Kenneth T. Urquhart of that Ilk, 7907 Birch Street, New Orleans, Louisiana 790118, USA

WALLACE: Ian F. Wallace of that Ilk, 5 Lennox Street, Edinburgh EH4 1QB

WEDDERBURN OF THAT ILK: The Master of Dundee, Birkhill, Cupar, Fife

WEMYSS: David Wemyss of that Ilk, Invermay, Fortviot, Perthshire

Decorations and Medals

PRINCIPAL DECORATIONS AND MEDALS
In order of precedence

VICTORIA CROSS (VC), 1856
GEORGE CROSS (GC), 1940

British Orders of Knighthood, etc. (for order in which worn, *see* pages 174–6)
BARONET'S BADGE
KNIGHT BACHELOR'S BADGE

Decorations
ROYAL RED CROSS CLASS I (RRC), 1883. For ladies
DISTINGUISHED SERVICE CROSS (DSC), 1914. For officers of RN below the rank of Captain, and Warrant Officers
MILITARY CROSS (MC), December 1914. Awarded to Captains, Lieutenants, and Warrant Officers (I and II) in the Army and Indian and Colonial forces
DISTINGUISHED FLYING CROSS (DFC), 1918. For officers and Warrant Officers in the RAF (and Fleet Air Arm from 1941) for acts of gallantry when flying in active operations against the enemy
AIR FORCE CROSS (AFC), 1918. Instituted as preceding, but for acts of courage or devotion to duty when flying, although not in active operations against the enemy (extended to Fleet Air Arm 1941)
ROYAL RED CROSS CLASS II (ARRC)
ORDER OF BRITISH INDIA
KAISAR-I-HIND MEDAL
ORDER OF ST JOHN

Medals for Gallantry and Distinguished Conduct
UNION OF SOUTH AFRICA QUEEN'S MEDAL FOR BRAVERY, in Gold
DISTINGUISHED CONDUCT MEDAL (DCM), 1854 Awarded to warrant officers, non-commissioned officers and men of the Army and RAF
CONSPICUOUS GALLANTRY MEDAL (CGM), 1874. Bestowed upon warrant officers and men of the RN and since 1942 of Mercantile Marine and RAF
THE GEORGE MEDAL (GM), 1940
QUEEN'S POLICE MEDAL FOR GALLANTRY
QUEEN'S FIRE SERVICE MEDAL FOR GALLANTRY
ROYAL WEST AFRICAN FRONTIER FORCE DISTINGUISHED CONDUCT MEDAL
KING'S AFRICAN RIFLES DISTINGUISHED CONDUCT MEDAL
INDIAN DISTINGUISHED SERVICE MEDAL
UNION OF SOUTH AFRICA QUEEN'S MEDAL FOR BRAVERY, in Silver
DISTINGUISHED SERVICE MEDAL (DSM), 1914. For chief petty officers, petty officers and men, of all branches of the Royal Navy, and since 1942 of Mercantile Marine; non-commissioned officers and men of the Royal Marines; all other persons holding corresponding positions in Her Majesty's service afloat
MILITARY MEDAL (MM), 1916. For warrant and non-commissioned officers and men and serving women
DISTINGUISHED FLYING MEDAL (DFM), 1918, and the AIR FORCE MEDAL (AFM). For warrant and non-commissioned officers and men for equivalent services as for DFC and AFC (extended to Fleet Air Arm 1941)
CONSTABULARY MEDAL (IRELAND)

MEDAL FOR SAVING LIFE AT SEA
INDIAN ORDER OF MERIT (Civil)
INDIAN POLICE MEDAL FOR GALLANTRY
CEYLON POLICE MEDAL FOR GALLANTRY
SIERRA LEONE POLICE MEDAL FOR GALLANTRY
SIERRA LEONE FIRE BRIGADES MEDAL FOR GALLANTRY
COLONIAL POLICE MEDAL FOR GALLANTRY (CPM)
QUEEN'S GALLANTRY MEDAL, 1974
ROYAL VICTORIAN MEDAL (RVM), Gold, Silver and Bronze
BRITISH EMPIRE MEDAL (BEM), (formerly the Medal of the Order of the British Empire, for Meritorious Service; also includes the Medal of the Order awarded before 29 December 1922)
QUEEN'S POLICE (QPM) AND QUEEN'S FIRE SERVICES MEDALS (QFSM) FOR DISTINGUISHED SERVICE
QUEEN'S MEDAL FOR CHIEFS

War Medals and Stars (in order of date)

Polar Medals (in order of date)

IMPERIAL SERVICE MEDAL

Police Medals for Valuable Service

BADGE OF HONOUR

Jubilee, Coronation and Durbar Medals

KING GEORGE V, KING GEORGE VI AND QUEEN ELIZABETH II LONG AND FAITHFUL SERVICE MEDALS

Efficiency and Long Service Decorations and Medals
MEDAL FOR MERITORIOUS SERVICE
LONG SERVICE AND GOOD CONDUCT MEDAL (Military)
NAVAL LONG SERVICE AND GOOD CONDUCT MEDAL
ROYAL MARINE MERITORIOUS SERVICE MEDAL
ROYAL AIR FORCE MERITORIOUS SERVICE MEDAL
ROYAL AIR FORCE LONG SERVICE AND GOOD CONDUCT MEDAL
MEDAL FOR LONG SERVICE AND GOOD CONDUCT (ULSTER DEFENCE REGIMENT)
POLICE LONG SERVICE AND GOOD CONDUCT MEDAL
FIRE BRIGADE LONG SERVICE AND GOOD CONDUCT MEDAL
COLONIAL POLICE AND FIRE BRIGADES LONG SERVICE MEDAL
COLONIAL PRISON SERVICE MEDAL
ARMY EMERGENCY RESERVE DECORATION (ERD), 1952
VOLUNTEER OFFICER'S DECORATION (VD)
VOLUNTEER LONG SERVICE MEDAL
VOLUNTEER OFFICER'S DECORATION for India and the Colonies
VOLUNTEER LONG SERVICE MEDAL for India and the Colonies
COLONIAL AUXILIARY FORCES OFFICER'S DECORATION
COLONIAL AUXILIARY FORCES LONG SERVICE MEDAL
MEDAL FOR GOOD SHOOTING (Naval)
MILITIA LONG SERVICE MEDAL
IMPERIAL YEOMANRY LONG SERVICE MEDAL
TERRITORIAL DECORATION (TD), 1908
EFFICIENCY DECORATION (ED)
TERRITORIAL EFFICIENCY MEDAL
EFFICIENCY MEDAL

SPECIAL RESERVE LONG SERVICE AND GOOD
  CONDUCT MEDAL
DECORATION FOR OFFICERS, ROYAL NAVY RESERVE
  (RD), 1910
DECORATION FOR OFFICERS, RNVR (VRD)
ROYAL NAVAL RESERVE LONG SERVICE AND GOOD
  CONDUCT MEDAL
RNVR LONG SERVICE AND GOOD CONDUCT MEDAL
ROYAL NAVAL AUXILIARY SICK BERTH RESERVE LONG
  SERVICE AND GOOD CONDUCT MEDAL
ROYAL FLEET RESERVE LONG SERVICE AND GOOD
  CONDUCT MEDAL
ROYAL NAVAL WIRELESS AUXILIARY RESERVE LONG
  SERVICE AND GOOD CONDUCT MEDAL
AIR EFFICIENCY AWARD (AE), 1942
ULSTER DEFENCE REGIMENT MEDAL
The QUEEN'S MEDAL For champion shots in the RN, RM,
  RNZN, Army, RAF
CADET FORCES MEDAL, 1950
COAST LIFE SAVING CORPS LONG SERVICE MEDAL,
  1911
SPECIAL CONSTABULARY LONG SERVICE MEDAL
ROYAL OBSERVER CORPS MEDAL
CIVIL DEFENCE LONG SERVICE MEDAL
ROYAL ULSTER CONSTABULARY SERVICE MEDAL
SERVICE MEDAL OF THE ORDER OF ST JOHN
BADGE OF THE ORDER OF THE LEAGUE OF MERCY
VOLUNTARY MEDICAL SERVICE MEDAL, 1932
WOMEN'S ROYAL VOLUNTARY SERVICE MEDAL
COLONIAL SPECIAL CONSTABULARY MEDAL

Foreign Orders, Decorations and Medals (in order of date)

THE VICTORIA CROSS (1856)
FOR CONSPICUOUS BRAVERY

VC

Ribbon, Crimson, for all Services (until 1918 it was blue for
Royal Navy)

Instituted on 29 January 1856, the Victoria Cross was
awarded retrospectively to 1854, the first being held by Lt.
C. D. Lucas, RN, for bravery in the Baltic Sea on 21 June
1854 (gazetted 24 February 1857). The first 62 Crosses were
presented by Queen Victoria in Hyde Park, London, on 26
June 1857.

The Victoria Cross is worn before all other decorations,
on the left breast, and consists of a cross-pattée of bronze,
one and a half inches in diameter, with the Royal Crown
surmounted by a lion in the centre, and beneath there is the
inscription *For Valour*. Holders of the VC receive a tax-free
annuity of £100, irrespective of need or other conditions. In
1911, the right to receive the Cross was extended to Indian
soldiers, and in 1920 to Matrons, Sisters and Nurses, and
the staff of the Nursing Services and other services
pertaining to hospitals and nursing, and to civilians of either
sex regularly or temporarily under the orders, direction or
supervision of the Naval, Military, or Air Forces of the
Crown.

SURVIVING RECIPIENTS OF THE VICTORIA CROSS
as at 31 August 1993

Agansing Rai, *Havildar*, MM (Gurkha Rifles)
  1944 *World War*
Ali Haidar, *Jemadar* (Frontier Force Rifles)
  1945 *World War*
Annand, *Capt.* R. W. (Durham Light Infantry)
  1940 *World War*
Bhan Bhagta Gurung, *Capt.* (2nd Gurkha Rifles)
  1945 *World War*
Bhandari Ram, *Capt.* (Baluch R.)
  1944 *World War*
Chapman, *Sgt.* E. T., BEM (Monmouthshire R.)
  1945 *World War*
Cruickshank, *Flt. Lt.* J. A. (RAFVR)
  1944 *World War*
Cutler, Sir Roden, AK, KCMG, KCVO, CBE (Australia)
  1941 *World War*
Ervine-Andrews, *Lt.-Col.* H. M. (E. Lancs. R.)
  1940 *World War*
Foote, *Maj.-Gen.* H. R. B., CB, DSO (R. Tank R.)
  1942 *World War*
Fraser, *Lt.-Cdr.* I. E., DSC (RNR)
  1945 *World War*
Gaje Ghale, *Subedar* (Gurkha Rifles)
  1943 *World War*
Ganju Lama, *Jemadar*, MM (Gurkha Rifles)
  1944 *World War*
Gardner, *Capt.* P. J., MC (RTR)
  1941 *World War*
Gian Singh, *Jemadar* (Punjab R.)
  1945 *World War*
Gould, *Lt.* T. W. (RN)
  1942 *World War*
Hinton, *Sgt.* J. D. (NZMF)
  1941 *World War*
Jackson, *WO* N. C. (RAFVR)
  1944 *World War*
Jamieson, *Maj.* D. A., CVO (R. Norfolk R.)
  1944 *World War*
Kenna, *Pte.* E. (Australian M. F.)
  1945 *World War*
Kenneally, *C-Q-M-S* J. P. (Irish Guards)
  1943 *World War*
Lachiman Gurung, *Rifleman* (Gurkha Rifles)
  1945 *World War*
Learoyd, *Wg Cdr.* R. A. B. (RAF)
  1940 *World War*
Merritt, *Lt.-Col.* C. C. I., CD (S. Saskatchewan R.)
  1942 *World War*
Norton, *Capt.* G. R., MM (SAMF)
  1944 *World War*
Payne, *WO* K. (Australian Army)
  1969 *Vietnam*
Place, *Rear-Adm.* B. C. G., CB, CVO, DSC (RN)
  1943 *World War*
Porteous, *Col.* P. A. (RA)
  1942 *World War*
Rambahadur Limbu, *Lt.*, MVO (Gurkha Rifles)
  1965 *Sarawak*
Reid, *Flt. Lt.* W. (RAFVR)
  1943 *World War*
Smith, *Sgt.* E. A., CD (Seaforth Highlanders of Canada)
  1944 *World War*
Smythe, *Capt.* Q. G. M. (SAMF)
  1942 *World War*
Speakman-Pitt, *Sgt.* W. (Black Watch)
  1951 *Korea*

Tulbahadur Pun, *WOI* (Gurkha Rifles)
　1944 *World War*
Umrao Singh, *Sub-Major* (IA)
　1944 *World War*
Upham, *Capt.* C. H. (and Bar, 1942), (NZMF)
　1941 *World War*
Watkins, *Maj. Rt. Hon.* Sir Tasker, GBE (Welch R.)
　1944 *World War*
Wilson, *Lt.-Col.* E. C. T. (E. Surrey R.)
　1940 *World War*

THE GEORGE CROSS (1940)
FOR GALLANTRY

GC

Ribbon, Dark blue, threaded through a bar adorned with laurel leaves

Instituted 24 September 1940 (with amendments, 3 November 1942).

The George Cross is worn before all other decorations (except the VC) on the left breast (when worn by a woman it may be worn on the left shoulder from a ribbon of the same width and colour fashioned into a bow). It consists of a plain silver cross with four equal limbs, the cross having in the centre a circular medallion bearing a design showing St George and the Dragon. The inscription *For Gallantry* appears round the medallion and in the angle of each limb of the cross is the Royal cypher 'G VI' forming a circle concentric with the medallion. The reverse is plain and bears the name of the recipient and the date of the award. The cross is suspended by a ring from a bar adorned with laurel leaves on dark blue ribbon one and a half inches wide.

The cross is intended primarily for civilians; awards to the fighting services are confined to actions for which purely military honours are not normally granted. It is awarded only for acts of the greatest heroism or of the most conspicuous courage in circumstances of extreme danger. From 1 April 1965, holders of the Cross have received a tax-free annuity of £100.

The royal warrant which ordained that the grant of the Empire Gallantry Medal should cease authorized holders of that medal to return it to the Central Chancery of the Orders of Knighthood and to receive in exchange the George Cross. A similar provision applied to posthumous awards of the Empire Gallantry Medal made after the outbreak of war in 1939. In October 1971 all surviving holders of the Albert Medal and the Edward Medal exchanged those decorations for the George Cross.

SURVIVING RECIPIENTS OF THE GEORGE CROSS
as at 31 August 1993

If the recipient originally received the Empire Gallantry Medal (EGM), the Albert Medal (AM) or the Edward Medal (EM), this is indicated by the initials in parenthesis.

Archer, *Col.* B. S. T., GC, OBE, ERD, 1941
Atkinson, T., GC (EGM), 1939
Baker, J. T., GC (EM), 1929
Baldwin, W. C. G., GC, Ph.D. (EM), 1943
Bamford, J., GC, 1952
Baxter, W. F., GC (EM), 1942

Beaton, J., GC, CVO, 1974
Biggs, *Maj.* K. A., GC, 1946
Bridge, *Cdr.* J., GC, GM, 1944
Butson, *Col.* A. R. C., GC, CD, MD (AM), 1948
Bywater, R. A. S., GC, GM, 1944
Durrani, *Lt.-Col.* M. K., GC, 1946
Easton, J. M. C., GC, 1941
Errington, H., GC, 1941
Fairfax, F. W., GC, 1953
Farrow, K., GC (AM), 1948
Flintoff, H. H., GC (EM), 1944
Gledhill, A. J., GC, 1967
Goad, W., GC (AM), 1943
Goldsworthy, *Lt.-Cdr.* L. V., GC, DSC, GM, 1944
Gregson, J. S., GC (AM), 1943
Hallowes, Mrs O. M. C., GC, MBE, Légion d'Honneur, 1946
Hawkins, E., GC (AM), 1943
Hodge, *Capt.* A. M., GC, VRD (EGM), 1940
Johnson, *WOI (SSM)* B., GC, 1990
Kinne, D. G., GC, 1954
Lowe, A. R., GC (AM), 1949
Lynch, J., GC, BEM (AM), 1948
McAloney, *Gp. Capt.* W. S., GC, OBE (AM), 1938
McClymont, J. M., GC (EGM), 1940
Malta, GC, 1942
Manwaring, T. G., GC (EM), 1949
May, P. R. S., GC (AM), 1947
Miller, *Lt.-Cdr.* J. B. P., GC, 1941
Moore, R. V., GC, 1940
Moss, B., GC, 1940
Naughton, F., GC (EGM), 1937
Nix, F. E., GC (EM), 1944
Patton, The Hon. John, GC, CBE, 1940
Pearson, Miss J. D. M., GC (EGM), 1940
Pratt, M. K., GC, 1978
Purves, Mrs M., GC (AM), 1949
Raweng, Awang anak, GC, 1951
Riley, G., GC (AM), 1944
Rimmer, R., GC (EGM), 1931
Rogerson, S., GC, 1946
Rowlands, *Air Marshal* Sir John, GC, KBE, 1943
Sinclair, *Air Vice-Marshal* Sir Laurence, GC, KCB, CBE, DSO,
　1941
Stevens, H. W., GC, 1958
Stronach, *Capt.* G. P., GC, 1943
Styles, *Lt.-Col.* S. G., GC, 1972
Sylvester, W. G., GC (EGM), 1940
Taylor, *Lt.-Cdr.* W. H., GC, MBE, 1941
Walker, C., GC, 1972
Walker, C. H., GC (AM), 1942
Walton, E. W. K., GC (AM), 1948
Western, D., GC (AM), 1948
Wilcox, C., GC (EM), 1949
Wiltshire, S. N., GC (EGM), 1930
Yates, P. W., GC (EM), 1932

Precedence

ENGLAND AND WALES

The Sovereign
The Prince Philip, Duke of Edinburgh
The Prince of Wales
The Sovereign's younger sons
The Sovereign's grandsons
The Sovereign's cousins
Archbishop of Canterbury
Lord High Chancellor
Archbishop of York
The Prime Minister
Lord President of the Council
Speaker of the House of Commons
Lord Privy Seal
Ambassadors and High
  Commissioners
Lord Great Chamberlain
Earl Marshal
Lord Steward of the Household
Lord Chamberlain of the Household
Master of the Horse
Dukes, according to their patent of
  creation:
  (1) of England
  (2) of Scotland
  (3) of Great Britain
  (4) of Ireland
  (5) those created since the Union
Ministers and Envoys
Eldest sons of Dukes of Blood Royal
Marquesses, according to their patent
  of creation:
  (1) of England
  (2) of Scotland
  (3) of Great Britain
  (4) of Ireland
  (5) those created since the Union
Dukes' eldest sons
Earls, according to their patent of
  creation:
  (1) of England
  (2) of Scotland
  (3) of Great Britain
  (4) of Ireland
  (5) those created since the Union
Younger sons of Dukes of Blood
  Royal
Marquesses' eldest sons
Dukes' younger sons
Viscounts, according to their patent of
  creation:
  (1) of England
  (2) of Scotland
  (3) of Great Britain
  (4) of Ireland
  (5) those created since the Union
Earls' eldest sons
Marquesses' younger sons
Bishops of London, Durham and
  Winchester
Other English Diocesan Bishops,
  according to seniority of
  consecration

Suffragan Bishops, according to
  seniority of consecration
Secretaries of State, if of the degree of
  a Baron
Barons, according to their patent of
  creation:
  (1) of England
  (2) of Scotland
  (3) of Great Britain
  (4) of Ireland
  (5) those created since the Union
Treasurer of the Household
Comptroller of the Household
Vice-Chamberlain of the Household
Secretaries of State under the degree
  of Baron
Viscounts' eldest sons
Earls' younger sons
Barons' eldest sons
Knights of the Garter
Privy Counsellors
Chancellor of the Exchequer
Chancellor of the Duchy of Lancaster
Lord Chief Justice of England
Master of the Rolls
President of the Family Division
Vice-Chancellor
Lords Justices of Appeal
Judges of the High Court
Viscounts' younger sons
Barons' younger sons
Sons of Life Peers
Baronets, according to date of patent
Knights of the Thistle
Knights Grand Cross of the Bath
Members of the Order of Merit
Knights Grand Commanders of the
  Star of India
Knights Grand Cross of St Michael
  and St George
Knights Grand Commanders of the
  Indian Empire
Knights Grand Cross of the Royal
  Victorian Order
Knights Grand Cross of the British
  Empire
Companions of Honour
Knights Commanders of the Bath
Knights Commanders of the Star of
  India
Knights Commanders of St Michael
  and St George
Knights Commanders of the Indian
  Empire
Knights Commanders of the Royal
  Victorian Order
Knights Commanders of the British
  Empire
Knights Bachelor
Vice-Chancellor of the County
  Palatine of Lancaster
Official Referees of the Supreme
  Court
Circuit judges and judges of the
  Mayor's and City of London Court
Companions of the Bath

Companions of the Star of India
Companions of St Michael and St
  George
Companions of the Indian Empire
Commanders of the Royal Victorian
  Order
Commanders of the British Empire
Companions of the Distinguished
  Service Order
Lieutenants of the Royal Victorian
  Order
Officers of the British Empire
Companions of the Imperial Service
  Order
Eldest sons of younger sons of Peers
Baronets' eldest sons
Eldest sons of Knights, in the same
  order as their fathers
Members of the Royal Victorian
  Order
Members of the British Empire
Younger sons of the younger sons of
  Peers
Baronets' younger sons
Younger sons of Knights, in the same
  order as their fathers
Naval, Military, Air, and other
  Esquires by office

SCOTLAND

The Sovereign
The Prince Philip, Duke of Edinburgh
The Lord High Commissioner to the
  General Assembly (while that
  Assembly is sitting)
The Duke of Rothesay (eldest son of
  the Sovereign)
The Sovereign's younger sons
The Sovereign's cousins
Lords Lieutenant of Counties
Lord Provosts of Counties of Cities
Sheriffs Principal, successively, within
  their own localities and during
  holding of office
Lord Chancellor of Great Britain
Moderator of the General Assembly of
  the Church of Scotland
The Prime Minister
Keepers of the Great Seal and of the
  Privy Seal, successively if Peers
Hereditary Lord High Constable of
  Scotland
Hereditary Master of the Household
Dukes, in same order as in England
Eldest sons of Dukes of the Blood
  Royal
Marquesses, as in England
Dukes' eldest sons
Earls, as in England
Younger sons of Dukes of Blood
  Royal
Marquesses' eldest sons
Dukes' younger sons

Keepers of the Great Seal and of the
    Privy Seal, successively if not Peers
Lord Justice General
Lord Clerk Register
Lord Advocate
Lord Justice Clerk
Viscounts, as in England
Earls' eldest sons
Marquesses' younger sons
Lord-Barons, as in England
Viscounts' eldest sons
Earls' younger sons
Lord-Barons' eldest sons
Knights of the Garter
Privy Counsellors
Senators of College of Justice (Lords of
    Session)
Viscounts' younger sons
Lord-Barons' younger sons
Sons of Life Peers
Baronets
Knights of the Thistle
Knights Grand Cross, Grand
    Commander, and Knight
    Commanders, as in England
Solicitor-General for Scotland
Lord Lyon King of Arms
Sheriffs Principal, except as shown
    above
Knights Bachelor
Sheriffs
Companions of Orders, as in England
Commanders of the Royal Victorian
    Order
Commanders of the British Empire
Eldest sons of younger sons of Peers
Companions of the Distinguished
    Service Order
Lieutenants of the Royal Victorian
    Order
Officers of the British Empire
Baronets' eldest sons
Knights' eldest sons, as in England
Members of the Royal Victorian
    Order
Members of the British Empire
Baronets' younger sons
Knights' younger sons
Queen's Counsel
Barons-feudal
Esquires
Gentlemen

WOMEN

Women take the same rank as their
husbands or as their brothers; but the
daughter of a peer marrying a commoner retains her title as Lady or
Honourable. Daughters of peers rank
next immediately after the wives of
their elder brothers, and before their
younger brothers' wives. Daughters of
peers marrying peers of lower degree
take the same order of precedence as
that of their husbands; thus the daughter of a Duke marrying a Baron
becomes of the rank of Baroness only,
while her sisters married to commoners
retain their rank and take precedence
of the Baroness. Merely official rank
on the husband's part does not give any
similar precedence to the wife.

Peeresses in their own right take the
same precedence as peers of the same
rank, i.e. from their date of creation.

LOCAL PRECEDENCE

England and Wales – No written code
of county or city order of precedence
has been promulgated, but in counties
the Lord Lieutenant stands first, and
secondly (normally) the Sheriff, and
therefore in cities and boroughs the
Lord Lieutenant has social precedence
over the Mayor; but at city or borough
functions the Lord Mayor or Mayor
will preside. At Oxford and Cambridge
the High Sheriff takes precedence of
the Vice-Chancellor.

Scotland – The Lord Provosts of the
city districts of Aberdeen, Dundee,
Edinburgh and Glasgow are Lord
Lieutenants for those districts ex officio
and take precedence as such.

Forms of address

It is only possible to cover here the forms of address for peers, baronets and knights, their wife and children, and Privy Counsellors. Greater detail should be sought in one of the publications devoted to the subject.

Both formal and social forms of address are given where usage differs; increasingly, the social form is preferred to the formal, though this is used for official documents and on very formal occasions.

F__ represents forename.

S__ represents surname.

BARON - *Envelope (formal)*, The Right Hon. Lord __ ; *(social)*, The Lord __ . *Letter (formal)*, My Lord; *(social)*, Dear Lord __ . *Spoken*, Lord __ .

BARON'S WIFE - *Envelope (formal)*, The Right Hon. Lady __ ; *(social)*, The Lady __ . *Letter (formal)*, My Lady; *(social)*, Dear Lady __ . *Spoken*, Lady __ .

BARON'S CHILDREN - *Envelope*, The Hon. F__S__. *Letter*, Dear Mr/Miss/Mrs S__. *Spoken*, Mr/Miss/Mrs [F__] S__.

BARONESS IN OWN RIGHT - *Envelope*, may be addressed in same way as a Baron's wife or, if she prefers *(formal)*, The Right Hon. the Baroness __ ; *(social)*, The Baroness __ . Otherwise as for a Baron's wife.

BARONET - *Envelope*, Sir F__S__, Bt. *Letter (formal)*, Dear Sir; *(social)*, Dear Sir F__. *Spoken*, Sir F__.

BARONET'S WIFE - *Envelope*, Lady S__. *Letter (formal)*, Dear Madam; *(social)*, Dear Lady S__. *Spoken*, Lady S__.

COUNTESS IN OWN RIGHT - As for an Earl's wife.

COURTESY TITLES - The heir apparent to a Duke, Marquess or Earl uses the highest of his father's other titles as a courtesy title. (For list, *see* pages 169–70.) The holder of a courtesy title is not styled The Most Hon. or The Right Hon., and in correspondence 'The' is omitted before the title. The heir apparent to a Scottish title may use the title 'Master' (*see* below).

DAME - *Envelope*, Dame F__S__, followed by appropriate post-nominal letters. *Letter (formal)*, Dear Madam; *(social)*, Dear Dame F__. *Spoken*, Dame F__.

DUKE - *Envelope (formal)*, His Grace the Duke of __ ; *(social)*, The Duke of __ . *Letter (formal)*, My Lord Duke; *(social)*, Dear Duke. *Spoken (formal)*, Your Grace; *(social)*, Duke.

DUKE'S WIFE - *Envelope (formal)*, Her Grace the Duchess of __ ; *(social)*, The Duchess of __ . *Letter (formal)*, Dear Madam; *(social)*, Dear Duchess. *Spoken*, Duchess.

DUKE'S ELDEST SON - *see* Courtesy titles.

DUKE'S YOUNGER SONS - *Envelope*, Lord F__S__. *Letter (formal)*, My Lord; *(social)*, Dear Lord F__. *Spoken (formal)*, My Lord; *(social)*, Lord F__.

DUKE'S DAUGHTER - *Envelope*, Lady F__S__. *Letter (formal)*, Dear Madam; *(social)*, Dear Lady F__. *Spoken*, Lady F__.

EARL - *Envelope (formal)*, The Right Hon. the Earl (of) __ ; *(social)*, The Earl (of) __ . *Letter (formal)*, My Lord; *(social)*, Dear Lord __ . *Spoken (formal)*, My Lord; *(social)*, Lord __ .

EARL'S WIFE - *Envelope (formal)*, The Right Hon. the Countess (of) __ ; *(social)*, The Countess (of) __ . *Letter (formal)*, Madam; *(social)*, Lady __ . *Spoken (formal)*, Madam; *(social)*, Lady __ .

EARL'S CHILDREN - *Eldest son, see* Courtesy titles. *Younger sons*, The Hon. F__S__ (for forms of address, *see* Baron's children). *Daughters*, Lady F__S__ (for forms of address, *see* Duke's daughter).

KNIGHT (BACHELOR) - *Envelope*, Sir F__S__. *Letter (formal)*, Dear Sir; *(social)*, Dear Sir F__. *Spoken*, Sir F__.

KNIGHT (ORDERS OF CHIVALRY) - *Envelope*, Sir F__S__, followed by appropriate post-nominal letters. Otherwise as for Knight Bachelor.

KNIGHT'S WIFE - As for Baronet's wife.

MARQUESS - *Envelope (formal)*, The Most Hon. the Marquess of __ ; *(social)*, The Marquess of __ . *Letter (formal)*, My Lord; *(social)*, Dear Lord __ . *Spoken (formal)*, My Lord; *(social)*, Lord __ .

MARQUESS'S WIFE - *Envelope (formal)*, The Most Hon. the Marchioness of __ ; *(social)*, The Marchioness of __ . *Letter (formal)*, Madam; *(social)*, Dear Lady __ . *Spoken*, Lady __ .

MARQUESS'S CHILDREN - *Eldest son, see* Courtesy titles. *Younger sons*, Lord F__S__ (for forms of address, *see* Duke's younger sons). *Daughters*, Lady F__S__ (for forms of address, *see* Duke's daughter).

MASTER - The title is used by the heir apparent to a Scottish peerage, though usually the heir apparent to a Duke, Marquess or Earl uses his courtesy title rather than 'Master'. *Envelope*, The Master of __ . *Letter (formal)*, Dear Sir; *(social)*, Dear Master of __ . *Spoken (formal)*, Master, or Sir; *(social)*, Master, or Mr S__.

MASTER'S WIFE - Addressed as for the wife of the appropriate peerage style, otherwise as Mrs S__.

PRIVY COUNSELLOR - *Envelope*, The Right (or Rt.) Hon. F__S__. *Letter*, Dear Mr/Miss/Mrs S__. *Spoken*, Mr/Miss/Mrs S__. It is incorrect to use the letters PC after the name, unless the Privy Counsellor is a peer below the rank of Marquess and so is styled The Right Hon. because of his rank. In this case the post-nominal letters may be used in conjunction with the prefix The Right Hon.

VISCOUNT - *Envelope (formal)*, The Right Hon. the Viscount __ ; *(social)*, The Viscount __ . *Letter (formal)*, My Lord; *(social)*, Dear Lord __ . *Spoken*, Lord __ .

VISCOUNT'S WIFE - *Envelope (formal)*, The Right Hon. the Viscountess __ ; *(social)*, The Viscountess __ . *Letter (formal)*, Madam; *(social)*, Dear Lady __ . *Spoken*, Lady __ .

VISCOUNT'S CHILDREN - As for Baron's children.

The Privy Council

The Sovereign in Council, or Privy Council, was the chief source of executive power until the system of Cabinet government developed in the 18th century. Now the Privy Council's main functions are to advise the Sovereign and to exercise its own statutory responsibilities independent of the Sovereign in Council (*see also* page 224).

Membership of the Privy Council is automatic upon appointment to certain government and judicial positions in the United Kingdom, e.g. Cabinet ministers must be Privy Counsellors and are sworn in on first assuming office. Membership is also accorded by The Queen to eminent people in the United Kingdom and independent countries of the Commonwealth of which Her Majesty is Queen, on the recommendation of the British Prime Minister. Membership of the Council is retained for life, except for very occasional removals.

The administrative functions of the Privy Council are carried out by the Privy Council Office (*see* page 344) under the direction of the Lord President of the Council, who is always a member of the Cabinet.

Lord President of the Council, The Rt. Hon. Antony Newton, OBE, MP
Clerk of the Council, N. H. Nicholls, CBE

MEMBERS *as at 31 August 1993*

As at 31 August 1993, the appointment of the following to the Privy Council had been announced but the new members had not been sworn: Sir Denis Henry; Sir John Higgins; Sir John Hobhouse; Sir Mark Saville

HRH The Duke of Edinburgh, 1951
HRH The Prince of Wales, 1977

Aberdare, Lord, 1974
Ackner, Lord, 1980
Adams-Schneider, Sir Lancelot, 1980
Airlie, Earl of, 1984
Aldington, Lord, 1954
Alebua, Ezekiel, 1988
Alison, Michael, 1981
Alport, Lord, 1960
Amery of Lustleigh, Lord, 1960
Anthony, Douglas, 1971
Archer of Sandwell, Lord, 1977
Armstrong, Ernest, 1979

Arnold, Sir John, 1979
Ashdown, Paddy, 1989
Ashley of Stoke, Lord, 1979
Avonside, Lord, 1962
Aylestone, Lord, 1962
Azikiwe, Nnamdi, 1960
Baker, Kenneth, 1984
Balcombe, Sir John, 1985
Barber, Lord, 1963
Barnett, Lord, 1975
Barwick, Sir Garfield, 1964
Beckett, Margaret, 1993
Beith, Alan, 1992
Beldam, Sir Roy, 1989
Belstead, Lord, 1983
Benn, Anthony, 1964
Bennett, Sir Frederic, 1985
Bevins, John, 1959
Biffen, John, 1979
Bingham, Sir Thomas, 1986
Birch, William, 1992
Bird, Vere, 1982
Bisson, Sir Gordon, 1987
Blaker, Sir Peter, 1983
Blanch, Lord, 1975
Blatch, Baroness, 1993
Bolger, James, 1991
Booth, Albert, 1976
Boothroyd, Betty, 1992
Boscawen, Hon. Robert, 1992
Bottomley, Lord, 1952
Bottomley, Virginia, 1992
Boyd-Carpenter, Lord, 1954
Boys, Michael, 1989
Boyson, Sir Rhodes, 1987
Braine, Lord, 1985
Braithwaite, Nicholas, 1991
Brandon of Oakbrook, Lord, 1978
Bridge of Harwich, Lord, 1975
Brightman, Lord, 1979
Brittan, Sir Leon, 1981
Brooke, Peter, 1988
Brown, Sir Simon, 1992
Brown, Sir Stephen, 1983
Browne, Sir Patrick, 1974
Browne-Wilkinson, Lord, 1983
Buckley, Sir Denys, 1970
Butler, Sir Adam, 1984
Butler-Sloss, Dame Elizabeth, 1988
Caithness, Earl of, 1990
Callaghan of Cardiff, Lord, 1964
Cameron of Lochbroom, Lord, 1984
Campbell of Croy, Lord, 1970
Canterbury, The Archbishop of, 1991
Carlisle of Bucklow, Lord, 1979
Carr of Hadley, Lord, 1963
Carrington, Lord, 1959
Casey, Sir Maurice, 1986
Castle of Blackburn, Baroness, 1964
Cato, Robert, 1981
Chalfont, Lord, 1964
Chalker of Wallasey, Baroness, 1987
Chan, Sir Julius, 1981

Channon, Paul, 1980
Charteris of Amisfield, Lord, 1972
Chataway, Christopher, 1970
Clark, Alan, 1991
Clark, Helen, 1990
Clark of Kempston, Lord, 1990
Clarke, Kenneth, 1984
Cledwyn of Penrhos, Lord, 1966
Cockfield, Lord, 1982
Cocks of Hartcliffe, Lord, 1976
Coggan, Lord, 1961
Colman, Fraser, 1986
Colnbrook, Lord, 1973
Colyton, Lord, 1952
Compton, John, 1983
Concannon, John, 1978
Cooke, Sir Robin, 1977
Cooper, Sir Frank, 1983
Cope, Sir John, 1988
Corfield, Sir Frederick, 1970
Cowen, Sir Zelman, 1981
Cradock, Sir Percy, 1993
Crawford and Balcarres, Earl of, 1972
Crickhowell, Lord, 1979
Croom-Johnson, Sir David, 1984
Cumming-Bruce, Sir Roualeyn, 1977
Cunningham, Jack, 1993
Davies, Denzil, 1978
Davison, Sir Ronald, 1978
Dean, Sir Paul, 1991
Deedes, Lord, 1962
Dell, Edmund, 1970
Denham, Lord, 1981
Denning, Lord, 1948
Devonshire, Duke of, 1964
Diamond, Lord, 1965
Dillon, Sir Brian, 1982
Donaldson of Lymington, Lord, 1979
Douglas, Sir William, 1977
du Cann, Sir Edward, 1964
Duff, Sir Antony, 1980
Dunn, Sir Robin, 1980
Eccles, Viscount, 1951
Eden of Winton, Lord, 1972
Eichelbaum, Sir Thomas, 1989
Emery, Sir Peter, 1993
Emslie, Lord, 1972
Ennals, Lord, 1970
Erroll of Hale, Lord, 1960
Esquivel, Manuel, 1986
Evans, Sir Anthony, 1992
Eveleigh, Sir Edward, 1977
Farquharson, Sir Donald, 1989
Fellowes, Sir Robert, 1990
Ferguson, Alan, 1992
Ferrers, Earl, 1982
Floissac, Sir Vincent, 1992
Foot, Michael, 1974
Foster, Derek, 1993
Fowler, Sir Norman, 1979
Fox, Sir Michael, 1981
Fraser, Malcolm, 1976
Fraser of Carmyllie, Lord, 1989

Rumbold, Dame Angela, 1991
Runcie, Lord, 1980
Russell, Sir Patrick, 1987
Ryder, Richard, 1990
Sainsbury, Hon. Timothy, 1992
St John of Fawsley, Lord, 1979
Sandiford, Erskine, 1989
Scarman, Lord, 1973
Scott, Nicholas, 1989
Scott, Sir Richard, 1992
Seaga, Edward, 1981
Seear, Baroness, 1985
Selkirk, Earl of, 1955
Shackleton, Lord, 1966
Shawcross, Lord, 1946
Shearer, Hugh, 1969
Sheldon, Robert, 1977
Shephard, Gillian, 1992
Shepherd, Lord, 1965
Shore, Peter, 1967
Simmonds, Kennedy, 1984
Simon of Glaisdale, Lord, 1961
Sinclair, Ian, 1977
Slade, Sir Christopher, 1982
Slynn of Hadley, Lord, 1992
Smith, John, 1978
Somare, Sir Michael, 1977
Somers, Sir Edward, 1981

Stanley, Sir John, 1984
Staughton, Sir Christopher, 1988
Steel, Sir David, 1977
Stephen, Sir Ninian, 1979
Stephenson, Sir John, 1971
Stewartby, Lord, 1989
Steyn, Sir Johan, 1992
Stocker, Sir John, 1986
Stodart of Leaston, Lord, 1974
Stott, Lord, 1964
Stuart-Smith, Sir Murray, 1988
Talboys, Sir Brian, 1977
Taylor of Gosforth, Lord, 1988
Tebbit, Lord, 1981
Templeman, Lord, 1978
Thatcher, Baroness, 1970
Thomas of Gwydir, Lord, 1964
Thomson, David, 1981
Thomson of Monifieth, Lord, 1966
Thorneycroft, Lord, 1951
Thorpe, Jeremy, 1967
Tizard, Robert, 1986
Tonypandy, Viscount, 1968
Tranmire, Lord, 1955
Trefgarne, Lord, 1989
Trumpington, Baroness, 1992
Varley, Lord, 1974
Waddington, Lord, 1987

Waite, Sir John, 1993
Wakeham, Lord, 1983
Waldegrave, William, 1990
Walker, Sir Harold, 1979
Walker of Worcester, Lord, 1970
Waller, Sir George, 1976
Watkins, Sir Tasker, 1980
Watkinson, Viscount, 1955
Weatherill, Lord, 1980
Wheeler, Sir John, 1993
Whitelaw, Viscount, 1967
Wilberforce, Lord, 1964
Williams, Alan, 1977
Williams of Crosby, Baroness, 1974
Wilson of Langside, Lord, 1967
Wilson of Rievaulx, Lord, 1947
Windlesham, Lord, 1973
Wingti, Paias, 1987
Withers, Reginald, 1977
Woodhouse, Sir Owen, 1974
Woolf, Lord, 1986
Wylie, *Hon.* Lord, 1970
York, The Archbishop of, 1983
Young, Baroness, 1981
Young, Sir George, 1993
Young of Graffham, Lord, 1984
Younger of Prestwick, Lord, 1979
Zacca, Edward, 1992

The Privy Council of Northern Ireland

The Privy Council of Northern Ireland had responsibilities in Northern Ireland similar to those of the Privy Council in Great Britain until the Northern Ireland Act 1974 instituted direct rule and a United Kingdom Cabinet minister became responsible for the functions previously exercised by the Northern Ireland government.

Membership of the Privy Council of Northern Ireland is retained for life. The postnominal initials PC(NI) are used to differentiate its members from those of the Privy Council.

MEMBERS *as at 31 August 1993*

Bailie, Robin, 1971
Bleakley, David, 1971
Bradford, Roy, 1969
Craig, William, 1963
Dobson, John, 1969
Glentoran, The Lord, 1953
Kelly, Sir Basil, 1969
Kirk, Herbert, 1962
Long, William, 1966
Lowry, The Lord, 1971
McConnell, Robert, 1964

McIvor, Basil, 1971
Morgan, William, 1961
Moyola, The Lord, 1966
Neill, Sir Ivan, 1950
Porter, Sir Robert, 1969
Rathcavan, The Lord, 1969
Simpson, Robert, 1969
Taylor, John, MP, 1970
West, Henry, 1960

Parliament

The United Kingdom constitution is not contained in any single document but has evolved in the course of time, formed partly by statute, partly by common law and partly by convention. A constitutional monarchy, the United Kingdom is governed by Ministers of the Crown in the name of the Sovereign, who is head both of the state and of the government.

The organs of government are the legislature (Parliament), the executive and the judiciary. The executive consists of HM Government (Cabinet and other Ministers) (*see* pages 280–1), government departments (*see* pages 282–369), local authorities (*see* Local Government), and public corporations operating nationalized industries or social or cultural services (*see* pages 282–369). The judiciary (*see* Law Courts and Offices) pronounces on the law, both written and unwritten, interprets statutes and is responsible for the enforcement of the law; the judiciary is independent of both the legislature and the executive.

THE MONARCHY

The Sovereign personifies the state and is, in law, an integral part of the legislature, head of the executive, head of the judiciary, the commander-in-chief of all armed forces of the Crown and the 'Supreme Governor' of the Church of England. The seat of the monarchy is in the United Kingdom. In the Channel Islands and the Isle of Man, which are Crown dependencies, the Sovereign is represented by a Lieutenant-Governor. In the member states of the Commonwealth of which the Sovereign is head of state, her representative is a Governor-General; in United Kingdom dependencies the Sovereign is usually represented by a Governor, who is responsible to the British Government.

Although the powers of the monarchy are now very limited, restricted mainly to the advisory and ceremonial, there are important acts of government which require the participation of the Sovereign. These include summoning, proroguing and dissolving Parliament, giving royal assent to Bills passed by Parliament, appointing important office-holders, e.g. government ministers, judges, bishops, and governors, conferring peerages, knighthoods and other honours, and granting pardon to a person wrongly convicted of a crime. An important function is appointing a Prime Minister, by convention the leader of the political party which enjoys, or can secure, a majority of votes in the House of Commons. In international affairs the Sovereign as head of state has the power to declare war and make peace, to recognize foreign states and governments, to conclude treaties and to annex or cede territory. However, as the Sovereign entrusts executive power to Ministers of the Crown and acts on the advice of her Ministers, which she cannot ignore, in practice royal prerogative powers are exercised by Ministers, who are responsible to Parliament.

Ministerial responsibility does not diminish the Sovereign's importance to the smooth working of government. She holds meetings of the Privy Council, gives audiences to her Ministers and other officials at home and overseas, receives accounts of Cabinet decisions, reads dispatches and signs state papers; she must be informed and consulted on every aspect of national life; and she must show complete impartiality.

In the event of the Sovereign's absence abroad, it is necessary to appoint Counsellors of State under letters patent to carry out the chief functions of the Monarch, including the holding of Privy Councils and giving royal assent to Acts passed by Parliament. The normal procedure is to appoint as Counsellors three or four members of the royal family among those remaining in the United Kingdom.

In the event of the Sovereign on accession being under the age of eighteen years, or at any time unavailable or incapacitated by infirmity of mind or body for the performance of the royal functions, provision is made for a regency.

THE PRIVY COUNCIL

The Sovereign in Council, or Privy Council, was the chief source of executive power until the system of Cabinet government developed. Now its main function is to advise the Sovereign to approve Orders in Council and to advise on the issue of royal proclamations. The Council's own statutory responsibilities (independent of the powers of the Sovereign in Council) include powers of supervision over the registering bodies for the medical and allied professions. A full Council is summoned only on the death of the Sovereign or when the Sovereign announces his or her intention to marry. (For full list of Counsellors, *see* pages 221–3)

There are a number of advisory Privy Council committees, whose meetings the Sovereign does not attend. Some are prerogative committees, such as those dealing with legislative matters submitted by the legislatures of the Channel Islands and the Isle of Man or with applications for charters of incorporation; and some are provided for by statute, e.g. those for the universities of Oxford and Cambridge and the Scottish universities.

The Judicial Committee of the Privy Council is the final court of appeal from courts of the United Kingdom dependencies, courts of independent Commonwealth countries which have retained the right of appeal, courts of the Channel Islands and the Isle of Man, some professional and disciplinary committees, and church sources. The Committee is composed of all Privy Counsellors who hold, or have held, high judicial office, although usually only three or five hear each case.

Administrative work is carried out by the Privy Council Office under the direction of the Lord President of the Council, a Cabinet Minister.

PARLIAMENT

Parliament is the supreme law-making authority and can legislate for the United Kingdom as a whole or for any parts of it separately (the Channel Islands and the Isle of Man are Crown dependencies and not part of the United Kingdom). The main functions of Parliament are to pass laws, to provide (by voting taxation) the means of carrying on the work of government and to scrutinize government policy and administration, particularly proposals for expenditure. International treaties and agreements are by custom presented to Parliament before ratification.

Parliament emerged during the late thirteenth and early fourteenth centuries. The officers of the King's household and the King's judges were the nucleus of early Parliaments, joined by such ecclesiastical and lay magnates as the King might summon to form a prototype 'House of Lords', and occasionally by the knights of the shires, burgesses and proctors of the lower clergy. By the end of Edward III's reign a 'House of Commons' was beginning to appear; the first known Speaker was elected in 1377.

Parliamentary procedure is based on custom and precedent, partly formulated in the Standing Orders of both Houses (see Standing Orders, page 230), and each House has the right to control its own internal proceedings and to commit for contempt. The system of debate in the two Houses is similar; when a motion has been moved, the Speaker proposes the question as the subject of a debate. Members speak from wherever they have been sitting. Questions are decided by a vote on a simple majority. Draft legislation is introduced, in either House, as a Bill. Bills can be introduced by a Government Minister or a private Member, but in practice the majority of Bills which become law are introduced by the Government. To become law, a Bill must be passed by each House (for parliamentary stages, see Bill, page 228) and then sent to the Sovereign for the royal assent, after which it becomes an Act of Parliament.

Proceedings of both Houses are public, except on extremely rare occasions. The minutes (called Votes and Proceedings in the Commons, and Minutes of Proceedings in the Lords) and the speeches (The Official Report of Parliamentary Debates, Hansard) are published daily. Proceedings are also recorded for transmission on radio and television and stored in the Parliamentary Recording Unit before transfer to the National Sound Archive. Television cameras have been allowed into the House of Lords since January 1985, and into the House of Commons since November 1989; committee meetings may also be televised.

By the Parliament Act of 1911, the maximum duration of a Parliament is five years (if not previously dissolved), the term being reckoned from the date given on the writs for the new Parliament. The maximum life has been prolonged by legislation in such rare circumstances as the two world wars (31 January 1911 to 25 November 1918; 26 November 1935 to 15 June 1945). Dissolution and writs for a general election are ordered by The Queen on the advice of the Prime Minister. The life of a Parliament is divided into sessions, usually of one year in length, beginning and ending most often in October or November.

THE HOUSE OF LORDS

London SW1A OPW
Tel 071-219 3000

The House of Lords consists of the Lords Spiritual and Temporal. The Lords Spiritual are the Archbishops of Canterbury and York, the Bishops of London, Durham and Winchester, and the 21 senior diocesan bishops of the Church of England. The Lords Temporal consist of all hereditary peers of England, Scotland, Great Britain and the United Kingdom who have not disclaimed their peerages, life peers created under the Life Peerages Act 1958, and those Lords of Appeal in Ordinary created life peers under the Appellate Jurisdiction Act 1876, as amended (law lords). Disclaimants of an hereditary peerage lose their right to sit in the House of Lords but gain the right to vote at Parliamentary elections and to offer themselves for election to the House of Commons (see also page 141). Those peers disqualified from sitting in the House include:

– aliens, i.e. any peer who is not a British citizen, a Commonwealth citizen (under the British Nationality Act 1981) or a citizen of the Republic of Ireland
– peers under the age of 21
– undischarged bankrupts or, in Scotland, those whose estate is sequestered
– peers convicted of treason

Peers who do not wish to attend sittings of the House of Lords may apply for leave of absence for the duration of a Parliament.

Until the beginning of this century the House of Lords had considerable power, being able to veto any Bill submitted to it by the House of Commons, but those powers were greatly reduced by the Parliament Act of 1911 and subsequently by the Parliament Act of 1949 (see Parliament Acts 1911 and 1949, page 229).

Combined with its legislative role, the House of Lords has judicial powers as the ultimate Court of Appeal for courts in Great Britain and Northern Ireland, except for criminal cases in Scotland. These powers are exercised by the Lord Chancellor and the law lords.

Members of the House of Lords are unpaid. However, they are entitled to reimbursement of travelling expenses on parliamentary business within the UK and certain other expenses incurred for the purpose of attendance at sittings of the House, within a maximum for each day of £69.00 for overnight subsistence, £31.00 for day subsistence and incidental travel, and £30.00 for secretarial costs, postage and certain additional expenses.

COMPOSITION as at 13 July 1993

Archbishops and Bishops, 26
Peers by succession, 760 (17 women)
Hereditary Peers of first creation (including the Prince of Wales), 15
Life Peers under the Appellate Jurisdiction Act 1876, 19
Life Peers under the Life Peerages Act 1958, 382 (59 women)
Total 1,202
Of whom:
   Peers without Writs of Summons, 84 (2 minors)
   Peers on leave of absence from the House, 85

STATE OF PARTIES as at 13 July 1993

About half of the members of the House of Lords take the whip of one of the political parties. The other members sit on the cross-benches or as independents.

Conservative, 470
Labour, 113
Liberal Democrats, 57
Cross-bench, 271
Other (including Bishops), 291

OFFICERS

The House is presided over by the Lord Chancellor, who is ex officio Speaker of the House. A panel of deputy Speakers is appointed by Royal Commission. The first deputy Speaker is the Chairman of Committees, appointed at the beginning of each session, a salaried officer of the House who takes the chair in committee of the whole House and in some select committees. He is assisted by a panel of deputy chairmen, headed by the salaried Principal Deputy Chairman of Committees, who is also chairman of the European Communities Committee of the House.

The permanent officers include the Clerk of the Parliaments, who is in charge of the administrative staff collectively known as the Parliament Office; the Gentleman Usher of the Black Rod, who is also Serjeant-at-Arms in attendance upon the Lord Chancellor and is responsible for security and for accommodation and services in the House of Lords; and the Yeoman Usher who is Deputy Serjeant-at-Arms and assists Black Rod in his duties.

Speaker (£15,532), The Rt. Hon. the Lord Mackay of Clashfern
Private Secretary, M. Ormerod
Chairman of Committees (£46,167), The Lord Ampthill, CBE
Principal Deputy Chairman of Committees (£42,188), The Lord Boston of Faversham, QC
Clerk of the Parliaments (£87,620), M. A. J. Wheeler-Booth
Clerk Assistant and Clerk of the Journals (£62,504–£73,216), J. M. Davies
Reading Clerk (£53,272–£61,280), P. D. G. Hayter, LVO
Counsel to Chairman of Committees (£62,504–£73,216), D. Rippengal, CB, QC
Second Counsel (£53,272–£61,280), Mrs E. Denza, CMG
Third Counsel (£53,272–£61,280), Sir James Nursaw, KCB, QC
Assistant Counsel (£42,689–£57,586), N. J. Adamson, CB, QC
Principal Clerks (£47,871–£61,280), J. A. Vallance White *(Judicial Office and Fourth Clerk at the Table)*; M. G. Pownall *(Committees)*; B. P. Keith *(Private Bills)*; D. R. Beamish *(Clerk of the Journals)*
Chief Clerks (£39,339–£51,540), C. A. J. Mitchell; R. H. Walters, D.Phil.; Dr F. P. Tudor
Senior Clerks (£27,080–£37,769), E. C. Ollard *(seconded as Secretary to the Leader of the House and Chief Whip)*; Mrs M. E. Ollard; A. Makower; E. J. J. Wells; T. V. Mohan; S. P. Burton
Clerks (£14,390–£25,013), Mrs M. B. Bloor; D. J. Batt
Clerk of the Records (£39,339–£51,540), D. J. Johnson, FSA
Deputy Clerk of the Records (£30,654–£46,140), S. K. Ellison
Accountant (£27,080–£46,140), C. Preece
Assistant Accountant (£19,832–£27,304), Miss J. M. Lansdown
Judicial Taxing Clerk (£19,832–£27,304), C. G. Osborne
Librarian (£39,339–£51,540), D. L. Jones
Deputy Librarian (£30,654–£46,140), P. G. Davis, Ph.D.
Senior Library Clerk (£27,080–£37,769), Miss I. L. Victory, Ph.D.
Examiners of Petitions for Private Bills, B. P. Keith; R. J. Willoughby
Gentleman Usher of the Black Rod and Serjeant-at-Arms (£53,272–£61,280), Adm. Sir Richard Thomas, KCB, OBE
Yeoman Usher of the Black Rod and Deputy Serjeant-at-Arms (£27,080–£37,769), Air Cdre A. C. Curry, OBE
Staff Superintendent, Maj. F. P. Horsfall, MBE
Shorthand Writer (fees), Mrs P. J. Woolger
Editor, Official Report (Hansard), (£37,084–£48,553), Mrs M. E. Villiers
Deputy Editor, Official Report (£27,764–£41,701), G. R. Goodbarne

THE HOUSE OF COMMONS

London SW1A 0AA
Tel 071-219 3000

The members of the House of Commons are elected by universal adult suffrage. For electoral purposes, the United Kingdom is divided into constituencies, each of which returns one member to the House of Commons, the member being the candidate who obtains the largest number of votes cast in the constituency. To ensure equitable representation the four Boundary Commissions keep constituency boundaries under review and recommend any redistribution of seats which may seem necessary because of population movements, etc.

The number of seats was raised to 640 in 1945, then reduced to 625 in 1948, and subsequently rose to 630 in 1955, 635 in 1970, 650 in 1983 and 651 in 1992. Of the present 651 seats, there are 524 for England, 38 for Wales, 72 for Scotland and 17 for Northern Ireland.

ELECTIONS

Elections are by secret ballot, each elector casting one vote; voting is not compulsory. When a seat becomes vacant between general elections, a by-election is held.

British subjects and citizens of the Irish Republic can stand for election as Members of Parliament (MPs) provided they are 21 or over and not subject to disqualification. Those disqualified from sitting in the House include:

– undischarged bankrupts
– people sentenced to more than one year's imprisonment
– clergy of the Church of England, Church of Scotland, Church of Ireland and Roman Catholic Church
– members of the House of Lords
– holders of certain offices listed in the House of Commons Disqualification Act 1975, e.g. members of the judiciary, Civil Service, regular armed forces, police forces, some local government officers and some members of public corporations and government commissions

For entitlement to vote in parliamentary elections, *see* Legal Notes section.

A candidate does not require any party backing but his or her nomination for election must be supported by the signatures of ten people registered in the constituency. A candidate must also deposit with the returning officer £500, which is forfeit if the candidate does not receive more than 5 per cent of the votes cast. All election expenses at a general election, except the candidate's personal expenses, are subject to a statutory limit of £4,330, plus 3.7 pence for each elector in a borough constituency or 4.9 pence for each elector in a county constituency.

See pages 234–41 for an alphabetical list of MPs, pages 243–73 for the results of the last General Election, and page 242 for the results of recent by-elections.

STATE OF PARTIES *as at 31 July 1993*

Conservative, 334 (19 women)
Labour, 270 (36 women)
Liberal Democrats, 22 (3 women)
Plaid Cymru, 4
Scottish Nationalist, 3 (1 woman)
Democratic Unionist, 3
Social Democratic and Labour, 4
Ulster Popular Unionist, 1
Ulster Unionist, 9
The Speaker, 1
Total, 651 (60 women)

BUSINESS

The week's business of the House is outlined each Thursday by the Leader of the House, after consultation between the Chief Government Whip and the Chief Opposition Whip. A quarter to a third of the time will be taken up by the Government's legislative programme, and the rest by other business, e.g. question time. As a rule, Bills likely to raise political controversy are introduced in the Commons before going on to the Lords, and the Commons claims exclusive control in respect of national taxation and expenditure. Bills such as the Finance Bill, which imposes taxation, and the Consolidated Fund Bills, which authorize expenditure, must begin in the Commons. A Bill of which the financial provisions are subsidiary may begin in the Lords; and the

Commons may waive its rights in regard to Lords' amendments affecting finance.

The Commons has a public register of MPs' financial and certain other interests. Members must also disclose any relevant financial interest or benefit in a matter before the House when taking part in a debate, in certain other proceedings of the House, or in consultations with other MPs, with Ministers or civil servants.

MEMBERS' PAY AND ALLOWANCES

Since 1911 members of the House of Commons have received salary payments; facilities for free travel were introduced in 1924. Members are entitled to claim income tax relief on expenses incurred in the course of their Parliamentary duties. Salary rates since 1911 are as follows:

1911	£400 p.a.	1979 June	£9,450 p.a.
1931	360	1980 June	11,750
1934	380	1981 June	13,950
1935	400	1982 June	14,510
1937	600	1983 June	15,308
1946	1,000	1984 Jan	16,106
1954	1,250	1985 Jan	16,904
1957	1,750	1986 Jan	17,702
1964	3,250	1987 Jan	18,500
1972 Jan	4,500	1988 Jan	22,548
1975 June	5,750	1989 Jan	24,107
1976 June	6,062	1990 Jan	26,701
1977 July	6,270	1991 Jan	28,970
1978 June	6,897	1992 Jan	30,854

In October 1969 MPs were granted an allowance for secretarial and research expenses. In 1987 this became known as the Office Costs Allowance. From April 1993 the allowance is £40,380.

Since January 1972 MPs can claim reimbursement for the additional cost of staying overnight away from their main residence while on Parliamentary business. This was set at £10,958 for the 1993–4 financial year. Since 1984 this has been non-taxable.

From April 1980 provision was made enabling each MP in receipt of Office Costs Allowance to contribute sums to an approved pension scheme for the provision of a pension, or other benefits, for or in respect of persons whose salary is met by him/her from the Office Costs Allowance.

The cost of travel allowances for 1992–3 was stated in June 1993 to be £7,041,663.

MEMBERS' PENSIONS

Pension arrangements for MPs were first introduced in 1964. The arrangements currently provide a pension of one-fiftieth of salary for each year of pensionable service with a maximum of two-thirds of salary at age 65. Pension is payable normally at age 65, for men and women, or on later retirement. Pensions may be paid earlier, e.g. on ill-health retirement. The widow/widower of a former MP receives a pension of five-eighths of the late MP's pension. Pensions are index-linked. Members currently contribute 6 per cent of salary to the pension fund; there is an Exchequer contribution, currently slightly more than the amount contributed by MPs.

The House of Commons Members' Fund provides for annual or lump sum grants to ex-MPs, their widows or widowers, and children whose incomes are below certain limits. Alternatively, payments of £2,033 per annum to ex-MPs with at least ten years' service and who left the House of Commons before October 1964, and £1,271 per annum to their widows or widowers are made as of right. Members contribute £24 per annum and the Exchequer £215,000 per annum to the fund. The net assets of the fund as at 30 September 1992 amounted to £2,061,301.

OFFICERS AND OFFICIALS

The House of Commons is presided over by the Speaker, who has considerable powers to maintain order in the House. A deputy, the Chairman of Ways and Means, and two Deputy Chairmen may preside over sittings of the House of Commons; they are elected by the House, and, like the Speaker, neither speak nor vote other than in their official capacity.

The staff of the House are employed by a Commission chaired by the Speaker. The heads of House of Commons departments are permanent officers of the House, not MPs. The Clerk of the House is the principal adviser to the Speaker on the privileges and procedures of the House, the conduct of the business of the House, and Committees. The Serjeant-at-Arms is responsible for security, ceremonial, and for accommodation in the Commons part of the Palace of Westminster.

Speaker (£63,047), The Rt. Hon. Betty Boothroyd, MP for West Bromwich West
Chairman of Ways and Means (£51,402), Michael Morris, MP for Northampton South
First Deputy Chairman of Ways and Means (£47,989), Geoffrey Lofthouse, MP for Pontefract and Castleford
Second Deputy Chairman of Ways and Means (£47,989), Dame Janet Fookes, DBE, MP for Plymouth Drake

OFFICES OF THE SPEAKER AND CHAIRMAN OF WAYS AND MEANS

Speaker's Secretary (£39,339–£44,474), N. Bevan, CB
Speaker's Counsel (£54,751–£62,990), H. Knorpel, CB, QC; T. J. G. Pratt, CB
Assistant to Speaker's Counsel (£29,410–£34,735), P. Harvey, CB
Chaplain to the Speaker, The Revd Canon D. Gray, TD
Secretary to the Chairman of Ways and Means, Ms P. A. Helme

DEPARTMENT OF THE CLERK OF THE HOUSE

Clerk of the House of Commons (£90,148), Sir Clifford Boulton, KCB
Clerk Assistant (£64,307–£75,238), D. W. Limon, CB
Clerk of Committees (£64,307–£75,238), J. F. Sweetman, CB, TD
Principal Clerks (£54,751–£62,990)
  Public Bills, W. R. McKay
  Table Office, C. B. Winnifrith
  Select Committees, R. B. Sands
  Overseas Office, G. Cubie
  Journals, A. J. Hastings
  Private Bills, R. J. Willoughby
  Second Clerk of Select Committees, D. G. Millar
  Standing Committees, M. R. Jack, PH.D.
  Domestic Committees, R. W. G. Wilson
  Financial Committees, W. A. Proctor
Deputy Principal Clerks (£39,339–£44,474), S. A. L. Panton; Mrs J. Sharpe; Ms A. Milner-Barry; F. A. Cranmer; R. J. Rogers; C. R. M. Ward, PH.D.; Ms H. E. Irwin; D. W. N. Doig; D. L. Natzler; E. P. Silk; A. R. Kennon; L. C. Laurence Smyth; S. J. Patrick; D. J. Gerhold; C. J. Poyser; D. F. Harrison; S. J. Priestley; A. H. Doherty; P. A. Evans; R. I. S. Phillips; R. G. James
Senior Clerks (£27,080–£31,957), Ms P. A. Helme; D. R Lloyd; R. A. Lambert; B. M. Hutton; J. S. Benger, D.Phil.; Ms E. C. Samson; N. P. Walker; M. D. Hamlyn; P. C. Seaward, D.Phil.; C. G. Lee; C. D. Stanton;

A. Y. A. Azad; H. R. Neilson (*acting*); D. Steel (*acting*);
D. J. Clarke (*acting*); P. Bolton (*acting*)
Clerks of Domestic Committees (£27,080–£31,957),
K. J. Brown; P. G. Moon
Examiners of Petitions for Private Bills, R. J. Willoughby;
B. P. Keith
Registrar of Members' Interests, R. B. Sands
Taxing Officer, R. J. Willoughby

Vote Office

Deliverer of the Vote (£39,339–£44,474), H. C. Foster
Deputy Deliverer of the Vote (£27,080–£31,957),
J. F. Collins

DEPARTMENT OF THE SERJEANT-AT-ARMS

Serjeant-at-Arms (£54,751–£62,990) Sir Alan Urwick, KCVO,
CMG
Deputy Serjeant-at-Arms (£39,339–£44,474),
P. N. W. Jennings
Assistant Serjeant-at-Arms (£30,654–£39,339),
M. J. A. Cummins
Deputy Assistant Serjeants-at-Arms (£27,080–£31,957),
P. A. J. Wright; J. M. Robertson

PARLIAMENTARY WORKS DIRECTORATE

Director of Works (£49,671), H. P. Webber
Deputy Director of Works (£39,339), B. C. Sewell
Principal Works Officers (£27,080–£31,957), A.
Makepeace; B. R. Hall; R. Bentley; C. Hillier;
M. Moone; G. Goode; J. F. Moore; M. Trott
Senior Professional and Technical Officers (£21,994–
£27,586), J. Stone; S. Howard; B. O'Boyle; C. Brown;
C. Cowell; J. Eaton; T. Fox; T. Jardine

DEPARTMENT OF THE LIBRARY

Librarian (£54,751–£62,990), Miss J. B. Tanfield
Deputy Librarian (£47,871–£49,671), Miss P. J. Baines
Assistant Librarians (£39,339–£44,474), S. Z. Young;
K. G. Cunninghame
Deputy Assistant Librarians (£30,654–£39,339),
Mrs J. M. Wainwright; C. C. Pond, PH.D.;
Mrs C. B. Andrews; R. C. Clements; Mrs J. M. Lourie;
R. J. Ware, D.PHIL.; C. R. Barclay; Mrs J. M. Fiddick; Mrs
C. M. Gillie; R. J. Twigger; Mrs G. L. Allen
Senior Library Clerks (£27,080–£31,957), Ms F. Poole;
T. N. Edmonds; R. J. Cracknell; Miss O. M. Gay;
Miss E. M. McInnes; B. K. Winetrobe; Miss M. Baber;
Ms A. Walker; Mrs H. V. Holden; Miss J. Seaton;
Mrs P. L. Carling; A. J. L. Crompton; Miss P. J.
Strickland; Miss V. A. Miller; Ms H. M. Jeffs; S. A. Wise

DEPARTMENT OF FINANCE AND ADMINISTRATION

Director of Finance and Administration (£54,751–£62,990),
J. Rodda
Accountant (£47,871–£49,671), A. J. Lewis
Deputy Accountant (£39,339–£44,474), A. R. Marskell
Assistant Accountants (£27,080–£31,957), M. Fletcher;
Mrs G. Crowther
Head of Establishments Office (£39,339–£44,474),
B. A. Wilson
Head of Finance Office (£30,654–£39,339), M. J. Barram
Financial Accountant (£27,080–£31,957), vacant
Management Accountant (£27,080–£31,957),
R. H. A. Russell
Deputy Head of Establishments Office (£30,654–£39,339),
J. A. Robb
Computer Officer (£39,339–£44,474), R. S. Morgan

Internal Auditor (£27,080–£31,957), A. A. Cameron
Staff Inspector (£30,654–£39,339), R. C. Collins

DEPARTMENT OF THE OFFICIAL REPORT

Editor (£47,871–£49,671), I. D. Church
Deputy Editor (£39,339–£44,474), P. Walker
Principal Assistant Editors (£30,654–£39,339), J. Gourley;
W. G. Garland; Miss H. Hales; R. V. Hadlow
Assistant Editors (£28,220–£34,735), Miss V. Grainger;
Miss V. A. A. Clarke; Miss G. L. Sutherland;
S. Hutchinson; Miss C. Fogarty

REFRESHMENT DEPARTMENT

Director of Catering Services (£39,339–£44,474),
Mrs S. J. Harrison
Catering Accountant (£27,080–£31,957), D. R. W. Wood
Operations Manager (£27,080–£31,957), N. M. Hutson

PARLIAMENTARY INFORMATION

The following is a short glossary of aspects of the work of
Parliament. Unless otherwise stated, references are to House
of Commons procedures.

ADJOURNMENT DEBATE – Usually a half-hour debate
introduced by a back-bencher at the end of business for the
day. The subjects raised are often local or personal issues.

BILL – Proposed legislation is termed a Bill. The stages of
a Public Bill (for Private Bills, *see* page 229) in the House of
Commons are as follows:
First Reading: There is no debate at this stage, which
nowadays merely constitutes an order to have the Bill printed
Second Reading: The debate on the principles of the Bill
Committee Stage: The detailed examination of a Bill, clause
by clause. In most cases this takes place in a Standing
Committee, or the whole House may act as a Committee. A
Special Standing Committee may take evidence before
embarking on detailed scrutiny of the Bill. Very rarely, a Bill
may be examined by a Select Committee (*see* page 230)
Report Stage: Detailed review of a Bill as amended in
Committee
Third Reading: Final debate on a Bill
Public Bills go through the same stages in the House of
Lords, except that in almost all cases the Committee stage is
taken in Committee of the Whole House.
A Bill may start in either House, and has to pass through
both Houses to become law. Both Houses have to agree the
same text of a Bill, so that the amendments made by the
second House are then considered in the originating House,
and if not agreed, sent back or themselves amended, until
agreement is reached.

CHILTERN HUNDREDS – A legal fiction, a nominal office
of profit under the Crown, the acceptance of which requires
an MP to vacate his seat. The Manor of Northstead is similar.
These are the only means by which an MP may resign.

CLOSURE AND GUILLOTINE – To prevent deliberate
waste of time of either House, a motion may be made that
the question be now put. In the House of Commons, if the
Speaker decides that the rights of a minority are not being
prejudiced and 100 members support the closure motion in
a division, if carried, the original motion is put to the House
without further debate.
The guillotine represents a more rigorous and systematic
application of the closure. Under this system, a Bill proceeds
in accordance with a rigid timetable and discussion is limited

to the time allotted to each group of clauses. The closure is hardly ever used in the Lords, and there is no procedure for a guillotine. The completion of business in the Lords is ensured by agreement from all sides of the House.

CONSOLIDATED FUND BILL – A Bill to authorize issue of money to maintain Government services. The Bill is dealt with without debate, but afterwards members may raise topics of public or local importance.

DELEGATED LEGISLATION – Many statutes empower Ministers to make delegated legislation, with little or no reference back to Parliament, usually by means of Statutory Instruments. These fall into four broad categories:
Affirmative Instruments, which are subject to approval by resolutions of both Houses before they can come into or remain in force
Negative Instruments, which are subject to annulment by resolution of either House
General Instruments, which include those not required to be laid before Parliament and those which are required to be so laid but are not subject to approval or annulment
Special Procedure Orders, against which parties outside Parliament may lodge petitions

DISSOLUTION – Parliament comes to an end either by dissolution by the Sovereign, on the advice of the Prime Minister, or on the expiration of the term of five years for which the House of Commons was elected. Dissolution is normally effected by a royal proclamation.

EARLY DAY MOTION – A motion put on the Notice Paper by an MP without in general the real prospect of its being debated. Such motions are expressions of back-bench opinion.

EMERGENCY DEBATE – In the Commons a method of obtaining prompt discussion of a matter of urgency is by moving the adjournment under Standing Order No. 20 for the purpose of discussing a specific and important matter that should have urgent consideration. A member may ask leave to make this motion by giving written notice to the Speaker, usually before 12 noon, and if the Speaker considers the matter of sufficient importance and the House agrees, it is discussed usually at 7 p.m. on the following day.

FATHER OF THE HOUSE – The Member whose continuous service in the House of Commons is the longest. The present Father of the House is the Rt. Hon. Sir Edward Heath, KG, MBE, MP, elected first in 1950.

GENERAL SYNOD MEASURE – A measure passed by the national assembly of the Church of England under the Church of England Assembly (Powers) Act 1919. These measures are considered by the Joint Ecclesiastical Committee, who make a report. They are then considered by both Houses and, if approved, sent for the royal assent.

HANSARD – The official report of debates in both Houses (and in Standing Committees) published by HMSO, normally on the day after the sitting concerned.

HOURS OF MEETING – The House of Commons meets Monday to Thursday at 2.30 p.m., and on Friday at 9.30 a.m. Changes to these hours are under consideration. The House of Lords normally meets at 2.30 p.m. Monday to Wednesday and at 3 p.m. on Thursday. In the latter part of the session, the House of Lords sometimes sits on Fridays at 11 a.m.

HYBRIDITY – Public Bill which is considered to affect specific private or local interests, as distinct from all such interests of a single category, is called a Hybrid Bill and is subject to a special form of scrutiny to enable people affected

to object. In the House of Lords, affirmative instruments (*see* Delegated Legislation above) may also be treated as hybrid.

LEADER OF THE OPPOSITION – In 1937 the office of Leader of the Opposition was recognized and a salary of £2,000 per annum was assigned to the post. Since January 1992 the salary has been £59,736 (including Parliamentary salary of £23,227). The present Leader of the Opposition is the Rt. Hon. John Smith, QC, MP.

THE LORD CHANCELLOR – The Lord High Chancellor of Great Britain is (*ex officio*) the Speaker of the House of Lords. Unlike the Speaker of the House of Commons, he is a member of the Government, takes part in debates and votes in divisions. He has none of the powers to maintain order that the Speaker in the Commons has, these powers being exercised in the Lords by the House as a whole. The Lord Chancellor sits in the Lords on one of the Woolsacks, couches covered with red cloth and stuffed with wool. If he wishes to address the House in any way except formally as Speaker, he leaves the Woolsack.

NAMING – When a member has been named by the Speaker for a breach of order, i.e. contrary to the practice of the House, called by surname and not addressed as the 'Hon. Member for . . . (her/his constituency)', the Leader of the House moves that the offender 'be suspended from the service of the House' for (in the case of a first offence) a period of five sitting days. Should the member offend again, the period of suspension is increased.

OPPOSITION DAY – A day on which the topic for debate is chosen by the Opposition. There are twenty such days in a normal session. On seventeen days, subjects are chosen by the Leader of the Opposition; on the remaining three days by the leader of the next largest opposition party.

PARLIAMENT ACTS 1911 AND 1949 – Under these Acts, Bills may become law without the consent of the Lords.
Since at least the eighteenth century the Commons have had the privilege of having Bills concerned with supply (i.e. taxation and money matters) passed without amendment by the Lords, though until 1911 the Lords retained the right to reject such Bills outright.
By the Parliament Act 1911, a Bill which has been endorsed by the Speaker of the House of Commons as a Money Bill, and has been passed by the Commons and sent up to the Lords at least one month before the end of a session, can become law without the consent of the Lords if it is not passed by them without amendment within a month.
Under the Parliament Acts 1911 and 1949, if the Lords reject any other Public Bill (except one to prolong the life of a Parliament) which has been passed by the Commons in two successive sessions, then that Bill shall (unless the Commons direct to the contrary) become law without the consent of the Lords. The Lords have power, therefore, to delay a Public Bill for thirteen months from its first Second Reading in the House of Commons.

PRIME MINISTER'S QUESTIONS – The Prime Minister answers questions from 3.15 to 3.30 p.m. on Tuesdays and Thursdays. Nowadays the 'open question' predominates. Members tend to ask the Prime Minister what are his or her official engagements for the day; a supplementary question on virtually any topic can then be put.

PRIVATE BILL – A Bill promoted by a body or an individual to give powers additional to, or in conflict with, the general law, and to which a special procedure applies to enable people affected to object.

PRIVATE MEMBERS' BILL – A Public Bill promoted by a Member who is not a member of the Government.

PRIVATE NOTICE QUESTION – A question adjudged of urgent importance on submission to the Speaker (in the Lords, the Leader of the House), answered at the end of oral questions, usually at 3.30 p.m.

PRIVILEGE – The following are covered by the privilege of Parliament:
(i) freedom from interference in going to, attending at, and going from, Parliament
(ii) freedom of speech in Parliamentary proceedings
(iii) the printing and publishing of anything relating to the proceedings of the two Houses is subject to privilege
(iv) each House is the guardian of its dignity and may punish any insult to the House as a whole

PROROGATION – The bringing to an end, by the Sovereign on the advice of the Government, of a session of Parliament. Public Bills which have not completed all their stages lapse on prorogation.

QUEEN'S SPEECH – The speech delivered by The Queen at the State Opening of Parliament, in which the Government's programme for the session is set forth. The speech is drafted by civil servants and approved by the Cabinet.

QUESTION TIME – Oral questions are answered by Ministers in the Commons from 2.30 to 3.30 p.m. every day except Friday. They are also taken at the start of the Lords sittings, with a daily limit of four oral questions.

ROYAL ASSENT – The royal assent is signified by letters patent to such Bills and Measures as have passed both Houses of Parliament (or Bills which have been passed under the Parliament Acts 1911 and 1949). The Sovereign has not given royal assent in person since 1854. On occasion, for instance in the prorogation of Parliament, royal assent may be pronounced to the two Houses by Lords Commissioners. More usually royal assent is notified to each House sitting separately in accordance with the Royal Assent Act 1967. The old French formulae for royal assent are then endorsed on the Acts by the Clerk of the Parliaments.

The power to withhold assent resides with the Sovereign but has not been exercised in the United Kingdom since 1707, in the reign of Queen Anne.

SELECT COMMITTEES – Consisting usually of 10–15 members of all parties, select committees are a means used by both Houses in order to investigate certain matters.

Most select committees in the House of Commons are now tied to departments; each committee investigates subjects within a government department's remit. There are other House of Commons select committees dealing with public accounts (i.e. the spending by the Government of money voted by Parliament) and European legislation, and also domestic committees dealing, for example, with privilege and procedure. Major select committees usually take evidence in public; their evidence and reports are published by HMSO.

The principal select committee in the House of Lords is that on the European Communities, which has, at present, six sub-committees dealing with all areas of Community policy. The House of Lords also has a select committee on science and technology, which appoints sub-committees to deal with specific subjects. In addition, *ad hoc* select committees have been set up from time to time to investigate specific subjects, e.g. overseas trade, murder and life imprisonment. There are also some joint committees of the two Houses, e.g. the Joint Committee on Statutory Instruments.

DEPARTMENTAL COMMITTEES
Agriculture – *Chair*, Sir Jerry Wiggin, MP; *Clerk*, Mr Walker
Defence – *Chair*, Sir Nicholas Bonsor, MP; *Clerks*, Mr Natzler; Mr Hennessy

Education – *Chair*, Sir Malcolm Thornton, MP; *Clerk*, Mr Harrison
Employment – *Chair*, Hon. Greville Janner, MP; *Clerk*, Mr Phillips
Environment – *Chair*, Robert Jones, MP; *Clerk*, Mr Priestley
Foreign Affairs – *Chair*, Rt. Hon. David Howell, MP; *Clerks*, Ms Irwin, Mr Hamlyn
Health – *Chair*, Marion Roe, MP; *Clerks*, Mr Evans, Mr Reid
Home Affairs – *Chair*, Sir Ivan Lawrence, MP; *Clerks*, Mr Silk; Mr Devine
National Heritage – *Chair*, Rt. Hon. Gerald Kaufman, MP; *Clerk*, Mrs Sharpe
Science and Technology – *Chair*, Sir Giles Shaw, MP; *Clerk*, Mrs Samson
Scottish Affairs – *Chair*, William McKelvey, MP; *Clerk*, Mr Doherty
Social Security – *Chair*, Frank Field, MP; *Clerk*, Mr Lloyd
Trade and Industry – *Chair*, Richard Caborn, MP; *Clerks*, Mr Gerhold, Ms Gardner
Transport – *Chair*, Rt. Hon. Paul Channon, MP; *Clerks*, Mr Doig, Mr Stanton
Treasury and Civil Service – *Chair*, John Watts, MP; *Clerks*, Mr Proctor, Mr Lee
Welsh Affairs – *Chair*, Gareth Wardell, MP; *Clerk*, Mr Hutton

NON-DEPARTMENTAL COMMITTEES
European Legislation – *Chair*, James Hood, MP; *Clerk*, Mr Rogers
Members' Interests – *Chair*, Sir Geoffrey Johnson Smith, MP; *Clerk*, Mr Sands
Parliamentary Commissioner – *Chair*, James Pawsey, MP; *Clerk*, Mr Azad
Procedure – *Chair*, Rt. Hon. Sir Peter Emery, MP; *Clerk*, Mr Kennon
Public Accounts – *Chair*, Rt. Hon. Robert Sheldon, MP; *Clerk*, Dr Benger

The Privileges committee had still to be reconstituted at the time of going to press.

THE SPEAKER – The Speaker of the House of Commons is the spokesman and president of the Chamber. He or she is elected by the House at the beginning of each Parliament or when the previous Speaker retires or dies. The Speaker neither speaks in debates nor votes in divisions except when the voting is equal.

STANDING ORDERS – Rules which have from time to time been agreed by each House of Parliament to regulate the conduct of its business. These orders may be amended or repealed, and are from time to time suspended or dispensed with.

STATE OPENING – This marks the start of each new session of Parliament. Parliament is normally opened, in the presence of both Houses, by The Queen in person, who makes the speech from the throne which outlines the Government's policies for the coming session (*see* Queen's Speech). In the absence of The Queen, Parliament is opened by Royal Commission, and The Queen's Speech is read by one of the Lords Commissioners specially appointed by letters patent for the occasion.

STRANGERS – Anyone who is not a Member or Officer of the House is a stranger. Visitors are generally admitted to debates of both Houses but may be excluded if the House so decides. In practice this happens only in time of war.

TEN MINUTE RULE – A colloquial term for Standing Order No. 19, under which back-benchers have an opportunity on Tuesdays and Wednesdays to state for about ten minutes why a Bill on a certain subject should be introduced. Time is also available for a short opposing speech.

VACANT SEATS – When a vacancy occurs in the House of Commons during a session of Parliament, the writ for the by-election is moved by a Whip of the party to which the member whose seat has been vacated belonged. If the House is in recess, the Speaker can issue a warrant for a writ, should two members certify to him that a seat is vacant.

WHIPS – In order to secure the attendance of Members of a particular party in Parliament on all occasions, and particularly on the occasion of an important vote, Whips (originally known as 'Whippers-in') are appointed. The written appeal or circular letter issued by them is also known as a 'whip', its urgency being denoted by the number of times it is underlined. Failure to respond to a three-line whip, headed 'Most important', is tantamount in the Commons to secession (at any rate temporarily) from the party. Whips are officially recognized by Parliament and are provided with office accommodation in both Houses. In both Houses, Government and some Opposition Whips receive salaries from public funds.

PUBLIC INFORMATION SERVICES

HOUSE OF COMMONS – Public Information Office, House of Commons, London SW1A 0AA. Tel: 071-219 4272
HOUSE OF LORDS – The Journal and Information Office, House of Lords, London SW1A 0PW. Tel: 071-219 3107

GOVERNMENT OFFICE

The Government is the body of Ministers responsible for the administration of national affairs, determining policy and introducing into Parliament any legislation necessary to give effect to government policy. The majority of Ministers are members of the House of Commons but members of the House of Lords or of neither House may also hold ministerial responsibility. The Lord Chancellor is always a member of the House of Lords. The Prime Minister is, by current convention, always a member of the House of Commons.

THE PRIME MINISTER
The office of Prime Minister, which had been in existence for nearly 200 years, was officially recognized in 1905 and its holder was granted a place in the table of precedence. The Prime Minister, by tradition also First Lord of the Treasury and Minister for the Civil Service, is appointed by the Sovereign and is usually the leader of the party which enjoys, or can secure, a majority in the House of Commons. Other Ministers are appointed by the Sovereign on the recommendation of the Prime Minister, who also allocates functions amongst Ministers and has the power to obtain their resignation or dismissal individually.

The Prime Minister informs the Sovereign of state and political matters, advises on the dissolution of Parliament, and makes recommendations for important Crown appointments, the award of honours, etc.

As the chairman of Cabinet meetings and leader of a political party, the Prime Minister is responsible for translating party policy into government activity. As leader of the Government, the Prime Minister is responsible to Parliament and to the electorate for the policies and their implementation.

The Prime Minister also represents the nation in international affairs, e.g. summit conferences.

THE CABINET
The Cabinet developed during the eighteenth century as an inner committee of the Privy Council, which was the chief source of executive power until that time. The Cabinet is composed of about twenty Ministers chosen by the Prime Minister, usually the heads of government departments (generally known as Secretaries of State unless they have a special title, e.g. Chancellor of the Exchequer), the leaders of the two Houses of Parliament, and the holders of various traditional offices.

The Cabinet's functions are the final determination of policy, control of government and co-ordination of government departments. The exercise of its functions is dependent upon enjoying majority support in the House of Commons. Cabinet meetings are held in private, taking place once or twice a week during parliamentary sittings and less often during a recess. Proceedings are confidential, the members being bound by their oath as Privy Counsellors not to disclose information about the proceedings.

The convention of collective responsibility means that the Cabinet acts unanimously even when Cabinet Ministers do not all agree on a subject. The policies of departmental Ministers must be consistent with the policies of the Government as a whole, and once the Government's policy has been decided, each Minister is expected to support it or resign.

The convention of ministerial responsibility holds a Minister, as the political head of his or her department, accountable to Parliament for the department's work. Departmental Ministers usually decide all matters within their responsibility, although on matters of political importance they normally consult their colleagues collectively. A decision by a departmental Minister is binding on the Government as a whole.

POLITICAL PARTIES

Before the reign of William and Mary the principal officers of state were chosen by and were responsible to the Sovereign alone and not to Parliament or the nation at large. Such officers acted sometimes in concert with one another but more often independently, and the fall of one did not, of necessity, involve that of others, although all were liable to be dismissed at any moment.

In 1693 the Earl of Sunderland recommended to William III the advisability of selecting a ministry from the political party which enjoyed a majority in the House of Commons and the first united ministry was drawn in 1696 from the Whigs, to which party the King owed his throne. This group became known as the Junto and was regarded with suspicion as a novelty in the political life of the nation, being a small section meeting in secret apart from the main body of Ministers. It may be regarded as the forerunner of the Cabinet and in course of time it led to the establishment of the principle of joint responsibility of Ministers, so that internal disagreement caused a change of personnel or resignation of the whole body of Ministers.

The accession of George I, who was unfamiliar with the English language, led to a disinclination on the part of the Sovereign to preside at meetings of his Ministers and caused the appearance of a Prime Minister, a position first acquired by Robert Walpole in 1721 and retained without interruption for 20 years and 326 days.

DEVELOPMENT OF PARTIES

In 1828 the old party of the Whigs became known as Liberals, a name originally given to it by its opponents to imply laxity of principles, but gradually accepted by the party to indicate its claim to be pioneers and champions of political reform and progressive legislation. In 1861 a Liberal Registration Association was founded and Liberal Associations became widespread. In 1877 a National Liberal Federation was formed, with headquarters in London. The Liberal Party was in power for long periods during the second half of the nineteenth century and for several years during the first quarter of the twentieth century, but after a split in the party the numbers elected were small from 1931. In March 1988, the Liberals and the Social Democratic Party merged under the title Social and Liberal Democrats. Since October 1989 they have been known as the Liberal Democrats.

Soon after the change from Whig to Liberal the Tory Party became known as Conservative, a name traditionally believed to have been invented by John Wilson Croker in 1830 and to have been generally adopted about the time of the passing of the Reform Act of 1832 to indicate that the preservation of national institutions was the leading principle of the party. After the Home Rule crisis of 1886 the dissentient Liberals entered into a compact with the Conservatives, under which the latter undertook not to contest their seats, but a separate Liberal Unionist organization was maintained until 1912, when it was united with the Conservatives.

Labour candidates for Parliament made their first appearance at the general election of 1892, when there were 27 standing as Labour or Liberal-Labour. In 1900 the Labour Representation Committee was set up in order to establish a distinct Labour group in Parliament, with its own whips, its own policy, and a readiness to co-operate with any party which might be engaged in promoting legislation in the direct interest of labour. In 1906 the LRC became known as The Labour Party.

The Council for Social Democracy was announced by four former Labour Cabinet Ministers on 25 January 1981. Subsequently a number of sitting Labour Members of Parliament, together with one Conservative, joined the new group, and on 26 March 1981 the Social Democratic Party was launched. Later that year the SDP and the Liberal Party formed an electoral alliance. In 1988 a majority of the SDP agreed on a merger with the Liberal Party (*see* above) but a minority continued as a separate party under the SDP title. In June 1990 it was decided to wind up the party organization and its three sitting MPs were known as independent social democrats. None were returned at the 1992 general election.

GOVERNMENT AND OPPOSITION

The government of the day is formed by the party which wins the largest number of seats in the House of Commons at a general election, or which has the support of a majority of members in the House of Commons. By tradition, the leader of the majority party is asked by the Sovereign to form a government, while the largest minority party becomes the official Opposition with its own leader and 'Shadow Cabinet'. Leaders of the Government and Opposition sit on the front benches of the Commons with their supporters (the backbenchers) sitting behind them.

When a party is in opposition and its leadership becomes vacant, it makes its free choice among the various personalities available; but if the party is in office, the Sovereign's choice may anticipate, and in a certain sense forestall, the decision of the party.

PARTIES

The parties included here are those with MPs sitting in the House of Commons in the present Parliament. Addresses of other political parties may be found in the Societies and Institutions section.

CONSERVATIVE AND UNIONIST PARTY
Central Office, 32 Smith Square, London SW1P 3HH
Tel 071-222 9000
Chairman, The Rt. Hon. Sir Norman Fowler, MP
Deputy Chairman, The Rt. Hon. Dame Angela Rumbold, DBE, MP; Gerald Malone, MP
Hon. Treasurers, C. Hambro; T. J. Smith, MP

SCOTTISH CONSERVATIVE AND UNIONIST CENTRAL OFFICE
Suite 1/1, 14 Links Place, Leith, Edinburgh EH6 7EX
Tel 031-555 2900
Chairman, Sir Michael Hirst
Vice-Chairmen, Miss A. Goldie; J. Carlow; R. Robertson, MP
Hon. Treasurers, P. Runciman, CBE; M. Tennant
Director of the Party in Scotland, R. Pratt

LABOUR PARTY
150 Walworth Road, London SE17 1JT
Tel 071-701 1234
Parliamentary Party Leader, The Rt. Hon. John Smith, QC, MP
Deputy Party Leader, The Rt. Hon. Margaret Beckett, MP
Leader in the Lords, The Lord Richard, PC, QC
Chair, A. Clarke
Vice-Chair, David Blunkett, MP
Treasurer, T. Burlison
General Secretary, L. Whitty

SHADOW CABINET *at July 1993*
Leader of the Opposition, The Rt. Hon. John Smith, QC, MP
Leader of the House, The Rt. Hon. Margaret Beckett, MP
Treasury and Economic Affairs, Gordon Brown, MP
Home Affairs, Tony Blair, MP
Trade and Industry, Robin Cook, MP
Employment, Frank Dobson, MP
Transport, John Prescott, MP
National Heritage, Ann Clwyd, MP
Chief Secretary to the Treasury, Harriet Harman, MP
Citizen's Charter and Women, Marjorie Mowlam, MP
Environmental Protection, Chris Smith, MP
Wales, Ron Davies, MP
Education, Ann Taylor, MP
Foreign and Commonwealth Affairs, The Rt. Hon. Jack Cunningham, MP
Development and Co-operation, Michael Meacher, MP
Social Security, Donald Dewar, MP
Health, David Blunkett, MP
Environment (Local Government), Jack Straw, MP
Scotland, Tom Clarke, MP
Defence, Disarmament and Arms Control, David Clark, MP
Food, Agriculture and Rural Affairs, Gavin Strang, MP
Northern Ireland, Kevin McNamara, MP
Chief Whip, The Rt. Hon. Derek Foster, MP
Chair of the Parliamentary Labour Party, Douglas Hoyle, MP

LABOUR WHIPS
House of Lords, The Lord Graham of Edmonton
House of Commons, The Rt. Hon. Derek Foster, MP

LIBERAL DEMOCRATS
4 Cowley Street, London SW1P 3NB
Tel 071-222 7999
President, Charles Kennedy, MP
Hon. Treasurer, T. Razzall

General Secretary, G. Elson
Parliamentary Party Leader, The Rt. Hon. Paddy Ashdown, MP
Leader in the Lords, The Rt. Hon. the Lord Jenkins of Hillhead

LIBERAL DEMOCRAT SPOKESMEN
Deputy Leader, Treasury and Civil Service, Alan Beith, MP
Trade and Industry, Malcolm Bruce, MP
Agriculture and Rural Affairs, Paul Tyler, MP
Environment and Natural Resources, Simon Hughes, MP
Transport, Nicholas Harvey, MP
Home Affairs and National Heritage, Robert Maclennan, MP
England, Local Government and Housing, Nigel Jones, MP
Citizen's Charter and Youth Issues, Matthew Taylor, MP
Women's Issues, Ray Michie, MP
Sport, Menzies Campbell, MP
Scotland, Jim Wallace, MP (also fisheries policy); Ray Michie, MP
Northern Ireland, Lord Holme of Cheltenham
Wales and Employment, Alex Carlile, MP
Social Security, Older People and Disabled People, Archy Kirkwood, MP
Health and Community Care, Liz Lynne, MP
Education and Training, Don Foster, MP
Foreign Affairs, Overseas Development, The Rt. Hon. Sir David Steel, MP
Defence and Disarmament, Menzies Campbell, MP
Europe and East-West Relations, Sir Russell Johnston, MP; Charles Kennedy, MP
Overseas Development, The Lord Bonham Carter

LIBERAL DEMOCRAT WHIPS
House of Lords, The Lord Tordoff
House of Commons, Archy Kirkwood, MP (*Chief Whip*); Simon Hughes, MP (*Deputy Whip*)

WELSH LIBERAL DEMOCRATS
57 St Mary Street, Cardiff CF1 1FE
Tel 0222-382210
Party President, Revd R. Roberts
Party Leader, Alex Carlile, QC, MP
Chairman, G. Williams
Treasurer, B. Lopez
Secretary, Ms K. Lloyd

SCOTTISH LIBERAL DEMOCRATS
4 Clifton Terrace, Edinburgh EH12 5DR
Tel 031-337 2314
Party President, Sir Russell Johnston, MP
Party Leader, Jim Wallace, MP
Chair, Ms S. Grieve
Vice-Chairs, M. Ford; D. Miller
Hon. Treasurer, N. Stephen
Secretary, Ms R. Grant

PLAID CYMRU
51 Cathedral Road, Cardiff CF1 9HD
Tel 0222-231944
Party President, Dafydd Wigley, MP
Chairman, J. Dixon
Hon. Treasurer, C. Bryant
Secretary, D. Williams

SCOTTISH NATIONAL PARTY
6 North Charlotte Street, Edinburgh EH2 4JH
Tel 031-226 3661
Parliamentary Party Leader, Margaret Ewing, MP
Chief Whip, Andrew Welsh, MP
National Convener, Alex Salmond, MP
Senior Vice-Convener, Dr A. Macartney

National Treasurer, T. Chalmers
National Secretary, J. Swinney

NORTHERN IRELAND

SOCIAL DEMOCRATIC AND LABOUR PARTY
Cranmore House, 611 Lisburn Road, Belfast BT9 7GT
Tel 0232-668100
Parliamentary Party Leader, John Hume, MP, MEP
Deputy Leader, Seamus Mallon, MP
Chief Whip, Eddie McGrady, MP
Chairman, M. Durkan
Vice-Chairs, J. Stephenson; Ms G. Leonard
Hon. Treasurer, Ms D. Field
Party Administrator, Mrs G. Cosgrove

ULSTER DEMOCRATIC UNIONIST PARTY
296 Albertbridge Road, Belfast BT5 4GX
Tel 0232-458597
Parliamentary Party Leader, I. Paisley, MP, MEP
Deputy Leader, Peter Robinson, MP
Chairman, W. J. McClure
Deputy Chairman, S. Gibson
Hon. Treasurer, D. F. Herron
General Secretary, N. Dodds

ULSTER UNIONIST COUNCIL
3 Glengall Street, Belfast BT12 5AE
Tel 0232-324601
President, J. Cunningham
Party Leader, The Rt. Hon. James Molyneaux, MP
Chief Whip, William Ross, MP
Chairman, J. Nicholson, MEP
Vice-Chairman, A. J. Wilson
Treasurer, J. Allen
Party Secretary, J. Wilson

MEMBERS OF PARLIAMENT AS AT 31 JULY 1993

For abbreviations, *see* page 243
* Denotes membership of the last Parliament

*Abbott, Ms Diane J. (*b.* 1953) *Lab.,* Hackney North and Stoke Newington, maj. 10,727
*Adams, Mrs Irene (*b.* 1948) *Lab.,* Paisley North, maj. 9,329
Ainger, Nicholas R. (*b.* 1949) *Lab., Pembroke,* maj. 755
Ainsworth, Peter M. (*b.* 1956) *C., Surrey East,* maj. 17,656
Ainsworth, Robert W. (*b.* 1952) *Lab., Coventry North East,* maj. 11,676
*Aitken, Jonathan W. P. (*b.* 1942) *C., Thanet South,* maj. 11,513
*Alexander, Richard T. (*b.* 1934) *C., Newark,* maj. 8,229
*Alison, Rt. Hon. Michael J. H. (*b.* 1926) *C., Selby,* maj. 9,508
*Allason, Rupert W. S. (*b.* 1951) *C., Torbay,* maj. 5,787
*Allen, Graham W. (*b.* 1953) *Lab., Nottingham North,* maj. 10,743
*Alton, David P. (*b.* 1951) *LD, Liverpool, Mossley Hill,* maj. 2,606
*Amess, David A. A. (*b.* 1952) *C., Basildon,* maj. 1,480
Ancram, Michael A. F. J. K. (Earl of Ancram) (*b.* 1945) *C., Devizes,* maj. 19,712
*Anderson, Donald (*b.* 1939) *Lab., Swansea East,* maj. 23,482
Anderson, Mrs Janet (*b.* 1949) *Lab., Rossendale and Darwen,* maj. 120
*Arbuthnot, James N. (*b.* 1952) *C., Wanstead and Woodford,* maj. 16,885
*Armstrong, Miss Hilary J. (*b.* 1945) *Lab., Durham North West,* maj. 13,987
*Arnold, Jacques A. (*b.* 1947) *C., Gravesham,* maj. 5,493
*Arnold, Sir Thomas (*b.* 1947) *C., Hazel Grove,* maj. 929
*Ashby, David G. (*b.* 1940) *C., Leicestershire North West,* maj. 979
*Ashdown, Rt. Hon. J. J. D. (Paddy) (*b.* 1941) *LD, Yeovil,* maj. 8,833
*Ashton, Joseph W. (*b.* 1933) *Lab., Bassetlaw,* maj. 9,997
*Aspinwall, Jack H. (*b.* 1933) *C., Wansdyke,* maj. 13,341
*Atkins, Robert J. (*b.* 1946) *C., South Ribble,* maj. 5,973
*Atkinson, David A. (*b.* 1940) *C., Bournemouth East,* maj. 14,823
Atkinson, Peter (*b.* 1943) *C., Hexham,* maj. 13,438
Austin-Walker, John E. (*b.* 1944) *Lab., Woolwich,* maj. 2,225
*Baker, Rt. Hon. Kenneth W., CH (*b.* 1934) *C., Mole Valley,* maj. 15,950
*Baker, Nicholas B. (*b.* 1938) *C., Dorset North,* maj. 10,080
*Baldry, Antony B. (*b.* 1950) *C., Banbury,* maj. 16,720
Banks, Matthew (*b.* 1961) *C., Southport,* maj. 3,063
*Banks, Robert G., MBE (*b.* 1937) *C., Harrogate,* maj. 12,589
*Banks, Tony L. (*b.* 1943) *Lab., Newham North West,* maj. 9,171
*Barnes, Harold (*b.* 1936) *Lab., Derbyshire North East,* maj. 6,270
*Barron, Kevin J. (*b.* 1946) *Lab., Rother Valley,* maj. 17,222
Bates, Michael W. (*b.* 1961) *C., Langbaurgh,* maj. 1,564
*Batiste, Spencer L. (*b.* 1945) *C., Elmet,* maj. 3,261
*Battle, John D. (*b.* 1951) *Lab., Leeds West,* maj. 13,828
Bayley, Hugh (*b.* 1952) *Lab., York,* maj. 6,342
*Beckett, Rt. Hon. Margaret M. (*b.* 1953) *Lab., Derby South,* maj. 6,936
*Beggs, Roy (*b.* 1936) *UUP, Antrim East,* maj. 7,422
*Beith, Rt. Hon. Alan J. (*b.* 1943) *LD, Berwick-upon-Tweed,* maj. 5,043
*Bell, Stuart (*b.* 1938) *Lab., Middlesbrough,* maj. 15,784

*Bellingham, Henry C. (*b.* 1955) *C., Norfolk North West,* maj. 11,564
*Bendall, Vivian W. H. (*b.* 1938) *C., Ilford North,* maj. 9,071
*Benn, Rt. Hon. Anthony N. W. (*b.* 1925) *Lab., Chesterfield,* maj. 6,414
*Bennett, Andrew F. (*b.* 1939) *Lab., Denton and Reddish,* maj. 12,084
*Benton, Joseph E. (*b.* 1933) *Lab., Bootle,* maj. 29,442
Beresford, Sir Paul (*b.* 1946) *C., Croydon Central,* maj. 9,650
*Bermingham, Gerald E. (*b.* 1940) *Lab., St Helens South,* maj. 18,209
Berry, Roger L., D.Phil (*b.* 1948) *Lab., Kingswood,* maj. 2,370
Betts, Clive J. C. (*b.* 1950) *Lab., Sheffield, Attercliffe,* maj. 15,480
*Biffen, Rt. Hon. John W. (*b.* 1930) *C., Shropshire North,* maj. 16,211
*Blackburn, John G., PH.D. (*b.* 1933) *C., Dudley West,* maj. 5,789
*Blair, Anthony C. L. (*b.* 1953) *Lab., Sedgefield,* maj. 14,859
*Blunkett, David (*b.* 1947) *Lab., Sheffield, Brightside,* maj. 22,681
*Boateng, Paul Y. (*b.* 1951) *Lab., Brent South,* maj. 9,705
*Body, Sir Richard (*b.* 1927) *C., Holland with Boston,* maj. 13,831
*Bonsor, Sir Nicholas, Bt. (*b.* 1942) *C., Upminster,* maj. 13,821
Booth, Hartley, PH.D. (*b.* 1946) *C., Finchley,* maj. 6,388
*Boothroyd, Rt. Hon. Betty (*b.* 1929) *The Speaker, West Bromwich West,* maj. 7,830
*Boswell, Timothy E. (*b.* 1942) *C., Daventry,* maj. 20,274
*Bottomley, Peter J. (*b.* 1944) *C., Eltham,* maj. 1,666
*Bottomley, Rt. Hon. Virginia H. B. M. (*b.* 1948) *C., Surrey South West,* maj. 14,975
*Bowden, Andrew, MBE (*b.* 1930) *C., Brighton, Kemptown,* maj. 3,056
*Bowis, John C., OBE (*b.* 1945) *C., Battersea,* maj. 4,840
Boyce, James (*b.* 1947) *Lab., Rotherham,* maj. 17,561
*Boyes, Roland (*b.* 1937) *Lab., Houghton and Washington,* maj. 20,808
*Boyson, Rt. Hon. Sir Rhodes (*b.* 1925) *C., Brent North,* maj. 10,131
*Bradley, Keith J. C. (*b.* 1950) *Lab., Manchester, Withington,* maj. 9,735
Brandreth, Gyles D. (*b.* 1948) *C., City of Chester,* maj. 1,101
*Bray, Jeremy W., PH.D. (*b.* 1930) *Lab., Motherwell South,* maj. 14,013
*Brazier, Julian W. H. (*b.* 1953) *C., Canterbury,* maj. 10,805
*Bright, Graham F. J. (*b.* 1942) *C., Luton South,* maj. 799
*Brooke, Rt. Hon. Peter L., CH (*b.* 1934) *C., City of London and Westminster South,* maj. 13,369
*Brown, J. Gordon, PH.D. (*b.* 1951) *Lab., Dunfermline East,* maj. 17,444
*Brown, Michael R. (*b.* 1951) *C., Brigg and Cleethorpes,* maj. 9,269
*Brown, Nicholas H. (*b.* 1950) *Lab., Newcastle upon Tyne East,* maj. 13,877
Browning, Mrs Angela F. (*b.* 1946) *C., Tiverton,* maj. 11,089
*Bruce, Ian C. (*b.* 1947) *C., Dorset South,* maj. 13,508
*Bruce, Malcolm G. (*b.* 1944) *LD, Gordon,* maj. 274
*Budgen, Nicholas W. (*b.* 1937) *C., Wolverhampton South West,* maj. 4,966

Burden, Richard (*b.* 1954) *Lab., Birmingham, Northfield,* maj. 630

*Burns, Simon H. M. (*b.* 1952) *C., Chelmsford,* maj. 18,260

*Burt, Alistair J. H. (*b.* 1955) *C., Bury North,* maj. 4,764

*Butcher, John P. (*b.* 1946) *C., Coventry South West,* maj. 1,436

Butler, Peter (*b.* 1951) *C., Milton Keynes North East,* maj. 14,176

*Butterfill, John V. (*b.* 1941) *C., Bournemouth West,* maj. 12,703

Byers, Stephen J. (*b.* 1953) *Lab., Wallsend,* maj. 19,470

*Caborn, Richard G. (*b.* 1943) *Lab., Sheffield Central,* maj. 17,294

*Callaghan, James (*b.* 1927) *Lab., Heywood and Middleton,* maj. 8,074

Campbell, Mrs Anne (*b.* 1940) *Lab., Cambridge,* maj. 580

*Campbell, Ronald (*b.* 1943) *Lab., Blyth Valley,* maj. 8,044

*Campbell, W. Menzies, CBE, QC (*b.* 1941) *LD, Fife North East,* maj. 3,308

*Campbell-Savours, Dale N. (*b.* 1943) *Lab., Workington,* maj. 10,449

*Canavan, Dennis A. (*b.* 1942) *Lab., Falkirk West,* maj. 9,812

Cann, James (*b.* 1946) *Lab., Ipswich,* maj. 265

*Carlile, Alexander C., QC (*b.* 1948) *LD, Montgomery,* maj. 5,209

*Carlisle, John R. (*b.* 1942) *C., Luton North,* maj. 13,094

*Carlisle, Kenneth M. (*b.* 1941) *C., Lincoln,* maj. 2,049

*Carrington, Matthew H. M. (*b.* 1947) *C., Fulham,* maj. 6,579

*Carttiss, Michael R. H. (*b.* 1938) *C., Great Yarmouth,* maj. 5,309

*Cash, William N. P. (*b.* 1940) *C., Stafford,* maj. 10,900

*Channon, Rt. Hon. H. Paul G. (*b.* 1935) *C., Southend West,* maj. 11,902

*Chapman, Sydney B. (*b.* 1935) *C., Chipping Barnet,* maj. 13,951

Chisholm, Malcolm (*b.* 1949) *Lab., Edinburgh, Leith,* maj. 4,985

*Churchill, Winston S. (*b.* 1940) *C., Davyhulme,* maj. 4,426

Clapham, Michael (*b.* 1943) *Lab., Barnsley West and Penistone,* maj. 14,504

Clappison, W. James (*b.* 1956) *C., Hertsmere,* maj. 18,735

*Clark, David G., PH.D. (*b.* 1939) *Lab., South Shields,* maj. 13,477

*Clark, Dr Michael (*b.* 1935) *C., Rochford,* maj. 26,036

Clarke, Eric L. (*b.* 1933) *Lab., Midlothian,* maj. 10,334

*Clarke, Rt. Hon. Kenneth H., QC (*b.* 1940) *C., Rushcliffe,* maj. 19,766

*Clarke, Thomas, CBE (*b.* 1941) *Lab., Monklands West,* maj. 17,065

*Clelland, David G. (*b.* 1943) *Lab., Tyne Bridge,* maj. 15,210

Clifton-Brown, Geoffrey R. (*b.* 1953) *C., Cirencester and Tewkesbury,* maj. 16,058

*Clwyd, Ms Ann (*b.* 1937) *Lab., Cynon Valley,* maj. 21,364

Coe, Sebastian N., OBE (*b.* 1956) *C., Falmouth and Camborne,* maj. 3,267

Coffey, Ms M. Ann (*b.* 1946) *Lab., Stockport,* maj. 1,422

*Cohen, Harry (*b.* 1949) *Lab., Leyton,* maj. 11,484

*Colvin, Michael K. B. (*b.* 1932) *C., Romsey and Waterside,* maj. 15,304

Congdon, David L. (*b.* 1949) *C., Croydon North East,* maj. 7,473

Connarty, Michael (*b.* 1949) *Lab., Falkirk East,* maj. 7,969

*Conway, Derek L. (*b.* 1953) *C., Shrewsbury and Atcham,* maj. 10,965

*Cook, Francis (*b.* 1935) *Lab., Stockton North,* maj. 10,474

*Cook, R. F. (Robin) (*b.* 1946) *Lab., Livingston,* maj. 8,105

*Coombs, Anthony M. V. (*b.* 1952) *C., Wyre Forest,* maj. 10,341

*Coombs, Simon C. (*b.* 1947) *C., Swindon,* maj. 2,826

*Cope, Rt. Hon. Sir John (*b.* 1937) *C., Northavon,* maj. 11,861

*Corbett, Robin (*b.* 1933) *Lab., Birmingham, Erdington,* maj. 4,735

*Corbyn, Jeremy B. (*b.* 1949) *Lab., Islington North,* maj. 12,784

*Cormack, Patrick T. (*b.* 1939) *C., Staffordshire South,* maj. 22,633

Corston, Ms Jean (*b.* 1942) *Lab., Bristol East,* maj. 2,692

*Couchman, James R. (*b.* 1942) *C., Gillingham,* maj. 16,638

*Cousins, James M. (*b.* 1944) *Lab., Newcastle upon Tyne Central,* maj. 5,288

*Cox, Thomas M. (*b.* 1930) *Lab., Tooting,* maj. 4,107

*Cran, James D. (*b.* 1944) *C., Beverley,* maj. 16,517

*Critchley, Julian M. G. (*b.* 1930) *C., Aldershot,* maj. 19,188

*Cryer, G. Robert (*b.* 1934) *Lab., Bradford South,* maj. 4,902

*Cummings, John S. (*b.* 1943) *Lab., Easington,* maj. 26,390

*Cunliffe, Lawrence F. (*b.* 1929) *Lab., Leigh,* maj. 18,827

Cunningham, James (*b.* 1941) *Lab., Coventry South East,* maj. 1,311

*Cunningham, Rt. Hon. Dr John A. (Jack) (*b.* 1939) *Lab., Copeland,* maj. 2,439

*Currie, Mrs Edwina (*b.* 1946) *C., Derbyshire South,* maj. 4,658

*Curry, David M. (*b.* 1944) *C., Skipton and Ripon,* maj. 19,330

Dafis, Cynog G. (*b.* 1938) *PC, Ceredigion and Pembroke North,* maj. 3,193

*Dalyell, Tam (Sir Thomas Dalyell of the Binns, Bt.) (*b.* 1932) *Lab., Linlithgow,* maj. 7,026

*Darling, Alistair M. (*b.* 1953) *Lab., Edinburgh Central,* maj. 2,126

Davidson, Ian (*b.* 1950) *Lab., Glasgow, Govan,* maj. 4,125

Davies, Bryan (*b.* 1939) *Lab., Oldham Central and Royton,* maj. 8,606

*Davies, Rt. Hon. D. J. Denzil (*b.* 1938) *Lab., Llanelli,* maj. 19,270

*Davies, J. Quentin (*b.* 1944) *C., Stamford and Spalding,* maj. 22,869

*Davies, Ronald (*b.* 1946) *Lab., Caerphilly,* maj. 22,672

*Davis, David M. (*b.* 1948) *C., Boothferry,* maj. 17,535

*Davis, Terence A. G. (*b.* 1938) *Lab., Birmingham, Hodge Hill,* maj. 7,068

*Day, Stephen R. (*b.* 1948) *C., Cheadle,* maj. 15,778

Denham, John V. (*b.* 1953) *Lab., Southampton, Itchen,* maj. 551

Deva, Niranjan J. A. (*b.* 1948) *C., Brentford and Isleworth,* maj. 2,086

*Devlin, Timothy R. (*b.* 1959) *C., Stockton South,* maj. 3,369

*Dewar, Donald C. (*b.* 1937) *Lab., Glasgow, Garscadden,* maj. 13,340

*Dickens, Geoffrey K. (*b.* 1931) *C., Littleborough and Saddleworth,* maj. 4,494

*Dicks, Terence P. (*b.* 1937) *C., Hayes and Harlington,* maj. 53

*Dixon, Donald (*b.* 1929) *Lab., Jarrow,* maj. 17,907

*Dobson, Frank G. (*b.* 1940) *Lab., Holborn and St Pancras,* maj. 10,824

Donohoe, Brian H. (*b.* 1948) *Lab., Cunninghame South,* maj. 10,680

*Dorrell, Stephen J. (*b.* 1952) *C., Loughborough,* maj. 10,883

*Douglas-Hamilton, Lord James (*b.* 1942) *C., Edinburgh West,* maj. 879

*Dover, Densmore (*b.* 1938) *C., Chorley,* maj. 4,246

Dowd, James P. (*b.* 1951) *Lab., Lewisham West,* maj. 1,809

Duncan, Alan J. C. (*b.* 1957) *C., Rutland and Melton,* maj. 25,535

Duncan-Smith, G. Iain (*b.* 1954) *C., Chingford,* maj. 14,938

*Dunn, Robert J. (*b.* 1946) *C., Dartford,* maj. 10,314

*Dunnachie, James F. (*b.* 1930) *Lab., Glasgow, Pollok,* maj. 7,883

*Dunwoody, Hon. Mrs Gwyneth P. (*b.* 1930) *Lab., Crewe and Nantwich,* maj. 2,695

*Durant, Sir Anthony (*b.* 1928) *C., Reading West,* maj. 13,298

*Dykes, Hugh J. (*b.* 1939) *C., Harrow East,* maj. 11,098

Eagle, Ms Angela (*b.* 1961) *Lab., Wallasey,* maj. 3,809

*Eastham, Kenneth (*b.* 1927) *Lab., Manchester, Blackley,* maj. 12,389

*Eggar, Timothy J. C. (*b.* 1951) *C., Enfield North,* maj. 9,430

Elletson, Harold D. H. (*b.* 1960) *C., Blackpool North,* maj. 3,040

*Emery, Rt. Hon. Sir Peter (*b.* 1926) *C., Honiton,* maj. 16,511

*Enright, Derek A. (*b.* 1935) *Lab., Hemsworth,* maj. 22,075

Etherington, William (*b.* 1941) *Lab., Sunderland North,* maj. 17,004

*Evans, David J. (*b.* 1935) *C., Welwyn Hatfield,* maj. 8,465

*Evans, John (*b.* 1930) *Lab., St Helens North,* maj. 16,244

Evans, Jonathan P. (*b.* 1950) *C., Brecon and Radnor,* maj. 130

Evans, Nigel M. (*b.* 1957) *C., Ribble Valley,* maj. 6,542

Evans, Roger (*b.* 1947) *C., Monmouth,* maj. 3,204

*Evennett, David A. (*b.* 1939) *C., Erith and Crayford,* maj. 2,339

*Ewing, Mrs Margaret A. (*b.* 1945) *SNP, Moray,* maj. 2,844

Faber, David J. C. (*b.* 1961) *C., Westbury,* maj. 12,606

Fabricant, Michael L. D. (*b.* 1950) *C., Staffordshire Mid,* maj. 6,236

*Fairbairn, Sir Nicholas, QC (*b.* 1933) *C., Perth and Kinross,* maj. 2,094

*Fatchett, Derek J. (*b.* 1945) *Lab., Leeds Central,* maj. 15,020

*Faulds, Andrew M. W. (*b.* 1923) *Lab., Warley East,* maj. 7,794

*Fenner, Dame Peggy, DBE (*b.* 1922) *C., Medway,* maj. 8,786

*Field, Barry J. A., TD (*b.* 1946) *C., Isle of Wight,* maj. 1,827

*Field, Frank (*b.* 1942) *Lab., Birkenhead,* maj. 17,613

*Fishburn, J. Dudley (*b.* 1946) *C., Kensington,* maj. 3,548

*Fisher, Mark (*b.* 1944) *Lab., Stoke-on-Trent Central,* maj. 13,420

*Flynn, Paul P. (*b.* 1935) *Lab., Newport West,* maj. 7,779

*Fookes, Dame Janet, DBE (*b.* 1936) *C., Plymouth, Drake,* maj. 2,013

*Forman, F. Nigel (*b.* 1943) *C., Carshalton and Wallington,* maj. 9,943

*Forsyth, Michael B. (*b.* 1954) *C., Stirling,* maj. 703

*Forsythe, Clifford (*b.* 1929) *UUP, Antrim South,* maj. 24,559

*Forth, Eric (*b.* 1944) *C., Worcestershire Mid,* maj. 9,870

*Foster, Rt. Hon. Derek (*b.* 1937) *Lab., Bishop Auckland,* maj. 10,087

Foster, Donald M. E. (*b.* 1937) *LD, Bath,* maj. 3,768

*Foulkes, George (*b.* 1942) *Lab., Carrick, Cumnock and Doon Valley,* maj. 16,626

*Fowler, Rt. Hon. Sir Norman (*b.* 1938) *C., Sutton Coldfield,* maj. 26,036

Fox, Dr Liam (*b.* 1961) *C., Woodspring,* maj. 17,509

*Fox, Sir Marcus, MBE (*b.* 1927) *C., Shipley,* maj. 12,382

*Fraser, John D. (*b.* 1934) *Lab., Norwood,* maj. 7,216

*Freeman, Rt. Hon. Roger N. (*b.* 1942) *C., Kettering,* maj. 11,154

*French, Douglas C. (*b.* 1944) *C., Gloucester,* maj. 6,058

*Fry, Peter D. (*b.* 1931) *C., Wellingborough,* maj. 11,816

*Fyfe, Mrs Maria (*b.* 1938) *Lab., Glasgow, Maryhill,* maj. 13,419

*Galbraith, Samuel L. (*b.* 1945) *Lab., Strathkelvin and Bearsden,* maj. 3,162

*Gale, Roger J. (*b.* 1943) *C., Thanet North,* maj. 18,210

Gallie, Philip (*b.* 1939) *C., Ayr,* maj. 85

*Galloway, George (*b.* 1954) *Lab., Glasgow, Hillhead,* maj. 4,826

Gapes, Michael J. (*b.* 1952) *Lab., Ilford South,* maj. 402

*Gardiner, Sir George (*b.* 1935) *C., Reigate,* maj. 17,664

*Garel-Jones, Rt. Hon. (W. A. T.) Tristan (*b.* 1941) *C., Watford,* maj. 9,590

Garnier, Edward (*b.* 1952) *C., Harborough,* maj. 13,543

*Garrett, John L. (*b.* 1931) *Lab., Norwich South,* maj. 6,181

*George, Bruce T. (*b.* 1942) *Lab., Walsall South,* maj. 3,178

Gerrard, Neil F. (*b.* 1942) *Lab., Walthamstow,* maj. 3,022

*Gilbert, Rt. Hon. Dr John W. (*b.* 1927) *Lab., Dudley East,* maj. 9,200

*Gill, Christopher J. F., RD (*b.* 1936) *C., Ludlow,* maj. 14,152

Gillan, Ms Cheryl E. K. (*b.* 1952) *C., Chesham and Amersham,* maj. 22,220

*Godman, Norman A., PH.D. (*b.* 1938) *Lab., Greenock and Port Glasgow,* maj. 14,979

Godsiff, Roger D. (*b.* 1946) *Lab., Birmingham, Small Heath,* maj. 13,989

*Golding, Mrs Llinos (*b.* 1933) *Lab., Newcastle under Lyme,* maj. 9,839

*Goodlad, Rt. Hon. Alistair R. (*b.* 1943) *C., Eddisbury,* maj. 12,697

*Goodson-Wickes, Dr Charles (*b.* 1945) *C., Wimbledon,* maj. 14,761

*Gordon, Mrs Mildred (*b.* 1923) *Lab., Bow and Poplar,* maj. 8,404

*Gorman, Mrs Teresa E. (*b.* 1931) *C., Billericay,* maj. 22,494

*Gorst, John M. (*b.* 1928) *C., Hendon North,* maj. 7,122

*Gould, Bryan C. (*b.* 1939) *Lab., Dagenham,* maj. 6,733

*Graham, Thomas (*b.* 1944) *Lab., Renfrew West and Inverclyde,* maj. 1,744

*Grant, Sir Anthony (*b.* 1925) *C., Cambridgeshire South West,* maj. 19,637

*Grant, Bernard A. M. (*b.* 1944) *Lab., Tottenham,* maj. 11,968

*Greenway, Harry (*b.* 1934) *C., Ealing North,* maj. 5,966

*Greenway, John R. (*b.* 1946) *C., Ryedale,* maj. 18,439

*Griffiths, Nigel (*b.* 1955) *Lab., Edinburgh South,* maj. 4,176

*Griffiths, Peter H. S. (*b.* 1928) *C., Portsmouth North,* maj. 13,881

*Griffiths, Winston J. (*b.* 1943) *Lab., Bridgend,* maj. 7,326

*Grocott, Bruce J. (*b.* 1940) *Lab., The Wrekin,* maj. 6,648

*Grylls, Sir Michael (*b.* 1934) *C., Surrey North West,* maj. 28,394

*Gummer, Rt. Hon. John S. (*b.* 1939) *C., Suffolk Coastal,* maj. 19,285

Gunnell, W. John (*b.* 1933) *Lab., Leeds South and Morley,* maj. 7,372

*Hague, William J. (*b.* 1961) *C., Richmond (Yorks)* maj. 23,504

*Hain, Peter G. (*b.* 1950) *Lab., Neath,* maj. 23,975

Hall, Michael T. (*b.* 1952) *Lab., Warrington South,* maj. 191

*Hamilton, Rt. Hon. Archibald G. (*b.* 1941) *C., Epsom and Ewell,* maj. 20,021

*Hamilton, M. Neil (*b.* 1949) *C., Tatton,* maj. 15,860

*Hampson, Dr Keith (*b.* 1943) *C., Leeds North West,* maj. 7,671

*Hanley, Jeremy J. (*b.* 1945) *C., Richmond and Barnes,* maj. 3,869

*Hannam, Sir John (*b.* 1929) *C., Exeter,* maj. 4,045

Hanson, David G. (*b.* 1957) *Lab., Delyn,* maj. 2,039

*Hardy, Peter (*b.* 1931) *Lab., Wentworth,* maj. 22,449

*Hargreaves, Andrew R. (*b.* 1955) *C., Birmingham, Hall Green,* maj. 3,665

*Harman, Ms Harriet (*b.* 1950) *Lab., Peckham,* maj. 12,005

*Harris, David A. (*b.* 1937) *C., St Ives,* maj. 1,645

Harvey, Nicholas B. (*b.* 1961) *LD, Devon North,* maj. 794

*Haselhurst, Alan G. B. (*b.* 1937) *C., Saffron Walden,* maj. 17,424

*Morris, Michael W. L. (b. 1936) C., Northampton South, maj. 16,973
*Moss, Malcolm D. (b. 1943) C., Cambridgeshire North East, maj. 15,093
*Mowlam, Dr Marjorie (b. 1949) Lab., Redcar, maj. 11,577
Mudie, George (b. 1945) Lab., Leeds East, maj. 12,697
*Mullin, Christopher J. (b. 1947) Lab., Sunderland South, maj. 14,501
*Murphy, Paul P. (b. 1948) Lab., Torfaen, maj. 20,754
*Needham, Richard F. (The Earl of Kilmorey) (b. 1942) C., Wiltshire North, maj. 16,388
*Nelson, R. Anthony (b. 1948) C., Chichester, maj. 20,887
*Neubert, Sir Michael (b. 1933) C., Romford, maj. 11,420
*Newton, Rt. Hon. Antony H., OBE (b. 1937) C., Braintree, maj. 17,494
*Nicholls, Patrick C. M. (b. 1948) C., Teignbridge, maj. 8,856
*Nicholson, David J. (b. 1944) C., Taunton, maj. 3,336
*Nicholson, Miss Emma H. (b. 1941) C., Devon West and Torridge, maj. 3,614
*Norris, Steven J. (b. 1945) C., Epping Forest, maj. 20,188
*Oakes, Rt. Hon. Gordon J. (b. 1931) Lab., Halton, maj. 18,204
O'Brien, Michael (b. 1954) Lab., Warwickshire North, maj. 1,454
*O'Brien, William (b. 1929) Lab., Normanton, maj. 8,950
*O'Hara, Edward (b. 1937) Lab., Knowsley South, maj. 22,011
Olner, William J. (b. 1942) Lab., Nuneaton, maj. 1,631
*O'Neill, Martin J. (b. 1945) Lab., Clackmannan, maj. 8,503
*Onslow, Rt. Hon. Sir Cranley, KCMG (b. 1926) C., Woking, maj. 19,842
*Oppenheim, Hon. Phillip A. C. L. (b. 1956) C., Amber Valley, maj. 712
*Orme, Rt. Hon. Stanley (b. 1923) Lab., Salford East, maj. 11,235
Ottaway, Richard G. J. (b. 1945) C., Croydon South, maj. 20,425
*Page, Richard L. (b. 1941) C., Hertfordshire South West, maj. 20,107
*Paice, James E. T. (b. 1949) C., Cambridgeshire South East, maj. 23,810
*Paisley, Revd Ian R. K. (b. 1926) DUP, Antrim North, maj. 14,936
*Parry, Robert (b. 1933) Lab., Liverpool, Riverside, maj. 17,437
*Patchett, Terry (b. 1940) Lab., Barnsley East, maj. 24,777
*Patnick, C. Irvine, OBE (b. 1929) C., Sheffield, Hallam, maj. 6,741
*Patten, Rt. Hon. John H. C. (b. 1945) C., Oxford West and Abingdon, maj. 3,539
*Pattie, Rt. Hon. Sir Geoffrey (b. 1936) C., Chertsey and Walton, maj. 22,819
*Pawsey, James F. (b. 1933) C., Rugby and Kenilworth, maj. 13,247
*Peacock, Mrs Elizabeth J. (b. 1937) C., Batley and Spen, maj. 1,408
*Pendry, Thomas (b. 1934) Lab., Stalybridge and Hyde, maj. 8,831
Pickles, Eric J. (b. 1952) C., Brentwood and Ongar, maj. 15,145
Pickthall, Colin (b. 1944) Lab., Lancashire West, maj. 2,077
*Pike, Peter L. (b. 1937) Lab., Burnley, maj. 11,491
Pope, Gregory J. (b. 1960) Lab., Hyndburn, maj. 1,960
*Porter, David J. (b. 1948) C., Waveney, maj. 6,702
*Porter, G. B. (Barry) (b. 1939) C., Wirral South, maj. 8,183
*Portillo, Rt. Hon. Michael D. X. (b. 1953) C., Enfield, Southgate, maj. 15,563
*Powell, Raymond (b. 1928) Lab., Ogmore, maj. 23,827
*Powell, William R. (b. 1948) C., Corby, maj. 342

Prentice, Mrs Bridget (b. 1952) Lab., Lewisham East, maj. 1,095
Prentice, Gordon (b. 1951) Lab., Pendle, maj. 2,113
*Prescott, John L. (b. 1938) Lab., Hull East, maj. 18,719
*Primarolo, Ms Dawn (b. 1954) Lab., Bristol South, maj. 8,919
Purchase, Kenneth (b. 1939) Lab., Wolverhampton North East, maj. 3,939
*Quin, Miss Joyce G. (b. 1944) Lab., Gateshead East, maj. 18,530
*Radice, Giles H. (b. 1936) Lab., Durham North, maj. 19,637
*Randall, Stuart J. (b. 1938) Lab., Hull West, maj. 10,585
*Rathbone, J. R. (Tim) (b. 1933) C., Lewes, maj. 12,175
Raynsford, W. R. N. (Nick) (b. 1945) Lab., Greenwich, maj. 1,357
*Redmond, Martin (b. 1937) Lab., Don Valley, maj. 13,534
*Redwood, Rt. Hon. John A. (b. 1951) C., Wokingham, maj. 25,709
*Reid, Dr John (b. 1947) Lab., Motherwell North, maj. 18,910
Rendel, David D. (b. 1949) LD, Newbury, maj. 22,055
*Renton, Rt. Hon. R. Timothy (b. 1932) C., Sussex Mid, maj. 20,528
Richards, Roderick (b. 1947) C., Clwyd North West, maj. 6,050
*Richardson, Ms Josephine (b. 1923) Lab., Barking, maj. 6,268
*Riddick, Graham E. G. (b. 1955) C., Colne Valley, maj. 7,225
*Rifkind, Rt. Hon. Malcolm L., QC (b. 1946) C., Edinburgh, Pentlands, maj. 4,290
Robathan, Andrew R. G. (b. 1951) C., Blaby, maj. 25,347
*Roberts, Rt. Hon. Sir Wyn (b. 1930) C., Conwy, maj. 995
*Robertson, George I. M. (b. 1946) Lab., Hamilton, maj. 16,603
Robertson, Raymond S. (b. 1959) C., Aberdeen South, maj. 1,517
*Robinson, Geoffrey (b. 1938) Lab., Coventry North West, maj. 6,432
Robinson, Mark N. F. (b. 1946) C., Somerton and Frome, maj. 4,341
*Robinson, Peter D. (b. 1948) DUP, Belfast East, maj. 7,787
Roche, Mrs Barbara M. R. (b. 1954) Lab., Hornsey and Wood Green, maj. 5,177
*Roe, Mrs Marion A. (b. 1936) C., Broxbourne, maj. 23,970
*Rogers, Allan R. (b. 1932) Lab., Rhondda, maj. 28,816
*Rooker, Jeffrey W. (b. 1941) Lab., Birmingham, Perry Barr, maj. 8,590
*Rooney, Terence H. (b. 1950) Lab., Bradford North, maj. 7,664
*Ross, Ernest (b. 1942) Lab., Dundee West, maj. 10,604
*Ross, William (b. 1936) UUP, Londonderry East, maj. 18,527
*Rowe, Andrew (b. 1935) C., Kent Mid, maj. 19,649
*Rowlands, Edward (b. 1940) Lab., Merthyr Tydfil and Rhymney, maj. 26,713
*Ruddock, Mrs Joan M. (b. 1943) Lab., Lewisham, Deptford, maj. 12,238
*Rumbold, Rt. Hon. Dame Angela, DBE (b. 1932) C., Mitcham and Morden, maj. 1,734
*Ryder, Rt. Hon. Richard A., OBE (b. 1949) C., Norfolk Mid, maj. 18,948
*Sackville, Hon. Thomas G. (b. 1950) C., Bolton West, maj. 1,079
*Sainsbury, Rt. Hon. Timothy A. D. (b. 1932) C., Hove, maj. 12,268
*Salmond, Alexander E. A. (b. 1954) SNP, Banff and Buchan, maj. 4,108
*Scott, Rt. Hon. Nicholas P., MBE (b. 1933) C., Chelsea, maj. 12,789

*Whitney, Raymond W., OBE (b. 1930) C., *Wycombe*, maj. 17,076

Whittingdale, John F. L., OBE (b. 1959) C., *Colchester South and Maldon*, maj. 21,821

Wicks, Malcolm H. (b. 1947) Lab., *Croydon North West*, maj. 1,526

*Widdecombe, Miss Ann N. (b. 1947) C., *Maidstone*, maj. 16,286

*Wiggin, Sir Jerry, TD (b. 1937) C., *Weston-super-Mare*, maj. 5,342

*Wigley, Dafydd (b. 1943) PC, *Caernarfon*, maj. 14,476

*Wilkinson, John A. D. (b. 1940) C., *Ruislip-Northwood*, maj. 19,791

Willetts, David L. (b. 1956) C., *Havant*, maj. 17,584

*Williams, Rt. Hon. Alan J. (b. 1930) Lab., *Swansea West*, maj. 9,478

*Williams, Dr Alan W. (b. 1945) Lab., *Carmarthen*, maj. 2,922

*Wilshire, David (b. 1943) C., *Spelthorne*, maj. 19,843

*Wilson, Brian D. H. (b. 1948) Lab., *Cunninghame North*, maj. 2,939

*Winnick, David J. (b. 1933) Lab., *Walsall North*, maj. 3,824

*Winterton, Mrs J. Ann (b. 1941) C., *Congleton*, maj. 11,120

*Winterton, Nicholas R. (b. 1938) C., *Macclesfield*, maj. 22,767

*Wise, Mrs Audrey (b. 1935) Lab., *Preston*, maj. 12,175

*Wolfson, G. Mark (b. 1934) C., *Sevenoaks*, maj. 19,154

*Wood, Timothy J. R. (b. 1940) C., *Stevenage*, maj. 4,888

*Worthington, Anthony (b. 1941) Lab., *Clydebank and Milngavie*, maj. 12,430

*Wray, James (b. 1938) Lab., *Glasgow, Provan*, maj. 10,703

Wright, Anthony W., D.Phil. (b. 1948) Lab., *Cannock and Burntwood*, maj. 1,506

*Yeo, Timothy S. K. (b. 1945) C., *Suffolk South*, maj. 17,289

*Young, David W. (b. 1930) Lab., *Bolton South East*, maj. 12,691

*Young, Rt. Hon. Sir George, Bt. (b. 1941) C., *Ealing, Acton*, maj. 7,007

MEMBERS WITH SMALL MAJORITIES

The following MPs were returned in April 1992 with majorities of fewer than 1,000 votes

*Denotes membership of last Parliament

	Maj.
Walter Sweeney, C., *Vale of Glamorgan*	19
*Michael Stern, C., *Bristol North West*	45
*Terry Dicks, C., *Hayes and Harlington*	53
Phil Gallie, C., *Ayr*	85
Janet Anderson, Lab., *Rossendale and Darwen*	120
Jonathan Evans, C., *Brecon and Radnor*	130
Estelle Morris, Lab., *Birmingham Yardley*	162
*Peter Thurnham, C., *Bolton North East*	185
Mike Hall, Lab., *Warrington South*	191
*David Martin, C., *Portsmouth South*	242
Jamie Cann, Lab., *Ipswich*	265
*Patrick Thompson, C., *Norwich North*	266
*Malcolm Bruce, LD, *Gordon*	274
*William Powell, C., *Corby*	342
Mike Gapes, Lab., *Ilford South*	402
*Sir Russell Johnston, LD, *Inverness, Nairn and Lochaber*	458
*Alice Mahon, Lab., *Halifax*	478
*John Watts, C., *Slough*	514
John Denham, Lab., *Southampton Itchen*	551

	Maj.
Anne Campbell, Lab., *Cambridge*	580
*James Hill, C., *Southampton Test*	585
Dr Joe Hendron, SDLP, *Belfast West*	589
*Dr Ian Twinn, C., *Edmonton*	593
Neville Trotter, C., *Tynemouth*	597
Richard Burden, Lab., *Birmingham Northfield*	630
*Ann Taylor, Lab., *Dewsbury*	634
*Michael Forsyth, C., *Stirling*	703
*Phillip Oppenheim, C., *Amber Valley*	712
Nick Ainger, Lab., *Pembroke*	755
*David Sumberg, C., *Bury South*	788
Nick Harvey, LD, *Devon North*	794
*Graham Bright, C., *Luton South*	799
*David Shaw, C., *Dover*	833
*Lord James Douglas-Hamilton, C., *Edinburgh West*	879
*Sir Tom Arnold, C., *Hazel Grove*	929
*Andrew Welsh, SNP, *Angus East*	954
*David Ashby, C., *Leicestershire North West*	979
*Sir Wyn Roberts, C., *Conwy*	995

NEWBURY
(6 May 1993)
E.81,081   T.71.25%

D. Rendel, *LD*	37,590
J. Davidson, *C*	15,535
S. Billcliffe, *Lab*	1,151
A. Sked, *Anti-Maastricht Anti Fed.*	601
A. Bannon, *Conservative Candidate*	561
S. Martin, *Commoners Party Movement*	435
Lord Sutch, *Loony*	432
J. Wallis, *Green*	341
R. Marlar, *Referendum*	338
J. Browne, *Conservative Rebel*	267
Ms L. St Clair, *Corrective*	170
W. Board, *Maastricht Referendum for Britain*	84
M. Grenville, *NLP*	60
J. Day. *People and Pensioners*	49
C. Palmer, *21st Century*	40
M. Grbin, *Defence of Children's Humanity Bosnia*	33
A. Page, *SDP*	33
Ms A. Murphy, *Comm. GB*	32
M. Stone, *Give Royal Billions to Schools*	21
LD majority	22,055

CHRISTCHURCH
(29 July 1993)
E.71,868   T.74.2%

Mrs D. Maddock, *LD*	33,164
R. Hayward, *C*	16,737
N. Lickley, *Lab*	1,453
A. Sked, *Anti-Maastricht Anti Fed.*	878
Lord Sutch, *Monster Raving Loony Rock-Roll*	404
A. Bannon, *Conservative Candidate*	357
P. Newman, *Sack Graham Taylor*	80
Ms T. B. Jackson, *Buy Daily Sport*	67
P. Hollyman, *Save NHS*	60
J. Crockard, *Highlander IV Wednesday Promotion Night*	48
M. Griffiths, *NLP*	45
M. Belcher, *Ian for King*	23
K. Fitzhugh, *Alfred Chicken*	18
J. Walley, *Rainbow Alliance Coalition*	16
LD majority	16,427

Speakers of the Commons since 1708

The date of appointment given is the day on which the Speaker was first elected by the House of Commons. The appointment requires Royal approbation before it is confirmed and this is usually given within a few days. The present Speaker is the 155th.

PARLIAMENT OF GREAT BRITAIN

Sir Richard Onslow (*Lord Onslow*), 16 November 1708
William Bromley, 25 November 1710
Sir Thomas Hanmer, 16 February 1714
Spencer Compton (*Earl of Wilmington*), 17 March 1715
Arthur Onslow, 23 January 1728
Sir John Cust, 3 November 1761
Sir Fletcher Norton (*Lord Grantley*), 22 January 1770
Charles Cornwall, 31 October 1780
Hon. William Grenville (*Lord Grenville*), 5 January 1789
Henry Addington (*Viscount Sidmouth*), 8 June 1789

PARLIAMENT OF UNITED KINGDOM

Sir John Mitford (*Lord Redesdale*), 11 February 1801

Charles Abbot (*Lord Colchester*), 10 February 1802
Charles Manners-Sutton (*Viscount Canterbury*), 2 June 1817
James Abercromby (*Lord Dunfermline*), 19 February 1835
Charles Shaw-Lefevre (*Viscount Eversley*), 27 May 1839
J. Evelyn Denison (*Viscount Ossington*), 30 April 1857
Sir Henry Brand (*Viscount Hampden*), 9 February 1872
Arthur Wellesley Peel (*Viscount Peel*), 26 February 1884
William Gully (*Viscount Selby*), 10 April 1895
James Lowther (*Viscount Ullswater*), 8 June 1905
John Whitley, 27 April 1921
Hon. Edward Fitzroy, 20 June 1928
Douglas Clifton-Brown (*Viscount Ruffside*), 9 March 1943
William Morrison (*Viscount Dunrossil*), 31 October 1951
Sir Harry Hylton-Foster, 20 October 1959
Horace King (*Lord Maybray-King*), 26 October 1965
Selwyn Lloyd (*Lord Selwyn-Lloyd*), 12 January 1971
George Thomas (*Viscount Tonypandy*), 2 February 1976
Bernard Weatherill (*Lord Weatherill*), 15 June 1983
Betty Boothroyd, 27 April 1992

PARLIAMENTARY CONSTITUENCIES AS AT 9 APRIL 1992

The results of voting in each parliamentary division at the General Election of 9 April 1992 are given below. The majority in the 1987 General Election, and any subsequent by-elections, is given below the 1992 result.

Symbols

E.	Total number of electors in the constituency at the 1992 General Election
T.	Turnout of electors at the 1992 General Election
*	Member of the last Parliament

Abbreviations

All.	Alliance Party (NI)
C.	Conservative
DUP	Democratic Unionist Party
Green	Green Party
Ind.	Independent
Lab.	Labour
L./All.	Liberal Alliance
LD	Liberal Democrat
Lib.	Liberal
PC	Plaid Cymru
SD	Social Democrat
SDLP	Social Democratic and Labour Party
SDP	Social Democrat Party
SF	Sinn Fein
SNP	Scottish National Party
UPUP	Ulster Popular Unionist Party
UUP	Ulster Unionist Party
ADS	After Dinner Speaker
AFE	Anti-Federal Europe
Alt.	Alternative
Anti Fed.	Anti Federalist League
Anti H.	Anti-Heseltine Independent
APAKBI	Anti-Paddy Ashdown Keep Britain Independent

AS	Anglo Saxon
Bastion	Bastion Party
BNP	British National Party
Brewer	Jolly Small Brewers Party
Brit. Ind.	British Independence Party
CD	Christian Democrat
Century	21st Century Party
Choice	People's Choice
CL	Communist League
Comm. GB	Communist Party of Great Britain
CRA	Chauvinist Raving Alliance
CSP	Common Sense Party
C. Thatch.	Conservative Thatcherite
DLC	Democrat Liberal Conservative
DOS	Doctor of Stockwell
EFRA	Epping Forest Residents Association
ERIP	Equal Representation in Parliament
EUVJJ	End Unemployment Vote Justice for the Jobless
FDP	Fancy Dress Party
Fellowship	Fellowship Party
FP	Feudal Party
FTA	Fair Trials Abroad
FTM	Forward to Mars Party
Fun	Funstermentalist
Gremloids	Gremloids
Hardcore	The Altern-8-ive (Hardcore) Party
Homeland	Independent British Homeland Defence
Hove C.	Official Conservative Hove Party
IFM	Irish Freedom Movement
ILP	Independent Labour Party
Ind. U.	Independent Unionist
Int. Comm.	International Communist Party
Islamic	Islamic Party
ISS	Illegal Sunday Shopping
JBR	Justice from British Rail

Loony	Official Monster Raving Loony Party
Loony G.	Loony Green
LP	Lodestar Party
LTU	Labour and Trade Union
MBI	Morecambe Bay Independent
NA	Noise Abatement
Nat.	Nationalist
NF	National Front
NLP	Natural Law Party
Pensioners	Pensioners' Party
PP	People's Party
PPP	Peoples' Peace Party
PR	Proportional Representation
Prog. Soc.	Independent Progressive Socialist
Prot. Ref.	Protestant Reformation Party
QFL	Quality for Life Party
RAVA	Rainbow Ark Voters Association
RCC	Revolutionary Christian Communist
Real Bean	Real Bean
Rev. Comm.	Revolutionary Communist
Rizz	Rizz Party - Rainbow
Scallywagg	Scallywagg
SML	Scottish Militant Labour
SOADDA	Struck Off and Die Doctor's Alliance
Soc.	Socialist
Soc. Lab.	Socialist Labour
True Lab.	True Labour
UTCHAP	Up The Creek Have A Party
WAR	Workers Against Racism
Wessex	Save Wessex
Whiplash	Whiplash Corrective
WP	Workers' Party
WRP	Workers' Revolutionary Party
WUWC	Wake Up Wokingham Campaign
YSOR	Young Socialist – Occupy Ravenscraig

ENGLAND

ALDERSHOT (Hants)
E.81,754 T.78.71%

*J. Critchley, C.	36,974
A. Collett, LD	17,786
J. Anthony Smith, Lab.	8,552
D. Robinson, Lib.	1,038
C. majority	19,188

(June 1987, C. maj. 17,784)

ALDRIDGE-BROWNHILLS (W. Midlands)
E.63,404 T.82.55%

*R. Shepherd, C.	28,431
N. Fawcett, Lab.	17,407
S. Reynolds, LD	6,503
C. majority	11,024

(June 1987, C. maj. 12,396)

ALTRINCHAM AND SALE (Greater Manchester)
E.65,897 T.80.66%

*Sir F. Montgomery, C.	29,066
Ms M. Atherton, Lab.	12,275
J. Mulholland, LD	11,601

J. Renwick, NLP	212
C. majority	16,791

(June 1987, C. maj. 14,228)

AMBER VALLEY (Derbys)
E.70,155 T.84.69%

*Hon. P. Oppenheim, C.	27,418
J. Cooper, Lab.	26,706
G. Brocklebank, LD	5,294
C. majority	712

(June 1987, C. maj. 9,500)

ARUNDEL (W. Sussex)
E.79,241 T.77.06%

*Sir M. Marshall, C.	35,405
Dr J. Walsh, LD	15,542
R. Nash, Lab.	8,321
Mrs D. Renson, Lib.	1,103
R. Corbin, Green	693
C. majority	19,863

(June 1987, C. maj. 18,880)

ASHFIELD (Notts)
E.75,075 T.77.70%

G. Hoon, Lab.	32,018
L. Robertson, C.	19,031
J. Turton, LD	7,291
Lab. majority	12,987

(June 1987, Lab. maj. 4,400)

ASHFORD (Kent)
E.71,767 T.79.20%

*K. Speed, C.	31,031
Ms C. Headley, LD	13,672
Ms D. Cameron, Lab.	11,365
Dr A. Porter, Green	773
C. majority	17,359

(June 1987, C. maj. 15,488)

ASHTON-UNDER-LYNE (Greater Manchester)
E.58,701 T.73.87%

*Rt. Hon. R. Sheldon, Lab.	24,550
J. Pinniger, C.	13,615
C. Turner, LD	4,005
C. Hall, Lib.	907

J. Brannigan, *NLP* 289
Lab. majority 10,935
(June 1987, Lab. maj. 9,286)

AYLESBURY (Bucks)
E.79,208   T.80.29%
D. Lidington, *C.* 36,500
Ms S. Bowles, *LD* 17,640
R. Priest, *Lab.* 8,517
N. Foster, *Green* 702
B. D'Arcy, *NLP* 239
C. majority 18,860
(June 1987, C. maj. 16,558)

BANBURY (Oxon)
E.71,840   T.81.51%
*A. Baldry, *C.* 32,215
Ms A. Billingham, *Lab.* 15,495
G. Fisher, *LD* 10,602
Dr R. Ticiiati, *NLP* 250
C. majority 16,720
(June 1987, C. maj. 17,330)

BARKING (Greater London)
E.50,454   T.69.99%
*Ms J. Richardson, *Lab.* 18,224
J. Kennedy, *C.* 11,956
S. Churchman, *LD* 5,133
Lab. majority 6,268
(June 1987, Lab. maj. 3,409)

BARNSLEY CENTRAL (S. Yorks)
E.55,373   T.70.53%
*E. Illsley, *Lab.* 27,048
D. Senior, *C.* 7,687
S. Cowton, *LD* 4,321
Lab. majority 19,361
(June 1987, Lab. maj. 19,051)

BARNSLEY EAST (S. Yorks)
E.54,051   T.72.73%
*T. Patchett, *Lab.* 30,346
J. Procter, *C.* 5,569
Ms S. Anginotti, *LD* 3,399
Lab. majority 24,777
(June 1987, Lab. maj. 23,511)

BARNSLEY WEST AND
PENISTONE (S. Yorks)
E.63,374   T.75.75%
M. Clapham, *Lab.* 27,965
G. Sawyer, *C.* 13,461
I. Nicolson, *LD* 5,610
D. Jones, *Green* 970
Lab. majority 14,504
(June 1987, Lab. maj. 14,191)

BARROW AND FURNESS
(Cumbria)
E.67,764   T.82.11%
J. Hutton, *Lab.* 26,568
*C. Franks, *C.* 22,990
C. Crane, *LD* 6,089
Lab. majority 3,578
(June 1987, Lab. maj. 3,928)

BASILDON (Essex)
E.67,585   T.79.61%
*D. Amess, *C.* 24,159
J. Potter, *Lab.* 22,679
G. Williams, *LD* 6,967
C. majority 1,480
(June 1987, C. maj. 2,649)

BASINGSTOKE (Hants)
E.82,952   T.82.79%
*A. Hunter, *C.* 37,521
D. Bull, *Lab.* 16,323
C. Curtis, *LD* 14,119
Ms V. Oldaker, *Green* 714
C. majority 21,198
(June 1987, C. maj. 17,893)

BASSETLAW (Notts)
E.58,583   T.92.97%
*J. Ashton, *Lab.* 29,061
Mrs C. Spelman, *C.* 19,064
M. Reynolds, *LD* 6,340
Lab. majority 9,997
(June 1987, Lab. maj. 5,613)

BATH (Avon)
E.63,689   T.82.54%
D. Foster, *LD* 25,718
*Rt. Hon. C. Patten, *C.* 21,950
Ms P. Richards, *Lab.* 4,102
D. McCanlis, *Green* 433
Ms M. Barker, *Lib.* 172
Dr A. Sked, *Anti Fed.* 117
J. Rumming, *Ind.* 79
LD majority 3,768
(June 1987, C. maj. 1,412)

BATLEY AND SPEN (W. Yorks)
E.76,417   T.79.63%
*Mrs E. Peacock, *C.* 27,629
Mrs E. Durkin, *Lab.* 26,221
G. Beever, *LD* 6,380
C. Lord, *Green* 628
C. majority 1,408
(June 1987, C. maj. 1,362)

BATTERSEA (Greater London)
E.68,218   T.76.63%
*J. Bowis, *C.* 26,390
A. Dubs, *Lab.* 21,550
R. O'Brien, *LD* 3,659
I. Wingrove, *Green* 584
W. Stevens, *NLP* 98
C. majority 4,840
(June 1987, C. maj. 857)

BEACONSFIELD (Bucks)
E.64,268   T.82.27%
*T. Smith, *C.* 33,817
Ms A. Purse, *LD* 10,220
G. Smith, *Lab.* 7,163
W. Foulds, *Ind. C.* 1,317
A. Foss, *NLP* 196
Ms J. Martin, *ERIP* 166
C. majority 23,597
(June 1987, C. maj. 21,339)

BECKENHAM (Greater London)
E.59,440   T.77.86%
P. Merchant, *C.* 26,323
K. Ritchie, *Lab.* 11,038
Ms M. Williams, *LD* 8,038
G. Williams, *Lib.* 643
P. Shaw, *NLP* 243
C. majority 15,285
(June 1987, C. maj. 13,464)

BEDFORDSHIRE MID
E.81,864   T.84.45%
*Rt. Hon. Sir N. Lyell, *C.* 40,230
R. Clayton, *Lab.* 15,092

N. Hills, *LD* 11,957
P. Cottier, *Lib.* 1,582
M. Lorys, *NLP* 279
C. majority 25,138
(June 1987, C. maj. 22,851)

BEDFORDSHIRE NORTH
E.73,789   T.80.03%
*Sir T. Skeet, *C.* 29,920
P. Hall, *Lab.* 18,302
M. Smithson, *LD* 10,014
Ms L. Smith, *Green* 643
B. Bench, *NLP* 178
C. majority 11,618
(June 1987, C. maj. 16,505)

BEDFORDSHIRE SOUTH WEST
E.79,662   T.82.39%
*W. D. Madel, *C.* 37,498
B. Elliott, *Lab.* 16,225
M. Freeman, *LD* 10,988
P. Rollings, *Green* 689
D. Gilmour, *NLP* 239
C. majority 21,273
(June 1987, C. maj. 22,305)

BERKSHIRE EAST
E.90,365   T.81.41%
*A. Mackay, *C.* 43,898
Ms L. Murray, *LD* 15,218
K. Dibble, *Lab.* 14,458
C. majority 28,680
(June 1987, C. maj. 22,626)

BERWICK-UPON-TWEED
(Northumberland)
E.54,919   T.79.12%
*A. Beith, *LD* 19,283
Dr A. Henfrey, *C.* 14,240
Dr G. Adam, *Lab.* 9,933
LD majority 5,043
(June 1987, L./All. maj. 13,945)

BETHNAL GREEN AND STEPNEY
(Greater London)
E.55,675   T.65.45%
*Rt. Hon. P. Shore, *Lab.* 20,350
J. Shaw, *LD* 8,120
Miss J. Emmerson, *C.* 6,507
R. Edmonds, *BNP* 1,310
S. Kelsey, *Comm. GB* 156
Lab. majority 12,230
(June 1987, Lab. maj. 5,284)

BEVERLEY (Humberside)
E.81,198   T.79.69%
*J. Cran, *C.* 34,503
A. Collinge, *LD* 17,986
C. Challen, *Lab.* 12,026
D. Hetherington, *NLP* 199
C. majority 16,517
(June 1987, C. maj. 12,595)

BEXHILL AND BATTLE (E. Sussex)
E.65,850   T.78.99%
*C. Wardle, *C.* 31,330
Ms S. Prochak, *LD* 15,023
F. Taylor, *Lab.* 4,883
J. Prus, *Green* 594
Mrs M. Smith, *CSP* 190
C. majority 16,307
(June 1987, C. maj. 20,519)

BEXLEYHEATH (Greater London)
E.57,684   T.82.17%
*C. Townsend, C.	25,606
J. Browning, Lab.	11,520
Ms W. Chaplin, LD	10,107
R. Cundy, Ind.	170
C. majority	14,086
(June 1987, C. maj. 11,687)

BILLERICAY (Essex)
E.80,388   T.82.34%
*Mrs T. Gorman, C.	37,406
F. Bellard, LD	14,912
Ms A. Miller, Lab.	13,880
C. majority	22,494
(June 1987, C. maj. 18,016)

BIRKENHEAD (Merseyside)
E.62,682   T.72.96%
*F. Field, Lab.	29,098
R. Hughes, C.	11,485
P. Williams, LD	4,417
Ms T. Fox, Green	543
Ms B. Griffiths, NLP	190
Lab. majority	17,613
(June 1987, Lab. maj. 15,372)

BIRMINGHAM EDGBASTON
(W. Midlands)
E.53,041   T.71.29%
*Dame J. Knight, C.	18,529
J. Wilton, Lab.	14,222
I. Robertson-Steel, LD	4,419
P. Simpson, Green	643
C. majority	4,307
(June 1987, C. maj. 8,581)

BIRMINGHAM ERDINGTON
(W. Midlands)
E.52,398   T.70.15%
*R. Corbett, Lab.	18,549
S. Hope, C.	13,814
Dr J. Campbell, LD	4,398
Lab. majority	4,735
(June 1987, Lab. maj. 2,467)

BIRMINGHAM HALL GREEN
(W. Midlands)
E.60,091   T.78.17%
*A. Hargreaves, C.	21,649
Ms J. Slowey, Lab.	17,984
D. McGrath, LD	7,342
C. majority	3,665
(June 1987, C. maj. 7,621)

BIRMINGHAM HODGE HILL
(W. Midlands)
E.57,651   T.70.82%
*T. Davis, Lab.	21,895
Miss E. Gibson, C.	14,827
S. Hagan, LD	3,740
E. Whicker, NF	370
Lab. majority	7,068
(June 1987, Lab. maj. 4,789)

BIRMINGHAM LADYWOOD
(W. Midlands)
E.56,970   T.65.92%
*Ms C. Short, Lab.	24,887
Mrs B. Ashford, C.	9,604
B. Worth, LD	3,068
Lab. majority	15,283
(June 1987, Lab. maj. 10,028)

BIRMINGHAM NORTHFIELD
(W. Midlands)
E.70,533   T.76.08%
R. Burden, Lab.	24,433
*R. King, C.	23,803
D. Cropp, LD	5,431
Lab. majority	630
(June 1987, C. maj. 3,135)

BIRMINGHAM PERRY BARR
(W. Midlands)
E.72,161   T.71.62%
*J. Rooker, Lab.	27,507
G. Green, C.	18,917
T. Philpott, LD	5,261
Lab. majority	8,590
(June 1987, Lab. maj. 6,933)

BIRMINGHAM SELLY OAK
(W. Midlands)
E.72,150   T.76.61%
Ms L. Jones, Lab.	25,430
*A. Beaumont-Dark, C.	23,370
D. Osborne, LD	5,679
P. Slatter, Green	535
C. Barwood, NLP	178
K. Malik, Rev Comm	84
Lab. majority	2,060
(June 1987, C. maj. 2,584)

BIRMINGHAM SMALL HEATH
(W. Midlands)
E.55,213   T.62.95%
R. Godsiff, Lab.	22,675
A. Qayyum Chaudhary, C.	8,686
H. Thomas, LD	2,575
Ms H. Clawley, Green	824
Lab. majority	13,989
(June 1987, Lab. maj. 15,521)

BIRMINGHAM SPARKBROOK
(W. Midlands)
E.51,677   T.66.80%
*Rt. Hon. R. Hattersley, Lab.	22,116
M. Khamisa, C.	8,544
D. Parry, LD	3,028
C. Alldrick, Green	833
Lab. majority	13,572
(June 1987, Lab. maj. 11,859)

BIRMINGHAM YARDLEY
(W. Midlands)
E.54,749   T.77.98%
Ms E. Morris, Lab.	14,884
*A. D. G. Bevan, C.	14,722
J. Hemming, LD	12,899
Miss P. Read, NF	192
Lab. majority	162
(June 1987, C. maj. 2,522)

BISHOP AUCKLAND (Durham)
E.72,572   T.76.52%
*D. Foster, Lab.	27,763
D. Williamson, C.	17,676
W. Wade, LD	10,099
Lab. majority	10,087
(June 1987, Lab. maj. 7,035)

BLABY (Leics)
E.81,790   T.83.39%
A. Robathan, C.	39,498
Ms E. Ranson, Lab.	14,151

Ms M. Lewin, LD	13,780
J. Peacock, BNP	521
Ms S. Lincoln, NLP	260
C. majority	25,347
(June 1987, C. maj. 22,176)

BLACKBURN (Lancs)
E.73,251   T.75.05%
*J. Straw, Lab.	26,633
R. Coates, C.	20,606
D. Mann, LD	6,332
R. Field, Green	878
Mrs M. Carmichael-Grimshaw, LP	334
W. Ayliffe, NLP	195
Lab. majority	6,027
(June 1987, Lab. maj. 5,497)

BLACKPOOL NORTH (Lancs)
E.58,087   T.77.55%
H. Elletson, C.	21,501
E. Kirton, Lab.	18,461
A. Lahiff, LD	4,786
Sir G. Francis, Loony	178
H. Walker, NLP	125
C. majority	3,040
(June 1987, C. maj. 7,321)

BLACKPOOL SOUTH (Lancs)
E.56,801   T.77.35%
N. Hawkins, C.	19,880
G. Marsden, Lab.	18,213
R. Wynne, LD	5,675
D. Henning, NLP	173
C. majority	1,667
(June 1987, C. maj. 6,744)

BLAYDON (Tyne & Wear)
E.66,044   T.77.69%
*J. McWilliam, Lab.	27,028
P. Pescod, C.	13,685
P. Nunn, LD	10,602
Lab. majority	13,343
(June 1987, Lab. maj. 12,488)

BLYTH VALLEY (Northumberland)
E.60,913   T.80.77%
*R. Campbell, Lab.	24,542
P. Tracey, LD	16,498
M. Revell, C.	7,691
S. Tyley, Green	470
Lab. majority	8,044
(June 1987, Lab. maj. 853)

BOLSOVER (Derbys)
E.66,693   T.78.94%
*D. Skinner, Lab.	33,973
T. James, C.	13,313
Ms S. Barber, LD	5,363
Lab. majority	20,660
(June 1987, Lab. maj. 14,120)

BOLTON NORTH EAST (Greater Manchester)
E.58,659   T.82.26%
*P. Thurnham, C.	21,644
D. Crausby, Lab.	21,459
B. Dunning, LD	4,971
P. Tong, NLP	181
C. majority	185
(June 1987, C. maj. 813)

BOLTON SOUTH EAST (Greater Manchester)
E.65,600　T.75.53%
*D. Young, Lab.　26,906
N. Wood-Dow, C.　14,215
D. Lee, LD　5,243
W. Hardman, Ind. Lab.　2,894
L. Walch, NLP　290
Lab. majority　12,691
(June 1987, Lab. maj. 11,381)

BOLTON WEST (Greater Manchester)
E.71,344　T.83.53%
*Hon. T. Sackville, C.　26,452
C. Morris, Lab.　25,373
Ms B. Ronson, LD　7,529
Ms J. Phillips, NLP　240
C. majority　1,079
(June 1987, C. maj. 4,593)

BOOTHFERRY (Humberside)
E.80,747　T.79.73%
*D. Davis, C.　35,266
Ms L. Coubrough, Lab.　17,731
J. Goss, LD　11,388
C. majority　17,535
(June 1987, C. maj. 18,970)

BOOTLE (Merseyside)
E.69,308　T.72.46%
*J. Benton, Lab.　37,464
C. Varley, C.　8,022
J. Cunningham, LD　3,301
Ms M. Hall, Lib.　1,174
T. Haynes, NLP　264
Lab. majority　29,442
(June 1987, Lab. maj. 24,477)
(May 1990, Lab. maj. 23,517)
(November 1990, Lab. maj. 19,465)

BOSWORTH (Leics)
E.80,234　T.84.13%
*D. Tredinnick, C.　36,618
D. Everitt, Lab.　17,524
G. Drozdz, LD　12,643
B. Fewster, Green　716
C. majority　19,094
(June 1987, C. maj. 17,016)

BOURNEMOUTH EAST (Dorset)
E.75,089　T.72.82%
*D. Atkinson, C.　30,820
N. Russell, LD　15,997
P. Brushett, Lab.　7,541
Ms S. Holmes, NLP　329
C. majority　14,823
(June 1987, C. maj. 14,683)

BOURNEMOUTH WEST (Dorset)
E.74,738　T.75.72%
*J. Butterfill, C.　29,820
Ms J. Dover, LD　17,178
B. Grower, Lab.　9,423
A. Springham, NLP　232
C. majority　12,642
(June 1987, C. maj. 12,651)

BOW AND POPLAR (Greater London)
E.56,685　T.65.84%
*Mrs M. Gordon, Lab.　18,487
P. Hughes, LD　10,083

S. Pearce, C.　6,876
J. Tyndall, BNP　1,107
S. Petter, Green　612
W. Hite, NLP　158
Lab. majority　8,404
(June 1987, Lab. maj. 4,631)

BRADFORD NORTH (W. Yorks)
E.66,719　T.73.38%
*T. Rooney, Lab.　23,420
M. Riaz, C.　15,756
D. Ward, LD　9,133
W. Beckett, Loony　350
M. Nasr, Islamic　304
Lab. majority　7,664
(June 1987, Lab. maj. 1,663)
(November 1990, Lab. maj. 9,514)

BRADFORD SOUTH (W. Yorks)
E.69,914　T.75.61%
*G. R. Cryer, Lab.　25,185
A. Popat, C.　20,283
B. Boulton, LD　7,243
M. Naseem, Islamic　156
Lab. majority　4,902
(June 1987, Lab. maj. 309)

BRADFORD WEST (W. Yorks)
E.70,016　T.69.90%
*M. Madden, Lab.　26,046
Dr A. Ashworth, C.　16,544
Dr. A. Griffiths, LD　5,150
P. Braham, Green　735
D. Pidcock, Islamic　471
Lab. majority　9,502
(June 1987, Lab. maj. 7,551)

BRAINTREE (Essex)
E.78,880　T.83.41%
*Rt. Hon. A. Newton, C.　34,415
I. Willmore, Lab.　16,921
Ms D. Wallis, LD　13,603
J. Abbott, Green　855
C. majority　17,494
(June 1987, C. maj. 16,857)

BRENT EAST (Greater London)
E.53,319　T.68.82%
*K. Livingstone, Lab.　19,387
D. Green, C.　13,416
M. Cummins, LD　3,249
Ms T. Dean, Green　548
Ms A. Murphy, Comm. GB　96
Lab. majority　5,971
(June 1987, Lab. maj. 1,653)

BRENT NORTH (Greater London)
E.58,917　T.70.57%
*Rt. Hon. Sir R. Boyson, C.　23,445
J. Moher, Lab.　13,314
P. Lorber, LD　4,149
T. Vipul, Ind.　356
T. Davids, NLP　318
C. majority　10,131
(June 1987, C. maj. 15,720)

BRENT SOUTH (Greater London)
E.56,034　T.64.10%
*P. Boateng, Lab.　20,662
R. Blackman, C.　10,957
M. Harskin, LD　3,658
D. Johnson, Green　479

C. Jani, NLP　166
Lab. majority　9,705
(June 1987, Lab. maj. 7,931)

BRENTFORD AND ISLEWORTH (Greater London)
E.70,880　T.76.22%
N. Deva, C.　24,752
Ms A. Keen, Lab.　22,666
Ms J. Salmon, LD　5,683
J. Bradley, Green　927
C. majority　2,086
(June 1987, C. maj. 7,953)

BRENTWOOD AND ONGAR (Greater London)
E.65,830　T.84.70%
E. Pickles, C.　32,145
Ms E. Bottomley, LD　17,000
F. Keohane, Lab.　6,080
Ms C. Bartley, Green　535
C. majority　15,145
(June 1987, C. maj. 18,921)

BRIDGWATER (Somerset)
E.71,567　T.79.51%
*Rt. Hon. T. King, C.　26,610
W. Revans, LD　16,894
P. James, Lab.　12,365
G. Dummett, Green　746
A. Body, Ind.　183
Ms G. Sanson, NLP　112
C. majority　9,716
(June 1987, C. maj. 11,195)

BRIDLINGTON (Humberside)
E.84,829　T.77.93%
*J. Townend, C.　33,604
J. Leeman, LD　17,246
S. Hatfield, Lab.　15,263
C. majority　16,358
(June 1987, C. maj. 17,321)

BRIGG AND CLEETHORPES (Humberside)
E.82,377　T.77.98%
*M. Brown, C.　31,673
I. Cawsey, Lab.　22,404
Ms M. Cockbill, LD　9,374
N. Jacques, Green　790
C. majority　9,269
(June 1987, C. maj. 12,250)

BRIGHTON KEMPTOWN (E. Sussex)
E.57,646　T.76.14%
*A. Bowden, C.　21,129
Ms G. Haynes, Lab.　18,073
P. Scott, LD　4,461
Ms E. Overall, NLP　230
C. majority　3,056
(June 1987, C. maj. 9,260)

BRIGHTON PAVILION (E. Sussex)
E.57,616　T.76.81%
D. Spencer, C.　20,630
D. Lepper, Lab.　16,955
T. Pearce, LD　5,606
I. Brodie, Green　963
Ms E. Turner, NLP　103
C. majority　3,675
(June 1987, C. maj. 9,142)

Bristol East (Avon)
E.62,577   T.80.40%

Ms J. Corston, *Lab.*	22,418
*J. Sayeed, *C.*	19,726
J. Kiely, *LD*	7,903
I. Anderson, *NF*	270
Lab. majority	2,692

(June 1987, C. maj. 4,123)

Bristol North West (Avon)
E.72,726   T.82.35%

*M. Stern, *C.*	25,354
D. Naysmith, *Lab.*	25,309
J. Taylor, *LD*	8,498
H. Long, *SD*	729
C. majority	45

(June 1987, C. maj. 6,952)

Bristol South (Avon)
E.64,309   T.78.04%

*Ms D. Primarolo, *Lab.*	25,164
J. Bercow, *C.*	16,245
P. Crossley, *LD*	7,892
J. Boxall, *Green*	756
N. Phillips, *NLP*	136
Lab. majority	8,919

(June 1987, Lab. maj. 1,404)

Bristol West (Avon)
E.70,579   T.74.37%

*Rt. Hon. W. Waldegrave, *C.*	22,169
C. Boney, *LD*	16,098
H. Bashforth, *Lab.*	12,992
A. Sawday, *Green*	906
D. Cross, *NLP*	104
B. Brent, *Rev. Comm.*	92
P. Hammond, *SOADDA*	87
T. Hedges, *Anti Fed.*	42
C. majority	6,071

(June 1987, C. maj. 7,703)

Bromsgrove (H & W)
E.71,111   T.82.49%

K. R. Thomason, *C.*	31,709
Ms C. Mole, *Lab.*	18,007
Ms A. Cassin, *LD*	8,090
J. Churchman, *Green*	856
C. majority	13,702

(June 1987, C. maj. 16,685)

Broxbourne (Herts)
E.72,116   T.79.95%

*Mrs M. Roe, *C.*	36,094
M. Hudson, *Lab.*	12,124
Mrs J. Davies, *LD*	9,244
G. Woolhouse, *NLP*	198
C. majority	23,970

(June 1987, C. maj. 22,995)

Broxtowe (Notts)
E.73,123   T.83.40%

*J. Lester, *C.*	31,096
J. Walker, *Lab.*	21,205
J. Ross, *LD*	8,395
D. Lukehurst, *NLP*	293
C. majority	9,891

(June 1987, C. maj. 16,651)

Buckingham
E.56,063   T.84.21%

*G. Walden, *C.*	29,496
T. Jones, *LD*	9,705

K. White, *Lab.*	7,662
L. Sheaff, *NLP*	353
C. majority	19,791

(June 1987, C. maj. 18,526)

Burnley (Lancs)
E.68,952   T.74.38%

*P. Pike, *Lab.*	27,184
Mrs B. Binge, *C.*	15,693
G. Birtwistle, *LD*	8,414
Lab. majority	11,491

(June 1987, Lab. maj. 7,557)

Burton (Staffs)
E.75,292   T.82.43%

*I. Lawrence, *C.*	30,845
Ms P. Muddyman, *Lab.*	24,849
R. Renold, *LD*	6,375
C. majority	5,996

(June 1987, C. maj. 9,830)

Bury North (Greater Manchester)
E.69,529   T.84.77%

*A. Burt, *C.*	29,266
J. Dobbin, *Lab.*	24,502
C. McGrath, *LD*	5,010
M. Sullivan, *NLP*	163
C. majority	4,764

(June 1987, C. maj. 6,929)

Bury South (Greater Manchester)
E.65,793   T.82.10%

*D. Sumberg, *C.*	24,873
Ms H. Blears, *Lab.*	24,085
A. Cruden, *LD*	4,832
Mrs N. Sullivan, *NLP*	228
C. majority	788

(June 1987, C. maj. 2,679)

Bury St Edmunds (Suffolk)
E.79,967   T.78.38%

R. Spring, *C.*	33,554
T. Sheppard, *Lab.*	14,767
J. Williams, *LD*	13,814
Ms J. Lillis, *NLP*	550
C. majority	18,787

(June 1987, C. maj. 21,458)

Calder Valley (W. Yorks)
E.74,417   T.82.09%

*Sir D. Thompson, *C.*	27,753
D. Chaytor, *Lab.*	22,875
S. Pearson, *LD*	9,842
Ms V. Smith, *Green*	622
C. majority	4,878

(June 1987, C. maj. 6,045)

Cambridge
E.69,022   T.73.18%

Mrs A. Campbell, *Lab.*	20,039
M. Bishop, *C.*	19,459
D. Howarth, *LD*	10,037
T. Cooper, *Green*	720
D. Brettell-Winnington, *Loony*	175
R. Chalmers, *NLP*	83
Lab. majority	580

(June 1987, C. maj. 5,060)

Cambridgeshire North East
E.79,935   T.79.38%

*M. Moss, *C.*	34,288
M. Leeke, *LD*	19,195
R. Harris, *Lab.*	8,746
C. Ash, *Lib.*	998
Mrs M. Chalmers, *NLP*	227
C. majority	15,093

(June 1987, C. maj. 1,428)

Cambridgeshire South East
E.78,600   T.80.57%

*J. Paice, *C.*	36,693
R. Wotherspoon, *LD*	12,883
M. Jones, *Lab.*	12,688
J. Marsh, *Green*	836
Ms B. Langridge, *NLP*	231
C. majority	23,810

(June 1987, C. maj. 17,502)

Cambridgeshire South West
E.84,418   T.81.10%

*Sir A. Grant, *C.*	38,902
Ms S. Sutton, *LD*	19,265
K. Price, *Lab.*	9,378
Ms L. Whitebread, *Green*	699
F. Chalmers, *NLP*	225
C. majority	19,637

(June 1987, C. maj. 18,251)

Cannock and Burntwood (Staffs)
E.72,600   T.84.21%

A. Wright, *Lab.*	28,139
*G. Howarth, *C.*	26,633
P. Treasaden, *LD*	5,899
M. Hartshorne, *Loony*	469
Lab. majority	1,506

(June 1987, C. maj. 2,689)

Canterbury (Kent)
E.75,181   T.78.12%

*J. Brazier, *C.*	29,827
M. Vye, *LD*	19,022
M. Whitemore, *Lab.*	8,936
Ms W. Arnall, *Green*	747
Ms S. Curphey, *NLP*	203
C. majority	10,805

(June 1987, C. maj. 14,891)

Carlisle (Cumbria)
E.55,140   T.79.39%

*E. Martlew, *Lab.*	20,479
C. Condie, *C.*	17,371
R. Aldersey, *LD*	5,740
Ms N. Robinson, *NLP*	190
Lab. majority	3,108

(June 1987, Lab. maj. 916)

Carshalton and Wallington (Surrey)
E.65,179   T.80.94%

*F. N. Forman, *C.*	26,243
T. Brake, *LD*	16,300
Ms M. Moran, *Lab.*	9,333
R. Steel, *Green*	614
D. Bamford, *Loony G.*	266
C. majority	9,943

(June 1987, C. maj. 14,409)

CASTLE POINT (Essex)
E.66,229 T.80.50%

Dr R. Spink, *C.*		29,629
D. Flack, *Lab.*		12,799
A. Petchey, *LD*		10,208
Ms I. Willis, *Green*		683
C. majority		16,830
(June 1987, C. maj. 19,248)		

CHEADLE (Greater Manchester)
E.66,131 T.84.43%

*S. Day, *C.*		32,504
Ms P. Calton, *LD*		16,726
Ms S. Broadhurst, *Lab.*		6,442
Ms P. Whittle, *NLP*		168
C. majority		15,778
(June 1987, C. maj. 10,631)		

CHELMSFORD (Essex)
E.83,441 T.84.61%

*S. Burns, *C.*		39,043
H. Nicholson, *LD*		20,783
Dr R. Chad, *Lab.*		10,010
Ms E. Burgess, *Green*		769
C. majority		18,260
(June 1987, C. maj. 7,761)		

CHELSEA (Greater London)
E.42,371 T.63.31%

*Rt. Hon. N. Scott, *C.*		17,471
Ms R. Horton, *Lab.*		4,682
Ms S. Broidy, *LD*		4,101
Ms N. Kortvelyessy, *Green*		485
D. Armstrong, *Anti Fed.*		88
C. majority		12,789
(June 1987, C. maj. 13,319)		

CHELTENHAM (Glos)
E.79,808 T.80.32%

N. Jones, *LD*		30,351
J. Taylor, *C.*		28,683
Ms P. Tatlow, *Lab.*		4,077
M. Rendall, *AFE*		665
H. Brighouse, *NLP*		169
M. Bruce-Smith, *Ind.*		162
LD majority		1,668
(June 1987, C. maj. 4,896)		

CHERTSEY AND WALTON (Surrey)
E.70,465 T.80.52%

*Rt. Hon. Sir G. Pattie, *C.*		34,163
A. Kremer, *LD*		11,344
Ms I. Hamilton, *Lab.*		10,791
Ms S. Bennell, *NLP*		444
C. majority		22,819
(June 1987, C. maj. 17,469)		

CHESHAM AND AMERSHAM (Bucks)
E.69,895 T.81.93%

Ms C. Gillan, *C.*		36,273
A. Ketteringham, *LD*		14,053
Ms C. Atherton, *Lab.*		5,931
Ms C. Strickland, *Green*		753
T. Griffith-Jones, *NLP*		255
C. majority		22,220
(June 1987, C. maj. 19,440)		

CHESTER, CITY OF
E.63,370 T.83.84%

G. Brandreth, *C.*		23,411
D. Robinson, *Lab.*		22,310

G. Smith, *LD*		6,867
T. Barker, *Green*		448
S. Cross, *NLP*		98
C. majority		1,101
(June 1987, C. maj. 4,855)		

CHESTERFIELD (Derbys)
E.71,783 T.77.98%

*A. Benn, *Lab.*		26,461
A. Rogers, *LD*		20,047
P. Lewis, *C.*		9,473
Lab. majority		6,414
(June 1987, Lab. maj. 8,577)		

CHICHESTER (W. Sussex)
E.82,124 T.77.77%

*R. A. Nelson, *C.*		37,906
P. Gardiner, *LD*		17,019
Ms D. Andrewes, *Lab.*		7,192
E. Paine, *Green*		876
Ms J. Weights, *Lib.*		643
Ms J. Jackson, *NLP*		238
C. majority		20,887
(June 1987, C. maj. 20,177)		

CHINGFORD (Greater London)
E.55,401 T.78.41%

G. I. Duncan-Smith, *C.*		25,730
P. Dawe, *Lab.*		10,792
S. Banks, *LD*		5,705
D. Green, *Lib.*		602
J. Baguley, *Green*		575
Revd C. John, *Ind.*		41
C. majority		14,938
(June 1987, C. maj. 17,955)		

CHIPPING BARNET (Greater London)
E.57,153 T.78.57%

*S. Chapman, *C.*		25,589
A. Williams, *Lab.*		11,638
D. Smith, *LD*		7,247
Ms D. Derksen, *NLP*		222
C. Johnson, *Fun.*		213
C. majority		13,951
(June 1987, C. maj. 14,871)		

CHISLEHURST (Greater London)
E.53,782 T.78.89%

*R. Sims, *C.*		24,761
I. Wingfield, *Lab.*		9,485
W. Hawthorne, *LD*		6,683
I. Richmond, *Lib.*		849
Dr F. Speed, *Green*		652
C. majority		15,276
(June 1987, C. maj. 14,507)		

CHORLEY (Lancs)
E.78,531 T.82.81%

*D. Dover, *C.*		30,715
R. McManus, *Lab.*		26,469
Ms J. Ross-Mills, *LD*		7,452
P. Leadbetter, *NLP*		402
C. majority		4,246
(June 1987, C. maj. 8,057)		

CHRISTCHURCH (Dorset)
E.71,438 T.80.70%

*R. Adley, *C.*		36,627
Revd D. Bussey, *LD*		13,612
A. Lloyd, *Lab.*		6,997
J. Barratt, *NLP*		243

A. Wareham, *CRA*		175
C. majority		23,015
(June 1987, C. maj. 22,374)		
See also page 242		

CIRENCESTER AND TEWKESBURY (Glos)
E.88,299 T.82.05%

G. Clifton-Brown, *C.*		40,258
E. Weston, *LD*		24,200
T. Page, *Lab.*		7,262
R. Clayton, *NLP*		449
P. Trice-Rolph, *Ind.*		287
C. majority		16,058
(June 1987, C. maj. 12,662)		

CITY OF LONDON AND WESTMINSTER SOUTH
E.55,021 T.63.08%

*Rt. Hon. P. Brooke, *C.*		20,938
C. Smith, *Lab.*		7,569
Ms J. Smithard, *LD*		5,392
G. Herbert, *Green*		458
P. Stockton, *Loony*		147
A. Farrell, *IFM*		107
R. Johnson, *NLP*		101
C. majority		13,369
(June 1987, C. maj. 12,034)		

COLCHESTER NORTH (Essex)
E.86,479 T.79.11%

Hon. B. Jenkin, *C.*		35,213
Dr J. Raven, *LD*		18,721
D. Lee, *Lab.*		13,870
M. Tariq Shabbeer, *Green*		372
M. Mears, *NLP*		238
C. majority		16,492
(June 1987, C. maj. 13,623)		

COLCHESTER SOUTH AND MALDON (Essex)
E.86,410 T.79.22%

J. Whittingdale, *C.*		37,548
I. Thorn, *LD*		15,727
C. Pearson, *Lab.*		14,158
M. Patterson, *Green*		1,028
C. majority		21,821
(June 1987, C. maj. 15,483)		

COLNE VALLEY (W. Yorks)
E.72,043 T.81.97%

*G. Riddick, *C.*		24,804
J. Harman, *Lab.*		17,579
N. Priestley, *LD*		15,953
R. Stewart, *Green*		443
Mrs M. Staniforth, *Loony*		160
J. Hasty, *Ind.*		73
J. Tattersall, *NLP*		44
C. majority		7,225
(June 1987, C. maj. 1,677)		

CONGLETON (Cheshire)
E.70,477 T.84.47%

*Mrs J. A. Winterton, *C.*		29,163
I. Brodie-Browne, *LD*		18,043
M. Finnegan, *Lab.*		11,927
P. Brown, *NLP*		399
C. majority		11,120
(June 1987, C. maj. 7,969)		

COPELAND (Cumbria)
E.54,911   T.83.54%
*Dr J. Cunningham, *Lab.*	22,328
P. Davies, *C.*	19,889
R. Putnam, *LD*	3,508
J. Sinton, *NLP*	148
Lab. majority	2,439

(June 1987, Lab. maj. 1,894)

CORBY (Northants)
E.68,333   T.82.88%
*W. Powell, *C.*	25,203
A. Feather, *Lab.*	24,861
M. Roffe, *LD*	5,792
Ms J. Wood, *Lib.*	784
C. majority	342

(June 1987, C. maj. 1,805)

CORNWALL NORTH
E.76,844   T.81.51%
P. Tyler, *LD*	29,696
*Sir G. Neale, *C.*	27,775
F. Jordan, *Lab.*	4,103
P. Andrews, *Lib.*	678
G. Rowe, *Ind.*	276
Mrs H. Treadwell, *NLP*	112
LD majority	1,921

(June 1987, C. maj. 5,682)

CORNWALL SOUTH EAST
E.73,027   T.82.14%
*R. Hicks, *C.*	30,565
R. Teverson, *LD*	22,861
Mrs L. Gilroy, *Lab.*	5,536
Miss M. Cook, *Lib.*	644
A. Quick, *Anti Fed.*	227
Miss R. Allen, *NLP*	155
C. majority	7,704

(June 1987, C. maj. 6,607)

COVENTRY NORTH EAST
(W. Midlands)
E.64,787   T.73.20%
R. Ainsworth, *Lab.*	24,896
K. Perrin, *C.*	13,220
V. McKee, *LD*	5,306
*J. Hughes, *Ind. Lab.*	4,008
Lab. majority	11,676

(June 1987, Lab. maj. 11,867)

COVENTRY NORTH WEST
(W. Midlands)
E.50,670   T.77.63%
*G. Robinson, *Lab.*	20,349
Mrs A. Hill, *C.*	13,917
Ms A. Simpson, *LD*	5,070
Lab. majority	6,432

(June 1987, Lab. maj. 5,663)

COVENTRY SOUTH EAST
(W. Midlands)
E.48,796   T.74.87%
J. Cunningham, *Lab.*	11,902
Mrs M. Hyams, *C.*	10,591
*D. Nellist, *Ind. Lab.*	10,551
A. Armstrong, *LD*	3,318
N. Tompkinson, *NF*	173
Lab. majority	1,311

(June 1987, Lab. maj. 6,653)

COVENTRY SOUTH WEST
(W. Midlands)
E.63,474   T.80.14%
*J. Butcher, *C.*	23,225
R. Slater, *Lab.*	21,789
G. Sewards, *LD*	4,666
R. Wheway, *Lib.*	989
D. Morris, *NLP*	204
C. majority	1,436

(June 1987, C. maj. 3,210)

CRAWLEY (W. Sussex)
E.78,277   T.79.16%
*Hon. A. N. Soames, *C.*	30,204
Ms L. Moffatt, *Lab.*	22,439
G. Seekings, *LD*	8,558
M. Wilson, *Green*	766
C. majority	7,765

(June 1987, C. maj. 12,138)

CREWE AND NANTWICH
(Cheshire)
E.74,993   T.81.87%
*Hon. Mrs G. Dunwoody, *Lab.*	28,065
B. Silvester, *C.*	25,370
G. Griffiths, *LD*	7,315
Ms N. Wilkinson, *Green*	651
Lab. majority	2,695

(June 1987, Lab. maj. 1,092)

CROSBY (Merseyside)
E.82,537   T.82.45%
*M. Thornton, *C.*	32,267
Ms M. Eagle, *Lab.*	17,461
Ms F. Clucas, *LD*	16,562
J. Marks, *Lib.*	1,052
S. Brady, *Green*	559
N. Paterson, *NLP*	152
C. majority	14,806

(June 1987, C. maj. 6,853)

CROYDON CENTRAL (Greater
London)
E.55,798   T.71.73%
Sir P. Beresford, *C.*	22,168
G. Davies, *Lab.*	12,518
Ms D. Richardson, *LD*	5,342
C. majority	9,650

(June 1987, C. maj. 12,617)

CROYDON NORTH EAST (Greater
London)
E.64,405   T.72.01%
D. Congdon, *C.*	23,835
Ms M. Walker, *Lab.*	16,362
J. Fraser, *LD*	6,186
C. majority	7,473

(June 1987, C. maj. 12,519)

CROYDON NORTH WEST (Greater
London)
E.57,241   T.70.76%
M. Wicks, *Lab.*	19,152
*H. Malins, *C.*	17,626
Ms L. Hawkins, *LD*	3,728
Lab. majority	1,526

(June 1987, C. maj. 3,988)

CROYDON SOUTH (Greater
London)
E.64,768   T.77.57%
R. Ottaway, *C.*	31,993
P. Billenness, *LD*	11,568

Miss H. Salmon, *Lab.*	6,444
M. Samuel, *Choice*	239
C. majority	20,425

(June 1987, C. maj. 19,063)

DAGENHAM (Greater London)
E.59,645   T.70.65%
*B. Gould, *Lab.*	22,027
D. Rossiter, *C.*	15,294
C. Marquand, *LD*	4,824
Lab. majority	6,733

(June 1987, Lab. maj. 2,469)

DARLINGTON (Durham)
E.66,094   T.83.60%
A. Milburn, *Lab.*	26,556
*M. Fallon, *C.*	23,758
P. Bergg, *LD*	4,586
Dr D. Clarke, *BNP*	355
Lab. majority	2,798

(June 1987, C. maj. 2,661)

DARTFORD (Kent)
E.72,366   T.83.14%
*B. Dunn, *C.*	31,194
Dr H. Stoate, *Lab.*	20,880
Dr P. Bryden, *LD*	7,584
A. Munro, *FDP*	262
Ms A. Holland, *NLP*	247
C. majority	10,314

(June 1987, C. maj. 14,929)

DAVENTRY (Northants)
E.71,824   T.82.75%
*T. Boswell, *C.*	34,734
Ms L. Koumi, *Lab.*	14,460
A. Rounthwaite, *LD*	9,820
R. France, *NLP*	422
C. majority	20,274

(June 1987, C. maj. 19,690)

DAVYHULME (Greater Manchester)
E.61,679   T.81.82%
*W. Churchill, *C.*	24,216
B. Brotherton, *Lab.*	19,790
Ms J. Pearcey, *LD*	5,797
T. Brotheridge, *NLP*	665
C. majority	4,426

(June 1987, C. maj. 8,199)

DENTON AND REDDISH (Greater
Manchester)
E.68,463   T.76.77%
*A. Bennett, *Lab.*	29,021
J. Horswell, *C.*	16,937
Dr F. Ridley, *LD*	4,953
M. Powell, *Lib.*	1,296
J. Fuller, *NLP*	354
Lab. majority	12,084

(June 1987, Lab. maj. 8,250)

DERBY NORTH
E.73,176   T.80.65%
*G. Knight, *C.*	28,574
R. Laxton, *Lab.*	24,121
R. Charlesworth, *LD*	5,638
E. Wall, *Green*	383
P. Hart, *NF*	245
N. Onley, *NLP*	58
C. majority	4,453

(June 1987, C. maj. 6,280)

DERBY SOUTH
E.66,328　T.75.52%
*Mrs M. Beckett, *Lab.* 25,917
N. Brown, *C.* 18,981
S. Hartropp, *LD* 5,198
Lab. majority 6,936
(June 1987, Lab. maj. 1,516)

DERBYSHIRE NORTH EAST
E.70,707　T.83.61%
*H. Barnes, *Lab.* 28,860
J. Hayes, *C.* 22,590
D. Stone, *LD* 7,675
Lab. majority 6,270
(June 1987, Lab. maj. 3,720)

DERBYSHIRE SOUTH
E.82,342　T.85.49%
*Mrs E. Currie, *C.* 34,266
M. Todd, *Lab.* 29,608
Ms D. Brass, *LD* 6,236
T. Mercer, *NLP* 291
C. majority 4,658
(June 1987, C. maj. 10,311)

DERBYSHIRE WEST
E.71,201　T.84.99%
*P. McLoughlin, *C.* 32,879
R. Fearn, *LD* 14,110
S. Clamp, *Lab.* 13,528
C. majority 18,769
(June 1987, C. maj. 10,527)

DEVIZES (Wilts)
E.89,745　T.81.67%
M. Ancram, *C.* 39,090
Ms J. Mactaggart, *LD* 19,378
Ms R. Berry, *Lab.* 13,060
S. Coles, *Lib.* 962
D. Ripley, *Green* 808
C. majority 19,712
(June 1987, C. maj. 17,830)

DEVON NORTH
E.68,998　T.84.36%
N. Harvey, *LD* 27,414
*A. Speller, *C.* 26,620
P. Donner, *Lab.* 3,410
Ms C. Simmons, *Green* 658
G. Treadwell, *NLP* 107
LD majority 794
(June 1987, C. maj. 4,469)

DEVON WEST AND TORRIDGE
E.76,933　T.81.46%
*Miss E. Nicholson, *C.* 29,627
D. McBride, *LD* 26,013
D. Brenton, *Lab.* 5,997
Dr F. Williamson, *Green* 898
D. Collins, *NLP* 141
C. majority 3,614
(June 1987, C. maj. 6,468)

DEWSBURY (W. Yorks)
E.72,839　T.80.18%
*Mrs W. A. Taylor, *Lab.* 25,596
J. Whitfield, *C.* 24,962
R. Meadowcroft, *LD* 6,570
Lady J. Birdwood, *BNP* 660
N. Denby, *Green* 471
Mrs J. Marsden, *NLP* 146
Lab. majority 634
(June 1987, Lab. maj. 445)

DONCASTER CENTRAL (S. Yorks)
E.68,890　T.74.24%
*Rt. Hon. H. Walker, *Lab.* 27,795
W. Glossop, *C.* 17,113
C. Hampson, *LD* 6,057
M. Driver, *WRP* 184
Lab. majority 10,682
(June 1987, Lab. maj. 8,196)

DONCASTER NORTH (S. Yorks)
E.74,732　T.73.92%
K. Hughes, *Lab.* 34,135
R. Light, *C.* 14,322
S. Whiting, *LD* 6,787
Lab. majority 19,813
(June 1987, Lab. maj. 19,938)

DON VALLEY (S. Yorks)
E.76,327　T.76.25%
*M. Redmond, *Lab.* 32,008
N. Paget-Brown, *C.* 18,474
M. Jevons, *LD* 6,920
S. Platt, *Green* 803
Lab. majority 13,534
(June 1987, Lab. maj. 11,467)

DORSET NORTH
E.76,718　T.81.79%
*N. Baker, *C.* 34,234
Ms L. Siegle, *LD* 24,154
J. Fitzmaurice, *Lab.* 4,360
C. majority 10,080
(June 1987, C. maj. 11,907)

DORSET SOUTH
E.75,788　T.76.91%
*I. Bruce, *C.* 29,319
B. Ellis, *LD* 15,811
Dr A. Chedzoy, *Lab.* 12,298
Mrs J. Nager, *Ind.* 673
M. Griffiths, *NLP* 191
C. majority 13,508
(June 1987, C. maj. 15,067)

DORSET WEST
E.67,256　T.81.18%
*Sir J. Spicer, *C.* 27,766
R. Legg, *LD* 19,756
J. Mann, *Lab.* 7,082
C. majority 8,010
(June 1987, C. maj. 12,364)

DOVER (Kent)
E.68,962　T.83.50%
*D. Shaw, *C.* 25,395
G. Prosser, *Lab.* 24,562
M. Sole, *LD* 6,212
A. Sullivan, *Green* 637
P. Sherred, *Ind.* 407
B. Philp, *Ind. C.* 250
C. Percy, *NLP* 127
C. majority 833
(June 1987, C. maj. 6,541)

DUDLEY EAST (W. Midlands)
E.75,355　T.74.96%
*Dr J. Gilbert, *Lab.* 29,806
J. Holland, *C.* 20,606
I. Jenkins, *LD* 5,400
G. Cartwright, *NF* 675
Lab. majority 9,200
(June 1987, Lab. maj. 3,473)

DUDLEY WEST (W. Midlands)
E.86,632　T.82.08%
*J. Blackburn, *C.* 34,729
K. Lomax, *Lab.* 28,940
G. Lewis, *LD* 7,446
C. majority 5,789
(June 1987, C. maj. 10,244)

DULWICH (Greater London)
E.55,141　T.67.91%
Ms T. Jowell, *Lab.* 17,714
*G. Bowden, *C.* 15,658
Dr A. Goldie, *LD* 4,078
Lab. majority 2,056
(June 1987, C. maj. 180)

DURHAM, CITY OF
E.68,165　T.74.61%
*G. Steinberg, *Lab.* 27,095
M. Woodroofe, *C.* 12,037
N. Martin, *LD* 10,915
Ms S. J. Banks, *Green* 812
Lab. majority 15,058
(June 1987, Lab. maj. 6,125)

DURHAM NORTH
E.73,694　T.76.08%
*G. Radice, *Lab.* 33,567
Ms E. Sibley, *C.* 13,930
P. Appleby, *LD* 8,572
Lab. majority 19,637
(June 1987, Lab. maj. 18,433)

DURHAM NORTH WEST
E.61,139　T. 75.58%
*Miss H. Armstrong, *Lab.* 26,734
Mrs T. May, *C.* 12,747
T. Farron, *LD* 6,728
Lab. majority 13,987
(June 1987, Lab. maj. 10,162)

EALING ACTON (Greater London)
E.58,687　T.76.03%
*Sir G. Young, *C.* 22,579
Ms Y. Johnson, *Lab.* 15,572
L. Rowe, *LD* 5,487
Ms A. Seibe, *Green* 554
T. Pitt-Aikens, *Ind. C.* 432
C. majority 7,007
(June 1987, C. maj. 12,233)

EALING NORTH (Greater London)
E.63,528　T.78.84%
*H. Greenway, *C.* 24,898
M. Stears, *Lab.* 18,932
P. Hankinson, *LD* 5,247
D. Earl, *Green* 554
C. Hill, *NF* 277
R. Davis, *CD* 180
C. majority 5,966
(June 1987, C. maj. 15,153)

EALING SOUTHALL (Greater London)
E.65,574　T.75.49%
P. Khabra, *Lab.* 23,476
P. Treleaven, *C.* 16,610
*S. Bidwell, *True Lab.* 4,665
Ms P. Nandhra, *LD* 3,790
N. Goodwin, *Green* 964
Lab. majority 6,866
(June 1987, Lab. maj. 7,977)

EASINGTON (Durham)
E.65,061   T.72.46%
*J. Cummings, *Lab.*	34,269
W. Perry, *C.*	7,879
P. Freitag, *LD*	5,001
Lab. majority	26,390
(June 1987, Lab. maj. 24,639)

EASTBOURNE (E. Sussex)
E.76,103   T.80.97%
N. Waterson, *C.*	31,792
*D. Bellotti, *LD*	26,311
I. Gibbons, *Lab.*	2,834
D. Aherne, *Green*	391
Ms T. Williamson, *Lib.*	296
C. majority	5,481
(June 1987, C. maj 16,923)
(October 1990, LD maj. 4,550)

EASTLEIGH (Hants)
E.91,736   T.82.91%
S. Milligan, *C.*	38,998
D. Chidgey, *LD*	21,296
Ms J. Sugrue, *Lab.*	15,768
C. majority	17,702
(June 1987, C. maj. 13,355)

ECCLES (Greater Manchester)
E.64,910   T.74.12%
*Miss J. Lestor, *Lab.*	27,357
G. Ling, *C.*	14,131
G. Reid, *LD*	5,835
R. Duriez, *Green*	521
Miss J. Garner, *NLP*	270
Lab. majority	13,226
(June 1987, Lab. maj. 9,699)

EDDISBURY (Cheshire)
E.75,089   T.82.55%
*A. Goodlad, *C.*	31,625
Ms N. Edwards, *Lab.*	18,928
D. Lyon, *LD*	10,543
A. Basden, *Green*	783
N. Pollard, *NLP*	107
C. majority	12,697
(June 1987, C. maj. 15,835)

EDMONTON (Greater London)
E.63,052   T.75.66%
*Dr I. Twinn, *C.*	22,076
A. Love, *Lab.*	21,483
E. Jones, *LD*	3,940
Ms E. Solley, *NLP*	207
C. majority	593
(June 1987, C. maj. 7,286)

ELLESMERE PORT AND NESTON
(Cheshire)
E.71,572   T.84.12%
A. Miller, *Lab.*	27,782
A. Pearce, *C.*	25,793
Ms E. Jewkes, *LD*	5,944
Dr M. Money, *Green*	589
Dr A. Rae, *NLP*	105
Lab. majority	1,989
(June 1987, C. maj. 1,853)

ELMET (W. Yorks)
E.70,558   T.82.53%
*S. Batiste, *C.*	27,677
C. Burgon, *Lab.*	24,416
Mrs A. Beck, *LD*	6,144

C. majority	3,261
(June 1987, C. maj. 5,356)

ELTHAM (Greater London)
E.51,989   T.78.72%
*P. Bottomley, *C.*	18,813
C. Efford, *Lab.*	17,147
C. McGinty, *LD*	4,804
A. Graham, *Ind. C.*	165
C. majority	1,666
(June 1987, C. maj. 6,460)

ENFIELD NORTH (Greater
London)
E.67,421   T.77.91%
*T. Eggar, *C.*	27,789
M. Upham, *Lab.*	18,359
Ms S. Tustin, *LD*	5,817
J. Markham, *NLP*	565
C. majority	9,430
(June 1987, C. maj. 14,015)

ENFIELD SOUTHGATE (Greater
London)
E.64,311   T.76.28%
*M. Portillo, *C.*	28,422
Ms K. Livney, *Lab.*	12,859
K. Keane, *LD*	7,080
Ms M. Hollands, *Green*	696
C. majority	15,563
(June 1987, C. maj. 18,345)

EPPING FOREST (Essex)
E.67,585   T.80.55%
*S. Norris, *C.*	32,407
S. Murray, *Lab.*	12,219
Mrs B. Austen, *LD*	9,265
A. O'Brien, *EFRA*	552
C. majority	20,188
(June 1987, C. maj. 21,513)
(December 1988, C. maj. 4,504)

EPSOM AND EWELL (Surrey)
E.68,138   T.80.14%
*Rt. Hon. A. Hamilton, *C.*	32,861
M. Emerson, *LD*	12,840
R. Warren, *Lab.*	8,577
G. Hatchard, *NLP*	334
C. majority	20,021
(June 1987, C. maj. 20,761)

EREWASH (Derbys)
E.75,627   T.83.78%
Mrs A. Knight, *C.*	29,907
S. Stafford, *Lab.*	24,204
P. Tuck, *LD*	8,606
L. Johnson, *BNP*	645
C. majority	5,703
(June 1987, C. maj. 9,754)

ERITH AND CRAYFORD (Kent)
E.59,213   T.79.66%
*D. Evennett, *C.*	21,926
N. Beard, *Lab.*	19,587
Ms F. Jamieson, *LD*	5,657
C. majority	2,339
(June 1987, C. maj. 6,994)

ESHER (Surrey)
E.58,840   T.80.80%
*I. Taylor, *C.*	31,115
J. Richling, *LD*	10,744
Ms J. Reay, *Lab.*	5,685

C. majority	20,371
(June 1987, C. maj. 19,068)

EXETER (Devon)
E.76,723   T.82.21%
*Sir J. Hannam, *C.*	26,543
J. Lloyd, *Lab.*	22,498
G. Oakes, *LD*	12,059
Ms A. Micklem, *Lib.*	1,119
T. Brenan, *Green*	764
M. Turnbull, *NLP*	98
C. majority	4,045
(June 1987, C. maj. 7,656)

FALMOUTH AND CAMBORNE
(Cornwall)
E.70,702   T.81.10%
S. Coe, *C.*	21,150
Ms T. Jones, *LD*	17,883
J. Cosgrove, *Lab.*	16,732
P. Holmes, *Lib.*	730
K. Saunders, *Green*	466
F. Zapp, *Loony*	327
A. Pringle, *NLP*	56
C. majority	3,267
(June 1987, C. maj. 5,039)

FAREHAM (Hants)
E.81,124   T.81.85%
*P. Lloyd, *C.*	40,482
J. Thompson, *LD*	16,341
Ms E. Weston, *Lab.*	8,766
M. Brimecome, *Green*	818
C. majority	24,141
(June 1987, C. maj. 18,795)

FAVERSHAM (Kent)
E.81,977   T.79.71%
*R. Moate, *C.*	32,755
Ms H. Brinton, *Lab.*	16,404
R. Truelove, *LD*	15,896
R. Bradshaw, *NLP*	294
C. majority	16,351
(June 1987, C. maj. 13,978)

FELTHAM AND HESTON (Greater
London)
E.81,221   T.73.90%
A. Keen, *Lab.*	27,660
*P. Ground, *C.*	25,665
M. Hoban, *LD*	6,700
Lab. majority	1,995
(June 1987, C. maj. 5,430)

FINCHLEY (Greater London)
E.52,907   T.77.64%
H. Booth, *C.*	21,039
Ms A. Marjoram, *Lab.*	14,651
Ms H. Leighter, *LD*	4,568
A. Gunstock, *Green*	564
Ms S. Johnson, *Loony*	130
J. Macrae, *NLP*	129
C. majority	6,388
(June 1987, C. maj. 8,913)

FOLKESTONE AND HYTHE (Kent)
E.65,856   T.79.61%
*Rt. Hon. M. Howard, *C.*	27,437
Mrs L. Cufley, *LD*	18,527
P. Doherty, *Lab.*	6,347
A. Hobbs, *NLP*	123
C. majority	8,910
(June 1987, C. maj. 9,126)

FULHAM (Greater London)
E.52,740   T.76.16%

*M. Carrington, C.	21,438
N. Moore, Lab.	14,859
P. Crystal, LD	3,339
Ms E. Streeter, Green	443
J. Darby, NLP	91
C. majority	6,579
(June 1987, C. maj. 6,322)	

FYLDE (Lancs)
E.63,573   T.78.50%

*M. Jack, C.	30,639
N. Cryer, LD	9,648
Ms C. Hughes, Lab.	9,382
P. Leadbetter, NLP	239
C. majority	20,991
(June 1987, C. maj. 17,772)	

GAINSBOROUGH AND HORNCASTLE (Lincs)
E.72,038   T.80.87%

*E. Leigh, C.	31,444
N. Taylor, LD	15,199
Ms F. Jones, Lab.	11,619
C. majority	16,245
(June 1987, C. maj. 9,723)	

GATESHEAD EAST (Tyne & Wear)
E.64,355   T.73.63%

*Miss J. Quin, Lab.	30,100
M. Callanan, C.	11,570
R. Beadle, LD	5,720
Lab. majority	18,530
(June 1987, Lab. maj. 17,228)	

GEDLING (Notts)
E.68,953   T.82.34%

*A. J. B. Mitchell, C.	30,191
V. Coaker, Lab.	19,554
D. George, LD	6,863
Ms A. Miszeweka, NLP	168
C. majority	10,637
(June 1987, C. maj. 16,539)	

GILLINGHAM (Kent)
E.71,851   T.80.32%

*J. Couchman, C.	30,201
P. Clark, Lab.	13,563
M. Wallbank, LD	13,509
C. MacKinlay, Ind.	248
D. Jolicoeur, NLP	190
C. majority	16,638
(June 1987, C. maj. 12,549)	

GLANFORD AND SCUNTHORPE (Humberside)
E.73,479   T.78.91%

*E. Morley, Lab.	30,623
Dr A. Saywood, C.	22,211
W. Paxton, LD	4,172
C. Nottingham, SD	982
Lab. majority	8,412
(June 1987, Lab. maj. 512)	

GLOUCESTER
E.80,578   T.80.24%

*D. French, C.	29,870
K. Stephens, Lab.	23,812
J. Sewell, LD	10,978
C. majority	6,058
(June 1987, C. maj. 12,035)	

GLOUCESTERSHIRE WEST
E.80,007   T.83.89%

*P. Marland, C.	29,232
Ms D. Organ, Lab.	24,274
L. Boait, LD	13,366
A. Reeve, Brit. Ind.	172
C. Palmer, Century	75
C. majority	4,958
(June 1987, C. maj. 11,679)	

GOSPORT (Hants)
E.69,638   T.76.79%

*P. Viggers, C.	31,094
M. Russell, LD	14,776
Ms M. Angus, Lab.	7,275
P. Ettie, Pensioners	332
C. majority	16,318
(June 1987, C. maj. 13,723)	

GRANTHAM (Lincs)
E.83,463   T.79.29%

*Hon. D. Hogg, C.	37,194
S. Taggart, Lab.	17,606
J. Heppell, LD	9,882
J. Hiley, Lib.	1,500
C. majority	19,588
(June 1987, C. maj. 21,303)	

GRAVESHAM (Kent)
E.70,740   T.83.48%

*J. Arnold, C.	29,322
G. Green, Lab.	23,829
D. Deedman, LD	5,269
A. Bunstone, Ind.	273
R. Khilkoff-Boulding, ILP	187
B. Buxton, Soc.	174
C. majority	5,493
(June 1987, C. maj. 8,792)	

GREAT GRIMSBY (Humberside)
E.67,427   T.75.28%

*A. V. Mitchell, Lab.	25,895
P. Jackson, C.	18,391
Ms P. Frankish, LD	6,475
Lab. majority	7,504
(June 1987, Lab. maj. 8,784)	

GREAT YARMOUTH (Norfolk)
E.68,263   T.77.94%

*M. Carttiss, C.	25,505
Ms B. Baughan, Lab.	20,196
M. Scott, LD	7,225
Ms P. Larkin, NLP	284
C. majority	5,309
(June 1987, C. maj. 10,083)	

GREENWICH (Greater London)
E.47,789   T.74.63%

W. R. N. Raynsford, Lab.	14,630
*Mrs R. Barnes, SD	13,273
Mrs A. McNair, C.	6,960
R. McCracken, Green	483
R. Mallone, Fellowship	147
M. Hardee, UTCHAP	103
J. Small, NLP	70
Lab. majority	1,357
(June 1987, SDP/All. maj. 2,141)	

GUILDFORD (Surrey)
E.77,265   T.78.48%

*Rt. Hon. D. Howell, C.	33,516

Mrs M. Sharp, LD	20,112
H. Mann, Lab.	6,781
A. Law, NLP	234
C. majority	13,404
(June 1987, C. maj. 12,607)	

HACKNEY NORTH AND STOKE NEWINGTON (Greater London)
E.54,655   T.63.53%

*Ms D. Abbott, Lab.	20,083
C. Manson, C.	9,356
K. Fitchett, LD	3,996
Ms H. Hunt, Green	1,111
J. Windsor, NLP	178
Lab. majority	10,727
(June 1987, Lab. maj. 7,678)	

HACKNEY SOUTH AND SHOREDITCH (Greater London)
E.57,935   T.63.82%

*B. Sedgemore, Lab.	19,730
A. Turner, C.	10,714
G. Wintle, LD	5,533
L. Lucas, Green	772
Ms G. Norman, NLP	226
Lab. majority	9,016
(June 1987, Lab. maj. 7,522)	

HALESOWEN AND STOURBRIDGE (W. Midlands)
E.77,644   T.82.28%

P. W. Hawksley, C.	32,312
A. Hankon, Lab.	22,730
V. Sharma, LD	7,941
T. Weller, Green	908
C. majority	9,582
(June 1987, C. maj. 13,808)	

HALIFAX (W. Yorks)
E.73,401   T.78.69%

*Ms A. Mahon, Lab.	25,115
T. Martin, C.	24,637
I. Howell, LD	7,364
R. Pearson, Nat.	649
Lab. majority	478
(June 1987, Lab. maj. 1,212)	

HALTON (Cheshire)
E.74,906   T.78.34%

*Rt. Hon. G. Oakes, Lab.	35,025
G. Mercer, C.	16,821
D. Reaper, LD	6,104
S. Herley, Loony	398
N. Collins, NLP	338
Lab. majority	18,204
(June 1987, Lab. maj. 14,578)	

HAMMERSMITH (Greater London)
E.47,229   T.71.90%

*C. Soley, Lab.	17,329
A. Hennessy, C.	12,575
J. Bates, LD	3,380
R. Crosskey, Green	546
K. Turner, NLP	89
Ms H. Szamuely, Anti Fed.	41
Lab. majority	4,754
(June 1987, Lab. maj. 2,415)	

HAMPSHIRE EAST
E.92,139   T.80.35%

*M. Mates, C.	47,541
Ms S. Baring, LD	18,376

J. Phillips, *Lab.* 6,840
I. Foster, *Green* 1,113
S. Hale, *RCC* 165
C. majority 29,165
(June 1987, C. maj. 23,786)

HAMPSHIRE NORTH WEST
*E.*73,101   *T.*80.75%
*Sir D. Mitchell, *C.* 34,310
M. Simpson, *LD* 16,462
M. Stockwell, *Lab.* 7,433
Ms D. Ashley, *Green* 825
C. majority 17,848
(June 1987, C. maj. 13,437)

HAMPSTEAD AND HIGHGATE
(Greater London)
*E.*58,203   *T.*73.04%
Ms G. Jackson, *Lab.* 19,193
O. Letwin, *C.* 17,753
D. Wrede, *LD* 4,765
S. Games, *Green* 594
Dr R. Prosser, *NLP* 86
Ms A. Hall, *RAVA* 44
C. Scallywag Wilson, *Scallywag* 44
Captain Rizz, *Rizz* 33
Lab. majority 1,440
(June 1987, C. maj. 2,221)

HARBOROUGH (Leics)
*E.*76,514   *T.*82.11%
E. Garnier, *C.* 34,280
M. Cox, *LD* 20,737
Ms C. Mackay, *Lab.* 7,483
A. Irwin, *NLP* 328
C. majority 13,543
(June 1987, C. maj. 18,810)

HARLOW (Essex)
*E.*68,615   *T.*82.56%
*J. Hayes, *C.* 26,608
W. Rammell, *Lab.* 23,668
Ms L. Spenceley, *LD* 6,375
C. majority 2,940
(June 1987, C. maj. 5,877)

HARROGATE (N. Yorks)
*E.*76,250   *T.*77.98%
*R. Banks, *C.* 32,023
T. Hurren, *LD* 19,434
A. Wright, *Lab.* 7,230
A. Warneken, *Green* 780
C. majority 12,589
(June 1987, C. maj. 11,902)

HARROW EAST (Greater London)
*E.*74,733   *T.*77.83%
*H. Dykes, *C.* 30,752
A. McNulty, *Lab.* 19,654
Ms V. Chamberlain, *LD* 6,360
P. Burrows, *Lib.* 1,142
Mrs S. Hamza, *NLP* 212
J. Lester, *Anti Fed.* 49
C. majority 11,098
(June 1987, C. maj. 18,273)

HARROW WEST (Greater London)
*E.*69,616   *T.*78.69%
*R. G. Hughes, *C.* 30,240
C. Moraes, *Lab.* 12,343
C. Noyce, *LD* 11,050
G. Aitman, *Lib.* 845

Mrs J. Argyle, *NLP* 306
C. majority 17,897
(June 1987, C. maj. 15,444)

HARTLEPOOL (Cleveland)
*E.*67,968   *T.*76.07%
P. Mandelson, *Lab.* 26,816
G. Robb, *C.* 18,034
I. Cameron, *LD* 6,860
Lab. majority 8,782
(June 1987, Lab. maj. 7,289)

HARWICH (Essex)
*E.*80,260   *T.*77.70%
I. Sproat, *C.* 32,369
Mrs P. Bevan, *LD* 15,210
R. Knight, *Lab.* 14,511
Mrs E. McGrath, *NLP* 279
C. majority 17,159
(June 1987, C. maj. 12,082)

HASTINGS AND RYE (E. Sussex)
*E.*71,838   *T.*74.86%
Ms J. Lait, *C.* 25,573
M. Palmer, *LD* 18,939
R. Stevens, *Lab.* 8,458
Ms S. Phillips, *Green* 640
T. Howell, *Loony* 168
C. majority 6,634
(June 1987, C. maj. 7,347)

HAVANT (Hants)
*E.*74,217   *T.*79.01%
D. Willetts, *C.* 32,233
S. van Hagen, *LD* 14,649
G. Morris, *Lab.* 10,968
T. Mitchell, *Green* 793
C. majority 17,584
(June 1987, C. maj. 16,510)

HAYES AND HARLINGTON
(Greater London)
*E.*54,449   *T.*79.70%
*T. Dicks, *C.* 19,489
J. McDonnell, *Lab.* 19,436
T. Little, *LD* 4,472
C. majority 53
(June 1987, C. maj. 5,965)

HAZEL GROVE (Greater
Manchester)
*E.*64,302   *T.*84.94%
*Sir T. Arnold, *C.* 24,479
A. Stunell, *LD* 23,550
C. McAllister, *Lab.* 6,390
M. Penn, *NLP* 204
C. majority 929
(June 1987, C. maj. 1,840)

HEMSWORTH (W. Yorks)
*E.*55,679   *T.*75.91%
*D. Enright, *Lab.* 29,942
G. Harrison, *C.* 7,867
Ms V. Megson, *LD* 4,459
Lab. majority 22,075
(June 1987, Lab. maj. 20,700)
(November 1991, Lab. maj. 11,087)

HENDON NORTH (Greater
London)
*E.*51,513   *T.*75.08%
*J. Gorst, *C.* 20,569
D. Hill, *Lab.* 13,447
P. Kemp, *LD* 4,136
Ms P. Duncan, *Green* 430
Ms P. Orr, *NLP* 95
C. majority 7,122
(June 1987, C. maj. 10,932)

HENDON SOUTH (Greater London)
*E.*48,401   *T.*72.38%
*J. Marshall, *C.* 20,593
Ms L. Lloyd, *Lab.* 8,546
J. Cohen, *LD* 5,609
J. Leslie, *NLP* 289
C. majority 12,047
(June 1987, C. maj. 11,124)

HENLEY (Oxon)
*E.*64,702   *T.*79.84%
*Rt. Hon. M. Heseltine, *C.* 30,835
D. Turner, *LD* 12,443
I. Russell-Swinnerton, *Lab.* 7,676
A. Plane, *Anti H.* 431
Ms S. Banerji, *NLP* 274
C. majority 18,392
(June 1987, C. maj. 17,082)

HEREFORD
*E.*69,676   *T.*81.29%
*C. Shepherd, *C.* 26,727
G. Jones, *LD* 23,314
Ms J. Kelly, *Lab.* 6,005
C. Mattingly, *Green* 596
C. majority 3,413
(June 1987, C. maj. 1,413)

HERTFORD AND STORTFORD
*E.*76,654   *T.*81.05%
*B. Wells, *C.* 35,716
C. White, *LD* 15,506
A. Bovaird, *Lab.* 10,125
J. Goth, *Green* 780
C. majority 20,210
(June 1987, C. maj. 17,140)

HERTFORDSHIRE NORTH
*E.*80,066   *T.*84.44%
O. Heald, *C.* 33,679
R. Liddle, *LD* 17,148
Ms S. Bissett Johnson, *Lab.* 16,449
B. Irving, *NLP* 339
C. majority 16,531
(June 1987, C. maj. 11,442)

HERTFORDSHIRE SOUTH WEST
*E.*70,836   *T.*83.76%
*R. Page, *C.* 33,825
Ms A. Shaw, *LD* 13,718
A. Gale, *Lab.* 11,512
C. Adamson, *NLP* 281
C. majority 20,107
(June 1987, C. maj. 15,784)

HERTFORDSHIRE WEST
*E.*78,573   *T.*82.36%
*R. Jones, *C.* 33,340
Mrs E. McNally, *Lab.* 19,400
M. Trevett, *LD* 10,464
J. Hannaway, *Green* 674

J. McAuley, *NF* 665
G. Harvey, *NLP* 175
C. majority 13,940
(June 1987, C. maj. 14,924)

HERTSMERE (Herts)
*E.*69,951　*T.*80.89%
W. J. Clappison, *C.* 32,133
Dr D. Souter, *Lab.* 13,398
Mrs Z. Gifford, *LD* 10,681
Ms D. Harding, *NLP* 373
C. majority 18,735
(June 1987, C. maj. 18,106)

HEXHAM (Northumberland)
*E.*57,812　*T.*82.37%
P. Atkinson, *C.* 24,967
I. Swithenbank, *Lab.* 11,529
J. Wallace, *LD* 10,344
J. Hartshorne, *Green* 781
C. majority 13,438
(June 1987, C. maj. 8,066)

HEYWOOD AND MIDDLETON
(Greater Manchester)
*E.*57,176　*T.*74.92%
*J. Callaghan, *Lab.* 22,380
E. Ollerenshaw, *C.* 14,306
Dr M. Taylor, *LD* 5,262
P. Burke, *Lib.* 757
Ms A. Scott, *NLP* 134
Lab. majority 8,074
(June 1987, Lab. maj. 6,848)

HIGH PEAK (Derbys)
*E.*70,793　*T.*84.62%
C. Hendry, *C.* 27,538
T. Levitt, *Lab.* 22,719
S. Molloy, *LD* 8,861
R. Floyd, *Green* 794
C. majority 4,819
(June 1987, C. maj. 9,516)

HOLBORN AND ST PANCRAS
(Greater London)
*E.*64,480　*T.*62.99%
*F. Dobson, *Lab.* 22,243
A. McHallam, *C.* 11,419
Ms J. Horne-Roberts, *LD* 5,476
P. Wolf-Light, *Green* 959
M. Hersey, *NLP* 212
R. Headicar, *Soc.* 175
N. Lewis, *WAR* 133
Lab. majority 10,824
(June 1987, Lab. maj. 8,853)

HOLLAND WITH BOSTON (Lincs)
*E.*67,900　*T.*77.93%
*Sir R. Body, *C.* 29,159
J. Hough, *Lab.* 15,328
N. Ley, *LD* 8,434
C. majority 13,831
(June 1987, C. maj. 17,595)

HONITON (Devon)
*E.*79,223　*T.*80.74%
*Sir P. Emery, *C.* 33,533
Ms J. Sharratt, *LD* 17,022
R. Davison, *Lab.* 8,142
D. Owen, *Ind. C.* 2,175
S. Hughes, *Loony G.* 1,442
G. Halliwell, *Lib.* 1,005

A. Tootill, *Green* 650
C. majority 16,511
(June 1987, C. maj. 16,562)

HORNCHURCH (Greater London)
*E.*60,522　*T.*79.78%
*R. Squire, *C.* 25,817
Ms L. Cooper, *Lab.* 16,652
B. Oddy, *LD* 5,366
T. Matthews, *SD* 453
C. majority 9,165
(June 1987, C. maj. 10,694)

HORNSEY AND WOOD GREEN
(Greater London)
*E.*73,491　*T.*75.85%
Mrs B. Roche, *Lab.* 27,020
A. Boff, *C.* 21,843
P. Dunphy, *LD* 5,547
Ms L. Crosbie, *Green* 1,051
P. Davies, *NLP* 197
W. Massey, *Rev. Comm.* 89
Lab. majority 5,177
(June 1987, C. maj. 1,779)

HORSHAM (W. Sussex)
*E.*84,158　*T.*81.27%
*Sir P. Hordern, *C.* 42,210
Ms J. Stainton, *LD* 17,138
S. Uwins, *Lab.* 6,745
Ms J. Elliott, *Lib.* 1,281
T. King, *Green* 692
J. Duggan, *PPP* 332
C. majority 25,072
(June 1987, C. maj. 23,907)

HOUGHTON AND WASHINGTON
(Tyne & Wear)
*E.*79,325　*T.*70.60%
*R. Boyes, *Lab.* 34,733
A. Tyrie, *C.* 13,925
O. Dumpleton, *LD* 7,346
Lab. majority 20,808
(June 1987, Lab. maj. 20,193)

HOVE (E. Sussex)
*E.*67,450　*T.*74.26%
*Hon. T. Sainsbury, *C.* 24,525
D. Turner, *Lab.* 12,257
A. Jones, *LD* 9,709
N. Furness, *Hove C.* 2,658
G. Sinclair, *Green* 814
J. Morilly, *NLP* 126
C. majority 12,268
(June 1987, C. maj. 18,218)

HUDDERSFIELD (W. Yorks)
*E.*67,604　*T.*72.32%
*B. Sheerman, *Lab.* 23,832
Ms J. Kenyon, *C.* 16,574
Ms A. Denham, *LD* 7,777
N. Harvey, *Green* 576
M. Cran, *NLP* 135
Lab. majority 7,258
(June 1987, Lab. maj. 7,278)

HULL EAST
*E.*69,036　*T.*69.29%
*J. Prescott, *Lab.* 30,092
J. Fareham, *C.* 11,373
J. Wastling, *LD* 6,050
C. Kinzell, *NLP* 323

Lab. majority 18,719
(June 1987, Lab. maj. 14,689)

HULL NORTH
*E.*71,363　*T.*66.71%
*J. K. McNamara, *Lab.* 26,619
B. Coleman, *C.* 11,235
A. Meadowcroft, *LD* 9,504
G. Richardson, *NLP* 253
Lab. majority 15,384
(June 1987, Lab. maj. 12,169)

HULL WEST
*E.*56,111　*T.*65.70%
*S. Randall, *Lab.* 21,139
D. Stewart, *C.* 10,554
R. Tress, *LD* 4,867
B. Franklin, *NLP* 308
Lab. majority 10,585
(June 1987, Lab. maj. 8,130)

HUNTINGDON (Cambs)
*E.*92,913　*T.*79.16%
*Rt. Hon. J. Major, *C.* 48,662
H. Seckleman, *Lab.* 12,432
A. Duff, *LD* 9,386
P. Wiggin, *Lib.* 1,045
Miss D. Birkhead, *Green* 846
Lord D. Sutch, *Loony* 728
M. Flanagan, *C. Thatch.* 231
Lord Buckethead, *Gremloids* 107
C. Cockell, *FTM* 91
D. Shepheard, *NLP* 26
C. majority 36,230
(June 1987, C. maj. 27,044)

HYNDBURN (Lancs)
*E.*58,539　*T.*83.97%
G. Pope, *Lab.* 23,042
*K. Hargreaves, *C.* 21,082
Ms Y. Stars, *LD* 4,886
S. Whittle, *NLP* 150
Lab. majority 1,960
(June 1987, C. maj. 2,220)

ILFORD NORTH (Greater London)
*E.*58,670　*T.*77.98%
*V. Bendall, *C.* 24,698
Ms L. Hilton, *Lab.* 15,627
R. Scott, *LD* 5,430
C. majority 9,071
(June 1987, C. maj. 12,090)

ILFORD SOUTH (Greater London)
*E.*55,741　*T.*76.83%
M. Gapes, *Lab.* 19,418
*N. Thorne, *C.* 19,016
G. Hogarth, *LD* 4,126
N. Bramachari, *NLP* 269
Lab. majority 402
(June 1987, C. maj. 4,572)

IPSWICH (Suffolk)
*E.*67,261　*T.*80.32%
J. Cann, *Lab.* 23,680
*M. Irvine, *C.* 23,415
J. White, *LD* 6,159
Ms J. Scott, *Green* 591
E. Kaplan, *NLP* 181
Lab. majority 265
(June 1987, C. maj. 874)

ISLE OF WIGHT
E.99,838   T.79.76%

*B. Field, C.	38,163
Dr P. Brand, LD	36,336
K. Pearson, Lab.	4,784
C. Daly, NLP	350
C. majority	1,827

(June 1987, C. maj. 6,442)

ISLINGTON NORTH (Greater London)
E.56,270   T.67.26%

*J. Corbyn, Lab.	21,742
Mrs L. Champagnie, C.	8,958
Ms S. Ludford, LD	5,732
C. Ashby, Green	1,420
Lab. majority	12,784

(June 1987, Lab. maj. 9,657)

ISLINGTON SOUTH AND FINSBURY (Greater London)
E.55,541   T.72.52%

*C. Smith, Lab.	20,586
M. Jones, C.	9,934
C. Pryce, LD	9,387
Ms R. Hersey, JBR	149
Ms M. Avino, Loony	142
M. Spinks, NLP	83
Lab. majority	10,652

(June 1987, Lab. maj. 805)

JARROW (Tyne & Wear)
E.62,611   T.74.44%

*D. Dixon, Lab.	28,956
T. Ward, C.	11,049
K. Orrell, LD	6,608
Lab. majority	17,907

(June 1987, Lab. maj. 18,795)

KEIGHLEY (W. Yorks)
E.66,358   T.82.58%

*G. Waller, C.	25,983
T. Flanagan, Lab.	22,387
I. Simpson, LD	5,793
M. Crowson, Green	642
C. majority	3,596

(June 1987, C. maj. 5,606)

KENSINGTON (Greater London)
E.42,129   T.73.29%

*J. D. Fishburn, C.	15,540
Ms A. Holmes, Lab.	11,992
C. Shirley, LD	2,770
Ms A. Burlingham-Johnson, Green	415
A. Hardy, NLP	90
Ms A. Bulloch, Anti Fed.	71
C. majority	3,548

(June 1987, C. maj. 4,447)
(July 1988, C. maj. 815)

KENT MID
E.74,459   T.79.66%

*A. Rowe, C.	33,633
T. Robson, Lab.	13,984
G. Colley, LD	11,476
G. Valente, NLP	224
C. majority	19,649

(June 1987, C. maj. 14,768)

KETTERING (Northants)
E.67,853   T.82.58%

*R. Freeman, C.	29,115
P. Hope, Lab.	17,961
R. Denton-White, LD	8,962
C. majority	11,154

(June 1987, C. maj. 11,327)

KINGSTON UPON THAMES (Greater London)
E.51,077   T.78.41%

*Rt. Hon. N. Lamont, C.	20,675
D. Osbourne, LD	10,522
R. Markless, Lab.	7,748
A. Amer, Lib.	771
D. Beaupre, Loony	212
G. Woollcoombe, NLP	81
A. Scholefield, Anti Fed.	42
C. majority	10,153

(June 1987, C. maj. 11,186)

KINGSWOOD (Avon)
E.71,727   T.83.85%

R. Berry, Lab.	26,774
*R. Hayward, C.	24,404
Ms J. Pinkerton, LD	8,960
Lab. majority	2,370

(June 1987, C. maj. 4,393)

KNOWSLEY NORTH (Merseyside)
E.48,761   T.72.81%

*G. Howarth, Lab.	27,517
S. Mabey, C.	5,114
J. Murray, LD	1,515
Mrs K. Lappin, Lib.	1,180
V. Ruben, NLP	179
Lab. majority	22,403

(June 1987, Lab. maj. 21,098)

KNOWSLEY SOUTH (Merseyside)
E.62,260   T.74.77%

*E. O'Hara, Lab.	31,933
L. Byrom, C.	9,922
I. Smith, LD	4,480
M. Raiano, NLP	217
Lab. majority	22,011

(June 1987, Lab. maj. 20,846)
(September 1990, Lab. maj. 11,367)

LANCASHIRE WEST
E.77,462   T.82.55%

C. Pickthall, Lab.	30,128
*K. Hind, C.	28,051
P. Reilly, LD	4,884
P. Pawley, Green	546
B. Morris, NLP	336
Lab. majority	2,077

(June 1987, C. maj. 1,353)

LANCASTER (Lancs)
E.58,714   T.78.78%

*Dame E. Kellett-Bowman, C.	21,084
Ms R. Henig, Lab.	18,131
J. Humberstone, LD	6,524
Ms G. Dowding, Green	433
R. Barcis, NLP	83
C. majority	2,953

(June 1987, C. maj. 6,453)

LANGBAURGH (Cleveland)
E.79,566   T.83.05%

M. Bates, C.	30,018
*A. Kumar, Lab.	28,454

P. Allen, LD 7,615
C. majority 1,564

(June 1987, C. maj. 2,088)
(November 1991, C. maj. 1,975)

LEEDS CENTRAL (W. Yorks)
E.62,058   T.61.29%

*D. Fatchett, Lab.	23,673
Mrs T. Holdroyd, C.	8,653
D. Pratt, LD	5,713
Lab. majority	15,020

(June 1987, Lab. maj. 11,505)

LEEDS EAST (W. Yorks)
E.61,695   T.70.02%

G. Mudie, Lab.	24,929
N. Carmichael, C.	12,232
P. Wrigley, LD	6,040
Lab. majority	12,697

(June 1987, Lab. maj. 9,526)

LEEDS NORTH EAST (W. Yorks)
E.64,372   T.76.89%

*T. Kirkhope, C.	22,462
F. Hamilton, Lab.	18,218
C. Walmsley, LD	8,274
J. Noble, Green	546
C. majority	4,244

(June 1987, C. maj. 8,419)

LEEDS NORTH WEST (W. Yorks)
E.69,406   T.72.84%

*Dr K. Hampson, C.	21,750
Ms B. Pearce, LD	14,079
Ms S. Egan, Lab.	13,782
D. Webb, Green	519
N. Nowosielski, Lib.	427
C. majority	7,671

(June 1987, C. maj. 5,201)

LEEDS SOUTH AND MORLEY (W. Yorks)
E.63,107   T.72.58%

W. J. Gunnell, Lab.	23,896
R. Booth, C.	16,524
Ms J. Walmsley, LD	5,062
R. Thurston, NLP	327
Lab. majority	7,372

(June 1987, Lab. maj. 6,711)

LEEDS WEST (W. Yorks)
E.67,084   T.71.14%

*J. Battle, Lab.	26,310
P. Bartlett, C.	12,482
G. Howard, LD	4,252
M. Meadowcroft, Lib.	3,980
Ms A. Mander, Green	569
R. Tenny, NF	132
Lab. majority	13,828

(June 1987, Lab. maj. 4,692)

LEICESTER EAST
E.63,434   T.78.40%

*N. K. A. S. Vaz, Lab.	28,123
J. Stevens, C.	16,807
Ms S. Mitchell, LD	4,043
M. Frankland, Green	453
D. Taylor, Homeland	308
Lab. majority	11,316

(June 1987, Lab. maj. 1,924)

LEICESTER SOUTH
E.71,120 T.75.09%
*J. Marshall, *Lab.*	27,934
Dr M. Dutt, *C.*	18,494
Ms A. Crumbie, *LD*	6,271
J. McWhirter, *Green*	554
Ms P. Saunders, *NLP*	154
Lab. majority	9,440

(June 1987, Lab. maj. 1,877)

LEICESTER WEST
E.65,510 T.73.66%
*Hon. G. Janner, *Lab.*	22,574
J. Guthrie, *C.*	18,596
G. Walker, *LD*	6,402
Ms C. Wintram, *Green*	517
Ms J. Rosta, *NLP*	171
Lab. majority	3,978

(June 1987, Lab. maj. 1,201)

LEICESTERSHIRE NORTH WEST
E.72,414 T.86.11%
*D. Ashby, *C.*	28,379
D. Taylor, *Lab.*	27,400
J. Beckett, *LD*	6,353
J. Fawcett, *NLP*	229
C. majority	979

(June 1987, C. maj. 7,828)

LEIGH (Greater Manchester)
E.70,064 T.75.02%
*L. Cunliffe, *Lab.*	32,225
J. Egerton, *C.*	13,398
R. Bleakley, *LD*	6,621
A. Tayler, *NLP*	320
Lab. majority	18,827

(June 1987, Lab. maj. 16,606)

LEOMINSTER (H & W)
E.70,873 T.81.69%
*P. Temple-Morris, *C.*	32,783
D. Short, *LD*	16,103
C. Chappell, *Lab.*	6,874
Ms F. Norman, *Green*	1,503
Capt. E. Carlise, *Anti Fed.*	640
C. majority	16,680

(June 1987, C. maj. 14,075)

LEWES (E. Sussex)
E.73,918 T.81.81%
*J. R. Rathbone, *C.*	33,042
N. Baker, *LD*	20,867
Ms A. Chapman, *Lab.*	5,758
A. Beaumont, *Green*	719
N. Clinch, *NLP*	87
C. majority	12,175

(June 1987, C. maj. 13,620)

LEWISHAM DEPTFORD (Greater London)
E.57,014 T.65.05%
*Mrs J. Ruddock, *Lab.*	22,574
Miss T. O'Neill, *C.*	10,336
Ms J. Brightwell, *LD*	4,181
Lab. majority	12,238

(June 1987, Lab. maj. 6,771)

LEWISHAM EAST (Greater London)
E.57,674 T.74.78%
Mrs B. Prentice, *Lab.*	19,576
*Hon. C. Moynihan, *C.*	18,481
J. Hawkins, *LD*	4,877
Ms G. Mansour, *NLP*	196
Lab. majority	1,095

(June 1987, C. maj. 4,814)

LEWISHAM WEST (Greater London)
E.59,317 T.73.11%
J. Dowd, *Lab.*	20,378
*J. Maples, *C.*	18,569
Ms E. Neale, *LD*	4,295
P. Coulam, *Anti Fed.*	125
Lab. majority	1,809

(June 1987, C. maj. 3,772)

LEYTON (Greater London)
E.57,271 T.67.38%
*H. Cohen, *Lab.*	20,334
Miss C. Smith, *C.*	8,850
J. Fryer, *LD*	8,180
L. de Pinna, *Lib.*	561
K. Pervez, *Green*	412
R. Archer, *NLP*	256
Lab. majority	11,484

(June 1987, Lab. maj. 4,641)

LINCOLN
E.78,905 T.79.15%
*K. Carlisle, *C.*	28,792
N. Butler, *Lab.*	26,743
D. Harding-Price, *LD*	6,316
Ms S. Wiggin, *Lib.*	603
C. majority	2,049

(June 1987, C. maj. 7,483)

LINDSEY EAST (Lincs)
E.80,026 T.78.07%
*Sir P. Tapsell, *C.*	31,916
J. Dodsworth, *LD*	20,070
D. Shepherd, *Lab.*	9,477
Ms R. Robinson, *Green*	1,018
C. majority	11,846

(June 1987, C. maj. 8,616)

LITTLEBOROUGH AND SADDLEWORTH (Greater Manchester)
E.65,576 T.81.61%
*G. Dickens, *C.*	23,682
C. Davies, *LD*	19,188
A. Brett, *Lab.*	10,649
C. majority	4,494

(June 1987, C. maj. 6,202)

LIVERPOOL BROADGREEN
E.60,080 T.69.59%
Mrs J. Kennedy, *Lab.*	18,062
Ms R. Cooper, *LD*	11,035
*T. Fields, *Soc. Lab.*	5,952
Mrs H. Roche, *C.*	5,405
S. Radford, *Lib.*	1,211
Mrs A. Brennan, *NLP*	149
Lab. majority	7,027

(June 1987, Lab. maj. 6,047)

LIVERPOOL GARSTON
E.57,538 T.70.60%
*E. Loyden, *Lab.*	23,212
J. Backhouse, *C.*	10,933
W. Roberts, *LD*	5,398
A. Conrad, *Lib.*	894
P. Chandler, *NLP*	187
Lab. majority	12,279

(June 1987, Lab. maj. 13,777)

LIVERPOOL MOSSLEY HILL
E.60,409 T.68.52%
*D. Alton, *LD*	19,809
N. Bann, *Lab.*	17,203
S. Syder, *C.*	4,269
B. Rigby, *NLP*	114
LD majority	2,606

(June 1987, L./All. maj. 2,226)

LIVERPOOL RIVERSIDE
E.49,595 T.54.57%
*R. Parry, *Lab.*	20,550
Dr A. Zsigmond, *C.*	3,113
M. Akbar Ali, *LD*	2,498
L. Brown, *Green*	738
J. Collins, *NLP*	169
Lab. majority	17,437

(June 1987, Lab. maj. 20,689)

LIVERPOOL WALTON
E.70,102 T.67.40%
*P. Kilfoyle, *Lab.*	34,214
B. Greenwood, *C.*	5,915
J. Lang, *LD*	5,672
T. Newall, *Lib.*	963
D. Carson, *Prot. Ref.*	393
Ms D. Raiano, *NLP*	98
Lab. majority	28,299

(June 1987, Lab. maj. 23,253)
(July 1991, Lab. maj. 6,860)

LIVERPOOL WEST DERBY
E.56,718 T.69.84%
*R. Wareing, *Lab.*	27,014
S. Fitzsimmons, *C.*	6,589
Ms G. Bundred, *LD*	4,838
D. Curtis, *Lib.*	1,021
C. Higgins, *NLP*	154
Lab. majority	20,425

(June 1987, Lab. maj. 20,496)

LOUGHBOROUGH (Leics)
E.75,450 T.78.52%
*S. Dorrell, *C.*	30,064
A. Reed, *Lab.*	19,181
A. Stott, *LD*	8,953
I. Sinclair, *Green*	817
P. Reynolds, *NLP*	233
C. majority	10,883

(June 1987, C. maj. 17,648)

LUDLOW (Salop)
E.68,935 T.80.87%
*C. Gill, *C.*	28,719
D. Phillips, *LD*	14,567
Ms B. Mason, *Lab.*	11,709
N. Appleton-Fox, *Green*	758
C. majority	14,152

(June 1987, C. maj. 11,699)

LUTON NORTH (Beds)
E.76,857 T.81.91%
*J. Carlisle, *C.*	33,777
A. McWalter, *Lab.*	20,683
Ms J. Jackson, *LD*	7,570
R. Jones, *Green*	633
K. Buscombe, *NLP*	292
C. majority	13,094

(June 1987, C. maj. 15,573)

LUTON SOUTH (Beds)
*E.*73,016   *T.*79.10%

*G. Bright, *C.*	25,900
W. McKenzie, *Lab.*	25,101
D. Rogers, *LD*	6,020
Ms L. Bliss, *Green*	550
D. Cooke, *NLP*	191
C. majority	799
(June 1987, C. maj. 5,115)	

MACCLESFIELD (Cheshire)
*E.*76,548   *T.*82.29%

*N. Winterton, *C.*	36,447
Mrs M. Longworth, *Lab.*	13,680
Dr P. Beatty, *LD*	12,600
Mrs C. Penn, *NLP*	268
C. majority	22,767
(June 1987, C. maj. 19,092)	

MAIDSTONE (Kent)
*E.*72,834   *T.*80.08%

*Miss A. Widdecombe, *C.*	31,611
Ms P. Yates, *LD*	15,325
Ms A. Logan, *Lab.*	10,517
Ms P. Kemp, *Green*	707
F. Ingram, *NLP*	172
C. majority	16,286
(June 1987, C. maj. 10,364)	

MAKERFIELD (Greater Manchester)
*E.*71,425   *T.*76.09%

*I. McCartney, *Lab.*	32,832
Mrs D. Dickson, *C.*	14,714
S. Jeffers, *LD*	5,097
Ms S. Cairns, *Lib.*	1,309
C. Davies, *NLP*	397
Lab. majority	18,118
(June 1987, Lab. maj. 15,558)	

MANCHESTER BLACKLEY
*E.*55,234   *T.*69.31%

*K. Eastham, *Lab.*	23,031
W. Hobhouse, *C.*	10,642
S. Wheale, *LD*	4,324
M. Kennedy, *NLP*	288
Lab. majority	12,389
(June 1987, Lab. maj. 10,122)	

MANCHESTER CENTRAL
*E.*56,446   *T.*56.90%

*R. Litherland, *Lab.*	23,336
P. Davies, *C.*	5,299
M. Clayton, *LD*	3,151
A. Buchanan, *CL*	167
Ms V. Mitchell, *NLP*	167
Lab. majority	18,037
(June 1987, Lab. maj. 19,867)	

MANCHESTER GORTON
*E.*62,410   *T.*60.84%

*Rt. Hon. G. Kaufman, *Lab.*	23,671
J. Bullock, *C.*	7,392
P. Harris, *LD*	5,327
T. Henderson, *Lib.*	767
M. Daw, *Green*	595
Ms P. Lawrence, *Rev. Comm.*	108
P. Mitchell, *NLP*	84
Ms C. Smith, *Int. Comm.*	30
Lab. majority	16,279
(June 1987, Lab. maj. 14,065)	

MANCHESTER WITHINGTON
*E.*63,838   *T.*71.27%

*K. Bradley, *Lab.*	23,962
E. Farthing, *C.*	14,227
G. Hennell, *LD*	6,457
B. Candeland, *Green*	725
C. Menhinick, *NLP*	128
Lab. majority	9,735
(June 1987, Lab. maj. 3,391)	

MANCHESTER WYTHENSHAWE
*E.*53,548   *T.*69.68%

*Rt. Hon. A. Morris, *Lab.*	22,591
K. McKenna, *C.*	10,595
S. Fenn, *LD*	3,633
G. Otten, *Green*	362
Ms E. Martin, *NLP*	133
Lab. majority	11,996
(June 1987, Lab. maj. 11,855)	

MANSFIELD (Notts)
*E.*66,964   *T.*82.23%

*J. A. Meale, *Lab.*	29,932
G. Mond, *C.*	18,208
S. Thompstone, *LD*	6,925
Lab. majority	11,724
(June 1987, Lab. maj. 56)	

MEDWAY (Kent)
*E.*61,736   *T.*80.22%

*Dame P. Fenner, *C.*	25,924
R. Marshall-Andrews, *Lab.*	17,138
C. Trice, *LD*	4,751
M. Austin, *Lib.*	1,480
P. Kember, *NLP*	234
C. majority	8,786
(June 1987, C. maj. 9,929)	

MERIDEN (W. Midlands)
*E.*76,994   *T.*78.85%

*I. Mills, *C.*	33,462
N. Stephens, *Lab.*	18,763
Ms J. Morris, *LD*	8,489
C. majority	14,699
(June 1987, C. maj. 16,820)	

MIDDLESBROUGH (Cleveland)
*E.*58,844   *T.*69.85%

*S. Bell, *Lab.*	26,343
P. Rayner, *C.*	10,559
Ms R. Jordan, *LD*	4,201
Lab. majority	15,784
(June 1987, Lab. maj. 14,958)	

MILTON KEYNES NORTH EAST
(Bucks)
*E.*62,748   *T.*80.95%

P. Butler, *C.*	26,212
Ms M. Cosin, *Lab.*	12,036
P. Gaskell, *LD*	11,693
A. Francis, *Green*	529
Mrs M. Kavanagh-Dowsett, *Ind. C.*	249
M. Simson, *NLP*	79
C. majority	14,176
(New constituency)	

MILTON KEYNES SOUTH WEST
(Bucks)
*E.*66,422   *T.*77%

B. Legg, *C.*	23,840
K. Wilson, *Lab.*	19,153

C. Pym, *LD*	7,429
Dr C. Field, *Green*	525
H. Kelly, *NLP*	202
C. majority	4,687
(New constituency)	

MITCHAM AND MORDEN
(Greater London)
*E.*63,723   *T.*80.32%

*Rt. Hon. A. Rumbold, *C.*	23,789
Ms S. McDonagh, *Lab.*	22,055
J. Field, *LD*	4,687
T. Walsh, *Green*	655
C. majority	1,734
(June 1987, C. maj. 6,183)	

MOLE VALLEY (Surrey)
*E.*66,949   *T.*81.97%

*Rt. Hon. K. Baker, *C.*	32,549
M. Watson, *LD*	16,599
Dr T. Walsh, *Lab.*	5,291
Ms J. Thomas, *NLP*	442
C. majority	15,950
(June 1987, C. maj. 16,076)	

MORECAMBE AND LUNESDALE
(Lancs)
*E.*56,426   *T.*78.35%

*Hon. M. Lennox-Boyd, *C.*	22,507
Ms J. Yates, *Lab.*	10,998
A. Saville, *LD*	9,584
M. Turner, *MBI*	916
R. Marriott, *NLP*	205
C. majority	11,509
(June 1987, C. maj. 11,785)	

NEWARK (Notts)
*E.*68,801   *T.*82.17%

*R. Alexander, *C.*	28,494
D. Barton, *Lab.*	20,265
P. Harris, *LD*	7,342
Ms P. Wood, *Green*	435
C. majority	8,229
(June 1987, C. maj. 13,543)	

NEWBURY (Berks)
*E.*80,252   *T.*82.75%

Mrs J. Chaplin, *C.*	37,135
D. Rendel, *LD*	24,778
R. Hall, *Lab.*	3,962
J. Wallis, *Green*	539
C. majority	12,357
(June 1987, C. maj. 16,658)	

See also page 242

NEWCASTLE UNDER LYME
(Staffs)
*E.*66,595   *T.*80.34%

*Mrs L. Golding, *Lab.*	25,652
A. Brierley, *C.*	15,813
A. Thomas, *LD*	11,727
R. Lines, *NLP*	314
Lab. majority	9,839
(June 1987, Lab. maj. 5,132)	

NEWCASTLE UPON TYNE
CENTRAL
*E.*59,973   *T.*71.32%

*J. Cousins, *Lab.*	21,123
M. Summersby, *C.*	15,835
L. Opik, *LD*	5,816
Lab. majority	5,288
(June 1987, Lab. maj. 2,483)	

NEWCASTLE UPON TYNE EAST
E.57,165 T.70.73%
*N. Brown, *Lab.*	24,342
J. Lucas, *C.*	10,465
A. Thompson, *LD*	4,883
G. Edwards, *Green*	744
Lab. majority	13,877

(June 1987, Lab. maj. 12,500)

NEWCASTLE UPON TYNE NORTH
E.66,187 T.76.80%
*D. Henderson, *Lab.*	25,121
I. Gordon, *C.*	16,175
P. Maughan, *LD*	9,542
Lab. majority	8,946

(June 1987, Lab. maj. 5,243)

NEW FOREST (Hants)
E.75,413 T.80.76%
*Sir P. McNair-Wilson, *C.*	37,986
Ms J. Vernon-Jackson, *LD*	17,581
M. Shutler, *Lab.*	4,989
Ms F. Carter, *NLP*	350
C. majority	20,405

(June 1987, C. maj. 21,732)

NEWHAM NORTH EAST (Greater London)
E.59,555 T.60.34%
*R. Leighton, *Lab.*	20,952
J. Galbraith, *C.*	10,966
J. Aves, *LD*	4,020
Lab. majority	9,986

(June 1987, Lab. maj. 8,236)

NEWHAM NORTH WEST (Greater London)
E.46,471 T.56.02%
*T. Banks, *Lab.*	15,911
M. Prisk, *C.*	6,740
A. Sawdon, *LD*	2,445
Ms A. Standford, *Green*	587
T. Jug, *Loony G.*	252
D. O'Sullivan, *Int. Comm.*	100
Lab. majority	9,171

(June 1987, Lab. maj. 8,496)

NEWHAM SOUTH (Greater London)
E.51,143 T.60.19%
*N. Spearing, *Lab.*	14,358
Ms J. Foster, *C.*	11,856
A. Kellaway, *LD*	4,572
Lab. majority	2,502

(June 1987, Lab. maj. 2,766)

NORFOLK MID
E.80,336 T.81.64%
*Rt. Hon. R. Ryder, *C.*	35,620
M. Castle, *Lab.*	16,672
J. Gleed, *LD*	13,072
Ms C. Waite, *NLP*	226
C. majority	18,948

(June 1987, C. maj. 18,008)

NORFOLK NORTH
E.73,780 T.80.84%
*R. Howell, *C.*	28,810
N. Lamb, *LD*	16,265
M. Cullingham, *Lab.*	13,850
Ms A. Zelter, *Green*	559

Ms S. Jackson, *NLP* 167
C. majority	12,545

(June 1987, C. maj. 15,310)

NORFOLK NORTH WEST
E.77,438 T.80.67%
*H. Bellingham, *C.*	32,554
Dr G. Turner, *Lab.*	20,990
A. Waterman, *LD*	8,599
S. Pink, *NLP*	330
C. majority	11,564

(June 1987, C. maj. 10,825)

NORFOLK SOUTH
E.81,647 T.83.99%
*Rt. Hon. J. MacGregor, *C.*	36,081
C. Brocklebank-Fowler, *LD*	18,516
C. Needle, *Lab.*	12,422
Ms S. Ross-Wagenknecht, *Green*	702
N. Clark, *NLP*	320
R. Peacock, *Ind.*	304
R. Watkins, *Ind. C.*	232
C. majority	17,565

(June 1987, C. maj. 12,418)

NORFOLK SOUTH WEST
E.77,652 T.79.30%
*Mrs G. Shephard, *C.*	33,637
Ms M. Page, *Lab.*	16,706
J. Marsh, *LD*	11,237
C. majority	16,931

(June 1987, C. maj. 20,436)

NORMANTON (W. Yorks)
E.65,562 T.76.35%
*W. O'Brien, *Lab.*	25,936
R. Sturdy, *C.*	16,986
M. Galdas, *LD*	7,137
Lab. majority	8,950

(June 1987, Lab. maj. 7,287)

NORTHAMPTON NORTH
E.69,139 T.78.52%
*A. Marlow, *C.*	24,865
Ms J. Thomas, *Lab.*	20,957
R. Church, *LD*	8,236
B. Spivack, *NLP*	232
C. majority	3,908

(June 1987, C. maj. 9,256)

NORTHAMPTON SOUTH
E.83,477 T.79.90%
*M. Morris, *C.*	36,882
J. Dickie, *Lab.*	19,909
G. Mabbutt, *LD*	9,912
C. majority	16,973

(June 1987, C. maj. 17,803)

NORTHAVON (Avon)
E.83,496 T.84.16%
*Rt. Hon. Sir J. Cope, *C.*	35,338
Ms H. Larkins, *LD*	23,477
Ms J. Norris, *Lab.*	10,290
Ms J. Greene, *Green*	789
P. Marx, *Lib.*	380
C. majority	11,861

(June 1987, C. maj. 14,270)

NORWICH NORTH (Norfolk)
E.63,308 T.81.82%
*H. P. Thompson, *C.*	22,419
I. Gibson, *Lab.*	22,153
D. Harrison, *LD*	6,706

L. Betts, *Green*	433
R. Arnold, *NLP*	93
C. majority	266

(June 1987, C. maj. 7,776)

NORWICH SOUTH (Norfolk)
E.63,603 T.80.60%
*J. Garrett, *Lab.*	24,965
D. Baxter, *C.*	18,784
C. Thomas, *LD*	6,609
A. Holmes, *Green*	803
B. Parsons, *NLP*	104
Lab. majority	6,181

(June 1987, Lab. maj. 336)

NORWOOD (Greater London)
E.52,496 T.65.87%
*J. Fraser, *Lab.*	18,391
J. Samways, *C.*	11,175
Ms S. Lawman, *LD*	4,087
S. Collins, *Green*	790
M. Leighton, *NLP*	138
Lab. majority	7,216

(June 1987, Lab. maj. 4,723)

NOTTINGHAM EAST
E.67,939 T.70.08%
J. Heppell, *Lab.*	25,026
*M. Knowles, *C.*	17,346
T. Ball, *LD*	3,695
A. Jones, *Green*	667
C. Roylance, *Lib.*	598
J. Ashforth, *NLP*	283
Lab. majority	7,680

(June 1987, C. maj. 456)

NOTTINGHAM NORTH
E.69,494 T.74.98%
*G. Allen, *Lab.*	29,052
I. Bridge, *C.*	18,309
A. Skelton, *LD*	4,477
A. Cadman, *NLP*	274
Lab. majority	10,743

(June 1987, Lab. maj. 1,665)

NOTTINGHAM SOUTH
E.72,796 T.74.22%
A. Simpson, *Lab.*	25,771
*M. Brandon-Bravo, *C.*	22,590
G. D. Long, *LD*	5,408
Ms J. Christou, *NLP*	263
Lab. majority	3,181

(June 1987, C. maj. 2,234)

NUNEATON (Warwicks)
E.70,906 T.83.70%
W. Olner, *Lab.*	27,157
*L. Stevens, *C.*	25,526
Ms R. Merritt, *LD*	6,671
Lab. majority	1,631

(June 1987, C. maj. 5,655)

OLD BEXLEY AND SIDCUP (Greater London)
E.49,449 T.81.94%
*Rt. Hon. E. Heath, *C.*	24,450
Ms D. Brierly, *Lab.*	8,751
D. Nicolle, *LD*	6,438
B. Rose, *Alt. C.*	733
R. Stephens, *NLP*	148
C. majority	15,699

(June 1987, C. maj. 16,274)

OLDHAM CENTRAL AND
ROYTON (Greater Manchester)
E.61,333   T.74.20%

B. Davies, *Lab.*	23,246
Mrs T. Morris, *C.*	14,640
Ms A. Dunn, *LD*	7,224
I. Dalling, *NLP*	403
Lab. majority	8,606

(June 1987, Lab. maj. 6,279)

OLDHAM WEST (Greater
Manchester)
E.54,063   T.75.65%

*M. Meacher, *Lab.*	21,580
J. Gillen, *C.*	13,247
J. Smith, *LD*	5,525
Ms S. Dalling, *NLP*	551
Lab. majority	8,333

(June 1987, Lab. maj. 5,967)

ORPINGTON (Greater London)
E.57,318   T.83.67%

J. Horam, *C.*	27,421
C. Maines, *LD*	14,486
S. Cowan, *Lab.*	5,512
R. Almond, *Lib.*	539
C. majority	12,935

(June 1987, C. maj. 12,732)

OXFORD EAST
E.63,075   T.74.59%

*A. Smith, *Lab.*	23,702
Dr M. Mayall, *C.*	16,164
M. Horwood, *LD*	6,105
Mrs C. Lucas, *Green*	933
Miss A. Wilson, *NLP*	101
K. Thompson, *Rev. Comm.*	48
Lab. majority	7,538

(June 1987, Lab. maj. 1,288)

OXFORD WEST AND ABINGDON
E.72,328   T.76.68%

*Rt. Hon. J. Patten, *C.*	25,163
Sir W. Goodhart, *LD*	21,624
B. Kent, *Lab.*	7,652
M. Woodin, *Green*	660
R. Jenking, *Lib.*	194
Miss S. Nelson, *Anti Fed.*	98
G. Wells, *NLP*	75
C. majority	3,539

(June 1987, C. maj. 4,878)

PECKHAM (Greater London)
E.58,269   T.53.87%

*Ms H. Harman, *Lab.*	19,391
C. Frazer, *C.*	7,386
Mrs R. Colley, *LD*	4,331
G. Dacres, *WRP*	146
V. Emmanuel, *Whiplash*	140
Lab. majority	12,005

(June 1987, Lab. maj. 9,489)

PENDLE (Lancs)
E.64,063   T.82.91%

G. Prentice, *Lab.*	23,497
*J. Lee, *C.*	21,384
A. Davies, *LD*	7,976
Mrs V. Thome, *Anti Fed.*	263
Lab. majority	2,113

(June 1987, Lab. maj. 2,639)

PENRITH AND THE BORDER
(Cumbria)
E.73,769   T.79.67%

*D. Maclean, *C.*	33,808
G. Walker, *LD*	15,359
J. Metcalfe, *Lab.*	8,871
R. Gibson, *Green*	610
I. Docker, *NLP*	129
C. majority	18,449

(June 1987, C. maj. 17,366)

PETERBOROUGH (Cambs)
E.87,638   T.75.12%

*B. Mawhinney, *C.*	31,827
Ms J. Owens, *Lab.*	26,451
Ms A. Taylor, *LD*	5,208
E. Murat, *Lib.*	1,557
R. Heaton, *BNP*	311
P. Beasley, *PP*	271
C. Brettell, *NLP*	215
C. majority	5,376

(June 1987, C. maj. 9,784)

PLYMOUTH DEVONPORT (Devon)
E.65,799   T.77.83%

D. Jamieson, *Lab.*	24,953
K. Simpson, *C.*	17,541
M. Mactaggart, *LD*	6,315
H. Luscombe, *SD*	2,152
F. Lyons, *NLP*	255
Lab. majority	7,412

(June 1987, SDP/All. maj. 6,470)

PLYMOUTH DRAKE (Devon)
E.51,667   T.75.56%

*Dame J. Fookes, *C.*	17,075
P. Telford, *Lab.*	15,062
Ms V. Cox, *LD*	5,893
D. Stanbury, *SD*	476
Ms A. Harrison, *Green*	441
T. Pringle, *NLP*	95
C. majority	2,013

(June 1987, C. maj. 3,125)

PLYMOUTH SUTTON (Devon)
E.67,430   T.81.17%

G. Streeter, *C.*	27,070
A. Pawley, *Lab.*	15,120
J. Brett-Freeman, *LD*	12,291
J. Bowler, *NLP*	256
C. majority	11,950

(June 1987, C. maj. 4,013)

PONTEFRACT AND
CASTLEFORD (W. Yorks)
E.64,648   T.74.25%

*G. Lofthouse, *Lab.*	33,546
A. Rockall, *C.*	10,051
D. Ryan, *LD*	4,410
Lab. majority	23,495

(June 1987, Lab. maj. 21,626)

POOLE (Dorset)
E.79,221   T.79.39%

*J. Ward, *C.*	33,445
B. Clements, *LD*	20,614
H. White, *Lab.*	6,912
M. Steen, *Ind. C.*	1,620
A. Bailey, *NLP*	303
C. majority	12,831

(June 1987, C. maj. 14,808)

PORTSMOUTH NORTH (Hants)
E.79,592   T.77.05%

*P. Griffiths, *C.*	32,240
A. Burnett, *Lab.*	18,359
A. Bentley, *LD*	10,101
Ms H. Palmer, *Green*	628
C. majority	13,881

(June 1987, C. maj. 18,401)

PORTSMOUTH SOUTH (Hants)
E.77,645   T.69.09%

*D. Martin, *C.*	22,798
M. Hancock, *LD*	22,556
S. Rapson, *Lab.*	7,857
A. Zivkovic, *Green*	349
W. Trend, *NLP*	91
C. majority	242

(June 1987, C. maj. 205)

PRESTON (Lancs)
E.64,158   T.71.74%

*Mrs A. Wise, *Lab.*	24,983
S. O'Toole, *C.*	12,808
W. Chadwick, *LD*	7,897
Ms J. Ayliffe, *NLP*	341
Lab. majority	12,175

(June 1987, Lab. maj. 10,645)

PUDSEY (W. Yorks)
E.70,847   T.80.14%

*Sir G. Shaw, *C.*	25,067
A. Giles, *Lab.*	16,095
D. Shutt, *LD*	15,153
Ms J. Wynne, *Green*	466
C. majority	8,972

(June 1987, C. maj. 6,436)

PUTNEY (Greater London)
E.61,914   T.77.91%

*Rt. Hon. D. Mellor, *C.*	25,188
Ms J. Chegwidden, *Lab.*	17,662
J. Martyn, *LD*	4,636
K. Hagenbach, *Green*	618
P. Levy, *NLP*	139
C. majority	7,526

(June 1987, C. maj. 6,907)

RAVENSBOURNE (Greater London)
E.57,259   T.81.24%

*Sir J. Hunt, *C.*	29,506
P. Booth, *LD*	9,792
E. Dyer, *Lab.*	6,182
I. Mouland, *Green*	617
P. White, *Lib.*	318
J. Shepheard, *NLP*	105
C. majority	19,714

(June 1987, C. maj. 16,919)

READING EAST (Berks)
E.72,151   T.75.02%

*Sir G. Vaughan, *C.*	29,148
Ms G. Parker, *Lab.*	14,593
D. Thair, *LD*	9,528
Ms A. McCubbin, *Green*	861
C. majority	14,555

(June 1987, C. maj. 16,217)

READING WEST (Berks)
E.67,937   T.77.98%

*Sir A. Durant, *C.*	28,048
P. Ruhemann, *Lab.*	14,750
K. Lock, *LD*	9,572

P. Unsworth, *Green* 613
C. majority 13,298
(June 1987, C. maj. 16,753)

REDCAR (Cleveland)
*E.*62,494 *T.*77.73%
*Dr M. Mowlam, *Lab.* 27,184
R. Goodwill, *C.* 15,607
C. Abbott, *LD* 5,789
Lab. majority 11,577
(June 1987, Lab. maj. 7,735)

REIGATE (Surrey)
*E.*71,853 *T.*78.54%
*Sir G. Gardiner, *C.* 32,220
B. Newsome, *LD* 14,556
Ms H. Young, *Lab.* 9,150
M. Dilcliff, *SD* 513
C. majority 17,664
(June 1987, C. maj. 18,173)

RIBBLE VALLEY (Lancs)
*E.*64,996 *T.*85.73%
N. Evans, *C.* 29,178
*M. Carr, *LD* 22,636
R. Pickup, *Lab.* 3,649
D. Beesley, *Loony G.* 152
Ms N. Holmes, *NLP* 112
C. majority 6,542
(June 1987, C. maj. 19,528)
(March 1991, LD maj. 4,641)

RICHMOND AND BARNES
(Greater London)
*E.*53,081 *T.*85.01%
*J. Hanley, *C.* 22,894
Dr J. Tonge, *LD* 19,025
D. Touhig, *Lab.* 2,632
Ms J. Maciejowska, *Green* 376
C. Cunningham, *NLP* 89
R. Meacock, *QFL* 62
Ms A. Ellis-Jones, *Anti Fed.* 47
C. majority 3,869
(June 1987, C. maj. 1,766)

RICHMOND (N. Yorks)
*E.*82,879 *T.*78.41%
*W. Hague, *C.* 40,202
G. Irwin, *LD* 16,698
R. Cranston, *Lab.* 7,523
M. Barr, *Ind.* 570
C. majority 23,504
(June 1987, C. maj. 19,576)
(Feb 1989, C. maj. 2,634)

ROCHDALE (Greater Manchester)
*E.*69,522 *T.*76.47%
Ms E. Lynne, *LD* 22,776
D. Williams, *Lab.* 20,937
D. Goldie-Scott, *C.* 8,626
K. Henderson, *BNP* 620
V. Lucker, *NLP* 211
LD majority 1,839
(June 1987, L./All. maj. 2,779)

ROCHFORD (Essex)
*E.*76,869 *T.*82.99%
*Dr M. Clark, *C.* 38,967
N. Harris, *LD* 12,931
D. Quinn, *Lab.* 10,537
Ms L. Farmer, *Lib.* 1,362
C. majority 26,036
(June 1987, C. maj. 19,694)

ROMFORD (Greater London)
*E.*54,001 *T.*78%
*Sir M. Neubert, *C.* 23,834
Ms E. Gordon, *Lab.* 12,414
Ms P. Atherton, *LD* 5,329
F. Gibson, *Green* 546
C. majority 11,420
(June 1987, C. maj. 13,471)

ROMSEY AND WATERSIDE
(Hants)
*E.*82,628 *T.*83.15%
*M. Colvin, *C.* 37,375
G. Dawson, *LD* 22,071
Mrs A. Mawle, *Lab.* 8,688
J. Spottiswood, *Green* 577
C. majority 15,304
(June 1987, C. maj. 15,272)

ROSSENDALE AND DARWEN
(Lancs)
*E.*76,909 *T.*83.06%
Mrs J. Anderson, *Lab.* 28,028
*D. Trippier, *C.* 27,908
K. Connor, *LD* 7,226
J. Gaffney, *Green* 596
P. Gorrod, *NLP* 125
Lab. majority 120
(June 1987, C. maj. 4,982)

ROTHERHAM (S. Yorks)
*E.*60,937 *T.*71.68%
J. Boyce, *Lab.* 27,933
S. Yorke, *C.* 10,372
D. Wildgoose, *LD* 5,375
Lab. majority 17,561
(June 1987, Lab. maj. 16,012)

ROTHER VALLEY (S. Yorks)
*E.*68,303 *T.*74.98%
*K. Barron, *Lab.* 30,977
T. Horton, *C.* 13,755
K. Smith, *LD* 6,483
Lab. majority 17,222
(June 1987, Lab. maj. 15,790)

RUGBY AND KENILWORTH
(Warwicks)
*E.*77,766 *T.*83.72%
*J. Pawsey, *C.* 34,110
J. Airey, *Lab.* 20,863
J. Roodhouse, *LD* 9,934
S. Withers, *NLP* 202
C. majority 13,247
(June 1987, C. maj. 16,264)

RUISLIP-NORTHWOOD (Greater
London)
*E.*54,151 *T.*81.91%
*J. Wilkinson, *C.* 28,097
Ms R. Brooks, *Lab.* 8,306
H. Davies, *LD* 7,739
M. Sheehan, *NLP* 214
C. majority 19,791
(June 1987, C. maj. 16,971)

RUSHCLIFFE (Notts)
*E.*76,253 *T.*83.04%
*Rt. Hon. K. Clarke, *C.* 34,448
A. Chewings, *Lab.* 14,682
Dr A. Wood, *LD* 12,660
S. Anthony, *Green* 775

M. Maelor-Jones, *Ind. C.* 611
D. Richards, *NLP* 150
C. majority 19,766
(June 1987, C. maj. 20,839)

RUTLAND AND MELTON (Leics)
*E.*80,976 *T.*80.82%
A. Duncan, *C.* 38,603
Ms J. Taylor, *Lab.* 13,068
R. Lustig, *LD* 12,682
J. Berreen, *Green* 861
R. Grey, *NLP* 237
C. majority 25,535
(June 1987, C. maj. 23,022)

RYEDALE (N. Yorks)
*E.*87,048 *T.*81.73%
*J. Greenway, *C.* 39,888
Mrs E. Shields, *LD* 21,449
J. Healey, *Lab.* 9,812
C. majority 18,439
(June 1987, C. maj. 9,740)

SAFFRON WALDEN (Essex)
*E.*74,878 *T.*83.21%
*A. Haselhurst, *C.* 35,272
M. Hayes, *LD* 17,848
J. Kotz, *Lab.* 8,933
M. Miller, *NLP* 260
C. majority 17,424
(June 1987, C. maj. 16,602)

ST ALBANS (Herts)
*E.*74,188 *T.*83.47%
*Rt. Hon. P. Lilley, *C.* 32,709
Ms M. Howes, *LD* 16,305
K. Pollard, *Lab.* 12,016
C. Simmons, *Green* 734
D. Lucas, *NLP* 161
C. majority 16,404
(June 1987, C. maj. 10,881)

ST HELENS NORTH (Merseyside)
*E.*71,261 *T.*77.35%
*J. Evans, *Lab.* 31,930
B. Anderson, *C.* 15,686
J. Beirne, *LD* 7,224
Ms A. Lynch, *NLP* 287
Lab. majority 16,244
(June 1987, Lab. maj. 14,260)

ST HELENS SOUTH (Merseyside)
*E.*67,507 *T.*73.77%
*G. Bermingham, *Lab.* 30,391
Mrs P. Buzzard, *C.* 12,182
B. Spencer, *LD* 6,933
Dr H. Jump, *NLP* 295
Lab. majority 18,209
(June 1987, Lab. maj. 13,801)

ST IVES (Cornwall)
*E.*71,152 *T.*80.29%
*D. Harris, *C.* 24,528
A. George, *LD* 22,883
S. Warran, *Lab.* 9,144
Dr G. Stephens, *Lib.* 577
C. majority 1,645
(June 1987, C. maj. 7,555)

SALFORD EAST (Greater
Manchester)
E.52,616   T.64.36%
*Rt. Hon. S. Orme, *Lab.*   20,327
D. Berens, *C.*   9,092
N. Owen, *LD*   3,836
M. Stanley, *Green*   463
C. Craig, *NLP*   150
Lab. majority   11,235
(June 1987, Lab. maj. 12,056)

SALISBURY (Wilts)
E.75,916   T.79.89%
*S. R. Key, *C.*   31,546
P. Sample, *LD*   22,573
S. Fear, *Lab.*   5,483
Dr S. Elcock, *Green*   609
S. Fletcher, *Ind.*   233
T. Abbott, *Wessex*   117
Ms A. Martell, *NLP*   93
C. majority   8,973
(June 1987, C. maj. 11,443)

SCARBOROUGH (N. Yorks)
E.76,364   T.77.18%
J. Sykes, *C.*   29,334
D. Billing, *Lab.*   17,600
B. Davenport, *LD*   11,133
Dr D. Richardson, *Green*   876
C. majority   11,734
(June 1987, C. maj. 13,626)

SEDGEFIELD (Durham)
E.61,024   T.77.06%
*A. Blair, *Lab.*   28,453
N. Jopling, *C.*   13,594
G. Huntington, *LD*   4,982
Lab. majority   14,859
(June 1987, Lab. maj. 13,058)

SELBY (N. Yorks)
E.77,178   T.80.16%
*Rt. Hon. M. Alison, *C.*   31,067
J. Grogan, *Lab.*   21,559
E. Batty, *LD*   9,244
C. majority   9,508
(June 1987, C. maj. 13,779)

SEVENOAKS (Kent)
E.71,050   T.81.35%
*G. M. Wolfson, *C.*   33,245
R. Walshe, *LD*   14,091
Ms J. Evans, *Lab.*   9,470
Ms M. Lawrence, *Green*   786
P. Wakeling, *NLP*   210
C. majority   19,154
(June 1987, C. maj. 17,345)

SHEFFIELD ATTERCLIFFE
(S. Yorks)
E.69,177   T.71.81%
C. Betts, *Lab.*   28,563
G. Millward, *C.*   13,083
Ms H. Woolley, *LD*   7,283
G. Ferguson, *Green*   751
Lab. majority   15,480
(June 1987, Lab. maj. 17,191)

SHEFFIELD BRIGHTSIDE
(S. Yorks)
E.63,810   T.66.26%
*D. Blunkett, *Lab.*   29,771
T. Loughton, *C.*   7,090

R. Franklin, *LD*   5,273
D. Hyland, *Int. Comm.*   150
Lab. majority   22,681
(June 1987, Lab. maj. 24,191)

SHEFFIELD CENTRAL (S. Yorks)
E.59,059   T.56.12%
*R. Caborn, *Lab.*   22,764
V. Davies, *C.*   5,470
A. Sangar, *LD*   3,856
G. Wroe, *Green*   750
M. Clarke, *EUVJJ*   212
Ms J. O'Brien, *CL*   92
Lab. majority   17,294
(June 1987, Lab. maj. 19,342)

SHEFFIELD HALLAM (S. Yorks)
E.76,584   T.70.83%
*C. I. Patnick, *C.*   24,693
Dr P. Gold, *LD*   17,952
Ms V. Hardstaff, *Lab.*   10,930
M. Baker, *Green*   473
R. Hurford, *NLP*   101
Ms T. Clifford, *Rev. Comm.*   99
C. majority   6,741
(June 1987, C. maj. 7,637)

SHEFFIELD HEELEY (S. Yorks)
E.70,953   T.70.89%
*W. Michie, *Lab.*   28,005
D. Beck, *C.*   13,051
P. Moore, *LD*   9,247
Lab. majority   14,954
(June 1987, Lab. maj. 14,440)

SHEFFIELD HILLSBOROUGH
(S. Yorks)
E.77,343   T.77.19%
Mrs H. Jackson, *Lab.*   27,568
D. Chadwick, *LD*   20,500
S. Cordle, *C.*   11,640
Lab. majority   7,068
(June 1987, Lab. maj. 3,286)

SHERWOOD (Notts)
E.73,354   T.85.48%
S. P. Tipping, *Lab.*   29,788
*A. Stewart, *C.*   26,878
J. Howard, *LD*   6,039
Lab. majority   2,910
(June 1987, C. maj. 4,495)

SHIPLEY (W. Yorks)
E.68,816   T.82.12%
*Sir M. Fox, *C.*   28,463
Ms A. Lockwood, *Lab.*   16,081
J. Cole, *LD*   11,288
C. Harris, *Green*   680
C. majority   12,382
(June 1987, C. maj. 12,630)

SHOREHAM (W. Sussex)
E.71,252   T.81.17%
B. M. L. Stephen, *C.*   32,670
M. King, *LD*   18,384
P. Godwin, *Lab.*   6,123
W. Weights, *Lib.*   459
J. Dreben, *NLP*   200
C. majority   14,286
(June 1987, C. maj. 17,070)

SHREWSBURY AND ATCHAM
(Salop)
E.70,620   T.82.45%
*D. Conway, *C.*   26,681
K. Hemsley, *LD*   15,716
Ms E. Owen, *Lab.*   15,157
G. Hardy, *Green*   677
C. majority   10,965
(June 1987, C. maj. 9,064)

SHROPSHIRE NORTH
E.82,675   T.77.68%
*Rt. Hon. J. Biffen, *C.*   32,443
J. Stevens, *LD*   16,232
R. Hawkins, *Lab.*   15,550
C. majority   16,211
(June 1987, C. maj. 14,415)

SKIPTON AND RIPON (N. Yorks)
E.75,628   T.81.34%
*D. Curry, *C.*   35,937
R. Hall, *LD*   16,607
Ms K. Allott, *Lab.*   8,978
C. majority   19,330
(June 1987, C. maj. 17,174)

SLOUGH (Berks)
E.73,889   T.78.24%
*J. Watts, *C.*   25,793
E. Lopez, *Lab.*   25,279
P. Mapp, *LD*   4,041
J. Clark, *Lib.*   1,426
D. Alford, *Ind. Lab.*   699
A. Carmichael, *NF*   290
M. Creese, *NLP*   153
Ms E. Smith, *ERIP*   134
C. majority   514
(June 1987, C. maj. 4,090)

SOLIHULL (W. Midlands)
E.77,303   T.81.61%
*J. Taylor, *C.*   38,385
M. Southcombe, *LD*   13,229
Ms N. Kutapan, *Lab.*   10,544
C. Hards, *Green*   925
C. majority   25,146
(June 1987, C. maj. 21,786)

SOMERTON AND FROME
(Somerset)
E.71,354   T.82.75%
M. Robinson, *C.*   28,052
D. Heath, *LD*   23,711
R. Ashford, *Lab.*   6,154
Ms L. Graham, *Green*   742
Ms J. Pollock, *Lib.*   388
C. majority   4,341
(June 1987, C. maj. 9,538)

SOUTHAMPTON ITCHEN (Hants)
E.72,104   T.76.93%
J. Denham, *Lab.*   24,402
*C. Chope, *C.*   23,851
J. Hodgson, *LD*   7,221
Lab. majority   551
(June 1987, C. maj. 6,716)

SOUTHAMPTON TEST (Hants)
E.72,932   T.77.40%
*S. J. A. Hill, *C.*   24,504
A. Whitehead, *Lab.*   23,919
Ms D. Maddock, *LD*   7,391

J. Michaelis, *Green* 535
D. Plummer, *NLP* 101
C. majority 585
(June 1987, C. maj. 6,954)

SOUTHEND EAST (Essex)
*E.*56,708   *T.*73.80%
*Sir E. Taylor, *C.* 24,591
G. Bramley, *Lab.* 11,480
Ms J. Horne, *LD* 5,107
B. Lynch, *Lib.* 673
C. majority 13,111
(June 1987, C. maj. 13,847)

SOUTHEND WEST (Essex)
*E.*64,198   *T.*77.80%
*Rt. Hon. P. Channon, *C.* 27,319
Ms N. Stimson, *LD* 15,417
G. Viney, *Lab.* 6,139
A. Farmer, *Lib.* 495
C. Keene, *Green* 451
P. Warburton, *NLP* 127
C. majority 11,902
(June 1987, C. maj. 8,400)

SOUTH HAMS (Devon)
*E.*83,061   *T.*81.09%
*A. Steen, *C.* 35,951
V. Evans, *LD* 22,240
Ms E. Cohen, *Lab.* 8,091
C. Titmuss, *Green* 846
Mrs L. Summerville, *NLP* 227
C. majority 13,711
(June 1987, C. maj. 13,146)

SOUTHPORT (Merseyside)
*E.*71,443   *T.*77.60%
M. Banks, *C.* 26,081
*R. Fearn, *LD* 23,018
J. King, *Lab.* 5,637
J. Walker, *Green* 545
G. Clements, *NLP* 159
C. majority 3,063
(June 1987, L./All. maj. 1,849)

SOUTH RIBBLE (Lancs)
*E.*78,173   *T.*82.99%
*R. Atkins, *C.* 30,828
Dr G. Smith, *Lab.* 24,855
S. Jones, *LD* 8,928
Dr R. Decter, *NLP* 269
C. majority 5,973
(June 1987, C. maj. 8,430)

SOUTH SHIELDS (Tyne & Wear)
*E.*59,392   *T.*70.07%
*D. Clark, *Lab.* 24,876
J. Howard, *C.* 11,399
A. Preece, *LD* 5,344
Lab. majority 13,477
(June 1987, Lab. maj. 13,851)

SOUTHWARK AND BERMONDSEY
(Greater London)
*E.*60,251   *T.*62.62%
*S. Hughes, *LD* 21,459
R. Balfe, *Lab.* 11,614
A. Raca, *C.* 3,794
S. Tyler, *BNP* 530
T. Blackham, *NF* 168
Dr G. Barnett, *NLP* 113
J. Grogan, *CL* 56

LD majority 9,845
June 1987, L./All. maj. 2,779

SPELTHORNE (Surrey)
*E.*69,343   *T.*80.36%
*D. Wilshire, *C.* 32,627
Ms A. Leedham, *Lab.* 12,784
R. Roberts, *LD* 9,202
Ms J. Wassell, *Green* 580
D. Rea, *Loony* 338
D. Ellis, *NLP* 195
C. majority 19,843
(June 1987, C. maj. 20,050)

STAFFORD
*E.*74,663   *T.*82.91%
*W. Cash, *C.* 30,876
D. Kidney, *Lab.* 19,976
Mrs J. Calder, *LD* 10,702
C. Peat, *Hardcore* 178
P. Lines, *NLP* 176
C. majority 10,900
(June 1987, C. maj. 13,707)

STAFFORDSHIRE MID
*E.*73,414   *T.*85.66%
M. Fabricant, *C.* 31,227
*Mrs S. Heal, *Lab.* 24,991
B. Stamp, *LD* 6,432
Ms D. Grice, *NLP* 239
C. majority 6,236
(June 1987, C. maj. 14,654)
(March 1990, Lab. maj. 9,449)

STAFFORDSHIRE MOORLANDS
*E.*75,036   *T.*83.66%
*D. Knox, *C.* 29,240
J. Siddelley, *Lab.* 21,830
Ms C. Jebb, *LD* 9,326
M. Howson, *Anti Fed.* 2,121
P. Davies, *NLP* 261
C. majority 7,410
(June 1987, C. maj. 14,427)

STAFFORDSHIRE SOUTH
*E.*82,758   *T.*81.54%
*P. Cormack, *C.* 40,266
B. Wylie, *Lab.* 17,633
I. Sadler, *LD* 9,584
C. majority 22,633
(June 1987, C. maj. 25,268)

STAFFORDSHIRE SOUTH EAST
*E.*70,199   *T.*82.05%
*D. Lightbown, *C.* 29,180
B. Jenkins, *Lab.* 21,988
Dr G. Penlington, *LD* 5,540
Miss J. Taylor, *SD* 895
C. majority 7,192
(June 1987, C. maj. 10,885)

STALYBRIDGE AND HYDE
(Greater Manchester)
*E.*68,189   *T.*73.46%
*T. Pendry, *Lab.* 26,207
S. Mort, *C.* 17,376
I. Kirk, *LD* 4,740
R. Powell, *Lib.* 1,199
D. Poyzer, *Loony* 337
E. Blomfield, *NLP* 238
Lab. majority 8,831
(June 1987, Lab. maj. 5,663)

STAMFORD AND SPALDING
(Lincs)
*E.*75,153   *T.*81.16%
*J. Q. Davies, *C.* 35,965
C. Burke, *Lab.* 13,096
B. Lee, *LD* 11,939
C. majority 22,869
(June 1987, C. maj. 14,007)

STEVENAGE (Herts)
*E.*70,233   *T.*83.03%
*T. Wood, *C.* 26,652
Ms J. Church, *Lab.* 21,764
A. Reilly, *LD* 9,668
A. Calcraft, *NLP* 233
C. majority 4,888
(June 1987, C. maj. 5,340)

STOCKPORT (Greater Manchester)
*E.*58,095   *T.*82.27%
Ms M. A. Coffey, *Lab.* 21,096
*A. Favell, *C.* 19,674
Ms A. Corris, *LD* 6,539
Ms J. Filmore, *Green* 436
D. Saunders, *NLP* 50
Lab. majority 1,422
(June 1987, C. maj. 2,853)

STOCKTON NORTH (Cleveland)
*E.*69,451   *T.*76.83%
*F. Cook, *Lab.* 27,918
S. Brocklebank-Fowler, *C.* 17,444
Ms S. Fletcher, *LD* 7,454
K. McGarvey, *Ind. Lab.* 550
Lab. majority 10,474
(June 1987, Lab. maj. 8,801)

STOCKTON SOUTH (Cleveland)
*E.*75,959   *T.*82.77%
*T. Devlin, *C.* 28,418
J. Scott, *Lab.* 25,049
Ms K. Kirkham, *LD* 9,410
C. majority 3,369
(June 1987, C. maj. 774)

STOKE-ON-TRENT CENTRAL
(Staffs)
*E.*65,527   *T.*68.12%
*M. Fisher, *Lab.* 25,897
N. Gibb, *C.* 12,477
M. Dent, *LD* 6,073
N. Pullen, *NLP* 196
Lab. majority 13,420
(June 1987, Lab. maj. 9,770)

STOKE-ON-TRENT NORTH
(Staffs)
*E.*73,141   *T.*73.42%
*Ms J. Walley, *Lab.* 30,464
L. Harris, *C.* 15,687
J. Redfern, *LD* 7,167
A. Morrison, *NLP* 387
Lab. majority 14,777
(June 1987, Lab. maj. 8,513)

STOKE-ON-TRENT SOUTH (Staffs)
*E.*71,316   *T.*74.33%
G. Stevenson, *Lab.* 26,380
R. Ibbs, *C.* 19,471
F. Jones, *LD* 6,870
Mrs E. Lines, *NLP* 291
Lab. majority 6,909
(June 1987, Lab. maj. 5,053)

STRATFORD-UPON-AVON
(Warwicks)
E.82,824   T.82.07%

*A. Howarth, *C.*	40,251
N. Fogg, *LD*	17,359
Ms S. Brookes, *Lab.*	8,932
R. Roughan, *Green*	729
A. Saunders, *Ind. C.*	573
M. Twite, *NLP*	130
C. majority	22,892

(June 1987, C. maj. 21,165)

STREATHAM (Greater London)
E.56,825   T.69.03%

K. Hill, *Lab.*	18,925
*Sir W. Shelton, *C.*	16,608
J. Pindar, *LD*	2,858
R. Baker, *Green*	443
A. Hankin, *Islamic*	154
Mrs C. Payne, *ADS*	145
J. Parsons, *NLP*	97
Lab. majority	2,317

(June 1987, C. maj. 2,407)

STRETFORD (Greater Manchester)
E.54,467   T.68.76%

*A. Lloyd, *Lab.*	22,300
C. Rae, *C.*	11,163
F. Beswick, *LD*	3,722
A. Boyton, *NLP*	268
Lab. majority	11,137

(June 1987, Lab. maj. 9,402)

STROUD (Glos)
E.82,553   T.84.49%

*R. Knapman, *C.*	32,201
D. Drew, *Lab.*	18,796
M. Robinson, *LD*	16,751
Ms S. Atkinson, *Green*	2,005
C. majority	13,405

(June 1987, C. maj. 12,375)

SUFFOLK CENTRAL
E.82,735   T.80.26%

*M. Lord, *C.*	32,917
Ms L. Henniker-Major, *LD*	16,886
J. Harris, *Lab.*	15,615
J. Matthissen, *Green*	800
Ms J. Wilmot, *NLP*	190
C. majority	16,031

(June 1987, C. maj. 16,290)

SUFFOLK COASTAL
E.79,333   T.81.62%

*Rt. Hon. J. Gummer, *C.*	34,680
P. Monk, *LD*	15,395
T. Hodgson, *Lab.*	13,508
A. Slade, *Green*	943
Ms F. Kaplan, *NLP*	232
C. majority	19,285

(June 1987, C. maj. 15,280)

SUFFOLK SOUTH
E.84,833   T.81.73%

*T. Yeo, *C.*	34,793
Ms K. Pollard, *LD*	17,504
S. Hesford, *Lab.*	16,623
T. Aisbitt, *NLP*	420
C. majority	17,289

(June 1987, C. maj. 16,243)

SUNDERLAND NORTH (Tyne &
Wear)
E.72,874   T.68.86%

W. Etherington, *Lab.*	30,481
Miss J. Barnes, *C.*	13,477
V. Halom, *LD*	5,389
Ms W. Lundgren, *Lib.*	841
Lab. majority	17,004

(June 1987, Lab. maj. 14,672)

SUNDERLAND SOUTH (Tyne &
Wear)
E.72,607   T.69.87%

*C. Mullin, *Lab.*	29,399
G. Howe, *C.*	14,898
J. Lennox, *LD*	5,844
T. Scouler, *Green*	596
Lab. majority	14,501

(June 1987, Lab. maj. 12,613)

SURBITON (Greater London)
E.42,421   T.82.44%

*R. Tracey, *C.*	19,033
Ms B. Janke, *LD*	9,394
R. Hutchinson, *Lab.*	6,384
W. Parker, *NLP*	161
C. majority	9,639

(June 1987, C. maj. 9,741)

SURREY EAST
E.57,878   T.82.53%

P. Ainsworth, *C.*	29,767
R. Tomlin, *LD*	12,111
Mrs G. Roles, *Lab.*	5,075
I. Kilpatrick, *Green*	819
C. majority	17,656

(June 1987, C. maj. 18,126)

SURREY NORTH WEST
E.83,648   T.78.27%

*Sir M. Grylls, *C.*	41,772
Mrs C. Clark, *LD*	13,378
M. Hayhurst, *Lab.*	8,886
Ms Y. Hockey, *Green*	1,441
C. majority	28,394

(June 1987, C. maj. 23,575)

SURREY SOUTH WEST
E.72,288   T.82.77%

*Mrs V. Bottomley, *C.*	35,008
N. Sherlock, *LD*	20,033
P. Kelly, *Lab.*	3,840
N. Bedrock, *Green*	710
K. Campbell, *NLP*	147
D. Newman, *AS*	98
C. majority	14,975

(June 1987, C. maj. 14,343)

SUSSEX MID
E.80,827   T.82.85%

*Rt. Hon. T. Renton, *C.*	39,524
Ms M. Collins, *LD*	18,996
Ms L. Gregory, *Lab.*	6,951
H. Stevens, *Green*	772
P. Berry, *Loony*	392
P. Hodkin, *PR*	246
Dr A. Hankey, *NLP*	89
C. majority	20,528

(June 1987, C. maj. 18,292)

SUTTON AND CHEAM (Greater
London)
E.60,949   T.82.39%

Lady O. Maitland, *C.*	27,710
P. Burstow, *LD*	16,954
G. Martin, *Lab.*	4,980
J. Duffy, *Green*	444
Ms A. Hatchard, *NLP*	133
C. majority	10,756

(June 1987, C. maj. 15,718)

SUTTON COLDFIELD
(W. Midlands)
E.71,410   T.79.51%

*Rt. Hon. Sir N. Fowler, *C.*	37,001
J. Whorwood, *LD*	10,965
Ms J. Bott-Obi, *Lab.*	8,490
H. Meads, *NLP*	324
C. majority	26,036

(June 1987, C. maj. 21,183)

SWINDON (Wilts)
E.90,067   T.81.46%

*S. Coombs, *C.*	31,749
J. D'Avila, *Lab.*	28,923
S. Cordon, *LD*	11,737
W. Hughes, *Green*	647
R. Gillard, *Loony G.*	236
V. Farrar, *Ind.*	78
C. majority	2,826

(June 1987, C. maj. 4,857)

TATTON (Cheshire)
E.71,085   T.80.83%

*M. N. Hamilton, *C.*	31,658
J. Kelly, *Lab.*	15,798
Ms C. Hancox, *LD*	9,597
M. Gibson, *FP*	410
C. majority	15,860

(June 1987, C. maj. 17,094)

TAUNTON (Somerset)
E.78,036   T.82.32%

*D. Nicholson, *C.*	29,576
Ms J. Ballard, *LD*	26,240
Ms J. Hole, *Lab.*	8,151
P. Leavey, *NLP*	279
C. majority	3,336

(June 1987, C. maj. 10,380)

TEIGNBRIDGE (Devon)
E.74,892   T.83.43%

*P. Nicholls, *C.*	31,272
R. Younger-Ross, *LD*	22,416
R. Kennedy, *Lab.*	8,128
A. Hope, *Loony*	437
N. Hayes, *NLP*	234
C. majority	8,856

(June 1987, C. maj. 10,425)

THANET NORTH (Kent)
E.70,978   T.76.02%

*R. Gale, *C.*	30,867
A. Bretman, *Lab.*	12,657
Ms J. Phillips, *LD*	9,563
Ms H. Dawe, *Green*	873
C. majority	18,210

(June 1987, C. maj. 17,480)

THANET SOUTH (Kent)
E.62,441   T.78.17%

*J. Aitken, *C.*	25,253
M. James, *Lab.*	13,740

W. Pitt, *LD*	8,948
Ms S. Peckham, *Green*	871
C. majority	11,513
(June 1987, C. maj. 13,683)	

THURROCK (Essex)
E.69,171　T.78.15%

A. MacKinlay, *Lab.*	24,791
*T. Janman, *C.*	23,619
A. Banton, *LD*	5,145
C. Rogers, *Pensioners*	391
P. Compobassi, *Anti Fed.*	117
Lab. majority	1,172
(June 1987, C. maj. 690)	

TIVERTON (Devon)
E.71,024　T.82.98%

Mrs A. Browning, *C.*	30,376
D. Cox, *LD*	19,287
Ms S. Gibb, *Lab.*	5,950
D. Morrish, *Lib.*	2,225
P. Foggitt, *Green*	1,007
B. Rhodes, *NLP*	96
C. majority	11,089
(June 1987, C. maj. 9,212)	

TONBRIDGE AND MALLING
(Kent)
E.77,292　T.82.66%

*Rt. Hon. Sir J. Stanley, *C.*	36,542
P. Roberts, *LD*	14,984
Ms M. O'Neill, *Lab.*	11,533
J. Tidy, *Green*	612
Mrs J. Hovarth, *NLP*	221
C. majority	21,558
(June 1987, C. maj. 16,429)	

TOOTING (Greater London)
E.68,306　T.74.79%

*T. Cox, *Lab.*	24,601
M. Winters, *C.*	20,494
B. Bunce, *LD*	3,776
Ms C. Martin, *Lib.*	1,340
P. Owens, *Green*	694
F. Anklesalria, *NLP*	119
M. Whitelaw, *CD*	64
Lab. majority	4,107
(June 1987, Lab. maj. 1,441)	

TORBAY (Devon)
E.71,171　T.80.63%

*R. Allason, *C.*	28,624
A. Sanders, *LD*	22,837
P. Truscott, *Lab.*	5,503
R. Jones, *NF*	268
Ms A. Thomas, *NLP*	157
C. majority	5,787
(June 1987, C. maj. 8,820)	

TOTTENHAM (Greater London)
E.68,319　T.65.60%

*B. Grant, *Lab.*	25,309
A. Charalambous, *C.*	13,341
A. L'Estrange, *LD*	5,120
P. Budge, *Green*	903
Ms M. Obomanu, *NLP*	150
Lab. majority	11,968
(June 1987, Lab. maj. 4,141)	

TRURO (Cornwall)
E.75,101　T.82.35%

*M. Taylor, *LD*	31,230
N. St Aubyn, *C.*	23,660

J. Geach, *Lab.*	6,078
L. Keating, *Green*	569
C. Tankard, *Lib.*	208
Ms M. Hartley, *NLP*	108
LD majority	7,570
(June 1987, L./All. maj. 4,753)	

TUNBRIDGE WELLS (Kent)
E.76,808　T.78.11%

*Rt. Hon. Sir P. Mayhew, *C.*	34,162
A. Clayton, *LD*	17,030
E. Goodman, *Lab.*	8,300
E. Fenna, *NLP*	267
R. Edey, *ISS*	236
C. majority	17,132
(June 1987, C. maj. 16,122)	

TWICKENHAM (Greater London)
E.63,072　T.84.27%

*T. Jessel, *C.*	26,804
Dr V. Cable, *LD*	21,093
M. Gold, *Lab.*	4,919
G. Gill, *NLP*	152
D. Griffith, *DLC*	103
A. Miners, *Lib.*	85
C. majority	5,711
(June 1987, C. maj. 7,127)	

TYNE BRIDGE (Tyne & Wear)
E.53,079　T.62.64%

*D. Clelland, *Lab.*	22,328
C. Liddell-Grainger, *C.*	7,118
J. Burt, *LD*	3,804
Lab. majority	15,210
(June 1987, Lab. maj. 15,573)	

TYNEMOUTH (Tyne & Wear)
E.74,955　T.80.39%

*N. Trotter, *C.*	27,731
P. Cosgrove, *Lab.*	27,134
P. Selby, *LD*	4,855
A. Buchanan-Smith, *Green*	543
C. majority	597
(June 1987, C. maj. 2,583)	

UPMINSTER (Greater London)
E.64,138　T.80.46%

*Sir N. Bonsor, *C.*	28,791
T. Ward, *Lab.*	14,970
T. Hurlstone, *LD*	7,848
C. majority	13,821
(June 1987, C. maj. 16,857)	

UXBRIDGE (Greater London)
E.61,744　T.78.87%

*J. M. Shersby, *C.*	27,487
R. Evans, *Lab.*	14,308
S. Carey, *LD*	5,900
I. Flindall, *Green*	538
M. O'Rourke, *BNP*	350
A. Deans, *NLP*	120
C. majority	13,179
(June 1987, C. maj. 15,970)	

VAUXHALL (Greater London)
E.62,473　T.62.35%

*Ms C. Hoey, *Lab.*	21,328
B. Gentry, *C.*	10,840
M. Tuffrey, *LD*	5,678
Ms P. Shepherd, *Green*	803
A. Khan, *DOS*	156
Ms S. Hill, *Rev. Comm.*	152

Lab. majority	10,488
(June 1987, Lab. maj. 9,019)	
(June 1989, Lab. maj. 9,766)	

WAKEFIELD (W. Yorks)
E.69,794　T.76.27%

*D. Hinchliffe, *Lab.*	26,964
D. Fanthorpe, *C.*	20,374
T. Wright, *LD*	5,900
Lab. majority	6,590
(June 1987, Lab. maj. 2,789)	

WALLASEY (Merseyside)
E.65,676　T.82.50%

Ms A. Eagle, *Lab.*	26,531
*Rt. Hon. L. Chalker, *C.*	22,722
N. Thomas, *LD*	4,177
Ms S. Davis, *Green*	650
G. Gay, *NLP*	105
Lab. majority	3,809
(June 1987, C. maj. 279)	

WALLSEND (Tyne & Wear)
E.77,941　T.74.12%

S. Byers, *Lab.*	33,439
Miss M. Gibbon, *C.*	13,969
M. Huscroft, *LD*	10,369
Lab. majority	19,470
(June 1987, Lab. maj. 19,384)	

WALSALL NORTH (W. Midlands)
E.69,604　T.74.98%

*D. Winnick, *Lab.*	24,387
R. Syms, *C.*	20,563
A. Powis, *LD*	6,629
K. Reynolds, *NF*	614
Lab. majority	3,824
(June 1987, Lab. maj. 1,790)	

WALSALL SOUTH (W. Midlands)
E.65,642　T.76.26%

*B. George, *Lab.*	24,133
L. Jones, *C.*	20,955
G. Williams, *LD*	4,132
R. Clarke, *Green*	673
J. Oldbury, *NLP*	167
Lab. majority	3,178
(June 1987, C. maj. 1,116)	

WALTHAMSTOW (Greater London)
E.49,140　T.72.35%

N. Gerrard, *Lab.*	16,251
*H. Summerson, *C.*	13,229
P. Leighton, *LD*	5,142
Ms J. Lambert, *Green*	594
V. Wilkinson, *Lib.*	241
A. Planton, *NLP*	94
Lab. majority	3,022
(June 1987, C. maj. 1,512)	

WANSBECK (Northumberland)
E.63,457　T.79.29%

*J. Thompson, *Lab.*	30,046
G. Sanderson, *C.*	11,872
B. Priestley, *LD*	7,691
N. Best, *Green*	710
Lab. majority	18,174
(June 1987, Lab. maj. 16,789)	

WANSDYKE (Avon)
E.77,156　T.84.33%

*J. Aspinwall, *C.*	31,389
D. Norris, *Lab.*	18,048

Ms D. Darby, *LD* — 14,834
F. Hayden, *Green* — 800
C. majority — 13,341
(June 1987, C. maj. 16,144)

WANSTEAD AND WOODFORD
(Greater London)
*E.*55,821   *T.*78.28%
*J. Arbuthnot, *C.* — 26,204
Ms L. Brown, *Lab.* — 9,319
G. Staight, *LD* — 7,362
F. Roads, *Green* — 637
A. Brickell, *NLP* — 178
C. majority — 16,885
(June 1987, C. maj. 16,412)

WANTAGE (Oxon)
*E.*68,328   *T.*82.68%
*R. Jackson, *C.* — 30,575
R. Morgan, *LD* — 14,102
V. Woodell, *Lab.* — 10,955
R. Ely, *Green* — 867
C. majority — 16,473
(June 1987, C. maj. 12,156)

WARLEY EAST (W. Midlands)
*E.*51,717   *T.*71.72%
*A. Faulds, *Lab.* — 19,891
G. Marshall, *C.* — 12,097
A. Harrod, *LD* — 4,547
A. Groucott, *NLP* — 561
Lab. majority — 7,794
(June 1987, Lab. maj. 5,585)

WARLEY WEST (W. Midlands)
*E.*57,164   *T.*73.90%
J. Spellar, *Lab.* — 21,386
Mrs S. Whitehouse, *C.* — 15,914
Ms E. Todd, *LD* — 4,945
Lab. majority — 5,472
(June 1987, Lab. maj. 5,393)

WARRINGTON NORTH (Cheshire)
*E.*78,548   *T.*77.38%
*E. D. H. Hoyle, *Lab.* — 33,019
C. Daniels, *C.* — 20,397
I. Greenhalgh, *LD* — 6,965
B. Davies, *NLP* — 400
Lab. majority — 12,622
(June 1987, Lab. maj. 8,013)

WARRINGTON SOUTH (Cheshire)
*E.*77,694   *T.*82.04%
M. Hall, *Lab.* — 27,819
*C. Butler, *C.* — 27,628
P. Walker, *LD* — 7,978
S. Benson, *NLP* — 321
Lab. majority — 191
(June 1987, C. maj. 3,609)

WARWICK AND LEAMINGTON
*E.*71,259   *T.*81.54%
*Sir D. Smith, *C.* — 28,093
M. Taylor, *Lab.* — 19,158
Ms S. Boad, *LD* — 9,645
Ms J. Alty, *Green* — 803
R. Newby, *Ind.* — 251
J. Brewster, *NLP* — 156
C. majority — 8,935
(June 1987, C. maj. 13,982)

WARWICKSHIRE NORTH
*E.*71,473   *T.*83.82%
M. O'Brien, *Lab.* — 27,599
*Hon. F. Maude, *C.* — 26,145
N. Mitchell, *LD* — 6,167
Lab. majority — 1,454
(June 1987, C. maj. 2,829)

WATFORD (Herts)
*E.*72,291   *T.*82.34%
*W. A. T. T. Garel-Jones, *C.* — 29,072
M. Jackson, *Lab.* — 19,482
M. Oaten, *LD* — 10,231
J. Hywel-Davies, *Green* — 566
L. Davis, *NLP* — 176
C. majority — 9,590
(June 1987, C. maj. 11,736)

WAVENEY (Suffolk)
*E.*84,181   *T.*81.81%
*D. Porter, *C.* — 33,174
E. Leverett, *Lab.* — 26,472
A. Rogers, *LD* — 8,925
D. Hook, *NLP* — 302
C. majority — 6,702
(June 1987, C. maj. 11,783)

WEALDEN (E. Sussex)
*E.*74,665   *T.*80.83%
*Sir G. Johnson Smith, *C.* — 37,263
M. Skinner, *LD* — 16,332
S. Billcliffe, *Lab.* — 5,579
I. Guy-Moore, *Green* — 1,002
Dr R. Graham, *NLP* — 182
C. majority — 20,931
(June 1987, C. maj. 20,110)

WELLINGBOROUGH (Northants)
*E.*73,875   *T.*81.89%
*P. Fry, *C.* — 32,302
P. Sawford, *Lab.* — 20,486
Ms J. Trevor, *LD* — 7,714
C. majority — 11,816
(June 1987, C. maj. 14,070)

WELLS (Somerset)
*E.*69,833   *T.*82.71%
*D. Heathcoat-Amory, *C.* — 28,620
H. Temperley, *LD* — 21,971
J. Pilgrim, *Lab.* — 6,126
M. Fenner, *Green* — 1,042
C. majority — 6,649
(June 1987, C. maj. 8,541)

WELWYN HATFIELD (Herts)
*E.*72,146   *T.*84.39%
*D. Evans, *C.* — 29,447
R. Little, *Lab.* — 20,982
R. Parker, *LD* — 10,196
Ms E. Lucas, *NLP* — 264
C. majority — 8,465
(June 1987, C. maj. 10,903)

WENTWORTH (S. Yorks)
*E.*64,914   *T.*74.03%
*P. Hardy, *Lab.* — 32,939
M. Brennan, *C.* — 10,490
Ms C. Roderick, *LD* — 4,629
Lab. majority — 22,449
(June 1987, Lab. maj. 20,092)

WEST BROMWICH EAST
(W. Midlands)
*E.*56,940   *T.*75.25%
*P. Snape, *Lab.* — 19,913
C. Blunt, *C.* — 17,100
M. Smith, *LD* — 5,360
J. Lord, *NF* — 477
Lab. majority — 2,813
(June 1987, Lab. maj. 983)

WEST BROMWICH WEST
(W. Midlands)
*E.*57,655   *T.*70.41%
*Miss B. Boothroyd, *Lab.* — 22,251
D. Swayne, *C.* — 14,421
Miss S. Broadbent, *LD* — 3,925
Lab. majority — 7,830
(June 1987, Lab. maj. 5,253)

WESTBURY (Wilts)
*E.*87,356   *T.*82.99%
D. Faber, *C.* — 36,568
Ms V. Rayner, *LD* — 23,962
W. Stallard, *Lab.* — 9,642
P. Macdonald, *Lib.* — 1,440
P. French, *Green* — 888
C. majority — 12,606
(June 1987, C. maj. 10,097)

WESTMINSTER NORTH (Greater
London)
*E.*58,847   *T.*75.75%
*Sir J. Wheeler, *C.* — 21,828
Ms J. Edwards, *Lab.* — 18,095
J. Wigoder, *LD* — 3,341
Ms A. Burke, *Green* — 1,017
J. Hinde, *NLP* — 159
M. Kelly, *Anti Fed.* — 137
C. majority — 3,733
(June 1987, C. maj. 3,310)

**WESTMORLAND AND
LONSDALE** (Cumbria)
*E.*71,865   *T.*77.76%
*Rt. Hon. M. Jopling, *C.* — 31,798
S. Collins, *LD* — 15,362
D. Abbott, *Lab.* — 8,436
R. Johnstone, *NLP* — 287
C. majority — 16,436
(June 1987, C. maj. 14,920)

WESTON-SUPER-MARE (Avon)
*E.*78,839   *T.*79.75%
*A. W. Wiggin, *C.* — 30,022
B. Cotter, *LD* — 24,680
D. Murray, *Lab.* — 6,913
Dr R. Lawson, *Green* — 1,262
C. majority — 5,342
(June 1987, C. maj. 7,998)

WIGAN (Greater Manchester)
*E.*72,739   *T.*76.16%
*R. Stott, *Lab.* — 34,910
E. Hess, *C.* — 13,068
G. Davies, *LD* — 6,111
K. White, *Lib.* — 1,116
Ms A. Taylor, *NLP* — 197
Lab. majority — 21,842
(June 1987, Lab. maj. 20,462)

WILTSHIRE NORTH
E.85,851   T.81.71%
*R. Needham, C.	39,028
Ms C. Napier, LD	22,640
Ms C. Reid, Lab.	6,945
Ms L. Howitt, Green	850
G. Hawkins, Lib.	622
S. Martienssen, Bastion	66
C. majority	16,388

(June 1987, C. maj. 10,939)

WIMBLEDON (Greater London)
E.61,917   T.80.23%
*Dr C. Goodson-Wickes, C.	26,331
K. Abrams, Lab.	11,570
Ms A. Willott, LD	10,569
V. Flood, Green	860
H. Godfrey, NLP	181
G. Hadley, Ind.	170
C. majority	14,761

(June 1987, C. maj. 11,301)

WINCHESTER (Hants)
E.79,218   T.83.46%
P. G. Malone, C.	33,113
A. Barron, LD	24,992
P. Jenks, Lab.	4,917
*J. Browne, Ind. C.	3,095
C. majority	8,121

(June 1987, C. maj. 7,479)

WINDSOR AND MAIDENHEAD
(Berks)
E.77,327   T.81.68%
Hon. M. Trend, C.	35,075
J. Hyde, LD	22,147
Ms C. Attlee, Lab.	4,975
R. Williams, Green	510
D. Askwith, Loony	236
Miss E. Bigg, Ind.	110
M. Grenville, NLP	108
C. majority	12,928

(June 1987, C. maj. 17,836)

WIRRAL SOUTH (Merseyside)
E.61,116   T.82.37%
*G. B. Porter, C.	25,590
Ms H. Southworth, Lab.	17,407
E. Cunniffe, LD	6,581
N. Birchenough, Green	584
G. Griffiths, NLP	182
C. majority	8,183

(June 1987, C. maj. 10,963)

WIRRAL WEST (Merseyside)
E.62,453   T.81.57%
*Rt. Hon. D. Hunt, C.	26,852
Ms H. Stephenson, Lab.	15,788
J. Thornton, LD	7,420
Ms G. Bowler, Green	700
N. Broome, NLP	188
C. majority	11,064

(June 1987, C. maj. 12,723)

WITNEY (Oxon)
E.78,521   T.81.89%
*Rt. Hon. D. Hurd, C.	36,256
J. Plaskitt, Lab.	13,688
I. Blair, LD	13,393
Ms C. Beckford, Green	716
Ms S. Catling, NLP	134
Miss M. Brown, FTA	119

C. majority	22,568

(June 1987, C. maj. 18,464)

WOKING (Surrey)
E.80,842   T.79.20%
*Rt. Hon. C. Onslow, C.	37,744
Mrs D. Buckrell, LD	17,902
J. Dalgleish, Lab.	8,080
Mrs T. Macintyre, NLP	302
C. majority	19,842

(June 1987, C. maj. 16,544)

WOKINGHAM (Berks)
E.85,914   T.82.41%
*J. Redwood, C.	43,497
P. Simon, LD	17,788
N. Bland, Lab.	8,846
P. Owen, Loony	531
P. Harriss, WUWC	148
C. majority	25,709

(June 1987, C. maj. 20,387)

WOLVERHAMPTON NORTH
EAST (W. Midlands)
E.62,695   T.78%
K. Purchase, Lab.	24,106
*Mrs M. Hicks, C.	20,167
M. Gwinnett, LD	3,546
K. Bullman, Lib.	1,087
Lab. majority	3,939

(June 1987, C. maj. 204)

WOLVERHAMPTON SOUTH EAST
(W. Midlands)
E.56,158   T.72.86%
*D. Turner, Lab.	23,215
P. Bradbourn, C.	12,975
R. Whitehouse, LD	3,881
Ms C. Twelvetrees, Lib.	850
Lab. majority	10,240

(June 1987, Lab. maj. 6,398)

WOLVERHAMPTON SOUTH
WEST (W. Midlands)
E.67,288   T.78.28%
*N. Budgen, C.	25,969
S. Murphy, Lab.	21,003
M. Wiggin, LD	4,470
C. Hallmark, Lib.	1,237
C. majority	4,966

(June 1987, C. maj. 10,318)

WOODSPRING (Avon)
E.77,534   T.83.21%
Dr L. Fox, C.	35,175
Ms N. Kirsen, LD	17,666
R. Stone, Lab.	9,942
N. Brown, Lib.	836
Ms R. Knifton, Green	801
B. Lee, NLP	100
C. majority	17,509

(June 1987, C. maj. 17,852)

WOOLWICH (Greater London)
E.55,977   T.70.91%
J. Austin-Walker, Lab.	17,551
*J. Cartwright, SD	15,326
K. Walmsley, C.	6,598
Ms S. Hayward, NLP	220
Lab. majority	2,225

(June 1987, SDP/All. maj. 1,937)

WORCESTER
E.74,211   T.80.99%
P. Luff, C.	27,883
R. Berry, Lab.	21,731
J. Caiger, LD	9,561
M. Foster, Green	592
M. Soden, Brewer	343
C. majority	6,152

(June 1987, C. maj. 10,453)

WORCESTERSHIRE MID
E.84,269   T.81.07%
*E. Forth, C.	33,964
Ms J. Smith, Lab.	24,094
D. Barwick, LD	9,745
P. Davis, NLP	520
C. majority	9,870

(June 1987, C. maj. 14,911)

WORCESTERSHIRE SOUTH
E.80,423   T.79.99%
*W. M. H. Spicer, C.	34,792
P. Chandler, LD	18,641
N. Knowles, Lab.	9,727
G. Woodford, Green	1,178
C. majority	16,151

(June 1987, C. maj. 13,645)

WORKINGTON (Cumbria)
E.57,597   T.81.52%
*D. Campbell-Savours, Lab.	26,719
S. Sexton, C.	16,270
Ms C. Neale, LD	3,028
D. Langstaff, Loony	755
Ms N. Escott, NLP	183
Lab. majority	10,449

(June 1987, Lab. maj. 7,019)

WORSLEY (Greater Manchester)
E.72,244   T.77.74%
*T. Lewis, Lab.	29,418
N. Cameron, C.	19,406
R. Boyd, LD	6,490
P. Connolly, Green	677
G. Phillips, NLP	176
Lab. majority	10,012

(June 1987, Lab. maj. 7,337)

WORTHING (W. Sussex)
E.77,540   T.77.41%
*Rt. Hon. T. Higgins, C.	34,198
Mrs S. Bucknall, LD	17,665
J. Deen, Lab.	6,679
Mrs P. Beever, Green	806
N. Goble, Lib.	679
C. majority	16,533

(June 1987, C. maj. 18,501)

THE WREKIN (Salop)
E.90,892   T.77.14%
*B. Grocott, Lab.	33,865
Mrs E. Holt, C.	27,217
A. West, LD	8,032
R. Saunders, Green	1,008
Lab. majority	6,648

(June 1987, Lab. maj. 1,456)

WYCOMBE (Bucks)
E.72,564   T.78.01%
*R. Whitney, C.	30,081
T. Andrews, LD	13,005
J. Huddart, Lab.	12,222

J. Laker, *Green*	686
A. Page, *SD*	449
T. Anton, *NLP*	168
C. *majority*	17,076
(June 1987, C. maj. 13,819)	

WYRE (Lancs)
*E.*67,778   *T.*79.54%

*K. Mans, *C.*	29,449
D. Borrow, *Lab.*	17,785
J. Ault, *LD*	6,420
R. Perry, *NLP*	260
C. *majority*	11,664
(June 1987, C. maj. 14,661)	

WYRE FOREST (H & W)
*E.*73,550   *T.*82.36%

*A. Coombs, *C.*	28,983
R. Maden, *Lab.*	18,642
M. Jones, *LD*	12,958
C. *majority*	10,341
(June 1987, C. maj. 7,224)	

YEOVIL (Somerset)
*E.*73,057   *T.*81.98%

*Rt. Hon. J. J. D. Ashdown, *LD*	30,958
J. Davidson, *C.*	22,125
Ms V. Nelson, *Lab.*	5,765
J. Risbridger, *Green*	639

D. Sutch, *Loony*	338
R. Simmerson, *APAKBI*	70
LD majority	8,833
(June 1987, L./All. maj. 5,700)	

YORK (N. Yorks)
*E.*79,242   *T.*80.97%

H. Bayley, *Lab.*	31,525
*C. Gregory, *C.*	25,183
Ms K. Anderson, *LD*	6,811
S. Kenwright, *Green*	594
Ms P. Orr, *NLP*	54
Lab. majority	6,342
(June 1987, C. maj. 147)	

WALES

ABERAVON (W. Glamorgan)
*E.*51,650   *T.*77.57%

*Rt. Hon. J. Morris, *Lab.*	26,877
H. Williams, *C.*	5,567
Mrs M. Harris, *LD*	4,999
D. Saunders, *PC*	1,919
Capt. Beany, *Real Bean*	707
Lab. majority	21,310
(June 1987, Lab. maj. 20,609)	

ALYN AND DEESIDE (Clwyd)
*E.*60,477   *T.*80.08%

*S. B. Jones, *Lab.*	25,206
J. Riley, *C.*	17,355
R. Britton, *LD*	4,687
J. Rogers, *PC*	551
V. Button, *Green*	433
J. Cooksey, *Ind.*	200
Lab. majority	7,851
(June 1987, Lab. maj. 6,383)	

BLAENAU GWENT
*E.*55,638   *T.*78.13%

L. Smith, *Lab.*	34,333
D. Melding, *C.*	4,266
A. Burns, *LD*	2,774
A. Davies, *PC*	2,099
Lab. majority	30,067
(June 1987, Lab. maj. 27,861)	

BRECON AND RADNOR (Powys)
*E.*51,509   *T.*85.94%

J. P. Evans, *C.*	15,977
*R. Livsey, *LD*	15,847
C. Mann, *Lab.*	11,634
Ms S. Meredudd, *PC*	418
H. Richards, *Green*	393
C. *majority*	130
(June 1987, L./All. maj. 56)	

BRIDGEND (Mid Glamorgan)
*E.*58,531   *T.*80.44%

*W. Griffiths, *Lab.*	24,143
D. Unwin, *C.*	16,817
D. Mills, *LD*	4,827
A. Lloyd Jones, *PC*	1,301
Lab. majority	7,326
(June 1987, Lab. maj. 4,380)	

CAERNARFON (Gwynedd)
*E.*46,468   *T.*78.15%

*D. Wigley, *PC*	21,439
P. Fowler, *C.*	6,963
Ms S. Mainwaring, *Lab.*	5,641

R. Arwel Williams, *LD*	2,101
G. Evans, *NLP*	173
PC majority	14,476
(June 1987, *PC maj. 12,812*)	

CAERPHILLY (Mid Glamorgan)
*E.*64,529   *T.*77.20%

*R. Davies, *Lab.*	31,713
H. Philpott, *C.*	9,041
L. Whittle, *PC*	4,821
S. Wilson, *LD*	4,247
Lab. majority	22,672
(June 1987, Lab. maj. 19,167)	

CARDIFF CENTRAL
(S. Glamorgan)
*E.*57,716   *T.*74.35%

J. O. Jones, *Lab.*	18,014
*I. Grist, *C.*	14,549
Ms J. Randerson, *LD*	9,170
H. Marshall, *PC*	748
C. von Ruhland, *Green*	330
B. Francis, *NLP*	105
Lab. majority	3,465
(June 1987, C. maj. 1,986)	

CARDIFF NORTH (S. Glamorgan)
*E.*56,721   *T.*84.15%

*G. H. Jones, *C.*	21,547
Ms J. Morgan, *Lab.*	18,578
Ms E. Warlow, *LD*	6,487
Ms E. Bush, *PC*	916
J. Morse, *BNP*	121
D. Palmer, *NLP*	86
C. *majority*	2,969
(June 1987, C. maj. 8,234)	

CARDIFF SOUTH AND PENARTH
(S. Glamorgan)
*E.*61,484   *T.*77.25%

*A. Michael, *Lab.*	26,383
T. Hunter Jarvie, *C.*	15,958
P. Verma, *LD*	3,707
Ms B. Anglezarke, *PC*	776
L. Davey, *Green*	676
Lab. majority	10,425
(June 1987, Lab. maj. 4,574)	

CARDIFF WEST (S. Glamorgan)
*E.*58,898   *T.*77.56%

*H. R. Morgan, *Lab.*	24,306
M. Prior, *C.*	15,015
Ms J. Gasson, *LD*	5,002
Ms P. Bestic, *PC*	1,177

A. Harding, *NLP*	184
Lab. majority	9,291
(June 1987, Lab. maj. 4,045)	

CARMARTHEN (Dyfed)
*E.*68,887 T. 82.70%

*Dr A. W. Williams, *Lab.*	20,879
R. Thomas, *PC*	17,957
S. Cavenagh, *C.*	12,782
Mrs J. Hughes, *LD*	5,353
Lab. majority	2,922
(June 1987, Lab. maj. 4,317)	

CEREDIGION AND PEMBROKE
NORTH (Dyfed)
*E.*66,180   *T.*77.36%

C. Dafis, *PC*	16,020
*G. Howells, *LD*	12,827
J. Williams, *C.*	12,718
J. Davies, *Lab.*	9,637
PC majority	3,193
(June 1987, L./All. maj. 4,700)	

CLWYD NORTH WEST
*E.*67,351   *T.*78.64%

R. Richards, *C.*	24,488
C. Ruane, *Lab.*	18,438
R. Ingham, *LD*	7,999
T. Neil, *PC*	1,888
Ms M. Swift, *NLP*	158
C. *majority*	6,050
(June 1987, C. maj. 11,781)	

CLWYD SOUTH WEST
*E.*60,607   *T.*81.52%

*M. Jones, *Lab.*	21,490
G. Owen, *C.*	16,549
G. Williams, *LD*	6,027
E. Lloyd Jones, *PC*	4,835
N. Worth, *Green*	351
Mrs J. Leadbetter, *NLP*	155
Lab. majority	4,941
(June 1987, Lab. maj. 1,028)	

CONWY (Gwynedd)
*E.*53,576   *T.*78.85%

*Rt. Hon. Sir W. Roberts, *C.*	14,250
Revd R. Roberts, *LD*	13,255
Ms E. Williams, *Lab.*	10,883
R. Davies, *PC*	3,108
O. Wainwright, *Ind. C.*	637
Ms D. Hughes, *NLP*	114
C. *majority*	995
(June 1987, C. maj. 3,024)	

CYNON VALLEY (Mid Glamorgan)
E.49,695   T.76.46%

*Ms A. Clwyd, *Lab.*	26,254
A. Smith, *C.*	4,890
T. Benney, *PC*	4,186
M. Verma, *LD*	2,667
Lab. majority	21,364

(June 1987, Lab. maj. 21,571)

DELYN (Clwyd)
E.66,591   T.83.40%

D. Hanson, *Lab.*	24,979
M. Whitby, *C.*	22,940
R. Dodd, *LD*	6,208
A. Drake, *PC*	1,414
Lab. majority	2,039

(June 1987, C. maj. 1,224)

GOWER (W. Glamorgan)
E.57,231   T.81.84%

*G. Wardell, *Lab.*	23,455
A. Donnelly, *C.*	16,437
C. Davies, *LD*	4,655
A. Price, *PC*	1,658
B. Kingzett, *Green*	448
G. Egan, *Loony G.*	114
M. Beresford, *NLP*	74
Lab. majority	7,018

(June 1987, Lab. maj. 5,764)

ISLWYN (Gwent)
E.51,079   T.81.48%

*Rt. Hon. N. Kinnock, *Lab.*	30,908
P. Bone, *C.*	6,180
M. Symonds, *LD*	2,352
Ms H. Jones, *PC*	1,636
Lord Sutch, *Loony*	547
Lab. majority	24,728

(June 1987, Lab. maj. 22,947)

LLANELLI (Dyfed)
E.65,058   T.77.80%

*Rt. Hon. D. Davies, *Lab.*	27,802
G. Down, *C.*	8,532
M. Phillips, *PC*	7,878
K. Evans, *LD*	6,404
Lab. majority	19,270

(June 1987, Lab. maj. 20,935)

MEIRIONNYDD NANT CONWY
(Gwynedd)
E.32,413   T.81.47%

E. Llwyd, *PC*	11,608
G. Lewis, *C.*	6,995
R. Williams, *Lab.*	4,978
Mrs R. Parry, *LD*	2,358
W. Pritchard, *Green*	471
PC majority	4,613

(June 1987, PC maj. 3,026)

MERTHYR TYDFIL AND
RHYMNEY (Mid Glamorgan)
E.58,430   T.75.84%

*E. Rowlands, *Lab.*	31,710
R. Rowland, *LD*	4,997
M. Hughes, *C.*	4,904
A. Cox, *PC*	2,704
Lab. majority	26,713

(June 1987, Lab. maj. 28,207)

MONMOUTH (Gwent)
E.59,147   T.86.06%

R. Evans, *C.*	24,059
*H. Edwards, *Lab.*	20,855
Mrs F. David, *LD*	5,562
M. Witherden, *Green/PC*	431
C. majority	3,204

(June 1987, C. maj. 9,350)
(May 1991, Lab. maj. 2,406)

MONTGOMERY (Powys)
E.41,386   T.79.87%

*A. Carlile, *LD*	16,031
Mrs J. France-Hayhurst, *C.*	10,822
S. Wood, *Lab.*	4,115
H. Parsons, *PC*	1,581
P. Adams, *Green*	508
LD majority	5,209

(June 1987, L./All. maj. 2,558)

NEATH (W. Glamorgan)
E.56,392   T.80.58%

*P. Hain, *Lab.*	30,903
D. Adams, *C.*	6,928
Dr D. Evans, *PC*	5,145
M. Phillips, *LD*	2,467
Lab. majority	23,975

(June 1987, Lab. maj. 20,578)
(April 1991, Lab. maj. 9,830)

NEWPORT EAST (Gwent)
E.51,603   T.81.21%

*R. J. Hughes, *Lab.*	23,050
Mrs A. Emmett, *C.*	13,151
W. Oliver, *LD*	4,991
S. Ainley, *Green/PC*	716
Lab. majority	9,899

(June 1987, Lab. maj. 7,064)

NEWPORT WEST (Gwent)
E.54,871   T.82.82%

*P. Flynn, *Lab.*	24,139
A. Taylor, *C.*	16,360
A. Toye, *LD*	4,296
P. Keelan, *PC*	653
Lab. majority	7,779

(June 1987, Lab. maj. 2,708)

OGMORE (Mid Glamorgan)
E.52,195   T.80.62%

*R. Powell, *Lab.*	30,186
D. Edwards, *C.*	6,359
J. Warman, *LD*	2,868
Ms L. McAllister, *PC*	2,667
Lab. majority	23,827

(June 1987, Lab. maj. 22,292)

PEMBROKE (Dyfed)
E.73,187   T.82.86%

N. Ainger, *Lab.*	26,253
*N. Bennett, *C.*	25,498
P. Berry, *LD*	6,625
C. Bryant, *PC*	1,627
R. Coghill, *Green*	484
M. Stoddart, *Anti Fed.*	158
Lab. majority	755

(June 1987, C. maj. 5,700)

PONTYPRIDD (Mid Glamorgan)
E.61,685   T.79.25%

*K. Howells, *Lab.*	29,722
Dr P. Donnelly, *C.*	9,925

Dr D. Bowen, *PC*	4,448
S. Belzak, *LD*	4,180
Ms E. Jackson, *Green*	615
Lab. majority	19,797

(June 1987, Lab. maj. 17,277)
(Feb. 1989, Lab. maj. 10,794)

RHONDDA (Mid Glamorgan)
E.59,955   T.76.61%

*A. Rogers, *Lab.*	34,243
G. Davies, *PC*	5,427
J. Richards, *C.*	3,588
P. Nicholls-Jones, *LD*	2,431
M. Fisher, *Comm. GB*	245
Lab. majority	28,816

(June 1987, Lab. maj. 30,596)

SWANSEA EAST (W. Glamorgan)
E.59,196   T.75.56%

*D. Anderson, *Lab.*	31,179
H. Davies, *C.*	7,697
R. Barton, *LD*	4,248
Ms E. Bonner-Evans, *PC*	1,607
Lab. majority	23,482

(June 1987, Lab. maj. 19,338)

SWANSEA WEST (W. Glamorgan)
E.59,785   T.73.34%

*Rt. Hon. A. Williams, *Lab.*	23,238
R. Perry, *C.*	13,760
M. Shrewsbury, *LD*	4,620
Dr D. Lloyd, *PC*	1,668
B. Oubridge, *Green*	564
Lab. majority	9,478

(June 1987, Lab. maj. 7,062)

TORFAEN (Gwent)
E.61,104   T.77.47%

*P. Murphy, *Lab.*	30,352
M. Watkins, *C.*	9,598
M. Hewson, *LD*	6,178
Dr J. Cox, *Green/PC*	1,210
Lab. majority	20,754

(June 1987, Lab. maj. 17,550)

VALE OF GLAMORGAN
(S. Glamorgan)
E.66,672   T.81.93%

W. Sweeney, *C.*	24,220
*J. Smith, *Lab.*	24,201
K. Davies, *LD*	5,045
D. Haswell, *PC*	1,160
C. majority	19

(June 1987, C. maj 6,251)
(May 1989, Lab. maj. 6,028)

WREXHAM (Clwyd)
E.63,720   T.80.71%

*J. Marek, *Lab.*	24,830
O. Paterson, *C.*	18,114
A. Thomas, *LD*	7,074
G. Wheatley, *PC*	1,415
Lab. majority	6,716

(June 1987, Lab. maj. 4,152)

YNYS MÔN (Gwynedd)
E.53,412   T.80.62%

*I. W. Jones, *PC*	15,984
G. Price Rowlands, *C.*	14,878
Dr R. Jones, *Lab.*	10,126
Ms P. Badger, *LD*	1,891
Mrs S. Parry, *NLP*	182
PC majority	1,106

(June 1987, PC maj. 4,298)

SCOTLAND

ABERDEEN NORTH (Grampian)
E.60,217   T.66.52%
*R. Hughes, *Lab.*	18,845
J. McGugan, *SNP*	9,608
P. Cook, *C.*	6,836
Dr M. Ford, *LD*	4,772
Lab. majority	9,237

(June 1987, Lab. maj. 16,278)

ABERDEEN SOUTH (Grampian)
E.58,881   T.69.78%
R. Robertson, *C.*	15,808
*F. Doran, *Lab.*	14,291
J. Davidson, *SNP*	6,223
Ms I. Keith, *LD*	4,767
C. majority	1,517

(June 1987, Lab. maj. 1,198)

ANGUS EAST (Tayside)
E.63,170   T.75.03%
*A. Welsh, *SNP*	19,006
Dr R. Harris, *C.*	18,052
G. Taylor, *Lab.*	5,994
C. McLeod, *LD*	3,897
D. McCabe, *Green*	449
SNP majority	954

(June 1987, SNP maj. 1,544)

ARGYLL AND BUTE (Strathclyde)
E.47,894   T.76.19%
*Mrs J. R. Michie, *LD*	12,739
J. Corrie, *C.*	10,117
Prof. N. MacCormick, *SNP*	8,689
D. Browne, *Lab.*	4,946
LD majority	2,622

(June 1987, L./All. maj. 1,394)

AYR (Strathclyde)
E.65,481   T.83.08%
P. Gallie, *C.*	22,172
A. Osborne, *Lab.*	22,087
Mrs B. Mullin, *SNP*	5,949
J. Boss, *LD*	4,067
R. Scott, *NLP*	132
C. majority	85

(June 1987, C. maj. 182)

BANFF AND BUCHAN (Grampian)
E.64,873   T.71.20%
*A. Salmond, *SNP*	21,954
S. Manson, *C.*	17,846
B. Balcombe, *Lab.*	3,803
Mrs R. Kemp, *LD*	2,588
SNP majority	4,108

(June 1987, SNP maj. 2,441)

CAITHNESS AND SUTHERLAND
(Highland)
E.30,905   T.71.93%
*R. Maclennan, *LD*	10,032
G. Bruce, *C.*	4,667
K. MacGregor, *SNP*	4,049
M. Coyne, *Lab.*	3,483
LD majority	5,365

(June 1987, SDP/All. maj. 8,494)

CARRICK, CUMNOCK AND
DOON VALLEY (Strathclyde)
E.55,330   T.76.94%
*G. Foulkes, *Lab.*	25,142
J. Boswell, *C.*	8,516

C. Douglas, *SNP*	6,910
Ms M. Paris, *LD*	2,005
Lab. majority	16,626

(June 1987, Lab. maj. 16,802)

CLACKMANNAN (Central)
E.48,963   T.78.34%
*M. O'Neill, *Lab.*	18,829
A. Brophy, *SNP*	10,326
J. Mackie, *C.*	6,638
Ms A. Watters, *LD*	2,567
Lab. majority	8,503

(June 1987, Lab. maj. 12,401)

CLYDEBANK AND MILNGAVIE
(Strathclyde)
E.47,337   T.77.79%
*A. Worthington, *Lab.*	19,637
G. Hughes, *SNP*	7,207
W. Harvey, *C.*	6,654
A. Tough, *LD*	3,216
Ms J. Barrie, *NLP*	112
Lab. majority	12,430

(June 1987, Lab. maj. 16,304)

CLYDESDALE (Strathclyde)
E.61,878   T.77.62%
*J. Hood, *Lab.*	21,418
Ms C. Goodwin, *C.*	11,231
I. Gray, *SNP*	11,084
Ms E. Buchanan, *LD*	3,957
S. Cartwright, *BNP*	342
Lab. majority	10,187

(June 1987, Lab. maj. 10,502)

CUMBERNAULD AND KILSYTH
(Strathclyde)
E.46,489   T.79.06%
*N. Hogg, *Lab.*	19,855
T. Johnston, *SNP*	10,640
I. Mitchell, *C.*	4,143
Ms J. Haddow, *LD*	2,118
Lab. majority	9,215

(June 1987, Lab. maj. 14,403)

CUNNINGHAME NORTH
(Strathclyde)
E.54,803   T.78.21%
*B. Wilson, *Lab.*	17,564
Ms E. Clarkson, *C.*	14,625
D. Crossan, *SNP*	7,813
D. Herbison, *LD*	2,864
Lab. majority	2,939

(June 1987, Lab. maj. 4,422)

CUNNINGHAME SOUTH
(Strathclyde)
E.49,010   T.75.88%
B. Donohoe, *Lab.*	19,687
R. Bell, *SNP*	9,007
S. Leslie, *C.*	6,070
B. Ashley, *LD*	2,299
W. Jackson, *NLP*	128
Lab. majority	10,680

(June 1987, Lab. maj. 16,633)

DUMBARTON (Strathclyde)
E.57,222   T.77.11%
*J. McFall, *Lab.*	19,255
T. Begg, *C.*	13,126

W. McKechnie, *SNP*	8,127
J. Morrison, *LD*	3,425
Ms D. Krass, *NLP*	192
Lab. majority	6,129

(June 1987, Lab. maj. 5,222)

DUMFRIES (D & G)
E.61,145   T.79.97%
*Sir H. Monro, *C.*	21,089
P. Rennie, *Lab.*	14,674
A. Morgan, *SNP*	6,971
N. Wallace, *LD*	5,749
G. McLeod, *Ind. Green*	312
T. Barlow, *NLP*	107
C. majority	6,415

(June 1987, C. maj. 7,493)

DUNDEE EAST (Tayside)
E.58,959   T.72.10%
*J. McAllion, *Lab.*	18,761
D. Coutts, *SNP*	14,197
S. Blackwood, *C.*	7,549
I. Yuill, *LD*	1,725
Ms S. Baird, *Green*	205
R. Baxter, *NLP*	77
Lab. majority	4,564

(June 1987, Lab. maj. 1,015)

DUNDEE WEST (Tayside)
E.59,953   T.69.82%
*E. Ross, *Lab.*	20,498
K. Brown, *SNP*	9,894
A. Spearman, *C.*	7,746
Ms E. Dick, *LD*	3,132
Ms E. Hood, *Green*	432
D. Arnold, *NLP*	159
Lab. majority	10,604

(June 1987, Lab. maj. 16,526)

DUNFERMLINE EAST (Fife)
E.50,179   T.75.62%
*J. G. Brown, *Lab.*	23,692
M. Tennant, *C.*	6,248
J. Lloyd, *SNP*	5,746
Ms T. Little, *LD*	2,262
Lab. majority	17,444

(June 1987, Lab. maj. 19,589)

DUNFERMLINE WEST (Fife)
E.50,948   T.76.44%
Ms R. Squire, *Lab.*	16,374
M. Scott-Hayward, *C.*	8,890
J. Smith, *SNP*	7,563
Ms E. Harris, *LD*	6,122
Lab. majority	7,484

(June 1987, Lab. maj. 9,402)

EAST KILBRIDE (Strathclyde)
E.64,080   T.80.01%
*A. Ingram, *Lab.*	24,055
Ms K. McAlorum, *SNP*	12,063
G. Lind, *C.*	9,781
Ms S. Grieve, *LD*	5,377
Lab. majority	11,992

(June 1987, Lab. maj. 12,624)

EAST LOTHIAN
E.66,699   T.82.37%
*J. Home Robertson, *Lab.*	25,537
J. Hepburne Scott, *C.*	15,501

G. Thomson, *SNP* 7,776
T. McKay, *LD* 6,126
Lab. majority 10,036
(June 1987, Lab. maj. 10,105)

EASTWOOD (Strathclyde)
E.63,685 *T*.80.97%
*J. A. Stewart, *C.* 24,124
P. Grant-Hutchison, *Lab.* 12,436
Miss M. Craig, *LD* 8,493
P. Scott, *SNP* 6,372
Dr L. Fergusson, *NLP* 146
C. majority 11,688
(June 1987, C. maj. 6,014)

EDINBURGH CENTRAL (Lothian)
E.56,527 *T*.69.26%
*A. Darling, *Lab.* 15,189
P. Martin, *C.* 13,063
Ms L. Devine, *SNP* 5,539
A. Myles, *LD* 4,500
R. Harper, *Green* 630
D. Wilson, *Lib.* 235
Lab. majority 2,126
(June 1987, Lab. maj. 2,262)

EDINBURGH EAST (Lothian)
E.45,687 *T*.73.89%
*G. Strang, *Lab.* 15,446
K. Ward, *C.* 8,235
D. McKinney, *SNP* 6,225
D. Scobie, *LD* 3,432
G. Farmer, *Green* 424
Lab. majority 7,211
(June 1987, Lab. maj. 9,295)

EDINBURGH LEITH (Lothian)
E.56,520 *T*.71.30%
M. Chisholm, *Lab.* 13,790
Ms F. Hyslop, *SNP* 8,805
M. Bin Ashiq Rizvi, *C.* 8,496
Mrs H. Campbell, *LD* 4,975
*R. Brown, *Ind. Lab.* 4,142
A. Swan, *NLP* 96
Lab. majority 4,985
(June 1987, Lab. maj. 11,327)

EDINBURGH PENTLANDS
(Lothian)
E.55,567 *T*.80.18%
*Rt. Hon. M. Rifkind, *C.* 18,128
M. Lazarowicz, *Lab.* 13,838
Ms K. Caskie, *SNP* 6,882
K. Smith, *LD* 5,597
D. Rae, *NLP* 111
C. majority 4,290
(June 1987, C. maj. 3,745)

EDINBURGH SOUTH (Lothian)
E.61,355 *T*.72.67%
*N. Griffiths, *Lab.* 18,485
S. Stevenson, *C.* 14,309
B. McCreadie, *LD* 5,961
R. Knox, *SNP* 5,727
G. Manclark, *NLP* 108
Lab. majority 4,176
(June 1987, Lab. maj. 1,859)

EDINBURGH WEST (Lothian)
E.58,998 *T*.82.67%
*Lord J. Douglas-Hamilton, *C.* 18,071
D. Gorrie, *LD* 17,192

Ms I. Kitson, *Lab.* 8,759
G. Sutherland, *SNP* 4,117
A. Fleming, *Lib.* 272
Ms L. Hendry, *Green* 234
D. Bruce, *BNP* 133
C. majority 879
(June 1987, C. maj. 1,234)

FALKIRK EAST (Central)
E.51,918 *T*.76.91%
M. Connarty, *Lab.* 18,423
R. Halliday, *SNP* 10,454
K. Harding, *C.* 8,279
Miss D. Storr, *LD* 2,775
Lab. majority 7,969
(June 1987, Lab. maj. 14,023)

FALKIRK WEST (Central)
E.50,126 *T*.76.77%
*D. Canavan, *Lab.* 19,162
W. Houston, *SNP* 9,350
M. Macdonald, *C.* 7,558
M. Reilly, *LD* 2,414
Lab. majority 9,812
(June 1987, Lab. maj. 13,552)

FIFE CENTRAL
E.56,152 *T*.74.33%
*H. McLeish, *Lab.* 21,036
Mrs T. Marwick, *SNP* 10,458
Ms C. Cender, *C.* 7,353
C. Harrow, *LD* 2,892
Lab. majority 10,578
(June 1987, Lab. maj. 15,709)

FIFE NORTH EAST
E.53,747 *T*.77.84%
*W. M. Campbell, *LD* 19,430
Mrs M. Scanlon, *C.* 16,122
D. Roche, *SNP* 3,589
Miss L. Clark, *Lab.* 2,319
T. Flynn, *Green* 294
D. Senior, *Lib.* 85
LD majority 3,308
(June 1987, L./All. maj. 1,447)

GALLOWAY AND UPPER
NITHSDALE (D & G)
E.54,474 *T*.81.66%
*Rt. Hon. I. Lang, *C.* 18,681
M. Brown, *SNP* 16,213
J. Dowson, *Lab.* 5,766
J. McKerchar, *LD* 3,826
C. majority 2,468
(June 1987, C. maj. 3,673)

GLASGOW CATHCART
(Strathclyde)
E.44,689 *T*.75.38%
*J. Maxton, *Lab.* 16,265
J. Young, *C.* 8,264
W. Steven, *SNP* 6,107
G. Dick, *LD* 2,614
Ms K. Allan, *Green* 441
Lab. majority 8,001
(June 1987, Lab. maj. 11,203)

GLASGOW CENTRAL (Strathclyde)
E.48,107 *T*.63.05%
*M. Watson, *Lab.* 17,341
B. O'Hara, *SNP* 6,322
E. Stewart, *C.* 4,208

Dr A. Rennie, *LD* 1,921
Ms I. Brandt, *Green* 435
T. Burn, *Comm. GB* 106
Lab. majority 11,019
(June 1987, Lab. maj. 17,253)
(June 1989, Lab. maj. 6,462)

GLASGOW GARSCADDEN
(Strathclyde)
E.41,289 *T*.71.13%
*D. Dewar, *Lab.* 18,920
R. Douglas, *SNP* 5,580
J. Scott, *C.* 3,385
C. Brodie, *LD* 1,425
W. Orr, *NLP* 61
Lab. majority 13,340
(June 1987, Lab. maj. 18,977)

GLASGOW GOVAN (Strathclyde)
E.45,822 *T*.76.03%
I. Davidson, *Lab.* 17,051
*J. Sillars, *SNP* 12,926
J. Donnelly, *C.* 3,458
R. Stewart, *LD* 1,227
D. Spaven, *Green* 181
Lab. majority 4,125
(June 1987, Lab. maj. 19,509)
(Nov. 1988, SNP maj. 3,554)

GLASGOW HILLHEAD
(Strathclyde)
E.57,223 *T*.68.80%
*G. Galloway, *Lab.* 15,148
C. Mason, *LD* 10,322
Ms A. Bates, *C.* 6,728
Miss S. White, *SNP* 6,484
Ms L. Collie, *Green* 558
Ms H. Gold, *Rev. Comm.* 73
D. Patterson, *NLP* 60
Lab. majority 4,826
(June 1987, Lab. maj. 3,251)

GLASGOW MARYHILL
(Strathclyde)
E.48,426 *T*.65.16%
*Mrs M. Fyfe, *Lab.* 19,452
C. Williamson, *SNP* 6,033
J. Godfrey, *C.* 3,248
J. Alexander, *LD* 2,215
P. O'Brien, *Green* 530
M. Henderson, *NLP* 78
Lab. majority 13,419
(June 1987, Lab. maj. 19,364)

GLASGOW POLLOK (Strathclyde)
E.46,139 *T*.70.74%
*J. Dunnachie, *Lab.* 14,170
T. Sheridan, *SML* 6,287
R. Gray, *C.* 5,147
G. Leslie, *SNP* 5,107
D. Jago, *LD* 1,932
Lab. majority 7,883
(June 1987, Lab. maj. 17,983)

GLASGOW PROVAN (Strathclyde)
E.36,560 *T*.65.31%
*J. Wray, *Lab.* 15,885
Ms A. MacRae, *SNP* 5,182
A. Rosindell, *C.* 1,865
C. Bell, *LD* 948
Lab. majority 10,703
(June 1987, Lab. maj. 18,372)

GLASGOW RUTHERGLEN
(Strathclyde)
E.52,709 T.75.23%
*T. McAvoy, *Lab.*   21,962
B. Cooklin, *C.*   6,692
J. Higgins, *SNP*   6,470
D. Baillie, *LD*   4,470
Ms B. Slaughter, *Int. Comm.*   62
Lab. majority   15,270
(June 1987, Lab. maj. 13,995)

GLASGOW SHETTLESTON
(Strathclyde)
E.51,910 T.68.91%
*D. Marshall, *Lab.*   21,665
Ms N. Sturgeon, *SNP*   6,831
N. Mortimer, *C.*   5,396
Ms J. Orskov, *LD*   1,881
Lab. majority   14,834
(June 1987, Lab. maj. 18,981)

GLASGOW SPRINGBURN
(Strathclyde)
E.45,842 T.65.65%
*M. Martin, *Lab.*   20,369
S. Miller, *SNP*   5,863
A. Barnett, *C.*   2,625
R. Ackland, *LD*   1,242
Lab. majority   14,506
(June 1987, Lab. maj. 22,063)

GORDON (Grampian)
E.80,103 T.73.86%
*M. Bruce, *LD*   22,158
J. Porter, *C.*   21,884
B. Adam, *SNP*   8,445
P. Morrell, *Lab.*   6,682
LD majority   274
(June 1987, L./All. maj. 9,519)

GREENOCK AND PORT
GLASGOW (Strathclyde)
E.52,053 T.73.72%
*N. Godman, *Lab.*   22,258
I. Black, *SNP*   7,279
Dr J. McCullough, *C.*   4,479
C. Lambert, *LD*   4,359
Lab. majority   14,979
(June 1987, Lab. maj. 20,055)

HAMILTON (Strathclyde)
E.61,531 T.76.15%
*G. Robertson, *Lab.*   25,849
W. Morrison, *SNP*   9,246
Ms M. Mitchell, *C.*   8,250
J. Oswald, *LD*   3,515
Lab. majority   16,603
(June 1987, Lab. maj. 21,662)

INVERNESS NAIRN AND
LOCHABER (Highland)
E.69,468 T.73.27%
*Sir R. Johnston, *LD*   13,258
D. Stewart, *Lab.*   12,800
F. Ewing, *SNP*   12,562
J. Scott, *C.*   11,517
J. Martin, *Green*   766
LD majority   458
(June 1987, L./All maj. 5,431)

KILMARNOCK AND LOUDOUN
(Strathclyde)
E.62,002 T.79.99%
*W. McKelvey, *Lab.*   22,210
A. Neil, *SNP*   15,231
R. Wilkinson, *C.*   9,438
Mrs K. Philbrick, *LD*   2,722
Lab. majority   6,979
(June 1987, Lab. maj. 14,127)

KINCARDINE AND DEESIDE
(Grampian)
E.66,617 T.78.74%
G. Kynoch, *C.*   22,924
*N. Stephen, *LD*   18,429
Dr A. Macartney, *SNP*   5,927
M. Savidge, *Lab.*   4,795
S. Campbell, *Green*   381
C. majority   4,495
(June 1987, C. maj. 2,063)
(Nov. 1991, LD maj. 7,824)

KIRKCALDY (Fife)
E.51,762 T.75.06%
*Dr L. Moonie, *Lab.*   17,887
S. Hosie, *SNP*   8,761
S. Wosley, *C.*   8,476
Ms S. Leslie, *LD*   3,729
Lab. majority   9,126
(June 1987, Lab. maj. 11,570)

LINLITHGOW (Lothian)
E.61,082 T.78.66%
*T. Dalyell, *Lab.*   21,603
K. MacAskill, *SNP*   14,577
Ms E. Forbes, *C.*   8,424
M. Falchikov, *LD*   3,446
Lab. majority   7,026
(June 1987, Lab. maj. 10,373)

LIVINGSTON (Lothian)
E.61,092 T.74.62%
*R. Cook, *Lab.*   20,245
P. Johnston, *SNP*   12,140
H. Gordon, *C.*   8,824
F. Mackintosh, *LD*   3,911
A. Ross-Smith, *Green*   469
Lab. majority   8,105
(June 1987, Lab. maj. 11,105)

MIDLOTHIAN
E.60,255 T.77.87%
E. Clarke, *Lab.*   20,588
A. Lumsden, *SNP*   10,254
J. Stoddart, *C.*   9,443
P. Sewell, *LD*   6,164
I. Morrice, *Green*   476
Lab. majority   10,334
(June 1987, Lab. maj. 12,253)

MONKLANDS EAST (Strathclyde)
E.48,391 T.75.07%
*Rt. Hon. J. Smith, *Lab.*   22,266
J. Wright, *SNP*   6,554
S. Walters, *C.*   5,830
P. Ross, *LD*   1,679
Lab. majority   15,712
(June 1987, Lab. maj. 16,389)

MONKLANDS WEST (Strathclyde)
E.49,269 T.77.45%
*T. Clarke, *Lab.*   23,384
K. Bovey, *SNP*   6,319

A. Lownie, *C.*   6,074
Ms S. Hamilton, *LD*   2,382
Lab. majority   17,065
(June 1987, Lab. maj. 18,333)

MORAY (Grampian)
E.63,255 T.72.46%
*Mrs M. Ewing, *SNP*   20,299
Ms R. Hossack, *C.*   17,455
C. Smith, *Lab.*   5,448
B. Sheridan, *LD*   2,634
SNP majority   2,844
(June 1987, SNP maj. 3,685)

MOTHERWELL NORTH
(Strathclyde)
E.57,290 T.76.71%
*Dr J. Reid, *Lab.*   27,852
D. Clark, *SNP*   8,942
R. Hargrave, *C.*   5,011
Miss H. Smith, *LD*   2,145
Lab. majority   18,910
(June 1987, Lab. maj. 23,595)

MOTHERWELL SOUTH
(Strathclyde)
E.50,042 T.76.17%
*J. Bray, *Lab.*   21,771
Mrs K. Ullrich, *SNP*   7,758
G. McIntosh, *C.*   6,097
A. Mackie, *LD*   2,349
D. Lettice, *YSOR*   146
Lab. majority   14,013
(June 1987, Lab. maj. 16,930)

ORKNEY AND SHETLAND
E.31,472 T.65.53%
*J. Wallace, *LD*   9,575
Dr P. McCormick, *C.*   4,542
J. Aberdein, *Lab.*   4,093
Mrs F. McKie, *SNP*   2,301
Ms C. Wharton, *NLP*   115
LD majority   5,033
(June 1987, L./All. maj. 3,922)

PAISLEY NORTH (Strathclyde)
E.46,403 T.73.39%
*Mrs I. Adams, *Lab.*   17,269
R. Mullin, *SNP*   7,940
D. Sharpe, *C.*   5,576
Miss E. McCartin, *LD*   2,779
D. Mellor, *Green*   412
N. Brennan, *NLP*   81
Lab. majority   9,329
(June 1987, Lab. maj. 14,442)
(Nov. 1990, Lab. maj. 3,770)

PAISLEY SOUTH (Strathclyde)
E.47,889 T.75.01%
*G. McMaster, *Lab.*   18,202
I. Lawson, *SNP*   8,653
Ms S. Laidlaw, *C.*   5,703
A. Reid, *LD*   3,271
S. Porter, *NLP*   93
Lab. majority   9,549
(June 1987, Lab. maj. 15,785)
(Nov. 1990, Lab. maj. 5,030)

PERTH AND KINROSS (Tayside)
E.65,410 T.76.86%
*Sir N. Fairbairn, *C.*   20,195
Ms R. Cunningham, *SNP*   18,101

M. Rolfe, *Lab.* 6,267
M. Black, *LD* 5,714
C. majority 2,094
(June 1987, C. maj. 5,676)

RENFREW WEST AND
INVERCLYDE (Strathclyde)
*E.*58,122   *T.*80.32%
*T. Graham, *Lab.* 17,085
Ms A. Goldie, *C.* 15,341
C. Campbell, *SNP* 9,444
S. Nimmo, *LD* 4,668
D. Maltman, *NLP* 149
Lab. majority 1,744
(June 1987, Lab. maj. 4,063)

ROSS, CROMARTY AND SKYE
(Highland)
*E.*55,524   *T.*73.90%
*C. Kennedy, *LD* 17,066
J. Gray, *C.* 9,436
R. Gibson, *SNP* 7,618
J. MacDonald, *Lab.* 6,275
D. Jardine, *Green* 642
LD majority 7,630
(June 1987, SDP/All. maj. 11,319)

ROXBURGH AND
BERWICKSHIRE (Borders)
*E.*43,485   *T.*77.71%
*A. Kirkwood, *LD* 15,852
S. Finlay-Maxwell, *C.* 11,595
M. Douglas, *SNP* 3,437
S. Lambert, *Lab.* 2,909
LD majority 4,257
(June 1987, L./All maj. 4,008)

STIRLING (Central)
*E.*58,266   *T.*82.29%
*M. Forsyth, *C.* 19,174
Ms K. Phillips, *Lab.* 18,471
G. Fisher, *SNP* 6,558
W. Robertson, *LD* 3,337
W. Thomson, *Green* 342
R. Sharp, *Loony* 68
C. majority 703
(June 1987, C. maj. 548)

STRATHKELVIN AND BEARSDEN
(Strathclyde)
*E.*61,116   *T.*82.33%
*S. Galbraith, *Lab.* 21,267
M. Hirst, *C.* 18,105
T. Chalmers, *SNP* 6,275
Ms B. Waterfield, *LD* 4,585
D. Whitley, *NLP* 90
Lab. majority 3,162
(June 1987, Lab. maj. 2,452)

TAYSIDE NORTH
*E.*55,969   *T.*77.64%
*W. Walker, *C.* 20,283
J. Swinney, *SNP* 16,288
S. Horner, *LD* 3,791
S. Maclennan, *Lab.* 3,094
C. majority 3,995
(June 1987, C. maj. 5,016)

TWEEDDALE, ETTRICK AND
LAUDERDALE (Borders)
*E.*39,493   *T.*78.04%
*Rt. Hon. Sir D. Steel, *LD* 12,296
L. Beat, *C.* 9,776
Mrs C. Creech, *SNP* 5,244
A. Dunton, *Lab.* 3,328
J. Hein, *Lib.* 177
LD majority 2,520
(June 1987, L./All. maj. 5,942)

WESTERN ISLES
*E.*22,784   *T.*70.35%
*C. MacDonald, *Lab.* 7,664
Ms F. MacFarlane, *SNP* 5,961
R. Heany, *C.* 1,362
N. Mitchison, *LD* 552
A. Price, *Ind.* 491
Lab. majority 1,703
(June 1987, Lab. maj. 2,340)

NORTHERN IRELAND

ANTRIM EAST
*E.*62,839   *T.*62.46%
*R. Beggs, *UUP* 16,966
N. Dodds, *DUP* 9,544
S. Neeson, *All.* 9,132
Miss M. Boal, *C.* 3,359
Ms A. Palmer, *NLP* 250
UUP majority 7,422
(June 1987, UUP maj. 15,360)

ANTRIM NORTH
*E.*69,124   *T.*65.82%
*Revd I. Paisley, *DUP* 23,152
J. Gaston, *UUP* 8,216
S. Farren, *SDLP* 6,512
G. Williams, *All.* 3,442
R. Sowler, *C.* 2,263
J. McGarry, *SF* 1,916
DUP majority 14,936
(June 1987, DUP maj. 23,234)

ANTRIM SOUTH
*E.*68,013   *T.*62.10%
*C. Forsythe, *UUP* 29,956
D. McClelland, *SDLP* 5,397
J. Blair, *All.* 5,224
H. Cushinan, *SF* 1,220
D. Martin, *Loony G.* 442
UUP majority 24,559
(June 1987, UUP maj. 19,587)

BELFAST EAST
*E.*52,833   *T.*67.74%
*P. Robinson, *DUP* 18,437
Dr J. Alderdice, *All.* 10,650
D. Greene, *C.* 3,314

Ms D. Dunlop, *Ind. U.* 2,256
J. O'Donnell, *SF* 679
J. Bell, *WP* 327
G. Redden, *NLP* 128
DUP majority 7,787
(June 1987, DUP maj. 9,798)

BELFAST NORTH
*E.*55,062   *T.*65.22%
*A. C. Walker, *UUP* 17,240
A. Maginness, *SDLP* 7,615
P. McManus, *SF* 4,693
T. Campbell, *All.* 2,246
Ms M. Redpath, *C.* 2,107
S. Lynch, *NA* 1,386
Ms M. Smith, *WP* 419
D. O'Leary, *NLP* 208
UUP majority 9,625
(June 1987, UUP maj. 8,560)

BELFAST SOUTH
*E.*52,032   *T.*64.54%
*Revd W. M. Smyth, *UUP* 16,336
Dr A. McDonnell, *SDLP* 6,266
J. Montgomery, *All.* 5,054
L. Fee, *C.* 3,356
S. Hayes, *SF* 1,123
P. Hadden, *LTU* 875
P. Lynn, *WP* 362
Ms T. Mullan, *NLP* 212
UUP majority 10,070
(June 1987, UUP maj. 11,954)

BELFAST WEST
*E.*54,609   *T.*73.19%
Dr J. Hendron, *SDLP* 17,415
*G. Adams, *SF* 16,826
F. Cobain, *UUP* 4,766
J. Lowry, *WP* 750
M. Kennedy, *NLP* 213
SDLP majority 589
(June 1987, SF maj. 2,221)

DOWN NORTH
*E.*68,662   *T.*65.47%
*J. Kilfedder, *UPUP* 19,305
Dr L. Kennedy, *C.* 14,371
Ms A. Morrow, *All.* 6,611
D. Vitty, *DUP* 4,414
A. Wilmot, *NLP* 255
UPUP majority 4,934
(June 1987, UPUP maj. 3,953)

DOWN SOUTH
*E.*76,093   *T.*80.92%
*E. McGrady, *SDLP* 31,523
D. Nelson, *UUP* 25,181
S. Fitzpatrick, *SF* 1,843
M. Healey, *All.* 1,542
Mrs S. McKenzie-Hill, *C.* 1,488
SDLP majority 6,342
(June 1987, SDLP maj. 731)

FERMANAGH AND SOUTH
TYRONE
*E.*70,192   *T.*78.53%
*K. Maginnis, *UUP* 26,923
T. Gallagher, *SDLP* 12,810
F. Molloy, *SF* 12,604

D. Kettyles, *Prog. Soc.*	1,094
E. Bullick, *All.*	950
G. Cullen, *NA*	747
UUP majority	14,113
(June 1987, UUP maj. 12,823)	

FOYLE

*E.*74,585 *T.*69.57%

*J. Hume, *SDLP*	26,710
G. Campbell, *DUP*	13,705
M. McGuinness, *SF*	9,149
Ms L. McIlroy, *All.*	1,390
G. McKenzie, *WP*	514
J. Burns, *NLP*	422
SDLP majority	13,005
(June 1987, SDLP maj. 9,860)	

LAGAN VALLEY

*E.*72,645 *T.*67.39%

*Rt. Hon. J. H. Molyneaux, *UUP*	
	29,772
S. Close, *All.*	6,207
H. Lewsley, *SDLP*	4,626
T. Coleridge, *C.*	4,423
P. Rice, *SF*	3,346
Ms A.-M. Lowry, *WP*	582
UUP majority	23,565
(June 1987, UUP maj. 23,373)	

LONDONDERRY EAST

*E.*75,559 *T.*69.79%

*W. Ross, *UUP*	30,370
A. Doherty, *SDLP*	11,843
Ms P. Davey-Kennedy, *SF*	5,320
P. McGowan, *All.*	3,613
A. Elder, *C.*	1,589
UUP majority	18,527
(June 1987, UUP maj. 20,157)	

NEWRY AND ARMAGH

*E.*67,508 *T.*77.87%

*S. Mallon, *SDLP*	26,073
J. Speers, *UUP*	18,982
B. Curran, *SF*	6,547
Mrs E. Bell, *All.*	972
SDLP majority	7,091
(June 1987, SDLP maj. 5,325)	

STRANGFORD

*E.*68,870 *T.*65.02%

*Rt. Hon. J. Taylor, *UUP*	19,517
S. Wilson, *DUP*	10,606
K. McCarthy, *All.*	7,585
S. Eyre, *C.*	6,782
D. Shaw, *NLP*	295
UUP majority	8,911
(June 1987, UUP maj. 20,646)	

ULSTER MID

*E.*69,071 *T.*79.28%

*Revd Dr R. T. W. McCrea, *DUP*	
	23,181
D. Haughey, *SDLP*	16,994
B. McElduff, *SF*	10,248
J. McLoughlin, *Ind.*	1,996
Ms A. Gormley, *All.*	1,506
H. Hutchinson, *LTU*	389
T. Owens, *WP*	285
J. Anderson, *NLP*	164
DUP majority	6,187
(June 1987, DUP maj. 9,360)	

UPPER BANN

*E.*67,446 *T.*67.43%

*W. D. Trimble, *UUP*	26,824
Mrs B. Rodgers, *SDLP*	10,661
B. Curran, *SF*	2,777
Dr W. Ramsey, *All.*	2,541
Mrs C. Jones, *C.*	1,556
T. French, *WP*	1,120
UUP majority	16,163
(June 1987, OUP maj. 17,361)	
(May 1990, OUP maj. 13,849)	

COMMONWEALTH PARLIAMENTARY ASSOCIATION (1911)

The Commonwealth Parliamentary Association consists of 122 branches in the national, state, provincial or territorial parliaments in the countries of the Commonwealth. Conferences and general assemblies are held every year in different countries of the Commonwealth.

President (1992–3), His Excellency Alexis Galanos, MP, President of the House of Representatives (*Cyprus*)
Vice-President (1992–3), Hon. John Fraser, PC, QC, MP, Speaker of the House of Commons (*Canada*)
Chairman of the Executive Committee (1990–3), Hon. Clive Griffiths, MLC, President of the Legislative Council (*Western Australia*)
Secretary-General, A. R. Donahoe, QC, 7 Old Palace Yard, London SW1P 3JY

UNITED KINGDOM BRANCH

Hon. Presidents, The Lord Chancellor; Madam Speaker
Chairman of Branch, The Rt. Hon. John Major, MP

Chairman of Executive Committee, C. Shepherd, MP
Secretary, P. Cobb, OBE, Westminster Hall, Palace of Westminster, London, SW1

THE INTER-PARLIAMENTARY UNION (1889)

To facilitate personal contact between members of all Parliaments in the promotion of representative institutions, peace and international co-operation.

Secretary-General, P. Cornillon, Place du Petit-Saconnex, BP 99, 1211 Geneva 19, Switzerland

BRITISH GROUP

Palace of Westminster, London SW1A 0AA

Hon. Presidents, The Lord Chancellor; Madam Speaker
President, The Rt. Hon. John Major, MP
Chairman, Dr M. Clark, MP
Secretary, D. Ramsay

European Parliament

* Denotes membership of the last Parliament

*Adam, Gordon J. (b. 1934), Lab., Northumbria, maj. 60,040

*Balfe, Richard A. (b. 1944), Lab. Co-op, London South Inner, maj. 45,018

Barton, Roger (b. 1945), Lab., Sheffield, maj. 69,276

*Beazley, Christopher J. P. (b. 1952), C., Cornwall and Plymouth, maj. 19,817

*Beazley, Peter G., CBE (b. 1922), C., Bedfordshire South, maj. 2,977

*Bethell, The Lord (b. 1938), C., London North West, maj. 7,400

*Bird, John A. W. (b. 1926), Lab. Co-op, Midlands West, maj. 42,364

Bowe, David (b. 1955), Lab., Cleveland and Yorkshire North, maj. 24,092

*Buchan, Mrs Janey O. (b. 1926), Lab., Glasgow, maj. 59,232

*Cassidy, Bryan M. D. (b. 1934), C., Dorset East and Hampshire West, maj. 61,774

*Catherwood, Sir Frederick (b. 1925), C., Cambridge and Bedfordshire North, maj. 32,321

Coates, Kenneth (b. 1939), Lab., Nottingham, maj. 14,513

*Collins, Kenneth D. (b. 1939), Lab., Strathclyde East, maj. 60,317

Crampton, Peter D. (b. 1932), Lab., Humberside, maj. 16,328

*Crawley, Mrs Christine M. (b. 1950), Lab., Birmingham East, maj. 46,948

*Daly, Mrs Margaret E. (b. 1938), C., Somerset and Dorset West, maj. 52,220

David, Wayne (b. 1957), Lab., Wales South, maj. 62,557

Donnelly, Alan J. (b. 1957), Lab., Tyne and Wear, maj. 95,780

*Elles, James E. M. (b. 1949), C., Oxford and Buckinghamshire, maj. 47,518

*Elliott, Michael N. (b. 1932), Lab., London West, maj. 14,808

*Ewing, Mrs Winifred M. (b. 1929), SNP, Highlands and Islands, maj. 44,695

*Falconer, Alec (b. 1940), Lab., Scotland Mid and Fife, maj. 52,157

Fletcher-Vane, see Inglewood

*Ford, J. Glyn (b. 1950), Lab., Greater Manchester East, maj. 34,501

Green, Ms Pauline (b. 1948), Lab. Co-op, London North, maj. 5,837

Harrison, Lyndon (b. 1947), Lab., Cheshire West, maj. 23,201

*Hindley, Michael J. (b. 1947), Lab., Lancashire East, maj. 39,148

*Hoon, Geoffrey W. (b. 1953), Lab., Derbyshire, maj. 33,388

*Howell, Paul F. (b. 1951), C., Norfolk, maj. 20,907

*Hughes, Stephen S. (b. 1952), Lab., Durham, maj. 86,848

*Hume, John, MP (b. 1937), SDLP, Northern Ireland, polled 136,335 votes

Inglewood, The Lord (Richard Fletcher-Vane) (b. 1951), C., Cumbria and Lancashire North, maj. 2,391

*Jackson, Mrs Caroline F. (b. 1946), C., Wiltshire, maj. 46,313

*Jackson, Christopher M. (b. 1935), C., Kent East, maj. 28,961

*Kellett-Bowman, Edward T. (b. 1931), C., Hampshire Central, maj. 27,674

*Lomas, Alfred (b. 1928), Lab., London North East, maj. 47,767

*McGowan, Michael (b. 1940), Lab., Leeds, maj. 42,518

McCubbin, Henry (b. 1942), Lab., Scotland North East, maj. 2,613

McIntosh, Miss Anne C. B. (b. 1954), C., Essex North East, maj. 39,398

*McMahon, Hugh R. (b. 1938), Lab., Strathclyde West, maj. 39,591

*McMillan-Scott, Edward H. C. (b. 1949), C., York, maj. 15,102

*Martin, David W. (b. 1954), Lab., Lothians, maj. 38,826

*Megahy, Thomas (b. 1929), Lab., Yorkshire South West, maj. 65,901

*Moorhouse, C. James O. (b. 1924), C., London South and Surrey East, maj. 30,816

*Morris, Revd David R. (b. 1930), Lab., Wales Mid and West, maj. 51,912

*Newens, A. Stanley (b. 1930), Lab. Co-op, London Central, maj. 11,542

*Newman, Edward (b. 1953), Lab., Greater Manchester Central, maj. 38,867

*Newton Dunn, William F. (b. 1941), C., Lincolnshire, maj. 20,650

Nicholson, James F. (b. 1945), UUP, Northern Ireland, polled 118,785 votes

Oddy, Ms Christine M. (b. 1955), Lab., Midlands Central, maj. 5,093

*O'Hagan, The Lord (b. 1945), C., Devon, maj. 57,298

*Paisley, Revd Ian R. K., MP (b. 1926), DUP, Northern Ireland, polled 160,110 votes

*Patterson, G. Benjamin (Ben) (b. 1939), C., Kent West, maj. 24,050

*Plumb, The Lord (b. 1925), C., The Cotswolds, maj. 45,678

Pollack, Ms Anita J. (b. 1946), Lab., London South West, maj. 518

*Prag, Derek (b. 1923), C., Hertfordshire, maj. 43,342

*Price, Peter N. (b. 1942), C., London South East, maj. 7,590

*Prout, Sir Christopher, TD, QC (b. 1942), C., Shropshire and Stafford, maj. 2,544

Rawlings, Miss Patricia (b. 1939), C., Essex South West, maj. 9,403

Read, Ms Mel (b. 1939), Lab., Leicester, maj. 15,322

*Scott-Hopkins, Sir James (b. 1921), C., Hereford and Worcester, maj. 25,665

*Seal, Barry H. (b. 1937), Lab., Yorkshire West, maj. 37,927

*Seligman, R. Madron (b. 1918), C., Sussex West, maj. 46,233

*Simmonds, Richard J. (b. 1944), C., Wight and Hampshire East, maj. 39,430

*Simpson, Anthony M. H., TD (b. 1935), C., Northamptonshire, maj. 20,447

Simpson, Brian (b. 1953), Lab., Cheshire East, maj. 1,864

Smith, Alexander (b. 1943), Lab., Scotland South, maj. 15,693

*Smith, Llewellyn T. (b. 1944), Lab., Wales South East, maj. 108,488

Spencer, Thomas N. B. (*b.* 1948), *C., Surrey West*, maj. 49,342

Stevens, John C. C. (*b.* 1955), *C., Thames Valley*, maj. 26,491

*Stevenson, George W. (*b.* 1938), *Lab., Staffordshire East*, maj. 31,769

*Stewart, Kenneth A. (*b.* 1925), *Lab., Merseyside West*, maj. 49,817

*Stewart-Clark, Sir John, Bt. (*b.* 1929), *C., Sussex East*, maj. 53,294

Titley, Gary (*b.* 1950), *Lab., Greater Manchester West*, maj. 50,135

*Tomlinson, John E. (*b.* 1939), *Lab., Birmingham West*, maj. 30,860

*Tongue, Miss Carole (*b.* 1955), *Lab., London East*, maj. 27,385

*Turner, Amédée E., QC (*b.* 1929), *C., Suffolk*, maj. 25,693

*Welsh, Michael J. (*b.* 1942), *C., Lancashire Central*, maj. 5,688

*West, Norman (*b.* 1935), *Lab., Yorkshire South*, maj. 91,784

White, Ian (*b.* 1947), *Lab., Bristol*, maj. 9,982

Wilson, Joseph (*b.* 1937), *Lab., Wales North*, maj. 4,460

Wynn, Terence (*b.* 1946), *Lab., Merseyside East*, maj. 76,867

UK CONSTITUENCIES AS AT 15 JUNE 1989

Corr.	Corrective Party
Grn.	Green
Hum.	Humanist Party
ICP	International Communist Party
Lab. RG	Labour for Regional Government
MK	Mebyon Kernow
W. Reg.	Wessex Regionalists

For other abbreviations, *see* page 243

BEDFORDSHIRE SOUTH
E. 569,506

*P. G. Beazley, *C.*	73,406
T. McWalter, *Lab.*	70,429
D. Everett, *Grn*	34,508
W. M. Johnston, *SLD*	8,748
R. Muller, *SDP*	3,067
C. majority	2,977

(June 1984, C. maj. 14,982)

BIRMINGHAM EAST
E. 531,081

*Mrs C. M. Crawley, *Lab.*	96,588
M. J. C. Harbour, *C.*	49,640
P. M. Simpson, *Grn.*	22,589
J. C. Binns, *SDP*	5,424
J. M. E. C. Roodhouse, *SLD*	4,010
M. Wingfield, *NF*	1,471
Lab. majority	46,948

(June 1984, Lab. maj. 21,383)

BIRMINGHAM WEST
E. 515,817

*J. E. Tomlinson, *Lab.*	86,545
C. F. Robinson, *C.*	55,685
J. D. Bentley, *Grn.*	21,384
S. Reynolds, *SLD*	7,673
Lab. majority	30,860

(June 1984, Lab. maj. 6,244)

BRISTOL
E. 562,277

I. White, *Lab.*	87,753
*R. J. Cottrell, *C.*	77,771
D. N. Wall, *Grn.*	39,436
C. Boney, *SLD*	16,309
G. McEwen *W. Reg.*	1,017
Lab. majority	9,982

(June 1984, C. maj. 17,644)

CAMBRIDGE AND
BEDFORDSHIRE NORTH
E. 562,539

*Sir F. Catherwood, *C.*	84,044
M. Strube, *Lab.*	51,723

Ms M. E. Wright, *Grn.*	37,956
A. N. Duff, *SLD*	15,052
C. majority	32,321

(June 1984, C. maj. 47,216)

CHESHIRE EAST
E. 518,311

B. Simpson, *Lab.*	74,721
*Sir T. Normanton, *C.*	72,857
C. C. White, *Grn.*	21,456
Mrs B. Fraenkel, *SLD*	12,344
Lab. majority	1,864

(June 1984, C. maj. 18,376)

CHESHIRE WEST
E. 543,256

L. Harrison, *Lab.*	102,962
*A. Pearce, *C.*	79,761
G. L. Nicholls, *Grn.*	25,933
J. Rankin, *SLD*	9,333
Lab. majority	23,201

(June 1984, C. maj. 9,692)

CLEVELAND AND YORKSHIRE
NORTH
E. 571,254

D. Bowe, *Lab.*	94,953
*Sir P. Vanneck, *C.*	70,861
O. Dumpleton, *Grn.*	17,225
T. M. Mawston, *SLD*	8,470
R. I. Andrew *SDP*	7,970
Lab. majority	24,092

(June 1984, C. maj. 2,625)

CORNWALL AND PLYMOUTH
E. 542,527

*C. J. P. Beazley, *C.*	88,376
P. A. Tyler, *SLD*	68,559
Ms D. Kirk, *Lab.*	41,466
H. Hoptrough, *Grn.*	24,581
C. Lawry, *MK*	4,224
C. majority	19,817

(June 1984, C. maj. 17,751)

THE COTSWOLDS
E. 558,115

*The Lord Plumb, *C.*	94,852
Mrs S. Limb, *Grn.*	49,174
T. Levitt, *Lab.*	48,180
L. A. Rowe, *SLD*	18,196
C. majority	45,678

(June 1984, C. maj. 48,942)

CUMBRIA AND LANCASHIRE
NORTH

E. 561,263	
W. R. Fletcher-Vane, *C.*	84,035
J. M. P. Hutton, *Lab.*	81,644
Mrs C. E. Smith, *Grn.*	21,262
E. E. Hill, *SLD*	12,590
J. Bates, *SDP*	4,206
C. majority	2,391

(June 1984, C. maj. 23,795)

DERBYSHIRE
E. 564,429

*G. W. Hoon, *Lab.*	105,018
P. Jenkinson, *C.*	72,630
E. Wall, *Grn.*	20,781
S. Molloy, *SLD*	4,613
Mrs A. M. Ayres, *SDP*	3,858
Lab. majority	33,388

(June 1984, Lab maj. 6,853)

DEVON
E. 596,671

*The Lord O'Hagan, *C.*	110,518
P. S. Christie, *Grn.*	53,220
W. J. Cairns, *Lab.*	40,675
M. Edmunds, *SLD*	23,306
R. Edwards, *SDP*	7,806
S. B. F. Hughes, *LM*	2,241
Lady Rous, *W. Reg.*	385
C. majority	57,298

(June 1984, C. maj. 56,610)

DORSET EAST AND HAMPSHIRE
WEST
E. 608,895

*B. M. D. Cassidy, *C.*	111,469
Ms K. I. Bradbury, *Grn.*	49,695
H. R. White, *Lab.*	38,011
H. R. Legg, *SLD*	21,809
C. majority	61,774

(June 1984, C. maj. 59,891)

DURHAM
E. 530,137

*S. S. Hughes, *Lab.*	124,448
R. Hull, *C.*	37,600
Ms H. I. Lennox, *Grn.*	18,770
P. Freitag, *SLD*	8,369
Lab. majority	86,848

(June 1984, Lab. maj. 61,227)

ESSEX NORTH EAST
E. 598,542

Miss A. C. B. McIntosh, *C.*	92,758
Ms H. J. Bryan, *Lab.*	53,360

C. R. Keene, *Grn.* 45,163
Miss D. P. Wallis, *SLD* 16,939
C. majority 39,398
(June 1984, C. maj. 54,302)

ESSEX SOUTH WEST
E. 569,011
Miss P. E. Rawlings, *C.* 77,408
J. W. Orpe, *Lab.* 68,005
Mrs M. E. Willis, *Grn.* 32,242
T. P. Allen, *SLD* 10,618
C. majority 9,403
(June 1984, C. maj. 16,021)

GLASGOW
E. 487,199
*Mrs J. O. Buchan, *Lab.* 107,818
A. Brophy, *SNP* 48,586
Mrs A. K. Bates, *C.* 20,761
D. L. Spaven, *Grn.* 12,229
J. Morrison, *SLD* 3,887
D. Chalmers, *Comm.* 1,164
J. Simons, *ICP* 193
Lab. majority 59,232
(June 1984, Lab. maj. 65,733)

GREATER MANCHESTER CENTRAL
E. 481,023
*E. Newman, *Lab.* 86,914
Miss C. E. Gillan, *C.* 48,047
B. Candeland, *Grn.* 19,742
J. H. Mulholland, *SLD* 9,437
S. M. Millson, *SDP* 2,769
S. Knight, *Hum.* 1,045
Lab. majority 38,867
(June 1984, Lab. maj. 28,077)

GREATER MANCHESTER EAST
E. 506,930
*J. G. Ford, *Lab.* 93,294
R. N. Greenwood, *C.* 58,793
M. J. Shipley, *Grn.* 19,090
A. B. Leah, *SLD* 16,645
Lab. majority 34,501
(June 1984, Lab. maj. 8,651)

GREATER MANCHESTER WEST
E. 522,476
G. Titley, *Lab.* 109,228
P. H. Twyman, *C.* 59,093
D. W. Milne, *Grn.* 22,778
A. H. Cruden, *SLD* 6,940
Mrs B. Archer, *SDP* 4,526
Lab. majority 50,135
(June 1984, Lab. maj. 37,698)

HAMPSHIRE CENTRAL
E. 546,630
*E. T. Kellett-Bowman, *C.* 78,651
Ms A. Mawle, *Lab.* 50,977
Mrs S. J. Penton, *Grn.* 33,186
D. W. G. Chidgey, *SLD* 18,418
C. majority 27,674
(June 1984, C. maj. 44,821)
(Dec. 1988, C. maj. 21,442)

HEREFORD AND WORCESTER
E. 595,504
*Sir James Scott-Hopkins, *C.* 87,898
C. A. Short, *Lab.* 62,233
Ms F. M. Norman, *Grn.* 49,296

Mrs J. D. Davies, *SLD* 13,569
C. majority 25,665
(June 1984, C. maj. 39,934)

HERTFORDSHIRE
E. 517,137
*D. N. Prag, *C.* 86,898
V. S. Anand, *Lab.* 43,556
M. F. Ames, *Grn.* 37,277
M. D. Phelan, *SLD* 13,456
Mrs C. Treves Brown, *SDP* 5,048
C. majority 43,342
(June 1984, C. maj. 45,932)

HIGHLANDS AND ISLANDS
E. 313,877
*Mrs W. M. Ewing, *SNP* 66,297
Sir A. McQuarrie, *C.* 21,602
N. MacAskill, *Lab.* 17,848
M. Gregson, *Grn.* 12,199
N. Michison, *SLD* 10,644
SNP majority 44,695
(June 1984, SNP maj. 16,277)

HUMBERSIDE
E. 504,219
P. D. Crampton, *Lab.* 74,163
*R. C. Battersby, *C.* 57,835
Mrs J. C. Clark, *Grn.* 23,835
F. L. Parker, *SLD* 3,989
S. W. Unwin, *SDP* 3,419
Lab. majority 16,328
(June 1984, C. maj. 8,015)

KENT EAST
E. 575,789
*C. M. Jackson, *C.* 85,667
G. N. J. Perry, *Lab.* 56,706
Ms P. A. Kemp, *Grn.* 36,931
A. F. C. Morris, *SLD* 15,470
C. majority 28,961
(June 1984, C. maj. 48,867)

KENT WEST
E. 569,725
*G. B. Patterson, *C.* 82,519
P. L. Sloman, *Lab.* 58,469
J. Tidy, *Grn.* 33,202
J. B. Doherty, *SLD* 16,087
C. majority 24,050
(June 1984, C. maj. 34,630)

LANCASHIRE CENTRAL
E. 537,610
*M. J. Welsh, *C.* 81,125
G. W. T. Smith, *Lab.* 75,437
Mrs H. Ingham, *Grn.* 28,777
Ms J. Ross-Mills, *SLD* 7,378
C. majority 5,688
(June 1984, C. maj. 26,195)

LANCASHIRE EAST
E. 529,740
*M. J. Hindley, *Lab.* 96,926
R. W. Sturdy, *C.* 57,778
S. Barker, *Grn.* 20,728
M. Hambley, *SLD* 12,661
Lab. majority 39,148
(June 1984, Lab. maj. 7,905)

LEEDS
E. 519,631
*M. McGowan, *Lab.* 97,385

J. W. Tweddle, *C.* 54,867
C. R. Lord, *Grn.* 22,558
Mrs J. Ewens, *SLD* 11,720
Lab. majority 42,518
(June 1984, Lab. maj. 10,357)

LEICESTER
E. 579,050
Ms I. M. Read, *Lab.* 90,798
*F. A. Tuckman, *C.* 75,476
C. J. Davis, *Grn.* 33,081
A. G. Barrett, *Ind. C.* 6,996
G. W. Childs, *SLD* 6,791
Lab. majority 15,322
(June 1984, C. maj. 2,892)

LINCOLNSHIRE
E. 586,156
*W. F. Newton Dunn, *C.* 92,043
S. Taggart, *Lab.* 71,393
Ms J. Steranka, *Grn.* 24,908
J. P. Heppell, *SLD* 14,341
C. majority 20,650
(June 1984, C. maj. 45,445)

LONDON CENTRAL
E. 486,558
*A. S. Newens, *Lab. Co-op.* 78,561
Ms H. S. Crawley, *C.* 67,019
Ms N. Kortvelyessy, *Grn.* 28,087
Miss S. A. Ludford, *SLD* 7,864
W. D. E. Mallinson, *SDP* 2,957
'Lord' D. E. Sutch, *LM* 841
Ms L. St-Claire, *Corr.* 707
S. Swinden, *Hum.* 304
Lab. Co-op majority 11,542
(June 1984, Lab. maj. 13,297)

LONDON EAST
E. 530,548
*Miss C. Tongue, *Lab.* 92,803
A. R. Tyrrell, *C.* 65,418
Ms E. L. Crosbie, *Grn.* 21,388
J. K. Gibb, *SLD* 7,341
D. A. O'Sullivan, *ICP* 717
Lab. majority 27,385
(June 1984, Lab. maj. 12,159)

LONDON NORTH
E. 573,043
Ms P. Green, *Lab. Co-op* 85,536
R. M. Lacey, *C.* 79,699
S. Clark, *Grn.* 30,807
Ms H. F. Leighter, *SLD* 8,917
P. Burns, *Ind.* 2,016
Ms L. Reith, *Comm.* 850
Lab. Co-op. majority 5,837
(June 1984, C. maj. 4,853)

LONDON NORTH EAST
E. 510,138
*A. Lomas, *Lab.* 76,085
M. Trend, *C.* 28,318
Mrs J. D. Lambert, *Grn.* 25,949
S. Banks, *SLD* 9,575
Ms N. C. Temple, *Comm.* 1,129
Lab. majority 47,767
(June 1984, Lab. maj. 52,665)

LONDON NORTH WEST
E. 506,707
*The Lord Bethell, *C.* 74,900

A. K. Toms, *Lab.* 67,500
I. E. Flindall, *Grn.* 28,275
C. D. Noyce, *SLD* 10,553
C. majority 7,400
(June 1984, C. maj. 7,422)

LONDON SOUTH AND SURREY
EAST
E. 495,942
*C. J. O. Moorhouse, *C.* 78,256
R. J. E. Evans, *Lab.* 47,440
G. F. Brand, *Grn.* 31,854
P. H. Billenness, *SLD* 14,967
C. majority 30,816
(June 1984, C. maj. 44,657)

LONDON, SOUTH EAST
E. 558,815
*P. N. Price, *C.* 80,619
D. J. Earnshaw, *Lab.* 73,029
Dr E. C. McPhee, *Grn.* 37,576
A. A. Kinch, *SDP* 10,196
Mrs M. C. Williams, *SLD* 9,052
W. E. Turner, *Ind.* 456
C. majority 7,590
(June 1984, C. maj. 20,015)

LONDON, SOUTH INNER
E. 528,188
*R. A. Balfe, *Lab Co-op* 90,378
R. J. Wheatley, *C.* 45,360
Ms P. A. Shepherd, *Grn.* 26,230
M. J. Pindar, *SLD* 10,277
P. N. Power, *Comm.* 1,277
Ms D. Weppler, *Comm. League* 323
Lab. Co-op majority 45,018
(June 1984, Lab. maj. 31,481)

LONDON SOUTH WEST
E. 486,412
Ms A. J. Pollack, *Lab.* 74,298
*Dame S. M. Roberts, *C.* 73,780
Ms M. A. Elson, *Grn.* 35,476
J. C. Field, *SLD* 10,400
Lab. majority 518
(June 1984, C. maj. 6,867)

LONDON WEST
E. 515,581
*M. N. Elliott, *Lab.* 92,959
B. Donnelly, *C.* 78,151
J. R. Hywell-Davies, *Grn.* 32,686
J. G. Parry, *SLD* 9,309
J. Rogers-Davies, *SDP* 2,877
Lab. majority 14,808
June 1984, Lab. maj. 5,229)

LOTHIANS
E. 523,506
*D. W. Martin, *Lab.* 90,840
Mrs C. M. Blight, *C.* 52,014
J. Smith, *SNP* 44,935
R. C. M. Harper, *Grn.* 22,983
K. Leadbetter, *SLD* 9,222
Lab. majority 38,826
(June 1984, Lab. maj. 25,924)

MERSEYSIDE EAST
E. 519,514
T. Wynn, *Lab.* 107,288
E. N. Farthing, *C.* 30,421
R. L. Georgeson, *Grn.* 20,018

R. M. Clayton, *SLD* 5,658
Lab. majority 76,867
(June 1984, Lab. maj. 49,039)

MERSEYSIDE WEST
E. 508,722
*K. A. Stewart, *Lab.* 93,717
M. D. Byrne, *C.* 43,900
L. Brown, *Grn.* 23,052
Mrs H. F. Clucas, *SLD* 16,327
D. J. E. Carson, *PRP* 1,747
Lab. majority 49,817
(June 1984, Lab. maj. 13,197)

MIDLANDS CENTRAL
E. 539,211
Ms C. M. Oddy, *Lab.* 76,736
*J. de Courcy Ling, *C.* 71,643
Ms J. A. Alty, *Grn.* 42,622
I. Cundy, *SLD* 8,450
Lab. majority 5,093
(June 1984, C. maj. 12,729)

MIDLANDS WEST
E. 529,505
*J. A. W. Bird, *Lab. Co-op.* 105,529
M. J. Whitby, *C.* 63,165
J. Raven, *Grn.* 21,787
Mrs F. M. Oborski, *SLD* 6,974
Lab. Co-op majority 42,364
(June 1984, Lab. maj. 19,685)
(March 1987, Lab. maj. 4,025)

NORFOLK
E. 577,576
*P. F. Howell, *C.* 92,385
Ms M. Page, *Lab.* 71,478
M. Macartney-Filgate, *Grn.* 40,575
R. A. Lawes, *SLD* 8,902
S. D. Maxwell, *SDP* 4,934
C. majority 20,907
(June 1984, C. maj. 36,857)

NORTHAMPTONSHIRE
E. 587,733
*A. M. H. Simpson, *C.* 86,695
M. Coyne, *Lab.* 66,248
Ms A. T. Bryant, *Grn.* 43,071
R. Church, *SLD* 11,619
C. majority 20,447
(June 1984, C. maj. 39,859)

NORTHUMBRIA
E. 514,083
*G. J. Adam, *Lab.* 110,688
P. Yeoman, *C.* 50,648
Ms A. Lipman, *Grn.* 24,882
Viscount Morpeth, *SLD* 10,983
Lab. majority 60,040
(June 1984, Lab. maj. 15,700)

NOTTINGHAM
E. 565,354
K. Coates, *Lab.* 92,261
*M. L. Kilby, *C.* 77,748
Mrs S. E. Blount, *Grn.* 34,097
A. Swift, *SLD* 6,693
Lab. majority 14,513
(June 1984, C. maj. 16,126)

OXFORD AND
BUCKINGHAMSHIRE
E. 560,730

*J. E. M. Elles, *C.* 92,483
R. Gifford, *Lab.* 44,965
T. H. Andrewes, *Grn.* 42,058
R. Johnston, *SLD* 14,405
R. C. Turner, *Ind.* 3,696
C. majority 47,518
June 1984, C. maj. 49,081)

SCOTLAND MID AND FIFE
E. 534,638
*A. Falconer, *Lab.* 102,246
K. W. MacAskill, *SNP* 50,089
A. Christie, *C.* 46,505
G. Moreton, *Grn.* 14,165
M. Black, *SLD* 8,857
Lab. majority 52,157
(June 1984, Lab. maj. 27,166)

SCOTLAND NORTH EAST
E. 554,408
H. McCubbin, *Lab.* 65,348
Dr A. Macartney, *SNP* 62,735
*J. L. C. Provan, *C.* 56,835
M. Hill, *Grn.* 15,584
S. Horner, *SLD* 12,704
Lab. majority 2,613
(June 1984, C. maj. 9,171)

SCOTLAND SOUTH
E. 491,865
A. Smith, *Lab.* 81,366
*A. H. Hutton, *C.* 65,673
M. Brown, *SNP* 35,155
J. Button, *Grn.* 11,658
J. E. McKercher, *SLD* 10,368
Lab. majority 15,693
(June 1984, C. maj. 3,137)

SHEFFIELD
E. 564,409
R. Barton, *Lab.* 109,677
T. S. R. Mort, *C.* 40,401
P. L. Scott, *Grn.* 26,844
A. H. Rogers, *SLD* 10,910
D. E. Hyland, *ICP* 657
Lab. majority 69,276
(June 1984, Lab. maj. 46,283)

SHROPSHIRE AND STAFFORD
E. 597,554
*C. J. Prout, *C.* 85,896
D. J. A. Hallam, *Lab.* 83,352
R. T. C. Saunders, *Grn.* 29,637
C. Hards, *SLD* 10,568
C. majority 2,544
(June 1984, C. maj. 24,932)

SOMERSET AND DORSET WEST
E. 582,098
*Mrs M. E. Daly, *C.* 106,716
Dr R. H. Lawson, *Grn.* 54,496
Ms D. M. Organ, *Lab.* 46,210
M. Mactaggart, *SLD* 28,662
A. P. B. Mockler *W. Reg.* 930
C. majority 52,220
(June 1984, C. maj. 40,251)

STAFFORDSHIRE EAST
E. 581,127
*G. W. Stevenson, *Lab.* 94,873
M. F. Spungin, *C.* 63,104
S. Parker, *Grn.* 23,415

R. C. Dodson, *SLD*	7,046
Lab. majority	31,769
(June 1984, Lab. maj. 7,867)	

STRATHCLYDE EAST
E. 494,274

*K. D. Collins, *Lab.*	109,170
G. A. Leslie, *SNP*	48,853
M. Dutt, *C.*	22,233
A. Whitelaw, *Grn.*	9,749
G. Lait, *SLD*	4,276
Lab. majority	60,317
(June 1984, Lab. maj. 63,462)	

STRATHCLYDE WEST
E. 493,067

*H. R. McMahon, *Lab.*	89,627
C. M. Campbell, *SNP*	50,036
S. J. Robin, *C.*	45,872
G. Campbell, *Grn.*	16,461
D. J. Herbison, *SLD*	8,098
Lab. majority	39,591
(June 1984, Lab. maj. 23,038)	

SUFFOLK
E. 550,131

*A. E. Turner, *C.*	82,481
M. D. Cornish, *Lab.*	56,788
A. C. Slade, *Grn.*	37,305
P. R. Odell, *SLD*	12,660
C. majority	25,693
(June 1984, C. maj. 47,098)	

SURREY WEST
E. 515,881

T. N. B. Spencer, *C.*	89,674
E. Haywood, *Grn.*	40,332
H. G. Trace, *Lab.*	28,313
A. Davies, *SLD*	18,042
B. M. Collignon, *SDP*	3,676
C. majority	49,342
(June 1984, C. maj. 52,588)	

SUSSEX EAST
E. 553,536

*Sir John Stewart-Clark, Bt., *C.*	96,388
Ms G. Roles, *Lab.*	43,094
Ms R. Addison, *Grn*	42,316
Mrs D. Venables, *SLD*	16,810
D. Howells, *LM*	1,181
C. majority	53,294
(June 1984, C. maj. 65,621)	

SUSSEX WEST
E. 554,664

*R. M. Seligman, *C.*	95,821
I. F. N. Bagnall, *Grn.*	49,588
M. Shrimpton, *Lab.*	32,006
Dr J. M. M. Walsh, *SLD*	24,855
C. majority	46,233
(June 1984, C. maj. 57,502)	

THAMES VALLEY
E. 542,855

J. C. C. Stevens, *C.*	73,070
Ms H. B. de Lyon, *Lab.*	46,579
P. Gordon, *Grn.*	36,865
D. B. Griffiths, *SLD*	14,603
C. majority	26,491
(June 1984, C. maj. 38,805)	

TYNE AND WEAR
E. 530,953

A. J. Donnelly, *Lab.*	126,682
N. C. Gibbon, *C.*	30,902
R. Stather, *Grn.*	18,107
P. J. Arnold, *SLD*	6,101
T. P. Kilgallon, *SPGB*	919
Lab. majority	95,780
(June 1984, Lab. maj. 49,414)	

WALES MID AND WEST
E. 547,740

*Revd D. R. Morris, *Lab.*	105,670
O. J. Williams, *C.*	53,758
Ms B. I. McPake, *Grn.*	29,852
Dr P. J. S. Williams, *PC*	26,063
G. A. Sinclair, *SLD*	10,031
Lab. majority	51,912
(June 1984, Lab. maj. 36,452)	

WALES NORTH
E. 540,230

J. Wilson, *Lab.*	83,638
*Miss B. A. Brookes, *C.*	79,178
Dr D. E. Thomas, *PC*	64,120
P. H. W. Adams, *Grn.*	15,832
R. K. Marshall, *SLD*	10,056
Lab. majority	4,460
(June 1984, C. maj. 12,278)	

WALES SOUTH
E. 520,911

W. David, *Lab.*	108,550
A. R. Taylor, *C.*	45,993
G. P. Jones, *Grn.*	25,993
P. J. Keelan, *PC*	10,727
P. K. Verma, *SLD*	4,037
D. A. T. Thomas, *SDP*	3,513
Lab. majority	62,557
(June 1984, Lab. maj. 44,258)	

WALES SOUTH EAST
E. 561,068

*L. T. Smith, *Lab.*	138,872
R. J. Young, *C.*	30,384
M. J. Witherden, *Grn.*	27,869
Ms J. Evans, *PC*	14,152
P. Nicholls-Jones, *SLD*	4,661
Lab. majority	108,488
(June 1984, Lab. maj. 95,557)	

WIGHT AND HAMPSHIRE EAST
E. 574,332

*R. J. Simmonds, *C.*	90,658
Dr A. D. Burnett, *Lab.*	51,228
S. L. Rackett, *Grn.*	40,664
Ms V. A. Rayner, *SLD*	19,569
C. majority	39,430
(June 1984, C. maj. 42,928)	

WILTSHIRE
E. 568,875

*Mrs C. F. Jackson, *C.*	93,200
G. A. Harris, *Lab.*	46,887
J. V. Hughes, *Grn.*	46,735
P. N. Crossley, *SLD*	18,302
J. A. Cade, *Ind.*	4,809
C. majority	46,313
(June 1984, C. maj. 26,469)	

YORK
E. 542,998

*E. H. C. McMillan-Scott, *C.*	81,453
J. T. Grogan, *Lab.*	66,351

R. Bell, *Grn.*	27,525
A. Collinge, *SLD*	12,542
C. majority	15,102
(June 1984, C. maj. 36,402)	

YORKSHIRE SOUTH
E. 518,995

*N. West, *Lab.*	121,060
W. J. Clappison, *C.*	29,276
A. Grace, *Grn.*	19,063
B. Boulton, *SLD*	5,039
Lab. majority	91,784
(June 1984, Lab. maj. 67,749)	

YORKSHIRE SOUTH WEST
E. 523,322

*T. Megahy, *Lab.*	108,444
G. T. Horton, *C.*	42,543
Mrs S. Leyland, *Grn.*	25,677
J. A. D. Ridgway, *SLD*	10,352
Lab. majority	65,901
(June 1984, Lab. maj. 44,173)	

YORKSHIRE WEST
E. 564,001

*B. H. Seal, *Lab.*	108,644
G. T. Hall, *C.*	70,717
N. Parrott, *Grn.*	28,308
P. Wrigley, *SLD*	9,765
Lab. majority	37,927
(June 1984, Lab. maj. 20,854)	

NORTHERN IRELAND
E. 1,105,551

*Revd I. R. K. Paisley, MP, *DUP*	160,110
*J. Hume, MP, *SDLP*	136,335
J. F. Nicholson, *UUP*	118,785
D. Morrison *SF*	48,914
J. T. Alderdice, *All.*	27,905
A. Kennedy, *C.*	25,789
M. H. Samuel, *Ecol.*	6,569
S. Lynch, *WP*	5,590
M. Langhammer, *Lab. RG*	3,540
B. Caul, *Lab.* 87	1,274

Revd I. R. K. Paisley, J. Hume and J. F. Nicholson were elected by the single transferable voting system.

Parliamentary statistics

PRINCIPAL PARTIES IN PARLIAMENT SINCE 1970

	1970	1974 Feb.	1974 Oct.	1979	1983	1987	1992
Conservative	330*	296	276	339	397	375	336
Labour	287	301	319	268	209	229	270
Liberal/LD	6	14	13	11	17	17	20
Social Democrat	—	1	—	—	6	5	—
Independent	5†	1	1	2	—	—	—
Plaid Cymru	—	2	3	2	2	3	4
Scottish Nationalist	1	7	11	2	2	3	3
Democratic Unionist	—	—	—	3	3	3	3
SDLP	—	1	1	1	1	3	4
Sinn Fein	—	—	—	—	1	1	—
Ulster Popular Unionist	—	—	—	—	1	1	1
Ulster Unionist‡	*	11	10	6	10	9	9
The Speaker	1	1	1	1	1	1	1
Total	630	635	635	635	650	650	651

* Including 8 Ulster Unionists
† Comprising: Independent Labour 1, Independent Unity 1, Protestant Unity 1, Republican Labour 1, Unity 1
‡ Comprises:
1974 (February) United Ulster Unionist Council 11
1974 (October) United Ulster Unionist 10
1979 Ulster Unionist 5, United Ulster Unionist 1
1983 Official Unionist 10

PARLIAMENTS SINCE 1970

Assembled	Dissolved	yr	m.	d.
29 June 1970	8 February 1974	3	7	10
6 March 1974	20 September 1974	0	6	14
22 October 1974	7 April 1979	4	5	16
9 May 1979	13 May 1983	4	0	4
15 June 1983	18 May 1987	3	11	3
17 June 1987	16 March 1992	4	8	28
27 April 1992				

Duration heading over yr m. d.

MAJORITIES IN THE HOUSE OF COMMONS SINCE 1970

Year	Party	Maj.
1970	Conservative	31
1974 Feb.	No majority	
1974 Oct.	Labour	5
1979	Conservative	43
1983	Conservative	144
1987	Conservative	102
1992	Conservative	21

VOTES CAST AT 1987 AND 1992 GENERAL ELECTIONS*

GENERAL ELECTION 1987

Conservative	13,760,525
Labour	10,029,944
Liberal/SDP Alliance	7,341,152
Scottish Nationalist	416,873
Plaid Cymru	123,589
†Green	89,753
Others	37,576

GENERAL ELECTION 1992

Conservative	14,048,283
Labour	11,559,735
Liberal Democrats	5,999,384
Scottish Nationalist	629,552
Plaid Cymru	154,439
Others	436,207

*Excluding Northern Ireland seats
†Excluding Ecology candidate in Northern Ireland

The Government

Prime Minister, First Lord of the Treasury and Minister for the Civil Service
The Rt. Hon. John Major, MP, since November 1990
Lord High Chancellor
The Lord Mackay of Clashfern, PC, since October 1987
Secretary of State for Foreign and Commonwealth Affairs
The Rt. Hon. Douglas Hurd, CBE, MP, since October 1989
Chancellor of the Exchequer
The Rt. Hon. Kenneth Clarke, QC, MP, since May 1993
Secretary of State for the Home Department
The Rt. Hon. Michael Howard, QC, MP, since May 1993
President of the Board of Trade and Secretary of State for Trade and Industry
The Rt. Hon. Michael Heseltine, MP, since April 1992
Secretary of State for Transport
The Rt. Hon. John MacGregor, OBE, MP, since April 1992
Secretary of State for Defence
The Rt. Hon. Malcolm Rifkind, QC, MP, since April 1992
Lord Privy Seal and Leader of the House of Lords
The Lord Wakeham, PC, since April 1992
Lord President of the Council and Leader of the House of Commons
The Rt. Hon. Antony Newton, OBE, MP, since April 1992
Secretary of State for National Heritage
The Rt. Hon. Peter Brooke, MP, since September 1992
Secretary of State for the Environment
The Rt. Hon. John Gummer, MP, since May 1993
Secretary of State for Employment
The Rt. Hon. David Hunt, MBE, MP, since May 1993
Secretary of State for Social Security
The Rt. Hon. Peter Lilley, MP, since April 1992
Chancellor of the Duchy of Lancaster and Minister of Public Service and Science
The Rt. Hon. William Waldegrave, MP, since April 1992
Secretary of State for Scotland
The Rt. Hon. Ian Lang, MP, since November 1990
Secretary of State for Northern Ireland
The Rt. Hon. Sir Patrick Mayhew, QC, MP, since April 1992
Secretary of State for Education
The Rt. Hon. John Patten, MP, since April 1992
Secretary of State for Health
The Rt. Hon. Virginia Bottomley, MP, since April 1992
Minister of Agriculture, Fisheries and Food
The Rt. Hon. Gillian Shephard, MP, since May 1993
Chief Secretary to the Treasury
The Rt. Hon. Michael Portillo, MP, since April 1992
Secretary of State for Wales
The Rt. Hon. John Redwood, MP, since May 1993

LAW OFFICERS

Attorney-General
The Rt. Hon. Sir Nicholas Lyell, QC, MP, since April 1992
Lord Advocate
The Lord Rodger of Earlsferry, PC, QC, since April 1992
Solicitor-General
Sir Derek Spencer, QC, MP, since April 1992

Solicitor-General for Scotland
Thomas Dawson, QC, since April 1992

MINISTERS OF STATE

Agriculture, Fisheries and Food
Michael Jack, MP
Defence
Jonathan Aitken, MP (*Defence Procurement*)
Jeremy Hanley, MP (*Armed Forces*)
Education
The Baroness Blatch, CBE, PC
Employment
Michael Forsyth, MP
Environment
The Rt. Hon. Sir George Young, MP (*Minister for Housing, Inner Cities and Construction*)
David Curry, MP (*Minister for Local Government and Planning*)
Timothy Yeo, MP (*Minister for Environment and Countryside*)
Foreign and Commonwealth Affairs
The Baroness Chalker of Wallasey, PC (*Minister for Overseas Development*)
The Rt. Hon. Douglas Hogg, QC, MP; The Rt. Hon. Alastair Goodlad, MP; David Heathcoat-Amory, MP
Health
Brian Mawhinney, MP (*Minister for Health*)
Home Office
The Earl Ferrers, PC; Peter Lloyd, MP; David Maclean, MP
Northern Ireland Office
Robert Atkins, MP; The Rt. Hon. Sir John Wheeler, MP
Scottish Office
The Lord Fraser of Carmyllie, PC, QC
Social Security
The Rt. Hon. Nicholas Scott, MBE, MP (*Minister for Social Security and Disabled People*)
Trade and Industry
The Rt. Hon. Timothy Sainsbury, MP (*Minister for Industry*)
Richard Needham, MP (*Minister for Trade*)
Timothy Eggar, MP (*Minister for Energy*)
Transport
The Earl of Caithness, PC (*Minister for Aviation and Shipping*)
The Rt. Hon. Roger Freeman, MP (*Minister for Public Transport*)
Treasury
Stephen Dorrell, MP (*Financial Secretary*)
The Rt. Hon. Sir John Cope, MP (*Paymaster-General*)
Anthony Nelson, MP (*Economic Secretary*)
Welsh Office
The Rt. Hon. Sir Wyn Roberts, MP

UNDER-SECRETARIES OF STATE

Agriculture, Fisheries and Food
The Earl Howe; the Hon. Nicholas Soames, MP

Office of the Minister for the Civil Service
David Davis, MP
Defence
Viscount Cranborne
Education
Eric Forth, MP; Timothy Boswell, MP; Robin Squire, MP
Employment
The Viscount Ullswater; Ann Widdecombe, MP
Environment
The Lord Strathclyde; Anthony Baldry, MP
Foreign and Commonwealth Affairs
The Hon. Mark Lennox-Boyd, MP
Health
The Baroness Cumberlege, CBE; The Hon. Thomas
Sackville, MP; John Bowis, OBE, MP
Home Office
Charles Wardle, MP
Lord Chancellor's Department
John Taylor, MP
National Heritage
Iain Sproat, MP
Northern Ireland
The Earl of Arran; Michael Ancram, MP
Scottish Office
Lord James Douglas-Hamilton, MP; Allan Stewart, MP;
Sir Hector Monro, MP
Social Security
The Lord Henley; Alistair Burt, MP; William Hague, MP
Trade and Industry
Neil Hamilton, MP (*Corporate Affairs*)
The Baroness Denton of Wakefield, CBE (*Consumer
Affairs and Small Firms*)
Patrick McLoughlin, MP (*Trade and Technology*)
Transport
Steven Norris, MP (*Minister for Transport in London*)
Robert Key, MP (*Minister for Roads and Traffic*)
Treasury
The Lords Commissioners, *see* Government Whips
Welsh Office
Gwilym Jones, MP

Lord Commissioners
Irvine Patnick, MP; Nicholas Baker, MP; Timothy Wood,
MP; Timothy Kirkhope, MP; Andrew MacKay, MP
Assistant Whips
Robert Hughes, MP; James Arbuthnot, MP; Andrew
Mitchell, MP; Michael Brown, MP; Derek Conway, MP

GOVERNMENT WHIPS

HOUSE OF LORDS

*Captain of the Honourable Corps of Gentlemen-at-Arms
(Chief Whip)*
The Lord Hesketh, PC
*Captain of The Queen's Bodyguard of the Yeomen of the
Guard (Deputy Chief Whip)*
The Earl of Strathmore and Kinghorne
Lords-in-Waiting
The Viscount Long, CBE; The Viscount Astor; The
Viscount St Davids; The Viscount Goschen
Baroness-in-Waiting
The Baroness Trumpington, PC

HOUSE OF COMMONS

Parliamentary Secretary to the Treasury (Chief Whip)
The Rt. Hon. Richard Ryder, OBE, MP
Treasurer of HM Household (Deputy Chief Whip)
Gregory Knight, MP
Comptroller of HM Household
David Lightbown, MP
Vice-Chamberlain of HM Household
Sydney Chapman, MP

Government Departments and Public Offices

MINISTERIAL SALARIES
as at 1 January 1993

Prime Minister	£53,007
Secretary of State	£39,820
Minister of State (Lords)	£44,945
Minister of State (Commons)	£28,175
Parliamentary Under-Secretary (Lords)	£37,689
Parliamentary Under-Secretary (Commons)	£21,384

Ministers who are Members of the House of Commons receive a reduced Parliamentary salary (£23,227 in 1993) in addition to this ministerial salary.

CIVIL SERVICE (BASIC) SALARIES *as at 1 April 1993*

*Secretary of the Cabinet and Head of the Home Civil Service	£112,083
*Permanent Secretary to the Treasury	£104,860
*Head of the Diplomatic Service	£104,860
*Grade 1	£90,148
*Grade 1A	£82,925
*Grade 2	£64,307–£75,328
*Grade 3	£51,360–£59,599
†Grade 4	£44,390–£49,790
†Grade 5	£36,019–£47,921
†Grade 6	£27,660–£42,724
†Grade 7	£24,239–£34,469
Senior Executive Officer	£17,535–£21,932
Higher Executive Officer (D)	£16,028–£20,163
Higher Executive Officer	£14,019–£17,895
Executive Officer	£8,260–£14,307
Administration Trainee	£12,760–£14,848
Administrative Officer	£5,167–£10,513
Administrative Assistant	£4,669–£8,878

London Rates

*Grade 3	£52,751–£60,990
†Grade 4	£46,121–£51,732
†Grade 5	£37,589–£49,790
†Grade 6	£28,904–£44,390
†Grade 7	£25,330–£36,019
Senior Executive Officer	£18,263–£22,844
Higher Executive Officer	£14,601–£18,639
Executive Officer	£8,602–£14,901
Administrative Officer	£5,529–£11,249
Administrative Assistant	£4,995–£9,499

*These grades do not attract London weighting. London weighting, since 1 April 1993, is:

Inner zone	£1,776 a year
Intermediate zone	£1,015 a year
Outer zone	£736 a year

†1992–3 salaries

The Home Civil Service's unified pay and grading structure for senior personnel represents the following:

Grade	Title
1	Permanent Secretary
1A	Second Permanent Secretary
2	Deputy Secretary
3	Under-Secretary
4	Chief Scientific Officer B, Professional and Technology Directing A
5	Assistant Secretary, Deputy Chief Scientific Officer, Professional and Technology Directing B
6	Senior Principal, Senior Principal Scientific Officer, Professional and Technology Superintending Grade
7	Principal

ADVISORY, CONCILIATION AND ARBITRATION SERVICE

27 Wilton Street, London SW1X 7AZ
Tel 071-210 3000

The Advisory, Conciliation and Arbitration Service (ACAS) is an independent organization set up under the Employment Protection Act 1975 (the provisions now being found in the Trade Union and Labour Relations (Consolidation) Act 1992). ACAS is directed by a Council consisting of a chairman and employer, trade union and independent members, all appointed by the Secretary of State for Employment. The functions of the Service are to provide facilities for conciliation, mediation and arbitration as means of avoiding and resolving industrial disputes, and to provide advisory services to industry on industrial relations and matters affecting the quality of working life.

ACAS also has main offices in Accrington, Birmingham, Bristol, Cardiff, Fleet, Glasgow, Leeds, Liverpool, Manchester, Newcastle upon Tyne and Nottingham, and 25 smaller offices in other parts of Great Britain.

Chairman, J. Hougham
Chief Conciliation Officer (G4), D. Evans
Director of Resources and General Policy Branch (G5), E. Norcross
Director of Conciliation and Arbitration Branch (G5), F. Noonan
Director of Advisory Services Branch (G5), P. Syson

MINISTRY OF AGRICULTURE, FISHERIES AND FOOD

*Whitehall Place, London SW1A 2HH
Tel 071-270 3000

The Ministry of Agriculture, Fisheries and Food is responsible for administering government policies on agriculture, horticulture and fisheries in England and policies relating to the safety and quality of food in the United Kingdom as a whole. In association with the Agriculture Departments of the Scottish, Welsh and Northern Ireland Offices and with the Intervention Board (*see* page 324), the Ministry is responsible for the negotiation and administration of the EC common agricultural and fisheries policies, for matters relating to the single European market, and for international agricultural and food trade policy. It commissions research to assist in the formulation and assessment of policy.

*Unless otherwise stated, this is the main address of divisions of the Ministry

The Ministry administers policies on the control and eradication of animal, plant and fish diseases, and on assistance to capital investment in farm and horticultural businesses; it also has responsibilities relating to the protection and enhancement of the countryside and the marine environment as well as to flood defence and other rural issues.

The Ministry is responsible for ensuring public health standards in the manufacture, preparation and distribution of basic foods, and for planning to safeguard essential food supplies in times of emergency. It is responsible for government relations with the UK food and drink manufacturing industries and the food and drink importing, distributive and catering trades.

The Food Safety Directorate is responsible for many aspects of food safety and quality. These include pesticide safety approval, biotechnology, meat hygiene, animal health and welfare, and related public health issues.

Minister, The Rt. Hon. Gillian Shephard, MP
Principal Private Secretary (G7), Miss E. J. Wordley
Private Secretary, D. C. Barnes
Special Advisers, Dr E. Cottrell; K. Leggatt
Parliamentary Private Secretary, S. Burns, MP
Minister of State, Michael Jack, MP *(Farming and Fisheries)*
Private Secretary, S. G. Cane
Parliamentary Private Secretary, Miss E. Nicholson, MP
Parliamentary Secretary (Lords), The Earl Howe
(*Countryside*)
Private Secretary, J. E. T. Hughes
Parliamentary Secretary, The Hon. Nicholas Soames, MP
(*Food*)
Private Secretary, S. C. Tanner
Parliamentary Clerk, Miss A. Evans
Permanent Secretary (G1), R. J. Packer
Private Secretary, P. Campbell

ESTABLISHMENT DEPARTMENT
Director of Establishments (G3), D. H. Griffiths

ESTABLISHMENTS (GENERAL) DIVISION
Victory House, 30–34 Kingsway, London WC2B 6TU
Tel 071-405 4310

Head of Division (G6), G. P. Hobrough

WELFARE BRANCH
Victory House, 30–34 Kingsway, London WC2B 6TU
Tel 071-405 4310

Chief Welfare Officer (SEO), D. J. Jones

PERSONNEL DIVISION
Victory House, 30–34 Kingsway, London WC2B 6TU
Tel 071-405 4310

Head of Division (G5), G. P. McLachlan

DEPARTMENTAL HEALTH AND SAFETY UNIT
Head of Unit (G7), Dr D. J. Knowles

†OFFICE SERVICES DIVISION
Head of Division (G5), P. A. Cocking

†STAFF TRAINING BRANCH
Principal (G7), Miss E. M. Berthoud

BUILDING AND ESTATE MANAGEMENT
Eastbury House, 30–34 Albert Embankment,
London SE1 7TL
Tel 071-238 3000

Head of Division (G5), J. S. Buchanan

†At Nobel/Ergon House, 17 Smith Square, London SW1P 3JR. Tel: 071-238 3000

INFORMATION DIVISION
Chief Information Officer (G5), S. Dugdale
Chief Press Officer (G7), M. Smith
Principal Librarian (G7), P. McShane

FINANCE DEPARTMENT
19–29 Woburn Place, London WC1H 0LU
Tel 071-917 1000

Principal Finance Officer (G3), A. R. Cruickshank

FINANCIAL PLANNING DIVISION
Head of Division (G5), P. P. Nash

FINANCIAL MANAGEMENT DIVISION
Head of Division (G5), A. G. Kuyk
Deputy Head of Financial Management (G6), J. M. Lowi

AUDIT CONSULTANCY AND MANAGEMENT SERVICES DIVISION
Director of Audit (G5), D. V. Fisher
Deputy Director of Audit (G6), D. J. Littler

MARKET TESTING AND PROCUREMENT ADVICE
Victory House, 30–34 Kingsway, London WC2B 6TU
Tel 071-405 4310
Director (G5), D. B. Rabey

LEGAL DEPARTMENT
55 Whitehall, London SW1A 2EY
Tel 071-270 3000

Legal Adviser and Solicitor (G2), G. J. Jenkins, CB, QC
Principal Assistant Solicitors (G3), B. T. Atwood; D. J. Pearson

LEGAL DIVISION A1
Assistant Solicitor (G5), Miss D. Wood

LEGAL DIVISION A2
Assistant Solicitor (G5), Mrs C. Davis

LEGAL DIVISION A3
Assistant Solicitor (G5), Miss C. A. Crisham

LEGAL DIVISION A4
Assistant Solicitor (G5), Miss E. A. Stephens

LEGAL DIVISION A5
Assistant Solicitor (G5), L. Gunatilleke

LEGAL DIVISION A6
Assistant Solicitor (G5), P. D. Davis

LEGAL DIVISION B1
Assistant Solicitor (G5), P. Hall

LEGAL DIVISION B2
Assistant Solicitor (G4), Ms S. B. Spence

LEGAL DIVISION B3
Assistant Solicitor (G5), A. I. Corbett

LEGAL DIVISION B4
Assistant Solicitor (G5), Dr M. R. Parke

INVESTIGATION UNIT
Chief Investigation Officer, L. R. Blake

AGRICULTURAL COMMODITIES, TRADE AND FOOD PRODUCTION
Deputy Secretary (G2), D. A. Hadley

EUROPEAN COMMUNITY
Under-Secretary (G3), P. W. Murphy

EUROPEAN COMMUNITY DIVISION I
Head of Division (G5), C. I. Llewelyn

EUROPEAN COMMUNITY DIVISION II
Head of Division (G6), L. G. Mitchell

ARABLE CROPS
Under-Secretary (G3), C. J. Barnes

CEREALS AND SET-ASIDE DIVISION
Head of Division (G5), Ms J. Allfrey

SUGAR, TOBACCO, OILSEEDS AND PROTEINS DIVISION
Head of Division (G5), Mrs A. M. Blackburn

†HORTICULTURE AND POTATOES DIVISION
Head of Division (G5), R. A. Saunderson

MEAT GROUP
Under-Secretary (G3), G. A. Hollis

BEEF DIVISION
Head of Division (G5), T. D. Rossington

SHEEP AND LIVESTOCK SUBSIDIES DIVISION
Head of Division (G5), J. R. Cowan

PIGS, EGGS AND POULTRY DIVISION
Head of Division (G5), G. W. Noble

MILK AND MILK PRODUCTS
Head of Division (G5), B. J. Harding

FOOD, MILK AND MARKETING POLICY
Under-Secretary (G3), J. W. Hepburn

MILK MARKETING AND LEGISLATION DIVISION
Head of Division (G5), P. Elliott

FOOD INDUSTRY, MARKETING AND COMPETITION POLICY DIVISION
Head of Division (G5), R. E. Melville

EXTERNAL RELATIONS AND TRADE PROMOTION DIVISION
Head of Division (G5), D. V. Orchard

TRADE POLICY AND TROPICAL FOODS
Head of Division (G5), D. P. Hunter

†MARKET TASK FORCE
Head of Division (G5), H. B. Brown

†ALCOHOLIC DRINKS DIVISION
Head of Division (G5), P. M. Boyling

FOOD SAFETY
Deputy Secretary (G2), C. W. Capstick, CB, CMG

†FOOD SAFETY GROUP
Under-Secretary (G3), B. H. B. Dickinson
Chief Scientist (Fisheries and Food) (G3),
  Dr W. H. B. Denner

CHEMICAL SAFETY OF FOOD DIVISION
Head of Division (G5), R. C. McKinley

CONSUMER PROTECTION DIVISION
Head of Division (G5), C. A. Cockbill

MICROBIOLOGICAL SAFETY OF FOOD DIVISION
Head of Division (G5), Mrs A. M. Pickering

FOOD SCIENCE DIVISION I
Head of Division (G5), Dr J. C. Sherlock

FOOD SCIENCE DIVISION II
Head of Division (G5), Dr J. R. Bell

FOOD SCIENCE LABORATORY
Norwich Research Park, Colney Lane, Norwich NR4 7UQ
Tel 0603-259350
Head of Laboratory (G5), Dr J. Gilbert

TORRY RESEARCH STATION
PO Box 31, 135 Abbey Road, Aberdeen AB9 8DG
Tel 0224-877071
Director (G5), K. Whittle, PH.D.

†CHIEF SCIENTIST'S GROUP (FOOD)
Head of Division (G6), Dr D. G. Lindsay

AGRICULTURAL INPUTS, PLANT PROTECTION AND EMERGENCIES
Under-Secretary (G3), Mrs E. A. J. Attridge

EMERGENCIES AND FOOD PROTECTION
Head of Division (G5), Dr J. R. Park

PLANT HEALTH DIVISION
Head of Division (G4), G. M. Trevelyan

PLANT VARIETY, RIGHTS OFFICE AND SEEDS DIVISION
White House Lane, Huntingdon Road, Cambridge CB3 OLF
Tel 0223-277151
Head of Division (G5), J. Harvey

†AGRICULTURAL RESOURCES POLICY DIVISION
Head of Division (G5), R. C. Lowson

ANIMAL HEALTH AND VETERINARY GROUP
Government Buildings, Hook Rise South, Tolworth,
Surbiton, Surrey KT6 7NF
Tel 081-330 4411
Under-Secretary (G3), M. T. Haddon
Chief Veterinary Officer (G3), K. C. Meldrum

ANIMAL HEALTH (ZOONOSES) DIVISION
Head of Division (G5), R. J. G. Cawthorne

ANIMAL HEALTH (DISEASE CONTROL) DIVISION
Head of Division (G5), T. E. D. Eddy

ANIMAL HEALTH (INTERNATIONAL TRADE) DIVISION
Head of Division (G5), R. A. Bell

MEAT HYGIENE DIVISION
Head of Division (G5), Mrs K. J. A. Brown

RESOURCE MANAGEMENT DIVISION
Head of Division (G6), R. A. Gregg

ANIMAL WELFARE DIVISION
Tolworth Tower, Surbiton, Surrey KT6 7DX
Tel 081-330 4411
Head of Division (G5), A. J. Perrins

STATE VETERINARY SERVICE
Government Buildings, Hook Rise South, Tolworth,
Surbiton, Surrey KT15 3NB
Tel 081-330 4411
Director of Veterinary Field Services (G3), I. Crawford

LASSWADE VETERINARY LABORATORY
East of Scotland College of Agriculture, The Bush Estate,
Penicuik, Midlothian EH26 0SA
Tel 031-445 5371

COUNTRYSIDE, MARINE ENVIRONMENT AND FISHERIES
Deputy Secretary (G2), C. R. Cann

LAND USE, CONSERVATION AND COUNTRYSIDE
†*Under-Secretary (G3)*, G. R. Waters

†Countryside Division
Head of Division (G5), R. C. McIvor

†Land Use and Tenure Division
Head of Division (G5), T. J. Osmond

†Conservation Policy Division
Head of Division (G5), C. R. Bodrell

†Environment Task Force
Head of Division (G5), J. Robbs

†Land Use Planning Unit
Head of Division (G5), J. R. Mathias

†FISHERIES DEPARTMENT
Fisheries Secretary (G3), S. Wentworth

Fisheries Division I
Head of Division (G5), I. C. Redfern

Fisheries Division II
Head of Division (G5), C. J. Ryder

Fisheries Division III
Head of Division (G5), R. S. Thomas

Fisheries Division IV
Head of Division (G6), B. S. Edwards

Sea Fisheries Inspectorate
Chief Inspector (G6), M. G. Jennings

Fisheries Research
Pakefield Road, Lowestoft, Suffolk NR33 0HT
Tel 0502-562244

Director of Fisheries Research and Development for Great Britain (G4), D. J. Garrod, PH.D.
Deputy Directors of Fisheries Research (G5),
Dr J. G. Shepherd; P. W. Greig-Smith

Fisheries Laboratory
Pakefield Road, Lowestoft, Suffolk NR33 0HT
Tel 0502-562244

Fisheries Laboratory
Remembrance Avenue, Burnham-on-Crouch, Essex
CM0 8HA
Tel 0621-782658

Fisheries Experiment Station
Benarth Road, Conwy, Gwynedd LL32 8UB
Tel 0492-593883

Fish Diseases Laboratory
33–33A Albany Road, Granby Industrial Estate,
Weymouth, Dorset DT4 9TU
Tel 0305-772137
Officer-in-Charge (Principal Scientific Officer) (G6),
B. J. Hill, PH.D.

ENVIRONMENT POLICY
Under-Secretary (G3), M. Madden

†At Nobel/Ergon House, 17 Smith Square, London SW1P 3JR. Tel: 071-238 3000

†Environmental Protection Division
Head of Division (G5), D. L. Dawson

†Marine Environmental Protection Division
Head of Division (G5), G. F. Meekings

†Salmon Whaling and Inland Fisheries
Head of Division (G5), A. R. Burne

Flood Defence Division
Eastbury House, 30–34 Albert Embankment, London
SE1 7TL
Tel 071-238 3000

Head of Division (G5), R. A. Hathaway

ECONOMICS AND STATISTICS
Under-Secretary (G3), R. E. Mordue

Economics (Farm Business) Division
Senior Economic Adviser (G5), J. P. Muriel

Economics (International) Division
Senior Economic Adviser (G5), Dr J. M. Slater

Economics (Resource Use) Division
Senior Economic Adviser (G5), R. W. Irving

Economics and Statistics (Food)
Senior Economic Adviser (G5), Dr P. J. Lund

†Statistics (Agricultural Commodities) Division
Chief Statistician (G5), D. Wallage

Statistics (Census and Prices) Division
Government Buildings, Epsom Road, Guildford,
Surrey GU1 2LD
Tel 0483-68121

Chief Statistician (G5), D. E. Bradbury

†CHIEF SCIENTIFIC ADVISER
Chief Scientific Adviser (G2), P. J. Bunyan, DSC, PH.D.
Chief Scientist (Agriculture and Horticulture) (G3),
D. W. F. Shannon, PH.D.
Assistant Chief Scientist (Agriculture and Horticulture) (G5),
Dr M. Parker
Scientific Liaison Officer (Fisheries) (G6), Dr D. G. Smith

Research Policy Co-ordination Division
Head of Division (G5), J. Suich

REGIONAL ORGANIZATION
†*Director of Regional Administration (G3)*, D. J. Coates

Regional Services and Agencies Support Division
†*Head of Division (G5)*, G. Belchamber

Resource Management Strategy Unit
Government Buildings, Epsom Road, Guildford, Surrey
GU1 2LD
Tel 0483 68121
Head of Division (G5), J. D. Garnett

Regional Service Centres
Anglia Region, Block B, Government Buildings,
Brooklands Avenue, Cambridge CB2 2DR. Tel: 0223-462727. *Regional Director (G5)*, D. A. Boreham
East Midlands Region, Government Buildings, Block
7, Chalfont Drive, Nottingham NG8 3SN. Tel: 0602-291191. *Regional Director (G5)*, M. J. Finnigan
North-East Region, Government Buildings, Crosby
Road, Northallerton, N. Yorks. DL6 1AD. Tel: 0609-773751. *Regional Director (G6)*, P. Watson

NORTHERN REGION, Eden Bridge House, Lowther Street, Carlisle, Cumbria CA3 8DX. Tel: 0228-23400. *Regional Director (G5)*, D. E. Jones
NORTH MERCIA REGION, Berkeley Towers, Nantwich Road, Crewe, Cheshire CW2 6PT. Tel: 0270-69211. *Regional Director (G6)*, R. Bettley-Smith
SOUTH-EAST REGION, Block A, Government Buildings, Coley Park, Reading, Berks. RG1 6DT. Tel: 0734-581222. *Regional Director (G5)*, R. Anderson
SOUTH MERCIA REGION, Block C, Government Buildings, Whittington Road, Worcester WR5 2LQ. Tel: 0905-763355. *Regional Director (G6)*, P. G. Gething
SOUTH-WEST REGION, Government Buildings, Alphington Road, Exeter EX2 8NQ. Tel: 0392-77951. *Regional Director (G6)*, M. R. W. Highman
WESSEX REGION, Block 3, Government Buildings, Burghill Road, Westbury-on-Trym, Bristol BS10 6NJ. Tel: 0272-591000. *Regional Director (G6)*, Mrs A. J. L. Ould

INFORMATION TECHNOLOGY DIRECTORATE
Government Buildings, Epsom Road, Guildford, Surrey GU1 2LD
Tel 0483-68121
Director (G4), D. Selwood
Assistant Directors (G5), A. G. Matthews; D. J. Dunthorne; (*G6*), D. D. Brown; R. F. Syrett

EXECUTIVE AGENCIES

CENTRAL VETERINARY LABORATORY
Woodham Lane, New Haw, Addlestone, Surrey KT15 3NB
Tel 0932-341111
The Central Veterinary Laboratory provides scientific and technical expertise in animal and public health.
Director and Chief Executive (G3), Dr T. W. A. Little
Director of Research (G4), Dr B. J. Shreeve
Director of Operations (G5), R. W. Saunders
Director of Business (G5), Dr J. A. Morris

VETERINARY MEDICINES DIRECTORATE
Woodham Lane, New Haw, Addlestone, Surrey KT15 3NB
Tel 0932-336911
The Veterinary Medicines Directorate is responsible for all aspects of licensing and control of animal medicines, including the protection of the consumer from hazardous or unacceptable residues.
Chief Executive and Director of Veterinary Medicines (G4), Dr J. M. Rutter
Director (Policy and Finance) (G5), C. J. Lawson
Director (Licensing) (G5), Dr K. N. Woodward
Licensing Manager, Pharmaceuticals and Feed Additives (G6), J. P. O'Brien
Licensing Manager, Immunologicals and Suspected Adverse Reactions (SARS) (G6), Dr A. M. T. Lee

CENTRAL SCIENCE LABORATORY
London Road, Slough, Berks. SL3 7HJ
Tel 0753-534626
Chief Executive (G3), Dr P. I. Stanley
Research Director (G5), Dr A. R. Hardy

AGRICULTURAL DEVELOPMENT AND ADVISORY SERVICE (ADAS)
ADAS Headquarters, Oxford Spires Business Park, The Boulevard, Kidlington, Oxon. OX5 1NZ
Tel 0865-842742

The Agricultural Development and Advisory Service (ADAS) provides a comprehensive range of consultancy services to the land-based industries. It also carries out research, performs certain statutory functions and provides advice on policy for MAFF and the Welsh Office.

Chief Executive (G2), Dr J. Walsh
Director of Operations (G3), P. Needham
Research Director (G4), Dr A. D. Hughes
Marketing Director (G5), D. N. Hall
Finance Director (G5), Dr C. Herring
Personnel Director (G5), Ms S. Nason
Director for Wales (G5), W. I. C. Davies
Non-Executive Directors, C. Bystram (*Chairman*); P. Christensen, CBE

PESTICIDES SAFETY DIRECTORATE
Ergon House, 17 Smith Square, London SW1P 3JR
Tel 071-238 6299
Rothamstead, Harpenden, Herts. AL5 2SS
Tel 0582-462100

The Pesticides Safety Directorate is responsible for the evaluation and approval of pesticides and the development of policies relating to them, in order to protect consumers, users and the environment.
Chief Executive (G4), G. K. Bruce
Director (Policy) (G5), J. A. Bainton
Director (Approvals) (G5), Dr A. D. Martin (*based at Harpenden*)

AGRICULTURAL AND FOOD RESEARCH COUNCIL
Polaris House, North Star Avenue, Swindon SN2 1UH
Tel 0793-413200

The Agricultural and Food Research Council (AFRC) is an independent body established by royal charter. It is funded by the Office of Science and Technology, receives commissions from the Ministry of Agriculture, Fisheries and Food, and does research for industry and other bodies.

The Council is responsible for research done in its institutes and in UK university departments funded through its research grants scheme. It advises the Scottish Office Agriculture and Fisheries Department (SOAFD) on research in the Scottish Agricultural Research Institutes. The institutes funded through AFRC and SOAFD, and the university groups supported, form the Agricultural and Food Research Service.

From April 1994, the Council will become the Biotechnology and Biological Sciences Research Council.
Chairman, Sir Alistair Grant
Deputy Chairman and Director-General, Prof. T. L. Blundell, FRS
Members, Dr P. J. Bunyan; C. R. Cann; Prof. E. C. D. Cocking, FRS; Prof. J. R. Coggins, FRSE; Sir Sam Edwards, FRS; D. F. R. George, OBE; A. B. N. Gill; Prof. R. M. Hicks, OBE; Prof. G. Horn, FRS; Prof. W. P. T. James, CBE; R. M. Knapman, MP; Prof. J. R. Krebs, FRS; Prof. C. J. Leaver, FRS; Dr T. Little; K. J. MacKenzie; Prof. T. Mansfield, FRS; J. L. C. Provan; G. T. Pryce; Dr D. W. F. Shannon; Prof. W. V. Shaw
Assessors, K. Meldrum; Dr C. McMurray; Prof. H. Smith, FRS; O. Rees, CB; Dr G. W. Robinson; D. Wilkinson; Dr E. Buttle; Prof. H. J. Newby; Dr D. A. Rees, FRS; Sir Mark Richmond, FRS

Director of Administration, Central Office (G3),
B. G. Jamieson, PH.D.
Heads of Divisions (G5), S. H. Visscher (Finance); R. J. Price
(Human Resources); Dr J. N. Wingfield (Science);
Dr A. V. Harrison (Policy)
Commercial Policy Section (G6), S. M. Lawrie
Principal Information Officer (G7), Dr M. A. Winstanley

AFRC COMPUTING DIVISION
West Common, Harpenden, Herts. AL5 2JE
Tel 0582-762271
Head of Division, A. Windram

For institutes and units of the Agricultural and Food Research
Service, see page 709

COLLEGE OF ARMS OR HERALDS
COLLEGE
Queen Victoria Street, London EC4V 4BT
Tel 071-248 2762

The College is the official repository of the arms and
pedigrees of English, Northern Irish and Commonwealth
families and their descendants, and its records include official
copies of the records of Ulster King of Arms, the originals of
which remain in Dublin. The 13 officers of the College
specialize in genealogical and heraldic work for their
respective clients.
Arms have been and still are granted by letters patent
from the Kings of Arms under authority delegated to them
by the Sovereign, such authority having been expressly
conferred on them since at least the fifteenth century. A right
to arms can only be established by the registration in the
official records of the College of Arms of a pedigree showing
direct male line descent from an ancestor already appearing
therein as being entitled to arms, or by making application
through the College of Arms for a grant of arms.
The College of Arms is open Mon.–Fri. 10–4, when an
Officer of Arms is in attendance to deal with enquiries by the
public, though such enquiries may also be directed to any of
the Officers of Arms, either personally or by letter.
Earl Marshal, His Grace the Duke of Norfolk, KG, GCVO, CB,
CBE, MC

KINGS OF ARMS
Garter, C. M. J. F. Swan, CVO, PH.D., FSA
Clarenceux, Sir Anthony Wagner, KCB, KCVO, FSA
Norroy and Ulster, J. P. B. Brooke-Little, CVO, FSA

HERALDS
Chester (and Registrar), D. H. B. Chesshyre, LVO, FSA
Windsor, T. D. Mathew
Lancaster, P. L. Gwynn-Jones
Somerset, T. Woodcock, FSA
Richmond, P. L. Dickinson
York, H. E. Paston-Bedingfeld

Earl Marshal's Secretary, Sir Walter Verco, KCVO, Surrey
Herald Extraordinary

PURSUIVANTS
Rouge Dragon, T. H. S. Duke
Bluemantle, R. J. B. Noel
Portcullis, W. G. Hunt, TD
Rouge Croix, vacant

COURT OF THE LORD LYON
HM New Register House, Edinburgh EH1 3YT
Tel 031-556 7255

The Court of the Lord Lyon is the Scottish Court of Chivalry
(including the genealogical jurisdiction of the Ri-Sennachie
of Scotland's Celtic Kings). It adjudicates rights to arms and
administers the Scottish Public Register of All Arms and
Bearings and the Public Register of All Genealogies. The
Lord Lyon presides and judicially establishes rights to
existing arms or succession to chiefship, or for cadets with
scientific 'differences' showing position in clan or family.
Pedigrees are also established by decrees of Lyon Court and
by letters patent. As Royal Commissioner in Armory, he
grants patents of arms (which constitute the grantee and
heirs noble in the Noblesse of Scotland) to 'virtuous and well-
deserving' Scotsmen and to petitioners (personal or corporate) in Her Majesty's overseas realms of Scottish connection,
and issues birthbrieves.
Lord Lyon King of Arms, Sir Malcolm Innes of Edingight,
KCVO, WS, FSA Scot

HERALDS
Albany, J. A. Spens, RD, WS
Rothesay, Sir Crispin Agnew of Lochnaw, Bt.
Ross, C. J. Burnett, FSA Scot

PURSUIVANTS
Kintyre, J. C. G. George, FSA Scot
Unicorn, Alastair Campbell of Airds, FSA Scot
Carrick, Mrs C. G. W. Roads, MVO, FSA Scot

Lyon Clerk and Keeper of Records, Mrs C. G. W. Roads,
MVO, FSA Scot
Procurator-Fiscal, I. R. Guild, CBE, FRSE, WS
Herald Painter, Mrs J. Phillips
Macer, A. M. Clark

ARTS COUNCIL OF GREAT BRITAIN
14 Great Peter Street, London SW1P 3NQ
Tel 071-333 0100

The Arts Council, an independent body established in 1946,
is the principal channel for the Government's support of the
arts. It funds the major arts organizations in England, the
Regional Arts Boards and the Scottish and Welsh Arts
Councils. From April 1994 the Scottish and Welsh Arts
Councils will become autonomous and will be funded directly
by the Scottish Office and Welsh Office respectively. The
Arts Council of Great Britain will then become the English
Arts Council (title to be confirmed).
The Arts Council also provides a service of advice,
information and help to artists, arts organizations and the
general public. Its objectives are to develop and improve the
understanding and practice of the arts and to increase their
accessibility to the public.
The Council distributes an annual grant from the
Department of National Heritage, and for the year 1993–4
the amount is £225.63 million.
Chairman, Lord Palumbo
Secretary-General, A. Everitt

REGIONAL ARTS BOARDS
EASTERN ARTS BOARD, Cherry Hinton Hall, Cherry
Hinton Road, Cambridge CB1 4DW. Tel: 0223-215355.
Chair, Prof. D. Hargreaves

EAST MIDLANDS ARTS BOARD, Mountfields House,
Forest Road, Loughborough, Leics. LEII 3HU. Tel: 0509-
218292. *Chair*, M. Hutchinson
LONDON ARTS BOARD, Elme House, 133 Long Acre,
London WC2E 9AF. Tel: 071-240 1313. *Chair*, C. Priestley
NORTHERN ARTS BOARD, 9–10 Osborne Terrace,
Newcastle upon Tyne NE2 INZ. Tel: 091-281 6334. *Chair*,
Mrs S. Robinson
NORTH-WEST ARTS BOARD, 12 Harter Street,
Manchester MI 6HY. Tel: 061-228 3062. *Chair* (acting),
A. Richardson
SOUTH-EAST ARTS BOARD, 10 Mount Ephraim,
Tunbridge Wells, Kent TN4 8AS. Tel: 0892-515210.
Chair, B. Nicholson
SOUTHERN ARTS BOARD, 13 St Clement Street,
Winchester SO23 9DQ. Tel: 0962-855099. *Chair*, D. Reid
SOUTH-WEST ARTS BOARD, Bradninch Place, Gandy
Street, Exeter EX4 3LS. Tel: 0392-218188. *Chair*, Ms
M. Guillebaud
WEST MIDLANDS ARTS BOARD, 82 Granville Street,
Birmingham BI 2LH. Tel: 021-631 3121. *Chair*,
R. Southgate
YORKSHIRE AND HUMBERSIDE ARTS BOARD, 21 Bond
Street, Dewsbury, W. Yorks. WFI3 IAX. Tel: 0924-
455555. *Chair*, E. Hall

SCOTTISH ARTS COUNCIL
12 Manor Place, Edinburgh EH3 7DD
Tel 031-226 6051
Chairman, W. Brown

WELSH ARTS COUNCIL
Holst House, 9 Museum Place, Cardiff CFI 3NX
Tel 0222-394 711
Chairman, M. Prichard, CBE

ARTS COUNCIL OF NORTHERN IRELAND
185 Stranmillis Road, Belfast BT9 5DU
Tel 0232-381591

The Arts Council of Northern Ireland is funded by the
Department of Education for Northern Ireland. Its function
is to develop and improve the accessibility of the arts to the
public and to disburse government funds in support of the
arts in Northern Ireland.
Chairman, D. Deeny, QC (*from Jan. 1994*)

ART GALLERIES, ETC

ROYAL FINE ART COMMISSION
7 St James's Square, London SWIY 4JU
Tel 071-839 6537

Established in 1924, the Commission is an autonomous
authority on the aesthetic implications of any project or
development, primarily but not exclusively architectural,
which affects the visual environment.
Chairman, The Lord St John of Fawsley, PC
Commissioners, R. D. Carter, CBE; Dame Elizabeth
Chesterton, DBE; Sir Philip Dowson, CBE, RA;
M. Girouard, PH.D.; The Duke of Grafton, KG, FSA;
D. Hamilton Fraser, RA; M. J. Hopkins, CBE, RA;
S. A. Lipton; R. MacCormac; H. T. Moggridge, OBE; Mrs
J. Nutting; Sir Philip Powell, CH, OBE, RA;

Prof. J. R. Steer, FSA; J. Sutherland; Miss W. Taylor, CBE;
Sir William Whitfield, CBE; J. Winter, MBE
Secretary (G6), S. Cantacuzino, CBE

ROYAL FINE ART COMMISSION FOR
SCOTLAND
9 Atholl Crescent, Edinburgh EH3 8HA
Tel 031-229 1109

The Commission was established in 1927 and advises
ministers and local authorities on the visual impact and
quality of design of construction projects. It is an independent
body and gives its opinions impartially.
Chairman, The Hon. Lord Prosser
Commissioners, Prof. G. Benson; Miss K. Borland;
W. A. Cadell; Mrs K. Dalyell; Dr Deborah Howard,
PH.D., FSA, FSA SCOT.; A. S. Matheson, FRIBA; G. Ogilvie-
Laing; Prof. T. Ridley; R. R. Steedman, RSA;
Prof. R. Webster; R. Wedgwood
Secretary, C. Prosser

NATIONAL GALLERY
Trafalgar Square, London WC2N 5DN
Tel 071-839 3321

Open weekdays 10–6, Sun. 2–6. Closed on Good Friday, 24–
26 December, New Year's Day and May Day Bank Holiday.
Admission free.
The National Gallery was founded in 1824, following a
parliamentary grant of £60,000 for the purchase and
exhibition of the Angerstein collection of pictures. The
present site was first occupied in 1838 and enlarged and
improved at various times throughout the years. A substantial
extension to the north of the building with a public entrance
in Orange Street was opened in 1975, and the Sainsbury wing
was opened in 1991. Government grant-in-aid for 1993–4 is
£17.9 million.

BOARD OF TRUSTEES
Chairman, N. H. Baring
Trustees, Sir Rex Richards, D.phil., FRS FRSC; The Lord
Alexander of Weedon, QC; F. St J. Gore, CBE;
B. Gascoigne, FRSL; P. Troughton; The Countess of
Airlie, CVO; Sir Derek Oulton, KCB, QC; E. Uglow; Sir
Keith Thomas, FBA; The Hon. Simon Sainsbury; Lady
Bingham

OFFICERS
Director (G3), R. N. MacGregor
Chief Curator (G5), Dr C. P. H. Brown
Senior Curators (G6), Dr N. Penny; *(G7)*, Dr S. Foister; Dr
D. Gordon; J. Leighton
Chief Restorer (G5), M. H. Wyld
Head of Exhibitions (G6), M. J. Wilson
Scientific Adviser (G6), Dr A. Roy
Director of Administration (G5), M. A. Cowdy
Head of Finance and Personnel (G5), T. Tarkowski
Head of Building, Mrs J. Evans
Head of Press and Public Relations, Miss J. Liddiard

NATIONAL PORTRAIT GALLERY
St Martin's Place, London WC2H OHE
Tel 071-306 0055

Open Mon.–Fri. 10–5, Sat. 10–6, Sun. 2–6. Closed on Good
Friday, May Day Bank Holiday, 24–26 December and New
Year's Day. Admission free.
A grant was made in 1856 to form a gallery of the portraits
of the most eminent persons in British history. The present
building was opened in 1896, an extension being opened in
1933. There are four outstations displaying portraits in

appropriate settings: Montacute House, Gawthorpe Hall, Beningbrough Hall and Bodelwyddan Castle.

Chairman, The Revd Prof. W. O. Chadwick, OM, KBE, FBA

Trustees, The Lord President of the Council (ex officio); The President of the Royal Academy of Arts (ex officio); Sir Oliver Millar, GCVO, FBA, FSA; J. Roberts, D.Phil.; The Lord Morris of Castle Morris, D.Phil.; H. Keswick; Prof. N. Lynton; The Lord Weidenfeld; Sir Eduardo Paolozzi; J. Tusa; Sir Antony Acland, GCMG, GCVO; Mrs J. E. Benson, LVO, OBE; Mrs W. Tumim; Sir David Scholey, CBE; Mrs C. Tomalin

Director (G3), J. T. Hayes, CBE, Ph.D., FSA *(until Jan. 1994)*

Keeper and Deputy Director (G5), M. Rogers, D.Phil.

TATE GALLERY
Millbank, London SW1P 4RG
Tel 071-821 1313

Open weekdays 10-5.50, Sun. 2-5.50. Closed New Year's Day, Good Friday, May Day Bank Holiday and 24-26 December. Admission free.

The Tate Gallery comprises the national collections of British painting and 20th-century painting and sculpture. The Gallery was opened in 1897, the cost of erection (£80,000) being defrayed by Sir Henry Tate, who also contributed the nucleus of the present collection. The Turner wing was opened in 1910, galleries to contain the collection of modern foreign painting in 1926, and a new sculpture hall in 1937. In 1979 a further extension was built; the latest extension to the Tate Gallery, the Clore Gallery for the Turner Collection, was opened in 1987. The Tate Gallery Liverpool, sited in the Albert Dock, opened in May 1988. The Tate Gallery St Ives opened in June 1993. Total government funding for 1993-4 is £17,075,000.

BOARD OF TRUSTEES
Chairman, D. Stevenson
Trustees, The Countess of Airlie, CVO; The Hon. Mrs J. de Botton; R. Deacon; D. Gordon; C. Le Brun; M. Craig-Martin; Sir Richard Carew Pole; Sir Rex Richards; Mrs P. Ridley; D. Verey

OFFICERS
Director (G3), N. Serota
Deputy Director (G5), F. Carnwath
Keeper of the British Collection (G5), A. Wilton
Keeper of the Modern Collection (G5), R. Morphet
Deputy Keepers (G6), L. A. Parris; J. Lewison

TATE GALLERY LIVERPOOL
Albert Dock, Liverpool L3 4BB
Tel 051-709 3223

Open Tues.–Sun., 10-6. Closed Mondays except Bank Holidays. Admission free.
Curator (G6), L. Biggs

TATE GALLERY ST IVES
Porthmeor Beach, St Ives, Cornwall TR26 1TG
Tel 0736-796226

Opening times vary. Closed Mondays Sept.–May except Bank Holidays, 24-26 December and 1 January. Admission £2.50 (inc. admission to Barbara Hepworth Museum and Sculpture Garden).
Curator (G6), M. Tooby

WALLACE COLLECTION
Hertford House, Manchester Square, London W1M 6BN
Tel 071-935 0687

Open weekdays 10-5, Sun. 2-5. Closed on Good Friday, 24-26 December, 1 January and May Day. Admission free.

The Wallace Collection was bequeathed to the nation by the widow of Sir Richard Wallace, Bt. on her death in 1897, and Hertford House was subsequently acquired by the Government. The collection includes pictures, drawings and miniatures, French furniture, sculpture, bronzes, porcelain, armour and miscellaneous *objets d'art.* The total net expenses for 1993-4 were estimated at £2,224,000.

Director, Miss R. J. Savill
Assistant to Director, P. Hughes
Head of Administration, A. W. Houldershaw

NATIONAL GALLERIES OF SCOTLAND
The Mound, Edinburgh EH2 2EL
Tel 031-556 8921

TRUSTEES
Chairman of the Trustees, A. M. Grossart, CBE
Trustees, J. Packer, OBE; A. R. Cole-Hamilton; Mrs L. W. Gibbs; Lord Macfarlane of Bearsden; Dr T. Johnston; Prof. A. A. Tait; E. Hagman; Prof. E. Fernie; M. Shea

OFFICERS
Director (G4), T. Clifford
Keeper of Conservation (G6), J. P. Dick
Keeper of Information (G7), Miss L. S. Callander
Keeper of Education (G7), M. Cassin
Registrar (G7), Miss A. Buddle
Secretary (G6), Ms S. Edwards
Buildings (G7), C. P. Fotheringham

NATIONAL GALLERY OF SCOTLAND
The Mound, Edinburgh
Tel 031-556 8921

Open Mon.–Sat. 10-5, Sun. 2-5. Closed 25, 26, 27, 31 December, 1-3 January. Admission free.
Keeper (G6), M. Clarke
Assistant Keepers (G7), Ms J. Lloyd Williams; R. M. M. Campbell; Miss H. Smailes

SCOTTISH NATIONAL PORTRAIT GALLERY
1 Queen Street, Edinburgh
Tel 031-556 8921

Hours as for National Gallery of Scotland
Keeper (G6), D. Thomson, Ph.D.
Assistant Keepers (G7), Miss R. K. Marshall, Ph.D.; J. E. Holloway
Curator of Photography, Miss S. F. Stevenson

SCOTTISH NATIONAL GALLERY OF MODERN ART
Belford Road, Edinburgh EH4 3DR
Tel 031-556 8921

Hours as for National Gallery of Scotland
Keeper (G6), R. Calvocoressi
Assistant Keepers (G7), K. S. Hartley; P. Elliott, Ph.D.

For other British Art Galleries, *see* Index

UNITED KINGDOM ATOMIC ENERGY AUTHORITY (AEA TECHNOLOGY)
Harwell, Oxfordshire OX11 0RA
Tel 0235-821111

The UKAEA was established by the Atomic Energy Authority Act 1954. Since April 1986 the UKAEA has been required by the Government to operate on a commercial footing and in 1990 it adopted the trading name AEA Technology. It provides scientific and technical services, products and consultancy in nuclear and non-nuclear fields to governments, utilities and industries world-wide. The UKAEA has six research and engineering centres. Many of the technical staff and activities of the Warren Spring Laboratory will be merged with the environmental capabilities of AEA Technology by mid-1994 to create a National Environmental Technology Centre based within AEA Technology.

Chairman (part-time), Sir Anthony Cleaver
Deputy Chairman and Chief Executive, Dr B. L. Eyre, CBE
Members (part-time), Prof. Sir Peter Hirsch, FRS; J. Bullock; R. Sanderson, OBE; Prof. Sir Roger Elliott, FRS; J. A. Gardiner; Mrs S. Shirley
Secretary, J. R. Bretherton
Executive Director, Finance, P. G. Daffern
Managing Director, Sites and Personnel, A. W. Hills
Managing Director, Industrial Business Group, Dr R. S. Nelson
Managing Director, Nuclear Business Group, Dr D. Pooley

AUDIT COMMISSION FOR LOCAL AUTHORITIES AND THE NATIONAL HEALTH SERVICE IN ENGLAND AND WALES
1 Vincent Square, London SW1P 2PN
Tel 071-828 1212

The Audit Commission was set up in 1983 with responsibility for the external audit of local authorities. This remit was extended from October 1990 to include the audit of the National Health Service bodies in England and Wales. The Commission appoints the auditors, who may be from the District Audit Service or from a private firm of accountants. The Commission is also responsible for promoting value for money in the services provided by local authorities and health bodies.

The Commission has 15–17 members appointed by the Secretary of State for the Environment in consultation with the Secretaries of State for Wales and for Health. Though appointed by the Secretary of State, the Commissioners are responsible to Parliament.

Chairman, Sir David Cooksey
Deputy Chairman, C. M. Stuart
Controller of Audit, A. Foster
Associate Controllers, P. Wilkinson; B. Willmor

COMMISSION FOR LOCAL AUTHORITY ACCOUNTS IN SCOTLAND
18 George Street, Edinburgh EH2 2QU
Tel 031-226 7346

The Commission was set up in 1975. It is responsible for securing the audit of the accounts of Scottish local authorities and certain joint boards and joint committees. Amongst its duties the Commission is required to deal with reports made by the Controller of Audit on items of account contrary to law; on incorrect accounting; and on losses due to misconduct, negligence and failure to carry out statutory duties. Since 1988 the Commission has had responsibility for value-for-money audits of authorities.

Members are appointed by the Secretary of State for Scotland.

Chairman, Prof. J. P. Percy
Controller of Audit, J. Broadfoot
Secretary, J. Ritchie

THE BANK OF ENGLAND
Threadneedle Street, London EC2R 8AH
Tel 071-601 4444

The Bank of England was incorporated in 1694 under royal charter. It is the banker of the Government, on whose behalf it executes monetary policy and manages the note issue and the national debt. It is also responsible for promoting the efficiency and competitiveness of financial services. As the central reserve bank of the country, the Bank keeps the accounts of British banks, who maintain with it a proportion of their cash resources, and of most overseas central banks. *(See also page 614).*

Governor, E. A. J. George
Deputy Governor, R. L. Pennant-Rea
Directors, Sir Adrian Cadbury; A. L. Coleby; Sir Colin Corness; A. D. Crockett; Mrs F. A. Heaton; Sir Christopher Hogg; Sir Martin Jacomb; Sir John Keswick; M. A. King; G. H. Laird, CBE; Sir David Lees; Sir Christopher Morse; B. Quinn; Sir David Scholey, CBE; Prof. Sir Roland Smith; Sir Colin Southgate
Associate Directors, P. H. Kent; H. C. E. Harris; I. Plenderleith
Advisers to the Governor, J. P. Charkham; Sir Peter Petrie; P. C. Peddie; I. G. Watt
Chief of Banking Department (Chief Cashier), G. E. A. Kentfield
Chief Registrar, D. A. Bridger
General Manager, Printing Works, A. W. Jarvis
Secretary, G. A. Croughton
Head of Information Division, J. R. E. Footman
The Auditor, M. J. W. Phillips

BOUNDARY COMMISSIONS

The Commissions are constituted under the Parliamentary Constituencies Act 1986. The Speaker of the House of Commons is ex-officio chairman of all four commissions in the United Kingdom. Each of the four commissions is required by law to keep the parliamentary constituencies in their part of the United Kingdom under review. Each of the three commissions in Great Britain is required by law to keep the European Parliamentary constituencies in their part of Great Britain under review.

ENGLAND
St Catherine's House, 10 Kingsway, London WC2B 6JP
Tel 071-242 0262
Deputy Chairman, The Hon. Mr Justice Knox
Joint Secretaries, R. McLeod; Mrs J. S. Morris

WALES
St Catherine's House, 10 Kingsway, London WC2B 6JP
Tel 071-242 0262
Deputy Chairman, The Hon. Mr Justice Pill
Joint Secretaries, R. McLeod; Mrs J. S. Morris

SCOTLAND
St Andrew's House, Edinburgh EH1 3DG
Tel 031-244 2196/3582
Deputy Chairman, The Hon. Lord Davidson
Secretary, D. K. C. Jeffrey

NORTHERN IRELAND
c/o Northern Ireland Office, Whitehall, London SW1A 2AZ
Tel 071-210 6569

Deputy Chairman, The Hon. Mr Justice Higgins
Secretary, J. R. Fisher

The Secretary, M. Stevenson
Legal Adviser, G. Roscoe

BRITISH BROADCASTING CORPORATION
Broadcasting House, London WIA IAA
Tel 071-580 4468
Television Centre, Wood Lane, London W12 7RJ
Tel 081-743 8000

The BBC was incorporated under royal charter as successor to the British Broadcasting Company Ltd, whose licence expired on 31 December 1926. Its present charter came into force on 1 August 1981, for 15 years (*see also* page 679). The Chairman, Vice-Chairman and other Governors are appointed by The Queen-in-Council. The BBC is financed by revenue from receiving licences for the home services and by grant-in-aid from Parliament for the external services. The total number of receiving licences in the UK at 31 March 1993 was 20,067,114, of which 1,036,320 were for monochrome receivers and 19,030,794 for colour receivers. Annual television licence fees are: monochrome £27.50; colour £83. For services, *see* Broadcasting section.

BOARD OF GOVERNORS *as at 1 July 1993*

Chairman (£57,360), M. Hussey
Vice-Chairman (£14,715), The Lord Cocks of Hartcliffe
National Governors (each £14,715), Sir Kenneth Bloomfield, KCB (*N. Ireland*); Dr G. Jones (*Wales*); Sir Graham Hills, FRSE (*Scotland*)
Governors (each £7,360), W. B. Jordan, CBE; Miss J. Glover, D.Phil.; Mrs S. Sadeque; Lord Nicholas Gordon Lennox, KCMG, KCVO; Mrs M. Spurr

BOARD OF MANAGEMENT
Director-General, J. Birt
Deputy Director-General and Managing Director, World Service, R. Phillis
Adviser to the Director-General, D. Hatch
Managing Directors, W. Wyatt (*Network Television*); Ms E. Forgan (*Network Radio*); R. Neil (*Regional Broadcasting*); T. Hall (*News and Current Affairs*); R. Lynch (*Resources and Engineering Services*)
Directors, Ms P. Taylor (*Corporate Affairs*); Ms M. Salmon (*Personnel*); Ms P. Hodgson (*Policy and Planning*); R. Baker-Bates (*Finance and Information Technology*)
Chief Executive, Enterprises, vacant

OTHER SENIOR STAFF
Controller, BBC1, A. Yentob
Controller, BBC2, M. Jackson
Assistant Managing Director, Network Television, Ms J. Drabble
Controller, Radio 1, M. Bannister
Controller, Radio 2, Ms F. Line
Controller, Radio 3, N. Kenyon
Controller, Radio 4, M. Green
Controller, Radio 5, Ms P. Ewing
Controller, Scotland, J. McCormick
Controller, Wales, G. Talfan Davies
Controller, N. Ireland, R. Walsh
Controller, European Services, A. Taussig
Controller, Overseas Services, S. Younger
Controller, English Services, Ms E. Smith
Chief Political Adviser, vacant
Controller, Editorial Policy, R. Ayre
Chief Executive Officer, BBC World Service TV, C. Irwin

BRITISH COAL CORPORATION
Hobart House, Grosvenor Place, London SWIX 7AE
Tel 071-235 2020

The British Coal Corporation (formerly the National Coal Board) was constituted in 1946 and took over the mines on 1 January 1947.
Chairman, J. N. Clarke
Deputy Chairman, A. Wheeler, CBE
Executive Members, R. Proctor (*Finance Director*); K. Hunt (*Employee Relations*); A. D. J. Horsler (*Marketing Director*)
Non-Executive Members, Dr D. V. Atterton, CBE; Dr T. J. Parker; D. B. Walker; J. P. Erbé; A. P. Hichens; Sir Robert Davidson, FEng.; Sir David Alliance, CBE
Secretary, M. S. Shelton

THE BRITISH COUNCIL
10 Spring Gardens, London SWIA 2BN
Tel 071-930 8466
Medlock Street, Manchester M15
Tel 061-957 7000

The British Council was established in 1934 and incorporated by royal charter in 1940. It is an independent, non-political organization which promotes Britain abroad. It provides access to British ideas, talents and experience in education and training, books and periodicals, the English language, the arts, the sciences and technology.
   The Council is represented in 98 countries and runs 187 offices, 116 libraries and 72 English language schools around the world.
   The Council's annual turnover in 1993–4 is estimated at £416 million, including grants from the Foreign and Commonwealth Office and the Overseas Development Administration. The Council's own revenue now exceeds £120 million.
Chairman, Sir Martin Jacomb
Deputy Chairman, The Lord Chorley
Director-General, J. Hanson, CBE

BRITISH FILM COMMISSION
70 Baker Street, London WIM IDJ
Tel 071-224 5000

The British Film Commission was established in 1992 to promote the use of British locations, production services, technicians and facilities. It is funded by the Department of National Heritage. It offers a free service to international producers and directs enquiries to local film commissions throughout the UK. It also encourages the development of local commissions where they do not already exist.
Commissioner and Chairman of the Board, S. W. Samuelson, CBE
Chief Executive, A. Patrick

BRITISH FILM INSTITUTE
21 Stephen Street, London w1p 1pl
Tel 071-255 1444

The British Film Institute was established in 1933 under royal charter. Its aims are to encourage the development of the art of film and its use as a record of contemporary life in Great Britain, and to foster the study, appreciation and use of films for television. It includes the National Film Archive, the National Film Theatre and the Museum of the Moving Image, and it supports a network of 40 regional film theatres. The BFI Library contains the world's largest collection of material relating to film and television. Total government funding for 1993–4 is £15 million.
Chairman, J. Thomas
Director, W. Stevenson

BRITISH PHARMACOPOEIA COMMISSION
Market Towers, 1 Nine Elms Lane, London sw8 5nq
Tel 071-273 0561

The British Pharmacopoeia Commission sets standards for medicinal products used in human and veterinary medicine. It is responsible for the British Pharmacopoeia (a publicly-available statement of the standard that a product must meet throughout its shelf-life), the British Pharmacopoeia (Veterinary) and the selection of British Approved Names. It also participates in the work of the European Pharmacopoeia on behalf of the United Kingdom. It has 18 members who are appointed by the Secretary of State for Health and the Minister for Agriculture, Fisheries and Food.
Chairman, Prof. D. Ganderton
Vice-Chairman, Prof. P. Turner, cbe
Secretary (G6), Dr R. C. Hutton

BRITISH RAILWAYS BOARD
Euston House, 24 Eversholt Street, PO Box 100, London
nw1 1dz
Tel 071-928 5151

The British Railways Board came into being in 1963 under the terms of the Transport Act 1962. The Board is responsible for the provision of railway services in Great Britain and for catering and other related services. For details of operations, *see* Transport section.
Chairman (£232,000), Sir Robert Reid
Members, P. Allen, cbe*; Miss K. T. Kantor*;
  J. B. Cameron, cbe*; D. E. Rayner, cbe;
  K. H. M. Dixon*; Sir Fred Holliday, cbe*; J. J. Jerram;
  E. Sanderson*; Dr P. Watson, obe; R. Horton*;
  A. Norman*; Miss J. Page*
* part-time members

BRITISH STANDARDS INSTITUTION (BSI)
2 Park Street, London w1a 2bs
Enquiry section: BSI, Linford Wood, Milton Keynes
mk14 6le
Tel 0908-221166

The British Standards Institution is the recognized authority in the UK for the preparation and publication of national standards for industrial and consumer products. In consulta-

tion with the interests concerned, BSI prepares standards relating to nearly every sector of the nation's industry and trade. It also represents the UK at European and international standards meetings. About 80 per cent of its standards work is now internationally linked.

British Standards are issued for voluntary adoption, though in a number of cases compliance with a British Standard is required by legislation. BSI operates certification schemes under which industrial and consumer products are certified as complying with the relevant British Standard and may carry the Institution's certification trade marks, known as the 'Kitemark' and the 'Safety Mark'. It assesses and registers companies which meet the requirements of the quality management standard, BS5750. BSI runs one of the largest testing laboratories in Europe and has an advisory service for exporters, Technical Help to Exporters.

BSI is financed by voluntary subscriptions, an annual government grant, the sale of its publications, and fees for testing and certification. There are more than 27,000 subscribing members of BSI.
Chief Executive, vacant

BRITISH TOURIST AUTHORITY
Thames Tower, Black's Road, London w6 9el
Tel 081-846 9000

Established under the Development of Tourism Act 1969, the British Tourist Authority has specific responsibility for promoting tourism to Great Britain from overseas. It also has a general responsibility for the promotion and development of tourism and tourist facilities within Great Britain as a whole, and for advising the Government on tourism matters.
Chairman (part-time), Ms A. Biss
Chief Executive (acting), A. Jefferson

BRITISH WATERWAYS
Willow Grange, Church Road, Watford, Herts. wd1 3qa
Tel 0923-226422

British Waterways is the navigational authority for over 2,000 miles of canals and river navigations in England, Scotland and Wales. Some 380 miles are maintained and are being developed as commercial waterways for use by freight-carrying vessels. Another 1,200 miles, the cruising waterways, are being developed for boating, fishing and other leisure activities. The remaining 500 miles, the remainder water-ways, are maintained with due regard to safety, public health and the preservation of amenities. Of this remaining mileage, nearly two-thirds is navigable or has been restored to navigation over the past twenty years.
Chairman (part-time), D. C. Ingman, cbe
Vice-Chairman (part-time), Sir Peter Hutchison, Bt.
Members (all part-time), J. Gordon; D. H. R. Yorke;
  M. Cairns; D. Porter; Viscountess Cobham
Chief Executive, B. C. Dice
Secretary and Solicitor, R. J. Duffy

BROADCASTING STANDARDS COUNCIL
5–8 The Sanctuary, London sw1p 3js
Tel 071-233 0544

The Council was set up in 1988 but received its statutory powers under the Broadcasting Act 1990. It monitors the

portrayal of violence, sex and matters of taste and decency in any television or radio programme or broadcast advertisement. The Council publishes a code of practice, considers complaints and undertakes relevant research. Members of the Council are appointed by the Secretary of State for National Heritage. The appointments are part-time.
Chair (£38,400), The Lady Howe of Aberavon
Deputy Chairman (£29,000), Dame Jocelyn Barrow, DBE
Members (each £11,550), R. Baker, OBE, RD; Ms R. Bevan; Dr Jean Curtis-Raleigh; Revd C. Robertson; M. Parris
Director, C. Shaw, CBE
Deputy Director, T. Cobley

THE BROADS AUTHORITY
Thomas Harvey House, 18 Colegate, Norwich NR3 1BQ
Tel 0603-610734

The Broads Authority is a special statutory authority set up under the Norfolk and Suffolk Broads Act 1988, with powers and responsibilities similar to those of National Park Authorities. The functions of the Authority are to conserve and enhance the natural beauty of the Broads; to promote the enjoyment of the Broads by the public; and to protect the interests of navigation.

The Authority comprises 35 members, appointed by Norfolk County Council (4); Suffolk County Council (2); Broadland District Council (2); Great Yarmouth Borough Council (2); North Norfolk District Council (2); Norwich City Council (2); South Norfolk District Council (2); Waveney District Council (2); the Countryside Commission (2); English Nature (1); the Great Yarmouth Port Authority (2); the National Rivers Authority (Anglian Region) (1); the Secretary of State for the Environment (9); and two from amongst members of the Authority's statutory Navigation Committee who are not already members of the Authority.
Chairman, J. S. Peel, MC
Chief Executive, M. A. Clark

THE CABINET OFFICE

The Cabinet Office comprises the Secretariat, who support Ministers collectively in the conduct of Cabinet business; and the Office of Public Service and Science (OPSS) which is responsible for the Citizen's Charter initiative, the Next Steps programme, policy on open government, senior Civil Service and public appointments, and the management and organization of the Civil Service and recruitment into it. The OPSS is also responsible for the Civil Service College, the Recruitment and Assessment Services Agency, the Occupational Health Service, HMSO, CCTA (the Government Centre for Information Systems), the Central Office of Information and the Chessington Computer Centre. The Office of Science and Technology also forms part of the OPSS.

The OPSS supports the Prime Minister in his capacity as Minister for the Civil Service, with responsibility for day-to-day supervision delegated to the Chancellor of the Duchy of Lancaster.

PRIME MINISTER'S OFFICE
Prime Minister and Minister for the Civil Service,
The Rt. Hon. John Major, MP
Principal Private Secretary to the Prime Minister (G3),
A. Allan

Private Secretaries to the Prime Minister, R. Lyne, CMG (*Overseas Affairs*); Mrs M. Francis (*Economic Affairs*); W. Chapman (*Parliamentary Affairs*); M. Adams (*Home Affairs*)
Diary Secretary to the Prime Minister, Miss S. Phillips
Secretary for Appointments (G5), J. Holroyd, CB
Foreign Affairs Adviser, Sir Rodric Braithwaite, KCMG
Efficiency and Competition Adviser, Sir Peter Levene, KBE
Political Secretary, J. Hill
Policy Unit, The Hon. Mrs S. Hogg; N. True, CBE; A. Rosling; The Lord Poole; Mrs K. Ramsey; Miss L. Neville-Rolfe; Ms J. Rutter; D. Green; D. Morris
Chief Press Secretary, A. T. O'Donnell
Deputy Chief Press Secretary, J. Haslam
Assistant Private Secretaries to the Prime Minister, Miss A. Hordern; Miss J. L. Wilkinson
Parliamentary Private Secretary, G. Bright, MP
Secretary of the Cabinet and Head of Home Civil Service,
Sir Robin Butler, GCB, CVO
Private Secretary, Miss M. J. Leech

SECRETARIAT
70 Whitehall, London SW1A 2AS
Tel 071-270 3000

Deputy Secretaries (G2), Miss L. Neville-Jones, CMG; P. F. Owen, CB; D. E. Fitchew, CMG
Under-Secretaries (G3), R. Bird; D. J. Gould; R. L. Niven; R. J. D. Carden
Grade 5, A. Sandall; J. Sibson; Brig. J. A. J. Budd; S. G. Eldon
Grade 6, R. Hope

ESTABLISHMENT OFFICER'S GROUP
Government Offices, Great George Street, London SW1P 3AL
Tel 071-270 3000

Principal Establishment and Finance Officer (G3),
R. W. D. Venning
Deputy Establishment Officer (G5), G. S. Royston
Senior Finance Officer (G6), Miss J. M. E. Buchan

HISTORICAL AND RECORDS SECTION
Hepburn House, Marsham Street, London SW1P 4HW
Tel 071-217 6032
Grade 5, Miss P. M. Andrews

CEREMONIAL OFFICER
53 Parliament Street, London SW1A 2NG
Tel 071-210 5056
Grade 6, J. H. Thompson, CB

OFFICE OF PUBLIC SERVICE AND SCIENCE (OPSS)
Horse Guards Road, London SW1P 3AL
70 Whitehall, London SW1A 2AS
Tel 071-270 5811

Chancellor of the Duchy of Lancaster and Minister of Public Service and Science, The Rt. Hon. William Waldegrave, MP
Principal Private Secretary, A. T. Cahn
Private Secretary, I. Dougal
Special Advisers, Dr J. Nicholson; Sir Peter Levene, KBE; I. Wilton
Parliamentary Private Secretary, I. Taylor, MBE, MP
Parliamentary Under-Secretary of State, David Davis, MP
Private Secretary, W. E. Jones
Second Permanent Secretary (G1A), R. C. Mottram
Private Secretary, G. R. Davies

Parliamentary Clerk, Miss T. N. Terry
Press Secretary (G5), P. Rose

CITIZEN'S CHARTER UNIT
Government Offices, Great George Street, London
SWIP 3AL
Tel 071-270 6343

Director (G2), B. Hilton, CB
Deputy Directors (G6), Mrs D. A. Goldsworthy; Mrs
E. Hunter-Johnson

EFFICIENCY UNIT
70 Whitehall, London SWIA 2AS
Tel 071-260 0273

Prime Minister's Adviser on Efficiency and Effectiveness,
Sir Peter Levene, KBE
Head of Unit (G3), J. Oughton
Deputy Head of Unit (G5), Ms D. Kahn

ADVISORY UNIT ON MINISTERS' AGENCIES
Adviser, C. M. Brendish
Grade 6, D. R. Wood

MANAGEMENT DEVELOPMENT GROUP
Under-Secretary (G3), vacant
Grade 5, R. D. J. Wright (*Security*); Mrs S. Britton (*Equal
Opportunities*); Miss S. C. Phippard (*Next Steps Project
Team*); C. J. Parry (*Development*)

TOP MANAGEMENT PROGRAMME
Director of Programme (G3), Miss M. T. Neville-Rolfe
Course Directors (G5), Mrs P. Clarkson; Mrs M. Chapman

SENIOR AND PUBLIC APPOINTMENTS GROUP AND
EUROPEAN STAFFING
Under-Secretary (G3), A. J. Merifield
Grade 5, D. Laughrin
Grade 6, J. K. Barron

MACHINERY OF GOVERNMENT
Grade 5, A. D. Whetnall

OFFICE OF THE CIVIL SERVICE COMMISSIONERS
(OCSC)
Alencon Link, Basingstoke, Hants. RG21 IJB
Tel 0256-29222

First Commissioner (G2), Mrs A. E. Bowtell, CB (*London*)
Commissioner (G3), M. D. Geddes (*Chief Executive, RAS*)
Commissioners (part-time), Ms U. Prashar; Mrs J. Rubin;
A. Maddrell; K. E. C. Sorensen
Secretary to the Commissioners and Head of the Office (G5),
Miss E. M. Goodison

INFORMATION OFFICER MANAGEMENT UNIT
Information Officer (G5), T. J. Perks

CCTA (THE GOVERNMENT CENTRE FOR
INFORMATION SYSTEMS)
Riverwalk House, 157–161 Millbank, London SWIP 4RT
Tel 071-217 3000
Gildengate House, Upper Green Lane, Norwich NR3 IDW
Tel 0603-694620

Director (G3), vacant
Deputy Director (G4), W. Houldsworth

OFFICE OF SCIENCE AND TECHNOLOGY
70 Whitehall, London SWIA 2AS
Tel 071-270 3000
Grove House, 16 Orange Street, London WC2H 7ED
Tel 071-270 6944
Sanctuary Buildings, Great Smith Street, London SWIP 3BT
Tel 071-925 5000

Chief Scientific Adviser and Head of Office, Prof.
W. D. P. Stewart, FRS, FRSE

Private Secretary (G7), Dr L. Drummond
Director-General of Research Councils (from Jan. 1994),
vacant

BRANCH A
Grade 3, R. Foster
Grade 5, Dr D. P. Walker (*Domestic science and technology
issues*); D. A. Warren (*International science and technology
issues*); Dr J. McGuinness (*ACOST Secretariat*)

BRANCH B
Grade 3, D. A. Wilkinson; Dr D. G. Libby
Grade 5, Dr J. Partington (*General Science Policy*);
R. P. Ritzema (*International Science*)
Grade 6, Dr K. Root (*Science Budget*); Dr R. Dowdell

EXECUTIVE AGENCIES

OCCUPATIONAL HEALTH SERVICE
18–20 Hill Street, Edinburgh EH2 3NB
Tel 031-220 4177
The Occupational Health Service provides services and
advice to all government departments and executive agencies,
and to other public bodies, on matters relating to the health
of their employees in their working environment.
Medical Adviser and Director, Dr E. C. McCloy
Deputy Medical Adviser, Dr P. Brown

CIVIL SERVICE COLLEGE
Sunningdale Park, Ascot, Berks. SL5 0QE
Tel 0344-634000
11 Belgrave Road, London SWIV IRB
Tel 071-834 6644
The College provides training in management and profes-
sional skills for civil servants and for those working in the
private sector.
Chief Executive (G3), Miss M. T. Neville-Rolfe
Director of Studies (G5), D. R. Smith
Director of Services and Resources (G5), I. Cameron
Business Group Directors (G5/G6), Ms C. M. Bentley; Ms
E. Chennells; J. G. Fuller; G. W. Llewellyn;
P. J. C. O'Connell; P. G. Tebby; Miss J. A. Topham
College Secretary (G6), Miss M. A. Wood

RECRUITMENT AND ASSESSMENT SERVICES (RAS)
Alencon Link, Basingstoke, Hants. RG21 IJB
Tel 0256-29222
24 Whitehall, London SWIA 2ED
Tel 071-210 3000
RAS provides professional recruitment and staff development
services to the Civil Service and other public sector bodies.
Chief Executive, M. D. Geddes
Grade 5, A. A. Carter (*London*)
Grade 6, F. D. Bedford (*London*); K. N. Bastin

CHESSINGTON COMPUTER CENTRE
Government Buildings, Leatherhead Road, Chessington,
Surrey KT9 2LT
Tel 081-391 3800

Director (G5), R. N. Edwards

CENTRAL ADJUDICATION SERVICES
Quarry House, Leeds LS2 7UB
Tel 0532-324000

The Chief Adjudication Officer and Chief Child Support
Officer are independent statutory authorities under the Social
Security Act 1975 (as amended) and the Child Support Act

1991. They are appointed by the Secretary of State for Social Security to give advice to adjudication officers and child support officers, to keep under review the operation of the systems of adjudication, and to report annually to the Secretary of State on adjudication standards.

Adjudication officers make decisions of first instance on all claims for social security cash benefits, and child support officers make decisions of first instance on applications for child maintenance made to the Child Support Agency. Officers of the Chief Adjudication Officer also enter written observations on all appeals made to the Social Security Commissioners, and officers of the Chief Child Support Officer make written observations on appeals to the Child Support Commissioners.

Chief Adjudication Officer and Chief Child Support Officer,
K. Bellamy, CBE

CENTRAL STATISTICAL OFFICE
Great George Street, London SW1P 3AQ
Tel 071-270 6363/6364

The work of the Central Statistical Office encompasses data collection from businesses; the preparation and publication of macro-economic statistics and social statistics abstracts; statistics relating to institutional sectors and financial statistics; the retail prices index and the family expenditure survey; liaison with international statistical bodies; and central management of the Government Statistical Service (GSS). The Central Statistical Office became an executive agency of the Treasury in November 1991.

Director and Head of the Government Statistical Service (G1A), W. McLennan
Private Secretary, Miss H. Shanks
Deputy Director and Director of National Accounts (G3), D. C. L. Wroe
Head of GSS and General Division (G3), R. G. Ward
Head of Business Statistics Division (G3), R. Norton
Head of Sector Accounts Division (G3), J. E. Kidgell
Head of Central Services Division (G4), Dr L. Mayhew
Head of Information (G5), I. Scott

GSS AND GENERAL DIVISION
Heads of Branches (G5), D. C. K. Stirling (*GSS policy and management*); Miss J. Church (*Social, regional and household expenditure*); Ms M. Haworth (*Retail Prices Index*); R. J. Scott (*Registers and materials inquiries*)

DEPUTY DIRECTOR'S OFFICE
Heads of Branches (G5), Miss S. P. Carter (*National accounts and economic assessment*); P. B. Kenny (*Statistical methods and quality*)

BUSINESS STATISTICS DIVISION
Heads of Branches (G5), K. Francombe (*Index of production*); C. J. Spiller (*Production censuses and capital expenditure inquiries*); G. D. Walker (*Distribution and services*); R. G. Lynch (*Product prices and sales*); K. Mansell (*Output and expenditure*)

SECTOR ACCOUNTS DIVISION
Heads of Branches (G5), G. Jenkinson (*Current account*); B. J. Buckingham (*Balance of payments*); Mrs P. Walker (*Company and personal sector accounts*); P. Turnbull (*Public sector and financial accounts*); S. Clark (*Financial institutions*)

CENTRAL SERVICES DIVISION
Heads of Branches (G5), Dr J. Ludley (*Information systems*); I. Scott (*Press and publications*); D. R. Lewis (*Personnel and finance*)

CERTIFICATION OFFICE FOR TRADE UNIONS AND EMPLOYERS' ASSOCIATIONS
27 Wilton Street, London SW1X 7AZ
Tel 071-210 3734/5

The Certification Office is an independent statutory authority. The Certification Officer is appointed by the Secretary of State for Employment and is responsible for receiving and scrutinizing annual returns from trade unions and employers' associations; for reimbursing certain costs of trade unions' postal ballots; for dealing with complaints concerning trade union elections; for ensuring observance of statutory requirements governing political funds and trade union mergers; and for certifying the independence of trade unions.
Certification Officer, E. G. Whybrew
Assistant Certification Officer, G. S. Osborne

SCOTLAND
58 Frederick Street, Edinburgh EH2 1LN
Tel 031-226 3224
Assistant Certification Officer for Scotland, J. L. J. Craig

CHARITY COMMISSION
St Alban's House, 57–60 Haymarket, London SW1Y 4QX
Tel 071-210 4477
Graeme House, Derby Square, Liverpool L2 7SB
Tel 051-227 3191
Woodfield House, Tangier, Taunton, Somerset TA1 4BL
Tel 0823-345000

The Charity Commission was established under the Charities Act 1960 with the general function of promoting the effective use of charitable resources in England and Wales. The Commissioners give information and advice to charity trustees to make the administration of their charity more effective, investigate misconduct and the abuse of charitable assets and take or recommend remedial action, and maintain a public register of charities. The Commission does not have at its disposal any funds with which to make grants to organizations or individuals.

At the end of 1992 the total number of registered charities was 170,357.
Chief Commissioner (G3), R. Fries
Commissioners (G3), J. Farquharson; R. M. C. Venables
Commissioners (part-time) (G4), M. Webber; Mrs D. H. Yeo
Deputy Commissioners (G5), J. A. Dutton; J. F. Claricoat; G. S. Goodchild; K. M. Dibble; S. Slack
Secretary and Executive Director (G4), Mrs E. A. Shaw
Director of Operations (G5), V. F. Mitchell
Grade 6, Mrs H. M. Phillips; Miss D. F. Taylor; S. K. Sen; P. P. White; N. M. Mackenzie; M. J. Harbottle; J. Tipping; R. E. Edwards; Miss V. A. Nuttall
Senior Legal Assistants, A. H. Bilbrough; I. M. Davies
Grade 7, R. E. Hatton; A. O. Polak; M. C. T. Seymour; K. M. Dickin; M. J. McManus; G. B. Ward; J. S. Holdsworth; M. Pearson; P. W. Somerfield; R. G. Dawes; Miss G. Fletcher; A. J. George; J. Thorne; I. Spencer; Mrs P. D. W. Holt; J. Kilby; R. Jones; Miss B. Lythgoe; R. A. V. Corden; J. M. Reid; Ms L. Matlock
Official Custodian for Charities (G6), Mrs S. E. Gillingham
Deputy Official Custodian (G7), M. Fry
Establishment Officer (G5), Mrs J. Cotton

The departments responsible for charities in Scotland and Northern Ireland are:

SCOTLAND – Scottish Home and Health Department, Charities Division, New St Andrews House, Edinburgh EHI 3DE. Tel: 031-244 2206

NORTHERN IRELAND – Department of Finance and Personnel, Charities Branch, Rosepark House, Upper Newtownards Road, Belfast BT4 3NR. Tel: 0232-484567

CHIEF ADJUDICATION OFFICER AND CHIEF CHILD SUPPORT OFFICER
— *see* Central Adjudication Services

CHURCH COMMISSIONERS
1 Millbank, London SWIP 3JZ
Tel 071-222 7010

The Church Commissioners were established in 1948 by the amalgamation of Queen Anne's Bounty (established 1704) and the Ecclesiastical Commissioners (established 1836).

The Commissioners are responsible for the management of most of the Church of England's assets, the income from which is predominantly used to pay, house and pension the clergy. The Commissioners own over 150,000 acres of agricultural land, a number of residential estates in central London, and commercial property in Great Britain and the USA. They also carry out administrative duties in connection with pastoral reorganization and redundant churches, and have been designated by the General Synod as the central stipends authority of the Church of England.

CONSTITUTION
The Commissioners are: the Archbishops of Canterbury and of York; the 41 diocesan bishops; five deans or provosts, ten other clergy and ten lay persons appointed by the General Synod; four lay persons nominated by The Queen; four persons nominated by the Archbishop of Canterbury; the Lord Chancellor; the Lord President of the Council; the First Lord of the Treasury; the Chancellor of the Exchequer; the Secretary of State for the Home Department; the Speaker of the House of Commons; the Lord Chief Justice; the Master of the Rolls; the Attorney-General; the Solicitor-General; the Lord Mayor and two Aldermen of the City of London; the Lord Mayor of York; and one representative from each of the Universities of Oxford and Cambridge.

INCOME AND EXPENDITURE
for year ended 31 December 1992

INCOME	£ million
Stock exchange investments	76.6
Property	63.2
Interest from loans, etc.	28.2
Diocesan/parish contributions for stipends	88.7
Total	£256.7

EXPENDITURE	
Clergy stipends	150.0
Clergy and widows' pensions	63.9
Clergy houses	10.2
Episcopal administration and payments to Chapters	10.8
Church buildings	2.6
Administrative expenses of the Commissioners and related bodies	11.2
Carried forward	8.0
Total	£256.7

Between 1988 and 1992, the value of the Church's assets fell by £800 million.

CHURCH ESTATES COMMISSIONERS
First, Sir Michael Colman, Bt.
Second, The Rt. Hon. Michael Alison, MP
Third, Mrs M. H. Laird

OFFICERS
Secretary, P. Locke
Assistant Secretaries:
The Accountant, G. C. Baines
Management Accountant, B. J. Hardy
Commercial Property, M. G. S. Farrell
Computer Manager, J. W. Ferguson
Secretariat, W. R. Herbert
Estates, P. H. P. Shaw, LVO
Houses, D. J. B. Long
Investments Manager, A. S. Hardy
Pastoral, and Redundant Churches, M. D. Elengorn
Stipends and Allocations, R. S. Hopgood
Senior Architect, J. A. Taylor
Principals, A. W. Atkins; Miss A. M. Mackie; G. Wills; J. A. W. Elloy; C. R. Bullen; D. W. H. Lewis; N. J. Neil-Smith; J. W. Wallace; R. A. Scott

LEGAL DEPARTMENT
Official Solicitor, J. P. Guy
Deputy Solicitor, Miss S. M. S. Jones
Solicitors, Miss J. M. Bland; J. D. Carter; Miss J. A. Egar; R. D. C. Murray; Ms A. R. Usher

CIVIL AVIATION AUTHORITY
CAA House, 45–59 Kingsway, London WC2B 6TE
Tel 071-379 7311

The CAA is responsible for the economic regulation of UK airlines by licensing air routes and air travel organizers and by approving fares; for the safety regulation of UK civil aviation by the certification of airlines and aircraft, and by licensing aerodromes, flight crew and aircraft engineers; and, through the National Air Traffic Services, for the provision of air traffic control and telecommunications services.
Chairman (part-time) (£60,606), The Rt. Hon. C. Chataway
Managing Director, T. Murphy, CBE
Secretary, Miss G. M. E. White

COMMONWEALTH DEVELOPMENT CORPORATION
1 Bessborough Gardens, London SWIV 2JQ
Tel 071-828 4488

The Commonwealth Development Corporation is charged with the task of assisting overseas countries in the development of their economies. Its main activity is providing long-term finance, as loans and risk capital, for projects. The Corporation's area of operations includes British dependent territories and, with ministerial approval, Commonwealth or other developing countries. At present, the Corporation is authorized to operate in more than 60 countries and territories. The Corporation is authorized to borrow up to £850 million.
Chairman (part-time), Sir Peter Leslie
Deputy Chairman (part-time), Sir Michael Caine
Members (part-time), Mrs A. Wright; Prof. M. Faber; E. B. Waide, OBE; M. D. McWilliam; Prof. I. Carruthers; J. Zochonis
Chief Executive, J. D. Eccles, CBE (*until May 1994*); Dr R. Reynolds (*from May 1994*)

COMMONWEALTH SECRETARIAT
— see Index

COMMONWEALTH WAR GRAVES COMMISSION
2 Marlow Road, Maidenhead, Berks. SL6 7DX
Tel 0628-34221

The Commonwealth War Graves Commission (formerly Imperial War Graves Commission) was founded by royal charter in 1917. It is responsible for the commemoration of 1,694,930 members of the forces of the Commonwealth who fell in the two world wars. More than one million graves are maintained in 23,071 burial grounds throughout the world. Over three-quarters of a million men and women who have no known grave or who were cremated are commemorated by name on memorials built by the Commission.

The funds of the Commission are derived from the six governments participating in its work, i.e. the UK, Australia, Canada, India, New Zealand and South Africa.
President, HRH The Duke of Kent, KG, GCMG, GCVO, ADC
Chairman, The Secretary of State for Defence in the UK
Vice-Chairman, Air Chief Marshal Sir Joseph Gilbert, KCB, CBE
Members, The Secretary of State for the Environment in the UK; The High Commissioners in London for Australia, Canada, India and New Zealand; the Ambassador in London for the Republic of South Africa; Dame Janet Fookes, DBE, MP; Sir Nigel Mobbs; Adm. Sir Nicholas Hunt, GCB, LVO; The Viscount Ridley, KG, TD; Prof. R. J. O'Neill, AO; Mrs L. Golding, MP; Sir Harold Walker, KCMG; Gen. Sir John Akenhurst, KCB, CBE
Director-General and Secretary to the Commission, D. Kennedy
Deputy Directors-General, T. F. Penfold (*Administration*); R. J. Dalley (*Operations*)
Directors, T. V. Reeves (*Finance*); A. Coombe (*Works*); D. C. Parker (*Horticulture*); H. Mackay (*Management Services*); D. R. Parker (*Personnel*); J. P. D. Gee (*Information and Secretariat*)
Legal Adviser and Solicitor, G. C. Reddie
Hon. Artistic Adviser, Prof. Sir Peter Shepheard, CBE
Hon. Botanical Adviser, Prof. G. T. Prance, D.Phil., FLS

IMPERIAL WAR GRAVES ENDOWMENT FUND
Trustees, H. U. A. Lambert (*Chairman*); Air Chief Marshal Sir Joseph Gilbert, KCB, CBE; The Lord Remnant, CVO
Secretary to the Trustees, T. V. Reeves

COUNTRYSIDE COMMISSION
John Dower House, Crescent Place, Cheltenham, Glos. GL50 3RA
Tel 0242-521381

The Countryside Commission was set up in 1968 and is an independent agency which promotes the conservation and enhancement of landscape beauty in England. It encourages the provision and improvement of facilities in the countryside, and works to secure access for open air recreation. Since 1982 the Commission has been funded by an annual grant from the Department of the Environment. Members of the Commission are appointed by the Secretary of State for the Environment.
Chairman, Sir John Johnson, KCMG

Director-General (*G3*), M. Dower
Directors (*G5*), R. Clarke (*Policy*); M. J. Kirby (*Operations*); M. Taylor (*Resources*)
National Heritage Adviser, P. Walshe
Head of Corporate Planning (*G7*), vacant
Head of Land Use Branch (*G7*), R. Roberts
Head of Recreation and Access Branch (*G7*), J. W. B. Worth
Head of Public Affairs (*G7*), Ms P. Palmer
Head of Finance and Establishments (*G7*), V. Ellis
Head of National Parks and Planning Branch (*G7*), R. Lloyd
Head of Environmental Protection Branch (*G7*), I. Mitchell
Regional Officers (*G7*), K. Buchanan, (*Newcastle*); Dr M. Carroll (*Cambridge*); Dr S. A. Bucknall (*Leeds*); E. Holdaway (*Bristol*); vacant (*Manchester*); D. E. Coleman (*London*); F. S. Walmsley (*Birmingham*)
Special Initiatives, Dr M. Rawson (*Community Forests*); S. Bell (*National Forest*); T. Allen (*Countryside Stewardship*)

COUNTRYSIDE COUNCIL FOR WALES/ CYNGOR CEFN GWLAD CYMRU
Plas Penrhos, Fford Penrhos, Bangor, Gwynedd LL57 2LQ
Tel 0248-370444

The Countryside Council for Wales took over the functions of the Nature Conservancy Council in Wales and the Countryside Commission in Wales in April 1991. It is the Government's statutory adviser on wildlife, countryside and maritime conservation matters in Wales, and it is the executive authority for the conservation of habitats and wildlife. It promotes the protection of the Welsh landscape and encourages opportunities for public access and enjoyment of the countryside. It provides grant aid to local authorities, voluntary organizations and individuals to pursue countryside management. It is funded by the Welsh Office and accountable to the Secretary of State for Wales, who appoints its members.
Chairman, E. M. W. Griffith, CBE
Chief Executive, Prof. I. Mercer
Director of Science and Policy Development, Prof. G. W. Jones
Director of Resources, R. J. Davies
Director of Operations, I. R. Bonner
Chief Ecologist, Dr M. E. Smith
Head of Interpretation and Education, Dr L. D. Gruffydd

COVENT GARDEN MARKET AUTHORITY
Covent House, New Covent Garden Market, London SW8 5NX
Tel 071-720 2211

The Covent Garden Market Authority is constituted under the Covent Garden Market Acts 1961 to 1977, the members being appointed by the Minister of Agriculture, Fisheries and Food. The Authority owns and operates the 56-acre New Covent Garden Markets (fruit, vegetables, flowers) which have been trading since 1974.
Chairman (*part-time*), W. P. Bowman, OBE
Members (*part-time*), P. J. Hunt; J. A. Harvey, CBE; R. Smith, OBE; Sir Peter Reynolds, CBE; Mrs A. M. Vinton
General Manager, Dr P. M. Liggins
Secretary, C. Farey

CRIMINAL INJURIES COMPENSATION BOARD

Blythswood House, 200 West Regent Street, Glasgow
G2 4SW
Tel 041-221 0945
Whittington House, 19 Alfred Place, London WC1E 7LG
Tel 071-355 6802

The Board was constituted in 1964 to administer the government scheme for *ex gratia* payments of compensation to victims of crimes of violence.

Chairman (part-time) (£27,385), The Lord Carlisle of Bucklow, PC, QC
Members, J. F. A. Archer, QC; D. Barker, QC, Sir Derek Bradbeer, OBE; D. Brennan, QC; Sir David Calcutt, QC; H. Carlisle, QC; B. W. Chedlow, QC; J. Cherry, QC; M. Churchouse; Miss B. Cooper, QC; Miss D. Cotton, QC; J. D. Crowley; His Hon. Judge da Cunha; T. A. K. Drummond, QC; C. Fawcett, QC; W. Gage, QC; Sir Richard Gaskell; E. Gee; G. M. Hamilton, QC; Sir Arthur Hoole; His Hon. Judge Kingham; J. Law, QC; M. E. Lewer, QC; M. Lewis, QC; C. Lindsay, QC; Lord Macaulay of Bragar, QC; J. M. McGhie, QC, D. Mackay, QC; N. Miscampbell, QC; I. M. S. Park, CBE; T. Preston, QC; Miss S. Ritchie, QC; D. B. Robertson, QC; C. Seagroatt, QC; E. Stone, QC; D. M. Thomas, OBE, QC; D. O. Thomas, QC; P. Weitzman, QC; His Hon. Sir David West-Russell; C. H. Whitby, QC; J. Leighton Williams, QC
Director, P. G. Spurgeon

CROFTERS COMMISSION

4-6 Castle Wynd, Inverness IV2 3EQ
Tel 0463-237231

The Crofters Commission is a statutory body established in 1955 which is responsible for reorganizing, developing and regulating crofting in the seven crofting (and former county) areas of Argyll, Caithness, Inverness, Orkney, Ross and Cromarty, Shetland and Sutherland. The Commission keeps under review all matters relating to crofting, advises the Secretary of State for Scotland on crofting matters and liaises with other relevant bodies. The Commission also administers the Crofting Counties Agricultural Grants (Scotland) Scheme 1988.

Chairman, H. A. M. Maclean
Members (part-time), B. T. Hunter; Fr. J. A. Macdonald; Mrs A. Rennie; P. Morrison; A. Cameron; W. Ritchie
Secretary (G6), M. Grantham

CROWN AGENTS FOR OVERSEA GOVERNMENTS AND ADMINISTRATIONS

St Nicholas House, St Nicholas Road, Sutton, Surrey SM1 1EL
Tel 081-643 3311

Incorporated by Act of Parliament, the Crown Agents are commercial, financial and professional agents for over 100 governments and over 300 public authorities, international bodies and other organizations, primarily in the public sector.
Chairman, D. H. Probert
Managing Director, P. F. Berry

CROWN ESTATE

16 Carlton House Terrace, London SW1Y 5AH
Tel 071-210 4377

The land revenues of the Crown in England and Wales have been collected on the public account since 1760, when George III surrendered them and received a fixed annual payment or Civil List. At the time of the surrender the gross revenues amounted to about £89,000 and the net return to about £11,000.

In the year ended 31 March 1993, the gross income from the Crown Estate totalled £119,924,000. The sum of £70,500,000 was paid to the Exchequer in 1992–3 as surplus revenue.

The land revenues in Ireland have been carried to the Consolidated Fund since 1820; from 1 April 1923, as regards the Republic of Ireland, they have been collected and administered by the Irish Government.

The land revenues in Scotland were transferred to the Crown Estate Commissioners in 1833.

First Commissioner and Chairman (part-time), The Earl of Mansfield and Mansfield
Second Commissioner and Chief Executive, C. K. Howes, CB
Commissioners (part-time), R. B. Caws, CBE; P. Sober; G. D. Inge-Innes-Lillingston, CVO, CBE; J. N. C. James, CBE; A. S. Macdonald, CBE; J. H. M. Norris, CBE
Deputy Chief Executives, D. E. Murray (*Property*); D. E. G. Griffiths (*Finance and Administration*)
Crown Estate Surveyor, C. F. Hynes
Asset Managers (Urban Estates), M. W. Dillon; J. S. Ellingford; B. T. O'Connoll; M. Tree
Housing Manager, R. Wyatt
Business Manager, Agricultural Estates, R. J. Mulholland
Asset Managers, Agricultural Estates, J. Stumbke; I. Gorwyn
Business Manager, Marine Estates, F. G. Parrish
Asset Managers, Marine Estates, P. Davies; A. Murray
Information Systems Manager, D. Kingston-Smith
Property Services and Technical Manager, P. Shearmur
Head of Valuation and Investment Analysis, R. Spence
Head of Building Services, R. Turner
Internal Audit Manager, J. E. Ford
Finance Manager, J. G. Lelliott
Corporate Services Manager, M. E. Beckwith
Legal Adviser, M. L. Davies
Deputy Legal Adviser, H. Turnsek
Solicitors, J. B. Postgate; R. T. Hayward; M. Drayton; P. Horner; D. R. Apthorpe
Senior Legal Assistant, M. A. J. Cordingley
Personnel Manager, R. J. Blake
Public Relations and Press Officer, Mrs G. Coates

SCOTLAND
10 Charlotte Square, Edinburgh EH2 4BR
Tel 031-226 2741
Crown Estate Receiver for Scotland, M. J. Gravestock
Asset Managers (Scottish Estates), N. Ruck Keene; I. Pritchard; Ms S. Harvey
Glenlivet Estate Ranger, A. Wells

WINDSOR ESTATE
The Great Park, Windsor, Berks. SL4 2HT
Tel 0753-860222
Surveyor and Deputy Ranger, A. R. Wiseman, MVO
Keeper of Gardens, J. Bond

CROWN PROSECUTION SERVICE

— *see* pages 378–9

BOARD OF CUSTOMS AND EXCISE
New King's Beam House, 22 Upper Ground, London
SE1 9PJ
Tel 071-620 1313

Commissioners of Customs were first appointed in 1671 and housed by the King in London. The Excise Department was formerly under the Inland Revenue Department and was amalgamated with the Customs Department in 1909.

HM Customs and Excise is responsible for collecting and administering customs and excise duties and value added tax, and advises the Chancellor of the Exchequer on any matters connected with them. The Department is also responsible for preventing and detecting the evasion of revenue laws and for enforcing a range of prohibitions and restrictions on the importation of certain classes of goods. In addition, the Department undertakes certain agency work on behalf of other departments, including the compilation of UK overseas trade statistics from customs import and export documents.

THE BOARD
Chairman (G1), Mrs V. P. M. Strachan, CB
  Private Secretaries, J. Wild; Miss J. C. Huneburg
Deputy Chairmen (G2), P. Jefferson Smith, CB;
  A. W. Russell
Commissioners (G3), P. R. H. Allen; D. F. O. Battle;
  A. C. Sawyer; L. J. Harris; Mrs E. Woods; M. J. Eland;
  M. R. Brown

HEADQUARTERS OFFICE
Head of Information Technology (G4), A. G. H. Paynter
Assistant Secretaries (G5), P. Kent; D. A. Walton; I. Walton;
  A. Killikelly; M. Peach; K. M. Romanski;
  B. E. G. Banks; D. C. Hewett; C. J. Holloway; P. Trevett;
  B. G. Dawbarn; Mrs M. Smith; J. Campbell;
  V. C. Whittington; C. Arnott; D. P. Child; R. Kellaway;
  M. F. Knox, CBE; F. A. D. Rush; W. L. Parker;
  L. I. Stark; A. P. Allen; J. Meyler; T. Byrne;
  A. Aitchison; D. Layton; S. Kingaby; M. Joyce;
  D. Chilver; A. Howard; B. Orr; H. Neuburger;
  J. Maclean; C. R. S. Talbot; R. McAfee; M. Norgrove
Head of Information (G7), Ms L. J. Sinclair

VAT CENTRAL UNIT
Controller (G5), D. E. J. Nissen

SOLICITOR'S OFFICE
Solicitor (G2), vacant
Principal Assistant Solicitors (G3), G. Fotherby;
  R. D. S. Wylie
Assistant Solicitors (G5), M. Michael; M. A. Cooper;
  M. C. K. Gasper; Miss A. E. Bolt; Miss S. G. Linton;
  J. A. Quinn; I. D. Napper; D. J. C. McIntyre;
  D. M. North; C. Allen; Mrs J. Clarke; J. Tester

ACCOUNTANT AND COMPTROLLER-GENERAL'S OFFICE
Accountant and Comptroller-General (G5), D. C. Hewitt
Deputy Accountants-General (G6), G. B. Fox; B. Wood;
  D. J. Coyne

STATISTICAL OFFICE
Controller (G5), A. H. Cowley

INVESTIGATION DIVISION
Chief Investigation Officer (G5), F. D. Tweddle

COLLECTORS OF CUSTOMS AND EXCISE (G5)
England and Wales:
Birmingham, R. A. Flavill
Dover, R. Crossley

East Anglia, R. C. Shepherd
East Midlands, M. D. Patten
Leeds, H. Peden
Liverpool, C. Roberts
London Airports, J. Bugge
London Central, Mrs F. Boardman
London North and West, J. Galloway, OBE
London Port, R. L. H. Lawrence
London South, T. S. Archer
Manchester, J. C. Bernard
Northampton, A. R. Ball
Northern England, J. A. Rigby
Southampton, C. J. Packman
South Wales and the Borders, W. I. Stuttle
South-west England, P. B. Grange
Thames Valley, A. Bowen

Scotland:
Edinburgh, W. F. Coghill
Glasgow and Clyde, T. F. Jessop

Northern Ireland:
Belfast, T. W. Logan

OFFICE OF THE DATA PROTECTION REGISTRAR
Wycliffe House, Water Lane, Wilmslow, Cheshire SK9 5AX
Tel 0625-535711 *(administration)*; 0625-535777 *(enquiries)*

The Office of the Data Protection Registrar was created by the Data Protection Act 1984. It is the Registrar's duty to compile and maintain the Register of Data Users and Computer Bureaux and to provide facilities for members of the public to examine the Register; to promote observance of data protection principles; to consider complaints made by data subjects; to disseminate information about the Act; to encourage the production of codes of practice by trade associations and other bodies; to guide data users in complying with data protection principles; to co-operate with other parties to the Council of Europe Convention and act as UK authority for the purposes of Article 13 of the Convention; and to report annually to Parliament on the performance of his functions.
Registrar, E. J. Howe, CBE

MINISTRY OF DEFENCE
— *see pages 392–5*

DESIGN COUNCIL
28 Haymarket, London SW1Y 4SU
Tel 071-839 8000

The Design Council's aim is to improve the design of British products and hence their competitiveness by advising companies on up-to-date practice in engineering and industrial design; presenting the annual British Design Awards; publishing information to help manufacturers, designers, and others professionally involved in design; and promoting improvements in design education and training at all levels. The headquarters and main exhibition area are in London and there are offices in Belfast, Birmingham, Glasgow, Leeds, Newcastle upon Tyne and Treforest in Wales. The Design Council is funded partly by a government grant-in-aid and partly by earned revenues.

Chairman (acting), C. Welch
Director-General, I. Owen, CBE

For research centres of the Economic and Social Science Research Council, *see* page 710.

THE DUCHY OF CORNWALL
10 Buckingham Gate, London SW1E 6LA
Tel 071-834 7346

The Duchy of Cornwall was instituted by Edward III in 1337 for the support of his eldest son, Edward, the Black Prince, and since 1503 the eldest surviving son of the Sovereign has, as heir apparent, succeeded to the dukedom by inheritance. It is the oldest of the English duchies. Before elevation to a dukedom, it was an earldom from 1227, when Richard, King of the Romans and younger brother of Henry III, was created Earl of Cornwall.

THE PRINCE'S COUNCIL
HRH The Prince of Wales, KG, KT, GCB; The Lord Ashburton, KCVO (*Lord Warden of the Stannaries*); The Earl Cairns, CBE (*Receiver-General*); R. J. A. Carnwath, QC (*Attorney-General to the Prince of Wales*); J. N. C. James, CBE (*Secretary and Keeper of the Records*); Earl of Shelburne; Cdr. R. J. Aylard, RN; J. E. Pugsley; A. M. J. Galsworthy; C. Howes; W. N. Hood, CBE; The Earl Peel

OTHER OFFICERS
Auditors, Sir Jeffery Bowman; I. Brindle; H. Hughes
Sheriff (1993–4), R. Gilbert

THE DUCHY OF LANCASTER
Lancaster Place, Strand, London WC2E 7ED
Tel 071-836 8277

The estates and jurisdiction known as the Duchy and County Palatine of Lancaster have been attached to the Crown since 1399, when John of Gaunt's son came to the throne as Henry IV. As the Lancaster inheritance it goes back to 1265. Edward III erected Lancashire into a County Palatine in 1351.
Chancellor of the Duchy of Lancaster, The Rt. Hon. William Waldegrave, MP
Attorney-General and Attorney and Serjeant within the County Palatine of Lancaster, T. A. W. Lloyd, QC
Receiver-General, Maj. Sir Shane Blewitt, KCVO
Vice-Chancellor, The Hon. Mr Justice Morritt, CVO
Clerk of the Council, M. K. Ridley, CVO
Solicitor, I. J. Dicker
Chief Clerk, Col. F. N. J. Davies

ECONOMIC AND SOCIAL RESEARCH COUNCIL
Polaris House, North Star Avenue, Swindon SN2 1UJ
Tel 0793-413000

The ESRC is an independent, government-funded body established by royal charter in 1965. It promotes and supports high-quality basic, strategic and applied social science research and related post-graduate training with the aim of increasing understanding of social and economic change and thereby enhancing the UK's industrial competitiveness and quality of life.
Chairman, Prof. H. Newby
Secretary, W. Solesbury

DEPARTMENT FOR EDUCATION
Sanctuary Buildings, Great Smith Street, London SW1P 3BT
Tel 071-925 5000

The Government Department of Education was, until the establishment of a separate office, a committee of the Privy Council appointed in 1839 to supervise the distribution of certain grants which had been made by Parliament since 1834. The Act of 1899 established the Board of Education, with a President and Parliamentary Secretary, and created a Consultative Committee. The Education Act of 1944 established the Ministry of Education. In April 1964 the office of the Minister of Science was combined with the Ministry to form the Department of Education and Science. In July 1992, responsibility for science was transferred to the Office of Public Service and Science and the department was re-named the Department for Education. It has overall responsibility for education in England, and for the Government's relations with universities in England, Wales and Scotland.

A review of the department's role and organization, and of its management, personnel and policies, was due to be completed in October 1993.
Secretary of State for Education, The Rt. Hon. John Patten, MP
 Private Secretary, Miss C. Bienkowska
 Special Adviser, C. Grantham
 Parliamentary Private Secretary, M. Carrington, MP
Minister of State, The Baroness Blatch, CBE, PC
 Private Secretary, T. Linden
 Parliamentary Private Secretary, D. Evennett, MP
Parliamentary Under-Secretaries of State, Erich Forth, MP; Tim Boswell, MP; Robin Squire, MP
Permanent Secretary (G1), Sir Geoffrey Holland, KCB
 Private Secretary, K. Hedger
Deputy Secretaries (G2), R. J. Dawe, CB, OBE; J. M. M. Vereker, CB; J. C. Hedger
Under-Secretaries (G3), P. A. Shaw (*Director of Establishments*); C. A. Clark; D. M. Forrester; R. D. Horne (*Accountant-General*); S. R. C. Jones; E. R. Morgan; B. M. Norbury; M. J. Richardson; R. N. Ricks (*Legal Adviser*); N. J. Sanders; C. H. Saville; N. Summers
Chief Architect (G4), P. Benwell

ESTABLISHMENTS AND ORGANIZATION BRANCH
Assistant Secretaries (G5), Mrs H. Douglas; M. F. Hipkins; A. K. C. Gibson
Senior Principals (G6), H. H. Barrick; G. H. N. Evans; S. Green
Principals (G7), R. Ward; K. R. Fitzgerald; Mrs M. J. Lawrence; S. J. Bishop; Mrs J. M. Craggs; M. L. Lyons; Miss B. M. Smart; A. W. Wilshaw

SCHOOLS BRANCH 1
Assistant Secretaries (G5), A. Clarke; A. J. Shaw; A. J. Sargent; J. W. Whitaker
Principals (G7), M. E. Malt; A. G. Short; T. C. Tarrant; Miss L. M. Clarke; N. R. Flint; Mrs A. C. Jeffery; Mrs S. G. Evans; Mrs R. M. King; Ms M. Pedersen; Mrs C. K. Saville; Ms A. Barlow; P. W. Fulford-Jones; Ms M. Moon; K. L. R. English; I. N. Walford

SCHOOLS BRANCH 2
Assistant Secretaries (G5), T. B. Jeffery; Ms
J. F. Cramphorn; Mrs P. A. Masters; P. S. Lewis
Principals (G7), C. Dowe; D. Noble; G. A. Holley;
M. Spearing; Miss S. A. Clarke; S. Dance; J. Ratcliff;
A. B. Thompson; Mrs M. Farthing; S. Jetha; R. Mace;
M. Williams

SCHOOLS BRANCH 3
Assistant Secretaries (G5), M. B. Baker; Mrs
C. M. Chattaway; M. F. Neale; S. R. Williams
Principals (G7), Mrs J. Baker; Ms G. Beauchamp; Ms
N. Bartman; J. Lawrence; Ms E. Casbon; I. C. Loveless;
B. D. Glickman; R. J. Wood

SCHOOLS BRANCH 4
Assistant Secretaries (G5), M. C. Stark; R. L. Smith;
A. D. Adamson; P. J. Thorpe; D. G. Halladay
Senior Principal (G6), Mrs J. M. Craggs
Principals (G7), Mrs P. Bailey; J. Browning; Mrs
L. J. Chapman; C. Dee; A. Eagleton; J. Ford;
R. A. V. Jacobs; J. Moore; Ms A. Rushton; A. Sevier; Ms
E. Slater; A. P. Smith; Mrs S. Todd; Mrs C. E. Treen;
Miss C. Trudgett

ARCHITECTS AND BUILDING BRANCH
Chief Architect (G4), A. J. Branton
Chief Quantity Surveyor (G5), B. G. Whitehouse
Superintending Architects (G5), G. J. Parker; J. J. Wilson
Principal Research Officer (G7), Dr G. B. Kenny
Principal Architects (G7), E. C. Bissell; Mrs D. Holt; Miss
E. J. Lloyd-Jones, OBE; P. Lenssen; D. S. Nightingale;
Miss B. M. T. Sanders; A. J. Benson-Wilson;
J. R. C. Brooke; A. C. Thompson; Miss S. A. Legg
Principal Quantity Surveyors (G7), A. A. Jones;
G. E. Wonnacott
Principal Engineer (G7), M. J. Patel
Principal Furniture Designer (G7), N. J. Carter
SPTO Architects, Miss L. Watson; T. J. Williamson;
W. Beadling; R. H. Bishop; A. V. Brock; R. A. Butler;
Miss F. A. Cowburn; T. Dicken; J. A. Ibikunle; P. Kemp;
Mrs H. C. Nicholls
SPTO Quantity Surveyors, D. F. Ashby; C. H. C. Marshall
SPTO Engineer, R. L. Daniels
SPTO Designer, Miss A. Wadsworth

FURTHER AND HIGHER EDUCATION BRANCH 1
Assistant Secretaries (G5), A. Woollard; R. D. Hull
Principals (G7), A. Sevier; A. Smyth; M. P. Markus;
P. Cohen; A. Callaghan

FURTHER AND HIGHER EDUCATION BRANCH 2
Head of FE Support Unit (G4), B. D. Short
Assistant Secretaries (G5), S. T. Crowne; Mrs I. Wilde
Senior Principals (G6), E. F. H. Brittain; B. J. Smeaton
Principals (G7), Ms S. P. Gane; G. Carters; S. E. Kershaw;
Mrs C. West; R. K. Read

FURTHER AND HIGHER EDUCATION BRANCH 3
Assistant Secretaries (G5), Miss P. Laidlaw; M. D. Phipps;
J. S. Street
Principals (G7), D. D. Cook; J. K. Bushnell; E. D. Foster;
Mrs P. Tansley; Miss J. Spatcher

INFORMATION BRANCH
Grade 4, J. W. Coe
Senior Principal Information Officers (G6), K. B. Kerslake;
M. Paterson
Chief Information Officer (G7), T. Cook
Marketing Manager (G7), J. M. Brown

INTERNATIONAL RELATIONS, YOUTH AND GENERAL
BRANCH
Assistant Secretaries (G5), R. W. Chattaway; Miss
C. E. Hodkinson; Miss M. d'Armenia
Principals (G7), Miss L. Hanmer; J. C. Sheridan; Ms
V. Berkeley; D. Barwick; R. Troedson; D. A. Robins;
N. Cornwell

TEACHERS BRANCH
Assistant Secretaries (G5), Ms S. L. Scales; A. J. Wye;
J. Wilde
Principals (G7), Mrs G. W. Dishart; S. A. Mellor;
M. Barker; P. B. Long; D. F. Miller; N. Cornwell;
T. Dracup; S. M. Hillier

INFORMATION SYSTEMS BRANCH
Assistant Secretary (G5), A. K. C. Gibson
Senior Principals (G6), P. D. Gott; E. Herbert; N. Rudd
Principals (G7), B. Lillburn; Mrs N. A. T. Malt;
M. Midwood; A. P. Thompson; D. Craggs; J. Winkle;
M. Young; J. Fitch; G. Trevena; K. Doherty

ANALYTICAL SERVICES BRANCH
Head of Branch (G4), D. Allnutt
Chief Statisticians (G5), J. W. Gardner; H. M. Dale;
S. J. Walton
Head of Economics (G5), D. J. Thompson
Head of Operations Research Unit (G5), R. B. Ladley
Statisticians (G7), A. J. Barnett; R. K. Jain; S. N. Kew;
J. Pascoe; T. C. Knight; M. J. Davidson; N. Rudoe; Mrs
H. E. Evans; S. K. Cook; Miss A. C. Kennedy; Mrs
J. Airs
Economics Advisers (G7), J. Tarsh; M. Thompson

LEGAL BRANCH
Legal Adviser (G3), R. Ricks
Assistant Legal Advisers (G5), D. J. Aries; A. D. Preston;
M. Harris
Assistant Solicitors (G6), Ms J. L. C. Brooks; A. K. Fraser
Senior Legal Assistant (G6), N. P. Beach

INFORMATION BUREAU AND LIBRARY
Chief Librarian, Miss M. Wilson

FINANCE BRANCH
Assistant Secretaries (G5), Mrs H. M. Williams; P. F. Slade;
R. J. Green; N. J. Thirtle
Senior Principal (G6), P. J. Edwards (*Assistant Accountant-
General*)
Principals (G7), P. L. Jones; D. R. Pollard; R. J. Gardner;
S. N. Jardine; K. Fleay; P. G. Dalgleish; P. V. D. Swift;
J. J. Watson; W. Irvine; S. D. James; S. M. Philpotts

TEACHERS PENSION AGENCY
Staindrop Road, Darlington, Co. Durham DL2 9EE
Tel 0325-392929

An executive agency of the Department for Education.
Chief Executive, Mrs D. Metcalfe
Directors, K. M. Miles; P. M. Bleasdale; A. Allison;
D. G. Sanders

OFFICE FOR STANDARDS IN EDUCATION
(OFSTED)
Elizabeth House, York Road, London SE1 7PH
Tel 071–925 6800

A non-ministerial government department established in
September 1992 to keep the Secretary of State informed
about the standards and management of schools in England,
and to establish and monitor a new independent inspection
system for maintained schools in England.
HM Chief Inspector (G2), Prof. S. Sutherland

Director of Administration (G3), T. Flescher
Director of Inspection (G3), Miss A. C. Millett

INFORMATION BRANCH
Senior Principal (G6), J. Lawson

FINANCE BRANCH
Assistant Secretary (G5), B. G. Townsend
Principals (G7), H. Candappa; I. Tough; P. J. Hodgman

PERSONNEL BRANCH
Assistant Secretary (G5), Miss J. M. Phillips
Principal (G7), Miss A. F. Brown

MANAGEMENT BRANCH
Assistant Secretary (G5), C. J. Payne
Principal (G7), P. Arkell

INSPECTION AND ANALYTICAL SERVICES BRANCH
Assistant Secretary (G5), J. Grewe
Chief Statistician (G6), C. Bryant
Principal (G7), Mrs A. Jolly

INFORMATION SYSTEMS BRANCH
Senior Principal (G6), M. L. Childs

COMPETITION AND COMPLIANCE BRANCH
Principal (G7), C. J. Bramley

WORK PROGRAMME BRANCH
Principal (G7), D. Bradley

HM INSPECTORATE
Deputy Directors of Inspection (G4), A. J. Rose;
M. J. Tomlinson
Assistant Directors of Inspection (G5), Mrs C. A. Agambar;
R. J. Brake; Miss D. H. Chorley; M. J. Convey; Miss
K. Cross; A. Dobson; Mrs G. Everson; R. C. Frost;
G. Goldstein; C. D. Gould; V. Green; J. A. Hertrich; Miss
B. J. Lewis; C. P. Marshall; B. E. Merton; Miss
E. L. Passmore; C. M. Richards; P. Singh; P. R. Smith;
D. E. Soulsby; D. W. Taylor; J. V. Townshend;
D. Trainor; D. E. Walker; D. L. West; T. Wylie
There are 218 Grade 6 Inspectors

OFFICE OF ELECTRICITY REGULATION
Hagley House, Hagley Road, Birmingham B16 8QG
Tel 021-456 2100
48 Vincent Street, Glasgow G2 5TS
Tel 041-248 5917

The Office of Electricity Regulation (OFFER) is the
regulatory body for the electricity supply industry in England,
Scotland and Wales. Headed by the Director-General of
Electricity Supply, OFFER was set up under the Electricity
Act 1989 but is independent of ministerial control.
Director-General of Electricity Supply, Prof. S. C. Littlechild
Deputy Director-General, Miss P. A. Boys
Deputy Director-General for Scotland, C. P. Carter

OFFICE OF ELECTRICITY REGULATION
NORTHERN IRELAND
Brookmount Buildings, 42 Fountain Street, Belfast BT1 5EE
Tel 0232-311575

OFFER NI is the regulatory body for the electricity supply
industry in Northern Ireland.
Director-General of Electricity Supply for Northern Ireland,
G. R. Horton
Deputy Director-General, C. H. Coulthard

EMPLOYMENT DEPARTMENT GROUP
Caxton House, Tothill Street, London SW1H 9NF
Tel 071-273 3000

The Employment Department Group is responsible for
government policies aimed at producing a competitive,
efficient and flexible labour market. Its main objectives are
to help people acquire and improve their skills, tb help
unemployed and other disadvantaged people into work, to
encourage industries to train their workforce, to protect
people at work and the public from industrial risks, and to
promote women's opportunities. The Secretary of State for
Employment is responsible for setting the strategic policy
framework in consultation with the Secretaries of State for
Scotland and Wales. From April 1994, responsibility for
training policy in Scotland and Wales within these strategic
aims will be transferred to the Scottish and Welsh Offices
respectively.

The Employment Department Group's policy interests
are carried out by three bodies, all reporting to the Secretary
of State for Employment. These are the Health and Safety
Commission (*see* page 312) and ACAS (*see* page 282) and,
within the Department, the Employment Service. The
training, enterprise and education functions of the Department are carried out by the Training, Enterprise and
Education Directorate, and the responsibility for planning
and delivering many government-funded training and
enterprise programmes rests with the network of 82
independent Training and Enterprise Councils in England
and Wales and with 22 Local Enterprise Companies in
Scotland (for addresses, see local telephone directories).
Secretary of State for Employment, The Rt. Hon. David
Hunt, MBE
  Principal Private Secretary (G5), D. Russell
  Special Adviser, M. McManus
  Parliamentary Private Secretary, N. Evans, MP
Minister of State, Michael Forsyth, MP
  Parliamentary Private Secretary, Mrs A. Browning, MP
Parliamentary Under-Secretaries of State, Ann Widdecombe,
MP; The Viscount Ullswater
  Private Secretaries, S. Wood; M. Daly; Ms C. Pride
Parliamentary Clerk, Ms M. East
Permanent Secretary (G1), N. Monck
  Private Secretary, A. Virgo
Deputy Secretaries (G2), N. W. Stuart, CB; G. Reid, CB;
I. Johnston
Legal Adviser (G3), H. R. L. Purse
Special Advisers, I. Wilton; Ms C. Stratton

THE EMPLOYMENT SERVICE
An executive agency within the Department of Employment.
The Employment Service is responsible for providing services
and administering programmes to help unemployed people
get back to work as quickly as possible and to make payments
to those entitled to benefit.
Chief Executive (G3+), M. E. G. Fogden
Deputy Chief Executive (G3), J. Turner
Director of Finance and Resources (G4), A. G. Johnson
Director of Field Operations (G4), R. Phillips
Director of Business Development (G4), J. Robertson
Director of Human Resources (G4), D. B. Price

TRAINING, ENTERPRISE AND EDUCATION
DIRECTORATE
Moorfoot, Sheffield S1 4PQ
Tel 0742-753275

Director-General (G2), I. Johnston
Director of Operations (G3), S. Loveman

Head of Financial Control Unit (G5), N. Gregory
Regional Directors (G5), Ms C. Johnson (Eastern);
P. Lauener (East Midlands); Ms B. Thomas (Greater
Manchester); W. Harris (London); K. Heslop (Northern);
Ms F. Everiss (North-west); D. Main (South-east); Ms
J. Henderson (South-west); P. Thomas (West Midlands);
J. Walker (Yorkshire and Humberside)

Youth and Education
Director (G3), Mrs V. Bayliss
Heads of Branches (G5); R. Wye (Schools and Partnerships
Policy); A. Davies (Careers Service); G. Dyche (Young
People and Work); K. Franklin (Further and Higher
Education)

Training Strategy and Infrastructure
Director (G3), D. Grover
Heads of Branches (G5), B. Shaw (Training Strategy and
Secretariat); P. Keen (Employer Investment); T. Down
(Learning Methods); C. Capella (European Training Policy,
Programmes and Funding); J. Fuller (Qualifications and
Industry Training Organizations)

Planning
Director (G4), K. White
Heads of Branches (G5), M. Nicholas (Operational Policy);
B. Heatley (Resource Planning); L. Ammon (Operational
Monitoring); M. Christie (The Field Systems)

Adult Learning
Director (G3), J. Lambert
Head of Branches (G5/G6), D. Tansley (Adult Training);
G. Macnair (Special Needs and Equal Opportunities);
J. Smith (Individual Commitment)

Quality Assurance
Director (G3), N. Schofield
Heads of Branches (G5), C. Williams (Financial Analysis and
Review); J. Blizard (Quality Assurance); T. Fellows
(Quality Policy and Networking)

National Advisory Council for Education and Training
Targets (NACETT)
Director (Special Adviser), Ms C. Stratton

INDUSTRIAL RELATIONS AND INTERNATIONAL
DIRECTORATE
Director (G2), G. Reid
International Division (G3), L. Lewis
Industrial Relations Division I (G3), C. Tucker
Industrial Relations Division II (G3), R. Hillier
Statistical Services Division (G3), P. Stibbard

RESOURCES AND STRATEGY DIRECTORATE
Director (G2), N. W. Stuart, CB
Finance and Resource Management Division (G3),
M. Addison
Economics, Research and Evaluation Division (G3), Ms
P. Meadows
Strategy and Employment Policy Division (G3), P. Makeham
Personnel and Development Division (G3), D. Normington
Business Services Division (G4), K. Jordan
Information Branch (G5), B. Sutlieff

ENGLISH HERITAGE
— see Historic Buildings and Monuments Commission for
England

ENGLISH NATURE
Northminster House, Peterborough PEI IUA
Tel 0733-340345

English Nature (the Nature Conservancy Council for
England) was established by Act of Parliament in 1991 as a
result of the dissolution of the Nature Conservancy Council
and the creation of three new independent bodies responsible
for promoting nature conservation in the three component
countries of Great Britain. English Nature is responsible for
advising the Government on nature conservation in England.
It promotes, directly and through others, the conservation of
England's wildlife and natural features. It selects, establishes
and manages National Nature Reserves and identifies and
notifies Sites of Special Scientific Interest. It provides advice
and information about nature conservation, and supports
and conducts research relevant to these functions. Through
the Joint Nature Conservation Committee (see page 339), it
works with its sister organizations in Scotland and Wales on
UK and international nature conservation issues.
Chairman, The Earl of Cranbrook
Chief Executive, Dr D. R. Langslow
Chief Scientist, Dr K. L. Duff
Director, Operations, E. T. Idle
Director, Corporate Services, Miss C. E. M. Wood
Director, Policy and Development, Mrs S. Collins
Director, Communications and Corporate Affairs, I. Dair
Environmental Audit Manager, M. R. Felton
Head of Lands, W. J. Hopkin

DEPARTMENT OF THE ENVIRONMENT
2 Marsham Street, London SWIP 3EB
Tel 071-276 3000

The Department of the Environment is responsible for
planning and land use; local government; housing and
construction; inner city areas; new towns; environmental
protection; conservation areas and countryside affairs; energy
efficiency; and property holdings.
Secretary of State for the Environment, The Rt. Hon. John
Gummer, MP
Private Secretary, A. G. Riddell
Special Advisers, T. Burke; Prof. P. Hall; K. Adams
Parliamentary Private Secretary, J. Paice, MP
Minister for Housing, Inner Cities and Construction, The Rt.
Hon. Sir George Young, Bt., MP
Private Secretary, R. Anderson
Parliamentary Private Secretary, Dr C. Goodson-Wickes,
MP
Minister for Local Government and Planning, David Curry,
MP
Private Secretary, Ms K. Jennings
Parliamentary Private Secretary, D. French, MP
Minister for Environment and Countryside, Timothy Yeo, MP
Private Secretary, Ms D. Lamb
Parliamentary Private Secretary, M. Trend, MP
Special Adviser to Ministers of State, J. Gray
Parliamentary Under-Secretaries of State, Tony Baldry, MP;
The Lord Strathclyde
Private Secretaries, Miss M. Cameron; Miss D. Butler
Lord-in-Waiting, The Viscount Goschen
Private Secretary, Miss A. Moore
Parliamentary Clerk, D. S. Demorais
Permanent Secretary (G1), R. Wilson, CB
Private Secretary, Mrs B. Houlden

ORGANIZATION AND ESTABLISHMENTS
Lambeth Bridge House, London SE1 7SB
Tel 071-238 3000

Principal Establishments and Finance Officer (G2), D. J. Burr

PERSONNEL
Director (G3), J. A. Owen
Grade 5, J. Adams; K. G. Arnold; L. B. Hicks
Grade 6, M. A. L. Ross; R. E. Vidler; Miss J. A. Clark;
  J. Kingdom
Chief Welfare Officer (G7), R. J. Lintern

FINANCE CENTRAL
Under-Secretary (G3), W. F. S. Rickett
Heads of Divisions (G5), B. L. Glicksman; I. H. Nicol;
  C. P. Evans; D. L. H. Roberts

ADMINISTRATION RESOURCES
Director (G3), D. A. R. Peel
Grade 4, B. G. Rosser
Grade 5, A. C. Allberry; I. S. Elrick
Grade 6, D. Tridgell; R. Bendall; M. J. Burt; G. Knowles,
  ISO; M. R. Haselip

INFORMATION
Director (G4), M. Granatt
Grade 5, J. Gee

PLANNING, RURAL AFFAIRS AND WATER
Deputy Secretary (G2), P. C. McQuail

PLANNING DIRECTORATE
Director (G3), J. F. Ballard
Grade 5, D. N. Donaldson; R. Jones; R. G. Wakeford;
  C. L. L. Braun; M. R. Ash; J. Zetter; R. C. Mabey;
  A. M. Oliver

DIRECTORATE OF RURAL AFFAIRS
Under-Secretary (G3), R. J. A. Sharp, CB
Grade 5, R. Bunce; R. M. Pritchard; Ms S. Carter

WATER DIRECTORATE
Director (G3), N. W. Summerton
Heads of Divisions (G5), N. Dorling; A. J. C. Simcock;
  J. Vaughan; M. Nelson

Drinking Water Inspectorate
Grade 5, M. G. Healey

PLANNING INSPECTORATE
Tollgate House, Houlton Street, Bristol BS2 9DJ
Tel 0272-218950

An executive agency within the Department of the
Environment.
Chief Executive and Chief Inspector of Planning (G3), S. Crow
Deputy Chief Inspector of Planning (G4), J. I. T. Dunlop
Director of Planning Appeals (G4), A. J. M. Morgan
Assistant Chief Planning Inspectors (G5), M. I. Montague-
  Smith; J. Acton; D. F. Harris; R. E. Wilson;
  M. C. Hurley; J. Greenfield; C. Jenkins; J. Waldron; Mrs
  S. Bruton
Head of Administration (G5), D. A. C. Marshall
Head of Finance and Management Services (G5), M. Brasher

MERSEYSIDE TASK FORCE
Director (G3), J. Stoker
Controllers (G5), S. P. Sage; I. Urquhart; J. Warnock

REGIONAL OFFICES

EASTERN, Bedford – *Regional Director (G3)*, P. F. Emms;
  Regional Controllers (G5), I. C. J. Dunabin; R. A. Bird

EAST MIDLANDS, Nottingham – *Regional Director (G4)*,
  D. J. Morrison; *Regional Controller (G6)*, G. Meynell,
  MBE; R. J. Smith
NORTHERN, Newcastle upon Tyne – *Regional Director
  (G3)*, P. A. Shaw; *Regional Controllers (G5)*, Ms
  D. Caudle; R. G. Bell
NORTH-WEST, Manchester – *Regional Director (G3)*,
  J. P. Plowman; *Regional Controllers (G5)*,
  B. C. Isherwood; P. Styche; *(G6)*, P. Walton; *Chairman,
  Mersey Basin Campaign*, B. Alexander
SOUTH-EAST, London W14 – *Regional Director (G3)*,
  J. W. Fellows; *Regional Controllers (G5)*, J. B. Wilson;
  T. E. Radice; *(G6)*, E. G. Everett
SOUTH-WEST, Bristol – *Regional Director (G3)*, Ms
  E. A. Hopkins; *Regional Controllers (G5)*, S. McQuillin;
  D. N. Donaldson
WEST MIDLANDS, Birmingham – *Regional Director (G3)*,
  D. R. Ritchie; *Regional Controllers (G5)*, J. E. Northover;
  J. Darlington; Mrs P. M. Holland
YORKSHIRE AND HUMBERSIDE, Leeds – *Regional Director
  (G3)*, J. P. Henry; *Regional Controllers (G5)*,
  I. H. Crowther; Mrs E. A. Kerry

LONDON REGIONAL OFFICE
Under-Secretary (G3), Mrs L. A. Heath
Grade 5, A. Buchanan; B. Strong; A. M. Wells; I. J. Scotter

HOUSING AND URBAN GROUP
Deputy Secretary (G2), Miss E. C. Turton
Secretariat (G7), P. G. Tobia

INNER CITIES
Director (G3), M. B. Gahagan
Heads of Divisions (G5), G. L. Laufer; P. F. Unwin; Mrs
  R. Le Guen; R. A. Beattie
Grade 6, D. Stroud

HOUSING POLICY AND PRIVATE SECTOR
Director (G4), N. A. J. Kinghan
Heads of Divisions (G5), P. D. Walton; J. E. Roberts; Mrs
  H. Ghosh
Grade 6, J. S. Gill

HOUSING MONITORING AND ANALYSIS
Under-Secretary (G3), N. J. Glass
Grade 5, J. E. Turner; A. E. Holmans, CBE; Mrs
  J. Littlewood; M. Hughes; D. A. C. Heigham, CBE

HOUSING RESOURCES AND MANAGEMENT
Under-Secretary (G3), Mrs M. McDonald
Heads of Divisions (G5), B. H. Leonard; R. S. Horsman;
  C. H. Bowder; Ms P. E. Alexander
Grade 6, R. Ryder

RELOCATION DIRECTORATE
Director (G3), D. A. McDonald
Grade 5, J. Whaley; J. P. Channing; J. Jacobs; A. M. Wells;
  J. A. McCarthy

PROPERTY HOLDINGS, CONSTRUCTION AND
CENTRAL SUPPORT SERVICES
Deputy Secretary (G2), Miss D. A. Nichols
Under-Secretary (G3), Mrs D. S. Phillips
Director, Property Holdings (G3), N. E. Borrett

DIRECTORATE OF ESTATE PLANNING
Grade 4, D. O. McCreadie
Grade 5, R. J. Dinwiddy
Grade 6, N. Lee; J. H. Bilsby; R. M. D. Smith; M. S. Jennett

DIRECTORATE OF ESTATE OPERATIONS
Head of Operations Division (G5), R. W. P. Brice
Head of Central London Division (G5), A. R. Edwards
Deputy Head of Central London Division (G6), J. Glen

Heads of Outstations (G6), Thames North, A. J. Partridge;
Thames South, C. G. H. Young
Heads of Outstations (G6), Midlands, M. J. Hathaway;
North-East, J. C. Lewis; *North-West,* A. R. Jones; *South-West/Wales,* R. M. Barry; *Scotland,* P. R. Stewart

FINANCE
Grade 5, B. Redfern

ADMINISTRATION DIVISION
Head of Division (G6), D. M. Gillen

CENTRAL POLICY DIVISION
Grade 5, M. H. Bowles

CONSTRUCTION POLICY DIRECTORATE
Under-Secretary (G3), P. D. Ward
Heads of Divisions (G5), J. N. Lithgow; P. F. Everall; Dr
J. F. A. Moore; J. G. Grevatt; M. Leigh-Pollitt
Grade 6, W. J. Marsh; R. F. Window

LOCAL GOVERNMENT
Deputy Secretary (G2), C. J. S. Brearley

LOCAL GOVERNMENT FINANCE POLICY
Director, Local Government Finance Policy (G3),
P. J. J. Britton
Heads of Divisions (G5), P. Rowsell; Mrs C. Wells;
M. H. Coulshed; Mrs H. J. Chipping; R. J. Gibson;
M. J. C. Faulkner

LOCAL GOVERNMENT
Under-Secretary (G3), R. U. Young
Heads of Divisions (G5), H. C. T. Fawcett; Miss L. F. Bell;
L. G. Packer
Grade 6, T. B. J. Crossley; J. R. Footit

LEGAL
Solicitor and Legal Adviser (G2), Mrs M. A. Morgan
Deputy Solicitors (G3), J. A. Catlin; Ms D. Unerman
Assistant Solicitors (G3), P. J. Szell; (G5), J. L. Comber;
P. J. Szell; I. D. Day; Mrs S. Headley; Miss R. A. Lester;
Mrs P. J. Conlon; Mrs G. Hedley-Dent; D. W. Jordan;
Miss D. C. S. Phillips; N. S. Lefton

ENVIRONMENT PROTECTION
Deputy Secretary (G2), F. A. Osborn, CB

HM INSPECTORATE OF POLLUTION
Director and Chief Inspector (G3), Dr D. H. Slater
Deputy Chief Inspector (G4), Dr A. Duncan
Heads of Division (G5), M. F. Tunnicliffe; Dr K. Speakman;
L. N. Stuffins; Dr D. J. Bryce; I. C. McBrayne

DIRECTORATE OF AIR, CLIMATE AND TOXIC
SUBSTANCES
Under-Secretary (G3), Dr D. J. Fisk
Heads of Division (G5), A. Davis; Dr N. J. King; R. Mills
Grade 6, Dr A. J. Apling; D. L. Pounder; Dr P. J. Corcoran;
Dr L. M. Smith; Dr M. Williams

CHIEF SCIENTIST
Chief Scientist (G3), Dr D. J. Fisk
Head of Division (G5), C. L. Robson

DIRECTORATE OF POLLUTION CONTROL AND WASTES
Under-Secretary (G3), R. S. Dudding
Heads of Division (G5), Mrs L. A. C. Simcock; N. Sanders;
Dr P. Hinchcliffe; J. Cleary; Dr N. Williams

ENVIRONMENTAL POLICY AND ANALYSIS
Director (G3), A. G. Watson
Heads of Division (G5), Mrs H. Hillier; J. S. Stevens;
A. Ramsey; J. W. M. Rogers

ENERGY EFFICIENCY UNIT
Director-General (G3), J. Hobson
Grade 5, Dr C. J. Myerscough; Dr J. Miles; A. D. Fagin
Grade 6, Mrs A. J. Wandsworth

OTHER EXECUTIVE AGENCIES

QUEEN ELIZABETH II CONFERENCE CENTRE
Broad Sanctuary, London SW1P 3EE
Tel 071-798 4010

Chief Executive (G5), M. C. Buck

BUILDING RESEARCH ESTABLISHMENT
Garston, Watford WD2 7JR
Tel 0923-894040

Chief Executive (G3), R. G. Courtney
Deputy Chief Executives (G4), N. O. Milbank; Dr
W. D. Woolley
Directors of Groups and Stations (G5), B. O. Hall; Dr
N. J. Cook, Dr V. H. C. Crisp; C. R. Durham

THE BUYING AGENCY
Royal Liver Building, Pier Head, Liverpool L3 1PE
Tel 051-227 4262

Chief Executive (G5), R. M. Powell

TRANSPORT AND SECURITY SERVICES
St Christopher House, Southwark Street, London SE1 0TE
Tel 071-921 3995

Chief Executive (G5), J. C. King

ROYAL COMMISSION ON ENVIRONMENTAL
POLLUTION
Church House, Great Smith Street, London SW1P 3BZ
Tel 071-276 2080

The Commission was set up in 1970 to advise on matters,
both national and international, concerning the pollution of
the environment; on the adequacy of research in this field;
and the future possibilities of danger to the environment.
Chairman, Sir John Houghton, CBE, FRS
Members, Sir Geoffrey Allen, FRS; Prof. H. Charnock, CBE,
FRS; Prof. Dame Barbara Clayton, DBE; H. R. Fell;
P. R. A. Jacques, CBE; Prof. J. H. Lawton, FRS;
Prof. R. Macrory, FRSA; Prof. J. G. Morris;
D. A. D. Reeve, CBE; Prof. E. M. Rothschild;
Prof. Z. A. Silberston, OBE
Secretary, D. R. Lewis

EQUAL OPPORTUNITIES COMMISSION
Overseas House, Quay Street, Manchester M3 3HN
Tel 061-833 9244

Press Office, Swan House, 53 Poland Street, London
W1V 3DF. Tel: 071-287 3953
Regional Offices, St Andrew House, 141 West Nile Street,
Glasgow G1 2RN. Tel: 041-332 8018; Caerwys House,
Windsor Place, Cardiff. Tel: 0222-343552

The Commission was set up by Parliament in 1975 as a result
of the passing of the Sex Discrimination Act. It works towards
the elimination of discrimination on the grounds of sex or
marital status and to promote equality of opportunity
between men and women generally.
Chair (£31,451), Ms K. Bahl
Deputy Chair (£28,119), Mrs J. Bridgeman

Members, Mrs M. Prosser; Lady Brittan; Mrs A. Hasan; Ms
B. Hillon; Ms A. Watts; Ms N. Bray; Ms A. Gibson; Mrs
B. Kelly; Ms C. Wells; C. Mather
Chief Executive, Ms V. Amos

EQUAL OPPORTUNITIES COMMISSION FOR NORTHERN
IRELAND
Chamber of Commerce House, 22 Great Victoria Street,
Belfast BT2 7BA
Tel 0232-242752
Chair and Chief Executive, Mrs J. Smyth

EXCHEQUER AND AUDIT DEPARTMENT
— *see* National Audit Office

ECGD (EXPORT CREDITS GUARANTEE
DEPARTMENT)
PO Box 2200, 2 Exchange Tower, Harbour Exchange
Square, London E14 9GS
Tel 071-512 7000

ECGD (Export Credits Guarantee Department), the official
export credit insurer, is a separate government department
responsible to the President of the Board of Trade and
functions under the Export and Investment Guarantees Act
1991. This enables ECGD to facilitate UK exports by making
available export credit insurance to British firms engaged in
selling overseas and to guarantee repayment to banks in
Britain providing finance for export credit for goods sold on
credit terms of two years or more. The Act also empowers
ECGD to insure British private investment overseas against
political risks such as war, expropriation and restrictions on
remittances.
Chief Executive, W. B. Willott
Group Directors (G3), M. T. Hawtin; J. R. Weiss;
T. M. Jaffray
Grade 5, R. P. Burnett; P. J. Callaghan; D. C. Cooper;
J. C. W. Croall; A. P. Fowell; R. Gotts; R. F. Lethbridge;
K. G. Lockwood; V. P. Lunn Rockliffe;
R. W. MacGregor; M. E. Maddox; M. D. Pentecost;
R. A. Ranson; J. W. Roberts; B. M. Sidwell, TD;
J. S. Snowdon
Grade 6, G. Cassell; F. O. H. Coulson;
R. O. L. Drummond; I. M. N. Ejiegbu; M. Foster;
N. Harington; G. G. Jones; L. S. W. Montgomery; Ms
S. Rice; D. I. Robbins; E. Walsby
Grade 7, Ms C. L. Anderson; J. S. Astruc; D. I. Calvert; Mrs
A. C. Cowie; D. M. Cox; G. P. Cox; A. B. Coyne;
M. J. Crane; M. Cranwell; R. P. D. Crick; S. R. Dodgson;
D. L. Dyke; A. C. Faulkner; R. X. Fear; G. C. Fisher;
P. C. Gaudoin; N. F. George; R. Hardy; P. F. Henson;
P. S. Hillman; M. R. Hodson; P. Jackson; S. J. Johnson;
K. Jones; R. Jones; N. A. Lambert; C. J. Leeds;
M. M. Leonard; D. J. M. Lucas; I. Mackay;
R. A. J. D. Mayer; S. Merchack; A. J. E. Muckersie;
P. L. Neal; G. A. Newhouse; J. K. Peacock; S. C. Pond;
P. J. Radford; A. B. Redmayne; D. M. Riley;
V. G. M. Robertson; S. Rosenthal; P. J. Rossington;
K. R. Smith; R. S. Summers; J. Sweeney; J. A. Sweet;
Miss V. M. Taylor; Ms A. V. Thomas; C. M. Thorogood;
T. West; J. M. Willis; I. Wilson; D. L. Wyatt; J. A. Youd;
G. A. Young

EXPORT GUARANTEES ADVISORY COUNCIL
Chairman, R. T. Fox, CBE
Deputy Chairman, A. G. Gormly, CBE

Other Members, Sir Robert Davidson; G. W. Lynch;
J. Melbourn; C. Smallwood; Sir Derek Thomas, KCMG;
The Viscount Weir

OFFICE OF FAIR TRADING
Field House, Bream's Buildings, London EC4A 1PR
Tel 071-242 2858

The Office of Fair Trading is a non-ministerial government
department, headed by the Director-General of Fair Trading.
It keeps commercial activities in the UK under review and
seeks to protect consumers against unfair trading practices.
The Director-General's consumer protection duties under
the Fair Trading Act 1973, together with his responsibilities
under the Consumer Credit Act 1974, the Estate Agents Act
1979, and Control of Misleading Advertisements Regulations
1988, are administered by the Office's Consumer Affairs
Division. The Competition Policy Division is concerned with
monopolies and mergers (under the Fair Trading Act 1973),
and the Director-General's other responsibilities for competition matters, including those under the Restrictive Trade
Practices Act 1976, the Resale Prices Act 1976, the
Competition Act 1980, the Financial Services Act 1986 and
the Broadcasting Act 1990. The Office is the UK competent
authority on the application of the European Commission's
competition rules, and also liaises with the Commission on
consumer protection initiatives.
Director-General, Sir Bryan Carsberg
Deputy Director-General (G2), J. W. Preston, CB

CONSUMER AFFAIRS DIVISION
Director (G3), J. F. Mills
Assistant Directors (G5), P. Casey; D. W. Lightfoot;
J. Chapman

COMPETITION POLICY DIVISION
Director (G3), Dr M. Howe
Assistant Directors (G5), A. J. White; D. Roots-Parsons;
H. L. Emden; C. J. C. Wright

LEGAL DIVISION
Director (G3), A. M. Inglese
Assistant Directors (G5), M. A. Khan; P. T. Rostron

Senior Economic Adviser (G5), D. Elliott
Establishment and Finance Officer (G5), Miss C. Banks
Chief Information Officer (G6), D. Hill

FOREIGN AND COMMONWEALTH
OFFICE
Downing Street, London SW1A 2AL
Tel 071-270 3000

The Foreign and Commonwealth Office provides, mainly
through diplomatic missions, the means of communication
between the British Government and other governments and
international governmental organizations for the discussion
and negotiation of all matters falling within the field of
international relations. It is responsible for alerting the
British Government to the implications of developments
overseas; for protecting British interests overseas; for
protecting British citizens abroad; for explaining British
policies to, and cultivating friendly relations with, governments overseas; and for the discharge of British responsibilities to the dependent territories.

DIPLOMATIC SERVICE SALARIES *since 1 April 1993*
Permanent Under-Secretary and Head of the

Diplomatic Service	£104,860
Senior Grade Salary Point 1 (SP1)	£90,148
Deputy Permanent Under-Secretary	£82,925
Senior Grade Salary Point 2 (SP2)	£75,328
Senior Grade Salary Point 3 (SP3)	£64,307
Senior Grade Salary Point 4 (SP4)	£58,347
Senior Grade Salary Point 5 (SP5)	£52,751
Diplomatic Service Grade 4 (DS4)	£37,589–£55,836

Secretary of State, The Rt. Hon. Douglas Hurd, CBE, MP
  Private Secretary, R. J. Sawers
  Social Secretary, Ms M. Hillsin
  Special Advisers, M. Maclay; M. Fraser
  Parliamentary Private Secretary, D. Martin, MP
Minister of State for Foreign and Commonwealth Affairs
  (Minister for Overseas Development), The Baroness
  Chalker of Wallasey, PC
  Private Secretary, M. Lowcock
  Parliamentary Private Secretary, M. Robinson, MP
Ministers of State for Foreign and Commonwealth Affairs, The
  Rt. Hon. Douglas Hogg, QC, MP; The Rt. Hon. Alastair
  Goodlad, MP; David Heathcoat-Amory, MP
  Private Secretaries, N. S. Archer; P. H. Tibber;
  T. M. Hitchens
  Parliamentary Private Secretaries:
  To Mr Hogg, H. Booth, MP
  To Mr Goodlad, G. Kynoch, MP
  To Mr Heathcoat-Amory, R. Richards, MP
Parliamentary Under-Secretary of State, The Hon. Mark
  Lennox-Boyd, MP
  Private Secretary, P. A. Speller
  Parliamentary Private Secretary, M. Robinson, MP
Parliamentary Relations Unit, R. Thomson (*Head*);
  J. P. Rodgers (*Deputy Head and Parliamentary Clerk*)
Permanent Under-Secretary of State and Head of the
  Diplomatic Service, Sir David Gillmore, KCMG
  Private Secretary, S. G. McDonald
Deputy Permanent Under-Secretary and Political Director,
  L. V. Appleyard, CMG
Deputy Under-Secretaries (SP2):
Chief Clerk; A. M. Wood, CMG
Economic Director, B. L. Crowe, CMG
M. Elliott, CMG; Sir John Coles, KCMG; Sir Timothy Daunt,
  KCMG
Assistant Under-Secretaries (SP5):
Deputy Chief Clerk and Principal Establishment and Security
  Officer, Mrs V. E. Sutherland, CMG
Deputy Political Director and UK Perm. Rep. on the Council
  of WEU, J. Greenstock, CMG
Director of Information Systems, J. Ling, CMG
Principal Finance Officer and Chief Inspector, R. J. S. Muir;
  R. J. Alston, CMG; A. J. Beamish, CMG; Sir Michael
  Burton, KCVO, CMG; M. H. Jay, CMG; R. B. Bone;
  A. M. Goodenough, CMG; D. C. B. Logan, CMG;
  C. O. Hum; J. T. Masefield, CMG; P. Lever, CMG
HM Vice-Marshal of the Diplomatic Corps,
  A. St J. H. Figgis, CMG
Legal Adviser (SP2), F. D. Berman, CMG, QC
Second Legal Adviser, D. H. Anderson, CMG
Deputy Legal Advisers, M. R. Eaton, CMG;
  K. J. Chamberlain, CMG
Legal Counsellors, A. Aust; Mrs A. Glover; Miss S. Brooks;
  Ms E. Wilmshurst; C. Whomersley

HEADS OF DEPARTMENTS (DS4)
*Aid Policy Department, S. Chakrabarti
Arms Control and Disarmament Department,
  P. W. M. Vereker
Aviation and Maritime Department, A. S. Collins
Central European Department, N. J. Thorpe

Commonwealth Co-ordination Department, D. Broad
Commonwealth Foreign and Security Policy Unit,
  A. D. R. Smith
Conference on Security and Co-operation in Europe Unit,
  C. A. Munro
Consular Department, S. F. Howarth
Cultural Relations Department, J. N. Elam
Eastern Adriatic Unit, A. Charlton
Eastern Department, D. G. Manning
*Economic Advisers Department, S. H. Broadbent
*Economic Relations Department, K. Tebbit
Environment Science and Energy Department, G. H. Boyce
Equatorial Africa Department, T. G. Harris
European Community Department (External),
  J. M. Macgregor
European Community Department (Internal), A. J. Cary
Far Eastern Department, G. Fry
Home Estate Department, D. Brown
Hong Kong Department, P. Ricketts
Honours Unit, D. E. Tarling
Human Rights Policy Unit, G. S. Hand
Information Department A. D. Harris, LVO
Information Systems Division (Operations), S. I. Soutar
Information Systems Division (Projects), K. Willis
Information Systems Division (Resources), M. Hodge, MBE
Internal Audit, R. Elias
Joint Assistance Unit (Central Europe), D. Coates
Joint Assistance Unit (Eastern Europe), M. McCulloch
†*Joint Directorate*, M. G. Dougal
Latin America Department, L. G. Faulkner
Library and Records Department, R. Bone
*Management Review Staff, E. C. Glover, MVO;
Medical and Welfare Unit, Miss D. M. Symes, OBE
Middle East Department, P. M. Nixon, CMG, OBE
Migration and Visa Department, D. I. Lewty
Narcotics Control and Aids Department, P. Thomson, CVO
Nationality, Treaty and Claims Department, M. F. Sullivan,
  MBE
Near East and North Africa Department, W. G. Ehrman
News Department, R. N. Culshaw
Non-Proliferation and Defence Department, J. B. Donnelly
North America Department, M. E. Pellew, LVO
Overseas Estate Department, M. H. R. Bertram
Overseas Inspectorate, R. J. S. Muir (*Chief Inspector and*
  Principal Finance Officer)
Overseas Police Adviser, L. Grundy (*Senior Police Adviser*)
Permanent Under-Secretary's Department, I. R. Callan, CMG
Personnel Management Department, P. J. Torry
Personnel Policy Department, J. Poston
Personnel Services Department, R. G. Short, MVO
Policy Planning Staff, R. D. Wilkinson
PROSPER, C. J. Edgerton, OBE
Protocol Department, D. C. B. Beaumont (*First Assistant*
  Marshal of the Diplomatic Corps)
Republic of Ireland Department, G. R. Archer
Research and Analysis Department, Director, B. S. Eastwood
Resource and Finance Department, J. W. Thorp
Royal Matters Unit, J. E. Brook
Security Department, J. W. Hodge
Security Co-ordination Department, J. P. G. Freeman
Security Policy Department, S. J. Gomersall
South Asian Department, L. B. Smith
South Atlantic and Antarctic Department, P. M. Newton
South-East Asian Department, G. Hewitt

---

*Joint Foreign and Commonwealth Office/Overseas Development
Administration department
†Joint Foreign and Commonwealth Office/Department of Trade and
Industry directorate

Southern Africa Department, D. R. C. Christopher
Southern European Department, D. C. A. Madden
South Pacific Department, M. R. J. Guest
Support Services Department, A. E. Gay
Technical Security Department, M. Buckland-Smith
Training Department, I. W. Mackley
United Nations Department, Miss M. G. D. Evans, CMG
Western European Department, M. L. H. Hope
West Indian and Atlantic Department, G. M. Baker

THE SECRET INTELLIGENCE SERVICE (MI6)
Director-General, Sir Colin McColl

GOVERNMENT COMMUNICATIONS
HEADQUARTERS (GCHQ)
Priors Road, Cheltenham, Glos. GL52 5AJ
Tel 0242-221491

GCHQ is an autonomous government department under the
Secretary of State for Foreign and Commonwealth Affairs.

CORPS OF QUEEN'S MESSENGERS
Foreign and Commonwealth Office, London SW1A 2AH
Tel 071-270 2779

Superintendent of the Corps of Queen's Messengers,
Maj. I. G. M. Bamber
Queen's Messengers, Maj. J. E. A. Andre;
  Cdr. D. H. Barraclough; Maj. A. N. D. Bols;
  Lt.-Cdr. K. E. Brown; Lt.-Col. W. P. A. Bush;
  Lt.-Col. M. B. de S. Clayton; Capt. G. Courtauld;
  Maj. P. C. H. Dening-Smitherman; Maj. P. T. Dunn;
  Sqn. Ldr. J. S. Frizzell; Capt. N. C. E. Gardner;
  Cdr. P. G. Gregson; Maj. D. A. Griffiths;
  Wg Cdr. J. O. Jewiss; Lt.-Col. P. S. Kerr-Smiley;
  Lt.-Col. J. M. C. Kimmins;
  Lt.-Col. R. C. Letchworth; G. F. Miller;
  Lt.-Col. A. R. Murray; Maj. D. R. Nevile;
  Maj. K. J. Rowbottom; Maj. M. R. Senior;
  Cdr. K. M. C. Simmons, AFC; Maj. P. M. O. Springfield;
  Maj. J. S. Steele; Col. D. W. F. Taylor

FOREIGN COMPENSATION COMMISSION
Old Admiralty Building, London SW1A 2AF
Tel 071-210 6158

The Commission was set up by the Foreign Compensation
Act 1950 primarily to distribute, under Orders in Council,
funds received from other governments in accordance with
agreements to pay compensation for expropriated British
property and other losses sustained by British nationals.
  The Commission also has the duty of registering claims
for British-owned property in contemplation of agreements
with other countries, and it has done so in seven instances
since 1950.
Chairman, A. W. E. Wheeler, CBE
Commissioner, J. A. S. Hall, DFC, QC
Secretary and Chief Examiner, D. H. Wright

FORESTRY COMMISSION
231 Corstorphine Road, Edinburgh EH12 7AT
Tel 031-334 0303

The Forestry Commission is the government department
responsible for forestry policy in Great Britain. It reports
directly to forestry ministers (i.e. the Minister of Agriculture,
Fisheries and Food, the Secretary of State for Scotland, and
the Secretary of State for Wales), to whom it is responsible
for advice on forestry policy and for the implementation of
that policy in Great Britain. There is a statutorily-appointed
Chairman and Board of Commissioners (four full-time and
seven part-time) with prescribed duties and powers. The full-
time Commissioners form the Executive Board.
  In 1992 the Commission implemented a reorganization to
distinguish between its departmental, regulatory and management functions. A Policy and Resources Group is
responsible for the parliamentary and policy aspects of the
Commission's duties as a government department. As the
Forestry Authority, the Commission provides advice and
sets the standards for the forestry industry, administers the
grant-aid schemes for private woodlands, carries out regulatory functions for plant health and felling control and
undertakes forest research. As the Forest Enterprise, the
Commission manages its forestry estate on a multi-use basis.
In discharging their functions, the Forestry Commissioners
have a statutory duty to endeavour to achieve a reasonable
balance between the needs of forestry and the environment.
  In April 1993, the Government set up a task force to
review options for the ownership and management of the
Commission's forestry estate.
Chairman (part-time) (£31,830), Sir Raymond Johnstone,
  CBE
Director-General and Deputy Chairman (G2), T. R. Cutler
Commissioner, Policy and Resources (G3), D. S. Grundy
Head of the Forestry Authority (G3), R. T. Bradley
Chief Executive, Forest Enterprise (G3), D. L. Foot
Secretary to the Commissioners (G4), P. J. Clarke, CBE

REGISTRY OF FRIENDLY SOCIETIES
15 Great Marlborough Street, London W1V 2AX
Tel 071-437 9992

The Registry of Friendly Societies is a government department serving three statutory bodies, the Building Societies
Commission, the Friendly Societies Commission, and the
Central Office of the Registry of Friendly Societies (together
with the Assistant Registrar of Friendly Societies for
Scotland).
  The Building Societies Commission was established by the
Building Societies Act 1986. The Commission is responsible
for the supervision of building societies and administers the
system of regulation. It also advises the Treasury and other
government departments on matters relating to building
societies.
  The Friendly Societies Commission was established by
the Friendly Societies Act 1992. Its responsibilities for
supervision of friendly societies parallel those of the Building
Societies Commission for building societies.
  The Central Office of the Registry of Friendly Societies
provides a public registry for mutual organizations registered
under the Building Societies Act 1986, Friendly Societies
Acts 1974 and 1992, and the Industrial and Provident
Societies Act 1965. It is responsible for the supervision of
friendly societies and credit unions, and advises the
Government on issues affecting those societies. The Chief
Registrar has certain powers to arbitrate in disputes between
members and registered societies, and acts as the Industrial
Assurance Commissioner.

BUILDING SOCIETIES COMMISSION
Chairman, Mrs R. E. J. Gilmore
Deputy Chairman, H. G. Walsh

Commissioners, T. F. Mathews; H. R. C. Walden, CBE; F. E. Worsley; F. G. Sunderland; N. Fox Bassett

FRIENDLY SOCIETIES COMMISSION
Chairman, D. W. Lee
Commissioners, F. da Rocha; A. Wilson; J. A. Geddes; P. E. Couse; Dr J. Dine

CENTRAL OFFICE
Chief Registrar, Mrs R. E. J. Gilmore
Assistant Registrars (G4), D. W. Lee; A. J. Perrett

THE REGISTRY
First Commissioner and Chief Registrar (G2), Mrs R. E. J. Gilmore

BUILDING SOCIETIES COMMISSION STAFF
Grade 3, H. G. Walsh
Grade 4, T. F. Mathews
Grade 5, D. A. W. Stevens; J. M. Palmer; W. Champion; R. K. Gabbertas
Grade 6, N. F. Digance

FRIENDLY SOCIETIES COMMISSION STAFF
Grade 4, D. W. Lee
Grade 6, F. da Rocha

CENTRAL SERVICES STAFF
Legal Adviser (G4), A. J. Perrett
Establishment and Finance Officer (G5), K. Blackburn
Legal Staff (G6), P. G. Ashcroft; Miss E. Long; R. Caune; C. Stallard

REGISTRY OF FRIENDLY SOCIETIES, SCOTLAND
58 Frederick Street, Edinburgh, EH2 1NB
Tel 031-226 3224
Assistant Registrar (G5), J. L. J. Craig, WS

GAMING BOARD FOR GREAT BRITAIN
Berkshire House, 168–173 High Holborn, London WC1V 7AA
Tel 071-240 0821

The Board was established in 1968 and its functions are to ensure that those involved in organizing gaming and lotteries are fit to do so and to keep criminals out of gaming; to ensure that gaming is run fairly and in accordance with the law; and to advise the Home Secretary on developments in gaming so that the law can respond to change.
Chairman (part-time) (£30,575), Lady Littler
Members (part-time) (each £12,260), Sir Richard Barratt, CBE, VRD; Lady Trethowan; W. B. Kirkpatrick; M. H. Hogan
Secretary, T. Kavanagh

OFFICE OF GAS SUPPLY
Stockley House, 130 Wilton Road, London SW1V 1LQ
Tel 071-828 0898

The Office of Gas Supply (Ofgas) is a regulatory body set up under the Gas Act 1986. It is headed by the Director-General of Gas Supply, who is independent of ministerial control.
The principal function of Ofgas is to monitor British Gas's activities as a public gas supplier and, where necessary, to enforce the conditions of that company's authorization to act as a public gas supplier. Other functions are to investigate complaints on matters where enforcement powers may be exercisable; to fix and publish maximum charges for reselling gas; to publish information and advice for the benefit of tariff customers; to keep under review developments concerning the gas supply industry, including competition; and to settle the terms on which other suppliers have access to British Gas pipelines in the event of disagreement.
Director-General, vacant
Deputy Director-General, J. Dorken
Legal Adviser, D. R. M. Long
Director, Competition and Tariffs, G. McGregor
Director, Public Affairs, I. Cooke
Director, Consumer Affairs, W. Macleod

GOVERNMENT ACTUARY'S DEPARTMENT
22 Kingsway, London WC2B 6LE
Tel 071-242 6828

The Government Actuary provides a consulting service to government departments, the public sector, and overseas governments. The actuaries advise on social security schemes and superannuation arrangements in the public sector at home and abroad, on population and other statistical studies, and on government supervision of insurance companies and friendly societies.
Government Actuary, C. D. Daykin, CB
Directing Actuaries, D. G. Ballantine; D. H. Loades; M. A. Pickford
Chief Actuaries, E. I. Battersby; J. L. Field; T. W. Hewitson; P. H. Hinton; A. I. Johnston; J. C. A. Rathbone; A. G. Young
Actuaries, W. D. B. Anderson; Ms W. M. Beaver; A. B. Chughtai; W. H. P. Davies; A. P. Gallop; Mrs B. J. Hall; C. A. Harris; V. P. Knowles; Mrs I. W. Lane; D. Lewis; A. J. Macnair; P. Merricks; P. Noonan; S. M. O'Ceallaigh; A. P. Pavelin; J. W. Peers; H. J. Prescott; D. E. Purchase; A. H. Silverman; J. G. Spain; D. I. Tomlinson; D. M. Webber

---

GOVERNMENT HOSPITALITY FUND
8 Cleveland Row, London SW1A 1DH
Tel 071-210 3000

The Government Hospitality Fund was instituted in 1908 for the purpose of organizing official hospitality on a regular basis, with a view to the promotion of international goodwill.
Minister in Charge, The Rt. Hon. Alastair Goodlad, MP
Secretary, Col. T. Earl

DEPARTMENT OF HEALTH
Richmond House, 79 Whitehall, London SW1A 2NS
Tel 071-210 3000

The Department of Health is responsible for the administration of the National Health Service in England and for the personal social services run by local authorities in England for children, the elderly, the infirm, the handicapped and other persons in need. It has functions relating to public and environmental health, food safety and nutrition. The Department is also responsible for the ambulance and emergency first aid services, under the Civil Defence Act 1948. The Department represents the UK at the World Health Organization.
Secretary of State for Health, The Rt. Hon. Virginia Bottomley, MP

Principal Private Secretary, R. M. Creighton
Private Secretary, Ms G. Wakeman
Special Adviser, R. Marsh
Parliamentary Private Secretary, K. Mans, MP
Minister of State, Dr Brian Mawhinney, MP
  Private Secretary, Ms T. Ing
  Parliamentary Private Secretary, P. Thompson, MP
Parliamentary Under-Secretaries of State, The Baroness
  Cumberlege, CBE; The Hon. Thomas Sackville, MP; John
  Bowis, OBE
Permanent Secretary (G1), G. A. Hart, CB
  Private Secretary, L. Wilkinson
Chief Medical Officer (G1A), Dr K. Calman
Director of Research and Development, Prof. M. Peckham

NATIONAL HEALTH SERVICE POLICY BOARD
Chairman, The Secretary of State
Deputy Chairman, Sir Roy Griffiths
Members, Dr K. Calman (*Chief Medical Officer*); Sir James
  Ackers; Dr B. Mawhinney, MP (*Minister of State*);
  Prof. C. Chantler; The Baroness Cumberlege, CBE; The
  Hon. T. Sackville, MP; J. Bowis, OBE, MP (*Parliamentary
  Under-Secretaries*); Sir Kenneth Durham; G. A. Hart, CB
  (*Permanent Secretary*); Sir Duncan Nichol, CBE; Sir Robert
  Scholey, CBE; P. Gummer; Mrs Y. Moores; Miss
  K. Jenkins; Ms S. Masters; Sir Timothy Chessels

NATIONAL HEALTH SERVICE MANAGEMENT
EXECUTIVE
Chief Executive, Sir Duncan Nichol, CBE (*until March 1994*)
*Deputy Chief Executive and Director of Performance
  Management*, A. Langlands
Director of Corporate Affairs, J. F. Shaw
Director of Personnel (acting), R. W. D. Venning
Director of Finance and Corporate Information,
  G. Greenshields
Medical Director, Dr G. Winyard
Chief Nursing Officer, Mrs Y. Moores
Director of Research and Development, Prof. M. Peckham

HEALTH AND PERSONAL SOCIAL SERVICES
GROUP
Deputy Secretary (G2), T. S. Heppell, CB

HEALTH ASPECTS OF THE ENVIRONMENT AND FOOD
Under-Secretary (G3), B. Bridges
Assistant Secretaries (G5), C. P. Kendall; R. Cunningham;
  Ms L. Lockyer
Senior Principal (G6), Mrs M. Fry

HEALTH CARE (ADMINISTRATIVE) DIVISION
Under-Secretary (G3), Miss R. D. B. Pease
Assistant Secretaries (G5), A. W. McCulloch; K. Jacobsen;
  I. Jewesbury; N. Boyd

COMMUNITY SERVICES DIVISION
Under-Secretary (G3), T. Luce
Assistant Secretaries (G5), Mrs A. De Peyer; J. A. Parker;
  R. P. S. Hughes, CBE; A. McKeon

HEALTH PROMOTION (ADMINISTRATIVE) DIVISION
Under-Secretary (G3), N. M. Hale, CB
Assistant Secretaries (G5), J. E. Knight; C. A. Muir;
  J. F. Sharpe; J. C. Middleton; R. Tyrrell

HEALTH CARE DIRECTORATE (PRIMARY
CARE)
Deputy Chief Medical Officer (G2), Dr G. Winyard

PERFORMANCE MANAGEMENT DIRECTORATE
(PRIMARY CARE)
Under-Secretary (G3), J. H. Barnes
Principal Medical Officer (G4), Dr P. Leech
Assistant Secretaries (G5), Miss H. Gwynn; D. Hewlett

P DIVISION
Under-Secretary (G3), M. Jeremiah
Assistant Secretaries (G5), S. J. Furniss; J. Thompson;
  M. Siswick; S. Alcock

NHS SUPPLIES AUTHORITY
Chairman, Sir Robin Buchanan
National Director of Supplies, T. Hunt
Directors, E. Sutherland (*Purchasing*); R. Chantler (*Finance
  and Information*); C. Uden (*Human Resources*); Mrs
  R. Sutton (*Communications*)

MEDICAL DEVICES DIRECTORATE
Director (G4), A. B. Barton

EUROPEAN AND STANDARDS BUSINESS
Head of Business (G5), Dr D. C. Potter

DEVICE TECHNOLOGY AND SAFETY
Head of Business (G5), Miss M. N. Duncan

DTS1 COMMUNITY HEALTH, NON-ACUTE AND
DIAGNOSTIC, IMAGING SERVICES
Group Manager (G6), A. D. C. Shipley

DTS2 ACUTE CARE SERVICES
Group Manager (G6), C. S. Bray

DEVICE EVALUATION AND PUBLICATIONS
Head of Business (G6), Dr N. A. Slark

MANUFACTURERS' REGISTRATION SCHEME
Head of Business (G6), R. W. B. Allen

CORPORATE MANAGEMENT
Head of Business (G6), T. F. Crawley

MEDICAL AND NURSING ADVICE
Senior Medical Officers (G5), Dr S. M. Ludgate; Dr
  S. P. Vahl
Nursing Officer (G6), Mrs P. A. Collinson

NHS MANAGEMENT EXECUTIVE
PERSONNEL GROUP
Director of Personnel (G2) (acting), R. W. D. Venning

DIVISION HAP
Under-Secretary (G3), R. M. Drury
Senior Principal (G6), A. W. Edwards
Assistant Secretaries (G5), M. G. Sturges; Miss S. Norman;
  M. Staniforth; J. Ashe; B. A. J. Bennett

INFORMATION SYSTEMS DIRECTORATE
Director of Information Systems (G4), Dr A. A. Holt
Deputy Director (G5), Mrs L. Masterman
Grade 6, Miss S. Blackburn; J. Wormald; P. Cobb;
  J. Watkins

RESEARCH AND DEVELOPMENT DIVISION
Director of Research and Development, Prof. M. Peckham
Director of Research Management (G4), Dr W. J. Burroughs
Deputy Director of Research Management (G4), Dr H. Pickles
Assistant Secretaries (G5), Miss M. Edwards; Mrs J. Griffin;
  Mrs B. Soper; Ms M. Woolley; Dr P. Greenaway
Senior Medical Officers (G5), Dr R. Singh; Dr G. Lewis;
  Dr J. Toy; Dr D. Sharp

Senior Principal Research Officers (G6), Ms A. Kauder;
Dr C. Davies; Ms J. Ennis; Dr C. Henshall
Nursing Officers (G6), Dr E. Meerabeau; Miss E. Scott

SOCIAL SERVICES INSPECTORATE
Chief Inspector (G2), H. Laming, CBE
Deputy Chief Inspectors (G4), D. C. Brand; Miss C. M. Hey
Assistant Chief Inspectors (HQ), Miss J. Baraclough;
J. Kennedy; S. Mitchell; J. G. Smith; Mrs W. Rose
Assistant Chief Inspectors (Regions), S. Allard;
J. K. Corcoran; J. Cypher; D. Gilroy; B. D. Harrison;
A. Jones; D. G. Lambert; Miss A. Taylor; Mrs P. K. Hall;
C. P. Brearley

MEDICAL DIVISIONS (HEALTH AND PERSONAL SOCIAL SERVICES)

Chief Medical Officer (G1A), Dr K. Calman
Deputy Chief Medical Officers (G2), Dr J. S. Metters; Dr
G. Winyard

MEDICAL DIVISIONS UNDER DR METTERS

DIVISIONS HP(M)1-3, CHMU, MEDICAL EDITORIAL
UNIT
Senior Principal Medical Officer (G3), Dr E. Rubery
Principal Medical Officers (G4), Dr G. Lewis; Dr D.
McInnes; Dr J. D. F. Bellamy
Senior Medical Officers (G5), Dr S. Turnbull; Dr
D. Salisbury; Dr J. Hilton; Dr J. Leese; Dr E. Tebbs; Dr
H. Williams; Dr M. Powlson; Dr H. Markowe; Dr
F. Harvey; Dr K. Binysh; Dr V. Press; Dr M. Thorley;
Dr C. M. Wein; Dr D. Ernaelsteen; Dr W. J. Modle; Dr
I. A. Lister-Cheese; Dr S. Shepherd; Dr D. Milner; Dr
R. Stanwell-Smith

DIVISION HEF(M)
Senior Principal Medical Officer (G3), Dr G. Jones
Principal Medical Officers (G4), Dr E. Smales; Dr
G. E. Diggle; Dr R. Skinner; Dr M. Wiseman
Senior Medical Officers (G5), Dr M. Waring; Dr N. Lazarus;
Dr R. L. Maynard; Dr T. Marrs; Dr A. Bulman; Dr
P. Clarke; Dr A. Dawson; Dr L. Robinson; Dr
C. Swinson; Dr A. Wight; Dr C. Van den Bosch; Dr
F. Kennedy; Dr S. Lader

DIVISION E
Principal Medical Officer (G4), Dr J. D. F. Bellamy

HEALTH CARE (MEDICAL) DIVISION
Senior Principal Medical Officer (G3), Dr J. L. Reed, CB
Principal Medical Officers (G4), Dr J. R. W. Hangartner; Dr
R. Jenkins
Senior Medical Officers (G5), Dr J. Ashwell; Dr
D. Rothman; Dr N. Halliday; Dr N. Melia; Dr E. Hills;
Dr P. Furnell; Dr A. Rejman; Dr E. Clissold; Dr
A. Rawson; Dr S. Munday; Dr D. Brooksbank; Dr
D. Kingdon; Dr E. Wilson; Dr P. Mason; Dr G. Parry;
Dr Y. Morris; Dr K. Lloyd; Prof. S. Hollins

MEDICAL DIVISIONS UNDER DR WINYARD

DIVISION HCD-PH
Principal Medical Officer (G4), Dr A. Lakhani
Senior Medical Officers (G5), Dr G. Pollock; Dr J. Rees; Dr
M. Campbell-Stern; Dr G. Thomas; Dr J. Dodge; Dr
B. Rana

DIVISION MME
Senior Principal Medical Officer (G3), Dr P. J. Bourdillon
Senior Medical Officers (G5), Dr R. Cairncross; Dr
R. Wilson; Dr P. I. M. Allen

Assistant Secretary (G5), S. D. Catling
Principals (G7), H. Tolland; T. G. Bennett; R. Haugh

DENTAL DIVISION
Chief Dental Officer, R. B. Mouatt
Senior Dental Officers, C. Howard; C. Audrey; K. A. Eaton

NURSING DIVISION
Chief Nursing Officer/Director of Nursing, Mrs Y. Moores
Deputy Director of Nursing, Mrs S. Williams, RGN, RSCN, RNT
Deputy Chief Nursing Officer, J. Tait, OBE
Principal Nursing Officer/Business Manager, M. Hill
Principal Nursing Officer, Miss S. Norman

PHARMACEUTICAL DIVISION
Chief Pharmaceutical Officer (G4), B. H. Hartley
Deputy Chief Pharmaceutical Officer (G5), J. R. V. Merrills
Senior Principal Pharmaceutical Officer (G6), P. E. Green

INFORMATION DIVISION
Director of Information (G4), Miss R. Christopherson
Deputy Directors (G6), C. P. Wilson (news); Mrs A. Rea
(publicity)

NATIONAL HEALTH SERVICE

REGIONAL HEALTH AUTHORITIES
The chairmen and members of Regional Health Authorities
are appointed by the Secretary of State for Health.

EAST ANGLIA, Union Lane, Chesterton, Cambridge CB4
1RF. Chairman, Sir Colin Walker, OBE; Regional General
Manager, A. Liddell
MERSEY, Hamilton House, 24 Pall Mall, Liverpool L3 6AL.
Chairman, Sir Donald Wilson; Regional General Manager,
G. Scaife
NORTH-EAST THAMES, 40 Eastbourne Terrace, London
W2 3QR. Chairman, Sir William Staveley, GCB; Regional
General Manager, B. Harrison
NORTHERN, Benfield Road, Walker Gate, Newcastle upon
Tyne NE6 4PY. Chairman, P. Carr, CBE; Regional General
Manager, Prof. L. Donaldson
NORTH-WESTERN, Gateway House, Piccadilly South,
Manchester M60 7LP. Chairman, Sir Bruce Martin, QC;
Regional General Manager, D. Allison, CB
NORTH-WEST THAMES, 40 Eastbourne Terrace, London
W2 3QR. Chairman, Sir William Doughty; Regional
General Manager, R. Kerr
OXFORD, Old Road, Headington, Oxford OX3 7LF.
Chairman, Dr S. Burgess, CBE; Regional General Manager,
Ms B. Stocking
SOUTH-EAST THAMES, Thrift House, Collington Avenue,
Bexhill-on-Sea, E. Sussex TN39 3NQ. Chairman,
P. Barker; Regional General Manager, G. Green
SOUTH-WESTERN, King Square House, 26-27 King
Square, Bristol BS2 8EF. Chairman, Ms R. Fritchie;
Regional General Manager, Ms P. Charlwood
SOUTH-WEST THAMES, 40 Eastbourne Terrace, London
W2 3QR. Chairman, Prof. M. Hicks, OBE; Regional General
Manager, C. Spry
TRENT, Fulwood House, Old Fulwood Road, Sheffield S10
3TH. Chairman, Sir Michael Carlisle; Regional General
Manager, Dr K. Woods
WESSEX, Highcroft, Romsey Road, Winchester, Hants.
SO22 5DH. Chairman, Sir Robin Buchanan; Regional
General Manager, K. Jarrold
WEST MIDLANDS, Arthur Thompson House, 146-150
Hagley Road, Birmingham B16 9PA. Chairman,
B. W. Baker; Regional General Manager, B. Edwards, CBE
YORKSHIRE, Park Parade, Harrogate HG1 5AH. Chairman,
Sir Bryan Askew; Regional General Manager, K. McLean

SPECIAL HEALTH AUTHORITIES

HEALTH EDUCATION AUTHORITY, Hamilton House, Mabledon Place, London WC1H 9TX. *Chairman,* Sir Donald Maitland, GCMG, OBE; *Chief Executive,* Dr Spencer Hagard

NHS SUPPLIES AUTHORITY, Apex Plaza, Forbury Road, Reading, Berks. RG1 1AX. *Chairman,* Sir Robin Buchanan

SPECIAL HOSPITALS SERVICE AUTHORITY, Charles House, Kensington High Street, London W14. The Special Hospitals Service is provided by four hospitals: Rampton, Broadmoor, Moss Side and Park Lane. *Chairman,* Dr D. E. Edmond; *Chief Executive,* C. Kaye

NATIONAL HEALTH SERVICE, SCOTLAND
—*see* Scottish Office entry

DEPARTMENTAL RESOURCES AND SERVICES GROUP
Deputy Secretary (G2), J. Pilling

FINANCE AND CORPORATE INFORMATION DIRECTORATE

FINANCIAL MANAGEMENT DIRECTORATE
Director of Finance NHSHE (G2), G. Greenshields

FINANCE BRANCH
Under-Secretary (Health) (G3), Ms M. E. Stuart
Assistant Secretaries (G5), J. M. Brownlee; K. J. Guinness; Miss A. Mithani; Ms G. Fletcher-Cook
Senior Principals (G6), R. J. Tredgett; R. Churchill; A. C. Symes; K. G. Gardner

FINANCE AND CORPORATE INFORMATION DIVISION A
Deputy Director (G3), Mrs J. Firth
Heads of Branch (G5), A. Simkins; C. Dobson; M. A. Harris; A. Angilley

FINANCE AND CORPORATE INFORMATION DIVISION B
Deputy Director (G3), B. Marsden
Heads of Branch (G5), J. Rushfirth; B. J. Derry; J. Tomlinson; M. Ruane; M. Gayton; *(G6),* R. M. Jordan; P. Macaulay; G. Smith; *(G7),* J. Dixon

FINANCE DIVISION D
Under-Secretary (Social Security) (G3), J. Tross
Assistant Secretaries (G5), S. Lord; Dr L. Mayhew; G. Foster

STATISTICS AND MANAGEMENT INFORMATION DIVISION (S7)
Director of Statistics and Management Information (G3), Mrs R. J. Butler
Chief Statisticians (G5), Miss P. W. Annesley; R. K. Willmer; G. J. O. Phillpotts

ECONOMICS AND OPERATIONAL RESEARCH DIVISION (HEALTH)
Chief Economic Adviser (G3), C. H. Smee
Senior Economic Advisers (G5), R. J. Churnside; J. W. Hurst

DEPARTMENTAL MANAGEMENT
Principal Establishment Officer (G3), M. G. Lillywhite
Assistant Secretaries (G5), Miss A. Stephenson; Ms P. Allen; Mrs S. Hughes; Ms P. A. Stewart

SOLICITOR'S OFFICE
Solicitor (G2), P. K. J. Thompson
Principal Assistant Solicitor (G3), A. D. Roberts
Proceedings Operational Director (G4), P. C. Nilsson

NHS TRUSTS UNIT
Head of Unit (G3), P. Garland
Operational Manager (G7), Dr V. Billingham

COMMITTEE ON THE SAFETY OF MEDICINES
Market Towers, 1 Nine Elms Lane, London SW8 5NQ
Tel 071-273 0451
Chairman, Prof. M. D. Rawlins

COMMITTEE ON DENTAL AND SURGICAL MATERIALS
Market Towers, 1 Nine Elms Lane, London SW8 5NQ
Tel 071-273 0502
Chairman, Prof. D. E. Poswillo, CBE

ADVISORY COMMITTEE ON THE MICROBIOLOGICAL SAFETY OF FOOD
Room 601A, Skipton House, 80 London Road, London SE1 6LW
Tel 071-972 5049
Chairman, Prof. H. M. Dick

CLINICAL STANDARDS ADVISORY GROUP
Room LG22, Wellington House, 133–155 Waterloo Road, London SE1 8UG
Tel 071-972 4926
Chairman, Sir Gordon Higginson

EXECUTIVE AGENCIES

NHS ESTATES
Euston Tower, 286 Euston Road, London NW1 3DN
Tel 071-388 1188

Chief Executive (G3), J. C. Locke
Estate Policy Director (G5), G. G. Mayers
Director of Business Development (G5), A. R. Tanner
Director of Resources (G5), L. J. Wardle
Head of Consultancy Services (G5), C. Davies
Chief Engineer (G5), L. W. M. Arrowsmith
Manager, Surveying Services (G6), A. Garbutt
Principal Nursing Adviser (G6), Mrs D. Vass

MEDICINES CONTROL AGENCY
Market Towers, 1 Nine Elms Lane, London SW8 5NQ
Tel 071-273 3000

Chief Executive, Dr K. H. Jones
Business Managers, D. O. Hagger; R. K. Alder; B. H. Hartley; Dr D. B. Jefferys; Dr S. M. Wood

NHS PENSIONS
Hesketh House, 200–220 Broadway, Fleetwood, Lancs. FY47 8LG
Tel 0253-774506

Chief Executive (G5), A. Cowan

HEALTH AND SAFETY COMMISSION
Baynards House, 1 Chepstow Place, Westbourne Grove, London W2 4TF
Tel 071-243 6000

The Health and Safety Commission was created under the Health and Safety at Work etc. Act 1974, with duties to reform health and safety law, to propose new regulations, and generally to promote the protection of people at work and of the public from hazards arising from industrial and commercial activity, including major industrial accidents and the transportation of hazardous materials.

The Commission members are appointed by the Secretary of State for Employment, although the Commission assists a number of Secretaries of State concerned with aspects of its functions. It is made up of representatives of employers, trades unions and local authorities, and has a full-time chairman.

The Commission can appoint agents, and it works in conjunction with local authorities who enforce the Act in such premises as offices and warehouses.

Chairman, vacant
Members, P. Jacques, CBE; A. Tuffin; R. Symons;
P. Gallagher; E. Carrick, Dame Rachel Waterhouse, DBE,
PH.D.; N. J. Pitcher; C. Chope; Dr G. Schofield
Secretary, T. Gates

HEALTH AND SAFETY EXECUTIVE
Baynards House, 1 Chepstow Place, Westbourne Grove,
London W2 4TF
Tel 071-243 6000

The Health and Safety Executive is the Health and Safety Commission's major instrument. Through its inspectorates it enforces health and safety law in the majority of industrial premises, to protect people at work and the public. The Executive advises the Commission in its major task of laying down safety standards through regulations and practical guidance for many industrial processes, liaising as necessary with government departments and other institutions. The Executive is also the licensing authority for nuclear installations. In carrying out its functions the Executive acts independently of the Government, guided only by the Commission as to general health and safety policy.

Director-General (G2), J. D. Rimington, CB (*at G1A*)
Deputy Directors-General (G2), D. C. T. Eves, CB;
Miss J. H. Bacon

HM FACTORY INSPECTORATE
HM Chief Inspector of Factories (G3), Dr J. T. Carter

HM AGRICULTURAL INSPECTORATE
HM Chief Agricultural Inspector (G3), F. D. Lindsay

HM MINES INSPECTORATE
HM Chief Inspector of Mines (G3), K. Twist

NUCLEAR SAFETY DIVISION
HM Chief Inspector of Nuclear Installations (G3),
Dr S. A. Harbison

HM RAILWAY INSPECTORATE
HM Chief Inspector of Railways (G3), S. S. J. Robertson

STRATEGY AND GENERAL DIVISION
Director (G3), Dr J. M. McQuaid

TECHNOLOGY AND HEALTH SCIENCES DIVISION
Includes HM Explosives Inspectorate
Director (G3), Dr A. Ellis

SAFETY POLICY DIVISION
Director (G3), R. S. Allison

RESEARCH AND LABORATORY SERVICES DIVISION
Director (G4), Dr A. Roberts

HEALTH POLICY DIVISION
Director of Medical Services (G3), A. W. Brown, CB

SOLICITOR'S OFFICE
Solicitor (G4), B. J. Ecclestone

RESOURCES AND PLANNING DIVISION
Including the Accident Prevention Advisory Unit
Director (G3), D. J. Hodgkins, CB

OFFSHORE SAFETY DIVISION
Chief Executive (G3), A. C. Barrell

HIGHLANDS AND ISLANDS ENTERPRISE
Bridge House, 20 Bridge Street, Inverness IV1 1QR
Tel 0463-234171

Highlands and Islands Enterprise (HIE) was set up in 1991 under the Enterprise and New Towns (Scotland) Act 1991. Its role is to design, direct and deliver enterprise development, training, environmental and social projects and services. In carrying out its role HIE operates through and in conjunction with ten Local Enterprise Companies (LECs) to which many of its individual functions are delegated, in particular those relating to the provision of Enterprise Assistance, Youth Training and the new Training for Work scheme. The LECs also design and develop initiatives at local level covering the wider range of economic and social development, training and environmental improvements.
Chairman, F. Morrison
Chief Executive, I. A. Robertson

HISTORIC BUILDINGS AND MONUMENTS COMMISSION FOR ENGLAND (ENGLISH HERITAGE)
Fortress House, 23 Savile Row, London W1X 1AB
Tel 071-973 3000

Under the National Heritage Act 1983, the duties of the Commission are to secure the preservation of ancient monuments and historic buildings; to promote the preservation and enhancement of conservation areas; and to promote the public's enjoyment of, and advance their knowledge of, ancient monuments and historic buildings and their preservation. The Commission has advisory committees on historic buildings and areas, ancient monuments, cathedrals and churches, and London.
Chairman, J. Stevens, CVO
Commissioners, HRH The Duke of Gloucester;
Miss J. A. Page (*Chief Executive*); Dr R. W. Brunskill;
The Lord Cavendish of Furness; Ms B. Cherry; Dr
N. Cossons; Sir Hugh Cubitt; T. Farrell; Sir David
Wilson; Mrs C. Lycett-Green; J. Seymour; R. Suddards;
G. Wilson

HISTORIC BUILDINGS COUNCIL FOR WALES
Brunel House, 2 Fitzalan Road, Cardiff CF2 1UY
Tel 0222-465511

The Council's function is to advise the Secretary of State for Wales through Cadw: Welsh Historic Monuments (*see* page 368), which is an executive agency within the Welsh Office.
Chairman, T. Lloyd, FSA
Members, W. Lindsay Evans; Prof. J. Eynon, OBE, FRIBA, FSA;
The Earl Lloyd George of Dwyfor; R. Haslam;
Dr P. Morgan
Secretary, R. W. Hughes

HISTORIC BUILDINGS COUNCIL FOR SCOTLAND
20 Brandon Street, Edinburgh EH3 5RA
Tel 031-244 2966

The Historic Buildings Council for Scotland is the advisory body to the Secretary of State for Scotland on matters related

to buildings of special architectural or historic interest and in particular to proposals for awards by him of grants for the repair of buildings of outstanding architectural or historic interest or lying within outstanding conservation areas.
Chairman, Sir Nicholas Fairbairn, QC, MP
Members, Sir Ilay Campbell, Bt.; Mrs P. Chalmers; Prof. J. D. Dunbar-Nasmith, CBE, FRSA, FRSE; M. Ellington; J. Hunter Blair; I. Hutchison, OBE; K. Martin; J. A. M. Mitchell, CB, CVO, MC; Miss G. Nayler; Revd C. Robertson; Prof. A. J. Rowan; Mrs F. Walker
Secretary, I. G. Dewar

ROYAL COMMISSION ON THE HISTORICAL MONUMENTS OF ENGLAND
Fortress House, 23 Savile Row, London WIX 2JQ
Tel 071-973 3500

The Royal Commission on the Historical Monuments of England was established in 1908. It is the national body charged with the recording and analysing of ancient and historical monuments and buildings. It compiles, preserves and makes publicly available the national archive of such material, which is housed in the National Monuments Record. The Commission is due to move to Swindon in the spring of 1994.
Chairman, The Baroness Park of Monmouth, CMG, OBE
Commissioners, Prof. R. Bradley, FSA; D. J. Keene, PH.D.; Prof. G. H. Martin, CBE, D.Phil., FSA; Prof. G. I. Meirion-Jones, PH.D., FSA; Prof. A. C. Thomas, CBE, D.Litt., FSA; Prof. M. Biddle, FBA, FSA; Mrs B. K. Cherry, FSA; R. D. H. Gem, PH.D., FSA; T. R. M. Longman; R. A. Yorke; Miss A. Riches, FSA; Dr M. Airs, FSA; Prof. M. Fulford, PH.D., FSA; Dr M. Palmer, FSA
Secretary, T. G. Hassall, FSA

ROYAL COMMISSION ON ANCIENT AND HISTORICAL MONUMENTS IN WALES
Crown Building, Plas Crug, Aberystwyth, Dyfed SY23 INJ
Tel 0970-624381

The Commission was established in 1908 to make an inventory of the ancient and historical monuments of Wales and Monmouthshire. It is currently empowered by a royal warrant of 1992 to survey, record, publish and maintain a database of ancient and historical sites, structures and landscapes in Wales. The Commission is also responsible for the National Monuments Record of Wales, which is open daily for public reference.
Chairman, Prof. J. B. Smith
Commissioners, R. W. Brunskill, OBE, PH.D., FSA; Prof. D. Ellis Evans, D.Phil., FBA; Prof. R. A. Griffiths, PH.D.; D. Gruffyd Jones; R. M. Haslam, FSA; Prof. G. B. D. Jones, D.Phil., FSA; Mrs A. Nicol; S. B. Smith; G. J. Wainwright, MBE, PH.D., FSA; E. Wiliam, PH.D., FSA
Secretary, P. R. White, FSA

ROYAL COMMISSION ON THE ANCIENT AND HISTORICAL MONUMENTS OF SCOTLAND
John Sinclair House, 16 Bernard Terrace, Edinburgh EH8 9NX
Tel 031-662 1446

The Commission was established in 1908 and is appointed to provide for the survey and recording of ancient and historical monuments connected with the culture, civilization and conditions of life of the people in Scotland from the earliest times. It compiles and maintains the National Monuments Record of Scotland as the national record of the archaeological and historical environment. The National Monuments Record is open for reference Mon.–Thurs. 9.30–4.30, Fri. 9.30–4.
Chairman, The Earl of Crawford and Balcarres, PC
Commissioners, Prof. J. M. Coles, PH.D., FBA; Prof. J. D. Dunbar-Nasmith, CBE, FRIBA; Prof. Rosemary Cramp, CBE, FSA; Mrs P. E. Durham; Prof. T. C. Smout, PH.D.; The Hon. Lord Cullen; Dr D. J. Howard, FSA; The Hon. P. D. E. M. Moncreiffe; R. A. Paxton
Secretary, R. J. Mercer, FSA

ANCIENT MONUMENTS BOARD FOR WALES
Brunel House, 2 Fitzalan Road, Cardiff CF2 IUY
Tel 0222-465511

The Ancient Monuments Board for Wales advises the Secretary of State for Wales on his statutory functions in respect of ancient monuments.
Chairman, Prof. G. Williams, CBE, FBA, FSA
Members, R. B. Heaton, OBE, FRIBA; Prof. R. R. Davies, FBA, D.Phil.; Dr S. H. R. Aldhouse-Green, FSA; R. G. Keen; Miss F. Lynch, FSA; Prof. W. H. Manning, PH.D., FSA; D. Moore, RD, FSA; Dr P. Smith, FSA; Prof. J. B. Smith
Secretary, S. Morris

ANCIENT MONUMENTS BOARD FOR SCOTLAND
20 Brandon Street, Edinburgh EH3 5RA
Tel 031-244 3108

The Ancient Monuments Board for Scotland advises the Secretary of State for Scotland on the exercise of his functions, under the Ancient Monuments and Archaeological Areas Act 1979, of providing protection for monuments of national importance. Protection may be provided by including a monument in a statutory list of protected monuments, by acquisition, or by guardianship in which the Secretary of State assumes responsibility for maintenance.
Chairman, Prof. E. C. Fernie, FSA, FSA SCOT.
Members, Prof. A. Fenton, CBE, FRSE, FSA SCOT.; J. Simpson, FSA SCOT.; Sir Jamie Stormonth Darling, CBE, MC, TD, WS; Mrs E. V. W. Proudfoot, FSA, FSA SCOT.; Mrs K. Dalyell; J. H. A. Gerrard, FRSA; T. R. H. Godden, FSA; L. J. Masters, FSA; Dr A. Richie; R. D. Kernohan, OBE; Dr J. Morgan, FSA SCOT.; Prof. C. D. Morris, FSA, FSA SCOT.; R. J. Mercer, FSA; W. D. H. Sellar, FSA SCOT.; Lady Jane Grosvenor
Secretary, R. A. J. Dalziel
Assessor, D. J. Breeze, PH.D., FSA

HOME-GROWN CEREALS AUTHORITY
Hamlyn House, Highgate Hill, London NI9 5PR
Tel 071-263 3391

Set up under the Cereals Marketing Act 1965, the Authority consists of nine members representing UK cereal growers, nine representing dealers in, or processors of, grain and three independent members. The Authority's functions are

to improve the production and marketing of UK-grown cereals through a research and development programme, to provide a market information service, and to promote UK cereals in export markets. The Authority also undertakes agency work for the Intervention Board in connection with the application in the UK of the Common Agricultural Policy for cereals.
Chairman, G. B. Nelson
General Manager, C. J. Ames

BRITISH CEREAL EXPORTS
Chairman, R. J. Cherrington
Manager, J. B. Rose

HOME OFFICE
50 Queen Anne's Gate, London SWIH 9AT
Tel 071-273 3000

The Home Office deals with those internal affairs in England and Wales which have not been assigned to other government departments. The Home Secretary is particularly concerned with the administration of justice; criminal law; the treatment of offenders, including probation and the prison service; the police; immigration and nationality; passport policy matters; community relations; certain public safety matters; and fire and civil emergencies services. The Home Secretary personally is the link between The Queen and the public, and exercises certain powers on her behalf, including that of the Royal Pardon.

Other subjects dealt with include electoral arrangements; addresses and petitions to The Queen; ceremonial and formal business connected with honours; requests for extradition of criminals; scrutiny of local authority byelaws; granting of licences for scientific procedures involving animals; cremations, burials and exhumations; firearms; dangerous drugs and poisons; general policy on laws relating to shops, liquor licensing, gaming and lotteries, charitable collections and marriage; theatre and cinema licensing; co-ordination of government action in relation to the voluntary social services; and race relations policy.

The Home Secretary is also the link between the UK government and the governments of the Channel Islands and the Isle of Man.
Secretary of State for the Home Department, The Rt. Hon. Michael Howard, QC, MP
Principal Private Secretary (G5), Miss J. MacNaughton
Private Secretaries, Mrs S. J. McCarthy; Ms J. D. Walker
Special Adviser, P. Rock
Parliamentary Private Secretary, Dr L. Fox, MP
Ministers of State, The Earl Ferrers, PC; Peter Lloyd, MP; David Maclean, MP
Special Adviser, D. Cameron
Parliamentary Private Secretaries:
To Mr Lloyd, D. Wilshire, MP
To Mr Maclean, J. Arnold, MP
Parliamentary Under-Secretary of State, Charles Wardle, MP
Parliamentary Clerk, Miss R. McCool
Permanent Under-Secretary of State (G1), Sir Clive Whitmore, GCB, CVO
Private Secretary, C. Dolphin
Chief Medical Officer (at Department of Health), Dr K. Calman

LEGAL ADVISER'S BRANCH
Legal Adviser (G2), M. L. Saunders, CB
Principal Assistant Legal Advisers (G3), D. J. Bentley, CB; Miss P. A. Edwards

Assistant Legal Advisers, R. J. Clayton; Mrs S. A. Evans; J. R. O'Meara; C. M. L. Osborne; D. Seymour
Senior Principal Legal Assistants, H. M. Carter; Ms M. Carter; Miss R. P. Davies; Mrs J. M. Jones; Mrs C. Price

CRIMINAL, RESEARCH AND STATISTICS DEPARTMENTS
Deputy Under-Secretary (G2), J. F. Halliday

CRIMINAL POLICY DEPARTMENT
Assistant Under-Secretary of State (G3), A. P. Wilson
Heads of Divisions (G5), Miss C. Macready; J. M. Potts; Miss C. J. Stewart; R. C. Stoate
Chief Inspector, Drugs Branch (G6), A. McFarlane
Senior Principals (G6), A. Norbury; T. C. Morris; M. Rumble
Principals (G7), R. Allen; Miss D. Collings; P. Dawson; R. G. W. Dyce; D. H. Evans; B. Gange; L. T. Hughes; Ms J. L. Hutcheon; N. Jordon; Mrs P. Lutterloch; Miss H. L. McKinnon; Mrs R. M. Mitev; M. J. Narey; R. D. Parsons; D. Rigby; Ms L. Rogerson; Miss A. M. Rutherford; G. H. H. Sonnenberg; Ms F. Taylor; J. R. Thew; P. Topping; P. F. Vallance

RESEARCH AND STATISTICS DEPARTMENT
Assistant Under-Secretary of State (G3), C. P. Nuttall

RESEARCH AND PLANNING UNIT
Head of Unit (G5), R. Tarling
Grade 6, J. M. Hough; P. J. Jordan; Mrs P. Mayhew; G. R. Walmsley
Principals (G7), A. C. Barton; D. C. Brown; J. A. Ditchfield; Dr P. J. Ekblom; Dr S. Field; Ms M. Fitzgerald; J. H. Graham; Dr P. Grove; Mrs K. E. Howard; T. Marshall; Ms P. M. Morgan; Miss J. W. Mott; Dr G. I. U. Mair; J. F. Mcleod; A. D. Moxon; F. P. E. Southgate; Dr I. P. Williamson

STATISTICS DEPARTMENT
Chief Statisticians (G5), K. Childs; C. G. Lewis; J. L. Walker
Grade 6, Mrs C. L. Lehmann; R. Pape; D. A. Povey; P. Sheriff; P. White
Grade 7, Ms A. Barber; G. G. Barclay; W. Burns; P. F. Collier; L. Davidoff; Mrs P. Dowdeswell; N. Frater; Z. Frosztega; I. Gaskell; Miss G. Goddard; Mrs A. James; K. M. Jackson; Mrs S. Keith; M. Lock; Miss A. Maxwell; Mrs P. A. Penneck; D. A. Povey; P. E. Ramell; P. Sheriff; R. M. Taylor; D. Turner; M. Uglow; P. White; Miss M. Wilkinson

CRIMINAL JUSTICE AND CONSTITUTIONAL DEPARTMENT
Assistant Under-Secretary of State (G3), R. M. Morris
Heads of Divisions (G5), E. A. Grant; P. J. Honour; Miss S. Marshall; P. R. C. Storr
Grade 6, M. P. Cook; R. G. Evans; Miss A. Fletcher; G. H. Marriage
Principals (G7), Mrs P. Baskerville; Mrs M. K. Branwell; Ms J. Cooke; S. L. Cox; Miss R. M. Fletton; J. Glaze; Ms M. Gorman; L. D. Hay; Mrs G. Hetherington; H. D. Hillier; Mrs S. J. McDougall; Mrs S. Mann; Miss S. E. Rae; K. E. R. Rogers; D. Ross; J. Wake; S. M. K. Willmington; R. W. Wootton
Chief Inspector of Probation (G4), G. W. Smith, CBE
Deputy Chief Inspector of Probation (G5), J. C. Haines

ANIMALS (SCIENTIFIC PROCEDURE) INSPECTORATE
Chief Inspector, Dr R. M. Watt

POLICE DEPARTMENT
Deputy Under-Secretary (G2), I. M. Burns, CB

POLICE DEPARTMENT
Assistant Under-Secretaries of State (G3), Miss
  M. A. Clayton; Miss C. Sinclair; J. Warne;
  G. J. Wasserman
Heads of Divisions (G5), Mrs P. G. W. Catto; Mrs
  C. Crawford; J. B. Duke-Evans; Mrs B. Fair;
  R. A. Harrington; K. H. Heal; D. A. Hill; A. Holt; Miss
  D. Loudon; N. C. Sanderson; E. Soden; R. R. Tilt
Senior Principals (G6), D. R. Birleson; D. Crick;
  R. A. Ginman; Dr G. K. Laycock; D. Rowe; Dr
  G. Turnbull
Principals (G7), Mrs J. Anderson; R. C. Barron; Dr
  B. J. Blain; Mrs J. Bonelle; J. W. Bradley; K. Brennan;
  R. Brett; D. Brown; G. Brown; Ms C. Checksfield; Mrs
  P. Cocks; G. T. Coulthard; N. Custanco; M. de Pulford;
  M. Dexter; Miss J. D. Erwteman; D. Faulks; A. Ford;
  N. Hancock; M. J. I. Hill; K. Hopley; G. R. Houghton;
  Mrs R. Johnson; A. N. Kent; Dr D. K. Laing;
  A. Maclean; E. Maclean; P. Martin; D. Massey;
  N. F. Montgomery-Pott; Mrs G. I. Moody; Mrs
  B. Moore; D. C. Moulton; M. Phillips; Mrs I. Posen;
  C. A. Pounds; P. W. Pugh; Mrs M. Rolfe; Miss
  J. B. Rumble; D. G. Skene; P. T. Smith; Mrs
  A. R. Stiling; R. Sutcliffe; D. Theobald; G. H. Thomas;
  P. Tomlinson; Mrs A. Underhill; R. H. Watt; B. Webb;
  P. D. White; G. A. Widdecombe; D. Wright; Dr
  J. Youell

POLICE SCIENTIFIC DEVELOPMENT BRANCH
Sandridge Laboratories, Woodcock Hill, Sandridge,
St Albans, Herts. AL4 9HQ
Tel 0727-865051

Head of Laboratory (G6)

Langhurst House, Langhurstwood Road, Nr. Horsham,
Sussex RH12 4WX
Tel 0403-55451

FORENSIC SCIENCE SERVICE HEADQUARTERS
Priory House, Gooch Street North, Birmingham B5 6QQ
Tel 021-666 6606

An executive agency within the Home Office.
Director-General (G3), Dr J. Thompson
Grade 5, vacant
Head of Personnel and Administration (G6), J. P. Emery
Grade 7, Mrs E. Sadler (*policy*); Mrs D. Grice

POLICE NATIONAL COMPUTER (HENDON DATA
CENTRE)
Aerodrome Road, Colindale, London NW9 5LN
Tel 081-200 2424

Head of Division (G6), J. Ladley
Principals (G7), J. A. Henderson; D. McGarry;
  L. D. Watson

DTELS (DIRECTORATE OF TELECOMMUNICATIONS)
DTELS House, Mereway, Ruddington, Nottingham
NG11 6JU
Tel 0602-406161

Head of Directorate (G5), N. F. K. Finlayson
Assistant Director (G6), J. F. Nicholson
Head of Operations (G6), vacant
Head of Marketing (G6), I. Aitken

Head of Engineering Consultancy (G6), vacant
Principals (G7), S. R. Cole; W. Hogg; A. Hulme;
  A. N. Kent; T. J. Logan; R. J. Sanders; K. Staves;
  R. Tuckley; L. T. Whiteside

HM INSPECTORATE OF CONSTABULARY
HM Chief Inspector of Constabulary (£83,944), T. A. Morris,
  CBE, QPM
HM Inspectors (£68,671–£75,899), G. J. Dear, QPM;
  D. Elliott, CBE, QPM; B. Hayes, CBE, QPM; Sir Philip
  Myers, OBE, QPM; D. J. O'Dowd, QPM; C. Smith, CVO, QPM

POLICE STAFF COLLEGE
Bramshill House, Basingstoke, Hants. RG27 0JW
Tel 025 126-2931

Commandant, Sir Robert Bunyard, KBE, QPM
Deputy Commandant and Director of Courses, J. A. Dickinson
National Director of Police Training, P. Ryan, QPM

THE SECURITY SERVICE (MI5)
PO Box 3255, London SW1P 1AE

The Security Service took over responsibility for mainland
intelligence about Irish terrorism in October 1992. Counter-
terrorism activities account for 70 per cent of its work;
25 per cent involves counter-espionage and counter-
proliferation activities, and the remaining 5 per cent involves
the monitoring of subversive organizations. The Service is
split into two sections, Operations and Administration.
Director-General, Mrs S. Rimington

EQUAL OPPORTUNITIES, IMMIGRATION
AND NATIONALITY DEPARTMENTS
Deputy Under-Secretary (G2), A. J. Langdon

EQUAL OPPORTUNITIES AND GENERAL DEPARTMENT
Assistant Under-Secretary of State (G3), M. E. Head, CVO
Heads of Divisions (G5), N. M. Johnson, CBE; R. Kornicki;
  A. Harding
Principals (G7), W. Brandon; Ms C. Dale;
  P. R. Edmundson; Mrs J. M. Flascher; Mrs
  D. D. Gonsalves; Mrs J. S. Morris; G. Sutton;
  R. A. Wright

Voluntary Services Unit
Assistant Secretary (G5), D. J. Hardwick
Principals (G7), R. G. W. Cook; Miss V. R. Hatcher;
  F. Smith; Ms N. Williams

IMMIGRATION AND NATIONALITY DEPARTMENT
Lunar House, 40 Wellesley Road, Croydon, Surrey, CR9 2BY
Tel 081-686 0688
Assistant Under-Secretaries of State (G3), W. A. Jeffrey;
  A. R. Rawsthorne
Heads of Divisions (G5), E. B. Nicholls; Mrs E. C. L. Pallett;
  K. D. Sutton; R. M. Whalley; P. N. Wrench; R. G. Yates
Senior Principals (G6), T. Farrage; C. J. Saunders;
  A. Walmsley
Principals (G7), C. A. Allison; G. Brindle; W. F. Bryant;
  D. Burgess; J. Casey; J. Couch; A. Cunningham;
  W. M. Dawnie; J. Gilbert; D. J. Hunt; Mrs C. Kellas;
  C. J. Kelly; B. D. C. Mennell; T. L. Neale; C. Passey; Ms
  C. Pelham; T. R. Peters; Miss G. M. Romney; Ms
  C. Stewart; J. Sweet; D. Truscott; Mrs F. Webster;
  R. B. Woodland

Immigration Service
Director (Ports) (G5), Miss K. J. Collins
Director (Immigration Service Enforcement) (G5),
  C. B. Manchip
Deputy Directors (G6), G. Boiling; J. M. de Llanos;
  D. J. McDonough

Assistant Directors (G7), B. R. Barrett; Miss G. M. Griffith;
V. Hogg; D. I. Ingham; G. Maguire; D. Mould;
P. Quibell; C. Passey; K. Richardson

EUROPEAN COMMUNITIES UNIT
Head of Division (G5), M. J. Gillespie
Grade 7, Dr S. Hadjipavlou

HM PRISON SERVICE
Cleland House, Page Street, London SW1P 4LN
Tel 071-217 3000

An executive agency within the Home Office.

NON-CIVIL SERVICE GRADE SALARIES

HM Chief Inspector of Prisons	£78,378
Prison Service Governor 1	£45,157
Prison Service Governor 2	£40,776
Prison Service Governor 3	£35,215
Prison Service Governor 4	£27,902–£30,285

THE PRISONS BOARD
Chairman, and Chief Executive of the Prison Service (G2),
D. C. Lewis
Director of Personnel and Finance (G3), A. J. Butler
Director of Inmate Administration (G3), I. Dunbar, CB
Director of Inmate Programmes (G3), A. J. Pearson
Director of Custody (G3), Miss P. C. Drew
Director of Services and Parole (G3), Ms J. Reisz
Director of Prison Health Care (G3), Dr R. Wool
Non-Executive Members, Mrs U. Banerjee; F. W. Bentley

PRISON SERVICE
Heads of Divisions (G5), I. Boon; J. I. Chisholm; Miss
L. F. Gill; Mrs E. J. Grimsey; G. E. Guy; Mrs
V. V. R. Harris; S. B. Hickson; R. C. Masefield;
H. H. Taylor; R. J. Weatherill; P. Wheatley; T. Wilson
Assistant Director of Prison Medical Services (G4), Dr
J. Sinclair
Principal Medical Officers (G4), Dr R. Gooch; Dr
R. Harkness; Dr M. Longfield; Dr P. B. Pattison; Dr
G. Penton; Dr R. Ralli; Dr D. Speed; Dr A. Todd
Senior Principals (G6), D. M. Ackland; Mrs P. Almond; Mrs
H. M. Bayne; P. Cook; R. E. Corrigan; C. F. Drewitt;
B. Johnson; R. W. Lockett; B. S. Luetchford; Dr
C. McDougall; P. Sleightholme; C. L. Spencer
Governors (1), J. W. Dring; G. Gregory-Smith; I. Ward;
C. J. Williams
Principals (G7), C. Allars; J. H. Attridge; A. J. Beasley;
A. D. Burgess; N. Burton; H. M. C. Crudge; P. Done;
J. A. Greenland; Mrs M. Haughey, MBE; N. F. M. Home;
G. P. Hopkins; C. Hudson; M. W. Jarvis; Mrs
V. Keating; R. S. H. Kettle; M. P. Loughlin; Ms
P. Lowe; K. MacKenzie; N. Maclean; K. Marshall;
C. R. Miller; Mrs E. Moody; D. S. Neal; Mrs A. Nelson;
N. Newcomen; J. S. Nottingham; J. Page; S. J. Rimmer;
J. S. Sarjantson; D. Shene; R. E. Smith; D. J. Tallock;
M. Todd; J. M. G. Toon; G. Utteridge; T. A. Ward; Miss
S. Weinel; S. C. Wells; W. F. Whiteing; Ms
A. Wickington; Mrs V. M. Wilsdon; A. Woolfenden;
R. J. Wood; P. Wright
Governors (2), Miss M. Carden; C. Lambert; Miss
S. F. McCormick; M. Morrison; C. Scott; D. Shaw;
A. G. Smith; D. Wilson
Chaplain-General and Archdeacon of the Prison Service,
Ven. D. Fleming
Chief Education Officer (G6), I. G. Benson
Chief Physical Education Officer (G6), M. W. Denton
Governors (3), M. Ainsworth; H. Bagshaw; T. Davies;
J. R. Dovell; W. S. Duff; Mrs M. Eagan; S. Eley; Mrs
S. Fielder; J. Forster; G. Gibson; D. Godfrey;

P. L. Hanaway; Ms U. McCollom; A. Mills; D. Myers;
P. Quinn; Miss P. Scriven; J. Talbot; P. Tebrey;
I. Truffet; R. W. Walker

DIRECTORATE OF WORKS
Abell House, John Islip Street, London SW1P 4LH
Tel 071-217 3000

Director of Works (G4), W. L. Sparks, CBE
Group Managers:
Superintending Architect (G6), S. Mahraj
Chief Civil Structural Engineer (G6), R. W. T. Haines
Chief Mechanical and Electrical Engineer (G6), R. Putland
Grade 6, B. Stickley
Principals (G7), O. Astaniotis; P. J. Attwater; B. J. Bleet;
C. F. Brown; J. K. Chamberlain; R. Chick; M. J. Davies;
J. B. Dawson; R. D'Cruz; J. A. Doohan; P. Enticknap;
J. V. Gleed; M. C. Hayes; G. E. Hickey; J. J. Hurley;
C. J. Lawton; L. P. Lumley; D. Newton; S. Richards;
M. Ryland; M. Sweeny; R. J. Tricker; A. Weeks

DSP3 (PRISON SERVICE INDUSTRIES AND FARMS)
Block A, Whitgift Centre, Wellesley Road, Croydon, Surrey
CR9 3LY
Tel 081-686 8710

Director (G5), P. R. A. Fulton
Group Managers (G6), R. K. Fisher; A. Sweeney; J. Weller
Governor (1), K. M. Brewer
Principals (G7), J. Cairns; R. Daw; J. W. Fallows;
B. D. Feist; P. J. Goulder; J. A. Gillcrist; C. Handley;
G. A. Merrett; D. E. Neville; T. Senior; A. S. Wilson;
R. M. Young

SUPPLY AND TRANSPORT BRANCH
Crown House, 52 Elizabeth Street, Corby, Northants
Tel 0536-202101

Director (G5), D. J. C. Kent
Grade 6, B. J. David
Principals (G7), R. C. Brett; D. J. Brown; M. Fitzgerald;
D. J. Miller

AREA MANAGERS (GOVERNORS 1)

Directorate of Custody (DOC)
East Anglia, T. G. Murtagh, OBE
Kent, J. Hunter
London North, Miss A. M. Edwards
London South, P. J. Kitteridge
South Coast, A. Rayfield

Directorate of Inmate Administration (DIA)
Central, J. Blakey
Mercia, D. Curtis
Chilterns, A. de Frisching
Wales and the West, J. Wilkinson
Wessex, R. J. May

Directorate of Inmate Programmes (DIP)
East Midland, J. C. Mullens
North-East, A. H. Papps
North-West, D. I. Lockwood
Trans-Pennine, T. Bone
Yorkshire, M. Codd

PRISONS
ACKLINGTON (DIP), Morpeth, Northumberland
NE65 9XF. *Governor*, F. P. Masserick
ALBANY (DOC), Newport, Isle of Wight PO30 5RS.
Governor, R. Mitchell
ALDINGTON (DOC), Ashford, Kent TN25 7BQ. *Governor*,
D. A. Bratton

ASHWELL (DIA), Oakham, Leics. LEI5 7LS. *Governor,*
H. Reid

*ASKHAM GRANGE (DIP), Askham Richard, York YO2 3PT.
Governor, H. E. Crew

BEDFORD (DOC), St Loyes Street, Bedford MK40 1HG.
Governor, S. P. Moore

BELMARSH (DOC), Western Way, Thamesmead, London
SE28 OEB. *Governor,* H. D. Jones

BIRMINGHAM (DIA), Winson Green Road, Birmingham
B18 4AS. *Governor,* C. B. Scott

BLAKENHURST (private prison), Hewell Lane, Redditch,
Worcs. B97 6QS. *Controller,* P. J. Hanglin

BLANTYRE HOUSE (DOC), Goudhurst, Cranbrook, Kent
TN17 2NH. *Governor,* J. Semple

BLUNDESTON (DOC), Lowestoft, Suffolk NR32 5BG.
Governor, S. Robinson

BRISTOL (DIA), Cambridge Road, Bristol BS7 8PS.
Governor, R. D. Dixon

BRIXTON (DOC), PO Box 369, Jebb Avenue, London
SW2 5XF. *Governor,* Dr A. Coyle

BROCKHILL (DIA), Redditch, Worcs. B97 6RD. *Governor,*
B. Stanhope

BULLINGDON (DIA), Padrick Haugh Road, Arncott,
Bicester, Oxon. OX6 0PZ. *Governor,* J. Thomas-Ferrand

*BULLWOOD HALL (DOC), High Road, Hockley, Essex
SS5 4TE. *Governor,* vacant

CAMP HILL (DOC), Newport, Isle of Wight PO30 5PB.
Governor, W. A. Wood

CANTERBURY (DOC), Longport, Canterbury, Kent CT1 1PJ.
Governor, J. L. Harrison

CARDIFF (DIA), Knox Road, Cardiff CF2 1UG. *Governor,*
N. D. Clifford

CASTINGTON (DIP), Morpeth, Northumberland NE65 9XF.
Governor, C. Harder

CHANNINGS WOOD (DIA), Denbury, Newton Abbott,
Devon TQ12 6DW. *Governor,* R. S. Brandon

CHELMSFORD (DOC), Springfield Road, Chelmsford,
Essex CM2 6LQ. *Governor,* D. B. Sinclair

COLDINGLEY (DIA), Bisley, Woking, Surrey GU24 9EX.
Governor, J. Capel

*COOKHAM WOOD (DOC), Cookham Wood, Rochester,
Kent MEI 3LU. *Governor,* Mrs C. Ellis

DARTMOOR (DIA), Princetown, Yelverton, Devon
PL20 6RR. *Governor,* J. Powls

DORCHESTER (DIA), North Square, Dorchester, Dorset
DTI 1JD. *Governor,* R. Walker

DOWNVIEW (DOC), Sutton Lane, Sutton, Surrey SM2 5PD.
Governor, D. Aram

*DRAKE HALL (DIA), Eccleshall, Staffs. ST21 6LQ. *Governor,*
R. J. Crouch

*DURHAM (DIP), Old Elvet, Durham DHI 3HU. *Governor,*
M. Mogg

*EAST SUTTON PARK (DOC), Sutton Valence, Maidstone,
Kent MEI7 3DF. *Governor,* W. S. Duff

*ELMLEY (DOC), Church Road, Eastchurch, Sheerness,
Kent MEI2 4DZ. *Governor,* W. J. Cooper

ERLESTOKE HOUSE (DIA), Devizes, Wilts. SNI0 5TU.
Governor, Ms A. J. Gomme

EVERTHORPE (DIP), Brough, North Humberside
HUI5 1RB. *Governor,* R. Smith

EXETER (DIA), New North Road, Exeter, Devon EX4 4EX.
Governor, D. Alderson

FEATHERSTONE (DIA), New Road, Featherstone,
Wolverhampton WVI0 7PU. *Governor,* L. M. Wiltshire

FORD (DOC), Arundel, W. Sussex BNI8 0BX. *Governor,*
Maj. B. Smith

FRANKLAND (DIP), Frankland, Brasside, Durham,
DHI 5YD. *Governor,* P. Buxton

FULL SUTTON (DIP), Full Sutton, York YO4 IPS. *Governor,*
J. W. Staples

GARTH (DIP), Ulnes Walton Lane, Leyland, Preston,
Lancs. PR5 3NE. *Governor,* W. Rose-Quirie

GARTREE (DIA), Leicester Road, Market Harborough,
Leics. LEI6 7RP. *Governor,* R. J. Perry

GLOUCESTER (DIA), Barrack Square, Gloucester GLI 2JN.
Governor, P. W. Winkley

GRENDON (DOC), Grendon Underwood, Aylesbury,
Bucks. HP18 0TL. *Governor,* T. C. Newell

HASLAR (DOC), Dolphin Way, Gosport, Hants. PO12 2AW.
Governor, J. R. Dovell

HAVERIGG (DIP), Haverigg Camp, Millom, Cumbria
LAI8 4NA. *Governor,* B. Wilson

HEWELL GRANGE (DIA), Redditch, Worcs. B97 6QQ.
Governor, D. W. Bamber

HIGH DOWN (DOC), Sutton Lane, Sutton, Surrey SM2 5PJ.
Governor, S. Pryor

HIGHPOINT (DOC), Stradishall, Newmarket, Suffolk
CB8 9YG. *Governor,* C. D. Sherwood

HINDLEY (DIP), Gibson Street, Bickershaw, Hindley,
Wigan, Lancs. WN2 5TH. *Governor,* D. Roberts

HOLLESLEY BAY COLONY (DOC), Hollesley, Woodbridge,
Suffolk IPI2 3JS. *Governor,* M. F. Clarke

*HOLLOWAY (DOC), Parkhurst Road, London N7 0NU.
Governor, T. M. O'Sullivan

HOLME HOUSE (DIP), Holme House Road, Stockton-on-
Tees, Cleveland TSI8 2QU. *Governor,* A. K. Rawson

HULL (DIP), Hedon Road, Hull, N. Humberside HU9 5LS.
Governor, R. Daly

KINGSTON (DOC), Milton Road, Portsmouth PO3 6AS.
Governor, R. Merricks

KIRKHAM (DIP), Preston, Lancs. PR4 2RA. *Governor,*
A. F. Jennings

KIRKLEVINGTON GRANGE (DIP), Yarm, Cleveland TSI5
9PA. *Governor,* M. K. Lees

LANCASTER (DIP), The Castle, Lancaster LAI IYL.
Governor, D. G. McNaughton

LATCHMERE HOUSE (DOC), Church Road, Ham
Common, Richmond, Surrey TWI0 5HH. *Governor,*
S. O'Neill

LEEDS (DIP), Armley, Leeds LSI2 2TJ. *Governor,*
A. J. Fitzpatrick

LEICESTER (DIA), Welford Road, Leicester LE2 7AJ.
Governor, G. Ross

LEWES (DOC), Brighton Road, Lewes, E. Sussex BN7 IEA.
Governor, J. F. Dixon

LEYHILL (DIA), Wotton-under-Edge, Glos. GLI2 8HL.
Governor, D. T. Williams

LINCOLN (DIP), Greetwell Road, Lincoln LN2 4BD.
Governor, D. Shaw

LINDHOLME (DIP), Bawtry Road, Hatfield, Woodhouse,
Doncaster DN7 6EE. *Governor,* P. Leonard

LITTLEHEY (DOC), Perry, Huntingdon, Cambs. PEI8 0SR.
Governor, M. L. Knight

LIVERPOOL (DIP), 68 Hornby Road, Liverpool L9 3DF.
Governor, R. H. Jacques

LONG LARTIN (DIA), South Littleton, Evesham, Worcs.
WRII 5TZ. *Governor,* P. Atherton

MAIDSTONE (DOC), County Road, Maidstone MEI4 IUZ.
Governor, P. J. Meakings

MANCHESTER (DIP), Southall Street, Manchester
M60 9AH. *Governor,* R. P. Halward

MOORLAND (DIP), Hatfield Woodhouse, Doncaster
DN7 6BW. *Governor,* C. R. Griffiths
MORTON HALL (DIP), Swinderby, Lincoln LN6 9PS.
Governor, C. P. A. Bushell
THE MOUNT (DIA), Molyneaux Avenue, Bovingdon,
Hemel Hempstead HP3 0NZ. *Governor,* Mrs M. Donnelly
*NEW HALL (DIP), Dial Wood, Flockton, Wakefield, W.
Yorks. WF4 4AX. *Governor,* D. England
NORTH SEA CAMP (DIP), Freiston, Boston, Lincs.
PE22 0QX. *Governor,* R. Reveley
NORWICH (DIP), Mousehold, Norwich NR1 4LU. *Governor,*
Miss J. M. Fowler
NOTTINGHAM (DIP), Perry Road, Sherwood, Nottingham
NG5 3AG. *Governor,* L. Lavender
OXFORD (DIA), New Road, Oxford OX1 1LZ. *Governor,*
R. J. Talbot
PARKHURST (DOC), Newport, Isle of Wight PO30 5NX.
Governor, J. R. Marriott
PENTONVILLE (DOC), Caledonian Road, London N7 8TT.
Governor, W. J. Abbott
PRESTON (DIP), 2 Ribbleton Lane, Preston, Lancs.
ORI 5AB. *Governor,* R. Doughty
RANBY (DIP), Ranby, Retford, Notts. DN22 8EU. *Governor,*
F. Abbott
*RISLEY (DIP), Warrington Road, Risley, Warrington
WA3 6BP. *Governor,* F. B. O'Friel.
ROCHESTER (DOC), Rochester, Kent ME1 3QS. *Governor,*
D. Wilson
RUDGATE (DIP), Wetherby, W. Yorks. LS23 7AZ.
Governor, H. Jones
SEND (DOC), Ripley Road, Send, Woking, Surrey
GU23 7LJ. *Governor,* A. French
SHEPTON MALLET (DIA), Cornhill, Shepton Mallet,
Somerset BA4 5LU. *Governor,* P. O'Sullivan
SHREWSBURY (DIA), The Dana, Shrewsbury, Salop
SY1 2HR. *Governor,* D. J. Bradley
STAFFORD (DIA), 54 Gaol Road, Stafford ST16 3AW.
Governor, vacant
STANDFORD HILL (DOC), Church Road, Eastchurch,
Sheerness, Kent ME12 4AA. *Governor,* D. M. Twiner
STOCKEN (DIP), Stocken Hall Road, Stretton, Nr Oakham,
Leics. LE15 7RD. *Governor,* D. Hall
STOCKE HEATH (DIA), Market Drayton, Shropshire
TF9 2JL. *Governor,* J. Alldridge
*STYAL (DIP), Wilmslow, Cheshire SK9 4HR. *Governor,*
G. Walker
SUDBURY (DIA), Sudbury, Derbys. DE6 5HW. *Governor,*
P. E. Salter
SWALESIDE (DOC), Eastchurch, Isle of Sheppey, Kent
ME12 4AX. *Governor,* R. Tasker
SWANSEA (DIA), Oystermouth Road, Swansea SA1 2SR.
Governor, J. Heyes
THORP ARCH (DIP), Wetherby, W. Yorks. LS23 7AY.
Governor, G. Barnard
USK (DIA), 29 Maryport Street, Usk, Gwent NP5 1XP.
Governor, N. J. Evans
THE VERNE (DIA), Portland, Dorset DT5 1EQ. *Governor,*
T. M. Turner
WAKEFIELD (DIP), Love Lane, Wakefield WF2 9AG.
Governor, R. S. Duncan
WANDSWORTH (DOC), PO Box 757, Heathfield Road,
London SW18 3HS. *Governor,* C. G. Clarke
WAYLAND (DOC), Wayland, Griston, Thetford, Norfolk
IP25 6RL. *Governor,* T. C. H. Newth
WELLINGBOROUGH (DOC), Millers Park, Doddington
Road, Wellingborough, Northants. NN8 2NH. *Governor,*
J. Whetton
WHATTON (DIP), Whatton, Notts. NG13 9FQ. *Governor,*
M. A. Lewis

WHITEMOOR (DOC), Longhill Road, March, Cambs.
PE15 0PR. *Governor,* A. J. Barclay
WINCHESTER (DOC), Romsey Road, Winchester, Hants.
SO22 5DF. *Governor,* M. K. Pascoe
WOODHILL (DOC), Tattenhoe Street, Milton Keynes
MK4 4DA. *Governor,* R. B. Clark
WORMWOOD SCRUBBS (DOC), PO Box 757, Du Cane
Road, London W12 0AE. *Governor,* J. F. Perris
WYMOTT (DIP), Moss Lane, Ulnes Walton, Leyland,
Preston, Lancs. PR5 3LW. *Governor,* J. W. Mullen

YOUNG OFFENDER INSTITUTIONS

AYLESBURY (DIA), Bierton Road, Aylesbury, Bucks.
HP20 1EH. *Governor,* C. Welsh
BRINSFORD (DIA), New Road, Featherstone,
Wolverhampton WV10 7PY. *Governor,* P. J. Earnshaw
*BULLWOOD HALL (DOC), High Road, Hockley, Essex
SS5 4TE. *Governor,* Miss S. Ryan
CASTINGTON (DIP), Morpeth, Northumberland NE65 9XF.
Governor, C. Harder
DEERBOLT (DIP), Bowes Road Barnard Castle, Co.
Durham DL12 9BG. *Governor,* W. J. Ginn
DOVER (DOC), The Citadel, Western Heights, Dover,
Kent CT17 9DR. *Governor,* B. W. Sutton
*DRAKE HALL (DIA), Eccleshall, Staffs. ST21 6LQ. *Governor,*
R. J. Crouch
*EAST SUTTON PARK (DOC), Sutton Valence, Maidstone,
Kent ME17 3DF. *Governor,* W. S. Duff
EASTWOOD PARK (DIA), Falfield, Wotton-under-Edge,
Glos. GL12 8DB. *Governor,* P. C. Mortimore
FELTHAM (DOC), Bedfont Road, Feltham, Middx.
TW13 4ND. *Governor,* J. Whitty
GLEN PARVA (DIA), Tigers Road, Wigston, Leics.
LE8 2TN. *Governor,* C. Williams
GUYS MARSH (DIA), Shaftesbury, Dorset SP7 0AH.
Governor, P. B. Tucker
HATFIELD (DIA), Hatfield, Doncaster DN7 6EL. *Governor,*
W. J. Clark
HOLLESLEY BAY COLONY (DOC), Hollesley, Woodbridge,
Suffolk IP12 3JS. *Governor,* M. F. Clarke
HUNTERCOMBE (DIA), Huntercombe Place, Nuffield,
Henley-on-Thames RG9 5SB. *Governor,* Miss A. W. Hair
LANCASTER FARMS (DIP), Stone Row Head, off
Quernmore Road, Lancaster LA1 3QZ. *Governor,*
D. J. Waplington
*NEW HALL (DIP), Dial Wood, Flockton, Wakefield
WF4 4AX. *Governor,* D. England
NORTHALLERTON (DIP), East Road, Northallerton,
N. Yorks. DL6 1NW. *Governor,* D. P. G. Appleton
ONLEY (DIA), Willoughby, Rugby, Warks. CV23 8AP.
Governor, J. O'Neill
PORTLAND (DIA), Easton, Portland, Dorset DT5 1DL.
Governor, D. Brisco
PRESCOED (DIA), 29 Maryport Street, Usk, Gwent
NP4 0TD. *Governor,* N. J. Evans
STOKE HEATH (DIA), Market Drayton, Salop TF9 2JL.
Governor, J. Alldridge
*STYAL (DIP), Wilmslow, Cheshire, SK9 4HR. *Governor,*
G. Walker
SWINFEN HALL (DIA), Lichfield, Staffs. WS14 9QS.
Governor, A. J. Davis
THORN CROSS (DIP), Arley Road, Appleton Thorn,
Warrington WA4 4RL. *Governor,* I. Windebank
WERRINGTON (DIA), Stoke-on-Trent ST9 0DX. *Governor,*
K. Naisbitt
WETHERBY (DIP), York Road, Wetherby, W. Yorks.
LS22 5ED. *Governor,* P. J. Atkinson

*Women's establishments/establishments with units for women

REMAND CENTRES

BRINSFORD (DIA), New Road, Featherstone,
Wolverhampton WV10 7PY. *Governor*, P. J. Earnshaw
CARDIFF (DIA), Knox Road, Cardiff CF2 1UG. *Governor*,
N. D. Clifford
EXETER (DIA), New North Road, Exeter, Devon EX4 4EX.
Governor, D. Alderson
FELTHAM (DOC), Bedfont Road, Feltham, Middx.
TW13 4ND. *Governor*, J. Whitty
GLEN PARVA (DIA), Tigers Road, Wigston, Leics.
LE8 2TN. *Governor*, C. Williams
LOW NEWTON (DIP), Brasside, Durham DH1 5SD.
Governor, A. Holman
NORWICH (DOC), Mousehold, Norwich, Norfolk NR1 4LU.
Governor, Miss J. M. Fowler
PUCKLECHURCH (DIA), Bristol BS17 3QJ. *Governor*,
P. Mortimore
READING (DIA), Forbury Road, Reading, Berks. RG1 3HY.
Governor, P. Dixon
STOKE HEATH (DIA), Market Drayton, Salop TF9 2JL.
Governor, J. Alldridge
THE WOLDS (private remand prison), Everthorpe, Brough,
N. Humberside HU15 2JZ. *Controller*, Mrs P. Midgley

INSPECTORATE OF PRISONS
HM Chief Inspector of Prisons, His Hon. Judge Tumim
HM Deputy Chief Inspector of Prisons (G5), B. V. Smith
HM Inspectors, C. Allen; J. Gallagher; E. Hornblow;
D. Longley; D. A. Strong; B. J. Wells
Principal (G7), S. E. Bass

ESTABLISHMENT, FINANCE, FIRE AND EMERGENCY PLANNING DEPARTMENTS

Deputy Under-Secretary (G2), T. C. Platt

ESTABLISHMENT DEPARTMENT
Assistant Under-Secretary of State (G3), C. L. Scoble
(*Personnel, Organization and Management Services*)
Heads of Divisions (G5), J. F. Acton; M. D. Boyle;
B. W. Buck; B. M. Caffarey; Mrs E. I. France
Senior Principals (G6), R. C. Case; J. G. Daly;
A. W. Gillman; D. J. Grant; D. C. Houghton;
S. E. Wharton
Principals (G7), Miss M. A. Allibone; K. Aylen;
F. Bannister; W. Black; P. Buley; M. Carr; A. Fishwick;
J. Fleming; Mrs S. Fleming; Mrs G. C. Hackett;
R. A. Hemmings; W. Heppolette; M. C. Jennings;
D. G. Jones; A. J. Lewis; R. T. Lewis; Ms
P. B. McFarlane; Miss F. Miller; Mrs J. Morgan; Mrs
B. Moxon; J. T. Neil; H. O'Connor; Miss A. Reece;
R. Ritchie; G. R. Sampher; T. Sargent; N. Shackleford;
A. Silver; P. A. Stanton; M. Walsh; T. Ward;
A. T. Williams; N. L. Willson; Mrs L. Wishart

ASSESSMENT CONSULTANCY UNIT
Director (G5), Miss S. E. Paul
Deputy Director (G6), G. J. Jones
Principal Psychologist (G7), D. J. Murray

PUBLIC RELATIONS BRANCH
Director of Information Services (G4), A. E. Moorey
Deputy Director of Information Services (G6), J. G. Blakeway
Head Publicity Officer (G6), C. Skinner

FINANCE DEPARTMENT
*Assistant Under-Secretary of State (Principal Finance Officer)
(G3)*, S. G. Norris
Heads of Divisions (G5), B. O. Bubbear; J. L. Haugh;
J. A. Ingman; G. C. Robertson
Senior Principals (G6), K. Cole; P. G. Davies;
T. A. S. Devon; R. Eagle; A. K. Holman; J. Nicholson

Principals (G7), B. D. Bishop; D. Burge; Mrs C. Burrows;
G. Cassell; K. I. Cole; Mrs M. Cooper; R. Daniels;
T. A. S. Daniels; C. I. Dickinson; G. J. Edwards;
F. H. Eggleston; B. Elliott; Mrs D. Grainger; C. Harnett;
C. Harwood; S. Hobbs; P. W. Jones; D. J. Kent;
G. Laing; M. Lee; S. Limpkin; Miss D. Loudon; Ms
C. Pelham; Mrs P. Poyton; R. P. Ritchie; C. Roden;
I. F. Rutherford; P. Sheehan; I. F. Smith; P. T. Smith;
Mrs F. Spencer; Mrs M. Thomas

FIRE AND EMERGENCY PLANNING DEPARTMENT
Assistant Under-Secretary of State (G3), W. J. A. Innes
Civil Emergencies Adviser, D. C. G. Brook, CB, CBE
Heads of Divisions (G5), P.E. Bolton; R. J. Miles; Dr
D. M. S. Peace
Grade 6, D. R. Dewick; D. Meakin
Principals (G7), Dr S. S. Athwal; D. Boyle; Dr G. A. Carr-
Hill; N. M. Clowes; E. Cook; Mrs P. E. Culley;
C. I. Dickinson; R. C. Eaton; J. A. Foster; Dr
J. A. Harwood; A. E. Mantle; M. A. Parker; D. A. Peters;
A. N. Pickersgill; Dr G. E. Scott; R. C. Stephen; Dr
M. D. Thomas; K. Wallace

HM FIRE SERVICE INSPECTORATE
HM Chief Inspector, Sir Reginald Doyle, CBE
HM Inspectors, S. D. Christian; B. T. A. Collins, OBE;
A. F. Kilford; N. Musselwhite, QFSM; E. G. Pearn, QFSM;
K. T. Phillips; D. Ritchie; A. V. Rule, QFSM; D. Spencer;
G. K. Tinley; A. C. Wells, QFSM; D. Wright
Senior Engineering Inspector, R. M. Simpson, OBE
Principal (G7), K. O'Sullivan

FIRE SERVICE COLLEGE
Moreton-in-Marsh, Glos. GL56 0RH
Tel 0608-50831

An executive agency within the Home Office
Chief Executive, B. Fuller, CBE
Deputy Chief Executive, A. Salisbury
Director of Studies, Dr R. Willis-Lee
Secretary (G7), J. A. Gundersen

EMERGENCY PLANNING COLLEGE
The Hawkhills, Easingwold, Yorks. YO6 3EG
Tel 0347-21406

Head of College (G5), J. B. Bettridge, CBE
Vice-Principal, Col. H. H. Evans

PASSPORT AGENCY
Clive House, Petty France, London SW1H 9HD
Tel 071-271 3000

An executive agency within the Home Office
Chief Executive (G5), J. E. Hayzelden
Deputy Chief Executive and Director of Operations (G6), Miss
A. Smith
Director of Planning and Resources (G6), N. S. Benger
Director of Systems (G6), T. Lonsdale
Principals (G7), J. Burgess; M. Copley; E. Downham;
R. G. Le Marechal; R. I. Henderson; J. McColl

HORSERACE TOTALISATOR BOARD
74 Upper Richmond Road, London SW15 2SU
Tel 081-874 6411

The Horserace Totalisator Board was established by the
Betting, Gaming and Lotteries Act 1963, as successor to the
Racecourse Betting Control Board. Its function is to operate
totalisators on approved racecourses in Great Britain, and it

also provides on- and off-course cash and credit offices. Under the Horserace Totalisator and Betting Levy Board Act 1972, it is further empowered to offer bets at starting price (or other bets at fixed odds) on any sporting event. The chairman and members of the Board are appointed by the Home Secretary.

Chairman (£92,000), The Lord Wyatt of Weeford
Members, B. McDonnell (*Chief Executive*); The Hon.
J. Deedes; T. J. Phillips (*Finance*); J. F. Sanderson;
The Hon. D. Sieff; The Lord Swaythling

HOUSING CORPORATION
149 Tottenham Court Road, London W1P 0BN
Tel 071-387 9466

Established by Parliament in 1964, the Housing Corporation registers, promotes, funds and supervises housing associations. The Corporation's duties were extended under the provisions of the Housing Act 1988 to cover the payment of capital and revenue grants to housing associations, advice for tenants interested in Tenants' Choice, and the approval and revocation of potential new landlords under this policy.

There are over 2,300 registered associations in England providing more than 600,000 homes for people in need of housing. Housing associations are non-profit making bodies run by voluntary committees. In 1992-3, 62,137 homes were made available for rent or low-cost sale.

Chairman, Sir Christopher Benson
Chief Executive, A. Mayer

HUMAN FERTILIZATION AND EMBRYOLOGY AUTHORITY
Paxton House, 30 Artillery Lane, London E1 7LS
Tel 071-377 5077

The Authority was established under the Human Fertilization and Embryology Act 1990. Its function is to license persons carrying out any of the following activities: the creation or use of embryos outside the body in the provision of infertility treatment services; the use of donated gametes in infertility treatment; the storage of gametes or embryos; and research on human embryos. The Authority also keeps under review information about embryos and, when requested to do so, gives advice to the Secretary of State for Health.

Chairman, Prof. C. Campbell
Deputy Chairman, Lady Brittan
Members, Prof. R. J. Berry; Prof. I. Cooke; Prof. A. Cox; Ms
J. Denton; Ms E. Forgan; Ms J. Harbison; Dr S. Hillier;
PH.D.; Prof. B. Hoggett, QC; The Most Revd
R. Holloway; Ms P. Keith; Ms A. Mays; Dr A. McLaren;
Dr J. Naish; Rabbi Julia Neuberger; Prof. R. W. Shaw;
D. Shilson; Prof. R. Snowden; Ms C. Walby;
Prof. D. Whittingham
Chief Executive, Mrs F. Goldhill

INDEPENDENT REVIEW SERVICE FOR THE SOCIAL FUND
Millbank Tower, 21–24 Millbank, London, SW1P 4QU
Tel 071-217 4799
4th Floor, Centre City Podium, 5 Hill Street,
Birmingham B5 4UB
Tel 021-631 4000

The Social Fund Commissioner is appointed by the Secretary of State for Social Security. The Commissioner appoints Social Fund Inspectors, who provide an independent review of decisions made by Social Fund Officers in the Benefits Agency of the Department of Social Security.

Social Fund Commissioner, Mrs R. Mackworth

INDEPENDENT TELEVISION COMMISSION
33 Foley Street, London W1P 7LB
Tel 071-255 3000

The Independent Television Commission replaced the Independent Broadcasting Authority at the beginning of 1991 under the terms of the Broadcasting Act 1990. The Commission is responsible for licensing and regulating all commercially funded UK television services.

Chairman (£56,809), Sir George Russell, CBE
Deputy Chairman, J. Stevens
Members, Earl of Dalkeith; Prof. J. F. Fulton; Ms
P. Mathias; Lady Popplewell; Prof. J. Ring; P. Sheth;
R. Goddard; Mrs E. Wynne Jones
Chief Executive, D. Glencross
Secretary, M. Redley

INDUSTRIAL INJURIES ADVISORY COUNCIL
6th Floor, The Adelphi, 1–11 John Adam Street, London
WC2N 6HT
Tel 071-962 8066

The Industrial Injuries Advisory Council is a statutory body under the Social Security Act 1975 which considers and advises the Secretary of State for Social Security on regulations and other questions relating to industrial injuries benefits or their administration.

Chairman, Prof. J. M. Harrington, CBE
Members, P. Arscott; Dr J. Asherson; Miss J. C. Brown; Mrs
J. Carter; Prof. M. J. Cinnamond; Dr D. Coggon;
Prof. A. Dayan; Dr C. P. Juniper; T. Mawer;
Prof. A. J. Newman Taylor; R. Pickering; Dr E. Roman;
Dr C. Taylor; O. Tudor; Ms M. Twomey
Secretary, R. Heigh

CENTRAL OFFICE OF INFORMATION
Hercules Road, London SE1 7DU
Tel 071-928 2345

The Central Office of Information (COI) is the government executive agency which provides publicity and information services to government departments, other executive agencies and public sector bodies. It provides consultancy, design, production, procurement and project management services for a wide range of publicity services in all media. Though the majority of COI's work is for government departments in the UK, it also produces a range of publicity materials for overseas consumption.

Administrative responsibility for the COI rests with the Minister of Public Service and Science, while the ministers whose departments it serves are responsible for the policy expressed in its work.

Chief Executive and Head of the Government Information Service (*G3*), G. M. Devereau
Private Secretary and Parliamentary Clerk, vacant
Senior Personal Secretary, Mrs J. Rodrigues

MANAGEMENT BOARD
Members, G. M. Devereau; J. Bolitho; K. Williamson;
R. Windsor; D. A. Low
Secretary, Miss K. Gliding

MARKETING AND CLIENT SERVICES GROUP
Group Director (G5), J. Bolitho
*Head, Business Development and Communications Services
(G7)*, W. Roberts

CAMPAIGNS GROUP
Group Director (G5), R. Windsor
Director, Advertising (G6), M. Brodie
Director, Research (G6), vacant
Director, Direct Marketing (G7), C. Noble

PUBLICATIONS, PRESS AND EXHIBITIONS
Group Director (G5), D. A. Low
Director, Press and PR (G6), vacant
Director, Publications (G6), J. Murray
Director, Reference and Translations (G6), D. Beynon
Director, Exhibitions and Pictures (G6), D. Beynon
Director, Films Television and Radio Division (G6),
M. Nisbet
Principal Finance Officer (G5), K. Williamson
Principal Establishment Officer (G6), M. Langhorne

NETWORK AND EMERGENCY PLANNING SERVICES
GROUP
Group Director (G5), J. Bolitho

NETWORK OFFICES
EASTERN, Three Crowns House, 72–80 Hills Road,
Cambridge CB2 ILL. *Network Director (G7)*, Mrs
V. Burdon
LONDON AND SOUTH-EAST, Lincoln House, Westminster
Bridge Road, London SEI 7DU. *Network Director (G6)*,
D. Smith
MIDLANDS, Five Ways Tower, Frederick Road,
Edgbaston, Birmingham BI5 ISH. *Network Director (G6)*,
O. J. B. Prince-White
NORTH-EAST, Wellbar House, Gallowgate, Newcastle
upon Tyne NEI 4TB. *Network Director (G7)*, H. Cozens
NORTH-WEST, Sunley Tower, Piccadilly Plaza,
Manchester MI 4BD. *Network Director (G7)*, Mrs E. Jones
SOUTH-WEST, The Pithay, Bristol BSI 2NF. *Network
Director (G7)*, B. Garner
YORKSHIRE AND HUMBERSIDE, City House, New Station
Street, Leeds LSI 4JG. *Network Director (G6)*,
R. P. Haslam

BOARD OF INLAND REVENUE
Somerset House, London WC2R ILB
Tel 071-438 6622

The Board of Inland Revenue was constituted under the
Inland Revenue Board Act 1849, by the consolidation of the
Board of Excise and the Board of Stamps and Taxes. In 1909
the administration of excise duties was transferred to the
Board of Customs. The Board of Inland Revenue administers
and collects direct taxes – mainly income tax, stamp duty,
development land tax and petroleum revenue tax – and
advises the Chancellor of the Exchequer on policy questions
involving them.
The Department is organized into a series of accountable
management units under the Next Steps programme. The
day-to-day operations in assessing and collecting tax and in
providing internal support services are carried out by 34

Executive Offices. The Department's Valuation Office is an
executive agency responsible for valuing property for tax
purposes, for compensation, for compulsory purchase, and
(in England and Wales) for local rating purposes. In 1991–2
the Inland Revenue collected over £79,675 million in tax.

THE BOARD
Chairman (G1), Sir Anthony Battishill, KCB
Private Secretary, G. Lloyd
Assistant Private Secretary, Miss F. Huskisson
Deputy Chairmen (G2), S. C. T. Matheson, CB;
L. J. H. Beighton, CB
Director-General (G2), C. W. Corlett

SUBJECT DIVISIONS
Directors (G3), E. McGivern; M. F. Cayley; B. Mace;
M. Templeman; P. Lewis; I. R. Spence; E. J. Gribbon
Senior Principal Inspectors of Taxes (G4), R. H. Allen;
R. E. Creed; R. N. Page, CBE; M. A. Keith; R. M. Elliss;
R. E. Haigh; D. L. Shaw; P. R. P. Stokes; A. J. O'Brien;
B. Sadler
Grade 5, R. B. Willis; L. E. Jaundoo; I. Stewart; C. Stewart;
Miss R. A. Dyall; M. T. Evans; M. D. R. Haigh;
R. Warden; C. D. Sullivan; J. P. B. Bryce; P. W. Fawcett;
J. B. Shepherd; M. J. G. Elliott; C. S. McNicol; Miss
S. P. B. Walker; P. A. Michael; Mrs C. B. Hubbard
Principal Inspectors of Taxes (G5), B. Jones; J. H. Keelty;
A. P. Beauchamp; Mrs M. E. Williams; R. S. Hurcombe;
J. E. Morris; M. D. Phelps; Mrs S. Waters; A. H. Williams;
P. H. Linford; J. F. McCormick; Mrs D. Hay; K. Hamer;
J. F. Gilhooly; S. P. Norris; Dr C. Howard; R. J. Gill;
R. Thomas

STATISTICS AND ECONOMICS OFFICE
Director (G3), J. R. Calder
Grade 5, Dr G. A. Keenay; Dr G. J. Parker; R. J. Eason;
E. Ko
Information Technology (G6), Dr R. James
Senior Economics Adviser (G5), W. M. McNie

INFORMATION TECHNOLOGY OFFICE
Director (G3), J. E. Yard
Director, Strategic Partnership Project (G3), G. H. Bush
Divisional Directors (G5), R. A. Assirati; P. W. Booth;
D. B. Topple; R. H. Wearing

PERSONNEL DIRECTORATE
Director of Personnel (G3), J. Gant
Deputy Directors (G4), R. Neilson; N. C. Munro
Assistant Directors (G5), A. Pardoe; J. Eastman; S. Mitha;
(G6), M. Jarrett; R. Cartwright; A. J. Walker

MANPOWER AND SUPPORT SERVICES
Director (G4), R. R. Martin
Assistant Directors (G5), J. Gray; R. P. R. Tilley;
D. E. Adam; T. A. Lawson; S. T. Ayling; *(G6)*,
M. K. Robins

TRAINING OFFICE
Royal Exchange House, Boar Lane, Leeds LSI 5PG
Controller (G5), D. J. Timmons

CENTRAL DIVISION
Director (G3), M. A. Johns
Grade 5, R. Golding; B. Glassberg

CHANGE MANAGEMENT GROUP
Head (G4), D. A. Smith

CORPORATE COMMUNICATIONS OFFICE
Controller (G5), B. Hooper
Press Secretary (G7), Mrs S. J. Bradley

FINANCE DIVISION
Principal Finance Officer (G3), J. M. Crawley, CB
Grade 5, J. H. Reed; J. R. Cavell; Miss M. A. Hill;
R. F. Moore

INTERNAL AUDIT OFFICE
22 Kingsway, London WC2B 6NR
Chief Internal Auditor (G5), N. R. Buckley

FINANCIAL SERVICES OFFICE
Barrington Road, Worthing, W. Sussex BN12 4XH
Controller (G6), J. D. Easey

FINANCIAL AND MANAGEMENT ACCOUNTING SYSTEMS
OFFICE
Barrington Road, Worthing, W. Sussex BN12 4XH
Controller (G6), C. R. F. Jury

SOLICITOR FOR INLAND REVENUE
Solicitor (G2), B. E. Cleave
Principal Assistant Solicitors (G3), J. D. H. Johnston;
J. G. H. Bates; G. F. Butt
Assistant Solicitors (G5), Miss M. P. E. Boland; A. J. Gunz;
A. K. S. Shaw; A. P. Douglas; W. J. Durrans; S. Bousher;
R. S. Waterson; R. F. Walters; Miss A. Hawkins;
K. Brown; R. W. Thornhill; Miss A. E. Wyman;
R. J. Alderman; Mrs M. A. Gilbert
Board's Advisory Accountant (G5), T. C. Carne

SOLICITOR OF INLAND REVENUE (SCOTLAND)
80 Lauriston Place, Edinburgh EH3 9SL
Solicitor, T. H. Scott

DIRECTORATE, OPERATIONS 1
Director (G3), K. V. Deacon
Deputy Directors (G4), D. W. Muir; R. Massingale
Assistant Directors (G5), T. R. Evans; J. M. Thomas;
J. W. Calder; E. C. Jones; A. McClure; S. J. McManus;
J. P. Gilbody; Dr E. A. Harrison; M. G. Oakley;
D. W. Swift; S. Hartlib

REGIONAL OFFICES
INLAND REVENUE EAST, Midgate House, Peterborough
PE1 1TD
INLAND REVENUE EAST LONDON, New Court, Carey
Street, London WC2A 2JE
INLAND REVENUE GREATER MANCHESTER, Apsley
House, Wellington Road North, Stockport SK4 1EY
INLAND REVENUE MIDLANDS, Chadwick House,
Blenheim Court, Solihull, W. Midlands B91 2AA
INLAND REVENUE NORTH, Corporation House, 73 Albert
Road, Middlesbrough, Cleveland TS1 2RZ
INLAND REVENUE NORTH AND WEST LONDON, New
Court, Carey Street, London WC2A 2JE
INLAND REVENUE NORTH-WEST, The Triad, Stanley
Road, Bootle, Merseyside L20 3PD
INLAND REVENUE SOUTH-EAST, Albion House, Chertsey
Road, Woking GU21 1BT
INLAND REVENUE SOUTH LONDON, New Court, Carey
Street, London WC2A 2JE
INLAND REVENUE SOUTH-WEST, Finance House,
Barnfield Road, Exeter EX1 1QX
INLAND REVENUE SOUTH YORKSHIRE, Sovereign
House, 110 Queen Street, Sheffield S1 2DU
INLAND REVENUE WALES, Ty Rodfa, Ty Glas Avenue,
Llanishen, Cardiff CF4 5TS
INLAND REVENUE SCOTLAND, 80 Lauriston Place,
Edinburgh EH3 9SL
INLAND REVENUE NORTHERN IRELAND, Dorchester
House, 52–58 Great Victoria Street, Belfast BT2 7QE

DIRECTORATE, OPERATIONS 2
Director (G3), J. H. Roberts
Deputy Director (G4), P. C. Fielder

SPECIAL COMPLIANCE OFFICE
Angel Court, 199 Borough High Street, London SE1 1HZ
Controller (G4), F. J. Brannigan
Grade 5, J. T. Cawdron; J. Mawson, D. F. Parrett;
G. W. Lunn
Board's Investigating Officer (G6), F. B. Dunbar

CLAIMS BRANCH
St John's House, Merton Road, Bootle L69 9BB
Controller (G5), D. A. Hartnett

CLAIMS BRANCH (SCOTLAND)
Trinity Park House, South Trinity Road, Edinburgh
EH5 3SD
Officer in Charge (G7), J. Duguid

PENSION SCHEMES OFFICE
Lynwood Road, Thames Ditton, Surrey KT7 0DP
Controller (G5), R. G. Lusk, CBE

THE STAMP OFFICE
South-West Wing, Bush House, Strand, London WC2B 4QN
Controller (G6), K. S. Hodgson

THE STAMP OFFICE (SCOTLAND)
Mulberry House, 16 Picardy Place, Edinburgh EH1 3NF
Controller, D. G. Hunter

CAPITAL TAXES OFFICE
Minford House, Rockley Road, London W14 0DF
Controller (G4), B. D. Kent
Deputy Controllers (G5), H. V. Capon; A. G. Nield;
R. J. Draper
Assistant Controllers (G6), D. J. Ferley; B. K. Lakhanpaul;
T. J. Plumb; P. R. Twiddy; C. A. Oldridge; F. A. Cook;
R. J. Shanks; N. S. Tant; M. J. Francis; A. D. Tytherleigh

CAPITAL TAXES OFFICE (SCOTLAND)
Mulberry House, 16 Picardy Place, Edinburgh, EH1 3NB
Registrar (G5), I. Fraser
Deputy Registrar (G6), W. Young
Chief Examiners (G7), Mrs J. A. Templeton; Miss
K. M. Patrick; D. McL. Paterson; T. E. Naysmith;
J. Telford; C. G. Hogg; Miss A. Forbes

OFFICE OF THE INSPECTOR OF FOREIGN DIVIDENDS
Lynwood Road, Thames Ditton, Surrey KT7 0DP
Inspector of Foreign Dividends (G6), T. R. Diggins

OIL TAXATION OFFICE
Melbourne House, Aldwych, London WC2B 4LL
Controller (G4), R. C. Mountain
Grade 5, K. Cartwright; I. M. Griffin; D. Newlyn;
D. J. Slattery; M. Wright

THE VALUATION OFFICE EXECUTIVE AGENCY
New Court, 48 Carey Street, London WC2A 2JE
Tel 071-324 1183/1057
Meldrum House, 15 Drumsheugh Gardens, Edinburgh
EH3 7UN
Tel 031-225 8511

Chief Executive (G2), R. R. B. Shutler, CB
Deputy Chief Executives (G3), A. J. Langford (*Management*);
R. J. Pawley (*Technical*)
Chief Valuer, Scotland (G5), A. MacLaren

INQUIRY INTO EXPORTS OF DEFENCE EQUIPMENT AND DUAL-USE GOODS TO IRAQ
Room 2.2.5, 1 Palace Street, London SW1E 5HE
Tel 071-238 3799; *Media:* 071-238 3809

Lord Justice Scott was asked by the President of the Board of Trade, after the collapse of the Matrix Churchill case in November 1992, to examine the facts in relation to the export from the United Kingdom of defence equipment and dual-use goods to Iraq between December 1984 and 1990 and the decisions reached on the export licence applications for such goods and the basis for them; to report on whether the relevant departments, agencies and responsible ministers operated in accordance with the policies of the Government; to examine and report on decisions taken by the prosecuting authority and by those signing public interest immunity certificates in R. v. Henderson and any other similar cases that Lord Justice Scott considers relevant to the issues of the inquiry; and to make recommendations.
Inquiry headed by The Rt. Hon. Lord Justice Scott
Secretary to the Inquiry (G5), C. P. J. Muttukumaru
Counsel to the Inquiry, Ms P. Baxendale, QC
Assistant Secretary (G7), P. Regan
Media Relations Officer (G6), D. Price

INTERCEPTION COMMISSIONER
c/o The Home Office, 50 Queen Anne's Gate, London SW1H 9AT

The Commissioner is appointed by the Prime Minister. He keeps under review the issue by the Home Secretary of warrants under the Interception of Communications Act 1985 and safeguards made in respect of intercepted material obtained through the use of such warrants. He is also required to give all such assistance as the Interception of Communications Tribunal may require to enable it to carry out its functions, and to submit an annual report to the Prime Minister with respect to the carrying out of his functions.
Commissioner, The Rt. Hon. Sir Thomas Bingham

INTERCEPTION OF COMMUNICATIONS TRIBUNAL
PO Box 44, London SE1 0TX

The Tribunal comprises senior members of the legal profession, who are appointed by The Queen. Under the Interception of Communications Act 1985, the Tribunal is required to investigate applications from any person who believes that communications sent to or by them have been intercepted in the course of their transmission by post or by means of a public telecommunications system.
President, The Hon. Mr Justice Macpherson of Cluny
Vice-President, Sir Cecil Clothier, KCB, QC
Members, Sir David Calcutt, QC; I. Guild, CBE; P. Scott, QC

INTERVENTION BOARD
Fountain House, Queen's Walk, Reading RG1 7QW
Tel 0734-583626

The Intervention Board was established as a government department in 1972 and became operational in 1973. It became an executive agency in April 1990. The Board is responsible for the implementation of European Community regulations covering the market support arrangements of the Common Agricultural Policy. Members of the Board are appointed by and are responsible to the Minister of Agriculture, Fisheries and Food and the Secretaries of State for Scotland, Wales and Northern Ireland.
Chairman, A. J. Ellis, CBE
Chief Executive (G3), G. Stapleton

HEADS OF DIVISIONS
Finance Division (G5), J. N. Diserens
External Trade Division (G5), G. N. Dixon
Crops Division (G5), H. MacKinnon
Livestock Products Division (G5), M. J. Griffiths
Corporate Services Division (G5), J. W. M. Peffers
Legal Division (G5), T. Middleton
Chief Accountant (G6), R. Bryant
External Operations (G6), J. P. Bradbury
Procurement and Supply (G6), P. J. Offer
Information Technology (G6), T. T. Simpson

LAND AUTHORITY FOR WALES
The Custom House, Customhouse Street, Cardiff CF1 5AP
Tel 0222-223444

The Authority is responsible for acquiring and disposing of land for private development in Wales.
Chairman (part-time) (£31,625), Sir Geoffrey Inkin, OBE
Chief Executive, B. Ryan, FRICS

LAND REGISTRIES

HM LAND REGISTRY
Lincoln's Inn Fields, London WC2A 3PH
Tel 071-917 8888

The registration of title to land was first introduced in England and Wales by the Land Registry Act 1862; HM Land Registry operates today under the Land Registration Acts 1925 to 1988. The object of registering title to land is to create and maintain a register of land owners whose title is guaranteed by the state and so to simplify the transfer, mortgage and other dealings with real property. Compulsory registration on sale was introduced in stages affecting only certain areas but it is now compulsory throughout England and Wales. The register, which used to be private and could only be inspected with the consent of the registered proprietor, became open to inspection by the public on 3 December 1990.

HM Land Registry is an executive agency administered under the Lord Chancellor by the Chief Land Registrar. The work is decentralized to a number of regional offices. The Chief Land Registrar is also responsible for the Land Charges Department and the Agricultural Credits Department.

HEADQUARTERS OFFICE
Chief Land Registrar and Chief Executive (G2), J. J. Manthorpe
Solicitor to Land Registry (G3), C. J. West
Senior Land Registrar (G5), Mrs J. G. Totty
Principal Establishment Officer (G4), E. G. Beardsall
Director of Operations (G5), G. N. French
Director of Information Technology (G5), R. J. Fenn
Director of Management Services (G6), P. J. Smith
Land Registrar (G5), M. L. Wood

Deputy Establishment Officer (G6), J. Hodder
Controller of Operations Development (G6), P. R. Laker

BIRKENHEAD DISTRICT LAND REGISTRY
Old Market House, Hamilton Street, Birkenhead L41 5FL
Tel 051-473 1110
District Land Registrar (G5), M. G. Garwood
Area Manager (G6), J. Eccles

COVENTRY DISTRICT LAND REGISTRY
Greyfriars Business Centre, 2 Eaton Road, Coventry CV1 2SD
Tel 0203-632442
District Land Registrar (G5), S. P. Kelway
Area Manager (G6), J. C. Lillistone

CROYDON DISTRICT LAND REGISTRY
Sunley House, Bedford Park, Croydon CR9 3LE
Tel 081-781 9100
District Land Registrar (G5), D. M. J. Moss
Area Manager (G6), V. J. C. Shorney

DURHAM DISTRICT LAND REGISTRY
Southfield House, Southfield Way, Durham DH1 5TR
Tel 091-301 3500
District Land Registrar (G5), C. W. Martin
Area Manager (G6), B. Warriner

GLOUCESTER DISTRICT LAND REGISTRY
Twyver House, Bruton Way, Gloucester GL1 1DQ
Tel 0452-511111
District Land Registrar (G5), W. W. Budden
Area Manager (G6), R. B. Johnson

HARROW DISTRICT LAND REGISTRY
Lyon House, Lyon Road, Harrow, Middx. HA1 2EU
Tel 081-427 8811
District Land Registrar (G5), J. V. Timothy
Area Manager (G6), M. J. Wyatt

KINGSTON UPON HULL DISTRICT LAND REGISTRY
Earle House, Portland Street, Hull HU2 8JN
Tel 0482-223244
District Land Registrar (G5), S. R. Coveney
Area Manager (G6), E. Howard

LAND CHARGES AND AGRICULTURAL CREDITS
DEPARTMENT
Burrington Way, Plymouth PL5 3LP
Tel 0752-779831
Superintendent of Land Charges (G7), H. Myers

LEICESTER DISTRICT LAND REGISTRY
Thames Tower, 99 Burleys Way, Leicester LE1 3UB
Tel 0533-654000
District Land Registrar (G6), Mrs J. A. Goodfellow
Area Manager (G7), G. M. Johns

LYTHAM DISTRICT LAND REGISTRY
Birkenhead House, Lytham St Annes, Lancs. FY8 5AB
Tel 0253-736999
District Land Registrar (G5), J. G. Cooper
Area Manager (G6), B. Elliott

NOTTINGHAM DISTRICT LAND REGISTRY
Chalfont Drive, Nottingham NG8 3RN
Tel 0602-291166
District Land Registrar (G5), P. J. Timothy
Area Manager (G6), W. Whitaker

PETERBOROUGH DISTRICT LAND REGISTRY
Touthill Close, City Road, Peterborough PE1 1XN
Tel 0733-288288
District Land Registrar (G5), L. M. Pope
Area Manager (G6), B. J. Andrews

PLYMOUTH DISTRICT LAND REGISTRY
Plumer House, Tailyour Road, Crownhill, Plymouth PL6 5HY
Tel 0752-701234
District Land Registrar (G5), A. J. Pain
Area Manager (G6), K. Robinson

PORTSMOUTH DISTRICT LAND REGISTRY
St Andrews Court, St Michael's Road, Portsmouth PO1 2JH
Tel 0705-865022
District Land Registrar (G6), S. R. Sehrawat
Area Manager (G7), A. W. Howarth

STEVENAGE DISTRICT LAND REGISTRY
Brickdale House, Swingate, Stevenage, Herts. SG1 1XG
Tel 0438-313003
District Land Registrar (G5), C. Tate
Area Manager (G6), A. D. Gould

SWANSEA DISTRICT LAND REGISTRY
Tybryn Glas, High Street, Swansea SA1 1PW
Tel 0792-458877
District Land Registrar (G5), G. A. Hughes
Area Manager (G6), R. T. Davis

TELFORD DISTRICT LAND REGISTRY
Parkside Court, Hall Park Way, Telford TF3 4LR
Tel 0952-290355
District Land Registrar (G5), M. A. Roche
Area Manager (G6), R. D. Moseley

TUNBRIDGE WELLS DISTRICT LAND REGISTRY
Curtis House, Hawkenbury, Tunbridge Wells, Kent TN2 5AQ
Tel 0892-510015
District Land Registrar (G5), G. R. Tooke
Area Manager (G6), B. S. Crozier

WEYMOUTH DISTRICT LAND REGISTRY
1 Cumberland Drive, Weymouth, Dorset DT4 9TT
Tel 0305-776161
District Land Registrar (G5), Mrs P. M. Reeson
Area Manager (G6), J. Dodd

YORK DISTRICT LAND REGISTRY
James House, James Street, York YO1 3YZ
Tel 0904-450000
District Land Registrar (G6), Mrs R. F. Lovel
Area Manager (G7), P. Wright

COMPUTER SERVICES DIVISION
Burrington Way, Plymouth PL5 3LP
Tel 0752-779831
Head of Services Division (G6), P. A. Maycock
Head of Development Division (G6), R. J. Smith

REGISTERS OF SCOTLAND (EXECUTIVE AGENCY)

Meadowbank House, 153 London Road, Edinburgh EH8 7AU
Tel 031-659 6111

The Registers of Scotland consist of: General Register of Sasines and Land Register of Scotland; Register of Deeds in the Books of Council and Session; Register of Protests; Register of Judgments; Register of Service of Heirs; Register of the Great Seal; Register of the Quarter Seal; Register of the Prince's Seal; Register of Crown Grants; Register of Sheriffs' Commissions; Register of the Cachet Seal; Register of Inhibitions and Adjudications; Register of Entails; Register of Hornings.

The General Register of Sasines and the Land Register of Scotland form the chief security in Scotland of the rights of land and other heritable (or real) property.
Keeper of the Registers of Scotland (G4), J. W. Barron
Senior Directors (G5), A. W. Ramage; A. G. Rennie

Senior Assistant Directors (*G6*), B. J. Corr; A. M. Falconer
Strategy Director (*G6*), D. Leslie
Assistant Directors (*G7*), D. G. Cant (*computers*); R. Glen
(*personnel*); J. Knox (*Land Register*); D. McCallum (*Land Register*); L. J. Mitchell (*management services*);
A. G. T. New (*Land Register*); I. M. Nicol (*finance*); Mrs
P. M. Stewart (*training*)
Assistant Keeper (*G7*), I. A. Davis
Grade 7, J. Anderson; J. F. Campbell; R. C. Clark; J. Cogle;
A. B. Farmer; J. S. McKinlay; D. Manson; J. B. Marshall;
Mrs A. Moore; W. F. Rankin; J. Rynn; M. J. Wilczynski

LAW COMMISSION
Conquest House, 37–38 John Street, Theobalds Road,
London WC1N 2BQ
Tel 071-411 1220

The Law Commission was set up in 1965, under the Law
Commissions Act 1965, to make proposals to the Government
for the examination of the law in England and Wales and for
its revision where it is unsuited for modern requirements,
obscure, or otherwise unsatisfactory. It recommends to the
Lord Chancellor programmes for the examination of different
branches of the law and suggests whether the examination
should be carried out by the Commission itself or by some
other body. The Commission is also responsible for the
preparation of Consolidation and Statute Law (Repeals) Bills.
Chairman, The Hon. Mr Justice Brooke
Members, J. Beatson; R. Buxton, QC; C. Harpum (*from Jan. 1994*)
Secretary, M. H. Collon

SCOTTISH LAW COMMISSION
140 Causewayside, Edinburgh EH9 1PR
Tel 031-668 2131

The Commission keeps the law in Scotland under review and
makes proposals for its development and reform.
Chairman, The Hon. Lord Davidson
Commissioners (*full-time*), Dr E. M. Clive; Sheriff
I. D. MacPhail, QC; (*part-time*) Prof. P. N. Love, CBE;
W. Nimmo Smith, QC
Secretary, K. F. Barclay

LAW OFFICERS' DEPARTMENTS
Attorney-General's Chambers, 9 Buckingham Gate,
London SW1E 6JP
Tel 071-828 7155
Attorney-General's Chambers, Royal Courts of Justice,
Belfast BT1 3JY
Tel 0232-235111

The Law Officers of the Crown for England and Wales are
the Attorney-General and the Solicitor-General. The Attorney-General, assisted by the Solicitor-General, is the chief
legal adviser to the Government and is also ultimately
responsible for all Crown litigation. He has overall responsibility for the work of the Law Officers' Departments (the
Treasury Solicitor's Department, the Crown Prosecution
Service, the Serious Fraud Office and the Legal Secretariat
to the Law Officers). He has a specific statutory duty to
superintend the discharge of their duties by the Director of

Public Prosecutions (who is head of the Crown Prosecution
Service) and the Director of the Serious Fraud Office. The
Director of Public Prosecutions for Northern Ireland is
responsible to the Attorney-General for the performance of
his functions. The Attorney-General has additional respon-
sibilities in relation to aspects of the civil and criminal law.
Attorney-General (**£42,314*), The Rt. Hon. Sir Nicholas
Lyell, QC, MP
Parliamentary Private Secretary, T. Devlin, MP
Solicitor-General (**£34,695*), Sir Derek Spencer, QC, MP
Parliamentary Private Secretary, G. Streeter, MP
Legal Secretary (*G2*), Miss J. L. Wheldon
Deputy Legal Secretary (*G4*), S. J. Wooler

LEGAL AID BOARD
5th and 6th Floors, 29–37 Red Lion Street, London WC1R 4PP
Tel 071-831 4209

The Legal Aid Board has the general function of ensuring
that advice, assistance and representation are available in
accordance with the Legal Aid Act 1988. In 1989 it took over
from the Law Society responsibility for administering legal
aid. The Board is a non-departmental government body
whose members are appointed by the Lord Chancellor.
Chairman, J. Pitts
Members, S. Orchard (*Chief Executive*); M. Acland; Ms
D. Beale; P. Jones; D. Sinker; J. Smith; Ms V. Boakes;
F. Collins; Ms K. Markus; G. Pulman, QC; A. Thomas

SCOTTISH LEGAL AID BOARD
44 Drumsheugh Gardens, Edinburgh EH3 7SW
Tel 031-226 7061

The Scottish Legal Aid Board was set up under the Legal
Aid (Scotland) Act 1986. It is responsible for ensuring that
advice, assistance and representation are available in
accordance with the Act. The Board is a non-departmental
government body whose members are appointed by the
Secretary of State for Scotland.
Chairman, Mrs C. A. M. Davis
Members, G. Barrie; Mrs P. A. M. Bolton; Miss L. Clark,
QC; A. Gilchrist; Prof. P. H. Grinyer; G. D. Holmes, CB;
D. A. Leitch; R. J. Livingstone; Mrs I. G. McColl;
C. N. McEachran, QC; Sheriff R. G. McEwan, QC; Mrs
G. M. Peebles; Mrs M. Tait
Chief Executive, A. E. M. Douglas

OFFICE OF THE LEGAL SERVICES OMBUDSMAN
22 Oxford Court, Oxford Street, Manchester M2 3WQ
Tel 061-236 9532

The Legal Services Ombudsman is appointed by the Lord
Chancellor under the Courts and Legal Services Act 1990 to
oversee the handling of complaints against solicitors,
barristers and licensed conveyancers by their professional
bodies. A complainant must first complain to the relevant
professional body before raising the matter with the
Ombudsman. The Ombudsman is independent of the legal
profession and his services are free of charge.

*Excluding reduced Parliamentary salary of £23,227

Legal Services Ombudsman, M. Barnes
Secretary (acting), S. Murray

LIBRARIES

THE BRITISH LIBRARY
2 Sheraton Street, London WIV 4BH
Tel 071-636 1544

The British Library is the UK's national library and occupies the central position in the library and information network. The Library aims to serve scholarship, research, industry, commerce and all other major users of information. Its services are based on collections which include over 18 million volumes, 1 million discs, and 55,000 hours of tape recordings, at 18 buildings in London and one complex in West Yorkshire. The British Library is in the process of moving to purpose-built accommodation at St Pancras, London NW1 (open to the public in 1996).

The British Library was established in 1973 and brought together the library departments of the British Museum, the National Central Library, the National Lending Library for Science and Technology, the British National Bibliography Ltd and, in 1974, the Office for Scientific and Technical Information. Subsequently the Library took responsibility for the India Office Library and Records, the HMSO Binderies, and the National Sound Archive.

Access to the Humanities and Social Sciences reading rooms in Great Russell Street is limited to holders of a British Library Reader's Pass, and information about eligibility is available from the Reader Admissions Office. The Aldwych and Holborn reading rooms of the Science Reference and Information Service are open to the general public without charge or formality. The Library's exhibition galleries are housed in the British Museum building in Great Russell Street.

BRITISH LIBRARY BOARD
96 Euston Road, London NW1 2DB
Tel 071-323 7262

Chairman, Sir Anthony Kenny, D.Phil., D.Litt., FBA
Chief Executive and Deputy Chairman (G2), B. Lang
Directors-General (G4), J. M. Smethurst; D. Russon
Part-time Members, The Lord Adrian, MD, FRS; The Lord Windlesham, CVO, PC; Prof. A. S. Forty, PH.D., D.SC.; Sir Robin Mackworth-Young, KCVO, FSA; R. E. Utiger, CBE; T. J. Rix; Dame Anne Warburton, DCVO, CMG; H. Heaney; D. Peake; The Rt. Revd M. A. Mann, KCVO; E. M. W. Griffith, CBE

BRITISH LIBRARY, BOSTON SPA
Boston Spa, Wetherby, W. Yorks. LS23 7BQ
Tel 0937-546000

Director-General (G4), D. Russon

DOCUMENT SUPPLY CENTRE
Tel 0937-546000
Director (G5), D. Bradbury

NATIONAL BIBLIOGRAPHIC SERVICE
Tel 0937-546585
Director (G6), S. J. Ede
London Unit, 2 Sheraton Street, London WIV 4BH. Tel: 071-323 7077

ACQUISITIONS PROCESSING AND CATALOGUING
Tel 0937-546000
Director (G5), Mrs J. E. Butcher

*COMPUTING AND TELECOMMUNICATIONS
2 Sheraton Street, London WIV 4BH
Tel 071-323 7210
Director (G5), J. R. Mahoney

BRITISH LIBRARY, LONDON
Great Russell Street, London WC1B 3DG
Tel 071-636 1544

Director-General (G4), J. M. Smethurst
St Pancras Project Director (G4), D. Lyman
Director of Project Services St Pancras Planning (G6), Dr R. Coman

ADMINISTRATION
2 Sheraton Street, London WIV 4BH
Tel 071-323 7132
Director (G5), R. Ball

PRESS AND PUBLIC RELATIONS
96 Euston Road, London NW1 2DB
Tel 071-323 7111
Head (G7), M. Jackson

PUBLIC SERVICES
Tel 071-323 7626
Director (G5), Dr D. Clements

EXHIBITIONS AND EDUCATION SERVICE. Tel: 071-323 7595

READER ADMISSIONS. Tel: 071-323 7677

HUMANITIES AND SOCIAL SCIENCES
Tel 071-323 7676
Director (G5), A. Phillips

WEST EUROPEAN COLLECTIONS, SLAVONIC AND EAST EUROPEAN COLLECTIONS, ENGLISH LANGUAGE COLLECTIONS. Tel: 071-323 7676
INFORMATION BRANCH, OFFICIAL PUBLICATIONS AND SOCIAL SCIENCE SERVICE. Tel: 071-323 7676
INFORMATION SCIENCES SERVICE (BLISS), Ridgmount Street, London WC1E 7AE. Tel: 071-323 7688
NEWSPAPER LIBRARY, Colindale Avenue, London NW9 5HE. Tel: 071-323 7353
NATIONAL SOUND ARCHIVE, 29 Exhibition Road, London SW7 2AS. Tel: 071-589 6603

COLLECTIONS AND PRESERVATION
Tel 071-323 7676
Director (G5), Dr M. Foot

PRESERVATION SERVICE (NATIONAL PRESERVATION OFFICE). Tel: 071-323 7612

SPECIAL COLLECTIONS
Tel 071-323 7513
Director (G5), Dr A. Prochaska

ORIENTAL AND INDIA OFFICE COLLECTIONS, 197 Blackfriars Road, London SE1 8NG. Tel: 071-412 7873
WESTERN MANUSCRIPTS. Tel: 071-323 7513
MAP LIBRARY. Tel: 071-323 7700

---

*Scheduled to relocate to Yorkshire by the mid-1990s

MUSIC LIBRARY. Tel: 071-323 7528
PHILATELIC COLLECTIONS. Tel: 071-323 7729

SCIENCE REFERENCE AND INFORMATION SERVICE
25 Southampton Buildings, London WC2A 1AW
Tel 071-323 7494
9 Kean Street, London WC2B 4AT
Tel 071-323 7288
Director (G5), A. Gomersall

RESEARCH AND DEVELOPMENT DEPARTMENT
2 Sheraton Street, London W1V 4BH
Tel 071-323 7060
Director (G6), B. J. Perry

NATIONAL LIBRARY OF SCOTLAND
George IV Bridge, Edinburgh EH1 1EW
Tel 031-226 4531

Opening hours: Reading Room, weekdays, 9.30–8.30 (Wed.,
10–8.30); Sat. 9.30–1. Map Library, weekdays, 9.30–5
(Wed., 10–5); Sat. 9.30–1. Exhibition, weekdays, 10–5; Sat.
10–5; Sun. 2–5. Scottish Science Library, weekdays, 9.30–5
(Wed., 9.30–8).

The Library, which was founded as the Advocates' Library
in 1682, became the National Library of Scotland by Act of
Parliament in 1925. It contains about 6,000,000 books and
pamphlets, 20,000 current periodicals, 230 newspaper titles
and 100,000 manuscripts. It has an unrivalled Scottish
collection.

The Reading Room is for reference and research which
cannot conveniently be pursued elsewhere. Admission is by
ticket issued to an approved applicant.

SALARIES

Librarian	£44,390–£49,790
Keeper	£27,760–£42,724
Curator Grade C	£24,239–£34,469

Chairman of the Trustees, The Earl of Crawford and
Balcarres, PC
Librarian and Secretary to the Trustees, I. D. McGowan
Secretary of the Library, M. C. Graham
Curators Grade C, A. Cameron; W. Jackson; J. E. McIntyre
Keepers of Printed Books, A. M. Marchbank, PH.D.; Ms
A. Matheson, PH.D.
Curators Grade C, T. A. Cherry; Ms A. E. Harvey Wood;
B. P. Hillyard, D.Phil.; S. Holland; W. A. Kelly;
J. M. Morris
Keeper of Manuscripts, I. C. Cunningham
Curators Grade C, I. G. Brown, PH.D., FSA; R. Duce;
I. F. Maciver; S. M. Simpson; Ms J. M. Wilkes; Ms
E. D. Yeo
Director of Computer Services and Research (Keeper),
B. Gallivan
Curator Grade C, R. F. Guy
Director of Scottish Science Library (Keeper), Ms A. J. Bunch

NATIONAL LIBRARY OF WALES/LLYFRGELL
GENEDLAETHOL CYMRU
Aberystwyth, Dyfed SY23 3BU
Tel 0970-623816

Readers' room open weekdays, 9.30–6 (Sat. 9.30–5); closed
first week of October. Admission by Reader's Ticket.

The National Library of Wales was founded by Royal
Charter in 1907, and is maintained by annual grant from the
Treasury. It contains about 4,000,000 printed books, 40,000
manuscripts, 4,000,000 deeds and documents, numerous
maps, prints and drawings, and an audio-visual collection. It
specializes in manuscripts and books relating to Wales and

the Celtic peoples. It is the repository for pre-1858 Welsh
probate records. It is approved by the Master of the Rolls as
a repository for manorial records and tithe documents, and
by the Lord Chancellor for certain legal records. It is the
Bureau of the Regional Libraries Scheme for Wales.
Librarian, B. F. Roberts, CBE, PH.D., FSA
Heads of Departments, M. W. Mainwaring (*Administration
and Technical Services*); G. Jenkins (*Manuscripts and
Records*); J. L. Madden (*Printed Books*); D. H. Owen
(*Pictures and Maps*)

LIGHTHOUSE AUTHORITIES

CORPORATION OF TRINITY HOUSE
Trinity House, Tower Hill, London EC3N 4DH
Tel 071-480 6601

Trinity House, the first general lighthouse and pilotage
authority in the kingdom, was a body of importance when
Henry VIII granted the institution its first charter in 1514.
The Corporation is the general lighthouse authority for
England, Wales and the Channel Islands, with certain
statutory jurisdiction over aids to navigation maintained by
local harbour authorities. It is also responsible for dealing
with wrecks dangerous to navigation, except those occurring
within port limits or wrecks of HM ships.

The Trinity House Lighthouse Service is maintained out
of the General Lighthouse Fund which is provided from light
dues levied on ships calling at ports of the UK and the
Republic of Ireland. The Corporation is also a deep-sea
pilotage authority and a charitable organization.

The affairs of the Corporation are controlled by a board of
Elder Brethren, who are master mariners with long
experience of command in the Royal Navy or merchant
navy, together with figures from the world of commerce, and
the Secretary. A separate board, which comprises Elder
Brethren, senior staff and outside representatives, currently
controls the Lighthouse Service. The Board is assisted by
administrative and technical staff. The Elder Brethren also
act as nautical assessors in marine cases in the Admiralty
Division of the High Court of Justice.

ELDER BRETHREN

Master, HRH The Duke of Edinburgh, KG, KT
Deputy Master, Capt. P. M. Edge
Elder Brethren, Capt. I. R. C. Saunders; Capt. P. F. Mason,
CBE; HRH The Prince of Wales, KG, KT; Capt. Sir George
Barnard, FRSA; Capt. R. N. Mayo, CBE; Capt. Sir David
Tibbits, DSC, RN; Capt. D. A. G. Dickens; Capt.
J. E. Bury; Capt. J. A. N. Bezant, DSC, RD, RNR; Capt.
D. J. Cloke; The Lord Wilson of Rievaulx, KG, OBE, PC,
FRS; Capt. Sir Miles Wingate, KCVO; The Rt. Hon. Sir
Edward Heath, KG, MBE, MP; Capt. T. Woodfield, OBE; Sir
Eric Drake, CBE; The Lord Simon of Glaisdale, PC;
Admiral of the Fleet the Lord Lewin, KG, GCB, LVO, DSC;
Capt. D. T. Smith, RN; Cdr. Sir Robin Gillett, GBE, RD,
RNR; The Lord Shackleton, KG, OBE, PC, FRS; Sir John
Cuckney; Capt. D. J. Orr; The Lord Carrington, KG,
GCMG, CH, MC, PC; Sir Brian Shaw; The Lord Mackay of
Clashfern, PC; Sir Adrian Swire; Capt. N. M. Turner, RD;
HRH The Duke of York, CVO, ADC; Capt. P. H. King;
Capt. The Lord Sterling of Plaistow, CBE, RNR; Cdr.
M. J. Rivett-Carnac, RN; Rear-Adm. P. B. Lowe, CBE, LVO

OFFICERS
Secretary and Director of Administration, M. J. Faulkner
Director of Finance, K. W. Clark

Director of Engineering, D. A. S. Vennings
Personnel and General Services Manager, Mrs B. C. Heesom
Navigation Manager, N. J. Cutmore
Legal and Information Manager, D. I. Brewer
General Manager Operations, Capt. J. M. Barnes
Operations Administration Manager, S. J. W. Dunning
Deputy Director of Engineering, F. E. J. Holden
Senior Inspector of Shipping, J. R. Dunnett
Manager, Corporate Department, R. Dobb
Information Officer, H. L. Cooper

COMMISSIONERS OF NORTHERN LIGHTHOUSES
84 George Street, Edinburgh EH2 3DA
Tel 031-226 7051

The Commissioners of Northern Lighthouses are the general lighthouse authority for Scotland and the Isle of Man. The present board owes its origin to an Act of Parliament passed in 1786. At present the Commissioners operate under the Merchant Shipping Act 1894 and are 19 in number.

The Commissioners control 15 major manned lighthouses, 69 major automatic lighthouses, 108 minor lights and many lighted and unlighted buoys. They have a fleet of two motor vessels.

COMMISSIONERS
The Lord Advocate; the Solicitor-General for Scotland; the Lord Provosts of Edinburgh, Glasgow and Aberdeen; the Provost of Inverness; the Chairman of Argyll and Bute District Council; the Sheriffs-Principal of North Strathclyde, Tayside, Central, Fife, Grampian, Highlands and Islands, South Strathclyde, Dumfries and Galloway, Lothians and Borders, and Glasgow and Strathkelvin; T. Macgill; Capt. A. F. Dickson, OBE; A. J. Struthers; W. F. Hay, CBE; J. Hann, CBE; Capt. D. M. Cowell

OFFICERS
Chief Executive, Capt. J. B. Taylor, RN
Secretary, I. A. Dickson
Engineer-in-Chief, W. Paterson

LOCAL COMMISSIONERS

COMMISSION FOR LOCAL ADMINISTRATION IN ENGLAND
21 Queen Anne's Gate, London SW1H 9BU
Tel 071-222 5622

Local Commissioners (local government ombudsmen) are responsible for investigating complaints from members of the public against local authorities (but not town and parish councils); police authorities; the Commission for New Towns and new town development corporations (housing functions); urban development corporations (town and country planning functions) and certain other authorities. The Commissioners are appointed by the Crown on the recommendation of the Secretary of State for the Environment.

Certain types of action are excluded from investigation, including personnel matters and commercial transactions unless they relate to the purchase or sale of land. Complaints can be sent direct to the Local Government Ombudsman or through a councillor, although the Local Government Ombudsman will not consider a complaint unless the council has had an opportunity to investigate and reply to a complainant.

A free booklet Complaint about the Council? How to Complain to the Local Government Ombudsman is available from the Commission's office.

Chairman of the Commission and Local Commissioner (£90,148), D. C. M. Yardley, LL D, D.Phil., FRSA
Vice-Chairman and Local Commissioner (£65,307), Mrs P. A. Thomas
Local Commissioner (£64,307), E. B. C. Osmotherly, CB
Member (ex officio), The Parliamentary Commissioner for Administration
Secretary (£45,447), G. D. Adams

COMMISSION FOR LOCAL ADMINISTRATION IN WALES
Derwen House, Court Road, Bridgend CF31 1BN
Tel 0656-661325

The Local Commissioner for Wales has similar powers to the Local Commissioners in England. The Commissioner is appointed by the Crown on the recommendation of the Secretary of State for Wales. A free booklet Your Local Ombudsman in Wales is available from the Commission's office.
Local Commissioner, E. R. Moseley
Secretary, D. Bowen
Member (ex officio), The Parliamentary Commissioner for Administration

COMMISSIONER FOR LOCAL ADMINISTRATION IN SCOTLAND
23 Walker Street, Edinburgh EH3 7HX
Tel 031-225 5300

The Local Commissioner for Scotland has similar powers to the Local Commissioners in England, and is appointed by the Crown on the recommendation of the Secretary of State for Scotland.
Local Commissioner, R. G. E. Peggie, CBE
Deputy and Secretary, Ms J. H. Renton

LONDON REGIONAL TRANSPORT
55 Broadway, London SW1H 0BD
Tel 071-222 5600

Subject to the financial objectives and principles approved by the Secretary of State for Transport, London Regional Transport has a general duty to provide or secure the provision of public transport services for Greater London.
Chairman (£111,030), Sir Wilfrid Newton
Deputy Chairman and Chief Executive (£100,000), Dr A. K. Watkins
Member (£79,390), A. J. Sheppeck

LORD ADVOCATE'S DEPARTMENT
2 Carlton Gardens, London SW1Y 5AA
Tel 071-210 3000

The Law Officers for Scotland are the Lord Advocate and the Solicitor-General for Scotland. The Lord Advocate's Department is responsible for drafting Scottish legislation, for providing legal advice to other departments on Scottish questions and for assistance to the Law Officers for Scotland in certain of their legal duties.
Lord Advocate (£50,638), The Lord Rodger of Earlsferry, PC, QC
Solicitor-General for Scotland (£44,342), Thomas C. Dawson, QC
Legal Secretary and First Scottish Parliamentary Counsel (G2), J. C. McCluskie, QC

Assistant Legal Secretaries and Scottish Parliamentary
  Counsel (G3), G. M. Clark; G. Kowalski; P. J. Layden, TD
Assistant Legal Secretaries and Depute Scottish Parliamentary
  Counsel (G5), J. D. Harkness; C. A. M. Wilson
Assistant Legal Secretary and Assistant Scottish Parliamentary
  Counsel (G6/7), Miss M. Mackenzie

LORD CHANCELLOR'S DEPARTMENT
House of Lords, London SWIA OPW
Tel 071-219 3000

The Lord Chancellor is responsible for promoting general reforms in the civil law, for the procedure of the civil courts and for the administration of the Supreme Court (Court of Appeal, High Court and Crown Court) and county courts in England and Wales, and for legal aid schemes. He also has ministerial responsibility for magistrates' courts, which are administered locally. He is advised and assisted in raising performance standards in the Service by the new Magistrates' Courts' Service Inspectorate.
The Lord Chancellor is responsible for advising the Crown on the appointment of judges and certain other officers and is himself responsible for the appointment of Masters and Registrars of the High Court, Judges of the Principal Registry of the Family Division, district judges and magistrates. He is responsible for ensuring that letters patent and other formal documents are passed in the proper form under the Great Seal of the Realm, of which he is the custodian. The work in connection with this is carried out under his direction in the Office of the Clerk of the Crown in Chancery.
Lord Chancellor (£114,083; draws only £110,940), The Lord Mackay of Clashfern, PC
  Private Secretary, M. Ormerod
Parliamentary Under-Secretary, John Taylor, MP
  Private Secretary, Ms S. Jones
Permanent Secretary (G1), Sir Thomas Legg, KCB, QC
  Private Secretary, Ms J. Hull

CROWN OFFICE
Clerk of the Crown in Chancery (G1), Sir Thomas Legg, KCB, QC
Deputy Clerk of the Crown in Chancery (G2), M. Huebner
Clerk of the Chamber, Miss J. L. Waine

JUDICIAL APPOINTMENTS GROUP
House of Lords, London SWIA OPW
Tel 071-219 4311

Head of Group (G3), R. E. E. Holmes
Grade 5, D. E. Staff; R. A. Vincent; R. V. Grobler; G. Norman; P. G. Taylor

LAW AND POLICY GROUPS
Trevelyan House, Great Peter Street, London SWIP 2BY
Tel 071-210 8734

Head of Group (G2), M. Malone-Lee
Grade 5, P. L. Jacob

LEGAL GROUP
Southside, 105 Victoria Street, London SWIE 6QJ
Tel 071-210 3508
Grade 3, R. H. H. White
Grade 5, R. Venne; J. Watherston; M. Kron; J. Gibson

POLICY AND LEGAL SERVICES GROUP
Trevelyan House, Great Peter Street, London SWIP 2BY
Tel 071-210 8769
Grade 3, C. Everett
Grade 5, D. M. Nooney; S. Smith; M. Sayers

COURT SERVICE
Trevelyan House, Great Peter Street, London SWIP 2BY
Tel 071-210 8719

Head (G2), M. Huebner

COURT SERVICE MANAGEMENT GROUP
Grade 3, J. F. Brindley
Grade 5, P. Handcock; R. Sams; Miss J. Killick; Mrs M. Pigott; P. White

ESTABLISHMENT AND FINANCE GROUP
Trevelyan House, Great Peter Street, London SWIP 2BY
Tel 071-210 8803

Head of Group (G3), Mrs N. A. Oppenheimer
Grade 5, Ms H. Tuffs; A. Cogbill; P. Matthews
Grade 6, Mrs J. Waters; J. Isaacs; K. Cregeen

MAGISTRATES' COURTS' SERVICE INSPECTORATE
Southside, 105 Victoria Street, London SWIE 6QJ
Tel 071-210 2169

Chief Inspector (G5), Mrs R. L. Melling

LORD CHANCELLOR'S ADVISORY COMMITTEE ON STATUTE LAW
6 Spring Gardens, London SWIA 2BP
Tel 071-389 3244

The Advisory Committee advises the Lord Chancellor on all matters relating to the revision, modernization and publication of the statute book.
Chairman, The Lord Chancellor
Members, Sir Thomas Legg, KCB, QC; M. A. J. Wheeler-Booth; Sir Clifford Boulton, KCB; The Hon. Mr Justice Brooke; The Hon. Lord Davidson; Sir Peter Graham, KCB, QC; J. C. McCluskie, QC; T. R. Erskine, CB; G. Hosker; R. Brodie, CB; R. H. H White; J. Gibson; Dr P. Freeman
Secretary, C. E. J. Carey

THE LORD CHANCELLOR'S ECCLESIASTICAL OFFICE
10 Downing Street, London SWIA 2AA
Tel 071-930 4433
Secretary for Ecclesiastical Patronage, J. W. Holroyd
Assistant Secretary for Ecclesiastical Patronage, N. C. Wheeler

See also Law Courts and Offices section

LORD GREAT CHAMBERLAIN'S OFFICE
House of Lords, London SWIA OAA
Tel 071-219 3100

The Lord Great Chamberlain is a Great Officer of State, the office being hereditary since the grant of Henry I to the family of De Vere, Earls of Oxford. The Lord Great Chamberlain is responsible for the Royal Apartments of the Palace of Westminster, i.e. The Queen's Robing Room, the Royal Gallery and, in conjunction with the Lord Chancellor and Madam Speaker, Westminster Hall. The Lord Great Chamberlain has particular responsibility for the internal administrative arrangements within the House of Lords for State Openings of Parliament.
Lord Great Chamberlain, The Marquess of Cholmondeley

Secretary to the Lord Great Chamberlain, Admiral Sir
Richard Thomas, KCB, OBE
Clerk to the Lord Great Chamberlain, Mrs S. E. Douglas

LORD PRIVY SEAL'S OFFICE
Privy Council Office, 68 Whitehall, London SW1A 2AT
Tel 071-270 3000

As leader of the House of Lords, the Lord Privy Seal is
responsible to the Prime Minister for the arrangement of
government business in the House. He also has a responsibility to the House itself to advise it on procedural matters
and other difficulties which arise. The Lord Privy Seal has
no departmental portfolio, but chairs a number of domestic
and economic Cabinet committees.
Lord Privy Seal, and Leader of the House of Lords, The Lord
Wakeham, PC
Private Secretary, Mrs J. M. Bailey
Private Secretary (House of Lords), E. C. Ollard

OFFICE OF MANPOWER ECONOMICS
22 Kingsway, London WC2B 6JY
Tel 071-405 5944

The Office of Manpower Economics was set up in 1971. It is
an independent non-statutory organization which is responsible for servicing independent review bodies which advise on
the pay of various public service groups (*see* Review Bodies,
page 348), the Pharmacists Review Panel and the Police
Negotiating Board. The Office is also responsible for servicing
ad hoc bodies of inquiry and for undertaking research into
pay and associated matters as requested by the Government.
Director, M. J. Horsman
Assistant Secretaries (G5), H. E. Miller; P. J. H. Edwards;
G. S. Charles; Mrs S. Webber

MEDICAL RESEARCH COUNCIL
20 Park Crescent, London W1N 4AL
Tel 071-636 5422

The Medical Research Council is the main government
agency for the promotion of medical and related biological
research. The council employs its own research staff and also
provides grants for other institutions and for individuals who
are not members of its own staff, thus complementing the
research resources of the universities and hospitals.
Chairman, Sir David Plastow
Deputy Chairman and Secretary, Sir David Rees, PH.D., D.SC.,
FRS
Members, Prof. I. V. Allen, D.SC., MD, FRCPath.; Prof.
D. T. Baird, D.SC., FRCP, FRCOG, FRSE; R. P. Bauman;
Prof. C. L. Berry, PH.D., FRCPath; Prof.
A. M. Breckenridge, MD, FRCP, FRCPE, FRSE;
K. C. Calman, MD, PH.D., FRCS(Glas.), FRCP, FRSE; Sir
Michael Carlisle; J. T. Carter, FRCP; P. Doyle, CBE, PH.D.;
Prof. C. R. W. Edwards, MD, FRCP, FRCPE; Prof.
J. Grimley Evans, MD, DM, FRCP, FFCM; R. E. Kendell,
CBE, MD, FRCP, FRCPsych., FRCPE; Prof. Sir Aaron Klug,
SC.D., FRS; Prof. M. J. Peckham, FRCP, FRCP(Glas.), FRCR;
Miss E. Nicholson, MP; Prof. J. R. Pattison, DM; Prof.
M. J. Peckham, FRCP, FRCP(Glas.), FRCR; Prof. Sir Michael

Rutter, CBE, MD, FRCP, FRCPsych., FRS; Prof. Sir David
Weatherall, MD, FRCP, FRCPath., FRS
Administrative Secretary, Ms N. F. Morris

NEUROSCIENCES AND MENTAL HEALTH BOARD
Chairman, Prof. Sir Michael Rutter, CBE, MD, FRCP,
FRCPsych., FRS

MOLECULAR AND CELLULAR MEDICINE BOARD
Chairman, Prof. M. Bobrow, D.SC., FRCP, FRCPath.

PHYSIOLOGICAL MEDICINE AND INFECTIONS BOARD
Chairman, Prof. J. R. Pattison, DM

HEALTH SERVICES AND PUBLIC HEALTH RESEARCH
BOARD
Chairman, Prof. J. Grimley Evans, DM, MD, FRCP, FFCM

HEADQUARTERS OFFICE
Second Secretary, D. Evered, MD, FRCP
Director of Finance, B. C. Dodd
Headquarters Office Services, J. E. A. Hay
Director of Human Resources, D. Smith, PH.D.
Director of Corporate Affairs, N. H. Winterton
Director of Research Management, D. Dunstan, PH.D.
Director of Research Planning, M. B. Davies, PH.D.
Director of Industrial Collaboration and Licensing,
D. A. A. Olsen, PH.D.
Research Policy Development Manager, M. B. Kemp, PH.D.
Research Business Manager, J. M. Lee
Executive Board Secretaries, P. Dukes, PH.D.; A. B. Stone,
D.Phil.; D. J. McLaren, D.SC.; R. D. Lang, D.Phil.;
A. C. Peatfield, PH.D.

For units of Medical Research Council, *see* pages 710–11

MENTAL HEALTH ACT COMMISSION
Maid Marian House, 56 Hounds Gate, Nottingham
NG1 6BG
Tel 0602-504040

The Mental Health Act Commission was established in 1983.
Its functions are to keep under review the operation of the
Mental Health Act 1983; to visit and interview patients
detained under the Act; to investigate complaints falling
within the Commission's remit; to operate the consent to
treatment safeguards in the Mental Health Act; to publish a
biennial report on its activities; to monitor the implementa-
tion of the Code of Practice; and to advise ministers.
Commissioners are appointed by the Secretary of State for
Health in the following categories: lay; legal; medical;
nursing; psychology; social worker; and specialist.
Chairman, Sir Louis Blom-Cooper, QC
Vice-Chairman, Prof. E. Murphy
Chief Executive (G6), W. Bingley

MONOPOLIES AND MERGERS COMMISSION
New Court, 48 Carey Street, London WC2A 2JT
Tel 071-324 1467

The Commission was established in 1948 as the Monopolies
and Restrictive Practices Commission and became the
Monopolies and Mergers Commission in 1973. The Commission has the duty of investigating and reporting on
questions referred to it with respect to the existence or
possible existence of monopolies not registrable under the
Restrictive Trade Practices Act 1976 and relating to the

supply of goods or services in the UK, or part of the UK, or to the supply of goods for export; to the transfer of a newspaper or newspaper's assets; and to the creation or possible creation of a merger qualifying for investigation within the meaning of the Fair Trading Act 1973. References may be made to the Commission on the general effect on the public interest of specified monopoly or other uncompetitive practices and of restrictive labour practices.

The Competition Act 1980 provides for the reference to the Commission of particular anti-competitive practices and of questions of efficiency, costs, service provided and possible abuse of monopolies in the public sector. In respect of recently-privatized industries, references to the Commission may be made in certain circumstances by the Director-General of Telecommunications, the Civil Aviation Authority, the Director-General of Gas Supply, the Director-General of Water Services and the Director-General of Electricity Supply, with regard to their respective industries.

Under the Broadcasting Act 1990 the Commission can investigate and report on the competition aspects of networking arrangements between holders of regional Channel 3 licences.

Chairman (£90,150), G. D. W. Odgers
Deputy Chairmen (£31,625), H. H. Liesner, CB; P. H. Dean, CBE; D. G. Goyder
Members (£12,735/*£8,490 each), A. G. Armstrong; C. C. Baillieu; I. Barter; Prof. M. E. Beesley, CBE; Mrs C. Blight; F. E. Bonner, CBE; *P. Brenan; J. S. Bridgeman; Prof. M. Bromwich; R. Davies; Prof. S. Eilon; J. Evans; A. Ferry, MBE; Sir Archibald Forster; Sir Ronald Halstead, CBE; Ms P. A. Hodgson; M. R. Hoffman; D. J. Jenkins, MBE; W. Johnson; *A. L. Kingshott; Miss P. K. R. Mann; G. C. S. Mather; *N. F. Matthews; Prof. J. S. Metcalfe, CBE; Mrs D. Miller, MBE; Prof. P. Minford; J. D. Montgomery; Dr D. J. Morris; B. C. Owens; *Prof. J. Pickering; *L. Priestley; Dr A. Robinson; J. K. Roe; D. P. Thomson; C. A. Unwin, MBE; Prof. G. Whittington
Secretary, S. N. Burbridge, CB

MUSEUMS

MUSEUMS AND GALLERIES COMMISSION
16 Queen Anne's Gate, London SW1H 9AA
Tel 071-233 4200

Established in 1931 as the Standing Commission on Museums and Galleries, the Commission was re-named and took up new functions in September 1981. Its sponsor department is the Department of National Heritage. The Commission advises the Government, including the Department of Education for Northern Ireland, the Scottish Education Department and the Welsh Office, on museum affairs. There are 15 Commissioners, appointed by the Prime Minister.

The Commission's executive functions include providing the services of the National Museums Security Adviser; the allocation of grants to the seven Area Museum Councils in England; funding and monitoring the work of the Museum Documentation Association; and directly administering a capital grant scheme for non-national museums, and various other grant schemes. The Commission administers the arrangements for government indemnities and the acceptance of works of art in lieu of inheritance tax, and it has responsibility for the two purchase grant funds for local museums managed on its behalf by the Victoria and Albert Museum and the Science Museum. The Commission's Conservation Unit advises on conservation and operates

grants schemes for conservators and an Environmental Adviser is drawing up guidelines on environmental standards in museums. A registration scheme for museums in the UK is being implemented by the Commission.

Chairman, G. Greene, CBE
Members, The Marchioness of Anglesey, DBE; F. Atkinson, OBE; J. Baer; The Baroness Brigstocke; The Viscountess Cobham; F. Dunning, OBE; R. Foster; J. Last, CBE; Prof. D. Michie; The Lord O'Neill, TD; The Lord Rees, PC, QC; R. H. Smith; Dame Margaret Weston, DBE; Adm. Sir David Williams, GCB
Director and Secretary, P. Longman

THE BRITISH MUSEUM
Great Russell Street, London WC1B 3DG
Tel 071-636 1555

The British Museum houses antiquities collections, coins and paper money, medals, and prints and drawings. Open daily 10–5; Sun. 2.30–6. Closed on Good Friday, 24–26 December, New Year's Day and the first Monday in May. Admission free. The ethnographical collections are displayed in the Museum of Mankind, 6 Burlington Gardens, London W1. Opening times as above.

The British Museum may be said to date from 1753, when Parliament approved the holding of a public lottery to raise funds for the purchase of the collections of Sir Hans Sloane and the Harleian manuscripts, and for their proper housing and maintenance. The building (Montagu House) was opened in 1759. The present buildings were erected between 1823 and the present day, and the original collection has increased to its present dimensions by gifts and purchases. Government grants for running costs and works and building projects were estimated at £34,102,000 in 1993–4.

BOARD OF TRUSTEES
Appointed by the Sovereign, HRH The Duke of Gloucester, GCVO
Appointed by the Prime Minister, The Lord Windlesham, CVO, PC (*Chairman*); Prof. Gillian Beer, FBA; Sir Matthew Farrer, KCVO; G. C. Greene, CBE; Prof. E. T. Hall, D.Phil., FSA, FBA; C. E. A. Hambro; Sir Peter Harrop, KCB; S. Keswick; Hon. Mrs Marten, OBE; Sir John Morgan, KCMG; The Rt. Hon. Sir Timothy Raison; S. Towneley, D.Phil.; Prof. G. H. Treitel, DCL, FBA, QC; The Lord Weinstock; Prof. Sir William Whitfield, CBE
Nominated by the Learned Societies, The Lord Adrian, MD, FRS (*Royal Society*); A. Jones, RA (*Royal Academy*); Sir Claus Moser, KCB, CBE, FBA (*British Academy*); The Lord Renfrew of Kaimsthorn, FBA, FSA (*Society of Antiquaries*)
Appointed by the Trustees of the British Museum, Sir David Attenborough, CVO, CBE, FRS; Prof. Rosemary Cramp, CBE, FSA; The Lord Egremont; Prof. Sir John Hale, FSA, FBA, FRHistS, FRSA; Prof. P. Lasko, CBE, FSA, FBA

OFFICERS
Director (*G2*), Dr R. G. W. Anderson
Deputy Director (*G4*), Miss J. M. Rankine
Secretary (*G6*), G. B. Morris
Assistant to the Director (*G7*), Ms M. L. Caygill, OBE
Head of Public Services (*G6*), G. A. L. House
Head of Design (*G6*), Miss M. Hall, OBE
Head of Education (*G7*), J. F. Reeve
Head of Press and Public Relations (*SIO*), A. E. Hamilton
Head of Administration (*G5*), C. E. I. Jones
Head of Building and Security Services (*G6*), K. T. Stannard
Head of Architectural and Building Services (*G7*), C. J. Walker
Head of Finance (*G7*), D. E. Williams

Head of Personnel and Office Services (G7),
Miss B. A. Hughes
Keeper of Prints and Drawings (G5), A. V. Griffiths
Keeper of Coins and Medals (G5), Dr A. M. Burnett
Keeper of Egyptian Antiquities (G5), W. V. Davies
Keeper of Western Asiatic Antiquities (G5), Dr J. E. Curtis
Keeper of Greek and Roman Antiquities (G5), Dr
D. J. R. Williams
Keeper of Medieval and Later Antiquities (G5),
N. M. Stratford
Keeper of Prehistoric and Romano-British Antiquities (G5),
Dr I. H. Longworth
Keeper of Japanese Antiquities (G5), L. R. H. Smith
Keeper of Oriental Antiquities (G5), Dr J. M. Rawson
Keeper of Ethnography (G5), B. J. Mack
Keeper of Scientific Research (G5), Dr S. G. E. Bowman
Keeper of Conservation (G5), W. A. Oddy

NATURAL HISTORY MUSEUM
Cromwell Road and Exhibition Road, London sw7 5BD
Tel 071-938 9123

Open Mon.-Sat. 10-6 (closed New Year's Day and 24-26 December), Sun. 11-6. Admission, £4.50.
The Natural History Museum originates from the natural history departments of the British Museum. During the 19th century the natural history collections grew extensively and in 1881 they were moved to South Kensington. In 1963 the Natural History Museum became completely independent with its own body of trustees. The Zoological Museum, Tring, bequeathed by the second Lord Rothschild, has formed part of the Museum since 1938. The Geological Museum merged with the Natural History Museum in 1985 (opening times are as given above). Research workers are admitted to the libraries and study collections by Student's Ticket, applications for which should be made in writing to the Director.
The grant-in-aid for 1992-3 was £28.9 million.

BOARD OF TRUSTEES
Appointed by the Prime Minister: Sir Walter Bodmer, FRS (*Chairman*); Sir Owen Green; The Baroness Blackstone, ph.D; E. N. K. Clarkson, FRS; Mrs J. M. d'Abo; Sir Denys Henderson; Prof. R. May, FRS; Sir Crispin Tickell, GCMG, KCVO
Nominated by the Royal Society, Prof. J. L. Harper, FRS
Appointed by the Trustees of the Natural History Museum,
R. J. Carter; Prof. B. K. Follett, FRS; Sir Anthony Laughton, FRS

OFFICERS
Director (G3), N. R. Chalmers, ph.D.
Associate Directors (Scientific Development) (G5),
Dr S. Blackmore; Dr P. Henderson
Secretary (G5), C. J. E. Legg
Assistant to the Director (G7), Miss R. P. Baillon
Head of Development and Marketing Department (G6),
Mrs R. Laughton-Scott
Marketing Manager (G6), Ms J. Batchelor
Science Marketing (G6), Mrs A. Wendelaar
Public Relations Manager (G6), Miss J. Bevan
Keeper of Zoology (G5), C. R. Curds, D.SC
Bird Section, Park Street, Tring, Herts. Tel: 044 282-4181. Grade 6, I. R. Bishop, OBE
Keeper of Entomology (G5), Dr R. P. Lane
Keeper of Botany (G5), S. Blackmore, ph.D.
Keeper of Palaeontology (G5), L. R. M. Cocks, D.SC
Keeper of Mineralogy (G5), P. Henderson, D.Phil
Head of Finance (G6), J. Card
Personnel Officer (G7), Mrs P. H. I. Orchard

Head of Library Services (G6), R. E. R. Banks
Head of Public Services (G5), R. S. Miles, D.SC
Head of Exhibition and Design (G7), R. M. Bloomfield, ph.D.

THE SCIENCE MUSEUM
South Kensington, London sw7 2DD
Tel 071-938 8000

Open Mon.-Sat. 10-6, Sun. 11-6. Closed 24-26 December. Admission charge. Library open Mon.-Fri. 9.30-7, Sat. 9.30-5.30. Closed on Sundays and Bank Holiday weekends.
The Science Museum, part of the National Museum of Science and Industry, houses the national collections of science, technology, industry and medicine. The Museum began as the science collection of the South Kensington Museum and first opened in 1857. In 1883 it acquired the collections of the Patent Museum and in 1909 the science collections were transferred to the new Science Museum, leaving the art collections with the Victoria and Albert Museum.
Some of the Museum's commercial aircraft, agricultural machinery, and road and rail transport collections are at Wroughton, near Swindon, Wilts., and are open for public viewing on selected weekends during the summer. The Museum is also responsible for the Concorde Exhibition at the Fleet Air Arm Museum, Yeovilton.
The total running expenses, including building costs, of the Museum, the Science Museum Library, the National Railway Museum and the National Museum of Photography, Film and Television are estimated at £26 million for 1993-4.

BOARD OF TRUSTEES
Chairman, Sir Austin Pearce, CBE
Members, HRH The Duke of Kent, KG, GCMG, GCVO, ADC; Dr Mary Archer; Prof. Sir Eric Ash, CBE, FRS, FEng.; The Lord Brabourne, CBE; The Viscount Downe; Miss M. S. Goldring, OBE; Mrs A. Higham; Mrs J. Kennedy; Dr Bridget Ogilvie; Sir Michael Quinlan, GCB; Sir Denis Rooke, CBE, FRS, FEng.; L. de Rothschild, CBE; Prof. Sir John Thomas, FRS; Sir Christopher Wates

OFFICERS
Director, Dr N. Cossons, OBE
Assistant Director and Head of Resource Management Division (G5), J. J. Defries
Head of Personnel and Training (G6), C. Gosling
Head of Finance (G6), Ms A. Caine
Assistant Director and Head of Collections Division (G5),
Dr T. Wright
Head of Physical Sciences Group (G5), Dr D. A. Robinson
Head of Life and Environmental Sciences Group (G5),
Dr R. F. Bud
Head of Technology Group (G5), Dr E. J. S. Becklake
Head of Collections Management Group (G6), Ms S. Keene
Assistant Director and Head of Public Affairs Division (G5),
C. M. Pemberton
Assistant Director and Head of Science Communication Division (G5), Prof. J. R. Durant
Head of Library and Information Services (G6), Dr L. D. Will
Head of Interpretation and Education (G6), Dr G. Farmelo
Assistant Director and Head of Project Development Division (G5), Mrs G. M. Thomas
Head of Design (G6), T. Molloy

NATIONAL RAILWAY MUSEUM
Leeman Road, York YO2 4XJ
Tel 0904-621261

Open Mon.-Sat. 10-6, Sun. 11-6. Admission charge. The Museum, opened in 1975, houses the national rail transport

collection. Locomotives, rolling stock and carriages are displayed to illustrate the technical, social and economic story of the development of railways in Britain.
Head of Museum (G5), A. R. G. Dow

NATIONAL MUSEUM OF PHOTOGRAPHY, FILM AND TELEVISION
Pictureville, Bradford BD1 1NQ
Tel 0274-727488

Open Tues.–Sun. 10.30–6, with special exhibition galleries open to 7.30. Admission free. The Museum, opened in 1983, collects, conserves and displays photography, film and television materials and equipment. It has the only IMAX cinema in the UK and the only public Cinerama theatre in the world.
Head of Museum (G5), vacant

VICTORIA AND ALBERT MUSEUM
South Kensington, London SW7 2RL
Tel 071-938 8500

Open Mon. 12–5.50, Tues.–Sun. 10–5.50. Closed 24–26 December, New Year's Day, Good Friday and May Day Bank Holiday. The National Art Library is open Tues.–Sat. 10–5 and the Print Room Tues.–Fri. 10–4.30, Sat. 10–1, 2–4.30. (The National Art Slide Library is now housed at De Montfort University, Leicester.) Admission free, but donations are invited.
A museum of all branches of fine and applied art and design, the Victoria and Albert Museum descends directly from the Museum of Manufactures, which opened in Marlborough House in 1852 after the Great Exhibition of 1851. The Museum was moved in 1857 to become part of the collective South Kensington Museum. It was renamed the Victoria and Albert Museum in 1899. The branch museum at Bethnal Green was opened in 1872 and the building is the most important surviving example of the type of glass and iron construction used by Paxton for the Great Exhibition. The Victoria and Albert Museum also administers the Wellington Museum (Apsley House), and the Theatre Museum.

BOARD OF TRUSTEES
Chairman, The Lord Armstrong of Ilminster, GCB, CVO
Deputy Chairman, Sir Michael Butler, GCMG
Members, The Lord Barnett, PC; Miss N. Campbell; Sir Clifford Chetwood; I. H. Davison; E. Dawe; R. Fitch, CBE; Prof. C. Frayling, PH.D.; Pamela, Lady Harlech; R. Gorlin; Sir Nevil Macready, Bt., CBE; Miss J. Muir, CBE; Miss A. Plowden; Prof. M. Podro, PH.D.; M. Saatchi; Prof. J. Steer, FSA
Secretary to the Board of Trustees (G7), P. A. Wilson

OFFICERS
Director (G3), Mrs E. A. L. Esteve-Coll
Assistant Directors (G5), vacant *(Collections);* J. W. Close *(Administration)*
Head of Buildings and Estate (G5), J. G. Charlesworth
Surveyor of Collections (G5), Mrs G. F. Miles
Head of Conservation Department (G5), Dr J. Ashley-Smith
Head of Finance and Central Services (G5), Miss R. M. Sykes
Development Director, Miss S. Mason
Curator, Ceramics Collection (G6), Dr O. Watson
Curator, Far Eastern Collection (G6), Miss R. Kerr
Curator, Furniture and Woodwork Collection (G6), C. Wilk
Curator, Indian and South-East Asian Collection (G6), Dr D. Swallow
Curator, Metalwork Collection (G6), Mrs P. Glanville
Head of Personnel (G6), Mrs G. Henchley

Curator, Prints, Drawings and Paintings Collection (G6), Miss S. B. Lambert
Head of Public Affairs (G5), R. Cole-Hamilton
Head of Marketing and Public Relations (G7), Miss R. Griffith-Jones
Head of Research (G5), Dr C. R. Saumarez Smith
Curator, Sculpture Collection (G6), P. E. D. Williamson
Curator, Textiles and Dress Collection (G6), Mrs V. D. Mendes
Managing Director, V. & A. Enterprises Ltd, M. Cass

NATIONAL ART LIBRARY
Curator and Chief Librarian (G5), J. F. van den Wateren

BETHNAL GREEN MUSEUM OF CHILDHOOD
Cambridge Heath Road, Bethnal Green, London E2 9PA
Tel 081-980 3204
Open Mon.–Thurs. and Sat. 10–6, Sun. 2.30–6. Closed every Friday, May Day Bank Holiday, 24–26 December and New Year's Day. Admission free but donations are invited.
Head of the Museum (G6), A. P. Burton

THEATRE MUSEUM
1E Tavistock Street, London WC2E 7PA
Tel 071-836 7891
Open Tues.–Sun. 11–7. Closed Mondays, 24–26 December, New Year's Day, Good Friday and May Day Bank Holiday. Admission charge.
Head of the Museum (G6), Ms M. Benton

WELLINGTON MUSEUM (APSLEY HOUSE)
149 Piccadilly, Hyde Park Corner, London W1V 9RA
Tel 071-499 5676
Open Tues.–Sun. 11–5. Closed Mondays. Apsley House is closed for essential works until the end of 1994.
Curator (E), J. R. S. Voak

MUSEUM OF LONDON
London Wall, London EC2Y 5HN
Tel 071-600 3699

Open Tues.–Sat. 10–6, Sun. 12–6. Closed Mondays and 24–25 December. Admission, £3 (three months), £6 (one year); concessions, £1.50.
The Museum of London opened in 1976. It is based on the amalgamation of the former Guildhall Museum and London Museum. The Museum is controlled by a Board of Governors, appointed (nine each) by the Government and the Corporation of London. The exhibition illustrates the history of London from prehistoric times to the present day.
Chairman of Board of Governors, P. Revell-Smith, CBE
Director, M. G. Hebditch, FSA

COMMONWEALTH INSTITUTE
Kensington High Street, London W8 6NQ
Tel 071-603 4535

Open Mon.–Sat. 10–5, Sun. 2–5. Closed Good Friday, May Day Bank Holiday, 24–26 December and New Year's Day. Admission £1.00; con. 50p.
The Commonwealth Institute is an independent statutory body funded by the British government with contributions from other Commonwealth governments. Its purpose is to increase knowledge and understanding of the Commonwealth in Britain. The Institute is controlled by a Board of Governors which includes the High Commissioners of all Commonwealth countries represented in London. It comprises the centre in London, a Northern Regional Centre in Bradford, and the autonomous Scottish Institute in Edinburgh. The Institute has permanent exhibitions on all Commonwealth nations, plus educational resource, information and conference centres.

Director-General, S. Cox
Director of Education, G. Brandt
Chief Administrative Officer, P. Kennedy
Head of Exhibitions, S. Brownlow

IMPERIAL WAR MUSEUM
Lambeth Road, London SE1 6HZ
Tel 071-416 5000

Open daily 10–6. Closed 24–26 December and New Year's Day. Admission £3.70; concessions £2.65/£1.85. Free admission after 4 p.m. daily. The Reference departments are open Mon.–Fri. 10–5, Sat. by appointment only.

The Museum, founded in 1917, illustrates and records all aspects of the two world wars and other military operations involving Britain and the Commonwealth since 1914. It was opened in its present home, formerly Bethlem Hospital or Bedlam, in 1936. The Museum also administers HMS *Belfast* in the Pool of London, Duxford Airfield near Cambridge and the Cabinet War Rooms in Westminster.

Expenses for 1993–4 are estimated at £21,058,000.
Director-General (G4), A. C. N. Borg, CBE, Ph.D., FSA
Deputy Director-General (G5), R. W. K. Crawford
Secretary (G6), J. J. Chadwick
Personnel Officer (G7), P. L. Cracknell
Finance Officer (G7), Mrs P. A. Whitfield
Museum Superintendent (G7), D. A. Needham
Information Systems Officer (G7), J. C. Barrett
Director of Duxford Airfield (G5), E. O. Inman
Director of HMS Belfast (G6), E. J. Wenzel

KEEPERS
Department of Museum Services (G6), C. Dowling, D.Phil
Department of Documents (G6), R. W. A. Suddaby
Department of Exhibits and Firearms (G6), D. J. Penn
Department of Printed Books (G6), G. M. Bayliss, Ph.D.
Department of Art (G6), Miss A. H. Weight
Department of Film (G6), R. B. N. Smither
Department of Photographs (G6), Miss K. J. Carmichael
Department of Sound Records (G6), Mrs M. A. Brooks
Department of Marketing and Training (G6), Miss A. Godwin
Curator of the Cabinet War Rooms (G7), P. Reed

NATIONAL MARITIME MUSEUM
Greenwich, London SE10 9NF
Tel 081-858 4422

Open Mon.–Sat., 10–6 (10–5 in winter); Sun. 12–6 (2–5 in winter). Closed 24–26 December. Admission charge. Reference Library open Mon.–Fri., 10–5; Sats. by appointment only; readers' tickets available on written application to the Librarian.

Established by Act of Parliament in 1934, the National Maritime Museum illustrates the maritime history of Great Britain in the widest sense, underlining the importance of the sea and its influence on the nation's power, wealth, culture, technology and institutions. The Museum is in three groups of buildings in Greenwich Park – the main building, the Queen's House (built by Inigo Jones, 1616–35) and the Old Royal Observatory (including Wren's Flamsteed House) – and also includes the *Cutty Sark* and a Special Exhibitions Centre. The collections include paintings, actual craft and ship models, ships' lines, prints and drawings, atlases and charts, navigational and astronomical instruments, clocks, uniforms and relics, books and MSS.
Director, R. L. Ormond

NATIONAL ARMY MUSEUM
Royal Hospital Road, London SW3 4HT
Tel 071-730 0717

Open daily, 10–5.30. Closed 24–26 December, New Year's Day, Good Friday and May Day Bank Holiday. Admission free.

The National Army Museum was established by royal charter in 1960. It covers the history of five centuries of the British Army, including the story of the Indian Army up to independence in 1947. The Indian Army room at the Royal Military Academy Sandhurst, Camberley, Surrey may be viewed by appointment.
Director, I. G. Robertson
Assistant Directors, D. K. Smurthwaite; A. J. Guy; Maj. P. R. Bateman

ROYAL AIR FORCE MUSEUM
Grahame Park Way, London NW9 5LL
Tel 081-205 2266

Open daily, 10–6. Closed 24–26 December and New Year's Day. Admission charge.

Situated on the former airfield at Hendon, the Museum illustrates the development of aviation from before the Wright brothers to the present-day RAF. More than 65 historic aircraft are on display. The complex includes the Bomber Command Hall and the 'Battle of Britain Experience'.
Director, Dr M. A. Fopp
Deputy Director, J. D. Freeborn
Keepers, D. C. R. Elliott; P. Elliott; D. F. Lawrence

NATIONAL MUSEUMS AND GALLERIES ON MERSEYSIDE
William Brown Street, Liverpool L3 8EN
Tel 051-207 0001

All museums and galleries are open all year except 24–26 December, New Year's Day and Good Friday. Opening times (except for the Maritime Museum and Museum of Liverpool Life) are Mon.–Sat. 10–5, Sun. 12–5. Admission free. Opening times for the Maritime Museum and Museum of Liverpool Life are 10.30–5.30 (last ticket sold 4.30). These two ventures have a joint admission charge.

The Board of Trustees of the National Museums and Galleries on Merseyside was established in 1986 to take over responsibility for the museums and galleries previously administered by Merseyside County Council. Various stores ancillary to the collections are also the responsibility of the body. It is grant-aided by the Department of National Heritage, and received about £14 million for 1993–4.
Chairman of the Board of Trustees, Sir Leslie Young, CBE
Director, R. Foster
Head of Central Services, P. Sudbury, Ph.D.
Keeper of Art Galleries, J. Treuherz
Keeper of Conservation, J. France

LIVERPOOL MUSEUM, William Brown Street, Liverpool L3 8EN. *Keeper*, E. Greenwood

MERSEYSIDE MARITIME MUSEUM, Albert Dock, Liverpool L3 4AA; and MUSEUM OF LIVERPOOL LIFE, Mann Island, Liverpool L3 1DG. *Keeper*, M. Stammers

WALKER ART GALLERY, William Brown Street, Liverpool L3 8EL

LADY LEVER ART GALLERY, Port Sunlight Village, Bebington, Wirral L62 5EQ

SUDLEY (ART GALLERY), Mossley Hill Road, Liverpool L18 5BX

NATIONAL MUSEUM OF WALES/
AMGUEDDFA GENEDLAETHOL CYMRU
Main Building, Cathays Park, Cardiff CF1 3NP
Tel 0222-397951

Open Tues.–Sat., 10–5. Sun. 2.30–5. Closed on Mondays (except Bank Holidays), 24–25 December and New Year's Day. Admission charge.
President, C. R. T. Edwards
Vice-President, M. C. T. Pritchard, CBE
Director, C. Ford, CBE
Head of Administration, T. Arnold
Keepers, M. G. Bassett, PH.D. *(Geology)*; B. A. Thomas, PH.D. *(Botany)*; P. M. Morgan *(Zoology)*; H. S. Aldhouse-Green, PH.D. *(Archaeology)*; T. J. Stevens, PH.D. *(Art)*

WELSH FOLK MUSEUM/AMGUEDDFA WERIN CYMRU
St Fagans, Nr. Cardiff
Open April–October, daily 10–5; November–March, Mon.–Sat. 10–5. Closed 24–25 December and New Year's Day. Admission charge.
Curator, Dr E. Williams
Keepers, E. Scourfield, PH.D.; J. W. Davies.

ROMAN LEGIONARY MUSEUM, CAERLEON
Caerleon, Gwent
Contains material found on the site of the Roman fortress of Isca and its suburbs. Open Mon.–Sat. 10–6, Sun. 2–6 (closes 4.30 p.m. mid-October to mid-March). Closed 24–25 December and New Year's Day. Admission charge.
Officer in Charge, D. Zienkiewicz

TURNER HOUSE ART GALLERY
Plymouth Road, Penarth, Nr. Cardiff
Open Tues.–Fri. 11–12.45 and 2–5, Sun. 2–5. Closed Mondays except Bank Holidays, Saturdays, 24–25 December and New Year's Day. Admission free.
Keeper in Charge, T. Stevens, PH.D.

MUSEUM OF THE NORTH
Llanberis, Gwynedd
A multi-media presentation of the history of Wales and the electricity supply industry. Open June to mid-September 9.30–6; mid-September–October and May, 10–5; November–April, pre-booked parties only. Closed 24–25 December and New Year's Day. Admission charge.
Keeper, D. Roberts, PH.D.

WELSH SLATE MUSEUM
Llanberis, Gwynedd
Open Easter–30 September daily 9.30–5.30. Admission charge.
Keeper in Charge, D. Roberts, PH.D.

SEGONTIUM ROMAN FORT MUSEUM
Beddgelert Road, Caernarfon, Gwynedd
Open weekdays at 9.30, Sundays at 2. Closes at 6 from May to September, at 5.30 in March, April and October (5 on Suns.), and at 4 from November to February. Closed 24–25 December and New Year's Day.
Officer in Charge, R. J. Brewer

MUSEUM OF THE WELSH WOOLLEN INDUSTRY
Dre-fach Felindre, nr. Llandysul, Dyfed
The museum occupies part of a working mill. Open April–September, Mon.–Sat. 10–5; October–March, Mon.–Fri. 10–5. Closed 24–25 December and New Year's Day. Admission charge.
Keeper in Charge, E. Scourfield, PH.D.

WELSH INDUSTRIAL AND MARITIME MUSEUM
Bute Street, Cardiff
Open Tues.–Sat. 10–5; Sun. 2.30–5. Closed Mondays, 24–25 December and New Year's Day. Admission charge.
Keeper, S. Owen-Jones, PH.D.

THE GRAHAM SUTHERLAND GALLERY AND PICTON CASTLE GROUNDS
The Rhos, Haverfordwest
Open Easter–end October, Tues.–Sun. 10.30–12.30, 1.30–5.00. Closed Mondays except Bank Holidays. Admission charge.
Officer in Charge, S. Moss

NATIONAL MUSEUMS OF SCOTLAND
Chambers Street, Edinburgh EH1 1JF
Tel 031-225 7534

BOARD OF TRUSTEES
Members, Prof. L. Bown, OBE; R. D. Cramond, CBE; Countess of Dalkeith; Sir Nicholas Fairbairn, QC, MP; Sir Alistair Grant; Dr H. A. P. Ingram; Prof. P. H. Jones; D. H. Pringle, CBE; R. Smith; Prof. T. C. Smout

OFFICERS
Director, M. Jones
Museums Administrator, I. Hooper
Keeper, Department of History and Applied Art (G5), Miss D. Idiens
Keeper, Department of Archaeology, D. V. Clarke, D.Phil
Keeper, Department of Geology (G5), W. D. I. Rolfe, PH.D.
Keeper, Department of Natural History (G5), M. Shaw, D.Phil
Keeper, Department of Science, Technology and Working Life (G5), D. J. Bryden
Head, Department of Public Affairs (G6), S. Brock, PH.D.
Head, Department of Museum Services (G6), S. R. Elson

ROYAL MUSEUM OF SCOTLAND
Chambers Street, Edinburgh
Open Mon.–Sat. 10–5, Sun. 12–5. Closed 25–26 December and 1–2 January. Admission free.

MUSEUM OF ANTIQUITIES
Queen Street, Edinburgh
Open Mon.–Sat. 10–5, Sun. 2–5. Closed 25–26 December and 1–2 January. Admission free.

SCOTTISH UNITED SERVICES MUSEUM
Edinburgh Castle
Open 1 April–30 September, Mon.–Sat. 9.30–5.50, Sun. 11–5.50; 1 October–31 March, Mon.–Sat. 9.30–5.05, Sun. 12.30–4.20. Closed 25–26 December and 1–2 January. Admission free.
Keeper, S. C. Wood

SCOTTISH AGRICULTURAL MUSEUM
Ingliston, Edinburgh
Open May and September Mon.–Fri. 10–4.30; June–August Mon.–Sat. 10–4.30. Admission free.
Curator, G. Sprott

MUSEUM OF FLIGHT
East Fortune Airfield, East Lothian
Open Easter–end September daily 10.30–4.30. Admission charge.
Curator, Sqn. Ldr. R. Major

BIGGAR GASWORKS MUSEUM
Biggar, Lanarkshire
Open June–September daily 2–5. Admission free.
Curator, J. Wood

SHAMBELLIE HOUSE MUSEUM OF COSTUME
New Abbey, nr Dumfries
Open Easter–October daily 11–5. Admission charge.
Keeper, Miss D. Idiens

NATIONAL ADVISORY COUNCIL FOR EDUCATION AND TRAINING TARGETS

Caxton House, Tothill Street, London SW1H 9NF
Tel 071-273 5695

The National Advisory Council for Education and Training Targets was established by the Government in March 1993. It will monitor progress towards the National Targets for Education and Training and advise the Secretaries of State for Employment, Education and Wales on performance and policies which influence progress towards them. It will also promote employer investment in the workforce and communicate the importance of continuous learning for all.
Chairman, P. Davis
Vice-Chairman, M. Heron
Members, Sir Christopher Harding; D. Cadbury; Ms C. Galley; A. Cann; M. Walker, OBE; W. Jordan; The Baroness Perry; M. Rowarth, OBE; R. Perks, OBE
Ex-officio, E. Roberts; Sir Brian Wolfson

NATIONAL AUDIT OFFICE

157–197 Buckingham Palace Road, London SW1W 9SP
Tel 071-798 7000

The National Audit Office came into existence under the National Audit Act 1983 to replace and continue the work of the former Exchequer and Audit Department. The Act reinforced the Office's total financial and operational independence from the Government and brought its head, the Comptroller and Auditor-General, into a closer relationship with Parliament as an officer of the House of Commons.

The National Audit Office provides independent information, advice and assurance to Parliament and the public about all aspects of the financial operations of government departments and many other bodies receiving public funds. This it does by examining and certifying the accounts of these organizations and by regularly publishing reports to Parliament on the results of its value for money investigations of the economy, efficiency and effectiveness with which public resources have been used. The National Audit Office is also the auditor by agreement of the accounts of certain international and other organizations. In addition, the Office authorizes the issue of public funds to government departments.
Comptroller and Auditor-General, Sir John Bourn, KCB
   Private Secretary, J. Rickleton
Deputy Comptroller and Auditor-General, R. N. Le Marechal
Assistant Auditors-General, D. A. Dewar; J. A. Higgins; L. H. Hughes; J. Marshall; M. C. Pfleger
Directors, A. G. Brown; C. L. Press; B. D. Baker; C. K. Beauchamp; R. M. Bennett; B. Hogg; G. G. Jones; A. R. Murray; J. Parsons; J. M. Pearce; A. G. Roberts; R. A. Skeen; R. E. Spurgeon; A. Fiander; Ms M. Bibby; M. Daynes; Miss C. Mawhood; R. J. Eales; J. Colman; B. Payne; G. R. L. Osborne
Associate Directors, C. J. Day; J. J. Jones; D. J. Woodward; A. Burchell; J. B. Cavanagh; J. Darling; P. R. Duncombe; D. A. Ferguson; N. Gale; T. Griffiths; K. Hawksell; Miss J. Lawler; J. S. McEwen; R. Parker; M. J. Reeves;

N. Sloan; P. G. Woodward; R. Goacher; M. Whitehouse; P. Cannon; R. Swan; M. Sinclair; R. P. Douglas

NATIONAL CONSUMER COUNCIL

20 Grosvenor Gardens, London SW1W ODH
Tel 071-730 3469

The National Consumer Council was set up by the Government in 1975 to give an independent voice to consumers in the UK. Its job is to advocate the consumer interest to decision-makers in business, industry, the public utilities, the professions, and central and local government. It does this through a combination of research and campaigning. It is funded by a grant-in-aid from the Department of Trade and Industry.
Chairman, Lady Wilcox
Vice-Chairman, Mrs A. Scully
Members, D. Arculus; Miss B. Brookes; A. Burton, OBE; Ms A. Daltrop; Prof. P. Fairest; Miss J. Francis; D. Gilchrist; J. Hughes; L. N. Hunter; Mrs D. Hutton; Prof. G. Jones; J. Mitchell; Ms M. McAnally; Lady McCollum; Mrs J. Varnam; Sir Geoffrey Allen
Director, R. Evans

NATIONAL DEBT OFFICE
— *see* National Investment and Loans Office

DEPARTMENT OF NATIONAL HERITAGE

2–4 Cockspur Street, London SW1Y 5DH
Tel 071-270 3000

The Department of National Heritage was established in 1992 and is responsible for aspects of government policy previously covered by six other government departments. It is responsible for government policy relating to the arts, broadcasting, the press, museums and galleries, libraries, sport and recreation, heritage and tourism. It funds the Arts Council of Great Britain and other arts bodies, including the National Heritage Memorial Fund. It also funds the Museums and Galleries Commission, the national museums and galleries in England, the British Library, the Sports Council, the British Tourist Authority and the English Tourist Board, and the British Film Institute. It is responsible for the issue of export licences on works of art, antiques and collector's items; the Government Art Collection; the built heritage, including the Royal Parks and Historic Royal Palaces Executive Agencies; and statistical services including the International Passenger Survey and broadcasting statistics. The Department is also responsible for policy and implementation of the National Lottery and the Millenium Fund.
Secretary of State for National Heritage, The Rt. Hon. Peter Brooke, MP
   Private Secretary, A. Davey
   Special Adviser, D. Loehnis
   Parliamentary Private Secretary, A. Steen, MP
Parliamentary Under-Secretary of State, Iain Sproat, MP
   Private Secretary, N. Mackenzie
Lord-in-Waiting, The Viscount Astor
Parliamentary Clerk, Ms S. Forsyth
Permanent Secretary (G1), G. H. Phillips, CB
   Private Secretary, Miss H. Wilkinson

ARTS GROUP
Head of Group (G3), Ms M. O'Mara
Head of Arts Division (G5), N. Kroll

Head of Libraries and Information Services Division (G5), P. Bolt
Director, British Library St Pancras Project (G5), J. Pardey
Head of Museums and Galleries Division (G5), P. Gregory
Director, Government Art Collection (G6), Dr Wendy Baron, OBE
Head of Cultural Property Unit (G7), Miss C. Morrison
Head of National Lottery Division (G5), Ms S. A. Booth

BROADCASTING, FILM AND SPORT GROUP
Head of Group (G3), P. Wright
Head of Broadcasting Policy Division (G5), Miss J. Goose, CBE
Head of Media Division (G5), P. Edwards
Head of Sport and Recreation Division (G5), Miss A. Stewart

HERITAGE AND TOURISM GROUP
Head of Group (G3), D. Chesterton
Head of Heritage Division (G5), A. Corner
Head of Royal Estate Division (G5), P. Douglas
Head of Tourism Division (G5), C. Leamy

RESOURCES AND SERVICES GROUP
Director (G4), N. Pittman
Director of Finance and Corporate Planning (G5), vacant
Director of Implementation and Review (G5), Dr K. Gray
Director of Personnel (G5), G. Jones

INFORMATION
Head of Information (G5), Miss A. MacLean

HISTORIC ROYAL PALACES AGENCY
The Birdwood Annexe, Hampton Court Palace, East Molesey, Surrey KT8 9AU
Tel 081-977 7222

An executive agency within the Department of National Heritage, the Historic Royal Palaces Agency manages the Tower of London, Hampton Court Palace, Kensington Palace, Kew Palace with Queen Charlotte's Cottage, and the Banqueting House, Whitehall.
Chief Executive (G3), D. C. Beeton.
Director of Finance and Resources (G5), Ms B. Darbyshire
Surveyor of the Fabric (G5), S. Bond.
Director of Marketing (G6), P. D. Hammond
Curator, Historic Royal Palaces (G6), Dr S. J. Thurley
Administrator, Hampton Court Palace (G6), D. J. C. MacDonald
Resident Governor, HM Tower of London (G5), Maj.-Gen. C. Tyler, CB (retd)
Administrator, Kensington Palace (G7), N. J. Arch

ROYAL PARKS EXECUTIVE AGENCY
The Royal Parks Headquarters, Hyde Park, London W2 2UH
Tel 071-298 2000

An executive agency within the Department of National Heritage
Chief Executive (G5), D. Welch

NATIONAL HERITAGE MEMORIAL FUND
10 St James's Street, London SW1A 1EF
Tel 071-930 0963

The National Heritage Memorial Fund is an independent body established in 1980 as a memorial to those who have died for the UK. The Fund is empowered by the National Heritage Act 1980 to give financial assistance towards the cost of acquiring, maintaining or preserving land, buildings,

works of art and other objects of outstanding interest which are also of importance to the national heritage. The Fund is administered by up to eleven trustees who are appointed by the Prime Minister. Its major source of funding is the Department of National Heritage, which gives an annual grant.

TRUSTEES
Chairman, The Lord Rothschild
Members, Sir Richard Carew Pole, Bt.; The Lord Crathorne; W. L. Evans; Sir Nicholas Goodison; Sir Martin Jacomb; The Lord Macfarlane of Bearsden; Prof. P. J. Newbould; Mrs J. Nutting; Mrs C. Porteous; Cdr. L. M. M. Saunders Watson
Director, Miss G. Nayler

NATIONAL INSURANCE JOINT AUTHORITY
The Adelphi, 1–11 John Adam Street, London WC2N 6HT
Tel 071-962 8000

The Authority's function is to co-ordinate the operation of social security legislation in Great Britain and Northern Ireland, including the necessary financial adjustments between the two National Insurance Funds.
Members, The Secretary of State for Social Security; the Head of the Department of Health and Social Services for Northern Ireland.
Secretary, Ms G. E. Taylor

NATIONAL INVESTMENT AND LOANS OFFICE
1 King Charles Street, London SW1A 2AP
Tel 071-270 3863

The National Investment and Loans Office was set up in 1980 by the merger of the National Debt Office and the Public Works Loan Board. The Office provides staff and services for the National Debt Commissioners and the Public Works Loan Commissioners.
Director, I. H. Peattie
Establishment Officer, A. G. Ladd

NATIONAL DEBT OFFICE
Comptroller-General, I. H. Peattie

PUBLIC WORKS LOAN BOARD
Chairman, Sir Robin Dent, KCVO
Deputy Chairman, Miss F. M. Cook, CBE
Other Commissioners, Miss V. J. Di Palma, OBE; G. Ross Russell; P. Brackfield; D. H. Adams; R. A. Chapman; A. Morton; G. G. Williams; R. G. Tettenborn; J. E. Scotford, CBE; A. Gillespie
Secretary, I. H. Peattie
Assistant Secretary, Miss L. M. Ashcroft

NATIONAL RADIOLOGICAL PROTECTION BOARD
Chilton, Didcot, Oxon. OX11 0RQ
Tel 0235-831600

The National Radiological Protection Board is an independent statutory body created by the Radiological Protection Act 1970. It is the national point of authoritative reference on radiological protection for both ionizing and non-ionizing radiations.

Chairman, Sir Richard Southwood, FRS
Director, Prof. R. H. Clarke

NATIONAL RIVERS AUTHORITY

Rivers House, Waterside Drive, Aztec West, Almondsbury, Bristol BS12 4UD
Tel 0454-624400

The National Rivers Authority (NRA) is an independent body set up under the Water Act 1989. Its responsibilities include monitoring the quality of water, controlling pollution, and the management of water resources, flood defence and fisheries. The NRA has a board of 14 members, two of whom are appointed by the Minister of Agriculture, Fisheries and Food, one by the Secretary of State for Wales, and the rest by the Secretary of State for the Environment.

Chairman, The Lord Crickhowell, PC.
Chief Executive, E. Gallagher
Chief Scientist, Dr J. Pentreath
Director, Water Management, Dr C. Swinnerton
Finance Director, N. Reader
Personnel Director, P. Humphreys
Director of Public Affairs, M. Wilson

DEPARTMENT FOR NATIONAL SAVINGS

Charles House, 375 Kensington High Street, London W14 8SD
Tel 071-605 9300

The Department for National Savings was established as a government department in 1969. The Department is responsible for the administration of a wide range of schemes for personal savers.
For details of schemes, *see* National Savings section.

Director of Savings (G2), C. D. Butler
Deputy Director (G3), D. Howard
Establishment Officer (G5), D. S. Speedie
Finance Officer (G5), M. A. Nicholls
Controllers (G5), Miss A. Nash (*Marketing and Information*);
  A. S. McGill; D. H. Monaghan; E. B. Senior;
  P. N. S. Hickman Robertson
Senior Principals (G6), D. W. Kellaway; W. J. Herd;
  I. Forsyth; M. A. Nicholls; D. Newton; T. Threlfall;
  P. Anderson; A. Muir; T. J. F. McMahon; J. W. Davison
Principals (G7), D. K. Paterson; A. J. V. Cummings;
  Dr A. Fort; W. J. Ferrier; H. Johnson; A. B. Wood;
  P. Finnie; C. E. Funk; I. Jordinson; A. Brown; B. Paley;
  H. Webster; J. Wheatley; C. McVey; R. A. Nichol;
  J. B. Dunphy; J. C. Foreman; D. Wilson; P. B. Robinson;
  G. V. Wise; A. S. Lamond; D. Jeffrey; J. Bolam;
  R. W. Day; C. Dodsworth; R. R. Hesketh;
  R. J. McLelland; M. J. Tan; M. McDade; I. Rich;
  Miss J. S. Clark; M. C. Richards; M. Taylor;
  J. M. Anderson; W. Brough; C. K. D. Conlan;
  S. F. Owen; W. Ward

NATURAL ENVIRONMENT RESEARCH COUNCIL

Polaris House, North Star Avenue, Swindon SN2 1EU
Tel 0793-411500

The Natural Environment Research Council was established in 1965 to encourage, plan and conduct research in the physical and biological sciences which relate to the natural environment and its resources. The Council carries out research and training through its own institutes and by grants, fellowships and post-graduate awards to universities and other institutions of higher education.

Chairman, Prof. J. Knill, PH.D., D.SC
Secretary, Dr Eileen Buttle
Director of Earth Sciences, Prof. J. C. Briden, PH.D.
Director of Terrestrial and Fresh Water Sciences, Prof.
  C. Arme
Director of Marine and Atmospheric Sciences, J. D. Woods,
  CBE, PH.D.

CENTRAL SERVICES
NERC SCIENTIFIC SERVICES, Polaris House, North Star Avenue, Swindon, Wilts. SN2 1EU. Tel: 0793-411500.
Director, B. J. Hinde, OBE

RESEARCH VESSEL SERVICES, No. 1 Dock, Barry, S. Glamorgan. Tel: 0446-737451. *Head,* Dr C. Fay

NERC COMPUTER SERVICE, Holbrook House, Station Road, Swindon, Wilts. SN1 1DE. Tel: 0793-411500. *Director,* H. J. Down

For research institutes and units of the Natural Environment Research Council, *see* page 711–12

JOINT NATURE CONSERVATION COMMITTEE

Monkstone House, City Road, Peterborough PE1 1JY
Tel 0733-62626

The Committee was established under the Environmental Protection Act 1990 and began work on 1 April 1991. It advises the Government and others on UK and international nature conservation issues and disseminates knowledge on these subjects. It establishes common standards for the monitoring of nature conservation and research, and analyses the resulting information. It commissions research relevant to these roles, and provides guidance to English Nature, Scottish Natural Heritage, the Countryside Council for Wales and the Department of the Environment for Northern Ireland.

Chairman, The Earl of Selborne, KBE, FRS
Chief Officer, C. R. Walker, CB
Director, Life Sciences and Resources, Dr M. W. Pienkowski
Director, Earth and Aquatic Sciences, C. Stevens

NORTHERN IRELAND OFFICE

Whitehall, London SW1A 2AZ
Tel 071-210 3000

The Northern Ireland Office is the office of the Secretary of State for Northern Ireland. It was established in 1972, when the Northern Ireland (Temporary Provisions) Act transferred the legislative and executive powers of the Northern Ireland Government and Parliament to the UK Parliament and a Secretary of State. The Northern Ireland Constitution Act 1973 provided for devolution in Northern Ireland through an assembly and executive, but agreement has not been reached on arrangements for involving locally-elected representatives in the government of Northern Ireland, and so responsibility still rests with the UK Parliament.

In 1985 the Governments of the United Kingdom and the Republic of Ireland signed the Anglo-Irish Agreement, establishing an intergovernmental conference in which the Irish Government may put forward views and proposals on certain aspects of Northern Ireland affairs.

Secretary of State for Northern Ireland, The Rt. Hon. Sir Patrick Mayhew, QC, MP
Special Adviser, J. Caine
Parliamentary Private Secretary, M. Moss, MP
Ministers of State, Robert Atkins, MP; The Rt. Hon. Sir John Wheeler, MP
Parliamentary Private Secretaries:
To Mr Atkins, J. Hayes, MP
To Sir John Wheeler, J. Evans, MP
Parliamentary Under-Secretaries of State, The Earl of Arran; Michael Ancram, MP
Permanent Under-Secretary of State(G1), J. A. Chilcot, CB
Second Permanent Under-Secretary of State, Head of the NICS, (G1A), D. Fell, CB

NORTHERN IRELAND CIVIL SERVICE (NICS), Stormont Castle, Belfast BT4 3TT. Tel: 0232-520700
DEPARTMENT OF AGRICULTURE FOR NORTHERN IRELAND, Dundonald House, Upper Newtownards Road, Belfast BT4 3SB. Tel: 0232-520100
DEPARTMENT OF ECONOMIC DEVELOPMENT NORTHERN IRELAND, Netherleigh, Massey Avenue, Belfast BT4 2JP. Tel: 0232-529900
DEPARTMENT OF EDUCATION FOR NORTHERN IRELAND, Rathgael House, Balloo Road, Bangor, Co. Down BT19 2PR. Tel: 0247-270077
DEPARTMENT OF THE ENVIRONMENT FOR NORTHERN IRELAND, Parliament Buildings, Stormont, Belfast BT4 3SS. Tel: 0232-520600
DEPARTMENT OF FINANCE AND PERSONNEL, Parliament Buildings, Stormont, Belfast BT4 3SW. Tel: 0232-520400
DEPARTMENT OF HEALTH AND SOCIAL SERVICES NORTHERN IRELAND, Dundonald House, Upper Newtownards Road, Belfast BT4 3SF. Tel: 0232-520500

OCCUPATIONAL PENSIONS BOARD
PO Box 2EE, Newcastle upon Tyne NE99 2EE
Tel 091-225 6414

The Occupational Pensions Board (OPB) is an independent statutory body set up under the Social Security Act 1973 to administer the contracting-out of occupational pensions from the State Earnings Related Pension Scheme (SERPS), and to advise the Secretary of State. Its functions have been extended by subsequent legislation and it is now also responsible for administering equal access, preservation and modification requirements and appropriate personal pension schemes. Following the Social Security Act 1990, the OPB was appointed as Registrar of Occupational and Personal Pension Schemes and granted powers to make grants to approved bodies in the field. The OPB now funds the operation of the Occupational Pensions Advisory Service (OPAS).

Chairman, Miss C. H. Dawes
Deputy Chairman, A. Pickering
Members, R. J. Amy; Mrs R. Brown; R. Ellison; A. U. Lyburn; W. M. R. Ramsey, D.Phil.; K. R. Thomas; A. S. Herbert; M. R. Slack
Secretary to the Board and General Manager of Executive Office (G6), A. Scaife

OMBUDSMAN
— see Local Commissioners *and* Parliamentary Commissioner. For non-statutory Ombudsmen, *see* Index

ORDNANCE SURVEY
Romsey Road, Maybush, Southampton SO9 4DH
Tel 0703-792000

The Ordnance Survey is the national mapping agency for Britain. It became an executive agency in May 1990 and reports to the Secretary of State for the Environment.

The Ordnance Survey has military origins. It produces over 220,000 large scale maps of the country at three basic scales. These are 1:1,250 (50 inches to 1 mile) for urban areas; 1:2,500 (25 inches to 1 mile) for rural areas; and 1:10,000 (6 inches to 1 mile) for mountain and moorland. In addition, Ordnance Survey produces a range of small scale maps and other products for general use.

Director-General, Prof. D. Rhind
Directors:
Surveys and Production, A. S. Macdonald
Marketing, Planning and Development, J. Leonard
Establishments and Finance, I. Lock
Heads of Functions:
Production, D. Davies
Topographic Surveys, D. Toft
Marketing, P. Wesley
Research and Development, I. T. Logan
Finance, D. James
Establishments, D. R. Evans
Information and Computer Service, B. W. Nanson
OS International, E. Gilbert

OVERSEAS DEVELOPMENT ADMINISTRATION
94 Victoria Street, London SW1E 5JL
Tel 071-917 7000
Abercrombie House, Eaglesham Road, East Kilbride, Glasgow G75 8EA
Tel 0355-844000

The Overseas Development Administration deals with British development assistance to overseas countries. This includes both capital aid on concessional terms and technical assistance (mainly in the form of specialist staff abroad and training facilities in the United Kingdom), whether provided directly to developing countries or through the various multilateral aid organizations, including the United Nations and its specialized agencies.

Minister for Overseas Development, The Baroness Chalker of Wallasey, PC
Private Secretary (G7), M. A. B. Lowcock
Permanent Secretary (G1A), T. P. Lankester
Private Secretary, Ms G. J. Lyons
Deputy Secretary (G2), R. M. Ainscow, CB
Under-Secretaries (G3), N. B. Hudson; B. R. Ireton; J. V. Kerby; R. G. Manning; A. J. Bennett; J. B. Wilmshurst; J. L. Faint; P. D. M. Freeman

ECONOMIC AND SOCIAL DIVISION
Head of the Economic Service (G3), J. B. Wilmshurst
Senior Economic Advisers (G5), J. C. H. Morris; B. P. Thomson; J. Roberts; M. Foster; P. Sandersley; P. J. Ackroyd
Economic Advisers (G6), P. L. Owen; (G7), P. D. Balacs; Dr F. C. Clift; J. G. Clarke; D. B. Crapper; P. J. Dearden; D. Donaldson; P. D. Grant; N. F. Gregory; Dr G. Haley; A. B. D. Hall; E. Hawthorn; N. Highton

Economists (G7), J. L. Hoy; W. Kingsmill; M. Lewis;
A. Moon; R. Teuten; Ms R. Turner; Mrs J. White;
A. Whitworth; Ms C. Laing; E. Cassidy;
Ms R. Phillipson; J. Burton; M. Surr; R. Moberly;
Ms J. Alston; P. G. Hill
Senior Small Enterprise Development Adviser (G6),
D. L. Wright
Small Enterprise Development Adviser (G7), J. R. Boulter
Small Business Adviser (G7), D. M. Spence
Chief Statistician (G5), R. M. Allen
Statisticians (G6), A. B. Williams; (G7), J. R. B. King;
P. J. Crook; Ms J. J. Church; M. Dyble
Principal Finance Management and Administration Adviser
(G5), K. L. Sparkhall
Senior Finance Management and Administration Advisers
(G6), Dr R. Thomas; Dr G. Glentworth
Finance Management and Administration Adviser (G7),
Dr M. Greaves
Senior Finance and Management Advisers (G6),
D. W. Heffer; D. J. Wood; D. W. Baker; S. Sharples;
J. G. Clarke
Overseas Policy Adviser (G6), L. Grundy
Chief Social Development Adviser (G5), Dr R. J. Eyben
Senior Social Development Adviser (G6), Dr S. Conlin
Social Development Advisers (G7), Ms P. Holden;
M. Schultz; R. H. Kinnear; Dr Anne Coles
Chief Health and Population Adviser (G5), Dr D. Nabarro
Senior Health and Population Adviser (G6), R. N. Grose
Forestry Adviser (G7), D. Chaffey
Purchasing Adviser (G7), R. H. Marriott

INFORMATION DEPARTMENT
Head of Information (G5), A. Bearpark
Principal Information Officer (G7), R. W. Fosker

ADMINISTRATIVE STAFF
Grade 5, Miss A. M. Archbold; M. Bawden; S. Chakrabarti;
J. H. S. Chard; Ms M. Cund; A. D. Davis; M. J. Dinham;
J. R. Drummond; R. Elias; D. S. Fish; R. M. Graham-
Harrison; B. W. Hammond; Mrs P. J. Hilton; J. Hodges;
Mrs S. Jay; Mrs B. M. Kelly; M. C. McCulloch;
J. C. Machin; V. J. McClean; C. Myhill; M. A. Power;
C. P. Raleigh; S. Ray; D. Sands-Smith; D. L. Stanton;
G. M. Stegmann; D. P. Turner; Ms S. E. Unsworth; Miss
M. Vowles; M. Wickstead; Mrs P. M. Wilkinson;
R. J. Wilson
Grade 6, J. A. Anning; D. R. Curran; K. D. Grimshaw;
D. Richards; D. Trotter; G. A. Williams
Grade 7, G. F. H. Aicken; J. D. Aitken; G. Alexander;
R. Allen; G. A. Armstrong; C. B. Austin; N. Bailey;
D. G. Bell; F. Black; H. Britton; W. A. Brownlie;
P. J. Burton; R. T. Calvert; P. H. Charters; D. J. Church;
Dr J. Cocking; T. F. G. Connor; R. G. Cousins;
G. Crabtree; A. O. Davies; M. J. Ellis; B. Foy;
J. R. Gilbert; M. A. Hammond; Ms V. M. Harris;
B. Hefferon; Ms A. C. Higginbottom; M. I. Holland;
N. Hoult; G. I. James; W. Jardine; Mrs J. Laurence;
D. Lawless; G. G. Leader; J. Lingham; I. M. McKendry;
M. Mallalieu; G. H. Malley; P. S. Mason; J. Maund;
C. A. Metcalf; J. C. H. Millett; D. J. Moran;
M. L. S. Mosselmans; J. D. Moye; G. A. Mustard;
J. Patel; P. T. Perris; V. R. Pheasant; R. J. Plumb;
G. M. Porter; Mrs J. Radice; C. N. Raynor;
S. R. J. Robbins; P. T. Rose; C. R. Roth;
Dr P. W. K. Rundell; Ms R. Schofield; D. A. Scott;
Mrs A. Scutt; S. J. Sharpe; R. J. Smith;
Miss R. B. Stevenson; M. J. Sexton; I. D. Stuart;
D. J. C. Taylor; E. C. N. Taylor; N. Thomas;
B. A. Thorpe; R. G. Toulmin; N. A. Tranter; R. Vernon;
Ms S. T. Wardell; C. W. Warren; R. S. White;

J. M. Winter; A. K. C. Wood; M. C. Wood;
Mrs G. B. Wright; M. S. S. Wyatt; P. L. Zoller

ADVISORY AND SPECIALIST STAFF
Chief Education Adviser (G5), Dr R. O. Iredale
Senior Education Advisers (G6), M. D. Francis;
Ms M. Harrison; Dr D. Pennycuick; M. E. Seath;
Dr D. G. Swift
Chief Engineering Adviser (G5), T. D. Pike
Senior Engineering Advisers (G6), A. G. Colley; C. I. Ellis;
D. Gillett; B. Dolton; H. B. Jackson;
P. W. D. H. Roberts; M. F. Sergeant
Engineering Advisers (G7), R. J. Cadwallader; A. Barker;
A. Smallwood; M. McCarthy; D. Robson; C. Hunt
Senior Renewable Energy and Research Adviser (G6), vacant
Senior Electrical and Mechanical Engineering Adviser (G6),
R. P. Jones
Senior Architectural and Physical Planning Advisers (G6),
M. W. Parkes; W. M. Housego-Woolgar
Chief Health and Population Advisers (G6), Dr P. Key, OBE;
Miss J. Isard; Dr M. Kapila; Ms S. Simmonds;
J. Lambert
Chief Natural Resources Adviser (G3), A. J. Bennett
Deputy Chief Natural Resources and Principal Agricultural
Adviser (G5), J. M. Scott
Deputy Chief Natural Resources Adviser (G5),
Dr J. C. Davies, OBE *(Research)*
Senior Natural Resources Advisers (G6), Ms L. C. Brown;
B. E. Grimwood; Dr I. Haines; J. R. F. Hansell;
J. A. Harvey; D. J. Salmon; A. J. Tainsh; D. Trotman;
M. J. Wilson; (G7), G. A. Gilman; Dr H. Potter;
Dr P. Dobie; T. Barrett
Animal Health Advisers (G6), G. G. Freeland;
Dr A. D. Irvin; Ms L. Bell
Senior Fisheries Advisers (G6), Dr J. Tarbit; R. W. Beales
Senior Forestry Advisers (G6), W. J. Howard; R. Jenkin;
P. Wood
Senior Procurement Adviser (G6), R. Davidson
Senior Technical Education Advisers (G6), C. Lewis;
Dr G. R. H. Jones
Industrial Training Advisers (G7), W. Wray; D. G. Marr
Population Adviser (G7), C. Allison
Agricultural Education and Training Adviser (G7), A. Hall

NATURAL RESOURCES INSTITUTE
Central Avenue, Chatham Maritime, Chatham, Kent
ME4 4TB
Tel 0634-880088

An executive agency within the ODA, the NRI provides
scientific and technical expertise in renewable natural
resources for the overseas aid programme.
Director and Chief Executive (G3), G. A. Beattie

OFFICE OF THE PARLIAMENTARY
COMMISSIONER AND HEALTH SERVICE
COMMISSIONER
Church House, Great Smith Street, London SW1P 3BW
Tel 071-276 3000

The Parliamentary Commissioner for Administration (the
Ombudsman) is responsible for investigating complaints
referred to him by Members of the House of Commons from
members of the public who claim to have sustained injustice
in consequence of maladministration by or on behalf of
government departments and certain non-departmental
public bodies. Certain types of action by government
departments or bodies are excluded from investigation.

Actions taken by other public bodies (such as local authorities, the police, the Post Office and nationalized industries) are outside the Commissioner's scope.

The Health Service Commissioners for England, for Scotland and for Wales are responsible for investigating complaints against National Health Service authorities that are not dealt with by those authorities to the satisfaction of the complainant. Complaints can be referred direct by the member of the public who claims to have sustained injustice or hardship in consequence of the failure in a service provided by a relevant body, failure of that body to provide a service or in consequence of any other action by that body. Certain types of action are excluded, in particular, action taken solely in consequence of the exercise of clinical judgment. The three offices are presently held by the Parliamentary Commissioner.

Parliamentary Commissioner and Health Service Commissioner (G1), W. K. Reid, CB
Deputy Parliamentary Commissioner (G3), J. E. Avery
Deputy Health Service Commissioner (G3), R. A. Oswald
Directors (G5), Mrs S. Maunsell; M. D. Randall;
J. C. Bateman; Mrs H. Bates; Mrs P. Newman;
Miss D. Fordham
Principals (G7), G. M. Keil; Mrs C. Bentley; T. J. Corkett;
T. J. Hull (*Establishment Officer*); S. J. Drummond;
B. P. Jones; K. O'Brien; D. Howard; Miss C. Corrigan;
D. S. Coleman; E. J. Drake; S. Lillington;
Miss S. Pearson; Mrs S. Skingley; Mrs L. Boulton;
G. Miller; Miss C. Rees-Jenkins, OBE

NORTHERN IRELAND PARLIAMENTARY COMMISSIONER FOR ADMINISTRATION AND NORTHERN IRELAND COMMISSIONER FOR COMPLAINTS
Progressive House, 33 Wellington Place, Belfast BT1 6HN
Tel 0232-233821

The Commissioner is appointed under legislation with powers to investigate complaints by people claiming to have sustained injustice in consequence of maladministration arising from action taken by a Northern Ireland government department, or any other public body within the Commissioner's remit. Senior executive staff are presently seconded from the Northern Ireland Civil Service.

Commissioner, Mrs J. McIvor, QSM
Senior Director, K. McWilliams
Director, G. R. Dawson
Deputy Directors, S. P. Hughes; D. Rodgers

PARLIAMENTARY COUNSEL
36 Whitehall, London SW1A 2AY
Tel 071-210 6633

Parliamentary Counsel draft all government Bills (i.e. primary legislation) except those relating exclusively to Scotland, the latter being drafted by the Lord Advocate's Department. They also advise on all aspects of parliamentary procedure in connection with such Bills and draft government amendments to them as well as any motions (including financial resolutions) necessary to secure their introduction into, and passage through, Parliament.

First Counsel (£82,780), Sir Peter Graham, KCB, QC
Second Counsel (£73,900), J. C. Jenkins, CB

Counsel (£59,020), J. S. Mason, CB; D. W. Saunders, CB;
E. G. Caldwell, CB; E. G. Bowman, CB; G. B. Sellers, CB;
E. R. Sutherland, CB; P. F. A. Knowles; S. C. Laws;
R. S. Parker

PAROLE BOARD FOR ENGLAND AND WALES
Abell House, John Islip Street, London SW1P 4LH
Tel 071-217 5314

The Board was constituted under the Criminal Justice Act 1967 and continued under the Criminal Justice Act 1991. Its duty is to advise the Secretary of State for the Home Department with respect to matters referred to it by him which are connected with the early release or recall of prisoners. Its functions include giving directions concerning the release on licence of prisoners serving discretionary life sentences and of certain prisoners serving long-term determinate sentences; and making recommendations to the Secretary of State concerning the early release on licence of other prisoners, the conditions of parole and licences and the variation and cancellation of such conditions, and the recall of long-term and life prisoners while on licence.

Chairman, The Lord Belstead, PC
Vice-Chairman, The Hon. Mr Justice Ian Kennedy
Secretary, T. E. Russell

PAROLE BOARD FOR SCOTLAND
Calton House, 5 Redheughs Rigg, Edinburgh EH12 9HW
Tel 031-244 8530

The Board advises the Secretary of State for Scotland on the release of prisoners on licence, and related matters.

Chairman, J. M. Scott
Vice-Chairman, I. McNee
Secretary, Miss W. M. Doonan

PATENT OFFICE
Cardiff Road, Newport, Gwent NP9 1RH
Tel 0633-814000

The Patent Office is an executive agency of the Department of Trade and Industry. The duties of the Patent Office consist in the administration of the Patent Acts, the Registered Designs Act and the Trade Marks Act, and in dealing with questions relating to the Copyright, Designs and Patents Act 1988. The Search and Advisory Service carries out commercial searches through patent information. In 1992 the Office granted 9,421 patents and registered 8,175 designs and 35,137 trade and service marks.

Comptroller-General (G3), P. R. S. Hartnack
Assistant Comptroller, Industrial Property and Copyright Department (G4), A. Sugden
Assistant Comptroller, Patents and Designs (G4),
R. J. Marchant
Assistant Registrar, Trade Marks (G4), Miss A. Brimelow
Head of Marketing and Information (Supt. Examiner),
E. F. Blake
Head of Administration and Resources (G5), T. Cassidy
Head of ADP Unit (G6), G. Bennett

OFFICE OF HM PAYMASTER-GENERAL
HM Treasury, Parliament Street, London SW1P 3AG
Tel 071-270 4349
Sutherland House, Russell Way, Crawley, W. Sussex
RH10 1UH
Tel 0293-560999

The Office of HM Paymaster-General was formed by the consolidation in 1835 of various separate pay departments then existing, some of which dated back at least to 1660. Its function is that of paying agent for government departments other than the revenue departments. Most of its payments are made through banks, to whose accounts the necessary transfers are made at the Bank of England. The payment of over 1.5 million public service pensions is an important feature of its work. The Office became an executive agency on 1 April 1993.
Paymaster-General, The Rt. Hon. Sir John Cope, MP
Assistant Paymaster-General/Chief Executive (G5),
  K. Sullens
Grade 6, G. Harbottle; G. Thomas; M. D. West
Grade 7, D. R. Alexander; Mrs D. F. Ambrose; M. L. Card;
  A. Edwards; T. R. George; R. G. Hollands; M. C. Kirk;
  D. Nunn; Mrs J. Parsons; C. A. Ulph

OFFICE OF THE PENSIONS OMBUDSMAN
11 Belgrave Road, London SW1V 1RB
Tel 071-834 9144

The Pensions Ombudsman is appointed by the Secretary of State for Social Security under the Social Security Act 1990 to deal with complaints against, and disputes with, occupational and personal pension schemes. He is completely independent.
Pensions Ombudsman, M. Platt

POLICE COMPLAINTS AUTHORITY
10 Great George Street, London SW1P 3AE
Tel 071-273 6450

The Police Complaints Authority was established under the Police and Criminal Evidence Act 1984 to introduce a further independent element into the procedure for dealing with complaints by members of the public against police officers in England and Wales. (In Scotland, complaints are investigated by independent public prosecutors.) The Authority has powers to supervise the investigation of certain categories of serious complaints and certain statutory functions in relation to the disciplinary aspects of complaints. It does not as a rule deal with complaints about police operations; these are usually dealt with by the Chief Constable of the relevant force.
Chairman, Sir Leonard Peach
Deputy Chairman (Investigations), J. Cartwright
Deputy Chairman (Discipline), P. W. Moorhouse
Members, Mrs L. Cawsey; M. Chapman; Miss L. Haye;
  G. V. Marsh; W. McCall; L. Spencer; Brig. A. Vivian;
  Miss B. Wallis; E. Wignall; A. Williams

POLITICAL HONOURS SCRUTINY COMMITTEE
Cabinet Office, 53 Parliament Street, London SW1A 2NG
Tel 071-210 5058

The function of the Political Honours Scrutiny Committee is set out in an Order of Council dated 31 May 1979. The Prime Minister submits certain particulars to the Committee about persons proposed to be recommended for honour for their political services. The Committee, after such enquiry as they think fit, report to the Prime Minister whether, so far as they believe, the persons whose names are submitted to them are fit and proper persons to be recommended.
Chairman, The Lord Pym, MC, PC
Members, The Lord Cledwyn of Penrhos, CH, PC; The Lord
  Thomson of Monifieth, KT, PC
Secretary, J. H. Thompson, CB

OFFICE OF POPULATION CENSUSES AND SURVEYS
St Catherine's House, 10 Kingsway, London WC2B 6JP
Tel 071-242 0262

The Office of Population Censuses and Surveys was created by the merger in 1970 of the General Register Office and the Government Social Survey Department. The Registrar-General controls the local registration service in England and Wales in the exercise of its registration and marriage duties. Copies of the original registrations of births, still births, marriages and deaths and a register of adopted children are kept at Southport. Central indexes are compiled annually and certified copies of entries may be obtained, on payment of certain fees, either by personal application from St Catherine's House or by post from Smedley Hydro, Southport PR8 2HH.

Since 1841 the Registrar-General has been responsible for taking the census of population. He also prepares and publishes a wide range of statistics and appropriate commentary relating to population, fertility, births, still births, marriages, deaths and cause of death and infectious diseases. The Registrar-General is also responsible for conducting surveys on a range of subjects for other government departments. He maintains, at Southport, the National Health Service Central Register.

Hours of access to Public Search Room, St Catherine's House, Mon.–Fri., 8.30–4.30.
Director and Registrar-General for England and Wales (G2),
  P. J. Wormald, CB
Deputy Director and Director of Statistics (G3),
  E. J. Thompson
Deputy Director and Chief Medical Statistician (G3),
  A. J. Fox, PH.D.
Deputy Registrar-General (G5), J. V. Ribbins
Principal Finance Officer (G5), B. S. Smith
Principal Establishment Officer (G6), N. E. Auckland
Principal Information Officer (G7), Miss S. Wallace
Heads of Division (G5), I. K. G. Arnold (*Information
  Technology*); M. F. G. Murphy (*Senior Medical
  Statistician*); R. Barnes (*Social Survey Division*); J. Craig
  (*Population Statistics*); Ms K. Dunnell (*Health Statistics*);
  B. H. Mahon (*Census*)
Heads of Division (G6), E. Barton (*NHS Central Register*);
  B. W. Meakings (*Data Services*)

Grade 6, B. S. T. Alcock; Mrs M. Bone; A. M. Clark;
J. Denton, OBE; W. Jenkins; I. B. Knight; D. L. Pearce;
R. McLeod; Mrs J. Martin; Ms J. Matheson
Grade 7, R. I. Armitage; F. L. Ashwood; R. A. P. Bailey;
N. Bateson; R. J. Beacham; D. E. Birch;
Mrs B. J. Botting; A. F. Bradbury; J. A. Brown;
L. Bulusu; D. Capron; R. J. Carpenter; J. R. H. Charlton;
J. Cloyne; B. C. Collett; C. J. Denham; T. L. F. Devis;
J. M. Dixie; Mrs J. C. Dobbs; Ms P. A. Dodd; D. Elliot;
Miss C. M. Ellis; Ms E. M. Goddard; Mrs J. R. Gregory;
P. C. Gregory; J. Haskey; A. J. H. Hayes (Chief Inspector
of Registration); P. J. Heady; G. Hughes; Mrs J. Humby;
J. Jackson; S. P. King; I. B. Knight; B. G. Little;
Miss C. S. J. Lloyd; D. Lockyer; W. F. Loomes;
Miss E. M. McCrossan; Mrs I. MacDonald-Davies;
Mrs M. Machin; A. J. Manners; V. A. Mason;
H. I. Meltzer; I. D. Mills; Miss D. Pace; A. Parr;
M. Quinn; A. P. Read; S. Robinson-Grindey;
C. I. Rooney; J. A. Salvetti; C. Savage; Ms J. M. Sharp;
Mrs S. M. Smyth; D. Stewart; P. Stickland;
Mrs L. M. Street; A. D. Teague; A. W. Tester;
Mrs M. J. Wagget; I. S. G. White; A. J. White;
E. W. Williams

PORT OF LONDON AUTHORITY
Devon House, 58–60 St Katharine's Way, London E1 9LB
Tel 071-265 2656

The Port of London Authority is a public trust constituted under the Port of London Act 1908 and subsequent legislation. The Board comprises a chairman and up to seven but not less than four non-executive members appointed by the Secretary of State for Transport, and up to four but not less than one executive members appointed by the Board.

The Port of London Authority is the governing body for the Port of London, covering the tidal portion of the River Thames from Teddington to the seaward limit.
Chairman, Sir Brian Shaw
Vice-Chairman, J. H. Kelly, CBE
Chief Executive, D. Jeffery
Secretary, G. E. Ennals

THE POST OFFICE
148 Old Street, London EC1V 9HQ
Tel 071-490 2888

Crown services for the carriage of government despatches were set up in about 1516. The conveyance of public correspondence began in 1635 and the mail service was made a parliamentary responsibility with the setting up of a Post Office in 1657. Telegraphs came under the Post Office control in 1870 and the Post Office Telephone Service began in 1880. The National Girobank service of the Post Office began in 1968. The Post Office ceased to be a government department in 1969 and responsibility for the running of the postal, telecommunications, giro and remittance services was transferred to a public authority called the Post Office. The 1981 British Telecommunications Act separated the functions of the Post Office, making it solely responsible for postal services and Girobank, which was privatized in 1990.

The chairman, chief executive and members of the Post Office Board are appointed by the Secretary of State for Trade and Industry but responsibility for the running of the Post Office as a whole rests with the Board in its corporate capacity.

FINANCIAL RESULTS	1991–2 £m	1992–3 £m
Post Office Group		
Turnover	5,149	5,345
Trading profit before tax	247	283
Royal Mail		
Turnover	3,911	4,048
Trading profit before tax and interest on long-term loans	205	216
Parcelforce		
Turnover	508	501
Trading loss before tax and interest on long-term loans	15	12
Post Office Counters		
Turnover	1,028	1,061
Trading profit before tax and interest on long-term loans	26	43

POST OFFICE BOARD
Chairman, M. Heron
Chief Executive, W. Cockburn, CBE, TD
Members, P. Howarth (Managing Director, Royal Mail);
M. Kitchener (Managing Director, Parcelforce); R. Dykes
(Managing Director, Post Office Counters Ltd); R. Close
(Managing Director, Finance)
Secretary, Miss M. MacDonald, CBE

PRIVY COUNCIL OFFICE
Whitehall, London SW1A 2AT
Tel 071-270 3000

The Office is responsible for the arrangements leading to the making of all royal proclamations and Orders in Council; for certain formalities connected with ministerial changes; for considering applications for the granting (or amendment) of royal charters; for the scrutiny and approval of by-laws and statutes of chartered bodies; and for the appointment of High Sheriffs and many Crown and Privy Council appointments to governing bodies.
Lord President of the Council (and Leader of the House of
Commons), The Rt. Hon. Antony Newton, OBE, MP
Private Secretary, G. D. S. Sandeman
Special Adviser, I. Stewart
Parliamentary Private Secretary, J. Marshall, MP
Clerk of the Council (G3), N. H. Nicholls, CBE
Deputy Clerk of the Council (G5), R. P. Bulling
Senior Clerk, J. Laverick

PROCURATOR FISCAL SERVICE
— see pages 381–2

PUBLIC HEALTH LABORATORY SERVICE
61 Colindale Avenue, London NW9 5DF
Tel 081-200 1295

The Public Health Laboratory Service comprises 53 regional or area laboratories in England and Wales, the Central Public Health Laboratory, the Communicable Disease Surveillance Centre, and the Centre for Applied Microbiology and Research. The PHLS provides diagnostic microbiological services to hospitals, and has reference facilities that are available nationally. It collates information on the incidence of infection, and when necessary it institutes special inquiries into outbreaks and the epidemiology of infectious disease. It also undertakes bacteriological surveillance of the quality of food and water for local authorities and others. The PHLS is often called upon to advise central and local government and the hospital service on many aspects of infectious disease. It maintains close contact with veterinary organizations in areas of mutual interest, and collaborates with the World Health Organization and with national laboratory and epidemiological services overseas.

THE BOARD
Chairman, Dr M. P. W. Godfrey, CBE, FRCP
Members, Prof. J. P. Arbuthnott, PH.D.; Dr W. Bogie;
D. F. R. Crofton; Prof. G. Crompton; A. E. Eames;
Prof. C. S. F. Easmon; Dr J. M. Forsythe; J. Godfrey;
A. Graham-Dixon, QC; Dr H. H. John; Prof. M. D. Lilly;
D. Noble, CBE; Dr M. J. Painter; Prof. J. R. Pattison;
Prof. I. Phillips; J. J. Skehel, PH.D., FRS; Prof. P. G. Smith,
D.SC.; Prof. L. Southgate

HEAD OFFICE
Director, Dr Diana Walford, FRCP, FRCPath.
Deputy Directors, Dr E. M. Cooke; Dr C. Roberts
Deputy Director (Administration) and Board Secretary,
K. M. Saunders
Deputy Board Secretary, J. M. Harker

CENTRAL PUBLIC HEALTH LABORATORY
Colindale Avenue, London NW9 5HT
Director, Dr M. C. Timbury

COMMUNICABLE DISEASES SURVEILLANCE CENTRE
Colindale Avenue, NW9 5EQ
Director, Dr C. L. R. Bartlett

CENTRE FOR APPLIED MICROBIOLOGY AND RESEARCH
Porton Down, Salisbury, Wilts. SP4 OJG
Director (acting), Prof. J. Melling, PH.D.

OTHER SPECIAL LABORATORIES AND UNITS
ANAEROBE REFERENCE UNIT, Public Health Laboratory,
Cardiff. Director, Prof. B. I. Duerden
CRYPTOSPROIDIUM REFERENCE UNIT, Public Health
Laboratory, Rhyl. Director, D. P. Casemore, PH.D.
GONOCOCCUS REFERENCE UNIT, Public Health
Laboratory, Bristol. Director, A. E. Jephcott, MD
LEPTOSPIRA REFERENCE LABORATORY, Public Health
Laboratory, Hereford. Director, I. R. Fergusson, TD
MALARIA REFERENCE LABORATORY, London School of
Hygiene and Tropical Medicine, London WC1. Directors,
Prof. D. J. Bradley, DM; D. C. Warhurst, PH.D., FRCPath.
MENINGOCOCCAL REFERENCE LABORATORY, Public
Health Laboratory, Manchester. Director,
D. M. Jones, OBE, MD
MYCOBACTERIUM REFERENCE UNIT, Public Health
Laboratory, Cardiff. Director, P. A. Jenkins, PH.D.
TOXOPLASMA REFERENCE LABORATORIES, Public
Health Laboratory, Leeds. Director, R. N. Peel; Public
Health Laboratory, Swansea. Director, D. H. M. Joynson;
Public Health Laboratory, Tooting, London. Director,
R. E. Holliman
WATER AND ENVIRONMENTAL LABORATORY, Public
Health Laboratory, Nottingham. Director,
J. V. Lee, PH.D.

REGIONAL LABORATORIES AND DIRECTORS
Birmingham, I. D. Farrell, PH.D.; Bristol, A. E. Jephcott;
Cambridge, U. Desselberger, MD, FRCP(G); Cardiff,
Prof. B. I. Duerden; Leeds, R. N. Peel; Liverpool,
J. H. Pennington, MD; Manchester, D. M. Jones, MD;
Newcastle, N. F. Lightfoot; Oxford, J. B. Selkon, TD;
Portsmouth, O. A. Okubadejo, MD; Sheffield, P. Norman

AREA LABORATORIES
Ashford, C. Dulake, TD; Bangor, T. Howard; Bath,
D. G. White; Brighton, B. T. Thom; Carlisle,
M. A. Knowles; Carmarthen, M. D. Simmons; Chelmsford,
R. E. Tettmar, D.Path.; Chester, P. Hunter, MD; Coventry,
P. R. Mortimer, MD; Dorchester, A. Rampling, PH.D.; Epsom,
S. A. Chambers; Exeter, J. G. Cruickshank, MD; Gloucester,
K. A. V. Cartwright; Guildford, Prof. R. Y. Cartwright;
Hereford, I. R. Ferguson, TD; Hull, S. L. Mawer; Ipswich,
P. H. Jones; Leicester, C. J. Mitchell; Lincoln, E. R. Youngs;
LONDON: Central Middlesex Hospital, M. S. Shafi (acting);
Dulwich, A. H. C. Uttley, PH.D.; Tooting,
Prof. A. R. M. Coates; Whipps Cross,
B. Chattopadhyay, MD; Luton, Dr S. A. Rousseau (acting);
Middlesbrough, E. McKay-Ferguson, MD; Norwich,
P. M. B. White; Nottingham, M. J. Lewis, MD;
Peterborough, R. S. Jobanputra, MD; Plymouth,
P. J. Wilkinson; Poole, W. L. Hooper; Preston,
D. N. Hutchinson, MD; Reading, J. V. Dadswell; Rhyl,
D. N. Looker; Salisbury, S. Patrick; Shrewsbury,
C. A. Morris, MD; Southampton, J. A. Lowes; Stoke-on-Trent,
J. Gray; Swansea, D. H. M. Joynson; Taunton,
J. V. S. Pether; Truro, W. A. Telfer Brunton; Watford,
M. T. Moulsdale; Wolverhampton, R. G. Thompson

REGISTRAR OF PUBLIC LENDING RIGHT
Bayheath House, Prince Regent Street,
Stockton-on-Tees, TS18 IDF
Tel 0642-604699

Under the Public Lending Right system, in operation since 1983, payment is made from public funds to authors whose books are lent out from public libraries. Payment is made once a year (in February) and the amount each author receives is proportionate to the number of times (established from a sample) that each registered book has been lent out during the previous year.

The Registrar of PLR, who is appointed by the Secretary of State for National Heritage, compiles the register of authors and books. Only living authors resident in the UK or Germany are eligible to apply. (The term 'author' covers writers, illustrators, translators, and some editors/compilers.)

A payment of 1.86 pence was made in 1992–3 for each estimated loan of a registered book, up to a top limit of £6,000 for the books of any one registered author; the money for loans above this level is used to augment the remaining PLR payments.

In February 1993, the sum of £3,945,000 was made available for distribution to 17,831 registered authors and assignees as the annual payment of PLR.

The PLR Advisory Committee advises the Secretary of State for National Heritage and the Registrar of Public Lending Right. Its members are appointed by the Secretary of State.
Chairman of Advisory Committee, D. H. Whitaker, OBE
Registrar, Dr J. Parker

PUBLIC RECORD OFFICE
— see pages 346–7

PUBLIC TRUST OFFICE
Stewart House, 24 Kingsway, London WC2B 6JX
Tel 071-269 7000

The Public Trustee is a trust corporation created to undertake the business of executorship and trusteeship; he can act as executor or administrator of the estate of a deceased person, or as trustee of a will or settlement. The Public Trustee is also responsible for the performance of all the administrative, but not the judicial, tasks required of the Court of Protection under Part VII of the Mental Health Act 1983, relating to the management and administration of the property and affairs of persons suffering from mental disorder. The Public Trustee also acts as Receiver when so directed by the Court, usually where there is no other person willing or able so to act.

The Accountant-General of the Supreme Court, through the Court Funds Office, is responsible for the investment and accounting of funds in court for persons under a disability, monies in court subject to litigation and statutory deposits.

The Court Funds Office is at 22 Kingsway, London WC2B 6LE. Tel: 071-936 6000
Public Trustee and Accountant-General, P. J. Farmer
Assistant Public Trustee, H. N. Mather
Investment Manager, H. Stevenson
Chief Property Adviser, A. Nightingale

CLIENT SERVICES SECTOR
Head, E. J. Dober
Receivership Division, Mrs H. Bratton
Protection Division, I. S. Price

INTERNAL SERVICES SECTOR
Head, I. J. MacBean
Court Funds Office, F. J. Eddy

PUBLIC WORKS LOAN BOARD
— *see* National Investment and Loans Office

COMMISSION FOR RACIAL EQUALITY
Elliot House, 10–12 Allington Street, London SW1E 5EH
Tel 071-828 7022

The Commission was established in 1977, under the Race Relations Act 1976, to work towards the elimination of discrimination and promote equality of opportunity and good relations between different racial groups.
Chairman, H. Ouseley
Deputy Chairs, A. Ward; R. Sondhi
Members, R. Kent; Revd E. A. Brown; Dr
M. C. K. Chan, MBE; T. A. Khan; A. Rose, OBE;
R. Purkiss; Dr D. Neil; Ms M. Cunningham; Dr
R. Chandran; Dr Z. Khan; M. Hastings
Chief Executive (acting), D. Sharma

THE RADIO AUTHORITY
Holbrook House, 14 Great Queen Street, London WC2B 5DG
Tel 071-430 2724

The Radio Authority was established in January 1991 under the Broadcasting Act 1990 as one of the two successor bodies to the Independent Broadcasting Authority. Its function is to plan frequencies, to grant licences for the provision of independent radio services, and to regulate the output of the services in accordance with published codes dealing with standards for programming, advertising and sponsorship.

Members of the Authority are appointed by the Secretary of State for National Heritage. Senior executive staff are appointed by the Authority.
Chairman, The Lord Chalfont OBE, MC, PC
Deputy Chairman, Mrs J. McIvor, QSM

Members, Mrs M. Corrigan; J. Grant; R. Hooper; R. Sondhi; M. Moriarty, CB
Chief Executive, P. Baldwin
Deputy Chief Executive and Head of Regulation, P. Brown
Head of Development, D. Vick
Head of Finance, N. Romain
Head of Engineering, M. Thomas
Secretary to the Authority, J. Norrington

RECORD OFFICES

ADVISORY COUNCIL ON PUBLIC RECORDS
Trevelyan House, Great Peter Street, London SW1P 2BY
Tel 071-210 8500

Council members are appointed by the Lord Chancellor, under the Public Records Act 1958, to advise him on matters concerning public records in general and, in particular, on those aspects of the work of the Public Record Office which affect members of the public who make use of it. The Council meets quarterly and produces an annual report which is published alongside the Report of the Keeper of Public Records as a House of Commons sessional paper.
Chairman, The Master of the Rolls
Members, Prof. B. W. E. Alford; Sir John Blelloch; Dr
A. Borg; Mrs L. Brindley; A. C. Carlile, QC, MP; Prof.
R. Chapman; T. A. G. Davis, MP; Prof. R. B. Dobson;
Miss A. Duncan; V. Gray; Mrs L. Lithgow; Prof. Shula
Marks; Prof. R. Skidelsky; D. Sumberg, MP; D. G. Vaisey
Assessor, Mrs S. Tyacke
Secretary, P. Kennedy

THE PUBLIC RECORD OFFICE
Ruskin Avenue, Kew, Richmond, Surrey TW9 4DU
Tel 081-876 3444
Chancery Lane, London WC2A 1LR
Tel 081-876 3444

The Office, originally established in 1838 under the Master of the Rolls, was placed by the Public Records Act 1958 under the direction of the Lord Chancellor. He appoints a Keeper of Public Records, whose duties are to co-ordinate and supervise the selection of records of government departments and the English law courts for permanent preservation, to safeguard the records and to make them available to the public.

The Office holds records of central government dating from the *Domesday Book* (1086) to the present. Under the Public Records Act 1967 they are normally open to inspection when 30 years old, and are then available, without charge, in the reading rooms, Mon.–Fri., 9.30–5. The museum at Chancery Lane is open Mon.–Fri., 10–5 and the Census rooms are open Mon.–Sat., 9.30–5.

The Public Records Office became an executive agency in 1992.
Keeper of Public Records (G3), Mrs S. Tyacke
Central Management Department (G6), Dr D. L. Thomas

PUBLIC SERVICES DIVISION
Director (G5), C. D. Chalmers
Reader Services Department (G6), Mrs A. Nicol
Editorial Services Department (G6), vacant
Publishing and Public Relations Department (G6), Dr
E. Hallam Smith
Preservation Department (G7), Dr H. Forde

ARCHIVAL SERVICES DIVISION
Director (G5), Dr N. G. Cox
Government Services Department (G6), J. L. Walford
Team Leaders (G7), A. H. W. Medlicott; E. J. Higgs;
K. J. Smith; Ms J. Rose

CORPORATE SERVICES DIVISION
Director (G5), Mrs S. E. Tyerman
IT Department (G7), Miss J. K. Lawlor
Finance Department (G7), Ms P. Ewens
Personnel Department (G7), N. J. Smedley
New PRO Sponsor (G7), Dr A. J. McDonald
Office Services Department (G7), J. S. Harley

HOUSE OF LORDS RECORD OFFICE
House of Lords, London SW1A OPW
Tel 071-219 3074

Since 1497, the records of Parliament have been kept within the Palace of Westminster. They are in the custody of the Clerk of the Parliaments. In 1946 a record department was established to supervise their preservation and their availability to the public. The search room of the office is open to the public Mon.–Fri., 9.30–5 (Tues. to 8, by appointment).

Some three million documents are preserved, including Acts of Parliament from 1497, journals of the House of Lords from 1510, minutes and committee proceedings from 1610, and papers laid before Parliament from 1531. Amongst the records are the Petition of Right, the Death Warrant of Charles I, the Declaration of Breda, and the Bill of Rights. The House of Lords Record Office also has charge of the journals of the House of Commons (from 1547), and other surviving records of the Commons (from 1572), which include plans and annexed documents relating to Private Bill legislation from 1818. Among other documents are the records of the Lord Great Chamberlain, the political papers of certain members of the two Houses, and documents relating to Parliament acquired on behalf of the nation. All the manuscripts and other records are preserved in the Victoria Tower of the Houses of Parliament. A permanent exhibition was established in the Royal Gallery in 1979.
Clerk of the Records (£37,589–£49,790), D. J. Johnson, FSA
Deputy Clerk of the Records (£28,904–£44,390),
S. K. Ellison
Assistant Clerk of the Records (£14,071–£21,798),
D. L. Prior

ROYAL COMMISSION ON HISTORICAL MANUSCRIPTS
Quality House, Quality Court, Chancery Lane, London WC2A 1HP
Tel 071-242 1198

The Commission was set up by royal warrant in 1869 to enquire and report on collections of papers of value for the study of history which were in private hands. In 1959 a new warrant enlarged these terms of reference to include all historical records, wherever situated, outside the Public Records and gave it added responsibilities as a central co-ordinating body to promote, assist and advise on their proper preservation and storage. The Commission has published over 200 volumes of reports.

It also maintains the National Register of Archives, which contains almost 36,000 unpublished lists and catalogues of manuscript collections describing the holdings of local record offices, national and university libraries, specialist repositories and others in the UK and overseas. The NRA can be searched using three computerised indices which are available in the Commission's search room.

The Commission also administers the Manorial and Tithe Documents Rules on behalf of the Master of the Rolls.
Chairman, G. E. Aylmer, FBA
Commissioners, The Lord Blake, FBA;
J. P. W. Ehrman, FBA, FSA; Prof. S. F. C. Milsom, FBA;
P. T. Cormack, FSA, MP; D. G. Vaisey, FSA; The Viscount of Arbuthnott, CBE, DSC; The Lord Camoys; The Lord Egremont and Leconfield; Mrs J. Thirsk, FBA;
Sir Matthew Farrer, KCVO; Miss B. Harvey, FBA, FSA;
Sir John Sainty, KCB, FSA; Prof. R. H. Campbell, PH.D.;
Very Revd H. E. C. Stapleton, FSA; Sir Keith Thomas
Secretary, C. J. Kitching, PH.D., FSA

SCOTTISH RECORD OFFICE
HM General Register House, Edinburgh EH1 3YY
Tel 031-556 6585

The history of the national archives of Scotland can be traced back to the 13th century. The present headquarters of the Scottish Record Office, the General Register House, was founded in 1774. Here are preserved the administrative records of pre-Union Scotland, the registers of central and local courts of law, the public registers of property rights and legal documents, and many collections of local and church records and private archives. Certain groups of records, mainly the modern records of government departments in Scotland, the Scottish railway records, the plans collection, and private archives of an industrial or commercial nature are preserved in the branch repository at the West Register House in Charlotte Square. The search rooms in both buildings open Mon.–Fri., 9–4.45. A permanent exhibition at the West Register House and changing exhibitions at the General Register House are open to the public on weekdays, 10–4. The National Register of Archives (Scotland), which is a branch of the Scottish Record Office, is based in the West Register House.

The Scottish Record Office became an executive agency of the Scottish Office in April 1993.
Keeper of the Records of Scotland, P. M. Cadell

CORPORATION OF LONDON RECORDS OFFICE
Guildhall, London EC2P 2EJ
Tel 071-332 1251

The Corporation of London Records Office contains the municipal archives of the City of London which are regarded as the most complete collection of ancient municipal records in existence. The collection includes charters of William the Conqueror, Henry II, and later kings and queens to 1957; ancient custumals: Liber Horn, Dunthorne, Custumarum, Ordinacionum, Memorandorum and Albus, Liber de Antiquis Legibus, and collections of Statutes; continuous series of judicial rolls and books from 1252 and Council minutes from 1275; records of the Old Bailey and Guildhall Sessions from 1603; financial records from the 16th century; the records of London Bridge from the 12th century; and numerous subsidiary series and miscellanea of historical interest. Readers' Room open Mon.–Fri., 9.30–4.45.
Keeper of the City Records, The Town Clerk
City Archivist, J. R. Sewell
Deputy City Archivist, Mrs J. M. Bankes

RED DEER COMMISSION
Knowsley, 82 Fairfield Road, Inverness IV3 5LH
Tel 0463-231751

The Red Deer Commission has the general functions of furthering the conservation and control of red and sika deer in Scotland and of keeping under review all matters relating to roe deer. It has the statutory duty, with powers, to prevent damage to agriculture and forestry by red and sika deer. The Commission also has the power to advise in the interest of conservation any owner of land on questions relating to the carrying of stocks of red deer, sika deer and roe deer on that land, and to carry out research into matters of scientific importance relating to deer.

Chairman (part-time), P. Gordon-Duff-Pennington, OBE
Secretary, A. Rinning
Senior Field Officer, R. W. Youngson

REVENUE ADJUDICATOR'S OFFICE
3rd Floor, Haymarket House, 28 Haymarket, London
SW1Y 4SP
Tel 071-930 2292

The Revenue Adjudicator is appointed by the Board of Inland Revenue to consider complaints about how the Inland Revenue or the Valuation Office Agency have handled someone's affairs. The Adjudicator's Office opened on 1 July 1993.

Revenue Adjudicator, Ms E. Filkin
Head of Office, D. I. Richardson

REVIEW BODIES

The secretariat for these bodies is provided by the Office of Manpower Economics (*see* page 331)

ARMED FORCES PAY

The Review Body on Armed Forces Pay was appointed in 1971 to advise the Prime Minister on the pay and allowances of members of naval, military and air forces of the Crown and of any women's service administered by the Defence Council.

Chairman, G. M. Hourston
Members, P. Ball, OBE; C. M. Bolton; J. C. L. Cox; J. Crosby; Ms B. Dean; Sir Richard Trant, KCB; Mrs D. Venables

DOCTORS' AND DENTISTS' REMUNERATION

The Review Body on Doctors' and Dentists' Remuneration was set up in 1971 to advise the Prime Minister on the remuneration of doctors and dentists taking any part in the National Health Service.

Chairman, C. B. Gough
Members, D. G. Boyd; Ms T. Boyden; D. Fredjohn, MBE; Dr E. Nelson; Prof. G. F. Thomason, CBE; A. J. P. Vineall

NURSING STAFF, MIDWIVES, HEALTH VISITORS AND PROFESSIONS ALLIED TO MEDICINE

The Review Body for nursing staff, midwives, health visitors and professions allied to medicine was set up in 1983 to advise the Prime Minister on the remuneration of nursing staff, midwives and health visitors employed in the National Health Service; and also of physiotherapists, radiographers, remedial gymnasts, occupational therapists, orthoptists, chiropodists, dietitians and related grades employed in the National Health Service.

Chairman, M. Bett, CBE
Members, J. Hildreth; Miss A. Mackie, OBE; Dame Anne Mueller, DCB; Mrs R. Pickavance;
Prof. G. F. Thomason, CBE; Miss D. Whittingham

SCHOOL TEACHERS

The School Teachers' Review Body (STRB) was established in 1991. It replaced an Interim Advisory Committee which made recommendations on school teachers' pay and conditions from 1988 to 1992. Unlike the other review bodies, the STRB is a statutory body, set up under the School Teachers' Pay and Conditions Act 1991. It is required to examine and report on such matters relating to the statutory conditions of employment of school teachers in England and Wales as may be referred to it by the Secretary of State for Education. The STRB's reports are submitted to the Prime Minister and the Secretary of State and the latter is required to publish them.

Chairman, Sir Graham Day
Members, Mrs B. Amey; Miss F. Cairncross; R. Carter, CBE; A. G. Cox, CBE; P. Halsey, CB, LVO; Mrs G. Rostron; Mrs A. Vinton

SENIOR SALARIES

A Top Salaries Review Body was set up in 1971 to advise the Prime Minister on the remuneration of the higher judiciary and other judicial appointments, senior civil servants, and senior officers of the armed forces. The Review Body was also asked on a number of occasions to advise on the remuneration of Members of Parliament and of Ministers and on the level of parliamentary allowances. In July 1993 its name was changed to the Senior Salaries Review Body, and its remit was officially extended to cover the pay, pensions and allowances of MPs, ministers and others whose pay is determined by a Ministerial and Other Salaries Order, and the allowances of peers. It will also be required to reward performance where appropriate, and to take into account equal opportunities policy.

Chairman, Sir David Nickson, KBE
Members, Prof. G. Bain; Ms L. Botting; Ms A. Burdus; Sir Peter Cazalet; Sir Cecil Clothier, KCB, QC; G. M. Hourston; H. S. Pigott; Sir Anthony Wilson

ROYAL BOTANIC GARDEN EDINBURGH
Inverleith Row, Edinburgh EH3 5LR
Tel 031-552 7171

The Royal Botanic Garden (RBG) Edinburgh originated as the Physic Garden, established in 1670 beside the Palace of Holyroodhouse. Since 1986, RBG Edinburgh has been administered by a Board of Trustees established under the National Heritage (Scotland) Act 1985.

RBG Edinburgh is an international centre for scientific research on plant diversity, maintaining collections of living plants and reference resources, including a herbarium of some two million specimens of preserved plants. Other statutory functions of RBG Edinburgh include the provision of education and information on botany and horticulture, and the provision of public access to the living plant collections.

The Garden moved to its present site at Inverleith, Edinburgh in 1821. There are also three specialist gardens: Younger Botanic Garden Benmore, near Dunoon, Argyllshire; Logan Botanic Garden, near Stranraer, Wigtownshire; and Dawyck Botanic Garden, near Stobo, Peeblesshire. Public opening hours: RBG Edinburgh, daily (except Christmas Day and New Year's Day) November–February 10–4; March–April and September–October 10–6; May–August 10–8; specialist gardens, March–October 10–6.

Chairman of the Board of Trustees, Sir Peter Hutchison, Bt., CBE

Regius Keeper, Prof. D. S. Ingram
Deputy Keeper, Dr D. J. Mann

ROYAL BOTANIC GARDENS KEW
Richmond, Surrey TW9 3AB
Tel 081-940 1171
Wakehurst Place, Ardingly, nr. Haywards Heath,
W. Sussex RH17 6TN
Tel 0444-892701

The Royal Botanic Gardens (RBG) Kew were founded in 1759 by HRH Princess Augusta. In 1965 the garden at Wakehurst Place was acquired; it is owned by the National Trust and managed by RBG Kew. Under the National Heritage Act 1983 a Board of Trustees was set up to administer the Gardens which in 1984 became an independent body supported by a grant-in-aid.

The functions of RBG Kew are to carry out research into plant sciences, to disseminate knowledge about plants and to provide the public with the opportunity to gain knowledge and enjoyment from the Gardens' collections. There are extensive national reference collections of living and preserved plants and a comprehensive library and archive. The main emphasis is on plant conservation and bio-diversity.

Open daily (except Christmas Day and New Year's Day) from 9.30 a.m. The closing hour varies from 4 p.m. in mid-winter to 6 p.m. on weekdays, and 7.30 p.m. on Sundays and Bank Holidays, in mid-summer. Admission (1993), £3.50. Concessionary schemes available. Museums open 9.30 a.m.; Glasshouses, 9.30–4.30 (weekdays); 9.30–5.30 (Sundays and Bank Holidays). No dogs except guide-dogs for the blind.

BOARD OF TRUSTEES
Chairman, R. A. E. Herbert
Members, R. P. Bauman; The Viscount Blakenham; Prof. W. G. Chaloner, FRS; Prof. E. C. D. Cocking, FRS; Sir Philip M. Dowson, CBE, RA; Sir Leslie Fowden, FRS; Mrs A. Lennox-Boyd; Prof. R. May, FRS; J. Pettifer; Jane Renfrew, PH.D.; Mrs V. R. Wakefield
Director, Dr G. T. Prance, FRS

ROYAL COMMISSION FOR THE EXHIBITION OF 1851
Sherfield Building, Imperial College of Science and Technology, London SW7 2AZ
Tel 071-225 6110

The Royal Commission was incorporated by supplemental charter as a permanent Commission after winding up the affairs of the Great Exhibition of 1851. Its object is to promote scientific and artistic education by means of funds derived from its Kensington estate, purchased with the surplus left over from the Great Exhibition.

President, HRH The Duke of Edinburgh, KG, KT, PC
Chairman, Board of Management, Sir Denis Rooke, CBE, FRS
Secretary to Commissioners, M. C. Neale, CB

ROYAL COMMISSION ON CRIMINAL JUSTICE

The setting up of a Royal Commission on Criminal Justice was announced in March 1991 and its members were announced in May 1991. Members were appointed by The Queen upon advice from the Home Secretary. The Commission undertook a review of the criminal justice system in England and Wales and completed its work in June 1993. For a summary of its recommendations, *see* Index.

Chairman, The Viscount Runciman of Doxford, CB, FBA
Members, Sir Robert Bunyard, CBE, QPM; Prof. Sir John Cadogan, CBE, FRS; Prof. J. Gunn; The Rt. Hon. Sir John May; Mrs Y. Newbold; Ms U. Prashar; Miss A. Rafferty, QC; Sir John Wickerson; Sir Philip Woodfield, KCB, CBE; Prof. M. Zander

---

THE ROYAL MINT
Llantrisant, nr Pontyclun, Mid Glamorgan CF7 8YT
Tel 0443-222111

The prime responsibility of the Royal Mint is the provision of United Kingdom coinage, but it actively competes in world markets for a share of the available circulating coin business and, on average, two-thirds of the 15,000 tonnes of coins produced annually is exported to more than 100 countries. The Mint also manufactures special proof and uncirculated quality coins in gold, silver and other metals; military and civil decorations and medals; commemorative and prize medals; and royal and official seals.

The Royal Mint became an executive agency responsible to the Chancellor of the Exchequer in April 1990.

Master of the Mint, The Chancellor of the Exchequer (ex officio)
Deputy Master and Comptroller, R. de L. Holmes

ROYAL NATIONAL THEATRE BOARD
South Bank, London, SE1 9PX
Tel 071-928 2033

Chairman, The Lady Soames, DBE
Members, The Hon. P. Benson; The Hon. Lady Cazalet; M. Codron, CBE; Dame Judi Dench, DBE; Sir John Hannam, MP; S. Lipton; Sir Derek Mitchell, KCB, CVO; D. Nandy; The Rt. Hon. Sir Michael Palliser, GCMG; L. Sieff, OBE; T. Stoppard, CBE; J. Whitney; S. Yassukovich, CBE
Company Secretary and Head of Finance, A. Blackstock
Board and Committee Secretary, M. McGregor

RURAL DEVELOPMENT COMMISSION
141 Castle Street, Salisbury, Wilts. SP1 3TP
Tel 0722-336255

The Rural Development Commission was formed in 1988 by the merger of the Development Commission for Rural England and the Council for Small Industries in Rural Areas. It is a statutory body funded by government grant-in-aid. It advises the Government on economic and social matters affecting rural areas, and its prime aim is to stimulate job creation and the provision of essential services in the countryside.

Chairman, The Lord Shuttleworth
Deputy Chairman, R. Thompson
Chief Executive, R. Butt
Deputy Chief Executive, J. Taylor

SCIENCE AND ENGINEERING RESEARCH COUNCIL
Polaris House, North Star Avenue, Swindon, Wilts. SN2 1ET
Tel 0793-411000

The Science and Engineering Research Council (SERC) is one of five research councils funded through the Office of Science and Technology. Its purposes are to develop the natural and social sciences, including engineering; to maintain a fundamental capacity of research and scholarship; and to support relevant postgraduate education. SERC's role is to encourage and support research and advanced training in UK higher education institutions in all the basic areas of science and engineering.

From 1 April 1994, the SERC will be split into the Engineering and Physical Sciences Research Council and the Particle Physics and Astronomy Research Council.
Chairman, Sir Mark Richmond, FRS
Members, Prof. P. G. Burke; D. A. Davis; Prof.
A. Donnachie; G. H. Fairtlough; Dr K. W. Gray;
Prof. R. E. Hester; Sir Gordon Higginson, FEng.;
Prof. C. J. Humphreys; Dr S. D. Iversen; Dr A. Ledwith;
Prof. J. S. Mason; D. P. Nash; Prof. Sir Ronald Oxburgh,
FRS; Dr G. W. Robinson; Prof. R. E. Smallman, FRS;
Prof. J. T. Stuart, FRS; Prof. J. O. Thomas, FRS;
Prof. D. J. Wallace, FRS; Prof. A. W. Wolfendale
For research establishments, *see* page 712

SCOTT INQUIRY
— *see* page 324

SCOTTISH COURTS ADMINISTRATION
— *see* page 380

SCOTTISH ENTERPRISE
120 Bothwell Street, Glasgow G2 7JP
Tel 041-248 2700

On 1 April 1991 Scottish Enterprise took over the economic development and environmental improvement functions of the Scottish Development Agency and the training functions of the Training Agency in lowland Scotland. Its remit is to further the development of Scotland's economy, to enhance the skills of the Scottish workforce, to promote Scotland's international competitiveness and to improve the environment. Many of its functions are contracted out to a network of local enterprise companies. Through Locate in Scotland, Scottish Enterprise is also concerned with attracting firms to Scotland.
Chairman, Prof. D. MacKay
Chief Executive, C. Beveridge
Senior Management Team, C. Aitken; R. Crawford;
R. Griggs; J. Langlands; J. Lord; R. Macfarlane;
A. Proctor; C. Woods

SCOTTISH HOMES
Thistle House, 91 Haymarket Terrace, Edinburgh EH12 5HE
Tel 031-313 0044

Scottish Homes, the national housing agency for Scotland, aims to improve the quality and choice of housing in Scotland by working in partnership with the public and private sectors.

The agency is a major funder of new and improved housing, as well as one of the biggest landlords in Scotland, with nearly 60,000 houses. Scottish Homes is involved in housing research and in piloting innovative housing solutions. Board Members are appointed by the Secretary of State for Scotland.
Chairman, Sir James Mellon
Deputy Chairman, J. Richards, CBE
Chief Executive, P. McKinlay

SCOTTISH NATURAL HERITAGE
12 Hope Terrace, Edinburgh EH9 2AS
Tel 031-447 4784

Scottish Natural Heritage came into existence on 1 April 1992 under the Natural Heritage (Scotland) Act 1991. It was created by the merger of the Countryside Commission for Scotland and the Nature Conservancy Council for Scotland and combines the functions of those bodies. It provides advice on nature conservation to all those whose activities affect wildlife, landforms and features of geological interest in Scotland, and seeks to develop and improve facilities for the enjoyment of the Scottish countryside.
Chairman, M. Magnusson, KBE
Chief Executive, R. Crofts
Chief Scientific Adviser, M. B. Usher

SCOTTISH OFFICE

The Secretary of State for Scotland is responsible in Scotland for a wide range of statutory functions which in England and Wales are the responsibility of a number of departmental ministers. He also works closely with ministers in charge of Great Britain departments on topics of special significance to Scotland within their fields of responsibility. His statutory functions are administered by five main departments: the Scottish Office Agriculture and Fisheries Department, the Scottish Office Education Department, the Scottish Office Environment Department, the Scottish Office Home and Health Department, and the Scottish Office Industry Department. These departments plus Central Services are collectively known as the Scottish Office.

In addition there are a number of other Scottish departments for which the Secretary of State has some degree of responsibility; these include the Scottish Courts Administration, the Department of the Registrar-General for Scotland (the General Register Office), the Scottish Record Office and the Department of the Registers of Scotland. The Secretary of State also bears ministerial responsibility for the activities in Scotland of several statutory bodies whose functions extend throughout Great Britain, such as the Training Commission and the Forestry Commission.

Dover House, Whitehall, London, SW1A 2AU
Tel 071-270 3000
Secretary of State for Scotland, The Rt. Hon. Ian Lang, MP
   Private Secretary (G5), A. W. Fraser
   Special Advisers, A. Young; G. Mackay
   Parliamentary Private Secretary, S. Coombs, MP
Minister of State, The Lord Fraser of Carmyllie, PC, QC
   (*Education, Health and Home Affairs, and General European Issues*)
   Private Secretary, Ms S. J. Morrell
Parliamentary Under-Secretaries of State, Lord James
   Douglas-Hamilton, MP; J. Allan Stewart, MP; Sir Hector
   Monro, MP

Private Secretaries, Ms H. A. Jones (Lord James Douglas-Hamilton); M. I. Pringle (J. Allan Stewart); A. E. Sim (Sir Hector Monro)
Parliamentary Clerk, I. Campbell
Permanent Under-Secretary of State (G1), Sir Russell Hillhouse, KCB
Private Secretary, J. Taylor
Liaison Staff:
Assistant Secretary (G5), E. W. Ferguson

St Andrew's House, Edinburgh EH1 3DG
Tel 031-556 8400

MANAGEMENT GROUP SUPPORT STAFF
Principal (G7), Ms M. M. A. McGinn

CENTRAL SERVICES
Grade 2, G. R. Wilson, CB

PERSONNEL GROUP
16 Waterloo Place Edinburgh, EH1 3DN
Tel 031-556 8400

Principal Establishment Officer (G3), C. C. MacDonald
Assistant Secretaries (G5), G. D. Calder; J. A. Rennie; W. R. J. McQueen
Senior Principals (G6), C. D. Henderson; I. C. Henderson; W. E. Bennet

ADMINISTRATIVE SERVICES
James Craig Walk, Edinburgh EH1 3BA
Tel 031-556 8400

Director of Administrative Services (G4), R. S. B. Gordon
Assistant Secretary (G5), D. Stevenson
Director of Information Technology (G5), A. M. Brown
Deputy Director (G6), I. W. Goodwin
Director of Telecommunications (G6), K. Henderson
Director of Office Management (G6), B. V. Surridge, ISO
Chief Estates Officer (G6), R. I. K. White, FRICS

FINANCE DIVISION
New St Andrew's House, Edinburgh EH1 3TG
Tel 031-556 8400

Principal Finance Officer (G3), Miss E. A MacKay
Assistant Secretaries (G5), J. S. Aldridge; P. A. Brady; S. F. Hampson; D. G. N. Reid; W. T. Tait
Director of Financial Systems Unit (G6), R. Smith

SOLICITOR'S OFFICE
For the Scottish departments and certain UK services, including HM Treasury, in Scotland

Solicitor (G2), R. Brodie, CB
Deputy Solicitor (G3), N. W. Boe
Divisional Solicitors (G5), J. B. Allan; K. F. Barclay (seconded to Scottish Law Commission); R. Bland; G. C. Duke; I. H. Harvie; R. M. Henderson; J. L. Jamieson; H. F. Macdiarmid; Mrs L. A. Wallace

SCOTTISH OFFICE INFORMATION DIRECTORATE
For the Scottish departments and certain UK services

Director (G5), Ms E. S. B. Drummond
Deputy Director (G6), W. A. McNeill

SCOTTISH OFFICE AGRICULTURE AND FISHERIES DEPARTMENT
Pentland House, 47 Robb's Loan, Edinburgh EH14 ITY
Tel 031-556 8400

Secretary (G2), K. J. MacKenzie
Under-Secretary (G3), T. A. Cameron
Fisheries Secretary (G3), G. Robson

Assistant Secretaries (G5), P. S. Collings; E. C. Davison; D. R. Dickson; J. Duffy; I. W. Gordon; R. A. Grant; A. K. MacLeod; K. W. Moore; A. J. Rushworth; I. M. Whitelaw
Chief Agricultural Officer (G4), J. F. Hutcheson
Deputy Chief Agricultural Officer (G5), W. A. Macgregor
Assistant Chief Agricultural Officers (G6), D. R. J. Craven; J. A. Hardie; J. G. Muir; A. Robb; J. I. Woodrow
Chief Agricultural Economist (G6), J. R. Wildgoose, D.phil.
Chief Meat and Livestock Inspector (G7), J. Miller
Chief Food and Dairy Officer (G7), D. J. MacDonald
Chief Surveyor (G6), N. Taylor, FRICS
Scientific Adviser (G5), T. W. Hegarty, ph.D.
Senior Principal Scientific Officers (G6), R. J. Dowdell, ph.D.; D. Thornton

AGRICULTURAL SCIENCE AGENCY
East Craigs, Edinburgh EH12 8NJ
Tel 031-556 8400

An executive agency within the Scottish Office
Director (G5), Dr R. K. M. Hay
Deputy Director (G6), R. S. Cooper
Senior Principal Scientific Officer (G6), M. J. Richardson

FISHERIES RESEARCH SERVICES
Marine Laboratory, PO Box 101,
Victoria Road, Torry, Aberdeen AB9 8DB
Tel 0224-876544

Director of Fisheries Research for Scotland (G4), Prof. A. D. Hawkins, ph.D., FRSE
Deputy Director (G5), D. N. MacLennan
Senior Principal Scientific Officers (G6), R. M. Cook, ph.D.; J. M. Davies, ph.D.; A. L. S. Munro, ph.D.; P. A. M. Stewart, ph.D.; C. S. Wardle, ph.D

Freshwater Fisheries Laboratory
Faskally, Pitlochry, Perthshire PH16 5LB
Tel 0796-472060

Senior Principal Scientific Officers (G6), R. G. J. Shelton, ph.D.; J. E. Thorpe, ph.D.
Inspector of Salmon and Freshwater Fisheries for Scotland (G7), R. B. Williamson

Scottish Fisheries Protection Agency
Pentland House, 47 Robb's Loan, Edinburgh EH14 ITW
Tel 031-556 8400

An executive agency within the Scottish Office
Chief Executive (G5), A. K. MacLeod
Director of Policy and Resources (G6), J. B. Roddin
Chief Inspector of Sea Fisheries (G6), J. F. Fenton
Marine Superintendent, Capt. R. M. Mill-Irving

SCOTTISH OFFICE ENVIRONMENT DEPARTMENT
New St Andrew's House, Edinburgh EH1 3TG
Tel 031-556 8400

Secretary (G2), H. H. Mills
Under-Secretaries (G3), J. S. Graham; J. F. Laing; A. M. Russell
Assistant Secretaries (G5), M. T. Affolter; M. Batho; C. M. Baxter; J. T. Birley; D. J. Chalmers; W. J. Fearnley; Dr J. M. Francis; I. C. Freeman; J. W. L. Lonie; K. W. McKay; D. F. Middleton; J. N. Randall; E. C. Reavley; A. M. Russell

PROFESSIONAL STAFF
Chief Engineer (G3), A. C. Paton
Deputy Chief Engineer (G5), T. D. Macdonald
Assistant Chief Engineers (G6), T. Bolton; D. MacFarlane; P. Wright

Director of Building and Chief Architect (G3), J. E. Gibbons,
PH.D., FSASCOt.
Deputy Director of Building and Deputy Chief Architect (G5),
vacant
Assistant Directors (G6), G. Gray; A. Higgins; A. J. Wyllie
Chief Planner (G4), A. Mackenzie
Deputy Chief Planner (G5), D. R. Dare
Assistant Chief Planners (G6), A. W. Denham; I. R. Duncan;
S. G. Fulton; T. Williamson
HM Chief Industrial Pollution Inspector (G5),
I. W. W. Wright

HISTORIC SCOTLAND
20 Brandon Street, Edinburgh EH3 5RA
Tel 031-244 3144
An executive agency within the Scottish Office
Chief Executive (G3), G. N. Munro
Directors (G5), F. J. Lawrie; D. Macniven, TD; I. Maxwell;
S. Rosie
Chief Inspector of Ancient Monuments, Dr D. J. Breeze
Chief Inspector, Building Division, D. M. Walker, OBE

LOCAL GOVERNMENT FINANCE GROUP
New St Andrew's House, Edinburgh EH1 3TB
Tel 031-556 8400

Assistant Secretaries (G5), C. M. Baxter; K. W. McKay

INQUIRY REPORTERS
16 Waterloo Place, Edinburgh EH1 3DN
Tel 031-556 8400

Chief Reporter (G3), Miss G. Pain
Deputy Chief Reporter (G5), R. M. Hickman

SCOTTISH OFFICE INDUSTRY
DEPARTMENT
New St Andrew's House, Edinburgh EH1 3TG
Tel 031-556 8400

Secretary (G2), P. MacKay, CB
Under-Secretaries (G3), A. D. F. Findlay; E. J. Weeple
Assistant Secretaries (G5), D. A. Brew; D. A. Campbell;
M. J. P. Cunliffe; J. W. Elvidge; I. F. Gray;
P. Heatherington; R. N. Irvine; R. MacEwan; R. Tait
Senior Economic Advisers (G5), A. Goudie; C. L. Wood

PROFESSIONAL STAFF
Director of Roads (G3), J. A. L. Dawson
Deputy Chief Engineers (Roads) (G5), J. A. Howison;
R. D. Udall
Deputy Chief Engineer (Bridges) (G5), J. Innes
Assistant Chief Engineers (G6), N. B. MacKenzie;
I. McIntosh

INDUSTRIAL EXPANSION
Alhambra House, 45 Waterloo Street, Glasgow G2 6AT
Tel 041-248 2855

Under-Secretary (G3), vacant
Industrial Adviser, Dr C. K. Benington
Scientific Adviser, I. McGhee
Assistant Secretaries (G5), J. McGhee; J. Meldrum;
J. Thornton

LOCATE IN SCOTLAND
120 Bothwell Street, Glasgow G2 7JP
Tel 041-248 2700

Director (G4), R. Crawford
Senior Principal (G6), W. Malone
Principal (G7), A. McCabe; J. Wilson
Director (North America), R. Crawford

SCOTTISH OFFICE EDUCATION
DEPARTMENT
New St Andrew's House, Edinburgh EH1 3TG
Tel 031-556 8400

Secretary (G2), G. R. Wilson, CB
Under-Secretaries (G3), W. A. P. Weatherston, CB;
J. S. B. Martin
Assistant Secretaries (G5), D. S. Henderson; R. D. Jackson;
T. J. Kelly; G. McHugh; Miss M. MacLean; K. Macrae;
*Mrs R. Menlowe; *Mrs V. MacNiven; *Mrs
N. S. Munro
Chief Statistician (G5), vacant

* part-time

HM INSPECTORS OF SCHOOLS
Senior Chief Inspector (G3), T. N. Gallacher
Deputy Senior Chief Inspectors (G4), W. T. Beveridge;
D. A. Osler
Chief Inspectors (G5), G. H. C. Donaldson; Miss
K. M. Fairweather; G. P. D. Gordon; R. H. Manser;
J. J. McDonald; A. S. McGlynn; M. Roebuck;
H. M. Stalker; R. M. S. Tuck
There are 96 Grade 6 Inspectors.

SCOTTISH OFFICE HOME AND HEALTH
DEPARTMENT
St Andrew's House, Edinburgh EH1 3DG
Tel 031-556 8400

Secretary (G2), J. Hamill
Under-Secretaries (G3), D. Belfall; N. G. Campbell;
D. J. Essery; Mrs G. M. Stewart
Assistant Secretaries (G5), Mrs M. H. Brannan; J. T. Brown;
Mrs M. B. Gunn; C. M. A. Lugton; C. K. McIntosh;
P. M. Russell; R. H. Scott
Senior Principal (G6), N. MacLeod

NATIONAL HEALTH SERVICE IN SCOTLAND
MANAGEMENT EXECUTIVE
Chief Executive, vacant
Private Secretary, vacant
Director of Strategic Management, G. A. Anderson
Director of Finance, M. Collier
Director of Administration, Dr D. Steel
Director of Information Services, C. B. Knox
Director of Manpower, A. J. Matheson
Assistant Secretaries (G5), W. J. Farquhar; Ms I. M. Low;
W. Moyes; Mrs A. Robson; G. M. D. Thomson;
G. W. Tucker
Assistant Director (G6), H. R. McCallum
Senior Principal (G6), Miss J. McGregor

MEDICAL SERVICES
Chief Medical Officer (G2), Prof. R. E. Kendell, CBE, MD
Deputy Chief Medical Officer (G3), Dr A. B. Young, FRCPE
Principal Medical Officers, Dr J. V. Basson;
Dr C. F. Fleming; Dr Margaret Hennigan; Dr Rosalind
Skinner; Dr Elizabeth Sowler
Senior Medical Officers, R. E. G. Aitken, TD; I. R. Bashford;
P. W. Brooks; S. Capewell; W. Dodd; Dr D. J. Ewing;
Dr A. Findlay; Ms E. Keel; Dr Sheila Lawson; Dr
Patricia Madden; Dr A. MacLeod; B. T. Potter; Dr
R. Simmons; Dr O. A. Thores; Dr M. I. Ullah
Chief Scientist, Prof. I. A. D. Bouchier, CBE, FRCP
Chief Dental Officer, J. R. Wild
Deputy Chief Dental Officer, vacant
Regional Dental Officers, K. J. McKenzie; M. G. Platt; Miss
A. J. Power; G. A. Reid
Chief Nursing Officer, Miss A. Jarvie
Chief Pharmacist (G5), W. Scott

Chief Research Officer, Dr C. P. A. Levein
Senior Principal Research Officers (G6), Mrs B. Doig; Dr
Jacqueline Tombs

SOCIAL WORK SERVICES GROUP
43 Jeffrey Street, Edinburgh EH1 1DN
Tel 031-556 8400

The Social Work Services Group administers the provisions
of the Social Work (Scotland) Act 1968.
Assistant Secretaries (G5), Ms L. J. Clare; J. W. Sinclair;
D. Wishart
Chief Inspector of Social Work Services, A. Skinner
Assistant Chief Inspectors, Mrs H. Dempster;
Ms M. L. Hunt; F. A. O'Leary; D. Pia; I. C. Robertson

MISCELLANEOUS APPOINTMENTS
HM Chief Inspector of Constabulary, Sir Colin
Sampson, KBE, QPM
HM Chief Inspector of Prisons , A. H. Bishop, CB
Commandant, Scottish Police College, H. I. Watson, QPM
HM Chief Inspector of Fire Services, N. Morrison
Commandant, Scottish Fire Service Training School,
C. F. McManus, QFSM
Secretary, Scottish Health Service Advisory Council,
W. J. Farquhar

SCOTTISH PRISON SERVICE
Calton House, 5 Redheughs Rigg, Edinburgh EH12 9HW
Tel 031-556 8400

An executive agency within the Scottish Office
Chief Executive of Scottish Prison Service (G3),
E. W. Frizzell
Deputy Chief Executive and Director of Prisons (G5),
A. R. Walker
Director, Human Resources (G5), J. D. Gallagher
Director, Strategy and Planning (G5), D. A. Stewart
Deputy Director, Regime Services and Supplies (G6),
N. Harvey
Deputy Director, Estates and Buildings (G6),
D. D. Sutherland
Area Director, South and West (G5), J. Milne
Area Director, North and East (G5), J. Pearce
Governor, Scottish Prison Service College, R. L. Houchin

Prisons

Aberdeen, Craiginches, Aberdeen AB9 2HN. *Governor,*
W. A. R. Rattray
Barlinnie, Barlinnie, Glasgow G33 2QX. *Governor,*
P. Withers
Barlinnie Special Unit, Barlinnie, Glasgow G33 2QX.
Governor, I. A. Bannatyne
Castle Huntly Young Offenders Institution, Castle Huntly,
Longforgan, nr Dundee DD2 5HL. *Governor,* Mrs
M. Wood
Cornton Vale, Cornton Road, Stirling FK9 5NY. *Governor,*
P. L. Abernethy
Dumfries Young Offenders Institution, Terregles Street,
Dumfries DG2 9AX. *Governor,* G. Taylor
Dungavel, Dungavel House, Strathaven, Lanarkshire
ML10 6RF. *Governor,* J. Bywalec
Edinburgh, Saughton, Edinburgh EH1 3LN. *Governor,*
J. Durno
Friarton, Friarton, Perth PH2 8DW. *Governor,* R. A. Findlay
Glenochil Prison and Young Offenders Institution, King
O'Muir Road, Tullibody, Clackmannanshire FK10 3AD.
Governor, L. McBain
Greenock, Gateside, Greenock PA16 9AH. *Governor,*
D. E. Gunn
Inverness, Porterfield, Inverness IV2 3HH. *Governor,*
W. Blyth

Longriggend Remand Institution, Longriggend, nr Airdrie,
Lanarkshire ML6 7TL. *Governor,* A. F. King
Low Moss, Low Moss, Bishopbriggs, Glasgow G64 2QB.
Governor, J. Collins
Noranside, Noranside, Fern, By Forfar, Angus DD8 3QY.
Governor, E. Brownsmith
Penninghame, Penninghame, Newton Stewart DG8 6RG.
Governor, H. Ross
Perth, 3 Edinburgh Road, Perth PH2 8AT. *Governor,* R. Kite
Peterhead, Salthouse Head, Peterhead, Aberdeenshire AB4
6YY. *Governor,* A. P. Spencer
Polmont Young Offenders Institution, Brightons, Falkirk,
Stirlingshire FK2 0AB. *Governor,* G. Shearer
Shotts, Shotts ML7 4LF. *Governor,* E. J. Campbell
Shotts Alternative Unit, Shotts ML7 4LF. *Governor,*
A. MacDonald

MENTAL WELFARE COMMISSION FOR SCOTLAND
25 Drumsheugh Gardens, Edinburgh EH3 7NS
Tel 031-225 7034

Chairman, Sheriff H. J. Aronson
Commissioners, Mrs A. Baxter; P. H. Brodie; R. G. Davis;
Mrs A. M. Glen; Ms A. M. Green; Mrs H. L. Grieve;
Mrs J. I. D. Isbister; Mrs M. Jeffcoat; Dr J. McCurley;
J. Murray; Miss L. M. Noble; M. O'Reilly;
J. G. Sutherland
Medical Commissioners, J. A. T. Dyer; A. A. McKechnie
Social Work Commissioner, J. H. L. Richards
Secretary, Mrs M. A. MacLeod

COUNSEL TO THE SECRETARY OF STATE FOR SCOTLAND
UNDER THE PRIVATE LEGISLATION PROCEDURE
(SCOTLAND) ACT 1936
50 Frederick Street, Edinburgh EH2 1EX
Tel 031-226 6499

Senior Counsel, G. S. Douglas, QC
Junior Counsel, N. M. P. Morrison

NATIONAL HEALTH SERVICE, SCOTLAND

HEALTH BOARDS
ARGYLL AND CLYDE, Gilmour House, Paisley. *Chairman,*
R. R. Reid; *General Manager,* I. C. Smith
AYRSHIRE AND ARRAN, PO Box 13, Hunters Avenue,
Ayr. *Chairman,* J. W. G. Donaldson, CBE; *General
Manager,* J. M. Eckford, OBE
BORDERS, Huntlyburn, Melrose, Roxburghshire.
Chairman, D. A. C. Kilshaw; *General Manager,*
D. A. Peters
DUMFRIES AND GALLOWAY, Nithbank, Dumfries.
Chairman, J. A. M. McIntyre, OBE; *General Manager,*
D. Banks
FIFE, Glenrothes House, North Street, Glenrothes.
Chairman, R. Baker, OBE; *General Manager,* vacant
FORTH VALLEY, 33 Spittal Street, Stirling. *Chairman,*
Mrs J. D. Isbister; *General Manager,* Miss L. Barrie
GRAMPIAN, 1–7 Albyn Place, Aberdeen. *Chairman,* Dr
C. MacLeod, CBE; *General Manager,* F. E. L. Hartnett,
OBE
GREATER GLASGOW, 112 Ingram Street, Glasgow.
Chairman, W. S. Fyfe, CBE; *General Manager,*
L. Peterken, CBE
HIGHLAND, Reay House, 17 Old Edinburgh Road,
Inverness. *Chairman,* J. D. M. Robertson, CBE; *General
Manager,* R. R. W. Stewart
LANARKSHIRE, 14 Beckford Street, Hamilton,
Lanarkshire. *Chairman,* I. Livingstone, OBE; *General
Manager,* F. Clark, CBE
LOTHIAN, 148 The Pleasance, Edinburgh. *Chairman,*
Dr J. W. Baynham; *General Manager,* J. Lusby

ORKNEY, Balfour Hospital, New Scapa Road, Kirkwall, Orkney. *Chairman*, J. Leslie; *General Manager*, Dr J. I. Cromarty

SHETLAND, 28 Burgh Road, Lerwick. *Chairman*, Mrs F. Grains; *General Manager*, B. J. Atherton

TAYSIDE, PO Box 75, Vernonholme, Riverside Drive, Dundee. *Chairman*, J. C. MacFarlane, OBE; *General Manager*, Dr R. C. Graham, CBE

WESTERN ISLES, 37 South Beach Street, Stornoway, Isle of Lewis. *Chairman*, A. Matheson; *General Manager*, J. J. Glover

HEALTH EDUCATION BOARD FOR SCOTLAND
Woodburn House, Canaan Lane, Edinburgh EH10 4SG
Chairman, E. Walker
General Manager, Dr A. Tannahill

STATE HOSPITAL
Carstairs Junction, Lanark ML11 8RP
Chairman, P. Hamilton-Grierson
General Manager, R. Manson

COMMON SERVICES AGENCY
Trinity Park House, South Trinity Road, Edinburgh
EH5 3SE
Chairman, vacant
General Manager, J. T. Donald

SCOTTISH OFFICE PENSIONS AGENCY
151 London Road, Edinburgh EH8 7TG
Tel 031-556 8400
An executive agency within the Scottish Office
Chief Executive, N. MacLeod

GENERAL REGISTER OFFICE
New Register House, Edinburgh EH1 3YT
Tel 031-334 0380

The General Register Office for Scotland is the office of the Registrar-General for Scotland, who has responsibility for civil registration and the taking of censuses in Scotland and has in his custody the following records: the statutory registers of births, deaths, still births, adoptions, marriages and divorces; the old parish registers (recording births, marriages, deaths, etc., before civil registration began in 1855); and records of censuses of the population in Scotland. Hours of public access: Mon.–Thurs. 9–4.30; Fri. 9–4.
Registrar-General (G4), Dr C. M. Glennie
Deputy Registrar-General (G5), B. V. Philp
Senior Principal (G6), D. A. Orr
Principals (G7), D. B. L. Brownlee; R. C. Lawson; F. D. Garvie
Statisticians (G7), J. Arrundale; G. W. L. Jackson; F. G. Thomas

SEA FISH INDUSTRY AUTHORITY
18 Logie Mill, Logie Green Road, Edinburgh EH7 4HG
Tel 031-558 3331

Chairman, The Lord Mackay of Ardbrecknish
Chief Executive, P. D. Chaplin
Assistant Secretary, D. Robertson
Technical Director, J. E. Tumilty
Marketing Director, R. M. Kennedy
Training Director, K. Waind

THE SECURITY SERVICE
COMMISSIONER
c/o The Home Office, 50 Queen Anne's Gate,
London SW1H 9AT

The Commissioner is appointed by the Prime Minister. He keeps under review the issue of warrants by the Home Secretary under the Security Service Act 1989, and is required to give the Security Service Tribunal help by investigating complaints which allege interference with property and by offering all such assistance in discharging its functions as it may require. He is also required to submit an annual report on the discharge of his functions to the Prime Minister.
Commissioner, The Rt. Hon. Lord Justice Stuart-Smith

SECURITY SERVICE TRIBUNAL
PO Box 18, London SE1 OTZ

The Security Service Act 1989 established a tribunal of three to five senior members of the legal profession, independent of the Government and appointed by The Queen, to investigate complaints from any person about anything which they believe the Security Service has done to them or to their property.
President, The Rt. Hon. Lord Justice Simon Brown
Vice-President, Sheriff J. McInnes, QC
Member, Sir Richard Gaskell

SERIOUS FRAUD OFFICE
Elm House, 10–16 Elm Street, London, WC1X OBJ
Tel 071-239 7272

The Serious Fraud Office is an autonomous department under the superintendence of the Attorney-General. Its remit is to investigate and prosecute serious and complex fraud. The scope of its powers covers England, Wales and Northern Ireland. The staff includes lawyers, accountants and other support staff; investigating teams work closely with the police.
Director, G. Staple
Deputy Director, J. Knox

DEPARTMENT OF SOCIAL SECURITY
Richmond House, 79 Whitehall, London, SW1A 2NS
Tel 071-210 3000

The Department of Social Security is responsible for the payment of benefits and the collection of contributions under the National Insurance and Industrial Injuries schemes, and for the payment of child benefit, one-parent benefit, Income Support and Family Credit. It administers the Social Fund, and is responsible for assessing the means of applicants for legal aid. It is also responsible for the payment of war pensions.
Secretary of State for Social Security, The Rt. Hon. Peter Lilley, MP
Private Secretary, Ms J. Rintoul
Special Adviser, P. Barnes
Parliamentary Private Secretary, P. Merchant, MP
Minister of State, Rt. Hon. Nicholas Scott, MBE, MP (*Social Security and Disabled People*)

Private Secretary, I. Spur
Parliamentary Private Secretary, M. Bates, MP
Parliamentary Under-Secretary of State (Lords), The Lord Henley
Private Secretary, Ms C. Poulson
Parliamentary Under-Secretaries of State (Commons), Alistair Burt, MP; William Hague, MP
Private Secretaries, Ms J. Simpson; Ms H. Nicholas
Parliamentary Private Secretary to all the Parliamentary Under-Secretaries, I. Bruce, MP
Permanent Secretary (G1), Sir Michael Partridge, KCB
Private Secretary, Ms H. Todd

RESOURCE MANAGEMENT AND PLANNING GROUP
Deputy Secretary (G2), B. Gilmore

CORPORATE, STRATEGIC AND PLANNING DIVISION
Grade 3, S. Hewitt

*ANALYTICAL SERVICES DIVISION
Director (G3), D. Stanton

FINANCE DIVISION
Grade 3, J. Tross

SOCIAL SECURITY POLICY GROUP
Deputy Secretary (G2), R. A. Birch

*SOCIAL SECURITY DIVISION A
Under-Secretary (G3), B. Walmsley
Assistant Secretaries (G5), N. Ward; K. Limm;
J. Groombridge; R. H. Layton; Mrs A. Lingwood

*SOCIAL SECURITY DIVISION B
Under-Secretary (G3), Miss M. Pierson
Assistant Secretaries (G5), J. Moor; Miss L. Richards;
C. Evans

*SOCIAL SECURITY DIVISION C
Under Secretary (G3), D. J. Clark
Assistant Secretaries (G5), Mrs C. Souter; Miss J. Liebling;
D. Hill; Ms J. Clayton

*SOCIAL SECURITY DIVISION D
Under-Secretary (G3), R. Brown
Assistant Secretaries (G5), P. Tansley; Miss N. Bastin;
D. Jackson; M. Lloyd

*SOCIAL SECURITY DIVISION E
Under-Secretary (G3), D. Brereton
Assistant Secretaries (G5), S. Wilcox; A. Woods;
B. Calderwood; Miss S. Fraenkel

MAXWELL PENSIONS UNIT
7 St James's Square, London SW1Y 4JU
Tel 071-839 3599
Director (G3), R. P. Cleasby

INFORMATION DIVISION
Head of Information (G5), S. Reardon
Deputy Head of Information (G6), T. Grace
Principal Information Officer (G7), J. Bretherton
Chief Publicity Officer (G7), Ms H. Midlane

SOLICITOR'S OFFICE
Solicitor (G2), P. K. J. Thompson

*At The Adelphi, 1–11 John Adam Street, London WC2N 6HT. Tel: 071-962 8000

SOLICITOR'S DIVISION A
New Court, 48 Carey Street, London WC2A 2LS
Tel 071-412 1342
Principal Assistant Solicitor (G3), Mrs G. S. Kerrigan

SOLICITOR'S DIVISION B
New Court, 48 Carey Street, London WC2A 2LS
Tel 071-412 1370
Proceedings Operational Director (G4), P. C. Nilsson

EXECUTIVE AGENCIES

BENEFITS AGENCY
Quarry House, Quarry Hill, Leeds LS2 7UA
Tel 0532-324000
Chief Executive (G2), M. Bichard
Private Secretary, S. G. Appleton
Directors (G3), D. Riggs (*finance*); G. Bardwell (*personnel*)

Benefits Agency Territories
SCOTLAND/NORTHERN ENGLAND, Sandyford House, Archbold Terrace, Newcastle upon Tyne NE2 1AA.
Director (G3), A. J. Laurance
SOUTHERN ENGLAND, Olympic House, Olympic Way, Wembley, Middx. HA9 0DL. *Director (G3)*, A. Cleveland
WALES/CENTRAL ENGLAND, Five Ways Tower, Frederick Road, Edgbaston, Birmingham B15 1ST.
Director (G3), I. Stewart

Benefits Agency Medical Services
Director (G3), Dr P. Castaldi
Principal Medical Officers, Dr M. Aylward; Dr P. Dewis; Dr C. Hudson; Dr P. Doughty

INFORMATION TECHNOLOGY SERVICES AGENCY
15th Floor, Euston Tower, 286 Euston Road, London NW1 3DN
Tel 071-306 5051
Chief Executive, I. Magee
Deputy Chief Executive, P. T. F. Dunn
Directors, Ms A. Cleveland; K. Caldwell; G. McCorkell; S. Williams; J. Thomas; U. Brennan; N. Haighton
Non-Executive Director, J. M. Bankier, CBE

CONTRIBUTIONS AGENCY
Room C1837, DSS Longbenton, Benton Park Road, Newcastle upon Tyne NE98 1YX
Tel 091-225 7665
Chief Executive (G4), Miss A. Chant
Deputy Chief Executive (G5), G. Bertram
Directors, K. Wilson; S. Heminsley; R. Roberts; D. Gatenby; A. Cass; I. Hutton
Non-Executive Director, R. Brimblecombe

RESETTLEMENT AGENCY
Euston Tower, 286 Euston Road, London, NW1 3DN
Tel 071-388 1188
Chief Executive (G6), A. J. Ward

CHILD SUPPORT AGENCY
Millbank Tower, 21–24 Millbank, London SW1P 4QU
Tel 071-210 3000
The Agency was set up in April 1993. It is responsible for setting maintenance payment levels and collecting and enforcing the payments where necessary.
Chief Executive (G4), Mrs R. Hepplewhite

WAR PENSIONS
An executive agency to be established in April 1994
Chief Executitive-designate, P. Mathison

Central Advisory Committee on War Pensions
Room 1138, The Adelphi, 1–11 John Adam Street, London
WC2N 6HT
Tel 071-962 8028
Secretary, S. Adams

SOCIAL SECURITY ADVISORY
COMMITTEE
New Court, Carey Street, London, WC2A 2LS
Tel 071-412 1507

The Social Security Advisory Committee (SSAC) was
established by the Social Security Act 1980 to advise the
Secretary of State for Social Security and the Department of
Health and Social Services for Northern Ireland on all social
security matters except those relating to benefits for industrial
injuries and diseases and occupational pensions. The Social
Security Housing Benefit Act 1982 added housing benefit to
the Committee's responsibilities.
Chairman, Sir Peter Barclay, CBE
Members, Mrs J. Anelay, OBE; A. Dilnot; Revd G. H. Good,
   OBE; D. Guereca; M. Hastings; P. F. Naish; Hon. Mrs
   R. H. P. Price; Lady Scott, CBE; Dr A. V. Stokes, OBE;
   Prof. Olive Stevenson; O. Tudor; R. G. Wendt
Secretary, L. C. Smith

SPORTS COUNCIL
16 Upper Woburn Place, London WC1H 0QP
Tel 071-388 1277

The Sports Council, created under royal charter, promotes
the development of sport and fosters the provision of facilities
for sport and recreation in Great Britain.
Chairman, Sir Peter Yarranton

HMSO (HER MAJESTY'S STATIONERY
OFFICE)
St Crispins, Duke Street, Norwich NR3 1PD
Tel 0603-622211

HMSO (Her Majesty's Stationery Office) was established in
1786 and is the government executive agency that provides
printing, binding and business supplies to government
departments and publicly funded organizations. HMSO is
also the Government's publisher, and has bookshops for the
sale of government publications in six major cities as well as
appointed agents in other cities. HMSO obtains most of its
supplies and printing from commercial sources by competitive tender, apart from about 20 per cent of its printing
requirement, such as Hansard and Bills and Acts of
Parliament, which are produced in its own printing works.
HMSO is a self-financing government trading fund and
competes for its business with other commercial suppliers.
Controller and Chief Executive, P. I. Freeman, CB
   Executive Assistant, Mrs J. B. Ward
Deputy Chief Executive, M. D. Lynn
Director-General of Corporate Services, P. J. Macdonald

HEADS OF DIVISIONS
Publications, C. N. Southgate
Business Supplies, A. J. Davies
Print Procurement, B. Ekers

Finance and Planning, C. J. Penn
Information Technology, D. C. Kerry
Technological Innovation, J. R. Eveson
Engineering and Estates, W. E. Scott
Human Resources, J. McDonald
Organization Development, V. C. Bell
Quality and Consultancy, A. M. Cole
BIRMINGHAM – *Bookshop*, 258 Broad Street, Birmingham
   B1 2HE
BRISTOL, Ashton Vale Road, Bristol BS3 2HN – *Bookshop*,
   33 Wine Street, Bristol BS1 2BQ
LONDON – *Publications Centre*, 51 Nine Elms Lane,
   London SW8 5DR. *Bookshop*, 49 High Holborn, London
   WC1V 6HB
MANCHESTER, Broadway, Chadderton, Oldham, Lancs.
   OL9 9QH – *Bookshop*, 9–21 Princess Street, Manchester
   M60 8AS
SCOTLAND, South Gyle Crescent, Edinburgh EH12 9EB.
   Director, Edinburgh, G. W. Bedford – *Bookshop*, 71
   Lothian Road, Edinburgh EH3 9AZ
NORTHERN IRELAND, IDB House, Chichester Street,
   Belfast BT1 4PS. *Director, Belfast*, M. McNeill – *Bookshop*,
   16 Arthur Street, Belfast BT1 4GD

STUDENT LOANS COMPANY LTD
100 Bothwell Street, Glasgow G2 7JD
Tel 041-306 2000

The Company was established in 1989 to administer the
student loans scheme on behalf of the Government. In
1992–3 more than 340,000 students took out loans with a
total value of more than £224 million.
Chief Executive, R. J. Harrison

OFFICE OF TELECOMMUNICATIONS
50 Ludgate Hill, London EC4M 7JJ
Tel 071-634 8700

The Office of Telecommunications (Oftel) is a non-ministerial
government department which is responsible for supervising
telecommunications activities in the UK. Its principal
functions are to ensure that holders of telecommunications
licences comply with their licence conditions; to maintain
and promote effective competition in telecommunications;
and to promote the interests of purchasers and other users of
telecommunication services and apparatus in respect of
prices, quality and variety.
   The Director-General has powers to deal with anti-
competitive practices and monopoly situations. He also has
a duty to consider all reasonable complaints and representations about telecommunication apparatus and services.
Director-General, D. G. Cruickshank
Director of Competition, Mrs A. Walker
Director of PTO Licensing, Mrs P. Sellers
Director of Consumer and International Affairs, D. G. Hyde
Head of Information, D. C. Redding

TOURIST BOARDS
(For British Tourist Authority, *see* page 292)

The English Tourist Board, the Scottish Tourist Board, the
Wales Tourist Board and the Northern Ireland Tourist Board

are responsible for developing and marketing the tourist industry in their respective countries. The Boards' main objectives are to promote holidays and to encourage the provision and improvement of tourist amenities.

ENGLISH TOURIST BOARD, Thames Tower, Black's Road, London W6 9EL. Tel: 081-846 9000. *Chief Executive*, J. East

SCOTTISH TOURIST BOARD, 23 Ravelston Terrace, Edinburgh EH4 3EU. Tel: 031-332 2433. *Chief Executive*, T. M. Band

WALES TOURIST BOARD, Brunel House, 2 Fitzalan Road, Cardiff CF2 1UY. Tel: 0222-499909. *Chief Executive*, P. Loveluck, CBE

NORTHERN IRELAND TOURIST BOARD, St Anne's Court, 59 North Street, Belfast BT1 1NB. Tel: 0232-231221. *Chief Executive*, I. Henderson

---

DEPARTMENT OF TRADE AND INDUSTRY

*Ashdown House, 123 Victoria Street, London SW1E 6RB
†Tel 071-215 5000

Enterprise Initiative: Tel 0800-500200
Business in Europe: Tel 0272-444888
Innovation Enquiry Line: Tel 0800-442001

The Department is responsible for:
(a) international trade policy, including the promotion of UK trade interests in the European Community, GATT, OECD, UNCTAD and other international organizations
(b) the promotion of UK exports and assistance to exporters
(c) policy in relation to industry and commerce, including policy towards small firms, regional policy and regional industrial assistance (some of this applying only to England), and policy in relation to British Shipbuilders and the Post Office
(d) competition policy and consumer protection, including relations with the Office of Fair Trading, the Office of Telecommunications and the Monopolies and Mergers Commission; co-ordination of policy on deregulation
(e) the development of national policies in relation to all forms of energy and the development of new sources of energy; international aspects of energy policy. Links with British Coal, the Atomic Energy Authority, the electricity supply industry, the nuclear power construction industry, and the oil and gas industries
(f) policy on science and technology research and development; space; standards, quality and design; the following executive agencies: the Laboratory of the Government Chemist, the National Engineering Laboratory, the National Physical Laboratory, the National Weights and Measures Laboratory, and Warren Spring Laboratory
(g) company legislation and the Companies House executive agency; the Insolvency Service executive agency; the regulation of insurance industries; the Radiocommunications Agency (executive agency); and the Patent Office and Accounts Services executive agencies

President of the Board of Trade and Secretary of State for Trade and Industry, The Rt. Hon. Michael Heseltine, MP
Principal Private Secretary, P. Smith
Private Secretaries, Ms E. Jones; N. Welch

Special Advisers, Lady Strathnever; Dr A. Kemp; Dr W. Eltis
Personal Advisers, The Lord Sainsbury of Preston Candover; Sir Peter Levene, KBE
Parliamentary Private Secretary, R. Ottaway, MP
Minister for Industry, The Rt. Hon. Timothy Sainsbury, MP
Private Secretary, M. Scott
Parliamentary Private Secretary, Mrs A. Knight, MP
Minister for Energy, Timothy Eggar, MP
Private Secretary, M. Baldwin
Parliamentary Private Secretary, P. Luff, MP
Minister for Trade, Richard Needham, MP
Private Secretary, J. Warren
Parliamentary Private Secretary, A. Rowe, MP
Parliamentary Under-Secretary of State for Trade and Technology, Patrick McLoughlin, MP
Principal Private Secretary, J. Walker
Parliamentary Under-Secretary of State for Corporate Affairs, Neil Hamilton, MP
Private Secretary, Ms K. Spall
Parliamentary Under-Secretary of State for Consumer Affairs and Small Firms, The Baroness Denton of Wakefield, CBE
Private Secretary, I. Gibbons
Parliamentary Clerk, T. Williams
British Overseas Trade Board Chairman, Sir Derek Hornby
Permanent Secretary (G1), Sir Peter Gregson, KCB
Private Secretary, C. Parker
Deputy Secretaries (G2), Dr G. Robinson (*Chief Adviser on Science and Technology*); C. W. Roberts, CB; R. Williams, CB; A. Lane, CB; A. Hammond, CB (*The Solicitor*); C. Henderson, CB; R. J. Priddle; A. C. Hutton; A. Macdonald, CB

DIVISIONAL ORGANIZATION

‡AEROSPACE DIVISION
Under-Secretary (G3), A. Nieduszynski
Heads of Branch (G5), Ms R. J. Anderson; M. Ralph; Dr G. Coleman

ATOMIC ENERGY
1 Palace Street, London SW1E 5HE

Under-Secretary (G3), Dr T. E. Walker
Heads of Branch (G5), Dr D. Hauser; P. H. Aggrell; Mrs H. Haddon; Dr D. Lumley; S. D. Spivey; Miss S. Haird

CHEMICALS AND BIOTECHNOLOGY DIVISION
Under-Secretary (G3), Dr E. Finer
Heads of Branch (G5), Ms G. Allister; Dr E. A. M. Baker; Dr J. M. Bird

COAL DIVISION
1 Palace Street, London SW1E 5HE
Under-Secretary (G3), W. I. MacIntyre, CB
Heads of Branch (G5), J. A. V. Collett; N. Hirst; A. Berry

COAL PRIVATIZATION UNIT
1 Palace Street, London SW1E 5HE
Under-Secretary (G3), P. Loughead
Grade 5, Ms F. S. Price

COMPANIES DIVISION
10–18 Victoria Street, London SW1H 0NN
Under-Secretary (G3), A. C. Russell, CB
Heads of Branch (G5), M. J. C. Butcher; N. D. Peace; J. Healey; F. C. Jenkins

---

COMPETITION POLICY DIVISION
Under-Secretary (G3), Dr C. E. D. Bell
Heads of Branch (G5), J. Alty; A. Cooper; C. C. Bridge

CONSUMER AFFAIRS DIVISION
10–18 Victoria Street, London SW1H 0NN
Under-Secretary (G3), C. Kerse
Heads of Branch (G5), D. Jones; P. D. Atkinson;
M. Oldham; D. W. Hellings

DEREGULATION UNIT
Director (G3), H. V. B. Brown
Heads of Branch (G5), R. M. Watson; Miss M. N. Carter

ECONOMICS AND STATISTICS DIVISION
Chief Economic Adviser (G3), D. R. Coates
Head of Industrial and Regional Economics (G4), Dr
J. A. S. Robertson
Heads of Energy Economics (G4), N. Hartley
Heads of Branch (G5), Dr D. S. Higham; C. B. Moir;
M. S. Bradbury; B. M. Nonhebel; J. M. Barber; Dr
R. Van Slooten; G. C. White; D. J. Hodgson; S. A. Price

ELECTRICITY DIVISION
1 Palace Street, London SW1E 5HE
Under-Secretary (G3), C. C. Wilcock
Heads of Branch (G5), S. F. D. Powell; J. H. T. Green; Dr
D. Fairmaner; G. G. Bevan; A. Steele; Dr P. Fenwick

‡ELECTRONICS AND ELECTRICAL ENGINEERING
DIVISION
Under-Secretary (G3), R. M. Rumbelow
Heads of Branch (G5), T. J. Soane; (G6) I. J. Lawrenson

ENTERPRISE INITIATIVE DIVISION
Kingsgate House, 66–74 Victoria Street, London SW1E 6SW
Under-Secretary (G3), Mrs S. Brown
Heads of Branch (G5), M. Garrod; Mrs E. Ryle

‡ENVIRONMENT DIVISION
Under-Secretary (G3), Dr D. Evans
Heads of Branch (G5), C. Brewer; M. Cohen; Dr
A. Eggington; G. Riggs

EUROPEAN COMMUNITY AND TRADE RELATIONS
DIVISION
Under-Secretary (G3), vacant
Heads of Branch (G5), J. Rhodes; D. I. Richardson;
M. D. C. Johnson

EXPORT SERVICES DIVISION
Kingsgate House, 66–74 Victoria Street, London SW1E 6SW
Director-General of Export Promotion (G3), F. R. Mingay,
CMG
Heads of Branch (G5), K. R. Timmins; (G6), L. B. Rabstaff;
A. E. Reynolds

EXPORTS TO ASIA, AFRICA AND AUSTRALASIA DIVISION
Kingsgate House, 66–74 Victoria Street, London SW1E 6SW
Under-Secretary (G3), M. M. Baker
Heads of Branch (G5), M. G. Petter; D. E. Love; G. Hopson

EXPORTS TO EUROPE AND THE AMERICAS DIVISION
Under-Secretary (G3), N. Thornton
Heads of Branch (G4), K. W. N. George; (G5),
K. D. Levinson; B. Hampton; J. V. Hagestadt

FINANCE AND RESOURCE MANAGEMENT DIVISION
Under-Secretary (G3), M. K. O'Shea
Heads of Branch (G5), W. Stow; D. T. Smith; Mrs M. Bloom

INDUSTRIAL COMPETITIVENESS DIVISION
Under-Secretary (G3), Dr R. Dobbie
Heads of Branch (G5), M. Gibson; G. Dart

INFORMATION DIVISION
Head of Information (G4), Ms J. M. Caines
Head of News (G6), A. Marre

Publicity
Bridge Place, 88–89 Eccleston Square, London SW1V 1PT
Grade 5, S. Lyle-Smythe

‡INNOVATION POLICY DIVISION
Under-Secretary, (G3), Dr C. Hicks
Heads of Branch (G5), R. King; I. C. Downing; Dr
R. Hinder; P. L. Bunn; J. Hobday; Mrs K. Elliott; (G6),
P. Hills

Innovation Unit
Grade 5, Dr A. Keddie

INSURANCE DIVISION
10–18 Victoria Street, London SW1H 0NN
Under-Secretary (G3), J. Spencer
Heads of Branch (G5), R. Allen; R. Hobbs; Ms S. Seymour;
Miss A. Lambert; Miss V. Evans

INTERNAL AUDIT
1 Palace Street, London SW1E 5HE
Head of Internal Audit (G5), A. C. Elkington

INTERNATIONAL ENERGY UNIT
1 Palace Street, London SW1E 5HE
Grade 4, S. W. Freemantle

INTERNATIONAL TRADE POLICY DIVISION
Under-Secretary (G3), J. Cooke
Heads of Branch (G5), J. Hunt; J. Startup; S. J. Bowen

INVESTIGATIONS DIVISION
Under-Secretary (G3), M. G. Roberts
Grade 4, Mrs T. J. Dunstan
Inspector of Companies (G4), G. Harp
Heads of Branch (G5), S. L. Parkinson; A. Mier; R. Burton;
H. Bradshaw; Mrs B. Chase; A. Robertshaw

JOINT DIRECTORATE (FCO/DTI)
Kingsgate House, 66–74 Victoria Street, London SW1E 6SW
Under-Secretary (G3), F. R. Mingay, CMG
Directors (G5), D. Saunders; (DS4) M. Dougal

‡MECHANICAL ENGINEERING DIVISION
Under-Secretary (G3), R. M. Rumbelow
Grade 5, Dr H. M. Sutton

OFFSHORE SUPPLIES OFFICE
Alhambra House, 45 Waterloo Street, Glasgow G2 6AS
Tel 041-221 8777
1 Palace Street, London SW1E 5HE
Tel 071-215 5000
Director-General (G3), J. E. d'Ancona
Heads of Branch (G5), A. E. Maule; Mrs R. E. Ebbers;
H. M. Whiteside; (G6), J. Roddie

OIL AND GAS DIVISION
1 Palace Street, London SW1E 5HE
Under-Secretary (G3), M. J. Michell
Heads of Branch (G5), M. H. Atkinson; J. R. Wakely;
W. C. F. Butler; (RES2), J. R. V. Brooks; B. Coleman;
(PS2), G. N. Marriott
Director of Petroleum Engineering (RES1), I. W. G. Hughes
Director of Oil and Gas Royalties Office (G5), J. F. Craven

Gas and Oil Measurement Branch
3 Tigers Road, Wigston, Leicester LEI8 4UX
Tel 0533-785354
Director (G5), J. Plant

OVERSEAS TRADE DIVISION 2
Kingsgate House, 66–74 Victoria Street, London SWIE 6SW
Under-Secretary (G3), R. J. Meadway
Grade 5, M. V. Coolican

PERSONNEL DIVISION
I Palace Street, London SWIE 5HE
Under-Secretary (G3), A. Titchener, CB
Heads of Branch (G5), J. Thompson; R. Rogers; H. Evans;
    A. Mantle

PROJECTS AND EXPORT POLICY DIVISION
Under-Secretary (G3), D. J. Hall
Heads of Branch (G5), C. Robbins; A. G. Atkinson;
    N. Worman

REGIONAL DEVELOPMENT AND INWARD INVESTMENT
DIVISION
Kingsgate House, 66–74 Victoria Street, London SWIE 6SW
Director (G3), B. Bender
Director, IDU (G3), P. Rew
Heads of Branch (G5), R. H. S. Wells; J. C. S. Priston;
    K. Holt; Mrs A. Taylor; Dr H. N. M. Stewart;
    M. A. Wilks; *(G6)*, M. P. Briggs

SERVICES MANAGEMENT DIVISION
Kingsgate House, 66–74 Victoria Street, London SWIE 6SW
Under-Secretary (G3), Dr R. Heathcote
Grade 4, R. J. Wheeler
Heads of Branch (G5), Miss D. Gane; K. M. Long

SMALL FIRMS DIVISION
c/o Employment Department, St Mary's House, Level 2,
Moorfoot, Sheffield SI 4PQ
Tel 0742-701356
Kingsgate House, 66–74 Victoria Street, London SWIE 6SW
Tel 071-215 5000
Under-Secretary (G3), Mrs S. Brown
Heads of Branch (G5), Miss S. C. Newton; J. M. Reid

SOLICITOR'S OFFICE
10–18 Victoria Street, London SWIH ONN
The Solicitor (G2), A. Hammond, CB
Grade 3, P. H. Bovey; R. Woolman; Miss K. Morton;
    J. M. Stanley
Assistant Solicitors (G5), H. D. M. Bailey; M. Bucknill; Mrs
    J. Darvell; R. D. Fayers; Miss P. A. E. Granados;
    R. D. B. Green; A. S. W. Hyett; D. H. M. Ingham;
    D. S. Mangat; I. K. Mathers; S. G. Milligan; R. Nicklen;
    Miss E. N. O'Flynn; S. A. Parker; R. C. Perkins; Miss
    G. Richmond; J. W. Roberts; A. M. Susman; B. Welch

‡STEEL, METALS AND MINERALS DIVISION
Under-Secretary (G3), M. Stanley
Head of Branch (G5), B. F. Harding; H. P. Brown

‡TECHNOLOGY PROGRAMMES AND SERVICES DIVISION
Director (G3), Dr K. C. Shotton
Heads of Branch (G5), C. W. Johnston; Dr I. G. Eddison; Dr
    D. K. Potter; B. N. Steele; J. C. Octon; R. L. Hird; Dr
    M. S. Draper; Dr K. F. Poulter

‡TELECOMMUNICATIONS AND POSTS DIVISION
Under-Secretary (G3), P. Salvidge
Grade 4, S. R. Temple

Heads of Branch (G5), D. D. Sibbick; Mrs L. Brown;
    P. Waller; N. McMillan; J. S. Neilson; D. A. Hendon

‡TEXTILES AND RETAILING DIVISION
Under-Secretary (G3), T. Muir
Heads of Branch (G5), C. M. Cruickshank; T. L. Roberts

‡VEHICLES DIVISION
Under-Secretary (G3), M. Stanley
Heads of Branch (G5), T. M. H. Shearer; H. J. Charman

BRITISH OVERSEAS TRADE BOARD
Kingsgate House, 66–74 Victoria Street, London SWIE 6SW
Tel 071-215 5000

President, The President of the Board of Trade
Chairman, Sir Derek Hornby
Vice-Chairman, HRH The Duke of Kent, KG, GCMG, GCVO
Members, Sir Hugh Bidwell, CBE; G. J. Bull; R. Burman, CBE;
    Sir Colin Chandler; Sir Alan Cockshaw; Mrs
    H. M. Cropper; B. L. Crowe, CMG; I. L. Dale, OBE;
    H. Davies; Mrs J. Hall; Dr A. Hayes, CBE; D. Lanigan;
    R. Mingay, CMG; H. B. G. Montgomery; The Rt. Hon.
    Sir Michael Palliser, GCMG; C. W. Roberts, CB;
    B. D. Taylor, CBE; B. W. Willott
Secretary (G5), D. Saunders

REGIONAL OFFICES

DTI EAST, Westbrook Centre, Milton Road, Cambridge
    CB4 IYG. Tel: 0223-461939. *Regional Director (G5)*,
    W. J. Hall
DTI EAST MIDLANDS, Severns House, 20 Middle
    Pavement, Nottingham NGI 7DW. Tel: 0602 506181.
    Regional Director (G5), E. Beston
DTI NORTH-EAST, Stanegate House, 2 Groat Market,
    Newcastle upon Tyne NEI IYN. Tel: 091-232 4722.
    Regional Director (G3), P. A. Denham; *Regional
    Industrial Adviser (G3)*, J. W. Armstrong
DTI NORTH-WEST, Sunley Tower, Piccadilly Plaza,
    Manchester MI 4BA. Tel: 061-236 2171. *Regional Director
    (G3)*, J. H. Pownall
DTI SOUTH-EAST, Bridge Place, 88–89 Eccleston Square,
    London SWIV IPT. Tel: 071-215 5000. *Regional Director
    (G5)*, I. Jones
DTI SOUTH-WEST, The Pithay, Bristol BSI 2PB. Tel:
    0272-272666. *Regional Director (G5)*, J. M. Bowder
DTI WEST MIDLANDS, 77 Paradise Circus, Queensway,
    Birmingham BI 2DT. Tel: 021-212 5000. *Regional
    Director (G3)*, S. G. Linstead
DTI YORKSHIRE AND HUMBERSIDE, 25 Queen Street,
    Leeds LSI 2TW. Tel: 0532 443171. *Regional Director (G3)*,
    H. M. Lanyon

EXECUTIVE AGENCIES

ACCOUNTS SERVICES AGENCY
PO Box 100, Caerleon House, Cleppa Park, Newport,
Gwent NPI 9YG
Tel 0633-652271
Director and Chief Executive (G5), D. M. Hoddinott

BRITISH NATIONAL SPACE CENTRE
Dean Bradley House, Horseferry Road, London SWIP 2AG
Tel 071-276 2688

Director-General (G3), D. R. Davis
Deputy Director-General (G4), J. S. Shrimplin

---

‡At 151 Buckingham Palace Road, London SWIW 9SS

Heads of Branch (G5), Prof. J. E. Harries; Dr R. Jude;
K. Inglis; *(G6)*, Dr G. W. D. Findlay; Dr D. Williams;
J. Thomas

COMPANIES HOUSE
Companies House, Crown Way, Cardiff CF4 3UZ
Tel 0222-388588
Registrar of Companies for England and Wales (G4),
D. Durham

London Search Room, 55–71 City Road, London ECIY IBB
Tel 071-253 9393

102 George Street, Edinburgh EH2 3DJ
Tel 031-225 5774

Registrar for Scotland, J. Henderson

THE INSOLVENCY SERVICE
Bridge Place, 88–89 Eccleston Square, London SWIV IPT
Tel 071-215 5000

*Inspector-General of the Insolvency Service and Chief
Executive*, P. R. Joyce
Deputy Inspectors-General, D. J. Flynn; Mrs J. K. Scoones;
Mrs K. D. St John-Brooks

LABORATORY OF THE GOVERNMENT CHEMIST
Queens Road, Teddington, Middx. TWII OLY
Tel 081-943 7000
Government Chemist (G3), Dr R. Worswick

NATIONAL ENGINEERING LABORATORY
East Kilbride, Glasgow G75 OQU
Tel 03552-20222
Chief Executive (G3), W. Edgar

NATIONAL PHYSICAL LABORATORY
Teddington, Middx. TWII OLW
Tel 081-977 3222
Chief Executive and Director (G3), Dr P. B. Clapham

NATIONAL WEIGHTS AND MEASURES LABORATORY
Stanton Avenue, Teddington, Middx. TWII OJZ
Tel 081-943 7272
Chief Executive (G5), Dr S. Bennett

PATENT OFFICE
— *see* page 342

RADIOCOMMUNICATIONS AGENCY
Waterloo Bridge House, Waterloo Road, London SEI 8UA
Tel 071-215 2150
Chief Executive (G3), J. Norton
Heads of Branch (G5), M. Goddard; R. Louth;
R. A. Bedford; D. Reed; R. M. Skiffins; *(G6)*,
B. A. Maxwell

WARREN SPRING LABORATORY
Gunnels Wood Road, Stevenage, Herts. SGI 2BX
Tel 0438-741122

(To form part of a new National Environmental Technology
Centre by mid-1994)
Director and Chief Executive (G3), Dr D. Cormack

DEPARTMENT OF TRANSPORT
2 Marsham Street, London SWIP 3EB
Tel 071-276 3000

The Department of Transport is responsible for land, sea
and air transport, including sponsorship of the rail and bus

industries; airports; domestic and international civil aviation;
shipping and the ports industry; navigational lights, pilotage,
HM Coastguard and marine pollution; motorways and other
trunk roads; oversight of road transport including vehicle
standards, registration and licensing, driver testing and
licensing, bus and road freight licensing, regulation of taxis
and private hire cars and road safety; and oversight of local
authorities transport planning, including payment of Transport Supplementary Grant.

Secretary of State for Transport, The Rt. Hon. John
MacGregor, OBE, MP
Private Secretary, P. J. Coby
Special Advisers, Mrs E. Laing; Sir Idris Pearce;
R. Salmon; J. Swift; Sir Christopher Foster
Parliamentary Private Secretary, G. Riddick, MP
Minister of State for Public Transport, The Rt. Hon. Roger
Freeman, MP
Private Secretary, Ms S. M. Watkins
Parliamentary Private Secretary, B. Wells, MP
Minister of State for Aviation and Shipping, The Earl of
Caithness, PC
Private Secretary, A. Ferguson
Parliamentary Private Secretary, B. Wells, MP
Parliamentary Under-Secretaries, Robert Key, MP
(Roads and Traffic); Steven Norris, MP *(Transport in
London)*
Private Secretaries, J. Nicholls; Miss S. Gray
*Parliamentary Private Secretary to Parliamentary Under-
Secretaries*, B. Wells, MP
Parliamentary Clerk, N. Duncan
Permanent Under-Secretary of State (G1), A. P. Brown
Private Secretary, Ms J. Osborne

INFORMATION
Head of Information (G5), M. J. Helm

CENTRAL SERVICES
Principal Establishment and Finance Officer (G2),
E. B. C. Osmotherley, CB

PERSONNEL
Lambeth Bridge House, London SEI 7SB
Tel 071-238 3000

Director of Personnel (G3), R. A. Allan
Grade 5, Mrs M. Clare; R. T. Bishop
Chief Welfare Officer (G7), Miss E. T. Haines
Grade 6, K. A. Wyatt; K. Wight; B. Meakins; B. Donaldson

FINANCE
Under-Secretary (G3), C. R. Grimsey
Heads of Division (G5), R. D. Bayly; M. N. Lambirth;
S. K. Reeves
Accounting Adviser (G4), A. R. Allum

EXECUTIVE AGENCIES DIRECTORATE
Under-Secretary (G3), J. Phillips
Grade 5, M. J. Fuhr; J. L. Gansler

INTERNAL AUDIT
Ashdown House, Sedlescombe Road North, Hastings,
E. Sussex TN37 7GA
Tel 0424-458306
Head of Branch (G5), M. J. Reece

CENTRAL SERVICES UNIT
Ashdown House, Sedlescombe Road North, Hastings,
E. Sussex TN37 7GA
Tel 0424-458306
Grade 4, M. R. Newey
Heads of Division (G5), D. E. Bridge; G. L. Jones
Grade 6, I. Harris

ECONOMICS
Chief Economic Adviser (G3), M. J. Spackman
Grade 5, T. E. Worsley; M. C. Mann

STATISTICS
Romney House, 43 Marsham Street, London SWIP 3PY
Tel 071-276 8513

Under-Secretary (G3), D. W. Flaxen
Grade 5, Miss B. J. Wood; H. Collings; P. J. Capell;
   R. P. Donachie

CHIEF SCIENTIST
Chief Scientist (G4), Dr D. H. Metz

PUBLIC TRANSPORT
Deputy Secretary (G2), N. L. J. Montagu, CB

RAILWAYS 1
Under-Secretary (G3), D. J. Rowlands, CB
Heads of Division (G5), A. Burchell; N. K. McDonald;
   M. R. Fawcett; S. P. Connolly

RAILWAYS 2
Under-Secretary (G3), P. Wood
Heads of Division (G5), A. T. Baker; P. H. McCarthy;
   B. Wadsworth; R. S. Peal; R. C. Bennett

PUBLIC TRANSPORT LONDON
Under-Secretary (G3), H. M. G. Stevens
Heads of Division (G5), A. B. Murray; G. J. Skinner

URBAN AND GENERAL
Under-Secretary (G3), J. R. Coates, CB
Heads of Division (G5), P. E. Pickering; D. R. Instone;
   M. R. Pitwood; C. C. Thame

HIGHWAYS, SAFETY AND TRAFFIC
Director-General, Highways (G2), J. W. S. Dempster

ROAD PROGRAMME
Friars House, Manor House Drive, Coventry CVI 2TV
Tel 0203-535117

Director (G3), A. Whitfield
Grade 5, N. E. Firkins

MOTORWAY WIDENING UNIT
Friars House, Manor House Drive, Coventry CVI 2TV
Tel 0203-535101

Director (G4), D. York
Grade 5, D. E. Oddy

CONSTRUCTION PROGRAMME DIVISION
EASTERN, Bedford – *Director (G4)*, J. A. Kerman; *Grade 5*,
   J. P. Boud
NORTH-WEST, Manchester – *Director (G4)*, A. J. Homer;
   Grade 5, E. A. Sherwin
SOUTH-EAST, Dorking – *Director (G4)*, B. A. Sperring;
   Grade 5, M. G. Quinn
SOUTH-WEST, Bristol – *Director (G4)*, P. E. Nutt; *Grade 5*,
   G. D. Rowe
WEST MIDLANDS, Birmingham – *Director (G4)*,
   P. E. Nutt; *Grade 5*, J. M. Bradley
YORKSHIRE AND HUMBERSIDE, Leeds – *Director (G4)*,
   A. J. Homer; *Grade 5*, R. R. Bineham

NETWORK MANAGEMENT AND CONSTRUCTION
EAST MIDLANDS, Nottingham – *Director (G5)*, S. Rose
NORTHERN, Newcastle upon Tyne – *Director (G5)*,
   D. W. Ward

NETWORK MANAGEMENT AND MAINTENANCE
2 Monck Street, London SWIP 2BQ
Tel 071-276 2716

Under-Secretary (G3), B. J. Billington
Heads of Division (G5), A. S. D. Whybrow; R. S. Wilson;
   Dr R. M. Kimber; M. R. Fawcett

HIGHWAYS POLICY AND RESOURCES
Grade 3, H. C. S. Derwent
Grade 5, D. J. Kershaw; J. B. W. Robins; R. W. Linnard;
   P. G. Collis; Mrs E. A. Baker; M. A. Walsh; Miss
   P. M. Williams

ENGINEERING POLICY
St Christopher House, Southwark Street, London SEI OTE
Tel 071-928 3666

Director and Chief Highway Engineer (G3), T. A. Rochester
Grade 5, P. H. Dawe; R. Eastman; N. S. Organ

ROAD AND VEHICLE SAFETY
Under-Secretary (G3), Miss S. J. Lambert
Heads of Division (G5), I. R. Jordan; Dr P. H. Martin;
   P. E. Butler
Grade 6, J. Winder
Departmental Medical Adviser (G4), Dr J. F. Taylor
Head of Medical Advisory Board (G5), Dr R. J. M. Irvine

TRAFFIC AREA OFFICES
Licensing Authorities and Traffic Commissioners
EASTERN (Nottingham and Cambridge), Brig. C. M. Boyd
NORTH-EASTERN (Newcastle upon Tyne and Leeds),
   K. R. Waterworth
NORTH-WESTERN (Manchester), M. S. Albu
SCOTTISH (Edinburgh), Brig. M. W. Betts
SOUTH-EASTERN AND METROPOLITAN (Eastbourne),
   Brig. M. H. Turner
SOUTH WALES (Cardiff), J. M. C. Pugh
WESTERN (Bristol), Air Vice-Marshal R. G. Ashford, CBE
WEST MIDLANDS (Birmingham), J. M. C. Pugh

CHIEF MECHANICAL ENGINEER'S OFFICE
Director and Chief Mechanical Engineer (G5), M. Fendick

LONDON REGION
Under-Secretary (G3), I. Yass, CB
Grade 4, D. A. Holland
Heads of Division (G5), R. J. Mance; Dr S. Chatterjee; Dr
   J. C. Miles; D. M. Smith; S. C. Whiteley; G. R. Emes

REGIONAL OFFICES

EASTERN, Bedford – *Regional Director (G3)*,
   P. F. Emms; *Director, Network Management (G5)*,
   R. T. Thorndike
EAST MIDLANDS, Nottingham – *Regional Director (G4)*,
   D. J. Morrison; *Director Network Management and
   Construction (G5)*, S. Rose
NORTHERN, Newcastle upon Tyne – *Regional Director
   (G3)*, B. H. Leonard; *Director, Network Management and
   Construction (G5)*, D. W. Ward
NORTH-WEST, Manchester – *Regional Director (G3)*,
   J. P. Plowman; *Director, Network Management (G5)*,
   M. M. Niven
SOUTH-EAST, London – *Regional Director (G3)*,
   J. W. Fellows; *Director, Network Management (G5)*,
   A. D. Rowland
SOUTH-WEST, Bristol – *Regional Director (G3)*,
   Ms E. A. Hopkins; *Director, Network Management (G5)*,
   A. P. Moss
WEST MIDLANDS, Birmingham – *Regional Director (G3)*,
   D. R. Ritchie; *Director, Network Management (G5)*,
   W. S. C. Wadrup

YORKSHIRE AND HUMBERSIDE, Leeds – *Regional Director (G3)*, J. P. Henry; *Director, Network Management (G5)*, J. R. Wilkins

AVIATION, SHIPPING AND INTERNATIONAL
Deputy Secretary (G2), G. R. Sunderland, CB

CIVIL AVIATION POLICY DIRECTORATE
Under-Secretary (G3), H. B. Wenban-Smith
Grade 5, E. C. Neve; A. G. Thorning; Ms A. Munro

INTERNATIONAL AVIATION DIRECTORATE
Under-Secretary (G3), A. J. Goldman
Heads of Division (G5), D. B. Cooke; M. L. Fielder; R. S. Balme

AIR ACCIDENTS INVESTIGATION BRANCH
Royal Aerospace Establishment, Farnborough, Hants. GU14 6TD
Tel 0252-510300
Chief Inspector of Air Accidents (G4), K. P. R. Smart
Grade 5, R. C. McKinlay

INTERNATIONAL AND FREIGHT DIRECTORATE
Under-Secretary (G3), J. D. Henes
Grade 5, P. D. Burgess; J. R. Fells
Grade 6, D. J. Blackman

CHANNEL TUNNEL SAFETY UNIT
Church House, Great Smith Street, London SW1P 3BL
Tel 071-276 2014
Grade 3, E. Ryder, CB
Deputy Chief Inspector of Mines and Quarries, A. Hall

SHIPPING POLICY, EMERGENCIES AND SECURITY DIRECTORATE
Under-Secretary (G3), R. E. Clarke
Heads of Division (G5), A. Fortnam; H. Ditmas; J. Jack, MBE; L. S. Moyle; J. F. Wall
Grade 7, A. Crosswell

MARINE DIRECTORATE
Spring Place, 105 Commercial Road, Southampton SO1 0ZD
Tel 0703-329100
Under-Secretary (G3), M. W. Jackson
Grade 5, P. R. Smith

MARINE EMERGENCY OPERATIONS AND MARINE POLLUTION CONTROL UNIT
Spring Place, 105 Commercial Road, Southampton SO1 0ZD
Tel 0703-329100
Director, and Chief Executive-designate of the Marine Emergency Operations Executive Agency (G4), C. J. Harris
Chief Coastguard (G5), Cdr. D. T. Ascona, RN (retd)
Surveyor-General, and Chief Executive-designate of the Surveyor-General's Organization Executive Agency (G4), R. M. Bradley
Grade 5, P. J. Hambling; W. A. Graham; Capt. D. Bell

MARINE ACCIDENTS INVESTIGATION BRANCH
5–7 Brunswick Place, Southampton SO1 2AN
Tel 0703-232424
Chief Inspector of Marine Accidents (G5), Capt. P. B. Marriott

EXECUTIVE AGENCIES

VEHICLE INSPECTORATE
Berkeley House, Croydon Street, Bristol BS5 0DA
Tel 0272-543274
Chief Executive (G4), R. J. Oliver

Deputy Chief Executive (G5), J. A. T. David
Director of Administration (G6), K. Walton

DRIVING STANDARDS AGENCY
Stanley House, Talbot Street, Nottingham NG1 5GU
Tel 0602-474222
Chief Executive (G5), Dr C. M. Woodman

TRANSPORT RESEARCH LABORATORY
Crowthorne, Berks. RG11 6AU
Tel 0344-773131
Chief Executive (G3), H. J. Wootton
Operations Director (G4), Dr R. S. Hinsley
Grade 5, Dr P. H. Bly; G. Maycock; J. Porter; D. H. Goody; D. A. Lynam; G. M. Clarke; P. B. Hunt

DRIVER AND VEHICLE LICENSING AGENCY
Longview Road, Morriston, Swansea SA6 7JL
Tel 0792-782318
Chief Executive (G3), S. R. Curtis
Heads of Division (G5), R. J. Verge; T. J. Horton; Dr R. J. M. Irvine; I. R. Heawood
Grade 6, P. G. Desborough

DRIVERS, VEHICLES AND OPERATORS INFORMATION TECHNOLOGY AGENCY
Oldway Centre, 36 Orchard Street, Swansea SA99 5AX
Tel 0792-304578
The agency is expected to be privatized by the end of 1993.
Chief Executive (G4), D. Evans
Grade 5, J. K. Griffiths

VEHICLE AND CERTIFICATION AGENCY
1 Eastgate Office Centre, Eastgate Road, Bristol BS5 6XX
Tel 0272-515151
Chief Executive (G5), D. W. Harvey

THE TREASURY
Parliament Street, London SW1P 3AG
Tel 071-270 3000

The Office of the Lord High Treasurer has been continuously in commission for well over 200 years. The Lord High Commissioners of HM Treasury consist of the First Lord of the Treasury (who is also the Prime Minister), the Chancellor of the Exchequer and five junior Lords. This Board of Commissioners is assisted at present by the Chief Secretary, a Parliamentary Secretary who is also the government Chief Whip, a Financial Secretary, an Economic Secretary, the Paymaster-General, and the Permanent Secretary.

The Prime Minister and First Lord is not primarily concerned in the day-to-day aspects of Treasury business. The junior lords are government whips in the House of Commons. The management of the Treasury devolves upon the Chancellor of the Exchequer and, under him, the Chief Secretary, the Financial Secretary, the Economic Secretary and the Paymaster-General.

The Chief Secretary is responsible for the control of public expenditure; pay in the public sector, including nationalized industries but excluding the Civil Service; parliamentary pay; export credit; and efficiency in the public sector.

The Financial Secretary discharges the traditional responsibility of the Treasury for the largely formal procedure for the voting of funds by Parliament. He also has responsibility for other parliamentary financial business; the legislative programme; Inland Revenue duties and taxes; privatization policy; competition and deregulation policy; and Civil Service pay, management and industrial relations.

The Paymaster-General is responsible for Customs and Excise duties and taxes; procurement policy; environment; women's issues; charities; the environment (including energy efficiency); the EC budget; general accounting issues; the Office of HM Paymaster-General; and ministerial correspondence.

The Economic Secretary has responsibility for monetary policy; the Royal Mint; the financial system (including banks, building societies and other financial institutions); the Central Office of Information; the Government Actuary's Department; Forward (the Civil Service catering organization); the Central Statistical Office; international financial business; Economic and Monetary Union; stamp duties; the Valuation Office; the Department for National Savings; the Registry of Friendly Societies; the National Investment and Loans Office; public expenditure casework; and the Treasury Bulletin and Economic Briefing.

The Office of HM Paymaster-General (*see* page 343) acts as a clearing bank and provides financial information for all government departments; it has particular responsibility for public sector pensions. All Treasury Ministers are concerned in tax matters.

Prime Minister and First Lord of the Treasury,
The Rt. Hon. John Major, MP
Chancellor of the Exchequer (*£39,820),
The Rt. Hon. Kenneth Clarke, QC, MP
Principal Private Secretary, J. Heywood
Private Secretary, O. M. Barder
Special Adviser, Mrs T. Keswick
Parliamentary Private Secretary, P. Oppenheim, MP
Chief Secretary to the Treasury (*£39,820), The
Rt. Hon. Michael Portillo, MP
Private Secretary, P. T. Wanless
Special Adviser, D. Ruffley
Parliamentary Private Secretary, D. Amess, MP
Financial Secretary to the Treasury (*£28,175), Stephen
Dorrell, MP
Private Secretary, W. Nye
Parliamentary Private Secretary, G. Brandreth, MP
Paymaster-General (*£28,175), The Rt. Hon. Sir John Cope,
MP
Private Secretary, D. Hubbard
Parliamentary Private Secretary, Dr I. Twinn, MP
Economic Secretary (*£21,384), Anthony Nelson, MP
Private Secretary, S. G. W. Jones
*Parliamentary Secretary to the Treasury and Government
Chief Whip* (*£33,142), The Rt. Hon. Richard Ryder,
OBE, MP
Private Secretary, M. Maclean
Treasurer of HM Household and Deputy Chief Whip
(*£28,175), Gregory Knight, MP
Lord Commissioners of the Treasury (*£28,175), I. Patnick,
OBE, MP; N. Baker, MP; T. Wood, MP; T. J. R. Kirkhope,
MP; A. J. MacKay, MP
Assistant Whips (*£18,130), R. Hughes, MP;
J. Arbuthnot, MP; A. Mitchell, MP; M. Brown, MP;
D. Conway, MP
Parliamentary Clerk, D. S. Martin
Panel of Independent Economic Advisers to the Treasury,
W. Godley; G. Davies; T. Congdon; A. Britton;
A. Sentance; D. Currie; P. Minford

*In addition to a reduced parliamentary salary of £23,227

Permanent Secretary to the Treasury (G1), Sir Terence Burns
Private Secretary, P. W. Owen
Second Permanent Secretaries (G1A), Sir Nigel Wicks, KCB,
CVO, CBE (*Overseas Finance*); A. Turnbull, CB, CVO (*Public
Expenditure*)

*Head of Government Economics Service and Chief Economic
Adviser to the Treasury,* Prof. A. Budd
*Head of Government Accountancy Service and Chief
Accountancy Adviser to the Treasury,* Sir Alan Hardcastle
Deputy Secretaries (G2), R. P. Culpin (*Public Finance*);
H. P. Evans, CB (*Overseas Finance*); A. J. C. Edwards
(*Public Services, and General Expenditure*); S. A. Robson
(*Industry*); R. Mountfield, CB (*Civil Service Management
and Pay*); Mrs J. R. Lomax (*Financial Services*)

CENTRAL DIVISIONS

ESTABLISHMENT AND ORGANIZATION DIVISION
Under-Secretary (G3), B. M. Fox
Assistant Secretaries (G5), E. I. Cooper; A. J. T. MacAuslan;
Dr R. Kosmin; Ms C. Slocock
Senior Principals (G6), J. W. Stevens; B. J. Porteus, OBE;
D. J. Baker; D. N. Walters; P. Tickner

INFORMATION DIVISION
Assistant Secretary (G5), A. Hudson
Deputy Head of Division (G6), D. Deaton

INDUSTRY

INDUSTRY, AGRICULTURE AND EMPLOYMENT GROUP
Under-Secretary (G3), M. L. Williams
Assistant Secretaries (G5), M. C. Mercer; D. Revolta;
C. R. Pickering; T. J. Sutton

PUBLIC ENTERPRISES GROUP
Under-Secretary (G3), I. P. Wilson
Assistant Secretaries (G5), S. Sargent; T. R. Fellgett

HOME AND EDUCATION GROUP
Under-Secretary (G3), M. Whippman
Assistant Secretaries (G5), J. Graham; D. J. Batt

PUBLIC SERVICES

SOCIAL SERVICES AND TERRITORIAL GROUP
Under-Secretary (G3), Miss G. M. Noble
Assistant Secretaries (G5), J. Halligan; J. W. Grice; S. Kelly

LOCAL GOVERNMENT GROUP
Under-Secretary (G3), J. Beastall
Assistant Secretaries (G5), N. J. Ilett; R. Bent

CENTRAL UNIT ON PURCHASING
Director, P. Forshaw, CBE
Deputy Director, M. J. Hoare

TREASURY OFFICER OF ACCOUNTS GROUP
Under-Secretary (G3), T. J. Burr
Assistant Secretary (G5), I. S. Thomson

GENERAL EXPENDITURE

GENERAL EXPENDITURE POLICY GROUP
Under-Secretary (G3), C. W. Kelly
Assistant Secretaries (G5), J. Hibberd; F. K. Jones;
I. W. V. Taylor

DEFENCE POLICY, MANPOWER AND MATERIEL GROUP
Under-Secretary (G3), Ms A. Perkins
Assistant Secretaries (G5), R. J. Devereux; M. E. Donnelly

OVERSEAS FINANCE

INTERNATIONAL FINANCE GROUP
Under-Secretary (G3), P. N. Sedgwick
Assistant Secretaries (G5), D. Owen; Ms E. Young;
J. S. Cunliffe

AID AND EXPORT FINANCE GROUP
Under-Secretary (G3), J. E. Mortimer
Assistant Secretaries (G5), S. N. Wood; M. G. Richardson

EUROPEAN COMMUNITY GROUP
Under-Secretary (G3), D. J. Bostock
Assistant Secretaries (G5), M. E. Corcoran; P. M. Rayner

GOVERNMENT ACCOUNTANCY SERVICE

MANAGEMENT UNIT AND ACCOUNTANCY ADVICE GROUP
Grade 4, D. Cooke
Assistant Secretaries (G5), D. Jamieson; K. E. Bradley
Senior Principals (G6), C. Butler; P. M. Rowley

TREASURY REPRESENTATIVES IN USA
Economic Minister and UK Representative IMF/IBRD,
  D. L. C. Peretz

CHIEF ECONOMIC ADVISER'S SECTOR

FORECASTS AND ANALYSIS GROUP
Under-Secretary (G3), C. J. Mowl
Senior Economic Advisers (G5), C. M. Kelly; S. Brooks

MEDIUM TERM AND POLICY ANALYSIS GROUP
Under-Secretary (G3), C. Riley
Assistant Secretaries (G5), D. Savage; S. W. Matthews

PUBLIC SERVICES ECONOMICS DIVISION
Under-Secretary (G3), Dr J. H. Rickard
Assistant Secretaries (G5), R. Weeden; M. A. Parsonage

ECONOMIC BRIEFING DIVISION
Assistant Secretary (G5), P. L. Patterson

PUBLIC FINANCE

FISCAL POLICY GROUP
Under-Secretary (G3), Mrs A. F. Case
Assistant Secretaries (G5), A. Sharples; R. P. Short

MONETARY GROUP
Under-Secretary (G3), P. R. C. Gray
Assistant Secretaries (G5), S. J. Davies; J. P. McIntyre

FINANCIAL INSTITUTIONS AND MARKETS GROUP

BANKING GROUP
Under-Secretary (G3), E. J. W. Gieve
Assistant Secretaries (G5), C. Farthing; J. M. G. Taylor

SECURITIES AND INVESTMENT GROUP
Under-Secretary (G3), A. Whiting
Grade 5, Dr J. P. Compton; Miss R. Thompson; Mrs
  P. C. Diggle

PUBLIC SECTOR FINANCE
Assistant Secretary (G5), A. W. Ritchie
Statistician (G7), S. C. Knight

CIVIL SERVICE MANAGEMENT AND PAY

CIVIL SERVICE PAY
Under-Secretary (G3), S. W. Boys-Smith
Assistant Secretaries (G5), Mrs S. D. Brown; R. J. Evans

PERSONNEL POLICY GROUP
Under-Secretary (G3), B. A. E. Taylor
Assistant Secretaries (G5), D. G. Pain; D. W. Rayson;
  J. Dixon; J. Strachan

MANAGEMENT POLICY
Under-Secretary (G3), R. I. G. Allen
Assistant Secretary (G5), M. Perfect

SPECIALIST SUPPORT GROUP
Grade 4, C. J. A. Chivers
Grade 5, J. B. Jones
Grade 6, J. A. Barker

FORWARD (CIVIL SERVICE CATERING)
Executive Director (G4) (acting), B. Bloxham

THE TREASURY SOLICITOR
DEPARTMENT OF HM PROCURATOR-GENERAL AND TREASURY SOLICITOR
Queen Anne's Chambers, 28 Broadway, London SW1H 9JS
Tel 071-210 3000

The Treasury Solicitor's Department provides legal services for many government departments. Those that do not have their own lawyers are given legal advice, and both they and other departments are provided with litigation and conveyancing services. The Department also deals with Bona Vacantia. The Treasury Solicitor is also the Queen's Proctor.
HM Procurator-General and Treasury Solicitor (G1),
  G. A. Hosker, CB, QC
Deputy Treasury Solicitor (G2), D. Hogg

CENTRAL ADVISORY DIVISION
Principal Assistant Solicitor (G3), M. A. Blythe
Assistant Solicitors (G5), Mrs P. A. Dayer; M. J. Hemming;
  Mrs V. Collett; Mrs I. G. Letwin
Grade 6, C. J. Gregory; Miss P. F. Henderson;
  C. A. R. Bird; A. K. Fraser; Ms S. Grundy; Ms
  S. Cochrane

LITIGATION DIVISIONS
Principal Assistant Solicitor (G3), P. Ridd
Grade 4, F. L. Croft; D. Brummell
Assistant Solicitors (G5), A. D. Lawton; A. Leithead;
  A. J. Sandal; P. F. O. Whitehurst; R. J. Phillips;
  M. Sturdy; P. R. Messer; J. B. C. Oliver; D. F. Pascho
Grade 6, A. P. M. Aylett; P. Carroll; Miss R. M. Caudwell;
  M. R. M. Davis; J. N. Desai; P. D. F. Grant;
  J. D. Howes; D. Palmer; Miss A. J. Rees;
  H. O. J. R. Shepheard; D. A. Stalker; A. Turek;
  R. J. Walter
Principals (G7), T. C. Adcock; C. Ashford; M. Benney;
  L. Blake; R. Brown; A. P. Chapman; J. M. Crane;
  H. Fassnidge; J. Gladysz; M. P. Gold; A. Goodfellow;
  L. John-Charles; Mrs K. Lester; Miss C. R. Manuel;
  J. B. Matthews; P. J. Moran; Miss J. A. Murnane;
  Miss C. R. Musaala-Mukasa; S. Nasser; L. Nicoll;
  A. C. Nwanodi; F. G. O'Connell; L. O'Dea;
  R. C. J. Opie; R. M. Pierce; M. E. Robinson;
  D. Trinchero; G. Tuttle; J. C. Youdell; J. Ziegel

QUEEN'S PROCTOR DIVISION
Queen's Proctor, G. A. Hosker, CB, QC
Assistant Queen's Proctor, Mrs D. Babar

ESTABLISHMENTS, FINANCE AND DEPARTMENTAL SERVICES DIVISION
*Principal Establishment and Finance and Security Officer
  (G5)*, A. J. E. Hollis
*Departmental Services Manager and Deputy Establishment
  and Security Officer (G7)*, P. Pegler
Departmental Personnel Manager (G7), Ms H. Donnelly
Chief Accountant (G7), R. B. Smith

Head of Information Systems Development (G7),
G. N. Younger
Business Support Manager (G7), P. Hoadly

BONA VACANTIA DIVISION
Assistant Solicitor (G5), Miss S. L. Sargant
Senior Legal Assistant, M. R. M. Davies
Grade 7, Mrs P. L. Woods; Mrs A. Evans; I. Adams;
D. Reid; N. Gajjar

EUROPEAN DIVISION
Principal Assistant Solicitor (G3), J. E. G. Vaux
Grade 5, J. E. Collins; D. Macrae
Grade 6, S. T. Harker; Miss R. Caudwell
Grade 7, Miss S. L. Hudson; J. D. Colahan

NATIONAL HERITAGE DIVISION
Grade 5, P. C. Jenkins
Grade 6, F. D. W. Clarke; C. A. R. Bird

OFFICE OF PUBLIC SERVICE AND SCIENCE DIVISION
Grade 5, M. C. Carpenter
Grade 6, P. Kilgarriff

MINISTRY OF DEFENCE BRANCH
Neville House, Page Street, London SW1P 4LS
Tel 071-218 4691

Principal Assistant Solicitor (G3), D. F. W. Pickup
Grade 5, J. R. J. Braggins; R. Batstone
Grade 6, Mrs A. Morris; P. Visagie; Miss V. F. Dewhurst
Grade 7, Miss E. Polledri; M. Truran; G. Brzezina;
M. Pulver; J. Cooper; J. Ziegel

DEPARTMENT FOR EDUCATION BRANCH
Sanctuary Buildings, Great Smith Street, London SW1P 3BT
Tel 071-925 5000
Principal Assistant Solicitor (G3), R. N. Ricks
Assistant Solicitors (G5), D. J. Aries; M. Harris;
A. D. Preston
Grade 6, Miss J. L. C. Brooks; A. K. Fraser; N. P. Beach
Grade 7, C. J. Reay; C. J. Hales

DEPARTMENT OF EMPLOYMENT BRANCH
Caxton House, Tothill Street, London SW1H 9NF
Tel 071-273 3000
Principal Assistant Solicitor (G3), H. R. L. Purse
Assistant Solicitors (G5), R. J. Baker; C. House;
Mrs A. Leale; N. A. D. Lambert
Grade 6, R. H. Britten; P. H. Kilgarriff; J. K. Winayak;
M. W. Smith; A. W. Stewart
Grade 7, Mrs K. Booth; S. J. Gibbon; Miss C. Smith;
R. Creasy

DEPARTMENT OF TRANSPORT BRANCH
2 Marsham Street, London SW1P 3EB
Tel 071-276 3000
Principal Assistant Solicitor (G3), M. C. P. Thomas
Assistant Solicitors (G5), R. G. Bellis; P. D. Coopman;
C. W. M. Ingram; A. G. Jones; R. Lines
Grade 6, G. W. M. Galliford; A. Lancaster;
A. M. H. Prosser; S. W. Rock; N. C. Thomas;
V. Edwards; J. Hall; G. Claydon; J. Jones; J. Jordan
Senior Legal Assistants, B. J. Hammersley; A. K. Johnston
Grade 7, R. C. Drabble; B. Golds; Mrs A. Heilpern;
R. J. R. Jones; N. Magyar; M. S. Esdale

GOVERNMENT PROPERTY LAWYERS
Riverside Chambers, Castle Street, Taunton, Somerset TA1 4AP
Tel 0823-345200
An executive agency within the Treasury Solicitor's Department

Chief Executive (G3), A. D. Osborne
Group Directors (G5), M. Benmayor; Miss G. Gilder;
P. L. Noble; P. F. Nockles; M. F. Rawlins; A. M. Scarfe
Director of Lands Advisory (G6), R. C. Paddock
Deputy Director of Lands Advisory (G7), T. P. Baker
Assistant Group Directors (G6), D. G. Ager; M. V. Cooper;
R. L. Coward; R. F. Good; R. D. Harris; P. K. Hicks;
J. B. Howe; R. S. Lugg; P. Page; I. Parker; A. W. Prior;
P. A. Redgrove; R. J. B. Stenhouse; T. Sylvester Jones;
B. D. Thurley
Senior Legal Assistants, T. Forrester; A. R. Lilleystone
Grade 7, S. R. Bould; Miss G. Bowles; A. M. Cross;
Ms J. K. Dabbs; H. S. Davis; Miss M. F. Davitt;
Mrs A. M. Foxhuntley; M. J. Hair; Q. J. Hawkes;
T. J. Howe; C. R. Irving; P. S. Jaskolski; J. H. Leggatt;
J. L. Leonard; Miss S. Lomas; P. J. Lowe; D. Roberts;
M. D. Savage; Miss J. C. Shotter; R. C. Stewart;
J. P. Trent
Finance and Personnel Director (G7), M. J. Robbins

COUNCIL ON TRIBUNALS
7th Floor, 22 Kingsway, London WC2B 6LE
Tel 071-936 7045

The Council on Tribunals is an independent statutory body.
It keeps under review the constitution and working of the
various tribunals which have been placed under its general
supervision, and considers and reports on administrative
procedures relating to statutory inquiries. It is consulted by
government departments on proposals for legislation affecting tribunals and inquiries, and on proposals where the need
for an appeals procedure may arise. It also offers advice on
draft primary legislation.
Some 60 tribunals are currently under the Council's
supervision. The matters with which they deal range from
agriculture to immigration, pensions, road traffic, taxation,
and the allocation of school places.
The Scottish Committee of the Council generally considers
Scottish tribunals and matters relating only to Scotland.
Members of the Council are appointed by the Lord
Chancellor and the Lord Advocate. The Scottish Committee
is composed partly of members of the Council designated by
the Lord Advocate and partly of others appointed by him.
The Parliamentary Commissioner for Administration is ex
officio a member of both the Council and the Scottish
Committee.
Chairman, The Lord Archer of Sandwell, PC, QC
Members, The Parliamentary Commissioner for
Administration; Mrs A. Anderson; G. A. Anderson;
T. N. Biggart, CBE, WS (*Chairman of the Scottish
Committee*); M. B. Dempsey; Prof. D. L. Foulkes;
Mrs S. Friend; T. R. H. Godden, CB; C. Heaps; B. Hill,
CBE; Prof. M. J. Hill; W. N. Hyde; R. H. Jones, CVO; Dr
C. A. Kaplan; L. F. Read, QC
Secretary, J. D. Saunders

SCOTTISH COMMITTEE
20 Walker Street, Edinburgh EH3 7HR
Tel 031-220 1236
Chairman, T. N. Biggart, CBE, WS
Members, The Parliamentary Commissioner for
Administration; G. A. Anderson; W. J. Campbell;
Mrs C. A. M. Davis; T. R. H. Godden, CB; J. Langan; Ms
M. Burns
Secretary, Ms L. Wilkie

TRIBUNALS
— see pages 384–7

UNRELATED LIVE TRANSPLANT
REGULATORY AUTHORITY
Department of Health, Room 520, Eileen House,
80–94 Newington Causeway, London SE1 6EF
Tel 071-972 2739

The Unrelated Live Transplant Regulatory Authority
(ULTRA) is a statutory body established on 1 January 1990.
In every case where the transplant of an organ within the
definition of the Human Organ Transplants Act 1989 is
proposed between a living donor and a recipient who are not
genetically related, the proposal must be referred to ULTRA.
Applications must be made by registered medical practi-
tioners.
    The Authority comprises a chairman and ten members
appointed by the Secretary of State for Health. The secretariat
is provided by Department of Health Officials.
Chairman, Prof. M. Bobrow
Members, Revd Prof. G. R. Dunstan; Dr P. A. Dyer;
    Mrs D. Eccles; Prof. M. G. McGeown; S. G. Macpherson;
    Dr N. P. Mallick; Prof. J. R. Salaman; Miss F. Smithers;
    Miss S. M. Taber; J. Wellbeloved
Administrative Secretary, P. Pudlo
Medical Secretary, Dr E. Hills

URBAN REGENERATION AGENCY
c/o Department of the Environment, 2 Marsham Street,
London SW1P 3EB
Tel 071-276 4704

The agency is likely to begin work during the second half of
1993, its primary aim being to bring 150,000 acres of vacant
and derelict land in towns and cities back into use and ease
the pressure for development in the countryside.
Chairman, The Lord Walker of Worcester, MBE, PC
Chief Executive, D. Taylor

WALES YOUTH AGENCY
Leslie Court, Lon-y-Llyn, Caerphilly, Mid Glamorgan
CF8 1BQ
Tel 0222-880088

The Wales Youth Agency is a non-departmental public body
funded by the Welsh Office. Its functions include the
encouragement and development of the partnership between
statutory and voluntary agencies relating to young people;
the promotion of staff development and training; and
the extension of marketing and information services in the
relevant fields. The board of directors is appointed by the
Secretary of State for Wales; directors do not receive a salary.
Chairman of the Board of Directors, G. Davies
Vice-Chairman of the Board of Directors, Dr H. Williamson
Executive Director, B. Williams

OFFICE OF WATER SERVICES
Centre City Tower, 7 Hill Street, Birmingham B5 4UA
Tel 021-625 1300

The Office of Water Services (Ofwat) was set up under the
Water Act 1989. Its role is to support the Director-General
of Water Services, who regulates the economic framework of
the water industry in England and Wales. His main duties
are to ensure that water companies (*see* page 508) comply
with the terms of their appointments (or licences) and to
protect the interests of water consumers. The Director-
General has established ten regional customer service
committees which investigate complaints and identify customer concerns. The Ofwat National Customer Council is a
non-statutory body set up by the Director-General in March
1993 to represent the views of water customers nationally.
    The Director-General is independent of ministerial control
and directly accountable to Parliament.
Director-General of Water Services, I. C. R. Byatt

WELSH DEVELOPMENT AGENCY
Pearl House, Greyfriars Road, Cardiff CF1 3XX
Tel 0222-222666

The Welsh Development Agency was established under the
Welsh Development Agency Act 1975 and came into
existence on 1 January 1976. Its remit is to help further the
regeneration of the economy and improve the environment
in Wales, a task that is carried out by business divisions
working from the Agency's head office in Cardiff and through
a network of six regional offices. The Agency's main activities
include helping to boost the growth, profitability and
competitiveness of indigenous Welsh companies; building
speculative and bespoke factories and encouraging investment by the private sector in site development; grant-aiding
land reclamation; and stimulating quality urban and rural
regeneration and development. Through Welsh Development International it also promotes inward investment into
Wales.
Chairman, D. Rowe-Beddoe
Deputy Chairman, Dr R. Bichan
Chief Executive, P. Head

WELSH OFFICE

The Welsh Office has responsibility in Wales for ministerial
functions relating to health and personal social services;
education, except for terms and conditions of service and
student awards; training, including training policy from April
1994; the Welsh language, arts and culture; the implementation of the Citizen's Charter in Wales; local government;
housing; water and sewerage; environmental protection;
sport; agriculture and fisheries; forestry; land use, including
town and country planning and countryside and nature
conservation; new towns; non-departmental public bodies
and appointments in Wales; ancient monuments and historic
buildings; and, from April 1994, the Welsh Arts Council;
roads; tourism; financial assistance to industry; the Strategic
Development Scheme in Wales and the Programme for the
Valleys; the operation of the European Regional Development Fund in Wales and other European Community
matters; civil emergencies; and all financial aspects of these
matters, including Welsh rate support grant. It has oversight
responsibilities for economic affairs and regional planning in
Wales.

Gwydyr House, Whitehall, London SW1A 2ER
Tel 071-270 3000
Secretary of State for Wales, The Rt. Hon. John Redwood,
MP
    Private Secretary, Miss J. C. Simpson
    Parliamentary Private Secretary, D. Evans, MP

Minister of State, The Rt. Hon. Sir Wyn Roberts, MP
  Private Secretary, H. O. Jones
Parliamentary Private Secretary, D. Tredinnick, MP
Parliamentary Under-Secretary, Gwilym Jones, MP
  Private Secretary, Ms J. Allen
Parliamentary Clerk, V. R. Watkin
Permanent Secretary (G1), M. C. Scholar, CB
  Private Secretary, R. Shearer

Cathays Park, Cardiff CF1 3NQ
Tel 0222-825111

LEGAL DIVISION
Legal Adviser (G3), D. G. Lambert
Assistant Solicitors (G5), P. J. Murrin; J. H. Turnbull
Lawyers (G6), H. D. Evans; J. D. H. Evans;
  Miss A. L. Ferguson; C. P. Jones; C. G. Longville;
  A. J. Park; Mrs A. T. Parkes; A. J. Watkins;
  A. Widdrington
Senior Legal Assistant, D. H. J. Williams
Lawyers (G7), Mrs K. R. Davies; T. R. E. Heywood;
  Ms T. L. Jones; Miss K. Nicholas; M. Partridge;
  Mrs P. Turnbull; Miss E. Stallard; Mrs R. J. Wiles

INFORMATION DIVISION
Director of Information (G5), H. G. Roberts
Chief Press Officer (G7), R. Lehnert
Principal Publicity Officer (G7), W. J. Edwards

ESTABLISHMENT GROUP
Principal Establishment Officer (G3), G. C. G. Craig
Heads of Divisions (G5), R. M. Abel; G. A. Thomas;
  Ms H. Angus
Senior Economic Adviser (G5), M. G. Phelps
Chief Statistician (G5), Dr M. P. G. Pepper
Head of Health Intelligence Unit (G6), M. R. Brand
Head of Training and Education Intelligence Unit (G6),
  J. D. Kinder
Principals (G7), R. J. Callen; J. F. Bowley; Mrs J. Leitch;
  P. Lunn; Mrs B. Hollick; M. Stevenson; P. H. Skellon;
  C. Tudor; D. D. Baird; Mrs J. Blamire
Economic Adviser (G7), V. W. F. McPherson
Principal Research Officers (G7), E. Darwin;
  Mrs M. A. J. Gronow
Statisticians (G7), P. J. Fullerton; E. Swires Hennessy;
  J. D. James; H. M. Jones; R. Jones; Mrs K. M. Phillips;
  Dr G. W. Thomas; Miss D. R. Carter; P. J. Demery;
  Miss C. M. Roberts; Mrs S. Leake; R. T. Kilpatrick
Medical Director of Cancer Registry, Dr M. Cotter
NHS (G9) Secondee, A. M. Jackson

FINANCE GROUP
Principal Finance Officer (G3), R. A. Wallace
Heads of Divisions (G5), D. W. Jones; L. A. Pavelin;
  Mrs E. A. Taylor
Grade 6, M. G. Horlock
Principals (G7), B. R. Davies; M. H. Harper; Mrs H. Usher;
  D. A. Powell; H. F. Rawlings; P. J. Higgins; W. F. Atwill
Head of Internal Audit (G7), D. Howarth

NATIONAL HEALTH SERVICE DIRECTORATE
Director of the NHS in Wales, J. W. Owen
Heads of Divisions (G5), D. H. Jones; D. A. Pritchard;
  N. E. Thomas; B. Wilcox; R. C. Williams
Senior Principal (G6), R. O'Sullivan
Principals (G7), Mrs J. D. Annand; M. A. C. Brooke;
  M. D. Chown; P. Davenport; J. Duggan; R. J. Dodd;
  J. Morgan; R. A. Williams; D. W. Evans; Mrs C. Lines;
  D. Boyland; I. Heppenstall; M. F. Webb; J. Toman;
  W. Evans; J. H. Grainger; E. J. McDonald; R. A. Jones;
  Ms J. Plastow; Mrs J. E. Wood; K. Orchard; K. S. Sleight

HEALTH AUTHORITIES
CLWYD, Preswylfa, Hendy Road, Mold, Clwyd CH7 1PZ.
  Chief Executive Director, B. F. Jones
EAST DYFED, Starling Park House, Johnstown,
  Carmarthen, Dyfed SA31 3HL. *Managing Director*,
  M. Ponton
GWENT, Brecon House, Mamhilad Park Estate, Pontypool,
  Gwent. *Joint Chief Executive*, J. Hallett
GWYNEDD, Coed Mawr, Bangor, Gwynedd LL57 4IP.
  District General Manager, C. H. Thomas
MID GLAMORGAN, District Headquarters, Albert Road,
  Pontypridd CF37 1LA. *District General Manager*,
  E. J. Thomas
PEMBROKESHIRE NHS TRUST, Meyler House, St
  Thomas Green, Haverfordwest, Dyfed SA61 1QP. *Chief
  Executive*, B. J. Davies
POWYS, Mansion House, Bronllys, Brecon, Powys LD3 0LS.
  District General Manager, Dr D. Bevan
SOUTH GLAMORGAN, Temple of Peace and Health,
  Cathays Park, Cardiff CF1 3NW. *District General Manager*,
  G. L. Harrhy
WEST GLAMORGAN, The Oldway Centre, 36 Orchard
  Street, Swansea SA1 5AQ. *Chief Executive Director*,
  A. Beddow

AGRICULTURE, INDUSTRY AND ECONOMIC
DEVELOPMENT AND TRAINING
Deputy Secretary (G2), J. F. Craig

AGRICULTURE DEPARTMENT
Head of Department (G3), O. Rees, CB
Heads of Divisions (G5), G. Podmore; D. R. Thomas;
  L. K. Walford
Principals (G7), Mrs B. Harding; A. G. Huws; Ms
  A. Jackson; R. F. Patterson; C. E. Taylor; B. E. Price;
  P. N. S. Wolfenden; A. Agett
Divisional Executive Officers (G7), W. K. Griffiths
  (*Carmarthen*); E. Hughes (*Caernarfon*); J. C. Alexander
  (*Llandrindod Wells*)

ECONOMIC DEVELOPMENT AND TRAINING GROUP
Head of Group (G3), M. J. Cochlin
Head of Training, Education and Enterprise Department (G4),
  C. L. Jones
Heads of Divisions (G5), M. E. Bevan; M. J. Clancy;
  Miss E. N. M. Davies; M. L. Evans; H. Evans
Senior Principals (G6), H. D. Brodie; M. Betenson;
  J. D. Kinder
Principals (G7), D. Beames; M. H. Bendon; C. J. Burdett;
  Dr M. C. Dunn; Ms J. M. Gordon; A. D. Lansdown;
  Miss J. E. Paulett; J. N. Roberts; M. A. J. Roberts;
  A. J. Davies; Dr J. Milligan; P. F. Brown; R. O. Evans;
  Mrs C. Fullerton; Dr I. I. Thomas; R. Keveren

INDUSTRY DEPARTMENT
Director (G3), C. D. Stevens
Industrial Director (G4), J. Cameron
Heads of Divisions (G5), D. T. Richards; G. T. Evans
Business Services Division Director (G6), Dr R. J. Loveland
Principals (G7), N. Barry; C. F. Francis; J. A. Grimes;
  G. Jones; J. A. Atkins; K. Smith; R. Waller;
  J. W. Wallington; G. Madden; I. Shuttleworth

EDUCATION, HOUSING, HEALTH AND SOCIAL
SERVICES, TRANSPORT, PLANNING AND
ENVIRONMENT
Deputy Secretary (G2), J. W. Lloyd, CB

EDUCATION DEPARTMENT
Head of Department (G3), S. H. Martin
Heads of Divisions (G5)°, W. G. Davies; H. Evans;
B. J. Mitchell; R. C. Simpson
Principals (G7)°, Mrs J. Booker; P. F. Brown; D. A. Bullen;
Mrs L. L. Changkee; B. Dare; R. O. Evans;
Mrs J. Hopkins; G. R. Jones; Mrs C. Peat;
M. G. Richards; D. M. Rolph

OFFICE OF HM CHIEF INSPECTOR FOR SCHOOLS IN
WALES
Chief Inspector (G4)°, R. L. James
Staff Inspectors (G5)°, S. J. Adams; J. R. N. Evans;
T. E. Parry; G. Thomas; P. Thomas; Mrs I. Thomas;
M. J. F. Wynn
There are 46 Grade 6 Inspectors.
Head of Administration (G7), Ms C. M. Owen

HOUSING, HEALTH AND SOCIAL SERVICES POLICY
GROUP
Head of Group (G3), R. W. Jarman
Heads of Divisions (G5), D. Adams; R. J. Davies;
Mrs B. J. M. Wilson; A. G. Thornton
Chief Inspector, Social Services Inspectorate (Wales) (G5),
D. G. Evans
Deputy Chief Inspectors, J. F. Mooney; R. C. Woodward
Grade 6, A. C. Elmer; M. J. Shanahan
Principals (G7), Mrs K. Cassidy; L. Conway; C. Coombs;
P. Godden-Kent; D. B. Hilbourne; D. Hobbs;
Miss E. M. Jones; J. Kilner; R. Norris; I. Price Jones
Social Services Inspectors (G7), D, Barker; D. A. Brushett;
G. H. Davies; Miss R. E. Evans; I. Forster;
Mrs J. Jenkins; C. D. Vyvyan; Mrs P. White
Principal Professional and Technology Officers (G7),
G. N. Harding; W. Ross

HEALTH PROFESSIONAL GROUP
Chief Medical Officer (G3), Dr D. J. Hine

Public Health Sub Group (HPG M1)
Deputy Chief Medical Officer (G4), Dr A. M. George
Senior Medical Officers (G5), Dr J. Ludlow; Dr B. Fuge; Dr
J. G. Avery

Hospital Services Sub Group (HPG M2)
Principal Medical Officer (acting) (G4), Dr D. W. Owen
Senior Medical Officers (G5), Dr B. Davies; Dr D. Salter;
(*part-time*) Dr J. N. P. Hughes

Community and Primary Care Services Sub Group (HPG M3)
Principal Medical Officer (G4), Dr J. K. Richmond
Senior Medical Officers (G5), Dr A. K. Thomas;
D. E. Davies; Dr R. Owen; Dr H. N. Williams

Divisional Medical Officer (G5), Dr D. E. Davies
Medical Officers (G6), Dr J. W. Crossley; Dr J. D. Andrews;
Dr H. Williams; Dr T. Lyons; Dr T. I. Evans;
Dr N. E. Thomas
Chief Dental Officer (G5), D. M. Heap
Senior Dental Officer (G5), vacant
Dental Officer (G6), J. D. O. Parkholm
Chief Scientific Adviser (G5), Dr J. A. V. Pritchard
Deputy Scientific Adviser (G6), Dr E. O. Crawley
Chief Pharmaceutical Adviser (G5), Dr G. B. A. Veitch
Deputy Pharmaceutical Adviser (G6), Mrs D. Kay Roberts
Chief Environmental Health Adviser (G5), R. Alexander
Deputy Environmental Health Adviser (G6), vacant

NURSING DIVISION
Chief Nursing Officer, Miss M. Bull
Deputy Chief Nursing Officer, Mrs B. Melvin
Nursing Officers, Mrs R. Cohen; Mrs S. M. Drayton;
P. Johnson; Mrs J. Sait; M. F. Tonkin

TRANSPORT, PLANNING AND ENVIRONMENT GROUP
Head of Group (G3), P. R. Gregory
Director of Highways (G4), K. J. Thomas°
Deputy Director of Highways (G5), J. G. Evans*
Heads of Divisions (G5), A. H. H. Jones; D. I. Westlake°;
H. R. Bollington°
Superintending Engineers (G6), J. R. Rees; B. H. Hawker,
OBE*
Chief Estates Adviser (G6), G. K. Hoad
Senior Principal (G6), P. R. Marsden
Scientific Adviser (G6), Dr H. Prosser
Chief Planning Adviser (G6), W. P. Roderick
Principals (G7), P. M. Bishop; M. D. Evans; T. W. Hunter;
H. R. Payne; Mrs C. R. Jones; G. R. Jones; D. Hadfield°;
R. D. Macey; G. Quarrell; D. C. Quinlan
Principal Planning Officers (G7), D. B. Courtier; L. Owen;
J. V. Spear
Principal Research Officers (G7), A. S. Dredge;
Ms L. J. Roberts
Principal Estates Officer (G7), R. W. Wilson
*Principal Professional and Technology Officers, Highways
Directorate (G7)*, M. J. Gilbert; I. A. Grindulais;
A. P. Howcroft; A. L. Perry; R. H. Powell; S. C. Shouler;
J. Collins; K. J. Alexander; R. H. Hooper; R. K. Cone;
J. Dawkins; T. Dorken; R. Shaw; M. J. A. Parker;
V. S. Pownall

LOCAL GOVERNMENT REORGANIZATION GROUP
Head of Group (G3), J. D. Shortridge
Principals (G7), I. R. Miller; A. C. Wood; Dr
H. F. Rawlings

HM INSPECTORATE OF POLLUTION FOR WALES
11th Floor, Brunel House, 2 Fitzalan Road, Cardiff CF2 1TI
Tel 0222-49558

Inspector, Hazardous Wastes (G7), G. Taylor
Inspector, Radiation and Chemicals (G7) (*acting*),
Dr C. Hardman
Inspector, Water (G7), A. A. Houlden

EXECUTIVE AGENCIES

CADW: WELSH HISTORIC MONUMENTS
Brunel House, Fitzalan Road, Cardiff CF2 1UY
Tel 0222-465511

Chief Executive, E. A. J. Carr
Director of Properties in Care, J. H. Pavitt
Director of Policy and Administration, R. W. Hughes
Conservation Architect (G6), J. D. Hogg
*Principal Inspector of Ancient Monuments and Historic
Buildings*, J. R. Avent
Inspectors of Ancient Monuments and Historic Buildings,
J. K. Knight; A. D. McLees; Dr S. E. Rees;
R. C. Turner; M. J. Yates

PLANNING INSPECTORATE
Cathays Park, Cardiff CF1 3NQ
Tel 0222-823892

Chief Executive and Chief Planning Officer (G3), H. S. Crow
Assistant Chief Planning Inspector (G5), D. F. Harris

Based at:
°Ty Glan Road, Llanishen, Cardiff CF4 5WE. Tel: 0222-761456
*Government Buildings, Dinerth Road, Rhos on Sea, Colwyn Bay
LL28 4UL. Tel: 0492-44261

WOMEN'S NATIONAL COMMISSION
Level 4, Caxton House, Tothill Street, London SW1H 9NF
Tel 071-273 5486

The Women's National Commission is an advisory committee to the Government whose remit is to ensure by all possible means that the informed opinions of women are given their due weight in the deliberations of the Government. The Commission's fifty members are all women who are elected or appointed by national organizations with a large and active membership of women. The organizations include the women's sections of the major political parties, trades unions, religious groups, professional women's organizations and other bodies broadly representative of women.
Government Co-Chairman, The Baroness Denton of Wakefield, CBE (*nominated by the Prime Minister* 1992)
Elected Co-Chairman, Ms M. Rooney (*elected* 1993)
Joint Secretaries, Ms J. Bailey; Ms W. Brown

WOMEN'S ROYAL VOLUNTARY SERVICE
234–244 Stockwell Road, London SW9 9SP
Tel 071-416 0146

The Women's Royal Voluntary Service (WRVS) assists government departments, local authorities and voluntary bodies in organizing and carrying out welfare and emergency work for the community on a nationwide network operated through divisional, county, metropolitan, district and London borough organizers. Activities include work for the elderly and handicapped, for young families, and for offenders and their families; non-medical work in hospitals; welfare work for HM Forces and for Service families; and trained teams to assist in international, national and local emergencies.
National Chairman, Mrs E. Toulson

Law Courts and Offices

THE JUDICIAL COMMITTEE OF THE PRIVY COUNCIL

The Judicial Committee of the Privy Council is the final court of appeal from courts of the United Kingdom dependencies and courts of independent Commonwealth countries which have retained the right of appeal (Antigua and Barbuda, the Bahamas, Barbados, Belize, Brunei, Dominica, The Gambia, Jamaica, Kiribati, Mauritius, New Zealand, Singapore, St Christopher and Nevis, St Lucia, St Vincent and the Grenadines, Trinidad and Tobago, and Tuvalu). The Committee also hears appeals from courts of the Channel Islands and the Isle of Man, the disciplinary and health committees of the medical and allied professions, and some ecclesiastical appeals under the Pastoral Measure 1983.

The Judicial Committee includes the Lord Chancellor, the Lords of Appeal in Ordinary (*see* below) and other members of the Privy Council who hold or have held high judicial office, and certain judges from the Commonwealth. Commonwealth appeals are usually heard by a board of five judges.

PRIVY COUNCIL OFFICE (JUDICIAL COMMITTEE), Downing Street, London SW1A 2AJ. Tel: 071-270 0483
Registrar of the Privy Council, D. H. O. Owen
Chief Clerk, K. N. Stringer

The Judicature of England and Wales

The legal system of England and Wales is separate from those of Scotland and Northern Ireland and differs from them in law, judicial procedure and court structure, although there is a common distinction between civil law (disputes between individuals) and criminal law (acts harmful to the community).

The supreme judicial authority for England and Wales is the House of Lords, which is the ultimate Court of Appeal from all courts in Great Britain and Northern Ireland (except criminal courts in Scotland). As a Court of Appeal it consists of the Lord Chancellor and the Lords of Appeal in Ordinary (Law Lords).

The Supreme Court of Judicature comprises the Court of Appeal, the Crown Court and the High Court of Justice. The High Court of Justice is the superior civil court and is divided into three divisions. The Chancery Division is concerned mainly with equity, bankruptcy and contentious probate business; the Queen's Bench Division deals with commercial and maritime law, with civil cases not assigned to other courts, and hears appeals from lower courts; and the Family Division deals with matters relating to family law. Sittings are held at the Royal Courts of Justice in London or at 26 Crown Court centres outside the capital. High Court judges sit alone to hear cases at first instance. Appeals from lower courts are heard by two or three judges, or by single judges of the appropriate division. The Restrictive Practices Court, set up under the Restrictive Trade Practices Act 1956, and the Official Referees' Courts, which deal almost exclusively with cases concerning the construction industry, are also part of the High Court.

Questions concerning the interpretation and application of European Community law, including preliminary rulings requested by British courts and tribunals, are decided by the European Court of Justice (*see* pages 761–2).

The decision to prosecute in the majority of cases rests with the Crown Prosecution Service, an independent prosecuting body established in 1986 to serve all of England and Wales (*see* pages 378–9). At the head of the service is the Director of Public Prosecutions, who discharges her duties under the superintendence of the Attorney-General. Certain categories of offence continue to require the Attorney-General's consent for prosecution.

Minor criminal offences (summary offences) are dealt with in magistrates' courts, which usually consist of three unpaid lay magistrates (Justices of the Peace) sitting without a jury, who are advised on points of law and procedure by a legally-qualified clerk to the justices. There were 29,686 Justices of the Peace at 1 January 1993. In busier courts a full-time, salaried and legally-qualified stipendiary magistrate presides alone. Cases involving people under 16 are heard in youth courts, specially constituted magistrates' courts which sit apart from other courts. Preliminary proceedings in a serious case to decide whether there is evidence to justify committal for trial in the Crown Court are also held in the magistrates' courts. Appeals from magistrates' courts against sentence or conviction are made to the Crown Court. Appeals upon a point of law are made to the High Court, and may go on to the House of Lords.

The Crown Court sits in about 90 centres, divided into six circuits, and is presided over by High Court judges, full-time circuit judges, and part-time recorders, sitting with a jury in all trials which are contested. It deals with trials of the more serious criminal offences, the sentencing of offenders committed for sentence by magistrates' courts (when the magistrates consider their own power of sentence inadequate), and appeals from lower courts. Magistrates usually sit with a circuit judge or recorder to deal with appeals and committals for sentence. Appeals from the Crown Court, either against sentence or conviction, are made to the Court of Appeal (Criminal Division), presided over by the Lord Chief Justice. A further appeal from the Court of Appeal to the House of Lords can be brought if a point of law of general public importance is considered to be involved.

Most minor civil cases are dealt with by the county courts, of which there are about 300 (details may be found in the local telephone directory). For cases involving small claims there are special arbitration facilities and simplified procedures. Where there are financial limits on county court jurisdiction, claims which exceed those limits may be tried in the county courts with the consent of the parties, or in certain circumstances on transfer from the High Court. Outside London, bankruptcy proceedings can be heard in designated county courts. Magistrates' courts can deal with certain classes of civil case and committees of magistrates license public houses, clubs and betting shops. For the implementation of the Children Act 1989, a new structure of hearing centres was set up in October 1991 for family proceedings cases, involving magistrates' courts (family proceedings courts), divorce county courts, family hearing centres and care centres.

Appeals in family matters heard in the family proceedings courts go to the Family Division of the High Court; affiliation appeals and appeals from decisions of the licensing committees of magistrates go to the Crown Court. Appeals from the High Court and county courts are heard in the Court of Appeal (Civil Division), presided over by the Master of the Rolls, and may go on to the House of Lords.

Coroners' courts investigate violent and unnatural deaths or sudden deaths where the cause is unknown. Cases may be brought before a local coroner (a senior lawyer or doctor) by doctors, the police, various public authorities or members of the public. Where a death is sudden and the cause is unknown, the coroner may order a post-mortem examination to determine the cause of death rather than hold an inquest in court.

THE HOUSE OF LORDS
AS FINAL COURT OF APPEAL

The Lord High Chancellor
  The Rt. Hon. the Lord Mackay of Clashfern, *born* 1927, *apptd* 1987

Lords of Appeal in Ordinary (each £103,790)

Rt. Hon. Lord Keith of Kinkel, *born* 1922, *apptd* 1977
Rt. Hon. Lord Templeman, MBE, *born* 1920, *apptd* 1982
Rt. Hon. Lord Goff of Chieveley, *born* 1926, *apptd* 1986
Rt. Hon. Lord Jauncey of Tullichettle, *born* 1925, *apptd* 1988
Rt. Hon. Lord Lowry, *born* 1919, *apptd* 1988 (until Jan. 1994)
Rt. Hon. Lord Browne-Wilkinson, *born* 1930, *apptd* 1991
Rt. Hon. Lord Mustill, *born* 1931, *apptd* 1992
Rt. Hon. Lord Slynn of Hadley, *born* 1930, *apptd* 1992
Rt. Hon. Lord Woolf, *born* 1933, *apptd* 1992
Rt. Hon. Lord Lloyd, *born* 1929, *apptd* 1993
Rt. Hon. Lord Nolan, *born* 1928, *apptd* 1994 (from Jan. 1994)
Registrar, The Clerk of the Parliaments (*see* page 228)

SUPREME COURT OF JUDICATURE

COURT OF APPEAL

The Master of the Rolls (£103,790), The Rt. Hon. Sir Thomas Bingham, *born* 1933, *apptd* 1992
Secretary, Miss V. Seymour
Clerk, D. G. Grimmett

Lords Justices of Appeal (each £99,510)

Rt. Hon. Sir Brian Dillon, *born* 1923, *apptd* 1982
Rt. Hon. Sir Brian Neill, *born* 1923, *apptd* 1985
Rt. Hon. Sir Martin Nourse, *born* 1932, *apptd* 1985
Rt. Hon. Sir Iain Glidewell, *born* 1924, *apptd* 1985
Rt. Hon. Sir John Balcombe, *born* 1925, *apptd* 1985
Rt. Hon. Sir Ralph Gibson, *born* 1922, *apptd* 1985
Rt. Hon. Sir Patrick Russell, *born* 1926, *apptd* 1987
Rt. Hon. Dame Elizabeth Butler-Sloss, DBE, *born* 1933, *apptd* 1988
Rt. Hon. Sir Murray Stuart-Smith, *born* 1927, *apptd* 1988
Rt. Hon. Sir Christopher Staughton, *born* 1933, *apptd* 1988
Rt. Hon. Sir Michael Mann, *born* 1930, *apptd* 1988
Rt. Hon. Sir Donald Farquharson, *born* 1928, *apptd* 1989
Rt. Hon. Sir Anthony McCowan, *born* 1928, *apptd* 1989

Rt. Hon. Sir Roy Beldam, *born* 1925, *apptd* 1989
Rt. Hon. Sir Andrew Leggatt, *born* 1930, *apptd* 1990
Rt. Hon. Sir Richard Scott, *born* 1934, *apptd* 1991
Rt. Hon. Sir Johan Steyn, *born* 1932, *apptd* 1992
Rt. Hon. Sir Paul Kennedy, *born* 1935, *apptd* 1992
Rt. Hon. Sir David Hirst, *born* 1925, *apptd* 1992
Rt. Hon. Sir Simon Brown, *born* 1937, *apptd* 1992
Rt. Hon. Sir Anthony Evans, *born* 1934, *apptd* 1992
Rt. Hon. Sir Christopher Rose, *born* 1937, *apptd* 1992
Rt. Hon. Sir Leonard Hoffman, *born* 1934, *apptd* 1992
Rt. Hon. Sir John Waite, *born* 1932, *apptd* 1993
Rt. Hon. Sir John Roch, *born* 1934, *apptd* 1993
Rt. Hon. Sir Peter Gibson, *born* 1934, *apptd* 1993
Rt. Hon. Sir John Hobhouse, *born* 1932, *apptd* 1993
Rt. Hon. Sir Denis Henry, *born* 1931, *apptd* 1993
Rt. Hon. Sir Mark Saville, *born* 1936, *apptd* 1994 (from Jan. 1994)
Ex officio Judges, The Lord High Chancellor; the Lord Chief Justice of England; the Master of the Rolls; the President of the Family Division; and the Vice-Chancellor

COURT OF APPEAL (CRIMINAL DIVISION)
Judges, The Lord Chief Justice of England; the Master of the Rolls; Lords Justices of Appeal; and Judges of the High Court of Justice

COURTS-MARTIAL APPEAL COURT
Judges, The Lord Chief Justice of England; the Master of the Rolls; Lords Justices of Appeal; and Judges of the High Court of Justice

HIGH COURT OF JUSTICE

CHANCERY DIVISION

President, The Lord High Chancellor
The Vice-Chancellor (£99,510), The Rt. Hon. Sir Donald Nicholls, *born* 1933, *apptd* 1991
Clerk, W. Northfield, BEM

Judges (each £90,148)

Hon. Sir John Vinelott, *born* 1923, *apptd* 1978
Hon. Sir Jean-Pierre Warner, *born* 1924, *apptd* 1981
Hon. Sir Jeremiah Harman, *born* 1930, *apptd* 1982
Hon. Sir John Knox, *born* 1925, *apptd* 1985
Hon. Sir Peter Millett, *born* 1932, *apptd* 1986
Hon. Sir Andrew Morritt, CVO, *born* 1938, *apptd* 1988
Hon. Sir William Aldous, *born* 1936, *apptd* 1988
Hon. Sir John Mummery, *born* 1938, *apptd* 1989
Hon. Sir Donald Rattee, *born* 1937, *apptd* 1989
Hon. Sir Francis Ferris, TD, *born* 1932, *apptd* 1990
Hon. Sir John Chadwick, ED, *born* 1941, *apptd* 1991
Hon. Sir Jonathan Parker, *born* 1937, *apptd* 1991
Hon. Sir John Lindsay, *born* 1935, *apptd* 1992
Hon. Dame Mary Arden, DBE, *born* 1947, *apptd* 1993
Hon. Sir Edward Evans-Lombe, *born* 1937, *apptd* 1993

HIGH COURT OF JUSTICE IN BANKRUPTCY
Judges, The Vice-Chancellor and judges of the Chancery Division of the High Court

COMPANIES COURT
Judges, The Vice Chancellor and judges of the Chancery Division of the High Court

PATENT COURT (APPELLATE SECTION)
Judges, The Hon. Mr Justice Aldous; The Hon. Mr Justice Mummery; The Hon. Mr Justice Morritt

QUEEN'S BENCH DIVISION

The Lord Chief Justice of England (£112,083) The Rt. Hon.
the Lord Taylor of Gosforth, *born* 1930, *apptd* 1992
Private Secretary, E. Adams
Clerk, J. Bond

Judges (each £90,148)

Hon. Sir Haydn Tudor Evans, *born* 1920, *apptd* 1974
Hon. Sir Ronald Waterhouse, *born* 1926, *apptd* 1978
Hon. Sir Maurice Drake, DFC, *born* 1923, *apptd* 1978
Hon. Sir Christopher French, *born* 1925, *apptd* 1979
Hon. Sir Charles McCullough, *born* 1931, *apptd* 1981
Hon. Sir John Leonard, *born* 1926, *apptd* 1981
Hon. Sir Oliver Popplewell, *born* 1927, *apptd* 1983
Hon. Sir William Macpherson, TD, *born* 1926, *apptd* 1983
Hon. Sir Philip Otton, *born* 1933, *apptd* 1983
Hon. Sir Michael Hutchison, *born* 1933, *apptd* 1983
Hon. Sir Swinton Thomas, *born* 1931, *apptd* 1985
Hon. Sir Richard Tucker, *born* 1931, *apptd* 1985
Hon. Sir Robert Gatehouse, *born* 1924, *apptd* 1985
Hon. Sir Patrick Garland, *born* 1929, *apptd* 1985
Hon. Sir Michael Turner, *born* 1931, *apptd* 1985
Hon. Sir John Alliott, *born* 1932, *apptd* 1986
Hon. Sir Harry Ognall, *born* 1934, *apptd* 1986
Hon. Sir Konrad Schiemann, *born* 1937, *apptd* 1986
Hon. Sir John Owen, *born* 1925, *apptd* 1986
Hon. Sir Humphrey Potts, *born* 1931, *apptd* 1986
Hon. Sir Richard Rougier, *born* 1932, *apptd* 1986
Hon. Sir Ian Kennedy, *born* 1930, *apptd* 1986
Hon. Sir Nicholas Phillips, *born* 1938, *apptd* 1987
Hon. Sir Robin Auld, *born* 1937, *apptd* 1988
Hon. Sir Malcolm Pill, *born* 1938, *apptd* 1988
Hon. Sir Stuart McKinnon, *born* 1938, *apptd* 1988
Hon. Sir Mark Potter, *born* 1937, *apptd* 1988
Hon. Sir Henry Brooke, *born* 1936, *apptd* 1988
Hon. Sir Igor Judge, *born* 1941, *apptd* 1988
Hon. Sir Edwin Jowitt, *born* 1929, *apptd* 1988
Hon. Sir Scott Baker, *born* 1937, *apptd* 1988
Hon. Sir Michael Morland, *born* 1929, *apptd* 1989
Hon. Sir Mark Waller, *born* 1940, *apptd* 1989
Hon. Sir Roger Buckley, *born* 1939, *apptd* 1989
Hon. Sir Anthony Hidden, *born* 1936, *apptd* 1989
Hon. Sir Michael Wright, *born* 1932, *apptd* 1990
Hon. Sir Charles Mantell, *born* 1937, *apptd* 1990
Hon. Sir John Blofeld, *born* 1932, *apptd* 1990
Hon. Sir Peter Cresswell, *born* 1944, *apptd* 1991
Hon. Sir Anthony May, *born* 1940, *apptd* 1991
Hon. Sir John Laws, *born* 1945, *apptd* 1992
Hon. Dame Ann Ebsworth, DBE, *born* 1937, *apptd* 1992
Hon. Sir Simon Tuckey, *born* 1941, *apptd* 1992
Hon. Sir David Latham, *born* 1942, *apptd* 1992
Hon. Sir John Kay, *born* 1943, *apptd* 1992
Hon. Sir Christopher Holland, *born* 1937, *apptd* 1992
Hon. Sir Richard Curtis, *born* 1933, *apptd* 1992
Hon. Sir Stephen Sedley, *born* 1939, *apptd* 1992
Hon. Dame Janet Smith, DBE, *born* 1940, *apptd* 1992
Hon. Sir Anthony Colman, *born* 1938, *apptd* 1992
Hon. Sir Anthony Clarke, *born* 1943, *apptd* 1993
Hon. Sir John Dyson, *born* 1943, *apptd* 1993
Hon. Sir Thayne Forbes, *born* 1938, *apptd* 1993
Hon. Sir Michael Sachs, *born* 1932, *apptd* 1993
Hon. Sir Stephen Mitchell, *born* 1941, *apptd* 1993
Hon. Sir Rodger Bell, *born* 1939, *apptd* 1993
Hon. Sir Michael Harrison, *born* 1939, *apptd* 1993
Hon. Sir Bernard Rix, *born* 1944, *apptd* 1993
Hon. Dame Anne Steel, DBE, *born* 1940, *apptd* 1993
Hon. Sir Richard Buxton, *born* 1938, *apptd* 1993

FAMILY DIVISION

President (£99,510) Rt. Hon. Sir Stephen Brown, *born* 1929,
apptd 1988
Secretary, Mrs S. Leung
Clerk, Mrs S. Bell

Judges (each £90,148)

Hon. Sir John Wood, MC, *born* 1922, *apptd* 1977
Hon. Dame Margaret Booth, DBE, *born* 1933, *apptd* 1979
Hon. Sir Anthony Ewbank, *born* 1925, *apptd* 1980
Hon. Sir Anthony Hollis, *born* 1927, *apptd* 1982
Hon. Sir Mathew Thorpe, *born* 1938, *apptd* 1988
Hon. Sir Edward Cazalet, *born* 1936, *apptd* 1988
Hon. Sir Alan Ward, *born* 1938, *apptd* 1988
Hon. Sir Robert Johnson, *born* 1933, *apptd* 1989
Hon. Sir Douglas Brown, *born* 1931, *apptd* 1989
Hon. Dame Joyanne Bracewell, DBE, *born* 1934, *apptd* 1990
Hon. Sir Michael Connell, *born* 1939, *apptd* 1991
Hon. Sir Peter Singer, *born* 1944, *apptd* 1993
Hon. Sir Nicholas Wall, *born* 1945, *apptd* 1993
Hon. Sir Andrew Kirkwood, *born* 1944, *apptd* 1993
Hon. Sir Nicholas Wilson, *born* 1945, *apptd* 1993
Hon. Sir Christopher Stuart-White, *born* 1933, *apptd* 1993

RESTRICTIVE PRACTICES COURT

Judge, The Hon. Mr Justice Warner
Lay Members, B. M. Currie; Sir Lewis Robertson, CBE;
R. Garrick, CBE; S. J. Ahearne; J. A. Graham;
Mrs D. H. Hatfield; S. McDowall; J. A. Scott

OFFICIAL REFEREES' COURTS
St Dunstan's House, 133–137 Fetter Lane, London
EC4A 1HD
Tel 071-936 7429

Judges (each £78,378)

His Hon. Judge Newey, QC (*Senior Official Referee*)
His Hon. Judge Lewis, QC
His Hon. Judge Fox-Andrews, QC
His Hon. Judge Bowsher, QC
His Hon. Judge Loyd, QC
His Hon. Judge Hicks, QC
His Hon. Judge Havery, QC

Chief Clerk, Miss B. Joy

LORD CHANCELLOR'S DEPARTMENT
— *see* Government Departments and Public Offices

SUPREME COURT DEPARTMENTS AND OFFICES
Royal Courts of Justice, London WC2A 2LL
Tel 071-936 6000

ADMINISTRATOR'S OFFICE
Administrator (G5), G. A. Calvett
Deputy Administrator (G6), I. Hyams
Secretary to the Family Division (G6), R. P. Knight

ADMIRALTY AND COMMERCIAL REGISTRY AND MARSHAL'S OFFICE
Registrar (£54,035), P. Miller
Marshal and Chief Clerk (G7), A. Ferrigno

BANKRUPTCY DEPARTMENT
Chief Registrar (£65,912), G. L. Pimm
Bankruptcy Registrars (£54,035), W. S. James;
  J. A. Simmonds; D. G. Scott
Chief Clerk (SEO), M. Brown

CENTRAL OFFICE OF THE SUPREME COURT
*Senior Master of the Supreme Court (QBD), and Queen's
  Remembrancer (£65,912)*, W. K. Topley
Masters of the Supreme Court (QBD) (£54,035),
  P. B. Creightmore; D. L. Prebble; G. H. Hodgson;
  R. L. Turner; J. Trench; M. Tennant; P. Miller;
  N. O. G. Murray; I. H. Foster; G. H. Rose; P. G. Eyre
Chief Clerk (Central Office) (G7), C. F. Jones

CHANCERY DIVISION
Chief Clerk (G7), P. Emery

CHANCERY CHAMBERS
Chief Master of the Supreme Court (£65,912),
  J. M. Dyson
Masters of the Supreme Court (£54,035), J. S. Gowers;
  G. A. Barratt; J. I. Winegarten; J. A. Moncaster
Chief Clerk (SEO), G. Robinson
Conveyancing Counsel of the Supreme Court, J. Monckton;
  S. G. Maurice; M. J. Roth

COMPANIES COURT
Registrar (£54,035), M. Buckley
Chief Clerk (SEO), A. Roberts

COURT OF APPEAL CIVIL DIVISION
Registrar (£65,912), J. D. R. Adams
Chief Clerk (SEO), Miss H. M. Goddard

COURT OF APPEAL CRIMINAL DIVISION
Registrar (£65,912), M. McKenzie, QC
Deputy Registrar (G5), M. N. Farmer
Chief Clerk (G7), K. M. Dickerson

COURTS-MARTIAL APPEALS OFFICE
Registrar (£65,912), M. McKenzie, QC
Chief Clerk (G7), K. M. Dickerson

CROWN OFFICE OF THE SUPREME COURT
*Master of the Crown Office, and Queen's Coroner and
  Attorney (£65,912)*, M. McKenzie, QC
Head of Crown Office (G5), Mrs L. Knapman
Chief Clerk (G7), K. M. Dickerson

EXAMINERS OF THE COURT
Empowered to take examination of witnesses in all
Divisions of the High Court
M. F. Meredith-Hardy; B. Rathbone; N. W. Briggs;
  R. Jacob

RESTRICTIVE PRACTICES COURT
Clerk of the Court, M. Buckley
Chief Clerk (SEO), A. Roberts

SUPREME COURT TAXING OFFICE
Chief Master (£65,912), P. T. Hurst
Masters of the Supreme Court (£54,035), C. R. N. Martyn;
  C. A. Prince; M. Ellis; T. H. Seager Berry (*Taxing
  Master*); C. C. Wright; P. A. Rogers
Chief Clerk (Administration) (G7), R. Cuthbert
Chief Taxing Officer (G7), T. J. Ryan

COURT OF PROTECTION
Stewart House, 24 Kingsway, London WC2B 6HD
Tel 071-269 7000
Master (£65,912), Mrs A. B. Macfarlane

ELECTION PETITIONS OFFICE
Room E218, Royal Courts of Justice, Strand, London
WC2A 2LL
Tel 071-936 6131
The office accepts petitions and deals with all matters relating
to the questioning of Parliamentary, European Parliament
and local government elections, and with applications for
relief under the Representation of the People legislation.
Prescribed Officer, W. K. Topley
Chief Clerk, C. I. P. Denyer

OFFICE OF THE LORD CHANCELLOR'S VISITORS
Trevelyan House, 30 Great Peter Street, London SW1P 2BY
Tel 071-210 8563
Legal Visitor, A. R. Tyrrell
Medical Visitors, A. G. Fullerton; F. E. Kenyon; K. Khan;
  P. A. Morris; D. Parr; J. Roberts

OFFICIAL RECEIVERS' DEPARTMENT
21 Bloomsbury Street, London WC1B 3SS
Tel 071-323 3090
Senior Official Receiver, J. R. Donnison
Official Receivers, M. J. Pugh; L. T. Cramp;
  M. W. A. Sanderson; G. J. A. Harp

OFFICIAL SOLICITOR'S DEPARTMENT
81 Chancery Lane, London WC2B 6HD
Tel 071-911 7105
Official Solicitor to the Supreme Court, P. M. Harris
Deputy Official Solicitor, H. J. Baker
Chief Clerk (G7), R. Lancaster

PRINCIPAL REGISTRY (FAMILY DIVISION)
Somerset House, London WC2R 1LP
Tel 071-936 6000
Senior District Judge (£65,912), G. B. N. A. Angel
District Judges (£54,035), T. G. Guest; J. E. Artro-Morris;
  R. B. Rowe; B. P. F. Kenworthy-Browne;
  Mrs K. T. Moorhouse; D. T. A. Davies; Mrs N. Pearce;
  M. J. Segal; R. Conn; Miss I. M. Plumstead; G. J. Maple;
  Miss H. C. Bradley; K. J. White; A. R. S. Bassett-Cross
Secretary (G6), R. P. Knight

District Probate Registrars
Birmingham and Stoke-on-Trent, C. Marsh
Brighton and Maidstone, M. N. Emery
Bristol, Exeter and Bodmin, P. L. Speyer
Ipswich, Norwich and Peterborough, E. R. Alexander
Leeds, Lincoln and Sheffield, A. P. Dawson
Liverpool, Lancaster and Chester, B. J. Thomas
Llandaff, Bangor, Carmarthen and Gloucester, R. F. Yeldam
Manchester and Nottingham, M. A. Moran
Newcastle, Carlisle, York and Middlesbrough, P. Sanderson
Oxford, R. R. Da Costa
Winchester, A. K. Biggs

OFFICE OF THE JUDGE ADVOCATE OF THE
FLEET
The Law Courts, Barker Road, Maidstone ME16 8EQ
Tel 0622-754966

Judge Advocate of the Fleet, His Hon. Judge Waley, VRD, QC

OFFICE OF THE JUDGE ADVOCATE-GENERAL
OF THE FORCES
(*Joint Service for the Army and the Royal Air Force*)
22 Kingsway, London WC2B 6LE
Tel 071-305 6649

Judge Advocate-General (£78,378), His Hon. Judge
J. W. Rant, QC
Vice-Judge Advocate-General (£65,912), G. L. Chapman
Assistant Judge Advocates-General (£42,850–£49,450),
E. G. Moelwyn-Hughes; A. P. Pitts; D. M. Berkson;
M. A. Hunter; T. R. King; T. G. Pontius; J. P. Camp
Deputy Judge Advocates (£30,000–£42,050), Miss S. E.
Woollam; R. C. C. Seymour

HIGH COURT AND CROWN COURT CENTRES

First-tier centres deal with both civil and criminal cases and
are served by High Court and circuit judges. Second-tier
centres deal with criminal cases only and are served by High
Court and circuit judges. Third-tier centres deal with criminal
cases only and are served only by circuit judges.

MIDLAND AND OXFORD CIRCUIT

First-tier – Birmingham, Lincoln, Nottingham, Oxford,
Stafford, Warwick
Second-tier – Leicester, Northampton, Shrewsbury,
Worcester
Third-tier – Coventry, Derby, Grimsby, Hereford,
Peterborough, Stoke-on-Trent, Wolverhampton
Circuit Administrator, L. Oates, 2 Newton Street,
Birmingham B4 7LU. Tel: 021–627 1700
Courts Administrators: Birmingham Group, V. C. Grove;
Nottingham Group, Mrs E. A. Folman; *Stafford Group*,
A. F. Parker

NORTH-EASTERN CIRCUIT

First-tier – Leeds, Newcastle upon Tyne, Sheffield, Teesside
Second-tier – York
Third-tier – Doncaster, Durham
Circuit Administrator, S. W. L. James, 17th Floor, West
Riding House, Albion Street, Leeds LS1 5AA. Tel: 0532–
441841
Courts Administrators: Leeds Group, P. Delany; *Newcastle
upon Tyne Group*, K. Budgen; *Sheffield Group*,
G. Bingham

NORTHERN CIRCUIT

First-tier – Carlisle, Liverpool, Manchester, Preston
Third-tier – Barrow-in-Furness, Bolton, Burnley, Lancaster
Circuit Administrator, R. A. Vincent, 15 Quay Street,
Manchester M60 9FD. Tel: 061-833 1005
Courts Administrators: Manchester Group, P. G. Walsh;
Liverpool Group, D. A. Beaumont; *Preston Group*,
Mrs A. Prior

SOUTH-EASTERN CIRCUIT

First-tier – Chelmsford, Lewes, Norwich
Second-tier – Ipswich, London (Central Criminal Court),
Luton, Maidstone, Reading, St Albans
Third-tier – Aylesbury, Bury St Edmunds, Cambridge,
Canterbury, Chichester, Guildford, King's Lynn, London
(Croydon, Harrow, Inner London Session House,

Isleworth, Kingston upon Thames, Knightsbridge,
Middlesex Guildhall, Snaresbrook, Southwark and Wood
Green, Woolwich), Southend
The High Court in Greater London sits at the Royal Courts
of Justice.
Circuit Administrator, B. Cooke, New Cavendish House,
18 Maltravers Street, London WC2R 3EU. Tel: 071–936
7235
Deputy Circuit Administrator, P. Stockton
Courts Administrators: Chelmsford Group, M. Littlewood;
Maidstone Group, Mrs H. Hartwell; *Kingston Group*,
J. L. Powell; *London (Civil)*, P. Risk; *London (Crime)*,
G. F. Addicott

WALES AND CHESTER CIRCUIT

First-tier – Caernarfon, Cardiff, Chester, Mold, Swansea
Second-tier – Carmarthen, Merthyr Tydfil, Newport,
Welshpool
Third-tier – Dolgellau, Haverfordwest, Knutsford,
Warrington
Circuit Administrator, D. Howe, Churchill House, Churchill
Way, Cardiff CF1 4HH. Tel: 0222–396925
Courts Administrators: Cardiff Group, G. Jones; *Chester
Group*, T. D. Beckett

WESTERN CIRCUIT

First-tier – Bristol, Exeter, Truro, Winchester
Second-tier – Dorchester, Gloucester, Plymouth
Third-tier – Barnstaple, Bournemouth, Devizes, Newport
(IOW), Portsmouth, Salisbury, Southampton, Swindon,
Taunton
Circuit Administrator, R. J. Clark, CBE, Bridge House, Sion
Place, Clifton, Bristol BS8 4BN. Tel: 0272–743763
Courts Administrators: Bristol Group, A. C. Butler; *Exeter
Group*, J. Ardern; *Winchester Group*, D. Ryan

CIRCUIT JUDGES

Senior Circuit Judges, each £78,378
Circuit Judges, each £65,912

MIDLAND AND OXFORD CIRCUIT

Senior Presiding Judge, Hon. Mr Justice Rougier
W. A. L. Allardice; F. A. Allen; Miss C. Alton;
B. J. Appleby, QC; M. J. Astill; R. S. A. Benson;
I. J. Black, QC; R. W. A. Bray; D. W. Brunning;
F. A. Chapman; F. L. Clark, QC; R. R. B. Cole; P. F. Crane;
P. J. Crawford, QC (Recorder of Birmingham);
I. T. R. Davidson, QC; P. N. de Mille; T. M. Dillon, QC;
C. H. Durman; J. F. Evans, QC; B. A. Farrer, QC;
Miss E. N. Fisher; J. E. Fletcher; R. J. H. Gibbs, QC;
H. G. A. Gosling; J. Hall; S. T. Hammond;
G. C. W. Harris, QC; M. K. Harrison-Hall; T. R. Heald;
J. R. Hopkin; R. H. Hutchinson; J. E. M. Irvine;
R. P. V. Jenkins; J. G. Jones; A. W. P. King; J. T. C. Lee;
M. H. Mander; K. Matthewman, QC; W. D. Matthews;
R. G. May; H. R. Mayor, QC; N. Micklem; P. R. Morrell;
A. J. H. Morrison; M. D. Mott; A. J. D. Nicholl;
R. T. N. Orme; J. F. F. Orrell; D. S. Perrett, QC;
C. J. Pitchers; R. F. D. Pollard; F. M. Potter; D. P. Pugsley;
J. R. Pyke; D. E. Roberts; J. A. O. Shand; J. R. S. Smyth;
P. J. Stretton; G. C. Styler; H. C. Taylor, QC; A. B. Taylor;
K. J. Taylor; M. B. Ward; R. L. Ward, QC; D. J. R. Wilcox;
H. Wilson; J. W. Wilson; K. S. W. Wilson Mellor, QC;
B. Woods; C. G. Young

NORTH-EASTERN CIRCUIT

Senior Presiding Judge, Hon. Mr Justice Waller
J. Altman; T. G. F. Atkinson; G. Baker, QC;
P. M. Baker, QC; T. W. Barber; J. M. A. Barker;

G. N. Barr Young; D. R. Bentley, QC; A. N. J. Briggs;
D. M. A. Bryant; J. W. M. Bullimore; B. Bush; M. C. Carr;
M. L. Cartlidge; P. J. Charlesworth; P. J. Cockroft;
G. J. K. Coles, QC; J. Crabtree; M. T. Cracknell;
W. H. R. Crawford, QC; Mrs J. Davies; E. J. Faulks;
P. J. Fox, QC; A. N. Fricker, QC; M. S. Garner;
S. P. Grenfell; W. Hannah; G. F. R. Harkins;
J. A. Henham; D. Herrod, QC; P. M. L. Hoffman; R. Hunt;
A. E. Hutchinson, QC; N. H. Jones, QC; G. H. Kamil;
T. D. Kent-Jones, TD; C. F. Kolbert; G. M. Lightfoot;
A. G. McCallum; A. C. Macdonald;
Miss M. B. M. MacMurray, QC; M. K. Mettyear;
A. L. Myerson, QC; D. A. Orde; Miss H. E. Paling;
*D. M. Savill, QC; R. M. Scott; A. Simpson; J. Stephenson;
*R. A. R. Stroyan, QC; Mrs L. Sutcliffe; R. C. Taylor;
G. M. Vos; M. Walker; P. H. C. Walker

NORTHERN CIRCUIT

Senior Presiding Judge, Hon. Mr Justice Morland
H. H. Andrew, QC; J. F. Appleton; A. W. Bell;
R. C. W. Bennett; Miss I. Bernstein; M. S. Blackburn;
R. Brown; I. B. Campbell; F. B. Carter, QC; B. I. Caulfield;
D. Clark; D. M. Clifton; G. P. Crowe, QC; *R. E. Davies, QC
(*Recorder of Manchester*); M. Dean, QC; Miss A. E. Downey;
B. R. Duckworth; S. B. Duncan; D. M. Evans, QC;
S. J. D. Fawcus; D. S. Gee; J. A. D. Gilliland, QC;
R. G. Hamilton; J. A. Hammond; R. J. Hardy;
F. D. Hart, QC; M. Hedley; T. D. T. Hodson;
F. R. B. Holloway; Miss M. Holt; N. J. G. Howarth;
G. W. Humphries; P. M. Kershaw, QC (*Commercial Circuit
Judge*); H. L. Lachs; C. N. Lees; J. M. Lever, QC;
R. J. D. Livesey, QC; R. Lockett; J. H. Lord; D. Lynch;
D. I. Mackay; D. G. Maddison; B. C. Maddocks;
C. J. Mahon; J. A. Morgan; M. O'Donoghue;
F. D. Owen, TD; R. E. I. Pickering; D. A. Pirie;
A. J. Proctor; J. H. Roberts; Miss G. D. Ruaux;
H. S. Singer; Miss E. M. Steel; I. R. Taylor, QC;
C. B. Tetlow; J. P. Townend; I. J. C. Trigger;
P. W. Urquhart; I. S. Webster; W. R. Wickham (*Recorder of
Liverpool*); B. Woodward

SOUTH-EASTERN CIRCUIT

Senior Presiding Judge, Hon. Mr Justice Garland (Hon. Mr
Justice Blofeld from Jan. 1994)
J. R. S. Adams; F. J. Aglionby; J. A. Baker; J. B. Baker, QC;
M. J. D. Baker; P. V. Baker, QC; A. F. Balston;
G. S. Barham; C. J. A. Barnett, QC; K. Bassingthwaighte;
G. A. Bathurst Norman; P. J. L. Beaumont, QC;
N. E. Beddard; G. J. Binns; J. E. Bishop; B. M. B. Black;
P. C. Bowsher; A. V. Bradbury; P. N. Brandt;
L. J. Bromley, QC; A. E. Brooks; R. G. Brown;
J. M. Bull, QC; G. N. Butler, QC; *N. M. Butter, QC;
H. J. Byrt, QC; C. V. Callman; B. E. Capstick, QC;
B. L. Charles, QC; A. W. Clark; D. J. Clarkson, QC;
P. C. Clegg; M. Cohen, QC; S. H. Colgan; P. H. Collins;
C. C. Colston, QC; S. S. Coltart; Viscount Colville of
Culross, QC; J. S. Colyer, QC; C. D. Compston;
T. A. C. Coningsby, QC; R. D. Connor; M. J. Cook;
R. A. Cooke; G. H. Coombe; M. R. Coombe; A. Cooray;
Dr E. Cotran; R. C. Cox; D. L. Croft, QC; G. L. Davies;
I. H. Davies, TD; W. L. M. Davies, QC; N. W. Denison, QC;
J. E. Devaux; K. M. Devlin; M. N. Devonshire, TD;
A. E. J. Diamond, QC; A. H. Durrant; C. M. Edwards;
Q. T. Edwards, QC; F. P. L. Evans; J. K. Q. Evans;
S. J. Evans; J. D. Farnworth; P. Fingret; J. J. Finney;
P. Ford; J. J. Fordham; G. C. F. Forrester; J. Fox-
Andrews, QC; Ms D. A. Freedman; R. Gee; L. Gerber;
Miss A. F. Goddard, QC; S. A. Goldstein; P. W. Goldstone;

M. B. Goodman; C. G. M. Gordon; J. B. Gosschalk;
J. H. Gower, QC; M. Graham, QC; B. S. Green, QC;
P. B. Greenwood; D. J. Griffiths; G. D. Grigson;
R. B. Groves, TD, VRD; N. T. Hague, QC;
A. B. R. Hallgarten, QC; Miss G. Hallon; P. J. Halnan;
J. Hamilton; R. E. Hammerton; C. R. H. Hardy;
B. Hargrove, OBE, QC; J. P. Harris, DSC, QC; M. F. Harris;
R. O. Havery, QC; R. G. Hawkins, QC; R. J. Haworth;
A. H. Head; J. C. Hicks, QC; A. N. Hitching; D. Holden;
A. C. W. Hordern, QC; R. W. Howe;
Sir David Hughes-Morgan, Bt., CB, CBE; J. G. Hull, QC;
J. Hunter; M. J. Hyam; D. A. Inman; Dr P. J. E. Jackson;
C. P. James; M. Kennedy, QC; A. M. Kenny; L. G. Krikler;
L. H. C. Lait; P. St J. H. Langan, QC;
Capt. J. B. R. L. Langdon, RN; G. F. B. Laughland, QC;
R. Laurie; T. Lawrence; D. M. Levy, QC; E. Lewis, QC;
D. T. Lloyd; F. R. Lockhart; D. B. D. Lowe; R. H. Lownie;
Mrs N. M. Lowry; R. J. Lowry, QC; J. A. T. Loyd, QC;
R. D. Lymbery, QC (*Common Serjeant*); Capt. S. Lyons;
K. M. McHale; K. A. Machin, QC; M. B. McMullan;
K. C. Macrae; J. R. Main, QC; B. A. Marder, QC;
F. J. M. Marr-Johnson; L. A. Marshall; N. A. Medawar, QC;
D. J. Mellor; G. D. Mercer; A. L. Mildon, QC; D. Q. Miller;
D. Morton Jack; J. I. Murchie; Mrs N. F. Negus;
M. H. D. Neligan; J. H. R. Newey, QC;
C. W. F. Newman, QC; Mrs M. F. Norrie;
Ms S. F. Norwood; P. W. O'Brien; C. R. Oddie;
M. A. Oppenheimer; D. A. Paiba; R. H. S. Palmer;
M. C. Parker, QC; Miss V. A. Pearlman; J. R. Peppitt, QC;
F. H. L. Petre; A. J. Phelan; N. A. J. Philpot; D. C. Pitman;
J. R. Platt; P. B. Pollock; H. C. Pownall, QC;
R. J. C. V. Prendergast; J. E. Previté, QC; B. H. Pryor, QC;
J. E. Pullinger; J. W. Rant, QC; E. V. P. Reece; G. K. Rice;
M. S. Rich, QC; K. A. Richardson, QC; G. Rivlin, QC;
J. H. P. Roberts; D. A. H. Rodwell, QC; J. W. Rogers, QC;
G. H. Rooke, TD, QC; P. C. R. Rountree; J. H. Rucker;
T. R. G. Ryland; R. B. Sanders;
Maj.-Gen. D. H. D. Selwood; J. L. Sessions; J. D. Sheerin;
D. R. A. Sich; A. G. Simmons; K. T. Simpson;
P. R. Simpson; M. Singh, QC; J. K. E. Slack, TD;
S. P. Sleeman; P. M. J. Slot; F. B. Smedley, QC;
C. M. Smith, QC; S. A. R. Smith; R. J. Southan;
S. B. Spence; *R. O. C. Stable, QC; E. Stockdale;
C. J. Sumner; W. F. C. Thomas; A. G. Y. Thorpe;
A. H. Tibber; C. H. Tilling; A. M. Troup; S. Tumim;
J. T. Turner; C. J. M. Tyrer; Mrs A. P. Uziell-Hamilton;
J. E. van der Werff; Sir Lawrence Verney, TD (*Recorder of
London*); A. O. R. Vick, QC; T. L. Viljoen;
Miss M. S. Viner, QC; A. F. Waley, VRD, QC; R. Walker;
D. B. Watling, QC; V. B. Watts; F. J. White;
S. R. Wilkinson; S. M. Willis; C. G. P. Woodford;
G. N. Worthington; E. G. Wrintmore; K. H. Zucker, QC

WALES AND CHESTER CIRCUIT

Senior Presiding Judge, Hon. Mr Justice Pill (Hon. Mr
Justice Curtis from Jan. 1994)
M. R. Burr; T. R. Crowther, QC; G. H. M. Daniel;
R. D. G. David, QC; J. B. S. Diehl, QC; D. E. H. Edwards;
G. O. Edwards, QC; Lord Elystan-Morgan; D. R. Evans, QC;
T. M. Evans, QC; *M. Gibbon, QC; D. M. Hughes;
G. J. Jones; H. D. H. Jones; G. E. Kilfoil;
T. E. I. Lewis-Bowen; D. G. Morgan; D. C. Morton;
T. H. Moseley, QC; D. A. Phillips; P. J. Price, QC;
E. J. Prosser, QC; H. W. J. ap Robert; H. E. P. Roberts, QC;
S. M. Stephens, QC; D. B. Williams, TD, QC;
H. V. Williams, QC; R. G. Woolley

WESTERN CIRCUIT

Senior Presiding Judge, Hon. Mr Justice Auld

M. F. Addison; S. T. Bates, QC; P. T. S. Batterbury;
J. F. Beashel; C. L. Boothman; M. J. L. Brodrick;
J. M. J. Burford, QC; R. D. H. Bursell, QC; J. R. Chalkley;
M. G. Cotterill; Ms H. Counsell; J. A. Cox;
S. C. Darwall Smith; Mrs S. P. Darwall Smith;
Mrs L. H. Davies; M. Dyer; *P. Fallon, QC; P. D. Fanner;
D. L. Griffiths; Mrs C. M. A. Hagen; I. S. Hill, QC;
G. B. Hutton; R. E. Jack, QC; A. G. H. Jones;
D. McCarraher, VRD; Miss S. M. D. McKinney;
I. S. McKintosh; I. G. McLean; J. G. McNaught;
T. J. Milligan; E. G. Neville; S. K. O'Malley;
S. K. Overend; R. C. Pryor, QC; J. N. P. Rudd;
R. M. Shawcross; D. A. Smith, QC; W. E. M. Taylor;
P. M. Thomas; A. A. R. Thompson, QC;
H. J. M. Tucker, QC; D. M. Webster, QC; J. H. Weeks, QC;
J. R. Whitley; J. A. J. Wigmore; K. M. Willcock, QC;
J. C. Willis; J. H. Wroath

RECORDERS (each £315 per day)

J. D. R. Adams; R. J. P. Aikens, QC; J. F. Akast;
I. D. G. Alexander, QC; C. D. Allen; M. P. Allweis;
W. P. Andreae-Jones, QC; P. J. Andrews, QC;
R. A. Anelay, QC; A. R. L. Ansell; J. T. Anthony;
Ms L. E. Appleby, QC; J. F. A. Archer, QC;
Lord Archer of Sandwell, PC, QC; A. J. Arlidge, QC;
E. K. Armitage; R. Ashton; P. Ashworth, QC;
J. M. Aspinall; E. G. Aspley; B. Atchley; N. J. Atkinson, QC;
M. G. Austin-Smith, QC; W. S. Aylen, QC;
J. F. Badenoch, QC; A. B. Baillie; M. F. Baker, QC;
N. R. J. Baker, QC; C. G. Ball, QC; A. Barker, QC;
B. J. Barker, QC; D. Barker, QC; G. E. Barling, QC;
R. O. Barlow; D. N. Barnard; D. M. W. Barnes, QC;
H. J. Barnes; T. P. Barnes; W. E. Barnett, QC;
R. A. Barratt, QC; J. E. Barry; R. Bartfield;
G. R. Bartlett, QC; J. C. T. Barton, QC; D. C. Bate;
S. D. Batten, QC; J. J. Baughan, QC; R. A. Bayliss;
C. H. Beaumont; C. O. M. Bedingfield, TD, QC;
C. O. J. Behrens; R. W. Belben; The Hon. M. J. Beloff, QC;
D. P. Bennett; H. P. D. Bennett, QC; J. M. Bennett;
P. Bennett, QC; K. C. Bentall; H. L. Bentham;
D. M. Berkson; M. Bethel, QC; J. P. V. Bevan;
J. C. Beveridge, QC; M. G. Binning; P. V. Birkett, QC;
W. J. Birtles; P. W. Birts, QC; H. O. Blacksell;
J. A. Blair-Gould; A. N. H. Blake; C. Bloom, QC;
D. J. Blunt, QC; J. G. Boal, QC; D. R. L. Bodey, QC;
G. T. K. Boney, QC; Miss J. A. M. Bonvin; D. J. Boulton;
S. N. Bourne-Arton; P. H. Bowers; J. J. Boyle;
W. T. S. Braithwaite, QC; G. B. Breen; D. J. Brennan, QC;
M. L. Brent, QC; G. J. B. G. Brice; J. N. W. Bridges-
Adams; A. J. Brigden; P. J. Briggs; R. P. Brittain;
J. Bromley-Davenport; S. C. Brown, QC; J. N. Browne;
A. J. N. Brunner; A. Bueno, QC; D. L. Bulmer;
J. P. Burgess; J. K. Burke, QC; J. P. Burke, QC;
H. W. Burnett, QC; M. J. Burton, QC; K. Bush;
A. J. Butcher, QC; A. N. L. Butterfield, QC; C. W. Byers;
M. D. Byrne; Mrs B. A. Calvert, QC; D. Calvert-Smith;
R. Camden Pratt, QC; Miss S. M. C. Cameron, QC;
A. N. B. Campbell; J. Q. Campbell; G. M. C. Carey, QC;
A. C. Carlile, QC, MP; The Lord Carlisle of Bucklow, PC, QC;
H. B. H. Carlisle, QC; J. J. Carter-Manning, QC;
R. Carus, QC; B. E. F. Catlin; J. J. Cavell; J. A. Chadwin, QC;
N. M. Chambers, QC; D. C. Champion; B. W. Chedlow, QC;
J. M. Cherry, QC; J. R. Cherryman, QC; C. F. Chruszcz, QC;
C. H. Clark, QC; C. S. C. S. Clarke, QC; D. C. Clarke, QC;
P. W. Clarke; S. P. Clarke; A. S. L. Cleary;
R. N. B. Clegg, QC; W. Clegg, QC; M. F. Coates;
W. P. Coates; D. J. Cocks, QC; J. J. Coffey; T. A. Coghlan;
W. J. Coker; J. R. Cole; N. J. Coleman; N. B. C. Coles, QC;

A. R. Collender, QC; P. N. Collier, QC; A. D. Collins, QC;
J. M. Collins; Ms M. Colton; Mrs J. R. Comyns;
G. D. Conlin; J. G. Connor; C. S. Cook; A. E. M. Cooper;
Miss B. P. Cooper, QC; P. J. Cooper, QC; P. E. Copley;
S. M. Corkhill; T. G. E. Corrie; P. J. Cosgrove;
G. W. A. Cottle; Miss D. R. Cotton, QC; J. S. Coward, QC;
P. R. Cowell; B. R. E. Cox, QC; P. J. Cox, DSC, QC;
D. I. Crigman, QC; M. L. S. Cripps; C. A. Critchlow;
J. F. Crocker; D. R. Crome; I. W. Crompton;
J. D. Crowley, QC; E. J. R. Crowther, OBE;
W. R. H. Crowther, QC; H. M. Crush; D. M. Cryan;
T. S. Culver; Miss E. A. M. Curnow, QC; J. T. Curran;
P. D. Curran; J. W. O. Curtis; M. J. Curwen; K. C. Cutler;
Ms J. M. P. Daley; A. J. G. Dalziel; G. W. Davey;
C. P. M. Davidson; A. R. M. Davies; D. T. A. Davies;
J. T. L. Davies; A. W. Dawson; D. H. Day, QC; J. J. Deave;
J. B. Deby, QC; P. G. Dedman; Mrs P. A. Deeley;
C. F. Dehn, QC; P. A. de la Piquerie; M. A. de Navarro, QC;
W. E. Denny, CBE, QC; R. L. Denyer, QC; S. C. Desch, QC;
H. A. D. de Silva; C. E. Dines; A. D. Dinkin, QC;
I. J. Dobkin; R. A. M. Doggett; Ms B. Dohmann, QC;
A. M. Donne, QC; A. K. Dooley; S. M. Duffield;
P. R. Dunkels, QC; W. H. Dunn, QC; R. T. Dutton;
D. Eady, QC; Ms D. B. Eaglestone; T. K. Earnshaw;
H. W. P. Eccles, QC; Miss S. M. Edwards, QC;
D. F. Elfer, QC; G. Elias, QC; B. J. Elliott; E. A. Elliott;
D. R. Ellis; C. Elwen; R. M. Englehart, QC; G. A. Ensor;
D. A. Evans, QC; D. H. Evans, QC; G. W. R. Evans;
Sir Graham Eyre, QC; W. D. Fairclough; R. B. Farley, QC;
D. J. Farrer, QC; K. J. Farrow; R. Fernyhough, QC;
P. S. Fish; D. P. Fisher; G. D. Flather, CBE, QC;
P. E. J. Focke, QC; J. D. Foley; R. A. Fordham, QC;
A. J. Forrest; R. Foster, QC; R. M. Foster;
R. H. K. Frisby, QC; J. H. Fryer-Spedding, OBE;
M. T. Fugard, CB; W. M. Gage, QC; M. Gale, QC;
C. J. E. Gardner; J. W. Gaskell; R. C. Gaskell;
S. A. G. L. Gault; J. R. B. Geake; A. C. Geddes;
A. H. Gee, QC; D. S. Geey; W. George; J. S. Gibbons;
C. A. H. Gibson; N. B. D. Gilmour, QC; L. Giovene;
A. T. Glass, QC; H. B. Globe; H. K. Goddard, QC;
H. A. Godfrey, QC; Ms L. S. Godfrey, QC;
J. J. Goldberg, QC; J. B. Goldring, QC; A. R. Goldsack, QC;
P. H. Goldsmith, QC; L. C. Goldstone, QC;
I. F. Goldsworthy; A. J. J. Gompertz, QC; A. A. Gordon;
J. P. Gorman, QC; T. J. C. Goudie, QC; C. O. G. Gould;
A. A. Goymer; G. Gozem; A. S. Grabiner, QC; R. A. Grant;
C. A. St J. Gray, QC; G. Gray, QC; J. M. Gray;
R. M. K. Gray, QC; H. Green, QC; J. C. Greenwood;
J. G. Grenfell; R. D. Grey, QC; J. Griffiths, CMG, QC;
J. P. G. Griffiths; L. Griffiths; J. D. Griggs; M. G. Grills;
M. S. E. Grime, QC; Mrs H. M. Grindrod, QC; P. Grobel;
M. A. W. Grundy; S. J. Gullick; A. S. Hacking, QC;
M. F. Haigh; J. W. Haines; D. R. Halbert; D. J. Hale;
V. E. Hall; J. P. N. Hallam; D. T. Hallchurch;
Ms H. C. Hallett, QC; A. W. Hamilton, QC;
D. R. D. Hamilton; G. M. Hamilton, TD, QC; J. Hampton;
J. L. Hand, QC; Miss R. S. A. Hare, QC; R. D. Harman, QC;
P. J. Harrington; D. M. Harris, QC; R. M. Harrison, QC;
H. M. Harrod; C. P. Hart-Leverton, QC; B. Harvey;
C. S. Harvey, MBE, TD; M. L. T. Harvey, QC;
T. S. A. Hawkesworth, QC; R. W. P. Hay;
Prof. D. J. Hayton; R. Hayward-Smith, QC; A. J. Healey;
M. J. Heath; T. B. Hegarty; G. E. Heggs;
R. A. Henderson, QC; R. H. Q. Henriques, QC;
P. J. M. Heppel; R. C. Herman; M. S. Heslop;
R. B. Hickman; B. J. Higgs, QC; E. M. Hill, QC;
J. W. Hillyer; A. J. H. Hilton, QC; Ms E. J. Hindley;
W. T. J. Hirst; J. D. Hitchen; S. A. Hockman, QC;
C. R. Hodson; The Hon. Mary Hogg, QC;

A. J. C. Hoggett, QC; Ms B. M. Hoggett, QC;
D. A. Hollis, VRD, QC; E. J. Holman, QC; R. C. Holman;
C. J. Holmes; J. F. Holt; R. M. Hone; A. T. Hoolahan, QC;
A. Hooper, QC; The Lord Hooson, QC; P. J. C. R. Hooton;
K. A. D. Hornby; M. Horowitz, QC; C. P. Hotten;
B. F. Houlder; R. Houlker, QC;
The Rt. Hon. M. Howard, QC, MP; M. N. Howard, QC;
C. I. Howells; M. J. Hubbard, QC; M. Hucker;
A. P. G. Hughes, QC; P. T. Hughes; R. P. Hughes;
T. M. Hughes; J. Hugill, QC; L. D. Hull; D. P. Hunt;
D. R. N. Hunt, QC; P. J. Hunt, QC; I. G. A. Hunter, QC;
M. Hussain, QC; B. A. Hytner, QC; A. B. Issard-Davies;
D. G. A. Jackson; M. R. Jackson; R. M. Jackson, QC;
I. E. Jacob; P. J. Jacobs; C. E. F. James;
N. F. B. Jarman; J. M. Jarvis, QC; A. H. Jeffreys;
D. A. Jeffreys, QC; J. Jeffs, QC; J. D. Jenkins, QC;
D. B. Johnson, QC; M. H. Johnson; G. R. Jones;
R. A. Jones; S. E. Jones; T. G. Jones; T. J. C. Joseph;
W. H. Joss; H. M. Joy; P. S. L. Joyce, QC;
M. D. L. Kalisher, QC; M. L. Kallipetis, QC; S. S. Katkhuda;
M. R. Kay, QC; M. L. Keane; D. N. Keating, QC;
K. R. Keen, QC; D. W. Keene, QC; B. R. Keith, QC;
C. L. Kelly; C. J. B. Kemp; D. A. M. Kemp, QC;
D. Kennett Brown; L. D. Kershen, QC; G. M. Khayat, QC;
R. I. Kidwell, QC; T. R. King; T. R. A. King, QC;
W. M. Kingston, QC; R. C. Klevan, QC; B. J. Knight, QC;
M. S. Knott; Miss P. E. Knowles; S. E. Kramer;
Miss L. J. Kushner, QC; P. E. Kyte; L. P. Laity;
P. M. Lakin; C. A. Lamb; D. G. Lane, QC;
G. J. H. Langley, QC; R. B. Latham, QC; S. W. Lawler, QC;
I. J. Lawrence, QC, MP; M. H. Lawson, QC; G. S. Lawson
Rogers; L. D. Lawton, QC; D. Lederman, QC;
M. K. Lee, QC; B. W. T. Leech; J. Leeming, QC;
C. H. de V. Leigh, QC; Sir Godfrey Le Quesne, QC;
A. P. Lester, QC; H. B. G. Lett; B. H. Leveson, QC;
S. Levine; A. E. Levy, QC; M. E. Lewer, QC;
A. K. Lewis, QC; B. W. Lewis; M. ap G. Lewis, QC;
R. S. Lewis; C. C. D. Lindsay, QC; S. J. Linehan, QC;
J. S. Lipton; B. J. E. Livesey, QC; C. G. Llewellyn-Jones, QC;
H. J. Lloyd, QC; S. H. Lloyd; J. Lloyd-Eley, QC;
A. J. C. Lodge, QC; A. C. Loughran, QC; D. C. Lovell-
Pank, QC; R. P. Lowden; G. W. Lowe; N. H. Lowe;
G. W. Lowther; F. D. L. Loy; G. Lumley;
Rt. Hon. Sir Nicholas Lyell, QC, MP; E. Lyons, QC;
D. L. McCarthy; A. W. McCreath; A. G. MacDuff, QC;
D. D. McEvoy, QC; R. D. Machell, QC; B. M. McIntyre;
C. C. Mackay, QC; T. N. MacKean; D. L. Mackie;
I. McLeod; N. R. B. Macleod, QC; N. J. C. McLusky;
J. B. MacMillan; T. Maher; A. R. Malcolm;
The Baroness Mallalieu, QC; J. H. Mance, QC;
M. E. Mann, QC; The Hon. G. R. J. Mansfield;
A. C. B. Markham-David; A. S. Marron, QC;
R. G. Marshall-Andrews, QC; D. N. N. Martineau;
H. R. A. Martineau; C. G. Masterman; D. Matheson, QC;
P. R. Matthews; P. B. Mauleverer, QC; R. B. Mawrey, QC;
R. Maxwell, QC; M. Meggeson; D. B. Meier;
N. F. Merriman, QC; J. T. Milford, QC; R. A. Miller;
S. M. Miller, QC; J. B. M. Milmo, QC;
N. A. Miscampbell, QC, MP; C. R. Mitchell; D. C. Mitchell;
F. I. Mitchell; N. J. Mitchell; J. E. Mitting, QC;
E. G. Moelwyn-Hughes; C. R. D. Moger, QC;
H. J. Montlake; R. J. Moore; M. J. Moore-Bick, QC;
M. G. C. Moorhouse; H. M. Morgan; G. E. Moriarty, QC;
T. R. A. Morison, QC; A. P. Morris, QC; D. G. Morris; The
Rt. Hon. J. Morris, QC, MP; J. I. Morris; W. P. Morris;
C. Morris-Coole; T. J. Mort; A. G. Moses, QC; C. J. Moss;
R. T. Moss; P. C. Mott, QC; R. W. Moxon-Browne, QC;
J. H. Muir; J. Mulcahy, QC; F. J. Muller, QC;
I. P. Murphy, QC; M. J. A. Murphy; N. J. Mylne, QC;

H. G. Narayan; T. M. E. Nash; R. F. Nelson, QC;
D. E. Neuberger, QC; R. E. Newbold;
A. R. H. Newman, QC; G. M. Newman, QC; G. Nice, QC;
C. A. A. Nicholls, QC; C. V. Nicholls, QC; M. C. Nicholson;
A. S. T. E. Nicol; B. Nolan, QC; Col. A. P. Norris, OBE;
P. H. Norris; J. G. Nutting; D. P. O'Brien, QC;
E. M. Ogden, QC; B. R. Oliver; S. Oliver-Jones;
C. P. L. Openshaw, QC; R. C. C. O'Rorke; G. V. Owen, QC;
R. M. Owen, QC; S. R. Page; D. C. J. Paget;
A. O. Palmer, QC; A. W. Palmer, QC; A. D. W. Pardoe, QC;
S. A. B. Parish; A. E. W. Park, QC; G. C. Parkins, QC;
G. E. Parkinson; M. P. Parroy, QC; D. J. Parry;
D. J. T. Parry; E. O. Parry; M. A. Parry Evans;
N. S. K. Pascoe, QC; A. Patience, QC; J. G. Paulusz;
Mrs N. Pearce; Prof. D. S. Pearl; R. J. Pearse Wheatley;
B. P. Pearson; D. H. Penry-Davey, QC; Sir Ian Percival, QC;
J. Perry, QC; M. Pert, QC; B. J. Phelvin; J. A. Phillips;
W. B. Phillips; J. C. Phipps; M. A. Pickering, QC;
C. J. Pitchford, QC; The Hon. B. M. D. Pitt; A. P. Pitts;
Miss E. F. Platt, QC; J. R. Playford, QC; A. G. S. Pollock, QC;
T. G. Pontius; D. A. Poole, QC; A. R. Porten, QC;
L. R. Portnoy; W. D. C. Poulton; M. J. Pratt, QC; S. Pratt;
T. W. Preston, QC; G. A. L. Price, QC; J. A. Price, QC;
N. P. L. Price, QC; R. N. M. Price; A. C. Pugh, QC;
G. V. Pugh, QC; C. P. B. Purchas, QC; R. M. Purchas, QC;
N. R. Purnell, QC; P. O. Purnell, QC; Q. C. W. Querelle;
D. A. Radcliffe; D. W. Radford; Ms A. J. Rafferty, QC;
A. Rankin, QC; A. D. Rawley, QC; P. R. Raynor;
L. F. Read, QC; A. R. F. Redgrave; J. Reeder, QC; P. Rees;
J. R. Reid, QC; P. C. Reid; M. P. Reynolds; P. C. Rhodes;
R. E. Rhodes, QC; D. G. Rice; D. W. Richards;
H. A. Richardson; N. P. Riddell; S. V. Riordan, QC;
Miss J. H. Ritchie, QC; Miss S. A. Ritchie, QC;
S. D. Robbins; J. A. Roberts, QC; J. D. Roberts;
J. M. G. Roberts, QC; P. B. Roberts; P. E. Robertshaw;
V. Robinson, QC; D. E. H. Robson, QC; G. W. Roddick, QC;
Miss D. J. Rodgers; J. M. T. Rogers, QC; K. S. Rokison, QC;
J. G. Ross Martyn; P. C. Rouch; J. J. Rowe, QC;
R. J. Royce, QC; R. J. Rubery; A. A. Rumbelow, QC;
A. P. Russell; R. R. Russell; A. Rutherford; G. C. Ryan, QC;
J. R. T. Rylance; J. E. A. Samuels, QC; A. T. Sander;
G. R. Sankey, QC; J. H. B. Saunders, QC; M. P. Sayers, QC;
R. J. Scholes, QC; A. R. G. Scott-Gall; R. J. Seabrook, QC;
C. Seagroatt, QC; H. M. Self, QC; M. R. Selfe; O. M. Sells;
J. S. Sennitt; D. Serota, QC; A. J. Seys-Llewellyn;
A. R. F. Sharp; P. P. Shears; S. J. Sher, QC;
J. M. Shorrock, QC; S. R. Silber, QC; P. F. Singer;
J. C. N. Slater, QC; E. Slinger; A. T. Smith, QC;
R. D. H. Smith, QC; R. S. Smith, QC; W. P. Smith;
Ms Z. P. Smith; S. M. Solley, QC; R. F. Solman; E. Somerset
Jones, QC; R. C. E. Southwell; Miss J. M. Southworth, QC;
M. H. Spence, QC; Sir Derek Spencer, QC, MP;
J. Spencer, QC; M. G. Spencer, QC; R. V. Spencer Bernard;
S. M. Spencer, QC; L. Spittle; J. A. C. Spokes, QC;
R. W. Spon-Smith; D. P. Stanley; D. W. Steel, QC;
D. Steer, QC; M. T. Steiger; D. H. Stembridge, QC;
Mrs L. J. Stern, QC; A. W. Stevenson, TD;
J. S. H. Stewart, QC; R. M. Stewart, QC; G. J. C. Still;
D. A. Stockdale; D. M. A. Stokes, QC; M. G. T. Stokes;
E. D. R. Stone, QC; P. L. Storr; T. M. F. Stow, QC;
D. M. A. Strachan, QC; J. M. Stuart-Moore, QC; F. R. C. Such;
A. B. Suckling, QC; J. M. Sullivan, QC; Ms L. E. Sullivan;
D. M. Sumner; J. P. C. Sumption, QC; P. J. Susman;
D. R. Swift; L. Swift, QC; M. R. Swift, QC; C. J. M. Symons;
J. A. Tackaberry, QC; R. K. K. Talbot; G. F. Tattersall, QC;
E. Taylor; N. Taylor, QC; J. J. Teare; A. D. Temple, QC;
V. B. A. Temple, QC; M. I. Tennant;
D. M. Thomas, OBE, QC; D. O. Thomas, QC;
R. J. L. Thomas, QC; R. L. Thomas; R. U. Thomas, QC;

P. J. Thompson; A. C. L. Thornton, QC; J. Tiley;
M. B. Tillett; J. W. Tinnion; R. N. Titheridge, QC;
J. K. Toulmin, QC; R. G. Toulson, QC; J. B. S. Townend, QC;
C. M. Treacy, QC; H. B. Trethowan; A. D. H. Trollope, QC;
H. W. Turcan; D. A. Turner, QC; P. A. Twigg, QC;
A. R. Tyrrell, QC; J. G. G. Ungley; N. P. Valios, QC;
A. R. Vandermeer, QC; M. J. D. Vere-Hodge;
C. D. Voelcker; J. P. Wadsworth, QC; D. St J. Wagstaff;
S. P. Waine; J. J. Wait; R. Wakefield; R. M. Wakerley, QC;
W. H. Waldron, QC; J. D. G. Walford; R. A. Walker, QC;
R. J. Walker, QC; T. E. Walker, QC; J. J. Walker-Smith;
S. P. Waller; B. Walsh, QC; C. T. Walton; J. C. Warner;
J. Warren; D. E. B. Waters; Sir James Watson, Bt.;
C. D. G. Waud; B. J. Waylen; A. R. Webb; R. S. Webb, QC;
P. A. Webster; M. Weisman; P. Weitzman, QC;
C. P. C. Whelon; G. Whitburn, QC; C. H. Whitby, QC;
W. J. M. White; D. R. B. Whitehouse, QC;
P. G. Whiteman, QC; P. J. M. Whiteman, TD;
A. Whitfield, QC; D. G. Widdicombe, QC; R. Wigglesworth;
J. S. Wiggs; A. D. F. Wilcken; K. H. P. Wilkinson;
N. V. M. Wilkinson; D. B. Williams;
G. H. G. Williams, QC; Lord Williams of Mostyn, QC;
J. G. Williams, QC; J. L. Williams, QC; The
Hon. J. M. Williams, QC; M. J. Williams;
W. L. Williams, QC; S. W. Williamson, QC;
A. M. Wilson, QC; C. Wilson-Smith, QC; G. W. Wingate-
Saul, QC; M. E. Wolff; J. S. Wolstenholme; H. Wolton, QC;
D. A. Wood, QC; D. R. Wood; N. A. Wood; W. R. Wood;
L. G. Woodley, QC; Miss S. Woodley; J. T. Woods;
W. C. Woodward, QC; D. R. Woolley, QC; N. G. Wootton;
A. M. Worrall, QC; N. J. Worsley, QC; P. F. Worsley, QC;
D. E. M. Young, QC

STIPENDIARY MAGISTRATES

PROVINCIAL (each £54,035)

Cheshire, P. K. Dodd, OBE, *apptd* 1991
East and West Sussex, P. C. Tain, *apptd* 1992
Greater Manchester, W. D. Fairclough, *apptd* 1982;
   C. T. Latham, OBE, *apptd* 1976; Miss J. E. Hayward,
   apptd 1991
Hampshire, T. G. Cowling, *apptd* 1989
Humberside, N. H. White, *apptd* 1985
Lancashire/Merseyside, J. Finestein, *apptd* 1992
Merseyside, N. G. Wootton, *apptd* 1976; D. R. G. Tapp,
   apptd 1992
Middlesex, N. A. McKittrick, *apptd* 1989; S. Somjee, *apptd*
   1991; S. N. Day, *apptd* 1991
Mid Glamorgan, B. R. Oliver, *apptd* 1983; J. T. Curran,
   apptd 1990
North-East London, G. E. Cawdron, *apptd* 1993
Nottinghamshire, P. F. Nuttall, *apptd* 1991; M. L. R. Harris,
   apptd 1991
South Glamorgan, vacant
South Yorkshire, I. W. Crompton, *apptd* 1983; J. A. Browne,
   apptd 1992; J. E. Barry, *apptd* 1985; W. D. Thomas,
   apptd 1989
Staffordshire, P. G. G. Richards, *apptd* 1991
West Midlands, W. M. Probert, *apptd* 1983; B. Morgan,
   apptd 1989; I. Gillespie, *apptd* 1991; M. F. James, *apptd*
   1991
West Yorkshire, F. D. L. Loy, *apptd* 1972; Mrs P. A. Hewitt,
   apptd 1990

METROPOLITAN
*Chief Metropolitan Stipendiary Magistrate and Chairman of
Committee of Magistrates for Inner London Area* (£69,924),
   P. G. N. Badge, *apptd* 1992 (*Bow Street*)

Magistrates (each £54,035)
Bow Street, The Chief Magistrate; R. D. Bartle, *apptd* 1972;
   J. G. Connor, *apptd* 1979; C. S. F. Black, *apptd* 1993
Camberwell Green, C. P. M. Davidson, *apptd* 1984;
   Mrs H. Mitcham, *apptd* 1986; T. H. Workman, *apptd*
   1986; H. Gott, *apptd* 1992; P. S. Wallis, *apptd* 1993
Clerkenwell, M. L. R. Romer, *apptd* 1972; C. J. Bourke,
   apptd 1972; B. Loosley, *apptd* 1989
Greenwich and Woolwich, Mrs K. R. Keating, *apptd* 1987;
   W. A. Kennedy, *apptd* 1991; D. A. Cooper, *apptd* 1991
Highbury Corner, D. Barr, *apptd* 1976; Miss D. Quick, *apptd*
   1986; G. Wicks, *apptd* 1987; D. B. Meier, *apptd* 1985
Horseferry Road, A. R. Davies, *apptd* 1985; R. T. Moss,
   apptd 1984; T. Maher, *apptd* 1983; G. Breen, *apptd* 1986
Marlborough Street, J. Q. Campbell, *apptd* 1981; Sir Bryan
   Roberts, KCMG, QC, *apptd* 1982
Marylebone, G. L. J. Noel, *apptd* 1975; A. C. Baldwin, *apptd*
   1990; T. English, *apptd* 1986; K. Maitland-Davies, *apptd*
   1984
Old Street, Miss G. B. Babington-Browne, *apptd* 1991;
   M. A. Johnstone, *apptd* 1980
South-Western, S. G. Clixby, *apptd* 1981; C. D. Voelcker,
   apptd 1982; A. Ormerod, *apptd* 1988
Thames, D. M. Fingleton, *apptd* 1980; Miss D. Wickham,
   apptd 1989; G. E. Parkinson, *apptd* 1982; N. Crichton,
   apptd 1987
Tower Bridge, Mrs J. R. Comyns, *apptd* 1982; R. D. Philips,
   apptd 1989; M. Kelly, *apptd* 1992
Wells Street, Miss A. M. Jennings, *apptd* 1972; I. M. Baker,
   apptd 1990; C. L. Pratt, *apptd* 1990
West London, H. J. Cook, *apptd* 1975; D. Kennett Brown,
   apptd 1982
Unattached Magistrates, D. L. Thomas, *apptd* 1990; I. Bing,
   apptd 1989; A. Evans, *apptd* 1990; D. Simpson, *apptd*
   1993; M. J. Read, *apptd* 1993

COMMITTEE OF MAGISTRATES FOR INNER
LONDON AREA
65 Romney Street, London SW1P 3RD
Tel 071–799 3332
Principal Chief Clerk and Clerk to the Committee (£53,023),
   I. Fowler, OBE
Chief Clerk (*Training*) (£47,848), P. Unwin

CROWN PROSECUTION SERVICE
50 Ludgate Hill, London EC4M 7EX
Tel 071–273 8000

The Crown Prosecution Service (CPS) is responsible for the
independent review and conduct of criminal proceedings
instituted by police forces in England and Wales (with the
exception of cases conducted by the Serious Fraud Office and
certain minor cases).
   The Director of Public Prosecutions is the head of the CPS
and discharges her statutory functions under the superintendence of the Attorney-General.
   The CPS comprises a headquarters office and 13 areas
covering England and Wales. Each of the CPS areas is
supervised by a Chief Crown Prosecutor.

For salaries, *see* page 282

Director of Public Prosecutions (G1), Mrs B. Mills, QC

Principal Establishment and Finance Officer (G3),
  D. J. Wiblin, CB
Director (Casework) (G3), C. Newell
Director (Operations) (G3), G. Duff
Director (Policy) (G3), K. Ashken

CPS AREAS

CPS ANGLIA, Queens House, 58 Victoria Street, St Albans
  ALI 3HZ. Tel: 0727–844753. *Chief Crown Prosecutor (G4)*,
  R. J. Chronnell
CPS EAST MIDLANDS, 2 King Edward Court, King
  Edward Street, Nottingham NGI IEL. Tel: 0602–480480.
  Chief Crown Prosecutor (G4), B. T. McArdle
CPS HUMBER, Belgrave House, 47 Bank Street, Sheffield
  SI 2EH. Tel: 0742–761601. *Chief Crown Prosecutor (G4)*,
  D. Adams
CPS LONDON, 24th Floor, Portland House, Stag Place,
  London SWIE 5BH. Tel: 071-828 9050. *Chief Crown
  Prosecutor (G3)*, G. D. Etherington
CPS MERSEY/LANCASHIRE, 7th Floor (South), Royal
  Liver Building, Pier Head, Liverpool L3 1HN. Tel: 051–
  236 7575. *Chief Crown Prosecutor (G4)*, E. C. Woodcock

CPS MIDLANDS, 6th Floor, Dale House, 31 Dale End,
  Birmingham B4 7LN. Tel: 021-233 3133. *Chief Crown
  Prosecutor (G4)*, T. M. McGowran
CPS NORTH, Benton House, 136 Sandyford Road,
  Newcastle upon Tyne NE2 1QE. Tel: 091–230 0800. *Chief
  Crown Prosecutor (G4)*, D. V. Dickenson
CPS NORTH-WEST, PO Box 377, 8th Floor, Sunlight
  House, Quay Street, Manchester M60 3LU. Tel: 061–837
  7402. *Chief Crown Prosecutor (G4)*, A. R. Taylor
CPS SEVERN/THAMES, Orchard House, Victoria Square,
  Droitwich, Worcester WR9 8QT. Tel: 0905–779502. *Chief
  Crown Prosecutor (G4)*, A. S. R. Clarke
CPS SOUTH-EAST, Stoke Mill, Woking Road, Guildford,
  Surrey GUI 1AQ. Tel: 0483-573255. *Chief Crown
  Prosecutor (G4)*, D. E. J. Dracup
CPS SOUTH-WEST, Hawkins House, Pynes Hill, Rydon
  Lane, Exeter EX2 5SS. Tel: 0392-422555. *Chief Crown
  Prosecutor (G4)*, P. Boeuf
CPS WALES, 21st Floor, Pearl Assurance House,
  Greyfriars Road, Cardiff CFI 3PL. Tel: 0222-382777.
  Chief Crown Prosecutor (G4), R. A. Prickett
CPS YORKSHIRE, 6th Floor, Ryedale Building, 60
  Piccadilly, York YOI INS. Tel: 0904-610726. *Chief Crown
  Prosecutor (G4)*, D. M. Sharp

The Scottish Judicature

Scotland has a legal system separate from and differing greatly from the English legal system in enacted law, judicial procedure and the structure of courts.

There is in Scotland a system of public prosecution headed by the Lord Advocate which is independent of the police, who have no say in the decision to prosecute. The Lord Advocate, discharging his functions through the Crown Office in Edinburgh, is responsible for prosecutions in the High Court, sheriff courts and district courts. Prosecutions in the High Court are prepared by the Crown Office and conducted in court by one of the law officers, by an advocate-depute, or by a solicitor advocate. In the inferior courts the decision to prosecute is made and prosecution is preferred by procurators fiscal, who are lawyers and full-time civil servants, subject to the directions of the Crown Office. A permanent legally-qualified civil servant known as the Crown Agent is responsible for the running of the Crown Office and the organization of the Procurator Fiscal Service, of which he is the head.

Scotland is divided into six Sheriffdoms, each with a full-time Sheriff Principal. The Sheriffdoms are further divided into sheriff court districts, each of which has a legally-qualified, resident sheriff or sheriffs, who are the judges of the court.

In criminal cases sheriffs principal and sheriffs have the same powers; sitting with a jury of 15 members, they may try more serious cases on indictment, or, sitting alone, may try lesser cases under summary procedure. Minor summary offences are dealt with in district courts which are administered by the district and the islands local government authorities and presided over by lay justices of the peace (of whom there are about 4,400) and, in Glasgow only, by stipendiary magistrates. Juvenile offenders (children under 16) may be brought before an informal children's hearing comprising three local lay people. The superior criminal court is the High Court of Justiciary which is both a trial and an appeal court. Cases on indictment are tried by a High

Court judge, sitting with a jury of 15, in Edinburgh and on circuit in other towns. Appeals from the lower courts against conviction or sentence are heard also by the High Court, which sits as an appeal court only in Edinburgh. There is no further appeal to the House of Lords in criminal cases.

In civil cases the jurisdiction of the sheriff court extends to most kinds of action. Appeal against decisions of the sheriff may be made to the Sheriff Principal and thence to the Court of Session, or direct to the Court of Session, which sits only in Edinburgh. The Court of Session is divided into the Inner and the Outer House. The Outer House is a court of first instance in which cases are heard by judges sitting singly, sometimes with a jury of 12. The Inner House, itself subdivided into two divisions of equal status, is mainly an appeal court. Appeals may be made to the Inner House from the Outer House as well as from the sheriff court. An appeal may be made from the Inner House to the House of Lords.

The judges of the Court of Session are the same as those of the High Court of Justiciary, the Lord President of the Court of Session also holding the office of Lord Justice General in the High Court. Senators of the College of Justice are Lords Commissioners of Justiciary as well as judges of the Court of Session.

The office of coroner does not exist in Scotland. The local procurator fiscal inquires privately into sudden and suspicious deaths and may report findings to the Crown Agent. In some cases a fatal accident inquiry may be held before the sheriff.

COURT OF SESSION AND HIGH COURT OF JUSTICIARY

The Lord President and Lord Justice General (£103,790)
  The Rt. Hon. Lord Hope (David Hope), *born* 1938, *apptd*
  1989

INNER HOUSE

Lords of Session (each £99,510)

FIRST DIVISION
The Lord President
Hon. Lord Allanbridge (William Stewart), *born* 1925, *apptd*
1977
Hon. Lord Cowie (William Cowie), *born* 1926, *apptd* 1977
Hon. Lord Mayfield (Ian MacDonald, MC), *born* 1921, *apptd*
1981

SECOND DIVISION
Lord Justice Clerk (£100,510), The Rt. Hon. Lord Ross
(Donald Ross), *born* 1927, *apptd* 1985
Rt. Hon. Lord Murray (Ronald Murray), *born* 1922, *apptd*
1979
Hon. The Lord McCluskey, *born* 1929, *apptd* 1984
Hon. Lord Morison (Alastair Morison), *born* 1931, *apptd*
1985

OUTER HOUSE

Lords of Session (each £90,148)

Hon. Lord Davidson (Charles Davidson) (*seconded to
Scottish Law Commission*), *born* 1929, *apptd* 1983
Hon. Lord Sutherland (Ranald Sutherland), *born* 1932,
apptd 1985
Hon. Lord Weir (David Weir), *born* 1931, *apptd* 1985
Hon. Lord Clyde (James Clyde), *born* 1932, *apptd* 1985
Hon. Lord Cullen (Douglas Cullen), *born* 1935, *apptd* 1986
Hon. Lord Prosser (William Prosser), *born* 1934, *apptd* 1986
Hon. Lord Kirkwood (Ian Kirkwood), *born* 1932, *apptd*
1987
Hon. Lord Coulsfield (John Cameron), *born* 1934, *apptd*
1987
Hon. Lord Milligan (James Milligan), *born* 1934, *apptd* 1988
Hon. The Lord Morton of Shuna, *born* 1930, *apptd* 1988
Hon. Lord Caplan (Philip Caplan), *born* 1929, *apptd* 1989
Rt. Hon. The Lord Cameron of Lochbroom, *born* 1931,
apptd 1989
Hon. Lord Marnoch (Michael Bruce), *born* 1938, *apptd* 1990
Hon. Lord MacLean (Ranald MacLean), *born* 1938, *apptd*
1990
Hon. Lord Penrose (George Penrose), *born* 1938, *apptd*
1990
Hon. Lord Osborne (Kenneth Osborne), *born* 1937, *apptd*
1990
Hon. Lord Abernethy (John Cameron), *born* 1938, *apptd*
1992

COURT OF SESSION AND HIGH COURT OF
JUSTICIARY
Parliament House, Parliament Square, Edinburgh EH1 1RQ
Tel 031-225 2595

Principal Clerk of Session and Justiciary (£36,019–£47,921),
H. S. Foley
Deputy Principal Clerk of Justiciary and Administration
(£27,660–£42,724), E. Cumming
Deputy Principal Clerk of Session and Principal Extractor
(£27,660–£42,724), M. Weir
Deputy Principal Clerk (Keeper of the Rolls) (£27,660–
£42,724), M. G. Bonar
Depute Clerks of Session and Justiciary (£17,535–£24,780),
T. D. McIntosh; A. Hogg; N. J. Dowie; J. M. Clark;
I. Smith; J. A. R. Cowie; T. Higgins; T. B. Cruickshank;
Q. Oliver; F. Shannly; R. D. Sinclair; Mrs A. Leighton;
T. M. Thomson; D. D. Mackay; A. S. Moffat;

J. Atkinson; D. J. Shand; G. Ellis; Mrs G. McKeand;
D. G. Lynn; R. Cockburn; W. Dunn; A. Finlayson

SCOTTISH COURTS ADMINISTRATION
26–27 Royal Terrace, Edinburgh EH7 5AH
Tel 031-556 0755

Director, G. Murray

SHERIFF COURT OF CHANCERY
16 North Bank Street, Edinburgh EH1 2NH
Tel 031-226 7181

The Court settles disputes related to unclaimed estates of
deceased persons, and other related matters.
Sheriff of Chancery, C. G. B. Nicholson, QC

HM COMMISSARY OFFICE
16 North Bank Street, Edinburgh EH1 2NJ
Tel 031-226 7181

The Office is responsible for issuing confirmation, a legal
document entitling a person to execute a deceased person's
will, and other related matters.
Commissary Clerk, I. E. Scott

SCOTTISH LAND COURT
1 Grosvenor Crescent, Edinburgh EH12 5ER
Tel 031-225 3595

The court deals with disputes relating to agricultural and
crofting land in Scotland.
Chairman (£78,378), The Hon. Lord Philip (Alexander
Philip), QC
Members, D. D. McDiarmid; D. M. MacDonald; J. Kinloch
(*part-time*)
Principal Clerk, K. H. R. Graham

SHERIFFDOMS

SALARIES
Sheriff Principal	£78,378
Sheriff	£65,912
Regional Sheriff Clerk	£27,660–£42,724
Sheriff Clerk	£14,019–£47,921

*Floating Sheriff

GRAMPIAN, HIGHLANDS AND ISLANDS
Sheriff Principal, D. J. Risk
Regional Sheriff Clerk, J. Robertson

SHERIFFS AND SHERIFF CLERKS
Aberdeen and Stonehaven, D. W. Bogie; G. C. Warner;
D. Kelbie; L. A. S. Jessop; *Sheriff Clerks*, J. Rodden;
W. A. Mouser
Peterhead and Banff, K. A. McLernan; *Sheriff Clerk*,
H. Hempseed; *Sheriff Clerk Depute*, W. H. Connon
Elgin, N. McPartlin; *Sheriff Clerk*, A. Lynch
*Inverness, Lochmaddy, Portree, Stornoway, Dingwall, Tain,
Wick and Dornoch*, W. J. Fulton; D. Booker-Milburn;
J. O. A. Fraser; E. Stewart; *Sheriff Clerk*, J. Robertson
Kirkwall and Lerwick, G. S. MacKenzie; *Sheriff Clerks
Depute*, Miss H. M. Phillips; A. C. Norris
Fort William, D. Noble (also *Oban and Campbeltown*);
Sheriff Clerk Depute, C. Morrison

TAYSIDE, CENTRAL AND FIFE

Sheriff Principal, J. J. Maguire, QC
Regional Sheriff Clerk, J. S. Doig

SHERIFFS AND SHERIFF CLERKS
Arbroath and Forfar, K. A. Veal; G. N. R. Stein; *Sheriff Clerks*, M. Herbertson; P. Dougan
Dundee, G. L. Cox; A. L. Stewart; *Sheriff Clerk*, J. S. Doig
Perth, J. F. Wheatley; J. C. McInnes, QC; *Sheriff Clerk*, W. Jones
Falkirk, A. V. Sheehan; A. J. Murphy; *Sheriff Clerk*, D. Nicoll
Stirling, A. Pollock; R. E. G. Younger; *Sheriff Clerk*, P. Crow
Alloa, R. E. G. Younger; *Sheriff Clerk*, J. M. Murphy
Cupar, C. Smith (also *Dundee*); *Sheriff Clerk*, B. Sullivan
Dunfermline, J. S. Forbes; W. M. Reid; *Sheriff Clerk*, J. Ross
Kirkcaldy, W. J. Christie; Mrs L. G. Patrick; *Sheriff Clerk*, I. Hay

LOTHIAN AND BORDERS

Sheriff Principal, C. G. B. Nicholson, QC
Regional Sheriff Clerk, I. E. Scott

SHERIFFS AND SHERIFF CLERKS
Edinburgh, N. E. D. Thomson; J. L. M. Mitchell; P. G. B. McNeill, PH.D., QC; Miss H. J. Aronson, QC; R. G. Craik, QC; G. I. W. Shiach; Miss I. A. Poole; R. J. D. Scott; A. M. Bell; J. M. S. Horsburgh, QC; G. W. S. Presslie; *J. A. Farrell; A. Lothian; *Sheriff Clerk*, I. E. Scott
Peebles, N. E. D. Thomson, CBE (also *Edinburgh*); *Sheriff Clerk*, I. E. Scott
Linlithgow, M. Stone; G. R. Fleming; *Sheriff Clerk*, R. Sinclair
Haddington, G. W. S. Presslie (also *Edinburgh*); *Sheriff Clerk*, B. W. S. Manthorpe
Jedburgh and Duns, J. V. Paterson; *Sheriff Clerk*, J. W. Williamson
Selkirk, J. V. Paterson; *Sheriff Clerk*, L. McFarlane

NORTH STRATHCLYDE

Sheriff Principal, R. C. Hay, CBE
Regional Sheriff Clerk, A. A. Brown

SHERIFFS AND SHERIFF CLERKS
Oban and Campbeltown, D. Noble (also *Fort William*); *Sheriff Clerk Deputes*, W. M. Cochrane; K. L. Graham
Dumbarton, J. T. Fitzsimons; T. Scott; S. W. H. Fraser; *Sheriff Clerk*, N. R. Weir
Paisley, R. G. Smith; C. N. Stoddart; J. Spy; C. K. Higgins; C. W. Palmer; *C. G. McKay; *Sheriff Clerk*, A. A. Brown
Greenock, J. Herald (also *Rothesay*); Sir Stephen Young; *Sheriff Clerk*, P. G. Corcoran
Kilmarnock, T. M. Croan; D. B. Smith; T. F. Russell; *Sheriff Clerk*, J. Shaw
Dunoon, A. Noble (also *Dumbarton*); *Sheriff Clerk Depute*, Mrs C. Carson

GLASGOW AND STRATHKELVIN

Sheriff Principal, N. D. MacLeod, QC
Regional Sheriff Clerk, C. McLay

SHERIFFS AND SHERIFF CLERKS
Glasgow, A. C. Horsfall, QC (*seconded to Scottish Lands Tribunal*); A. A. Bell, QC; B. Kearney; G. H. Gordon, QC;

A. C. McKay; J. C. M. Jardine; Mrs D. J. B. Robertson; B. A. Lockhart; I. G. Pirie; Mrs A. L. A. Duncan; W. G. Stevenson, QC; G. J. Evans; E. H. Galt; F. J. Keane; A. C. Henry; J. K. Mitchell; A. G. Johnston; J. P. Murphy; M. Sischy; S. A. O. Raeburn; A. B. Wilkinson; *Sheriff Clerk*, C. McLay

SOUTH STRATHCLYDE, DUMFRIES AND GALLOWAY

Sheriff Principal, J. S. Mowat, QC
Regional Sheriff Clerk, H. Findlay

SHERIFFS AND SHERIFF CLERKS
Hamilton, L. S. Lovat; A. C. MacPherson; W. F. Lunny; D. G. Russell; V. J. Canavan (also *Airdrie*); W. E. Gibson; H. Stirling; *C. B. Miller; *Sheriff Clerk*, J. Cumming
Lanark, J. D. Allan; *Sheriff Clerk*, D. M. Cameron
Ayr, N. Gow, QC; R. G. McEwan, QC; *Sheriff Clerk*, G. W. Waddell
Stranraer and Kirkcudbright, J. R. Smith; *Sheriff Clerk*, N. L. Hodgson; *Sheriff Clerk Depute*, B. Lindsay
Dumfries, K. G. Barr; L. Cameron; *Sheriff Clerk*, P. McGonigle
Airdrie, J. H. Stewart; V. J. Canavan (also *Hamilton*); R. H. Dickson; I. C. Simpson; *Sheriff Clerk*, H. Findlay

STIPENDIARY MAGISTRATES

GLASGOW
R. Hamilton, *apptd* 1984; J. B. C. Nisbet, *apptd* 1984; R. B. Christie, *apptd* 1985; Mrs J. A. M. MacLean, *apptd* 1990

PROCURATOR FISCAL SERVICE

CROWN OFFICE
Regent Road, Edinburgh EH7 5BL
Tel 031-557 3800
Crown Agent (£67,600), J. D. Lowe
Deputy Crown Agent (†£46,122), A. D. Vannet

PROCURATORS FISCAL

†SALARIES

Regional Procurator Fiscal–grade 3	£48,000
Regional Procurator Fiscal–grade 4	£46,122
Procurator Fiscal–upper level	£34,667–£39,402
Procurator Fiscal–lower level	£24,928–£33,921

†as at August 1992

GRAMPIAN, HIGHLANDS AND ISLANDS REGION
Regional Procurator Fiscal, S. W. Lockhart, CBE (*Aberdeen*)
Procurators Fiscal, E. K. Barbour (*Stonehaven*); A. J. M. Colley (*Banff*); I. S. McNaughtan (*Peterhead*); G. K. Buchanan (*Elgin*); A. N. MacDonald (*Wick*); C. B. McClory (*Portree and Lochmaddy*); Mrs D. Wilson (*Stornoway*); H. T. Westwater (*Dornoch and Tain*); W. W. Orr (*Inverness*); D. K. Adam (*Kirkwall and Lerwick*); Mrs A. Neizer (*Fort William*); D. R. Hingston (*Dingwall*)

TAYSIDE, CENTRAL AND FIFE REGION
Regional Procurator Fiscal, B. K. Heywood (*Dundee*)
Procurators Fiscal, Mrs B. Bott (*Arbroath*); A. L. Ingram
(*Forfar*); I. A. McLeod (*Perth*); G. E. Scott (*Falkirk*);
K. Valentine (*Stirling*); I. D. Douglas (*Alloa*);
E. B. Russell (*Cupar*); R. T. Hamilton (*Dunfermline*);
F. R. Crowe (*Kirkcaldy*)

LOTHIAN AND BORDERS REGION
Regional Procurator Fiscal, R. F. Lees (*Edinburgh*)
Procurators Fiscal, R. F. Lees (*Peebles*); H. R. Annan
(*Linlithgow*); A. J. P. Reith (*Haddington*); A. R. G. Fraser
(*Duns* and *Jedburgh*); D. McNeill (*Selkirk*)

NORTH STRATHCLYDE REGION
Regional Procurator Fiscal, J. D. Friel (*Paisley*)
Procurators Fiscal, I. Henderson (*Campbeltown*); J. Cardle
(*Dumbarton*); C. C. Donnelly (*Greenock* and *Rothesay*);
D. L. Webster (*Dunoon*); J. G. MacGlennan
(*Kilmarnock*); B. R. Maguire (*Oban*)

GLASGOW AND STRATHKELVIN REGION
Regional Procurator Fiscal, A. C. Normand (*Glasgow*)

SOUTH STRATHCLYDE, DUMFRIES AND
GALLOWAY REGION
Regional Procurator Fiscal, W. G. Carmichael (*Hamilton*)
Procurators Fiscal, S. R. Houston (*Lanark*); N. G. O'Brien
(*Ayr*); F. Walkingshaw (*Stranraer*); D. J. Howdle
(*Dumfries* and *Kirkcudbright*); A. T. Wilson (*Airdrie*)

Northern Ireland Judicature

In Northern Ireland the legal system and the structure of courts closely resemble those of England and Wales; there are, however, often differences in enacted law.

The Supreme Court of Judicature of Northern Ireland comprises the Court of Appeal, the High Court of Justice and the Crown Court. The practice and procedure of these courts is similar to that in England. The superior civil court is the High Court of Justice, from which an appeal lies to the Northern Ireland Court of Appeal; the House of Lords is the final civil appeal court.

The Crown Court, served by High Court and county court judges, deals with criminal trials on indictment. Cases are heard before a judge and, except those involving offences specified under emergency legislation, a jury. Appeals from the Crown Court against conviction or sentence are heard by the Northern Ireland Court of Appeal; the House of Lords is the final court of appeal.

The decision to prosecute in cases tried on indictment and in summary cases of a serious nature rests in Northern Ireland with the Director of Public Prosecutions, who is responsible to the Attorney-General. Minor summary offences are prosecuted by the police.

Minor criminal offences are dealt with in magistrates' courts by a full-time, legally qualified resident magistrate and, where an offender is under 17, by juvenile courts each consisting of a resident magistrate and two lay members specially qualified to deal with juveniles (at least one of whom must be a woman). There are 974 Justices of the Peace in Northern Ireland. Appeals from magistrates' courts are heard by the county court, or by the Court of Appeal on a point of law or an issue as to jurisdiction.

Magistrates' courts in Northern Ireland can deal with certain classes of civil case but most minor civil cases are dealt with in county courts. Judgments of all civil courts are enforceable through a centralized procedure administered by the Enforcement of Judgments Office.

SUPREME COURT OF JUDICATURE
The Royal Courts of Justice, Belfast BT1 3JF
Tel 0232-235111

Lord Chief Justice of Northern Ireland (£103,790),
The Rt. Hon. Sir Brian Hutton, *born* 1931, *apptd* 1988

Lords Justices of Appeal (each £99,510)
Rt. Hon. Sir Basil Kelly, *born* 1920, *apptd* 1984
Rt. Hon. Sir John MacDermott, *born* 1927, *apptd* 1987
Rt. Hon. Sir John Higgins, *born* 1927, *apptd* 1993

Puisne Judges (each £90,147)
Hon. Sir Robert Carswell, *born* 1934, *apptd* 1984
Hon. Sir Michael Nicholson, *born* 1933, *apptd* 1986
Hon. Sir William McCollum, *born* 1933, *apptd* 1987
Hon. Sir Anthony Campbell, *born* 1936, *apptd* 1988
Hon. Sir John Sheil, *born* 1938, *apptd* 1989
Hon. Sir Brian Kerr, *born* 1948, *apptd* 1993
Hon. Sir John Pringle, *born* 1929, *apptd* 1993

LORD CHIEF JUSTICE'S OFFICE
Principal Secretary to the Lord Chief Justice and Clerk of the Crown for Northern Ireland, J. A. L. McLean, QC
Legal Secretary to the Lord Chief Justice,
Mrs. D. M. Kennedy

MASTERS OF SUPREME COURT (each £54,035)
Master, Queen's Bench and Appeals, J. W. Wilson, QC
Master, High Court, vacant
Master, Office of Care and Protection, F. B. Hall
Master, Chancery Office, vacant
Master, Bankruptcy and Companies Office, J. B. C. Glass
Master, Probate and Matrimonial Office, R. T. Millar
Master, Taxing Office, J. C. Napier

COUNTY COURTS

RECORDERS (each £78,377)
Belfast, vacant
Londonderry, Judge Higgins, QC

JUDGES (each £78,377)
Rt. Hon. Judge Sir Robert Porter, QC; Judge Russell, QC;
Judge Curran, QC; Judge McKee, QC; Judge Gibson, QC;
Judge Hart, QC; Judge Petrie, QC; Judge Smyth, QC;
Judge Martin, QC; Judge Burgess

MAGISTRATES COURTS

RESIDENT MAGISTRATES (each £54,035)
There are 17 resident magistrates in Northern Ireland.

CROWN SOLICITOR'S OFFICE
PO Box 410, Royal Courts of Justice, Belfast BT1 3JY
Tel 0232–235111

Crown Solicitor, N. P. Roberts

DEPARTMENT OF THE DIRECTOR OF PUBLIC
PROSECUTIONS
Royal Courts of Justice, Belfast BT1 3NX
Tel 0232–235111

Director of Public Prosecutions, A. Fraser, CB, QC
Deputy Director of Public Prosecutions, D. Magill

Ecclesiastical Courts

Original jurisdiction is exercised by the consistory court of each diocese in England, presided over by the Chancellor of that diocese. Appellate jurisdiction is exercised by the provincial courts detailed below, by the Court for Ecclesiastical Causes Reserved, and by commissions of review (the membership of these being newly constituted for each case).

COURT OF ARCHES (PROVINCE OF CANTERBURY)
Registry, 16 Beaumont Street, Oxford OX1 2LZ
Tel 0865–241974
Dean of the Arches, The Rt. Worshipful Sir John Owen

COURT OF THE VICAR-GENERAL OF THE
PROVINCE OF CANTERBURY
Registry, 16 Beaumont Street, Oxford OX1 2LZ
Tel 0865–241974
Vicar-General, The Rt. Worshipful Miss S. Cameron, QC

CHANCERY COURT OF YORK
Registry, 1 Peckitt Street, York YO1 1SG
Tel 0904–623487
Auditor, The Rt. Worshipful Sir John Owen

THE VICAR-GENERAL OF THE PROVINCE OF YORK
Registry, 1 Peckitt Street, York YO1 1SG
Tel 0904–623487
Vicar-General, His Honour the Worshipful Judge
    T. A. C. Coningsby, QC

COURT OF FACULTIES
Registry, 1 The Sanctuary, London SW1P 3JT
Tel 071–222 5381
Office for the use of special and common marriage licences, appointment of notaries public, etc. Office hours, Monday–Friday, 10–4.
Master of the Faculties, The Rt. Worshipful Sir John Owen

Tribunals

AGRICULTURAL LAND TRIBUNALS
c/o Land Use and Tenure Division, Ministry of Agriculture,
Fisheries and Food, Nobel House, 17 Smith Square,
London SW1P 3JR
Tel 071–238 3000

Agricultural Land Tribunals were set up under the Agriculture Act 1947 and settle disputes and other issues between agricultural landlords and tenants. They also settle drainage disputes between neighbours.

There are seven tribunals covering England and one covering the whole of Wales. For each tribunal the Lord Chancellor appoints a chairman and one or more deputies, who must be barristers or solicitors of at least seven years standing. The Lord Chancellor also appoints lay members to three statutory panels of members: the 'landowners' panel, the 'farmers' panel and the 'drainage' panel.

Each of the eight tribunals is an independent statutory body with jurisdiction only within its own area. A separate tribunal is constituted for each case, and consists of a chairman (who may be the chairman or one of the deputy chairmen) and two lay members nominated by the chairman. The chairmen and deputy chairmen are entitled to claim a fee of £221 per day.

Chairmen (England), W. D. Greenwood; K. J. Fisher; The Hon. Mr Justice Evans-Lombe; C. H. Beaumont; N. J. Worsley; G. L. Newsom; His Hon. Judge Robert Taylor
Chairman (Wales), W. J. Owen

COMMONS COMMISSIONERS
Golden Cross House, Duncannon Street, London WC2N 4JF
Tel 071–210 4584

The Commons Commissioners are responsible for deciding disputes arising under the Commons Registration Act 1965 and the Common Land (Rectification of Registers) Act 1989. They also enquire into the ownership of unclaimed common land. Commissioners are appointed by the Lord Chancellor.
Chief Commons Commissioner (£78,377), M. Roth
Commissioners, I. L. R. Romer; D. M. Burton; P. G. Langdon-Davies
Clerk, Miss F. A. A. Buchan

COPYRIGHT TRIBUNAL
Room 4/6, Hazlitt House, 45 Southampton Buildings,
London WC2A 1AR
Tel 071–438 4776

The Copyright Tribunal is the successor to the Performing Right Tribunal which was established by the Copyright Act 1956 to resolve various classes of copyright dispute, principally in the field of collective licensing. Its jurisdiction was extended by the Copyright, Designs and Patents Act 1988 and the Broadcasting Act 1990.

The chairman and two deputy chairmen are appointed by the Lord Chancellor. Up to eight ordinary members are appointed by the Secretary of State for Trade and Industry.

Chairman, J. M. Bowers
Secretary, Mrs K. M. Adams

DATA PROTECTION TRIBUNAL
c/o The Home Office, Queen Anne's Gate, London
SW1H 9AT
Tel 071–273 3755

The Data Protection Tribunal was established under the Data Protection Act 1984 to determine appeals against decisions of the Data Protection Registrar. The chairman and two deputy chairmen are appointed by the Lord Chancellor and must be legally qualified. Lay members are appointed by the Home Secretary to represent the interests of data users or data subjects.

A tribunal consists of a legally-qualified chairman sitting with equal numbers of the lay members appointed to represent the interests of data users and data subjects. The chairman and members receive an *ad hoc* daily fee when the tribunal is sitting.
Chairman, J. A. C. Spokes, QC
Secretary, S. Bucher-Jones

EMPLOYMENT APPEAL TRIBUNAL
Central Office, Audit House, 58 Victoria Embankment,
London EC4Y 0DS
Tel 071–273 1041
Divisional Office, 11 Melville Crescent, Edinburgh
EH3 7LU
Tel 031–225 3963

The Employment Appeal Tribunal was established as a superior court of record under the provisions of the Employment Protection Act 1975, hearing appeals on a question of law arising from any decision of an industrial tribunal.

A tribunal consists of a legally-qualified chairman and two lay members, one from each side of industry. They are appointed by The Queen on the recommendation of the Lord Chancellor and the Secretary of State for Employment.
President, The Hon. Mr Justice Wood
Scottish Chairman, The Hon. Lord Coulsfield
Registrar, Miss V. J. Selio

IMMIGRATION APPELLATE AUTHORITIES
Thanet House, 231 Strand, London WC2R 1DA
Tel 071–353 8060

The Immigration Appeal Adjudicators hear appeals from immigration decisions concerning the need for, and refusal of, leave to enter or remain in the UK, decisions to make deportation orders and directions to remove persons subject to immigration control from the UK. The Immigration Appeal Tribunal hears appeals direct from decisions to make deportation orders in matters concerning conduct contrary to the public good. Its principal jurisdiction is, however, the hearing of appeals from adjudicators by the party (Home

Office or individual) who is aggrieved by the decision. Appeals are subject to leave being granted by the tribunal.

An adjudicator sits alone. The tribunal sits in divisions of three – normally a legally qualified member and two lay members. Members of the tribunal and adjudicators are appointed by the Lord Chancellor.

IMMIGRATION APPEAL TRIBUNAL
President (£64,064), G. W. Farmer
Vice-Presidents, Prof. D. C. Jackson; Mrs J. Chatwani

IMMIGRATION APPEAL ADJUDICATORS
Chief Adjudicator (£63,103) M. Patey, MBE
Deputy Chief Adjudicator, R. G. Care

INDEPENDENT TRIBUNAL SERVICE
City Gate House, Finsbury Square, London EC2A 1UU
Tel 071-814 6500

The service is the administrative authority which exercises judicial and administrative control over the independent social security and child support appeal tribunals, medical appeal tribunals, vaccine damage tribunals and disability appeal tribunals.
President (£69,500), His Hon. Judge Thorpe
Chief Executive, Mrs V. Willcocks

INDUSTRIAL TRIBUNALS

CENTRAL OFFICE (ENGLAND AND WALES)
93 Ebury Bridge Road, London SW1W 8RE
Tel 071-730 9161

Industrial Tribunals for England and Wales sit in 11 regions. The tribunals deal with matters of employment law, redundancy, dismissal, sexual and racial discrimination and related areas of dispute which may arise in the workplace. The tribunals are funded by the Department of Employment.

Chairmen, who may be full-time or part-time, are legally qualified. They are appointed by the Lord Chancellor. Tribunal members are nominated by the CBI and TUC, and appointed by the Secretary of State for Employment.
President (£78,377), His Hon. Judge T. Lawrence

CENTRAL OFFICE (SCOTLAND)
St Andrew House, 141 West Nile Street, Glasgow G1 2RU
Tel 041-331 1601

Tribunals in Scotland have the same remit as those in England and Wales. Chairmen are appointed by the Lord President of the Court of Session and lay members by the Secretary of State for Employment.
President (£65,250), Mrs D. Littlejohn

INDUSTRIAL TRIBUNALS AND THE FAIR EMPLOYMENT TRIBUNAL (NORTHERN IRELAND)
Long Bridge House, 20–24 Waring Street, Belfast BT1 2EB
Tel 0232-327666

The industrial tribunal system in Northern Ireland was set up in 1965 and is similar to the system operating in the rest of the UK. The main legislation in Northern Ireland giving jurisdiction to industrial tribunals to hear complaints relating to employment matters corresponds to legislation enacted in

Great Britain, except that there is no equivalent legislation to the Race Relations Act.

Since 1 January 1990 there has been a separate Fair Employment Tribunal in Northern Ireland. The Fair Employment Tribunal hears and determines individual cases of alleged religious or political discrimination in employment. Employers can also appeal to the Fair Employment Tribunal if they consider the directions of the Fair Employment Commission to be unreasonable, inappropriate or unnecessary, and the Fair Employment Commission can make application to the Tribunal for the enforcement of undertakings or directions with which an employer has not complied.

The president, vice-president and part-time chairmen of the Fair Employment Tribunal are appointed by the Lord Chancellor. The full-time chairman and the part-time chairmen of the industrial tribunals and the panel members to both the industrial tribunals and the Fair Employment Tribunal are appointed by the Department of Economic Development Northern Ireland.
President of the Industrial Tribunals and the Fair Employment Tribunal (£78,377), J. Maguire
Vice-President of the Industrial Tribunals and the Fair Employment Tribunal (£65,912), Mrs M. Perceval-Price
Secretary, J. Murphy

LANDS TRIBUNAL
48–49 Chancery Lane, London WC2A 1JR
Tel 071-936 7200

The Lands Tribunal is an independent judicial body constituted by the Lands Tribunal Act 1949 for the purpose of determining a wide range of questions relating to the valuation of land, rating appeals from local valuation courts and the discharge or modification of restrictive covenants. The Act also empowers the tribunal to accept the function of arbitration under references by consent. The tribunal consists of a president and a number of other members, who are appointed by the Lord Chancellor.
President (£69,412), His Hon. Judge Marder, QC
Members (£65,912), Dr T. Hoyes, FRICS; M. S. J. Hopper, FRICS
Members (part-time) (£300 per day), J. C. Hill, TD; His Hon. Judge O'Donoghue; His Hon. Judge Rich, QC; A. P. Musto, FRICS; P. H. Clarke, FRICS
Registrar, C. A. McMullan

LANDS TRIBUNAL FOR SCOTLAND
1 Grosvenor Crescent, Edinburgh EH12 5ER
Tel 031-225 7996

The Lands Tribunal for Scotland was constituted by the Lands Tribunal Act 1949. Its remit is the same as the tribunal for England and Wales but also covers questions relating to tenants rights. The president is appointed by the Lord President of the Court of Session.
President (£78,377), The Hon. Lord Philip, QC
Members (£65,912), Sheriff A. C. Horsfall, QC; A. R. MacLeary; J. Devine (*full-time*); R. A. Edwards, CBE, WS (*part-time*)
Clerk, D. Pentland

MENTAL HEALTH REVIEW TRIBUNALS

The Mental Health Review Tribunals are independent judicial bodies established under the Mental Health Act 1959 and which now operate under the Mental Health Act 1983. They are responsible for reviewing the cases of patients compulsorily detained under the Act's provisions. They have the power to discharge the patient and, in the case of unrestricted patients, to re-classify the patient, to recommend leave of absence, delayed discharge, transfer to another hospital, or that a guardianship order be made. There are 14 Tribunals in England, each headed by a regional chairman who is appointed by the Lord Chancellor's Department on a part-time basis. In practice there are ten chairmen covering the 14 regions, some with more than one region. Each tribunal is made up of at least three members, and must include a lawyer, who acts as president (£221 per day), a medical member (£217.40 per day) and a lay member (£91 per day).

The Medical Health Review Tribunals' secretariat is based in five regional offices:

LONDON (NORTH), Spur 5, Block 1, Government Buildings, Honeypot Lane, Stanmore, Middx. HA7 1AY. Tel: 071-972 2373. *Clerk,* P. Barnett
LONDON (SOUTH), Spur B, Block 3, Crown Offices, Kingston Bypass Road, Surbiton, Surrey KT6 5QN. Tel: 081-398 4166. *Clerk,* Mrs J. Innes
LIVERPOOL, 3rd Floor, Cressington House, 249 St Mary's Road, Garston, Liverpool L19 0NF. Tel: 051-494 0095. *Clerk,* Mrs B. Foot
NOTTINGHAM, Spur A, Block 5, Government Buildings, Chalfont Drive, Western Boulevard, Nottingham NG8 3RZ. Tel: 0602-294222. *Clerk,* M. Chapman
WALES, 1st Floor, New Crown Buildings, Cathays Park, Cardiff CF1 3NQ. Tel: 0222-825328. *Clerk,* Mrs C. Thomas

NATIONAL HEALTH SERVICE TRIBUNAL

The NHS Tribunal inquires into representations that the continued inclusion of a family practitioner (doctor, dentist, pharmacist or optician) on a Family Practitioner Committee's list would be prejudicial to the efficiency of the services concerned. The tribunal sits when required, about eight times a year, and usually in London.
Chairman, R. Bell, QC
Clerk, I. D. Keith, East Hookers, Twineham, nr Haywards Heath, W. Sussex RH17 5NN. Tel: 0444-881345

NATIONAL HEALTH SERVICE TRIBUNAL (SCOTLAND)
33 Queen Street, Edinburgh EH2 1LE
Tel 031-226 6541

The tribunal was set up under the National Health Service (Scotland) Act 1978, and exists to consider representations that the continued inclusion of a registered medical practitioner, dental practitioner, optometrist or pharmacist on a health board's list would be prejudicial to the continuing efficiency of the service in question.

The tribunal meets when required and is composed of a chairman, one lay member, and one practitioner member drawn from a representative professional panel. The chairman is appointed by the Lord President of the Court of Session, and the lay member and the members of the professional panel are appointed by the Secretary of State for Scotland. The chairman and members receive an *ad hoc* daily fee when the tribunal is sitting.

Chairman, W. C. Galbraith, QC
Lay member, J. D. M. Robertson
Clerk to the Tribunal, D. G. Brash, WS

PENSIONS APPEAL TRIBUNALS

CENTRAL OFFICE (ENGLAND AND WALES)
48–49 Chancery Lane, London WC2A 1JR
Tel 071-936 7034

The Pensions Appeal Tribunals are responsible for hearing appeals from ex-servicemen or women and widows who have had their claims for a war pension rejected by the Secretary of State for Social Security. The Entitlement Appeal Tribunals hear appeals in cases where the Secretary of State has refused to grant a war pension. The Assessment Appeal Tribunals hear appeals against the Secretary of State's assessment of the degree of disablement caused by an accepted condition.

The tribunal members are appointed by the Lord Chancellor.
President (£55,777), J. R. T. Holt
Secretary, Miss A. Gibson

PENSIONS APPEAL TRIBUNALS FOR SCOTLAND
20 Walker Street, Edinburgh EH3 7HS
Tel 031-220 1404
President, A. C. Hamilton, QC

OFFICE OF THE SOCIAL SECURITY AND CHILD SUPPORT COMMISSIONERS
Harp House, 83–86 Farringdon Street, London EC4A 4DH
Tel 071-353 5145

23 Melville Street, Edinburgh EH3 7PW
Tel 031-225 2201

The Social Security Commissioners are the final statutory authority to decide appeals relating to entitlement to social security benefits. The Child Support Commissioners are the final statutory authority to decide appeals relating to child support. Appeals may be made in relation to both matters only on a point of law. The Commissioners' jurisdiction covers England, Wales and Scotland. The commissioners are all qualified lawyers.
Chief Social Security Commissioner and Chief Child Support Commissioner (£78,000), His Hon. Judge Machin, QC
Secretary, Mrs M. White (*London*); R. Lindsay (*Edinburgh*)

OFFICE OF THE SOCIAL SECURITY AND CHILD SUPPORT COMMISSIONERS FOR NORTHERN IRELAND
Lancashire House, 5 Linenhall Street, Belfast BT2 8AA
Tel 0232-332344

The role of Northern Ireland Social Security and Child Support Commissioners is similar to that of the Commissioners in Great Britain.
Chief Commissioner (£78,377), His Hon. Judge Chambers, QC
Registrar of Appeals, W. D. Pollock

THE SOLICITORS' DISCIPLINARY TRIBUNAL
16 Bell Yard, London WC2A IPL
Tel 071-242 0219

The Solicitors' Disciplinary Tribunal was constituted under the provisions of the Solicitors Act 1974. It is an independent statutory body whose members are appointed by the Master of the Rolls. The tribunal considers applications made to it alleging either professional misconduct and/or a breach of the statutory rules by which solicitors are bound against an individually named solicitor, former solicitor, or registered foreign lawyer. The tribunal's jurisdiction extends to solicitor's clerks, in respect of whom they may make an order restricting that clerk's employment by solicitors.
President, G. B. Marsh
Clerk, Mrs S. C. Elson

SPECIAL COMMISSIONERS OF INCOME TAX
15-19 Bedford Avenue, London WCIB 3AS
Tel 071-631 4242

The Special Commissioners are an independent body appointed by the Lord Chancellor to hear appeals concerning income taxes, etc.
Presiding Special Commissioner (£78,378), His Hon.
Stephen Oliver, QC
Special Commissioners (£54,035), T. H. K. Everett;
D. A. Shirley
Deputy Special Commissioners, D. C. Potter, QC;
R. H. Widdows, CB
Clerk (£22,618), R. P. Lester

TRAFFIC COMMISSIONERS
c/o Western Traffic Area, The Gaunt's House, Denmark Street, Bristol BSI 5DR
Tel 0272-755065

The Traffic Commissioners are responsible for the licensing of operators of heavy goods and public service vehicles, and they also have responsibility for appeals relating to the licensing of operators and for disciplinary cases involving the conduct of drivers of these vehicles. There are seven Commissioners in the eight traffic areas covering Great Britain. For Traffic Area Offices and Commissioners, *see* page 361. Each Traffic Commissioner constitutes a tribunal for the purposes of the Tribunals and Inquiries Act 1971.
Senior Traffic Commissioner, Air Vice-Marshal
R. G. Ashford, CBE

TRANSPORT TRIBUNAL
48-49 Chancery Lane, London, WC2A IJR
Tel 071-936 7494

The Transport Tribunal was set up in 1947 and hears appeals against decisions made by Traffic Commissioners at public inquiries. The tribunal consists of a legally-qualified president, two legal members who may sit as chairmen, and four lay members. The president and legal members are appointed by the Lord Chancellor and the lay members are appointed by the Secretary of State for Transport.

President (part-time), His Hon. Judge H. Wilson
Legal members (£221 per day), His Hon. Judge Brodrick
(*part-time*); R. Owen, QC
Lay members (£177 per day), T. W. Hall; J. W. Whitworth;
G. Simms; Miss E. B. Haran
Secretary, P. Harris

VALUATION TRIBUNALS
c/o Warwickshire Valuation Tribunal, 2nd Floor, Walton House, 11 Parade, Leamington Spa, Warks. CV32 4DG
Tel 0926-421875

The Valuation Tribunals hear appeals concerning the council tax, non-domestic rating and land drainage rates in England and Wales. They also have residual jurisdiction to hear appeals concerning the community charge, the pre-1990 rating list, disabled rating and mixed hereditaments. There are 56 Valuation Tribunals in England, and eight in Wales. Each tribunal is a separate independent body; those in England are funded by the Department of the Environment and those in Wales by the Welsh Office. A separate tribunal is constituted for each hearing, and normally consists of a chairman and two other members. Members are appointed by the local authority/authorities, and serve on a voluntary basis. A National Committee of Valuation Tribunals considers all matters affecting Valuations Tribunals in England, and the Council of Wales, Valuation Tribunal Presidents, performs the same function in Wales.
President, National Committee of Valuation Tribunals,
A. W. H. Kennard
Secretary, National Committee of Valuation Tribunals,
B. P. Massen
President, Council of Wales, Valuation Tribunal Presidents,
T. W. Jones

VAT TRIBUNALS
15-19 Bedford Avenue, London WCIB 3AS
Tel 071-631 4242

VAT Tribunals are administered by the Lord Chancellor's Department in England and Wales, and by the Secretary of State in Scotland. They are independent and decide disputes between taxpayers and the Commissioners of Customs and Excise, who manage VAT. In England and Wales, the president and chairmen are appointed by the Lord Chancellor, and members are appointed by the Treasury. Chairmen in Scotland are appointed by the Lord President of the Court of Session.
President (£78,378), His Hon. Stephen Oliver, QC
Vice-President, Scotland (£54,035), R. A. Bennett, CBE, QC
Registrar, R. P. Lester

TRIBUNAL CENTRES
LONDON (including Belfast), 15-19 Bedford Avenue,
London WCIB 3AS. Tel: 071-631 4242
EDINBURGH, 44 Palmerston Place, Edinburgh EHI2 5BJ.
Tel: 031-226 3551
MANCHESTER, Warwickgate House, Warwick Road, Old
Trafford, Manchester MI6 0GP. Tel: 061-872 6471

The Police Service

There are 52 police forces in the United Kingdom, each responsible for law enforcement in its area. Most forces' area is conterminous with an English or Welsh county or Scottish region, though there are several combined forces. Law enforcement in London is carried out by the Metropolitan Police and the City of London Police; in Northern Ireland by the Royal Ulster Constabulary; and by the Isle of Man, States of Jersey, and Guernsey forces in their respective islands and bailiwicks. The National Criminal Intelligence Service (*see* below) was set up in April 1992.

Each police force is maintained by a police authority. The authorities of English and Welsh forces comprise committees of local councillors and magistrates; in Scotland, the regional and islands councils are the authorities. The authority for the Metropolitan Police is the Home Secretary. In Northern Ireland the Secretary of State appoints the police authority.

Police authorities are financed by central and local government. Subject to the approval of the Home Secretary and to regulations, they appoint the chief constable, decide the maximum size of the force and provide buildings and equipment.

The Home Secretary and the Secretaries of State for Scotland and Northern Ireland are responsible for the organization, administration and operation of the police service. They make regulations covering matters such as police ranks, discipline, hours of duty, and pay and allowances.

All police forces (including the Metropolitan Police at the request of the Commissioner) are subject to inspection by HM Inspectors of Constabulary, who report to the respective Secretary of State.

The investigation of a serious complaint against a police officer is supervised by the Police Complaints Authority (*see* page 343) in England and Wales. An officer may appeal against the finding of an investigation, or against the resulting punishment, to the Home Secretary; appeals are heard by private Police Appeal tribunals consisting of a chairman (a barrister or solicitor) and two retired police officers appointed on an *ad hoc* basis. In Scotland, complaints are investigated by independent public prosecutors, and in Northern Ireland by the Independent Commission for Police Complaints.

For details of the government White Paper on the police and the Sheehy report on police pay and conditions, *see* Index.

BASIC RATES OF POLICE PAY
as at 1 September 1993

Chief Constable	£56,313–£71,580
Deputy Chief Constable	£49,605–£57,264
Assistant Chief Constable	£47,241
Chief Superintendent	£40,071–£42,549
Superintendent	£36,042–£39,135
Chief Inspector	£26,496–£29,472
Inspector	£23,337–£26,496
Sergeant	£20,343–£23,337
Constable	£12,744–£21,267

Metropolitan Police
(excluding London weighting and London allowance)

Metropolitan Commissioner	£90,148
Deputy Commissioner	£76,266
Assistant Commissioner	£67,281
Deputy Assistant Commissioner	£53,826

Commander	£47,241
Chief Superintendent	£40,071–£42,549
Superintendent	£36,960–£39,135
Chief Inspector	£27,768–£30,732
Inspector	£24,591–£27,768
Sergeant	£20,343–£23,337
Constable	£12,744–£21,267

THE SPECIAL CONSTABULARY

The Special Constabulary is the part-time volunteer branch of the police force. Special Constables have full police powers within their force area and undertake regular officers' routine policing duties when required, thus freeing regulars at times of emergency for those tasks which only they can perform. There were 19,243 Special Constables in England and Wales at the end of 1992.

NATIONAL CRIMINAL INTELLIGENCE SERVICE
Headquarters: PO Box 8000, Spring Gardens, Tinworth Street, London SE11 5EN
Tel 071-238 8000

The function of the National Criminal Intelligence Service (NCIS) is to gather, collate and disseminate information and intelligence on serious crime of a regional, national and international nature. It is independent of any other police organization.
Director-General, A. H. Pacey, QPM
Director (Intelligence), S. R. W. Crawshaw, QPM
Director, Drugs Division, S. Wesley
Director of Resources, R. Creedon

POLICE AUTHORITIES

Strength: actual strength of force as at mid June 1993
Chair: Chairman/Convener of the Police Authority/Police Committee

ENGLAND

AVON AND SOMERSET CONSTABULARY, *HQ,* PO Box 37, Valley Road, Portishead, Bristol BS20 8QJ. Tel: 0272-818181. *Strength,* 3,056; *Chief Constable,* D. J. Shattock, QPM; *Chair,* D. Heath

BEDFORDSHIRE POLICE, *HQ,* Woburn Road, Kempston, Bedford MK43 9AX. Tel: 0234-841212. *Strength,* 1,173; *Chief Constable,* A. Dyer, QPM; *Chair,* elected at each meeting

CAMBRIDGESHIRE CONSTABULARY, *HQ,* Hinchingbrooke Park, Huntingdon, Cambs. PE18 8NP. Tel: 0480-456111. *Strength,* 1,224; *Chief Constable,* I. H. Kane, QPM; *Chair,* J. Fitch

CHESHIRE CONSTABULARY, *HQ,* Castle Esplanade, Chester, CH1 2PP. Tel: 0244-350000. *Strength,* 1,892; *Chief Constable,* J. M. Jones, QPM; *Chair,* J. H. Collins, OBE

CLEVELAND CONSTABULARY, *HQ,* PO Box 70, Ladgate Lane, Middlesbrough, Cleveland TS8 9EH. Tel: 0642-326326. *Strength,* 1,466; *Chief Constable,* B. D. D. Shaw; *Chair,* I. Jeffrey

CUMBRIA CONSTABULARY, *HQ*, Carleton Hall, Penrith, Cumbria CA10 2AU. Tel: 0768-64411. *Strength*, 1,196; *Chief Constable*, A. G. Elliott; *Chair*, R. Watson

DERBYSHIRE CONSTABULARY, *HQ*, Butterley Hall, Ripley, Derbyshire DE5 3RS. Tel: 0773-570100. *Strength*, 1,811; *Chief Constable*, J. F. Newing, QPM; *Chair*, E. H. Swain

DEVON AND CORNWALL CONSTABULARY, *HQ*, Middlemoor, Exeter EX2 7HQ. Tel: 0392-52101. *Strength*, 2,960; *Chief Constable*, J. S. Evans, QPM; *Chair*, O. A. May

DORSET POLICE FORCE, *HQ*, Winfrith, Dorchester, Dorset DT2 8DZ. Tel: 0929-462727. *Strength*, 1,302; *Chief Constable*, B. H. Weight, QPM; *Chair*, Sir Stephen Hammick, Bt.

DURHAM CONSTABULARY, *HQ*, Aykley Heads, Durham DH1 5TT. Tel: 091-386 4929. *Strength*, 1,376; *Chief Constable*, F. W. Taylor, QPM; *Chair*, J. Richardson

ESSEX POLICE, *HQ*, PO Box 2, Springfield, Chelmsford CM2 6DA. Tel: 0245-491491. *Strength*, 2,955; *Chief Constable*, J. H. Burrow, CBE; *Chair*, G. W. Rice

GLOUCESTERSHIRE CONSTABULARY, *HQ*, Holland House, Lansdown Road, Cheltenham, Glos. GL51 6QH. Tel: 0242-521321. *Strength*, 1,137; *Chief Constable*, A. J. P. Butler, PH.D.; *Chair*, C. Hay

GREATER MANCHESTER POLICE, *HQ*, PO Box 22 (S. West PDO), Chester House, Boyer Street, Manchester M16 ORE. Tel: 061-872 5050. *Strength*, 7,039; *Chief Constable*, D. Wilmot, QPM; *Chair*, S. Murphy

HAMPSHIRE CONSTABULARY, *HQ*, West Hill, Winchester, Hants. SO22 5DB. Tel: 0962-868133. *Strength*, 3,267; *Chief Constable*, J. C. Hoddinott, QPM; *Chair*, vacant

HERTFORDSHIRE CONSTABULARY, *HQ*, Stanborough Road, Welwyn Garden City, Herts. AL8 6XF. Tel: 0707-331177. *Strength*, 1,684; *Chief Constable*, B. H. Skitt, BEM, QPM; *Chair*, F. Peacock

HUMBERSIDE POLICE, *HQ*, Queens Gardens, Kingston upon Hull, N. Humberside HU1 3DJ. Tel: 0482-26111. *Strength*, 2,027; *Chief Constable*, D. A. Leonard, QPM; *Chair*, I. A. Cawsey

KENT CONSTABULARY, *HQ*, Sutton Road, Maidstone, Kent ME15 9BZ. Tel: 0622-690690. *Strength*, 3,140; *Chief Constable*, J. D. Phillips; *Chair*, Sir John Grugeon

LANCASHIRE CONSTABULARY, *HQ*, PO Box 77, Hutton, Preston PR4 5SB. Tel: 0772-614444. *Strength*, 3,188; *Chief Constable*, R. B. Johnson, CBE, QPM; *Chair*, Mrs R. B. Henig

LEICESTERSHIRE CONSTABULARY, *HQ*, PO Box 999, Leicester LE99 1AZ. Tel: 0533-530066. *Strength*, 1,833; *Chief Constable*, K. Povey, QPM; *Chair*, B. Singh

LINCOLNSHIRE POLICE, *HQ*, PO Box 999, Lincoln LN5 7PH. Tel: 0522-532222. *Strength*, 1,196; *Chief Constable*, vacant; *Chair*, B. Fippard

MERSEYSIDE POLICE, *HQ*, PO Box 59, Canning Place, Liverpool L69 1JD. Tel: 051-709 6010. *Strength*, 4,766; *Chief Constable*, J. Sharples, QPM; *Chair*, G. Bundred, CBE

NORFOLK CONSTABULARY, *HQ*, Martineau Lane, Norwich NR1 2DJ. Tel: 0603-768769. *Strength*, 1,428; *Chief Constable*, K. R. Williams, QPM; *Chair*, vacant

NORTHAMPTONSHIRE POLICE, *HQ*, Wootton Hall, Northampton NN4 0JQ. Tel: 0604-700700. *Strength*, 1,190; *Chief Constable*, E. Crew, QPM; *Chair*, Dr M. Dickie

NORTHUMBRIA POLICE, *HQ*, Ponteland, Newcastle upon Tyne NE20 OBL. Tel: 0661-872555. *Strength*, 3,620; *Chief Constable*, J. A. Stevens, QPM; *Chair*, G. Gill

NORTH YORKSHIRE POLICE, *HQ*, Newby Wiske Hall, Newby Wiske, Northallerton, N. Yorks. DL7 9HA. Tel: 0609-783131. *Strength*, 1,386; *Chief Constable*, D. M. Burke, QPM; *Chair*, elected at each meeting

NOTTINGHAMSHIRE CONSTABULARY, *HQ*, Sherwood Lodge, Arnold, Nottingham NG5 8PP. Tel: 0602-670999. *Strength*, 2,357; *Chief Constable*, D. Crompton, QPM; *Chair*, C. P. Winterton

SOUTH YORKSHIRE POLICE, *HQ*, Snig Hill, Sheffield S3 8LY. Tel: 0742-768522. *Strength*, 3,400; *Chief Constable*, R. Wells, QPM; *Chair*, Sir John Layden

STAFFORDSHIRE POLICE, *HQ*, Cannock Road, Stafford ST17 0QG. Tel: 0785-57717. *Strength*, 2,165; *Chief Constable*, C. H. Kelly, CBE, QPM; *Chair*, T. J. Meir

SUFFOLK CONSTABULARY, *HQ*, Martlesham Heath, Ipswich IP5 7QS. Tel: 0473-613500. *Strength*, 1,234; *Chief Constable*, A. T. Coe, QPM; *Chair*, C. C. Jones

SURREY POLICE, *HQ*, Mount Browne, Sandy Lane, Guildford, Surrey GU3 1HG. Tel: 0483-571212. *Strength*, 1,763; *Chief Constable*, D. J. Williams, QPM; *Chair*, A. C. Tisdall

SUSSEX POLICE, *HQ*, Malling House, Church Lane, Lewes, E. Sussex BN7 2DZ. Tel: 0273-475432. *Strength*, 2,994; *Chief Constable*, P. Whitehouse, QPM; *Chair*, J. P. Sheridan

THAMES VALLEY POLICE, *HQ*, Oxford Road, Kidlington, Oxon. OX5 2NX. Tel: 0865-846000. *Strength*, 3,944; *Chief Constable*, C. Pollard, QPM; *Chair*, C. F. Robinson, OBE

WARWICKSHIRE CONSTABULARY, *HQ*, PO Box 4, Leek Wootton, Warwick CV35 7QB. Tel: 0926-415000. *Strength*, 1,037; *Chief Constable*, P. D. Joslin, QPM; *Chair*, M. Singh

WEST MERCIA CONSTABULARY, *HQ*, PO Box 55, Hindlip Hall, Hindlip, Worcester WR3 8SP. Tel: 0905-723000. *Strength*, 2,048; *Chief Constable*, D. C. Blakey, QPM; *Chair*, P. H. Fallows, TD

WEST MIDLANDS POLICE, *HQ*, PO Box 52, Lloyd House, Colmore Circus, Queensway, Birmingham B4 6NQ. Tel: 021-626 5000. *Strength*, 7,092; *Chief Constable*, R. Hadfield, QPM; *Chair*, L. V. Jones

WEST YORKSHIRE POLICE, *HQ*, PO Box 9, Laburnum Road, Wakefield, W. Yorks. WF1 3QP. Tel: 0924-375222. *Strength*, 5,024; *Chief Constable*, K. Hellawell, QPM; *Chair*, T. Brennan

WILTSHIRE CONSTABULARY, *HQ*, London Road, Devizes, Wilts. SN10 2DN. Tel: 0380-722341. *Strength*, 1,163; *Chief Constable*, W. R. Girven, QPM; *Chair*, Mrs J. M. Wood

WALES

DYFED–POWYS POLICE, *HQ*, PO Box 99, Llangunnor, Carmarthen, Dyfed SA31 2PF. Tel: 0267-236444. *Strength*, 969; *Chief Constable*, R. White, QPM; *Chair*, D. R. Irving

GWENT CONSTABULARY, *HQ*, Croesyceiliog, Cwmbran, Gwent NP44 2XJ. Tel: 0633-838111. *Strength*, 995; *Chief Constable*, J. E. Over, QPM, CPM; *Chair*, B. Sutton

NORTH WALES POLICE, *HQ*, Glan-y-Don, Colwyn Bay, Clwyd LL29 8AW. Tel: 0492-517171. *Strength*, 1,369; *Chief Constable*, D. Owen, CBE, QPM; *Chair*, W. E. Conway

SOUTH WALES CONSTABULARY, *HQ*, Cowbridge Road, Bridgend, Mid Glamorgan CF31 3SU. Tel: 0656-655555. *Strength*, 3,172; *Chief Constable*, W. R. Lawrence, QPM; *Chair*, R. Jones

SCOTLAND

CENTRAL SCOTLAND POLICE, *HQ*, Randolphfield, Stirling FK8 2HD. Tel: 0786-456000. *Strength*, 651; *Chief Constable*, W. J. M. Wilson, QPM; *Convener*, H. Brown

DUMFRIES AND GALLOWAY CONSTABULARY, *HQ*, Cornwall Mount, Dumfries DG1 1PZ. Tel: 0387-52112.

Strength, 384; *Chief Constable*, G. A. Esson, QPM; *Chair*, R. Brown

FIFE CONSTABULARY, *HQ*, Wemyss Road, Dysart, Kirkcaldy, Fife KY1 2YA. Tel: 0592-652611. *Strength*, 772; *Chief Constable*, W. M. Moodie, CBE, QPM; *Chair*, C. J. Groom

GRAMPIAN POLICE, *HQ*, Queen Street, Aberdeen AB9 1BA. Tel: 0224-639111. *Strength*, 1,174; *Chief Constable*, I. T. Oliver, QPM, PH.D.; *Chair*, Dr J. K. A. Thomaneck

LOTHIAN AND BORDERS POLICE, *HQ*, Fettes Avenue, Edinburgh EH4 1RB. Tel: 031-311 3131. *Strength*, 2,500; *Chief Constable*, Sir William Sutherland, QPM; *Chair*, R. B. Martin

NORTHERN CONSTABULARY, *HQ*, Perth Road, Inverness IV2 3SY. Tel: 0463-239191. *Strength*, 654; *Chief Constable*, H. C. MacMillan, QPM; *Chair*, Mrs I. C. Rhind

STRATHCLYDE POLICE, *HQ*, 173 Pitt Street, Glasgow G2 4JS. Tel: 041-204 2626. *Strength*, 6,805; *Chief Constable*, L. Sharp, QPM; *Chair*, J. Jennings

TAYSIDE POLICE, *HQ*, PO Box 59, West Bell Street, Dundee DD1 9JU. Tel: 0382-23200. *Strength*, 1,093; *Chief Constable*, J. W. Bowman, CBE, QPM; *Chair*, W. Smith

NORTHERN IRELAND

ROYAL ULSTER CONSTABULARY, *HQ*, Brooklyn, Knock Road, Belfast BT5 6LE. Tel: 0232-650222. *Strength*, 8,468; *Chief Constable*, Sir Hugh Annesley, QPM; *Chair*, T. Rainey

ISLANDS

ISLAND POLICE FORCE, *HQ*, St Peter Port, Guernsey, Channel Islands. Tel: 0481-725111. *Strength*, 149; *Chief Officer*, M. Le Moignan, QPM; *President, States Committee for Home Affairs*, M. Torode

STATES OF JERSEY POLICE, *HQ*, Rouge Bouillon, PO Box 789, St Helier, Jersey, Channel Islands JE2 3ZA. Tel: 0534-69996. *Strength*, 232; *Chief Officer*, R. H. Le Breton; *Chair*, M. Wavell

ISLE OF MAN CONSTABULARY, *HQ*, Glencrutchery Road, Douglas, Isle of Man. Tel: 0624-631212. *Strength*, 212; *Chief Constable*, R. E. N. Oake; *Minister for Home Affairs*, The Hon. A. A. Callin

---

METROPOLITAN POLICE SERVICE
New Scotland Yard, Broadway, London SW1H OBG
Tel 071-230 1212

Establishment, 28,472
Commissioner, P. Condon, QPM
Deputy Commissioner, J. A. Smith, QPM
Receiver, G. L. Angel

TERRITORIAL OPERATIONS DEPARTMENT
Assistant Commissioner, R. A. Hunt, OBE, QPM
Deputy Assistant Commissioner, T. J. Siggs, OBE
Commanders, J. J. Allinson; D. N. Stevens, QPM

AREA HEADQUARTERS
Deputy Assistant Commissioners, M. B. Taylor, QPM; D. J. Osland, QPM; A. G. Fry, QPM; L. T. Roach, QPM; A. J. Speed, QPM; D. Flanders; M. J. Sullivan, QPM; W. J. R. Johnston, QPM
Commanders, T. O. Jones, MBE; J. A. Coo, QPM; L. J. Poole; D. M. T. Kendrick, QPM; J. F. Purnell, CGM; B. J. Luckhurst; T. D. Laidlaw; A. V. Comben;

B. S. Plaxton; J. Townshend; H. N. L. Blenkin; R. C. Adams; C. R. Pearman; A. L. Rowe

SPECIALIST OPERATIONS DEPARTMENT
Assistant Commissioner, W. Taylor, QPM
Deputy Assistant Commissioners, D. M. Meynell, OBE; J. A. Hawley, QPM; D. C. Veness
Commanders, K. G. Churchill-Coleman, QPM; P. R. Nove; R. A. Penrose, QPM; D. C. Stockley; D. Buchanan; R. C. Marsh, QPM; D. M. Tucker; B. G. Moss; J. G. D. Grieve

Metropolitan Police Laboratory
Director, Dr B. Sheard
Deputy Directors, G. J. O. Lee; M. R. Loveland; P. D. Martin; Dr W. D. C. Wilson

PERSONNEL DEPARTMENT
Director of Personnel, E. Mitchell, QPM
Director of Civil Staff Personnel Management, R. M. Gregory
Director of Police Personnel Management, C. A. Couch
Director of Manpower Planning and Personnel Policy, J. S. Steele
Director of Catering, A. Thompson
Director of Occupational Health, Dr A. Johnson

MEDICAL AND DENTAL BRANCH
Chief Medical Officer, Dr E. C. A. Bott, CBE

INSPECTION AND REVIEW
Assistant Commissioner, P. J. J. Winship, QPM
Deputy Assistant Commissioner, J. E. Metcalfe
Commander, J. D. Gibson

COMPLAINTS INVESTIGATION BUREAU
Commander, E. Humphrey, QPM

CENTRAL STAFF
Commander, M. Briggs

DIRECTORATE OF PUBLIC AFFAIRS
Director of Public Affairs, Ms S. Cullum

DIRECTORATE OF PERFORMANCE REVIEW AND MANAGEMENT SERVICES
Director, Mrs S. M. Merchant

SOLICITOR'S DEPARTMENT
Solicitor, C. S. Porteous, CBE

FINANCE DEPARTMENT
Director of Finance, J. A. Crutchlow

PROPERTY SERVICES DEPARTMENT
Director of Property Services, T. G. Lawrence

DEPARTMENT OF TECHNOLOGY
Director of Technology, N. Boothman

CITY OF LONDON POLICE
26 Old Jewry, London EC2R 8DJ
Tel 071-601 2222

Strength (June 1993), 862
Commissioner (£74,745), O. Kelly, QPM
Assistant Commissioner (£56,841), C. Coxall, QPM
Commander (£47,709), H. J. Moore, QPM
Chief Superintendents (£39,480–£42,540):
   'B' Division, G. Marshall
   'C' Division, P. Eskriett
   CID, T. Dickinson

Company Fraud, R. Knevett
Management Support, R. Friend
Operational Support, T. Hillier

BRITISH TRANSPORT POLICE
15 Tavistock Place, London WC1H 9SJ
Tel 071-388 7541

Strength (August 1993), 2,123
The Force provides a policing service to the British Railways
Board and London Underground Ltd. Police stations are
located throughout England, Wales and Scotland. The Chief
Constable reports to the British Transport Police Committee,
a statutory body set up under the Transport Act 1962. The
members of the Committee are appointed by the British
Railways Board and London Underground Ltd.
Chief Constable, D. O'Brien, OBE, QPM
Deputy Chief Constable, A. Parker
Assistant Chief Constables:
  Support Services, G. K. Miller
  Operations, W. I. McGregor, QPM
  Scottish Area, S. Mannion
  Communications and Technology, A. Horn

MINISTRY OF DEFENCE POLICE
Ministry of Defence, Empress State Building,
Lillie Road, London SW6 1TR
Tel 071-385 1244

Strength (May 1993), 5,035
The Ministry of Defence Police is a statutory police force
directly responsible to the Secretary of State for Defence for
the policing of all military land, stations and establishments
in the United Kingdom. It is due to become a defence agency
in 1994.
Chief Constable, J. Reddington, QPM
Deputy Chief Constable, W. E. E. Boreham, OBE
Head of Secretariat, J. A. Smallwood
Assistant Chief Constables:
  Corporate Development, S. G. Edwards, QPM
  Operations, R. E. Murray
  Personnel and Training, B. J. Smith
  Scotland, J. Reade
  Support, P. A. Bedwell

ROYAL PARKS CONSTABULARY
The Old Police House, Hyde Park, London W2 2UH
Tel 071-298 2054

Strength (August 1993), 190
The Royal Parks Constabulary is maintained by the
Department of National Heritage and is responsible for the
policing of 21 Royal Parks in and around London. These
comprise an area in excess of 6,300 acres. Officers of the
Force are appointed under the Parks Regulations Act 1872,
as amended by the Parks Regulations (Amendment) Act
1974.
Chief Officer, W. Ross
Deputy Chief Officer, M. J. Loader

UNITED KINGDOM ATOMIC ENERGY
AUTHORITY CONSTABULARY
Building E6, Culham Laboratory, Abingdon,
Oxon. OX14 3DB
Tel 0235-463760

Strength (June 1993), 509
The Constabulary is responsible for policing United Kingdom
Atomic Energy Authority and British Nuclear Fuels PLC
establishments and for escorting nuclear material between
establishments.
The Chief Constable is responsible, through the Atomic
Energy Authority Police Committee, to the President of the
Board of Trade.
Chief Constable, H. J. McMorris, QPM
Deputy Chief Constable, E. H. Miller

STAFF ASSOCIATIONS

ASSOCIATION OF CHIEF POLICE OFFICERS OF
ENGLAND, WALES AND NORTHERN IRELAND, Room
311, Wellington House, 67–73 Buckingham Gate,
London SW1E 6BE. Tel: 071-230 7148. Represents the
Chief Constables, Deputy Chief Constables and Assistant
Chief Constables of England, Wales and Northern
Ireland, and officers of the rank of Commander and
above in the Metropolitan and City of London Police.
General Secretary, Miss M. C. E. Barton
THE POLICE SUPERINTENDENTS' ASSOCIATION OF
ENGLAND AND WALES, 67A Reading Road,
Pangbourne, Reading RG8 7JD. Tel: 0734-844005.
Represents officers of the rank of Superintendent and
Chief Superintendent. *Secretary*, Chief Supt. P. G. Wall
THE POLICE FEDERATION OF ENGLAND AND WALES,
15–17 Langley Road, Surbiton, Surrey KT6 6LP. Tel: 081-
399 2224. Represents officers up to and including the
rank of Chief Inspector. *General Secretary*, L. Williams;
Chairman, R. Coyles
ASSOCIATION OF CHIEF POLICE OFFICERS IN
SCOTLAND, Police Headquarters, Fettes Avenue,
Edinburgh EH4 1RB. Tel: 031-311 3051. Represents the
Chief Constables, Deputy Chief Constables and Assistant
Chief Constables of the Scottish police forces. *Hon.
Secretary*, Sir William Sutherland, QPM
THE ASSOCIATION OF SCOTTISH POLICE
SUPERINTENDENTS, Secretariat, 173 Pitt Street,
Glasgow G2 4JS. Tel: 041-221 5796. Represents officers of
the rank of Superintendent and Chief Superintendent.
Hon. Secretary, Chief Supt. J. Urquhart
THE SCOTTISH POLICE FEDERATION, 5 Woodside Place,
Glasgow G3 7QF. Tel: 041-332 5234. Represents officers
up to and including the rank of Chief Inspector. *General
Secretary*, D. J. Keil
THE SUPERINTENDENT ASSOCIATION OF NORTHERN
IRELAND, Ormiston House, Hawthornden Road, Belfast
BT4 3JW. Tel: 0232-700129. Represents Superintendents
and Chief Superintendents in the RUC. *Hon. Secretary,*
Chief Supt. A. Donald
THE POLICE FEDERATION FOR NORTHERN IRELAND,
Royal Ulster Constabulary, Garnerville, Garnerville
Road, Belfast BT4 2NX. Tel: 0232-760831. Represents
officers up to and including the rank of Chief Inspector.
Secretary, D. A. McClurg

Defence

MINISTRY OF DEFENCE
Main Building, Whitehall, London SWIA 2HB
Tel 071-218 9000

The Ministry of Defence is concerned with the control, administration, equipment and support of the Armed Forces of the Crown. The research, development, production and purchase of weapons systems and equipment is the concern of the Procurement Executive.

SALARIES 1993–4

Secretary of State	£39,820*
Minister of State	£28,175*
Parliamentary Under-Secretary	£37,689*
Grade 1	£90,148
Grade 1A	£82,925
Grade 2	£64,307–£75,328
Grade 3	£51,360–£59,599†
Grade 4	£44,390–£49,790†‡
Grade 5	£36,178–£47,921†‡

*In addition to a reduced parliamentary salary of £23,227
†Plus London weighting (see page 282); Grade 3s in London also receive a £2,000 London allowance
‡1992–3 figures
For Services salaries, see pages 402–4

Secretary of State for Defence, The Rt. Hon. Malcolm Rifkind, QC, MP
 Private Secretary (G5), J. Pitt-Brooke
 Special Advisers, C. Blunt; C. Littmoden
 Parliamentary Private Secretary, H. Bellingham, MP
Minister of State for the Armed Forces, Jeremy Hanley, MP
 Private Secretary (G7), Miss O. Muirhead
 Parliamentary Private Secretary, R. Gale, MP
Minister of State for Defence Procurement, The Rt. Hon. Jonathan Aitken, MP
 Private Secretary (G7), J. Wright
 Parliamentary Private Secretary, S. Milligan, MP
Parliamentary Under-Secretary of State, Viscount Cranborne
 Private Secretary (SEO), Miss H. Davies
Permanent Under-Secretary of State (G1), Sir Christopher France, KCB
 Private Secretary (G7), B. R. Mann
Chief of the Defence Staff, Marshal of the RAF Sir Peter Harding, GCB, ADC

THE DEFENCE COUNCIL

The Defence Council is responsible for running the Armed Forces. It is chaired by the Secretary of State for Defence and consists of: the Ministers of State; the Permanent Under-Secretary of State; the Chief of the Defence Staff and the Vice-Chief of the Defence Staff; the Parliamentary Under-Secretary of State; the Chief Scientific Adviser; the Chief of Defence Procurement; the Second Permanent Under-Secretary of State; the Chief of the Naval Staff; the Chief of the General Staff; and the Chief of the Air Staff.

DEFENCE STAFF

Vice-Chief of the Defence Staff, Adm. Sir Jock Slater, GCB, LVO
Deputy Under-Secretary (Policy) (G2), D. B. Omand
Defence Services Secretary, Maj.-Gen. B. T. Pennicott
Deputy CDS (Commitments), Vice-Adm. the Hon. Sir Nicholas Hill-Norton, KCB

Asst Under-Secretary (Commitments) (G3), W. D. Reeves, CB
Asst CDS (Overseas), Air Vice-Marshal N. B. Baldwin
Asst CDS (Logistics), Rear-Adm. F. B. Goodson
Deputy CDS (Systems), Air Marshal Sir Roger Austin, KCB, AFC
Head of Manpower Structure Study Team, Air Vice-Marshal A. L. Roberts, CBE, AFC
Asst CDS, Operational Requirements (Sea), Rear-Adm. R. F. Cobbold
Asst CDS, Operational Requirements (Land), Maj.-Gen. S. Cowan, CBE
Asst CDS, Operational Requirements (Air), Air Vice-Marshal I. D. Macfadyen, CB, OBE
Asst CDS (CIS), Maj.-Gen. W. J. P. Robins, OBE
Asst CDS (Policy and Nuclear), Rear-Adm. J. J. R. Tod, CBE
Asst Under-Secretary (Policy) (G3), I. D. Dawson
Deputy CDS (Programmes and Personnel), Lt.-Gen. the Hon. Sir Thomas Boyd-Carpenter, KBE
Asst CDS (Programmes), Air Vice-Marshal T. Garden
Surgeon-General and Director-General, Army Medical Services, Lt.-Gen. Sir Peter Beale, KBE, QHP
Deputy Surgeon-General (Health Services) and Director-General, Medical Services (RAF), Air Vice-Marshal J. M. Brook, QHS
Deputy Surgeon-General (Ops. and Plans) and Medical Director-General (Naval), Surgeon Rear-Adm. A. L. Revell
Director, Defence Nursing Services and Director, Nursing Services (Royal Navy), Commandant Nursing Officer Miss J. Titley
Director, Army Nursing Services, Brig. H. S. Dixon-Nuttal, QHNS
Director, Defence Dental Services, Air Vice-Marshal J. Mackey, QHDS
Head of Medical Services (Finance and Secretariat Division) (G5), P. G. Schulte
Director, Army Medicine and Consultant Physician, Brig. G. O. Cowan, OBE, QHP
Director, Army Surgery and Consultant Surgeon, Brig. I. R. Haywood
Director, Army Psychiatry and Consultant Psychiatrist, Col. R. M. L. Anderson

DEFENCE INTELLIGENCE STAFF

Director, Defence Intelligence (Secretariat) (G5), P. Bailey

NAVAL DEPARTMENT

Chief of the Naval Staff and First Sea Lord, Adm. Sir Benjamin Bathurst, KCB
Asst Chief of Naval Staff, Rear-Adm. J. R. Brigstocke
Commandant-General Royal Marines, Lt.-Gen. R. J. Ross, CB, OBE
Chief of Naval Personnel and Second Sea Lord, Vice-Adm. Sir Michael Layard, KCB, CBE
Naval Secretary, Rear-Adm. M. G. Rutherford, CBE
Director-General, Naval Manpower and Training, Rear-Adm. N. J. Wilkinson
Asst Under-Secretary (Naval Personnel) (G3), J. M. Moss
Chief of Fleet Support, Vice-Adm. Sir Neville Purvis, KCB
Asst Under-Secretary (Fleet Support) (G3), A. J. D. Pawson
Director-General, Ship Refitting (G3), B. V. Babbington
Director-General, Supplies and Transport (N) (G3), D. G. Jones

Principal Director, Supplies and Transport (Ops.) (G4),
W. N. Cooke
Principal Director, Supplies and Transport (Stores and
Victualling) (G4), G. E. Miller
Principal Director, Supplies and Transport (Armaments)
(G4), M. A. Holder
Director-General, Fleet Support (Operations and Plans), Rear-
Adm. J. H. Dunt
Director, Naval Shore Telecommunications (G5), M. Frowde
Director-General, Aircraft (Navy), Rear-Adm.
R. C. Moylan-Jones
Chaplain of The Fleet, Ven. M. W. Bucks, QHC

HYDROGRAPHIC OFFICE
Taunton, Somerset TAI 2DN
Tel 0823-337900

The Hydrographic Office was established as a defence
support agency in April 1990 and provides charts and
publications for the Royal Navy and other customers in the
UK and overseas.
Hydrographer of the Royal Navy and Chief Executive,
Hydrographic Office, Rear-Adm. J. A. L. Myres, CB *(until*
Feb. 1994); Rear-Adm. N. R. Essenhigh *(from Feb. 1994)*

ARMY DEPARTMENT
Chief of the General Staff, Gen. Sir Peter Inge, KCB, ADC
(Gen.)
Asst Chief of the General Staff, Maj.-Gen. M. J. D. Walker
Director-General, TA, Maj.-Gen. A. I. J. Kennedy, CBE
Director-General, Army Training, Maj.-Gen.
R. W. M. McAfee
Inspector-General, Doctrine and Training, Lt.-Gen.
P. R. Duffell, CBE, MC
Director, Royal Armoured Corps, Maj.-Gen. R. J. Hayman-
Joyce, CBE *(until Jan. 1994)*
Director, Royal Artillery, Maj.-Gen. M. T. Tennant
Director, Infantry, Maj.-Gen. B. H. Dutton, CBE
Director, Army Air Corps, Maj.-Gen. S. W. St J. Lytle
Engineer in Chief (Army), Maj.-Gen. G. W. Field
Director-General, Communications and Information Systems
(Army) and Signals Officer in Chief (Army), Maj.-Gen.
A. H. Boyle
Military Secretary, Maj.-Gen. R. J. Hayman-Joyce, CBE
(from Jan. 1994)
Adjutant-General, Gen. Sir Michael Wilkes, KCB, CBE
Asst Under-Secretary (Command Secretary, HQ UK Land
Forces) (G3), D. Dreher
Director-General, Army Manning and Recruiting, Maj.-Gen.
J. F. Deverell
Director, Staff and Personal Services (Army), Brig. C. Geal,
OBE
Director-General, Personal Services (Army), Maj.-Gen.
M. D. Jackson, MBE
Provost Marshal (Army), Brig. I. Cameron
Director, Army Legal Services, Maj.-Gen. M. H. F. Clarke
Director, Educational and Training Services (Army), Brig.
J. M. Macfarlane
Quartermaster-General, Lt.-Gen. the Hon. Sir William
Rous, KCB, OBE *(from Jan. 1994)*
Asst Under-Secretary (Quartermaster) (G3), N. J. Beaumont
Director-General, Logistics Policy (Army), Maj.-Gen.
P. J. Sheppard, CBE
Director, Royal Army Veterinary Corps, Brig. A. H. Parker-
Bowles, OBE
Director-General, Management and Support of Intelligence,
Maj.-Gen. A. L. Meier, OBE
Director-General, Equipment Support (Army), Maj.-Gen.
M. S. Heath

Director, Women, Brig. J. M. Roulstone
Chaplain General, Revd J. Harkness, OBE, QHC

MILITARY SURVEY
Elmwood Avenue, Feltham, Middx. TWI3 7AH
Tel 081-890 3622

Military Survey was established as a defence support agency
in April 1991. Its role is to give the armed forces the
geographic support required to enable them to plan, train
and fight effectively.
Director-General, Maj.-Gen. R. Wood

AIR FORCE DEPARTMENT
Chief of the Air Staff, Air Chief Marshal Sir Michael
Graydon, GCB, CBE
Asst Chief of Air Staff, Air Vice-Marshal A. J. C. Bagnall
Chief Executive, National Air Traffic Services (G3),
D. J. McLauchlan
Director-General, Policy and Planning, Air Vice-Marshal
M. J. Gibson, OBE
Air Member for Personnel, Air Chief Marshal Sir Andrew
Wilson, KCB, AFC, ADC
Air Secretary, Air Vice-Marshal R. J. Honey, CB, CBE
Director-General, Training and Personnel (RAF), Air Vice-
Marshal P. G. Beer, CBE, LVO
Director, Legal Services (RAF) Air Vice-Marshal
G. W. Carleton
Asst Under-Secretary (Personnel (Air)) (G3), M. D. Tidy
Air Member for Supply and Organization, Air Chief Marshal
Sir Michael Alcock, KCB
Director-General, Support Services (RAF), Air Vice-Marshal
R. H. Kyle, MBE
Director-General, Support Management (RAF), Air Vice-
Marshal C. G. Terry, OBE
Asst Under-Secretary (Supply and Organization (Air)) (G3),
H. Griffiths
Chaplain-in-Chief (RAF), Ven. B. H. Lucas, CB, QHC

RAF SUPPORT COMMAND MAINTENANCE GROUP
RAF Brampton, Huntingdon, Cambs. PEI8 8QL
Tel 0480-52151

The Group became a defence support agency in April 1991.
It supplies engineering, warehousing, transportation and
communications services to the RAF and some other UK
and NATO services.
Chief Executive, Air Vice-Marshal D. R. French, CB

DEFENCE SCIENTIFIC STAFF
Chief Scientific Adviser (G1A), Prof. D. Davies, CBE
Deputy Chief Scientific Adviser (G2), Dr G. G. Pope, CB
Asst Chief Scientific Advisers (G3), Dr G. D. Coley
(Projects); G. H. B. Jordan *(Capabilities);* P. M. Sutcliffe
(Research); (G4) A. L. C. Quigley *(Nuclear)*
Chief Executive, Defence Operational Analysis Centre (G3),
Dr D. Leadbeater
Director, Science Ballistic Missile Defence Directorate (G5),
P. Varnish

OFFICE OF MANAGEMENT AND BUDGET
Second Permanent Under-Secretary of State (G1A),
J. M. Stewart, CB
Deputy Under-Secretaries (G2), J. F. Howe, OBE *(Civilian*
Management); R. L. L. Facer, CB *(Personnel and Logistics);*
R. T. Jackling, CBE *(Resources and Programmes);* vacant
(Security and Common Services)
Asst Under-Secretaries (G3), T. J. Brack *(General Finance);*
I. D. Fauset *(Civilian Management (Personnel));*
Dr M. J. Harte *(Resources);* A. J. Cragg *(Director-General*
of Management Audit); A. Walker *(Service Personnel);*

vacant (*Programmes*); D. Fisher (*Systems*); B. F. Rule (*Director-General, Information Technology Services*); B. W. Stanley (*Director, Works Services*); T. F. W. B. Knapp (*Infrastructure and Logistics*)
Chief Statistical Adviser and Chief Executive of Defence Analytical Services Agency, P. Altobell
Chief of Ministry of Defence Police, J. Reddington, QPM

DIRECTORATE-GENERAL OF DEFENCE ACCOUNTS
Warminster Road, Bath BA1 5AA
Tel 0225-828106
This defence support agency was established in April 1991 and is responsible for providing accounting services to the MOD.
Chief Executive (G4), M. J. Dymond

PUBLIC RELATIONS
Chief of Public Relations (G4), Ms G. Samuel
Deputy Chief of Public Relations (G5), A. Armstrong
Director, Public Relations (Navy), Capt. C. Esplin-Jones
Director, Public Relations (Army), Brig. P. Trousdell
Director, Public Relations (RAF), Air Cdre G. McRobbie

PROCUREMENT EXECUTIVE

Chief of Defence Procurement (G1), Dr M. K. McIntosh
Private Secretary (G7), S. H. Lowe

PROCUREMENT EXECUTIVE POLICY AND ADMINISTRATION
Deputy Under-Secretary (Defence Procurement) (G2), M. J. V. Bell
Asst Under-Secretary (Business Strategy) (G3), J. A. Gulvin
Asst Under-Secretary (Finance) (G3), Ms D. J. Seammen
President of the Ordnance Board, Maj.-Gen. C. R. S. Notley, CBE
Director-General, Test and Evaluation (G3), B. Miller
Director-General, Defence Contracts (G3), G. E. Roe
Principal Director, Pricing and Quality Services (G4), J. V. A. Crawford
Director, Intellectual Property Rights (G4), D. J. Isaaks
Director, Test and Evaluation (Air Systems), Air Cdre J. E. Houghton, AFC

DEFENCE RESEARCH AGENCY
Farnborough, Hants. GU14 6TD
Tel 0252-392000
The Defence Research Agency (DRA) was set up on 1 April 1991. It incorporated the Royal Aerospace Establishment, the Admiralty Research Establishment, the Royal Armament Research and Development Establishment, and the Royal Signals and Radar Establishment.
Chief Executive (G2), J. A. R. Chisholm
Directors (G3), Dr A. L. Mears (*technical and quality*); Dr D. C. Tyte (*rationalization*); M. Goodfellow (*commercial*); Dr D. J. L. Smith (*group services*); G. Love (*finance*); (*G5*), R. Hack (*personnel*)
Managing Director, Maritime Division (G3), P. D. Ewins
Managing Director, Military and Aeronautics Division (G3), Dr R. H. Warren
Managing Director, Electronics Division (G3), Dr V. G. Roper
Managing Director (Operations) (G3), P. D. Ewins
Head of Marketing Intelligence, Dr B. Milsom
Company Secretary (G5), Mrs E. Peace

CHEMICAL AND BIOLOGICAL DEFENCE ESTABLISHMENT
Porton Down, Salisbury, Wilts. SP4 0JQ
Tel 0980-613000
This defence support agency was established in April 1991 and is the United Kingdom's scientific and technical authority on chemical and biological defence matters. It carries out research, provides advice and support to the MOD and other government departments, and assists the development and production in industry of appropriate equipment for the armed forces.
Chief Executive (G3), Dr G. S. Pearson, CB

NUCLEAR PROGRAMMES
Deputy Controller (Nuclear) (G3), G. N. Beaven
Chief Executive, Atomic Weapons Establishment (G2), B. H. Richards

SEA SYSTEMS CONTROLLERATE
Controller of the Navy, Adm. Sir Kenneth Eaton, KCB
Head of Material Co-ordination (Naval) (G5), vacant
Principal Director, Navy and Nuclear Contracts (G4), A. T. Phipps
Director-General, Submarines and Deputy Controller, Rear-Adm. R. Walmsley
Director-General, Surface Ships (G3), C. V. Betts
Director-General, Surface Weapons (G4), Cdre F. P. Scourse, MBE
Naval Ships Acceptance, Cdre S. Taylor
Director (Finance and Secretariat), Underwater Systems (G3), J. A. Kenny
Director-General, Underwater Weapons (G4), D. McArthur
Director, Naval Architect (G5), P. Davies
Chief, Strategic Systems Executive, Rear-Adm. R. D. Irwin
Deputy Chief, Strategic Systems Executive, Cdre N. R. Hodgson
Director-General, Strategic Weapons Systems, Dr J. P. Catchpole
Director (Finance and Secretariat), Strategic Systems (G5), D. M. T. Lewis
Director, Naval Support Command Implementation (G5), J. Read
Director (Finance and Secretariat), Abovewater Systems (G5), J. C. Cox
Director, Future Projects (G5), P. C. Bryan

LAND SYSTEMS CONTROLLERATE
Master-General of the Ordnance, Lt.-Gen. Sir Jeremy Blacker, KCB, CBE
Director-General, Policy and Special Projects, J. G. H. Walker
Principal Director, Contracts (Ordnance) (G4), R. C. Harford
Director-General, Guided Weapons and Electronic Systems (G3), J. D. Maines
Director-General, Land Fighting Systems, Maj.-Gen. A. C. P. Stone

AIR SYSTEMS CONTROLLERATE
Controller, Aircraft, Sir Donald Spiers, CB, TD
Principal Director, Contracts (Air) (G4), S. L. Porter
Director-General, Aircraft 1, (G3), J. A. Gordon
Director-General, Aircraft 2, Air Vice-Marshal P. C. Norriss, AFC
Director-General, Avionics Weapons and Information Systems (G3), J. C. Mabberley

DEFENCE EXPORT SERVICES ORGANIZATION
Head of Defence Export Services (G2), Sir Alan Thomas
Military Deputy to Head of DES, Rear-Adm. J. F. T. G. Salt

Director-General, Saudi Armed Forces Project, Air Marshal Sir William Wratten, KBE, CB, AFC
Director-General, Marketing (G3), N. Paren
Asst Under-Secretary (Export Policy and Finance) (G3), C. T. Sandars
Malaysian Project Office (G5), J. B. Taylor

METEOROLOGICAL OFFICE
London Road, Bracknell, Berks. RG12 2SZ
Tel 0344-420242

The Meteorological Office is the national meteorological service. It became an executive support agency within the Ministry of Defence in April 1990. It provides meteorological services for the Services departments and civilian aviation, shipping, public services, the press, industry and the general public. It collects, distributes and publishes meteorological information from all parts of the world and undertakes research related to meteorology and climate.
Chief Executive (G2), Prof. J. Hunt, FRS
Director of Operations (G3), Dr P. Ryder
Director of Research (G4), Dr P. Mason

The Royal Navy

LORD HIGH ADMIRAL OF THE UNITED KINGDOM, HM The Queen

ADMIRALS OF THE FLEET
HRH The Prince Philip, Duke of Edinburgh, KG, KT, OM, GBE, AC, QSO, PC, apptd 1953
Sir Varyl Begg, GCB, DSO, DSC, apptd 1968
The Lord Hill-Norton, GCB, apptd 1971
Sir Michael Pollock, GCB, LVO, DSC, apptd 1974
Sir Edward Ashmore, GCB, DSC, apptd 1977
The Lord Lewin, KG, GCB, LVO, DSC, apptd 1979
Sir Henry Leach, GCB, apptd 1982
Sir William Staveley, GCB, apptd 1989
Sir Julian Oswald, GCB, apptd 1993

ADMIRALS
Bathurst, Sir Benjamin, GCB, ADC (Chief of the Naval Staff and First Sea Lord)
Slater, Sir Jock, GCB, LVO, (Vice-Chief of the Defence Staff)
Kerr, Sir John, GCB, ADC (C.-in-C. Naval Home Command)
White, Sir Hugo, KCB, CBE (C.-in-C. Fleet)
Eaton, Sir Kenneth, KCB (Controller of the Navy)

VICE-ADMIRALS
Coward, Sir John, KCB, DSO (Commandant, Royal College of Defence Studies)
Hill-Norton, The Hon. Sir Nicholas, KCB (Deputy CDS (Commitments))
Purvis, Sir Neville, KCB (Chief of Fleet Support)
Dobson, Sir David, KBE (Chief of Staff to Commander, Allied Naval Forces Southern Europe)
Newman, Sir Roy, KCB (Flag Officer Plymouth and Naval Base Comd. Devonport)
Woodhead, Sir Peter, KCB
Layard, Sir Michael, KCB, CBE (Chief of Naval Personnel and Second Sea Lord)
Biggs, Sir Geoffrey, KCB (Deputy Comd. Fleet)
Morgan, C. C. (Flag Officer Scotland and N. Ireland)
Frere, R. T. (Flag Officer Submarines and Comd. Sub. Area East Atlantic, until Dec. 1993)
Abbott, P. C. (Deputy Supreme Allied Commander Atlantic)

REAR-ADMIRALS
Tod, J. J. R., CBE (Asst CDS (Policy and Nuclear))
Walmsley, R. (Director-General, Submarines)
Myres, J. A. L., CB (Hydrographer of the Navy and Chief Executive, Hydrographic Office Defence Support Agency, until Feb. 1994)
Hoddinott, A. P., OBE (Commander, British Naval Staff Washington, Naval Attaché Washington and UK National Liaison Representative to SACLANT)
Woodard, R. N. (Flag Officer Royal Yachts)
Moore, M. A. C., LVO (Maritime Adviser to the Supreme Allied Commander Europe)
Wilkinson, N. J. (Director-General, Naval Manpower and Training)
Brigstocke, J. R. (Asst Chief of Naval Staff)
Cobbold, R. F. (Asst CDS Operational Requirements (Sea Systems))
Boyce, M. C., OBE (Flag Officer Surface Flotilla)
Shiffner, J. R. (Director-General, Fleet Support (Equipment and Systems))
Lang, J. S. (Director-General, Intelligence (Assessments))
Sanders, J. T., OBE (Flag Officer Gibraltar)
Moylan-Jones, R. C. (Director-General, Aircraft (Navy))
Rankin, N. E., CBE (Flag Officer Portsmouth)
England, T. J. (Chief Staff Officer (Support)/Fleet)
Tolhurst, J. G. (Flag Officer Sea Training)
Garnett, I. D. G. (Flag Officer Naval Aviation)
Rutherford, M. G., CBE (Naval Secretary)
Irwin, R. O. (Chief, Strategic Systems Executive)
Goodson, F. B., OBE (Asst CDS (Logistics))
Blackham, J. J. (Chief of Staff to C.-in-C. NAVHOME)
Gretton, M. P. (Commander, UK Task Group)
Dunt, J. H. (Director-General, Fleet Support (Operations and Plans))
Lane-Nott, R. C. (Flag Officer Submarines, from Dec. 1993)
Essenhigh, N. R. (Hydrographer of the Navy and Chief Executive, Hydrographic Office Defence Support Agency, from Feb. 1994)

HM FLEET AS AT 1 APRIL 1993

SUBMARINES

TRIDENT
Operational: Vanguard

POLARIS
Operational: Renown, Repulse, Resolution

FLEET
Operational: Sceptre, Spartan, Splendid, Superb, Talent, Tireless, Torbay, Trenchant, Triumph, Turbulent, Valiant
Refitting/standby: Sovereign, Trafalgar

TYPE 2400
Operational: Unicorn*, Upholder†
Refitting/standby: Unseen, Ursula

OBERON CLASS
Operational: Opossum, Opportune
Refitting/standby: Oracle

ANTI-SUBMARINE WARFARE (ASW) CARRIERS

Operational: Ark Royal, Invincible
Refitting/standby: Illustrious

ASSAULT SHIPS

Operational: Fearless
Refitting/standby: Intrepid

DESTROYERS

TYPE 42
Operational: Birmingham, Cardiff, Edinburgh, Exeter,
  Glasgow, Liverpool, Manchester, Newcastle,
  Nottingham, Southampton, York
Refitting/standby: Gloucester

FRIGATES

TYPE 23
Operational: Argyll, Iron Duke†, Lancaster†, Marlborough,
  Monmouth†, Montrose*, Norfolk, Westminster*

TYPE 22
Operational: Battleaxe, Beaver, Boxer, Brazen, Brilliant,
  Broadsword, Campbeltown, Chatham, Cornwall,
  Coventry, Cumberland, London, Sheffield
Refitting/standby: Brave

TYPE 21
Operational: Active, Alacrity, Amazon, Ambuscade, Arrow,
  Avenger

LEANDER CLASS
Operational: Andromeda, Scylla

OFFSHORE PATROL

CASTLE CLASS
Operational: Dumbarton Castle, Leeds Castle

ISLAND CLASS
Operational: Alderney, Anglesey, Guernsey, Jersey,
  Lindisfarne, Orkney, Shetland

MINESWEEPERS

RIVER CLASS[1]
Operational: Arun, Blackwater, Carron, Dovey, Helford,
  Humber, Itchen, Orwell, Spey, Waveney
Refitting/standby: Helmsdale, Ribble

MINEHUNTERS TON CLASS
Operational: Brinton, Nurton, Sheraton, Wilton (Dartmouth
  Navigation Training Ship)
Refitting/standby: Iveston, Kellington

HUNT CLASS
Operational: Atherstone, Berkeley, Bicester, Brocklesby,
  Cattistock, Chiddingfold, Cottesmore, Dulverton,
  Hurworth, Ledbury, Middleton, Quorn
Refitting/standby: Brecon

SINGLE ROLE MINEHUNTER
Operational: Bridport*, Cromer†, Inverness†, Sandown,
  Walney†

PATROL CRAFT

BIRD CLASS
Operational: Cygnet, Kingfisher, Redpole

COASTAL TRAINING CRAFT[2]
Operational: Biter, Blazer, Charger, Dasher, Puncher,
  Pursuer
Refitting/standby: Archer, Smiter

PEACOCK CLASS
Operational: Peacock, Plover, Starling

GIBRALTAR SEARCH AND RESCUE CRAFT
Operational: Ranger, Trumpeter

ROYAL YACHT/HOSPITAL SHIP

Operational: Britannia

TRAINING SHIPS

FLEET TENDERS
Operational: Messina

ICE PATROL SHIP

Operational: Endurance

SURVEY SHIPS

Operational: Bulldog, Gleaner, Hecla, Herald, Roebuck
Refitting/standby: Beagle

SOLD/DECOMMISSIONED 1992–3

Argonaut, Ariadne, Blue Rover, Hermione, Juno, Jupiter,
Minerva, Osiris, Regent, Revenge, Sentinel, Sirius

* Under construction at 1 April 1993 and planned to enter
  service 1993–4
† Engaged in trials or training at 1 April 1993
1 River Class vessels, apart from HMS *Blackwater*, are
  operated by the RNR
2 Coastal training craft are operated by the RNR and
  University Royal Naval Units

ROYAL FLEET AUXILIARY (RFA)

The Royal Fleet Auxiliary supplies ships of the fleet with
fuel, food, water, spares and ammunition while at sea. Its
ships are manned by merchant seamen.

FLEET AIR ARM

The Fleet Air Arm was established in 1937 and operates
aircraft and helicopters for the Royal Navy.

ROYAL NAVAL RESERVE (RNR)

The Royal Naval Reserve is a totally integrated part of the
Royal Navy. It comprises about 6,000 men and women
nationwide who volunteer to train in their spare time for a
variety of sea and shore tasks which they would carry out in
time of tension or war.
Chief Staff Officer, Capt. C. W. Pile

ROYAL NAVAL AUXILIARY SERVICE (RNXS)

The RNXS is a uniformed, unarmed and, in peacetime,
volunteer civilian service of some 2,700 men and women,
under the direction of the Commander-in-Chief Naval Home
Command. Members train in their spare time in units around
the coasts of the United Kingdom for duties in times of
tension and war. Their role includes manning port headquarters in support of the Naval Control of Shipping Organization,
and providing crews for vessels engaged in the defence of
ports and anchorages.
Patron and Hon. Auxiliary Commodore, HRH Prince
  Michael of Kent
Captain, Capt. J. M. Neville-Rolfe, RN

ROYAL MARINES

The Army

The Corps of Royal Marines was formed in 1664 and is part of the Naval Service. The Royal Marines provide Britain's sea soldiers and in particular 3 Commando Brigade Royal Marines, which is trained and equipped for arctic warfare. Royal Marines also serve in HM Ships, provide landing craft crews, special boat sections and other detachments for naval and amphibious operations. They also provide the Naval Band Service. The Corps is about 7,000 strong.
Commandant-General, Royal Marines, Lt.-Gen. R. J. Ross, CB, OBE
Major-Generals, A. M. Keeling (*MGRM*); J. S. Chester, OBE (*Royal College Defence Studies*)

ROYAL MARINES RESERVE (RMR)

The Royal Marines Reserve is a force of commando-trained volunteers who train to combat-readiness in order to support the regular Royal Marines should the need arise. About 50 per cent are trained and equipped for arctic warfare and most regular Royal Marine specializations are open to the reservist. There are RMR centres in London, Glasgow, Bristol, Liverpool and Newcastle, each with a number of outlying detachments. The present strength of the RMR is about 1,200.
Director, Brig. R. S. Tailyour

QUEEN ALEXANDRA'S ROYAL NAVAL NURSING SERVICE

The first nursing sisters were appointed to naval hospitals in 1884 and the Queen Alexandra's Royal Naval Nursing Service (QARNNS) gained its current title under the patronage of Queen Alexandra in 1902. Nursing ratings were introduced in 1960 and men were integrated into the Service in 1982; both men and women serve as officers and ratings. Female medical assistants were introduced in 1987. Qualified staff and learners are mainly based at the UK Royal Naval Hospitals, and continue their responsibility for the health and fitness of naval personnel. The strength is about 600.
Patron, HRH Princess Alexandra, the Hon. Lady Ogilvy
Matron-in-Chief, Commandant Nursing Officer Miss J. Titley

WOMEN'S ROYAL NAVAL SERVICE

Originally founded in 1917, the Women's Royal Naval Service (WRNS) was temporarily disbanded between the First and Second World Wars. The contribution of the Service is now established as a professional and integral part of the Royal Navy with personnel serving in the United Kingdom and abroad in a wide range of specialist roles. From 6 February 1990, the role of the WRNS was expanded to include sea service, and from 1 January 1991 to include aircrew. WRNS officers adopted Royal Navy rank titles from 1 December 1990. The strength of the WRNS is about 4,500. Commandant Spencer is not being replaced when she retires in October 1993, and it is thought that the WRNS will then be abolished as a separate Service.
Chief Commandant, HRH The Princess Royal
Director, Commandant A. C. Spencer, ADC (*retires Oct. 1993*)

THE QUEEN

FIELD MARSHALS
HRH The Prince Philip, Duke of Edinburgh, KG, KT, OM, GBE, AC, QSO, PC, *apptd* 1953
Sir James Cassels, GCB, KBE, DSO, *apptd* 1968
The Lord Carver, GCB, CBE, DSO, MC, *apptd* 1973
Sir Roland Gibbs, GCB, CBE, DSO, MC, *apptd* 1979
The Lord Bramall, KG, GCB, OBE, MC, *apptd* 1982
Sir John Stanier, GCB, MBE, *apptd* 1985
Sir Nigel Bagnall, GCB, CVO, MC, *apptd* 1988
Sir Richard Vincent, GBE, KCB, DSO (*Chairman of NATO's Military Committee*), *apptd* 1991
Sir John Chapple, GCB, CBE (*Governor and C.-in-C. Gibraltar*), *apptd* 1992
HRH The Duke of Kent, KG, GCMG, GCVO, ADC, *apptd* 1993

GENERALS
Inge, Sir Peter, GCB, ADC (*Gen.*), Col. Green Howards, Col. Cmdt. APTC (*Chief of the General Staff*)
Waters, Sir John, KCB, CBE, ADC (*D. SACEUR*)
Guthrie, Sir Charles, KCB, LVO, OBE, ADC (*Gen.*), Col. Cmdt. Int. Corps (*C.-in-C. BAOR and Comdt, Northern Army Group*)
Jones, Sir Edward, KCB, CBE, Col. Cmdt. 2 RGJ (*UK Military Rep. to NATO*)
Learmont, Sir John, KCB, CBE, Col. Cmdt. AAC, Col. Cmdt. RA (*Quartermaster-General, until Jan. 1994*)
Johnson, Sir Garry, KCB, OBE, Col. 10 GR, Col. Cmdt. The Light Division (*C.-in-C. AFNORTH*)
Wilkes, Sir Michael, KCB, CBE, Col. Cmdt. Hon. Artillery Company (TA) (*Adjutant-General*)
Wilsey, Sir John, KCB, CBE, Col. Cmdt POW Division, Col. Cmdt. Royal Logistic Corps (*C.-in-C. UK Land Forces*)

LIEUTENANT-GENERALS
Swinburn, Sir Richard, KCB (*GOC S District*)
Blacker, Sir Jeremy, KCB, CBE, Col. Cmdt. RTR, Col. Cmdt. RAC (*Master-General of the Ordnance*)
Rous, The Hon. Sir William, KCB, OBE (*Quartermaster-General, from Jan. 1994*)
Mackenzie, Sir Jeremy, KCB, OBE, Col. Cmdt. AG Corps (*Cmdt. NATO Rapid Reaction Corps*)
Duffell, Sir Peter, KCB, CBE, MC (*Inspector-General, Doctrine and Training*)
Beale, Sir Peter, KBE, QHP (*Surgeon-General*)
Boyd-Carpenter, the Hon. Sir Thomas, KBE (*Deputy CDS (Programmes and Personnel)*)
Wheeler, Sir Roger, KCB, CBE (*GOC Northern Ireland*)
Rose, H. M., CBE, QGM (*Comd. UK Land Forces*)

MAJOR-GENERALS
Corbett, R. J. S., CB (*GOC London District*)
Hayman-Joyce, R. J., CBE (*Military Secretary, from Jan. 1994*)
Cowan, S., CBE, Col. QGS (*Asst Chief of the Defence Staff OR (Land)*)
Pennicott, B. T. (*Defence Services Secretary*)
Barr, J. A. J. P., CB, CBE, Col. Cmdt. Corps of Royal Engineers
Crawford, I. P., GM, QHP, FFCM
Grist, R. D., OBE, Col. Gloucesters (*Director-General, AG Corps*)

Thomson, D. P., CB, CBE, MC, Col. The Argyll and Sutherland Highlanders (Princess Louise's) (*Senior Army Member, Royal College of Defence Studies*)

Denison-Smith, A. A., MBE (*GOC 4 Armd Division*)

Field, G. W., CB, OBE, Col. Cmdt. Royal Logistic Corps (*Engineer-in-Chief (Army)*)

Stone, A. C. P., CB, Col. Cmdt. Royal Regiment of Artillery (*Director-General, Land Fighting Systems*)

Wallace, C. B. Q., OBE, Col. Cmdt. RMP (*Comdt. Staff College*)

Harley, A. G. H., CB, OBE (*Comd. British Forces Cyprus*)

Baskervyle-Glegg, J., MBE (*SBLSO RAO*)

Smith, R. A., DSO, OBE, QGM, Col. Cmdt. Parachute Regiment, Col. Cmdt. REME Equipment Support Organization (*Asst CDS (Operations/Security)*)

Wood, R., FRICS (*Director-General, Military Survey*)

Courage, W. J., MBE (*Chief of Joint Services Liaison Organization Bonn*)

Mayes, F. B., QHS, FRCS (*Director-General, Army Medical Services*)

Toyne Sewell, T. P. (*Cmdt. RMAS*)

Tennant, M. T. (*Director, Royal Artillery*)

Heath, M. S., CBE (*Director-General, Equipment Support (Army)*)

Burton, E. F. G., OBE (*Cmdt. RMCS*)

Grove, D. A., OBE (*Team Leader, AG Study Group*)

Meier, A. L., OBE (*Director-General, Management and Support of Intelligence, MOD*)

Pett, R. A., MBE (*Deputy Chief of Staff (Support) AFNORTH*)

Grant, S. C. (*Team Leader, Command Structure Review*)

Gordon, J., CBE (*Chief of Staff HQ UK Land Forces*)

Sheppard, P. J., CBE (*Director-General, Logistics Policy (Army)*)

Walker, M. J. D., CBE, Col. Cmdt. The Queen's Division (*Asst Chief of General Staff*)

Regan, M. D., OBE (*GOC Wales and W District*)

Freer, I. L., CBE, Col. Staffords (*CLF and DD Ops. N. Ireland*)

Foley, J. P., CB, OBE, MC (*Comd. BFHK and Maj.-Gen. Brigade of Gurkhas*)

Hollands, G. S. (*Cmdt. Artillery 1 (Br) Corps*)

Lytle, S. W. St J. (*Director, Army Air Corps*)

Notley, C. R. S., CBE (*President, Ordnance Board*)

Dutton, B. H., CBE (*Director, Infantry*)

Pike, H. W. R., DSO, MBE, Col. SASC (*GOC UK Division*)

Carr-Smith, S. R. (*Chief C3 NACISA*)

Clarke, M. F. H. (*Director, Army Legal Services*)

Jackson, M. D., CBE (*Director-General, Personal Services (Army)*)

Kennedy, A. I. G., CBE (*Director-General, TA*)

Burden, D. L., CBE (*Director-General, Logistic Support (Army)*)

Craig, R. P., MD, FRCS, QHS (*Cmdt. MED. UK Land Forces*)

Boyle, A. H. (*Director-General, CCCIS (Army) and Signal Officer-in-Chief (Army)*)

Cordingley, P. A. J., DSO (*GOC E District*)

Robins, W. J. P., OBE (*Asst CDS (CCCIS)*)

Willcocks, M. A. (*Director-General, Land Warfare*)

McAfee, R. W. M. (*Director-General, Army Training*)

Scott, M. I. E., CBE, DSO, Col. Cmdt. The Scottish Division (*GOC Scotland*)

Deverell, J. F., OBE (*Director-General, Army Manning and Recruiting*)

Mackay-Dick, I. C., MBE (*Comd. British Forces Falkland Islands*)

Pigott, A. D., CBE (*Chief of Staff HQ ACE Rapid Reaction Corps*)

White, M. S., CBE (*Director of Support LANDCENT*)

Cowan, G. O. (*Cmdt. Royal Army Medical College*)

Cordy-Simpson, R. A. (*Chief of Staff HQ BAOR*)

CONSTITUTION OF THE BRITISH ARMY

The regular forces include the following arms, branches and corps. Soldiers' record offices are shown at the end of each group; records of officers are maintained at the Ministry of Defence.

THE ARMS

HOUSEHOLD CAVALRY – The Household Cavalry Regiment (The Blues and Royals and The Life Guards). *Records*, Horse Guards, London SW1.

ROYAL ARMOURED CORPS – Cavalry Regiments: 1st The Queen's Dragoon Guards; The Royal Scots Dragoon Guards (Carabiniers and Greys); The Royal Dragoon Guards; The Queen's Royal Hussars (The Queen's Own and Royal Irish); 9th/12th Royal Lancers (Prince of Wales's); The King's Royal Hussars; The Light Dragoons; The Queen's Royal Lancers; Royal Tank Regiment comprising two regular regiments. *Records*, Queen's Park, Chester.

ARTILLERY – Royal Regiment of Artillery. *Records*, Imphal Barracks, Fulford Road, York.

ENGINEERS – Corps of Royal Engineers. *Records*, Kentigern House, Brown Street, Glasgow.

SIGNALS – Royal Corps of Signals. *Records*, Kentigern House, Brown Street, Glasgow.

THE INFANTRY

The Foot Guards and Regiments of Infantry of the Line are grouped in Divisions as follows:

GUARDS DIVISION – Grenadier, Coldstream, Scots, Irish and Welsh Guards. *Divisional HQ*, HQ Household Division, Horse Guards, London SW1. *Depot*, Pirbright Camp, Brookwood, Surrey. *Records*, Imphal Barracks, Fulford Road, York.

SCOTTISH DIVISION – The Royal Scots (The Royal Regiment); The Royal Highland Fusiliers (Princess Margaret's Own Glasgow and Ayrshire Regiment); The King's Own Scottish Borderers; The Black Watch (Royal Highland Regiment); Queen's Own Highlanders (Seaforth and Camerons); The Gordon Highlanders; The Argyll and Sutherland Highlanders (Princess Louise's). *Divisional HQ*, The Castle, Edinburgh. *Depots*, Scottish Divisional Depots, Glencorse, Milton Bridge, Midlothian; Albemarle Barracks, Ouston, Newcastle. *Records*, Imphal Barracks, Fulford Road, York.

QUEEN'S DIVISION – The Princess of Wales's Royal Regiment (Queen's and Royal Hampshire's); The Royal Regiment of Fusiliers; The Royal Anglian Regiment. *Divisional HQ and Depot*, Bassingbourn Barracks, Royston, Herts. *Records*, Higher Barracks, Exeter, Devon.

KING'S DIVISION – The King's Own Royal Border Regiment; The King's Regiment; The Prince of Wales's Own Regiment of Yorkshire; The Green Howards (Alexandra, Princess of Wales's Own Yorkshire Regiment); The Queen's Lancashire Regiment; The Duke of Wellington's Regiment (West Riding). *Divisional HQ*, Imphal Barracks, York. *Depots*, The King's Division Depot (Yorkshire), Queen Elizabeth Barracks, Strensall, Yorks.; Albemarle Barracks, Ouston, Newcastle. *Records*, Imphal Barracks, Fulford Road, York.

PRINCE OF WALES'S DIVISION – The Devonshire and Dorset Regiment; The Cheshire Regiment; The Royal

Welch Fusiliers; The Royal Regiment of Wales (24th/41st Foot); The Gloucestershire Regiment; The Worcestershire and Sherwood Foresters Regiment (29th/45th Foot); The Staffordshire Regiment (The Prince of Wales's); The Duke of Edinburgh's Royal Regiment (Berkshire and Wiltshire). *Divisional HQ* and *Depot*, Whittington Barracks, Lichfield, Staffs. *Records*, Imphal Barracks, Fulford, York.

LIGHT DIVISION – The Light Infantry; The Royal Green Jackets. *Divisional HQ* and *Depot*, Sir John Moore Barracks, Winchester, Hants. *Records*, Higher Barracks, Exeter.

BRIGADE OF GURKHAS – 2nd King Edward VII's Own Gurkha Rifles (The Sirmoor Rifles); 6th Queen Elizabeth's Own Gurkha Rifles; 7th Duke of Edinburgh's Own Gurkha Rifles; 10th Princess Mary's Own Gurkha Rifles; The Queen's Gurkha Engineers; Queen's Gurkha Signals; Gurkha Transport Regiment. *Brigade HQ*, HMS *Tamar*, Hong Kong, BFPO 1. *Depot*, Training Depot, Brigade of Gurkhas, Malaya Lines, Sek Kong, BFPO 1. *Records*, Record Office, Brigade of Gurkhas, Hong Kong, BFPO 1.

THE ROYAL IRISH REGIMENT (two general service and seven home service battalions) – 27th (Inniskilling), 83rd, 87th and the Ulster Defence Regiment. *Depot*, St Patrick's Barracks, Ballymena, N. Ireland. *Records*, Imphal Barracks, Fulford Road, York.

THE PARACHUTE REGIMENT (three regular battalions) – *Depot*, Browning Barracks, Aldershot, Hants. *Records*, Higher Barracks, Exeter.

SPECIAL AIR SERVICE REGIMENT – *Regimental HQ*, Duke of York's Headquarters, Sloane Square, London SW3. *Depot*, Stirling Lines, Hereford. *Records*, Higher Barracks, Exeter, Devon.

ARMY AIR CORPS – Regimental HQ and *Depot*, Middle Wallop, Hants. *Records*, Higher Barracks, Exeter.

THE SERVICES

Royal Army Chaplain's Department – *Regimental HQ* and *Depot*, Bagshot Park, Surrey.

Royal Logistic Corps – formed in April 1993 to subsume the functions of the Royal Corps of Transport, the Royal Army Ordnance Corps, the Royal Pioneer Corps, the Army Catering Corps, and the Postal and Courier Service of the Royal Engineers.

Royal Army Medical Corps, Royal Army Dental Corps and Queen Alexandra's Royal Army Nursing Corps. – *Records*, Queen's Park, Chester.

Adjutant-General's Corps – *Depot*, Worthy Down, Winchester, Hants. *Records*, Queen's Park, Chester.

Corps of Royal Electrical and Mechanical Engineers Equipment Support Organization – *Records*, Glen Parva Barracks, Saffron Road, Wigston, Leicester.

Small Arms School Corps – *Records*, Higher Barracks, Exeter.

General Service Corps – *Records*, Imphal Barracks, Fulford Road, York.

Corps of Royal Military Police, Royal Army Pay Corps, Royal Army Veterinary Corps, Intelligence Corps, Army Physical Training Corps, Sandhurst, Officers Training Corps – *Records*, Higher Barracks, Exeter, Devon.

THE TERRITORIAL ARMY (TA)

The Territorial Army is designed to provide a highly-trained and well-equipped force which will complete the Regular Army order of battle in a time of national emergency. Its establishment is approximately 91,000, reducing to 65,000, due to TA restructuring, by 1995.

QUEEN ALEXANDRA'S ROYAL ARMY NURSING CORPS

The Queen Alexandra's Royal Army Nursing Corps (QARANC) was founded in 1902 as Queen Alexandra's Imperial Military Nursing Service (QAIMNS) and gained its present title in 1949. The QARANC has trained nurses for the register and roll since 1950 and has eight other employment categories. A non-nursing officer element was introduced in 1959 for personnel work. Since 1 April 1992 men have been eligible to join the QARANC. The Corps provides service in military hospitals in the United Kingdom (including Northern Ireland), BAOR, Hong Kong, Cyprus, Falkland Islands and Belize.

Colonel-in-Chief, HRH The Princess Margaret, Countess of Snowdon, GCVO, CI

Matron-in-Chief (Army) and Director, Army Nursing Services, Brig. H. Dixon-Nuttal

WOMEN'S ROYAL ARMY CORPS

Formed 1 February 1949; disbanded April 1992.

The Royal Air Force

THE QUEEN

MARSHALS OF THE ROYAL AIR FORCE

HRH The Prince Philip, Duke of Edinburgh, KG, KT, OM, GBE, AC, QSO, PC, *apptd* 1953
Sir John Grandy, GCB, GCVO, KBE, DSO, *apptd* 1971
Sir Denis Spotswood, GCB, CBE, DSO, DFC, *apptd* 1974
Sir Michael Beetham, GCB, CBE, DFC, AFC, *apptd* 1982
Sir Keith Williamson, GCB, AFC, *apptd* 1985
Lord Craig of Radley, GCB, OBE, *apptd* 1988
Sir Peter Harding, GCB, ADC (*Chief of the Defence Staff*), *apptd* 1993

AIR CHIEF MARSHALS

Graydon, Sir Michael, GCB, CBE (*Chief of the Air Staff*)
Stear, Sir Michael, KCB, CBE (*Deputy C.-in-C. Allied Forces Central Europe*)
Thomson, Sir John, KCB, CBE, AFC (*AOC.-in-C. Strike Command and C.-in-C. UK Air Forces*)
Wilson, Sir Andrew, KCB, AFC, ADC (*Air Member for Personnel*)
Alcock, Sir Michael, KCB (*Air Member for Supply and Organization*)

AIR MARSHALS

Walker, Sir John, KCB, CBE, AFC (*Chief of Defence Intelligence*)
Austin, Sir Roger, KCB, AFC (*Deputy CDS (Systems)*)
Harris, Sir John, KCB, CBE (*AOC No. 18 Group*)
Wratten, Sir William, KBE, CB, AFC (*Director-General, Saudi Armed Forces Project*)
Willis, Sir John, KCB, CBE (*AOC.-in-C. RAF Support Command*)
Johns, R. E., CB, CBE, LVO (*Chief of Staff and Deputy C.-in-C. Strike Command*)

AIR VICE-MARSHALS

Roberts, A. L., CB, CBE, AFC (*Head of Manpower Structure Study Team*)

Honey, R. J., CB, CBE (*Air Secretary and AOC RAF Personnel Management Centre*)

Blackley, A. B., CBE, AFC (*Air Officer Scotland and N. Ireland*)

Harding, P. J., CB, CBE, AFC (*Deputy Chief of Staff (Operations) Allied Air Forces Central Europe*)

Cousins, D., CB, AFC (*Cmdt. RAF College, Cranwell*)

Allison, J. S., CBE (*AOC No. 11 Group*)

Dodworth, P., OBE, AFC (*Defence Attaché and Head of British Defence Staff, Washington*)

Garden, T., CB (*Asst CDS (Programmes)*)

Baird, J. A., QHP (*Principal Medical Officer Strike Command*)

Beer, P. G., CBE, LVO (*Director-General, Training and Personnel (RAF)*)

Clark, P. D., CB (*Air Officer Engineering Strike Command*)

Ferguson, G. M., CB, CBE (*Air Officer Admin. Strike Command*)

French, D. R., CB, MBE (*Chief Executive, RAF Support Command Maintenance Group*)

Gibson, M. J., OBE (*Director-General, Policy and Planning*)

Macfadyen, I. D., CB, OBE (*Asst CDS Operational Requirements (Air)*)

Saunders, D. J., CBE (*Asst CDS (Logistics)*)

Squire, P. T., DFC, AFC (*AOC No. 1 Group*)

Robertson, G. A., CBE (*AOC No. 2 Group*)

Lucas, Ven. B. H., QHC (*Chaplain-in Chief (RAF)*)

Davison, D. J., QHS (*Dean of Air Force Medicine*)

Brook, J. M., CB, QHS (*Director-General, Medical Services (RAF)*)

Chapple, R., QHP (*Principal Medical Officer, RAF Support Command*)

Cheshire, J. A., CBE (Asst COS (*Policy*), SHAPE)

Kyle, R. H., MBE (*Director-General, Support Services (RAF)*)

Mackey, J., QHDS (*Director, Defence Dental Services*)

Norriss, P. C., AFC (*Director-General, Aircraft 2*)

Rae, W. M., CB (*Senior Director of Staff, Royal College of Defence Studies*)

Sherrington, T. B., OBE (*Air Officer Admin., RAF Support Command*)

Carleton, G. W. (*Director, Legal Services (RAF)*)

Coville, C. C. C. (*Air Officer Training RAF Support Command*)

O'Brien, R. P., OBE (*Cmdt. Joint Service Defence College*)

May, J. A. G., CBE

Bagnall, A. J. C., OBE (*Asst Chief of Air Staff*)

Baldwin, N. B., CBE (*Asst CDS (Overseas)*)

Donaldson, M. P., MBE (*Cmdt. RAF Staff College, Bracknell*)

Terry, C. G., OBE (*Director-General, Support Management (RAF)*)

CONSTITUTION OF THE ROYAL AIR FORCE

The RAF currently consists of two Commands: Strike Command and Support Command. On 1 April 1993 RAF Germany became No. 2 Group of Strike Command. From April 1994, the RAF will consist of Strike Command, Logistics Command, and Personnel and Training Command. The two new Commands will take over the functions of Support Command, the Air Member for Personnel, and the Air Member for Supply and Organization. Strike Command is the RAF's operational command for the UK and designated locations abroad (including Germany); its roles include

strike/attack, air defence, control and reporting, maritime surveillance, air reconnaissance, air-to-air refuelling, offensive support, air transport, aero-medical facilities, and search and rescue. Logistics Command will be responsible for all logistics, engineering support, and maintenance. Personnel and Training Command will be responsible for air and ground training, hospitals, and personnel administration.

To carry out its tasks, the Royal Air Force is equipped (as at 1 April 1993) with:

Aircraft – 8 Victor, 274 Tornado, 24 Buccaneer, 6 Hunter, 7 Sentry, 56 Harrier, 53 Jaguar, 19 Canberra, 29 Nimrod, 19 VC10, 9 Tristar, 55 Hercules, 118 Hawk, 30 Jet Provost, 104 Tucano, 63 Chipmunk, 118 Bulldog

Helicopters – 37 Puma, 37 Wessex, 17 Sea King, 26 Chinook, 28 Gazelle

Miscellaneous communications aircraft, etc.

Rapier missiles

ROYAL AUXILIARY AIR FORCE (RAUXAF)

Formed in 1924, the Auxiliary Air Force served with great distinction in the Second World War and in recognition of its war record King George VI conferred the prefix 'Royal' in 1947. Following a major reduction of units in the late 1950s, the benefits to be gained by using auxiliary forces in certain roles has resulted in a subsequent expansion. Today, the Royal Auxiliary Air Force supports the RAF in maritime air operations, air and ground defence of major airfields, air movements and aero-medical evacuation.

Air Commodore-in-Chief, HM The Queen

Director of Personnel Management (Airmen) and Director of Reserve Forces (RAF), Air Cdre D. T. Davies

ROYAL AIR FORCE VOLUNTEER RESERVE (RAFVR)

The Royal Air Force Volunteer Reserve was created in 1936 with the object of providing training for the increased number of aircrew who were seen as necessary for the forthcoming conflict. The RAFVR was reconstituted in 1947 following war service and today is a small but important part of the Air Force Reserve. The RAFVR provides specialist personnel who fill specific wartime intelligence support, photo interpretation and public relations appointments. A small number of RAFVR aircrew are employed to augment regular crews on Nimrod (Maritime Reconnaissance) aircraft in wartime.

Director of Personnel Management (Airmen) and Director of Reserve Forces (RAF), Air Cdre D. T. Davies

PRINCESS MARY'S ROYAL AIR FORCE NURSING SERVICE

The Princess Mary's Royal Air Force Nursing Service (PMRAFNS) is open to both male and female candidates. Commissions are offered to those who are Registered General Nurses (RGN) with a minimum of two years experience after obtaining RGN and normally with a second qualification. RGNs with no additional experience or qualification are also recruited as non-commissioned officers in the grade of Staff Nurse.

Air Chief Commandant, HRH Princess Alexandra, the Hon. Lady Ogilvy, GCVO

Matron-in-Chief, Group Captain V. M. Hand (*from Jan. 1994*)

WOMEN'S ROYAL AIR FORCE

Formed on 1 April 1918, the Women's Royal Air Force (WRAF) was disbanded on 1 April 1920 and re-formed on 1 February 1949 from the Women's Auxiliary Air Force, the Second World War service which had been formed on 28 June 1939, and from the RAF companies of the Auxiliary Territorial Service.

WRAF officers and airwomen serve in most of the RAF branches and trades including as aircrew and as pilots of combat jets. WRAF personnel are employed at RAF stations and higher formations at home and abroad, and they compete on equal terms with their RAF counterparts for appointments, promotion and places on training courses.

Commandant-in-Chief, HM Queen Elizabeth The Queen Mother

Air Chief Commandant, HRH Princess Alice, Duchess of Gloucester

Director, Air Commodore R. M. B. Montague, ADC

ROYAL OBSERVER CORPS
Established in 1925; stood down 31 March 1992

ARMED FORCES STRENGTHS

AS AT 1 JULY 1993

All Services	270,912
Men	252,148
Women	18,764
Royal Naval Services	58,513
Men	54,092
Women	4,421
Army	133,058
Men	125,507
Women	7,551
Royal Air Force	79,341
Men	72,549
Women	6,792

DEFENCE CUTS

Cuts and restructuring are intended to achieve the following strengths by the mid 1990s:

Royal Navy	52,500
Army	119,000
Royal Air Force	70,000

SERVICE SALARIES AND PENSIONS

The following rates of pay have been introduced as part of the 1993 pay award for service personnel.

The increasing integration of women in the armed services is reflected in equal pay for equal work and the X factor addition is now the same for men and women (11.5 per cent).

Annual salaries are derived from daily rates in whole pence and rounded to the nearest £.

The pay rates shown are for Army personnel. The rates apply also to personnel of equivalent rank and pay band in the other services.

OFFICERS' SALARIES

MAIN SCALE

Rank	Daily	Annual	Rank	Daily	Annual
Second Lieutenant	£34.55	£12,611	Special List Lieutenant-Colonel	£101.03	£36,876
Lieutenant			Lieutenant-Colonel		
On appointment	45.69	16,677	On appointment with less		
After 1 year in the rank	46.88	17,111	than 19 years service	102.79	37,518
After 2 years in the rank	48.08	17,549	After 2 years in the rank or with		
After 3 years in the rank	49.28	17,987	19 years service	105.50	38,508
After 4 years in the rank	50.48	18,425	After 4 years in the rank or with		
Captain			21 years service	108.21	39,497
On appointment	58.14	21,221	After 6 years in the rank or with		
After 1 year in the rank	59.71	21,794	23 years service	110.92	40,486
After 2 years in the rank	61.29	22,371	After 8 years in the rank or with		
After 3 years in the rank	62.86	22,944	25 years service	113.63	41,475
After 4 years in the rank	64.43	23,517	Colonel		
After 5 years in the rank	66.01	24,094	On appointment	119.72	43,698
After 6 years in the rank	67.58	24,667	After 2 years in the rank	122.87	44,848
Major			After 4 years in the rank	126.01	45,994
On appointment	73.27	26,744	After 6 years in the rank	129.16	47,143
After 1 year in the rank	75.09	27,408	After 8 years in the rank	132.31	48,293
After 2 years in the rank	76.91	28,072	Brigadier	146.85	53,600
After 3 years in the rank	78.72	28,733	Major-General	155.37	56,710
After 4 years in the rank	80.54	29,397	Lieutenant-General	177.65	64,842
After 5 years in the rank	82.36	30,061	General	246.98	90,148
After 6 years in the rank	84.17	30,722	Field Marshal	307.08	112,084
After 7 years in the rank	85.99	31,386			
After 8 years in the rank	87.81	32,051			

SALARIES OF OFFICERS COMMISSIONED FROM THE RANKS (LIEUTENANTS AND CAPTAINS ONLY)

YEARS OF COMMISSIONED SERVICE	YEARS OF NON-COMMISSIONED SERVICE FROM AGE 18					
	Less than 12 years		12 years but less than 15 years		15 years or more	
	Daily	Annual	Daily	Annual	Daily	Annual
On appointment	£63.89	£23,320	£67.14	£24,506	£70.39	£25,692
After 1 year service	65.52	23,915	68.77	25,101	71.45	26,079
After 2 years service	67.14	24,506	70.39	25,692	72.50	26,462
After 3 years service	68.77	25,101	71.45	26,079	73.56	26,849
After 4 years service	70.39	25,692	72.50	26,462	74.61	27,233
After 5 years service	71.45	26,079	73.56	26,849	75.67	27,620
After 6 years service	72.50	26,462	74.61	27,233	76.72	28,003
After 8 years service	73.56	26,849	75.67	27,620	77.78	28,390
After 10 years service	74.61	27,233	76.72	28,003	77.78	28,390
After 12 years service	75.67	27,620	77.78	28,390	77.78	28,390
After 14 years service	76.72	28,003	77.78	28,390	77.78	28,390
After 16 years service	77.78	28,390	77.78	28,390	77.78	28,390

The pay structure below officer level is divided into pay bands. Jobs at each rank are allocated to bands according to their score in the job evaluation system.

Scale A: committed to serve/have completed less than 6 years
Scale B: committed to serve/have completed 6 years but less than 9 years
Scale C: committed to serve/have completed more than 9 years

Daily rates of pay effective from 1 April 1993 are:

SALARIES OF WARRANT OFFICERS AND SENIOR NCOs

Rank	Scale A				Scale B				Scale C			
	Band 4	Band 5	Band 6	Band 7	Band 4	Band 5	Band 6	Band 7	Band 4	Band 5	Band 6	Band 7
Sergeant	£42.47	£46.69	£51.31	£ —	£42.77	£46.99	£51.61	£ —	£43.23	£47.45	£52.07	£ —
Staff Sergeant	44.90	49.13	53.75	59.34	45.21	49.43	54.06	59.64	45.66	49.89	54.52	60.10
Warrant Officer												
Class 2	48.02	52.24	57.95	63.64	48.32	52.55	58.25	63.95	48.78	53.00	58.71	64.40
Class 1	51.21	55.43	61.19	66.89	51.51	55.73	61.50	67.19	51.97	56.19	61.96	67.65

SALARIES OF ADULT PERSONNEL OF THE RANK OF CORPORAL AND BELOW

Rank	Scale A			Scale B			Scale C		
	Band 1	Band 2	Band 3	Band 1	Band 2	Band 3	Band 1	Band 2	Band 3
Private									
Class 4	£21.62	£ —	£ —	£21.92	£ —	£ —	£22.38	£ —	£ —
Class 3	24.22	28.13	32.46	24.52	28.43	32.76	24.98	28.89	33.22
Class 2	27.09	31.01	35.34	27.39	31.31	35.65	27.85	31.77	36.10
Class 1	29.39	33.30	37.64	29.70	33.61	37.94	30.16	34.06	38.40
Lance-Corporal									
Class 3	29.39	33.30	37.64	29.70	33.61	37.94	30.16	34.06	38.40
Class 2	31.40	35.32	40.00	31.71	35.63	40.31	32.17	36.08	40.76
Class 1	33.79	37.71	42.39	34.09	38.01	42.69	34.55	38.47	43.15
Corporal									
Class 2	36.29	40.19	44.88	36.59	40.50	45.19	37.05	40.96	45.64
Class 1	38.95	42.86	47.55	39.25	43.17	47.86	39.71	43.62	48.31

Relative Rank – Armed Forces

Royal Navy	Army	Royal Air Force
1 Admiral of the Fleet	1 Field Marshal	1 Marshal of the RAF
2 Admiral (Adm.)	2 General (Gen.)	2 Air Chief Marshal
3 Vice-Admiral (Vice-Adm.)	3 Lieutenant-General (Lt.-Gen.)	3 Air Marshal
4 Rear-Admiral (Rear-Adm.)	4 Major-General (Maj.-Gen.)	4 Air Vice-Marshal
5 Commodore (1st & 2nd Class) (Cdre)	5 Brigadier (Brig.)	5 Air Commodore (Air Cdre)
6 Captain (Capt.)	6 Colonel (Col.)	6 Group Captain (Gp Capt)
7 Commander (Cdr.)	7 Lieutenant-Colonel (Lt.-Col.)	7 Wing Commander (Wg Cdr.)
8 Lieutenant-Commander (Lt.-Cdr.)	8 Major (Maj.)	8 Squadron Leader (Sqn. Ldr.)
9 Lieutenant (Lt.)	9 Captain (Capt.)	9 Flight Lieutenant (Flt. Lt.)
10 Sub-Lieutenant (Sub-Lt.)	10 Lieutenant (Lt.)	10 Flying Officer (FO)
11 Acting Sub-Lieutenant (Acting Sub-Lt.)	11 Second Lieutenant (2nd Lt.)	11 Pilot Officer (PO)

SERVICE RETIRED PAY ON COMPULSORY RETIREMENT

Those who leave the services having served at least five years, but not long enough to qualify for the appropriate immediate pension, now qualify for a preserved pension and terminal grant, both of which are payable at age 60. The tax-free resettlement grants shown below are payable on release to those who qualify for a preserved pension and who have completed nine years service from age 21 (officers) or 12 years from age 18 (other ranks).

The annual rates for army personnel are given. The rates apply also to personnel of equivalent rank in the other services, including the nursing services.

OFFICERS (applicable to officers who give full pay service on the active list on or after 31 March 1993)

No. of years reckonable service over age 21	Capt. and below*	Major*	Lt.-Col.	Col.	Brigadier	Major-General	Lieutenant-General	General
16	£ 7,030	£ 8,378	£10,975	£ —	£ —	£ —	£ —	£ —
17	7,354	8,776	11,483	—	—	—	—	—
18	7,678	9,174	11,991	13,964	—	—	—	—
19	8,003	9,573	12,498	14,555	—	—	—	—
20	8,327	9,971	13,006	15,146	—	—	—	—
21	8,651	10,369	13,514	15,738	—	—	—	—
22	8,975	10,767	14,022	16,329	18,849	—	—	—
23	9,300	11,165	14,529	16,920	19,445	—	—	—
24	9,624	11,563	15,037	17,511	20,040	21,203	—	—
25	9,948	11,962	15,545	18,102	20,636	21,833	—	—
26	10,272	12,360	16,053	18,693	21,232	22,463	—	—
27	10,596	12,758	16,561	19,284	21,827	23,093	26,405	—
28	10,921	13,156	17,068	19,875	22,423	23,723	27,125	—
29	11,245	13,554	17,576	20,466	23,018	24,354	27,846	—
30	11,569	13,952	18,084	21,058	23,614	24,984	28,566	39,716
31	11,893	14,351	18,592	21,649	24,209	25,614	29,287	40,718
32	12,218	14,749	19,099	22,240	24,805	26,244	30,007	41,719
33	12,542	15,147	19,607	22,831	25,400	26,874	30,728	42,721
34	12,866	15,545	20,115	23,422	25,996	27,504	31,448	43,722

Field Marshal – active list retired pay at the rate of £54,361 a year

*Including Quartermaster

WARRANT OFFICERS, NCOS AND PRIVATES (applicable to soldiers who give full pay service on or after 21 March 1993)

Number of years reckonable service	Below Corporal	Corporal	Sergeant	Staff Sergeant	Warrant Officer Class II	Warrant Officer Class I
22	£4,082	£5,216	£5,732	£6,524	£ 6,744	£ 7,452
23	4,224	5,398	5,932	6,752	6,983	7,720
24	4,367	5,580	6,132	6,979	7,222	7,988
25	4,509	5,762	6,332	7,207	7,461	8,256
26	4,652	5,944	6,532	7,435	7,700	8,524
27	4,794	6,126	6,732	7,663	7,939	8,792
28	4,937	6,308	6,932	7,890	8,178	9,060
29	5,079	6,490	7,132	8,118	8,417	9,328
30	5,222	6,673	7,333	8,346	8,656	9,595
31	5,364	6,855	7,533	8,574	8,895	9,863
32	5,507	7,037	7,733	8,801	9,134	10,131
33	5,649	7,219	7,933	9,029	9,375	10,399
34	5,792	7,401	8,133	9,257	9,612	10,667
35	5,934	7,583	8,333	9,485	9,851	10,935
36	6,077	7,765	8,533	9,712	10,090	11,203
37	6,219	7,947	8,733	9,940	10,329	11,471

TERMINAL GRANTS AND GRATUITIES

Terminal grants are in each case three times the rate of retired pay or pension. There are special rates of retired pay for chaplains and certain other ranks not shown above. Lower rates are payable in cases of voluntary retirement.

A gratuity of £2,355 is payable for officers with short service commissions for each year completed. Resettlement grants are: officers £8,101; non-commissioned ranks £5,357.

The Christian Churches

The Church of England

The Church of England is the established (i.e. state) church in England and the mother church of the Anglican Communion. It originated in the conflicts between church and state throughout the Middle Ages, culminating in the Act of Supremacy issued by Henry VIII in 1534. This repudiated papal supremacy and declared the King to be the supreme head of the Church in England. Since 1559 the English monarch has been termed the Supreme Governor of the Church of England. The Thirty-Nine Articles, a set of doctrinal statements defining the position of the Church of England, were adopted in their final form in 1571 and include the emphasis on personal faith and the authority of the scriptures common to the Protestant Reformation throughout Europe.

The Church of England is divided into the two provinces of Canterbury and York, each under an archbishop. The two provinces are subdivided into 44 dioceses. Decisions on matters concerning the Church of England are made by the General Synod, established in 1970. It also discusses and expresses opinion on any other matter of religious or public interest. The General Synod has 574 members in total, divided between three houses: the House of Bishops, the House of Clergy and the House of Laity. It is presided over jointly by the Archbishops of Canterbury and York and normally meets twice a year. The Synod has the power, delegated by Parliament, to frame statute law (known as a Measure) on any matter concerning the Church of England. A Measure must be laid before both Houses of Parliament, who may accept or reject it but cannot amend it. Once accepted the Measure is submitted for Royal Assent and then has the full force of law. The Synod appoints a number of committees, boards and councils which deal with, or advise on, a wide range of matters. In addition to the General Synod, there are synods of clergy and laity at diocesan level.

In 1990 the Church of England had an electoral roll membership of 1.4 million, of whom about 1.1 million regularly attended Sunday services. There are (1992 figures) two archbishops, 104 diocesan, suffragan and (stipendiary) assistant bishops, 10,141 male and 707 female full-time stipendiary clergy, and over 16,000 churches and places of worship. (The Diocese in Europe is not included in these figures.)

THE ORDINATION OF WOMEN

On 11 November 1992, the General Synod of the Church of England voted to permit the ordination of women as priests. In the House of Bishops there were 39 votes (75 per cent) in favour of the legislation and 13 (25 per cent) against; in the House of Clergy, 176 (70.4 per cent) in favour and 74 (29.6 per cent) against; and in the House of Laity, 169 (67.3 per cent) in favour and 82 (32.7 per cent) against. The legislation therefore received the required two-thirds majority in all three houses.

The most important stages leading to the legislation being passed were:

1975 A motion that 'there are no fundamental objections to the ordination of women to the priesthood' was passed in the General Synod

1984 The General Synod agreed to 'bring forward legislation to permit the ordination of women to the priesthood'

1985 A motion permitting the ordination of women as deacons was carried

1987 A motion asking the standing committee to prepare draft legislation was carried
      The first women deacons were ordained

1988 Draft legislation to enable the ordination of women to the priesthood was approved and sent to a revision committee

1989 The revised legislation was amended and carried

1990 A majority of the 44 diocesan synods approved the legislation in the Diocesan House of Clergy and the Diocesan House of Laity

1992
June The House of Bishops of the General Synod debated the final draft of the legislation and passed it on unaltered

July The legislation was 'claimed' for debate and approved on a simple majority in the separate Houses of the Convocations of Canterbury and York (which together form the House of Bishops and the House of Clergy of the General Synod) and in the House of Laity of the General Synod

Nov   Final Approval debate and vote in the General Synod (*see* above)

The case for the ordination of women as priests was supported by the Archbishop of Canterbury (Dr George Carey), who said in the General Synod debate that this would not be a break with tradition, and that 'we must draw on all available talent if we are to be a credible church engaged in a mission to an increasingly confused and lost world'. Supporters of the legislation appealed to scripture to show that both men and women are made in the image of God, and said that the legislation should be passed for theological, practical and financial reasons. Opposition to the measure was led by the Bishop of London (Dr David Hope), who said that he was committed to women's full-time ministry, but was not convinced that this should be in the context of the ministerial priesthood and episcopate. Other opponents said that the legislation was confused and divisive, and that 2,000 years of tradition should not be broken, and that the maleness of Christian priesthood was supported by scripture.

The legislation was presented to the Ecclesiastical Committee of Parliament in early 1993. The Committee found the legislation expedient, and it will be debated in both Houses of Parliament in the autumn of 1993. If either House votes the legislation down, the General Synod has the right to present it for a second time. If the legislation receives royal assent, the petition to promulgate the canon will be submitted to the Crown. When the canon has been promulged (proclaimed) in the General Synod, which is likely to be in February 1994, the first women may be ordained as priests.

A clause of the Priests (Ordination of Women) Measure allows the bishop of a diocese to declare that women may not be ordained within his diocese, and that a woman ordained outside the diocese may not officiate or act as a priest within it. After the measure was passed, organizations opposed to women priests proposed that a system of 'alternative episcopal oversight' be set up, under which priests in dioceses where the bishop ordained women would be able to petition the nearest diocesan bishop opposed to women priests to oversee their ministry. This was rejected by the House of Bishops, who in January 1993 unanimously agreed a plan to appoint up to three 'provincial visitors' to work with those who are unable to accept the ministry of bishops ordaining women priests. The provincial visitors, who would be suffragan bishops, would be allowed to carry out confirmations and ordinations in parishes opposed to women priests, as long as they had the permission of the diocesan bishop. Diocesan bishops would also be able to depute a suffragan to ordain women; authorize a suffragan to minister to clergy and parishes whose views differ from his own; or make similar arrangements with bishops in neighbouring dioceses. The plan was welcomed by all the Anglo-Catholic diocesan bishops, and by the Archbishop of Canterbury, who said: 'We want to reject the idea of a church within a church, and to retain the geographical unity of each diocese'.

In June 1993 the House of Bishops drew up a draft Act of Synod setting out the practical arrangements to provide pastoral care for all, irrespective of their views on the ordination of women to the priesthood. The draft Act will go before the General Synod in November 1993 but will not be enshrined in a supplementary Measure which would be put before Parliament. Clergy who still feel compelled to leave the ministry will be entitled to generous financial assistance.

GENERAL SYNOD OF THE CHURCH OF ENGLAND, Church House, Dean's Yard, London SW1P 3NZ. Tel: 071-222 9011. *Secretary-General*, P. Mawer
HOUSE OF BISHOPS: *Chairman*, The Archbishop of Canterbury; *Vice-Chairman*, The Archbishop of York
HOUSE OF CLERGY: *Joint Chairmen*, The Archdeacon of Leicester; Canon J. Stanley
HOUSE OF LAITY: *Chairman*, Prof. J. D. McClean; *Vice-Chairman*, Dr Christina Baxter

STIPENDS 1993–4

Archbishop of Canterbury	£43,550
Archbishop of York	£38,150
Bishop of London	£35,560
Bishop of Durham	£31,380
Bishop of Winchester	£26,160
Other Diocesan Bishops	£23,610
Suffragan Bishops	£19,410
Deans and Provosts	£19,410
Residentiary Canons	£15,870

Province of Canterbury

CANTERBURY

103RD ARCHBISHOP AND PRIMATE OF ALL ENGLAND
Most Revd and Rt. Hon. George L. Carey, PH.D., *cons.* 1987, *trans.* 1991, *apptd* 1991; Lambeth Palace, London SE1 7JU. *Signs* George Cantuar:

BISHOPS SUFFRAGAN
Dover, Rt. Revd John R. A. Llewellin, *cons.* 1985, *apptd* 1992; Upway, St Martin's Hill, Canterbury, CT1 1PR
Maidstone, Rt. Revd Gavin H. Reid, *cons.* 1992, *apptd* 1992; Bishop's House, Pett Lane, Charing, Ashford TN27 0DL

ASSISTANT BISHOPS
Rt. Revd Ross Hook, MC, *cons.* 1965, *apptd* 1986; Rt. Revd William Franklin, OBE, *cons.* 1972, *apptd* 1987; Rt. Revd Richard Say, KCVO, *cons.* 1961, *apptd* 1988

DEAN
Very Revd John Arthur Simpson, *apptd* 1986

CANONS RESIDENTIARY
J. H. R. De Sausmarez, *apptd* 1981; P. Brett, *apptd* 1983; Ven. M. Till, *apptd* 1986
Organist, D. Flood, FRCO, *apptd* 1988

ARCHDEACONS
Canterbury, Ven. M. Till, *apptd* 1986
Maidstone, Ven. P. Evans, *apptd* 1989

Stipendiary Male Clergy, 189
Stipendiary Women Deacons, 11

Vicar-General of Province and Diocese, Chancellor S. Cameron, QC
Commissary-General, His Honour Judge Newey, QC, *apptd* 1971
Joint Registrars of the Province, F. E. Robson, OBE, 16 Beaumont Street, Oxford; B. J. T. Hanson, Church House, Dean's Yard, London SW1P 3NZ
Registrar of the Diocese of Canterbury, A. O. E. Davies, 9 The Precincts, Canterbury CT1 2EE

LONDON

131ST BISHOP
Rt. Revd and Rt. Hon. David M. Hope, D.Phil., *cons.* 1985, *trans.* 1991, *apptd* 1991; 8 Barton Street, London SW1P 3NE. *Signs* David Londin:

AREA BISHOPS
Edmonton, Rt. Revd Brian J. Masters, *cons.* 1982, *apptd* 1984; 1 Regent's Park Terrace, London NW1 7EE
Kensington, Rt. Revd John Hughes, PH.D., *cons.* 1987, *apptd* 1987; 19 Campden Hill Square, London W8 7JY
Stepney, Rt. Revd Richard C. Chartres; 63 Coborn Road, London E3 2DB
Willesden, Rt. Revd Graham G. Dow; 173 Willesden Lane, London NW6 7YN

BISHOP SUFFRAGAN
Fulham, Rt. Revd C. John Klyberg, *cons.* 1985, *apptd* 1985; 4 Cambridge Place, London W8 5PB

ASSISTANT BISHOPS
Rt. Revd Maurice Wood, DSC, *cons.* 1971, *apptd* 1985; Rt. Revd Michael Marshall, *cons.* 1975, *apptd* 1984

DEAN OF ST PAUL'S
Very Revd T. Eric Evans, *apptd* 1988

CANONS RESIDENTIARY
Ven. G. Cassidy, *apptd* 1987; C. J. Hill, *apptd* 1989; R. J. Halliburton, *apptd* 1990; M. J. Saward, *apptd* 1991
Registrar and Receiver of St Paul's, Brig. R. W. Acworth, CBE
Organist, J. Scott, FRCO, *apptd* 1990

ARCHDEACONS
Charing Cross, Rt. Revd C. J. Klyberg, *apptd* 1989
Hackney, Ven. C. Young, *apptd* 1992
Hampstead, Ven. R. A. W. Coogan, *apptd* 1985
London, Ven. G. Cassidy, *apptd* 1987
Middlesex, Ven. T. J. Raphael, *apptd* 1983
Northolt, Ven. M. Colclough, *apptd* 1992

Stipendiary Male Clergy, 568
Stipendiary Women Deacons, 49

Chancellor and Commissary of the Dean and Chapter, Miss S. Cameron, QC, *apptd* 1992
Registrar, D. W. Faull, OBE, 35 Great Peter Street, London SW1P 3LR

WESTMINSTER
The Collegiate Church of St Peter (A Royal Peculiar)

DEAN
Michael Clement Otway Mayne, *apptd* 1986

SUB DEAN AND ARCHDEACON
A. E. Harvey, *apptd* 1987

CANONS OF WESTMINSTER
A. E. Harvey, *apptd* 1982; D. C. Gray, *apptd* 1987;
C. D. Semper, *apptd* 1987; P. S. Bates, *apptd* 1990

Chapter Clerk and Receiver-General, Rear-Adm. K. A. Snow,
CB, *apptd* 1987
Organist, M. Neary, FRCO, *apptd* 1988
Legal Secretary, C. L. Hodgetts, *apptd* 1973
Registrar, S. J. Holmes, MVO, *apptd* 1984, 20 Dean's Yard,
London SW1P 3PA

WINCHESTER

95TH BISHOP
Rt. Revd Colin C. W. James, *cons.* 1973, *trans.* 1977 and
1985, *apptd* 1985; Wolvesey, Winchester SO23 9ND. *Signs*
Colin Winton:

BISHOPS SUFFRAGAN
Basingstoke, vacant; Bishop's Lodge, Skippetts Lane West,
Basingstoke RG21 3HP
Southampton, Rt. Revd John F. Perry, *cons.* 1989, *apptd*
1989; Ham House, The Crescent, Romsey SO51 7NG

ASSISTANT BISHOPS
Rt. Revd Hassan Dehqani-Tafti, *cons.* 1961, *apptd* 1982; Rt.
Revd Leslie Rees, *cons.* 1980, *apptd* 1986

DEAN
Very Revd Trevor R. Beeson, *apptd* 1987

Dean of Jersey (A Peculiar), Very Revd John Seaford, *apptd*
1993
Dean of Guernsey (A Peculiar), Very Revd Jeffery Fenwick,
apptd 1989

CANONS RESIDENTIARY
E. G. Job, *apptd* 1979; P. A. Britton, *apptd* 1980;
A. K. Walker, *apptd* 1987; Ven. A. F. Knight, *apptd* 1991

Organist, D. Hill, FRCO, *apptd* 1988

ARCHDEACONS
Basingstoke, Ven. A. F. Knight, *apptd* 1990
Winchester, Ven. A. G. Clarkson, *apptd* 1984

Stipendiary Male Clergy, 252
Stipendiary Women Deacons, 9

Chancellor, C. Clark, *apptd* 1993
Registrar and Legal Secretary, P. M. White, 19 St Peter
Street, Winchester SO23 8BU

BATH AND WELLS

76TH BISHOP
Rt. Revd James L. Thompson, *cons.* 1978, *apptd* 1991; The
Palace, Wells BA5 2PD. *Signs* James Bath & Wells

BISHOP SUFFRAGAN
Taunton, Rt. Revd J. H. Richard Lewis, *cons.* 1992, *apptd*
1992; Sherford Farm House, Sherford, Taunton TA1 3RF

DEAN
Very Revd Richard Lewis, *apptd* 1990

CANONS RESIDENTIARY
C. E. Thomas, *apptd* 1983; P. de N. Lucas, *apptd* 1988;
G. O. Farran, *apptd* 1985
Organist, A. Nethsingha, FRCO, *apptd* 1993

ARCHDEACONS
Bath, Ven. J. E. Burgess, *apptd* 1975
Taunton, Ven. R. M. C. Frith, *apptd* 1992
Wells, Ven. R. Ackworth, *apptd* 1993

Stipendiary Male Clergy, 253
Stipendiary Women Deacons, 13

Chancellor, T. Briden, *apptd* 1993
Registrar, Secretary and Chapter Clerk, T. Berry, Diocesan
Registry, Market Place, Wells BA5 2RE

BIRMINGHAM

7TH BISHOP
Rt. Revd Mark Santer, *cons.* 1981, *apptd* 1987; Bishop's
Croft, Harborne, Birmingham B17 0BG. *Signs* Mark
Birmingham

BISHOP SUFFRAGAN
Aston, Rt. Revd John Austin, *cons.* 1992, *apptd* 1992;
Strensham House, 8 Strensham Hill, Moseley,
Birmingham B13 8AG

STIPENDIARY ASSISTANT BISHOP
Rt. Revd Michael Whinney, *cons.* 1982, *apptd* 1989

ASSISTANT BISHOP
Rt. Revd Anthony Dumper, *cons.* 1977, *apptd* 1993

PROVOST
Very Revd Peter A. Berry, *apptd* 1986

CANONS RESIDENTIARY
Ven. C. J. G. Barton, *apptd* 1990; A. H. F. Luff, *apptd* 1992
Organist, M. Huxley, FRCO, *apptd* 1986

ARCHDEACONS
Aston, Ven. C. J. G. Barton, *apptd* 1990
Birmingham, Ven. J. F. Duncan, *apptd* 1985
Coleshill, Ven. J. L. Cooper, *apptd* 1990

Stipendiary Male Clergy, 210
Stipendiary Women Deacons, 15

Chancellor, His Honour Judge Aglionby, *apptd* 1970
Registrar and Legal Secretary, H. Carslake, St Philip's
House, St Philip's Place, Birmingham B3 2PP

BRISTOL

54TH BISHOP
Rt. Revd Barry Rogerson, *cons.* 1979, *apptd* 1985; Bishop's
House, Clifton Hill, Bristol BS8 1BW. *Signs* Barry Bristol

BISHOP SUFFRAGAN
Malmesbury, Rt. Revd Peter J. Firth, *cons.* 1983, *apptd* 1983;
7 Ivywell Road, Bristol BS9 1NX

DEAN
Very Revd Dr A. Wesley Carr, *apptd* 1987

CANONS RESIDENTIARY
J. Rogan, *apptd* 1983; A. L. J. Redfern, *apptd* 1987;
J. L. Simpson, *apptd* 1989; P. F. Johnson, *apptd* 1990

Organist, C. Brayne, *apptd* 1990

ARCHDEACONS
Bristol, Ven. D. J. Banfield, *apptd* 1990
Swindon, Ven. M. Middleton, *apptd* 1992

Stipendiary Male Clergy, 162
Stipendiary Women Deacons, 19

Chancellor, Sir David Calcutt, QC, *apptd* 1971
Registrar and Secretary, T. R. Urquhart, 30 Queen Charlotte
Street, Bristol BS13 8HE

CHELMSFORD

7TH BISHOP
Rt. Revd John Waine, *cons.* 1975, *apptd* 1986; Bishopscourt,
Margaretting, Ingatestone CM4 0HD. *Signs* John
Chelmsford

BISHOPS SUFFRAGAN
Barking, Rt. Revd Roger F. Sainsbury, *cons.* 1991, *apptd*
1991; 110 Capel Road, Forest Gate, London E7 0JS
Bradwell, Rt. Revd Laurence Green, *cons.* 1993, *apptd* 1993;
The Vicarage, Orsett Road, Horndon-on-the-Hill,
Stanford-le-Hope, Essex SS17 8NS
Colchester, Rt. Revd Michael E. Vickers, *cons.* 1988, *apptd*
1988; 1 Fitzwalter Road, Lexden, Colchester CO3 3SS

PROVOST
Very Revd John H. Moses, PH.D., *apptd* 1982

CANONS RESIDENTIARY
P. G. Brett, *apptd* 1985; P. G. Southwell-Sander, *apptd* 1985;
T. Thompson, *apptd* 1988; B. P. Thompson, *apptd* 1988

Organist, Dr G. Elliott, PH.D., FRCO, *apptd* 1981

ARCHDEACONS
Colchester, Ven. E. C. F. Stroud, *apptd* 1983
Harlow, Ven. M. J. Fox, *apptd* 1993
Southend, Ven. D. Jennings, *apptd* 1992
West Ham, Ven. T. J. Stevens, *apptd* 1991

Stipendiary Male Clergy, 496
Stipendiary Women Deacons, 27

Chancellor, Miss S. M. Cameron, QC, *apptd* 1970
Diocesan Registrar, B. Hood, 53 New Street, Chelmsford
CM1 1NG

CHICHESTER

102ND BISHOP
Rt. Revd Eric W. Kemp, DD, *cons.* 1974, *apptd* 1974; The
Palace, Chichester PO19 1PY. *Signs* Eric Cicestr:

BISHOPS SUFFRAGAN
Horsham, Rt. Revd John W. Hind, *cons.* 1991, *apptd* 1991;
Bishop's Lodge, Worth, nr. Crawley RH10 4RT
Lewes, Rt. Revd Ian P. M. Cundy, *cons.* 1992, *apptd* 1992;
Beacon House, Berwick, Polegate BN26 6ST

ASSISTANT BISHOPS
Rt. Revd William Hunt, *cons.* 1955, *apptd* 1980; Rt. Revd
Mark Green, *cons.* 1972, *apptd* 1982; Rt. Revd Simon

Phipps, *cons.* 1968, *apptd* 1987; Rt. Revd Edward Knapp-
Fisher, *cons.* 1960, *apptd* 1987; Rt. Revd Morris Maddocks,
cons. 1972, *apptd* 1987; Rt Revd Christopher Luxmoore,
cons. 1984, *apptd* 1991; Rt. Revd Michael Marshall, *cons.*
1975, *apptd* 1992

DEAN
Very Revd John D. Treadgold, LVO, *apptd* 1989

CANONS RESIDENTIARY
R. T. Greenacre, *apptd* 1975; J. F. Hester, *apptd* 1985

Organist, A. J. Thurlow, FRCO, *apptd* 1980

ARCHDEACONS
Chichester, Ven. M. Brotherton, *apptd* 1991
Horsham, Ven. W. C. L. Filby, *apptd* 1983
Lewes and Hastings, Ven. H. Glaisyer, *apptd* 1991

Stipendiary Male Clergy, 362
Stipendiary Women Deacons, 5

Chancellor, His Honour Judge Q. T. Edwards, QC, *apptd*
1978
Legal Secretary to the Bishop, and Diocesan Registrar,
C. L. Hodgetts, 5 East Pallant, Chichester PO19 1TS

COVENTRY

7TH BISHOP
Rt. Revd Simon Barrington-Ward, *cons.* 1985, *apptd* 1985;
The Bishop's House, 23 Davenport Road, Coventry
CV5 6PW. *Signs* Simon Coventry

BISHOP SUFFRAGAN
Warwick, Rt. Revd George C. Handford, *cons.* 1990, *apptd*
1990; 139 Kenilworth Road, Coventry CV4 7AF

ASSISTANT BISHOPS
Rt. Revd John Daly, *cons.* 1935, *apptd* 1968; Rt. Revd
Vernon Nicholls, *cons.* 1974, *apptd* 1984

PROVOST
Very Revd John F. Petty, *apptd* 1987

CANONS RESIDENTIARY
P. Oestreicher, *apptd* 1986; M. Sadgrove, *apptd* 1987;
G. T. Hughes, *apptd* 1989

Organist, A. P. Leddington Wright (from March 1994)

ARCHDEACONS
Coventry, Ven. H. I. L. Russell, *apptd* 1989
Warwick, Ven. M. J. J. Paget-Wilkes, *apptd* 1990

Stipendiary Male Clergy, 186
Stipendiary Women Deacons, 12

Chancellor, W. M. Gage, *apptd* 1980
Registrar, D. J. Dumbleton, 8 The Quadrant, Coventry
CV1 2EL

DERBY

5TH BISHOP
Rt. Revd Peter S. Dawes, *cons.* 1988, *apptd* 1988; The
Bishop's House, 6 King Street, Duffield, Derby
DE56 4EU. *Signs* Peter Derby

BISHOP SUFFRAGAN
Repton, Rt. Revd F. Henry A. Richmond, *cons.* 1986, *apptd*
1986; Repton House, Lea, Matlock DE4 1JP

PROVOST
Very Revd Benjamin H. Lewers, *apptd* 1981

CANONS RESIDENTIARY
G. A. Chesterman, *apptd* 1989; Ven. I. Gatford, *apptd* 1992;
G. O. Marshall, *apptd* 1992; R. M. Parsons, *apptd* 1993
Organist, P. Gould, *apptd* 1982

ARCHDEACONS
Chesterfield, Ven. G. R. Phizackerley, *apptd* 1978
Derby, Ven. I. Gatford, *apptd* 1992

Stipendiary Male Clergy, 201
Stipendiary Women Deacons, 12

Chancellor, J. W. M. Bullimore, *apptd* 1981
Registrar, J. S. Battie, Derby Church House, Full Street,
Derby DEI 3DR

ELY

67TH BISHOP
Rt. Revd Stephen W. Sykes, *cons.* 1990, *apptd* 1990; The
Bishop's House, Ely CB7 4DW. *Signs* Stephen Ely

BISHOP SUFFRAGAN
Huntingdon, Rt. Revd William G. Roe, D.Phil., *cons.* 1980,
apptd 1980; 14 Lynn Road, Ely, Cambs. CB6 IDA

DEAN
Very Revd Michael Higgins, *apptd* 1991

CANONS RESIDENTIARY
D. J. Green, *apptd* 1980; J. Rone, *apptd* 1989
Organist, P. Trepte, FRCO, *apptd* 1991

ARCHDEACONS
Ely, Ven. J. Watson, *apptd* 1993
Huntingdon, Ven. R. K. Sledge, *apptd* 1978
Wisbech, Ven. D. Fleming, *apptd* 1984

Stipendiary Male Clergy, 170
Stipendiary Women Deacons, 7

Chancellor, W. Gage, QC
Registrar, W. H. Godfrey, 18 The Broadway, St Ives,
Huntingdon PEI7 4BS
Joint Registrar (Legal Secretary), P. F. B. Beesley, 1 The
Sanctuary, London SWIP 3JT

EXETER

69TH BISHOP
Rt. Revd G. Hewlett Thompson, *cons.* 1974, *apptd* 1985;
The Palace, Exeter EXI 1HY. *Signs* Hewlett Exon:

BISHOPS SUFFRAGAN
Crediton, Rt. Revd Peter E. Coleman, *cons.* 1984, *apptd*
1984; 10 The Close, Exeter EXI 1EZ
Plymouth, Rt. Revd Richard S. Hawkins, *cons.* 1988, *apptd*
1988; 31 Riverside Walk, Tamerton Foliot, Plymouth PL5
4AQ

ASSISTANT BISHOPS
Rt. Revd Ronald Goodchild, *cons.* 1964, *apptd* 1983; Rt.
Revd Philip Pasterfield, *cons.* 1974, *apptd* 1984; Rt. Revd
Richard Cartwright, *cons.* 1972, *apptd* 1988; Rt. Revd Colin
Docker, *cons.* 1975, *apptd* 1991

DEAN
Very Revd Richard Montague Stephens Eyre, *apptd* 1981

CANONS RESIDENTIARY
A. C. Mawson, *apptd* 1979; Ven. J. Richards, *apptd* 1981;
K. C. Parry, *apptd* 1991
Organist, L. A. Nethsingha, FRCO, *apptd* 1973

ARCHDEACONS
Barnstaple, Ven. T. Lloyd, *apptd* 1989
Exeter, Ven. J. Richards, *apptd* 1981
Plymouth, Ven. R. G. Ellis, *apptd* 1982
Totnes, Ven. A. F. Tremlett, *apptd* 1988

Stipendiary Male Clergy, 280
Stipendiary Women Deacons, 10

Chancellor, Sir David Calcutt, QC, *apptd* 1971
Registrar, R. K. Wheeler, 18 Cathedral Yard, Exeter
EXI IHE

GIBRALTAR IN EUROPE

BISHOP
Vacant; 5A Gregory Place, London W8 4NG. *Signs* –
Gibraltar

BISHOP SUFFRAGAN
In Europe, Rt. Revd Edward Holland, *apptd* 1986

AUXILIARY BISHOPS
Rt. Revd E. M. H. Capper, OBE, *cons.* 1967, *apptd* 1973; Rt.
Revd D. de Pina Cabral, *cons.* 1967, *apptd* 1976; Rt. Revd
A. W. M. Weeks, CB, *cons.* 1977, *apptd* 1988; Rt. Revd E.
Devenport, *apptd* 1992

Vicar-General, Revd W. G. Reid
Bishop's Commissaries, Canon L. Tyzack; Canon
J. D. Beckwith; Canon D. H. Palmer; A. M. Apostol
Dean, Cathedral Church of the Holy Trinity, Gibraltar, Very
Revd B. W. Horlock, OBE
Chancellor, Pro-Cathedral of St Paul, Valletta, Malta, Canon
P. Cousins
*Chancellor, Pro-Cathedral of the Holy Trinity, Brussels,
Belgium,* vacant

ARCHDEACONS
Aegean, Ven. G. B. Evans
North-West Europe, Ven. G. G. Allen
North France, Ven. M. B. Lea
Gibraltar, Rt. Revd D. de Pina Cabral
Italy, Rt. Revd E. Devenport
Riviera, Ven. J. Livingstone
Scandinavia, Ven. G. A. C. Brown
Switzerland, Ven. P. J. Hawker

Chancellor, Sir David Calcutt, QC
Diocesan Registrar and Legal Secretary, J. G. Underwood,
37A Walbrook, London EC4 8BS

GLOUCESTER

39TH BISHOP
Rt. Revd David Bentley, *cons.* 1986, *apptd* 1993;
Bishopscourt, Gloucester GLI 2BQ. *Signs* David Gloucester

BISHOP SUFFRAGAN
Tewkesbury, Rt. Revd G. D. Jeremy Walsh, *cons.* 1986,
apptd 1986; Green Acre, Hempsted, Gloucester GL2 6LG

DEAN
Very Revd Kenneth N. Jennings, *apptd* 1982

CANONS RESIDENTIARY
R. D. M. Grey, *apptd* 1982; R. P. Greenwood, *apptd* 1986;
N. Chatfield, *apptd* 1992

Organist, Dr J. D. Sanders, FRCO, *apptd* 1967

ARCHDEACONS
Cheltenham, Ven. J. A. Lewis, *apptd* 1988
Gloucester, Ven. C. J. H. Wagstaff, *apptd* 1982

Stipendiary Male Clergy, 185
Stipendiary Women Deacons, 12

Chancellor and Vicar-General, Ms D. J. Rogers, *apptd* 1990
Registrar, C. G. Peak, 34 Brunswick Road, Gloucester
GLI IJJ

GUILDFORD

7TH BISHOP
Rt. Revd Michael E. Adie, *cons.* 1983, *apptd* 1983; Willow
Grange, Woking Road, Guildford GU4 7QS. *Signs* Michael
Guildford

BISHOP SUFFRAGAN
Dorking, Rt. Revd David P. Wilcox, *cons.* 1986, *apptd* 1986;
13 Pilgrims Way, Guildford GU4 8AD

DEAN
Very Revd Alexander G. Wedderspoon, *apptd* 1987

CANONS RESIDENTIARY
F. S. Telfer, *apptd* 1973; P. G. Croft, *apptd* 1983;
R. D. Fenwick, *apptd* 1990

Organist, A. Millington, FRCO, *apptd* 1982

ARCHDEACONS
Dorking, Ven. C.W. Herbert, *apptd* 1990
Surrey, Ven. J. S. Went, *apptd* 1989

Stipendiary Male Clergy, 194
Stipendiary Women Deacons, 15

Chancellor, His Hon. Judge Goodman
Legal Secretary and Registrar, P. F. B. Beesley, 1 The
Sanctuary, London SW1P 3JT

HEREFORD

103RD BISHOP
Rt. Revd John Oliver (until Dec. 1993), *cons.* 1990, *apptd*
1990; The Palace, Hereford HR4 9BN. *Signs* John
Hereford

BISHOP SUFFRAGAN
Ludlow, Rt. Revd Ian M. Griggs, *cons.* 1987, *apptd* 1987;
Bishop's House, Halford, Craven Arms, Shropshire SY7
9BT

DEAN
Very Revd Robert A. Willis, *apptd* 1992

CANONS RESIDENTIARY
P. Iles, *apptd* 1983; J. Tiller, *apptd* 1984

Organist, Dr R. Massey, FRCO, *apptd* 1974

ARCHDEACONS
Hereford, Ven. L. G. Moss, *apptd* 1992
Ludlow, Ven. J. C. Saxbee, *apptd* 1992

Stipendiary Male Clergy, 129
Stipendiary Women Deacons, 9

Chancellor, J. M. Henty
Joint Registrars, V. T. Jordan, 44 Bridge Street, Hereford;
P. Beesley, 1 The Sanctuary, London SW1P 3JT

LEICESTER

5TH BISHOP
Rt. Revd Thomas F. Butler, PH.D., *cons.* 1985, *apptd* 1991;
Bishop's Lodge, 10 Springfield Road, Leicester LE2 3BD.
Signs Thomas Leicester

STIPENDIARY ASSISTANT BISHOP
Rt. Revd Godfrey Ashby, *cons.* 1980, *apptd* 1988

ASSISTANT BISHOP
Rt. Revd John Mort, CBE, *cons.* 1952, *apptd* 1972

PROVOST
Very Revd Derek Hole, *apptd* 1992

CANONS RESIDENTIARY
M. T. H. Banks, *apptd* 1988; M. Wilson, *apptd* 1988

Organist, P. G. White, FRCO, *apptd* 1968

ARCHDEACONS
Leicester, Ven. R. D. Silk, *apptd* 1980
Loughborough, Ven. I. Stanes, *apptd* 1992

Stipendiary Male Clergy, 180
Stipendiary Women Deacons, 12

Chancellor, N. Seed, *apptd* 1989
Registrars, P. C. E. Morris, 35 Great Peter Street, London
SW1P 3LR; R. H. Bloor, 23 Friar Lane, Leicester LE1 5QQ

LICHFIELD

97TH BISHOP
Rt. Revd Keith N. Sutton, *cons.* 1978, *apptd* 1984; Bishop's
House, The Close, Lichfield WS13 7LG. *Signs* Keith
Lichfield

BISHOPS SUFFRAGAN
Shrewsbury, Rt. Revd John D. Davies, *cons.* 1987, *apptd*
1987; Athlone House, 68 London Road, Shrewsbury SY2
6PG
Stafford, Rt. Revd Michael C. Scott-Joynt, *cons.* 1987, *apptd*
1987; Ash Garth, Broughton Crescent, Barlaston ST12
9DD
Wolverhampton, Rt. Revd Michael G. Bourke, *cons.* 1993,
apptd 1993; 61 Richmond Road, Wolverhampton WV3
9JH

ASSISTANT BISHOPS
Rt. Revd Ronald O. Bowlby, *cons.* 1973, *apptd* 1991; Rt.
Revd Kenneth C. Oram, *cons.* 1974, *apptd* 1987

DEAN
Very Revd Tom Wright, *apptd* 1993 (from Dec. 1993)

CANONS RESIDENTIARY
Ven. R. B. Ninis, *apptd* 1974; A. N. Barnard, *apptd* 1977;
W. J. Turner, *apptd* 1983; J. Howe, *apptd* 1988

Organist, A. Lumsden, *apptd* 1992

ARCHDEACONS
Lichfield, Ven. R. B. Ninis, *apptd* 1974
Salop, Ven. G. Frost, *apptd* 1987

Stoke-on-Trent, Ven. D. Ede, *apptd* 1989

Stipendiary Male Clergy, 406
Stipendiary Women Deacons, 41

Chancellor, His Honour Judge Shand
Diocesan Registrar, J. P. Thorneycroft, St Mary's House, The Close, Lichfield WS13 7LD

LINCOLN

70TH BISHOP
Rt. Revd Robert M. Hardy, *cons.* 1980, *apptd* 1987; Bishop's House, Eastgate, Lincoln LN2 1QQ. *Signs* Robert Lincoln

BISHOPS SUFFRAGAN
Grantham, Rt. Revd William Ind, *cons.* 1987, *apptd* 1987; Fairacre, Barrowby High Road, Grantham NG31 8NP
Grimsby, Rt. Revd David Tustin, *cons.* 1979, *apptd* 1979; Bishop's House, Church Lane, Irby-upon-Humber, Grimsby DN37 7JR

ASSISTANT BISHOPS
Rt. Revd Gerald Colin, *cons.* 1966, *apptd* 1979; Rt. Revd Harold Darby, *cons.* 1975, *apptd* 1989

DEAN
Very Revd Brandon D. Jackson, *apptd* 1989

CANONS RESIDENTIARY
B. R. Davis, *apptd* 1977; A. J. Stokes, *apptd* 1992

Organist, C. S. Walsh, FRCO, *apptd* 1988

ARCHDEACONS
Lincoln, Ven. M. P. Brackenbury, *apptd* 1988
Lindsey, Ven. J. H. C. Laurence, *apptd* 1985
Stow, Ven. R. J. Wells, *apptd* 1989

Stipendiary Male Clergy, 244
Stipendiary Women Deacons, 21

Chancellor, His Honour Judge Goodman, *apptd* 1971
Registrar and Legal Secretary, D. M. Wellman, 28 West Parade, Lincoln LN1 1JT

NORWICH

70TH BISHOP
Rt. Revd Peter J. Nott, *cons.* 1977, *apptd* 1985; Bishop's House, Norwich, NR3 1SB. *Signs* Peter Norvic:

BISHOPS SUFFRAGAN
Lynn, vacant; The Old Vic, Castle Acre, King's Lynn PE32 2AA
Thetford, Rt. Revd Hugo F. de Waal, *cons.* 1992, *apptd* 1992; Rectory Meadow, Bramerton, Norwich NR14 7DW

DEAN
Very Revd John P. Burbridge, *apptd* 1983

CANONS RESIDENTIARY
M. S. McLean, *apptd* 1986; M. F. Perham, *apptd* 1992

Organist, M. B. Nicholas, FRCO, *apptd* 1971

ARCHDEACONS
Lynn, Ven. A. C. Foottit, *apptd* 1987
Norfolk, Ven. A. M. Handley, *apptd* 1993
Norwich, vacant

Stipendiary Male Clergy, 237
Stipendiary Women Deacons, 10

Chancellor, His Honour J. H. Ellison, VRD, *apptd* 1955
Registrar and Secretary, J. W. F. Herring, Francis House, 3–7 Redwell Street, Norwich NR2 4TJ

OXFORD

41ST BISHOP
Rt. Revd Richard D. Harries, *cons.* 1987, *apptd* 1987; Diocesan Church House, North Hinksey, Oxford OX2 0NB. *Signs* Richard Oxon:

AREA BISHOPS
Buckingham, Rt. Revd Simon H. Burrows, *cons.* 1974, *apptd* 1974; Sheridan, Grimms Hill, Great Missenden HP16 9BD
Dorchester, Rt. Revd Anthony J. Russell, *cons.* 1988, *apptd* 1988; Holmby House, Sibford Ferris, Banbury, Oxon. OX15 5RG
Reading, Rt. Revd John F. E. Bone, *cons.* 1989, *apptd* 1989; Greenbanks, Old Bath Road, Sonning, Reading RG4 0SY

ASSISTANT BISHOPS
Rt. Revd Kenneth Cragg, DD, *cons.* 1970, *apptd* 1982; Rt. Revd Leonard Ashton, CB, *cons.* 1974, *apptd* 1984; Rt. Revd Richard Watson, *cons.* 1970, *apptd* 1988; Rt. Revd Peter Walker, *cons.* 1972, *apptd* 1990; Rt. Revd Maurice Wood, *cons.* 1971, *apptd* 1991; Rt. Revd Stephen Verney, *cons.* 1977, *apptd* 1991

DEAN OF CHRIST CHURCH
Very Revd John H. Drury, *apptd* 1991

CANONS RESIDENTIARY
Ven. F. V. Weston, *apptd* 1982; O. M. T. O'Donovan, D.Phil., *apptd* 1982; J. M. Pierce, *apptd* 1987; J. S. K. Ward, *apptd* 1991; Rt. Revd A. R. M. Gordon, *apptd* 1991

Organist, S. Darlington, FRCO, *apptd* 1985

ARCHDEACONS
Berkshire, Ven. M. A. Hill, *apptd* 1992
Buckingham, Ven. J. A. Morrison, *apptd* 1989
Oxford, Ven. F. V. Weston, *apptd* 1982

Stipendiary Male Clergy, 449
Stipendiary Women Deacons, 36

Chancellor, P. T. S. Boydell, QC, *apptd* 1958
Registrar and Legal Secretary, Dr F. E. Robson, OBE, 16 Beaumont Street, Oxford OX1 2LZ

WINDSOR
The Queen's Free Chapel of St George within Her Castle of Windsor (A Royal Peculiar)

DEAN
Very Revd Patrick R. Mitchell, FSA, *apptd* 1989

CANONS RESIDENTIARY
J. A. White, *apptd* 1982; D. M. Stanesby, PH.D., *apptd* 1985; A. A. Coldwells, *apptd* 1987; M. A. Moxon, *apptd* 1990

Chapter Clerk, Lt.-Col. N. J. Newman, *apptd* 1990
Organist, J. Rees-Williams, FRCO, *apptd* 1991

PETERBOROUGH

36TH BISHOP
Rt. Revd William J. Westwood, *cons.* 1975, *apptd* 1984; The Palace, Peterborough PE1 1YA. *Signs* William Petriburg:

BISHOP SUFFRAGAN
Brixworth, Rt. Revd Paul E. Barber, *cons.* 1989, *apptd* 1989; 4 The Avenue, Dallington, Northampton NN1 4RZ

DEAN
Very Revd Michael Bunker, *apptd* 1992

CANONS RESIDENTIARY
T. R. Christie, *apptd* 1980; J. Higham, *apptd* 1983; T. Willmott, *apptd* 1989

Organist, C. S. Gower, FRCO, *apptd* 1977

ARCHDEACONS
Northampton, Ven. M. R. Chapman, *apptd* 1991
Oakham, Ven. B. Fernyhough, *apptd* 1977

Stipendiary Male Clergy, 186
Stipendiary Women Deacons, 9
Chancellor, T. A. C. Coningsby, QC, *apptd* 1989
Registrar and Legal Secretary, R. Hemingray, 4 Holywell Way, Longthorpe, Peterborough PE3 6SS

PORTSMOUTH

7TH BISHOP
Rt. Revd Timothy J. Bavin, *cons.* 1974, *apptd* 1985; Bishopswood, Fareham, Hants. PO14 1NT. *Signs* Timothy Portsmouth

PROVOST
Vacant

CANONS RESIDENTIARY
M. D. Doe, *apptd* 1989; C. J. Bradley, *apptd* 1990; D. T. Isaac, *apptd* 1990; Jane Hedges, *apptd* 1993

Organist, A. Lucas, FRCO, *apptd* 1990

ARCHDEACONS
Isle of Wight, Ven. A. H. M. Turner, *apptd* 1986
Portsmouth, Ven. G. P. Knowles, *apptd* 1993

Stipendiary Male Clergy, 138
Stipendiary Women Deacons, 9
Chancellor, His Honour Judge Aglionby, *apptd* 1978
Registrar, Miss H. A. G. Tyler, 132 High Street, Portsmouth PO1 2HR

ROCHESTER

105TH BISHOP
Rt. Revd Michael A. Turnbull, *cons.* 1988, *apptd* 1988; Bishopscourt, Rochester ME1 1TS. *Signs* Michael Roffen:

BISHOP SUFFRAGAN
Tonbridge, Rt. Revd Brian A. Smith, *cons.* 1993, *apptd* 1993; Bishop's Lodge, St Botolph's Road, Sevenoaks TN13 3AG

ASSISTANT BISHOP
Rt. Revd Colin Buchanan, *cons.* 1985, *apptd* 1989

DEAN
Very Revd Edward F. Shotter, *apptd* 1990

CANONS RESIDENTIARY
E. R. Turner, *apptd* 1981; R. J. R. Lea, *apptd* 1988; J. Armson, *apptd* 1989; N. Warren, *apptd* 1989
Organist, B. Ferguson, FRCO, *apptd* 1977

ARCHDEACONS
Bromley, Ven. E. R. Francis, *apptd* 1979
Rochester, Ven. N. L. Warren, *apptd* 1989
Tonbridge, Ven. R. J. Mason, *apptd* 1977

Stipendiary Male Clergy, 226
Stipendiary Women Deacons, 20

Chancellor, His Honour Judge M. B. Goodman, *apptd* 1971
Registrar, O. R. Woodfield, The Precinct, Rochester ME1 1SZ

ST ALBANS

8TH BISHOP
Rt. Revd John B. Taylor, *cons.* 1980, *apptd* 1980; Abbey Gate House, St Albans AL3 4HD. *Signs* John St Albans

BISHOPS SUFFRAGAN
Bedford, vacant; 168 Kimbolton Road, Bedford MK41 8DN
Hertford, Rt. Revd Robin J. N. Smith, *cons.* 1990, *apptd* 1990; Hertford House, Abbey Mill Lane, St Albans AL3 4HE

ASSISTANT BISHOPS
Rt. Revd The Lord Runcie, *cons.* 1970, *apptd* 1991; Rt. Revd David J. Farmbrough, *cons.* 1981, *apptd* 1994 (from 1994)

DEAN
Very Revd Christopher Lewis, *apptd* 1993

CANONS RESIDENTIARY
C. B. Slee, *apptd* 1982; C. Garner, *apptd* 1984; G. R. S. Ritson, *apptd* 1987; M. Sansom, *apptd* 1988
Organist, Dr B. Rose, *apptd* 1988

ARCHDEACONS
Bedford, vacant
St Albans, Ven. P. B. Davies, *apptd* 1987

Stipendiary Male Clergy, 323
Stipendiary Women Deacons, 26

Chancellor, His Honour Judge Bursell, QC, *apptd* 1992
Registrar and Legal Secretary, D. N. Cheetham, Holywell Lodge, 41 Holywell Hill, St Albans AL1 1HE

ST EDMUNDSBURY AND IPSWICH

8TH BISHOP
Rt. Revd John Dennis, *cons.* 1979, *apptd* 1986; Bishop's House, 4 Park Road, Ipswich IP1 3ST. *Signs* John St Edmundsbury and Ipswich

BISHOP SUFFRAGAN
Dunwich, Rt. Revd Jonathan S. Bailey, *cons.* 1992, *apptd* 1992; The Old Vicarage, Stowupland, Stowmarket IP14 4BQ

PROVOST
Very Revd Raymond Furnell, *apptd* 1981

CANONS RESIDENTIARY
A. M. Shaw, *apptd* 1989; M. E. Mingins, *apptd* 1993

ARCHDEACONS
Ipswich, Ven. T. A. Gibson, *apptd* 1987
Sudbury, Ven. R. Garrard, *apptd* 1992
Suffolk, Ven. N. Robinson, *apptd* 1987

Stipendiary Male Clergy, 192
Stipendiary Women Deacons, 11

Chancellor, His Honour Sir John Blofeld, QC, *apptd* 1974
Registrar, J. D. Mitson, 22–28 Museum Street, Ipswich IP1 1JA

SALISBURY

77TH BISHOP
Rt. Revd David S. Stancliffe, *cons.* 1993, *apptd* 1993 (to be enthroned early 1994); South Canonry, The Close, Salisbury SP1 2ER. *Signs* David Sarum

BISHOPS SUFFRAGAN
Ramsbury, Rt. Revd Peter St G. Vaughan, *cons.* 1989, *apptd* 1989; Bishop's House, Urchfont, Devizes, Wilts. SN10 4QH
Sherborne, Rt. Revd John D. G. Kirkham, *cons.* 1976, *apptd* 1976; Little Bailie, Sturminster Marshall, Wimborne BH21 4AD

ASSISTANT BISHOP
Rt. Revd John Cavell, *cons.* 1972, *apptd* 1988

DEAN
Very Revd the Hon. Hugh G. Dickinson, *apptd* 1986

CANONS RESIDENTIARY
D. J. C. Davies, *apptd* 1985; J. R. Stewart, *apptd* 1990; D. M. K. Durston, *apptd* 1992

Organist, R. G. Seal, FRCO, *apptd* 1968

ARCHDEACONS
Dorset, Ven. G. E. Walton, *apptd* 1982
Sarum, Ven. B. J. Hopkinson, *apptd* 1986
Sherborne, Ven. P. C. Wheatley, *apptd* 1991
Wilts, Ven. B. J. Smith, *apptd* 1980

Stipendiary Male Clergy, 260
Stipendiary Women Deacons, 11

Chancellor of the Diocese, His Honour J. H. Ellison, VRD, *apptd* 1955
Registrar and Legal Secretary, F. M. Broadbent, 42 Castle Street, Salisbury SP1 3TX

SOUTHWARK

8TH BISHOP
Rt. Revd Robert K. Williamson, *cons.* 1984, *trans.* 1991, *apptd* 1991; Bishop's House, 38 Tooting Bec Gardens, London SW16 1QZ. *Signs* Robert Southwark

BISHOPS SUFFRAGAN
Croydon, Rt. Revd Wilfred D. Wood, DD, *cons.* 1985, *apptd* 1985; St Matthew's House, George Street, Croydon CR0 1PE
Kingston upon Thames, Rt Revd Martin Wharton, *cons.* 1992, *apptd* 1992; *Office*, Whitelands College, West Hill, London SW15 3SN

Woolwich, Rt. Revd Albert P. Hall, *cons.* 1984, *apptd* 1984; 8B Hilly Fields Crescent, London SE4 1QA

ASSISTANT BISHOPS
Rt. Revd Edmund Capper, OBE, *cons.* 1967, *apptd* 1981; Rt. Revd John Hughes, *cons.* 1956, *apptd* 1986; Rt. Revd Hugh Montefiore, *cons.* 1970, *apptd* 1987; Rt. Revd Simon Phipps, *cons.* 1976, *apptd* 1987; Rt. Revd Michael Nazir-Ali, *cons.* 1984, *apptd* 1990

PROVOST
Very Revd David L. Edwards, *apptd* 1983

CANON RESIDENTIARY
D. Painter, *apptd* 1991

Organist, P. Wright, FRCO, *apptd* 1989

ARCHDEACONS
Croydon, vacant
Lambeth, Ven. C. R. B. Bird, *apptd* 1988
Lewisham, Ven. G. Kuhrt, *apptd* 1989
Reigate, Ven. P. B. Coombs, *apptd* 1988
Southwark, Ven. D. L. Bartles-Smith, *apptd* 1985
Wandsworth, Ven. D. Gerrard, *apptd* 1989

Stipendiary Male Clergy, 404
Stipendiary Women Deacons, 34

Chancellor, R. M. K. Gray, QC, *apptd* 1990
Joint Registrars, D. W. Faull, OBE, and P. Morris, 35 Great Peter Street, London SW1P 3LR

TRURO

13TH BISHOP
Rt. Revd Michael T. Ball, *cons.* 1980, *apptd* 1990; Lis Escop, Truro TR3 6QQ. *Signs* Michael Truro

BISHOP SUFFRAGAN
St Germans, Rt. Revd Graham R. James, *cons.* 1993, *apptd* 1993; 32 Falmouth Road, Truro TR1 2HX

ASSISTANT BISHOP
Rt. Revd Conrad Meyer, *cons.* 1979, *apptd* 1991

DEAN
Very Revd David J. Shearlock, *apptd* 1982

CANONS RESIDENTIARY
Ven. R. L. Ravenscroft, *apptd* 1988; R. O. Osborne, *apptd* 1988

Organist, D. J. Briggs, FRCO, *apptd* 1989

ARCHDEACONS
Cornwall, Ven. R. L. Ravenscroft, *apptd* 1988
Bodmin, Ven. R. D. C. Whiteman, *apptd* 1989

Stipendiary Male Clergy, 149
Stipendiary Women Deacons, 2

Chancellor, P. T. S. Boydell, QC, *apptd* 1957
Registrar and Secretary, M. J. Follett, Messrs Follett Stock, Riverside Business Centre, Malpas Road, Truro TR1 1QH

WORCESTER

111TH BISHOP
Rt. Revd Philip H. E. Goodrich, *cons.* 1973, *apptd* 1982; The Bishop's House, Hartlebury Castle, Kidderminster DY11 7XX. *Signs* Philip Worcester

BISHOP SUFFRAGAN
Dudley, Rt. Revd Dr Rupert Hoare, *cons.* 1993, *apptd* 1993;
The Bishop's House, Brooklands, Halesowen Road,
Cradley Heath B64 7JF

ASSISTANT BISHOPS
Rt. Revd John Maund, CBE, MC, *cons.* 1950, *apptd* 1984; Rt.
Revd Kenneth Woollcombe, *cons.* 1971, *apptd* 1989; Rt.
Revd George Briggs, *cons.* 1973, *apptd* 1990; Rt. Revd
Derek Bond, *cons.* 1976, *apptd* 1992

DEAN
Very Revd Robert M. C. Jeffery, *apptd* 1987

CANONS RESIDENTIARY
Ven. F. Bentley, *apptd* 1984; D. G. Thomas, *apptd* 1987;
I. M. MacKenzie, *apptd* 1989

Organist, Dr D. Hunt, FRCO, *apptd* 1975

ARCHDEACONS
Dudley, Ven. J. Gathercole, *apptd* 1987
Worcester, Ven. F. Bentley, *apptd* 1984

Stipendiary Male Clergy, 150
Stipendiary Women Deacons, 14

Chancellor, P. T. S. Boydell, QC, *apptd* 1959
Registrar, M. Huskinson, Diocesan Registry, 8 Sansome
Walk, Worcester WRI ILW

Province of York

YORK

95TH ARCHBISHOP AND PRIMATE OF ENGLAND
Most Revd and Rt. Hon. John S. Habgood, PH.D., *cons.*
1973, *trans.* 1983, *apptd* 1983; Bishopthorpe, York
YO2 IQE. *Signs* John Ebor:

BISHOPS SUFFRAGAN
Hull, Rt. Revd Donald G. Snelgrove, TD, *cons.* 1981, *apptd*
1981; Hullen House, Woodfield Lane, Hessle, Hull HU13
OES
Selby, Rt. Revd Humphrey V. Taylor, *cons.* 1991, *apptd*
1991; 10 Precentor's Court, York YOI 2ES
Whitby, Rt. Revd Gordon Bates, *cons.* 1983, *apptd* 1983;
60 West Green, Stokesley, Middlesbrough TS9 5BD

ASSISTANT BISHOPS
Rt. Revd George Cockin, *cons.* 1959, *apptd* 1969; Rt. Revd
Richard Wimbush, *cons.* 1963, *apptd* 1977; Rt. Revd
Richard Wood, *cons.* 1973, *apptd* 1985; Rt. Revd Graham
Foley, *cons.* 1982, *apptd* 1989; Rt. Revd David Galliford,
cons. 1975, *apptd* 1991; Rt. Revd Clifford Barker, *cons.* 1976,
apptd 1991

DEAN
Very Revd John E. Southgate, *apptd* 1984

CANONS RESIDENTIARY
R. A. Hockley, *apptd* 1976; R. Mayland, *apptd* 1982; J. Toy,
PH.D., *apptd* 1983; R. Metcalfe, *apptd* 1988

Organist, P. Moore, FRCO, *apptd* 1983

ARCHDEACONS
Cleveland, Ven. C. J. Hawthorn, *apptd* 1991
East Riding, Ven. H. F. Buckingham, *apptd* 1988
York, Ven. G. B. Austin, *apptd* 1988

Stipendiary Male Clergy, 329

Stipendiary Women Deacons, 23

Official Principal and Auditor of the Chancery Court,
J. A. D. Owen, QC
Chancellor of the Diocese, His Honour Judge Coningsby, QC,
apptd 1977
*Vicar-General of the Province and Official Principal of the
Consistory Court*, His Honour Judge Coningsby, QC
Registrar and Legal Secretary, L. P. M. Lennox, I Peckitt
Street, York YOI ISG

DURHAM

92ND BISHOP
Rt. Revd David E. Jenkins (until June 1994), *cons.* 1984,
apptd 1984; Auckland Castle, Bishop Auckland DLI4 7NR.
Signs David Dunelm:

BISHOP SUFFRAGAN
Jarrow, Rt. Revd Alan Smithson, *cons.* 1990, *apptd* 1990;
The Old Vicarage, Hallgarth, Pittington, Durham
DH6 IAB

DEAN
Very Revd John R. Arnold, *apptd* 1989

CANONS RESIDENTIARY
M. C. Perry, *apptd* 1970; R. L. Coppin, *apptd* 1974; Ven. J.
D. Hodgson, *apptd* 1983; D. W. Brown, *apptd* 1990;
G. S. Pedley, *apptd* 1993

Organist, J. B. Lancelot, FRCO, *apptd* 1985

ARCHDEACONS
Auckland, Ven. G. G. Gibson, *apptd* 1993
Durham, Ven. J. D. Hodgson, *apptd* 1993

Stipendiary Male Clergy, 266
Stipendiary Women Deacons, 22

Chancellor, His Honour Judge Bursell, QC, *apptd* 1989
Registrar and Legal Secretary, D. M. Robertson, Diocesan
Registry, Auckland Castle, Bishop Auckland DLI4 7QJ

BLACKBURN

7TH BISHOP
Rt. Revd Alan D. Chesters, *cons.* 1989, *apptd* 1989; Bishop's
House, Ribchester Road, Blackburn BBI 9EF. *Signs* Alan
Blackburn

BISHOPS SUFFRAGAN
Burnley, vacant; Dean House, 449 Padiham Road, Burnley
BBI2 6TE
Lancaster, Rt. Revd John Nicholls, *cons.* 1990, *apptd* 1990;
Wheatfields, 7 Dallas Road, Lancaster LAI ITN

PROVOST
Very Revd David Frayne, *apptd* 1992

CANONS RESIDENTIARY
J. M. Taylor, *apptd* 1976; G. I. Hirst, *apptd* 1987;
M. A. Kitchener, *apptd* 1990

Organist, D. A. Cooper, FRCO, *apptd* 1983

ARCHDEACONS
Blackburn, Ven. W. D. Robinson, *apptd* 1986
Lancaster, Ven. K. H. Gibbons, *apptd* 1981

Stipendiary Male Clergy, 262

Stipendiary Women Deacons, 8

Chancellor, J. W. M. Bullimore, *apptd* 1990
Registrar, T. A. Hoyle, Diocesan Registry, Cathedral Close,
Blackburn BB1 5AB

BRADFORD

8TH BISHOP
Rt. Revd David J. Smith, *cons.* 1987, *apptd* 1992;
Bishopscroft, Ashwell Road, Heaton, Bradford BD9 4AU.
Signs David Bradford

PROVOST
Very Revd John S. Richardson, *apptd* 1990

CANONS RESIDENTIARY
K. H. Cook, *apptd* 1977; C. G. Lewis, *apptd* 1993
Organist, A. Horsey, FRCO, *apptd* 1986

ARCHDEACONS
Bradford, Ven. D. H. Shreeve, *apptd* 1984
Craven, vacant

Stipendiary Male Clergy, 134
Stipendiary Women Deacons, 11

Chancellor, D. M. Savill, QC, *apptd* 1976
Registrar and Secretary, J. G. H. Mackrell, 6–14 Devonshire
Street, Keighley BD21 2AY

CARLISLE

65TH BISHOP
Rt. Revd Ian Harland, *cons.* 1985, *apptd* 1989; Rose Castle,
Dalston, Carlisle CA5 7BZ. *Signs* Ian Carliol:

BISHOP SUFFRAGAN
Penrith, Rt. Revd George L. Hacker, *cons.* 1979, *apptd*
1979; The Rectory, Great Salkeld, Penrith CA11 9NA

DEAN
Very Revd Henry E. C. Stapleton, *apptd* 1988

CANONS RESIDENTIARY
R. A. Chapman, *apptd* 1978; R. C. Johns, *apptd* 1989;
D. T. I. Jenkins, *apptd* 1991; Ven. D. C. Turnbull, *apptd*
1993
Organist, J. Suter, FRCO, *apptd* 1991

ARCHDEACONS
Carlisle, Ven. D. C. Turnbull, *apptd* 1993
West Cumberland, Ven. J. R. Packer, *apptd* 1991
Westmorland and Furness, Ven. L. J. Peat, *apptd* 1989

Stipendiary Male Clergy, 169
Stipendiary Women Deacons, 8

Chancellor, His Honour Judge Aglionby, *apptd* 1991
Registrar and Secretary, Mrs S. Holmes, Woodside, Great
Corby, Carlisle CA4 8LL

CHESTER

39TH BISHOP
Rt. Revd Michael A. Baughen, *cons.* 1982, *apptd* 1982;
Bishop's House, Chester CH1 2JD. *Signs* Michael Cestr:

BISHOPS SUFFRAGAN
Birkenhead, Rt. Revd Michael L. Langrish, *cons.* 1993,
apptd 1993; 67 Bidston Road, Oxton, Birkenhead L43
6TR
Stockport, Rt. Revd Frank P. Sargeant, *cons.* 1984, *apptd*
1984; Bishop's Lodge, Back Lane, Dunham Town,
Altrincham, Cheshire WA14 4SG

DEAN
Very Revd Stephen S. Smalley, *apptd* 1986

CANONS RESIDENTIARY
R. M. Rees, *apptd* 1990; C. J. Bennetts, *apptd* 1990;
O. A. Conway, *apptd* 1991
Organist, R. Fisher, FRCO, *apptd* 1968

ARCHDEACONS
Chester, Ven. G. M. Turner, *apptd* 1993
Macclesfield, Ven. J. S. Gaisford, *apptd* 1986

Stipendiary Male Clergy, 300
Stipendiary Women Deacons, 13

Chancellor, H. H. Lomas, *apptd* 1977
Registrar and Legal Secretary, A. K. McAllester, Friars,
20 White Friars, Chester CH1 1XS

LIVERPOOL

6TH BISHOP
Rt. Revd David S. Sheppard, *cons.* 1969, *apptd* 1975;
Bishop's Lodge, Woolton Park, Liverpool L25 6DT. *Signs*
David Liverpool

BISHOP SUFFRAGAN
Warrington, Rt. Revd Michael Henshall, *cons.* 1976, *apptd*
1976; Martinsfield, Elm Avenue, Great Crosby, Liverpool
L23 2SX

ASSISTANT BISHOPS
Rt. Revd Graham Chadwick, *cons.* 1976, *apptd* 1990; Rt.
Revd James Roxburgh, *cons.* 1983, *apptd* 1991

DEAN
Very Revd Rhys D. C. Walters, *apptd* 1983

CANONS RESIDENTIARY
M. M. Wolfe, *apptd* 1982; D. J. Hutton, *apptd* 1983;
K. J. Riley, *apptd* 1983; H. Thomas, *apptd* 1988
Organist, Prof. I. Tracey, *apptd* 1980

ARCHDEACONS
Liverpool, Ven. S. Durant, *apptd* 1991
Warrington, Ven. C. D. S. Woodhouse, *apptd* 1981

Stipendiary Male Clergy, 274
Stipendiary Women Deacons, 23

Chancellor, R. G. Hamilton
Registrar and Cathedral Chapter Clerk, R. H. Arden,
1 Hanover Street, Liverpool L1 3DW

MANCHESTER

10TH BISHOP
Rt. Revd Christopher J. Mayfield, *cons.* 1985, *apptd* 1993;
Bishopscourt, Bury New Road, Manchester M7 0LE. *Signs*
Christopher Manchester

BISHOPS SUFFRAGAN
Bolton, Rt. Revd David Bonser, *cons.* 1991, *apptd* 1991;
   4 Sandfield Drive, Lostock, Bolton BL6 4DU
Hulme, Rt. Revd Colin J. F. Scott, *cons.* 1984, *apptd* 1984;
   1 Raynham Avenue, Didsbury, Manchester M20 0BW
Middleton, vacant; The Hollies, Manchester Road,
   Rochdale OL11 3QY

ASSISTANT BISHOP
Rt. Revd Edward Wickham, *cons.* 1959, *apptd* 1982

DEAN
Vacant

CANONS RESIDENTIARY
Ven. R. B. Harris, *apptd* 1980; J. R. Atherton, PH.D., *apptd*
1984; B. Duncan, *apptd* 1986; A. E. Radcliffe, *apptd* 1991

Organist, C. Stokes, *apptd* 1992

ARCHDEACONS
Bolton, Ven. L. M. Davies, *apptd* 1992
Manchester, Ven. R. B. Harris, *apptd* 1980
Rochdale, Ven. J. M. M. Dalby, *apptd* 1991

Stipendiary Male Clergy, 377
Stipendiary Women Deacons, 16

Chancellor, G. C. H. Spafford, *apptd* 1976
Registrar and Bishop's Secretary, M. Darlington,
   90 Deansgate, Manchester M3 2GH

NEWCASTLE

10TH BISHOP
Rt. Revd Andrew A. K. Graham, *cons.* 1977, *apptd* 1981;
   Bishop's House, 29 Moor Road South, Gosforth,
   Newcastle upon Tyne NE3 1PA. *Signs* A. Newcastle

ASSISTANT BISHOP
Rt. Revd Kenneth Gill, *cons.* 1972, *apptd* 1980

PROVOST
Very Revd Nicholas G. Coulton, *apptd* 1990

CANONS RESIDENTIARY
R. Langley, *apptd* 1985; P. R. Strange, *apptd* 1986;
I. F. Bennett, *apptd* 1988; Ven. P. Elliott, *apptd* 1993

Organist, T. G. Hone, FRCO, *apptd* 1987

ARCHDEACONS
Lindisfarne, Ven. M. E. Bowering, *apptd* 1987
Northumberland, Ven. P. Elliott, *apptd* 1993

Stipendiary Male Clergy, 175
Stipendiary Women Deacons, 10

Chancellor, His Honour A. J. Blackett-Ord, CVO, *apptd* 1971
Registrar and Secretary, R. R. V. Nicholson, 46 Grainger
   Street, Newcastle upon Tyne NE1 5LB

RIPON

11TH BISHOP
Rt. Revd David N. de L. Young, *cons.* 1977, *apptd* 1977;
   Bishop Mount, Ripon HG4 5DP. *Signs* David Ripon

BISHOP SUFFRAGAN
Knaresborough, Rt. Revd Malcolm J. Menin, *cons.* 1986,
   apptd 1986; 16 Shaftesbury Avenue, Roundhay, Leeds
   LS8 1DT

ASSISTANT BISHOPS
Rt. Revd Ralph Emmerson, *cons.* 1972, *apptd* 1986; Rt.
   Revd Derek A. Rawcliffe, *cons.* 1974, *apptd* 1991

DEAN
Very Revd Christopher R. Campling, *apptd* 1984

CANONS RESIDENTIARY
D. G. Ford, *apptd* 1980; P. J. Marshall, *apptd* 1985;
M. R. Glanville-Smith, *apptd* 1990

Organist, R. Perrin, FRCO, *apptd* 1966

ARCHDEACONS
Leeds, Ven. J. M. Oliver, *apptd* 1992
Richmond, Ven. K. Good, *apptd* 1993

Stipendiary Male Clergy, 174
Stipendiary Women Deacons, 17

Chancellor, His Honour Judge Grenfell, *apptd* 1992
Registrar and Legal Secretary, J. R. Balmforth, York House,
   York Place, Knaresborough HG5 0AD
Diocesan Secretary, G. M. Royal, Diocesan Office, St Mary's
   Street, Leeds LS9 7DP

SHEFFIELD

5TH BISHOP
Rt. Revd David R. Lunn, *cons.* 1980, *apptd* 1980;
   Bishopscroft, Snaithing Lane, Sheffield S10 3LG. *Signs*
   David Sheffield

BISHOP SUFFRAGAN
Doncaster, Rt. Revd. Michael F. Gear, *cons.* 1993, *apptd*
   1993; Bishops Lodge, Hooton Roberts, Rotherham S65
   4PF

ASSISTANT BISHOPS
Rt. Revd Kenneth Skelton, CBE, *cons.* 1962, *apptd* 1984; Rt.
   Revd Kenneth Pillar, *cons.* 1982, *apptd* 1989

PROVOST
Very Revd John W. Gladwin, *apptd* 1988

CANONS RESIDENTIARY
T. M. Page, *apptd* 1982; Ven. S. R. Lowe, *apptd* 1988;
C. M. Smith, *apptd* 1991; Jane E. M. Sinclair, *apptd* 1993

Organist, P. Brough, FRCO, *apptd* 1991

ARCHDEACONS
Doncaster, Ven. D. Carnelley, *apptd* 1985
Sheffield, Ven. S. R. Lowe, *apptd* 1988

Stipendiary Male Clergy, 216
Stipendiary Women Deacons, 16

Chancellor, Prof. J. D. McClean, *apptd* 1992
Registrar and Legal Secretary, C. P. Rothwell, 30 Bank
   Street, Sheffield S1 2DS

SODOR AND MAN

79TH BISHOP
Rt. Revd Noel D. Jones, CB, *cons.* 1989, *apptd* 1989; The
   Bishop's House, Quarterbridge Road, Douglas, IOM.
   Signs Noel Sodor and Man

CANONS
B. H. Kelly, *apptd* 1980; B. H. Partington, *apptd* 1985;
J. Sheen, *apptd* 1991; F. H. Bird, *apptd* 1993

ARCHDEACON
Isle of Man, Ven. D. A. Willoughby, *apptd* 1982

Stipendiary Male Clergy, 21

Vicar-General and Registrar, P. W. S. Farrant, 24 Athol Street, Douglas, IOM

SOUTHWELL

9TH BISHOP
Rt. Revd Patrick B. Harris, *cons.* 1973, *apptd* 1988; Bishop's Manor, Southwell NG25 0JR. *Signs* Patrick Southwell

BISHOP SUFFRAGAN
Sherwood, Rt. Revd Alan W. Morgan, *cons.* 1989, *apptd* 1989; Sherwood House, High Oakham Road, Mansfield NG18 5AJ

PROVOST
Very Revd David Leaning, *apptd* 1991

CANONS RESIDENTIARY
D. P. Keene, *apptd* 1981; I. G. Collins, *apptd* 1985; M. Austin, *apptd* 1992

Organist, P. Hale, *apptd* 1981

ARCHDEACONS
Newark, Ven. D. C. Hawtin, *apptd* 1992
Nottingham, Ven. T. O. Walker, *apptd* 1991

Stipendiary Male Clergy, 212
Stipendiary Women Deacons, 9

Chancellor, J. Shand, *apptd* 1981
Registrar, C. C. Hodson, Diocesan Office, Westgate, Southwell NG25 0JL

WAKEFIELD

11TH BISHOP
Rt. Revd Nigel S. McCulloch, *cons.* 1986, *apptd* 1992; Bishop's Lodge, Woodthorpe Lane, Wakefield WF2 6JL. *Signs* Nigel Wakefield

BISHOP SUFFRAGAN
Pontefract, Rt. Revd John T. Finney, *cons.* 1993, *apptd* 1993; Pontefract House, Manygates Lane, Wakefield WF2 6AX

PROVOST
Very Revd John E. Allen, *apptd* 1982

CANONS RESIDENTIARY
R. D. Baxter, *apptd* 1986; I. C. Knox, *apptd* 1989; D. O'Connor, *apptd* 1992; G. Nairn-Briggs, *apptd* 1992

Organist, J. Bielby, FRCO, *apptd* 1972

ARCHDEACONS
Halifax, Ven. D. Hallatt, *apptd* 1989
Pontefract, Ven. J. Flack, *apptd* 1992

Stipendiary Male Clergy, 196
Stipendiary Women Deacons, 14

Chancellor, P. Collier, QC, *apptd* 1992
Registrar and Secretary, E. Chapman, Burton Street, Wakefield WF1 2DA

The Anglican Communion

The Anglican Communion consists of 30 independent provincial or national Christian Churches throughout the world, many of which are in Commonwealth countries and originated from missionary activity by the Church of England. There is no single world authority linking the Communion, but all recognize the leadership of the Archbishop of Canterbury and have strong ecclesiastical and historical links with the Church of England. Every ten years all the bishops in the Communion meet at the Lambeth Conference, convened by the Archbishop of Canterbury. The Conference has no policy-making authority but is an important forum for the discussion of issues of common concern. The Anglican Consultative Council was set up in 1968 to function between conferences and the meeting of the Primates every two years.

There are about 70 million Anglicans and 700 archbishops and bishops world-wide.

THE CHURCH IN WALES

The Anglican Church was the established church in Wales from the 16th century until 1920, when the estrangement of the majority of Welsh people from Anglicanism, in particular in favour of Presbyterianism, resulted in disestablishment. Since then the Church in Wales has been an autonomous province consisting of six sees, with one of the diocesan bishops being elected Archbishop of Wales by an electoral college comprising elected lay and clerical members.

The legislative body of the Church in Wales is the Governing Body, which has 347 members in total, divided between the three orders of bishops, clergy and laity. It is presided over by the Archbishop of Wales and meets twice annually. Its decisions are binding upon all members of the Church. There are 105,661 members of the Church in Wales, with six bishops, about 700 clergy and 1,142 parishes.

THE GOVERNING BODY OF THE CHURCH IN WALES, 39 Cathedral Road, Cardiff CF1 9XF. Tel: 0222–231638. *Secretary-General,* J. W. D. McIntyre

10TH ARCHBISHOP OF WALES, Most Revd Alwyn R. Jones (Bishop of St Asaph), *elected* 1991

THE RT. REVD BISHOPS
Bangor (79th), Rt. Revd Barry C. Morgan, *b.* 1947, *cons.* 1993, *apptd* 1992; Tŷ'r Esgob, Bangor LL57 2SS. *Signs* Barry Bangor. *Stipendiary clergy,* 69
Llandaff (101st), Rt. Revd Roy T. Davies, *b.* 1934, *cons.* 1985, *apptd* 1985; Llys Esgob, The Cathedral Green, Llandaff, Cardiff CF5 2YE. *Signs* Roy Landav. *Stipendiary clergy,* 168
Monmouth (8th), Rt. Revd Rowan D. Williams, *b* 1950, *cons.* 1992, *apptd* 1992; Bishopstow, Stow Hill, Newport NP9 4EA. *Signs* Rowan Monmouth. *Stipendiary clergy,* 110
St Asaph (74th), Most Revd Alwyn R. Jones, *b.* 1934, *cons.* 1982, *apptd* 1982; Esgobty, St Asaph, Clwyd LL17 0TW. *Signs* Alwyn Cambrensis. *Stipendiary clergy,* 112
St David's (125th), Rt. Revd J. Ivor Rees, *b.* 1926, *cons.* 1988, *apptd* 1991; Llys Esgob, Abergwili, Dyfed SA31 2JG. *Signs* Ivor St Davids. *Stipendiary clergy,* 132
Swansea and Brecon (7th), Rt. Revd Dewi M. Bridges, *b.* 1933, *cons.* 1988, *apptd* 1988; Ely Tower, Brecon, Powys LD3 9DE. *Signs* Dewi Swansea & Brecon. *Stipendiary clergy,* 100

The stipend of a diocesan bishop of the Church in Wales is £23,610 a year from 1994.

THE EPISCOPAL CHURCH IN SCOTLAND

The Episcopal Church in Scotland was founded after the Act of Settlement (1690) established the presbyterian nature of the Church of Scotland. The Episcopal Church is in full communion with the Church of England but is autonomous. The governing authority is the General Synod, an elected body of 160 members which meets once a year. The diocesan bishop who convenes and presides at meetings of the General Synod is called the Primus and is elected by his fellow bishops.

There are 56,742 members of the Episcopal Church in Scotland, of whom 34,909 are communicants. There are seven bishops, 207 clergy, and 341 churches and places of worship.

THE GENERAL SYNOD OF THE EPISCOPAL CHURCH IN SCOTLAND, 21 Grosvenor Crescent, Edinburgh EH12 5EE. Tel: 031-225 6357. *Secretary-General*, J. Simpson

PRIMUS OF THE EPISCOPAL CHURCH IN SCOTLAND, Most Revd Richard F. Holloway (Bishop of Edinburgh), *elected* 1992

THE RT. REVD BISHOPS
Aberdeen and Orkney, A. Bruce Cameron, *b.* 1941, *cons.* 1992, *apptd* 1992. *Clergy* 14
Argyll and the Isles, Douglas M. Cameron, *b.* 1935, *cons.* 1992, *apptd* 1992. *Clergy* 10
Brechin, Robert T. Halliday, *b.* 1932, *cons.* 1990, *apptd* 1990. *Clergy* 15
Edinburgh, Richard F. Holloway, *b.* 1933, *cons.* 1986, *apptd* 1986. *Clergy* 65
Glasgow and Galloway, John M. Taylor, *b.* 1932, *cons.* 1991, *apptd* 1991. *Clergy* 45
Moray, Ross and Caithness, vacant. *Clergy* 16
St Andrews, Dunkeld and Dunblane, Michael G. Hare-Duke, *b.* 1925, *cons.* 1969, *apptd* 1969. *Clergy* 30

The stipend of a diocesan bishop of the Episcopal Church in Scotland was £16,840 in 1993

THE CHURCH OF IRELAND

The Anglican Church was the established church in Ireland from the 16th century but never secured the allegiance of a majority of the Irish and was disestablished in 1871. The Church in Ireland is divided into the provinces of Armagh and Dublin, each under an archbishop. The provinces are subdivided into 12 dioceses.

The legislative body is the General Synod, which has 660 members in total, divided between the House of Bishops and the House of Representatives. The Archbishop of Armagh is elected by the House of Bishops; other episcopal elections are made by an electoral college.

There are about 375,000 members of the Church of Ireland, with two archbishops, ten bishops, about 600 clergy and about 1,000 churches and places of worship.

CENTRAL OFFICE, Church of Ireland House, Church Avenue, Rathmines, Dublin 6. Tel: 0001-978422. *Assistant Secretary of the General Synod*, J. F. Buttimore

PROVINCE OF ARMAGH

ARCHBISHOP OF ARMAGH AND PRIMATE OF ALL IRELAND, Most Revd Robert H. A. Eames, PH.D., *b.* 1937, *cons.* 1975, *trans.* 1986. *Clergy* 57

THE RT. REVD BISHOPS
Clogher, Brian D. A. Hannon, *b.* 1936, *cons.* 1986, *apptd* 1986. *Clergy* 33
Connor, Samuel G. Poyntz, PH.D., *b.* 1926, *cons.* 1978, *trans.* 1987. *Clergy* 116
Derry and Raphoe, James Mehaffey, PH.D., *b.* 1931, *cons.* 1980, *apptd* 1980. *Clergy* 54
Down and Dromore, Gordon McMullan, PH.D., *b.* 1934, *cons.* 1980, *trans.* 1986. *Clergy* 111
Kilmore, Elphin and Ardagh, Michael H. G. Mayes, *b.* 1941, *cons.* 1993, *apptd* 1993. *Clergy* 30
Tuam, Killala and Achonry, John R. W. Neill, *b.* 1945, *cons.* 1986, *apptd* 1986. *Clergy* 9

PROVINCE OF DUBLIN

ARCHBISHOP OF DUBLIN, BISHOP OF GLENDALOUGH, AND PRIMATE OF IRELAND, Most Revd Donald A. Caird, DD, *b.* 1925, *cons.* 1970, *trans.* 1976, 1985. *Clergy* 92

THE RT. REVD BISHOPS
Cashel and Ossory, Noel V. Willoughby, *b.* 1926, *cons.* 1980, *apptd* 1980. *Clergy* 38
Cork, Cloyne and Ross, Robert A. Warke, *b.* 1930, *cons.* 1988, *apptd* 1988. *Clergy* 24
Limerick and Killaloe, Edward F. Darling, *b.* 1933, *cons.* 1985, *apptd* 1985. *Clergy* 22
Meath and Kildare, Most Revd Walton N. F. Empey, *b.* 1934, *cons.* 1981, *trans.* 1985. *Clergy* 21

Anglican Communion Overseas

ANGLICAN CHURCH OF AOTEAROA, NEW ZEALAND AND POLYNESIA

PRIMATE AND ARCHBISHOP OF NEW ZEALAND, The Most Revd Brian N. Davis (Bishop of Wellington), *cons.* 1980, *apptd* 1986

THE RT. REVD BISHOPS
Aotearoa, Whakahuhui Vercoe, *cons.* 1981, *apptd* 1981
Auckland, Bruce Gilberd, *cons.* 1985, *apptd* 1985
Christchurch, David Coles, *cons.* 1990, *apptd* 1990
Dunedin, Penelope Jamieson, *cons.* 1990, *apptd* 1990
Nelson, Derek Eaton, *cons.* 1990, *apptd* 1990
Polynesia, Jabez Bryce, *cons.* 1975, *apptd* 1975
Waiapu, Murray Mills, *cons.* 1991, *apptd* 1991
Waikato, David Moxon, *cons.* 1993, *apptd* 1993
Wellington, see above

ANGLICAN CHURCH OF AUSTRALIA

PRIMATE OF AUSTRALIA, The Most Revd Keith Rayner (Archbishop of Melbourne), *cons.* 1969, *apptd* 1991

PROVINCE OF NEW SOUTH WALES

METROPOLITAN
Archbishop of Sydney, The Most Revd R. Harry Goodhew, *cons.* 1982, *apptd* 1993

THE RT. REVD BISHOPS
Armidale, Peter Chiswell, *cons.* 1976, *apptd* 1976
Bathurst, Bruce W. Wilson, *cons.* 1984, *apptd* 1989

Canberra and Goulburn, George V. Browning, *apptd* 1993
Grafton, Bruce A. Schultz, *cons.* 1985, *apptd* 1985
Newcastle, Roger A. Herft, *apptd* 1993
Riverina, Bruce Q. Clark, *apptd* 1993

PROVINCE OF QUEENSLAND

METROPOLITAN
Archbishop of Brisbane, The Most Revd Peter Hollingworth,
cons. 1985, *apptd* 1990

THE RT. REVD BISHOPS
Carpentaria, Anthony F. B. Hall-Matthews, *cons.* 1984
North Queensland, John Lewis, *cons.* 1971
Northern Territory, Richard F. Appleby, *cons.* 1992
Rockhampton, George A. Hearn, *cons.* 1981

PROVINCE OF SOUTH AUSTRALIA

METROPOLITAN
Archbishop of Adelaide, The Most Revd Ian G. C. George,
cons. 1989, *apptd* 1991

THE RT. REVD BISHOPS
The Murray, Graham H. Walden, *cons.* 1981, *apptd* 1989
Willochra, W. David H. McCall, *cons.* 1987, *apptd* 1987

PROVINCE OF VICTORIA

METROPOLITAN
Archbishop of Melbourne, The Most Revd Keith Rayner,
cons. 1969, *apptd* 1990 *(see above)*

THE RT. REVD BISHOPS
Ballarat, vacant
Bendigo, vacant
Gippsland, Colin D. Sheumack, *cons.* 1987, *apptd* 1987
Wangaratta, Robert G. Beal, *cons.* 1985, *apptd* 1985

PROVINCE OF WESTERN AUSTRALIA

METROPOLITAN
Archbishop of Perth, The Most Revd Peter F. Carnley,
PH.D., *cons.* 1981, *apptd* 1981

THE RT. REVD BISHOPS
Bunbury, Hamish J. U. Jamieson, *cons.* 1974, *apptd* 1984
North-West Australia, Anthony Nicholls, *cons.* 1992, *apptd*
1992

EXTRA-PROVINCIAL DIOCESE

Bishop of Tasmania, Rt. Revd Phillip K. Newell, AO, *cons.*
1982, *apptd* 1982

EPISCOPAL ANGLICAN CHURCH OF BRAZIL
Igreja Episcopal Anglicana Do Brasil

PRIMATE *(acting),* The Most Revd Claudio V. S. Gastal
(Bishop of Southern Brazil), *cons.* 1984, *acting since* 1993

THE RT. REVD BISHOPS
Brasília, Almir dos Santos, *cons.* 1989, *apptd* 1989
Central Brazil, Sydney A. Ruiz, *cons.* 1985, *apptd* 1985
Northern Brazil, Clovis E. Rodrigues, *cons.* 1985, *apptd* 1986
Pelotas, Luiz O. P. Prado, *cons.* 1987, *apptd* 1989
South Central Brazil, Glauco Soares de Lima, *cons.* 1989,
apptd 1989
Southern Brazil, see above, apptd 1984

South-Western Brazil, Jubal P. Neves, *cons.* 1993, *apptd*
1993

CHURCH OF THE PROVINCE OF BURUNDI

ARCHBISHOP OF PROVINCE, The Most Revd Samuel
Sindamuka (Bishop of Matana), *cons.* 1975, *apptd* 1989

THE RT. REVD BISHOPS
Bujumbura, Pie Ntukamazina, *cons.* 1990, *apptd* 1990
Buye, Samuel Ndayisenga, *apptd* 1979
Gitega, Jean Nduwayo, *apptd* 1985
Matana, see above

ANGLICAN CHURCH OF CANADA

ARCHBISHOP AND PRIMATE, The Most Revd Michael
G. Peers, *cons.* 1977, *trans.* 1986

PROVINCE OF BRITISH COLUMBIA

METROPOLITAN
vacant

THE RT. REVD BISHOPS
British Columbia, Barry Jenks, *cons.* 1992, *elected* 1992
Caledonia, John Hannen, *cons.* 1981, *elected* 1981
Cariboo, James Cruickshank, *cons.* 1992, *elected* 1992
Kootenay, David Crawley, *cons.* 1990, *elected* 1990
New Westminster, vacant
Yukon, Ronald Ferris, *cons.* 1981, *elected* 1981

PROVINCE OF CANADA

METROPOLITAN
Archbishop of Western Newfoundland, Most Revd Stewart
S. Payne, *cons.* 1978, *elected* 1990

THE RT. REVD BISHOPS
Central Newfoundland, Edward Marsh, *cons.* 1990, *elected*
1990
Eastern Newfoundland and Labrador, Donald Harvey, *cons.*
1993, *elected* 1992
Fredericton, George Lemon, *cons.* 1989, *elected* 1989
Montreal, Andrew Hutchison, *cons.* 1990, *elected* 1990
Nova Scotia, Arthur Peters, *cons.* 1982, *elected* 1982
Quebec, Bruce Stavert, *cons.* 1991, *elected* 1991
Western Newfoundland, see above

PROVINCE OF ONTARIO

METROPOLITAN
Archbishop of Huron, The Most Revd Percival O'Driscoll,
cons. 1987, *elected* 1993

THE RT. REVD BISHOPS
Algoma, Leslie Peterson, *cons.* 1983, *elected* 1983
Huron, see above
Moosonee, Caleb Lawrence, *cons.* 1980, *elected* 1980
Niagara, Walter Asbil, *cons.* 1990, *elected* 1990
Ontario, Peter Mason, *cons.* 1992, *elected* 1992
Ottawa, John Baycroft, *cons.* 1985, *elected* 1993
Toronto, Terence Finlay, *cons.* 1986, *elected* 1990

PROVINCE OF RUPERT'S LAND

METROPOLITAN
Archbishop of Rupert's Land, The Most Revd Walter
H. Jones, *cons.* 1970, *elected* 1988

THE RT. REVD BISHOPS
Arctic, J. C. R. Williams, *cons.* 1987, *elected* 1991
Athabasca, John Clarke, *cons.* 1992, *elected* 1992
Brandon, Malcolm Harding, *cons.* 1992, *elected* 1992
Calgary, Barry Curtis, *cons.* 1983, *elected* 1983
Edmonton, Kenneth Genge, *cons.* 1988, *elected* 1988
Keewatin, Thomas Collings, *cons.* 1991, *elected* 1991
Qu' Appelle, Eric Bays, *cons.* 1986, *elected* 1986
Rupert's Land, see above
Saskatchewan, vacant
Saskatoon, Thomas Morgan, *cons.* 1985, *elected* 1993

CHURCH OF THE PROVINCE OF CENTRAL AFRICA

ARCHBISHOP OF PROVINCE, The Most Revd Walter
P. K. Makhulu (Bishop of Botswana), *cons.* 1979, *apptd*
1980

THE RT. REVD BISHOPS
Botswana, see above
Central Zambia, Clement Shaba, *cons.* 1984, *apptd* 1984
Harare, Ralph Hatendi, *cons.* 1979, *apptd* 1981
Lake Malawi, Peter Nyanja, *cons.* 1978, *apptd* 1978
The Lundi, Jonathan Siyachitema, *cons.* 1981, *apptd* 1981
Lusaka, Stephen Mumba, *cons.* 1981, *apptd* 1981
Manicaland, Elijah Masuko, *cons.* 1981, *apptd* 1981
Matabeleland, Theophilus Naledi, *cons.* 1987, *apptd* 1987
Northern Zambia, Bernard Malango, *cons.* 1988, *apptd* 1988
Southern Malawi, Nathaniel Aipa, *cons.* 1987, *apptd* 1987

CHURCH OF THE PROVINCE OF THE INDIAN OCEAN

ARCHBISHOP OF PROVINCE, The Most Revd French
Chang-Him (Bishop of Seychelles), *cons.* 1979, *apptd*
1984

THE RT. REVD BISHOPS
Antananarivo, Remi Rabenirina, *cons.* 1984, *apptd* 1984
Antsiranana, Keith Benzies, OBE, *cons.* 1982, *apptd* 1982
Mauritius, Rex Donat, *cons.* 1984, *apptd* 1984
Seychelles, see above
Toamasina, Donald Smith, *cons.* 1990, *apptd* 1990

THE HOLY CATHOLIC CHURCH IN JAPAN
Nippon Sei Ko Kai

PRIMATE, The Most Revd Christopher I. Kikawada
(Bishop of Osaka), *cons.* 1975, *apptd* 1986

THE RT. REVD BISHOPS
Chubu, Samuel W. Hoyo, *cons.* 1987, *apptd* 1987
Hokkaido, Augustine H. Amagi, *cons.* 1987, *apptd* 1987
Kita Kanto, James T. Yashiro, *cons.* 1985, *apptd* 1985
Kobe, John J. Furumoto, *cons.* 1992, *apptd* 1992
Kyoto, John T. Okano, *cons.* 1991, *apptd* 1991
Kyushu, Joseph N. Iida, *cons.* 1982, *apptd* 1982

Okinawa, Paul S. Nakamura, *cons.* 1972, *apptd* 1972
Osaka, see above
Tohoku, William T. Murakami, *cons.* 1993, *apptd* 1993
Tokyo, John M. Takeda, *cons.* 1988, *apptd* 1988
Yokohama, Raphael S. Kajiwara, *cons.* 1984, *apptd* 1984

THE EPISCOPAL CHURCH IN JERUSALEM AND THE MIDDLE EAST

PRESIDENT-BISHOP, Rt. Revd Samir Kafity, *apptd* 1986

THE RT. REVD BISHOPS
Jerusalem, Samir Kafity, *cons.* 1984
Iran, Iraj Mottahedeh, *cons.* 1990
Egypt, Ghais A. Malik, *cons.* 1984
Cyprus and the Gulf, John Brown, *cons.* 1986

CHURCH OF THE PROVINCE OF KENYA

ARCHBISHOP OF PROVINCE, The Most Revd Manasses
Kuria (Bishop of Nairobi), *cons.* 1970, *apptd* 1980

THE RT. REVD BISHOPS
Eldoret, Stephen Kewasis, *apptd* 1992
Embu, Moses Njue
Katakwa, Eliud Okiring
Kirinyaga, David Gitari, *cons.* 1975, *apptd* 1975
Machakos, Benjamin Nzimbi, *cons.* 1985, *apptd* 1985
Maseno North, James Mundia, *cons.* 1970, *apptd* 1970
Maseno South, Henry Okullu, *cons.* 1974, *apptd* 1974
Maseno West, Joseph Wesonga, *apptd* 1991
Mombasa, Crispus Nzano, *cons.* 1975, *apptd* 1981
Mount Kenya Central, John Mahiaini, *cons.* 1984, *apptd* 1984
Mount Kenya South, George Njuguna, *cons.* 1984, *apptd*
1985
Nairobi, see above
Nakuru, Stephen M. Nijihia, *apptd* 1992
Nambale, Isaac Namango, *cons.* 1984, *apptd* 1987

CHURCH OF THE PROVINCE OF KOREA

ARCHBISHOP OF PROVINCE, The Most Revd Bundo Kim
(Bishop of Pusan), *apptd* 1993

THE RT. REVD BISHOPS
Pusan, see above, *apptd* 1988
Seoul, Simon Kim
Taejon, Paul Hwan Yoon, *apptd* 1988

CHURCH OF THE PROVINCE OF MELANESIA

ARCHBISHOP OF PROVINCE, The Most Revd Amos
S. Waiaru (Bishop of Central Melanesia), *cons.* 1981,
apptd 1988

THE RT. REVD BISHOPS
Central Melanesia, see above
Hanuato'o, James Mason, *cons.* 1991, *apptd* 1991
Malaita, Raymond Aumae, *cons.* 1990, *apptd* 1990
Temotu, Lazarus Munamua, *cons.* 1987, *apptd* 1987
Vanuatu, Michael Tavoa, *cons.* 1990, *apptd* 1990
Ysabel, Ellison Pogo, *cons.* 1981, *apptd* 1981

CHURCH OF THE PROVINCE OF MYANMAR

ARCHBISHOP OF PROVINCE, The Most Revd Andrew
  Mya Han (Bishop of Yangon), *cons.* 1988, *apptd* 1988

THE RT. REVD BISHOPS
Hpa'an, Daniel Hoi Kyin, *cons.* 1992, *apptd* 1992
Mandalay, Andrew Hla Aung, *cons.* 1988, *apptd* 1988
Myitkyina, Timothy Mya Wah, *cons.* 1984, *apptd* 1984
Sittwe, Barnabas Theaung Hawi, *cons.* 1978, *apptd* 1980
Taungoo, George Kyaw Mya, *cons.* 1979, *apptd* 1979
Yangon (Rangoon), see above

CHURCH OF THE PROVINCE OF NIGERIA

ARCHBISHOP OF THE PROVINCE, The Most Revd Joseph
  Adetiloye (Bishop of Lagos), *apptd* 1991

THE RT. REVD BISHOPS
Aba, A. O. Iwuagwu, *apptd* 1985
Abuja, Peter Akinole, *apptd* 1989
Akoko, J. O. K. Olowokure, *apptd* 1986
Akure, Emmanuel Gbonigi, *apptd* 1983
Asaba, Roland Nwosu, *apptd* 1977
Awka, Maxwell Anikwenwa, *apptd* 1987
Bauchi, Emmanuel O. Chukwuma, *apptd* 1990
Benin, John George, *apptd* 1985
Calabar, W. G. Ekprikpo
Egbado, Timothy Bolaji
Egba-Egbado, T. I. Akintayo, *apptd* 1977
Ekiti, C. A. Akinbola, *apptd* 1986
Enugu, Gideon Otubelu, *apptd* 1969
Ibadan, Gideon Olajide, *apptd* 1988
Ife, Gabriel Oloniyo
Ijebu, Abraham Olowoyo, *apptd* 1990
Ijebu Remo, E. O. I. Ogundana, *apptd* 1984
Ilesha, E. A. Ademowo, *apptd* 1989
Jos, B. A. Kwashi
Kaduna, Titus Ogbonyomi, *apptd* 1975
Kafanchan, William Diya, *apptd* 1990
Kano, B. O. Omoseibi, *apptd* 1990
Katsina, J. S. Kwasu, *apptd* 1990
Kwara, Herbert Haruna, *apptd* 1974
Lagos, see above, *apptd* 1985
Maiduguri, E. K. Mani, *apptd* 1990
Makurdi, Nathan Nyom
Minna, Nathaniel Yisa, *apptd* 1990
The Niger, Jonathan Onyemelukwe, *apptd* 1975
Niger Delta, Samuel Elenwo, *apptd* 1981
Okigwe/Orlu, Samuel Ebo, *apptd* 1984
Ondo, Samuel Aderin, *apptd* 1981
Osun, Seth Fagbemi, *apptd* 1987
Owerri, Benjamin Nwankiti, *apptd* 1968
Owo, Abraham Awosan, *apptd* 1983
Sokoto, J. A. Idowu-Fearon, *apptd* 1990
Uyo, Ebenezar Nglass
Warri, Nathaniel Enuku
Yola, Chris O. Efobi, *apptd* 1990

ANGLICAN CHURCH OF PAPUA NEW GUINEA

ARCHBISHOP OF PROVINCE, The Most Revd Bevan
  Meredith (Bishop of New Guinea Islands), *cons.* 1967,
  elected 1990

THE RT. REVD BISHOPS
Aipo Rongo, Paul Richardson, *cons.* 1987, *elected* 1987
Dogura, Tevita Talanoa, *cons.* 1992, *elected* 1992
New Guinea Islands, see above, *elected* 1977
Popondota, Walter Siba, *cons.* 1990, *elected* 1990
Port Moresby, Isaac Gadebo, *cons.* 1983, *elected* 1983

PHILIPPINE EPISCOPAL CHURCH

PRIME BISHOP, The Most Revd Narciso V. Ticobay, *cons.*
  1986, *apptd* 1993

THE RT. REVD BISHOPS
Central Philippines, Manuel C. Lumpias, *cons.* 1977, *apptd*
  1978
North Central Philippines, Joel A. Pachao, *cons.* 1993, *apptd*
  1993
Northern Luzon, Ignacio C. Soliba, *cons.* 1990, *apptd* 1990
Northern Philippines, Robert L. Longid, *cons.* 1983, *apptd*
  1986
Southern Philippines, James B. Manguramas, *cons.* 1993,
  apptd 1993

CHURCH OF THE PROVINCE OF RWANDA

ARCHBISHOP OF THE PROVINCE, The Most Revd
  Augustin Nshamihigo (Bishop of Shyira), *apptd* 1992

THE RT. REVD BISHOPS
Butare, Justin Ndandali, *apptd* 1992
Byunba, Onesphore Rwaje
Cyangugu, Daniel Nduhura
Kigali, Adonia Sebununguri, *cons.* 1965
Kigeme, Norman Kayumba
Shyira, see above, *apptd* 1984
Shyogwe, Samuel Musubyinare

CHURCH OF THE PROVINCE OF SOUTHERN AFRICA

METROPOLITAN
Archbishop of Cape Town, The Most Revd Desmond
  M. B. Tutu, *cons.* 1976, *trans.* 1986

THE RT. REVD BISHOPS
Bloemfontein, Thomas Stanage, *cons.* 1978, *apptd* 1982
Christ the King, Peter Lee, *cons.* 1990, *apptd* 1990
George, Derek Damant, *cons.* 1985, *apptd* 1985
Grahamstown, David Russell, *cons.* 1986, *apptd* 1987
Johannesburg, Duncan Buchanan, *cons.* 1986, *apptd* 1986
Kimberley and Kuruman, W. N. Ndungane, *cons.* 1991,
  apptd 1991
Klerksdorp, David Nkwe, *cons.* 1990, *apptd* 1990
Lebombo, Dinis Sengulane, *cons.* 1976, *apptd* 1976
Lesotho, Philip Mokuku, *cons.* 1978, *apptd* 1978
Namibia, James Kauluma, *cons.* 1978, *apptd* 1981
Natal, Michael Nuttall, *cons.* 1975, *apptd* 1982
Niassa, Paulino Manhique, *cons.* 1986, *apptd* 1986
Port Elizabeth, Eric Pike, *cons.* 1989, *apptd* 1993
Pretoria, Richard Kraft, *cons.* 1982, *apptd* 1982
St Helena, John Ruston, *cons.* 1985, *apptd* 1991
St John's, Jacob Dlamini, *cons.* 1980, *apptd* 1985
St Mark the Evangelist, Rollo Le Feuvre, *cons.* 1987, *apptd*
  1987

South-Eastern Transvaal, David Beetge, *cons.* 1990, *apptd* 1990
Swaziland, Lawrence Zulu, *cons.* 1975, *apptd* 1993
Umzimvubu, Geoffrey Davies, *cons.* 1987, *apptd* 1991
Zululand, Peter Harker, *cons.* 1993, *apptd* 1993

Order of Ethiopia, Sigqibo Dwane, *cons.* 1983, *apptd* 1983

ANGLICAN CHURCH OF THE SOUTHERN CONE OF AMERICA

PRESIDING BISHOP, Rt. Revd Colin Bazley (Bishop of Chile), *cons.* 1969

THE RT. REVD BISHOPS
Argentina, David Leake, *cons.* 1969, *apptd* 1990
Chile, see above, *apptd* 1977
Northern Argentina, Maurice Sinclair, *cons.* 1990, *apptd* 1990
Paraguay, John Ellison, *cons.* 1988, *apptd* 1988
Peru, Alan Winstanley, *cons.* 1988, *apptd* 1988
Uruguay, Harold Godfrey, *cons.* 1986, *apptd* 1986

PROVINCE OF THE EPISCOPAL CHURCH OF THE SUDAN

ARCHBISHOP OF PROVINCE, The Most Revd Benjamin W. Yugusuk (Bishop of Juba)

THE RT. REVD BISHOPS
Bor, Nathaniel Garang
Juba, see above
Kadugli, Mubarek Khamis
Kajokeji, Manaseh Dawidi
Khartoum, Bulus Idris
Malakal, Kedekia Mabior
Maridi, Joseph Marona
Mundri, Eluzai Munda
Red Sea, Butrus Kowa Kori
Rumbek, Gabriel Jur
Wau, Henry Riak
Yambio, Daniel Zindo, *cons.* 1984, *apptd* 1984
Yei, Seme Solomona

CHURCH OF THE PROVINCE OF TANZANIA

ARCHBISHOP OF PROVINCE, The Most Revd John A. Ramadhani (Bishop of Zanzibar and Tanga), *cons.* 1980, *apptd* 1984

THE RT. REVD BISHOPS
Central Tanganyika, Godfrey Mhogolo, *cons.* 1989, *apptd* 1989
Dar es Salaam, Basil Sambano, *cons.* 1992, *apptd* 1992
Kagera, Edwin Nyang'ubi, *cons.* 1993, *apptd* 1993
Mara, Gershom Nyaronga, *cons.* 1985, *apptd* 1985
Masasi, Christopher Sadiki, *cons.* 1992, *apptd* 1992
Morogoro, Dudley Mageni, *cons.* 1987, *apptd* 1987
Mount Kilimanjaro, Simon Makundi, *cons.* 1991, *apptd* 1991
Mpwapwa, Simon Chiwanga, *cons.* 1991, *apptd* 1991
Rift Valley, Alpha Mohamed, *cons.* 1982, *apptd* 1991
Ruaha, Donald Mtetemela, *cons.* 1982, *apptd* 1990
Ruvuma, Stanford Shauri, *cons.* 1989, *apptd* 1989
South-West Tanganyika, Charles Mwaigoga, *cons.* 1983, *apptd* 1983

Tabora, Francis Ntiruka, *cons.* 1989, *apptd* 1989
Victoria Nyanza, John Changae, *cons.* 1993, *apptd* 1993
Western Tanganyika, George Mpango, *cons.* 1983, *apptd* 1983
Zanzibar and Tanga, see above

CHURCH OF THE PROVINCE OF UGANDA

ARCHBISHOP OF THE PROVINCE, The Most Revd Dr Yona Okoth (Bishop of Kampala), *cons.* 1972, *apptd* 1984

THE RT. REVD BISHOPS
Bukedi, Nicodemus Okille, *apptd* 1984
Bunyoro-Kitara, Wilson Turumanya, *apptd* 1981
Busoga, Cyprian Bamwoze, *apptd* 1972
East Ankole, Elisha Kyamugambi, *cons.* 1992, *apptd* 1992
Kampala, see above
Karamoja, Peter Lomongin, *apptd* 1987
Kigezi, William Rukirande
Lango, Melchizedek Otim, *apptd* 1976
Luwero, M. Bugimbi, *cons.* 1990, *apptd* 1990
Madi and West Nile, Caleb Nguma, *apptd* 1991
Mbale, Israel Koboyi, *cons.* 1992, *apptd* 1992
Mityana, Wilson Mutebi, *apptd* 1977
Muhabura, Ernest M. Shalita, *cons.* 1990, *apptd* 1990
Mukono, Livingstone Mpalanyi-Nkoyoyo, *apptd* 1985
Namirembe, Misaeri Kauma, *apptd* 1985
Nebbi, Henry L. Orombi, *cons.* 1993, *apptd* 1993
North Mbale, Peter Mudonyi, *cons.* 1992, *apptd* 1992
North Kigezi, Yustasi Ruhindi, *apptd* 1981
Northern Uganda, Allan Oboma
Ruwenzori, Eustace Kamanyire, *apptd* 1981
Soroti, Geresom Ilukor, *apptd* 1976
South Ruwenzori, Zebidee Masereka
West Ankole, Yorumu Bamunoba, *apptd* 1977
West Buganda, Christopher Senyonjo, *apptd* 1974

EPISCOPAL CHURCH IN THE USA

PRESIDING BISHOP AND PRIMATE, Most Revd Edmond Lee Browning, DD, *cons.* 1968, *apptd* 1986

RT. REVD BISHOPS
(*missionary diocese)

Province I
Connecticut, Clarence Coleridge, *cons.* 1981, *apptd* 1994
Maine, Edward C. Chalfant, *cons.* 1984, *apptd* 1986
Massachusetts, David E. Johnson, *cons.* 1985, *apptd* 1986
New Hampshire, Douglas E. Theuner, *cons.* 1986, *apptd* 1986
Rhode Island, George N. Hunt, *cons.* 1980, *apptd* 1980
Vermont, Mary A. Mcleod, *cons.* 1993, *apptd* 1993
Western Massachusetts, Robert S. Denig, *cons.* 1993, *apptd* 1993

Province II
Albany, David S. Ball, *cons.* 1984, *apptd* 1984
Central New York, David B. Joslin, *cons.* 1991, *apptd* 1992
Europe, Convocation of American Churches in, Matthew P. Bigliardi, *cons.* 1974, *apptd* 1988
*Haiti, Zaché Duracin, *cons.* 1993, *apptd* 1994
Long Island, Orris Walker, *cons.* 1988, *apptd* 1991
New Jersey, G. P. Mellick Belshaw, *cons.* 1975, *apptd* 1983
New York, Richard Grein, *cons.* 1981, *apptd* 1989

Newark, John S. Spong, *cons.* 1976, *apptd* 1979
Rochester, William G. Burrill, *cons.* 1984, *apptd* 1984
Virgin Islands, Don. E. Taylor, *cons.* 1987, *apptd* 1987
Western New York, David C. Bowman, *cons.* 1986, *apptd* 1987

Province III

Bethlehem, J. Mark Dyer, *cons.* 1982, *apptd* 1983
Central Pennsylvania, Charlie F. McNutt, *cons.* 1980, *apptd* 1982
Delaware, C. Cabell Tennis, *cons.* 1986, *apptd* 1986
Easton, Martin G. Townsend, *cons.* 1992, *apptd* 1993
Maryland, A. Theodore Eastman, *cons.* 1982, *apptd* 1986
North-Western Pennsylvania, Robert D. Rowley jun., *cons.* 1989, *apptd* 1991
Pennsylvania, Allen L. Bartlett, *cons.* 1986, *apptd* 1987
Pittsburgh, Alden M. Hathaway, *cons.* 1981, *apptd* 1983
Southern Virginia, Frank Vest, *cons.* 1985, *apptd* 1991
South-Western Virginia, Arthur H. Light, *cons.* 1979, *apptd* 1979
Virginia, Peter J. Lee, *cons.* 1984, *apptd* 1985
Washington, Ronald Haines, *cons.* 1986, *apptd* 1990
West Virginia, John H. Smith, *cons.* 1989, *apptd* 1989

Province IV

Alabama, Robert O. Miller, *cons.* 1988, *apptd* 1988
Atlanta, Frank K. Allen, *cons.* 1988, *apptd* 1989
Central Florida, John Howe, *cons.* 1989, *apptd* 1990
Central Gulf Coast, Charles F. Duvall, *cons.* 1981, *apptd* 1981
East Carolina, B. Sidney Sanders, *cons.* 1979, *apptd* 1983
East Tennessee, Robert G. Tharp, *cons.* 1991, *apptd* 1992
Florida, Frank S. Cerveny, *cons.* 1974, *apptd* 1975
Georgia, Harry W. Shipps, *cons.* 1984, *apptd* 1985
Kentucky, David B. Reed, *cons.* 1964, *apptd* 1974
Lexington, Don A. Wimberley, *cons.* 1984, *apptd* 1985
Louisiana, James B. Brown, *cons.* 1976, *apptd* 1976
Mississippi, Alfred C. Marble jun., *cons.* 1991, *apptd* 1993
North Carolina, Robert W. Estill, *cons.* 1980, *apptd* 1983
South Carolina, Edward Salmon jun., *cons.* 1990, *apptd* 1990
South-East Florida, Calvin O. Schofield jun., *cons.* 1979, *apptd* 1980
South-West Florida, Roger Harris, *cons.* 1989, *apptd* 1989
Tennessee, Bertram N. Herlong, *cons.* 1993, *apptd* 1993
Upper South Carolina, William A. Beckham, *cons.* 1979, *apptd* 1979
West Tennessee, Alex D. Dickson jun., *cons.* 1983, *apptd* 1983
Western Louisiana, Robert Hargrove jun., *cons.* 1989, *apptd* 1990
Western North Carolina, Robert Johnson, *cons* 1989, *apptd* 1990

Province V

Chicago, Frank T. Griswold III, *cons.* 1985, *apptd* 1987
Eau Claire, William C. Wantland, *cons.* 1980, *apptd* 1980
Fond Du Lac, William L. Stevens, *cons.* 1980, *apptd* 1980
Indianapolis, Edward W. Jones, *cons.* 1977, *apptd* 1977
Michigan, R. Stewart Wood, *cons.* 1990, *apptd* 1990
Milwaukee, Roger J. White, *cons.* 1984, *apptd* 1985
Missouri, Hayes Rockwell, *cons.* 1991, *apptd* 1993
Northern Indiana, Francis C. Gray, *cons.* 1986, *apptd* 1987
Northern Michigan, Thomas K. Ray, *cons.* 1982, *apptd* 1982
Ohio, James R. Moodey, *cons.* 1983, *apptd* 1984
Quincy, Edward Macburney, *cons.* 1988, *apptd* 1988
Southern Ohio, Herbert Thompson jun., *cons.* 1988, *apptd* 1992
Springfield, Donald M. Hultstrand, *cons.* 1982, *apptd* 1982
Western Michigan, Edward L. Lee jun., *cons.* 1989, *apptd* 1989

Province VI

Colorado, William Winterrowd, *cons.* 1991, *apptd* 1991
Iowa, C. Christopher Epting, *cons.* 1988, *apptd* 1988
Minnesota, James Jelinek, *cons.* 1993, *apptd* 1993
Montana, Charles I. Jones, *cons.* 1986, *apptd* 1986
Nebraska, James E. Krotz, *cons.* 1989, *apptd* 1989
North Dakota, Andrew H. Fairfield, *cons.* 1990, *apptd* 1990
South Dakota, vacant
Wyoming, Bob G. Jones, *cons.* 1977, *apptd* 1977

Province VII

Arkansas, vacant
Dallas, James Stanton, *cons.* 1993, *apptd* 1993
Fort Worth, Clarence C. Pope jun., *cons.* 1985, *apptd* 1986
Kansas, William E. Smalley, *cons.* 1989, *apptd* 1989
North-West Texas, Sam B. Hulsey, *cons.* 1980, *apptd* 1980
Oklahoma, Robert M. Moodey, *cons.* 1988, *apptd* 1989
Rio Grande, Terence Kelshaw, *cons.* 1989, *apptd* 1989
Texas, Maurice M. Benitez, *cons.* 1980, *apptd* 1980
West Missouri, John C. Buchanan, *cons.* 1989, *apptd* 1989
West Texas, John H. MacNaughton, *cons.* 1986, *apptd* 1987
Western Kansas, John F. Ashby, *cons.* 1981, *apptd* 1981

Province VIII

Alaska, Stephen Charleston, *cons.* 1991, *apptd* 1991
Arizona, Robert R. Shahan, *cons.* 1992, *apptd* 1993
California, William E. Swing, *cons.* 1979, *apptd* 1980
El Camino Real, Richard L. Skimpfky, *cons.* 1990, *apptd* 1990
Eastern Oregon, Rustin R. Kimsey, *cons.* 1980, *apptd* 1980
Hawaii, Donald P. Hart, *cons.* 1986, *apptd* 1986
Idaho, John Thornton, *cons.* 1990, *apptd* 1990
Los Angeles, Frederick L. Borsch, *cons.* 1988, *apptd* 1988
Navajoland Area Mission, Steven T. Plummer, *cons.* 1989, *apptd* 1989
Nevada, Stewart C. Zabriskie, *cons.* 1986, *apptd* 1986
Northern California, Jerry A. Lamb, *cons.* 1991, *apptd* 1992
Olympia, Vincent W. Warner, *cons.* 1989, *apptd* 1990
Oregon, Robert L. Ladehoff, *cons.* 1985, *apptd* 1986
San Diego, Gethin B. Hughes, *cons.* 1992, *apptd* 1992
San Joaquin, John-David Schofield, *cons.* 1988, *apptd* 1989
Spokane, Frank Terry, *cons.* 1990, *apptd* 1991
Taiwan, John C. T. Chien, *cons.* 1988, *apptd* 1988
Utah, George E. Bates, *cons.* 1986, *apptd* 1986

Province IX

Central Ecuador, Neptali L. Moreno, *cons.* 1990, *apptd* 1990
Colombia, Bernardo Merino-Botero, *cons.* 1979, *apptd* 1979
Cuernavaca, Jose G. Saucedo, *cons.* 1958, *apptd* 1989
Dominican Republic, Julio C. Holguin, *apptd* 1991
Guatemala, Armando Guerra-Soria, *cons.* 1982, *apptd* 1982
Honduras, Leopold Frade, *cons.* 1984, *apptd* 1984
Mexico, Sergio Cananga-Gomez, *cons.* 1989, *apptd* 1989
Nicaragua, Sturdie W. Downs, *cons.* 1985, *apptd* 1985
Northern Mexico, German Martinez, *cons.* 1987, *apptd* 1987
Panama, James H. Ottley, *cons.* 1984, *apptd* 1984
El Salvador, Martin Barahona, *cons.* 1992, *apptd* 1992
South-East Mexico, Claro H. Rames, *cons.* 1980, *apptd* 1989
Western Mexico, Samuel Espinoza-Venegas, *cons.* 1981, *apptd* 1983

Extra-Provincial

Costa Rica, Cornelius J. Wilson, *cons.* 1978, *apptd* 1978
Puerto Rico, David Alvarez, *cons.* 1987, *apptd* 1987
Venezuela, Onell A. Soto, *cons.* 1987, *apptd* 1987

CHURCH OF THE PROVINCE OF WEST AFRICA

ARCHBISHOP OF PROVINCE, vacant

THE RT. REVD BISHOPS
Accra, Francis Thompson, *cons.* 1983, *apptd* 1983
Bo, Michael Keili, OBE, *cons.* 1981, *apptd* 1981
Cape Coast, Kobina Quashie, *apptd* 1992
Freetown, Prince Thompson, *cons.* 1981, *apptd* 1981
Gambia, Solomon Johnson, *cons.* 1990, *apptd* 1990
Guinea, vacant
Koforidua, Robert Okine, *cons.* 1981, *apptd* 1981
Kumasi, Edmund Yeboah, *cons.* 1985, *apptd* 1985
Liberia, vacant
Sekondi, Theophilus Annobil, *cons.* 1981, *apptd* 1981
Sunyani/Tamale, Joseph Dadson, *cons.* 1981, *apptd* 1981

The Anglican Church of Cameroon is a missionary area of the Province

CHURCH IN THE PROVINCE OF THE WEST INDIES

ARCHBISHOP OF PROVINCE, The Most Revd Orland Lindsay (Bishop of North-Eastern Caribbean and Aruba), *cons.* 1970, *apptd* 1986

THE RT. REVD BISHOPS
Barbados, Drexel Gomez, *cons.* 1972, *apptd* 1972
Belize, Desmond Smith, *cons.* 1989, *apptd* 1989
Guyana, Randolph George, *cons.* 1976, *apptd* 1980
Jamaica, Neville de Souza, *cons.* 1973, *apptd* 1979
Nassau and the Bahamas, Michael Eldon, CMG, *cons.* 1971, *apptd* 1972
North-Eastern Caribbean and Aruba, see above
Trinidad and Tobago, Clive Abdulah, *cons.* 1970, *apptd* 1970
Windward Islands, Philip Elder, *cons.* 1966

CHURCH OF THE PROVINCE OF ZAIRE

ARCHBISHOP OF THE PROVINCE, The Most Revd Byanka Njojo (Bishop of Boga-Zaire), *apptd* 1992

THE RT. REVD BISHOPS
Boga-Zaire, see above, *apptd* 1980
Bukavu, Balufuga Dirokpa, *apptd* 1982
Kisangani, Sylvestre Mugera, *apptd* 1980
Nord Kivu, Methusela Musubaho
Shaba, Emmanuel Mbona

OTHER CHURCHES AND EXTRA-PROVINCIAL DIOCESES

ANGLICAN CHURCH OF BERMUDA, Rt. Revd William Down, *apptd* 1990
EPISCOPAL CHURCH OF CUBA, Rt. Revd Emilio H. Albalate
HONG KONG AND MACAO, Rt. Revd Peter Kwong
KUCHING, Rt. Revd Datuk John Leong Chee Yun
SABAH, Rt. Revd Yong Ping Chung, *apptd* 1991
SINGAPORE, Rt. Revd Moses Leng Kong Tay, *apptd* 1982

WEST MALAYSIA, Rt. Revd Tan Sri John Savarimuthu, *apptd* 1973
LUSITANIAN CHURCH *(Portuguese Episcopal Church),* Rt. Revd Fernando Soares, *apptd* 1971
SPANISH REFORMED CHURCH, Rt. Revd Arturo Sánchez Galan, *apptd* 1982

The Church of Scotland

The Church of Scotland is the established (i.e. state) church of Scotland. The Church is Reformed and evangelical in doctrine, and presbyterian in constitution. In 1560 the jurisdiction of the Roman Catholic Church in Scotland was abolished and the first assembly of the Church of Scotland ratified the Confession of Faith, drawn up by a committee including John Knox. In 1592 Parliament passed an Act guaranteeing the liberties of the Church and its presbyterian government. James VI (James I of England) and later Stuart monarchs attempted to restore episcopacy, but a presbyterian church was finally restored in 1690 and secured by the Act of Settlement (1690) and the Act of Union (1707). The Free Church of Scotland was formed in 1843 in a dispute over patronage and state interference; in 1900 most of its ministers joined with the United Presbyterian Church (formed in 1847) to form the United Free Church of Scotland. In 1929 most of this body rejoined the Church of Scotland to form the united Church of Scotland.

The Church of Scotland is presbyterian in its organization, i.e. based on a hierarchy of councils of ministers and elders and, since 1990, of members of a diaconate. At local level the kirk session consists of the parish minister and ruling elders. At district level the presbyteries, of which there are 47, consist of all the ministers in the district, one ruling elder from each congregation, and those members of the diaconate who qualify for membership. The General Assembly is the supreme authority, and is presided over by a Moderator chosen annually by the Assembly. The Sovereign, if not present in person, is represented by a Lord High Commissioner who is appointed each year by the Crown.

The Church of Scotland has about 753,000 members, 1,260 ministers and 1,700 churches. There are about 100 ministers and other personnel working overseas.

Lord High Commissioner (1993), The Lord Macfarlane of Bearsden
Moderator of the General Assembly (1993), Rt. Revd J. L. Weatherhead
Principal Clerk, Revd A. G. McGillivray
Deputy Clerk, Revd F. A. J. MacDonald
Procurator, A. Dunlop, QC
Law Agent and Solicitor of the Church, R. A. Paterson
Parliamentary Agent, I. McCulloch *(London)*
General Treasurer, W. G. P. Colledge
CHURCH OFFICE, 121 George Street, Edinburgh EH2 4YN. Tel: 031-225 5722

PRESBYTERIES
Clerks

Edinburgh, Revd W. P. Graham
West Lothian, Revd D. Shaw
Lothian, Revd J. Ritchie

Melrose and Peebles, Revd C. A. Duncan
Duns, Revd I. G. Wotherspoon
Jedburgh, Revd N. R. Combe

Annandale and Eskdale, Revd C. B. Haston

Dumfries and Kirkcudbright, Revd G. M. A. Savage
Wigtown and Stranraer, Revd D. Dutton

Ayr, Revd J. Crichton
Irvine and Kilmarnock, Revd C. G. F. Brockie
Ardrossan, Revd D. Broster

Lanark, Revd I. D. Cunningham
Paisley, Revd J. P. Cubie
Greenock, Revd D. Mill
Glasgow, Revd A. Cunningham
Hamilton, Revd J. H. Wilson
Dumbarton, Revd D. P. Munro

South Argyll, Revd R. H. McNidder
Dunoon, Revd R. Samuel
Lorn and Mull, Revd W. M. Ritchie

Falkirk, Revd D. E. McClements
Stirling, Revd G. A. McCutcheon

Dunfermline, Revd W. E. Farquhar
Kirkcaldy, Revd B. L. Tomlinson
St Andrews, Revd J. W. Patterson

Dunkeld and Meigle, Revd A. F. Chisholm
Perth, Revd G. G. Stewart
Dundee, Revd J. A. Roy
Angus, Revd A. F. M. Downie

Aberdeen, Revd A. M. Douglas
Kincardine and Deeside, Revd J. W. S. Brown
Gordon, Revd I. U. Thomson
Buchan, Revd R. Neilson
Moray, Revd J. T. Stuart

Abernethy, Revd J. A. I. MacEwan
Inverness, Revd R. J. V. Logan
Lochaber, Revd A. Ramsay

Ross, Revd R. M. MacKinnon
Sutherland, Revd J. L. Goskirk
Caithness, Revd M. G. Mappin
Lochcarron/Skye, Revd A. I. Macarthur
Uist, Revd A. P. J. Varwell
Lewis, Revd T. S. Sinclair

Orkney (Finstown), Revd D. A. Williams
Shetland (Lerwick), Revd M. Cheyne
England (London), Revd W. A. Cairns

Europe (Portugal), Revd R. Hill

The Roman Catholic Church

The Roman Catholic Church is one world-wide Christian Church acknowledging as its head the Bishop of Rome, known as the Pope (Father). The Pope is held to be the successor of St Peter and thus invested with the power which was entrusted to St Peter by Jesus Christ. A direct line of succession is therefore claimed from the earliest Christian communities. Papal authority over the doctrine and jurisdiction of the Church in western Europe developed early and was unrivalled after the split with the Eastern Orthodox Church until the Protestant Reformation in the 16th century. With the fall of the Roman Empire the Pope also became an important political leader. His temporal power is now limited to the 107 acres of the Vatican City State.

The Pope exercises spiritual authority over the Church with the advice and assistance of the Sacred College of Cardinals, the supreme council of the Church. He is also advised about the concerns of the Church locally by his ambassadors, who liaise with the Bishops' Conference in each country.

In addition to advising the Pope, those members of the Sacred College of Cardinals who are under the age of 80 also elect a successor following the death of a Pope. The assembly of the Cardinals at the Vatican for the election of a new Pope is known as the Conclave in which, in complete seclusion, the Cardinals elect by a secret ballot; a two-thirds majority is necessary before the vote can be accepted as final. When a Cardinal receives the necessary votes, the Dean of the Sacred College formally asks him if he will accept election and the name by which he wishes to be known. On his acceptance of the office the Conclave is dissolved and the First Cardinal Deacon announces the election to the assembled crowd in St Peter's Square. On the first Sunday or Holyday following the election, the new Pope assumes the pontificate at High Mass in St Peter's Square. A new pontificate is dated from the assumption of the pontificate.

The number of cardinals was fixed at 70 by Pope Sixtus V in 1586, but has been steadily increased since the pontificate of John XXIII and now stands at 153 (as at May 1993). The Roman Catholic Church universally and the Vatican City State are run by the Curia, which is made up of the Secretariat of State, the Sacred Council for the Public Affairs of the Church, and various congregations, secretariats and tribunals assisted by commissions and offices. The congregations are permanent commissions for conducting the affairs of the Church and are made up of cardinals, one of whom occupies the office of prefect. Below the Secretariat of State and the congregations are the secretariats and tribunals, all of which are headed by cardinals. (The Curial cardinals are analagous to ministers in charge of government departments.)

The Vatican State has its own diplomatic service, with representatives known as nuncios. Papal nuncios with full diplomatic recognition are given precedence over all other ambassadors to the country to which they are appointed; where precedence is not recognized, as in Britain, the Papal representative is known as a pro-nuncio. Where the representation is only to the local churches and not to the government of a country, the Papal representative is known as an apostolic delegate. The Roman Catholic Church has an estimated 890,907,000 adherents world-wide.

SOVEREIGN PONTIFF

His Holiness Pope John Paul II (Karol Wojtyla), *born* Wadowice, Poland, 18 May 1920; *ordained priest* 1946; *appointed Archbishop* of Krakow 1964; *created Cardinal* 1967; *assumed pontificate* 16 October 1978

SECRETARIAT OF STATE

Secretary of State, HE Cardinal Angelo Sodano
First Section (General Affairs), Mgr G. Re, Archbishop of Vescovio
Second Section (Relations with other states), Mgr J. L. Tauran, Archbishop of Telepte

BISHOPS' CONFERENCE

The Roman Catholic Church in England and Wales is governed by the Bishops' Conference, membership of which includes the Diocesan Bishops, the Apostolic Exarch of the Ukrainians, the Bishop of the Forces and the Auxiliary Bishops. The Conference is headed by the President (Cardinal Basil Hume, Archbishop of Westminster) and Vice-President (the Archbishop of Liverpool). There are five departments, each with an episcopal chairman: the Department for Christian Life and Worship (the Archbishop of Southwark), the Department for Mission and Unity (the Bishop of East Anglia), the Department for Catholic Education and Formation (the Bishop of Leeds), the Department for Christian Responsibility and Citizenship (the Bishop of Middlesbrough), and the Department for International Affairs (the Bishop of Salford).

The Bishops' Standing Committee, made up of all the Archbishops and the chairman of each of the above departments, has general responsibility for continuity and policy between the plenary sessions of the Conference. It prepares the Conference agenda and implements its decisions. It is serviced by a General Secretariat. There are also agencies and consultative bodies affiliated to the Conference.

The Bishops' Conference of Scotland has as its president Archbishop Winning of Glasgow and is the permanently constituted assembly of the Bishops of Scotland. To promote its work, the Conference establishes various agencies which have an advisory function in relation to the Conference. The more important of these agencies are called Commissions and each one has a Bishop President who, with the other members of the Commissions, are appointed by the Conference.

The Irish Episcopal Conference has as its acting president Archbishop Connell of Dublin. Its membership comprises all the Archbishops and Bishops of Ireland and it appoints various Commissions to assist it in its work. There are three types of Commissions: (a) those made up of lay and clerical members chosen for their skills and experience, and staffed by full-time expert secretariats; (b) Commissions whose members are selected from existing institutions and whose services are supplied on a part-time basis; and (c) Commissions of Bishops only.

The Roman Catholic Church in Britain and Ireland has an estimated 8,992,092 members, 11 archbishops, 67 bishops, 12,698 priests, and 8,588 churches and chapels open to the public.

Bishops' Conferences secretariats:

ENGLAND AND WALES, 39 Eccleston Square, London SWIV IPD. Tel: 071-630 8220. *General Secretary*, Revd Philip Carroll

SCOTLAND, Candida Casa, 8 Corsehill Road, Ayr, Scotland KA7 2ST. Tel: 0292-256750. *General Secretary*, Rt. Revd Maurice Taylor, Bishop of Galloway

IRELAND, Iona, 67 Newry Road, Dundalk, Co. Louth. *Executive Secretary*, Revd Gerard Clifford

---

GREAT BRITAIN

APOSTOLIC PRO-NUNCIO TO THE UNITED KINGDOM OF GREAT BRITAIN AND NORTHERN IRELAND
The Most Revd Luigi Barbarito

ENGLAND AND WALES

THE MOST REVD ARCHBISHOPS
Westminster, HE Cardinal Basil Hume, *cons.* 1976
Auxiliary, Victor Guazzelli, *cons.* 1970
Auxiliary, Vincent Nichols, *cons.* 1992
Auxiliary, James J. O'Brien, *cons.* 1977
Auxiliary, Patrick O'Donoghue, *cons.* 1983
Clergy, 839
Birmingham, Maurice Couve de Murville, *cons.* 1982, *apptd* 1982
Auxiliary, Terence Brain, *cons.* 1991
Auxiliary, Philip Pargeter, *cons.* 1989
Clergy, 426
Cardiff, John A. Ward, *cons.* 1981, *apptd* 1983
Clergy, 163
Liverpool, Derek Worlock, *cons.* 1965, *apptd* 1976
Auxiliary, John Rawsthorne, *cons.* 1981

Auxiliary, Vincent Malone, *cons.* 1989
Clergy, 515
Southwark, Michael Bowen, *cons.* 1970, *apptd* 1977
Auxiliary, Charles Henderson, *cons.* 1972
Auxiliary, Howard Tripp, *cons.* 1980
Auxiliary, John Jukes, *cons.* 1980
Clergy, 518

THE RT. REVD BISHOPS
Arundel and Brighton, Cormac Murphy-O'Connor, *cons.* 1977. *Clergy*, 255
Brentwood, Thomas McMahon, *cons.* 1980, *apptd* 1980. *Clergy*, 188
Clifton, Mervyn Alexander, *cons.* 1972, *apptd* 1975. *Clergy*, 242
East Anglia, Alan Clark, *cons.* 1969, *apptd* 1976. *Clergy*, 112
Hallam, Gerald Moverley, *cons.* 1968, *apptd* 1980. *Clergy*, 100
Hexham and Newcastle, Michael Ambrose Griffiths, *cons.* 1992. *Clergy*, 309
Auxiliary, Owen Swindelhurst, *cons.* 1977
Lancaster, John Brewer, *cons.* 1971, *apptd* 1985. *Clergy*, 228
Leeds, David Konstant, *cons.* 1977, *apptd* 1985. *Clergy*, 225
Menevia (Wales), Daniel Mullins, *cons.* 1970, *apptd* 1987. *Clergy*, 59
Middlesbrough, John Crowley, *cons.* 1986, *apptd* 1992. *Clergy*, 201
Auxiliary, Thomas O'Brien, *cons.* 1981
Northampton, Patrick Leo McCartie, *cons.* 1977. *Clergy*, 123
Nottingham, James McGuinness, *cons.* 1972, *apptd* 1975. *Clergy*, 224
Plymouth, Christopher Budd, *cons.* 1986. *Clergy*, 168
Portsmouth, F. Crispian Hollis, *cons.* 1987, *apptd* 1989. *Clergy*, 282
Salford, Patrick Kelly, *cons.* 1984. *Clergy*, 455
Shrewsbury, Joseph Gray, *cons.* 1969, *apptd* 1980. *Clergy*, 226
Wrexham (Wales), James Hannigan, *cons.* 1983, *apptd* 1987. *Clergy*, 94

SCOTLAND

THE MOST REVD ARCHBISHOPS
St Andrews and Edinburgh, Keith Patrick O'Brian, *cons.* 1985
Auxiliary, Kevin Rafferty, *cons.* 1990
Clergy, 213
Glasgow, Thomas Winning, *cons.* 1971, *apptd* 1974
Clergy, 338

THE RT. REVD BISHOPS
Aberdeen, Mario Conti, *cons.* 1977. *Clergy*, 59
Argyll and the Isles, Roderick Wright, *cons.* 1990. *Clergy*, 35
Dunkeld, Vincent Logan, *cons.* 1981. *Clergy*, 67
Galloway, Maurice Taylor, *cons.* 1981. *Clergy*, 75
Motherwell, Joseph Devine, *cons.* 1977, *apptd* 1983. *Clergy*, 190
Paisley, John A. Mone, *cons.* 1984, *apptd* 1988. *Clergy*, 98

IRELAND

There is one hierarchy for the whole of Ireland. Several of the dioceses have territory partly in the Republic of Ireland and partly in Northern Ireland.

NUNCIO TO IRELAND
Most Revd Emanuele Gerada (titular Archbishop of Nomenta)

THE MOST REVD ARCHBISHOPS
Armagh, HE Cardinal Cahal B. Daly, *cons.* 1990
  Auxiliary, Gerard Clifford, *cons.* 1991
  Clergy, 271
Cashel, Dermot Clifford, *cons.* 1986
  Clergy, 122
Dublin, Desmond Connell, *cons.* 1988, *apptd* 1988
  Auxiliary, Donal Murray, *cons.* 1982
  Auxiliary, Dermot O'Mahony, *cons.* 1975
  Auxiliary, James Moriarty, *cons.* 1992
  Auxiliary, Eamonn Walsh, *cons.* 1990
  Auxiliary, Desmond Williams, *cons.* 1985
  Clergy, 994
Tuam, Joseph Cassidy, *cons.* 1979, *apptd* 1987
  Auxiliary, Michael Neary, *cons.* 1992
  Clergy, 165

THE MOST REVD BISHOPS
Achonry, Thomas Flynn, *cons.* 1975. *Clergy,* 55
Ardagh and Clonmacnois, Colm O'Reilly, *cons.* 1983.
  Clergy, 108
Clogher, Joseph Duffy, *cons.* 1979. *Clergy,* 124
Clonfert, Joseph Kirby, *cons.* 1988. *Clergy,* 76
Cloyne, John Magee, *cons.* 1987. *Clergy,* 155
Cork and Ross, Michael Murphy, *cons.* 1976. *Clergy,* 360
  Auxiliary, John Buckley, *cons.* 1984
Derry, Edward Daly, *cons.* 1974. *Clergy,* 149
  Auxiliary, Francis Lagan, *cons.* 1988
Down and Connor, Patrick J. Walsh, *cons.* 1991. *Clergy,* 324
  Auxiliary, Anthony Farquhar, *cons.* 1983
  Auxiliary, William Philbin, *cons.* 1991
Dromore, Francis Brooks, *cons.* 1976. *Clergy,* 71
Elphin, Dominic Conway, *cons.* 1970. *Clergy,* 104
Ferns, Brendon Comiskey, *cons.* 1980. *Clergy,* 148
Galway and Kilmacduagh, James McLoughlin, *cons.* 1993
Kerry, Dermot O'Sullivan, *cons.* 1985. *Clergy,* 143
Kildare and Leighlin, Laurence Ryan, *cons.* 1984.
  Clergy, 225
Killala, Thomas Finnegan, *cons.* 1970. *Clergy,* 51
Killaloe, Michael Harty, *cons.* 1967. *Clergy,* 186
Kilmore, Francis McKiernan, *cons.* 1972. *Clergy,* 103
Limerick, Jeremiah Newman, *cons.* 1974. *Clergy,* 234
Meath, Michael Smith, *cons.* 1984, *apptd* 1990. *Clergy,* 270
Ossory, Laurence Forristal, *cons.* 1980. *Clergy,* 125
Raphoe, Seamus Hegarty, *cons.* 1984. *Clergy,* 102
Waterford and Lismore, Michael Russell, *cons.* 1965.
  Clergy, 206

RESIDENTIAL ARCHBISHOPRICS THROUGHOUT THE WORLD

This list is set out with the name of the relevant country first; then the name of the diocese; and finally the Archbishop's name. It does not include England and Wales, Scotland or Ireland which are above.

ALBANIA
Durrës-Tirana, Brok K. Mirdita
Shkodër, Frano Illia

ALGERIA
Algiers, Henri Teissier

ANGOLA
Huambo, Francisco Viti
Luanda, HE Cardinal Alexandre do Nascimento
Lubango, Manuel Franklin da Costa

ARGENTINA
Bahia Blanca, Romulo Garcia
Buenos Aires, HE Cardinal Antonio Quarracino
Córdoba, HE Cardinal Raúl Francisco Primatesta
Corrientes, Fortunato A. Rossi
La Plata, Carlos Galán
Mendoza, Candido Genaro Rubiolo
  Coadjutor, Jose M. Grancibia
Paraná, Estanislao Esteban Karlic
Resistencia, vacant
Rosario, Jorge Manuel López
Salta, Moises J. Blanchoud
San Juan de Cuyo, Italo Severino Di Stefano
Santa Fe, Edgardo Gabriel Storni
Tucumán, Horatio A. Bozzoli

AUSTRALIA
Adelaide, Leonard Anthony Faulkner
Brisbane, John A. Bathersby
Canberra, Francis P. Carroll
Hobart, Joseph E. D'Arcy
Melbourne, Thomas Francis Little
Perth, Barry J. Hickey
Sydney, HE Cardinal Edward B. Clancy

AUSTRIA
Salzburg, Georg Eder
Vienna, HE Cardinal Hans Hermann Groer

BANGLADESH
Dhaka, Michael Rozario

BELARUS
Minsk-Mohilev Archdiocese, Kazimierz Swiatek

BELGIUM
Malines-Bruxelles, HE Cardinal Godfried Danneels

BENIN
Cotonou, Isidore de Souzá

BOLIVIA
Cochabamba, Rene Fernandez Apaza
La Paz, Luis Sainz Hinojosa
Santa Cruz de la Sierra, Julio T. Sandoval
Sucre, Jesus G. Pérez Rodriguez

BOSNIA HERCEGOVINA
Vrhbosna, Sarajevo, Vinko Pubjić

BRAZIL
Aparacida, Geraldo Maria de Morais Penido
Aracaju, Luciano José Cabral Duarte
Bélem do Pará, Vicente Joaquim Zico
Belo Horizonte, Serafim Fernandes de Araújo
Botucatu, Antonio M. Mucciolo
Brasilia, HE Cardinal Jose Freire Falcao
Campinas, Gilberto Pereira Lopes
Campo Grande, Vitorio Pavanello
Cascavel, Armando Cirio
Cuiaba, Bonifacio Piccinini
Curitiba, Pedro Antonio Fedalto
Diamantina, Geraldo Majelo Reis
Florianópolis, Eusebio Oscar Scheid
Fortaleza, HE Cardinal Aloisio Lorscheider
Goiania, Antonio Ribeiro de Oliveira
Juiz de Fora, Clovis Frainer
Londrina, Albano Bortoletto Cavallin
Maceió, Edvaldo G. Amaral
Manaus, Luiz S. Vieira
Mariana, Luciano Mendes de Almeida
Maringá, Jaime Luis Coelho
Natal, Alair V. Fernandes de Melo

Niteroi, Carlos A. Navarro
Olinda and Recife, José Cardoso Sobrinho
Paraiba, José M. Pires
Porto Alegre, Altamiro Rossato
Porto Velho, José Martins da Silva
Pouso Alegre, João Bergese
Ribeirão Preto, Arnaldo Ribeiro
São Luis do Maranhão, Paulo Eduardo de Andrade Ponte
São Paulo, HE Cardinal Paulo Evaristo Arns
São Salvador da Bahia, HE Cardinal Lucas Moreira Neves
São Sebastião do Rio de Janeiro, HE Cardinal Eugenio de Araújo Sales
Sorocaba, José Lambert
Teresina, Miguel F. Camara Filho
Uberaba, Benedito de Ulhôa Vieira
Vitória, Silvestre L. Scandian

BURKINA
Ouagadougou, HE Cardinal Paul Zoungrana

BURUNDI
Gitega, Joachim Ruhuna

CAMEROON
Bamenda, Paul Verdzekov
Douala, HE Cardinal Christian W. Tumi
Garoua, Antoine Ntalou
Yaoundé, Jean Zoa

CANADA
Edmonton, Joseph N. MacNeil
Gatineau-Hull, Roger Ebacher
Grouard-McLennon, Henri Légaré
Halifax, Austin-Emile Burke
Keewatin-Le Pas, Peter Alfred Sutton
Kingston, Francis John Spence
Moncton, Donat Chiasson
Montreal, Jean-Claude Turcotte
Ottawa, Marcel A. Gervais
Quebec, Maurice Couture
Regina, Charles Halpin
Rimouski, Bertrand Blanchet
St Boniface, Antoine Hacault
St Johns, Newfoundland, James H. MacDonald
Sherbrooke, Jean Marie Fortier
Toronto, Aloysius Matthew Ambrosic
Vancouver, Adam J. Exner
Winnipeg, Leonard J. Wall; (Ukrainian Rite), Michael Bzdel

CENTRAL AFRICAN REPUBLIC
Bangui, Joachim N'Dayen

CHAD
Ndjamena, Charles Vandame

CHILE
Antofagasta, Patricio Infante Alfonso
Concepción, Antonio M. Casamitjana
La Serena, Francisco J. Cox Huneeus
Puerto Montt, Savino B. Cazzaro Bertollo
Santiago de Chile, Carlos Oviedo Cavada

CHINA
Anking, Huai-Ning, vacant
Canton, Dominic Tang Yee-Ming
Changsha, vacant
Chungking, vacant
Foochow, Min-Hou, vacant
Hangchow, vacant
Hankow, vacant
Kaifeng, vacant
Kunming, vacant
Kweyang, vacant

Lanchow, vacant
Mukden, vacant
Nanchang, vacant
Nanking, vacant
Nanning, vacant
Peking (Beijing), vacant
Sian, vacant
Suiyūan, Francis Wang Hsueh-Ming
Taiyuan, vacant
Tsinan, vacant

COLOMBIA
Barranquilla, Felix Maria Torres Parra
Bogotá, HE Cardinal Mario Revollo Bravo
Bucaramanga, Dario Castrillon Hoyos
Cali, Pedro Rubiano Sáenz
Cartagena, Carlos José Ruiseco Vieira
Ibague, Juan S. Jaramillo
Manizales, José de Jesús Pimiento Rodriguez
Medellin, Hector Rueda Hernández
Nueva Pamplona, Rafael Sarmiento Peralta
Popayán, Alberto G. Jaramillo
Santa Fe de Antioquia, Ignacio Gomez Afistizabal
Tunja, Augusto Trujillo Arango

CONGO
Brazzaville, Barthélémy Batantu

COSTA RICA
San José, Román Arrieta Villalobos

CÔTE D'IVOIRE
Abidjan, HE Cardinal Bernard Yago

CROATIA
Rijeka-Senj, Anton Tamarut
Split-Makarska, Ante Juric
Zadar, Marijan Oblak
Zagreb, HE Cardinal Franjo Kuharić

CUBA
San Cristóbal de la Habana, Jaime Lucas Ortega y Alamino
Santiago de Cuba, Pedro Meurice Estiu

CYPRUS
Cyprus (Maronite Seat at Nicosia), Boutros Gemayel

CZECH REPUBLIC
Olomouc, Jan Graubner
Praha, Miloslav Vlk

DOMINICAN REPUBLIC
Santo Domingo, HE Cardinal Nicolás de Jesús López Rodriguez

ECUADOR
Cuenca, Alberto Luna Tobar
Guayaquil, Ignacio Larrea Holguin
Quito, Antonio J. González Zumárraga

EQUATORIAL GUINEA
Malabo, Idlefonso Obama Obono

ETHIOPIA
Addis Ababa, HE Cardinal Paul Tzadua

FRANCE
Aix, Bernard Panafieu
Albi, Roger Meindre
Auch, Gabriel Vanel
Avignon, Raymond Bouchex
Besançon, Lucien Daloz
Bordeaux, Pierre Eyt
Bourges, Pierre Plateau
Cambrai, Jacques Delaporte

Chambéry, Claude Feidt
Lyon, HE Cardinal Albert Decourtray
Marseilles, HE Cardinal Robert Coffy
Paris, HE Cardinal J. M. Lustiger
Reims, Jean Balland
Rennes, Jacques Jullien
Rouen, Joseph Duval
Sens, Gérard Defois
Strasbourg, Charles Amarin Brand
Toulouse, André Collini
Tours, Jean Honoré

FRENCH POLYNESIA
Papeete, Michel Coppenrath

GABON
Libreville, André Fernand Anguilé

GERMANY
Bamberg, Elmar Maria Kredel
Cologne, HE Cardinal Joachim Meisner
Freiburg im Breisgau, Oskar Saier
Munich and Freising, HE Cardinal Friedrich Wetter
Paderborn, Johannes Joachim Degenhardt

GHANA
Accra, Dominic K. Andoh
Cape Coast, Peter Kodwo A. Turkson
Tamale, Peter Poreiku Dery

GREECE
Athens, Nicholaos Foscolos
Corfu, Antonio Varthalitis
Naxos, Nicolaos Printesis
Rhodes, vacant (Apostolic Administrator, Nicholaos Foscolos)

GUATEMALA
Guatemala, Prospero Penados del Barrio

GUINEA
Conakry, Robert Sarah

HAITI
Cap-Haitien, François Gayot
Port au Prince, François-Wolff Ligondé

HONDURAS
Tegucigalpa, Oscar A. Maradiaga

HONG KONG
Hong Kong, HE Cardinal J. B. Wu Cheng Chung

HUNGARY
Eger, Istvan Seregely
Esztergom, HE Cardinal Laslo Paskai
Kalocsa, Laszlo Danko

INDIA
Agra, Cecil de Sa
Bangalore, Alphonsus Mathias
Bhopal, Eugene D' Souza
Bombay, HE Cardinal I. Pimenta
Calcutta, Henry Sebastian D'Souza
Changanacherry, Joseph Powathil
Cuttack-Bhubaneswar, Raphael Cheenath
Delhi, Alan de Lastic
Ernakulam, HE Cardinal Anthony Padiyara
Goa and Daman, Raul Nicolau Gonsalves
Hyderabad, Saminini Arulappa
Madras and Mylapore, Casimir Gnanadickam
Madurai, Marianus Arokiasamy
Nagpur, Leobard D'Souza
Pondicherry and Cuddalore, Michael Augustine
Ranchi, Telesphore P. Toppo

Shillong-Gauhati, Hubert D'Rosario
Trivandrum (Syrian Melekite Rite), Benedict Varghese Gregorios Thangalathil
Verapoly, Cornelius Elanjikal

INDONESIA
Ende, Donatus Djagom
Jakarta, Leo Soekoto
Kupang, Gregorius Manteiro
Medan, Alfred Gonti Pius Datubara
Merauke, Jacobus Duivenvoorde
Pontianak, Hieronymus Herculanus Bumbun
Semarang, Julius R. Darmaatmadja
Ujung Pandang, R. P. Francis van Roessel

IRAN
Ahváz, Hanna Zora
Tehran, Youhannan Semaan Issayi
Urmyá, Thomas Meram

IRAQ
Arbil, Stephane Babaca
Baghdad (Latin Rite), Paul Dahdah; (Syrian Rite), Athanase M. S. Matoka; (Armenian Rite), Paul Coussa
Basra, Yousif Thomas
Kirkuk, André Sana
Mosul, Georges Garmo

ISRAEL
Akka (Greek Melekite Catholic Rite), Maximos Salloum

ITALY
Acerenza, Michele Scandiffio
Amalfi, Beniamino De Palma
Ancona, Franco Festorazzi
Bari, Mariano Magrassi
Benevento, Serafino Sprovieri
Bologna, HE Cardinal Giacomo Biffi
Brindisi, Settimio Todisco
Cagliari, Otterino Pietro Alberti
Camerino, vacant
Campobasso-Boiano, Ettore Di Filippo
Capua, Luigi Diligenza
Catania, Luigi Bommarito
Catanzaro, Antonio Cantisani
Chieti, Antonio Valentini
Conza, Mario Milano
Cosenza, Dino Trabalzini
Crotone-Santa Severina, Giuseppe Agostino
Fermo, Cleto Bellucci
Ferrara, Luigi Maverna
Florence, HE Cardinal Silvano Piovanelli
Foggia, Giuseppe Casale
Gaeta, Vincenzo Farano
Genoa, HE Cardinal Giovanni Canestri
Gorizia and Gradisca, Antonio Vitale Bommarco
Lanciano, Enzio d'Antonio
L'Aquila, Mario Peressin
Lecce, Cosmo F. Ruppi
Lucca, Bruno Tommasi
Manfredonia, Vincenzo D'Addario
Matera, Antonio Ciliberti
Messina, Ignazio Cannavó
Milan, HE Cardinal Carlo Maria Martini
Modena, Santo B. Quadri
Monreale, Salvatore Cassisa
Naples, HE Cardinal Michele Giordano
Oristano, Pier Luigi Tiddia
Otranto, Francesco Cacucci
Palermo, HE Cardinal Salvatore Pappalardo
Perugia, Ennio Antonelli

Pescara-Penne, Francesco Cuccarese
Pisa, Alessandro Plotti
Potenza, Ennio Appignanesi
Ravenna, Luigi Amaducci
Reggio Calabria, Vittorio L. Mondello
Rossano-Cariati, Andrea Cassone
Salerno, Gerardo Pierro
Sassari, Salvatore Isgrò
Siena, Gaetano Bonicelli
Siracusa, Giuseppe Costanzo
Sorrento, Felice Cece
Spoleto, Antonio Ambrosanio
Taranto, Luigi Papa
Turin, HE Cardinal Giovanni Saldarini
Trani and Barletta, Carmelo Cassati
Trento, Giovanni Sartori
Udine, Alfredo Battisti
Urbino, Donato U. Bianchi
Vercelli, Tarcisio Bertone

JAMAICA
Kingston, Samuel Emmanuel Carter

JAPAN
Nagasaki, Francis Xavier Shimamoto
Osaka, Paul Hisao Yasuda
Tokyo, Peter Seiichi Shirayanagi

JORDAN
Petra and Filadelfia (Greek Melekite Catholic Rite), George
El-Murr

KAZAKHSTAN
Karaganda Apostolic Administration (Latin Rite), Apostolic
Administrator, Mgr Jan Lenga (titular Bishop of Arba)

KENYA
Kisumu, Zaccharus Okoth
Mombasa, John Njenga
Nairobi, HE Cardinal Maurice Otunga
Nyeri, Nicodemus Kirima

KOREA
Kwangju, Victorinus Kong-Hi Youn
Seoul, HE Cardinal Stephen Sou Hwan Kim
Taegu, Paul Moun-Hi Ri

LATVIA
Riga, Jānis Pujats

LEBANON
Antelias (Maronite Rite), Joseph Mohsen Bechara
Baalbek, Eliopoli (Greek Melekite Catholic Rite), Salim
Bustros
Baniyas (Greek Melekite Catholic Rite), Antoine Hayek
Beirut (Greek Melekite Catholic Rite), Habib Bacha;
(Maronite Rite), Khalil Abinader
Saïda (Greek Melekite Catholic Rite), Georges Kwaiter
Tripoli (Maronite Rite), Antoine Joubeir; (Greek Melekite
Catholic Rite), Elias Nijmé
Tyre (Greek Melekite Catholic Rite), Jean A. Haddad;
(Maronite Rite), Maroun Sader
Zahle and Furzol (Greek Melekite Catholic Rite), Andre
Haddad

LESOTHO
Maseru, Bernard Mohlalisi

LIBERIA
Monrovia, Michael Kpakala Francis

LITHUANIA
Kaunas, HE Cardinal Vincentas Sladkevicius
Vilnius, Audris J. Bačkis

LUXEMBOURG
Luxembourg, Fernand Franck

MADAGASCAR
Antananarive, HE Cardinal Victor Razafimahatratra
Antsiranana, Albert Joseph Tsiahoana
Fianarantsoa, Philibert Randriambololona

MALAYSIA
Kuala Lumpur, Anthony S. Fernandez
Kuching, Peter Chung Hoan Ting

MALI
Bamako, Luc Auguste Sangaré

MALTA
Malta, Joseph Mercieca

MARTINIQUE
Fort de France, Maurice Marie-Sainte

MAURITIUS
Port Louis, HE Cardinal Jean Margeot

MEXICO
Acapulco, Rafael Bello Ruiz
Antequera, Bartolomé Carrasco Briseno
Chihuahua, José Fernández Arteaga
Durango, José M. Perez
Guadalajara, vacant
Hermosillo, Carlos Quintero Arce
Jalapa, Sergio Obeso Rivera
Mexico City, HE Cardinal Ernesto Corripio Ahumada
Monterrey, Adolfo Suarez Rivera
Morelia, Estanislao Alcarez Figueroa
Puebla de los Angeles, Rosendo Huesca Pacheco
San Luis Potosi, Arturo A. Szymanski Ramirez
Tlalnepantla, Manuel P. Gil Gonzalez
Yucatán, Manuel Castro Ruiz

MONACO
Monaco, Joseph-Marie Sardou

MOROCCO
Rabat, Hubert Michon
Tangier, Antonio J. Peteiro Freire

MOZAMBIQUE
Beira, Jaime P. Goncalves
Maputo, HE Cardinal Alexandre José Maria dos Santos
Nampula, Manuel Vieira Pinto

MYANMAR (BURMA)
Mandalay, Alphonse U. Than Aung
Yangon (Rangoon), Gabriel Thohey Mahn Gaby

NETHERLANDS
Utrecht, HE Cardinal Adrianus J. Simonis

NEW ZEALAND
Wellington, HE Cardinal Thomas Stafford Williams

NICARAGUA
Managua, HE Cardinal Miguel Obando Bravo

NIGERIA
Kaduna, Peter Yariyok Jatau
Lagos, Anthony Okogie
Onitsha, Stephen Nweke Ezeanya

OCEANIA
Agaña, Anthony Sablan Apuron
Honiara, Adrian Thomas Smith
Nouméa, Michel-Marie-Bernard Calvet
Samoa, Apia and Tokelau, HE Cardinal Pio Taofino'u
Suva, Petero Mataca

PAKISTAN
Karachi, HE Cardinal Joseph Cordeiro
  Coadjutor, Simeon Pereira

PANAMA
Panama, Marcos Gregorio McGrath

PAPUA NEW GUINEA
Madang, Benedict To Varpin
Mount Hagen, Michael Meier
Port Moresby, Peter Kurongku
Rabaul, Karl Hesse

PARAGUAY
Asuncion, Felipe Santiago B. Avalos

PERU
Arequipa, Fernando Vargas Ruiz de Somocurcio
Ayacucho o Huamanga, vacant
Cuzco, Alcides Mendoza Castro
Huancayo, vacant
Lima, Augusto Vargas Alzamora
Piura, Oscar Rolando Cantuarias Pastor
Trujillo, Manuel Prado Pérez-Rosas

PHILIPPINES
Caceres, Leonardo Legazpi
Cagayan de Oro, Jesus B. Tuquib
Capiz, Onesimo C. Gordoncillo
Cebu, HE Cardinal Ricardo Vidal
Cotabato, Philip Frances Smith
Davao, Antonio Mabutas
Jaro, Alberto J. Piamonte
Lingayen-Dagupan, Oscar V. Cruz
Lipa, Gaudencio B. Rosales
Manila, HE Cardinal Jaime L. Sin
Nueva Segovia, Orlando Quevedo
Ozamiz, Jesus Dosado
Palo, Pedro R. Dean
San Fernando, Paciano Aniceto
Tuguegarao, Diosdado A. Talamayan
Zamboanga, Francisco Raval Cruces

POLAND
Bialystok, Stanislaw Szymecki
Czestochowa, Stanislaw Nowak
Gdańsk, Tadeusz Goclowski
Gniezno, Henryk Muszyński
Katowice, Damian Zimoń
Kraków, HE Cardinal Franciszek Macharski
Lodz, Wladyslaw Ziolek
Lublin, Boleslaw Pylak
Poznań, Jerzy Stroba
Przemyśl of the Latins, Jozef Michalik
Szczecin-Kamień, Marian Przykucki
Warmia, Edmund Piszcz
Warsaw, HE Cardinal Józef Glemp
Wroclaw, HE Cardinal Henryk Roman Gulbinowicz

PORTUGAL
Braga, Eurico Dias Nogueira
Evora, Maurilio Jorge Quintal de Gouveia

PUERTO RICO
San Juan, HE Cardinal Luis Aponte Martinez

ROMANIA
Alba Julia (Latin Rite), Lajos Balint
Bucareşti, Ioan Robu
Fagaras and Alba Julia (Romanian Byzantine Rite), HE
  Cardinal Alexandru Todea

RUSSIA
Moscow Apostolic Administration (covering European
  Russia), Apostolic Administrator, Archbishop Tadeusz
  Kondrusiewicz
Novosibirsk Apostolic Administration (covering Siberia),
  Apostolic Administrator, Mgr Joseph Werth, SJ (titular
  Bishop of Bulna)

RWANDA
Kigali, Vincent Nsengiyumva

EL SALVADOR
San Salvador, Arturo Rivera Damas

SENEGAL
Dakar, HE Cardinal Hyacinthe Thiandoum

SIERRA LEONE
Freetown and Bo, Joseph Ganda

SINGAPORE
Singapore, Gregory Yong Sooi Ngean

SLOVAK REPUBLIC
Trnava, Jan Sokol

SLOVENIA
Ljubljana, Alojzij Suštar

SOUTH AFRICA
Bloemfontein, Peter John Butelezi
Cape Town, Lawrence Patrick Henry
Durban, Wilfrid Fox Napier
Pretoria, George Francis Daniel

SPAIN
Barcelona, Ricardo Maria Carles Gordó
Burgos, Santiago Martinez Acebes
Granada, José Méndez Asensio
Madrid, HE Cardinal Angel Suquia Goicoechea
Oviedo, Gabino Diaz Merchán
Pamplona, Fernando S. Aquilar
Santiago de Compostela, Antonio Rouco Varela
Sevilla, Carlos Amigo Vallejo
Tarragona, Ramon Torrella Cascante
Toledo, HE Cardinal Marcelo González Martin
Valencia, Agustin Garcia-Gasco Vicente
Valladolid, José Delicado Baeza
Zaragoza, Elíaz Yanez Alvarez

SRI LANKA
Colombo, Nicholas Marcus Fernando

SUDAN
Khartoum, Gabriel Zubeir Wako

SYRIA
Alep, Beroea, Halab (Greek Melekite Catholic Rite),
  Néophytes Edelby; (Syrian Rite), Raboula A. Beylouni;
  (Maronite Rite), Pierre Callaos; (Armenian Rite),
  Boutros Marayati
Baniyas (Greek Melekite Catholic Rite), Antoine Hayek
Bosra, Bostra, Boulos Nassif Borkhoche
Damascus (Greek Melekite Catholic Rite), vacant; (Syrian
  Rite), Eustache J. Mounayer; (Maronite Rite), Hamid A.
  Mourany
Hassaké-Nisibi, Georges Habib Hafouri
Homs, Emesa (Greek Melekite Catholic Rite), Abraham
  Nehmé; (Syrian Catholic Rite), Jean Dahi
Laodicea (Greek Melekite Catholic Rite), Michel Yatim

TAIWAN
Taipei, Joseph Ti-Kang

TANZANIA
Dar es Salaam, Polycarp Pengo
Mwanza, Antony Mayala

Songea, Norbert W. Mtega
Tabora, Mario E. A. Mgulunde

THAILAND
Bangkok, HE Cardinal Michael Michai Kitbunchu
Tharé and Nonseng, Lawrence Khai Saen-Phon-On

TOGO
Lomé, Philippe F. K. Kpodzro

TRINIDAD
Port of Spain, Gordon Anthony Pantin

TURKEY
Diarbekir, Paul Karatas
Istanbul (Constantinople), Jean Tcholakian
Izmir, Giuseppe G. Bernardini

UGANDA
Kampala, Emmanuel Wamala

UKRAINE
Lvov (Latin Rite), Marian Jaworski (Archbishop of Lvov of the Latins); (Ukrainian Rite), HE Cardinal Myroslav I. Lubachivsky (Major Archbishop of Lvov of the Ukrainians)

URUGUAY
Montevideo, José Gottardi Cristelli

USA
Anchorage, Francis Thomas Hurley
Atlanta, vacant
Baltimore, William Henry Keeler
Boston, HE Cardinal Bernard F. Law
Chicago, HE Cardinal Joseph L. Bernardin
Cincinnati, Daniel E. Pilarczyk
Denver, James Francis Stafford
Detroit, Adam J. Maida
Dubuque, Daniel W. Kucera
Hartford, Daniel A. Cronin
Indianapolis, Daniel Mark Buechlein
Kansas City, Ignatius J. Strecker
Los Angeles, HE Cardinal Roger M. Mahony
Louisville, Thomas C. Kelly
Miami, Edward A. McCarthy
Milwaukee, Rembert G. Weakland
Mobile, Oscar H. Lipscomb
Newark, Theodore E. McCarrick
New Orleans, Francis B. Schulte
New York, HE Cardinal John J. O'Connor
Oklahoma City, Eusebius Joseph Beltran
Omaha, Elden Curtiss
Philadelphia, HE Cardinal Anthony J. Bevilacqua; (Ukrainian Rite), Stephen Sulyk
Pittsburgh (Byzantine Rite), Thomas V. Dolinay
Portland (Oregon), William J. Levada
St Louis (Missouri), vacant
St Paul and Minneapolis, John Robert Roach
San Antonio, Patrick F. Flores
San Francisco, John R. Quinn
Santa Fe, Administrator, Michael Sheehan
Seattle, Thomas J. Murphy
Washington, HE Cardinal James A. Hickey

VENEZUELA
Barquisimeto, Julio Manuel Chirivella Varela
Caracas, HE Cardinal José Ali Lebrún Moratinos; (Greek Melekite Catholic Rite), Pierre Rai
Ciudad Bolivar, Medardo Luzardo Romero
Cumana, Alfredo J. R. Figueroa
Maracaibo, Ramon O. Perez Morales
Mérida, Baltazar P. Cardozo
Valencia, Jorge Liberato Urosa Savino

VIETNAM
Hanoi, vacant
Hue, vacant
Thanh-Phô Hôchiminh, Paul Nguyên Van Binh

WEST INDIES
Castries, Kelvin Edward Felix, OBE

YUGOSLAV FEDERAL REPUBLIC
Bar, Petar Perkolić
Belgrade, Franc Perko

ZAIRE
Bukavu, Mulindwa Mutabesha Mweru
Kananga, Bakole wa Ilunga
Kinshasa, HE Cardinal Frederick Etsou-Nzabi-Bamungwabi
Kisangani, Laurent Monsengwo Pasinya
Lubumbashi, Kabanga Songasonga
Mbandaka-Bikoro, Joseph Kumuondala Mbimba

ZAMBIA
Kasama, James Spaita
Lusaka, Adrian Mungandu

ZIMBABWE
Harare, Patrick Chakaipa

PATRIARCHS IN COMMUNION WITH THE ROMAN CATHOLIC CHURCH

Alexandria, HB Stephanos II Ghattas (Patriarch for Catholic Copts)
Antioch, HB Ignace Antoine II Hayek (Patriarch for Syrian Rite Catholics); HB Maximos V. Hakim (Patriarch for Greek Melekite Rite Catholics); HB Nasrallah Pierre Sfeir (Patriarch for Maronite Rite Catholics)
Jerusalem, HB Michel Sabbah (Patriarch for Latin Rite Catholics)
Babilonia of the Chaldeans, HB Raphael I Bidawid
Cilicia of the Armenians, HB Jean Pierre XVIII Kasparian (Patriarch for Armenian Rite Catholics)
Oriental India, Archbishop Raul Nicolau Gonsalves
Lisbon, HE Cardinal Antonio Ribeiro
Venice, HE Cardinal Marco Ce

Other Churches in the UK

AFRICAN AND AFRO-CARIBBEAN CHURCHES

There are more than 160 Christian churches or groups of African or Afro-Caribbean origin in the United Kingdom. These include the Apostolic Faith Church, the Cherubim and Seraphim Church, the New Testament Church Assembly, the New Testament Church of God and the Wesleyan Holiness Church.

The Council of African and Allied Churches was initiated by the Most Revd Father Olu Abiola in 1979 to give one voice to the various Christian churches of African origin in the UK. Membership increased in the early 1980s and some churches of Caribbean origin also joined, resulting in 1986 in the change of name to the Council of African and Afro-Caribbean Churches UK. The Council is the medium through which the member churches can work jointly to provide services they cannot easily provide individually.

There are about 68,500 adherents of African and Afro-Caribbean churches in the United Kingdom, and about 950 churches. The Council has 30 member churches, with 70 congregations, 12,000 members and 200 ministers.
Council Chairman, His Grace The Most Revd Father Olu A. Abiola, 31 Norton House, Sidney Road, London SW9 0UJ. Tel: 071-274 5589

ASSOCIATED PRESBYTERIAN CHURCHES OF SCOTLAND

The Associated Presbyterian Churches came into being in 1989 as a result of a division within the Free Presbyterian Church of Scotland. Following two controversial disciplinary cases, the culmination of deepening differences within the Church, a Deed of Separation was drawn up by several members of the Church's synod. This held that the Church, in contravention of its constitution, had denied its members freedom of judgement in matters relating to the application of the Christian faith to daily living. A presbytery was formed calling itself the Associated Presbyterian Churches (APC). The APC claims that it represents the Free Presbyterian Church of Scotland as constituted in 1893. The Associated Presbyterian Churches has about 20 churches, 1,000 members and 13 ministers.
Clerk of the Scottish Presbytery, D. K. Laing, 1 Golden Square, Aberdeen AB9 1HA. Tel: 0862-87541

THE BAPTIST CHURCH

Baptists trace their origins to John Smyth, who in 1609 in Amsterdam reinstituted the baptism of conscious believers as the basis of the fellowship of a gathered church. Members of Smyth's church established the first Baptist church in England in 1612. They came to be known as 'General' Baptists and their theology was Arminian, whereas a later group of Calvinists who adopted the baptism of believers came to be known as 'Particular' Baptists. The two sections of the Baptists were united into one body, the Baptist Union of Great Britain and Ireland, in 1891. In 1988 the title was changed to the Baptist Union of Great Britain.

Baptists emphasize the complete independence of the local church, although individual churches are linked in various kinds of associations. There are international bodies (such as the Baptist World Alliance) and national bodies, but many Baptist churches belong to neither. However, in Great Britain the majority of churches and associations belong to the Baptist Union of Great Britain. There are also Baptist Unions in Wales, Scotland and Ireland which are much smaller than the Baptist Union of Great Britain, and there is some overlap of membership.

There are over 38 million Baptist church members world-wide; in the Baptist Union of Great Britain there are 160,000 members, 1,779 pastors and 2,118 churches. In the Baptist Union of Scotland there are 16,212 members, 130 pastors and 166 churches. In the Baptist Union of Wales there are 27,700 members, 117 pastors and 560 churches. In the Baptist Union of Ireland there are 8,505 members, 72 pastors and 103 churches.
President of the Baptist Union of Great Britain (1993–4), Revd Dr B. Haymes
General Secretary, Revd D. R. Coffey, Baptist House, PO Box 44, 129 Broadway, Didcot, Oxon. OX11 8RT. Tel: 0235-512077

THE CHURCH OF CHRIST, SCIENTIST

The Church of Christ, Scientist, was founded by Mary Baker Eddy in the United States of America in 1879 to 'reinstate primitive Christianity and its lost element of healing'. Christian Science is concerned with spiritual regeneration and salvation from sin, but is best known for its reliance on prayer alone in the healing of sickness. Adherents believe that such healing is in direct line with that practised by Jesus Christ (revered, not as God, but as the Son of God) and by the early Christian Church.

The denomination consists of the First Church of Christ, Scientist, in Boston, Massachusetts, USA (the Mother Church) and its branch churches in over 60 countries world-wide. Branch churches are democratically governed by their members. There is also a five-member Board of Directors which oversees Church matters. There are no clergy. Those engaged in full-time healing ministry are called practitioners, of whom there are 3,500 world-wide.

No membership figures are available, since Mary Baker Eddy felt that numbers are no measure of spiritual vitality and ruled that such statistics should not be published. There are over 2,500 branch churches world-wide, including 210 in the United Kingdom.
CHRISTIAN SCIENCE COMMITTEE ON PUBLICATION, 108 Palace Gardens Terrace, London W8 4RT. Tel: 071-221 5650. *District Manager for Great Britain and Ireland*, G. Phaup

THE CONGREGATIONAL FEDERATION

The Congregational Federation was founded by members of Congregational churches in England and Wales who did not join the United Reformed Church (q.v.) in 1972. There are also churches in Scotland and Australia. The Federation exists to encourage congregations of believers to worship in free assembly, to give them no authority over them and emphasizes their right to independence and self-government.

The Federation has 9,455 members, 117 ministers, 36 pastors, about 330 lay preachers and 287 churches.
President of the Federation (1993–4), Revd Dr R. W. Cleaves
General Secretary, G. M. Adams, The Congregational Centre, 4 Castle Gate, Nottingham NG1 7AS. Tel: 0602–413801

THE FREE CHURCH OF ENGLAND

The Free Church of England, also known as the Reformed Episcopal Church, traces its beginnings to a dispute over the influence of the Oxford Movement in the established church between the Bishop of Exeter and one of his clergy, James Shore, in 1843. The Church defined its beliefs in 1863, accepting the Church of England's Thirty-Nine Articles and recognizing the legitimacy of the principle of episcopacy. Although its government was at first presbyterian, the Church later became affiliated to the Reformed Episcopal Church in the USA (a connection which has not been maintained) and adopted episcopal organization.

The Free Church of England has 1,700 members, 35 ministers and 30 churches in England. It also has three churches and three ministers in New Zealand, and one church and one minister in St Petersburg, Russia.

General Secretary, Revd W. J. Lawler, 45 Broughton Road, Wallasey, Merseyside L45 1JP. Tel: 051-638 2564

THE FREE CHURCH OF SCOTLAND

The Free Church of Scotland was formed in 1843 when over 400 ministers withdrew from the Church of Scotland as a result of interference in the internal affairs of the church by the civil authorities. In 1900, all but 26 ministers joined with others to form the United Free Church (most of which rejoined the Church of Scotland in 1929). In 1904 the remaining 26 ministers were recognized by the House of Lords as continuing the Free Church of Scotland.

The Church maintains strict adherence to the Westminster Confession of Faith (1648) and accepts the Bible as the sole rule of faith and conduct. Its General Assembly meets annually. It also has links with Reformed Churches overseas. The Free Church of Scotland has about 20,000 members, 110 ministers and 140 churches.

General Treasurer, I. D. Gill, The Mound, Edinburgh EH1 2LS. Tel: 031-226 5286

THE FREE PRESBYTERIAN CHURCH OF SCOTLAND

The Free Presbyterian Church of Scotland was formed in 1893 by two ministers of the Free Church of Scotland who refused to accept a Declaratory Act passed by the Free Church General Assembly in 1892. The Free Presbyterian Church of Scotland is Calvinistic in doctrine and emphasizes observance of the Sabbath. It adheres strictly to the Westminster Confession of Faith of 1648.

The Church has about 4,000 members in Scotland and about 11,000 in overseas congregations. It has 22 ministers and 34 churches.

Moderator, Revd D. MacLean, 104 Barronald Drive, Glasgow G12 0HE. Tel: 041-357 2315.

Clerk of Synod, Revd D. B. MacLeod, 8 Colinton Road, Edinburgh EH10 5DS. Tel: 031-447 1920

THE INDEPENDENT METHODIST CHURCHES

The Independent Methodist Churches seceded from the Wesleyan Methodist Church in 1805 and remained independent when the Methodist Church in Great Britain was formed in 1932. They are mainly concentrated in the industrial areas of the north of England.

The churches are Methodist in doctrine but their organization is congregational. All the churches are members of the Independent Methodist Connexion of Churches. The controlling body of the Connexion is the Annual Meeting, to which churches send delegates. The Connexional President is elected annually. Between annual meetings the affairs of the Connexion are handled by departmental committees. Ministers are appointed by the churches and trained through the Connexion. The ministry is open to both men and women and is unpaid.

There are 3,600 members, 126 ministers and 103 churches in Great Britain.

Connexional President (1993–4), H. Porter

General Secretary, Revd J. M. Day, The Old Police House, Croxton, Stafford ST21 6PE. Tel: 063-082 671

THE LUTHERAN CHURCH

Lutheranism is based on the teachings of Martin Luther, the German leader of the Protestant Reformation. The authority of the scriptures is held to be supreme over Church tradition and creeds, and the key doctrine is that of justification by faith alone.

Lutheranism is one of the largest Protestant denominations and it is particularly strong in northern Europe and the USA. Some Lutheran churches are episcopal, while others have a synodal form of organization; unity is based on doctrine rather than structure. Most Lutheran churches are members of the Lutheran World Federation, based in Geneva.

Lutheran services in Great Britain are held in many languages to serve members of different nationalities. English-language congregations are members either of the Lutheran Church in Great Britain–United Synod, or of the Evangelical Lutheran Church of England. The United Synod and most of the various national congregations are members of the Lutheran Council of Great Britain.

There are over 70 million Lutherans world-wide; in Great Britain there are 27,000 members, 45 ministers and 100 churches.

Chairman of the Lutheran Council of Great Britain, Very Revd R. J. Patkai, 8 Collingham Gardens, London SW5 0HW. Tel: 071-373 1141

THE METHODIST CHURCH

The Methodist movement started in England in 1729 when the Revd John Wesley, an Anglican priest, and his brother Charles met with others in Oxford and resolved to conduct their lives and study by 'rule and method'. In 1739 the Wesleys began evangelistic preaching and the first Methodist chapel was founded in Bristol in the same year. In 1744 the first annual conference was held, at which the Articles of Religion were drawn up. Doctrinal emphases included repentance, faith, the assurance of salvation, social concern and the priesthood of all believers. After John Wesley's death in 1791 the Methodists withdrew from the established Church to form the Methodist Church. Methodists gradually drifted into many groups, but in 1932 the Wesleyan Methodist Church, the United Methodist Church and the Primitive Methodist Church united to form the Methodist Church in Great Britain as it now exists.

The governing body and supreme authority of the Methodist Church is the Conference, but there are also 33 district synods, consisting of all the ministers and selected lay people in each district, and circuit meetings of the ministers and lay people of each circuit.

There are over 54 million Methodists world-wide; in Great Britain (1992 figures) there are 408,107 members, 3,601 ministers, 10,414 lay preachers and 6,950 churches.

President of the Conference in Great Britain (1993–4), Revd B. E. Beck

Vice-President of the Conference (1993–4), Mrs S. M. Howdle

Secretary of the Conference, Revd B. E. Beck, Methodist Church, Conference Office, 1 Central Buildings, Storeys Gate, London SW1H 9NH. Tel: 071-222 8010

THE METHODIST CHURCH IN IRELAND

The Methodist Church in Ireland is closely linked to British Methodism but is autonomous. It has 19,217 members, 196 ministers, 296 lay preachers and 234 churches.

President of the Conference in Ireland (1993–4), Revd R. H.
Taylor
Secretary of the Conference in Ireland, Revd
E. T. I. Mawhinney, 1 Fountainville Avenue, Belfast
BT9 6AN. Tel: 0232-324554

THE ORTHODOX CHURCH

The Orthodox Church (or Eastern Orthodox Church) is a
communion of self-governing Christian churches recognizing
the honorary primacy of the Oecumenical Patriarch of
Constantinople.

In the first millennium of the Christian era the faith was
slowly formulated. Between AD 325 and 787 there were
seven Oecumenical Councils at which bishops from the entire
Christian world assembled to resolve various doctrinal
disputes which had arisen. The estrangement between East
and West began after Constantine moved the centre of the
Roman Empire from Rome to Constantinople, and it gained
momentum after the temporal administration was divided.
Linguistic and cultural differences between Greek East and
Latin West served to encourage separate ecclesiastical
developments which became pronounced in the tenth and
early eleventh centuries.

The administration of the church was divided between five
ancient patriarchates: Rome and all the West, Constantinople
(the imperial city – the 'New Rome'), Jerusalem and all
Palestine, Antioch and all the East, and Alexandria and all
Africa. Of these, only Rome was in the Latin West and after
the Great Schism in 1054, Rome developed a structure of
authority centralized on one source, the Papacy, while the
Orthodox East maintained the style of localized administration.

To the older patriarchates were later added the Patriar-
chates of Russia, Georgia, Serbia, Bulgaria and Romania.
The Orthodox Church also includes autocephalous (self-
governing) national churches in Greece, Cyprus, Poland,
Albania, Czechoslovakia and Sinai, and autonomous national
churches in Finland and Japan. The Estonian and Latvian
Orthodox Churches are in practice part of the Moscow
Patriarchate. The Belorussians and Ukrainians have recently
been given greater autonomy by Moscow, but some
Ukrainians have broken away to establish an independent
Ukrainian Patriarchate. In Macedonia the local hierarchy has
declared itself independent of the Serbian Patriarchate. The
Russian dioceses in the diaspora fall into four groups: those
under the direct control of the Moscow Patriarchate; the
Russian Orthodox Church Outside Russia, sometimes known
as the Synod in Exile; the Russian Archdiocese centred at
the cathedral in rue Daru, Paris, which is part of the
Patriarchate in Constantinople; and the Orthodox Church in
America, which was granted autocephalous status in 1970.

The position of Orthodox Christians is that the faith was
fully defined during the period of the Oecumenical Councils.
In doctrine it is strongly trinitarian, and stresses the mystery
and importance of the sacraments. It is episcopal in
government. The structure of the Orthodox Christian year
differs from that of Western Churches (*see* page 82).

Orthodox Christians throughout the world are estimated
to number about 150 million.

PATRIARCHS
*Archbishop of Constantinople, New Rome and Oecumenical
Patriarch*, Bartholomew, *elected* 1991
Pope and Patriarch of Alexandria and All Africa, Parthenios
III, *elected* 1987

Patriarch of Antioch and All the East, Ignatios IV, *elected*
1979
Patriarch of Jerusalem and All Palestine, Diodoros, *elected*
1981
Patriarch of Moscow and All Russia, Alexei II, *elected* 1990
*Archbishop of Tbilisi and Mtskheta, Catholicos-Patriarch of
All Georgia*, Ilia II, *elected* 1977
*Archbishop of Pec, Metropolitan of Belgrade and Karlovci,
Patriarch of Serbia*, Paul, *elected* 1990
Archbishop of Bucharest and Patriarch of Romania, Teoctist,
elected 1986
Metropolitan of Sofia and Patriarch of Bulgaria, Maxim,
elected 1971
Patriarch of Kiev and All Ukraine, Mstyslav, *elected* 1990
(not officially recognized by other national Orthodox
churches)

ORTHODOX CHURCHES IN THE UK

THE GREEK ORTHODOX CHURCH (PATRIARCHATE OF
CONSTANTINOPLE)
The presence of Greek Orthodox Christians in Britain dates
back to 1677 when Archbishop Joseph Geogirenes of Samos
fled from Turkish persecution and came to London, where a
church was built for him in Soho. The present Greek cathedral
in Moscow Road, Bayswater, was opened for public worship
in 1879 and the Diocese of Thyateira and Great Britain was
established in 1922. There are now 87 parishes in Great
Britain, served by eight bishops and 87 churches.

In Great Britain the Patriarchate of Constantinople is
represented by Archbishop Gregorios of Thyateira and Great
Britain, 5 Craven Hill, London W2 3EN. Tel: 071-723 4787.

THE RUSSIAN ORTHODOX CHURCH (PATRIARCHATE
OF MOSCOW) AND THE RUSSIAN ORTHODOX CHURCH
OUTSIDE RUSSIA
The earliest records of Russian Orthodox Church activities
in Britain date from the visit to England of Tsar Peter I at
the beginning of the 18th century. Clergy were sent from
Russia to serve the chapel established to minister to the staff
of the Imperial Russian Embassy in London.

After 1917 the Church of Russia was persecuted. The
Patriarch of Moscow, St Tikhon the New Martyr, anathema-
tized both the atheistic persecutors of the Church and all who
collaborated with them. Because of the civil war normal
administrative contact with Russian Orthodox Christians
outside the country was impossible, and he therefore
authorized the establishment of a higher church administration, i.e. a synod in exile, by Russian bishops who were then
outside Russia. This is the origin of the Russian Orthodox
Church Outside Russia. The attitude of the Church of Russia
to the former Soviet regime was always a source of contention
between the two hierarchies; tensions are now lessening but
remain unresolved.

In Britain the Patriarchate of Moscow is represented by
Metropolitan Anthony of Sourozh, 67 Ennismore Gardens,
London SW7 1NH. Tel: 071-584 0096. He is assisted by one
archbishop, one bishop and about 13 priests. There are 15
parishes.

The Russian Orthodox Church Outside Russia is represented by Archbishop Mark of Richmond and Great Britain
(who is also Archbishop of Berlin and Germany), 14 St
Dunstan's Road, London W6 8RB. Tel: 081-748 4232. There
are eight parishes and two monasteries, served by six priests.

THE SERBIAN ORTHODOX CHURCH (PATRIARCHATE OF
SERBIA)
There was a small congregation of Orthodox Christian Serbs
in London before the Second World War, but most Serbian

parishes in Britain have been established since 1945. There is no resident bishop as the parishes are part of the Serbian Orthodox Diocese of Western Europe, which has its centre in Germany. There are five main parishes in Britain and several smaller communities served by seven priests.

In Britain the Patriarchate of Serbia is represented by the Episcopal Vicar, the Very Revd Milun Kostic, 89 Lancaster Road, London WII 1QQ. Tel: 071-727 8367.

OTHER NATIONALITIES

Latvian, Polish and some Belorussian Orthodox parishes in Britain are under the care of the Patriarchate of Constantinople. The Patriarchates of Antioch, Bulgaria and Romania are represented by one priest each. Both the Ukrainian Autocephalous Orthodox Church and the Belorussian Autocephalic Orthodox Church have a few parishes in Britain.

ORTHODOX CHURCH PUBLIC RELATIONS OFFICE, St George Orthodox Information Service, 64 Prebend Gardens, London W6 0XU. Tel: 081-741 9624. *Secretary,* A. Bond

PENTECOSTAL CHURCHES

Pentecostalism is inspired by the descent of the Holy Spirit upon the apostles at Pentecost. The movement began in Los Angeles, USA, in 1906 and is characterized by baptism with the Holy Spirit, divine healing, speaking in tongues (glossolalia), and a literal interpretation of the scriptures. The Pentecostal movement in Britain dates from 1907. Initially, groups of Pentecostalists were led by laymen and did not organize formally. However, in 1915 the Elim Foursquare Gospel Alliance (more usually called the Elim Pentecostal Church) was founded in Ireland by George Jeffreys and in 1924 about 70 independent assemblies formed a fellowship, the Assemblies of God in Great Britain and Ireland. The Apostolic Church grew out of the 1904–5 revivals in South Wales and was established in 1916, and the New Testament Church of God was established in England in 1953. In recent years many aspects of Pentecostalism have been adopted by the growing charismatic movement within the Roman Catholic Church and Protestant and Eastern Orthodox churches.

There are about 22 million Pentecostalists world-wide, with about 115,000 adult adherents in Great Britain and Ireland.

THE APOSTOLIC CHURCH, International Administration Offices, PO Box 389, 24–27 St Helens Road, Swansea, West Glamorgan SA1 1ZH. Tel: 0792-473992. *President,* Pastor P. Cawthorne; *Administrator,* Pastor M. Davies. The Apostolic Church has about 130 churches, 5,500 adherents and 83 ministers

THE ASSEMBLIES OF GOD IN GREAT BRITAIN AND IRELAND, General Offices, 106–114 Talbot Street, Nottingham NG1 5GH. Tel: 0602-474525. *General Superintendent,* W. Shenton; *General Administrator,* B. D. Varnam. The Assemblies of God has 614 churches, about 70,000 adherents (including children) and 627 accredited ministers

THE ELIM PENTECOSTAL CHURCH, PO Box 38, Cheltenham, Glos. GL50 3HN. Tel: 0242-519904. *General Superintendent,* Pastor I. W. Lewis; *Administrator,* Pastor B. Hunter. The Elim Pentecostal Church has about 470 churches, 50,000 adherents and 475 accredited ministers

THE NEW TESTAMENT CHURCH OF GOD, Main House, Overstone Park, Overstone, Northampton NN6 0AD. Tel: 0604-645944. *National Overseer,* Revd Dr S. E. Arnold. The New Testament Church of God has

106 organized congregations, 7,042 baptized members, about 20,000 adherents and 216 accredited ministers

THE PRESBYTERIAN CHURCH IN IRELAND

The Presbyterian Church in Ireland is Calvinistic in doctrine and presbyterian in constitution. Presbyterianism was established in Ireland as a result of the Ulster plantation in the early 17th century, when English and Scottish Protestants settled in the north of Ireland.

There are 21 presbyteries and five regional synods under the chief court known as the General Assembly. The General Assembly meets annually and is presided over by a Moderator who is elected for one year. The ongoing work of the Church is undertaken by 18 boards under which there are a number of specialist committees.

There are about 330,000 Presbyterians in Ireland, mainly in the north, in 562 congregations and with 400 ministers.

Moderator (1993–4), Rt. Revd Dr A. Rodgers
Clerk of Assembly and General Secretary, Revd S. Hutchinson, Church House, Belfast BT1 6DW. Tel: 0232-322284

THE PRESBYTERIAN CHURCH OF WALES

The Presbyterian Church of Wales or Calvinistic Methodist Church of Wales is Calvinistic in doctrine and presbyterian in constitution. It was formed in 1811 when Welsh Calvinists severed the relationship with the established church by ordaining their own ministers. It secured its own confession of faith in 1823 and a Constitutional Deed in 1826, and since 1864 the General Assembly has met annually, presided over by a Moderator elected for a year. The doctrine and constitutional structure of the Presbyterian Church of Wales was confirmed by Act of Parliament in 1931–2.

The Church has 57,876 members, 118 ministers and 971 churches.

Moderator (1993–4), A. C. Davies
General Secretary, Revd D. H. Owen, 53 Richmond Road, Cardiff CF2 3UP. Tel: 0222-494913

THE RELIGIOUS SOCIETY OF FRIENDS (QUAKERS)

Quakerism is a movement, not a church, which was founded in the 17th century by George Fox and others in an attempt to revive what they saw as 'primitive Christianity'. The movement was based originally in the Midlands, Yorkshire and north-west England, but there are now Quakers in 36 countries around the world. The colony of Pennsylvania, founded by William Penn, was originally Quaker.

Emphasis is placed on the experience of God in daily life rather than on sacraments or religious occasions. There is no church calendar. Worship is largely silent and there are no appointed ministers; the responsibility for conducting a meeting is shared equally among those present. Social reform and religious tolerance have always been important to Quakers, together with a commitment to non-violence in resolving disputes.

There are 213,800 Quakers world-wide, with over 19,000 in Great Britain and Ireland. There are 464 meeting houses in Great Britain.
CENTRAL OFFICES: (GREAT BRITAIN) Friends House, Euston Road, London NW1 2BJ. Tel: 071-387 3601; (IRELAND) Swanbrook House, Morehampton Road, Dublin 4. Tel: 0001-683684

THE SALVATION ARMY

The Salvation Army was founded by a Methodist minister, William Booth, in the east end of London in 1865, and has since become established in 95 countries world-wide. It was first known as the Christian Mission, and took its present name in 1878 when it adopted a quasi-military command structure intended to inspire and regulate its endeavours and to reflect its view that the Church was engaged in spiritual warfare. Salvationists emphasize evangelism, social work and the relief of poverty.

The world leader, known as the General, is elected by a High Council composed of the Chief of the Staff and senior ranking officers known as commissioners.

There are about 1.5 million soldiers, 16,455 active officers (full-time ordained ministers) and 14,068 corps (churches) world-wide. In Great Britain and Ireland there are 55,000 soldiers, 1,807 active officers and 992 worship centres.
International Leader, B. Tillsley
UK Territorial Commander, Commissioner D. Pender
INTERNATIONAL AND TERRITORIAL HEADQUARTERS, PO Box 249, 101 Queen Victoria Street, London EC4P 4EP. Tel: 071-236 5222

THE SEVENTH-DAY ADVENTIST CHURCH

The Seventh-day Adventist Church was founded in 1863 in the USA. Its members look forward to the second coming of Christ and observe the Sabbath as a day of rest, worship and ministry. The Church bases its faith and practice wholly on the Bible and has developed 27 fundamental beliefs.

The World Church is divided into 12 divisions, each made up of unions of churches. The Seventh-day Adventist Church in the British Isles is known as the British Union of Seventh-day Adventists and is a member of the Trans-European Division. In the British Isles the administrative organization of the church is arranged in three tiers: the local churches; the regional conferences for south England, north England, Wales, Scotland and Ireland, which are held every three years; and the national 'union' conference which is held every five years.

There are over 7 million Adventists and 34,363 churches in 201 countries world-wide. In the United Kingdom and Ireland there are 18,200 members, 155 ministers and 242 churches.
President of the British Union Conference (1991–6), Pastor C. Perry
BRITISH ISLES HEADQUARTERS, Stanborough Park, Watford WD2 6JP. Tel: 0923-672251

UNDEB YR ANNIBYNWYR CYMRAEG
The Union of Welsh Independents

The Union of Welsh Independents was formed in 1872 and is a voluntary association of Welsh Congregational Churches

and personal members. It is entirely Welsh-speaking. Congregationalism in Wales dates back to 1639 when the first Welsh Congregational Church was opened in Gwent. Member Churches are Calvinistic in doctrine and congregationalist in organization. Each church has complete independence in the government and administration of its affairs.

The Union has 48,000 members, 120 ministers and 610 chapels.
President of the Union (1993–4), Revd J. G. Jones
General Secretary, Revd D. Morris Jones, Tŷ John Penry, 11 Heol Sant Helen, Swansea SA1 4AL. Tel: 0792-467040

UNITARIAN AND FREE CHRISTIAN CHURCHES

Unitarianism has its historical roots in the Judaeo-Christian tradition but denies the exclusive divinity of Christ and the doctrine of the trinity. It allows the individual to embrace insights from all the world's faiths and philosophies, as there is no formal creed. It is accepted that beliefs may evolve in the light of personal experience.

Unitarian communities first became established in Poland and Transylvania in the 16th century. The first avowedly Unitarian place of worship in the British Isles opened in London in 1774. The General Assembly of Unitarian and Free Christian Churches came into existence in 1928 as the result of the amalgamation of two earlier organizations.

There are about 10,000 Unitarians in Great Britain and Ireland, and 150 Unitarian ministers. About 250 self-governing congregations and fellowship groups, including a small number overseas, are members of the General Assembly.
GENERAL ASSEMBLY OF UNITARIAN AND FREE CHRISTIAN CHURCHES, Essex Hall, 1–6 Essex Street, Strand, London WC2R 3HY. Tel: 071-240 2384. *General Secretary*, Dr R. W. Smith

---

THE UNITED REFORMED CHURCH

The United Reformed Church was formed by the union of most of the Congregational churches in England and Wales with the Presbyterian Church of England in 1972.

Congregationalism dates from the mid 16th century. It is Calvinistic in doctrine, and its followers form independent self-governing congregations bound under God by covenant, a principle laid down in the writings of Robert Browne (1550–1633). From the late 16th century the movement was driven underground by persecution, but the cause was defended at the Westminster Assembly in 1643 and the Savoy Declaration of 1658 laid down its principles. Congregational churches formed county associations for mutual support and in 1832 these associations merged to form the Congregational Union of England and Wales.

The Presbyterian Church in England also dates from the mid 16th century, and was Calvinistic and evangelical in its doctrine. It was governed by a hierarchy of courts.

In the 1960s there was close co-operation locally and nationally between Congregational and Presbyterian Churches. This led to union negotiations and a Scheme of Union, supported by Act of Parliament in 1972. In 1981 a further unification took place, with the Reformed Association of Churches of Christ becoming part of the URC. In its basis the United Reformed Church reflects local church initiative and responsibility with a conciliar pattern of oversight. The

General Assembly is the central body, and is made up of equal numbers of ministers and lay members.

The United Reformed Church is divided into 12 Provinces, each with a Provincial Moderator who chairs the Synod, and 70 Districts. There are 115,000 members, 730 full-time ministers and 1,800 local churches.

General Secretary, Revd A. G. Burnham, 86 Tavistock Place, London WC1H 9RT. Tel: 071-916 2020

THE WESLEYAN REFORM UNION

The Wesleyan Reform Union was founded by Methodists who left or were expelled from Wesleyan Methodism in 1849 following a period of internal conflict. Its doctrine is Methodist but its organization is congregational, each church having complete independence in the government and administration of its affairs. The main concentration of churches is in Yorkshire.

The Union has 2,698 members, 20 ministers, 143 lay preachers and 122 churches.

President (1993–4), B. S. Pratt

General Secretary, Revd E. W. Downing, Wesleyan Reform Church House, 123 Queen Street, Sheffield S1 2DU. Tel: 0742-721928

Popes since 1800

The family name is in italics

Pius VII, *Chiaramonti*, elected 1800
Leo XII, *della Genga*, elected 1823
Pius VIII, *Castiglioni*, elected 1829
Gregory XVI, *Cappellari*, elected 1831
Pius IX, *Mastai-Ferretti*, elected 1846
Leo XIII, *Pecci*, elected 1878
Pius X, *Sarto*, elected 1903
Benedict XV, *della Chiesa*, elected 1914
Pius XI, *Ratti*, elected 1922

Pius XII, *Pacelli*, elected 1939
John XXIII, *Roncalli*, elected 1958
Paul VI, *Montini*, elected 1963
John Paul I, *Luciani*, elected 1978
John Paul II, *Wojtyla*, elected 1978

Adrian IV is the only Englishman to be elected pope. He was born Nicholas Breakspear at Langley, near St Albans, and was elected Pope in 1154 on the death of Anastasius IV. He died in 1159.

Archbishops of Canterbury since 1414

Henry Chichele (1362–1443), translated 1414
John Stafford (?–1452), translated 1443
John Kemp (c.1380–1454), translated 1452
Thomas Bourchier (c.1410–86), translated 1454
John Morton (c.1420–1500), translated 1486
Henry Deane (?–1503), translated 1501
William Warham (1450–1532), translated 1503
Thomas Cranmer (1489–1556), translated 1533
Reginald Pole (1500–58), translated 1556
Matthew Parker (1504–75), translated 1559
Edmund Grindal (c. 1519–83), translated 1576
John Whitgift (c.1530–1604), translated 1583
Richard Bancroft (1544–1610), translated 1604
George Abbot (1562–1633), translated 1611
William Laud (1573–1645), translated 1633
William Juxon (1582–1663), translated 1660
Gilbert Sheldon (1598–1677), translated 1663
William Sancroft (1617–93), translated 1678
John Tillotson (1630–94), translated 1691
Thomas Tenison (1636–1715), translated 1695
William Wake (1657–1737), translated 1716

John Potter (c. 1674–1747), translated 1737
Thomas Herring (1693–1757), translated 1747
Matthew Hutton (1693–1758), translated 1757
Thomas Secker (1693–1768), translated 1758
Hon. Frederick Cornwallis (1713–83), translated 1768
John Moore (1730–1805), translated 1783
Charles Manners-Sutton (1755–1828), translated 1805
William Howley (1766–1848), translated 1828
John Bird Sumner (1780–1862), translated 1848
Charles Longley (1794–1868), translated 1862
Archibald Campbell Tait (1811–82), translated 1868
Edward White Benson (1829–96), translated 1883
Frederick Temple (1821–1902), translated 1896
Randall Thomas Davidson (1848–1930), translated 1903
Cosmo Gordon Lang (1864–1945), translated 1928
William Temple (1881–1944), translated 1942
Geoffrey Fisher (1887–1972), translated 1945
Arthur Ramsey (1904–88), translated 1961
Donald Coggan (1909–), translated 1974
Robert Runcie (1921–), translated 1980
George Carey (1935–), translated 1991

Archbishops of York since 1606

Tobias Matthew (1546–1628), translated 1606
George Montaigne (1569–1628), translated 1628
Samuel Harsnett (1561–1631), translated 1629
Richard Neile (1562–1640), translated 1632
John Williams (1582–1650), translated 1641
Accepted Frewen (1588–1664), translated 1660
Richard Sterne (1596–1683), translated 1664
John Dolben (1625–86), translated 1683
Thomas Lamplugh (1615–91), translated 1688
John Sharp (1645–1714), translated 1691
William Dawes (1671–1724), translated 1714
Launcelot Blackburn (1658–1743), translated 1724
Thomas Herring (1693–1757), translated 1743
Matthew Hutton (1693–1758), translated 1747
John Gilbert (1693–1761), translated 1757
Robert Hay Drummond (1711–76), translated 1761

William Markham (1719–1807), translated 1777
Edward Venables Vernon Harcourt (1757–1847), translated 1808
Thomas Musgrave (1788–1860), translated 1847
Charles Longley (1794–1868), translated 1860
William Thomson (1819–90), translated 1862
William Connor Magee (1821–91), translated 1891
William Dalrymple Maclagan (1826–1910), translated 1891
Cosmo Gordon Lang (1864–1945), translated 1909
William Temple (1881–1944), translated 1929
Cyril Garbett (1875–1955), translated 1942
Arthur Ramsey (1904–88), translated 1956
Donald Coggan (1909–), translated 1961
Stuart Blanch (1918–), translated 1975
John Habgood (1927–), translated 1983

Non-Christian Faiths

BUDDHISM

Buddhism originated in northern India, in the teachings of Siddharta Gautama, who was born near Kapilavastu about 560 BC. After a long spiritual quest he experienced enlightenment beneath a tree at the place now known as Bodhgaya, and began missionary work.

Fundamental to Buddhism is the concept that there is no such thing as a permanent soul or self; when someone dies, consciousness is the only one of the elements of which they were composed which is lost. All the other elements regroup in a new body and carry with them the consequences of the conduct of the earlier life (known as the law of *karma*). This cycle of death and rebirth is broken only when the state of *nirvana* has been reached. Buddhism steers a middle path between belief in personal immortality and belief in death as the final end.

The Four Noble Truths of Buddhism (*dukkha*, suffering; *tanha*, a thirst or desire for continued existence which causes dukkha; *nirvana*, the final liberation from desire and ignorance; and *ariya*, the path to nirvana) are all held to be universal and to sum up the *dhamma* or true nature of life. Necessary qualities to promote spiritual development are *sila* (morality), *samadhi* (meditation) and *panna* (wisdom).

There are two main schools of Buddhism: *Theravada* Buddhism, the earliest extant school, which is more traditional, and *Mahayana* Buddhism, which began to develop about 100 years after the Buddha's death and is more liberal; it teaches that all people may attain Buddahood. Important schools which have developed within Mahayana Buddhism are *Zen* Buddhism, *Nichiren* Buddhism and Pure Land Buddhism or *Amidism*. There are also distinctive Tibetan forms of Buddhism. Buddhism began to establish itself in the West at the beginning of the 20th century.

The scripture of Theravada Buddhism is the *Pali Canon*, which dates from the first century BC. Mahayana Buddhism uses a Sanskrit version of the Pali Canon but also has many other works of scripture.

There is no set time for Buddhist worship, which may take place in a temple or in the home. Worship centres around *paritta* (chanting), acts of devotion centring on the image of the Buddha, and, where possible, offerings to a relic of the Buddha. Buddhist festivals vary according to local traditions and within Theravada and Mahayana Buddhism. For religious purposes Buddhists use solar and lunar calendars, the New Year being celebrated in April. Other festivals mark events in the life of the Buddha.

There is no supreme governing authority in Buddhism. In the United Kingdom communities representing all schools of Buddhism have developed and operate independently. The Buddhist Society was established in 1924; it runs courses and lectures, and publishes books about Buddhism. It represents no one school of Buddhism.

There are estimated to be at least 300 million Buddhists world-wide, with about 200 groups, an estimated 25,000 adherents and 15 temples or monasteries in the United Kingdom.

THE BUDDHIST SOCIETY, 58 Eccleston Square, London SWIV IPH. Tel: 071-834 5858. *General Secretary,* R. C. Maddox

HINDUISM

Hinduism has no historical founder but is known to have been highly developed in India by about 1200 BC. Its adherents originally called themselves Aryans; Muslim invaders first called the Aryans 'Hindus' (derived from the word 'Sindhu', the name of the river Indus) in the eighth century.

Hinduism's evolution has been complex and it embraces many different religious beliefs, mythologies and practices. Most Hindus hold that *satya* (truthfulness), *ahimsa* (non-violence), honesty, physical labour and tolerance of other faiths are essential for good living. They believe in one supreme spirit (*Brahman*), and in the transmigration of *atman* (the soul). Most Hindus accept the doctrine of *karma* (consequences of actions), the concept of *samsara* (successive lives) and the possibility of all atmans achieving *moksha* (liberation from samsara) through *jnana* (knowledge), *yoga* (meditation), *karma* (work or action) and *bhakti* (devotion).

Most Hindus offer worship to *murtis* (images or statues) representing different aspects of Brahman, and follow their *dharma* (religious and social duty) according to the traditions of their *varna* (social class), *ashrama* (stage in life), *jati* (caste) and *kula* (family).

Hinduism's sacred texts are divided into *shruti* ('heard' or divinely inspired), including the *Vedas*; or *smriti* ('remembered' tradition), including the *Ramayana*, the *Mahabharata*, the *Puranas* (ancient myths), and the sacred law books. Most Hindus recognize the authority of the *Vedas*, the oldest holy books, and accept the philosophical teachings of the *Upanishads*, the *Vedanta Sutras* and the *Bhagavad-Gita*.

Brahman is formless, limitless and all-pervading, and is represented in worship by murtis which may be male or female and in the form of a human, animal or bird. Brahma, Vishnu and Shiva are the most important gods worshipped by Hindus; their respective consorts are Saraswati, Lakshmi and Durga or Parvati, also known as Shakti. There are held to have been ten *avatars* (incarnations) of Vishnu, of whom the most important are Rama and Krishna. Other popular gods are Ganesha, Hanuman and Subrahmanyam. All gods are seen as aspects of the supreme God, not as competing deities.

Orthodox Hindus revere all gods and goddesses equally, but there are many sects, including the Hare-Krishna movement (ISKCon), the Arya Samaj, the Swami Narayan Hindu mission and the Satya Sai-Baba movement. Worship in the sects is concentrated on one deity to the exclusion of others. In some sects a human *guru* (spiritual teacher), usually the head of the organization, is revered more than the deity, while in other sects the guru is seen as the source of spiritual guidance.

Hinduism does not have a centrally-trained and ordained priesthood. The pronouncements of the *shankaracharyas* (heads of monasteries) of Shringeri, Puri, Dwarka and Badrinath are heeded by the orthodox but may be ignored by the various sects.

The commonest form of worship is a *puja*, in which offerings of red and yellow powders, rice grains, water, flowers, food, fruit, incense and light are made to the image of a deity. Puja may be done either in a home shrine or a *mandir* (temple). For details of the Hindu calendar, main festivals etc, *see* pages 84–5.

The largest communities of Hindus in Britain are in Leicester, London, Birmingham and Bradford, and developed as a result of immigration from India, east Africa and Sri Lanka. Many Hindus now are British by birth, with English as their first language; the main ethnic languages are Gujarati, Hindi, Punjabi, Tamil, Bengali and Marathi.

There are an estimated 650 million Hindus world-wide; there are about 350,000 adherents and over 150 temples in the UK.

ARYA PRATINIDHI SABHA (UK), 69A Argyle Road, London W13 OLY

BHARATIYA VIDYA BHAVAN, Old Church Building, 4A Castletown Road, London W14 9HQ. Tel: 071-381 3086

INTERNATIONAL SOCIETY FOR KRISHNA CONSCIOUSNESS (ISKCon), Bhakti Vedanta Manor, Radlett, Herts. Tel: 0923-857244

NATIONAL COUNCIL OF HINDU TEMPLES, 559 St Alban's Road, Watford, Herts. WD2 6JH

SWAMI NARAYAN HINDU MISSION, 54 Meadow Garth, London NW10 8HD. Tel: 081-965 2651

VISHVA HINDU PARISHAD (UK), 5 Rosemary Drive, Redbridge, Ilford, Essex IG4 5JD

ISLAM

Islam (which means 'peace arising from submission to the wisdom of Allah' in Arabic) is a monotheistic religion which originated in Arabia through the prophet Muhammad, who was born in Mecca in AD 570. Islam spread to Egypt, North Africa, Spain and the borders of China in the century following the prophet's death, and is now the predominant religion in Indonesia, the Near and Middle East, North and parts of West Africa, Pakistan, Bangladesh, Malaysia and some of the republics of the former Soviet Union. There are also large Muslim communities in many other countries.

For Muslims (adherents of Islam), God (*Allah*) is one and holds absolute power. His commands were revealed to mankind through the prophets, who include Abraham, Moses and Jesus, but his message was gradually corrupted until revealed finally and in perfect form to Muhammad by the angel *Jibril* (Gabriel) over a period of 23 years. This last, incorruptible message has been recorded in the *Qur'an* (Koran), which contains 114 divisions called *surahs*, each made up of *ayahs*, and is held to be the essence of all previous scriptures. The *Hadith* is the record of the prophet Muhammad's deeds and sayings (the *Sunnah*) as recounted by his immediate followers. A culture and a system of law and theology based on the Hadith and the Qur'an gradually developed to form a distinctive Islamic civilization. Islam makes no distinction between sacred and worldly affairs and provides rules for every aspect of human life.

The 'five pillars of Islam' are *shahada* (a declaration of faith in the oneness and supremacy of Allah); *salat* (formal prayer, to be performed five times a day facing the holy city of Mecca); *zakat* (alms-giving); *saum* (fasting during the month of Ramadan); and *hajj* (pilgrimage to Mecca); some Muslims would add *jihad* (striving for the cause of good and resistance to evil). Together with other prescriptions, the five pillars make up the *Shari'a* (sacred law) of Islam.

Two main groups, with distinct legal and theological characteristics, developed among Muslims. *Sunni* Muslims accept the legitimacy of Muhammad's first four *caliphs* (successors as head of the Muslim community) and of the authority of the Muslim community as a whole. About 90 per cent of Muslims are *Sunni* Muslims. *Shi'ites* recognize

only Muhammad's son-in-law Ali as his rightful successor and the *Imams* (descendants of Ali, not to be confused with *imams* (prayer leaders or religious teachers)) as the principal legitimate religious authority. The largest group within *Shi'ism* is *Twelver Shi'ism*, which has been the official religion of Iran since the 16th century, and other subsects include the *Ismailis* and the *Druze* (the latter being an offshoot of the Ismailis and differing considerably from the main body of Muslims).

There is no organized priesthood, but holy men such as *ulama, imams* and *ayatollahs* are accorded great respect. The *Sufis* are the mystics of Islam. Mosques are centres for worship and teaching and also for social and welfare activities. For details of the Muslim calendar and festivals, *see* page 86.

Islam was first known in western Europe in the eighth century AD when 800 years of Muslim rule began in Spain. Later, Islam spread to eastern Europe. More recently, Muslims came to Europe from Africa, the Middle East and Asia in the late 19th century. Both the Sunni and Shi'ah traditions are represented in Britain, but the majority of Muslims in Britain adhere to Sunni Islam.

The largest communities are in London, Liverpool, Manchester, Birmingham, Bradford, Cardiff, Edinburgh and Glasgow. There is no central organization, but the Islamic Cultural Centre, which is the London Central Mosque, and the Imams and Mosques Council are influential bodies; there are many other Muslim organizations in Britain.

There are at least 700 million Muslims world-wide. The estimated number of adherents in Britain is between one and two million, with over 350 mosques.

ISLAMIC CULTURAL CENTRE, 146 Park Road, London NW8 7RG. Tel: 071-724 3363. *Director,* Dr M. A. al-Ghamdi

IMAMS AND MOSQUES COUNCIL, 20–22 Creffield Road, London W5 3RP. Tel: 081-992 6636. *Director of the Council and Principal of the Muslim College,* Dr M. A. Z. Badawi

JUDAISM

Judaism is the oldest monotheistic faith. The primary authority of Judaism is the Hebrew Bible or *Tanakh*, which records how the descendants of Abraham were led by Moses out of their slavery in Egypt to Mount Sinai where God's law (*Torah*) was revealed to them as the chosen people. The *Talmud*, which consists of commentaries on the *Mishnah* (the first text of rabbinical Judaism), is also held to be authoritative, and may be divided into two main categories: the *halakah* (dealing with legal and ritual matters) and the *Aggadah* (dealing with theological and ethical matters not directly concerned with the regulation of conduct). The *Midrash* comprises rabbinic writings containing biblical interpretations in the spirit of the *Aggadah*. The *halakah* has become a source of division; Orthodox Jews regard Jewish law as derived from God and therefore unalterable; Reform and Liberal Jews seek to interpret it in the light of contemporary considerations; and Conservative Jews aim to maintain most of the traditional rituals but to allow changes in accordance with that tradition. Reconstructionist Judaism, a 20th-century movement, regards Judaism as a culture rather than a theological system and therefore accepts all forms of Jewish practice.

The family is the basic unit of Jewish ritual, with the synagogue playing an important role as the centre for public worship and religious study. A synagogue is led by a group of laymen who are elected to office; there are no priestly roles. The Rabbi is primarily a teacher and spiritual guide. The Sabbath is the central religious observance. For details of the Jewish calendar, fasts and festivals, see page 85. Most British Jews are descendants of either the *Ashkenazim* of central and eastern Europe or the *Sephardim* of Spain and Portugal.

The Chief Rabbi of the United Hebrew Congregations of the Commonwealth is appointed by a Chief Rabbinate Conference, and is the rabbinical authority of the Orthodox sector of the Ashkenazi Jewish community. His authority is not recognized by the Reform Synagogues of Great Britain (the largest progressive group), the Union of Liberal and Progressive Synagogues, the Union of Orthodox Hebrew Congregations, the Federation of Synagogues, the Sephardi community, or the Assembly of Masorti Synagogues. He is, however, generally recognized both outside the Jewish community and within it as the public religious representative of the totality of British Jewry.

The *Beth Din* (Court of Judgment) is the rabbinic court. The *Dayanim* (Assessors) adjudicate in disputes or on matters of Jewish law and tradition; they also oversee dietary law administration. The Chief Rabbi is President of the *Beth Din* of the United Synagogue.

The Board of Deputies of British Jews was established in 1760 and is the representative body of British Jewry. The basis of representation is mainly synagogal, but communal organizations are also represented. It watches over the interests of British Jewry and seeks to counter anti-Jewish discrimination.

There are over 12.5 million Jews world-wide; in Great Britain and Ireland there are an estimated 300,000 adherents and about 350 synagogues. Of these, 185 congregations and about 150 rabbis and ministers are under the jurisdiction of the Chief Rabbi. A further 99 orthodox congregations have a more independent status, and 72 congregations do not recognize the authority of the Chief Rabbi.

Chief Rabbi, Dr Jonathan Sacks
CHIEF RABBINATE, Adler House, Tavistock Square, London WC1H 9HN. Tel: 071-387 1066. *Executive Director*, J. Kestenbaum
BETH DIN (COURT OF THE CHIEF RABBI), Adler House, Tavistock Square, London WC1H 0EP. Tel: 071-387 5772. *Registrar*, J. Phillips; *Dayanim*, Rabbi C. Ehrentreu; Rabbi I. Binstock; Rabbi C. D. Kaplin; Rabbi I. D. Berger
UNITED SYNAGOGUE HEAD OFFICE, Woburn House, Tavistock Square, London WC1H 0EZ. Tel: 071-387 4300. *Chief Executive*, J. M. Lew
REFORM SYNAGOGUES OF GREAT BRITAIN, The Sternberg Centre, Manor House, 80 East End Road, London N3 2SY. Tel: 081-349 4731. *Executive Director*, R. M. Goldman
UNION OF LIBERAL AND PROGRESSIVE SYNAGOGUES (JEWISH RELIGIOUS UNION), 109 Whitfield Street, London W1P 5RP. Tel: 071-580 1663. *Director*, Mrs R. Rosenberg
UNION OF ORTHODOX HEBREW CONGREGATIONS, 40 Queen Elizabeth's Walk, London N16 0HH. Tel: 081-802 6226. *Executive Director*, B. Steinhart
FEDERATION OF SYNAGOGUES, 65 Watford Way, London NW4 3AQ. Tel: 081-202 2263. *Administrator*, G. Kushner
SPANISH AND PORTUGUESE JEWS' CONGREGATION, 2 Ashworth Road, London W9 1JY. Tel: 071-289 2573. *Chief Executive*, Mrs J. Velleman
ASSEMBLY OF MASORTI SYNAGOGUES, 766 Finchley Road, London NW11 7TH. Tel: 081-201 8772. *Administrator*, Mrs G. Miller

BOARD OF DEPUTIES OF BRITISH JEWS, Woburn House, Tavistock Square, London WC1H 0EZ. Tel: 071-387 3952. *President*, His Hon. I. Finestein, QC; *Chief Executive*, N. A. Nagler

SIKHISM

The Sikh religion dates from the birth of Guru Nanak in the Punjab in 1469. The word 'guru' means teacher, but in Sikh tradition it has come to represent the divine presence of God giving inner spiritual guidance. Nanak's role as the human vessel of the divine guru was passed on to nine successors, the last of whom (Guru Gobind Singh) died in 1708. The immortal guru is now held to reside in the sacred scripture, *Guru Granth Sahib*, and so to be present in all Sikh gatherings.

Guru Nanak taught that there is one God and that different religions are like different roads leading to the same destination. He condemned religious conflict, ritualism and caste prejudices. The fifth Guru, Guru Arjan, compiled the Sikh Holy Book, a collection of hymns (*gurbani*) known as the *Adi Granth*. It contains the writings of the first five Gurus and selected writings of Hindu and Muslim saints whose views are in accord with the Guru's teachings. Guru Arjan also built the Golden Temple at Amritsar, the centre of Sikhism. The tenth Guru, Guru Gobind Singh, passed on the guruship to the sacred scripture, Guru Granth Sahib. He also founded the *Khalsa*, an order intended to fight against tyranny and injustice. Male initiates to the order added 'Singh' to their given names and women added 'Kaur'. Guru Gobind Singh also made five symbols obligatory: *kaccha* (a special undergarment), *kara* (a steel bangle), *kirpan* (a small sword), *kesh* (long unshorn hair, and consequently the wearing of a turban), and *kangha* (a comb). These practices are still compulsory for those Sikhs who are initiated into the *Khalsa* (the *Amritdharis*). Those who do not seek initiation are known as *Sahajdharis*.

There are no professional priests in Sikhism; anyone with a reasonable proficiency in the Punjabi language can conduct a service. Worship can be offered individually or communally, and in a private house or a *gurdwara* (temple). Sikhs are forbidden to eat meat prepared by ritual slaughter; they are also asked to abstain from smoking, alcohol and other intoxicants. For details of the Sikh calendar and main celebrations, see page 86.

Sikhs first came to Britain in the 1950s, mainly for economic and political reasons. The largest Sikh communities are in London, Bradford, Leeds, Huddersfield, Birmingham, Nottingham, Coventry and Wolverhampton. Every gurdwara manages its own affairs and there is no central body in the UK. The Sikh Missionary Society UK works for the advancement of Sikhism and provides an information service.

There are about 12.5 million Sikhs world-wide and an estimated 400,000 adherents and 170 gurdwaras in Great Britain.

SIKH MISSIONARY SOCIETY UK, 10 Featherstone Road, Southall, Middx. UB2 5AA. Tel: 081-574 1902. *Hon. General Secretary*, H. S. Kular

Education

For addresses of national education departments, *see* Government Departments and Public Offices. For other addresses, *see* Education Directory

Responsibility for education in the United Kingdom is largely decentralized. Overall responsibility for all aspects of education in England lies with the Secretary of State for Education; in Wales with the Secretary of State for Wales; in Scotland with the Secretary of State for Scotland acting through the Scottish Office Education Department; and in Northern Ireland with the Secretary of State for Northern Ireland.

The main concerns of the education departments (the Department for Education (DFE), the Welsh Office, the Scottish Office Education Department (SOED), and the Department of Education for Northern Ireland (DENI)) are the formulation of national policies for education, and the maintenance of consistency in educational standards. They are responsible for the broad allocation of resources for education, for the rate and distribution of educational building and for the supply, training and superannuation of teachers. Hitherto, none of the education departments have run any schools or colleges directly, nor employed any teachers. However, under the provisions of the Education Reform Act 1988 and the Self-Governing Schools etc. (Scotland) Act 1989, the Department for Education in England until March 1994, the Welsh office and the Scottish Office Education Department fund individual schools which have opted out of local education authority control and applied for direct funding from the Secretaries of State. In addition, the Department for Education, in association with sponsors from industry, funds the new City Technology Colleges (CTCs) and the City Colleges for the Technology of the Arts. Technology Academies are proposed on a similar basis in Scotland.

Schools in Northern Ireland providing integrated education are able to apply for grant-maintained status from the Department of Education for Northern Ireland.

EXPENDITURE

The Department for Education, the Welsh Office, the Scottish Office and the Northern Ireland Office act within a framework of estimates approved by Parliament.

In real terms expenditure on education by central government departments was as follows (£ million):

	1992–3 estimated outturn	1993–4 planned
DFE	7,200	9,523
Welsh Office	151.5	403.6
SOED	678	1,182
DENI	1,199	1,234

The discontinuity between the expenditure profiles of the DFE, Welsh Office and SOED for the years 1992–3 and 1993–4 is due to the transfer of resources to the Higher Education Funding Councils and the Further Education Funding Councils.

In the United Kingdom in 1990-1, central government provisional expenditure on education was apportioned as follows (£million):

Schools	15,579
Further and higher education	6,833
Other education and related expenditure	2,458

Most of this expenditure is incurred by local authorities, which make their own expenditure decisions according to their local situations and needs and which, until April 1993, were also responsible for funding most further education courses. The bulk of direct expenditure by the DFE, the Welsh Office and SOED is directed towards supporting higher education in universities and colleges through the three Higher Education Funding Councils and further education and sixth form colleges through the Further Education Funding Councils in England and Wales and directly from central government in Scotland. In addition, the DFE funds grant-maintained schools (from April 1994 through the Funding Agency for Schools (FAS)) and CTCs in the schools sector.

The Welsh Office also funds grants for higher and further education, grant-maintained schools, educational services and research and supports bilingual education and the Welsh language.

In Scotland, as in England and Wales, the bulk of expenditure on education is at a local level by the regional and islands councils. In addition to those outlined above, the main elements of central government expenditure are grant-aided special schools, self-governing schools, student awards, curriculum development, special educational needs and community education.

The Department of Education for Northern Ireland finances higher education, teacher education, teacher salaries and superannuation, student awards, grant-maintained integrated schools, and voluntary grammar schools. Remaining expenditure is by education and library boards at local level.

Current net expenditure on education by local education authorities in England and Wales, regional and islands councils in Scotland, and education and library boards in Northern Ireland is as follows (£million):

	1992–3 estimated outturn	1993–4 planned
England	22,576	16,854
Wales	1,336.5	1,234.4
Scotland	2,583	2,425
Northern Ireland	856	880

LOCAL EDUCATION ADMINISTRATION

The education service at present is a national service in which the provision of most school education is locally administered; its administration is still largely decentralized.

ENGLAND AND WALES – In England and Wales the education service is administered by local education authorities (LEAs), which carry the day-to-day responsibility for providing most state primary and secondary education in their areas, although the planning and supply of school places is to be shared with the newly established Funding Agency for Schools (FAS) as the number of pupils in grant-maintained schools grows. They also share with the FEFCs the duty to provide adult education to meet the needs of their areas.

Each local education authority was formerly required by statute to appoint an education committee, or committees, authorized to exercise on its behalf any of the authority's functions with respect to education, except the power to borrow money, but the passing of the Education Act 1993 removed this requirement and LEAs are now free to organize themselves as they think fit.

The LEAs own and maintain schools and colleges, build new ones and provide equipment. Most of the public money spent on education is disbursed by the local authorities. LEAs are financed largely from the council tax and Aggregate External Finance (AEF) from the Department of the Environment in England and the Welsh Office in Wales.

The powers of local education authorities as regards the control of schools have been modified in recent years. The Education (No. 2) Act 1986 legislated for equal numbers of parents and local authority representatives as governors in most maintained schools. The process was continued by the Education Reform Act 1988, which delegated control of their budgets directly to all schools by April 1994. It also provided for schools to opt out of local authority control and to be funded by central government, from April 1994 through the Funding Agency for Schools in England. The Schools Funding Council for Wales will take over from the Welsh Office when the number of grant-maintained schools warrants the change. The Education Act 1993 has facilitated this process and also enabled primary schools to apply for grant-maintained status as a group as well as individually. It also provided for an Education Association to be set up to take over the management of failing schools where both the LEA and the governing body have not brought about the improvements identified as necessary.

SCOTLAND – The duty of providing education locally in Scotland rests with the nine regional and three islands councils. They are responsible for the construction of buildings, the employment of teachers and other staff, and the provision of equipment and materials, but management is to be devolved to the schools themselves by April 1996. Their responsibility for the curricula taught in schools is shared with headteachers under the guidance of the Secretary of State for Scotland and the Scottish Consultative Council on the Curriculum.

The powers of local authorities over educational institutions under their control have been reduced also in Scotland. Under the School Boards (Scotland) Act 1988, education authorities are required to establish school boards consisting of parents and teachers as well as co-opted members, responsible among other things for the appointment of staff. The Self-Governing Schools etc. (Scotland) Act 1989 provides for schools to withdraw from local authority control and become self-governing; for the institution of Technology Academies directly funded by central government; and for the composition of further education college councils on which at least half the members are employers, and for the delegation of substantial functions to these new councils.

NORTHERN IRELAND – Education is administered locally in Northern Ireland by five education and library boards, although a review of educational administration is taking place. All grant-aided schools include elected parents and teachers on their boards of governors. Provision has been made for schools wishing to provide integrated education to have grant-maintained integrated status from the outset. All secondary schools and colleges of further education, and most primary schools, have full responsibility for their own budgets, including staffing costs. Full delegation was phased in for the remaining primary schools from April 1993.

The Council for Catholic Maintained Schools forms an upper tier of management for Catholic schools and provides advice on matters relating to management and administration.

THE INSPECTORATE

Under the Education (Schools) Act 1992, the Office for Standards in Education (OFSTED), headed by HM Chief Inspector of Schools in England (HMCI), was created separately from the DFE. Its counterpart in Wales is the Office of HM Chief Inspector of Schools in Wales (OHMCISW). OFSTED's remit is to inspect, report on and improve standards of achievement and quality of education through regular independent inspection, public reporting and informed advice. OFSTED's major and most urgent task is to set up the new system of inspection by independent registered inspectors. The new system provides a full inspection for all state schools every four years, beginning in September 1993 for secondary schools and one year later for primary and special schools. OFSTED will select the teams of independent inspectors following bids for the contracts. A summary of the inspection report must be sent to parents of each pupil, followed by a copy of the governors' action plan thereon. HM Inspectorate in Scotland carries out the inspection of schools in that country, and in addition requires schools to produce a document setting out their educational targets for the two years ahead and a report on progress over the previous two years. The inspection of further and higher education is the responsibility of inspectors appointed to the Further and Higher Education Funding Councils. Inspection is carried out in Northern Ireland by the Education and Training Inspectorate of the Department of Education which also performs an advisory function to the Secretary of State for Northern Ireland.

There were, in 1992–3, 300 HMIs in England, 58 in Wales, 108 in Scotland and 61 members of the Inspectorate in Northern Ireland.

Schools and Pupils

Schooling is compulsory in the United Kingdom for all children between five and 16 years. Some provision is made for children under five and many pupils remain at school after the minimum leaving age. No fees are charged in any publicly maintained school in England, Wales and Scotland. In Northern Ireland, fees are paid by pupils in preparatory departments of grammar schools, but pupils admitted to the secondary departments of grammar schools do not pay fees.

In the United Kingdom, parents have a right to express a preference for a particular school and have a right to appeal if dissatisfied. Parental choice has been increased by the introduction of a policy known as more open enrolment whereby schools are required to admit children up to the limit of their capacity if there is a demand for places, and to publish their criteria for selection if they are over-subscribed, in which case parents have a right of appeal.

Schools are now required to make available information about themselves, their public examination and key stage 2 national curriculum test results, truancy rates, and destination of leavers. Corporal punishment is no longer legal in publicly maintained schools in the United Kingdom.

FALL AND RISE IN NUMBERS

In primary education, and increasingly in secondary education, pupil numbers in the United Kingdom have declined. In nursery and primary schools pupil numbers reached their lowest figure of 4.5 million in 1990. Numbers are expected to increase gradually year by year until by 2000 they reach about 5.5 million. In secondary schools pupil numbers rose to 4.6 million in 1981. They stood at 3.5 million in 1991 and are projected to rise to 4 million in 2000.

ENGLAND AND WALES

There are two main categories of school in England and Wales: those maintained by local education authorities, which charge no fees; and independent schools, which charge fees (*see* page 447). To these categories may be added two more as a result of the Education Reform Act 1988, consisting of grant-maintained schools funded directly by the Secretary of State in England until March 1994, thereafter through the Funding Agency for Schools (FAS), and by the Welsh office in Wales. These comprise primary and secondary schools which, although still providing free education, have applied to opt out of local education authority control in favour of grant-maintained status; and City Technology Colleges (*see* below). There are 32,119 schools in the maintained sector and 2,508 independent schools.

Maintained schools are of two types: (i) county schools (16,958 in 1992) which are owned by LEAs and wholly funded by them. They are non-denominational and provide primary and secondary education; (ii) voluntary schools (7,538 in 1992) which also provide primary and secondary education. Although the buildings are in many cases provided by the voluntary bodies (mainly religious denominations) they are financially maintained by an LEA.

Voluntary schools are of three kinds: controlled (3,132), aided (4,406) and special agreement (67). In controlled schools the LEA bears all costs. In aided schools the building is usually provided by the voluntary body. The managers or governors are responsible for repairs to the outside of the school building and for improvements and alterations to it, though the Department for Education may reimburse part of approved capital expenditure, while the LEA pays for internal maintenance and other running costs. Special agreement schools are those where the LEA may, by special agreement, pay between one-half and three-quarters of the cost of building a new, or extending an existing, voluntary school, almost always a secondary school. There are no special agreement schools in Wales. In voluntary schools the majority of the managers or governors are appointed by the voluntary body and at least one by the LEA. The managers or governors control the appointment of teachers. Expenditure is normally apportioned between the authority and the voluntary body.

All publicly maintained schools have a governing body usually made up of a number of parent representatives, governors appointed by the LEA if the school is LEA maintained, the headteacher (unless he or she chooses otherwise), and serving teachers. The passing of the Education Act 1993 allows schools to appoint up to four sponsor governors from business who will be expected to provide financial and managerial assistance. Parental involvement in the running of schools has increased considerably in recent years, and parents have also been given the power to decide by ballot whether their child's school should opt out of local authority control and become self-governing (grant-maintained). Governors are responsible for the overall policies of schools and their academic aims and objectives; they also now control matters of school discipline and the appointment and dismissal of staff. Under the Education (Schools) Act 1992, governing bodies select inspectors for their schools, are responsible for action as a result of inspection reports and are required to make these reports and their action plans thereon available to parents. The Education Reform Act 1988 delegated control of the administration of the major part of school budgets, including staffing costs, from LEAs directly to schools under an initiative known as Local Management of Schools (LMS).

Technology schools and Technology Colleges – The technology schools initiative, launched in December 1991, provides capital and project funding for a network of schools committed to offering innovative technology teaching of a vocational nature. In 1993–4 £23 million of capital funding has been made available to 122 schools which submitted successful bids. A similar initiative was launched for Wales in May 1993 for which funding of £2.24 million has been earmarked for

the financial years 1993–4 and 1994–5. In autumn 1993 the Government will publish a detailed prospectus for schools wishing to become Technology Colleges which will specialize in the teaching of technology, mathematics and science.

Grant-maintained (GM) schools (self-governing state schools) – All secondary and primary schools are eligible to apply for grant-maintained status, subject to a ballot of parents. GM schools are maintained directly by the Secretary of State and the Welsh office, not the LEA, and are wholly run by their own governing body. The Funding Agency for Schools (FAS) is being set up from April 1944 to take over the payment of grants to grant-maintained schools in England. The Schools Funding Council for Wales will be instituted when the number of GM schools justifies the change in funding arrangements. By April 1994 there are projected to be at least 1,000 GM schools. Of the 493 schools operating in June 1993, 388 were secondary schools, and 105 were primary schools.

City Technology Colleges (CTCs) and *City Colleges for the Technology of the Arts (CCTAs)* are state-aided but independent of LEAs. Their aim is to widen the choice of secondary education in disadvantaged urban areas and to teach a broad curriculum with an emphasis on science, technology, business understanding and arts technologies. Capital costs are shared by government and sponsors from industry and commerce, and running costs are covered by a per capita grant from the DFE in line with comparable costs in an LEA maintained school.

The first city technology college opened in September 1988 in Solihull. By September 1993 there were fifteen. The first CCTA, known as Britschool, opened in Croydon in September 1991.

SCOTLAND

Schools in Scotland fall into three main categories: education authority schools (3,796) (known as public schools), which are managed by the regional and islands councils and financed jointly by the councils and central government; grant-aided schools (8), conducted by voluntary managers who receive grants direct from the Scottish Office Education Department; and independent schools (123), which receive no direct grant and charge fees, but are subject to inspection and registration. An additional category is created under the provisions of the Self-Governing Schools etc. (Scotland) Act 1989, of schools opting to be managed entirely by a board of management consisting of the headmaster, parent and staff representatives and co-opted members. The change of status will require a ballot of parents and the publication of proposals by the board, and the achievement of self-government is subject to a final decision by the Secretary of State. These schools will remain in the public sector and will be funded by direct government grant set to match the resources the school would have received under education authority management. None has yet been established.

Under the School Boards (Scotland) Act 1988, education authorities are required to establish school boards to participate in the administration and management of schools. These boards consist of elected parents and staff members as well as co-opted members.

Technology Academies (TAs) – The Self-Governing Schools etc. (Scotland) Act 1989 provides for setting up technology academies in areas of urban deprivation. These secondary schools are intended to be so placed as to draw on a wide catchment, and will offer a broad curriculum with an emphasis on science and technology. They are to be founded and managed in partnership with industrial sponsors, with central government meeting the running costs by grant-aid thereafter. None has yet been set up.

NORTHERN IRELAND

There are three main categories of grant-aided school in Northern Ireland: controlled schools (706), which are controlled by the education and library boards with all costs paid from public funds; voluntary maintained schools (584), mainly under Roman Catholic management, which receive grants towards capital costs and running costs in whole or in part; and voluntary grammar schools (52), which may be under Roman Catholic or non-denominational management and receive grants from the Department of Education for Northern Ireland. All grant-aided schools include elected parents and teachers on their boards of governors, whose responsibilities also include financial management under the Local Management of Schools (LMS) initiative. Legislation is being brought forward under which voluntary maintained and voluntary grammar schools will be able to apply for designation as a new category of voluntary school, which will be eligible for 100 per cent grant. Such schools will be managed by a board of governors on which no single interest group will have a majority of nominees. There are also 17 independent schools in Northern Ireland.

The majority of children in Northern Ireland are educated in schools which in practice are segregated on religious lines. The Education Reform (Northern Ireland) Order 1989, however, makes provision for parents to opt for integrated education more easily. These provisions include arrangements to fund new integrated schools from the outset and procedures for balloting parents in existing segregated schools to determine whether they want instead to have integrated schools. By September 1993, 21 integrated schools had been established, four of them secondary.

THE STATE SYSTEM

NURSERY EDUCATION – Nursery education is for children from two to five years and is not compulsory. In the United Kingdom it takes place in nursery schools or nursery classes in primary schools. In 1990-1, 799,100 pupils under five years of age were receiving education in maintained nursery and primary schools, an increase of 30,000 on the previous year. Of the total, 84,400 were in nursery schools, 660,500 in primary schools, and 47,800 in non-maintained nursery schools. Expressed as a percentage of the population aged three and four years, the 799,100 represented 53 per cent, compared to 51 per cent in the previous year.

Many children also attend pre-school playgroups organized by parents and voluntary bodies such as the Pre-School Playgroups Association.

PRIMARY EDUCATION – Primary education begins at five years and is almost always co-educational. In England, Wales and Northern Ireland the transfer to secondary school is generally made at 11 years. In Scotland, the primary school course lasts for seven years and pupils transfer to secondary courses at about the age of 12.

Primary schools consist mainly of infants' schools for children aged five to seven, junior schools for those aged seven to 11, and combined junior and infant schools for both age groups. First schools in some parts of England cater for ages five to ten as the first stage of a three-tier system: first, middle and secondary. Many primary schools provide nursery classes for children under five (see above).

The number of primary schools in the United Kingdom in 1990-1 was 24,135, which was 133 fewer than in 1989-90, with 4,989,000 full- and part-time pupils, of which 660,500 were under five. Between 1990 and 2000 primary school pupil numbers are projected to rise by about 10 per cent.

Pupil-teacher ratios in maintained primary schools in the United Kingdom are:

	1989–90	1990–1
England	21.8	22.0
Wales	22.3	22.3
Scotland	19.7	19.5
Northern Ireland	23.2	22.9
UK	21.7	21.8

The average size of classes 'as taught' fell to 23.8 in 1991 but rose to 25.5 in 1992.

MIDDLE SCHOOLS – Middle schools (which take children from first schools), mostly in England, cover varying age ranges between eight and 14 and usually lead on to comprehensive upper schools.

SECONDARY EDUCATION – Secondary schools are for children aged 11 to 16 and for those who choose to stay on to 18. At 16, many students prefer to move on to tertiary or sixth form colleges (see page 451). Most secondary schools in England, Wales and Scotland are co-educational. The largest secondary schools have over 2,000 pupils but only 2.8 per cent of the schools take over 1,000 pupils.

In England and Wales the main types of secondary schools are: comprehensive schools (85.7 per cent of pupils in England, 99.2 in Wales), whose admission arrangements are without reference to ability or aptitude; middle deemed secondary schools for children aged variously between eight and 14 years who then move on to senior comprehensive schools at 12, 13 or 14 (6.4 per cent of pupils in England only); secondary modern schools (3.3 per cent of pupils in England only) providing a general education with a practical bias; secondary grammar schools (3.6 per cent of pupils in England only) with selective intake providing an academic course from 11 to 16–18 years; and technical schools (0.1 per cent in England only), providing an integrated academic and technical education.

In January 1991 there were in England and Wales 3,154,000 pupils in maintained secondary schools, including 12.2 per cent in England and 12.1 per cent in Wales who were 16 or over. After falling by 16 per cent between 1987 and 1991, numbers are projected to rise 10.3 per cent by 2000.

Pupil-teacher ratios improved steadily from 15.7 in 1987 to 15.3 in 1990 in England and Wales, then rose to 15.7 again in 1992. The average class size in England was 21.2 in 1992. In Wales the average class size in 1992 was 21.5.

In Scotland all pupils in education authority secondary schools attend schools with a comprehensive intake. Most of these schools provide a full range of courses appropriate to all levels of ability from first to sixth year. In 1991-2 there were 296,446 pupils in education authority schools, of whom 21.9 per cent were 16 or over. Numbers are projected to increase to 326,000 in 2000. Pupil-teacher ratios worsened from 12.4 in 1991 to 12.6 in 1992. The average class size in 1992 was 18.9.

In most areas of Northern Ireland there is a selective system of secondary education with pupils transferring either to grammar schools or secondary schools at 11–12 years of age. Parents can choose the school they would like their children to attend and all those who apply must be admitted if they meet the criteria. If a school is over-subscribed beyond its statutory admissions number, selection is on the basis of published criteria, which, for most grammar schools, place emphasis on performance in the transfer procedure tests which are centrally administered by the Department for Education. When parents consider that a school has not applied its criteria fairly they have access to independent appeals tribunals. Grammar schools provide an academic type of secondary education with A-levels at the end of the seventh year, while secondary non-grammar schools follow a curriculum suited to a wider range of aptitudes and abilities.

In 1992 there were 143,300 pupils in public sector secondary schools, of whom 87,525 (61.1 per cent) attended non-grammar secondary and 55,770 (38.9 per cent) attended grammar schools. Of all pupils 35.4 per cent were 16 or over. Pupil-teacher ratios in Northern Ireland were 15.3 in 1992.

SPECIAL EDUCATION – Special education is provided for children with special educational needs, usually because they have a disability which either prevents or hinders them from making use of educational facilities of a kind generally provided for children of their age in schools within the area of the local authority concerned. However, wherever possible, such children are now educated in ordinary schools, taking the parents' wishes into account and schools are required to publish their policy for pupils with special educational needs. Maintained special schools are run by education authorities which pay all the costs of maintenance, and by April 1994 Local Management of Schools (LMS) will be extended to those that are able and wish to manage their own budgets. Non-maintained special schools are run by voluntary bodies; they may receive some grant from central government for capital expenditure and for equipment, but their current expenditure is met primarily from the fees charged to the education authorities for pupils placed in the schools. Some independent schools provide education wholly or mainly for children with special educational needs and are required to meet similar standards to those for maintained and non-maintained special schools. The national curriculum also applies to children with a statement of special needs, but there is provision for them to be exempt from it, or for it to be modified to suit their capabilities. The Education Act 1993 gives parents greater choice of schools and extends their right of appeal by establishing the Special Educational Needs (SEN) Tribunal.

In January 1991 in the United Kingdom there was a total of 111,700 full-time pupils in special schools (of whom 900 were in hospital schools in England, Wales and Northern Ireland). Of the total, 94,500 were in England, 3,600 in Wales, 8,700 in Scotland and 4,000 in Northern Ireland. Numbers have decreased since 1975–6 as education authorities in England, Wales and Northern Ireland must now ensure that children with special needs are educated as far as possible in ordinary schools with support teaching.

In Scotland, school placing is a matter of agreement between education authorities and parents. Parents have the right to say which school they want their child to attend, and a right of appeal where their wishes are not being met. Whenever possible, children with special needs are integrated into ordinary schools. However, for those who require a different environment or specialized facilities, there are special schools, both grant-aided by central government and independent, and special classes within ordinary schools. The Self-Governing Schools etc. (Scotland) Act 1989 obliges education authorities to respond to reasonable requests for independent special schools, and provides for them to send children with special needs to schools outside Scotland if appropriate provision is not available within the country. A new centre has been opened which practices conductive education methods for children with motor impairments.

ALTERNATIVE PROVISION

There is no legal obligation on parents in the United Kingdom to educate their children at school provided that the local education authority is satisfied that the child is receiving full-time education suited to its age, abilities and aptitudes. The education authority need not be informed that a child is being educated at home unless the child is already registered at a state school. In this case the parents must arrange for the child's name to be removed from the school's register (by writing to the headteacher) before education at home can begin. Failure to de-register a child leaves the parents liable to prosecution for condoning non-attendance.

In most cases an initial visit is made by an education adviser or education welfare officer, and sometimes subsequent inspections are made, but practice varies according to the individual education authority. There is no requirement for parents educating their children at home to be in possession of a teaching qualification.

Further advice on educating children other than at school can be obtained from Education Otherwise (*see* page 460).

INDEPENDENT SCHOOLS

Independent schools receive no grants from public funds. They charge fees, and are owned and managed under special trusts, with profits being used for the benefit of the schools concerned. There is a wide variety of provision, from kindergartens to large day and boarding schools, and from experimental schools to traditional institutions. A number of independent schools have been instituted by religious and ethnic minorities.

All independent schools in the United Kingdom are open to inspection by approved inspectors (*see* page 444) and must register with the appropriate government education department. The education departments lay down certain minimum standards and can make schools remedy any unacceptable features of their building or instruction and exclude any unsuitable teacher or proprietor. Most independent schools offer a similar range of courses to state schools and enter pupils for the same public examinations. Introduction of the national curriculum and the associated education targets and assessment procedures is not obligatory in the independent sector.

The term public schools is often applied to those independent schools in membership of the Headmasters' Conference, the Governing Bodies Association or the Governing Bodies of Girls' Schools Association. Most public schools are single-sex (about half of them for girls) but there are some mixed schools and an increasing number of schools have mixed sixth forms.

Preparatory schools are so-called because they prepare children for the Common Entrance Examination to senior independent schools. Most cater for boys from about seven to 13 years, some are for girls, and an increasing number are co-educational. The Common Entrance Examination is set by the Common Entrance Examination Board, but marked by the independent school to which the pupil intends to go. It is taken at 13 by boys, and from 11 to 13 by girls.

In 1992 there were in England 2,256 independent schools with 566,700 full-time pupils and a pupil-teacher ratio of 10.6.

In Wales in 1991–2 there were 68 independent schools, with 11,913 pupils and a pupil-teacher ratio of 9.7.

In Scotland in 1991–2 there were 123 registered independent schools with 33,500 pupils and a pupil-teacher ratio of 11.4. Most independent schools in Scotland follow the English examination system, i.e. GCSE followed by A-levels, although some take the Scottish Education Certificate at Ordinary/Standard grade followed by Highers.

There are 17 independent schools in Northern Ireland with 1,023 pupils and a pupil-teacher ratio of 11.9.

ASSISTED PLACES SCHEME

The Assisted Places Scheme enables children to attend independent secondary schools which their parents could not otherwise afford. The scheme provides help with tuition fees and other expenses, except boarding costs, on a sliding scale depending on the family's income. The take-up rate for places available at age 11 to 13 at the 303 participating schools in England and Wales is around 99 per cent, and the proportion of pupils receiving full fee remission is about 36 per cent. Over 35,000 places were offered in England and Wales in the academic year 1992–3. The 58 participating schools in Scotland admitted about 3,000 pupils on the scheme in 1992–3, which, unlike that in England and Wales, is cash-limited. The proportion of pupils receiving full fee remission is expected to be about 50 per cent.

The scheme is administered and funded in England by the Department for Education, in Wales by the Welsh Office, and in Scotland by the Scottish Office Education Department. The scheme does not operate in Northern Ireland as the independent sector admits non-fee-paying pupils. There is, however, a similar scheme known as the Talented Children's Scheme to help pupils gifted in music and dance.

Further information can be obtained from the Independent Schools Information Service (see page 460).

THE CURRICULUM

ENGLAND AND WALES

The Education Reform Act 1988 legislated for the progressive introduction of a national curriculum in primary and secondary schools from autumn 1989. During the period of compulsory schooling for children aged five to 16 the curriculum includes mathematics, English and science as core subjects and history, geography, technology, music, art, physical education and (for pupils in secondary schools) a modern foreign language as foundation subjects. For the core and foundation subjects attainment targets have been identified and standard assessment tests (known as SATS) are being instituted at the end of each key stage, at the ages of 7, 11, 14 and 16. It was planned to use the SATS results in compiling publicly available comparative tables of schools, but this has met with resistance from schools and is being reconsidered. The first assessment tests took place in 1991 for seven year-olds. Pilot tests were carried out in 1992 for 14 year-olds and are planned in 1994 for 11 year-olds. Teachers have, however, expressed dissatisfaction with the tests since their inception. In response to their concerns the Government's interim review of the manageability of the national curriculum and the testing system has announced that there will be fewer and shorter tests and that the compulsory curriculum will be reduced. A final report is due in December 1993. The 1993 tests were boycotted by many schools, some of which substituted their own examinations, while others carried out the tests but did not report the results. At 16 the GCSE will be the main form of assessment. It is intended that pupils with special educational needs should have access to as much of the national curriculum as possible. Religious education is required to be available in schools, with the curriculum devised locally, but parents have the right to remove their children if they wish.

In Wales in 1991–2 the Welsh language was in use as the main or secondary medium of instruction in 33.3 per cent of primary and 31.4 per cent of secondary schools. Following the introduction of the national curriculum it will constitute a core subject in Welsh-speaking schools and a foundation subject in the others, although there is provision for exemptions to be made.

In England the School Curriculum and Assessment Authority (SCAA), funded by the Department for Education, is responsible for the promotion and support of curriculum development, in addition to advising the Secretary of State on the national curriculum. The Authority replaced the National Curriculum Council and the School Examinations and Assessment Council in October 1993. In Wales its functions are performed by the Curriculum Council for Wales, funded by the Welsh Office, which will undertake additional functions and be renamed the Curriculum and Assessment Authority for Wales from April 1994.

SCOTLAND

The content and management of the curriculum in Scotland is the responsibility of education authorities and individual headteachers. Advice and guidance is provided by the Scottish Office Education Department and the Scottish Consultative Council on the Curriculum. Scotland effectively has a national curriculum for 14–16 year-olds, who are required to study English, mathematics and a science subject plus five other subjects. These form the core area, supplemented by other activities forming the elective area. There is a recommended percentage of class time to be devoted to each area over the two years. Provision is made for teaching in Gaelic in Gaelic-speaking areas.

The Scottish Consultative Council on the Curriculum, which is responsible for development and advisory work on the curriculum in Scotland, has undertaken a major review of the balance of the primary curriculum, and produced new guidelines for each of the subject areas for the age group five to 14. There are new guidelines on assessment across the whole curriculum, and standardized tests are being phased in for English language and mathematics at five stages for this age group which are taken when teachers think the pupils are ready. For 16–18 year-olds, there is available a modular system of vocational courses in addition to academic courses.

NORTHERN IRELAND

Major programmes of curriculum review and development are in progress in primary and secondary schools. A curriculum common to all schools is being introduced over a four-year period to 1994–5, with six broad areas of study within which ten subjects will be compulsory; religious education will also be a compulsory part of the curriculum. The Irish language will be a compulsory subject in Irish-medium primary schools and can be chosen as the compulsory foreign language in secondary schools. Arrangements for the assessment of pupils, broadly in line with those in England and Wales, are proposed at the ages of eight, 11, 14 and 16. Voluntary pilot assessments were carried out by June 1993 for 11 and 14 year-olds and in May 1994 for 8 year-olds. In Northern Ireland, as in England and Wales, teachers are dissatisfied with the assessment arrangements.

The Northern Ireland Curriculum Council (NICC) advises the Government on all matters concerning the curriculum for grant-aided schools in Northern Ireland. From April 1994 it will amalgamate with the Northern Ireland Schools Examination and Assessment Council (NISEAC) to form the Northern Ireland Council for the Curriculum, Assessment and Examinations (NICCAE).

RECORDS OF ACHIEVEMENT

The National Records of Achievement sets down the range of a school-leaver's achievements and activities both inside and outside the classroom, including those not tested by examination. It is issued to all those leaving school in England

and Wales and will be introduced in Scotland. Under the Education (Schools) Act 1992, parents in England and Wales must receive a written yearly progress report on all aspects of their children's achievements. There is a similar commitment for Northern Ireland. In Scotland the school report card has been reformed to give parents more information on their children's progress; the new format was introduced in schools in September 1993.

TECHNICAL AND VOCATIONAL EDUCATION INITIATIVE
The Technical and Vocational Education Initiative (TVEI), administered and funded by the Department of Employment in England, the Welsh Office in Wales and the Scottish Office Industry Department in Scotland, operates across the curriculum within a framework of general education. It aims to make the secondary curriculum more relevant to adult life and work. Following pilot projects, it is now a national scheme with newly established criteria which complement and are compatible with the requirements of the new national curriculum in England and Wales. Participation is voluntary, and is open to all maintained schools and colleges providing for young people of all abilities aged 14–18. TVEI is not an examination or a qualification.

THE PUBLIC EXAMINATION SYSTEM

ENGLAND, WALES AND NORTHERN IRELAND
Until the end of 1987, secondary school pupils at the end of compulsory schooling around the age of 16, and others, took the General Certificate of Education (GCE) Ordinary-level or the Certificate of Secondary Education (CSE). From 1988 these were replaced by a single system of examinations, the General Certificate of Secondary Education (GCSE), which is usually taken after five years of secondary education. The first examinations took place in summer 1988. From summer 1994, the GCSE will be used to assess the performance of pupils in all national curriculum subjects required to be assessed at the end of compulsory schooling and the structure of the exam is being adapted in accordance with national curriculum requirements.

The GCSE differs from its predecessors in that there are syllabuses based on national criteria covering course objectives, content and assessment methods; differentiated assessment (i.e. different papers or questions for different ranges of ability); and grade-related criteria (i.e. grades awarded on absolute rather than relative performance).

The GCSE certificates are at present awarded on a seven-point scale, A to G, although a ten-level scale is under discussion. Grades A to C are the equivalent of the corresponding O-level grades A to C, or CSE grade 1. Grades D, E, F and G record achievement at least as high as that represented by CSE grades 2 to 5. There is no restriction on entry to any examination. All GCSE syllabuses, assessments and grading procedures are monitored by the School Curriculum and Assessment Authority (see pages 448, 450) to ensure that they conform to the national criteria.

Of school leavers in the United Kingdom who left school without A-levels or SCE H-grades in 1990–1, 48.9 per cent had achieved one or more graded GCSE or SCE O or Standard grade results.

From September 1991, many maintained schools have offered BTEC Firsts (see page 452) and it is hoped that more schools will offer BTEC Nationals than do so at present. National Vocational Qualifications in the form of General NVQs have been available to students in schools from September 1992 (see page 453).

Advanced levels – Advanced (A-level) examinations are taken by those who choose to continue their education after GCSE. A-level courses last two years and have traditionally provided the foundation for entry to higher education. A-levels are marked on a seven-point scale, from A to E, N (narrow failure) and U (unclassified), which latter grade will not be certificated.

Advanced Supplementary levels – As an alternative to, and to complement, A-level examinations, Advanced Supplementary level (AS-level) examinations were introduced in September 1987, with the first examinations taking place in summer 1989. AS-levels are for full-time A-level students but are also open to other students. An AS-level syllabus covers not less than half the amount of ground covered by the corresponding A-level syllabus and, where possible, is related to it. An AS-level course lasts two years and requires not less than half the teaching time of the corresponding A-level course, and two AS-levels are equivalent to one A-level. AS-level courses are intended to supplement and broaden A-level studies, and examinations are held at the same time as A-levels. AS-level passes are graded A to E, with grade standards related to the A-level grades.

A mixture of A-level courses in the subjects to be specialized in and AS-levels will form the standard for admission to higher education.

In the United Kingdom in 1990–1, 28 per cent of all 17 year-olds (26 per cent of boys, 30 per cent of girls) achieved one or more A-level or SCE H-grade result. This figure includes those continuing their education in maintained further education establishments including tertiary colleges, as well as school leavers.

Of school leavers alone (661,000), 23.2 per cent achieved at least one A-level or SCE H-grade (21.7 per cent of boys, 24.7 per cent of girls). Of those in Great Britain obtaining two or more A-levels, or three or more SCE H-grades, 13 per cent studied sciences (18 per cent of boys, 8 per cent of girls), 45 per cent studied arts/social studies (35 per cent of boys, 54 per cent of girls), and 43 per cent (47 per cent of boys, 38 per cent of girls) studied a combination of science and arts/social studies.

S-levels – Most examining boards allow the option of an additional paper of greater difficulty to be taken by A-level candidates to obtain what is known as a Special-level or Scholarship-level qualification. S-level papers are available in most of the traditional academic subjects and are marked on a three-point scale, grade A or 1, grade B or 2, and unclassified.

The Diploma of Vocational Education – The City and Guilds Diploma of Vocational Education superseded Foundation programmes and the Certificate of Pre-Vocational Education (CPVE) in schools and colleges in England, Wales and Northern Ireland from September 1992. It is intended for a wide ability range, including pupils who might not go on to A-levels but would like to continue their education on completion of compulsory secondary schooling. The qualification is offered by the City and Guilds of London Institute.

The City and Guilds Diploma of Vocational Education provides recognition of achievement at three levels: foundation, intermediate and national; the two latter broadly corresponding to the one- and two-year CPVE programmes, and linked with the GNVQ (see page 453) at levels 2 and 3. Within guidelines schools and colleges design their own courses, which stress activity-based learning, core skills of application of numbers, communication and information technology, and work experience. The City and Guilds Diploma of Vocational Education is mainly for those who want to find out what aptitudes they may have and to prepare themselves for work, but who are not yet committed to a particular occupation. It can be taken alongside other courses such as GCSEs, A- or AS-levels. The City and Guilds Diploma of Vocational Education will be phased out at intermediate and national levels as GNVQs are introduced. The Diploma at foundation level will continue.

CO-ORDINATION AND ADVISORY BODIES

The School Curriculum and Assessment Authority (SCAA) advises the Government on all school curriculum examination and assessment matters in England. It was formed by the amalgamation of the Schools Examination and Assessment Council with the National Curriculum Council in October 1993 and is funded wholly by the Department for Education.

The Curriculum Council for Wales advises on the curriculum in Wales. From April 1994 it will take on additional functions from SCAA and be renamed the Curriculum and Assessment Authority for Wales.

The Northern Ireland Schools Examinations and Assessment Council (NISEAC) performs the same function in Northern Ireland. In April 1994 it will amalgamate with the Northern Ireland Curriculum Council (NICC) to form a single new body the Northern Ireland Council for the Curriculum, Assessment and Examinations (NICCEA). Both NISEAC and its successor are funded by the Department for Education for Northern Ireland.

SCOTLAND

The system of public examinations in Scotland is different from that elsewhere in the United Kingdom. At the end of the fourth year of secondary education (equivalent to the fifth year in the rest of the United Kingdom), at about the age of 16, pupils take either the Ordinary grade of the Scottish Certificate of Education Examination (corresponding to the old GCE Ordinary level) or the Standard grade. By 1994–5, the Ordinary grade will have been replaced by Standard grade courses and examinations, which have been designed to suit every level of ability, with assessment against nationally determined standards of performance.

For most courses there are three separate examination papers at the end of the two-year Standard grade course. They are set at Credit (leading to awards at grade 1 or 2), General (leading to awards at grade 3 or 4) and Foundation (leading to awards at grade 5 or 6) levels. Grade 7 is available to those who, although they have completed the course, have shown no significant level of attainment. Normally pupils will take examinations covering two pairs of grades, either grades 1–4 or grades 3–6.

Pupils may attempt as many of a wide range of subjects as they are capable of, on either the Ordinary/Standard grades, or on the Higher grade which is normally taken one year after Ordinary/Standard grades, at the age of 17 or thereabouts. The shorter course means that Higher grades are normally studied to a lesser depth than A-levels; on the other hand it is common for pupils to be presented for four or more Higher grades at a single diet of the examination.

The Certificate of Sixth Year Studies (CSYS) is designed to give direction and purpose to sixth-year work by encouraging pupils who have completed their main subjects at Higher grade to study a maximum of three of these subjects in depth. Pupils may also use the sixth year to gain improved or additional Higher grades or Ordinary/Standard grades. The Scottish Office Education Department is proposing a number of changes in the system of Highers and CSYS as a result of recommendations made in the report of the Howie Committee in 1992.

The examining body for the Scottish Certificate of Education and the Certificate of Sixth Year Studies is the Scottish Examination Board.

National Certificates – National Certificates were introduced in 1984–5 as an alternative to, and to complement, Highers and CSYS. They are awarded to pupils normally over the age of 16 who have successfully completed a programme of vocational courses based on modular study units, and the assessment system is based on national criteria. National Certificates are validated by the Scottish Vocational Education Council (*see also* page 452).

THE INTERNATIONAL BACCALAUREATE

The International Baccalaureate is an internationally recognized two-year pre-university course designed to facilitate the mobility of students and to promote international understanding. Candidates must offer one subject from each of six subject groups, at least three at higher level and the remainder at subsidiary level. Single subjects can be offered, for which a certificate is received. There are 27 schools and colleges in the United Kingdom which offer the International Baccalaureate diploma.

TEACHERS

ENGLAND AND WALES

Teachers are appointed by local education authorities, school governing bodies, or school managers. Those in publicly maintained schools must be approved as qualified by the Department for Education. To become a qualified teacher it is necessary to have successfully completed a course of initial teacher training, usually either a Bachelor of Education (B.Ed.) degree or the Postgraduate Certificate of Education (PGCE), but a one-year course is being considered which will qualify certain non-graduates to teach at nursery and infant level. Teacher training has hitherto been largely integrated with the rest of higher education, with training places concentrated in universities and institutes or colleges of education, but it is now to become largely school-based, with student teachers on secondary PGCE courses spending two-thirds of their training in the classroom by September 1994. From September 1993 secondary schools or consortia of schools and CTCs will be invited to bid for funds from the DFE to carry out their own teacher training, including recruitment of students, subject to approval of their proposed training programme. Funds will be given to schools to meet the costs of designing and delivering the courses, and students will receive flat-rate bursaries equivalent in value to the PGCE student grant plus loan. Changes are also to be introduced by September 1994 in primary phase teacher training with a view to making it more school-based and giving schools a role in course design and delivery. Under the articled teacher scheme, graduates are paid a bursary in addition to a salary to complete a school-based PGCE course over two years involving a progressively increasing teaching load. From September 1993, this scheme was restricted to primary phase teacher training only.

With certain exceptions the profession at present has an all-graduate entry. Teachers in further education are not required to have qualified teacher status, though roughly half have a teaching qualification and most have industrial, commercial or professional experience.

The licensed teacher scheme is designed to attract into the teaching profession entrants over 24 years of age without formal teaching qualifications but with relevant training and experience. All licensees are required to have the equivalent of two years' higher education in the United Kingdom and the equivalent of grade C in GCSE maths and English. Local education authorities will be involved in devising a suitable two-year training programme for any licensed teachers they may appoint to their schools; for grant-maintained schools and City Technology Colleges this will be a matter for the schools themselves. LEAs have discretion to recommend qualified teacher status after one year for a licensee with at least two years' experience as an instructor prior to becoming a licensed teacher.

SCOTLAND

All teachers in maintained schools must be registered with the General Teaching Council for Scotland. They are registered provisionally for a two-year probationary period which can be extended if necessary. Only graduates are accepted as entrants to the teaching profession in Scotland. As a result of a review of initial teacher training instituted in 1992 a greater proportion of training is to be classroom-based. The colleges of education provide both in-service and pre-service training for teachers and are funded by the Scottish Higher Education Funding Council.

NORTHERN IRELAND

Teacher training in Northern Ireland is provided by the two universities and two colleges of education. The colleges are concerned with teacher education mainly for the primary school sector. They also provide B.Ed. courses for intending secondary school teachers of religious education, commercial studies, and craft, design and technology. With these exceptions, the training of teachers for secondary schools is provided in the education departments of the universities. A review of primary and secondary teacher training is taking place.

ACCREDITATION OF TRAINING INSTITUTIONS

The Council for the Accreditation of Teacher Education (CATE) advises central government on the accreditation, content and quality of initial teacher training courses in England, Wales and Northern Ireland, monitoring and disseminating good practice.

In Scotland all training courses in colleges of education must be approved by the Scottish Office Education Department and a validating body.

NEWLY-TRAINED TEACHERS

Of teachers who in 1990 had successfully completed initial training courses in the United Kingdom, 10,800 had completed a postgraduate course and 7,000 a course for non-graduates.

Because of a shortage of teachers in a number of secondary subjects, a tax-free bursary scheme for trainee teachers on one- or two-year courses has been introduced. The subjects are: physics, chemistry, biology, or any combination of these three; mathematics; modern languages (including Welsh in Wales); technology; craft, design and technology (CDT). The bursary is £1,000 a year.

SERVING TEACHERS

In 1990–1 there were 560,000 teachers (full-time and full-time equivalent) in public sector schools and establishments of further education in the United Kingdom. Of these, 463,000 were in maintained schools and 91,000 in further education. There were 210,000 full-time teachers in public sector primary schools, 234,000 in public sector secondary schools and 19,000 in special schools.

SALARIES

Qualified teachers in England and Wales, other than heads and deputy heads, are paid on an 18-point scale ranging from £11,244 to £18,837 (September 1993 figures). Entry points and placement depend on qualifications, experience, responsibilities, excellence and recruitment and retention factors as calculated by the relevant body, i.e. in grant-maintained

schools and LEA schools with delegated budgets, the governing body; otherwise the LEA. Headteachers' salaries range from £23,505 to £50,682 and deputy headteachers' salaries range from £22,404 to £36,855. Qualified teachers in Northern Ireland are paid on a ten-point scale as of April 1993 ranging from £11,244 to £18,942. Salaries for principals range from £23,505 to £46,398 and vice-principals from £22,404 to £33,789. There is a statutory superannuation scheme in maintained schools.

Teachers in Scotland are paid (April 1993 figures) on a ten-point scale from £11,562 to £19,218. The entry point depends on type of qualification, and additional allowances are payable under certain circumstances. Headteachers are paid on a scale from £24,375 to £45,150 and deputy headteachers from £24,375 to £33,783, depending on whether the school is primary or secondary and the size of school roll.

Further Education

The Education Reform Act 1988 defines further education as all provision outside schools to people aged over 16 of education up to and including A-level and its equivalent. The Further Education Funding Councils for England and Wales, the Scottish Office Education Department and the Education and Library Boards in Northern Ireland have a duty to secure provision of adequate facilities for further education in their territories.

ENGLAND AND WALES

The Further and Higher Education Act 1992 removed all further education and sixth form colleges from local authority control as of April 1993, and provided for them to be funded directly by central government through the Further Education Funding Council for England (FEFC) and the Further Education Funding Council for Wales (FEFCW). These councils are also responsible for the assessment of quality. The colleges are controlled by autonomous further education corporations with substantial representation from business, which own their own assets and employ their own staff. Their funding is determined in part by the number of students recruited.

In England and Wales further education courses are taught at a variety of institutions. These range from universities which were formerly polytechnics and colleges of higher education and colleges of further education (most of which also offer higher education courses) to tertiary colleges and sixth form colleges, which concentrate on the provision of normal sixth form school courses as well as a range of vocational courses. A number of institutions specific to a particular form of training, e.g. the Royal College of Music, are also involved. Until April 1993, all such courses were funded by local education authorities, including further education courses in universities and colleges of higher education. Funding is now provided by the Further Education Funding Councils.

Every institution providing full-time further education under a further education scheme is required to appoint a board of governors which has the power to appoint staff and manage budgets under the local management of further and higher education colleges initiative, duties devolved from local eduction authorities in 1989. From April 1993, governing boards and principals have had total responsibility and accountability for their institutions. At least half the governors must represent employment interests or be independent of local authority or college interests.

Teaching staff in further education establishments are not necessarily required to have teaching qualifications although many do so, but they are subject to regular appraisal of teaching performance.

Much of the post-school provision outside the higher education sector is broadly vocational in purpose. It ranges from lower-level technical and commercial courses through courses for those aiming at higher-level posts in industry, commerce and administration, to professional courses. Facilities for GCSE courses, Diploma of Vocational Education, AS-levels and A-level courses are also provided (*see* page 449). These courses can form the foundation for progress to higher education qualifications (*see* below).

The main courses and examinations in the vocational field, all of which link in with the NVQ framework, are offered by the following bodies, but there are also many others:

The Business and Technology Education Council (BTEC) provides programmes of study across a wide range of subject areas. The main qualifications are: the BTEC First Certificate; the BTEC First Diploma; the BTEC National Certificate and the BTEC National Diploma; BTEC intermediate and advanced GNVQs (which are being introduced progressively in 14 vocational sectors over the next few years); and BTEC foundation, intermediate and advanced GNVQs in some vocational areas.

City and Guilds of London Institute (C&G) offers a wide range of technical and vocational qualifications all of which link in with the GNVQ framework, and has sole responsibility for administering the Diploma of Vocational Education (*see* page 449). Most courses are part-time for students already in employment, but some full-time courses are available.

RSA (Royal Society of Arts) Examinations Board schemes cover a wide range of vocational qualifications, including business administration, management, language schemes, information technology and teaching qualifications. Many schemes are offered at levels matching those established by the NCVQ (*see* below), and a policy operates of credit accumulation, so that candidates can take a single unit or complete qualifications.

There are 413 further education establishments in England and Wales and 2,656 adult education centres. In 1991–2 there were 495,000 full-time and sandwich students and 808,000 part-time students on further education courses.

SCOTLAND

Further education comprises non-advanced courses up to SCE Highers grade, GCE A-level and SCOTVEC vocational courses. Under the Further and Higher Education (Scotland) Act 1992 funding of further education colleges was transferred to central government from the education authorities in April 1993; a further education funding council is proposed at a later stage. Courses are taught mainly at colleges of further education, including technical colleges, and in some schools.

The Self-Governing Schools etc. (Scotland) Act 1989 legislated for Further Education College Councils to be set up with extensive powers to run their colleges; from April 1993 when the colleges became self-governing the Councils became boards of management. These run the colleges and employ staff. They include the Principal and staff and student representatives among their 10–16 members, and at least half the members must have experience of commerce, industry or the practice of a profession.

The Scottish Vocational Education Council (SCOTVEC) provides qualifications for most occupations (paralleling the work of the Business and Technology Education Council, City and Guilds of London Institute, the Royal Society of Arts and other bodies in England, Wales and Northern Ireland). It provides at non-advanced level the National Certificate which is completely comprehensive and covers

the whole range of non-advanced further education provision in Scotland. Students may study for the National Certificate on a full-time, part-time, open learning or work-based learning basis. The system is based on modules and National Certificate modules and modular programmes can be taken in further education colleges, secondary schools and other centres, normally from the age of 16 onwards. SCOTVEC also offers modular advanced level HNC/HND qualifications and a few post-graduate or post-experience qualifications which are available in further education colleges and higher education institutions. Scottish Vocational Qualifications (SVQs) combine programmes of SCOTVEC's National Certificate modules or Higher National Units. They correspond to the system of NVQs which operates in the rest of the UK and were introduced in schools, further education colleges and other centres from August 1992.

The Record of Education and Training (RET) has been introduced to provide a single certificate recording SCOT-VEC achievements; an updated version is provided as and when necessary.

In 1990–1 there were 37,923 full-time and sandwich students and 93,981 part-time students on non-advanced vocational courses of further education in the 49 further education colleges, 15 central institutions and five colleges of education then in existence.

NORTHERN IRELAND

The Education and Library Boards are obliged to prepare and submit for approval to the Department of Education for Northern Ireland, schemes setting out the principles to be applied by the boards in planning the further education provision to be made by colleges under their management.

The colleges of further education are at present maintained by the Education and Library Boards, but financial powers and responsibilities are delegated to the boards of governors of the colleges. The boards of governors must include at least 50 per cent membership from the professions, local business or industry, or other fields of employment relevant to the activities of the college. The review of further education provision which took place during 1992–3 recommended that from 1995 further education should be planned and funded centrally and that college and course provision should be rationalized by the amalgamation of some colleges from March 1994.

On reaching school-leaving age, pupils may attend colleges of further education to pursue the same type of vocational courses as are provided in colleges in England and Wales, administered by the same examining bodies.

Northern Ireland has 24 institutions of further education with 309 out-centres. In 1990–1 there were 20,468 full-time students and 55,440 part-time students on non-advanced vocational courses of further education.

COURSE INFORMATION

Applications for further education courses are generally made directly to the colleges concerned. Information on further education courses in the United Kingdom and addresses of colleges can be found in the *Directory of Further Education* published annually by the Careers Research and Advisory Centre.

NATIONAL COUNCIL FOR VOCATIONAL QUALIFICATIONS

The National Council for Vocational Qualifications (NCVQ) was set up by the Government in October 1986 to achieve a coherent national framework for vocational qualifications in England, Wales and Northern Ireland. The Council does not award qualifications but works with and through the established examining and awarding bodies to reform the existing vocational qualifications system and introduce simplified arrangements. SCOTVEC (*see* above) performs similar functions in Scotland, but its role includes the awarding of qualifications.

The name and style National Vocational Qualification is accorded to qualifications accredited by NCVQ. The NVQ framework is currently based on five levels incorporating qualifications up to and including the Higher National standard. From September 1992 General National Vocational Qualifications were introduced into colleges and schools. They cover broad categories in the NVQ framework and are aimed at those wishing to familiarize themselves with a range of opportunities. Advanced GNVQ or the vocational A-level (formerly level 3) is designed to be equivalent to two A-levels; intermediate (formerly level 2) is equivalent to four or five good GCSEs. Foundation GNVQs (formerly level 1) are being piloted.

The National Record of Achievement (NRA) replaced the National Record of Vocational Achievement (NRVA) in autumn 1993. The NRA is intended to be a record of achievement, both formal and informal, in education, training and employment, in a single format.

Higher Education

The term higher education is used to describe education above A-level, Higher grade and their equivalent, which is provided mainly in universities and colleges of higher education.

The Further and Higher Education Act 1992 and parallel legislation in Scotland marked the end of the so-called 'binary' system in higher education in Great Britain; a unitary system has always existed in Northern Ireland, where the funding of higher education is undertaken by DENI. The Acts removed the distinction between higher education provided by the universities, which were funded by the Universities Funding Council (UFC), and that provided in England and Wales by the polytechnics and colleges of higher education, funded by the Polytechnics and Colleges Funding Council (PCFC), and in Scotland by the central institutions and other institutions funded by central government. All are now brought under a single funding structure, the Higher Education Funding Councils for England, Wales and Scotland. The HEFCs took over from the UFC, PCFC and Scottish Office in April 1993. The Acts also provided for other changes to bring the non-university sector in line with the universities, including the right for all polytechnics, and other higher education institutions which satisfy the necessary criteria, to award their own taught course and research degrees and to adopt the title of university, subject to Privy Council approval of the proposed new name. The change of name does not affect the legal constitution of the institutions.

In 1990-1, there were 748,600 full-time and sandwich students in higher education in the United Kingdom, of whom 80,200 were from overseas. The number of part-time students in the United Kingdom, including the Open University, was 428,000. The proportion of 16- to 20-year-olds entering full-time higher education in Great Britain rose from 16.1 per cent in 1985-6 to 19.9 per cent in 1990-1. The number of mature entrants (those aged 21 and over when starting an undergraduate course and 25 and over when starting a postgraduate course) to higher education in Great Britain in 1990 (excluding those at the Open University) was 237,000, up by 77 per cent on 1980. The number of full-time students on science courses in 1990-1 was 124,700, of whom 43,700 were female.

UNIVERSITIES AND COLLEGES

The universities are self-governing institutions established by royal charter or Act of Parliament. They have academic freedom and are responsible for their own academic appointments, curricula and student admissions and award their own degrees.

Responsibility for universities in England rests with the Secretary of State for Education, and in their territories with the Secretaries of State for Scotland, Wales and Northern Ireland. Advice to the Government on matters relating to the universities is provided by the Higher Education Funding Councils for England, Wales and Scotland, and by the Northern Ireland Higher Education Council. The HEFCs receive a block grant from central government which they allocate to the universities and colleges. The grant is allocated directly by central government in Northern Ireland.

There are now 86 universities in the United Kingdom, where only 48 existed prior to the Further and Higher Education Acts 1992. Of these 86, 70 are in England (including one federal university), two (one a federal institution) in Wales, 12 in Scotland and two in Northern Ireland.

The universities which pre-date the 1992 Acts each have their own system of internal government, but broad similarities exist. Most are run by two main bodies: the senate, which deals primarily with academic issues and consists of members elected from within the university; and the council, which is the supreme body and is responsible for all appointments and promotions, and bidding for and allocation of financial resources. At least half the members of the council are drawn from outside the university. Joint committees of senate and council are becoming increasingly common.

In 1991-2, at the 48 universities which then existed in the United Kingdom (two in Northern Ireland, eight in Scotland, a single federal university in Wales) there were 401,657 full-time students (19,369 from EC countries; 44,044 from other overseas countries) and 66,438 part-time students. Women formed 44.3 per cent of the full-time total and 44.7 per cent of the part-time total.

Those universities which were formerly polytechnics and the colleges of higher education are run by Higher Education Corporations (HECs), which are controlled by boards of governors whose members were initially appointed by the Secretaries of State but which will subsequently make their own appointments. At least half the members of each board must be drawn from industry, business, commerce and the professions.

In England and Wales, there were 336,637 students in the 33 polytechnics in 1990-1. Of these, 324,301 were on higher education courses, of whom 225,794 were full-time or sandwich course students. In the 50 colleges of higher education in England and Wales in 1990-1, there were 619,313 students, 131,296 of these on higher education courses and of whom 83,201 were full-time or sandwich course students.

In 1990-1 there were 413 major establishments in higher education (maintained, assisted by LEAs, in receipt of direct grant from the DFE, or voluntary) outside the PCFC sector. In England and Wales in 1990-1 they catered for 114,575 students on higher education courses funded by the PCFC, including 23,548 on full-time or sandwich courses. The higher education courses in these establishments are now, as a result of the 1992 Act, funded by the HEFCs for England and Wales, while their further education courses are funded through the FEFCs.

The non-residential Open University provides courses nationally leading to degrees. Teaching is through a combination of television and radio programmes, correspondence, tutorials, short residential courses and local audio-visual centres. No qualifications are needed for entry. The Open University offers a modular programme of undergraduate courses by credit accumulation and post-experience and postgraduate courses, including a programme of higher degrees which comprise B.Phil., M.Phil. and Ph.D. through research, and MA, MBA and M.Sc. through taught courses. The Open University throughout the UK is funded by the Higher Education Funding Council for England. In 1993, about 86,000 undergraduates were registered at the Open University, of whom about 41,000 were women and 43,000 were men. Estimated cost (year 1993) of a six-credit degree was around £2,750.

The independent University of Buckingham provides a two-year course leading to a bachelor's degree and its tuition fees were £8,456 for 1993. It receives no capital or recurrent income from the Government but its students are eligible for mandatory awards from local education authorities. Its academic year consists of four terms of ten weeks each.

ACADEMIC STAFF

Each university and college appoints its own academic staff on its own conditions. There is, however, a common salary structure and, except for Oxford and Cambridge, a common career structure in universities; and a common salary structure for the former PCFC sector. The Education Reform Act 1988 appointed the University Commissioners to secure changes to university statutes abolishing the granting of tenure, thus enabling staff to be dismissed for good cause and for redundancy.

The Education Reform Act 1988 took polytechnics and higher education colleges in England and Wales out of local education authority control, turning them into employers on their own account. The Polytechnics and Colleges Employers' Forum was set up to look after terms and conditions of employment and has negotiated the introduction of an academic contract similar to that obtaining in the universities which pre-dated the Higher and Further Education Act 1992.

Teaching staff in higher education require no formal teaching qualification, but teacher trainers are required to spend a certain amount of time in schools to ensure that they have sufficient recent practical experience.

In 1991–2, when the binary system still operated, there were 57,600 full-time and part-time academic staff in universities in the United Kingdom and 125,927 in public sector further and higher education.

Salary scales for staff in the pre-existing universities differ from those in the former polytechnics and colleges; it is hoped to amalgamate them over the next three years. The 1993–4 salary scales for non-clinical academic staff in universities are:

lecturer grade A, £13,601–£18,855
lecturer grade B, £19,642–£25,107
senior lecturer, £26,359–£29,788
professor, £30,358 (minimum)
The salaries of clinical academic staff are kept broadly comparable to those of doctors and dentists in the National Health Service.

Salary scales for lecturers in the former polytechnics, now universities, and colleges of further and higher education are (September 1992):

lecturer, £11,163–£20,235
senior lecturer, £19,536–£24,423
principal, from £25,986
The same scales apply in Northern Ireland. The salary scales for staff in Scotland are (April 1993):

lecturer, £13,875–£24,903
senior lecturer, £22,842–£29,526
head of department/professorial, from £30,453

FINANCE

Although universities and colleges are expected to look to a much wider range of funding sources than before, and to generate additional revenue in collaboration with industry, they are still largely financed, directly or indirectly, from government resources.

In the academic year 1991–2 the total recurrent income of the 48 universities then existing in the United Kingdom was £4,870 million (£4,422 million in 1990–1). The exchequer grant was £1,564 million (£1,590 million in 1990–1), forming 32.1 per cent of total income (36.6 per cent in 1990–1), compared to 1976–7 when it formed 75 per cent. Income from research grants and contracts in 1991–2 was £941 million, an increase of 7.3 per cent on the previous year.

In the academic year 1991–2 the PCFC recurrent grant to institutions and LEAs for higher education courses was £842 million (£988.8 million in 1990–1).

COURSES

In the United Kingdom all universities, including the Open University, and some colleges award their own degrees and other qualifications and can act as awarding and validating bodies for neighbouring colleges which are not yet accredited. These functions, and the accreditation of institutions to award their own degrees, were formerly effected by the Council for National Academic Awards until it ceased to operate in October 1992. The Higher Education Quality Council (HEQC), to be funded by institutional contributions, has now been set up to advise the Secretaries of State on applications for degree-awarding powers.

Higher education courses last full-time for at least four weeks or, if part-time, involve more than 60 hours of instruction. Facilities exist for full-time and part-time study, day release, sandwich or block release. Credit Accumulation and Transfer (CATS) is a system of study which is now becoming widely available. It allows a student to achieve a final qualification by accumulating credits for courses of study successfully achieved, or even professional experience, over a period. Credit transfer information and values are carried on an electronic database called ECCTIS 2000, which is available in most careers offices and many schools and colleges.

Higher education courses include: first degree and postgraduate (including research); Diploma in Higher Education (Dip.HE); Higher National Diploma (HND) and Higher National Certificate (HNC); preparation for professional examinations; and the in-service training of teachers.

The Diploma of Higher Education (Dip.HE) is a two-year diploma usually intended to serve as a stepping-stone to a degree course or other further study. The Dip.HE is awarded by the institution itself if it is accredited; by an accredited institution of its choice if not. The BTEC Higher National Certificate (HNC) is awarded after two years part-time study. The BTEC Higher National Diploma (HND) is awarded after two years full-time, or three years sandwich or part-time study.

With the exception of certain Scottish universities where master is sometimes used for a first degree in arts subjects, undergraduate courses lead to the title of Bachelor – Bachelor of Arts (BA) and Bachelor of Science (B.Sc.) being the most common – and for a higher degree, Master of Arts (MA), Master of Science (M.Sc.) (usually taught courses) and the research degrees of Master of Philosophy (M.Phil.) and Doctor of Philosophy (Ph.D. or, at a few universities, D.Phil.).

Most undergraduate programmes at British universities and colleges of higher education run for three years, except in Scotland and at the University of Keele where they may take four years. Professional courses in subjects such as medicine, dentistry and veterinary science take longer. Details of courses on offer and of predicted entry requirements for the following year's intake are provided in *University and College Entrance* published annually by Universities and Colleges Admissions Service (UCAS), which includes degree, Dip.HE and HND courses at all universities (excluding the Open University) and most colleges of HE (for address, see page 462).

Postgraduate programmes vary in length. Taught courses which lead to certificates, diplomas or master's degrees usually take one year full-time or two years part-time. Research degrees take from two to three years full-time and much longer if completed on a part-time basis. Details of taught courses and research degree opportunities can be found in *Graduate Studies* published annually for the Careers Research and Advisory Centre (CRAC) by Hobsons Publishing PLC (for address, see page 462).

Post-experience short courses are forming an increasing part of higher education provision, reflecting the need to update professional and technical training. Most of these courses fund themselves.

ADMISSIONS

Apart from quotas for medical, dental and veterinary students, there are no limits set for student intakes and the individual university or college decides which students to accept. The formal entry requirements to most degree courses are two A-levels at grade E or above (or equivalent), and to HND courses one A-level (or equivalent). In practice, most offers of places require qualifications in excess of this, higher requirements usually reflecting the popularity of a course. These requirements do not, however, exclude applications from students with a variety of non-GCSE qualifications or unquantified experience and skills.

For admission to a degree, Dip.HE or HND, potential students apply through a central clearing house. All universities and most colleges providing higher education courses in the United Kingdom are members of the Universities and Colleges Admission Service (UCAS), which operates for the first time for 1994 entry and replaces the former Universities Central Council on Admissions (UCCA) and Polytechnics Central Admissions System (PCAS). (The only exception among universities is the Open University, which conducts its own admissions.) Applicants are supplied with an application form and a *UCAS Handbook*, available from schools, colleges and careers offices or direct from UCAS, and may apply to a maximum of eight institutions on the UCAS form.

There are a number of studio-based art and design courses for which applications should be made through the Art and Design Admissions Registry. Initial teacher training courses in Scotland are at present applied to through the Teacher Education Admissions Clearing House (TEACH), which will, however, be wound up after handling the intake for session 1994–5. Applications for undergraduate teacher training courses will thereafter be made through UCAS; procedures for admission to postgraduate teacher training courses have yet to be decided.

For admission as a postgraduate student, universities and colleges normally require a good first degree in a subject related to the proposed course of study or research, but other experience and qualifications will be considered on merit. Most applications are made to individual institutions but there are two clearing houses of relevance. Postgraduate teacher training courses in England, Wales and Northern Ireland utilise the Graduate Teacher Training Registry (see page 462) and for social work the Social Work Admissions System operates (see page 462).

SCOTLAND

As a result of changes brought about by the Further and Higher Education (Scotland) Act 1992, the Scottish Higher Education Funding Council (SHEFC) now funds 23 institutions of higher education, including 12 universities. The universities are broadly managed as described above and each institution of higher education is managed by an independent governing body which includes representatives of industrial, commercial, professional and educational interests. Most of the courses outside the universities have a vocational orientation and a substantial number are sandwich courses.

In 1990–1, there were 77,475 students enrolled on courses of higher education outside the universities. Of these, 36,924 attended the 15 central institutions, 6,999 the five colleges of education, and 33,164 the 49 education authority colleges. Of the total number, 55 per cent were on full-time or sandwich courses.

Applications to institutions of higher education in Scotland are made through UCAS, except for applications for teacher training which are made through TEACH (see page 462) up to and including student intake for the session 1994–5. Details of initial teacher training courses can be obtained from colleges of education and those universities offering such courses, and from the Committee of Scottish Higher Education Principals (COSHEP).

NORTHERN IRELAND

In Northern Ireland advanced courses are provided by 24 institutions of further education and by the two universities. As well as offering first and postgraduate degrees, the University of Ulster offers courses leading to the BTEC Higher National Diploma and professional qualifications. Applications to undertake courses of higher education other than degree courses are made to the institutions direct. Applications for degree courses are made through UCAS.

In 1990–1, 4,095 students were enrolled on advanced courses of higher education in the institutions of further education, 43.5 per cent of whom were women. There were 951 students on full-time or sandwich courses.

FEES

The tuition fees for students with mandatory awards (*see* page 456) are paid by the grant-awarding body. Students from member states of the European Community pay fees at home student rates. Since 1980–1 students from outside the EC have paid fees that are meant to cover the cost of their education, but financial help is available under a number of schemes. Information about these schemes is available from British Council offices world-wide.

Although universities are free to set their own charges, the Committee of Vice-Chancellors and Principals recommend minimum fees for students from non-EC countries which, however, do not apply to those institutions formerly in the PCFC sector. Fees for 1993–4 are £5,550 for arts students, £7,360 for science students, and £13,550 for students following clinical courses in medicine, dentistry and veterinary science. These compare with undergraduate fees for home and EC students of £1,300 for arts courses, £2,770 for laboratory or workshop based courses, mainly science, and £4,985 for clinical courses in the academic year 1993–4.

All institutions of higher education charge the same fees for home students and EC nationals.

For postgraduate students, the maximum tuition fee that will be reimbursed through the awards system is £2,260 in 1993–4.

GRANTS FOR STUDENTS

Students in the United Kingdom who plan to take a full-time or sandwich course of further study after leaving school may be eligible for a grant. A parental contribution is deductible on a sliding scale dependent on income. For married students this may be deducted from their spouse's income instead. However, parental contribution is not deducted from the grant to students over 25 years of age who have been self-supporting for at least three years. The main rates of mandatory grant have been frozen from 1991–2, as it is envisaged that students will increasingly support themselves by loans (*see* below). Tuition fees are paid in full for all students in receipt of a grant, regardless of parental income, and they are usually paid direct to the university or college by the education authority.

Grants are paid by local education authorities in England, Wales and Northern Ireland, which are reimbursed for 100 per cent of the cost by central government, and by the Scottish Office Education Department in Scotland. Applications are made to the authority in the area in which the student normally lives. Applications should not, however, be made earlier than the January preceding the start of the course.

TYPES OF GRANT

Grants are of two kinds: mandatory and discretionary. Mandatory grants are those which awarding authorities must pay to students who are attending designated courses (*see* below) and who can satisfy certain other conditions. Such a grant is awarded normally to enable the student to attend only one designated course and there is no general entitlement to an award for any particular number of years. Discretionary grants are those for which each awarding authority has discretion to decide its own policy.

Designated courses are those full-time or sandwich courses leading to: a degree; the Diploma of Higher Education; the BTEC Higher National Diploma; initial teacher-training courses, including those for the postgraduate certificate of education and the art teachers' certificate or diploma; a university certificate or diploma lasting at least three years; other qualifications which are specifically designated as being comparable to first degree courses; and the SCOTVEC Higher National Diploma.

To be eligible for a mandatory grant, students admitted to a designated course must usually have been ordinarily resident in the United Kingdom for the three years immediately preceding the academic year in which the course begins; have not previously attended a course of advanced further education of more than two years' duration; and apply for the grant before the end of the first term of the course. The local education authority should be consulted for advice about eligibility.

Students taking designated courses who do not satisfy the residency condition may be eligible for a mandatory grant if they come from other member states of the EC and can establish migrant worker status, or their parents are migrant workers; or if they, or their spouse and children, are asylees or refugees.

A means-tested maintenance grant, usually paid once a term, covers periods of attendance during term as well as the Christmas and Easter vacations, but not the summer vacation. It is subject to deduction on account of the student's own income and her/his parents' or spouse's income. The basic grant rates are: £2,845 if living in a hall of residence or lodgings and studying within the London area; £2,265 as above but outside the London area; £1,795 if living at the parental home. Additional allowances are available if, for example, the course requires a period of study abroad.

Education authority and Scottish Office Education Department expenditure on student fees and maintenance in 1991–2 was £2,368 million; 649,360 mandatory awards were made.

STUDENT LOANS

The Education (Student Loans) Act 1990 legislated for interest-free but indexed top-up loans of up to £940 in 1993–4 to be made available to eligible students in the United Kingdom. The government expects that at least £276.8 million will be taken up in loans in 1993–4.

Students apply direct to the Student Loans Company Ltd (see page 356), which will require a certificate of eligibility from their place of study. Loans are available to students on designated courses within the scope of mandatory awards and the same residency conditions apply. Repayment is normally over five to seven years, although it can be deferred if income is low.

ACCESS FUNDS

Access Funds are allocated by education departments to the appropriate Funding Councils in England, Wales and Scotland and administered by further and higher education institutions. In Northern Ireland they are allocated by central government to the institutions direct. They are available to students whose access to higher education might otherwise be inhibited by financial considerations or where real financial difficulties are faced. For the academic year 1993–4, provision in the United Kingdom will be £29.7 million. The purpose and operation of access funds was under review in late 1993.

POSTGRADUATE AWARDS

Unlike funding for undergraduates, which is mandatory for most degree and equivalent level courses, grants for postgraduate study are usually discretionary. Grants are also often dependent on the class of first degree, especially for research degrees.

A number of schemes of postgraduate bursaries or studentships for residents in England and Wales are funded by the Department for Education, the five government research councils, the Ministry of Agriculture, Fisheries and Food, and the British Academy, which awards grants for study in the humanities.

In Scotland postgraduate funding is provided by the Scottish Office Education Department, the Scottish Office Agriculture and Fisheries Department, and the research councils as in England and Wales.

Awards in Northern Ireland are made by the Department of Education for Northern Ireland, the Department of Agriculture for Northern Ireland, and the Medical Research Council.

In 1990–1 in the United Kingdom 26,200 awards were made. The national rates for twelve-month studentships in 1993–4 were: £5,340 in college or lodgings in London; £4,245 in college or lodgings outside London; £3,130 for those living with parents or spouse's parents. The rates for 30-week bursaries for 1993–4 were: £3,170 in college or lodgings in London; £2,500 in college or lodgings outside London; £1,890 if living with parents or spouse's parents.

Adult and Continuing Education

The term adult education covers a broad spectrum of educational activities ranging from non-vocational courses of general interest, through the acquiring of special vocational skills needed in industry or commerce, to study for a degree at the Open University.

Until the passing of the Further and Higher Education Act 1992, local education authorities were the main providers of adult and continuing education in England and Wales and had a statutory duty to do so. The Further Education Funding Councils are now responsible for, and fund, those courses which take place in their sector and lead to academic and vocational qualifications, prepare students to undertake further or higher education courses, or confer basic skills. Advanced courses of continuing education are funded by the Higher Education Funding Councils. Courses which do not fall within the remit of the funding councils continue to be the responsibility of the LEAs. Arrangements for funding in Scotland and Northern Ireland are unchanged, through the regional and islands education authorities in Scotland and the education and library boards in Northern Ireland.

PROVIDERS

Courses specifically for adults are provided by many bodies. They include, in the statutory sector: local education authorities in England and Wales; the regional and islands education authorities in Scotland and the Scottish Office Education Department; education and library boards in Northern Ireland; further education colleges; higher education colleges; universities, especially the Open University and Birkbeck College of the University of London; residential colleges; the BBC, independent television and local radio stations. There are also a number of voluntary bodies.

The local education authorities in England and Wales operate through 'area' adult education centres (2,656 in 1991), institutes or colleges, and the adult studies departments of colleges of further education. The regional and islands education authorities in Scotland fund adult education, including that provided by the universities and the Workers' Educational Association, at vocational further education colleges (46 in 1991). In addition, the Scottish Office Education Department provides grants to a number of voluntary organizations. Provision in the statutory sector in Northern Ireland is the responsibility of the universities and the education and library boards, which operate 24 further education colleges and a number of community schools.

The involvement of universities in adult education and continuing education has diversified considerably and is supported by a variety of administrative structures ranging from dedicated departments to a devolved approach. Birkbeck College in the University of London caters solely for part-time students. Those institutions and colleges formerly in the PCFC sector in England and Wales, because of their range of courses and flexible patterns of student attendance, provide opportunities in the field of adult and continuing education. The New Universities and Polytechnics Association for Continuing Education promotes collaboration between institutions of higher education active in this area. The Open University, in partnership with the BBC, provides distance teaching leading to first degrees, and also offers post-experience and higher degree courses (see page 470).

Of the voluntary bodies, the biggest is the Workers' Educational Association (WEA) which operates throughout the United Kingdom, reaching about 180,000 adult students annually. The Further Education Funding Councils for England and Wales, Scottish Office Education Department, Department of Education for Northern Ireland and local education authorities make grants towards provision.

The National Institute of Adult Continuing Education (England and Wales) (NIACE) provides information and advice to organizations and individuals on all aspects of adult continuing education. NIACE conducts research, project and development work, and is funded by the DFE, the Welsh Office, the LEAs and other funding bodies. The Welsh committee, NIACE Cymru, receives financial support from the Welsh Office, support in kind from the Welsh Joint Education Committee, and advises government, voluntary bodies and education providers on adult continuing education and training matters in Wales. In Scotland advice on adult and community education, and promotion thereof, is provided by the Scottish Community Education Council. The Northern Ireland Council for Adult Education has an advisory role. Its membership includes representatives of the education and library boards and of most organizations involved in the field, together with an assessor appointed by DENI.

Membership of the Universities Association for Continuing Education is open to any university or university college in the United Kingdom. It promotes university continuing education, facilitates the interchange of information, and supports research and development work in continuing education.

COURSES

Although lengths vary, most courses are part-time. Long-term residential colleges grant-aided by the DFE, the Welsh Office or the Scottish Office provide full-time courses lasting one or two years. Some colleges and centres offer short-term residential courses, lasting from a few days to a few weeks, in a wide range of subjects. Local education authorities directly sponsor many of the colleges, while others are sponsored by universities or voluntary organizations. A list, *Residential Short Courses*, is published by NIACE.

GRANTS

Although full-time courses at degree level attract mandatory awards, for courses below that level all students over the age of 19 must pay a fee. However, discretionary grants may be available. Adult education bursaries for students at the long-term residential colleges of adult education are the responsibility of the colleges themselves. The awards are administered for the colleges by the Awards Officer of the Residential Colleges Committee for students resident in England and are funded by the Further Education Funding Council for England in English colleges; for colleges in Wales they are funded and administered by the Further Education Funding Council for Wales; for colleges in Scotland by the Scottish Office Education Department; and for colleges in Northern Ireland by the Department of Education for Northern Ireland. A booklet *Adult Education Bursaries* can be obtained from the Awards Officer, Adult Education Bursaries, c/o Ruskin College (see page 473).

NUMBERS

There are no comprehensive statistics covering all aspects of adult education. However, enrolments on evening courses in the United Kingdom numbered 1,791,000 in 1990–1 (66.7 per cent women). This number included 1,026,000 students at adult education centres. In 1991–2, liberal adult education and professional updating short courses organized by university departments were attended by 870,491 students, an increase of 8.8 per cent on the previous year.

Education Directory

LOCAL EDUCATION AUTHORITIES

ENGLAND

COUNTY COUNCILS

AVON, PO Box 57, Avon House North, St James Barton, Bristol BS99 7EB. Tel: 0272-290777. *Director,* G. Badman

BEDFORDSHIRE, County Hall, Cauldwell Street, Bedford MK42 9AP. Tel: 0234-363222. *Director,* D. G. Wadsworth

BERKSHIRE, Shire Hall, Shinfield Park, Reading RG2 9XE. Tel: 0734-233401. *Chief Education Officer,* S. R. Goodchild

BUCKINGHAMSHIRE, County Hall, Aylesbury HP20 1UZ. Tel: 0296-395000. *Chief Education Officer,* S. Sharp

CAMBRIDGESHIRE, Castle Court, Shire Hall, Cambridge CB3 0AP. Tel: 0223-317667. *Director,* J. Ferguson

CHESHIRE, County Hall, Chester CH1 1SF. Tel: 0244-602424. *Director,* D. Cracknell

CLEVELAND, Woodlands Road, Middlesbrough TS1 3BN. Tel: 0642-248155. *County Education Officer,* B. Worthy

CORNWALL, County Hall, Truro TR1 3AY. Tel: 0872-74282. *Secretary of Education,* D. W. Fryer

CUMBRIA, 5 Portland Square, Carlisle CA1 1PU. Tel: 0228-23456. *Director,* Ms P. Black

DERBYSHIRE, County Offices, Matlock DE4 3AG. Tel: 0629-580000. *Chief Education Officer (acting),* R. Taylor

DEVON, County Hall, Exeter EX2 4QG. Tel: 0392-382059. *Chief Education Officer,* S. W. Jenkin

DORSET, County Hall, Dorchester DT1 1XJ. Tel: 0305-251000. *Director,* R. H. Ely

DURHAM, County Hall, Durham DH1 5UJ. Tel: 091-386 4411. *Director,* K. Mitchell

EAST SUSSEX, PO Box 4, County Hall, St Anne's Crescent, Lewes BN7 1SG. Tel: 0273-481000. *County Education Officer,* D. Mallen

ESSEX, Threadneedle House, Market Road, Chelmsford CM1 1LD. Tel: 0245-492211. *County Education Officer,* R. M. Sharp

GLOUCESTERSHIRE, Shire Hall, Gloucester GL1 2TP. Tel: 0452-425301. *Director,* K. D. Anderson

HAMPSHIRE, The Castle, Winchester SO23 8UJ. Tel: 0962-841841. *County Education Officer,* P. J. Coles

HEREFORD AND WORCESTER, Castle Street, Worcester WR1 3AG. Tel: 0905-763763. *County Education Officer,* vacant

HERTFORDSHIRE, County Hall, Hertford SG13 8DF. Tel: 0992-555827. *County Education Officer,* Mrs H. du Quesnay

HUMBERSIDE, County Hall, Cross Street, Beverley HU17 9BA. Tel: 0482-867131. *Director,* Dr M. W. Garnett

ISLE OF WIGHT, County Hall, Newport PO30 1UD. Tel: 0983-823400. *Director,* Dr J. A. Williams

KENT, Springfield, Maidstone ME14 2LJ. Tel: 0622-671411. *Director,* R. Pryke

LANCASHIRE, PO Box 61, County Hall, Preston PR1 8RJ. Tel: 0772-254868. *Chief Education Officer,* A. J. Collier

LEICESTERSHIRE, County Hall, Glenfield, Leicester LE3 8RF. Tel: 0533-323232. *Director,* K. H. Wood-Allum

LINCOLNSHIRE, County Offices, Newland, Lincoln LN1 1YL. Tel: 0522-552222. *Director,* A. M. Ridings

NORFOLK, County Hall, Martineau Lane, Norwich NR1 2DL. Tel: 0603-222300. *Director,* M. H. Edwards

NORTHAMPTONSHIRE, Northampton House, Northampton NN1 2HX. Tel: 0604-236236. *Director,* R. Atkinson

NORTHUMBERLAND, County Hall, Morpeth NE61 2EF. Tel: 0670-533000. *Director,* C. C. Tipple

NORTH YORKSHIRE, County Hall, Racecourse Lane, Northallerton DL7 8AE. Tel: 0609-780780. *Director,* F. F. Evans

NOTTINGHAMSHIRE, County Hall, West Bridgford, Nottingham NG2 7QP. Tel: 0602-823823. *Director,* P. J. Housden

OXFORDSHIRE, Macclesfield House, New Road, Oxford OX1 1NA. Tel: 0865-815449. *Chief Education Officer,* Mrs J. Stephens

SHROPSHIRE, The Shirehall, Abbey Foregate, Shrewsbury SY2 6ND. Tel: 0743-254302. *County Education Officer,* P. B. Cates

SOMERSET, County Hall, Taunton TA1 4DY. Tel: 0823-333451. *Chief Education Officer,* Mrs J. Wisker

STAFFORDSHIRE, Tipping Street, Stafford ST16 2DH. Tel: 0785-223121. *Chief Education Officer,* Dr P. J. Hunter

SUFFOLK, St Andrew House, County Hall, St Helen Street, Ipswich IP4 2JS. Tel: 0473-230000. *County Education Officer,* D. J. Peachey

SURREY, County Hall, Penrhyn Road, Kingston upon Thames KT1 2DJ. Tel: 081-541 9501. *County Education Officer,* Ms J. H. Burrow

WARWICKSHIRE, PO Box 24, 22 Northgate Street, Warwick CV34 4SR. Tel: 0926-410410. *Director,* Ms M. Maden

WEST SUSSEX, County Hall, Chichester PO19 1RF. Tel: 0243-777100. *Director,* R. D. C. Bunker

WILTSHIRE, County Hall, Trowbridge BA14 8JB. Tel: 0225-753641. *Director,* Dr K. Robinson

METROPOLITAN DISTRICT COUNCILS

BARNSLEY, Berneslai Close, Barnsley. Tel: 0226-770770. *Director (acting),* M. Warrington

BIRMINGHAM, Council House, Margaret Street, B3 3BU. Tel: 021-235 2590/2872. *Chief Education Officer,* T. Brighouse

BOLTON, Paderborn House, Civic Centre, BL1 1JW. Tel: 0204-22311. *Education Officer,* B. Hughes

BRADFORD, Flockton House, Flockton Road, BD4 7RY. Tel: 0274-751700. *Education Officer,* Mrs S. Conway

BURY, Athenaeum House, Market Street, BL9 0BN. Tel: 061-705 5000. *Chief Education Officer,* J. Beech

CALDERDALE, Northgate House, Halifax HX1 1UN. Tel: 0422-357257. *Director,* Miss J. Tonge

COVENTRY, The Council House, Earl Street, CV1 5RR. Tel: 0203-831500. *Chief Education Officer,* C. Farmer

DONCASTER, PO Box 266, The Council House, DN1 3AD. Tel: 0302-737222. *Director,* A. M. Taylor

DUDLEY, Westox House, 1 Trinity Road, DY1 1JB. Tel: 0384-452200. *Chief Education Officer,* R. K. Westerby

GATESHEAD, Civic Centre, Regent Street, NE8 1HH. Tel: 091-477 1011. *Director,* D. Arbon

KIRKLEES, Oldgate House, 2 Oldgate, Huddersfield HD1 6QW. Tel: 0484-422133. *Chief Education Officer,* Ms J. Devlin

KNOWSLEY, Huyton Hey Road, Huyton, Merseyside L36 5YH. Tel: 051-443 3220. *Education Officer,* A. Culley

LEEDS, Merrion House, 110 Merrion Centre, LS2 8DT. Tel: 0532-348080. *Chief Education Officer,* Mrs J. A. M. Strong

LIVERPOOL, 14 Sir Thomas Street, LI 6BJ. Tel: 051-227 3911. *Director*, M. F. Cogley
MANCHESTER, Cumberland House, Crown Square, M60 3BB. Tel: 061-234 7121. *Education Officer*, R. Jobson
NEWCASTLE UPON TYNE, Civic Centre, NE99 2BN. Tel: 091-232 8520. *Education Officer*, N. Purser
NORTH TYNESIDE, Stephenson House, Stephenson Street, North Shields NE30 1QA. Tel: 091-257 5544. *Education Officer*, C. Benneworth
OLDHAM, Old Town Hall, Middleton Road, Chadderton, OL9 6PP. Tel: 061-678 4200. *Education Officer*, W. R. Kneen, PH.D.
ROCHDALE, PO Box 70, Municipal Offices, Smith Street, OL16 1YD. Tel: 0706-47474. *Director*, Mrs D. Cavanagh
ROTHERHAM, Norfolk House, Walker Place, Rotherham, S60 1QT. Tel: 0709-382121. *Education Officer*, B. H. Yemm
ST HELENS, Rivington Centre, Rivington Road WA10 4ND. Tel: 0744-24061. *Director*, B. M. Mainwaring
SALFORD, Chapel Street, M3 5LT. Tel: 061-832 9751. *Chief Education Officer*, D. Johnston
SANDWELL, PO Box 41, Shaftesbury House, 402 High Street, West Bromwich B70 9LT. Tel: 021-525 7366. *Director*, S. Gallacher
SEFTON, Town Hall, Oriel Road, Bootle, Merseyside L20 7AE. Tel: 051-933 6003. *Education Officer*, J. A. Marsden
SHEFFIELD, PO Box 67, Leopold Street, SI 1RJ. Tel: 0742-734420/1. *Director*, Ms A. Muller
SOLIHULL, PO Box 20, Council House, B91 3QU. Tel: 021-704 6674. *Director*, C. J. Trinick
SOUTH TYNESIDE, Town Hall and Civic Offices, Westoe Road, South Shields NE33 2RL. Tel: 091-427 1717. *Education Officer*, I. L. Reid
STOCKPORT, Stopford House, Piccadilly, SK1 3XE. Tel: 061-474 3808. *Director*, M. K. J. Hunt
SUNDERLAND, PO Box 101, Civic Centre, SR2 7DN. Tel: 091-567 6161. *Education Officer*, D. A. Bowers
TAMESIDE, Council Offices, Wellington Road, Ashton-under-Lyne OL6 6DL. Tel: 061-342 8355. *Director*, A. M. Webster
TRAFFORD, Town Hall, Tatton Road, Sale M33 1YR. Tel: 061-872 2101. *Director*, A. Lee
WAKEFIELD, County Hall, WF1 2QW. Tel: 0924-290900. *Education Officer*, A. Lenney
WALSALL, Civic Centre, Darwall Street, WS1 1DQ. Tel: 0922-650000. *Education Officer*, M. J. Quinn
WIGAN, Gateway House, Standishgate, WN1 1AE. Tel: 0942-44991. *Education Officer*, J. K. Hampson
WIRRAL, Hamilton Building, Conway Street, Birkenhead L41 4FD. Tel: 051-666 2121. *Director*, D. Rigby
WOLVERHAMPTON, Civic Centre, St Peter's Square, WV1 1RR. Tel: 0902-27811. *Director*, Ms C. Adams

LONDON

*Inner London borough

BARKING AND DAGENHAM, Town Hall, Barking, Essex IG11 7LU. Tel: 081-592 4500. *Education Officer*, A. Larbalastier
BARNET, Town Hall, Friern Barnet Lane, Friern Barnet, N11 3DL. Tel: 081-368 1255. *Education Officer*, vacant
BEXLEY, Hill View, Hill View Drive, Welling, Kent DA16 5RY. Tel: 081-303 7777. *Director*, P. McGee
BRENT, Chesterfield House, 9 Park Lane, Wembley, Middx. HA9 7RW. Tel: 081-900 5443. *Director*, G. Benham
BROMLEY, Town Hall, Widmore Road, Bromley, Kent BR1 1SB. Tel: 081-464 3333. *Director*, A. Baxter

*CAMDEN, Crowndale Centre, 218–220 Eversholt Street, NW1 1BD. Tel: 071-911 1525. *Education Officer*, P. Mitchell
*CITY OF LONDON, Education Department, Corporation of London, PO Box 270, Guildhall, EC2P 2EJ. Tel: 071-332 1750. *City Education Officer*, D. Smith
*CITY OF WESTMINSTER, City Hall, Victoria Street, SW1E 6QP. Tel: 071-828 8070. *Education Officer*, Mrs D. Tuck
CROYDON, Taberner House, Park Lane, CR9 1TP. Tel: 081-686 4433. *Director*, P. Benians
EALING, Perceval House, 14–18 Uxbridge Road, W5 2HL. Tel: 081-579 2424. *Director*, M. Herrman
ENFIELD, PO Box 56, Civic Centre, Silver Street, EN1 3XQ. Tel: 081-967 9257. *Director*, G. Hutchinson
*GREENWICH, Riverside House, Woolwich High Street, Woolwich, SE18 6DN. Tel: 081-854 8888. *Director*, J. Kramer
*HACKNEY, Edith Cavell Building, Enfield Road, N1 5AZ. Tel: 071-214 8400. *Director*, G. John
*HAMMERSMITH AND FULHAM, Cambridge House, Cambridge Grove, W6 4LE. Tel: 081-748 3020. *Director*, Ms C. Whatford
HARINGEY, 48 Station Road, N22 4TY. Tel: 081-975 9700. *Director*, R. L. Jones
HARROW, PO Box 22, Civic Centre, Harrow HA1 2UW. Tel: 081-863 5611. *Director*, Mrs C. Gilbert
HAVERING, Mercury House, Mercury Gardens, Romford RM1 3DR. Tel: 0708-766999. *Director*, C. Hardy
HILLINGDON, Civic Centre, Uxbridge, Middx. UB8 1UW. Tel: 0895-250528. *Education Officer*, Ms K. Higgins
HOUNSLOW, Civic Centre, Lampton Road, TW3 4DN. Tel: 081-862 5301. *Director*, J. D. Trickett
*ISLINGTON, Laycock Street, N1 1TH. Tel: 071-457 5753. *Education Officer*, C. Webb
*KENSINGTON AND CHELSEA, Town Hall, Hornton Street, W8 7NX. Tel: 071-937 5464. *Education Officer*, M. Stoten
KINGSTON UPON THAMES, Guildhall, KT1 1EU. Tel: 081-547 5280. *Director*, W. Dickinson
*LAMBETH, Blue Star House, 234–244 Stockwell Road, SW9 9SP. Tel: 071-926 2248. *Chief Education Officer*, Mrs B. Burchell
*LEWISHAM, Laurence House, 1 Catford Road, SE6 4RY. Tel: 081-695 6000. *Director*, L. Fullick
MERTON, Civic Centre, London Road, Morden, Surrey SM4 5DX. Tel: 081-545 3251. *Director*, Ms L. Kant
NEWHAM, Broadway House, 322 High Street, E15 1AJ. Tel: 081-555 5552. *Director*, I. Harrison
REDBRIDGE, Lynton House, 255–259 High Road, Ilford, IG1 1NN. Tel: 081-478 3020. *Director*, K. G. M. Ratcliffe
RICHMOND UPON THAMES, Regal House, London Road, Twickenham, TW1 3QB. Tel: 081-891 1411. *Director*, G. Alexander
*SOUTHWARK, 1 Bradenham Close, SE17 2QA. Tel: 071-525 5000. *Education Officer*, G. Mott
SUTTON, The Grove, Carshalton, Surrey SM5 3AL. Tel: 081-770 5000. *Director*, C. Blurton
*TOWER HAMLETS, Mulberry Place, 5 Clove Crescent, E14 2BG. Tel: 071-512 4200. *Education Officer*, Mrs A. Sofer
WALTHAM FOREST, Municipal Offices, High Road, Leyton E10 5QJ. Tel: 081-527 5544. *Director*, A. Lockhart
*WANDSWORTH, Town Hall, Wandsworth High Street, SW18 2PU. Tel: 081-871 7890. *Director*, D. Naismith

WALES

COUNTY COUNCILS

CLWYD, Shire Hall, Mold CH7 6ND. Tel: 0352-702500. *Director*, K. McDonogh

DYFED, Pibwrlwyd, Carmarthen SA31 2NH. Tel: 0267-233333. *Director*, J. G. Ellis
GWENT, County Hall, Cwmbran NP44 2XD. Tel: 0633-838838. *Director*, J. D. Griffiths
GWYNEDD, County Offices, Caernarfon LL55 1SH. Tel: 0286-672255. *Director*, G. E. Humphreys
MID GLAMORGAN, County Hall, Cathays Park, Cardiff CFI 3NE. Tel: 0222-820820. *Director*, E. Roberts
POWYS, County Hall, Llandrindod Wells LDI 5LG. Tel: 0597-826000. *Director*, M. R. J. Barker
SOUTH GLAMORGAN, County Hall, Atlantic Wharf, Cardiff CFI 5UW. Tel: 0222-872000. *Director*, T. Parry Davies
WEST GLAMORGAN, County Hall, Swansea SAI 3SN. Tel: 0792-471111. *Director*, H. G. Roberts

SCOTLAND

REGIONAL AND ISLANDS COUNCILS

BORDERS, Regional Headquarters, Newtown St Boswells, Melrose TD6 0SA. Tel: 0835-23301. *Director*, I. Dutton
CENTRAL, Regional Council Offices, Viewforth, Stirling FK8 2ET. Tel: 0786-442000. *Director*, I. Collie
DUMFRIES AND GALLOWAY, 30 Edinburgh Road, Dumfries DGI 1JQ. Tel: 0387-61234. *Director*, W. C. Fordyce
FIFE, Fife House, North Street, Glenrothes KY7 5LT. Tel: 0592-754411. *Director*, B. Welsh
GRAMPIAN, Summerhill Education Centre, Stronsay Drive, Aberdeen AB2 6JA. Tel: 0224-664600. *Director*, J. Graham
HIGHLAND, Regional Buildings, Glenurquhart Road, Inverness IV3 5NX. Tel: 0463-702081. *Director*, Dr C. E. Stewart
LOTHIAN, 40 Torphichen Street, Edinburgh EH8 8JB. Tel: 031-229 9166. *Director*, Ms E. Reid
ORKNEY, Council Offices, Kirkwall KW15 INY. Tel: 0856-873535. *Director*, J. Anderson
SHETLAND, 1 Harbour Street, Lerwick ZEI OLS. Tel: 0595-3535. *Director*, J. Halcrow
STRATHCLYDE, 20 India Street, Glasgow G2 4PF. Tel: 041-249 4150. *Director*, F. Pignatelli
TAYSIDE, Tayside House, 28 Crichton Street, Dundee DDI 3RJ. Tel: 0382-23281. *Director*, A. B. Watson
WESTERN ISLES, Council Offices, Sandwick Road, Stornoway, Isle of Lewis PA87 2BW. Tel: 0851-703773. *Director*, N. R. Galbraith

NORTHERN IRELAND

EDUCATION AND LIBRARY BOARDS

BELFAST, Board Headquarters, 40 Academy Street, Belfast BTI 2NQ. Tel: 0232-329211. *Chief Executive*, T. G. J. Moag
NORTH EASTERN, County Hall, 182 Galgorm Road, Ballymena, Co. Antrim BT42 1HN. Tel: 0266-653333. *Chief Executive*, G. Topping
SOUTH EASTERN, 18 Windsor Avenue, Belfast BT9 6EF. Tel: 0232-381188. *Chief Executive*, T. Nolan, OBE
SOUTHERN, 3 Charlemont Place, The Mall, Armagh BT61 9AX. Tel: 0861-523811. *Chief Executive*, J. G. Kelly
WESTERN, 1 Hospital Road, Omagh, Co. Tyrone BT79 0AW. Tel: 0662-240240. *Chief Executive*, M. H. F. Murphy, OBE

ISLANDS

GUERNSEY, PO Box 32, Grange Road, St Peter Port. Tel: 0481-710821. *Director*, J. D. Stephenson

JERSEY, PO Box 142, St Saviour JE4 8QJ. Tel: 0534-509500. *Director*, B. Grady
ISLE OF MAN, Department of Education, Murray House, Mount Havelock, Douglas. Tel: 0624-685685. *Director*, G. Baker
ISLES OF SCILLY, Town Hall, St Mary's TR21 0LW. Tel: 0720-22537. *Secretary for Education*, P. S. Hygate

---

ADVISORY BODIES

SCHOOLS

EDUCATION OTHERWISE, PO Box 120, Leamington Spa, Warks. CV32 7ER. *Helpline*, tel: 0926-886828
INTERNATIONAL BACCALAUREATE, Examinations Office, Pascal Close, St Mellons, Cardiff CF3 0YP. Tel: 0222-770770. *Director of Examinations*, C. Carthew

INDEPENDENT SCHOOLS

ASSISTED PLACES COMMITTEE, 26 Queen Anne's Gate, London SWIH 9AN. Tel: 071-222 9595. *Secretary*, Mrs M. L. Shaw
COMMON ENTRANCE BOARD, Jordan House, Christchurch Road, New Milton, Hants. BH25 6QJ. Tel: 0425-621111. *Secretary*, Mrs J. Williams
GOVERNING BODIES ASSOCIATION, Windleshaw Lodge, Withyham, Nr. Hartfield, E. Sussex TN7 4DB. Tel: 0892-770879. *Secretary*, D. G. Banwell
GOVERNING BODIES OF GIRLS' SCHOOLS ASSOCIATION, Windleshaw Lodge, Withyham, Nr. Hartfield, E. Sussex TN7 4DB. Tel: 0892-770879. *Secretary*, D. G. Banwell
INDEPENDENT SCHOOLS INFORMATION SERVICE, 56 Buckingham Gate, London SWIE 6AG. Tel: 071-630 8793. *National Director*, D. J. Woodhead

FURTHER EDUCATION

FURTHER EDUCATION UNIT, Unit 3, Citadel Place, Tinworth Street, London SEII 5BR. Tel: 071-962 1280. *Chief Officer*, G. Stanton
NATIONAL COUNCIL FOR VOCATIONAL QUALIFICATIONS, 222 Euston Road, London NWI 2BZ. Tel: 071-387 9898. *Chief Executive*, J. Hillier

Regional Advisory Councils

ASSOCIATION OF COLLEGES IN THE EASTERN REGION, Merlin Place, Milton Road, Cambridge CB4 4DP. Tel: 0223-424022. *Chief Officer*, A. Young
CENTRA (NORTH WESTERN REGIONAL ADVISORY COUNCIL FOR FURTHER EDUCATION), Walkden Road, Worsley, Manchester M28 4QE. Tel: 061-702 8700. *Manager*, R. S. Welsh
EMFEC (EAST MIDLAND FURTHER EDUCATION COUNCIL), Robins Wood House, Robins Wood Road, Aspley, Nottingham NG8 3NH. Tel: 0602-293291. *Chief Executive*, R. Ainscough
LASER ADVISORY COUNCIL (LONDON AND SOUTH EAST), Chenies House, 21 Bedford Square, London WCIB 3HH. Tel: 071-637 3073. *Director*, L. South
NORTHERN COUNCIL FOR FURTHER EDUCATION, 5 Grosvenor Villas, Grosvenor Road, Newcastle upon Tyne NE2 2RU. Tel: 091-281 3242. *Director*, J. F. Pearce
SOUTHERN REGIONAL COUNCIL FOR EDUCATION AND TRAINING, The Mezzanine Suite, Civic Centre, Reading RGI 7TD. Tel: 0734-390592. *Chief Officer*, B. J. Knowles
SOUTH WEST ASSOCIATION FOR FURTHER EDUCATION AND TRAINING, Bishops Hull House, Bishops Hull,

Taunton, Somerset TA1 5RA. Tel: 0823-335491. *Secretary,*
F. S. Fisher

WELSH JOINT EDUCATION COMMITTEE, 245 Western
Avenue, Cardiff CF5 2YX. Tel: 0222-561231. *Secretary,*
C. Heycock

YORKSHIRE AND HUMBERSIDE ASSOCIATION FOR
FURTHER AND HIGHER EDUCATION, 13 Wellington
Road East, Dewsbury, W. Yorks. WF13 1XG. Tel: 0924-
450900. *Chief Executive,* Ms P. Cole

HIGHER EDUCATION

ASSOCIATION OF COMMONWEALTH UNIVERSITIES, John
Foster House, 36 Gordon Square, London WC1H 0PE.
Tel: 071-387 8572. *Secretary-General,* Dr A.
Christodoulou, CBE

COMMITTEE OF VICE-CHANCELLORS AND PRINCIPALS
OF THE UNIVERSITIES OF THE UNITED KINGDOM,
29 Tavistock Square, London WC1H 9EZ. Tel: 071-387
9231. *Chairman,* Dr K. Edwards

HIGHER EDUCATION QUALITY COUNCIL, 344–354
Gray's Inn Road, London WC1X 8BP. Tel: 071-837 2223.
Company Secretary, G. L. Middleton

NORTHERN IRELAND HIGHER EDUCATION COUNCIL,
c/o Department of Education for Northern Ireland,
Rathgael House, Balloo Road, Bangor BT19 7PR. Tel:
0247–270077. *Chairman,* Sir Kenneth Bloomfield

CURRICULUM COUNCILS, ETC.

CURRICULUM COUNCIL FOR WALES/CURRICULUM AND
ASSESSMENT AUTHORITY FOR WALES, Castle
Buildings, Womanby Street, Cardiff CF1 9SX. Tel: 0222-
344946. *Chief Executive,* B. Jones

NORTHERN IRELAND CURRICULUM COUNCIL,
Stranmillis College, Stranmillis Road, Belfast BT9 5DY.
Tel: 0232-381414. *Chief Executive,* Mrs C. Coxhead

SCHOOL CURRICULUM AND ASSESSMENT AUTHORITY,
Newcombe House, 45 Notting Hill Gate, London
W11 3JB. Tel: 071-243 9238. *Chairman,* Sir Ron Dearing.
Chief Executive, C. Woodhead

SCOTTISH CONSULTATIVE COUNCIL ON THE
CURRICULUM, Gardyne Road, Broughty Ferry, Dundee
DD5 1NY. Tel: 0382-455053. *Chief Executive,*
C. E. Harrison

TVEI UNIT, Training Agency, Employment Department,
Room E435, Moorfoot, Sheffield S1 4PQ. Tel: 0742-
593857

EXAMINING BODIES

GCSE

NORTHERN EXAMINATIONS AND ASSESSMENT BOARD,
Devas Street, Manchester M15 6EX. Tel: 061-953 1180.
Chief Executive, Ms K. Tattersall

NORTHERN IRELAND SCHOOLS EXAMINATIONS AND
ASSESSMENT COUNCIL, Beechill House, 42 Beechill
Road, Belfast BT8 4RS. Tel: 0232-704666. *Chief
Executive,* W. J. Caves

SOUTHERN EXAMINING GROUP, Stag Hill House,
Guildford, Surrey GU2 5XJ. Tel: 0483-506506/0865-
510085. *Joint Secretaries,* J. A. Day; J. Pailing

UNIVERSITY OF LONDON EXAMINATIONS AND
ASSESSMENT COUNCIL, The Lindens, 139 Lexden
Road, Colchester CO3 3RL. Tel: 0206-549595; Stewart
House, 32 Russell Square, London WC1B 5DN. Tel: 071-
331 4000. *Chief Executive,* A. Smith

WELSH JOINT EDUCATION COMMITTEE, 245 Western
Avenue, Cardiff CF5 2YX. Tel: 0222-561231. *Secretary,*
C. Heycock

WEST MIDLANDS EXAMINATIONS BOARD, Mill Wharf,
Mill Street, Birmingham B6 4BU. Tel: 021-628 2000.
Secretary, B. Swift

A-LEVEL

ASSOCIATED EXAMINING BOARD, Stag Hill House,
Guildford, Surrey GU2 5XJ. Tel: 0483-506506. *Secretary-
General,* J. A. Day

NORTHERN EXAMINATIONS AND ASSESSMENT BOARD,
Devas Street, Manchester M15 6EX. Tel: 061-953 1180.
Chief Executive, Ms K. Tattersall

NORTHERN IRELAND SCHOOLS EXAMINATIONS AND
ASSESSMENT COUNCIL, Beechill House, 42 Beechill
Road, Belfast BT8 4RS. Tel: 0232-704666. *Chief
Executive,* W. J. Caves

OXFORD AND CAMBRIDGE SCHOOLS EXAMINATION
BOARD, Purbeck House, Purbeck Road, Cambridge
CB2 2PU. Tel: 0223-411211. *Secretary-General,* H. F. King

OXFORD AND CAMBRIDGE SCHOOLS EXAMINATION
BOARD, Elsfield Way, Oxford OX2 8EP. Tel: 0865-54421.
Secretary (acting), J. G. Lloyd

UNIVERSITY OF CAMBRIDGE LOCAL EXAMINATIONS
SYNDICATE, Syndicate Buildings, 1 Hills Road,
Cambridge CB1 2EU. Tel: 0223-61111. *Secretary,*
M. P. Halstead

UNIVERSITY OF LONDON EXAMINATIONS AND
ASSESSMENT COUNCIL, Stewart House, 32 Russell
Square, London WC1B 5DN. Tel: 071-331 4000. *Chief
Executive,* A. Smith

UNIVERSITY OF OXFORD DELEGACY OF LOCAL
EXAMINATIONS, Ewert House, Ewert Place,
Summertown, Oxford OX2 7BZ. Tel: 0865-54291.
Secretary, J. Pailing

WELSH JOINT EDUCATION COMMITTEE, 245 Western
Avenue, Cardiff CF5 2YX. Tel: 0222-561231. *Secretary,*
C. Heycock

SCOTLAND

SCOTTISH EXAMINATION BOARD, Ironmills Road,
Dalkeith, Midlothian EH22 1LE. Tel: 031-663 6601. *Chief
Executive,* H. A. Long, PH.D.

SCOTTISH VOCATIONAL EDUCATION COUNCIL,
Hanover House, 24 Douglas Street, Glasgow G2 7NQ.
Tel: 041-248 7900. *Chief Executive,* T. J. McCool

FURTHER EDUCATION

BUSINESS AND TECHNOLOGY EDUCATION COUNCIL,
Central House, Upper Woburn Place, London
WC1H 0HH. Tel: 071-413 8400. *Chief Executive,*
J. E. Sellars

CITY AND GUILDS OF LONDON INSTITUTE, 76 Portland
Place, London W1N 4AA. Tel: 071-278 2468. *Director-
General,* Dr N. Carey

RSA EXAMINATIONS BOARD, Westwood Way, Coventry
CV4 8HS. Tel: 0203-470033. *Chief Executive,* M. F. Cross

VOCATIONAL EDUCATION UNIT, 46 Britannia Street,
London WC1X 9RG. Tel: 071-278 2468. *Chairman,*
P. Wates; *Division Manager,* Ms H. Aylett

FUNDING COUNCILS

SCHOOLS

FUNDING AGENCY FOR SCHOOLS, Albion Wharf,
25 Skeldergate, York YO1 2XL. Comes into operation in
April 1994

FURTHER EDUCATION

FURTHER EDUCATION FUNDING COUNCIL FOR ENGLAND, Sheriffs Orchard, Greyfriars Road, Coventry CU1 3PJ. Tel: 0203-530300. *Chief Executive,* W. H. Stubbs

SCOTTISH FURTHER EDUCATION FUNDING UNIT, Scottish Office Education Department, 43 Jeffrey Street, Edinburgh EH1 IDN. *Director,* J. G. Henderson

WELSH FUNDING COUNCIL, FURTHER EDUCATION DIVISION, Lambourne House, Cardiff Business Park, Llanishen, Cardiff CF4 5GL. Tel: 0222-761861. *Chief Executive,* Prof. J. A. Andrews

HIGHER EDUCATION

HIGHER EDUCATION FUNDING COUNCIL FOR ENGLAND, Northavon House, Coldharbour Lane, Bristol BS16 IQD. Tel: 0272-317317. *Chief Executive,* Prof. G. Davies, FEng.

SCOTTISH HIGHER EDUCATION FUNDING COUNCIL, Donaldson House, 97 Haymarket Terrace, Edinburgh EH12 5HD. Tel: 031-244 5345. *Chief Executive,* Prof. J. Sizer

WELSH FUNDING COUNCIL, HIGHER EDUCATION DIVISION, Lambourne House, Cardiff Business Park, Llanishen, Cardiff CF4 5GL. Tel: 0222-761861. *Chief Executive,* Prof. J. A. Andrews

ADMISSIONS AND COURSE INFORMATION

ART AND DESIGN ADMISSIONS REGISTRY, Penn House, 9 Broad Street, Hereford HR4 9AP. Tel: 0432-266653. *Registrar,* T. W. M. Gourdie

CAREERS RESEARCH AND ADVISORY CENTRE (CRAC), Sheraton House, Castle Park, Cambridge CB3 OAX. Tel: 0223-460277. *Director,* D. Blandford. *Publishers,* Hobsons Publishing PLC, Bateman Street, Cambridge CB2 ILZ

COMMITTEE OF SCOTTISH HIGHER EDUCATION PRINCIPALS (COSHEP), St Andrews House, 141 West Nile Street, Glasgow G2 2RN. Tel: 041-353 1880. *Secretary,* Dr R. L. Crawford

GRADUATE TEACHER TRAINING REGISTRY, Fulton House, Jessop Avenue, Cheltenham, Glos. GL50 3SH

SOCIAL WORK ADMISSIONS SYSTEM, Fulton House, Jessop Avenue, Cheltenham GL50 3SH. Tel: 0242-225977. *Admissions Officer,* Ms M. Griffiths

TEACHER EDUCATION ADMISSIONS CLEARING HOUSE (TEACH) (Scotland only), PO Box 165, Holyrood Road, Edinburgh EH8 8AT. *Registrar,* Miss R. C. Williamson

UNIVERSITIES AND COLLEGES ADMISSIONS SERVICE, Fulton House, Jessop Avenue, Cheltenham GL50 3SH. Tel: 0242-222444. *Chief Executives,* M. A. Higgins (*Corporate Affairs*); P. A. Oakley (*Applications*). Application materials from PO Box 67, Cheltenham GL50 3SF

UNIVERSITIES

THE UNIVERSITY OF ABERDEEN (1495)
Regent Walk, Aberdeen AB9 1FX
Tel 0224-272000
Full-time Students (1992–3), 8,600

Chancellor, Sir Kenneth Alexander, FRSE (1987)
Principal, Prof. J. Maxwell Irvine, PH.D.
Secretary, N. R. D. Begg
Rector, vacant

ANGLIA POLYTECHNIC UNIVERSITY (1992)
Victoria Road South, Chelmsford, Essex CM1 ILL
Tel 0245-493131
Full-time Students (1992–3), 7,863
Chancellor, The Lord Prior, PC
Vice-Chancellor, M. J. Salmon
Head of Student Administration, D. Davis

ASTON UNIVERSITY (1966)
Aston Triangle, Birmingham B4 7ET
Tel 021-359 3611
Full-time Students (1992–3), 4,240
Chancellor, Sir Adrian Cadbury (1979)
Vice-Chancellor, Prof. Sir Frederick Crawford, PH.D., D.ENG., D.SC., FEng.
Registrar and Secretary, R. D. A. Packham

THE UNIVERSITY OF BATH (1966)
Claverton Down, Bath BA2 7AY
Tel 0225-826826
Full-time Students (1992–3), 5,000
Chancellor, Sir Denys Henderson (1993)
Vice-Chancellor, Prof. V. D. VanderLinde
Secretary and Registrar, R. M. Mawditt, OBE, FRSA

THE UNIVERSITY OF BIRMINGHAM (1900)
Edgbaston, Birmingham B15 2TT
Tel 021-414 3344
Full-time Students (1992–3), 13,000
Chancellor, Sir Alexander Jarratt, CB (1983)
Vice-Chancellor, Prof. Sir Michael Thompson, D.SC.
Registrar and Secretary, D. R. Holmes

BOURNEMOUTH UNIVERSITY (1992)
(formerly Bournemouth Polytechnic)
Poole House, Talbot Campus, Fern Barrow,
Dorset BH12 5BB
Tel 0202-524111
Full-time Students (1992–3), 8,000
Chancellor, The Baroness Cox (1992)
Vice-Chancellor, Dr B. R. MacManus
Secretary and Registrar, Miss B. Chamberlain

THE UNIVERSITY OF BRADFORD (1966)
Bradford BD7 IDP
Tel 0274-733466
Full-time Students (1992–3), 5,765
Chancellor, Sir Trevor Holdsworth (1992)
Vice-Chancellor, Prof. D. J. Johns, PH.D., D.SC. (1989)
Registrar and Secretary, D. W. Granger, MBE

THE UNIVERSITY OF BRIGHTON (1992)
(formerly Brighton Polytechnic)
Mithras House, Lewes Road, Brighton BN2 4AT
Tel 0273-600900
Full-time Students (1992–3), 8,806
Chairman of the Board, M. J. Aldrich
Director, Prof. D. J. Watson
Deputy Director, D. E. House

THE UNIVERSITY OF BRISTOL (1909)
Senate House, Tyndall Avenue, Bristol BS8 ITH
Tel 0272-303030
Full-time Students (1992–3), 10,000

Chancellor, Sir Jeremy Morse, KCMG (1989)
Vice-Chancellor, Sir John Kingman, FRS
Registrar, vacant
Secretary, J. H. M. Parry

BRUNEL UNIVERSITY (1966)
Uxbridge, Middx. UB8 3PH
Tel 0895-274000
Full-time Students (1992–3), 5,690
Chancellor, The Earl of Halsbury, FRS (1966)
Vice-Chancellor, Prof. M. J. H. Sterling
Secretary-General and Registrar, D. Neave

THE UNIVERSITY OF BUCKINGHAM (1983)
Founded 1976 as University College at Buckingham
Buckingham MK18 1EG
Tel 0280-814080
Full-time Students (1992–3), 908
Chancellor, The Baroness Thatcher, OM, PC, FRS (1992)
Vice-Chancellor, The Rt. Hon. Sir Richard Luce (1992)
Registrar and Secretary, M. Lavis, PH.D.

THE UNIVERSITY OF CAMBRIDGE
University Offices, The Old Schools, Cambridge CB2 1TN
Tel 0223-337733
Number of undergraduates in residence 1993–4: *Men*,
   6,108; *Women*, 4,348

UNIVERSITY OFFICERS, ETC.
Chancellor, HRH The Duke of Edinburgh, KG, KT, OM, GBE,
   PC (1977)
Vice-Chancellor, Prof. Sir David Williams (*Wolfson*) (1989)
High Steward, The Lord Runcie, PC, DD (1991)
Deputy High Steward, The Lord Richardson of
   Duntisbourne, PC, MBE, TD (1983)
Commissary, The Lord Oliver of Aylmerton, PC (*Trinity
   Hall*) (1989)
Proctors, P. Echlin (*Clare Hall*); F. J. J. Leeper (*Emmanuel*) (1993)
Orator, A. J. Bowen (*Jesus*) (1993)
Registrary, S. G. Fleet, PH.D. (*Downing*) (1983)
Deputy Registrary, N. J. B. A. Branson, PH.D. (*Darwin*)
   (1993)
Librarian, F. W. Ratcliffe, PH.D. (*Corpus Christi*) (1980)
Treasurer, Ms J. Womack (*Trinity*) (1993)
Secretary-General of the Faculties, D. A. Livesey,
   PH.D. (*Emmanuel*) (1992)
Director of the Fitzwilliam Museum, S. S. Jervis (*Corpus
   Christi*) (1990)

COLLEGES AND HALLS, ETC.
with dates of foundation

CHRIST'S (1505), *Master*, Prof. Sir Hans Kornberg, PH.D.,
   D.SC., SC.D., FRS (1983)
CHURCHILL (1960), *Master*, Prof. A. N. Broers, PH.D., FRS
   (1990)
CLARE (1326), *Master*, Prof. B. A. Hepple (1993)
CLARE HALL (1966), *President*, Prof. D. A. Low, PH.D.
   (1987)
CORPUS CHRISTI (1352), *Master*, M. W. McCrum (1980)
DARWIN (1964), *Master*, Prof. G. E. R. Lloyd, PH.D., FBA
   (1989)
DOWNING (1800), *Master*, P. Mathias, CBE, Litt.D., FBA
   (1987)
EMMANUEL (1584), *Master*, The Lord St John of Fawsley,
   PC, PH.D. (1991)
FITZWILLIAM (1966), *Master*, Prof. A. W. Cuthbert, PH.D.,
   FRS (1991)

GIRTON (1869), *Mistress*, Mrs J. J. d'A. Campbell, CMG
   (1992)
GONVILLE AND CAIUS (1348), *Master*, Prof. P. Gray, SC.D.,
   FRS (1988)
HOMERTON (1824) (for B.Ed. students), *Principal*,
   Mrs K. B. Pretty, PH.D. (1991)
HUGHES HALL (1885), (for post-graduate students),
   President, J. T. Dingle, D.SC. (1993)
JESUS (1496), *Master*, Prof. the Lord Renfrew of
   Kaimsthorn, SC.D. (1986)
KING'S (1441), *Provost*, Prof. P. P. G. Bateson, SC.D., FRS
   (1987)
*LUCY CAVENDISH COLLEGE (1965) (for women research
   students and mature and affiliated undergraduates),
   President, Dame Anne Warburton, DCVO, CMG (1985)
MAGDALENE (1542), *Master*, Sir David Calcutt, QC (1985)
*NEW HALL (1954), *President*, Mrs V. L. Pearl, PH.D. (1981)
*NEWNHAM (1871), *Principal*, Ms O. S. O'Neill (1992)
PEMBROKE (1347), *Master*, Sir Roger Tomkys, KCMG (1992)
PETERHOUSE (1284), *Master*, Prof. Sir John Meurig
   Thomas, FRS (1993)
QUEENS' (1448), *President*, Revd J. C. Polkinghorne, SC.D.,
   FRS (1989)
ROBINSON (1977), *Warden*, Prof. the Lord Lewis of
   Newnham, SC.D., FRS (1977)
ST CATHARINE'S (1473), *Master*, Prof. Sir Terence English
   (1993)
ST EDMUND'S (1896), *Master*, R. M. Laws, CBE, PH.D.
   (1986)
ST JOHN'S (1511), *Master*, Prof. R. A. Hinde, SC.D., FRS
   (1989)
SELWYN (1882), *Master*, D. Harrison, CBE, SC.D., F.Eng.
   (1993)
SIDNEY SUSSEX (1596), *Master*, Prof. G. Horn, SC.D., FRS
   (1992)
TRINITY (1546), *Master*, Sir Michael Atiyah, PH.D., FRS,
   FRSE (1990)
TRINITY HALL (1350), *Master*, Sir John Lyons, PH.D.
   (1984)
WOLFSON (1965), *President*, J. Tusa (1993)
*Colleges for women only

THE UNIVERSITY OF CENTRAL ENGLAND
IN BIRMINGHAM (1992)
(formerly Birmingham Polytechnic)
Perry Barr, Birmingham B42 5SU
Tel 021-331 5000
Full-time Students (1992–3), 11,900
Vice-Chancellor, Dr P. C. Knight
Secretary and Registrar, Ms M. Penlington

THE UNIVERSITY OF CENTRAL LANCASHIRE
(1992)
(formerly Lancashire Polytechnic)
Preston PR1 2TQ
Tel 0772-201201
Full-time Students (1992–3), 11,102
Rector and Chief Executive, B. Booth
Secretary, Ms P. M. Ackroyd

THE CITY UNIVERSITY (1966)
Northampton Square, London EC1V 0HB
Tel 071-477 8000
Full-time Students (1992–3), 5,833
Chancellor, The Rt. Hon. the Lord Mayor of London
Vice-Chancellor and Principal, Prof. R. N. Franklin, D.Phil.,
   D.SC.
Registrar, A. H. Seville, PH.D.
Secretary, M. M. O'Hara

COVENTRY UNIVERSITY (1992)
(formerly Coventry Polytechnic)
Priory Street, Coventry CVI 5FB
Tel 0203-631313
Full-time Students (1992–3), 14,000
Vice-Chancellor, M. Goldstein, PH.D., D.SC.
Registrar, J. Gledhill, PH.D.
Secretary, Ms L. Arlidge

DE MONTFORT UNIVERSITY (1992)
(formerly Leicester Polytechnic)
The Gateway, Leicester LEI 9BH
Tel 0533-551551
Full-time Students (1991–2), 14,500
Chancellor, Dame Anne Mueller
Vice-Chancellor and Chief Executive, Prof. K. Barker
Registrar, J. Wools
Secretary, A. Denny

THE UNIVERSITY OF DERBY (1993)
(formerly Derbyshire College of Higher Education)
Kedleston Road, Derby DE22 1GB
Tel 0332-622222
Full-time Students (1992–3), *c.* 5,700
Vice-Chancellor, Prof. R. Waterhouse
Academic Registrar, Mrs J. Fry

THE UNIVERSITY OF DUNDEE (1967)
Dundee DDI 4HN
Tel 0382-23181
Full-time Students (1992–3), 6,340
Chancellor, Sir James Black, FRCP, FRS (1992)
Vice-Chancellor, Prof. M. J. Hamlin, FRSE, FEng.
Secretary, R. Seaton
Rector, S. Fry (1992–5)

THE UNIVERSITY OF DURHAM
Founded 1832; re-organized 1908, 1937 and 1963
Old Shire Hall, Durham DHI 3HP
Tel 091-374 2000
Full-time Students (1992–3), 6,742
Chancellor, Sir Peter Ustinov, CBE, FRSL
Vice-Chancellor and Warden, Prof. E. A. V. Ebsworth, PH.D., D.SC., FRSE
Registrar and Secretary, J. C. F. Hayward

COLLEGES

COLLINGWOOD, *Principal*, G. H. Blake, PH.D.
GRADUATE SOCIETY, *Principal*, M. Richardson, PH.D.
GREY, *Master*, V. E. Watts
HATFIELD, *Master*, J. P. Barber, PH.D.
ST AIDAN'S, *Principal*, R. J. Williams
ST CHAD'S, *Principal*, E. Halladay
ST CUTHBERT'S SOCIETY, *Principal*, S. G. C. Stoker
ST HILD AND ST BEDE, *Principal*, J. V. Armitage, PH.D.
ST JOHN'S, *Principal*, D. V. Day
ST MARY'S, *Principal*, Miss J. M. Kenworthy
TREVELYAN, *Principal*, Miss D. Lavin
UNIVERSITY, *Master*, E. C. Salthouse, PH.D.
USHAW, *President*, Rt. Revd Mgr R. Atherton, OBE
VAN MILDERT, *Principal*, Dr J. Turner

THE UNIVERSITY OF EAST ANGLIA (1963)
Norwich NR4 7TJ
Tel 0603-56161
Full-time Students (1992–3), 5,751

Chancellor, Revd Prof. W. O. Chadwick, OM, KBE, DD, FBA (1985)
Vice-Chancellor, Prof. D. C. Burke, PH.D.
Registrar and Secretary, M. G. E. Paulson-Ellis, OBE

THE UNIVERSITY OF EAST LONDON (1992)
(formerly Polytechnic of East London)
Romford Road, London EI5 4LZ
Tel 081-590 7722
Full-time Students (1992–3), 8,200
Vice-Chancellor, Prof. F. Gould
Registrar, Ms S. Millard

THE UNIVERSITY OF EDINBURGH (1583)
Old College, South Bridge, Edinburgh EH8 9YL
Tel 031-667 1011
Full-time Students (1992–3), 13,700
Chancellor, HRH The Prince Philip, Duke of Edinburgh, KG, KT, OM, GBE, PC, FRS (1952)
Vice-Chancellor and Principal, Sir David Smith, D.Phil., FRS, FRSE
Registrar and Secretary, M. J. B. Lowe, PH.D.
Rector, D. Munro (1991–4)

THE UNIVERSITY OF ESSEX (1964)
Wivenhoe Park, Colchester CO4 3SQ
Tel 0206-873333
Full-time Students (1992–3), 4,580
Chancellor, The Rt. Hon. Sir Patrick Nairne, GCB, MC (1983)
Vice-Chancellor, Prof. R. J. Johnston, PH.D.
Registrar and Secretary, A. F. Woodburn

THE UNIVERSITY OF EXETER (1955)
Northcote House, The Queen's Drive, Exeter EX4 4QJ
Tel 0392-263263
Full-time Students (1992–3), 7,409
Chancellor, Sir Rex Richards, D.SC., FRS (1981)
Vice-Chancellor, D. Harrison, CBE, PH.D., SC.D., FEng.
Academic Registrar and Secretary, I. H. C. Powell

GLAMORGAN UNIVERSITY (1992)
(formerly Polytechnic of Wales)
Pontypridd, Mid Glamorgan CF37 IDL
Tel 0443-480480
Full-time Students (1992–3), 7,664
Vice-Chancellor, Prof. A. L. Webb
Academic Registrar, J. O'Shea
Secretary, J. L. Bracegirdle

THE UNIVERSITY OF GLASGOW (1451)
Glasgow G12 8QQ
Tel 041-339 8855
Full-time Students (1991–2), 13,054
Chancellor, Sir Alexander Cairncross, KCMG, FBA (1972)
Vice-Chancellor, Sir William Fraser, GCB, LL D, FRSE
Registrar, J. M. Black
Secretary, R. Ewen, OBE, TD
Rector, J. Ball (1993–6)

GLASGOW CALEDONIAN UNIVERSITY
Cowcaddens Road, Glasgow G4 OBA
Tel 041-331 3000
Full-time Students (1992–3), 8,800
Chancellor, Sir David Nickson, KBE
Vice-Chancellor, Prof. J. S. Mason
Secretary, B. M. Fraser, PH.D.

THE UNIVERSITY OF GREENWICH (1992)
(formerly Thames Polytechnic)
Wellington Street, Woolwich, London SE18 6PF
Tel 081-316 8000
Full-time Students (1991–2), 9,700
Chancellor, The Baroness Young
Vice-Chancellor, Dr D. Fussey
Academic Registrar, A. I. Mayfield
Secretary, J. Charles

HERIOT-WATT UNIVERSITY (1966)
Riccarton, Edinburgh EH14 4AS
Tel 031-449 5111
Full-time Students (1992–3), c.8,550
Chancellor, The Lord Mackay of Clashfern, PC, QC, FRSE
(1979)
Principal and Vice-Chancellor, Prof. A. G. J. MacFarlane,
CBE, Ph.D., FRS, FRSE, FEng. (1989)
Registrar, D. Sturgeon
Secretary, P. L. Wilson

THE UNIVERSITY OF HERTFORDSHIRE
(1992)
(formerly Hatfield Polytechnic)
College Lane, Hatfield, Herts. AL10 9AB
Tel 0707-279000
Full-time Students (1992–3), 10,128
Chancellor, Sir Brian Corby
Vice-Chancellor, Prof. N. K. Buxton
Registrar and Secretary, P. G. Jeffreys

THE UNIVERSITY OF HUDDERSFIELD (1992)
(formerly Polytechnic of Huddersfield)
Queensgate, Huddersfield HD1 3DH
Tel 0484-422288
Full-time Students (1992–3), 8,520
Chancellor, R. C. Cross, OBE
Vice-Chancellor and Rector, Prof. K. J. Durrands, CBE
Academic Registrar, M. E. Bond
Secretary, D. J. Lock

THE UNIVERSITY OF HULL (1954)
Cottingham Road, Hull HU6 7RX
Tel 0482-46311
Full-time Students (1992–3), 8,289
Chancellor, The Lord Wilberforce, CMG, OBE, PC (1978)
Vice-Chancellor, Prof. D. Dilks, FRSL
Registrar and Secretary, P. A. Bolton

THE UNIVERSITY OF HUMBERSIDE (1992)
(formerly Humberside Polytechnic)
Cottingham Road, Hull HU6 7RT
Tel 0482-440552
Full-time Students (1992–3), 10,085
Pro-Chancellor, Dr Harry Hooper
Vice-Chancellor, Prof. R. King
Registrar, Mrs P. Jackson
Secretary, Miss M. Harries-Jenkins

THE UNIVERSITY OF KEELE (1962)
Keele, Newcastle under Lyme, Staffs. ST5 5BG
Tel 0782-621111
Full-time Students (1992–3), 4,925
Chancellor, Sir Claus Moser, KCB, CBE, FBA (1986)
Vice-Chancellor, Prof. B. E. Fender, CMG, Ph.D.
Registrar, D. Cohen, Ph.D.

THE UNIVERSITY OF KENT AT CANTERBURY
(1965)
Tanglewood, Giles Lane, Canterbury CT2 7LX
Tel 0227-764000
Full-time Students (1992–3), 5,982
Chancellor, R. Horton (1990)
Vice-Chancellor, D. J. E. Ingram, CBE, D.Phil., D.SC.
Registrar, T. Mead, Ph.D.

KINGSTON UNIVERSITY (1992)
(formerly Kingston Polytechnic)
Penrhyn Road, Kingston upon Thames,
Surrey KT1 2EE
Tel 081-547 2000
Full-time Students (1992–3), 8,804
Vice-Chancellor, R. C. Smith, CBE, Ph.D.
Academic Registrar, Miss A. Hynes
Secretary, E. Lang

THE UNIVERSITY OF LANCASTER (1964)
Lancaster LA1 4YW
Tel 0524-65201
Full-time Students (1992–3), 6,133
Chancellor, HRH Princess Alexandra, the Hon. Lady
Ogilvy, GCVO (1964)
Vice-Chancellor, Prof. H. J. Hanham, Ph.D.
Secretary, G. M. Cockburn

THE UNIVERSITY OF LEEDS (1904)
Leeds LS2 9JT
Tel 0532-431751
Full-time Students (1992–3), 15,210
Chancellor, HRH The Duchess of Kent, GCVO (1966)
Vice-Chancellor, Prof. A. G. Wilson
Registrar, E. Newcomb

LEEDS METROPOLITAN UNIVERSITY
(formerly Leeds Polytechnic)
Calverley Street, Leeds LS1 3HE
Tel 0532-832600
Full-time Students (1992–3), 13,777
Principal and Chief Executive, C. Price
Secretary, M. Wilkinson

THE UNIVERSITY OF LEICESTER (1957)
Leicester LE1 7RH
Tel 0533-522522
Full-time Students (1992–3), 7,551
Chancellor, The Lord Porter of Luddenham, OM, Ph.D.,
SC.D., FRS (1985)
Vice-Chancellor, K. J. R. Edwards, Ph.D.
Registrar, K. J. Julian

THE UNIVERSITY OF LIVERPOOL (1903)
PO Box 147, Liverpool L69 3BX
Tel 051-794 2000
Full-time Students (1992–3), 11,560
Chancellor, The Viscount Leverhulme, KG, TD (1980)
Vice-Chancellor, Prof. P. N. Love, CBE
Registrar and Secretary, M. D. Carr

LIVERPOOL JOHN MOORES UNIVERSITY
(1992)
(formerly Liverpool Polytechnic)
Rodney House, 70 Mount Pleasant, Liverpool L3 5UX
Tel 051-231 2121
Full-time Students (1992–3), 19,000
Chancellor, vacant
Vice-Chancellor, Prof. P. Toyne
Registrar, Ms A. Richardson
Secretary, P. Blackburn

THE UNIVERSITY OF LONDON (1836)
Senate House, London WCIE 7HU
Tel 071-636 8000
Internal Students (1992–3), 64,744, External Students,
16,807
Visitor, HM The Queen in Council
Chancellor, HRH The Princess Royal, GCVO, FRS (1981)
Vice-Chancellor, Prof. S. R. Sutherland
Chairman of the Court, The Lord Rippon of Hexham, PC, QC
Chairman of Convocation, Prof. C. D. Cowan, CBE, Ph.D.
Principal, P. Holwell

SCHOOLS OF THE UNIVERSITY
BIRKBECK COLLEGE, Malet Street, London
WCIE 7HX. *Master,* The Baroness Blackstone, Ph.D.
GOLDSMITHS' COLLEGE, Lewisham Way, New Cross,
London SE14 6NW. *Warden,* Prof. K. J. Gregory, Ph.D.
IMPERIAL COLLEGE OF SCIENCE, TECHNOLOGY AND
MEDICINE (includes St Mary's Hospital Medical School),
Prince Consort Road, London SW7 2AZ. *Rector,* Prof. Sir
Ronald Oxburgh, KBE, FRS
INSTITUTE OF EDUCATION, 20 Bedford Way, London
WCIH OAL. *Director,* Sir Peter Newsam
KING'S COLLEGE LONDON (includes King's College
School of Medicine and Dentistry), Strand, London
WC2R 2LS. *Principal,* Prof. A. Lucas, Ph.D.
LONDON SCHOOL OF ECONOMICS AND POLITICAL
SCIENCE, Houghton Street, London WC2A 2AE. *Director,*
J. M. Ashworth, Ph.D., D.SC.
QUEEN MARY AND WESTFIELD COLLEGE, Mile End
Road, London E1 4NS. *Principal,* Prof. G. Zellick, Ph.D.
ROYAL HOLLOWAY, Egham Hill, Egham, Surrey TW20
OEX. *Principal,* Prof. N. Gowar
ROYAL VETERINARY COLLEGE, Royal College Street,
London NW1 OTU. *Principal and Dean,*
Prof. L. E. Lanyon, Ph.D.
SCHOOL OF ORIENTAL AND AFRICAN STUDIES,
Thornhaugh Street, London WCIH OXG. *Director,*
M. D. McWilliam
SCHOOL OF PHARMACY, 29–39 Brunswick Square,
London WCIN 1AX. *Dean,* Prof. A. T. Florence, Ph.D.,
FRSE
UNIVERSITY COLLEGE LONDON (including UCL Medical
School), Gower Street, London WCIE 6BT. *Provost,*
Dr D. H. Roberts, CBE, FRS
WYE COLLEGE, Wye, Ashford, Kent TN25 5AH. *Principal,*
Prof. J. H. D. Prescott, Ph.D.
*HEYTHROP COLLEGE, Kensington Square, London
W8 5HQ. *Principal,* Revd B. A. Callaghan, SJ

*Not in receipt of HEFCE grants

MEDICAL SCHOOLS
CHARING CROSS AND WESTMINSTER MEDICAL
SCHOOL, The Reynolds Building, St Dunstan's Road,
London W6 8RP. *Dean,* J. E. H. Pendower, FRCS
THE LONDON HOSPITAL MEDICAL COLLEGE, Turner
Street, London E1 2AD. *Dean,* Prof. R. Duckworth, CBE,
MD, FRCS, FRCPath
ROYAL FREE HOSPITAL SCHOOL OF MEDICINE,
Rowland Hill Street, London NW3 2PF. *Dean,*
Prof. A. J. Zuckerman, MD, FRCP
ST BARTHOLOMEW'S HOSPITAL MEDICAL COLLEGE,
West Smithfield, London EC1A 7BE. *Dean,* L. H. Rees,
MD, FRCP
ST GEORGE'S HOSPITAL MEDICAL SCHOOL, Cranmer
Terrace, London SW17 ORE. *Dean,* Prof. A. W. Asscher,
MD, FRCP, FRCPath.

UNITED MEDICAL AND DENTAL SCHOOLS OF GUY'S
AND ST THOMAS' HOSPITALS, Guy's, London Bridge,
London SE1 9RT; St Thomas', Lambeth Palace Road,
London SE1 7EH. *Principal,* Prof. C. Chantler

POSTGRADUATE MEDICAL INSTITUTIONS
LONDON SCHOOL OF HYGIENE AND TROPICAL
MEDICINE, Keppel Street, London WCIE 7HT. *Dean,*
Prof. R. G. Feachem, Ph.D, D.SC.(med)
ROYAL POSTGRADUATE MEDICAL SCHOOL, Du Cane
Road, London W12 OSH. *Dean,* Prof. Sir Colin
Dollery, FRCP
BRITISH POSTGRADUATE MEDICAL FEDERATION
(University of London), 33 Millman Street, London
WCIN 3EJ. *Director,* Dr M. Green, DM, FRCP
Comprises:
HUNTERIAN INSTITUTE, Royal College of Surgeons of
England, Lincoln's Inn Fields, London
WC2A 3PN. *Master,* Prof. Sir Stanley Peart, FRS, FRCP;
Academic Dean, Dr N. Wedderburn
INSTITUTE OF CANCER RESEARCH, Royal Cancer
Hospital, 17A Onslow Gardens, London
SW7 3AL. *Director,* Prof. P. B. Garland, Ph.D., FRSE
INSTITUTE OF CHILD HEALTH, 30 Guilford Street,
London WCIN 1EH. *Dean,* Prof. R. J. Levinsky, MD, FRCP
INSTITUTE OF DENTAL SURGERY, Eastman Dental
Hospital, Gray's Inn Road, London WCIX 8LD. *Dean,*
Prof. G. B. Winter, D.ch.
INSTITUTE OF NEUROLOGY, National Hospital, Queen
Square, London WCIN 3BG. *Dean,* Prof. D. N. Landon
INSTITUTE OF OPHTHALMOLOGY, 11–43 Bath Street,
London ECIV 9EL. *Dean,* N. S. C. Rice, MD, FRCS
INSTITUTE OF PSYCHIATRY, De Crespigny Park,
Denmark Hill, London SE5 8AF. *Dean,* S. A. Checkley,
FRCPsych.
NATIONAL HEART AND LUNG INSTITUTE, Dovehouse
Street, London SW3 6LI. *Dean,* Prof. T. Clark, MD, FRCP

SENATE INSTITUTES
BRITISH INSTITUTE IN PARIS, 9–11 Rue de Constantine,
75007, Paris. *Director,* Prof. C. L. Campos, L-ès-L., Ph.D.
London office: Senate House, Malet Street, London
WCIE 7HU
CENTRE FOR DEFENCE STUDIES, King's College London,
Strand, London WC2R 2LS. *Director,* Prof. L. Freedman
COURTAULD INSTITUTE OF ART, North Block, Somerset
House, Strand, London WC2R 2LS. *Director,*
Prof. C. M. Kauffmann, Ph.D, FSA
INSTITUTE OF ADVANCED LEGAL STUDIES, Charles
Clore House, 17 Russell Square, London
WCIB 5DR. *Director,* Prof. T. C. Daintith
INSTITUTE OF CLASSICAL STUDIES, 31–34 Gordon
Square, London WCIH OPY. *Director,*
Prof. R. R. K. Sorabji, FBA
INSTITUTE OF COMMONWEALTH STUDIES, 27–28
Russell Square, London WCIB 5DS. *Director,* Prof. Shula
E. Marks, Ph.D.
INSTITUTE OF GERMANIC STUDIES, 29 Russell Square,
London WCIB 5DP. *Hon. Director,* Prof. M. W. Swales,
Ph.D.
INSTITUTE OF HISTORICAL RESEARCH, Senate House,
Malet Street, London WCIE 7HU. *Director,*
Prof. P. K. O'Brien, D.Phil.
INSTITUTE OF LATIN AMERICAN STUDIES, 31 Tavistock
Square, London WCIH 9HA. *Director,* Prof. V. G. Bulmer-
Thomas, D.phil.

INSTITUTE OF ROMANCE STUDIES, Senate House, Malet Street, London WCIE 7HU. *Hon. Director*, Prof. A. Lavers, L-ès-L, Ph.D.
INSTITUTE OF UNITED STATES STUDIES, Senate House, Malet Street, London WCIE 7HU. *Director*, G. L. McDowell, PH.D.
INSTITUTE OF ZOOLOGY, Royal Zoological Society, Regent's Park, London NWI 4RY. *Director*, Prof. A. P. F. Flint, PH.D., D.SC.
SCHOOL OF SLAVONIC AND EAST EUROPEAN STUDIES, Senate House, Malet Street, London WCIE 7HU. *Director*, Prof. M. A. Branch, PH.D.
WARBURG INSTITUTE, Woburn Square, London WCIH OAB. *Director*, Prof. C. N. J. Mann, PH.D.

INSTITUTIONS HAVING RECOGNIZED TEACHERS
JEWS' COLLEGE, 44A Albert Road, London NW4 2SJ. *Principal*, Rabbi Dr I. Jacobs
LONDON BUSINESS SCHOOL, Sussex Place, London NWI 4SA. *Principal*, Prof. G. Bain, D.Phil.
ROYAL ACADEMY OF MUSIC, Marylebone Road, London NWI 5HT. *Principal*, L. Harrell
ROYAL COLLEGE OF MUSIC, Prince Consort Road, London SW7 2BS. *Director*, M. G. Matthews, FRSA, FRCM
TRINITY COLLEGE OF MUSIC, Mandeville Place, London WIM 6AQ. *Principal*, P. Jones, CBE, FRCM

LONDON GUILDHALL UNIVERSITY
31 Jewry Street, London EC3N 2EY
Tel 071-320 1000
Full-time Students (1992–3), 8,235
Provost, Prof. R. Floud, D.Phil.
Registrar, B. High

LOUGHBOROUGH UNIVERSITY OF TECHNOLOGY (1966)
Loughborough LEII 3TU
Tel 0509-263171
Full-time Students (1992–3), 7,688
Chancellor, Sir Denis Rooke, CBE, FRS, FEng (1989)
Vice-Chancellor, Prof. D.Wallace, PH.D., FRS, FRSE
Registrar, D. E. Fletcher, PH.D.
Academic Secretary, N. A. McHard

UNIVERSITY OF LUTON (1993)
(formerly Luton College of Higher Education)
Park Square, Luton LUI 3JU
Tel 0582-34111
Full-time Students (1992–3), 10,825
Chancellor, Sir David Plastow
Vice-Chancellor, Dr A. Wood
Admissions Tutor, P. Vachon

THE UNIVERSITY OF MANCHESTER
(Founded 1851; re-organized 1880 and 1903)
Oxford Road, Manchester MI3 9PL
Full-time Students (1992–3), c.14,000
Chancellor, B. Redhead
Vice-Chancellor, Prof. M. B. Harris, CBE, PH.D.
Registrar and Secretary, K. E. Kitchen

UNIVERSITY OF MANCHESTER INSTITUTE OF SCIENCE AND TECHNOLOGY (1824)
PO Box 88, Manchester M60 IQD
Tel 061-236 3311
Full-time Students (1992–3), 5,635
President, Sir John Mason, CB, D.SC., FRS (1986)
Principal, Prof. H. C. A. Hankins, PH.D.
Secretary and Registrar, P. C. C. Stephenson

MANCHESTER METROPOLITAN UNIVERSITY
(formerly Manchester Polytechnic)
All Saints, Manchester MI5 6BH
Tel 061-247 2000
Full-time Students (1992–3), 21,354
Chancellor, The Duke of Westminster
Director, Sir Kenneth Green
Registrar, J. Karczewski-Slowikowski
Secretary, R. O. Yeo

MIDDLESEX UNIVERSITY (1992)
(formerly Middlesex Polytechnic)
White Hart Lane, London NI7 8HR
Tel 081-362 5000
Full-time Students (1992–3), 13,500
Chancellor, The Baroness Platt of Writtle
Vice-Chancellor, Prof. D. Melville, PH.D.
Registrar, G. Jones

NAPIER UNIVERSITY (1992)
(formerly Napier Polytechnic)
219 Colinton Road, Edinburgh EHI4 IDJ
Tel 031-444 2266
Full-time Students (1992–3), 7,500
Chancellor, The Lord Younger of Prestwick, KCVO, TD, PC, FRSE
Vice-Chancellor, Prof. W. Turmeau, CBE, FRSE
Secretary and Registrar, I. J. Miller

THE UNIVERSITY OF NEWCASTLE UPON TYNE
(Founded 1852; re-organized 1908, 1937 and 1963)
6 Kensington Terrace, Newcastle upon Tyne NEI 7RU
Tel 091-222 6000
Full-time Students (1992–3), 10,943
Chancellor, The Viscount Ridley, KG, TD (1989)
Vice-Chancellor, J. R. G. Wright
Registrar, D. E. T. Nicholson

THE UNIVERSITY OF NORTH LONDON (1992)
(formerly Polytechnic of North London)
166–220 Holloway Road, London N7 8DB
Tel 071-607 2789
Full-time Students (1992–3), 9,770
Vice-Chancellor, L. Wagner
Academic Registrar, Dr M. Storey
Secretary, C. Wragg

THE UNIVERSITY OF NORTHUMBRIA AT NEWCASTLE
(formerly Newcastle upon Tyne Polytechnic)
Newcastle upon Tyne NEI 8ST
Tel 091-232 6002
Full-time Students (1992–3), 12,000
Chancellor, The Lord Glenamara, CH, PC
Vice-Chancellor, Prof. L. Barden, CBE, PH.D., D.SC.
Registrar and Secretary, R. A. Bott

THE UNIVERSITY OF NOTTINGHAM (1948)
University Park, Nottingham NG7 2RD
Tel 0602-484848
Full-time Students (1992–3), 10,500
Chancellor, Sir Ron Dearing, CB (1993)
Vice-Chancellor, Prof. C. M. Campbell
Registrar, G. E. Chandler

NOTTINGHAM TRENT UNIVERSITY
Burton Street, Nottingham NGI 4BU
Tel 0602-418418

Full-time Students (1991–2), 12,260
Vice-Chancellor, Prof. R. Cowell, PH.D.
Academic Registrar, A. E. Foster

THE UNIVERSITY OF OXFORD
University Offices, Wellington Square, Oxford OX1 2JD
Tel 0865-270001
Number of students in residence 1992–3:
Men, 8,871; *Women*, 5,723

UNIVERSITY OFFICERS, ETC.

Chancellor, The Lord Jenkins of Hillhead, PC
   (*Balliol*), elected 1987
High Steward, The Lord Goff of Chieveley, PC (*Lincoln* and
   New College), elected 1990
Vice-Chancellor, Dr P. M. North, CBE, FBA (*Jesus*), elected
   1993
Proctors, P. A. Allen (*St Cross*); Ms E. A. Fallaize (*St
   John's*), elected 1993
Assessor, J. S. Rowett, D.phil. (*Brasenose*), elected 1993
Public Orator, J. Griffin (*Balliol*), elected 1992
Bodley's Librarian, D. G. Vaisey (*Exeter*), elected 1986
Keeper of Archives, J. Hackney (*Wadham*), elected 1988
Director of the Ashmolean Museum, C. J. White (*Worcester*),
   elected 1985
Registrar of the University, A. J. Dorey, D.phil. (*Linacre*),
   elected 1979
Surveyor to the University, P. M. R. Hill, elected 1993
Secretary of Faculties, A. P. Weale (*Worcester*), elected 1984
Secretary of the Chest, I. G. Thompson (*Merton*), elected 1986
Deputy Registrar (Administration), P. W. Jones (*Green*),
   elected 1991

OXFORD COLLEGES AND HALLS
with dates of foundation

ALL SOULS (1438), *Warden*, Sir Patrick Neill, QC (1977)
BALLIOL (1263), *Master*, B. S. Blumberg (1989)
BRASENOSE (1509), *Principal*, The Lord Windlesham, CVO,
   PC (1989)
CHRIST CHURCH (1546), *Dean*, Very Revd J. H. Drury
   (1991)
CORPUS CHRISTI (1517), *President*, Prof. Sir Keith
   Thomas, FBA (1986)
EXETER (1314), *Rector*, vacant
GREEN (1979), *Warden*, Sir Crispin Tickell, GCMG, KCVO
   (1990)
HERTFORD (1874), *Principal*, Prof. Sir Erik Zeeman, KBE,
   FRS (1988)
JESUS (1571), *Principal*, Dr P. M. North, CBE, FBA (1984)
KEBLE (1868), *Warden*, G. B. Richardson, CBE (1989)
LADY MARGARET HALL (1878), *Principal*, D. M. Stewart
   (1979)
LINACRE (1962), *Principal*, Sir Bryan Cartledge, KCMG
   (1988)
LINCOLN (1427), *Rector*, Sir Maurice Shock (1987)
MAGDALEN (1458), *President*, A. D. Smith, CBE (1988)
MERTON (1264), *Warden*, J. M. Roberts, D.phil. (1985)
NEW COLLEGE (1379), *Warden*, H. McGregor, QC, DCL
   (1985)
NUFFIELD (1937), *Warden*, Sir David Cox, FRS (1988)
ORIEL (1326), *Provost*, E. W. Nicholson, DD, FBA (1990)
PEMBROKE (1624), *Master*, Prof. R. Stevens, DCL (1993)
QUEEN'S (1340), *Provost*, G. Marshall (1993)
REWLEY HOUSE (1990), *President*, G. P. Thomas,
   ph.D. (1990)
ST ANNE'S (1952) (Originally Society of Oxford Home-
   Students (1879)), *Principal*, Mrs R. L. Deech (1991)
ST ANTONY'S (1950), *Warden*, The Lord Dahrendorf, KBE,
   ph.D., FBA (1987)

ST CATHERINE'S (1962), *Master*, G. C. K. Peach (*acting*)
ST CROSS (1965), *Master*, R. C. Repp, D.phil. (1987)
ST EDMUND HALL (*c.* 1278), *Principal*, J. C. B. Gosling
   (1983)
*ST HILDA'S (1893), *Principal*, Miss E. Llewellyn-Smith, CB
   (1990)
ST HUGH'S (1886), *Principal*, D. Wood, QC (1991)
ST JOHN'S (1555), *President*, W. Hayes, D.phil. (1987)
ST PETER'S (1929), *Master*, J. P. Barron, D.phil. (1991)
SOMERVILLE (1879), *Principal*, Mrs C. E. Hughes, CMG
   (1989)
TRINITY (1554), *President*, Sir John Burgh, KCMG, CB (1987)
UNIVERSITY (1249), *Master*, W. J. Albery, D.phil., FRS
   (1989)
WADHAM (1612), *Warden*, J. S. Flemming (1993)
WOLFSON (1966), *President*, Sir David Smith, D.phil. (1994)
WORCESTER (1714), *Provost*, R. G. Smethurst (1991)
CAMPION HALL (1896), *Master*, Revd J. A. Munitiz (1989)
GREYFRIARS (1910), *Warden*, Revd M. W. Sheehan,
   D.phil. (1990)
MANCHESTER (1786), *Principal*, Revd R. Waller, ph.D.
   (1990)
MANSFIELD (1886), *Principal*, D. J. Trevelyan, CB (1989)
REGENT'S PARK (1810), *Principal*, Revd P. S. Fiddes,
   D.phil. (1989)
ST BENET'S HALL (1897), *Master*, Revd H. Wansbrough,
   OSB (1991)

* College for women only

OXFORD BROOKES UNIVERSITY
Headington, Oxford OX3 0BP
Tel 0865-741111
Full-time Students (1992–3), 8,500
Chancellor, vacant
Vice-Chancellor, Dr C. Booth
Registrar, R. M. Tulloch
Secretary, B. Summers

THE UNIVERSITY OF PAISLEY (1992)
(formerly Paisley College of Technology)
High Street, Paisley PA1 2BE
Tel 041-848 3000
Full-time Students (1992–3), 5,107
Chancellor, Sir Robert Easton, CBE
Vice-Chancellor, Prof. R. W. Shaw
Registrar, D. Rigg
Secretary, J. Fraser

UNIVERSITY OF PLYMOUTH (1992)
(formerly Polytechnic SouthWest)
Drake Circus, Plymouth PL4 8AA
Tel 0752-600600
Full-time Students (1992–3), 15,000
Vice-Chancellor, Prof. J. Bull
Registrar, Dr C. J. Sparrow
Deputy Vice-Chancellor (Secretariat), Dr R. M. Thorpe

PORTSMOUTH UNIVERSITY (1992)
(formerly Portsmouth Polytechnic)
University House, Winston Churchill Avenue, Portsmouth
POI 2UP
Tel 0705-827681
Full-time Students (1992–3), 10,298
Chancellor, The Lord Palumbo
Vice-Chancellor, N. Merritt
Academic Registrar, R. Moore
Secretary, D. Hunt

THE QUEEN'S UNIVERSITY OF BELFAST
(1908)
Belfast BT7 INN
Tel 0232-245133
Full-time Students (1992–3), 9,875
Chancellor, Sir David Orr
President and Vice-Chancellor, G. Beveridge, ph.d., FRSE
Academic Secretary, Dr G. Baird

THE UNIVERSITY OF READING (1926)
Whiteknights, PO Box 217, Reading RG6 2AH
Tel 0734-875123
Full-time Students (1992–3), 8,816
Chancellor, The Lord Carrington, KG, GCMG, CH, MC, PC
(1992)
Vice-Chancellor, Prof. E. Williams
Registrar, D. C. R. Frampton

THE ROBERT GORDON UNIVERSITY (1992)
(formerly Robert Gordon Institute of Technology)
Schoolhill, Aberdeen AB9 IFR
Tel 0224-262000
Full-time Students (1992–3), 5,239
Chancellor, Sir Bob Reid
Vice-Chancellor and Principal, Dr D. A. Kennedy
Academic Registrar, Mrs H. Douglas
Secretary, D. Caldwell

THE UNIVERSITY OF ST ANDREWS (1411)
College Gate, St Andrews KY16 9AJ
Tel 0334-76161
Full-time Students (1992–3), 4,461
Chancellor, Sir Kenneth Dover, D.Litt., FRSE, FBA (1981)
Vice-Chancellor, Prof. S. Arnott, ph.d., FRS, FRSE
Registrar, R. Douglas
Secretary of Court, D. J. Corner
Rector, N. Campbell (1991–4)

THE UNIVERSITY OF SALFORD (1967)
Salford M5 4WT
Tel 061-745 5000
Full-time Students (1992–3), 5,538
Chancellor, HRH The Duchess of York (1990)
Vice-Chancellor, Prof. T. M. Husband, ph.d, FEng.
Registrar (acting), M. D. Winton, ph.d.

THE UNIVERSITY OF SHEFFIELD (1905)
Western Bank, Sheffield S10 2TN
Tel 0742-768555
Full-time Students (1991–2), 10,723
Chancellor, The Lord Dainton, ph.d., sc.d., FRS (1979)
Vice-Chancellor, Prof. G. G. Roberts
Registrar and Secretary, Dr J. S. Padley

SHEFFIELD HALLAM UNIVERSITY
(formerly Sheffield Polytechnic)
Pond Street, Sheffield S1 IWB
Tel 0742-720911
Full-time Students (1992–3), 15,417
Chancellor, Sir Bryan Nicholson
Vice-Chancellor, J. Stoddart
Registrar, Ms J. Tory
Secretary, Ms S. Neocosmos

THE UNIVERSITY OF SOUTHAMPTON (1952)
Highfield, Southampton SO9 5NH
Tel 0703-595000
Full-time Students (1992–3), 9,160

Chancellor, The Earl Jellicoe, KBE, DSO, MC, PC, FRS (1984)
Vice-Chancellor, Sir Gordon Higginson, Ph.D, FEng.
Secretary and Registrar, J. F. D. Lauwerys
Academic Registrar, Miss A. E. Clarke

SOUTH BANK UNIVERSITY (1992)
(formerly South Bank Polytechnic)
103 Borough Road, London SE1 OAA
Tel 071-928 8989
Full-time Students (1991–2), 10,627
Chairman of the Board of Governors, C. McLaren
Vice-Chancellor, Prof. G. Bernbaum
Registrar, N. Andrew
Secretary, Ms L. Gander

STAFFORDSHIRE UNIVERSITY (1992)
(formerly Staffordshire Polytechnic)
College Road, Stoke-on-Trent ST4 2DE
Tel 0782-744531
Full-time Students (1992–3), 9,169
Chancellor, The Lord Ashley of Stoke, CH, PC
Vice-Chancellor, K. B. Thompson
Academic Registrar, Miss F. Francis
Secretary, K. Sproston

THE UNIVERSITY OF STIRLING (1967)
Stirling FK9 4LA
Tel 0786-73171
Full-time Students (1992–3), 4,510
Chancellor, The Lord Balfour of Burleigh, FRSE (1988)
Principal and Vice-Chancellor, Prof. A. J. Forty, CBE, ph.d.,
D.SC., FRSE
Registrar, D. J. Farrington, D.phil.
Secretary, R. G. Bomont

THE UNIVERSITY OF STRATHCLYDE (1964)
16 Richmond Street, Glasgow G1 IXQ
Tel 041-552 4400
Full-time Students (1992–3), 12,246
Chancellor, The Lord Tombs, LL D, D.SC., FEng. (1990)
Principal and Vice-Chancellor, Prof. J. P. Arbuthnott
Secretary, P. W. A. West

THE UNIVERSITY OF SUNDERLAND (1992)
(formerly Sunderland Polytechnic)
Langham Tower, Ryhope Road, Sunderland SR2 7EE
Tel 091-515 2000
Full-time Students (1992–3), 10,060
Vice-Chancellor, A. Wright, ph.d.
Registrar, S. Porteous
Secretary, J. D. Pacey

THE UNIVERSITY OF SURREY (1966)
Guildford, Surrey GU2 5XH
Tel 0483-300800
Full-time Students (1992–3), 5,255
Chancellor, HRH The Duke of Kent, KG, GCMG, GCVO
(1977)
Vice-Chancellor, Prof. A. Kelly, CBE, SC.D., FRS, FEng.
Secretary, H. W. B. Davies

THE UNIVERSITY OF SUSSEX (1961)
Falmer, Brighton BN1 9RH
Tel 0273-678416
Full-time Students (1992–3), 7,346
Chancellor, The Duke of Richmond and Gordon (1985)
Vice-Chancellor, Prof. G. Conway
Registrar and Secretary, G. Lockwood, D.phil.

THE UNIVERSITY OF TEESSIDE (1992)
(formerly Teesside Polytechnic)
Middlesbrough, Cleveland TS1 3BA
Tel 0642-218121
Full-time Students (1992–3), 6,995
Chancellor, Sir Leon Britten
Vice-Chancellor, Prof. D. Fraser
University Secretary, J. M. McClintock

THAMES VALLEY UNIVERSITY (1992)
(formerly Polytechnic of West London)
St Mary's Road, Ealing, London W5 5RF
Tel 081-579 5000
Full-time Students (1992–3), 10,393
Chancellor, P. Hamlyn
Vice-Chancellor, Dr M. Fitzgerald
Secretary, Ms M. Joyce

THE UNIVERSITY OF ULSTER (1984)
(Amalgamation of New University of Ulster and Ulster
Polytechnic)
Cromore Road, Coleraine BT52 1SA
Tel 0265-44141
Full-time Students (1992–3), 13,234
Chancellor, vacant
Vice-Chancellor, Prof. T. A. Smith
Academic Registrar, K. Millar, PH.D.
Secretary, J. A. Hunter

THE UNIVERSITY OF WALES (1893)
King Edward VII Avenue, Cathays Park, Cardiff CF1 3NS
Tel 0222-382656
Chancellor, HRH The Prince of Wales, KG, KT, GCB, PC
(1976)
Vice-Chancellor, Prof. K. O. Morgan, D.Phil., FBA
Acting Registrar, J. D. Pritchard

COLLEGES

ST DAVID'S UNIVERSITY COLLEGE, Lampeter, Dyfed
SA48 7ED. Tel: 0570-422351. *Principal*, Prof. K. Robbins,
D.Litt., D.Phil., FRSE (1992)
UNIVERSITY COLLEGE OF NORTH WALES, Bangor,
Gwynedd LL57 2DG. Tel: 0248-351151. *Principal*, Prof.
E. Sunderland, PH.D. (1984)
UNIVERSITY COLLEGE OF SWANSEA, Singleton Park,
Swansea SA2 8PP. Tel: 0792-205678. *Principal*, Prof.
B. L. Clarkson, PH.D. (1982)
UNIVERSITY COLLEGE OF WALES, Old College, King
Street, Aberystwyth, Dyfed SY23 2AX. Tel: 0970-623111.
Principal, Prof. K. O. Morgan, D.Phil., FBA (1979)
UNIVERSITY OF WALES COLLEGE OF CARDIFF, PO Box
920, Cardiff CF1 3XP. Tel: 0222-874000. *Principal*,
E. B. Smith, PH.D. (1993)
UNIVERSITY OF WALES COLLEGE OF MEDICINE, Heath
Park, Cardiff CF4 4XN. Tel: 0222-747747. *Provost*, Prof.
Sir Herbert Duthie, MD, Ch.M., FRCS (1979)

THE UNIVERSITY OF WARWICK (1965)
Coventry CV4 7AL
Tel 0203-523523
Full-time Students (1992–3), 9,666
Chancellor, Sir Shridath Surendranath Ramphal, GCMG, QC
(1989)
Vice-Chancellor, Sir Brian Follett, FRS, D.SC.
Registrar, M. L. Shattock, OBE

THE UNIVERSITY OF WESTMINSTER (1992)
(formerly Polytechnic of Central London)
309 Regent Street, London W1R 8AL
Tel 071-911 5000
Full-time Students (1992–3), 6,000
Rector, Prof. T. E. Burlin
Deputy-Rector, Dr G. M. Copland
Registrar, Ms J. Hopkinson

THE UNIVERSITY OF THE WEST OF
ENGLAND, BRISTOL (BRISTOL UWE) (1992)
(formerly Bristol Polytechnic)
Coldharbour Lane, Frenchay, Bristol BS16 1QY
Tel 0272-656261
Full-time Students (1992–3), 10,625
Vice-Chancellor, A. C. Morris
Academic Registrar, Ms M. J. Carter
Secretary, W. Evans

THE UNIVERSITY OF WOLVERHAMPTON
(1992)
(formerly Wolverhampton Polytechnic)
Molineux Street, Wolverhampton WV1 1SB
Tel 0902-321000
Full-time Students (1992–3), 15,128
Chancellor, The Earl of Shrewsbury and Waterford
Vice-Chancellor/Director, Prof. M. J. Harrison

THE UNIVERSITY OF YORK (1963)
Heslington, York YO1 5DD
Tel 0904-430000
Full-time Students (1992–3), 5,026
Chancellor, Dame Janet Baker, DBE
Vice-Chancellor, Prof. R. U. Cooke
Registrar, D. J. Foster

CRANFIELD UNIVERSITY (1969)
Cranfield, Bedford MK43 0AL
Tel 0908-672974
Cranfield University (formerly the Cranfield Institute of
Technology) grants degrees in applied science, engineering,
technology and management.
Full-time Students (1992–3), 2,120
Chancellor, The Lord Kings Norton, PH.D., FEng. (1969)
Vice-Chancellor, Prof. F. R. Hartley, D.SC.
Secretary and Registrar, J. K. Pettifer

THE OPEN UNIVERSITY (1969)
Walton Hall, Milton Keynes MK7 6AA
Tel 0908-274066
Students and clients (1993), 200,000
Tuition by correspondence linked with special radio and
television programmes, video and audio cassettes, residential
schools and a locally-based tutorial and counselling service.
The University awards degrees of BA, B.Phil., MA, MBA, M.SC.,
M.Phil., Ph.D., D.SC. and D.Litt. There are eight faculties: arts;
education; health, welfare and community education; man-
agement; mathematics and computing; science; social sci-
ences; technology; and a wide range of qualification courses
and study packs.
Chancellor, The Lord Briggs, FBA (1978)
Vice-Chancellor, Dr J. S. Daniel
Secretary, D. J. Clinch

THE ROYAL COLLEGE OF ART (1837)
Kensington Gore, London SW7 2EU
Tel 071-584 5020
Under royal charter (1967) the Royal College of Art grants
the degrees of Doctor, Doctor of Philosophy, Master of Arts,

Master of Design and Master of Design (Engineering)
(RCA).
Students (1991–2), 700 (all postgraduate)
Provost, The Earl of Gowrie, PC (1986)
Registrar, A. Selby

SCOTTISH CENTRALLY-FUNDED COLLEGES

DUNCAN OF JORDANSTONE COLLEGE OF ART, Perth
Road, Dundee DD1 4HT. Tel: 0382-23261. *Principal*, Dr
C. Carter
DUNDEE INSTITUTE OF TECHNOLOGY, Bell Street,
Dundee DD1 1HG. Tel: 0382-308012. *Principal*,
Prof. B. King
EDINBURGH COLLEGE OF ART, Lauriston Place,
Edinburgh EH3 9DF. Tel: 031-229 9311. *Principal*,
Prof. A. J. Rowan, PH.D.
GLASGOW SCHOOL OF ART, 167 Renfrew Street, Glasgow
G3 6RQ. Tel: 041-332 9797. *Director*, Prof. D. Cameron
QUEEN MARGARET COLLEGE, Clerwood Terrace,
Edinburgh EH12 8TS. Tel: 031-317 3000. *Principal*, Prof.
D. F. Leach
ROYAL SCOTTISH ACADEMY OF MUSIC AND DRAMA,
100 Renfrew Street, Glasgow G2 3DB. Tel: 041-332 4101.
Principal, Dr P. Ledger, CBE, FRSE
SAC: THE NATIONAL COLLEGE FOR FOOD, LAND AND
ENVIRONMENTAL STUDIES, Central Office, West
Mains Road, Edinburgh EH9 3JG. Tel: 031-662 1303.
Campuses at Aberdeen, Auchincruive, and Edinburgh.
Principal and Chief Executive, Prof. P. C. Thomas
SCOTTISH COLLEGE OF TEXTILES, Netherdale,
Galashiels, Selkirkshire TD1 3HF. Tel: 0896-3351.
Principal, Prof. C. E. R. Maddox, PH.D.

COLLEGES

It is not possible to name here all the colleges offering courses
of higher or further education. The list of English colleges
that follows is confined to those in the Higher Education
Funding Council for England sector; there are many more
colleges in England providing higher education courses,
some with HEFCFE funding.
The list of colleges in Wales, Scotland and Northern
Ireland includes institutions providing at least one full-time
course leading to a first degree granted by an accredited
validating body. It does not include colleges forming part of
a polytechnic or a university, nor does it include Scottish
centrally-funded colleges.

ENGLAND

BATH COLLEGE OF HIGHER EDUCATION, Newton Park,
Newton St Loe, Bath BA2 9BN. Tel: 0225-873701.
Director and Chief Executive, B. L. Gomes da Costa
BISHOP GROSSETESTE COLLEGE, Lincoln LN1 3DY. Tel:
0522-527347. *Principal*, Prof. L. Marsh, OBE, D.phil.
BOLTON INSTITUTE OF HIGHER EDUCATION, Deane
Road, Bolton BL3 5AB. Tel: 0204-28851. *Principal*,
R. Oxtoby, ph.D.
BRETTON HALL, West Bretton, Wakefield,
W. Yorks. WF4 4LG. Tel: 0924-830261. *Principal*,
Prof. G.H. Bell

BUCKINGHAMSHIRE COLLEGE, Queen Alexandra Road,
High Wycombe, Bucks. HP11 2JZ. Tel: 0494-522141.
Director, P. B. Mogford
CANTERBURY CHRIST CHURCH COLLEGE, North
Holmes Road, Canterbury, Kent CT1 1QU. Tel: 0227-
767700. *Principal*, M. H. A. Berry, TD
THE CENTRAL SCHOOL OF SPEECH AND DRAMA,
Embassy Theatre, Eton Avenue, London NW3 3HY. Tel:
071-722 8183. *Principal*, R. S. Fowler
CHELTENHAM AND GLOUCESTER COLLEGE OF HIGHER
EDUCATION, PO Box 220, The Park, Cheltenham, Glos.
GL50 2QF. Tel: 0242-532700. *Director*, Miss J. O. Trotter,
OBE
CHESTER COLLEGE, Cheyney Road, Chester CH1 4BJ. Tel:
0244-375444. *Principal*, Revd E. V. Binks
COLLEGE OF ST MARK AND ST JOHN, Derriford Road,
Plymouth PL6 8BH. Tel: 0752-761110. *Principal*,
J. E. Anderson
DARTINGTON COLLEGE OF ARTS, Totnes, Devon
TQ9 6EJ. Tel: 0803-862224. *Principal*, Prof.
K. Thompson
EDGE HILL COLLEGE OF HIGHER EDUCATION,
St Helens Road, Ormskirk, Lancs. L39 4QP. Tel: 0695-
575171. *Director*, Prof. R. Gee
FALMOUTH SCHOOL OF ART AND DESIGN, Woodlane,
Falmouth, Cornwall TR11 4RA. Tel: 0326-211077.
Principal, Prof. A. G. Livingston
HARPER ADAMS AGRICULTURAL COLLEGE, Newport,
Shropshire TF10 8NB. Tel: 0952-820280. *Principal*,
A. G. Harris, OBE
HOMERTON COLLEGE, Cambridge CB2 2PH. Tel: 0223-
411141. *Principal*, Mrs K. Pretty, ph.D.
INSTITUTE OF ADVANCED NURSING, Royal College of
Nursing, 20 Cavendish Square, London W1M 0AB. Tel:
071-355 1396. *Principal*, J. C. A. Wells
KENT INSTITUTE OF ART AND DESIGN, Oakwood Park,
Oakwood Road, Maidstone ME16 8AG (*also* New Dover
Road, Canterbury CT1 3AN; and Fort Pitt, Rochester
ME1 1DZ). Tel: 0622-757286. *Director*, P. I. Williams
KING ALFRED'S COLLEGE, Winchester SO22 4NR. Tel:
0962-841515. *Principal*, Prof. J. P. Dickinson
LIVERPOOL INSTITUTE OF HIGHER EDUCATION,
PO Box 6, Stand Park Road, Liverpool L16 9JD. Tel: 051-
737 3000. *Rector*, J. Burke, OBE, ph.D.
THE LONDON INSTITUTE, 65 Davies Street, London
W1Y 2AA. *Rector*, Prof. J. C. McKenzie
Comprising:
Camberwell College of Arts, Peckham Road, London SE5 8UF
Central St Martins College of Art and Design, Southampton
Row, London WC1B 4AP
Chelsea College of Art and Design, Manresa Road, London
SW3 6LS
London College of Fashion, 20 John Prince's Street, London
W1M 9HE
London College of Printing and Distributive Trades, Elephant
and Castle, London SE1 6SB
LOUGHBOROUGH COLLEGE OF ART AND DESIGN,
Radmoor, Loughborough, Leics. LE11 3BT. Tel: 0509-
261515. *Principal*, I. Pugh
LSU COLLEGE OF HIGHER EDUCATION, The Avenue,
Southampton SO9 5HB. Tel: 0703-228761. *Principal*,
Dr A. C. Chitnis
NENE COLLEGE, Park Campus, Boughton Green Road,
Northampton NN2 7AL. Tel: 0604-735500. *Director*,
S. M. Gaskell, ph.D.
NEWMAN COLLEGE, Genners Lane, Bartley Green,
Birmingham B32 3NT. Tel: 021-476 1181. *Principal*,
Joan S. Cuming, ph.D.

RAVENSBOURNE COLLEGE OF DESIGN AND COMMUNICATION, Walden Road, Chislehurst, Kent BR7 5SN. Tel: 081-468 7071. *Director*, N. J. Frewing
ROEHAMPTON INSTITUTE, Senate House, Roehampton Lane, London SW15 5PU. Comprises Digby Stuart College, Froebel Institute College, Southlands College and Whitelands College. Tel: 081-392 3000. *Rector*, S. C. Holt, PH.D
ROSE BRUFORD COLLEGE OF SPEECH AND DRAMA, Lamorbey Park, Burnt Oak Lane, Sidcup, Kent DA15 9DF. Tel: 081-300 3024. *Principal*, R. Ely
ROYAL ACADEMY OF MUSIC, Marylebone Road, London NW1 5HT. Tel: 071-935 5461. *Principal*, L. Harrell
ROYAL COLLEGE OF MUSIC, Prince Consort Road, London SW7 2BS. Tel: 071-589 3643. *Director*, J. Ritterman, PH.D.
ROYAL NORTHERN COLLEGE OF MUSIC, 124 Oxford Road, Manchester M13 9RD. Tel: 061-273 6283. *Principal*, Sir John Manduell, CBE
S. MARTIN'S COLLEGE, Lancaster LA1 3JD. Tel: 0524-63446. *Principal*, D. Edynbry, PH.D.
ST MARY'S COLLEGE, Strawberry Hill, Twickenham TW1 4SX. Tel: 081-892 0051. *Principal*, Dr A. Naylor
SALFORD COLLEGE OF TECHNOLOGY, Frederick Road, Salford M6 6PU. Tel: 061-736 6541. *Principal*, J. Squires
SOUTHAMPTON INSTITUTE OF HIGHER EDUCATION, East Park Terrace, Southampton SO9 4WW. Tel: 0703-229381. *Director*, D. G. Leyland
TRINITY AND ALL SAINTS' COLLEGE, Brownberrie Lane, Horsforth, Leeds LS18 5HD. Tel: 0532-584341. *Principal*, Dr G. L. Turnbull
TRINITY COLLEGE OF MUSIC, 11–13 Mandeville Place, London W1M 6AQ. Tel: 071-935 5773. *Principal*, P. Jones, CBE
UNIVERSITY COLLEGE OF RIPON AND YORK ST JOHN, Lord Mayor's Walk, York YO3 7EX. Tel: 0904-656771. *Principal*, Prof. G. P. McGregor
UNIVERSITY COLLEGE SCARBOROUGH, THE NORTH RIDING COLLEGE, Filey Road, Scarborough, N. Yorks. YO11 3AZ. Tel: 0723-362392. *Principal*, R. A. Withers, PH.D.
WESTHILL COLLEGE, Hamilton Building, Weoley Park Road, Selly Oak, Birmingham B29 6LL. Tel: 021-472 7245. *Principal*, Dr J. G. Priestley
WEST LONDON INSTITUTE OF HIGHER EDUCATION, Lancaster House, Borough Road, Isleworth, Middx. TW7 5DU. Tel: 081-568 8741/891 0121. *Principal*, Prof. J. E. Kane, OBE, PH.D.
WESTMINSTER COLLEGE, Oxford OX2 9AT. Tel: 0865-247644. *Principal*, Revd Dr K. B. Wilson, OBE
WEST SURREY COLLEGE OF ART AND DESIGN, Falkner Road, The Hart, Farnham, Surrey GU9 7DS. Tel: 0252-722441. *Director*, N. J. Taylor
WEST SUSSEX INSTITUTE OF HIGHER EDUCATION, College Lane, Chichester, West Sussex PO19 4PE. Tel: 0243-787911. *Director*, Dr J. F. Wyatt
WINCHESTER SCHOOL OF ART, Park Avenue, Winchester, Hants. SO23 8DL. Tel: 0962-842500. *Principal*, M. Sadler-Forster
WORCESTER COLLEGE OF HIGHER EDUCATION, Henwick Grove, Worcester WR2 6AJ. Tel: 0905-748080. *Principal*, Ms D. Urwin

WALES

BANGOR NORMAL COLLEGE OF HIGHER EDUCATION, Bangor, Gwynedd LL57 2PX. Tel: 0248-370171. *Principal*, R. Williams

CARDIFF INSTITUTE OF HIGHER EDUCATION, Western Avenue, Llandaff, Cardiff CF5 2YB. Tel: 0222-551111. *Director*, J. D. Winslow
GWENT COLLEGE OF HIGHER EDUCATION, College Crescent, Caerleon, Newport, Gwent NP6 1XJ. Tel: 0633-430088. *Principal*, Dr K. J. Overshott
INSTITUTE OF HEALTH CARE STUDIES, University Hospital of Wales, Heath Park, Cardiff CF4 4XW. TEL: 0222-747747. *Manager*, J. Connelly
THE NORTH EAST WALES INSTITUTE (NEWI Plas Coch), Mold Road, Wrexham, Clwyd LL11 2AW. Tel: 0978-290666. Also NEWI Cartrefle at Cefn Road, Wrexham LL13 9NL, NEWI College of Art and Design Technology at Regent Street, Wrexham LL11 and NEWI Deeside at Kelsterton Road, Connah's Quay, Deeside CH5 4BR. *Principal*, Prof. J. O. Williams, PH.D, D.SC.
SWANSEA INSTITUTE OF HIGHER EDUCATION, Townhill Road, Swansea SA2 0UT. Tel: 0792-203482. *Principal*, Prof. G. Stockdale
TRINITY COLLEGE, Carmarthen, Dyfed, SA31 3EP. Tel: 0267-237971. *Principal*, D. C. Jones-Davies, OBE
WELSH AGRICULTURAL COLLEGE, Llanbadarn Fawr, Aberystwyth, Dyfed SY23 3AL. Tel: 0970-624471. *Principal*, Dr J. H. Harries
WELSH COLLEGE OF MUSIC AND DRAMA, Castle Grounds, Cathays Park, Cardiff CF1 3ER. Tel: 0222-342854. *Principal*, E. Fivet

SCOTLAND

BELL COLLEGE OF TECHNOLOGY, Almada Street, Hamilton, Lanarkshire ML3 0JB. Tel: 0698-283100. *Principal*, J. Reid
MORAY HOUSE COLLEGE OF EDUCATION, Holyrood Campus, Holyrood Road, Edinburgh EH8 8AQ. Tel: 031-556 8455. *Principal*, Prof. G. Kirk
NORTHERN COLLEGE OF EDUCATION, Hilton Place, Aberdeen AB9 1FA. Tel: 0224-283500; Gardyne Road, Dundee DD5 1NY. Tel: 0382-464000. *Principal*, D. A. Adams
ST ANDREW'S COLLEGE OF EDUCATION, Duntocher Road, Bearsden, Glasgow G61 4QA. Tel: 041-943 1424. *Principal*, B. J. McGettrick

NORTHERN IRELAND

ST MARY'S COLLEGE, 191 Falls Road, Belfast BT12 6FE. Tel: 0232-327678. *Principal*, Revd M. O'Callaghan
STRANMILLIS COLLEGE, Stranmillis Road, Belfast BT9 5DY. Tel: 0232-381271. *Principal*, Dr R. McMinn

---

ADULT AND CONTINUING EDUCATION

NATIONAL INSTITUTE OF ADULT CONTINUING EDUCATION, 19B De Montfort Street, Leicester LE1 7GE. Tel: 0533-551451. *Director*, A. Tuckett
NIACE CYMRU, 245 Western Avenue, Cardiff CF5 2YX. Tel: 0222-571201. *National Officer for Wales*, Ms A. Poole
NORTHERN IRELAND COUNCIL FOR ADULT EDUCATION, c/o Western Education and Library Board, 1 Hospital Road, Omagh, Co. Tyrone BT79 0AW. Tel: 0662-240240. *Chairman*, M. H. F. Murphy, OBE
THE NEW UNIVERSITIES AND POLYTECHNICS ASSOCIATION FOR CONTINUING EDUCATION, Educational Development Officer, Polytechnic of Wales, Pontypridd, Mid Glam. CF37 1DL. Tel: 0443-480480. *Secretary*, P. Race

THE RESIDENTIAL COLLEGES COMMITTEE, c/o Ruskin College, Oxford OX1 2HE. Tel: 0865-56360. *Awards Officer*, Mrs F. A. Bagchi

SCOTTISH COMMUNITY EDUCATION COUNCIL, Rosebery House, 9 Haymarket Terrace, Edinburgh EH12 5EZ. Tel: 031-313 2488. *Executive Director*, C. McConnell

THE UNIVERSITIES ASSOCIATION FOR CONTINUING EDUCATION, Department of Continuing Education, Westwood Site, The University of Warwick, Coventry CV4 7AL. Tel: 0203-523835/27. *Hon. Secretary*, Prof. C. Duke, PH.D.

THE WORKER'S EDUCATIONAL ASSOCIATION, Temple House, 17 Victoria Park Square, London E2 9PB. Tel: 081-983 1515. *General Secretary*, R. Lochrie

LONG-TERM RESIDENTIAL COLLEGES FOR ADULT EDUCATION

COLEG HARLECH, Harlech, Gwynedd LL46 2PU. Tel: 0766-780363. *Warden*, J. W. England

CO-OPERATIVE COLLEGE, Stanford Hall, Loughborough, Leics. LE12 5QR. Tel: 0509-852333. *Principal*, Dr R. Houlton

FIRCROFT COLLEGE, 1018 Bristol Road, Selly Oak, Birmingham B29 6LH. Tel: 021-472 0116. *Principal*, K. Jackson

HILLCROFT COLLEGE, South Bank, Surbiton, Surrey KT6 6DF. Tel: 081-399 2688. For women only. *Principal*, Ms E. Aird

NEWBATTLE ABBEY COLLEGE, Dalkeith, Midlothian EH22 3LL. Tel: 031-663 1921. *Principal*, W. M. Conboy

NORTHERN COLLEGE, Wentworth Castle, Stainborough, Barnsley, S. Yorks. S75 3ET. Tel: 0226-285426. *Principal*, R. H. Fryer

PLATER COLLEGE, Pullens Lane, Oxford OX3 0DT. Tel: 0865-741676. *Principal*, M. Blades

RUSKIN COLLEGE, Walton Street, Oxford OX1 2HE. Tel: 0865-54331. *Principal*, S. Yeo, D.Phil.

Professional Education

Excluding postgraduate study

The organizations listed below are those which, by providing specialist training or conducting examinations, control entry into a profession, or organizations responsible for maintaining a register of those with professional qualifications in their sector.

Many professions now have a largely graduate entry, and possession of a first degree can exempt entrants from certain of the professional examinations. Enquiries about obtaining professional qualifications should be made to the relevant professional organization(s). Details of higher education providers of first degrees may be found in *University and College Entrance*.

ACCOUNTANCY

The main bodies granting membership on examination after a period of practical work are:

INSTITUTE OF CHARTERED ACCOUNTANTS IN ENGLAND AND WALES, Chartered Accountants' Hall, PO Box 433, Moorgate Place, London EC2P 2BJ. Tel: 071-920 8100. *Secretary and Chief Executive*, A. J. Colquhoun

INSTITUTE OF CHARTERED ACCOUNTANTS OF SCOTLAND, 27 Queen Street, Edinburgh EH2 1LA. Tel: 031-479 4809. *Chief Executive*, P. W. Johnston

CHARTERED ASSOCIATION OF CERTIFIED ACCOUNTANTS, 29 Lincoln's Inn Fields, London WC2A 3EE. Tel: 071-242 6855. *Secretary*, Mrs A. L. Rose

CHARTERED INSTITUTE OF MANAGEMENT ACCOUNTANTS, 63 Portland Place, London WIN 4AB. Tel: 071-637 2311. *Secretary*, Sir George Vallings, KCB

CHARTERED INSTITUTE OF PUBLIC FINANCE AND ACCOUNTANCY, 3 Robert Street, London WC2N 6BH. Tel: 071-895 8823. *Secretary*, N. P. Hepworth, OBE

ACTUARIAL SCIENCE

Two professional organizations grant qualifications after examination:

INSTITUTE OF ACTUARIES, Staple Inn Hall, High Holborn, London WC1V 7QJ. Tel: 071-242 0106. *Secretary-General*, A. G. Tait. Enquiries to Actuarial Education Service, Napier House, 4 Worcester Street, Oxford OX1 2AW. Tel: 0865-794144

FACULTY OF ACTUARIES IN SCOTLAND, 23 St Andrew Square, Edinburgh EH2 1AQ. Tel: 031-557 1575. *Secretary*, W. W. Mair

ARCHITECTURE

The Education and Professional Development Committee of the Royal Institute of British Architects sets standards and guides the whole system of architectural education throughout the United Kingdom. Courses at Schools recognized by the RIBA exempt students from the RIBA's own examinations.

THE ROYAL INSTITUTE OF BRITISH ARCHITECTS, 66 Portland Place, London WIN 4AD. Tel: 071-580 5533. *President*, Dr F. Duffy; *Director-General*, The Lord Rodgers of Quarry Bank, PC

Schools of architecture outside the universities include:

THE ARCHITECTURAL ASSOCIATION, 34–36 Bedford Square, London WC1B 3ES. *Secretary*, E. A. Le Maistre

BANKING

Professional organizations granting qualifications after examination are:

CHARTERED INSTITUTE OF BANKERS, 10 Lombard Street, London EC3V 9AS. Tel: 071-623 3531. *Secretary-General*, E. Glover

CHARTERED INSTITUTE OF BANKERS IN SCOTLAND, 19 Rutland Square, Edinburgh EH1 2DE. Tel: 031-229 9869. *Chief Executive*, Dr C. W. Munn

BIOLOGY, CHEMISTRY, PHYSICS

Professional qualifications are awarded by:

INSTITUTE OF BIOLOGY, 20–22 Queensberry Place, London SW7 2DZ. Tel: 071-581 8333. *President*, Prof. C. R. W. Spedding, CBE; *General Secretary*, Dr R. H. Priestley

ROYAL SOCIETY OF CHEMISTRY, Burlington House, Piccadilly, London WIV 0BN. Tel: 071-437 8656. *President*, Prof. C. W. Rees, FRS; *Secretary-General*, Dr T. Inch

INSTITUTE OF PHYSICS, 47 Belgrave Square, London SW1X 8QX. Tel: 071-235 6111. *Chief Executive,* Dr A. Jones

BUILDING

Examinations are conducted by:
CHARTERED INSTITUTE OF BUILDING, Englemere, King's Ride, Ascot, Berks. SL5 8BJ. Tel: 0344-23355. *Chief Executive,* K. Banbury
INSTITUTE OF BUILDING CONTROL, 21 High Street, Ewell, Epsom, Surrey KT17 ISB. Tel: 081-393 6860. *Director,* Ms R. Raywood
INSTITUTE OF CLERKS OF WORKS OF GREAT BRITAIN, 41 The Mall, London W5 3TJ. Tel: 081-579 2917/8. *Secretary,* A. P. Macnamara

BUSINESS, MANAGEMENT AND ADMINISTRATION

Professional bodies conducting training and/or examinations in business, administration, management or commerce include:
AMETS (ASSOCIATION FOR MANAGEMENT EDUCATION AND TRAINING IN SCOTLAND), c/o University of Stirling, Stirling FK9 4LA. Tel: 0786-450906. *Vice-Chairman,* M. Makower
CAM FOUNDATION (COMMUNICATIONS, ADVERTISING AND MARKETING EDUCATION FOUNDATION), Abford House, 15 Wilton Road, London SW1V INJ. Tel: 071-828 7506. *Registrar,* Ms K. Hutchinson
CHARTERED INSTITUTE OF MARKETING, Moor Hall, Cookham, Maidenhead, Berks. SL6 9QH. Tel: 0628-524922. *Director-General,* J. McAinsh
CHARTERED INSTITUTE OF PURCHASING AND SUPPLY, Easton House, Easton on the Hill, Stamford, Lincs. PE9 3NZ. Tel: 0780-56777. *Director-General,* P. Thomson
CHARTERED INSTITUTE OF TRANSPORT, 80 Portland Place, London W1N 4DP. *Director-General,* R. P. Botwood
FACULTY OF SECRETARIES AND ADMINISTRATORS, PO Box 7, Godalming, Surrey GU7 1PR. Tel: 0483-425144. *Secretary,* Mrs D. M. Rummery
INSTITUTE OF ADMINISTRATIVE MANAGEMENT, 40 Chatsworth Parade, Petts Wood, Orpington, Kent BR5 1RW. Tel: 0689-875555. *Chief Executive,* Ms C. Hayhurst
INSTITUTE OF CHARTERED SECRETARIES AND ADMINISTRATORS, 16 Park Crescent, London W1N 4AH. Tel: 071-580 4741. *Secretary,* M. J. Ainsworth
INSTITUTE OF CHARTERED SHIPBROKERS, 3 Gracechurch Street, London EC3V OAT. Tel: 071-626 3058. *Secretary,* J. H. Parker
INSTITUTE OF EXPORT, Export House, 64 Clifton Street, London EC2A 4HB. Tel: 071-247 9812. *Director-General,* I. J. Campbell
INSTITUTE OF HEALTH SERVICES MANAGEMENT, 75 Portland Place, London W1N 4AN. Tel: 071-580 5041. *Director,* R. Rowden
INSTITUTE OF HOUSING, Octavia House, Westwood Business Park, Westwood Way, Coventry CV4 8JP. Tel: 0203-694433. *Chief Executive,* P. McGurk
INSTITUTION OF MANAGEMENT, Management House, Cottingham Road, Corby, Northants. NN17 1TT. Tel: 0536-204222. *Chief Executive,* R. Young

INSTITUTE OF PERSONNEL MANAGEMENT, IPM House, Camp Road, London SW19 4UX. Tel: 081-946 9100. *Director-General,* G. Armstrong
INSTITUTE OF PRACTITIONERS IN ADVERTISING, 44 Belgrave Square, London SW1X 8QS. Tel: 071-235 7020. *Secretary,* J. Raad
HENLEY MANAGEMENT COLLEGE, Greenlands, Henley-on-Thames, Oxon. RG9 3AU. Tel: 0491-571454. *Principal,* Prof. R. Wild
LONDON BUSINESS SCHOOL, Sussex Place, Regent's Park, London NW1 4SA. Tel: 071-262 5050. *Principal,* Prof. G. Bain, Ph.D.
MANCHESTER BUSINESS SCHOOL, Booth Street West, Manchester M15 6PB. Tel: 061-275 6333. *Director,* Prof. A. Cockerill
LONDON CHAMBER OF COMMERCE AND INDUSTRY EXAMINATIONS BOARD, Marlowe House, Station Road, Sidcup, Kent DA15 7BJ. Tel: 081-302 0261. *Chief Executive,* L. Swords

DANCE

ROYAL ACADEMY OF DANCING, 36 Battersea Square, London SW11 3RA. Tel: 071-223 0091. *Chief Executive,* D. Watchman; *Artistic Director,* J. Byrne
ROYAL BALLET SCHOOL, 155 Talgarth Road, London W14 9DE. Tel: 081-748 6335. Also at White Lodge, Richmond Park, Surrey TW10 5HR. Tel: 081-876 5547. *Director,* Dame Merle Park, DBE
IMPERIAL SOCIETY OF TEACHERS OF DANCING, Euston Hall, Birkenhead Street, London WC1H 8BE. Tel: 071-837 9967. *General Secretary,* M. J. Browne

DEFENCE

ROYAL NAVAL COLLEGES
ROYAL NAVAL COLLEGE, Greenwich, London SE10 9NN. Tel: 081-858 2154. *Admiral President,* Vice-Adm. Sir Michael Layard, KCB, CBE; *Dean of the College,* Prof. D. C. C. Gibbs
BRITANNIA ROYAL NAVAL COLLEGE, Dartmouth, Devon TQ6 OHJ. Tel: 0803-832141. Provides general and academic officer training. *Captain,* Capt. S. Moore
ROYAL NAVAL ENGINEERING COLLEGE, Manadon, Plymouth PL5 3AQ. Provides BA, B.Eng., M.Sc. and specialist training in naval engineering. Students are selected uniformed officers of the Royal Navy, Commonwealth and foreign navies, and civilians. *Captain,* Capt. D. G. Littlejohns, CBE; *Dean,* Capt. B. M. Leavey; *Executive Officer,* Cdr. S. P. C. Westwood

MILITARY COLLEGES
STAFF COLLEGE, Camberley, Surrey GU15 4NP. Tel: 0276-412691. *Commandant,* Maj.-Gen. C. B. Q. Wallace, OBE
ROYAL MILITARY ACADEMY SANDHURST, Camberley, Surrey GU15 4PQ. Tel: 0276-63344. *Commandant,* Maj.-Gen. T. P. Toyne Sewell
ROYAL MILITARY COLLEGE OF SCIENCE, Shrivenham, Swindon, Wilts. SN6 8LA. Tel: 0793-785434. Students from UK and overseas study from degree to postgraduate levels in management, science and technology. There is an increasing range of research and consultancy activity as the College is now a Faculty of Cranfield University.

Commandant, Maj.-Gen. E. F. B. Burton, OBE; *Principal*,
Prof. A. C. Baynham, PH.D.
DIRECTORATE OF EDUCATIONAL AND TRAINING
SERVICES, Director-General Adjutant General's Corp,
Worthydown, Winchester, Hants SO21 2RG. Tel: 0962-
887672/3. *Director*, Brig. J. M. Macfarlane

ROYAL AIR FORCE COLLEGES
ROYAL AIR FORCE STAFF COLLEGE, Bracknell,
Berks. RG12 3DD. Prepares selected senior officers for
high-grade command and staff appointments. Two-thirds
of the students are RAF officers; the others are officers
from the other UK Services and overseas air forces. *Air
Officer Commanding and Commandant*, Air Vice-Marshal
M. P. Donaldson
ROYAL AIR FORCE COLLEGE, Cranwell, Sleaford, Lincs.
NG34 8HB. Provides initial officer training for officers of
the RAF, WRAF and PMRAFNS. The initial specialist
training for officers of the Engineer and Supply Branches,
advanced specialist training for officers of the General
Duties, Engineer and Supply Branches and basic flying
training for pilots of the General Duties Branch are also
conducted at Cranwell. *Air Officer Commanding and
Commandant*, Air Vice-Marshal D. Cousins, CB, AFC
ROYAL AIR FORCE SCHOOL OF EDUCATION AND
TRAINING SUPPORT, RAF Newton, Nottingham
NG13 8HL. Tel: 0949-20771. *Commanding Officer*,
Gp Capt J. Rennie

DENTISTRY

To be entitled to be registered in the Dentists Register, a
person must hold the degree or diploma in dental surgery of
a university in the United Kingdom or the diploma of any
of the licensing authorities (The Royal College of Surgeons
of England and of Edinburgh, and the Royal College of
Physicians and Surgeons of Glasgow). Nationals of an EC
member state holding an appropriate European diploma,
and holders of certain overseas diplomas, may also be
registered. The Dentists Register is maintained by:
THE GENERAL DENTAL COUNCIL, 37 Wimpole Street,
London WIM 8DQ. Tel: 071-486 2171. *Registrar*,
N. T. Davies, MBE

DIETETICS
See also FOOD AND NUTRITION SCIENCE

The professional association is The British Dietetic Associa-
tion. Full membership is open to dietitians holding a
recognized qualification, who may also become State
Registered Dietitians through the Council for Professions
Supplementary to Medicine (*see* Medicine)
THE BRITISH DIETETIC ASSOCIATION, 7th Floor,
Elizabeth House, 22 Suffolk Street, Queensway,
Birmingham BI ILS. Tel: 021-643 5483

DRAMA

The national validating body for courses providing training
in drama for the professional theatre is the National Council
for Drama Training. It currently has accredited courses at
the following: Academy of Live and Recorded Arts; Arts
Educational Schools; Birmingham School of Speech Training
& Dramatic Art; Bristol Old Vic Theatre School; Central
School of Speech and Drama; Drama Centre, London;
Drama Studio; Guildford School of Acting; Guildhall School
of Music and Drama; London Academy of Music and
Dramatic Art; Manchester Polytechnic School of Theatre;
Mountview Theatre School; Rose Bruford College of Speech
and Drama; Royal Academy of Dramatic Art; Royal Scottish
Academy of Music and Drama; Webber Douglas Academy
of Dramatic Art; Welsh College of Music and Drama.
   The accreditation of a course in a school does not
necessarily imply that other courses of different type or
duration in the same school are also accredited
THE NATIONAL COUNCIL FOR DRAMA TRAINING,
5 Tavistock Place, London WC1H 9SS. *Secretary*,
Miss E. M. McKay

ENGINEERING

The Engineering Council supervises the engineering profes-
sion through the 42 nominated engineering institutions who
are represented on its Board for Engineers' Registration.
Working with and through the institutions, the Council sets
the standards for the registration of individuals, and also the
accreditation for academic courses in universities and colleges
and the practical training in industry.
THE ENGINEERING COUNCIL, 10 Maltravers Street,
London WC2R 3ER. Tel: 071-240 7891. *Secretary*,
L. Chelton
The principal qualifying bodies are:
BRITISH COMPUTER SOCIETY, PO Box 1454, Station
Road, Swindon SN1 ITG. Tel: 0793 480269. *Chief
Executive*, G. Kirkpatrick
CHARTERED INSTITUTION OF BUILDING SERVICES
ENGINEERS, Delta House, 222 Balham High Road,
London SW12 9BS. Tel: 081-675 5211. *Secretary*,
A. V. Ramsay
INSTITUTION OF CHEMICAL ENGINEERS, The Davis
Building, 165–171 Railway Terrace, Rugby,
Warks. CV21 3HQ. Tel: 0788-578214. *General Secretary*,
Dr T. J. Evans
INSTITUTION OF CIVIL ENGINEERS, Great George Street,
London SW1P 3AA. Tel: 071-222 7722. *Secretary*,
R. Dobson
INSTITUTION OF ELECTRICAL ENGINEERS, Savoy Place,
London WC2R OBL. Tel: 071-240 1871. *Secretary*, Dr
J. C. Williams, FENG.
INSTITUTE OF ENERGY, 18 Devonshire Street, London
WIN 2AU. Tel: 071-580 7124. *Secretary*, J. E. H. Leach
INSTITUTION OF GAS ENGINEERS, 17 Grosvenor
Crescent, London SW1X 7ES. Tel: 071-245 9811. *Secretary*,
D. J. Chapman
INSTITUTE OF MARINE ENGINEERS, The Memorial
Building, 76 Mark Lane, London EC3R 7JN. Tel: 071-481
8493. *Secretary*, J. E. Sloggett
INSTITUTE OF MATERIALS, I Carlton House Terrace,
London SW1Y 5DB. Tel: 071-839 4071. *Secretary*, Dr
J. A. Catterall
INSTITUTE OF MEASUREMENT AND CONTROL, 87 Gower
Street, London WCIE 6AA. Tel: 071-387 4949. *Secretary*,
M. J. Yates
INSTITUTION OF MECHANICAL ENGINEERS, I Birdcage
Walk, London SW1H 9JJ. Tel: 071-222 7899. *Director-
General*, Dr R. Pike
INSTITUTION OF MINING ENGINEERS, Danum House,
6a South Parade, Doncaster DN1 2DY. Tel: 0302-320486.
Secretary, W. J. W. Bourne, OBE

INSTITUTION OF MINING AND METALLURGY, 44 Portland Place, London WIN 4BR. Tel: 071-580 3802. *Secretary*, M. J. Jones

INSTITUTION OF STRUCTURAL ENGINEERS, 11 Upper Belgrave Street, London SWIX 8BH. Tel: 071-235 4535. *Secretary*, D. J. Clark

ROYAL AERONAUTICAL SOCIETY, 4 Hamilton Place, London WIV OBQ. Tel: 071-499 3515. *Director*, R. J. Kennett

ROYAL INSTITUTION OF NAVAL ARCHITECTS, 10 Upper Belgrave Street, London SWIX 8BQ. Tel: 071-235 4622. *Secretary*, J. Rosewarn

FOOD AND NUTRITION SCIENCE
See also DIETETICS

Scientific and professional bodies include:

INSTITUTE OF FOOD SCIENCE & TECHNOLOGY, 5 Cambridge Court, 210 Shepherd's Bush Road, London W6 7NL. Tel: 071-603 6316. *Executive Secretary*, Ms H. G. Wild

NUTRITION SOCIETY, 10 Cambridge Court, 210 Shepherds Bush Road, London W6 7NJ. Tel: 071-602 0228. *Hon. Secretary*, Dr R. F. Grimble

FORESTRY AND TIMBER STUDIES

Professional organizations include:

ROYAL FORESTRY SOCIETY OF ENGLAND, WALES AND NORTHERN IRELAND, 102 High Street, Tring, Herts., HP23 4AF. Tel: 0442-822028. *Director*, J. E. Jackson, PH.D.

ROYAL SCOTTISH FORESTRY SOCIETY, Camsie House, Charlestown, Dunfermline, Fife KY11 3EE. Tel: 0383-873014. *Director*, M. Osborne

INSTITUTE OF CHARTERED FORESTERS, 7A St Colme Street, Edinburgh EH3 6AA. Tel: 031-225 2705. *Secretary*, Mrs M. W. Dick

COMMONWEALTH FORESTRY ASSOCIATION, c/o Oxford Forestry Institute, South Parks Road, Oxford OXI 3RB. Tel: 0865-275072. *Chairman*, P. J. Wood

FUEL AND ENERGY SCIENCE

The principal professional bodies are:

INSTITUTE OF ENERGY, 18 Devonshire Street, London WIN 2AU. Tel: 071-580 7124. *Secretary*, J. Leach

INSTITUTION OF GAS ENGINEERS, 17 Grosvenor Crescent, London SWIX 7ES. Tel: 071-245 9811. *Secretary*, D. J. Chapman

INSTITUTE OF PETROLEUM, 61 New Cavendish Street, London WIM 8AR. Tel: 071-636 1004. *Director-General*, I. Ward

HOTELKEEPING, CATERING AND INSTITUTIONAL MANAGEMENT
See also DIETETICS, and FOOD and NUTRITION SCIENCE

The qualifying professional body in the subjects is:

HOTEL CATERING AND INSTITUTIONAL MANAGEMENT ASSOCIATION, 191 Trinity Road, London SWI7 7HN. Tel: 081-672 4251. *Chief Executive*, J. Logie

INDUSTRIAL AND VOCATIONAL TRAINING

There are 120 Industry Training Organizations, employer-led independent organizations whose role includes setting the standards of National and Scottish Vocational Qualifications.

NATIONAL COUNCIL OF INDUSTRY TRAINING ORGANIZATIONS, 5 George Lane, Royston, Herts. SG8 9AR. Tel: 0763-247285. *Chairman*, P. Morley; *Administrator*, Mrs C. Armstrong

INSURANCE

Organizations conducting examinations and awarding diplomas are:

ASSOCIATION OF AVERAGE ADJUSTERS, HQS *Wellington*, Temple Stairs, Victoria Embankment, London WC2R 2PN. Tel: 071-240 5516. *Secretary*, Mrs P. J. Albano

CHARTERED INSURANCE INSTITUTE, 20 Aldermanbury, London EC2V 7HY. Tel: 071-606 3835. *Director-General*, Dr D. E. Bland

CHARTERED INSTITUTE OF LOSS ADJUSTERS, Manfield House, 376 The Strand, London WC2R OLR. Tel: 071-240 1496. *Director*, A. F. Clack

JOURNALISM

Courses for trainee newspaper journalists are available at 20 centres. One-year full-time courses are available for selected students. Particulars of all these courses are available from the National Council for the Training of Journalists. Short courses for experienced journalists are also arranged by the National Council.

For periodical journalists, there are six centres running courses approved by the Periodicals Training Council.

THE NATIONAL COUNCIL FOR TRAINING OF JOURNALISTS, Latton Bush Centre, Southern Way, Harlow, Essex CMI8 7BL. Tel: 0279-430009. *Chief Executive*, K. Hall

THE PERIODICALS TRAINING COUNCIL, Imperial House, 15–19 Kingsway, London WC2B 6UN. Tel: 071-836 8798. *Executive Director*, D. Longbottom, MBE

LAW

THE BAR

Admission to the Bar of England and Wales is controlled by the Inns of Court and admission to the Bar of Northern Ireland by the Honorable Society of the Inn of Court of Northern Ireland, which are the governing bodies of barristers in England and Wales and Northern Ireland respectively. Admission as an Advocate of the Scottish Bar is controlled by the Faculty of Advocates.

THE GENERAL COUNCIL OF THE BAR, 3 Bedford Row, London WCIR 4DB. Tel: 071-242 0082. The governing body of the barristers' branch of the legal profession in England and Wales. *Chairman*, J. Rowe, QC; *Chief Executive*, J. Mottram, CB, LVO, OBE

The Inns of Court

THE INNER TEMPLE, London EC4Y 7HL. Tel: 071-797
8175/7. *Treasurer,* The Rt. Hon. Sir John May; *Sub-
Treasurer,* Capt. P. T. Sheehan, CBE, RN.
THE MIDDLE TEMPLE, London EC4Y 9AT. *Treasurer,*
Rear-Adm. J. R. Hill; *Deputy Treasurer,* M. J. P. Spain
GRAY'S INN, 8 South Square, London WCIR 5EU. *Treasurer,*
C. Sparrow, QC, FSA; *Under-Treasurer,* D. Machin
LINCOLN'S INN, London WC2A 3TL. Tel: 071-405 1393.
Treasurer, The Lord Oliver of Aylmerton, PC; *Under-
Treasurer,* Capt. P. M. Carver, RN

The education and examination of students for the Bar of
England and Wales is superintended by the COUNCIL OF
LEGAL EDUCATION, Inns of Court School of Law, 39 Eagle
Street, London WCIR 4AJ. Tel: 071-404 5787. *Chairman,* The
Hon. Mr Justice Phillips; *Dean, Inns of Court School of Law,*
Mrs M. A. Phillips
FACULTY OF ADVOCATES, Advocates Library, Parliament
House, Edinburgh EHI IRF. Tel: 031-226 5071. *Dean,*
A. C. M. Johnston, QC; *Clerk,* J. R. Doherty
THE HONORABLE SOCIETY OF THE INN OF COURT OF
NORTHERN IRELAND, Royal Courts of Justice, Belfast
BTI 3JF. Tel: 0232-235111. *Treasurer* (1993), The Hon. Mr
Justice Campbell; *Under-Treasurer,* J. A. L. McLean, QC

SOLICITORS

Qualifications for solicitor are obtainable only from one of
the Law Societies, which control the education and examina-
tion of articled clerks, and the admission of solicitors.
LAW SOCIETY OF ENGLAND AND WALES, 113 Chancery
Lane, London WC2A IPL. Tel: 071-242 1222. *President*
(1993-4), R. J. Pannone; *Vice-President* (1993-4),
R. C. Elly; *Secretary-General,* J. W. Hayes
THE COLLEGE OF LAW provides courses for the Law
Society examinations at Braboeuf Manor, St Catherine's,
Guildford, Surrey GU3 IHA; 14 Store Street, London
WCIE 7DE; Christleton Hall, Chester CH3 7AB;
Bishopthorpe Road, York YO2 IQA
THE SOLICITORS COMPLAINTS BUREAU, Victoria Court,
8 Dormer Place, Leamington Spa, Warks CV31 IHE. Tel:
0926-820082. The Bureau is an independent arm of the
Law Society set up to handle complaints about solicitors.
LAW SOCIETY OF SCOTLAND, Law Society's Hall, 26
Drumsheugh Gardens, Edinburgh EH3 7YR. Tel: 031-226
7411. *President* (1993-4), I. D. Dunbar; *Secretary,*
K. W. Pritchard, OBE
LAW SOCIETY OF NORTHERN IRELAND, Law Society
House, 90-106 Victoria Street, Belfast BTI 3JZ. Tel: 0232-
231614. *Secretary,* M. C. Davey

LIBRARIANSHIP AND INFORMATION
SCIENCE/MANAGEMENT

The Library Association accredits degree and/or postgraduate courses in library and information science which are
offered by 16 universities in the UK. A full list of accredited
degree and postgraduate courses is available from the
Education Department. The Association also maintains a
professional register of Chartered Members open to graduate
ordinary members of the Association.
THE LIBRARY ASSOCIATION, 7 Ridgmount Street,
London WCIE 7AE. Tel: 071-636 7543. *Chief Executive,*
R. Shimmon

MATERIALS STUDIES

The qualifying body is:
INSTITUTE OF MATERIALS, I Carlton House Terrace,
London SWIY 5DB. Tel: 071-839 4071. *Secretary,* Dr
J. A. Catterall

MEDICINE

LICENSING CORPORATIONS GRANTING DIPLOMAS
SOCIETY OF APOTHECARIES OF LONDON, Black Friars
Lane, London EC4V 6EJ. Tel: 071-236 1189. *Clerk,*
Maj. J. C. O'Leary; *Registrar,* A. M. Wallington-Smith
SCOTTISH TRIPLE QUALIFICATION BOARD, Nicolson
Street, Edinburgh EH8 9DW, tel: 031-556 6206; and 242
St Vincent Street, Glasgow, tel: 041-221 6072

COLLEGES HOLDING POSTGRADUATE MEMBERSHIP
AND DIPLOMA EXAMINATIONS
ROYAL COLLEGE OF ANAESTHETISTS, 48-49 Russell
Square, London WCIB 4JY. Tel: 071-813 1900. *President,*
Prof. A. Spence, CBE. *Chief Executive,* Sir Geoffrey de
Deney, KCVO
ROYAL COLLEGE OF GENERAL PRACTITIONERS, 14
Princes Gate, London SW7 IPU. Tel: 071-581 3232.
President, Dr A. Donald; *Secretary,* Dr M. McBride
ROYAL COLLEGE OF OBSTETRICIANS AND
GYNAECOLOGISTS, 27 Sussex Place, London NWI 4RG.
Tel: 071-262 5425. *President,* Prof. G. V. P. Chamberlain,
RD, FRCOG; *Secretary,* Prof. W. Dunlop, FRCOG
ROYAL COLLEGE OF PATHOLOGISTS, 2 Carlton House
Terrace, London SWIY 5AF. Tel: 071-930 5863. *President,*
Prof. A. J. Bellingham, FRCP, FRCPath.; *Secretary,*
K. Lockyer
ROYAL COLLEGE OF PHYSICIANS, II St Andrews Place,
London NWI 4LE. Tel: 071-935 1174. *President,*
Prof. L. A. Turnberg; *Secretary,* D. B. Lloyd
ROYAL COLLEGE OF PHYSICIANS OF EDINBURGH,
9 Queen Street, Edinburgh EH2 IJQ. Tel: 031-225 7324.
President, Dr A. D. Toft; *Secretary,* Dr J. StJ. Thomas
ROYAL COLLEGE OF PHYSICIANS AND SURGEONS OF
GLASGOW, 234-242 St Vincent Street, Glasgow G2 5RJ.
Tel: 041-221 6072. *President,* Prof. D. Campbell, CBE;
Hon. Secretary, Dr B. Williams
ROYAL COLLEGE OF PSYCHIATRISTS, 17 Belgrave
Square, London SWIX 8PG. Tel: 071-235 2351. *President,*
Dr F. Caldicott; *Secretary,* Mrs V. Cameron
ROYAL COLLEGE OF RADIOLOGISTS, 38 Portland Place,
London WIN 3DG. Tel: 071-636 4432. *President,*
Dr C. H. Paine; *Secretary,* A. J. Cowles
ROYAL COLLEGE OF SURGEONS OF ENGLAND, 35-43
Lincoln's Inn Fields, London WC2A 3PN. Tel: 071-405
3474. *President,* Prof. N. L. Browse, PRCS; *Secretary,*
R. H. E. Duffett
ROYAL COLLEGE OF SURGEONS OF EDINBURGH,
Nicolson Street, Edinburgh EH8 9DW. Tel: 031-556 6206.
President, Prof. P. S. Boulter; *Secretary,* I. B. Macleod,
FRCSEd.

PROFESSIONS SUPPLEMENTARY TO
MEDICINE

The standard of professional education in chiropody,
dietetics, medical laboratory sciences, occupational therapy,
orthoptics, physiotherapy and radiography is the

responsibility of seven professional boards, which also publish an annual register of qualified practitioners. The work of the Boards is co-ordinated by the Council for Professions Supplementary to Medicine.
THE COUNCIL FOR PROFESSIONS SUPPLEMENTARY TO MEDICINE, Park House, 184 Kennington Park Road, London SE11 4BU. Tel: 071-582 0866. *Registrar*, R. Pickis

CHIROPODY

Professional recognition is granted by the Society of Chiropodists and Podiatrists to students who are awarded B.Sc. degrees in Podiatry or Podiatric medicine after attending a course of full-time training for three or four years at one of the 14 recognized schools in the UK (11 in England and Wales, two in Scotland and one in Northern Ireland). Qualifications granted and degrees recognized by the Society are approved by the Chiropodists Board for the purpose of State Registration, which is a condition of employment within the National Health Service.
THE SOCIETY OF CHIROPODISTS AND PODIATRISTS, 53 Welbeck Street, London W1M 7HE. Tel: 071-486 3381. *General Secretary*, J. G. C. Trouncer

See also DIETETICS

MEDICAL LABORATORY SCIENCES

Qualifications from higher or further education establishments and training in medical laboratories are required for progress to the professional examinations and qualifications of the INSTITUTE OF MEDICAL LABORATORY SCIENCES, 12 Queen Anne Street, London W1M 0AU. Tel: 071-636 8192. *Chief Executive*, A. Potter

OCCUPATIONAL THERAPY

Professional qualifications are awarded by the College of Occupational Therapists upon completion of one of the 27 training courses approved by the College
THE COLLEGE OF OCCUPATIONAL THERAPISTS, 6–8 Marshalsea Road, London SE1 1HL. Tel: 071-357 6480. *Secretary*, M. D. Hall, OBE, GM

See also OPHTHALMIC OPTICS

ORTHOPTICS

Orthoptics undertake the diagnosis and treatment of all types of squint and other anomalies of binocular vision, working in close collaboration with ophthalmologists. The training and maintenance of professional standards are the responsibility of the Orthoptists Board of the Council for the Professions Supplementary to Medicine. The professional body is the British Orthoptic Society. Training is at degree level.
THE BRITISH ORTHOPTIC SOCIETY, Tavistock House North, Tavistock Square, London WC1H 9HX. *Secretary*, Mrs A. Charnock

PHYSIOTHERAPY

Full-time three- or four-year degree courses are available at 31 recognized schools in the UK. Information about courses leading to eligibility for Membership of the Chartered Society of Physiotherapy and to State Registration is available from THE CHARTERED SOCIETY OF PHYSIOTHERAPY, 14 Bedford Row, London WC1R 4ED. Tel: 071-242 1941. *Secretary*, T. Simon

RADIOGRAPHY AND RADIOTHERAPY

In order to practise both diagnostic and therapeutic radiography in the United Kingdom, it is necessary to have successfully completed a course of education and training recognized by the Privy Council. Such courses are offered by universities and colleges throughout the United Kingdom and lead to the award of either a degree in radiography or the Diploma of the College of Radiographers. Further information is available from THE COLLEGE OF RADIOGRAPHERS, 14 Upper Wimpole Street, London W1M 8BN. Tel: 071-935 5726. *Chief Executive*, B. Macey

MERCHANT NAVY TRAINING SCHOOLS

OFFICERS

MARITIME OPERATIONS CENTRE, Southampton Institute of Higher Education, Newtown Road, Warsash, Southampton SO3 9ZL. Tel: 0489-576161. *Head of Centre*, Capt. G. B. Angas

SEAFARERS

INDEFATIGABLE SCHOOL, Plas Llanfair, Llanfairpwll, Anglesey LL61 6NT. Tel: 0248-714338. *Headmaster*, Capt. P. White
NATIONAL SEA TRAINING COLLEGE, Denton, Gravesend, Kent DA12 2HR. Tel: 0474-363656. *Principal*, M. Bolton

MUSIC

ASSOCIATED BOARD OF THE ROYAL SCHOOLS OF MUSIC, 14 Bedford Square, London WC1B 3JG. Conducts music examinations in centres throughout the world for the Royal Academy of Music and the Royal College of Music in London, the Royal Northern College of Music, Manchester and the Royal Scottish Academy of Music and Drama, Glasgow. *Chief Executive*, R. Morris
ROYAL ACADEMY OF MUSIC, Marylebone Road, London NW1 5HT. Tel: 071-935 5461. *Principal*, L. Harrell
ROYAL COLLEGE OF MUSIC, Prince Consort Road, London SW7 2BS. Tel: 071-589 3643. *Director*, Dr J. Ritterman
ROYAL NORTHERN COLLEGE OF MUSIC, 124 Oxford Road, Manchester M13 9RD. Tel: 061-273 6283. *Principal*, Sir John Manduell, CBE
ROYAL SCOTTISH ACADEMY OF MUSIC AND DRAMA, 100 Renfrew Street, Glasgow G2 3DB. Tel: 041-332 4101. *Principal*, Dr P. Ledger, CBE
ROYAL COLLEGE OF ORGANISTS, 7 St Andrew Street, London EC4A 3LQ. Tel: 071-936 3606. *Clerk*, V. Waterhouse
GUILDHALL SCHOOL OF MUSIC AND DRAMA, Silk Street, London EC2Y 8DT. Tel: 071-628 2571. *Principal*, I. Horsbrugh
LONDON COLLEGE OF MUSIC, Thames Valley University, St Mary's Road, London W5 5RF. Tel: 081-231 2364. *General Manager*, R. D. Roberts
TRINITY COLLEGE OF MUSIC, 11–13 Mandeville Place, London W1M 6AQ. Tel: 071-935 5773. *Principal*, P. Jones, CBE

NURSING

Courses leading to registration as a nurse are at least three years in length. There are also some programmes which are combined with degrees. Students study in colleges of nursing or in institutions of higher education. Courses offer a combination of theoretical and practical experience in a wide variety of settings. Depending on the type of course, students will register in adult, child, mental health or mental handicap (learning disabilities) nursing. A wide variety of specialist programmes are available after registration, for example in district nursing or occupational health nursing.

UK CENTRAL COUNCIL FOR NURSING, MIDWIFERY AND HEALTH VISITING, 23 Portland Place, London WIN 3AF. Tel: 071-637 7181. *Registrar and Chief Executive,* C. Ralph

ENGLISH NATIONAL BOARD FOR NURSING, MIDWIFERY AND HEALTH VISITING, Victory House, 170 Tottenham Court Road, London WIP OHA. Tel: 071-388 3131. *Chief Executive Officer,* A. P. Smith

WELSH NATIONAL BOARD FOR NURSING, MIDWIFERY AND HEALTH VISITING, Floor 13, Pearl Assurance House, Greyfriars Road, Cardiff CFI 3AG. Tel: 0222-395535. *Chief Executive Officer,* D. A. Ravey

NATIONAL BOARD FOR NURSING, MIDWIFERY AND HEALTH VISITING FOR SCOTLAND, 22 Queen Street, Edinburgh EH2 1JX. Tel: 031-226 7371. *Chief Executive Officer,* Mrs L. Mitchell

NATIONAL BOARD FOR NURSING, MIDWIFERY AND HEALTH VISITING FOR NORTHERN IRELAND, RAC House, 79 Chichester Street, Belfast BTI 4JE. Tel: 0232-238152. *Chief Executive Officer,* Dr O. D'A. Slevin.

OPHTHALMIC OPTICS

Professional bodies are:

THE BRITISH COLLEGE OF OPTOMETRISTS, IO Knaresborough Place, London SW5 OTG. Tel: 071-373 7765. Grants qualifications as an optometrist. *General Secretary,* P. D. Leigh

THE ASSOCIATION OF BRITISH DISPENSING OPTICIANS, 6 Hurlingham Business Park, Sulivan Road, London SW6 3DU. Tel: 071-736 0088. Grants qualifications as a dispensing optician. *Registrar,* D. G. Baker

PHARMACY

Information may be obtained from the Secretary and Registrar, ROYAL PHARMACEUTICAL SOCIETY OF GREAT BRITAIN, I Lambeth High Street, London SEI 7JN. *Secretary and Registrar,* J. Ferguson

PHOTOGRAPHY

The professional body is:

BRITISH INSTITUTE OF PROFESSIONAL PHOTOGRAPHY, Fox Talbot House, 2 Amwell End, Ware, Herts. SG12 9HN. Tel: 0920-464011. *Chief Executive,* A. Mair

PRINTING

Details of courses in general and technical design can be obtained from the Institute of Printing and the British Printing Industries Federation. In addition to these examining and organizing bodies, examinations are held by various independent regional examining boards in further education.

BRITISH PRINTING INDUSTRIES FEDERATION, II Bedford Row, London WCIR 4DX. Tel: 071-242 6904. *Director-General,* C. Stanley

INSTITUTE OF PRINTING, 8 Lonsdale Gardens, Tunbridge Wells, Kent TNI INU. Tel: 0892-538118. *Secretary-General,* C. F. Partridge

SOCIAL WORK

The Central Council for Education and Training in Social Work promotes education and training for social work and social care throughout the UK. It approves education and training programmes, including those leading to its qualifying award, the Diploma in Social Work.

THE CENTRAL COUNCIL FOR EDUCATION AND TRAINING IN SOCIAL WORK, Derbyshire House, St Chad's Street, London WCIH 8AD. Tel: 071-278 2455. *Chairman,* J. Greenwood; *Director,* T. Hall

SPEECH THERAPY

The College of Speech and Language Therapists provides details of courses leading to qualification as a speech and language therapist. The College also sponsors advanced clinical courses. Other professionals may become Associates of the College. A directory of registered members is published annually.

THE COLLEGE OF SPEECH AND LANGUAGE THERAPISTS, 7 Bath Place, London EC2A 3DR. Tel: 071-613 3855. *Director,* Mrs S. Davis

SURVEYING

The qualifying professional bodies include:

ROYAL INSTITUTION OF CHARTERED SURVEYORS (incorporating The Institute of Quantity Surveyors), Surveyor Court, Westwood Way, Coventry CV4 8JE. Tel: 0203-694757. *Chief Executive,* M. Pattison

ARCHITECTS AND SURVEYORS INSTITUTE, 15 St Mary Street, Chippenham, Wilts. SN15 3JN. Tel: 0249-444505. *Chief Executive.,* B. A. Hunt

ASSOCIATION OF BUILDING ENGINEERS, Jubilee House, Billing Brook Road, Weston Favell, Northampton NN3 4NW. Tel: 0604-404121. *Chief Executive,* B. D. Hughes

INSTITUTE OF REVENUES, RATING AND VALUATION, 41 Doughty Street, London WCIN 2LF. Tel: 071-831 3505. *Director,* C. Farrington

INCORPORATED SOCIETY OF VALUERS AND AUCTIONEERS (1968), 3 Cadogan Gate, London SWIX OAS. Tel: 071-235 2282. *Chief Executive,* H. Whitty

TEACHING

To become a qualified teacher it is necessary to have successfully completed a course of initial teacher training. Non-graduates usually qualify by way of a three- or four-year course leading to a Bachelor of Education (B.Ed.) honours degree, but some universities offer first degree courses (BA, B.Sc.) taken concurrently with a certificate of education.

Graduates take a one-year postgraduate certificate of education (PGCE). Increasingly, it is possible to train in schools whilst working as a teacher.

Details of courses in England and Wales are contained in the *Handbook of Degree and Advanced Courses* published annually by the National Association of Teachers in Further and Higher Education.

Applications for B.Ed. courses in England and Wales at institutions other than universities are made through UCAS. For all PGCE courses in England and Wales, applications are handled by the Graduate Teacher Training Registry. (For addresses, *see* page 462).

Details of courses in Scotland can be obtained from the colleges of education and from TEACH through which applications are made (*see* page 462). Details of courses in Northern Ireland can be obtained from the Department of Education for Northern Ireland. Applications for teacher training courses in Northern Ireland are made to the institutions direct.

TEXTILES

THE TEXTILE INSTITUTE, 10 Blackfriars Street, Manchester M3 5DR. Tel: 061-834 8457. *Chief Executive,* R. G. Denyer

---

THEOLOGICAL COLLEGES

The number of students training for the ministry for the academic year 1992-3 is shown in parenthesis.

ANGLICAN

CHICHESTER THEOLOGICAL COLLEGE, Chichester, W. Sussex PO19 1SG. (25). *Principal,* Revd Canon P. Atkinson
CRANMER HALL, St John's College, Durham DH1 3RJ. (77). *Warden,* Revd J. Pritchard
LINCOLN THEOLOGICAL COLLEGE, Drury Lane, Lincoln LN1 3BP. (65). *Warden,* Revd Canon W. M. Jacob, PH.D.
OAK HILL COLLEGE, Chase Side, London N14 4PS. (87). *Principal,* Revd Canon G. Bridger
COLLEGE OF THE RESURRECTION, Mirfield, W. Yorks. WF14 0BW. (37). *Principal,* Revd Dr D. J. Lane
RIDLEY HALL, Cambridge CB3 9HG. (60). *Principal,* Revd G. A. Cray
RIPON COLLEGE, Cuddesdon, Oxford OX9 9EX. (65). *Principal,* Revd Canon J. H. Garton
ST JOHN'S COLLEGE, Chilwell Lane, Bramcote, Nottingham NG9 3DS. (120). *Principal,* Revd Dr J. Goldingay
ST MICHAEL'S THEOLOGICAL COLLEGE, Llandaff, Cardiff CF5 2YJ. (38). *Warden,* Revd Canon J. H. L. Rowlands
ST STEPHEN'S HOUSE, 16 Marston Street, Oxford OX4 1JX. (55). *Principal,* Revd E. R. Barnes
SALISBURY AND WELLS THEOLOGICAL COLLEGE, 19 The Close, Salisbury SP1 2EE. (60). *Principal,* Revd Canon P. A. Crowe
THEOLOGICAL INSTITUTE OF THE SCOTTISH EPISCOPAL CHURCH, Coates Hall, Rosebery Crescent, Edinburgh EH12 5JT. (45). *Principal,* Revd Canon K. Mason
TRINITY COLLEGE, Stoke Hill, Bristol BS9 1JP. (130). *Principal (acting),* Revd M. Roberts

WESTCOTT HOUSE, Jesus Lane, Cambridge CB5 8BP. (50). *Principal,* Revd Dr R. W. N. Hoare
WYCLIFFE HALL, 54 Banbury Road, Oxford OX2 6PW. (70). *Principal,* Revd Dr R. T. France

BAPTIST

BRISTOL BAPTIST COLLEGE, Woodland Road, Bristol BS8 1UN. (24). *Principal,* vacant
NORTHERN BAPTIST COLLEGE, Northern Federation for Training in Ministry, Luther King House, Brighton Grove, Rusholme, Manchester M14 5JP. (40). *Principal,* Revd Dr B. Haymes
NORTH WALES BAPTIST COLLEGE, Ffordd Ffriddoedd, Bangor, Gwynedd LL57 2EH. (3). *Principal,* Revd J. R. Rowlands
REGENT'S PARK COLLEGE, Oxford OX1 2LB. (25). *Principal,* Revd Dr P. S. Fiddes
THE SCOTTISH BAPTIST COLLEGE, 12 Aytoun Road, Glasgow G41 5RT. (14). *Principal,* Revd Dr I. J. W. Oakley
SOUTH WALES BAPTIST COLLEGE, 54 Richmond Road, Cardiff CF2 3UR. (23). *Principal,* Revd D. H. Matthews
SPURGEON'S COLLEGE, South Norwood Hill, London SE25 6DJ. (140). *Principal,* Revd M. Quicke

CHURCH OF SCOTLAND

CHRIST'S COLLEGE, Aberdeen AB1 1YD. (28). *Master,* Revd Prof. A. Main, TD, PH.D.
NEW COLLEGE, Mound Place, Edinburgh EH1 2LU. (54). *Principal,* Revd Prof. D. B. Forrester
TRINITY COLLEGE, 4 The Square, University of Glasgow, Glasgow G12 8QQ. (65). *Principal,* Revd Prof. G. M. Newlands

CONGREGATIONAL

COLLEGE OF THE WELSH INDEPENDENTS, 38 Pier Street, Aberystwyth, Dyfed. *Principal,* Revd Dr E. S. John
SCOTTISH CONGREGATIONAL COLLEGE, Rosebery Crescent, Edinburgh EH12 5YN. (12). *Principal,* Revd Dr J. W. S. Clark

ECUMENICAL

QUEEN'S COLLEGE, Somerset Road, Edgbaston, Birmingham B15 2QH. (75). *Principal,* Revd Dr J. B. Walker

METHODIST

EDGHILL THEOLOGICAL COLLEGE, 9 Lennoxvale, Belfast BT9 5BY. (13). *Principal,* Revd D. Cooke, PH.D.
HARTLEY VICTORIA COLLEGE, Northern Federation for Training in Ministry, Luther King House, Brighton Grove, Manchester M14 5JP. (24). *Principal,* Revd G. Slater
LINCOLN THEOLOGICAL COLLEGE, Drury Lane, Lincoln LN1 3BP. (65). *Warden,* Revd Canon W. M. Jacob, PH.D.
WESLEY COLLEGE, College Park Drive, Henbury Road, Bristol BS10 7QD. (62). *Principal,* Dr H. McKeating
WESLEY HOUSE, Cambridge CB5 8BJ. (34). *Principal,* Revd Dr I. H. Jones
WESLEY STUDY CENTRE, 55 The Avenue, Durham DH1 4EB. (18). *Director,* Revd P. Luscombe, PH.D.

NON-DENOMINATIONAL

ST MARY'S COLLEGE, The University, St Andrews, Fife KY16 9JU. (180). *Principal,* Dr R. A. Piper

PRESBYTERIAN

UNION THEOLOGICAL COLLEGE, Belfast BT7 1JT. (76). *Principal,* Revd Prof. T. S. Reid

PRESBYTERIAN CHURCH OF WALES
UNITED THEOLOGICAL COLLEGE, Aberystwyth SY23 2LT.
(58). *Principal*, Revd Prof. E. ap Nefydd Roberts

ROMAN CATHOLIC
ALLEN HALL COLLEGE, 28 Beaufort Street, London
SW3 5AA. (63). *Principal*, Revd K. Barltrop, STL
CAMPION HOUSE COLLEGE, 112 Thornbury Road,
Isleworth, Middx. TW7 4NN. (35). *Principal*,
Revd M. Barrow, SJ
OSCOTT COLLEGE, Chester Road, Sutton Coldfield,
W. Midlands B73 5AA. (67). *Rector*, Rt. Revd
Mgr P. McKinney, STL
SCOTUS COLLEGE, 2 Chesters Road, Bearsden, Glasgow
G61 4AG. (50). *Rector*, Rt Revd Mgr M. J. Conway
ST JOHN'S SEMINARY, Wonersh, Guildford, Surrey
GU5 0QX. (35). *Rector*, Rt. Revd Mgr P. Smith
USHAW COLLEGE, Durham DH7 9RH. (92). *Principal*,
Rt. Revd Mgr R. Atherton, OBE

UNITARIAN
UNITARIAN COLLEGE, Northern Federation for Training
in Ministry, Luther King House, Brighton Grove,
Rusholme, Manchester M14 5JP. (5). *Principal*, Revd
L. Smith, PH.D.

UNITED REFORMED
BALA-BANGOR INDEPENDENT COLLEGE, Bangor
LL57 2EH. (15). *Principal*, R. T. Jones, D.Phil., DD
MANSFIELD COLLEGE, Mansfield Road, Oxford OX1 3TF.
(27). *Principal*, D. J. Trevelyan, CB
NORTHERN COLLEGE, Northern Federation for Training
in Ministry, Luther King House, Brighton Grove,
Rusholme, Manchester M14 5JP. (34). *Principal*, Revd Dr
D. R. Peel
WESTMINSTER COLLEGE, Madingley Road, Cambridge
CB3 0AA. (35). *Principal*, Revd M. H. Cressey

JEWISH
JEWS' COLLEGE, Albert Road, London NW4 2SJ. (20).
Principal, Rabbi Dr I. Jacobs
LEO BAECK COLLEGE, Sternberg Centre for Judaism, 80
East End Road, London N3 2SY. (22). *Principal*, Rabbi
Dr J. Magonet

TOWN AND COUNTRY PLANNING

Degree and diploma courses in town planning are accredited
by the Royal Town Planning Institute.
THE ROYAL TOWN PLANNING INSTITUTE, 26 Portland
Place, London W1N 4BE. Tel: 071-636 9107. *Secretary-
General*, D. Fryer

TRANSPORT

Qualifying examinations in transport management and
logistics leading to chartered professional status are con-
ducted by the Chartered Institute of Transport.
THE CHARTERED INSTITUTE OF TRANSPORT, 80
Portland Place, London W1N 4DP. Tel: 071-636 9952.
Director, A. M. J. Pomeroy

Independent Schools

The following pages list those independent schools whose Head is a member of the Headmasters' Conference, the Society of Headmasters and Headmistresses of Independent Schools or the Girls' Schools Association

THE HEADMASTERS' CONFERENCE

Chairman (1994), R. J. Wilson (Trinity School, Surrey)
Secretary, V. S. Anthony, 130 Regent Road, Leicester
LEI 7PG. Tel: 0533-854810
Membership Secretary, R. N. P. Griffiths, 1 Russell House, Bepton Road, Midhurst, W. Sussex GU29 9NB. Tel: 0730-815635. The annual meeting is, as a rule, held at the end of September

* Woodard Corporation School, 1 The Sanctuary, London SWIP 3JT. Tel: 071-222 5381
† Girls in VI form
‡ Co-educational
° 1992 figures

Name of School	Foun- ded	No. of pupils	Annual fees £ Boarding	Day	Head (with date of appointment)
ENGLAND AND WALES			Boarding	Day	
Abbotsholme School, Staffs.	1889	240‡	10,251	6,906	D. J. Farrant (1984)
Abingdon School, Oxon.	1256	750	9,036	4,794	M. St J. Parker (1975)
Ackworth School, W. Yorks.	1779	430‡	8,673	5,022	D. S. Harris (1989)
Aldenham School, Herts.	1597	350†	10,600	7,200	M. Higginbottom (1983)
Alleyn's School, London SE22	1619	903‡	—	5,340	Dr C. H. R. Niven (1992)
Allhallows School, Dorset	1515	240‡	10,686	5,343	P. S. Larkman, LVO (1983)
Ampleforth College (RC), Yorks.	1802	632	10,860	5,700	Revd G. F. L. Chamberlain, OSB (1993)
*Ardingly College, W. Sussex	1858	447‡	10,710	8,505	J. W. Flecker (1980)
Arnold School, Blackpool	1896	815‡	6,837	3,385	W. T. Gillen (1993)
Ashville College, Harrogate	1877	368‡	8,172	4,386	M. H. Crosby (1987)
Bablake School, Coventry	1560	804†	—	3,312	Dr S. Nuttall (1991)
Bancroft's School, Essex	1727	716‡	—	5,094	Dr P. C. D. Southern (1985)
Barnard Castle School, Co. Durham	1883	500†	7,614	4,506	F. S. McNamara (1980)
Batley Grammar School, W. Yorks.	1612	595	—	3,228	C. S. Parker (1986)
Bedales School, Hants.	1893	374‡	11,901	8,529	R. E. I. Newton (1992)
Bedford School	1552	713	10,080	6,300	Dr I. P. Evans (1990)
Bedford Modern School	1566	980	7,632	3,987	P. J. Squire (1977)
Berkhamsted School, Herts.	1541	651	10,083	6,198	Revd K. H. Wilkinson (1989)
Birkenhead School, Merseyside	1860	750	—	3,234	S. J. Haggett (1988)
Bishop's Stortford College, Herts.	1868	°360†	°9,520	°6,880	S. G. G. Benson (1984)
*Bloxham School, Oxon.	1860	340†	10,665	7,995	D. K. Exham (1991)
Blundell's School, Devon	1604	380†	10,500	6,250	J. Leigh (1992)
Bolton School	1524	870	—	4,191	A. W. Wright (1983)
Bootham School, York	1823	340‡	9,500	6,300	I. M. Small (1988)
Bradfield College, Berks.	1850	580‡	11,475	8,606	P. B. Smith (1985)
Bradford Grammar School	1662	1,000†	—	3,666	D. A. G. Smith (1974)
Brentwood School, Essex	1557	1,038†	9,156	5,232	J. A. B. Kelsall (1993)
Brighton College, E. Sussex	1845	480‡	10,800	7,101	J. D. Leach (1987)
Bristol Cathedral School	1542	483†	—	3,789	K. J. Riley (1994)
Bristol Grammar School	1532	1,220‡	—	3,591	C. E. Martin (1986)
Bromsgrove School, Worcs.	1553	610‡	9,285	5,805	T. M. Taylor (1986)
Bryanston School, Dorset	1928	650‡	12,255	8,169	T. D. Wheare (1983)
Bury Grammar School, Lancs.	1634	690	—	3,432	K. Richards (1990)
Canford School, Dorset	1923	494†	11,440	8,580	J. D. Lever (1992)
Caterham School, Surrey	1811	450†	9,513	5,181	S. R. Smith (1974)
Charterhouse, Surrey	1611	700†	11,910	9,825	P. Hobson (1993)
Cheadle Hulme School, Cheshire	1855	910‡	—	3,780	D. J. Wilkinson (1990)
Cheltenham College, Glos.	1841	559†	11,370	8,595	P. D. V. Wilkes (1990)
Chetham's School of Music, Manchester	1653	274‡	14,844	11,496	Revd P. F. Hullah (1992)
Chigwell School, Essex	1629	400†	8,844	5,817	A. R. M. Little (1989)
Christ College, Brecon	1541	366†	8,697	6,591	S. W. Hockey (1982)
Christ's Hospital, W. Sussex	1553	835‡	varies	—	R. C. Poulton (1987)

Name of School	Founded	No. of pupils	Annual fees £ Boarding	Day	Head (with date of appointment)
Churcher's College, Hants.	1722	561‡	8,700	4,650	G. W. Buttle (1988)
City of London, London EC4	1442	850	—	5,391	B. G. Bass (1990)
City of London Freemen's School, Surrey	1854	365‡	8,370	5,373	D. C. Haywood (1987)
Clifton College, Bristol	1862	660‡	11,355	7,962	H. Monro (1990)
Colfe's School, London SE12	1652	710†	—	4,455	Dr D. Richardson (1990)
Colston's Collegiate School, Bristol	1710	350†	8,130	4,905	S. B. Howarth (1988)
Cranleigh School, Surrey	1863	545†	11,625	8,715	A. Hart (1984)
Culford School, Suffolk	1881	357‡	9,156	5,952	J. Richardson (1992)
Dame Allan's School, Newcastle upon Tyne	1705	460†	—	3,276	T. A. Willcocks (*Principal*) (1988)
Dauntsey's School, Wiltshire	1543	615‡	9,717	5,985	C. R. Evans (1985)
Dean Close School, Cheltenham	1884	439‡	11,070	7,740	C. J. Bacon (1979)
*Denstone College, Staffs.	1873	290‡	9,972	7,110	H. C. K. Carson (1990)
Douai School (*RC*), Berks.	1903	238‡	9,735	6,270	Revd E. Power (1993)
Dover College, Kent	1871	300‡	10,500	5,970	M. P. G. Wright (1991)
Downside School (*RC*), Somerset	1607	378	10,320	7,118	Dom. A. Bellenger (1991)
Dulwich College, London SE21	1619	1,250	11,670	5,835	A. C. F. Verity (*Master*) (1986)
Durham School	1414	362†	10,815	7,209	M. A. Lang (1982)
Eastbourne College, E. Sussex	1867	512†	10,908	8,067	C. M. P. Bush (1993)
*Ellesmere College, Shropshire	1884	350†	9,600	6,600	D. R. du Croz (1988)
Eltham College, London SE9	1842	580†	10,558	4,998	D. M. Green (1990)
Emanuel School, London SW11	1594	760	—	4,215	P. F. Thomson (1984)
Epsom College, Surrey	1855	664†	10,620	7,890	A. H. Beadles (1993)
Eton College, Berks.	1440	1,270	11,934	—	Dr W. E. K. Anderson (1980)
Exeter School	1633	735†	7,116	3,756	N. W. Gamble (1992)
Felsted School, Essex	1564	350†	11,418	9,018	S. C. Roberts (1993)
Forest School, London E17	1834	810‡	7,923	5,046	A. Boggis (*Warden*) (1992)
Framlingham College, Suffolk	1864	440‡	9,000	5,775	J. F. X. Miller (1989)
Frensham Heights, Surrey	1925	295‡	10,920	6,990	P. de Voile (1993)
Giggleswick School, N. Yorks.	1512	304‡	10,776	7,086	A. P. Millard (1993)
Gresham's School, Norfolk	1555	456‡	10,800	7,550	J. H. Arkell (1991)
Haberdashers' Aske's School, Herts.	1690	1,118	—	5,028	K. Dawson (1987)
Haileybury, Herts.	1862	626†	11,775	8,535	D. J. Jewell (1987)
Hampton School, Middx.	1557	909	—	4,254	G. G. Able (1988)
Harrow School, Middx.	1571	780	12,360	—	N. R. Bomford (1991)
Hereford Cathedral School	1384	586‡	7,365	4,185	Dr H. C. Tomlinson (1988)
Highgate School, London N6	1565	575	10,416	6,525	R. P. Kennedy (1989)
Hulme Grammar School, Oldham	1611	740	—	3,315	G. F. Dunkin (1987)
*Hurstpierpoint College, W. Sussex	1849	350	10,605	8,475	S. A. Watson (1986)
Hymers College, Hull	1889	940	—	3,180	J. C. Morris (1990)
Ipswich School, Suffolk	1390	620†	7,839	4,581	I. G. Galbraith (1993)
John Lyon School, Middx.	1876	520	—	4,950	Revd T. J. Wright (1986)
Kelly College, Devon	1877	305‡	10,485	6,750	C. H. Hirst (1985)
Kent College, Canterbury	1885	540‡	9,183	5,145	R. J. Wicks (1980)
Kimbolton School, Cambs.	1600	550‡	8,175	4,740	R. V. Peel (1987)
King Edward VI School, Southampton	1553	956†	—	4,305	T. R. Cookson (1990)
King Edward VII School, Lytham	1908	530	—	3,345	P. J. Wilde (1993)
King Edward's School, Bath	1552	680†	—	3,744	P. J. Winter (1993)
King Edward's School, Birmingham	1552	870	—	4,074	H. R. Wright (*Chief Master*) (1991)
King Edward's School, Witley, Surrey	1553	515‡	8,295	5,085	R. J. Fox (1988)
King Henry VIII School, Coventry	1545	830‡	—	3,312	G. R. James (1991)
*King's College, Taunton	1880	465‡	10,500	7,290	R. S. Funnell (1988)
King's College School, London SW19	1829	680	—	5,760	R. M. Reeve (1980)
King's School, Bruton, Somerset	1519	308†	10,245	7,260	R. I. Smyth (1993)
King's School, Canterbury	600	700‡	11,820	8,160	Revd Canon A. C. J. Phillips (1986)
King's School, Chester	1541	500	—	4,048	A. R. D. Wickson (1981)
King's School, Ely, Cambs.	970	379‡	10,413	6,975	R. H. Youdale (1992)
King's School, Macclesfield	1502	1,000†	—	3,875	A. G. Silcock (1987)
King's School, Rochester, Kent	604	311†	10,167	5,955	Dr I. R. Walker (1986)
King's School, Tynemouth	1860	900‡	—	3,309	Dr D. Younger (1993)
King's School, Worcester	1541	770‡	8,439	4,917	Dr J. M. Moore (1983)
Kingston Grammar School, Surrey	1561	590‡	—	4,890	C. D. Baxter (1991)

Name of School	Foun-ded	No. of pupils	Annual fees £		Head (with date of appointment)
			Boarding	Day	
Kingswood School, Bath	1748	446‡	10,164	6,609	G. M. Best (1987)
*Lancing College, W. Sussex	1848	532†	11,175	8,400	C. J. Saunders (1993)
Latymer Upper School, London w6	1642	970	—	5,055	C. Diggory (1991)
Leeds Grammar School	1552	1,130	—	3,909	B. W. Collins (1986)
Leighton Park School, Reading	1890	350†	10,350	7,767	J. A. Chapman (1986)
The Leys School, Cambridge	1875	400†	11,070	8,190	Revd J. C. A. Barrett (1990)
Liverpool College	1840	650‡	—	3,702	B. R. Martin (1992)
Llandovery College, Dyfed	1848	245‡	8,463	5,523	Dr C. E. Evans (*Warden*) (1988)
Lord Wandsworth College, Hants.	1912	435†	8,712	6,804	G. de W. Waller (1993)
Loughborough Grammar School	1495	920	7,587	4,068	D. N. Ireland (1984)
Magdalen College School, Oxford	1480	500	—	4,380	P. M. Tinniswood (*Master*) (1991)
Malvern College, Worcs.	1865	669‡	11,400	8,295	R. de C. Chapman (1983)
Manchester Grammar School	1515	1,450	—	3,792	J. G. Parker (*High Master*) (1985)
Marlborough College, Wilts.	1843	816‡	11,658	8,219	E. J. H. Gould (1993)
Merchant Taylors' School, Liverpool	1620	728	—	3,456	S. J. R. Dawkins (1986)
Merchant Taylors' School, Middx.	1561	725	10,050	6,130	J. R. Gabitass (1991)
Mill Hill School, London nw7	1807	570†	10,584	7,014	E. A. M. MacAlpine (1992)
Monkton Combe School, Bath	1868	325‡	10,860	7,695	M. J. Cuthbertson (1990)
Monmouth School, Gwent	1614	546	7,596	4,560	R. D. Lane (1982)
Mount St Mary's College (*RC*), Sheffield	1842	320‡	8,343	5,637	P. Fisher (1991)
Newcastle under Lyme School	1874	1,185‡	—	3,276	Dr R. M. Reynolds (*Principal*) (1990)
Norwich School	1250	593	7,680	4,080	C. D. Brown (1984)
Nottingham High School	1513	840	—	4,119	D. T. Witcombe, ph.d. (1970)
Oakham School, Rutland	1584	800‡	10,530	5,820	G. Smallbone (1985)
The Oratory School (*RC*), Berks.	1859	365	10,926	7,635	S. W. Barrow (1992)
Oundle School, Northants	1556	820‡	12,021	—	D. B. McMurray (1984)
Pangbourne College, Berks.	1917	360†	10,440	7,320	A. B. E. Hudson (1988)
Perse School, Cambridge	1615	486†	—	4,044	Dr G. M. Stephen (1986)
Plymouth College	1877	621	7,935	4,140	A. J. Morsley (1992)
Pocklington School, York	1514	600‡	7,995	4,368	J. N. D. Gray (1992)
Portsmouth Grammar School	1732	775‡	—	4,035	A. C. V. Evans (1983)
Prior Park College (*RC*), Bath	1830	449‡	9,423	5,211	J. W. R. Goulding (1989)
Queen Elizabeth GS, Wakefield	1591	744†	—	3,792	R. P. Mardling (1985)
Queen Elizabeth's GS, Blackburn	1567	1,100†	—	3,788	P. F. Johnston (1978)
Queen Elizabeth's Hospital, Bristol	1590	520	6,360	3,624	Dr R. Gliddon (1985)
Queen's College, Taunton	1843	650‡	8,475	5,535	C. T. Bradnock (1991)
Radley College, Oxon.	1847	607	11,430	—	R. M. Morgan (*Warden*) (1991)
Ratcliffe College (*RC*), Leicester	1844	462‡	8,409	5,607	Revd K. A. Tomlinson (1993)
Reading Blue Coat School	1646	560†	8,535	4,680	Revd A. Sanders (1974)
Reed's School, Surrey	1813	350†	9,468	7,155	D. E. Prince (1983)
Reigate Grammar School, Surrey	1675	815†	—	4,425	J. G. Hamlin (1982)
Rendcomb College, Glos.	1920	230‡	9,639	7,632	J. Tolputt (1987)
Repton School, Derby	1557	600‡	10,770	8,070	G. E. Jones (1987)
RNIB New College, Worcester	1987	126‡	20,400	13,600	Revd B. R. Manthorp (1980)
Rossall School, Lancs.	1844	460‡	10,500	5,250	R. D. W. Rhodes (1987)
Royal Grammar School, Guildford	1552	820	—	5,274	T. M. S. Young (1992)
Royal Grammar School, Newcastle upon Tyne	1545	973	—	3,312	A. S. Cox (1972)
Royal Grammar School, Worcester	1291	780	—	4,104	W. A. Jones (1993)
Rugby School, Warwicks.	1567	655‡	11,865	8,898	M. B. Mavor, cvo (1990)
Rydal School, Clwyd	1885	333‡	9,039	6,819	N. W. Thorne (1991)
Ryde School, Isle of Wight	1921	424‡	7,716	3,864	M. D. Featherstone (1990)
St Albans School, Herts.	1570	640†	—	4,920	A. R. Grant (1993)
St Ambrose College, Cheshire	1946	680	—	2,928	G. E. Hester (1991)
St Anselm's College (*RC*), Birkenhead	1933	630	—	2,967	C. Cleugh (1993)
St Bede's College (*RC*), Manchester	1876	944‡	—	3,543	J. Byrne (1983)
St Bees School, Cumbria	1583	285‡	9,609	6,612	P. A. Chamberlain (1988)
St Benedict's School (*RC*), London w5	1902	592†	—	4,425	Dr A. J. Dachs (1987)
St Dunstan's College, London se6	1888	570	—	4,836	J. D. Moore (1993)
St Edmund's College (*RC*), Herts.	1568	475‡	8,586	5,493	D. J. J. McEwen (1984)

Name of School	Foun-ded	No. of pupils	Annual fees £		Head (with date of appointment)
			Boarding	Day	
St Edmund's School, Canterbury	1749	315‡	11,820	7,230	J. V. Tyson (1978)
St Edward's College (RC), Liverpool	1853	660‡	—	°3,150	J. E. Waszek (1992)
St Edward's School, Oxford	1863	571†	11,430	8,595	D. Christie (Warden) (1988)
St George's College (RC), Surrey	1869	475†	—	6,075	P. A. Johnson, D.Phil. (1992)
St John's School, Surrey	1851	400†	9,300	6,600	C. H. Tongue (1993)
St Lawrence College, Kent	1879	360‡	10,200	6,870	J. H. Binfield (1983)
St Mary's College (RC), Merseyside	1919	564‡	—	3,402	W. Hammond (1991)
St Paul's School, London SW13	1509	750	11,685	7,485	R. S. Baldock (High Master) (1992)
St Peter's School, York	627	470‡	9,576	5,700	R. N. Pittman (1985)
Sedbergh School, Cumbria	1525	460	10,770	7,537	Dr R. G. Baxter (1982)
Sevenoaks School, Kent	1418	940‡	10,701	6,507	R. P. Barker (1981)
Sherborne School, Dorset	1550	650	11,700	8,940	P. H. Lapping (1988)
Shrewsbury School	1552	680	11,388	8,034	F. E. Maidment (1988)
Silcoates School, W. Yorks.	1820	492‡	8,772	5,022	A. P. Spillane (1991)
Solihull School, Warwicks	1560	820†	—	3,931	A. Lee (1983)
Stamford School, Lincs.	1532	572	7,446	3,723	G. J. Timm (1978)
Stockport Grammar School	1487	1,005‡	—	3,636	D. R. J. Bird (1985)
Stonyhurst College (RC), Lancs.	1593	397†	10,608	6,342	Dr R. G. G. Mercer (1985)
Stowe School, Bucks.	1923	570†	12,000	8,400	J. G. L. Nichols (1989)
Sutton Valence School, Kent	1576	340‡	10,341	6,621	M. R. Haywood (1980)
Taunton School	1847	515‡	10,650	6,810	B. B. Sutton (1987)
Tettenhall College, Staffs.	1863	300‡	8,670	5,340	W. J. Dale (1968)
Tonbridge School, Kent	1553	640	11,820	8,340	J. M. Hammond (1990)
Trent College, Derbys.	1868	756‡	9,630	5,871	J. S. Lee (1988)
Trinity School, Surrey	1596	840	—	4,722	R. J. Wilson (1972)
Truro School	1879	890‡	7,950	4,269	G. A. G. Dodd (1993)
University College School, London NW3	1830	520	—	6,270	G. D. Slaughter (1983)
Uppingham School, Leics.	1584	620†	11,850	7,110	S. C. Winkley (1991)
Warwick School	914	800	8,985	4,185	P. J. Cheshire (1988)
Wellingborough School, Northants.	1595	413‡	8,130	4,890	F. R. Ullmann (1993)
Wellington College, Berks.	1856	807†	11,505	8,400	C. J. Driver (1989)
Wells Cathedral School, Somerset	1180	620‡	8,196	4,815	J. S. Baxter (1986)
West Buckland School, Devon	1858	459‡	8,142	4,416	M. Downward (1979)
Westminster School, London SW1	1560	664†	11,850	8,850	D. M. Summersale (1986)
Whitgift School, Surrey	1596	960	—	5,034	C. A. Barnett, D.Phil. (1991)
William Hulme's GS, Manchester	1887	790‡	—	3,816	P. A. Briggs (1987)
Winchester College, Hants.	1382	664	12,270	9,204	J. P. Sabben-Clare (1985)
Wisbech Grammar School, Cambs.	1379	630‡	—	4,125	R. S. Repper (1988)
Wolverhampton Grammar School	1512	655‡	—	4,269	B. St J. Trafford (1990)
Woodbridge School, Suffolk	1662	520‡	8,208	4,998	S. H. Cole (1994)
Woodhouse Grove School, Bradford	1812	560‡	7,995	4,785	D. W. Welsh (1991)
*Worksop College, Notts.	1895	350‡	9,876	6,816	R. D. V. Knight (1990)
Worth School (RC), W. Sussex	1959	311	10,880	8,100	Fr C. Jamison (1994)
Wrekin College, Shropshire	1880	320‡	10,470	7,185	P. Johnson (1991)
Wycliffe College, Glos.	1882	301‡	11,085	7,740	D. C. M. Prichard (1994)

SCOTLAND

Name of School	Foun-ded	No. of pupils	Annual fees £		Head (with date of appointment)
Daniel Stewart's and Melville College, Edinburgh	1832	785	7,500	3,843	P. J. F. Tobin (Principal) (1989)
Dollar Academy, Clackmannanshire	1818	750‡	7,869	3,549	L. Harrison (Rector) (1984)
Dundee High School	1239	1,100‡	—	3,549	R. Nimmo, OBE (Rector) (1977)
The Edinburgh Academy	1824	851†	10,194	4,821	A. J. D. Rees (Rector) (1992)
Fettes College, Edinburgh	1870	343‡	11,385	7,650	M. T. Thyne (1988)
George Heriot's School, Edinburgh	1659	978‡	—	3,489	K. P. Pearson (1983)
George Watson's College, Edinburgh	1741	1,256‡	7,578	3,798	F. E. Gerstenberg (Principal) (1985)
Glasgow Academy	1845	605‡	—	3,900	C. W. Turner (Rector) (1983)
Glenalmond College, Perthshire	1841	274†	11,100	7,395	I. G. Templeton (Warden) (1992)
Gordonstoun School, Moray	1934	465‡	11,160	7,200	M. C. S.-R. Pyper (1990)
Hutchesons' Grammar School, Glasgow	1641	1,117‡	—	3,303	D. R. Ward (Rector) (1987)
Kelvinside Academy, Glasgow	1878	630	—	4,050	J. H. Duff (Rector) (1980)

Name of School	Foun-ded	No. of pupils	Annual fees £		Head (with date of appointment)
			Boarding	Day	
Loretto School, E. Lothian	1827	312†	10,575	7,050	Revd N. W. Drummond (1984)
Merchiston Castle School, Edinburgh	1833	380	10,590	6,870	D. M. Spawforth (1981)
Morrison's Academy, Crieff	1860	690‡	9,192	3,321	H. A. Ashmall (*Rector*) (1979)
Robert Gordon's College, Aberdeen	1729	928‡	7,700	3,500	G. A. Allan (1978)
Strathallan School, Perthshire	1913	400‡	9,990	6,660	A. McPhail (1993)
NORTHERN IRELAND					
Bangor Grammar School, Co. Down	1856	900	—	354	T. W. Patton (1979)
Belfast Royal Academy	1785	1,320‡	—	185	W. M. Sillery (1980)
Campbell College, Belfast	1894	650	4,900	900	Dr R. J. I. Pollock (1987)
Coleraine Academical Institution	1856	850	5,120	2,285	R. S. Forsythe (1984)
Methodist College, Belfast	1868	1,727‡	5,016	2,316	T. W. Mulryne (1988)
Portora Royal School, Enniskillen	1618	420	2,901	nil	R. L. Bennett (1983)
Royal Belfast Academical Institution	1810	990	—	300	R. M. Ridley (1990)
CHANNEL ISLANDS AND ISLE OF MAN					
Elizabeth College, Guernsey	1563	570†	5,760	2,280	J. H. F. Doulton (1988)
King William's College, Isle of Man	1668	298‡	9,825	7,020	S. A. Westley (1989)
EUROPE					
Aiglon College, Switzerland	1949	273‡	Fr.40,485	Fr.27,825	P. Parsons (1976)
British School in the Netherlands	1935	540‡	—	Gld.18,350	M. J. Cooper (*Principal*) (1990)
British School of Brussels	1970	1,020‡	—	Fr.561,000	Ms J. M. Bray (1993)
British School of Paris, France	1954	°280‡	—	Fr.68,825	A. Slesser (1992)
The English School, Nicosia, Cyprus	1900	830‡	—	C£1,500	A. M. Hudspeth (1988)
The International School of Geneva	1924	2,750‡	Fr.40,000	Fr.17,000	G. Walker, OBE (*Director-General*) (1991)
The International School of Paris	1964	210‡	—	Fr.75,000	N. M. Prentki (1988)
St Columba's College, Dublin	1843	291‡	IR£5,310	IR£2,970	T. E. Macey (*Warden*) (1988)
St George's English School, Rome	1958	450‡	—	L17.3m	Dr R. B. Guthrie (*acting*)
Sir James Henderson School, Milan	1969	°170†	—	°L12.4m	C. T. G. Leech (1986)

OTHER OVERSEAS MEMBERS

AFRICA

FALCON COLLEGE, PO Esigodini, Zimbabwe. *Head*, P. N. Todd

HILTON COLLEGE, Natal 3245, SA. *Head*, P. Marsh

MICHAELHOUSE, Balgowan, Natal 3275, SA. *Head*, J. H. Pluke

PETERHOUSE, Marondera, Zimbabwe. *Head*, Revd Dr A. J. Megahey

ST GEORGE'S COLLEGE, Harare, Zimbabwe. *Head*, M. F. Hackett

DIOCESAN COLLEGE, Rondebosch, SA. *Head*, J. B. Gardener

ST JOHN'S COLLEGE, Johannesburg, SA. *Head*, W. Macfarlane

ST STITHIAN'S COLLEGE, Randburg, SA. *Head*, D. B. Wylde

AUSTRALIA

ANGLICAN CHURCH GRAMMAR SCHOOL, Brisbane. *Head*, C. V. Ellis

BRIGHTON GRAMMAR SCHOOL, Brighton, Victoria. *Head*, R. L. Rofe

CAMBERWELL GRAMMAR SCHOOL, Balwyn, Victoria 3101. *Head*, C. F. Black

CANBERRA GS, Red Hill, ACT 2603. *Head*, T. C. Murray

CAULFIELD GRAMMAR SCHOOL, East St Kilda, Victoria. *Head*, Revd A. S. Holmes

CHRIST CHURCH GRAMMAR SCHOOL, Claremont 6010, W. Australia. *Head*, J. J. S. Madin

CHURCH OF ENGLAND GRAMMAR SCHOOL, Melbourne. *Head*, A. J. de V. Hill

CHURCH OF ENGLAND GRAMMAR SCHOOL, Sydney, NSW. *Head*, R. A. I. Grant

CRANBROOK SCHOOL, Sydney, NSW. *Head*, Dr B. N. Carter

GEELONG CHURCH OF ENGLAND GRAMMAR SCHOOL, Corio. *Head*, J. E. Lewis

THE GEELONG COLLEGE, Geelong, Victoria. *Head*, A. P. Sheahan

GUILDFORD GRAMMAR SCHOOL, W. Australia. *Head*, J. M. Moody

HAILEYBURY COLLEGE, Keysborough, Victoria 3175. *Head*, A. H. M. Aikman

HALE SCHOOL, Wembley Downs, W. Australia. *Head*, K. G. Tregonning

KING'S SCHOOL, Parramatta, NSW. *Head*, J. A. Wickham

KINROSS WOLAROI SCHOOL, NSW. *Head*, A. E. S. Anderson

KNOX GS, Wahroonga 2076, NSW. *Head*, Dr I. Paterson

NEWINGTON COLLEGE, Stanmore, NSW. *Head*, A. J. Rae

THE PENINSULA SCHOOL, Mt Eliza, Victoria. *Head*, H. A. Macdonald

ST PETER'S COLLEGE, St Peter's, S. Australia. *Head,*
Dr A. J. Shinkfield
SCOTCH COLLEGE, Adelaide, S. Australia. *Head,*
W. M. Miles
SCOTCH COLLEGE, Hawthorn, Melbourne, Victoria. *Head,*
Dr F. G. Donaldson
SCOTCH COLLEGE, Swanbourne, W. Australia. *Head,*
W. R. Dickinson
SCOTS COLLEGE, Sydney, NSW. *Head,* G. A. W. Renney
THE SOUTHPORT SCHOOL, Southport, Queensland. *Head,*
B. A. Cook
SYDNEY GRAMMAR SCHOOL, NSW. *Head,*
Dr R. D. Townsend
WESLEY COLLEGE, Melbourne. *Head,* D. H. Prest

CANADA
BRENTWOOD COLLEGE SCHOOL, Vancouver, BC. *Head,*
W. T. Ross
GLENLYON-NORFOLK SCHOOL, Victoria, BC. *Head,*
D. Brooks
HILLFIELD-STRATHALLAN COLLEGE, Hamilton, Ontario.
Head, M. B. Wansbrough
PICKERING COLLEGE, Newmarket, Ontario. *Head,*
S. H. Clark
ST ANDREW'S COLLEGE, Aurora, Ontario. *Head,*
R. P. Bedard
TORONTO FRENCH SCHOOL. *Head,* A. S. Troubetzkoy
TRINITY COLLEGE SCHOOL, Port Hope, Ontario. *Head,*
R. C. N.Wright
UPPER CANADA COLLEGE, Toronto. *Head,* J. D. Blakey

HONG KONG
ISLAND SCHOOL, Borrett Road. *Head,* D. J. James
KING GEORGE V SCHOOL, Kowloon. *Head,*
M. J. Behennah

INDIA
BIRLA PUBLIC SCHOOL, Pilani 333 031, Rajasthan. *Head,*
B. K. Sood
LAWRENCE SCHOOL, Lovedale, Nilgiris. *Head,*
B. S. Bhatnagar
LAWRENCE SCHOOL, Sanawar. *Head,* Sumer Singh
THE SCINDIA SCHOOL, GWALIOR. *Head,* Dr S. D. Singh

NEW ZEALAND
CHRIST'S COLLEGE, Christchurch, Canterbury. *Head,*
Dr M. J. Rosser
KING'S COLLEGE, Auckland. *Head,* J. S. Taylor
ST ANDREW'S COLLEGE, Christchurch, Canterbury. *Head,*
Dr A. J. Rentoul
RATHKEALE COLLEGE, Masterton. *Head,* B. R. Levick
THE COLLEGIATE SCHOOL, Wanganui. *Head,*
T. S. McKinlay
WAITAKI BOYS' HIGH SCHOOL, Oamaru. *Head,*
B. R. Gollop

SOUTH AMERICA
ACADEMIA BRITANICA CUSCATLECA, El Salvador. *Head,*
A. J. McGuiggan
MARKHAM COLLEGE, Lima, Peru. *Head,* W. J. Baker
ST ANDREW'S SCOTS SCHOOL, Argentina. *Head,* K. Prior
ST GEORGE'S COLLEGE, Quilmes, Argentina. *Head,*
N. P. O. Green
ST PAULS' SCHOOL, São Paulo, Brazil. *Head,*
M. T. M. C. McCann
THE BRITISH SCHOOLS, Montevideo, Uruguay. *Head,*
J. H. Sidwell

ADDITIONAL MEMBERS

The headteachers of some maintained schools are by
invitation Additional Members of the HMC. They include
the following:

DURHAM JOHNSTONE SCHOOL, Durham. *Head,*
J. Dunford
EGG BUCKLAND COMMUNITY COLLEGE, Plymouth.
Head, H. Green
HABERDASHERS' ASKE'S HATCHAM BOYS' SCHOOL,
Pepys Road, London SE14 5SF. *Head,* G. J. Walker
HAYWARDS HEATH SIXTH FORM COLLEGE, W. Sussex.
Head, B. W. Derbyshire
THE JUDD SCHOOL, Tonbridge, Kent. *Head,*
K. A. Starling
KING EDWARD VI CAMP HILL SCHOOL FOR BOYS,
Birmingham. *Head,* R. Dancey
LISKEARD SCHOOL, Cornwall. *Head,* A. D. Wood
THE LONDON ORATORY SCHOOL, London SW6. *Head,*
J. C. McIntosh
PRESCOT SCHOOL, Merseyside. *Head,* P. A. Barlow
PRINCE HENRY'S GRAMMAR SCHOOL, Otley, W Yorks.
Head, M. Franklin
PRINCE WILLIAM SCHOOL, Oundle, Cambs. *Head,*
C. J. Lowe
THE ROYAL GRAMMAR SCHOOL, Lancaster. *Head,*
P. J. Mawby
ST BARTHOLOMEW'S SCHOOL, Newbury, Bucks. *Head,*
R. P. H. Mermagen
ST JOHN'S SCHOOL, Marlborough, Wilts. *Head,* J. Price
STOWMARKET HIGH SCHOOL, Suffolk. *Head,*
Dr R. J. Montgomery
WESTMINSTER CITY SCHOOL, London SW1. *Head,*
M. Billingham

SOCIETY OF HEADMASTERS AND HEADMISTRESSES OF INDEPENDENT SCHOOLS

The Society was founded in 1961 and, in general, represents smaller boarding schools.

Hon. Secretary, A. E. R. Dodds, Mantons, Park Road, Winchester, Hants. SO23 7BE. Tel: 0962-862579

Headmasters of the following schools are members of both HMC and SHMIS; details of these schools appear in the HMC list: Abbotsholme School, Ackworth School, Bedales School, Churcher's College, City of London Freemen's School, Colston's Collegiate School, King's School, Tyne-

mouth, Lord Wandsworth College, Pangbourne College, Reading Blue Coat School, Reed's School, Rendcomb College, Ryde School, St George's College, Silcoates School, Tettenhall College, West Buckland School, Wisbech Grammar School, Woodbridge School

* Woodard Corporation School
† Girls in VI form
‡ Co-educational

Name of School	Founded	No. of pupils	Annual fees £		Head (with date of appointment)
			Boarding	Day	
Austin Friars School (*RC*), Carlisle	1951	302‡	6,915	4,132	Revd T. Lyons, OSA (1981)
Bearwood College, Berks.	1827	265	9,300	5,175	Dr R. J. Belcher (1993)
Bedstone College, Shropshire	1948	165‡	9,000	5,610	M. S. Symonds (1990)
Belmont Abbey (*RC*), Hereford	1926	180	8,115	4,680	Revd D. C. Jenkins, OSB (1988)
Bembridge School, Isle of Wight	1919	180‡	8,490	4,230	J. High (1986)
Bentham School, N. Yorks	1726	260‡	7,794	3,891	N. K. D. Ward (1992)
Bethany School, Kent	1866	275‡	8,814	5,640	W. M. Harvey (1988)
Box Hill School, Surrey	1959	297‡	9,390	5,820	Dr R. A. S. Atwood (1987)
Carmel College (*Jewish*), Oxon.	1948	224‡	12,450	7,200	P. D. Skelker (1984)
Claremont Fan Court School, Surrey	1932	377‡	8,340	5,250	J. H. Scott (1987)
Clayesmore School, Dorset	1896	301‡	10,440	7,305	D. J. Beeby (1986)
Cokethorpe School, Oxon.	1957	200‡	10,950	7,200	D. G. Crawford (1989)
Duke of York's Royal Military School, Dover	1803	473	—	—	Col. G. H. Wilson (1992)
Embley Park School, Romsey, Hants.	1946	225†	8,885	5,490	D. F. Chapman (1987)
Ewell Castle School, Surrey	1926	320†	—	3,900	R. A. Fewtrell (1983)
Friends' School, Essex	1702	270‡	9,126	5,664	Miss S. H. Evans (1989)
Fulneck Boys' School, W. Yorks.	1753	317†	8,310	4,365	I. D. Cleland (1980)
*Grenville College, Devon	1954	250	9,030	4,428	M. C. V. Cane, PH.D. (1992)
Halliford School, Middx.	1956	320†	—	4,020	J. R. Crook (1984)
Hipperholme Grammar School, Halifax	1648	362‡	—	3,024	C. C. Robinson (1988)
Keil School, Dumbarton	1915	225‡	8,082	4,527	J. A. Cummings (1993)
Kingham Hill School, Oxon.	1886	195‡	8,181	4,908	M. Payne (*Warden*) (1990)
King's School, Gloucester	1541	350‡	8,100	4,800	P. Lacey (1993)
Kirkham Grammar School, Lancs.	1549	510‡	6,147	3,276	B. Stacey (1991)
Licensed Victuallers' School, Ascot, Berks.	1803	670‡	8,910	5,010	Mrs P. M. Cowley (1992)
Lord Mayor Treloar College, Hants.	1908	228‡	33,384	25,038	H. Heard (1990)
Milton Abbey School, Dorset	1954	250	10,620	7,080	R. H. Hardy (1987)
Oswestry School, Shropshire	1407	283‡	8,340	4,920	J. V. Light (1992)
Pierrepont School, Surrey	1947	170‡	9,465	5,699	N. Taylor (1993)
The Purcell School (music), Middx.	1962	150‡	13,446	7,950	K. J. Bain (1984)
Rannoch School, Perthshire	1959	270‡	9,585	5,430	M. Barratt (1982)
Rishworth School, W. Yorks.	1724	475‡	8,610	4,455	M. J. Elford (1992)
Rougemont School, Gwent	1919	236‡	—	4,227	G. R. Sims (1991)
Royal Hospital School, Ipswich	1712	602‡	7,200	—	M. A. B. Kirk (1983)
Royal Russell School, Surrey	1853	450‡	9,150	4,830	R. D. Balaam (1981)
Royal School, Dungannon, N. Ireland	1614	650‡	5,505	85	P. D. Hewitt (1984)
Royal Wolverhampton School	1850	320‡	8,310	4,755	P. Gorring (1985)
Ruthin School, Clwyd	1574	170‡	8,985	5,685	J. S. Rowlands (1993)
St Bede's School, E. Sussex	—	360‡	10,455	6,450	R. A. Perrin (1978)
St David's College, Gwynedd	1965	235	8,640	5,625	W. Seymour (1991)
Scarborough College, N. Yorks.	1898	418‡	8,775	4,758	D. S. Hempsall, PH.D. (1985)
Seaford College, W. Sussex	1884	300†	9,030	5,550	R. C. Hannaford (1990)
Shebbear College, Devon	1841	260‡	8,460	4,620	R. J. Buley (1983)
Shiplake College, Oxon.	1959	325	10,500	7,350	N. V. Bevan (1988)
Sidcot School, Avon	1808	300‡	8,925	5,355	C. J. Greenfield (1986)
Stafford Grammar School, Staffs.	1982	290‡	—	3,636	M. James (1992)
Stanbridge Earls School, Hants.	1952	180‡	10,785	8,100	H. Moxon (1984)
Warminster School, Wilts.	1707	323‡	8,310	4,905	T. D. Holgate (1990)
Yarm School, Cleveland	1978	430†	—	4,350	R. Neville Tate (1978)

GIRLS' SCHOOLS ASSOCIATION

THE GIRLS' SCHOOLS ASSOCIATION, 130 Regent Road, Leicester LEI 7PG. Tel: 0533-541619
President (1993–4), Miss J. Jefferson
Secretary, Miss A. C. Parkin

CSC Church Schools Company, IA Doughty Street, London WCIN 2PH. Tel: 071-404 3134
§ Girls Public Day School Trust, 26 Queen Anne's Gate, London SWIH 9AN. Tel: 071-222 9595
* Woodard Corporation School
† Boys in VI form
‡ Co-educational
° 1992 figures

Name of School	Foun-ded	No. of pupils	Annual fees £ Boarding	Day	Head (with date of appointment)
ENGLAND AND WALES			Boarding	Day	
Abbey School, Reading	1887	760	—	3,780	Miss B. C. L. Sheldon (1991)
Abbot's Hill, Herts.	1912	170	9,435	5,565	Mrs J. Kingsley (1979)
Adcote School, Shropshire	1907	70	8,385	4,725	Mrs S. B. Cecchet (1979)
Alice Ottley School, Worcester	1883	600	—	4,260	Miss C. Sibbit (1986)
Amberfield School, Ipswich	1952	179	—	3,630	Mrs L. A. Lewis (1992)
Ashford School, Kent	1910	428	8,178	4,716	Mrs P. Metham (1992)
Atherley School, Southampton (*CSC*)	1926	320	—	3,915	Mrs M. Williams (1988)
Badminton School, Bristol	1858	355	10,350	5,700	C. J. T. Gould (1981)
§Bath High School	1875	407	—	3,600	Miss M. A. Winfield (1985)
Battle Abbey School, E. Sussex	1912	120‡	8,565	5,295	D. J. A. Teall (1982)
Bedford High School	1882	800	8,101	4,282	Mrs D. M. Willis (1987)
Bedgebury School, Kent	1860	373	9,879	6,114	Mrs M. E. A. Kaye (1987)
Beechwood School (*RC*), Kent	1915	152	9,810	5,775	J. A. Fallon, ph.D. (1979)
§Belvedere School, Liverpool	1880	439	—	3,600	Mrs C. H. Evans (1992)
Benenden School, Kent	1923	418	11,730	—	Mrs G. D. duCharme (1985)
Berkhamsted School, Herts.	1888	454	8,472	4,986	Miss V. E. M. Shepherd (1980)
§Birkenhead High School	1901	732	—	3,600	Mrs K. R. Irving (1986)
§Blackheath High School, London SE3	1880	341	—	4,200	Miss R. K. Musgrave (1989)
Bolton School, Lancs.	1877	936	—	4,190	Mrs M. A. Spurr (1979)
Bradford Girls' Grammar School	1875	646	—	3,744	Mrs L. J. Warrington (1986)
§Brighton and Hove High School	1876	500	—	3,600	Miss R. A. Woodbridge (1989)
Brigidine School, Windsor	1948	260	—	3,993	Mrs M. B. Cairns (1987)
§Bromley High School, Kent	1883	552	—	4,200	Mrs E. J. Hancock (1989)
Bruton School, Somerset	1900	510	6,201	3,357	Mrs J. M. Wade (1987)
Burgess Hill School, W. Sussex	1906	365	8,280	4,980	Mrs R. F. Lewis (1992)
Bury Grammar School, Lancs.	1884	820	—	3,432	Miss J. M. Lawley (1987)
Casterton School, Cumbria	1823	335	8,388	5,256	A. F. Thomas (1990)
§Central Newcastle High School	1895	582	—	3,600	Mrs A. M. Chapman (1985)
Channing School, London N6	1885	310	—	5,235	Mrs I. R. Raphael (1984)
§Charters-Ancaster School, E. Sussex	1906	220	8,220	4,080	Mrs K. Lewis (1990)
Cheltenham Ladies' College, Glos.	1853	830	10,725	6,810	Miss E. Castle (*Principal*) (1987)
City of London School for Girls, London EC2	1894	538	—	4,626	Lady France (1986)
Clifton High School, Bristol	1877	463	7,710	4,035	Mrs J. D. Walters (1985)
Cobham Hall, Kent	1962	175	11,520	7,731	Mrs R. J. McCarthy (1989)
Colston's Girls' School, Bristol	1891	600	—	3,273	Mrs J. P. Franklin (1989)
Combe Bank School, Kent	1868	415	—	5,010	Miss N. Spurr (1993)
Commonweal Lodge School, Surrey	1916	150	—	4,125	Miss J. M. Brown (1982)
Cranford House School, Oxon.	1931	195	—	4,260	Mrs A. B. Gray (1992)
Croft House School, Dorset	1941	130	8,910	6,288	M. P. Hawkins (1993)
Croham Hurst School, Surrey	1899	330	—	3,900	Miss J. M. Shelmerdine (1986)
§Croydon High School, Surrey	1874	706	—	4,200	Mrs P. E. Davies (1990)
Dame Alice Harpur School, Bedford	1882	780	—	3,765	Mrs R. Randle (1990)
Dame Allan's Girls' School, Newcastle upon Tyne	1705	453†	—	3,267	T. A. Willcocks (*Principal*) (1988)

Name of School	Foun-ded	No. of pupils	Annual fees £		Head (with date of appointment)
			Boarding	Day	
Derby High School	1892	316	—	3,990	Dr G. H. Goddard (1983)
Downe House, Berks.	1907	520	11,385	8,250	Miss S. Cameron (1989)
Dunottar School, Surrey	1926	295	—	4,020	Miss J. Burnell (1985)
Durham High School	1884	271	—	3,630	M. L. Walters (1992)
Edgbaston Church of England College	1886	215	—	4,020	Mrs A. Varley-Tipton (1992)
Edgbaston High School	1876	521	—	3,960	Mrs S. J. Horsman (1992)
Edgehill College, Devon	1884	368	8,505	4,635	Mrs E. M. Burton (1987)
Elmslie Girls' School, Lancs.	1918	300	—	3,516	Miss E. M. Smithies (1978)
Eothen School, Surrey (CSC)	1892	160	—	4,407	Mrs A. Coutts (1992)
Farlington School, W. Sussex	1896	234	8,400	5,190	Mrs P. Mawer (1992)
Farnborough Hill, Hants.	1889	500	—	3,873	Sr E. McCormack (1988)
Farringtons, Kent	1911	280	8,379	4,587	Mrs B. J. Stock (1987)
Felixstowe College, Suffolk	1929	200	10,155	6,330	Mrs B. Patterson (1993)
Fernhill Manor School, Hants.	1890	144	7,500	4,770	Revd A. J. Folks (1985)
Francis Holland School, London NW1	1878	365	—	4,710	Mrs P. H. Parsonson (1988)
Francis Holland School, London SW1	1881	170	—	5,205	Mrs J. A. Anderson (1982)
Gateways School, Leeds	1941	200	—	3,240	Miss L. M. Brown (1984)
Godolphin School, Wilts.	1726	360	9,900	5,880	Mrs H. Fender (1990)
Godolphin and Latymer School, London W6	1905	703	—	5,190	Miss M. Rudland (1986)
Greenacre School, Surrey	1933	°376	—	°4,272	Mrs P. M. Wood (1990)
The Grove School, Hindhead, Surrey	1877	206	8,862	5,544	C. Brooks (1984)
Guildford High School (CSC)	1888	450	—	4,611	Mrs S. H. Singer (1991)
Haberdashers' Aske's School for Girls, Herts.	1873	847	—	3,015	Mrs P. Penney (1991)
Haberdashers' Monmouth School, Gwent	1891	543	7,380	4,065	Mrs D. L. Newman (1992)
Harrogate Ladies' College	1893	395	8,325	5,595	Mrs J. A. Smith (1993)
Headington School, Oxford	1915	545	8,181	4,335	Miss E. M. Tucker (1982)
Heathfield School, Ascot, Berks.	1900	210	11,415	—	Mrs J. Benammar (1992)
§Heathfield School, Pinner, Middx.	1900	344	—	4,200	Mrs J. Merritt (1988)
Hethersett Old Hall School, Norwich	1928	207	7,560	3,945	Mrs V. M. Redington (1983)
Highclare School, W. Midlands	1932	261†	—	3,380	Mrs C. A. Hanson (1973)
Hollygirt School, Nottingham	1877	185	—	3,330	Mrs M. R. Banks (1985)
Holy Child School, Birmingham	1933	200	—	4,065	Mrs J. Hill (acting)
Holy Trinity College, Bromley	1886	280	—	3,846	Sr B. Wetz (1986)
Holy Trinity School, Kidderminster	1903	180	—	4,050	Mrs S. M. Bell (1990)
Howell's School, Denbigh, Clwyd	1859	220	9,330	6,039	Mrs M. Steel (1991)
§Howell's School, Llandaff, Cardiff	1860	571	—	3,600	Mrs C. J. Fitz (1991)
Hull High School (CSC)	1890	163	5,795	3,648	Miss C. M. B. Radcliffe (1976)
Hulme Grammar School, Oldham	1895	520	—	3,315	Miss M. S. Smolenski (1992)
§Ipswich High School	1878	419	—	3,600	Miss V. MacCuish (1993)
James Allen's Girls' School, London SE22	1741	745	6,732	4,190	Mrs B. Davies (1984)
Kent College	1885	234‡	10,020	5,940	Miss B. Crompton (1990)
King Edward VI High School for Girls, Birmingham	1883	548	—	3,780	Miss E. W. Evans (1977)
King's HS for Girls, Warwick	1879	556	—	3,582	Mrs J. M. Anderson (1987)
Kingsley School, Warwicks.	1884	431	—	3,855	Mrs M. A. Webster (1988)
Lady Eleanor Holles School, Middx.	1711	630	—	4,530	Miss E. M. Candy (1981)
La Retraite School, Wilts.	1953	200	—	°3,840	Mrs M. Paisey (1986)
La Sagesse Convent High School, Newcastle upon Tyne	1906	350	—	3,381	Mrs D. C. Parker (1988)
La Sagesse Convent School, Hants.	1896	°125	—	°2,600	Sr Thomas Cox (1977)
Lavant House School, W. Sussex	1952	126	9,150	5,595	Mrs Y. Graham (1990)
Lawnside, Worcs.	1818	100	9,585	5,685	Miss J. Harvey (1991)
Leeds Girls' High School	1876	615	—	3,954	Miss P. A. Randall (1977)
Leicester High School	1906	304	—	3,750	Mrs P. A. Watson (1992)
Loughborough High School	1850	525	5,793	3,663	Miss J. E. L. Harvatt (1978)
Luckley-Oakfield School, Berks.	1895	304	7,470	4,647	R. C. Blake (1984)
Malvern Girls' College, Worcs.	1893	485	10,602	7,068	Dr V. B. Payne (1986)
Manchester High School	1874	725	—	3,600	Miss M. M. Moon (1983)
Manor House School, Little Bookham, Surrey	1927	260	—	4,974	Mrs L. Mendes (1989)
Maynard School, Exeter	1877	553	—	3,684	Miss F. Murdin (1980)
Merchant Taylors' School, Liverpool	1888	640	—	3,456	Miss E. J. Panton (1988)
Micklefield School, E. Sussex	1910	120	9,270	5,325	E. Reynolds (1987)
Moira House School, E. Sussex	1875	300	9,630	6,216	A. R. Underwood (1975)

Name of School	Foun-ded	No. of pupils	Annual fees £		Head (with date of appointment)
			Boarding	Day	
More House School, London SW1	1953	240	—	5,040	Miss M. Connell (1991)
Moreton Hall, Shropshire	1913	275	10,125	7,020	J. Forster (1992)
Mount School, York	1831	252	9,060	6,030	Miss B. J. Windle (1986)
Newcastle upon Tyne Church HS	1885	399	—	3,330	Miss P. E. Davies (1974)
New Hall School, Essex	1642	450	9,864	6,318	Sr Margaret Mary Horton (1986)
Northampton High School	1878	535	—	3,825	Mrs L. A. Mayne (1988)
North Foreland Lodge, Hants.	1909	180	9,900	—	Miss D. L. Matthews (1983)
North London Collegiate School	1850	725	—	4,401	Mrs J. L. Clanchy (1987)
Northwood College, Middx.	1878	525	—	4,428	Mrs J. A. Mayou (1991)
§Norwich High School	1875	641	—	3,600	Mrs V. C. Bidwell (1985)
§Nottingham High School	1875	807	—	3,600	Mrs C. Bowering (1984)
§Notting Hill and Ealing High School	1873	560	—	4,200	Mrs S. M. Whitfield (1991)
Ockbrook School, Derby	1799	220	5,802	3,156	Ms M. Rennie, PH.D. (1987)
Old Palace School, Surrey	1887	600	—	3,570	Miss K. L. Hilton (1974)
§Oxford High School	1875	559	—	3,600	Mrs J. Townsend (1981)
Palmers Green High School, London N21	1905	320	—	3,675	Mrs S. Grant (1989)
Park School, Somerset	1851	°93	°7,620	°4,380	Mrs M. J. Hannon (1987)
Parsons Mead, Surrey	1897	250	8,610	4,485	Miss E. B. Plant (1990)
Penrhos College, Clwyd	1880	236	8,670	5,940	C. M. J. Allen (1993)
Perse School for Girls, Cambridge	1881	530	—	4,020	Miss H. S. Smith (1989)
*Peterborough High School	1939	200	7,560	3,765	Mrs A. Storey (1977)
Pipers Corner School, Bucks.	1930	370	8,535	5,100	Dr M. M. Wilson (1986)
Polam Hall, Co. Durham	1848	350	8,223	4,023	Mrs H. C. Hamilton (1987)
§Portsmouth High School	1882	542	—	3,600	Mrs J. M. Dawtrey (1984)
Princess Helena College, Herts.	1820	150	9,240	6,450	Miss H. Davidson-Wall (1990)
Prior's Field, Surrey	1902	230	8,685	5,685	Mrs J. M. McCallum (1987)
§Putney High School, London SW15	1893	571	—	4,200	Mrs E. Merchant (1991)
Queen Anne's School, Berks.	1698	373	10,200	6,450	Mrs D. Forbes (1993)
Queen Ethelburga's College, York	1912	250	9,085	5,685	Mrs G. L. Richardson (1993)
Queen Margaret's School, York	1901	355	9,375	5,940	Dr G. A. H. Chapman (1993)
Queen Mary School, Lytham, Lancs.	1930	550	—	3,345	Miss M. C. Ritchie (1981)
Queen's College, London W1	1848	390	6,570	5,370	Lady Goodhart (1991)
Queen's Gate School, London SW7	1891	210	—	4,710	Mrs A. M. Holyoak (Principal) (1987)
Queen's School, Chester	1878	416	—	3,879	Miss D. M. Skilbeck (1989)
Queenswood, Herts.	1894	406	10,680	6,318	Mrs A. M. B. Butler (1981)
Redland High School, Bristol	1882	480	—	3,633	Mrs C. Lear (1989)
Red Maids' School, Bristol	1634	500	6,990	3,525	Miss S. Hampton (1987)
Rickmansworth Masonic School, Herts.	1788	520	7,677	4,401	Mrs I. M. Andrews (1992)
Roedean School, Brighton	1885	440	11,985	—	Mrs A. R. Longley (1984)
Rosemead, W. Sussex	1919	130	8,970	5,160	Mrs H. Kingham (Principal) (1991)
Royal Naval School, Surrey	1840	250	8,820	5,598	Dr J. L. Clough (1987)
Royal School, Bath	1864	305	10,371	6,615	Mrs E. McKendrick (1994)
Runton and Sutherland School, Norfolk	1875	120	9,705	5,670	Mrs D. J. Buckenham (1993)
Rye St Antony School (RC), Oxford	1930	400	7,725	4,650	Miss A. M. Jones (1990)
St Albans High School, Herts.	1889	520	—	4,299	Miss E. M. Diggory (1983)
St Andrew's School, Bedford	1897	170	—	3,012	Mrs J. E. Stephen (1991)
St Anne's School, Cumbria	1863	265	8,685	5,760	C. M. G. Jenkins (1993)
St Antony's-Leweston School (RC), Dorset	1891	285	9,363	6,105	Miss C. Denley Lloyd (1993)
St Catherine's School, Surrey	1885	450	8,580	5,235	J. R. Palmer (1982)
*School of St Clare, Penzance	1889	100	7,665	4,050	I. Halford (1986)
St David's School, Middx.	1716	246†	8,295	4,785	Mrs J. G. Osborne (1985)
St Dunstan's Abbey, Devon	1850	210	7,399	5,089	R. A. Bye (1991)
St Elphin's School, Derbys.	1844	180	9,111	5,307	A. P. C. Pollard (1979)
St Felix School, Suffolk	1897	265	9,627	6,189	Mrs S. R. Campion (1991)
St Francis' College (RC), Herts.	1933	205	8,850	4,575	Miss M. Hegarty (1993)
S. Gabriel's School, Berks.	1929	170	—	4,497	D. Cobb (1990)
St George's School, Ascot, Berks.	1923	295	10,950	6,150	Mrs A. M. Griggs (1989)
School of S. Helen and S. Katharine, Oxon.	1903	520	—	3,750	Mrs C. L. Hall (1993)
St Helen's School, Middx.	1899	571	8,187	4,341	Mrs Y.A. Burne, PH.D. (1987)
*S. Hilary's School, Cheshire	1880	188	—	3,735	Mrs J. Tracey (1985)

Name of School	Foun-ded	No. of pupils	Annual fees £		Head (with date of appointment)
			Boarding	Day	
St James's and the Abbey, Worcs.	1896	200	9,600	6,399	Miss E. M. Mullenger (1986)
St Joseph's Convent School (RC), Berks.	1909	420	—	3,540	Mrs V. Brookes (1990)
St Joseph's School, Lincoln	1905	210	7,245	3,645	Mrs A. Scott (1983)
St Leonards-Mayfield School, E. Sussex	1850	525	9,360	6,240	Sr J. Sinclair (1980)
St Margaret's School, Bushey, Herts.	1749	380	8,040	5,085	Miss M. de Villiers (1993)
*St Margaret's School, Exeter	1904	370	5,805	3,540	Mrs M. D'Albertanson (1993)
St Martin's School, Solihull, W. Midlands	1941	245	—	4,230	Mrs S. J. Williams (1989)
*School of St Mary and St Anne, Abbots Bromley, Staffs.	1874	240	9,900	6,597	A. Grigg (1989)
St Mary's Convent School, Worcester	1934	350	—	3,075	Mrs M. Kilbride (1986)
St Mary's Hall, Brighton	1836	227	8,487	5,439	Mrs P. J. James (1992)
St Mary's School (RC), Ascot, Berks.	1885	338	10,995	6,597	Sr M. M. Orchard (1982)
St Mary's School, Calne, Wilts.	1872	321	10,530	6,240	Miss D. H. Burns (1985)
St Mary's School, Cambridge	1898	590	6,180	3,450	Miss M. Conway (1989)
St Mary's School, Colchester	1908	260	—	3,336	Mrs G. M. G. Mouser (1981)
St Mary's School, Gerrards Cross	1872	325	—	4,575	Mrs J. P. G. Smith (1984)
St Mary's School (RC), Shaftesbury	1945	290	8,970	5,730	Sr M. Campion Livesey (1985)
St Mary's School, Wantage, Oxon.	1873	270	9,900	—	Revd Mrs P. H. Johns (1980)
St Maur's Convent School, Weybridge	1898	750	—	4,500	Mrs M. E. Dodds (1991)
*S. Michaels Burton Park, W. Sussex	1844	130	8,970	5,970	Mrs L. J. Griffin (1991)
St Michael's, Limpsfield, Surrey	1850	131	9,521	5,528	Ms M. J. Hustler, ph.d. (1989)
St Paul's Girls' School, London w6	1904	620	—	5,538	Miss J. Gough (High Mistress) (1992)
St Swithun's School, Winchester	1884	448	10,275	6,210	Miss J. E. Jefferson (1986)
St Teresa's School, Dorking	1928	360	9,330	4,590	L. Allan (1987)
Selwyn School, Glos.	—	230	8,025	4,575	A. Beatson (1990)
§Sheffield High School	1878	540	—	3,600	Mrs M. A. Houston (1989)
Sherborne School for Girls, Dorset	1899	457	10,350	6,900	Miss J. M. Taylor (1985)
§Shrewsbury High School	1885	406	—	3,600	Miss S. Gardner (1990)
Sir William Perkins's School, Surrey	1725	504	—	°3,315	Mrs A. F. Darlow (1982)
§South Hampstead High School, London NW3	1876	593	—	4,200	Mrs J. G. Scott (1993)
Stamford High School, Lincs.	1876	730	7,488	3,744	Miss G. K. Bland (1978)
Stonar School, Wilts.	1921	450	8,910	4,935	Mrs S. Hopkinson (1986)
Stover School, Devon	1932	260	°7,290	°3,825	Mrs W. E. Lunel (1984)
Stratford House School, Kent	1912	230	—	4,260	Mrs A. A. Williamson (1974)
§Streatham Hill and Clapham High School, London sw2	1887	391	—	4,200	Miss G. M. Ellis (1979)
Sunderland High School (CSC)	1884	230‡	—	3,600	Miss C. Rendle-Short (1993)
Surbiton High School (CSC), Surrey	1884	510	—	4,428	Miss G. Perry (1993)
§Sutton High School, Surrey	1884	557	—	4,200	Miss A. E. Cavendish (1980)
§Sydenham High School, London se26	1887	488	—	4,200	Mrs G. Baker (1988)
Talbot Heath, Dorset	1886	439	7,911	4,509	Mrs C. Dipple (1991)
Teesside High School, Cleveland	1970	375	—	3,393	Mrs H. Coles (1982)
Tormead School, Surrey	1905	450	—	4,635	Mrs H. E. M. Alleyne (1992)
Truro High School	1880	350	7,341	4,023	J. Graham-Brown (1992)
Tudor Hall School, Oxon.	1850	262	9,510	5,925	Miss N. Godfrey (1984)
Upper Chine, Isle of Wight	1799	138	8,415	4,485	Dr H. Harvey (1990)
Ursuline Convent School, Kent	1904	300	7,881	4,596	Sr M. Murphy (1977)
Ursuline High School, Ilford	1903	408	—	4,020	Miss J. Reddington (1990)
Wadhurst College, E. Sussex	1930	165	9,855	6,270	Miss A. M. Phillips (1991)
Wakefield Girls' High School	1878	900	—	3,792	Mrs P. A. Langham (1987)
Walthamstow Hall, Kent	1838	375	9,810	5,280	Mrs J. S. Lang (1984)
Wentworth Milton Mount, Dorset	1962	280	8,064	5,040	Miss S. Coe (1991)
Westfield School, Newcastle upon Tyne	1962	205	—	3,771	Mrs M. Farndale (1990)
West Heath, Kent	1867	129	10,500	7,380	Mrs R. A. Ditchburn (1993)
Westholme School, Lancs.	1923	650	—	3,195	Mrs L. Croston (Principal) (1988)
Westonbirt, Glos.	1928	250	9,975	6,420	Mrs G. Hylson-Smith (1986)
§Wimbledon High School, London sw19	1880	539	—	4,200	Mrs E. M. Baker (1992)
Wispers School, Surrey	1946	165	8,442	5,442	L. H. Beltran (1979)
Withington Girls' School, Manchester	1890	480	—	3,465	Mrs M. Kenyon (1986)

Name of School	Foun-ded	No. of pupils	Annual fees £		Head (with date of appointment)
			Boarding	Day	
Woldingham School, Surrey	1842	453	10,404	6,300	Ms P. Dineen, PH.D. (1985)
Wroxall Abbey School, Warwick	1872	100	9,075	5,325	Mrs J. M. Gowen (1993)
Wychwood School, Oxford	1897	160	6,420	4,020	Mrs M. L. Duffill (1981)
Wycombe Abbey School, Bucks.	1896	485	11,538	—	Mrs J. M. Goodland (1989)
Wykeham House School, Fareham, Hants.	1913	250	—	3,546	Mrs E. M. Moore (1983)
York College for Girls (*CSC*)	1908	147	—	4,041	Mrs J. L. Clare (1982)
SCOTLAND					
Kilgraston School, Perthshire	1930	236	8,700	4,725	Mrs J. L. Austin (1993)
Laurel Bank School, Glasgow	1903	385	—	3,870	Miss L. G. Egginton (1984)
Mary Erskine School, Edinburgh	1694	630	7,750	3,843	P. F. J. Tobin (*Principal*) (1989)
Park School, Glasgow	1880	365	—	3,627	Mrs M. E. Myatt (1986)
St Denis and Cranley School, Edinburgh	1858·	150	8,400	4,170	Mrs J. M. Munro (1984)
St George's School, Edinburgh	1888	540	7,926	4,101	Dr J. McClure (1994)
St Leonards School, St Andrews	1877	270	11,100	5,850	Mrs L. E. James (1988)
St Margaret's School, Aberdeen	1846	218	—	3,360	Miss L. M. Ogilvie (1989)
St Margaret's School, Edinburgh	1890	400	7,759	3,782	Mrs M. J. Cameron (1984)
Wellington School for Girls, Ayr	1849	°300	°8,160	°4,095	Mrs D. A. Gardner (1988)
CHANNEL ISLANDS					
The Ladies' College, Guernsey	1872	346	—	1,890	Miss M. Macdonald (1992)

Social Welfare

National Health Service

and Local Authority Personal Social Services

The National Health Service came into being on 5 July 1948, as a result of the National Health Service Act 1946. The Act placed a duty on the Secretary of State for Social Services to promote the establishment in England and Wales of a comprehensive health service designed to secure improvement in the mental and physical health of the people and the prevention, diagnosis and treatment of illness. The Secretary of State for Wales administers the National Health Service in Wales. There are separate Acts for Scotland and Northern Ireland, where the health services are run on very similar lines and the respective Secretaries of State are responsible to Parliament.

The National Health Service covers a comprehensive range of hospital, specialist, family practitioner (medical, dental, ophthalmic and pharmaceutical), artificial limb and appliance, ambulance, and community health services. Everyone normally resident in this country is entitled to use any of these services, there are no contribution conditions and the charges made (except those for amenity beds) are reduced or waived in cases of hardship.

In addition, the Secretary of State for Social Services is responsible under the Local Authority Social Services Act 1970 for the provision by local authorities of social services for the elderly, the disabled, those with mental disorders and for families and children.

The NHS is financed mainly from taxation and the cost met from moneys voted by Parliament. The present level of expenditure is £30.5 billion per annum.

STRUCTURE

The National Health Service and Community Care Act 1990 introduced wide-ranging reforms in management and patient care. The Act provides for more streamlined Regional and District Health Authorities and Family Health Services Authorities, and for the establishment of NHS Trusts, which operate as self-governing health care providers. One result of the Act is that health care is provided through NHS contracts, where one body (the purchaser) is responsible for obtaining the appropriate health care for its population from another body (the provider). From 1 April 1993, the Community Care Reforms introduced major changes in the way care is administered for the elderly, the mentally ill, the physically handicapped and people with learning disabilities.

The 14 Regional Health Authorities (RHAs) in England are responsible for regional planning, the allocation of resources to District Health Authorities, Family Health Services Authorities and general practitioner fundholders, and the promotion of national policies and priorities. They are directly accountable to the Secretary of State for Health and provide the link between the DHAs and FHSAs, and the NHS Management Executive.

The 145 District Health Authorities (DHAs) are responsible for purchasing health care for the people who live within their areas, and for the operational management of health services and planning within regional and national strategic guidelines. DHAs' resources are allocated by RHAs, to which they are also accountable for their performance. As a result of the reforms, some DHAs have merged to form larger bodies, allowing them to increase their purchasing power and make better use of resources.

THE HEALTH SERVICES

FAMILY DOCTOR SERVICE

In England and Wales the Family Doctor Service (or General Medical Services) is managed by 90 Family Health Services Authorities (FHSAs) which also organize the general dental, pharmaceutical and ophthalmic services for their areas. There is a Family Health Services Authority for one or more District Health Authorities. In England the chairman is appointed by the Secretary of State and the non-executive members by the Regional Health Authority. In Wales the chairman and non-executive members are appointed by the Secretary of State. There are nine non-executive members: a general medical practitioner, a general dental practitioner, a community pharmacist, a nurse, and five lay members.

Any doctor may take part in the Family Doctor Service (provided the area in which he/she wishes to practise has not already an adequate number of doctors) and most general practitioners in England and Wales do so. They may at the same time have private fee-paying patients. Family doctors are paid for their Health Service work in accordance with a scheme of remuneration which includes *inter alia* a basic practice allowance, capitation fees, reimbursement of certain practice expenses and payments for out-of-hours work.

The National Health Service and Community Care Act 1990 enables general practitioner practices with at least 7,000 patients to apply for fundholding status (a number of smaller practices form units in order to achieve fundholding status). This makes the practice responsible for its own NHS budget for a specified range of goods and services. There are currently 1,120 fundholding units, comprising 1,235 practices. Fundholding practices are monitored by the FHSAs on behalf of the Regional Health Authorities.

Everyone aged 16 or over can choose their doctor (parents or guardians choose for children under 16) and the doctor is also free to accept a person or not as he or she chooses. A person may change their doctor if they wish, by going to the surgery of a general practioner of their choice who is willing to accept them, and either handing in their medical card to register or filling in a form. When people are away from home they can still use the Family Doctor Service if they ask to be treated as temporary residents, and in an emergency, if a person's own doctor is not available, any doctor in the service will give treatment and advice.

Patients are treated either in the doctor's surgery or, when necessary, at home. Doctors may prescribe for their patients all drugs and medicines which are medically necessary for their treatment and also a certain number of surgical appliances (the more elaborate being provided through hospitals).

DENTAL SERVICE

Dentists, like doctors, may take part in the National Health Service and also have private patients. About 16,000 of the dentists available for general practice in England provide

NHS general dental services. They are responsible to the Family Health Services Authorities in whose areas they provide services.

Patients are free to go to any dentist who is taking part in the Service and willing to accept them. Dentists are paid a capitation fee for patients registered with them who are under 18 years of age. They receive payment for items of treatment for individual adult patients and, in addition, a continuing care payment for those registered with them.

Patients are asked to pay 80 per cent of the cost of NHS dental treatment. The maximum charge for a course of treatment is £250. There is no charge for arrest of bleeding, repairs to dentures, home visits by the dentist or re-opening a surgery in an emergency (in these two cases, payment will be for treatment given in the normal way). The following are exempt from dental charges:

(i)   young people under 18
(ii)   full time students under 19
(iii)   expectant mothers who were pregnant when accepted for treatment
(iv)   women who have had a child in the previous 12 months

People receiving Income Support or Family Credit, and members of the same family as someone receiving Income Support or Family Credit, are automatically entitled to full remission of charges.

Leaflet AB11 available from post offices and leaflet D11 available from local social security offices explain how other people on a low income can, depending on their financial circumstances, get free treatment or help with charges.

PHARMACEUTICAL SERVICE

Patients may obtain medicines, appliances and oral contraceptives prescribed under the NHS from any pharmacy whose owner has entered into arrangements with the Family Health Services Authority to provide this service. Almost all pharmacy owners have done so and display notices that they dispense under the NHS; the number of these pharmacies in England and Wales at the end of 1990 was about 10,400. There are also some appliance suppliers who only provide special appliances. In country areas where access to a pharmacy may be difficult, patients may be able to obtain medicines, etc., from their doctor.

Except for contraceptives (for which there is no charge), a charge of £4.25 is payable for each item supplied unless the patient is exempt and the declaration on the back of the prescription form is completed. Exemptions cover:

(i)   children under 16
(ii)   full-time students under 19
(iii)   men aged 65 and over
(iv)   women aged 60 and over
(v)   pregnant women
(vi)   mothers who have had a baby within the last 12 months
(vii)   people suffering from certain medical conditions
(viii) people who receive Income Support or Family Credit and their dependants
(ix)   people who hold an AG2 certificate issued by the Health Benefits Unit, and their dependants
(x)   war pensioners (for their accepted disablements)

Prepayment certificates (£22 valid for four months, £60.60 valid for a year) may be purchased by those patients not entitled to exemption who require frequent prescriptions. Further information about the exemption and prepayment arrangements is given in leaflet P11.

GENERAL OPHTHALMIC SERVICES

General Ophthalmic Services, which are administered by Family Practitioner Committees, form part of the ophthalmic services available under the National Health Service. The NHS sight test is available free to:

(i)   children under 16
(ii)   full-time students under the age of 19
(iii)   people in receipt of Income Support and Family Credit, and their partners
(iv)   people prescribed complex lenses
(v)   the registered blind and partially sighted
(vi)   diagnosed diabetic and glaucoma patients
(vii)   close relatives aged 40 or over of diagnosed glaucoma patients

Those on a low income may qualify for help with the cost.

Certain groups are automatically entitled to help with the purchase of glasses under an NHS voucher scheme:

(i)   children under 16
(ii)   full-time students under 19
(iii)   people in receipt of Income Support or Family Credit, and their partners
(iv)   people wearing certain complex lenses
(v)   people whose spectacles are lost or damaged as a result of their disability, injury or illness

The value of the voucher depends on the lenses required. Vouchers may be used to help pay for the glasses or contact lenses of the patient's choice. People with a low income may claim help on form AG1. Glasses or contact lenses should not be purchased until the result of a claim is known as no refunds can be given. Booklet G11 gives further details.

Diagnosis and specialist treatment of eye conditions is available through the Hospital Eye Service as well as the provision of glasses of a special type. Testing of sight may be carried out by any ophthalmic medical practitioner or ophthalmic optician and can cost up to £18. The optician must hand the prescription, and a voucher if eligible, to the patient who can take this to any supplier of glasses of his/her choice to have dispensed. However, only registered opticians can supply glasses to children and to people registered as blind or partially sighted.

PRIMARY HEALTH CARE SERVICES

Primary health care services include the general medical, dental, ophthalmic and pharmaceutical services and the family doctor service. They also include community services run by district health authorities, health centres and clinics, family planning outside the hospital service, and preventive activities in the community including vaccination, immunization and fluoridation.

The district nursing and health visiting services include community psychiatric nursing for mentally ill people living outside hospital, and school nursing for the health surveillance of schoolchildren of all ages. Ante- and post-natal care and chiropody are also an integral part of the primary health care service.

COMMUNITY CHILD HEALTH SERVICES

Pre-school services, usually at child health clinics, provide regular surveillance of children's physical, mental and emotional health and development, and advice to parents on their children's health and welfare.

The School Health Service provides for the medical and dental examination of schoolchildren, and advises the local education authority, the school, the parents and the pupil of any health factors which may require special consideration during the pupil's school life. GPs are increasingly undertaking child health surveillance to improve the preventive health care of children.

HOSPITALS AND OTHER SERVICES

The Secretary of State for Health has a duty to provide, to such extent as he/she considers necessary to meet all reasonable requirements, hospital and other accommodation; medical, dental, nursing and ambulance services; other facilities for the care of expectant and nursing mothers and young children; facilities for the prevention of illness and the care and after-care of persons suffering from illness; and such other services as are required for the diagnosis and treatment of illness. Rehabilitation services (occupational therapy, physiotherapy and speech therapy) may also be provided for those who need it and surgical and medical appliances are supplied in appropriate cases.

Specialists and consultants who take part in the Health Service can engage in private practice, including the treatment of their private patients in NHS hospitals.

Trusts

The National Health Service and Community Care Act 1990 enables hospitals and other providers of health care, to become independent of health authority control as self-governing NHS Trusts run by boards of directors. The Trusts derive their income principally from contracts to provide health services to health authorities and fund-holding general practitioners. In April 1993 there were 292 NHS Trusts, and applications from hospitals wishing to become Trusts in April 1994 are currently under consideration.

Charges

In a number of hospitals, accommodation is available for the treatment of private in-patients who undertake to pay the full costs of hospital accommodation and services and (usually) separate medical fees to a specialist as well. The amount of the medical fees is a matter for agreement between doctor and patient. Hospital charges for private resident patients are determined by District Health Authorities or Trusts, either on a local basis or in line with a central 'model' list.

Certain hospitals have accommodation in single rooms or small wards which, if not required for patients who need privacy for medical reasons, may be made available to patients who desire it as an amenity. These patients are still NHS patients and are treated as such.

There is no charge for drugs supplied to National Health hospital in-patients but out-patients pay £4.25 per item unless they are exempt.

With certain exceptions, hospital out-patients have to pay fixed charges for dentures, contact lenses and certain appliances. Glasses may be obtained either from the hospital or an optician and the charge will be related to the type of lens prescribed and the choice of frame.

LOCAL AUTHORITY PERSONAL SOCIAL SERVICES

Local authorities are responsible for the organization, management and administration of the personal social services and each authority has a Director of Social Services and a Social Services Committee responsible for the social services functions placed upon them by the Local Authority Social Services Act 1970.

National Insurance and Related Cash Benefits

The State insurance and assistance schemes, comprising schemes of national insurance and industrial injuries insurance, national assistance, and non-contributory old age pensions came into force from 5 July 1948. The Ministry of Social Security Act 1966 replaced national assistance and non-contributory old age pensions with a scheme of non-contributory benefits, termed supplementary allowances and pensions. These, and subsequent measures relating to social security provision in Great Britain, were consolidated by the Social Security Act 1975; the Social Security (Consequential Provisions) Act 1975; and the Industrial Injuries and Diseases (Old Cases) Act 1975. Corresponding measures were passed for Northern Ireland. The Social Security Pensions Act 1975 introduced a new State pensions scheme, which came into force on 6 April 1978, and the graduated pension scheme 1961 to 1975 has been wound up, existing rights being preserved. The Pensioners' Payments and Social Security Act 1979 provided for a £10 bonus for pensioners in 1979 and for the payment of a bonus in succeeding years at levels then to be determined. The Child Benefit Act 1975 replaced family allowances (introduced 1946) with child benefit and one parent benefit.

Some of the above legislation has been superseded by the provisions of the Social Security Acts 1968 to 1992.

NATIONAL INSURANCE SCHEME

The National Insurance scheme operates under the Social Security Contributions and Benefits Act 1992 and the Social Security Administration Act 1992, and orders and regulations made thereunder. The scheme is financed by contributions payable by earners, employers and others (such as non-employed persons, paying voluntary contributions). It provides the funds required for paying benefits payable under the Social Security Acts out of the National Insurance Fund and not out of other public money and for the making of payments towards the cost of the National Health Service. In 1991 the Redundancy Fund was absorbed into the National Insurance Fund. The yearly Treasury supplement to the National Insurance Fund was abolished in April 1989.

CONTRIBUTIONS

Contributions are of four classes:

Class 1 contributions

These are earnings-related, based on a percentage of the employee's earnings.

(a) primary Class 1 contributions are payable by employed earners and office-holders over age 16 with gross earnings at or above the lower earnings limit of £56.00 per week. For those with gross earnings at or above this level, contributions are payable on all earnings up to an upper limit of £420.00 per week. 'Gross earnings' include overtime pay, commission, bonus, etc., without deduction of any superannuation contributions.

(b) secondary Class 1 contributions are payable by employers of employed earners, and by the appropriate authorities in the case of office-holders. On 6 October 1985 the upper earnings limit for employers' contributions was abolished and secondary contributions are payable on all the employee's earnings if they reach or exceed £56.00 per week.

Women who marry for the first time no longer have a right to elect not to pay the full contribution rate. Married women and widows who before 12 May 1977 elected not to pay contributions at the full rate retain the right to pay a reduced rate over the same earnings range, which includes a contribution to the National Health Service. They lose this right if, after 5 April 1978, there are two consecutive tax years in which they receive no earnings on which primary Class 1 contributions are payable and in which they have not been at any time self-employed earners. No primary contributions are due on earnings paid for a period on or after the employee's pension age, even when retirement is deferred.

Primary contributions are deducted from earnings by the employer and are paid, together with the employer's contributions, to the Inland Revenue along with income tax collected under the PAYE system. On 6 October 1985 several lower percentage rates of contribution for lower paid employees and their employers were introduced.

Class 2 contributions

These are flat-rate, paid weekly by self-employed earners over age 16. Those with earnings below £3,140 a year for the tax year 1993-4 can apply for exemption from liability to pay Class 2 contributions. People who while self-employed are exempted from liability to pay contributions on the grounds of small earnings may pay either Class 2 or Class 3 contributions voluntarily. Self-employed earners (whether or not they pay Class 2 contributions) may also be liable to pay Class 4 contributions based on profits or gains within certain limits. There are special rules for those who are concurrently employed and self-employed.

Married women and widows can no longer choose not to pay Class 2 contributions. Those who elected not to pay Class 2 contributions before 12 May 1977 retain the right until there is a period of two consecutive tax years after 5 April 1978 in which they were not at any time either self-employed earners or had earnings on which primary Class 1 contributions were payable.

Class 2 contributions may be paid by direct debit through a bank or National Giro account or by stamping a contribution card.

Class 3 contributions

These are voluntary flat-rate contributions payable by persons over school-leaving age who would otherwise be unable to qualify for retirement pension and certain other benefits because they have an insufficient record of Class 1 or Class 2 contributions. Married women and widows who on or before 11 May 1977 elected not to pay Class 1 (full rate) or Class 2 contributions cannot pay Class 3 contributions while they retain this right.

Payment may be made by stamping a contribution card or by direct debit through a bank or National Giro account.

Class 4 contributions

These are payable by self-employed earners, whether or not they pay Class 2 contributions, on annual profits or gains from a trade, profession or vocation chargeable to income tax under Schedule D, where these fall between £6,340 and £21,840 a year. The maximum Class 4 contribution, payable on profits or gains of £21,840 or more, is £976.50.

Class 4 contributions are generally assessed and collected by the Inland Revenue along with Schedule D income tax. Self-employed persons under 16, or who at the beginning of a tax year are over pension age even where retirement is deferred, are not liable to pay Class 4 contributions. There

are special rules for people who have more than one job, or who pay Class 1 contributions on earnings which are chargeable to income tax under Schedule D.

Regulations state the cases in which earners may be exempted from liability to pay contributions, and the conditions upon which contributions are credited to persons who are exempted. Leaflet NI 208 is obtainable from local social security offices.

The Secretary of State for Social Services is empowered by the Social Security Acts to alter certain rates of contributions by order approved by both Houses of Parliament, and is required by the same enactments to make annual reviews of the general level of earnings in order to determine whether such an order should be made.

For the period 6 April 1993 to 5 April 1994 the earnings brackets determining Class 1 contributions are:

	Weekly earnings
1	£56.00– 94.99
2	95.00–139.99
3	140.00–194.99
4	195.00–420.00
5	over 420.00

Contribution rates for the period 6 April 1993 to 5 April 1994 are:

CLASS 1 CONTRIBUTIONS – NOT CONTRACTED OUT

Employee's rates

Earnings bracket	Percentage of reckonable income		On earnings from	
	On first £56.00		£56.00–£420.00	
	standard	reduced	standard	reduced
1	2	3.85	9	3.85
2	2	3.85	9	3.85
3	2	3.85	9	3.85
4	2	3.85	9	3.85
5	*2	*3.85	*9	*3.85

*to a maximum of £420.00 per week

The employee's rate is scheduled to go up to 10 per cent from 7 April 1994

CLASS 1 CONTRIBUTIONS – CONTRACTED OUT

(*see also* page 499)

Employee's rates

Earnings bracket	On first £56.00		On earnings from £56.00–£420.00	
	standard	reduced	standard	reduced
1	2	3.85	7.2	3.85
2	2	3.85	7.2	3.85
3, 4, 5	2	3.85	7.2	3.85

Employer's rates

Earnings bracket	On first £56.00	On earnings from £56.00–£420.00	On any earnings over £420.00
1	4.6	1.6	0
2	6.6	3.6	0
3	8.6	5.6	0
4	10.4	7.4	0
5	10.4	7.4	10.4

	Weekly flat rate
CLASS 2 CONTRIBUTIONS	£5.55

CLASS 3 CONTRIBUTIONS   £5.45

CLASS 4 CONTRIBUTIONS   6.3% of profits or gains
                         (7.4% from 7 April 1994)

From 5 October 1989 there was a change in the assessment of National Insurance contributions for employees. Where earnings were paid or were due to be paid on or after 5 October 1989, employees' contributions were paid at 2 per cent of earnings at the lower earnings limit (£56.00 a week or equivalent) plus 9 per cent (not contracted out) or 7.2 per cent (contracted out) of earnings between the lower earnings limit up to and including the employees' upper earnings limit (£420.00 a week or equivalent). Employees contributing at the reduced rate continue to pay contributions at 3.85 per cent on all earnings up to and including the employees' upper earnings limit.

The Social Security (Contributions) Act 1991 added a new class of contributions: 1A, payable in respect of car fuel by persons liable to pay secondary Class 1 contributions. It has effect with regard to the 1991–2 tax year and thereafter.

Employees earning less than the lower earnings limit continue not to pay any contributions.

There was no change in the assessment of employers' contributions.

THE STATE EARNINGS RELATED
PENSION SCHEME (SERPS)

The Social Security Pensions Act 1975, which came into force in April 1978, aims to reduce reliance upon means-tested benefit in old age, in widowhood and in chronic ill-health by providing better pensions; to ensure that occupational pension schemes which are contracted out of part of the State scheme fulfil the conditions of a good scheme; that pensions are adequately protected against inflation; and that in both the State and occupational schemes men and women are treated equally. Retirement, widow's and invalidity pensions under the new scheme started to be paid in April 1979. Since 6 April 1979 flat-rate retirement and other State pensions have been augmented for employed earners by additional pensions related to earnings, but it will be twenty years before these additional pensions become payable at the full rate.

Under the scheme, retirement, invalidity and widow's pensions for employees are related to the earnings on which national insurance contributions have been paid. For employees of either sex with a complete insurance record, the scheme provides a category A retirement pension in two parts, a basic and an additional pension. The basic pension corresponds to the old personal flat-rate national insurance pension. The additional pension is 1.25 per cent of average earnings between the lower weekly earnings limit for Class 1 contribution liability and the upper earnings limit for each year of such earnings under the scheme, and will thus build up to 25 per cent in twenty years.

The additional pension will be calculated in a different way for individuals who reach pension age after 6 April 1999. The changes are to be phased in over ten years. From 2010 a lifetime's earnings will be included in the calculation and for years from 1988–9 onwards the accrual rate on these surplus earnings will be 20 per cent. The accrual rate on surplus earnings for the years from 1978–9 to 1987–8 will remain at 25 per cent.

Actual earnings are to be revalued in terms of the earnings level current in the last complete tax year before pension age (or death or incapacity). Both components of pensions in

payment will be uprated annually in line with the movement of prices. Graduated retirement pensions in payment, and rights to such pensions earned by people who are still working, will be brought into the annual review of benefits.

Self-employed persons pay contributions towards the basic pension. The non-employed and employees with earnings below the lower limit may contribute voluntarily for basic pension. Although no primary Class 1 contributions or Class 2 or Class 4 contributions are payable by persons who work beyond pension age (65 for men, 60 for women), the employer's liability for secondary Class 1 contributions continues if earnings are at or above the lower earnings limit. Class 4 contributions are still payable up to the end of the tax year during which pension age is reached.

Widows will get the whole of any additional pensions earned by their husbands with their widowed mother's allowances or widow's pensions; and can add to the retirement pensions earned by their own contributions any additional pensions earned by their husbands up to the maximum payable on one person's contributions. Men whose wives die when they are both over pension age can add together their own and their wives' pension rights in the same way as widows.

Among the steps taken to give women equal treatment in benefit provision, the State scheme permits years of home responsibilities to reduce the number of qualifying years (since 1978) needed for retirement pension, widowed mother's allowance and widow's pension; and the 'half-test', by which a married woman who married before age 55 could not qualify for a Category A retirement pension unless she had contributed on earnings at the basic level in at least half the years between marriage and pension age, has been abolished with effect from 22 December 1984. The range of short-term social security benefits and industrial injury benefits under the Social Security Act 1975 continues with only minor changes.

CONTRACTED-OUT AND PERSONAL
PENSION SCHEMES

Members of occupational pension schemes which meet the standards laid down in the Social Security Pensions Act 1975 can be contracted-out of the earnings related part of the state scheme relating to retirement and widows' benefits. Regulations made under the Act require employers to consult employees and their organizations and inform them of their intention to contract out. (Leaflets relating to pensions and guidance for employers about contracting-out are available from local social security offices.) The Act also contains provisions ensuring equal access to membership of schemes for men and women.

Until 6 April 1988 occupational pension schemes could only contract out if they promised a pension that was related to earnings. These are known as contracted-out salary related schemes. They must provide a pension that is not less than the guaranteed minimum pension (GMP), which is broadly equivalent to the state earnings related pension. However, new options were introduced by the Social Security Act 1986. Since 6 April 1988 occupational pension schemes which promise a minimum level of contributions have also been able to contract out. These are known as contracted-out money purchase schemes. They provide a pension based on the fund built up in the scheme over the years plus the results of the way they have been invested.

In addition, since July 1988 employees whose employers do not provide a pension scheme have been able to start their own personal pension instead of staying in the state earnings related pension scheme. Since 6 April 1988, this choice has been open to all employees even if their employer does have a pension scheme. A personal pension, like a contracted-out money purchase scheme, provides a pension based on the fund built up in the scheme over the years plus the results of the way they have been invested.

The decision on whether or not an occupational pension scheme may become contracted-out lies with the Occupational Pension Board, an independent statutory body which has a general responsibility for supervising contracting-out. They also consider and approve personal pension schemes which can be used instead of state additional pension.

The State earnings related pension payable to a member of a contracted-out salary related scheme, or his widow, will be reduced by the amount of GMP payable (which in the case of a widow must be at least half of the late husband's GMP entitlement). Members of contracted-out money purchase schemes and personal pension schemes, or their widows, have no GMP entitlement as such. But the state earnings related pension payable will be reduced by an amount equivalent to a GMP (or widow's GMP).

Since 6 April 1988 contracted-out salary related schemes must also provide a widower's GMP which must be at least half of the late wife's GMP entitlement built up from 6 April 1988. (A scheme need not provide entitlement to a GMP for widowers of earners dying before April 1989.) Contracted-out money purchase schemes and personal pension schemes must provide half-rate widower's benefit.

In contracted-out schemes, both the employee and the employer pay the full ordinary rate of contribution on the first £56.00 (1993–4 figure) of earnings but earnings above that amount attract a lower rate of contribution from the employee, and from the employer where the employee's earnings are under £420.00; where the employee's earnings exceed this amount, the full ordinary rate of contribution is payable only by the employer and the employee has no liability for contributions on these earnings (*see also* page 497).

An employee who chooses a personal pension in place of SERPS or their employer's pension scheme must pay National Insurance contributions at the full ordinary rate (the employer's share must also be paid at the same rate). The DSS pays the difference between the lower contracted-out rate and the full ordinary rate directly into the personal pension scheme.

NATIONAL INSURANCE FUND

The National Insurance Fund receives all social security contributions (less only the National Health Service and Redundancy Fund and Maternity Pay Fund allocations and the National Insurance surcharge for taxation purposes) and it bears the cost of all contributory benefits provided by the Social Security Acts and the cost of administration.

Approximate receipts and payments of the National Insurance Fund for the year ended 31 March 1992, were as follows:

Receipts	£'000
Balance, 1 April 1991	11,791,856
Contributions under the Social Security Acts (net of SSP/SMP)	32,474,390
Compensation from Consolidated Fund for SSP/SMP recoveries	1,055,000
Income from investments	1,109,426
Other receipts	37,284
	46,467,956

Payments	£'000	£'000
Unemployment benefit	1,603,815	
Sickness benefit	273,512	
Invalidity benefit	5,485,418	
Maternity allowance	30,951	
Widow's benefit	1,010,599	
Guardian's allowance and child's special allowance	1,471	
Retirement pension	25,543,024	
Pensioners' lump sum payments	114,324	34,063,114
Personal pensions		2,451,867
Transfers to Northern Ireland		125,000
Administration		1,201,541
Other payments		9,682
Redundancy payments		283,452
Balance, 31 March 1992		8,333,300
		46,467,956

NB: There have been changes to the National Insurance Fund. Payments will no longer be paid into surcharges or the Maternity Pay Fund. However, residual payments are still being paid in respect of late paid contributions for premium years.

BENEFITS

The benefits payable under the Social Security Acts are as follows:

CONTRIBUTORY BENEFITS

Unemployment benefit
Sickness benefit
Invalidity pension and allowance
Maternity allowance
Widow's benefit, comprising widow's payment, widowed mother's allowance and widow's pension
Retirement pensions, categories A and B

NON-CONTRIBUTORY BENEFITS

Child benefit
One parent benefit
Guardian's allowance
Invalid care allowance
Mobility allowance
Severe disablement allowance
Attendance allowance
Disability Living Allowance
Disability Working Allowance
Retirement pensions, categories C and D
Income Support
Family Credit
Social Fund

BENEFITS FOR INDUSTRIAL INJURIES, DISABLEMENT AND DEATH

OTHER

Statutory sick pay
Statutory maternity pay

Leaflets relating to the various benefits and payments are obtainable from local social security offices.

The Social Security Acts empower the Secretary of State to increase certain rates of benefit by order approved by both Houses of Parliament, and require him to increase certain rates by such an order if an annual review shows that they have not retained their value in relation to the general level of prices obtaining in Great Britain as measured by the Retail Price Index.

The latest order providing for increases in benefit rates took effect from the week commencing 6 April 1993. It did not apply to all benefits.

CONTRIBUTORY BENEFITS

Entitlement to contributory benefits depends on contribution conditions being satisfied either by the client or by some other person (depending on the kind of benefit). The class or classes of contribution which for this purpose are relevant to each benefit are as follows:

Short-term benefits

Unemployment benefit	Class 1
Sickness benefit	Class 1 or 2
Maternity allowance	Class 1 or 2

Long-term benefits

Widow's benefits	
Category A retirement pension	} Class 1, 2 or 3
Category B retirement pension	
Invalidity benefit	Class 1 or 2

The system of contribution conditions relates to yearly levels of earnings on which contributions have been paid. The contribution conditions for different benefits are set out in summary form in leaflets available at local social security offices.

UNEMPLOYMENT BENEFIT

Benefit is payable in a period of interruption of employment for up to 312 days (a year, excluding Sundays). Spells of unemployment and sickness not separated by more than eight weeks count as one period of interruption of employment. A person who has exhausted benefit requalifies when he/she has again worked as an employed earner for at least 16 hours a week for 13 weeks. These weeks need not be consecutive but must generally fall within 26 weeks prior to the date of the claim.

There are disqualifications from receiving benefit, e.g. for a period not exceeding 26 weeks if a person has lost their employment through misconduct, or has voluntarily left employment without just cause, or has, without good cause, refused an offer of employment or training.

SICKNESS BENEFIT

Sickness benefit is payable for up to 28 weeks of sickness in a period of interruption of employment and is then replaced by invalidity benefit (*see* below).

There are disqualifications from receiving sickness or invalidity benefit for a period not exceeding six weeks if a person has become incapable of work through his/her own misconduct or fails without good cause to attend for or submit himself/herself to prescribed medical or other examination or treatment, or observe prescribed rules of behaviour.

Statutory sick pay (SSP) was introduced from 6 April 1983 and was payable for up to eight weeks. Since 6 April 1986 employers are responsible for paying SSP to their employees for up to 28 weeks of sickness in any period of incapacity for work. SSP replaces the employee's entitlement to State Sickness Benefit, which is not payable as long as any SSP liability remains. SSP is subject to PAYE and to NI deductions. From 6 April 1991 employers can recover 80 per cent (previously 100 per cent) of the SSP they have paid out. Employees who cannot get SSP can claim State Sickness Benefit instead.

INVALIDITY BENEFIT

Normally, after 28 weeks of sickness, sickness benefit (or SSP where the underlying conditions for sickness benefit are satisfied) is replaced by an invalidity pension. In addition, an invalidity allowance is payable if incapacity for work begins more than five years before pension age. The allowance varies according to the age at which invalidity began, and if still in payment at pension age will continue as an addition to retirement pension. From 16 September 1985 invalidity allowance has been offset by entitlement to an additional earnings-related pension and/or a guaranteed minimum pension.

MATERNITY BENEFIT

Statutory maternity pay (SMP) is administered by employers. The state maternity allowance scheme covers women who are self-employed or otherwise do not qualify for SMP.

In general, employers pay SMP to pregnant women who have been employed by them for at least 26 weeks and earned at least the lower earnings limit for the payment of NI contributions. For those who have been employed for at least two years, payment of SMP for the first six weeks is related to earnings, followed by up to twelve weeks at a standard rate of £47.95. Those who have been employed for at least 26 weeks but less than two years receive payment at standard rate only for the 18 weeks. Part-time working women also qualify for the earnings-related element if employed for at least five years. Women have some choice in deciding when to begin maternity leave but SMP is not payable for any week in which work is done.

A woman may qualify for maternity allowance (MA) if she has been working and paying contributions at the full rate for at least 26 weeks in the 52-week period which ends 15 weeks before the baby is due. She also has an element of choice in deciding when to stop work and receive MA, which is not payable for any period she works.

WIDOW'S BENEFITS

Only the late husband's contributions of any class count for widow's benefit in any of its three forms.

Widow's Payment – may be received by a woman who at her husband's death is under 60, or whose husband was not entitled to a Category A retirement pension when he died.

Widowed Mother's Allowance – payable to a widow if she is entitled or treated as entitled to child benefit, or if she is expecting her husband's baby.

Widow's Pension – a widow may receive this pension if aged 45 or over at the time of her husband's death or when her widowed mother's allowance ends. If aged 55 or over she will receive the full widow's pension rate.

Widow's benefit of any form ceases upon re-marriage or during a period in which she lives with a man as his wife.

RETIREMENT PENSION – CATEGORIES A AND B

A Category A pension is payable for life to men or women on their own contributions if they are over pension age (65 for a man and 60 for a woman).

Where a person defers making a claim at 65 (60 for a woman) or later opts to be treated as if he/she had not made a claim, and does not draw a Category A pension, the weekly rate of pension is increased, when he or she finally makes a claim or reaches the age of 70 (65 for a woman), in respect of weeks when pension is forgone during the five years after reaching minimum pension age. Details of the increase in the rate of pension due to deferred retirement are given in leaflet NP46, available at social security offices. If a married man defers his own Category A pension, his wife has to defer receiving her Category B pension based on his contribution record. During this time she earns increments to the

Category B pension, provided she does not claim retirement pension or Graduated Retirement Benefit in her own right, which is payable to her (and not her husband) when they both claim their pensions.

A Category B pension is normally payable for life to a woman on her husband's contributions when he has claimed, or is over 70, and has qualified for his own Category A pension, and she has reached 60. It is also payable on widowhood after 60 whether or not the late husband had retired and qualified for his own pension. The weekly pension is payable at the rate of the increase for a wife while the husband is alive, and at the single person's rate on widowhood after 60. Where a woman is widowed before she reaches 60, a Category B pension is paid to her on reaching 60 at the same weekly rate as her widow's pension if she claims. If a woman qualifies for a pension of each category she receives whichever pension is the larger. Details of the increase in the rate of pension due to deferred retirement are given in leaflet NP46, available at social security offices.

The earnings rule which stated that a man aged 65 to 70, or a woman aged 60 to 65, who has qualified for pension would have it reduced if he or she earned more than a certain amount was abolished on 1 October 1989. Where an adult dependant is living with the client, an Adult Dependants Allowance will only be payable if the dependant's earnings do not exceed the standard rate of unemployment benefit for a single person under pensionable age (*see* below). For the purpose of the dependency rule only, earnings will include payments by way of occupational or personal pension. The earnings of a separated spouse affect the increase of retirement pension if they exceed £31.25 a week.

Unemployment, sickness or invalidity benefit is payable to men between 65 and 70, and women between 60 and 65 who have not claimed their retirement pension and who would have been entitled to a retirement pension if they had claimed at pension age. This applies in the case of sickness and invalidity benefit if incapacity for work is the result of an industrial accident or prescribed disease. These rates of benefit for people over pension age are shown in leaflet NI 196. A retirement pension will be increased by the amount of any invalidity allowance the pensioner was getting within the period of eight weeks and one day before reaching minimum pension age but this will be offset against any Additional Pension or Guaranteed Minimum Pension. An age addition of 25p per week is payable if a retirement pensioner is aged 80 or over.

GRADUATED RETIREMENT BENEFIT

Graduated National Insurance contributions were first payable from April 1961 and were calculated as a percentage of earnings between certain bands. They were discontinued in April 1975. Any graduated pension which an employed person over 18 and under 70 (65 for a woman) had earned by paying graduated contributions will be paid when the contributor claims retirement pension or at 70 (65 for a woman), in addition to any retirement pension for which he or she qualifies.

Graduated retirement benefit is at the rate of 7.35p a week (April 1993) for each 'unit' of graduated contributions paid by the employee (half a unit or more counts as a whole unit). A unit of contributions is £7.50 for men and £9.00 for women of graduated contributions paid.

A wife can get a graduated pension in return for her own graduated contributions, but not for her husband's. A widow, or a widower whose wife died after 5 April 1979 when they were both over pensionable age, gets a graduated addition to his/her retirement pension equal to half of any graduated additions earned by his/her late spouse, plus any additions earned by his/her own graduated contributions. If a person

defers making a claim beyond 65 (60 for a woman), entitlement may be increased by one seventh of a penny per £1 of its weekly rate for each complete week of deferred retirement, as long as the retirement is deferred for a minimum of seven weeks.

RATES OF BENEFITS
from week commencing 6 April 1993

	Weekly rate
Unemployment Benefit: standard rate	
Person under pension age	£44.65
Increase for wife/other adult dependant	27.55
*Person over pension age	56.10
Increase for wife/other adult dependant	33.70
Sickness Benefit: standard rate	
Person under pension age	42.70
Increase for wife/other adult dependant	26.40
*Person over pension age	53.80
Increase for wife/other adult dependant	32.30
Invalidity Pension	
Person (under or over pension age)	56.10
Increase for wife or adult dependant	33.70
Invalidity Allowance: maximum amount payable	
Higher rate	11.95
Middle rate	7.50
Lower rate	3.75
Maternity Allowance	43.75
Widow's Benefits	
Widow's Payment (lump sum)	1,000.00
*Widowed Mother's Allowance	56.10
*Widow's Pension	56.10
Retirement pension: categories A and B	
Single person	56.10
Increase for wife or adult dependant	33.70

*These benefits attract an increase for each dependent child (in addition to child benefit) of £9.80 for the first or only child and £10.95 for each subsequent child

NON-CONTRIBUTORY BENEFITS

CHILD BENEFIT

Child benefit is payable for virtually all children aged under 16, and for those aged 16 to 18 who are studying full-time up to and including A-level or equivalent standard. It is also payable for a short period if the child has left school recently and is registered for work or youth training at a careers office.

ONE PARENT BENEFIT

This benefit may be paid to a person in receipt of Child Benefit who is responsible for bringing up one or more children on his/her own. It is a flat rate non-means tested, non-contributory benefit payable for the eldest child.

GUARDIAN'S ALLOWANCE

Where the parents of a child are dead, the person who has the child in his/her family may claim a guardian's allowance in addition to child benefit. The allowance, in exceptional circumstances, is payable on the death of only one parent.

INVALID CARE ALLOWANCE

Invalid care allowance is payable to persons of working age, who are not gainfully employed because they are regularly and substantially engaged in caring for a severely disabled person who is receiving attendance allowance, the middle or highest rate of disability living allowance or constant attendance allowance with either a war or services pension, industrial disablement workman's compensation, or an allowance under the Pneumoconiosis, Byssinosis and Miscellaneous Diseases Benefit Scheme.

SEVERE DISABLEMENT ALLOWANCE

Persons under pensionable age who have been continuously incapable of work for a period of at least 28 weeks but who do not qualify for a contributory invalidity pension may be entitled to severe disablement allowance. People who first become incapable of work after their twentieth birthday must be at least 80 per cent disabled.

ATTENDANCE ALLOWANCE

This is payable to disabled people over 65 who need a lot of care or supervision because of physical or mental disability for a period of at least six months. People not expected to live for six months because of an illness do not have to wait six months. The allowance has two rates: the lower rate is for day or night care, and the higher rate is for day and night care.

DISABILITY LIVING ALLOWANCE

This is payable to disabled people under 65 who have personal care and mobility needs because of an illness or disability for a period of at least three months. People not expected to live for six months because of an illness do not have to wait three months. The allowance has two components: the care component, which has three rates of help, and the mobility component, which has two rates. The amount payable depends on the care and mobility needs of the claimant. The mobility component is payable only to those aged five or over.

DISABILITY WORKING ALLOWANCE

This is a tax-free, income-related benefit for people who are working 16 hours a week or more but have an illness or disability which puts them at a disadvantage in getting a job. To qualify a person must be aged 16 or over and must, at the date of the claim, have one of the 'qualifying benefits', such as Disability Living Allowance. The amount payable depends on the size of the family and weekly income. DWA is not payable if any savings exceed £16,000.

NON-CONTRIBUTORY RETIREMENT PENSION – CATEGORIES C AND D

A Category C pension is provided, subject to a residence test, for persons who were over pensionable age on 5 July 1948, and for women whose husbands are so entitled if they are over pension age, with increases for adult and child dependants. A Category D pension is provided for others when they reach 80 if they are not already getting a retirement pension of any category or if they are getting that pension at less than these rates. An age addition of 25p per week is payable if persons entitled to retirement pension are aged 80 or over.

RATES OF BENEFITS

from week commencing 6 April, 1993

	Weekly rate
Child Benefit (first child)	£10.00
Each subsequent child	8.10
One Parent Benefit	
First or only child of certain lone parents	6.05
Guardian's Allowance (eldest child)	9.80
Each subsequent child	10.95

	Weekly rate
*Severe Disablement Allowance	
†Basic rate	£33.70
Under 40	11.95
40–49	7.50
50–59	3.75
Increase for wife/other adult dependant	20.15
*Invalid Care Allowance	33.70
Increase for wife/other adult dependant	20.15
Attendance Allowance	
Higher rate	44.90
Lower rate	30.00
Disability Living Allowance	
Care component	
Higher rate	44.90
Middle rate	30.00
Lower rate	11.95
Mobility component	
Higher rate	31.40
Lower rate	11.95
Disability Working Allowance	
Single person	43.95
Couple or single parent	60.95
Child aged under 11	10.75
aged 11–15	17.85
aged 16–17	22.20
aged 18	31.00
‡*Applicable amount* (income threshold)	
Single person	41.40
Couple or single parent	69.00
Retirement Pension: Categories *C and D	
Single person	33.70
Increase for wife/other adult dependant	20.15
(not payable with Category D pension)	

* These benefits attract an increase for each dependent child (in addition to child benefit) of £9.80 for the first or only child and £10.95 for each subsequent child
† The age addition applies to the age when incapacity began
‡ 70 pence is deducted from the maximum DWA payable (this is obtained by adding up the appropriate allowance for each person in the family) for every pound coming in each week over the appropriate applicable amount. Where weekly income is below the applicable amount, maximum DWA is payable

INCOME SUPPORT

Income Support is a benefit for those aged 18 and over (although certain vulnerable 16- and 17-year-olds may be eligible) whose income is inadequate and who are unemployed. Others who may be eligible include people who are: over 60; bringing up children alone; unable to work through sickness; caring for a disabled person; or working part-time. Except in special cases Income Support is not available to those who work for more than 16 hours per week or who have a partner who works for more than 16 hours per week.

Income Support is not payable if the claimant, or claimant and partner, have capital or savings in excess of £8,000. The rate of benefits is affected by possession of capital or savings in excess of £3,000 and may be affected by a claimant's earnings.

Sums payable depend on fixed allowances laid down by law for people in different circumstances. Special rates may apply to some people living in residential care or nursing homes. Details are available from local social security offices.

Applications for Income Support are made on form IS1, available from post offices; Income Support claim forms, available from social security offices; or on form B1 (for the unemployed), available from unemployment benefit offices. If both partners are entitled to Income Support, either may claim it for the couple. People receiving Income Support will be able to receive Housing Benefit, help with mortgage or home loan interest and help with health care. They may also be eligible for help with exceptional expenses, from the Social Fund. Leaflet IS20 gives a detailed explanation of Income Support.

INCOME SUPPORT PREMIUMS

Income Support Premiums are additional weekly payments for those with special needs. They are payable as part of the Income Support scheme. People qualifying for more than one premium will normally only receive the highest single premium for which they qualify. However Family Premium, Disabled Child's Premium, Severe Disability Premium and Carer Premium are payable in addition to other premiums.

People with children qualify for a Family Premium if they have at least one child; a Disabled Child's Premium if they have a child who receives Attendance Allowance or certain components of Disability Living Allowance or is registered blind; or a Lone Parent Premium if they are bringing up one or more children alone. If someone receives Invalid Care Allowance, they qualify for the Carer Premium.

Long-term sick or disabled people qualify for a Disability Premium if they or their partner are receiving certain benefits because they are disabled or cannot work; are registered blind; or if the claimant, but not their partner, has been sending in doctor's statements for at least 28 weeks stating inability to work through sickness. If someone is living alone and they are in receipt of Attendance Allowance or Disability Living Allowance, without anyone receiving Invalid Care Allowance for looking after them, they may qualify for a Severe Disability Premium in addition to a Disability Premium.

People qualify for a Pensioner Premium if they or their partner are aged between 60 and 79, and for a Higher Pensioner Premium if they or their partner are aged 80 or over. A Higher Pensioner Premium is also payable to people aged between 60 and 79 who receive Attendance Allowance, Mobility Allowance, Invalidity Benefit or Severe Disablement Allowance, or who are registered blind. A Higher Pensioner Premium may be paid as well as a Severe Disability Premium. Enhanced Pensioner Premium is payable to pensioners aged between 75 and 79 in addition to Pensioner Premium.

RATES OF BENEFIT

from week commencing 6 April 1993

	Weekly rate
Income Support	
Single people	
aged 16–17	£26.45
aged 16–17 (certain circumstances)	34.80
aged 18–24	34.80
aged 25 and over	44.00
aged 18 and over and a single parent	44.00
Couples*	
both under 18	52.40
both aged 18 or over	69.00
For each child in a family	
under 11	15.05
aged 11–15	22.15
†aged 16–17	26.45
†aged 18 and over	34.80

	Weekly rate
Premiums	
Family Premium	9.65
Disabled Child's Premium	18.45
Lone Parent Premium	4.90
Disability Premium	
Single	18.45
Couple	26.45
Severe Disability Premium	
Single	33.70
Couple (one person qualified)	33.70
Couple (both qualified)	67.40
Pensioner Premium	
Single	17.30
Couple	26.25
Higher Pensioner Premium	
Single	23.55
Couple	33.70
Enhanced Pensioner Premium	
Single	19.30
Couple	29.00

*Where one or both partners are aged under 18, their personal allowance will depend on their situation
†If in full-time education up to A-level or equivalent standard

FAMILY CREDIT

Family Credit is a tax-free benefit for working families with children. It is not a loan and does not have to be paid back. To qualify, a family must include at least one child under 16 (under 19 if in full-time education up to A-level or equivalent standard), and the claimant, or partner (if there is one), must be working for at least 16 hours per week. It does not matter which partner is working and they may be employed or self-employed. The right to Family Credit does not depend on NI contributions and the same rates of benefit are paid to one- and two-parent families. Family Credit is not payable if the claimant, or claimant and partner, have capital or savings in excess of £8,000. The rate of benefit is affected if capital or savings in excess of £3,000 are held. The rate of benefit payable depends upon the claimant's (and partner's) net income (excluding Child Benefit), number of children, and children's ages. Family Credit, One Parent Benefit, and the first £15.00 of any maintenance in payment are paid for 26 weeks and the amount payable will usually remain the same throughout this period, regardless of change of circumstances. Payment is made weekly via post offices or every four weeks directly into a bank or building society account. Family Credit is claimed by post. A claim pack FC1 which includes a claim form can be obtained at a post office or social security office or call the Family Credit Helpline on 0253-500050. In two-parent families the woman should claim.

RATES OF BENEFIT

from week commencing 6 April 1993

The maximum amount will be payable where net income is no more than £69.00 per week. Where net income exceeds that amount, the maximum credit is reduced by 70 per cent of the excess and the result is the Family Credit payable. The maximum rate consists of:

	Weekly rate
Adult credit (for one or two parents)	£42.50
plus for each child	
aged under 11	10.75
aged 11–15	17.85
aged 16–17	22.20
aged 18	31.00

CLAIMS AND QUESTIONS

With a few exceptions, claims and questions relating to Social Security benefits are decided by statutory authorities who act independently of the Department of Social Security and Department of Employment.

The first of the statutory authorities, the Adjudication Officer, determines entitlement to benefit. A client who is dissatisfied with that decision has the right of appeal to a Social Security Appeal Tribunal. There is a further right of appeal to a Social Security Commissioner against the Tribunal's decision but leave to appeal must first be obtained. Appeals to the Commissioner must be on a point of law. Provision is also made for the determination of certain questions by the Secretary of State for Social Services.

Disablement questions are decided by adjudicating medical authorities or Medical Appeal Tribunals. Appeal to the Commissioner against a tribunal's decision is with leave and on a point of law only.

Leaflet NI246, which is available from social security offices, explains how to appeal, and leaflet NI260 is a guide to reviews and appeals.

THE SOCIAL FUND

The Social Fund helps people with expenses which are difficult to meet from regular income. Regulated Maternity, Funeral and Cold Weather payments are decided by Adjudication Officers and are not cash-limited. Discretionary Community Care Grants, and Budgeting and Crisis Loans are decided by Social Fund Officers and come out of a yearly budget which is allocated to each district (1993–4, grants £95 million; loans £250 million).

REGULATED PAYMENTS

Maternity Payments

A payment of up to £100 for each baby expected, born or adopted. It is payable to people on Income Support and Family Credit and is non-repayable.

Funeral Payments

Payable for reasonable funeral expenses incurred by people receiving Income Support, Family Credit or Housing Benefit. It is recoverable from the estate of the deceased.

Cold Weather Payments

£6 for any consecutive seven days when the average temperature is 0°C or below. Paid to people on Income Support who are pensioners, disabled or parents with a child under the age of five. It is non-repayable.

DISCRETIONARY PAYMENTS

Community Care Grants

They are intended to help people on Income Support to move into the community or avoid institutional care; ease exceptional pressures on families; and/or meet certain essential travelling expenses. They are usually non-repayable.

Budgeting Loans

These are interest-free loans to people who have been receiving Income Support for at least six months, for intermittent expenses that may be difficult to budget for.

Crisis Loans

These are interest-free loans to anyone, whether receiving benefit or not, who is without resources in an emergency, where there is no other means of preventing serious risk or damage to health or safety.

Loans are normally repaid over a period of up to 78 weeks at 15, 10 or 5 per cent of Income Support (less housing costs), depending on other commitments.

SAVINGS

Savings over £500 (£1,000 for people aged 60 or over) are taken into account for Maternity and Funeral Payments, Community Care Grants and Budgeting Loans. All savings are taken into account for crisis loans.

APPEALS AND REVIEWS

For regulated payment there is a right of appeal to an independent Social Security Appeal and thereafter to a Social Security Commissioner. For discretionary payments there is a review system where persons can ask for a review at the local office with a further right of review to an independent Social Fund Inspector.

INDUSTRIAL INJURIES, DISABLEMENT AND DEATH BENEFITS

The Industrial Injuries scheme, administered under the Social Security Contributions and Benefits Act 1992, provides a range of benefits designed to compensate for disablement resulting from an industrial accident (i.e. an accident arising out of and in the course of an employed earner's employment) or from a prescribed disease due to the nature of a person's employment. Rates of benefit are increased periodically.

BENEFITS

Disablement Benefit is normally payable 15 weeks (90 days) after the date of accident or onset of disease if the employed earner suffers from loss of physical or mental faculty such that the resulting disablement is assessed at not less than 14 per cent. The amount of disablement benefit payable varies according to the degree of disablement (in the form of a percentage) assessed by an adjudicating medical authority or medical appeal tribunal.

Disablement assessed at less than 14 per cent does not normally attract basic benefit except for certain chest diseases. A weekly pension is payable where the assessment of disablement is between 14 and 100 per cent (assessments of 14 to 19 per cent are payable at the 20 per cent rate). Payment can be made for a limited period or for life.

The basic rates are applicable to adults and to juveniles entitled to an increase for a child or adult dependant; other juveniles receive lower rates.

Basic rates of pension are not related to the pensioner's loss of earning power, and are payable whether he/she is in work or not. There is provision for increases of pension if the pensioner requires constant attendance or if his/her disablement is exceptionally severe. A pensioner may draw SSP, sickness or invalidity benefit as appropriate, in addition to disablement pension, during spells of incapacity for work.

Regulations impose certain obligations on clients and beneficiaries and on employers, including, in the case of clients for disablement benefit, that of submitting themselves for medical examination.

SUPPLEMENTARY ALLOWANCES

Special schemes under the Industrial Injuries and Diseases (Old Cases) Act 1975 provide supplementary allowances to those entitled to receive weekly payments of workmen's compensation for loss of earnings due to injury at work, or disease contracted during employment before 5 July 1948 when the Industrial Injuries scheme was introduced. Other schemes under the Act provide allowances to those who contracted slowly-developing diseases during employment before July 1948 where neither workmen's compensation nor Industrial Injuries Benefits are payable. A lump sum death benefit of up to £300 may also be payable to a dependant of such a person. Leaflet NI196 provides details relating to these allowances.

RATES OF BENEFITS

from April 1993

	Weekly rate
Disablement Benefit/Pension	
Degree of disablement	
100 per cent	£91.60
90	82.44
80	73.28
70	64.12
60	54.96
50	45.80
40	36.64
30	27.48
20	18.32
†Unemployability supplement	56.10
Addition for adult dependant (subject to earnings rule)	33.70
Reduced earnings allowance (maximum)	35.36
Constant Attendance allowance (normal maximum rate)	36.70
Exceptionally severe disablement allowance	36.70

*There is a weekly benefit for those under 18 with no dependants which is set at a lower rate
†This benefit attracts an increase for each dependent child (in addition to child benefit) of £9.80 for the first child and £10.95 for each subsequent child

CLAIMS AND QUESTIONS

Provision is made for the determination of certain questions by the Secretary of State for Social Security, and of 'disablement questions' by a medical board (or a single doctor) or, on appeal, by a medical appeal tribunal. An appeal on a point of law against a medical appeal tribunal decision is determined by the Social Security Commissioner.

Claims for benefit and certain questions arising in connection with a claim for or award of benefit (e.g. whether the accident arose out of and in the course of the employment) are determined by an adjudication officer appointed by the Secretary of State, or a Social Security Appeal Tribunal, or in certain circumstances, on further appeal, by the Commissioners.

War Pensions

War pensions are awarded under The Naval, Military and Air Forces, Etc. (Disablement and Death) Service Pensions Order 1983, which was a consolidation of the previous Royal Warrants, Orders in Council and Orders by Her Majesty.

The Department of Social Security (DSS) awards war pensions to members of the armed forces in respect of the periods 4 August 1914 to 30 September 1921 and subsequent to 3 September 1939 (including present members of the armed forces). There is also a scheme for civilians and civil defence workers in respect of the 1939-45 war, and other schemes for groups such as merchant seamen, and Polish armed forces who served under British command.

War pensions for the period 1 October 1921 to 2 September 1939 are dealt with by the Ministry of Defence, which is also responsible for the Armed Forces Pension Scheme.

PENSIONS

War disablement pension is awarded for the disabling effects of any injury, wound or disease which is attributable to, or has been aggravated by, conditions of service in the armed forces. It cannot be paid until the serviceman or woman has left the armed forces.

Disablement is assessed by comparison of the disabled person's health with that of a normal, healthy person of the same age and sex, without taking into account the disabled person's earning capacity or occupation, and is expressed on a percentage scale up to 100 per cent. Disablement of 20 per cent and above, for which a pension is awarded, is assessed in steps of 10 per cent. Maximum assessment does not necessarily imply total incapacity. For assessment of less than 20 per cent a lump sum is payable. No award is made where disablement in respect of noise-induced sensorineural hearing loss is assessed at less than 20 per cent.

The Dependency Allowance, formerly payable in respect of a wife or child, was abolished in April 1992 and an equivalent amount incorporated into the basic War Disablement Pension.

War widow's pension is awarded where death occurs as a result of service or where a war disablement pensioner was receiving constant attendance allowance at the time of his death, or would have been receiving it if he were not in hospital, in which case his widow has automatic entitlement to a war widow's pension, regardless of the cause of death.

Additional allowances are payable for dependent children, in addition to child benefit.

A reduced weekly rate is payable to war widows of men below the rank of Lieutenant-Colonel who are under the age of 40, without children and capable of maintaining themselves. This is increased to the standard rate at age 40.

Rank additions and gratuities to disablement and widow's pensions may be paid where the rank held was above that of private (or equivalent).

CLAIMS

Where a claim is made no later than seven years after the termination of service, the client does not have to prove that the disablement or death on which the claim is based is related to service and receives the benefit of any reasonable doubt. Where a claim is made more than seven years after the termination of service the claimant has to show that disablement or death is related to service. However, the claim succeeds if reliable evidence is produced which raises a reasonable doubt whether or not disablement or death is related to service. There is no time limit for making a claim for war pension.

SUPPLEMENTARY ALLOWANCES

A number of supplementary allowances may be awarded to a war pensioner which are intended to meet the various needs such as mobility, unemployability, constant nursing care, which may result from disablement or death and take account of its particular effect on the pensioner or spouse.

The principal supplementary allowances are:

Unemployability supplement – with additional allowances for dependants, this may be paid to a war pensioner whose pensioned disablement is so serious as to make him unemployable. In addition, an invalidity allowance may be payable if the incapacity for work began more than five years before normal retirement age.

Allowance for lowered standard of occupation – this may be awarded to a partially disabled pensioner whose pensioned disablement permanently prevents him from following his pre-service occupation and from doing another job of equivalent financial standard. The allowance, together with the basic war disablement pension, must not exceed pension at the 100 per cent rate.

Constant attendance allowance – this may be awarded if the pensioner is receiving a pension at the 80 per cent rate or more and needs a great deal of care because of the disability.

Widow's age allowance – this is paid at three different rates according to age, 65–69, 70–79 and over 80.

Widow's child's allowance – this may be paid in addition to child benefit.

Other supplementary allowances include exceptionally severe disablement allowance, severe disablement occupational allowance, mobility supplement, comforts allowance, clothing allowance, age allowance and education allowance. There is a supplementary rent allowance available on a war widow's pension.

Decisions on supplementary allowances are made on a discretionary basis on behalf of the Secretary of State and there is no provision for a statutory right of appeal against them. However, war pensioners may discuss any aspect of their pension position with their local War Pensions Committee, which may be able to arrange help or make representations to the DSS.

WAR PENSIONERS ABROAD

The DSS is responsible for the payment of war pensions, and, where necessary, meeting the cost of treatment for accepted disablement, to pensioners who reside overseas. They receive the same pension rates as war pensioners in this country and benefit from the same annual upratings.

SOCIAL SECURITY BENEFITS

When a war disablement pensioner is sick, unemployed or retired, the appropriate social security benefits are paid in addition to the basic war disablement pension.

Any sickness, invalidity, unemployment benefit or retirement pension for which a war widow qualifies on her own contributions, and any graduated retirement benefit, or additional earnings related pension inherited from her husband, can be paid in addition to her war widow's pension.

A war pensioner or war widow who claims Income Support, Family Credit or Disability Working Allowance has the first £10 of pension disregarded. A similar provision operates for housing benefit and council tax benefit; but the local authority may, at its discretion, disregard any or all of the balance.

PENSIONS APPEAL TRIBUNALS

There are independent Pensions Appeal Tribunals, set up by the Lord Chancellor's office, which hear appeals against the decisions of the DSS on entitlement, and assessment of disablement, in respect of the 1939–45 war and subsequent service cases. There are no time limits within which an entitlement appeal must be made but there are time limits within which an assessment appeal should be made. However, there are now no rights of appeal in the 1914–21 war disablement cases, the great majority of which were given final assessment in the 1920s with a 12 months' right of appeal at the time. An appeal by a 1914 war widow must be made within twelve months of the date on which the rejection of the claim is notified.

WAR PENSIONERS WELFARE SERVICE

The DSS operates a war pensioners welfare service to advise and assist war pensioners and their widows on any matters affecting their welfare. Welfare officers are attached to War Pensioners' Welfare Offices located in the major towns, and work closely with central and local government agencies as well as the various ex-service organizations. The service is available on call to any war pensioner or war widow who needs it.

RATES OF PENSIONS AND ALLOWANCES

from week commencing 6 April 1993

	Weekly rates
War Disablement pension	
(for Private or equivalent rank)	
Degree of disablement:	
100 per cent	£97.20
90 per cent	87.48
80 per cent	77.76
70 per cent	68.04
60 per cent	58.32
50 per cent	48.60
40 per cent	38.88
30 per cent	29.16
20 per cent	19.44
Unemployability supplement	
Personal allowance	59.55
Increase for wife/other adult dependant	33.70
Increase for first child	9.80
Increase for other children	10.95
Allowance for lowered standard of occupation	
(maximum)	36.64
Widow's pension	
(widow of Private or equivalent rank)	
Standard rate	72.90
Increase for first child	13.85
Increase for other children	15.00
Childless widow under 40	16.83
Widow's age allowance	
aged 65–69	8.35
aged 70–79	16.10
aged 80 and over	23.95

The current rates of all war pensions and allowances are listed in leaflet MPL154 *Rates of War Pensions and Allowances*, obtainable from War Pensioners Welfare Offices or the Leaflets Unit, PO Box 21, Stanmore, Middx. HA7 1AY, or phone the War Pension Helpline on 0253-858858.

New Towns in Great Britain

COMMISSION FOR THE NEW TOWNS
Glen House, Stag Place, London SW1E 5AJ
Tel 071-828 7722

The Commission was established under the New Towns Act 1959. Its remit is to:
(a) take over and, with a view to its eventual disposal, to hold, manage and turn to account the property of development corporations transferred to the Commission
(b) dispose of property so transferred and any other property held by it, as soon as it considers it expedient to do so
In carrying out its remit the Commission must have due regard to the convenience and welfare of persons residing, working or carrying on business there and, until disposal, the maintenance and enhancement of the value of the land held and return obtained from it.

The Commission has such responsibilities in Basildon, Bracknell, Central Lancashire, Corby, Crawley, Harlow, Hatfield, Hemel Hempstead, Milton Keynes, Northampton, Peterborough, Redditch, Skelmersdale, Stevenage, Telford, Warrington and Runcorn, Washington, and Welwyn Garden City. These properties are administered through four regional offices.

The Commission has minimal responsibilities (principally financial and litigation) in Aycliffe and Peterlee, and Cwmbran following the wind-up of their development corporations in 1988.

Chairman, Sir Neil Shields, MC
Deputy Chairman, The Lord Finsberg, MBE
Members, R. B. Caws, CBE; W. J. Mackenzie, OBE;
Sir Gordon Roberts, CBE; The Lord Bellwin; Sir Brian Jenkins, GBE; M. H. Mallinson; R. W. P. Luff;
F. C. Graves, OBE; J. Trustram Eve; Ms W. Luscombe;
Lady Marsh
Chief Executive, N. J. Walker

REGIONAL OFFICES

NORTH (Central Lancashire, Skelmersdale, Warrington and Runcorn, Washington, Aycliffe and Peterlee) –
Office, New Town House, Buttermarket Street, Warrington WA1 2LF. Tel: 0925-51144. *Director*, J. Leigh
MILTON KEYNES – *Office*, Saxon Court, 502 Avebury Boulevard, Central Milton Keynes MK9 3HS. Tel: 0908-692692. *Director*, J. Napleton
WEST MIDLANDS (Redditch, Telford) – *Office*, Jordan House West, Hall Court, Hall Park Way, Telford TF3 4NN. Tel: 0952-293131. *Director*, C. Mackrell

SOUTH (Basildon, Bracknell, Corby, Crawley, Harlow, Hatfield, Hemel Hempstead, Northampton, Peterborough, Stevenage, Welwyn Garden City) – *Office*, Glen House, Stag Place, London SW1E 5AJ. Tel: 071-828 7722. *Director*, G. D. Johnston

DEVELOPMENT CORPORATIONS

WALES
DEVELOPMENT BOARD FOR RURAL WALES – Formed 1977. *Chairman*, G. Davies. *Offices*, Ladywell House, Newtown, Powys SY16 1JB. Tel: 0686-626965

SCOTLAND
CUMBERNAULD, Strathclyde – Formed 1956. *Chairman*, D. W. Mitchell, CBE. *Chief Executive*, D. Millan. *Headquarters*, Cumbernauld House, Cumbernauld G67 3JH. Area, 7,788 acres. Population, 50,600. Estimated eventual population, 60,000
EAST KILBRIDE, Strathclyde – Formed 1947. *Chairman*, J. A. Denholm, CBE. *Managing Director*, J. C. Shaw. *Offices*, Atholl House, East Kilbride, Glasgow G74 1LU. Area, 10,250 acres. Population, 70,300. Estimated eventual population, 71,600
GLENROTHES, Fife – Formed 1948. *Chairman*, Prof. C. Blake, CBE. *General Manager*, J. A. F. McCombie. *Offices*, Balgonie Road, Markinch, Glenrothes KY7 6AH. Area, 5,760 acres. Population, 38,950. Estimated eventual population, 48,000
IRVINE, Ayrshire – Formed, 1966. *Chairman*, M. Crichton. *Managing Director*, Brig. R. A. Rickets. *Offices*, Perceton House, Irvine, Ayrshire KA11 2AL. Area, 16,000 acres. Population, 56,000. Estimated eventual population, 70,000
LIVINGSTON, West Lothian – Formed 1962. *Chairman*, R. S. Watt, CBE. *Chief Executive*, J. A. Pollock. *Offices*, Sidlaw House, Almondvale, Livingston, West Lothian EH54 6QA. Area, 6,868 acres. Population, 44,800. Estimated eventual population, 70,000

The Water Industry

ENGLAND AND WALES

In England and Wales the Secretaries of State for the Environment and for Wales and the Director-General of Water Services are responsible for the general oversight of the industry and for ensuring that the private water companies fulfil their statutory obligation to provide water supply and sewerage services.

The Minister of Agriculture, Fisheries and Food and the Secretary of State for Wales are responsible for policy relating to land drainage, flood protection, sea defences and the protection and development of fisheries.

The National Rivers Authority is responsible for water quality and the control of pollution, the management of water resources and nature conservation. The Drinking Water Inspectorate and local authorities are responsible for the quality of drinking water.

THE WATER COMPANIES

Until the end of 1989, nine regional water authorities in England and the Welsh Water Authority in Wales were responsible for water supply and the development of water resources, sewerage and sewage disposal, pollution control, freshwater fisheries, flood protection, water recreation, and environmental conservation. The Water Act 1989 provided for the creation of a privatized water industry under public regulation.

Of the 99 per cent of the population of England and Wales who are connected to a public water supply, 75 per cent are supplied by the water companies (through their principal operating subsidiaries, the water service companies), which have replaced the regional water authorities. The remaining 25 per cent are supplied by statutory water companies which were already in the private sector. Most of these have now converted to public limited company (PLC) status. The ten water service companies are also responsible for sewerage and sewage disposal throughout England and Wales.

Water Service Companies

ANGLIAN WATER SERVICES LTD, Compass House, Chivers Way, Histon, Cambs. CB4 4ZY

DWR CYMRU (WELSH WATER), Cambrian Way, Brecon, Powys LD3 7HP

NORTHUMBRIAN WATER LTD, Abbey Road, Pity Me, Durham DH1 5FS

NORTH WEST WATER LTD, Dawson House, Liverpool Road, Great Sankey, Warrington WA5 3LW

SEVERN TRENT WATER LTD, 2297 Coventry Road, Sheldon, Birmingham B26 3PU

SOUTHERN WATER SERVICES LTD, Southern House, Yeoman Road, Worthing, W. Sussex BN13 3NX

SOUTH WEST WATER SERVICES LTD, Peninsula House, Rydon Lane, Exeter EX2 7HR

THAMES WATER UTILITIES LTD, Nugent House, Vastern Road, Reading RG1 8DB

WESSEX WATER SERVICES LTD, Wessex House, Passage Street, Bristol BS2 0JQ

YORKSHIRE WATER SERVICES LTD, West Riding House, 67 Albion Street, Leeds LS1 5AA

REGULATORY BODIES

The Director-General of Water Services is appointed by the Secretaries of State for the Environment and for Wales. Independent of ministers and directly accountable to Parliament, his main duties are to ensure that the water companies comply with the terms of their appointments (or licences) and to protect the interests of the consumer. All the water companies are subject to a system of price control which sets a limit on the average increase in their prices each year. The Office of Water Services (*see* page 366) was set up to support the director-general's activities.

An independent national body, the National Rivers Authority (*see* page 339) was established under the Water Act 1989 to take over the regulatory and river management functions of the regional water authorities. It has statutory duties and powers in relation to water resources, pollution control, flood defence, fisheries, recreation, conservation and navigation in England and Wales.

The Drinking Water Inspectorate (*see* page 304) was established under the Water Act 1989, and is responsible for assessing the quality of the drinking water supplied by all the water companies in England and Wales and for inspecting the companies themselves. The inspectors look at records, check operational manuals, visit laboratories and water treatment works, and question company officials. They also investigate any accidents affecting drinking water quality. The Chief Inspector presents an annual report to the Secretaries of State for the Environment and for Wales.

METHODS OF CHARGING

In England and Wales, most householders have up to now paid for domestic water supply and sewerage services through charges based on the assessed value of their property under the old domestic rating system. Industrial and most commercial users are charged according to consumption, which is recorded by meter.

The abolition of domestic rates necessitated new methods of charging the private consumer for water and sewerage services. The Water Industry Act 1991 gives the water companies until the end of the century to decide on and introduce a suitable method of charging. Three options under consideration are a flat-rate licence fee, property banding, and metering. Trials of domestic metering are currently taking place.

SCOTLAND

Overall responsibility for national water policy in Scotland rests with the Secretary of State for Scotland. Most aspects of water policy are administered through the Scottish Office Environment Department, but fisheries and certain aspects of land drainage are the responsibility of the Scottish Office Agriculture and Fisheries Department. The supply of water and sewerage services and the development of water resources are administered by separate authorities from those responsible for the control of water pollution.

Water supply and sewerage services are at present local authority responsibilities and are provided by the nine Regional Councils and the three Islands Councils.

In November 1992 the Government published a consultation paper which set out eight options for the future structure of water and sewerage services in Scotland, ranging from privatization to retention of the services in local authority control. Following the consultation, the Secretary of State announced in July 1993 that three public water authorities would be established to own and operate current water and sewerage assets and to arrange new investment to maximize private sector involvement. The authorities will be in place by April 1996, with a new independent representative body being set up to protect consumers' interests.

Seven river purification boards and the Islands Councils of Orkney, Shetland and the Western Isles have the specific duty of promoting the cleanliness of Scotland's rivers, lochs and coastal waters and conserving water resources. They are responsible for the prevention and control of pollution within their own areas.

The Central Scotland Water Development Board was established in 1967 with the main statutory function of developing new sources of water supply for the purpose of providing water in bulk to water authorities whose limits of supply are within the board's area, i.e. Central, Fife, Lothian, Strathclyde and Tayside Regional Councils.

Along with the council tax, which was introduced in April 1993, a council water charge is set by each Regional and Islands Council.

CENTRAL SCOTLAND WATER DEVELOPMENT BOARD, Balmore, Torrance, Glasgow G64 4AJ. *Director,* W. G. Mitchell

NORTHERN IRELAND

In Northern Ireland ministerial responsibility for water services lies with the Secretary of State for Northern Ireland. The Department of the Environment for Northern Ireland, operating through the Water Executive, is responsible for policy and co-ordination with regard to supply and distribution of water, and provision and maintenance of sewerage services.

The Water Executive is divided into four regions, the Eastern, Northern, Western and Southern Divisions. These are based in Belfast, Ballymena, Londonderry and Craigavon respectively.

On major issues the Department of the Environment for Northern Ireland seeks the views of the Northern Ireland Water Council, a body appointed to advise the Department on the exercise of its water and sewerage functions. The Council includes representatives from agriculture, angling, industry, commerce, tourism, trade unions and local government.

Usually householders do not pay directly for water and sewerage services; the costs of these services are allowed for in the Northern Ireland regional rate. Water consumed by industry, commerce and agriculture in excess of 100 cubic metres (22,000 gallons) per half year is charged through meters. Traders operating from industrially derated premises are required to pay for the treatment and disposal of the trade effluent which they discharge into the public sewerage system.

HM Coastguard

Founded in 1822, originally to guard the coasts against smuggling, HM Coastguard's role today is the very different one of guarding and saving life at sea. The Service is responsible for co-ordinating all civil marine search and rescue operations around the 2,500 mile coastline of Great Britain and Northern Ireland and 1,200 miles into the Atlantic. In addition, it co-operates with search and rescue organizations of neighbouring countries in western Europe and around the Atlantic seaboard. The Service maintains a 24-hour radar watch on the Dover Strait, providing a Channel navigation information service for all shipping in one of the busiest sea lanes in the world. The Service is administered by the Department of Transport.

Since 1978 HM Coastguard has been organized into six regions, each with a Regional Controller, operating from a Maritime Rescue Co-ordination Centre. Each region is subdivided into districts under District Controllers, operating from Maritime Rescue Sub-Centres. In all there are 21 of these centres. They are on 24-hour watch and are fitted with a comprehensive range of communications and rescue equipment. They are supported by some 350 smaller stations manned by Auxiliary Coastguards under the direction of Regulars, each of which keeps its parent centre fully informed of day-to-day casualty risk, particularly on the more remote danger spots around the coast.

Between 1 January and 31 December 1992, the 500 Regular and 4,000 Auxiliary Coastguards co-ordinated 8,532 incidents requiring search and rescue facilities, resulting in assistance being given to 14,528 persons. All distress telephone and radio calls are centralized on the 21 centres, which are on the alert for people or vessels in distress, shipping hazards and oil slicks. Using modern telecommunications equipment, including satellite, they can alert and co-ordinate the most appropriate rescue facilities; RNLI lifeboats, Royal Navy, RAF or Coastguard helicopters, fixed-wing aircraft, naval vessels, ships in the vicinity, or Coastguard shore and cliff rescue teams.

For those who regularly sail in local waters or make longer passages, the Coastguard Yacht and Boat Safety Scheme provides a valuable free service. Its aim is to give the Coastguard a record of the details of craft, their normal operating areas and their passage plans. Yacht and Boat Safety Scheme cards are available from all Coastguard stations, harbourmasters' offices, and most yacht clubs and marinas.

Members of the public who see an accident or a potentially dangerous incident on or around the coast should dial 999 and ask for the Coastguard.

Energy

COAL: SUPPLY AND DEMAND   *million tonnes*

	1986	1987	1988	1989	1990	1991
Supply						
Production of deep-mined coal	90.4	86.0	83.8	79.6	72.9	73.4
Production of opencast coal	14.3	15.8	17.9	18.7	18.1	18.6
Recovered slurry, fines, etc.	3.5	2.8	2.4	2.8	3.4	4.2
Imports	10.6	9.8	11.7	12.1	14.8	19.5
Change in colliery stocks	+0.3	−1.1	+0.7	+1.3	−0.9	+2.8
Change in stocks at opencast sites	−0.8	−1.5	+0.5	+1.5	−0.1	−0.8
Total supply	119.2	116.9	114.6	110.6	108.1	117.6
Home consumption						
Electricity supply industry	82.7	86.2	82.5	80.6	82.6	82.0
Coke ovens	11.1	10.9	10.9	10.8	10.9	10.0
Low temperature carbonization plants	1.0	1.0	0.8	0.8	0.8	0.8
Manufactured fuel plants	1.0	1.0	1.2	0.9	0.8	0.7
Railways	—	—	—	—	—	—
Collieries	0.3	0.2	0.2	0.1	0.1	0.1
Industry (disposals to users)	8.2	8.0	8.1	7.5	7.4	7.0
Domestic (disposals to users)	8.4	7.2	6.6	5.7	4.5	5.7
Public services	1.3	1.2	1.0	0.9	0.9	0.8
Miscellaneous	0.2	0.2	0.2	0.2	0.3	0.3
Total home consumption	114.2	115.9	111.5	107.6	108.3	107.5
Overseas shipments and bunkers	2.7	2.4	1.8	2.0	2.5	1.7
Total consumption and shipments	116.9	118.2	113.3	109.6	110.8	109.2
*Change in distributed stocks	+4.0	−2.8	+1.7	+0.4	−0.4	+3.6
†Balance	−1.8	+1.3	−0.4	+0.6	−2.3	+4.8

*Stock change excludes industrial and domestic stocks
†This is the balance between supply and consumption, shipments and changes in known distributed stocks

Source: HMSO - *Annual Abstract of Statistics 1993*

FUEL INPUT AND GAS OUTPUT: GAS SALES   *million therms*

	1986	1987	1988	1989	1990	1991
Fuel input to gas industry						
Petroleum (*million tonnes*)	0.1	0.1	—	—	—	—
*Petroleum gases	36	6	1	3	1	1
Natural gas	—	—	—	—	—	—
Coke oven gas	—	—	—	—	—	—
Total to gas works	55	20	6	3	1	1
Natural gas for direct supply	19,747	20,198	19,083	18,826	19,231	21,087
Total fuel input	19,802	20,218	19,089	18,829	19,232	21,083
Gas output and sales						
Gas output:						
Town gas	18	13	4	1	1	1
Natural gas supplied direct	19,775	20,205	19,083	18,826	19,231	21,087
Gross total available	19,793	20,218	19,087	18,827	19,232	21,088
Own use	−152	−137	−120	−101	−81	−103
†Statistical difference	−613	−708	−328	−377	−223	−691
Total sales	18,496	19,373	18,639	18,349	18,928	20,294
Analysis of gas sales						
Power stations	75	357	381	395	396	467
Final users:						
Iron and steel industry	419	465	446	467	461	404
Other industries	4,804	4,997	4,515	4,606	4,779‡	4,519
Domestic	10,242	10,500	10,255	9,914	10,250	11,395
Public administration	1,286	1,326	1,242	1,188	1,204	1,365
Agriculture	24	29	30	32	34	35
Miscellaneous	1,597	1,636	1,725	1,699	1,760	2,050

*Butane, propane, ethane and refinery tail gases
†Supply greater than recorded demand (−). Includes losses in distribution

‡Includes 27 million therms by independent gas suppliers
Source: HMSO - *Annual Abstract of Statistics 1993*

THE ELECTRICITY SUPPLY INDUSTRY

Under the Electricity Act 1989 twelve new public electricity supply companies were formed from the twelve Area Electricity Boards in England and Wales. These companies were floated on the stock market in 1990. Four new companies were formed from the Central Electricity Generating Board: three new generating companies (National Power PLC, Nuclear Electric PLC and PowerGen PLC) and the National Grid Company PLC. National Power PLC and PowerGen PLC were floated on the stock market in 1991, the Government retaining a 40 per cent holding in both companies.

In Scotland, there are three new companies: Scottish Power PLC, Scottish Hydro-Electric PLC and Scottish Nuclear Ltd. Flotation of Scottish Power PLC and Scottish Hydro-Electric PLC on the stock market took place in 1991.

A new trade and representational organization, the Electricity Association, was created by the newly formed British electricity companies; its principal subsidiaries were Electricity Association Services Ltd (for representational and professional services) and Electricity Association Technology Ltd (for distribution and utilization research, development and technology transfer). Electricity Association Technology Ltd (now renamed EA Technology Ltd) left the Electricity Association group of companies in April 1993.

ELECTRICITY ASSOCIATION SERVICES LTD, 30 Millbank, London SW1P 4RD. Tel: 071-344 5700. *Chief Executive*, R. Farrance
EA TECHNOLOGY LTD, Capenhurst, Chester CH1 6ES. Tel: 051-339 4181. *Managing Director*, Dr S. F. Exell

CEGB SUCCESSOR COMPANIES
THE NATIONAL GRID COMPANY PLC, National Grid House, Kirby Corner Road, Coventry CV4 8JY. Tel: 0203-537777. *Chief Executive*, B. Kerss
NATIONAL POWER PLC, Senator House, 85 Queen Victoria Street, London EC4V 4DP. Tel: 071-454 9494. *Chief Executive*, J. Baker
NUCLEAR ELECTRIC PLC, Barnett Way, Barnwood, Glos GL4 7RS. Tel: 0452-652222. *Chairman*, J. Collier
POWERGEN PLC, 53 New Broad Street, London EC2M 1JJ. Tel: 071-638 5742. *Chief Executive*, E. Walliss

REGIONAL ELECTRICITY COMPANIES
EASTERN ELECTRICITY PLC, PO Box 40, Wherstead, Ipswich IP2 9AQ
EAST MIDLANDS ELECTRICITY PLC, PO Box 4 North PDO, 398 Coppice Road, Arnold, Nottingham NG5 7HX
LONDON ELECTRICITY PLC, Templar House, 81–87 High Holborn, London WC1V 6NU
MANWEB PLC, Sealand Road, Chester CH1 4LR
MIDLANDS ELECTRICITY PLC, Mucklow Hill, Halesowen, W. Midlands B62 8BP
NORTHERN ELECTRIC PLC, Carliol House, Newcastle upon Tyne NE99 1SE
NORWEB PLC, Talbot Road, Manchester M16 0MQ
SEEBOARD PLC, Grand Avenue, Hove, E. Sussex BN3 2LS
SOUTHERN ELECTRIC PLC, Littlewick Green, Maidenhead, Berks SL6 3QB
SOUTH WALES ELECTRICITY PLC, St Mellons, Cardiff CF3 9XW
SOUTH WESTERN ELECTRICITY PLC, 800 Park Avenue, Aztec West, Almondsbury, Avon BS12 4SE
YORKSHIRE ELECTRICITY GROUP PLC, Scarcroft, Leeds LS14 3HS

SCOTTISH COMPANIES
SCOTTISH HYDRO-ELECTRIC PLC, 16 Rothesay Terrace, Edinburgh EH3 7SE. Tel: 031-225 1361. *Chief Executive*, R. Young
SCOTTISH NUCLEAR LTD, Minto Building, 6 Inverlair Avenue, Glasgow G44 4AD. Tel: 041-633 1166. *Chief Executive*, Dr R. C. Jeffrey
SCOTTISH POWER PLC, Cathcart House, Spean Street, Glasgow G44 4BE. Tel: 041-637 7177. *Chief Executive*, Dr I. Preston

GENERATION, SUPPLY AND CONSUMPTION
gigawatt-hours

	1990	1991
Electricity generated		
All generating companies: total	318,979	322,132
Conventional steam stations	245,732	245,227
Nuclear stations	65,747	70,543
Gas turbines and oil engines	432	355
Hydro-electric stations:		
Natural flow	5,080	4,482
Pumped storage	1,982	1,523
Other (mainly wind)	4	3
Electricity used on works: total	19,583	20,083
Major generating companies	17,891	18,420
Other generators	1,691	1,663
Electricity supplied (gross)		
All generating companies: total	299,396	302,050
Conventional steam stations	233,366	233,042
Nuclear stations	58,664	62,761
Gas turbines and oil engines	403	310
Hydro-electric stations:		
Natural flow	5,067	4,469
Pumped storage	1,892	1,465
Other (mainly wind)	3	3
Electricity used in pumping		
Major generating companies	2,626	2,109
Electricity supplied (net): total	296,770	299,942
Major generating companies	277,978	280,649
Other generators	18,792	19,293
Net imports	11,943	16,407
Electricity available	308,713	316,349
Losses in transmission, etc	24,293	25,508
Electricity consumption: total	284,420	290,841
Fuel industries	9,986	9,794
Final users: total	274,434	281,048
Industrial sector	100,643	99,570
Domestic sector	93,793	98,098
Other sectors	79,997	83,380

Source: HMSO - Annual Abstract of Statistics 1993

THE GAS INDUSTRY

The gas industry in the United Kingdom was nationalized in 1949 under the Gas Act 1948, and operated as the Gas Council. The Gas Act 1972 replaced the Gas Council with the British Gas Corporation and led to greater centralization of the industry. The British Gas Corporation was privatized in 1986 as British Gas PLC and remains the main supplier of gas in Great Britain.

The principal business of British Gas is the purchase, transmission and sale of natural gas to domestic, industrial and commercial customers in Great Britain. British Gas has hydrocarbon exploration and production operations offshore and onshore, both in Great Britain and overseas, and it has an interest in gas-related activities world-wide.

BRITISH GAS PLC, Rivermill House, 152 Grosvenor Road, London SW1V 3JL. Tel: 071-821 1444. *Chairman*, R. Evans, CBE; *Chief Executive*, C. H. Brown

REGIONS

The Regions are largely concerned with the management of the gas business locally, including distribution and sale of gas, installation and servicing of appliances, meter reading, and the maintenance of emergency services.

EASTERN, Star House, Potters Bar, Herts. EN6 2PD
EAST MIDLANDS, PO Box 145, De Montfort Street, Leicester LEI 9DB
NORTH-EASTERN, New York Road, Leeds LS2 7PE
NORTHERN, PO Box 1GB, Killingworth, Newcastle upon Tyne NE99 1GB
NORTH THAMES, North Thames House, London Road, Staines, Middx. TW18 4AE
NORTH-WESTERN, Welman House, Altrincham, Cheshire WA15 8AE
SCOTLAND, Granton House, 4 Marine Drive, Edinburgh EH5 1YB
SOUTH-EASTERN, Katherine Street, Croydon CR9 1JU
SOUTHERN, 80 St Mary's Road, Southampton SO9 7GL
SOUTH-WESTERN, Riverside, Temple Street, Keynsham, Bristol BS19 1EQ
WALES, Helmont House, Churchill Way, Cardiff CF1 4NB
WEST MIDLANDS, Wharf Lane, Solihull, W. Midlands B91 2JP

SUPPLY AND TRANSMISSION

British Gas obtains natural gas from fields on mainland Britain, in coastal waters and in the North Sea. It also imports gas from other countries. In 1992 total production from UK continental shelf fields of gas contracted to British Gas was 55,666 million cubic metres, of which 55,397 million cubic metres was offshore production and 289 million cubic metres was onshore production.

The mainland national transmission system is operated by British Gas, with other gas suppliers entering contracts with British Gas to use the system. British Gas operates six reception terminals. The length of mains in use in 1992 was 255,200 km: 242,900 km of distribution mains and 17,900 km of transmission mains.

SALES 1992

Total gas sold and used:	GWh
Domestic	330,100
Commercial	92,625
Industrial	132,081
Released	2,651
Used for own purposes	3,547
Total	561,004

Charges for domestic use from 1 Oct. 1992:	*pence*
Standing charge per day	10.10
Unit charges	*pence per kilowatt hour*
Annual consumption	
First 146,536 KWh	1.477
146,537–293,071 KWh	1.409
293,072–439,607 KWh	1.375
439,608–732,678 KWh	1.341

BRITISH GAS FINANCE

	1991	*£ million* 1992
Turnover		
UK gas supply	8,423	8,129
Overseas gas supply	879	883
Exploration and production	980	995
UK marketing activities	774	786
Other activities	105	184
Less: intra-group sales	(676)	(723)
Total	10,485	10,254
Operating costs include:		
UK gas supply (includes levy)	3,834	3,033
Overseas gas supply	581	567
Payroll costs	1,647	1,672
Current cost depreciation less replacement expenditure	786	772
Current cost working capital adjustments	88	50
Total	8,812	8,825
Current cost operating profit	1,673	1,429
Gearing adjustment	39	41
Net interest payable	(243)	(311)
Current cost profit before tax	1,469	846
Current cost profit after tax	913	475
Minority shareholders' interest	8	(2)
Current cost profit attributable to British Gas shareholders	921	473
Dividends	(571)	(613)
Current cost profit retained	350	(140)

Transport

GOODS TRANSPORT IN GREAT BRITAIN

	1986	1987	1988	1989	1990	1991
TOTAL TONNE KILOMETRES (*thousand millions*)	187.2	195.2	218.8	222.8	218.8	212.2
Road	105.4	113.3	130.2	137.8	136.3	130.0
Rail (British Rail only)	16.6	17.3	18.2	17.3	15.8	15.2
Water: coastwise oil products*	33.9	31.6	34.2	34.1	32.1	31.3†
Water: other*	20.9	22.5	25.1	23.8	23.6	24.6†
Pipelines (except gases)	10.4	10.5	11.1	9.8	11.0	11.1
TOTAL (*million tonnes*)	1,836	1,909	2,163	2,206	2,163	1,984
Road	1,473	1,542	1,758	1,812	1,749	1,600
Rail (British Rail only)	140	141	150	146	141	135
Water: coastwise oil products*	46	43	47	46	44	44†
Water: other*	98	100	109	109	108	100†
Pipelines (except gases)	79	83	99	93	121	105

*'Coastwise' includes all sea traffic within the UK, Isle of Man and Channel Islands. 'Other' means other coastwise plus inland waterway traffic and one-port traffic

†provisional
Source: HMSO – *Annual Abstract of Statistics 1993*

SEAPORT TRAFFIC OF GREAT BRITAIN   *Million gross tonnes*

	1986	1987	1988	1989	1990	1991
FOREIGN TRAFFIC: *Imports*						
Bulk fuel traffic	61.7	57.3	62.9	64.2	75.1	78.0
Other bulk traffic	37.3	42.0	45.0	47.0	45.1	43.1
Container and roll-on traffic	31.1	34.0	38.0	40.9	40.5	40.2
Semi-bulk traffic	15.8	16.9	18.9	18.1	17.3	15.5
Conventional traffic	1.5	1.6	1.6	1.2	1.8	1.3
All imports	147.4	151.8	166.4	171.4	179.8	178.1
FOREIGN TRAFFIC: *Exports*						
Bulk fuel traffic	101.9	100.2	91.1	72.9	80.3	84.7
Other bulk traffic	21.1	20.4	18.5	19.5	19.0	19.6
Container and roll-on traffic	22.1	23.9	26.5	29.4	30.8	32.4
Semi-bulk traffic	4.0	5.0	4.6	4.6	4.3	5.1
Conventional traffic	1.2	1.2	1.0	0.7	1.1	0.9
All exports	150.4	150.6	141.7	127.1	135.7	142.7
DOMESTIC TRAFFIC						
Bulk fuel traffic	112.3	108.3	115.5	108.5	101.7	102.1
Other bulk traffic	32.7	34.8	41.1	45.5	44.0	41.1
Container and roll-on traffic	6.2	7.3	7.6	8.1	8.0	8.2
Semi-bulk traffic	0.2	0.2	0.3	0.3	0.3	0.4
Conventional traffic	0.3	0.3	0.3	0.4	0.3	0.4
Non-oil traffic with UK offshore installations	3.3	3.5	3.9	4.2	5.5	4.8
All domestic traffic	154.9	154.4	168.8	166.9	159.8	157.0
TOTAL FOREIGN AND DOMESTIC TRAFFIC	452.7	456.8	476.9	465.4	475.3	477.8

Source: HMSO – *Annual Abstract of Statistics 1993*

PASSENGER TRANSPORT IN GREAT BRITAIN   *Thousand million passenger kilometres (estimated)*

		1986	1987	1988	1989	1990	1991†
TOTAL		568	604	640	684	694	689
Air		4	4	5	5	5	5
Rail*		37	39	41	40	41	38
Road:	Public service vehicles	47	47	46	47	46	45
	Cars, vans and taxis	467	501	536	581	591	590
	Motorcycles	8	7	7	6	6	6
	Pedal cycles	5	6	5	5	5	5

*Including London Regional Transport and Passenger Transport Executive railway systems

†provisional
Source: HMSO – *Annual Abstract of Statistics 1993*

AIR PASSENGERS BY TYPE OF OPERATOR 1992

	Total terminal & transit	*Scheduled		*Charter	
		Terminal	Transit	Terminal	Transit
ALL UK AIRPORTS: TOTAL	107,803,780	78,820,169	1,229,081	27,303,183	451,347
LONDON AREA AIRPORTS: TOTAL	69,744,368	57,921,836	309,313	11,364,742	148,477
Battersea Heliport	3,959	—	—	3,959	—
Gatwick	19,968,401	10,934,103	32,466	8,070,378	94,964
Heathrow	45,242,604	44,742,141	272,649	225,841	1,973
London City	186,175	183,334	22	2,819	—
Luton	1,976,179	443,185	1,402	1,499,875	31,717
Southend	16,460	419	—	16,011	30
Stansted	2,354,549	1,618,654	2,774	713,328	19,793
OTHER UK AIRPORTS: TOTAL	38,055,453	20,898,333	919,768	15,934,482	302,870
Aberdeen	2,182,117	1,250,502	27,924	902,980	711
Barrow-in-Furness	627	243	—	384	—
Belfast	2,257,361	1,793,853	715	447,422	15,371
Belfast City	612,110	611,076	—	1,034	—
Bembridge	77	—	—	59	18
Benbecula	34,499	31,735	1,733	1,031	—
Birmingham	3,827,659	2,003,288	153,163	1,648,320	22,888
Blackpool	109,815	68,887	1,009	39,767	152
Bournemouth	109,104	24,723	723	80,211	3,447
Bristol	1,068,604	343,231	28,600	682,679	14,094
Cambridge	23,329	19,266	—	4,063	—
Cardiff	698,623	127,704	19,480	525,232	26,207
Carlisle	955	—	—	934	21
Coventry	9,299	7,436	241	1,622	—
Dundee	21,362	11,188	8,307	1,859	8
East Midlands	1,264,782	450,898	3,837	799,644	10,403
Edinburgh	2,678,937	2,324,642	137,321	213,914	3,060
Exeter	174,372	73,868	875	93,347	6,282
Glasgow	4,785,181	3,114,876	75,699	1,554,169	40,437
Gloucester/Cheltenham	9,646	4,297	1,263	4,075	11
Hawarden	1,185	—	—	1,166	19
Humberside	174,131	82,877	22,233	67,713	1,308
Inverness	229,318	210,543	16,079	2,606	90
Islay	18,989	17,590	624	775	—
Isle of Man	475,365	455,243	15,205	4,375	542
Isles of Scilly–St Mary's	102,318	102,318	—	—	—
–Tresco	21,675	20,445	1,230	—	—
Kirkwall	115,486	98,593	9,822	6,399	672
Leeds/Bradford	708,868	481,255	1,299	217,949	8,365
Lerwick (Tingwall)	5,062	2,305	126	2,604	27
Liverpool	455,869	408,254	9,848	36,778	989
Londonderry	27,567	26,568	—	999	—
Lydd	4,592	2,546	—	2,046	—
Manchester	12,051,220	4,779,651	292,323	6,898,285	80,961
Manston	7,385	633	79	5,826	847
Newcastle	1,996,998	799,289	31,946	1,142,268	23,495
Norwich	189,215	131,843	4,932	51,314	1,126
Penzance Heliport	89,719	89,041	176	502	—
Plymouth	84,362	65,564	16,634	2,164	—
Prestwick	17,134	4,791	950	6,340	5,053
Scatsta	14,112	—	—	14,097	15
Shoreham	2,087	277	—	1,810	—
Southampton	404,954	383,682	997	20,098	177
Stornoway	85,898	85,627	36	235	—
Sumburgh	440,937	93,822	61	312,452	34,602
Teesside	336,628	255,440	25,486	54,274	1,428
Tiree	6,026	5,078	843	105	—
Unst	80,194	2,131	15	78,048	—
Wick	39,700	31,214	7,934	508	44
CHANNEL IS. AIRPORTS: TOTAL	2,484,976	2,275,469	54,446	153,297	1,764
Alderney	78,550	78,280	1	266	3
Guernsey	787,354	744,383	32,723	10,034	214
Jersey	1,619,072	1,452,806	21,722	142,997	1,547

*UK and overseas   Source: Civil Aviation Authority

AERODROMES/AIRPORTS

The following aerodromes in the UK, the Isle of Man and the Channel Islands are either state owned or licensed for use by civil aircraft. A number of unlicensed aerodromes not included in this list are also available for private use by special permission. Aerodromes designated as Customs airports are printed in small capitals. Customs facilities are available at certain other aerodromes by special arrangement.

BAA Owned by BAA PLC
H   Licensed for helicopters
HIAL Operated by Highland and Islands Airports Ltd
J   Military aerodromes – civil availability by prior permission
M   Owned by municipal authority
P   Private ownership
S   Government owned and operated

ENGLAND AND WALES
Aberporth, Dyfed   J
Andrewsfield, Essex
Barrow (Walney Island), Cumbria
Bedford/Thurleigh   J
Bembridge, IOW
Benson, Oxon   J
Beverley/Linley Hill, N. Humberside
BIGGIN HILL, Kent   P
BIRMINGHAM, W. Midlands   P
Blackbushe, Hants
BLACKPOOL, Lancs   P
Bodmin, Cornwall
Boscombe Down, Wilts   S
Bourn, Cambridge
BOURNEMOUTH, Dorset   P
BRISTOL, Avon   P
Brize Norton, Oxford   J
Brough, N. Humberside
Caernarfon, Gwynedd
CAMBRIDGE   P
CARDIFF, S. Glamorgan   P
Carlisle, Cumbria   M
Chichester (Goodwood), Sussex
Chivenor, Devon   J
Church Fenton, N. Yorks   J
Clacton, Essex
Compton Abbas, Dorset
Cosford, Wolverhampton   J
COVENTRY, W. Midlands   M
Cranfield, Beds
Cranwell, Lincs   J
Crowfield, Suffolk
Culdrose, Cornwall   J
Deenethorpe, Northants
Denham, Bucks
Dishforth, N. Yorks   J
Dunkeswell, Devon
Dunsfold, Surrey   M
Duxford, Cambs   M
Eaglescott, Devon
Earls Colne, Halstead
EAST MIDLANDS, Derbys   P

Elstree, Herts
EXETER, Devon
Fairoaks, Surrey
Farnborough, Hants   S
Fenland, Lincs
Filton, Bristol
Finningley, S. Yorks   J
Fowlmere, Cambs
Gloucestershire (Staverton)   P
Great Yarmouth (North Denes), Norfolk   H
Halfpenny Green, Staffs
Halton, Bucks   J
Hatfield, Herts
Haverfordwest, Dyfed   M
Hawarden, Clywd
Hucknall, Notts
HUMBERSIDE   P
Ipswich, Suffolk
Isle of Wight/Sandown
Land's End (St Just), Cornwall
Lashenden, Headcorn, Kent
Leavesden, Herts
LEEDS/BRADFORD, Yorks   P
Lee-on-Solent, Hants   J
Leicester, Leics
Linton-on-Ouse, Yorks   J
Little Gransden, Beds
LIVERPOOL, Merseyside   P
Llanbedr, Gwynedd   J
LONDON/CITY
LONDON/GATWICK   BAA
LONDON/HEATHROW   BAA
LONDON/STANSTED   BAA
London/Westland Heliport   H
LUTON, Beds   P
LYDD, Kent
Lyneham, Wilts   J
MANCHESTER   P
Manchester (Barton)
MANSTON, Kent   J
Marston Moor, York
Mona, Gwynedd   J
Netherthorpe, S. Yorks
NEWCASTLE, Tyne and Wear   P
Newton, Notts   J
Northampton (Sywell), Northants
Northolt, Middx   J
NORWICH, Norfolk   M
Nottingham, Notts
Old Sarum, Wilts
Oxford (Kidlington), Oxfordshire
Penzance, Cornwall   H
Perranporth, Cornwall
Peterborough (Conington)
Peterborough (Sibson), Cambs
PLYMOUTH (ROBOROUGH), Devon
Portland Naval, Dorset   JH
Redhill, Surrey
Retford/Gamston, Notts
Rochester, Kent
St Mawgan, Cornwall   J
Sandtoft, Humberside
Scilly Isles (St Mary's)   M
Seething, Norfolk
Shawbury, Shropshire   J
Sherburn-in-Elmet, N. Yorks
Shipdham, Norfolk
Shobdon, Herefordshire
SHOREHAM, W. Sussex   P

Silverstone, Northants
Sleap, Shropshire
SOUTHAMPTON/Eastleigh, Hants   P
SOUTHEND, Essex   P
Stapleford, Essex
Sturgate, Lincs
Swansea, W. Glam   M
TEESSIDE, Cleveland   P
Thruxton, Hants
Tresco, Isles of Scilly   H
Turweston, Northants
Valley, Gwynedd   J
Warton, Lancs
Wattisham, Suffolk   J
Wellesbourne Mountford, Warwick
Welshpool, Powys
Weston, Avon   H
White Waltham, Berks
Wickenby, Lincs
Woodford, Gtr Manchester
Woodvale, Merseyside   J
Wycombe Air Park (Booker), Bucks
Yeovil, Somerset
Yeovilton, Somerset   J

SCOTLAND
ABERDEEN (DYCE)   BAA
Barra, Hebrides
Benbecula, Hebrides   HIAL
Cumbernauld, Strathclyde
Dounreay (Thurso)   S
Dundee, Angus   M
Eday   M
EDINBURGH   BAA
Fair Isle
Fife/Glenrothes   M
Flotta, Orkneys
GLASGOW   BAA
Inverness (Dalcross)   HIAL
Islay (Port Ellen)   HIAL
Kirkwall   HIAL
Lerwick (Tingwall)   M
Leuchars, Fife   J
Machrihanish, Kintyre   J
North Ronaldsay, Orkneys   M
Papa Westray, Orkneys   M
Perth (Scone)
PRESTWICK,   BAA
Sanday, Orkneys   M
Scatsta
Stornoway, Hebrides   HIAL
Stronsay, Orkneys   M
SUMBURGH, Shetlands   HIAL
Tiree   HIAL
Unst, Shetlands   M
West Freugh, Dumfries   S
Westray, Orkneys   M
Whalsay, Shetlands
Wick   HIAL

NORTHERN IRELAND
BELFAST (ALDERGROVE)   S
Belfast (City)
Enniskillen (St Angelo)   P
Londonderry (Eglinton)   M
Newtownards

ISLANDS
ALDERNEY, CI   S
GUERNSEY, CI   S
JERSEY, CI   S
RONALDSWAY, IOM   S

RAILWAYS

The British Railways Board was set up by the Transport Act 1962, and assumed its responsibilities on 1 January 1963. (For members, *see* Government Departments and Public Offices section.)

Management of the railways is organized into the business sectors of InterCity, Network SouthEast, Regional Railways, Trainload Freight and Railfreight Distribution. A new organization, European Passenger Services Ltd, has been set up to manage international rail services through the Channel Tunnel. Under the Government's plans for the privatization of British Rail, ownership of track and land would be vested in a new body, Railtrack. Operation of passenger and freight rail services would be divided into a number of train-operating units, which would gradually be transferred to the private sector by franchising or sale.

FINANCIAL RESULTS

The profit and loss account for 1992–3 showed a deficit of £163.9 million after interest and extraordinary items, compared with a deficit of £144.7 million in 1991–2. The railway operating surplus was £13.4 million compared with a deficit of £101.4 million for the previous year.

	£ million
Railways	1992–3
Gross receipts	
Passenger (including grants)	2,862.6
Freight (incl. parcels and mails)	751.4
Other	109.3
Total	3,723.3
Working expenses	
Train services	1,669.8
Terminals	464.5
Miscellaneous traffic expenses	186.3
Track and signalling	625.8
General expenses	360.4
Depreciation	246.3
Other expenses	156.8
Total expenditure	3,709.9
Railway operating surplus	13.4
Interest and exceptional items	(177.3)
Group deficit	(163.9)

STAFF

On 31 March 1993 British Rail employed 124,791 staff (133,060 at 31 March 1992). Including subsidiaries, the group total at 31 March 1993 was 129,990 (138,001 at 31 March 1992).

OPERATING STATISTICS

At 31 March 1993, British Rail had 23,446 miles of standard gauge lines and sidings in use, representing 10,270 miles of route of which 3,051 miles were electrified. Standard rail on main line has a weight of 110 lb per yard. British Rail had 1,991 locomotives (2 diesel, 1,754 diesel-electric and 235 electric); 1,925 diesel multiple-unit vehicles, 6,629 electric multiple-unit vehicles and 2,630 locomotive-hauled vehicles. Loaded train miles run in passenger service totalled 228.3 million. Passenger journeys made during the year totalled 744.8 million, including 361.3 million made by holders of season tickets. The average distance of each passenger journey on ordinary fare was 36.1 miles; and on season ticket, 16.2 miles. Passenger stations in use in 1993 numbered 2,482 and freight terminals 61.

FREIGHT

There were 15,912 freight vehicles and 1,241 other vehicles in the non-passenger-carrying stock. Train miles run in freight service totalled 31 million.

ACCIDENTS ON RAILWAYS

	1990*	1991–2
Train accidents: total	1,283	960
Persons killed: total	4	11
Passengers	0	2
Railway staff	1	2
Others	3	7
Persons injured: total	243	391
Passengers	157	307
Railway staff	73	65
Others	13	19
Other accidents through movement of railway vehicles		
Persons killed	75	73
Persons injured	2,658	2,360
Other accidents on railway premises		
Persons killed	4	10
Persons injured	6,815	6,900
Trespassers and suicides		
Persons killed	285	242
Persons injured	123	92

* Calendar year

ROADS

HIGHWAY AUTHORITIES

The powers and responsibilities of highway authorities in England and Wales are set out in the Highways Acts 1980; for Scotland there is separate legislation.

Responsibility for trunk road motorways and other trunk roads in Great Britain rests in England with the Secretary of State for Transport, in Scotland with the Secretary of State for Scotland, and in Wales with the Secretary of State for Wales. The costs of construction, improvement and maintenance are paid for by central government. The highway authority for non-trunk roads in England and Wales is, in general, the county council, metropolitan district council or London borough council in whose area the roads lie, and in Scotland the regional or islands council. In Northern Ireland the Northern Ireland Department of the Environment is responsible for public roads and their maintenance and construction.

EXPENDITURE

Transport Supplementary Grant (TSG) is a block grant and was introduced in England and Wales in 1975 to replace a variety of specific grants paid towards local transport expenditure.

In England grant was paid towards capital and current spending on transport by county councils and the GLC from 1975–6 to 1984–5. Since 1985 TSG has only been paid towards capital spending on highways and the regulation of traffic, current expenditure having been subsumed by rate support grant. Since the abolition of the GLC and the metropolitan county councils in 1986, grant has been paid to London boroughs, the Common Council of the City of London and metropolitan district councils. Since 1991 TSG has also been paid towards capital spending on bridge assessment and strengthening; since 1992 towards structural maintenance on the Primary Route Network; and since 1 April 1993 towards all principal 'A' roads. In Wales grant was also paid to the Welsh county councils towards current and capital expenditure on transport. In 1982 TSG became payable on capital expenditure only, current expenditure having been subsumed by rate support grant. In 1990 the grant for Wales was renamed Transport Grant.

Grant rates are determined by the respective Secretaries of State; at present, grant is paid at 50 per cent of expenditure accepted for grant in England and Wales.

For the financial year 1993–4 local authorities in England will receive £431 million in TSG. Total estimated expenditure on building and maintaining motorways and trunk roads in 1991–2 was £1.85 billion in England; estimated outturn for 1992–3 is £1.98 billion.

In the financial year 1993–4, local authorities in Wales will receive £36.5 million in TG. Total expenditure on roads in Wales in 1991–2 was £268 million.

Total capital expenditure on local roads in 1991–2 was £156 million in Scotland, and total expenditure on building and maintaining trunk roads was £208 million.

ROAD LENGTHS (in miles) as at April 1992

	Total roads	Trunk roads (including motorways)	Motorways*
England	171,924	6,571	1,684
Wales	20,836	1,063	74
Scotland	32,343	1,987	167
N. Ireland	15,039	1,373†	69
UK	240,142	10,994	1,994

*There were in addition 42 miles of local authority motorway in England and 15 miles in Scotland
†'A' roads; there are no designated trunk roads in N. Ireland

MOTORWAYS

The network in England and Wales is based on five main routes:

M1	London to Yorkshire
M4	London to South Wales
M5	Birmingham, Bristol, Exeter
M6	Birmingham to Carlisle
M62	Lancashire to North Humberside

Other important motorways include:

M2	Medway towns
M3	London to Winchester
M11	London to Cambridge
M18	Rotherham to Goole
M20	London to Folkestone
M25	London orbital route
M40	London to Birmingham
M56	North Cheshire
M180	South Humberside

Motorways in Scotland include:

M8	Edinburgh, Glasgow, Greenock
M9	Edinburgh to Stirling
M73	Maryville to Mollisburn
M74	Nether Abington to Maryville
M80	Stirling to Haggs/Glasgow (M8) to Stepps
M85	Perth to Friarton Bridge
M90	Perth to Inverkeithing
M876	Dennyloanhead to Kincardine Bridge

DRIVING TESTS

The number of driving tests conducted in Great Britain in 1992 was 1,650,436, of which 50.38 per cent resulted in a pass. In addition a total of 67,034 LGV/PCV (Large goods vehicle/Passenger carrying vehicle) tests were undertaken, of which 53 per cent were successful.

MOTOR VEHICLES

The number of vehicles in Great Britain with current licences in 1992 was:

Private and light goods	22,344,000
Motor cycles, scooters, mopeds	688,000
Public transport vehicles	108,000
Heavy goods vehicles	437,000
Agricultural tractors	324,000
Others	59,000
Total	24,851,000

This total includes 891,000 Crown vehicles and vehicles exempt from licensing.

BUSES AND COACHES 1991–2 (Great Britain)

Number of vehicles (31 March 1992)	71,200
Vehicle kilometres (millions)	3,873
Local bus passenger journeys (millions)	4,669
Passenger receipts (£ million)	2,966

ROAD ACCIDENTS 1992

Road accidents	233,025
Vehicles involved:	
Pedal cycles	25,285
Motor vehicles	391,311
Total casualties	310,673
Pedestrians	51,587
Vehicle users	259,086
Killed*	4,229
Pedestrians	1,347
Pedal cycles	204
All two-wheeled motor vehicles	469
Cars and taxis	1,978
Others	231

*Died within 30 days of accident

	Killed	Injured
1965	7,952	389,985
1970	7,499	355,869
1975	6,366	318,584
1980	6,010	323,000
1985	5,165	312,359
1990	5,217	335,924
1991	4,568	306,701
1992	4,229	306,444

LICENCES

VEHICLE LICENSES

Since 1974 registration and first licensing of vehicles has been through local offices (known as Vehicle Registration Offices) of the Department of Transport's Driver and Vehicle Licensing Centre in Swansea. The records of existing vehicles are held at Swansea. Local facilities for relicensing are available as follows:

(i) with a licence reminder (form V11) in person at any post office which deals with vehicle licensing, or post it to the post office shown on the form

(ii) with a vehicle licence renewal (form V10). You may normally apply in person at any licensing post office. You will need to take your vehicle registration document with you; if this is not available you must complete form V62 which is held at post offices. Postal applications can be made to the post offices shown on form V100, available at any post office. This form also provides guidance on registering and licensing vehicles.

Details of the present duties chargeable on motor vehicles are available at post offices and Vehicle Registration Offices. The Vehicles (Excise) Act 1971 provides *inter alia* that any vehicle kept on a public road but not used on roads is chargeable to excise duty as if it were in use.

Rates of duty for motor car and motor cycle licences are shown below.

	12 months £	6 months £
Motor Cars		
Those first constructed before 1 January		
1947	70.00	38.50
Others	125.00	68.75
Motor Cycles		
With or without sidecar, not exceeding		
150 cc	15.00	—
With or without sidecar, 150–250 cc	35.00	—
Others	55.00	30.25
Three Wheelers		
Not over 150 cc	15.00	—
Others	55.00	30.25
Hackney Carriages		
Seating less than 9 persons	125.00	68.75
Seating 9–16 persons	150.00	82.50
Seating 17–35 persons	200.00	110.00
Seating 36–60 persons	300.00	165.00
Seating over 60 persons	450.00	247.50

DRIVING LICENCE FEES
On or after 1 February 1993

Full Licence

First full licence	£21.00
Changing a provisional to a full licence after passing a driving test	free
Renewal of licence issued after 30 September 1982	£6.00
Medical renewal	free
Medical renewal (over 70)	£6.00
Removing endorsements	£6.00
New licence after a period of disqualification	£12.00

Provisional Licence

First provisional licence	£21.00
Renewal of provisional licence issued before 1 October 1982	£21.00

Duplicate Licence	£6.00
Exchange Licence	£6.00

The minimum age for driving motor cars, light goods vehicles and motor cycles is 17 (moped, 16).

DRIVING TEST FEES (weekday rate/Saturday rate)

For cars	£26/£36
*For motor cycles	£34/£45
For lorries, buses	£60/£77.50
For invalid carriages	free

*The first part of the motor cycle test, now known as Compulsory Basic Training, is no longer conducted by the Department of Transport but by appointed motor cycle training organizations, who conduct the majority of Basic Training tests within the framework of their own training courses and are free to set their own fee. The fee for a certificate of completion of a Compulsory Basic Training course is £5.

An extended driving test was introduced in 1992 for those convicted of dangerous driving. The fee is £48.50/£77.50 (car) or £57/£92 (motorcycle)

MoT TESTING

Cars, motor cycles, motor caravans, light goods and dual-purpose vehicles more than three years old must be covered by a current MoT test certificate. Copies of the legislation governing MoT testing can be obtained from any bookshop which stocks HMSO publications. The legislation comprises the Road Traffic Act 1988 (Sections 45 and 46), the Motor Vehicles (Test) Regulations 1981, and subsequent amendments.

PRINCIPAL MERCHANT FLEETS OF THE WORLD

Flag	1982		1987		1991		1992	
	No.	Gross tonnage	No.	Gross tonnage	No.	Gross tonnage	No.	Gross tonnage
Liberia	2,189	70,718,439	1,574	51,412,029	1,605	52,426,516	1,672	55,166,948
Panama	5,032	32,600,278	5,136	43,254,716	4,953	44,949,330	5,217	49,629,986
Japan	10,652	41,593,612	9,822	35,932,177	10,063	26,406,930	10,091	25,403,270
Greece	3,501	40,035,204	1,948	23,559,852	1,863	22,752,919	1,872	24,542,087
Norway	2,409	21,861,635	1,979	6,359,349	2,577	23,585,661	2,499	22,583,133
Cyprus	557	2,149,869	1,341	15,650,207	1,359	20,297,661	1,416	20,385,718
Bahamas	96	432,502	469	9,105,182	973	17,541,196	1,061	20,054,161
China, People's Republic of	1,108	8,056,849	1,773	12,341,477	2,382	14,298,912	2,390	13,946,326
China, Republic of (Taiwan)	511	2,225,377	594	4,512,749	644	5,888,100	649	6,103,581
*United States of America	6,133	1,911,092	6,427	20,178,236	6,222	20,290,520	5,737	18,228,470
Russia	—	—	—	—	—	—	4,543	15,632,698
Malta	93	425,563	271	1,725,984	702	6,916,325	889	10,126,848
Singapore	849	7,183,326	700	7,098,116	854	8,488,172	946	9,247,352
Philippines	882	2,773,855	1,394	8,681,227	1,465	8,625,561	1,499	8,448,711
(USSR)	—	—	—	—	—	—	2,272	8,109,752
Italy	1,663	10,374,966	1,571	7,817,353	1,652	8,121,595	1,636	7,730,054
Korea (South)	1,652	5,529,398	1,899	7,214,070	2,136	7,820,532	2,138	7,518,485
Hong Kong	255	3,498,512	409	8,034,668	355	5,875,825	387	6,925,724
India	644	6,213,489	803	6,725,776	890	6,516,780	888	6,457,275
United Kingdom	2,826	22,505,265	2,165	8,504,605	1,949	6,610,633	1,747	6,016,868
Denmark	1,152	5,214,063	1,256	4,873,465	1,290	5,870,589	1,276	5,780,551
Brazil	666	5,678,111	718	6,324,059	669	5,882,528	635	5,573,175
Germany	1,782	7,706,661	1,414	4,317,616	1,522	5,971,254†	1,375	5,552,094†
Iran	235	1,312,734	370	3,976,873	401	4,583,179	403	4,558,219
Saint Vincent	34	25,966	145	699,947	698	2,709,794	881	4,380,956
Netherlands	1,228	5,393,104	1,307	3,908,231	1,249	3,872,301	1,230	4,250,456
France	1,171	10,770,880	954	5,371,273	910	3,988,072	890	4,205,310
Turkey	631	2,127,921	852	3,336,093	880	4,107,075	880	4,186,083
Romania	345	2,203,317	430	3,263,823	469	3,828,034	439	3,266,168
Spain	2,635	8,130,693	2,350	4,949,387	2,305	3,617,151	2,190	3,224,604
Poland	816	3,650,615	719	3,469,670	673	3,348,443	644	3,162,140
Bermuda	68	474,402	105	1,925,297	100	3,036,987	94	3,139,164
Sweden	697	3,787,567	642	2,269,541	684	3,174,274	664	3,081,166
Australia	558	1,875,316	690	2,404,559	714	2,571,867	695	2,676,087
Canada	1,299	3,212,562	1,238	2,971,155	1,204	2,684,614	1,185	2,642,795
Indonesia	1,319	1,846,824	1,734	2,120,531	1,991	2,336,880	2,014	2,338,604
Vanuatu	9	3,035	88	540,088	287	2,172,621	280	2,154,913
Marshall Islands	—	—	—	—	28	1,698,051	35	2,098,671
Malaysia	329	1,195,411	498	1,688,523	508	1,755,279	552	2,015,562
Kuwait	217	2,014,379	236	2,087,856	197	1,372,976	209	1,910,180
Luxembourg	—	—	—	—	51	1,703,482	54	1,580,695
Bulgaria	193	1,248,210	205	1,551,176	226	1,366,792	222	1,346,085
Latvia	—	—	—	—	—	—	261	1,235,573
Egypt	341	635,801	428	1,074,192	444	1,256,641	444	1,200,054
Finland	354	2,376,995	257	1,122,249	266	1,052,980	263	1,186,691
Mexico	545	1,251,630	651	1,532,485	649	1,195,517	635	1,109,683
Saudi Arabia	347	4,301,789	349	2,692,044	309	1,321,464	301	1,016,127

*Including ships of the United States Reserve Fleet
†Including the former German Democratic Republic

Classification with Lloyd's Register of Shipping: As at 30 June 1992, 8,620 ships with an aggregate gross tonnage of 96 million were classed or were to be classed with Lloyd's Register

Source: Lloyd's Register of Shipping

MERCHANT SHIPS COMPLETED DURING 1992

Country of Build	Total		For Registration in	Total	
	No.	Gross tonnage		No.	Gross tonnage
Japan	568	7,581,728	Liberia	117	4,947,193
Korea (South)	105	4,766,704	Panama	160	3,958,543
*China, People's Republic of	38	360,735	Japan	378	1,366,909
China, Republic of (Taiwan)	13	698,932	Norway	54	1,236,128
Germany	94	903,555	Singapore	60	731,805
Denmark	40	599,878	Bahamas	32	713,010
Spain	70	478,971	China, People's Republic of	28	146,175
Italy	43	391,735	China, Republic of (Taiwan)	10	425,408
Croatia	12	384,186	Germany	70	479,438
Poland	44	340,728	Kuwait	4	449,513
Brazil	11	285,668	Cyprus	24	447,387
Romania	18	200,634	Italy	54	442,040
Finland	9	196,385	Denmark	40	375,852
Netherlands	55	173,860	Netherlands	43	244,110
Norway	54	168,967	France	19	204,316
United Kingdom	28	152,307	Finland	7	192,252
*Ukraine	7	129,333	Hong Kong	12	189,397
France	17	116,161	Korea (South)	19	147,671
Belgium	9	108,114	United Kingdom	25	142,078
Portugal	10	93,057	Malaysia	19	139,481
Singapore	42	66,866	Poland	10	136,495
Bulgaria	6	60,004	Bermuda	2	125,878
India	10	57,060	Russia	20	125,758
Turkey	15	56,657	Saint Vincent	2	122,634
United States of America	27	54,033	Greece	5	121,410
Indonesia	8	23,902	Belgium	11	118,314
Malaysia	29	23,017	India	14	116,341
Sweden	6	22,791	Brazil	9	115,808
*Russia	3	20,863	Sweden	7	113,310
Other countries	115	116,056	Other countries	251	558,233
World Total	1,506	18,632,887	World Total	1,506	18,632,887

*Information incomplete

Of the ships completed in the world during the year
2,909,865 gross tonnage (15.6 per cent) was to be classed
with Lloyd's Register

Source: Lloyd's Register of Shipping

Communications

Postal Services

On 1 October 1969 the Post Office ceased to be a government department. The responsibility for running postal services was transferred to a public authority called the Post Office, which also administered telecommunications in the United Kingdom. The British Telecommunications Act 1981 separated the postal and telecommunications functions and gave the Secretary of State for Trade and Industry powers to suspend the monopoly of the Post Office in certain areas and to issue licences to other bodies to provide an alternative service. Non-Post Office bodies are now permitted to transfer mail between document exchanges and to deliver letters, provided that a minimum fee of £1 per letter is charged. Charitable organizations are allowed to carry and deliver Christmas and New Year cards.

INLAND POSTAL SERVICES AND REGULATIONS

INLAND LETTER POST RATES*

Not over	1st class	2nd class
60 g	24p	18p
100 g	36p	28p
150 g	45p	34p
200 g	54p	41p
250 g	64p	49p
300 g	74p	58p
350 g	85p	66p
400 g	96p	75p
450 g	£1.08	84p
500 g	£1.20	93p
600 g	£1.50	£1.15
700 g	£1.80	£1.35
750 g	£1.95	£1.40 (not
800 g	£2.05	admissible
900 g	£2.25	over 750 g)
1,000 g	£2.40	
Each extra 250 g or part thereof	60p	

Postcards travel at the same rates

UK PARCEL RATES

Not over		Not over	
1 kg	£2.60	8 kg	£5.50
2 kg	£3.25	10 kg	£6.50
4 kg	£4.25	30 kg	£8.10
6 kg	£4.80		

STAMPS

There is a two-tier postal delivery system in the UK with first class letters normally being delivered the following day and second class post within three days.

Postage stamps are sold in values of 1p, 2p, 3p, 4p, 5p, 6p, 10p, 18p, 20p, 24p, 28p, 30p, 33p, 34p, 35p, 39p, 50p, 75p, £1, £1.50, £2.00, £5.00, and £10.00.

*The Post Office has proposed an increase in 1st and 2nd class inland letter post (to 25p and 18p respectively) and in rates for other services from 1 November 1993. At the time of going to press no decision had been made

Books of stamps costing 50p or £1, or single first or second class stamps, are available from electronic vending machines at some main post offices. At post office counters books are sold containing ten first class stamps (£2.40) and ten second class stamps (£1.80). Rolls of 24p and 18p stamps are also sold. Mixed value rolls are only available on special order from post offices. The sale of postage stamps has been extended to outlets other than post offices, including stationers and newsagents.

PREPAID STATIONERY

Aerogrammes to all destinations, 34p.
Forces Aerogrammes, free to certain destinations. Other mail charged at a concessionary rate.
Registered Prepaid Letter Envelopes in three sizes:
G, 156 × 95mm, £2.30
H, 203 × 120mm, £2.35
K, 292 × 152mm, £2.45
Printed postage stamps cut from envelopes, postcards, newspaper wrappers, etc., may be used as stamps in payment of postage, provided that they are not imperfect or defaced.

POSTAL ORDERS

Postal Orders (British pattern) are issued and paid at nearly all post offices in the UK. They are also paid in the Irish Republic, and issued and/or paid in many other countries overseas.

Postal orders are printed with a counterfoil for denominations of 50p and £1, followed by £1 steps to £10, £15 and £20. Postage stamps may be affixed in the space provided to increase the value of the postal order by up to 49p.

Charges (in addition to the value of the postal order): Up to £1, 25p; £2–£4, 42p; £5–£7, 55p; £8–£10, 60p; £15, 75p; £20, 80p.

The name of the payee must be inserted on the postal order. If not presented within six months of the last day of the month of issue, orders must be sent to the local customer services manager of Post Office Counters Ltd (the address and telephone number can be found in the telephone directory), to ascertain whether the order may still be paid, although if the counterfoil has been retained postal orders not more than four years out of date may be paid when presented with the counterfoil at a post office.

OTHER SERVICES

Cash on Delivery Service
(Inland, excluding Irish Republic and HM ships). A trade charge (amount to be collected) up to £500 can, under certain conditions, be collected from addresses and remitted to the sender of a parcel containing an invoice. Invoice values of over £100 are only collectable at Post Office premises.

Charge per parcel (exclusive of postage and registration): Customers under contract, £1.70; other customers, £2.00; COD enquiry, £1.70.

Certificate of Posting
Issued free on request at time of posting.

Compensation
(Royal Mail inland only): compensation up to a maximum of £24 may be paid where it can be shown that a letter was

damaged or lost in the post due to the fault of the Post Office, its employees or agents. The onus of making up properly any parcel sent by post lies with the sender. The Post Office does not accept any responsibility for loss arising from faulty packing.

Parcelforce: compensation up to £20 per parcel will be paid for loss or damage if a certificate of posting has been obtained. A Compensation Fee Certificate of Posting can also be obtained; 65p, up to £150 compensation, £1.15, up to £500 compensation.

Newspaper Post

Copies of newspapers registered at the Post Office may be posted by the publisher or their agents in wrappers open at both ends, in unsealed envelopes approved by the Post Office, or without covers and tied by string which can be removed without cutting. Wrappers and envelopes must be prominently marked 'newspaper post' in the top left-hand corner. No writing or additional printing is permitted, other than the words 'with compliments', name and address of sender, request for return if undeliverable and a reference to a page. Items receive first class letter service.

Newspapers posted by the public, or supplements to registered newspapers dispatched apart from their ordinary publications, are transmitted under the conditions governing the first or second class letter services.

Prohibited Articles

Prohibitions include offensive or dangerous articles, packets likely to impede Post Office sorters, and certain kinds of advertisement.

Recorded Delivery

The recorded delivery service provides a record of posting and delivery of inland letters and ensures a signature on delivery. No compensation is available for money or jewellery sent by this service. Charge, 55p. To confirm delivery, call LocalCall 0645-272100 and quote the number on the bar-coded receipt. (Also for Registered and Special Delivery.)

Redirection

(i) By agent of addressee – mail other than parcels, business reply and freepost items may be reposted free not later than the day after delivery (not counting Sundays and public holidays) if unopened and if original addressee's name is unobscured. Parcels may be redirected free of charge within the same time limits only if the original and substituted address are in the same local parcel delivery area (or within the London postal area). Registered packets, which must be taken to a post office, are re-registered free only up to the day after delivery.

(ii) By the Post Office – requests for redirection of mail should be made on printed forms obtainable from the Post Office and must be signed by the person to whom the letters are to be addressed. A fee is payable for each different surname on the application form.

Charges: Up to 1 calendar month, £3.50; up to 3 calendar months, £7.75; up to 12 calendar months, £18.75; up to 12 calendar months where redirection has already been in operation for 12 months or more, £65.00.

Registration

(Inland first class letters only). All packets intended for registration must be handed to the post office and a certificate of posting obtained. The registration fee is £3.00, which includes a 30p compensation premium (for up to a £500 claim). Registered Plus service is available for items worth between £500 and £2,200.

Consequential Loss Insurance provides cover up to £10,000 for items worth more than their material value:

Compensation up to	Standard fee in addition to registered fee and postage
£1,000	£0.45
£2,500	£0.60
£5,000	£0.85
£7,500	£1.10
£10,000	£1.35

Compensation in respect of currency or other forms of monetary worth is given only if money is sent by registered letter post in one of the special envelopes sold officially (*see* Prepaid Stationery). Compensation cannot be paid in the case of any packet containing anything not legally transmissible by post. Compensation is paid for fragile articles only if they have been adequately packed. No compensation is paid for deterioration due to delay of perishable articles or for damage to exceptionally fragile articles.

Special Delivery

Offers the same next-day delivery service as Registered Post but with no compensation service. Charge, £2.70.

Undelivered Mail

Undelivered mail is returned to the sender provided the return address is indicated either on the outside of the envelope or inside. If the sender's address is not available, items not containing property are destroyed. If the packet contains something of value it is retained for up to three months. Exceptionally, items in the minimum weight step on which a rebate of postage has been allowed are destroyed unopened unless there is a return address shown on the outside of the cover. In addition, undeliverable second class mail which contains newspapers, magazines or commercial advertising is destroyed.

Unpaid Mail

All unpaid or underpaid letters are treated as second class mail. The recipient is charged the amount of underpayment plus 14p per item. The same rates apply to parcels.

SPECIAL DELIVERY SERVICES

Datapost

A guaranteed service for the delivery of documents and packages: (i) Datapost Sameday offers same-day collection and delivery in many areas; (ii) Datapost 10 and Datapost 12 offer next day delivery nationwide. Datapost 10 for delivery before 10 a.m. and Datapost 12 for delivery before noon are available to certain destinations only. Items may be collected or handed in at post offices. There are also Datapost links with a number of overseas countries. Parcelforce 24 and 48 offer a similar guaranteed service to Datapost, 24 being delivered the following day and 48 the day after.

Royal Mail Special Delivery

This service offers special messenger treatment, where necessary, to ensure next day delivery of first class letters and packets. The fee of £2.70 is refunded if next working day delivery is not achieved, provided that items are posted before latest recommended posting times.

Swiftair

Express delivery of airmail letters and packets up to 2 kg anywhere in the world. Items normally arrive at least one day in advance of normal air mail. Charge (in addition to postage), £2.70.

OVERSEAS POSTAL SERVICES AND REGULATIONS

OVERSEAS SURFACE MAIL RATES
Letters and Postcards

Not over		Not over	
20 g	28p	450 g	£2.44
60 g	48p	500 g	£2.70
100 g	69p	750 g	£4.00
150 g	92p	1,000 g	£5.30
200 g	£1.18	1,250 g	£6.60
250 g	£1.42	1,500 g	£7.90
300 g	£1.66	1,750 g	£9.20
350 g	£1.92	2,000 g	£10.50
400 g	£2.18		

AIRMAIL LETTER RATES
Europe: Letters and Postcards

Not over		Not over	
20 g	24p	260 g	£1.60
20 g non EC	28p	280 g	£1.71
40 g	39p	300 g	£1.82
60 g	50p	320 g	£1.93
80 g	61p	340 g	£2.04
100 g	72p	360 g	£2.15
120 g	83p	380 g	£2.26
140 g	94p	400 g	£2.37
160 g	£1.05	420 g	£2.48
180 g	£1.16	440 g	£2.59
200 g	£1.27	460 g	£2.70
220 g	£1.38	480 g	£2.81
240 g	£1.49	*500 g	£2.92

* Max. 2 kg

Outside Europe: Letters

	Not over 10 g	Not over 20 g	Each extra 20 g
Zone 1	39p	57p	32p
Zone 2	39p	57p	42p

For airmail letter zones outside Europe, *see* pages 527–8

OTHER SERVICES
Cash on Delivery

Applicable to parcels only, but not to all countries, nor to British naval, military and RAF forces serving overseas.

A charge starting at £5.00 per parcel must be prepaid in addition to the postage for outward parcels. The trade charge (amount to be collected) may not exceed £1,500 but to most non-European countries the limit is lower. The addressee has also to pay on delivery, besides Customs charges if any, a further charge which is not prepayable. If the trade charge cannot be collected special rules apply for undeliverable COD parcels.

Compensation

If a certificate of posting is produced, compensation may be given for loss or damage in the UK to uninsured parcels to or from most overseas countries. No compensation will be paid for any loss or damage due to the action of the Queen's Enemies.

Export Restrictions

Under Department of Trade and Industry regulations the exportation of some goods by post is prohibited except under Department of Trade licence. Enquiries should be addressed to the Export Data Branch, Overseas Trade Divisions, Department of Trade and Industry, 1 Victoria Street, London SW1H 0ET. Tel: 071-215 5000.

Insurance

Packets containing valuable papers, documents or articles such as jewellery can be insured as letters, or as parcels if the country of destination does not accept dutiable goods in the letter post. For HM ships abroad and also members of the Army and RAF overseas using BFPO numbers, parcels only are insurable up to £140 at a fee of £1.20.

Charges: Cover up to £150, £1.90; up to £300, £2.15; up to £450, £2.40; up to £600, £2.65; to a limit of £3.90 for £1,500 coverage.

International Reply Coupons

Coupons are used to prepay replies to letters. They are exchangeable abroad for stamps representing the minimum surface mail letter rate from the country concerned to the UK. Charge, 60p each.

Poste Restante

Solely for the convenience of travellers and for three months only in any one town. A packet may be addressed to any post office, except town sub-offices, and should have the words 'Poste Restante' or 'to be called for' in the address. Redirection from a Poste Restante is undertaken for up to three months. Letters at a seaport for an expected ship are kept for two months; otherwise letters are kept for two weeks, or for one month if originating from abroad. At the end of this period mail is treated as undeliverable, unless bearing a request for return.

Registration

(Except for parcels and printed paper items posted in bulk). Registration is available to all countries except the British Indian Ocean Territory and the Republic of the Maldives. No compensation is payable for loss or damage to valuable articles sent in an unregistered letter. Charge in addition to postage, £3.00.

Small Packets Post

This service permits the transmission of goods up to 2 kg to all countries, in the same mails as printed papers (NB: To Australia, Cuba, Myanmar (Burma) and Papua New Guinea there is a limit of 500 g, and to Italy 1 kg). Packets can be sealed and can contain personal correspondence if it relates to the contents of the packet. Registration is allowed as insurance as long as the item is packed in a way which complies with appropriate insurance regulations. A customs declaration is required and the packet must be endorsed 'small packet' and marked with a return address.

Instructions for the disposal of undelivered packets must be given at the time of posting. A packet which cannot be delivered will be returned to the sender at his/her expense.

SMALL PACKETS POST RATES
Surface Mail: World-wide

Not over		Not over	
100 g	45p	450 g	£1.50
150 g	60p	500 g	£1.65
200 g	75p	750 g	£2.30
250 g	90p	1,000 g	£2.95
300 g	£1.05	1,500 g	£4.15
350 g	£1.20	2,000 g	£5.35
400 g	£1.35		

Public Telecommunications Services

Under the British Telecommunications Act 1981 the functions of the Post Office were divided between two separate organizations. The Post Office retained control of postal services and British Telecom (now BT) was created to provide a telecommunications service. The Act also provided for a limited relaxation of the telecommunications monopoly. This was further advanced by the Telecommunications Act 1984, which removed BT's monopoly on running the public telecommunications system. British Telecom was privatized as a public limited company in 1984.

The Telecommunications Act 1984 also established the Office of Telecommunications (Oftel) as the independent regulatory body for the telecommunications industry. (*See also* Government Departments and Public Offices.)

PUBLIC TELECOMMUNICATIONS OPERATORS

Until recently there were three licensed fixed-link public telecommunications operators (PTOs) in the UK: BT, Mercury Communications Ltd, and Kingston Communications (Hull) PLC. In 1988 the Government announced its intention to license up to six other operators to provide one-way satellite communications systems; during 1989 three of these operators were granted temporary licences and the Government announced that such operators could offer services throughout Europe, rather than in the UK only, as previously indicated. In March 1991 the Government announced that it was opening up the existing duopoly of the two major fixed-link operators and would be encouraging applications for telecommunications licences. Since then there have been four recipients of major licences (Ionica, COLT, Energis, and Scottish Hydro-Electric) included in the 23 licences issued by the Department of Trade and Industry. There are 35 applications under consideration.

BT's obligations under its operating licence include the provision of a universal telecommunications service; a service in rural areas; and essential services, such as public call boxes and emergency services.

Mercury Communications is licensed to provide national and international public telecommunications services for residential and business customers. These services utilize the digital network created by Mercury. Mercury can also provide the following services: (i) public and private telephone services; (ii) national and international telex; (iii) international switched data services; (iv) electronic messaging (electronic mail and access to telex via a personal computer); (v) data network services; (vi) customer equipment; (vii) mobile communications services; and (viii) Mercury paging.

PRIVATE TELEPHONE SERVICES

There are over 260 private telephone companies which offer information on a variety of subjects such as the weather, stock market analysis, horoscopes, etc., on the BT network. Other services are available on Mercury's network.

The lines and equipment are provided by BT under condition that services adhere to the codes of practice of the Independent Committee for the Supervision of Standards of Telephone Information Practice. All services are charged at 48p per minute (peak and standard rate) or 36p per minute (cheap rate).

MOBILE TELEPHONE SYSTEMS

Cellular telephone network systems, in existence since 1985, allow calls to be made to and from mobile telephones. The two companies licensed by the Department of Trade and Industry to provide competing cellular telephone systems

are Cellnet, jointly owned by BT and Securicor, and Racal Vodafone Ltd, owned by the Racal Electronics Group. Cellular phones can be identified by the number prefixes 0831, 0836, 0850, 0860, or 0881 and calls to them are charged at the 'm' rate.

INLAND TELEPHONES

Since December 1986 an individual customer can install an extension telephone socket or apparatus in their own home without the need to buy the items from any of the licensed public telecommunications operators. However, it is necessary to possess a special style of master-socket which must be supplied by the public network operator. Although an individual need not buy or rent an apparatus from a PTO, a telephone bought from a retail outlet must be of an approved standard compatible with the public network (indicated by a green disc on the label).

BT CHARGES

EXCHANGE LINE RENTALS (*excluding VAT*)

	Per quarter
Residential, exclusive	£19.54
Supportline, exclusive	£9.77
Business, exclusive	£31.65

Telephone apparatus rental	
Residential	from £3.80
Business	from £4.70
Private payphone	from £36.50

EXCHANGE LINE CONNECTION AND TAKE-OVER CHARGES (*including VAT*)

	Residential	Business
New customer	£116.32	£116.32
Removing customer	£116.32	£116.32
Take-over of existing lines	£0.00	£0.00
Non-simultaneous take-over of lines	£36.78	£36.78

Local and dialled national calls are charged in 4.2p units when made from ordinary lines and in 10p units when made from payphones. All charges are subject to VAT except those from payphones which are VAT inclusive. VAT charges on ordinary lines are calculated as a percentage of the total quarterly bill.

The length of time per unit depends on the distance of the call and the time of day:

*Local rate

'a' rate – up to 35 miles (56 km)
'b1' rate – frequently used routes over 35 miles (56 km)
'b' rate – over 35 miles (56 km) (incl. Channel Islands and Isle of Man)
'm' rate – dialled calls to mobile phones
'p1' rate – calls to Callstream service

*Greater London has an exceptionally large 'local' call area

Peak rate: Monday to Friday, 9 a.m.–1 p.m.
Standard rate: Monday to Friday, 8 a.m.–9 a.m and 1 p.m.–6 p.m.

Cheap rate: Monday to Friday, 6 p.m.–8 a.m. All day
Saturday and Sunday and also Christmas Day, Boxing
Day and New Year's Day

DIALLED CALL UNIT TIME (*excluding VAT*)

	Seconds per unit at 4.2p
Local rate	
Peak	57.5
Standard	80
Cheap	220
'a' rate	
Peak	27
Standard	36.15
Cheap	80.8
'b1' rate	
Peak	23.9
Standard	32
Cheap	50.35
'b' rate	
Peak	19.2
Standard	25.6
Cheap	37.9
'm' rate	
Peak	7.61
Standard	7.61
Cheap	11.4
'p1' rate	
Peak	6.2
Standard	6.2
Cheap	8.25

PREFIXED CALL CHARGES

0800 – free
0345 – charged at the local rate
0831, 0860 and Callstream 0077 services – charged at 'm'
rate (and some 0836 calls also)
0839, 0898 and 08364 – charged at 'p1' rate

OPERATOR-CONNECTED CALLS

Operator-connected calls from ordinary lines are generally
subject to a three-minute minimum charge (and thereafter
by the minute) which varies with distance and time of day.
Operator-connected calls from payphones are charged in
three-minute periods at the payphone tariff. For calls that
have to be placed through the operator because a dialled call
has failed, the charge is equivalent to the dialled rate,
subject normally to the three-minute minimum.

Higher charges apply to other operator-connected calls,
including special services calls and those to mobile phones,
the Irish Republic and the Channel Islands.

PHONECARDS

Phonecards to the value of £2, £4, £10 and £20 are
available from post offices and other outlets for use in
specially designated public telephone boxes. Each
phonecard unit is equivalent to a 10p coin in a payphone.

Special public payphones at major railway stations and
airports also accept commercial credit cards.

INTERNATIONAL TELEPHONES

All UK customers have access to International Direct
Dialling (IDD) and can dial direct to numbers on most
exchanges in over 200 countries world-wide. Details about
how to make calls are given in dialling code information and
in the International Telephone Guide.

For countries without IDD, calls have to be made through
the International Operator. All operator-connected calls are
subject to a three-minute minimum charge. Thereafter the
call is charged by the minute.

Countries which can be called on IDD fall into one of 13
international charge bands depending on location. Charges
in each band also vary according to the time of day; cheap
rate dialled calls are available to all countries at certain
times, but there is no reduced rate for operator-connected
calls. Details of current international telephone charges can
be obtained from the International Operator.

For International Dialling Codes, *see* pages 527–8

OTHER TELECOMMUNICATIONS SERVICES

Telex Service

There are now 208 countries that can be reached by the BT
telex service from the UK, over 200 of them by direct
dialling.

For most customers, direct dialled calls to international
destinations are charged in six-second units. Units cost
between 4.5p and 13.5p depending upon the country called.
Calls via the BT operator are charged in one-minute steps
with a three-minute minimum, plus a surcharge of £1.30 a
call. Operator-connected calls are charged at between 39p
and £1.60 a minute depending upon the country called.

Calls made via BT's Telex Plus store and forward facility
attract normal telex charges and a handling charge of 13p for
inland delivered messages and 30p for international delivered
messages.

Telemessage

Telemessages can be sent by telephone or telex within the
UK for 'hard copy' delivery the next working day, including
Saturdays. To achieve this, a telemessage must be tele-
phoned/telexed before 10 p.m. Monday to Saturday (7 p.m.
Sundays and Bank Holidays). Dial 100 (190 in London,
Birmingham and Glasgow) and ask for the Telemessage
Service or see the telex directory for codes.

A telemessage costs £5 for the first 50 words and £2.75
for each subsequent group of 50 words – the name and
address are free. A sender's copy costs 85p. A selection of
cards is available for special occasions at 80p per card. All
prices are subject to VAT.

International Telemessage

Telemessage is also available to the USA. For next working
day delivery a telemessage must be filed by 10 p.m. UK time
Monday to Saturday (7 p.m. Sundays and Bank Holidays).
US addresses must include the ZIP code. Charges are £7.25
for the first 50 words and £3.60 for each subsequent group
of 50 words. The name and address are free but all charges
are subject to VAT.

BT SERVICES

OPERATOR SERVICES – 100
For difficulties
For the following call services: alarm calls (booking
charge £2.15); advice of duration and charge (charge
75p); charge card calls (charge 25p); freefone calls;
international personal calls (charge £2.15–£4.30);
transferred charge calls (charge 40p); subscriber
controlled transfer (All charges exclude VAT)

INTERNATIONAL OPERATOR – 155
DIRECTORY ENQUIRIES
For numbers in the London postal area, 142
For numbers outside the London postal area, including
the Irish Republic, 192
INTERNATIONAL DIRECTORY ENQUIRIES – 153
EMERGENCY SERVICES – 999
Services include fire service; police service; ambulance
service; coastguard; lifeboat; cave rescue; mountain
rescue
FAULTS – 151
TELEMESSAGE – 100 (190 in London, Birmingham and
Glasgow)

INTERNATIONAL TELEMESSAGE – 100 (190 in London,
Birmingham and Glasgow). The service is only available
to the USA
INTERNATIONAL TELEGRAMS – 100 (190 in London,
Birmingham and Glasgow). The service is available
world-wide
MARITIME SERVICES – 100
Includes Ship's Telegram Service and Ship's Telephone
Service
BT INMARSAT SATELLITE SERVICE – 155
ALL OTHER CALL ENQUIRIES – 191

Forecast Services

WEATHERCALL SERVICE

To obtain local weather forecasts, dial the prefix code
0891 500 followed by the appropriate regional code

Greater London	401
Kent, Surrey and Sussex	402
Dorset, Hampshire and IOW	403
Devon and Cornwall	404
Wiltshire, Glos., Avon and Somerset	405
Berks., Bucks. and Oxfordshire	406
Beds., Herts. and Essex	407
Norfolk, Suffolk and Cambridgeshire	408
West, Mid and South Glamorgan and Gwent	409
Salop, Hereford and Worcester	410
Central Midlands	411
East Midlands	412
Lincolnshire and Humberside	413
Dyfed and Powys	414
Gwynedd and Clwyd	415
North-west England	416
West and South Yorkshire	417
North-east England	418
Cumbria and the Lake District	419
South-west Scotland	420
West Central Scotland	421
Edinburgh, South Fife, Lothian and Borders	422
East Central Scotland	423
Grampian and East Highlands	424
North-west Scotland	425
Caithness, Orkney and Shetland	426
Northern Ireland	427
Yorkshire Dales	748

Calls are charged at 36p per minute cheap rate, 48p at all
other times, as at June 1993

MARINECALL SERVICE

To obtain information about weather conditions up to twelve
miles off the coast, dial the prefix code 0891 500, followed
by the appropriate area code

Scotland North	451
Scotland East	452
North-east	453
East	454
Anglia	455
Channel East	456
Mid-Channel	457
South-west	458
Bristol Channel	459
Wales	460
North-west	461
Clyde	462
Caledonia	463
Minch	464
Ulster	465
Southern North Sea	991
English Channel	992

Calls are charged at 36p per minute cheap rate, 48p at all
other times, as at June 1993

Airmail and IDD Codes

AIRMAIL ZONES (AZ)
The table includes airmail letter zones for countries outside Europe, and destinations to which European and European Community airmail letter rates apply (*see also* page 523). (*Source: Post Office*)

1 airmail zone 1
2 airmail zone 2
e Europe
ec European Community

INTERNATIONAL DIRECT DIALLING (IDD)
International dialling codes are composed of four elements which are dialled in sequence:

(i)   the international code
(ii) the country code (*see* below)
(iii) the area code
(iv) the customer's telephone number

Calls to some countries must be made via the international operator. (*Source: BT*)

† Calls must be made via the international operator
p A pause in dialling is necessary whilst waiting for a second tone
p* Only in Bruges, Ostende and Veurne
° Second tone may not always be audible
* Varies in some areas

Country	AZ	IDD from UK	IDD to UK
Afghanistan	1	010 93	†
Albania	e	010 355	†
Algeria	1	010 213	00p44
Andorra	ec	010 33 628	0p44
Angola	1	010 244	†
Anguilla	1	010 1 809	001 44
Antigua and Barbuda	1	010 1 809	011 44
Argentina	1	010 54	00 44
Armenia	e	010 7	810 44
Aruba	1	010 297	†
Ascension Island	1	010 247	
Australia	2	010 61	00 11 44
Austria	e	010 43	00 44
Azerbaijan	e	010 7	810 44
Azores	ec	010 351	00 44
Bahamas	1	010 1 809	011 44
Bahrain	1	010 973	0 44
Bangladesh	1	010 880	00 44
Barbados	1	010 1 809	011 44
Belarus	e	010 7	810 44
Belgium	ec	010 32	00p44*
Belize	1	010 501	†
Benin	1	010 229	00p44
Bermuda	1	010 1 809	1 44
Bhutan	1	010 975	00 44
Bolivia	1	010 591	00 44
Bosnia-Hercegovina	e	010 38	99 44
Botswana	1	010 267	00 44
Brazil	1	010 55	00 44
British Virgin Islands	1	010 1 809 49	011 44
Brunei	1	010 673	00 44
Bulgaria	e	010 359	00 44
Burkina Faso	1	010 226	
Burundi	1	010 257	90 44
Cambodia	1	†	†
Cameroon	1	010 237	00 44

Country	AZ	IDD from UK	IDD to UK
Canada	1	010 1	011 44
Canary Islands	ec	010 34	07p44
Cape Verde	e	010 238	†
Cayman Islands	1	010 1 809	0 44
Central African Republic	1	010 236	†
Chad	1	010 235	†
Chile	1	010 56	00 44
China	2	010 86	00 44
Colombia	1	010 57	90 44
Comoros	1	010 269	†
Congo	1	010 242	00 44
Cook Islands	2	010 682	00 44
Costa Rica	1	010 506	00 44
Côte d'Ivoire	1	010 225	00 44
Croatia	e	010 38	99 44
Cuba	1	010 53	
Cyprus	e	010 357	00 44
Czech Republic	e	010 42	00 44
Denmark	ec	010 45	009 44
Djibouti	1	010 253	00 44
Dominica	1	010 1 809	011 44
Dominican Republic	1	010 1 809	†
Ecuador	1	010 593	00 44
Egypt	1	010 20	00 44
Equatorial Guinea	1	010 240	†
Estonia	e	010 7	810 44
Ethiopia	1	010 251	
Falkland Islands	1	010 500	01 44
Faroe Islands	e	010 298	009 44
Fiji	2	010 679	05 44
Finland	e	010 358	990 44
France	ec	010 33	19p44°
French Guiana	1	010 594	†
French Polynesia	2	010 689	00 44
Gabon	1	010 241	00 44
The Gambia	1	010 220	00 44
Georgia	e	010 7	810 44
Germany	ec	010 49	00 44
Ghana	1	010 233	
Gibraltar	ec	010 350	00 44
Greece	ec	010 30	00 44
Greenland	e	010 299	009 44
Grenada	1	010 1 809	011 44
Guadeloupe	1	010 590	†
Guam	2	010 671	00 44
Guatemala	1	010 502	00 44
Guinea	1	010 224	†
Guinea-Bissau	1	010 245	†
Guyana	1	010 592	011 44
Haiti	1	010 509	†
Honduras	1	010 504	00 44
Hong Kong	1	010 852	001 44
Hungary	e	010 36	00 44
Iceland	e	010 354	90 44
India	1	010 91	00 44
Indonesia	1	010 62	00 44
Iran	1	010 98	00 44
Iraq	1	010 964	00 44
Irish Republic	ec	010 353	00 44
Dublin		0001	
Israel	1	010 972	00 44
Italy	ec	010 39	00 44
Jamaica	1	010 1 809	†
Japan	2	010 81	001 44
Jordan	1	010 962	00 44*
Kazakhstan	e	010 7	810 44

Country	AZ	IDD from UK	IDD to UK
Kenya	1	010 254	000 44
Kiribati	2	010 686	09 44
Korea, North	2	010 850	†
Korea, South	2	010 82	001 44
Kuwait	1	010 965	00 44
Kyrgystan	e	010 7	810 44
Laos	1	†	†
Latvia	e	010 7	810 44
Lebanon	1	010 961	00 44
Lesotho	1	010 266	00 44
Liberia	1	010 231	00 44
Libya	1	010 218	00 44
Liechtenstein	e	010 41 75	00 44
Lithuania	e	010 7	810 44
Luxembourg	ec	010 352	00 44
Macao	1	010 853	00 44
Madagascar	1	010 261	†
Madeira	ec	010 351 91	00 44*
Malawi	1	010 265	101 44
Malaysia	1	010 60	00 44
Maldives	1	010 960	
Mali	1	010 223	00 44
Malta	e	010 356	00 44
Mariana Islands, Northern	2	010 670	
Marshall Islands	2	010 692	
Martinique	1	010 596	†
Mauritania	1	010 222	†
Mauritius	1	010 230	
Mayotte	1	010 269	
Mexico	1	010 52	98 44
Micronesia, Federated States of	2	010 691	
Moldova	e	010 7	810 44
Monaco	ec	010 33 93	19p44
Mongolia	2	†	†
Montserrat	1	010 1 809	†
Morocco	1	010 212	00p44
Mozambique	1	010 258	†
Myanmar	1	010 95	†
Namibia	1	010 264	091 44
Nauru	2	010 674	00 44
Nepal	1	010 977	00 44
Netherlands	ec	010 31	09p44
Netherlands Antilles	1	010 599	00 44
New Caledonia	2	010 687	00 44
New Zealand	2	010 64	00 44
Nicaragua	1	010 505	00 44
Niger	1	010 227	00 44
Nigeria	1	010 234	009 44
Niue	2	010 683	
Norfolk Island	2	010 672	
Norway	e	010 47	095 44
Oman	1	010 968	00 44
Pakistan	1	010 92	00 44
Palau	2	010 6809	
Panama	1	010 507	00 44
Papua New Guinea	2	010 675	31 44
Paraguay	1	010 595	002 44 / 003 44
Peru	1	010 51	00 44
Philippines	2	010 63	00 44
Poland	e	010 48	0p044
Portugal	ec	010 351	00 44
Puerto Rico	1	010 1 809	135 44
Qatar	1	010 974	044
Réunion	1	010 262	19p44
Romania	e	010 40	

Country	AZ	IDD from UK	IDD to UK
Russia	e	010 7	810 44
Rwanda	1	010 250	†
St Helena	1	010 290	†
St Kitts and Nevis	1	010 1 809	†
St Lucia	1	010 1 809	0 44
St Pierre and Miquelon	1	010 508	†
St Vincent and the Grenadines	1	010 1 809	0 44
El Salvador	1	010 503	00 44
Samoa, American	2	010 684	144
San Marino	ec	010 39 549	00 44
São Tomé and Príncipe	1	010 23 912	†
Saudi Arabia	1	010 966	00 44
Senegal	1	010 221	00p44
Seychelles	1	010 248	0 44
Sierra Leone	1	010 232	†
Singapore	1	010 65	005 44
Slovak Republic	e	010 42	00 44
Slovenia	e	010 38	99 44
Solomon Islands	2	010 677	00 44
Somalia	1	010 252	†
South Africa	1	010 27	09 44
Spain	ec	010 34	07p44
Sri Lanka	1	010 94	00 44
Sudan	1	010 249	†
Suriname	1	010 597	001 44
Swaziland	1	010 268	00 44
Sweden	e	010 46	009 44p
Switzerland	e	010 41	00 44
Syria	1	010 963	00 44
Taiwan	2	010 886	002 44
Tajikistan	e	010 7	810 44
Tanzania	1	010 255	†
Thailand	1	010 66	001 44
Tibet	1	010 86	00 44
Togo	1	010 228	
Tonga	2	010 676	0 44
Trinidad and Tobago	1	010 1 809	01 44
Tristan da Cunha	1	†	
Tunisia	1	010 216	00 44
Turkey	e	010 90	9p944
Turkmenistan	e	010 7	810 44
Turks and Caicos Islands	1	010 1 809	†
Tuvalu	2	010 688	†
Uganda	1	010 256	†
Ukraine	e	010 7	810 44
United Arab Emirates	1	010 971	00 44
Uruguay	1	010 598	00 44
USA	1	010 1	011 44
Alaska		010 1 907	
Hawaii		010 1 808	
Uzbekistan	e	010 7	810 44
Vanuatu	2	010 678	†
Vatican City State	ec	010 39 66982	
Venezuela	1	010 58	00 44
Vietnam	1	010 84	†
Virgin Islands (US)	1	010 1 809	011 44
Western Samoa	2	010 685	†
Yemen			
north	1	010 967	00 44
south	1	010 969	00 44
Yugoslav Fed. Rep.	e	010 38	99 44
Zaire	1	010 243	00 44
Zambia	1	010 260	00 44
Zimbabwe	1	010 263	110 44

Local Government

The Local Government Acts of 1972 and 1985, the Local Government (Scotland) Act 1973 and the London Government Act 1963 are the main Acts which have brought about the present structure of local government in Great Britain. This structure has been in effect in England and Wales since 1974, with alterations in 1986 with the abolition of the metropolitan counties and the Greater London Council; and in Scotland since 1975.

The structure is based on two tiers of local authorities (county or regional councils and district councils) in the non-metropolitan areas; and a single tier of metropolitan and London borough councils in the six metropolitan areas of England and in London respectively.

The two-tier structure of local government in England is currently being reviewed by the Local Government Commission. The Government has published proposals for the establishment of a single tier of unitary authorities in Wales and Scotland.

Local authorities are empowered or required by various Acts of Parliament to carry out functions in their areas. The legislation concerned comprises public general Acts and 'local' Acts which local authorities have promoted as private bills.

ELECTIONS

Local elections are normally held on the first Thursday in May. Generally, all British subjects or citizens of the Republic of Ireland of 18 years or over who are resident on the qualifying date in the area for which the election is being held, are entitled to vote at local government elections. A register of electors is prepared and published annually by local electoral registration officers.

A returning officer has the overall responsibility for an election. Voting takes place at polling stations, arranged by the local authority and under the supervision of a presiding officer specially appointed for the purpose. Candidates, who are subject to various statutory qualifications and disqualifications designed to ensure that they are suitable persons to hold office, must be nominated by electors for the electoral area concerned.

In England, the Local Government Boundary Commission keeps the areas and electoral arrangements under review, and makes proposals to the Secretary of State for changes found necessary. In Wales and Scotland there are separate Local Government Boundary Commissions which carry out this task.

INTERNAL ORGANIZATION

The council as a whole is the final decision-making body within any authority. Councils are free to a great extent to make their own internal organizational arrangements.

Normally, questions of major policy are settled by the full council, while the administration of the various services is the responsibility of committees of councillors. Day-to-day decisions are delegated to the council's officers, who act within the policies laid down by the councillors.

FINANCE

Local government in England, Wales and Scotland is financed from three sources: the council tax, non-domestic rates and government grants. (For arrangements in Northern Ireland, see page 533.)

COUNCIL TAX

Under the Local Government Finance Act 1992, from 1 April 1993 the council tax replaced the community charge (which had been introduced in April 1989 in Scotland and April 1990 in England and Wales in place of domestic rates).

The council tax is a local tax levied by each local council. Liability for the council tax bill usually falls on the owner-occupier or tenant of a dwelling which is their sole or main residence. Council tax bills may be reduced because of the personal circumstances of people resident in a property, and there are discounts in the case of dwellings occupied by fewer than two adults.

In England and Wales, each county council and each district council sets its own council tax rate. The district councils collect the combined council tax and the county councils claim their share from the district councils' collection funds. In Scotland the regional and islands councils levy the council tax and the district councils claim a share.

The tax relates to the value of the dwelling. Each dwelling is placed in one of eight valuation bands, ranging from A to H, based on the property's estimated market value as at 1 April 1991.

The valuation bands and ranges of values in England, Wales and Scotland are:

England

A	Up to £40,000	E	£88,001–£120,000
B	£40,001–£52,000	F	£120,001–£160,000
C	£52,001–£68,000	G	£160,001–£320,000
D	£68,001–£88,000	H	Over £320,000

Wales

A	Up to £30,000	E	£66,001–£90,000
B	£30,001–£39,000	F	£90,001–£120,000
C	£39,001–£51,000	G	£120,001–£240,000
D	£51,001–£66,000	H	Over £240,000

Scotland

A	Up to £27,000	E	£58,001–£80,000
B	£27,001–£35,000	F	£80,001–£106,000
C	£35,001–£45,000	G	£106,001–£212,000
D	£45,001–£58,000	H	Over £212,000

The council tax within a local area varies between the different bands according to proportions laid down by law. The charge attributable to each band as a proportion of the Band D charge set by the council is:

A	67%	E	122%
B	78%	F	144%
C	89%	G	167%
D	100%	H	200%

The band D rate is given in the tables on pages 551–7 (England), 563 (London), 566 (Wales), and 570–1 (Scotland). There may be variations from the given figure within each district council area because of different parish precepts being levied.

NON-DOMESTIC RATES

Non-domestic (business) rates have been collected since 1 April 1990 by billing authorities, i.e. district councils in England and Wales, and regional and islands councils in Scotland. The Local Government Finance Act 1988 provides for liability for rates to be assessed on the basis of a poundage (multiplier) tax on the rateable value of property (hereditaments). The multiplier is set by central government and rates are collected by the billing authority for the area where a property is located. Rate income collected by billing authorities is paid into a national non-domestic rating (NNDR) pool and redistributed to individual authorities on the basis of the adult population figure as prescribed by the Secretary of State. For the years 1990–1 to 1994–5 actual payment of rates in certain cases are subject to transitional arrangements, to phase in the larger increases and reductions in rates resulting from the combined effects of the 1990 revaluation and the introduction of a uniform national business rate (UBR). The transitional arrangements were altered in 1992–3 and 1993–4 to freeze the increases for those going towards higher bills and ensure those going towards lower bills reached their true bill sooner.

Rateable values for the rating lists came into force on 1 April 1990. They are derived from the rental value of property as at 1 April 1988 and determined on certain statutory assumptions by valuation officers of the Valuation Office Agency. New property which is added to the list, and significant changes to existing property, necessitate amendments to the rateable value on the same basis. Rating lists remain in force until the next general revaluation, which is scheduled for 1 April 1995.

Certain types of property are exempt from rates, e.g. agricultural land and buildings, and places of public religious worship. Charities and other non-profit-making organizations may receive full or partial relief. Specified classes of empty property are liable to pay rates at 50 per cent.

GOVERNMENT GRANTS

In addition to specific grants in support of revenue expenditure on particular services, central government pays revenue support grant to local authorities. This grant is paid to each county/regional and district council so that if each authority spends at a level sufficient to provide a standard level of service, it can set the same council tax.

COMPLAINTS

Commissioners for Local Administration in England, Wales and Scotland (*see* page 329) are responsible for investigating complaints from members of the public who claim to have suffered injustice as a consequence of maladministration in local government.

The Northern Ireland Commissioner for Complaints fulfils a similar function in Northern Ireland, investigating complaints about local authorities and certain public bodies.

QUEEN'S REPRESENTATIVES

The Lord Lieutenant of a county is the permanent local representative of the Crown and as such takes precedence in the county. The Lord Lieutenant is appointed by the Sovereign on the recommendation of the Prime Minister. The title was created in 1557, when the Lord Lieutenant was given a range of responsibilities including the maintenance of an efficient militia. Some of the rights and duties of the post were abolished in 1871, but the Lord Lieutenant's duties still include attending on royalty during official visits to the county, acting as head of the county's commission of the peace (which recommends the appointment of magistrates for the county bench), raising the militia in times of need, and appointing deputy lieutenants. Lord Lieutenants must retire at the age of 75 if they do not choose to do so before reaching that age.

The office of Sheriff (from the Old English shire-reeve) of a county was created in the tenth century. The Sheriff was the special nominee of the Sovereign, and the office reached the peak of its influence under the Norman kings. The Provisions of Oxford (1258) laid down a yearly tenure of office. Since the mid-16th century the office has been purely civil, with military duties taken over by the Lord Lieutenant of the county. The Sheriff (commonly known as 'High Sheriff') attends on royalty during official visits to the county, acts as the returning officer during parliamentary elections in county constituencies, attends the opening ceremony when a High Court judge goes on circuit, executes High Court writs, and appoints under-sheriffs to act as deputies. The appointments and duties of the High Sheriffs in England and Wales are laid down by the Sheriffs Act 1887.

The serving High Sheriff submits a list of names of possible future sheriffs to a tribunal which chooses three names to put to the Sovereign. The tribunal nominates the High Sheriff annually on 12 November and the Sovereign pricks the name of the Sheriff to succeed in the following year. The term of office runs from 25 March to the following 24 March (the civil and legal year before 1752). No person may be chosen twice in three years if there is any other suitable person in the county.

CIVIC DIGNITIES

District councils may petition for a royal charter granting borough or 'City' status to the district.

In England and Wales the chairman of a borough council may be called a mayor, and the chairman of a city council a Lord Mayor. Parish councils in England and Wales may call themselves 'town councils', in which case their chairman is the town mayor.

In Scotland the chairman of a district council may be known as a convenor; a provost is the equivalent of a mayor. The chairmen of the councils for the cities of Aberdeen, Dundee, Edinburgh and Glasgow are Lord Provosts.

ENGLAND
(For London, *see* below)

England outside Greater London is divided into counties. Each county is divided into districts. There are 39 non-metropolitan counties; each of these is divided into non-metropolitan districts, of which there are 296. These districts have populations broadly in the range of 60,000 to 100,000; some however, have larger populations, because of the need to avoid dividing large towns, and some in mainly rural areas have smaller populations.

Six metropolitan counties cover the main conurbations outside Greater London; Tyne and Wear, West Midlands, Merseyside, Greater Manchester, West Yorkshire and South Yorkshire. They are divided into 36 metropolitan districts, most of which have a population of over 200,000.

There are also about 10,000 parishes, in 219 of the non-metropolitan and 18 of the metropolitan districts.

ELECTIONS

For districts, non-metropolitan counties, and for about 8,000 parishes, there are elected councils, consisting of directly elected councillors. The councillors elect annually one of their number as chairman.

Generally, councillors serve four years and there are no elections of district and parish councillors in county election years. In metropolitan districts, one-third of the councillors for each ward are elected each year except in the year of county elections. Non-metropolitan districts can choose whether to have elections by thirds or whole council elections. In the former case, one-third of the council, as nearly as may be, is elected in each year of metropolitan district elections.

If whole council elections are chosen, these are held in the year midway between county elections.

FUNCTIONS

In non-metropolitan areas, functions are divided between the districts and counties, those requiring the larger area or population for their efficient performance going to the county. The metropolitan district councils, with the larger population in their areas, already had wider functions than non-metropolitan councils, and following abolition of the metropolitan county councils were given most of their functions also. A few functions continue to be exercised over the larger area by joint bodies, made up of councillors from each district.

The allocation of functions is as follows:

County councils: education; strategic planning; traffic, transport and highways; police; fire service; consumer protection; refuse disposal; smallholdings; social services; libraries

Non-metropolitan district councils: local planning; housing; highways (maintenance of certain urban roads and off-street car parks); building regulations; environmental health; refuse collection; cemeteries and crematoria

Metropolitan district councils: their functions are all those listed above, except that fire, civil defence, police and passenger transport (and in some cases, refuse disposal) are exercised by joint bodies

Concurrently by county and district councils: recreation (parks, playing fields, swimming pools); museums; encouragement of the arts, tourism and industry

PARISH COUNCILS

Parishes with 200 or more electors must generally have parish councils, which means that over three-quarters of the parishes have councils. A parish council comprises at least five members, the number being fixed by the district council. Elections are held every four years, in the year in which the local district council is elected. All parishes have parish meetings, comprising the electors of the parish. Where there is no council, the meeting must be held at least twice a year.

Parish council functions include: allotments; encouragement of arts and crafts; community halls, recreational facilities (e.g. open spaces, swimming pools), cemeteries and crematoria; and many minor functions. They must also be given an opportunity to comment on planning applications. They may, like county and district councils, spend limited sums for the general benefit of the parish. They levy a precept on the district councils for their funds.

FINANCE

Aggregate external finance for 1993-4 was originally determined at £33,180 million. Of this, specific grants were estimated at £3,981 million and special grants at £588 million (mainly the community charge special grant). £17,051 million was in respect of revenue support grant and £11,559 million was support from the national non-domestic rate pool. Total standard spending by local authorities considered for grant purposes was £41,168 million.

The average council taxes, expressed in terms of Band C, two-adult properties for 1993-4, were: inner London boroughs £502; outer London boroughs £492; London £496; metropolitan districts £566; non-metropolitan districts £488. The average for England was £505.

National non-domestic rate (or uniform business rate) for 1993-4 is 41.6p. The amount estimated to be raised is £11.8 billion. Total rateable value held on local authority lists at 31 December 1992 was £31.1 billion.

EXPENDITURE

Local authority budgeted net revenue expenditure for 1992-3 was (1992-3 cash prices):

Service	£m
Education	18,531
School catering	410
Libraries, museums and art galleries	721
Personal social services	5,698
Police	5,513
Fire	1,197
Other Home Office services	768
Local transport	2,378
Local environmental services	5,098
Agricultural services	34
Consumer protection and trading standards	135
Employment	183
Non-housing revenue account housing	380
Housing benefits	3,418
Parish precepts	108
New net current expenditure	44,574
Capital charges	2,788
Capital charged to revenue	588
Other non-current expenditure	2,830
Interest receipts	−732
Gross revenue expenditure	50,048
Specific grants outside AEF	−7,399
Other income	−61
Revenue expenditure	42,588
Specific grants inside AEF	−4,563
Net revenue expenditure	38,025

AEF = aggregate external finance

LONDON

Since the abolition of the Greater London Council in 1986, the Greater London area has not had a single local government body. The area is divided into 32 borough councils, which have a status similar to the metropolitan district councils in the rest of England, and the Corporation of the City of London.

LONDON BOROUGH COUNCILS

The London boroughs have whole council elections every four years, in the year immediately following the county council election year. The next elections will be held on 6 May 1994.

The borough councils have responsibility for the following functions: building regulations; cemeteries and crematoria; consumer protection; education; youth employment; environmental health; electoral registration; food; drugs; housing; leisure services; libraries; local planning; local roads; museums; parking; recreation (parks, playing fields, swimming pools); refuse collection and street cleansing; social services; town planning; and traffic management.

THE CORPORATION OF THE CITY OF LONDON
(*see also* pages 558–60)

The Corporation of the City of London is the local authority for the City of London. Its legal definition is 'The Mayor and Commonalty and Citizens of the City of London'. It is governed by the Court of Common Council, which consists of the Lord Mayor, 24 other aldermen, and 132 common councilmen. The Lord Mayor and two sheriffs are nominated annually by the City guilds (the livery companies) and elected by the Court of Aldermen. Aldermen and councilmen are elected by businesses in the 25 wards into which the City is divided; councilmen must stand for re-election annually. The Council is a legislative assembly, and there are no political parties.

The Corporation has the same functions as the London borough councils. In addition, it runs the City of London Police; is the health authority for the Port of London; has health control of animal imports throughout Greater London, including at Heathrow airport; owns and manages public open spaces throughout Greater London; runs the Central Criminal Court; and runs Billingsgate, Smithfield and Spitalfields markets.

THE CITY GUILDS (LIVERY COMPANIES)

The livery companies of the City of London grew out of early medieval religious fraternities and began to emerge as trade and craft guilds, retaining their religious aspect, in the 12th century. From the early 14th century, only members of the trade and craft guilds could call themselves citizens of the City of London. The guilds began to be called livery companies, because of the distinctive livery worn by the most prosperous guild members on ceremonial occasions, in the late 15th century.

By the early 19th century the power of the companies within their trades had begun to wane, but those wearing the livery of a company continued to play an important role in the government of the City of London. Liverymen still have the right to nominate the Lord Mayor and sheriffs, and most members of the Court of Common Council are liverymen (*see also* page 560).

GREATER LONDON SERVICES

After the abolition of the Greater London Council (GLC) in 1986, the London boroughs took over most of its functions. Successor bodies have also been set up for certain functions.

The London Residuary Body (LRB) was set up in 1986 to deal with residual matters of the GLC which could not easily be transferred elsewhere. The LRB completed its work in relation to the GLC in 1990, when it became responsible for residual matters relating to the Inner London Education Authority, which was abolished on 1 April 1990. The LRB has now transferred most residual greater London-wide matters to the London Borough of Bromley and inner London-wide matters to the Royal Borough of Kensington and Chelsea. Its sole remaining responsibility is the disposal of County Hall.

LONDON RESIDUARY BODY, c/o Town Hall, Royal Borough of Kensington and Chelsea, Hornton Street, London w8 7NX. Tel: 071-938 4028.

WALES

Since 1974 Wales, including the former Monmouthshire, has been divided into eight counties. Each county is divided into districts, of which there are 37.

The arrangements for Welsh counties and districts are generally similar to those for English non-metropolitan counties and districts. There are some differences in functions; Welsh district councils have refuse disposal as well as refuse collection functions, and they may provide on-street as well as off-street car parks with the consent of the county council. A few districts have also been designated as library authorities.

COMMUNITY COUNCILS

In Wales parishes have been replaced by communities. Unlike England, where many areas are not in any parish, communities have been established for the whole of Wales, approximately 865 communities in all. Community meetings may be convened as and when desired.

Community councils exist in 734 communities and further councils may be established at the request of a community meeting. Community councils have broadly the same range of powers as English parish councils. Community councillors are elected en bloc at the same time as a district council election and for a term of four years.

FINANCE

Aggregate external finance for 1993–4 is £2,344.2 million. This comprises revenue support grant of £1,669.3 million, specific grants of £204.7 million, and support from the national non-domestic rate pool of £470.2 million. Total standard spending by local authorities considered for grant purposes is £2,599.8 million.

The average council tax levied in Wales for 1993–4 is £328, comprising county councils £267 and district councils £61.

National non-domestic rates (or uniform business rate) in Wales for 1993–4 is 44p. The amount estimated to be raised is £470.2 million. Total rateable value held on local authority lists at 31 December 1992 was £1,087 million.

SCOTLAND

Since 1975, mainland Scotland has been divided for local government purposes into nine regions within which there are 53 districts. In the three islands areas, Orkney, Shetland and the Western Isles, there are single-tier islands councils responsible for most local authority functions.

ELECTIONS

For the regional, islands and district councils, there are councils consisting of directly elected councillors. The councillors serve for four years, elections to district councils taking place midway between regional council elections. The next elections for regional councils are in 1994. In 1995 there will be elections for the shadow unitary authorities in advance of local government reform.

In 1993 the register showed 3,930,286 electors in Scotland.

FUNCTIONS

Regional councils: education; social work; strategic planning; the provision of infrastructure such as roads, water and sewerage; consumer protection; flood prevention; coast protection; valuation and rating; the police and fire services; civil defence; electoral registration; public transport; registration of births, deaths and marriages

District councils: housing; leisure and recreation, including tourism, parks, libraries, museums and galleries; development control and building control; environmental health, including cleansing, refuse collection and disposal, food hygiene, inspection of shops, offices and factories, clean air, markets and slaughterhouses, burial and cremation; licensing, including liquor, cinemas and theatres, taxis, street traders, betting and gaming, and charitable collections; allotments; public conveniences; the administration of district courts

COMMUNITY COUNCILS

Unlike the parish councils of England or community councils of Wales, Scottish community councils are not local authorities. Their purpose as defined in statute is to ascertain and express the views of the communities which they represent, and to take in the interests of their communities such action as appears to be expedient or practicable. Over 1,000 community councils have been established under schemes drawn up by district and islands councils in Scotland.

FINANCE

In 1991–2 a total of £1,332.9 million was received from non-domestic rates by local authorities. The average non-domestic rate levied was 58.1p. Total non-domestic water rate income was £17,611,000 and the average non-domestic water rate levied was 4.9p. Income from the non-domestic sewerage rate was £93,115,000 and the average non-domestic sewerage rate levied was 4.5p. Total metered water income was £77,961,000 and the average metered water rate levied was 36.7p.

The 1991–2 community charge income received by local authorities totalled £790,801,000 and the average personal community charge levied was £247.36 (after the £140 reduction). The community water charge receipts were £88,828,000 and the average community water charge levied was £28.64.

Provisional figures for 1992–3 show total receipts from non-domestic rates of £1,137.07 million and £982.33 million from the community charge. The average non-domestic rate per £ levied for 1992–3 was 55p and the average personal community charge payable in Scotland was £297.46.

rateable value). Rates are collected by the Department of the Environment for Northern Ireland and consist of a regional rate made by the Department of Finance and Personnel and a district rate made by individual district councils.

In 1991–2 a total of £321 million was raised in domestic rates in Northern Ireland and the total rateable value was £203.6 million. The average domestic poundage levied was 145.44p and the average non-domestic rate poundage was 239.44p.

NORTHERN IRELAND

For the purpose of local government Northern Ireland has a system of 26 single-tier district councils.

ELECTIONS

There are 566 members of the councils, elected for periods of four years at a time on the principle of proportional representation.

FUNCTIONS

The district councils have three main roles. These are:

Executive: responsibility for a wide range of local services including building regulations; community services; consumer protection; cultural facilities; environmental health; miscellaneous licensing and registration provisions, including dog control; litter prevention; recreational and social facilities; refuse collection and disposal; street cleansing; and tourist development

Representative: nominating representatives to sit as members of the various statutory bodies responsible for the administration of regional services such as drainage, education, electricity, fire, health and personal social services, and libraries

Consultative: acting as the medium through which the views of local people are expressed on the operation in their area of other regional services, notably conservation (including water supply and sewerage services), planning, and roads, provided by those departments of central government which have an obligation, statutory or otherwise, to consult the district councils about proposals affecting their areas

FINANCE

Local government in Northern Ireland is funded by a system of rates (a local property tax calculated by using the rateable value of a property multiplied by an amount per pound of

Political Composition of Local Councils

AS AT END MAY 1993

Abbreviations:

C.	Conservative
Com.	Communist
Dem.	Democrat
Green	Green
Ind.	Independent
Lab.	Labour
Lib.	Liberal
LD	Liberal Democrat
MK	Mebyon Kernow
NP	Non-political/Non-party
PC	Plaid Cymru
RA	Ratepayers'/Residents' Associations
SD	Social Democrat
SNP	Scottish National Party

ENGLAND

COUNTY COUNCILS

Avon	*Lab.* 33, *C.* 25, *LD* 18
Bedfordshire	*Lab.* 31, *C.* 28, *LD* 13, *Ind.* 1
Berkshire	*LD* 33, *Lab.* 24, *C.* 16, *Ind.* 2, *Lib.* 1
Buckinghamshire	*C.* 39, *LD* 16, *Lab.* 13, *Ind.* 2, *RA* 1
Cambridgeshire	*C.* 33, *Lab.* 21, *LD* 21, *Ind.* 1, *Lib.* 1
Cheshire	*Lab.* 35, *C.* 22, *LD* 14
Cleveland	*Lab.* 51, *C.* 14, *LD* 12
Cornwall	*LD* 42, *Ind.* 21, *Lab.* 8, *C.* 6, *Lib.* 1, *MK* 1
Cumbria	*Lab.* 39, *C.* 28, *LD* 14, *Ind.* 2
Derbyshire	*Lab.* 55, *C.* 21, *LD* 7, *Ind.* 1
Devon	*LD* 40, *Lab.* 21, *C.* 19, *Ind.* 4, *Lib.* 1
Dorset	*LD* 38, *C.* 29, *Lab.* 6, *Ind.* 4
Durham	*Lab.* 56, *C.* 6, *LD* 6, *Ind.* 4
East Sussex	*LD* 30, *C.* 22, *Lab.* 18
Essex	*Lab.* 33, *C.* 32, *LD* 32, *Ind.* 1
Gloucestershire	*LD* 30, *Lab.* 18, *C.* 10, *Ind.* C. 2, *Others* 3
Hampshire	*LD* 48, *C.* 29, *Lab.* 24, *Ind.* 1
Hereford and Worcester	*C.* 25, *Lab.* 24, *LD* 23, *Ind.* 4
Hertfordshire	*Lab.* 30, *C.* 27, *LD* 19, *Ind. RA* 1
Humberside	*Lab.* 43, *C.* 22, *LD* 10
Isle of Wight	*LD* 28, *C.* 9, *Ind.* 4, *Others* 2
Kent	*C.* 41, *Lab.* 30, *LD* 28
Lancashire	*Lab.* 52, *C.* 35, *LD* 10, *vacant* 2
Leicestershire	*Lab.* 37, *C.* 31, *LD* 17
Lincolnshire	*C.* 32, *Lab.* 25, *LD* 15, *Ind.* 4
Norfolk	*C.* 33, *Lab.* 32, *LD* 16, *Ind.* 2
Northamptonshire	*Lab.* 36, *C.* 27, *LD* 5
Northumberland	*Lab.* 40, *C.* 14, *LD* 11, *Ind.* 1
North Yorkshire	*LD.* 35, *C.* 29, *Lab.* 23, *Ind.* 8, *Ind. Lab.* 1
Nottinghamshire	*Lab.* 58, *C.* 24, *LD* 6
Oxfordshire	*C.* 25, *Lab.* 24, *LD* 20, *Green* 1

Shropshire	*C.* 26, *Lab.* 23, *LD* 14, *Ind.* 2, *Ind. Lab.* 1
Somerset	*LD* 41, *C.* 13, *Lab.* 2, *Ind.* 1
Staffordshire	*Lab.* 53, *C.* 22, *LD* 4, *Ind.* 1, *RA* 1, *Ratepayer* 1
Suffolk	*Lab.* 31, *C.* 26, *LD* 19, *Ind.* 4
Surrey	*C.* 34, *LD* 29, *Lab.* 8, *RA* 3, *Ind.* 2
Warwickshire	*Lab.* 30, *C.* 19, *LD* 10, *Ind.* 3
West Sussex	*LD* 34, *C.* 26, *Lab.* 10, *Ind.* 1
Wiltshire	*LD* 33, *C.* 18, *Lab.* 17

METROPOLITAN DISTRICT COUNCILS

GREATER MANCHESTER

Bolton	*Lab.* 39, *C.* 16, *Lib.* 4, *LD* 1
Bury	*Lab.* 24, *C.* 22, *LD* 2
Manchester	*Lab.* 78, *LD* 14, *C.* 5, *Ind. Lab.* 2
Oldham	*Lab.* 32, *LD* 19, *C.* 7, *Ind. Lab.* 1, *Ind. LD* 1
Rochdale	*Lab.* 23, *LD* 20, *C.* 16, *Ind.* 1
Salford	*Lab.* 53, *C.* 6, *vacant* 1
Stockport	*LD* 26, *C.* 17, *Lab.* 17, *Ind.* 3
Tameside	*Lab.* 46, *C.* 8, *Others* 2, *vacant* 1
Trafford	*C.* 37, *Lab.* 22, *LD* 4
Wigan	*Lab.* 63, *LD* 6, *C.* 2, *Ind. Lab.* 1

MERSEYSIDE

Knowsley	*Lab.* 59, *C.* 3, *Ind.* 2, *Ind. Lab.* 1, *vacant* 1
Liverpool	*Lab.* 40, *LD* 37, *C.* 2, *Lib.* 1, *SD* 1, *Others* 18
St Helens	*Lab.* 29, *LD* 14, *C.* 6, *Others* 5
Sefton	*Lab.* 27, *C.* 25, *LD* 17
Wirral	*Lab.* 31, *C.* 29, *LD* 6

SOUTH YORKSHIRE

Barnsley	*Lab.* 61, *C.* 2, *Ind.* 1, *vacant* 2
Doncaster	*Lab.* 54, *C.* 9
Rotherham	*Lab.* 63, *C.* 3
Sheffield	*Lab.* 65, *C.* 11, *LD* 11

TYNE AND WEAR

Gateshead	*Lab.* 55, *LD* 8, *C.* 1, *Ind.* 1, *Lib.* 1
Newcastle upon Tyne	*Lab.* 61, *LD* 11, *C.* 6
North Tyneside	*Lab.* 36, *C.* 16, *LD* 8
South Tyneside	*Lab.* 56, *LD* 3, *Ind.* 1
Sunderland	*Lab.* 64, *C.* 8, *LD* 3

WEST MIDLANDS

Birmingham	*Lab.* 61, *C.* 43, *LD* 13
Coventry	*Lab.* 40, *C.* 13, *vacant* 1
Dudley	*Lab.* 37, *C.* 35
Sandwell	*Lab.* 42, *C.* 24, *LD* 6
Solihull	*C.* 24, *Lab.* 15, *LD* 6, *RA* 6
Walsall	*C.* 23, *Lab.* 23, *LD* 9, *Ind.* 4, *vacant* 1
Wolverhampton	*Lab.* 29, *C.* 28, *LD* 3

WEST YORKSHIRE

Bradford	*Lab.* 50, *C.* 38, *LD* 2
Calderdale	*C.* 24, *Lab.* 22, *LD* 7, *Ind.* C. 1
Kirklees	*Lab.* 41, *C.* 18, *LD* 10, *RA* 2, *Others* 1
Leeds	*Lab.* 67, *C.* 23, *LD* 8, *Ind.* 1
Wakefield	*Lab.* 55, *C.* 6, *Ind.* 2

NON-METROPOLITAN DISTRICT COUNCILS

* denotes councils where one-third of councillors retire each year except the year of county council elections

*Adur	*LD* 22, *C.* 14, *RA* 2, *Lab.* 1
Allerdale	*Lab.* 30, *C.* 11, *Ind.* 11, *LD* 3
Alnwick	*LD* 15, *C.* 7, *Ind.* 5, *Lab.* 2
*Amber Valley	*Lab.* 21, *C.* 16, *Ind.* 3, *Others* 2, *vacant* 1
Arun	*C.* 36, *LD* 12, *Lab.* 7, *Ind.* 1
Ashfield	*Lab.* 32, *C.* 1
Ashford	*C.* 29, *LD* 12, *Lab.* 4, *Ind.* 1, *Others* 3
Aylesbury Vale	*C.* 27, *LD* 24, *Ind.* 6, *Lab.* 1
Babergh	*C.* 16, *Ind.* 9, *Lab.* 6, *LD* 5, *Others* 6
*Barrow-in-Furness	*C.* 18, *Lab.* 18, *Ind.* 2
*Basildon	*C.* 25, *Lab.* 13, *LD* 3, *vacant* 1
*Basingstoke and Deane	*C.* 35, *Lab.* 11, *LD* 7, *Ind.* 2, *Others* 2
*Bassetlaw	*Lab.* 30, *C.* 17, *Ind.* 2, *LD* 1
*Bath	*C.* 24, *LD* 17, *Lab.*7
Berwick-upon-Tweed	*LD* 11, *Ind.* 7, *C.* 5, *Lab.* 1, *Others* 4
Beverley	*C.* 31, *Lib.* 19, *Lab.* 2, *Ind.* 1
Blaby	*C.* 30, *LD* 4, *Ind.* 3, *Lab.* 1
*Blackburn	*Lab.* 36, *C.* 19, *LD* 4, *Ind.* 1
Blackpool	*Lab.* 27, *C.* 11, *LD* 5, *vacant* 1
Blyth Valley	*Lab.* 30, *LD* 17
Bolsover	*Lab.* 35, *RA* 2
Boothferry	*C.* 18, *Lab.* 12, *Ind.* 5
Boston	*C.* 12, *Lab.* 8, *LD* 8, *Ind.* 6
Bournemouth	*LD* 25, *C.* 21, *Lab.* 6, *Ind.* 5
Bracknell Forest	*C.* 32, *Lab.* 7, *LD* 1
Braintree	*C.* 24, *Lab.* 21, *Ind.* 9, *LD* 6
Breckland	*C.* 33, *Ind.* 12, *Lab.* 8
*Brentwood	*LD* 24, *C.* 13, *Ind.* 1, *Lab.* 1
Bridgnorth	*C.* 12, *Ind.* 8, *LD* 3, *Ind. Lab.* 2, *NP* 2, *Lab.* 1, *Others* 5
*Brighton	*Lab.* 25, *C.* 22, *Ind. Lab.* 1
*Bristol	*Lab.* 38, *C.* 22, *LD* 6, *Others* 2
*Broadland	*C.* 27, *Ind.* 8, *LD* 8, *Lab.* 6
Bromsgrove	*C.* 26, *Lab.* 14, *LD* 1
*Broxbourne	*C.* 36, *Lab.* 4, *LD* 2
Broxtowe	*C.* 27, *Lab.* 15, *LD* 6, *Ind.* 1
*Burnley	*Lab.* 33, *C.* 8, *LD* 7
*Cambridge	*Lab.* 20, *LD* 12, *C.* 9, *vacant* 1
*Cannock Chase	*Lab.* 30, *C.* 8, *Dem.* 2, *Ind.* 1, *Ind. Lib.* 1
Canterbury	*LD* 22, *C.* 19, *Lab.* 8
Caradon	*Ind.* 21, *LD* 8, *C.* 7, *RA* 4, *Lab.* 1
*Carlisle	*Lab.* 30, *C.* 18, *LD* 2, *Ind.* 1
Carrick	*LD* 20, *C.* 9, *Ind.* 8, *Lab.* 4, *Ind. C.* 1, *Others* 2, *vacant* 1
Castle Morpeth	*Ind.* 9, *Lab.* 9, *LD* 9, *C.* 7
Castle Point	*C.* 37, *Lab.* 2
Charnwood	*C.* 35, *Lab.* 15, *Ind.* 1, *LD* 1
Chelmsford	*C.* 29, *LD* 21, *Ind.* 4, *Lab.* 2
*Cheltenham	*LD* 23, *C.* 12, *Ind.* 3, *Lab.* 3
*Cherwell	*C.* 33, *Lab.* 15, *LD* 3, *Ind.* 1
*Chester	*C.* 23, *Lab.* 19, *LD* 16, *Ind.* 2
Chesterfield	*Lab.* 31, *LD* 12, *C.* 3, *vacant* 1
Chester-le-Street	*Lab.* 27, *Ind.* 5, *C.* 1
Chichester	*C.* 33, *LD* 14, *Ind.* 3
Chiltern	*C.* 39, *LD* 9, *RA* 2
*Chorley	*Lab.* 22, *C.* 20, *LD* 3, *Ind. C.* 2, *Ind.* 1
Christchurch	*C.* 13, *Ind.* 12

Cleethorpes	*Lab.* 16, *C.* 13, *LD* 10, *Ind.* 1, *vacant* 1
*Colchester	*LD* 30, *C.* 21, *Lab.* 7, *RA* 2
*Congleton	*LD* 19, *C.* 16, *Lab.* 9, *vacant* 1
Copeland	*Lab.* 28, *C.* 19, *Ind.* 3, *vacant* 1
Corby	*Lab.* 23, *C.* 2, *Ind.* 1, *LD* 1
Cotswold	*Ind.* 15, *C.* 10, *LD* 6, *Lab.* 1, *Others* 13
*Craven	*C.* 13, *LD* 10, *Ind.* 5, *Lab.* 3, *Ind. C.* 1, *Lib.* 1, *vacant* 1
*Crawley	*Lab.* 22, *C.* 8, *Ind.* 1, *LD* 1
*Crewe and Nantwich	*Lab.* 31, *C.* 24, *LD* 2
Dacorum	*C.* 37, *Lab.* 16, *LD* 4, *Ind. C.* 1
Darlington	*Lab.* 30, *C.* 18, *Ind.* 2, *SD* 2
Dartford	*C.* 25, *Lab.* 20, *RA* 2
*Daventry	*C.* 19, *Lab.* 11, *LD* 3, *Ind.* 2
*Derby	*C.* 22, *Lab.* 22
Derbyshire Dales	*C.* 26, *LD* 9, *Lab.* 4
Derwentside	*Lab.* 37, *Ind.* 14, *C.* 2, *vacant* 2
Dover	*C.* 28, *Lab.* 20, *LD* 6, *Ind.* 1, *vacant* 1
Durham	*Lab.* 29, *LD* 14, *Ind.* 6
Easington	*Lab.* 40, *Ind.* 4, *Lib.* 4, *Ind. Lab.* 3
*Eastbourne	*LD* 17, *C.* 12, *vacant* 1
East Cambridgeshire	*Ind.* 24, *C.* 5, *LD* 5, *Ind. C.* 1, *Lab.* 1, *vacant* 1
East Devon	*C.* 41, *LD* 11, *Green* 2, *Ind.* 2, *Ind. C.* 1, *Lib.* 1, *Others* 2
East Dorset	*C.* 18, *LD* 14, *RA* 2, *Others* 2
East Hampshire	*LD* 21, *C.* 15, *Ind.* 6
East Hertfordshire	*C.* 33, *LD* 11, *Ind.* 3, *Lab.* 2, *RA* 1
*Eastleigh	*C.* 20, *LD* 19, *Lab.* 5
East Lindsey	*Ind.* 44, *C.* 6, *LD* 5, *Lab.* 4, *Green* 1
East Northamptonshire	*C.* 24, *Lab.* 9, *LD* 3
East Staffordshire	*Lab.* 23, *C.* 18, *LD* 4, *vacant* 1
East Yorkshire	*C.* 16, *Ind.* 13, *LD* 6, *Lab.* 5, *SD* 3
Eden	*Ind.* 32, *LD* 4, *vacant* 1
*Ellesmere Port and Neston	*Lab.* 30, *C.* 11
*Elmbridge	*C.* 22, *RA* 19, *LD* 10, *Lab.* 8, *Ind.* 1
*Epping Forest	*C.* 31, *Lab.* 13, *RA* 10, *LD* 3, *SD* 2
Epsom and Ewell	*RA* 30, *Lib.* 6, *Lab.* 3
Erewash	*Lab.* 27, *C.* 22, *Ind.* 2, *LD* 1
*Exeter	*Lab.* 16, *C.* 14, *LD* 5, *Lib.* 1
*Fareham	*C.* 30, *LD* 8, *Lab.* 4
Fenland	*C.* 25, *Lab.* 6, *Ind.* 4, *LD* 3, *vacant* 2
Forest Heath	*C.* 12, *Ind.* 9, *LD* 3, *Lab.* 1
Forest of Dean	*Lab.* 25, *Ind.* 16, *LD* 7, *Others* 1
Fylde	*C.* 23, *Ind.* 11, *RA* 9, *LD* 4, *Green* 1, *Lab.* 1
Gedling	*C.* 38, *Lab.* 15, *LD* 3, *Ind.* 1
*Gillingham	*C.* 16, *LD* 15, *Lab.* 9, *Ind.* *LD* 2
Glanford	*C.* 22, *Ind.* 9, *Lab.* 7, *Green* 3
*Gloucester	*Lab.* 16, *C.* 13, *LD* 5, *Ind.* 1
*Gosport	*LD* 16, *C.* 8, *Ind.* 3, *Lab.* 3
Gravesham	*C.* 22, *Lab.* 22
*Great Grimsby	*Lab.* 28, *C.* 13, *LD* 2, *Ind.* 1, *vacant* 1
*Great Yarmouth	*Lab.* 29, *C.* 18, *LD* 1
Guildford	*C.* 20, *LD* 18, *Lab.* 6, *Ind.* 1
*Halton	*Lab.* 44, *LD* 7, *C.* 2

Hambleton	*C.* 24, *Ind.* 13, *LD* 5, *SD* 3, *Lab.* 2
Harborough	*C.* 18, *LD* 12, *Ind.* 4, *Lab.* 3
*Harlow	*Lab.* 31, *C.* 8, *LD* 3
*Harrogate	*LD* 31, *C.* 22, *Lab.* 4, *Ind.* 2, *Green* 1
*Hart	*C.* 16, *LD* 12, *Ind.* 7
*Hartlepool	*Lab.* 28, *C.* 12, *LD* 6, *Ind.* 1
*Hastings	*C.* 14, *Lab.* 9, *LD* 9
*Havant	*C.* 19, *Lab.* 12, *LD* 6, *Ind.* 5
*Hereford	*LD* 22, *Lab.* 4, *C.* 1
*Hertsmere	*C.* 23, *Lab.* 12, *LD* 3, *Ind.* 1
High Peak	*Lab.* 17, *C.* 14, *LD* 10, *Ind.* 3
Hinckley and Bosworth	*C.* 22, *LD* 8, *Lab.* 3, *Ind.* 1
Holderness	*Ind.* 24, *LD* 6, *vacant* 1
Horsham	*C.* 27, *LD* 14, *Ind.* 2
Hove	*C.* 21, *Lab.* 6, *LD* 3
*Huntingdonshire	*C.* 41, *LD* 7, *Lab.* 4, *Ind.* 1
*Hyndburn	*Lab.* 31, *C.* 12, *LD* 3, *vacant* 1
*Ipswich	*Lab.* 33, *C.* 15
Kennet	*C.* 17, *Ind.* 13, *LD* 8, *Lab.* 1, *vacant* 1
Kerrier	*LD* 15, *Lab.* 12, *Ind.* 10, *C.* 5, *Lib.* 2
Kettering	*Lab.* 18, *C.* 11, *LD* 8, *Ind.* 6, *Others* 2
King's Lynn and West Norfolk	*C.* 38, *Lab.* 15, *LD* 5, *Ind.* 1, *vacant* 1
*Kingston upon Hull	*Lab.* 56, *LD* 3, *C.* 1
Kingswood	*Lab.* 25, *C.* 18, *LD* 5, *Ind.* 1, *Ind. Lab.* 1
Lancaster	*Lab.* 24, *C.* 15, *Ind. Lab.* 11, *LD* 6, *Ind.* 2, *Ind. C.* 1
Langbaurgh on Tees	*Lab.* 29, *C.* 22, *LD* 7, *Ind. Lab.* 1
Leicester	*Lab.* 37, *C.* 12, *LD* 7
*Leominster	*Ind.* 24, *LD* 9, *Lab.* 2, *Green* 1
Lewes	*LD* 27, *C.* 18, *Ind.* 3
Lichfield	*C.* 37, *Lab.* 15, *Ind. Lab.* 3, *Ind.* 1
*Lincoln	*Lab.* 30, *C.* 3
Luton	*Lab.* 29, *C.* 9, *LD* 9, *Ind. C.* 1
*Macclesfield	*C.* 34, *LD* 13, *Lab.* 10, *RA* 3
*Maidstone	*C.* 26, *LD* 15, *Lab.* 8, *Ind.* 6
Maldon	*C.* 14, *Ind.* 11, *LD* 4, *vacant* 1
Malvern Hills	*Ind.* 17, *LD* 16, *C.* 15, *Lab.* 1, *Others* 1
Mansfield	*Lab.* 39, *C.* 5, *LD* 2
Medina	*C.* 18, *LD* 13, *Ind.* 2, *Lab.* 2, *vacant* 1
Melton	*C.* 18, *LD* 8
Mendip	*LD* 19, *C.* 13, *Ind.* 7, *Lab.* 3, *vacant* 1
Mid Bedfordshire	*C.* 43, *LD* 4, *Ind.* 3, *Lab.* 3
Mid Devon	*Ind.* 28, *LD* 8, *Lib.* 2, *Lab.* 1, *Ind. SD* 1
Middlesbrough	*Lab.* 37, *C.* 9, *LD* 5, *Ind.* 1, *vacant* 1
Mid Suffolk	*C.* 17, *LD* 10, *Lab.* 9, *Ind. C.* 4
*Mid Sussex	*C.* 34, *LD* 13, *Ind.* 5, *Lab.* 2
*Milton Keynes	*Lab.* 21, *C.* 15, *LD* 9, *Ind.* 1
*Mole Valley	*LD* 18, *C.* 13, *Ind.* 9, *Lab.* 1
Newark and Sherwood	*Lab.* 28, *C.* 18, *LD* 5, *Ind.* 3
Newbury	*LD* 24, *C.* 20, *vacant* 1
*Newcastle under Lyme	*Lab.* 36, *C.* 10, *LD* 10
New Forest	*LD* 30, *C.* 22, *Ind.* 6
Northampton	*Lab.* 21, *C.* 18, *LD* 4
Northavon	*LD* 25, *C.* 20, *Lab.* 11, *Ind.* 1
*North Bedfordshire	*C.* 25, *Lab.* 15, *LD* 10, *Ind.* 3

North Cornwall	*Ind.* 29, *LD* 6, *Lab.* 2, *C.* 1
North Devon	*LD* 29, *Ind.* 12, *C.* 3
North Dorset	*Ind.* 21, *LD* 12
North East Derbyshire	*Lab.* 34, *C.* 12, *Ind.* 4, *LD* 3
*North Hertfordshire	*C.* 27, *Lab.* 16, *LD* 3, *RA* 3, *Ind.* 1
North Kesteven	*NP* 26, *Lab.* 6, *LD* 5, *Ind.* 2
North Norfolk	*C.* 16, *LD* 7, *Ind.* 6, *Lab.* 6, *Others* 11
North Shropshire	*Ind.* 31, *C.* 5, *Lab.* 4
North Warwickshire	*Lab.* 20, *C.* 12, *Ind.* 2
North West Leicestershire	*Lab.* 26, *C.* 11, *Ind.* 3
North Wiltshire	*LD* 30, *C.* 15, *Ind.* 3, *Lab.* 3, *Others* 1
*Norwich	*Lab.* 35, *LD* 10, *C.* 3
Nottingham	*Lab.* 37, *C.* 17, *Green* 1
*Nuneaton and Bedworth	*Lab.* 36, *C.* 9
*Oadby and Wigston	*LD* 19, *C.* 7
Oswestry	*Ind.* 10, *C.* 9, *Lab.* 6, *LD* 4
*Oxford	*Lab.* 35, *C.* 10, *LD* 5, *Ind. LD* 1
*Pendle	*Lab.* 27, *Lib.* 17, *C.* 7
*Penwith	*C.* 12, *Lab.* 9, *Ind.* 8, *LD* 3, *Ind. Lab.* 1, *MK* 1
*Peterborough	*C.* 21, *Lab.* 18, *Lib.* 6, *Ind.* 3
Plymouth	*Lab.* 41, *C.* 18, *LD* 1
Poole	*LD* 20, *C.* 16
*Portsmouth	*C.* 17, *Lab.* 14, *LD* 7, *vacant* 1
*Preston	*Lab.* 32, *C.* 20, *LD* 5
*Purbeck	*C.* 12, *Ind.* 5, *LD* 5
*Reading	*Lab.* 29, *C.* 11, *LD* 4, *Others* 1
*Redditch	*Lab.* 20, *C.* 9
*Reigate and Banstead	*C.* 24, *Lab.* 11, *LD* 10, *RA* 3, *Ind.* 1
Restormel	*LD* 29, *Ind.* 12, *C.* 2, *Lab.* 1
Ribble Valley	*C.* 23, *LD* 15, *Lab.* 1
Richmondshire	*Ind.* 26, *C.* 4, *LD* 4
Rochester upon Medway	*C.* 22, *Lab.* 21, *LD* 7
*Rochford	*LD* 18, *C.* 12, *Ind. Lab.* 7, *RA* 2, *Ind.* 1
*Rossendale	*Lab.* 21, *C.* 15
Rother	*C.* 18, *LD* 16, *Ind.* 8, *Lab.* 3
*Rugby	*C.* 19, *Lab.* 16, *Ind.* 8, *LD* 3, *Ind. C.* 1, *vacant* 1
*Runnymede	*C.* 28, *Lab.* 7, *Ind.* 6, *Green* 1
Rushcliffe	*C.* 43, *LD* 6, *Lab.* 5
*Rushmoor	*C.* 30, *LD* 9, *Lab.* 6
Rutland	*Ind.* 9, *C.* 7, *LD* 4
Ryedale	*LD* 20, *Ind.* 14, *C.* 6, *Lab.* 2
*St Albans	*LD* 24, *C.* 22, *Lab.* 8, *Ind.* 1, *vacant* 2
St Edmundsbury	*C.* 26, *Lab.* 11, *LD* 5, *Ind.* 2
Salisbury	*C.* 33, *Ind.* 11, *LD* 8, *Lab.* 6
Scarborough	*C.* 16, *Lab.* 16, *Ind.* 9, *LD* 8
*Scunthorpe	*Lab.* 33, *C.* 6, *SD* 1
Sedgefield	*Lab.* 31, *LD* 8, *Ind.* 4, *C.* 2, *Others* 2, *vacant* 2
Sedgemoor	*C.* 26, *Lab.* 12, *LD* 7, *Ind.* 4
Selby	*C.* 22, *Lab.* 13, *Ind.* 10, *LD* 3, *Ind. Lab.* 2
Sevenoaks	*C.* 31, *LD* 11, *Ind.* 9, *Others* 2
Shepway	*LD* 32, *C.* 19, *Lab.* 3, *Ind.* 2
*Shrewsbury and Atcham	*C.* 20, *Lab.* 17, *Ind.* 6, *LD* 5
*Slough	*Lab.* 28, *C.* 5, *Lib.* 5, *vacant* 1
*Southampton	*Lab.* 30, *C.* 8, *LD* 6, *vacant* 1
*South Bedfordshire	*C.* 37, *Lab.* 9, *LD* 6, *Ind.* 1
South Bucks	*C.* 30, *Ind.* 10, *LD* 1
*South Cambridgeshire	*C.* 26, *Ind.* 21, *Lab.* 5, *LD* 3

South Derbyshire — *Lab.* 20, *C.* 11, *Ind.* 2, *Others* 1
*Southend-on-Sea — *C.* 25, *LD* 8, *Lab.* 6
South Hams — *C.* 24, *Ind.* 8, *NP* 6, *LD* 4, *Ind. C.* 1, *Lab.* 1
*South Herefordshire — *Ind.* 29, *C.* 5, *LD* 4, *RA* 1
South Holland — *Lab.* 10, *C.* 7, *Ind.* 2, *Others* 19
South Kesteven — *C.* 24, *Lab.* 13, *Ind.* 10, *LD* 9, *Lib.* 1
*South Lakeland — *C.* 17, *LD* 15, *Ind.* 14, *Lab.* 6
South Norfolk — *C.* 22, *LD.* 22, *Ind.* 3
South Northamptonshire — *C.* 29, *Ind.* 9, *Lab.* 2
South Oxfordshire — *C.* 28, *LD* 8, *Ind.* 5, *Lab.* 5, *RA* 3, *vacant* 1
South Ribble — *C.* 33, *Lab.* 15, *LD* 6
South Shropshire — *NP* 25, *C.* 5, *Ind.* 5, *LD* 3, *Ind. C.* 1, *Lab.* 1
South Somerset — *LD* 41, *C.* 14, *Ind.* 5
South Staffordshire — *C.* 37, *Lab.* 9, *LD* 3, *Ind.* 1
South Wight — *LD* 10, *C.* 7, *Ind.* 7
Spelthorne — *C.* 33, *Lab.* 4, *LD* 2, *Ind.* 1
Stafford — *C.* 29, *Lab.* 18, *LD* 11, *Ind.* 2
Staffordshire Moorlands — *RA* 24, *C.* 13, *Lab.* 8, *Ind.* 5, *Lib.* 4, *Others* 1, *vacant* 1
*Stevenage — *Lab.* 32, *C.* 4, *LD* 3
Stockton-on-Tees — *Lab.* 26, *C.* 17, *LD* 11, *Ind. Lab.* 1
*Stoke-on-Trent — *Lab.* 49, *C.* 11
*Stratford-upon-Avon — *C.* 27, *LD* 19, *Ind.* 6, *Ind. C.* 1, *Lab.* 1, *vacant* 1
*Stroud — *C.* 22, *Lab.* 14, *LD* 10, *Green* 5, *Ind.* 3, *vacant* 1
Suffolk Coastal — *C.* 37, *Ind.* 7, *Lab.* 6, *LD* 5
Surrey Heath — *C.* 31, *LD* 4, *Lab.* 1
*Swale — *C.* 20, *Lab.* 14, *LD* 14, *Ind.* 1
*Tamworth — *Lab.* 21, *C.* 8, *Ind.* 1
*Tandridge — *C.* 20, *LD* 18, *Lab.* 4
Taunton Deane — *LD* 29, *C.* 13, *Lab.* 7, *Ind.* 4
Teesdale — *Ind.* 21, *Lab.* 8, *C.* 2
Teignbridge — *Ind.* 22, *C.* 18, *Lib.* 14, *Lab.* 4
Tendring — *LD* 21, *C.* 19, *Lab.* 12, *Ind.* 8
Test Valley — *C.* 26, *LD* 16, *Ind.* 1, *NP* 1
Tewkesbury — *Ind.* 20, *C.* 7, *LD* 6, *Lab.* 3
*Thamesdown — *Lab.* 34, *C.* 13, *LD* 6, *Ind.* 1
Thanet — *C.* 30, *Lab.* 14, *Ind.* 8, *LD* 2
*Three Rivers — *C.* 21, *LD* 18, *Lab.* 9
*Thurrock — *Lab.* 29, *C.* 7, *Ind. C.* 2, *Others* 1
*Tonbridge and Malling — *C.* 32, *LD* 17, *Lab.* 6
*Torbay — *LD* 20, *C.* 13, *Lab.* 2, *Others* 1
Torridge — *Ind.* 16, *C.* 5, *LD* 5, *Lab.* 4, *Ind. C.* 5, *Green* 1, *Others* 2
*Tunbridge Wells — *C.* 29, *LD* 15, *Lab.* 3, *Ind.* 1
Tynedale — *C.* 18, *Lab.* 14, *LD* 9, *Ind.* 6
Uttlesford — *C.* 23, *LD* 12, *Ind.* 6, *Lab.* 1
Vale of White Horse — *C.* 30, *LD* 17, *Ind.* 2, *Lab.* 2
Vale Royal — *Lab.* 31, *C.* 24, *LD* 3, *Ind.* 1, *vacant* 1
Wansbeck — *Lab.* 44, *Lib.* 2
Wansdyke — *C.* 22, *Lab.* 20, *Ind.* 3, *LD* 2
Warrington — *Lab.* 42, *LD* 9, *C.* 8, *Ind. Lab.* 1
Warwick — *C.* 24, *Lab.* 10, *LD* 8, *RA* 3
*Watford — *Lab.* 22, *C.* 10, *LD* 4
*Waveney — *Lab.* 26, *C.* 17, *LD* 5
Waverley — *C.* 28, *LD* 27, *Lab.* 2
Wealden — *C.* 44, *LD* 9, *Ind.* 5
Wear Valley — *LD* 28, *Lab.* 8, *Ind.* 4
Wellingborough — *C.* 19, *Lab.* 12, *Ind.* 3
*Welwyn Hatfield — *C.* 24, *Lab.* 23
West Devon — *Ind.* 16, *LD* 7, *C.* 5, *Green* 1, *Lab.* 1

West Dorset — *C.* 17, *LD* 12, *Ind.* 7, *Lab.* 3, *SD* 1, *Others* 15
*West Lancashire — *C.* 27, *Lab.* 27, *LD* 1
*West Lindsey — *Ind.* 11, *C.* 10, *LD* 9, *Ind. Lab.* 7
*West Oxfordshire — *Ind.* 20, *C.* 14, *LD* 8, *Lab.* 6, *vacant* 1
West Somerset — *Ind.* 23, *C.* 5, *Lab.* 3, *LD* 1
West Wiltshire — *LD* 23, *C.* 9, *Lib.* 5, *Ind.* 2, *Lab.* 2, *Others* 1, *vacant* 1
*Weymouth and Portland — *C.* 10, *Lab.* 10, *LD* 10, *Ind.* 5
*Winchester — *C.* 24, *LD* 22, *Lab.* 6, *Ind.* 3
Windsor and Maidenhead — *C.* 26, *LD* 25, *RA* 7
*Woking — *C.* 19, *LD* 11, *Lab.* 5
*Wokingham — *C.* 33, *LD* 19, *Lab.* 1, *vacant* 1
Woodspring — *C.* 36, *LD* 15, *Ind.* 4, *Lab.* 3, *Green* 1
*Worcester — *C.* 22, *Lab.* 12, *Ind.* 1, *LD* 1
*Worthing — *C.* 22, *LD* 14
Wrekin — *Lab.* 33, *C.* 10, *LD* 2, *Ind.* 1
Wychavon — *C.* 32, *LD* 10, *Lab.* 6, *Ind.* 1
Wycombe — *C.* 37, *LD* 11, *Lab.* 9, *Ind.* 2, *RA* 1
Wyre — *C.* 32, *Lab.* 17, *LD* 5, *Ind.* 1, *RA* 1
*Wyre Forest — *Lab.* 21, *LD* 11, *C.* 9, *Ind.* 1
*York — *Lab.* 34, *C.* 7, *LD* 4

GREATER LONDON BOROUGHS

Barking and Dagenham — *Lab.* 44, *RA* 3, *LD* 1
Barnet — *C.* 39, *Lab.* 18, *LD* 3
Bexley — *C.* 34, *Lab.* 18, *LD* 9, *Ind.* 1
Brent — *C.* 33, *Lab.* 22, *LD* 7, *Ind.* 2, *Green* 1, *vacant* 1
Bromley — *C.* 42, *Lab.* 11, *LD* 7
Camden — *Lab.* 42, *C.* 15, *LD* 2
City of Westminster — *C.* 45, *Lab.* 15
Croydon — *C.* 40, *Lab.* 30
Ealing — *C.* 39, *Lab.* 31
Enfield — *C.* 35, *Lab.* 31
Greenwich — *Lab.* 42, *C.* 12, *SD* 4, *Ind.* 2, *LD* 2
Hackney — *Lab.* 41, *C.* 8, *LD* 7, *Ind. Lab.* 2, *Others* 1, *vacant* 1
Hammersmith and Fulham — *Lab.* 27, *C.* 22, *vacant* 1
Haringey — *Lab.* 43, *C.* 16
Harrow — *C.* 35, *Lab.* 13, *LD* 12, *Ind.* 3
Havering — *Lab.* 26, *C.* 19, *RA* 13, *LD* 5
Hillingdon — *C.* 35, *Lab.* 34
Hounslow — *Lab.* 44, *C.* 15, *LD* 1
Islington — *Lab.* 47, *LD* 4, *C.* 1
Kensington and Chelsea — *C.* 39, *Lab.* 15
Kingston upon Thames — *C.* 25, *LD* 18, *Lab.* 7
Lambeth — *Lab.* 26, *C.* 18, *LD* 9, *Others* 10, *vacant* 1
Lewisham — *Lab.* 58, *C.* 6, *LD* 3
Merton — *Lab.* 29, *C.* 22, *RA* 2, *Ind. Lab.* 1, *Others* 3
Newham — *Lab.* 54, *C.* 4, *LD* 2
Redbridge — *C.* 43, *Lab.* 17, *LD* 3
Richmond upon Thames — *LD* 49, *C.* 3
Southwark — *Lab.* 35, *LD* 22, *C.* 6, *Ind.* 1
Sutton — *LD* 32, *C.* 18, *Lab.* 6
Tower Hamlets — *LD* 29, *Lab.* 21
Waltham Forest — *Lab.* 30, *C.* 15, *LD* 11, *Ind.* 1
Wandsworth — *C.* 48, *Lab.* 13

WALES

COUNTY COUNCILS

Clwyd	*Lab.* 32, *Ind.* 15, *C.* 8, *Others* 8, *vacant* 1
Dyfed	*Ind.* 31, *Lab.* 22, *LD* 8, *PC* 7, *C.* 1, *RA* 1
Gwent	*Lab.* 55, *C.* 6, *LD* 1, *PC* 1
Gwynedd	*Ind.* 27, *PC* 18, *Lab.* 9, *LD* 7, *C.* 1
Mid Glamorgan	*Lab.* 60, *PC* 10, *Ind.* 3, *C.* 1
Powys	*Ind.* 35, *Lab.* 6, *LD* 4, *Others* 1
South Glamorgan	*Lab.* 40, *C.* 12, *LD* 8, *Ind. Lab.* 1, *PC* 1
West Glamorgan	*Lab.* 47, *Ind.* 5, *C.* 3, *LD* 3, *PC* 1, *RA* 1, *SD* 1

DISTRICT COUNCILS

Aberconwy	*Lab.* 11, *LD* 10, *C.* 9, *Ind.* 6, *PC* 1, *Others* 4
Alyn and Deeside	*Lab.* 27, *C.* 8, *Ind.* 5, *LD* 2, *Ind. Lab.* 1
Arfon	*Ind.* 14, *PC* 14, *Lab.* 8, *LD* 2, *Others* 1
Blaenau Gwent	*Lab.* 32, *RA* 5, *Ind.* 3, *PC* 2, *C.* 1, *Lib.* 1
Brecknock	*Ind.* 29, *Lab.* 13, *LD* 2
Cardiff	*Lab.* 39, *C.* 16, *LD* 9, *Ind.* 1
Carmarthen	*Ind.* 27, *Lab.* 6, *PC* 2, *LD* 1, *RA* 1
Ceredigion	*Ind.* 30, *LD* 9, *PC* 4, *Lab.* 1
Colwyn	*LD* 12, *Ind.* 11, *C.* 7, *Lab.* 3, *vacant* 1
Cynon Valley	*Lab.* 25, *PC* 10, *Ind. Lab.* 2, *Others* 1
Delyn	*Ind.* 22, *Lab.* 12, *Others* 8
Dinefwr	*Lab.* 15, *PC* 5, *Ind. Lab.* 2, *NP* 1
Dwyfor	*PC* 7, *Others* 22
Glyndŵr	*Ind.* 26, *Lab.* 6, *LD* 2, *PC* 1
Islwyn	*Lab.* 30, *PC* 5
Llanelli	*Lab.* 19, *LD* 4, *Green* 2, *PC* 2, *Ind.* 1, *Others* 7
Lliw Valley	*Lab.* 22, *Green* 5, *PC* 4, *C.* 1, *Others* 1
Meirionnydd	*PC* 13, *Lab.* 5, *Ind.* 1, *Others* 22
Merthyr Tydfil	*Lab.* 20, *RA* 8, *Ind.* 2, *PC* 1, *Others* 2
Monmouth	*C.* 22, *Lab.* 14, *Ind.* 3, *LD* 1
Montgomeryshire	*Ind.* 38, *LD* 4, *Lab.* 2, *C.* 1, *PC* 1
Neath	*Lab.* 25, *PC* 5, *LD* 2, *Ind.* 1, *Others* 1
Newport	*Lab.* 40, *C.* 7
Ogwr	*Lab.* 38, *C.* 9, *Ind. Lab.* 1, *LD* 1
Port Talbot	*Lab.* 21, *RA* 6, *SD* 2, *Ind.* 1, *LD* 1
Preseli Pembrokeshire	*Ind.* 36, *Lab.* 2, *C.* 1, *LD* 1
Radnorshire	*NP* 26, *Lab.* 4, *LD* 2, *Green* 1
Rhondda	*Lab.* 26, *PC* 4, *RA* 3
Rhuddlan	*Ind.* 21, *Lab.* 11
Rhymney Valley	*Lab.* 27, *PC* 13, *Ind.* 3, *NP* 3
South Pembrokeshire	*NP* 26, *Lab.* 2, *PC* 2
Swansea	*Lab.* 30, *C.* 10, *Ind.* 6, *LD* 6
Taff-Ely	*Lab.* 19, *PC* 14, *Ind.* 4, *C.* 2, *LD* 2, *RA* 1, *SD* 1
Torfaen	*Lab.* 36, *Ind.* 3, *LD* 3, *C.* 1, *Others* 1

Vale of Glamorgan	*Lab.* 20, *C.* 18, *PC* 3, *Others* 4, *vacant* 1
Wrexham Maelor	*Lab.* 29, *Ind.* 6, *LD* & *Lib.* 6, *C.* 4, *PC* 1
Ynys Môn	*Ind.* 25, *PC* 8, *Lab.* 5, *C.* 1

SCOTLAND

REGIONAL AND ISLANDS COUNCILS

Borders	*Ind.* 14, *LD* 5, *C.* 2, *SNP* 2
Central	*Lab.* 22, *SNP* 6, *C.* 5, *Ind.* 1
Dumfries and Galloway	*Lab.* 11, *Ind.* 9, *NP* 6, *SNP* 4, *Lib.* 2, *C.* 1, *Ind. Lab.* 1, *Others* 1
Fife	*Lab.* 29, *LD* 11, *C.* 2, *SNP* 2, *Com.* 1, *Ind.* 1
Grampian	*Lab.* 17, *SNP* 14, *C.* 13, *LD* 9, *Ind.* 3, *Ind. Lab.* 1
Highland	*Ind.* 34, *Lab.* 10, *LD* 3, *SNP* 2, *C.* 1, *Green* 1, *Ind. LD* 1
Lothian	*Lab.* 34, *C.* 12, *LD* 2, *SNP* 1
Orkney	*Ind.* 23, *SNP* 1
Shetland	*Ind.* 17, *Lab.* 2, *Others* 6
Strathclyde	*Lab.* 87, *C.* 5, *LD* 4, *Ind.* 3, *Ind. Lab.* 2, *SNP* 2
Tayside	*Lab.* 18, *C.* 13, *SNP* 10, *LD* 3, *Ind.* 1, *Ind. Lab.* 1
Western Isles	*NP* 30

DISTRICT COUNCILS

Aberdeen	*Lab.* 27, *LD* 13, *C.* 10, *SNP* 2
Angus	*SNP* 11, *C.* 7, *Ind.* 2, *Others* 1
Annandale and Eskdale	*LD* 10, *NP* 5, *Lab.* 1
Argyll and Bute	*Ind.* 10, *NP* 6, *C.* 4, *LD* 3, *SNP* 2, *Lab.* 1
Badenoch and Strathspey	*Ind. C.* 11
Banff and Buchan	*Ind.* 11, *SNP* 7
Bearsden and Milngavie	*C.* 5, *LD* 4, *Lab.* 1
Berwickshire	*C.* 7, *Ind.* 3, *LD* 1, *vacant* 1
Caithness	*Ind.* 14, *Ind. Lib.* 1, *Lab.* 1
Clackmannan	*Lab.* 8, *SNP* 3, *C.* 1
Clydebank	*Lab.* 8, *SNP* 2, *C.* 1, *Ind.* 1
Clydesdale	*Lab.* 7, *SNP* 4, *C.* 3, *Ind.* 2
Cumbernauld and Kilsyth	*Lab.* 7, *SNP* 5
Cumnock and Doon Valley	*Lab.* 10
Cunninghame	*Lab.* 20, *C.* 6, *SNP* 3, *Ind.* 1
Dumbarton	*Lab.* 8, *C.* 5, *SNP* 2, *NP* 1
Dundee	*Lab.* 26, *C.* 12, *SNP* 6
Dunfermline	*Lab.* 22, *LD* 5, *SNP* 4, *C.* 2, *Others* 1
East Kilbride	*Lab.* 12, *C.* 2, *SNP* 2
East Lothian	*Lab.* 9, *C.* 7, *SNP* 1
Eastwood	*C.* 8, *RA* 2, *Lab.* 1, *LD* 1
Edinburgh	*Lab.* 30, *C.* 23, *LD* 7, *SNP* 2
Ettrick and Lauderdale	*Ind.* 15, *SNP* 1
Falkirk	*Lab.* 16, *SNP* 12, *Ind.* 5, *C.* 3
Glasgow	*Lab.* 54, *C.* 5, *Ind.* 4, *SNP* 2, *LD* 1
Gordon	*Ind.* 9, *LD* 5, *C.* 2
Hamilton	*Lab.* 15, *C.* 2, *LD* 2, *Ind. Lab.* 1
Inverclyde	*Lab.* 11, *LD* 8, *C.* 1
Inverness	*Ind.* 13, *Lab.* 8, *LD* 5, *Lib.* 1, *SNP* 1
Kilmarnock and Loudoun	*Lab.* 8, *SNP* 7, *C.* 3

Kincardine and Deeside	*C.* 5, *Ind.* 5, *LD* 1, *SNP* 1
Kirkcaldy	*Lab.* 24, *SNP* 7, *Ind.* 3, *C.* 2, *LD* 2, *Others* 2
Kyle and Carrick	*C.* 16, *Lab.* 9
Lochaber	*Ind.* 8, *Lab.* 3, *SNP* 3, *Ind. Lab.* 1
Midlothian	*Lab.* 12, *C.* 2, *SNP* 1
Monklands	*Lab.* 17, *SNP* 3
Moray	*Ind.* 9, *SNP* 7, *C.*1, *Lab.* 1
Motherwell	*Lab.* 22, *SNP* 4, *C.* 2, *Ind.* 1, *NP* 1
Nairn	*Ind.* 8, *C.* 1, *SNP* 1
Nithsdale	*Lab.* 9, *Ind.* 8, *C.* 5, *SNP* 5, *LD* 1
North East Fife	*LD* 13, *C.* 4, *Ind.* 1
Perth and Kinross	*C.* 16, *SNP* 5, *Ind.* 3, *Lab.* 3, *Lib.* 2
Renfrew	*Lab.* 22, *SNP* 12, *C.* 8, *LD* 2, *Ind.* 1
Ross and Cromarty	*Ind.* 15, *SNP* 4, *Lab.* 2, *C.* 1
Roxburgh	*Ind.* 8, *LD* 5, *C.* 2, *SNP* 1
Skye and Lochalsh	*Ind.* 10, *SNP* 1
Stewartry	*Ind.* 11, *C.* 1
Stirling	*C.* 10, *Lab.* 10
Strathkelvin	*Lab.* 8, *C.* 6, *vacant* 1
Sutherland	*Ind.* 14
Tweeddale	*Ind.* 6, *LD* 2, *Lab.* 1, *SNP* 1
West Lothian	*Lab.* 11, *SNP* 10, *C.* 2, *Ind.* 1
Wigtown	*Ind.* 10, *SNP* 2, *C.* 1, *Lab.* 1

England

The Kingdom of England lies between 55° 46′ and 49° 57′ 30″ N. latitude (from a few miles north of the mouth of the Tweed to the Lizard), and between 1° 46′ E. and 5° 43′ W. (from Lowestoft to Land's End). England is bounded on the north by the Cheviot Hills; on the south by the English Channel; on the east by the Straits of Dover (Pas de Calais) and the North Sea; and on the west by the Atlantic Ocean, Wales and the Irish Sea. It has a total area of 50,377 sq. miles (130,478 sq. km): land 50,085 sq. miles (129,720 sq. km); inland water 293 sq. miles (758 sq. km).

POPULATION

The population at the 1991 Census was 46,382,050 (males 22,469,707; females 23,912,343). The average density of the population in 1991 was 3.6 persons per hectare.

FLAG

The cross of St George, the patron saint of England (cross gules in a field argent), has been used since the 13th century.

RELIEF

There is a marked division between the upland and lowland areas of England. In the extreme north the Cheviot Hills (highest point, The Cheviot, 2,674 ft) form a natural boundary with Scotland. Running south from the Cheviots, though divided from them by the Tyne Gap, is the Pennine range (highest point, Cross Fell, 2,930 ft), the main orological feature of the country. The Pennines culminate in the Peak District of Derbyshire (Kinder Scout, 2,088 ft). West of the Pennines are the Cumbrian mountains, which include Scafell Pike (3,210 ft), the highest peak in England, and to the east are the Yorkshire Moors, their highest point being Urra Moor (1,490 ft).

In the west, the foothills of the Welsh mountains extend into the bordering English counties of Shropshire (the Wrekin, 1,334 ft; Long Mynd, 1,694 ft) and Hereford and Worcester (the Malvern Hills – Worcestershire Beacon, 1,394 ft). Extensive areas of high land and moorland are also to be found in the south-western peninsula formed by Somerset, Devon and Cornwall: principally Exmoor (Dunkery Beacon, 1,704 ft), Dartmoor (High Willhays, 2,038 ft) and Bodmin Moor (Brown Willy, 1,377 ft). Ranges of low, undulating hills run across the south of the country, including the Cotswolds in the Midlands and south-west, the Chilterns to the north of London, and the North (Kent) and South (Sussex) Downs of the south-east coastal areas.

The lowlands of England lie in the Vale of York, East Anglia and the area around the Wash. The lowest-lying are the Cambridgeshire Fens in the valleys of the Great Ouse and the River Nene, which are below sea-level in places. Since the 17th century extensive drainage has brought much of the Fens under cultivation. The North Sea coast between the Thames and the Humber, low-lying and formed of sand and shingle for the most part, is subject to erosion and defences against further incursion have been built along many stretches.

HYDROGRAPHY

The Severn is the longest river in Great Britain, rising in the north-eastern slopes of Plynlimon (Wales) and entering England in Shropshire with a total length of 220 miles (354 km) from its source to its outflow into the Bristol Channel, where it receives on the east the Bristol Avon, and on the west the Wye, its other tributaries being the Vyrnwy, Tern,

Stour, Teme and Upper (or Warwickshire) Avon. The Severn is tidal below Gloucester, and a high bore or tidal wave sometimes reverses the flow as high as Tewkesbury (13½ miles above Gloucester). The scenery of the greater part of the river is very picturesque and beautiful, and the Severn is a noted salmon river, some of its tributaries being famous for trout. Navigation is assisted by the Gloucester and Berkeley Ship Canal (16¾ miles), which admits vessels of 350 tons to Gloucester. The Severn Tunnel was begun in 1873 and completed in 1886 at a cost of £2,000,000 and after many difficulties from flooding. It is 4 miles 628 yards in length (of which 2¼ miles are under the river). The Severn road bridge between Haysgate, Gwent, and Almondsbury, Glos., with a centre span of 3,240 ft, was opened in 1966.

The longest river wholly in England is the Thames, with a total length of 215 miles (346 km) from its source in the Cotswold hills to the Nore, and is navigable by ocean-going ships to London Bridge. The Thames is tidal to Teddington (69 miles from its mouth) and forms county boundaries almost throughout its course; on its banks are situated London, Windsor Castle, the oldest royal residence still in regular use, Eton College, the first of the public schools, and Oxford, the oldest university in the kingdom.

Of the remaining English rivers those flowing into the North Sea are the Tyne, Wear, Tees, Ouse and Trent from the Pennine Range, the Great Ouse (160 miles), which rises in Northamptonshire, and the Orwell and Stour from the hills of East Anglia. Flowing into the English Channel are the Sussex Ouse from the Weald, the Itchen from the Hampshire Hills, and the Axe, Teign, Dart, Tamar and Exe from the Devonian hills. Flowing into the Irish Sea are the Mersey, Ribble and Eden from the western slopes of the Pennines and the Derwent from the Cumbrian mountains.

The English Lakes, noteworthy for their picturesque scenery and poetic associations, lie in Cumbria, the largest being Windermere (10 miles long), Ullswater and Derwentwater.

ISLANDS

The Isle of Wight is separated from Hampshire by the Solent. The capital, Newport, stands at the head of the estuary of the Medina, Cowes (at the mouth) being the chief port. Other centres are Ryde, Sandown, Shanklin, Ventnor, Freshwater, Yarmouth, Totland Bay, Seaview and Bembridge.

Lundy (the name means Puffin Island), 11 miles north-west of Hartland Point, Devon, is about two miles long and about half a mile broad (average), with a total area of about 1,116 acres, and a population of about 20. It became the property of the National Trust in 1969 and is now principally a bird sanctuary.

The Isles of Scilly consist of about 140 islands and skerries (total area, 6 sq. miles/10 sq. km) situated 28 miles south-west of Land's End. Only five are inhabited: St Mary's, St Agnes, Bryher, Tresco and St Martin's. The population is 1,978. The entire group has been designated a Conservation Area, a Heritage Coast, and an Area of Outstanding Natural Beauty, and has been given National Nature Reserve status by the Nature Conservancy Council because of its unique flora and fauna. Tourism and the winter/spring flower trade for the home market form the basis of the economy of the Isles. The island group is a recognized rural development area.

EARLY HISTORY

Prehistoric Inhabitants

Archaeological evidence suggests that England has been inhabited since at least the Palaeolithic period, though the extent of the various Palaeolithic cultures was dependent upon the degree of glaciation. The succeeding Neolithic and Bronze Age cultures have left abundant remains throughout the country, the best-known of these being the henges and stone circles of Stonehenge (ten miles north of Salisbury, Wilts.) and Avebury (Wilts.), both of which are believed to have been of religious significance. In the latter part of the Bronze Age the Goidels, a people of Celtic race, and in the Iron Age other Celtic races of Brythons and Belgae, invaded the country and brought with them Celtic civilization and dialects, place names in England bearing witness to the spread of the invasion over the whole kingdom.

The Roman Conquest

The Roman conquest of Gaul (57–50 BC) brought Britain into close contact with Roman civilization, but although Julius Caesar raided the south of Britain in 55 BC and 54 BC, conquest was not undertaken until nearly 100 years later. In AD 43 the Emperor Claudius dispatched Aulus Plautius, with a well-equipped force of 40,000, and himself followed with reinforcements in the same year. Success was delayed by the resistance of Caratacus (Caractacus), the British leader from AD 48–51, who was finally captured and sent to Rome, and by a great revolt in AD 61 led by Boudicca (Boadicea), Queen of the Iceni; but the south of Britain was secured by AD 70, and Wales and the area north to the Tyne by about AD 80.

In AD 122, the Emperor Hadrian visited Britain and built a continuous rampart, since known as Hadrian's Wall, from Wallsend to Bowness (Tyne to Solway). The work was entrusted by the Emperor Hadrian to Aulus Platorius Nepos, legate of Britain from AD 122 to 126, and it was intended to form the northern frontier of the Roman Empire.

The Romans administered Britain as a province under a Governor, with a well-defined system of local government, each Roman municipality ruling itself and surrounding territory, while London was the centre of the road system and the seat of the financial officials of the Province of Britain. Colchester, Lincoln, York, Gloucester and St Albans stand on the sites of five Roman municipalities, and Wroxeter, Caerleon, Chester, Lincoln and York were at various times the sites of legionary fortresses. Well-preserved Roman towns have been uncovered at (or near) Silchester (*Calleva Atrebatum*), ten miles south of Reading, Wroxeter (*Viroconium Cornoviorum*), near Shrewsbury, and St Albans (*Verulamium*) in Hertfordshire.

Four main groups of roads radiated from London, and a fifth (the Fosse) ran obliquely from Lincoln through Leicester, Cirencester and Bath to Exeter. Of the four groups radiating from London, one ran south-east to Canterbury and the coast of Kent, a second to Silchester and thence to parts of western Britain and south Wales, a third (later known as Watling Street) ran through Verulamium to Chester, with various branches, and the fourth reached Colchester, Lincoln, York and the eastern counties.

In the fourth century Britain was subject to raids along the east coast by Saxon pirates, which led to the establishment of a system of coast defence from the Wash to Southampton Water, with forts at Brancaster, Burgh Castle (Yarmouth), Walton (Felixstowe), Bradwell, Reculver, Richborough, Dover, Lympne, Pevensey and Porchester (Portsmouth). The Irish (Scoti) and Picts in the north were also becoming more aggressive; from about AD 350 incursions became more

frequent and more formidable. As the Roman Empire came under attack increasingly towards the end of the fourth century, many troops were removed from Britain for service in other parts of the empire. The island was eventually cut off from Rome by the Teutonic conquest of Gaul, and with the withdrawal of the last Roman garrison early in the fifth century, the Romano-British were left to themselves.

Saxon Settlement

According to legend, the British King Vortigern called in the Saxons to defend him against the Picts, the Saxon chieftains being Hengist and Horsa, who landed at Ebbsfleet, Kent, and established themselves in the Isle of Thanet; but the events during the one and a half centuries between the final break with Rome and the re-establishment of Christianity are unclear. However, it would appear that in the course of this period the raids turned into large-scale settlement by invaders traditionally known as Angles (England north of the Wash and East Anglia), Saxons (Essex and southern England) and Jutes (Kent and the Weald), which pushed the Romano-British into the mountainous areas of the north and west, Celtic culture outside Wales and Cornwall surviving only in topographical names. Various kingdoms were established at this time which attempted to claim overlordship of the whole country, hegemony finally being achieved by Wessex (capital, Winchester) in the ninth century. This century also saw the beginning of raids by the Vikings (Danes), which were resisted by Alfred the Great (871–899), who fixed a limit to the advance of Danish settlement by the Treaty of Wedmore (878), giving them the area north and east of Watling Street, on condition that they adopt Christianity.

In the tenth century the kings of Wessex recovered the whole of England from the Danes, but subsequent rulers were unable to resist a second wave of invaders. England paid tribute (*Danegeld*) for many years, and was invaded in 1013 by the Danes and ruled by Danish kings from 1016 until 1042, when Edward the Confessor was recalled from exile in Normandy. On Edward's death in 1066 Harold Godwinson (brother-in-law of Edward and son of Earl Godwin of Wessex) was chosen King of England. After defeating (at Stamford Bridge, Yorkshire, 25 September) an invading army under Harald Hadraada, King of Norway (aided by the outlawed Earl Tostig of Northumbria, Harold's brother), Harold was himself defeated at the Battle of Hastings on 14 October 1066, and the Norman conquest secured the throne of England for Duke William of Normandy, a cousin of Edward the Confessor.

Christianity

Christianity reached the Roman province of Britain from Gaul in the third century (or possibly earlier); Alban, traditionally Britain's first martyr, was put to death as a Christian during the persecution of Diocletian (22 June 303), at his native town Verulamium; and the Bishops of Londinium, Eboracum (York), and Lindum (Lincoln) attended the Council of Arles in 314. However, the Anglo-Saxon invasions submerged the Christian religion in England until the sixth century when conversion was undertaken in the north from 563 by Celtic missionaries from Ireland led by St Columba, and in the south by a mission sent from Rome in 597 which was led by St Augustine, who became the first archbishop of Canterbury. England appears to have been converted again by the end of the seventh century and followed, after the Council of Whitby in 663, the practices of the Roman Church, which brought the kingdom into the mainstream of European thought and culture.

PRINCIPAL CITIES

BIRMINGHAM

Birmingham (West Midlands) is Britain's second city. It is a focal point in national communications networks with a rapidly expanding International Airport. The generally accepted derivation of 'Birmingham' is the *ham* (dwelling-place) of the *ing* (family) of *Beorma*, presumed to have been a Saxon. During the Industrial Revolution the town grew into a major manufacturing centre. In 1889 Birmingham was granted City status.

Despite the decline in manufacturing, Birmingham is still a major hardware trade and motor component industry centre. As well as the National Exhibition Centre and the Aston Science Park, recent developments include the International Convention Centre and the National Indoor Arena. An Urban Development Agency was set up in 1986.

The principal buildings are the Town Hall (1832-4); the Council House (1879); Victoria Law Courts (1891); the University (1909); the 13th century Church of St Martin-in-the-Bullring (rebuilt 1873); the Cathedral (formerly St Philip's Church) (1711) and the Roman Catholic Cathedral of St Chad (1839-41).

BRADFORD

Bradford (West Yorkshire) lies on the southern edge of the Yorkshire Dales National Park, including within its boundaries the village of Haworth, home of the Brontë sisters, and Ilkley Moor.

Originally a Saxon township, Bradford received a market charter in 1251 but developed only slowly until the industrialization of the textile industry brought rapid growth during the 19th century. The prosperity of that period is reflected in much of the city's architecture, particularly the public buildings: City Hall (1873), Wool Exchange (1867), St George's Hall (Concert Hall, 1853), Cartwright Hall (Art Gallery, 1904) and the Technical College (1882). Other chief buildings are the Cathedral (15th century) and Bolling Hall (14th century).

Textiles still play an important part in the city's economy but industry is now more broadly based, including engineering and micro-electronics. The city has a strong financial services sector, and a growing tourism industry.

BRISTOL

Bristol (Avon) was a Royal Borough before the Norman Conquest. The earliest form of the name is *Bricgstow*. In 1373 it received from Edward III a charter granting it county status.

The chief buildings include the 12th century Cathedral (with later additions), with Norman chapter house and gateway, the 14th century Church of St Mary Redcliffe, Wesley's Chapel, Broadmead, the Merchant Venturers' Almshouses, the Council House (1956), Guildhall, Exchange (erected from the designs of John Wood in 1743), Cabot Tower, the University and Clifton College. The Roman Catholic Cathedral at Clifton was opened in 1973.

The Clifton Suspension Bridge, with a span of 702 feet over the Avon, was projected by Brunel in 1836 but was not completed until 1864. Brunel's SS *Great Britain*, the first ocean-going propeller-driven ship, is now being restored in the City Docks from where she was launched in 1843. The docks themselves have been extensively restored and redeveloped.

CAMBRIDGE

Cambridge, a settlement far older than its ancient University, lies on the River Cam or Granta. The city is a county town and regional headquarters. Its industries include electronics, flour milling, cement making, the manufacture of scientific instruments and the growing area of biotechnology. Among its open spaces are Jesus Green, Sheep's Green, Coe Fen, Parker's Piece, Christ's Pieces, the University Botanic Garden, and the Backs, or lawns and gardens through which the Cam winds behind the principal line of college buildings. East of the Cam, King's Parade, upon which stand Great St Mary's Church, Gibbs' Senate House and King's College Chapel with Wilkins' screen, joins Trumpington Street to form one of the most beautiful throughfares in Europe.

University and college buildings provide the outstanding features of Cambridge architecture but several churches (especially St Benet's, the oldest building in the City, and St Sepulchre's, the Round Church) also are notable. The modern Guildhall (1939) stands on a site of which at least part has held municipal buildings since 1224.

CANTERBURY

Canterbury, the Metropolitan City of the Anglican Communion, has a history going back to prehistoric times. It was the Roman *Durovernum Cantiacorum* and the Saxon *Cant-wara-byrig* (stronghold of the men of Kent). Here in 597 St Augustine began the conversion of the English to Christianity, when Ethelbert, King of Kent, was baptized.

Of the Benedictine St Augustine's Abbey, burial place of the Jutish Kings of Kent (whose capital Canterbury was), only extensive ruins remain. St Martin's Church, on the eastern outskirts of the city, is stated by Bede to have been the place of worship of Queen Bertha, the Christian wife of King Ethelbert, before the advent of St Augustine.

In 1170 the rivalry of Church and State culminated in the murder in Canterbury Cathedral, by Henry II's knights, of Archbishop Thomas Becket, whose shrine became a great centre of pilgrimage, as described by Chaucer in his *Canterbury Tales*. After the Reformation pilgrimages ceased, but the prosperity of the city was strengthened by an influx of Huguenot refugees, who introduced weaving. The Elizabethan poet and playwright Christopher Marlowe was born and reared in Canterbury, and there are literary associations also with Defoe, Dickens, Joseph Conrad and Somerset Maugham.

The Cathedral, with architecture ranging from the 11th to 15th centuries, is world famous. Modern pilgrims are attracted particularly to the Martyrdom, the Black Prince's Tomb, the Warriors' Chapel and the many examples of medieval stained glass.

The medieval city walls are built on Roman foundations and the 14th century West Gate is one of the finest buildings of its kind in the country.

The 1,000 seat Marlowe Theatre is the base for the Canterbury International Festival of the Arts each autumn.

CARLISLE

Carlisle is situated at the confluence of the River Eden and River Caldew, 309 miles north-west of London and about ten miles from the Scottish border. It was granted a charter in 1158.

The city stands at the western end of Hadrian's Wall and dates from the original Roman settlement of *Luguvalium*. Granted to Scotland in the tenth century, Carlisle is not included in the Domesday Book. William Rufus reclaimed the area in 1092 and the castle and city walls were built to guard Carlisle and the western border; the citadel is a Tudor addition to protect the south of the city. Until the Union of the Crowns in 1603, Carlisle changed hands several times and was frequently besieged. During the Civil War the city remained Royalist; in 1745 it supported the Young Pretender.

The Cathedral, originally a 12th century Augustinian priory, was enlarged in the 13th and 14th centuries after the diocese was created in 1133. To the south is a restored Tithe Barn and nearby the 18th century church of St Cuthbert, the third to stand on a site dating from the seventh century.

Carlisle is the major shopping, commercial and agricultural centre for the area, and industries include the manufacture of metal goods, biscuits and textiles. However, the largest employer is the services sector, notably in retailing and transport. The city has an important communications position at the centre of a network of major roads, as an important stage on the main west coast rail services, and with its own airport at Crosby.

CHESTER

Chester is situated on the River Dee, and was granted Borough and City status in 1974. Its recorded history dates from the first century when the Romans founded the fortress of *Deva*. The city's name is derived from the Latin *castra* (a camp or encampment). During the Middle Ages, Chester was the principal port of north-west England but declined with the silting of the Dee estuary and competition from Liverpool. The city was also an important military centre, notably during Edward I's Welsh campaigns and the Elizabethan Irish campaigns. During the Civil War, Chester supported the King and was besieged from 1643 to 1646. Chester's first charter was granted *c.*1175 and the city was incorporated in 1506. The office of Sheriff is the earliest created in the country (*c.*1120s), and in 1992 the Mayor was granted the title of Lord Mayor. He/she also enjoys the title 'Admiral of the Dee'.

The city's architectural features include the city walls (an almost complete two-mile circuit), the unique Rows (covered galleries above the street-level shops), the Victorian Gothic Town Hall (1869), the Castle (rebuilt 1788 and 1822) and numerous half-timbered buildings. The Cathedral was a Benedictine abbey until the Dissolution. Remaining monastic buildings include the chapter house, refectory and cloisters and there is a modern free-standing bell tower. The Norman church of St John the Baptist was a cathedral church in the early Middle Ages.

Chester is primarily a regional service centre and has considerable tourist appeal. In 1984 the city was awarded Development Area status, which has attracted a range of nationally-known companies to expand or locate in Chester.

COVENTRY

Coventry (West Midlands) is an important industrial centre, producing vehicles, machine tools, agricultural machinery, man-made fibres, aerospace components and telecommunications equipment. New investment has come from the financial services, power transmission, professional services and educational sectors.

The city owes its beginning to Leofric, Earl of Mercia, and his wife Godiva who, in 1043, founded a Benedictine monastery. The guildhall of St Mary dates from the 14th century, three of the city's churches date from the 14th and 15th centuries, and 16th century almshouses may still be seen. Coventry's first cathedral was destroyed at the Reformation, its second in the 1940 blitz (the walls and spire remain) and the new cathedral designed by Sir Basil Spence, consecrated in 1962, now draws innumerable visitors.

Coventry is the home of the University of Warwick and its Science Park, Coventry University, the rapidly-expanding

Westwood Business Park and the Museum of British Road Transport.

DERBY

Derby stands on the banks of the River Derwent, and its name dates back to 880 when the Danes settled in the locality and changed the original Saxon name of *Northworthy* to *Deoraby*.

Derby has a wide range of industries: its products include aero engines, pipework, specialized mechanical engineering equipment, textiles, chemicals, plastics and the Royal Crown Derby porcelain. The city is an established railway centre, the site of British Rail's Technical Centre with its research laboratories.

Buildings of interest include St Peter's Church and the Old Abbey Building (14th century), the Cathedral (1525), St Mary's Roman Catholic Church (1839) and the Industrial Museum, formerly the Old Silk Mill (1721). The traditional city centre is complemented by the new Eagle Centre and 'out-of-centre' retail developments. In addition to the Derby Playhouse, the Assembly Rooms are a multi-purpose venue.

The first charter granting a Mayor and Aldermen was that of Charles I in 1637. Previous charters date back to 1154. It was granted City status in 1977.

DURHAM

The city of Durham is a district in the county of Durham and a major tourist attraction because of its prominent Norman Cathedral and Castle set high on a wooded peninsula overlooking the River Wear. The Cathedral was founded as a shrine for the body of St Cuthbert in 995. The present building dates from 1093 and among its many treasures is the tomb of the Venerable Bede (673–735). Durham's Prince Bishops had unique powers up to 1836, being lay rulers as well as religious leaders. As a palatinate Durham could have its own army, nobility, coinage and courts. The Castle was the main seat of the Prince Bishops for nearly 800 years; it is now used as a college by the University. The University, founded on the initiative of Bishop William Van Mildert, is England's third oldest. Its students live in 14 colleges spread across the city.

Among other buildings of interest is the Guildhall in the Market Place which dates originally from the 14th century. Much work has been carried out to conserve this area, forming part of the city's major contribution to the Council of Europe's Urban Renaissance Campaign. Annual events include Durham's Regatta in June (claimed to be the oldest rowing event in Britain) and the Annual Gala (formerly Durham Miners' Gala) in July.

In the past 20 years the economy of Durham has undergone a significant change with the replacement of mining as the dominant industry by 'white collar' employment. Although still a predominantly rural area, the industrial and commercial sector is growing and a wide range of manufacturing and service industries are based on industrial estates in and around the city.

EXETER

Exeter lies on the River Exe ten miles from the sea. It was granted a Royal Charter by Henry II. The Romans founded *Isca Dumnoniorum* in the first century AD, and in the third century a stone wall (most of which remains) was built, providing protection against Saxon, and then Danish invasions. After the Conquest, the city led resistance to William in the west, until reduced by siege. The Normans built the ringwork castle of Rougemont, the gatehouse and one tower of which remain, although the rest was pulled down in 1784. The first bridge across the Exe was built in the 13th century. The city's role as a port declined due to the silting of the river, but was somewhat restored by the construction in the 1560s of the first true canal in England. Exeter was the Royalist headquarters in the west during the Civil War.

The diocese of Exeter was established by Edward the Confessor in 1050, although a minster existed near the Cathedral site from the late seventh century. A new cathedral was built in the 12th century but the present building was begun c.1275, although incorporating the Norman towers, and completed about a century later. The Guildhall dates from the 12th century and there are many other medieval buildings in the city, as well as architecture in the Georgian and Regency styles, and the Custom House (1680). Damage suffered by bombing in 1942 led to the redevelopment of the city centre.

Exeter's prosperity from medieval times was based on trade in wool and woollen cloth (commemorated by Tuckers Hall), which remained at its height until the late 18th century when export trade was hit by the French wars. Subsequently Exeter has developed as an administrative and commercial centre, notably in the distributive trades, light manufacturing industries and tourism.

KINGSTON UPON HULL

Hull (officially Kingston upon Hull) lies in the mostly rural county of Humberside, at the junction of the River Hull with the Humber, 22 miles from the North Sea. It is one of the great seaports of the United Kingdom. It has docks covering a water area of 172 acres, equipped to handle cargoes by unit-load techniques, and is a departure point for car ferry services to continental Europe. There is a great variety of industry and service industries, as well as increasing tourism and conference business.

The city, restored after very heavy air raid damage during the Second World War, has good office and administrative buildings, its municipal centre being the Guildhall, its educational centre the University of Hull and its religious centre the Parish Church of the Holy Trinity. The old town area is being renovated and includes a new marina and shopping complex. Just west of the city is the Humber Bridge, the world's longest single span suspension bridge.

Kingston upon Hull was so named by Edward I. City status was accorded in 1897 and the office of Mayor raised to the dignity of Lord Mayor in 1914.

LEEDS

Leeds (West Yorkshire), situated in the lower Aire Valley, is a junction for road, rail, canal and air services and an important commercial centre. Seventy-three per cent of employment is in services, notably the distributive trades, public administration, medical services and business services. The main manufacturing industries are mechanical engineering, printing and publishing, metal goods and furniture.

The principal buildings are the Civic Hall (1933), the Town Hall (1858), the Municipal Buildings and Art Gallery (1884) with the Henry Moore Gallery (1982), the Corn Exchange (1863) and the University. The Parish Church (St Peter's) was rebuilt in 1841; the 17th century St John's Church has a fine interior with a famous English Renaissance screen; the last remaining 18th century church in the city is Holy Trinity in Boar Lane (1727). Kirkstall Abbey (about three miles from the centre of the city), founded by Henry de Lacy in 1152, is one of the most complete examples of Cistercian houses now remaining. Temple Newsam, birthplace of Lord Darnley, was acquired by the Council in 1922. The present house was largely rebuilt by Sir Arthur Ingram in about

1620. Adel Church, about five miles from the centre of the city, is a fine Norman structure.

Leeds was first incorporated by Charles I in 1626. The earliest forms of the name are *Loidis* or *Ledes*, the origins of which are obscure.

LEICESTER

Leicester is situated geographically in the centre of England. It dates back to pre-Roman times and was one of the five Danish *Burghs*. In 1589 Queen Elizabeth I granted a Charter to the City and the ancient title was confirmed by Letters Patent in 1919. Under local government reorganization Leicester retained its designation as a City.

The principal industries of the city are hosiery, knitwear, footwear manufacturing and engineering. The growth of Leicester as a hosiery centre increased rapidly from the introduction there of the first stocking frame in 1670 and today it has some of the largest hosiery factories in the world.

The principal buildings in the city are the Town Hall, the New Walk Centre, the University of Leicester, De Montfort University, De Montfort Hall, one of the finest concert halls in the provinces seating over 2,750 people, and the Granby Halls, an indoor sports facility. The ancient Churches of St Martin (now Leicester Cathedral), St Nicholas, St Margaret, All Saints, St Mary de Castro, and buildings such as the Guildhall, the 14th century Newarke Gate, the Castle and the Jewry Wall Roman site still exist. The Haymarket Theatre was opened in 1973 and The Shires, a new shopping centre, was opened in 1992.

LINCOLN

Situated 40 miles inland on the River Witham, Lincoln derives its name from a contraction of *Lindum Colonia*, the settlement founded in AD 48 by the Romans to command the crossing of Ermine Street and Fosse Way. Sections of the third century Roman city wall can be seen, including an extant gateway (Newport Arch), and excavations have discovered traces of a sewerage system unique in Britain. The Romans also drained the surrounding fenland and created a canal system, laying the foundations of Lincoln's agricultural prosperity, and also of the city's importance in the medieval wool trade as a port and Staple town.

As one of the Five Boroughs of the Danelaw, Lincoln was an important trading centre in the ninth and tenth centuries and medieval prosperity from the wool trade lasted until the 14th century, enabling local merchants to build parish churches (of which three survive), and attracting in the 12th century a Jewish community (Jew's House and Court, Aaron's House). However, the removal of the Staple to Boston in 1369 heralded a decline from which the city only recovered fully in the 19th century when improved fen drainage made Lincoln agriculturally important, and improved canal and rail links led to industrial development, mainly in the manufacture of machinery, components and engineering products.

The castle was built shortly after the Conquest and is unusual in having two mounds; on one motte stands a Keep (Lucy's Tower) added in the 12th century. The Cathedral was begun c.1073 when the first Norman bishop moved the see of Lindsey to Lincoln, but was mostly destroyed by fire and earthquake in the 12th century. Rebuilding was begun by St Hugh and completed over a century later. The Wren library contains manuscripts including one of the four surviving originals of the Magna Carta. Other notable architectural features of the city are the 12th century High Bridge, the oldest in Britain still to carry buildings, and the Guildhall situated above the 15th–16th century Stonebow gateway.

LIVERPOOL

Liverpool (Merseyside) on the right bank of the River Mersey, three miles from the Irish Sea, is the United Kingdom's foremost port for the Atlantic trade. Tunnels link Liverpool with Birkenhead and Wallasey.

There are 2,100 acres of dockland on both sides of the river and the Gladstone and Royal Seaforth Docks can accommodate the largest vessels afloat. Annual tonnage of cargo handled is approximately 27.8 million tonnes. The main imports are crude oil, grain, ores, edible oils, timber, containers and break-bulk cargo. Liverpool Free Port, Britain's largest, was opened in 1984.

Liverpool was created a free borough in 1207 and a city in 1880. From the early 18th century it expanded rapidly with the growth of industrialization and the Atlantic trade. Surviving buildings from this date include the Bluecoat Chambers (1717, formerly the Bluecoat School), the Town Hall (1754, rebuilt to the original design 1795), and buildings in Rodney Street, Canning Street and the suburbs. Notable from the 19th and 20th centuries are the Anglican Cathedral, built from the designs of Sir Giles Gilbert Scott (the foundation stone was laid in 1904, and the building was completed only in 1980), the Catholic Metropolitan Cathedral (designed by Sir Frederick Gibberd, consecrated 1967) and St George's Hall (1838–54), regarded as one of the finest modern examples of classical architecture. The recently refurbished Albert Dock (designed by Jesse Hartley) contains the Merseyside Maritime Museum and Tate Gallery, Liverpool.

In 1852 an Act was obtained for establishing a public library, museum and art gallery: as a result Liverpool had one of the first public libraries in the country. The Brown, Picton and Hornby libraries now form one of the country's major libraries. The Victoria Building of Liverpool University, the Royal Liver, Cunard and Mersey Docks & Harbour Company buildings at the Pier Head, the Municipal Buildings and the Philharmonic Hall are other examples of the City's fine buildings. Britain's first International Garden Festival was held in Liverpool in 1984.

MANCHESTER

Manchester (the *Mamucium* of the Romans, who occupied it in AD 79) is a commercial and industrial centre with a population engaged in the engineering, chemical, clothing, food processing and textile industries and in education. Banking, insurance and a growing leisure industry are among the prime commercial activities. The city is connected with the sea by the Manchester Ship Canal, opened in 1894, 35½ miles long, and accommodating ships up to 15,000 tons. Manchester Airport handles more than 11 million passengers yearly.

The principal buildings are the Town Hall, erected in 1877 from the designs of Alfred Waterhouse, together with a large extension of 1938; the Royal Exchange (1869, enlarged 1921); the Central Library (1934); Heaton Hall; the 17th century Chetham Library; the Rylands Library (1900), which includes the Althorp collection; the University precinct; the 15th century Cathedral (formerly the parish church); G-MEX and the Free Trade Hall. Manchester is the home of the Hallé Orchestra, the Royal Northern College of Music, the Royal Exchange Theatre and seven public art galleries. Metrolink, the new light rail system, opened in 1992.

The town received its first charter of incorporation in 1838 and was created a city in 1853. The title of City was retained under local government reorganization.

NEWCASTLE UPON TYNE

Newcastle upon Tyne (Tyne and Wear), on the north bank of the River Tyne, is eight miles from the North Sea. A Cathedral and University city, it is the administrative, commercial and cultural centre for north-east England and the principal port. It is an important manufacturing centre with a wide variety of industries.

The principal buildings include the Castle Keep (12th century), Black Gate (13th century), Blackfriars (13th century), West Walls (13th century), St Nicholas's Cathedral (15th century, fine lantern tower), St Andrew's Church (12th–14th century), St John's (14th–15th century), All Saints (1786 by Stephenson), St Mary's Roman Catholic Cathedral (1844), Trinity House (17th century), Sandhill (16th century houses), Guildhall (Georgian), Grey Street (1834–9), Central Station (1846–50), Laing Art Gallery (1904), University of Newcastle Physics Building (1962) and Medical Building (1985), Civic Centre (1963), Central Library (1969) and Eldon Square Shopping Development (1976). Open spaces include the Town Moor (927 acres) and Jesmond Dene. Eight bridges span the Tyne at Newcastle.

The City derives its name from the 'new castle' (1080) erected as a defence against the Scots. In 1400 it was made a County, and in 1882 a City.

NORWICH

Norwich (Norfolk) grew from an early Anglo-Saxon settlement near the confluence of the Rivers Yare and Wensum, and now serves as provincial capital for the predominantly agricultural region of East Anglia. The name is thought to relate to the most northerly of a group of Anglo-Saxon villages or *wics*. The city's first known Charter was granted in 1158 by Henry II.

Norwich serves its surrounding area as a market town and commercial centre, banking and insurance being prominent among the city's businesses. From the 14th century until the Industrial Revolution, Norwich was the regional centre of the woollen industry, but now the biggest single industry is financial services and principal trades are engineering, printing, shoemaking, double glazing, and the production of chemicals, clothing, confectionery and other foodstuffs. Norwich is accessible to seagoing vessels by means of the River Yare, entered at Great Yarmouth, 20 miles to the east.

Among many historic buildings are the Cathedral (completed in the 12th century and surmounted by a 15th century spire 315 feet in height), the keep of the Norman castle (now a museum and art gallery), the 15th century flint-walled Guildhall (now a tourist information centre), some thirty medieval parish churches, St Andrew's and Blackfriars' Halls, the Tudor houses preserved in Elm Hill and the Georgian Assembly House. The University of East Anglia is located on a site at Earlham on the city's western boundary.

NOTTINGHAM

Nottingham stands on the River Trent in one of the most valuable coalfields of the country and connected by canal with the Atlantic Ocean and the North Sea. *Snotingaham* or *Notingeham*, literally the homestead of the people of Snot, is the Anglo-Saxon name for the Celtic settlement of *Tigguoco-bauc*, or the house of caves. In 878, Nottingham became one of the Five Boroughs of the Danelaw following a treaty signed by Alfred the Great and the Danish King Guthrum. William the Conqueror ordered the construction of Nottingham Castle, while the town itself developed rapidly under Norman rule. Its laws and rights were later formally recognized by Henry II's Charter in 1155. The Castle became a favoured residence of King John. In 1642 King Charles I raised his personal standard at Nottingham Castle at the start of the Civil War.

Nottingham is a major sporting centre, home to Nottingham Forest FC, Notts County FC (the world's oldest Football league side), Nottingham Racecourse and the National Watersports Centre. The principal industries include textiles, pharmaceuticals, food manufacturing, engineering and telecommunications. There are two universities within the city boundaries.

Architecturally, Nottingham has a wealth of notable buildings, particularly those designed in the Victorian era by T. C. Hine and Watson Fothergill. The City Council owns the Castle, of Norman origin but restored in 1878, Wollaton Hall (1580–8), Newstead Abbey (home of Lord Byron), the Guildhall (1888) and Council House (1929). St Mary's, St Peter's and St Nicholas's Churches of interest, as is the Roman Catholic Cathedral (Pugin, 1842–4).

Nottingham was granted City status in 1897.

OXFORD

Oxford is a University city, an important industrial centre, and a market town. Industry played a minor part in Oxford until the motor industry was established in 1912.

It is for its architecture that Oxford is of most interest to the visitor, its oldest specimens being the reputedly Saxon tower of St Michael's church, the remains of the Norman castle and city walls, and the Norman church at Iffley. It is chiefly famous, however, for its Gothic buildings, such as the Divinity Schools, the Old Library at Merton College, William of Wykeham's New College, Magdalen College and Christ Church and many other college buildings. Later centuries are represented by the Laudian quadrangle at St John's College, the Renaissance Sheldonian Theatre by Wren, Trinity College Chapel, and All Saints Church; Hawksmoor's mock-Gothic at All Souls College, and the 18th century Queen's College. In addition to individual buildings, High Street and Radcliffe Square, just off it, both form architectural compositions of great beauty. Most of the Colleges have gardens, those of Magdalen, New College, St John's (designed by 'Capability' Brown) and Worcester being the largest.

PLYMOUTH

Plymouth is situated on the borders of Devon and Cornwall at the confluence of the Rivers Tamar and Plym. The city has a long maritime history; it was the home port of Sir Francis Drake and the starting point for his circumnavigation of the world, as well as the last port of call for the *Mayflower* when the Pilgrim Fathers sailed for the New World in 1620. Today Plymouth is host to many international yacht races. The Barbican harbour area has many Elizabethan buildings and on Plymouth Hoe stands Smeaton's lighthouse, the third to be built on the Eddystone Rocks 13 miles offshore.

Following extensive war damage, the city centre, comprising a large shopping centre, municipal offices, law courts and public buildings, has been rebuilt. The main employment is provided at the naval base, though many new industrial firms and service industries have become established in the post-war period and the city is a growing tourism centre. In 1982 the Theatre Royal was opened. In conjunction with the Cornwall County Council, the Tamar Bridge was constructed linking the city by road with Cornwall.

PORTSMOUTH

Portsmouth occupies Portsea Island, Hampshire, with boundaries extending to the mainland. It is a centre of industry and commerce, including many high technology and manufacturing industries. It is the British headquarters of several major international companies. The Royal Navy base still has a substantial work force, although this has decreased in recent years. The commercial port and continental ferry port is owned and run by the City Council, and carries passengers and vehicles to France and northern Spain.

A major port since the 16th century, Portsmouth is also a thriving seaside resort catering for thousands of visitors annually. Among many historic attractions are Lord Nelson's flagship, HMS *Victory*, the Tudor warship *Mary Rose*, Britain's first 'ironclad', HMS *Warrior*, the D-Day Museum, Charles Dickens' birthplace at 393 Old Commercial Road, the Royal Naval and Royal Marine museums, Southsea Castle (built by Henry VIII), the Round Tower and Point Battery, which for hundreds of years have guarded the entrance to Portsmouth Harbour, Fort Nelson on Portsdown Hill and the Sealife Centre.

ST ALBANS

The origins of St Albans, situated on the River Ver, stem from the Roman town of *Verulamium*. Named after the first Christian martyr in Britain, who was executed here, St Albans has developed around the Norman Abbey and Cathedral Church (consecrated 1115), built partly of materials from the old Roman city. The museums house Iron Age and Roman artefacts and the Roman Theatre, unique in Britain, has a stage as opposed to an amphitheatre. Archaeological excavations in the city centre continue also to reveal evidence of pre-Roman, Saxon and medieval occupation.

The town's significance grew to the extent that it was a signatory and venue for the drafting of the Magna Carta. It was also the scene of riots during the Peasants' Revolt, the French King John was imprisoned there after the Battle of Poitiers, and heavy fighting took place there during the Wars of the Roses.

Previously controlled by the Abbot, the town achieved a Royal Charter in 1553 and City status in 1877. The street market, first established in 1553, is still an important feature of the city, as are many hotels and inns which survive from the days when St Albans was an important coach stop. Tourist attractions include historic churches and houses, and a 15th century clock tower.

The city now contains a wide range of firms, with special emphasis on micro-technology and electronics, particularly in the medical field. In addition, it is the home of the Royal National Rose Society, and of Rothamsted Park, the agricultural research centre.

SHEFFIELD

Sheffield (South Yorkshire), the centre of the special steel and cutlery trades, is situated at the junction of the Sheaf, Porter, Rivelin and Loxley valleys with the River Don. Though its cutlery, silverware and plate have long been famous, Sheffield has other and now more important industries: special and alloy steels, engineering, tool-making and financial services. Research in glass, metallurgy and other fields is carried out.

The parish church of St Peter and St Paul, founded in the 12th century, became the Cathedral Church of the Diocese of Sheffield in 1914. The Roman Catholic Cathedral Church of St Marie (founded 1847) was created Cathedral for the new diocese of Hallam in 1980. Parts of the present building date from c.1435. The principal buildings are the Town Hall (1897, 1923 and 1977), the Cutlers' Hall (1832), the University (1905 and recent extensions, including 19-storey Arts Tower), City Hall (1932), Graves Art Gallery (1934), Mappin Art Gallery and the Crucible Theatre. The restored 19th century Lyceum theatre opened in 1990.

Sheffield was created a city in 1893 and in 1974 retained its city status.

Master Cutler (1993–4) *of the Company of Cutlers in Hallamshire*, Derrick Willingham

SOUTHAMPTON

Southampton is the leading British deep-sea port on the Channel and is situated on one of the finest natural harbours in the world. The first Charter was granted by Henry II and Southampton was created a county of itself in 1447. In 1964 it was granted city status by Royal Charter.

There were Roman and Saxon settlements on the site of the city, which has been an important port since the time of the Conquest due to its natural deep-water harbour. The oldest church is St Michael's (1070) which has a black tournai marble font and an unusually tall spire built in the 18th century as a landmark for navigators of Southampton Water. Other buildings and monuments within the city walls are the Tudor House, God's House Tower, Bargate Museum, the Tudor Merchants Hall, the Weigh-house, West Gate, King John's House, Long House, Wool House, the ruins of Holy Rood Church, St Julien's Church and the Mayflower Memorial. The medieval town walls, built for artillery, are among the most complete in Europe. Public open spaces total over 1,000 acres in extent and comprise 9 per cent of the city's area. The Common covers an area of 328 acres in the central district of the city and is mostly natural parkland.

STOKE-ON-TRENT

Stoke-on-Trent (Staffordshire), standing on the River Trent and familiarly known as The Potteries, is the main centre of employment for the population of North Staffordshire. The city is the largest clayware producer in the world (china, earthenware, sanitary goods, refractories, bricks and tiles) and has a considerable coal mining output drawn from one of the richest coalfields in western Europe. The city has steelworks, foundries, chemical works, engineering plants, rubber works, paper mills, and a very wide range of manufactures. Extensive reconstruction has been carried out in recent years.

The city was formed by the federation in 1910 of the separate municipal authorities of Tunstall, Burslem, Hanley, Stoke, Fenton, and Longton, all of which are now combined in the present City of Stoke-on-Trent.

WINCHESTER

Winchester, the ancient capital of England, is situated on the River Itchen. The city is rich in architecture of all types but the Cathedral takes pride of place. The longest Gothic cathedral in the world, it was built in 1079–93 and exhibits examples of Norman, Early English and Perpendicular styles. Winchester College, founded in 1382, is one of the most famous public schools, the original building (of 1393) remaining largely unaltered. St Cross Hospital, another great medieval foundation, lies one mile south of the city. The almshouses were founded in 1136 by Bishop Henry de Blois, and Cardinal Henry Beaufort added a new almshouse of 'Noble Poverty' in 1446. The chapel and dwellings are of great architectural interest, and visitors may still receive the 'Wayfarer's Dole' of bread and ale.

Recent excavations have done much to clarify the origins and development of Winchester. Part of the forum and several of the streets of the Roman town have been discovered; and excavations in the Cathedral Close have uncovered the entire site of the Anglo-Saxon cathedral (known as the Old Minster) and parts of the New Minster, built by Alfred's son Edward the Elder and the burial place of the Alfredian

dynasty. The original burial place of St Swithun, before his remains were translated to a site in the present cathedral, was also uncovered.

Excavations in other parts of the city have thrown much light on Norman Winchester, notably on the site of the Royal Castle, adjacent to which the new Law Courts have been built, and in the grounds of Wolvesey Castle, where the great house built by Bishops Giffard and Henry de Blois in the 12th century has been uncovered. The Great Hall, built by Henry III between 1222 and 1236 survives. It houses the Arthurian Round Table.

YORK

The city of York (North Yorkshire) is an archiepiscopal seat. Its recorded history dates from AD 71, when the Roman Ninth Legion established a base under Petilius Cerealis which later became the fortress of *Eburacum*. In Anglo-Saxon times the city was the royal and ecclesiastical centre of Northumbria, and after capture by a Viking army in AD 866 it became the capital of the Viking kingdom of Jorvik. By the 14th century the city had become a great mercantile centre, mainly owing to its control of the wool trade, and was used as the chief base against the Scots. Under the Tudors its fortunes declined, though Henry VIII made it the headquarters of the Council of the North. Recent excavations on many sites, including Coppergate, have greatly expanded knowledge of Roman, Viking and medieval urban life.

With its development as a railway centre in the 19th century the commercial life of York expanded. The principal industries are the manufacture of chocolate, railway coaches, scientific instruments, and sugar. It is the location of several government departments.

The city is rich in examples of architecture of all periods. The earliest church was built in AD 627 and, in the 12th to 15th centuries, the present Minster was built in a succession of styles. Other examples within the city are the medieval city walls and gateways, churches and guildhalls. Domestic architecture includes the Georgian mansions of The Mount, Micklegate and Bootham. Its museums include York Castle Museum, the National Railway Museum and the Jorvik Viking Centre.

English Counties and Shires

LORD LIEUTENANTS AND HIGH SHERIFFS

County/Shire	Lord Lieutenant	High Sheriff, 1993–4
Avon	Sir John Wills, Bt., TD	H. H. Bayntun-Coward
Bedfordshire	S. C. Whitbread	E. Fountain, OBE
Berkshire	J. R. Henderson, CVO, OBE	Maj. T. C. Gore
Buckinghamshire	Cdr. the Hon. J. T. Fremantle	D. V. Palmer
Cambridgeshire	J. G. P. Crowden	The Hon. Lady Hastings
Cheshire	W. Bromley-Davenport	The Hon. R. H. Cornwall-Legh
Cleveland	The Lord Gisborough	D. Manners
Cornwall	The Viscount Falmouth	R. J. Gilbert
Cumbria	Maj. Sir Charles Graham, Bt.	Mrs M. H. Washington
Derbyshire	Col. Sir Peter Hilton, KCVO, MC	R. H. Turner
Devon	Lt.-Col. the Earl of Morley	Sir John Boles, MBE
Dorset	The Lord Digby	R. G. G. de Pelet
Durham	D. J. Grant, CBE	Mrs E. A. Jennings
East Sussex	Adm. Sir Lindsay Bryson, KCB	A. K. Stewart-Roberts
Essex	The Lord Braybrooke	C. S. Gosling
Gloucestershire	H. W. G. Elwes	C. G. M. Lloyd-Baker
Greater London	Field Marshal the Lord Bramall, GCB, OBE, MC	A. C. Everett, OBE
Greater Manchester	Col. J. B. Timmins, OBE, TD	L. D. Lawton
Hampshire	Lt.-Col. Sir James Scott, Bt.	C. N. Wilson
Hereford and Worcester	Capt. T. R. Dunne	S. Webb
Hertfordshire	S. A. Bowes Lyon	F. E. Harvey
Humberside	R. A. Bethell	P. W. Barker, CBE
Isle of Wight	*The Lord Mottistone, CBE	D. B. B. Cheverton, OBE
Kent	The Lord Kingsdown, PC	Hon. R. Dennison-Pender
Lancashire	S. Towneley	Col. R. R. Craik, OBE, TD
Leicestershire	T. G. M. Brooks	R. H. Murray-Philipson
Lincolnshire	Capt. Sir Henry N. Nevile, KCVO	A. G. Jarvis
Merseyside	vacant	Cdre R. H. Walker
Norfolk	T. J. Colman	R. E. Buscall
Northamptonshire	J. L. Lowther, CBE	J. G. Church
Northumberland	The Viscount Ridley, KG, TD	R. Errington
North Yorkshire	Sir Marcus Worsley, Bt.	M. D. Abrahams, MBE
Nottinghamshire	Sir Andrew Buchanan, Bt.	Mrs J. L. Mortensen
Oxfordshire	Sir Ashley Ponsonby, Bt., KCVO, MC	Sir David Black, Bt.
Shropshire	J. R. S. Dugdale	Capt. R. M. Gabb
Somerset	Col. Sir Walter Luttrell, KCVO, MC	The Hon. J. H. Jolliffe
South Yorkshire	J. H. Neill, CBE, TD	C. S. Barker
Staffordshire	J. A. Hawley, TD	C. H. Mitchell
Suffolk	Sir Joshua Rowley, Bt.	C. J. H. Gurney
Surrey	R. E. Thornton, OBE	Rear-Adm. Sir Peter Anson, Bt., CB
Tyne and Wear	Sir Ralph Carr-Ellison, TD	Sir David Chapman, Bt.
Warwickshire	Capt. the Viscount Daventry	D. C. Wasdell
West Midlands	The Earl of Aylesford	J. I. Westwood
West Sussex	The Duke of Richmond and Gordon	R. H. Goring
West Yorkshire	J. Lyles	G. F. Armitage
Wiltshire	Field Marshal Sir Roland Gibbs, GCB, CBE, DSO, MC	Lt.-Gen. Sir Maurice Johnston, KCB, OBE

* Lord Lieutenant and Governor

COUNTY COUNCILS: AREA, POPULATION, FINANCE

Council	Administrative headquarters	Area (hectares)	Population 1991	Total demand upon collection fund 1993
Avon	Avon House North, St James Barton, Bristol	134,628	962,000	£158,000,000
Bedfordshire	County Hall, Bedford	123,468	534,200	349,276,000
Berkshire	Shire Hall, Reading	125,901	752,500	124,853,000
Buckinghamshire	County Hall, Aylesbury	188,279	640,200	104,300,000
Cambridgeshire	Shire Hall, Cambridge	340,181	669,900	94,507,000
Cheshire	County Hall, Chester	233,325	966,400	165,860,256
Cleveland	Municipal Buildings, Middlesbrough	59,079	557,500	78,948,287
Cornwall	County Hall, Truro	356,442*	475,200	74,807,000
Cumbria	The Courts, Carlisle	682,451	489,700	80,638,000
Derbyshire	County Offices, Matlock	263,098	939,700	150,448,263
Devon	County Hall, Exeter	671,096	1,040,000	594,058,743
Dorset	County Hall, Dorchester	265,433	662,900	107,242,800
Durham	County Hall, Durham	243,369	604,300	76,801,000
East Sussex	Pelham House, St Andrews Lane, Lewes	179,530	716,500	113,826,000
Essex	County Hall, Chelmsford	367,167	1,548,800	229,324,000
Gloucestershire	Shire Hall, Gloucester	264,270	538,700	84,226,000
Hampshire	The Castle, Winchester	378,022	1,578,700	916,000,000
Hereford and Worcester	County Hall, Worcester	392,650	686,000	101,442,107
Hertfordshire	County Hall, Hertford	163,601	989,500	162,612,000
Humberside	County Hall, Beverley, N. Humberside	351,256	874,500	266,000,000
Isle of Wight	County Hall, Newport, IOW	38,063	126,600	21,072,626
Kent	County Hall, Maidstone	373,063	1,538,800	233,000,000
Lancashire	County Hall, Preston	306,957	1,408,300	219,567,974
Leicestershire	County Hall, Leicester	255,297	890,800	114,978,900
Lincolnshire	County Offices, Lincoln	591,791	592,600	82,355,560
Norfolk	County Hall, Norwich	537,482	759,400	110,225,196
Northamptonshire	County Hall, Northampton	236,721	587,100	77,822,400
Northumberland	County Hall, Morpeth	503,165	307,100	47,000,000
North Yorkshire	County Hall, Northallerton	831,236	720,800	108,500,000
Nottinghamshire	County Hall, Nottingham	216,090	1,015,400	151,611,000
Oxfordshire	County Hall, Oxford	260,798	579,600	93,800,000
Shropshire	The Shirehall, Shrewsbury	349,013	412,600	59,346,000
Somerset	County Hall, Taunton	345,233	469,400	75,449,200
Staffordshire	County Buildings, Stafford	271,616	1,047,400	135,344,200
Suffolk	County Hall, Ipswich	379,664	661,900	484,000,000
Surrey	County Hall, Kingston upon Thames	167,924	1,035,500	181,000,000
Warwickshire	Shire Hall, Warwick	198,052	489,900	82,832,315
West Sussex	County Hall, Chichester	198,935	713,600	385,700,000
Wiltshire	County Hall, Trowbridge	347,883	575,100	90,135,000

* Including Isles of Scilly

THE ISLES OF SCILLY

The islands of the Scillies group are administered by the Council of the Isles of Scilly, a 21-member non-political body, which combines the powers and duties of a county council and a district council under the Local Government Act 1972 and the Isles of Scilly Orders 1978. Legislation is specifically applied to the Isles of Scilly by Special Order. The Council is responsible for education, fire services, highways, planning, social services, water, and the airport. The police service is administered by the Devon and Cornwall Police Authority, of which the Council is a member. The Isles are part of the St Ives electoral division.

Administrative Headquarters, Town Hall, St Mary's, Isles of Scilly TR21 0LW

Chairman of the Council, J. P. Greenlaw

Clerk and Chief Executive, P. S. Hygate

Chief Technical Officer, B. M. Lowen

COUNTY COUNCILS: Officers and Chairman

Council	Chief Executive	County Treasurer	Chairman of County Council
Avon	B. D. Smith	D. G. Morgan	T. Walker
Bedfordshire	D. Cleggett	‡B. Phelps	A. Brewer
Berkshire	A. J. Allen	vacant	R. J. Day
Buckinghamshire	C. M. Garrett	J. Beckerlegg	C. F. Robinson
Cambridgeshire	A. G. Lister	‡D. Earle	C. Bradford
Cheshire	M. E. Pitt	J. E. H. Whiteoak	P. Walker
Cleveland	B. Stevenson	†P. Riley	E. Wood
Cornwall	G. K. Burgess	S. F. Nicol	P. B. Locks, CBE
Cumbria	J. E. Burnet	R. F. Mather	R. Strike
Derbyshire	*J. S. Raine	P. Swaby	J. McKay
Devon	R. D. Clark	J. Glasby	D. W. Lentell
Dorset	P. K. Harvey	A. P. Peel	Mrs P. A. Hymers
Durham	°K. W. Smith	J. Kirkby	J. Mackintosh
East Sussex	R. M. Beechey	J. Davies	D. Bellotti
Essex	R. W. Adcock, CBE	K. D. Neale	Mrs B. A. Barton
Gloucestershire	M. Honey	J. R. Cockroft	F. R. Thompson
Hampshire	A. R. Hodgson	J. E. Scotford	J. Maynard
Hereford and Worcester	J. W. Turnbull	P. Middleborough	J. W. Wardle, MBE
Hertfordshire	B. Briscoe	‡W. D. Ogley	M. D. Colne
Humberside	J. A. Parkes	‡G. T. Southern	D. Rose
Isle of Wight	J. S. Horsnell	J. B. W. Proctor	Mrs V. A. Anderson
Kent	P. R. Sabin	‡P. Martin	B. Clark
Lancashire	G. A. Johnson	B. G. Aldred	H. Caunce
Leicestershire	D. Prince	R. Hale	D. Lucas
Lincolnshire	R. J. D. Procter	M. Spink	R. Rainsforth
Norfolk	B. J. Capon, CBE	R. D. Summers	J. F. B. Donaldson
Northamptonshire	A. J. Greenwell, CBE	‡R. Paver	Mrs E. M. Dicks
Northumberland	K. Morris	‡K. Morris	W. E. Ashbridge
North Yorkshire	R. A. Leyland	D. Martin	F. Robson
Nottinghamshire	M. T. Lyons	R. Latham	Mrs N. Smedley
Oxfordshire	J. Harwood	C. Gray	J. E. Jones
Shropshire	A. Barnish	N. Pursey	G. Raxster
Somerset	B. M. Tanner	C. N. Bilsland	C. Clarke
Staffordshire	B. A. Price	R. G. Tettenborn	J. O'Leary
Suffolk	P. F. Bye	P. B. Atkinson	Maj. L. A. Henniker
Surrey	D. J. Thomas	R. Wolstenholme	Mrs C. Gerard
Warwickshire	I. G. Caulfield	S. R. Freer	J. Haynes
West Sussex	B. Fieldhouse	D. P. Rigg	C. Robinson
Wiltshire	I. A. Browning	‡D. Chalker	Mrs P. Rugg

* County Director
° Principal Executive Officer
‡ Director of Finance
† County Finance Officer

Metropolitan Councils

Council	Population 1991	Band D charge 1993	Chief Executive	Mayor (a) Lord Mayor 1993-4
Greater Manchester	2,561,600			
Bolton	262,900	£594.12	B. Collinge	C. Benjamin
Bury	179,100	607.81	D. J. Burton	G. Sharkey
MANCHESTER	432,700	738.00	A. Sandford	(a) W. Risby
Oldham	219,700	621.00	C. Smith	B. J. Mather
Rochdale	205,200	664.90	J. F. D. Pierce	A. Bagnall
SALFORD	227,400	706.87	J. C. Willis	R. Heron
Stockport	288,100	646.11	A. L. Wilson	B. P. Harrison
Tameside	220,000	698.40	M. Greenwood	A. E. Hatton
Trafford	216,000	513.00	W. A. Lewis	R. E. Crosbie
Wigan	310,500	650.00	S. M. Jones	J. Clarke
Merseyside	1,441,000			
Knowsley	154,500	654.99	D. G. Henshaw	G. Bundred, CBE
LIVERPOOL	474,600	725.20	P. Bounds	(a) M. Black
St Helens	180,800	612.32	Mrs C. A. Hudson	J. Molyneux
Sefton	295,100	618.78	G. J. Haywood	G. H. Mann
Wirral	336,100	690.15	A. White	P. Corcoran
South Yorkshire	1,292,700			
Barnsley	224,200	595.94	J. A. Edwards, OBE	G. Hadfield
Doncaster	293,600	577.46	J. P. Hale	J. Quinn
Rotherham	254,700	686.34	J. Bell	C. A. Kelly
SHEFFIELD	520,300	639.90	Mrs P. Gordon	(a) Q. Hussain
Tyne and Wear	1,125,500			
Gateshead	203,100	693.00	L. N. Elton	S. Henderson
NEWCASTLE UPON TYNE	273,300	791.81	G. N. Cook	(a) J. M. Lamb
North Tyneside	195,400	706.90	*B. Drew	K. Conroy
			*J. Foster	
			*V. Gallant	
			*C. Roberts	
			*D. Wright	
South Tyneside	157,200	654.66	S. Clark	T. A. Bamford
SUNDERLAND	296,300	600.01	C. Sinclair	(a) B. Charlton
West Midlands	2,619,000			
BIRMINGHAM	994,500	657.00	R. M. W. Taylor	(a) P. Tilsley
COVENTRY	306,300	685.80	I. Roxburgh	(a) A. Boyd
Dudley	309,200	582.99	A. V. Astling	Miss M. Whitehouse
Sandwell	295,100	611.43	F. N. Summers	G. I. Wyton
Solihull	201,400	510.00	J. Scampion	P. Llewellyn
Walsall	263,400	591.48	D. C. Winchurch	E. Moorman
Wolverhampton	249,200	554.40	N. H. Perry, PH.D.	R. F. Whitehouse
West Yorkshire	2,066,200			
BRADFORD	468,700	517.65	R. Penn	(a) R. Sowman
Calderdale	194,100	613.02	M. Ellison	A. D. J. Mazey
Kirklees	381,200	627.00	R. V. Hughes	J. Mernagh
LEEDS	706,300	599.65	J. P. Smith	(a) K. Loudon
WAKEFIELD	315,900	635.84	R. Mather	H. Clark

* Lead Officer

Non-Metropolitan Councils

SMALL CAPITALS denote CITY status
§ denotes Borough status

Council	Population 1991	Band D charge 1993	Chief Executive	Chairman 1993–4 (a) Mayor (b) Lord Mayor
Adur, West Sussex	58,900	£575.74	F. M. G. Staden	Mrs S. Bucknall
Allerdale, Cumbria	96,700	573.66	*C. J. Hart	(a) J. E. Fryer
Alnwick, Northumberland	30,600	621.01	L. St Ruth	Mrs S. E. Bolam
§Amber Valley, Derbyshire	112,800	585.72	P. M. Carney	(a) C. Cutting
Arun, West Sussex	131,500	505.87	I. Sumnall	G. E. Bird
Ashfield, Nottinghamshire	109,700	586.54	S. Beedham	D. Shooter
§Ashford, Kent	93,800	487.15	E. H. W. Mexter	(a) G. H. Turner
Aylesbury Vale, Bucks.	148,300	480.20	B. J. Quoroll	W. G. Lapham
Babergh, Suffolk	80,600	450.75	D. C. Bishop	C. M. Spence
§Barrow-in-Furness, Cumbria	73,700	696.48	T. O. Campbell (acting)	(a) D. H. Edwards
Basildon, Essex	162,400	656.73	°J. C. Rosser	T. G. Leask
§Basingstoke and Deane, Hants.	146,300	434.49	D. W. Pilkington, RD	(a) K. J. Brant
Bassetlaw, Notts.	105,200	597.82	M. S. Havenham	B. Yeoman
BATH, Avon	84,600	510.31	N. C. Abbott	(a) Mrs E. H. Bradley
§Berwick-upon-Tweed, Northumberland	26,900	579.72	E. D. Cawthorn	(a) P. Herdman
§Beverley, Humberside	113,600	601.42	M. Rice	(a) T. B. Pearson
Blaby, Leics.	83,500	479.96	†E. Hemsley	A. C. M. Pullen
§Blackburn, Lancs.	137,800	620.65	G. L. Davies	(a) P. N. Browne
§Blackpool, Lancs.	150,100	649.53	D. Wardman	(a) J. L. Preston
§Blyth Valley, Northumberland	80,300	676.14	D. Crawford	(a) R. B. Anderson
Bolsover, Derbys.	71,300	611.64	J. R. Fotherby	R. Brooks
§Boothferry, Humberside	64,800	558.79	J. W. Barber	(a) M. Deneley
§Boston, Lincs.	53,700	524.27	I. Ward	(a) K. Dobson
§Bournemouth, Dorset	159,100	504.00	D. Newell	(a) R. Whittaker
§Bracknell Forest, Berks.	98,500	519.16	A. J. Targett	(a) Mrs I. Mattick
Braintree, Essex	119,800	513.57	C. R. Daybell	M. F. Hall
Breckland, Norfolk	108,600	485.27	R. Garnett	D. R. M. Sanyer
Brentwood, Essex	70,900	500.58	C. P. Sivell	(a) L. Bottomley
Bridgnorth, Salop	50,800	524.98	A. L. Bain	M. G. Pate
§Brighton, East Sussex	153,900	535.91	G. Jones	(a) D. Lepper
BRISTOL, Avon	392,600	699.11	M. Robinson	(b) J. Channon
Broadland, Norfolk	107,400	505.89	J. H. Bryant	H. Bowyer
Bromsgrove, Hereford and Worcs.	92,300	503.54	R. P. Bradshaw	M. J. Scanlan
§Broxbourne, Herts.	82,400	527.86	M. J. Walker	(a) K. G. Holliday, DFC
§Broxtowe, Notts.	108,800	557.55	M. Brown	(a) Mrs L. Ball
§Burnley, Lancs.	92,100	627.59	R. Ellis	(a) J. Greenwood
CAMBRIDGE	105,700	575.05	R. Hammond	(a) A. Maceachern
Cannock Chase, Staffs.	90,000	567.65	M. G. Kemp	C. H. Harris
CANTERBURY, Kent	130,700	542.86	C. Gay	(b) R. Ruston
Caradon, Cornwall	77,500	556.54	J. Neal	B. E. de St Paër-Gotch
CARLISLE, Cumbria	102,000	618.16	R. S. Brackley	(a) Miss J. Prewitt
Carrick, Cornwall	84,000	558.47	P. M. Talbot	D. C. Hancock
§Castle Morpeth, Northumberland	50,300	641.35	P. Wilson	(a) G. M. Green
§Castle Point, Essex	87,200	624.66	B. Rollinson	Mrs E. V. M. Wood
§Charnwood, Leics.	147,900	552.86	S. M. Peatfield	R. J. Shepherd
§Chelmsford, Essex	154,400	527.22	R. M. C. Hartley	(a) C. J. C. Kingsley
§Cheltenham, Glos.	107,700	588.01	C. Nye	(a) R. Wilson
Cherwell, Oxon.	125,700	500.67	G. J. Handley	N. A. Matthews
CHESTER, Cheshire	118,300	606.26	P. F. Durham	(b) M. Byatt
§Chesterfield, Derbyshire	100,300	624.94	D. R. Shaw	(a) G. A. Wright
Chester-le-Street, Co. Durham	53,200	574.33	J. A. Greensmith	M. G. Briscoe
Chichester, West Sussex	103,100	447.89	C. E. Evans	Capt. S. A. Stuart, CBE
Chiltern, Bucks.	89,900	532.33	D. G. Sainsbury	A. Dibbo
§Chorley, Lancs.	97,100	613.00	J. W. Davies	(a) D. E. Simkin

* General Manager
° Town Manager
† Finance and General Manager

Council	Population 1991	Band D charge 1993	Chief Executive	Chairman 1993–4 (a) Mayor (b) Lord Mayor
§Christchurch, Dorset	41,300	£491.20	C. H. Dewsnap	(a) Mrs J. J. Payne
§Cleethorpes, Humberside	69,800	666.12	P. Daniel	(a) K. M. Bradley
§Colchester, Essex	146,600	531.76	J. Cobley	(a) I. Truster
§Congleton, Cheshire	85,300	575.28	Miss C. L. Pointer	(a) G. Baxendale
§Copeland, Cumbria	72,000	600.00	R. G. Smith	(a) C. Blair
Corby, Northants.	53,600	522.21	T. Simmons	(a) R. Telfer
Cotswold, Glos.	75,200	586.48	D. A. Sketchley	Mrs M. F. Brown
Craven, North Yorks.	50,800	498.67	††H. H. Crabtree	Mrs V. M. Cutter
§Crawley, West Sussex	88,700	544.36	M. D. Sander	(a) A. G. Nickson
§Crewe and Nantwich, Cheshire	105,300	601.20	A. Wenham	(a) R. Ellwood
§Dacorum, Herts.	133,900	510.02	K. Hunt	(a) Mrs Appleby
§Darlington, Co. Durham	100,000	588.35	H. R. C. Owen	(a) E. A. Richmond
§Dartford, Kent	81,000	525.17	C. R. Shepherd	(a) Mrs A. Allen
Daventry, Northants.	63,200	479.58	R. J. Symons, RD	C. J. Over
DERBY	222,500	582.50	R. H. Cowlishaw	(a) R. Wood
Derbyshire Dales	67,900	602.21	D. Wheatcroft	Mrs P. V. Edwards, MBE
Derwentside, Co. Durham	87,000	702.54	N. F. Johnson	E. Coulson
Dover, Kent	105,700	532.72	J. P. Moir, TD	R. R. Chesterfield
DURHAM	86,000	552.12	C. G. Firmin	(a) M. Cranthorne
Easington, Co. Durham	99,000	633.21	*P. Innes	J. Goodwin
§Eastbourne, East Sussex	85,200	591.40	Dr M. Blanch	A. E. Leggett
East Cambridgeshire	61,300	456.33	T. T. G. Hardy	L. W. Neal
East Devon	118,700	497.34	F. J. Vallender	F. A. C. Pinney, OBE
East Dorset	79,300	514.84	A. Breakwell	Mrs P. H. Batstone
East Hampshire	104,700	469.15	B. P. Roynon	S. M. E. Halstead
East Hertfordshire	118,000	514.97	R. J. Bailey	R. J. F. Tucker
§Eastleigh, Hants.	107,100	478.48	C. Tapp	(a) M. Kyrle
East Lindsey, Lincs.	118,800	469.51	‡P. Haigh	R. F. Dickinson
East Northamptonshire	69,000	468.40	R. K. Heath	H. E. Gregory
East Staffordshire	98,500	434.22	F. W. Saunders	G. Callister
§East Yorkshire, Humberside	85,400	558.00	J. H. Gibson	(a) J. Ireland
Eden, Cumbria	46,000	589.45	I. W. Bruce	E. S. C. Wooff
§Ellesmere Port and Neston, Cheshire	81,500	616.14	S. Ewbank	(a) J. A. Sherlock
§Elmbridge, Surrey	114,700	600.15	D. W. L. Jenkins	(a) D. A. S. Brooke
Epping Forest, Essex	117,100	517.69	J. Burgess	W. A. G. Easton, OBE
§Epsom and Ewell, Surrey	68,000	524.85	D. J. Smith	(a) H. H. Upton
§Erewash, Derbyshire	107,400	726.00	R. M. Fletcher	(a) Mrs M. E. Henshaw
EXETER, Devon	104,700	543.44	B. Frowd	(a) M. J. Rich
§Fareham, Hants.	100,600	443.97	A. A. Davies	(a) Mrs D. Burton-Jenkins
Fenland, Cambs.	75,600	511.86	N. R. Topliss	A. R. German
Forest Heath, Suffolk	65,300	460.19	S. W. Catchpole	W. J. Bishop
Forest of Dean, Glos.	76,200	619.00	‡R. A. Willis	B. W. Hobman
§Fylde, Lancs.	72,600	594.94	J. P. Johnson	(a) Miss J. Wilding
§Gedling, Notts.	111,100	590.13	W. Brown	(a) Mrs E. M. Hindle
§Gillingham, Kent	96,600	504.86	J. A. McBride	(a) K. Webber
§Glanford, Humberside	72,400	603.98	D. D. H. Cameron	(a) K. Vickers
GLOUCESTER	103,600	526.69	G. Garbett	(a) Mrs E. Hedge
§Gosport, Hants.	77,200	492.36	M. S. Friend	(a) M. G. Russell
§Gravesham, Kent	93,800	475.78	E. V. J. Seager	(a) F. J. Eve
§Great Grimsby, Humberside	91,800	685.00	R. S. G. Bennett	(a) S. J. Norton
§Great Yarmouth, Norfolk	89,000	519.20	vacant	(a) C. Burrows
§Guildford, Surrey	126,900	543.38	D. T. Watts	(a) R. Marks
§Halton, Cheshire	124,700	645.00	M. Cuff	(a) J. Pimblett
Hambleton, North Yorks.	80,200	435.00	C. Spencer	R. G. Horner
Harborough, Leics.	68,200	569.87	B. B. Bowen (acting)	J. Shaw
Harlow, Essex	75,500	724.56	*D. Byrne	H. Talbot
§Harrogate, North Yorks.	146,300	579.00	P. M. Walsh	(a) R. M. Whitfield
Hart, Hants.	81,700	438.10	G. R. Jelbart	P. Carr
§Hartlepool, Cleveland	91,400	655.05	B. J. Dinsdale	(a) B. Smith
§Hastings, East Sussex	83,700	536.37	R. A. Carrier	(a) R. Stevens

* General Manager
‡ Director of Central Services
†† Head of Paid Service

Council	Population 1991	Band D charge 1993	Chief Executive	Chairman 1993-4 (a) Mayor (b) Lord Mayor
§Havant, Hants.	120,600	£512.28	D. E. Ridley	(a) Mrs J. Carruthers
HEREFORD	51,300	497.50	C. E. S. Willis	(a) R. E. G. Alford
§Hertsmere, Hertfordshire	88,900	537.22	†P. Copland	(a) A. R. Gattward
§High Peak, Derbyshire	86,000	602.19	R. P. H. Brady	(a) J. Francis
§Hinckley and Bosworth, Leics.	97,200	427.44	vacant	(a) Mrs A. Wainwright
§Holderness, Humberside	51,400	590.13	A. Johnson	(a) F. J. Gledhill
Horsham, West Sussex	110,400	460.63	M. J. Pearson	G. Godwin
§Hove, East Sussex	90,000	525.20	J. P. Teasdale	(a) P. B. Martin
Huntingdonshire, Cambs.	149,600	422.29	T. J. Gee	Mrs J. Day
§Hyndburn, Lancs.	79,000	633.96	M. J. Wedgeworth	(a) Mrs S. M. Bramley-Haworth
§Ipswich, Suffolk	118,800	632.43	J. D. Hehir	(a) Mrs M. D. Alderton
Kennet, Wilts.	70,400	490.67	P. L. Owens	D. J. Godwin
Kerrier, Cornwall	89,400	572.24	G. G. Cox	G. J. J. Stephens
§Kettering, Northants.	77,000	515.70	P. S. Williams	(a) C. J. Groome
§King's Lynn and West Norfolk	132,300	495.47	A. E. Pask	(a) C. A. Matkin
KINGSTON UPON HULL, Humberside	262,900	633.81	D. Stephenson	(b) L. Harvey
§Kingswood, Avon	90,600	582.43	A. Smith	(a) C. A. Rickards
LANCASTER, Lancs.	130,300	615.45	W. Pearson	(a) Mrs J. Taylor
§Langbaurgh-on-Tees, Cleveland	146,400	528.31	K. Abigail	(a) V. Teesdale
LEICESTER	280,500	650.89	I. Farookhi	(b) H. Dundhy
Leominster, Hereford and Worcs.	40,000	505.67	G. R. Chilton	Mrs G. Wright
Lewes, East Sussex	88,700	540.57	J. N. Crawford	Mrs A. D. G. Stiles
Lichfield, Staffs.	93,500	507.80	J. T. Thompson	M. B. Hession
LINCOLN	83,600	525.22	C. J. Thomas	(a) W. Crumblehulme
§Luton, Beds.	174,600	511.77	J. C. Southwell	(a) Mrs J. Fensome
§Macclesfield, Cheshire	151,500	584.51	B. W. Longden	(a) C. H. T. Cleaver
§Maidstone, Kent	137,700	541.09	J. D. Makepeace	(a) P. Oldham
Maldon, Essex	53,000	508.74	E. A. P. Plumridge	F. Delderfield
Malvern Hills, Hereford and Worcs.	89,200	540.63	M. J. Jones	D. J. Young
Mansfield, Notts.	101,600	677.59	R. P. Goad	Mrs F. Spate
§Medina, Isle of Wight	72,100	536.38	*J. Sprake	(a) Mrs R. Hames
§Melton, Leics.	45,600	480.14	°P. J. G. Herrick	(a) M. C. R. Graham
Mendip, Somerset	97,900	541.61	G. Jeffs	W. Mackay
Mid Bedfordshire	113,300	511.43	C. A. Tucker	Mrs C. M. Barnes
Mid Devon	65,300	533.81	M. I. R. Bull	Mrs M. E. Turner
§Middlesbrough, Cleveland	144,500	637.22	J. R. Foster	(a) Mrs I. Berryman
Mid Suffolk	79,600	482.73	H. McFarlane	Air Cdre. J. B. Wellingham
Mid Sussex	122,700	496.24	B. J. Grimshaw	W. E. Knighton
§Milton Keynes, Bucks.	178,800	580.03	M. J. Murray	(a) L. B. Hostler
Mole Valley, Surrey	79,800	517.35	A. A. Huggins	H. M. Sewill
Newark and Sherwood, Notts.	103,700	630.63	†R. G. Dix	T. P. Crewe
Newbury, Berks.	139,900	520.00	P. E. McMahon	K. H. Lock
§Newcastle under Lyme, Staffs.	122,100	543.62	D. F. Hill	(a) Mrs E. Ashley, OBE
New Forest, Hants.	162,200	464.45	P. A. D. Hyde	Mrs J. K. Vernon-Jackson, MBE
§Northampton	184,400	541.80	R. J. B. Morris	(a) A. Howes
Northavon, Avon	132,900	585.41	F. Maude	R. M. McGurk
§North Bedfordshire	137,400	505.42	L. W. Gould	(a) D. A. Jones
North Cornwall	74,400	521.40	D. H. Westwell	K. F. White
North Devon	85,700	450.32	R. D. Hall	M. J. Edmunds
North Dorset	54,100	443.95	A. J. Bridgeman	B. R. Clarke
North East Derbyshire	98,700	632.20	Mrs C. A. Gilbey	Mrs T. M. Lide
North Hertfordshire	113,200	517.84	S. Philp	R. S. Flatman
North Kesteven, Lincs.	81,400	500.00	S. Lamb	T. E. Ball, MBE
North Norfolk	92,600	495.11	T. V. Nolan	P. D. Blaxell
North Shropshire	54,000	545.57	K. Flood	Mrs S. Lewis
§North Warwickshire	61,300	643.72	D. Monks	(a) P. F. Morson
North West Leicestershire	81,400	487.06	J. E. White	D. T. Williamson
North Wiltshire	114,600	498.47	H. Miles	A. S. R. Jackson

* General Manager
† Managing Director
° Clerk

Council	Population 1991	Band D charge 1993	Chief Executive	Chairman 1993–4 (a) Mayor (b) Lord Mayor
NORWICH, Norfolk	125,200	£595.61	J. R. Packer	(b) R. Durrant
NOTTINGHAM	276,000	630.56	E. F. Cantle	(b) M. Ibrahim
§Nuneaton and Bedworth, Warwicks.	118,100	658.37	‡‡J. Walton	(a) M. Kedwards
§Oadby and Wigston, Leics.	53,100	534.78	Mrs R. E. Hyde	(a) M. Griffiths
§Oswestry, Shropshire	34,600	529.55	D. A. Towers	(a) W. S. Keable
OXFORD	127,600	587.79	R. S. Block	(b) J. G. Power
§Pendle, Lancs.	85,700	652.55	S. Barnes	(a) R. Clarkson
Penwith, Cornwall	60,000	551.99	‡M. J. Furneaux	T. A. Harvey
PETERBOROUGH, Cambs.	155,200	531.73	W. E. Samuel	(a) Mrs K. Coppen
PLYMOUTH, Devon	254,500	565.02	Mrs A. Stone	(b) J. Richards
§Poole, Dorset	135,400	481.50	J. W. Brooks	(a) B. R. V. Grant-Braham
PORTSMOUTH, Hants.	185,200	454.95	N. Gurney	(b) A. M. Bentley
§Preston, Lancs.	129,900	651.82	G. Driver	(a) K. J. Hudson
Purbeck, Dorset	43,400	468.51	P. B. Croft	D. B. Humphry
§Reading, Berks.	134,600	607.76	Ms S. Pierce	(a) R. Sohpal
§Redditch, Hereford and Worcs.	78,900	558.75	Ms S. Manzie	(a) K. L. Somner
§Reigate and Banstead, Surrey	119,000	554.11	M. Bacon	(a) N. Spiers
§Restormel, Cornwall	88,000	541.79	D. Brown	(a) G. H. Netherton
§Ribble Valley, Lancs.	52,100	597.22	O. Hopkins	(a) T. Jackson
Richmondshire, North Yorks.	46,200	492.49	H. Tabiner	K. Jones
ROCHESTER UPON MEDWAY, Kent	147,100	498.00	R. I. Gregory	(a) R. D. Cox
Rochford, Essex	75,900	497.34	P. W. Hughes	T. Fawell
§Rossendale, Lancs.	66,100	668.61	J. S. Hartley	(a) G. Atkinson
Rother, East Sussex	83,200	541.44	D. F. Powell	G. A. Swift
§Rugby, Warwicks.	86,000	590.35	J. S. R. Lawton	(a) Mrs C. A. Lane
§Runnymede, Surrey	74,900	470.00	T. N. Williams	(a) Mrs E. W. Meany
§Rushcliffe, Notts.	99,300	569.95	J. Saxton	(a) E. J. Bonham
§Rushmoor, Hants.	86,000	455.05	R. Upton	(a) T. R. Davies
Rutland, Leics.	33,400	517.27	K. R. Emslie	P. R. Holloway
Ryedale, North Yorks.	92,000	480.38	M. Walker	K. J. R. Binks
ST ALBANS, Herts.	126,900	644.51	E. A. Hackford	(a) Mrs S. Burton
§St Edmundsbury, Suffolk	93,100	499.47	G. R. N. Toft	(a) E. G. Spooner
Salisbury, Wilts.	107,900	474.38	D. R. J. Rawlinson	W. R. Moss
§Scarborough, North Yorks.	109,600	495.00	J. M. Trebble	(a) E. W. Dixon
§Scunthorpe, Humberside	62,500	653.23	I. M. Hutchinson	(a) Mrs C. Pearson
Sedgefield, Co. Durham	91,500	561.49	A. J. Roberts	G. Ferguson
Sedgemoor, Somerset	99,400	532.99	A. G. Lovell	P. H. Daniel
Selby, North Yorks.	92,500	490.00	J. C. Edwards	J. W. Bramall
Sevenoaks, Kent	109,600	527.00	B. C. Cova, MBE	M. H. L. Whitehouse
Shepway, Kent	93,800	560.86	R. J. Thompson	P. Rossiter
§Shrewsbury and Atcham	92,800	520.66	D. Bradbury	(a) L. N. Morris
§Slough, Berks.	102,400	468.00	°A. Bhattacharya	(a) Mrs S. Thorpe
SOUTHAMPTON, Hants.	204,500	500.00	E. A. Urquhart	(a) J. Martin
South Bedfordshire	109,900	543.88	T. D. Rix	Mrs E. A. Luckhurst-Matthews
South Bucks.	62,600	502.63	C. Furness	Prof. C. A. Hogarth
South Cambridgeshire	122,500	442.93	J. S. Ballantyne	E. W. Bullman
South Derbyshire	72,900	587.40	T. Day	G. S. Knight
§Southend-on-Sea, Essex	162,900	516.72	°D. Moulson	(a) J. Tobin
South Hams, Devon	78,700	493.10	F. G. Palmer	D. J. Andrews
South Herefordshire	52,400	484.34	A. Hughes	E. R. Vines
South Holland, Lincs.	67,900	504.31	C. J. Simpkins	Mrs A. M. Newton
South Kesteven, Lincs.	110,200	499.50	K. R. Cann	R. Briggs
South Lakeland, Cumbria	99,300	608.29	°A. F. Winstanley	Mrs E. M. Braithwaite
South Norfolk	104,100	484.82	A. G. T. Kellett	Mrs K. Rogers
South Northamptonshire	71,600	537.32	K. Whitehead	F. Pinny
South Oxfordshire	120,800	539.98	R. Watson	Mrs E. A. Ducker
§South Ribble, Lancs.	102,900	602.46	J. B. R. Leadbetter	(a) J. C. Hughes
South Shropshire	38,700	511.59	G. C. Biggs	J. McCormick

° Clerk
‡‡ Borough Manager
‡Director of Central Services

Council	Population 1991	Band D charge 1993	Chief Executive	Chairman 1993–4 (a) Mayor (b) Lord Mayor
South Somerset	144,000	£539.90	M. Usher	R. Madelin
South Staffordshire	106,400	434.22	L. Barnfild	B. R. Edwards
§South Wight, IOW	54,500	547.10	D. W. Jaggar	(a) Mrs A. E. Cardew
§Spelthorne, Surrey	91,400	528.43	M. B. Taylor	(a) G. Paterson-Borland
§Stafford	120,300	508.26	°J. K. M. Krawiec	(a) A. B. Compton
Staffordshire Moorlands	96,000	553.25	A. W. Law	A. R. Williamson
§Stevenage, Herts.	76,000	605.83	H. L. Miller	(a) R. A. Clark
§Stockton-on-Tees, Cleveland	175,300	628.54	°F. F. Theobalds	(a) J. Vaughan
STOKE-ON-TRENT, Staffs.	249,700	562.05	B. Smith	(b) Mrs M. Beckett
Stratford-upon-Avon, Warwicks.	106,200	562.66	I. B. Prosser	J. W. Sharp
Stroud, Glos.	104,700	615.22	R. M. Ollin	Mrs S. M. Bruce
Suffolk Coastal	116,000	479.16	T. K. Griffin	K. R. Burnett
§Surrey Heath	80,200	527.91	N. M. Pughe	(a) D. A. V. Martell
§Swale, Kent	116,900	487.57	W. Croydon, CBE	(a) B. Austen
§Tamworth, Staffs.	70,900	507.24	G. Morrell	(a) B. D. Jenkins
Tandridge, Surrey	77,600	540.88	P. J. D. Thomas	M. J. Kelly
§Taunton Deane, Somerset	95,900	489.33	*Mrs S. Douglas	(a) T. G. Smith
Teesdale, Co. Durham	24,500	464.84	C. E. Fell	E. T. Scott
Teignbridge, Devon	110,200	542.13	P. B. Young	K. A. Beer
Tendring, Essex	127,200	530.63	D. Mitchell-Gears	J. Hewitt
§Test Valley, Hants.	103,400	444.56	G. Blythe	(a) G. E. King
§Tewkesbury, Glos.	71,500	458.53	R. A. Wheeler	(a) D. M. M. Davies
§Thamesdown, Wilts.	173,000	561.10	D. M. Kent	(a) G. D. Dart
Thanet, Kent	127,300	526.16	I. G. Gill	Mrs M. Mortlock
Three Rivers, Herts.	79,600	562.14	A. Robertson	T. Palmer
§Thurrock, Essex	129,600	549.51	K. Barnes	(a) P. Rice
§Tonbridge and Malling, Kent	102,700	528.30	T. Thompson	(a) Mrs M. Cole
§Torbay, Devon	122,800	567.00	D. P. Hudson	(a) B. Spencer
Torridge, Devon	53,200	515.71	R. K. Brasington	Mrs P. D. Biggs
§Tunbridge Wells, Kent	102,200	536.02	R. J. Stone	(a) Mrs A. Sturley
Tynedale, Northumberland	57,500	610.12	A. Baty	A. Rubery
Uttlesford, Essex	66,200	507.46	K. Ivory	J. A. Wright
Vale of White Horse, Oxon.	113,200	510.34	D. J. Heavens	K. H. Davies
§Vale Royal, Cheshire	114,700	611.26	W. R. T. Woods	(a) J. S. Chesworth
Wansbeck, Northumberland	61,500	691.99	A. G. White	J. Smith
Wansdyke, Avon	80,800	616.81	*P. May	D. Hamblin
§Warrington, Cheshire	185,100	575.88	M. I. M. Sanders	(a) J. Taylor
Warwick	118,200	575.00	J. V. Picking	A. W. Boxley
§Watford, Herts.	75,800	570.65	D. Plank	M. Jackson
Waveney, Suffolk	108,500	493.02	M. Berridge	J. Reynolds
§Waverley, Surrey	116,100	536.00	G. W. Nuttall	(a) Mrs C. Savage
Wealden, East Sussex	132,000	548.50	D. R. Holness	P. Clifford
Wear Valley, Co. Durham	63,400	628.10	†Mrs E. M. Ashness	H. Russell
§Wellingborough, Northants.	68,500	244.71	W. B. Veal	(a) A. W. Robertson
Welwyn Hatfield, Herts.	94,900	587.70	D. Riddle	F. Matthews
§West Devon	46,200	521.14	J. S. Ligo	(a) R. B. Tait
West Dorset	87,500	503.63	R. C. Rennison	Mrs J. D. Cockerill
West Lancashire	109,100	609.75	B. A. Knight	B. Gannaway-James
West Lindsey, Lincs.	77,000	522.12	R. W. Nelsey	Mrs J. E. Tilney-Bassett
West Oxfordshire	92,400	491.47	N. J. B. Robson	C. R. M. Fox
West Somerset	32,200	495.10	C. Rockall	N. Edwards
West Wiltshire	109,200	517.80	D. G. Latham	J. B. Wesley
§Weymouth and Portland, Dorset	62,800	535.46	M. N. Ashby	(a) A. Martindale
WINCHESTER, Hants.	99,300	432.37	D. H. Cowan	(a) Mrs S. Glasspool
§Windsor and Maidenhead, Berks.	135,100	499.50	G. B. Blacker	(a) M. Scott
§Woking, Surrey	87,200	532.11	P. Russell	(a) Mrs R. Sharpley
Wokingham, Berks.	141,800	550.39	N. B. J. Gurney	G. Parkinson
Woodspring, Avon	180,500	599.60	C. A. Stephens	Mrs J. W. B. Young
WORCESTER	83,900	550.51	††D. Wareing	(a) Mrs H. S. License
§Worthing, West Sussex	98,200	523.23	M. J. Ball	(a) P. Bennett
Wrekin, Shropshire	141,700	629.54	D. G. Hutchinson	Mrs J. Noel

* General Manager
† Director of Administration
° Clerk
††Head of Paid Service

Council	Population 1991	Band D charge 1993	Chief Executive	Chairman 1993-4 (a) Mayor (b) Lord Mayor
Wychavon, Hereford and Worcs.	102,400	£498.94	T. Du Sautoy	P. Coley
Wycombe, Bucks.	160,500	510.11	R. J. Cummins	(a) D. Morris
§Wyre, Lancs.	103,300	601.41	M. Brown	(a) Mrs S. Preston
Wyre Forest, Hereford and Worcs.	95,700	547.49	A. S. Dick	J. L. Gordon
YORK, North Yorks.	103,300	516.29	J. Cairns	(b) Mrs A. Reid

The Cinque Ports

As their name implies, the Cinque Ports were originally five in number: Hastings, New Romney, Hythe, Dover and Sandwich. They were formed during the eleventh century to defend the Channel coast and, after the Norman Conquest, were recognized as a Confederation by a charter of 1278. The "antient towns" of Winchelsea and Rye were added at some time after the Conquest. The other members of the Confederation, known as Limbs, are Lydd, Faversham, Folkestone, Deal, Tenterden, Margate and Ramsgate.

Until 1855 the duty of the Cinque Ports was to provide ships and men for the defence of the state in return for considerable privileges, such as tax exemptions and the framing of by-laws. Of these privileges only jurisdiction in Admiralty remains.

The Barons of the Cinque Ports have the ancient privilege of attending the Coronation ceremony and are allotted special places in Westminster Abbey.

Lord Warden of the Cinque Ports, HM Queen Elizabeth the Queen Mother

Judge, Court of Admiralty, G. Darling, RD, QC

Registrar, I. G. Gill, LVO, PO Box 9, Margate, Kent CT9 1XZ. Tel: 0843-225511

LORD WARDENS OF THE CINQUE PORTS since 1904

The Marquess Curzon	1904
The Prince of Wales	1905
The Earl Brassey	1908
The Earl Beauchamp	1913
The Marquess of Reading	1934
The Marquess of Willingdon	1936
Winston Churchill	1941
Sir Robert Menzies	1965
HM Queen Elizabeth the Queen Mother	1978

Roman Names of English Towns and Cities

Bath	Aquae Sulis
Canterbury	Durovernum Cantiacorum
Carlisle	Luguvalium
Chelmsford	Caesaromagus
Chester	Deva
Chichester	Noviomagus Regnensium
Cirencester	Corinium Dobunnorum
Colchester	Camulodunum
Doncaster	Danum
Dorchester	Durnovaria
Dover	Dubris
Exeter	Isca Dumnoniorum
Gloucester	Glevum

Leicester	Ratae Corieltauvorum
Lincoln	Lindum
London	Londinium
Manchester	Mamucium
Newcastle upon Tyne	Pons Aelius
Pevensey	Anderetium
Rochester	Durobrivae
St Albans	Verulamium
Salisbury (Old Sarum)	Sorviodunum
Silchester	Calleva Atrebatum
Winchester	Venta Belgarum
Wroxeter	Viroconium Cornoviorum
York	Eburacum

London

THE CORPORATION OF LONDON
(see also page 531)

The City of London is the historic centre at the heart of London known as 'the square mile' around which the vast metropolis has grown over the centuries. The City's residential population is 4,100 (1991 Census). The civic government is carried on by the Corporation of the City of London through the Court of Common Council.

The City is the financial and business centre of London and includes the head offices of the principal banks, insurance companies and mercantile houses, in addition to buildings ranging from the historic interest of the Roman Wall and the 15th century Guildhall, to the massive splendour of St Paul's Cathedral and the architectural beauty of Wren's spires.

The City of London was described by Tacitus in AD 62 as 'a busy emporium for trade and traders'. Under the Romans it became an important administration centre and hub of the road system. Little is known of London in Saxon times, when it formed part of the kingdom of the East Saxons. In 886 Alfred recovered London from the Danes and reconstituted it a burgh under his son-in-law. In 1066 the citizens submitted to William the Conqueror who in 1067 granted them a charter, which is still preserved, establishing them in the rights and privileges they had hitherto enjoyed.

THE MAYORALTY

The Mayoralty was probably established about 1189, the first Mayor being Henry Fitz Ailwyn who filled the office for 23 years and was succeeded by Fitz Alan (1212–14). A new charter was granted by King John in 1215, directing the Mayor to be chosen annually, which has ever since been done, though in early times the same individual often held the office more than once. A familiar instance is that of 'Whittington, thrice Lord Mayor of London' (in reality four times, 1397, 1398, 1406, 1419); and many modern cases have occurred. The earliest instance of the phrase 'Lord Mayor' in English is in 1414. It was used more generally in the latter part of the 15th century and became invariable from 1535 onwards. At Michaelmas the liverymen in Common Hall choose two Aldermen who have served the office of Sheriff for presentation to the Court of Aldermen, and one is chosen to be Lord Mayor for the following mayoral year.

LORD MAYOR'S DAY

The Lord Mayor of London was previously elected on the feast of St Simon and St Jude (28 October), and from the time of Edward I, at least, was presented to the King or to the Barons of the Exchequer on the following day, unless that day was a Sunday. The day of election was altered to 16 October in 1346, and after some further changes was fixed for Michaelmas Day in 1546, but the ceremonies of admittance and swearing-in of the Lord Mayor continued to take place on 28 and 29 October respectively until 1751. In 1752, at the reform of the calendar, the Lord Mayor was continued in office until 8 November, the 'New Style' equivalent of 28 October. The Lord Mayor is now presented to the Lord Chief Justice at the Royal Courts of Justice on the second Saturday in November to make the final declaration of office, having been sworn in at Guildhall on the preceding day. The procession to the Royal Courts of Justice is popularly known as the Lord Mayor's Show.

REPRESENTATIVES

Aldermen are mentioned in the 11th century and their office is of Saxon origin. They were elected annually between 1377 and 1394, when an Act of Parliament of Richard II directed them to be chosen for life.

The Common Council, elected annually on the first Friday in December, was, at an early date, substituted for a popular assembly called the Folkmote. At first only two representatives were sent from each ward, but the number has since been greatly increased.

OFFICERS

Sheriffs were Saxon officers; their predecessors were the wicreeves and portreeves of London and Middlesex. At first they were officers of the Crown, and were named by the Barons of the Exchequer; but Henry I (in 1132) gave the citizens permission to choose their own Sheriffs, and the annual election of Sheriffs became fully operative under King John's charter of 1199. The citizens lost this privilege, as far as the election of the Sheriff of Middlesex was concerned, by the Local Government Act 1888; but the liverymen continue to choose two Sheriffs of the City of London, who are appointed on Midsummer Day and take office at Michaelmas. The office of Chamberlain is an ancient one, the first contemporary record of which is 1237. The Town Clerk (or Common Clerk) is mentioned in 1274.

ACTIVITIES

The work of the Corporation is assigned to a number of committees which present reports to the Court of Common Council. These Committees are: City Lands and Bridge House Estates, Policy and Resources, Finance, Planning and Communications, Central Markets, Billingsgate and Leadenhall Markets, Spitalfields Market, Police, Port and City of London Health and Social Services, Libraries, Art Galleries and Records, Boards of Governors of Schools, Music and Drama (Guildhall School of Music and Drama), Establishment, Housing, Gresham (City side), Hampstead Heath Management, Epping Forest and Open Spaces, West Ham Park, Privileges, Barbican Residential and Barbican Centre (Barbican Arts and Conference Centre).

The City's estate, in the possession of which the Corporation of London differs from other municipalities, is managed by the City Lands and Bridge House Estates Committee, the chairmanship of which carries with it the title of Chief Commoner. Chairman (1993), C. D. Woodward, OBE.

The Honourable the Irish Society (The Irish Chamber), Guildhall, London EC2P 2EJ. Clerk, S. J. Murrells), which manages the Corporation's estates in Ulster, consists of a Governor and five other Aldermen, the Recorder, and 19 Common Councilmen, of whom one is elected Deputy Governor.

THE LORD MAYOR 1992–3*

The Rt. Hon. the Lord Mayor (1992-3), Sir Francis McWilliams, GBE
Secretary, Air Vice-Marshal M. Dicken, CB

THE SHERIFFS 1993–4

L. J. Chalstrey (Alderman, Vintry) and J. M. B. Gotch; elected, 8 July 1993; assumed office, 28 September 1993

OFFICERS

Town Clerk, S. Jones, apptd 1991
Chamberlain, B. P. Harty, apptd 1983

* The Lord Mayor for 1993-4 was elected on Michaelmas Day. See Stop-press

THE ALDERMEN

Name and Ward	CC	Ald.	Shff.	Lord Mayor
Cdr. Sir Robin Gillett, Bt., GBE, RD, *Bassishaw*	1965	1969	1973	1976
Sir Peter Gadsden, GBE, *Farringdon Wt.*	1969	1971	1970	1979
Sir Christopher Leaver, GBE, *Dowgate*	1973	1974	1979	1981
Sir Alan Traill, GBE, *Langbourn*	1970	1975	1982	1984
Sir David Rowe-Ham, GBE, *Bridge*	—	1976	1984	1986
Sir Greville Spratt, GBE, TD, *Castle Baynard*	—	1978	1984	1987
Sir Christopher Collett, GBE, *Broad Street*	1973	1979	1985	1988
Sir Hugh Bidwell, GBE, *Billingsgate*	—	1979	1986	1989
Sir Alexander Graham, GBE, *Queenhithe*	1978	1979	1986	1990
Sir Brian Jenkins, GBE, *Cordwainer*	—	1980	1987	1991
Sir Francis McWilliams, GBE, *Aldersgate*	1978	1980	1988	1992

All the above have passed the Civic Chair

Paul Newall, TD, *Walbrook*	1980	1981	1989
Christopher Walford, *Farringdon Wn.*	—	1982	1990
Neil Young, *Bread Street*	1980	1982	1991
Roger Cork, *Tower*	1978	1983	1992
Bryan Toye, *Lime Street*	—	1983	
Richard Nichols, *Candlewick*	1983	1984	
Peter Bull, *Cheap*	1968	1984	
Sir Peter Levene, KBE, *Portsoken*	1983	1984	
Leonard Chalstrey, *Vintry*	1981	1984	1993
Clive Martin, OBE, TD, *Aldgate*	—	1985	
David Howard, *Cornhill*	1972	1986	
James Oliver, *Bishopsgate*	1980	1987	
Gavyn Arthur, *Cripplegate*	1988	1991	
Robert Finch, *Coleman Street*	—	1992	

THE COMMON COUNCIL OF LONDON

Deputy: Each Common Councilman so described serves as deputy to the Alderman of her/his ward

Angell, E. H. (1991) — *Cripplegate Wt.*
Anstee, N. J. (1987) — *Aldersgate*
Archibald, *Deputy* W. W. (1986) — *Cornhill*
Ballard, K. A., MC (1969) — *Castle Baynard*
Balls, *Deputy* H. D. (1970) — *Cripplegate Wt.*
Barker, J. A. (1981) — *Cripplegate Wt.*
Barnes-Yallowley, H. M. F. (1986) — *Coleman Street*
Beale, M. J. (1979) — *Lime Street*
Bird, J. L. (1977) — *Bridge*
Biroum-Smith, P. L. (1988) — *Dowgate*
Block, S. A. A. (1983) — *Cheap*
Bradshaw, D. J. (1991) — *Cripplegate Wn.*
Bramwell, F. M. (1983) — *Langbourn*
Brewer, D. W. (1992) — *Bassishaw*
Brighton, R. L. (1984) — *Portsoken*
Brooks, W. I. B. (1988) — *Billingsgate*
Brown, *Deputy* D. T. (1971) — *Walbrook*
Cassidy, *Deputy* M. J. (1989) — *Coleman Street*
Catt, B. F. (1982) — *Farringdon Wn.*
Challis, G. H., CBE (1978) — *Langbourn*
Clements, *Deputy* G. E. I. (1960) — *Farringdon Wt.*
Cohen, Mrs C. M. (1986) — *Lime Street*
Cole, Lt.-Col. Sir Colin, KCB, KCVO, TD (1964) — *Castle Baynard*

Collinson, Miss A. H. (1991) — *Farringdon Wt.*
Cope, Dr J. (1963) — *Farringdon Wt.*
Cotgrove, C. B. (1991) — *Lime Street*
Coven, *Deputy* Mrs E. O., CBE (1972) — *Dowgate*
Currie, Miss S. E. M. (1985) — *Cripplegate Wt.*
Daily-Hunt, R. B. (1989) — *Cripplegate*
David, C. P. (1984) — *Aldgate*
Davis, C. B. (1991) — *Bread Street*
de Silva, D., QC (1980) — *Farringdon Wt.*
Dowson, G. R. (1992) — *Cripplegate Wn.*
Dunitz, A. A. (1984) — *Portsoken*
Edwards, R. D. K. (1978) — *Bassishaw*
Eskenzi, A. N. (1970) — *Farringdon Wn.*
Evans, Mrs J. (1975) — *Farringdon Wt.*
Eve, R. A. (1980) — *Cheap*
Everett, K. M. (1984) — *Candlewick*
Falk, F. A., TD (1984) — *Farringdon Wt.*
Farthing, R. B. C. (1981) — *Aldgate*
Fell, J. A. (1982) — *Queenhithe*
FitzGerald, R. C. A. (1981) — *Bread Street*
Floyd-Ewin, *Deputy* Sir David, LVO, OBE (1963) — *Castle Baynard*
Forbes, G. B. (1993) — *Bishopsgate*
Frankenberg, P. B. (1989) — *Cordwainer*
Frappell, *Deputy* C. E. (1973) — *Bread Street*
Fraser, W. B. (1981) — *Vintry*
Frazer, C. M. (1986) — *Farringdon Wt.*
Galloway, A. D. (1981) — *Broad Street*
Ginsburg, S. (1990) — *Bishopsgate*
Gold, R. (1965) — *Castle Baynard*
Gowman, Miss A. (1991) — *Dowgate*
Graves, A. C. (1985) — *Bishopsgate*
Halliday, Mrs P. (1992) — *Walbrook*
Harding, N. H. (1970) — *Farringdon Wn.*
Hardwick, Dr P. B. (1987) — *Aldgate*
Hart, *Deputy* M. G. (1970) — *Bridge*
Haynes, J. E. H. (1986) — *Cornhill*
Henderson, *Deputy* J. S., OBE (1975) — *Langbourn*
Henderson-Begg, M. (1977) — *Coleman Street*
Hill-Smith, A. G. L. (1992) — *Farringdon Wt.*
Holland, *Deputy* J. (1972) — *Aldgate*
Horlock, *Deputy* H. W. S. (1969) — *Farringdon Wn.*
Hughesdon, J. S. (1991) — *Bread Street*
Ide, W. R. (1972) — *Castle Baynard*
Jackson, L. St J. T. (1978) — *Bassishaw*
Jennings, I. G. (1988) — *Cripplegate Wn.*
Keep, Mrs B. (1987) — *Cripplegate Wn.*
Kellett, Mrs M. W. F. (1986) — *Tower*
Kemp, D. L. (1984) — *Coleman Street*
Knowles, S. K. (1984) — *Candlewick*
Langmead, A. D. G., TD (1982) — *Tower*
Langton Way, J. H. (1992) — *Cripplegate Wt.*
Lawrence, D. W. O., TD (1979) — *Bridge*
Lawson, G. C. H. (1971) — *Portsoken*
MacLellan, A. P. W. (1989) — *Walbrook*
McNeil, I. D. (1977) — *Lime Street*
Malins, J. H., QC (1981) — *Farringdon Wt.*
Martin, R. C. (1986) — *Queenhithe*
Mayhew, Miss J. (1986) — *Queenhithe*
Mitchell, C. R. (1971) — *Castle Baynard*
Mizen, *Deputy* D. H. (1979) — *Broad Street*
Mobsby, D. J. L. (1985) — *Billingsgate*
Morgan, *Deputy* B. L., CBE (1963) — *Bishopsgate*
Moss, A. D. (1989) — *Tower*
Nash, *Deputy* Mrs J. C. (1983) — *Aldersgate*
Neary, J. E. (1982) — *Aldgate*
Newman, Mrs P. B. (1989) — *Aldersgate*
Northall-Laurie, P. D. (1975) — *Walbrook*
Owen, Mrs J. (1975) — *Langbourn*
Owen-Ward, J. R. (1983) — *Bridge*

Packard, Brig. J. J. (1972)	Cripplegate Wn.
Parmley, A. C. (1992)	Vintry
Pembroke, Deputy Mrs A. M. F. (1978)	Cheap
Ponsonby of Shulbrede, The Lady (1981)	Farringdon Wt.
Pulman, G. A. G. (1983)	Tower
Reed, Deputy J. L., MBE (1967)	Farringdon Wn.
Revell-Smith, Deputy P. A., CBE (1959)	Vintry
Rigby, P. P., CBE (1972)	Farringdon Wn.
Robinson, Mrs D. C. (1989)	Bishopsgate
Rodgers, Miss E. H. L. (1987)	Vintry
Roney, Deputy E. P. T., CBE (1974)	Bishopsgate
Samuel, Deputy Mrs I. (1971)	Portsoken
Sargant, K. A. (1991)	Cornhill
Saunders, Deputy R. (1975)	Candlewick
Savory, M. B. (1980)	Broad Street
Scriven, R. G. (1984)	Candlewick
Sellon, S. A., TD, OBE (1990)	Cordwainer
Shalit, D. M. (1972)	Farringdon Wn.
Sharp, Deputy Mrs I. M. (1974)	Queenhithe
Sherlock, M. R. C. (1992)	Dowgate
Shindler, Deputy A. B. (1966)	Billingsgate
Simpson, A. S. J. (1987)	Aldersgate
Simpson, Mrs S. G. (1992)	Aldersgate
Smithers, H. J. (1986)	Billingsgate
Snyder, M. J. (1986)	Cordwainer
Spanner, J. H., TD (1984)	Broad Street
Stitcher, Deputy G. M., CBE (1966)	Farringdon Wt.
Swan, N. E. B. (1985)	Coleman Street
Taylor, J. A. F., TD (1991)	Bread Street
Walsh, S. (1989)	Farringdon Wt.
White, J. W. (1986)	Cornhill
Williams, G. M. E. (1985)	Aldersgate
Willoughby, P. J. (1985)	Bishopsgate
Wilmot, Deputy R. T. D. (1973)	Cordwainer
Wilson, A. B., CBE (1984)	Cheap
Wixley, G. R. A., TD (1964)	Bassishaw
Woodward, Deputy C. D., OBE (1971)	Cripplegate Wn.
Wooldridge, F. D. (1988)	Farringdon Wn.

The City Guilds (Livery Companies)

The constitution of the livery companies has been unchanged for centuries. There are three ranks of membership; freemen, liverymen and assistants. A person can become a freeman by patrimony (through a parent having been a freeman); by servitude (through having served an apprenticeship to a freeman); or by redemption (by purchase).

Election to the livery is the prerogative of the company, who can elect any of its freemen as liverymen. Assistants are usually elected from the livery and form a Court of Assistants which is the governing body of the company. The Master (in some companies called the Prime Warden) is elected annually from the assistants.

As at June 1993, 22,995 liverymen of the guilds were entitled to vote at elections at Common Hall.

The order of precedence, omitting extinct companies, is given in parenthesis after the name of each company in the list below.

THE TWELVE GREAT COMPANIES
In order of civic precedence

MERCERS (*1*). *Hall*, Ironmonger Lane, London EC2V 8HE. *Livery*, 250. *Clerk*, G. M. M. Wakeford. *Master*, F. R. Baden-Powell

GROCERS (*2*). *Hall*, Princes Street, London EC2R 8AD. *Livery*, 305. *Clerk*, C. G. Mattingley, CBE. *Master*, Viscount Glenapp

DRAPERS (*3*). *Hall*, Throgmorton Street, London EC2N 2DQ. *Livery*, 238. *Clerk*, A. L. Lang, MBE. *Master*, R. P. St G. Cazalet

FISHMONGERS (*4*). *Hall*, London Bridge, London EC4R 9EL. *Livery*, 363. *Clerk*, M. R. T. O'Brien. *Prime Warden*, D. T. Young

GOLDSMITHS (*5*). *Hall*, Foster Lane, London EC2V 6BN. *Livery*, 276. *Clerk*, R. D. Buchanan-Dunlop, CBE. *Prime Warden*, Dr A. M. Stirling.

MERCHANT TAYLORS (*6/7*). *Hall*, 30 Threadneedle Street, London EC2R 8AY. *Livery* 317. *Clerk*, Capt. D. A. Wallis, RN. *Master*, Sir Edward Studd, Bt.

SKINNERS (*6/7*). *Hall*, 8 Dowgate Hill, London EC4R 2SP. *Livery*, 370. *Clerk*, Capt. D. H. Dyke, CBE, LVO, RN. *Master*, Sir John Leahy, KCMG

HABERDASHERS (*8*). *Hall*, Staining Lane, London EC2V 7DD. *Livery*, 300. *Clerk*, Capt. M. E. Barrow, DSO, RN. *Master*, B. E. Sturgess

SALTERS (*9*). *Hall*, 4 Fore Street, London EC2Y 5DE. *Livery*, 153. *Clerk*, Col. M. P. Barneby. *Master*, The Lord Porter of Luddenham, OM, FRS

IRONMONGERS (*10*). *Hall*, Shaftesbury Place, Barbican, London EC2Y 8AA. *Livery*, 217. *Clerk*, J. A. Oliver. *Master*, R. B. Brayne, MBE

VINTNERS (*11*). *Hall*, Upper Thames Street, London EC4V 3BJ. *Livery*, 324. *Clerk*, Brig. G. Read, CBE. *Master*, C. de C. P. Paynter

CLOTHWORKERS (*12*). *Hall*, Dunster Court, Mincing Lane, London EC3R 7AH. *Livery*, 185. *Clerk*, M. G. T. Harris. *Master*, G. P. Purefoy

OTHER CITY GUILDS
In alphabetical order

ACTUARIES (*91*). *Livery*, 175. *Clerk*, P. D. Esslemont, 16A Cadogan Square, London SW1X 0JU. *Master*, A. V. Hall

AIR PILOTS AND AIR NAVIGATORS, GUILD OF (*81*). *Livery*, 390. *Grand Master*, HRH The Prince Philip, Duke of Edinburgh, KG, KT. *Clerk*, Gp Capt J. W. Tritton, AFC, Cobham House, 291 Gray's Inn Road, London WC1X 8QF. *Master*, Capt. C. E. Elton

APOTHECARIES, SOCIETY OF (*58*). *Hall*, Black Friars Lane, London EC4V 6EJ. *Livery*, 1,250. *Clerk*, Lt.-Col. R. J. Stringer. *Master*, M. P. Ward, CBE, MD, FRCS

ARBITRATORS (*93*). *Livery*, 190. *Clerk*, Lt.-Col. I. R. P. Green, 2 Bolts Hill, Castle Camps, Cambs. CB1 6GL. *Master*, A. P. G. Borley

ARMOURERS AND BRASIERS (*22*). *Hall*, 81 Coleman Street, London EC2R 5BJ. *Livery*, 120. *Clerk*, Lt.-Col. R. R. F. Cowe. *Master*, Brig. G. L. D. Duckworth

BAKERS (*19*). *Hall*, Harp Lane, London EC3R 6DP. *Livery*, 415. *Clerk (acting)*, J. W. Tompkins. *Master*, H. Gould

BARBERS (*17*). *Hall*, Monkwell Square, London EC2Y 5BL. *Livery*, 224. *Clerk*, Col. A. B. Harfield, CBE. *Master*, R. J. Pincham, CBE

BASKETMAKERS (*52*). *Livery*, 430. *Clerk*, A. Gillett, 7 Kinghorn Street, London EC1A 7HT. *Prime Warden*, A. K. Brown, MBE, MB, FRCS

BLACKSMITHS (*40*). *Livery*, 275. *Clerk*, R. C. Jorden, 27 Cheyne Walk, Grange Park, London N21 1DB. *Prime Warden*, Lt.-Col. D. D. Dennis, OBE

BOWYERS (*38*). *Livery*, 107. *Clerk*, A. Black, CBE, 2 Serjeant's Inn, Fleet Street, London EC4Y 1LL. *Master*, C. Ballenden

BREWERS (*14*). *Hall*, Aldermanbury Square, London EC2V 7HR. *Livery*, 130. *Clerk*, C. W. Dallmeyer. *Master*, J. H. Morgan

BRODERERS (*48*). *Livery*, 156. *Clerk*, P. J. C. Crouch, 11 Bridge Road, East Molesey, Surrey KT8 9EU. *Master*, D. N. Smedley

BUILDERS MERCHANTS (*88*). *Livery*, 215. *Clerk*, Miss S. Robinson, TD, 14 Charterhouse Square, London EC1M 6AX. *Master*, M. Pares

BUTCHERS (*24*). *Hall*, 87 Bartholomew Close, London EC1A 7EB. *Livery*, 800. *Clerk*, A. H. Emus. *Master*, F. J. Mallion

CARMEN (*77*). *Livery*, 447. *Clerk*, Lt.-Col. G. T. Pearce, MBE, 35–37 Ludgate Hill, London EC4M 7JN. *Master*, E. R. Britt

CARPENTERS (*26*). *Hall*, 1 Throgmorton Avenue, London EC2N 2JJ. *Livery*, 150. *Clerk*, Maj.-Gen. P. T. Stevenson, OBE. *Master*, V. F. Browne

CHARTERED ACCOUNTANTS (*86*). *Livery*, 345. *Clerk*, G. H. Kingsmill, The Grove, Hinton Parva, Swindon SN4 0DH. *Master*, Mrs B. M. Culverhouse

CHARTERED ARCHITECTS (*98*). *Livery*, 118. *Clerk*, L. W. Groome, OBE, 5 Claylands Place, London SW8 1NZ. *Master*, B. A. Barker, OBE

CHARTERED SECRETARIES AND ADMINISTRATORS (*87*). *Livery*, 235. *Hon. Clerk*, G. H. Challis, CBE, St Dunstan's House, Carey Lane, London EC2V 8AA. *Master*, F. J. Bergin

CHARTERED SURVEYORS (*85*). *Livery*, 340. *Clerk*, Mrs A. L. Jackson, 16 St Mary-at-Hill, London EC3R 8EE. *Master*, A. Gordon-James

CLOCKMAKERS (*61*). *Livery*, 285. *Hall*, St Dunstan's House, Carey Lane, London EC2Y 8AA. *Clerk*, P. H. Gibson, MBE. *Master*, J. N. W. Smith

COACHMAKERS AND COACH-HARNESS MAKERS (*72*). *Livery*, 400. *Clerk*, Maj. W. H. Wharfe, 149 Banstead Road, Ewell, Epsom, Surrey KT17 3HL. *Master*, P. C. K. O'Ferrall, OBE

CONSTRUCTORS (*99*). *Livery*, 105. *Clerk*, A. W. J. Appleton, Graves End House, Woodbury, Salterton, Exeter EX5 1PG. *Master*, R. H. Rooley

COOKS (*35*). *Livery*, 75. *Clerk*, M. C. Thatcher, 35 Great Peter Street, London SW1P 3LR. *Master*, S. J. Herbage

COOPERS (*36*). *Hall*, 13 Devonshire Square, London EC2M 4TH. *Livery*, 260. *Clerk*, J. A. Newton. *Master*, C. S. Griffin

CORDWAINERS (*27*). *Livery* 150. *Clerk*, Cdr. C. Shears, CVO, OBE, Eldon Chambers, 30 Fleet Street, London EC4Y 1AA. *Master*, T. M. A. Upfill-Brown

CURRIERS (*29*). *Livery*, 93. *Clerk*, Gp Capt F. J. Hamilton, Kestrel Cottage, East Knoyle, Salisbury SP3 6AD. *Master*, M. Simmonds

CUTLERS (*18*). *Hall*, Warwick Lane, London EC4M 7GR. *Livery*, 100. *Clerk*, K. S. G. Hinde, TD. *Master*, P. R. W. Roberts

DISTILLERS (*69*). *Livery*, 250. *Clerk*, C. V. Hughes, 71 Lincoln's Inn Fields, London WC2A 3JF. *Master*, N. C. Strofton

DYERS (*13*). *Hall*, Dowgate Hill, London EC4R 2ST. *Livery*, 125. *Clerk*, J. R. Chambers. *Prime Warden*, D. G. Mathieson

ENGINEERS (*94*). *Livery*, 286. *Clerk*, Cdr. B. D. Gibson, 1 Carlton House Terrace, London SW1Y 5DB. *Master*, G. Clerehugh, OBE

ENVIRONMENTAL CLEANERS (*97*). *Livery*, 185. *Clerk*, S. J. Holt, Whitethorns, Rannoch Road, Crowborough, E. Sussex TN6 1RA. *Master*, J. A. Howard

FAN MAKERS (*76*). *Livery*, 216. *Clerk*, Lt.-Col. I. R. P. Green, 2 Bolts Hill, Castle Camps, Cambs. CB1 6GL. *Master*, J. R. P. Hammond

FARMERS (*80*). *Hall*, 3 Cloth Street, London EC1A 7LD. *Livery*, 278. *Clerk*, vacant. *Master*, A. Tritton

FARRIERS (*55*). *Livery*, 375. *Clerk*, H. W. H. Ellis, 37 The Uplands, Loughton, Essex IG10 1NQ. *Master*, R. J. D. Thompson

FELTMAKERS (*63*). *Livery*, 170. *Clerk*, Lt.-Col. C. J. Holroyd, Providence Cottage, Chute Cadley, Andover, Hants. SP11 9EB. *Master*, B. D. S. Burgess

FLETCHERS (*39*). *Hall*, 3 Cloth Street, London EC1A 7LD. *Livery*, 102. *Clerk*, J. R. Garnett. *Master*, P. L. Whiting

FOUNDERS (*33*). *Hall*, 1 Cloth Fair, London EC1A 7HT. *Livery*, 170. *Clerk*, A. J. Gillett. *Master*, B. D. Farmer

FRAMEWORK KNITTERS (*64*). *Livery*, 212. *Clerk*, D. A. Tate, Apothecaries' Hall, Black Friars Lane, London EC4V 6EL. *Master*, R. A. Wessel

FRUITERERS (*45*). *Livery*, 275. *Clerk*, Cdr. M. T. H. Styles, Denmead Cottage, Chawton, Alton, Hants. GU34 1SB. *Master*, M. C. Wallis

FUELLERS (*95*). *Livery*, 85. *Clerk*, Wg Cdr. H. F. C. Squire, OBE, 4 Maycross Avenue, Morden, Surrey SM4 4DA. *Master*, Dr P. W. Glover

FURNITURE MAKERS (*83*). *Livery*, 268. *Clerk*, Wg Cdr. G. Acklam, MBE, 30 Harcourt Street, London W1H 2AA. *Master*, B. Perring

GARDENERS (*66*). *Livery*, 243. *Clerk*, Col. N. G. S. Gray, 25 Luke Street, London EC2A 4AR. *Master*, E. M. Upward

GIRDLERS (*23*). *Hall*, Basinghall Avenue, London EC2V 5DD. *Livery*, 80. *Clerk*, N. Wyldbore-Smith. *Master*, I. W. Fairclough

GLASS-SELLERS (*71*). *Livery*, 167. *Hon. Clerk*, B. J. Rawles, 43 Aragon Avenue, Thames Ditton, Surrey KT7 0PY. *Master*, P. C. Northam

GLAZIERS AND PAINTERS OF GLASS (53). *Hall*, 9 Montague Close, London SE1 9DD. *Livery*, 281. *Clerk*, P. R. Batchelor. *Master*, N. Burston

GLOVERS (62). *Livery*, 287. *Clerk*, Mrs M. Hood, 71 Ifield Road, London SW10 9AU. *Master*, C. J. Wood

GOLD AND SILVER WYRE DRAWERS (74). *Livery*, 330. *Clerk*, J. R. Williams, 50 Cheyne Avenue, London E18 2DR. *Master*, N. E. B. Swan

GUNMAKERS (73). *Livery*, 269. *Clerk*, F. B. Brandt, The Proof House, 48–50 Commercial Road, London E1 1LP. *Master*, Dr C. Swan, CVO, FSA

HORNERS (54). *Livery*, 290. *Clerk*, S. J. Holt, Whitethorns, Rannoch Road, Crowborough, E. Sussex TN6 1RA. *Master* J. D. Spofforth

INFORMATION TECHNOLOGISTS (100). *Livery*, 225. *Clerk*, R. A. Laidlaw, Epworth House, 25 City Road, London EC1Y 1AA. *Master*, P. R. E. Monson

INNHOLDERS (32). *Hall*, College Street, London EC4R 2SY. *Livery*, 135. *Clerk*, J. R. Edwardes Jones. *Master*, Sir Malcolm Chaplin, CBE

INSURERS (92). *Hall*, 20 Aldermanbury, London EC2V 7HY. *Livery*, 360. *Clerk*, V. D. Webb. *Master*, J. S. Greig

JOINERS AND CEILERS (41). *Livery*, 139. *Clerk*, D. A. Tate, Parkville House, Bridge Street, Pinner, Middx. HA5 3JD. *Master*, W. E. Gale

LAUNDERERS (89). *Hall*, 9 Montague Close, London SE1 9DD. *Livery*, 193. *Clerk*, P. E. Coombe. *Master*, J. G. Crisp

LEATHERSELLERS (15). *Hall*, 15 St Helen's Place, London EC3A 6DQ. *Livery*, 150. *Clerk*, Rear-Adm. P. B. Rowe, CBE, LVO. *Master*, J. G. Curtis

LIGHTMONGERS (96). *Livery*, 122. *Clerk*, S. H. Birch, 53 Leithcote Gardens, London SW16 2UX. *Master*, R. J. Seabrook

LORINERS (57). *Livery*, 380. *Clerk*, J. R. Williams, 50 Cheyne Avenue, London E18 2DR. *Master*, R. C. A. Fitzgerald

MAKERS OF PLAYING CARDS (75). *Livery*, 145. *Clerk*, M. J. Smyth, 6 The Priory, Godstone, Surrey RH9 8NL. *Master*, C. J. F. Latham

MARKETORS (90). *Livery*, 240. *Clerk*, B. F. Catt, 42 Tottenham Lane, London N8 7EA. *Master*, J. A. E. Hathrell, OBE

MASONS (30). *Livery*, 125. *Clerk*, T. F. Ackland, 261 Green Lanes, London N13 4XS. *Master*, R. A. Waters

MASTER MARINERS, HONOURABLE COMPANY OF (78). HQS *Wellington*, Temple Stairs, London WC2R 2PN. *Livery*, 253. *Clerk*, J. A. V. Maddock. *Admiral*, HRH The Duke of Edinburgh, KG, KT. *Master*, Capt. A. D. Braithwaite, RD

MUSICIANS (50). *Livery*, 307. *Clerk*, M. J. G. Fletcher, 1 The Sanctuary, Westminster, London SW1P 3JT. *Master*, J. C. Iles

NEEDLEMAKERS (65). *Livery*, 250. *Clerk*, M. G. Cook, 17 Southampton Place, London WC1A 2EH. *Master*, D. S. Anslow-Wilson

PAINTER-STAINERS (28). *Hall*, 9 Little Trinity Lane, London EC4V 2AD. *Livery*, 380. *Clerk*, Wg Cdr. B. C. Pratt. *Master*, M. L. Giles

PATTENMAKERS (70). *Livery*, 200. *Clerk*, P. Merritt, 25 Wellesley Road, London W4 4BU. *Master*, G. R. A. Andrews

PAVIORS (56). *Livery*, 267. *Clerk*, R. F. Coe, 154 Dukes Avenue, New Malden, Surrey KT3 4HR. *Master*, V. J. Willey

PEWTERERS (16). *Hall*, Oat Lane, London EC2V 7DE. *Livery*, 107. *Clerk*, Maj.-Gen. J. St J. Grey, CB. *Master*, Sir Frank Layfield, QC

PLAISTERERS (46). *Hall*, 1 London Wall, London EC2Y 5JU. *Livery*, 209. *Clerk*, H. Mott. *Master*, G. C. Grover

PLUMBERS (31). *Livery*, 360. *Clerk*, Cdr. A. J. Roberts, OBE, 49 Queen Victoria Street, London EC4N 4SE. *Master*, G. E. Banks

POULTERS (34). *Livery*, 178. *Clerk*, A. W. Scott, 23 Orchard Drive, Chorleywood, Herts. WD3 5QN. *Master*, D. C. Butcher

SADDLERS (25). *Hall*, 40 Gutter Lane, London EC2V 6BR. *Livery*, 70. *Clerk*, K. M. Oliver. *Master*, A. D. G. Welch

SCIENTIFIC INSTRUMENT MAKERS (84). *Hall*, 9 Montague Close, London SE1 9DD. *Livery*, 208. *Clerk*, F. G. Everard. *Master*, D. R. Coleman

SCRIVENERS (44). *Livery*, 146. *Clerk*, H. J. W. Harman, Westminster Bank Chambers, 11 Bridge Road, East Molesey, Surrey KT8 9EU. *Master*, B. J. Ducker

SHIPWRIGHTS (59). *Livery*, 450. *Clerk*, Capt. R. F. Channon, RN, Ironmongers' Hall, Barbican, London EC2Y 8AA. *Permanent Master*, HRH The Duke of Edinburgh, KG, KT. *Prime Warden*, Sir Brian Shaw

SOLICITORS (79). *Livery*, 287. *Clerk*, Miss S. M. Robinson, TD, 14 Charterhouse Square, London EC1M 6AX. *Master*, C. R. Walford

SPECTACLE MAKERS (60). *Livery*, 360. *Clerk*, C. J. Eldridge, Apothecaries' Hall, Black Friars Lane, London EC4V 6EL. *Master*, M. Jalie

STATIONERS AND NEWSPAPER MAKERS (47). *Hall*, Ave Maria Lane, London EC4M 7DD. *Livery*, 450. *Clerk*, Capt. P. Hames, RN. *Master*, P. T. Rippon

TALLOW CHANDLERS (21). *Hall*, 4 Dowgate Hill, London EC4R 2SH. *Livery*, 180. *Clerk*, Brig. W. K. L. Prosser, CBE, MC. *Master*, D. G. Milne, CBE

TIN PLATE WORKERS alias Wire Workers (67). *Livery*, 150. *Clerk*, S. J. Holt, Whitethorns, Rannoch Road, Crowborough, E. Sussex TN6 1RA. *Master*, R. G. Vincent

TOBACCO PIPE MAKERS AND TOBACCO BLENDERS (82). *Livery*, 180. *Clerk*, I. J. Kimmins, Bouverie House, 154 Fleet Street, London EC4A 2HX. *Master*, G. A. Alton

TURNERS (51). *Livery*, 152. *Clerk*, R. G. Woodwark, DSC, 33A Hill Avenue, Amersham, Bucks. HP6 5BX. *Master*, P. F. W. Venn

TYLERS AND BRICKLAYERS (37). *Livery*, 130. *Clerk*, F. A. G. Rider, 6 Martin Lane, Cannon Street, London EC4R ODP. *Master*, N. H. Carter

UPHOLDERS (49). *Livery*, 200. *Clerk*, W. R. Wallis, Charrington House, The Causeway, Bishop's Stortford CH23 2EW. *Master*, Judge R. Cole

WAX CHANDLERS (20). *Hall*, Gresham Street, London EC2V 7AD. *Livery*, 80. *Clerk*, T. Wood. *Master*, H. R. C. Riches, FRCP

WEAVERS (42). *Livery*, 125. *Clerk*, J. G. Ouvry, 1 The Sanctuary, Westminster, London SW1P 3JT. *Upper Bailiff*, G. E. L. Yeandle

WHEELWRIGHTS (68). *Livery*, 246. *Clerk*, M. R. Francis, Greenup, Milton Avenue, Gerrards Cross, Bucks. SL9 8QW. *Master*, K. A. Wells

WOOLMEN (43). *Livery*, 125. *Clerk*, F. Allen, Hollands, Hedsor Road, Bourne End, Bucks. SL8 5EE. *Master*, R. J. R. Cousins

PARISH CLERKS (No livery). *Members*, 104. *Clerk*, B. J. N. Coombes, 1 Dean Trench Street, London SW1P 3HB. *Master*, L. R. R. Miller

WATERMEN AND LIGHTERMEN (No livery). *Craft Owning Freemen*, 350. *Hall*, 16 St Mary-at-Hill, London EC3R 8EE. *Clerk*, Lt.-Col. C. P. Cameron, MC. *Master*, P. D. T. Roberts

In certain companies the election of Master or Prime Warden for the year does not take place till the autumn. In such cases the Master or Prime Warden for 1992–3 is given.

LONDON BOROUGH COUNCILS

Council	Municipal offices	Population 1991	Band D charge 1993	Chief Executive (*Managing Director)	Mayor (a) Lord Mayor 1993-4
Barking and Dagenham	°Dagenham, RMIO 7BN	145,200	£504.00	W. C. Smith	J. White
Barnet	†The Burroughs, Hendon, NW4 4BG	298,200	549.52	M. M. Caller	V. Lyon
Bexley	‡Bexleyheath, Kent DA6 7LB	218,100	515.00	T. Musgrave	A. W. Charlton
Brent	†Forty Lane, Wembley, HA9 9EZ	247,200	597.60	C. Wood	A. Steel
Bromley	°Bromley, BRI 3UH	293,000	510.00	N. T. Palk	R. Egington
§Camden	†Euston Road, NWI 2RU	177,900	717.54	J. Smith	R. Bhattacharyya
§CITY OF WESTMINSTER	City Hall, Victoria Street, SWIE 6QP	182,400	295.00	*M. C. Montacute	(a) Mrs J. Bianco
Croydon	Taberner House, Park Lane, Croydon CR9 3JS	317,200	515.00	D. Wechsler	P. Hecks
Ealing	°Uxbridge Road, W5 2HL	280,100	570.00	Ms J. Hunt	M. Mallam
Enfield	°Enfield, ENI 3XA	261,500	587.50	Ms M. Arnold	Ms N. Conway
§Greenwich	†Wellington Street, SEI8 6PW	212,000	696.00	C. Roberts	Ms A. Barratt
§Hackney	†Mare Street, E8 IEA	183,500	698.54	J. White	J. Lamb
§Hammersmith and Fulham	†King Street, W6 9JU	152,000	548.74	N. Newton (acting)	Ms J. Caruana
Haringey	°Wood Green, N22 4LE	206,800	726.55	G. Singh	R. Rice
Harrow	°Harrow, HAI 2UH	203,000	553.00	A. G. Redmond	E. W. H. Feakins
Havering	†Romford, RMI 3BD	231,200	535.00	D. R. Bradley	Mrs M. Edwards
Hillingdon	°Uxbridge, UB8 IUW	235,300	525.00	C. Rippingale	G. Booth
Hounslow	°Lampton Road, Hounslow, TW3 4DN	207,700	612.99	R. Kerslake	L. Bawn
§Islington	†Upper Street, NI 2UD	169,600	697.08	E. W. Dear	Ms A. Gilman
§Kensington and Chelsea (RB)	†Hornton Street, W8 7NX	141,300	489.00	R. A. Taylor	D. Harney, OBE
Kingston upon Thames (RB)	Guildhall, Kingston upon Thames KTI IEU	136,800	522.66	T. Hornsby	Ms J. Smith
§Lambeth	†Brixton Hill, SW2 IRW	249,900	629.84	H. Gilby	Ms M. Schumann
§Lewisham	†Catford, SE6 4RU	235,700	515.99	T. Hanafin	S. Mani
Merton	°London Road, Morden, SM4 5DX	170,800	496.81	Ms H. Rabbats	M. de Villiers
Newham	†East Ham, E6 2RP	217,000	599.00	D. Stevenson	Ms J. Reeves
Redbridge	†Ilford, IGI IDD	229,800	525.00	M. J. Frater	R. J. Watts
Richmond upon Thames	°York Street, Twickenham, TWI 3AA	163,400	540.79	R. L. Harbord	Ms G. Mackinney
§Southwark	†Peckham Road, SE5 8UB	222,200	756.00	Ms A. Whyatt	C. Lothian
Sutton	‡St Nicholas Way, Sutton, SMI IEA	170,300	520.74	Ms P. Hughes	F. Sharp
§Tower Hamlets	107 Commercial Street, EI 6BG	165,100	631.55	A. Golding	J. Snooks
Waltham Forest	†Forest Road, Walthamstow, EI7 4JF	216,200	589.50	A. Tobias	N. S. Matharoo
§Wandsworth	†Wandsworth, SWI8 2PU	258,700	145.89	G. K. Jones	M. Johnson

§ Inner London Borough
RB Royal Borough
° Civic Centre
† Town Hall
‡ Civic Offices

Wales

The Principality of Wales (Cymru) occupies the extreme west of the central southern portion of the island of Great Britain, with a total area of 8,018 sq. miles (20,766 sq. km): land 7,968 sq. miles (20,636 sq. km); inland water 50 sq. miles (130 sq. km). It is bounded on the north by the Irish Sea, on the south by the Bristol Channel, on the east by the English counties of Cheshire, Shropshire, Hereford and Worcester, and Gloucestershire, and on the west by St George's Channel.

Across the Menai Straits is the Welsh island of Ynys Môn (Anglesey) (276 sq. miles), communication with which is facilitated by the Menai Suspension Bridge (1,000 ft. long) built by Telford in 1826, and by the tubular railway bridge (1,100 ft. long) built by Stephenson in 1850. Holyhead harbour, on Holy Isle (north-west of Anglesey), provides accommodation for ferry services to Dublin (70 miles).

POPULATION

The population at the 1991 Census was 2,811,865 (males 1,356,886; females 1,454,979). The average density of population in 1991 was 1.36 persons per hectare.

RELIEF

Wales is a country of extensive tracts of high plateau and shorter stretches of mountain ranges deeply dissected by river valleys. Lower-lying ground is largely confined to the coastal belt and the lower parts of the valleys. The highest mountains are those of Snowdonia in the north-west (Snowdon, 3,559 ft), Berwyn (Aran Fawddwy, 2,971 ft), Cader Idris (Pen y Gadair, 2,928 ft), Dyfed (Plynlimon, 2,467 ft), and the Black Mountain, Brecon Beacons and Black Forest ranges in the south-east (Carmarthen Van, 2,630 ft, Pen y Fan, 2,906 ft, Waun Fâch, 2,660 ft).

HYDROGRAPHY

The principal river rising in Wales is the Severn (see page 540), which flows from the slopes of Plynlimon to the English border. The Wye (130 miles) also rises in the slopes of Plynlimon. The Usk (56 miles) flows into the Bristol Channel, through Gwent. The Dee (70 miles) rises in Bala Lake and flows through the Vale of Llangollen, where an aqueduct (built by Telford in 1805) carries the Pontcysyllte branch of the Shropshire Union Canal across the valley. The estuary of the Dee is the navigable portion, 14 miles in length and about five miles in breadth, and the tide rushes in with dangerous speed over the 'Sands of Dee'. The Towy (68 miles), Teifi (50 miles), Taff (40 miles), Dovey (30 miles), Taf (25 miles) and Conway (24 miles), the last named broad and navigable, are wholly Welsh rivers.

The largest natural lake in Wales is Bala (Llyn Tegid) in Gwynedd, nearly four miles long and about one mile wide. Lake Vyrnwy is an artificial reservoir, about the size of Bala, and forms the water supply of Liverpool; Birmingham is supplied from a chain of reservoirs in the Elan and Claerwen valleys.

WELSH LANGUAGE

According to the 1991 Census results, the percentage of persons of three years and over able to speak Welsh was:

Clwyd	18.2	Powys	20.2
Dyfed	43.7	S. Glamorgan	6.5
Gwent	2.4	W. Glamorgan	15.0
Gwynedd	61.0		
Mid Glamorgan	8.5	Wales	18.7

The 1991 figure represents a slight decline from 18.9 per cent in 1981 (1971, 20.8 per cent; 1961, 26 per cent).

FLAG

A red dragon on a field divided white over green (per fess Argent and Vert a dragon passant Gules). The flag was augmented in 1953 by a royal badge on a shield encircled with a riband bearing the words *Ddraig Goch Ddyry Cychwyn* and imperially crowned. Only the unaugmented flag is flown on Government offices in Wales and, where appropriate, in London. Both flags continue to be used elsewhere.

EARLY HISTORY

CELTS AND ROMANS

The earliest inhabitants of whom there is any record appear to have been subdued or exterminated by the Goidels (a people of Celtic race) in the Bronze Age. A further invasion of Celtic Brythons and Belgae followed in the ensuing Iron Age. The Roman conquest of southern Britain and Wales was for some time successfully opposed by Caratacus (Caractacus or Caradog), chieftain of the Catuvellauni and son of Cunobelinus (Cymbeline). South-east Wales was subjugated and the legionary fortress at Caerleon-on-Usk established by about AD 75–77; the conquest of Wales was completed by Agricola about AD 78. Communications were opened up by the construction of military roads from Chester to Caerleon-on-Usk and Caerwent, and from Chester to Conwy (and thence to Carmarthen and Neath). Christianity was introduced during the Roman occupation, in the fourth century.

ANGLO-SAXON ATTACKS

The Anglo-Saxon invaders of southern Britain drove the Celts into the mountain stronghold of Wales, and into Strathclyde (Cumberland and south-west Scotland) and Cornwall, giving them the name of *Waelisc* (Welsh), meaning 'foreign'. The West Saxons' victory of Deorham (AD 577) isolated Wales from Cornwall and the battle of Chester (AD 613) cut off communication with Strathclyde and northern Britain. In the eighth century the boundaries of the Welsh were further restricted by the annexations of Offa, King of Mercia, and counter-attacks were largely prevented by the construction of an artificial boundary from the Dee to the Wye (Offa's Dyke).

In the ninth century Rhodri Mawr (844–878) united the country and successfully resisted further incursions of the Saxons by land and raids of Norse and Danish pirates by sea, but at his death his three provinces of Gwynedd (north), Powys (mid) and Deheubarth (south) were divided among his three sons, Anarawd, Mervyn and Cadell. Cadell's son Hywel Dda ruled a large part of Wales and codified its laws but the provinces were not united again until the rule of Llewelyn ap Seisyllt (husband of the heiress of Gwynedd) from 1018 to 1023.

THE NORMAN CONQUEST

After the Norman conquest of England, William I created palatine counties along the Welsh frontier, and the Norman barons began to make encroachments into Welsh territory. The Welsh princes recovered many of their losses during the civil wars of Stephen's reign and in the early 13th century Owen Gruffydd, prince of Gwynedd, was the dominant figure in Wales. Under Llywelyn ap Iorwerth (1194–1240) the Welsh united in powerful resistance to English incursions and Llywelyn's privileges and *de facto* independence were recognized in Magna Carta. His grandson, Llywelyn ap Gruffydd, was the last native prince; he was killed in 1282 during hostilities between the Welsh and English, allowing Edward I of England to establish his authority over the country. On 7 February 1301, Edward of Caernarvon, son of Edward I, was created Prince of Wales, a title which has subsequently been borne by the eldest son of the sovereign.

Strong Welsh national feeling continued, expressed in the early 15th century in the rising led by Owain Glyndŵr, but the situation was altered by the accession to the English throne in 1485 of Henry VII of the Welsh House of Tudor. Wales was politically assimilated to England under the Act of Union of 1535, which extended English laws to the Principality and gave it parliamentary representation for the first time.

EISTEDDFOD

The Welsh are a distinct nation, with a language and literature of their own, and the national bardic festival (Eisteddfod), instituted by Prince Rhys ap Griffith in 1176, is still held annually (for date, *see* page 12). These *Eisteddfodau* (sessions) form part of the *Gorsedd* (assembly), which is believed to date from the time of Prydian, a ruling prince in an age many centuries before the Christian era.

PRINCIPAL CITIES

CARDIFF

Cardiff (South Glamorgan), at the mouth of the Rivers Taff, Rhymney and Ely, is the capital city of Wales and one of

Britain's major administrative, commercial and business centres. It has many industries, including steel and cigars, and is a flourishing port with a substantial and varied trade.

There are many fine buildings in the civic centre, including the City Hall, the National Museum of Wales, University Buildings, Law Courts, Welsh Office, County Hall, Police Headquarters and the Temple of Peace and Health. Also in the city are Llandaff Cathedral, the Welsh National Folk Museum at St Fagans, Cardiff Castle, the New Theatre, the Sherman Theatre and the Cardiff College of Music and Drama. New buildings include St David's Hall, a concert and conference hall, and the Welsh National Ice Rink.

SWANSEA

Swansea (*Abertawe*) is a city and a seaport of West Glamorgan. The Gower peninsula was brought within the city boundary under local government reform in 1974. The trade of the port includes coal, steel products, containerized goods and the import and export of petroleum products and petrochemicals.

The principal buildings are the Norman Castle (rebuilt *c.*1330), the Royal Institution of South Wales, founded in 1835 (including Library), the University College at Singleton, and the Guildhall, containing the Brangwyn panels. New buildings include the Industrial and Maritime Museum, the new Maritime Quarter and Marina and the leisure centre.

Swansea was chartered by the Earl of Warwick, *c.*1158–84, and further charters were granted by King John, Henry III, Edward II, Edward III and James II, Cromwell (two) and the Marcher Lord William de Breos.

Welsh Counties

LORD LIEUTENANTS AND HIGH SHERIFFS

County	Lord Lieutenant	High Sheriff, 1993-4
Clwyd	Sir William Gladstone, Bt.	P. Cauldfield
Dyfed	D. C. Mansel Lewis	Mrs P. Rooney
Gwent	R. Hanbury-Tenison	S. Boyle
Gwynedd	R. E. Meuric Rees, CBE	Sir Richard Williams-Bulkeley, Bt.
Mid Glamorgan	M. A. McLaggan	B. M. Ladbrooke
Powys	M. L. Bourdillon	A. J. Gibson-Watt
South Glamorgan	Capt. N. Lloyd-Edwards	J. Curteis
West Glamorgan	Lt.-Col. Sir Michael Llewellyn, Bt.	A. Aylesbury, OBE

COUNTY COUNCILS: AREA, POPULATION, FINANCE

Council	Administrative headquarters	Area (hectares)	Population 1991	Total demand upon collection fund 1993
Clwyd	Shire Hall, Mold	243,015	413,700	£41,619,000
Dyfed	County Hall, Carmarthen	576,575	350,800	38,400,000
Gwent	County Hall, Cwmbran	137,652	446,900	35,171,900
Gwynedd	County Offices, Caernarfon	386,331	240,000	23,310,000
Mid Glamorgan	County Hall, Cathays Park, Cardiff	101,749	541,500	36,532,782
Powys	County Hall, Llandrindod Wells	507,716	118,600	11,310,000
South Glamorgan	County Hall, Atlantic Wharf, Cardiff	41,622	405,800	31,576,000
West Glamorgan	County Hall, Swansea	81,960	368,700	34,847,000

COUNTY COUNCILS: Officers and Chairman

Council	Chief Executive *County Clerk	County Treasurer	Chairman of County Council
Clwyd	E. R. Davies	A. Bell	H. O. Clarke
Dyfed	W. J. Phillips	H. Morse	H. Jones
Gwent	M. J. Perry	J. P. Walsh	P. Geraghty
Gwynedd	H. V. Thomas	T. D. Heald	T. I. Morris
Mid Glamorgan	*D. H. Thomas, CBE	L. M. James	L. Lewis
Powys	N. M. Pringle	†J. Wrightson	D. M. J. James
South Glamorgan	B. Davies	K. Bray	D. J. Francies
West Glamorgan	A. G. Corless	°S. G. Dunster	V. C. Alexander

† County Finance Officer
° Director of Finance

District Councils

Small capitals denote City status
§ denotes Borough status

Council	Population 1991	Band D charge 1993	Chief Executive	Chairman 1993-4 (a) Mayor (b) Lord Mayor
§Aberconwy, Gwynedd	53,900	£335.00	A. G. Carr	(a) Miss E. Jones
Alyn and Deeside, Clwyd	74,500	382.72	D. Salisbury	E. Bagnall
§Arfon, Gwynedd	56,100	315.19	D. L. Jones	(a) H. Jones
§Blaenau Gwent, Gwent	76,900	296.90	R. Leadbeter	(a) M. Mochan
§Brecknock, Powys	41,600	304.99	R. O. Doylend	(a) E. T. Morgan
CARDIFF, South Glamorgan	290,000	289.56	R. E. Paine	(b) V. Riley
Carmarthen, Dyfed	56,100	316.38	R. R. Morgan	J. R. Davies
Ceredigion, Dyfed	66,700	354.00	D. Morgan	H. G. Evans
§Colwyn, Clwyd	56,600	359.44	C. D. Barker	(a) T. Stott
§Cynon Valley, Mid Glamorgan	65,800	285.66	T. B. Roberts	(a) P. M. David
§Delyn, Clwyd	68,300	381.82	P. J. McGreevy	(a) Mrs H. E. D. Jones
§Dinefwr, Dyfed	39,100	340.69	E. W. Harries	(a) D. R. Harris
Dwyfor, Gwynedd	27,200	313.67	E. M. Royles	D. B. Evans
Glyndŵr, Clwyd	42,300	350.30	J. H. Parry	E. C. Edwards
§Islwyn, Gwent	66,900	306.00	B. Bird	(a) S. Jenkins
§Llanelli, Dyfed	75,300	406.32	D. B. Parry-Jones	(a) H. W. Jenkins
§Lliw Valley, West Glamorgan	63,700	351.74	G. C. Sambrook	(a) D. Lewis
Meirionnydd, Gwynedd	33,100	344.86	G. W. Hughes	E. Williams
§Merthyr Tydfil, Mid Glamorgan	59,900	281.30	R. V. Morris	(a) Mrs L. Matthews
§Monmouth, Gwent	76,600	317.40	G. Cummings	(a) A. W. Breeze
Montgomeryshire, Powys	53,200	290.15	N. J. Bardsley	D. R. Jones
§Neath, West Glamorgan	66,000	389.15	S. Penny	(a) K. C. Palmer
§Newport, Gwent	135,500	309.86	R. D. Blair	(a) Mrs J. Jepps
§Ogwr, Mid Glamorgan	133,600	285.04	J. G. Cole	(a) K. F. King
§Port Talbot, West Glamorgan	51,300	351.10	I. K. Lewis	(a) T. P. Crowley
Preseli Pembrokeshire, Dyfed	71,300	327.45	I. W. R. David	W. H. Hitchings
Radnorshire, Powys	24,000	289.64	G. C. Read	L. V. Lewis
§Rhondda, Mid Glamorgan	79,300	280.05	G. Evans	(a) D. Morgan
§Rhuddlan, Clwyd	55,300	367.68	E. O. Lake	(a) P. E. Williams
Rhymney Valley, Mid Glamorgan	104,500	278.66	P. A. Bennett	L. R. Rees
South Pembrokeshire, Dyfed	42,400	309.38	G. H. James	M. Williams
SWANSEA, West Glamorgan	187,700	360.79	A. K. B. Boatswain	(b) W. Dyer
§Taff-Ely, Mid Glamorgan	98,400	288.86	D. Gethin	(a) C. Hughes
§Torfaen, Gwent	91,200	300.30	M. B. Mehta	(a) F. H. Bacon
§Vale of Glamorgan, South Glamorgan	115,800	275.02	M. P. A. Smith	(a) Mrs L. S. Hughes
§Wrexham Maelor, Clwyd	116,700	361.88	R. J. Dutton, CBE	(a) Mrs W. Williams
§Ynys Môn (Isle of Anglesey), Gwynedd	69,800	335.00	E. L. Gibson	(a) J. M. Davies

Scotland

POSITION AND EXTENT

The Kingdom of Scotland occupies the northern portion of the main island of Great Britain and includes the Inner and Outer Hebrides, and the Orkney, Shetland, and many other islands. It lies between 60° 51′ 30″ and 54° 38′ N. latitude and between 1° 45′ 32″ and 6° 14′ W. longitude, with England to the south, the Atlantic Ocean on the north and west, and the North Sea on the east.

The greatest length of the mainland (Cape Wrath to the Mull of Galloway) is 274 miles, and the greatest breadth (Buchan Ness to Applecross) is 154 miles. The customary measurement of the island of Great Britain is from the site of John o' Groats house, near Duncansby Head, Caithness, to Land's End, Cornwall, a total distance of 603 miles in a straight line and approximately 900 miles by road.

The total area of Scotland is 30,420 sq. miles (78,789 sq. km); land 29,767 sq. miles (77,097 sq. km), inland water 653 sq. miles (1,692 sq. km).

POPULATION

The population at the 1991 Census was 4,998,567 (males 2,391,961; females 2,606,606). The average density of the population in 1991 was 0.65 persons per hectare.

RELIEF

There are three natural orographic divisions of Scotland. The southern uplands have their highest points in Merrick (2,766 ft), Rhinns of Kells (2,669 ft), and Cairnsmuir of Carsphairn (2,614 ft), in the west; and the Tweedsmuir Hills in the east (Hartfell 2,651 ft, Dollar Law 2,682 ft, Broad Law 2,756 ft).

The central lowlands, formed by the valleys of the Clyde, Forth and Tay, divide the southern uplands from the northern Highlands, which extend almost from the extreme north of the mainland to the central lowlands, and are divided into a northern and a southern system by the Great Glen.

The Grampian Mountains, which entirely cover the southern Highland area, include in the west Ben Nevis (4,406 ft), the highest point in the British Isles, and in the east the Cairngorm Mountains (Cairn Gorm 4,084 ft, Braeriach 4,248 ft, Ben Macdui 4,296 ft). The north-western Highland area contains the mountains of Wester and Easter Ross (Carn Eige 3,880 ft, Sgurr na Lapaich 3,775 ft).

Created, like the central lowlands, by a major geological fault, the Great Glen (60 miles long) runs between Inverness and Fort William, and contains Loch Ness, Loch Oich and Loch Lochy. These are linked to each other and to the north-east and south-west coasts of Scotland by the Caledonian Canal, providing a navigable passage between the Moray Firth and the Inner Hebrides.

HYDROGRAPHY

The western coast of Scotland is fragmented by peninsulas and islands, and indented by fjords (sea-lochs), the longest of which is Loch Fyne (42 miles long) in Argyll. Although the east coast tends to be less fractured and lower, there are several great drowned inlets (firths), e.g. Firth of Forth, Firth of Tay, Moray Firth, as well as the Firth of Clyde in the west.

The lochs are the principal hydrographic feature of Scotland. The largest in Scotland and in Great Britain is Loch Lomond (27 sq. miles), in the Grampian valleys; the longest and deepest is Loch Ness (24 miles long and 800 feet deep), in the Great Glen; and Loch Shin (20 miles long) and Loch Maree in the northern Highlands.

The longest river in Scotland is the Tay (117 miles), noted for its salmon. It flows into the North Sea, with Dundee on the estuary, which is spanned by the Tay Bridge (10,289 ft) opened in 1887 and the Tay Road Bridge (7,365 ft) opened in 1966. Other noted salmon rivers are the Dee (90 miles) which flows into the North Sea at Aberdeen, and the Spey (110 miles), the swiftest flowing river in the British Isles, which flows into Moray Firth. The Tweed, which gave its name to the woollen cloth produced along its banks, marks in the lower stretches of its 96-mile course the border between Scotland and England.

The most important river commercially is the Clyde (106 miles), formed by the junction of the Daer and Portrail water, which flows through the city of Glasgow to the Firth of Clyde. During its course it passes over the picturesque Falls of Clyde, Bonnington Linn (30 ft), Corra Linn (84 ft), Dundaff Linn (10 ft) and Stonebyres Linn (80 ft), above and below Lanark. The Forth (66 miles), upon which stands Edinburgh, the capital, is spanned by the Forth (Railway) Bridge (1890), which is 5,330 feet long, and the Forth (Road) Bridge (1964), which has a total length of 6,156 feet (over water) and a single span of 3,000 feet.

The highest waterfall in Scotland, and the British Isles, is Eas a'Chùal Aluinn with a total height of 658 feet (200 m), which falls from Glas Bheinn in Sutherland. The Falls of Glomach, on a head-stream of the Elchaig in Wester Ross, have a drop of 370 feet.

GAELIC LANGUAGE

According to the 1991 Census, 1.4 per cent of the population of Scotland, mainly in the Highlands and western coastal regions, were able to speak the Scottish form of Gaelic.

FLAG

A white diagonal cross (the cross of St Andrew, the patron saint of Scotland) on a blue field (saltire Argent in a field Azure).

THE SCOTTISH ISLANDS

The Hebrides did not become part of the Kingdom of Scotland until 1266, when they were ceded to Alexander III by Magnus of Norway. Orkney and Shetland fell to the Scottish Crown for the unpaid dowry of Margaret of Denmark, wife of James III, in 1468, the Danish claims to suzerainty being relinquished in 1590 when James VI married Anne of Denmark.

ORKNEY

The Orkney Islands (total area 375¼ sq. miles) lie about six miles north of the mainland, separated from it by the Pentland Firth. Of the 90 islands and islets (holms and skerries) in the group, about one-third are inhabited.

The total population at the 1981 Census was 19,040; the 1981 populations of the islands shown here include those of smaller islands forming part of the same civil parish.

Mainland, 14,299	Shapinsay, 345
Eday, 154	South Ronaldsay, 1,188
Hoy and Graemsay, 80	Stronsay, 462
Papa Westray, 94	Walls and Flotta, 761
Rousay and Egilsay, 264	Westray, 741
Sanday and North Ronaldsay, 652	

The islands are rich in Pictish and Scandinavian remains, the most notable being the Stone Age village of Skara Brae, the burial chamber of Maeshowe, the many brochs (Pictish towers) and St Magnus Cathedral. Scapa Flow, between the Mainland and Hoy, was the war station of the British Grand Fleet from 1914 to 1919 and the scene of the scuttling of the surrendered German High Seas Fleet (21 June 1919).

Most of the islands are low-lying and fertile, and farming (principally beef cattle) is the main industry. Flotta, to the south of Scapa Flow, is now the site of the oil terminal for the Piper, Claymore and Tartan fields in the North Sea. The capital is Kirkwall (population 6,881) on Mainland.

SHETLAND

The Shetland Islands have a total area of 551 sq. miles and a population at the 1981 Census of 27,271. They lie about 50 miles north of the Orkneys, with Fair Isle about half-way between the two groups. Out Stack, off Muckle Flugga, one mile north of Unst, is the most northerly part of the British Isles (60° 51′ 30″ N. lat.).

There are over 100 islands, of which 16 are inhabited. Populations at the 1981 census were:

Mainland, 22,184	Muckle Roe, 101
Bressay, 335	Out Skerries, 79
East and West Burra	Papa Stour, 29
and Trondra, 930	Unst, 1,206
Fair Isle, 69	Whalsay, 1,026
Fetlar, 102	Yell, 1,168
Foula, 39	

Shetland's many archaeological sites include Jarlshof, Mousa and Clickhimin, and its long connection with Scandinavia has resulted in a strong Norse influence on its place-names and dialect. Industries include fishing, knitwear and farming. In addition to the fishing fleet there are fish processing factories, while the traditional handknitting of Fair Isle and Unst is supplemented now with machine-knitted garments. Farming is mainly crofting, with sheep being raised on the moorland and hills of the islands. Latterly the islands have become an important centre of the North Sea oil industry, with pipelines from the Brent and Ninian fields running to the terminal at Sullom Voe, the largest of its kind in Europe. Lerwick is the main centre for supply services for offshore oil exploration and development.

The capital is Lerwick (population 7,901) on Mainland.

THE HEBRIDES

Until the closing years of the 13th century the Hebrides included other Scottish islands in the Firth of Clyde, the peninsula of Kintyre (Argyllshire), the Isle of Man, and the (Irish) Isle of Rathlin. The origin of the name is stated to be the Greek *Eboudai*, latinized as *Hebudes* by Pliny, and corrupted to its present form. The Norwegian name *Sudreyjar* (Southern Islands) was latinized as *Sodorenses*, a name that survives in the Anglican bishopric of Sodor and Man.

There are over 500 islands and islets, of which about 100 are inhabited, though mountainous terrain and extensive peat bogs mean that only a fraction of the total area is under cultivation. Stone, Bronze and Iron Age settlement has left many remains, including those at Callanish on Lewis, and Norse colonization has influenced language, customs and place-names. Occupations include farming (mostly crofting and stock-raising), fishing and the manufacture of tweeds and other woollens. Tourism is also an important factor in the economy.

The Inner Hebrides lie off the west coast of Scotland and relatively close to the mainland. The largest and best-known is Skye (area 643 sq. miles; pop. 8,139; chief town, Portree), which contains the Cuillin Hills (Sgurr Alasdair 3,257 ft), the Red Hills (Beinn na Caillich 2,403 ft), Bla Bheinn (3,046 ft) and The Storr (2,358 ft). Skye is also famous as the refuge of the Young Pretender in 1746. Other islands in the Highland Region include Raasay (pop. 182), Rum, Eigg and Muck.

Islands in the Strathclyde Region include Arran (pop. 4,726) containing Goat Fell (2,868 ft); Coll and Tiree (pop. 933); Colonsay and Oronsay (pop. 137); Islay (area 235 sq. miles; pop. 3,997); Jura (area 160 sq. miles; pop. 239) with a range of hills culminating in the Paps of Jura (Beinn-an-Oir, 2,576 ft, and Beinn Chaolais, 2,477 ft); and Mull (area 367 sq. miles; pop. 2,605; chief town Tobermory) containing Ben More (3,171 ft).

The Outer Hebrides, separated from the mainland by the Minch, now form the Western Isles Islands Council area (area 1,119 sq. miles; population at the 1981 Census 31,842). The main islands are Lewis with Harris (area 770 sq. miles, pop. 23,390), whose chief town, Stornoway (pop. 13,409), is the administrative headquarters; North Uist (pop. 1,454); South Uist (pop. 2,223); Benbecula (pop. 1,988) and Barra (pop. 1,232). Other inhabited islands include Bernera (292), Berneray (134), Eriskay (219), Grimsay (206), Scalpay (461) and Vatersay (108).

EARLY HISTORY

PREHISTORIC INHABITANTS

The Picts, believed to be of non-Aryan origin, seem to have inhabited the whole of northern Britain and to have spread over the north of Ireland. Remains are most frequent in Caithness and Sutherland and the Orkney Islands.

Celts arrived from Belgic Gaul during the latter part of the Bronze Age and in the early Iron Age, and except in the extreme north of the mainland and in the islands, the civilization and speech of the people were definitely Celtic at the time of the Roman invasion of Britain.

THE ROMAN INVASION

In AD 79–80 Julius Agricola extended the Roman conquests in Britain by advancing into Caledonia and building a line of fortifications across the isthmus between the Forth and Clyde, but after a victory at Mons Graupius he was recalled. Hadrian's Wall, mostly complete by AD 130, marked the frontier until about AD 143 when the frontier moved north to the Forth–Clyde isthmus and was secured by the Antonine Wall. From about AD 155 the Antonine Wall was damaged by frequent attacks and by the end of the second century the northern limit of Roman Britain had receded to Hadrian's Wall.

THE SCOTS

After the withdrawal or absorption of the Roman garrison of Britain there were many years of tribal warfare between the Picts and Scots (the Gaelic tribe then dominant in Ireland), the Brythonic Waelisc (Welsh) of Strathclyde (south-west Scotland and Cumberland), and the Anglo-Saxons of Lothian. The Waelisc were isolated from their kinsmen in Wales by the victory of the West Saxons at Chester (613), and towards the close of the ninth century the Scots under Kenneth Mac Alpin became the dominant power in Caledonia. In the reign of Malcolm I (943–954) Strathclyde was brought into subjection, the English lowland kingdom (Lothian) being conquered by Malcolm II (1005–1034).

From the late 11th century until the mid 16th century there were constant wars between Scotland and England, the outstanding figures in the struggle being William Wallace, who defeated the English at Stirling Bridge (1297) and Robert Bruce, who won the victory of Bannockburn (1314). James IV and many of his nobles fell at the disastrous battle of Flodden (1513).

THE JACOBITE REVOLTS

In 1603 James VI of Scotland succeeded Elizabeth I on the throne of England (his mother, Mary Queen of Scots, was the great-granddaughter of Henry VII), his successors reigning as sovereigns of Great Britain, although political union of the two countries did not occur until 1707. After the abdication (by flight) in 1688 of James VII and II, the crown devolved upon William III (grandson of Charles I) and Mary (elder daughter of James VII and II). In 1689 Graham of Claverhouse roused the Highlands on behalf of James VII and II, but died after a military success at Killiecrankie.

After the death of Anne (younger daughter of James VII and II), the throne devolved upon George I (great-grandson of James VI and I). In 1715, armed risings on behalf of James Stuart (the Old Pretender) led to the indecisive battle of Sheriffmuir, and the Jacobite movement died down until 1745, when Charles Stuart (the Young Pretender) defeated the Royalist troops at Prestonpans and advanced to Derby (1746). From Derby, the adherents of 'James VIII and III' (the title claimed for his father by Charles Stuart) fell back on the defensive, and the movement was finally crushed at Culloden (16 April 1746).

PRINCIPAL CITIES

ABERDEEN

Aberdeen, 130 miles north-east of Edinburgh, received its charter as a Royal Burgh from William the Lion in 1179. Scotland's third largest city, Aberdeen is the second largest Scottish fishing port and the main centre for offshore oil exploration. It is also an ancient university town and distinguished research centre. Other industries include engineering, shipbuilding, food processing, textiles, paper manufacturing and chemicals.

Places of interest include King's College, St Machar's Cathedral, Brig o' Balgownie, Duthie Park and Winter Gardens, Hazlehead Park, the Kirk of St Nicholas, Mercat Cross, Marischal College and Marischal Museum, Provost Skene's House, Art Gallery, James Dun's House (children's museum), Satrosphere Hands-On Discovery Centre, and Provost Ross's House (maritime museum).

DUNDEE

Dundee, a Royal Burgh, is situated on the north bank of the Tay estuary. The city's port and dock installations are important to the offshore oil industry and the airport also provides servicing facilities. Principal industries include textiles, computers and other electronic industries, lasers, printing, tyre manufacture, food processing, carpets, engineering and clothing manufacture. Six sites have Enterprise Zone status, including the Technology Park, airport and port.

The unique City Churches – three churches under one roof, together with the 15th century St Mary's Tower – are the most prominent architectural feature. RRS *Discovery*, the ship which took Captain Scott to the Antarctic and which was built in Dundee in 1901, is berthed in Discovery Quay.

EDINBURGH

Edinburgh is the capital of and seat of government in Scotland. The city is built on a group of hills and contains in Princes Street one of the most beautiful thoroughfares in the world.

The principal buildings are the Castle, which includes St Margaret's Chapel, the oldest building in Edinburgh, and near it, the Scottish National War Memorial; the Palace of Holyroodhouse; Parliament House, the present seat of the judicature; three universities (Edinburgh, Heriot-Watt, Napier); St Giles' Cathedral (restored 1879–83); St Mary's (Scottish Episcopal) Cathedral (Sir Gilbert Scott); the General Register House (Robert Adam); the National and the Signet Libraries; the National Gallery; the Royal Scottish Academy; and the National Portrait Gallery.

GLASGOW

Glasgow, a Royal Burgh, is the principal commercial and industrial centre in Scotland. The city occupies the north and south banks of the Clyde, formerly one of the chief commercial estuaries in the world. The principal industries include engineering, electronics, finance, chemicals and printing. The city has also developed recently as a tourism and conference centre.

The chief buildings are the 13th century Gothic Cathedral, the University (Sir Gilbert Scott), the City Chambers, the Royal Concert Hall, St Mungo Museum of Religious Life and Art, Pollok House, the School of Art (Mackintosh), Kelvingrove Art Galleries, the Burrell Collection museum and the Mitchell Library. The city is home to the Scottish National Orchestra, Scottish Opera and Scottish Ballet.

LORD LIEUTENANTS

Region	Title	Name
Borders	Berwickshire	Maj.-Gen. Sir John Swinton, KCVO, OBE
	Roxburgh, Ettrick and Lauderdale	The Duke of Buccleuch and Queensberry, KT, VRD
	Tweeddale	Lt.-Col. A. M. Sprot of Haystoun, MC
Central	Clackmannan	The Earl of Mar and Kellie
	Stirling and Falkirk	Lt.-Col. J. Stirling of Garden, CBE, TD
Dumfries and Galloway	Dumfries	Capt. R. C. Cunningham-Jardine
	The Stewartry of Kirkcudbright	Sir Michael Herries, OBE, MC
	Wigtown	Maj. E. S. Orr Ewing
Fife	Fife	The Earl of Elgin and Kincardine, KT
Grampian	Aberdeenshire	Capt. C. A. Farquharson
	Banffshire	J. A. S. McPherson, CBE
	Kincardineshire	The Viscount of Arbuthnott, CBE, DSC, FRSE
	Morayshire	Capt. Sir Iain Tennant, KT

Region	Title	Name
Highland	Caithness	The Viscount Thurso
	Inverness	Lt.-Cdr. L. R. D. Mackintosh of Mackintosh, OBE
	Nairn	The Earl of Leven and Melville
	Ross and Cromarty	Capt. R. W. K. Stirling of Fairburn, TD
	Sutherland	Maj.-Gen. D. Houston, CBE
Lothian	East Lothian	Sir Hew Hamilton-Dalrymple, Bt., KCVO
	Midlothian	Capt. G. W. Burnett, LVO
	West Lothian	The Earl of Morton
Strathclyde	Argyll and Bute	vacant
	Ayrshire and Arran	Maj. R. Y. Henderson, TD
	Dumbartonshire	Brig. D. D. G. Hardie, TD
	Lanarkshire	H. B. Sneddon, CBE
	Renfrewshire	Maj. J. D. M. Crichton Maitland
Tayside	Angus	The Earl of Airlie, KT, GCVO, PC
	Perth and Kinross	Maj. Sir David Butter, KCVO, MC
Orkney	Orkney	Brig. M. G. Dennison
Shetland	Shetland	M. M. Shearer
Western Isles	Western Isles	The Earl Granville, MC

The Lord Provosts of the four city districts of Aberdeen, Dundee, Edinburgh and Glasgow are Lord Lieutenants for those districts *ex officio*

Scottish Regions and Islands

REGIONAL AND ISLANDS COUNCILS: Area, Population, Finance

Council	Administrative headquarters	Area (hectares)	Population (latest estimate)	Band D charge 1993	Band D water charge per household 1993
Borders	Newtown St Boswells	471,253	103,881	£365.00	£86.00
Central	Stirling	263,455	272,800	416.00	47.00
Dumfries and Galloway	Dumfries	639,561	148,400	378.00	84.00
Fife	Glenrothes	131,201	345,900	445.00	59.00
Grampian	Aberdeen	869,772	514,400	389.00	89.00
Highland	Inverness	2,539,759	204,004	396.00	81.00
Lothian	Edinburgh	171,595	750,500	730.30	70.00
Orkney	Kirkwall	97,581	19,580	400.00	116.00
Shetland	Lerwick	143,268	22,522	397.62	106.05
Strathclyde	Glasgow	1,350,283	2,306,000	371.00	75.00
Tayside	Dundee	749,165	383,848	415.00	64.00
Western Isles	Stornoway, Lewis	289,798	29,600	463.00	183.00

REGIONAL AND ISLAND COUNCILS: Officers and Conveners

Council	Chief Executive	Director of Finance	Convener
Borders	K. J. Clark, CBE	P. Jeary	The Earl of Minto, OBE
Central	D. Sinclair	S. C. Craig	Mrs A. Wallace
Dumfries and Galloway	I. F. Smith	J. C. Stewart	D. R. Robinson
Fife	Dr J. A. Markland	A. E. Taylor	R. Gough, CBE
Grampian	A. G. Campbell	A. McLean	R. Middleton
Highland	R. H. Stevenson	J. W. Bremner	D. J. McPherson, CBE
Lothian	G. M. Bowie, CBE	D. B. Chynoweth	E. Milligan
Orkney	R. H. Gilbert	R. H. Gilbert	J. A. Tait
Shetland	M. E. Green	A. Matthews	E. Thomason, OBE
Strathclyde	N. McIntosh	A. Gillespie	Dr D. Sanderson
Tayside	R. W. Black	I. B. McIver	Dr G. W. Buckman
Western Isles	B. W. Stewart	R. Bennie	D. Macleod

District Councils

Council	Administrative headquarters	Population (latest estimate)	Band D charge 1993	Chief Executive	Chairman (a) Convener (b) Provost (c) Lord Provost
Aberdeen City (5)	Aberdeen	211,080	£155.50	D. MacDonald	(c) J. Wyness
Angus (9)	Forfar	94,480	99.00	P. B. Regan	(b) B. M. C. Milne
Annandale and Eskdale (3)	Annan	36,361	118.00	W. J. Davidson	(a) D. T. R. Wilson
Argyll and Bute (8)	Lochgilphead	65,140	170.00	M. A. J. Gossip, CBE	G. McMillan
Badenoch and Strathspey (6)	Kingussie	11,900	99.00	Mrs J. M. Fraser	A. Gordon
Banff and Buchan (5)	Banff	85,020	94.50	R. M. Blackburn	(a) W. R. Cruickshank, OBE
Bearsden and Milngavie (8)	Bearsden	40,900	126.00	I. C. Laurie	(b) I. J. Miller
Berwickshire (1)	Duns	19,120	64.80	R. A. Christie	Capt. J. Evans
Caithness (6)	Wick	26,790	96.00	A. Beattie	(a) J. M. Young, OBE
Clackmannan (2)	Alloa	47,470	165.03	R. Allan	(a) J. Watson
Clydebank (8)	Clydebank	44,700	193.00	J. T. McNally	(b) A. Macdonald
Clydesdale (8)	Lanark	46,000	198.00	P. W. Daniels	(a) Mrs E. Logan
Cumbernauld and Kilsyth (8)	Cumbernauld	64,100	145.00	J. Hutton	(b) C. Combe
Cumnock and Doon Valley (8)	Cumnock	42,950	118.22	K. W. Inch	(a) E. Ross
Cunninghame (8)	Irvine	138,069	154.00	B. Devine	(a) S. Dewar
Dumbarton (8)	Dumbarton	77,173	199.00	‡M. J. Watters	(b) P. O'Neill
Dundee City (9)	Dundee	172,120	208.00	A. Stephen	(c) T. M. McDonald
Dunfermline (4)	Dunfermline	130,000	117.00	K. Drennan	(b) Ms M. Millar
East Kilbride (8)	East Kilbride	82,777	171.00	D. Liddell	(b) S. Crawford
East Lothian (7)	Haddington	84,114	135.00	M. Duncan	G. M. Wanless
Eastwood (8)	Giffnock	62,380	79.00	M. D. Henry	(b) L. M. Rosin
Edinburgh City (7)	Edinburgh	418,914	219.30	P. Lowenberg	(c) Rt. Hon. N. Irons
Ettrick and Lauderdale (1)	Galashiels	34,000	100.80	C. M. Anderson	(b) W. Hardie
Falkirk (2)	Falkirk	143,200	80.00	W. Weir	(b) J. Constable
Glasgow City (8)	Glasgow	689,210	234.00	T. J. Monaghan	(c) Rt. Hon. R. Innes
Gordon (5)	Inverurie	77,130	86.00	M. C. Barron	(b) R. G. Bisset
Hamilton (8)	Hamilton	105,202	156.00	M. Docherty	(b) S. Casserly
Inverclyde (8)	Greenock	91,600	167.00	R. McPherson	(b) A. Robertson
Inverness (6)	Inverness	62,490	90.00	B. Wilson	(b) W. A. E. Fraser
Kilmarnock and Loudoun (8)	Kilmarnock	81,350	155.14	R. W. Jenner	(b) D. Coffey
Kincardine and Deeside (5)	Stonehaven	53,710	58.50	T. Hyder	(a) Mrs D. Ewing
Kirkcaldy (4)	Kirkcaldy	147,053	150.00	§D. A. Watt	(a) R. King, OBE
Kyle and Carrick (8)	Ayr	112,658	220.42	I. R. D. Smillie	(b) G. T. Macdonald
Lochaber (6)	Fort William	20,000	141.00	D. A. B. Blair	D. Purdon
Midlothian (7)	Dalkeith	79,990	125.00	T. Muir	(a) D. Molloy
Monklands (8)	Coatbridge	102,379	200.00	M. V. P. Hart	(b) R. Gilson
Moray (5)	Elgin	83,616	90.00	L. Morgan	(a) E. Aldridge
Motherwell (8)	Motherwell	144,750	166.00	J. Bonomy	(b) W. Wilson
Nairn (6)	Nairn	10,420	108.00	†A. M. Kerr	(b) J. Cattanach
Nithsdale (3)	Dumfries	57,140	129.00	T. Orr	(b) Mrs J. McMurdo
North-East Fife (4)	Cupar	65,100	158.00	R. G. Brotherton	Mrs I. M. Carter
Perth and Kinross (9)	Perth	128,369	110.00	H. Robertson	(b) Mrs J. McCormack
Renfrew (8)	Paisley	201,030	180.00	*A. I. Cowe	(b) W. Orr
Ross and Cromarty (6)	Dingwall	49,197	136.00	R. Mair	(a) Maj. A. Cameron, MBE
Roxburgh (1)	Hawick	35,340	99.00	K. W. Cramond	Mrs M. S. Turnbull
Skye and Lochalsh (6)	Portree	12,541	109.00	D. H. Noble	J. F. Munro
Stewartry (3)	Kirkcudbright	23,550	67.50	J. C. Howie	(a) J. Nelson, MBE, TD
Stirling (2)	Stirling	81,280	186.00	G. Bonner	(a) Mrs P. Greenhill
Strathkelvin (8)	Kirkintilloch	85,191	199.00	C. Mallon	(b) R. M. Coyle
Sutherland (6)	Golspie	13,050	102.00	†J. Allison	Mrs A. Magee
Tweeddale (1)	Peebles	15,375	95.00	G. H. T. Garvie	D. Suckling
West Lothian (7)	Bathgate	146,430	87.00	A. M. Linkston	(a) J. McGinley
Wigtown (3)	Stranraer	30,254	123.00	A. Geddes	W. Service

‡ District Secretary
§ General Manager
* Managing Director
† Director of Administration

Regions
(1) Borders
(2) Central
(3) Dumfries and Galloway
(4) Fife
(5) Grampian
(6) Highland
(7) Lothian
(8) Strathclyde
(9) Tayside

Northern Ireland

Northern Ireland has a total area of 5,461 sq. miles (14,144 sq. km): land, 5,215 sq. miles (13,506 sq. km); inland water and tideways, 246 sq. miles (638 sq. km). The population of Northern Ireland at the 1991 Census was 1,577,836 (males, 769,071; females, 808,765). The average density of population in 1991 was 1.11 persons per hectare.

In 1991 the number of persons in the various religious denominations (expressed as percentages of the total population) were: Roman Catholic, 38.4; Presbyterian, 21.4; Church of Ireland, 17.7; Methodist, 3.8; others 7.7; none, 3.7; not stated, 7.3.

PRINCIPAL CITIES

BELFAST

Belfast, the administrative centre of Northern Ireland, is situated at the mouth of the River Lagan at its entrance to Belfast Lough. The city grew, owing to its easy access by sea to Scottish coal and iron, to be a great industrial centre.

The principal buildings are of a relatively recent date and include the Parliament Buildings at Stormont, the City Hall, the Law Courts, the Public Library and the Museum and Art Gallery.

Belfast received its first charter of incorporation in 1613 and was created a city in 1888; the title of Lord Mayor was conferred in 1892.

LONDONDERRY

Londonderry, situated on the River Foyle, was reputedly founded in AD 546 by St Columba. Londonderry (formerly Derry) has important associations with the City of London. The Irish Society, under its royal charter of 1613, fortified the city and was for long closely associated with its administration.

The city is famous for the great siege of 1688–9, when for 105 days the town held out against the forces of James II until relieved by sea. The city walls are still intact and form a circuit of almost a mile around the old city.

Interesting buildings are the Protestant Cathedral of St Columb's (1633) and the Guildhall, reconstructed in 1912 and containing a number of beautiful stained glass windows, many of which were presented by the livery companies of London.

CONSTITUTION AND GOVERNMENT

As part of the United Kingdom, Northern Ireland is subject to the same fundamental constitutional provisions which apply to the rest of the United Kingdom. However, the Northern Ireland Constitution Act 1973 and the Northern Ireland Act 1982 provide for a measure of devolved government in Northern Ireland. This arrangement was last in force in January 1974, following agreement between the Northern Ireland political parties to form a power-sharing executive. However, this arrangement collapsed in May 1974 and there has been no devolution since.

In the interim, Northern Ireland continues to be governed by direct rule under the provisions of the Northern Ireland

Act 1974. This allows Parliament to approve all laws for Northern Ireland and places the Northern Ireland departments under the direction and control of the Secretary of State for Northern Ireland.

Attempts have been made by successive governments to find a means of restoring a widely acceptable form of devolved government to Northern Ireland. A 78-member Assembly was elected by proportional representation in 1982. However, four years later it was dissolved after it ceased to discharge its responsibilities of making proposals for the resumption of devolved government and of monitoring the work of the Northern Ireland Departments.

In January 1990 further dialogue between the Government and the constitutional political parties in Northern Ireland was established as a means of exploring the extent of the common ground which existed between them at that time. A formula, known as the three-stranded approach, for political talks about the future of Northern Ireland and its relationship with the United Kingdom and the Republic of Ireland was agreed in 1991. Strand 1 of the new talks between the Government and the four main local constitutional political parties began in April 1992. Strand 2, involving the government of the Republic of Ireland, began in July 1992. Though a settlement had not been reached when the talks ended in November 1992, progress had been made and the Government hopes that discussions will restart soon. (*See also* Events of the Year.)

FLAG

The official national flag is the Union Flag. The flag formerly in use (a white, six-pointed star in the centre of a red cross on a white field, enclosing a red hand and surmounted by a crown) has not been used since the imposition of direct rule.

FINANCE

Taxation in Northern Ireland is largely imposed and collected by the United Kingdom government. After deducting the cost of collection and of Northern Ireland's contributions to the European Community the balance, known as the Attributed Share of Taxation, is paid over to the Northern Ireland Consolidated Fund. Northern Ireland's revenue is insufficient to meet its expenditure and is supplemented by a grant-in-aid.

	1992–3*	1993–4**
Public income	£5,300,604,492	£5,982,100,000
Public expenditure	5,319,603,886	5,982,100,000
* Outturn		
** Estimate		

PRODUCTION

The products of the engineering, shipbuilding and aircraft industries, which employed 33,500 persons in 1990, were valued at £1,695 million. The textile industries, employing about 10,500 persons, produced products valued at approximately £412 million. The food and drink industry, employing about 20,700 persons, produced goods valued at £3,355 million.

In 1991 1,316 persons were employed in mining and quarrying operations in Northern Ireland and the minerals raised (19,073,832 tonnes) were valued at £37,567,234.

COMMUNICATIONS

SEAPORTS

The total tonnage handled by Northern Ireland ports in 1992 was 17.5 million. Regular ferry, freight and container services operate to ports in Great Britain and Europe from 18 ports including Belfast, Coleraine, Larne, Londonderry and Warrenpoint.

ROAD AND RAIL

The Northern Ireland Transport Holding Company is largely responsible for the supervision of the subsidiary companies, Ulsterbus and Citybus (which operate the public road passenger services) and Northern Ireland Railways. Road freight services are also provided by a large number of hauliers operating competitively under licence.

AIR

Belfast International Airport, which is due to be privatized during 1994, is operated by Northern Ireland Airports Ltd, a subsidiary of the Northern Ireland Transport Holding Company. It has substantial passenger and freight handling facilities and provides scheduled and chartered services on domestic and international routes.

Scheduled services also operate from Belfast City Airport to 19 UK destinations and from Eglinton Airport to two UK destinations.

Northern Ireland Counties

County	Area* (sq. miles)	Lord Lieutenant	High Sheriff, 1993
Antrim	1,093	Sir Richard Dobbs, KCVO	P. D. Cooke
‡Belfast City	25	Col. J. E. Wilson, OBE	J. Walker
Armagh	484	The Earl of Caledon	J. N. Greenlee
Down	945	Col. W. S. Brownlow	S. B. Cunningham
Fermanagh	647	The Earl of Erne	W. R. Dickson
†Londonderry	798	Col. M. W. McCorkell, OBE, TD	K. H. Greeves
‡Londonderry City	3.4	J. T. Eaton, CBE, TD	T. E. W. Huey
Tyrone	1,211	The Duke of Abercorn	G. R. A. Darling, QC

* Excluding inland waters and tideways
‡ Denotes County Borough
† Excluding the City of Londonderry

District Councils

§ Denotes Borough Council

Council	Population (30 June 1991)	Net Annual Value	Council Clerk	Chairman †Mayor 1993
§Antrim, Co. Antrim	45,400	£6,611,649	S. J. Magee	†T. E. Wallace
§Ards, Co. Down	65,000	7,663,758	D. J. Fallows	†W. Magill
Armagh, Co. Armagh	51,800	5,185,016	D. R. D. Mitchall	P. Brannigan
§Ballymena, Co. Antrim	56,600	8,293,838	M. G. Rankin	†Revd R. Coulter
§Ballymoney, Co. Antrim	24,200	2,626,353	J. C. Alderdice	†C. J. Cousley
Banbridge, Co. Down	33,500	3,651,303	R. Gilmore	J. F. Dobson
Belfast, Co. Antrim and Co. Down	287,100	55,270,064	I. Macdonald	R. Empey (Lord Mayor)
§Carrickfergus, Co. Antrim	33,100	4,478,264	R. Boyd	†J. L. Neeson
§Castlereagh, Co. Down	61,500	8,175,226	J. White	†T. Jeffers
§Coleraine, Co. Londonderry	51,200	7,566,221	W. E. Andrews	†D. McClarty
Cookstown, Co. Tyrone	30,900	3,108,381	M. McGuckin	S. A. Glasgow
§Craigavon, Co. Armagh	75,400	10,565,555	E. A. McKinley	†Mrs A. A. J. Savage
Derry, Co. Londonderry	97,100	12,046,002	J. Keanie	†Mrs A. Courtney
Down, Co. Down	58,800	6,019,037	O. O'Connor	Miss M. M. Ritchie
Dungannon, Co. Tyrone	45,300	4,562,524	W. J. Beattie	P. Daly
Fermanagh, Co. Fermanagh	54,400	5,619,283	G. Burns, MBE	B. Kerr
§Larne, Co. Antrim	29,500	3,969,281	G. McKinley	†Mrs R. G. Armstrong
§Limavady, Co. Londonderry	29,700	2,896,569	J. K. Stevenson	†A. Doherty

Council	Population (30 June 1991)	Net Annual Value	Council Clerk	Chairman †Mayor 1993
§Lisburn, Co. Antrim and Co. Down	101,100	13,251,541	M. S. Fielding	†S. A. Close
Magherafelt, Co. Londonderry	36,100	3,585,929	J. A. McLaughlin	P. A. Kilpatrick
Moyle, Co. Antrim	14,700	1,514,384	R. G. Lewis	M. McSparran
Newry and Mourne, Co. Down and Co. Armagh	83,100	8,273,433	K. O'Neill	J. Savage
§Newtownabbey, Co. Antrim	74,500	11,234,637	J. Campbell	†J. A. Kell
§North Down, Co. Down	72,900	9,472,934	A. McDowell	†B. A. S. Wilson
Omagh, Co. Tyrone	46,000	4,494,364	J. P. McKinney	P. J. McGowan, MBE
Strabane, Co. Tyrone	35,500	3,135,065	Dr V. R. Eakin	E. Turner

Patron Saints

ST GEORGE
Patron Saint of England

St George is believed to have been born in Cappadocia, of Christian parents, in the latter part of the third century and to have served with distinction as a soldier under the Emperor Diocletian, including a visit to England on a military mission. When the persecution of Christians was ordered, St George sought a personal interview to remonstrate with the Emperor and after a profession of faith resigned his military commission. Arrest and torture followed and he was martyred at Nicomedia on 23 April 303, a day ordered to be kept in remembrance as a national festival by the Council of Oxford in 1222, although it was not until the reign of Edward III that he was made patron saint of England.

St George's connection with a dragon seems to date from the close of the sixth century and to be due to the transfer of his remains from Nicomedia to Lydda, close to the scene of the legendary exploit of Perseus in rescuing Andromeda and slaying the sea monster, credit for which became attached to the Christian martyr.

ST DAVID
Patron Saint of Wales

St David is believed to have been born towards the beginning and to have died towards the end of the sixth century. St David was an eloquent preacher, who founded the monastery at Menevia, now St David's. He became the patron of Wales,

but there is no record of any papal canonization before 1181. His annual festival is observed on 1 March.

ST ANDREW
Patron Saint of Scotland

St Andrew, one of the Christian Apostles and brother of Simon Peter, was born at Bethsaida on the Sea of Galilee and lived at Capernaum. He preached the Gospel in Asia Minor and in Scythia along the shores of the Black Sea and became the patron saint of Russia. It is believed that he suffered crucifixion at Patras in Achaea, on a *crux decussata* (now known as St Andrew's Cross) and that his relics were removed from Patras to Constantinople and thence to St Andrews, probably in the eighth century, since which time he has been the patron saint of Scotland. The festival of St Andrew is held on 30 November.

ST PATRICK
Patron Saint of Ireland

St Patrick was born, probably in England, about 389 and was carried off to Ireland as a slave about 16 years later, escaping to Gaul at the age of 22. He was ordained deacon at Auxerre and having been consecrated Bishop in 432 was despatched to Wicklow to reorganize the Christian communities in Ireland. He founded the see of Armagh and introduced Latin into Ireland as the language of the Church. He died *c.*461 and his festival is celebrated on 17 March.

The Isle of Man

Ellan Vannin

The Isle of Man is an island situated in the Irish Sea, in latitude 54° 3'–54° 25' N. and longitude 4° 18'–4° 47' W., nearly equidistant from England, Scotland and Ireland. Although the early inhabitants were of Celtic origin, the Isle of Man was part of the Norwegian Kingdom of the Hebrides until 1266, when this was ceded to Scotland. Subsequently granted to the Stanleys (Earls of Derby) in the 15th century and later to the Dukes of Atholl, it was brought under the administration of the Crown in 1765. The island forms the bishopric of Sodor and Man.

The total land area is 221 sq. miles (572 sq. km). The report on the 1991 Census showed a resident population of 69,788 (males, 33,693; females, 36,095). The main language in use is English. There are no remaining native speakers of Manx Gaelic but 643 people are able to speak the language. CAPITAL – ΨDouglas; population (1991), 22,214. ΨCastletown (3,152) is the ancient capital; the other towns are ΨPeel (3,829) and ΨRamsey (6,496)

FLAG – Three conjoined armoured legs in white and gold on a red ground

TYNWALD DAY – 5 July.

GOVERNMENT

The Isle of Man is a self-governing Crown dependency, having its own parliamentary, legal and administrative system. The British Government is responsible for international relations and defence. The island has a limited relationship with the European Community (UK Act of Accession, Protocol 3). The Lieutenant-Governor is The Queen's personal representative in the island.

The legislature, Tynwald, is the oldest parliament in the world in continuous existence. It has two branches: the Legislative Council and the House of Keys. The Council consists of the President of Tynwald, the Bishop of Sodor and Man, the Attorney-General (who does not have a vote) and eight members elected by the House of Keys. The House of Keys has 24 members, elected by universal adult suffrage. The branches sit separately to consider legislation and sit together, as Tynwald Court, for most other parliamentary purposes.

The presiding officer in Tynwald Court is the President of Tynwald, elected by the members, who also presides over sittings of the Legislative Council. The presiding officer of the House of Keys is Mr Speaker, who is elected by members of the House.

The principal members of the Manx Government are the Chief Minister and nine departmental ministers, who comprise the Council of Ministers.

Lieutenant-Governor, His Excellency Air Marshal Sir Laurence Jones, KCB, AFC
ADC to the Lieutenant-Governor, M. M. Wood
President of Tynwald, The Hon. Sir Charles Kerruish, OBE
Speaker, House of Keys, The Hon. J. C. Cain
The First Deemster and Clerk of the Rolls, His Honour J. W. Corrin
Clerk of Legislative Council, T. A. Bawden
Clerk of Tynwald, Secretary to the House of Keys and Counsel to the Speaker, Prof. T. St J. N. Bates
Attorney-General, T. W. Cain, QC
Chief Minister, The Hon. M. R. Walker
Chief Secretary, J. F. Kissack
Chief Financial Officer, J. A. Cashen

ECONOMY

Most of the income generated in the island is earned in the services sector with financial and business services being considerably larger than the traditional industry of tourism. Manufacturing industry is also a major generator of income whilst the island's other traditional industries of agriculture and fishing now play a smaller role in the economy.

Under the terms of Protocol 3, the island has free access to EC markets for its products.

A 20-acre freeport has been developed adjacent to the main airport at Ronaldsway.

The island's unemployment rate is approximately 4 per cent and price inflation is around 2 per cent per annum.

FINANCE

The island's Budget for 1993–4 provided for net expenditure of £202,046,000. The principal sources of government revenue are taxes on income and expenditure. Income tax is payable at a rate of 15 per cent on the first £17,000 of taxable income of resident individuals and 20 per cent on the balance, after personal allowances. The rate of income tax is 20 per cent on the whole taxable income of non-residents and companies. By agreement with the British Government, the island keeps most of its rates of indirect taxation (Value Added Tax and duties) the same as those in the United Kingdom, but this agreement may be terminated by either party. A reciprocal agreement on national insurance benefits and pensions exists between the Governments of the Isle of Man and the United Kingdom. Taxes are also charged on property (rates), but these are comparatively low.

The major government expenditure items are health, social security and education, which account for 59 per cent of the government budget. The island makes a voluntary annual contribution to the United Kingdom for defence and other external services.

Although the island has a limited relationship with the European Community, it neither contributes money to nor receives funds from the EC Budget.

The Channel Islands

The Channel Islands, situated off the north-west coast of France (at distances of from ten to thirty miles), are the only portions of the Dukedom of Normandy now belonging to the Crown, to which they have been attached ever since the Conquest. The islands consist of Jersey (28,717 acres/11,630 ha), Guernsey (15,654 acres/6,340 ha), and the dependencies of Guernsey: Alderney (1,962 acres/795 ha), Brechou (74/30), Great Sark (1,035/419), Little Sark (239/97), Herm (320/130), Jethou (44/18) and Lihou (38/15) – a total of 48,083 acres/19,474 ha, or 75 sq. miles/121 sq. km. In 1991 the population of Jersey was 84,082; and of Guernsey, 58,867; Alderney, 2,297 and Sark, 575.

GOVERNMENT

The islands are Crown dependencies with their own legislative assemblies (the States in Jersey, Guernsey and Alderney, and the Court of Chief Pleas in Sark), and systems of local administration and of law, and their own courts. Acts passed by the States require the sanction of The Queen-in-Council. The British Government is responsible for defence and international relations.

In both Bailiwicks the Lieutenant-Governor and Commander-in-Chief, who is appointed by the Crown, is the personal representative of The Queen and the channel of communication between the Crown (via the Privy Council) and the island's government.

The Bailiffs of Jersey and Guernsey, also appointed by the Crown, are President of the States and of the Royal Courts of their respective islands.

The government of each Bailiwick is conducted by committees appointed by the States. Justice is administered by the Royal Courts of Jersey and Guernsey, each consisting of the Bailiff and 12 elected Jurats.

Each Bailiwick constitutes a deanery under the jurisdiction of the Bishop of Winchester (see Index).

ECONOMY

A mild climate and good soil have led to the development of intensive systems of agriculture and horticulture, which form a significant part of the economy of the Channel Islands. Equally important are invisible earnings, principally from the tourist trade and from banking and finance, the low rate of income tax (20p in the £ in Jersey and Guernsey; no tax of any kind in Sark) and the absence of super-tax and death duties making the Channel Islands a popular tax-haven.

Principal exports are agricultural produce and flowers; imports are chiefly machinery, manufactured goods, food, fuel and chemicals. Trade with the UK is regarded as internal trade.

British currency is legal tender in the Channel Islands but each Bailiwick issues its own coins, and some notes (see page 613). They also issue their own postage stamps; UK stamps are not valid.

LANGUAGE

The official languages are English and French, but French is gradually being supplanted by English, which is the language in daily use. In country districts of Jersey and Guernsey and throughout Sark a Norman-French *patois* is also in use, though to a declining extent.

JERSEY

Lieutenant-Governor and Commander-in-Chief of Jersey, His Excellency Air Marshal Sir John Sutton, KCB, *apptd* 1990
  Secretary and ADC, Cdr. D. M. L. Braybrooke, LVO
Bailiff of Jersey, Sir Peter Crill, CBE
Deputy Bailiff, vacant
Attorney-General and Receiver-General, P. M. Bailhache, QC
Solicitor-General, T. C. Sowden, QC
Greffier of the States, G. H. C. Coppock
States Treasurer, G. M. Baird

FINANCE

Year to 31 Dec.	1991	1992
Revenue	£354,010,485	£377,235,237
Revenue expenditure	297,812,924	377,331,511
Capital expenditure	62,701,000	51,106,748
Public debt	0	0

CHIEF TOWN – ΨSt Helier, on the south coast of Jersey
FLAG – A white field charged with a red saltire cross, and the coat of arms of Jersey in the upper centre

GUERNSEY AND DEPENDENCIES

Lieutenant-Governor and Commander-in-Chief of the Bailiwick of Guernsey and its Dependencies, His Excellency Lt.-Gen. Sir Michael Wilkins, KCB, OBE, *apptd* 1990
  Secretary and ADC, Capt. D. P. L. Hodgetts
Bailiff of Guernsey, Sir Graham Dorey
Deputy Bailiff, de V. G. Carey
HM Procureur and Receiver-General, A. C. K. Day, QC
HM Comptroller, G. R. Rowland, QC
States Supervisor, M. J. Brown

FINANCE

Year to 31 Dec.	1991	1992
Revenue	£149,453,687	£157,145,000
Expenditure	132,621,840	140,661,000

CHIEF TOWNS – Ψ St Peter Port, on the east coast of Guernsey; St Anne on Alderney
FLAG – White, bearing a red cross of St George, with a gold cross overall in the centre

ALDERNEY

President of the States, J. Kay-Mouat
Clerk of the States, D. V. Jenkins
Clerk of the Court, A. Johnson

SARK

Seigneur of Sark, J. M. Beaumont
The Seneschal, L. P. de Carteret
The Greffier, J. P. Hamon

OTHER DEPENDENCIES

Brechou, Lihou and Jethou are leased by the Crown. Herm is leased by the States of Guernsey.

Conservation and Heritage

Countryside Conservation

NATIONAL PARKS

ENGLAND AND WALES

The ten National Parks of England and Wales were established in the 1950s under the provisions of the National Parks and Access to the Countryside Act 1949. The National Parks were set up to conserve and protect scenic landscapes from inappropriate development and to provide access to the land for public enjoyment.

The Countryside Commission is the statutory body which has the power to designate National Parks in England and the Countryside Council for Wales is responsible for National Parks in Wales. The designation of National Parks in England is considered and confirmed by the Secretary of State for the Environment, and the designation of National Parks in Wales by the Secretary of State for Wales. The designation of a National Park does not affect the ownership of the land, nor does it remove the rights of the local community. Although the parks are administered through local government, the majority of the land is owned by private landowners (74 per cent) or by other bodies like the National Trust (7 per cent) and the Forestry Commission (7 per cent). The National Park Authorities own only 2.3 per cent of the land in the National Parks.

Under the Local Government Act 1972, National Park Authorities (NPAs) are the authorities responsible for park administration. They also influence land use and development, and deal with planning applications.

Two-thirds of the members of each authority are appointed by the county and district councils within whose boundaries the parks lie. One-third of the members are appointed by the Secretary of State for the Environment or the Secretary of State for Wales with advice from the Countryside Commission or the Countryside Council for Wales.

In the Peak District and the Lake District the NPAs are special boards: the Peak Park Joint Planning Board and the Lake District Special Planning Board. These are autonomous authorities which are financially independent, unlike the authorities in the other eight parks which are county council committees. The NPAs appoint the National Park Officer for the National Park they administer.

Central government provides 75 per cent of the funding for the parks through the National Park Supplementary Grant. The remaining 25 per cent is supplied by the local authorities concerned. Forecast net expenditure for all National Parks in England and Wales in 1993-4 was £28,241,660.

The Countryside Commission has stated that other areas are regarded as being worthy of National Parks status. Two areas considered as having equivalent status are the Broads and the New Forest (see page 578).

The National Parks in England and Wales (with date designation confirmed) are:

BRECON BEACONS (1957), 1,351 sq. km/522 sq. miles – The park lies in Powys (66 per cent), Dyfed, Gwent and Mid Glamorgan. The park is centred on the Beacons, Pen y Fan, Corn Du and Cribyn, but also includes the valley of the Usk and the Cribyn, but also includes the valley of the Usk and the Black Mountains to the east and the Black Mountain to the west. There are information

centres at Brecon, Craig-y-nos Country Park, Abergavenny and Llandovery, a study centre at Danywenallt and a day visitor centre near Libanus. *Information Office*, 7 Glamorgan Street, Brecon, Powys LD3 7DP. Tel: 0874-624437. *National Park Officer*, M. Fitton

DARTMOOR (1951), 954 sq. km/368 sq. miles – Dartmoor lies wholly in Devon. Dartmoor consists of moorland and rocky granite tors, and is rich in prehistoric remains. There are information centres at Newbridge, Tavistock, Bovey Tracey, Steps Bridge, Princetown and Postbridge. *Information Office*, Parke, Haytor Road, Bovey Tracey, Devon TQ13 9JQ. Tel: 0626-832093. *National Park Officer*, N. Atkinson

EXMOOR (1954), 693 sq. km/268 sq. miles – Exmoor lies in Somerset (71 per cent) and Devon. Exmoor is a moorland plateau inhabited by wild ponies and red deer. There are many ancient remains and burial mounds. There are information centres at Lynmouth, County Gate, Dulverton and Combe Martin. *Information Office*, Exmoor House, Dulverton, Somerset TA22 9HL. Tel: 0398-23665. *National Park Officer*, K. Bungay

LAKE DISTRICT (1951), 2,292 sq. km/885 sq. miles – The Lake District lies wholly in Cumbria. The Lake District includes England's highest mountains (Scafell Pike, Helvellyn and Skiddaw) but it is most famous for its glaciated lakes. There are information centres at Keswick, Waterhead, Hawkshead, Seatoller, Bowness, Grasmere, Coniston, Glenridding and Pooley Bridge, an information van at Gosforth and a park centre at Brockhole, Windermere. *Information Office*, Busher Walk, Kendal, Cumbria LA9 4RH. Tel: 0539-724555. *National Park Officer*, J. Toothill

NORTHUMBERLAND (1956), 1,049 sq. km/405 sq. miles – The Northumberland National Park lies wholly in Northumberland. The park is an area of hill country stretching from Hadrian's Wall to the Scottish Border. There are information centres at Ingram, Once Brewed, Rothbury, Housesteads, Harbottle and Kielder, and an information caravan at Cawfields. *Information Office*, Eastburn, South Park, Hexham, Northumberland NE46 1BS. Tel: 0434-605555. *National Park Officer*, G. Taylor

NORTH YORK MOORS (1952), 1,436 sq. km/554 sq. miles – The North York Moors lie in North Yorkshire (96 per cent) and Cleveland. The park consists of woodland and moorland, and includes the Hambleton Hills and the Cleveland Way. There are information centres at Danby, Pickering, Sutton Bank, Ravenscar, Helmsley and Hutton-le-Hole, and a day study centre at Danby. *Information Office*, The Old Vicarage, Bondgate, Helmsley, York YO6 5BP. Tel: 0439-70657. *National Park Officer*, D. Statham

PEAK DISTRICT (1951), 1,438 sq. km/555 sq. miles – The Peak District lies in Derbyshire (64 per cent), Staffordshire, South Yorkshire, Cheshire, West Yorkshire and Greater Manchester. The Peak District is composed of the gritstone moors of the 'dark peak' and the limestone dales of the 'white peak'. There are information centres at Bakewell, Edale, Fairholmes and Castleton, and information points at Torside (in the Longdendale Valley) and at Hartington (former station). *Information Office*, Aldern House, Baslow Road, Bakewell, Derbyshire DE45 1AE. Tel: 0629-814321. *National Park Officer*, C. Harrison

PEMBROKESHIRE COAST (1952), 584 sq. km/225 sq. miles – The Pembrokeshire Coast National Park lies wholly in Dyfed. The park consists of cliffs, open moorland and Skomer Island. There are information centres at Tenby, St David's, Pembroke, Newport, Kilgetty, Haverfordwest and Broad Haven. *Information Office*, County Offices, Haverfordwest, Dyfed SA61 1QZ. Tel: 0437-764591. *National Park Officer*, N. Wheeler

SNOWDONIA (1951), 2,142 sq. km/817 sq. miles – Snowdonia lies wholly in Gwynedd. It is an area of deep valleys and rugged mountains in northern Wales. There are information centres at Aberdovey, Bala, Betws y Coed, Blaenau Ffestiniog, Conwy, Harlech, Dolgellau and Llanberis. *Information Office*, Penrhyndeudraeth, Gwynedd LL48 6LS. Tel: 0766-770274. *National Park Officer*, A. Jones

YORKSHIRE DALES (1954), 1,769 sq. km/683 sq. miles – The Yorkshire Dales National Park lies in North Yorkshire (88 per cent) and Cumbria. The Yorkshire Dales are composed primarily of limestone overlaid in places by millstone grit. The three peaks of Ingleborough, Whernside and Pen-y-Ghent are within the park. There are information centres at Clapham, Grassington, Hawes, Aysgarth Falls, Malham and Sedbergh. *Information Office*, Yorebridge House, Bainbridge, Leyburn, North Yorkshire DL8 3BP. Tel: 0969-50456. *National Park Officer*, R. Harvey

Two other areas considered to have equivalent status to national parks are the Broads and the New Forest. The Broads Authority, a special statutory authority, was established in 1989 to develop, conserve and manage the Norfolk and Suffolk Broads (*see also* Government Departments and Public Offices). The Government declared in 1992 its intention of giving the New Forest a status equivalent to that of a National Park by declaring it an 'area of national significance'.

THE BROADS (1989), 303 sq. km/117 sq. miles – The Broads are located between Norwich and Great Yarmouth on the flood plains of the five rivers flowing through the area to the sea. The area is one of fens, winding waterways, woodland and marsh. The forty or so broads are man-made, the flooded remains of medieval peat pits, and are connected to the rivers by dykes, providing over 200 km of navigable waterways. There are information centres at Beccles, Hoveton, North-west Tower (Yarmouth), Ranworth and Toad Hole. *Broads Authority*, Thomas Harvey House, 18 Colegate, Norwich NR3 1BQ. Tel: 0603-610734. *Chief Executive*, A. Clark

THE NEW FOREST, 376 sq. km/145 sq. miles – The area has been protected since 1079 when it was declared a royal hunting forest. The landscape consists of forest, ancient woodland and heathland which is grazed by New Forest ponies and cattle. Much of the Forest is managed by the Forestry Commission, which provides several camp-sites. The main villages are Brockenhurst, Burley and Lyndhurst, which has a visitor centre.

The Forestry Commission, Office of the Deputy Surveyor of the New Forest, The Queen's House, Lyndhurst, Hants. SO43 7NH. Tel: 0703-284149

SCOTLAND AND NORTHERN IRELAND

The National Parks and Access to the Countryside Act 1949 dealt only with England and Wales, and made no provision for Scotland or Northern Ireland. Although there are no national parks in these two countries, there is power to designate them in Northern Ireland under the Amenity Lands Act 1965 and the Nature Conservation and Amenity Lands Order (Northern Ireland) 1985; and in 1989 the Scottish Office asked Scottish Natural Heritage to report on whether national parks should be designated in Scotland.

AREAS OF OUTSTANDING NATURAL BEAUTY

ENGLAND AND WALES

Under the National Parks and Access to the Countryside Act 1949, provision was made for the designation of Areas of Outstanding Natural Beauty (AONBs) by the Countryside Commission. The Countryside Act 1968 further defines the role of AONBs, suggesting that they should show due regard for the interests of other land users, such as agriculture and forestry groups. The Countryside Commission continues to be responsible for AONBs in England but since April 1991 the Countryside Council for Wales has been responsible for the Welsh AONBs. Designations in England are confirmed by the Secretary of State for the Environment and those in Wales by the Secretary of State for Wales.

Although less emphasis is placed upon the provision of open-air enjoyment for the public than in the national parks, AONBs are seen as areas which are no less beautiful and require the same degree of protection to conserve and enhance the natural beauty of the countryside. This includes protecting flora and fauna, geological and other landscape features.

In AONBs planning and management responsibilities are split between county and district councils (there are 17 which cross county boundaries). Finance for the AONBs is provided by grant-aid.

Thirty-nine Areas of Outstanding Natural Beauty have been designated since 1956. They are (with date designation confirmed):

ANGLESEY (1967), 221 sq. km/85 sq. miles – The designated area extends along the entire coastline of the island, except for breaks around the urban areas and in the vicinity of Wylfa

ARNSIDE AND SILVERDALE (1972), 75 sq. km/29 sq. miles – The area embraces the upper half of Morecambe Bay, the Kent estuary, and includes extensive tidal flats in the Bay

BLACKDOWN HILLS (1991), 370 sq. km/143 sq. miles – An area of greensand ridges in Devon and Somerset extending from Cullompton in the west to Chard in the east, south of Taunton to north of Honiton

CANNOCK CHASE (1958), 68 sq. km/26 sq. miles – An area of high heathland in Staffordshire. Deer continue to roam over the Chase

CHICHESTER HARBOUR (1964), 74 sq. km/29 sq. miles – The area extends from Hayling Island to Apuldram and includes Thorney Island

CHILTERNS (1965; extended 1990), 833 sq. km/322 sq. miles – Chalk downlands running from South

Oxfordshire north-eastwards to Bedfordshire, including the outlying group of hills beyond Luton

CLWYDIAN RANGE (1985), 157 sq. km/61 sq. miles – A prominent ridge extending southwards from Prestatyn on the north Wales coast. Offa's Dyke runs along the crest of the range

CORNWALL (1959; Camel estuary 1983), 958 sq. km/370 sq. miles – A number of separate areas including Bodmin Moor, most of the Land's End peninsula, the coast between St Michael's Mount and St Austell (with Falmouth omitted), the Fowey estuary; in north Cornwall most of the coast to Bedruthan Steps and between Perranporth and Godrevy Towans, plus the Camel estuary

COTSWOLDS (1966; extended 1990), 2,038 sq. km/787 sq. miles – The area of limestone hills above the Vales of Gloucester and Evesham

CRANBORNE CHASE AND WEST WILTSHIRE DOWNS (1983), 983 sq. km/379 sq. miles – A mainly chalkland and greensand area covering parts of Wiltshire, Dorset, Hampshire and Somerset, including the wooded remnants of the ancient Chase

DEDHAM VALE (1970; extended 1978, 1991), 90 sq. km/35 sq. miles – The area on the Essex/Suffolk border where John Constable painted

EAST DEVON (1963), 268 sq. km/103 sq. miles – The coastline between Exmouth and Lyme Regis, with Sidmouth, Beer and Seaton omitted. Inland, Gittisham Hill, East Hill and Woodbury and Aylebeare Commons are included

NORTH DEVON (1960), 171 sq. km/66 sq. miles – Includes most of the North Devon coastline, from just north of Bude to the boundary of the Exmoor National Park

SOUTH DEVON (1960), 337 sq. km/130 sq. miles – Includes the coast between Bolt Head and Bolt Tail, Salcombe, Slapton Sands and Dartmouth, and the estuaries and valleys of the Yealm, Erme, Avon and Dart

DORSET (1959), (1,129 sq. km/436 sq. miles – The coastline between Lyme Regis and Poole, with the Isle of Portland and Weymouth omitted, stretching inland to include the Purbeck Hills and the downs of Hardy country

FOREST OF BOWLAND (1964), 802 sq. km/310 sq. miles – A moorland area mostly in Lancashire running westward from the River Ribble, with a small outlying area east of the Ribble which includes Pendle Hill

GOWER (1956), 188 sq. km/73 sq. miles – A peninsula in West Glamorgan, South Wales, known for its coastline

EAST HAMPSHIRE (1962), 383 sq. km/148 sq. miles – A chalkland area stretching from the outskirts of Winchester to the Sussex border at a distance of about 10 miles inland

SOUTH HAMPSHIRE COAST (1967), 77 sq. km/30 sq. miles – 14 miles of coastline between Hurst Castle and Calshot Castle, extending inland up the River Beaulieu for about six miles

HIGH WEALD (1983), 1,460 sq. km/564 sq. miles – The area covers parts of East and West Sussex, Kent and Surrey. It is predominantly wooded, and includes larger heathland areas like Ashdown Forest, the remnants of the old Wealden forests

HOWARDIAN HILLS (1987), 204 sq. km/79 sq. miles – Wooded hills which rise above the Vales of York and Pickering

KENT DOWNS (1968), 878 sq. km/339 sq. miles – Running east and south-east from the Surrey border near Westerham to the coast near Dover and Folkestone, with a coastal outlier at South Foreland and a narrow strip of the old sea cliff escarpment west of Hythe overlooking Romney Marsh

LINCOLNSHIRE WOLDS (1973), 558 sq. km/215 sq. miles – The area extends in a south-east direction from Laceby and Caistor in the north to the region of Spilsby, about ten miles west of the coast

LLEYN (1957), 161 sq. km/62 sq. miles – The peninsula forming the westernmost part of the county of Gwynedd

MALVERN HILLS (1959), 105 sq. km/40 sq. miles – The whole range of the Malvern Hills in the county of Hereford and Worcester, just touching Gloucestershire

MENDIP HILLS (1972; extended 1989), 198 sq. km/76 sq. miles – Comprising over half of the Mendip Hills, the area stretches from Bleadon Hill to the A39 road north of Wells and includes Cheddar Gorge and Wookey Hole

NORFOLK COAST (1968), 451 sq. km/174 sq. miles – An almost continuous coastal strip three to five miles in depth from Hunstanton to Bacton, with a further small strip between Sea Palling and Winterton-on-Sea. The area includes part of the Sandringham estate

NORTH PENNINES (1988), 1,998 sq. km/766 sq. miles – The northern limit of the Pennine chain, covering parts of Cumbria, Co. Durham and Northumberland

NORTHUMBERLAND COAST (1958), 135 sq. km/52 sq. miles – Stretches from just south of Berwick to Amble and includes Holy Island and the Farne Islands

QUANTOCK HILLS (1957), 99 sq. km/38 sq. miles – A range of sandstone hills in Somerset

ISLES OF SCILLY (1976), 16 sq. km/6 sq. miles – About 140 islands and skerries in the Scillies group of which only five are inhabited. There are a number of Sites of Special Scientific Interest

SHROPSHIRE HILLS (1959), 804 sq. km/310 sq. miles – Most of south-west Shropshire between the Welsh border and the boundary with Hereford and Worcester, including the region around Clun, the area of the Stiperstones, the Long Mynd and Wenlock Edge, with the tongues of land running north-east to the Wrekin and south towards Ludlow

SOLWAY COAST (1964), 115 sq. km/44 sq. miles – A stretch of coastline in Cumbria from Maryport to the estuaries of the Rivers Eden and Esk (with Silloth omitted) backed by the Solway Plain

SUFFOLK COAST AND HEATHS (1970), 403 sq. km/156 sq. miles – The area includes 38 miles of coastline and parts of the Stour and Orwell estuaries, while the Rivers Deben, Alde and Blyth flow through it

SURREY HILLS (1958), 419 sq. km/162 sq. miles – An area of hills to the east and south of Guildford, including the Hog's Back and the ridge of the North Downs

SUSSEX DOWNS (1966), 983 sq. km/379 sq. miles – The area includes the chalk escarpment of the South Downs from Beachy Head to the Hampshire border, and stretches down to the coast between Eastbourne and Seaford

NORTH WESSEX DOWNS (1972), 1,730 sq. km/668 sq. miles – An upland area in Hampshire, Wiltshire, Oxfordshire and Berkshire, bounded by the Marlborough and Lambourn Downs in the west, the Chiltern Hills in the east and Salisbury Plain in the south

ISLE OF WIGHT (1963), 189 sq. km/73 sq. miles – A number of separate areas comprising stretches of coastline, the Yar Valley, the high downland behind Ventnor and the chalk ridge which runs from Newport to Culver Cliff and Foreland

WYE VALLEY (1971), 326 sq. km/126 sq. miles – The deep, wooded, river valley running through the counties of Gwent, Gloucestershire, and Hereford and Worcester

Proposals for further designations include: the Tamar valley, Devon/Cornwall and Nidderdale, North Yorkshire.

NORTHERN IRELAND

The Department of the Environment for Northern Ireland, with advice from the Council for Nature Conservation and the Countryside, designates Areas of Outstanding Natural Beauty in Northern Ireland. At present there are nine and these cover a total area of approximately 284,948 hectares (704,121 acres).

ANTRIM COAST AND GLENS, Co. Antrim, 70,600 ha/ 174,452 acres
CAUSEWAY COAST, Co. Antrim, 4,200 ha/10,378 acres
LAGAN VALLEY, Co. Down, 2,072 ha/5,119 acres
LECALE COAST, Co. Down, 3,108 ha/7,679 acres
MOURNE, Co. Down, 57,012 ha/140,876 acres
NORTH DERRY, Co. Londonderry, 12,950 ha/31,999 acres
RING OF GULLION, Co. Armagh, 15,353 ha/37,938 acres
SPERRIN, Co. Tyrone/Co. Londonderry, 101,006 ha/ 249,585 acres
STRANGFORD LOUGH, Co. Down, 18,647 ha/46,077 acres

NATIONAL SCENIC AREAS

No Areas of Outstanding Natural Beauty are designated in Scotland. However, National Scenic Areas have a broadly equivalent status.

Scottish Natural Heritage recognizes areas of national scenic significance. At present there are 40, covering a total area of 1,001,800 hectares (2,475,448 acres).

Development within National Scenic Areas is dealt with by the local planning authority, who are required to consult Scottish Natural Heritage for certain categories of development within these areas. Land management uses can also be modified in the interest of scenic conservation. The Secretary of State for Scotland has limited powers of intervention should a planning authority and Scottish Natural Heritage disagree.

	hectares	acres
BORDER		
Eildon and Leaderfoot	3,600	8,896
Upper Tweeddale	10,500	25,945
CENTRAL		
*Loch Lomond	11,200	27,675
*Loch Rannoch and Glen Lyon	1,300	3,212
The Trossachs	4,600	11,367
DUMFRIES AND GALLOWAY		
East Stewartry Coast	4,500	11,119
Fleet Valley	5,300	13,096
Nith Estuary	9,300	22,980
GRAMPIAN		
*The Cairngorm Mountains	29,800	73,636
*Deeside and Lochnagar	32,200	79,566
HIGHLAND		
Assynt-Coigach	90,200	222,884
*Ben Nevis and Glen Coe	79,600	196,692
*The Cairngorm Mountains	37,400	92,415
The Cuillin Hills	21,900	54,115
Dornoch Firth	7,500	18,532
Glen Affric	19,300	47,690
Glen Strathfarrar	3,800	9,390
Kintail	15,500	38,300
Knoydart	39,500	97,604
Kyle of Tongue	18,500	45,713
Loch Shiel	13,400	33,111
Morar, Moidart and Ardna-murchan	13,500	33,358
North-west Sutherland	20,500	50,655
The Small Isles	15,500	38,300
Trotternish	5,000	12,355
Wester Ross	145,300	359,036
ORKNEY ISLANDS		
Hoy and West Mainland	14,800	36,571
SHETLAND ISLANDS		
Shetland	11,600	28,664
STRATHCLYDE		
*Ben Nevis and Glen Coe	17,500	43,242
Jura	21,800	53,868
Knapdale	19,800	48,926
Kyles of Bute	4,400	10,872
*Loch Lomond	16,200	40,030
Loch na Keal, Isle of Mull	12,700	31,382
Lynn of Lorn	4,800	11,861
North Arran	23,800	58,810
Scarba, Lunga and the Garvel-lachs	1,900	4,692
TAYSIDE		
*Ben Nevis and Glen Coe	4,500	11,119
*Deeside and Lochnagar	7,800	19,274
*Loch Rannoch and Glen Lyon	47,100	116,384
Loch Tummel	9,200	22,733
River Earn	3,000	7,413
River Tay	5,600	13,838
WESTERN ISLES		
St Kilda	900	2,224
South Lewis, Harris and North Uist	109,600	270,821
South Uist Machair	6,100	15,073
TOTAL	1,001,800	2,475,448

*National Scenic Areas in more than one region

Nature Conservation Areas

SITES OF SPECIAL SCIENTIFIC INTEREST

Site of Special Scientific Interest (SSSI) is a legal designation applied to land in England, Scotland or Wales which English Nature (EN), Scottish Natural Heritage (SNH), or the Countryside Council for Wales (CCW) identifies as being of special interest because of its flora, fauna, geological or physiographical features. In some cases, SSSI are managed as nature reserves.

EN, SNH and CCW must notify the designation of a SSSI to the local planning authority, every owner/occupier of the land, and the Secretary of State for the Environment (or Secretary of State for Scotland or for Wales where applicable). Forestry and agricultural departments and a number of other bodies are also informed of this designation.

Objections to the designation of a SSSI can be made and ultimately considered at a full meeting of the Council of EN or the Site Safeguard Committee of CCW. In Scotland an objection will be dealt with by the appropriate regional board or the main board of SNH, depending on the nature of the objection. Unresolved objections on scientific grounds must be referred to the Advisory Committee for SSSI.

The protection of these sites depends on the co-operation of individual landowners and occupiers. Owner/occupiers must consult EN, SNH or CCW and gain written consent before they can undertake certain listed activities on the site. Funds are available through management agreements and grants to assist owners and occupiers in conserving sites' interests. As a last resort a site can be purchased.

As at 31 March 1993 there were 5,927 SSSI in Britain, covering 1,861,558 hectares (4,599,909 acres).

	no.	hectares	acres
England	3,707	839,309	2,073,932
Scotland	1,350	816,596	2,017,808
Wales	870	205,653	508,168

NORTHERN IRELAND

In Northern Ireland 41 Areas of Special Scientific Interest (ASSIs) have been established by the Department of the Environment for Northern Ireland. These cover a total area of 47,832 hectares (118,145 acres).

NATIONAL NATURE RESERVES

National Nature Reserves are defined in the National Parks and Access to the Countryside Act 1949 as land designated for the study and preservation of flora and fauna, or of geological or physiographic features.

English Nature (EN), Scottish Natural Heritage (SNH) or the Countryside Council for Wales (CCW) can designate as a National Nature Reserve land which is being managed as a nature reserve under an agreement with one of the statutory nature conservation agencies; land held and managed by EN, SNH or CCW; or land held and managed as a nature reserve by another approved body. EN, SNH or CCW can turn to the appropriate Secretary of State to impose by-laws for the protection of the reserves from undesirable development.

As at 31 March 1993 there were 258 National Nature Reserves in Britain, covering 182,795 hectares (451,686 acres).

	no.	hectares	acres
England	140	57,151	141,220
Scotland	69	112,247	277,362
Wales	49	13,397	33,103

NORTHERN IRELAND

National Nature Reserves are established and managed by the Department of the Environment for Northern Ireland, with advice from the Council for Nature Conservation and the Countryside. There are 45 National Nature Reserves covering 4,574 hectares (11,297 acres).

LOCAL NATURE RESERVES

Local Nature Reserves are defined in the National Parks and Access to the Countryside Act 1949 as land designated for the study and preservation of flora and fauna, or of geological or physiographical features. The Act gives local authorities in England and Wales and district councils in Scotland the power to acquire, declare and manage local nature reserves in consultation with English Nature, Scottish Natural

Heritage and the Countryside Council for Wales. Conservation trusts can also own and manage non-statutory local nature reserves.

As at 31 March 1993 there were 364 designated Local Nature Reserve areas in Britain, covering 20,266 hectares (50,077 acres).

	no.	hectares	acres
England	337	13,977	34,537
Scotland	8	2,866	7,081
Wales	19	3,423	8,458

An additional 17.19 km of linear trails are designated as Local Nature Reserves.

FOREST NATURE RESERVES

Forest Enterprise (part of the Forestry Commission) has created Forest Nature Reserves from conservation sites within its estate. These are like other nature reserves in that their purpose is to protect and conserve special forms of natural habitat, flora and fauna existing in forested areas.

Forest Enterprise has 397 SSSI on its estates and has chosen 46 as Forest Nature Reserves. They extend in size from under 50 hectares (124 acres) to 500 hectares (1,236 acres). The largest include the Black Wood of Rannoch, by Loch Rannoch; Cannop Valley Oakwoods, Forest of Dean; Culbin Forest, near Forres; Glen Affric, near Fort Augustus; Kylerhea, Skye; Pembrey, Carmarthen Bay; Starr Forest, in Galloway Forest Park; and Wyre Forest, near Kidderminster.

NORTHERN IRELAND

There are 36 Forest Nature Reserves in Northern Ireland, covering 1,759 hectares (4,346 acres). They are designated and administered by the Forest Service, a division of the Department of Agriculture for Northern Ireland. There are also 15 National Nature Reserves on Forest Service-owned property.

MARINE NATURE RESERVES

The Wildlife and Countryside Act 1981 gives the Secretary of State for the Environment (and the Secretaries of State for Wales and for Scotland where appropriate) power to designate Marine Nature Reserves, and English Nature, Scottish Natural Heritage and the Countryside Council for Wales powers to select and manage these reserves. Interested parties at a national and at a local level are consulted prior to the confirmation of an area.

Marine Nature Reserves provide protection for marine flora and fauna, and geological and physiographical features on land covered by tidal waters or parts of the sea in or adjacent to Great Britain. Reserves also provide opportunities for study and research.

Statutory Marine Nature Reserves are:

LUNDY (1986), Bristol Channel
SKOMER (1990), Dyfed

Other areas proposed for designation as reserves are: the Isles of Scilly, the Menai Strait, Bardsey Island, and part of the Lleyn peninsula, Gwynedd.

A number of non-statutory marine reserves have been set up by conservation groups.

Wildlife Conservation

PROTECTED SPECIES

The Wildlife and Countryside Act 1981 gives legal protection to a wide range of animals and wild plants. Subject to parliamentary approval, the Secretary of State for the Environment may vary the animals and plants given legal protection. The most recent variation of Schedules 5 and 8 came into effect in October 1992.

ANIMALS, ETC.

Under Schedule 5 of the Act it is illegal without a licence to kill, injure, take, possess or sell any of the animals mentioned below (whether alive or dead) and to disturb its place of shelter and protection or to destroy that place.

†Adder (*Vipera berus*)
§Allis shad (*alosa alosa*)
Anemone, Ivell's Sea (*Edwardsia ivelli*)
Anemone, Startlet Sea (*Nematosella vectensis*)
Apus (*Triops cancriformis*)
Bat, Horseshoe (*Rhinolophidae*, all species)
Bat, Typical (*Vespertilionidae*, all species)
Beetle (*Graphoderus zonatus*)
Beetle (*Hypebaeus flavipes*)
Beetle (*Paracymus aeneus*)
Beetle, Lesser Silver Water (*Hydrochara caraboides*)
§§Beetle, Mire Pill (*Curimopsis nigrita*)
Beetle, Rainbow Leaf (*Chrysolina cerealis*)
Beetle, Violet Click (*Limoniscus violaceus*)
Burbot (*Lota lota*)
*Butterfly, Adonis Blue (*Lysandra bellargus*)
*Butterfly, Black Hairstreak (*Strymonidia pruni*)
*Butterfly, Brown Hairstreak (*Thecla betulae*)
*Butterfly, Chalkhill Blue (*Lysandra coridon*)
*Butterfly, Chequered Skipper (*Carterocephalus palaemon*)
*Butterfly, Duke of Burgundy Fritillary (*Hamearis lucina*)
*Butterfly, Glanville Fritillary (*Melitaea cinxia*)
Butterfly, Heath Fritillary (*Mellicta athalia* (or *Melitaea athalia*))
Butterfly, High Brown Fritillary (*Argynnis adippe*)
Butterfly, Large Blue (*Maculinea arion*)
*Butterfly, Large Copper (*Lycaena dispar*)
*Butterfly, Large Heath (*Coenonympha tullia*)
*Butterfly, Large Tortoiseshell (*Nymphalis polychloros*)
*Butterfly, Lulworth Skipper (*Thymelicus acteon*)
*Butterfly, Marsh Fritillary (*Eurodryas aurinia*)
*Butterfly, Mountain Ringlet (*Erebia epiphron*)
*Butterfly, Northern Brown Argus (*Aricia artaxerxes*)
*Butterfly, Pearl-bordered Fritillary (*Boloria euphrosyne*)
*Butterfly, Purple Emperor (*Apatura iris*)
*Butterfly, Silver Spotted Skipper (*Hesperia comma*)
*Butterfly, Silver-studded Blue (*Plebejus argus*)
*Butterfly, Small Blue (*Cupido minimus*)
Butterfly, Swallowtail (*Papilio machaon*)
*Butterfly, White Letter Hairstreak (*Stymonida w-album*)

*the offence relates to 'sale' only
**the offence relates to 'taking' and 'sale' only
†the offence relates to 'killing and injuring' only
‡the offence relates to 'killing, injuring and sale'
§the offence relates to 'killing, injuring and taking'
§§the offence relates only to damaging, destroying or obstructing access to a shelter or protection, or disturbing during occupation of such

*Butterfly, Wood White (*Leptidea sinapis*)
Cat, Wild (*Felis silvestris*)
Cicada, New Forest (*Cicadetta montana*)
**Crayfish, Atlantic Stream (*Austropotamobius pallipes*)
Cricket, Field (*Gryllus campestris*)
Cricket, Mole (*Gryllotalpa gryllotalpa*)
Dolphin (*Cetacea*)
Dormouse (*Muscardinus avellanarius*)
Dragonfly, Norfolk Aeshna (*Aeshna isosceles*)
*Frog, Common (*Rana temporaria*)
Grasshopper, Wart-biter (*Decticus verrucivorus*)
Hatchet Shell, Northern (*Thyasira gouldi*)
Lagoon Snail (*Paludinella littorina*)
Lagoon Snail, De Folin's (*Caecum armoricum*)
Lagoon Worm, Tentacled (*Alkmaria romijni*)
Leech, Medicinal (*Hirudo medicinalis*)
Lizard, Sand (*Lacerta agilis*)
‡Lizard, Viviparous(*Lacerta vivipara*)
Marten, Pine (*Martes martes*)
Moth, Barberry Carpet (*Pareulype berberata*)
Moth, Black-veined (*Siona lineata* (or *Idaea lineata*))
Moth, Essex Emerald (*Thetidia smaragdaria*)
Moth, New Forest Burnet (*Zygaena viciae*)
Moth, Reddish Buff (*Acosmetia caliginosa*)
Moth, Sussex Emerald (*Thalera fimbrialis*)
Moth, Viper's Bugloss (*Hadena irregularis*)
Mussel, Freshwater Pearl (*Margaritifera margaritifera*)
Newt, Great Crested (or Warty) (*Triturus cristatus*)
*Newt, Palmate (*Triturus helveticus*)
*Newt, Smooth (*Triturus vulgaris*)
Otter, Common (*Lutra lutra*)
Porpoise (*Cetacea*)
Sandworm, Lagoon (*Armandia cirrhosa*)
Sea Fan, Pink (*Eunicella verrucosa*)
Sea-Mat, Trembling (*Victorella pavida*)
Sea Slug, Lagoon (*Tenellia adspersa*)
Shrimp, Fairy (*Chirocephalus diaphanus*)
Shrimp, Lagoon Sand (*Gammarus insensibilis*)
‡Slow-worm (*Anguis fragilis*)
Snail, Glutinous (*Myxas glutinosa*)
Snail, Sandbowl (*Catinella arenaria*)
‡Snake, Grass (*Natrix natrix* (*Natrix helvetica*))
Snake, Smooth (*Coronella austriaca*)
Spider, Fen Raft (*Dolomedes plantarius*)
Spider, Ladybird (*Eresus niger*)
Squirrel, Red (*Sciurus vulgaris*)
Sturgeon (*Acipenser sturio*)
*Toad, Common (*Bufo bufo*)
Toad, Natterjack (*Bufo calamita*)
Turtle, Marine (*Dermochelyidae* and *Cheloniidae*, all species)
Vendace (*Coregonus albula*)
Walrus (*Odobenus rosmarus*)
Whale (*Cetacea*)
Whitefish (*Coregonus lavaretus*)

PLANTS

Under Schedule 8 of the Wildlife and Countryside Act 1981 it is illegal without a licence to pick, uproot, sell or destroy any of the plants mentioned below and, unless authorized, to uproot any wild plant.

Adder's tongue, Least (*Ophioglossum lusitanicum*)
Alison, Small (*Alyssum alyssoides*)
Blackwort (*Southbya nigrella*)
Broomrape, Bedstraw (*Orobanche caryophyllacea*)
Broomrape, Oxtongue (*Orobanche loricata*)

Broomrape, Thistle (*Orobanche reticulata*)
Cabbage, Lundy (*Rhynchosinapis wrightii*)
Calamint, Wood (*Calamintha sylvatica*)
Caloplaca, Snow (*Caloplaca nivalis*)
Catapyrenium, Tree (*Catapyrenium psoromoides*)
Catchfly, Alpine (*Lychnis alpina*)
Catillaria, Laurer's (*Catellaria laureri*)
Centaury, Slender (*Centaurium tenuiflorum*)
Cinquefoil, Rock (*Potentilla rupestris*)
Cladonia, Upright Mountain (*Cladonia stricta*)
Clary, Meadow (*Salvia pratensis*)
Club-rush, Triangular (*Scirpus triquetrus*)
Colt's-foot, Purple (*Homogyne alpina*)
Cotoneaster, Wild (*Cotoneaster integerrimus*)
Cottongrass, Slender (*Eriophorum gracile*)
Cow-wheat, Field (*Melampyrum arvense*)
Crocus, Sand (*Romulea columnae*)
Crystalwort, Lizard (*Riccia bifurca*)
Cudweed, Broad-leaved (*Filago pyramidata*)
Cudweed, Jersey (*Gnaphalium luteoalbum*)
Cudweed, Red-tipped (*Filago lutescens*)
Diapensia (*Diapensia lapponica*)
Dock, Shore (*Rumex rupestris*)
Earwort, Marsh (*Jamesoniella undulifolia*)
Eryngo, Field (*Eryngium campestre*)
Fern, Dickie's bladder (*Cystopteris dickieana*)
Fern, Killarney (*Trichomanes speciosum*)
Flapwort, Norfolk (*Leiocolea rutheana*)
Fleabane, Alpine (*Erigeron borealis*)
Fleabane, Small (*Pulicaria vulgaris*)
Frostwort, Pointed (*Gymnomitrion apiculatum*)
Galingale, Brown (*Cyperus fuscus*)
Gentian, Alpine (*Gentiana nivalis*)
Gentian, Dune (*Gentianella uliginosa*)
Gentian, Early (*Gentianella anglica*)
Gentian, Fringed (*Gentianella ciliata*)
Gentian, Spring (*Gentiana verna*)
Germander, Cut-leaved (*Teucrium botrys*)
Germander, Water (*Teucrium scordium*)
Gladiolus, Wild (*Gladiolus illyricus*)
Goosefoot, Stinking (*Chenopodium vulvaria*)
Grass-poly (*Lythrum hyssopifolia*)
Grimmia, Blunt-leaved (*Grimmia unicolor*)
Gyalecta, Elm (*Gyalecta ulmi*)
Hare's-ear, Sickle-leaved (*Bupleurum falcatum*)
Hare's-ear, Small (*Bupleurum baldense*)
Hawk's-beard, Stinking (*Crepis foetida*)
Hawkweed, Northroe (*Hieracium northroense*)
Hawkweed, Shetland (*Hieracium zetlandicum*)
Hawkweed, Weak-leaved (*Hieracium attenuatifolium*)
Heath, Blue (*Phyllodoce caerulea*)
Helleborine, Red (*Cephalanthera rubra*)
Helleborine, Young's (*Epipactis youngiana*)
Horsetail, Branched (*Equisetum ramosissimum*)
Hound's-tongue, Green (*Cynoglossum germanicum*)
Knawel, Perennial (*Scleranthus perennis*)
Knotgrass, Sea (*Polygonum maritimum*)
Lady's-slipper (*Cypripedium calceolus*)
Lecanactis, Churchyard (*Lecanactis hemisphaerica*)
Lecanora, Tarn (*Lecanora archariana*)
Lecidea, Copper (*Lecidea inops*)
Leek, Round-headed (*Allium sphaerocephalon*)
Lettuce, Least (*Lactuca saligna*)
Lichen, Arctic Kidney (*Nephroma arcticum*)
Lichen, Ciliate Strap (*Heterodermia leucomelos*)
Lichen, Coralloid Rosette (*Heterodermia propagulifera*)
Lichen, Ear-lobed Dog (*Peltigera lepidophora*)
Lichen, Forked Hair (*Bryoria furcellata*)
Lichen, Golden Hair (*Teloschistes flavicans*)

Lichen, Orange Fruited Elm (*Caloplaca luteoalba*)
Lichen, River Jelly (*Collema dichotomum*)
Lichen, Scaly Breck (*Squamarina lentigera*)
Lichen, Stary Breck (*Buellia asterella*)
Lily, Snowdon (*Lloydia serotina*)
Liverwort (*Petallophyllum ralfsi*)
Liverwort, Lindenberg's Leafy (*Adelanthus lindenbergianus*)
Marsh-mallow, Rough (*Althaea hirsuta*)
Marshwort, Creeping (*Apium repens*)
Milk-parsley, Cambridge (*Selinum carvifolia*)
Moss (*Drepanocladius vernicosus*)
Moss, Alpine Copper (*Mielichoferia mielichoferi*)
Moss, Baltic Bog (*Sphagnum balticum*)
Moss, Blue Dew (*Saelania glaucescens*)
Moss, Blunt-leaved Bristle (*Orthotrichum obtusifolium*)
Moss, Bright Green Cave (*Cyclodictyon laetevirens*)
Moss, Cordate Beard (*Barbula cordata*)
Moss, Cornish Path (*Ditrichum cornubicum*)
Moss, Derbyshire Feather (*Thamnobryum angustifolium*)
Moss, Dune Thread (*Bryum mamillatum*)
Moss, Glaucous Beard (*Barbula glauca*)
Moss, Green Shield (*Buxbaumia viridis*)
Moss, Hair Silk (*Plagiothecium piliferum*)
Moss, Knothole (*Zygodon forsteri*)
Moss, Large Yellow Feather (*Scorpidium turgescens*)
Moss, Millimetre (*Micromitrium tenerum*)
Moss, Multifruited River (*Cryphaea lamyana*)
Moss, Nowell's Limestone (*Zygodon gracilis*)
Moss, Rigid Apple (*Bartramia stricta*)
Moss, Round-leaved Feather (*Rhyncostegium rotundifolium*)
Moss, Schleicher's Thread (*Bryum schleicheri*)
Moss, Triangular Pygmy (*Acaulon triquetrum*)
Moss, Vaucher's Feather (*Hypnum vaucheri*)
Mudwort, Welsh (*Limosella australis*)
Naiad, Holly-leaved (*Najas marina*)
Naiad, Slender (*Najas flexilis*)
Orache, Stalked (*Halimione pedunculata*)
Orchid, Early Spider (*Ophrys sphegodes*)
Orchid, Fen (*Liparis loeselii*)
Orchid, Ghost (*Epipogium aphyllum*)
Orchid, Lapland Marsh (*Dactylorhiza lapponica*)
Orchid, Late Spider (*Ophrys fuciflora*)
Orchid, Lizard (*Himantoglossum hircinum*)
Orchid, Military (*Orchis militaris*)
Orchid, Monkey (*Orchis simia*)
Pannaria, Caledonia (*Pannaria ignobilis*)
Parmelia, New Forest (*Parmelia minarum*)
Parmentaria, Oil Stain (*Parmentaria chilensis*)
Pear, Plymouth (*Pyrus cordata*)
Penny-cress, Perfoliate (*Thlaspi perfoliatum*)
Pennyroyal (*Mentha pulegium*)
Pertusaria, Alpine Moss (*Pertusaria bryontha*)
Physcia, Southern Grey (*Physcia tribacioides*)
Pigmyweed (*Crassula aquatica*)
Pine, Ground (*Ajuga chamaepitys*)
Pink, Cheddar (*Dianthus gratianopolitanus*)
Pink, Childling (*Petroraghia nanteuilii*)
Plantain, Floating Water (*Luronium natans*)
Pseudocyphellaria, Ragged (*Pseudocyphellaria lacerata*)
Psora, Rusty Alpine (*Psora rubiformis*)
Ragwort, Fen (*Senecio paludosus*)
Ramping-fumitory, Martin's (*Fumaria martinii*)
Rampion, Spiked (*Phyteuma spicatum*)
Restharrow, Small (*Ononis reclinata*)
Rock-cress, Alpine (*Arabis alpina*)
Rock-cress, Bristol (*Arabis stricta*)
Rustworth, Western (*Marsupella profunda*)
Sandwort, Norwegian (*Arenaria norvegica*)
Sandwort, Teesdale (*Minuartia stricta*)

Saxifrage, Drooping (*Saxifraga cernua*)
Saxifrage, Marsh (*Saxifrage hirulus*)
Saxifrage, Tufted (*Saxifraga cespitosa*)
Solenopsora, Serpentine (*Solenopsora liparina*)
Solomon's-seal, Whorled (*Polygonatum verticillatum*)
Sow-thistle, Alpine (*Cicerbita alpina*)
Spearwort, Adder's-tongue (*Ranunculus ophioglossifolius*)
Speedwell, Fingered (*Veronica triphyllos*)
Speedwell, Spiked (*Veronica spicata*)
Star-of-Bethlehem, Early (*Gagea bohemica*)
Starfruit (*Damasonium alisma*)
Stonewort, Bearded (*Chara canescens*)
Stonewort, Foxtail (*Lamprothamnium papulosum*)
Strapwort (*Corrigiola litoralis*)
Turpswort (*Geocalyx graveolens*)
Violet, Fen (*Viola persicifolia*)
Viper's-grass (*Scorzonera humilis*)
Water-plantain, Ribbon-leaved (*Alisma gramineum*)
Wood-sedge, Starved (*Carex depauperata*)
Woodsia, Alpine (*Woodsia alpina*)
Woodsia, Oblong (*Woodsia ilvensis*)
Wormwood, Field (*Artemisia campestris*)
Woundwort, Downy (*Stachys germanica*)
Woundwort, Limestone (*Stachys alpina*)
Yellow-rattle, Greater (*Rhinanthus serotinus*)

WILD BIRDS

The Wildlife and Countryside Act 1981 lays down a close season for wild birds (other than game birds) from 1 February to 31 August inclusive, each year. Exceptions to these dates are made for:
Capercaillie and (except Scotland) *Woodcock* – 1 February–30 September
Snipe – 1 February–11 August
Wild Duck and *Wild Goose* (below high water mark) – 21 February–31 August

Birds which may be killed or taken outside the close season (except on Sundays and on Christmas Day in Scotland, and on Sundays in prescribed areas of England and Wales) are the above-named, plus coot, certain wild duck (gadwall, goldeneye, mallard, pintail, pochard, shoveler, teal, tufted duck, wigeon), certain wild geese (Canada, greylag, pink-footed, white-fronted (in England and Wales only)), moorhen, golden plover and woodcock.

Certain wild birds may be killed or taken at any time by authorized persons: crow, collared dove, gull (great and lesser black-backed or herring), jackdaw, jay, magpie, pigeon (feral or wood), rook, sparrow (house), and starling.

All other British birds are fully protected by law throughout the year.

HUNTING AND GROUND GAME

There is no statutory close time for fox-hunting or rabbit-shooting, nor for hares. However, by an Act passed in 1892 the sale of hares or leverets in Great Britain is prohibited from 1 March to 31 July inclusive under a penalty of £1. The recognized date for the opening of the fox-hunting season is 1 November, and it continues till the following April.

DEER

The statutory close seasons for deer (all dates inclusive) are:

	England and Wales	Scotland
Fallow deer		
Male	1 May–31 July	1 May–31 July
Female	1 Mar.–31 Oct.	16 Feb.–20 Oct.
Red deer		
Male	1 May–31 July	21 Oct.–30 June
Female	1 Mar.–31 Oct.	16 Feb.–20 Oct.
Roe deer		
Male	1 Nov.–31 Mar.	21 Oct.–31 Mar.
Female	1 Mar.–31 Oct.	1 April–20 Oct.
Sika deer		
Male	1 May–31 July	21 Oct.–30 June
Female	1 Mar.–31 Oct.	16 Feb.–20 Oct.
Red/Sika hybrids		
Male	—	21 Oct.–30 June
Female	—	16 Feb.–20 Oct.

ANGLING

Where local by-laws neither specify nor dispense with an annual close season, the following are statutory close times (dates inclusive):
Coarse fishing - 15 March–15 June
Game fishing - Trout, 1 October–end February; salmon, 1 November–31 January

Close seasons vary in accordance with local by-laws. It is now necessary in all cases to check with the National Rivers Authority regional office covering the area (details can be found in the local telephone directory).

The NRA introduced in 1992 an annual national rod fishing licence which replaced more than 100 regional licences, as well as removing the need for separate licences for game and coarse fish. Purchase of a national rod fishing licence is legally required of anglers wishing to fish with rod and line for salmon, migratory trout (sea trout), trout, char, grayling and other freshwater fish (coarse fish) and eels, in all waters within the area of the NRA. The full licence, valid 1 April to 31 March, costs £13.25 in 1993-4. Seven day licences and concessionary licences (for senior citizens aged 60 and over, registered disabled and juniors aged 12–16) are available at £6.75.

CLOSE SEASONS AND TIMES

GAME BIRDS

In each case the dates are inclusive:

Black game – 11 December–19 August (31 August in Somerset, Devon and New Forest)
★*Grouse* – 11 December–11 August
★*Partridge* – 2 February–31 August
★*Pheasant* – 2 February–30 September
★*Ptarmigan* – (Scotland only) 11 December–11 August

★ It is also unlawful in England and Wales to kill this game on a Sunday or Christmas Day

Historic Monuments

ENGLAND

The following is a select list of monuments, most of which are in the care of English Heritage or the National Trust. Charges for admission are those obtaining in 1993–4. Concessionary rates are available for children, etc. Standard hours of opening are:

| 1 April–30 September | 10–6 |
| 1 October–31 March | 10–4 |

* Monuments open all year. Other monuments open from 1 April to 30 September only. All monuments are closed on 24–26 December and 1 January. Some smaller sites may close for the lunch-hour, which is normally 1–2 p.m. During the winter season, many English Heritage monuments are closed on Mondays.

*AVEBURY, Wilts. Adm. free. Remains of stone circles constructed 4,000 years ago surrounding the later village of Avebury. Also AVEBURY MUSEUM, adm. £1.30

*BATTLE ABBEY, E. Sussex. £2.70. Remains of the abbey founded by William the Conqueror on the site of the Battle of Hastings

*BEESTON CASTLE, Cheshire. £2.00. Thirteenth-century inner ward with gatehouse and towers, and considerable remains of large outer ward

*BOLSOVER CASTLE, Derbyshire. £2.00. Notable for its interesting 17th-century buildings

*BOSCOBEL HOUSE, Shropshire. £3.00. Timber-framed early 17th-century hunting lodge with later alterations. A descendent of Charles II's 'Royal Oak' is nearby

BRINKBURN PRIORY, Northumberland. £1.20. A house of Augustinian canons; the church (c.1200, repaired 1858) and parts of the cloister buildings survive

*BYLAND ABBEY, North Yorkshire. £1.20. Considerable remains of church and conventual buildings date from the abbey's foundation in 1177 by the Cistercians

*CARISBROOKE CASTLE, Isle of Wight. £3.20. Norman castle, the prison of Charles I from 1647–8

*CARLISLE CASTLE, Cumbria. £2.00. Medieval castle, prison of Mary Queen of Scots. Inner and outer wards enclosing a 12th century keep

*CASTLE ACRE PRIORY, Norfolk. £2.00. Extensive remains include the 12th century church and the prior's lodgings

*CASTLE RISING CASTLE, Norfolk. £1.20. A 12th century keep standing in a massive earthwork with its gatehouse and bridge

*CHESTERS ROMAN FORT, Northumberland. £2.00. Fine example of a Roman cavalry fort

*CHYSAUSTER ANCIENT VILLAGE, Cornwall. £1.30. Romano–Cornish village, 2nd and 3rd century AD, probably on a late Iron Age site

*CLEEVE ABBEY, Somerset. £1.70. Much of the claustral buildings survive including timber-roofed frater, but only foundations of the church

*CLIFFORD'S TOWER, York. £1.20. Thirteenth-century tower built on a mound

*CORBRIDGE ROMAN SITE, Northumberland. £2.00. Excavations have revealed the central area of a Roman town and successive military bases

*CORFE CASTLE, Dorset. £2.80. Feb.–Oct., daily. Nov.– Jan., weekends only, PM. Ruined former royal castle dating back to the 11th century

*DEAL CASTLE, Kent. £2.00. The largest and most complete of the forts erected by Henry VIII for coastal defence

*DOVER CASTLE, Kent. £5.00. One of the strongest British castles, with Roman, Saxon and Norman features

*DUNSTANBURGH CASTLE, Northumberland. £1.20. The 14th century castle standing on a cliff above the sea has a substantial gatehouse-keep

*FARLEIGH HUNGERFORD CASTLE, Somerset. £1.20. Late 14th century castle of two courts. The chapel contains fine tomb of Sir Thomas Hungerford

FARNHAM CASTLE KEEP, Surrey. £1.50. Built by the Bishops of Winchester, the motte of the castle is dominated by a large 12th century shell keep. Foundations of a Norman tower

*FOUNTAINS ABBEY, nr. Ripon, North Yorkshire. £3.50. Closed Fri. Nov.–Jan. Ruined monastery founded by Cistercian monks in 1132. Eighteenth-century landscaped garden at Studley Royal

*FRAMLINGHAM CASTLE, Suffolk. £1.70. Impressive castle (c.1200) with high curtain walls enclosing an almshouse of 1639

*FURNESS ABBEY, Cumbria. £2.00. Founded in 1123 by Stephen, afterwards King of England; extensive remains of church and conventual buildings

*GLASTONBURY ABBEY, Somerset. £2.00. Ruined abbey built in AD 708 by the Saxon Ina, on the site of an earlier monastery

*GOODRICH CASTLE, Hereford and Worcester. £1.70. Extensive remains of 13th and 14th century castle incorporating 12th century keep

*GRIMES GRAVES, Norfolk. £1.20. Extensive group of flint mines dating from the Neolithic period. One shaft can be descended

*HAILES ABBEY, Gloucestershire. £1.80. Ruins of a Cistercian monastery founded in 1246. Museum contains some fine architectural fragments

*HELMSLEY CASTLE, North Yorkshire. £1.70. Twelfth century keep and curtain wall with 16th century domestic buildings. Spectacular earthwork defences

*HOUSESTEADS ROMAN FORT, Northumberland. £2.00. Excavation has exposed this infantry fort on Hadrian's Wall with its extra-mural civilian settlement

*KENILWORTH CASTLE, Warwickshire. £1.70. One of the most extensive castles in Britain, showing many styles of building from 1155 to 1649

LANERCOST PRIORY, Cumbria. 80p. The nave of the Augustinian priory church, c.1166, is still used and there are remains of other claustral buildings

*LINDISFARNE PRIORY, Northumberland. £2.00 (subject to tide). The bishopric of the Northumbrian kingdom destroyed by the Danes; re-established in 11th century as a Benedictine priory, now ruined

*LULLINGSTONE ROMAN VILLA, Kent. £1.70. A large villa occupied through much of the Roman period; fine mosaics

*MIDDLEHAM CASTLE, North Yorkshire. £1.20. Childhood home of Richard III. The 12th century keep stands within later fortifications and domestic buildings

*MOUNT GRACE PRIORY, North Yorkshire. £2.00. Carthusian monastery, founded 1398, with remains of monastic buildings

NETLEY ABBEY, Hampshire. £1.20. Extensive remains of Cistercian abbey, founded 1239, with ruined Tudor house

*OLD SARUM, Wiltshire. £1.30. Large earthworks enclosing the excavated remains of the castle and the first Salisbury cathedral, begun in 1078

*ORFORD CASTLE, Suffolk. £1.70. Circular keep of c.1170 and remains of coastal defence castle built by Henry II

*PENDENNIS CASTLE, Cornwall. £2.00. Well-preserved castle erected by Henry VIII for coastal defence

*PEVENSEY CASTLE, East Sussex. £1.70. Walls of a 4th century Roman fort enclosing remains of an 11th century castle

*PEVERIL CASTLE, Derbyshire. £1.20. In a picturesque and nearly impregnable position, this 12th century castle is defended on two sides by precipitous rocks

*PORTCHESTER CASTLE, Hampshire. £1.70. Walls of a late Roman fort enclosing a Norman keep and an Augustinian priory church

*RICHBOROUGH CASTLE, Kent. £1.70. The landing-site of the Claudian invasion in AD 43, with massive 3rd century stone walls

*RICHMOND CASTLE, North Yorkshire. £1.70. This 12th century keep, with 11th century curtain wall and gatehouse, commands Swaledale

*RIEVAULX ABBEY, North Yorkshire. £2.00. Founded c.1132. Extensive remains include an early Cistercian nave and fine 13th century choir and claustral buildings

*ROCHESTER CASTLE, Kent. £1.70. Eleventh century castle partly founded on the Roman city wall, with a square keep of c.1130

*ST AUGUSTINE'S ABBEY, Kent. £1.20. Remains of Benedictine monastery, with Norman church, on site of abbey founded by St Augustine in AD 598

*ST MAWES CASTLE, Cornwall. £1.30. Coastal defence castle built by Henry VIII consisting of central tower and three bastions

*SCARBOROUGH CASTLE, North Yorkshire. £1.70. Remains of 12th century keep and curtain walls dominating the town

*STONEHENGE, Wiltshire. £2.70. Prehistoric monument consisting of a series of concentric stone circles surrounded by a ditch and bank

*TILBURY FORT, Essex. £1.70. One of Henry VIII's coastal forts, extended by Charles II

*TINTAGEL CASTLE, Cornwall. £2.00. 12th century castle on cliff top. Dark Age settlement site

*TYNEMOUTH PRIORY and CASTLE, Tyne and Wear. £1.20. Remains of a Benedictine priory, founded 1090, on Saxon monastic site. Coastal batteries with reconstructed First World War magazine

*WALMER CASTLE, Kent. £2.70. (Closed when Lord Warden is in residence.) One of Henry VIII's coastal defence castles, now the residence of the Lord Warden of the Cinque Ports

*WALTHAM ABBEY, Essex. Adm. free. Ruined abbey including the nave of the former Abbey church c.1120, 'Harold's Bridge' and late 14th-century gatehouse. Traditionally, burial place of Harold II (1066)

*WARKWORTH CASTLE, Northumberland. £1.70. 15th century keep amidst earlier ruins with a 14th century hermitage upstream

*WHITBY ABBEY, North Yorkshire. £1.20. 13th and 14th century Benedictine church on site of monastery founded in AD 657

*WROXETER ROMAN CITY, Shropshire. £1.70. The 2nd century public baths and part of the forum remain of the Roman town of Viroconium

WALES

The following is a select list of monuments under the control of Cadw: Welsh Historic Monuments. Charges for admission are those obtaining in 1993–4; concessionary rates are available for children, etc.

Standard hours of admission:

	Weekdays	Sundays
29 March–24 October	9.30–6.30	9.30–6.30
25 October–28 March	9.30–4.00	2.00–4.00

All monuments are closed on Christmas Eve, Christmas Day, Boxing Day and New Year's Day.

BEAUMARIS CASTLE, Anglesey, Gwynedd. £1.50. The finest example of the concentrically planned castle in Britain, it is still almost intact

CAERLEON ROMAN AMPHITHEATRE, Gwent. £1.25. Late 1st century oval arena surrounded by bank for spectators

CAERLEON ROMAN FORTRESS BATHS, Gwent. £1.25, joint ticket £2.00 (with National Museum of Wales). Rare example of a legionary bath-house

CAERNARFON CASTLE, Gwynedd. £3.50. The most important of the Edwardian castles, built together with the town wall between 1283 and 1330

CAERPHILLY CASTLE, Mid Glamorgan. £2.00. Concentrically planned castle (c.1270) notable for its great scale and use of water defences

CASTELL COCH, S. Glamorgan. £2.00. Rebuilt 1875–90 on medieval foundations

CHEPSTOW CASTLE, Gwent. £2.90. Fine rectangular keep in the middle of extensive fortifications

CONWY CASTLE, Gwynedd. £2.90. Built by Edward I to guard the Conwy ferry

CRICCIETH CASTLE, Gwynedd. £1.80. A native Welsh castle of the early 13th century, much altered by Edward I

DENBIGH CASTLE, Clwyd. £1.50. The remains of the castle, which dates from 1282–1322, include an unusual triangular gatehouse

HARLECH CASTLE, Gwynedd. £2.90. Well-preserved Edwardian castle with a concentric plan sited on a rocky outcrop above the former shore-line

RAGLAN CASTLE, Gwent. £1.80. Extensive remains of 15th century castle with moated hexagonal keep

ST DAVID'S, BISHOP'S PALACE, Dyfed. £1.50. Extensive remains of principal residence of Bishop of St David's dating from 1280–1350

TINTERN ABBEY, Gwent. £2.00. Extensive remains of 13th century church and conventual buildings of this Cistercian monastery

TRETOWER COURT, Powys. £1.80. Medieval house with remains of castle nearby

SCOTLAND

The following is a select list of monuments under the control of Historic Scotland.

Except where indicated differently, charges are: adults £1.00, concessions (con.) 50p.

Monuments open at any reasonable time are indicated by *. Standard hours of opening (marked †) are:

	Weekdays	Sundays
April–September	9.30–6.30	2.00–6.30
October–March	9.30–4.30	2.00–4.30

*ABERLEMNO SCULPTURED STONES, Tayside. Adm. free. Four Pictish stones

*ANTONINE WALL, Central and Strathclyde regions. Adm. free. Built about AD 142, consists of ditch, turf rampart and road, with forts every two miles

†BLACKHOUSE ARNOL, Western Isles. Closed Sun. £1.50, con. 80p. Traditional Lewis thatched house

†BONAWE IRONWORKS, Strathclyde. Closed in winter. £1.50, con. 80p. Charcoal-fuelled ironworks

*BROCH OF BIRSAY, Orkney. Adm. free. Remains of Norse church

†CAERLAVEROCK CASTLE, Dumfries and Galloway. £1.70, con. 90p. One of the finest examples of early classical Renaissance building in Scotland

†CAIRNPAPPLE HILL, Lothian. Closed in winter. A prehistoric ritual complex and Bronze Age cairn

*CALLANISH, Western Isles. Adm. free. Standing stones in a cross-shaped setting, dating back to 3000 BC

*CATERTHUNS (BROWN AND WHITE), Tayside. Adm. free. Iron Age hill forts

*CLAVA CAIRNS, Highland. Adm. free. Late Neolithic or early Bronze Age cairns

†DRYBURGH ABBEY, Borders. £2.00, con. £1.00. Twelfth-century abbey containing tomb of Sir Walter Scott

EDINBURGH CASTLE, including Scottish National War Memorial, Scottish United Services Museum and historic apartments. Open April–September 9.30–6, October–March 9.30–5. Adm. to War Memorial, free; to all other areas £4.00, con. £2.00

†EDZELL CASTLE, Tayside. Closed Tuesday p.m. and Friday in winter. £1.70, con. 90p. A late medieval tower house incorporated into a 16th-century courtyard mansion. Walled garden

†ELGIN CATHEDRAL, Grampian. Closed Thursday p.m. and Friday in winter. £1.20, con. 60p. Thirteenth-century cathedral with fine chapterhouse

†FORT GEORGE, Highland.£2.30, con. £1.20. A complete view of the defensive system of an 18th-century artillery fort

†GLASGOW CATHEDRAL, Strathclyde. Adm. free. Medieval cathedral with elaborately vaulted crypt

*GLENELG BROCHS, Highland. Adm. free. Two broch towers with well-preserved structural features

†HERMITAGE CASTLE, Borders. Closed weekdays in winter. £1.20, con. 60p. Extensive ruined castle dating back to the 14th century

†HUNTLY CASTLE, Grampian. Closed Thursday p.m. and Friday in winter. £1.70, con. 90p. Ruin of a house built in the 16th and 17th centuries

†JARLSHOF, Shetland. Closed all winter. £1.70, con. 90p. Remains of Bronze Age village

†JEDBURGH ABBEY, Borders. £2.00, con. £1.00. Romanesque and early Gothic style church founded about 1138

†KELSO ABBEY, Borders. Adm. free. Remains of west end of great abbey church founded 1128

†LINLITHGOW PALACE, Lothian. £1.70, con. 90p. Ruin of royal palace set in its own park. Birthplace of Mary , Queen of Scots

*LOANHEAD STONE CIRCLE, Grampian. Adm. free. Recumbent stone circle enclosing a ring cairn

†MAES HOWE, Orkney. £1.70, con. 90p. Prehistoric tomb

†MEIGLE MUSEUM, Tayside. Closed all winter. Pictish stones

†MELROSE ABBEY, Borders. £2.00, con. £1.00p. Ruin of Cistercian abbey founded about 1136

*MOUSA BROCH, Shetland. Adm. free. Finest surviving Iron Age broch tower

*NETHER LARGIE CAIRNS, Argyll and Bute. Adm. free. Bronze Age and Neolithic cairns

†NEW ABBEY CORN MILL, Dumfries and Galloway. Closed Thursday p.m. and Friday in winter. £1.50, con. 80p. Water-powered oatmeal mill in working order

*RING OF BROGAR, Orkney. Adm. free. Late Neolithic circle of upright stones with an enclosing ditch spanned by causeways

*RUTHWELL CROSS, Dumfries and Galloway. Adm. free. Seventh-century Anglian cross

†ST ANDREWS CASTLE AND CATHEDRAL, Fife. Separate adm. fee for Cathedral; £1.50, con. 80p. Ruins of 13th-century castle and remains of the largest cathedral in Scotland

†SKARA BRAE, Orkney. £2.00, con. £1.00. Prehistoric village

†SMAILHOLM TOWER, Borders. Closed in winter. £1.50, con. 80p. Well-preserved rectangular tower

STIRLING CASTLE, Central. Open April–September 9.30–6, October–March 9.30–5. £2.50, con. £1.30/£1.00. Great Hall and gatehouse of James IV, palace of James V, Chapel Royal remodelled by James VI, artillery fortifications

†TANTALLON CASTLE, Lothian. £1.70, con. 90p. Closed Thursday p.m. and Friday in winter. Fortification with earthwork defences and a 14th-century curtain wall with towers

†THREAVE CASTLE, Dumfries and Galloway. Adm. includes ferry trip. Closed in winter. £1.20, con. 60p. Late 14th-century tower with an artillery fortification. On an island; approached by boat, long walk to castle

Historic Houses and Castles

Dates of opening and admission fees shown are those which obtained in 1993, and are subject to modification. Specific opening hours are not given but may be checked by telephone. Most houses have concessionary rates for certain categories of visitor.

Space permits only a selection of some of the more noteworthy houses in the UK which are open to the public.
*Property of the National Trust
Adm. admission
PM open in afternoons only

*A LA RONDE, Exmouth. 1 April–31 Oct. Sun.–Thurs. Adm. £3.00. Tel: 0395–265514. Unique 16-sided house built in 1796
ALNWICK CASTLE, Northumberland. Maundy Thursday– mid Oct. Adm. £3.60. Tel: 0665–510777. The second largest inhabited castle in England, with Italian Renaissance-style interior
ALTHORP, Northants. Opening times and prices subject to change. Contact Lord Spencer. House originally built in early 16th century. Fine art collection
*ANGLESEY ABBEY, Cambs. 27 March–17 Oct. Wed.–Sun. and Bank Holiday Mons. Closed Good Fri. PM. Adm. £4.50. Gardens only Adm. £2.50. Tel: 0223–811200. House built about 1600; bought by Lord Fairhaven in early 20th century. Outstanding grounds with unique statuary
ARUNDEL CASTLE, W. Sussex. 1 April–29 Oct. daily (not Sat.). PM. Adm. charge. Tel: 0903–883136. Castle dating from the Norman Conquest. Seat of the Dukes of Norfolk
BALMORAL CASTLE, Grampian. 1 May–31 July, daily (not Sun.). Adm. £1.75. Tel: 03397–42334. Mid 19th-century Baronial-style castle built for Queen Victoria and Prince Albert. The Queen's private Highland residence
BANQUETING HOUSE, Whitehall, London. Daily (not Sun. or Bank Holidays). Adm. £2.75. Tel: 071-839 3787. Designed by Inigo Jones; ceiling paintings by Rubens. Site of the execution of Charles I
*BASILDON PARK, Berks. April–Oct. (not Mon. except Bank Holidays; not Tues., not Good Friday). Adm. £3.50. Grounds £2.50. Tel: 0734–843040. Palladian house built in 1776; unusual octagonal room
BEAULIEU, Hants. Daily (not Christmas). Adm. charge. Tel: 0590–612345. House and gardens, Beaulieu abbey and exhibition of monastic life, National Motor Museum (see also page 592)
*BELTON HOUSE, Grantham. April–Oct. Wed.–Sun. and Bank Holiday Mons. Closed Good Friday. PM. Adm. £4.00. Tel: 0476–66116. Fine 17th-century country house in landscaped park
BELVOIR CASTLE, nr. Grantham. 1 April–1 Oct. daily (not Mon., Fri. except Bank Holidays). Adm. £3.50. Tel: 0476–870262. Seat of the Dukes of Rutland; early 19th-century Gothic-style castle
BERKELEY CASTLE, Glos. April–Sept. daily (not Mon. except Bank Holidays). PM only except May–Aug., Tues.–Sat. and Bank Holidays 11–5. Oct. Sun. PM only. Adm. £3.70. Tel: 0453–810332. Completed 1153; site of the murder of Edward II in 1327. Elizabethan terraced gardens and tropical butterfly house
BLAIR CASTLE, Tayside. April–last Fri. in Oct. daily (Sun. April, May and Oct PM.). Adm. £4.00. Tel: 0796– 481207. Seat of the Duke of Atholl; mid 18th-century mansion with 13th-century tower
BLENHEIM PALACE, Oxon. Mid-March–31 Oct. daily. Adm. charge. Tel: 0993–811325. Seat of the Duke of

Marlborough and Winston Churchill's birthplace; designed by Vanbrugh
BOUGHTON HOUSE, Northants. Aug.–1 Sept. daily PM. Staterooms by prior booking. Grounds 1 May–30 Sept. daily (not Fri.). PM. Adm. charge. Tel: 0536–515731. French-style 17th-century house with fine state apartments
BOWHILL, Selkirk. House 1 July–31 July daily PM; Grounds early May to late summer daily (not Fri.) PM. Adm. £3, Grounds only, £1. Tel: 0750–20732. Seat of the Duke of Buccleuch and Queensberry. Fine collection of paintings including portrait miniatures
BROADLANDS, Hants. Easter–end Sept. daily (not Fri. except Aug. and Good Friday). Adm. £5.00 Tel: 0794– 516878. Palladian mansion set in Capability Brown parkland. Mountbatten exhibition
BRONTË PARSONAGE, Haworth, W. Yorks. Daily (not Christmas or mid Jan.–mid Feb.). Adm. £3.50. Tel: 0535–642323. Home of the Brontë sisters; museum and memorabilia
BROUGHTON CASTLE, Oxon. 19 May–12 Sept. Wed., Sun. (also Thurs. in July and Aug.) and Bank Holiday Suns and Mons PM. Adm. £3.00. Tel: 0295–262624. Moated medieval mansion; important Civil War role
BUCKFAST ABBEY, Devon. Daily. Adm. free. Tel: 0364– 43301. Abbey church erected between 1907 and 1938
BUCKINGHAM PALACE, London SW1. Open daily for eight weeks from early August, annually until further notice. Adm. £8. Tel: 071–930 5526. The Queen's official London residence. Eighteen state rooms on view, including the throne room and dining-room; also the picture gallery, housing the Royal Collection
*BUCKLAND ABBEY, Devon. 1 April–31 Oct. daily except Thurs. Nov.–March Wed., Sat., Sun. (Wed. pre-booked parties only) PM. Adm. £4.00. Tel: 0822–853607. Thirteenth-century Cistercian monastery. Home of Sir Francis Drake
BURGHLEY HOUSE, Stamford. 1 April–3 Oct. (closed 4 Sept) daily. Adm. £4.80. Tel: 0780–52451. Late Elizabethan house; vast state apartments
*CALKE ABBEY, Derbyshire. 3 April–end Oct., Sat.–Wed. Closed Good Friday. PM. Adm. £4.20 by timed ticket only. Tel: 0332–863822. Baroque early 18th-century mansion
CARDIFF CASTLE . Daily (not Christmas, New Year). Adm. charge. Tel: 0222–822086. Castle built on the site of a Roman fort; spectacular towers and rich interior
*CARLYLE'S HOUSE, Chelsea, London. April–end Oct. Wed.–Sun. and Bank Holiday Mons (not Good Friday). Adm. £2.50. Tel: 071–352 7087. Home of Thomas Carlyle, Scottish historian and philosopher
*CASTLE COOLE, Enniskillen. Easter period, daily; June, July, Aug. daily (not Thurs.); Sat., Sun. and Bank Holidays in April, May, Sept. PM. Adm. £2.30, Grounds April–Sept. free. Tel: 0365–322690. Eighteenth-century mansion by James Wyatt
*CASTLE DROGO, Devon. April–Oct. daily except Fri. Adm. £4.60. Grounds only £2.00. Tel: 064743–3306. Granite castle designed by Lutyens
CASTLE HOWARD, N. Yorks. 19 March–31 Oct., daily. Adm. £5.50. Tel: 065384–333. Designed by Vanbrugh 1699–1726; mausoleum designed by Hawksmoor
CAWDOR CASTLE, Inverness. May–3 Oct., daily. Adm. £3.50, Grounds £1.80. Tel: 06677–615. Fourteenth-century tower-house with mainly 17th-century additions

*CHARTWELL, Kent. Open three days each week. Times vary. Adm. £4.20, Grounds only £2.00. Tel: 0732-866368. Home of Sir Winston Churchill

CHATSWORTH, Derbyshire. 21 March–31 Oct. daily. Grounds 21 March–3 Oct., daily. Adm. charge. Tel: 0246-582204. Tudor mansion with later additions, in magnificent parkland

CHICHELEY HALL, nr. Newport Pagnell. 11 April–30 May, Aug. Sun. and Bank Holidays PM. Adm. £3.00. Tel: 023065-252. Early Georgian house with notable brickwork and a Palladian hall

*CLIVEDEN, Maidenhead. House, April–31 Oct., Thurs. and Sun. PM. Gardens March–Dec. daily. Adm. £3.50, £1.00 extra for house. Tel: 0628-605069. Former home of the Astors, now an hotel. About 375 acres of garden and woodland

*COMPTON CASTLE, nr. Paignton. April–31 Oct. Mon., Wed., Thurs. daily. Adm. £2.60. Tel: 0803-872112. Fortified manor house with notable façade

*CROFT CASTLE, Herefordshire. Easter Bank Holiday weekend (not Fri.), May–Sept. Wed.–Sun., Bank Holiday Mons., April and Oct. weekends. PM. Adm. £2.80. Tel: 056885-246. Border castle mentioned in the Domesday Book; Georgian-Gothic interior

DICKENS HOUSE, London, WCI. Daily (not Sun., Christmas and Bank Holidays). Adm. £2.00. Tel: 071-405 2127. House occupied by Dickens 1837–9; manuscripts, furniture and portraits

DR JOHNSON'S HOUSE, London, EC4. Daily (not Sun. and Bank Holidays). Adm. £2.00. Tel: 071-353 3745. Home of Samuel Johnson, built in 1700

DRUMLANRIG CASTLE, Dumfries. May–Aug., daily (not Thurs.). Sun., PM. Adm. charge. Tel: 0848-31682. Castle with baroque decorative features and notable art and furniture collections

GLAMIS CASTLE, Tayside. 4 April–11 Oct., daily. Adm. £4.00, grounds only £2.00. Tel: 03078-4-242. A royal residence and seat of the Lyon family (later earls of Strathmore and Kinghorne) since 1372

GREENWICH, London SE10. ROYAL OBSERVATORY, daily (Sun., PM). Closed 24–26 Dec. Adm. charge. Former Royal Observatory (founded 1675) where the time ball and zero meridian of longitude can be seen. THE QUEEN'S HOUSE, daily (Sun., PM). Closed 24–26 Dec. Adm. charge. Tel: 081-858 4422. Designed for Anne of Denmark, wife of James I, by Inigo Jones; begun in 1616. PAINTED HALL AND CHAPEL, daily (not Thurs.), PM. Visitors are also admitted to Sunday service in the Chapel at 11 a.m. except during Royal Naval College vacations

HADDON HALL, Derbyshire. 1 April–30 Sept. Tues.–Sun., and Bank Holidays. Closed Sun. in July and Aug. (except Bank Holiday weekends). Adm. £3.40. Tel: 0629-812855. Well-preserved 12th-century manor house

*HAM HOUSE, Richmond, Surrey. House re-opens after restoration on 3 April 1994. April–Oct. Sat.–Wed. Nov.–Dec. weekends only. Adm. free. Tel: 081-940 1950. Stuart house with fine interior decoration

HAMPTON COURT PALACE, East Molesey, Surrey. Daily (closed 24–26 Dec.). Adm. £5.90. Tel: 081-781 9500. Sixteenth-century palace built by Cardinal Wolsey, with additions by Sir Christopher Wren. Beautiful gardens with maze; Tudor tennis court (summer only)

*HARDWICK HALL, Derbyshire. 1 April–31 Oct. House Wed., Thurs., Sat., Sun., Bank Holiday Mons. Garden daily to end Oct. (not Good Friday). PM. Adm. £5.00, Garden only, £2.00. Tel: 0246-850430. Built 1591–7 by Bess of Hardwick; notable furniture and tapestries

HAREWOOD HOUSE, Leeds. 3 April–31 Oct. daily. Adm. charge. Tel: 0532-886331. Eighteenth-century house designed by John Carr and Robert Adam; park landscaped by Capability Brown

HATFIELD HOUSE, Herts. 25 March–10 Oct. daily (not Mon. except Bank Holidays, not Good Friday). PM except Bank Holidays. Grounds, times vary. Adm. charge. Tel: 0707-262823. Jacobean house built by Robert Cecil, and the family home of the Cecils. Surviving wing of Royal Palace of Hatfield (1497)

HEVER CASTLE, Kent. 16 March–7 Nov., daily PM. Grounds 11–6. Adm. charge. Tel: 0732-865224. Thirteenth-century double-moated castle, childhood home of Anne Boleyn

HOLKER HALL, Cumbria. 1 April–31 October daily (not Sat.). Adm. charge. Tel: 05395-58328. Former home of the Dukes of Devonshire; award-winning gardens

HOLKHAM HALL, Norfolk. 30 May–30 Sept. Sun.–Thurs. and Easter, Spring and Summer Bank Holidays. PM, except Bank Holidays. Adm. £2.70. Tel: 0328-710227. Fine Palladian mansion

HOPETOUN HOUSE, nr. Edinburgh. 9 April–3 October, daily. Adm. £3.50. Tel: 031-331 2451. House designed by Sir William Bruce, enlarged by William Adam

HOUGHTON HALL, Norfolk. Easter Sun.–27 Sept., Sun., Thurs. and Bank Holidays. Opening times to be announced. Adm. £4.00. Tel: 0485-528569. Home of the Marquess of Cholmondeley; built for Sir Robert Walpole in the 18th century; fine example of Palladian architecture

*HUGHENDEN MANOR, High Wycombe. April–end Oct. (not Good Friday), Wed.–Sun. and Bank Holiday Mons PM. March, weekends only. Adm. £3.30. Tel: 0494-532580. Home of Benjamin Disraeli; small formal garden

INVERARAY CASTLE, Argyll. 1st Sat. in April–2nd Sun. in Oct. daily (not Fri., except July–Aug.), Sun., PM. Adm. £3.00. Woods open all year. Tel: 0499-2203. Seat of the Dukes of Argyll; Gothic-style 18th-century castle

IONA ABBEY, Inner Hebrides. Daily. Adm. £2.00. Tel: 06817-404. Monastery founded by St Columba in AD 563 and restored by the Iona community

JANE AUSTEN'S HOUSE, Chawton, Hants. April–Oct. daily, Jan. and Feb. weekends, Nov., Dec. and March, Wed.–Sun. (not Christmas). Adm. £1.50. Tel: 0420-83262. Jane Austen's home from 1809 until 1817

KEATS HOUSE, Hampstead, London. April–Oct. daily (Sun. and Bank Holidays, PM). Nov.–March, daily (Mon.–Fri. and Sun., PM). (Not Christmas, New Year, Good Friday, Easter Eve, 4 May). Adm. free. Tel: 071-435 2062. Home of John Keats from 1818 to 1820

KELMSCOTT MANOR, nr. Lechlade, Glos. April–Sept., Wed. only. Thurs., Fri. by written application. Adm. (Wed.) £4.50. Summer home of William Morris, containing many products of Morris and Co. Tel: 0367-252486

KENSINGTON PALACE, London W8. Daily (closed 24–26 Dec., 1 Jan. and Good Friday). Adm. £3.90. Tel: 071-937 9561. Built in 1605 and bought by William and Mary in 1689; enlarged by Wren. Birthplace of Queen Victoria

KENWOOD, Hampstead Heath, London. Daily (closed 24–25 Dec.). Adm. free. Tel: 081-348 1286. Adam villa housing the Iveagh Bequest of paintings and furniture. Open air concerts in summer

KEW PALACE, Surrey. April–Sept. daily. Adm. £1.20. Tel: 081-940 3321. Built in 1631 as the Dutch House; residence of George III. Also QUEEN CHARLOTTE'S COTTAGE. April–Sept., weekends and Bank Holidays only. Adm. 70p. Joint ticket Palace and Cottage £1.50

*KINGSTON LACY HOUSE, Dorset. 3 April–31 Oct., PM.
Sat.–Wed. Adm. £5.00, Grounds only £2.00. Tel: 0202–
883402. Seventeenth-century house with 18th- and 19th-
century alterations; important collection of paintings
KNEBWORTH HOUSE, Herts. 3 April–31 May, Sat., Sun.,
School and Bank Holidays, 1 June–5 Sept. daily (not
Mon.). PM. Weekends only to 3 Oct. (Closed 16–19 July).
Adm. £4.00, Grounds only, £2.50. Tel: 0438–812661.
Tudor manor house concealed by 19th-century Gothic
decoration; Lutyens gardens
*KNOLE, Kent. April–Oct. Wed., Fri.–Sun. and Bank
Holiday Mons. Thurs., PM. Adm. £4.00, Garden 50p.
Tel: 0732–450608. House dating from 15th century set
in magnificent parkland; fine art treasures
LEEDS CASTLE, Kent. 15 March–end Oct. daily. Nov.–
March, weekends only. Adm. charge. Tel: 0622–765400.
Castle dating from 9th century, on two small islands in
the middle of a lake. Former royal palace
LINCOLN CASTLE, Daily (closed 25–26 Dec.). Adm. £1.40.
Tel: 0522–511068. Built by William the Conqueror in
1068
*LITTLE MORETON HALL, Cheshire. April–30 Sept.,
Wed.–Sun. and Bank Holiday Mons (not Good Friday).
Oct. weekends, Wed. PM. Adm. £2.50, weekends and
Bank Holidays. £3.50. Tel: 0260–272018. Timber-
framed moated manor house with a knot garden
LONGLEAT HOUSE, Warminster. House daily (not
Christmas). Safari Park mid-March–Oct. Adm. charge.
Tel: 0985–844551. Elizabethan house (1580) in the
Italian Renaissance style
LUTON HOO, Beds. April–Oct., Fri.–Sun., PM and Bank
Holiday Mondays. Adm. £4.50. Tel: 0582–22955.
Houses the Wernher collection of china, glass, pictures
and other *objets d'art*
MARBLE HILL HOUSE, Twickenham, Middx. All year,
daily (not 24, 25 Dec.). Adm. free. Tel: 081–892 5115.
English Palladian villa with early Georgian paintings and
furniture
MICHELHAM PRIORY, E. Sussex. 25 March–31 Oct. daily.
Nov. and March, Sun. only. Adm. £3.30. Tel: 0323–
844224. Tudor house built onto an Augustinian priory
*MONTACUTE HOUSE, Yeovil. 1 April–31 Oct. daily (not
Tues.) PM. Closed Good Friday. Grounds open all year
(not Tues.). Adm. £4.60, Grounds only £2.50. Tel:
0935–823289. Elizabethan house built of Ham Hill stone
*MOUNT STEWART, Co. Down. Times vary. Adm. House,
Garden, Temple £3.30, Garden and Temple only £2.70.
Tel: 024774–387. Eighteenth-century house, childhood
home of Lord Castlereagh
OSBORNE HOUSE, IOW. 1 April–31 Oct. daily. Adm.
£5.40. Tel: 0983–200022. Queen Victoria's seaside
residence
*OSTERLEY PARK HOUSE, Isleworth, Middx. April–Oct.
Wed.–Sat. PM. Sun., Bank Holiday Mon. 11–5. (Closed
Good Fri.). Adm. £3.50, Grounds (open all year) free.
Tel: 081–560 3918. Elizabethan mansion set in parkland
PALACE OF HOLYROODHOUSE, Edinburgh. Open daily
(not Sun. in winter, and not when The Queen is in
residence). Adm. charge. Tel: 031–556 7371. The
Queen's official Scottish residence. Main part of the
palace built 1671–9
*PENRHYN CASTLE, Bangor. 1 April–31 Oct. daily (not
Tues.) PM. Adm. £4.20, Garden £2.00. Tel: 0248–
353084. Neo-Norman castle built in the 19th century.
Industrial Railway Museum
PENSHURST PLACE, Kent. 27 March–4 Oct. daily PM.
Adm. £4.50, Grounds only £3.00. Tel: 0892–870307.
Stately home with medieval Baron's Hall and 14th-
century gardens

*PETWORTH HOUSE, W. Sussex. April–Oct. Tues.–Sun.,
Bank Holiday Mons., Good Friday. PM. Adm. £4.00. Tel:
0798–42207. Late 17th-century house set in deer park
*POLESDEN LACY, Surrey. April–Oct. Wed.–Sun., also
Bank Holidays and preceding Suns. March and Nov.,
weekends only. PM. Grounds open daily all year. Adm.
charge. Tel: 0372–458203. Regency villa remodelled in
the Edwardian era. Fine paintings, tapestries and
furniture
PORTMEIRION, Gwynedd. All year daily. Adm. £2.90
(April–Oct.) £1.45 (Nov.–March). Tel: 0766–770228.
Village in Italianate style
POWDERHAM CASTLE, Exeter. Easter–Oct. Sun.–Fri.
Adm. charge. Tel: 0626–890243. Medieval castle with
18th- and 19th-century alterations
*POWIS CASTLE, Powys. 1 April–30 June, 1 Sept.–31 Oct.
Wed.–Sun.; July and Aug. Tues.–Sun. Open Bank
Holiday Mons. PM. Adm. £5.80, Museum, garden £3.60.
Tel: 0938–554336. Medieval castle with interior in
variety of architectural styles. Fine 17th-century gardens
and Clive of India museum
RABY CASTLE, Durham. Easter (Sat.–Wed.), 1 May–30
June, Wed. and Sun., July–Sept. daily (not Sat.). Also
Bank Holiday Sat.–Tues. PM. Adm. £3.00, Grounds
£1.00. Tel: 0833–60202. Fourteenth-century castle with
extensive walled gardens
RAGLEY HALL, Warks. 10 April–26 Sept. daily (not Mon.,
Fri.). PM. Open Bank Holidays. Adm. £4.50, Garden
£3.50. Tel: 0789–762090. Seventeenth-century house
with gardens, park and lake
ROCKINGHAM CASTLE, Northants. Easter Sunday–30
Sept., Sun., Thurs., (also Bank Holiday Mon. and Tues.
and Tues. in Aug.). PM. Adm. £3.50, Gardens only
£2.00. Tel: 0536–770240. Built by William the
Conqueror; former royal castle
ROYAL PAVILION, Brighton. Daily (closed 24–25 Dec.).
Adm. charge. Tel: 0273–603005. Palace of George IV.
Chinoiserie interiors with much of the original furniture
*RUFFORD OLD HALL, Lancashire. 1 April–31 Oct. daily
(not Fri.). PM. Adm. £2.70. Tel: 0704–821254. Fifteenth-
century hall with unique screen
*ST MICHAEL'S MOUNT, Cornwall. April–Oct. Mon.–Fri.
Nov.–March, guided tours or free flow as tide, weather
and circumstances permit (no regular ferry service in
winter). Adm. £2.90. Tel: 0736–710507. Fourteenth-
century castle with later additions and alterations, off the
coast at Marazion
SANDRINGHAM, Norfolk. 11 April–3 Oct. (closed 19 July–7
Aug.) Daily; Sun. PM. Closed when Royal Family in
residence. Adm. £3.00, Grounds only £2.00. Tel: 0553–
772675. The Queen's private residence; a neo-Jacobean
house built in 1870 with attractive gardens
SCONE PALACE, Perth. Good Friday–mid Oct., daily. Sun.,
PM except July and Aug. Adm. £4.00. Tel: 0738–52300.
House built between 1802 and 1813 on the site of a former
medieval palace
SHERBORNE CASTLE, Dorset. Easter Sat.–end Sept.
Thurs., Sat., Sun. and Bank Holiday Mons. PM. Adm.
charge. Tel: 0935–813182. Built by Sir Walter Raleigh
*SHUGBOROUGH, Staffs. 27 March–31 Oct., daily. Adm.
£7.50 (House, Museum, Farm; House only, £3.00). Tel:
0889–881388. Elegant house set in 18th-century park
with monuments, temples and pavilions in the Greek
Revival style
SKIPTON CASTLE, N. Yorks. Open all year (not Christmas
Day). Daily. (Sun., PM). Adm. £2.60. Tel: 0756–792442.
D-shaped castle with six round towers and beautiful inner
courtyard

*SMALLHYTHE PLACE, Kent. April–Oct. Sat.–Wed. PM.
Open Good Friday. Adm. £2.50. Tel: 05806–2334. Half-
timbered 16th-century house; home of Ellen Terry 1899–
1928
STANFORD HALL, Leics. Easter Sat.–end Sept. Sat., Sun.,
Bank Holidays (Mon. and Tues.). PM. Adm. £2.90. Tel:
0788–860250. Elegant William and Mary house with
unique collection of Stuart portraits. Motorcycle museum
STONELEIGH ABBEY, Warks. Open by prior appointment
only, Mon.–Fri. Tel: 0926–52116. Italianate mansion
built in the early 18th century on the site of a former
Cistercian abbey
STONOR PARK, Oxon. Times vary. Adm. £3.30. Tel: 0491–
63587. Large medieval house with Georgian façade.
Centre of Roman Catholicism after the Reformation
*STOURHEAD, Wilts. 3 April–31 Oct., Sat.–Wed. PM.
Gardens all year, daily. Adm. House £4.00, Gardens
£4.00. Tel: 0747–840348. English Palladian mansion
with famous Italian landscape gardens
STRATFIELD SAYE HOUSE, nr. Reading. 1 May–last Sun.
in Sept. daily (not Fri.). Wellington Country Park
March–Oct. daily, Nov.–Feb. weekends only. Adm.
charge. Tel: 0256–882882. House built between 1630
and 1640; home of the Dukes of Wellington since 1817
SUDELEY CASTLE, Glos. April–Oct. daily, PM. Adm. £4.75.
Tel: 0242–602308. Castle built in 1442; a royal palace
between 1469 and 1547. Restored in the 19th century
SULGRAVE MANOR, Northants. March–31 Dec., daily (not
Wed.), Closed Christmas. Adm. £3.00. Tel: 0295–
760205. Sixteenth-century manor house
SYON HOUSE, Brentford, Middx. 1 April–29 Sept., Wed.–
Sun. and Bank Holiday Mons. Also Sun. in Oct. PM. Adm.
charge. Tel: 081–560 0881. Built on the site of a former
monastery; magnificent Adam interior
TOWER OF LONDON. Daily, March–Oct. 9–6, Nov.–Feb.
9.30–5. Closed 1 Jan., Good Friday and 24–26 Dec.
(Jewel House closed all Jan.). Adm. charge. Tel: 071–709
0765. Royal palace and fortress begun by William the
Conqueror in 1078. Home of the Crown Jewels since the
reign of Henry III, and of the national collection of arms
and armour
*TRERICE, Cornwall. 1 April–31 Oct. daily (not Tues.).
Adm. £3.60. Tel: 0637–875404. Small Elizabethan
manor house
WARWICK CASTLE. Daily (not Christmas Day). Adm.
£6.75. Tel: 0926–408000. Fine medieval castle in
Capability Brown parkland
WILTON HOUSE, Wilts. 5 April–17 Oct. daily 11–6, Sun.
PM. Adm. £5.00. Tel: 0722–743115. Grey stone house
completed in 1653 on site of former Tudor house and
Saxon abbey
WINDSOR CASTLE, Berks. Daily (but State apartments
closed when The Queen is in residence). Adm. charge,
including the castle precincts. Tel: 0753–868286. Official
residence of The Queen and the oldest royal residence
still in regular use. State apartments, Queen Mary's
Dolls' House, Exhibition of The Queen's Presents and
Royal Carriages. Restoration work in progress on fire-
damaged state rooms (which may still be viewed). Also
ST GEORGE'S CHAPEL. Tel: 0753-865538. Adm. free.
Also ROYAL MAUSOLEUM, Frogmore Gardens. Tel:
0753-831118 for recorded information
WOBURN ABBEY, Beds. 29 March–31 Oct. daily. 1 Jan.–28
March, weekends only. Adm. £6.00. Tel: 0525–290666.
Built on site of a former Cistercian abbey; home of the
Dukes of Bedford since the 17th century. Important art
collection; deer park with wildlife

Museums and Galleries

Adm. admission; con. concessionary rate (prices are mostly those obtaining in 1993)

BARNARD CASTLE, Co. Durham – *The Bowes Museum.* European art from the late medieval period to 19th century. Fine porcelain and glass, tapestries and furniture. Music and costume galleries. English period rooms from Elizabeth I to Victoria; French decorative arts of 18th and 19th centuries; local antiquities. Temporary exhibitions. Open weekdays: May–Sept., 10–5.30, March, April, Oct., 10–5, Nov.–Feb., 10–4. Sun., 2–5 (summer); 2–4 (winter). Adm. charge

BATH – *Roman Baths Museum.* Roman baths complex of 1st century AD. Open daily, 9–6. Adm. (including adjoining 18th century Pump Room), £4.00, con. £1.90
Museum of Costume, Assembly Rooms. Fashion from 16th century to date. Adm. £2.50, con. £1.30
American Museum in Britain, Claverton Manor. American decorative arts from late 17th to mid 19th centuries. Open end March to end Oct., daily (not Mon.), 2–5, Bank Hol. Mons. and preceding Suns. 11–5. During winter only on application. Adm. charge
Victoria Art Gallery, Bridge Street. Open Mon.–Fri. 10–5.30, Sat. 10–5. Closed Sun., Bank Hols. Adm. free

BEAMISH – *The North of England Open Air Museum,* Beamish, Co. Durham. Re-creates northern life c.1900. Local buildings have been rebuilt and furnished, including the Town with houses, shops, etc., the Colliery Village, the Railway Station and Home Farm complete with agricultural machinery, animals and exhibitions. Open daily: 14 March–31 Oct., 10–6, 1 Nov.–13 March, 10–4 (not Mon. or Fri.). Check for Christmas opening

BEAULIEU – *National Motor Museum.* Displays of vehicles dating from 1895 to present. Open daily (not Christmas Day), 10–6 (winter, 10–5). Adm. charge

BELFAST – *Ulster Museum,* Botanic Gardens. Collections of Irish antiquities, natural and local history, fine and applied arts. Open Mon.–Fri. 10–5, Sat. 1–5, Sun. 2–5
Ulster Folk and Transport Museum, Holywood. Indoor and outdoor exhibits. Open Oct.–March, weekdays 9.30–4, weekends 12.30–4.30 (April–Sept. 9.30–5, Sat. 10.30–6, Sun. 12–6). July, Aug. 10.30–6, Sun. 12–6. Adm. £2.60, con. £1.30

BEVERLEY, N. Humberside. – *Museum of Army Transport.* Exhibits include field workshop, amphibious assault landing, railway section and aircraft. Open 10–5. Closed Christmas period. Adm. £2.50, con. £1.50

BIRMINGHAM – *City Museum and Art Gallery.* European art 14th to 20th centuries (particularly Pre-Raphaelites), sculpture, European gold, silver and jewellery, metalwork, glass, pottery and porcelain, furniture, textiles and costume, archaeology, local and natural history. Open Mon.–Sat. 9.30–5, Sun. 2–5. Closed Christmas Day, Boxing Day and New Year's Day. Adm. free
Museum of Science and Industry, Newhall Street. From the Industrial Revolution to the present; many working machines. Open Mon.–Sat. 9.30–5, Sun. 2–5. Adm. free
Also *Aston Hall, Blakesley Hall, Birmingham Nature Centre, Jewellery Quarter Discovery Centre, Sarehole Mill,* and *Weoley Castle*

BRADFORD – *Cartwright Hall Art Gallery,* Lister Park. British 19th and 20th century fine art
Bolling Hall, off Wakefield Road, a furnished period house, mainly 17th and 18th century

Industrial and Horses at Work Museum, Moorside Road, illustrates the local industries and transport in an old mill, with mill owner's and workers' houses and stables with shire horses
Cliffe Castle, Keighley. Natural history, minerals and folk life material, and period rooms
Manor House, Ilkley. Archaeology, local history and contemporary fine art. Open 10–5 (April–Sept. 10–6, except Industrial Museum). Closed Good Friday, Christmas Day, Boxing Day and Mon. (except Bank Hols.). Adm. free

BRIGHTON – *Museum and Art Gallery,* Church Street. Old master paintings; Willett pottery and porcelain collection, 20th century art and furniture, ethnography, archaeology, local history, musical instruments, costume gallery. Open Mon.–Sat. 10–5, Sun. 2–5. Closed Wed., Good Friday, 25, 26 Dec. and 1 Jan. Adm. free
Preston Manor, Preston Park. Thomas-Stanford/ Macquoid bequests of English period furniture, china and silver. Servants quarters. Open Tues.–Sat. and Bank Hol. Mon. 10–5, Sun. 2–5. Closed Mon., 25, 26 Dec. and Good Friday. Adm. charge
The Booth Museum of Natural History, Dyke Road. Open 10–5, Sun. 2–5. Closed Thurs., Good Friday, 25, 26 Dec. and 1 Jan. Adm. free

BRISTOL – *City Museum and Art Gallery,* Queen's Road. Collections include geology, natural history, archaeology, Egyptology, ethnography, applied art, fine art, and oriental art. Displays include Bristol ceramics and the Bristol school of artists, silver, Japanese and Chinese ceramics
Also *Red Lodge, Blaise Castle House Museum, Georgian House, Bristol Industrial Museum, Maritime Heritage Centre.* Adm. charges. Times vary, tel: 0272–223571

CAMBRIDGE – *Fitzwilliam Museum.* Egyptian, Greek, Near Eastern and Roman antiquities, coins and medals, medieval manuscripts, paintings and drawings, prints, sculpture, Oriental and Occidental fans, pottery and porcelain, textiles, arms and armour, medieval and renaissance objects of art, and a library. Open Tues.–Sat., Lower Galleries 10–2, Upper Galleries 2–5; Sun. 2.15–5. Closed 24 Dec.–1 Jan., Good Friday, Mon. incl. May Day Bank Hol. but not Easter and Bank Hol. Mons. Adm. free

CANTERBURY – *Royal Museum and Art Gallery,* and *Buffs Regimental Museum.* Military artefacts and pictures. Open Mon.–Sat. 10–5. Adm. free
Canterbury Heritage, a museum of the city's history in the medieval Poor Priest's Hospital, Stour Street. Open Mon.–Sat. 10.30–5, Sun. (June–Oct.) 1.30–5. Adm. £1.40, con. £1.00
Roman Museum. Open Mon.–Sat., 10.30–5, Sun. (June–Oct.) 1.30–5. Adm. £1.40, con. £1.00
West Gate Museum. Arms and armour and views of the city from the battlements. Open Mon.–Sat., 11–12.30 and 1.30–3.30. Adm. 60p, con. 40p

CARLISLE – *Tullie House Museum and Art Gallery,* Castle Street. Collections of archaeology, natural and social history, fine and decorative arts in Jacobean house with Victorian and modern extensions. Open Mon.–Sat. 10–5, Sun. 12–5
Guildhall Museum, Greenmarket. Civic and guild history and artefacts. Contact Tullie House Museum for information. Tel: 0228–34781

CHESTER – *Grosvenor Museum*, Grosvenor Street. Roman collections, silver gallery, natural history, art and folk-life. Open weekdays 10.30–5, Sun. 2–5
Chester Heritage Centre, St Michael's Church, Bridge Street Row. Displays Chester's history and architecture. Open weekdays 11–5, Sun. 12–5. Adm. charge
King Charles Tower, City Walls. Civil War displays
Water Tower, City Walls. Camera obscura. Open Mon.–Sat. 11–5, Sun. 12–5. Adm. charge
COLCHESTER – *Colchester Castle*. Local archaeological antiquities, especially from Roman Colchester. Tours of Roman vaults, castle walls, chapel and prisons. Open Mon.–Sat. 10–5, Sun. March–Nov., 2–5. Closed 24–26 Dec. Adm. £2.00, con. £1.00
Hollytrees Museum. 18th and 19th century costume, toys and social history. Open Tues.–Sat. 10–5. Closed Good Friday and Christmas period. Adm. free
Natural History Museum, All Saints Church. Open April–Oct.–Tues.–Sat., 10–5. Adm. free
Social History Museum, Holy Trinity Church. Domestic life and crafts. Open as Natural History Museum
Tymperleys Clock Museum. Open as Natural History Museum. Adm. free
COVENTRY – *Herbert Art Gallery and Museum*, Jordan Well. City's history exhibition, natural history gallery, fine and decorative art. Open weekdays 10–5.30, Sun. 2–5. Closed Christmas period
Museum of British Road Transport, St Agnes Lane, Hales Street. Open daily 10–5. Adm. £2.95, con. £1.95
Lunt Roman Fort, Baginton. Open Easter–mid-July, Sat.–Sun., 10–5, mid-July–end Sept., Wed.–Sun., 10–5. Adm. £2.50, con. £1.25
CRICH, nr. Matlock, Derbyshire – *National Tramway Museum*. Open-air working museum with tram-rides. Open April–Oct. weekends and Bank Hols. 10–6.30. May–Sept., open daily (not Fri. in May and Sept.) 10–5.30
DERBY – *Museum and Art Gallery*, The Strand. Archaeology, geology, military, natural history, paintings by Joseph Wright of Derby, Derby porcelain. Open Mon. 11–5, Tues.–Sat. 10–5, Sun. and Bank Hols. 2–5. Adm. free
Industrial Museum, Silk Mill, Full Street. Rolls-Royce collection of aero engines, a railway engineering gallery. Open as above. Adm. 30p, con. 10p
Pickford's House, Friargate. 18th and 19th century period room settings, social history, decorative arts, costume and textiles. Open as above. Adm. 30p, con. 10p
DORCHESTER – *Dorset County Museum*. Geology, archaeology, local and natural history and rural crafts of Dorset. Collection of Thomas Hardy's manuscripts, books, notebooks and drawings. Open Mon.–Sat. 10–5, closed 24, 25 Dec. Adm. £1.95, con. 95p
DURHAM – *Light Infantry Museum and Art Gallery*. Display of County regiment's 200-year history, arts and crafts exhibitions. Open weekdays (except Mon.) 10–5, Sun. and Bank Hol. Mon. 2–5. Closed Christmas Day and Boxing Day. Adm. 75p, con. 35p
Oriental Museum, Elvet Hill. Collections ranging from Ancient Egypt to China and Japan
Cathedral Treasury and Dormitory Museum. Relics of St Cuthbert, church plate, medieval seals, manuscripts and vestments. Open weekdays 10–4.30, Sun. 2–4.30. Adm. 80p, con. 20p
Old Fulling Mill Museum. Archaeological material from local excavations. Open Nov.–March, daily 12.30–3, April–Oct., daily 11–4. Adm. 50p, con. 25p
EDINBURGH – *City Art Centre*, 2 Market Street. Late 19th and 20th century art, mostly Scottish, and temporary

exhibitions. Open weekdays 10–5 (June–Sept. 10–6). Adm. free
People's Story, Canongate Tolbooth, Canongate. Courthouse and prison, now museum of Edinburgh life. Open weekdays 10–5 (June–Sept. 10–6). Adm. free
Huntly House, Canongate. Local history, collections of Edinburgh silver, glass and Scottish pottery. Open weekdays 10–5 (June–Sept. 10–6). Adm. free
Lady Stair's House, Lawnmarket. Mon.–Sat. 10–5 (June–Sept. 10–6)
Lauriston Castle, Cramond Road South. April–Oct. daily (except Fri.), 11–5; Nov.–March, weekends only
Museum of Childhood, High Street. Open weekdays 10–5 (June–Sept. 10–6). Adm. free
For *National Galleries of Scotland* and *National Museums of Scotland*, see Government Departments and Public Offices section
EXETER – *Exeter Maritime Museum*, The Haven. Collection of boats. Open daily, April–Sept., 10–5. Adm. charge
Royal Albert Memorial Museum and Art Gallery, Queen Street. Fine art, Exeter silver, ceramics, ethnography, natural and local history. Open Tues.–Sat. 10–5.30. Adm. free
Underground Passages, High Street. Medieval water supply
Connections Discovery Centre, Rougemont House. Hands-on centre for schools and groups
St Nicholas' Priory, The Mint. Norman priory
FORT WILLIAM – *West Highland Museum*, Cameron Square. Historical, natural history and folk exhibits, including those of the 1745 Rising. Daily (except Sun.) 10–5; July and Aug. 9.30–5.30, Sun 2–5. Closed lunchtime in winter
GLASGOW – *Art Gallery and Museum*, Kelvingrove. Old Masters, 19th century French paintings, archaeology and natural history, collection of armour
People's Palace, Glasgow Green. History of city from 1175 to present
The Burrell Collection, Pollok Country Park. Textiles, furniture, ceramics, stained glass, silver and paintings, especially 19th century
Pollok House, Pollok Country Park. Spanish paintings, furniture, silver, ceramics
Haggs Castle Museum, St Andrews Drive. Children's museum with activity workshops
Provand's Lordship, Castle Street. Oldest house in Glasgow, period furniture displays
Rutherglen Museum, King Street. History of former royal burgh of Rutherglen
Museum of Transport, Kelvin Hall
St Mungo Museum of Religious Life and Art, Castle Street
All open Mon.–Sat. 10–5, Sun. 11–5. Adm. free
Also *McLellan Galleries*, Sauchiehall Street. Major exhibition venue for large-scale temporary exhibitions. Adm. charge
HULL – *Ferens Art Gallery*. European art, especially Dutch 17th century, British portraits from 17th to 20th centuries, Humberside marine paintings, live art space and changing exhibitions
Wilberforce House. Jacobean merchant's house, birthplace of Wilberforce; slavery relics, period furniture, costume and ceramics
Streetlife. Museum of Transport; public service vehicles from the stage-coach to the last surviving Hull tram
Hull and East Riding Museum. Closed for two years from 8 Sept. 1993
Town Docks Museum. Whaling, fishing, trawling, ships and shipping

Old Grammar School. Hull's oldest secular building with story of Hull displays
Spurn Lightship, built 1927, restored 1986. Closed Mon. and Tues. in winter
All open Mon.–Sat. 10–5, Sun. 1.30–4.30
HUNTINGDON – *Cromwell Museum.* Remaining portion of the 12th century Hospital of St John; portraits of Cromwell, his family and parliamentary notables, and Cromwelliana. Open April–Oct., Tues.–Fri. 11–5, Sat, Sun. 11–4 (closed 1–2); Nov.–March, Tues.–Fri. 1–4, Sat. 11–1, 2–4, Sun. 2–4. Closed 1–2, Bank Hols. other than Good Friday. Adm. free
IPSWICH – *Ipswich Museum.* Suffolk geology, archaeology, natural history and ethnology. Temporary exhibitions. Open Tues.–Sat. 10–5
Christchurch Mansion. Tudor house containing furniture, Suffolk portraits, English porcelain, pottery and glass. Collections of paintings (local artists, Gainsborough, Constable). Victorian room displays
Wolsey Art Gallery, temporary exhibitions. Open Tues.–Sat. 10–5, Sun. and Bank Hol. Mons 2.30–4.30. Closed Good Friday, 24–26 Dec., 1 Jan. Adm. free
LEEDS – *City Art Gallery.* English watercolours. British and European painting, modern sculpture, Henry Moore gallery, Print Room. Open Tues.–Fri. 10–5.30, Sat. 9.30–4
Temple Newsam House. Tudor/Jacobean house, furnished in style of 17th and 18th centuries; silver, European porcelain and pottery, pictures, etc. Open daily (not Mon. except Bank Hols.) 10.30–6.15, Weds. (May–Sept.) 10.30–8.30. Adm. £1.00, con. 45p
Lotherton Hall, Gascoigne art and silver collection, oriental gallery, costume collection, 19th century furniture, ceramics; park and gardens. Open daily (not Mon. except Bank Hols.) 10.30–6.15, Thurs. (May–Sept.) 10.30–8.30. Adm. £1.00, con. 45p
Abbey House Museum. Folk museum including three full-sized streets. Open Mon.–Sat. 9.30–5. Sun. 2–5
City Museum. Geology, archaeology, ethnography and natural history
Also *Armley Mills Industrial Museum, Thwaite Mills*
LEICESTER – *Leicestershire Museum and Art Gallery*, New Walk. Natural history, geology, Egyptology, 15th–20th century European art, ceramics, silver
Newarke Houses, The Newarke. Social history of Leicestershire from 1485, musical instruments, local clocks, Gimson furniture collection
Jewry Wall Museum, St Nicholas Circle. Archaeology, Roman Jewry Wall and Baths, mosaics
Belgrave Hall, Church Road. Queen Anne house with furniture and garden
Museum of the Royal Leicestershire Regiment, Oxford Street
Museum of Technology, Corporation Road. Horse-drawn and motor vehicles, beam engines, motive power galleries, site narrow gauge railway
Wygston's House Museum of Costume, Applegate. Costume from 1789 to the present
All museums open weekdays 10–5.30, Sun. 2–5.30. Closed Christmas Day, Boxing Day and Good Friday.
Snibston Discovery Park, Ashby Road, Colville. Science and industry museum on site of historic coal mine. Open daily (except 25, 26 Dec.) 10–6. Adm. charge
LEWES – *Museum of Sussex Archaeology*, Barbican House, near Castle. Open weekdays, 10–5.30, Sun. 11–5.30. Adm. (including Castle and Lewes Living History Model) £2.80, con. £1.50
Museum of Local History, Anne of Cleves House, Southover. Local history and folk museum. Open April–

Oct., weekdays 10–5.30, Sun. 2–5.30. Adm. £1.60, con. 80p
LINCOLN – *Usher Gallery.* Watches, miniatures, porcelain, silver, etc., Peter de Wint collection of oils and watercolours, Lincolnshire topographical drawings, personalia associated with Tennyson family. Open weekdays 10–5.30, Sun. 2.30–5
City and County Museum, Broadgate. Geology and archaeology of Lincolnshire. Open Mon.–Fri. 10–5.30, Sun. 2.30–5
Museum of Lincolnshire Life. Covers the last 200 years; large agricultural collection. Open weekdays 10–5.30, Sun. 2–5.30
National Cycle Museum, Brayford Wharf. Vintage cycles. Open daily, except Christmas week, 10–5
Lincoln Castle, 11th century, features Victorian Silent System Prison Chapel, Magna Carta. Open daily
LIVERPOOL – For *National Museums and Galleries on Merseyside, see* Government Departments and Public Offices section
LONDON: GALLERIES – *Courtauld Institute Galleries*, Somerset House, Strand, WC2. The galleries of the University of London containing many collections of major works of art. Open weekdays 10–6, Sun. 2–6. Adm. £3.00, con. £1.50
Dulwich Picture Gallery, College Road, SE21. Built by Sir John Soane to house the Bourgeois collection. Open Tues.–Fri. 10–1, 2–5, Sat. 11–5, Sun. 2–5. Adm. £2.00, con. £1.00
Percival David Foundation of Chinese Art, 53 Gordon Square, WC1. Open Mon.–Fri. 10.30–5. Adm. free
The Queen's Gallery, Buckingham Palace, SW1. Changing selection of works of art from the royal collection. Open Tues.–Sat. and Bank Hols. 10–5, Sun. 2–5. Adm. charge
Ranger's House, Chesterfield Walk (Greenwich Park), SE10. The villa houses the Suffolk collection of English portraits and the Dolmetsch Collection of musical instruments. Open daily 1 Oct.–Maundy Thursday 10–4 (not 24, 25 Dec.), Good Friday–30 Sept. 10–6. Adm. free
Whitechapel Art Gallery, Whitechapel High Street, E1. Temporary exhibitions, mainly of modern art. Open Tues.–Sun. 11–5, Wed. 11–8. Adm. free for most exhibitions
For *National Gallery, National Portrait Gallery, Tate Gallery* and *Wallace Collection, see* Government Departments and Public Offices section
LONDON: MUSEUMS – *Bank of England Museum*, public entrance Bartholomew Lane, EC2. History of the Bank from 1694. Open Mon.–Fri. 10–5, Sun. and Bank Hols. (summer only) 11–5. Adm. free
Design Museum, Butlers Wharf, SE1. Illustrates development of design and mass-production of consumer objects. Open Mon.–Fri. 10.30–5.30, Sat.–Sun. 10.30–6.30. Adm. £3.50, con. £2.50
Geffrye Museum, Kingsland Road, E2. Series of English period rooms dating from 1600 to 1939 with decorative arts exhibits. Open Tues.–Sat. 10–5, Sun. and Bank Hols. 2–5. Adm. free
Horniman Museum and Gardens, London Road, SE23. Museum of ethnography, musical instruments, and natural history. Reference library (not Mon.). Free concerts and lectures (autumn and spring). Open Mon.–Sat. 10.30–5.30, Sun. 2–5.30 (not Christmas). Adm. free
Jewish Museum. Moves from Woburn House, Tavistock Square, WC1 to 129 Albert Street, NW1 in 1994, reopening June. Illustrates Jewish life, history and religion. Tues.–Thurs. 10–4; Fri., Sun. 10–1. Adm. £1. Closed public and Jewish holidays

London Transport Museum, Covent Garden, WC2.
Reopens Dec. 1993, daily 10–6. Adm. charge
MCC Museum, Lord's Ground, St John's Wood Road,
NW8. Open match days, Mon.–Sat. 10.30–5, Sun. 1–5.
Adm. £1.00, con. 50p. Conducted tours by appointment
with Tours Manager
Museum of the Moving Image, South Bank, SE1. The
history of the moving image in cinema and television.
Open daily 10–6 (not 24–26 Dec.). Adm. £5.50, con. £4/
4.70
The Royal Mews, Buckingham Palace, SW1. Open 5 Jan.–
23 March Wed. 12–4, 29 March–29 Sep. Tues.–Thurs.
12–4, 5 Oct.–21 Dec. Wed. 12–4. Adm. charge.
Information line: 071-799 2331
Sherlock Holmes Museum, 221B Baker Street, NW1. Open
daily 10–6. Adm. £5.00, con. £3.00
Sir John Soane's Museum, 13 Lincoln's Inn Fields, WC2.
Containing Sir John Soane's collections of art and
antiques. Open Tues.–Sat., first Tues. in month 6–
9. Adm. free. Tours must be booked in advance
Tower Bridge Walkway and Museum, SE1. Centenary
exhibition, panoramic high-level viewing gallery, original
Victorian steam machinery. Open daily from 10 (not
Christmas Eve). Adm. £3.50, con. £2.50
Wellington Museum, Apsley House, 149 Piccadilly, W1
(Hyde Park Corner). Known as 'No. 1 London', the home
of the 1st Duke of Wellington, housing paintings,
sculptures, services of porcelain and silver plate and
personal relics. Reopening June 1994. Adm. charge
Wimbledon Lawn Tennis Museum, Church Road, SW19.
Open Tues.–Sat. 10.30–5, Sun. 2–5. Adm. £2.00, con.
£1.00
For the *British Museum, Natural History Museum,
Museum of London, Science Museum, Victoria and Albert
Museum, Imperial War Museum, National Maritime
Museum, National Army Museum* and *RAF Museum, see*
Government Departments and Public Offices section
MANCHESTER – *City Art Galleries*, Mosley Street and
Princess Street. Old Masters, Turner, Pre-Raphaelites;
sculpture, furniture, porcelain, silver. Changing
exhibitions. Weekdays 10–5.45, Sun. 2–5.45
Whitworth Art Gallery, University of Manchester, Oxford
Road. Watercolours, drawings, prints, textiles and
wallpaper collections, 20th century British art. Mon.–Sat.
10–5 (Thurs. 10–9), closed Suns, Good Friday and
Christmas week. Adm. free
Museum of Science and Industry, Liverpool Road,
Castlefield. Working machinery and displays in world's
oldest passenger railway station. Open daily 10–5
Gallery of English Costume, Platt Hall, Platt Fields,
Rusholme. Exhibits from 16th century to present. Times
vary
Also *Heaton Hall*, Prestwich, *Wythenshawe Hall*,
Northenden. Times vary, tel: 061-236 5244
NEWCASTLE UPON TYNE – *Laing Art Gallery*, Higham
Place. Fine art from 17th century, pottery, glass, silver
and metalwork. Open Tues.–Fri. 10–5.30, Sat. 10–4.30,
Sun. 2.30–5.30
Castle Keep, St Nicholas Street. Oct.–March, Tues.–Sun.
9.30–4.30 (April–Sept. 9.30–5.30)
Trinity Maritime Centre and *Trinity House*, Broad Chare.
Centre open April–Oct., Mon.–Fri. 11–4, 16–30 Oct. 11–
2.30. Trinity House, April–Nov. (chapel and entrance
hall only) Tues.–Thurs. 2–4
Museum of Science and Engineering, West Blandford
Square. Tues.–Fri. 10–5.30, Sat. 10–4.30

Newburn Hall Motor Museum, Townfield Gardens.
Tues.–Sun. 10–6
NEWMARKET – *National Horseracing Museum*. Six galleries
of displays relating to horseracing, horses and people
connected with the sport. Sporting art galleries. Equine
Tours. Open April–Dec., Tues.–Sat. 10–5, Sun. 12–5.
Closed Mon. except Bank Hols, July, Aug. Adm. £2.50,
con. £1.50/75p
NORWICH – *Castle Museum*. Exhibits of art (including
Norwich school), archaeology, natural history, silver and
glass, Twining teapot gallery, battlement and dungeon
tours. Open Mon.–Sat., 10–5, Sun. 2–5
Strangers' Hall, Charing Cross. Medieval mansion with
period room settings from Tudor to Victorian times, toy
display and costumes. Open Mon.–Sat. 10–5
Bridewell Museum of Local Industries, Bridewell Alley.
Open Mon.–Sat. 10–5
St Peter Hungate Church Museum, Princes Street. 15th
century church used for display of church art and
antiquities. Brass rubbing centre. Open Mon.–Sat. 10–5
Royal Norfolk Regimental Museum, Market Avenue.
History of the regiment from 1685 to the present. Open
Mon.–Sat., 10–5, Sun. 2–5
NOTTINGHAM – *Castle Museum and Art Gallery*. Paintings
and drawings 17th–20th centuries. Selection of decorative
arts, interactive 'Story of Nottingham' exhibition, and
Sherwood Foresters' regimental collection. Conducted
tours of Mortimer's Hole caves
Industrial Museum, Wollaton Park. Lacemaking
machinery, steam engines, transport
Canal Museum, Canal Street. History of local canals and
river transport
Natural History Museum, Wollaton Hall. Tudor building
and park
Museum of Costumes and Textiles, Castlegate
Brewhouse Yard Museum, Castle Boulevard. Everyday life
from the 17th century to the present
Green's Mill and Science Centre, Sneinton. Working
windmill and interactive science centre
Also the *Lace Hall* and the *Robin Hood Centre*
OAKHAM – *Rutland County Museum*, Catmos Street.
Archaeology, local history, craft tools and agricultural
implements. Open Mon.–Sat. 10–5, Sun. (April–Oct.) 2–
5 (Nov.–March) 2–4
OXFORD – *Ashmolean Museum*, Beaumont Street. The
University's collections of European and Oriental fine
and applied arts, Classical and Near-Eastern archaeology
and numismatics. Open Tues.–Sat. 10–4, Sun. 2–4. Bank
Hol. Mons. 2–5. Adm. free
PLYMOUTH – *City Museum and Art Gallery*, Drake Circus.
Fine art including Reynolds' portraits, Plymouth
porcelain, archaeology, local and natural history. Tues.–
Sat. 10–5.30, Sun. 2–5. Also Bank Holiday Mons. Adm.
free
Elizabethan House, 32 New Street
Merchant's House, 33 St Andrew's Street. 16th century
The Dome, the Hoe. Maritime history museum
PORTSMOUTH – *City Museum*, Museum Road
Natural Science Museum and Butterfly House, Eastern
Parade
Southsea Castle and Museum, D-Day Museum, Clarence
Esplanade
All open daily 10.30–5.30, except 24–26 Dec. Adm.
charge
Charles Dickens' Birthplace Museum, Old Commercial
Road. Open 1 March–31 Oct., daily 10.30–5.30. Adm.
charge

Naval Heritage Area. Tells the story of the Royal Navy using Henry VIII's *Mary Rose*, HMS *Victory* and the ironclad HMS *Warrior* (1860)
Royal Naval Museum. Open daily (except Christmas Day). Adm. charge

ST ALBANS – *Museum of St Albans*, Hatfield Road. Story of St Albans since Roman times. Open weekdays 10–5, Sun. 2–5
Verulamium Museum, St Michael's. Iron Age and Roman Verulamium including wall plasters, jewellery, mosaics. Open weekdays 10–5.30, Sun. 2–5.30. Adm. £2.40, con. £1.40

SHEFFIELD – *City Museum*, Weston Park. Includes the Bateman collection of antiquities from Peak District, cutlery and old Sheffield plate, local geology and wildlife
Mappin Art Gallery, Weston Park. Paintings and sculpture of 18th–20th centuries (mainly British school) and contemporary works
Abbeydale Hamlet, Abbeydale Road South. A late 18th to early 19th century scythe and steel works with associated housing
Kelham Island Industrial Museum. Sheffield's industrial past
Shepherd Wheel, Whiteley Wood. Water-powered cutlery grinding establishment
Bishops' House, Meersbrook Park. Museum of local history in Tudor yeoman's house. Opening times vary. Tel: 0742–768588

STOKE-ON-TRENT – *City Museum and Art Gallery*, Bethesda Street, Hanley. Major ceramic collections. Open daily 10–5, Sun. 2–5
Chatterley Whitfield Mining Museum, Tunstall. Guided tours underground. Open March–Oct. 10–5; Nov.–Feb., Tues.–Sat. 11–4, Sun. 10–5
Gladstone Pottery Museum, Longton. A working Victorian pottery
Pottery factory tours are available Mon.–Fri., except during factory holidays, at the following: *Royal Doulton*, Nile Street, Burslem; *Spode*, Church Street, Stoke; *Beswick*, Gold Street, Longton; *Royal Grafton China*, Marlborough Road, Longton; *Coalport*, Park Street, Fenton, *Wedgwood's*, Barlaston; *Aynsley*, Uttoxeter Road, Longton

STRATFORD-UPON-AVON – *Shakespeare's Birthplace*. Period furniture, rare books, MSS and memorabilia; Shakespeare Centre nearby
Anne Hathaway's Cottage, Shottery. Home of Shakespeare's wife
Mary Arden's House, Wilmcote. Tudor farmhouse home of Shakespeare's mother
New Place, where Shakespeare died
Hall's Croft. Shakespeare's daughter's home
Grammar School attended by Shakespeare
Royal Shakespeare Theatre. Burnt down 1926, rebuilt 1932. *Swan Theatre*, opened in 1986

STYAL – *Quarry Bank Mill*, Cheshire. History of the cotton industry, weaving demonstrations at water-powered cotton mill. Restored Apprentice House. Open all year. Closed Mon., Oct.–March. Open Bank Hols. Adm. charge

WINCHESTER – *City Museum*. Weekdays 10–5, Sun. 2–5 (closed Mon. in winter)
Cathedral Library and *Triforium Gallery*. Illuminated manuscripts, sculpture, wood- and metalwork from 12th to 19th centuries. Times vary. Closed Mon. morning and Suns. Adm. charge

WORCESTER – *City Museum and Art Gallery*. Natural history of Worcestershire, changing art exhibitions; also

military museum. Open Mon.–Wed., Fri. 9.30–6, Sat. 9.30–5
The Commandery, Sidbury. Civil War centre. Weekdays 10.30–5, Sun. 1.30–5.30
Tudor House Museum, Friar Street. Local history. Mon.–Wed., Fri., Sat. 10.30–5
Dyson Perrins Museum and Royal Worcester Porcelain Works, Severn Street. Mon.–Fri. 9.30–5, Sat. 10–5

YORK – *Castle Museum*. Everyday life of the last three centuries. Open weekdays 9.30–5.30, Sun. 10–5.30 (closes 6.30 April–Oct., 4.45 Nov.–March). Adm. £3.80, con. £2.70
Jorvik Viking Centre, Coppergate. Reconstruction of Viking York. Open daily. Adm. £3.80, con. £1.90
Yorkshire Museum and Gardens, Museum Street, Roman Life gallery, archaeology, decorative arts, geology, natural history. Open weekdays 10–5, Sun. 1–5. Adm. £2.50, con. £1.25, family ticket £6.00. Gardens, Roman, Anglian and medieval ruins. Open weekdays 7.30–dusk (summer 7.30–8), Sun. 10–dusk
Art Gallery, Exhibition Square. European paintings, 14th to 20th century; watercolours and prints of Yorkshire; modern English stoneware pottery. Open weekdays 10–5, Sun. 2.30–5. Adm. free
Treasurer's House, Chapter House Street. Open 26 March–30 Oct. 10.30–5. Adm. £3.00, con. £1.50

Sights of London

ALEXANDRA PALACE AND PARK, Wood Green, London N22 4AY. The Victorian Palace was severely damaged by fire in 1980 but has been restored and was reopened in January 1988. Alexandra Palace provides modern facilities for exhibitions, sports, conferences and leisure activities. There is an ice rink, open daily.

BARBICAN CENTRE, Silk Street, London EC2Y 8DS. Owned, funded and managed by the Corporation of London, the Barbican Centre was opened in 1982 and is the largest complex of its kind in western Europe. It houses the 1,166 seat Barbican Theatre, the London base of the Royal Shakespeare Company, along with a 200 seat studio theatre (The Pit), and the 2,026 seat Barbican Hall, the home of the London Symphony Orchestra. There are also three cinemas, an art gallery, a sculpture court, a lending library, trade exhibition and conference facilities, and bars and restaurants.

BLACKHEATH, London SE10. Morden College, founded in 1695 as a home for 'decayed Turkey merchants', is near the south-east corner of the parkland. The building was designed by Wren and its chapel doors have carvings attributed to Grinling Gibbons. Not open to the public. Concerts and poetry recitals are held at Rangers House.

BRIDGES. The bridges over the Thames (from east to west) are:

The Queen Elizabeth II Bridge, opened 1991, from Dartford to Thurrock
Tower Bridge, opened 1894 (*see also* page 595)
London Bridge, opened after rebuilding by Rennie, 1831; the new London Bridge completed and opened 1973
Southwark Bridge (Rennie), opened 1819; rebuilt 1922
Blackfriars Bridge, opened 1769; rebuilt 1869; widened 1909
Waterloo Bridge (Rennie), opened 1817; rebuilt 1944
Hungerford Bridge (railway bridge with footbridge), opened 1863
Westminster Bridge (width 84 ft), built 1750; rebuilt 1862
Lambeth Bridge, built 1862; rebuilt 1932
Vauxhall Bridge, built 1811–16; rebuilt 1906
Chelsea Bridge, built and widened 1937
Albert Bridge, built 1873
Battersea Bridge, opened 1890
Wandsworth Bridge, opened 1873; rebuilt 1940
Putney Bridge, built 1729; rebuilt 1884; widened 1933; starting point of Oxford and Cambridge Boat Race
Hammersmith Bridge, rebuilt 1887
Barnes Bridge (pedestrian bridge), opened 1933
Chiswick Bridge, opened 1933
King Edward VII Bridge, Kew, rebuilt 1902, opened 1903
Twickenham Lock Bridge
Twickenham Bridge, opened 1933
Richmond Bridge, opened 1777
Kingston Bridge, built 1828; widened 1914
Hampton Court Bridge, rebuilt 1933

BUCKINGHAM PALACE, London SWIA IAA. Purchased by King George III in 1762 from the heir of the Duke of Buckingham, the Palace has been the London home of the Sovereign since Queen Victoria's accession in 1837. It was altered by Nash for King George IV, and refronted in stone by Sir Aston Webb in 1913.

CATHOLIC CENTRAL LIBRARY, St Francis Friary, 47 Francis Street, London SWIP IQR. Founded as a private library in 1914, it was taken over in 1959 by the Franciscan Friars of the Atonement. It is a lending and research library of over 55,000 volumes and 150 periodicals, for the general reader, student and ecumenist. Books are sent by post when required. Open Mon.-Fri. 10–5, Sat. 10–1.30.

CEMETERIES. *Kensal Green Cemetery*, London W10 (70 acres), tombs of Thackeray, Trollope, Sydney Smith, Wilkie Collins, Tom Hood, George Cruikshank, Leigh Hunt, I. K. Brunel and Charles Kemble. *Highgate Cemetery*, London N6, tombs of George Eliot, Herbert Spencer, Faraday and Marx. Guided tours only, £2. *Abney Park Cemetery*, Stoke Newington, London N16, tomb of General Booth, founder of the Salvation Army, and memorials to many Nonconformist divines. *South Metropolitan Cemetery*, Norwood, London SE27, tombs of Sir Henry Bessemer, Sir Hiram Maxim, Mrs Beeton, Sir Henry Tate and Joseph Whitaker (*Whitaker's Almanack*). Churchyard of the former *Marylebone Chapel*, Charles Wesley and his son Samuel Wesley (musician) buried; chapel demolished in 1949. Crematoria. *Ilford* (City of London); *Norwood*; *Hendon*; *Streatham Park*; *Finchley* (St Marylebone) and *Golders Green* (12 acres), with 'Garden of Rest' and memorials to famous men and women.

CENOTAPH, Whitehall, London SWI (Literally 'empty tomb'.) Monument erected 'To the Glorious Dead', as a memorial to all ranks of the sea, land and air forces who gave their lives in the service of the Empire during the First World War. Designed by Sir Edwin Lutyens. Erected as a temporary memorial in 1919 and replaced by a permanent structure unveiled by George V on Armistice Day 1920. An additional inscription was made after the Second World War to commemorate those who gave their lives in that conflict.

CHARTERHOUSE, Sutton's Hospital, Charterhouse Square, London ECIM 6AN. A Carthusian monastery from 1371 to 1537, when it came into the possession of Sir Edward (later first Lord) North, who sold it in 1565 to the fourth Duke of Norfolk. After Norfolk's execution in 1572 following the Ridolfi Plot (hatched at Charterhouse), it was granted by Queen Elizabeth I in 1587 to Norfolk's second son, Thomas Howard, later Earl of Suffolk. In 1611 he sold it to Thomas Sutton, who endowed it as a hospital for aged men 'of gentle birth' and a school for poor scholars (removed to Godalming in 1872). The buildings are partly 15th but mainly 16th and 17th century. Parts of the building were damaged by bombing in 1941 but have been largely restored and now accommodate some 40 pensioners. Roger Williams, founder and governor of Rhode Island, was a scholar of the foundation. Among other famous pupils were John Wesley, Lord Baden-Powell, the poets and writers Crashaw, Lovelace and Thackeray. Visitors are shown round on Wednesdays at 2.15 (April–July). Admission £2.00.

Master, E. E. Harrison, FSA; *Registrar and Clerk to the Governors*, Lt.-Col. I. Macdonald.

CHELSEA PHYSIC GARDEN, 66 Royal Hospital Road, London SW3 4HS. A garden of general botanical research, maintaining a wide range of rare and unusual plants. The garden was established in 1673 by the Society of Apothecaries. Open Wed. and Sun. p.m. during summer months. All enquiries to the Curator.

CITY BUSINESS LIBRARY (Corporation of London), 1 Brewers Hall Garden, London EC2V 5BX. Open Mon.-Fri. 9.30-5.00. Public information, tel: 071-638 8215.

COLLEGE OF ARMS OR HERALDS' COLLEGE, Queen Victoria Street, London EC4V 4BT. The Sovereign's Officers of Arms (Kings, Heralds and Pursuivants of Arms) were first incorporated by Richard III, and granted Derby House (on the site of the present College building) by Philip and Mary. The building now in use dates from 1671–88. The powers vested by the Crown in the Earl Marshal (The Duke of Norfolk) with regard to state ceremonial are largely exercised through the College, which is also the official repository of English pedigrees and all Arms granted to subjects of The Queen, except in Scotland and (since 1988) Canada. Enquiry may be made to the officer on duty in the Public Office, Mon.-Fri. 10–4.

COMMONWEALTH INSTITUTE, Kensington High Street, London W8 6NQ. A cultural and educational centre promoting knowledge and understanding of the Commonwealth through permanent exhibitions on the Commonwealth countries, and diverse cultural and educational programmes. Facilities include the resource centre, conference and events centre. (*See also* page 334). The Institute opened its first regional centre, the Northern Regional Centre in Saltaire, Bradford, in September 1991. Open Mon.-Sat. 10–5, Sun. 2–5. Admission £1.00, concessions 50p. Closed 24–26 Dec., 1 Jan., Good Friday and May Day.

DOWNING STREET, London SW1. Number 10 Downing Street is the official town residence of the Prime Minister, No. 11 is the Chancellor of the Exchequer and No. 12 is the office of the Government Whips. The street was named after Sir George Downing, Bt., soldier and diplomatist, who was MP for Morpeth from 1660 to 1684. *Chequers*, a Tudor mansion in the Chilterns, about three miles from Princes Risborough, was presented by Lord and Lady Lee of Fareham in 1917 to serve, from 1 January 1921, as a country residence for the Prime Minister of the day. The mansion contains a famous collection of Cromwellian portraits and relics.

ELTHAM, London SE9. Contains remains of 13th- to 15th-century Eltham Palace, the birthplace of John of Eltham (1316), son of Edward II. The hall, built by Edward IV, has a hammer-beam roof of chestnut. In the churchyard of St John the Baptist is the tomb of Thomas Doggett, the comedian and founder of the Thames Watermen's championship (Doggett's Coat and Badge).

GEORGE INN, Borough High Street, London SE1. The last galleried inn in London, built in 1677. Now run as ordinary public house.

GREENWICH, London SE10. Greenwich Hospital (since 1873, the Royal Naval College) was built by Charles II, largely from designs by John Webb, and by Queen Anne and William III, from designs by Wren. It stands on the site of an ancient royal palace, and of the more recent Palace of Placentia, an enlarged edition of the palace, constructed by Humphrey, Duke of Gloucester (1391–1447), son of Henry IV. Henry VIII, Mary I and Elizabeth I were born in the royal palace (which reverted to the Crown in 1447) and Edward VI died there. In the principal quadrangle is a marble statue of George II by Rysbraeck. (For National Maritime Museum, *see* Index.) *Greenwich Park* (196½ acres) was enclosed by Humphrey, Duke of Gloucester, and laid out by Charles II, from the designs of Le Nôtre. On a hill in Greenwich Park is the former Royal Observatory (founded 1675). Part of its buildings at Greenwich have been taken over by the Maritime Museum and named Flamsteed House, after John Flamsteed (1646–1719), the first Astronomer Royal. *Charlton House* was built in the early 17th century (1607–12) for Adam Newton, tutor to Prince Henry, brother to Charles I. It is largely in the Jacobean style of architecture. *Cutty Sark*, the last of the famous tea clippers, which has been preserved as a memorial to ships and men of a past era, is fully restored and re-rigged, with a museum of sail

on board. Open weekdays 11–5 (summer 11–6), Sundays and Boxing Day 2.30–5. The yacht *Gipsy Moth IV* in which Sir Francis Chichester sailed single-handed round the world 1966–7, is preserved alongside the *Cutty Sark*.

GUILDHALL, Gresham Street, London EC2. Centre of civic government for the City for more than a thousand years. Built c.1440; façade built 1788–9; damaged in the Great Fire, 1666, and by incendiary bombs, 1940. The main hall and crypt have been restored. Events in Guildhall include the annual election of Lord Mayor, election of Sheriffs, receptions in honour of sovereigns and heads of state, and the meetings of the Court of Common Council. Open weekdays and Sun. (May to Sept.) 10–5. Admission free. *Keeper of the Guildhall*, J. H. Lucioni.

The *Guildhall Library* (reference) and the Library and Museum of the Clockmakers' Company are housed in new premises. Library open Mon.-Sat. 9.30–5, Museum open Mon.-Fri. 9.30–4.45. Admission free (entrance in Aldermanbury). The Library contains plans of London, 1570; Deed of Sale with Shakespeare's signature; first, second and fourth folios of Shakespeare's plays, etc.

HONOURABLE ARTILLERY COMPANY'S HEADQUARTERS, City Road, London EC1Y 2BQ. The HAC received its charter of incorporation from Henry VIII in 1537, and has occupied its present ground since 1641. The Armoury House dates from 1735. The castellated barracks date from 1860. The HAC is the senior regiment of the Territorial Army Volunteer Reserves, and maintains a headquarters, four squadrons and a gun troop. It also provides the Company of Pikemen and Musketeers, the Light Cavalry Troop and a detachment of Metropolitan Special Constabulary. *Chief Executive*, Brig. M. R. N. Bray, CBE.

HORSE GUARDS, Whitehall, London SW1. Archway and offices built about 1753. The mounting of the guard at 11 a.m. (10 a.m. on Sundays) and the dismounted inspection at 4 p.m. are picturesque ceremonies. Only those on the Lord Chamberlain's list may drive through the gates and archway into *Horse Guards' Parade* (230,000 sq. ft), where the Colour is 'trooped' on The Queen's Official Birthday.

THE HOUSES OF PARLIAMENT, Westminster, London SW1. The royal palace of Westminster, originally built by Edward the Confessor (Westminster Hall (*q.v.*) being added by William Rufus), was the normal meeting place of Parliament from about 1340. St Stephen's Chapel was used from about 1550 for the meetings of the House of Commons, which had previously been held in the Chapter House or Refectory of Westminster Abbey. The House of Lords met in an apartment of the royal palace. The fire of 1834 destroyed much of the palace and the present Houses of Parliament were erected on the site from the designs of Sir Charles Barry and Augustus Welby Pugin between 1840 and 1867. The Chamber of the House of Commons was destroyed by bombing in 1941 and a new Chamber designed by Sir Giles Gilbert Scott was used for the first time on 26 October 1950.

The Victoria Tower of the House of Lords is about 330 ft high, and when Parliament is sitting the Union Flag flies by day from its flagstaff. *The Clock Tower* of the House of Commons is about 320 ft high and contains 'Big Ben', the hour bell said to be named after Sir Benjamin Hall, First Commissioner of Works when the original bell was cast in 1856. This bell, which weighed 16 tons 11 cwt, was found to be cracked in 1857. The present bell (13½ tons) is a recasting of the original and was first brought into use in July 1859. The dials of the clock are 23 ft in diameter, the hands being 9 ft and 14 ft long (including balance piece). A light is displayed from the Clock Tower at night when Parliament is sitting.

For security reasons tours of the Houses of Parliament are available only to those who have made advance arrangements through a Member or Peer.

Admission to the Strangers' Gallery of the House of Lords is arranged by a Peer or by queue via St Stephen's Entrance. Admission to the Strangers' Gallery of the House of Commons is by Members' order (Members' orders should be sought several weeks in advance), or by queue via St Stephen's Entrance. Queues are usually shorter after 6 p.m., Mon.–Thurs. Overseas visitors may obtain cards of introduction from their Embassy or High Commission.

INNS OF COURT. The *Inner* and *Middle Temple*, Fleet Street/Victoria Embankment, London EC4, have occupied since the early 14th century the site of the buildings of the Order of Knights Templars. *Inner Temple Hall* is open Mon.–Fri. 10.30–11.30 and 3–4 on application to Treasurer's Office during law sittings. *Middle Temple Hall* (1562–70) is open when not in use, Mon.–Fri. 10–12 and 3–4; closed on public holidays. In Middle Temple Gardens (not open to the public) Shakespeare (Henry VI, Part I) places the incident which led to the 'Wars of the Roses' (1455–85).

Temple Church, London EC4, has a nave which forms one of five remaining round churches in England (the others being at Cambridge, Northampton, Little Maplestead (Essex) and Ludlow Castle). Open weekdays 10–4. Services: 8.30 and 11.15 a.m. except in August and September. *Master of the Temple*, Revd Canon J. Robinson.

Lincoln's Inn, Chancery Lane/Lincoln's Inn Fields, London WC2, occupies the site of the palace of a former Bishop of Chichester and of a Black Friars monastery. Records show the Society as being in existence in 1422. The Hall and Library Buildings are of 1845, although the Library is first mentioned in 1474; the old Hall (early 16th century) and the Chapel were rebuilt c.1619–23. Halls open by appointment, Chapel and Gardens, Mon.–Fri. 12–2.30. Chapel services Sunday 11.30 a.m. during law terms.

Lincoln's Inn Fields (7 acres). The Square was laid out by Inigo Jones.

Gray's Inn, Holborn/Gray's Inn Road, London WC1. Early 14th century. Hall 1556–8. Chapel services 11.15 a.m. (during law dining terms only). Holy Communion first Sunday in every month except Aug.–Sept. Gardens open to the public at certain times. Tel: 071-405 8164

No other 'Inns' are active, but what remains of *Staple Inn* is worth visiting as a relic of Elizabethan London; it retains a picturesque gabled front on Holborn (opposite Gray's Inn Road). *Clement's Inn* (near St Clement Danes Church), *Clifford's Inn*, Fleet Street, and *Thavies Inn*, Holborn Circus, are all rebuilt. *Serjeants' Inn*, Fleet Street and another (demolished 1910) of the same name in Chancery Lane, were composed of Serjeants-at-Law, the last of whom died in 1922.

KEW, Surrey. A favourite home of the early Hanoverian monarchs. Kew House, the residence of Frederick, Prince of Wales, and later of his son, George III, was pulled down in 1803, but the earlier Dutch House, now known as Kew Palace, survives. The famous Kew Gardens (*see* Index) were originally laid out as a private garden for Kew House for George III's mother in 1759 and were much enlarged in the 19th century, notably by the inclusion of the grounds of the former Richmond Lodge.

LAMBETH PALACE, London SE1. The official residence of the Archbishop of Canterbury; the oldest part is 13th century, the house itself being early 19th century. For leave to visit the historical portions, applications should be made by letter to the Archbishop's Chaplain.

LLOYD'S, Lime Street, London EC3M 7HA. Society of private underwriters which evolved during the 18th century from

Lloyds Coffee House. Housed in the Royal Exchange for 150 years and in Leadenhall Street and Lime Street from 1928 to 1986. The present building was opened for business in May 1986, and houses the Lutine Bell. Underwriting is on four floors with a total area of 114,000 sq. ft. A visitors' gallery is open Mon.–Fri. for pre-booked groups.

LONDON PLANETARIUM, Marylebone Road, London NW1 5LR. Open daily (except Christmas Day), star show and Space Trail 12.20–4.40. Admission charge.

LORD'S CRICKET GROUND, St John's Wood Road, London NW8 8QN. The headquarters since 1814 of the Marylebone Cricket Club, the premier cricket club in England (founded 1787), Lord's is the scene of some of the principal matches of the season and Middlesex County headquarters.

MADAME TUSSAUD'S, Marylebone Road, London NW1 5LR. Waxwork exhibition. Open daily (except Christmas Day) 10–5.30. Admission charge.

MANSION HOUSE, London EC4. Built 1739–53, reconstructed 1930–1. The official residence of the Lord Mayor; the Egyptian Hall and Ballroom are the chief attractions. Group visits only by arrangement with the Principal's Assistant.

MARKETS. The London markets (administered by the Corporation of the City of London) provide foodstuffs for 8–9 million people. *Central Meat, Fish, Fruit, Vegetable, and Poultry Markets, Smithfield* (built 1866) the site of St Bartholomew's Fair from 9th to 19th century; *Leadenhall Market* (meat and poultry), built 1881, part recently demolished; *Billingsgate* (fish), Thames Street, built 1875, part recently demolished, a market site for over 1,000 years (moved to the Isle of Dogs, January 1982); *Spitalfields*, E1 (vegetables, fruit, etc.), enlarged 1928 (moved to Leyton, May 1991); *London Fruit Exchange*, Brushfield Street, built by Corporation of London 1928–9; *Covent Garden* (vegetables, fruit, flowers, etc.), (now moved to Nine Elms) established in 1661 under a charter of Charles II; *Borough Market*, SE1 (vegetables, fruit, flowers, etc.).

MARLBOROUGH HOUSE, Pall Mall, London SW1A 2AF. Built by Wren for the first Duke of Marlborough and completed in 1711, the house reverted to the Crown in 1835. Prince Leopold lived there until 1831, and Queen Adelaide from 1837 until her death in 1849. In 1863 it became the London house of the Prince of Wales and was the London home of Queen Mary until her death in 1953. The Queen's Chapel, Marlborough Gate, begun in 1623 from the designs of Inigo Jones for the Infanta Maria of Spain, and completed for Queen Henrietta Maria, is open to the public for services on Sundays at 8.30 a.m. and 11.15 a.m. between Easter Day and end July (*see* St James's Palace for winter services in The Chapel Royal). In 1959 Marlborough House was given by The Queen as a centre for Commonwealth government conferences and it was opened as such in 1962.

LONDON MONUMENT (commonly called The Monument), Monument Street, London EC3. Built from designs of Wren, 1671–7, to commemorate the Great Fire of London, which broke out in Pudding Lane on 2 September 1666. The fluted Doric column is 120 ft high; the moulded cylinder above the balcony supporting a flaming vase of gilt bronze is an additional 42 ft; and the column is based on a square plinth 40 ft high (with fine carvings on the west face) making a total height of 202 ft. Splendid views of London from gallery at top of column (311 steps). As total refurbishment planned for 1993 onwards, check with Town Clerk's office for access. Tel: 071-606 3030.

MONUMENTS (sculptor's name in parenthesis). *Albert Memorial*, South Kensington; *Royal Air Force*, Victoria Embankment; *Viscount Alanbrooke*, Whitehall; *Beaconsfield*, Parliament Square; *Beatty, Jellicoe* and *Cunningham*,

Trafalgar Square; *Belgian Gratitude* (Blomfield), Victoria Embankment; *Boadicea* (or Boudicca), Queen of the Iceni (Thornycroft), Westminster Bridge; *Brunel* (Marochetti), Victoria Embankment; *Burghers of Calais* (Rodin), Victoria Tower Gardens, Westminster; *Burns*, Embankment Gardens; *Carlyle* (Boehm), Cheyne Walk, Chelsea; *Cavalry*, Hyde Park; *Edith Cavell* (Frampton), St Martin's Place; *Cenotaph* (Lutyens), Whitehall; *Charles I*, Trafalgar Square; *Charles II*, inside the Royal Exchange; *Churchill*, Parliament Square; *Cleopatra's Needle* (68½ ft high, c.1500 BC, erected on the Thames Embankment in 1877-8; the Sphinxes are Victorian; *Clive*, Whitehall; *Captain Cook* (Brock), The Mall; *Crimean*, Broad Sanctuary; *Oliver Cromwell* (Thornycroft), outside Westminster Hall; *Gen. Charles de Gaulle*, Carlton Gardens; *Lord Dowding* (Faith Winter), Strand; *Duke of Cambridge*, Whitehall; *Duke of York* (124 ft), Carlton House Terrace; *Edward VII* (Mackennal), Waterloo Place; *Elizabeth I* (1586, oldest outdoor statue in London; from Ludgate), Fleet Street; *Eros* (Shaftesbury Memorial) (Gilbert), Piccadilly Circus; *Marechal Foch*, Grosvenor Gardens; *Charles James Fox*, Bloomsbury Square; *George III*, Cockspur Street; *George IV* (Chantrey), riding without stirrups, Trafalgar Square; *George V*, Old Palace Yard; *George VI*, Carlton Gardens; *Gladstone*, Strand; *Guards'* (Crimea), Waterloo Place; (Great War), Horse Guards' Parade; *Haig* (Hardiman), Whitehall; *Sir Arthur (Bomber) Harris* (Faith Winter), Strand; *Irving* (Brock), north side of National Portrait Gallery; *James II*, Trafalgar Square; *Samuel Johnson*, opposite St Clement Danes; *Kitchener*, Horse Guards' Parade; *Abraham Lincoln*, Parliament Square; *Milton*, St Giles, Cripplegate; *The Monument* (see above); *Mountbatten*, Foreign Office Green; *Nelson* (170 ft 2 in), Trafalgar Square, with Landseer's lions (cast from guns recovered from the wreck of the *Royal George*); *Florence Nightingale*, Waterloo Place; *Palmerston*, Parliament Square; *Peel*, Parliament Square; *Pitt* (Chantrey), Hanover Square; *Portal*, Embankment Gardens; *Prince Consort*, Holborn Circus; *Queen Elizabeth Gate*, Hyde Park Corner; *Raleigh*, Whitehall; *Richard Coeur de Lion* (Marochetti), Old Palace Yard; *Roberts*, Horse Guards' Parade; *Franklin D. Roosevelt* (Dick), Grosvenor Square; *Royal Artillery* (South Africa), The Mall; (Great War), Hyde Park Corner; *Captain Scott* (Lady Scott), Waterloo Place; *Shackleton*, Kensington Gore; *Shakespeare*, Leicester Square; *Smuts* (Epstein), Parliament Square; *Sullivan*, Victoria Embankment; *Trenchard*, Victoria Embankment; *Victoria Memorial*, in front of Buckingham Palace; *George Washington* (Houdon copy), Trafalgar Square; *Wellington*, Hyde Park Corner; *Wellington* (Chantrey) riding without stirrups, Royal Exchange; *John Wesley*, City Road; *William III*, St James's Square; *Wolseley*, Horse Guards' Parade.

PORT OF LONDON. The Port of London covers the tidal portion of the River Thames from Teddington to the seaward limit (Tongue light vessel), a distance of 150 km. The governing body is the Port of London Authority (PLA). Eighty-eight per cent of the total port traffic is handled at riverside berths between Vauxhall and Canvey Island, the rest at the enclosed dock at Tilbury, 40 km below London Bridge. The docks perform every type of cargo-handling operation. Tilbury is principally used by vessels to and from Australia, the Americas, India, Middle and Far East, Scandinavia, Russia and continental Europe. Passenger vessels and cruise liners can be handled at moorings at Greenwich, Tower Bridge and Tilbury. The latter provides accommodation for liners at all states of the tide.

ROMAN REMAINS. Sections of the city wall are the most striking remains to be seen of Roman *Londinium*, although even these are largely medieval because of the Roman wall being rebuilt during the medieval period. Sections may be seen near the White Tower in the Tower of London; at Tower Hill; at Coopers' Row; at All Hallows, London Wall, its vestry being built on the remains of a semi-circular Roman bastion; at St Alphage, London Wall, showing a striking succession of building repairs from the Roman until the late medieval period, and at St Giles, Cripplegate. Excavations in the Cripplegate area have revealed that a Roman fort was built there c.AD 100-120. It was later incorporated into the city wall when this was built c.AD 200.

The administrative centre of the Roman city was the great forum and basilica, more than 165 metres square, sections of which have been encountered during excavations in the area of Leadenhall, Gracechurch Street and Lombard Street. Excavations during the past few years have revealed Roman activity along the river. Traces of a massive riverside wall, built in the late Roman period, have been found and a succession of Roman timber quays have been excavated along Lower and Upper Thames Street, helping to prove that Roman London was a thriving commercial centre.

Other major buildings found are the Provincial Governor's Palace in Cannon Street; remains of a bath-building, preserved in Lower Thames Street; and the Temple of Mithras in Walbrook. The fine sculptures from this temple are displayed in the Museum of London (*see* Index) where many other relics from the Roman city may be seen.

ROYAL ALBERT HALL, Kensington Gore, London SW7 2AP. The elliptical hall, one of the largest in the world, was completed in 1871, and since 1941 has been the venue each summer for the Promenade Concerts founded in 1895 by Sir Henry Wood. Other events include pop and classical music concerts, dance, opera, sporting events, conferences and banquets. *Chief Executive*, P. Deuchar.

ROYAL EXCHANGE, London EC3V 3LS. Founded by Sir Thomas Gresham, 1569, opened as 'The Bourse' and proclaimed 'The Royal Exchange' by Queen Elizabeth I, 1571, rebuilt 1667-9 and 1842-4. It was enlarged and reopened by The Queen in 1991. The building houses the corporate head office of the Guardian Royal Exchange Assurance and is administered by the Gresham Committee. *Clerk*, Mercers' Hall, Ironmonger Lane, London EC2V 8HE.

ROYAL GEOGRAPHICAL SOCIETY, Kensington Gore, London SW7 2AR. Map room open to public, admission free. Advice for scientific expeditions abroad by appointment only.

ROYAL HOSPITAL, CHELSEA, Royal Hospital Road, London SW3 4SL. Founded by Charles II in 1682, and built by Wren; opened in 1692 for old and disabled soldiers. Open Mon.-Sat. 10-12, daily 2-4. The extensive grounds include the former Ranelagh Gardens, and are the venue for the Chelsea Flower Show held each May by the Royal Horticultural Society. *Governor*, General Sir Brian Kenny, GCB, CBE; *Lt.-Governor and Secretary*, Maj.-Gen. F. G. Sugden, CB, CBE.

ROYAL OPERA HOUSE, Covent Garden, London WC2E 9DD. Home of The Royal Ballet (1931) and The Royal Opera (1946). The Royal Opera House is the third theatre to be built on the site, opening 1858; the first was opened 7 December 1732. The season of the resident companies runs mid September to August. *General Director*, J. Isaacs.

ST JAMES'S PALACE, Pall Mall, London SW1. Built by Henry VIII; the Gatehouse and Presence Chamber remain; later alterations were made by Wren and Kent. The Chapel

Royal is open for services on Sundays at 8.30 a.m. and 11.15 a.m. between the beginning of October and Good Friday (see Marlborough House for summer services in The Queen's Chapel). Representatives of Foreign Powers are still accredited 'to the Court of St James's'. *Clarence House* (1825) in the palace precinct is the home of The Queen Mother.

ST PAUL'S CATHEDRAL, London EC4M 8AD. Built 1675–1710, cost £747,660. The cross on the dome is 365 ft above the ground level, the inner cupola 218 ft above the floor. 'Great Paul' in the south-west tower weighs nearly 17 tons. Organ by Father Smith (enlarged by Willis and rebuilt by Mander) in a case carved by Grinling Gibbons, who also carved the choir stalls. The choir and high altar were restored in 1958 after war damage and the north transept in 1962. The American War Memorial Chapel was consecrated in 1958. The chapel of the Order of the British Empire in the Crypt of the Cathedral was dedicated in 1960. Open for sightseeing Mon.–Sat. 8.30–4.15. Admission to cathedral and crypt: £2.50, children £1.50; Galleries £2.50/£1.50. Services: Sundays, 8, 10.30, 11.30 and 3.15. Weekdays, 7.30, 8, 12.30 and 5 (Sat. Mattins 10 a.m.).

SOMERSET HOUSE, Strand and Victoria Embankment, London WC2. The river façade (600 ft. long) was built in 1776–86 from the designs of Sir William Chambers; the eastern extension, which houses part of King's College, was built by Smirke in 1829. Somerset House was property of Lord Protector Somerset, at whose attainder in 1552 the palace passed to the Crown, and it was a royal residence until 1692.

SOUTH BANK, London SE1. The arts complex on the south bank of the River Thames includes the South Bank Centre, owned and managed by the South Bank Board, which consists of the 2,903-seat *Royal Festival Hall* (opened 1951 for the Festival of Britain), the adjacent 1,056-seat *Queen Elizabeth Hall*, the 368-seat *Purcell Room*, accommodating smaller-scale performances, and the 77-seat Voice Box.

The *National Film Theatre* (opened 1958), administered by the British Film Institute, has three auditoria showing almost 2,000 films a year. The London Film Festival is held here every November.

The *National Theatre* opened in 1976 and stages classical, modern, new and neglected plays in its three auditoria: the 1,160-seat Olivier theatre (open stage), the 890-seat Lyttelton theatre (proscenium stage) and the Cottesloe theatre (adaptable stage) which seats up to 400.

SOUTHWARK CATHEDRAL, London SE1 9DA. Mainly 13th century, but the nave is largely rebuilt. The tomb of John Gower (1330–1408) is between the Bunyan and Chaucer memorial windows in the north aisle; Shakespeare's effigy backed by a view of Southwark and the Globe Theatre in the south aisle; the altar screen (erected 1520) has been restored; the tomb of Bishop Andrews (died 1626) is near the screen. The Early English lady chapel (behind the choir), restored 1930, was the scene of the consistory courts of the reign of Mary (Gardiner and Bonner) and is still used as a consistory court. John Harvard, after whom Harvard University is named, was baptized here in 1607, and the chapel by the north choir aisle is his memorial chapel. Open 8.30–6, admission free. Services: Sundays, 11, 3. Weekdays, 12.45, 5.30 (sung on Tuesdays and Fridays), Saturdays, 12 noon.

STOCK EXCHANGE, London EC2. The market floor of the present Stock Exchange building in London opened for trading in June 1973. A tower 331 feet high and the new Market replace the complex of buildings started in 1801 on the same site. Information on how the Exchange works can be obtained from Public Information, The London Stock Exchange, Old Broad Street, London EC2N 1HP. Tel: 071-797 1000.

THAMES EMBANKMENTS. The *Victoria Embankment*, on the north side from Westminster to Blackfriars, was constructed by Sir Joseph Bazalgette for the Metropolitan Board of Works, 1864–70; the seats, of which the supports of some are a kneeling camel, laden with spicery, and of others a winged sphinx, were presented by the Grocers' Company and by Rt. Hon. W. H. Smith, MP, in 1874; the *Albert Embankment*, on the south side from Westminster Bridge to Vauxhall, 1866–9; the *Chelsea Embankment*, 1871–4. The total cost exceeded £2,000,000. Bazalgette (1819–91) also inaugurated the London main drainage system, 1858–65. A medallion has been placed on a pier of the Victoria Embankment to commemorate the engineer (*Flumini vincula posuit*).

THAMES FLOOD BARRIER. Officially opened in May 1984, though first used in February 1983, the barrier consists of ten rising sector gates which span 570 yards from bank to bank of the Thames at Woolwich Reach. When not in use the gates lie horizontally, allowing shipping to navigate the river normally; when the barrier is closed, the gates turn through 90 degrees to stand vertically more than 50 feet above the river bed. The barrier took eight years to complete and can be raised within about 30 minutes.

THAMES TUNNELS. The *Rotherhithe Tunnel*, opened 1908, connects Commercial Road, London E14, with Lower Road, Rotherhithe; it is 1 mile 332 yards long, of which 474 yards are under the river. The first *Blackwall Tunnel* (northbound vehicles only), opened 1897, connects East India Dock Road, Poplar, with Blackwall Lane, East Greenwich. A second tunnel (for southbound vehicles only) opened 1967. The lengths of the tunnels measured from East India Dock Road to the Gate House on the south side are 6,215 ft (old tunnel) and 6,152 ft. *Greenwich Tunnel* (pedestrians only), opened 1902, connects the Isle of Dogs, Poplar, with Greenwich; it is 406 yards long. The *Woolwich Tunnel* (pedestrians only), opened 1912, connects North and South Woolwich below the passenger and vehicular ferry from North Woolwich Station, London E16, to High Street, Woolwich, London SE18; it is 552 yards long.

WALTHAM HOLY CROSS, Essex. At Waltham Cross, one mile from Waltham Abbey, is one of the crosses (partly restored) erected by Edward I to mark a resting place of the corpse of Queen Eleanor on its way to Westminster Abbey. Ten crosses were erected, but only those at Geddington, Northampton and Waltham survive; 'Charing' Cross originally stood near the spot now occupied by the statue of Charles I at Whitehall.

WESTMINSTER ABBEY, London SW1. Built between 1050 and 1745; contains the chapel of Henry VII, chapter house and cloisters; Edward the Confessor's shrine, AD 1269, tombs of kings and queens (Henry III, Edward I, Edward III, Henry V, Mary Queen of Scots, Elizabeth I), and many other monuments, including the grave of 'The Unknown Warrior' and Poets' Corner. The Coronation Chair encloses the Stone of Scone, removed from Scotland by Edward I in 1296. Open on weekdays 9.20–6 (9.20–7.45 Wed.). Admission to the Royal Chapels, Poets' Corner, Quire and Statesmen's Aisle £3.00, con. £1.50/£1.00. Last admission Mon.–Fri. 4 p.m., Sat. 5 p.m. Wed. 6–8 p.m. free. Nave open on Sundays between services. Services: Sundays, 8, 10, 11.15, 3, 6.30 (generally preceded by an organ recital). Monday–Friday, 7.30, 8, 12.30, 5. Saturdays, 8, 9.20, 3.

WESTMINSTER CATHEDRAL, Ashley Place, London SW1P 1QW. Built 1895–1903 from the designs of J. F. Bentley.

The campanile is 283 feet high. Cathedral open 6.45 a.m.–8 p.m. Masses: Sundays, 7, 8, 9, 10.30 (sung), 12, 5.30 and 7; Solemn Vespers and Benediction 3.30. Monday–Friday, 7, 8, 8.30, 9, 10.30, 12.30, 1.05 and 5.30 (sung). Morning Prayer 7.40, Vespers 5. Saturdays 7, 8, 8.30, 9, 10.30 (sung), 12.30 and 6, Morning Prayer 7.40, Vespers 5.30. Holy days of obligation, Low Masses 7, 8, 8.30, 9, 10.30, 12.30, 1.05, 5.30 (sung) and 7.

WESTMINSTER HALL, London SW1A 0AA. The only part of the old Palace of Westminster to survive the fire of 1834, Westminster Hall is adjacent to and incorporated in the Houses of Parliament. Westminster Hall was built by William Rufus 1097–9 and altered by Richard II 1394–9. It is about 240 ft long, 68 ft wide and 92 ft high; the hammerbeam roof of carved oak dates from 1396–8. The Hall was the scene of the trial of Charles I. Westminster Hall is included on the route followed by those who have arranged a visit to the Houses of Parliament with their MP.

ZOOLOGICAL GARDENS (London Zoo), Regent's Park, London NW1. Opened in 1828. Open daily (except Christmas Day) March–September 10–5.30, 10–4 in winter. Admission £6.00, con. £5.00/£4.00.

LONDON TOURISM BOARD AND CONVENTION BUREAU, Tourist Information Centre, Victoria Station Forecourt, London SW1V 1JU. Tel: 071-730 3488

PARKS, SPACES AND GARDENS

Maintained by the Crown

BUSHY PARK (1,099 acres), Surrey. Adjoining Hampton Court, contains avenue of horse-chestnuts enclosed in a fourfold avenue of limes planted by William III. 'Chestnut Sunday' (when the trees are in full bloom with their 'candles') is usually about 1 to 15 May

GREEN PARK (49 acres), London W1. Between Piccadilly and St James's Park with Constitution Hill, leading to Hyde Park Corner

GREENWICH PARK (196¼ acres), London SE10

HAMPTON COURT GARDENS (54 acres), Surrey

HAMPTON COURT GREEN (17 acres), Surrey

HAMPTON COURT PARK (622 acres), Surrey

HYDE PARK (341 acres), London W1/W2. From Park Lane to Kensington Gardens, containing the Serpentine. Fine gateway at Hyde Park Corner, with Apsley House, the Achilles Statue, Rotten Row and the Ladies' Mile. To the north-east is the Marble Arch, originally erected by George IV at the entrance to Buckingham Palace and re-erected in the present position in 1851

KENSINGTON GARDENS (275 acres), London W2. From the western boundary of Hyde Park to Kensington Palace, containing the Albert Memorial

KEW, ROYAL BOTANIC GARDENS *see* Index

REGENT'S PARK and PRIMROSE HILL (464 acres), London NW1. From Marylebone Road to Primrose Hill surrounded by the Outer Circle and divided by the Broad Walk leading to the Zoological Gardens

RICHMOND PARK (2,469 acres), Surrey

ST JAMES'S PARK (93 acres), London SW1. From Whitehall to Buckingham Palace. Ornamental lake of 12 acres. The original suspension bridge built in 1857 was replaced in 1957. The Mall leads from the Admiralty Arch to Buckingham Palace, Birdcage Walk from Storey's Gate to Buckingham Palace

Maintained by the Corporation of London

ASHTEAD COMMON (500 acres), Surrey

BURNHAM BEECHES and FLEET WOOD (540 acres), Bucks. Purchased by the Corporation for the benefit of the public in 1880, Fleet Wood (65 acres) being presented in 1921

COULSDON COMMON (133 acres), Surrey

EPPING FOREST (6,000 acres), Essex. Purchased by the Corporation and opened to the public in 1882. The present Forest is 12 miles long by 1 to 2 miles wide, about one-tenth of its original area

FARTHING DOWNS (121 acres), Surrey

HAMPSTEAD HEATH (789 acres), London NW3. Including Golders Hill (36 acres) and Parliament Hill (271 acres)

HIGHGATE WOOD (70 acres), London

KENLEY COMMON (138 acres), Surrey

QUEEN'S PARK (30 acres), London

RIDDLESDOWN (90 acres), Surrey

SPRING PARK (51 acres), Kent

WEST HAM PARK (77 acres), London

WEST WICKHAM COMMON (25 acres), Kent

WOODREDON AND WARLIES PARK ESTATE (740 acres), Waltham Abbey

Also smaller open spaces within the City of London, including FINSBURY CIRCUS GARDENS

Hallmarks

Hallmarks are the symbols stamped on gold, silver or platinum articles to indicate that they have been tested at an official Assay Office and that they conform to one of the legal standards. With certain exceptions, all gold, silver, or platinum articles are required by law to be hallmarked before they are offered for sale. Hallmarking was instituted in England in 1300 under a statute of Edward I.

MODERN HALLMARKS

Normally a complete modern hallmark consists of four symbols – the sponsor's mark, the assay office mark, the standard mark and the date letter. Additional marks have been authorized from time to time.

SPONSOR'S MARK

Instituted in England in 1363, the sponsor's mark was originally a device such as a bird or fleur-de-lis. Now it consists of the initial letters of the name or names of the manufacturer or firm. Where two or more sponsors have the same initials, there is a variation in the surrounding shield or style of letters.

STANDARD MARK

The standard mark indicates that the content of the precious metal in the alloy from which the article is made, is not less than the legal standard. The legal standard is the minimum content of precious metal by weight in parts per thousand, and the standards are:

Gold	916.6	(22 carat)
	750	(18 carat)
	585	(14 carat)
	375	(9 carat)
Silver	958.4	(Britannia)
	925	(sterling)
Platinum	950	

The metals are marked as follows, if they are manufactured in the United Kingdom:

GOLD – a crown followed by the millesimal figure for the standard, e.g. 916 for 22 carat (see table above)

SILVER – Britannia silver: a full-length figure of Britannia. Sterling silver: a lion passant (England) or a lion rampant (Scotland)

 Britannia Silver

 Sterling Silver (England)

 Sterling Silver (Scotland)

PLATINUM – an orb

ASSAY OFFICE MARK

This mark identifies the particular assay office at which the article was tested and marked. The existing assay offices in Britain are:

LONDON, Goldsmiths' Hall, London EC2V 8AQ.
Tel: 071-606 8975

BIRMINGHAM, Newhall Street, Birmingham B3 1SB.
Tel: 021-236 6951

 Gold and platinum

 Silver

SHEFFIELD, 137 Portobello Street, Sheffield S1 4DS.
Tel: 0742-755111

EDINBURGH, 9 Granton Road, Edinburgh EH5 3QJ.
Tel: 031-551 2189

Assay offices formerly existed in other towns, e.g. Chester, Exeter, Glasgow, Newcastle, Norwich and York, each having its own distinguishing mark.

DATE LETTER

The date letter shows the year in which an article was assayed and hallmarked. Each alphabetical cycle has a distinctive style of lettering or shape of shield. The date letters were different at the various assay offices and the particular office must be established from the assay office mark before reference is made to tables of date letters.

The table on page 604 shows specimen shields and letters used by the London Assay Office on silver articles in each period from 1498. The same letters are found on gold articles but the surrounding shield may differ. Since 1 January 1975, each office has used the same style of date letter and shield for all articles.

OTHER MARKS

FOREIGN GOODS

Since 1842 foreign goods imported into Britain have been required to be hallmarked before sale. The marks consist of the importer's mark, a special assay office mark, the figure denoting fineness (fineness mark) and the annual date letter.

The following are the assay office marks for gold imported articles. For silver and platinum the symbols remain the same but the shields differ in shape.

 London

 Birmingham

 Sheffield

 Edinburgh

CONVENTION HALLMARKS

Special marks at authorized assay offices of the signatory countries of the International Convention (Austria, Denmark, Finland, Ireland, Norway, Portugal, Sweden, Switzerland and the UK) are legally recognized in the United Kingdom as approved hallmarks. These consist of a sponsor's mark, a common control mark, a fineness mark (arabic numerals showing the standard in parts per thousand), and an assay office mark. There is no date letter.

The fineness marks are:

Gold	750	(18 carat)
	585	(14 carat)
	375	(9 carat)
Silver	925	(sterling)
Platinum	950	

The common control marks are:

 Gold (18 carat)

 Silver

 Platinum

DUTY MARKS

In 1784 an additional mark of the reigning sovereign's head was introduced to signify that the excise duty had been paid. The mark became obsolete on the abolition of the duty in 1890.

COMMEMORATIVE MARKS

There are three other marks to commemorate special events, the Silver Jubilee of King George V and Queen Mary in 1935, the Coronation of Queen Elizabeth II in 1953, and her Silver Jubilee in 1977.

LONDON (GOLDSMITHS' HALL) DATE LETTERS FROM 1498

		from	*to*
	Black letter, small	1498–9	1517–8
	Lombardic	1518–9	1537–8
	Roman and other capitals	1538–9	1557–8
	Black letter, small	1558–9	1577–8
	Roman letter, capitals	1578–9	1597–8
	Lombardic, external cusps	1598–9	1617–8
	Italic letter, small	1618–9	1637–8
	Court hand	1638–9	1657–8

		from	*to*
	Black letter, capitals	1658–9	1677–8
	Black letter, small	1678–9	1696–7
	Court hand	1697	1715–6
	Roman letter, capitals	1716–7	1735–6
	Roman letter, small	1736–7	1738–9
	Roman letter, small	1739–40	1755–6
	Old English, capitals	1756–7	1775–6
	Roman letter, small	1776–7	1795–6
	Roman letter, capitals	1796–7	1815–6
	Roman letter, small	1816–7	1835–6
	Old English, capitals	1836–7	1855–6
	Old English, small	1856–7	1875–6
	Roman letter, capitals [A to M *square* shield N to Z as shown]	1876–7	1895–6
	Roman letter, small	1896–7	1915–6
	Black letter, small	1916–7	1935–6
	Roman letter, capitals	1936–7	1955–6
	Italic letter, small	1956–7	1974
	Italic letter, capitals	1975	

Government Finance

GENERAL GOVERNMENT RECEIPTS

£ billion

	Outturn 1991–2	Budget forecast 1992–3	Latest forecast
Tax, community charge and royalty receipts	170.7	177.8	169.4
Social security receipts	36.9	38.7	37.9
Interest and dividends	6.2	5.5	5.0
Other receipts	8.1	7.7	10.7
Total general government receipts	221.9	229.8	223.1
of which:			
North Sea revenues	1.0	1.2	1.2

Source: HM Treasury – *Autumn Statement 1992*

THE NEW CONTROL TOTAL AND GENERAL GOVERNMENT EXPENDITURE
(EXCLUDING PRIVATIZATION PROCEEDS)

£ million

	Estimated outturn 1992–3	Plans/ projections 1993–4
Central government expenditure	158,700	166,100
Central government support for local authorities	58,900	58,700
Local authority self-financed expenditure	10,900	11,100
Financing requirements of nationalized industries	3,360	3,880
Reserve	—	4,000
Adjustment	100	
New control total	232,000	243,800
Cyclical social security	13,000	15,500
Central government debt interest	17,700	20,000
Accounting adjustments	6,000	7,500
General government expenditure excluding privatization proceeds	268,800	286,600
GGE excluding privatization proceeds as a percentage of GDP	44¾%	45¼%

Source: HM Treasury – *Autumn Statement 1992*

CENTRAL GOVERNMENT EXPENDITURE WITHIN THE NEW CONTROL TOTAL
BY DEPARTMENT

£ million

	Estimated outturn 1992–3	New plans 1993–4
Defence	23,800	23,520
Foreign Office	1,360	1,220
Overseas Development	2,250	2,270
Agriculture, Fisheries and Food	2,390	2,960
Trade and Industry	1,450	1,370
ECGD	110	−30
Employment	3,210	3,350
Transport	2,630	2,740
DoE – Housing	3,590	2,810
DoE – Environment	840	730
DoE – PSA	60	120
DoE – Local government	240	230
Home Office	2,530	2,490
Legal departments	2,100	2,270
Education	3,770	6,330
National Heritage	980	980
Health	28,060	29,120
Social Security	56,300	59,600
Scotland	6,530	7,270
Wales	3,040	3,400
Northern Ireland	6,520	6,850
Chancellor of the Exchequer's departments	3,560	3,390
Cabinet Office– OPSS	1,140	1,250
Cabinet Office – other, etc.	450	480
European Communities	1,770	1,410
Total	158,700	166,100
of which		
Financing requirements of trading funds and public corporations	1,770	1,400

Source: HM Treasury – *Autumn Statement 1992*

FINANCING REQUIREMENTS OF NATIONALIZED INDUSTRIES
BY DEPARTMENT AND INDUSTRY

	Estimated outturn 1992–3	£ million Plans 1993–4
Trade and Industry	190	1,210
British Coal	540	1,900
British Shipbuilders	−10	−10
Nuclear Electric	−280	−500
Post Office	−70	−180
Transport	3,100	2,600
British Rail	2,000	1,500
Civil Aviation Authority	70	100
London Transport	1,040	1,010
DoE – Environment	50	50
British Waterways Board	50	50
Scotland	30	30
Caledonian MacBrayne Ltd	10	10
Scottish Nuclear	10	−30
Scottish Transport Group	0	40
Total	3,360	3,880

Source: HM Treasury - *Autumn Statement 1992*

PUBLIC SECTOR BORROWING REQUIREMENT

	Outturn 1991–2	Budget forecast 1992–3	£ billion Latest forecast
PSBR	13.7	28.1	37.0
Percentage of GDP	2¼	4½	6¼
PSBR excluding privatization proceeds	21.7	36.1	45.0
Percentage of GDP	3¾	5¾	7½

Source: HM Treasury - *Autumn Statement 1992*

CENTRAL GOVERNMENT SUPPORT FOR LOCAL AUTHORITIES

	Estimated outturn 1992–3	£ million Plans 1993–4
CURRENT		
Aggregate External Finance and transitional arrangements		
England		
National non-domestic rate payments	12,310	
Revenue support grant	16,680	
Specific grants	4,160	
Community charge grant	210	
Transitional relief	1,020	
Total	34,380	33,520†
Scotland		
National non-domestic rate payments	1,220	
Revenue support grant	3,500	
Specific grants	330	
Community charge grant	20	
Transitional relief	100	
Total	5,180	5,200†
Wales		
National non-domestic rate payments	540	
Revenue support grant	1,620	
Specific grants	190	
Community charge grant	30	
Transitional relief	40	
Total	2,420	2,340†
TOTAL	41,970	41,070
Other current grants	10,780	11,780
TOTAL CURRENT	52,800	52,900
CAPITAL		
Capital grants	1,600	1,650
Credit approvals	4,570	4,210
Total capital	6,170	5,860
TOTAL	58,900	58,700

†Breakdown of total not available
Source: HM Treasury - *Autumn Statement 1992*

GROSS DOMESTIC PRODUCT BY INDUSTRY BEFORE DEPRECIATION BUT AFTER STOCK APPRECIATION

	1986	1987	1988	1989	1990	£ million 1991
Agriculture, forestry and fishing	6,565	6,918	7,008	8,139	8,753	8,772
Energy and water supply	24,386	25,266	23,122	23,771	25,456	28,273
Manufacturing	77,638	82,868	92,368	99,702	105,808	104,283
Construction	20,718	24,083	28,988	32,084	35,616	33,686
Distribution; hotels and catering; repairs	46,435	50,557	58,510	64,651	71,865	73,024
Transport and communication	23,601	25,968	28,465	31,073	33,487	34,755
Banking, finance, insurance, business services and leasing	51,611	59,511	67,351	82,776	87,151	88,179
Ownership of dwellings	19,490	20,988	23,180	25,915	30,254	34,839
Public administration, national defence and compulsory social security	23,062	24,972	27,103	28,447	31,647	34,786
Education and health services	30,030	33,179	37,555	41,156	44,815	49,643
Other services	20,627	23,286	26,836	29,474	30,431	33,915
Total	344,163	377,596	420,486	467,188	505,283	524,155
less adjustment for financial services	16,033	16,997	19,359	26,052	26,159	27,171
Statistical discrepancy (income adjustment)	–	–	–	–	328	17
Gross domestic product	328,130	360,599	401,127	441,136	479,452	497,001

Source: HMSO - *Annual Abstract of Statistics 1993*

Unemployment

UNEMPLOYMENT IN THE UNITED KINGDOM
AT JULY EACH YEAR

	1990	1991	1992
Total unemployed and claiming benefit	1,623,900	2,362,500	2,760,100

Source: HMSO - *Annual Abstract of Statistics 1993*

RATES OF UNEMPLOYMENT BY STANDARD
REGIONS SEASONALLY ADJUSTED

Annual averages	1989	1990	Percentages 1991
United Kingdom	6.3	5.8	8.1
North	9.9	8.7	10.4
Yorkshire and Humberside	7.4	6.7	8.7
East Midlands	5.4	5.1	7.2
East Anglia	3.6	3.7	5.8
South East	3.9	4.0	7.0
South West	4.5	4.4	7.1
West Midlands	6.6	5.9	8.6
North West	8.5	7.7	9.4
England	6.2	5.8	8.0
Wales	7.3	6.6	8.7
Scotland	9.3	8.1	8.7
Northern Ireland	14.6	13.4	13.7

NOTE: Percentages calculated using mid-year estimates of total employees in employment, unemployed, self-employed and HM Forces, and participants in work-related government training schemes
Source: HMSO - *Annual Abstract of Statistics 1993*

HOUSEHOLDS AND THEIR EXPENDITURE[1] UNITED KINGDOM

	1988	1989	1990	1991
NUMBER OF HOUSEHOLDS SUPPLYING DATA	7,265	7,410	7,046	7,056
Total number of persons	18,280	18,590	17,437	17,089
Total number of adults[2]	13,640	13,850	12,939	12,934
HOUSEHOLD PERCENTAGE DISTRIBUTION BY TENURE (PER CENT)				
Rented unfurnished	30.3	30.3	29.2	27.7
Rented furnished	2.8	3.0	3.4	3.3
Rent-free	1.7	1.4	1.3	2.0
Owner-occupied	65.1	65.3	66.1	67.0
AVERAGE NUMBER OF PERSONS PER HOUSEHOLD				
All persons	2.516	2.509	2.475	2.422
Males	1.229	1.217	1.193	1.169
Females	1.288	1.292	1.281	1.253
Adults[2]	1.877	1.869	1.836	1.833
Persons under 65	1.504	1.500	1.459	1.455
Persons 65 and over	0.374	0.369	0.378	0.378
Children[2]	0.639	0.640	0.638	0.589
Children under 2	0.073	0.084	0.075	0.077
Children 2 and under 5	0.111	0.117	0.119	0.112
Children 5 and under 18	0.455	0.439	0.444	0.400
Persons economically active	1.168	1.167	1.195	1.171
Persons not economically active	1.348	1.342	1.280	1.251
Men 65 and over, women 60 and over	0.406	0.401	0.405	0.408
Others	0.942	0.940	0.875	0.843
AVERAGE WEEKLY HOUSEHOLD EXPENDITURE ON COMMODITIES AND SERVICES (£)				
Housing[3]	35.81	38.44	44.42	50.24
Fuel, light and power	10.48	10.58	11.11	12.25
Food	38.28	41.67	44.81	46.13
Alcoholic drink	9.19	9.53	10.01	10.83
Tobacco	4.45	4.77	4.82	5.15
Clothing and footwear	14.52	15.25	16.03	15.80
Household goods	15.01	19.17	20.00	20.13
Household services	9.80	9.73	12.28	13.00
Personal goods and services	8.13	8.48	9.47	9.97
Motoring expenditure	25.31	30.42	33.83	34.12
Fares and other travel costs	4.88	5.35	6.19	5.58
Leisure goods	9.65	10.97	11.28	12.06
Leisure services	18.13	19.02	21.54	22.20
Miscellaneous	0.78	0.93	1.37	1.59
Total	204.41	224.32	247.16	259.04
EXPENDITURE ON COMMODITY OR SERVICE AS A PERCENTAGE OF TOTAL EXPENDITURE (PER CENT)				
Housing[3]	17.5	17.1	18.0	19.4
Fuel, light and power	5.1	4.7	4.5	4.7
Food	18.7	18.6	18.1	17.8
Alcoholic drink	4.5	4.2	4.1	4.2
Tobacco	2.2	2.1	2.0	2.0
Clothing and footwear	7.1	6.8	6.5	6.1
Household goods	7.3	8.5	8.1	7.8
Household services	4.8	4.3	5.0	5.0
Personal goods and services	4.0	3.8	3.8	3.8
Motoring expenditure	12.4	13.6	13.7	13.2
Fares and other travel costs	2.4	2.4	2.5	2.2
Leisure goods	4.7	4.9	4.6	4.7
Leisure services	8.9	8.5	8.7	8.6
Miscellaneous	0.4	0.4	0.6	0.6
Total	100.0	100.0	100.0	100.0

[1] Information derived from the Family Expenditure Survey
[2] Adults = all persons 18 and over and married persons under 18
  Children = all unmarried persons under 18
[3] Excludes mortgage payments but includes imputed expenditure (i.e.
  the weekly equivalent of rateable value)

Source: HMSO - *Annual Abstract of Statistics 1993*

Trade

BALANCE OF PAYMENTS   £ MILLION

	1987	1988	1989	1990	1991
CURRENT ACCOUNT					
Visible trade					
Exports (fob)	79,153	80,346	92,154	101,718	103,413
Imports (fob)	90,735	101,826	116,837	120,527	113,703
Visible balance	−11,582	−21,480	−24,683	−18,809	−10,290
Invisibles					
Credits	79,826	87,739	107,778	115,150	116,164
Debits	72,726	82,438	104,821	113,370	112,195
Invisibles balance	7,099	5,302	2,956	1,778	3,969
of which:					
Services balance	6,745	4,397	4,039	4,581	4,990
Interest, profits and dividends balance	3,754	4,423	3,495	2,094	328
Transfers balance	−3,400	−3,518	−4,578	−4,897	−1,349
CURRENT BALANCE	−4,482	−16,179	−21,726	−17,029	−6,321
*TRANSACTIONS IN EXTERNAL ASSETS AND LIABILITIES					
Investment overseas by UK residents					
Direct	−19,239	−20,944	−21,515	−9,553	−10,261
Portfolio	5,163	−11,239	−35,486	−15,844	−30,908
Total UK investment overseas	−14,076	−32,183	−57,001	−25,397	−41,169
Investment in the UK by overseas residents					
Direct	9,449	12,006	18,567	18,634	12,045
Portfolio	19,535	15,564	14,603	5,276	16,627
Total overseas investment in UK	28,984	27,570	33,170	23,910	28,672
Foreign currency lending abroad by UK banks	−45,867	−15,064	−25,689	−37,440	27,394
Foreign currency borrowing abroad by UK banks	43,566	20,447	32,338	34,992	−14,802
Net foreign currency transactions of UK banks	−2,301	5,383	6,649	−2,448	12,592
Sterling lending abroad by UK banks	−4,633	−4,626	−2,923	−3,800	4,837
Sterling borrowing and deposit liabilities abroad of UK banks	8,867	13,641	12,401	12,620	−9,222
Net sterling transactions of UK banks	4,234	9,015	9,478	8,820	−4,385
Deposits with and lending to banks abroad by UK non-bank private sector	−4,914	−4,025	−9,334	−8,280	−3,580
Borrowing from banks abroad by:					
UK non-bank private sector	2,075	3,973	8,017	10,006	13,032
Public corporations	−166	−253	−1,726	−127	−49
General government	104	−10	529	−363	−65
Official reserves (additions to −, drawings on +)	−12,012	−2,761	5,440	−79	−2,662
Other external assets of:					
UK non-bank private sector and public corporations	93	1,070	1,468	−3,479	−4,707
General government	−796	−887	−873	−1,025	−894
Other external liabilities of:					
UK non-bank private sector and public corporations	1,382	1,664	21,191	8,272	10,710
General government	1,725	842	2,252	1,281	−2,246
NET TRANSACTIONS IN ASSETS AND LIABILITIES	4,334	9,396	19,259	11,091	5,249
BALANCING ITEM	148	6,783	2,467	5,938	1,072

* Assets: increase −/decrease +
Liabilities: increase +/decrease −

Source: HMSO - *Annual Abstract of Statistics 1993*

VALUE OF UNITED KINGDOM IMPORTS (cif) 1991* BY SECTIONS AND DIVISIONS

	£ million		£ million
TOTAL UK IMPORTS	118,786.0	Manufactured goods classified chiefly by material	20,519.9
		Leather, leather manufactures, nes, and	
Food and live animals chiefly for food	10,389.3	dressed furskins	185.9
Live animals chiefly for food	203.3	Rubber manufactures, nes	872.2
Meat and meat preparations	1,845.0	Cork and wood manufactures (excluding	
Dairy products and birds' eggs	871.0	furniture)	821.2
Fish, crustaceans and molluscs, and		Paper, paperboard, and articles of paper	
preparations thereof	978.5	pulp, of paper or of paperboard	3,868.4
Cereals and cereal preparations	818.5	Textile yarn, fabrics, made-up articles, nes,	
Vegetables and fruit	3,002.6	and related products	3,738.0
Sugar, sugar preparations and honey	681.2	Non-metallic mineral manufactures, nes	3,332.9
Coffee, tea, cocoa, spices, and manufactures		Iron and steel	2,620.2
thereof	869.7	Non-ferrous metals	2,557.9
Feeding-stuff for animals (not including		Manufactures of metal, nes	2,523.1
unmilled cereals)	619.1		
Miscellaneous edible products and		Machinery and transport equipment	43,101.6
preparations	500.4	Power generating machinery and	
		equipment	3,345.5
Beverages and tobacco	1,936.1	Machinery specialized for particular	
Beverages	1,464.8	industries	3,005.6
Tobacco and tobacco manufactures	471.3	Metalworking machinery	860.7
		General industrial machinery and	
Crude materials, inedible, except fuels	4,678.3	equipment, nes, and machine parts, nes	4,202.8
Hides, skins and furskins, raw	68.8	Office machines and automatic data	
Oil seeds and oleaginous fruit	224.0	processing equipment	7,586.5
Crude rubber (including synthetic and		Telecommunications, sound recording and	
reclaimed)	223.6	reproducing apparatus and equipment	3,351.2
Cork and wood	1,043.7	Electrical machinery, apparatus and	
Pulp and waste paper	608.0	appliances, nes, and electrical parts thereof	
Textile fibres (other than wool tops) and		(including non-electrical counterparts, nes,	
their wastes (not manufactured into yarn or		of electrical household type equipment)	7,078.4
fabric)	452.6	Road vehicles (including air cushion	
Crude fertilizers and crude minerals		vehicles)	10,227.2
(excluding coal, petroleum and precious		Other transport equipment	3,443.7
stones)	284.8		
Metalliferous ores and metal scrap	1,232.7	Miscellaneous manufactured articles	17,559.3
Crude animal and vegetable materials	540.1	Sanitary, plumbing, heating and lighting	
		fixtures and fittings, nes	368.3
Mineral fuels, lubricants and related materials	7,510.7	Furniture and parts thereof	1,004.7
Petroleum, petroleum products and related		Travel goods, handbags and similar	
materials	5,773.6	containers	285.1
Coal, coke, gas and electric current	1,737.1	Articles of apparel and clothing accessories	4,128.5
		Footwear	1,169.0
Animal and vegetable oils, fats and waxes	387.5	Professional, scientific and controlling	
		instruments and apparatus, nes	2,525.1
Total manufactured goods	92,159.4	Photographic apparatus, equipment and	
		supplies and optical goods, nes, watches and	
Chemicals and related products	10,978.6	clocks	1,565.5
Organic chemicals	2,618.4	Miscellaneous manufactured articles, nes	6,513.3
Inorganic chemicals	1,033.5		
Dyeing, tanning and colouring materials	620.9	Commodities and transactions not classified	
Medicinal and pharmaceutical products	1,371.2	elsewhere	1,724.7
Essential oils and perfume materials; toilet,			
polishing and cleansing materials	798.1		
Fertilizers, manufactured	283.0		
Plastics in primary forms	2,053.1		
Plastics in non-primary forms	976.6		
Chemical materials	1,223.7		

* provisional
nes not elsewhere specified

Source: HMSO – Annual Abstract of Statistics 1993

VALUE OF UNITED KINGDOM EXPORTS (fob) 1991* BY SECTIONS AND DIVISIONS

	£ million
TOTAL UK EXPORTS	104,877.0
Food and live animals chiefly for food	4,715.8
Live animals chiefly for food	288.4
Meat and meat preparations	672.6
Dairy products and birds' eggs	451.9
Fish, crustaceans and molluscs, and preparations thereof	574.4
Cereals and cereal preparations	1,102.8
Vegetables and fruit	298.5
Sugar, sugar preparations and honey	247.5
Coffee, tea, cocoa, spices and manufactures thereof	465.2
Feeding-stuff for animals (not including unmilled cereals)	302.6
Miscellaneous edible products and preparations	311.7
Beverages and tobacco	3,031.8
Beverages	2,251.7
Tobacco and tobacco manufactures	780.3
Crude materials, inedible, except fuels	1,919.7
Hides, skins and furskins, raw	135.1
Oil seeds and oleaginous fruit	52.6
Crude rubber (including synthetic and reclaimed)	198.1
Cork and wood	27.9
Pulp and waste paper	38.8
Textile fibres (other than wool tops) and their wastes (not manufactured into yarn or fabric)	466.2
Crude fertilizers and crude minerals (excluding coal, petroleum and precious stones)	365.5
Metalliferous ores and metal scrap	526.9
Crude animal and vegetable materials	108.5
Mineral fuels, lubricants and related materials	7,169.0
Petroleum, petroleum products and related materials	6,814.1
Coal, coke, gas and electric current	355.0
Animal and vegetable oils, fats and waxes	95.9
Total manufactured goods	86,137.2
Chemicals and related products	13,788.6
Organic chemicals	3,468.4
Inorganic chemicals	1,000.6
Dyeing, tanning and colouring materials	1,216.4
Medicinal and pharmaceutical products	2,556.1
Essential oils and perfume materials; toilet, polishing and cleansing materials	1,298.4
Fertilizers, manufactured	103.2
Plastics in primary forms	1,332.9
Plastics in non-primary forms	786.9
Chemical materials	2,025.7

	£ million
Manufactured goods classified chiefly by material	15,581.1
Leather, leather manufactures, nes, and dressed furskins	258.0
Rubber manufactures, nes	887.9
Cork and wood manufactures (excluding furniture)	116.4
Paper, paperboard, and articles of paper pulp, of paper or of paperboard	1,623.8
Textile yarn, fabrics, made-up articles, nes, and related products	2,349.0
Non-metallic mineral manufactures, nes	3,177.1
Iron and steel	3,011.3
Non-ferrous metals	1,975.2
Manufactures of metal, nes	2,182.4
Machinery and transport equipment	43,627.1
Power generating machinery and equipment	5,073.1
Machinery specialized for particular industries	3,922.1
Metalworking machinery	812.5
General industrial machinery and equipment, nes, and machine parts, nes	4,520.6
Office machines and automatic data processing equipment	6,590.9
Telecommunications and sound recording and reproducing apparatus and equipment	2,942.8
Electrical machinery, apparatus and appliances, nes, and electrical parts thereof (including non-electrical counterparts, nes, of electrical household type equipment)	5,709.7
Road vehicles (including air cushion vehicles)	8,555.4
Other transport equipment	5,500.2
Miscellaneous manufactured articles	13,140.4
Sanitary, plumbing, heating and lighting fixtures and fittings, nes	267.3
Furniture and parts thereof	564.2
Travel goods, handbags and similar containers	72.4
Articles of apparel and clothing accessories	1,920.1
Footwear	314.8
Professional, scientific and controlling instruments and apparatus, nes	2,992.7
Photographic apparatus, equipment and supplies and optical goods, nes, watches and clocks	1,266.1
Miscellaneous manufactured articles, nes	5,742.9
Commodities and transactions not classified elsewhere	1,807.6

* provisional
nes not elsewhere specified

Source: HMSO – *Annual Abstract of Statistics 1993*

Finance

British Currency

COIN

Gold Coins
*One hundred pounds £100
*Fifty pounds £50
*Twenty-five pounds £25
*Ten pounds £10
Five pounds £5
Two pounds £2
Sovereign £1
Half-Sovereign 50p

Silver Coins
†Maundy Money
Fourpence 4p
Threepence 3p
Twopence 2p
Penny 1p

Nickel-Brass Coins
Two pounds £2
One pound £1

Cupro-Nickel Coins
Crown £5 (since 1990)
50 pence 50p
Crown 25p (pre-1990)
20 pence 20p
‡10 pence 10p
§5 pence 5p

Bronze Coins
2 pence 2p
1 penny 1p

Copper-plated Steel Coins
2 pence 2p
1 penny 1p

*Britannia gold bullion coins, introduced in October 1987
†Gifts of special money distributed by the Sovereign annually on Maundy Thursday to the number of aged poor men and women corresponding to the Sovereign's own age
‡New 10 pence coin introduced on 30 September 1992
§New 5 pence coin introduced on 27 June 1990

GOLD COIN

Gold ceased to circulate during the First World War. An Order of 27 April 1966 made it illegal for UK residents to continue holding more than four gold coins minted after 1837, or to acquire such coins unless they had been licensed as genuine collectors by the Bank of England. This Order was revoked on 1 April 1971 by the Exchange Control (Gold Coins Exemption) Order 1971, whereby residents of the United Kingdom, Channel Islands and the Isle of Man may freely buy, sell and hold gold coins.

The 1971 Order was revoked on 15 April 1975 by the Exchange Control (Gold Coins Exemption) Order 1975. Under this Order, Section 1 of the Exchange Control Act 1947 (which prohibits dealings in gold or foreign currency except with Treasury permission) was exempted for gold coins minted in or before 1837. The import of gold coins minted after 1837 was prohibited except by authorized dealers in gold with individual import licences from the Department of Trade and Industry, and dealing between other UK residents was restricted to coins already held in the UK.

Under an amendment, dated 16 December 1977, the exemptions contained in the 1975 Order were extended to cover gold coins minted in or before 1937.

The 1975 controls over the import of and dealing in gold coins were abolished on 13 June 1979 under the Exchange Control (Gold Coins Exemption) Order 1979. Gold coins may now be imported and exported without restriction, except gold coins which are more than fifty years old and valued at a sum in excess of £8,000; these cannot be exported without specific authorization from the Department of Trade and Industry.

SILVER COIN

Prior to 1920 silver coins were struck from sterling silver, an alloy of which 925 parts in 1,000 were silver. In 1920 the proportion of silver was reduced to 500 parts. From 1 January 1947 all 'silver' coins, except Maundy money, have been struck from cupro-nickel, an alloy of copper 75 parts and nickel 25 parts, except for the 20p, composed of copper 84 parts, nickel 16 parts. Maundy coins continue to be struck from sterling silver.

BRONZE COIN

Bronze, introduced in 1860 to replace copper, is currently an alloy of copper 97 parts, zinc 2.5 parts and tin 0.5 part. These proportions have been subject to slight variations in the past.

The 'remedy' is the amount of variation from standard permitted in weight and fineness of coins when first issued from the Mint.

Copper-plated steel was introduced in September 1992.

LEGAL TENDER

Gold, dated 1838 onwards, if not below least current weight, is legal tender to any amount. £5 (Crown 1990), £2 and £1 coins are legal tender to any amount; 50p and 20p coins are legal tender up to £10; 10p and 5p coins are legal tender up to £5, and bronze coins are legal tender for amounts up to 20p.

Farthings ceased to be legal tender on 31 December 1960, the halfpenny on 1 August 1969, the halfcrown on 1 January 1970, the threepence and penny on 31 August 1971, the sixpence on 30 June 1980, the decimal halfpenny on 31 December 1984, the old 5p on 31 December 1990, and the old 10p on 30 June 1993.

The decimal system was introduced on 15 February 1971. Since 1982 the word 'new' in 'new pence' displayed on decimal coins has been dropped.

The Channel Islands and the Isle of Man issue their own coinage, which are legal tender only in the island of issue. For denominations, *see* page 613.

	Metal	Standard weight (g)	Standard diameter (cm)
Penny	bronze	3.564	2.032
Penny	copper-plated steel	3.564	2.032
2 pence	bronze	7.128	2.591
2 pence	copper-plated steel	7.128	2.591
5p	cupro-nickel	3.25	1.80
10p	cupro-nickel	6.5	2.45
20p	cupro-nickel	5.0	2.14
25p Crown	cupro-nickel	28.276	3.861
50p	cupro-nickel	13.5	3.0
£1	copper/nickel/zinc	9.5	2.25
£2	copper/nickel/zinc	15.98	2.84
£5 Crown	cupro-nickel	28.28	3.861

BANKNOTES

Bank of England notes are currently issued in denominations of £5, £10, £20 and £50 for the amount of the fiduciary note issue, and are legal tender in England and Wales. Banknotes which are no longer legal tender are payable when presented at the head office of the Bank of England in London.

The old white notes for £10, £20, £50, £100, £500 and £1,000, which were issued until April 1943, ceased to be legal tender in May 1945, and the old white £5 note in March 1946.

The white £5 note issued between October 1945 and September 1956, the £5 notes issued between 1957 and 1963, (bearing a portrait of Britannia) and the first series to bear a portrait of The Queen, issued between 1963 and 1971, ceased to be legal tender in March 1961, June 1967 and September 1973 respectively.

The series of £1 notes issued during the years 1928 to 1960 and the 10s. notes of the same type issued from 1928 to 1961 (those without the royal portrait) ceased to be legal tender in May and October 1962 respectively. The £1 note first issued in March 1960 (bearing on the back a representation of Britannia) and the £10 note first issued in February 1964 (bearing a lion on the back) both bearing a portrait of The Queen on the front ceased to be legal tender in June 1979. The £1 note first issued in 1978 ceased to be legal tender on 11 March 1988. The 10s. note was replaced by the 50p coin in October 1969, and ceased to be legal tender on 21 November 1970.

The first of the D series of banknotes was a £20 note issued on 9 July 1970 and this was followed by the £5 note on 11 November 1971. These noted ceased to be legal tender on 19 March 1993 and 29 November 1991 respectively. The D series £10 note was issued on 20 February 1975, £1 note on 9 February 1978 and £50 note on 20 March 1981. The £1 coin was introduced on 21 April 1983 to replace the £1 note. The predominant identifying feature of each note is the portrayal on the back of a prominent figure from Britain's history, namely:

£5	The Duke of Wellington
£10	Florence Nightingale
£20	William Shakespeare
£50	Sir Christopher Wren

A new series of notes was introduced in June 1990 when a new £5 was issued, followed by a £20 note in June 1991 and the £10 note in April 1992. This new series will eventually replace the D series. The historical figures portrayed in this series to date are:

£5	George Stephenson
£10	Charles Dickens
£20	Michael Faraday

The £50 note will be issued in 1994 to commemorate the tercentenary of the Bank of England, and will carry a portrait of Sir John Houblon, the first governor.

NOTE CIRCULATION

Note circulation is highest at the two peak spending periods of the year, around Christmas and during the summer holiday period. A peak of £19,059 million was reached immediately prior to Christmas 1992, a 1.8 per cent increase on the previous year.

The proportion of the total value of £1 notes in circulation at end February 1993 compared with the previous year was down 0.1 per cent to 0.3 per cent. £5 notes fell from 7.2 per cent to 6.9 per cent. £10 notes decreased from 35.6 per cent to 31.5 per cent. £20 and £50 notes increased from 32.8 per

cent and 15.6 per cent to 36.0 per cent and 16.1 per cent respectively.

On 26 February 1993 the values of notes in circulation were:

£1	£58,184,661
£5	£1,162,573,290
£10	£5,347,583,910
£20	£6,101,588,120
£50	£2,732,012,850

OTHER BANKNOTES

SCOTLAND – Banknotes are issued by three Scottish banks. The Royal Bank of Scotland and the Bank of Scotland issue notes for £5, £10, £20 and £100. The Royal Bank of Scotland also issues £1 notes. The Clydesdale Bank issues notes for £5, £10, £20, £50, £100. Scottish notes are not legal tender in Scotland but they enjoy there a status comparable to that of the Bank of England note.

NORTHERN IRELAND – Banknotes are issued by four banks in Northern Ireland. The Northern Bank and the Ulster Bank issue notes for £5, £10, £20, £50 and £100. The Allied Irish Bank and the Bank of Ireland issue notes for £5, £10, £20 and £100. Northern Ireland notes are not legal tender in Northern Ireland but they circulate widely and enjoy a status comparable to that of Bank of England notes.

CHANNEL ISLANDS – The States of Jersey issues its own currency notes and coinage. The note denominations are for £1, £5, £10, £20 and £50. The seven denominations of coin are: 1p, 2p, 5p, 10p, 20p, 50p and £1. The States of Guernsey issues its own currency notes and coinage. The notes are for £1, £5, £10 and £20. The eight denominations of coin are 1p, 2p, 5p, 10p, 20p, 50p, £1 and £2.

THE ISLE OF MAN – The Isle of Man Government issues notes for £1, £5, £10, £20 and £50. Although these notes are only legal tender in the Isle of Man, they are accepted at face value in branches of the clearing banks in the United Kingdom. The Isle of Man issues coins for 1p, 2p, 5p, 10p, 20p, 50p, £1, £2 and £5.

Although none of the series of notes specified above is legal tender in the United Kingdom, they are generally accepted by the banks irrespective of their place of issue. At one time the banks made a commission charge for handling Scottish and Irish notes but this was abolished some years ago.

Banking

Deposit-taking institutions may be broadly divided into two sectors: the monetary sector, which is predominantly banks and is supervised by the Bank of England; and those institutions outside the monetary sector, of which the most important are the building societies and the National Savings Bank.

The main institutions within the British banking system are the Bank of England (the central bank), the clearing banks (the major retail banks), the merchant banks, the overseas banks, and the discount houses.

The Banking Act 1987 established a single category of authorized institutions eligible to carry out banking business. Under the 1987 Act, the Bank of England exercises a regulatory role over the banking system, and ensures the efficient functioning of payment and settlement systems and efficient services. In its role as the central bank, the Bank of England also acts as banker to the Government and as a note-issuing authority. It is responsible for executing monetary policy and therefore sets the base rates.

BANK BASE RATES 1992-3

5 May 1992	10.0%
16 September 1992	12%, 15%, 12%
17 September 1992	10%
22 September 1992	9%
16 October 1992	8%
13 November 1992	7%
26 January 1993	6%

CLEARING BANKS

The clearing banks are Abbey National, Bank of Scotland, Barclays, Clydesdale, Co-operative, Coutts, Girobank, Lloyds, Midland, National Westminster, the Royal Bank of Scotland Group, the TSB and the Yorkshire Bank.

Banking hours differ throughout Great Britain. Many banks in England and Wales are experimenting with longer hours and Saturday morning opening, and hours vary from branch to branch. Current minimum opening hours are:
ENGLAND AND WALES: Monday–Friday 9.30–3.30 (City of London town clearers 9.30–3)
SCOTLAND: Monday–Wednesday, Friday, 9.15–4.45; Thursday 9.15–5.30

NORTHERN IRELAND: Open four days a week 10–3; open one day a week 9.30–5

CLEARING SERVICES

The Association for Payment Clearing Services (APACS) manages the payment clearing systems and oversees money transmission in the UK. It is an umbrella organization for three separate companies:

BACS Ltd is the UK's automated clearing house for bulk clearing of electronic debits and credits (e.g. direct debits and salary credits).

The Cheque and Credit Clearing Company Ltd operates bulk clearing systems for inter-bank cheques and paper credit items.

CHAPS and Town Clearing Company Ltd provides same-day clearing for high value electronic funds transfers or cheques.

Membership of APACS and the operational clearing companies is open to any appropriately regulated financial institution providing payment services and meeting the relevant membership criteria. As at June 1993, APACS had 21 members, comprising the major banks and building societies.

ASSOCIATION FOR PAYMENT CLEARING SERVICES (APACS), Mercury House, Triton Court, 14 Finsbury Square, London EC2A 1BR. Tel: 071–711 6200. *Head of Public Affairs*, R. Tyson-Davies
BACS LTD, De Havilland Road, Edgware, Middlesex HA8 5QA. *Chief Executive*, A. E. Robinson
CHEQUE AND CREDIT CLEARING COMPANY LTD, Mercury house, Triton Court, 14 Finsbury Square, London EC2A 1BR. *Chief Inspector*, P. M. Rowe
CHAPS AND TOWN CLEARING COMPANY LTD, Mercury House, Triton Court, 14 Finsbury Square, London EC2A 1BR. *Chief Inspector*, P. M. Rowe

BANKING SERVICES

Retail banks now offer a wide variety of financial services to companies and individuals, including current and deposit accounts, loan facilities, automated teller (cashpoint) machines, cheque guarantee cards, credit cards and debit cards.

FINANCIAL RESULTS 1992

Bank Group	P/L before taxation £m	P/L after taxation £m	Total assets £m	Number of UK branches
Abbey National	564	317	71,812	680
*Bank of Scotland	125.3	78	28,809	484
Barclays	− 242	− 285	149,118	2,272
Clydesdale	59.05	37.65	5,753	330
Co-operative	9.85	6.27	3,081.4	107
Coutts & Co.	46	n/a	11,035	18
Girobank	64.4	45.3	2,820.2	20,000
Lloyds	801	521	53,997	1,888
Midland	178	91	61,354	1,740
National Westminster	405	210	143,216	2,684
The Royal Bank of Scotland Group PLC	20.9	32	34,497.7	750
†Yorkshire Bank	64.6	46.1	4,239.3	266

*For year ended 28 February 1993
†Nine months only

AUTHORIZED INSTITUTIONS

Banking in the United Kingdom is regulated by the Banking Act 1987 as amended by the European Community's Second Banking Co-ordination Directive, which came into effect on 1 January 1993.

The Directive permits banks incorporated in one EC member state to carry on certain banking activities in another member state without the need for authorization by that state. Consequently, the Bank of England no longer authorizes banks incorporated in other EC states with branches in the UK so that they may accept deposits in the UK; the authorization of their home state supervisor is sufficient provided that certain notification requirements are met. However, UK-incorporated subsidiaries of banks incorporated in other EC states which wish to accept deposits in the UK continue to need authorization by the Bank of England.

As at 28 February 1993, a total of 508 institutions were authorized to carry out business in the UK:

Authorized under the Banking Act 1987	429
UK-incorporated	253
Incorporated outside the EC	176
European authorized institutions	79
TOTAL	508

The following lists show the institutions authorized or entitled to accept deposits in the UK and covered by the UK's deposit protection scheme, as at 3 September 1993.

AUTHORIZED BY THE BANK OF ENGLAND

UK-INCORPORATED
(Including partnerships formed under the law of any part of the UK)
*In administration

ABC International Bank PLC
ANZ Grindlays Bank PLC
AY Bank Ltd
Abbey National PLC
Abbey National Treasury Services PLC
Adam & Company PLC
Afghan National Credit & Finance Ltd
Airdrie Savings Bank
Aitken Hume Bank PLC
Alexanders Discount PLC
Alliance Trust (Finance) Ltd
Allied Bank Philippines (UK) PLC
Allied Trust Bank Ltd
Anglo-Romanian Bank Ltd
Henry Ansbacher & Co. Ltd
Assemblies of God Property Trust
Associates Capital Corporation Ltd
Avco Trust PLC

Bank Leumi (UK) PLC
Bank of America International Ltd
Bank of Boston Ltd
Bank of Cyprus (London) Ltd
The Bank of Edinburgh PLC
Bank of Montreal Europe Ltd
Bank of Scotland
Bank of Scotland Treasury Services PLC
Bank of Tokyo International Ltd
Bank of Wales PLC
Bankers Trust International PLC
Banque Nationale de Paris PLC

The Baptist Union Corporation Ltd
Barclays Bank PLC
Barclays Bank Trust Company Ltd
Barclays de Zoete Wedd Ltd
Baring Brothers & Co. Ltd
Belmont Bank Ltd
Beneficial Bank PLC
*British and Commonwealth Merchant Bank PLC
The British Bank of the Middle East
The British Linen Bank Ltd
British Railways Savings Company Ltd
Brown, Shipley & Co. Ltd
Bunge Finance Ltd

CIBC Bank PLC
CLF Municipal Bank PLC
Caledonian Bank PLC
Cater Allen Ltd
Central Hispano Bank (UK) Ltd
The Charities Aid Foundation Money Management Company Ltd
Chartered Trust PLC
Charterhouse Bank Ltd
Chase Investment Bank Ltd
Chemical Investment Bank Ltd
Chesterfield Street Trust Ltd
Citibank International PLC
Citibank Trust Ltd
City Merchants Bank Ltd
City Trust Ltd
Clive Discount Company Ltd
Close Brothers Ltd
Clydesdale Bank PLC
Combined Capital Ltd
Commercial Bank Trust PLC
Commercial Bank of London PLC
Confederation Bank Ltd
Consolidated Credits Bank Ltd
The Co-operative Bank PLC
County NatWest Ltd
Coutts & Co.
Credit Suisse Financial Products

Daiwa Europe Bank PLC
Dalbeattie Finance Co. Ltd
Dao Heng Bank (London) PLC
Davenham Trust PLC
Den norske Bank PLC
The Dorset, Somerset & Wilts. Investment Society Ltd
Dryfield Finance Ltd
Dunbar Bank PLC
Duncan Lawrie Ltd

Eccles Savings and Loans Ltd
Enskilda Securities-Skandinaviska Enskilda Ltd
*Equatorial Bank PLC
Exeter Bank Ltd

FIBI Bank (UK) PLC
Fairmount Trust Ltd
FennoScandia Bank Ltd
Financial & General Bank PLC
James Finlay Bank Ltd
First National Bank PLC
First National Commercial Bank PLC
The First Personal Bank PLC
First Trust Bank (AIB Group Northern Ireland PLC)
Robert Fleming & Co. Ltd
Ford Credit Europe PLC
Foreign & Colonial Management Ltd

Forward Trust Ltd
Forward Trust Personal Finance Ltd
Frizzell Banking Services Ltd

Gartmore Money Management Ltd
Gerrard & National Ltd
Girobank PLC
Goldman Sachs Ltd
Granville Trust Ltd
Gresham Trust PLC
Greyhound Bank PLC
Guinness Mahon & Co. Ltd

HFC Bank PLC
HSBC Investment Banking Ltd
Habibsons Bank Ltd
Hambros Bank Ltd
Hampshire Trust PLC
The Hardware Federation Finance Co. Ltd
Harrods Bank Ltd
Harton Securities Ltd
Havana International Bank Ltd
The Heritable & General Investment Bank Ltd
Hill Samuel Bank Ltd
C. Hoare & Co.
Julian Hodge Bank Ltd
Humberclyde Finance Group Ltd
Hungarian International Bank Ltd

3i PLC
3i Group PLC
IBJ International PLC
International Mexican Bank Ltd
Iran Overseas Investment Bank Ltd
Italian International Bank PLC

Jordan International Bank PLC
Leopold Joseph & Sons Ltd

KDB Bank (UK) Ltd
KEXIM Bank (UK) Ltd
King & Shaxson Ltd
Kleinwort Benson Ltd
Kleinwort Benson Investment Management Ltd
Korea Long Term Credit Bank International Ltd

LTCB International Ltd
Lazard Brothers & Co. Ltd
Lloyds Bank PLC
Lloyds Bank (BLSA) Ltd
Lloyds Bowmaker Ltd
Lloyds Private Banking Ltd
Lombard Bank Ltd
Lombard & Ulster Ltd
Lombard North Central PLC
London Scottish Bank PLC
London Trust Bank PLC
Lordsvale Finance PLC

MBNA International Bank Ltd
McDonnell Douglas Bank Ltd
McNeill Pearson Ltd
W. M. Mann & Co. (Investments) Ltd
Marks and Spencer Financial Services Ltd
Mase Westpac Ltd
Matheson Bank Ltd
Matlock Bank Ltd
Meghraj Bank Ltd
Mellon Europe Ltd
Mercury Provident PLC
Merrill Lynch International Bank Ltd
The Methodist Chapel Aid Association Ltd
Midland Bank PLC

Midland Bank Trust Company Ltd
Minories Finance Ltd
Minster Trust Ltd
Samuel Montagu & Co. Ltd
Morgan Grenfell & Co. Ltd
Moscow Narodny Bank Ltd
*Mount Banking Corporation Ltd
Mutual Trust and Savings Ltd

NIIB Group Ltd
NWS Bank PLC
National Bank of Egypt International Ltd
National Bank of Kuwait (International) PLC
The National Mortgage Bank PLC
National Westminster Bank PLC
NationsBank Europe Ltd
The Nikko Bank (UK) PLC
Noble Grossart Ltd
Nomura Bank International PLC
Northern Bank Ltd
Northern Bank Executor & Trustee Company Ltd
Nykredit Mortgage Bank PLC

Omega Trust Co. Ltd

PaineWebber International Bank Ltd
People's Bank PLC
Pointon York Ltd
The Private Bank and Trust Company Ltd
Provincial Bank PLC

Ralli Investment Company Ltd
R. Raphael & Sons PLC
Rathbone Bros. & Co. Ltd
Rea Brothers Ltd
Reliance Bank Ltd
Riggs AP Bank Ltd
Riyad Bank Europe Ltd
N. M. Rothschild & Sons Ltd
Royal Bank of Canada Europe Ltd
The Royal Bank of Scotland PLC
RoyScot Trust PLC

SBI European Bank Ltd
Sabanci Bank PLC
Sanwa International PLC
Saudi American Bank (UK) Ltd
Saudi International Bank (Al-Bank Al-Saudi Al-Alami Ltd)
Schroder Leasing Ltd
J. Henry Schroder Wagg & Co. Ltd
Scotiabank (UK) Ltd
Scottish Amicable Money Managers Ltd
Seccombe Marshall & Campion PLC
Secure Homes Ltd
Singer & Friedlander Ltd
Smith & Williamson Securities
Southsea Mortgage & Investment Co. Ltd
Standard Bank London Ltd
Standard Chartered Bank
Svenska International PLC

TSB Bank PLC
TSB Bank Scotland PLC
Tokai Bank Europe Ltd
Toronto Dominion Bank Europe Ltd
Turkish Bank (UK) Ltd
Tyndall Bank PLC

UBAF Bank Ltd
UCB Bank PLC
ULC Trust Ltd
Ulster Bank Ltd

Unibank PLC
Union Discount Company Ltd
The United Bank of Kuwait PLC
United Dominions Trust Ltd
Unity Trust Bank PLC

Wagon Finance Ltd
S. G. Warburg & Co. Ltd
Wesleyan Savings Bank Ltd
Western Trust & Savings Ltd
West Merchant Bank Ltd
Whiteaway Laidlaw Bank Ltd
Wimbledon & South West Finance PLC
Wintrust Securities Ltd
Woodchester Credit Lyonnais PLC

Yamaichi Bank (UK) PLC
Yorkshire Bank PLC

INCORPORATED OUTSIDE THE EC
(Including partnerships or other unincorporated associations
formed under the law of any member state of the European
Community other than the UK)
†Provisional liquidator appointed

ABSA Bank Ltd
Allied Bank of Pakistan Ltd
American Express Bank Ltd
Arab African International Bank
Arab Bank PLC
Arab Banking Corporation BSC
Arab National Bank
Asahi Bank Ltd
Ashikaga Bank Ltd
Australia & New Zealand Banking Group Ltd

BSI – Banca della Svizzera Italiana
Banca Serfin SA
Banco de la Nación Argentina
Banco do Brasil SA
Banco do Estado de São Paulo SA
Banco Mercantil de São Paulo SA
Banco Nacional de México SNC
Banco Real SA
Bancomer SA
Bangkok Bank Ltd
Bank Julius Baer & Co. Ltd
Bank Bumiputra Malaysia Berhad
PT Bank Ekspor Impor Indonesia (Persero)
Bank Handlowy w Warszawie SA
Bank Hapoalim BM
Bank Mellat
Bank Melli Iran
PT Bank Negara Indonesia (Persero)
Bank of America NT & SA
Bank of Baroda
The Bank of N. T. Butterfield & Son Ltd
Bank of Ceylon
Bank of China
The Bank of East Asia Ltd
The Bank of Fukuoka Ltd
Bank of India
Bank of Montreal
The Bank of New York
Bank of New Zealand
The Bank of Nova Scotia
Bank of Oman Ltd
Bank of Seoul
The Bank of Tokyo Ltd
The Bank of Yokohama Ltd
Bank Saderat Iran

Bank Sepah-Iran
Bank Tejarat
Bank von Ernst & Co. Ltd
Bankers Trust Company
Beirut Riyad Bank SAL
Boston Safe Deposit and Trust Company

Canadian Imperial Bank of Commerce
Canara Bank
Chang Hwa Commercial Bank Ltd
The Chase Manhattan Bank NA
Chemical Bank
The Chiba Bank Ltd
Cho Hung Bank
Christiania Bank og Kreditkasse
The Chuo Trust & Banking Co. Ltd
Citibank NA
Commercial Bank of Korea Ltd
Commonwealth Bank of Australia
Continental Bank, National Association
CoreStates Bank NA
Crédit Suisse
Creditanstalt-Bankverein
Cyprus Credit Bank Ltd
The Cyprus Popular Bank

The Dai-Ichi Kangyo Bank Ltd
The Daiwa Bank Ltd
Den norske Bank A/S
The Development Bank of Singapore Ltd
Discount Bank and Trust Company

Emirates Bank International Ltd

First Bank of Nigeria PLC
First Commercial Bank
First Fidelity Bank NA Pennsylvania
The First National Bank of Boston
The First National Bank of Chicago
Fleet Bank of Massachusetts, NA
French Bank of Southern Africa Ltd
The Fuji Bank Ltd

Ghana Commercial Bank
Girocredit Bank Aktiengesellschaft der Sparkassen
Gota Bank
Gulf International Bank BSC

Habib Bank AG Zurich
Habib Bank Ltd
Hanil Bank
Harris Trust and Savings Bank
The Hiroshima Bank Ltd
The Hokkaido Takushoku Bank Ltd
The Hokuriku Bank Ltd
The Hongkong and Shanghai Banking Corporation Ltd

The Industrial Bank of Japan Ltd

The Joyo Bank Ltd

Kansallis-Osake-Pankki
Korea Exchange Bank
Korea First Bank

The Long-Term Credit Bank of Japan Ltd

Malayan Banking Berhad
Mellon Bank NA
Merchants National Bank & Trust Company of Indianapolis
  (National City Bank, Indiana)
The Mitsubishi Bank Ltd
The Mitsubishi Trust and Banking Corporation
The Mitsui Trust & Banking Co. Ltd
Morgan Guaranty Trust Company of New York
Multibanco Comermex SA

NBD Bank, NA
National Australia Bank Ltd
National Bank of Abu Dhabi
National Bank of Canada
The National Bank of Dubai Ltd
National Bank of Pakistan
NationsBank of North Carolina NA
Nedcor Bank Ltd
The Nippon Credit Bank Ltd
Nordbanken
The Norinchukin Bank
The Northern Trust Company

Oversea-Chinese Banking Corporation Ltd
Overseas Trust Bank Ltd
Overseas Union Bank Ltd

Philippine National Bank
Postipankki Ltd

Qatar National Bank SAQ

R&I Bank of Western Australia Ltd
†Rafidain Bank
Raiffeisen Zentralbank Osterreich AG
Republic National Bank of New York
The Riggs National Bank of Washington DC
Riyad Bank
Royal Bank of Canada

The Sakura Bank Ltd
The Sanwa Bank Ltd
Saudi American Bank
Shanghai Commercial Bank Ltd
Shinhan Bank
The Siam Commercial Bank Ltd
Skandinaviska Enskilda Banken
Sonali Bank
State Bank of India
State Bank of New South Wales Ltd
State Bank of South Australia
State Street Bank and Trust Company
The Sumitomo Bank Ltd
The Sumitomo Trust & Banking Co. Ltd
Svenska Handelsbanken
SwedBank
Swiss Bank Corporation
Syndicate Bank

TC Ziraat Bankasi
The Thai Farmers Bank Ltd
The Tokai Bank Ltd
The Toronto-Dominion Bank
The Toyo Trust & Banking Company Ltd
Türkiye Iş Bankasi AŞ

Uco Bank
Union Bancaire Privée CBI-TDB
Union Bank of Finland Ltd
Union Bank of Nigeria PLC
Union Bank of Switzerland
United Bank Ltd
United Mizrahi Bank Ltd
United Overseas Bank Ltd

Westpac Banking Corporation

The Yasuda Trust & Banking Co. Ltd

Z-Länderbank Bank Austria AG
Zambia National Commercial Bank Ltd
Zivnostenská Banka AS

EUROPEAN AUTHORIZED INSTITUTIONS

The following are entitled to establish branches in the UK for the purpose of accepting deposits in the UK. The country of the home state supervisory authority is in parenthesis.

ABN AMRO Bank NV (Netherlands)
AIB Capital Markets PLC (Republic of Ireland)
AIB Finance Ltd (Republic of Ireland)
ASLK-CGER Bank NV-SA (Belgium)
Allied Irish Banks PLC (Republic of Ireland)
Anglo Irish Bank Corporation PLC (Republic of Ireland)

BfG Bank AG (Germany)
Banca Cassa di Risparmio di Torino SpA (Italy)
Banca Commerciale Italiana (Italy)
Banca di Roma SpA (Italy)
Banca Nazionale dell'Agricoltura SpA (Italy)
Banca Nazionale del Lavoro SpA (Italy)
Banca Popolare di Milano (Italy)
Banca Popolare di Novara (Italy)
Banco Ambrosiano Veneto SpA (Italy)
Banco Bilbao-Vizcaya (Spain)
Banco Central Hispanoamericano SA (Spain)
Banco de Sabadell (Spain)
Banco di Napoli SpA (Italy)
Banco di Sicilia SpA (Italy)
Banco Español de Crédito SA (Spain)
Banco Espirito Santo e Comercial de Lisboa (Portugal)
Banco Exterior de España SA (Spain)
Banco Nacional Ultramarino SA (Portugal)
Banco Português do Atlântico (Portugal)
Banco Santander (Spain)
Banco Totta & Açores SA (Portugal)
The Bank of Ireland (Republic of Ireland)
Banque Arabe et Internationale d'Investissement (France)
Banque Banorabe (France)
Banque Brussels Lambert (Belgium)
Banque Française de l'Orient (France)
Banque Française du Commerce Extérieur (France)
Banque Indosuez (France)
Banque Internationale à Luxembourg SA (Luxembourg)
Banque Nationale de Paris (France)
Banque Paribas (France)
Banque Worms (France)
Bayerische Hypotheken-und Wechsel-Bank AG (Germany)
Bayerische Landesbank Girozentrale (Germany)
Bayerische Vereinsbank AG (Germany)
Belgolaise SA (Belgium)
Berliner Bank AG (Germany)
Berliner Handels-und Frankfurter Bank (Germany)
Byblos Bank Belgium SA (Belgium)

CARIPLO (Cassa di Risparmio delle Provincie Lombarde SpA) (Italy)
Caisse Nationale de Crédit Agricole (France)
Cassa di Risparmio di Verona Vicenza Belluno e Ancona SpA (Italy)
Commerzbank AG (Germany)
Compagnie Financière de CIC et de l'Union Européenne (France)
Confederacion Española de Cajas de Ahorros (Spain)
Crédit Commercial de France (France)
Crédit du Nord (France)
Crédit Lyonnais (France)
Crédit Lyonnais Bank Nederland NV (Netherlands)
Credito Italiano (Italy)

Den Danske Bank Aktieselskab (Denmark)
Deutsche Bank AG (Germany)
Deutsche Genossenschaftsbank (Germany)
Dresdner Bank AG (Germany)

Ergobank SA (Greece)

First National Building Society (Republic of Ireland)

Generale Bank (Belgium)

Hamburgische Landesbank Girozentrale (Germany)

ICS Building Society (Republic of Ireland)
Internationale Nederlanden Bank NV (Netherlands)
Irish Permanent Building Society (Republic of Ireland)
Istituto Bancario San Paolo di Torino SpA (Italy)

Jyske Bank (Denmark)

Kas-Associatie NV (Netherlands)
Kredietbank NV (Belgium)

Landesbank Hessen-Thüringen Girozentrale (Germany)

MeesPierson NV (Netherlands)
Monte dei Paschi di Siena (Italy)

National Bank of Greece SA (Greece)
Norddeutsche Landesbank Girozentrale (Germany)

Rabobank Nederland (Coöperatieve Centrale Raiffeisen-
Boerenleenbank BA) (Netherlands)

Société Générale (France)
Südwestdeutsche Landesbank Girozentrale (Germany)

Ulster Investment Bank Ltd (Republic of Ireland)

Westdeutsche Landesbank Girozentrale (Germany)

The National Debt

Net central government borrowing each year represents an addition to the National Debt. At the end of March 1992 the National Debt amounted to some £214,500 million of which about £9,400 million was in currencies other than sterling. Of the £205,100 million sterling debt, £134,400 million consisted of gilt-edged stock; of this, 30 per cent had a maturity of up to five years, 46 per cent a maturity of over five years and up to 15 years, and 24 per cent a maturity of over 15 years or undated. The remaining sterling debt was made up mainly of national savings (£34,500 million), certificates of tax deposits, Treasury bills, and Ways and Means advances (very short-term internal government borrowing).

Sizeable trust funds have been established over the past fifty years for the purpose of reducing the National Debt. The National Fund was established in 1927 with an original gift of £499,878. At 31 March 1992 it was valued at £77,977,907; it is administered by Baring Brothers & Co. Ltd. The Elsie Mackay Fund was established in 1929 with an original gift of £527,809 to run for 45–50 years. It was wound up on 19 January 1979, when it was valued at £4,902,864. The John Buchanan Fund was established in 1932 with gifts totalling £36,702 to run for 50 years. It was wound up on 28 February 1982, when it was valued at £204,138.

Slang Terms for Money
(Reproduced from *Whitaker's Almanack* 1891)

In addition to the ordinary terms there are others which, although puzzling to a foreigner, are tolerably well understood in this country. In Scotland, a man who flies 'kites' may not be worth a 'bodle', and in England not worth a 'mag' – coins which no one ever saw. Such a man will toss you for a 'bob'. He, of course, would be shunned by the lady who lost a 'pony' on last year's Oaks, and by her husband who lost a 'monkey' on the Derby at Epsom a day or two previously. A gentleman who is worth a 'plum' (£100,000) need never be short of 'tin'; while the outcast who begs a few 'coppers' in

order to procure a bed generally has no 'blunt'. The following words are commonly in use:

A Joey = 4d.
A Tanner = 6d.
A Bob = 1s.
Half a Bull = 2s. 6d.
A Bull = 5s.
A Quid = £1

A Pony = £25
A Monkey = £500
A Kite = An accommodation Bill
Browns = Copper or bronze
Tin = Money generally
Blunt = Silver, or money in general

The Cost of Living

The first cost-of-living index to be calculated in Great Britain was the one which took July 1914 as 100 and was based on the pattern of expenditure of working class families in 1904. Since 1947 the General Index of Retail Prices has superseded the cost-of-living index, although the older term is still often popularly applied to it. This index is designed to reflect the month-by-month changes in the average level of retail prices of goods and services purchased by the 'majority' of households in the United Kingdom, including practically all wage-earners and most small and medium salary-earners. For spending coming within the scope of the index, a representative list of items is selected and the prices actually charged for these items are collected at regular intervals. In working out the index figure, the price changes are 'weighted' – that is, given different degrees of importance – in accordance with the pattern of consumption of the average family.

A more widely used guide when considering changes in the average level of prices of all consumer goods and services, particularly over a number of years, is the consumer price index, now renamed the consumers' expenditure deflator. This index, which has been calculated back to 1938, covers the expenditure of all consumers as defined for national income purposes, and compares the price of goods and services actually purchased in a given year with the prices of the same goods and services in a base year.

During 1973 the Central Statistical Office constructed an annual index of prices of consumer goods and services over the period 1914 to 1972. This index has been constructed by linking together the pre-war cost-of-living index for the period 1914–38, the consumers' expenditure deflator for the period 1938 and 1946–62 and the General Index of Retail Prices for the period 1962–72.

In August 1979, the tax and price index (TPI) was introduced in order to provide a statistic which incorporates the effects of direct and indirect taxation, as well as prices, on taxpayers. The TPI is not directly concerned with the purchasing power of money, however, but with the purchasing power of pre-tax income. The General Index of Retail Prices thus retains its function of measuring the changes in the prices of goods and services purchased by households (from their post-tax income), and therefore as an indicator of the purchasing power of money.

	Long term index of consumer goods and services (Jan. 1987 = 100)	Comparable purchasing power of £1 in 1992
1914	2.8	49.46
1915	3.5	39.57
1920	7.0	19.79
1925	5.0	27.70
1930	4.5	30.78
1935	4.0	34.63
1938	4.4	31.48
There are no official figures for 1939–45		
1946	7.4	18.72
1950	9.0	15.39
1955	11.2	12.37
1960	12.6	10.99
1965	14.8	9.36
1970	18.5	7.49
1975	34.2	4.05
1976	39.8	3.48
1977	46.1	3.00
1978	50.0	2.77
1979	56.6	2.45
1980	66.8	2.07
1981	74.8	1.85
1982	81.2	1.71
1983	84.9	1.63
1984	89.2	1.55
1985	94.6	1.46
1986	97.8	1.42
1987	101.9	1.36
1988	106.9	1.30
1989	115.2	1.20
1990	126.1	1.10
1991	133.5	1.04
1992	138.5	1.00

By employing this table an annual purchasing power of the pound index may be derived by taking the inverse of the price index. So, for example, if the purchasing power of the pound is taken to be 100p in 1975, then its comparable purchasing power in 1992 would be:

$$100 \times \frac{34.2}{138.5} = 24.7p$$

It should be noted that these figures can only be approximate.

Mutual Societies

FRIENDLY SOCIETIES IN BRITAIN

Friendly societies are voluntary mutual organizations, the main purposes of which are the provision of relief or maintenance during sickness, unemployment or retirement, and the provision of life assurance. Many of the older traditional societies complement their business activities by social activity and a general care for individual members in ways normally outside the scope of a purely commercial organization. There are three main categories of friendly societies: societies with separately registered branches, commonly called orders; centralized societies, which conduct business directly with members (having no separately registered branches); and collecting societies. Collecting societies conduct industrial assurance business and are subject to the requirements of the Industrial Assurance Acts in addition to the Friendly Societies Acts. Industrial assurance is life assurance for which the premiums are payable at intervals of less than two months and are received by means of collectors who make house-to-house visits for the purpose.

Long before the term 'friendly society' came into use, the seeds of voluntary mutual insurance had been sown in the ancient religious and trade guilds. Guilds had become widespread in Britain by the 14th century. By then, the purely charitable character of the original guilds had largely changed with the emergence of numerous small institutions adopting primitive mutual insurance methods of a regular flat rate contribution to insure relief when sick or in old age and a payment to the widow in the event of death. The present register of friendly societies includes several societies which have been in existence for more than 200 years, the oldest, operating in Scotland, being the Incorporation of Carters in Leith, established in 1555.

The first Act for the encouragement and protection of friendly societies in this country was not passed until 1793, but various amending Acts were passed during the next century as the result of the recommendations of successive select committees (including a Royal Commission in 1871). The rules and other documents of societies deposited with local justices passed into the custody of the Registrar of Friendly Societies following the Act of 1846. Those relating to some societies no longer on the register have been transferred to the Public Record Office for permanent preservation.

The Friendly Societies Act 1974 allows three other main classes of society to be registered: benevolent societies, working men's clubs and specially authorized societies. Benevolent societies are established for any charitable or benevolent purpose, to provide the same type of benefits as would be permissible for a friendly society, but in contrast the benefits must be for persons who are not members instead of, or in addition to, members. Working men's clubs provide social and recreational facilities for members. Specially authorized societies are registered for any purpose authorized by the Treasury as a purpose to which some or all of the provisions of the 1974 Act ought to be extended. Examples are societies for the promotion of science, literature and the fine arts, or to enable members to pursue an interest in sports and games.

The most recent legislation, the Friendly Societies Act 1992, creates a new legislative framework for friendly societies, enabling them to provide a wider range of services to their members and allowing them to compete on more equal terms with other financial institutions. At the same time it provides for more flexible prudential supervision to safeguard members of societies.

The Act enables friendly societies to incorporate and establish subsidiaries to provide various financial and other services to their members and the public. The activities which subsidiaries will be able to conduct as the relevant provisions come into force under subordinate legislation include those: to establish and manage unit trust schemes and Personal Equity Plans; to arrange for the provision of credit, whether as agents or providers; to carry on long-term or general insurance business; to provide insurance intermediary services; to provide fund management services for trustees of pension funds; to administer estates and execute trusts of wills; and to establish and manage sheltered housing, residential homes for the elderly, hospitals and nursing homes.

The Act establishes a new framework to oversee friendly societies, including a Friendly Societies Commission, whose principal functions will be to regulate the activities of friendly societies, promote their financial stability and protect members' funds. All friendly societies carrying on insurance or non-insurance business will require authorization by the Commission, which will have a broad range of prudential powers. Friendly societies will also be brought within the scope of the Policyholders Protection Act 1975, the statutory investor protection scheme covering insurance policyholders.

The principal statistics at the end of 1991 are given in the table below.

	No. of societies	No. of members 000s	Benefits paid £000s	Total funds £000s
Orders and branches	1,335*	342†	6,375†	179,848†
Collecting societies	30	13,575‡	227,112	2,763,470
Other centralized societies	384	2,872	261,425	2,540,073
Benevolent societies	80	324	4,163	28,344
Working men's clubs	2,373	1,274†	n/a	162,793†
Specially authorized societies				
Loans	8	15	n/a	328
Others	139	99	916	20,323

* 18 orders, 1,317 branches
† 1990 figure
‡ Assurances

INDUSTRIAL AND PROVIDENT SOCIETIES IN BRITAIN

The familiar 'Co-op' societies are amongst the wide variety which are registered under the Industrial and Provident Societies Act 1965. This consolidating Act, which is administered by the Chief Registrar of Friendly Societies, provides for the registration of societies and lays down the broad framework within which they must operate. Internal relations of societies are governed by their registered rules.

Registration under the Act confers upon a society corporate status by its registered name with perpetual succession and a common seal, and limited liability. A society qualifies for registration if it is carrying on an industry, business or trade, and it satisfies the Registrar either (a) that it is a bona fide co-operative society, or (b) that in view of the fact that its business is being, or is intended to be, conducted for the benefit of the community, there are special reasons why it should be registered under the Act rather than as a company under the Companies Act.

The Credit Unions Act 1979 added a new class of society registerable under the 1965 Act. It also made provision for the supervision of these savings and loan bodies. Unlike other classes, where the role of the Registry is solely that of a registration authority, it is for credit unions the prudential supervisor, seeking to encourage the prudent safekeeping of investors' money.

During 1991 the number of registered societies of all classes decreased by 4 to 11, 11,388 but the number of credit unions increased by 52 to 327. The largest group in terms of turnover was that consisting of the retail societies, which includes those trading under the 'Co-op' sign, with sales in 1991 of £5,150 million. The principal statistics at the end of 1991 are given in the table below.

	No. of societies	No. of members 000s	Funds of members £000s	Total assets £000s
Retail	184	6,985	1,207,225	2,535,225
Wholesale and productive	200	183	468,867	1,212,832
Agricultural	1,105	306	215,278	513,848
Fishing	95	6	4,955	15,250
Social and recreational clubs	3,766	1,952	205,084	331,916
General service	1,135	503	5,312,369	6,493,737
Housing	4,552	195	14,481,884	20,749,474
Credit unions	327	69	22,163	23,473
TOTAL	11,388	10,198	21,917,825	31,875,755

BUILDING SOCIETIES IN THE UK

The Building Societies Act 1986 gave building societies a completely new legal framework, the first since the initial comprehensive building society legislation in 1874. The new Act applies to societies throughout the United Kingdom.

The 1986 Act made provision for a Building Societies Commission to promote the protection of shareholders and depositors, the financial stability of societies, and to administer the system of regulation of building societies provided under the Act. The First Commissioner and Chairman of the Commission is also Chief Registrar of Friendly Societies (see Index). Much of the Act is concerned with the powers of control of the Commission and provision in relation to the management of societies, accounts, audit and so on. But the greatest impact flowed from the new powers which societies could adopt, leading to an increased range of services which they might provide. There were also some significant changes in relation to members' rights.

Under an earlier Act, raising funds to make loans was the only purpose for which a building society could exist. Under the 1986 Act that has only to be its principal purpose. The constitutional provisions include the right of members to have access to the register of members, entitlement to have notices of meetings and to vote, and the right of members to have a resolution circulated.

In addition to traditional mortgage business, the power of societies to lend in respect of shared ownership, index-linked and equity-linked schemes is given. Societies may also lend the deposit, lend on registered land before the borrower is registered as the owner and on other equitable interests. Provision is also made for societies to make advances secured on land outside the United Kingdom. Larger societies were able, for the first time, to make unsecured loans, and make loans on mobile homes.

Under the 1962 Act building societies could only hold land for the purposes of running their business. The 1986 Act gave building societies power to hold and develop land as a commercial asset. However, the land has to be primarily for residential purposes, or adjoining land, or for purposes incidental to the holding of residential land.

An investor protection scheme and the Investor Protection Board which administers it were established under the Act. The Scheme comes into operation on the insolvency of a building society and protects the first £20,000 of a person's shares. Joint holdings are split between the holders so that, for example, a husband and wife can each have £20,000 of protected investments. The Board determines the percentage of protected investment in each case; there is a statutory maximum of 90 per cent.

Societies were also empowered to offer for the first time the following services:

(a) Money transmission services
(b) Foreign exchange services
(c) Making or receiving of payments as agents
(d) Management, as agents, of mortgage investments
(e) Management, as agents, of land (larger societies only)
(f) Arranging for the provision of services relating to the acquisition or disposal of investments for individuals
(g) Establishment and management of personal equity plans
(h) Arranging for the provision of credit to individuals
(i) Establishment and management of unit trust schemes for the provision of pensions (through a subsidiary)
(j) Establishment and administration of pension schemes
(k) Arranging for the provision of insurance of any description
(l) Giving advice on insurance of any description
(m) Estate agency service (through a subsidiary)
(n) Surveys and valuations of land
(o) Conveyancing services

Technical problems emerged in relation to these services and in June 1988 Parliament made Orders which allowed societies to have the power to own up to 100 per cent of a life assurance company, 15 per cent of a general insurance company, 100 per cent of a stockbroking company and to offer an additional range of financial services including executorship and trusteeship, hire purchase, and leasing and safe deposit facilities. The Orders also included an increase in the limit on unsecured personal loans from £5,000 to £10,000.

On mergers, the main difference is that borrowers have a vote. For a merger to be approved at least 50 per cent of borrowers who exercise their right to vote must vote in favour, as well as 75 per cent of qualifying share investors who vote. Provision is also made for a society to convert to company status. During 1989 the Abbey National became the first, and as yet the only, building society to complete the process of conversion to a company. During the year ended 31 March 1992 six mergers between societies were completed.

OMBUDSMAN SCHEME

Societies must belong to an ombudsman scheme for the investigation of complaints. Matters to be covered by the scheme include operation of share and deposit accounts, loans (but not the making of new loans), money transmission services, foreign exchange services, agency payments and receipts, and the provision of credit. Grounds for complaint include breach of the Act or contract, unfair treatment or maladministration, and where the complainant has suffered pecuniary loss or expense or inconvenience. A society must agree to be bound by decisions of the adjudicator unless it agrees to give notice to its members and the public of its reasons for not doing so. For address of the Building Societies Ombudsman scheme, *see* Index.

BUILDING SOCIETIES 1991–2

	1991	1992
No. of societies – total	110	105
– authorized	94	88
No. of shareholders (000s)	37,925	37,533
No. of depositors (000s)	4,698	3,879
No. of borrowers (000s)	6,998	7,055
Share balances (£m)	177,519	187,108
Deposit balances (£m)	49,517	57,068
Mortgage balances (£m)	196,946	210,995
Total assets (£m)	243,980	262,515
Advances during year		
No. (000s)	1,492	1,187
Amount (£m)	42,948	34,989

MORTGAGE ARREARS AND REPOSSESSIONS

The economic recession has resulted in a sharp rise in mortgage arrears and repossessions, with more than 75,000 properties repossessed in 1991. That total fell by 7,000 in 1992 as a result of a greater willingness by societies to enter into arrangements with borrowers. However, the number of loans where repayments were six months or more in arrears increased from 275,000 at the end of 1991 to 352,000 at the end of 1992. Details of loans outstanding and properties repossessed for recent years are shown below.

	1986	1987	1988	1989	1990	1991	1992
No. of loans at end year (000s)	8,138	8,283	8,564	9,125	9,415	9,815	9,922
Properties repossessed in year							
number	24,090	26,390	18,510	15,810	43,890	75,540	68,540
%	0.30	0.32	0.22	0.17	0.47	0.77	0.70

INTEREST RATES – MORTGAGE AND SHARE

The interest rates prevailing on mortgage lending and share investment vary from society to society and in relation to the type or amount of loan or investment. General rate changes are made in response to market conditions and recent rates, with the dates of change, are given below.

The interval between the payments or compounding of interest is crucial in determining the competitiveness of particular societies' accounts. In order to make a true comparison of interest rates, the annual percentage rate or APR, which should appear in all advertisements and leaflets, must be used.

	May '91	July '91	Sept. '91	Jan. '92	May '92	Sept. '92	Oct. '92	Nov. '92	Jan. '93
Gross average rate for all share accounts %	11.16	10.20	9.77	9.73	8.93	8.41	7.52	6.59	6.25
Predominant mortgages rate %	12.45	11.95	11.50	10.95	10.70	9.95	9.34	8.55	8.09

SOCIETIES WITH TOTAL ASSETS EXCEEDING £1 MILLION

AT END OF FINANCIAL YEAR 1992

Name of Society (abbreviated*) and head office address	Share investors	Total assets £'000
Alliance and Leicester, 49 Park Lane, London WIY 4EQ	2,875,000	20,529,500
Barnsley, Regent Street, Barnsley, South Yorks S70 2EH	29,901	169,165
Bath Investment, 20 Charles Street, Bath BA1 1HY	12,480	47,945
Beverley, 57 Market Place, Beverley, N. Humberside HU17 8AA	5,623	34,005
Bexhill-on-Sea, 2 Devonshire Square, Bexhill-on-Sea, East Sussex TN40 1AE	2,924	17,229
Birmingham Midshires, PO Box 81, 35–49 Lichfield Street, Wolverhampton WV1 1EL	647,094	3,822,811
Bradford and Bingley, Crossflatts, Bingley, West Yorks. BD16 2UA	1,269,932	13,048,693
Bristol and West, Broad Quay, Bristol BS99 7AX	979,430	7,731,961
Britannia, Newton House, Cheadle Road, Leek, Staffs. ST13 5RG	1,205,052	10,517,300
Buckinghamshire, High Street, Chalfont St Giles, Bucks. HP8 4QB	5,750	48,531
Cambridge, 32 St Andrew's Street, Cambridge CB2 3AR	40,500	293,128
Catholic, 7 Strutton Ground, London SW1P 2HY	3,279	22,330
Century, 23 Albany Street, Edinburgh EH1 3QW	1,227	9,406
Chelsea, Thirlestaine Hall, Thirlestaine Road, Cheltenham, Glos. GL53 7AL	208,955	2,294,900
Cheltenham and Gloucester, Barnett Way, Gloucester GL4 7RL	1,102,000	16,067,200
Chesham, 12 Market Square, Chesham, Bucks. HP5 1ER	9,750	68,643
Cheshire, Castle Street, Macclesfield, Chesire SK11 6AH	231,119	1,236,491
Chorley and District, 49–51 St Thomas's Road, Chorley, Lancs. PR7 1JL	8,410	54,340
City and Metropolitan, 219 High Street, Bromley, Kent BR1 1PR	9,197	89,363
Clay Cross Benefit, Eyre Street, Clay Cross, Chesterfield S45 9NS	3,200	14,380
Coventry, PO Box 9, High Street, Coventry CV1 5QN	440,373	2,694,511
Cumberland, Cumberland House, Castle Street, Carlisle CA3 8RX	119,802	507,566
Darlington, Tubwell Row, Darlington, Co. Durham DL1 1NX	42,866	248,613
Derbyshire, Duffield Hall, Duffield, Derby DE56 1AG	285,206	1,515,936
Dudley, Dudley House, Stone Street, Dudley DY1 1NP	16,715	72,967
Dunfermline, 12 East Port, Dunfermline, Fife KY12 7LD	137,748	720,012
Earl Shilton, 22 The Hollow, Earl Shilton, Leicester LE9 7NB	9,489	52,039
Ecology, 18 Station Road, Cross Hills, Keighley, West Yorks BD20 7EH	2,873	10,334
Furness, 51–55 Duke Street, Barrow-in-Furness LA14 1RT	61,746	314,680
Gainsborough, 26 Lord Street, Gainsborough, Lincs. DN21 2DB	4,638	23,621
Greenwich, 279–283 Greenwich High Road, London SE10 8NL	26,600	145,388
Halifax, Trinity Road, Halifax, West Yorks HX1 2RG	7,739,800	62,775,400
Hanley Economic, Granville House, Festival Park, Hanley, Stoke-on-Trent, Staffs. ST1 5TB	27,879	162,619
Harpenden, 14 Station Road, Harpenden, Herts. AL5 4SE	8,669	39,809
Heart of England, Olympus Avenue, Tachbrook Park, Warwick CV34 6NQ	190,520	1,039,175
Hinckley and Rugby, Upper Bond Street, Hinckley, Leics. LE10 1DG	39,594	240,410
Holmesdale, 43 Church Street, Reigate, Surrey RH2 0AE	5,630	57,470
Ilkeston Permanent, 24–26 South Street, Ilkeston, Derby DE7 5HQ	4,103	16,828
Ipswich, 44 Upper Brook Street, Ipswich IP4 1DP	27,844	155,255
Kent Reliance, Reliance House, Manor Road, Chatham, Kent ME4 6AF	44,759	225,728
Lambeth, 118–120 Westminster Bridge Road, London SE1 7XE	50,333	525,720
Leeds and Holbeck, 105 Albion Street, Leeds LS1 5AS	287,525	2,431,550
Leeds Permanent, Permanent House, 1 Lovell Park Road, Leeds LS1 1NS	3,448,420	18,318,500
Leek United, 50 St Edward Street, Leek, Staffs. ST13 5DH	47,827	301,435
Londonderry Provident, 7 Castle Street, Londonderry BT48 6HQ	1,011	6,086
Loughborough, 6 High Street, Loughborough, Leics. LE11 2QB	12,486	87,573
Manchester, 18–20 Bridge Street, Manchester M3 3BU	8,616	76,768
Mansfield, Regent House, Regent Street, Mansfield, Notts. NG18 1SS	18,453	101,659
Market Harborough, Welland House, The Square, Market Harborough, Leics. LE16 7PD	29,470	193,013
Marsden, 6–20 Russell Street, Nelson, Lancs. BB9 7NJ	40,300	244,844
Melton Mowbray, 39 Nottingham Street, Melton Mowbray, Leics. LE13 1NR	32,369	183,599
Mercantile, 75 Howard Street, North Shields, Tyne and Wear NE30 1AQ	21,608	124,465
Monmouthshire, John Frost Square, Newport, Gwent NP9 1PX	22,947	139,075
National and Provincial, Provincial House, Bradford BD1 1NL	2,101,310	12,036,100
National Counties, National Counties House, Church Street, Epsom, Surrey KT17 4NL	16,000	356,263
Nationwide, Nationwide House, Pipers Way, Swindon SN38 1NW	6,256,214	34,996,000
Newbury, 17–20 Bartholomew Street, Newbury, Berks. RG14 5LY	28,293	213,917
Newcastle, Grainger Chambers, Hood Street, Newcastle upon Tyne NE1 6JP	139,847	1,077,544
North of England, 50 Fawcett Street, Sunderland SR1 1SA	216,576	1,420,740
Northern Rock, Northern Rock House, Gosforth, Newcastle upon Tyne NE3 4PL	839,634	6,017,368
Norwich and Peterborough, Peterborough Business Park, Lynchwood, Peterborough PE2 6WZ	168,067	1,368,651
Nottingham, 5–13 Upper Parliament Street, Nottingham NG1 2BX	135,500	783,924

Name of Society (abbreviated*) and head office address	Share investors	Total assets £'000
Nottingham Imperial, Imperial Building, 29 Bridgford Road, West Bridgford, Nottingham NG2 6AU	6,412	35,925
Penrith, 7 King Street, Penrith, Cumbria CA11 7AR	6,548	45,277
Portman, Portman House, Richmond Hill, Bournemouth, Dorset BH2 6EP	479,073	2,816,745
Principality, PO Box 89, Principality Buildings, Queen Street, Cardiff CF1 1UA	230,511	1,115,438
Progressive, 33–37 Wellington Place, Belfast BT1 6HH	40,261	278,603
Saffron Walden, Herts. and Essex, 1A Market Street, Saffron Walden, Essex CB10 1HX	35,183	197,528
St Pancras, 200 Finchley Road, London NW3 6DA	10,122	95,509
Scarborough, Prospect House, 442/444 Scalby Road, Scarborough, North Yorks. YO12 6EE	62,410	398,026
Scottish, 23 Manor Place, Edinburgh EH3 7XE	16,526	96,449
Shepshed, Bull Ring, Shepshed, Loughborough, Leics. LE12 9QD	7,034	30,288
Skipton, The Bailey, Skipton, North Yorks. BD23 1DN	222,183	3,008,512
Stafford Railway, 4 Market Square, Stafford ST16 2JH	7,676	38,765
Staffordshire, Jubilee House, PO Box 66, 84 Salop Street, Wolverhampton WV3 0SA	182,414	912,557
Standard, 64 Church Way, North Shields, Tyne and Wear NE29 0AF	2,375	14,593
Stroud and Swindon, Rowcroft, Stroud, Glos. GL5 3BG	93,677	504,213
Surrey, Sentinel House, 10–12 Massetts Road, Horley, Surrey RH6 7DE	8,829	78,524
Swansea, 11 Cradock Street, Swansea SA1 3EW	3,241	26,398
Teachers, Allenview House, Hanham Road, Wimborne, Dorset BH21 1AG	9,300	115,183
Tipton and Coseley, 70 Owen Street, Tipton, West Midlands DY4 8HG	16,061	81,963
Tynemouth, 53–55 Howard Street, North Shields, Tyne and Wear NE30 1AN	6,779	46,261
Universal, Universal House, Kings Manor, Newcastle upon Tyne NE1 6PA	24,900	173,544
Vernon, 19 St Petersgate, Stockport, Cheshire SK1 1HF	26,803	112,707
West Bromwich, 374 High Street, West Bromwich, West Midlands B70 8LR	269,280	1,239,825
West Cumbria, Cumbria House, Murray Road, Workington CA14 2AD	6,650	35,390
Woolwich, Watling Street, Bexleyheath, Kent DA6 7RR	3,247,000	23,263,100
Yorkshire, Yorkshire House, Yorkshire Drive, Bradford BD5 8LJ	754,766	4,846,656

* 'Building Society' are the last words in every society's name

National Savings

NATIONAL SAVINGS BANK

On 31 May 1993, there were about 15,881,000 active accounts with the sum of approximately £1,444.5 million due to depositors in ordinary accounts and about 4,848,000 active accounts with the sum of approximately £8,911.5 million due to depositors in investment accounts.

Interest is earned at 3.75 per cent per year on each ordinary account for every complete calendar month in which the balance is £500 or more, provided the account is kept open for the whole of 1993 (31 December 1992 to 1 January 1994); and at 2.5 per cent per year for other months or for accounts opened or closed during 1993. The minimum deposit is £10; maximum balance £10,000 plus interest credited. On 31 May 1993 the average amount held in ordinary accounts was approximately £91.

The investment account pays a higher rate of interest (the current rate can be found at any post office). The minimum deposit is £20; maximum balance £100,000 plus interest credited. On 31 May 1993 the average amount held in investment accounts was approximately £1,838.

PREMIUM BONDS

Premium Bonds are a Government security which were first introduced on 1 November 1956. Premium Bonds enable savers to enter a regular draw for tax-free prizes, while retaining the right to get their money back. A sum equivalent to interest on each bond is put into a prize fund and distributed by weekly and monthly prize draws. (The rate of interest is 5 per cent a year from 1 March 1993). The prizes are drawn by ERNIE (electronic random number indicator equipment) and are free of all UK income tax and capital gains tax.

Bonds are in units of £1, with a minimum purchase of £100; above this, purchases must be in multiples of £10, up to a maximum holding limit of £20,000 per person. Winners of £50 prize warrants will be invited to return their prize warrants to National Savings, Lytham, if they wish to reinvest. This transaction cannot be made through the Post Office. Bonds can only be held in the name of an individual and not by organizations.

Bonds become eligible for prizes once they have been held for three clear calendar months following the month of purchase. Each £1 unit can win only one prize per draw, but it will be awarded the highest for which it is drawn. Bonds remain eligible for prizes until they are repaid. When a holder dies, bonds remain eligible for prizes up to and including the twelfth monthly draw after the month in which the holder dies.

By April 1993 bonds to the value of £5,574 million had been sold. Of these £2,910 million had been cashed, leaving £2,663 million still invested. By the April 1993 prize draw, 42.36 million prizes totalling £2,484 million had been distributed since the first prize draw in June 1957.

INCOME BONDS

National Savings Income Bonds were introduced in 1982. They are particularly suitable for those who want to receive regular monthly payments of interest while preserving the full cash value of their capital. The bonds are sold in multiples of £1,000. The minimum holding is £2,000 and the maximum £250,000 (sole or joint holding).

Interest is calculated on a day-to-day basis and paid monthly. Interest is taxable, but is paid without deduction of tax at source. The bonds have a guaranteed life of ten years, but may be repaid at par before maturity on giving three

months' notice. If repayment of a bond is made within the first year of purchase, interest from the date of purchase to the date of repayment is earned at half rate. If the sole or sole surviving holder dies, however, no fixed period of notice is required and there is no loss of interest for repayment made within the first year.

Net investment in National Savings Income Bonds was £9,970 million at the end of April 1993.

INDEXED INCOME BONDS

Indexed Income Bonds were withdrawn from sale on 28 August 1987. Existing holders will continue to receive monthly income in accordance with the prospectus.

CHILDREN'S BONUS BONDS

Children's Bonus Bonds were introduced in July 1991. The latest issue, Issue E, was introduced on 7 December 1992. They can be bought for any child under 16 and will go on growing in value until he or she is 21. The bonds are sold in multiples of £25. The minimum holding is £25, the maximum £1,000 per child (excluding interest and bonuses) in all issues. Bonds for children under 16 must be held by a parent or guardian.

Children's Bonus Bonds (Issue E) earn 5 per cent a year over five years. A bonus (18.28 per cent) of the purchase price is added at the fifth anniversary. This is equal to 7.85 per cent a year compound. All returns are totally exempt from UK income tax. No interest is earned on bonds cashed in before the first anniversary of purchase. Bonuses are only payable if the bond is held until the next bonus date. Bonds over five years old continue to earn interest and bonuses until the holder is 21, when they should be cashed in. If bonds are not cashed in on the holder's 21st birthday, they earn no interest after that birthday.

FIRST OPTION BONDS

FIRST (Fixed Interest Rate Savings Tax-paid) Option Bonds were introduced in July 1992. They offer guaranteed rates without the need for long-term commitment for personal savers over 16. They can be held indefinitely and will continue to grow in value at rates of interest fixed for 12 months at a time. Tax is deducted from the interest at source. The minimum purchase is £1,000 and the maximum holding is £250,000. Withdrawals can be made without penalty at any anniversary date and there is no formal notice period for repayment. No interest is earned on repayments before the first anniversary.

CAPITAL BONDS

National Savings Capital Bonds were introduced in January 1989. The latest series, Series G, was introduced on 7 December 1992. Capital Bonds offer capital growth over five years with guaranteed returns at fixed rates. The interest is taxable each year (for those who pay income tax) but is not deducted at source. The minimum purchase is £100, with larger purchases in multiples of £100. There is a maximum holding limit of £250,000 from Series B onwards.

Capital Bonds will be repaid in full with all interest gained at the end of five years. No interest is earned on bonds repaid in the first year.

DEPOSIT BONDS

National Savings Deposit Bonds were withdrawn from sale on 19 November 1988. All Deposit Bonds purchased on or before that date may continue to be held, and will earn interest, beyond the tenth anniversary of purchase.

YEARLY PLAN

The National Savings Yearly Plan was introduced on 2 July 1984. It offers a guaranteed tax-free return. Applicants agree to make 12 monthly payments, leading to the issue of a Yearly Plan Certificate. The maximum guaranteed rate of interest is earned if the certificate is held for a full four years. Applications may be made by any individuals aged seven or over; in the name of children under seven years; and by not more than two trustees for a sole beneficiary.

Payments must be made on the same date every month by standing order from a bank or other acceptable account. Only one payment may be made in any one month and must be in multiples of £5. Minimum monthly contribution is £20, maximum £400. Net investment in National Savings Yearly Plan was £511,628,797 at 30 April 1993.

GILTS ON THE NATIONAL SAVINGS STOCK REGISTER

Government stock or 'Gilts' are Stock Exchange securities issued by the Government. They usually have a life of between five and 20 years and most pay a guaranteed fixed rate of interest twice a year throughout this period. When they reach the end of this period they are 'redeemed' (which means repaid) at their face value.

The National Savings Stock Register (NSSR) enables investors to buy and sell Gilts by post. It is now possible to have most new issues of Gilts registered on the NSSR. Interest on Gilts held on the NSSR, although taxable, is paid in full without deduction of tax at source.

NATIONAL SAVINGS CERTIFICATES

RECENT ISSUES

The amount, including accrued interest, index-linked increase or bonus remaining to the credit of investors in National Savings Certificates on 30 April 1993 was approximately £17,010.3 million. In 1992–3, approximately £3,494.7 million was subscribed and £1,096.1 million (excluding interest, index-linked increase or bonus) was repaid. Interest, index-linked increase, bonus or other sum payable is free of UK income tax (including investment income surcharge) and capital gains tax.

RETIREMENT ISSUE
2 June 1975–15 November 1980
Maximum holding: 120 units
Unit cost: £10
Interest per unit: unlike conventional issues where interest is accrued periodically, the repayment value of Index-Linked Certificates, subject to their being held a year, is related to the movement of the UK General Index of Retail prices.**

Certificates of the Retirement Issue were only on sale to men aged 65 years or over and women aged 60 years or over, but may now be transferred to anyone

SECOND INDEX-LINKED ISSUE
17 November 1980–29 June 1985
Maximum holding: 1,000 units
Unit cost: £10
Interest per unit: the repayment value, subject to their being held a year, is related to the movement of the UK General Index of Retail Prices**

THIRD INDEX-LINKED ISSUE
1 July 1985–31 July 1986
Maximum holding: 200 units

Unit cost: £25
Interest per unit: the repayment value, subject to their being held for one year, is related to the movement of the UK General Index of Retail Prices.

In addition, there is guaranteed extra interest of 2.5 per cent for the first year; 2.75 per cent for the second year; 3.25 per cent for the third year; 4 per cent for the fourth year, and 5.25 per cent for the fifth year. This interest is worth 3.54 per cent compound over a full five years. Certificates held beyond the fifth anniversary earn index-linking plus half a per cent interest on each following anniversary*

FOURTH INDEX-LINKED ISSUE
1 August 1986–30 June 1990
Maximum holding: 200 units
Unit cost: £25
Interest per unit: the repayment value, subject to their being held for one year, is related to the movement of the UK General Index of Retail Prices.

In addition, there is guaranteed extra interest of 3 per cent for the first year; 3.25 per cent for the second year; 3.5 per cent for the third year; 4.5 per cent for the fourth year, and 6 per cent for the fifth year. This interest is worth 4.04 per cent compound over a full five years. Certificates held beyond the fifth anniversary earn index-linking plus half a per cent interest on each following anniversary*

THIRTY-FOURTH ISSUE
22 July 1988–16 June 1990
Maximum holding: 40 units, plus facilities to hold up to a further 400 units
Unit cost: £25
Value after five years: £35.89
Interest per unit: after one year the repayment value increases by 6 per cent for ordinarily held 34th Issue. However, 34th Issue Reinvestment Certificates earn interest during the first year at a rate of 6 per cent a year for each three-month period. Thereafter, all 34th Issue earn 6.25 per cent after two years; 6.5 per cent after three years; 7 per cent after four years; and 7.5 per cent after five years*

THIRTY-FIFTH ISSUE
18 June 1990–14 March 1991
Maximum holding: 40 units, plus special facilities to hold up to a further 400 units
Unit cost: £25
Value after five years: £39.36
Interest per unit: after one year the repayment value increases by 6.5 per cent for ordinarily held 35th Issue. However, 35th Issue Reinvestment Certificates earn interest during the first year at a rate of 6.5 per cent a year. Thereafter, all 35th Issue earn 7 per cent after two years; 7.75 per cent after three years; 8.5 per cent after four years; and 9.5 per cent after five years

FIFTH INDEX-LINKED ISSUE
2 July 1990–12 November 1992
Maximum holding: 400 units, plus special facilities to hold up to a further 400 units
Unit cost: £25
Interest per unit: the repayment value, subject to their being held for one year, is related to the movement of the UK General Index of Retail Prices. In addition, there is guaranteed extra interest which is paid from the date of purchase for each full year the certificates are held. After the first year the return is the Retail Price Index (RPI) only. Certificates repaid before the first anniversary date earn RPI for each complete month held from the

purchase date. For the second year, the RPI plus 0.5 per cent; for the third, the RPI plus 1 per cent; for the fourth, the RPI plus 2 per cent; and at the fifth anniversary, RPI plus 4.5 per cent

SIXTH INDEX-LINKED ISSUE
7 December 1992–
Maximum holding: 400 units, plus special facilities to hold up to a further 800
Unit cost: £100; reinvestment certificates £25
Interest per unit: the repayment value, subject to their being held for one year, is related to the movement of the UK General Index of Retail Prices. In addition, there is a guaranteed extra interest of 1.5 per cent for the first year; 2 per cent for the second year; 2.75 per cent for the third year; 3.75 per cent for the fourth year; and 6.32 per cent for the fifth year. This is worth 3.25 per cent compound over the full five years. Certificates repaid before the first anniversary date earn RPI plus extra interest of 1.5 per cent a year for each complete month

THIRTY-SIXTH ISSUE
2 April 1991–2 May 1992
Maximum holding: 400 units, plus special facilities to hold up to a further 400
Unit cost: £25
Value after five years: £37.59
Interest per unit: after one year the repayment value increases by 5.5 per cent for ordinarily held 36th Issue. However, 36th Issue Reinvestment Certificates earn interest during the first year at a rate of 5.5 per cent a year. Thereafter, all 36th Issue earn 6 per cent after two years; 6.75 per cent after three years; 7.5 per cent after four years; and 8.5 per cent after five years

THIRTY-SEVENTH ISSUE
13 May 1992–5 August 1992
Maximum holding: 300 units, plus special facilities to hold up to a further 400
Unit cost: £25
Value after five years: £36.74
Interest per unit: after one year the repayment value increases by 5.5 per cent for ordinarily held 37th Issue. However, 37th Issue Reinvestment Certificates earn interest during the first year at a rate of 5.5 per cent a year. After one year, £1.38 is added; during the second year, 41 pence per completed three months; during the third year, 56 pence per completed three months; during the fourth year, 71 pence per completed three months; and during the fifth year, 91 pence per completed three months

THIRTY-EIGHTH ISSUE
24 August 1992–22 September 1992
Maximum holding: 200 units, plus special facilities to hold up to a further 400
Unit cost: £25
Value after five years: £35.89
Interest per unit: after one year the repayment value increases by 5.25 per cent for ordinarily held 38th Issue. However, 38th Issue Reinvestment Certificates earn interest during the first year at a rate of 5.25 per cent a year. After one year, £1.31 is added; during the second year, 41 pence per completed three months; during the third year, 50 pence per completed three months; during the fourth year, 63 pence per completed three months; and during the fifth year, 86 pence per completed three months

THIRTY-NINTH ISSUE
5 October 1992–12 November 1992
Maximum holding: 50 units, plus special facilities to hold up to a further 100
Unit cost: £100
Value after five years: £138.63
Interest per unit: after one year the repayment value increases by 4.6 per cent for ordinarily held 39th Issue. However, 39th Issue Reinvestment Certificates earn interest during the first year at a rate of 4.6 per cent a year. After one year, £4.60 is added; during the second year, £1.37 per completed three months; during the third year, £1.86 per completed three months; during the fourth year, £2.32 per completed three months; and during the fifth year, £2.96 per completed three months

FORTIETH ISSUE
7 December 1992–
Maximum holding: 400 units, plus special facilities to hold up to a further 800
Unit cost: £100; reinvestment certificates £25
Value after five years: £132.25
Interest per unit: after one year the repayment value increases by 4 per cent for ordinarily held 40th Issue. However, 40th Issue Reinvestment Certificates earn interest during the first year at a rate of 4 per cent a year. On a £100 unit after one year, £4 is added; during the second year, £1.15 per completed three months; during the third year, £1.56 per completed three months; during the fourth year, £1.54 per completed three months; and during the fifth year, £2.42 per completed three months

*As announced by the Treasury
†From June 1982, savings certificates of the 7th to 34th Issues will be extended on general extension rates as they reach the end of their existing extension periods. The percentage interest rate is determined by the Treasury and any change in this general extension rate will be applicable from the first of the month following its announcement. Under the system, a certificate earns interest for each complete period of three months beyond the expiry of the previous extension terms. Within each three-month period, interest is calculated separately for each month at the rate applicable from the beginning of that month. The interest for each month is one-twelfth of the annual rate (i.e. it does not vary with the number of days in the month) and is capitalized annually on the anniversary of the date of purchase. The current rate of interest under the general extension rate is given in leaflets available at post offices
**Index-linked certificates of the Retirement and 2nd Issues were eligible for annual supplements to index-linking. Seven supplements were introduced, the final one for 1988–9. At the fifth anniversary there is a bonus of 4 per cent of the purchase price, and at the tenth anniversary there is a second bonus of 4 per cent of the capitalized value at the fifth anniversary. All supplements and bonuses are fully index-linked once earned

Insurance

Section Three of the Insurance Companies Act 1982 empowers the Department of Trade and Industry (Insurance Division, 10–18 Victoria Street, London SW1H 0NN) to authorize corporate bodies to transact insurance in the United Kingdom provided they comply with the financial and other regulations detailed in the Act.

At the end of 1992 there were 836 insurance companies with authorization to transact one or more classes of insurance business in the UK.

REGULATION OF COMPANIES

Under the Financial Services Act 1986, the Securities and Investments Board (SIB) is empowered to make, monitor and enforce rules about the conduct of investment business.

The SIB has, in turn, set up a number of self-regulating organizations (SROs) dealing with different sectors of the investment market. Insurance companies offering long-term contracts like life insurance, pensions, unit trusts and annuities can either obtain authorization directly from SIB or from the main SRO dealing with the marketing of life insurance and pensions, the Life And Unit Trust Regulatory Organization (LAUTRO). Insurance companies may offer other investment services, which may mean authorization by other SROs such as the Investment Management Regulatory Organization (IMRO). For addresses, *see* Investment Business Regulation section.

In 1991 SIB announced a review of retail regulation which proposed the formation of a new body, the Personal Investment Authority. This new self-regulating organization will cover all retail investment matters and replace LAUTRO, FIMBRA, some parts of IMRO, and a small amount of direct regulation by SIB. Discussions about the formation of this authority continue.

THE EUROPEAN COMMUNITY

In 1986 the European Community's Heads of Government signed the Single European Act, which set out a programme of over 300 EC directives intended to achieve the removal of barriers to a free market within the community.

Sir Leon Brittan, the EC Commissioner responsible for financial services and competition, outlined in November 1989 proposals for a 'single licence' system (already applying to banks and investment services) for the insurance sector. He also announced a timetable for draft directives to give effect to these plans. The single licence concept envisages the supervisor in the insurer's home country carrying out all the financial supervision necessary. This would mean a UK insurer, authorized by the Department of Trade, would automatically satisfy the supervisory authority in all other EC countries. During the year, the Life and Non-Life Framework Directives were adopted. They will be implemented in July 1994 when the essential supervisory elements will be in place for the single European insurance market for insurance in Europe to become a reality.

Despite this advance many other matters remain to be finalized, including taxation provisions and the regulation of intermediaries.

ASSOCIATION OF BRITISH INSURERS

Ninety per cent of the world-wide business of insurance companies is transacted by the 450 members of the Association of British Insurers (51 Gresham Street, London EC2V 7HQ), a trade association which represents both life and general insurers. On general insurance (motor, household,

holiday, etc.), ABI acts as a regulatory organization for insurance intermediaries who do not qualify to be registered brokers.

INSURANCE BROKERS

The Insurance Brokers Registration Act 1977 empowers the Insurance Brokers Registration Council (15 St Helen's Place, London EC3A 6DS) as the statutory body responsible for the registration of insurance brokers. The Council is responsible for the registration and training of insurance brokers, conduct of business, and discipline, and it lays down rules relating to such matters as accounting practice, staff qualifications, advertising, etc.

It is possible to act as an insurance intermediary without being registered with the IBRC but unregistered intermediaries are forbidden to use the words 'Insurance Broker' as a title.

IBRC Registered Brokers

	1992
Registered individuals	13,501
Limited companies registered	2,161
Sole traders and partnerships	2,888
(containing 1,331 partners and directors)	

INVISIBLE EARNINGS OF INSURANCE

	1990	1991
Insurance	£2,152m	£3,293m

GENERAL INSURANCE

General insurance results for 1992 showed a dramatic improvement over 1991 but the industry still traded at an overall loss for the third year running. The world-wide overall trading result showed a small loss of 2.3 per cent in 1992 compared with the 1991 loss of 12 per cent. This turnaround was brought about by reduced operating expenses, loss prevention initiatives (including a campaign against insurance fraud), and rating increases.

In the UK a significant reduction in overall losses was achieved by a 12 per cent increase in premiums, reduced operating expenses, a fall in the frequency of claims, and a reduction in the rate of increase in motor crime. Fire and accident premiums increased by 11 per cent but the main reasons for reduced losses were a 13 per cent fall in commercial theft claims, a 20 per cent drop in commercial fire claims and a massive 52 per cent fall in subsidence claims. Domestic mortgage indemnity losses were in the region of £750 million (a fall from £1,200 million in 1991).

Overseas the results improved slightly, influenced by the weakening of the pound. In the USA the average premium increase of 24 per cent would have been only 4 per cent but for devaluation.

Major overseas losses included damage from Hurricane Andrew and the serious flooding across Europe, particularly in France, in September.

WORLD-WIDE GENERAL BUSINESS UNDERWRITING RESULT

	1991				1992			
	UK	USA	Other	Total	UK	USA	Other	Total
Fire and Accident								
Premiums (£m)	9,709	1,614	3,021	14,345	10,597	1,970	3,247	15,814
Profit/loss (£m)	−3,306	−241	−441	−3,989	−1,627	−333	−496	−2,455
% of premiums	−34.1	−14.9	−14.6	−27.8	−15.4	−16.9	−15.3	−15.5
Motor								
Premiums (£m)	5,098	1,271	2,555	8,924	5,715	1,610	2,751	10,077
Profit/loss (£m)	−1,171	−135	−210	−1,515	−570	−132	−213	−915
% of premiums	−23.0	−10.6	−8.2	−17.0	−10.0	−8.2	−7.7	−9.1

NET PREMIUM INCOME BY TERRITORY 1992

	UK £m	Other EC countries £m	USA £m	Other overseas £m	Total (world-wide) £m	Increase %
Fire and Accident (non-motor)	11,376	1,405	2,070	3,637	18,488	+12.5
Motor	5,850	1,324	1,611	1,589	10,375	+14.1
Marine, Aviation and Transport	1,723	232	161	145	2,260	+26.2
Total general business	18,950	2,961	3,842	5,371	31,123	+13.9
Ordinary long-term	41,760	2,798	2,923	3,465	50,946	+10.5
Industrial long-term	1,380	—	—	—	1,380	+0.3
Total long-term business	43,140	2,798	2,923	3,465	52,327	+10.2
Total	62,090	5,759	6,765	8,836	83,450	+11.6

BRITISH INSURANCE COMPANIES IN 1992

The following insurance company figures refer to members of the Association of British Insurers, and also to certain non-members.

CLAIMS STATISTICS

	1991 £m	1992 £m
Fire claims		
Commercial fires	774.6	613.1 (−20.8%)
Domestic fires	243.5	237.1 (−2.6%)
Theft claims		
Commercial theft (inc. money)	316.6	276.2 (−12.8%)
Domestic theft	590.7	749.2 (+26.8%)

WORLD-WIDE GENERAL BUSINESS TRADING RESULT

	1991 £m	1992 £m
Net written premiums	27,321	31,123
Underwriting profit/loss for one year account business		
Motor	−1,532	−915
Fire and Accident	−3,975	−2,455
Transfer to profit and loss account for other business		
Marine, Aviation, Transport	−685	−630
Other	−770	−744
Total underwriting result	−6,961	−4,745
Investment income	3,691	4,038
Overall trading profit	−3,270	−707
Profit as % of premium income	−12.0%	−2.3%

LLOYD'S OF LONDON

Lloyd's of London is an incorporated society of private underwriters who provide an international market for almost all types of insurance.

Lloyd's currently earns a gross premium income of around £7,000 million for underwriters each year. Much of this business comes from outside Great Britain and makes a valuable contribution to the balance of payments.

Today, as it was three centuries ago, a policy is underwritten at Lloyd's by private individuals with unlimited liability. Now that Lloyd's members are numbered in their thousands, however, the method of underwriting is the same only in principle. Specialist underwriters accept insurance risks at Lloyd's on behalf of members (often referred to as 'names') grouped in syndicates. There are currently around 20,000 members in some 388 syndicates of varying sizes, some with over 2,000 names, each managed by an underwriting agent approved by the Council of Lloyd's.

Lloyd's membership is drawn from many sources. Industry, commerce and the professions are strongly represented, while many members work at Lloyd's either for brokerage firms or for underwriting agencies. Underwriting membership of Lloyd's is open to anyone provided they meet the stringent financial requirements of the Corporation of Lloyd's. Substantial financial assets have to be shown and a deposit lodged with the Corporation as security for underwriting liabilities. This deposit, which must be in the form of approved securities, is determined at 30 per cent of the member's annual premium income and showing nominal means.

Lloyd's is incorporated by an Act of Parliament (Lloyd's Acts 1871–1982) and is governed by a Council of 20 members. In 1992 the Council accepted the recommendation of a working party chaired by Sir Jeremy Morse that there should be a separation of the business and regulatory functions of the Society. The result will be a Market Board consisting of 18 members (eight working members of the Council, the chief executive, four further working members, three external members and two other executives) and a Regulatory Board with 16 members (six nominated members of the Council, five external members of the Council, four working members and the Solicitor to the Corporation).

The Corporation is a non-profit making body chiefly financed by its members' subscriptions. It provides the premises, administrative staff and services enabling Lloyd's underwriting syndicates to conduct their business. It does not, however, assume corporate liability for the risks accepted by its members, who remain responsible to the full extent of their personal means for their underwriting affairs.

Lloyd's syndicates have no direct contact with the public. All business is transacted through insurance brokers accredited by the Corporation of Lloyd's. In addition, non-Lloyd's brokers in the United Kingdom, when guaranteed by Lloyd's brokers, are able to deal directly with Lloyd's motor syndicates, a facility which has made the Lloyd's market more accessible to the insuring public.

Lloyd's also provides the most comprehensive shipping intelligence service available in the world. The enormous volume of shipping and other information received from Lloyd's agents, shipowners, news agencies and other sources throughout the world, is collated and distributed to the media as well as to the maritime and commercial sectors in general. *Lloyd's List* is London's oldest daily newspaper and contains news of general commercial interest as well as shipping information. *Lloyd's Shipping Index*, also published daily, lists some 25,000 ocean-going vessels in alphabetical order and gives the latest known report of each.

DEVELOPMENTS IN 1992

The biggest challenge facing the Lloyd's market during the year was the action of the names who, faced with record losses which could mean total financial ruin, have become increasingly angry and vociferous. It is estimated that about 2,000 names applied to Lloyd's 'hardship' committee for assistance in dealing with debts, and some 17,000 have joined various action groups seeking different forms of compensation through publicity and legal campaigns.

Forty-seven syndicates lost more than £10 million before personal expenses, with the largest loss amounting to £127 million. At the other end of the spectrum, five syndicates made a profit of more than £10m, with the highest surplus being £26 million.

Despite the market's record losses, a brighter future is still possible with increasing premium rates bringing better levels of profitability, the new Lloyd's Business Plan (devised by chairman David Rowland and chief executive Peter Middleton) and moves to bring corporate investors into the market.

LLOYD'S GLOBAL ACCOUNTS *as at 31 December 1992*

	1989 £000	1990 £000
Gross premiums	7,074,348	9,325,817
Premiums in respect of reinsurance ceded	3,108,827	4,045,318
Net premiums	3,965,521	5,280,499
Reinsurance premiums received from previous accounts	6,183,897	9,060,143
Total premiums	10,149,418	14,340,642
Gross claims	13,599,934	16,722,073
Reinsurance recoveries	9,368,961	10,817,870
Net claims	4,230,973	5,904,203
Reinsurance premiums paid to close the accounts	7,820,489	10,854,091
Total claims	12,051,462	16,758,294
Underwriting result	(1,902,044)	(2,417,652)
Gross investment income	554,794	590,612
Gross investment appreciation	181,188	155,414
Gross investment return	735,982	746,026
Profit/(loss) on currency exchange	(56,769)	(90,013)
Total income	679,213	656,013
Result before syndicate expenses	(1,222,831)	(1,761,639)
Syndicate expenses	548,499	696,408
Closed year of account loss/profit	(1,771,330)	(2,458,047)
Names' personal expenses	291,836	456,845
(Loss attributable) profit available to names before tax	(2,063,166)	(2,914,892)

LLOYD'S RESULTS 1990

	Marine 1989 £m	Marine 1990 £m	Non-Marine 1989 £m	Non-Marine 1990 £m
Net premiums	1,326	1,703.4	1,762	2,619.1
Underwriting result	(821)	(1,332.3)	(1,149)	(1,046.7)

	Aviation 1989 £m	Aviation 1990 £m	Motor 1989 £m	Motor 1990 £m
Net premiums	281	324.0	597	634.0
Underwriting result	16	(47.5)	52	8.9

LLOYD'S MEMBERSHIP AND CAPACITY

	1990	1991	1992
Membership	28,770	26,539	22,259
Gross market capacity	£11,070m	£11,382m	£10,046m
Average capacity per member	£385,000	£455,000	£451,000

LIFE INSURANCE AND PENSIONS

Record levels of life and pensions premiums were paid to insurance companies in 1992. UK ordinary long-term premium income rose by 9.2 per cent with very strong growth in single premium life business (up 29 per cent) and single premium personal pensions (up 19.6 per cent). The particularly strong growth in single premium products was thought to have been because of the increase in the number of people with single lump sums to invest – mainly inheritance proceeds or redundancy payments.

Both single and yearly annuity premiums fell back from the high levels of 1991; yearly annuity premiums fell 33 per cent and single premiums by 15 per cent.

Total payments to UK policyholders also reached record levels, increasing by 16.5 per cent to £27.7 billion. For life policies surrenders rose 8 per cent, death claims were up 11 per cent and maturities increased by 20 per cent.

The pensions industry has been watching developments on two major topics during the year. Neither has been resolved. First, the Government has not yet announced its proposals for equalizing state pension ages. Secondly, in September 1992, the Pension Law Review (the Goode Committee) published its consultation document on the Law and Regulation of Occupational Pension Schemes. Written submissions and oral evidence continue to be considered by the Committee. Its findings are expected during 1993.

PREMIUM INCOME FOR WORLD-WIDE LONG-TERM INSURANCE BUSINESS

	1991 £m	1992 £m	Increase %
Ordinary Branch:			
Yearly premiums for life insurances, annuities and pensions in the UK	18,207	19,267	+6.6
Single premiums for life insurances, annuities and pensions in the UK	19,610	22,100	+11.5
Premiums for permanent health and other long-term insurances in the UK	331	393	+14.5
Overseas premium income	7,472	9,186	+17.1
Industrial Branch:			
Premium income (UK only)	2,127	1,380	+0.3

WORLD-WIDE LONG-TERM INSURANCE BUSINESS – OUTGO

	1991 £m	1992 £m	Increase %
Ordinary Branch:			
Total payments made to UK policyholders	21,576	25,452	+17.7
Total payments made to overseas policyholders	3,924	5,135	+23.8
Industrial Branch:			
Total payments made to UK policyholders	2,127	2,214	+4.2

Percentages shown are increases of 1992 figures over those for 1991

NB: Payments to policyholders include death claims, maturities, annuities, surrenders (including planned cashing-in of linked and other similar savings policies and surrenders of bonus and bonuses in cash), refunds under pension schemes and payments under PHI and other long-term contracts

INDIVIDUAL PENSIONS: NEW BUSINESS 1991-2

Personal or self-employed pensions	New annual premiums £m			New single premiums £m			DSS rebates* £m	
	Non-linked	Linked	Total	Non-linked	Linked	Total	Non-linked	Linked
1991								
1st quarter	130	134	264	446	407	853	64	82
2nd quarter	174	164	338	593	526	1,119	64	76
3rd quarter	137	128	265	518	538	1,056	44	56
4th quarter	131	136	267	575	561	1,136	39	50
1992								
1st quarter	144	153	297	683	550	1,233	39	54
2nd quarter	157	155	312	818	587	1,406	37	57
3rd quarter	127	129	257	739	615	1,354	35	62
4th quarter	127	124	251	664	606	1,270	29	46
12 months to:								
31 December 1991	516	599	1,114	2,173	1,825	3,998	186	253
31 December 1992	556	561	1,117	2,905	2,358	5,263	140	219

*The figures shown here are the best estimate of one year's DSS rebates and incentives to be received under policies effected in the quarter, whether received or not

INVESTMENTS OF INSURANCE COMPANIES 1992

Investment of funds	Long-term business £m	General business £m
Index-linked British Government securities	5,253	520
British Government authority securities (excluding those in line 1)	45,331	7,475
Other government, provincial and municipal stocks	25,143	12,752
Debentures, loan stocks, preference and guaranteed stocks and shares	31,859	8,583
Ordinary stocks and shares	183,021	13,216
Mortgages	16,143	1,359
Real property and ground rents	32,789	3,913
Other invested assets	22,432	9,499
'Net current assets'	1,328	9,318
Total net assets	363,299	66,636
Gross income for year on investment holdings (gross of tax and interest paid)	21,251	4,305
Interest payable in year	395	267

DIRECTORY OF INSURANCE COMPANIES

Classes of insurance undertaken
A Accident (which includes Motor, Employers' Liability, etc.)
F Fire (including Burglary)
L Life
M Marine
Re Reinsurance

Group membership
(CU) Commercial Union
(ES) Eagle Star
(GA) General Accident
(GRE) Guardian Royal Exchange
(NU) Norwich Union
(R) Royal
(SA) Sun Alliance & London

Nature of business	Name of company	Head Office address
L	Abbey Life	80 Holdenhurst Road, Bournemouth BH8 8AL
AFLM Re	AGF Holdings (UK)	41 Botolph Lane, London EC3R 8DL
AFM Re	Albion	9–13 Fenchurch Buildings, London EC3M 5HR
AFLM	Alliance Assurance (SA)	1 Bartholomew Lane, London EC2N 2AB
L	Allied Dunbar	Allied Dunbar Centre, Swindon SN1 1EL
L	American Life	2–8 Altyre Road, Croydon CR9 2LG
AF	Ansvar	31 St Leonards Road, Eastbourne BN21 3UR
AFM	Atlas (GRE)	Royal Exchange, London EC3V 3LS
AFL Re	Avon	Arden Street, Stratford-upon-Avon CV37 6WA
AF	Baptist	1 Merchant Street, London E3 4LY
L	Barclays	94 St Paul's Churchyard, London EC4M 8EH
AFM	Bedford General	Zurich House, Stanhope Road, Portsmouth
AFLM Re	Black Sea and Baltic	65 Fenchurch Street, London EC3M 4EV
AFLM	Bradford (SA)	North Park, Halifax HX1 2TU
L	Britannia Life	190 West George Street, Glasgow G2 2PA
AFL	Britannic	Moor Green, Moseley, Birmingham B13 8QF
M	British & Foreign Marine (R)	New Hall Place, Liverpool
Engineering	British Engine (R)	Longridge House, Manchester M60 4DT
AFLM	British Equitable (GRE)	Royal Exchange, London EC3V 3LS
L	British Life Office	Reliance House, Mount Ephraim, Tunbridge Wells, Kent TN4 8BL
FM	British Oak (GRE)	Royal Exchange, London EC3V 3LS
A	Builders' Accident	Inigo Place, 31–33 Bedford Street, London, WC2E 9EL
L	Caledonian (GRE)	Royal Exchange, London EC3V 3LS
AFM	Cambrian (GRE)	Royal Exchange, London EC3V 3LS
L	Canada Life	Canada Life House, Potters Bar, Herts EN6 5BA
L	Cannon Assurance	1 Olympic Way, Wembley HA9 0NB
AFM	Car & General (GRE)	Royal Exchange, London EC3V 3LS
AL	Cigna Employee Benefits	PO Box 42, Greenock, Renfrewshire PA15 1AB
L	Citibank Life	21–23 Perrymount Road, Haywards Heath, W. Sussex RH16 3TP
L	City of Glasgow Friendly	200 Bath Street, Glasgow G2 4HJ
L	Clerical, Medical Group	Narrow Plain, Bristol BS2 0JH
L	Colonial Mutual	PO Box 60, 24 Ludgate Hill, London EC4P 4BD
AFLM Re	Commercial Union	St Helen's, 1 Undershaft, London EC3P 3DQ
L	Confederation	Lytton Way, Stevenage, Herts SG1 2NN
AF	Congregational and General	Currer House, Currer Street, Bradford BD1 5BA
AFLM	Co-operative	Miller Street, Manchester M60 0AL
AFLM Re	Cornhill	32 Cornhill, London EC3V 3LJ
L	Crown Financial Management	Crown House, Crown Square, Woking GU21 1XW
A	Crusader	Woodhatch, Reigate, Surrey RH2 8BL

Nature of business	Name of company	Head Office address
AFM	Dominion	52–54 Leadenhall Street, London EC3A 2AQ
AFLM Re	Eagle Star	60 St Mary Axe, London EC3A 8JQ
AFL	Ecclesiastical	Beaufort House, Brunswick Road, Gloucester
AFL	Economic	Economic House, 25 London Road, Sittingbourne ME10 1PE
AFM	Employers' Liability (CU)	St Helen's, 1 Undershaft, London EC3
Animal Ins.	Equine and Livestock	PO Box 100, Ouseburn, York YO5 9SZ
L	Equitable Life	4 Coleman Street, London EC2R 5AP
L	Equity & Law	Amersham Road, High Wycombe, Bucks HP13 5AL
AFM	Essex & Suffolk (GRE)	Royal Exchange, London EC3V 3LS
A	Federation	29 Linkfield Lane, Redhill, Surrey RHI IJH
AF	Fine Art & General (CU)	St Helen's, 1 Undershaft, London EC3
L	Friends' Provident	Pixham End, Dorking, Surrey
L	FS Assurance	190 West George Street, Glasgow
AFM Re	General Accident	Pitheavlis, Perth, Scotland PH2 0NH
L Re	General Accident Life	2 Rougier Street, York YO1 1HR
AF	Gresham Fire & Accident	11 Queen Victoria Street, London EC4N 4XP
L	Gresham Life	2–6 Prince of Wales Road, Bournemouth BH4 9HD
AFM	Guarantee Society (GA)	42–47 Minories, London EC3N 1NX
L	Guardian Assurance (GRE)	Royal Exchange, London EC3V 3LS
AFLM Re	Guardian Royal Exchange (GRE)	Royal Exchange, London EC3V 3LS
AFM	Hibernian	Haddington Road, Dublin 4
L	Hill Samuel	NLA Tower, Addiscombe Road, Croydon
FL	Ideal	Pitmaston, Birmingham B13
L	Irish Life	Lower Abbey Street, Dublin 2
AF	Iron Trades	Iron Trades House, 21–24 Grosvenor Place, London SW1V 7JA
L	LAS Group	113 Dundas Street, Edinburgh EH3 5EB
L	Laurentian Life	Laurentian House, Barnwood, Glos GL4 7RZ
AFLM Re	Legal and General	Temple Court, 11 Queen Victoria Street, London EC4N 4TP
L	Liberty Life	Liberty House, Station Road, New Barnet EN5 1PA
AF	Licenses & General	15 Bonhill Street, London EC2A 4BY
AFM	Liverpool Marine & General (SA)	1 Bartholomew Lane, London EC2N 2AB
L	Liverpool Victoria Friendly	Victoria House, Southampton Row, London WC1B 4DB
AFM	Local Government Guarantee (GRE)	Royal Exchange, London EC3V 3LS
AFM Re	Lombard Continental Insurance	182 High Street, Tonbridge, Kent
AFM	London & Edinburgh	The Warren, Worthing, W. Sussex BN14 9QD
AFM	London & Lancashire	New Hall Place, Liverpool
L	London & Manchester	Winslade Park, Exeter, Devon EX5 1DS
AFM	London & Scottish (CU)	St Helen's, 1 Undershaft, London EC3
L	London Life	100 Temple Street, Bristol
L	M & G Assurance	M & G House, Victoria Road, Chelmsford
L	Manufacturers Life	St George's Way, Stevenage
M	Marine (R)	34–36 Lime Street, London EC3
M	Maritime (NU)	Surrey Street, Norwich NR1 3NS
L	Medical, Sickness, Annuity and Life	7–10 Chandos Street, Cavendish Square, London W1A 2LN
Re	Mercantile & General	Moorfields House, Moorfields, London EC2Y 9AL
L	Merchant Investors (MI Group)	91 Wimpole Street, London W1M 7DA
M	Merchants' Marine (CU)	St Helen's, 1 Undershaft, London EC3
AF	Methodist	Brazennose House, Brazennose Street, Manchester M2 5AS
L	MGM Assurance	MGM House, Heene Road, Worthing BN11 2DY
AFM	Minster	Minster House, Arthur Street, London EC4
AF	Motor Union (GRE)	Royal Exchange, London EC3V 3LS
FL	Nalgo Insurance Association	137 Euston Road, London NW1 2AU
Fidelity Guar.	National Guarantee & Suretyship (CU)	St Helen's, 1 Undershaft, London EC3
L	National Mutual Life	The Priory, Hitchin, Herts. SG5 2DW
L	National Provident Institution	NP House, Tunbridge Wells, Kent TN1 2UE
Machinery	National Vulcan Eng. Ins. Group (SA)	St Mary's Parsonage, Manchester M60 9AP
Naval Officers' risks, etc.	Navigators & General (ES)	113 Queens Road, Brighton BN1 3XN
L	NEL	Milton Court, Dorking, Surrey RH4 3LZ
AFL Re	NFU Mutual	Tiddington Road, Stratford-upon-Avon CV37 7BJ
AF	Nig Skandia	Crown House, 145 City Road, London EC1V 1LP
L	NM Financial Management	Enterprise House, Isambard Brunel Road, Portsmouth PO1 2AW
AFLM	North British & Mercantile (CU)	St Helen's, 1 Undershaft, London EC3
AFLM	Northern (CU)	St Helen's, 1 Undershaft, London EC3
AFM Re	Norwich Union Fire	Surrey Street, Norwich
L	Norwich Union Life	Surrey Street, Norwich

Nature of business	Name of company	Head Office address
Re	NRG Victory Reinsurance	Castle Hill Avenue, Folkestone CT20 2TF
AFM	Ocean Accident (CU)	St Helen's, 1 Undershaft, London EC3
M	Ocean Marine (CU)	Room 115, ILU, Leadenhall Street, London EC3
AFM Aviation	Orion Personal Insurances Ltd	Orion House, Bouverie Road West, Folkestone, Kent CT20 2RW
AFM Re	Palatine	77 Leadenhall Street, London EC3
AFLM Re	Pearl	The Pearl Centre, Lynchwood, Peterborough PE2 6FY
A L Sickness	Permanent	7–10 Chandos Street, Cavendish Square, London W1
AFLM	Phoenix (SA)	1 Bartholomew Lane, London EC2N 2AB
L	Prolific Life and Pensions	Bridge Mills, Stramongate, Kendal LA9 4UB
L	Property Growth	Leon House, High Street, Croydon
L	Provident Life Association	Provident Way, Basingstoke, Hants RG21 2SZ
L	Provident Mutual Life	25–31 Moorgate, London EC2R 6BA
F	Provincial	Stramongate, Kendal, Cumbria LA9 4BE
AFLM Re	Prudential	142 Holborn Bars, London EC1N 2NH
L	Prudential Holborn	30 Old Burlington Street, London W1
AF	Railway Passengers (CU)	St Helen's, 1 Undershaft, London EC3
AFL	Refuge	Refuge House, Alderley Road, Wilmslow, Cheshire SK9 1PF
AFM	Reliance Marine (GRE)	Royal Exchange, London EC3V 3LS
L	Reliance Mutual	Reliance House, Mount Ephraim, Tunbridge Wells, Kent
AF	Road Transport & General (GA)	Pitheavlis, Perth
AF	Royal Exchange	Royal Exchange, London EC3V 3LS
L	Royal Heritage Life	Royal Insurance House, Business Park, Peterborough PE2 6GG
L	Royal Life	PO Box 30, New Hall Place, Liverpool L69 3HS
L	Royal Liver Friendly	Royal Liver Building, Pier Head, Liverpool L3 1HT
AFL	Royal London	Royal London House, Middleborough, Colchester CO1 1RA
L	Royal National Pension Fund for Nurses	Burdett House, 15 Buckingham Street, Strand, London WC2N 6ED
F	Salvation Army	117–121 Judd Street, London WC1H 9NN
L	Save & Prosper	1 Finsbury Avenue, London EC2M
L	Scottish Amicable	150 St Vincent Street, Glasgow G2 5NQ
Engineering	Scottish Boiler (GA)	Pitheavlis, Perth, Scotland
L	Scottish Equitable	28 St Andrew Square, Edinburgh EH2 1YF
M	Scottish General (GA)	100 West Nile Street, Glasgow G12
L	Scottish Legal	95 Bothwell Street, Glasgow G2 7HY
L	Scottish Life	19 St Andrew Square, Edinburgh EH2 2YA
L	Scottish Mutual	109 St Vincent Street, Glasgow G2 5HN
L	Scottish Provident Institution	6 St Andrew Square, Edinburgh EH2 2YA
AFLM	Scottish Union & National (NU)	Surrey Street, Norwich
L	Scottish Widows'	15 Dalkeith Road, Edinburgh EH16 5BU
AFM	Sea (SA)	1 Bartholomew Lane, London EC2N 2AB
L	Sentinel Life	2 Eyre Street Hill, London EC1
L	Stalwart Assurance	Stalwart House, 142 South Street, Dorking RH4 2EV
L	Standard Life	3 George Street, Edinburgh EH2 2X2
AFM	State Assurance (GRE)	Royal Exchange, London EC3V 3LS
AFLM	Sun Alliance and London	1 Bartholomew Lane, London EC2N 2AB
AFM	Sun Insurance Office (SA)	1 Bartholomew Lane, London EC2N 2AB
L	Sun Life Assurance Group	Sun Life Court, Bristol BS99 7SL
L Re	Sun Life of Canada	Basing View, Basingstoke, Hants RG21 2DZ
AL	Swiss Pioneer Life	16 Crosby Road North, Waterloo, Liverpool L22 0NY
FL	Teacher's Assurance	12 Christchurch Road, Bournemouth BH1 3LW
L	Tunstall & District	Station Chambers, Tunstall, Stoke-on-Trent ST6 6DU
M	Ulster Marine (GA)	Pitheavlis, Perth
AFM	Union Assurance (CU)	St Helen's, 1 Undershaft, London EC3
AFM	Union Insurance Society of Canton (GRE)	Royal Exchange, London EC3V 3LS
M	Union Marine	4–5 King William Street, London EC4
AFL	United Friendly	42 Southwark Bridge Road, London SE1
L	UK Life Assurance	UK House, Worthing Road, Horsham
L	University	4 Coleman Street, London EC2R 5AP
AF	Welsh Insurance Corporation (CU)	St Helen's, 1 Undershaft, London EC3
AFL Re	Wesleyan Assurance	Colmore Circus, Birmingham B4 6AR
AFLM	Western Australian	Swan Court, Mansel Road, Wimbledon, London SW19
AF	West of Scotland (CU)	26 George Street, Edinburgh 2
AF	White Cross (CU)	St Helen's, 1 Undershaft, London EC3
AL	Windsor Life	Windsor House, Telford, Salop TF3 4NB
AFM	World Marine & General (CU)	Dunster House, Mark Lane, London EC3
AFM Re	Zurich	Zurich House, Stanhope Road, Portsmouth

The Stock Exchange

The International Stock Exchange of the United Kingdom and Republic of Ireland Ltd serves the needs of government, industry and investors by providing facilities for raising capital and a central market-place for securities trading. There are 7,468 securities listed on the London Stock Exchange, which have a value of approximately £2,605,093.5 million. In 1992 securities worth some £2,089,425.3 million changed hands. This central market-place covers not only government stocks (called gilts) and UK and overseas company shares (called equities and fixed interest stocks) but other investment instruments such as traded options on equities and indices.

Big Bang

During 1986 the London Stock Exchange went through the greatest period of change in its two-hundred year history. In March 1986 it opened its doors for the first time to overseas and corporate membership of the Exchange, allowing banks, insurance companies and overseas securities houses to become members of the Exchange and to buy existing member firms. On 27 October 1986, three major reforms took place, changes which became known as 'Big Bang':

1 Abolition of scales of minimum commissions, allowing clients to negotiate freely with their brokers about the charge for their services
2 Abolition of the separation of member firms into brokers and jobbers. Under the new system, firms are broker/dealers, able to act as agents on behalf of clients; to act as principals buying and selling shares for their own account; and to become registered market makers, making continuous buying and selling prices in specific securities
3 The introduction of the Stock Exchange Automated Quotations (SEAQ) system. Market makers input their buying and selling prices into SEAQ, which displays the competing quotations on a composite page onscreen. For all but the smallest, least frequently traded UK companies, the volume of shares traded is also updated continuously throughout the day

Of all these changes, the implementation of SEAQ has had the most visible effect. Dealing in stocks and shares now takes place via the telephone in the firms' own dealing rooms, rather than face to face on the floor of the Exchange. The new systems also provide increased investor protection. All deals taking place via the Exchange's SEAQ system are recorded on a database which can be used to resolve disputes or to carry out investigations.

Members of the London Stock Exchange buy and sell shares on behalf of the public, as well as institutions such as pension funds or insurance companies. In return for transacting the deal, the broker will charge a commission, which is usually based upon the value of the transaction. The market makers, or wholesalers, in each security do not charge a commission for their services, but will quote the broker two prices, a price at which they will buy and a price at which they will sell. It is the middle of these two prices which is published in lists of Stock Exchange prices in newspapers.

Regulatory Bodies

On 12 November 1986 members of the Exchange agreed to merge with members of the international broking community in London, based outside the Exchange, in order to form two new bodies: the International Stock Exchange of the United Kingdom and Republic of Ireland Ltd, and the Securities and Futures Authority. These two regulatory bodies were formed under the provisions of the Financial Services Act 1986, which requires investment businesses to be authorized and regulated by a self-regulating organization (SRO) of which the Securities and Futures Authority is one. The Act also requires business to be conducted through a recognized investment exchange (RIE). The London Stock Exchange is an RIE, regulating three main markets: UK equities, international equities and gilts.

Primary Markets

The Exchange serves the needs of industry by providing a mechanism where companies can raise capital for development and growth through the issue of listed securities. For a company entering the market for the first time there are two possible Stock Exchange markets, depending upon the size, history and requirements of the company. The first is the listed market, which exists for well-established companies, which must comply with stringent criteria relating to all aspects of their operations. At present, companies coming to this market require a three-year trading record with a minimum of 25 per cent of the shares held in public hands. The Unlisted Securities Market was established in 1980 with less rigorous entry requirements designed with the smaller and newer company in mind. Companies at present are required to provide a two-year trading record and a minimum of 10 per cent of the shares must be in public hands. Owing to the lack of distinction between the two markets, it is proposed that the Unlisted Securities Market be closed by the end of 1996.

Once admitted to the Exchange, all companies are obliged to keep their shareholders informed of their progress, making announcements of a price-sensitive nature through the Exchange's company announcements department.

The Governing Board

The International Stock Exchange has its headquarters in London, and representative offices around the UK and the Republic of Ireland. At present there are 395 member firms.

The interests of the membership of the London Stock Exchange are reflected in the governing board, whose members are responsible for overall policy and the strategic direction of the Exchange. The board consists of representatives drawn from listed companies, investors and other major users, elected at the annual general meeting, and the Government Broker, the Chief Executive and up to five senior executives of the Stock Exchange.

The London Stock Exchange, Old Broad Street, London EC2N 1HP. Tel: 071-797 1000
Chairman, Sir Andrew Hugh Smith
Chief Executive, vacant

Investment Business Regulation

The growth of Britain's financial services industry in the 1970s and 1980s left the regulatory structure existing at that time inadequate to deal with the new competitive climate or to provide the necessary safeguards for the investing public. Under the Financial Services Act 1986, a new supervisory framework was set up to regulate companies conducting investment business and new criminal offences were created. The Act came into force on 29 April 1988, when it became a criminal offence to conduct investment business without authorization, unless specifically exempt from the authorization requirement.

SECURITIES AND INVESTMENTS BOARD LTD
Gavrelle House, 2–14 Bunhill Row, London ECIY 8RA
Tel 071-638 1240

The Securities and Investments Board (SIB) is the designated agency under the Financial Services Act 1986 for regulating the activities of investment businesses in the UK. Although not a statutory body, the SIB has statutory powers under the Act to recognize self-regulating organizations, professional bodies, investment exchanges and clearing houses, and directly to authorize firms to undertake investment business in the UK.

The SIB oversees the regulation of all investment business in the UK. It is not responsible for areas involving public issues, takeovers and mergers, and insider dealing investigation. Its area of authority overlaps with that of the Bank of England, the Department of Trade and Industry (for insurance companies) and the Building Societies Commission where their respective member bodies are carrying out investment business.

The regulatory sanctions of the SIB are as follows:

1 It may issue public or private reprimands
2 It may restrict business
3 It may suspend authorization
4 It may withdraw authorization
5 In certain cases it may take out a civil injunction
6 It may petition the courts for the winding up of companies

CENTRAL REGISTER
Checkline 071-929 3652

The SIB maintains a register (the Central Register) of all firms who are authorized to carry on investment business. The entry for each firm gives its name, address and telephone number; an SIB reference number; its authorization status; its appropriate regulatory body; and whether it can handle client money.

INVESTORS COMPENSATION SCHEME
The Investors Compensation Scheme, run by a management company as part of the overall investor protection offered by the SIB, comes into play when authorized firms become insolvent owing money to private investors. It is funded by means of a levy on all member firms, according to their size and category. The maximum compensation that the scheme can pay to an investor is £48,000.

SELF-REGULATING ORGANIZATIONS

The SIB recognizes self-regulating organizations (SROs), which are responsible to the SIB for ensuring financial supervision in their respective sectors of investment business. Most members of the financial services industry obtain their authorization by being members of an SRO.

The following are recognized by the SIB as being able to provide proper regulation of the investment business carried out by their members, and the necessary standard of investor protection:

FIMBRA (Financial Intermediaries, Managers and Brokers Regulatory Organization), Hertsmere House, Hertsmere Road, London E14 4AB. Tel: 071-538 8860
IMRO (Investment Management Regulatory Organization), Broadwalk House, Appold Street, London EC2A 2LL. Tel: 071-628 6022
LAUTRO (Life Assurance and Unit Trust Regulatory Organization), Centre Point, 103 New Oxford Street, London WC1A 1QH. Tel: 071-379 0444
SFA (Securities and Futures Authority Ltd), Cottons Centre, Cottons Lane, London SE1 2QB. Tel: 071-378 9000

IMRO and LAUTRO also regulate the activities of friendly societies.

There are plans to reduce the number of SROs to four with the creation of a new SRO for the private investor, to be called PIA (Personal Investment Authority). This new SRO will replace FIMBRA and LAUTRO, possibly in 1994.

RECOGNIZED PROFESSIONAL BODIES

The SIB is also empowered to recognize professional bodies (RPBs) who, as a result, can authorize their members for investment business. Such business must not form the whole or main part of the total business undertaken by the firm.

INSTITUTE OF CHARTERED ACCOUNTANTS IN ENGLAND AND WALES, Chartered Accountants Hall, PO Box 433, Moorgate Place, London EC2P 2BJ. Tel: 071-920 8100
INSTITUTE OF CHARTERED ACCOUNTANTS OF SCOTLAND, 27 Queen Street, Edinburgh EH2 1LA. Tel: 031-225 5673
INSTITUTE OF CHARTERED ACCOUNTANTS IN IRELAND, 11 Donegall Square South, Belfast BT1 5JE. Tel: 0232-321600
CHARTERED ASSOCIATION OF CERTIFIED ACCOUNTANTS, 29 Lincoln's Inn Fields, London WC2A 3EE. Tel: 071-242 6855
THE LAW SOCIETY, Law Society House, 50–52 Chancery Lane, London WC2A 1SX. Tel: 071-242 1222
LAW SOCIETY OF SCOTLAND, Law Society's Hall, 26 Drumsheugh Gardens, Edinburgh EH3 7YR. Tel: 031-226 7411
LAW SOCIETY OF NORTHERN IRELAND, Law Society's House, 90–106 Victoria Street, Belfast BT1 3JZ. Tel: 0232-231614
INSTITUTE OF ACTUARIES, Staple Inn Hall, High Holborn, London WC1V 7QJ. Tel: 071-242 0106
INSURANCE BROKERS REGISTRATION COUNCIL, 15 St Helen's Place, London EC3A 6DS. Tel: 071-588 4387

RECOGNIZED INVESTMENT EXCHANGES

Investment exchanges are exempt from needing authorization from the SIB as an investment business. However, to be a recognized investment exchange (RIE), each must fulfil the following requirements:

1 Adequate financial resources
2 Proper conduct of business rules
3 A proper market in its products
4 Procedures for recording transactions
5 Effective monitoring and enforcement of rules
6 Proper arrangements for the clearing and performance of contracts

INTERNATIONAL PETROLEUM EXCHANGE (IPE), International House, 1 St Katharine's Way, London E1 9UN. Tel: 071-481 0643
INTERNATIONAL STOCK EXCHANGE OF THE UNITED KINGDOM AND THE REPUBLIC OF IRELAND (LSE), Old Broad Street, London EC2N 1HP. Tel: 071-588 2355
LONDON COMMODITY EXCHANGE LTD, 1 Commodity Quay, St Katharine Docks, London E1 9AX. Tel: 071-481 2080
LONDON INTERNATIONAL FINANCIAL FUTURES AND OPTIONS EXCHANGE (LIFFE), Cannon Bridge, London EC4R 3XX. Tel: 071-623 0444
LONDON METAL EXCHANGE LTD (LME), Plantation House, Fenchurch Street, London EC3M 3AP. Tel: 071-626 3311
THE LONDON SECURITIES AND DERIVATIVES EXCHANGE LTD (OMLX), 107 Cannon Street, London EC4N 5AD. Tel: 071-283 0678

The following overseas exchanges are recognized by the Treasury as offering adequate investor protection:

CHICAGO BOARD OF TRADE (CBOT), European Office, 52–54 Gracechurch Street, London EC3V 0EH. Tel: 071-929 0021
CHICAGO MERCANTILE EXCHANGE (CME), 27 Throgmorton Street, London EC2N 2AN. Tel: 071-920 0722
NATIONAL ASSOCIATION OF SECURITIES DEALERS INCORPORATED (NASDAQ), 43 London Wall, London EC2M 5TB. Tel: 071-538 5656
NEW YORK MERCANTILE EXCHANGE (NYMEX), 35 Piccadilly, W1V 9PB. Tel: 071-437 2933
SYDNEY FUTURES EXCHANGE LTD, 30–32 Grosvenor Street, Sydney, NSW 2000, Australia. Tel: 010–2 256 0555

RECOGNIZED CLEARING HOUSES

A recognized clearing house (RCH) must satisfy the same kind of criteria to obtain recognition as the RIEs. There is one RCH which acts as a clearing house for some of the above RIEs:

LONDON CLEARING HOUSE LTD (LCH), Roman Wall House, 1–2 Crutched Friars, London EC3N 2AN. Tel: 071-265 2000

DESIGNATED INVESTMENT EXCHANGES

The SIB has drawn up a list of 41 overseas exchanges (known as DIEs) who appear to have operating procedures broadly equivalent to those of the RIEs. Designation merely shows that an exchange meets certain basic criteria but carries no guarantee.

OMBUDSMEN SCHEMES

Independent ombudsmen schemes have been set up for banks, building societies, and insurance companies. They provide an independent and impartial method of resolving disputes that arise between a company and its customer. In each ombudsman scheme there is a council which appoints and supervises the Ombudsman. The Ombudsman Council is composed of people representing public and consumer interests and member companies. The schemes are funded in various ways: annual subscription from member companies, a levy on member companies according to the size of their assets, or a charge for each complaint handled against a particular company.

The Investment Management Regulatory Organization (IMRO) has also appointed an independent ombudsman, known as the Investment Ombudsman. The Ombudsman is responsible for resolving disputes that arise between a customer and a member company of IMRO. The Investment Ombudsman scheme is funded by IMRO, but operates independently.

The Pensions Ombudsman is appointed by the Secretary of State for Social Security under the Social Security Act 1990, and is responsible to Parliament. He can resolve grievances between an individual and his/her pension scheme (but not National Insurance Benefits). His decisions are binding on both parties. A statutory levy on pension schemes, based on the number of members therein, contributes to the funding of the scheme.

THE OFFICE OF THE BANKING OMBUDSMAN, 70 Gray's Inn Road, London WC1X 8NB. Tel: 071-404 9944. *Banking Ombudsman*, L. Shurman
THE OFFICE OF THE BUILDING SOCIETIES OMBUDSMEN, 35–37 Grosvenor Gardens, London SW1X 7AW. Tel: 071-931 0044. *Building Societies Ombudsmen*, S. Edell; B. Murphy
THE INSURANCE OMBUDSMAN BUREAU, City Gate One, 135 Park Street, London SE1 9EA. Tel: 071-928 7600. *Insurance Ombudsman*, Dr J. T. Farrand; *Deputy Ombudsman*, L. Slade
INVESTMENT OMBUDSMAN, 6 Frederick's Place, London EC2R 8BT. Tel: 071-796 3065. *Investment Ombudsman*, R. Youard
THE PENSIONS OMBUDSMAN, 11 Belgrave Road, London SW1V 1RB. Tel: 071-834 9144. *Pensions Ombudsman*, M. Platt

THE TAKEOVER PANEL

PO Box 226, The Stock Exchange Building, London EC2P 2JX
Tel 071-382 9026

The Takeover Panel was set up in 1968 in response to concern about practices unfair to shareholders in takeover bids for public and certain private companies. Its principal objective is to ensure equality of treatment, and fair opportunity for all shareholders to consider on its merits an offer that would result in the change of control of a company. It is a non-statutory body that operates the City Code on Takeovers and Mergers.

The chairman, deputy chairmen and two lay members of the panel are appointed by the Bank of England. The remainder are representatives of the following: British Bankers' Association; Association of British Insurers; Association of Investment Trust Companies; British Merchant Banking and Securities House Association corporate finance committee; Confederation of British Industry; IMRO Ltd; Institute of Chartered Accountants in England and Wales; London Stock Exchange; National Association of Pension Funds; SFA Ltd; Association of Unit Trusts and Investment Funds.
Chairman, Sir David Calcutt, QC

Taxation

INCOME TAX

Income tax is charged on the total income of individuals for a year of assessment commencing on 6 April and ending on the following 5 April. The rates of tax and the calculation of liability will frequently differ, sometimes substantially, as between one year of assessment and another. The following information is confined to the year of assessment 1993–4, ending on 5 April 1994.

Liability to income tax is determined by establishing the taxable income for a year of assessment. The income will be reduced by an individual's personal allowances and other reliefs. The first £2,500 of taxable income remaining is assessable to income tax at the lower rate of 20 per cent and the next £21,200 at the basic rate of 25 per cent. Should any excess remain over £23,700 (£2,500 plus £21,200) this will be taxable at the higher rate of 40 per cent.

The three rates apply to the assessment of both earned and investment income. Indeed, there is little distinction between the two classes, although the receipt of earned income may produce an entitlement to some allowances not available against investment income. Special rules, first coming into operation in April 1993, apply to tax on company dividends.

The tables on the following page show the income tax payable for 1993–4 by an individual on the amount of income specified, after deducting the personal allowance and married couple's allowance also, where appropriate. Elderly persons over the age of 74 years may pay less tax. The taxpayer may also be entitled to transitional allowances and other reliefs which reduce the tax payable below the amount shown by the tables.

Trustees administering settled property are chargeable to income tax at the basic rate of 25 per cent. Where the trustees retain discretionary powers or income is accumulated, there will also be liability to the additional rate of 10 per cent. Companies residing in the United Kingdom are not liable to income tax but suffer corporation tax on income, profits and gains.

The charge to income tax broadly arises on all taxable income accruing from sources in the United Kingdom. Individuals who are resident in this territory may also become liable on income arising overseas. An individual is resident in the United Kingdom if he or she normally resides here. Persons not normally residing in the United Kingdom may become resident if they visit this territory for periods which average three months or more throughout a period of years, or are present for at least 183 days in a particular year.

Income arising overseas will often incur liability to foreign taxation. If that income is also chargeable to United Kingdom income tax, excessive liability could well arise. The United Kingdom has concluded double taxation agreements with many overseas territories and these ensure that the same slice of income is not doubly assessed. In the absence of such an agreement, foreign tax suffered can usually be relieved under the domestic code when calculating liability to United Kingdom income tax.

INDEPENDENT TAXATION

For many years the income of a married woman 'living with' her husband was treated as that of the husband for income tax purposes. This did not generally apply in the year of marriage and it remained possible for the couple to exercise the right of separate assessment or for the wife to be separately assessed as a single person on her earned income. However, the husband was usually responsible for submitting income tax returns, for discharging income tax on the combined incomes and dealing generally with taxation matters.

This practice ceased to apply on 6 April 1990 with the introduction of independent taxation. A husband and wife are now independently taxed, with each entitled to a personal allowance. In most situations any unused personal allowance available to one spouse cannot be transferred to the other. A married man 'living with' his wife can obtain a married couple's allowance. This allowance must, if possible, be set against the husband's income but where that income is insufficient, any balance of the married couple's allowance may be transferred to the wife. From 6 April 1993 it became possible for a married woman to claim half the basic married couple's allowance as of right. In addition, the entire basic allowance may be obtained by the wife, if her husband so agrees.

Each spouse may obtain other allowances and reliefs where the underlying conditions are satisfied. Income must be accurately allocated between a husband and wife by reference to the individual beneficially entitled to that income. Where income arises from jointly-held assets, this must be apportioned equally between husband and wife. In those cases where the beneficial interests in jointly-held assets are not equal, a special declaration can be made to apportion income by reference to the actual interests in that income.

INCOME TAXABLE

Income tax is assessed and collected under several Schedules. Each Schedule determines the extent of liability and establishes the amount to be included in taxable income. In some instances the actual income arising in a year of assessment will be charged to income tax for that year. A different basis of assessment may arise for income taxable under Cases I to V of Schedule D. Frequently, income assessable under these Cases will be that arising in a previous year or period but there are special rules where a new source is acquired or an existing source discontinued.

Following the withdrawal of income tax liability for most commercial woodlands in the United Kingdom, Schedule B no longer applies. The contents of the remaining schedules are shown below.

Schedule A

Tax is charged on annual profits arising from the ownership or occupation of land in the United Kingdom. This will include rents, ground rents and other income from land. Expenditure incurred by the landlord on maintenance, repairs, insurance and management can be subtracted from the annual profits. This Schedule does not include profits from farming, market gardening or woodlands, nor does it extend to mineral rents and royalties. Premiums arising on the grant of a lease for a period not exceeding fifty years are assessed to income tax as rent. However, the amount of the taxable premium may be reduced by 2 per cent for each complete year, after the first year, of the leasing period. Income from furnished lettings is assessable under Case VI of Schedule D, unless an option is exercised for such income to be assessed under Schedule A. Where income arises from furnished holiday lettings, additional expenditure may be

SINGLE PERSONS AND MARRIED WOMEN

Income £	Persons under 65 Income tax £	Average rate %	Persons 65 or over* Income tax £	Average rate %
4,000	111	2.8	—	—
5,000	311	6.2	160	3.2
6,000	514	8.6	360	6.0
7,000	764	10.9	575	8.2
8,000	1,014	12.7	825	10.3
9,000	1,264	14.0	1,075	11.9
10,000	1,514	15.1	1,325	13.3
12,000	2,014	16.8	1,825	15.2
14,000	2,514	18.0	2,325	16.6
16,000	3,014	18.8	3,014	18.8
18,000	3,514	19.5	3,514	19.5
20,000	4,014	20.1	4,014	20.1
25,000	5,264	21.1	5,264	21.1
30,000	6,942	23.1	6,942	23.1
40,000	10,942	27.4	10,942	27.4
50,000	14,942	29.9	14,942	29.9
60,000	18,942	31.6	18,942	31.6
100,000	34,942	34.9	34,942	34.9

* Persons aged 75 or over suffer less tax on income falling below £16,000 on this table

MARRIED MEN

Income £	Couples under 65 Income tax £	Average rate %	Couples 65 or over† Income tax £	Average rate %
4,000	—	—	—	—
5,000	—	—	—	—
6,000	167	2.8	—	—
7,000	367	5.2	67	1.0
8,000	584	7.3	267	3.3
9,000	834	9.3	467	5.2
10,000	1,084	10.8	709	7.1
12,000	1,584	13.2	1,209	10.1
14,000	2,084	14.9	1,709	12.2
16,000	2,584	16.1	2,434	15.2
18,000	3,084	17.1	3,084	17.1
20,000	3,584	17.9	3,584	17.9
25,000	4,834	19.3	4,834	19.3
30,000	6,254	20.8	6,254	20.8
40,000	10,254	25.6	10,254	25.6
50,000	14,254	28.5	14,254	28.5
60,000	18,254	30.4	18,254	30.4
100,000	34,254	34.3	34,254	34.3

† Persons aged 75 or over suffer less tax on income falling below £18,000 on this table

included in calculating income chargeable to tax. Income from furnished holiday lettings is treated as earned income.

Receipts not exceeding £3,250 annually and received by an individual from letting property furnished in his or her own home are not chargeable to tax.

Schedule C

This Schedule is confined to interest or dividends on government or public authority funds and certain payments made out of the public revenues of overseas countries.

Schedule D

This Schedule is divided into six Cases, as follows:

Cases I and II – Profits arising from trades, professions and vocations, including farming and market gardening. Capital expenditure incurred on assets used for business purposes will often produce an entitlement to capital allowances which reduce the profits chargeable. These profits may also be reduced following the submission of claims for loss relief and other matters.

Case III – Interest on government stocks not taxed at source (e.g. War Loan and British Savings Bonds), interest on National Savings Bank deposits and discounts. Interest up to £70 on ordinary National Savings Bank deposits is exempt from income tax. The exemption applies to both husband and wife separately. Interest on National Savings Bank Special Investment accounts is not exempt.

Cases IV and V – Interest from overseas securities, rents, dividends and all other income accruing outside the United Kingdom. Assessment is based on the full amount of income arising, whether remitted to the United Kingdom or retained overseas, but individuals who are either not domiciled in the United Kingdom or who are ordinarily resident overseas may be taxed on a remittance basis. Overseas pensions are taxable but the amount arising may be reduced by 10 per cent for assessment purposes. From April 1993 dividends on overseas investments are chargeable only at the lower rate of 20 per cent and the higher rate of 40 per cent.

Case VI – Sundry profits and annual receipts not assessed under any other Case or Schedule. These may include

insurance commissions, post-cessation receipts, income from furnished lettings, and numerous other receipts specifically charged under Case VI.

Schedule E

All emoluments from an office or employment are assessable under this Schedule. There are three Cases, as follows:

Case I – This applies to all emoluments of an individual resident and ordinarily resident in the United Kingdom.

Case II – Of application where the individual is not resident or not ordinarily resident and extends to emoluments for duties undertaken in the United Kingdom.

Case III – Applies in rare situations to other emoluments remitted to the United Kingdom.

Although earnings for overseas duties may be assessable under Case I where the employee is resident and ordinarily resident in the United Kingdom, a foreign earnings deduction of 100 per cent may be available, which reduces the overseas assessable earnings to nil. This deduction can be obtained where duties are performed overseas for a continuous period reaching or exceeding 365 days and is confined to earnings from the overseas activity.

A 'receipts basis' applies for determining the year of assessment in which earnings must be taxed. Where emoluments are assessable under Case I or Case II, the date of receipt will comprise the earlier of:

(a) the date of payment
(b) the date entitlement arises

In the case of company directors it is the earliest of the two dates given above with the addition of the following three which establish the time of receipt:

(c) the date emoluments are credited in the company's books
(d) where emoluments for a period are determined after the end of that period, the date of determination
(e) where emoluments for a period are determined in that period, the last day of that period

The emoluments assessable under Schedule E include all salaries, wages, director's fees and other money sums. In addition, there are a wide range of benefits which must be added to taxable emoluments. These include the provision of living accommodation on advantageous terms and advantages arising from the use of vouchers.

Further taxable benefits accrue to directors and employees receiving emoluments of £8,500 or more in the year of assessment. These benefits include the reimbursement of expenses, the availability of motor cars for private motoring, the provision of petrol or other fuel for private motoring, the use of vans, the provision of interest-free loans, and other benefits provided at the employer's expense. The cost of providing a limited range of child care facilities may be excluded.

In arriving at the amount to be assessed under Schedule E, all expenses incurred wholly, exclusively and necessarily in the performance of the duties may be deducted. This includes fees and subscriptions paid to certain professional bodies and learned societies. Fees paid to managers by entertainers, actors and others assessable under Schedule E may be deducted, up to a maximum of 17.5 per cent of earnings.

Compensation for loss of office and other sums received on the termination of an office or employment are assessable to tax. However, the first £30,000 may be excluded with only the balance remaining chargeable, unless the compensatory payment is linked with the retirement of the recipient.

Earnings received from an approved profit-related pay scheme are exempt from income tax.

Schedule F

This Schedule is concerned with company dividends and distributions. A United Kingdom resident company paying a dividend or making a distribution must account to the Inland Revenue for advance corporation tax. A shareholder residing in the United Kingdom obtains the dividend or distribution together with a tax credit equal to one-quarter of the sum received for 1993–4. The dividend or distribution is regarded as having suffered income tax, equal to the tax credit, at the lower rate of 20 per cent. Where the shareholder is not liable, or not fully liable, at that rate a repayment can be obtained. Dividends or distributions are not liable to tax at the difference between the lower rate of 20 per cent and the basic rate of 25 per cent. However, shareholders liable at the higher rate of 40 per cent will incur further liability on the grossed-up equivalent of the sum received at the rate of 40 per cent, less the tax credit of 20 per cent.

Some payments made by an unquoted trading company to redeem or purchase its own shares are not treated as distributions.

Building society interest and bank interest

Many payments of interest by building societies and banks are received after the deduction of income tax at the basic rate of 25 per cent. However, those not liable to income tax at the basic rate may arrange to receive interest gross, with no tax being deducted on payment. Others who suffer income tax by deduction can obtain a repayment in whole or in part if they are not fully liable at the basic rate.

INCOME NOT TAXABLE

This includes interest on National Savings Certificates, most scholarship income, bounty payments to members of the armed services and annuities payable to the holders of certain awards. Dividend income arising from investments in personal equity plans may be exempt from tax. Income received under most maintenance agreements and court orders made after 30 June 1988 will not be liable to tax. Nor will payments made under many deeds of covenant executed after 14 March 1988 be recognized for tax purposes, unless

the recipient is a charity. Interest arising on a Tax Exempt Special Savings Account (TESSA) opened with a building society or bank will be exempt from tax, if the account is maintained throughout a five-year period.

SOCIAL SECURITY BENEFITS

Many social security benefits are not liable to income tax. These include income support, family credit, maternity allowance, long-term sickness benefit, child benefit, war widow's pension, disability living allowance and numerous others. Among the limited range of benefits which are taxable is the retirement pension, widow's pension, widowed mother's allowance, and unemployment benefits. Short-term sick pay and maternity pay payable by an employer are also chargeable to tax.

PAY AS YOU EARN

The Pay As You Earn system is not an independent form of taxation but has been designed to collect income tax by deduction from most emoluments. When paying emoluments to employees, an employer is usually required to deduct income tax and account for that tax to the Inland Revenue. In many cases this deduction procedure will fully exhaust the individual's liability to income tax, unless there is other income. The date of 'receipt' used for assessment purposes (*see* above) also identifies the date of 'payment' when establishing liability for PAYE.

ALLOWANCES

The allowances available to individuals for 1993–4 are outlined below.

Personal allowance

Each individual receives a basic personal allowance of £3,445. This is increased to £4,200 for individuals over the age of 64 on 5 April 1994, and further increased to £4,370 for those over the age of 74 on the same date. The increased allowance is available for those who died during the year of assessment but who would otherwise have achieved the appropriate age not later than 5 April 1994.

The amount of the increased personal allowance for older taxpayers will be reduced by one-half of total income in excess of £14,200. This reduction in the allowance will continue until it has been reduced to the basic personal allowance of £3,445.

Apart from limited transitional matters mentioned below, any unused part of the personal allowance of one spouse cannot be transferred to the other.

Married couple's allowance

A married man who was 'living with' his wife at any time in the year ending on 5 April 1994 is entitled to a married couple's allowance. The basic allowance is £1,720. This may be increased to £2,465 if either the husband or the wife is 65 years or over at any time in the year ending on 5 April 1994. A further increase to £2,505 can be obtained where either party to the marriage was 75 or over on 5 April 1994. Where an individual would otherwise have reached either age by 5 April 1994, but who died earlier in the year, the increased allowance is given.

The amount of the increased married couple's allowance may be reduced where the income of the husband (excluding the income of the wife) exceeds £14,200. The reduction will comprise:

(a) one-half of the husband's total income in excess of £14,200, less
(b) the amount of any reduction made when calculating the husband's increased personal allowance

This reduction in the married couple's allowance cannot reduce that allowance below the basic amount of £1,720.

If husband and wife were married during 1993-4 the married couple's allowance of £1,720, or any increased sum, must be reduced by one-twelfth for each complete month commencing on 6 April 1993, and preceding the date of marriage.

In the absence of any further action the married couple's allowance will be given to the husband. If he is unable to utilize all or any part of that allowance, due to an absence of income, the husband may transfer the unused portion to his wife. The decision whether or not to transfer remains at the discretion of the husband.

However, for 1993-4 and future years a wife may file an election to obtain one-half of the basic married couple's allowance as of right, leaving the husband with the balance of that allowance. Alternatively, the couple may jointly elect that the entire basic allowance should be allocated to the wife only. Except in the year of marriage, the election must be made before the commencement of the year of assessment to which it is to apply. Should either spouse be unable to utilize his or her share of the married couple's allowance the unused part may be transferred to the other spouse.

Additional personal allowance

An allowance of £1,720 is available to a single person who has a qualifying child resident with him or her in 1993-4. The allowance can also be obtained by a married man whose wife is totally incapacitated by physical or mental infirmity throughout the year.

A 'qualifying child' for 1993-4 must be born during the year, be under the age of 16 years at the commencement of the year, or be over the age of 16 at the commencement of the year and either receiving full-time instruction at a university, college, school or other educational establishment or undergoing training for a trade, profession or vocation throughout a minimum period of two years. It is also necessary that the child is the claimant's own, a stepchild of the claimant, an illegitimate child if the parents married after the child's birth, or an adopted child under the age of 18 at the time of adoption. Alternatively it must be shown that the child was either born during 1993-4 or under the age of 18 at the commencement of the year and maintained by the claimant at his or her own expense during the whole of the succeeding twelve-month period.

Only one additional personal allowance of £1,720 can be obtained by an individual notwithstanding the number of children involved. Where an unmarried couple are living together as husband and wife, it is not possible for both to obtain the additional personal allowance.

Widow's bereavement allowance

For the year of assessment in which a husband dies his surviving widow may obtain a widow's bereavement allowance which is £1,720 for 1993-4. It is a requirement that the parties were 'living together' immediately before the husband's death. A similar allowance will be available in the year following death, unless the widow remarried in the year of death. No widow's bereavement allowance can be obtained for future years.

Blind person's allowance

An allowance of £1,080 is available to an individual if at any time during the year ending on 5 April 1994, he or she was registered as blind on a register maintained by a local authority. If the individual is 'living with' a wife or husband, any unused part of the blind person's allowance can be transferred to the other spouse.

Transitional allowances

There are three limited transitional allowances which are intended to ensure that the introduction of independent taxation on 6 April 1990 does not increase liability to income tax for subsequent years. These allowances comprise:
(a) an increased personal allowance available to a wife where the husband cannot fully use that allowance in 1993-4
(b) a special personal allowance available to a husband where his wife falls into a higher age group, namely over 64 or over 74
(c) a married couple's allowance available to a separated husband not 'living with' his wife if the separation occurred before 6 April 1990

LIFE ASSURANCE RELIEF

Life assurance deduction relief is limited to premiums paid on policies made before 14 March 1984. No relief is available for policies issued after this date. Where the terms of a policy made before 14 March 1984 are subsequently varied or extended to produce increased benefits, future premiums paid may no longer qualify for relief.

When paying premiums under a qualifying policy made before 14 March 1984, the payer will deduct and retain income tax at the rate of 12.5 per cent. The ability to retain deductions made in this manner is not affected by the payer's liability to income tax on taxable income. No restriction to the deduction procedure arises if aggregate premiums paid during a year of assessment do not exceed £1,500 (calculated before deducting tax). Should premiums exceed this amount, relief will be confined to £1,500 or one-sixth of total income, whichever is the greater. Where sums deducted exceed the maximum limit, the excess must be accounted for to the Inland Revenue.

OTHER DEDUCTIONS

In addition to personal and other allowances, which reduce taxable income, further deductions may be available to an individual. These include payments of interest.

In some instances, interest paid by a business proprietor may be included when calculating profits chargeable to income tax under Case I or Case II of Schedule D. Many private individuals cannot obtain relief in this manner and must satisfy stringent requirements before relief will be forthcoming. In general terms, before interest can qualify for relief it must be annual, as opposed to short, interest or paid to a bank, stockbroker or discount house. Relief will not be available to the extent that interest exceeds a reasonable commercial rate and no relief is forthcoming for interest on an overdraft.

For 1993-4 relief will be available on the following payments:
(a) Interest on a loan to purchase, develop or improve an interest in land owned by the individual and used as the only or main residence of that individual. 'Land' includes large houseboats and also caravans used for residential purposes. No relief is available for interest on loans applied after 5 April 1988 for the development or improvement of land, unless the work involves the construction of a new building. Relief is available for interest paid on a loan applied to acquire a property which is the only or main residence of a dependent relative, a separated spouse or a divorced former spouse, but only where that person occupied the property before 6 April 1988. Relief may also be forthcoming for interest on a loan used to acquire some other property, perhaps to be used as the only or main residence on retirement, by an individual who is compelled to occupy property by reason of his or her work. If the loan, or aggregate of several loans, exceeds £30,000, relief is restricted to

interest on that amount. Where two or more persons apply loans after 31 July 1988 to acquire interests in a single building, those persons cannot, collectively, obtain relief for interest on more than £30,000 in relation to that building. Relief is confined to income tax at the basic rate. There can be no relief at the higher rate in excess of 25 per cent. It is proposed that relief should be limited to the lower rate of 20 per cent for interest paid after 5 April 1994

(b) Interest on a loan to purchase or improve an interest in land which is let or available for letting at a commercial rent. This interest is only capable of being deducted from rental income

(c) Interest on a loan made to acquire an interest in a close company or in a partnership, or to advance money to such a person

(d) Interest on a loan to a member of a partnership to acquire machinery or plant for use in the partnership business

(e) Interest on a loan to an employed person to acquire machinery or plant for the purposes of his/her employment

(f) Interest on a loan made for the purpose of contributing capital to an industrial co-operative

(g) Interest on a loan applied for investment in an employee-controlled company

(h) Interest on a loan made to elderly persons for the purchase of an annuity where the loan is secured on land. If the loan exceeds £30,000, relief is limited to interest on this amount. This relief also is restricted to income tax at the basic rate

(i) Interest on a loan to personal representatives to provide funds for the payment of capital transfer tax or inheritance tax

Relief for many payments of mortgage interest is obtained through a special scheme known as MIRAS (mortgage interest relief at source). This applies to interest paid to a building society, bank, insurance company and certain other approved persons. When making payments of this nature in 1993–4 the payer will deduct and retain income tax at the basic rate. This will provide the payer with full relief at the basic rate and no other relief will be necessary. Qualifying payments of interest outside the MIRAS scheme continue to produce relief by deduction from income chargeable to income tax at the basic rate.

Many employees pay contributions to an approved occupational pension scheme. The amount of their contributions may be deducted when establishing emoluments assessable under Schedule E. Relief should also be available for any additional voluntary contributions paid.

Self-employed individuals and those receiving earnings not covered by an occupational pension scheme may contribute under personal pension scheme arrangements. These individuals may also pay premiums under retirement annuity schemes, if the arrangements were concluded before 1 July 1988. Contributions paid under both headings may obtain income tax relief, subject to maximum limits.

Subject to a maximum of £40,000 in any one year, the cost of subscribing for shares in an unquoted company may qualify as a deduction from taxable income under the Business Expansion Scheme. Many requirements must be satisfied before this relief can be obtained, but husband and wife may each take advantage of the £40,000 annual maximum. The relief is being withdrawn and will cease to be available for subscriptions made after 31 December 1993.

CAPITAL GAINS TAX

A person is chargeable to capital gains tax on chargeable gains which accrue to him or her during a year of assessment ending on 5 April. The application of the tax has been amended substantially in recent years and the following information is confined to the year of assessment 1993–4, ending on 5 April 1994.

Liability extends to persons who are either resident or ordinarily resident for the year but special rules apply where a person permanently leaves the United Kingdom or comes to this territory for the purpose of acquiring residence. Non-residents are not liable to capital gains tax unless, exceptionally, they carry on a business in the United Kingdom through a branch or agency.

Chargeable gains accruing to companies are assessable to corporation tax and not to capital gains tax.

Capital gains tax is chargeable on the total of chargeable gains which accrue to a person in a year of assessment, after subtracting allowable losses arising in the same year. Unused allowable losses brought forward from some earlier year may be offset against current chargeable gains but in the case of individuals this must not reduce the net chargeable gains for 1993–4 below £5,800. It is possible to utilize trading losses against chargeable gains where those losses have not been offset against income.

RATE OF TAX

Where the net chargeable gains accruing to an individual during 1993–4 do not exceed £5,800 there will be no liability to capital gains tax. If the net gains exceed £5,800 the excess is chargeable at the taxpayer's marginal rate of income tax. This is achieved by adding to the amount of income chargeable to income tax the excess net chargeable gains. The rate attributable to this top slice will disclose the rate of capital gains tax payable, which may be at 20 per cent, 25 per cent, 40 per cent or a combination of the three. Although the income tax rates are used, capital gains tax remains a separate tax.

Capital gains tax for 1993–4 normally falls due for payment on or before 1 December 1994. If the return or other information recording chargeable gains is delayed, interest may become chargeable.

HUSBAND AND WIFE

Following the introduction of independent taxation on 6 April 1990 a husband and wife 'living together' are separately assessed to capital gains tax. Each spouse must independently calculate his or her gains and losses, with each entitled to the annual exemption of £5,800.

No liability to capital gains tax arises from the transfer of assets between husband and wife 'living together'.

DISPOSAL OF ASSETS

Before liability to capital gains tax can arise a disposal, or deemed disposal, of an asset must take place. This occurs not only where assets are sold or exchanged but applies on the making of a gift. There is also a disposal of assets where any capital sum is derived from assets, for example, where compensation is received for loss or damage to an asset.

The date on which a disposal must be treated as having taken place will determine the year of assessment into which the chargeable gain or allowable loss falls. In those cases where a disposal is made under an unconditional contract, the time of disposal will be that when the contract was entered into and not the subsequent date of conveyance or transfer. A disposal under a conditional contract or option is treated as taking place when the contract becomes unconditional or the option is exercised. Disposals by way of gift are undertaken when the gift becomes effective.

VALUATION OF ASSETS

The amount actually received as consideration for the disposal of an asset will be the sum from which very limited outgoings must be deducted for the purpose of establishing the gain or loss. In some cases, however, the consideration passing will not accurately reflect the value of the asset and a different basis must be used. This applies, in particular, where an asset is transferred by way of gift or otherwise than by a bargain made at arm's length. Such transactions are deemed to take place for a consideration representing market value, which will determine both the disposal proceeds accruing to the transferor and the cost of acquisition to the transferee.

Market value represents the price which an asset might reasonably be expected to fetch on a sale in the open market. In the case of unquoted shares or securities, it is to be assumed that the hypothetical purchaser in the open market would have available all the information which a prudent prospective purchaser of shares or securities might reasonably require if he were proposing to purchase them from a willing vendor by private treaty and at arm's length. This is an important consideration as the amount of information deemed to be available to a hypothetical purchaser may materially affect the price 'reasonably' offered in an open market situation. The market value of unquoted shares or securities will usually be established following negotiations with the Shares Valuation Division of the Capital Taxes Office. The valuation of land and interests in land in the United Kingdom will be dealt with by the District Valuer. Special rules apply to determine the market value of shares quoted on the Stock Exchange.

DEDUCTION FOR OUTGOINGS

Once the actual or notional disposal proceeds have been determined, it only remains to subtract eligible outgoings for the purpose of computing the gain or loss. There is the general rule that any outgoings deducted, or which are available to be deducted, when calculating income tax liability must be ignored. Subject to this, deductions will usually be limited to:

(a) the cost of acquiring the asset, together with incidental costs wholly and exclusively incurred in connection with the acquisition
(b) expenditure incurred wholly and exclusively on the asset in enhancing its value, being expenditure reflected in the state or nature of the asset at the time of the disposal, and any other expenditure wholly and exclusively incurred in establishing, preserving or defending title to, or a right over, the asset
(c) the incidental costs of making the disposal

Where the disposal concerns a leasehold interest having less than 50 years to run, any expenditure falling under (a) and (b) must be written off throughout the duration of the lease. This recognizes that a lease is a wasting asset which, at the termination of the leasing period, will retain no value.

ASSETS HELD ON 31 MARCH 1982

Where the disposal relates to assets held on 31 March 1982, the actual cost of acquisition will not usually enter into the calculation of gain. It is to be assumed that such assets were acquired on 31 March 1982 for a consideration representing market value on that date. The increase in value, if any, occurring before 31 March 1982 will not be assessable to capital gains tax.

INDEXATION ALLOWANCE

An indexation allowance will be available when calculating the chargeable gain or allowable loss. This allowance is based on percentage increases in the retail prices index between the month of March 1982 or, if later, the month in which expenditure is incurred, and the month of disposal. The increase is applied to the items of expenditure in (a) and (b) above to determine the amount of the indexation allowance. However, if the asset was acquired before 31 March 1982, the allowance will be based on market value at 31 March 1982.

The amount of the indexation allowance must be subtracted from the gain, or added to the loss, to calculate the chargeable gain or allowable loss arising on disposal.

EXEMPTIONS

There is a general exemption from liability to capital gains tax where the net gains of an individual for 1993–4 do not exceed £5,800. This general exemption applies separately to a husband and to his wife where the parties are 'living together'.

The disposal of many assets will not give rise to chargeable gains or allowable losses and these assets include:

(a) private motor cars
(b) government securities
(c) loan stock and other securities (but not shares)
(d) options and contracts relating to securities within (b) and (c)
(e) National Savings Certificates, Premium Bonds, Defence Bonds and National Development Bonds
(f) currency of any description acquired for personal expenditure outside the United Kingdom
(g) decorations awarded for valour
(h) betting wins and pools, lottery or games prizes
(i) compensation or damages for any wrong or injury suffered by an individual in his/her person or in his/her profession or vocation
(j) life assurance and deferred annuity contracts where the person making the disposal is the original beneficial owner
(k) dwelling-houses and land enjoyed with the residence which is an individual's only or main residence
(l) tangible movable property, the consideration for the disposal of which does not exceed £6,000
(m) certain tangible movable property which is a wasting asset having a life not exceeding 50 years
(n) assets transferred to charities and other bodies
(o) works of art, historic buildings and similar assets
(p) assets used to provide maintenance funds for historic buildings
(q) assets transferred to trustees for the benefit of employees

DWELLING-HOUSES

Exemption from capital gains tax will usually be available for any gain which accrues to an individual from the disposal of, or of an interest in, a dwelling-house or part of a dwelling-house which has been his/her only or main residence. The exemption extends to land which has been occupied and enjoyed with the residence as its garden or grounds. Some restriction may be necessary where the land exceeds half a hectare.

The gain will not be chargeable to capital gains tax if the dwelling-house, or part, has been the individual's only or main residence throughout the period of ownership, or throughout the entire period except for all or any part of the last three years. A proportionate part of the gain will be exempt in other cases if the dwelling-house has been the individual's only or main residence for part only of the period of ownership. In the case of property acquired before 31

March 1982, the period of ownership is treated as commencing on this date.

Where part of the dwelling-house has been used exclusively for business purposes, that part of the gain attributable to business use will not be exempt. It will be comparatively unusual for any part to be used exclusively for such a purpose, except perhaps in the case of doctors' or dentists' surgeries.

In those cases where part of a qualifying dwelling-house has been used to provide rented residential accommodation this non-personal use may frequently be ignored when calculating exemption from capital gains tax, unless relatively substantial sums are involved.

Dwellings occupied by dependent relatives or separated or divorced former spouses, may also qualify for the exemption, but only where occupation commenced before 6 April 1988.

ROLL-OVER RELIEF – BUSINESS ASSETS

Persons carrying on business will often undertake the disposal of an asset and use the proceeds to finance the acquisition of a replacement asset. Where this situation arises a claim for roll-over relief may be available. The broad effect of such a claim is that all or part of the gain arising on the disposal of the old asset may be disregarded. The gain or part is then subtracted from the cost of acquiring the replacement asset. As this cost is reduced, any gain arising from the future disposal of the replacement asset will be correspondingly increased, unless of course a further roll-over situation then develops.

It remains a requirement that both the old and the replacement asset must be used for the purpose of the taxpayer's business. Relief will only be available if the acquisition of the replacement asset takes place within a period commencing twelve months before, and ending three years after, the disposal of the old asset, although the Board of Inland Revenue retain a discretion to extend this period where the circumstances were such that it was impossible for the taxpayer to acquire the replacement asset before the expiration of the normal time limit.

Whilst many business assets qualify for roll-over relief there are exceptions.

ROLL-OVER RELIEF – SHARES

An additional form of roll-over relief was introduced for disposals taking place after 15 March 1993. This enables certain gains arising from the disposal of unquoted shares to be rolled over and subtracted from the cost of acquiring unquoted shares in a different company. It is a requirement that the individual making the disposal retained at least 5 per cent of the issued share capital and was also a full-time working officer or employee of the company concerned. An unusual feature of this additional roll-over relief is that the individual may select the amount of the gain he or she wishes to roll-over, subject to upper limits. The ability to select may enable part of the gain arising on disposal to be offset against available losses or used to absorb the annual exemption of £5,800.

HOLD-OVER RELIEF – GIFTS

The gift of an asset is treated as a disposal made for a consideration equal to market value, with a corresponding acquisition by the transferee at an identical value. In the case of gifts made by individuals and a limited range of trustees to a transferee resident in the United Kingdom, a form of hold-over relief may be available. Relief is limited to the transfer of certain assets, including the following:

(a) assets used for the purposes of a trade or similar activity carried on by the transferor or his/her personal company

(b) shares or securities of a trading company which is neither quoted on a stock exchange nor dealt in on the Unlisted Securities Market

(c) shares or securities of a trading company which is quoted or listed but which is the transferor's personal company

(d) many interests in agricultural property qualifying for business property relief or agricultual property relief for inheritance tax purposes

(e) assets involved in transactions which are lifetime transfers for inheritance tax purposes, other than potentially exempt transfers

The effect of the claim is similar to that following a claim for roll-over relief on the disposal of business assets, but adjustments will be necessary where some consideration is given for the transfer, the asset has not been used for business purposes throughout the period of ownership, or not all assets of a company are used for business purposes.

RETIREMENT RELIEF

Retirement relief is available to an individual who disposes by way of sale or gift of the whole or part of a business. It does not necessarily follow that the isolated disposal of assets will represent the disposal of the whole or part of a business. The main condition for granting this relief is that throughout a period of at least one year the business has been owned either by the individual or by a trading company in which the individual retained a sufficient shareholding interest. The relief extends also to cases where an individual disposes by way of sale or gift of shares or securities of a company. It must be demonstrated that the company was a trading company, that the individual retained a sufficient shareholding interest, and that he/she was engaged as a full-time working officer or employee.

An individual who has attained the age of 55 years at the time of a disposal may obtain retirement relief up to a maximum of £375,000. The amount of this relief must be reduced if the conditions have not been satisfied throughout a ten-year period. With a single exception no retirement relief can be obtained if the disposal occurs before the individual's 55th birthday. This exception arises where an individual is compelled to retire early on the grounds of ill-health. The normal retirement relief may then be obtained. Any retirement relief must be subtracted from the net gains arising on disposal, leaving the balance remaining, if any, chargeable to capital gains tax in the normal manner.

DEATH

No capital gains tax is chargeable on the value of assets retained at the time of death. However, the personal representatives administering the deceased's estate are deemed to acquire those assets for a consideration representing market value on death. This ensures that any increase in value occurring before the date of death will not be chargeable to capital gains tax. If a legatee or other person acquires an asset under a will or intestacy no chargeable gain will accrue to the personal representatives, and the person taking the asset will also be treated as having acquired it at the time of death for its then market value.

INHERITANCE TAX

Substantial changes to the former capital transfer tax were introduced for events occurring after 17 March 1986. In recognition of these changes the tax was renamed inheritance tax. The nature and scope of inheritance tax is outlined below, but the comments made have little application to events occurring before 18 March 1986 when capital transfer tax applied.

Liability to inheritance tax may arise on a limited range of lifetime gifts and other dispositions and also on the value of assets retained, or deemed to be retained, at the time of death. An individual's domicile at the time of any gift or on death is an important matter. Domicile will generally be determined by applying normal rules, although special considerations may be necessary where an individual was previously domiciled in the United Kingdom but subsequently acquired a domicile of choice overseas. Where a person was domiciled in the United Kingdom at the time of a disposition or on death the location of assets is immaterial and full liability to inheritance tax arises. Individuals domiciled outside the United Kingdom are, however, chargeable to inheritance tax only on transactions affecting assets located in the United Kingdom.

The assets of husband and wife are not merged for inheritance tax purposes. Each spouse is treated as a separate individual entitled to receive the benefit of his or her exemptions, reliefs and rates of tax. Where husband and wife retain similar assets, for example shares in the same family company, special 'related property' provisions may require the merger of those assets for valuation purposes only.

LIFETIME GIFTS AND DISPOSITIONS

Gifts and dispositions made during lifetime fall under four broad headings, namely:
(a) dispositions which are not transfers of value
(b) exempt transfers
(c) potentially exempt transfers
(d) chargeable transfers

Dispositions which are not transfers of value

Several lifetime transactions are not treated as transfers of value and may be entirely disregarded for inheritance tax purposes. These include transactions not intended to confer gratuitous benefit, the provision of family maintenance, the waiver of the right to receive remuneration or dividends, and the grant of agricultural tenancies for full consideration.

Exempt transfers

Certain other transfers are treated as exempt transfers and incur no liability to inheritance tax. The main exempt transfers are listed below:

Transfers between spouses – Transfers between husband and wife are usually exempt. However, if the transferor is, but the transferee spouse is not, domiciled in the United Kingdom, transfers will be exempt only to the extent that the total does not exceed £55,000. Unlike the requirement used for income tax and capital gains tax purposes, it is immaterial whether husband and wife are living together.

Annual exemption – The first £3,000 of gifts and other dispositions made in a year ending on 5 April is exempt. If the exemption is not used, or not wholly used, in any year the balance may be carried forward to the following year only. The annual exemption will only be available for a potentially exempt transfer if that transfer subsequently becomes chargeable by reason of the donor's death.

Small gifts – Outright gifts of £250 or less to any person in one year ending 5 April are exempt.

Normal expenditure – A transfer made during lifetime and comprising normal expenditure is exempt. To obtain this exemption it must be shown that:
(a) the transfer was made as part of the normal expenditure of the transferor
(b) taking one year with another, the transfer was made out of income

(c) after allowing for all transfers of value forming part of normal expenditure the transferor was left with sufficient income to maintain his or her usual standard of living

Gifts in consideration of marriage – These are exempt if they satisfy certain requirements. The amount allowed will be governed by the relationship between the donor and a party to the marriage. The allowable amounts comprise:
(a) gifts by a parent, £5,000
(b) gifts by a grandparent, £2,500
(c) gifts by a party to the marriage, £2,500
(d) gifts by other persons, £1,000

Gifts to charities – Gifts to charities are exempt from liability.

Gifts to political parties – Gifts to political parties which satisfy certain requirements are generally exempt.

Gifts for national purposes – Gifts made to an extensive list of bodies are exempt from liability. These include, among others:
(a) the National Gallery
(b) the British Museum
(c) the National Trust
(d) the National Art Collections Fund
(e) the National Heritage Memorial Fund
(f) the Historic Buildings and Monuments Commission for England (English Heritage)
(g) any local authority
(h) any university or university college in the United Kingdom

A number of other gifts made for the public benefit are also exempt.

Potentially exempt transfers

Lifetime gifts and dispositions which are neither to be ignored nor comprise exempt transfers incur possible liability to inheritance tax. However, relief is available for a range of potentially exempt transfers. These comprise gifts made by an individual to:
(a) a second individual
(b) trustees administering an accumulation and maintenance trust
(c) trustees administering a disabled person's trust

The accumulation and maintenance trust mentioned in (b) must provide that on reaching a specified age, not exceeding 25 years, a beneficiary will become absolutely entitled to trust assets or obtain an interest in possession in the income of those assets.

Additions to the above list affect settled property administered by trustees where an individual, or individuals, retain an interest in possession. The transfer of assets to, the removal of assets from, or the rearrangement of interests in such property comprise potentially exempt transfers if the person transferring an interest and the person benefiting from the transfer are both individuals.

No immediate liability to inheritance tax will arise on the making of a potentially exempt transfer. Should the donor survive for a period of seven years, immunity from liability will be confirmed. However, the donor's death within the seven-year *inter vivos* period produces liability, as explained later, if the amounts involved are sufficiently substantial.

Chargeable transfers

Any remaining lifetime gifts or dispositions which are neither to be ignored nor represent exempt transfers or potentially exempt transfers, incur liability to inheritance tax. The range of such chargeable transfers is severely limited and is broadly confined to transfers made to or affecting discretionary trusts, transfers to non-individuals and transfers involving companies.

GIFTS WITH RESERVATION

A lifetime gift of assets made at any time after 17 March 1986 may incur additional liability to inheritance tax if the donor retains some interest in the subject matter of the gift. This may arise, for example, where a parent transfers a dwelling-house to a son or daughter and continues to occupy the property or to enjoy some benefit from that property. The retention of a benefit may be ignored where it is enjoyed in return for full consideration, perhaps a commercial rent, or where the benefit arises from changed circumstances which could not have been foreseen at the time of the original gift. The gift with reservation provisions will not usually apply to most exempt transfers.

There are three possibilities which may arise where the donor reserves or enjoys some benefit from the subject matter of a previous gift and subsequently dies, namely:

(a) if no benefit is enjoyed within a period of seven years before death there can be no further liability

(b) if the benefit ceased to be enjoyed within a period of seven years before the date of death, the original donor is deemed to have made a potentially exempt transfer representing the value of the asset at the time of cessation

(c) if the benefit is enjoyed at the time of death, the value of the asset must be included in the value of the deceased's estate on death

It must be emphasized that the existence of a benefit enjoyed at any time within a period of seven years before death will establish liability to tax on gifts with reservation, notwithstanding that the gift may have been made many years earlier, providing it was undertaken after 17 March 1986.

DEATH

Immediately before the time of death an individual is deemed to make a transfer of value. This transfer will comprise the value of assets forming part of the deceased's estate after subtracting most liabilities. Any exempt transfers may, however, be excluded. These include transfers for the benefit of a surviving spouse, a charity and a qualifying political party, together with bequests to approved bodies and for national purposes.

Death may also trigger three additional liabilities, namely:

(a) A potentially exempt transfer made within the period of seven years ending on death loses its potential status and becomes chargeable to inheritance tax

(b) The value of gifts made with reservation may incur liability if any benefit was enjoyed within a period of seven years preceding death

(c) Additional tax may become payable for chargeable lifetime transfers made within seven years before death

VALUATIONS

The valuation of assets is an important matter as this will establish the value transferred for lifetime dispositions and also the value of a person's estate at the time of death. The value of property will represent the price which might reasonably be expected from a sale in the open market. This price cannot be reduced on the grounds that, should the whole property be placed on the market simultaneously, values would be depressed.

In some cases it may be necessary to incorporate the value of 'related property'. This will include property comprised in the estate of the transferor's spouse and certain property previously transferred to charities. The purpose of the related property valuation rules is not to add the value of the property to the estate of the transferor. Related property must be merged to establish the aggregate value of the respective interests and this value is then apportioned, usually on a *pro rata* basis, to the separate interests.

The value of shares and securities quoted on the Stock Exchange will be determined by extracting figures from the daily list of official prices.

Where quoted shares and securities are sold or the quotation is suspended within a period of twelve months following the date of death, a claim may be made to substitute the proceeds or subsequent value for the value on death. This claim will only be beneficial if the gross proceeds realized are lower or the value has fallen below market value at the time of death. A similar claim may be available for interests in land sold within a period of four years following death.

RELIEF FOR ASSETS

Special relief is made available for certain assets, notably woodlands, agricultural property and business property. The effect of this relief is summarized below.

Woodlands

Where woodlands pass on death the value will usually be included in the deceased's estate. However, an election may be made in respect of land in the United Kingdom on which trees or underwood is growing to delete the value of those assets. Relief is confined to the value of trees or underwood and does not extend to the land on which they are growing. Liability to inheritance tax will arise if and when the trees or underwood are sold on a future occasion.

Agricultural property

Relief is available for the agricultural value of agricultural property. Such property must be occupied and used for agricultural purposes and relief is confined to the agricultural value.

The value transferred, either on a lifetime gift or on death, must be determined. This value may then be reduced by a percentage. The percentage has changed from time to time but for events taking place after 9 March 1992 a 100 per cent deduction will be available if the transferor retained vacant possession or could have obtained that possession within a period of twelve months following the transfer. In other cases, notably including land let to tenants, a lower deduction of 50 per cent is available.

It remains a requirement that the agricultural property was either occupied by the transferor for the purposes of agriculture throughout a two-year period ending on the date of the transfer, or was owned by him/her throughout a period of seven years ending on that date and also occupied for agricultural purposes.

Business property

Where the value transferred is attributable to relevant business property, that value may be reduced by a percentage. The reduction in value applies to:

(a) property consisting of a business or an interest in a business

(b) shares or securities of an unquoted company which provided the transferor with control

(c) unquoted shares or securities not falling within (b) which provided the transferor with more than 25 per cent of voting rights

(d) other unquoted shares or securities not falling within (c)

(e) shares or securities of a quoted company which provided the transferor with control

(f) any land, building, machinery or plant which, immediately before the transfer, was used wholly or mainly for the purposes of a business carried on by a company of which the transferor had control

(g) any land, building, machinery or plant which, immediately before the transfer, was used wholly or mainly for the purposes of a business carried on by a partnership of which the transferor was a partner

(h) any land, building, machinery or plant which, immediately before the transfer, was used wholly or mainly for the purposes of a business carried on by the transferor and was then settled property in which he retained an interest in possession

Here also the percentage deductions have changed, but for events occurring after 9 March 1992 a deduction of 100 per cent is available for assets falling within (a), (b) or (c). A reduced deduction of 50 per cent can be obtained for assets within (d) to (h).

It is a general requirement that the property must have been retained for a period of two years before the transfer or death and restrictions may be necessary if the property has not been used wholly for business purposes. The same slice of property cannot obtain both business property relief and the relief available for agricultural property.

CALCULATION OF TAX PAYABLE

The calculation of inheritance tax payable adopts the use of a cumulative total. Each chargeable lifetime transfer is added to the total with a final addition made on death. The top slice added to the total for the current event determines the rate at which inheritance tax must be paid. However, the cumulative total will only include transfers made within a period of seven years before the current event and those undertaken outside this period must be excluded. Although inheritance tax was only introduced on 18 March 1986, the seven-year cumulative total will include chargeable lifetime gifts made before that date, subject to the seven-year limitation.

Lifetime chargeable transfers

The value transferred by the limited range of lifetime chargeable transfers must be added to the seven-year cumulative total to calculate the amount of inheritance tax due. The tax is imposed at one-half of the rate shown below. However, if the donor dies within a period of seven years from the date of the chargeable lifetime transfer, additional tax may be due. This is calculated by applying tax at the full rate (in substitution for the one-half rate previously used). The amount of tax is then reduced to a percentage by applying tapering relief. This percentage is governed by the number of years from the date of the lifetime gift to the date of death and is as follows:

Period of years before death

Not more than 3	100%
More than 3 but not more than 4	80%
More than 4 but not more than 5	60%
More than 5 but not more than 6	40%
More than 6 but not more than 7	20%

Should this exercise produce liability greater than that previously paid at the one-half rate on the lifetime transfer, additional tax, representing the difference, must be discharged. Where the calculation shows an amount falling below tax paid on the lifetime transfer, no additional liability can arise nor will the deficiency become repayable.

Potentially exempt transfers

Where a potentially exempt transfer loses immunity from liability, due to the donor's death within the seven-year *inter vivos* period, the value transferred becomes liable to inheritance tax. Liability is calculated by applying the full rate shown below, reduced to the percentage governed by tapering relief if the original transfer occurred more than three years before death.

Death

The final addition to the seven-year cumulative total will comprise the value of an estate on death. Inheritance tax will be calculated by applying the full rate shown below. No tapering relief can be obtained.

RATES OF TAX

In earlier times there were several rates of inheritance tax which progressively increased as the value transferred grew in size. However, for events taking place after 9 March 1992, a nil rate applies to the initial slice of £150,000. Any excess is charged at the single positive rate of 40 per cent.

Only one-half of the 40 per cent rate (namely 20 per cent) will be applicable for chargeable lifetime transfers.

The above rate and rateband is likely to be amended on future occasions.

PAYMENT OF TAX

Inheritance tax usually falls due for payment six months after the end of the month in which the chargeable transaction takes place. Where a transfer, other than that made on death, occurs after 5 April and before the following 1 October, tax falls due on the following 30 April, although there are some exceptions to this general rule.

Inheritance tax attributable to the transfer of certain land, controlling shareholding interests, unquoted shares, businesses and interests in businesses, together with agricultural property, may usually be satisfied by instalments spread over ten years. Except in the case of non-agricultural land, where interest is charged on outstanding instalments, no liability to interest arises where tax is paid on the due date. In all cases, delay in the payment of tax may incur liability to interest.

SETTLED PROPERTY

Complex rules apply to establish inheritance tax liability on settled property. Where a person is beneficially entitled to an interest in possession, that person is effectively deemed to own the property in which the interest subsists. It follows that where the interest comes to an end during the beneficiary's lifetime and some other person becomes entitled to the property or interest, the beneficiary is treated as having made a transfer of value. However, this will usually comprise a potentially exempt transfer. In addition, no liability will arise where the property vests in the absolute ownership of the previous beneficiary. The death of a person entitled to an interest in possession will require the value of the underlying property to be added to the value of the deceased's estate.

In the case of other settled property where there is no interest in possession (e.g. discretionary trusts), liability to tax will arise on each ten-year anniversary of the trust. There will also be liability if property ceases to be held on discretionary trusts before the first ten-year anniversary date is reached or between anniversaries. The rate of tax suffered will be governed by several considerations, including previous dispositions made by the settlor, transactions concluded by the trustees, and the period throughout which property has been held in trust.

Accumulation and maintenance settlements which require assets to be distributed, or interests in income to be created, not later than a beneficiary's twenty-fifth birthday may be exempt from any liability to inheritance tax.

CORPORATION TAX

Profits, gains and income accruing to companies resident in the United Kingdom incur liability to corporation tax. Non-resident companies are immune from this tax unless they carry on a trade in the United Kingdom through a permanent establishment, branch or office. Companies residing outside the United Kingdom may be liable to income tax at the basic rate on other income arising in the United Kingdom, perhaps from letting property. The following comments are confined to companies resident in the United Kingdom and have little application to those residing overseas.

Liability to corporation tax is governed by the profits, gains or income for an accounting period. This is usually the period for which financial accounts are made up, and in the case of companies preparing accounts to the same accounting date annually will comprise successive periods of twelve months.

RATE OF TAX

The amount of profits or income for an accounting period must be determined on normal taxation principles. The special rules which apply to individuals where a source of income is acquired or discontinued are ignored and consideration is confined to the actual profits or income for an accounting period.

The rate of corporation tax is fixed for a financial year ending on 31 March. Where the accounting period of a company overlaps this date and there is a change in the rate of corporation tax, profits and income must be apportioned.

In recent years the rate of corporation tax has been as follows:

Financial year

12 months ending 31 March 1987, 1988, 1989, 1990	35%
31 March 1991	34%
31 March 1992, 1993, 1994	33%

SMALL COMPANIES RATE

Where the profits of a company do not exceed stated limits, corporation tax becomes payable at the following small companies rate. It is the amount of profits and not the size of the company which governs the application of this rate.

Financial year

12 months ending 31 March 1988	27%
31 March 1989, 1990 1991, 1992, 1993, 1994	25%

The level of profits which a company may derive without losing the benefit of the small companies rate has been frequently changed. For each of the years ending on 31 March 1992, 31 March 1993 and 31 March 1994, the limit was £250,000. However, if profits do exceed £250,000 but fall below £1,250,000, marginal small companies rate relief applies. The broad effect of marginal relief is that the first £250,000 of profits is taxed at the appropriate small companies rate. Profits falling in the margin then incur liability at the marginal rate of 35 per cent. Different upper limits and marginal rates applied for earlier years. Where the accounting period of a company overlaps 31 March, profits must be apportioned to establish the appropriate rate for each part of those profits.

The lower limit of £250,000 and the upper limit of £1,250,000 applies for a period of twelve months in duration and must be proportionately reduced for shorter periods. Some restriction in the small companies rate and the marginal rate may be necessary if there are two or more associated companies, namely companies under common control.

The small companies rate is not available for close investment-holding companies. These are mainly investment companies, other than those receiving most of their income from letting land and property.

CAPITAL GAINS

Chargeable gains arising to a company are calculated in a manner similar to that used for individuals. However, companies cannot obtain the annual exemption of £5,800, nor are they assessed to capital gains tax. In place of this tax companies suffer liability to corporation tax on chargeable gains. Tax is suffered on the full chargeable gain, after subtracting relief for losses, if any.

DISTRIBUTIONS

Dividends and other qualifying distributions made by a United Kingdom resident company are not satisfied after deduction of income tax. However, when making a distribution a company is required to account to the Inland Revenue for advance corporation tax. The amount of this tax is based on the distribution and changes in the rate are being made throughout a three-year period as follows:

Distribution	*Rate*
Year ending 5 April 1993	one third
Year ending 5 April 1994	nine thirty-firsts
Year ending 5 April 1995	one quarter

Advance corporation tax accounted for in this manner in relation to distributions made in an accounting period may usually be set against a company's corporation tax liability for the same period. Some restrictions are imposed on the amount which can be offset but any surplus may be carried forward, or perhaps carried backwards, and set against corporation tax paid or due for other accounting periods.

A United Kingdom resident shareholder receiving a qualifying distribution also obtains a tax credit based on the distribution made. Over the same three-year period the tax credit will be calculated as follows:

Distribution	*Rate*
Year ending 5 April 1993	one third
Year ending 5 April 1994	one quarter
Year ending 5 April 1995	one quarter

The total income of the individual therefore comprises the aggregate of the distribution and the tax credit. It will particularly be noted that whilst the rate of advance corporation tax and the amount of the tax credit are identical for the first and last of the three years, the amounts differ in 1993-4.

For 1993-4 a distribution is treated as having suffered income tax at the lower rate of 20 per cent. If the individual is not liable, or not fully liable, to income tax at this rate all or part of the tax credit can be refunded by the Inland Revenue. There is no liability on distributions at the basic rate of 25 per cent. However, individuals with substantial income incur liability to income tax at the higher rate of 40 per cent on the aggregate of the distribution and the tax credit. With tax deemed to have been suffered at the lower rate of 20 per cent the additional liability will be limited to the excess over this rate, which is also 20 per cent.

PAYMENT OF TAX

Corporation tax, less any relief for advance corporation tax, falls due for payment nine months following the end of the accounting period to which the tax relates. Companies which were carrying on business before 1966 previously had a later due and payable date, but this has now been phased out to achieve a common nine-month period for all companies.

INTEREST

On making many payments of interest a company is required to deduct income tax at the basic rate and account for the tax deducted to the Inland Revenue. The gross amount of interest paid will usually comprise a charge on income to be offset against profits on which corporation tax becomes payable.

GROUPS OF COMPANIES

Each company within a group is separately charged to corporation tax on profits, gains and income. However, where one group member realizes a loss, other than a capital loss, a claim may be made to offset the deficiency against profits of some other member of the same group.

Claims are also available to avoid the payment of advance corporation tax on distributions, or the deduction of income tax on the payment of interest, for transactions between members of a group of companies. The transfer of capital assets from one member of a group to a fellow member will incur no liability to tax on chargeable gains.

PAY AND FILE

For accounting periods ending after 30 September 1993 a new 'pay and file' system will affect all companies. Under this system tax will have to be paid on a self-assessment basis nine months following the end of the accounting period involved, with accounts and returns being submitted three months later. Failure to satisfy corporation tax or to submit documents within these time limits will result in a liability to interest and penalties.

VALUE ADDED TAX

Unlike income tax, capital gains tax, inheritance tax and corporation tax, which are collected and administered by the Inland Revenue, value added tax is the responsibility of Customs and Excise. Value added tax is charged on the value of the supplies made by a registered trader and extends to both the supply of goods and the supply of services. For many years liability to account for value added tax also arose on the value of goods imported into the United Kingdom. This liability remains where goods are imported from many overseas sources.

However, substantial changes were introduced with the commencement of the European 'single market' on 1 January 1993. Where goods are imported by a trader from a member state of the European Community there is no value added tax on importation. In place of importation tax there is an acquisition tax whereby a trader who acquires goods must include the acquisition with his normal value added tax return and account for the tax due. A United Kingdom trader who exports goods to a member state will not be required to account for value added tax on the supply, if that trader observes the requirements laid down by regulation.

REGISTRATION

All traders, including professional men and women, together with companies, making taxable supplies of a value exceeding stated limits are required to register for value added tax purposes. Taxable supplies represent the supply of goods and services potentially chargeable with value added tax. The limits which govern mandatory registration are amended annually but from 16 March 1993 an unregistered trader must register:

(a) at any time, if there are reasonable grounds for believing that the value of taxable supplies in the next 30 days will exceed £37,600

(b) at the end of any month if the value of taxable supplies in the last 12 months then ending has exceeded £37,600.

Liability to register under (b) may be avoided if it can be shown that the value of supplies in the period of 12 months

then beginning will not exceed £36,000. There may, however, be liability to register immediately where a business is taken over from another trader as a 'going concern'.

Where the limits governing mandatory registration have been exceeded, it is necessary for the trader to notify Customs and Excise. Failure to provide prompt notification may have unfortunate results as the person concerned will be required to account for value added tax from the proper registration date.

A trader whose taxable supplies do not reach the mandatory registration limits may apply for voluntary registration. This step may be thought advisable to recover input tax or to compete with other registered traders.

A registered trader may submit an application for de-registration if the value of taxable supplies subsequently falls. From 1 May 1993, an application for de-registration can be made if the value of taxable supplies for the year beginning on the application date is not expected to exceed £36,000.

INPUT TAX

A registered trader will both suffer tax (input tax) when obtaining goods or services for the purposes of his business and also become liable to account for tax (output tax) on the value of goods and services which he supplies. Relief can usually be obtained for input tax suffered, either by setting that tax against output tax due or by repayment. Most items of input tax can be relieved in this manner but there are exceptions including the prohibition of relief for the cost of business entertaining. Where a registered trader makes both exempt supplies and also taxable supplies to his customers or clients, there may be some restriction in the amount of input tax which can be recovered.

OUTPUT TAX

When making a taxable supply of goods or services a registered trader must account for output tax, if any, on the value of the supply. Usually the price charged by the registered trader will be increased by adding value added tax but failure to make the required addition will not remove liability to account for output tax.

EXEMPT SUPPLIES

No value added tax is chargeable on the supply of goods or services which are treated as exempt supplies. These include the provision of burial and cremation facilities, insurance, finance and education. The granting of a lease to occupy land or the sale of land will usually comprise an exempt supply, but there are numerous exceptions. In particular, the sale of new non-domestic buildings or certain buildings used by charities cannot be treated as exempt supplies.

A taxable person may elect to tax rents and other supplies of buildings and agricultural land not used for residential or charitable purposes.

Exempt supplies do not enter into the calculation of taxable supplies which governs liability to mandatory registration. Such supplies made by a registered trader may, however, limit the amount of input tax which can be relieved. It is for this reason that the election may be useful.

RATES OF TAX

Two rates of value added tax have applied since 1 April 1991, namely:

(a) a zero, or nil, rate

(b) a standard rate of 17.5 per cent

Although no tax is due on a zero-rated supply, this does comprise a taxable supply which must be included in the calculation governing liability to register.

ZERO-RATING

A large number of supplies are zero-rated, including, among others:

(a) the supply of many items of food and drink for human consumption. This does not include ice creams, chocolates, sweets, potato crisps and alcoholic drinks. Nor does it extend to supplies made in the course of catering or to items supplied for consumption in a restaurant or café. Whilst the supply of cold items, e.g. sandwiches, for consumption away from the supplier's premises, is zero-rated, the supply of hot food, for example fish and chips, is not

(b) animal feeding stuffs

(c) sewerage and water, unless supplied for industrial purposes

(d) books, brochures, pamphlets, leaflets, newspapers, maps and charts

(e) talking books for the blind and handicapped, and wireless sets for the blind

(f) electricity, gas and coal, but supplies are limited to domestic use. Zero rating under this heading is being removed on 1 April 1994. Supplies made after this date will be subject to tax at the rate of 8 per cent, increasing to 17.5 per cent 12 months later

(g) supplies of services, other than professional services, when constructing a new domestic building or a building to be used by a charity. The supply of materials for such a building is also zero-rated, together with the sale or the grant of a long lease for these buildings. Alterations to some protected buildings are also zero-rated

(h) the transportation of persons in a vehicle, ship or aircraft designed to carry not less than twelve persons

(i) supplies of drugs, medicines and other aids for the handicapped

(j) supplies of clothing and footwear for young persons

(k) exports

This list is not exhaustive but indicates the wide range of supplies which may be zero-rated.

COLLECTION OF TAX

Registered traders submit value added tax returns for accounting periods. Each accounting period is usually three months in duration but arrangements can be made to submit returns on a monthly basis. Very large traders must account for tax on a monthly basis from October 1992 but this does not affect the three-monthly return. The return will show both the output tax due for supplies made by the trader in the accounting period and also the input tax for which relief is claimed. If the output tax exceeds input tax the balance must be remitted with the value added tax return. Where input tax suffered exceeds the output tax due the registered trader may claim recovery of the excess from Customs and Excise.

This basis for collecting tax explains the structure of value added tax. Where supplies are made between registered traders the supplier will account for an amount of tax which will usually be identical to the tax recovered by the person to whom the supply is made. However, where the supply is made to a person who is not a registered trader there can be no recovery of input tax and it is on this person that the final burden of value added tax eventually falls.

In those cases where goods are acquired by a United Kingdom trader from a supplier within a member state of the European Community the trader must also account for the tax due on acquisition.

An optional scheme is available for registered traders having an annual turnover of taxable supplies not exceeding £350,000. Such traders may, if they wish, render returns annually. Nine equal payments of value added tax will be paid on account, with a final balancing payment accompanying submission of the return.

BAD DEBTS

Many retailers operate special retail schemes for calculating the amount of value added tax due. These schemes are, broadly, based on the volume of consideration received in an accounting period. Should a customer fail to pay for goods or services supplied, there will be no consideration on which value added tax falls to be calculated.

To avoid the problem of bad debts incurred by traders not operating a special retail scheme, an optional system of cash accounting is available. This scheme, confined to traders with annual taxable supplies not exceeding £350,000, enables returns to be made on a cash basis, in substitution for the normal supply basis. Traders using such a scheme will not, of course, include bad debts in the calculation of cash receipts.

Where neither the cash accounting arrangements nor the special retail scheme applies, output tax falls due on the value of the supply and liability is not affected by failure to receive consideration. However, where a debt is more than 12 months old and is written off in the supplier's books, relief for bad debts will be forthcoming.

OTHER SPECIAL SCHEMES

In addition to the schemes for retailers, there are several special schemes applied to calculate the amount of value added tax due and which also limit the ability to recover input tax. These schemes apply to the supply of second-hand motor cars, motor cycles, caravans, boats, electronic organs, aircraft and firearms, together with works of art, antiques and collectors' pieces.

FARMERS

Farmers may elect to apply a special flat rate scheme. This scheme is available to farmers who are not registered traders. Under the scheme a flat-rate addition of 4 per cent may be made on sales, with the amount of the addition being retained by the farmer. Registered traders to whom such a supply is made may treat the 4 per cent addition as recoverable input tax.

Stamp Duties

Stamp duty is a tax on documents. There are a number of separate duties, under different heads of charge. The Finance Act 1990 included provisions abolishing all the stamp duty charges on transactions in shares from a date to be fixed by Treasury order (which has not yet been made). The Finance Act 1991 removed the stamp duty charges on documents relating to all other types of property except land and buildings, again from a date to be specified (no date yet specified). In the list of documents which follows, those which will be affected by the above provisions are indicated with an asterisk*.

AGREEMENT FOR LEASE, *see* LEASES

AGREEMENT FOR SALE OF PROPERTY
Charged with *ad valorem* duty as if an actual conveyance on sale, with certain exceptions, e.g. agreements for the sale of land, stocks and shares, goods, wares or merchandise, or a ship (*see* S. 59 (1), Stamp Act 1891). If *ad valorem* duty is paid on an agreement in accordance with this provision, the subsequent conveyance or transfer is not chargeable with any *ad valorem* duty and the Commissioners will upon application either place a denoting stamp on such conveyance or transfer or will transfer the *ad valorem* duty thereto. Further, if such an agreement is rescinded, not performed, etc., the Commissioners will return the *ad valorem* duty paid.

AGREEMENT UNDER SEAL
Subject to exemptions, 50p

ASSIGNMENT
By way of sale, *see* CONVEYANCE
By way of gift, *see* VOLUNTARY DISPOSITION

ASSURANCE, *see* INSURANCE POLICIES

*BEARER INSTRUMENT
Inland bearer instrument, i.e. share warrant, stock certificate to bearer or any other instrument to bearer by which stock can be transferred, issued by a company or body formed or established in the UK, 1.5%

Overseas bearer instrument, i.e. such an instrument issued in Great Britain by a company formed out of the UK, 1.5%

BILL OF SALE, ABSOLUTE, *see* CONVEYANCE ON SALE

CAPITAL DUTY
This was charged at 1 per cent on every £100 or fraction of £100 of the actual value of assets contributed by the members of a company provided the place of effective management of the company was in Great Britain, or its registered office was in Great Britain but the place of its effective management was outside the EC (Finance Act 1973). The tax was abolished by the Finance Act 1988 in respect of transactions entered into on or after 16 March 1988.

CONTRACT, *see* AGREEMENT

*CONTRACT OR GRANT FOR PAYMENT OF A SUPERANNUATION ANNUITY
For every £10 or fractional part of £10, 5p

CONVEYANCE OR TRANSFER ON SALE
(In the case of a Voluntary Disposition, *see* below)

Conveyance or transfer on sale of any property (except stock or marketable securities), where the conveyance or transfer contains a certificate of value certifying that the transaction does not form part of a larger transaction or a series of transactions in respect of which the aggregate amount or value of the consideration exceeds £60,000, *nil*

Exceeds £60,000 (for every £100 or fraction of £100), £1

The limit was increased from £30,000 to £60,000 for documents executed after 15 March 1993

If the conveyance or transfer on sale does not contain the appropriate statement, duty at the full rate of £1 for every £100 or fraction of £100 will be payable whatever the amount of the consideration.

However, if the consideration does not exceed £500, and the instrument does not contain a certificate of value, there are graduated duties ranging from 50p to £5.

Conveyances to charities are exempt from duty under this head provided the instrument is stamped with a denoting stamp.

CONVEYANCE OR TRANSFER OF ANY OTHER KIND
Fixed duty, 50p

However, under the Stamp Duty (Exempt Instruments) Regulations 1987, instruments which would otherwise fall under this head are exempt from stamp duty provided the document is duly certified. The certificate must contain a sufficient description of the category into which the instrument falls, and must be signed by the transferor, his solicitor or agent: 'I/We hereby certify that this instrument falls within category . . . in the Schedule to the Stamp Duty (Exempt Instruments) Regulations 1987.'

COVENANT, for original creation and sale of any annuity, *see* CONVEYANCE

DECLARATION OF TRUST
Not being a will or settlement, 50p

DEMISE, *see* LEASES

DUPLICATE OR COUNTERPART
Same duty as original, but not to exceed, 50p

GIFT, *see* VOLUNTARY DISPOSITION

*GUARANTEE
If under seal, 50p

INSURANCE POLICIES, LIFE
Exceeding £50 and not exceeding £1,000, for every £100 or part of £100, 5p

Exceeding £1,000, for every £1,000 or any fractional part of £1,000, 50p

Made after 1 August 1966 for period not exceeding two years, 5p

The Finance Act 1989 abolished this charge for policies made after 31 December 1989.

LEASES (INCLUDING AGREEMENTS FOR LEASES)

Lease or tack for any definite term less than a year of any furnished dwelling-house or apartments where the rent for such term exceeds £500, £1

Of any lands, tenements, etc., in consideration of any rent, according to the following:

Annual rent not exceeding	†Term not exceeding 7 yrs	35 yrs	100 yrs	Exceeding 100 yrs
£	£ p	£ p	£ p	£ p
5	Nil	0.10	0.60	1.20
10	Nil	0.20	1.20	2.40
15	Nil	0.30	1.80	3.60
20	Nil	0.40	2.40	4.80
25	Nil	0.50	3.00	6.00
50	Nil	1.00	6.00	12.00
75	Nil	1.50	9.00	18.00
100	Nil	2.00	12.00	24.00
150	Nil	3.00	18.00	36.00
200	Nil	4.00	24.00	48.00
250	Nil	5.00	30.00	60.00
300	Nil	6.00	36.00	72.00
350	Nil	7.00	42.00	84.00
400	Nil	8.00	48.00	96.00
450	Nil	9.00	54.00	108.00
500	Nil	10.00	60.00	120.00
Exceeding £500, for every £50 or fraction thereof	0.50	1.00	6.00	12.00

†If the term is indefinite the same duty is payable as if the term did not exceed seven years.

Where a consideration other than rent is payable, the same rule applies where the consideration does not exceed £60,000 as under conveyance or transfer on sale (except stock or marketable securities), provided that any rent payable does not exceed £600 a year and a certificate of value is included in the conveyance or transfer.

Leases to charities are exempt from duty under this head provided the instrument is stamped with a denoting stamp.

MORTGAGES, exempt.

RECEIPTS FOR SALARIES, WAGES AND SUPERANNUATION, AND OTHER LIKE ALLOWANCES, exempt.

*TRANSFER OF STOCK AND SHARES BY SALE, 0.5%

*UNIT TRUST INSTRUMENT

Any trust instrument of a unit trust scheme, for every £100 or fraction of £100 of the amount or value of the property subject to the trusts created or recorded by the instrument, 25p

By the Finance Act 1989, the transfer of units in certain authorized unit trusts is no longer subject to duty.

VOLUNTARY DISPOSITION, *inter vivos*, 50p

The Commissioners as a general rule allow deeds, etc., to be stamped after execution:

WITHOUT PENALTY, ON PAYMENT OF DUTY ONLY

Deeds and instruments not otherwise excepted, within 30 days of first execution.

NB. Where wholly executed abroad, the period begins to run from the date of arrival in the UK.

PENALTIES ENFORCEABLE ON STAMPING IN ADDITION TO DUTY

Instruments presented after the proper time (subject to special provisions in some cases and subject to the Commissioner's power to mitigate), a penalty equal to the unpaid duty (and interest thereon if duty exceeds £10) plus £10

Legal Notes

IMPORTANT

The purpose of these notes is to outline some of the more common parts of the law as they may affect the average person. They are believed to be correct at the time of going to press. However, the law is constantly developing and changing, and it is always best to take expert advice. Anyone who does not have a solicitor already and is unable to find one through the recommendation of a friend, can contact the Citizens' Advice Bureau (whose address can be obtained from the telephone directory or from any post office or town hall). Each CAB has a list of solicitors in the area who deal with particular types of problem. Alternatively, assistance can be sought from The Law Society, 113 Chancery Lane, London WC2A 1PL or The Law Society of Scotland, 26 Drumsheugh Gardens, Edinburgh EH3 7YR.

The legal aid and legal advice and assistance schemes exist to make the help of the trained lawyer available to those who would not otherwise be able to afford legal advice. The best policy is to go to a solicitor without delay; timely advice will set your mind at rest but sitting on your rights can mean that you lose them.

It is not necessary for a dispute to have arisen before advice is sought from a solicitor; the legal advice and assistance scheme enables a solicitor to advise you on your rights, for instance under a tenancy agreement, the estate of a deceased person or in connection with matrimonial and consumer matters, and to write letters or take other steps on your behalf. Entitlement to take advantage of the scheme depends on your means (*see* pages 673, 674, 675) but a solicitor or Citizens' Advice Bureau will be able to advise about entitlement.

BRITISH CITIZENSHIP

There are three types of citizenship: British Citizenship; Citizenship of the British Dependent Territories; and British Overseas Citizenship.

Acquisition of citizenship on change of law

The British Nationality Act 1981 which came into force on 1 January 1983 made substantial changes to the law of citizenship, which before that date did not distinguish between the three types of citizenship referred to above. Almost all persons who were then both citizens of the UK and colonies and who had a right of abode in the UK became British citizens when the Act came into force. Most UK and colonies citizens who did not have a right of abode in the UK became Citizens of the British Dependent Territories. This type of citizenship was, broadly speaking, conferred on citizens of the UK and colonies by birth, naturalization or registration in dependent territories. Dependent territories include Hong Kong, Gibraltar, the Falkland Islands, and St Helena and its dependencies. Any UK and colonies citizen who, on 1 January 1983, did not acquire either British or British Dependent Territories Citizenship became a British Overseas Citizen.

Later acquisition of British citizenship

British citizenship is acquired automatically by those born in the UK (including, for this purpose, the Channel Islands and the Isle of Man) who have a parent who is a British citizen or a parent who is settled in the UK. Certain other categories of children born in the UK also acquire this type of citizenship, i.e. foundlings, those whose parents subsequently settle in the UK, those who live in the UK for ten years from birth and those adopted in the UK.

A person born outside the UK may acquire British citizenship in the following ways:
(a) if one of his/her parents is a British citizen otherwise than by descent, e.g. parent was born in the UK
(b) if one of his/her parents is a British citizen serving the Crown overseas
(c) if the Secretary of State consents to his/her registration while he/she is a minor
(d) if he/she is a Citizen of the British Dependent Territories, a British Overseas Citizen, a British subject or a British Protected Person (these last two are residual categories of people who have not acquired one of the three new types of citizenship) and has been lawfully resident in the UK for five years without any time restriction
(e) if he/she is a British Dependent Territories Citizen who is a national of the UK for the purposes of the EC (i.e. a Gibraltarian)
(f) if he/she is naturalized. Naturalization may be applied for only by adults and the Secretary of State has a discretion whether to permit it. The basic requirements are five years' residence, good character, sufficient knowledge of the English or Welsh language, and an intention to reside in the UK permanently. The requirements are somewhat less restrictive in the case of an applicant who is married to a British citizen

Acquisition of British Dependent Territories and British Overseas Citizenship after the Act

These citizenships are intended for persons connected with certain Commonwealth countries other than the UK. In the case of dependent territories the rules are very similar to those for acquiring British citizenship, except that the connection is with the dependent territory rather than with the UK. British Overseas Citizenship may be acquired by the wife and minor children of a British Overseas Citizen in certain circumstances.

Retention of nationality by persons born in or who are citizens of the Republic of Ireland

By the Ireland Act 1949, a person who was born before 6 December 1922 in what is now the Republic of Ireland (Eire) and was a British subject immediately before 1 January 1949, is not deemed to have ceased to be a British subject unless either he/she (a) was domiciled in the Irish Free State on 6 December 1922, (b) was on or after 10 April 1935 and before 1 January 1949 permanently resident there, or (c) had before 1 January 1949 been registered as a citizen of Eire under the laws of that country.

In addition, by the British Nationality Act 1948, any citizen of Eire who immediately before 1 January 1949 was also a British subject can retain that status by submitting at any time a claim to the Home Secretary on any of the following grounds:
(a) he/she has been in the service of the United Kingdom government
(b) he/she holds a British passport issued in the United Kingdom or in any colony, protectorate, United Kingdom mandated or trust territory

(c) he/she has associations by way of descent, residence or otherwise with any such place

(d) on complying with similar legislation in any of the 'dominions'

The British Nationality Act 1981 provides that persons who have made a claim may continue to be British subjects. Any citizen of Eire who was a British subject before 1 January 1949 and who has not yet made a claim may do so provided that:

(a) he/she is or has been in Crown service under the government of the United Kingdom

(b) he/she has associations by way of descent, residence or otherwise with the United Kingdom or any dependent territory

Renunciation and resumption

A person may cease to be a British citizen by renouncing his/her citizenship (with the consent of the Secretary of State in wartime). The renunciation is required to be registered with the Secretary of State and will be revoked if no new citizenship or nationality is acquired within six months. Once renounced, citizenship may be reacquired if the renunciation was necessary to retain or acquire some other citizenship or nationality. Similar rules as to renunciation and reacquisition apply in the case of British Dependent Territories Citizenships and of renunciation (but not reacquisition) in the case of British Overseas Citizenship.

Status of aliens

Property may be held by an alien in the same manner as by a natural-born British subject, but he/she may not hold public office, exercise the franchise or own a British ship or aircraft. The Republic of Ireland Act 1949 declares that the Republic, though not part of HM Dominions, is not a foreign country, and any reference in an Act of Parliament to foreigners, aliens, foreign countries, etc., shall be construed accordingly.

CONSUMER LAW

THE SUPPLY OF GOODS AND SERVICES

(1) The Sale of Goods Act 1979 provides protection to the purchaser of goods, by implying certain terms into every contract for the sale of goods. These implied terms are:

(a) A condition that the seller will pass good title to the buyer (unless the seller agrees to transfer only such title as he or his principal has) and warranties that the goods will be free from undisclosed encumbrances, and that the buyer will enjoy quiet possession of the goods

(b) Where there is a sale of goods by description, a condition that the goods will correspond with that description, and where the sale is by sample and description, a condition that the bulk of the goods shall correspond with both sample and description

(c) Where the seller sells goods in the course of a business, a condition that the goods will be of merchantable quality, unless before the contract is made, the buyer has examined the goods and ought to have noticed the defect, bearing in mind the purchaser's knowledge of the goods and the extent of the examination, or unless the seller has specifically drawn the attention of the buyer to the defect. Merchantable quality means fit for the purpose for which goods of the kind are commonly bought, taking into account any description applied to them, the price and other relevant circumstances

(d) A condition that where the seller sells goods in the course of a business, the goods are reasonably fit for any purpose made known to the seller by the buyer, unless the buyer does not rely on the seller's skill and judgment, or it would be unreasonable for him to do so

(e) Where there is a sale of goods by sample, conditions that the bulk of the goods shall correspond with the sample in quality, that the buyer will have a reasonable opportunity of comparing the bulk with the sample, and that the goods are free from any defect rendering them unmerchantable, which would not be apparent from the sample

For these purposes, the broad difference between a condition and a warranty is that the remedy for a breach of an implied condition may enable the buyer to reject the goods and recover damages if he has suffered loss, whereas the remedy for a breach of warranty will only enable the buyer to recover damages.

It is possible for a seller to exclude some of the above terms from a contract, subject to restrictions imposed by the Unfair Contract Terms Act 1977 as given below. These restrictions give more protection where the buyer 'deals as consumer'. In a contract of sale of goods, a buyer 'deals as consumer' where there is a sale by a seller in the course of a business, where the goods are of a type ordinarily bought for private use or consumption, and where the goods are sold to a person who does not buy or hold himself out as buying them in the course of a business. A buyer in a sale by auction or competitive tender never 'deals as consumer'.

The 1977 Act prohibits the exclusion of the implied terms given in (b) to (e) above, where the buyer 'deals as consumer'. In sales where the buyer does not 'deal as consumer', terms purporting to exclude these implied terms may be relied upon only to the extent that it would be reasonable to allow reliance. The Act provides guidelines for determining whether it would be reasonable to allow reliance. The implied terms in (a) above cannot be excluded whether the buyer 'deals as consumer' or not.

(2) Similar terms to those implied in contracts of sale of goods are implied into contracts of hire-purchase by the Supply of Goods (Implied Terms) Act 1973, and the 1977 Act limits the exclusion of these implied terms in a similar manner.

(3) Under the Supply of Goods and Services Act 1982, terms similar to those in the Sale of Goods Act relating to quiet possession, compliance with description, merchantable quality, fitness for purpose and correspondence with sample are implied into other types of contract under which ownership of goods passes (e.g. a contract for 'work and materials' such as a supply of new parts during the servicing of a motor car) and also into contracts for the hire of goods. In the case of contracts under which ownership of goods is to pass, there is also an implied condition as to title.

The 1977 Act limits the exclusion of these implied terms in a similar manner to the implied terms in the Sale of Goods Act.

(4) The Supply of Goods and Services Act 1982 also implies into a contract for the supply of services terms that the supplier will use reasonable care and skill, carry out the service within a reasonable time (unless the time is agreed) and make a reasonable charge (unless the charge is agreed).

(5) The Trade Descriptions Act 1968 provides that it is a criminal offence for a trader or businessman to apply a false trade description to any goods, or to supply or offer to supply any goods to which a false trade description has been applied. A trade description includes a description as to quantity, size, method, place and date of manufacture, other history, composition, other physical characteristics, fitness for purpose, behaviour or accuracy, testing or approval. It is also an

offence to give a false indication as to the price of goods. Prosecutions are brought by trading standards inspectors.

(6) The Fair Trading Act 1973 is also designed to protect the consumer. It provides for the appointment of a Director-General of Fair Trading, whose duties include keeping under review commercial activities in the UK relating to the supply of goods or services to consumers, and to collect information to discover practices that may adversely affect the economic interests of the consumer. He may refer certain consumer trade practices to the Consumer Protection Advisory Committee, or of his own initiative take proceedings against firms that are trading unfairly. He may also publish information and advice to consumers. Examples of practices which have been prohibited by virtue of references made under this Act include the use of certain void exclusion clauses in contracts for the sale of goods and hire-purchase, and advertisements by traders appearing to sell as private persons.

(7) The Consumer Protection Act 1987 makes the producer of a product liable for any damage exceeding £275 caused by a defect in that product, subject to certain defences.

(8) The Consumer Protection (Cancellation of Contracts Concluded away from Business Premises) Regulations 1987 allow consumers a seven-day period in which to cancel most contracts for supply of goods or services exceeding £35 in cost, where these contracts have been made following an unsolicited visit to the consumer's home or workplace.

Scotland

The Sale of Goods Act 1979, a consolidating Act, applies with some modification to Scotland. For example, it is not necessary in Scotland to distinguish between the words condition and warranty. The remedies of the buyer in both cases are the same, i.e. the buyer can either within a reasonable time reject the goods and treat the contract as repudiated, or retain the goods and treat the failure to perform such material part as a breach which may give rise to a claim for compensation or damages.

CONSUMER CREDIT

The Consumer Credit Act 1974 provides a system for the protection of the consumer, of licensing and control of all matters relating to the provision of credit or to the supply of goods on hire or hire-purchase, administered by the Director-General of Fair Trading. A licence is required to carry on a consumer credit or consumer hire business, or to deal in credit brokerage, debt adjusting, counselling or collecting, for which group licences are available. Any 'fit' person may apply to the Director-General of Fair Trading for a licence which is normally renewable after ten years. A licence is not necessary if such types of business are only transacted 'occasionally' or if exempt agreements only are involved.

For the Act's provisions to apply, the agreement must be 'regulated', i.e. be to individuals or partnerships only; must not be exempt, e.g. certain loans by local authorities or building societies; and the total credit must not exceed £15,000. The terms of a regulated agreement can be varied by the creditor, but only if the agreement gives him the right to do so and the debtor receives notice in the prescribed form.

To be enforceable the agreement must be properly executed, and the specified information must be given during the antecedent negotiations for the contract. These are conducted by the creditor, credit broker or supplier (these being the creditor's agents) and begin when the parties first begin discussions.

The agreement must state certain information such as the amount of credit, the annual percentage rate of interest, and the amount and timing of repayments.

An agreement is cancellable under the Act if oral representations were made in the debtor's presence during antecedent negotiations and the debtor signed the agreement other than at the creditor's (or credit-broker's or negotiator's) place of business. Time for cancellation expires five clear days after the debtor receives a second copy of the agreement. The agreement must inform the debtor of his right to cancel and how to cancel.

Where there are arrangements or connections between the creditor and supplier, the former is generally liable for any misrepresentation or breach of contract by the latter, and will thus be liable to indemnify the debtor.

If the debtor is in arrears or is otherwise in breach of the agreement, the creditor may not enforce the agreement, e.g. by repossessing goods, without serving a default notice on the debtor. This notice will give the debtor a chance to remedy the default. Even if the default is not remedied by the debtor, if the agreement is a hire-purchase or conditional sale agreement, the creditor cannot repossess the goods without an order of the court if the debtor has paid one-third of the total price of the goods.

Where the agreement requires the debtor to make grossly exorbitant payments or is contrary to the ordinary principles of fair dealing, the court can reopen it either at the debtor's request or during enforcement proceedings and (*inter alia*) alter the terms of the contract or set aside any obligations it imposes so as to do justice between the parties. Whether an agreement is such an extortionate credit bargain is decided by reference (*inter alia*) to interest rates prevailing at the date of agreement, the pressure for finance the debtor was under, etc.

If a credit reference agency was used to check the debtor's financial standing the creditor must give the agency's name to the debtor, who is entitled to see the agency's file on him/her on payment of a fee of £1.

Scotland

The Consumer Credit Act also extends to Scotland and goes far in assimilating the Scots law on this topic with English law. The Supply of Goods (Implied Terms) Act 1973 also applies to Scotland. Parts II and III only of the Unfair Contract Terms Act 1977 apply to Scotland.

RECEIPTS

The law on receipts in Scotland is governed by the Prescription and Limitations (Scotland) Act 1973, which for this purpose came into force on 25 July 1976. Receipts need only be kept for a period of five years and if a creditor does not make a relevant claim within that period no action can be raised.

THE CROWN – PROCEEDINGS AGAINST

Before 1947, proceedings against the Crown were generally possible only by a procedure known as a petition of right, which placed the litigant at a considerable disadvantage. However, by the Crown Proceedings Act 1947, which came into operation on 1 January 1948, the Crown, in its public capacity, is largely placed in the same position as a subject, although some procedural disadvantages remain, e.g. the enforcement of judgments against the Crown.

Scotland

The Act as amended extends to Scotland and has the effect of bringing the practice of the two countries as closely together as the different legal systems will permit. While formerly actions against the Crown, when permissible, were confined to the Court of Session, proceedings may now be brought in the Sheriff Court.

The Act lays down that arrestment of money in the hands of the Crown or of a government department is competent in any case where arrestment in the hands of a subject would have been competent, but an exception is made in respect of National Savings Bank deposits. Section 2 (1) of the Law Reform (Miscellaneous Provisions) (Scotland) Act 1966 removes the privilege whereby the wages of Crown servants, other than serving members of the armed forces, are exempt from arrestment in execution.

DEATHS

REGISTRATION
(For Certificates, *see* page 664)

England and Wales

When a death takes place, information of it must be given in person to the local Registrar of Births and Deaths, and the register signed in his/her presence by a relative of the deceased present at the death or in attendance during the last illness; or by some other relative of the deceased; in default of any relatives by (a) a person present at the death, or the occupier of the house in which the death happened, or (b) an inmate of the house, or (c) the person arranging the disposal of the body.

The registration must be made within five days of the death, or within the same time written notice of the death must be sent to the Registrar. If the deceased was attended during his/her last illness by a registered medical practitioner, a certificate of cause of death must be sent by the doctor to the Registrar. The doctor must give to the informant of the death a written notice of the signing of the certificate, which must be delivered to the Registrar.

If the death is not registered within five days (or fourteen days if written notice of the occurrence of the death is sent to him/her), the Registrar may require any one of the above-mentioned persons to attend to register at a stated time and place. Failure to comply involves a penalty. The registration of a death is free of charge. After twelve months no death can be registered without the Registrar-General's consent.

Whenever the death of a child is registered, particulars of the name and occupation of the mother are to be entered in the register.

It is essential that a certificate for disposal should be obtained from the Registrar before the funeral or cremation. No fee is chargeable for this certificate. A body must not be disposed of until either the Registrar has given a certificate to the effect that he/she has registered or received notice of the death, or until the Coroner has made a disposal order.

A person disposing of a body must within ninety-six hours deliver to the Registrar a notification as to the date, place, and means of the disposal of the body.

Still births: see page 663.

Death at sea: the master of a British ship must record any death on board and send particulars to the Registrar-General of Shipping.

Death abroad: consular officers are authorized to register deaths of British subjects occurring abroad. Certificates are obtainable at the Registrar-General's Office, London. If the deceased was of Scottish domicile, particulars are sent to the Registrar-General for Scotland.

With regard to the registration of deaths of members of the armed forces and deaths occurring on HM ships and aircraft, *see* the Registration of Births, etc. Act 1957.

Scotland

The Registration of Births, Deaths and Marriages (Scotland) Act 1965 supersedes provisions in former Acts.

Personal notification within eight days must be given to the Registrar of either the registration district in which the death took place, or any registration district in which the deceased was ordinarily resident immediately before his/her death. When a body is found and the place of death is not known, notification must be given to the Registrar of either the registration district in which the body was found or any other registration district appropriate by virtue of the preceding sentence. When a person dies (in or out of Scotland) in a ship, aircraft or land vehicle during a journey and the body is conveyed therein to any place in Scotland the death shall, unless the Registrar-General otherwise directs, be deemed to have occurred at that place.

The register must be signed in the presence of the Registrar by one of the following: (a) any relative of the deceased; (b) any person present at the death; (c) the deceased's executor or other legal representative; (d) the occupier, at the time of the death, of the premises where the death took place; (e) if these fail, any other person having knowledge of the particulars to be registered. Failure to comply involves a penalty.

The medical practitioner who attended the deceased during the last illness must sign a certificate of the cause of death within seven days. If there is no such medical practitioner, any medical practitioner who is able to do so may sign the certificate. At the time of registering the death the Registrar shall, without charge, give the informant a certificate of registration, and the person to whom the certificate is given must hand it to the undertaker before cremation. A body may, however, be interred before the death is registered, in which case the undertaker must deliver a certificate of burial to the Registrar within three days.

BURIAL

The duty of burial is placed on the deceased person's executors (if any appointed); it is also a recognized obligation of the parent of a child, and of a householder where the body lies. Funeral expenses of a reasonable amount will be repayable out of the deceased's estate in priority to any other claims. Directions as to place and mode of burial are frequently contained in the deceased's will, in some memorandum placed with private papers, or may have been communicated verbally to a relative. Consequently, steps should immediately be taken to ascertain the deceased's wishes from the above sources. If the wishes are considered objectionable, they are not necessarily enforceable; legal advice should be taken. A person may legally leave directions for the anatomical examination of his/her body. As to the place of burial, the parish churchyard is the normal burying place for parishioners or any person dying in the parish, but nowadays this will apply only in villages and smaller towns. In populous districts cemeteries and crematoria have been established, either by the local council or a private company, and burials will take place there in accordance with the regulations. For an exclusive right to a burial space in the churchyard, a faculty is required from the Ecclesiastical Court. Poor persons may be buried at the public expense by the local authority. As to the necessity for obtaining a

Registrar's certificate or authority from the Coroner for disposal, see above.

CREMATION

Under the Cremation Acts 1902 and 1952, regulations are made by the Home Secretary dealing fully with the cremation of a body, disposal of ashes, etc., and containing numerous safeguards.

If cremation is desired it is advisable for instructions to be left in writing to that effect. However, in Scotland, even if the deceased wished his/her body to be cremated or anatomically dissected, relatives can still veto his/her wishes.

To arrange for cremation, the executor or near relative should instruct the undertaker to that effect and obtain from him the forms required by statute.

INTESTACY

As regards deaths on or after 15 March 1977, the position is governed by the Administration of Estates Act 1925, as amended by the Intestates' Estates Act 1952, the Family Provision Act 1966 and Orders made thereunder. If the intestate leaves a spouse and issue, the spouse takes:
(a) the 'personal chattels'
(b) £75,000 with interest at 6 per cent from death until payment
(c) a life interest in half of the rest of the estate

This life interest can be capitalized at the option of the spouse. Personal chattels are articles of household use or ornament (including motor cars), not used for business purposes. The rest of the estate goes to the issue.

If the intestate leaves a spouse and no issue, but leaves a parent or brother or sister of the whole blood or issue of such brothers and sisters the spouse takes
(a) the 'personal chattels'
(b) £125,000 with interest at 6 per cent from death until payment
(c) half of the rest of the estate absolutely

The other half of the rest of the estate goes to the parents, equally if more than one, or, if none, to the brothers and sisters of the whole blood or issue of such brothers and sisters.

If the intestate leaves a spouse, no issue, no parents and no brothers or sisters of the whole blood or their issue, the spouse takes the whole estate absolutely.

If resident therein at the intestate's death, the surviving spouse may generally require the personal representatives to appropriate the interest of the intestate in the matrimonial home in or towards satisfaction of any absolute interest of the spouse, including the capitalized value of a life interest. In certain cases, leave of court is required. On a partial intestacy any benefit (other than personal chattels specifically bequeathed) received by the surviving spouse under the will must be brought into account against the statutory legacy of £75,000 or £125,000, as the case may be. If there is no surviving spouse, the estate is distributed among those who survive the intestate in the following order (those entitled under earlier numbers taking to the exclusion of those entitled under later numbers):
(1) children
(2) father or mother (equally, if both alive)
(3) brothers and sisters of the whole blood
(4) brothers and sisters of the half blood
(5) grandparents (equally, if more than one alive)
(6) uncles and aunts of the whole blood
(7) uncles and aunts of the half blood
(8) the Crown

In cases (1), (3), (4), (6) and (7), the persons entitled lose their interests unless they or their issue not only survive the intestate, but also attain eighteen or marry under that age, their shares going to the persons (if any) within the same group who do attain eighteen or marry. Moreover, in the same cases, succession is not per capita, but per stirpes, i.e. by stocks or families. Thus, if the intestate leaves one child and two grandchildren, being the children of a child of the intestate who predeceased the intestate, the two grandchildren represent their deceased parent and take between them one-half of the issue's share, the remaining half going to the surviving child. Similarly, nephews and nieces represent a deceased brother, and so on.

When the deceased died partially intestate (i.e. leaving a will which disposed of only part of his/her property), the above rules apply to the intestate part.

Children must bring into account (hotchpot) any substantial advances received from the intestate during his/her lifetime before claiming any further share under the intestacy. Special hotchpot provisions apply to partial intestacy.

In respect of deaths occurring on or after 4 April 1988, Section 18 of the Family Law Reform Act 1987 provides that references to any relationship between two persons shall, unless the contrary intention appears, be construed without regard to whether or not the father and mother of either of them, or the father and mother of any person through whom the relationship is deduced, have or had been married to each other at any time.

In respect of deaths after March 1976 the provisions of the Inheritance (Provision for Family and Dependants) Act 1975 may allow other persons to claim provision out of the estate. See page 659.

For personal application for letters of administration, see page 660.

Scotland

The Succession (Scotland) Act 1964, provides that the whole estate of any person dying intestate shall devolve without distinction between heritable and moveable property. By that Act the surviving spouse of an intestate may, as a prior right (in addition to legal rights, see below), claim the matrimonial home to a maximum of £65,000, or a choice of one matrimonial home if more than one (or in certain circumstances the value thereof), with its furniture and plenishings not exceeding £12,000 in value, plus the sum of £21,000 if the deceased left issue or, if no issue, the sum of £35,000. These figures have applied since 1 May 1988 and may be increased from time to time by order of the Secretary of State.

The fact that a person was born illegitimate no longer has any effect in their rights of succession as against a legitimate child, by virtue of the Law Reform (Parent and Child) (Scotland) Act 1986.

Legal rights, referred to above, are:
Jus relicti(ae) – the right of a surviving spouse to one half of the deceased's net moveable estate after satisfaction of prior rights if there are no surviving children, or to one-third if there are any surviving children
Legitim – the right of surviving children to one-half of the net moveable estate of deceased parents if no surviving spouse, or one-third of the net moveable estate of deceased parents after satisfaction of prior rights where there is a surviving spouse.

There are no legal rights in heritage.

In general, the lines of succession are:
(1) descendants
(2) collaterals
(3) ascendants and their collaterals, and so on in the ascending scale

The Crown is *ultimus haeres*

The right of representation, i.e. the right of the issue of a person who would have succeeded if he/she had survived the intestate, is open to any line of succession where previously it was limited to apply only when there were next of kin or the issue of predeceasing next of kin. The surviving mother of an intestate now has equal rights of succession with the surviving father, where formerly these were restricted. The intestate's maternal relations, who prior to the Act had no rights of succession, are now on an equal footing with the paternal relations. Where the intestate is survived only by parents and by brothers and sisters (collaterals), half of the estate is taken by the parents and the other half by the brothers and sisters, those of the whole blood being preferred to those of the half blood. Where, however, succession opens to collaterals (which expression can include the brothers and sisters of an ancestor of the intestate) of the half blood, they shall rank equally amongst themselves, whether related to the intestate (or his/her ancestor) through their father or their mother.

WILLS

The following notes and those on intestacy must be read subject to the provisions of the Inheritance (Provision for Family and Dependants) Act 1975, which can affect the estate of anyone dying domiciled in England and Wales after March 1976. Very broadly, a spouse, former spouse who has not remarried, a child of the deceased or one treated by the deceased as a child of his/her family, or any person maintained by him/her at his/her death may apply to the Court under the Act. If the Court thinks that the will or the law of intestacy or both do not make reasonable provision for the applicant, it may order payment out of the net estate of maintenance or a lump sum. It may also order the transfer of property or vary certain trusts, and the powers can affect property disposed of by the deceased in his/her lifetime intending to defeat the Act. It is up to the applicant to take the initiative, and the application must generally be made within six months of the grant of probate or letters of administration.

MAKING A WILL

Every person over the age of 18 should make a will. However small the estate, the rules of intestacy (*see* above) may not reflect a person's wishes as to his/her property. In any case a will can do more than just deal with property. It can in particular appoint executors, give directions as to the disposal of the body and appoint guardians to take care of children in the event of the parents' death. For the wealthier person an appropriately drawn will can operate to reduce the burden of inheritance tax.

It is considered desirable for a will to be properly drawn up by a solicitor. Although normally the making of a will is not one of the services which can be provided under the legal advice and assistance scheme, it can be provided for certain special categories of person such as the aged and infirm (*see* below).

In no circumstances should one person prepare a will for another person where the former is to take any benefit under it. This can easily lead to a suggestion of undue influence, which may cause the will to be held bad.

Assuming a lawyer is not employed, a person having resolved to make a will must remember that it is only after a person is dead, and cannot explain his/her meaning, that his/her will can be open to dispute. It is the more necessary, therefore, to express what is meant in language of the utmost clarity, avoiding the use of any word or expression that admits of another meaning than the one intended. Avoid the use of legal terms, such as heirs and issue, when the same thing may be expressed in plain language. If in writing the will a mistake is made, it is better to rewrite the whole. Before a will is executed (*see* page 660), an alteration may be made by striking through the words with a pen, but opposite to such alteration the testator and witnesses should write their names or place their initials. Never scratch out a word with a knife or other instrument; no alteration of any kind whatever must be made after the will is executed. If the testator afterwards wishes to change the disposition of his/her estate, it is best to make a new will, revoking the old one. The use of codicils should be left to a lawyer.

A will should be written in ink and very legibly, on a single sheet of paper. Although forms of wills must vary to suit different cases, the following forms may be found useful to those who, in cases of emergency, are called upon to draw up wills, either for themselves or others. Nothing more complicated should be attempted. The forms should be studied in conjunction with the following notes:

This is the last will and testament of me [*Thomas Smith*] of [*Vine Cottage, Silver Street, Reading, Berks.*] which I make this [*thirteenth*] day of [*February* 1994] and whereby I revoke all previous wills and testamentary dispositions.

1. I hereby appoint [*John Green of_____ and Richard Brown of_____*] to be the executor(s) of this my will.

2. I give all my property real and personal to [*my wife Mary* or *my sons Raymond and David equally* or as the case may be].

Signed by the testator in the presence of us both present at the same time who, at his request, in his presence and in the presence of each other have hereunto set our names as witnesses.

Thomas Smith
Signature of Testator;

William Jones (*signed*)
of Green Gables, South Street, Reading, tailor.

Henry Morgan (*signed*)
of 16 North Street, Reading, butcher.

Should it be desired to give legacies and/or gifts of specific property, instead of giving the whole estate to one or more persons, the form above should be used with the substitution for clause 2 of the following clauses:

2. I give to_____ of_____ the sum of £_____ and to_____ of_____ the sum of £_____ and to_____ of_____ all my books [*or as the case may require*].

3. All the residue of my property real and personal I give to_____ of_____.

Terms

Real property includes freehold land and houses, while personal property includes debts due, arrears of rents, money, leasehold property, house furniture, goods, assurance policies, stocks and shares in companies, and the like. The words 'my money', apart from the context, will normally only include actual real money. The expression 'goods and chattels' should not be used. In giving particular property, ordinary language is sufficient, e.g. my house, Vine Cottage, Silver Street, Reading, Berks. Such specific gifts fail if not owned by the testator at his/her death.

Residuary legatees

It is well in all cases where legacies or specific gifts are made, to leave to some person or persons 'the residue of my property', although it may be thought that the whole of the property has been disposed of in legacies, etc., already mentioned in the will. It should be remembered that a will operates on property owned at the time of death.

Execution of a will, and witnesses

The testator should sign his/her name at the foot or end of the will, in the presence of two witnesses, who will immediately afterwards sign their names in the testator's and in each other's presence. A person who has been left any gift or share of residue in the will, or whose wife or husband has been left such a gift, should not be an attesting witness. Their attestation would be good, but they would forfeit the gift. It is better that a person named as executor should not be a witness. Husband and wife may both be witnesses, provided neither is a legatee. If a solicitor be appointed executor, it is lawful to direct that his/her ordinary fees and charges shall be paid; but in this case the solicitor (as an interested party) must not be a witness to the will.

It is desirable that the witnesses should be fully described, as they may possibly be wanted at some future time. If the testator should be too ill to sign, even by a mark, another person may sign the testator's name to the will for him/her, in his/her presence and by his/her direction, and in this case it should be shown that the testator knew the contents of the document. The attestation clause should therefore be worded:

Signed by Thomas Brown, by the direction and in the presence of the testator, Thomas Smith, in the joint presence of us, who thereupon signed our names in his presence and in the presence of each other, the will having been first read over to the testator, who appeared fully to understand the same.

Where there is any suspicion that the testator is not, by reason of age or infirmity, fully in command of his/her faculties it is desirable to ask his/her doctor to act as a witness (*see* Testamentary capacity below).

A blind person may make a will in braille. If the testator is blind the will should be read aloud to him/her in the presence of the witnesses, and the fact mentioned in the attestation clause. A blind person cannot witness a will.

If by inadvertence the testator should have signed his/her will without the witnesses being present, then the attestation should be: 'The testator acknowledged his signature already made as his signature to his last will and testament, in the joint presence,' etc. Any omission in the observance of these details may invalidate the will. The stringency of the law as to signature and witnessing of a will is only relaxed in favour of soldiers, sailors and airmen in certain circumstances.

Executors

It is usual to appoint two executors, although one is sufficient; any number up to and including four may be appointed. The name and address of each executor should be given in full. An executor may be a legatee. Thus a child of full age or wife to whom the whole or a portion of the estate is left may be appointed sole executor, or one of two executors. The addresses of the executors are not essential, but it is desirable here as elsewhere, to avoid ambiguity or vagueness.

Lapsed legacies

If a legatee dies in the lifetime of the testator, the legacy generally lapses and falls into the residue. Where a residuary legatee predeceases the testator, his/her share of the residuary estate will not generally pass to the other residuary legatees, but will pass to the persons entitled on the deceased's intestacy. In all such cases it is desirable to make a new will.

An important exception to the general rule of lapse stated above is contained in the Administration of Justice Act 1982, where there is a gift to a child or remoter issue of the testator

who dies before the testator leaving issue who survive the testator. In such a case the gift will pass to the issue of the deceased child.

Testamentary capacity

A person under the age of 18 cannot make a will (except for soldiers, sailors and airmen in exceptional circumstances).

So far as mental capacity is concerned the testator must be able to understand and appreciate the nature and effect of making a will, the property of which he/she can dispose and the claims to which he/she ought to give effect. If a person is not mentally able to make a will, provision exists (under the Mental Health Act 1983) for the Court to do this for him/her.

REVOCATION

A later will revokes an earlier will if it expressly says so, or is completely inconsistent with it. Otherwise the earlier one is revoked only in so far as it is inconsistent with the later one. A will may also be revoked by burning, tearing or otherwise destroying the will with the intention of revoking it. Such destruction must either be by the testator or by some other person in the testator's presence and at his/her direction. It is not sufficient to obliterate the will with a pen. Marriage in every case acts as the revocation of a will, except that under the Administration of Justice Act 1982, there is a provision to the effect that if it appears from a will that at the time it was made the testator was expecting to be married to a particular person and that he/she intended that the will (or a disposition in the will) should not be revoked by the marriage to that person, the will will not be revoked by marriage to that person. The Act also provides that where after a testator has made a will the testator's marriage is terminated by a decree of divorce or nullity, any gift to a spouse shall lapse and any appointment of the spouse as executor shall be omitted from the will unless the will shows a contrary intention.

PROBATE OR LETTERS OF ADMINISTRATION

Application for probate or for letters of administration may be made in person at the Personal Application Department of the Principal Registry of the Family Division, a district probate registry or sub-registry, or a probate office, by the executors or persons entitled to a grant of administration. Applicants should bring (a) the will, if any; (b) a certificate of death; (c) particulars of all property and assets left by the deceased; and (d) a list of debts and funeral expenses.

Intending applicants, before attending at a registry or probate office, should write or telephone to the nearest probate registry or sub-registry for the necessary forms. Postal or telephone applications cannot be dealt with at the local probate offices, which are part-time only.

Certain property can be disposed of on death without a grant of probate or administration, or in pursuance of a nomination made by the deceased, provided the amount involved does not exceed £5,000. (See The Administration of Estates (Small Payments) Act 1965.)

WHERE TO FIND A PROVED WILL

A will proved since 1858 must have been proved either at the Principal Registry at Somerset House, or a district registry. In the former case the original will itself is preserved at Somerset House, the copy of which probate has been granted is in the hands of the executors who proved the will, and another copy for Parliament is bound up in a folio volume of wills made by testators of that initial and date. The indices to these volumes may be examined at Somerset House and a copy of any will read. In the latter case, the original will proved in the district registry is kept there and may be seen or a copy obtained, but a copy is sent to and filed at Somerset House, where also it may be seen. A general index of grants, both probates and administrations, is prepared and printed annually in lexicographical form, and may be seen at either the Principal Registry or a district registry. This index is usually ready by about October of the following year.

Recent deaths

A system introduced in 1975 enables a person to discover when a grant of probate or letters of administration is made which may be invaluable to a creditor of the deceased or applicant under the Inheritance (Provision for Family and Dependants) Act 1975 (*see* page 659). A standing search may be made by sending a request in the form set out below to the Record Keeper at the Principal Registry of the Family Division with a small fee. The searcher will receive particulars of any grant made in the previous 12 months or the following six months, including names and addresses of the executors or administrators and the registry in which the grant was made.

Form of search

In the High Court of Justice
Family Division
The Principal Registry (Probate)
I/We apply for the entry of a standing search so that there shall be sent to me/us an office copy of every grant of representation in England and Wales in the estate of:
Full name of deceased:
Alternative or alias name
Full address
Exact date of death

Which either has issued not more than twelve months before the entry of this application or issues within six months hereafter
Signed ———— (full address).

SCOTLAND

A domiciled Scotsman, unlike a domiciled Englishman, cannot in certain circumstances dispose effectively of the entirety of his estate. If he leave a widow and children, the widow is entitled to a one-third share in the whole of the moveable estate (her *jus relictae*), and the children are entitled to another one-third share equally between them (their *legitim*). If he leave a widow but no children, or children but no widow, the *jus relictae* or *legitim* is increased to a one-half share of the net moveable estate. The remaining portion is known as the dead's part. A surviving husband and children have comparable rights (*jus relicti* and *legitim*) in the wife's estate. The dead's part is the only portion of which the testator can freely dispose. Legacies and bequests are payable only out of the dead's part. All debts are payable out of the whole estate before any division.

Pupils, i.e. a girl up to the age of 12 or a boy up to the age of 14, cannot make wills. Formerly a minor could dispose only of moveables but since the passing of the Succession (Scotland) Act 1964, a minor has a like capacity to test on heritable property.

A will must be in writing and may be typewritten or even in pencil. A will may be either:
(a) holograph, i.e. written, dated and subscribed by the testator himself/herself, in which case no witnesses are necessary; a printed form filled up by the testator or a typewritten document is not necessarily a holograph but may become so if the testator writes, in hand, at the foot of the form or document the words 'adopted as holograph' followed by his/her signature and the date. Words written on erasure or marginal additions or interlineations in holograph writings, if proved to be in the handwriting of the maker of the deed, are valid
(b) attested, i.e. signed in presence of two witnesses. It is not necessary that these witnesses should sign in the presence of one another, or even that they should see the testator signing so long as the testator acknowledges his/her signature to the witnesses

The Conveyancing and Feudal Reform (Scotland) Act 1970, whilst altering generally the rules for the subscription of deeds, specifically (s. 44 (2)) makes no change in the rules applying to wills, which must still be signed by the testator on every page. If the testator cannot write or is blind, the will may be authenticated by a law agent, notary public or justice of the peace and two witnesses. It is better that the will is not witnessed by a beneficiary thereunder, although this circumstance will not invalidate the attestation of the will or (as it would in England) the gift. A parish minister may act as a notary for the purpose of subscribing a will in his own parish.

Wills may be registered in the Books of the Sheriffdom in which the deceased died domiciled, or in the Books of Council and Session at HM General Register House, Edinburgh. The original deed may be inspected on payment of a small fee and a certified official copy may be obtained. A Scottish will is not revoked by the subsequent marriage of the testator. The subsequent birth of a child for whom no testamentary provision has been made may revoke a will. A will may be revoked by a subsequent will, either expressly or by implication; but in so far as the two can be read together, both wills have effect. If a subsequent will is revoked, the earlier will is revived.

CONFIRMATION

Confirmation, the Scottish equivalent of probate, is obtained in the sheriff court of the sheriffdom in which the deceased was domiciled at the date of his/her death or, where the deceased had no fixed domicile or died abroad, in the Commissariat of Edinburgh. Executors are either 'nominate' or 'dative'. An executor nominate is one nominated by the deceased in the will or, where such person has predeceased the testator, by the residuary beneficiary. An executor dative is one appointed by the court in the case of intestacy or where the deceased had failed to name an executor in the will and there is no residuary beneficiary. In the former case the deceased's next-of-kin are all entitled to be declared executors dative. An inventory of the deceased's estate and a schedule of debts, together with an affidavit, must first be given up. In estates under £17,000 gross, confirmation is obtained under a simplified procedure at reduced fees.

PRESUMPTION OF SURVIVORSHIP

The Succession (Scotland) Act 1964 provides, by s. 31, that where two persons die in circumstances indicating that they died simultaneously or if it is uncertain which was the survivor, the younger will be deemed to have survived the elder unless the elder person left testamentary provision in favour of the younger, whom failing in favour of a third person, the younger person having died intestate (partially or wholly); but if the persons so dying were husband and wife, neither shall be presumed to have survived the other.

EMPLOYMENT

WAGES AND SICK PAY

Under the Wages Act 1986, subject to certain exceptions, employers may not make deductions from an employee's wages unless authorized by statute or contract or with the employee's prior written consent. There is an upper limit of one-tenth of gross pay for deductions from retail workers' wages on account of cash or stock shortages.

Under the Social Security and Housing Benefits Act 1982 as amended, an employee absent from work because of illness or injury is entitled to receive Statutory Sick Pay from the employer for a maximum period of 28 weeks in any period of three years. No payment is made for the first three days of any period of illness. Employers can recoup the payments from their National Insurance contributions.

The Equal Pay Act 1970, which extends to Scotland, prevents discrimination as regards terms and conditions of employment between men and women employed on like work in the same employment.

PARTICULARS OF TERMS OF EMPLOYMENT

Under the Employment Protection (Consolidation) Act 1978, an employer must give each full-time employee within 13 weeks of the beginning of the employment a written statement containing the following particulars of the contract between them:

(a) the date when the employment began (when continuous employment began if previous work counts as continuous with this job)
(b) the rate of remuneration (or how it is calculated)
(c) the intervals at which wages are paid
(d) the hours of work
(e) the employee's entitlement to holidays (including public holidays) and holiday pay
(f) the title of the employee's job
(g) terms relating to sickness, injury and sick pay
(h) details of any pension scheme
(i) the length of notice which the employee should give and receive in order to terminate the contract

In addition, the written particulars must specify any disciplinary rules; and also must identify the person to whom the employee can apply if dissatisfied with any disciplinary decision or to seek redress of any grievance, and what further steps may ensue.

TERMINATION OF EMPLOYMENT

An employee may be dismissed without notice if guilty of gross breach of contract, such as disobedience to a lawful order or dishonesty. The employee is then entitled only to wages accrued due at the date of dismissal.

In other cases, the employee is entitled to reasonable notice which, under the Employment Protection (Consolidation) Act 1978, must not be less than one week if he/she has been continuously employed for four weeks but less than two years; after two years it is two weeks' notice, increasing by one week's notice for each further full year worked up to a maximum of 12 weeks' notice after 12 years' service.

An employer who wrongfully dismisses an employee (i.e. with less than the length of notice to which he/she is entitled) is generally liable to pay wages for the period of proper notice.

An employee who has a fixed term contract has no claim against his/her employer for breach of contract (wrongful dismissal) if the contract is not renewed when it expires. If he/she is wrongfully dismissed before the contract expires, he/she is generally entitled to remuneration payable over the full period of the contract.

An employee may be entitled to a redundancy payment or to compensation for unfair dismissal if the employment has been terminated by the employer (with or without proper notice) or he/she has a fixed term contract which expires without being renewed or the employment has been terminated by the employee by reason of the employer's breach of contract.

Under the Employment Protection (Consolidation) Act 1978, an employee who satisfies the foregoing conditions and has been continuously employed for two years and who is dismissed by reason of redundancy may be entitled to a redundancy payment calculated by reference to his/her age, pay and length of service.

The Employment Protection (Consolidation) Act 1978 also enables an employee who is unfairly dismissed to complain to an industrial tribunal (generally within three months of dismissal). The onus will then be on the employer to prove that the dismissal was due to capability, conduct, redundancy, illegality or some other substantial reason justifying dismissal. The tribunal must decide whether the employer acted reasonably in dismissing the employee. If the employer fails to prove that the dismissal was due to one or more of the above five reasons, or the tribunal decides that the employer did not act reasonably in dismissing the employee, the dismissal will be unfair, in which case the tribunal can:

(a) order re-engagement or reinstatement
(b) award compensation consisting of a basic and a compensatory award

For an employee to bring himself/herself within the unfair dismissal provisions, he/she must have been continuously employed for a period of two years.

All complaints of unfair dismissal are referred to a conciliation officer or the Department of Employment and a very high proportion of complaints are disposed of in this way.

DISCRIMINATION

Discrimination on the grounds of sex or marital status is made unlawful by the Sex Discrimination Act 1975. The provisions of the Sex Discrimination Act are similar to those of the Race Relations Act 1976 which make discrimination on 'racial grounds' unlawful. 'Racial grounds' include colour, race, nationality, or ethnic or national origins. The Equal Opportunities Commission and the Commission for Racial Equality have the function of eliminating such discriminations and may provide assistance in pursuing allegations of discrimination.

FAMILY LAW

ADOPTION OF CHILDREN

In England and Wales the adoption of children is mainly governed by the Adoption Act 1976, as amended by the Children Act 1989. A court order is necessary to legalize the adoption, which, when completed, has the effect of making the adopted child the child of the adopter as if he or she had been born to the adopter in lawful wedlock, and the original rights and duties of the natural parents are thereby cut. The adopter has full rights as to residence, education, etc., and the child is treated as his/hers for the purpose of any devolution of property on an intestacy occurring or under any disposition made after the adoption order. The application may be made to the High Court (Family Division) or to a county court or family proceedings court.

Orders may be made in favour of married couples, single, widowed or divorced persons, but not of one party to a marriage alone unless the other spouse cannot be found, is physically or mentally incapable of making an application, or they are separated in circumstances likely to be permanent. A person aged under 21 cannot adopt.

The child's parents or guardians must consent unconditionally to the making of the order unless the court dispenses with the consent, which it may do if the parent cannot be found or is incapable of giving consent, is withholding consent unreasonably, or has neglected or ill-treated the child.

Restrictions are placed on societies which may arrange adoptions.

An adopted person aged over 18 may apply to the Registrar-General for information to enable him/her to obtain a full certificate of his/her birth, but before being supplied with the information he/she will be informed that counselling services are available to him/her. The 1989 Act provides for the creation of a new register (the Adoption Contact Registrar) in which details of those who have had their children adopted, and of adopted persons themselves, may be recorded.

An adopter and the adopted child are within the prohibited degrees for the purposes of marriage to one another.

All adoptions in Great Britain are registered in the Registers of Adopted Children kept by the Registrars-General in London and Edinburgh respectively. Certificates from these registers, including short certificates which contain no reference to adoptions, can be obtained on conditions similar to those relating to birth certificates (*see* below).

Scotland

The law is consolidated in the Adoption (Scotland) Act 1978 as amended by the Children Act 1989. The law relating to fostering is consolidated in the Foster Children (Scotland) Act 1984. A petition for adoption is presented either to the sheriff court or the Court of Session. As in England, the petitioner(s) must be 21 or over and may be a married couple or one person who, if married, is living apart permanently from his or her spouse. The consent of the child's natural parents/guardians is required unless dispensed with, or the child is already free for adoption.

The Succession (Scotland) Act 1964 gives the adopted child the same rights of succession as a child born to the adopter in wedlock but deprives him/her of any such rights in the estates of his natural parents.

BIRTHS (REGISTRATION)

When a birth takes place, personal information of it must be given to the Registrar of Births and Deaths for the sub-district in which the birth occurred, and the register signed in his/her presence by the father or mother of the child; or, if they fail, by (a) the occupier of the house in which the birth happened; (b) a person present at the birth; or (c) the person having charge of the child. The duty of attending to the registration therefore rests firstly on the parents. The mother is responsible for the registration of the birth of an illegitimate child.

The registration is required to be made within 42 days of the birth. Failure to do this without reasonable cause involves liability to a penalty. The registration of a birth is free. In England or Wales, the informant, instead of attending before the registrar of the sub-district where the birth occurred, may make a declaration of the particulars required to be registered in the presence of any registrar. Under the National Health Service Act 1977, notice of every birth must be given by the father, or person in attendance on the mother, to the district medical officer of health by post within 36 hours of the birth. This is in addition to the registration already mentioned.

Still birth: a still birth must be registered, and a certificate signed by the doctor or midwife who was present at the birth or who has examined the body of the child must be produced to the registrar. The certificate must, where possible, state the cause of death and the estimated duration of the pregnancy. A still birth may only be registered within three months of the birth.

Re-registration: the re-registration of the birth of a person legitimated by the subsequent marriage of the parents is provided for in the Births and Deaths Registration Act 1953, as amended by the Family Law Reform Act 1987. Special provisions apply to the registration and re-registration of births of abandoned children, and the re-registration of births of illegitimate children showing the father's name; the mother must normally be party to the latter application.

Birth at sea: the master of a British ship must record any birth on board and send particulars to the Registrar-General of Shipping.

Birth abroad: consular officers are authorized to register births of British subjects occurring abroad. Certificates are obtainable in due course at the Registrar-General's Office, London.

The registration of births occurring out of the United Kingdom among members of the armed forces or occurring on board HM ships and aircraft, is provided for by the Registration of Births, Deaths and Marriages (Special Provisions) Act 1957, applicable also to Scotland.

Scotland

The Registration of Births, Deaths and Marriages (Scotland) Act 1965 supersedes former Acts. Personal notification within 21 days of any birth must be given to the registrar of either the registration district in which the birth took place, or any registration district in which the mother of the child was ordinarily resident at the time of the birth. In the case of a foundling child, dead or alive, when the place of birth is not known, notification must be given to the registrar of the registration district in which the child, or the body, was found, within two months from the date on which the child was found. When a child is born (in or out of Scotland) in a ship, aircraft or land vehicle during a journey and the child is conveyed therein to any place in Scotland, the birth shall, unless the Registrar-General otherwise directs, be deemed to have occurred at that place.

The register must be signed in the presence of the registrar by the father or mother of the child; or, if they fail, by (a) any relative of either parent who has knowledge of the birth; (b) the occupier of the premises in which the child was, to the knowledge of that occupier, born; (c) any person present at the birth; (d) any person having charge of the child. Failure without reasonable cause involves a penalty.

The name of the father of a child born out of wedlock may be entered in the register of births at the time of registration if jointly requested by the mother and father, and the latter's name may also be recorded at a later date on declaration by both parents. A free abbreviated certificate of birth will be issued to the informant at the time of registration.

Still birth: a still birth must be registered and a certificate, signed by the doctor or certified midwife present at the birth or who has examined the body of the child, must be produced.

Re-registration: provision is made for the re-registration of the birth of a person made legitimate by the subsequent marriage of the parents or whose birth entry is affected by any matter respecting status or paternity, or has been so made as to imply that he/she is a foundling.

CERTIFICATES OF BIRTHS, DEATHS, OR MARRIAGES

Certificates of births, deaths or marriages in England and Wales can be obtained at the Office of Population Censuses and Surveys, St Catherine's House, 10 Kingsway, London WC2B 6JP, or from the Superintendent Registrar having the legal custody of the register containing the entry of which a certificate is required. Certificates of marriage can also be obtained from the incumbent of the church in which the marriage took place, or from the Nonconformist minister (or other authorized person) where the marriage takes place in a registered building.

A standard certificate of birth, death or marriage may be obtained from the Superintendent Registrar for a fee of £5.50 or from the registrar for a fee of £2.50. One short birth certificate is issued free of charge at registration. The fee for the issue of a short birth certificate by the Superintendent Registrar is £3.50 and by a registrar, £2.00. Certificates of birth, death or marriage for special purposes cost £2.00.

When a certificate is required, the nearest register office will be able to advise on the best way of obtaining it and any fees payable. For a general search in the indexes of not more than six successive hours and where the object is not stated, the fee is £15.00. No fee is payable for a search in the indexes when a particular entry in the register is specified.

Records of births, deaths and marriages registered in England and Wales since 1837 are kept at the Office of Population Censuses and Surveys, St Catherine's House, 10 Kingsway, London WC2B 6JP. The Society of Genealogists, 14 Charterhouse Buildings, Goswell Road, London ECIM 7BA, possesses many records of baptisms, marriages and deaths prior to 1837, including copies in whole or in part of about 4,000 parish registers.

Scotland

Certificates of births, deaths or marriages registered from 1855 (when compulsory registration commenced in Scotland) can be obtained personally at the General Register Office, New Register House, Edinburgh EHI 3YT, or from the appropriate local registrar, on payment of the fee of £8.50 for a full extract entry of birth, death or marriage (£11.50 by post), and £8.50 for an abbreviated certificate of birth (£11.50 by post). An abbreviated certificate of registration of death is issued free of charge for National Insurance purposes in certain cases. A Register of Divorces (which includes decrees of declaration of nullity of marriage) is kept by the Registrar-General at the General Register Office. The fee for an extract decree is £8.50 (£11.50 by post).

There are also available at the General Register Office old parish registers of the date prior to 1855, which were formerly kept under the administration of the established Church of Scotland. An extract of an entry in these registers may be obtained for a fee of £14.00 (which includes the search fee).

The Registration of Presumed Deaths (Prescription of Particulars) (Scotland) Regulations 1978 as read with Presumption of Death (Scotland) Act 1977 prescribe the particulars to be notified by the clerk of court to the Registrar-General after a decree or variation order has been granted in an action of declarator of death of a missing person.

DIVORCE, SEPARATION AND ANCILLARY MATTERS

Matrimonial suits may be conveniently divided into two classes: those in which it is sought to annul the marriage because of some defect; and those in which, the marriage being admitted, it is sought to end the marriage or the duties

arising from it. By virtue of the Matrimonial and Family Proceedings Act 1984, all matrimonial causes are commenced in one of the divorce county courts designated by the Lord Chancellor or in the Divorce Registry in London. If the suit becomes defended, it may be transferred to the High Court.

NULLITY OF MARRIAGE

Nullity of marriage is now mainly governed as to England and Wales by the Matrimonial Causes Act 1973. A marriage is void *ab initio* if the parties were within the prohibited degrees of affinity; were not male and female; if it was bigamous; if one of the parties was under the age of consent, i.e. 16; or, in the case of a polygamous marriage entered into outside England and Wales, if either party was at the time of the marriage domiciled in England or Wales. Where the formalities of the marriage were defective, the marriage is generally void if both parties knew of the defect (e.g. where marriage took place otherwise than in an authorized building). However, absence of the consent of parents or guardians (or of the court or other authority, in lieu thereof) in the case of minors does not invalidate the marriage.

A marriage is voidable (i.e. a decree of nullity may be obtained but until such time the marriage remains valid) on the following grounds:

(a) incapacity of either party to consummate
(b) respondent's wilful refusal to consummate
(c) that either party did not validly consent to the marriage, whether in consequence of duress, mistake, unsoundness of mind or otherwise
(d) that either party at the time of marriage was a mentally disordered person
(e) that at the time of marriage the respondent was suffering from communicable venereal disease
(f) that at the time of the marriage the respondent was pregnant by another man

In cases (e) and (f), the petitioner must have been ignorant of the grounds at the date of the marriage. In cases (c), (d), (e) and (f) proceedings must be instituted within three years of the marriage, although leave may be obtained to petition outside this period in the case of certain persons suffering from mental illness. In all cases the court shall not grant a decree where the petitioner has led the respondent to believe that he/she would not seek a decree and it would be unjust for it to be granted.

The 1973 Act provides that a decree of nullity in a voidable marriage only annuls the marriage from the date of the decree. The marriage remains valid until the decree, and any children of the marriage are legitimate. Children of a void marriage are illegitimate unless the father was domiciled in England or Wales at the child's birth (or father's death, if earlier); and at the time of conception (or marriage if later) both or either of the parents reasonably believed the marriage was valid.

A spouse's insistence upon the use of contraceptives will not constitute wilful refusal to consummate within (b) above, even though there has been no normal intercourse, but it may in certain circumstances constitute unreasonable behaviour for the purpose of divorce (*see* below). Further, it has been allowed as a defence to a charge of desertion against the aggrieved party.

JUDICIAL SEPARATION AND DIVORCE

The second class of suit includes a suit for judicial separation (which does not dissolve a marriage) and a suit for divorce (which, if successful, dissolves the marriage altogether and leaves the parties at liberty to marry again). Either spouse may petition for judicial separation. It is not necessary to prove that the marriage has broken down irretrievably and the facts listed below are grounds for judicial separation.

DIVORCE

The sole ground on which a divorce is obtained by either husband or wife is the irretrievable breakdown of the marriage. However, the court is precluded from holding that a marriage has irretrievably broken down unless it is satisfied of one or more of the following facts:

(a) that the respondent has committed adultery since the marriage and the petitioner finds it intolerable to live with the respondent

(b) that the respondent has behaved in such a way that the petitioner cannot reasonably be expected to continue cohabitation

(c) desertion by the respondent for two years immediately before the petition

(d) five years' separation immediately before the petition (but only two years where the respondent consents to the decree). Matrimonial Causes Act 1973

The foregoing is subject to a clause prohibiting any petition for divorce (but not for judicial separation) before the lapse of one year from the date of the marriage.

Desertion may be defined as a voluntary withdrawal from cohabitation by one spouse without just cause and against the wishes of the other. Where one spouse is guilty of conduct of a serious nature which forces the other to leave, the party at fault is said to be guilty of constructive desertion.

Encouragement of reconciliation

The 1973 Act requires the solicitor for the petitioner in certain cases to certify whether the possibility of a reconciliation has been discussed with the petitioner and whether or not the solicitor has given the petitioner the names and addresses of persons qualified to help effect a reconciliation.

A total period of less than six months during which the parties have resumed living together is to be disregarded in determining whether the prescribed period of desertion or separation has been continuous. Similar provision for effecting a reconciliation exists in relation to the other proofs of breakdown, but a petitioner cannot rely on an act of adultery by the other party if they have lived together for more than six months after discovery of that act of adultery.

Obtaining the decree nisi

Where the suit is defended, i.e. the respondent opposes the dissolution or the fact/ground on which the petitioner seeks it, the petition will be heard by a judge in open court, the parties giving oral evidence. Where the suit is undefended, the evidence will normally take the form of a sworn written statement made by the petitioner which will be sent to the court and read over by a district judge. If the district judge is satisfied that the petitioner has proved the contents of the petition, he/she will simply fix a date for the pronouncement of the decree nisi in open court, it being unnecessary for either party to attend. Only if the district judge is not satisfied as above will he/she order that the petition be heard formally by the judge.

Children

After giving his/her certificate in relation to the decree nisi, the district judge must consider whether he/she should exercise any of his/her powers under the Children Act 1989. If the district judge thinks it may be necessary to exercise those powers, he/she can in exceptional circumstances delay the grant of the decree absolute.

Decree absolute

Every decree of divorce or nullity is in the first instance a decree nisi, and the marriage subsists until the decree is made absolute, usually six weeks after decree nisi on the petitioner's application. After the decree absolute either party is free to remarry.

Maintenance, etc

The court has wide powers to order either party to the marriage to make financial provision (e.g. periodical payments, a lump sum, the transfer of property) for the other party or, in certain circumstances, any child of the family, having regard to the party's means, the recipient's needs and all the important aspects of the case. These so-called ancillary matters often present more difficulty than the divorce itself, especially where they affect the home, and may go on long after the marriage is dissolved. There is, however, nothing to stop financial matters being negotiated by the parties through their solicitors before the divorce goes through.

The jurisdiction of the court to make child maintenance orders has been restricted by the Child Support Act 1991. Under this Act, a government agency, the Child Support Agency, has become responsible for assessing the maintenance that absent parents should pay for their natural children.

The court may, where the husband has neglected to provide reasonable maintenance for the wife or children, order the husband to make provision for the wife and, in certain circumstances, the children, even though no matrimonial suit is pending between the parties to the marriage, and while such an order is in force the court may also make orders relating to the children.

ORDERS REGARDING CHILDREN

The Court may make orders in respect of children in connection with a suit for divorce, nullity or judicial separation (see above), or with an application to the family proceedings court (see below) whether the suit succeeds or not. In addition, if there is no other matrimonial suit involved, a parent may apply for orders under the Children Act 1989, and any person interested may apply to the High Court for the child to be made a ward of court.

In all cases the welfare of the child is the paramount consideration. The categories of child who may be covered by any particular type of proceedings differ according to the nature of those proceedings and to the nature of the particular relief sought, but it should be borne in mind that in connection with divorce, nullity and judicial separation a child which has been treated by the spouses as a child of the family may be included as a 'child of the family' as well as the children of the spouses themselves. This also applies to most maintenance cases in the family proceedings court (see below). It should be borne in mind that where there is financial need (because of continuing education or disability, for instance), maintenance may be ordered for children even beyond the age of majority.

Any dispute relating to the above matters should be placed in the hands of a solicitor without delay.

SEPARATION BY AGREEMENT

Husband and wife may enter into an agreement to separate and live apart but the agreement, to be valid, must be followed by an immediate separation. It is most desirable to consult a solicitor in every such case, who will often advise obtaining a court order by consent.

FAMILY PROCEEDINGS COURT

For many years the law relating to domestic proceedings in magistrates' courts (now family proceedings courts) was out of line with the divorce law which was reformed in 1969. The Domestic Proceedings and Magistrates' Courts Act 1978 took effect in early 1981 and now contains the relevant law.

A husband or wife can apply to a family proceedings court for a matrimonial order on the grounds that the other spouse: (a) has failed to pay reasonable maintenance for the applicant; (b) has failed to make a proper contribution towards the reasonable maintenance of a child of the family; (c) has deserted the applicant; or (d) has behaved in such a way that the applicant cannot reasonably be expected to live with the respondent.

If the case is proved the court can order: (a) periodical payments for the applicant; (b) periodical payments for a child of the family (except where the court's jurisdiction has been superseded by the Child Support Agency, *see* above); or (c) a lump sum (not exceeding £1,000) for the benefit of the applicant and/or for any child of the family.

In deciding what orders (if any) to make, the court must consider a number of guidelines which are similar to those governing financial orders on divorce. There are also special provisions relating to consent orders and separation by agreement. The court also has powers to make orders relating to a child of the family and these orders together with orders for child maintenance can be made even though the court makes no order for spouse maintenance. Other provisions of the Act relate to interim orders, and variation, discharge and revival of orders. An order may be enforceable even though the parties are living together, but in some cases it will cease to have effect if they continue to do so for six months. The hearing of matrimonial disputes is separate from ordinary court business, and the public are not admitted.

DOMESTIC VIOLENCE

The Domestic Violence and Matrimonial Proceedings Act 1976, the Domestic Proceedings and Magistrates' Courts Act 1978 (the former not being applicable to Scotland and the latter only to a limited extent; *see* page 667) and the Matrimonial Homes Act 1983 have made it easier for one spouse who has been subjected to violence by the other to obtain an order to restrain further violence and if need be to have the other excluded from the home. Such orders can be obtained very quickly, and a person disobeying them is liable to be imprisoned for contempt of court. There are some differences of detail between the three Acts; in particular the 1976 Act also applies to unmarried couples. Such orders may also be obtained in the course of suits for divorce and judicial separation.

SCOTLAND

NULLITY OF MARRIAGE

A declaration of nullity of marriage may be obtained on the ground of any impediment, such as consanguinity and affinity, subsistence of a previous marriage, nonage of one of the parties, incapacity or insanity of one of the parties, or by the absence of genuine consent. The financial provisions on divorce contained in the Family Law (Scotland) Act 1985 also apply to an action for declaration of nullity of marriage.

JUDICIAL SEPARATION

Under the Divorce (Scotland) Act 1976, a decree of judicial separation can be obtained by proof of the same facts necessary to obtain decree of divorce, except that for the principle of irretrievable breakdown there is substituted that of grounds justifying separation. This type of action is competent in both the Court of Session and the sheriff court.

DIVORCE

Actions of divorce could formerly only be raised in the Court of Session, having jurisdiction to entertain such actions only if either of the parties to the marriage in question is domiciled in Scotland on the date when the action is begun, or was habitually resident in Scotland throughout the period of one year ending with that date. As from 1 May 1984, however, when the Divorce Jurisdiction, Court Fees and Legal Aid (Scotland) Act 1983 came into force, actions of divorce may also be raised in the sheriff courts provided the above conditions are complied with, and provided either party to the marriage was resident in the sheriffdom for a period of forty days ending with the date the action was begun, or was resident in the sheriffdom for a period of not less than forty days ending not more than forty days before the date the action was begun.

The Scots law of divorce is now governed by the Divorce (Scotland) Act 1976, which for the purposes of divorce came into force on 1 January 1977. The sole ground of divorce is now irretrievable breakdown of the marriage. This can be established only in one of the following ways:

(a) The defending spouse has committed adultery since the date of the marriage. It is not necessary for the pursuing spouse to prove that the fact of adultery made it intolerable to live with the defending spouse

(b) The defending spouse has behaved in such a way that the pursuing spouse cannot reasonably be expected to cohabit with him or her. It is immaterial whether or not the conduct founded upon is active or passive

(c) The defending spouse has deserted the pursuing spouse for a continuous period of two years. There must be no question of the pursuing spouse having refused a genuine and reasonable offer to adhere. Nor is irretrievable breakdown established if cohabitation is resumed for a period of more than three months after the two-year period has expired

(d) There has been no cohabitation at any time during a continuous period of two years immediately preceding the action between the parties to the action, and the defending spouse consents to the divorce being granted

(e) There has been no cohabitation at any time during a continuous period of five years, as in (d), except that on the expiry of the five-year period, the consent of the defending spouse is not required

The facts of desertion and separation are not interrupted by the parties cohabiting for a period or periods not exceeding six months. However, such a period or periods of cohabitation would not be included in the calculation of the two-year or five-year periods.

Encouragement of reconciliation

The burden of promoting a reconciliation between spouses in a divorce action in Scotland falls upon the court by virtue of the 1976 Act. Where an action of divorce has been raised, it may be postponed by the court to enable the parties to seek to effect a reconciliation, if the court feels that there may be a reasonable prospect of such reconciliation. If the parties do cohabit during such postponement, no account shall be taken of such cohabitation if the action later proceeds.

Maintenance, etc.

The 1976 Act also provides that either party to a marriage can apply to the court at any time prior to decree being granted for: (a) an order for interim custody of all or some of the children of the marriage under 16 years of age; (b) an order for access to all or some of the children of the marriage under 16 years of age in the custody of the other party.

The financial provisions on divorce in the 1976 Act have been superseded by the Family Law (Scotland) Act 1985, which allows either party to the marriage to apply to the court for an order for payment of a capital sum or for a periodical allowance or for an incidental order. The Act sets out principles to be applied by the court, one of these being that the financial provisions awarded to a party who has been dependent for financial support on the other party should be given over a period of not more than three years.

The Act also defines the rights and obligations of aliment between parents and children, thereby excluding aliment between grandparents and grandchildren and of children to parents, and provides that a child is entitled to aliment up to the age of 18 or to 25 if in full-time further education, and for the claiming of aliment whether in connection with an action of divorce, etc., or independently.

Procedure

Appearance in court at a proof in an undefended divorce action has been rendered unnecessary since April 1978. A full proof is still necessary if the action is defended in any respect. In place of court appearance, affidavits (statements sworn before a notary public) by the pursuer and any witnesses are lodged in the court together with a Minute by the solicitor craving decree.

A new simplified procedure for 'do-it-yourself' divorce was introduced in January 1983 for certain divorces. Thus, if the action is based on (d) or (e) above and will not be opposed, and if there are no children under 16 and no financial claims, then the applicant can write directly to the local sheriff court or to the Court of Session, Divorce Section (SP), Parliament House, Edinburgh, for the appropriate forms to enable him or her to proceed. The fee is £40 unless the applicant receives Income Support, Family Credit or legal advice and assistance, in which case there is no fee.

CUSTODY OF CHILDREN

In actions for divorce and separation, the court has a discretion in awarding the custody of the children of the parties. The welfare of the children is the paramount consideration, and the mere fact that a spouse, by reason of his or her behaviour, brought about the breakdown of the marriage does not of itself preclude him or her from being awarded custody. The Children Act 1975, as amended, also applies to Scotland.

DOMESTIC VIOLENCE

The Matrimonial Homes (Family Protection) (Scotland) Act 1981, as amended, provides that one spouse, whether or not he or she has title to the matrimonial home, can obtain an exclusion order suspending the other spouse's occupancy rights in the matrimonial home. The court (either Court of Session or sheriff court) is empowered to make such an order if satisfied that it is necessary to protect the applicant or any child of the family from any conduct, actual or threatened or reasonably apprehended, of the other spouse which would be injurious to the physical or mental health of the applicant or child. In making the order the court may include a warrant for the summary ejection of the non-applicant spouse from the matrimonial home and for an interdict prohibiting him/her from entering it.

ILLEGITIMACY AND LEGITIMATION

The Children Act 1989 gives the mother parental responsibility for her child when not married to the father. The father can acquire parental responsibility by agreement with her (in prescribed form) or by court order.

Prima facie every child born of a married woman during a marriage is legitimate; and this presumption can only be rebutted by strong evidence. However, under the Family Law Reform Act 1969, any presumption of law as to the legitimacy (or illegitimacy) of any person may in civil proceedings be rebutted by evidence showing that it is more probable than not that the person is illegitimate (or legitimate) and in any proceedings where paternity is in question, blood tests may be ordered. If, however, the husband and wife are separated under an order of the court, a child conceived by the wife during such separation is presumed not to be the husband's child.

LEGITIMATION

The Legitimacy Act 1976 consolidates earlier legislation dating back to 1 January 1927. Where the parents of an illegitimate person marry, or have married, whether before or after that date, the marriage, if the father is at the date thereof domiciled in England or Wales, renders that person, if living, legitimate as from 1 January 1927, or from the date of the marriage, whichever last happens. Marriage legitimates a person even though the father or mother was married to a third person at the time when the illegitimate person was born. It is the duty of the parents to supply to the Registrar-General information for re-registration of the birth of a legitimate child.

Declarations of legitimacy

A person claiming that he, his parents, or any remoter ancestor has become legitimated, may petition the High Court or the county court for the necessary declaration.

Rights and duties of legitimated persons

A legitimated person, his/her spouse or children may take property under an intestacy occurring after the date of legitimation, or under any disposition (e.g. a will) coming into operation after such date, as if he/she had been legitimate. He/she must maintain all persons whom he/she would be bound to maintain had he/she been born legitimate, and he/she is entitled to the benefit of any Act of Parliament which confers rights on legitimate persons to recover damages or compensation. The Act specially provides that nothing therein contained is to render any person capable of succeeding to or transmitting a right to any dignity or title.

PROPERTY RIGHTS OF ILLEGITIMATE CHILDREN

By the Family Law Reform Act 1969 the rights of an illegitimate child on intestacy were broadly equated with those of a legitimate child, and in any disposition made after 31 December 1969, any reference to children or other relatives was, unless the contrary intention appears, to be construed as including any person who is illegitimate or who is related through another person who is illegitimate. However, these provisions of the 1969 Act have been replaced by the general provision of the Family Law Reform Act 1987 (*see* page 658).

SCOTLAND

The Law Reform (Parent and Child) Scotland Act 1986 implements the Scottish Law Commission's report on illegitimacy. The Act contains a general provision granting equal status to all persons whatever the marital status of their parents. The mother of an illegitimate child may raise an action of affiliation and aliment against the father, either in the Court of Session or, more usually, in the sheriff court. Where in any such action the court finds that the defender is the father of the child, the court shall, in awarding expenses, or aliment, have regard to the means of the parties and the whole circumstances of the case. The court may, upon application by the mother or by the father of any illegitimate child, or in any action for aliment for an illegitimate child, make such order as it may think fit regarding the custody of such child and the right of access thereto of either parent, having regard to the welfare of the child and to the conduct of the parents and to the wishes as well of the mother as of the father and may on the application of either parent recall or vary such order. The obligation of the mother and of the father of an illegitimate child to provide aliment for such child shall (without prejudice to any obligation attaching at common law) endure until the child attains the age of sixteen.

LEGITIMATION

By Scottish law an illegitimate child is legitimated by and on the date of the subsequent marriage of its parents and there is no objection to there having been an impediment to the marriage of the parents at the time of the child's conception; see the Legitimation (Scotland) Act 1968, which came into operation on 8 June 1968, on which date thousands of existing illegitimate children were regarded as legitimated. By the Registration of Births, Deaths and Marriages (Scotland) Act 1965, a child so legitimated who has already been registered as illegitimate may be re-registered as legitimate. The consent of the father of an illegitimate child to its adoption is not required unless he has been awarded parental rights by the court.

MARRIAGE

MARRIAGE ACCORDING TO RITES OF THE
CHURCH OF ENGLAND

Marriage by banns

The Marriage Act 1949 prescribes audible publication according to the rubric, on three Sundays preceding the ceremony during morning service or, if there is no morning service on a Sunday on which the banns are to be published, during evening service. Where the parties reside in different parishes, the banns must be published in both. Under the Act, banns may be published and the marriage solemnized in the parish church, which is the usual place of worship of the persons to be married or either of them, although neither of such persons dwells in such parish; but this publication of banns is in addition to any other publication required by law and does not apply if the church or the residence of either party is in Wales. The Act provides specially for the case where one of the parties resides in Scotland and the other in England, the publication being then in the parish in England in which one party resides, and, according to the law and custom in Scotland, in the place where the other party resides. After the lapse of three months from the last time of publication, the banns become useless, and the parties must either obtain a licence (*see* below), or submit to the republication of banns.

Marriage by licence

Marriage licences are of two kinds:
Common Licence: a common licence, dispensing with the necessity for banns, is granted by the archbishops and bishops through their surrogates, for marriages in any church or chapel duly licensed for marriages. A common licence can be obtained in London by application at the Faculty Office (1 The Sanctuary, London SW1 3JT) and (for marriages in London) at the Bishop of London's Diocesan Registry (1 The Sanctuary, London SW1 3JT), by one of the parties about to be married. In the country they may be obtained at the offices of the bishop's registrars, but licences obtained at the bishop's diocesan registry only enable the parties to be married in the diocese in which they are issued; those procured at the Faculty Office are available for all England and Wales. No instructions, either verbal or in writing, can

be received, except from one of the parties. Affidavits are prepared from the personal instructions of one of the parties about to be married, and the licence is delivered to the party upon payment of a fee (*see* page 670). Before a licence can be granted one of the parties must make an affidavit that there is no legal impediment to the intended marriage; and also that one of such parties has had his or her usual place of abode for the space of fifteen days immediately preceding the issuing of the licence within the parish or ecclesiastical district of the church in which the marriage is to be solemnized, or that the church in which the marriage is to be solemnized is the usual place of worship of the parties or one of them. In the country there may generally be found a parochial clergyman (surrogate) before whom the affidavit may be taken, and whose office it is to deliver the licence personally to the applicant. (In some dioceses it is necessary for the surrogate to procure the licence from the bishop's registry.) The licence continues in force for three months from its date.

Special Licence: a special licence is granted by the Archbishop of Canterbury, in special circumstances, for marriage at any place with or without previous residence in the district, or at any time, etc.; but the reasons assigned must meet with the archbishop's approval. Application must be made to the Faculty Office. For fee, *see* page 670.

Marriage under Superintendent Registrar's certificate

A marriage may be performed in church on the Superintendent Registrar's certificate (*see* below) without banns, provided that the incumbent's consent is obtained. One of the parties must be resident within the ecclesiastical parish of the church in which the marriage is to take place unless the church is the usual place of worship of the parties or one of them.

MARRIAGE UNDER SUPERINTENDENT REGISTRAR'S
CERTIFICATE

The following marriages may be solemnized on the authority of a Superintendent Registrar's certificate (either with or without a licence):

(a) a marriage in a registered building, e.g. a Nonconformist church registered for the solemnization of marriages therein
(b) a marriage in a register office
(c) a marriage according to the usages of the Society of Friends (commonly called Quakers)
(d) a marriage between two persons professing the Jewish religion according to the usages of the Jews
(e) a marriage according to the rites of the Church of England (*see* above – in this case the marriage can only be without licence)
(f) a marriage of a person who is housebound or is detained at the place where he or she normally resides (*see* page 669)

Notice of the intended marriage must be given as follows:
Marriage by certificate (without licence): if both parties reside in the same registration district, they must both have resided there for seven days before the notice can be given. It may then be given by either party. If the parties reside in different registration districts, notice must be given by each to the Superintendent Registrar of the district in which he or she resides, and the preliminary residential qualification of seven days must be fulfilled by each before either notice can be given.

Marriage by certificate (with licence): one notice only is necessary, whether the parties live in the same or in different registration districts. Either party may give the notice, which must be given to the Superintendent Registrar of any registration district in which one of the parties has resided for the period of fifteen days immediately preceding the giving of notice, but both parties must be resident in England or Wales on the day notice is given.

The notice (in either case) must be in the prescribed form and must contain particulars as to names, marital status, occupation, residence, length of residence, and the building in which the marriage is to take place. The notice must also contain or have added at the foot thereof a solemn declaration that there is no legal impediment to the marriage, and, in the case of minors, that the consent of the person whose consent to the marriage is required by law (*see* Minors, page 670) has been duly given, and that the residential qualifications mentioned above have been complied with. A person making a false declaration renders himself or herself liable to prosecution for perjury. The notice is entered in the marriage notice book.

Issue of certificate

Without licence: the notice (or an exact copy thereof) is affixed in some conspicuous place in the Superintendent Registrar's office for 21 days next after the notice was entered in the marriage notice book. After the lapse of this period the Superintendent Registrar may, provided no impediment is shown his certificate for the marriage which can then take place at any time within three months from the date of the entry of the notice.

With licence: the notice in this case is not affixed in the office of the Superintendent Registrar. After the lapse of one whole day (other than a Sunday, Christmas Day or Good Friday) from the date of entry of the notice, the Superintendent Registrar may, provided no impediment is shown, issue his certificate and licence for the marriage, which can then take place on any day within three months from the date of entry of the notice.

SOLEMNIZATION OF THE MARRIAGE

In a registered building

The marriage must generally take place at a building within the district of residence of one of the parties, but if the usual place of worship of either is outside the district of his or her residence, it may take place in such usual place of worship. Further, if there is not within the district of residence of one of the parties a registered building within which marriages are solemnized according to the rites and ceremonies which the parties desire to adopt in solemnizing their marriage, it may take place in an appropriate registered building in the nearest district.

The presence of a Registrar of Marriages is not necessary at marriages at registered buildings which have adopted the provisions of section 43 of the Marriage Act 1949. This section provides for the appointment of an authorized person (a person, usually the minister or an official of the building, certified by the trustees or governing body as having been duly authorized for the purpose) who must be present and must register the marriage.

The marriage must be solemnized between the hours of 8 a.m. and 6 p.m., with open doors, in the presence of two or more witnesses. The parties must at some time during the ceremony make the following declaration: 'I do solemnly declare that I know not of any lawful impediment why I, A. B., may not be joined in matrimony to C. D.' Also each of the parties must say to the other: 'I call upon these persons here present to witness that I, A. B., do take thee, C. D., to be my lawful wedded wife [or husband],' or, if the marriage is solemnized in the presence of an authorized person without the presence of a registrar, each party may say in lieu thereof:

'I, A. B., do take thee, C. D., to be my wedded wife [or husband].'

In a register office

The marriage may be solemnized in the office of the Superintendent Registrar to whom notice of the marriage has been given. The marriage must be solemnized between the hours of 8 a.m. and 6 p.m., with open doors, in the presence of the Superintendent Registrar or a registrar of the registration district of that Superintendent Registrar, and in the presence of two witnesses. The parties must make the following declaration: 'I do solemnly declare that I know not of any lawful impediment why I, A. B., may not be joined in matrimony to C. D.,' and each party must say to the other: 'I call upon these persons here present to witness that I, A. B., do take thee, C. D., to be my lawful wedded wife [or husband].'

No religious ceremony may take place in the register office, though the parties may, on production of their marriage certificate, go through a subsequent religious ceremony in any church or persuasion of which they are members.

Other cases

If both parties are members of the Society of Friends (Quakers), or if, not being in membership, they have been authorized by the Society of Friends to solemnize their marriage in accordance with its usages, they may be married in a Friends' meeting-house. The marriage must be registered by the registering officer of the Society appointed to act for the district in which the meeting-house is situated. The presence of a Registrar of Marriages is not necessary.

If both parties are Jews they may marry according to their usages in a synagogue which has a certified marriage secretary, or in a private dwelling-house at any hour; the building may be situated within or without the district of residence. The marriage must be registered by the secretary of the synagogue of which the man is a member. The presence of a Registrar of Marriages is not necessary.

MARRIAGE UNDER REGISTRAR-GENERAL'S LICENCE

The main purpose of the Marriage (Registrar-General's Licence) Act 1970, which came into force on 1 January 1971, is to enable non-Anglicans to be married in unregistered premises where one of the persons to be married is seriously ill, is not expected to recover, and cannot be moved to registered premises.

DETAINED AND HOUSEBOUND PERSONS

The Marriage Act 1983 (which does not extend to Scotland) enables marriages of detained persons and housebound persons to be solemnized at their place of residence . The Act came into operation on 1 May 1984.

MARRIAGE IN ENGLAND OR WALES WHEN ONE PARTY LIVES IN SCOTLAND OR NORTHERN IRELAND

Notice for a marriage by a Superintendent Registrar's certificate in a register office or registered building may be given in the usual way by the party resident in England. As regards Scotland, the party there should give notice of intention to marry to the Registrar. As regards Northern Ireland, the party there, after a residence of seven days, must give notice to the District Registrar of Marriages. Notice cannot be given for such marriages to take place by certificate with licence of the Superintendent Registrar.

Marriage of such parties may take place in a church of the Church of England after the publication of banns, or by ecclesiastical licence.

670 Legal Notes

CIVIL FEES from 1 April 1993

Marriage by Superintendent Registrar's certificate

If both parties live in same district
 In register office, £35.00
 In a registered building when presence of registrar is
 required, £47.00
If the parties live in different districts
 In register office, £52.00
 In a registered building when presence of registrar is
 required, £64.00

Marriage by Superintendent Registrar's licence

In register office, £80.00
In a registered building when presence of registrar is
required, £92.00

Total fees for the preliminaries to marriage by Registrar-
General's licence, £15.00

Marriage of a housebound or detained person

For attendance of Superintendent Registrar at residence of
 housebound or detained person to attest notice of
 marriage, £32.00
For attendance of Superintendent Registrar at residence of
 housebound or detained person, £32.00
For attendance of registrar at residence of housebound or
 detained person, £30.00

In the case of a registered building, further fees may be
payable to the minister or the authorities of the building.

ECCLESIASTICAL FEES from 1 April 1993

Marriage after banns

Parties residing in same parish, £80.00
Parties residing in different parishes, £93.00

Marriages by common licence

Fee for licence varies, but usually £42.00
Fee to Church authorities for ceremony, £72.00

*Marriage on the authority of the Superintendent Registrar's
certificate*

Parties residing in same registration district, £89.00
Parties residing in different districts, £106.00

Marriage by special licence

Fee payable at Faculty Office, £90.00

Marriage of a housebound or detained person

For attendance of a Superintendent Registrar at residence
 of a housebound or detained person to attest marriage,
 £32.00
*For entering notice of marriage, £17.00

*Two notices are required to be given if the parties reside in
different registration districts
Further fees may be payable for additional facilities at the
marriage, e.g. the organist's fee
Some of the above fees may not apply to the Church in
Wales

MISCELLANEOUS NOTES

Consanguinity and affinity

A marriage between persons within the prohibited degrees
of consanguinity or affinity is void. Relaxations have,
however, been made by various statutes which have now
been replaced by the Marriage Act 1949 (see 1st Schedule to
the Act) and the Marriage (Enabling) Act 1960. It is now
permitted to contract a marriage with:

(a) Sister, aunt or niece of a former wife (whether living or
 not)
(b) Former wife of brother, uncle or nephew (whether
 living or not)
 No clergyman can be compelled to solemnize any of the
foregoing marriages, but he may allow his church to be used
for the purpose by another minister.
 The Marriage (Prohibited Degrees of Relationship) Act
1986 makes further provision with regard to the marriage of
persons related by affinity, e.g. after section 1 of the Act
came into force, a marriage between a man and the daughter
or granddaughter of his former wife will not be void by
reason only of that relationship if both parties have attained
21 at the time of the marriage and the younger party has not
at any time before attaining 18 been a child of the family in
relation to the other party.

Minors

Persons under 18 years of age are generally required to
obtain the consent of certain persons (Marriage Act 1949,
section 3 and 2nd Schedule as amended by the Children Act
1989). Where both parents are living, both must consent.
Where one is dead, the survivor, or, if there is a guardian
appointed by the deceased parent, the guardian and the
survivor must consent. (For the position where the parents
of the child were not married to each other at the time of the
birth, see Schedule 12, paragraph 5 to the Children Act
1989.) No consent is required in the case of a minor's second
marriage. In certain exceptional cases consent may be
dispensed with, e.g. the insanity of a parent.
 If consent is refused the court may, on application being
made, consent to the marriage; application can be made for
this purpose to the High Court, the county court, or a court
of summary jurisdiction. The Act prohibits any marriage
where either party is under 16 years of age.

SCOTLAND

According to the law of Scotland, marriage is a contract
which is completed by the mutual consent of parties. The
Marriage (Scotland) Act 1977, which came into force on 1
January 1978, states or restates the law in convenient form.
References in this section are to that Act.

IMPEDIMENTS TO MARRIAGE

These are: (a) nonage, i.e. where either party is under the
age of 16; (b) forbidden degrees of relationship (Section 2) as
amended by the Marriage Prohibited Degrees of Relationship Act 1986; (c) subsisting previous marriage; (d) incapacity
to understand the nature of the contract; (e) both parties of
the same sex; (f) non-residence, i.e. if the requirements of
prior residence of one or other of the parties in Scotland have
not been complied with.
 The Act also states the grounds on which certain marriages
may be declared void, but this is amended by the Law
Reform (Miscellaneous Provisions) (Scotland) Act 1980
which prevents a marriage being rendered void solely due to
the failure to comply with certain formalities, provided that
particulars of that marriage are entered in a register of
marriages by or at the behest of an appropriate registrar.

REGULAR AND IRREGULAR MARRIAGES

Regular marriages

A regular marriage is one which is celebrated by a minister
of religion or authorized registrar or other celebrant specified

in the Act. The parties must submit to the district registrar a statutory notice of intention to marry, the fee for which is £10.00 each. The registrar will then enter the parties' names and particulars in the marriage notice book which must also show the intended date of the marriage. The registrar must then display the notice of intention to marry in a prominent public place until the intended date, and any person claiming an interest may lodge written objections thereto with the registrar (Section 5). The registrar, after 14 clear days of receipt of the marriage notice and on being satisfied that there are no legal impediments to the marriage, will issue to either or both parties a marriage schedule. The 14-day period may be shortened in exceptional circumstances. The marriage schedule must be produced to the celebrant of the marriage. The fee for the solemnization ceremony in a register office is £30.00. After the ceremony the marriage must be registered within three days with the Registrar-General for inclusion in the Register of Births, Deaths and Marriages. Within one month of the ceremony, the fee for an extract marriage certificate is £6.00; thereafter it is £8.50.

Irregular marriages

Since the Marriage (Scotland) Act 1939 the only form of irregular marriage to be recognized by law, marriage by habit and repute, remains competent under the 1977 Act. If the parties live together constantly as husband and wife and are held to be such by the general repute of the neighbourhood and among their friends and relations, then there may arise a presumption from which marriage can be inferred. Before such a marriage can be registered, however, a decree of declarator of marriage must be obtained from the Deputy Principal Clerk of the Court of Session. It is the duty of the Deputy Principal Clerk to register the decree as soon as it is granted.

JURY SERVICE

Every parliamentary or local elector between the ages of 18 and 70 who has resided in the United Kingdom, Channel Islands or Isle of Man for at least five years since he/she attained the age of 13 will be qualified to serve on a jury unless he/she is ineligible or disqualified.

Ineligible persons include those who have at any time been judges, magistrates and certain senior court officials, those who within the previous ten years have been concerned with the law (such as barristers and solicitors and their clerks, court officers, coroners, police, prison and probation officers); priests of any religion and vowed members of religious communities; and certain sufferers from mental illness.

Disqualified persons are those who have at any time been sentenced by a court in the United Kingdom, Channel Islands or Isle of Man, to a term of imprisonment of five years or more, or a person who in the last ten years has (a) served any part of a sentence of imprisonment, youth custody or detention; (b) been detained in a Borstal institution; (c) had passed on him/her or made in respect of him/her a suspended sentence of imprisonment or order for detention; or (d) had made in respect of him/her a community service order. A person who at any time in the last five years has been placed on probation is also disqualified.

Some others are excusable as of right. These include persons over 65, members and officers of the Houses of Parliament, full-time serving members of the armed forces,

registered and practising members of the medical, dental, nursing, veterinary and pharmaceutical professions, and any person who has served on a jury in the two years before he/she is summoned. In other cases the court may excuse a juror at its discretion, e.g. where the service would be a hardship to the juror.

If a person serves on a jury knowing himself/herself to be disqualified or ineligible, he/she is liable to be fined up to £2,000 or £400 respectively.

A juror is entitled to subsistence and travelling expenses, compensation for other expenses incurred in consequence of attendance for jury service, loss of earnings and loss of national insurance benefits, but certain maximum figures (which are revised from time to time) are laid down.

A verdict of a jury must normally be unanimous but after two hours' consideration (or such longer period as the court thinks reasonable), a majority verdict is acceptable if ten jurors agree to it (or nine if the size of the jury has been reduced to ten, e.g. by illness during the trial).

Jury trial is now very unusual in civil cases but a person charged with any but the least serious crimes is entitled to be tried by a jury. The defendant may object to any juror if he/she can show that that juror ought not to be on the jury, e.g. because he/she is ineligible or is biased against him/her.

The Coroners' Juries Act 1983 (which does not extend to Scotland) makes provision in relation to qualification to serve on coroners' juries.

Scotland

It is the duty of the sheriff principal of each sheriffdom, in respect of each sheriff court district in the sheriffdom, to maintain a book (the general jury book) containing the names and designations of persons within the district who are qualified and liable to serve as jurors. The book, which is compiled from information which every householder is required to provide, is kept open for the inspection by any person, upon payment of a nominal fee, at the sheriff clerk's office for the district.

Under s.1 of the Law Reform (Miscellaneous Provisions) (Scotland) Act 1980, every man or woman between the ages of 18 and 65 who is for the time being registered as a parliamentary or local government elector and who has been ordinarily resident in the United Kingdom, the Channel Islands or the Isle of Man for any period of at least five years since attaining the age of 13 years, is qualified to serve on a jury.

Ineligible persons include those who at any time within the past ten years have been judges of the supreme courts, sheriffs and certain other senior court officials, those who at any time within the past five years have been concerned with the administration of justice (such as advocates and their clerks, solicitors, court staff, police officers, prison officers, sheriff officers, procurator fiscals, and members of parole boards and children's panels), and certain sufferers from mental illness.

The same rules for disqualified persons operate in Scotland as in England.

Those excusable as of right are members and officers of the Houses of Parliament, full-time serving members of the armed forces, registered and practising members of the medical, dental, nursing, veterinary and pharmaceutical professions, ministers of religion and other persons in holy orders, and any person who has attended for jury service in the past five years.

If a person serves on a jury knowing himself/herself to be disqualified or ineligible, he/she is liable to be fined up to £2,000 or £400 respectively. Jurors failing to attend without good cause are liable to a maximum fine of £200.

Part II of the Juries Act 1949 (amended by regulations following thereon and by the Law Reform (Miscellaneous Provisions) (Scotland) Act 1980) applies only to Scotland and provides, *inter alia*, for the payment of travelling expenses and subsistence allowances to jurors and for loss of earnings.

The number of a jury in a civil cause in the Court of Session is 12 and in the sheriff court seven. In a criminal trial the number is 15.

LANDLORD AND TENANT

Although basically the relationship between the parties to a lease is governed by the lease itself, the position is complicated by numerous statutory provisions. The few points dealt with may show the desirability of seeking professional assistance in these matters. Important provisions include the following:

(1) The Agricultural Holdings Act 1986, among other things, regulates the length of notice necessary to determine an agricultural tenancy, the tenant's right to remove fixtures on the land, his right to compensation for damage done by game, for improvements and for disturbance, and his right to require the consent of the Agricultural Land Tribunal to the operation of a notice to quit.

(2) The Landlord and Tenant Acts 1927 and 1954, as amended: Part II of the 1954 Act gives security of tenure to the tenant of most business premises, and in effect the tenant can only be ousted on one or more of the seven grounds set out in the Act. In some cases, where the landlord can resume possession, the tenant is entitled to compensation.

(3) The complicated mass of legislation regarding dwelling-houses is embodied in the Rent Act 1977 and the Housing Act 1988.

If a tenancy of a house is within the Rent Act, the tenant has a personal right to reside there, and may only be ousted on certain grounds. Tenancies with full Rent Act protection are known as regulated tenancies. The maximum rent recoverable under such a tenancy is the rent agreed between the landlord and tenant, unless a fair rent has been registered, in which case that is the maximum. Application for the registration of a fair rent may be made by either the landlord or tenant, to the local rent officer, and appeal against his decision lies to the rent assessment committee.

Since the Housing Act 1988 came into force on 15 January 1989, it has not generally been possible to create a new regulated tenancy, although the above protection remains for existing regulated tenancies. Tenancies granted on or after 15 January 1989 are known as assured tenancies provided they satisfy certain conditions, which are broadly the same as those for regulated tenancies under the 1977 Act. However, the rent payable by an assured tenant is either that agreed with the landlord or the open market rent fixed by the Rent Assessment Committee.

(4) The Protection from Eviction Act 1977, as amended by the Housing Act 1988, provides that if any person with intent to cause the residential occupier of any premises to give up the occupation thereof does any act calculated to interfere with the peace or comfort of the residential occupier or members of the household, that person shall be guilty of an offence. A further provision prevents a landlord enforcing without a court order a right to possession against a tenant who is not protected by any security of tenure legislation, and there are special rules in such cases relating to agricultural employees.

(5) A notice to quit any dwelling-house must be given at least four weeks before it is to take effect, and must be in writing and in the prescribed statutory form.

(6) Part I of the Landlord and Tenant Act 1954 applies to most tenancies of houses for over 21 years at a ground rent. Where it applies, the contractual tenancy is continued until brought to an end in the manner prescribed by the Act, and in effect the landlord can only get possession on limited grounds.

Further, under the Leasehold Reform Act 1967, tenants of houses under leases for over 21 years at a low rent are in most cases given a right to purchase the freehold or to take an extended lease for a term of fifty years, provided the tenant at the time when he/she seeks to exercise the right has been occupying the house as his/her residence for the last three years or for periods amounting to three years in the last ten years.

(7) Full Rent Act or Housing Act protection is available only if a dwelling-house is let on a tenancy. If the occupier of a dwelling-house has a mere licence to occupy, he/she does not have protection. Further, even if he/she has a tenancy, he/she will not be protected if a low rent is payable. For these reasons, many occupants of houses owned by farmers and occupied by farm workers did not enjoy full security of tenure. The Rent (Agriculture) Act 1976 contains detailed provisions conferring security of tenure on certain agricultural workers housed by their employers and on their successors on death.

(8) Under the Landlord and Tenant Act 1985 (which does not extend to Scotland), in a lease of a dwelling-house granted for a term of less than seven years, there is implied a covenant by the landlord (a) to keep in repair the structure and exterior of the house and (b) to keep in repair and proper working order the installations in the house for the supply of water, gas and electricity, for sanitation, and for space heating or heating water.

(9) The Housing Act 1985 gives security of tenure to many tenants of local authorities and certain other bodies. Further, and subject to certain conditions, such tenants may have the right to purchase their houses or to take a long lease of their flats.

(10) Tenants of flats and other dwellings are given a number of special rights by the Landlord and Tenant Act 1987, as amended by the Housing Act 1988.

Scotland

A lease is a contract, the relationship of the parties being governed by the terms thereof. As is also the case in England, legislation has played an important part in regulating that relationship. Thus, what at common law was an agreement binding only the parties to the deed, becomes in virtue of the Leases Act 1449, a contract binding the landlord's successors, as purchasers or creditors, provided the following four conditions are observed: (a) the lease, if for more than one year, must be in writing; (b) there must be a rent; (c) there must be a term of expiry; and (d) the tenant must have entered into possession.

It would be impracticable to enter here upon a general discussion of this branch of the law. A few important provisions include:

(1) The Agricultural Holdings (Scotland) Act 1991 is a consolidating Act applicable to Scotland. It contains provisions similar to those in the English Act alluded to in the preceding section.

The Small Landholders Act 1911 provided for the setting up of the Land Court, which has jurisdiction over a large proportion of agricultural and pastoral land in Scotland.

(2) In Scotland business premises are not controlled by statute to so great an extent as in England, but the Tenancy of Shops (Scotland) Act 1949 gives a measure of security to tenants of shops. This Act enables the tenant of a shop who is threatened with eviction to apply to the sheriff for a renewal of the tenancy. If the landlord has offered to sell the property to the tenant at an agreed price the application for a renewal of the tenancy may be dismissed. Reference should be made to Section 1 (3) of the 1949 Act for particulars of other circumstances in which the sheriff has a discretion to dismiss an application. The Act extends to premises held by the Crown or government departments, either as landlord or tenant.

(3) Many leases contain references to the term and quarter days in connection with the expiry of the lease payment dates or for rent reviews. At common law these days and dates are respectively Candlemas (2 February), Whitsunday (15 May), Lammas (1 August) and Martinmas (11 November). The Term and Quarter Days (Scotland) Act 1990 amends these dates to 28 February, 28 May, 28 August and 28 November respectively, with effect from 13 July 1991, unless, in the case of a deed executed before that date an application had been made to a sheriff for a declaration that a date other than the statutory date should apply. Where a pre-existing deed contains a reference to a specific date instead of or in addition to a day, then it is that date which shall apply.

(4) The Housing (Scotland) Act 1987 consolidates previous legislation in regard to the extensive powers and duties to local authorities in relation to housing. Included therein is the general provision regarding the rights of public sector tenants to purchase the houses which they occupy and the restrictions regarding this right in certain circumstances where the house has been designed or adapted for occupation by the elderly. This Act also makes provision for secure tenancies for public sector tenants.

(5) The Housing (Scotland) Act 1988 creates, with certain exceptions, two new forms of tenancy for tenancies created after 2 January 1989: assured tenancies, and short assured tenancies. The assured tenancy significantly reduces the concept of security of tenure and abolishes any method of regulating rent other than market forces. The short assured tenancy lasts for at least six months and if properly constituted will allow the landlord to recover possession on its expiry. Provision is made for a tenant to apply to the Rent Assessment Committee to fix a rent based on the rent a landlord might reasonably expect for a short assured tenancy of the property.

(6) For most tenancies created before 2 January 1989, the Rent (Scotland) Act 1984 will continue to apply. It defines regulated tenancies, which may be either furnished or unfurnished, and lays down the system by which a landlord or tenant may obtain from the Rent Office registration of a fair rent. The Act gives to tenants of either furnished or unfurnished lets a substantial degree of security of tenure. There are, however, certain exceptions; they do not apply to tenancies where the interest belongs to the Crown or to a government department or to a local authority, a development corporation of a new town or a housing corporation. There must be a true tenancy for the Act to apply. It does not apply to licencees such as lodgers or persons allowed to occupy houses on a grace and favour basis or to services occupiers.

The Act regulates the short tenancy, a category of let under which, on compliance with certain conditions, the landlord can be assured of recovering possession on the expiry of the stipulated period of let. The Act defines the circumstances in which generally a landlord may apply for increased rent as a consequence of having carried out improvements to the property, and also lays down the system of phasing such rent increases. On the death of a statutory successor to a tenancy, the tenancy may pass for a second time to a member of the family or a relative who has been in residence in the house for a period of at least six months. The Act further lays down the duties and functions of rent officers and rent assessment committees with regard to unfurnished accommodation and of rent tribunals for furnished accommodation.

The Secretary of State for Scotland is given power in the 1988 Act to repeal or amend those sections of the 1984 Act relating to the phasing of rent increases. The other major features of the 1988 Act are to establish Scottish Homes, and to permit public sector properties to be transferred to Scottish Homes or a landlord approved by Scottish Homes.

LEGAL AID

The Legal Aid Act 1988 (as amended) is designed to make legal aid and advice more readily available for persons of small and moderate means. The main structure of the service is contained in the Act itself and the regulations made thereunder, administered by the Legal Aid Board.

CIVIL PROCEEDINGS

Legal aid is available for proceedings (including matrimonial causes) in the House of Lords, Court of Appeal, High Court, county courts, Lands Tribunal, Employment Appeal Tribunal, Restrictive Practices Court, before the Commons Commissioners, and civil proceedings in magistrates' courts. In any event, an application for legal aid will not be approved if it appears that the applicant would gain only a trivial advantage from the proceedings. Further, proceedings wholly or partly in respect of defamation are excepted from the scheme, as are also relator actions and election petitions. Legal aid is not available for proceedings before tribunals, other than those mentioned above. It is generally not available for obtaining the decree in undefended divorce and judicial separation, although the legal advice and assistance scheme (see below) is, and legal aid is still available to deal with property, disputes over children, etc., arising in the suit.

Where a person is concerned in proceedings only in a representative, fiduciary or official capacity, his/her personal resources are not to be taken into account in considering eligibility for legal aid. In certain public law proceedings under the Children Act 1989, non-means tested legal aid is available. Apart from this, eligibility in civil proceedings depends upon an applicant's disposable income and disposable capital. The figures change frequently; particulars can be obtained from a solicitor, the Law Society or a Citizens' Advice Bureau. Disposable income is calculated by making deductions from gross income in respect of certain matters such as dependants, interest on loans, income tax, rent and other matters for which the applicant must or reasonably may provide. Disposable capital is calculated by excluding from gross capital part of the value of the house in which the applicant resides, furniture and household possessions; allowances are made in respect of dependants. Except in cases where they are living apart or have a contrary interest, any resources of a person's wife or husband or cohabitee are to be treated as that person's resources. These figures will be assessed by the Department of Social Security and will be referred to the Legal Aid Board, who will determine whether reasonable grounds exist for the grant of a civil aid certificate. Appeal from refusal of a certificate lies to an area committee. A person resident in England or Wales desiring legal aid should apply for a certificate to the appropriate area director for the area in which he or she resides; if resident elsewhere, application should be made to an area director in London. If a certificate is granted, the applicant may select his/her solicitor, and, if necessary, counsel from a panel. The costs of the assisted person's solicitor and counsel will be paid out of the legal aid fund. When, however, damages or property are recovered or preserved by the assisted person, the legal aid fund has a charge over them in respect of these costs less any contribution towards costs recovered from the unsuccessful party. In matrimonial cases, maintenance is exempt, as is the first £2,500 of any property settlement. The court may order that the costs of a successful unassisted party shall be paid out of the legal aid fund.

In an urgent case, e.g. domestic violence or to restrain the kidnapping abroad of a child, legal aid may be granted without the applicant's means being fully investigated beforehand. If on a full examination later he/she is found financially ineligible, he/she is liable to pay all the costs incurred on his/her behalf.

LEGAL ADVICE AND ASSISTANCE

The scheme is governed by the Legal Aid Act 1988. Under the legal advice and assistance scheme a client may obtain such advice or assistance as is normally provided by a solicitor. If necessary, the advice of a barrister may be obtained but, with the exception of domestic proceedings in a family proceedings court and certain other proceedings (*see* below), the scheme does not extend to taking any step in any proceedings before any court or tribunal. Where legal aid is available for civil proceedings (*see* above) or in criminal cases (*see* below), the scheme covers work done in making application for such legal aid.

A person (other than one receiving advice and assistance at a police station or from a duty solicitor) is eligible for advice or assistance under the scheme provided his/her disposable capital and his/her disposable income do not exceed limits in force from time to time or if he/she is eligible for Income Support or Family Credit. In calculating disposable income, income tax and National Insurance contributions are deducted. For a married man or person with children or other dependants, further deductions will be made from both income and capital. It is intended that the financial limits shall approximate to those applying for legal aid in civil proceedings (*see* page 673). Except when they are separated or have conflicting interests, the means of husband and wife or cohabiting couple will be aggregated for the purpose of determining financial eligibility. As in the case of legal aid, depending on his/her means, a person may be called upon to pay a contribution towards the costs of work done for him/her. Particulars may be obtained from a solicitor, the Law Society or a Citizens' Advice Bureau.

A solicitor cannot do more than two hours' work, or three hours' in the case of divorce (where acting for the petitioner), without leave of the area legal aid committee. The solicitor's costs are paid out of the client's contribution and any monies recovered in respect of costs or damages from another party (although this may be waived by leave of the area committee in cases of hardship) and the balance will be paid by the legal aid fund.

The Act also extends the scheme to cover the costs of a solicitor who is present within the precincts of a family proceedings court or county court and is requested by the court to advise or represent a person who is in need of help.

In April 1980 the scheme was enlarged to cover the cost of representation in domestic proceedings in a magistrates' court. It has since been extended to cover the representation of patients before Mental Health Review Tribunals. Subject to financial eligibility limits, application is made to the area

or local committee for 'approval of assistance by way of representation' which will replace legal aid for such proceedings. The two-hour limit referred to above will not apply. An applicant who is outside the financial limits but eligible for legal aid will still have to apply for a legal aid certificate as before. Free advice and assistance, and assistance by way of representation from a duty solicitor, are also available in limited circumstances to persons appearing before a magistrates' court charged with a criminal offence.

In January 1986 the scheme was further extended to provide free advice and assistance to all suspects detained at a police station, whether arrested or merely helping police with their enquiries, and free representation for all arrested persons who are the subject of an application for a warrant of further detention under the Police and Criminal Evidence Act 1984. Such persons may instruct a solicitor of their choice or take advantage of the duty solicitor scheme which has now been extended to cover police stations.

CRIMINAL PROCEEDINGS

The Legal Aid Act 1988 provides for legal aid in criminal proceedings. A criminal court (e.g. magistrates' court, Crown Court) has power to order legal aid to be granted where it appears desirable to do so in the interests of justice. The court shall make an order in certain cases, e.g. where a person is committed for trial on a charge of murder. However, the court may not make an order unless it appears to the court that the person's disposable income and capital are such that he/she requires assistance in meeting the costs of the particular proceedings in question. Application should be made to the appropriate court where proceedings are to take place.

An applicant shall be required to make a contribution towards the costs of his/her case if his/her disposable income and capital exceed certain prescribed limits. Persons in receipt of Income Support are automatically exempt. In order to ascertain the amount of this contribution an applicant will have to produce written evidence of his/her means. Investigation of means will be carried out by the court. Any person who falls into arrears with the payment of contribution is liable to have the order revoked.

Any practising barrister or solicitor may act for a legally aided person in criminal proceedings unless excluded by reason of misconduct. In general, where legal aid is given it will normally include representation by both counsel and solicitor. However, in connection with magistrates' courts, representation will be by solicitor alone unless the offence is a serious one.

Where any doubt arises about the grant of a legal aid order, that doubt is to be resolved in favour of the applicant. The court also has power to amend or revoke a legal aid order. Legal aid may also be granted in connection with appellate proceedings, e.g. on appeal to the Criminal Division of the Court of Appeal under the Criminal Appeal Act 1968.

SCOTLAND

Legal aid in Scotland is governed by the Legal Aid (Scotland) Act 1986 and the regulations made thereunder. This Act established the Scottish Legal Aid Board, which has the general function of securing that legal aid and legal advice and assistance are available in accordance with the Act, and of administering the Scottish Legal Aid Fund.

CIVIL PROCEEDINGS

Civil legal aid is available in relation to civil proceedings in the House of Lords in appeals from the Court of Session, in the Court of Session, the Lands Valuation Appeal Court, the Scottish Land Court, the sheriff court, the Lands Tribunal for Scotland, the Employment Appeals Tribunal and to the European Court of Human Rights. Civil legal aid is granted if, on application to the Board, the Board is satisfied that there is *probabilis causa litigandi* and that it is reasonable in the particular circumstances of the case that legal aid should be awarded. As in England, eligibility and any contribution required from an applicant is dependent on their disposable income and disposable capital. Information on current financial limits can be obtained from the Scottish Legal Aid Board, a solicitor, or a Citizens' Advice Bureau.

A person believing himself/herself to be eligible may instruct any solicitor of his/her own choice. If a court action is not immediately contemplated, application will be made for legal advice and assistance which operates in a similar manner to the legal advice and assistance scheme in England. If proceedings are contemplated then a formal application for civil legal aid will be made and there are special provisions for emergency applications in appropriate circumstances.

If proceedings are decided against a person in receipt of legal aid the court shall determine a reasonable sum in the circumstances as an appropriate award of expenses to be made against the applicant. The court may make an award out of the fund only if proceedings were instituted by the legally assisted person and the court is satisfied that the resisting party would suffer severe financial hardship unless the order is made, and if the court is satisfied that in all the circumstances it is just and equitable that an award be made. If monies are recovered by a legally assisted person these fall to be paid to the Scottish Legal Aid Board who will then determine the appropriate level of contribution from the sums received which should be made to the expenses of their litigation.

CRIMINAL PROCEEDINGS

Legal aid in criminal causes is also administered under the Legal Aid (Scotland) Act 1986. The procedure for application for criminal legal aid is dependent on the circumstances of each case. In serious cases heard before a jury under solemn procedure it is for the court to decide whether to grant legal aid. Applications for legal aid must normally be made on the prescribed forms to the clerk of the court in question and an applicant is required to provide therein particulars of the merits of his/her case and his/her financial circumstances. In summary criminal causes, however, the procedure is dependent on whether the applicant is in custody; if so he/she is entitled to automatic free legal aid from the duty solicitor. If the applicant is not in custody and wishes to plead guilty, he/she is ineligible for full legal aid but may be entitled to criminal legal advice and assistance, and in some circumstances may qualify for assistance by way of representation which will enable his/her solicitor to appear and make a plea in mitigation on his/her behalf. If he/she is not in custody and wishes to plead not guilty, he/she can apply to the Scottish Legal Aid Board for criminal legal aid on the prescribed form not later than fourteen days after the first court appearance at which he/she made the plea, and legal aid shall be granted only if the Board is satisfied that the accused cannot meet the expenses of the case without undue hardship and that it is in the interest of justice as defined by the 1986 Act.

liberty of an owner of land to develop and use it at will. A person has generally to get planning permission from the local planning authority before carrying out any development on the land.

Development includes:

(a) carrying out of building, engineering, mining or other operations

(b) making a material change in use

It is expressly provided that if one dwelling-house is converted into two or more dwelling-houses, this involves a material change in use.

The following do not constitute 'development':

(a) maintaining, improving or altering the interior of a building, provided there is no material change to the exterior, with the exception that any expansion, or works begun for the expansion, of a building below ground level constitutes development

(b) changing the use of property within the curtilage of a dwelling-house for a purpose incidental to the use of the dwelling-house as such. (It will, however, be development if building operations are carried out)

Application can be made to the local planning authority to determine whether or not an operation or change of use constitutes development.

PLANNING PERMISSION

Application for planning permission is not always necessary, as the Secretary of State may make development orders giving general permission for a specified type of development, e.g. enlargement of a dwelling-house (including erection of a garage), so long as the cubic content of the original dwelling (external measurement) is not exceeded by more than 70 cubic metres or 15 per cent, whichever is greater, subject to a maximum of 115 cubic metres. However, in the case of a terraced house, the limitation is 50 cubic metres or 10 per cent, whichever is the greater, subject to the maximum of 115 cubic metres.

Appeal against refusal of permission lies to the Secretary of State and from his decision, in limited circumstances, to the High Court. If the result of the appeal is unsatisfactory, an applicant may in certain circumstances require the local authority to purchase the land.

SCOTLAND

The Town and Country Planning (Scotland) Act 1972 consolidates the statute law relating to town and country planning in Scotland.

The uses of buildings are classified by the Town and Country Planning (Use Classes) (Scotland) Order 1988. Changes in use prior to 31 December 1984 are immune from enforcement proceedings.

Development normally requires to be commenced within five years from the date of granting permission.

The 1972 Act contains provisions for an appeal to the Secretary of State against the refusal of planning permission. The decision of the Secretary of State is final.

Sections 87 and 92 of the Local Government, Planning and Land Act 1980 contain important provisions on planning applications and, unlike certain parts of this Act, extend to Scotland.

TOWN AND COUNTRY PLANNING

The Town and Country Planning Act 1990 (consolidating earlier Acts) as amended by the Planning and Compensation Act 1991, contains far-reaching provisions affecting the

VOTERS' QUALIFICATIONS

The franchise is governed by the Representation of the People Acts 1983 and 1985. Those entitled to vote as electors at a parliamentary election in any constituency are all persons resident there on the qualifying date who, at that date and on the date of the poll, are Commonwealth citizens or citizens of the Republic of Ireland and who are not subject to any legal incapacity to vote and who on the date of the poll are at least 18 years of age. However, a person is not entitled to vote at a parliamentary election in any constituency in Northern Ireland unless he/she was resident in Northern Ireland during the whole of the period of three months ending on the qualifying date for that election. Also, no person can use his/her vote unless he/she is on the register of electors kept for the constituency. A person who is of voting age on the date of the poll at a parliamentary or local government election is entitled to vote, whether or not he/she was of voting age on the qualifying date. Accordingly, a qualified person will be entitled to be registered in a register of parliamentary electors or a register of local government electors if he/she will attain voting age within twelve months from the date on which the register is required to be published. Subject to certain conditions, the 1985 Act extends the franchise to British citizens overseas.

The register is prepared by the registration officer in each constituency in Great Britain. It is the registration officer's duty to have a house-to-house or other official inquiry made as to the persons entitled to be registered and to publish preliminary electors' lists showing the persons appearing to him/her to be entitled to be registered. Any person whose name is omitted may claim registration, and any person on the list may object to the inclusion therein of other persons' names; the registration officer determines the claims and objections.

Voters at a parliamentary or local government election must generally vote in person at the allotted polling station, except for those entitled to vote by post or at any polling station, and those for whom proxies have been appointed. Certain people can apply to be treated as absent voters at a parliamentary election and thus able to vote by post; among these are registered service voters, those unable by reason of blindness or other physical incapacity to go in person to the polling station, and those unable to go in person from their qualifying address to the polling station without making a journey by air or sea.

Unless entitled to vote by post, a person registered as a service voter may vote by proxy at a parliamentary or local government election. A proxy may also be appointed by a registered elector, where the registration officer is satisfied that the applicant's circumstances on the date of the poll are likely to be such that he/she cannot reasonably be expected to vote in person at the allotted polling station. The appointment of a person to vote as proxy at parliamentary elections has effect also for the purposes of local government elections.

The Probation Service

ENGLAND AND WALES

The Probation Service is employed in each area (55 in total) by an independent committee of justices and it provides a professional social work agency in the courts, with responsibility for a wide range of duties which include:
(a) a social enquiry service for the criminal courts
(b) provision of a range of non-custodial measures involving the supervision of offenders in the community
(c) supervisory aftercare for offenders released from custody, together with social work in penal establishments and help for the families of those serving sentences
(d) an enquiry, conciliation and supervision service in the divorce and domestic courts
(e) support for and promotion of preventive and containment measures in the community designed to reduce the level of crime and domestic breakdown
It is a direct grant service funded 80 per cent from the Home Office and 20 per cent from the relevant local authority.
Its national representative bodies are:

THE CENTRAL COUNCIL OF PROBATION COMMITTEES, 38 Belgrave Square, London SW1X 8NT. Tel: 071-245 9364. *Secretary*, I. Miles
THE ASSOCIATION OF CHIEF OFFICERS OF PROBATION, 20–30 Lawefield Lane, Wakefield WF2 8SP. Tel: 0924–361156. *General Secretary*, W. R. Weston
THE NATIONAL ASSOCIATION OF PROBATION OFFICERS, 3 Chivalry Road, London SW11 1HT. Tel: 071-223 4887. *General Secretary*, Ms J. McKnight

SCOTLAND

The probation service in Scotland is a statutory duty of local authorities under s. 27 of the Social Work (Scotland) Act 1968. Social workers have to supervise and provide advice, guidance and assistance to those persons living in their area who are subject to a court's supervision order. This is done by social workers as part of their normal duties and not by a separate probation staff.

Intellectual Property

COPYRIGHT

Copyright protects all original literary, dramatic, musical and artistic works, published editions of works, computer programs, sound recordings, films (including video) and broadcasts (including cable and satellite broadcasts). Under copyright the creators of these works can control the various ways in which their material may be exploited, the rights broadly covering copying, adapting, issuing copies to the public, performing in public, and broadcasting the material.

Copyright protection in the United Kingdom is automatic and there is no registration system. The normal term of copyright protection in literary, dramatic, musical and artistic works is the life of the author plus 50 years. Other forms of copyright usually last for 50 years or less.

The main international treaties protecting copyright are the Berne Convention for the Protection of Literary and Artistic Works, the Rome Convention for the Protection of Performers, Producers of Phonograms and Broadcasting Organizations, and the Universal Copyright Convention (UCC); the United Kingdom is a signatory to these conventions. Copyright material created by UK nationals or residents is protected in each country which is a member of the conventions by the national law of that country. A full list of participating countries may be obtained from the Patent Office.

LICENSING

Reproduction of copyright material without seeking permission in each instance is permitted under licence. In the UK the Copyright Licensing Agency, formed in 1982 by the Authors' Licensing and Collecting Society and the Publishers Licensing Society, licenses the reprographic copying of literary works. The International Federation of Reproduction Rights Organizations facilitates agreements between its member licensing agencies and on behalf of its members with organizations such as the World Intellectual Property Organization, UNESCO, the European Community and the Council of Europe.

LEGAL DEPOSIT

Publishers are legally obliged to send one copy of a new publication to each of the copyright deposit libraries within one month of publication. The aim of legal deposit is to keep a complete national archive of published works as a current reference and information source. The copyright deposit libraries are the British Library, the Bodleian Library in Oxford, Cambridge University Library, the National Library of Scotland, the National Library of Wales, and Trinity College Library in Dublin.

The duties of the British Library's Legal Deposit Office are split between two locations. Books and other publications are deposited at Boston Spa, and newspapers and periodicals at the Newspaper Legal Deposit Office in London. All publications for the other four copyright libraries in the UK are dealt with by the Agent for Copyright Libraries.

PATENTS

A patent is a document issued by the Patent Office relating to an invention and giving the proprietor monopoly rights, effective within the United Kingdom (including the Isle of Man). In return the patentee pays a fee to cover the costs of processing the patent and publicly discloses details of the invention.

To qualify for a patent an invention must be new, must exhibit an inventive step, and must be capable of industrial application. The patent is valid for a maximum of 20 years from the date on which the application was filed, subject to payment of annual fees from the end of the fourth year.

The Patent Office, established in 1852, is responsible for ensuring that all stages of an application comply with the Patents Act 1977, and that the invention meets the criteria for a patent. Patent Office Examiners check that the invention is new and innovative by searching previously published documents on the Patent Office databank, which contains details of some two million British patents, together with published international and European applications. The contents of the databank and of the Science Reference Library, which developed from the library established at the Patent Office, are available to the public.

The World Intellectual Property Organization (WIPO), a United Nations body, is responsible for administering many of the international conventions on intellectual property. The Patent Co-operation Treaty allows inventors to file a single application for patent rights in some or all of the 60 contracting states. This application is searched by an International Searching Authority and published by the International Bureau of WIPO. It may also be the subject of an (optional) international preliminary examination. Applicants must then deal directly with the patent offices in the countries where they are seeking patent rights.

The European Patent Convention, linked to the Patent Co-operation Treaty, allows inventors to obtain patent rights in all 17 contracting states by filing a single European patent application which is processed by the European Patent Office (EPO). Once granted, the patent is subject to national laws in each signatory country. To comply with security requirements, an applicant resident in the UK must file a European patent application with the UK Patent Office unless the Patent Office gives permission for it to be filed directly with the EPO. The EPO office for international patent documentation (Inpadoc) is based in Vienna and acts as an information, collection and reference centre for patent offices around the world.

TRADE AND SERVICE MARKS

The trade mark and the service mark are a means of identification, whether a word or device or a combination of both, which enable traders to make their goods or services readily distinguishable from those supplied by other traders. Registration prevents other traders using the same or a similar trade or service mark for products or services for which the mark is registered.

In order to qualify for registration in the United Kingdom

a mark should be distinctive but it should not describe the product or use geographical, laudatory or any non-distinctive expressions. It should be non-deceptive and not easily confused with a mark that has already been registered for the same or similar goods or services.

Trade and service marks are registered at the Patent Office. The Trade Marks Registry was established at the Patent Office in 1876, and the standards for registration have remained essentially unchanged since then. The relevant current legislation is the Trade Marks Act 1938 (as amended).

It is possible to obtain an international trade mark registration, effective in over 30 countries, under the Madrid Agreement. Since, however, the UK is not a party to this agreement, British companies are unable to use this system. A White Paper setting out the UK Government's proposals for reforming the law on trade marks, including adherence to the Madrid system, was published in 1990; the proposals have not yet been implemented because parliamentary time has not been available.

There is not, as yet, a trade mark registration organization in Europe which is administered by one body; a trader must apply to each country individually for registration, though Belgium, Luxembourg and the Netherlands have a common system. Proposals have been put forward for a European Community trade marks office which would be separate from each of the national registries.

DESIGN REGISTRATION

Design registration protects the outward appearance of an article including any decorative ornamentation that appears on it. It does not protect the materials or methods used to make the article, or its function; shapes dictated solely by the function of the article are specifically excluded. Artistic matter, such as sculpture, medals, wall plaques, etc., are generally covered by copyright and are not eligible for design registration.

In order to qualify for registration a design must be new and materially different from other published designs in the United Kingdom at the date of application. To obtain a valid registration the proprietor must apply before selling or offering for sale articles manufactured in quantity or piece goods bearing the design. Registration lasts for five years, after which additional fees are payable for further five-year registration periods up to a maximum of 25 years. Only the proprietor or proprietors may apply for design registration.

The Designs Registry, part of the Patent Office, was set up early in the nineteenth century in response to a growing demand from Britain's textile manufacturers for statutory protection for the design of their products. Nowadays many applications for design registrations are for toys and games. The current legislation is the Registered Designs Act 1949 (as amended).

There is no international design registry available to UK applicants, so separate applications must be made in each country in which protection is sought. Under the terms of the Paris Convention for the Protection of Industrial Property, if application for registration is first made in a convention country, priority to protect the same design in any other convention country can be claimed up to six months later. The UK is a convention country.

There are a number of countries, mainly members of the Commonwealth, which have enacted legislation whereby the UK registration of a design is accepted as an independent registration in the country concerned.

ORGANIZATIONS

AGENT FOR THE COPYRIGHT LIBRARIES, 100 Euston Street, London NW1 2HQ. Tel: 071-380 0240. *Agent* A. T. Smail

AUTHORS' LICENSING AND COLLECTING SOCIETY, 33 Alfred Place, London WC1E 7DP. Tel: 071-255 2034

CHARTERED INSTITUTE OF PATENT AGENTS, Staple Inn Buildings, London WC1V 7PZ. Tel: 071-405 9450

COPYRIGHT LICENSING AGENCY LTD, 90 Tottenham Court Road, London WIP 9HE. Tel: 071-436 5931

DESIGNS REGISTRY, The Patent Office, Cardiff Road, Newport, Gwent NP9 1RH. Tel: 0633-814000

EUROPEAN PATENT OFFICE, *Headquarters*, Erhardstrasse 27, D-8000 Munich 2, Germany

INPADOC, Schottenfeldgasse 29, Pastfach 82, A-1072, Vienna, Austria

INTERNATIONAL FEDERATION OF REPRODUCTION RIGHTS ORGANIZATIONS (IFFRO), Goethestrasse 49, D-8000 Munich 2, Germany

LEGAL DEPOSIT OFFICE, The British Library, Boston Spa, Wetherby, West Yorkshire LS23 7BY. Tel: 0937-546600

NEWSPAPER LEGAL DEPOSIT OFFICE, The British Library, 120 Colindale Avenue, London NW9 5LF. Tel: 071-323 7353

THE PATENT OFFICE, Cardiff Road, Newport, Gwent NP9 1RH. Tel: 0633-814000

PUBLISHERS LICENSING SOCIETY, 90 Tottenham Court Road, London WIP 9HE. Tel: 071-436 5931

SCIENCE REFERENCE LIBRARY, 25 Southampton Buildings, London WC2A 1AW. Tel: 071-323 7494

TRADE MARKS REGISTRY, The Patent Office, Cardiff Road, Newport, Gwent NP9 1RH. Tel: 0633-814000

WORLD INTELLECTUAL PROPERTY ORGANIZATION (WIPO), 34 chemin des Colombettes, 1211 Geneva 20, Switzerland

The Media

Broadcasting

FUTURE OF THE BBC

The BBC's present charter expires in 1996. In anticipation of this the Government has initiated a debate about the future of public service broadcasting.

A Green Paper, *The Future of the BBC*, was presented to Parliament by the Secretary of State for National Heritage (Peter Brooke) on 24 November 1992. The Green Paper reaffirmed the role of the BBC as a major broadcasting organization with special responsibilities for public service broadcasting. It outlined a range of options for change when the BBC's royal charter comes up for renewal in 1996, and invited comments by 30 April 1993; a White Paper will be published in 1994.

The Green Paper questioned all aspects of the BBC's role, objectives, operations and financing, and specifically:
- what should be the aims of public service broadcasting in the future?
- should the BBC continue to broadcast a comprehensive range of programmes, or concentrate on programmes unlikely to be broadcast by other television channels or radio stations?
- should all the current BBC television and radio channels be retained?
- should the BBC continue to carry out all its other current functions, e.g. arts patronage, transmission, research and development, training and publishing?
- how can the BBC's organization become more flexible and efficient?
- should the BBC continue to be funded only by the licence fee; if so, should the present system continue unaltered? If not, what other methods could be used?
- what should be the role of the governors of the BBC?

The BBC published a charter review document, *Extending Choice*, on 26 November 1992. The director-general designate of the BBC (John Birt) said that a series of public meetings would be held to discuss the role and future of the BBC. The document outlined the BBC's view of its future and made the following points:
- the expansion of commercial broadcasting serves more clearly to limit and define the role of public service broadcasting
- the BBC's role should be to guarantee access to programmes which might be at risk in a purely commercial market. Its activities should therefore concentrate on four key areas: news and current affairs; programmes reflecting both traditional and contemporary British culture, including drama, comedy, the arts, sport and children's programmes; educational programmes; and programmes which communicate between the United Kingdom and the rest of the world (including World Service radio and television), programmes which reflect the rest of the world to British audiences, and an increasing involvement in international programme sales and co-productions. Material widely available on commercial channels should be phased out

- the BBC must ensure that its programming is distinctive, intelligent and innovative, rather than aiming at attracting a large audience for its own sake
- *licence fee income should be used exclusively by the BBC and should not be distributed to other broadcasters by a Public Service Broadcasting Council
- BBC1 should be the main television channel, with BBC2 being more innovative and experimental. Radios 3 and 4 should appeal to a wider audience, and Radios 1 and 2 and BBC local radio should broadcast more spoken word programmes in order to be distinctive
- the BBC should continue to be funded mainly by the licence fee, but should also increase its role in activities which supplement its licence fee income
- the *Producer Choice* scheme will allow programme-makers to choose whether to use internal BBC resources or those of outside providers
- the BBC should continue with functions such as patronage of the arts, research and development, training
- the role of the BBC's governors should be more clearly defined and separated from that of the Board of Management

On 27 May 1993, after a period of consultation and debate, the BBC published *Responding to the Green Paper*. It expanded on *Extending Choice* and took into account the results of consultation with viewers and listeners and of a MORI poll commissioned by *Reader's Digest*. It also included a separate report, prepared by McKinsey & Co., comparing the political, commercial, financial and regulatory backgrounds of public service broadcasters from 11 countries.

Responding to the Green Paper made the following main points:
- the public debate had revealed strong support for the continuation of a publicly-funded BBC independent of government, party political and commercial pressures and more responsive to the needs of its audience
- the BBC's principal objectives should be to provide programmes solely with viewers and listeners in mind; to ensure the highest quality, diversity and choice of programmes; to schedule its services to deliver programmes of quality to large audiences and maximize choice at peak times; to develop and apply the very best programme-making skills; to maintain high standards of editorial integrity and independence; to reflect regional diversity; to ensure efficiency and value for money; to reflect the UK's traditions, history, culture and values; to bring credit to Britain; and to ensure full and direct accountability to licence payers
- the BBC had set up a Programme Strategy Review to ensure that its programmes would embody the principles set out in *Extending Choice*; the results of the review would be published at the end of 1993
- the BBC was committed to further developing its commercial potential in both domestic and international markets, within new guidelines to ensure that it would compete fairly and that its commercial policies would be consistent with its public purpose
- the licence fee should continue to provide the greater part of the BBC's income, since it is the only method of funding able to guarantee freedom from commercial pressures to maximize audience ratings or political influence
- the BBC would ensure that in future the roles of its governors, board and management would be clearly differentiated

TELEVISION

The British Broadcasting Corporation (*see* page 291) is responsible for public service broadcasting in the United Kingdom. Its constitution and finances are governed by royal charter and by a licence and agreement. Its role is to provide high-quality programmes with wide-ranging appeal that educate, inform and entertain.

The Independent Television Commission (*see* page 321) is the regulator and licenser for independent television companies. The ITV franchises for the 15 regional companies and for breakfast television came up for renewal at the end of 1992; new ten-year licences from January 1993 were allocated by the ITC in 1991.

A new independent national television channel was due to be established by the autumn of 1993, but the ITC decided not to award the licence to Channel Five Holdings Ltd, the only applicant. The ITC is now examining further options, including re-advertising the licence.

All channels are broadcast in colour on 625 lines UHF from a network of transmitting stations which are owned and operated by National Transcommunications Ltd. Transmissions are available to more than 99 per cent of the population.

BBC TELEVISION
Television Centre, Wood Lane, London W12 7RJ
Tel 081-743 8000

The BBC's experiments in television broadcasting started in 1929 and in 1936 the BBC began the world's first public service of high-definition television from Alexandra Palace.

The BBC broadcasts two national television services, BBC 1 and BBC 2 (outside England these services are designated BBC Scotland on 1, BBC Scotland on 2, BBC 1 Northern Ireland, BBC 2 Northern Ireland, BBC Wales on 1 and BBC Wales on 2).

BBC WORLD SERVICE TELEVISION
80 Wood Lane, London W12 0TT
Tel 081-576 2000

BBC World Service Television is a wholly-owned subsidiary of the BBC, established in March 1991 to create a global television news service and assume responsibility for all the BBC's satellite television interests. Adopting the BBC's existing European subscription channel, BBC TV Europe, it developed it into an entertainment channel featuring the best of BBC1 and BBC2 programming. In November 1991 it launched the BBC's first 24-hour news and information channel throughout Asia. The service offers international news bulletins every hour, world weather and business reports, and a range of feature programmes including current affairs and documentary series. This channel was introduced to Africa in April 1992, and in November 1992 'CBC Newsworld' began rebroadcasting the company's news programmes in Canada. Programme sales are made to Russia and various countries in eastern Europe as well as to several airlines for their in-flight service.

BBC World Service Television is entirely self-funding; it receives no revenue from the British licence fee or the World Service parliamentary grant-in-aid.

INDEPENDENT TELEVISION

INDEPENDENT TELEVISION NETWORK CENTRE
200 Gray's Inn Road, London WC1X 8HF
Tel 071-843 8000

The ITV Network Centre is wholly owned by the ITV companies and undertakes the commissioning and schedul-

ing of those television programmes which are shown across the ITV network. As successor to the ITV Association it also provides a range of services to the ITV companies where a common approach is required.

Programmes for the network are commissioned from the ITV companies as well as from independent producers. As the Centre has no legal status as a broadcaster, commissions must then be contracted jointly with one of the ITV companies. The scheduling of all networked programmes is submitted for general approval to the network companies' heads of broadcasting, who sit on the ITV Broadcast Board.

ITV's governing body is Council, comprising the heads of the ITV companies and chaired by the chief executive of the Network Centre.

Chief Executive, A. Quinn
Network Director, M. Plantin

INDEPENDENT TELEVISION NETWORK COMPANIES
ANGLIA TELEVISION (*eastern England*), Anglia House, Norwich NR1 3JG. Tel: 0603-615151
BORDER TELEVISION PLC (*the Borders*), Television Centre, Carlisle CA1 3NT. Tel: 0228-25101
CARLTON TELEVISION LTD (*London (weekdays)*), 101 St Martin's Lane, London WC2N 4AZ. Tel: 071-240 4000
CENTRAL INDEPENDENT TELEVISION (*the Midlands*), Central House, Broad Street, Birmingham B1 2JP. Tel: 021-643 9898
CHANNEL TELEVISION (*Channel Islands*), The Television Centre, St Helier, Jersey JE2 3ZD. Tel: 0534-73999
GRAMPIAN TELEVISION (*northern Scotland*), Queen's Cross, Aberdeen AB9 2XJ. Tel: 0224-646464
GRANADA TELEVISION (*north-west England*), Granada TV Centre, Quay Street, Manchester M60 9EA. Tel: 061-832 7211
HTV (*Wales and western England*), HTV Wales, Television Centre, Cardiff CF5 6XJ. Tel: 0222-590590
LONDON WEEKEND TELEVISION (*London (weekends)*), London Television Centre, Upper Ground, London SE1 9LT. Tel: 071-620 1620
MERIDIAN BROADCASTING LTD (*south and south-east England*), 8 Montague Close, London SE1 9RD. Tel: 071-378 7898
SCOTTISH TELEVISION (*central Scotland*), Cowcaddens, Glasgow G2 3PR. Tel: 041-332 9999
TYNE TEES TELEVISION (*north-east England*), The Television Centre, City Road, Newcastle upon Tyne NE1 2AL. Tel: 091-261 0181
ULSTER TELEVISION (*Northern Ireland*), Havelock House, Ormeau Road, Belfast BT7 1EB. Tel: 0232-328122
WESTCOUNTRY TELEVISION LTD (*south-west England*), c/o Brittany Ferries, Millbay Docks, Plymouth PL1 3EW. Tel: 0752-253322
YORKSHIRE TELEVISION LTD (*Yorkshire*), The Television Centre, Leeds LS3 1JS. Tel: 0532-438283

OTHER INDEPENDENT TELEVISION COMPANIES
CHANNEL FOUR TELEVISION COMPANY LTD, 60 Charlotte Street, London W1P 2AX. Tel: 071-631 4444. Provides a service to the UK except Wales, and is charged to cater for interests under-represented by the ITV network companies
GMTV LTD (*breakfast television*), The London Television Centre, Upper Ground, London SE1 9LT. Tel: 071-827 7000
INDEPENDENT TELEVISION NEWS LTD, ITN House, 200 Gray's Inn Road, London WC1X 8XD. Tel: 071-833 3000

TELETEXT UK LTD, 101 Farm Lane, London SW6 1QJ. Tel: 071-386 5000. Provides teletext services for the ITV companies and Channel 4

WELSH FOURTH CHANNEL AUTHORITY (Sianel Pedwar Cymru), Parc Ty Glas, Llanishen, Cardiff CF4 5DU. Tel: 0222-747444. S4C schedules Welsh language programmes and also relays most Channel 4 programmes

DIRECT BROADCASTING BY SATELLITE TELEVISION

BRITISH SKY BROADCASTING, 6 Centaurs Business Park, Grant Way, Isleworth, Middx. TW7 5QD. Tel: 071-705 3000. Broadcasts six channels (*Sky One, Sky News, Sky Sports, The Movie Channel, Sky Movies Plus* and *Sky Movies Gold*). A multi-channel package is to be launched in autumn 1993.

RADIO

The BBC provides both national and local radio services. The Radio Authority (*see* page 346) is the regulator and licenser for independent radio companies.

Under the Broadcasting Act 1990, the Radio Authority was empowered to allocate licences for three national radio stations. The first national licence was awarded to Classic FM in September 1991 and the second was awarded to Independent Music Radio (now Virgin 1215) in April 1992. The third national licence will be advertised by early 1994.

Three out of five new independent regional local radio licences have now been awarded (*see* page 683); the licences for the West Midlands and Central Scotland have not yet been awarded.

Since January 1991 the Authority has awarded more than 35 new local radio licences, and is continuing to advertise about one new licence a month. By the end of 1993 it will also have re-advertised 54 local licences, with a further 74 to be re-advertised by the end of 1995. A total of 48 applications has been received by the Authority for two new and six re-advertised London licences, and a decision on the award of these licences will be made in autumn 1993.

BBC RADIO

Broadcasting House, Portland Place, London W1A 1AA
Tel 071-580 4468

BBC Radio broadcasts five national services to the United Kingdom, Isle of Man and the Channel Islands; a 24-hour radio news network will be broadcast from early 1994 on a frequency to be decided. There is also a tier of national regional services in Wales, Scotland and Northern Ireland and 39 local radio stations in England and the Channel Islands. In Wales there are two regional services based on the Welsh and English languages respectively.

The national services are:

RADIO 1 (Pop and rock music) – 24 hours a day. *Frequencies:* FM 97.6–99.8 MHz, coverage 96%; MW 1053 khz/285m and 1089 khz/275m, plus two local fillers, 6 a.m. to 12 midnight only

RADIO 2 (Popular music, entertainment, comedy and the arts) – 24 hours a day. *Frequency:* FM 88–90.2 MHz, coverage 98%

RADIO 3 (Classical music, drama, documentaries, poetry, and cricket in season) – 6.55 a.m.–12.35 a.m. daily. *Frequencies:* FM 90.2–92.4 MHz, coverage 98%

RADIO 4 (News, documentaries, drama and entertainment) – 5.55 a.m. to 12.40 a.m. daily. *Frequencies:* FM in

England 92.4–94.6 MHz, elsewhere 92.4–96.1 and 103.5–105 MHz, coverage 97%; LW 198khz/1515m, plus eight local fillers on MW

RADIO 5 (Speech radio for the family, with sport, education, children and youth programmes and elements of World Service) – 6 a.m.–12.05 a.m. daily. *Frequencies:* MW 693 khz/433m and 909 khz/330m, plus one local filler

The national regional services are:

RADIO SCOTLAND *Frequencies:* MW 810 khz/370m plus two local fillers; FM 92.4–96.1 and 103.5–105 MHz, coverage 94%. Local programmes on FM as above: RADIO ABERDEEN (also MW 990 khz/303m); RADIO HIGHLAND; RADIO NAN GAIDHEAL; RADIO ORKNEY; RADIO SHETLAND; RADIO SOLWAY (also MW 585 khz/513m); RADIO TWEED

RADIO ULSTER *Frequencies:* MW 1341 khz/224m, plus two local fillers; FM 92.4–96.1 MHz, coverage 96%. Local programmes on RADIO FOYLE *Frequencies:* MW 792 khz/379m; FM 93.1 MHz

RADIO WALES *Frequency:* MW 882 khz/340m plus two local fillers, coverage 96% (day) and 63% (night). Local programmes on RADIO CLWYD *Frequency:* MW 657 khz/457m

RADIO CYMRU (Welsh-language) *Frequencies:* FM 92.4–96.1 and 103.5–105 MHz, coverage 96%

BBC LOCAL RADIO STATIONS

There are 39 local stations serving England and the Channel Islands:

BBC 3 COUNTIES RADIO, PO Box 3CR, Luton, Beds. LU1 5XL. Tel: 0582-441000. *Frequencies:* MW 258/476 m, 1161/630 kHz, 95.5/103.8FM

BERKSHIRE, Broadcasting House, 42A Portman Road, Reading, Berks. RG3 1NB. Tel: 0734-567056. *Frequencies:* 94.6/95.4/104.1/104.4 FM

BRISTOL, 3 Tyndalls Park Road, Bristol BS8 1PP. Tel: 0272-741111. *Frequencies:* MW 194m, 1548 kHz, 95.5/104.6 FM

CAMBRIDGESHIRE, Broadcasting House, 104 Hills Road, Cambridge CB2 1LD. Tel: 0223-259696. *Frequencies:* MW 207/292m, 1449/1026 kHz, 96.0/95.7 FM

CLEVELAND, PO Box 1548, Broadcasting House, Newport Road, Middlesbrough, Cleveland TS1 5DG. Tel: 0642-225211. *Frequencies:* 95.0/95.8 FM

CORNWALL, Phoenix Wharf, Truro, Cornwall TR1 1UA. Tel: 0872-75421. *Frequencies:* MW 476/457m, 630/657 kHz, 95.2/96.0/103.9 FM

CUMBRIA, Annetwell Street, Carlisle CA3 8BB. Tel: 0228-31661. *Frequencies:* MW 397/206/358m, 756/1458/837 kHz, 95.2/95.6/96.1/104.2 FM

CWR (COVENTRY AND WARWICKSHIRE RADIO), 25 Warwick Road, Coventry CV1 2WR. Tel: 0203-559911. *Frequencies:* 94.8/103.7 FM; 104 FM (Nuneaton area)

DERBY, 56 St Helen's Street, Derby DE1 3HY. Tel: 0332-361111. *Frequencies:* MW 269m, 1116 kHz, 94.2/95.3/104.5 FM

DEVON, PO Box 100, Walnut Gardens, St David's, Exeter EX4 4DB. Tel: 0392-215651. *Frequencies:* MW 351/303/206/375m, 855/990/1458/801 kHz, 103.4/96.0/95.8/94.8 FM

ESSEX, PO Box 765, 198 New London Road, Chelmsford CM2 9AB. Tel: 0245-262393. *Frequencies:* MW 392/196/412m, 765/729/1530 kHz, 103.5/95.3 FM

GLOUCESTERSHIRE, London Road, Gloucester GL1 1SW. Tel: 0452-308585. *Frequencies:* 95.0/95.8/104.7 FM

GLR (GREATER LONDON RADIO), 35C Marylebone High Street, London W1A 4LG. Tel: 071-224 2424. *Frequencies:* MW 206m, 1458 kHz, 94.9 FM

GMR (GREATER MANCHESTER RADIO), New Broadcasting House, Oxford Road, Manchester M60 ISJ. Tel: 061-200 2000. *Frequencies:* MW 206m, 1458 kHz, 95.1 FM

GUERNSEY, Commerce House, Les Banques, St Peter Port, Guernsey. Tel: 0481-728977. *Frequencies:* MW 269m, 1116 kHz, 93.2 FM

HEREFORD AND WORCESTER, 43 Broad Street, Hereford HR4 9HH; and Hylton Road, Worcester WR2 5ww. Tel: 0905-748485. *Frequencies:* MW 406/366 m, 738/ 819 kHz, 104.6/104.0/94.7 FM

HUMBERSIDE, 9 Chapel Street, Hull HUI 3NU. Tel: 0482-23232. *Frequencies:* MW 202m, 1485 kHz, 95.9 FM

JERSEY, Broadcasting House, Rouge Bouillon, St Helier, Jersey. Tel: 0534-70000. *Frequencies:* MW 292m, 1026 kHz, 88.8 FM

KENT, Sun Pier, Chatham, Kent ME4 4EZ. Tel: 0634-830505. *Frequencies:* MW 290/388/187m, 1035/774/ 1602 kHz, 96.7 FM

LANCASHIRE, 20–26 Darwen Street, Blackburn BB2 2EA. Tel: 0254-62411. *Frequencies:* MW 351/193m, 855/1557 kHz, 95.5/104.5/103.9 FM

LEEDS, Broadcasting House, Woodhouse Lane, Leeds LS2 9PN. Tel: 0532-442131. *Frequencies:* MW 388m, 774 kHz, 92.4/95.3/103.9 FM

LEICESTER, Epic House, Charles Street, Leicester LEI 3SH. Tel: 0533-516688. *Frequencies:* MW 358m, 837 kHz, 104.9 FM

LINCOLNSHIRE, Radion Buildings, Newport, Lincoln LNI 3BU. Tel: 0522-511411. *Frequencies:* MW 358m, 837 kHz, 104.9 FM

MERSEYSIDE, 55 Paradise Street, Liverpool LI 3BP. Tel: 051-708 5500. *Frequencies:* MW 202m, 1485 kHz, 95.8 FM

NEWCASTLE, Broadcasting Centre, Barrack Road, Fenham, Newcastle upon Tyne NE99 IRN. Tel: 091-232 4141. *Frequencies:* MW 206m, 1458 kHz, 95.4/104.4/96.0 FM

NORFOLK, Norfolk Tower, Surrey Street, Norwich NRI 3PA. Tel: 0603-617411. *Frequencies:* MW 351/343m, 855/ 873 kHz, 95.1/104.4 FM

NORTHAMPTON, Broadcasting House, Abington Street, Northampton NNI 2BH. Tel: 0604-239100. *Frequencies:* 104.2/106.3 FM

NOTTINGHAM, York House, Mansfield Road, Nottingham NGI 3JB. Tel: 0602-415161. *Frequencies:* MW 189/197m, 1584/1521 kHz, 103.8/95.5 FM

OXFORD, 269 Banbury Road, Oxford OX2 7DW. Tel: 0865-311444. *Frequency:* 95.2 FM

SHEFFIELD, Ashdell Grove, 60 Westbourne Road, Sheffield SIO 2QU. Tel: 0742-686185. *Frequencies:* MW 290m, 1035 kHz, 94.7/104.1/88.6 FM

SHROPSHIRE, 2–4 Boscobel Drive, Shrewsbury SYI 3TT. Tel: 0743-248484. *Frequencies:* MW 189m, 1584 kHz, 95.0/96.0 FM

SOLENT, Broadcasting House, Havelock Road, Southampton SOI OXR. Tel: 0703-631311. *Frequencies:* MW 221/300m, 999/1359 kHz, 96.1 FM

STOKE-ON-TRENT, Conway House, Cheapside, Hanley, Stoke-on-Trent STI IJJ. Tel: 0782-208080. *Frequencies:* MW 200m, 1503 kHz, 94.6 FM

SUFFOLK, Broadcasting House, St Matthew's Street, Ipswich IPI 3EP. Tel: 0473-250000. *Frequencies:* 95.5/ 103.9/104.6 FM

SURREY, Broadcasting House, Guildford, Surrey GU2 5AP. Tel: 0483-306113. *Frequency:* 104.6 FM

SUSSEX, Marlborough Place, Brighton BNI ITU. Tel: 0273-680231. *Frequencies:* MW 202/258/219m, 1485/1161/ 1368 kHz, 95.0/95.1/95.3/104.5/104.0 FM

WILTSHIRE SOUND, Broadcasting House, 56–58 Prospect Place, Swindon SNI 3RW. Tel: 0793-513626. *Frequencies:* MW 225/219m, 1332/1368 kHz, 103.6/103.4/103.5 FM

WM (WEST MIDLANDS), Pebble Mill Road, Birmingham B5 7SD. Tel: 021-414 8484. *Frequencies:* MW 362/206m, 828/1458 kHz, 95.6 FM

YORK, 20 Bootham Row, York YO3 7BR. Tel: 0904-641351. *Frequencies:* MW 450/238m, 666/1260 kHz, 103.7/ 104.3/95.5 FM

BBC WORLD SERVICE
Bush House, Strand, London WC2R 4PX
Tel 071-240 3456

The BBC World Service broadcasts over 870 hours of programmes a week in 39 languages including English. Eighty-four transmitters are used, 37 of them in the UK and 47 at relay stations overseas. In addition the World Service supplies about 362 hours of programmes a week for other radio stations.

WORLD SERVICE IN ENGLISH, 24 hours a day, directed to all parts of the world, and with additional streams of programmes specially designated for audiences in Africa, south-east Asia, Europe, the Caribbean and the Falklands at appropriate peak listening times

AFRICAN SERVICE, which broadcasts in Swahili, Somali and Hausa

ARABIC SERVICE, on the air for ten and a half hours a day to the Middle East and North Africa

CENTRAL EUROPEAN SERVICE, in Czech, Slovak, Hungarian, Polish and Finnish

CHINESE SERVICE, in Cantonese and Mandarin

EASTERN SERVICE, which broadcasts in Bengali, Hindi, Nepali, Pashto, Persian, Sinhalese, Tamil and Urdu

FRENCH AND PORTUGUESE SERVICE, directed to Europe and Africa

GERMAN SERVICE, directed to Germany, Austria, and German-speaking Switzerland

LATIN AMERICAN SERVICE, in Spanish and Portuguese

RUSSIAN AND UKRAINIAN SERVICE, on the air for eight and a quarter hours a day in Russian and one hour a day in Ukrainian

SOUTH-EAST ASIAN SERVICE, in Burmese, Indonesian, Thai and Vietnamese.

SOUTH-EAST EUROPEAN SERVICE, in Albanian, Bulgarian, Romanian, Serbian, Croatian, Slovene, Greek and Turkish

BBC ENGLISH teaches English to learners outside Britain through radio, television and a wide range of published courses

BBC MONITORING provides regional summaries and a teleprinted news service from the output of overseas radio and television stations

TOPICAL TAPES provides a variety of programmes on tape for overseas radio stations and produces 'Caribbean Report' and 'Calling the Falklands'

BBC TRANSCRIPTION produces and sells to overseas radio stations recorded programmes drawn from the whole range of BBC Radio

INDEPENDENT RADIO

INDEPENDENT NATIONAL RADIO STATIONS

CLASSIC FM, Academic House, 24–28 Oval Road, London NWI 7DQ. Tel: 071-284 3000. 24 hours a day. *Frequencies:* 99.9–101.9 FM

VIRGIN 1215, 1 Golden Square, London WIR 4DJ. Tel: 071-434 1215. 24 hours a day. *Frequencies:* MW 241/245/247/ 251 m, 1242/1266/1215/1197 kHz

INDEPENDENT REGIONAL LOCAL RADIO STATIONS
(from September 1994)

GALAXY RADIO (*Severn Estuary*), Broadcast Centre,
Portland Square, Bristol BS2 8RZ. Tel: 0272-240111

JAZZ FM (*North-west*), The Jazz House, 26–27 Castlereagh
Street, London W1H 5YR. Tel: 071–706 4100.

RADIO NORTH-EAST (*North-east*), 63 Woodbine Road,
Gosforth, Newcastle upon Tyne NE3 1DE. Tel: 091-285
7426

INDEPENDENT LOCAL RADIO STATIONS

AIRE FM, PO Box 2000, Leeds LS3 1LR. Tel: 0532-
452299. *Frequency:* 96.3 FM

THE BAY, PO Box 969, St George's Quay, Lancaster LA1
3LD. Tel: 0524-848747. *Frequencies:* 96.9/103.2 FM

BEACON RADIO, 267 Tettenhall Road, Wolverhampton
WV6 0DQ. Tel: 0902-757211. *Frequency:* 97.2/103.1 FM

BREEZE AM, PO Box 300, Southend-on-Sea, Essex SS1 1SY.
Tel: 0702-430966. *Frequency:* MW 221/209m, 1359/1431
kHz

BRMB FM, Aston Road North, Birmingham B6 4BX. Tel:
021-359 4481. *Frequency:* 96.4 FM

BROADLAND FM, St George's Plain, 47–49 Colegate,
Norwich NR3 1DB. Tel: 0603-630621. *Frequencies:* MW
260m, 1152 kHz, 102.4 FM

BRUNEL CLASSIC GOLD, PO Box 2000, Swindon SN4 7EX.
Tel: 0793-848600; PO Box 2000, Bristol BS99 7SN. Tel:
0272-279911. *Frequencies:* MW 238m, 1260 kHz (Bristol);
258m, 1161 kHz (Swindon); 320m, 936 kHz (West Wilts)

BUZZ FM, The Spencers, 20 Augusta Street, Hockley,
Birmingham B18 6JA. Tel: 021-236 4888. *Frequency:* 102.4
FM

CAPITAL RADIO PLC, Euston Tower, London NW1 3DR.
Tel: 071-608 6080. *Frequencies:* MW 194m, 1548 kHz,
95.8 FM

CENTRAL FM, Stirling Enterprise Park, Kerse Road,
Stirling FK7 7YJ. Tel: 0786-451188. *Frequency:* 96.7 FM

CFM, PO Box 964, Carlisle, Cumbria CA1 3NG. Tel: 0228-
818964. *Frequency:* 96.4 FM

CHANNEL 103, 6 Tunnell Street, St Helier, Jersey JE2 4LU.
Tel: 0543-888103. *Frequency:* 103 FM

CHILTERN RADIO PLC, Broadcast Centre, Chiltern Road,
Dunstable, Bedfordshire LU6 1HQ. Tel: 0582-666001.
Frequencies: 362m, 828 kHz, 97.6 FM(Luton), 379m, 792
kHz, 96.9 FM (Bedford)

CHOICE FM, 16–18 Trinity Gardens, London SW9 8DP.
Tel: 071-738 7969. *Frequency:* 96.9 FM

CITY FM, PO Box 967, Liverpool L69 1TQ. Tel: 051-227
5100. *Frequency:* 96.7 FM

CLYDE 1 and 2, Clydebank Business Park, Clydebank,
Glasgow G81 2RX. Tel: 041-306 2200. *Frequencies:* FM
261m, 1152 kHz, 102.5 FM

CN FM (Cambridge and Newmarket), PO Box 1000, The
Vision Park, Chivers Way, Histon, Cambridge CB4 4WW.
Tel: 0223-235255. *Frequencies:* 103.0/97.4 FM

COLCHESTER FM, East Anglian Radio, 47–49 Colegate,
Norwich NR3 1DB. Tel: 0603-630621. (From autumn
1993.)

COOL FM, Newtownards, Co. Down BT23 4ES. Tel: 0247-
815555. *Frequency:* 97.4 FM

COUNTY SOUND AM, Broadfield House, Brighton Road,
Crawley, W. Sussex RH11 9TT. Tel: 0293-519161.
Frequencies: MW 203/197m, 1476/1521 kHz

DEVONAIR RADIO, 35–37 St David's Hill, Exeter EX4
4DA. Tel: 0392-430703. *Frequencies:* MW 450m,
666 kHz, 97.0 FM (Exeter); 314m, 954 kHz, 96.4 FM
(Torbay); 103 FM (East Devon)

DOWNTOWN RADIO, Kiltonga Industrial Estate,
Newtownards, Co. Down BT23 4ES. Tel: 0247-815555.
Frequencies: MW 293m, 1026 kHz, 96.6/96.4/102.4 FM

ESSEX RADIO PLC, Radio House, Clifftown Road,
Southend-on-Sea, Essex SS1 1SX. Tel: 0702-333711.
Frequencies: 96.3 FM (Southend), 102.6 FM (Chelmsford)

FOX FM, Brush House, Pony Road, Cowley, Oxford OX4
2XR. Tel: 0865-748787. *Frequencies:* 102.6 FM (Oxford);
97.4 FM (Banbury)

GALAXY RADIO, 25 Portland Square, Bristol BS2 8RZ. Tel:
0272-240111. *Frequency:* 97.2 FM

GEM-AM, 29–31 Castle Gate, Nottingham NG1 7AP. Tel:
0602-581731. *Frequencies:* MW 238m, 1260 kHz
(Leicester); 300m, 999 kHz (Nottingham); 317m, 945
kHz (Derby)

GREAT NORTH RADIO, Newcastle upon Tyne NE99 1BB.
Tel: 091-496 0377. *Frequencies:* MW 260m, 1152 kHz
(Tyne and Wear); 256m, 1170 kHz (Teesside)

GREAT YORKSHIRE RADIO, PO Box 777, Sheffield, Hull
and Bradford. Tel: 0742-852121. *Frequencies:* MW 194/
230/303m, 1548/1305/990 kHz (S. Yorks); 235/196m,
1278/1530 kHz (W. Yorks); 258m, 1161 kHz
(Humberside)

GWR FM (EAST), PO Box 2000, Swindon SN4 7EX. Tel:
0793-853222. *Frequencies:* 96.5 FM (Marlborough); 97.2
FM (Swindon); 102.2 FM (West Wilts)

GWR FM (WEST), PO Box 2000, Bristol BS99 7SN. Tel:
0272-279900. *Frequency:* 96.3/103.0 FM

HALLAM FM, Radio House, 900 Herries Road,
Hillsborough, Sheffield S6 1RH. Tel: 0742-853333.
Frequencies: 97.4 FM (Sheffield); 96.1 FM (Rotherham);
102.9 FM (Barnsley); 103.4 FM (Doncaster)

HEARTLAND FM, Lower Oakfield, Pitlochry, Perthshire
PH16 2DS. Tel: 0796-474040. *Frequency:* 97.5 FM

HEREWARD RADIO LTD, PO Box 225, Queensgate
Centre, Peterborough PE1 1XJ. Tel: 0733-46225.
Frequency: 102.7 FM

HORIZON RADIO, Broadcast Centre, Crownhill, Milton
Keynes, Bucks. MK8 0AB. Tel: 0908-269111. *Frequency:*
103.3 FM

INVICTA FM, Radio House, John Wilson Business Park,
Whitstable, Kent CT5 3QX. Tel: 0227-772004.
Frequencies: MW 241/497m, 1242/603 kHz, 102.8/95.9/
97.0/96.1/103.1 FM

ISLAND FM, 12 Westerbrook, St Sampsons, Guernsey,
Channel Islands. Tel: 0481-42000. *Frequency:* 104.7 FM

ISLE OF WIGHT RADIO, Dodnor Park, Newport, Isle of
Wight PO30 5XE. Tel: 0983-822557. *Frequency:* MW
241m, 1242 kHz

JAZZ FM, 26–27 Castlereagh Street, London W1H 5YR. Tel:
071-706 4100. *Frequency:* 102.2 FM

KCBC (Kettering), PO Box 1530, Kettering, Northants.
NN16 8PU. Tel: 0536-412413. *Frequency:* MW 189m, 1584
kHz

KISS 100 FM, Kiss House, 80 Holloway Road, London N7
8JG. Tel: 071-700 6100. *Frequency:* 100.0 FM

KL.FM, 18 Blackfriars Street, King's Lynn, Norfolk PE30
1NN. Tel: 0553-772777. *Frequency:* 96.7 FM

LANTERN RADIO, Light House, 17 Market Place,
Bideford, N. Devon EX39 2DR. Tel: 0237-424444.
Frequency: 96.2 FM

LBC NEWSTALK (London Broadcasting Company Ltd),
Crown House, 72 Hammersmith Road, London W14 8YE.
Tel: 071-603 2400. *Frequency:* 97.3 FM

LEICESTER SOUND FM, Granville House, Granville Road,
Leicester LE1 7RW. Tel: 0533-551616. *Frequency:*
103.2 FM

LINCS FM, Witham Park, Waterside South, Lincoln LN5
7JN. Tel: 0522-549900. *Frequency:* 102.2 FM

LONDON GREEK RADIO, Florentia Village, Vale Road,
London N4 1TD. Tel: 081-800 8001. *Frequency:* 103.3 FM

LONDON TALKBACK RADIO, Crown House,
72 Hammersmith Road, London W14 8YE. Tel: 071-333
0003. *Frequency:* MW 260m, 1152 kHz

MAGIC 828, PO Box 2000, Leeds LS3 ILR. Tel: 0532-452299. *Frequency:* MW 362m, 828 kHz
MARCHER COAST FM, The Studios, Conwy Road, Colwyn Bay, Clwyd. Tel: 0978-752202. *Frequency:* 96.3 FM
MARCHER GOLD, The Studios, Mold Road, Wrexham, Clwyd LL11 4AF. Tel: 0978-752202. *Frequencies:* MW 238m, 1260 kHz
MAX AM, Forth House, Forth Street, Edinburgh EH1 3LF. Tel: 031-556 9255. *Frequency:* MW 194m, 1548 kHz
MELLOW 1557, 21–23 Walton Road, Frinton-on-Sea, Essex CO13 OAA. Tel: 0255-675303. *Frequency:* MW 192m, 1557 kHz
MELODY RADIO, 180 Brompton Road, London SW3 1HF. Tel: 071-584 1049. *Frequency:* 104.9 FM
MERCIA FM, Hertford Place, Coventry CV1 3TT. Tel: 0203-633933. *Frequencies:* 97.0/102.9 FM
METRO FM, Long Rigg, Swalwell, Newcastle upon Tyne NE99 1BB. Tel: 091-488 3131. *Frequencies:* 97.1/103.0 FM
MFM, The Studios, Mold Road, Wrexham, Clwyd LL11 4AF. Tel: 0978-752202. *Frequencies:* 103.4/97.1 FM
MINSTER FM, PO Box 123, Dunnington, York YO1 5ZX. Tel: 0904-488888. *Frequency:* 104.7 FM
MORAY FIRTH RADIO, PO Box 271, Inverness IV3 6SF. Tel: 0463-224433. *Frequencies:* MW 271m, 1107 kHz, 97.4 FM
96.7 BCR, Russell Court, Claremont Street, Lisburn Road, Belfast BT9 6JX. Tel: 0232-438500. *Frequency:* 96.7 FM
NORTHANTS RADIO, Broadcast Centre, The Enterprise Park, Boughton Green Road, Northampton NN2 7AH. Tel: 0604-792411. *Frequencies:* MW 193m, 1557 kHz, 96.6 FM
NORTH SOUND RADIO, 45 Kings Gate, Aberdeen AB2 6BL. Tel: 0224-632234. *Frequencies:* MW 290m, 1035 kHz, 96.9 FM
OCEAN FM, Radio House, Whittle Avenue, Segensworth West, Fareham, Hants. PO15 5PA. Tel: 0489-589911. *Frequencies:* 97.5/96.7 FM
ORCHARD FM, Haygrove House, Shoreditch, Taunton TA3 7BT. Tel: 0823-338448. *Frequencies:* 102.6/97.1 FM
PICCADILLY RADIO LTD, 127-131 The Piazza, Piccadilly Plaza, Manchester M1 4AW. Tel: 061-236 9913. *Frequencies:* MW 261m, 1152 kHz, 103.0 FM
PIRATE FM, Carn Brea Studios, Wilson Way, Redruth, Cornwall TR15 3XX. Tel: 0209-314400. *Frequencies:* 102.2/102.8 FM
PLYMOUTH SOUND LTD, Earl's Acre, Alma Road, Plymouth PL3 4HX. Tel: 0752-27272. *Frequencies:* MW 261m, 1152 kHz, 97.0 FM
POWERFM, Radio House, Whittle Avenue, Segensworth West, Fareham, Hants. PO15 5PA. Tel: 0489-589911. *Frequency:* 103.2 FM
THE PULSE, PO Box 3000, Bradford BD1 5NE. Tel: 0274-731521. *Frequencies:* 97.5/102.5 FM
Q96, 26 Lady Lane, Paisley PA1 2LG. Tel: 041-887 9630. *Frequency:* 96.3 FM
RADIO BORDERS, Tweedside Park, Galashiels TD1 3TD. Tel: 0896-59444. *Frequencies:* 96.8/97.5/103.1/103.4 FM
RADIO CEREDIGION, PO Box 600, Aberystwyth, Dyfed SY23 1PE. Tel: 0970-627999. *Frequencies:* 103.3/96.6 FM
RADIO CITY GOLD, PO Box 967, Liverpool L69 1TQ. Tel: 051-227 5100. *Frequency:* MW 194m, 1548 kHz
RADIO FORTH RFM, Forth House, Forth Street, Edinburgh EH1 3LF. Tel: 031-556 9255. *Frequencies:* 97.3/97.6 FM
RADIO HARMONY, Ringway House, Hill Street, Coventry CV1 4AN. Tel: 0203-525656. *Frequency:* 102.6 FM
RADIO IN TAVISTOCK, Earls Acre, Plymouth PL3 4HX. Tel: 0752-227272. *Frequency:* 96.6 FM

RADIO MALDWYN, The Studios, The Park, Newtown, Powys SY16 2NZ. Tel: 0686-623555. *Frequency:* MW 397m, 756 kHz
RADIO MERCURY (EAST), Broadfield House, Brighton Road, Crawley, W. Sussex. Tel: 0293-519161. *Frequency:* 102.7 FM
RADIO MERCURY (WEST), The Friary, Guildford, Surrey GU1 4YX. Tel: 0428-61019. *Frequencies:* 96.4/97.1 FM
RADIO TAY, PO Box 123, 6 North Isla Street, Dundee DD1 9UF. Tel: 0382-200800. *Frequencies:* MW 258m, 1161 kHz, 102.8 FM (Dundee); 189m, 1584 kHz, 96.4 FM (Perth)
RADIO TFM, Yale Crescent, Thornaby, Stockton-on-Tees, Cleveland TS17 6AA. Tel: 0642-615111. *Frequency:* 96.6 FM
RADIOWAVE, 965 Mowbray Drive, Blackpool, Lancs. FY3 7JR. Tel: 0253-304965. *Frequency:* 96.5 FM
RADIO WYE, 5 East Drive, Totteridge, High Wycombe, Bucks. HP13 6JN. Tel: 0494-446611. *Frequency:* MW 256m, 1170 kHz.
RADIO WYVERN, 5–6 Barbourne Terrace, Worcester WR1 3JZ. Tel: 0905-612212. *Frequencies:* MW 314m, 954 kHz, 97.6 FM (Hereford); 196m, 1530 kHz, 102.8 FM (Worcester)
RED DRAGON FM, Radio House, West Canal Wharf, Cardiff CF1 5XJ. Tel: 0222-384041. *Frequencies:* 97.4/103.2 FM
RED ROSE GOLD, PO Box 999, St Paul's Square, Preston, Lancashire PR1 1XR. Tel: 0772-556301. *Frequency:* MW 301m, 999 kHz
RED ROSE ROCK FM, PO Box 974, St Paul's Square, Preston PR1 1XS. Tel: 0772-200500. *Frequency:* 97.4 FM
RTM, 19 Tavy Bridge, Thamesmead, London SE2 9UG. Tel: 081-311 3112. *Frequency:* 103.8 FM
SEVERN SOUND, Broadcast Centre, 67 Southgate Street, Gloucester GL1 2DQ. Tel: 0452-423791. *Frequencies:* MW 387m, 774 kHz, 103.0/102.4 FM
SGR-FM, PO Box 250, Ipswich IP1 5AR. Tel: 0473-461000. *Frequencies:* MW 256m, 1170 kHz, 97.1 FM (Ipswich); 240m, 1251 kHz, 96.4 FM (Bury)
SIBC, Market Street, Lerwick, Shetland ZE1 OJN. Tel: 0595-5299. *Frequency:* 96.2 FM
SIGNAL CHESHIRE, Regent House, Heaton Lane, Stockport SK4 1BX. Tel: 061-480 5445. *Frequencies:* 104.9/96.4 FM
SIGNAL RADIO, Studio 257, Stoke Road, Stoke-on-Trent ST4 2SR. Tel: 0782-747047. *Frequencies:* MW 257m, 1170 kHz, 102.6/96.9 FM
603 RADIO, Churchill Studios, Churchill Road, Cheltenham, Glos. GL53 7EP. Tel: 0242-255023. *Frequency:* MW 497m, 603 kHz
SOUTH COAST RADIO, Radio House, Whittle Avenue, Segensworth West, Fareham, Hants. PO15 5PA. Tel: 0489-589911; Radio House, PO Box 2000, Brighton BN41 2SS. Tel: 0273-430111. *Frequencies:* MW 256/192/226m, 1170/1557/1323 kHz
SOUTHERN FM, Radio House, PO Box 2000, Brighton BN41 2SS. Tel: 0273-430111. *Frequencies:* 103.5 FM (Brighton); 96.9 FM (Newhaven); 102.4 FM (Eastbourne); 102.0 FM (Hastings)
SOUTH WEST SOUND, Campbell House, Bankend Road, Dumfries DG1 4TH. Tel: 0387-50999. *Frequency:* 97.2 FM
SPECTRUM INTERNATIONAL RADIO, Endeavour House, Brent Cross, London NW2 1JT. Tel: 081-905 5000. *Frequency:* MW 537m, 558 kHz
SPIRE FM, City Hall Studios, Malthouse Lane, Salisbury, Wilts. Tel: 0722-416644. *Frequency:* 102.0 FM
STAR FM, The Observatory, Slough, Berks. SL1 ILH. Tel: 0753-551016. *Frequency:* 101.6 FM
SUNRISE EAST MIDLANDS, Granville House, Granville Road, Leicester LE1 7RW. Tel: 0533-543002. *Frequency:* MW 238m, 1260 kHz

SUNRISE FM, 30 Chapel Street, Little Germany, Bradford BDI 5DN. Tel: 0274-735043. *Frequency:* 103.2 FM
SUNRISE RADIO, Sunrise House, Sunrise Road, Southall, Middx. UB2 4AU. Tel: 081-574 6666. *Frequency:* MW 212m, 1413 khz
SUNSET RADIO, 23 New Mount Street, Manchester M4 4DE. Tel: 061-953 5353. *Frequency:* 102.0 FM
SUNSHINE 855, Sunshine House, Waterside, Ludlow, Shropshire SY8 1PE. Tel: 0584-877855. *Frequency:* MW 351m, 855 khz
SWANSEA SOUND, Victoria Road, Gowerton, Swansea SA4 3AB. Tel: 0792-893751. *Frequencies:* MW 257m, 1170 khz, 96.4 FM
TEN 17, Latton Bush Centre, Southern Way, Harlow, Essex CM18 7BU. Tel: 0279-432415. *Frequency:* 101.7 FM
1332 THE WORLD'S GREATEST MUSIC STATION, Queensgate Centre, Peterborough PE1 1XJ. Tel: 0733-346225. *Frequency:* MW 225m, 1332 khz
TOUCH AM, PO Box 99, Cardiff CF1 5YJ. Tel: 0222-237878. *Frequencies:* MW 221m, 1359 khz (Cardiff); 230m, 1305 khz (Newport)
TRENT-FM (DERBY), The Market Place, Derby DE1 3AA. Tel: 0332-292945. *Frequency:* 102.8 FM
TRENT-FM (NOTTINGHAM), 29–31 Castle Gate, Nottingham NG1 7AP. Tel: 0602-581731. *Frequencies:* 96.2/96.5 FM
2CR RADIO, 5 Southcote Road, Bournemouth BH1 3LR. Tel: 0202-294881. *Frequencies:* MW 362m, 828 khz, 102.3 FM
210 CLASSIC GOLD RADIO, PO Box 2020, Reading, Berks. RG3 5RZ. Tel: 0734-413131. *Frequency:* MW 209m, 1431 khz
2 TEN FM, PO Box 210, Reading, Berks. RG3 5RZ. Tel: 0734-413131. *Frequency:* 97.0 FM (Reading); 102.9 FM (Basingstoke and Andover)
VIKING FM, Commercial Road, Hull HU1 2SG. Tel: 0482-25141. *Frequency:* 96.9 FM
WABC, 267 Tettenhall Road, Wolverhampton WV6 0DQ. Tel: 0902-757211. *Frequencies:* MW 303m, 990 khz (Wolverhampton); 295m, 1017 khz (Shrewsbury and Telford)
WEAR FM, Forster Building, Chester Road, Sunderland SRI 3SD. Tel: 091-515 2103. *Frequency:* 103.4 FM
WESSEX FM, Radio House, Trinity Street, Dorchester, Dorset DT1 1DJ. Tel: 0305-250333. *Frequency:* 97.2 FM
WEST SOUND RADIO, Radio House, 54 Holmston Road, Ayr KA7 3BE. Tel: 0292-283662. *Frequencies:* MW 290m, 1035 khz, 96.7 FM
WEY VALLEY 102, Prospect Place, Mill Lane, Alton, Hants. GU34 2SY. Tel: 0420-544444. *Frequency:* 102 FM
WNK, 185B High Road, Wood Green, London N22 6BA. Tel: 081-889 1547. *Frequency:* 103.3 FM
XTRA-AM, Radio House, Aston Road North, Birmingham B6 4BX. Tel: 021-359 4481. *Frequencies:* MW 260m, 1152 khz (Birmingham); 221m, 1359 khz (Coventry)

ASSOCIATION OF INDEPENDENT RADIO COMPANIES, 46 Westbourne Grove, London W2 5SH. Tel: 071-727 2646. *Director,* B. West

THE BROADCASTING COMPLAINTS COMMISSION
Grosvenor Gardens House, 35–37 Grosvenor Gardens, London SW1W 0BS
Tel 071-630 1966

The Broadcasting Complaints Commission's function and authority derive from the Broadcasting Act 1990. Its task is to consider and adjudicate upon complaints of unjust or unfair treatment or unwarranted infringement of privacy in sound or television programmes broadcast by the BBC, S4C, the Independent Television Commission, the Radio Authority or their licensees as appropriate. This function extends to all sound, television and cable advertisements and teletext transmissions, and programmes broadcast by the BBC's World Services.

The members of the Commission are appointed by the Secretary of State for National Heritage.
Chairman, Canon P. Pilkington
Members, D. Allen, CMG; T. Christopher, CBE; J. Leighton
Legal Adviser, Sir James Nursaw, KCB, QC
Secretary, R. M. Hargreaves

SERVICES SOUND AND VISION CORPORATION (Incorporating BFBS)
Chalfont Grove, Gerrards Cross, Bucks. SL9 8TN
Tel 0494-874461

The Services Sound and Vision Corporation (SSVC) is the official organization providing the Ministry of Defence, HM Forces and their families with radio and television broadcasting, audio-visual and electronic training and educational support, training film production, and entertainment. The SSVC is a private limited company and registered charity with 1,100 employees and an annual turnover approaching £50 million; financial surpluses are donated to Services' welfare.

The Corporation's radio arm, British Forces Broadcasting Service, operates stations in London, Germany, Gibraltar, Cyprus, the Falklands, Hong Kong, Brunei and Belize. BFBS provides programmes from London for inclusion with local input by its overseas staff, and broadcasts to overseas stations by satellite throughout the year.

SSVC television broadcasts its own, BBC and ITV programmes in Germany, Cyprus, Gibraltar and the Falkland Islands. Up to 70 isolated detachments of HM Forces (including ships at sea and the Service Children's Education Authority schools overseas), receive daily television programmes on cassette.

All SSVC services are available to other organizations and are provided to overseas governments and many UK companies.
Managing Director, Air Vice-Marshal D. O. Crwys-Williams, CB

The Press

The newspaper and periodical press in the UK is large and diverse, catering for a wide variety of views and interests. There is no state control or censorship of the press, though it is subject to the laws on publication and the Press Complaints Commission (*see* below) was set up by the industry as a means of self-regulation. Self-regulation was reviewed in 1992–3 (*see* below).

The press is not state-subsidized and receives few tax concessions. The income of most newspapers and periodicals is derived largely from sales and from advertising; the press is the largest advertising medium in Britain.

REVIEW OF PRESS SELF-REGULATION

The *Calcutt Review of Press Self-Regulation* was presented to Parliament by the Secretary of State for National Heritage (Peter Brooke) on 14 January 1993.

When the report of the Committee on Privacy and Related Matters, chaired by David Calcutt, QC, was published in June 1990, the then Home Secretary (David Waddington) said that the Government would review the performance of a non-statutory Press Complaints Commission after 18 months of operation to determine whether statutory measures were required. The Press Complaints Commission began work on 1 January 1991, and in July 1992 the then Secretary of State for National Heritage (David Mellor) asked Sir David Calcutt, QC, to conduct the review.

The review principally considered three matters: whether self-regulation of the press, primarily by the Press Complaints Commission, had been effective; what criminal offences should be enacted in order to provide better protection against physical intrusion; and whether a new statutory tort of infringement of privacy should be introduced.

The review came to the following conclusions:

- the Press Complaints Commission had not been an effective regulator of the press; it did not hold the balance fairly between the press and the individual; it was not truly independent; and it was operating a code of practice over-favourable to the press
- too many fundamental changes to the present arrangements would be needed to provide a commission which would command public confidence and would fairly hold the balance between the press and the individual; the review considered that the press would not, in any case, be willing to make the necessary changes
- accordingly, the Government should set up a statutory press complaints tribunal with a range of functions and powers, including drawing up and keeping under review a code of practice; receiving and inquiring into complaints, and initiating investigations without a complaint; attempting conciliation; ruling on alleged breaches of the code of practice; requiring the printing of apologies, corrections and replies; awarding compensation; and imposing fines
- the criminal offences proposed by the original report should, with modifications, now be enacted in order to provide better protection against physical intrusion. The new offences would relate to entering private property, placing or using surveillance devices, and taking photographs or recording voices without consent and with a view to publication. Alternatively, the substance of the proposed criminal offences could be incorporated into the statutory tribunal's code of practice

- the Government should give further consideration to the introduction of a new tort of infringement of privacy
- the Government should give further consideration to the extent to which the Data Protection Act may contain provisions which are relevant for purposes of misrepresentation or intrusion into personal privacy by the press
- the Government should give further consideration to amending and clarifying the legislation on the non-identification of minors in England and Wales
- in any criminal proceedings, the court should have the power to prohibit the publication of the name and address or other matters which could lead to the identification of the alleged victim(s)
- the Government should give further consideration to the legislation covering interception of telecommunications, identify all significant gaps, and determine whether any further legislation is needed

A report, *Privacy and Media Intrusion*, by the national heritage select committee of the House of Commons was published on 24 March 1993. It made the following proposals:

- a statutory press ombudsman should be appointed with the power to impose fines and demand corrections and compensation from offending newspapers
- a protection of privacy bill should be introduced, creating new civil and criminal offences
- a new Press Commission should replace the Press Complaints Commission and be charged with upholding press freedom, maintaining ethical standards and enforcing a revised code of practice. The commission's functions would in some areas overlap with those of the ombudsman
- a complaints hotline should be set up by the Press Commission
- strict controls on the sale of surveillance equipment should be considered
- legal aid should be extended to cases of defamation

THE PRESS COMPLAINTS COMMISSION

1 Salisbury Square, London EC3Y 8AE
Tel 071-353 1248

The Press Complaints Commission was founded by the newspaper and magazine industry in January 1991 to replace the Press Council (established in 1953). It is a voluntary, non-statutory body set up to operate the press's self-regulation system, and funded by the industry through the Press Standards Board of Finance.

The Commission's objects are to consider, adjudicate, conciliate, and resolve complaints of unfair treatment by the press; and to ensure that the press maintains the highest professional standards with respect to generally recognized freedoms, including freedom of expression, the public's right to know, and the right of the press to operate free from improper pressure. The Commission judges newspaper and magazine conduct by a code of practice drafted by editors, agreed by the industry and ratified by the Commission. The code of practice has recently been updated to include a clause on the publication of information obtained by the use of listening devices and long lens cameras.

In future, seven of the Commission's members will be editors of national, regional and local newspapers and magazines, and nine, including the chairman, will be drawn from other fields.

Chairman, Lord McGregor of Durris
Members (currently under review), Ms I. Burton; Lady
Elizabeth Cavendish, LVO; The Lord Colnbrook, KCMG,
PC; Dame Mary Donaldson, GBE; Sir David English; G.
McKechnie; K. Parker; Prof. R. Pinker; P. Preston; Prof.
L. Rees, FRCP, FRCPath
Director, M. Bolland

NEWSPAPERS

Newspapers are usually financially independent of any
political party, though most adopt a political stance in their
editorial comments, usually reflecting proprietorial influence.
Ownership of the national and regional daily newspapers is
concentrated in the hands of large corporations whose
interests cover publishing and communications. However,
there are strict rules on cross-media ownership to prevent
undue concentration of newspaper ownership.

There are 15 daily national papers and 10 Sunday national
papers, about 80 regional daily papers, and several hundred
local papers that are published weekly or twice-weekly.
Scotland, Wales and Northern Ireland all have at least one
daily and one Sunday national paper.

Newspapers are usually published in either broadsheet or
tabloid format. The 'quality' daily papers, i.e. those providing
detailed coverage of a wide range of public matters, have a
broadsheet format. The tabloid papers take a more popular
approach and are more illustrated.

NATIONAL DAILY NEWSPAPERS

DAILY EXPRESS, Ludgate House, 245 Blackfriars Road,
London SE1 9UX. Tel: 071-928 8000.
DAILY MAIL, Northcliffe House, 2 Derry Street, London
W8 5TT. Tel: 071-938 6000.
DAILY MIRROR, Holborn Circus, London EC1P 1DQ. Tel:
071-353 0246.
DAILY SPORT, 19 Great Ancoats Street, Manchester M60
4BT. Tel: 061-236 4466.
DAILY TELEGRAPH, 1 Canada Square, Canary Wharf,
London E14 5DT. Tel: 071-538 5000.
FINANCIAL TIMES, 1 Southwark Bridge, London SE1 9HL.
Tel: 071-873 3000.
THE GUARDIAN, 119 Farringdon Road, London EC1R 3ER.
Tel: 071-278 2332.
THE INDEPENDENT, 40 City Road, London EC1Y 2DB. Tel:
071-253 1222.
MORNING STAR, 1–3 Ardleigh Road, London N1 4HS. Tel:
071-254 0033.
RACING POST, 112–120 Coombe Lane, London SW20 0BA.
Tel: 081-879 3377.
THE SPORTING LIFE, Orbit House, 1 New Fetter Lane,
London EC4A 1AR. Tel: 071-822 2119.
THE STAR, Ludgate House, 245 Blackfriars Road,
London SE1 9UX. Tel: 071-928 8000.
THE SUN, 1 Virginia Street, London E1 9XR. Tel: 071-
782 4000.
THE TIMES, 1 Pennington Street, London E1 9XN. Tel: 071-
782 5000.
TODAY, 1 Virginia Street, London E1 9BD. Tel: 071-
782 4600.

REGIONAL DAILY NEWSPAPERS

Aberdeen: PRESS AND JOURNAL, and EVENING EXPRESS,
PO Box 43, Lang Stracht, Mastrick, AB9 8AF.

Ashford, Kent: KENT TODAY, 67 Middle Row, Maidstone
ME14 1TJ.
Barrow-in-Furness: NORTH-WEST EVENING MAIL,
Newspaper House, Abbey Road, LA14 5QS.
Bath: BATH EVENING CHRONICLE, 33–34 Westgate
Street, BA1 1EW.
Belfast: BELFAST TELEGRAPH, 124–144 Royal Avenue, BT1
1EB; IRISH NEWS AND BELFAST MORNING NEWS,
113–117 Donegall Street, BT1 2GE; NEWS LETTER,
51–59 Donegall Street, BT1 2GB.
Birmingham: THE BIRMINGHAM POST, and BIRMINGHAM
EVENING MAIL, 28 Colmore Circus, Queensway, B4
6AX.
Blackburn: LANCASHIRE EVENING TELEGRAPH,
Newspaper House, High Street, BB1 1HT.
Blackpool: WEST LANCASHIRE EVENING GAZETTE,
PO Box 20, FY4 4AU.
Bolton: BOLTON EVENING NEWS, Newspaper House,
Churchgate, BL1 1DL.
Bournemouth: EVENING ECHO, Richmond Hill, BH2 6HH.
Bradford: TELEGRAPH AND ARGUS, Hall Ings, BD1 1JR.
Brighton: EVENING ARGUS, Argus House, 89 North Road,
BN1 4AU.
Bristol: BRISTOL EVENING POST, and WESTERN DAILY
PRESS, Temple Way, BS99 7HD.
Burton-on-Trent: BURTON MAIL, 65–68 High Street, DE14
1LE.
Cambridge: CAMBRIDGE EVENING NEWS, 51 Newmarket
Road, CB5 8EJ.
Cardiff: SOUTH WALES ECHO, and WESTERN MAIL,
Thomson House, Havelock Street, CF1 1WR.
Cheltenham: GLOUCESTERSHIRE ECHO, 1 Clarence
Parade, GL50 3NZ.
Colchester: EVENING GAZETTE, Oriel House, 43–44 North
Hill, CO1 1TZ.
Coventry: COVENTRY EVENING TELEGRAPH, Corporation
Street, CV1 1FP.
Darlington: NORTHERN ECHO, Priestgate, DL1 1NF.
Derby: DERBY EVENING TELEGRAPH, Northcliffe House,
Meadow Road, DE1 2DW.
Dundee: COURIER AND ADVERTISER, and EVENING
TELEGRAPH AND POST, 2 Albert Square, DD1 9QJ.
Edinburgh: THE SCOTSMAN, and EVENING NEWS, 20
North Bridge, EH1 1YT.
Exeter: EXPRESS AND ECHO, Sidwell House, 160 Sidwell
Street, EX4 6RS.
Glasgow: DAILY RECORD, 40 Anderston Quay, G3 8DA;
HERALD, and EVENING TIMES, 195 Albion Street, G1
1QP.
Gloucester: THE GLOUCESTERSHIRE CITIZEN, St John's
Lane, GL1 2AY.
Greenock: GREENOCK TELEGRAPH, 2 Crawford Street,
PA15 1LH.
Grimsby: GRIMSBY EVENING TELEGRAPH, 80 Cleethorpe
Road, DN31 3EH.
Guernsey: GUERNSEY EVENING PRESS AND STAR, PO
Box 57, Braye Road, Vale.
Halifax: EVENING COURIER, PO Box 19, Courier
Buildings, King Cross Street, HX1 2SF.
Hartlepool: HARTLEPOOL MAIL, Clarence Road, TS24 8BU.
Huddersfield: HUDDERSFIELD DAILY EXAMINER, PO Box
A26, Queen Street South, HD1 2TD.
Hull: HULL DAILY MAIL, Blundell's Corner, Beverley
Road, HU3 1XS.
Ipswich: EAST ANGLIAN DAILY TIMES, and EVENING
STAR, 30 Lower Brook Street, IP4 1AN.
Jersey: JERSEY EVENING POST, PO Box 582, Five Oaks, St
Saviour.

Kettering: NORTHAMPTONSHIRE EVENING TELEGRAPH, Northfield Avenue, NN16 9TT.
Leeds: YORKSHIRE EVENING POST, and YORKSHIRE POST, PO Box 168, Wellington Street, LS1 1RF.
Leicester: LEICESTER MERCURY, St George Street, LEI 9FQ.
Lincoln: LINCOLNSHIRE ECHO, Brayford Wharf East, LN5 7AT.
Liverpool: DAILY POST, and LIVERPOOL ECHO, PO Box 48, Old Hall Street, L69 3EB.
London: THE EVENING STANDARD, 2 Derry Street, W8 5EE.
Maidstone: KENT EVENING POST, 67 Middle Row, MEI4 1TJ.
Manchester: MANCHESTER EVENING NEWS, 164 Deansgate, M60 2RR.
Middlesbrough: EVENING GAZETTE, Gazette Building, Borough Road, TS1 3AZ.
Newcastle upon Tyne: EVENING CHRONICLE, and THE JOURNAL, Thomson House, Groat Market, NE1 1ED.
Newport: SOUTH WALES ARGUS, Cardiff Road, Maesglas, NP9 1QW.
Northampton: CHRONICLE AND ECHO, Upper Mounts, NN1 3HR.
Norwich: EASTERN DAILY PRESS, and EASTERN EVENING NEWS, Prospect House, Rouen Road, NR1 1RE.
Nottingham: EVENING POST, PO Box 99, Forman Street, NG1 4AB.
Nuneaton: NUNEATON EVENING TRIBUNE, 1 New Century Way, CV11 5NE.
Oldham: EVENING CHRONICLE, 172 Union Street, OL1 1EQ.
Oxford: OXFORD MAIL, Newspaper House, Osney Mead, OX2 0EJ.
Paisley: PAISLEY DAILY EXPRESS, 195 Albion Street, Glasgow G1 1QP.
Peterborough: PETERBOROUGH EVENING TELEGRAPH, New Priestgate House, 57 Priestgate, PE1 1JW.
Plymouth: WESTERN MORNING NEWS, and EVENING HERALD, 65 New George Street, PL1 1RE.
Portsmouth: THE NEWS, The News Centre, Hilsea, PO2 9SX.
Preston: LANCASHIRE EVENING POST, Oliver's Place, Fulwood, PR2 4ZA.
Reading: EVENING POST, 8 Tessa Road, RG1 8NS.
Scarborough: SCARBOROUGH EVENING NEWS, 17–23 Aberdeen Walk, YO11 1BB.
Scunthorpe: SCUNTHORPE EVENING TELEGRAPH, Telegraph House, Doncaster Road, DN15 7RE.
Sheffield: THE STAR, York Street, S1 1PU.
South Shields: SHIELDS GAZETTE, Chapter Row, NE33 1BL.
Southampton: SOUTHERN EVENING ECHO, 45 Above Bar, SO9 7BA.
Stoke-on-Trent: EVENING SENTINEL, Sentinel House, Etruria, ST1 5SS.
Sunderland: SUNDERLAND ECHO, Echo House, Pennywell Estate, SR4 9ER.
Swansea: SOUTH WALES EVENING POST, Adelaide Street, SA1 1QT.
Swindon: EVENING ADVERTISER, Newspaper House, 100 Victoria Road, SN1 3BE.
Telford: SHROPSHIRE STAR, Ketley, TF1 4HU.
Torquay: HERALD EXPRESS, Harmsworth House, Barton Hill Road, TQ2 8JN.
Weymouth: DORSET EVENING ECHO, 57 St Thomas Street, DT4 8EU.
Wolverhampton: EXPRESS AND STAR, 51–53 Queen Street, WV1 3BU.
Worcester: EVENING NEWS, Hylton Road, WR2 5JX.

York: YORKSHIRE EVENING PRESS, PO Box 29, 76–86 Walmgate, YO1 1YN.

WEEKLY NEWSPAPERS

AL MAJALLA, Arab Press House, 184 High Holborn, London WC1V 7AP. Tel: 071-831 8181.
ASIAN TIMES, Tower House, 139–149 Fonthill Road, London N4 3HF. Tel: 071-281 1191.
CARIBBEAN TIMES, Tower House, 139–149 Fonthill Road, London N4 3HF. Tel: 071-281 1191.
THE EUROPEAN, Orbit House, 5 New Fetter Lane, London EC4A 1AP. Tel: 071-822 2002.
THE GUARDIAN WEEKLY, 119 Farringdon Road, London EC1R 3ER. Tel: 071-278 2332.
THE INDEPENDENT ON SUNDAY, 40 City Road, London EC1Y 2DB. Tel: 071-253 1222.
INDIA TIMES, Suites F and G, 2nd Floor, Liberty Shopping Centre, 14 South Road, Southall, Middx. UB1 1RT. Tel: 081-843 1605.
THE MAIL ON SUNDAY, Northcliffe House, 2 Derry Street, London W8 5TS. Tel: 071-938 6000.
NEWS OF THE WORLD, 1 Virginia Street, London E1 9XR. Tel: 071-782 4000.
THE OBSERVER, 119 Farringdon Road, London EC1R 3ER. Tel: 071-278 2332.
THE PEOPLE, Holborn Circus, London EC1P 1DQ. Tel: 071-353 0246.
SCOTLAND ON SUNDAY, 20 North Bridge, Edinburgh EH1 1YT. Tel: 031-225 2468.
THE SCOTSMAN, 20 North Bridge, Edinburgh EH1 1YT. Tel: 031-225 2468.
SUNDAY EXPRESS, Ludgate House, 245 Blackfriars Road, London SE1 9UX. Tel: 071-928 8000.
SUNDAY MAIL, 40 Anderston Quay, Glasgow G3 8DA. Tel: 041-248 7000.
SUNDAY MIRROR, Holborn Circus, London EC1P 1DQ. Tel: 071-353 0246.
SUNDAY NEWS, 51–59 Donegall Street, Belfast BT1 2GB. Tel: 0232-680040.
SUNDAY POST, Courier Place, Dundee DD1 9QJ. Tel: 0382-23131.
SUNDAY SPORT, 3rd Floor, Marten House, 39–47 East Road, London N1 6AH. Tel: 071-251 2544.
SUNDAY TELEGRAPH, Peterborough Court at South Quay, 181 Marsh Wall, London E14 9SR. Tel: 071-538 5000.
THE SUNDAY TIMES, 1 Pennington Street, London E1 9XN. Tel: 071-782 5000.
THE VOICE, 370 Coldharbour Lane, London SW9 8PL. Tel: 071-737 7377.
WALES ON SUNDAY, Thomson House, Havelock Street, Cardiff CF1 1WR. Tel: 0222-223333.
WEEKLY NEWS, Courier Place, Dundee, Angus DD1 9QJ. Tel: 0382-23131.
WEEKLY TELEGRAPH, 1 Canada Square, Canary Wharf, London E14 5DT. Tel: 071-538 6298.

RELIGIOUS PAPERS

Alt. = Alternate; *M.* = Monthly; *Q.* = Quarterly; *W.* = Weekly

BAPTIST TIMES, PO Box 54, 129 The Broadway, Didcot, Oxon OX11 8XB. *W.*
CATHOLIC HERALD, Herald House, Lamb's Passage, Bunhill Row, London EC1Y 8TQ. *W.*
CHALLENGE: THE GOOD NEWS PAPER, Revenue Buildings, Chapel Road, Worthing, W. Sussex BN11 1BQ. *M.*

CHRISTIAN HERALD, Herald House, 96 Dominion Road, Worthing, W. Sussex BN14 8JP. *W.*

CHRISTIAN SCIENCE MONITOR, 20 Beulah Road, London SW19 3SU. *W.*

CHURCH OF ENGLAND NEWSPAPER, 77–79 Farringdon Road, London EC1M 3JY. *W.*

CHURCH OF IRELAND GAZETTE, 36 Bachelor's Walk, Lisburn, Co. Antrim, BT28 1XN. *W.*

CHURCH TIMES, 33 Upper Street, London N1 0PW. *W.*

ENGLISH CHURCHMAN, 22 Lesley Avenue, Canterbury, Kent CT1 3LF. *Alt. W.*

THE FRIEND, Drayton House, 30 Gordon Street, London WC1H 0BQ. *W.*

THE INQUIRER, 1–6 Essex Street, London WC2R 3HY. *Alt. W.*

JEWISH CHRONICLE, 25 Furnival Street, London EC4A 1JT. *W.*

JEWISH GAZETTE, 27 Bury Old Road, Prestwich, Manchester M25 8EY. *W.*

JEWISH TELEGRAPH, Telegraph House, 11 Park Hill, Bury Old Road, Prestwich, Manchester M25 8HH. *W.*

LIFE AND WORK, Church of Scotland, 121 George Street, Edinburgh EH2 4QS. *M.*

METHODIST RECORDER, 122 Golden Lane, London EC1Y 0TL. *W.*

ORTHODOX NEWS, 64 Prebend Gardens, London W6 0XU. *Alt. M.*

PRESBYTERIAN HERALD, Church House, Fisherwick Place, Belfast BT1 6DW. *M.*

QUAKER MONTHLY, Friends House, Euston Road, London NW1 2BJ. *M.*

REFORM, 86 Tavistock Place, London WC1H 9RT. *Eleven times a year.*

SIKH MESSENGER, 43 Dorset Road, London SW19 3EZ. *Q.*

THE TABLET, 1 King Street Cloisters, Clifton Walk, London W6 0QZ. *W.*

THE UNIVERSE, 1st Floor, St James Building, Oxford Street, Manchester M1 6FP. *W.*

THE WAR CRY, 101 Queen Victoria Street, London EC4P 4EP. *W.*

PERIODICALS

There are about 6,700 periodicals published in Britain. These are classified as consumer, i.e. general interest, or as trade, professional or academic.

CONSUMER PERIODICALS

Alt. = Alternate; *M.* = Monthly; *Q.* = Quarterly; *W.* = Weekly

AMATEUR PHOTOGRAPHER, King's Reach Tower, Stamford Street, London SE1 9LS. *W.*

ANGLING TIMES, Bretton Court, Bretton, Peterborough PE3 8DZ. *W.*

ANNABEL, 80 Kingsway East, Dundee, Angus DD4 8SL. *M.*

THE ANTIQUE COLLECTOR, National Magazine House, 72 Broadwick Street, London W1V 2BP. *M.*

APOLLO MAGAZINE, 29 Chesham Place, London SW1X 8HB. *M.*

ARENA, 3rd Floor, Block A, Exmouth House, Pine Street, London EC1R 0JL. *Alt. M.*

THE ARTIST, Caxton House, 63–65 High Street, Tenterden, Kent TN30 6BD. *M.*

ASTRONOMY NOW, 193 Uxbridge Road, London W12 9RA. *M.*

ATHLETICS WEEKLY, Bretton Court, Bretton, Peterborough PE3 8DZ. *W.*

AUTOCAR AND MOTOR, 38–42 Hampton Road, Teddington, Middx. TW11 0JE. *W.*

BBC GARDENER'S WORLD, 101 Bayham Street, London NW1 0AG. *M.*

BBC GOOD FOOD, 101 Bayham Street, London NW1 0AG. *M.*

BBC WILDLIFE MAGAZINE, Woodlands, 80 Wood Lane, London W12 0TT. *M.*

BELFAST GAZETTE (*Official*), 129 IDB House, 64 Titchester Street, Belfast BT1 4PS. *W.*

BELLA, 2nd Floor, Shirley House, 25–27 Camden Road, London NW1 9LL. *W.*

BEST, 10th Floor, Portland House, Stag Place, London SW1E 5AU. *W.*

BIRDS, RSPB, The Lodge, Sandy, Beds. SG19 2DL. *Q.*

BIRD WATCHING, Bretton Court, Bretton, Peterborough PE3 8DZ. *M.*

BOXING NEWS, PO Box 300, London SW15 5QF. *W.*

BRIDES & SETTING UP HOME, Vogue House, Hanover Square, London W1R 0AD. *Alt. M.*

BRITISH BOOK NEWS, The British Council, 65 Davies Street, London W1Y 2AA. *M.*

THE BURLINGTON MAGAZINE, 6 Bloomsbury Square, London WC1A 2LP. *M.*

CAMPING & CARAVANNING, Greenfields House, Westwood Way, Coventry CV4 8JH. *M.*

CAR, Bushfield House, Orton Centre, Peterborough PE2 0UW. *M.*

CAT WORLD, 10 Western Road, Shoreham-by-Sea, W. Sussex BN43 5WD. *M.*

CD REVIEW, PO Box 381, Millharbour, London E14 9TW. *M.*

CHAT, King's Reach Tower, Stamford Street, London SE1 9LS. *W.*

CITY LIMITS, 3rd Floor, 115 Shaftesbury Avenue, London WC2H 8ED. *W.*

CLASSICAL MUSIC, 241 Shaftesbury Avenue, London WC2H 8EH. *Alt. W.*

CLASSIC AND SPORTSCAR, 60 Waldegrave Road, Teddington, Middx. TW11 8LG. *M.*

CLOTHES SHOW MAGAZINE, 101 Bayham Street, London NW1 0AG. *M.*

COARSE ANGLER, 281 Ecclesall Road, Sheffield S11 8NX. *M.*

COIN NEWS, 105 High Street, Honiton, Devon EX14 8PE. *M.*

COMPANY, 72 Broadwick Street, London W1V 2BP. *M.*

COMPETITORS JOURNAL, PO Box 300, London SW15 5QF. *Alt. W.*

COMPUTER AND VIDEO GAMES, Priory Court, 30–32 Farringdon Road, London EC1R 3AU. *M.*

COSMOPOLITAN, 72 Broadwick Street, London W1V 2BP. *M.*

COUNTRY HOMES AND INTERIORS, King's Reach Tower, Stamford Street, London SE1 9LS. *M.*

COUNTRY LIFE, King's Reach Tower, Stamford Street, London SE1 9LS. *W.*

COUNTRY LIVING, 72 Broadwick Street, London W1V 2BP. *Alt. M.*

THE COUNTRYMAN, Link House, Dingwall Avenue, Croydon, Surrey CR9 2TA. *Alt. M.*

CRICKETER INTERNATIONAL, Beech Hanger, Ashurst, Tunbridge Wells, Kent TN3 9ST. *M.*

CYCLING WEEKLY, King's Reach Tower, Stamford Street, London SE1 9LS. *W.*

THE DALESMAN, Dalesman Publishing Company Ltd, Clapham, Lancaster LE2 8EB. *M.*

DALTONS WEEKLY, CI Tower, St George's Square, New Malden, Surrey KT3 4JA. *W.*

DANCE AND DANCERS, 214 Panther House, 38 Mount Pleasant, London WCIX OAP. *M.*

DANCING TIMES, Clerkenwell House, 45–47 Clerkenwell Green, London ECIR OBE. *M.*

DOGS TODAY, 10 Sheet Street, Windsor, Berks. SL4 1BG. *M.*

DOG WORLD, 9 Tufton Street, Ashford, Kent TN23 1QN. *W.*

DO IT YOURSELF, Link House, Dingwall Avenue, Croydon, Surrey CR9 2TA. *M.*

THE ECOLOGIST, Agriculture House, Bath Road, Sturminster Newton, Dorset DT10 1DU. *Alt. M.*

THE ECONOMIST, 25 St James's Street, London SWIA 1HG. *W.*

EDINBURGH GAZETTE (*Official*), HMSO, PO Box 276, London SW8 5DT. *Twice a week.*

ELLE, 20 Orange Street, London WC2H 7ED. *M.*

EMPIRE, 42–48 Great Portland Street, London WIN 5AH. *M.*

ESQUIRE, 72 Broadwick Street, London WIV 2BP. *M.*

ESSENTIALS, Garden House, 57–59 Long Acre, London WC2E 9JL. *M.*

EVERYWOMAN, 34 Islington Green, London NI 8DU. *M.*

EXCHANGE AND MART, Link House, West Street, Poole, Dorset BHI5 ILL. *W.*

THE FACE, 3rd Floor, Block A, Exmouth House, Pine Street, London ECIR OJL. *M.*

FAMILY CIRCLE, King's Reach Tower, Stamford Street, SEI 9LS. *Thirteen times a year.*

THE FIELD, 10 Sheet Street, Windsor, Berks. SL4 1BG. *M.*

FILM REVIEW, 214 Panther House, 38 Mount Pleasant, London WCIX OAP. *M.*

FOR HIM, 9–11 Curtain Road, London EC2A 3LT. *Ten times a year.*

GARDEN NEWS, Apex House, Oundle Road, Peterborough PE2 9NP. *W.*

GAY TIMES, Worldwide House, 116–134 Bayham Street, London NWI OBA. *M.*

GEOGRAPHICAL MAGAZINE, 80 Wood Lane, London WI2 OTT. *M.*

GIBBONS STAMP MONTHLY, 5 Parkside, Christchurch Road, Ringwood, Hants. BH24 3SH. *M.*

GOLF ILLUSTRATED WEEKLY, 37–39 Millharbour, London EI4 9TX. *W.*

GOLF WORLD, Advance House, 37–39 Millharbour, London EI4 9TX. *M.*

GOOD HOLIDAY MAGAZINE, 1–2 Dawes Court, 93 High Street, Esher, Surrey KTIO 9QD. *Q.*

GOOD HOUSEKEEPING, 72 Broadwick Street, London WIV 2BP. *M.*

GQ, Vogue House, Hanover Square, London WIR OAD. *M.*

GRAMOPHONE, 177–179 Kenton Road, Harrow, Middx. HA3 OHA. *M.*

GRANTA, 2–3 Hanover Yard, Noel Road, London NI 8BE. *Q.*

GREEN MAGAZINE, PO Box 381, London EI4 9TW. *M.*

GUIDING, 17–19 Buckingham Palace Road, London SWIW OPT. *M.*

HANSARD, *see* Parliamentary Debates.

HARPERS AND QUEEN, 72 Broadwick Street, London WIV 2BP. *M.*

HELLO, 69–71 Upper Ground, London SEI 9PQ. *W.*

HOMES AND GARDENS, King's Reach Tower, Stamford Street, London SEI 9LS. *M.*

HORSE AND HOUND, King's Reach Tower, Stamford Street, London SEI 9LS. *W.*

HOUSE AND GARDEN, Vogue House, Hanover Square, London WIR OAD. *M.*

HOUSE BEAUTIFUL, 72 Broadwick Street, London WIV 2BP. *M.*

i–D MAGAZINE, 134–146 Curtain Road, London EC2A 3AR. *M.*

IDEAL HOME, King's Reach Tower, Stamford Street, London SEI 9LS. *M.*

ILLUSTRATED LONDON NEWS, 20 Upper Ground, London SEI 9PF. *Alt. M.*

IN BRITAIN, 3rd Floor, Greater London House, Hampstead Road, London NWI 7QQ. *M.*

INDIAMAIL, Heron House, 109 Wembley Hill, Wembley, Middx. HA9 8DH. *W.*

INVESTORS CHRONICLE, Greystoke Place, Fetter Lane, London EC4A IND. *W.*

IRISH POST, 464 Uxbridge Road, Hayes, Middx. UB4 OSP. *W.*

JAZZ JOURNAL INTERNATIONAL, 1–5 Clerkenwell Road, London ECIM 5PA. *M.*

JUST 17, 20 Orange Street, London WC2H 7ED. *W.*

LABOUR RESEARCH, 78 Blackfriars Road, London SEI 8HF. *M.*

THE LADY, 39–40 Bedford Street, London WC2E 9ER. *W.*

LAND AND LIBERTY, 177 Vauxhall Bridge Road, London SWIV IEU. *Alt. M.*

LITERARY REVIEW, 51 Beak Street, London WIR 3LF. *M.*

LIVING, King's Reach Tower, Stamford Street, London SEI 9LS. *Thirteen times a year.*

LONDON GAZETTE (*Official*) Room 413, HMSO, 51 Nine Elms Lane, London SW8 5DR. *Five times a week.*

LONDON REVIEW OF BOOKS, Tavistock House South, Tavistock Square, London WCIH 9JZ. *Alt. W.*

LONDON WEEKLY ADVERTISER, 137 George Lane, London EI8 IAJ. *W.*

MAJESTY, 26–28 Hallam Street, London WIN 5LF. *M.*

MARIE CLAIRE, 195 Knightsbridge, London SWI. *M.*

ME, 57–59 Long Acre, London WC2E 9JL. *W.*

MELODY MAKER (MM), King's Reach Tower, Stamford Street, London SEI 9LS. *W.*

METEOROLOGICAL MAGAZINE, HMSO, PO Box 276, London SW8 5DT. *M.*

MIZZ, King's Reach Tower, Stamford Street, London SEI 9LS. *Alt. W.*

MODEL BOATS, Argus House, Boundary Way, Hemel Hempstead, Herts. HP2 7ST. *M.*

MONEYWISE, 10 Old Bailey, London EC4M 7NB. *M.*

MORE!, 20 Orange Street, London WC2H 7ED. *W.*

MOTHER AND BABY, Victory House, 14 Leicester Place, London WC2H 7BP. *M.*

MOTOR CYCLE NEWS, Bushfield House, Orton Centre, Peterborough PE2 OUW. *W.*

MOTORING NEWS, Standard House, Bonhill Street, London EC2A 4DA. *W.*

MOTOR SPORT, Standard House, Bonhill Street, London EC2A 4DA. *M.*

MY WEEKLY, 80 Kingsway East, Dundee DD4 8SL. *W.*

NATIONAL STUDENT EXTRA, Bleaklow House, Howard Town Mill, Mill Street, Glossop, Derbys. SKI3 8PT. *Three times a year.*

NATURE, 4 Little Essex Street, London WC2R 3LF. *W.*

NEEDLECRAFT, Beaufort Court, 30 Monmouth Street, Bath BAI 2BW. *M.*

NEW INTERNATIONALIST, 55 Rectory Road, Oxford OX4 IBW. *M.*

NEW SCIENTIST, King's Reach Tower, Stamford Street, London SEI 9LS. *W.*

NEW STATESMAN AND SOCIETY, Foundation House, Perseverance Works, 38 Kingsland Road, London E2 8DQ. *W.*

NEWSWEEK INTERNATIONAL, 25 Upper Brook Street, London WIY 2AB. *W.*

NEW WOMAN, 20 Orange Street, London WC2H 7ED. *M.*

19, King's Reach Tower, Stamford Street, London SE1 9LS. *M.*

NME, King's Reach Tower, Stamford Street, London SE1 9LS. *W.*

THE OLDIE, 26 Charlotte Street, London W1P 1HJ. *Alt. W.*

OPERA, 1A Mountgrove Road, London N5 2LU. *M.*

OPERA NOW, 9 Grape Street, London WC2H 8DR. *M.*

OPTIONS, King's Reach Tower, Stamford Street, London SE1 9LS. *M.*

OUR DOGS, 5 Oxford Road, Station Approach, Manchester M60 1SX. *W.*

PARENTS, Victory House, 14 Leicester Place, London WC2H 7BP. *M.*

PARLIAMENTARY DEBATES (COMMONS) (Hansard), HMSO, PO Box 276, London SW8 5DT. *Daily or weekly during Session.*

PARLIAMENTARY DEBATES (LORDS) (Hansard), HMSO, PO Box 276, London SW8 5DT. *Daily or weekly during Session.*

PEOPLE'S FRIEND, 80 Kingsway East, Dundee DD4 8SL. *W.*

PLAYS AND PLAYERS, 18 Friern Park, London N12 9DA. *M.*

POETRY REVIEW, 22 Betterton Street, London WC2H 9BU. *Q.*

PONY, 296 Ewell Road, Surbiton, Surrey KT6 7AQ. *M.*

PRACTICAL BOAT OWNER, Westover House, West Quay Road, Poole, Dorset BH15 1JG. *M.*

PRACTICAL CARAVAN, 38–42 Hampton Road, Teddington, Middx. TW11 0JE. *M.*

PRACTICAL GARDENING, Apex House, Oundle Road, Peterborough PE2 9NP. *M.*

PRACTICAL PARENTING, King's Reach Tower, Stamford Street, London SE1 9LS. *M.*

PRACTICAL PHOTOGRAPHY, Apex House, Oundle Road, Peterborough PE2 9NP. *M.*

PRIMA, Portland House, Stag Place, London SW1E 5AU. *M.*

PRIVATE EYE, 6 Carlisle Street, London W1V 5RG. *Alt. W.*

PROGRESS (*Braille type*), RNIB, Orton, Southgate, Peterborough PE2 0XU. *M.*

THE PUZZLER, Glenthorne House, Hammersmith Grove, London W6 0LG. *M.*

Q, Meed House, 21 John Street, London WIN 2BP. *M.*

RACING CALENDAR, The Jockey Club, Weatherbys, Sanders Road, Wellingborough, Northants. NN8 4BX. *W.*

RADIO TIMES, 80 Wood Lane, London W12 0TT. *W.*

RAILWAY MAGAZINE, King's Reach Tower, Stamford Street, London SE1 9LS. *M.*

RAILWAY MODELLER, Peco Publications, Beer, Seaton, Devon EX12 3NA. *M.*

READER'S DIGEST, Berkeley Square House, Berkeley Square, London W1X 6AB. *M.*

RIDING, Corner House, Foston, Grantham, Lincs. NG32 2JU. *M.*

RUGBY LEAGUER, Martland Mill, Martland Mill Lane, Wigan, Lancs. WN5 0LX. *W.*

RUGBY WORLD AND POST, Weirbank, Bray, Maidenhead, Berks. SL6 2ED. *M.*

SCOTS MAGAZINE, 2 Albert Square, Dundee, Angus DD1 9QJ. *M.*

SCOTTISH FIELD, 7th Floor, The Plaza Tower, East Kilbride, Glasgow G74 1LW. *M.*

SCOUTING, Baden-Powell House, Queen's Gate, London SW7 5JS. *M.*

SEA ANGLER, Bretton Court, Bretton, Peterborough PE3 8DZ. *M.*

SHE, 72 Broadwick Street, London W1V 2BP. *M.*

SHOOT, King's Reach Tower, Stamford Street, London SE1 9LS. *W.*

SHOOTING TIMES AND COUNTRY MAGAZINE, 10 Sheet Street, Windsor, Berks. SL4 1BG. *W.*

SKY MAGAZINE, 5th Floor, Mappin House, London W1N 7AR. *M.*

SLIMMING MAGAZINE, Victory House, 14 Leicester Place, London WC2H 7BP. *Ten times a year.*

SMASH HITS, Meed House, 21 John Street, London W1N 2BP. *Alt. W.*

THE SPECTATOR, 56 Doughty Street, London WC1N 2LL. *W.*

THE STRAD, 214 Panther House, 38 Mount Pleasant, London WC1X 0AP. *M.*

TATLER, Vogue House, Hanover Square, London W1R 0AD. *Ten times a year.*

TENNIS WORLD, The Spendlove Centre, Enstone Road, Charlbury, Oxon. OX7 3PQ. *M.*

THIS ENGLAND, Alma House, Rodney Road, Cheltenham, Glos. GL50 1YQ. *Q.*

TIME INTERNATIONAL, Time Life Building, 153 New Bond Street, London W1Y 0AA. *W.*

TIME OUT, Tower House, Southampton Street, London WC2E 7HD. *W.*

THE TIMES EDUCATIONAL SUPPLEMENT, Priory House, St John's Lane, London EC1M 4BX. *W.*

THE TIMES HIGHER EDUCATION SUPPLEMENT, Priory House, St John's Lane, London EC1M 4BX. *W.*

THE TIMES LITERARY SUPPLEMENT, Priory House, St John's Lane, London EC1M 4BX. *W.*

TRIBUNE, 308 Gray's Inn Road, London WC1X 8DY. *W.*

TROUT AND SALMON, Bretton Court, Bretton, Peterborough PE3 8DZ. *M.*

TRUE ROMANCES, 2–4 Leigham Court Road, London SW16 2PD. *M.*

TRUE STORY, 2–4 Leigham Court Road, London SW16 2PD. *M.*

TV TIMES, King's Reach Tower, Stamford Street, London SE1 9LS. *W.*

VACHER'S PARLIAMENTARY COMPANION, 113 High Street, Berkhamsted, Herts. HP4 2DJ. *Q.*

VANITY FAIR, Vogue House, Hanover Square, London W1R 0AD. *M.*

VIZ COMIC, The Boat House, Crabtree Lane, London SW6 8NJ. *Alt. M.*

VOGUE, Vogue House, Hanover Square, London W1R 0AD. *M.*

VOX, King's Reach Tower, Stamford Street, London SE1 9LS. *M.*

WEATHER, 104 Oxford Road, Reading RG1 7LJ. *M.*

WELSH NATION, 51 Cathedral Road, Cardiff CF1 9HD. *Alt. M.*

WHICH?, 2 Marylebone Road, London NW1 4DX. *M.*

WOMAN, King's Reach Tower, Stamford Street, London SE1 9LS. *W.*

WOMAN AND HOME, King's Reach Tower, Stamford Street, London SE1 9LS. *M.*

WOMAN'S JOURNAL, King's Reach Tower, Stamford Street, London SE1 9LS. *M.*

WOMAN'S OWN, King's Reach Tower, Stamford Street, London SE1 9LS. *W.*

WOMAN'S REALM, King's Reach Tower, Stamford Street, London SE1 9LS. *W.*

WOMAN'S WEEKLY, King's Reach Tower, Stamford Street, London SE1 9LS. *W.*

WORLD OF INTERIORS, Vogue House, Hanover Square, London W1R 0AD. *Eleven times a year.*

YACHTING MONTHLY, King's Reach Tower, Stamford Street, London SE1 9LS. *M.*

TRADE, PROFESSIONAL AND ACADEMIC PERIODICALS

Alt. = Alternate; *M.* = Monthly; *Q.* = Quarterly; *W.* = Weekly

ACCOUNTANCY, Institute of Chartered Accountants, 40 Bernard Street, London WCIN ILD. *M.*

ACCOUNTANCY AGE, 32–34 Broadwick Street, London WIA 2HG. *W.*

ACCOUNTANTS' MAGAZINE, Institute of Chartered Accountants of Scotland, 27 Queen Street, Edinburgh EH2 ILA. *M.*

THE ACTUARY, Garrets Building, Cathles Road, London SW12 9LD. *M.*

AGRICULTURE INTERNATIONAL, Yew Tree House, Horne, Horley, Surrey RH6 9JP. *Alt. M.*

ANTIQUARIES JOURNAL, Oxford University Press, Walton Street, Oxford OX2 6DP. *Twice a year.*

ANTIQUE DEALER AND COLLECTORS' GUIDE, PO Box 805, London SE10 8TD. *M.*

ANTIQUES TRADE GAZETTE, 17 Whitcomb Street, London WC2H 7PL. *W.*

ARCHITECTS' JOURNAL, 33–39 Bowling Green Lane, London ECIR ODA. *W.*

ARCHITECTURAL REVIEW, 33–39 Bowling Green Lane, London ECIR ODA. *M.*

ARMED FORCES DEFENCE INTERNATIONAL, 21 Hawley Road, London NWI 8RP.

THE AUTHOR, Society of Authors, 84 Drayton Gardens, London SW10 9SB. *Q.*

THE BANKER, Greystoke Place, Fetter Lane, London EC4A IND. *M.*

BANKING WORLD (Chartered Institute of Bankers), Greater London House, Hampstead Road, London NWI 7QQ. *M.*

THE BIOCHEMIST, The Biochemist Society, 59 Portland Place, London WIN 3AJ. *Alt. M.*

BIOLOGIST, Institute of Biology, 20 Queensberry Place, London SW7 2DZ. *Five times a year.*

THE BOOKSELLER, 12 Dyott Street, London WCIA IDF. *W.*

BRAIN, Oxford University Press, Walton Street, Oxford OX2 6DP. *Alt. M.*

BREWING AND DISTILLING INTERNATIONAL, Peel House, Lichfield Street, Burton-on-Trent, Staffs. DE14 3RH. *M.*

BRITISH BAKER, Maclaren House, 19 Scarbrook Road, Croydon CR9 IQH. *W.*

BRITISH DENTAL JOURNAL, BMA House, Tavistock Square, London WCIH 9JR. *Alt. W.*

BRITISH FOOD JOURNAL, MCB University Press Ltd, 62 Toller Lane, Bradford BD8 9BY. *Nine times a year.*

BRITISH JEWELLER & WATCHBUYER, Wentworth House, Wentworth Street, Peterborough PEI IDS. *M.*

BRITISH JOURNAL FOR THE PHILOSOPHY OF SCIENCE, Oxford University Press, Walton Street, Oxford OX2 6DP. *Q.*

BRITISH JOURNAL OF PHOTOGRAPHY, 58 Fleet Street, London EC4Y IJU. *W.*

BRITISH JOURNAL OF PSYCHIATRY, Royal College of Psychiatrists, 17 Belgrave Square, London SWIX 8PG. *M.*

BRITISH JOURNAL OF PSYCHOLOGY, British Psychological Society, 13A Church Lane, London N2 8DX. *Q.*

BRITISH JOURNAL OF SOCIAL WORK, Oxford University Press, Walton Street, Oxford OX2 6DP. *Six times a year.*

BRITISH MEDICAL JOURNAL, British Medical Association, BMA House, Tavistock Square, London WCIH 9JR. *W.*

BRITISH PRINTER, Maclean Hunter House, Chalk Lane, Cockfosters Road, Barnet, Herts. EN4 0BU. *M.*

BRITISH TAX REVIEW, South Quay Plaza, 183 Marsh Wall, London E14 9FT. *Alt. M.*

BRITISH VETERINARY JOURNAL, 24–28 Oval Road, London NWI 7DX. *Alt. M.*

BUILDING, Builder House, 1 Millharbour, London E14 9RA. *W.*

BUILDING TRADE & INDUSTRY, 131–133 Duckmoor Road, Bristol BS3 2BH. *M.*

BUSINESS CONNECTIONS, Node Court, Drivers End, Codicote, Hitchin, Herts. SG4 8TR. *Alt. M.*

BUSINESS EDUCATION TODAY, 128 Long Acre, London WC2E 9AN. *M.*

CABINET MAKER AND RETAIL FURNISHER, Sovereign Way, Tonbridge, Kent TN9 IRW. *W.*

CAMPAIGN, 22 Lancaster Gate, London W2 3LY. *W.*

CARPET AND FLOORCOVERINGS REVIEW, PO Box 20, Sovereign Way, Tonbridge, Kent TN9 IRW. *Alt. W.*

CATERER AND HOTELKEEPER, Quadrant House, The Quadrant, Sutton, Surrey SM2 5AS. *W.*

CHEMIST AND DRUGGIST, PO Box 20, Sovereign Way, Tonbridge, Kent TN9 IRW. *W.*

CHEMISTRY AND INDUSTRY, 14 Belgrave Square, London SWIX 8PS. *Alt. W.*

CHEMISTRY IN BRITAIN, Royal Society of Chemistry, Thomas Graham House, Science Park, Milton Road, Cambridge CB4 4WF. *M.*

CHILD EDUCATION, Villiers House, Clarendon Avenue, Leamington Spa, Warks. CV32 5PR. *M.*

CLASSICAL QUARTERLY, Oxford University Press, Walton Street, Oxford OX2 6DP. *Twice a year.*

CLASSICAL REVIEW, Oxford University Press, Walton Street, Oxford OX2 6DP. *Twice a year.*

COMPUTER SHOPPER, 19 Bolsover Street, London WI. *M.*

COMPUTER WEEKLY, Quadrant House, The Quadrant, Sutton, Surrey SM2 5AS. *W.*

COMPUTING, VNU House, 32–34 Broadwick Street, London WIA 2HG. *W.*

CONSTRUCTION NEWS, 100 Avenue Road, London NW3 3TP. *W.*

CONSTRUCTION WEEKLY, Morgan-Grampian House, Calderwood Street, London SE18 6QH. *W.*

CONTAINERISATION INTERNATIONAL, 72 Broadwick Street, London WIV 2BP. *M.*

CONTRACT JOURNAL, Quadrant House, The Quadrant, Sutton, Surrey SM2 5AS. *W.*

CONTROL AND INSTRUMENTATION, Morgan-Grampian House, 30 Calderwood Street, London SE18 6QH. *M.*

CRAFTS MAGAZINE, Crafts Council, 44A Pentonville Road, London NI 9BY. *Alt. M.*

CRIMINOLOGIST, East Row, Little London, Chichester, W. Sussex PO19 IPG. *Q.*

DAIRY FARMER AND DAIRY BEEF PRODUCER, Wharfedale Road, Ipswich IPI 4LG. *M.*

DAIRY INDUSTRIES INTERNATIONAL, Wilmington House, Church Hill, Wilmington, Dartford, Kent DA2 7EF. *M.*

THE DENTIST, 20 Leas Road, Guildford, Surrey GUI 4QT. *Eleven times a year.*

DESIGN, The Design Council, 28 Haymarket, London SWIY 4SU. *M.*

DESIGN WEEK, St Giles House, 49–50 Poland Street, London WIV 4AX. *W.*

DIRECTOR, Institute of Directors, Mountbarrow House, 6–20 Elizabeth Street, London SWIW 9RB. *M.*

ECONOMIC JOURNAL, 108 Cowley Road, Oxford OX4 1JF. *Alt. M.*

EDUCATION, 21–27 Lamb's Conduit Street, London WC1N 3NJ. *W.*

ELECTRICAL AND RADIO TRADING, Quadrant House, The Quadrant, Sutton, Surrey SM2 5AS. *W.*

ELECTRICAL REVIEW, Quadrant House, The Quadrant, Sutton, Surrey SM2 5AS. *Alt. W.*

ELECTRICAL TIMES, Quadrant House, The Quadrant, Sutton, Surrey SM2 5AS. *Ten times a year.*

ELECTRONIC ENGINEERING, Morgan-Grampian House, 30 Calderwood Street, London SE18 6QH. *M.*

ENERGY MANAGEMENT, Maclean Hunter House, Chalk Lane, Cockfosters Road, Barnet, Herts. EN4 0BU. *Alt. M.*

THE ENGINEER, Morgan-Grampian House, 30 Calderwood Street, London SE18 6QH. *W.*

ENGINEERING, 28 Haymarket, London SW1Y 4SU. *Eleven times a year.*

ENGLISH HISTORICAL REVIEW, Longman House, Burnt Mill, Harlow, Essex CM20 2JE. *Q.*

ENGLISH TODAY, Cambridge University Press, The Edinburgh Building, Shaftesbury Road, Cambridge CB2 2RU. *Q.*

THE ENVIRONMENTALIST, 12 Clarence Road, Kew, Surrey TW29 3NL. *Q.*

EQUITY JOURNAL, Guild House, Upper St Martin's Lane, London WC2H 9EG. *Q.*

ESTATES GAZETTE, 151 Wardour Street, London W1V 4BN. *W.*

FAIRPLAY INTERNATIONAL SHIPPING WEEKLY, 20 Ullswater Crescent, Ullswater Business Park, Coulsdon, Surrey CR5 2HR. *W.*

FARMERS WEEKLY, Quadrant House, The Quadrant, Sutton, Surrey SM2 5AS. *W.*

FASHION WEEKLY, Greater London House, Hampstead Road, London NW1 7SD. *W.*

FIRE, Queensway House, 2 Queensway, Redhill, Surrey RH1 1QS. *M.*

FIRE PREVENTION, 140 Aldersgate Street, London EC1A 4HX. *Ten times a year.*

FISH, Institute of Fisheries Management, 151 Cove Road, Farnborough, Hants. GU14 0HQ. *Q.*

FISH TRADER, Queensway House, 2 Queensway, Redhill, Surrey RH1 1QS. *Alt. W.*

FLIGHT INTERNATIONAL, Quadrant House, The Quadrant, Sutton, Surrey SM2 5AS. *W.*

FOOD TRADE REVIEW, Station House, Hortons Way, Westerham, Kent TN16 1BZ. *M.*

FORESTRY AND BRITISH TIMBER, Sovereign Way, Tonbridge, Kent TN9 1RW. *M.*

FOUNDRY TRADE JOURNAL, Queensway House, 2 Queensway, Redhill, Surrey RH1 1QS. *Alt. W.*

FROZEN AND CHILLED FOODS, Queensway House, 2 Queensway, Redhill, Surrey RH1 1QS. *M.*

FUEL, Linacre House, Jordan Hill, Oxford OX2 8DP. *M.*

GARDEN TRADE NEWS, Apex House, Oundle Road, Peterborough PE2 9NP. *M.*

GAS WORLD, PO Box 105, 25–31 Ironmonger Row, London EC1V 3PN. *Q.*

GEOGRAPHY, Geographical Association, 343 Fulwood Road, Sheffield S10 3BP. *Q.*

GEOLOGICAL MAGAZINE, Cambridge University Press, The Edinburgh Building, Shaftesbury Road, Cambridge CB2 2RU. *Alt. M.*

GLASS AND GLAZING PRODUCTS, 19 Scarbrook Road, Croydon CR9 1QH. *M.*

GREECE AND ROME, Oxford University Press, Walton Street, Oxford OX2 6DP. *Twice a year.*

THE GROCER, Broadfield Park, Crawley, West Sussex RH11 9RT. *W.*

THE GROWER, 50 Doughty Street, London WC1N 2LS. *W.*

HAIRDRESSERS' JOURNAL INTERNATIONAL, Quadrant House, The Quadrant, Sutton, Surrey SM2 5AS. *W.*

THE HEALTH SERVICE JOURNAL, 4 Little Essex Street, London WC2R 3LF. *W.*

HEALTH VISITOR, BMA House, Tavistock Square, London WC1H 9JR. *M.*

HEATING, VENTILATING AND PLUMBING, PO Box 13, Hereford House, Bridle Path, Croydon CR9 4NL. *M.*

HISTORY TODAY, 83–84 Berwick Street, London W1V 3PJ. *M.*

INDEPENDENT RETAILER, 14 Pierpoint Street, Worcester WR1 1TA. *M.*

INDUSTRIAL EXCHANGE AND MART, Link House, West Street, Poole, Dorset BH15 1LL. *W.*

INDUSTRIAL RELATIONS JOURNAL, 108 Cowley Road, Oxford OX4 1JF. *Q.*

INTERNATIONAL AFFAIRS, Cambridge University Press, The Edinburgh Building, Shaftesbury Road, Cambridge CB2 2RU. *Q.*

JANE'S DEFENCE WEEKLY, Sentinel House, 163 Brighton Road, Coulsdon, Surrey CR5 2NH. *W.*

THE JOURNALIST, National Union of Journalists, Acorn House, 314 Gray's Inn Road, London WC1X 8DP. *M.*

JOURNAL OF ALTERNATIVE AND COMPLEMENTARY MEDICINE, 53A High Street, Bagshot, Surrey GU19 5AH. *M.*

JOURNAL OF THE BRITISH ASTRONOMICAL ASSOCIATION, Burlington House, Piccadilly, London W1V 9AG. *Alt. M.*

JOURNAL OF THE CHEMICAL SOCIETY, Thomas Graham House, Science Park, Milton Road, Cambridge CB4 4WF. *Five parts each M.*

JUSTICE OF THE PEACE, East Row, Little London, Chichester, W. Sussex PO19 1PG. *W.*

THE LANCET, 42 Bedford Square, London WC1B 3SL. *W.*

LAW QUARTERLY REVIEW, South Quay Plaza, 183 Marsh Wall, London E14 9FT. *Q.*

THE LAW REPORTS, 3 Stone Buildings, Lincoln's Inn, London WC2A 3XN. *M.*

LAW SOCIETY GAZETTE, 50 Chancery Lane, London WC2A 1SX. *W.*

LEATHER, Sovereign Way, Tonbridge, Kent TN9 1RW. *M.*

LIBRARY ASSOCIATION RECORD, 7 Ridgmount Street, London WC1E 7AE. *M.*

LLOYD'S LOADING LIST, Collwyn House, Sheepen Place, Colchester, Essex CO3 3LP. *W.*

LLOYD'S SHIPPING INDEX, Collwyn House, Sheepen Place, Colchester, Essex CO3 3LP. *W.*

LOCAL GOVERNMENT CHRONICLE, 122 Minories, London EC3N 1NT. *W.*

MACHINERY AND PRODUCTION ENGINEERING, Franks Hall, Franks Lane, Horton Kirby, Dartford, Kent DA4 9LL. *Alt. W.*

MACHINERY MARKET, 6 Blyth Road, Bromley, Kent BR1 3RX. *W.*

MANAGEMENT ACCOUNTING, Chartered Institute of Management Accountants, 63 Portland Place, London W1N 4AB. *M.*

MANAGEMENT TODAY, 32 Lancaster Gate, London W2 3LY. *M.*

MANUFACTURING CHEMIST, Morgan-Grampian House, 30 Calderwood Street, London SE18 6QH. *M.*

MARKETING, 22 Lancaster Gate, London W2 3LY. *W.*

MARKETING WEEK, St Giles House, 49–50 Poland Street, London W1V 4AX. *W.*

MATERIALS RECLAMATION WEEKLY, Maclaren House, 19 Scarbrook Road, Croydon CR9 1QH. *W.*

MEAT TRADES' JOURNAL, Greater London House, Hampstead Road, London NW1 7SD. *W.*

MEDIA WEEK, 33–39 Bowling Green Lane, London ECIR ODA. *W.*

METALS AND MATERIALS, Institute of Materials, 1 Carlton House Terrace, London SW1Y 5DB. *M.*

METALS INDUSTRY NEWS, Queensway House, 2 Queensway, Redhill, Surrey RHI 1QS. *M.*

MIND, Oxford University Press, Walton Street, Oxford OX2 6DP. *Q.*

MINING JOURNAL, 60 Worship Street, London EC2A 2HD. *W.*

MOTOR TRANSPORT, Quadrant House, The Quadrant, Sutton, Surrey SM2 5AS. *W.*

MUNICIPAL JOURNAL, 32 Vauxhall Bridge Road, London SW1V 2SS. *W.*

MUNICIPAL REVIEW AND AMA NEWS, 35 Great Smith Street, London SW1P 3BJ. *Ten times a year.*

MUSEUMS JOURNAL, Museums Association, 42 Clerkenwell Close, London ECIR OPP. *M.*

THE MUSICAL TIMES, 214 Panther House, 38 Mount Pleasant, London WC1X OAP. *M.*

MUSIC AND LETTERS, Oxford University Press, Walton Street, Oxford OX2 6DP. *Q.*

MUSIC WEEK, Ludgate House, 245 Blackfriars Road, London SE1 9UR. *W.*

NOTES AND QUERIES, Oxford University Press, Walton Street, Oxford OX2 6DP. *Q.*

NUCLEAR ENGINEERING INTERNATIONAL, Quadrant House, The Quadrant, Sutton, Surrey SM2 5AS. *M.*

NURSING TIMES & NURSING MIRROR, 4 Little Essex Street, London WC2R 3LF. *W.*

OFF-LICENCE NEWS, Broadfield Park, Crawley, W. Sussex RHII 9RT. *W.*

OPTICIAN, Quadrant House, The Quadrant, Sutton, Surrey SM2 5AS. *W.*

OPTOMETRY TODAY, 11 Somerset Place, Glasgow G3 7JT. *Alt. W.*

PACKAGING WEEK, PO Box 20, Sovereign Way, Tonbridge, Kent TN9 IRW. *W.*

PAPER, PO Box 20, Sovereign Way, Tonbridge, Kent TN9 IRW. *M.*

PC PLUS, 30 Monmouth Street, Bath BAI 2BW. *M.*

PERSONAL COMPUTER WORLD, 32–34 Broadwick Street, London W1A 2HG. *M.*

PERSONNEL MANAGEMENT (Institute of Personal Management), 17 Britton Street, London ECIM 5NQ. *M.*

PHARMACEUTICAL JOURNAL, 1 Lambeth High Street, London SE1 7JN. *W.*

PHILOSOPHY, Cambridge University Press, The Edinburgh Building, Shaftesbury Road, Cambridge CB2 2RU. *Q.*

THE PHOTOGRAPHER, Fox Talbot House, Amwell End, Ware, Herts. SG12 9HN. *M.*

PHYSICS WORLD, Techno House, Redcliffe Way, Bristol BS1 6NX. *M.*

PLUMBING AND HEATING NEWS, Peterson House, Northbank, Berryhill Industrial Estate, Droitwich, Worcs. WR9 9BL. *M.*

POLICE REVIEW, South Quay Plaza 2, 183 Marsh Wall, London E14 9FS. *W.*

THE PRACTITIONER, Morgan-Grampian House, 30 Calderwood Street, London SE18 6QH. *M.*

PRINTING WORLD, PO Box 20, Sovereign Way, Tonbridge, Kent TN9 IRW. *W.*

PROBATION JOURNAL, 3–4 Chivalry Road, London SW11 IHT. *Q.*

PROFESSIONAL CARE OF MOTHER AND CHILD, Media Medica, 1 The Chambers, Chapel Street, Chichester, W. Sussex PO19 IDL. *Ten times a year.*

THE PSYCHOLOGIST, The British Psychological Society, St Andrews House, 48 Princess Road East, Leicester LEI 7DR. *M.*

QUARRY MANAGEMENT, 7 Regent Street, Nottingham NGI 5BY. *M.*

RAILWAY GAZETTE INTERNATIONAL, Quadrant House, The Quadrant, Sutton, Surrey SM2 5AS. *M.*

RATING & VALUATION REPORTER, 4 Breams Buildings, London EC4A 1AQ. *M.*

RETAIL NEWSAGENT, Robert Taylor House, 11 Angel Gate, City Road, London ECIV 2PT. *W.*

RETAIL WEEK, 19 Scarbrook Road, Croydon CR9 1QH. *W.*

THE REVIEW, Audit House, Field End Road, Eastcote, Ruislip, Middx. HA4 9LT. *M.*

REVIEW OF ENGLISH STUDIES, Oxford University Press, Walton Street, Oxford OX2 6DP. *Q.*

RUSI JOURNAL, Royal United Services Institute for Defence Studies, Whitehall, London SW1A 2ET. *Q.*

SHIPPING WORLD & SHIPBUILDER, 4 Hubbard Road, Houndsmill, Basingstoke, Hants. RG21 2UH. *Ten times a year.*

SHOE & LEATHER NEWS, Greater London House, Hampstead Road, London NW1 7QZ. *M.*

SMALLHOLDER, High Street, Stoke Ferry, King's Lynn, Norfolk PE33 9SF. *M.*

SOCIOLOGICAL REVIEW, 108 Cowley Road, Oxford OX4 IJF. *Q.*

SOLICITORS' JOURNAL, 21–27 Lamb's Conduit Street, London WCIN 3NJ. *W.*

SPORTS RETAILING, 147 Temple Chambers, Temple Avenue, London EC4Y ODT. *M.*

THE STAGE AND TELEVISION, 47 Bermondsey Street, London SE1 3XT. *W.*

STRUCTURAL ENGINEER, 11 Upper Belgrave Street, London SW1X 8BH. *Alt. W.*

SURVEYOR, Quadrant House, The Quadrant, Sutton, Surrey SM2 5AS. *W.*

TAXATION PRACTITIONER, Institute of Taxation, 12 Upper Belgrave Street, London SW1X 8BB. *M.*

TAXI, 9–11 Woodfield Road, London W9 2BA. *Alt. W.*

THE TEACHER, National Union of Teachers, Hamilton House, Mabledon Place, London WCIH 9BD. *Eight times a year.*

TEACHING HISTORY, 108 Cowley Road, Oxford OX4 IJF. *Q.*

TELEVISION, Quadrant House, The Quadrant, Sutton, Surrey SM2 5AS. *M.*

TEXTILE HORIZONS, 10 Blackfriars Street, Manchester M3 5DR. *Alt. W.*

TEXTILE MONTH, 76 Kirkgate, Bradford, W. Yorkshire BDI ITB. *M.*

TIMBER TRADES JOURNAL, PO Box 20, Sovereign Way, Tonbridge, Kent TN9 IRW. *W.*

TOBACCO, Queensway House, 2 Queensway, Redhill, Surrey RHI 1QS. *Alt. M.*

TOWN AND COUNTRY PLANNING, 17 Carlton House Terrace, London SW1Y 5AH. *M.*

TOWN PLANNING REVIEW, Liverpool University Press, PO Box 147, Liverpool L69 3BX. *Q.*

TOY TRADER, 171 High Street, Rickmansworth, Herts WD3 ISN. *M.*

TRADE MARKS JOURNAL, Patent Office, 25 Southampton Buildings, London WC2A 1AY. *W.*

THE TRADER, Link House, West Street, Poole, Dorset BHI5 ILL. *M.*

TRAVEL TRADE GAZETTE (UK & IRELAND), Morgan-
Grampian House, 30 Calderwood Street, London SE18
6QH. *W.*

UK PRESS GAZETTE, Maclean Hunter House, Chalk
Lane, Cockfosters Road, Barnet, Herts. EN4 0BU. *W.*

WEEKLY LAW REPORTS, 3 Stone Buildings, Lincoln's Inn,
London WC2A 3XN. *W.*

WOODCARVING, 166 High Street, Lewes, E. Sussex
BN7 1XU. *Alt. M.*

WORLD'S FAIR, 2 Daltry Street, Oldham OL1 4BB. *W.*

NEWS AGENCIES IN LONDON

News agencies provide general, business, sport and television
news to a variety of subscribers including the press, other
media, and industrial, commercial, financial and business
users.

THE ASSOCIATED PRESS LTD, 12 Norwich Street, London
EC4A 4BP. Tel: 071-353 8118.

CENTRAL PRESS FEATURES LTD, 20 Spectrum House,
32-34 Gordon House Road, London NW5 1LP. Tel: 071-
284 1433.

EXTEL FINANCIAL LTD, 13-17 Epworth Street, London
EC2A 4DL. Tel: 071-251 3330.

HAYTERS, 4-5 Gough Square, EC4A 3DE. Tel: 071-353
0971.

PARLIAMENTARY AND EEC NEWS SERVICE, 19 Douglas
Street, London SW1P 4PA. Tel: 071-233 8283.

PRESS ASSOCIATION, 85 Fleet Street, London EC4P 4BE.
Tel: 071-353 7440.

REUTERS LTD, 85 Fleet Street, London EC4P 4AJ. Tel:
071-250 1122.

UNITED PRESS INTERNATIONAL (UK) LTD,
2 Greenwich View, Millharbour, London E14 9NN. Tel:
071-538 0932.

UNIVERSAL NEWS SERVICE LTD, 210 Old Street, London
EC1V 9UN. Tel: 071-490 8111.

Book Publishers

More than 15,000 firms, individuals and societies have published one or more books in recent years. The list which follows is a selective one comprising, in the main, those firms whose names are most familiar to the general public. A fuller list, *Publishers in the United Kingdom and Their Addresses*, containing some 2,500 names and addresses is published annually in April by the publishers of *Whitaker's Almanack*.

ALLAN (IAN), Coombelands House, Coombelands Lane, Addlestone KT15 1HY. Tel: 0932-855909

ALLEN (J. A.), 1 Lower Grosvenor Place, London SW1W 0EL. Tel: 071-834 0090

ALLEN (W. H.), *see* Virgin Publishing

ANAYA PUBLISHERS, 44–50 Osnaburgh Street, London NW1 3ND. Tel: 071-383 2997

APPLE PRESS, 6 Blundell Street, London N7 9BH. Tel: 071-700 6700

ARGUS BOOKS, Argus House, Boundary Way, Hemel Hempstead, Herts. HP2 7ST. Tel: 0442-66551

ARMADA BOOKS, 77 Fulham Palace Road, London W6 8JB. Tel: 081-741 7070

ARMS & ARMOUR PRESS, 41 Strand, London WC2N 5JE. Tel: 071-839 4900

ARNOLD (EDWARD), Mill Road, Dunton Green, Sevenoaks TN13 2YA. Tel: 0732-450111

ARROW BOOKS, 20 Vauxhall Bridge Road, London SW1V 2SA. Tel: 071-973 9700

ATHLONE PRESS, 1 Park Drive, London NW11 7SG. Tel: 081-458 0888

AURUM PRESS, 25 Bedford Avenue, London WC1B 3AT. Tel: 071-637 3225

AUTOMOBILE ASSOCIATION, Fanum House, Basingstoke, Hants. RG21 2EA. Tel: 0256-491524

BAILLIÈRE TINDALL, 24 Oval Road, London NW1 7DX. Tel: 071-267 4466

BANTAM BOOKS, 61 Uxbridge Road, London W5 5SA. Tel: 081-579 2652

BARRIE & JENKINS, 20 Vauxhall Bridge Road, London SW1V 2SA. Tel: 071-973 9690

BARTHOLOMEW, 77 Fulham Palace Road, London W6 8JB. Tel: 081-741 7070

BATSFORD (B. T.), 4 Fitzhardinge Street, London W1H 0AH. Tel: 071-486 8484

BBC BOOKS, 80 Wood Lane, London W12 0TT. Tel: 081-576 2536

BINGLEY (CLIVE), 7 Ridgmount Street, London WC1E 7AE. Tel: 071-636 7543

BLACK (A. & C.), 35 Bedford Row, London WC1R 4JH. Tel: 071-242 0946

BLACKIE CHILDREN'S BOOKS, 27 Wright's Lane, London W8 5TZ. Tel: 071-938 2200

BLACKWELL PUBLISHERS, 108 Cowley Road, Oxford OX4 1JF. Tel: 0865-791100

BLANDFORD PRESS, 41 Strand, London WC2N 5JE. Tel: 071-839 4900

BLOOMSBURY PUBLISHING, 2 Soho Square, London W1V 5DE. Tel: 071-494 2111

BODLEY HEAD, 20 Vauxhall Bridge Road, London SW1V 2SA. Tel: 071-973 9730

BOXTREE, 21 Broadwall, London SE1 9PL. Tel: 071-928 9696

BOYARS (MARION), 24 Lacy Road, London SW15 1NL. Tel: 081-788 9522

BRIMAX BOOKS, 4 Studlands Park Industrial Estate, Exning Road, Newmarket, Suffolk CB8 7AU. Tel: 0638-664611

BRITISH MUSEUM PRESS, 46 Bloomsbury Street, London WC1B 3QQ. Tel: 071-323 1234

BUTTERWORTH & CO., Borough Green, Sevenoaks TN15 8PH. Tel: 0732-884567

CADOGAN BOOKS, Letts of London House, Parkgate Road, London SW11 4NQ. Tel: 071-738 1961

CALDER PUBLICATIONS, 9–15 Neal Street, London WC2H 9TU. Tel: 071-497 1741

CAMBRIDGE UNIVERSITY PRESS, The Edinburgh Building, Cambridge CB2 2RU. Tel: 0223-312393

CAPE (JONATHAN), 20 Vauxhall Bridge Road, London SW1V 2SA. Tel: 071-973 9730

CASSELL, 41 Strand, London WC2N 5JE. Tel: 071-839 4900

CENTAUR PRESS, Fontwell, Arundel, W. Sussex BN18 0TA. Tel: 0243-543302

CENTURY PUBLISHING CO., *see* Random House UK

CHAMBERS (W. & R.), 43 Annandale Street, Edinburgh EH7 4AZ. Tel: 031-557 4571

CHAPMAN & HALL, 2 Boundary Row, London SE1 8HN. Tel: 071-865 0066

CHAPMAN (GEOFFREY), 41 Strand, London WC2N 5JE. Tel: 071-839 4900

CHAPMANS PUBLISHERS, 5 Upper St Martin's Lane, London WC2H 9EA. Tel: 071-240 3444

CHATTO & WINDUS, 20 Vauxhall Bridge Road, London SW1V 2SA. Tel: 071-973 9740

CHIVERS PRESS, Windsor Bridge Road, Bath BA2 3AX. Tel: 0225-335336

CHURCH HOUSE PUBLISHING, Church House, Great Smith Street, London SW1P 3NZ. Tel: 071-222 9011

CHURCHILL LIVINGSTONE, 1–3 Baxter's Place, Leith Walk, Edinburgh EH1 3AF. Tel: 031-556 2424

COLLINS (WILLIAM), *see* HarperCollins Publishers

CONSTABLE & CO., 3 The Lanchesters, 162 Fulham Palace Road, London W6 9ER. Tel: 081-741 3663

CONSUMERS' ASSOCIATION, 2 Marylebone Road, London NW1 4DF. Tel: 071-486 5544

CORGI BOOKS, 61 Uxbridge Road, London W5 5SA. Tel: 081-579 2652

DARTON, LONGMAN & TODD, 1 Spencer Court, 140 Wandsworth High Street, London SW18 4JJ. Tel: 081-875 0155

DAVID & CHARLES, Brunel House, Newton Abbot, Devon TQ12 4PU. Tel: 0626-61121

DEAN & SON, 81 Fulham Road, London SW3 6RB. Tel: 071-581 9393

DENT (J. M.) & SONS, 5 Upper St Martin's Lane, London WC2H 9EA. Tel: 071-240 3444

DEUTSCH (ANDRE), 105 Great Russell Street, London WC1B 3LJ. Tel: 071-580 2746

DORLING KINDERSLEY, 9 Henrietta Street, London WC2E 8PS. Tel: 071-836 5411

DOUBLEDAY, 61 Uxbridge Road, London W5 5SA. Tel: 081-579 2652

DUCKWORTH & CO., 48 Hoxton Square, London N1 6PB. Tel: 071-729 5986

EBURY PRESS, 20 Vauxhall Bridge Road, London SW1V 2SA. Tel: 071-973 9690

ELEMENT BOOKS, The Old School House, The Courtyard, Bell Street, Shaftesbury, Dorset SP7 8BP. Tel: 0747-51448

ELLIOT RIGHT WAY BOOKS, Kingswood Building, Kingswood, Tadworth, Surrey KT20 6TD. Tel: 0737-832202

ENCYCLOPAEDIA BRITANNICA INTERNATIONAL, Carew House, Station Approach, Wallington, Surrey SM6 ODA. Tel: 081-669 4355

EPWORTH PRESS, c/o SCM Press, 26 Tottenham Road, London NI 4BZ. Tel: 071-249 7262

EVANS BROS, 2A Portman Mansions, Chiltern Street, London WIM ILE. Tel: 071-935 7160

EVERYMAN'S LIBRARY, 79 Berwick Street, London WIV 3PF. Tel: 071-287 0035

FABER & FABER, 3 Queen Square, London WCIN 3AU. Tel: 071-465 0045

FONTANA, 77 Fulham Palace Road, London W6 8JB. Tel: 081-741 7070

FOULIS (G. T.), Sparkford, Yeovil, Somerset BA22 7JJ. Tel: 0963-40635

FOULSHAM (W.) & CO., Yeovil Road, Slough SLI 4JH. Tel: 0753-526769

FOURTH ESTATE, 289 Westbourne Grove, London WII 2QA. Tel: 071-727 8993

FRENCH (SAMUEL), 52 Fitzroy Street, London WIP 6JR. Tel: 071-387 9373

GAIA BOOKS, 20 High Street, Stroud GL5 IAS. Tel: 0453-752985

GIBBONS (STANLEY), 5 Parkside, Christchurch Road, Ringwood, Hants. BH24 3SH. Tel: 0425-472363

GIBSON (ROBERT), 17 Fitzroy Place, Glasgow G3 7SF. Tel: 041-248 5674

GINN & CO., Prebendal House, Parson's Fee, Aylesbury, Bucks. HP20 2QZ. Tel: 0296-88411

GLASGOW (MARY), 140 Freston Road, London WIO 6TR. Tel: 071-792 3644

GOLLANCZ (VICTOR), 41 Strand, London WC2N 5JE. Tel: 071-839 4900

GOWER PUBLISHING CO., Croft Road, Aldershot, Hants. GUII 3HR. Tel: 0252-331551

GRAFTON BOOKS, 77 Fulham Palace Road, London W6 8JB. Tel: 081-741 7070

GRANTA BOOKS, 2 Hanover Yard, London NI 8BE. Tel: 071-704 9776

GREEN (W.), 21 Alva Street, Edinburgh EH2 4PS. Tel: 031-225 4879

GUINNESS PUBLISHING, 33 London Road, Enfield, Middx. EN2 6DJ. Tel: 081-367 4567

HALE (ROBERT), 45 Clerkenwell Green, London ECIR OHT. Tel: 071-251 2661

HAMILTON (HAMISH), 27 Wright's Lane, London W8 5TZ. Tel: 071-416 3100

HAMLYN (PAUL), 81 Fulham Road, London SW3 6RB. Tel: 071-581 9393

HARCOURT BRACE, 24 Oval Road, London NWI 7DX. Tel: 071-267 4466

HARPERCOLLINS PUBLISHERS, 77 Fulham Palace Road, London W6 8JB. Tel: 081-741 7070

HARRAP, 43 Annandale Street, Edinburgh EH7 4AZ. Tel: 031-557 4571

HARVESTER WHEATSHEAF, Campus 400, Maylands Avenue, Hemel Hempstead HP2 7EZ. Tel: 0442-881900

HAYNES (J. H.), Sparkford, Yeovil, Somerset BA22 7JJ. Tel: 0963-40635

HEADLINE BOOK PUBLISHING, 79 Great Titchfield Street, London WIP 7FN. Tel: 071-631 1687

HEINEMANN (WILLIAM), 81 Fulham Road, London SW3 6RB. Tel: 071-581 9393

HIPPO BOOKS, 7 Pratt Street, London NWI OAE. Tel: 071-284 4474

HMSO, PO Box 276, London SW8 5DT. Tel: 071-873 0011

HODDER & STOUGHTON, 47 Bedford Square, London WCIB 3DP. Tel: 071-636 9851

HOGARTH PRESS, 20 Vauxhall Bridge Road, London SWIV 2SA. Tel: 071-973 9740

HUTCHINSON, see Random House UK

JANE'S INFORMATION GROUP, 163 Brighton Road, Coulsdon, Surrey CR5 2NH. Tel: 081-763 1030

JARROLD PUBLISHING, Whitefriars, Norwich NR3 ITR. Tel: 0603-763300

JORDAN PUBLISHING, 21 St Thomas Street, Bristol BSI 6JS. Tel: 0272-230600

JOSEPH (MICHAEL), 27 Wright's Lane, London W8 5TZ. Tel: 071-416 3200

KAYE & WARD, 38 Hans Crescent, London SWIX OLZ. Tel: 071-581 9393

KEGAN PAUL INTERNATIONAL, PO Box 256, London WCIB 3SW. Tel: 071-580 5511

KELLY'S, Windsor Court, East Grinstead House, East Grinstead, W. Sussex RHI9 IXB. Tel: 0342-326972

KIMPTON MEDICAL, 82 Great King Street, Edinburgh EH3 6QY. Tel: 031-332 8764

KINGFISHER BOOKS, 24 Great Titchfield Street, London WIP 7AD. Tel: 071-631 0878

KINGSWAY PUBLICATIONS, Lottbridge Drove, Eastbourne BN23 6NT. Tel: 0323-410930

KOGAN PAGE, 120 Pentonville Road, London NI 9JN. Tel: 071-278 0433

LADYBIRD BOOKS, Beeches Road, Loughborough LEII 2NQ. Tel: 0509-268021

LASCELLES (ROGER), 47 York Road, Brentford, Middx TW8 OQP. Tel: 081-847 0935

LAWRENCE & WISHART, 144A Old South Lambeth Road, London SW8 IXX. Tel: 071-820 9281

LENNARD PUBLISHING ,Windmill Cottage, Mackerye End, Harpenden AL5 5DR. Tel: 0582-715866

LETTS (CHARLES), Parkgate Road, London SWII 4NQ. Tel: 071-407 8891

LINCOLN (FRANCES), 5 Charlton Kings Road, London NW5 2SB. Tel: 071-482 3302

LION PUBLISHING, Peter's Way, Oxford OX4 5HG. Tel: 0865-747550

LITTLE, BROWN & CO., 165 Great Dover Street, London SEI 4YA. Tel: 071-334 4800

LONGMAN GROUP, Burnt Mill, Harlow, Essex CM20 2JE. Tel: 0279-426721

LUND HUMPHRIES, I Russell Gardens, London NWII 9NN. Tel: 081-458 6314

LUTTERWORTH PRESS, PO Box 60, Cambridge CBI 2NT. Tel: 0223-350865

MACDONALD & EVANS, 128 Long Acre, London WC2E 9AN. Tel: 071-379 7383

McGRAW-HILL, Shoppenhangers Road, Maidenhead, Berks. SL6 2QL. Tel: 0628-23432

MACMILLAN PUBLISHERS, 4 Little Essex Street, London WC2R 3LF. Tel: 071-836 6633

MACRAE (JULIA), 20 Vauxhall Bridge Road, London SWIV 2SA. Tel: 071-973 9750

MAMMOTH, 38 Hans Crescent, London SWIX OLZ. Tel: 071-581 9393

MANDALA, see HarperCollins Publishers

MANDARIN, 81 Fulham Road, London SW3 6RB. Tel: 071-581 9393

MARSHALL CAVENDISH, 119 Wardour Street, London WIV 3TD. Tel: 071-734 6710

METHODIST PUBLISHING HOUSE, 20 Ivatt Way, Peterborough PE3 7PG. Tel: 0733-332202

METHUEN LONDON, 81 Fulham Road, London SW3 6RB. Tel: 071-581 9393

MILLS & BOON, 18 Paradise Road, Richmond, Surrey TW9 ISR. Tel: 081-948 0444

MITCHELL BEAZLEY, 81 Fulham Road, London SW3 6RB. Tel: 071-581 9393

MOWBRAY, 41 Strand, London WC2N 5JE. Tel: 071-839 4900

MURRAY (JOHN), 50 Albemarle Street, London WIX 4BD. Tel: 071-493 4361

NATIONAL CHRISTIAN EDUCATION COUNCIL, Robert Denholm House, Nutfield, Redhill RHI 4HW. Tel: 0737-822411

NELSON (THOMAS), Mayfield Road, Walton-on-Thames KTI2 5PL. Tel: 0932-252211

NEW ENGLISH LIBRARY, 47 Bedford Square, London WCIB 3DP. Tel: 071-636 9851

NISBET & CO., 78 Tilehouse Street, Hitchin, Herts. SG5 2DY. Tel: 0462-438331

NOVELLO & CO., 3 Primrose Mews, IA Sharpleshall Street, London NWI 8YL. Tel: 071-483 2161

OCTOPUS BOOKS, 81 Fulham Road, London SW3 6RB. Tel: 071-581 9393

OLIVER & BOYD, Longman House, Burnt Mill, Harlow, Essex CM20 2JE. Tel: 0279-426721

O'MARA (MICHAEL) BOOKS, 9 Lion Yard, Tremadoc Road, London SW4 7NQ. Tel: 071-720 8643

ORCHARD BOOKS, 96 Leonard Street, London EC2A 4RH. Tel: 071-739 2929

ORION PUBLISHING GROUP, 5 Upper St Martin's Lane, London WC2H 9EA. Tel: 071-240 3444

OWEN (PETER), 73 Kenway Road, London SW5 ORE. Tel: 071-373 5628

OXFORD UNIVERSITY PRESS, Walton Street, Oxford OX2 6DP. Tel: 0865-56767

PALADIN BOOKS, *see* HarperCollins Publishers

PAN BOOKS, Cavaye Place, London SWIO 9PG. Tel: 071-373 6070

PELHAM BOOKS, 27 Wright's Lane, London W8 5TZ. Tel: 071-416 3200

PENGUIN BOOKS, Bath Road, Harmondsworth, Middx. UB7 ODA. Tel: 081-759 1984

PERGAMON PRESS, Headington Hill Hall, Oxford OX3 0BW. Tel: 0865-794141

PHAIDON PRESS, 140 Kensington Church Street, London W8 4BN. Tel: 071-221 5656

PHARMACEUTICAL PRESS, 1 Lambeth High Street, London SEI 7JN. Tel: 071-735 9141

PHILIP (GEORGE), 81 Fulham Road, London SW3 6RB. Tel: 071-581 9393

PIATKUS BOOKS, 5 Windmill Street, London WIP IHF. Tel: 071-631 0710

PICCADILLY PRESS, 5 Castle Road, London NWI 8PR. Tel: 071-267 4492

PITKIN PICTORIALS, Healey House, Dene Road, Andover, Hants. SPIO 2AA. Tel: 0264-334303

PITMAN PUBLISHING, 128 Long Acre, London WC2E 9AN. Tel: 071-379 7383

PUTNAM & CO., 101 Fleet Street, London EC4Y IDE. Tel: 071-583 2412

QUARTET BOOKS, 27 Goodge Street, London WIP IFD. Tel: 071-636 3992

QUILLER PRESS, 46 Lillie Road, London SW6 ITN. Tel: 071-499 6529

RANDOM HOUSE UK, 20 Vauxhall Bridge Road, London SWIV 2SA. Tel: 071-973 9000

READER'S DIGEST, 25 Berkeley Square, London WIX 6AB. Tel: 071-629 8144

RELIGIOUS & MORAL EDUCATION PRESS, St Mary's Works, St Mary's Plain, Norwich NR3 3BH. Tel: 0603-615995

ROUTLEDGE, 11 New Fetter Lane, London EC4P 4EE. Tel: 071-583 9855

ST ANDREW PRESS, 121 George Street, Edinburgh EH2 4YN. Tel: 031-225 5722

SCM PRESS, 26 Tottenham Court Road, London NI 4BZ. Tel: 071-249 7262

SCRIPTURE UNION, 130 City Road, London ECIV 2NJ. Tel: 071-782 0013

SECKER & WARBURG, 81 Fulham Road, London SW3 6RB. Tel: 071-581 9393

SERPENT'S TAIL PUBLISHING, 4 Blackstock Mews, London N4 2BT. Tel: 071-354 1949

SEVERN HOUSE, 9 Sutton High Street, Sutton SMI IDF. Tel: 081-770 3930

SHELDON PRESS, Holy Trinity Church, Marylebone Road, London NWI 4DU. Tel: 071-387 5282

SIDGWICK & JACKSON, Cavaye Place, London SWIO 9PG. Tel: 071-373 6070

SIMON & SCHUSTER, Campus 400, Maylands Avenue, Hemel Hempstead HP2 7EZ. Tel: 0442-881900

SINCLAIR-STEVENSON, 81 Fulham Road, London SW3 6RB. Tel: 071-581 9393

SOUVENIR PRESS, 43 Great Russell Street, London WCIB 3PA. Tel: 071-580 9307

SPCK, Holy Trinity Church, Marylebone Road, London NWI 4DU. Tel: 071-387 5282

SPON (E. & F. N.), 2 Boundary Row, London SEI 8HN. Tel: 071-865 0066

STEPHENS (PATRICK), Sparkford, Yeovil BA22 7JJ. Tel: 0963-40635

SWEET & MAXWELL, 183 Marsh Wall, London EI4 9FT. Tel: 071-538 8686

THAMES & HUDSON, 30 Bloomsbury Street, London WCIB 3QP. Tel: 071-636 5488

THORSONS, 77 Fulham Palace Road, London W6 8JB. Tel: 081-741 7070

TIMES BOOKS, 77 Fulham Palace Road, London W6 8JB. Tel: 081-741 7070

UNIVERSITY OF WALES PRESS, 6 Gwennyth Street, Cardiff CF2 4YD. Tel: 0222-231919

VIKING, 27 Wright's Lane, London W8 5TZ. Tel: 071-938 2200

VIRAGO PRESS, 20–23 Mandela Street, London NWI OHQ. Tel: 071-383 5150

VIRGIN PUBLISHING, 33–34 Grand Union Centre, 332 Ladbroke Grove, London WIO 5AH. Tel: 081-968 7554

WALKER BOOKS, 87 Vauxhall Walk, London SEII 5HJ. Tel: 071-793 0909

WARD LOCK, 41 Strand, London WC2N 5JE. Tel: 071-839 4900

WARD LOCK EDUCATIONAL CO., 1 Christopher Road, East Grinstead, W. Sussex RHI9 3BT. Tel: 0342-318980

WARNE (FREDERICK), *see* Penguin

WATTS (FRANKLIN), 96 Leonard Street, London EC2A 4RH. Tel: 071-739 2929

WEBB & BOWER, 3 Cathedral Close, Exeter EXI IEZ. Tel: 0392-435362

WEIDENFELD & NICOLSON, 5 Upper St Martin's Lane, London WC2H 9EA. Tel: 071-240 3444

WHITAKER (J.), 12 Dyott Street, London WCIA IDF. Tel: 071-836 8911

WILDWOOD HOUSE, Gower House, Croft Road, Aldershot, Hants. GUII 3HR. Tel: 0252-331551

WISDEN (JOHN), 25 Down Road, Merrow, Guildford GUI 2PY. Tel: 0483-570358

WITHERBY (H. F. & G.), 41 Strand, London WC2N 5JE. Tel: 071-839 4900

Annual Reference Books

If the address of the editorial office of a publication differs from the address to which orders should be sent, the address given is usually the one for orders

ADVERTISER'S ANNUAL, East Grinstead House, East Grinstead, W. Sussex RH19 IXA. 3V, £167.00

ALLIED DUNBAR INVESTMENT AND SAVINGS GUIDE, PO Box 88, Harlow, Essex CMI9 5SR. £21.95

ALLIED DUNBAR TAX GUIDE, PO Box 88, Harlow, Essex CMI9 5SR. £19.99

ANNUAL ABSTRACT OF STATISTICS, PO Box 276, London SW8 5DT. (Feb.) £22.50

ANNUAL REGISTER OF WORLD EVENTS, PO Box 88, Harlow, Essex CMI9 5SR. £89.00

ANTIQUE SHOPS OF BRITAIN, GUIDE TO THE, 5 Church Street, Woodbridge, Suffolk IP12 IDS. £14.50

ART SALES INDEX, I Thames Street, Weybridge, Surrey KTI 8JG. £95.00

ART WORLD DIRECTORY, Park House, I Russell Gardens, London NWII 9NN. (Jan.) £13.95

ASSOCIATION OF CONSULTING ENGINEERS DIRECTORY OF MEMBERS FIRMS, Alliance House, 12 Caxton Street, London SWIH 0QL. £10.00

ASTRONOMICAL ALMANAC, HMSO, PO Box 276, London SW8 5DT. £15.00

ATHLETICS ANNUAL, 10 Sheet Street, Windsor, Berks. SL4 IBG. (May) £13.95

AUTOMOBILE YEAR, Star Road, Partridge Green, Horsham, W. Sussex RH13 8LD. £29.95

BAILY'S HUNTING DIRECTORY, 10 Sheet Street, Windsor, Berks. SL4 IBG. (Nov.) £29.00

BANKER'S ALMANAC AND YEAR BOOK, East Grinstead House, East Grinstead, W. Sussex RH19 IXE. (Feb.) 3v. £219.00

BENEDICTINE AND CISTERCIAN MONASTIC YEAR BOOK, Ampleforth Abbey, York YO6 4EN. (Dec.) £1.75

BENN'S DO-IT-YOURSELF TRADE BUYERS GUIDE, PO Box 20, Sovereign Way, Tonbridge, Kent TN9 IRQ. £58.00

BENN'S MEDIA DIRECTORY, PO Box 20, Sovereign Way, Tonbridge, Kent TN9 IRQ. 3V. £225.00

BIRMINGHAM POST AND MAIL YEAR BOOK AND WHO'S WHO, 137 Newhall Street, Birmingham B3 ISF. (Sept.) £21.70

BPIF SERVICES AND LIST OF MEMBERS, II Bedford Row, London WCIR 4DX. £90.00

BRITAIN: AN OFFICIAL HANDBOOK, HMSO, PO Box 276, London SW8 5DT. (Jan.) £19.50

BRITANNICA BOOK OF THE YEAR, Carew House, Station Approach, Wallington, Surrey SM6 0DA. (April) £56.00

BRITISH CLOTHING INDUSTRY YEAR BOOK, II The Swan Courtyard, Charles Edward Road, Yardley, Birmingham B26 IBU. £49.00

BRITISH EXPORTS, East Grinstead House, East Grinstead, W. Sussex RH19 IXB. £135.00

BRITISH MUSIC WORLDWIDE, 241 Shaftesbury Avenue, London WC2H 8EH. £20.00, £15.00

BRITISH PERFORMING ARTS YEAR BOOK, 241 Shaftesbury Avenue, London WC2H 8EH. (Jan.) £15.95

BRITISH PLASTICS AND RUBBER DIRECTORY, Catalyst House, 159 Clapham High Street, London SW4 7SS. £10.00

BROWN'S NAUTICAL ALMANACK DAILY TIDE TABLES, 4-10 Darnley Street, Glasgow G4I 2SD. (Sept.) £33.00

BUILDING AND CONSERVATION INDEX, PO Box 20, Sovereign Way, Tonbridge, Kent TN9 IRQ. (May) £48.00

BUILDING SOCIETIES YEAR BOOK, South Quay Plaza, 183 Marsh Wall, London EI4 9FS. £58.00

BUSES YEARBOOK, Terminal House, Station Approach, Shepperton, Middx. TWI7 8AS. £20.00

BUTTERWORTHS LEGAL SERVICES DIRECTORY, Borough Green, Sevenoaks, Kent TNI5 8PH. (Feb.) £28.00

CARPET ANNUAL, PO Box 20, Sovereign Way, Tonbridge, Kent TN9 IRQ. £72.00

CATERING BUYERS GUIDE, PO Box 20, Sovereign Way, Tonbridge, Kent TN9 IRQ. (Jan.) £60.00

CATHOLIC DIRECTORY OF ENGLAND AND WALES, 18 Crosby Road North, Liverpool L22 4QF. £17.50

CDS AND BRASSEY'S DEFENCE YEAR BOOK, PO Box 87, Osney Mead, Oxford OX2 0DT. £40.00

CHARITIES DIGEST, 501-505 Kingsland Road, London E8 4AU. £14.95

CHEMICAL INDUSTRY, EUROPE, PO Box 20, Sovereign Way, Tonbridge, Kent TN9 IRQ. £99.00

CHEMIST AND DRUGGIST DIRECTORY, PO Box 20, Sovereign Way, Tonbridge, Kent TN9 IRQ. £86.00

CHRISTIES' REVIEW OF THE SEASON, I Stewart's Court, 220 Stewart's Road, London SW8 4UD. (Dec.) £30.00

CHURCH OF ENGLAND YEAR BOOK, Church House, Great Smith Street, London SWIP 3NZ. (Jan.) £18.00

CHURCH OF SCOTLAND YEAR BOOK, 121 George Street, Edinburgh EH2 4YN. (April) £9.95

CITY OF LONDON DIRECTORY AND LIVERY COMPANIES GUIDE, Seatrade House, 42-48 North Station Road, Colchester, Essex COI IRB. £19.00, £17.00

CIVIL SERVICE YEAR BOOK, HMSO, PO Box 276, London SW8 5DT. (Feb.) £19.50

COMMONWEALTH UNIVERSITIES YEAR BOOK, 36 Gordon Square, London WCIH 0PF. (Sept.) £136.00

COMMONWEALTH YEAR BOOK, HMSO, PO Box 276, London SW8 5DT. (May) £22.50

COMPUTER USERS' YEAR BOOK, 32-34 Broadwick Street, London WIA 2HG. 4V. £146.50

CONCRETE YEAR BOOK, Thomas Telford House, I Heron Quay, London EI4 9XF. £55.00

CURRENT LAW YEAR BOOK, South Quay Plaza, 183 Marsh Wall, London EI4 9FT. £95.00

DEBRETT'S PEOPLE OF TODAY, 73-77 Britannia Road, PO Box 357, London SW6 2JY. (April) £96.00

DIPLOMATIC SERVICE LIST, HMSO, PO Box 276, London SW8 5DT. (April) £18.50

DIRECTORY OF DIRECTORS, East Grinstead House, East Grinstead, W. Sussex RH19 IXE. (April) 2V. £168.00

DIRECTORY OF FURTHER EDUCATION, Bateman Street, Cambridge CB2 ILZ. (June) £46.95, £41.95

DIRECTORY OF HIGHER EDUCATION, Bateman Street, Cambridge CB2 ILZ. (June) £46.95, £41.95

DIRECTORY OF OFFICIAL ARCHITECTURE AND PLANNING, PO Box 88, Harlow, Essex CMI9 5SR. £63.00

DOD'S PARLIAMENTARY COMPANION, Hurst Green, Etchingham, E. Sussex TNI9 7PX. £70.00

EDUCATION AUTHORITIES' DIRECTORY AND ANNUAL, Derby House, Bletchingley Road, Merstham, Surrey RHI 3DN. (Jan.) £58.00, £52.00

EDUCATION YEAR BOOK, PO Box 88, Harlow, Essex CMI9 5SR. £69.00

ELECTRICAL AND ELECTRONICS TRADES DIRECTORY, Michael Faraday House, Six Hills Way, Stevenage, Herts. SG1 2AY. (Feb.) £69.00

ELECTRICITY SUPPLY HANDBOOK, Quadrant House, The Quadrant, Sutton, Surrey SM2 5AS. (Feb.) £35.00

EUROPA WORLD YEAR BOOK, 18 Bedford Square, London WC1B 3JN. 2v. £290.00

EUROPEAN FOOD TRADES DIRECTORY, 32 Vauxhall Bridge Road, London SW1V 2SS. 2v. £130.00

EUROPEAN GLASS DIRECTORY AND BUYER'S GUIDE, 2 Queensway, Redhill, Surrey RH1 1QS. £83.00

FAIRPLAY WORLD SHIPPING YEARBOOK, PO Box 96, Coulsdon, Surrey CR5 2TE. £89.00

FLIGHT INTERNATIONAL DIRECTORY, PO Box 1315, Potters Bar, Herts. EN6 1PU. 2v. £44.00, £40.00

FROZEN AND CHILLED FOODS YEAR BOOK, 2 Queensway, Redhill, Surrey RH1 1QS. £69.20

FURNISHING TRADE, DIRECTORY TO THE, PO Box 20, Sovereign Way, Tonbridge, Kent TN9 1RQ. £90.00

GAS INDUSTRY DIRECTORY, PO Box 20, Sovereign Way, Tonbridge, Kent TN9 1RQ. (Jan.) £74.00

GIBBONS' STAMPS OF THE WORLD CATALOGUE, 5 Parkside, Christchurch Road, Ringwood, Hants. BH24 3SH. (Oct.) 3v. £19.95, £19.95, £17.95

GOOD FOOD GUIDE, PO Box 6, Mill Road, Dunton Green, Sevenoaks, Kent TN13 2YA. £14.99

GOOD HOTEL GUIDE, Brunel Road, Houndmills, Basingstoke, Hants. RG21 2XS. £14.99

GOVERNMENT AND MUNICIPAL BUYERS GUIDE, PO Box 20, Sovereign Way, Tonbridge, Kent TN9 1RQ. (June) £50.00

GRADUATE STUDIES, Bateman Street, Cambridge CB2 1LZ. (May) £99.75

GUINNESS BOOK OF ANSWERS, 33 London Road, Enfield EN2 6DJ. £13.99

GUINNESS BOOK OF RECORDS, 33 London Road, Enfield EN2 6DJ. (Oct.) £14.99

HEALTH CARE BUYERS GUIDE, PO Box 20, Sovereign Way, Tonbridge, Kent TN9 1RQ. £65.00

HISTORIC HOUSES, CASTLES AND GARDENS IN GREAT BRITAIN AND IRELAND, East Grinstead House, East Grinstead, W. Sussex RH19 1XA. (March) £7.45

HOLLIS PRESS AND PR ANNUAL, Contact House, Lower Hampton Road, Sunbury-on-Thames TW16 5HG. (Oct.) £65.00

HOSPITALS AND HEALTH SERVICES YEARBOOK AND DIRECTORY OF HOSPITAL SUPPLIERS, 75 Portland Place, London W1N 4AN. £80.00

HUTCHINS' PRICED SCHEDULES, 33 Station Road, Bexhill-on-Sea, E. Sussex TN40 1RG. £45.00

INDEPENDENT SCHOOLS YEAR BOOK, 35 Bedford Row, London WC1R 4JH. £19.99

INSURANCE DIRECTORY AND YEAR BOOK, 58 Fleet Street, London EC4Y 1JU. (Jan.) £85.00

INTERNATIONAL PAPER DIRECTORY, PHILLIPS', PO Box 20, Sovereign Way, Tonbridge, Kent TN9 1RQ. £107.00

INTERNATIONAL WHO'S WHO, 18 Bedford Square, London WC1R 4JH. (Sept.) £130.00

INTERNATIONAL YEARBOOK AND STATESMAN'S WHO'S WHO, East Grinstead House, East Grinstead, W. Sussex RH19 1XE. (April) £147.00

JANE'S ALL THE WORLD'S AIRCRAFT, Sentinel House, 163 Brighton Road, Coulsdon, Surrey CR5 2NH. (Oct.) £145.00

JANE'S ARMOUR AND ARTILLERY, Sentinel House, 163 Brighton Road, Coulsdon, Surrey CR5 2NH. (Nov.) £145.00

JANE'S CONTAINERIZATION DIRECT, Sentinel House, 163 Brighton Road, Coulsdon, Surrey CR5 2NH. (Nov.) £159.00

JANE'S FIGHTING SHIPS, Sentinel House, 163 Brighton Road, Coulsdon, Surrey CR5 2NH. £145.00

JANE'S HIGH SPEED MARINE CRAFT AND AIR CUSHION VEHICLES, Sentinel House, 163 Brighton Road, Coulsdon, Surrey CR5 2NH. £159.00

JANE'S INFANTRY WEAPONS, Sentinel House, 163 Brighton Road, Coulsdon, Surrey CR5 2NH. (Aug.) £145.00

JANE'S NAVAL WEAPON SYSTEMS, Sentinel House, 163 Brighton Road, Coulsdon, Surrey CR5 2NH. £250.00

JANE'S WORLD RAILWAYS, Sentinel House, 163 Brighton Road, Coulsdon, Surrey CR5 2NH. £159.00

JEWISH YEAR BOOK, 25 Furnival Street, London EC4A 1JT. (Jan.) £14.00

KELLY'S BUSINESS DIRECTORY, East Grinstead House, East Grinstead, W. Sussex RH19 1XB. £155.00

KEMPE'S ENGINEERS YEAR BOOK, PO Box 20, Sovereign Way, Tonbridge, Kent TN9 1RQ. £99.00

KEMP'S INTERNATIONAL MUSIC BOOK, 12 Felix Avenue, London N8 9TL. £28.00

KIME'S INTERNATIONAL LAW DIRECTORY, PO Box 88, Harlow, Essex CM19 5SR. (Dec.) £48.00

LAXTON'S BUILDING PRICE BOOK, East Grinstead House, East Grinstead, W. Sussex RH19 1XE. £83.50

LIBRARY ASSOCIATION YEARBOOK, 7 Ridgmount Street, London WC1E 7AE. (May) £35.00

LLOYD'S LIST OF SHIPOWNERS, 71 Fenchurch Street, London EC3M 4BS. (Sept.) £115.00

LLOYD'S MARITIME DIRECTORY, Sheepen Place, Colchester CO3 3LP. (Jan.) £135.00

LLOYD'S NAUTICAL YEAR BOOK, Sheepen Place, Colchester CO3 3LP. (Sept.) £37.50

LLOYD'S REGISTER OF SHIPS, 71 Fenchurch Street, London EC3M 4BS. (July). 3v. £425.00

LYLE'S OFFICIAL ANTIQUES PRICE GUIDE, Glenmayne, Galashiels TDI 3NR. £16.95

LYLE'S PAINTINGS PRICE GUIDE, Glenmayne, Galashiels TDI 3NR. £16.95

MACMILLAN AND SILK CUT NAUTICAL ALMANACK, Brunel Road, Houndmills, Basingstoke, Hants. RG21 2XS. £21.99

MAGISTRATES' COURT GUIDE, Borough Green, Sevenoaks, Kent TN15 8PH. £18.95

MEDICAL ANNUAL, Falcon House, Queen Square, Lancaster LA1 1RN. £25.00

MEDICAL DIRECTORY, PO Box 88, Harlow, Essex CM19 5SR. (April) 3v. £149.00

MEDICAL REGISTER, 44 Hallam Street, London W1N 6AE. (March) 3v. £90.00

MIDDLE EAST AND NORTH AFRICA, 18 Bedford Square, London WC1B 3JN. (Oct.) £145.00

MILLER'S ANTIQUES PRICE GUIDE, The Cellars, 5 High Street, Tenterden, Kent TN30 6BN. £19.99

MINING ANNUAL REVIEW, PO Box 10, Edenbridge, Kent TN8 5NE. £60.00

MINING INTERNATIONAL YEAR BOOK, PO Box 88, Harlow, Essex CM19 5SR. (June) £140.00

MOTOR INDUSTRY OF GREAT BRITAIN WORLD AUTOMOTIVE STATISTICS, Forbes House, Halkin Street, London SW1X 7DS. (Oct.) £75.00

MOTOR SHIP DIRECTORY, Quadrant House, The Quadrant, Sutton, Surrey SM2 5AS. £80.00

MUNICIPAL YEARBOOK AND PUBLIC SERVICES DIRECTORY, 32 Vauxhall Bridge Road, London SW1V 2SS. (Dec.) 2v. £120.00

MUSEUMS AND GALLERIES IN GREAT BRITAIN AND IRELAND, East Grinstead House, East Grinstead, W. Sussex RH19 1XA. (Oct.) £6.90

NAUTICAL ALMANAC, HMSO, PO Box 276, London SW8 5DT. (Oct.) £17.50

PACKAGING INDUSTRY DIRECTORY, PO Box 20, Sovereign Way, Tonbridge, Kent TN9 1RQ. £68.00

PEARS CYCLOPEDIA, 27 Wright's Lane, London W8 5TZ. £14.99

PHOTOGRAPHY YEAR BOOK, Queensborough House, 2 Claremont Road, Surbiton, Surrey KT6 4QU. £18.95

POLYMERS, PAINT AND COLOUR YEAR BOOK, 2 Queensway, Redhill, Surrey RH1 1QS. £82.00

PORTS OF THE WORLD, Sheepen Place, Colchester, Essex CO3 3LP. £130.00

PRINTING TRADES DIRECTORY, PO Box 20, Sovereign Way, Tonbridge, Kent TN9 1RQ. £86.00

PUBLIC AUTHORITIES DIRECTORY, 122 Minories, London EC3N 1NT. (Jan.) £69.00

PUBLIC SERVICES DIRECTORY, Cheriton House, North Way, Andover, Hants SP10 5BE. (April) £19.95

PUBLISHING, DIRECTORY OF, Artillery House, Artillery Row, London SW1P 1RT. (Oct.) £45.00

RAC EUROPEAN HOTEL GUIDE, PO Box 100, RAC House, Lansdowne Road, Croydon CR9 2JA. (Jan.) £9.99

RAC HOTEL GUIDE, PO Box 100, RAC House, Lansdowne Road, Croydon CR9 2JA. (Nov.) £15.99, £12.99

RAILWAY DIRECTORY AND YEAR BOOK, Quadrant House, The Quadrant, Sutton, Surrey SM2 5AS. (Dec.) £50.00

REGIONAL TRENDS, PO Box 276, London SW8 5DT. (July) £26.00

RETAIL DIRECTORY OF THE UNITED KINGDOM, 32 Vauxhall Bridge Road, London SW1V 2SS. £128.00

RIBA DIRECTORY OF PRACTICES, Royal Institute of British Architects, 39 Moreland Street, London EC1V 8BB. (Oct.) £45.00

ROTHMANS FOOTBALL YEAR BOOK, 39 Milton Park, Abingdon, Oxon. OX14 4TD. (Aug.) £27.50, £16.99

ROTHMAN'S RUGBY LEAGUE YEAR BOOK, 39 Milton Park, Abingdon, Oxon OX14 4TD. (Sept.) £14.99

ROTHMAN'S RUGBY UNION YEAR BOOK, 39 Milton Park, Abingdon, Oxon OX14 4TD. (Sept.) £14.99

ROYAL SOCIETY YEAR BOOK, 6 Carlton House Terrace, London SW1Y 5AG. (Feb.) £16.00

RUFF'S GUIDE TO THE TURF AND SPORTING LIFE ANNUAL, Orbit House, 1 New Fetter Lane, London EC4A 1AR. (Jan.) £55.00

SALVATION ARMY YEAR BOOK, 117–121 Judd Street, London WC1H 9NN. (April) £4.25

SCOTTISH CURRENT LAW YEAR BOOK, 21 Alva Street, Edinburgh EH2 4PS. £320.00

SCOTTISH LAW DIRECTORY, 59 George Street, Edinburgh EH2 2LQ. £32.00

SELL'S AEROSPACE EUROPE, PO Box 20, Sovereign Way, Tonbridge, Kent TN9 1RQ. £63.00

SELL'S DIRECTORY OF PRODUCTS AND SERVICES, PO Box 20, Sovereign Way, Tonbridge, Kent TN9 1RQ. (June) £72.00

SHEET METAL INDUSTRIES YEAR BOOK, 2 Queensway, Redhill, Surrey RH1 1QS. £57.00

SOCIAL SERVICES YEAR BOOK, PO Box 88, Harlow, Essex CMI9 5SR. (April) £68.00

SOCIAL TRENDS, PO Box 276, London SW8 5DT. (Jan.) £26.00

SOLICITORS AND BARRISTERS DIRECTORY, 50 Chancery Lane, London WC2A 1SX. £50.00

SPON'S ARCHITECTS' AND BUILDERS' PRICE BOOK, 2–6 Boundary Row, London SE1 8HN. £59.50

SPON'S MECHANICAL AND ELECTRICAL SERVICES PRICE BOOK, 2–6 Boundary Row, London SE1 8HN. £65.00

STATESMAN'S YEARBOOK, Brunel House, Houndmills, Basingstoke, Hants. RG21 2XS. (Aug.) £40.00

STOCK EXCHANGE OFFICIAL YEAR BOOK, Brunel House, Houndmills, Basingstoke, Hants. RG21 2XS. £195.00

STONE'S JUSTICES' MANUAL, Borough Green, Sevenoaks, Kent TN15 8PH. 3V. (May) £165.00

TANKER REGISTER, 12 Camomile Street, London EC3A 7BP. (May) £145.00

TIMBER TRADE ADDRESS BOOK, PO Box 20, Sovereign Way, Tonbridge, Kent TN9 1RQ. £52.00

TRAINING DIRECTORY, 120 Pentonville Road, London N1 9JN. £25.00

TRAVEL TRADE DIRECTORY, PO Box 20, Sovereign Way, Tonbridge, Kent TN9 1RQ. (March) £65.00

UK KOMPASS REGISTER, East Grinstead House, East Grinstead, W. Sussex RH19 1XD. 5V. £780.00

UNITED KINGDOM MINERALS YEARBOOK, British Geological Survey, Keyworth, Nottingham NG12 5GG. £27.50

UNITED REFORMED CHURCH YEAR BOOK, 86 Tavistock Place, London WC1H 9RT. (Sept.) £8.50, £7.50

UNIT TRUST YEAR BOOK, 7th Floor, 50–64 Broadway, London SW1H 0DB. (March) £95.00

UNIVERSITY AND COLLEGE ENTRANCE, 14 Cooper's Row, London EC3N 2BH. (June) £10.00

VETERINARY ANNUAL, Osney Mead, Oxford OX2 0EL. £65.00

WATER SERVICES YEAR BOOK, 2 Queensway, Redhill, Surrey RH1 1QS. (Oct.) £56.00

WHITAKER'S ALMANACK, 12 Dyott Street, London WC1A 1DF. (Nov.) £40.00, £25.00

WHITAKER'S BOOKS IN PRINT, 12 Dyott Street, London WC1A 1DF. (Jan.) £250.00

WHITAKER'S CONCISE ALMANACK, 12 Dyott Street, London WC1A 1DF. (Nov.) £9.95

WHITAKER'S PUBLISHERS IN THE UNITED KINGDOM AND THEIR ADDRESSES, 12 Dyott Street, London WC1A 1DF. (March) £9.50

WHO OWNS WHOM? – Holmers Farm Way, High Wycombe, Bucks. HP12 4UL. 2V. £325.00

WHO'S WHO, 35 Bedford Row, London WC1R 4JH. £88.00

WILLING'S PRESS GUIDE, East Grinstead House, East Grinstead, W. Sussex RH19 1XE. (Feb.) 2V. £145.00

WISDEN CRICKETERS' ALMANACK, 13–14 Eldon Way, Lineside Estate, Littlehampton, W. Sussex BN17 7HE. (April) £22.50, £19.50

WORLD HOTEL DIRECTORY, PO Box 88, Harlow, Essex CM19 5SR. £89.00

WORLD INSURANCE, PO Box 88, Harlow, Essex CM19 5SR. £125.00

WORLD MINERAL STATISTICS, British Geological Survey, Keyworth, Notts. NG12 5GG. (Sept.) £50.00

WORLD OF LEARNING, 18 Bedford Square, London WC1B 3JN. (Jan.) 2V. £180.00

WRITERS' AND ARTISTS' YEAR BOOK, 35 Bedford Row, London WC1R 4JH. (Oct.) £9.99

Employers' and Trade Associations

At 31 December 1992 there were 128 employers' associations listed by the Certification Officer (*see* page 295). Most national employers' associations are members of the Confederation of British Industry (CBI). For ACAS, the Certification Office, the Commission for Racial Equality, the Equal Opportunities Commission, the Health and Safety Commission, the Industrial Tribunals and Review Bodies, *see* Index.

CONFEDERATION OF BRITISH INDUSTRY
Centre Point, 103 New Oxford Street, London WC1A 1DU
Tel 071-379 7400

The Confederation of British Industry was founded in 1965 and is an independent non-party political body financed by industry and commerce. It exists primarily to ensure that the Government understands the intentions, needs and problems of British business. It is the recognized spokesman for the business viewpoint and is consulted as such by the Government.

The CBI represents, directly and indirectly, some 250,000 companies, large and small, from all sectors.

The governing body of the CBI is the 400-strong Council, which meets monthly in London under the chairmanship of the President. It is assisted by some 27 expert standing committees which advise on the main aspects of policy. There are 13 regional councils and offices covering the administrative regions of England, Wales, Scotland and Northern Ireland. There is also an office in Brussels.
President, Sir Michael Angus
Director-General, H. Davies
Secretary, M. W. Hunt

ASSOCIATIONS

ADVERTISING ASSOCIATION, Abford House, 15 Wilton Road, London SW1V 1NJ. Tel: 071-828 2771. *Director-General*, R. L. Wade
AEROSPACE COMPANIES LTD, SOCIETY OF BRITISH, 29 King Street, London SW1Y 6RD. Tel: 071-839 3231. *Director*, Sir Barry Duxbury, KCB, CBE
APPAREL AND TEXTILE CONFEDERATION, BRITISH, British Apparel and Textile Centre, 7 Swallow Place, London WIR 7AA. Tel: 071-408 0020. *Director-General*, J. R. Wilson
BAKERS, FEDERATION OF, 20 Bedford Square, London WC1B 3HF. Tel: 071-580 4252. *Director*, A. Casdagli, CBE
BANKERS' ASSOCIATION, BRITISH, 10 Lombard Street, London EC3V 9EL. Tel: 071-623 4001. *Director-General*, The Lord Inchyra
BLIND AND DISABLED INC., NATIONAL ASSOCIATION OF INDUSTRIES FOR THE, Triton House, 43A High Street South, Dunstable, Beds. LU6 3RZ. Tel: 0582-606796. *Hon. Secretary*, G. J. Entwistle
BREWERS' SOCIETY, 42 Portman Square, London WIH 0BB. Tel: 071-486 4831. *Director*, R. W. Simpson
BRUSH MANUFACTURERS' ASSOCIATION, BRITISH, Brooke House, 4 The Lakes, Bedford Road, Northampton NN4 0YD. Tel: 0604-22023. *Secretary*, A. N. Nisbet

BUILDING EMPLOYERS' CONFEDERATION, 82 New Cavendish Street, London WIM 8AD. Tel: 071-580 5588. *Director-General*, I. A. Deslandes
BUILDING MATERIAL PRODUCERS, NATIONAL COUNCIL OF, 26 Store Street, London WC1E 7BT. Tel: 071-323 3770. *Director-General*, N. M. Chaldecott, OBE
BUS AND COACH COUNCIL, Sardinia House, 52 Lincoln's Inn Fields, London WC2A 3LZ. Tel: 071-831 7546. *Director-General*, Mrs A. V. M. Palmer, MBE
CHAMBER OF SHIPPING LTD, Minories House, 2-5 Minories, London EC3N 1BJ. Tel: 071-702 1100. *Director-General*, Adm. Sir Nicholas Hunt, GCB, LVO
CHEMICAL INDUSTRIES ASSOCIATION LTD, Kings Buildings, Smith Square, London SW1P 3JJ. Tel: 071-834 3399. *Director-General*, J. C. L. Cox
CLOTHING INDUSTRY ASSOCIATION LTD, BRITISH, British Apparel and Textile Centre, 7 Swallow Place, London WIR 7AA. Tel: 071-408 0020. *Director*, J. R. Wilson
DAIRY TRADE FEDERATION, 19 Cornwall Terrace, London NW1 4QP. Tel: 071-486 7244. *Director-General*, J. P. Price
ELECTROTECHNICAL AND ALLIED MANUFACTURERS' ASSOCIATIONS, FEDERATION OF BRITISH (BEAMA), Leicester House, 8 Leicester Street, London WC2H 7BN. Tel: 071-437 0678. *Director-General*, J. G. Gaddes
ENGINEERING EMPLOYERS' FEDERATION, Broadway House, Tothill Street, London SW1H 9NQ. Tel: 071-222 7777. *Director-General*, N. A. Johnson, OBE
FARMERS' UNION, NATIONAL (NFU), 22 Long Acre, London WC2E 9LY. Tel: 071-235 5077. *Director-General*, D. Evans, CBE
FARMERS' UNION OF SCOTLAND, NATIONAL, Rural Centre-West Mains, Ingliston, Newbridge, Midlothian EH28 8LT. Tel: 031-335 3111. *Chief Executive*, D. S. Johnston, OBE
FARMERS' UNION, ULSTER, Dunedin, 475-477 Antrim Road, Belfast BT15 3DA. Tel: 0232-370222. *Director-General*, A. MacLaughlin
FINANCE AND LEASING ASSOCIATION, 18 Upper Grosvenor Street, London WIX 9PB. Tel: 071-491 2783. *Director*, N. A. D. Grant, CBE
FOOD AND DRINK FEDERATION, 6 Catherine Street, London WC2B 5JJ. Tel: 071-836 2460. *Director-General*, M. P. Mackenzie
FREIGHT TRANSPORT ASSOCIATION LTD, Hermes House, 157 St John's Road, Tunbridge Wells, Kent TN4 9UZ. Tel: 0892-526171. *Director-General*, D. C. Green
INSURERS, ASSOCIATION OF BRITISH, 51 Gresham Street, London EC2V 7HQ. Tel: 071-600 3333. *Director-General*, M. Boléat
KNITTING INDUSTRIES FEDERATION LTD, 53 Oxford Street, Leicester LE1 5XY. Tel: 0533-541608. *Director*, J. P. Harrison
LEATHER CONFEDERATION, BRITISH, Leather Trade House, Kings Park Road, Moulton Park, Northampton NN3 1JD. Tel: 0604-494131. *Chief Executive*, Dr K. T. W. Alexander
LEATHER PRODUCERS' ASSOCIATION, Leather Trade House, Kings Park Road, Moulton Park, Northampton NN3 1JD. Tel: 0604-494131. *National Secretary*, J. Purvis

MANAGEMENT CONSULTANCIES ASSOCIATION, 11 West Halkin Street, London SW1X 8JL. Tel: 071-235 3897. *Executive Director*, B. O'Rorke

MARINE INDUSTRIES FEDERATION, BRITISH, Meadlake Place, Thorpe Lea Road, Egham, Surrey TW20 8HE. Tel: 0784-473377. *Executive Chairman*, A. V. Beechey

MASTER BUILDERS, FEDERATION OF, Gordon Fisher House, 14–15 Great James Street, London WC1N 3DP. Tel: 071-242 7583. *Director-General*, J. D. Maiden

MOTOR MANUFACTURERS AND TRADERS LTD, SOCIETY OF, Forbes House, Halkin Street, London SW1X 7DS. Tel: 071-235 7000. *Chief Executive*, Sir Hal Miller

NEWSPAPER PUBLISHERS ASSOCIATION LTD, 34 Southwark Bridge Road, London SE1 9EU. Tel: 071-928 6928. *Director*, D. Pollock

NEWSPAPER SOCIETY, Bloomsbury House, 74–77 Great Russell Street, London WC1B 3DA. Tel: 071-636 7014. *Director*, D. Nisbet-Smith

OFFICE SYSTEMS AND STATIONERY FEDERATION, BRITISH, 6 Wimpole Street, London W1M 8AS. Tel: 071-637 7692. *Director*, D. F. Hall

PAPER AND BOARD INDUSTRY FEDERATION, BRITISH, Papermakers House, Rivenhall Road, Westlea, Swindon SN5 7BD. Tel: 0793-886086. *Director-General*, W. J. Bartlett

PLASTICS FEDERATION, BRITISH, 5 Belgrave Square, London SW1X 8PD. Tel: 071-235 9483. *Director*, D. R. Jones

PORTS FEDERATION, BRITISH, Victoria House, Vernon Place, London WC1B 4LL. Tel: 071-242 1200. *Managing Director*, J. Sharples

PRINTING INDUSTRIES FEDERATION, BRITISH, 11 Bedford Row, London WC1R 4DX. Tel: 071-242 6904. *Director-General*, C. Stanley

PUBLISHERS ASSOCIATION, THE, 19 Bedford Square, London WC1B 3HJ. Tel: 071-580 6321. *Chief Executive*, C. Bradley

RADIO COMPANIES LTD, ASSOCIATION OF INDEPENDENT, Radio House, 46 Westbourne Grove, London W2 5SH. Tel: 071-727 2646. *Chief Executive*, B. West

RETAIL CONSORTIUM, BRITISH, Bedford House, 69–79 Fulham High Street, London SW6 3JW. Tel: 071-371 5185. *Director-General*, J. N. W. May

RETAIL NEWSAGENTS, NATIONAL FEDERATION OF, Yeoman House, Sekforde Street, London EC1R 0HD. Tel: 071-253 4225. *Chief Executive*, K. E. J. Peters

ROAD FEDERATION, BRITISH, Pillar House, 194–202 Old Kent Road, London SE1 5TG. Tel: 071-703 9769. *Director*, R. Diment

ROAD HAULAGE ASSOCIATION LTD, Roadway House, 35 Monument Hill, Weybridge, Surrey KT13 8RN. Tel: 0932-841515. *Director-General*, D. B. H. Colley, CB, CBE

RUBBER MANUFACTURERS' ASSOCIATION LTD, BRITISH, 90 Tottenham Court Road, London W1P 0BR. Tel: 071-580 2794. *Director*, W. R. Pollock

SPORTS AND ALLIED INDUSTRIES FEDERATION LTD, BRITISH, 23 Brighton Road, Croydon CR2 4EA. Tel: 081-681 1242. *Chief Executive*, L. F. Standen

TIMBER GROWERS' UNITED KINGDOM, 5 Dublin Street, Lane South, Edinburgh EH1 3PX. Tel: 031-557 0944. *Chief Executive*, P. H. Wilson

TIMBER MERCHANTS' ASSOCIATION, BRITISH, Stocking Lane, Hughenden Valley, High Wycombe, Bucks. HP14 4JZ. Tel: 0494-563602. *Secretary*, R. T. Allcorn

TIMBER TRADE FEDERATION, Clareville House, 26–27 Oxendon Street, London SW1Y 4EL. Tel: 071-839 1891. *Director-General*, P. G. Harris

UK OFFSHORE OPERATORS ASSOCIATION LTD, 3 Hans Crescent, London SW1X 0LN. Tel: 071-589 5255. *Director-General*, Dr H. W. D. Hughes, OBE

UK PETROLEUM INDUSTRY ASSOCIATION LTD, 9 Kingsway, London WC2B 6XH. Tel: 071-240 0289. *Director-General*, D. Parker

Trade Unions

At 31 December 1992 there were 302 trade unions listed by the Certification Officer (*see* page 295). In 1991 9,489,034 people were members of listed trade unions, representing about 33 per cent of the total labour force and about 36 per cent of the labour force in employment. Over 80 per cent of trade union members belong to the 69 unions affiliated to the TUC (*see* below).

The Central Arbitration Committee arbitrates in industrial disputes between trade unions and employers, and determines disclosure of information complaints. The Commissioner for the Rights of Trade Union Members provides assistance to individuals taking action against their trade union when they have not been afforded their statutory rights or when specific union rules have been breached.

For ACAS, the Certification Office, the Commission for Racial Equality, the Equal Opportunities Commission, the Health and Safety Commission, the Industrial Tribunals and Review Bodies, *see* Index.

THE CENTRAL ARBITRATION COMMITTEE, 39 Grosvenor Place, London SW1X 7BD. Tel: 071-210 3737/8. *Chairman*, Prof. Sir John Wood, CBE; *Secretary*, S. Gouldstone

THE COMMISSIONER FOR THE RIGHTS OF TRADE UNION MEMBERS, 1st Floor, Bank Chambers, 2A Rylands Street, Warrington, Cheshire WA1 1EN. Tel: 0925-415771. *Commissioner*, Mrs G. Rowlands

---

TUC-AFFILIATED TRADE UNIONS

TRADES UNION CONGRESS (TUC)
Congress House, 23–28 Great Russell Street, London WC1B 3LS
Tel 071-636 4030

The Trades Union Congress, founded in 1868, is an independent association of trade unions. Its main job is to help unions achieve together things which they could not do alone. It draws up common policies and promotes and publicizes them. It makes representations to government, to employers and, increasingly, to international bodies such as the European Community. The TUC also carries out research, campaigns and a programme of trade union education. Resolving disputes between unions is another task it undertakes. TUC representatives sit on many public bodies at national and international level.

The governing body of the TUC is the annual Congress. Between Congresses, business is conducted by a General Council which meets monthly and appoints specialist policy committees. The full-time staff is headed by the General Secretary who is elected by Congress and is a permanent member of the General Council.

Affiliated unions (in 1992–3) totalled 69 with an aggregate membership of 7,757,000.
President (1993–4), J. Knapp (RMT)
General Secretary, J. Monks, *elected* 1993

SCOTTISH TRADES UNION CONGRESS
16 Woodlands Terrace, Glasgow G3 6DF
Tel 041-332 4946

The Congress was formed in 1897 and acts as a national centre for the trade union movement in Scotland. In 1993 it consisted of 53 unions with a membership of 768,183 and 40 directly affiliated Trades Councils.

The Annual Congress in April elects a 34-member General Council on the basis of eight industrial sections.
Chairperson, H. McLevy
General Secretary, C. Christie

AFFILIATED UNIONS *as at 1 September 1993*
(Number of members in parentheses)

AMALGAMATED ENGINEERING AND ELECTRICAL UNION (AEEU) (at present, only the Engineering section of the union has TUC membership) (884,463; Engineering section 541,367), 110 Peckham Road, London SE15 5EL. Tel: 071-703 4231. *General Secretary*, G. H. Laird, CBE

ASSOCIATED SOCIETY OF LOCOMOTIVE ENGINEERS AND FIREMEN (ASLEF) (18,866), 9 Arkwright Road, London NW3 6AB. Tel: 071-431 0275. *Secretary*, D. Fullick (L. Adams, from Jan. 1994)

ASSOCIATION OF FIRST DIVISION CIVIL SERVANTS (9,642), 2 Caxton Street, London SW1H 0QH. Tel: 071-222 6242. *General Secretary*, Ms E. Symons

ASSOCIATION OF UNIVERSITY TEACHERS (31,000), United House, 1 Pembridge Road, London W11 3JY. Tel: 071-221 4370. *General Secretary*, D. Triesman

BAKERS, FOOD AND ALLIED WORKERS' UNION (32,122), Stanborough House, Great North Road, Stanborough, Welwyn Garden City, Herts. AL8 7TA. Tel: 0707-260150. *General Secretary*, J. R. Marino

BANKING, INSURANCE AND FINANCE UNION (153,562), Sheffield House, 1B Amity Grove, London SW20 0LG. Tel: 081-946 9151. *General Secretary*, L. A. Mills

BRITISH ACTORS' EQUITY ASSOCIATION (45,000), Guild House, Upper St Martin's Lane, London WC2H 9EG. Tel: 071-379 6000. *General Secretary*, I. McGarry

BRITISH AIR LINE PILOTS ASSOCIATION, THE (8,059), 81 New Road, Harlington, Hayes, Middx. UB3 5BG. Tel: 081-759 9331. *General Secretary*, C. Darke

BRITISH ASSOCIATION OF COLLIERY MANAGEMENT, THE (5,796), BACM House, 317 Nottingham Road, Old Basford, Nottingham NG7 7DP. Tel: 0602-785819. *General Secretary*, J. D. Meads

BROADCASTING, ENTERTAINMENT, CINEMATOGRAPH AND THEATRE UNION (BECTU) (42,092), 111 Wardour Street, London W1V 4AY. Tel: 071-437 8506. *General Secretary*, D. A. Hearn (until Nov. 1993)

CARD SETTING MACHINE TENTERS' SOCIETY (88), 48 Scar End Lane, Staincliffe, W. Yorks. WF12 4NY. Tel: 0924-400206. *Secretary*, A. Moorhouse

CERAMIC AND ALLIED TRADES UNION, THE (23,122), Hillcrest House, Garth Street, Stoke-on-Trent ST1 2AB. Tel: 0782-272755. *General Secretary*, A. W. Clowes

CHARTERED SOCIETY OF PHYSIOTHERAPY, THE (24,924), 14 Bedford Row, London WC1R 4ED. Tel: 071-242 1941. *Secretary*, T. Simon

CIVIL AND PUBLIC SERVICES ASSOCIATION, THE (126,000), 160 Falcon Road, London SW11 2LN. Tel: 071-924 2727. *General Secretary*, B. Reamsbottom

COMMUNICATION MANAGERS' ASSOCIATION (15,474), CMA House, Ruscombe Road, Twyford, Reading RG10 9JD. Tel: 0734-342300. *General Secretary*, T. L. Deegan

EDUCATIONAL INSTITUTE OF SCOTLAND, THE (46,803), 46 Moray Place, Edinburgh EH3 6BH. Tel: 031-225 6244. *General Secretary*, J. B. Martin

ELECTRICAL AND PLUMBING INDUSTRIES UNION (4,000), Park House, 64–66 Wandsworth Common North Side, London SW18 2SH. Tel: 081-874 0458. *General Secretary*, J. Aitkin

ENGINEERING AND FASTENER TRADE UNION (240), 42 Galton Road, Warley, West Midlands, B67 5JU. Tel: 021-429 2594. *General Secretary*, J. Burdis

ENGINEERS' AND MANAGERS' ASSOCIATION (38,350), Flaxman House, Gogmore Lane, Chertsey, Surrey KT16 9JS. Tel: 0932-564131. *General Secretary*, D. A. Cooper

FILM ARTISTES' ASSOCIATION (2,000) 61 Marloes Road, London W8 6LE. Tel: 071-937 4567. *General Secretary*, G. Avory

FIRE BRIGADES UNION, THE (48,970), Bradley House, 68 Coombe Road, Kingston upon Thames, Surrey KT2 7AE. Tel: 081-541 1765. *General Secretary*, K. Cameron

FURNITURE, TIMBER AND ALLIED TRADES UNION (31,642), Fairfields, Roe Green, London NW9 0PT. Tel: 081-204 0273. *General Secretary*, C. A. Christopher

GENERAL UNION OF ASSOCIATIONS OF LOOM OVERLOOKERS, THE (502), 9 Wellington Street, St Johns, Blackburn, Lancs. BB1 8AF. Tel: 0254-51760. *President*, D. J. Rishton

GMB (formerly GENERAL, MUNICIPAL, BOILERMAKERS AND ALLIED TRADES UNION) (862,785), 22–24 Worple Road, London SW19 4DD. Tel: 081-947 3131. *General Secretary*, J. Edmonds

GRAPHICAL, PAPER AND MEDIA UNION (270,023), 63–67 Bromham Road, Bedford MK40 2AG. Tel: 0234-351521. *General Secretary*, A. D. Dubbins

HOSPITAL CONSULTANTS AND SPECIALISTS ASSOCIATION, THE (2,301), 1 Kingsclere Road, Overton, Hants. RG25 3JP. Tel: 0256-771777. *Chief Executive*, S. J. Charkham

INLAND REVENUE STAFF FEDERATION (59,044), Douglas Houghton House, 231 Vauxhall Bridge Road, London SW1V 1EH. Tel: 071-834 8254. *General Secretary*, C. Brooke

INSTITUTION OF PROFESSIONALS, MANAGERS AND SPECIALISTS (90,008), 75–79 York Road, London SE1 7AQ. Tel: 071-928 9951. *General Secretary*, W. Brett

IRON AND STEEL TRADES CONFEDERATION, THE (45,000), Swinton House, 324 Gray's Inn Road, London WC1X 8DD. Tel: 071-837 6691. *General Secretary*, D. K. Brookman

MANUFACTURING, SCIENCE AND FINANCE UNION (MSF) (604,000), Park House, 64–66 Wandsworth Common North Side, London SW18 2SH. Tel: 081-871 2100. *General Secretary*, R. Lyons

MILITARY AND ORCHESTRAL MUSICAL INSTRUMENT MAKERS' TRADE SOCIETY (48), 2 Whitehouse Avenue, Borehamwood, Herts. WD6 1HD. Tel: 081-952 7711. *General Secretary*, F. McKenzie

MUSICIANS' UNION (36,979), 60–62 Clapham Road, London SW9 0JJ. Tel: 071-582 5566. *General Secretary*, D. Scard

NATIONAL ASSOCIATION OF COLLIERY OVERMEN, DEPUTIES AND SHOTFIRERS (5,750), Simpson House, 48 Nether Hall Road, Doncaster DN1 2PZ. Tel: 0302-368015. *Secretary*, P. McNestry

NATIONAL ASSOCIATION OF CO-OPERATIVE OFFICIALS (4,042), Coronation House, Arndale Centre, Manchester M4 2HW. Tel: 061-834 6029. *General Secretary*, L. W. Ewing

NATIONAL ASSOCIATION OF LICENSED HOUSE MANAGERS (10,000), 9 Coombe Lane, London SW20 8NE. Tel: 081-947 3080. *General Secretary*, J. Madden

NATIONAL ASSOCIATION OF PROBATION OFFICERS (7,526), 3–4 Chivalry Road, London SW11 1HT. Tel: 071-223 4887. *Secretary*, Ms J. McKnight

NATIONAL ASSOCIATION OF SCHOOLMASTERS AND UNION OF WOMEN TEACHERS (NAS/UWT) (190,637), Hillscourt Education Centre, Rose Hill, Rednal, Birmingham B45 8RS. Tel: 021-453 6150. *General Secretary*, N. De Gruchy

NATIONAL ASSOCIATION OF TEACHERS IN FURTHER AND HIGHER EDUCATION (73,517), 27 Britannia Street, London WC1X 9JP. Tel: 071-837 3636. *General Secretary*, G. Woolf

NATIONAL COMMUNICATIONS UNION (150,703), Greystoke House, 150 Brunswick Road, London W5 1AW. Tel: 081-998 2981. *General Secretary*, A. I. Young

NATIONAL LEAGUE OF THE BLIND AND DISABLED, THE (2,371), 2 Tenterden Road, London N17 8BE. Tel: 081-808 6030. *Secretary*, M. A. Barrett

NATIONAL UNION OF CIVIL AND PUBLIC SERVANTS (NUCPS) (111,831), 124–130 Southwark Street, London SE1 0TU. Tel: 071-928 9671. *General Secretary*, J. Sheldon

NATIONAL UNION OF DOMESTIC APPLIANCES AND GENERAL OPERATIVES, THE (2,400), 6–8 Imperial Buildings, Corporation Street, Rotherham, S. Yorks. S60 1PB. Tel: 0709-382820. *General Secretary*, A. McCarthy

NATIONAL UNION OF INSURANCE WORKERS (16,200), 27 Old Gloucester Street, London WC1N 3AF. Tel: 071-405 6798. *General Secretary*, K. Perry

NATIONAL UNION OF JOURNALISTS (NUJ) (25,000), Acorn House, 314–320 Gray's Inn Road, London WC1X 8DP. Tel: 071-278 7916. *General Secretary*, J. Foster

NATIONAL UNION OF KNITWEAR, FOOTWEAR AND APPAREL TRADES (51,636), The Grange, 108 Northampton Road, Earls Barton, Northampton NN6 0JH. Tel: 0604-810326. *General Secretary*, Mrs H. McGrath

NATIONAL UNION OF LOCK AND METAL WORKERS (4,666), Bellamy House, Wilkes Street, Willenhall, W. Midlands WV13 2BS. Tel: 0902-366651. *General Secretary*, M. Bradley

NATIONAL UNION OF MARINE, AVIATION AND SHIPPING TRANSPORT OFFICERS, THE (18,730), Oceanair House, 750–760 High Road, Leytonstone, London E11 3BB. Tel: 081-989 6677. *General Secretary*, B. Orrell

NATIONAL UNION OF MINEWORKERS (NUM) (33,000), Holly Street, Sheffield S1 2GT. Tel: 0742-766900. *President*, A. Scargill

NATIONAL UNION OF RAIL, MARITIME AND TRANSPORT WORKERS (RMT) (110,000), Unity House, Euston Road, London NW1 2BL. Tel: 071-381 4771. *General Secretary*, J. Knapp

NATIONAL UNION OF SCALEMAKERS (712), Queensway House, 57 Livery Street, Birmingham B3 1HA. Tel: 021-236 8998. *General Secretary*, C. D. Wicks

NATIONAL UNION OF TEACHERS (NUT) (162,192), Hamilton House, Mabledon Place, London WC1H 9BD. Tel: 071-388 6191. *General Secretary*, D. McAvoy

NORTHERN CARPET TRADES' UNION (715), 22 Clare Road, Halifax, W. Yorks. HX1 2HX. Tel: 0422-360492. *General Secretary*, K. Edmondson

POWER LOOM CARPET WEAVERS' AND TEXTILE WORKERS' UNION, THE (2,050), Callows Lane,

Kidderminster, Worcs. DY10 2JG. Tel: 0562-823192. *General Secretary,* R. White

PRISON OFFICERS' ASSOCIATION, THE (29,077), Cronin House, 245 Church Street, London N9 9HW. Tel: 081-803 0255. *General Secretary,* D. Evans

ROSSENDALE UNION OF BOOT, SHOE AND SLIPPER OPERATIVES, THE (2,239), Taylor House, 7 Tenterfield Street, Waterfoot, Rossendale, Lancs. BB4 7BA. Tel: 0706-215657. *General Secretary,* M. Murray

SCOTTISH PRISON OFFICERS' ASSOCIATION (4,200) 21 Calder Road, Edinburgh EH11 3PF. Tel: 031-443 8105. *General Secretary,* W. Goodall

SCOTTISH UNION OF POWER-LOOM OVERLOOKERS (60), 3 Napier Terrace, Dundee DD2 2SL. Tel: 0382-612196. *Secretary,* J. D. Reilly

SHEFFIELD WOOL SHEAR WORKERS' UNION (14), 50 Bankfield Road, Malin Bridge, Sheffield S6 4RD. Tel: 0742-333688. *Secretary,* J. H. R. Cutler

SOCIETY OF RADIOGRAPHERS (12,815), 14 Upper Wimpole Street, London W1M 8BN. Tel: 071-935 5726. *General Secretary,* B. Macey

SOCIETY OF TELECOM EXECUTIVES (22,143), 1 Park Road, Teddington, Middx. TW11 0AR. Tel: 081-943 5181. *General Secretary,* S. Petch

TRANSPORT AND GENERAL WORKERS' UNION (TGWU) (1,126,631), Transport House, Smith Square, London SW1P 3JB. Tel: 071-828 7788. *General Secretary,* B. Morris

TRANSPORT SALARIED STAFFS' ASSOCIATION (40,874), Walkden House, 10 Melton Street, London NW1 2EJ. Tel: 071-387 2101. *General Secretary,* R. A. Rosser

UNION OF COMMUNICATION WORKERS, THE (UCW) (182,418), UCW House, Crescent Lane, London SW4 9RN. Tel: 071-622 9977. *General Secretary,* A. Johnson

UNION OF CONSTRUCTION, ALLIED TRADES AND TECHNICIANS (UCATT) (202,000), UCATT House, 177 Abbeville Road, London SW4 9RL. Tel: 071-622 2442. *Secretary,* G. Brumwell

UNION OF SHOP, DISTRIBUTIVE AND ALLIED WORKERS (USDAW) (316,491), Oakley, 188 Wilmslow Road, Fallowfield, Manchester M14 6LJ. Tel: 061-224 2804. *Secretary,* D. G. Davies

UNION OF TEXTILE WORKERS (1,704), Foxlowe, Market Place, Leek, Staffs. ST13 6AD. Tel: 0538-382068. *General Secretary,* A. Hitchmough

UNISON (1,400,000), Unison Centre, Holborn Towers, 137 High Holborn, London WC1V 6FL. Tel: 071-404 1884. *General Secretary,* A. Jinkinson

UNITED ROAD TRANSPORT UNION (18,000), 76 High Lane, Chorlton, Manchester M21 1FD. Tel: 061-881 6245. *General Secretary,* D. Higginbottom

WRITERS' GUILD OF GREAT BRITAIN, THE (1,670), 430 Edgware Road, London W2 1EH. Tel: 071-723 8074. *General Secretary,* Ms A. Gray

MERGERS, ETC, 1992–3

The Electrical, Electronics, Telecommunications and Plumbing Union (EETPU) merged with the Amalgamated Engineering Union in May 1992 to form the Amalgamated Engineering and Electrical Union (AEEU). Only the Engineering section is affiliated to the TUC at present. In April 1993 the EETPU section voted in favour of re-affiliating with the TUC and the question of re-affiliation will be put to Congress in September 1993.

The Confederation of Health Service Employees (COHSE), the National and Local Government Officers' Association (NALGO) and the National Union of Public Employees (NUPE) merged to form UNISON on 1 July 1993.

MERGERS UNDER CONSIDERATION

The Furniture, Timber and Allied Trade Union will ballot its members in September 1993 regarding a merger with the GMB. If the vote is in favour, the merger will take place on 1 January 1994.

NON-AFFILIATED TRADE UNIONS

ASSOCIATION OF CAREER TEACHERS, Hillsborough, Castledine Street, Loughborough, Leics. LE11 2DX. Tel: 0509-214617. *General Secretary,* Miss R. Yaffé

BRITISH DENTAL ASSOCIATION, 64 Wimpole Street, London W1M 8AL. Tel: 071-935 0875. *Chief Executive,* J. M. G. Hunt

NATIONAL ASSOCIATION OF HEAD TEACHERS (NAHT), 1 Heath Square, Boltro Road, Haywards Heath, W. Sussex RH16 1BL. Tel: 0444-458133. *General Secretary,* D. Hart, OBE

NATIONAL SOCIETY FOR EDUCATION IN ART AND DESIGN, The Gatehouse, Corsham Court, Corsham, Wilts. SN13 0BZ. Tel: 0249-714825. *General Secretary,* J. H. M. Steers

PATTERN WEAVERS SOCIETY, 38 St Paul's Road, Kirkheaton, Huddersfield HD5 0EY. Tel: 0484-424988. *General Secretary,* K. Bradley

RETAIL BOOK, STATIONERY AND ALLIED TRADES EMPLOYEES' ASSOCIATION, 8–9 Commercial Road, Swindon SN1 5RB. Tel: 0793-615811. *General Secretary,* J. Windust

ROYAL COLLEGE OF MIDWIVES, 15 Mansfield Street, London W1M OBE. Tel: 071-580 6523. *General Secretary,* Miss R. M. Ashton, OBE

SCOTTISH SECONDARY TEACHERS' ASSOCIATION, 15 Dundas Street, Edinburgh EH3 6QG. Tel: 031-556 5919. *General Secretary,* A. A. Stanley

SECONDARY HEADS ASSOCIATION, 130 Regent Road, Leicester LE1 7PG. Tel: 0533-471797. *General Secretary,* J. Sutton

SOCIETY OF AUTHORS, 84 Drayton Gardens, London SW10 9SB. Tel: 071-373 6642. *General Secretary,* M. Le Fanu

SOCIETY OF SHUTTLEMAKERS, 211 Burnley Road, Colne, Lancs. BB8 8JD. Tel: 0282-866716. *General Secretary,* L. Illingworth

National Academies of Scholarship

The British Academy is an independent, self-governing learned society for the promotion of historical, philosophical and philological studies. It supports advanced academic research in the humanities and social sciences, and is the recognized channel outside the universities for the Government's support of research in the humanities and social sciences.

The Fellows are scholars who have attained distinction in one of the branches of study that the Academy exists to promote. Candidates must be nominated by existing Fellows. At 1 June 1993 there were 588 Fellows, 15 Honorary Fellows, and 293 Corresponding Fellows overseas.

President, Sir Keith Thomas, PBA
Treasurer, Dr E. A. Wrigley, FBA
Foreign Secretary, Prof. J. B. Trapp, FBA
Publications Officer, Prof. D. E. Luscombe, FBA
Secretary, P. W. H. Brown

The Royal Academy of Arts is an independent, self-governing society devoted to the encouragement and promotion of the fine arts.

Membership of the Academy is limited to 80 Royal Academicians, all being painters, engravers, sculptors or architects. Candidates are nominated and elected by the existing Academicians. There is also a limited class of honorary membership and there were 9 honorary members as at mid-1993.

President, Sir Roger de Grey, KCVO, PRA
Treasurer, Sir Philip Powell, CH, OBE, RA
Keeper, Prof. N. Adams, RA
Secretary, P. Rodgers

The Royal Academy of Engineering was established as the Fellowship of Engineering in 1976. It was granted a Royal Charter in May 1983 and its present title in 1992. It is an independent, self-governing body whose object is the pursuit, encouragement and maintenance of excellence in the whole field of engineering, in order to promote the advancement of the science, art and practice of engineering for the benefit of the public.

Election to the Fellowship is by invitation only from nominations supported by the body of Fellows. Fellows are chosen from among chartered engineers of all disciplines. The Royal Charter states that the total number of Fellows may not exceed 1,000. At July 1993 there were 943 Fellows, nine Honorary Fellows and 50 Foreign Members. The Duke of Edinburgh is the Senior Fellow and the Duke of Kent is a Royal Fellow.

President, Sir William Barlow, FEng
Senior Vice-President, B. F. Street, FEng
Vice-Presidents, Dr A. Denton, FEng; Dr A. M. Neville, MC, FEng, FRSE; B. W. Manley, FEng
Hon. Treasurer, G. A. Lee, FEng
Hon. Secretaries, R. Garrick, CBE, FEng, FRSE (*Mechanical Engineering*); R. H. Rooley, FEng (*Civil Engineering*); D. G. Jefferies, CBE, FEng (*Electrical Engineering*); Dr G. S. G. Beveridge, FEng, FRSE (*Process Engineering*); Dr A. A. Denton, FEng (*Overseas Affairs*); B. W. Manley, FEng (*Education, Training and Competence to Practise*)
Executive Secretary, J. R. Appleton.

The Scottish Academy was founded in 1826 to arrange exhibitions for contemporary paintings and to establish a society of fine art in Scotland. The Academy was granted a Royal Charter in 1838.

Members are elected from the disciplines of painting, sculpture, architecture and printmaking. Elections are from nominations put forward by the existing membership. At mid-1993 there were 11 Senior Academicians, 37 Academicians, 40 Associates, three non-resident Associates and 20 Honorary Members.

President, W. J. L. Baillie, PRSA
Secretary, I. McKenzie Smith, RSA
Treasurer, J. Morris, RSA
Librarian, P. Collins, RSA
Administrative Secretary, W. T. Meikle

The Royal Society is the United Kingdom's national academy of science. It is an independent, self-governing body under a Royal Charter, promoting and advancing all fields of physical and biological sciences, of mathematics and engineering, medical and agricultural sciences, their applications and place in society.

Election to Fellowship of the Royal Society is limited to those distinguished for original scientific work. Each year up to 40 new Fellows and six Foreign Members are elected from the most distinguished scientists. In addition, the Council can recommend for election members of the Royal family and, on average, one person each year for conspicuous service to the cause of science. At July 1993, there were 1,100 Fellows and 100 Foreign Members.

President, Sir Michael Atiyah, OM, FRS
Treasurer, Prof. J. H. Horlock, F.Eng, FRS
Biological Secretary, Prof. P. J. Lackmann, FRS
Physical Secretary, Sir Francis Graham-Smith, FRS
Foreign Secretary, Dr A. L. McLaren, DBE, FRS
Executive Secretary, Dr P. T. Warren

THE ROYAL SOCIETY OF EDINBURGH (1783)
22–24 George Street, Edinburgh EH2 2PQ
Tel 031-225 6057

The Royal Society of Edinburgh is Scotland's premier learned society. The Society was founded by Royal Charter in 1783 for 'the advancement of Learning and Useful Knowledge', and its principal role is the promotion of scholarship in all its branches. It provides a forum for broadly-based interdisciplinary activity in Scotland, including organizing public lectures, conferences and specialist research seminars;

providing advice to Parliament and government; administering a range of research fellowships held in Scotland; and publishing learned journals.

Fellows are elected by ballot after being nominated by at least four existing Fellows. At 31 May 1993 there were 1,035 Ordinary Fellows and 64 Honorary Fellows.

President, Sir Alastair Currie, FRCP, FRCPE, FRCPG, FRCSE, FRCPath.
Treasurer, The Lord Balfour of Burleigh
General Secretary, Prof. V. B. Proudfoot
Executive Secretary, Dr W. Duncan

Royal Academicians

The category of Associate was abolished in June 1991 and all the Associates became Royal Academicians
*Senior Academician

1991	Abrahams, Ivor
1991	Ackroyd, Norman
1972	Adams, Norman
1988	Aitchison, Craigie
1991	Armfield, Diana
1991	Ayres, Gillian, OBE
1991	Bellany, John
1992	Berg, Adrian
1976	Blackadder, Elizabeth, OBE
1981	Blake, Peter, CBE
1975	*Blamey, Norman
1978	Blow, Sandra
1975	Bowey, Olwyn
1981	Bowyer, William
1972	Brown, Ralph
1972	Butler, James
1975	*Cadbury-Brown, H. T., OBE
1984	Camp, Jeffery
1970	*Casson, Sir Hugh, CH, KCVO
1989	Christopher, Ann
1976	Clarke, Geoffrey
1973	Clatworthy, Robert
1972	Coker, Peter
1972	Cooke, Jean
1990	Crosby, Theo
1991	Cullinan, Edward, CBE
1974	Cuming, Frederick
1992	Cummins, Gus
1983	Dannatt, Trevor
1969	de Grey, Sir Roger, KCVO

1976	Dickson, Jennifer
1985	Dowson, Sir Philip, CBE
1991	Draper, Kenneth
1968	Dunstan, Bernard
1986	Eyton, Anthony
1992	*Fedden, Mary
1991	Flanagan, Barry, OBE
1991	Foster, Sir Norman
1985	Fraser, Donald Hamilton
1991	Freeth, Peter
1992	*Frost, Terry
1972	*Gore, Frederick, CBE
1977	Green, Anthony
1970	Hayes, Colin
1961	*Hepple, Norman
1990	*Herman, Josef, OBE
1991	Hockney, David
1984	Hogarth, Paul, OBE
1992	Hopkins, Michael, CBE
1991	Howard, Ken
1991	Hoyland, John
1991	Huxley, Paul
1991	Jacklin, Bill
1991	*Jellicoe, Sir Geoffrey
1986	Jones, Allen
1986	Kenny, Michael
1991	Kiff, Ken
1988	King, Phillip, CBE
1991	Kitaj, R. B.
1974	Kneale, Bryan
1991	Koralek, Paul, CBE
1991	*Lasdun, Sir Dennis, CBE
1991	Lawson, Sonia
1986	*Lessore, Helen, OBE

1986	Levene, Ben
1991	McComb, Leonard
1956	*Machin, Arnold, OBE
1979	*Manasseh, Leonard, OBE
1985	*Martin, Sir Leslie
1985	*Medley, Robert, CBE
1991	Mistry, Dhruva
1992	Neiland, Brendan
1979	Paolozzi, Sir Eduardo, CBE
1988	Partridge, John, CBE
1983	*Pasmore, Victor, CH, CBE
1989	Phillips, Tom
1977	Powell, Sir Philip, CH, OBE
1973	*Roberts-Jones, Ivor, CBE
1984	Rogers, Sir Richard
1991	Rooney, Michael
1969	*Rosoman, Leonard, OBE
1989	Sandle, Michael
1969	*Soukop, Willi
1986	Stephenson, Ian
1988	Sutton, Philip
1991	Symons, Patrick
1991	Tilson, Joe
1979	Tindle, David
1991	Titchell, John
1992	Tucker, William
1965	Ward, John, CBE
1965	*Weight, Carel, CBE
1989	Whishaw, Anthony
1974	Williams, Kyffin, OBE
1991	Wilson, Colin St J.
1991	Wragg, John

The Research Councils

The Government funds basic and applied civil science research mostly through the five research councils, which are supported by the Office of Public Service and Science (OPSS) at the Cabinet Office. The councils conduct research through their own establishments (listed below) and by supporting selected research, study and training in universities and other higher education establishments. They also receive income for research commissioned by government departments and the private sector. In May 1993 the Government published a White Paper on science, engineering and technology in which changes were planned to the role of the research councils (*see* page 1173).

AGRICULTURAL AND FOOD RESEARCH COUNCIL*

HEADQUARTERS, Polaris House, North Star Avenue, Swindon SN2 1UH. Tel: 0793-413200

AFRC BABRAHAM INSTITUTE
Director of Research, Prof. R. B. Heap, FRS, Babraham Hall, Babraham, Cambridge CB2 4AT. Tel: 0223-832312

AFRC INSTITUTE FOR ANIMAL HEALTH
Director of Research, Prof. F. J. Bourne, PH.D., Compton, Newbury, Berks. RG16 0NN. Tel: 0635-578411
AFRC AND MRC NEUROPATHOGENESIS UNIT, Ogston Building, West Mains Road, Edinburgh EH9 3JF. Tel: 031-667 5204/5. *Head*, vacant
COMPTON LABORATORY, Compton, Newbury, Berks. RG16 0NN. Tel: 0635-578411. *Head of Division in Charge*, Dr P. Jones
PIRBRIGHT LABORATORY, Ash Road, Pirbright, Woking, Surrey GU24 0NF. Tel: 0483-232441. *Head*, Dr A. I. Donaldson

AFRC INSTITUTE OF ARABLE CROPS RESEARCH
Director of Research, Dr B. Miflin, Rothamsted Experimental Station, Harpenden, Herts. AL5 2JQ. Tel: 0582-763133
BROOM'S BARN EXPERIMENTAL STATION, Higham, Bury St Edmunds, Suffolk IP28 6NP. Tel: 0284-810363. *Head*, Prof. T. H. Thomas, PH.D., D.SC.
LONG ASHTON RESEARCH STATION, Long Ashton, Bristol BS18 9AF. Tel: 0275-392181. *Head*, Prof. P. R. Shewry
ROTHAMSTED EXPERIMENTAL STATION, Harpenden, Herts. AL5 2JQ. Tel: 0582-763133. *Head*, Prof. T. Lewis, PH.D., D.SC.

AFRC INSTITUTE OF FOOD RESEARCH
Director of Research, Prof. D. L. Georgala, CBE, PH.D., Earley Gate, Whiteknights Road, Reading RG6 2EF. Tel: 0734-357055
NORWICH LABORATORY, Norwich Research Park, Colney Lane, Norwich NR4 7UA. Tel: 0603-56122. *Head*, Prof. P. S. Belton

READING LABORATORY, Earley Gate, Whiteknights Road, Reading RG6 2EF. Tel: 0734-357000. *Head*, Prof. B. E. B. Moseley, PH.D.

AFRC INSTITUTE OF GRASSLAND AND ENVIRONMENTAL RESEARCH
Director of Research, Dr C. J. Pollock, Plas Gogerddan, Aberystwyth, Dyfed SY23 3EB. Tel: 0970-828255
ABERYSTWYTH RESEARCH CENTRE, Plas Gogerddan, Aberystwyth, Dyfed SY23 3EB. Tel: 0970-828255. *Head*, Prof. D. Wilson, PH.D.
NORTH WYKE RESEARCH STATION, Okehampton, Devon EX20 2SB. Tel: 0837-82558. *Head*, Prof. R. J. Wilkins, PH.D.

AFRC INSTITUTE OF PLANT SCIENCE RESEARCH
Director, Prof. R. B. Flavell, John Innes Institute, Colney Lane, Norwich NR4 7UH. Tel: 0603-52571
IPSR CAMBRIDGE LABORATORY, Colney Lane, Norwich NR4 7UH. Tel: 0603-52571. *Head (acting)*, Dr M. D. Gale
IPSR NITROGEN FIXATION LABORATORY, University of Sussex, Brighton BNI 9RQ. Tel: 0273-678252. *Head*, Prof. B. E. Smith, PH.D.
JOHN INNES INSTITUTE, Colney Lane, Norwich NR4 7UH. Tel: 0603-52571. *Director*, Prof. R. B. Flavell

AFRC ROSLIN INSTITUTE
Director of Research, Prof. G. Bulfield, Roslin, Midlothian EH25 9PS. Tel: 031-440 2726

AFRC SILSOE RESEARCH INSTITUTE
Director of Research, Prof. B. J. Legg, Wrest Park, Silsoe, Bedford MK45 4HS. Tel: 0525-860000

SCOTTISH AGRICULTURAL RESEARCH INSTITUTES

HANNAH RESEARCH INSTITUTE, Ayr KA6 5HL. Tel: 0292-76013. *Director*, Prof. M. Peaker
MACAULAY LAND USE RESEARCH INSTITUTE, Craigiebuckler, Aberdeen AB9 2QJ. Tel: 0224-318611. *Director*, Prof. T. J. Maxwell, PH.D.
MOREDUN RESEARCH INSTITUTE, 408 Gilmerton Road, Edinburgh EH17 7JH. Tel: 031-664 3262. *Director*, Prof. I. D. Aitken, PH.D.
ROWETT RESEARCH INSTITUTE, Greenburn Road, Bucksburn, Aberdeen AB2 9SB. Tel: 0224-712751. *Director*, Prof. W. P. T. James, CBE
SCOTTISH AGRICULTURAL STATISTICS SERVICE, University of Edinburgh, James Clerk Maxwell Building, The King's Buildings, Mayfield Road, Edinburgh EH9 3JZ. Tel: 031-650 4900. *Director*, R. A. Kempton
SCOTTISH CROP RESEARCH INSTITUTE, Invergowrie, Dundee DD2 5DA. Tel: 0382-562731. *Director*, Prof. J. Hillman, PH.D., FRSE

---

*In April 1994 the AFRC will become the Biotechnology and Biological Sciences Research Council

ECONOMIC AND SOCIAL RESEARCH COUNCIL

HEADQUARTERS, Polaris House, North Star Avenue, Swindon SN2 1UJ. Tel: 0793-413000

RESEARCH CENTRES

CAMBRIDGE GROUP FOR THE HISTORY OF POPULATION AND SOCIAL STRUCTURE, 27 Trumpington Street, Cambridge CB2 1QA. Tel: 0223-333186. *Director*, Dr R. Schofield

CENTRE FOR ECONOMIC PERFORMANCE, London School of Economics, Houghton Street, London WC2A 2AE. Tel: 071-955 7048. *Director*, Prof. R. Layard

CENTRE FOR EDUCATIONAL SOCIOLOGY, University of Edinburgh, 7 Buccleuch Place, Edinburgh EH8 9LW. Tel: 031-650 4190. *Director*, Prof. A. McPherson

CENTRE FOR HOUSING RESEARCH, University of Glasgow, 25 Bute Gardens, Hillhead, Glasgow G12 8LE. Tel: 041-339 8855. *Director*, Prof. D. MacLennan, PH.D.

CENTRE FOR MICRO-ECONOMIC ANALYSIS OF FISCAL POLICY, Institute for Fiscal Studies, 7 Ridgmount Street, London WC1E 7AE. Tel: 071-636 3784. *Director*, Prof. R. Blundell

CENTRE FOR RESEARCH IN DEVELOPMENT IN STRUCTURE AND TRAINING, Department of Psychology, University of Nottingham, Nottingham NG7 2RD. Tel: 0602-515312. *Director*, Prof. D. J. Wood

CENTRE FOR RESEARCH IN ETHNIC RELATIONS, University of Warwick, Gibbet Hill Road, Coventry CV4 7AL. Tel: 0203-523523. *Director*, Prof. M. Anwar, PH.D.

CENTRE FOR SCIENCE TECHNOLOGY, ENERGY AND ENVIRONMENTAL POLICY, Science Policy Research Unit, University of Sussex, Mantell Building, Falmer, Brighton BN1 9RF. Tel: 0273-686758. *Director*, Prof. M. Gibbons

CENTRE FOR SOCIAL AND ECONOMIC RESEARCH ON THE GLOBAL ENVIRONMENT, School of Environmental Sciences, University of East Anglia, Norwich NR4 7TJ. Tel: 0603-593176. *Director*, Prof. R. K. Turner

CENTRE FOR SOCIAL WORK RESEARCH, University of Stirling, Stirling FK9 4LA. Tel: 0786-467724. *Director*, Prof. J. Cheetham

CENTRE FOR SOCIO-LEGAL STUDIES, Wolfson College, University of Oxford, Oxford OX2 6UD. Tel: 0865-52967. *Director*, D. Harris

CENTRE FOR THE STUDY OF AFRICAN ECONOMIES, St Cross Building, Manor Road, Oxford OX1 3UL. Tel: 0865-271084. *Director*, Prof. P. Collier

HUMAN COMMUNICATION RESEARCH CENTRE, University of Edinburgh, 2 Buccleuch Place, Edinburgh EH8 9LW. Tel: 031-650 4444. *Director*, Prof. K. Stenning

INDUSTRIAL RELATIONS RESEARCH UNIT, School of Industrial and Business Studies, University of Warwick, Gibbet Hill Road, Coventry CV4 7AL. Tel: 0203-523523. *Director*, Prof. K. Sisson

JOINT UNIT FOR THE STUDY OF SOCIAL TRENDS, Social and Community Planning Research, 35 Northampton Square, London EC1V 0AX. Tel: 071-250 1866. *Director*, Prof. R. Jowell

MRC/ESRC SOCIAL AND APPLIED PSYCHOLOGY UNIT, Department of Psychology, University of Sheffield, Sheffield S10 2TN. Tel: 0742-756600. *Director*, Prof. P. Warr

NORTHERN IRELAND ECONOMIC RESEARCH CENTRE, 46–48 University Road, Belfast BT7 1NJ. Tel: 0232-325594. *Director*, Dr G. Gudgin

RESEARCH CENTRE IN MICRO-SOCIAL CHANGE, University of Essex, Wivenhoe Park, Colchester, Essex CO4 3SQ. Tel: 0206-872957. *Director*, Prof. J. Gershuny

RESEARCH UNIT IN HEALTH AND BEHAVIOURAL CHANGE, University of Edinburgh, 24 Buccleuch Place, Edinburgh EH8 9LN. Tel: 031-650 6192. *Director (acting)*, Dr C. Currie

RESOURCE CENTRES

CENTRE FOR ECONOMIC POLICY RESEARCH, 25–28 Old Burlington Street, London W1X 1LB. Tel: 071-734 9110. *Director*, Prof. R. Portes

ESRC DATA ARCHIVE, University of Essex, Wivenhoe Park, Colchester, Essex CO4 3SQ. Tel: 0206-872001. *Director*, Prof. D. Lievesley

---

MEDICAL RESEARCH COUNCIL

HEADQUARTERS, 20 Park Crescent, London W1N 4AL. Tel: 071-636 5422

CLINICAL RESEARCH CENTRE, Watford Road, Harrow, Middx. HA1 3UJ. Tel: 081-864 3232. *Administrative Director*, Dr K. E. Kirkham, OBE, PH.D.

LABORATORY OF MOLECULAR BIOLOGY, Hills Road, Cambridge CB2 2QH. Tel: 0223-248011. *Director*, Prof. Sir Aaron Klug, PH.D., FRS

MRC CLINICAL SCIENCES CENTRE, Royal Postgraduate Medical School, Du Cane Road, London W12 0NN. Tel: 081-743 7117. *Director of Research*, Prof. K. E. Davies, D.Phil.

NATIONAL INSTITUTE FOR MEDICAL RESEARCH, The Ridgeway, Mill Hill, London NW7. Tel: 081-959 3666. *Director*, J. Skehel, PH.D., FRS

RESEARCH UNITS

AFRC/MRC NEUROPATHOGENESIS UNIT, Ogston Building, West Mains Road, Edinburgh EH9 3JF. Tel: 031-667 5204. *Director*, vacant

ANATOMICAL NEUROPHARMACOLOGY UNIT, Mansfield Road, Oxford OX1 3TH. Tel: 0865-271865. *Hon. Director*, Prof. A. D. Smith, D.Phil.

APPLIED PSYCHOLOGY UNIT, 15 Chaucer Road, Cambridge CB2 2EF. Tel: 0223-355294. *Director*, A. D. Baddeley, PH.D.

BIOSTATISTICS UNIT, Institute of Public Health, University Forvie Site, Robinson Way, Cambridge CB2 2SR. Tel: 0223-330366. *Hon. Director*, Prof. N. E. Day, PH.D.

BLOOD GROUP UNIT, University College, London, Wolfson House, 4 Stephenson Way, London NW1 2HE. Tel: 071-388 7752. *Director*, P. Tippett, PH.D.

BLOOD PRESSURE UNIT, Western Infirmary, Glasgow G11 6NT. Tel: 041-339 8822 ext. 4065. *Director*, A. F. Lever, FRCP, FRSE

BRAIN METABOLISM UNIT, University Department of Pharmacology, 1 George Square, Edinburgh EH8 9JZ. Tel: 031-650 3548. *Director*, Prof. G. Fink, MD, D.Phil., FRSE

CELL MUTATION UNIT, University of Sussex, Falmer, Brighton BN1 9RR. Tel: 0273-678123. *Director*, Prof. B. A. Bridges, PH.D., FIBiol.

CELLULAR IMMUNOLOGY UNIT, Sir William Dunn School of Pathology, Oxford OX1 3RE. Tel: 0865-275594. *Director (acting)*, D. W. Mason

CHILD PSYCHIATRY UNIT, Institute of Psychiatry, De Crespigny Park, Denmark Hill, London SE5 8AF. Tel: 071-703 5411. *Hon. Director*, Prof. Sir Michael Rutter, CBE, FRS, MD, FRCP, FRCPsych.

CLINICAL ONCOLOGY AND RADIOTHERAPEUTICS UNIT, MRC Centre, Hills Road, Cambridge CB2 2QH. Tel: 0223-245133. *Hon. Director*, Prof. N. M. Bleehen, FRCP, FRCR

CLINICAL PHARMACOLOGY UNIT, University Department of Clinical Pharmacology, Radcliffe Infirmary, Woodstock Road, Oxford OX2 6HE. Tel: 0865-311188 ext. 24524. *Hon. Director*, Prof. D. G. Grahame-Smith, CBE, Ph.D., FRCP

COGNITIVE DEVELOPMENT UNIT, 17 Gordon Street, London WC1H 0AH. Tel: 071-387 4692. *Director*, Prof. J. Morton, Ph.D.

CYCLOTRON UNIT, Hammersmith Hospital, Du Cane Road, London W12 0HS. Tel: 081-743 2030. *Director (acting)*, T. Jones, D.SC., MD

DUNN NUTRITION UNIT, Downhams Lane, Milton Road, Cambridge CB4 1XJ. Tel: 0223-426356. *Director*, R. G. Whitehead, CBE, Ph.D.

ENVIRONMENTAL EPIDEMIOLOGY UNIT, Southampton General Hospital, Southampton SO9 4XY. Tel: 0703-777624. *Director*, Prof. D. J. P. Barker, MD, Ph.D, FRCP

EPIDEMIOLOGY AND MEDICAL CARE UNIT, Wolfson Institute of Preventive Medicine, St Bartholomew's Medical College, Charterhouse Square, London EC1M 6BQ. Tel: 071-982 6000. *Director*, Prof. T. W. Meade, DM, FRCP

EPIDEMIOLOGY UNIT (SOUTH WALES), Llandough Hospital, Penarth, South Glamorgan CF6 1XX. Tel: 0222-711404. *Director*, P. C. Elwood, MD, FRCP

EXPERIMENTAL EMBRYOLOGY AND TERATOLOGY UNIT, St George's Hospital Medical School, Cranmer Terrace, London SW17 0RE. Tel: 081-672 9944 ext. 56309. *Director*, D. G. Whittingham, D.SC., FRCVS, FIBiol.

HUMAN BIOCHEMICAL GENETICS UNIT, The Galton Laboratory, University College London, Wolfson House, 4 Stephenson Way, London NW1 2HE. Tel: 071-387 7050. *Director*, Prof. D. A. Hopkinson, MD

HUMAN GENETICS UNIT, Western General Hospital, Crewe Road, Edinburgh EH4 2XU. Tel: 031-332 2471. *Director*, Prof. H. J. Evans, Ph.D., FIBiol., FRCPE, FRSE

IMMUNOCHEMISTRY UNIT, University Department of Biochemistry, South Parks Road, Oxford OX1 3QU. Tel: 0865-275354. *Director*, K. B. M. Reid, Ph.D.

INSTITUTE OF HEARING RESEARCH, University of Nottingham, Nottingham NG7 2RD. Tel: 0602-223431. *Director*, Prof. M. P. Haggard, Ph.D.

MEDICAL SOCIOLOGY UNIT, 6 Lilybank Gardens, Glasgow G12 8QQ. Tel: 041-357 3949. *Director*, S. Macintyre, Ph.D.

MOLECULAR HAEMATOLOGY UNIT, Institute of Molecular Medicine, John Radcliffe Hospital, Headington, Oxford OX3 9DU. Tel: 0865-222359. *Hon. Director*, Prof. Sir David Weatherall, MD, FRCP, FRCPath., FRS

MRC BIOCHEMICAL AND CLINICAL MAGNETIC RESONANCE UNIT, University Department of Biochemistry, South Parks Road, Oxford OX1 3QU. Tel: 0865-275274. *Hon. Director*, Prof. G. K. Radda, CBE, D.Phil., FRS

MRC COLLABORATIVE CENTRE, 1–3 Burtonhole Lane, Mill Hill, London NW7 1AD. Tel: 081-906 3811. *Director*, C. C. G. Hentschel, Ph.D.

MRC/ESRC SOCIAL AND APPLIED PSYCHOLOGY UNIT, Dept. of Psychology, University of Sheffield, Sheffield S10 2TN. Tel: 0742-756600. *Director*, Prof. P. B. Warr, Ph.D.

MRC HUMAN MOVEMENT AND BALANCE UNIT, Institute of Neurology, National Hospital for Neurology and Neuro-surgery, Queen Square, London WC1 3BG. Tel: 071-387 3611. *Hon. Director*. Prof. C. D. Marsden, D.SC., FRCP, FRS

MRC LABORATORIES, THE GAMBIA, PO Box 273, Banjul, The Gambia, W. Africa. *Director*, B. M. Greenwood, CBE, MD, FRCP

MRC LABORATORIES, JAMAICA, University of the West Indies, Mona, Kingston 7, Jamaica. *Director*, Prof. G. R. Serjeant, CMG, MD, FRCP

MRC MOLECULAR IMMUNOPATHOLOGY UNIT, MRC Centre, University Medical School, Hills Road, Cambridge CB2 2QH. Tel: 0223-245133. *Hon. Director*, Prof. P. J. Lachmann, Ph.D., SC.D., FRCP, FRCPath., FRS

MRC MUSCLE AND CELL MOTILITY UNIT, Division of Biomedical Sciences, King's College London, 26–29 Drury Lane, London WC2B 5RL. Tel: 071-836 8851. *Hon. Director*, Prof. R. M. Simmons, Ph.D.

MRC PROTEIN FUNCTION AND DESIGN UNIT, Department of Chemistry, University of Cambridge, Lensfield Road, Cambridge CB2 1EW. Tel: 0223-336341. *Hon. Director*, Prof. A. R. Fersht, Ph.D., FRS

MRC PROTEIN PHOSPHORYLATION UNIT, Department of Biochemistry, Medical Sciences Institute, University of Dundee, Dundee DD1 4HN. Tel: 0382-307238. *Hon. Director*, Prof. P. Cohen, Ph.D., FRS, FRSE

MRC TOXICOLOGY UNIT, Hodgkin Building, University of Leicester, PO Box 138, Lancaster Road, Leicester LE1 9HN. Tel: 0533-525544. *Director*, Dr L. Smith

NEUROCHEMICAL PATHOLOGY UNIT, Newcastle General Hospital, Westgate Road, Newcastle upon Tyne NE4 6BE. Tel: 091-273 5251. *Director*, Prof. J. A. Edwardson, Ph.D.

RADIOBIOLOGY UNIT, Chilton, Didcot, Oxon. OX11 0RD. Tel: 0235-834393. *Director*, Prof. G. E. Adams, Ph.D., D.SC.

REPRODUCTIVE BIOLOGY UNIT, Centre for Reproductive Biology, 37 Chalmers Street, Edinburgh EH3 9EW. Tel: 031-229 2575. *Director*, Prof. D. W. Lincoln, D.SC., FRSE

SOCIAL AND COMMUNITY PSYCHIATRY UNIT, Institute of Psychiatry, De Crespigny Park, Denmark Hill, London SE5 8AF. Tel: 071-703 5411. *Director*, Prof. J. P. Leff, MD, FRCPsych.

TUBERCULOSIS AND RELATED INFECTIONS UNIT, RPMS, Hammersmith Hospital, Du Cane Road, London W12 0HS. Tel: 081-743 2030. *Director*, Prof. J. Ivanyi, MD, Ph.D.

UK HUMAN GENOME MAPPING PROJECT RESOURCE CENTRE, Clinical Research Centre, Watford Road, Harrow, Middx. HA1 3UJ. Tel: 081-869 3446. *Manager*, Dr K. Gibson

VIROLOGY UNIT, Institute of Virology, Church Street, Glasgow G11 5JR. Tel: 041-330 4017. *Hon. Director*, Prof. J. H. Subak-Sharpe, CBE, Ph.D., FRSE

NATURAL ENVIRONMENT RESEARCH COUNCIL

HEADQUARTERS, Polaris House, North Star Avenue, Swindon SN2 1EU. Tel: 0793-411500

BRITISH ANTARCTIC SURVEY, Madingley Road, Cambridge CB3 0ET. Tel: 0223-61188. *Director*, Dr D. J. Drewry

BRITISH GEOLOGICAL SURVEY, Nicker Hill, Keyworth, Nottingham NG12 5GG. Tel: 0602-363100. *Director*, Dr P. Cook

CENTRE FOR POPULATION BIOLOGY, Imperial College, Silwood Park, Ascot, Berks. SL5 7PY. Tel: 0344-294223. *Director*, Prof. J. Lawton

DUNSTAFFNAGE MARINE LABORATORY, PO Box 3, Oban, Argyll PA34 4AD. Tel: 0631-62244. *Director*, Prof. J. B. L. Matthews

INSTITUTE OF FRESHWATER ECOLOGY, The Ferry House, Far Sawrey, Ambleside, Cumbria LA22 0LP. Tel: 05394-42468. *Director*, Prof. J. G. Jones

INSTITUTE OF HYDROLOGY, Maclean Building, Crowmarsh Gifford, Wallingford, Oxon. OX10 8BB. Tel: 0491-838800. *Director*, Prof. W. B. Wilkinson

INSTITUTE OF OCEANOGRAPHIC SCIENCES, Deacon Laboratory, Wormley, nr. Godalming, Surrey GU8 5UB. Tel: 042868-4141. *Director*, Dr C. Summerhayes

INSTITUTE OF TERRESTRIAL ECOLOGY (NORTH), Bush Estate, Penicuik, Midlothian EH26 0QB. Tel: 031-445 4343. *Director*, Prof. O. W. Heal

INSTITUTE OF TERRESTRIAL ECOLOGY (SOUTH), Monks Wood, Abbots Ripton, Huntingdon PE17 2LS. Tel: 04873-381/8. *Director*, Dr T. M. Roberts

INSTITUTE OF VIROLOGY AND ENVIRONMENTAL MICROBIOLOGY, Mansfield Road, Oxford OX1 3SR. Tel: 0865-512361. *Director*, Prof. D. H. L. Bishop

JAMES RENNELL CENTRE FOR OCEAN CIRCULATION, Gamma House, Chilworth Research Centre, Chilworth, Southampton SO1 7NS. Tel: 0703-766184. *Head of Centre*, Dr R. Pollard

NERC UNIT FOR THEMATIC INFORMATION SYSTEMS, Department of Geography, Reading University, Whiteknights, PO Box 227, Reading RG6 2AB. Tel: 0734-318741. *Officer in Charge*, Prof. R. Gurney

PLYMOUTH MARINE LABORATORY, Prospect Place, The Hoe, Plymouth PL1 3DH; Citadel Hill, Plymouth PL1 2PB. Tel: 0752-222772. *Director*, Dr B. L. Bayne; *Assistant Director*, Dr P. N. Claridge

PROUDMAN OCEANOGRAPHIC LABORATORY, Bidston, Birkenhead L43 7RA. Tel: 051-653 8633. *Director*, Dr B. S. McCartney

SEA MAMMAL RESEARCH UNIT, c/o British Antarctic Survey (*see above*). Tel: 0223-311354. *Head*, J. Harwood, Ph.D.

UNIT OF AQUATIC BIOCHEMISTRY, Stirling University, FK9 4LA. Tel: 0786-73171. *Director*, Prof. J. R. Sargent

UNIT OF COMPARATIVE PLANT ECOLOGY, Department of Animal and Plant Biology and Ecology, Sheffield University, Sheffield S10 2TN. Tel: 0742-768555. *Head of Unit*, Prof. J. P. Grime

---

SCIENCE AND ENGINEERING RESEARCH COUNCIL*

HEADQUARTERS, Polaris House, North Star Avenue, Swindon SN2 1ET. Tel: 0793-411000

DARESBURY LABORATORY, Keckwick Lane, Daresbury, Warrington, Cheshire WA4 4AD. Tel: 0925-603000. *Director*, Prof. A. J. Leadbetter

ROYAL GREENWICH OBSERVATORY, Madingley Road, Cambridge CB3 0EZ. Tel: 0223-374700. *Director*, Prof. A. Boksenberg, FRS

ROYAL OBSERVATORY, EDINBURGH, Blackford Hill, Edinburgh EH9 3HJ. Tel: 031-668 8100. *Director*, Dr P. Murdin, OBE

RUTHERFORD APPLETON NUCLEAR PHYSICS LABORATORY, Chilton, Didcot, Oxon OX11 0QX. Tel: 0235-821900. *Director*, Dr P. R. Williams

*In April 1994 the SERC will be split into two councils – *see* page 1173.

Research Associations

The following industrial and technological research bodies are members of the Association of Independent Research and Technology Organizations (AIRTO), PO Box 330, Cambridge CB5 8DU. Tel: 0223-467831

ADVANCED MANUFACTURING TECHNOLOGY RESEARCH INSTITUTE, Hulley Road, Macclesfield, Cheshire SK10 2NE. Tel: 0625-425421. *Chief Executive (acting)*, I. G. Bruce

AIRCRAFT RESEARCH ASSOCIATION LTD, Manton Lane, Bedford MK41 7PF. Tel: 0234-350681. *Chief Executive*, Dr J. E. Green

BHR GROUP LTD (BRITISH HYDRO-MECHANICS RESEARCH GROUP), Cranfield, Bedford MK43 0AJ. Tel: 0234-750422. *Chief Executive*, I. Cooper

BIBRA TOXICOLOGY INTERNATIONAL, Woodmansterne Road, Carshalton, Surrey SM5 4DS. Tel: 081-643 4411. *Director*, Dr S. E. Jaggers

BRITISH CERAMIC RESEARCH LTD, Queen's Road, Penkhull, Stoke-on-Trent ST4 7LQ. Tel: 0782-45431. *Chief Executive*, Dr N. E. Sanderson

BRITISH GLASS, Northumberland Road, Sheffield S10 2UA. Tel: 0742-686201. *Research Director*, Dr G. J. Copley

BRITISH LEATHER CONFEDERATION, Leather Trade House, Kings Park Road, Moulton Park, Northants. NN3 1JD. Tel: 0604-494131. *Technical Director*, Dr K. Alexander

BRITISH MARITIME TECHNOLOGY LTD, Orlando House, 1 Waldegrave Road, Teddington, Middx. TW11 8LZ. Tel: 081-943 5544. *Chief Executive*, D. Goodrich

BRITISH TEXTILE TECHNOLOGY GROUP, Wira House, West Park Ring Road, Leeds LS16 6QL. Tel: 0532-781381. *Managing Director*, Dr D. N. Munro

BUILDING SERVICES RESEARCH AND INFORMATION ASSOCIATION, Old Bracknell Lane West, Bracknell, Berks. RG12 4AH. Tel: 0344-426511. *Chief Executive*, G. J. Baker

CAMBRIDGE CONSULTANTS LTD (*Product and process development of technology applications in business*), Science Park, Milton Road, Cambridge CB4 4DW. Tel: 0223-420024. *Managing Director*, Dr J. P. Auton

CAMPDEN FOOD AND DRINK RESEARCH ASSOCIATION, Chipping Campden, Glos. GL55 6LD. Tel: 0386-840319. *Director-General*, Prof. C. Dennis

CIRIA (THE CONSTRUCTION INDUSTRY RESEARCH AND INFORMATION ASSOCIATION), 6 Storey's Gate, London SW1P 3AU. Tel: 071-222 8891. *Director-General*, Dr P. L. Bransby

CUTLERY AND ALLIED TRADES RESEARCH ASSOCIATION, Henry Street, Sheffield S3 7EQ. Tel: 0742-769736. *Director of Research*, R. C. Hamby

EA TECHNOLOGY, Capenhurst, Chester CH1 6ES. Tel: 051-339 4181. *Managing Director*, Dr S. F. Exell

ERA TECHNOLOGY LTD (*Electronic and electrical engineering*), Cleeve Road, Leatherhead, Surrey KT22 7SA. Tel: 0372-374151. *Chief Executive*, M. J. Withers

FLOUR MILLING AND BAKING RESEARCH
ASSOCIATION, Chorleywood, Herts. WD3 5SH. Tel:
0923-284111. *Director-General*, Dr A. D. B. Malcolm

FURNITURE INDUSTRY RESEARCH ASSOCIATION,
Maxwell Road, Stevenage, Herts. SG1 2EW. Tel: 0438-
313433. *Director and Chief Executive*, Dr
C. A. Aitkenhead

INTERNATIONAL RESEARCH AND DEVELOPMENT LTD
(*Electronics and mechanical and electrical engineering*),
Fossway, Newcastle upon Tyne NE6 2YD. Tel: 091-265
0451. *General Manager*, W. Carpenter

LAMBEG INDUSTRIAL RESEARCH ASSOCIATION
(*Textiles*), Lambeg, Lisburn, Co. Antrim, N. Ireland BT27
4RJ. Tel: 0846-662255. *Director of Operations*,
J. R. Haycock

LEATHERHEAD FOOD RESEARCH ASSOCIATION,
Randalls Road, Leatherhead, Surrey KT22 7RY. Tel:
0372-376761. *Director*, Dr M. P. J. Kierstan

MOTOR INDUSTRY RESEARCH ASSOCIATION, Watling
Street, Nuneaton, Warks. CV10 0TU. Tel: 0203-348541.
Managing Director, J. R. Wood

THE NATIONAL COMPUTING CENTRE LTD, Oxford
Road, Manchester M1 7ED. Tel: 061-228 6333. *Chief
Executive*, N. Bannister

PAINT RESEARCH ASSOCIATION, 8 Waldegrave Road,
Teddington, Middx. TW11 8LD. Tel: 081-977 4427.
Managing Director, J. A. Bernie

PERA INTERNATIONAL (*Multi-disciplinary research,
design, development and consultancy*), Melton Mowbray,
Leics. LE13 0PB. Tel: 0664-501501. *Director-General*,
R. A. Armstrong

PIRA INTERNATIONAL (*Paper and board, printing,
publishing and packaging*), Randalls Road, Leatherhead,
Surrey KT22 7RU. Tel: 0372-376161. *Managing Director*,
B. W. Blunden

RAPRA TECHNOLOGY LTD (*Polymer materials*),
Shawbury, Shrewsbury SY4 4NR. Tel: 0939-250383. *Chief
Executive*, Dr M. Copley

RICARDO AEROSPACE LTD, Bowling Hill, Chipping
Sodbury, Bristol BS17 6JX. Tel: 0454-325288. *Managing
Director*, P. H. Wells

SATRA FOOTWEAR TECHNOLOGY CENTRE, Satra
House, Rockingham Road, Kettering, Northants. NN16
9JH. Tel: 0536-410000. *Chief Executive*,
Dr R. E. Whittaker

SHIPOWNERS REFRIGERATED CARGO RESEARCH
ASSOCIATION, 140 Newmarket Road, Cambridge CB5
8HE. Tel: 0223-65101. *Technical Director*, R. D. Heap

SIRA LTD (*Instrumentation and systems technology*), South
Hill, Chislehurst, Kent BR7 5EH. Tel: 081-467 2636.
Managing Director, R. A. Brook

SMITH SYSTEM ENGINEERING LTD, Surrey Research
Park, Guildford, Surrey GU2 5YP. Tel: 0483-505565.
Chairman, Dr B. G. Smith

SPRING RESEARCH AND MANUFACTURERS'
ASSOCIATION, Henry Street, Sheffield S3 7EQ. Tel: 0742-
760771. *Director*, D. Saynor

TIMBER RESEARCH AND DEVELOPMENT ASSOCIATION,
Stocking Lane, Hughenden Valley, High Wycombe,
Bucks. HP14 4ND. Tel: 0494-563091. *Director*, Dr C. J.
Gill

TWI (WELDING), Abington Hall, Abington, Cambridge
CB1 6AL. Tel: 0223-891162. *Chief Executive*,
A. B. M. Braithwaite, OBE

WRC (WATER RESEARCH) PLC, Henley Road,
Medmenham, PO Box 16, Marlow, Bucks. SL7 2HD. Tel:
0491-571531. *Managing Director*, Dr J. Moss

Sports Bodies

Bodies which are the governing body for their sport are indicated by *

Sports Councils

THE SPORTS COUNCIL, 16 Upper Woburn Place, London WCIH OQP. Tel: 071-388 1277. *Director-General*, vacant

SCOTTISH SPORTS COUNCIL, Caledonia House, South Gyle, Edinburgh EH12 9DQ. Tel: 031-317 7200. *Chief Executive*, F. A. L. Alstead, CBE

SPORTS COUNCIL FOR WALES, Sophia Gardens, Cardiff CFI 9SW. Tel: 0222-397571. *Chief Executive*, L. Tatham

SPORTS COUNCIL FOR NORTHERN IRELAND, House of Sport, Upper Malone Road, Belfast BT9 5LA. Tel: 0232-381222. *Director*, J. E. Miller

CENTRAL COUNCIL OF PHYSICAL RECREATION, Francis House, Francis Street, London SWIP IDE. Tel: 071-828 3163. *General Secretary*, P. Lawson

Alpine Skiing

*BRITISH SKI FEDERATION, 258 Main Street, East Calder, Livingston, West Lothian EH53 OEE. Tel: 0506-884343. *Chairman*, J. Blyth

Angling

*NATIONAL FEDERATION OF ANGLERS, Halliday House, 2 Wilson Street, Derby DEI IPG. Tel: 0332-362000. *Chief Administration Officer*, K. E. Watkins

Archery

*GRAND NATIONAL ARCHERY SOCIETY, 7th Street, National Agricultural Centre, Stoneleigh, Kenilworth, Coventry CV8 2LG. Tel: 0203-696631. *Chief Executive*, J. S. Middleton

Association Football

*THE FOOTBALL ASSOCIATION, 16 Lancaster Gate, London W2 3LW. Tel: 071-262 4542. *Chief Executive*, R. H. G. Kelly

FOOTBALL LEAGUE LTD, 319 Clifton Drive South, Lytham St Annes, Lancs. FY8 1JG. Tel: 0253-729421. *Secretary*, J. D. Dent

*SCOTTISH FOOTBALL ASSOCIATION, 6 Park Gardens, Glasgow G3 7YF. Tel: 041-332 6372. *Chief Executive*, J. Farry

SCOTTISH FOOTBALL LEAGUE, 188 West Regent Street, Glasgow G2 4RY. Tel: 041-248 3844. *Secretary*, P. Donald

*FOOTBALL ASSOCIATION OF WALES, Plymouth Chambers, 3 Westgate Street, Cardiff CFI IDD. Tel: 0222-372325. *Secretary*, A. E. Evans

*IRISH FOOTBALL ASSOCIATION, 20 Windsor Avenue, Belfast BT9 6EE. Tel: 0232-669458. *General Secretary*, D. I. Bowen

IRISH FOOTBALL LEAGUE, 96 University Street, Belfast BT7 IHE. Tel: 0232-242888. *Chief Executive*, H. Wallace

*WOMEN'S FOOTBALL ASSOCIATION, 448–450 Hanging Ditch, The Corn Exchange, Manchester M4 3ES. Tel: 061-832 5911. *Chief Executive*, Ms L. Whitehead

Athletics

*BRITISH ATHLETIC FEDERATION, 225A Bristol Road, Edgbaston, Birmingham B5 7UB. Tel: 021-440 5000. *Chief Executive*, vacant

AMATEUR ATHLETIC ASSOCIATION OF ENGLAND, 225A Bristol Road, Edgbaston, Birmingham B5 7UB. Tel: 021-440 5000. *Chief Executive*, vacant

Badminton

*BADMINTON ASSOCIATION OF ENGLAND LTD, National Badminton Centre, Bradwell Road, Loughton Lodge, Milton Keynes MK8 9LA. Tel: 0908-568822. *Chief Executive*, G. Snowdon

*SCOTTISH BADMINTON UNION, Cockburn Centre, 40 Bogmoor Place, Glasgow G51 4TQ. Tel: 041-445 1218. *Chief Executive*, Miss A. Smillie

*WELSH BADMINTON UNION, Fourth Floor, 3 Westgate Street, Cardiff CFI IDD. Tel: 0222-222082. *Chief Executive*, L. Williams

Baseball

*BRITISH BASEBALL FEDERATION, 66 Belvedere Road, Hessle, N. Humberside HUI3 9JJ. Tel: 0482-643551. *Secretary*, K. Macadam

Basketball

*ENGLISH BASKETBALL ASSOCIATION, 48 Bradford Road, Stanningley, Leeds LS28 6DF. Tel: 0532-361166. *Chief Executive*, D. Ransom

*SCOTTISH BASKETBALL ASSOCIATION, Caledonia House, South Gyle, Edinburgh EH12 9DQ. Tel: 031-317 7260. *Technical Director*, K. Johnston

*BASKETBALL ASSOCIATION OF WALES, Connies House, Rhymney River Bridge Road, Cardiff CF3 7YZ. Tel: 0222-454395. *Administrator*, L. Beck

Billiards

*WORLD PROFESSIONAL BILLIARDS AND SNOOKER ASSOCIATION, 27 Oakfield Road, Clifton, Bristol BS8 2AT. Tel: 0272-744491. *Company Secretary*, M. D. Blake

*WORLD LADIES BILLIARDS AND SNOOKER ASSOCIATION, 3 Sywell Grove, Elm, Wisbech, Cambs. PEI4 OBN. Tel: 0945-860545. *Secretary*, Ms M. Fisher

Bobsleigh

*BRITISH BOBSLEIGH ASSOCIATION, Springfield House, 7 Woodstock Road, Coulsdon, Surrey CR5 3HS. Tel: 0737-555152. *Secretary*, vacant

Bowls

*BRITISH ISLES BOWLING COUNCIL, 28 Woodford Park, Lurgan, Co. Armagh BT66 7HA. Tel: 0762-322036. *Hon. Secretary*, W. A. Gracey

*BRITISH ISLES INDOOR BOWLING COUNCIL, 41 Montfode Court, Ardrossan KA22 7NJ. Tel: 0294-68372. *Secretary*, J. Barclay

*BRITISH ISLES WOMEN'S BOWLING COUNCIL, 2 Case Gardens, Seaton, Devon EX12 2AP. Tel: 0297-21317. *Hon. Secretary*, Ms N. Colling

*BRITISH ISLES WOMEN'S INDOOR BOWLS COUNCIL, 16 Windsor Crescent, Radyr, Cardiff CF4 8AE. Tel: 0222-842391. *Hon. Secretary*, Ms J. Johns

*ENGLISH BOWLING ASSOCIATION, Lyndhurst Road, Worthing, W. Sussex BNII 2AZ. Tel: 0903-820222. *Secretary*, D. Johnson

*ENGLISH WOMEN'S BOWLING ASSOCIATION, 2 Case Gardens, Seaton, Devon EX12 2AP. Tel: 0297-21317. *Hon. Secretary*, Ms N. Colling

Boxing
*AMATEUR BOXING ASSOCIATION OF ENGLAND LTD,
Francis House, Francis Street, London SW1P 1DE. Tel:
071-976 5361. *Secretary*, C. Brown
*BRITISH BOXING BOARD OF CONTROL LTD, Jack
Petersen House, 52A Borough High Street, London SE1
1XW. Tel: 071-403 5871. *General Secretary*, J. Morris
*BRITISH AMATEUR BOXING ASSOCIATION, 96 High
Street, Lochee, Dundee DD2 3AY. Tel: 0382-611412. *Chief
Executive*, F. Hendry

Canoeing
*BRITISH CANOE UNION, Adbolton Lane, West Bridgford,
Nottingham NG2 5AS. Tel: 0602-821100. *Director*, P.
Owen

Clay Pigeon Shooting
*CLAY PIGEON SHOOTING ASSOCIATION, 107 Epping
New Road, Buckhurst Hill, Essex IG9 5TQ. Tel: 081-505
6221. *Director*, B. G. Carter

Cricket
MCC, Lords, London NW8 8QN. Tel: 071-289 1611.
President D. R. W. Silk; *Secretary*, Lt.-Col.
J. R. Stephenson, OBE (*from Jan.* 1994, R. Knight)
TEST AND COUNTY CRICKET BOARD, Lord's, London
NW8 8QZ. Tel: 071-286 4405. *Chairman* (1993–4),
W. R. F. Chamberlain; *Chief Executive*, A. C. Smith
*CRICKET COUNCIL, Lord's, London NW8 8QZ. Tel: 071-
286 4405. *Chairman*, W. R. F. Chamberlain; *Secretary*,
A. C. Smith

Croquet
*CROQUET ASSOCIATION, c/o The Hurlingham Club,
Ranelagh Gardens, London SW6 3PR. Tel: 071-736 3148
Secretary, L. W. D. Antenen

Cycling
*BRITISH CYCLING FEDERATION, 36 Rockingham Road,
Kettering, Northants. NN16 8HG. Tel: 0536-412211. *Chief
Executive*, J. Hendry
*ROAD TIME TRIALS COUNCIL, 77 Arlington Drive,
Pennington, Leigh, Lancs. WN7 3QP. Tel: 0942-603976.
National Secretary, P. Heaton

Equestrianism
*BRITISH EQUESTRIAN FEDERATION, British Equestrian
Centre, Stoneleigh Park, Kenilworth, Warks. CV8 2LR.
Tel: 0203-696697. *Director-General*, Maj. M. Wallace

Eton Fives
*ETON FIVES ASSOCIATION, Welches, Bentley, Farnham,
Surrey GU10 5HZ. Tel: 0420-22107. *Hon. Secretary*,
M. P. Powell

Fencing
*AMATEUR FENCING ASSOCIATION, 1 Barons Gate,
33–35 Rothschild Road, London W4 5HT. Tel: 081-742
3032. *Secretary*, Miss G. Kenneally

Gliding
*BRITISH GLIDING ASSOCIATION, Kimberley House,
Vaughan Way, Leicester LE1 4SE. Tel: 0533-531051.
Secretary, B. Rolfe

Golf
*ROYAL AND ANCIENT GOLF CLUB, St Andrews, Fife
KY16 9JD. Tel: 0334-72112. *Secretary*,
M. F. Bonallack, OBE
*LADIES' GOLF UNION, The Scores, St Andrews, Fife KY16
9AT. Tel: 0334-75811. *Administrator*, Mrs E. A. Mackie

Greyhound Racing
*NATIONAL GREYHOUND RACING CLUB LTD, 24–28
Oval Road, London NW1 7DA. Tel: 071-267 9256. *Senior
Stipendiary Steward*, F. Melville

Gymnastics
*BRITISH AMATEUR GYMNASTICS ASSOCIATION, Ford
Hall, Lilleshall National Sports Centre, nr. Newport,
Shropshire TF10 9NB. Tel: 0952-820330. *Promotions
Officer*, S. Dangerfield

Hockey
*HOCKEY ASSOCIATION, Norfolk House, 102 Saxon Gate
West, Milton Keynes MK9 2EP. Tel: 0908-241100. *Chief
Executive*, S. P. Baines
*ALL ENGLAND WOMEN'S HOCKEY ASSOCIATION,
51 High Street, Shrewsbury SY1 1ST. Tel: 0743-233572.
Executive Director, Miss T. Morris
*SCOTTISH HOCKEY UNION, 48 Pleasance, Edinburgh EH8
9TJ. Tel: 031-650-8170. *Chairman*, Mrs E. Raistrick
*WELSH HOCKEY ASSOCIATION, 1 White Hart Lane,
Caerleon, Gwent NP6 1AB. Tel: 0633-420326. *Secretary*,
J. G. Williams
*WELSH WOMEN'S HOCKEY ASSOCIATION, Welsh
Hockey Office, Deeside Leisure Centre, Chester Road
West, Deeside, Clwyd CH5 1SA. Tel: 0244-811825.
President, Miss A. Ellis, MBE

Horseracing
*BRITISH HORSERACING BOARD, 42 Portman Square,
London W1H 0EN. Tel: 071-396 0011. *Chairman*,
Marquess of Hartington; *Chief Executive*, T. Ricketts
THE JOCKEY CLUB, 42 Portman Square, London W1H 0EN.
Tel: 071-486 4921. *Senior Steward*, Marquess of
Hartington

Ice Hockey
*BRITISH ICE HOCKEY ASSOCIATION, Second Floor
Offices, 517 Christchurch Road, Boscombe,
Bournemouth BH1 4AG. Tel: 0202-303946. *General
Secretary*, D. Pickles

Ice Skating
*NATIONAL SKATING ASSOCIATION OF THE UNITED
KINGDOM LTD, 15–27 Gee Street, London EC1V 3RE.
Tel: 071-253 3824. *President*, C. J. L. Jones, OBE

Judo
*BRITISH JUDO ASSOCIATION, 7A Rutland Street,
Leicester LE1 1RB. Tel: 0533-559669. *Office Manager*,
Ms S. Startin

Lacrosse
*ENGLISH LACROSSE UNION, 70 High Road, Rayleigh,
Essex SS6 7AD. Tel: 0268-770758. *Hon. Secretary*, R. Balls
*ALL ENGLAND WOMEN'S LACROSSE ASSOCIATION,
4 Western Court, Bromley Street, Digbeth, Birmingham
B9 4AN. Tel: 021-773 4422. *Administrator*, Miss A. Mason

Lawn Tennis
*LAWN TENNIS ASSOCIATION, The Queen's Club, London
W14 9EG. Tel: 071-381 7000. *Secretary*, J. C. U. James

Lugeing
*GREAT BRITAIN LUGE ASSOCIATION, Mortimer House,
Holmer Road, Hereford HR4 9SB. Tel: 0432-353539.
General Secretary, J. G. Evans

Martial Arts
MARTIAL ARTS COMMISSION, Broadway House,
15–16 Deptford Broadway, London SE8 4PE. Tel: 081-691
8711. *Chairman* (*acting*), R. Thomas

Motor Sports
*AUTO-CYCLE UNION, ACU House, Wood Street, Rugby, Warks. CV21 2YX. Tel: 0788-540519. *Chief Executive,* D. R. Barnfield
*RAC MOTOR SPORTS ASSOCIATION LTD, Motor Sports House, Riverside Park, Colnbrook, Slough SL3 0HG. Tel: 0753-681736. *Chief Executive,* J. R. Quenby
*SCOTTISH AUTO CYCLE UNION LTD, Block 2, Unit 6, Whiteside Industrial Estate, Bathgate, West Lothian EH48 2RX. Tel: 0506-630262. *Secretary,* A. M. Brownlie

Mountaineering
*BRITISH MOUNTAINEERING COUNCIL, Crawford House, Precinct Centre, Booth Street East, Manchester M13 9RZ. Tel: 061-273 5835. *General Secretary,* D. Walker

Multi-Sport Bodies
BRITISH OLYMPIC ASSOCIATION, I Wandsworth Plain, London SW18 1EH. Tel: 081-871 2677. *General Secretary,* R. Palmer, OBE
COMMONWEALTH GAMES FEDERATION, Walkden House, 3–10 Melton Street, London NW1 2EB. Tel: 071-383 5596. *Hon. Secretary,* D. Dixon
BRITISH COLLEGES SPORTS ASSOCIATION, 11 Allcock Street, Birmingham B9 4DY. Tel: 021-766 8855. *Hon. Administrative Secretary,* P. Rhodes
BRITISH UNIVERSITIES SPORTS FEDERATION, 11 Allcock Street, Birmingham B9 4DY. Tel: 021-766 8855. *General Secretary,* P. Rhodes

Netball
*ALL ENGLAND NETBALL ASSOCIATION, Netball House, 9 Paynes Park, Hitchin, Herts. SG5 1EH. Tel: 0462-442344. *Chief Executive,* Mrs E. M. Nicholl
*SCOTTISH NETBALL ASSOCIATION, Kelvin Hall Sports Complex, Argyle Street, Glasgow G3 8AW. Tel: 041-334 3650. *Administrator,* Ms M. Spence
*WELSH NETBALL ASSOCIATION, 82 Cathedral Road, Cardiff CF1 9LN. Tel: 0222-237048. *Chairman,* Mrs P. J. Lane

Orienteering
*BRITISH ORIENTEERING FEDERATION, Riversdale, Dale Road North, Darley Dale, Matlock, Derbyshire DE4 2HX. Tel: 0629-734042. *Manager,* Mrs H. Gregson

Polo
*HURLINGHAM POLO ASSOCIATION, Winterlake, Kirtlington, Oxford OX5 3HG. Tel: 0869-50044. *Secretary,* J. W. M. Crisp

Rackets and Real Tennis
*TENNIS AND RACKETS ASSOCIATION, c/o The Queen's Club, Palliser Road, London W14 9EQ. Tel: 071-381 4746. *Chief Executive,* Brig. A. D. Myrtle, CB, CBE

Rifle Shooting
*NATIONAL RIFLE ASSOCIATION, Bisley Camp, Brookwood, Woking GU24 0PB. Tel: 0483-797777. *Chief Executive,* Col. C. A. Ewing, OBE
*NATIONAL SMALL-BORE RIFLE ASSOCIATION, Lord Roberts House, Bisley Camp, Brookwood, Woking GU24 0NP. Tel: 0483-476969. *Secretary,* Gp Capt D. King, MBE

Rowing
*AMATEUR ROWING ASSOCIATION LTD, The Priory, 6 Lower Mall, London W6 9DJ. Tel: 081-748 3632. *Senior Administrative Officer,* Mrs R. E. Webb
HENLEY ROYAL REGATTA, Regatta Headquarters, Henley-on-Thames, Oxon. RG9 2LY. Tel: 0491-572153. *Secretary,* R. S. Goddard

SCOTTISH AMATEUR ROWING ASSOCIATION, 134 Newton Street, Greenock PA16 8SJ. Tel: 0475-22996. *Secretary,* Mrs M. Pow
*WELSH AMATEUR ROWING ASSOCIATION, c/o 30 Lady Mary Road, Cardiff CF2 5NT. Tel: 0222-754259. *Hon. Secretary,* Dr G. R. H. Greaves

Rugby Fives
*RUGBY FIVES ASSOCIATION, The Old Forge, Sutton Valence, Maidstone, Kent ME17 3AW. Tel: 0622-842278. *Secretary,* M. F. Beaman

Rugby League
*RUGBY FOOTBALL LEAGUE, 180 Chapeltown Road, Leeds LS7 4HT. Tel: 0532-624637. *Chief Executive,* M. P. Lindsay
*BRITISH AMATEUR RUGBY LEAGUE ASSOCIATION, West Yorkshire House, 4 New North Parade, Huddersfield HD1 5JP. Tel: 0484-544131. *Chief Executive,* M. F. Oldroyd

Rugby Union
*RUGBY FOOTBALL UNION, Twickenham TW1 1DZ. Tel: 081-892 8161. *Secretary,* D. E. Wood
*SCOTTISH RUGBY UNION, Murrayfield, Edinburgh EH12 5PJ. Tel: 031-337 2346. *Chief Executive,* I. A. L. Hogg
*WELSH RUGBY UNION, Cardiff Arms Park, PO Box 22, Cardiff CF1 1JL. Tel: 0222-390111. *Secretary,* D. P. Evans.
*IRISH RUGBY FOOTBALL UNION, 62 Lansdowne Road, Dublin 4, Republic of Ireland. Tel: 010-353-16-684601. *Secretary,* P. J. O'Donoghue
*WOMEN'S RUGBY FOOTBALL UNION, Meadow House, Springfield Farm, Shipston-on-Stour, Warks. CV36 4HQ. Tel: 0608-663336. *Secretary,* Ms R. Golby

Snooker
*WORLD PROFESSIONAL BILLIARDS AND SNOOKER ASSOCIATION, 27 Oakfield Road, Clifton, Bristol BS8 2AT. Tel: 0272-744491. *Company Secretary,* M. D. Blake
*WORLD LADIES BILLIARDS AND SNOOKER ASSOCIATION, 3 Felsted Avenue, Wisbech, Cambs. PE13 3SL. Tel: 0945-589589. *Chairman,* Ms M. Fisher

Speedway
*SPEEDWAY CONTROL BOARD, 57 Villa Crescent, Bulkington, Nuneaton CV12 9NF. Tel: 0203-643336. *Manager,* J. Eglese

Squash Rackets
*SQUASH RACKETS ASSOCIATION, Westpoint, 33–34 Warple Way, London W3 0RQ. Tel: 081-746 1616. *Chief Executive,* Ms J. Goodacre
*SCOTTISH SQUASH, Caledonia House, South Gyle, Edinburgh EH12 9DQ. Tel: 031-317 7343. *Secretary,* N. Brydon
*WELSH SQUASH RACKETS FEDERATION, 7 Kymin Terrace, Penarth, South Glamorgan CF6 1AP. Tel: 0222-704096. *Chairman,* D. Gadsby
BRITISH SQUASH PROFESSIONALS' ASSOCIATION, Apartment 4, Claudius Court, St Peter's Street, Colchester, Essex CO1 1EW. Tel: 0206-765195. *Chief Executive,* C. Walker

Swimming
*AMATEUR SWIMMING ASSOCIATION, Harold Fern House, Derby Square, Loughborough, Leics. LE11 0AL. Tel: 0509-230431. *Secretary,* D. A. Reeves
*SCOTTISH AMATEUR SWIMMING ASSOCIATION, Holmhills Farm, Greenlees Road, Cambuslang, Glasgow G72 8DT. Tel: 041-641 8818. *General Secretary,* W. Black
*WELSH AMATEUR SWIMMING ASSOCIATION, Wales Empire Pool, Wood Street, Cardiff CF1 1PP. Tel: 0222-342201. *Hon. General Secretary,* P. Rees

*BRITISH SUB-AQUA CLUB, Telfords Quay, Ellesmere
Port, South Wirral, Cheshire L65 4FY. Tel: 051-357 1951.
Chairman, H. Painter

Table Tennis
*ENGLISH TABLE TENNIS ASSOCIATION, Queensbury
House, Havelock Road, Hastings TN34 1HF. Tel: 0424-
722525. *Chief Executive*, Miss E. Shaw

Volleyball
*ENGLISH VOLLEYBALL ASSOCIATION, 27 South Road,
West Bridgford, Nottingham NG2 7AG. Tel: 0602-
816324. *National Director*, G. Bulman
*SCOTTISH VOLLEYBALL ASSOCIATION, 48 Pleasance,
Edinburgh EH8 9TJ. Tel: 031-556 4633. *Director*,
N. Moody
*WELSH VOLLEYBALL ASSOCIATION, 6 Redwood Close,
St Mellons, Cardiff CF3 9BX. Tel: 0222-798110.
Chairperson, Miss J. Thompson

Walking
*RACE WALKING ASSOCIATION. Hufflers, Heard's Lane,
Shenfield, Brentwood, Essex CM15 0SF. Tel: 0277-
220687. *Hon. Secretary*, P. J. Cassidy

Water Skiing
*BRITISH WATER SKI FEDERATION, 390 City Road,
London EC1V 2QA. Tel: 071-833 2855. *Secretary*, Ms G.
Hill

Weightlifting
*BRITISH AMATEUR WEIGHTLIFTERS ASSOCIATION, 3
Iffley Turn, Oxford OX4 4DU. Tel: 0865-778319. *Hon.
Secretary*, W. Holland, OBE

Wrestling
*BRITISH AMATEUR WRESTLING ASSOCIATION, 41 Great
Clowes Street, Salford, Manchester M7 9RQ. Tel: 061-832
9209. *Secretary*, R. Tomlinson

Yachting
*ROYAL YACHTING ASSOCIATION, RYA House, Romsey
Road, Eastleigh, Hants. SO5 4YA. Tel: 0703-629962.
Secretary-General, R. Duchesne, OBE

Clubs

LONDON CLUBS

ALPINE CLUB (1857), 55 Charlotte Road, London EC2A 3QT. Tel: 071-613 0755. *Hon. Secretary*, Dr M. J. Esten

AMERICAN WOMEN'S CLUB (1899), Connaught Rooms, Great Queen Street, London WC2B 5DA. Tel: 071-831 6660. *Secretary*, Ms K. Fales

ANGLO-BELGIAN CLUB (1955), 60 Knightsbridge, London SW1X 7LF. Tel: 071-235 2121. *Secretary*, Baronne van Havre

ARMY AND NAVY CLUB (1837), 36–39 Pall Mall, London SW1Y 5JN. Tel: 071-930 9721. *Secretary*, Maj. D. B. Taylor

ARTS CLUB (1863), 40 Dover Street, London W1X 3RB. Tel: 071-499 8581. *Secretary*, Mrs J. Downing

ARTS THEATRE CLUB (1927), 50 Frith Street, London W1V 5TE. Tel: 071-287 9236. *Secretary*, R. Thornton

THE ATHENAEUM (1824), 107 Pall Mall, London SW1Y 5ER. Tel: 071-930 4843. *Secretary*, R. R. T. Smith

AUTHORS' CLUB (1892), 40 Dover Street, London W1X 3RB. Tel: 071-499 8581. *Secretary*, Mrs A. Carter

BEEFSTEAK CLUB (1876), 9 Irving Street, London WC2H 7AT. Tel: 071-930 5722. *Secretary*, Sir John Lucas-Tooth, Bt.

BOODLE'S (1762), 28 St James's Street, London SW1A 1HJ. Tel: 071-930 7166. *Secretary*, R. J. Edmonds

BROOKS'S (1764), St James's Street, London SW1A 1LN. Tel: 071-493 4411. *Secretary*, vacant

BUCK'S CLUB (1919), 18 Clifford Street, London W1X 1RG. Tel: 071-734 2337. *Secretary*, Capt. P. Murison, RN

CALEDONIAN CLUB (1891), 9 Halkin Street, London SW1X 7DR. Tel: 071-235 5162. *Secretary*, P. J. Varney

CANNING CLUB (1910), 42 Half Moon Street, London W1Y 8DS. Tel: 071-499 5163. *Secretary*, T. M. Harrington

CARLTON CLUB (1832), 69 St James's Street, London SW1A 1PJ. Tel: 071-493 1164. *Secretary*, R. N. Linsley

CAVALRY AND GUARDS CLUB (1893), 127 Piccadilly, London W1V 0PX. Tel: 071-499 1261. *Secretary*, N. J. Walford

CHELSEA ARTS CLUB (1891), 143 Old Church Street, London SW3 6EB. Tel: 071-376 3311. *Secretary*, D. Winterbottom

CITY LIVERY CLUB (1914), Sion College, Victoria Embankment, London EC4Y 0DN. Tel: 071-353 2431/2. *Hon. Secretary*, B. L. Morgan, CBE

CITY OF LONDON CLUB (1832), 19 Old Broad Street, London EC2N 1DS. Tel: 071-588 7991. *Manager*, G. S. Jones

CITY UNIVERSITY CLUB (1895), 50 Cornhill, London EC3V 3PD. Tel: 071-626 8571. *Secretary*, Miss R. C. Graham

EAST INDIA CLUB (1849), 16 St James's Square, London SW1Y 4LH. Tel: 071-930 1000. *Secretary*, J. G. F. Stoy

FARMERS CLUB (1842), 3 Whitehall Court, London SW1A 2EL. Tel: 071-930 3751. *Secretary*, Lt.-Col. G. B. Murray

FLYFISHERS' CLUB (1884), 24A Old Burlington Street, London W1X 1RG. Tel: 071-734 9229. *Secretary*, Cdr. N. T. Fuller (retd)

GARRICK CLUB (1831), 15 Garrick Street, London WC2E 9AY. Tel: 071-379 6478. *Secretary*, M. J. Harvey

GREEN ROOM CLUB (1877), 9 Adam Street, London WC2N 6AA. Tel: 071-836 7453. *Secretary*, J. Booth

GROUCHO CLUB (1985), 45 Dean Street, London W1V 5AP. Tel: 071-439 4685. *Company Secretary*, Miss Z. Noordin

HUNTERS CLUB (1981), 3 London Wall Buildings, London EC2M 5PD. Tel: 071-638 0363. *Secretary*, R. A. Sanders

HURLINGHAM CLUB (1869), Ranelagh Gardens, London SW6 3PR. Tel: 071-736 8411. *Secretary*, P. H. Covell

KEMPTON PARK CLUB (1878), Kempton Park Racecourse, Sunbury-on-Thames, Middx., TW16 5AQ. Tel: 0932-782292. *Secretary*, Mrs C. Milburn-Lee

KENNEL CLUB (1873), 1–5 Clarges Street, London W1Y 8AB. Tel: 071-493 6651. *Secretary*, Mrs B. E. Ormerod

LANSDOWNE CLUB (1934), 9 Fitzmaurice Place, London W1X 6JD. Tel: 071-629 7200. *Secretary*, Lt.-Cdr. T. P. Havers (retd)

LONDON ROWING CLUB (1856), Embankment, Putney, London SW15 1LB. Tel: 081-788 1400. *Hon. Secretary*, N. A. Smith

MCC (MARYLEBONE CRICKET CLUB) (1787), Lord's Cricket Ground, London NW8 8QN. Tel: 071-289 1611. *Secretary*, Lt.-Col. J. R. Stephenson, OBE

NATIONAL CLUB (1845), 234 Kilburn High Road, London NW6 4JR. Tel: 071-328 3141. *Secretary*, I. E. Nash

NATIONAL LIBERAL CLUB (1882), Whitehall Place, London SW1A 2HE. Tel: 071-930 9871. *Secretary*, S. J. Roberts

NAVAL AND MILITARY CLUB (1862), 94 Piccadilly, London W1V 0BP. Tel: 071-499 5163. *Secretary*, Cdr. J. A. Holt, MBE

NAVAL CLUB (1946), 38 Hill Street, London W1X 8DP. Tel: 071-493 7672. *Chief Executive*, Capt. R. J. Husk, CBE, RN (retd)

NEW CAVENDISH CLUB (1984), (formerly VAD), 44 Great Cumberland Place, London W1H 8BS. Tel: 071-723 0391. *Secretary*, J. Malone-Lee

DEN NORSKE KLUB (1924), Norway House, 21–24 Cockspur Street, London SW1Y 5BN. Tel: 071-930 4084. *Secretary*, Ms J. P. Holm

ORIENTAL CLUB (1824), Stratford House, Stratford Place, London W1N 0ES. Tel: 071-629 5126. *Secretary*, S. C. Doble

PORTLAND CLUB (1816), 42 Half Moon Street, London W1Y 7RD. Tel: 071-499 1523. *Secretary*, R. B. Little

PRATT'S CLUB (1841), 14 Park Place, London SW1A 1LP. Tel: 071-493 0397. *Secretary*, Capt. P. W. E. Parry, MBE

QUEEN'S CLUB, THE (1886), Palliser Road, London W14 9EQ. Tel: 071-385 3421. *Secretary*, J. A. S. Edwardes

RAILWAY CLUB (1899), Room 208, 25 Marylebone Road, London NW1 5JS. *Hon. Secretary*, A. G. Wells

REFORM CLUB (1836), 104–105 Pall Mall, London SW1Y 5EW. Tel: 071-930 9374. *Secretary*, R. A. M. Forrest

ROEHAMPTON CLUB (1901), Roehampton Lane, London SW15 5LR. Tel: 081-876 5505. *Chief Executive*, M. Yates

ROYAL AIR FORCE CLUB (1918), 128 Piccadilly, London W1V 0PY. Tel: 071-499 3456. *Secretary*, P. N. Owen

ROYAL AUTOMOBILE CLUB (1897), 89–91 Pall Mall, London SW1Y 5HS. Tel: 071-930 2345. *General Secretary*, M. J. Limb

ROYAL OCEAN RACING CLUB (1925), 20 St James's Place, London SW1A 1NN. Tel: 071-493 2248. *General Manager*, D. J. Minords, OBE

ROYAL OVER-SEAS LEAGUE (1910), Over-Seas House, Park Place, St James's Street, London SW1A 1LR. Tel: 071-408 0214. *Secretary*, R. F. Newell

ROYAL THAMES YACHT CLUB (1775), 60 Knightsbridge, London SW1X 7LF. Tel: 071-235 2121. *Secretary*, Capt. D. Goldson, RN (retd)

ST STEPHEN'S CONSTITUTIONAL CLUB (1870), 34 Queen Anne's Gate, London SW1H 9AB. Tel: 071-222 1382. *Secretary*, L. D. Mawby

SAVAGE CLUB (1857), 1 Whitehall Place, London SW1A 2HD. Tel: 071-930 8118. *Hon. Secretary*, D. Stirling

SAVILE CLUB (1868), 69 Brook Street, London W1Y 2ER. Tel: 071-629 5462. *Secretary*, N. Storey

SKI CLUB OF GREAT BRITAIN (1903), 118 Eaton Square, London SW1W 9AF. Tel: 071-245 1033. *Chief Executive*, Ms I. Grimsey

THAMES ROWING CLUB (1860), Embankment, Putney, London SW15 1LB. Tel: 081-788 0676. *Hon. Secretary*, Ms K. Watson

TRAVELLERS' CLUB (1819), 106 Pall Mall, London SW1Y 5EP. Tel: 071-930 8688. *Secretary*, M. S. Allcock

TURF CLUB (1868), 5 Carlton House Terrace, London SW1Y 5AQ. Tel: 071-930 8555. *Secretary*, J. Rigby, OBE

UNITED OXFORD AND CAMBRIDGE UNIVERSITY CLUB (1972), 71 Pall Mall, London SW1Y 5HD. Tel: 071-930 5151. *General Secretary*, D. McDougall

UNIVERSITY WOMEN'S CLUB (1886), 2 Audley Square, London W1Y 6DB. Tel: 071-499 2268. *Secretary*, Mrs P. A. Burtwell

VICTORIA CLUB (1863), 1 North Court, Great Peter Street, London SW1P 3LL. Tel: 071-222 2357. *Secretary*, Ms H. David

VICTORY SERVICES CLUB (1907), 63–79 Seymour Street, London W2 2HF. Tel: 071-723 4474. *General Manager*, Capt. G. F. Taylor

WHITE'S CLUB (1693), 37–38 St James's Street, London SW1A 1JG. Tel: 071-493 6671. *Secretary*, D. C. Ward

WIG AND PEN CLUB (1908), 229–230 Strand, London WC2R 1BA. Tel: 071-583 7255. *Administrator*, J. Reynolds

---

CLUBS OUTSIDE LONDON

Bath: BATH AND COUNTY CLUB (1865), Queens Parade, Bath, BA1 2NJ. Tel: 0225-423732. *Secretary*, Mrs G. M. Jones

Birmingham: BIRMINGHAM CLUB (1872), Winston Churchill House, 8 Ethel Street, Birmingham B2 4BG. Tel: 021-643 3357. *Hon. Secretary*, T. R. Pepper
ST PAUL'S CLUB (1859), 34 St Paul's Square, Birmingham B3 1QZ. Tel: 021-236 1950. *Hon. Secretary*, E. A. Fellowes

Bishop Auckland: THE CLUB (1868), 1 Victoria Avenue, Bishop Auckland, Co. Durham DL14 7JH. Tel: 0388-603219. *Hon. Secretary*, R. Kellett

Blackburn: DISTRICT AND UNION CLUB (1849), Northwood, 1 West Park Road, Blackburn BB2 6DE. Tel: 0254-51474. *Hon. Secretary*, B. Haydock

Bristol: CLIFTON CLUB (1882), 22 The Mall, Clifton, Bristol BS8 4DS. Tel: 0272-735527. *Secretary*, H. B. Peckham

Cambridge: AMATEUR DRAMATIC CLUB (1855), ADC Theatre, Park Street, Cambridge CB5 8AS. Tel: 0223-359547. *Secretary*, S. Brown
THE UNION (1815), Bridge Street, Cambridge CB2 1UB. Tel: 0223-61521. *Chief Clerk*, B. Thoday

Canterbury: KENT AND CANTERBURY CLUB (1868), 17 Old Dover Road, Canterbury CT1 3JB. Tel: 0227-462181. *Secretary*, H. V. Brown, LVO, QPM, CPM

Cheltenham: NEW CLUB (1874), Montpellier Parade, Cheltenham GL50 1UD. Tel: 0242-523285. *Hon. Secretary*, J. A. Warhurst, OBE

Chester: CITY CLUB (1807), St Peter's Churchyard, Chester CH1 2AG. *Secretary*, C. Hodkinson

Chichester: WEST SUSSEX COUNTY CLUB (1872), 5 Stirling Road, Chichester, W. Sussex PO19 2EW. *Secretary*, Mrs P. Green

Colchester: THE COLCHESTER CLUB (1874), 3–5 Culver Street, Colchester CO1 1LE. *Secretary*, D. G. Congdon

Devizes: DEVIZES AND DISTRICT CLUB (1932), 27 St John Street, Devizes, Wilts. SN10 1BN. *Secretary*, D. J. J. Cox

Durham: COUNTY CLUB (1890), 52 Old Elvet, Durham. Tel: 091-384 1679. *Secretary*, Mrs C. Arnot
DURHAM UNION SOCIETY (1842), 24 North Bailey, Durham DH1 3EP. Tel: 091-384 3724. *Secretary*, Mrs E. M. Hardcastle

Eastbourne: DEVONSHIRE CLUB (1872), Hartington Place, Eastbourne, E. Sussex BN21 3RN. *Hon. Secretary*, D. G. Matthews

Guildford: COUNTY CLUB, 158 High Street, Guildford GU1 3HF. Tel: 0483-575370. *Hon. Secretary*, R. W. D. Hemingway

Harrogate: THE CLUB (1857), 36 Victoria Avenue, Harrogate, N. Yorks. *Hon. Secretary*, C. L. Leslie

Henley-on-Thames: LEANDER CLUB (1818), Henley-on-Thames, Oxon. RG9 2LP. Tel: 0491-575782. *Hon. Secretary*, J. Beveridge
PHYLLIS COURT CLUB (1906), Marlow Road, Henley, Oxon. RG9 2HT. Tel: 0491-574366. *Secretary*, D. M. Brockett

Hove: HOVE CLUB (1882), 28 Fourth Avenue, Hove, E. Sussex BN3 2PJ. Tel: 0273-730872. *Secretary*, J. C. Ager, RD

Leamington: TENNIS COURT CLUB (1846), 50 Bedford Street, Leamington, Warks. CV32 5DT. Tel: 0926-424977. *Hon. Secretary*, O. D. R. Dixon

Leeds: LEEDS CLUB (1850), 3 Albion Place, Leeds LS1 6JL. Tel: 0532-421591. *Manager*, Mrs C. Myers

Leicester: LEICESTERSHIRE CLUB (1873), 9 Welford Place, Leicester LE1 6ZH. Tel: 0533-540399. *Hon. Secretary*, G. C. Jones

Liverpool: THE ATHENAEUM (1797), Church Alley, Liverpool L1 3DD. Tel: 051-709 7770. *Permanent Secretary*, B. B. P. Kinsman

Macclesfield: OLD BOYS' AND PARK GREEN CLUB, 7 Churchside, Macclesfield, Cheshire SK10 1HG. Tel: 0625-423292. *Hon. Secretary*, Dr P. R. Baker, MBE

Manchester: ST JAMES'S CLUB, St James's House, Charlotte Street, Manchester M1 4DZ. Tel: 061-236 2235. *Hon. Secretary*, R. H. C. Nichols

Newcastle upon Tyne: NORTHERN CONSTITUTIONAL CLUB (1882), 37 Pilgrim Street, Newcastle upon Tyne NE1 6QE. Tel: 091-232 0884. *Hon. Secretary*, J. L. Browne

Northampton: NORTHAMPTON AND COUNTY CLUB (1873), George Row, Northampton NN1 1DF. Tel: 0604-32962. *Secretary*, J. Coley

Norwich: NORFOLK CLUB (1770), 17 Upper King Street, Norwich NR3 1RB. Tel: 0603-610652. *Secretary*, A. J. M. Williamson

Nottingham: NOTTINGHAM AND NOTTS UNITED SERVICES CLUB (1920), Newdigate House, Castle Gate, Nottingham NG1 6AF. Tel: 0602-472138. *Hon. Secretary*, A. C. Ready

Oxford: FREWEN CLUB (1869), 98 St Aldate's, Oxford OX1 1BT. Tel: 0865-243816. *Hon. Secretary*, W. H. Miller, BEM
OXFORD UNION SOCIETY (1823), Frewin Court, Oxford OX1 3JB. *Secretary*, S. Green

VINCENT'S CLUB (1863), 1A King Edward Street, Oxford OX1 4HS. Tel: 0865-722984. *Secretary,* J. B. Bailey

Paignton: PAIGNTON CLUB (1882), The Esplanade, Paignton, Devon TQ4 6ED. Tel: 0803-559682. *Hon. Secretary,* P. Grafton

Peterborough: CITY AND COUNTIES CLUB (1867), Priestgate, Peterborough PE6 7LT. *Secretary,* J. R. Fillingham

Reading: BERKSHIRE ATHENAEUM CLUB (1972), 53 Blagrave Street, Reading, Berks. *Hon. Secretary,* W. J. Stuck

Rye: DORMY HOUSE CLUB (1896), Rye, E. Sussex TN31 7LD. Tel: 0797-222338. *Hon. Secretary,* P. G. Armitage

Shrewsbury: SALOP CLUB (1974), The Old House, Dogpole, Shrewsbury SY1 1EP. Tel: 0743-362182. *Secretary,* J. W. Rouse

Stourbridge: STOURBRIDGE OLD EDWARDIAN CLUB (1898), Drury Lane, Stourbridge, West Midlands DY8 1BL. Tel: 0384-395635. *Hon. Secretary,* J. V. Sanders

Teddington: ROYAL CANOE CLUB (1866), Trowlock Island, Teddington, Middx. TW11 9QZ. Tel: 081-977 5269. *Hon. Secretary,* Mrs J. S. Evans

Worcester: UNION AND COUNTY CLUB (1861), 40 Foregate Street, Worcester. *Secretary,* M. G. Maton

York: YORKSHIRE CLUB (1839), 17 Museum Street, York YO1 2DW. Tel: 0904-624116. *Hon. Secretary,* D. E. Gabbitas

WALES

Cardiff: CARDIFF AND COUNTY CLUB (1866), Westgate Street, Cardiff CF1 1DA. Tel: 0222-220846. *Hon. Secretary,* Cdr. J. E. Payn, RD

SCOTLAND

Aberdeen: ROYAL NORTHERN AND UNIVERSITY CLUB (1854/1889, amal. 1979), 9 Albyn Place, Aberdeen AB1 1YE. Tel: 0224-583292. *Secretary,* Miss R. A. Black

Ayr: COUNTY CLUB (1872), Savoy Park Hotel, Ayr KA7 2XA. *Hon. Secretary,* J. K. Templeton

Edinburgh: CALEDONIAN CLUB (1825), 32 Abercromby Place, Edinburgh EH3 6QE. Tel: 031-557 2675. *Secretary,* Ms F. Fowler

NEW CLUB (1787), 86 Princes Street, Edinburgh EH2 2BB. Tel: 031-226 4881. *Secretary,* A. D. Orr Ewing

Glasgow: GLASGOW ART CLUB (1867), 135 Wellington Street, Glasgow G2 2XE. Tel: 041-248 5210. *Secretary,* L. J. McIntyre

ROYAL SCOTTISH AUTOMOBILE CLUB (1899), 11 Blythswood Square, Glasgow G2 4AG. Tel: 041-221 3850. *Secretary,* J. C. Lord

WESTERN CLUB (1825), 32 Royal Exchange Square, Glasgow G1 3AB. Tel: 041-221 2016. *Secretary,* D. H. Gifford

NORTHERN IRELAND

Belfast: ULSTER REFORM CLUB (1885), 4 Royal Avenue, Belfast BT1 1DA. Tel: 0232-323411. *Secretary,* Miss M. P. Mackintosh

CHANNEL ISLANDS

Guernsey: UNITED CLUB (1870), St Peter Port, Guernsey. Tel: 0481-725722. *Secretary,* J. G. Doggart

Jersey: VICTORIA CLUB (1853), Beresford Street, St Helier, Jersey. Tel: 0534-23381. *Secretary,* Miss C. Rynd

YACHT CLUBS

Bembridge: BEMBRIDGE SAILING CLUB (1886), Embankment Road, Bembridge, IOW, PO35 5NR. Tel: 0983-872237. *Hon. Secretary,* B. J. B. Sloley

Birkenhead: ROYAL MERSEY YACHT CLUB (1844), Bedford Road East, Rock Ferry, Birkenhead, Merseyside L42 1LS. Tel: 051-645 3204. *Hon. Secretary,* A. Tetley

Bridlington: ROYAL YORKSHIRE YACHT CLUB (1847), 1 Windsor Crescent, Bridlington, N. Humberside YO15 3HX. Tel: 0262-672041. *Secretary,* J. H. Evans

Burnham-on-Crouch: ROYAL CORINTHIAN YACHT CLUB (1872), Burnham-on-Crouch, Essex CM0 8AX. Tel: 0621-782105. *Hon. Secretary,* K. W. Bushell

Cowes: ROYAL YACHT SQUADRON (1815), The Castle, Cowes, IOW, PO31 7QT. Tel: 0983-292191. *Secretary,* Maj. R. P. Rising, RM

ROYAL LONDON YACHT CLUB (1838), The Parade, Cowes, IOW, PO31 7QS. Tel: 0983-299727. *Secretary,* Lt.-Col. R. J. Freeman-Wallace (retd)

Dover: ROYAL CINQUE PORTS YACHT CLUB (1872), 5 Waterloo Crescent, Dover, Kent CT16 1LA. Tel: 0304-206262. *Secretary,* Mrs H. Moors

Fishbourne: ROYAL VICTORIA YACHT CLUB (1844), Fishbourne Lane, Ryde, IOW, PO33 4EU. Tel: 0983-882325. *Hon. Secretary,* Ms H. Vrba

Fowey: ROYAL FOWEY YACHT CLUB (1881), Whitford Yard, Fowey, Cornwall PL23 1BH. Tel: 0726-833573. *Hon. Secretary,* E. P. Warren

Harwich: ROYAL HARWICH YACHT CLUB (1843), Woolverstone, Ipswich IP9 1AT. Tel: 0473-780319. *Secretary,* I. A. Murdoch

Kingswear: ROYAL DART YACHT CLUB (1866), Priory Street, Kingswear, Dartmouth, Devon TQ6 0AB. Tel: 0803-752496. *Hon. Secretary,* Dr N. Baxter

Leigh-on-Sea: ESSEX YACHT CLUB (1890), HQS Bembridge, Foreshore, Leigh-on-Sea, Essex SS9 1BD. Tel: 0702-78404. *Hon. Secretary,* A. Manning

London: THE CRUISING ASSOCIATION (1908), Ivory House, St Katharine Dock, London E1 9AT. Tel: 071-481 0881. *General Secretary,* Mrs L. Hammett

ROYAL CRUISING CLUB (1880), c/o Royal Thames Yacht Club, 60 Knightsbridge, London SW1X 7LF. Tel: 0276-65946. *Hon. Secretary,* P. Price

Lowestoft: ROYAL NORFOLK AND SUFFOLK YACHT CLUB (1859), Royal Plain, Lowestoft, Suffolk NR33 0AQ. Tel: 0502-566726. *Hon. Secretary,* J. M. Brown

Lymington: ROYAL LYMINGTON YACHT CLUB (1922), Bath Road, Lymington, Hants SO41 9SE. Tel: 0590-672677. *Secretary,* Gp Capt J. D. Hutchinson (retd)

Plymouth: ROYAL WESTERN YACHT CLUB (1827), Queen Anne's Battery, Plymouth PL4 0TW. Tel: 0752-660077. *Secretary,* Maj. J. Lewis, RM

ROYAL PLYMOUTH CORINTHIAN YACHT CLUB (1877), Madeira Road, Plymouth PL1 2NY. Tel: 0752-664327. *Hon. Secretary,* V. J. De Boo

Poole: EAST DORSET SAILING CLUB (1875), 352 Sandbanks Road, Poole, Dorset BH14 8HY. Tel: 0202-706111. *Hon. Secretary,* P. Neely

PARKSTONE YACHT CLUB (1895), Pearce Avenue, Parkstone, Poole, Dorset BH14 8EH. Tel: 0202-743610. *Secretary,* D. E. Norman

POOLE HARBOUR YACHT CLUB (1949), 38 Salterns Way, Lilliput, Poole, Dorset BH14 8JR. Tel: 0202-707321. *Secretary,* J. N. J. Smith

POOLE YACHT CLUB (1865), New Harbour Road West, Hamworthy, Poole, Dorset BH15 4AQ. Tel: 0202-672687. *Secretary/Manager*, Miss L. Clark

Portsmouth: ROYAL NAVAL CLUB AND ROYAL ALBERT YACHT CLUB (1867), 17 Pembroke Road, Portsmouth PO1 2NT. Tel: 0705-824491. *Secretary*, Lt.-Cdr. C. J. Howe

Ramsgate: ROYAL TEMPLE YACHT CLUB (1857), 6 Westcliff Mansions, Ramsgate, Kent CT11 9HY. Tel: 0843-591766. *Hon. Secretary*, G. F. Randell

Southampton: ROYAL AIR FORCE YACHT CLUB (1932), Riverside House, Rope Walk, Hamble, Southampton SO3 5HD. Tel: 0703-452208. *Secretary*, Miss A. R. Prees

ROYAL SOUTHAMPTON YACHT CLUB, 1 Channel Way, Ocean Village, Southampton SO1 1XE. Tel: 0703-223352. *Hon. Secretary*, R. Higgs

ROYAL SOUTHERN YACHT CLUB (1837), Hamble, Southampton SO3 5HB. Tel: 0703-453271. *Secretary*, Mrs J. A. Atkins

Southend: ALEXANDRA YACHT CLUB (1873), Clifton Terrace, Southend-on-Sea SS1 1DT. *Hon. Secretary*, D. C. Osborn

Torquay: ROYAL TORBAY YACHT CLUB (1863), Beacon Hill, Torquay, Devon TQ1 2BQ. Tel: 0803-292006. *Hon. Secretary*, J. N. Carleton-Stiff, TD

Westcliff-on-Sea: THAMES ESTUARY YACHT CLUB (1895), 3 The Leas, Westcliff-on-Sea, Essex SS0 7ST. Tel: 0702-345967. *Hon. Secretary*, D. Howard

Weymouth: ROYAL DORSET YACHT CLUB (1875), 11 Custom House Quay, Weymouth, Dorset DT4 8BG. Tel: 0305-786258. *Secretary*, Mrs K. Mead

Windermere: ROYAL WINDERMERE YACHT CLUB (1860), Fallbarrow Road, Bowness-on-Windermere, Windermere, Cumbria LA23 3DJ. Tel: 05394-43106. *Hon. Secretary*, M. C. Bentley

Yarmouth: ROYAL SOLENT YACHT CLUB (1878), Yarmouth, IOW, PO41 0NS. Tel: 0983-760256. *Secretary*, Mrs S. Tribe

WALES

Beaumaris: ROYAL ANGLESEY YACHT CLUB (1802), 6–7 Green Edge, Beaumaris, Gwynedd LL58 8BY. Tel: 0248-810295. *Hon. Secretary*, V. G. Keep

Caernarfon: ROYAL WELSH YACHT CLUB (1847), Porth-Yr-Aur, Caernarfon, Gwynedd LL55 1SW. Tel: 0286-672599. *Hon. Secretary*, G. Tecwyn Evans

Penarth: PENARTH YACHT CLUB (1880). The Esplanade, Penarth, S. Glamorgan CF64 3AU. Tel: 0222-708196. *Hon. Secretary*, R. S. McGregor

Swansea: BRISTOL CHANNEL YACHT CLUB (1875), 744 Mumbles Road, Mumbles, Swansea SA3 4EL. Tel: 0792-366000. *Hon. Secretary*, B. G. T. Rees

SCOTLAND

Dundee: ROYAL TAY YACHT CLUB (1885), 34 Dundee Road, Broughty Ferry, Dundee DD5 1LX. Tel: 0382-77516. *Hon. Secretary*, Dr G. R. Foster

Edinburgh: ROYAL FORTH YACHT CLUB (1868), Middle Pier, Granton Harbour, Edinburgh EH5 1HF. Tel: 031-552 8560. *Hon. Secretary*, D. Skinner

Glasgow: ROYAL WESTERN YACHT CLUB (1875), Lochaber, 20 Barclay Drive, Helensburgh, Dunbartonshire G84 9RB. Tel: 0436-72088. *Hon. Secretary*, D. G. M. Watson

Oban: ROYAL HIGHLAND YACHT CLUB (1881), West Manse House, Kilchrenan, Taynuilt, Argyll PA35 1HG. Tel: 08663-213. *Secretary*, Mrs J. D. Carr

Rhu: ROYAL NORTHERN AND CLYDE YACHT CLUB (1824, amal. 1978), Rhu, Helensburgh, Dunbartonshire G84 8NG. Tel: 0436-820322. *Hon. Secretary*, B. C. Staig

NORTHERN IRELAND

Bangor: ROYAL ULSTER YACHT CLUB (1866), 101 Clifton Road, Bangor, Co. Down BT20 5HY. Tel: 0247-270568. *Hon. Secretary*, T. O'Hara

CHANNEL ISLANDS

Jersey: ROYAL CHANNEL ISLANDS YACHT CLUB (1862), Le Boulevard, Bulwarks, St Aubin, Jersey. Tel: 0534-41023. *Hon. Secretary*, D. C. Dale

Societies and Institutions

Although this section is arranged in alphabetic order, organizations are usually listed by the keyword in their title. The date in parenthesis after the organization's title is the year of its foundation.

ABBEYFIELD SOCIETY, 186–192 Darkes Lane, Potters Bar, Herts. EN6 IAB. Tel: 0707-644845. Housing for elderly people. *Chief Executive*, F. Murphy

ACCOUNTANTS, CHARTERED ASSOCIATION OF CERTIFIED (1904), 29 Lincoln's Inn Fields, London WC2A 3EE. Tel: 071-242 6855. *Secretary*, Mrs A. L. Rose

ACCOUNTANTS, INSTITUTE OF COMPANY (1974), 40 Tyndalls Park Road, Bristol BS8 IPL. Tel: 0272-738261. *Director-General*, B. T. Banks

ACCOUNTANTS, INSTITUTE OF FINANCIAL (1916), Burford House, 44 London Road, Sevenoaks, Kent TN13 IAS. Tel: 0732-458080. *Chief Executive*, D. Gurney

ACCOUNTANTS IN ENGLAND AND WALES, INSTITUTE OF CHARTERED (1880), PO Box 433, Chartered Accountants' Hall, Moorgate Place, London EC2P 2BJ. Tel: 071-628 7060. *Secretary*, A. J. Colquhoun

ACCOUNTANTS IN IRELAND, INSTITUTE OF CHARTERED (1888), Chartered Accountants House, 87–89 Pembroke Road, Dublin 4. Tel: Dublin 6680400/Belfast 321600. *Director*, R. F. Hussey

ACCOUNTANTS OF SCOTLAND, THE INSTITUTE OF CHARTERED (1854), 27 Queen Street, Edinburgh EH2 ILA. Tel: 031-479 4809. *Chief Executive*, P. W. Johnston

ACCOUNTING TECHNICIANS, ASSOCIATION OF (1980), 154 Clerkenwell Road, London ECIR 5AD. Tel: 071-837 8600. *Secretary*, J. Hanson

ACE STUDY TOURS (formerly Association for Cultural Exchange), Babraham, Cambridge CB2 4AP. Tel: 0223-835055. *General Secretary*, P. B. Barnes

ACTION RESEARCH (1952), Vincent House, North Parade, Horsham, W. Sussex RHI2 2DA. Tel: 0403-210406. *Director-General*, Mrs A. Luther

ACTORS' BENEVOLENT FUND (1882), 6 Adam Street, London WC2N 6AA. Tel: 071–836 6378. *General Secretary*, Mrs R. Stevens

ACTORS' CHARITABLE TRUST (1896), 19–20 Euston Centre, London NWI 3JH. Tel: 071-608 6212. *Administrative Secretary*, Ms A. Stewart

ACTORS' CHURCH UNION (1899), St Paul's Church, Bedford Street, London WC2E 9ED. Tel: 071-836 5221. *Senior Chaplain*, Canon W. Hall

ACTUARIES, INSTITUTE OF (1848), Staple Inn Hall, High Holborn, London WCIV 7QJ. Tel: 071-242 0106. *Secretary-General*, A. G. Tait

ACTUARIES IN SCOTLAND, THE FACULTY OF (1856), 23 St Andrew Square, Edinburgh EH2 IAQ. Tel: 031-557 1575. *Secretary*, W. W. Mair

ADMINISTRATIVE MANAGEMENT, INSTITUTE OF (1915), 40 Chatsworth Parade, Petts Wood, Orpington, Kent BR5 IRW. Tel: 0689-875555. *Chief Executive*, Ms C. Hayhurst

ADULT SCHOOL ORGANIZATION, NATIONAL (1899), MASU Centre, Gaywood Croft, Cregoe Street, Birmingham BI5 2ED. Tel: 021-622 3400. *General Secretary*, W. J. Scarle

ADVERTISING BENEVOLENT SOCIETY, NATIONAL (1913), 199–205 Old Marylebone Road, London NWI 5QP. Tel: 071-723 8028. *Director*, Mrs D. Larkin

ADVERTISING, INSTITUTE OF PRACTITIONERS IN (1927), 44 Belgrave Square, London SWIX 8QS. Tel: 071-235 7020. *Director-General*, N. Phillips

ADVERTISING STANDARDS AUTHORITY (1962), Brook House, 2–16 Torrington Place, London WCIE 7HN. Tel: 071-580 5555. *Director-General*, Mrs M. Alderson

AERONAUTICAL SOCIETY, ROYAL (1866), 4 Hamilton Place, London WIV OBQ. Tel: 071-499 3515. *Director*, R. J. Kennett

AFRICAN INSTITUTE, INTERNATIONAL (1926), London School of Economics, Connaught House, Houghton Street, London WC2A 2AE. Tel: 071-831 3068. *Hon. Director*, Prof. D. Parkin

AFRICAN MEDICAL AND RESEARCH FOUNDATION, II Waterloo Street, Clifton, Bristol BS8 4BT. Tel: 0272-238424. *Executive Director*, Mrs E. Young

AGE CONCERN ENGLAND (1940), Astral House, 1268 London Road, London SWI6 4ER. Tel: 081-679 8000. *Director*, Lady Greengross, OBE

AGE CONCERN NORTHERN IRELAND (1976), 6 Lower Crescent, Belfast BT2 7BG. Tel: 0232-245729. *Director*, C. J. Common

AGE CONCERN SCOTLAND (1943), 54A Fountainbridge, Edinburgh EH3 9PT. Tel: 031-228 5656. *Director*, M. Cairns

AGE CONCERN WALES, 4th Floor, I Cathedral Road, Cardiff CFI 9SD. Tel: 0222-371566. *Operations Manager*, R. W. Taylor

AGED POOR SOCIETY, *see* ST JOSEPH'S SOCIETY FOR THE RELIEF OF THE AGED POOR

AGEING, CENTRE FOR POLICY ON (1947), 25–31 Ironmonger Row, London ECIV 3QP. Tel: 071-253 1787. *Director*, Ms K. Herbst, PH.D.

AGEING, RESEARCH INTO (1978), Baird House, 15–17 St Cross Street, London ECIN 8UN. Tel: 071-404 6878. *Director*, Mrs E. Mills

AGRICULTURAL BENEVOLENT INSTITUTION, ROYAL (1860), Shaw House, 27 West Way, Oxford OX2 OQH. Tel: 0865-724931. *Chief Executive*, A. G. Staniforth, CBE

AGRICULTURAL BENEVOLENT INSTITUTION, ROYAL SCOTTISH (1897), Ingliston, Edinburgh, EH28 8NB. Tel: 031-333 1023. *Director*, I. C. Purves-Hume

AGRICULTURAL ENGINEERS ASSOCIATION (1875), Samuelson House, Paxton Road, Orton Centre, Peterborough PE2 OLT. Tel: 0733-371381. *Director-General*, J. Vowles

AGRICULTURAL SOCIETY, EAST OF ENGLAND, East of England Showground, Peterborough PE2 6XE. Tel: 0733-234451. *Chief Executive*, T. Gibson, OBE

AGRICULTURAL SOCIETY OF ENGLAND, ROYAL (1838), National Agricultural Centre, Stoneleigh Park, Warks. CV8 2LZ. Tel: 0203-696969. *Chief Executive*, C. Runge

AGRICULTURAL SOCIETY OF THE COMMONWEALTH, ROYAL (1957), 55 Sleaford Street, London SW8 5AB. Tel: 071-627 2111. *Hon. Secretary*, F. R. Francis, LVO, MBE

AGRICULTURAL SOCIETY, ROYAL ULSTER (1826), The King's Hall, Balmoral Show Grounds, Belfast BT9 6GW. Tel: 0232-665225. *Chief Executive*, W. H. Yarr, OBE

AIR LEAGUE, THE (1909), 4 Hamilton Place, London WIV OBQ. Tel: 071-491 0470. *Secretary-General*, Air Cdre J. C. Atkinson, CBE

ALCOHOLICS ANONYMOUS (1947), PO Box 1, Stonebow House, Stonebow, York YO1 2NJ. Tel: 0904-644026. *General Secretary*, J. Keeney

ALEXANDRA ROSE DAY (1912), 1 Castelnau, Barnes, London SW13 9RP. Tel: 081-748 4824. *National Director*, Mrs G. Greenwood

ALLOTMENT AND LEISURE GARDENERS LIMITED, NATIONAL SOCIETY OF (1930), Hunters Road, Corby, Northants NN17 1JE. Tel: 0536-66576. *National Secretary*, G. W. Stokes

ALMSHOUSES, NATIONAL ASSOCIATION OF (1946), Billingbear Lodge, Wokingham, Berks. RG11 5RU. *Director*, D. M. Scott

ALZHEIMER'S DISEASE SOCIETY (1979), Gordon House, 10 Greencoat Place, London SW1P 1PH. Tel: 071-306 0606. *Director*, H. Cayton

AMNESTY INTERNATIONAL (1961), 99–119 Rosebery Avenue, London EC1R 4RE. Tel: 071-814 6200. *Director*, D. Bull

ANAESTHETISTS OF GREAT BRITAIN AND IRELAND, ASSOCIATION OF (1932), 9 Bedford Square, London WC1B 3RA. Tel: 071-631 1650. *Hon. Secretary*, Dr R. S. Vaughan

ANCIENT BUILDINGS, SOCIETY FOR THE PROTECTION OF (1877), 37 Spital Square, London E1 6DY. Tel: 071-377 1644. *Secretary*, P. Venning

ANCIENT MONUMENTS SOCIETY (1924), St Ann's Vestry Hall, 2 Church Entry, London EC4V 5HB. Tel: 071-236 3934. *Secretary*, M. J. Saunders

ANGLO-ARAB ASSOCIATION (1961), The Arab British Centre, 21 Collingham Road, London SW5 0NU. Tel: 071-373 8414. *Executive Director*, A. Lee

ANGLO-BELGIAN SOCIETY (1982), 45 West Common, Haywards Heath, W. Sussex RH16 2AJ. *Hon. Secretary*, Mrs A. M. Woodhead

ANGLO-BRAZILIAN SOCIETY (1943), 32 Green Street, London W1Y 3FD. Tel: 071-493 8493. *Secretary*, C. H. Seaward, CBE

ANGLO-DANISH SOCIETY (1924), 25 New Street Square, London EC4A 3LN Tel: 0753-884846. *Chairman*, Sir Andrew Stark, KCMG, CVO

ANGLO-NORSE SOCIETY (1918), 25 Belgrave Square, London SW1X 8QD. Tel: 071-235 7151. *Chairman*, Mrs A. Dixon

ANGLO-THAI SOCIETY (1962). *Hon. Secretary*, J. A. Bradstreet, 500 Grovely Lane, Birmingham B45 8PD

ANIMAL CONCERN (SCOTLAND) (1988), 62 Old Dumbarton Road, Glasgow G3 8RE. Tel: 041-334 6014. *Organizing Secretary*, J. F. Robins

ANIMAL HEALTH TRUST (1942), PO Box 5, Newmarket, Suffolk CB8 7DW. Tel: 0638-661111. *Director*, A. J. Higgins, PH.D.

ANTHROPOLOGICAL INSTITUTE, ROYAL (1843), 50 Fitzroy Street, London W1P 5HS. Tel: 071-387 0455. *Director*, J. C. M. Benthall

ANTHROPOSOPHICAL SOCIETY IN GREAT BRITAIN (1923), Rudolf Steiner House, 35 Park Road, London NW1 6XT. Tel: 071-723 4400. *General Secretary*, N. C. Thomas

ANTIQUARIES OF LONDON, SOCIETY OF (1717), Burlington House, Piccadilly, London W1V OHS. Tel: 071-734 0193. *General Secretary*, D. M. Evans

ANTIQUARIES OF SCOTLAND, SOCIETY OF (1780), Royal Museum of Scotland, Queen Street, Edinburgh EH2 1JD. Tel: 031-225 7534, ext. 327. *Director*, Mrs F. Ashmore

ANTI-SLAVERY INTERNATIONAL FOR THE PROTECTION OF HUMAN RIGHTS (1839), 180 Brixton Road, London SW9 6AT. Tel: 071-582 4040. *Director*, Miss L. Roberts

ANTI-VIVISECTION: BRITISH UNION FOR THE ABOLITION OF VIVISECTION (1898), 16A Crane Grove, London N7 8LB. Tel: 071-700 4888. *Executive Director*, P. Knowles

ANTI-VIVISECTION SOCIETY, NATIONAL (1875), 261 Goldhawk Road, London W12 9PE. Tel: 081-846 9777. *Director*, Ms J. Creamer

APOSTLESHIP OF THE SEA (1920), Stella Maris, 66 Dock Road, Tilbury, Essex RM18 7BX. Tel: 0375-845641. *National Director*, Revd J. Maguire

APOTHECARIES OF LONDON, SOCIETY OF (1617), Black Friars Lane, London EC4V 6EJ. Tel: 071-236 1189. *Registrar*, A. M. Wallington-Smith

ARBITRATORS, CHARTERED INSTITUTE OF (1915), 24 Angel Gate, City Road, London EC1V 2RS. Tel: 071-837 4483. *Secretary*, K. R. K. Harding

ARCHAEOLOGICAL ASSOCIATION, CAMBRIAN (1846), The Laurels, Westfield Road, Newport, Gwent NP9 4ND. Tel: 0633-262449. *General Secretary*, Dr J. M. Hughes

ARCHAEOLOGICAL INSTITUTE, ROYAL (1843), c/o Society of Antiquaries of London, Burlington House, Piccadilly, London W1V OHS. *Secretary*, J. G. Coad

ARCHAEOLOGY, COUNCIL FOR BRITISH (1944), Bowes Morrell House, 111 Walmgate, York YO1 2UA. Tel: 0904-671417. *Director*, R. K. Morris

ARCHITECTS, ROYAL INSTITUTE OF BRITISH (1834), 66 Portland Place, London W1N 4AD. Tel: 071-580 5533. *President*, Dr F. Duffy; *Director-General*, The Lord Rodgers of Quarry Bank, PC

ARCHITECTS AND SURVEYORS INSTITUTE (1926), 15 St Mary Street, Chippenham, Wilts. SN15 3JN. Tel: 0249-444505. *Chief Executive*, B. A. Hunt

ARCHITECTS BENEVOLENT SOCIETY (1850), 66 Portland Place, London W1N 4AD. *Hon. Secretary*, R. J. Double

ARCHITECTS IN SCOTLAND, ROYAL INCORPORATION OF (1922), 15 Rutland Square, Edinburgh EH1 2BE. Tel: 031-229 7545. *Secretary*, C. A. McKean

ARCHITECTS REGISTRATION COUNCIL OF THE UNITED KINGDOM (1931), 73 Hallam Street, London W1N 6EE. Tel: 071-580 5861. *Registrar*, D. S. Smart

ARCHITECTURAL ASSOCIATION INC. (1847), 34–36 Bedford Square, London WC1B 3ES. TEL: 071-636 0974. *Secretary*, E. Le Maistre

ARCHITECTURAL HERITAGE FUND, THE (1976), 27 John Adam Street, London WC2N 6HX. Tel: 071-925 0199. *Secretary*, Lady Weir

ARCHIVISTS, SOCIETY OF (1947), Information House, 20–24 Old Street, London EC1V 9AP. Tel: 071-253 5087. *Executive Secretary*, P. S. Cleary

ARK ENVIRONMENTAL FOUNDATION, THE (1988), 8 Bourdon Street, London W1X 9HX. Tel: 071-409 2638. *Director*, Miss R. Orosz

ARLIS/UK AND IRELAND, THE ART LIBRARIES SOCIETY (1969). *Administrator*, Ms S. French, 18 College Road, Bromsgrove, Worcs. B60 2NE. Tel: 0527-579298 579298

ARMY BENEVOLENT FUND (1944), 41 Queen's Gate, London SW7 5HR. Tel: 071-584 5232/8684. *Controller*, Maj.-Gen. G. M. G. Swindells, CB

ARMY CADET FORCE ASSOCIATION (1930), E Block, Duke of York's HQ, London SW3 4RR. Tel: 071-730 9733. *General Secretary*, Brig. R. B. MacGregor-Oakford, CBE, MC

ART, ROYAL CAMBRIAN ACADEMY OF (1882), Crown Lane, Conwy, Gwynedd LL32 8BH. Tel: 0492-593413. *Curator and Secretary*, L. H. S. Mercer

ART COLLECTIONS FUND, NATIONAL (1903), 20 John Islip Street, London SW1P 4JX. Tel: 071-821 0404. *Director*, D. Barrie

ARTHRITIS AND RHEUMATISM COUNCIL FOR RESEARCH (1936), Copeman House, St Mary's Court, St Mary's Gate, Chesterfield, Derbys. S41 7TD. Tel: 0246-558033. *General Secretary*, J. Norton

ARTHRITIS CARE (1949), 18 Stephenson Way, London NW1 2HD. Tel: 071-916 1500. *Secretary*, J. R. Collins

ARTISTS' GENERAL BENEVOLENT INSTITUTION (1814) AND ARTISTS' ORPHAN FUND (1871), Burlington House, Piccadilly, London W1V 0DJ. *Secretary*, Mrs C. M. Rees

ARTISTS, FEDERATION OF BRITISH, 17 Carlton House Terrace, London SW1Y 5BD. Tel: 071-930 6844. *Chairman*, J. Walton

ART WORKERS' GUILD (1884), 6 Queen Square, London WC1N 3AR. Tel: 071-837 3474. *Secretary*, H. Krall

ASIAN FAMILY COUNSELLING SERVICE (1985), 74 The Avenue, London W13. Tel: 081-997 5749. *National Director*, R. Atma

ASLIB, The Association for Information Management (1924), Information House, 20-24 Old Street, London EC1V 9AP. Tel: 071-253 4488. *Chief Executive*, R. Bowes

ASTHMA CAMPAIGN, NATIONAL (1927), Providence House, Providence Place, London N1 0NT. Tel: 071-226 2260. *Chairman*, Rt. Hon. Sir Peter Emery, MP

ASTRONOMICAL ASSOCIATION, BRITISH (1890), Burlington House, Piccadilly, London W1V 9AG. Meetings at 23 Savile Row, London W1X 1AB. *Assistant Secretary*, Miss P. M. Barber

ASTRONOMICAL SOCIETY, ROYAL (1820), Burlington House, Piccadilly, London W1V 0NL. Tel: 071-734 3307. *President*, Prof. Sir Martin Rees, FRS; *Executive Secretary*, J. E. Lane

ATS/WRAC BENEVOLENT FUNDS (1964), PO Box 212, Guildford, Surrey GU2 6ZD. Tel: 0252-355562. *Secretaries*, Mrs A. H. S. Matthews; Lt.-Col. D. Dunn

AUDIT BUREAU OF CIRCULATIONS LTD (1931), Black Prince Yard, 207-209 High Street, Berkhamsted, Herts. HP4 1AD. Tel: 0442-870800. *Secretary*, J. Beadell

AUTHORS, SOCIETY OF (1884), 84 Drayton Gardens, London SW10 9SB. Tel: 071-373 6642. *General Secretary*, M. Le Fanu

AUTOMOBILE ASSOCIATION (1905), Fanum House, Basingstoke, Hants. RG21 2EA. Tel: 0256-20123. *Director-General*, S. Dyer

AVICULTURAL SOCIETY (1894), c/o Bristol Zoological Gardens, Clifton, Bristol BS8 3HA. *Hon. Secretary*, G. R. Greed

AYRSHIRE CATTLE SOCIETY OF GREAT BRITAIN AND IRELAND (1877), 1 Racecourse Road, Ayr KA7 2DE. Tel: 0292-267123. *General Secretary*, S. J. Thomson

BALTIC AIR CHARTER ASSOCIATION (1949), 6 The Office Village, Romford Road, London E15 4EA. Tel: 081-519 6967. *Hon. Executive*, D. Shepherd

BALTIC EXCHANGE LTD, THE (1903), St Mary Axe, London EC3A 8BH. Tel: 071-623 5501. *Chief Executive*, J. Buckley

BALTIC EXCHANGE CHARITABLE SOCIETY (1978), 14-20 St Mary Axe, London EC3A 8BH. Tel: 071-369 1643. *Secretary*, D. A. Painter

BALZAN FOUNDATION – PRIZE, INTERNATIONAL (1956), Piazzetta U. Giordano 4, Milan 20122, Italy. Tel: 02-7600 2212. Awards prizes for literature; moral sciences and the arts; physical, mathematical and natural sciences; medicine; humanity, peace and brotherhood. *Secretary-General*, Dr F. M. Tedeschi

BANKERS, CHARTERED INSTITUTE OF (1879), 10 Lombard Street, London EC3V 9AS. Tel: 071-623 3531. *Secretary-General*, E. Glover

BANKERS IN SCOTLAND, CHARTERED INSTITUTE OF (1875), 19 Rutland Square, Edinburgh EH1 2DE. Tel: 031-229 9869. *Chief Executive*, Dr C. W. Munn

BAPTIST MISSIONARY SOCIETY (1792), Baptist House, PO Box 49, 129 Broadway, Didcot, Oxon. OX11 8XA. Tel: 0235-512077. *General Secretary*, Revd R. G. S. Harvey

BAR ASSOCIATION FOR LOCAL GOVERNMENT AND THE PUBLIC SERVICE (1945), 23 Wentworth Way, Bletchley, Milton Keynes MK3 7RW. Tel: 0908-682205. *Chairman*, P. G. Stivadoros

BARNARDO'S (1866), Tanners Lane, Barkingside, Ilford, Essex IG6 1QG. Tel: 081-550 8822. *Senior Director*, R. Singleton

BARONETAGE, STANDING COUNCIL OF THE (1898), The Church House, Bibury, Cirencester, Glos. GL7 5NR. *Hon. Secretary*, R. B. Snow, ISO

BARRISTERS' BENEVOLENT ASSOCIATION (1873), 14 Gray's Inn Square, London WC1R 5JP. Tel: 071-242 4761. *Secretary*, Mrs A. Ashley

BEECHAM TRUST, SIR THOMAS (1946), Denton House, Denton, Harleston, Norfolk IP20 0AA. Tel: 098 686-780. *Secretary*, Shirley, Lady Beecham

BEE-KEEPERS' ASSOCIATION, BRITISH (1874), National Agricultural Centre, Stoneleigh Park, Warks. CV8 2LZ. Tel: 0203-696679. *General Secretary*, J. K. Law

BIBLE SOCIETY, BRITISH AND FOREIGN (1804), Stonehill Green, Westlea, Swindon SN5 7DG. Tel: 0793-513713. *Executive Director*, N. Crosbie

BIBLIOGRAPHICAL SOCIETY (1892), British Library, Great Russell Street, London WC1B 3DG. *Hon. Secretary*, Dr M. M. Foot

BIBLIOGRAPHICAL SOCIETY, EDINBURGH (1890), c/o New College Library, Mound Place, Edinburgh EH1 2LU. Tel: 031-225 8400, ext. 256. *Hon. Secretary*, Dr M. C. T. Simpson

BIOCHEMICAL SOCIETY (1911), 59 Portland Place, London W1N 3AJ. Tel: 071-580 5530. *Executive Secretary*, G. D. Jones

BIOLOGICAL ENGINEERING SOCIETY (1960), Royal College of Surgeons, Lincoln's Inn Fields, London WC2A 3PN. Tel: 071-242 7750. *Hon. Secretary*, Dr R. E. Trotman

BIOLOGY, INSTITUTE OF (1950), 20–22 Queensberry Place, London SW7 2DZ. Tel: 071-581 8333. *General Secretary*, Dr. R. H. Priestley

BIRD PRESERVATION, INTERNATIONAL COUNCIL FOR (BRITISH SECTION) (1922), c/o RSPB, The Lodge, Sandy, Beds. SG19 2DL. Tel: 0767-680551. *Executive Secretary*, A. Gammell

BIRMINGHAM AND MIDLAND INSTITUTE (1854) and PRIESTLEY LIBRARY (1779), Margaret Street, Birmingham B3 3BS. Tel: 021-236 3591. *Administrator*, J. Hunt

BIRTHDAY TRUST FUND, NATIONAL (1928), 27 Sussex Place, London NW1 4RG.Tel: 071-706 3903. For extension of maternity services

BLIND, GUIDE DOGS FOR THE, *see* GUIDE DOGS FOR THE BLIND ASSOCIATION

BLIND PEOPLE, ACTION FOR (1857), 14–16 Verney Road, London SE16 3DZ. Tel: 071-732 8771. *Director*, A. Kent

BLIND, NATIONAL LIBRARY FOR THE (1882), Cromwell Road, Bredbury, Stockport, Cheshire SK6 2SG. Tel: 061-494 0217. *Director-General*, A. Leach

BLIND, ROYAL LONDON SOCIETY FOR THE (1838), 105–9 Salusbury Road, London NW6 6RH. Tel: 071-624 8844. *Chief Executive*, P. Talbot

BLIND, ROYAL NATIONAL COLLEGE FOR THE (1872), College Road, Hereford HR1 1EB. Tel: 0432-265725. *Principal*, C. Housby-Smith, PH.D.

BLIND, ROYAL NATIONAL INSTITUTE FOR THE, *see* ROYAL NATIONAL INSTITUTE FOR THE BLIND

BLIND, ROYAL SCHOOL FOR THE (1799), 56–66 Highlands Road, Leatherhead, Surrey KT22 8NR. Tel: 0372-373086. *Chief Executive*, R. M. Perkins

BLOOD TRANSFUSION ASSOCIATION, SCOTTISH NATIONAL (1940), Erskine House, 68–73 Queen Street, Edinburgh EH2 4NH. Tel: 031-226 4488. *Secretary*, P. C. Taylor

BLOOD TRANSFUSION SERVICE, NATIONAL (1948), National Directorate, Gateway House, Piccadilly South, Manchester M60 7LP. Tel: 0923-212121. *Chief Executive*, J. Adey

BLUE CROSS (1897), Shilton Road, Burford, Oxon. OX18 4PF. Tel: 0993-822651. *Secretary*, A. Kennard, MBE

BODLEIAN, FRIENDS OF THE (1925), Bodleian Library, Oxford OX1 3BG. Tel: 0865-277023. *Secretary*, G. Groom

BOOKSELLERS ASSOCIATION OF GREAT BRITAIN AND IRELAND (1895), Minister House, 272 Vauxhall Bridge Road, London SW1V 1BA. Tel: 071-834 5477. *Chief Executive*, T. E. Godfray

BOOK TRADE BENEVOLENT SOCIETY (1967), Dillon Lodge, The Retreat, Kings Langley, Herts. WD4 8LT. Tel: 0923-263128. *Executive Secretary*, Mrs A. R. Brown

BOOK TRUST (1986), Book House, 45 East Hill, London SW18 2QZ. Tel: 081-870 9055. *Chief Executive*, Mrs B. Anderson

BOTANICAL SOCIETY OF THE BRITISH ISLES (1836), The Natural History Museum, Cromwell Road, London SW7 5BD. Tel: 071-938 9026. *Hon. General Secretary*, Mrs M. Briggs, MBE

BOTANICAL SOCIETY OF SCOTLAND, c/o Royal Botanic Garden, Inverleith Row, Edinburgh EH3 5LR. *Hon. General Secretary*, R. Galt

BOY SCOUTS ASSOCIATION, *see* SCOUT ASSOCIATION

BOYS' BRIGADE (1883), Felden Lodge, Felden, Hemel Hempstead HP3 0BL. Tel: 0442-231681. *Brigade Secretary*, S. Jones.

BOYS' CLUBS, NATIONAL ASSOCIATION OF (1925), 369 Kennington Lane, London SE11 5QY. Tel: 071-793 0787. *National Director*, D. James

BOYS' CLUBS OF NORTHERN IRELAND (1940), 2nd Floor, 38 Dublin Road, Belfast BT2 7HN. Tel: 0232-241924. *General Secretary*, K. Culbert

BREWING, INSTITUTE OF (1886), 33 Clarges Street, London W1Y 8EE. Tel: 071-499 8144. *Chief Executive*, P. W. E. Istead

BRIDEWELL ROYAL HOSPITAL (1553), Witley, Godalming, Surrey GU8 5SG. *Registrar*, Mrs J. Benyon

BRITAIN-NEPAL SOCIETY (1960), 24 Carthew Villas, London W6 0BS. *Hon. Secretary*, Mrs J. Thomas

BRITAIN-RUSSIA CENTRE (1959), 14 Grosvenor Place, London SW1X 7HW. Tel: 071-235 2112. *Director*, I. Elliot

BRITISH AND FOREIGN SCHOOL SOCIETY (1808), Richard Mayo Hall, Eden Street, Kingston upon Thames, Surrey KT1 1HZ. Tel: 081-546 2379. *Secretary*, S. M. A. Banister

BRITISH INSTITUTE IN EASTERN AFRICA (1959), 1 Kensington Gore, London SW7 2AR. Tel: 071-584 4653. *London Secretary*, Mrs J. Moyo

BRITISH INSTITUTE OF ARCHAEOLOGY AT ANKARA (1948), c/o British Academy, 20–21 Cornwall Terrace, London NW1 4QP. Tel: 071-388 2361. *London Secretary*, Mrs F. Ligonnet

BRITISH INSTITUTE OF PERSIAN STUDIES (1961), 38 Thomas More House, Barbican, London EC2Y 8BT. Tel: 071-638 4674. *Secretary*, Miss D. Morgan

BRITISH INTERPLANETARY SOCIETY (1933), 27–29 South Lambeth Road, London SW8 1SZ. Tel: 071-735 3160. *Executive Secretary*, Ms S. A. Jones

BRITISH ISRAEL WORLD FEDERATION (1919), 8 Blades Court, Deodar Road, London SW15 2NU. Tel: 081-877 9010. *Secretary*, A. E. Gibb

BRITISH LEGION, ROYAL (1921), 48 Pall Mall, London SW1Y 5JY. Tel: 071-973 0633. *General Secretary*, Lt.-Col. P. C. E. Creasy, OBE

BRITISH LEGION SCOTLAND, ROYAL (1921), New Haig House, Logie Green Road, Edinburgh EH7 4HR. Tel: 031-557 2782. *General Secretary*, Brig. R. W. Riddle, OBE

BRITISH MEDICAL ASSOCIATION (1832), BMA House, Tavistock Square, London WC1H 9JP. Tel: 071-387 4499. *Chairman*, Dr A. Macara; *Secretary*, Dr E. M. Armstrong

BRITISH RED CROSS (1870), 9 Grosvenor Crescent, London SW1X 7EJ. Tel: 071-235 5454. *Director-General*, M. R. Whitlam

BRITISH SCHOOL OF ARCHAEOLOGY IN JERUSALEM (1919), 21 Buccleuch Place (Top Flat), University of Edinburgh, Edinburgh EH8 9LN. Tel: 031-650 3975. *President*, P. R. S. Moorey, PH.D., FBA

BRITISH TECHNOLOGY GROUP, 101 Newington Causeway, London SE1 6BU. Tel: 071-403 6666. *Chief Executive*, I. A. Harvey

BTCV (BRITISH TRUST FOR CONSERVATION VOLUNTEERS) (1970), 36 St Mary's Street, Wallingford, Oxon. OX10 0EU. Tel: 0491-839766. *Chief Executive*, T. Flood

BUDDHIST SOCIETY, THE (1924), 58 Eccleston Square, London SW1V 1PH. Tel: 071-834 5858. *General Secretary*, R. C. Maddox

BUDGERIGAR SOCIETY, THE (1925), 49–53 Hazelwood Road, Northampton NN1 1LG. Tel: 0604-24549. *General Secretary*, A. C. Crook

BUILDING, CHARTERED INSTITUTE OF (1834), Englemere, Kings Ride, Ascot, Berks. SL5 8BJ. Tel: 0344-23355. *Chief Executive*, K. Banbury

BUILDING ENGINEERS, ASSOCIATION OF (1925), Jubilee House, Billing Brook Road, Weston Favell, Northampton NN3 4NW. Tel: 0604-404121. *Chief Executive*, B. D. Hughes

BUILDING SERVICES ENGINEERS, CHARTERED INSTITUTION OF (1897), Delta House, 222 Balham High Road, London SW12 9BS. Tel: 081-675 5211. *Secretary*, A. V. Ramsay

BUILDING SOCIETIES ASSOCIATION (1936), 3 Savile Row, London WIX 1AF. Tel: 071-437 0655. *Director-General*, A. Coles

BUSINESS AND PROFESSIONAL WOMEN, UNITED KINGDOM FEDERATION OF (1938), 23 Ansdell Street, London W8 5BN. Tel: 071-938 1729. *General Secretary*, Mrs R. Bangle

BUSINESS ARCHIVES COUNCIL (1934), 185 Tower Bridge Road, London SE1 2UF. Tel: 071-407 6110. *Secretary-General*, W. S. Quinn-Robinson

CADET FORCE ASSOCIATION, COMBINED (1952), 'E' Block, The Duke of York's HQ, London SW3 4RR. Tel: 071-730 9733. *Secretary*, Brig. R. B. MacGregor-Oakford, CBE, MC

CAFOD (CATHOLIC FUND FOR OVERSEAS DEVELOPMENT) (1962), 2 Romero Close, Stockwell Road, London SW9 9TY. Tel: 071-733 7900. *Director*, J. Filochowski

CALOUSTE GULBENKIAN FOUNDATION (1956), 98 Portland Place, London WIN 4ET. Tel: 071-636 5313. *Director*, B. Whitaker

CAMBRIDGE PRESERVATION SOCIETY (1929), Wandlebury Ring, Gog Magog Hills, Babraham, Cambridge CB2 4AE. Tel: 0223-243830. *Secretary*, G. Brewster

CAMERON FUND, THE (1971), Tavistock House North, Tavistock Square, London WC1H 9JP. Tel: 071-388 0796. *Secretary*, Mrs J. Martin

CAMPAIGN FOR NUCLEAR DISARMAMENT (CND) (1958), 162 Holloway Road, London N7 8DQ. Tel: 071-700 2393. *General Secretary*, G. Lefley

CANCER RELIEF MACMILLAN FUND (1911), Anchor House, 15–19 Britten Street, London SW3 3TZ. Tel: 071-351 7811. *Chief Executive*, D. Scott

CANCER RESEARCH CAMPAIGN, 10 Cambridge Terrace, London NW1 4JL. Tel: 071-224 1333. *Director-General*, D. de Peyer

CANCER RESEARCH FUND, IMPERIAL (1902), PO Box 123, Lincoln's Inn Fields, London WC2A 3PX. Tel: 071-242 0200. *Secretary*, Miss M. J. Craggs

CANCER RESEARCH, INSTITUTE OF, Royal Cancer Hospital, 17A Onslow Gardens, London SW7 3AL. Tel: 071-352 8133. *Chief Executive*, Prof. P. Garland

CANCER PATIENTS, BRITISH ASSOCIATION OF (BACUP) (1985), 3 Bath Place, Rivington Street, London EC2A 3JR. Tel: 071-696 9003. *Chief Executive*, A. Watson

CARERS NATIONAL ASSOCIATION (1988), 20–25 Glasshouse Yard, London EC1A 4JS. Tel: 071-490 8818. *Director*, Ms J. Pitkeathley, OBE

CARNEGIE DUNFERMLINE TRUST (1903), Abbey Park House, Dunfermline KY12 7PB. Tel: 0383-723638. *Secretary*, W. C. Runciman

CARNEGIE HERO FUND TRUST (1908). Abbey Park House, Dunfermline KY12 7PB. Tel: 0383-723638. *Secretary*, W. C. Runciman

CARNEGIE UNITED KINGDOM TRUST (1913), Comely Park House, Dunfermline KY12 7EJ. Tel: 0383-721445. *Secretary*, C. J. Naylor

CATHEDRALS FABRIC COMMISSION FOR ENGLAND (1949), 83 London Wall, London EC2M 5NA. Tel: 071-638 0971. *Secretary*, Dr. R. Gem

CATHOLIC MARRIAGE ADVISORY COUNCIL (1946), Clitherow House, 1 Blythe Mews, Blythe Road, London W14 0NW. Tel: 071-371 1341. *Chief Executive*, Mrs M. Corbett

CATHOLIC RECORD SOCIETY (1904), c/o 114 Mount Street, London W1Y 6AH. *Hon. Secretary*, Miss R. Rendel

CATHOLIC TRUTH SOCIETY (1868), 38–40 Eccleston Square, London SW1V 1PD. Tel: 071-834 4392. *General Secretary*, D. Murphy

CATHOLIC UNION OF GREAT BRITAIN (1872), St Maximilian Kolbe House, 63 Jeddo Road, London W12 9EE. Tel: 081-749 1321. *President*, The Duke of Norfolk, KG, GCVO, CB, CBE, MC; *Hon. Secretary*, Mrs J. Stuyt, MBE

CATTLE BREEDERS' ASSOCIATION, NATIONAL, Lawford Grange, Lawford Heath, Rugby, Warks. CV23 9HG. Tel: 0788-565264. *Secretary*, R. W. Kershaw-Dalby

CATTLE BREEDER'S CLUB LTD, BRITISH (1945), Lavenders, Isfield, Uckfield, E. Sussex TN22 5TX. Tel: 0825-750356. *Secretary*, C. R. Stains

CENTRAL AND CECIL HOUSING TRUST (1926), 2 Priory Road, Kew, Richmond, Surrey TW9 3DG. Tel: 081-940 9828. *Secretary*, G. Brighton

CENTRAL BUREAU (for educational visits and exchanges) (1948), Seymour Mews House, Seymour Mews, London WIH 9PE. Tel: 071-486 5101. *Director* A. H. Male

CERAMICS, INSTITUTE OF (1955), Shelton House, Stoke Road, Shelton, Stoke-on-Trent ST4 2DR. *President*, Dr. D. W. F. James

CHADWICK TRUST (1895), Department of Civil and Environmental Engineering, University College, Gower Street, London WC1E 6BT. Tel: 071-380 7327/7766. For the promotion of health and prevention of disease. *Secretary to the Trustees*, I. K. Orchardson PH.D.

CHANTREY BEQUEST (1875), Royal Academy of Arts, Burlington House, Piccadilly, London W1V 0DS. Tel: 071-439 7438. *Secretary*, P. Rodgers

CHARITIES AID FOUNDATION (1974), 48 Pembury Road, Tonbridge, Kent TN9 2JD. Tel: 0732-771333. *Executive Director*, M. Brophy

CHARTERED SECRETARIES AND ADMINISTRATORS, INSTITUTE OF (1891), 16 Park Crescent, London WIN 4AH. Tel: 071-580 4741. *Secretary*, M. J. Ainsworth

CHEMICAL ENGINEERS, INSTITUTION OF (1922), The Davis Building, 165–171 Railway Terrace, Rugby, Warks. London CV21 3HQ. Tel: 0788-578214. *General Secretary*, Dr. T. J. Evans

CHEMISTRY, ROYAL SOCIETY OF, Burlington House, Piccadilly, London W1V 0BN. Tel: 071-437 8656. *Secretary-General*, Dr. J. S. Gow, FRSE

CHESHIRE (LEONARD) FOUNDATION, *see* LEONARD CHESHIRE FOUNDATION

CHESS FEDERATION, BRITISH (1904), 9A Grand Parade, St Leonards-on-Sea, E. Sussex TN38 0DD. Tel: 0424-442500. *General Secretary*, Mrs G. White

CHEST, HEART AND STROKE ASSOCIATION, *see* STROKE ASSOCIATION, THE

CHIEF EMERGENCY PLANNING OFFICERS' SOCIETY (1966), Emergency Planning Department, County Hall, Trowbridge, Wilts. BA14 8JE. Tel: 0225-753641, ext. 3511. *Hon. Secretary,* N. B. Knocker, OBE

CHILDBIRTH TRUST, NATIONAL (1956), Alexandra House, Oldham Terrace, London W3 6NH. Tel: 081-992 8637. *Chief Executive,* Ms S. Dobson

CHILDMINDING ASSOCIATION, NATIONAL (1977), 8 Masons Hill, Bromley, Kent BR2 9EY. Tel: 081-464 6164. *Director,* Mrs J. Burnell

CHILDREN'S HOME, NATIONAL (1869), 85 Highbury Park, London N5 IUD. Tel: 071-226 2033. *Principal,* T. White, CBE

CHILDREN'S SOCIETY, THE (1881), Edward Rudolf House, Margery Street, London WCIX OJL. Tel: 071-837 4299. *Director,* I. Sparks

CHINA ASSOCIATION, THE (1889), Swire House, 59 Buckingham Gate, London SW1E 6AJ. Tel: 071-821 3220/1. *Executive Director,* Brig. B. G. Hickey, OBE, MC

CHIROPODISTS AND PODIATRISTS, SOCIETY OF (1945), 53 Welbeck Street, London WIM 7HE. Tel: 071-486 3381. *General Secretary,* J. G. C. Trouncer

CHOIRS SCHOOLS ASSOCIATION (1921), Wells Cathedral, Wells, Somerset BA5 2ST. Tel: 0749-672117. *Hon. Secretary,* J. S. Baxter

CHRISTIAN ACTION, St Anselm's Church Hall, Kennington Cross, Kennington Road, London SEII 5DU. Tel: 071-735 2372. *Hon. Director,* Revd Canon E. James

CHRISTIAN AID (1945), PO Box 100, London SEI 7RT. Tel: 071-620 4444. *Director,* Revd M. H. Taylor

CHRISTIAN EDUCATION COUNCIL, NATIONAL (1809), Robert Denholm House, Nutfield, Redhill RHI 4HW. Tel: 0737-822411. *Executive Officer,* Revd J. Gear

CHRISTIAN EDUCATION MOVEMENT (1965), Royal Buildings, Victoria Street, Derby DEI IGW. Tel: 0332-296655. *General Secretary,* Revd Dr. S. Orchard

CHRISTIAN EVIDENCE SOCIETY (1870), St Stephen's House, St Stephen's Crescent, Brentwood, Essex CM13 2AT. Tel: 0277-214623. *Administrator,* Mrs G. M. Ryeland

CHRISTIAN KNOWLEDGE, SOCIETY FOR PROMOTING (SPCK) (1698), Holy Trinity Church, Marylebone Road, London NWI 4DU. Tel: 071-387 5282. *General Secretary,* P. Chandler

CHRISTIANS AND JEWS, COUNCIL OF (1942), 1 Dennington Park Road, London NW6 IAX. Tel: 071-794 8178. *Executive Director,* M. Latham

CHURCH ARMY (1882), Independents Road, London SE3 9LG. Tel: 081-318 1226. *Chief Secretary,* Capt. P. Johanson

CHURCH BUILDING SOCIETY, INCORPORATED (1818), Fulham Palace, London SW6 6EA. Tel: 071-736 3054. *Secretary,* Capt. R. H. C. Heptinstall, RN

CHURCH EDUCATION CORPORATION, Bedgebury School, Goudhurst, Cranbrook, Kent TNI7 2SH. Tel: 0580-211630. *Secretary,* Col. C. G. Champion

CHURCH HOUSE, THE CORPORATION OF (1888), Dean's Yard, London SWIP 3NZ. Tel: 071-222 9011. *Secretary,* C. D. L. Menzies

CHURCH LADS' AND CHURCH GIRLS' BRIGADE (1891), 2 Barnsley Road, Wath upon Dearne, Rotherham, S. Yorks. S63 6PY. Tel: 0709-876535. *General Secretary,* J. S. Cresswell

CHURCH MISSIONARY SOCIETY (1799), 157 Waterloo Road, London SEI 8UU. Tel: 071-928 8681. *General Secretary,* Rt. Revd M. Nazir-Ali

CHURCH MUSIC, ROYAL SCHOOL OF (1927), Addington Palace, Croydon CR9 5AD. Tel: 081-654 7676. *Chief Executive,* R. Lawrence

CHURCH OF ENGLAND PENSIONS BOARD (1926), 7 Little College Street, London SWIP 3SF. Tel: 071-222 2091. *Secretary,* R. G. Radford

CHURCH UNION (1859), Faith House, 7 Tufton Street, London SWIP 3QN. Tel: 071-222 6952. *General Secretary,* A. Leggatt

CHURCHES, COUNCIL FOR THE CARE OF (1921), 83 London Wall, London EC2M 5NA. Tel: 071-638 0971. *Secretary,* Dr. T. Cocke

CHURCHES FOR BRITAIN AND IRELAND, COUNCIL OF (1942), Inter-Church House, 35-41 Lower Marsh, London SEI 7RL. Tel: 071-620 4444. *General Secretary,* Revd J. P. Reardon

CHURCHES, FRIENDS OF FRIENDLESS (1957), 12 Edwardes Square, London W8 6HG. Tel: 071-602 6267. *Hon. Director,* I. Bulmer-Thomas

CHURCHES MAIN COMMITTEE (1941), Fielden House, Little College Street, London SWIP 3JZ. Tel: 071-222 4984. *Secretary,* J. D. Taylor Thompson, CB

CHURCHES TOGETHER IN ENGLAND (1990), Inter-Church House, 35-41 Lower Marsh, London SEI 7RL. Tel: 071-620 4444. *General Secretary,* Canon M. Reardon

CHURCHES TOGETHER IN SCOTLAND, ACTION OF (1990), Scottish Churches House, Kirk Street, Dunblane FKI5 OAJ. Tel: 0786-823588. *General Secretary,* Revd M. Craig

CITIZENS' ADVICE BUREAUX, NATIONAL ASSOCIATION OF (1931), Myddelton House, 115-123 Pentonville Road, London NI 9LZ. Tel: 071-833 2181. *Chief Executive,* Ms A. Abraham

CITY PAROCHIAL FOUNDATION (1891), 6 Middle Street, London ECIA 7PH. Tel: 071-606 6145. *Clerk,* T. Cook

CIVIC TRUST, THE (1957), 17 Carlton House Terrace, London SWIY 5AW. Tel: 071-930 0914. *Director,* M. C. Bradshaw

CIVIL DEFENCE AND DISASTER STUDIES, INSTITUTE OF (1938), Bell Court House, 11 Blomfield Street, London EC2M 7AY. Tel: 071-588 3700. *Hon. General Secretary,* V. G. B. Atwater

CIVIL ENGINEERS, INSTITUTION OF (1818), Great George Street, London SWIP 3AA. Tel: 071-222 7722. *Secretary,* R. S. Dobson, OBE

CIVIL LIBERTIES, NATIONAL COUNCIL FOR, *see* LIBERTY

CLASSICAL ASSOCIATION (1903), Department of Classics, University of Keele, Keele, Newcastle under Lyme, Staffs. ST5 5BG. Tel: 0782-583049. *Hon. Treasurer,* R. Wallace

CLEAN AIR AND ENVIRONMENTAL PROTECTION, NATIONAL SOCIETY FOR (1899), 136 North Street, Brighton BNI IRG. Tel: 0273-326313. *Secretary-General,* Dr T. Crossett

CLERGY ORPHAN CORPORATION (1749), 57B Tufton Street, London SWIP 3QL. Tel: 071-222 1812. *Secretary,* Miss J. Buncher

CLERKS OF WORKS OF GREAT BRITAIN INC., INSTITUTE OF (1882), 41 The Mall, London W5 3TJ. Tel: 081-579 2917/8. *Secretary*, A. P. Macnamara

COACHING CLUB (1871), West Compton House, West Compton, Shepton Mallet, Somerset BA4 4PD. Tel: 0749-890633. *Secretary*, D. H. Clarke

COMMERCE, BRITISH CHAMBERS OF (1860), 9 Tufton Street, London SW1P 3QB. Tel: 071-222 1555. *Director-General*, R. G. Taylor, CBE

COMMERCE, ASSOCIATION OF SCOTTISH CHAMBERS OF, 30 George Square, Glasgow G2 1EQ. Tel: 041-204 2121. *Director*, E. Marwick

COMMERCE AND INDUSTRY, LONDON CHAMBER OF (1881), Swan House, 33 Queen Street, London EC4R 1AP. Tel: 071-248 4444. *Chief Executive*, S. G. Sperryn

COMMERCE AND MANUFACTURERS, EDINBURGH CHAMBER OF (1786), 3 Randolph Crescent, Edinburgh EH3 7UD. Tel: 031-225 5851. *Chief Executive*, I. Brown

COMMERCE AND MANUFACTURERS, GLASGOW CHAMBER OF (1783), 30 George Square, Glasgow G2 1EQ. Tel: 041-204 2121. *Chief Executive (acting)*, J. A. McLaughlin

COMMERCE, CANADA UNITED KINGDOM CHAMBER OF (1921), 3 Regent Street, London SW1Y 4NZ. Tel: 071-930 7711. *Executive Director*, G. F. Bacon

COMMERCIAL AND INDUSTRIAL EDUCATION, BRITISH ASSOCIATION FOR (BACIE) (1919), 35 Harbour Exchange Square, Off Marsh Wall, London E14 9GE. Tel: 071-987 8989. *Director*, B. V. Murphy

COMMERCIAL TRAVELLERS' BENEVOLENT INSTITUTION (1849), Gable End, Mill Hill Road, Arnesby, Leics. LE8 3WG. Tel: 0533-478647. *Secretary*, M. N. Bown

COMMISSIONAIRES, THE CORPS OF (1859), Market House, 85 Cowcross Street, London EC1B 6BP. Tel: 071-490 1125. *Managing Director*, C. J. Salt

COMMONWEALTH TRUST (linking the Royal Commonwealth Society and the Victoria League for Commonwealth Friendship), Commonwealth House, 18 Northumberland Avenue, London WC2N 5BJ. Tel: 071-930 6733. *Director-General*, Maj.-Gen. Sir David Thorne, KBE

COMPLEMENTARY AND ALTERNATIVE MEDICINE, COUNCIL FOR (1985), 179 Gloucester Place, London NW1 6DX. Tel: 071-724 9103. *Secretary*, Ms C. Daglish

COMPLEMENTARY MEDICINE, INSTITUTE FOR (1856), 4 Tavern Quay, Plough Way, Surrey Quays, London SE16 1QZ. Tel: 071-237 5165. *Director*, A. Baird

COMPOSERS' GUILD OF GREAT BRITAIN (1945), 34 Hanway Street, London W1P 9DE. Tel: 071-436 0007. *General Secretary*, Ms H. Rosenblatt

COMPUTER SOCIETY, BRITISH (1957), PO Box 1454, Station Road, Swindon SN1 1TG. Tel: 0793-480269. *Chief Executive*, G. Kirkpatrick

CONSERVATION OF HISTORIC AND ARTISTIC WORKS, INTERNATIONAL INSTITUTE FOR (1950), 6 Buckingham Street, London WC2N 6BA. Tel: 071-839 5975. *Secretary-General*, Prof. H. W. M. Hodges

CONSULTING ECONOMISTS' ASSOCIATION, INTERNATIONAL (1986), 1C Barnes High Street, London SW13 9LB. Tel: 081-876 2299. *Chairman*, P. Prynne

CONSULTING ENGINEERS, ASSOCIATION OF (1913), Alliance House, 12 Caxton Street, London SW1H 0QL. Tel: 071-222 6557. *Secretary*, H. C. Woodrow

CONSULTING SCIENTISTS, ASSOCIATION OF (1958), 2-3 Bosworth House, High Street, Thorpe-le-Soken, Clacton-on-Sea, Essex CO16 0EA. Tel: 0255-862412. *Hon. Secretary*, W. G. Simpson

CONSUMERS' ASSOCIATION (1957), c/o The Association for Consumer Research, 2 Marylebone Road, London NW1 4DF. Tel: 071-830 6000. *Director*, Dr J. Beishon

CONTEMPORARY APPLIED ARTS (1948), 43 Earlham Street, London WC2H 9LD. Tel: 071-836 6993. *Director*, Ms T. Peters

CONVEYANCERS, COUNCIL FOR LICENSED (1986), Suite 3, Cairngorm House, 203 Marsh Wall, London E14 9YT. Tel: 071-537 2953. *Secretary*, A. Viner

CO-OPERATIVE PARTY, 342 Hoe Street, London E17 9PX. Tel: 081-520 3580. *Secretary*, P. Clarke

CO-OPERATIVE STUDIES, PLUNKETT FOUNDATION FOR (1919), 23 Hanborough Business Park, Long Hanborough, Oxford OX8 8LH. Tel: 0993-883636. *Director*, E. Parnell

CO-OPERATIVE UNION LTD (1869), Holyoake House, Hanover Street, Manchester M60 0AS. Tel: 061-832 4300. *Chief Executive*, D. L. Wilkinson

CO-OPERATIVE WHOLESALE SOCIETY LTD (CWS) (1863), PO Box 53, New Century House, Manchester M60 4ES. Tel: 061-834 1212. *Chief Executive*, D. Skinner

COPYRIGHT COUNCIL, BRITISH (1953), 29-33 Berners Street, London W1P 4AA. *Secretary*, G. V. Adams

CORONERS' SOCIETY OF ENGLAND AND WALES (1846). *Hon. Secretary*, Dr. J. D. K. Burton, CBE, 7 Orchard Rise, Richmond, Surrey TW10 5BX. Tel: 071-371 9938

CORPORATE TREASURERS, ASSOCIATION OF (1979), 12 Devereux Court, London WC2R 3JJ. Tel: 071-936 2354. *Secretary*, Ms G. Pierpoint

CORPORATE TRUSTEES, ASSOCIATION OF (1974), 2 Withdean Rise, Brighton BN1 6YN. Tel: 0273-504276. *Secretary*, L. C. Howes

CORRESPONDENCE COLLEGES, ASSOCIATION OF BRITISH (1955), 6 Francis Grove, London SW19 4DT. Tel: 081-544 9559. *Secretary*, Mrs H. Owen

CORRYMEELA COMMUNITY (1965), Corrymeela House, 8 Upper Crescent, Belfast BT7 1NT. Tel: 0232-325008. *Director*, Revd T. Williams

COTTON GROWING ASSOCIATION, BRITISH (1904), 13 Upper High Street, Thame, Oxon. OX9 3ER. Tel: 0844-261447. *Chairman*, J. R. Wilson

COUNCIL FOR THE PROTECTION OF RURAL ENGLAND, see RURAL

COUNSEL AND CARE (1954), Twyman House, 16 Bonny Street, London NW1 9PG. Tel: 071-485 1566. *General Manager*, J. Smith

COUNTRY HOUSES ASSOCIATION (1955), 41 Kingsway, London WC2B 6UB. Tel: 071-836 1624. *Chief Executive*, R. D. Bratby

COUNTRY LANDOWNERS ASSOCIATION (1907), 16 Belgrave Square, London SW1X 8PQ. Tel: 071-235 0511. *Director-General*, J. Anderson

COUNTY CHIEF EXECUTIVES, ASSOCIATION OF (1974), PO Box 9, Shire Hall, Warwick CV34 4RR. Tel: 0926-412559. *Hon. Secretary*, I. G. Caulfield

COUNTY COUNCILS, ASSOCIATION OF (1890), Eaton House, 66A Eaton Square, London SW1W 9BH. Tel: 071-235 1200. *Secretary*, R. G. Wendt

COUNTY EMERGENCY PLANNING OFFICERS' SOCIETY, *see* CHIEF EMERGENCY PLANNING

COUNTY SECRETARIES, SOCIETY OF (1974), County Hall, Chester CHI ISF. Tel: 0234-228911. *Hon. Secretary*, R. C. Wilkinson

COUNTY SURVEYORS' SOCIETY (1884), Transportation and Engineering Department, County Hall, Dorchester DTI IXJ. Tel: 0305-224741. *Hon. Secretary*, D. A. Hutchinson

COUNTY TREASURERS, SOCIETY OF (1903), PO Box 4, County Hall, Chelmsford, Essex CMI IJZ. Tel: 0245-431000. *Hon. Secretary*, K. D. Neale

CRISIS (1967), 7 Whitechapel Road, London EI IDU. Tel: 071-377 0489. *Director*, M. Scothern

CROSSLINKS (1922), 251 Lewisham Way, London SE4 IXF. Tel: 081-691 6111. *General Secretary*, Canon J. M. Ball

CRUEL SPORTS, THE LEAGUE AGAINST (1924), 83 Union Street, London SEI ISG. Tel: 071-403 6155. *Executive Director*, J. Barrington

CRUELTY TO ANIMALS, SOCIETY FOR THE PREVENTION OF, *see* ROYAL and SCOTTISH

CRUELTY TO CHILDREN, SOCIETY FOR THE PREVENTION OF, *see* NATIONAL and ROYAL SCOTTISH

CRUSE – BEREAVEMENT CARE (1959), 126 Sheen Road, Richmond, Surrey TW9 IUR. Tel: 081-940 4818. *Director*, R. Pearce

CURWEN INSTITUTE (1875), 5 Bigbury Close, Styvechale, Coventry CV3 5AJ. Tel: 0203-413010. *General Secretary*, vacant

CWMNI URDD GOBAITH CYMRU (1922), Swyddfa'r Urdd, Aberystwyth, Dyfed SY23 IEN. Tel: 0970-623744. *Director*, J. E. Williams

CYCLISTS' TOURING CLUB (1878), Cotterell House, 69 Meadrow, Godalming, Surrey GU7 3HS. Tel: 0483-417217. *Director*, A. Harlow

CYMMRODORION, THE HONOURABLE SOCIETY OF (1751), 30 Eastcastle Street, London WIN 7PD. *Hon. Secretary*, Dr. T. Wyn Jones

CYSTIC FIBROSIS RESEARCH TRUST (1964), Alexandra House, 5 Blyth Road, Bromley BRI 3RS. Tel: 081-464 7211. *Executive Director*, G. J. Edkins

CYTUN (CHURCHES TOGETHER IN WALES) (1990), 21 St Helen's Road, Swansea SAI 4AP. Tel: 0792-460876. *General Secretary*, Revd N. A. Davies

DAIRY ASSOCIATION, UNITED KINGDOM (1950), Giggs Hill Green, Thames Ditton, Surrey KT7 OEL. Tel: 081-398 4101, ext. 2436. *Secretary*, Mrs J. M. Newton

DAIRY FARMERS, ROYAL ASSOCIATION OF BRITISH (1876), 55 Sleaford Street, London SW8 5AB. Tel: 071-627 2111. *Chief Executive*, P. M. Gilbert

DAIRY TECHNOLOGY, SOCIETY OF (1943), 72 Ermine Street, Huntingdon, Cambs. PEI8 6EZ. Tel: 0480-450741. *National Secretary*, Mrs R. Gale

DATA (DESIGN AND TECHNOLOGY ASSOCIATION), 16 Wellesbourne House, Walton Road, Wellesbourne, Warks. CV35 9JB. Tel: 0789-470007. *Director*, G. Warren

D-DAY AND NORMANDY FELLOWSHIP (1968), 9 South Parade, Southsea, Hants. PO5 2JB. Tel: 0705-812180. *Hon. Secretary*, Mrs L. R. Reed

DEAF, COMMONWEALTH SOCIETY FOR THE (1959), Dilke House, Malet Street, London WCIE 7JA. Tel: 071-631 5311. *Chairman*, C. Holborow, OBE, TD, MD, FRCS

DEAF ASSOCIATION, BRITISH (1890 *formerly* BRITISH DEAF AND DUMB ASSOCIATION), 38 Victoria Place, Carlisle CAI IHU. Tel: 0228-48844. *Chief Executive*, Ms E. Wincott

DEAF CHILDREN, ROYAL SCHOOL FOR (1792), Victoria Road, Margate, Kent CT9 INB. Tel: 0843-227561. *Secretary*, D. E. Downs

DEAF PEOPLE, FOLEY HOUSE RESIDENTIAL HOME FOR (1851), Foley House, 115 High Garrett, Braintree, Essex CM7 5NU. Tel: 0376-326652. *Director*, Mrs N. Hartard

DEAF PEOPLE, ROYAL ASSOCIATION IN AID OF (1841), 27 Old Oak Road, London W3 7HN. Tel: 081-743 6187. *Chief Executive*, Ms R. Brotherwood

DEAF PEOPLE, ROYAL NATIONAL INSTITUTE FOR (1911), 105 Gower Street, London WCIE 6AH. Tel: 071-387 8033. *Chief Executive*, S. Etherington

DEFENCE STUDIES, ROYAL UNITED SERVICES INSTITUTE FOR (1831), Whitehall, London SWIA 2ET. Tel: 071-930 5854. *Director*, Gp. Capt. D. Bolton

DEMOCRATIC LEFT (1991), 6 Cynthia Street, London NI 9JF. Tel: 071-278 4443. *Secretary*, Ms N. Temple.

DENTAL ASSOCIATION, BRITISH (1880), 64 Wimpole Street, London WIM 8AL. Tel: 071-935 0875. *Chief Executive*, J. M. G. Hunt

DENTAL COUNCIL, GENERAL (1956), 37 Wimpole Street, London WIM 8DQ. Tel: 071-486 2171. *Registrar*, N. T. Davies, MBE

DENTAL HOSPITALS OF THE UNITED KINGDOM, ASSOCIATION OF (1942), Birmingham Dental Hospital, St Chad's Queensway, Birmingham B4 6NN. Tel: 021-236 8611. *Hon. Secretary*, Mrs P. Harrington

DESIGN AND INDUSTRIES ASSOCIATION (1915), 17 Lawn Crescent, Kew Gardens, Surrey TW9 3NR. Tel: 081-940 4925. *Secretary-General*, N. Chamberlain

DESIGNERS FOR INDUSTRY, FACULTY OF ROYAL (1936), RSA, 8 John Adam Street, London WC2N 6EZ. Tel: 071-930 5115. *Secretary*, C. Lucas

DESIGNERS, CHARTERED SOCIETY OF (1930), 29 Bedford Square, London WCIB 3EG. Tel: 071-631 1510. *Director*, B. Lymbery

DIABETIC ASSOCIATION, BRITISH (1934), 10 Queen Anne Street, London WIM OBD. Tel: 071-323 1531. *Director*, M. Cooper

DICKENS FELLOWSHIP (1902), Dickens House, 48 Doughty Street, London WCIN 2LF. Tel: 071-405 2127. *Hon. General Secretary*, E. Preston

DIRECTORS, INSTITUTE OF (1903), 116 Pall Mall, London SWIY 5ED. Tel: 071-839 1233. *Director-General*, P. Morgan

DIRECTORS OF PUBLIC HEALTH, ASSOCIATION OF (1982), South Manchester Health Authority, 293A Upper Brook Street, Manchester MI3 OFW. Tel: 061-257 3459. *Hon. Secretary*, Dr. M. Spencely

DISPENSING OPTICIANS, ASSOCIATION OF BRITISH (1925), 6 Hurlingham Business Park, Sulivan Road, London SW6 3DU. Tel: 071-736 0088. *Registrar*, D. S. Baker

DISTRESSED GENTLEFOLKS' AID ASSOCIATION (1897), Vicarage Gate House, Vicarage Gate, London W8 4AQ. Tel: 071-229 9341. *General Secretary*, N. B. M. Clack

DISTRICT COUNCILS, ASSOCIATION OF (1974), 26 Chapter Street, London SWIP 4ND. Tel: 071-233 6868. *Secretary*, G. Filkin

DISTRICT SECRETARIES, ASSOCIATION OF (1974), 9 Margaret Road, Bishopsworth, Bristol BSI3 9DQ. Tel: 0272-647299. *Hon. Secretary*

DITCHLEY FOUNDATION, Ditchley Park, Enstone, Chipping Norton, Oxon. OX7 4ER. Tel: 0608-677346. *Director,* Sir Michael Quinlan, GCB

DOMESTIC SERVANTS' BENEVOLENT INSTITUTION (1846), Royal Bank of Scotland PLC, 7 Burlington Gardens, London W1A 3DD. *Secretary,* A. J. Gibson

DOWNS SYNDROME ASSOCIATION (1970), 155 Mitcham Road, London SW17 9PG. Tel: 081-682 4001. *Director,* Ms A. Khan

DOWSERS, BRITISH SOCIETY OF (1933), Sycamore Barn, Hastingleigh, Ashford, Kent TN25 5HW. Tel: 0233-750253. *Secretary,* M. D. Rust

DRAINAGE AUTHORITIES, ASSOCIATION OF (1937), The Mews, 3 Royal Oak Passage, High Street, Huntingdon, Cambs. PE18 6EA. Tel: 0480-411123. *Secretary,* D. Noble

DRINKING FOUNTAIN AND CATTLE TROUGH ASSOCIATION, METROPOLITAN (1859), 105 Wansunt Road, Bexley, Kent DA5 2DN. Tel: 0322-528062. *Secretary,* D. R. W. Randall

DRIVING SOCIETY, BRITISH (1957), 27 Dugard Place, Barford, Warwick CV35 8DX. Tel: 0926-624420. *Secretary,* Mrs J. M. Dillon

DRUG DEPENDENCE, INSTITUTE FOR THE STUDY OF (1968), 1–4 Hatton Place, London ECIN 8ND. Tel: 071-430 1991. *Director,* Ms A. Bradley

DUKE OF EDINBURGH'S AWARD SCHEME (1956), Gulliver House, Madeira Walk, Windsor, Berks. SL4 1EU. Tel: 0753-810753. *Director,* Maj.-Gen. M. F. Hobbs, CBE

DYERS AND COLOURISTS, SOCIETY OF (1884), Perkin House, PO Box 244, 82 Grattan Road, Bradford BD1 2JB. Tel: 0274-725138. *General Secretary,* J. D. Watson

DYSLEXIA INSTITUTE (1972), 133 Gresham Road, Staines, Middx TW18 2AJ. Tel: 0784-463851. *Executive Director,* Mrs E. J. Brooks

EARLY CHILDHOOD EDUCATION, BRITISH ASSOCIATION FOR (1923), 111 City View House, 463 Bethnal Green Road, London E2 9QY. Tel: 071-739 7594. *Secretary,* Mrs B. Boon

ECCLESIASTICAL HISTORY SOCIETY (1961), School of History, University of Birmingham, Edgbaston, Birmingham B15 2TT. Tel: 021-414 5748. *Secretary,* Dr R. Swanson

ECCLESIOLOGICAL SOCIETY (1839), Underedge, Back Lane, Hathersage, Derbys. S30 1AR. *Hon. Secretary,* Prof. K. H. Murta

EDUCATION OFFICERS, SOCIETY OF (1971), 20 Bedford Way, London WCIH 0AL. Tel: 071-612 6388. *General Secretary,* J. Hendy

EDUCATION OFFICERS' SOCIETY, COUNTY (1889). *Hon. Secretary,* S. Sharp, Education Department, County Hall, Aylesbury, Bucks. Tel: 0296-382105

EDUCATIONAL RESEARCH IN ENGLAND AND WALES, NATIONAL FOUNDATION FOR (1946), The Mere, Upton Park, Slough SL1 2DQ. Tel: 0753-574123. *Director,* Ms C. Burstall, PH.D., D.SC.

EGYPT EXPLORATION SOCIETY (1882), 3 Doughty Mews, London WCIN 2PG. Tel: 071-242 1880. *Secretary,* Dr P. A. Spencer

ELECTORAL REFORM SOCIETY OF GREAT BRITAIN AND IRELAND, 6 Chancel Street, London SE1 0UU. Tel: 071-928 1622. *President,* The Lord Blake, FBA; *Administrator,* Miss A. M. Kruthoffer

ELECTRICAL ENGINEERS, INSTITUTION OF (1871), Savoy Place, London WC2R 0BL. Tel: 071-240 1871. *Secretary,* J. C. Williams, PH.D., FEng.

ELGAR FOUNDATION (1973), 23 Meadow Hill Road, King's Norton, Birmingham B38 8DE. Tel: 021-458 2747. *Secretary to the Trustees,* J. G. Hughes

ELGAR SOCIETY (1951), 20 Geraldine Road, Malvern, Worcs. WR14 3PA. Tel: 0684-568822. *Secretary,* Mrs C. Holt

ENERGY ASSOCIATION, BRITISH (1924), 34 St James's Street, London SW1A 1HD. Tel: 071-930 1211. *Director,* M. Jefferson.

ENERGY, INSTITUTE OF (1927), 18 Devonshire Street, London W1N 2AU. Tel: 071-580 7124. *Secretary,* J. E. H. Leach

ENGINEERING COUNCIL, THE (1981), 10 Maltravers Street, London WC2R 3ER. Tel: 071-240 7891. *Secretary,* L. Chelton

ENGINEERING DESIGNERS, INSTITUTE OF (1945), Courtleigh, Westbury Leigh, Westbury, Wilts. BA13 3TA. Tel: 0373-822801. *Secretary,* M. J. Osborne

ENGINEERING INDUSTRIES ASSOCIATION (1941), 16 Dartmouth Street, London SW1H 9BL. Tel: 071-222 2367. *Director-General,* Col. W. T. Williams

ENGINEERS, INSTITUTION OF BRITISH (1928), Royal Liver Building, 6 Hampton Place, Brighton BN1 3DD. Tel: 0273-734274. *Secretary,* Mrs D. Henry

ENGINEERS, SOCIETY OF (INCORPORATED) (1854), Guinea Wiggs, Nayland, Colchester CO6 4NF. Tel: 0206-263332. *Secretary,* Mrs C. A. Wright

ENGLISH ASSOCIATION, THE (1906), The Vicarage, Priory Gardens, London W4 1TT. Tel: 081-995 4236. *Secretary,* Dr R. Fairbanks-Joseph

ENGLISH FOLK DANCE AND SONG SOCIETY (1932), Cecil Sharp House, 2 Regent's Park Road, London NW1 7AY. Tel: 071-485 2206. *Executive Officer,* Mrs B. Godrich

ENGLISH PLACE-NAME SOCIETY (1923), Department of English, The University, Nottingham NG7 2RD. Tel: 0602-515919. *Hon. Director,* Ms V. E. Watts

ENGLISH-SPEAKING UNION OF THE COMMONWEALTH, THE (1918), Dartmouth House, 37 Charles Street, London W1X 8AB. Tel: 071-493 3328. *Director-General,* D. Thorp

ENTOMOLOGICAL SOCIETY OF LONDON, ROYAL (1833), 41 Queen's Gate, London SW7 5HR. Tel: 071-584 8361. *Registrar,* G. G. Bentley

ENVIRONMENTAL HEALTH OFFICERS, INSTITUTION OF (1883), 16 Great Guildford Street, London SE1 0ES. Tel: 071-928 6006. *Secretary,* T. Brunt

ENVIRONMENT COUNCIL (1969), 21 Elizabeth Street, London SW1W 9RP. Tel: 071-824 8411. *Chief Executive,* S. Robinson

EPILEPSY ASSOCIATION, BRITISH (1949), Anstey House, 40 Hanover Square, Leeds LS3 1BE. Tel: 0532-439393. *Chief Executive,* T. J. O'Leary

EPILEPSY, NATIONAL SOCIETY FOR (1892), Chalfont St Peter, Gerrards Cross, Bucks. SL9 0RJ. Tel: 0494-873991. *Chief Executive,* Col. D. W. Eking

EQUESTRIAN FEDERATION, BRITISH (1972), Stoneleigh, Kenilworth, Warks. CV8 2LR. Tel: 0203-696697. *Director-General,* Maj. M. Wallace

ESPERANTO ASSOCIATION OF BRITAIN (1977), 140 Holland Park Avenue, London W11 4UF. Tel: 071-727 7821. *Hon. Secretary,* W. Green

ESTATE AGENTS, NATIONAL ASSOCIATION OF (1962), Arbon House, 21 Jury Street, Warwick CV34 4EH. Tel: 0926-496800. *General Secretary,* A. B. Clark

ESTATE AGENTS, OMBUDSMAN FOR CORPORATE (1990), PO Box 1114, Salisbury, Wilts. SP1 1YQ. Tel: 0722-333306. *Ombudsman*, D. Quayle, CB

EUGENICS SOCIETY, *see* GALTON INSTITUTE

EVANGELICAL ALLIANCE (1846), Whitefield House, 186 Kennington Park Road, London SE11 4BT. Tel: 071-582 0228. *General Director*, Revd C. R. Calver

EVANGELICAL LIBRARY, THE (1928), 78A Chiltern Street, London W1M 2HB. Tel: 071-935 6997. *Librarian*, S. J. Taylor

EXECUTIVES ASSOCIATION OF GREAT BRITAIN LTD (1929), Suite 87–89, The Hop Exchange, 24 Southwark Street, London SE1 1TY. Tel: 071-403 3653. *Secretary*, Lt.-Col. J. J. Langdon-Mudge

EXPORT, INSTITUTE OF (1935), Export House, 64 Clifton Street, London EC2A 4HB. Tel: 071-247 9812. *Director-General*, I. J. Campbell

EX-SERVICES LEAGUE, BRITISH COMMONWEALTH (1921), 48 Pall Mall, London SW1Y 5JG. Tel: 071-973 0633. *Secretary-General*, Brig. M. J. Doyle, MBE

EX-SERVICES MENTAL WELFARE SOCIETY (1919), Broadway House, The Broadway, London SW19 1RL. Tel: 081-543 6333. *Director*, Brig. A. K. Dixon

FABIAN SOCIETY (1884), 11 Dartmouth Street, London SW1H 9BN. Tel: 071-222 8877. *General Secretary*, S. Crine

FAIR ISLE BIRD OBSERVATORY TRUST (1948), 21 Regent Terrace, Edinburgh EH7 5BT. Tel: 031-556 6226. *Secretary*, Mrs A. M. Legg

FAMILY HISTORY SOCIETIES, FEDERATION OF (1974), The Benson Room, Birmingham and Midland Institute, Margaret Street, Birmingham B3 3BS. *Administrator*, Mrs P. A. Saul

FAMILY MEDIATION AND CONCILIATION SERVICES, THE NATIONAL ASSOCIATION OF (1982), Shaftesbury Centre, Percy Street, Swindon SN2 2AZ. Tel: 0793-514055. *Chairman*, Prof. B. Hoggett, QC

FAMILY PLANNING ASSOCIATION (1939), 27–35 Mortimer Street, London W1N 7RJ. Tel: 071-636 7866. *Director*, Ms D. E. Massey

FAMILY WELFARE ASSOCIATION (1869), 501–505 Kingsland Road, London E8 4AU. Tel: 081-254 6251. *Director*, Ms L. Berry

FAUNA AND FLORA PRESERVATION SOCIETY (1903), 1 Kensington Gore, London SW7 2AR. Tel: 071-823 8899. *Administrator*, Miss A. Hillier

FELLOWSHIP HOUSES TRUST (1937), Clock House, 192 High Road, Byfleet, Surrey KT14 7RN. Tel: 0932-343172. *Secretary*, Mrs A. J. Elliot

FIELD ARCHAEOLOGISTS, INSTITUTE OF (1982), University of Birmingham, Edgbaston, Birmingham B15 2TT. Tel: 021-471 2788. *Secretary*, S. M. Walls

FIELD SPORTS SOCIETY, BRITISH (1930), 59 Kennington Road, London SE1 7PZ. Tel: 071-928 4742. *Director*, P. Smith

FIELD STUDIES COUNCIL (1943), Preston Montford, Montford Bridge, Shrewsbury SY4 1HW. Tel: 0743-850674. *Director*, A. D. Thomas

FILM CLASSIFICATION, BRITISH BOARD OF (1912), 3 Soho Square, London W1V 5DE. Tel: 071-439 7961. *Director*, J. Ferman

FIRE ENGINEERS, INSTITUTION OF (1918), 148 New Walk, Leicester LE1 7QB. Tel: 0533-553654. *General Secretary*, D. Evans

FIRE PROTECTION ASSOCIATION (1946), 140 Aldersgate Street, London EC1A 4HX. Tel: 071-606 3757. *Director*, A. S. Kidd

FIRE SERVICES ASSOCIATION, BRITISH (1949), 86 London Road, Leicester LE2 0QR. Tel: 0533-542879. *General Secretary*, D. Stevens

FIRE SERVICES NATIONAL BENEVOLENT FUND (1943), Marine Court, Fitzalan Road, Littlehampton, W. Sussex BN17 5NF. Tel: 0903-717185. *General Manager*, R. A. Spackman

FLEET AIR ARM OFFICERS ASSOCIATION (1957), 94 Piccadilly, London W1V 0BP. Tel: 071-499 0360. *Chairman*, Capt. A. J. Leahy, CBE, DSC, RN (retd)

FOLKLORE SOCIETY, c/o University College, Gower Street, London WC1E 6BT. Tel: 071-387 5894. *Hon. Secretary*, T. W. Brown

FOOD FROM BRITAIN (1983), 301–344 Market Towers, New Covent Garden Market, London SW8 5NQ. Tel: 071-720 2144. *Chairman (acting)*, G. John

FOOD SCIENCE AND TECHNOLOGY, INSTITUTE OF (1964), 5 Cambridge Court, 210 Shepherd's Bush Road, London W6 7NL. Tel: 071-603 6316. *Executive Secretary*, Ms H. G. Wild

FORCES HELP SOCIETY AND LORD ROBERTS WORKSHOPS (1899), 122 Brompton Road, London SW3 1JE. Tel: 071-589 3243. *Comptroller and Secretary*, Col. A. W. Davis, MBE

FOREIGN PRESS ASSOCIATION IN LONDON (1888), 11 Carlton House Terrace, London SW1Y 5AJ. Tel: 071-930 0445. *Secretary*, Mrs D. Crole

FORENSIC SCIENCE SOCIETY, THE (1959), Clarke House, 18A Mount Parade, Harrogate, N. Yorks HG1 1BX. Tel: 0423-506068. *Hon. Secretary*, B. W. J. Rankin (*until Nov. 1993*)

FORENSIC SCIENCES, BRITISH ACADEMY OF (1959), Anaesthetic Unit, The London Hospital Medical College, Turner Street, London E1 2AD. Tel: 071-377 9201. *Secretary-General*, Dr P. J. Flynn

FORESTERS, INSTITUTE OF CHARTERED (1982), 22 Walker Street, Edinburgh EH3 7HR. *Secretary*, Mrs M. W. Dick

FORESTRY ASSOCIATION, COMMONWEALTH (1921), c/o Oxford Forestry Institute, South Parks Road, Oxford OX1 3RB. Tel: 0865-275072. *Chairman*, P. J. Wood

FORESTRY SOCIETY OF ENGLAND, WALES AND NORTHERN IRELAND, ROYAL (1882), 102 High Street, Tring, Herts. HP23 4AF. Tel: 044 282-2028. *Director*, J. E. Jackson, PH.D.

FORESTRY SOCIETY, ROYAL SCOTTISH (1854), Camsie House, Charlestown, Dunfermline, Fife KY11 3EE. Tel: 0383-873014. *Director*, M. Osborne

FOUNDRYMEN, INSTITUTE OF BRITISH (1904), Bordesley Hall, The Holloway, Alvechurch, Birmingham B48 7QA. Tel: 0529-596100. *Secretary*, G. A. Schofield

FRANCO-BRITISH SOCIETY (1924), Room 623, Linen Hall, 162–168 Regent Street, London W1R 5TB. Tel: 071-734 0815. *Executive Secretary*, Mrs M. Clarke

FREE CHURCH FEDERAL COUNCIL (1940), 27 Tavistock Square, London WC1H 9HH. Tel: 071-387 8413. *General Secretary*, Revd D. Staple

FREEDOM ASSOCIATION (1975), 35 Westminster Bridge Road, London SE1 7JB. Tel: 071-928 9925. *Chairman*, Mrs P. North

FREEMASONS, GRAND LODGE OF ANTIENT FREE AND ACCEPTED MASONS OF SCOTLAND (1736), Freemasons' Hall, 96 George Street, Edinburgh EH2 3DH. Tel: 031-225 5304. *Grand Master Mason of Scotland*, The Lord Burton; *Grand Secretary*, A. O. Hazel

FREEMASONS, UNITED GRAND LODGE OF ENGLAND (1717), Freemasons' Hall, Great Queen Street, London WC2B 5AZ. Tel: 071-831 9811. *Grand Master*, HRH The Duke of Kent, KG, GCMG, GCVO; *Grand Secretary*, Cdr. M. B. S. Higham

FREEMEN OF ENGLAND AND WALES (1966), 10 Wyngate Road, Hale, Altrincham, Cheshire WA15 0LZ. Tel: 061-904 9304. *Secretary*, R. J. M. Bishop

FREEMEN'S GUILDS:

City of Coventry Freemen's Guild (1946), 5 Adare Drive, Styvechale, Coventry CV3 6AD. *Hon. Clerk*, J. H. Bradbury

Guild of Freemen of the City of London (1908), PO Box 153, 40A Ludgate Hill, London EC4M 7DE. Tel: 071-223 7638. *Clerk*, Col. D. Ivy

Gild of Freemen of the City of York (1953), 29 Albemarle Road, York YO2 1EW. Tel: 0904-653698. *Hon. Clerk*, R. Lee

FRIENDLY SOCIETIES, NATIONAL CONFERENCE OF (1887), Park Gate, 2 Tothill Street, London SW1H 9LL. Tel: 071-976 0717. *General Secretary*, Miss M. Poole

FRIENDS OF CATHEDRAL MUSIC (1956), c/o Addington Palace, Croydon, Surrey CR9 5AD. *Secretary*, V. Waterhouse

FRIENDS OF THE CLERGY CORPORATION, THE (1972), 27 Medway Street, London SW1P 2BD. Tel: 071-222 2288. *Secretary*, J. M. Greany

FRIENDS OF THE EARTH (1971), 26–28 Underwood Street, London N1 7JQ. Tel: 071-490 1555. *Director*, C. Secrett

FRIENDS OF THE ELDERLY AND GENTLEFOLK'S HELP (1905), 42 Ebury Street, London SW1W 0LZ. Tel: 071-730 8263. *General Secretary*, Revd J. Schofield

FRIENDS OF THE NATIONAL LIBRARIES (1931), c/o The British Library, London WC1B 3DG. Tel: 071-323 7559. *Hon. Secretary*, Mrs A. Payne

FURNITURE HISTORY SOCIETY (1964), 1 Mercedes Cottages, St John's Road, Haywards Heath, W. Sussex RH16 4EH. Tel: 0444-413845. *Membership Secretary*, Dr B. Austen

GALLIPOLI ASSOCIATION (1915), Earlydene Orchard, Earlydene, Ascot, Berks. SL5 9JY. Tel: 0344-26523. *Hon. Secretary*, J. C. Watson Smith

GALTON INSTITUTE, THE (formerly The Eugenics Society) (1907), 19 Northfields Prospect, London SW18 1PE. Tel: 081-874 7257. *General Secretary*, Mrs L. Brooks

GAMBLERS ANONYMOUS (1954), PO Box 88, London SW10 0EU. Tel: 081-741 4181

GAME CONSERVANCY TRUST, THE (1969), Fordingbridge, Hants. SP6 1EF. Tel: 0425-652381. *Director-General*, G. R. Potts, PH.D., D.SC.

GARDEN HISTORY SOCIETY (1965), 5 The Knoll, Hereford HR1 1RU. Tel: 0432-354479. *Hon. Membership Secretary*, Mrs A. Richards

GARDENERS' ASSOCIATION, THE GOOD (1968), Pinetum, Churcham, Glos. GL2 8AD. Tel: 0452-750554. *Hon. Director*, R. Shewell-Cooper

GARDENERS' ROYAL BENEVOLENT SOCIETY, THE (1839), Bridge House, 139 Kingston Road, Leatherhead, Surrey KT22 7NT. Tel: 0372-373962. *Secretary-Administrator*, C. R. C. Bunce

GAS CONSUMERS COUNCIL (1986), 6th Floor, Abford House, 15 Wilton Road, London SW1V 1LT. Tel: 071-931 0977. *Director*, I. W. Powe

GAS ENGINEERS, INSTITUTION OF (1863), 17 Grosvenor Crescent, London SW1X 7ES. Tel: 071-245 9811. *Secretary*, D. J. Chapman

GEMMOLOGICAL ASSOCIATION OF GREAT BRITAIN (1931), 1st Floor, 27 Greville Street, London EC1N 8SU. Tel: 071-404 3334. *Director*, R. R. Harding

GENEALOGICAL RESEARCH SOCIETY, IRISH (1936), c/o The Irish Club, 82 Eaton Square, London SW1W 9AJ. *Hon. Secretary*, vacant

GENEALOGISTS AND RECORD AGENTS, ASSOCIATION OF (1968), 29 Badgers Close, Horsham, W. Sussex RH12 5RU. *Secretaries*, Mr and Mrs D. A. Young

GENEALOGISTS, SOCIETY OF (1911), 14 Charterhouse Buildings, Goswell Road, London EC1M 7BA. Tel: 071-251 8799. *Director*, A. J. Camp

GENERAL PRACTITIONERS, ROYAL COLLEGE OF (1952), 14 Princes Gate, London SW7 1PU. Tel: 071-581 3232. *Secretary*, Dr M. McBride

GENTLEPEOPLE, GUILD OF AID FOR (1904), 10 St Christopher's Place, London W1M 6HY. Tel: 071-935 0641. *Secretary*, vacant

GEOGRAPHICAL ASSOCIATION, 343 Fulwood Road, Sheffield S10 3BP. Tel: 0742-670666. *Senior Administrator*, Miss F. Soar

GEOGRAPHICAL SOCIETY, ROYAL (1830), 1 Kensington Gore, London SW7 2AR. Tel: 071-589 5466. *President*, The Earl Jellicoe; *Director*, Dr J. Hemming

GEOGRAPHICAL SOCIETY, ROYAL SCOTTISH (1884), Hills Building, 50 George Street, Glasgow G1 1XN. *Director*, A. B. Cruickshank

GEOLOGICAL SOCIETY (1807), Burlington House, Piccadilly, London W1V 0JU. Tel: 071-434 9944. *Executive Secretary*, R. M. Bateman

GEOLOGISTS' ASSOCIATION (1858), Burlington House, Piccadilly, London W1V 9AG. Tel: 071-434 9298. *Hon. General Secretary*, Prof. R. Stoneley

GEORGIAN GROUP (1937), 37 Spital Square, London E1 6DY. Tel: 071-377 1722. *Director*, M. Cudlipp

GIFTED CHILDREN, NATIONAL ASSOCIATION FOR (1966), Park Campus, Boughton Green Road, Northampton NN2 7AL. Tel: 0604-792300. *Executive Director*, M. Short

GILBERT AND SULLIVAN SOCIETY (1924), 31A Kenmere Gardens, Wembley, Middx. HA0 1TD. *Hon. Secretary*, Miss B. Dove

GINGERBREAD, AN ASSOCIATION FOR ONE PARENT FAMILIES (1970), 35 Wellington Street, London WC2E 7BN. Tel: 071-240 0953. *Chief Executive*, Ms M. Honeyball

GIRL GUIDES ASSOCIATION (1910), 17–19 Buckingham Palace Road, London SW1W 0PT. Tel: 071-834 6242. *Chief Commissioner*, Mrs J. Garside; *Chief Executive*, Ms H. Williams

GIRLS' BRIGADE, THE, Girls' Brigade House, 62 Foxhall Road, Didcot, Oxon. OX11 7BQ. Tel: 0235-510425. *Brigade Secretary*, Miss D. M. Cosser (*from 1 Jan. 1994* Mrs S. Bunting)

GIRLS' FRIENDLY SOCIETY AND TOWNSEND FELLOWSHIP (1875), 126 Queens Gate, London SW7 5LQ. Tel: 071-589 9628. *General Secretary,* Mrs H. Crompton

GIRLS' VENTURE CORPS AIR CADETS (1964), Redhill Aerodrome, Kings Mill Lane, South Nutfield, Redhill RH1 5JY. Tel: 0737-823345. *Corps Director,* Mrs M. Rowland

GLASS ENGRAVERS, GUILD OF (1975), 8 Rathcoole Avenue, London N8 9NA. Tel: 081-348 8772. *Secretary,* Mrs J. Orsler

GLASS TECHNOLOGY, SOCIETY OF (1916), Thornton, 20 Hallam Gate Road, Sheffield S10 5BT. Tel: 0742-663168. *Administration Manager,* Miss J. Costello

GLIDING ASSOCIATION, BRITISH (1930), Kimberley House, Vaughan Way, Leicester LE1 4SE. Tel: 0533-531051. *Secretary,* B. Rolfe

GOAT SOCIETY, BRITISH (1879), 34–36 Fore Street, Bovey Tracey, Newton Abbot, Devon TQ13 9AD. Tel: 0626-833168. *Secretary,* Ms S. Knowles

GRAPHIC FINE ART, SOCIETY OF (1919), 9 Newburgh Street, London W1V 1LH. *Secretary,* Ms J. Caesar

GRAPHOLOGISTS, BRITISH INSTITUTE OF (1983), 4th Floor, Bell Court House, 11 Blomfield Street, London EC2M 7AY. *Chairman,* Dr C. Molander

GREEK INSTITUTE (1969), 34 Bush Hill Road, London N21 2DS. Tel: 081-360 7968. *Director,* Dr K. Tofallis

GREEN PARTY, THE (1973), 10 Station Parade, Balham High Road, London SW12 9AZ. Tel: 081-673 0045. *Office Manager,* J. Bishop

GREENPEACE UK (1971), Canonbury Villas, London N1 2PN. Tel: 071-354 5100. *Executive Director,* The Lord Melchett

GROCERS ASSOCIATION, BRITISH INDEPENDENT (1890), Federation House, 17 Farnborough Street, Farnborough, Hants. GU14 8AG. Tel: 0252-515001. *National Secretary,* A. Taylor

GUIDE DOGS FOR THE BLIND ASSOCIATION (1931), Hillfields, Burghfield, Reading RG7 3YG. Tel: 0734-835555. *Director-General,* J. C. Oxley

GULBENKIAN FOUNDATION, *see* CALOUSTE GULBENKIAN FOUNDATION

HAEMOPHILIA SOCIETY, THE (1950), 123 Westminster Bridge Road, London SE1 7HR. Tel: 071-928 2020. *General Secretary,* D. G. Watters

HAKLUYT SOCIETY (1846), c/o Map Library, The British Library, Great Russell Street, London WC1B 3DG. Tel: 0986-86359. *Joint Hon. Secretaries,* Dr W. F. Ryan; Mrs S. Tyacke

HANSARD SOCIETY FOR PARLIAMENTARY GOVERNMENT, THE (1944), St Philips Building North, Sheffield Street, London WC2A 2EX. Tel: 071-955 7478. *Director,* D. Harris

HARD OF HEARING, BRITISH ASSOCIATION OF THE (1948), 7–11 Armstrong Road, London W3 7JL. Tel: 081-743 1110. *Chairman,* P. J. Phillips

HARVEIAN SOCIETY OF EDINBURGH (1782), Department of Medicine, The Royal Infirmary, Edinburgh EH3 9YW. Tel: 031-229 2477, ext. 3166. *Joint Secretaries,* A. B. MacGregor; Dr A. D. Toft

HARVEIAN SOCIETY OF LONDON (1831), 11 Chandos Street, London W1M 0EB. Tel: 071-580 1043. *Executive Secretary,* M. Griffiths

HEALTH AUTHORITIES AND TRUSTS, NATIONAL ASSOCIATION OF (1974), Birmingham Research Park, Vincent Drive, Birmingham B15 2SQ. Tel: 021-471 4444. *Director,* P. Hunt

HEALTH CARE ASSOCIATION, BRITISH (1931), 24A Main Street, Garforth, Leeds LS25 1AA. Tel: 0532-320903. *National Secretary,* Ms C. Bell

HEALTH EDUCATION, INSTITUTE OF (1962), 14 High Elm Road, Hale Barns, Altrincham, Cheshire WA15 0HS. Tel: 061-980 8276. *Hon. Secretary,* Prof. L. Baric, PH.D.

HEALTH, GUILD OF (1904), Edward Wilson House, 26 Queen Anne Street, London W1M 9LB. Tel: 071-580 2492. *National Director,* W. R. Booth

HEALTH SERVICES MANAGEMENT, INSTITUTE OF (1902), 75 Portland Place, London W1N 4AN. Tel: 071-580 5041. *Director,* R. Rowden

HEART FOUNDATION, BRITISH (1963), 14 Fitzhardinge Street, London W1H 4DH. Tel: 071-935 0185. *Director-General,* Maj.-Gen. L. F. H. Busk, CB

HEDGEHOG PRESERVATION SOCIETY, BRITISH (1982), Knowbury House, Knowbury, Ludlow, Shropshire SY8 3LQ. Tel: 0584-890287. *Founder,* Maj. A. H. Coles

HELLENIC STUDIES, SOCIETY FOR THE PROMOTION OF (1879), 31–34 Gordon Square, London WC1H 0PP. Tel: 071-387 7495. *Secretary,* Dr L. Rodley

HELP THE AGED (1960), St James's Walk, Clerkenwell Green, London EC1R 0BE. Tel: 071-253 0253. *Director-General,* Col. J. Mayo, OBE

HERALDIC AND GENEALOGICAL STUDIES, INSTITUTE OF (1961), 79–82 Northgate, Canterbury, Kent CT1 1BA. Tel: 0227-768664. *Registrar,* J. Parker

HERALDRY SOCIETY, THE (1947), 44–45 Museum Street, London WC1A 1LY. Tel: 071-430 2172. *Secretary,* Mrs M. Miles, MBE

HERPETOLOGICAL SOCIETY, BRITISH (1947), c/o Zoological Society of London, Regent's Park, London NW1 4RY. Tel: 081-452 9578. *Secretary,* Mrs M. Green

HIGHWAYS AND TRANSPORTATION, INSTITUTION OF (1930), 3 Lygon Place, Ebury Street, London SW1W 0JS. Tel: 071-370 5245. *Secretary,* Dr M. R. Cragg

HISPANIC AND LUSO BRAZILIAN COUNCIL (1943), Canning House, 2 Belgrave Square, London SW1X 8PJ. Tel: 071-235 2303. *Director-General,* Sir Michael Simpson-Orlebar, KCMG

HISTORICAL ASSOCIATION, THE (1906), 59A Kennington Park Road, London SE11 4JH. Tel: 071-735 3901. *Secretary,* Mrs M. Stiles

HISTORICAL SOCIETY, ROYAL (1868), University College, Gower Street, London WC1E 6BT. Tel: 071-387 7532. *Executive Secretary,* Mrs J. N. McCarthy

HOMOEOPATHIC ASSOCIATION, BRITISH (1902), 27A Devonshire Street, London W1N 1RJ. Tel: 071-935 2163. *General Secretary,* Mrs E. Segall

HONG KONG ASSOCIATION (1961), Swire House, 59 Buckingham Gate, London SW1E 6AJ. Tel: 071-821 3220. *Executive Director,* Brig. B. G. Hickey, OBE, MC

HOROLOGICAL INSTITUTE, BRITISH (1858), Upton Hall, Upton, Newark, Notts. NG23 5TE. Tel: 0636-813795. *Secretary,* W. M. G. Evans

HOROLOGICAL SOCIETY, ANTIQUARIAN (1953), New House, High Street, Ticehurst, Wadhurst, E. Sussex TN5 7AL. Tel: 0580-200155. *Secretary,* Mrs M. A. Collins

HORSE SOCIETY, BRITISH (1947) (incorporating The Pony Club), British Equestrian Centre, Kenilworth, Warks. CV8 2LR. Tel: 0203-696697. *Chief Executive*, Col. T. Eastwood

HOSPITAL FEDERATION, INTERNATIONAL (1947), 4 Abbot's Place, London NW6 4NP. Tel: 071-372 7181. *Director-General*, Dr E. N. Pickering

HOSPITAL SATURDAY FUND, THE (1873), 24 Upper Ground, London SE1 9PQ. Tel: 071-928 6662. *Chief Executive*, K. R. Bradley

HOSPITAL SAVING ASSOCIATION, THE, Hambleden House, Andover, Hants. SP10 1LQ. Tel: 0264-353211. *General Secretary*, J. A. Young

HOSPITALITY ASSOCIATION, BRITISH (1907), 40 Duke Street, London WIM 6HR. Tel: 071-499 6641. *Chief Executive*, R. Lees, CB, MBE

HOTEL, CATERING AND INSTITUTIONAL MANAGEMENT ASSOCIATION (1971), 191 Trinity Road, London SW17 7HN. *Director*, Miss E. Gadsby

HOUSE OF ST BARNABAS-IN-SOHO (1846), 1 Greek Street, London WIV 6NQ. Tel: 071-437 1894. For homeless women in London. *Director*, D. G. Saunders

HOUSING, INSTITUTE OF, Octavia House, Westwood Business Park, Westwood Way, Coventry CV4 8JP. Tel: 0203-694433. *Director*, P. McGurk

HOUSING AID SOCIETY, CATHOLIC (1956), 189A Old Brompton Road, London SW5 0AR. Tel: 071-373 4961. *Director*, Ms R. Rafferty

HOUSING AND TOWN PLANNING COUNCIL, NATIONAL (1900), 14–18 Old Street, London EC1V 9AB. Tel: 071-251 2363. *Director*, Ms A. Holmes

HOUSING ASSOCIATION FOR OFFICERS' FAMILIES (1916), Alban Dobson House, Green Lane, Morden, Surrey SM4 5NS. Tel: 081-648 0335. *General Secretary*, J. B. Holt

HOVERCRAFT SOCIETY, THE (1971), 24 Jellicoe Avenue, Alverstoke, Gosport, Hants. PO12 2PE. Tel: 0705-601310. *Chairman*, M. J. Cox

HOWARD LEAGUE FOR PENAL REFORM (1866), 708 Holloway Road, London N19 3NL. Tel: 071-281 7722. *Director*, Ms F. Crook

HUGUENOT SOCIETY OF GREAT BRITAIN AND IRELAND (1885), The Huguenot Library, University College, Gower Street, London WC1E 6BT. Tel: 071-380 7094. *Hon. Secretary*, Mrs M. Bayliss

HUMANE RESEARCH TRUST, (1974), Brook House, 29 Bramhall Lane South, Bramhall, Stockport, Cheshire SK7 2DN. Tel: 061-439 8041. *Chairman*, K. Cholerton

HYDROGRAPHIC SOCIETY (1972), c/o University of East London, Longbridge Road, Dagenham, Essex RM8 2AS. Tel: 081-597 1946. *Hon. Secretary*, V. J. Abbott

HYMN SOCIETY OF GREAT BRITAIN AND IRELAND (1936), St Nicholas Rectory, Glebe Fields, Curdworth, Sutton Coldfield, W. Midlands B76 9ES. Tel: 0675-470384. *Secretary*, Revd M. Garland

IMMIGRANTS ADVISORY SERVICE, UK (1970), 190 Great Dover Street, London SE1 4YB. Tel: 071-357 6917. *Director*, T. Sullivan

INDEPENDENT BRITAIN, CAMPAIGN FOR AN (1976), 81 Ashmole Street, London SW8 1NF. Tel: 081-340 0314. *Hon. Secretary*, Sir Robin Williams, Bt.

INDEPENDENT SCHOOL BURSARS' ASSOCIATION (1933), Woodlands, Closewood Road, Denmead, Waterlooville, Hants PO7 6JD. Tel: 0705-264506. *Secretary*, D. J. Bird

INDEPENDENT SCHOOLS CAREERS ORGANIZATION (1942), 12A–18A Princess Way, Camberley, Surrey GU15 3SP. *Director*, G. W. Searle

INDEPENDENT SCHOOLS INFORMATION SERVICE (ISIS) (1972), 56 Buckingham Gate, London SW1E 6AG. Tel: 071-630 8793. *Director*, D. J. Woodhead

INDEPENDENT SCHOOLS JOINT COUNCIL (1974), Grosvenor Gardens House, 35–37 Grosvenor Gardens, London SW1W 0BS. Tel: 071-630 0144. *General Secretary*, Dr A. G. Hearnden, OBE

INDEXERS, SOCIETY OF (1957), 38 Rochester Road, London NW1 9JJ. Tel: 071-916 7809. *Secretary*, Mrs C. Troughton

INDUSTRIAL CHRISTIAN FELLOWSHIP (1877), Dukes Meadow, 1 One Tree Lane, Beaconsfield, Bucks. HP9 2BU. Tel: 071-283 6120. *Director*, Revd R. Holloway

INDUSTRIAL EDITORS, BRITISH ASSOCIATION OF, (1949), 3 Locks Yard, High Street, Sevenoaks, Kent, TN13 1LT. Tel: 0732-459331. *Chief Executive*, C. Pedersen

INDUSTRIAL MARKETING RESEARCH ASSOCIATION (IMRA) (1963), 11 Bird Street, Lichfield, Staffs. WS13 6PW. Tel: 0543-263448. *Executive Officer*, M. Berry

INDUSTRIAL SOCIETY, THE (1918), Robert Hyde House, 48 Bryanston Square, London WIH 7LN. Tel: 071-262 2401. *Director*, Mrs R. Chapman

INDUSTRY AND PARLIAMENT TRUST, 1 Buckingham Place, London SW1E 6HR. Tel: 071-976 5311. *Director*, F. R. Hyde-Chambers

INDUSTRY TRAINING ORGANIZATIONS, NATIONAL COUNCIL OF (1988), 5 George Lane, Royston, Herts. SG8 9AR. Tel: 0763-247285. *Administrator*, Mrs C. Armstrong

INFANT DEATHS, FOUNDATION FOR THE STUDY OF (1971), 35 Belgrave Square, London SW1X 8QB. Tel: 071-235 0965/1721. *Secretary-General*, Mrs J. Epstein

INFORMATION SCIENTISTS, INSTITUTE OF (1958), 44–45 Museum Street, London WC1A 1LY. Tel: 071-831 8003. *Executive Secretary*, Mrs S. A. Carter

INNER WHEEL CLUBS IN GREAT BRITAIN AND IRELAND, ASSOCIATION OF (1934), 51 Warwick Square, London SW1V 2AT. Tel: 071-834 4600. *General Secretary*, Miss J. Dobson

INSURANCE AND INVESTMENT BROKERS' ASSOCIATION, BRITISH, BIIBA House, 14 Bevis Marks, London EC3A 7NT. Tel: 071-623 9043. *Director-General*, Mrs I. R. Rooley

INSURANCE BROKERS REGISTRATION COUNCIL, 15 St Helen's Place, London EC3A 6DS. Tel: 071-588 4387. *Registrar*, Miss E. J. Rees

INSURANCE INSTITUTE, CHARTERED (1897), 20 Aldermanbury, London EC2V 7HY. Tel: 071-606 3835. *Director-General*, Dr D. E. Bland

INSURERS, ASSOCIATION OF BRITISH (1985), 51 Gresham Street, London EC2V 7HQ. Tel: 071-600 3333. *Director-General*, M. Boléat

INTERCON (INTERCONTINENTAL CHURCH SOCIETY) (1823), 175 Tower Bridge Road, London SE1 2AQ. Tel: 071-407 4588. *General Secretary*, Deaconess P. K. L. Schmiegelow

INTERNATIONAL AFFAIRS, ROYAL INSTITUTE OF (1920), Chatham House, 10 St James's Square, London SW1Y 4LE. Tel: 071-957 5700. *Director*, Prof. L. Martin

INTERNATIONAL FRIENDSHIP LEAGUE (1931), 3 Creswick Road, London W3 9HE. Tel: 081-992 0221. *Secretary*, Mrs B. Macdonald

INTERNATIONAL LAW ASSOCIATION (1873), Charles Clore House, 17 Russell Square, London WCIB 5DR. Tel: 071-323 2978. *Hon. Secretary-General*, B. Mauleverer, QC

INTERNATIONAL POLICE ASSOCIATION (British Section) (1950), 1 Fox Road, West Bridgford, Nottingham NG2 6AJ. Tel: 0602-813638. *Chief Executive Officer*, A. F. Carter

INTERNATIONAL STUDENTS HOUSE (1962), 229 Great Portland Street, London WIN 5HD. Tel: 071-631 3223. *Secretary*, P. Anwyl

INTERNATIONAL TIN RESEARCH INSTITUTE (1932), Kingston Lane, Uxbridge, Middx. UB8 3PJ. Tel: 0895-72406. *Director*, Dr B. T. K. Barry

INTERNATIONAL VOLUNTARY SERVICE (1920), 162 Upper New Walk, Leicester LEI 7QA. *General Secretaries*, P. Ticher; D. T. Huggins

INTERSERVE (1852), 325 Kennington Park Road, London SEII 4QH. Tel: 071-735 8227. *General Director*, A. M. S. Pont

INTER VARSITY CLUBS, ASSOCIATION OF (1946), 2nd Floor, Grosvenor House, 94–96 Grosvenor Square, Manchester MI 7HL. Tel: 061-273 2316. *Secretary*, D. Bousfield

INVALID CHILDREN'S AID NATIONWIDE (I CAN)(1888), 10 Bowling Green Lane, London ECIR OBD. Tel: 071-253 9111. *Director*, B. J. Jones

INVALIDS-AT-HOME (1966), 17 Lapstone Gardens, Kenton, Harrow HA3 OEB. *Executive Officer*, Ms S. Lomas

INVISIBLES, BRITISH (1983), Windsor House, 39 King Street, London EC2V 8DQ. Tel: 071-600 1198. *Director-General*, Mrs A. Wright

INVOLVEMENT AND PARTICIPATION ASSOCIATION (1884), 42 Colebrook Row, London NI 8AF. Tel: 071-354 8040. *Director*, B. C. Stevens

IRAN SOCIETY (1936), 2 Belgrave Square, London SWIX 8PJ. Tel: 071-235 5122. *Hon. Secretary*, A. D. Ashmole

JACQUELINE DU PRÉ MEMORIAL FUND (1988), 14 Ogle Street, London WIP 7LG. Tel: 071-436 3173. *Chairman*, Lord Goodman, CH

JAPAN ASSOCIATION, THE (1950), Swire House, 59 Buckingham Gate, London SWIE 6AJ. Tel: 071-821 3220. *Executive Director*, Brig. B. G. Hickey, OBE, MC

JERUSALEM AND THE MIDDLE EAST CHURCH ASSOCIATION, THE (1887), 1 Hart House, The Hart, Farnham, Surrey GU9 7HA. Tel: 0252-726994. *Secretary*, Mrs V. Wells

JEWISH HISTORICAL SOCIETY OF ENGLAND (1893), 33 Seymour Place, London WIH 5AP. Tel: 071-723 4404. *Hon. Secretary*, C. M. Drukker

JEWISH YOUTH, ASSOCIATION FOR (1899), 128 East Lane, Wembley, Middx. HAO 3NL. Tel: 081-908 4747. *Executive Director*, M. Shaw

JEWS, CHURCH'S MINISTRY AMONG THE (1809), 30C Clarence Road, St Albans, Herts. ALI 4JJ. Tel: 0727-833114. *General Director*, Revd J. M. V. Drummond

JOURNALISTS, THE CHARTERED INSTITUTE OF (1883), 2 Dock Offices, Surrey Quays, Lower Road, London SEI6 2XL. Tel: 071-252 1187. *Director*, W. Tadd

JUSTICE (British Section of the International Commission of Jurists) (1957), 95A Chancery Lane, London WC2A IDT. *Director*, Ms A. Owers

JUSTICES' CLERKS' SOCIETY (1839), The Law Courts, Petters Way, Yeovil, Somerset BA20 ISW. Tel: 0935-21912. *Hon. Secretary*, L. G. C. Cramp

KING EDWARD'S HOSPITAL FUND FOR LONDON (THE KING'S FUND) (1897), 14 Palace Court, London W2 4HT. Tel: 071-727 0581. *Director*, Dr R. J. Maxwell

KING GEORGE'S FUND FOR SAILORS (1917), 8 Hatherley Street, London SWIP 2YY. *Director-General*, The Lord Burnham

KIPLING SOCIETY, THE (1927), 2nd Floor, Schomberg House, 80–82 Pall Mall, London SWIY 5ET. Tel: 0428-652709. *Hon. Secretary*, N. Entract

LADIES IN REDUCED CIRCUMSTANCES, SOCIETY FOR THE ASSISTANCE OF (1886), Lancaster House, 25 Hornyold Road, Malvern, Worcs. WRI4 IQQ. Tel: 0684-574645. *Secretary*

LANDSCAPE INSTITUTE (1929), 6–7 Barnard Mews, London SWII IQU. Tel: 071-738 9166. *Registrar*, P. R. Broadbent, OBE

LAND-VALUE TAXATION AND FREE TRADE, INTERNATIONAL UNION FOR, 177 Vauxhall Bridge Road, London SWIV IEU. Tel: 071-834 4266. *President*, Mrs B. P. Sobrielo

LANGUAGE LEARNING, ASSOCIATION FOR (1990), 16 Regent Place, Rugby CV21 2PN. Tel: 0788-546443. *General Secretary*, Mrs C. Wilding

LAW REPORTING FOR ENGLAND AND WALES, INCORPORATED COUNCIL OF (1865), 3 Stone Buildings, Lincoln's Inn, London WC2A 3XN. Tel: 071-242 6471. *Secretary*, B. Symondson

LEAGUE OF THE HELPING HAND (1908), Baileys, Church Street, Charlbury, Oxford OX7 3PR. *Secretary*, Mrs I. Goodlad

LEAGUE OF WELLDOERS (1893), 119–121 Limekiln Lane, Liverpool L5 8SN. Tel: 051-207 1984. *Warden and Secretary*, K. H. Stanton

LEATHER AND HIDE TRADES' BENEVOLENT INSTITUTION (1860), 60 Wickham Hill, Hurstpierpoint, Hassocks, W. Sussex BN6 9NP. Tel: 0273-843488. *Secretary*, Mrs G. M. Stapleton, MBE

LEGAL EXECUTIVES, INSTITUTE OF (1892), Kempston Manor, Kempston, Bedford MK42 7AB. Tel: 0234-841000. *Secretary-General*, L. A. Evans

LEONARD CHESHIRE FOUNDATION (1955), 26–29 Maunsel Street, London SWIP 2QN. Tel: 071-828 1822. *Director*, J. Stanford

LEPROSY MISSION, THE (England and Wales) (1874), Goldhay Way, Orton Goldhay, Peterborough PE2 OGZ. Tel: 0733-370505. *Executive Director*, Revd J. A. Lloyd

LEUKAEMIA RESEARCH FUND (1962), 43 Great Ormond Street, London WCIN 3JJ. Tel: 071-405 0101. *Director*, D. L. Osborne

LIBERAL PARTY (1877; relaunched 1989), Gayfere House, 22 Gayfere Street, London SWI 3HP. Tel: 071-233 2124. *Secretary-General*, N. Ashton

LIBERTY (NATIONAL COUNCIL FOR CIVIL LIBERTIES) (1934), 21 Tabard Street, London SEI 4LA. Tel: 071-403 3888. *General Secretary*, A. Puddephatt

LIBRARY ASSOCIATION (1877), 7 Ridgmount Street, London WCIE 7AE. Tel: 071-636 7543. *Chief Executive*, R. Shimmon

LIFEBOATS, *see* ROYAL NATIONAL LIFEBOAT INSTITUTION

LIGHT HORSE BREEDING SOCIETY, NATIONAL (1885), 96 High Street, Edenbridge, Kent TN8 5AR. Tel: 0732-866277. *Secretary*, G. W. Evans

LINGUISTS, INSTITUTE OF (1910), 24A Highbury Grove, London N5 2EA. Tel: 071-359 7445. *Director,* Ms E. H. F. Ostarhild

LINNAEAN SOCIETY OF LONDON (1788), Burlington House, Piccadilly, London W1V OLQ. Tel: 071-434 4479. *President,* Prof. J. G. Hawkes; *Executive Secretary,* Dr J. C. Marsden

LIONS CLUBS INTERNATIONAL (British Isles and Ireland) (1949), 257 Alcester Road South, Kings Heath, Birmingham B14 6BT. Tel: 021-441 4510. *General Secretary,* P. Jay

LLOYD'S OF LONDON, 1 Lime Street, London EC3M 7HA. Tel: 071-327 6224. *Chief Executive,* P. J. Middleton

LLOYD'S PATRIOTIC FUND (1803), Lloyd's, Lime Street, London EC3M 7HA. Tel: 071-327 5558. *Secretary,* Miss B. A. Lowden

LOCAL AUTHORITY CHIEF EXECUTIVES, SOCIETY OF (1974), Kensington Town Hall, Hornton Street, London W8 7NX. Tel: 071-938 3400. *Hon. Secretary,* A. Taylor

LOCAL COUNCILS, NATIONAL ASSOCIATION OF (1947), 108 Great Russell Street, London WC1B 3LD. Tel: 071-637 1865. *Secretary,* J. Clark

LOCAL GOVERNMENT INTERNATIONAL BUREAU (1913), *also* COUNCIL OF EUROPEAN MUNICIPALITIES AND REGIONS (British Section) and INTERNATIONAL UNION OF LOCAL AUTHORITIES (British Section) (1951), 35 Great Smith Street, London SW1P 3BJ. Tel: 071-222 1636. *Secretary-General,* P. N. Bongers

LOCAL HISTORY, BRITISH ASSOCIATION FOR (1843), 24 Lower Street, Harnham, Salisbury, Wilts. SP2 8EY. Tel: 0722-320115. *Secretary,* M. Cowan

LONDON APPRECIATION SOCIETY (1932), 17 Manson Mews, London SW7 5AF. *Hon. Secretary,* H. L. B. Peers, PH.D.

LONDON BOROUGHS ASSOCIATION (1964), College House, Great Peter Street, London SW1P 3LN. Tel: 071-799 2477. *Secretary,* J. Hall

LONDON CITY MISSION (1835), 175 Tower Bridge Road, London SE1 2AH. Tel: 071-407 7585. *General Secretary,* Revd J. McAllen

LONDON COURT OF INTERNATIONAL ARBITRATION (1892), 2–5 Minories, London EC3N 1BJ. Tel: 071-702 9599. *Registrar,* B. W. Vigrass, OBE, VRD

LONDON FLOTILLA (1937), Marden Rise, 81 Lower Road, Fetcham, Leatherhead, Surrey KT22 9HG. Tel: 0372-453059. *Hon. Secretary,* Lt. Cdr. P. A. G. Norman, RD, RNR

LONDON LIBRARY, THE (1841), 14 St James's Square, London SW1Y 4LG. Tel: 071-930 7705. *Librarian,* A. S. Bell

LONDON MAGISTRATES' CLERKS' ASSOCIATION (1889), c/o Marlborough Street Magistrates' Court, 21 Great Marlborough Street, London W1A 4EY. Tel: 071-287 4525, ext. 3842. *Hon. Secretary,* K. W. Burman

LONDON PLAYING FIELDS SOCIETY, THE (1890), Boston Manor Playing Field, Boston Gardens, Brentford, Middx. TW8 9LR. Tel: 081-560 3667. *Secretary,* D. Northwood

LONDON SOCIETY, THE (1912), 4th Floor, Senate House, Malet Street, London WC1E 7HU. Tel: 071-580 5537. *Hon. Secretary,* Mrs B. Jones

LORD'S DAY OBSERVANCE SOCIETY, THE (1831), 6 Sherman Road, Bromley, Kent BR1 3JH. Tel: 081-313 0456. *General Secretary,* J. G. Roberts

LORD'S TAVERNERS, THE (1950), 22 Queen Anne's Gate, London SW1H 9AA. Tel: 071-222 0707. *Director,* P. Shervington

LOTTERIES COUNCIL, THE (1979), 81 Mansel Street, Swansea SA1 5TT. Tel: 0792-462845. *Hon. Secretary,* J. H. Solly

MAGISTRATES' ASSOCIATION, THE (1920), 28 Fitzroy Square, London W1P 6DD. Tel: 071-387 2353. *Secretary,* T. R. P. Rudin

MAIL USERS' ASSOCIATION (1976), 3 Pavement House, The Pavement, Hay-on-Wye, Hereford HR3 5BU. Tel: 0497-821357. *Chairman,* L. K. Morelli

MALAYSIAN RUBBER PRODUCERS' RESEARCH ASSOCIATION (1938), Tun Abdul Razak Laboratory, Brickendonbury, Hertford SG13 8NL. Tel: 0992-584966. *Director,* Dr C. S. L. Baker

MALCOLM SARGENT CANCER FUND FOR CHILDREN (1968), 14 Abingdon Road, London W8 6AF. Tel: 071-937 4548. *General Administrator*

MALONE SOCIETY (for the publication of scholarly editions and facsimiles of early English dramatic texts). *Executive Secretary,* Prof. J. Creaser, Royal Holloway and Bedford New College, Egham Hill, Egham, Surrey TW20 OEX

MANAGEMENT, INSTITUTE OF (1992), Management House, Cottingham Road, Corby, Northants NN17 1TT. Tel: 0536-204222. *Director-General,* R. Young

MANAGEMENT AND PROFESSIONAL STAFFS, ASSOCIATION OF (1972), Parkgates, Bury New Road, Prestwich, Manchester M25 8JX. Tel: 061-773 8621. *Executive Secretary,* A. J. Casey

MANAGEMENT SERVICES, INSTITUTE OF, 1 Cecil Court, London Road, Enfield, Middx. EN2 6DD. Tel: 081-363 7452. *General Secretary,* F. O'Connolly

MANIC DEPRESSION FELLOWSHIP (1983), 13 Rosslyn Road, Twickenham, Surrey TW1 2AR. Tel: 081-892 2811. *Director,* Ms M. Fulford

MANORIAL SOCIETY OF GREAT BRITAIN (1906), 104 Kennington Road, London SE11 6RE. Tel: 071-735 6633. *Hon. Chairman,* R. A. Smith

MANPOWER SOCIETY (1969), 39 Apple Tree Walk, Climping, Littlehampton, W. Sussex BN17 5QN. Tel: 0903-731728. *Administrator,* Mrs H. Gale

MARIE CURIE MEMORIAL FOUNDATION (1948), 28 Belgrave Square, London SW1X 8QG. Tel: 071-235 3325. *Scottish Office,* 21 Rutland Street, Edinburgh EH1 2AH. *Director-General,* Maj.-Gen. M. E. Carleton-Smith, CBE

MARINE ARTISTS, ROYAL SOCIETY OF (1939), 17 Carlton House Terrace, London SW1Y 5BD. Tel: 071-930 6844. *Secretary,* D. Curtis

MARINE BIOLOGICAL ASSOCIATION OF THE UK (1884), Citadel Hill, Plymouth PL1 2PB. Tel: 0752-222772. *Secretary,* Dr M. Whitfield

MARINE ENGINEERS, INSTITUTE OF (1889), The Memorial Building, 76 Mark Lane, London EC3R 7JN. Tel: 071-481 8493. *Secretary,* J. E. Sloggett

MARINE SCIENCE, THE SCOTTISH ASSOCIATION FOR (1914), PO Box 3, Oban, Argyll PA34 4AD. Tel: 0631-62244. *Secretary,* Prof. J. B. L. Matthews, FRSE

MARINE SOCIETY, THE (1756), 202 Lambeth Road, London SE1 7JW. Tel: 071-261 9535. *General Secretary,* Lt. Cdr. R. M. Frampton

MARIO LANZA EDUCATIONAL FOUNDATION (1976), 7 Lionsfield Avenue, Allesley Village, Coventry CV5 9GN. *Hon. Secretary,* Miss P. Barron

MARKET AUTHORITIES, NATIONAL ASSOCIATION OF BRITISH (1948), 19 Derwent Avenue, Milnrow, Rochdale, Lancs. OL16 3UD. Tel: 0706-57740. *Secretary*, B. Ormshaw

MARKETING, CHARTERED INSTITUTE OF (1911), Moor Hall, Cookham, Maidenhead, Berks. SL6 9QH. Tel: 0628-524922. *Director-General*, J. McAinsh

MARKET TRADERS' FEDERATION, NATIONAL (1899), Hampton House, Hawshaw Lane, Hoyland, Barnsley S74 0HA. Tel: 0226-749021. *General Secretary*, D. E. Feeny

MARK MASTER MASONS, GRAND LODGE OF (1856), Mark Masons' Hall, 86 St James's Street, London SW1A 1PL. Tel: 071-839 5274. *Grand Master*, HRH Prince Michael of Kent, KCVO; *Grand Secretary*, P. G. Williams

MASONIC BENEVOLENT INSTITUTION, ROYAL (1842), 20 Great Queen Street, London WC2B 5BG. Tel: 071-405 8341. *Chief Executive*, Ms J. Reynolds

MASONIC BENEVOLENT INSTITUTIONS IN IRELAND, 17–19 Molesworth Street, Dublin 2. Tel: 0001-679 6799. *Secretary*, M. R. McWilliam

MASONIC TRUST FOR GIRLS AND BOYS (1985), 31 Great Queen Street, London WC2B 5AG. Tel: 071-405 2644. *Secretary*, Col. R. K. Hind

MASTERS OF FOXHOUNDS ASSOCIATION (1881). *Secretary*, A. H. B. Hart, Parsloes Cottage, Bagendon, Cirencester, Glos. GL7 7DU

MASTERS OF WINE, INSTITUTE OF (1955), Five Kings House, 1 Queen Street Place, London EC4R 1QS. Tel: 071-236 4427. *Executive Director*, D. F. Stevens

MATERNAL AND CHILD WELFARE, NATIONAL ASSOCIATION FOR (1911), 40–42 Osnaburgh Street, London NW1 3ND. Tel: 071-383 4115. *Administrator*, Mrs F. N. Kapadia

MATERIALS, INSTITUTE OF (1985), 1 Carlton House Terrace, London SW1Y 5DB. Tel: 071-839 4071. *Secretary*, Dr J. A. Catterall

MATERNITY ALLIANCE, THE (1980), 15 Britannia Street, London WC1X 9JP. Tel: 071-837 1265. *Chair*, A. Phillips

MATHEMATICAL ASSOCIATION (1871), 259 London Road, Leicester LE2 3BE. Tel: 0533-703877. *Executive Secretary*, Ms H. Whitby

MATHEMATICS AND ITS APPLICATIONS, INSTITUTE OF (1964), 16 Nelson Street, Southend-on-Sea SS1 1EF. Tel: 0702-354020. *Registrar*

MEASUREMENT AND CONTROL, INSTITUTE OF, 87 Gower Street, London WC1E 6AA. Tel: 071-387 4949. *Secretary*, M. Yates

MECHANICAL ENGINEERS, INSTITUTION OF (1847), 1 Birdcage Walk, London SW1H 9JJ. Tel: 071-222 7899. *Director-General*, Dr R. Pike

MEDIC-ALERT FOUNDATION, 12 Bridge Wharf, 156 Caledonian Road, London N1 9UU. Tel: 071-833 3034. *Chief Executive*, Mrs R. Evans

MEDICAL COUNCIL, GENERAL (1858), 44 Hallam Street, London W1N 6AE. Tel: 071-580 7642. *Registrar*, P. L. Towers, CBE

MEDICAL SOCIETY OF LONDON (1773), 11 Chandos Street, London W1M 0EB. Tel: 071-580 1043. *Registrar*, M. Griffiths, TD

MEDICAL WOMEN'S FEDERATION (1917), Tavistock House North, Tavistock Square, London WC1H 9HX. *Hon. Secretary*, Dr I. Weinreb

MEMORIAL FUND FOR DISASTER RELIEF, 3 Throgmorton Avenue, London EC2N 2WW. Tel: 071-638 6442. *Director*, R. Kandt

MENCAP (THE ROYAL SOCIETY FOR MENTALLY HANDICAPPED CHILDREN AND ADULTS) (1946), 123 Golden Lane, London EC1Y 0RT. Tel: 071-454 0454. *Chief Executive*, F. Heddell

MENTAL AFTER CARE ASSOCIATION (1879), 25 Bedford Square, London WC1B 3HW. Tel: 071-436 6194. *Director*, B. G. Garner

MENTAL HEALTH FOUNDATION, THE (1949), 37 Mortimer Street, London W1N 7RS. Tel: 071-580 0145. *Director-General*, Ms J. McKerrow

MERCHANT NAVY WELFARE BOARD (1948), 19–21 Lancaster Gate, London W2 3LN. Tel: 071-723 3642. *General Secretary*

METAL TRADES BENEVOLENT SOCIETY, ROYAL (1843), Kelvin House, 1 Totteridge Avenue, High Wycombe, Bucks. HP13 6XG. Tel: 0494-530430. *General Secretary*, A. Whittle, MBE

METEOROLOGICAL SOCIETY, ROYAL (1850), 104 Oxford Road, Reading, Berks. RG1 7LJ. Tel: 0734-568500. *Executive Secretary*, R. P. C. Swash

METROPOLITAN AND CITY POLICE ORPHANS FUND (1870), 30 Hazlewell Road, London SW15 6LH. Tel: 081-788 5140. *Secretary*, R. Duff-Cole, BEM

METROPOLITAN AUTHORITIES, ASSOCIATION OF (1974), 35 Great Smith Street, London SW1P 3BJ. Tel: 071-222 8100. *Secretary*, R. Brooke

METROPOLITAN HOSPITAL-SUNDAY FUND (1872), 40 High Street, Teddington, Middx. TW11 8EW. Tel: 081-977 4154. *Secretary*, D. A. B. Lynch

MIDDLE EAST ASSOCIATION, THE (1961), Bury House, 33 Bury Street, London SW1Y 6AX. Tel: 071-839 2137. *Director-General*, J. R. Grundon

MIDWIVES, ROYAL COLLEGE OF (1881), 15 Mansfield Street, London W1M 0BE. Tel: 071-580 6523. *General Secretary*, Miss R. M. Ashton, OBE

MIGRAINE ASSOCIATION, BRITISH (1958), 178A High Road, Byfleet, Weybridge, Surrey KT14 7ED. Tel: 0932-352468. *Director*, Mrs J. Liddell

MIGRAINE TRUST (1965), 45 Great Ormond Street, London WC1N 3HD. Tel: 071-278 2676. *Director*, Ms A. Rush

MILITARY HISTORICAL SOCIETY, National Army Museum, Royal Hospital Road, London SW3 4HT. Tel: 081-460 7341. *Hon. Secretary*, J. Gaylor

MIND (NATIONAL ASSOCIATION FOR MENTAL HEALTH), 22 Harley Street, London W1N 2ED. Tel: 071-673 0741. *Director*, Ms J. Clements

MINERALOGICAL SOCIETY (1876), 41 Queen's Gate, London SW7 5HR. Tel: 071-584 7516. *Hon. General Secretary*, Dr G. M. Manby

MINES OF GREAT BRITAIN, FEDERATION OF SMALL, 29 King Street, Newcastle under Lyme, Staffs. ST5 1ER. Tel: 0782-614618. *Secretary*, R. W. Bladen

MINIATURE PAINTERS, SCULPTORS AND GRAVERS, ROYAL SOCIETY OF (1895), Burwood House, 15 Union Street, Wells, Somerset BA5 2PU. Tel: 0749-674472. *Executive Secretary*, Mrs S. M. Burton

MINING AND METALLURGY, THE INSTITUTION OF (1892), 44 Portland Place, London W1N 4BR. Tel: 071-580 3802. *Secretary*, M. J. Jones

MINING ENGINEERS, INSTITUTION OF (1889), Danum House, 6A South Parade, Doncaster, S. Yorks. DN1 2DY. Tel: 0302-320486. *Secretary*, W. Bourne, OBE

MISSING PERSONS BUREAU (1992), Parkway House, Sheen Lane, London SW14 8LS. Tel: 081-392 2000. *Chairman*, R. Samuels

MISSION TO DEEP SEA FISHERMEN, ROYAL NATIONAL (1881), 43 Nottingham Place, London W1M 4BX. Tel: 071-487 5101. *Chief Executive*, A. D. Marsden

MISSIONS TO SEAMEN, THE (1856), St Michael Paternoster Royal, College Hill, London EC4R 2RL. Tel: 071-248 5202. *Secretary-General*, Revd Canon G. Jones

MODERN CHURCHPEOPLE'S UNION (1898), St Martin's Vicarage, 25 Birch Grove, London W3 9SP. Tel: 081-752 0919. *Hon. Secretary*, Revd N. Henderson

MONUMENTAL BRASS SOCIETY (1887), 57 Leeside Crescent, London NW11 0HA. *Hon. Secretary*, W. Mendelsson

MORAVIAN MISSIONS, LONDON ASSOCIATION IN AID OF (1817), Moravian Church House, 5–7 Muswell Hill, London N10 3TJ. Tel: 081-883 3409. *Secretary*, Revd F. Linyard

MOTHERS' UNION, THE (1876), Mary Sumner House, 24 Tufton Street, London SW1P 3RB. Tel: 071-222 5533. *Central Secretary*, Mrs A. Ridler

MOTOR INDUSTRY, INSTITUTE OF THE, Fanshaws, Brickendon, Hertford SG13 8PQ. Tel: 0992-511521. *Secretary*, F. W. Janes

MOUNTBATTEN MEMORIAL TRUST (1979), 1 Grosvenor Crescent, London SW1X 7EF. Tel: 071-235 5231. *Director*, J. Boyd-Brent

MOUNTBATTEN TRUST, THE EDWINA (1960), 1 Grosvenor Crescent, London SW1X 7EF. Tel: 071-235 5231. *Secretary*, J. Boyd-Brent

MULTIPLE SCLEROSIS SOCIETY (1953), 25 Effie Road, London SW6 1EE. Tel: 071-736 6267. *General Secretary*, J. Walford

MUNICIPAL ENGINEERS, ASSOCIATION OF, Institution of Civil Engineers, 1–7 Great George Street, London SW1P 3AA. Tel: 071-222 7722. *Director*, K. J. Marchant

MUSEUMS ASSOCIATION (1889), 42 Clerkenwell Close, London EC1R 0PA. Tel: 071-250 1836. *Director*, M. Taylor

MUSIC HALL SOCIETY, BRITISH (1963), Brodie and Middleton Ltd, 68 Drury Lane, London WC2B 5SP. Tel: 071-836 3289. *Hon. Secretary*, Mrs J. D. Masterton

MUSICIANS BENEVOLENT FUND (1921), 16 Ogle Street, London W1P 7LG. Tel: 071-636 4481. *Secretary*, M. B. M. Williams

MUSICIANS, INCORPORATED SOCIETY OF (1882), 10 Stratford Place, London W1N 9AE. Tel: 071-629 4413. *Chief Executive*, N. Hoyle

MUSICIANS OF GREAT BRITAIN, ROYAL SOCIETY OF (1738), 10 Stratford Place, London W1N 9AE. Tel: 071-629 6137. *Administrator*, Mrs M. Gibb

MUSIC INFORMATION CENTRE, BRITISH (1967), 10 Stratford Place, London W1N 9AE. Tel: 071-499 8567. *Administrator*, R. Montgomery

MUSIC SOCIETIES, NATIONAL FEDERATION OF (1935), Francis House, Francis Street, London SW1P 1DE. Tel: 071-828 7320. *Director*, R. Jones

MYALGIC ENCEPHALOMYELITIS ASSOCIATION (1976), Stanhope House, High Street, Stanford-le-Hope, Essex SS17 0HA. Tel: 0375-642466. *Chief Executive*, Ms V. Airs

NACRO (NATIONAL ASSOCIATION FOR THE CARE AND RESETTLEMENT OF OFFENDERS) (1966), 169 Clapham Road, London SW9 0PU. Tel: 071-582 6500. *Director*, Ms V. Stern

NATIONAL AND UNIVERSITY LIBRARIES, STANDING CONFERENCE OF (SCONUL) (1950), 102 Euston Street, London NW1 2HA. Tel: 071-387 0317. *Secretary*, Miss G. M. Pentelow

NATIONAL BENEVOLENT INSTITUTION (1812), 61 Bayswater Road, London W2 3PG. Tel: 071-723 0021. *Secretary*, Gp Capt D. St J. Homer, MVO

NATIONAL COUNCIL FOR VOLUNTARY ORGANIZATIONS (1919), Regent's Wharf, 8 All Saints Street, London N1 9RL. Tel: 071-713 6161. *Director*, Ms J. Weleminsky

NATIONAL COUNCIL OF WOMEN OF GREAT BRITAIN (1895), 36 Danbury Street, London N1 8JU. Tel: 071-354 2395. *President*, Mrs P. Purdy

NATIONAL LISTENING LIBRARY, 12 Lant Street, London SE1 1QH. Tel: 071-407 9417. *Executive Director*, G. A. Hepworth

NATIONAL SOCIETY, THE, (1811), Church House, Great Smith Street, London SW1P 3NZ. Tel: 071-222 1672. For promoting religious education. *General Secretary*, G. Duncan

NATIONAL SOCIETY FOR THE PREVENTION OF CRUELTY TO CHILDREN (NSPCC) (1884), 67 Saffron Hill, London EC1N 8RS. Tel: 071-242 1626. *Director*, C. Brown

NATIONAL TRUST, THE (1895), 36 Queen Anne's Gate, London SW1H 9AS. Tel: 071-222 9251. *Chairman*, Lord Chorley; *Director-General*, A. Stirling

NATIONAL TRUST FOR SCOTLAND (1931), 5 Charlotte Square, Edinburgh EH2 4DU. Tel: 031-226 5922. *Director*, Rear-Adm. D. Dow, CB

NATIONAL UNION OF STUDENTS (1922), Nelson Mandela House, 461 Holloway Road, London N7 6LJ. Tel: 071-272 8900. *National President*, Ms L. Fitzsimons

NATIONAL VIEWERS' AND LISTENERS' ASSOCIATION (1964), Ardleigh, Colchester CO7 7RH. Tel: 0206-230123. *President*, Mrs M. Whitehouse, CBE

NATIONAL WOMEN'S REGISTER (1960), 9 Bank Plain, Norwich, Norfolk NR2 4SL. Tel: 0603-765392. *National Organizer*, Mrs A. Dickinson

NATION'S FUND FOR NURSES (1917), 3 Albemarle Way, London EC1V 4JB. Tel: 071-490 4227. *Administrator*, Mrs P. Bagnall

NATURALISTS' ASSOCIATION, BRITISH (1905), 1 Bracken Mews, Chingford, London E4 7HE. *Hon. Membership Secretary*, Mrs Y. H. Griffiths

NATURE CONSERVATION, ROYAL SOCIETY FOR, *see* RSNC

NAUTICAL RESEARCH, SOCIETY FOR (1911), c/o National Maritime Museum, Greenwich, London SE10 9NF. Tel: 071-873 2139. *Hon. Secretary*, D. G. Law

NAVAL, MILITARY AND AIR FORCE BIBLE SOCIETY (1780), Radstock House, 3 Eccleston Street, London SW1W 9LZ. Tel: 071-730 2155. *General Secretary*, R. Kennedy

NAVAL ARCHITECTS, ROYAL INSTITUTION OF (1860), 10 Upper Belgrave Street, London SW1X 8BQ. Tel: 071-235 4622. *Secretary*, J. Rosewarn

NAVIGATION, ROYAL INSTITUTE OF (1947), 1 Kensington Gore, London SW7 2AT. Tel: 071-589 5021. *Director*, Gp Capt D. W. Broughton, MBE

NAVY RECORDS SOCIETY (1893), c/o Barclays Bank PLC, Murray House, 1 Royal Mint Court, London EC3N 4HH. Tel: 071-382 5400. *Hon. Secretary*, A. J. McMillan

NEEDLEWORK, ROYAL SCHOOL OF (1872), Apartment 12A, Hampton Court Palace, East Molesey, Surrey KT8 9AU. Tel: 081-943 1432. *Principal*, Mrs E. Elvin

NEWCOMEN SOCIETY (1920), The Science Museum, London SW7 2DD. Tel: 071-589 1793. For the study of the history of engineering and technology. *Executive Secretary*, C. Ellam

NEWSPAPER EDITORS, GUILD OF BRITISH (1946), Bloomsbury House, Bloomsbury Square, 74–77 Great Russell Street, London WC1B 3DA. Tel: 071-636 7014. *Secretary*, Ms V. L. Hird

NEWSPAPER PRESS FUND (1864), Dickens House, 35 Wathen Road, Dorking, Surrey RH4 1JY. Tel: 0306-887511. *Director*, P. W. Evans

NEWSVENDORS' BENEVOLENT INSTITUTION (1839), PO Box 306, Dunmow, Essex CM6 1HY. Tel: 0371-874198. *Director*, B. Buckingham

NOISE ABATEMENT SOCIETY (1959), PO Box 8, Bromley, Kent BR2 0UH. Tel: 081-460 3146. *Chairman*, J. Connell, OBE

NON-SMOKERS, NATIONAL SOCIETY OF, *see* QUIT

NORWOOD CHILD CARE (1795), Norwood House, Harmony Way, Victoria Road, London NW4 2DR. Tel: 081-203 3030. *Executive Director*, S. Brier

NOTARIES' SOCIETY (1907), 7 Lower Brook Street, Ipswich IP4 1AF. Tel: 0473-214762. *Secretary*, A. G. Dunford

NUCLEAR ENERGY SOCIETY, BRITISH (1962), 1–7 Great George Street, London SW1P 3AA. Tel: 071-222 7722. *Executive Officer*, P. Bacos

NUFFIELD FOUNDATION (1943), 28 Bedford Square, London WC1B 3EG. Tel: 071-631 0566. *Director*, R. Hazell

NUFFIELD PROVINCIAL HOSPITALS TRUST (1939), 59 New Cavendish Street, London W1M 7RD. Tel: 071-485 6632. *Secretary*, Dr M. Ashley-Miller

NUMISMATIC SOCIETY, BRITISH (1903), c/o Royal Mint, Llantrisant, Pontyclun, Mid Glamorgan CF7 8YT. Tel: 0443-222111, ext. 521. *Hon. Secretary*, G. P. Dyer

NUMISMATIC SOCIETY, ROYAL (1836), c/o Department of Coins and Medals, The British Museum, Great Russell Street, London WC1B 3DG. Tel: 071-323 8585. *Hon. Secretaries*, J. E. Cribb; R. G. Bland

NURSES' NATIONAL HOME, RETIRED (1934), Riverside Avenue, Bournemouth BH7 7EE. Tel: 0202-396418. *Chairman*, G. J. Rowlett

NURSES, ROYAL NATIONAL PENSION FUND FOR, Burdett House, 15 Buckingham Street, London WC2N 6ED. Tel: 071-839 6785. *General Manager*, V. G. West

NURSING, MIDWIFERY AND HEALTH VISITING, UK CENTRAL COUNCIL FOR, 23 Portland Place, London W1N 3AF. Tel: 071-637 7181. *Registrar and Chief Executive*, C. Ralph

NURSING, MIDWIFERY AND HEALTH VISITING, ENGLISH NATIONAL BOARD FOR, Victory House, 170 Tottenham Court Road, London W1P 0HA. Tel: 071-388 3131. *Chief Executive Officer*, A. P. Smith

NURSING, MIDWIFERY AND HEALTH VISITING, WELSH NATIONAL BOARD FOR, Floor 13, Pearl Assurance House, Greyfriars Road, Cardiff CF1 3AG. Tel: 0222-395535. *Chief Executive*, D. A. Ravey

NURSING, MIDWIFERY AND HEALTH VISITING FOR SCOTLAND, NATIONAL BOARD FOR, 22 Queen Street, Edinburgh EH2 1JX. Tel: 031-226 7371. *Chief Executive*, Mrs L. Mitchell

NURSING, MIDWIFERY AND HEALTH VISITING FOR NORTHERN IRELAND, NATIONAL BOARD FOR, RAC House, 79 Chichester Street, Belfast BT1 4JE. Tel: 0232-238152. *Chief Executive*, Dr O. D'A. Slevin

NURSING, ROYAL COLLEGE OF (1916), 20 Cavendish Square, London W1M 0AB. Tel: 071-409 3333. *General Secretary*, Miss C. Hancock

NUTRITION FOUNDATION, BRITISH (1967), 15 Belgrave Square, London SW1X 8PG. Tel: 071-235 4904. *Director-General*, Dr D. M. Conning

NUTRITION SOCIETY (1941), 10 Cambridge Court, 210 Shepherds Bush Road, London W6 7NJ. Tel: 071-602 0228. *Hon. Secretary*, Dr R. F. Grimble

OBSTETRICIANS AND GYNAECOLOGISTS, ROYAL COLLEGE OF (1929), 27 Sussex Place, London NW1 4RG. Tel: 071-262 5425. *Secretary*, Prof. W. Dunlop, FRCOG

OCCUPATIONAL PENSIONS ADVISORY SERVICE (1982), 11 Belgrave Road, London SW1V 1RB. Tel: 071-233 8080. *Chief Executive*, D. Hall

OCCUPATIONAL SAFETY AND HEALTH, INSTITUTION OF (1946), 222 Uppingham Road, Leicester LE5 0QG. Tel: 0533-768424. *Chief Executive*, J. R. Barrell

OFFICERS' ASSOCIATION, THE (1920), 48 Pall Mall, London SW1Y 5JY. Tel: 071-930 0125. *General Secretary*, Brig. P. D. Johnson

OFFICERS' PENSIONS SOCIETY LTD (1946), 68 South Lambeth Road, London SW8 1RL. Tel: 071-820 9988. *General Secretary*, Maj.-Gen. Sir Laurence New, CB, CBE

OIL PAINTERS, ROYAL INSTITUTE OF (1883), 17 Carlton House Terrace, London SW1Y 5BD. Tel: 071-930 6844. *Secretary*, Ms O. Tarrant

OILSEED, OIL AND FEEDINGSTUFFS TRADES BENEVOLENT ASSOCIATION, 14–20 St. Mary Axe, London EC3A 8BU. Tel: 071-623 5501. *Secretary*, D. A. Painter

ONE PARENT FAMILIES, NATIONAL COUNCIL FOR, 255 Kentish Town Road, London NW5 2LX. Tel: 071-267 1361. *Director*, Miss S. Slipman

OPEN-AIR MISSION, THE (1853), 19 John Street, London WC1N 2DL. Tel: 071-405 6135. *Secretary*, A. J. Greenbank

OPEN SPACES SOCIETY (1865), 25A Bell Street, Henley-on-Thames, Oxon. RG9 2BA. Tel: 0491-573535. *General Secretary*, Miss K. Ashbrook

OPERATIC AND DRAMATIC ASSOCIATION, NATIONAL (1899), NODA House, 1 Crestfield Street, London WC1H 8AU. Tel: 071-837 5655. *General Administrator*, M. Thorburn

OPTICAL COUNCIL, GENERAL (1958), 41 Harley Street, London W1N 2DJ. Tel: 071-580 3898. *Registrar*, R. Wilshin

OPTOMETRISTS, BRITISH COLLEGE OF, 10 Knaresborough Place, London SW5 0TG. Tel: 071-373 7765. *General Secretary*, P. D. Leigh

ORDERS AND MEDALS RESEARCH SOCIETY (1942), 123 Turnpike Link, Croydon CR0 5NU. Tel: 081-680 2701. *General Secretary*, N. G. Gooding

ORIENTAL CERAMIC SOCIETY (1921), 31B Torrington Square, London WC1E 7LJ. Tel: 071-636 7985. *Secretary*, Mrs J. Martin

ORNITHOLOGISTS' CLUB, SCOTTISH (1936), 21 Regent Terrace, Edinburgh EH7 5BT. Tel: 031-556 6042. *Administrator*, M. H. Murphy

ORNITHOLOGISTS' UNION, BRITISH (1858), c/o Natural History Museum, Sub-department of Ornithology, Tring, Herts. HP23 6AP. Tel: 0442-890080. *Administrative Secretary*, Mrs G. Bonham

ORNITHOLOGY, BRITISH TRUST FOR (1932) National Centre for Ornithology, The Nunnery, Thetford, Norfolk IP24 2PU. Tel: 0842-750050. *Director of Services*, A. Elvin

ORTHOPAEDIC ASSOCIATION, BRITISH (1918), c/o The Royal College of Surgeons, 35–43 Lincoln's Inn Fields, London WC2A 3PN. Tel: 071-405 6507. *Hon. Secretary*, M. K. d'A. Benson, FRCS

OSTEOPATHIC MEDICINE, LONDON COLLEGE OF, 8–10 Boston Place, London NW1 6QH

OSTEOPOROSIS SOCIETY, NATIONAL (1986), PO Box 10, Radstock, Bath BA3 3YB. *General Secretary*, Ms V. Collier

OUTWARD BOUND TRUST LTD (1941), Chestnut Field, Regent Place, Rugby, Warks. CV21 2PJ. Tel: 0788-560423. *Director*, I. L. Fothergill

OVERSEAS DEVELOPMENT INSTITUTE (1960), Regent's College, Inner Circle, Regent's Park, London NW1 4NS. Tel: 071-487 7413. *Director*, Dr J. Howell

OVERSEAS SERVICE PENSIONERS' ASSOCIATION (1960), 138 High Street, Tonbridge, Kent TN9 1AX. Tel: 0732-363836. *Secretary*, D. LeBreton, CBE

OVERSEAS SETTLEMENT (1925), Church of England Board for Social Responsibility, Great Smith Street, London SW1P 3NZ. Tel: 071-222 9011. *Administration Secretary*, Miss P. J. Hallett

OXFAM (1942), 274 Banbury Road, Oxford OX2 7DZ. Tel: 0865-311311. *Director*, D. Bryer

OXFORD PRESERVATION TRUST (1927), 10 Turn Again Lane, St Ebbes, Oxford OX1 1QL. Tel: 0865-242918. *Secretary*, Mrs M. Haynes

OXFORD SOCIETY (1932), 41 Wellington Square, Oxford OX1 2JF. Tel: 0865-270088. *Secretary*, Dr H. A. Hurren

PAEDIATRIC ASSOCIATION, BRITISH (1928), 5 St Andrew's Place, London NW1 4LB. Tel: 071-486 6151. *Hon. Secretary*, Dr R. MacFaul

PAINTER-PRINTMAKERS, ROYAL SOCIETY OF (1880), Bankside Gallery, 48 Hopton Street, London SE1 9JH. Tel: 071-928 7521. *Secretary*, J. Winkelman

PAINTERS IN WATER COLOURS, ROYAL INSTITUTE OF (1831), 17 Carlton House Terrace, London SW1Y 5BD. Tel: 071-930 6844. *Secretary*, R. Spurrier

PALAEONTOGRAPHICAL SOCIETY (1847) c/o British Geological Survey, Keyworth, Nottingham NG12 5GG. *Secretary*, S. P. Tunnicliff

PALAEONTOLOGICAL ASSOCIATION (1957), c/o British Antarctic Survey, High Cross, Madingley Road, Cambridge CB3 0ET. Tel: 0223-61188, ext. 261. *Secretary*, Dr J. A. Crame

PARKINSON'S DISEASE SOCIETY (1969), 22 Upper Woburn Place, London WC1H 0RA. Tel: 071-383 3513. *Chief Executive*, M. Whelan

PARLIAMENTARY AND SCIENTIFIC COMMITTEE (1939), 16 Great College Street, London SW1P 3RX. Tel: 071-222 7085. *Secretary*, A. Butler

PASTORAL PSYCHOLOGY, GUILD OF (1936), PO Box 1107, London W3 6ZP. Tel: 081-993 8366. *Administrator*, Mrs N. Stanley

PATENT AGENTS, CHARTERED INSTITUTE OF (1882), Staple Inn Buildings, High Holborn, London WC1V 7PZ. Tel: 071-405 9450. *Secretary*, M. C. Ralph

PATENTEES AND INVENTORS, INSTITUTE OF (1919), Suite 505A, Triumph House, 189 Regent Street, London W1R 7WF. Tel: 071-242 7812. *Secretary*, R. Magnus

PATHOLOGISTS, ROYAL COLLEGE OF, 2 Carlton House Terrace, London SW1Y 5AF. Tel: 071-930 5863. *Secretary*, K. Lockyer

PATIENTS ASSOCIATION (1963), 18 Victoria Park Square, London E2 9PF. Tel: 081-981 5676. *Director*, Mrs L. Lamont

PEACE COUNCIL, NATIONAL (1908), 88 Islington High Street, London N1 8EG. Tel: 071-354 5200. *Co-ordinator*, A. McLeod

PEAK AND NORTHERN FOOTPATHS SOCIETY (1894), 15 Parkfield Drive, Tyldesley, Manchester M29 8NR. Tel: 061-790 4383. *Hon. General Secretary*, D. Taylor

PEARSON'S HOLIDAY FUND, THE, Bishops Waltham, Hants SO3 1ZE. Tel: 0489-893260. *General Secretary*, R. Heasman

PEDESTRIANS ASSOCIATION (1929), 126 Aldersgate Street, London EC1A 4JQ. Tel: 071-490 0750. *Chairman*, Ms F. Lawson

PEN, INTERNATIONAL (1921), 9–10 Charterhouse Buildings, Goswell Road, London EC1M 7AT. Tel: 071-253 4308. World association of writers. *International Secretary*, A. Blokh

PENSION FUNDS LTD, NATIONAL ASSOCIATION OF (1923), 12–18 Grosvenor Gardens, London SW1W 0DH. Tel: 071-730 0585. *Director-General*, M. A. Elton

PEOPLE'S DISPENSARY FOR SICK ANIMALS (PDSA) (1917), Whitechapel Way, Priorslee, Telford, Shropshire TF2 9PQ. Tel: 0952-290999. *Director-General*, M. R. Curtis, MBE

PERFORMING RIGHT SOCIETY LTD (1914), 29–33 Berners Street, London W1P 4AA. Tel: 071-580 5544. *Chief Executive*, M. J. Freegard

PERIODICAL PUBLISHERS ASSOCIATION LTD (1913), Imperial House, 15–19 Kingsway, London WC2B 6UN. Tel: 071-379 6268. *Chief Executive*, I. Locks

PESTALOZZI CHILDREN'S VILLAGE TRUST (1959), Sedlescombe, Battle, E. Sussex TN33 0RR. Tel: 0424-870444. *Director*, C. C. Wagstaff

PETROLEUM, INSTITUTE OF (1913), 61 New Cavendish Street, London W1M 8AR. Tel: 071-636 1004. *Director-General*, I. Ward

PHARMACEUTICAL SOCIETY OF GREAT BRITAIN, ROYAL (1841), 1 Lambeth High Street, London SE1 7JN. *Secretary and Registrar*, J. Ferguson

PHARMACOLOGICAL SOCIETY, BRITISH (1931), Medical College, Charterhouse Square, London EC1M 6BQ. Tel: 071-982 6170. *Hon. General Secretary*, Dr J. Maclagan

PHILOLOGICAL SOCIETY (1842), School of Oriental and African Studies, University of London, Thornhaugh Street, London WC1H 0XG. Tel: 071-323 6357. *Hon. Secretary*, Prof. R. J. Hayward

PHILOSOPHY, ROYAL INSTITUTE OF (1925), 14 Gordon Square, London WC1H 0AG. Tel: 071-387 4130. *Director*, Prof. A. Phillips Griffiths

PHOTOGRAPHY, BRITISH INSTITUTE OF PROFESSIONAL (1901), Fox Talbot House, Amwell End, Ware, Herts. SG12 9HN. Tel: 0920-464011. *Chief Executive*, A. M. Berkeley

PHYSICAL RECREATION, CENTRAL COUNCIL OF (1935), Francis House, Francis Street, London SWIP IDE. Tel: 071-828 3163/4. *General Secretary*, P. Lawson

PHYSICIANS, ROYAL COLLEGE OF (1518), 11 St Andrew's Place, London NWI 4LE. Tel: 071-935 1174. *Secretary*, D. B. Lloyd

PHYSICIANS AND SURGEONS OF GLASGOW, ROYAL COLLEGE OF (1599), 234–242 St Vincent Street, Glasgow G2 5RJ. Tel: 041-221 6072. *Hon. Secretary*, Dr B. Williams

PHYSICIANS OF EDINBURGH, ROYAL COLLEGE OF (1681), 9 Queen Street, Edinburgh EH2 1JQ. Tel: 031-225 7324. *Secretary*, Dr J. St J. Thomas

PHYSICS, INSTITUTE OF (1874), 47 Belgrave Square, London SWIX 8QX. Tel: 071-235 6111. *Chief Executive*, Dr A. Jones

PHYSIOLOGICAL SOCIETY (1876), PO Box 506, Oxford OXI 3XE. Tel: 0865-798498. *Hon. Secretary*, Dr C. A. R. Boyd

PHYSIOTHERAPY, CHARTERED SOCIETY OF (1894), 14 Bedford Row, London WCIR 4ED. Tel: 071-242 1941. *Secretary*, T. Simon

PIG ASSOCIATION, BRITISH (1884), 7 Rickmansworth Road, Watford, Herts. WDI 7HE. Tel: 0923-234377. *Chief Executive*, G. E. Welsh

PILGRIM TRUST, THE (1930), Fielden House, Little College Street, London SWIP 3SH. Tel: 071-222 4723. *Secretary*, Hon. A. Hoyer Millar

PILGRIMS OF GREAT BRITAIN, THE (1902), Savoy Hotel, London WC2R OEU. *Hon. Secretary*, M. P. S. Barton

PLANT ENGINEERS, INSTITUTION OF, 77 Great Peter Street, London SWIP 2EZ. Tel: 071-233 2855. *Secretary-General*, R. S. Pratt

PLAYING CARD SOCIETY, INTERNATIONAL (1972), 188 Sheen Lane, London SW14 8LF. *Secretary*, C. C. Rayner

PLAYING FIELDS ASSOCIATION, NATIONAL (1925), 25 Ovington Square, London SW3 ILQ. Tel: 071-584 6445. *Director*, Ms E. Davies

POETRY SOCIETY, THE (1909), 22 Betterton Street, London WC2H 9BU. Tel: 071-240 4810. *Director and General Secretary*, C. Green

POLICY STUDIES INSTITUTE (1978), 100 Park Village East, London NWI 3SR. Tel: 071-387 2171. *Director*, Ms P. Meadows

POLIO FELLOWSHIP, BRITISH (1939), Bell Close, West End Road, Ruislip, Middx. HA4 6LP. Tel: 0895-675515. *General Secretary*, M. Drake

PORTRAIT PAINTERS, ROYAL SOCIETY OF (1891), 17 Carlton House Terrace, London SWIY 5BD. Tel: 071-930 6844. *Secretary*, J. Stultiens

POST OFFICE USERS' NATIONAL COUNCIL (1970), Waterloo Bridge House, Waterloo Road, London SEI 8UA. Tel: 071-928 9458. *Secretary*, K. Hall

POULTRY CLUB OF GREAT BRITAIN, THE (1877). *General Secretary*, Mrs E. A. Aubrey-Fletcher, Cliveden, Sandy Bank Farm, Chipping, Preston, Lancs. PR3 2GA

PRAYER BOOK SOCIETY, THE (1975), St James Garlickhythe, Garlick Hill, London EC4V 2AL. Tel: 081-958 8769. *Hon. Secretary*, Mrs. M. Thompson

PRECEPTORS, COLLEGE OF (1846), Coppice Row, Theydon Bois, Epping, Essex CMI6 7DN. Tel: 0992-812727. *Chief Executive Officer*, T. Wheatley

PRE-SCHOOL PLAYGROUPS ASSOCIATION, 61–63 Kings Cross Road, London WCIX 9LL. Tel: 071-833 0991. *Chief Executive Officer*, Ms M. Lochrie

PRESS UNION, COMMONWEALTH (1909), Studio House, 184 Fleet Street, London EC4A 2DU. Tel: 071-242 1056. *Director*, R. MacKichan

PREVENTION OF ACCIDENTS, ROYAL SOCIETY FOR THE (1916), Cannon House, Priory Queensway, Birmingham B4 6BS. Tel: 021-200 2461. *Chief Executive*, A. Edwards

PRINCESS LOUISE SCOTTISH HOSPITAL (Erskine Hospital) (1916), Bishopton, Renfrewshire PA7 5PU. Tel: 041-812 1100. For disabled ex-servicemen and women. *Commandant*, Col. W. K. Shepherd

PRINCESS ROYAL TRUST FOR CARERS (1990), 16 Byward Street, London EC3R 5BA. *Chief Executive*, Dr E. Nelson

PRINCE'S SCOTTISH YOUTH BUSINESS TRUST, THE (1989), 6th Floor, Mercantile Chambers, 53 Bothwell Street, Glasgow G2 6TS. Tel: 041-248 4999. *Director*, D. W. Cooper

PRINCE'S TRUST, THE (1976) and THE ROYAL JUBILEE TRUSTS (1935, 1977), 8 Bedford Row, London WCIR 4BA. Tel: 071-430 0524. *Director*, T. Shebbeare

PRINCE'S YOUTH BUSINESS TRUST, THE, 5 Cleveland Place, London SWIY 6JJ. Tel: 071-321 6500. *Chief Executive*, J. Pervin

PRINTERS' CHARITABLE CORPORATION (1827), Victoria House, Harestone Valley Road, Caterham, Surrey CR3 6HY. Tel: 0883-345331. *Director*, H. J. Court

PRINTING HISTORICAL SOCIETY (1964), St Bride Institute, Bride Lane, London EC4Y 8EE. *Hon. Secretary*, Dr M. Smith

PRINTING, INSTITUTE OF (1961), 8 Lonsdale Gardens, Tunbridge Wells, Kent TNI INU. Tel: 0892-538118. *Secretary-General*, C. F. Partridge

PRISONERS ABROAD (1978), 72–82 Rosebery Avenue, London ECIR 4RR. Tel: 071-833 3467. *Director*, K. Best

PRISON VISITORS, NATIONAL ASSOCIATION OF (1922), 46B Hartington Street, Bedford MK41 7RP. Tel: 0234-359763. *General Secretary*, Mrs A. G. McKenna

PRIVATE LIBRARIES ASSOCIATION (1957), Ravelston, South View Road, Pinner, Middx. HA5 3YD. *Hon. Secretary*, F. Broomhead

PROCURATORS IN GLASGOW, ROYAL FACULTY OF (1600), 12 Nelson Mandela Place, Glasgow G2 1BT. Tel: 041-204 3213. *Clerk*, J. H. Sinclair

PROFESSIONAL CLASSES AID COUNCIL (1921), 10 St Christopher's Place, London WIM 6HY. Tel: 071-935 0641. *Secretary*

PROFESSIONAL ENGINEERS, UK ASSOCIATION OF (1969), Hayes Court, West Common Road, Bromley BR2 7AU. Tel: 081-462 7755. *National Secretary*, J. M. Dalgleish

PROFESSIONAL FOOTBALLERS' ASSOCIATION, 2 Oxford Court, Bishopsgate, Manchester M2 3WQ. Tel: 061-236 0575. *Chief Executive*, G. Taylor

PROFESSIONS SUPPLEMENTARY TO MEDICINE, THE COUNCIL FOR, Park House, 184 Kennington Park Road, London SEII 4BU. Tel: 071-582 0866. *Registrar*, R. Pickis

PROTECTION OF THE UNBORN CHILD, SOCIETY FOR THE (1967), 7 Tufton Street, London SWIP 3QN. Tel: 071-222 5845. *Director*, Mrs P. Bowman

PROTESTANT ALLIANCE, THE (1845), 77 Ampthill Road, Flitwick, Bedford MK45 1BD. Tel: 0525-712348. *General Secretary,* Dr S. J. Scott-Pearson

PSORIASIS ASSOCIATION (1968), 7 Milton Street, Northampton NN2 7JG. Tel: 0604-711129. *National Secretary,* Mrs L. Henley

PSYCHIATRISTS, ROYAL COLLEGE OF (1971), 17 Belgrave Square, London SW1X 8PG. Tel: 071-235 2351. *Secretary,* Mrs V. Cameron

PSYCHICAL RESEARCH, SOCIETY FOR (1882), 49 Marloes Road, London W8 6LA. Tel: 071-937 8984. *President,* Prof. A. E. Roy

PSYCHOLOGICAL SOCIETY, BRITISH (1901), St Andrews House, 48 Princess Road East, Leicester LE1 7DR. Tel: 0533-549568. *Executive Secretary,* C. V. Newman, PH.D.

PUBLIC FINANCE AND ACCOUNTANCY, CHARTERED INSTITUTE OF (1885), 3 Robert Street, London WC2N 6BH. Tel: 071-895 8823. *Director,* N. P. Hepworth, OBE

PUBLIC HEALTH AND HYGIENE, ROYAL INSTITUTE OF (1937), 28 Portland Place, London WIN 4DE. Tel: 071-580 2731. *Secretary,* R. A. Smith

PUBLIC RELATIONS, INSTITUTE OF (1948), The Old Trading House, 15 Northburgh Street, London EC1V OPR. Tel: 071-253 5151. *Executive Director,* J. B. Lavelle

PUBLIC TEACHERS OF LAW, SOCIETY OF (1908), All Souls College, Oxford OX1 4AL. Tel: 0865-279379. *Hon. Secretary,* Prof. P. B. H. Birks

PURCHASING AND SUPPLY, CHARTERED INSTITUTE OF (1967), Easton House, Easton on the Hill, Stamford, Lincs. PE9 3NZ. Tel: 0780-56777. *Director-General,* P. Thomson

PURE WATER ASSOCIATION, NATIONAL (1960), Meridan, Cae Goody Lane, Ellesmere, Shrops. SY12 9DW. Tel: 0691-623015. *Secretary,* N. Brugge

QUAKER SOCIAL RESPONSIBILITY AND EDUCATION, Friends House, Euston Road, London NW1 2BJ. Tel: 071-387 3601. *General Secretary,* Ms B. Smith

QUALITY ASSURANCE, INSTITUTE OF, PO Box 712, 61 Southwark Street, London SE1 1SB. Tel: 071-401 7227. *Secretary-General,* D. Campbell

QUARRIER'S HOMES (1871), Bridge of Weir, Renfrewshire PA11 3SA. Tel: 0505-612224. *Director of Social Work,* G. E. Lee

QUARRYING, INSTITUTE OF (1917), 7 Regent Street, Nottingham NG1 5BY. Tel: 0602-411315. *Secretary,* M. J. Arthur

QUEEN ELIZABETH'S FOUNDATION FOR DISABLED PEOPLE (1967), Leatherhead Court, Leatherhead, Surrey KT22 OBN. Tel: 0372-842204. *Director,* M. B. Clark, PH.D.

QUEEN VICTORIA CLERGY FUND (1897), Church House, Dean's Yard, London SW1P 3NZ. Tel: 071-222 5261. *Secretary,* C. D. L. Menzies

QUEEN VICTORIA SCHOOL (1908), Dunblane, Perthshire FK15 OJY. Tel: 0786-822288. *Headmaster,* J. D. Hankinson

QUEEN'S ENGLISH SOCIETY, THE (1972), 104 Drive Mansions, Fulham Road, London SW6 5JH. Tel: 071-371 7530. *Hon. Membership Secretary,* M. Plumbe

QUEEN'S NURSING INSTITUTE (1887), 3 Albemarle Way, London EC1V 4JB. Tel: 071-490 4227. *Director,* Mrs P. Bagnall

QUEKETT MICROSCOPICAL CLUB (1865). *Hon. Business Secretary,* B. Scott, 237 Petts Hill, Northolt, Middx. UB5 4NR

QUIT (NATIONAL SOCIETY OF NON-SMOKERS) (1926), 102 Gloucester Place, London W1H 3DA. Tel: 071-487 2858. *Director,* Ms S. Wilson

RADAR (ROYAL ASSOCIATION FOR DISABILITY AND REHABILITATION) (1977), 25 Mortimer Street, London WIN 8AB. Tel: 071-637 5400. *Director,* B. Massie, OBE

RADIOLOGISTS, ROYAL COLLEGE OF (1934), 38 Portland Place, London WIN 3DG. Tel: 071-636 4432. *Secretary,* A. J. Cowles

RADIOLOGY, BRITISH INSTITUTE OF (1897), 36 Portland Place, London WIN 4AT. Tel: 071-580 4085. *Chief Executive,* Ms M. A. Piggott

RAILWAY AND CANAL HISTORICAL SOCIETY, 17 Clumber Crescent North, The Park, Nottingham NG7 1EY. Tel: 0602-414844. *Hon. Secretary,* G. H. R. Gwatkin

RAILWAY BENEVOLENT INSTITUTION (1858), 67 Ashbourne Road, Derby DE22 3FS. Tel: 0332-363067. *Director,* R. B. Boiling

RAINER FOUNDATION (1876), 89 Blackheath Hill, London SE10 8TJ. Tel: 081-694 9497. Provides community-based services for young people who are homeless, offending or in difficulty with their families. *Director,* Dr R. Kay

RAMBLERS' ASSOCIATION (1935), 1–5 Wandsworth Road, London SW8 2XX. Tel: 071-582 6878. *Director,* A. Mattingly

RANFURLY LIBRARY SERVICE (1954), 2 Coldharbour Place, 39–41 Coldharbour Lane, London SE5 9NR. Tel: 071-733 3577. *Director,* Mrs S. Harrity

RARE BREEDS SURVIVAL TRUST (1973), National Agricultural Centre, Kenilworth, Warks. CV8 2LG. Tel: 0203-696551. *Executive Director,* L. Alderson

RATHBONE SOCIETY, THE (1919), 1st Floor, Princess House, 105–107 Princess Street, Manchester M1 6DD. Tel: 061-236 5358. Helps people with learning difficulties. *Chief Executive,* Ms A. Weinstock, CBE

RECORD SOCIETY, SCOTTISH (1897), Department of Scottish History, University of Glasgow, Glasgow G12 8QH. Tel: 041-339 8855, ext. 5682. *Hon. Secretary,* J. Kirk, PH.D.

RECORDS ASSOCIATION, BRITISH (1932), 18 Padbury Court, London E2 7EH. Tel: 071-729 1415. *Secretary,* T. Davies

RED CROSS SOCIETY, BRITISH, *see* BRITISH RED CROSS

RED POLL CATTLE SOCIETY (1888), The Market Hill, Woodbridge, Suffolk IP12 4LU. Tel: 0394-380643. *Secretary,* P. Ryder-Davies

REFRIGERATION, INSTITUTE OF (1899), Kelvin House, 76 Mill Lane, Carshalton, Surrey SM5 2JR. Tel: 081-647 7033. *Secretary,* M. J. Horlick

REFUGEE COUNCIL, BRITISH (1981), Bondway House, 3–9 Bondway, London SW8 1SJ. Tel: 071-582 6922. *Director,* A. Dubs

REGIONAL STUDIES ASSOCIATION (1965), Wharfdale Projects, 15 Micawber Street, London N1 7TB. Tel: 071-490 1128. *Director,* Mrs S. Hardy

REGULAR FORCES EMPLOYMENT ASSOCIATION (1885), 25 Bloomsbury Square, London WC1A 2LN. Tel: 071-637 3918. *General Manager,* Maj.-Gen. D. T. Crabtree, CB

RELATE: NATIONAL MARRIAGE GUIDANCE (1938), Herbert Gray College, Little Church Street, Rugby, Warks. CV21 3AP. Tel: 0788-573241. *Director,* D. French

RENT OFFICERS, INSTITUTE OF (1966), Beaufort House, Hamble Lane, Bursledon, Southampton SO3 8BR. Tel: 0703-403716. *Hon. Secretary*, A. E. Corcoran

RESEARCH DEFENCE SOCIETY (1908), 58 Great Marlborough Street, London W1V 1DD. Tel: 071-287 2818. *Executive Director*, Dr M. Matfield

RESIDENTS' ASSOCIATIONS, NATIONAL UNION OF (1921). *Hon. General Secretary*, Mrs B. Reith, 35 Clement Way, Upminster, Essex RM14 2NX

RETIREMENT PENSIONS ASSOCIATIONS, NATIONAL FEDERATION OF (1938), 14 St Peter Street, Blackburn BB2 2HD. Tel: 0254-52606. *General Secretary*, R. Stansfield

REVENUES, RATING AND VALUATION, INSTITUTE OF (1882), 41 Doughty Street, London WCIN 2LF. Tel: 071-831 3505. *Director*, C. Farrington

RICHARD III SOCIETY (1924), 4 Oakley Street, London SW3 5NN. *Secretary*, Miss E. M. Nokes

ROAD SAFETY OFFICERS, INSTITUTE OF (1971), 31 Heather Grove, Hollingworth, via Hyde, Cheshire SK14 8JL. Tel: 061-474 4876. *Secretary*, B. Wilkinson

ROAD TRANSPORT ENGINEERS, INSTITUTE OF (1945), 1 Cromwell Place, London SW7 2JF. Tel: 071-589 3744. *Executive Secretary*, A. F. Stroud

ROMAN STUDIES, SOCIETY FOR PROMOTION OF (1910), 31–34 Gordon Square, London WCIH OPP. Tel: 071-387 8157. *Secretary*, Dr H. M. Cockle

ROTARY INTERNATIONAL IN GREAT BRITAIN AND IRELAND (1914), Kinwarton Road, Alcester, Warks. B49 6BP. Tel: 0789-765411. *Secretary*, G. S. Large

ROUND TABLES OF GREAT BRITAIN AND IRELAND, NATIONAL ASSOCIATION OF (1927), Marchesi House, 4 Embassy Drive, Calthorpe Road, Edgbaston, Birmingham B15 ITP. Tel: 021-456 4402. *General Secretary*, R. H. Renold

ROYAL AFRICAN SOCIETY (1901), 18 Northumberland Avenue, London WC2N 5BJ. Tel: 071-930 1662. *Secretary*, Mrs L. Allan

ROYAL AIR FORCE BENEVOLENT FUND (1919), 67 Portland Place, London W1N 4AR. Tel: 071-580 8343. *Controller*, Air Chief Marshal Sir Roger Palin, KCB, OBE

ROYAL AIR FORCES ASSOCIATION (1943), 43 Grove Park Road, London W4 3RX. Tel: 081-994 8504. *Secretary-General*, J. G. Hargreaves, CBE

ROYAL ALEXANDRA AND ALBERT SCHOOL (1758), Gatton Park, Reigate, Surrey RH2 OTW. Tel: 0737-642576. *Secretary*, Capt. A. J. Walsh, RN

ROYAL ALFRED SEAFARERS' SOCIETY (1865), Weston Acres, Woodmansterne Lane, Banstead, Surrey SM7 3HB. Tel: 0737-352231. *General Secretary*, A. R. Quinton

ROYAL ARMOURED CORPS WAR MEMORIAL BENEVOLENT FUND (1946), c/o RHQ RTR, Bovington Camp, Wareham, Dorset BH20 6JA. Tel: 0929-403331. *Secretary*, Maj. R. Clooney (retd)

ROYAL ARTILLERY ASSOCIATION, Old Royal Military Academy, Artillery House, Woolwich, London SE18 4DN. Tel: 081-319 4052. *General Secretary*, Lt.-Col. M. J. Darmody

ROYAL ASIATIC SOCIETY (1823), 60 Queen's Gardens, London W2 3AF. Tel: 071-724 4741/2. *Secretary*, Miss L. Collins

ROYAL BRITISH LEGION, *see* BRITISH LEGION, ROYAL

ROYAL CALEDONIAN SCHOOLS (1815), Aldenham Road, Bushey, Watford, Herts. WD2 3TS. Tel: 0923-226642. *Master*, Capt. D. F. Watts, RN

ROYAL CELTIC SOCIETY (1820), 23 Rutland Street, Edinburgh EH1 2RN. Tel: 031-228 6449. *Secretary*, J. G. Cameron, WS

ROYAL CHORAL SOCIETY (1871), 8 Wendell Road, London W12 9RT. Tel: 081-740 4273. *General Manager*, M. Heyland

ROYAL ENGINEERS ASSOCIATION, RHQ Royal Engineers, Brompton Barracks, Chatham, Kent ME4 4UG. Tel: 0634-847005. *Controller*, Lt.-Col. J. W. Ray

ROYAL ENGINEERS, INSTITUTION OF (1875), Brompton Barracks, Chatham, Kent ME4 4UG. Tel: 0634-842669. *Secretary*, Col. R. I. Reive, OBE

ROYAL HIGHLAND AND AGRICULTURAL SOCIETY OF SCOTLAND (1784), Royal Highland Centre, Ingliston, Edinburgh EH28 8NF. Tel: 031-333 2444. *Secretary*, J. R. Good

ROYAL HORTICULTURAL SOCIETY (1804), PO Box 313, 80 Vincent Square, London SW1P 2PE. Tel: 071-834 4333. *Secretary*, D. P. Hearn

ROYAL HOSPITAL AND HOME, PUTNEY (1854), West Hill, London SW15 3SW. Tel: 081-788 4511. *Chief Executive*, Brig. V. J. Beauchamp

ROYAL HUMANE SOCIETY (1774), Brettenham House, Lancaster Place, London WC2E 7EP. Tel: 071-836 8155. *Secretary*, Maj. A. J. Dickinson

ROYAL INSTITUTION, THE (1799), 21 Albemarle Street, London W1X 4BS. Tel: 071-409 2992. *Director*, Prof. P. Day, FRS

ROYAL LIFE SAVING SOCIETY UK (1891), Mountbatten House, Studley, Warks. B80 7NN. Tel: 0527-853943. *Director*, Ms C. J. Godsall

ROYAL LITERARY FUND (1790), 144 Temple Chambers, Temple Avenue, London EC4Y ODA. Tel: 071-353 7150. *Secretary*, Mrs F. M. Clark

ROYAL MEDICAL BENEVOLENT FUND (1836), 24 King's Road, London SW19 8QN. Tel: 081-540 9194. *Secretary*, Mrs G. A. R. Wells

ROYAL MEDICAL SOCIETY (1737), Students Centre, 5/5 Bristo Square, Edinburgh EH8 9AL. Tel: 031-650 2672. *Secretary*, G. Robertson

ROYAL MICROSCOPICAL SOCIETY (1839), 37–38 St Clements, Oxford OX4 1AJ. Tel: 0865-248768. *Administrator*, P. B. Hirst

ROYAL MUSICAL ASSOCIATION (1874), Faculty of Music, St Aldates, Oxford OX1 1DB. Tel: 0865-276125. *Secretary*, E. West

ROYAL NATIONAL INSTITUTE FOR THE BLIND (1868), 224 Great Portland Street, London W1N 6AA. Tel: 071-388 1266. *Director-General*, I. Bruce

ROYAL NATIONAL LIFEBOAT INSTITUTION (1824), West Quay Road, Poole, Dorset BH15 1HZ. Tel: 0202-671133. *Director*, Lt.-Cdr. B. Miles, RD

ROYAL NAVAL AND ROYAL MARINES CHILDREN'S TRUST (1834), HMS *Nelson*, Portsmouth, POI 3HH. Tel: 0705-817435. *Secretary*, Mrs M. Bateman

ROYAL NAVAL ASSOCIATION (1950), 82 Chelsea Manor Street, London SW3 5QJ. Tel: 071-352 6764. *General Secretary*, Capt. J. W. Rayner, RMR

ROYAL NAVAL BENEVOLENT SOCIETY (1739), 1 Fleet Street, London EC4Y IBD. Tel: 071-353 4080. *Secretary*, Cdr P. J. F. Moore, RN

ROYAL NAVAL BENEVOLENT TRUST (1922), 1 High Street, Brompton, Gillingham, Kent ME7 5QZ. Tel: 0634-842743. *General Secretary*, Lt.-Cdr. D. C. Lawrence (retd)

ROYAL NAVY OFFICERS, ASSOCIATION OF (1920), 70 Porchester Terrace, London W2 3TP. Tel: 071-402 5231. *Secretary*, Lt.-Cdr. I. M. P. Coombes

ROYAL OVER-SEAS LEAGUE (1910), Over-Seas House, Park Place, St James's Street, London SW1A 1LR. Tel: 071-408 0214. *Director-General*, R. F. Newell

ROYAL PATRIOTIC FUND CORPORATION (1854), Golden Cross House, Duncannon Street, London WC2N 4JR. Tel: 071-930 9370. *Secretary*, Brig. T. G. Williams, CBE

ROYAL PHILATELIC SOCIETY, THE (1869), 41 Devonshire Place, London W1N 1PE. Tel: 071-486 1044. *Hon. Secretary*, Prof. B. Jay

ROYAL PHOTOGRAPHIC SOCIETY (1853), Milsom Street, Bath BA1 1DN. Tel: 0225-462841. *Secretary*, Mrs A. Nevill

ROYAL PINNER SCHOOL FOUNDATION, 110 Old Brompton Road, London SW7 3RB. Tel: 071-373 6168. *Secretary*, D. Crawford

ROYAL SAILORS' RESTS (1876), 2A South Street, Gosport, Hants. PO12 1ES. Tel: 0705-589551. *General Secretary*, A. A. Lockwood

ROYAL SCOTTISH SOCIETY FOR PREVENTION OF CRUELTY TO CHILDREN (1884), 41 Polwarth Terrace, Edinburgh EH11 1NU. Tel: 031-337 8539. *Chief Executive*, A. M. M. Wood, OBE

ROYAL SIGNALS INSTITUTION (1950), 56 Regency Street, London SW1P 4AD. Tel: 071-414 8421. *Secretary*, Col. A. N. de Bretton-Gordon

ROYAL SOCIETY FOR ASIAN AFFAIRS (1901), 2 Belgrave Square, London SW1X 8PJ. Tel: 071-235 5122. *Secretary*, Miss M. FitzSimons

ROYAL SOCIETY FOR THE ENCOURAGEMENT OF ARTS, MANUFACTURES AND COMMERCE (RSA) (1754), 8 John Adam Street, London WC2N 6EZ. Tel: 071-930 5115. *Director*, C. Lucas

ROYAL SOCIETY FOR THE PREVENTION OF CRUELTY TO ANIMALS (RSPCA) (1824), Causeway, Horsham, W. Sussex RH12 1HG. Tel: 0403-264181. *Director-General*, P. R. Davies, CB

ROYAL SOCIETY FOR THE PROTECTION OF BIRDS (1889), The Lodge, Sandy, Beds. SG19 2DL. Tel: 0767-680551. *Chief Executive*, Ms B. Young

ROYAL SOCIETY OF HEALTH, THE (1876), RSH House, 38 St George's Drive, London SW1V 4BH. Tel: 071-630 0121. *Secretary*, D. Goad

ROYAL SOCIETY OF LITERATURE (1823), 1 Hyde Park Gardens, London W2 2LT. Tel: 071-723 5104. *Secretary*, Ms M. Parham

ROYAL SOCIETY OF MEDICINE (1805), 1 Wimpole Street, London W1M 8AE. Tel: 071-408 2119. *Executive Director*, Dr J. T. Green

ROYAL SOCIETY OF ST GEORGE, (1894), Dartmouth House, 37 Charles Street, London W1X 8AB. Tel: 071-499 5430. *Chairman*, G. Andrews

ROYAL STAR AND GARTER HOME FOR DISABLED SAILORS, SOLDIERS AND AIRMEN (1916), Richmond, Surrey TW10 6RR. Tel: 081-940 3314. *Chief Executive*, I. Lashbrooke

ROYAL STATISTICAL SOCIETY (1834), 25 Enford Street, London W1H 2BH. Tel: 071-723 5882. *Executive Secretary*, I. Goddard

ROYAL TANK REGIMENT BENEVOLENT FUND (1919), RHQ RTR Centre, Bovington Camp, Wareham, Dorset BH20 6JA. Tel: 0929-403331. *Regimental Secretary*, Maj. R. Clooney (retd)

ROYAL TELEVISION SOCIETY (1927), Holborn Hall, 100 Gray's Inn Road, London WC1X 8AL. Tel: 071-430 1000. *Executive Director*, M. Bunce

ROYAL UNITED KINGDOM BENEFICENT ASSOCIATION (1863), 6 Avonmore Road, London W14 8RL. Tel: 071-602 6274. *Director*, W. Rathbone

RSNC (ROYAL SOCIETY FOR NATURE CONSERVATION), THE WILDLIFE TRUSTS PARTNERSHIP (1912), The Green, Witham Park, Lincoln LN5 7JR. Tel: 0522-544400. *Chief Executive*, T. S. Cordy

RURAL ENGLAND, COUNCIL FOR THE PROTECTION OF (CPRE) (1926), Warwick House, 25 Buckingham Palace Road, London SW1W 0PP. Tel: 071-976 6433. *Director*, Ms F. Reynolds

RURAL SCOTLAND, ASSOCIATION FOR THE PROTECTION OF (1926), 3rd Floor, Gladstone's Land, 483 Lawnmarket, Edinburgh EH1 2NT. Tel: 031-225 7012/3. *Director*, Mrs E. J. Garland

RURAL WALES, CAMPAIGN FOR THE PROTECTION OF (1928), Tŷ Gwyn, 31 High Street, Welshpool, Powys SY21 7JP. Tel: 0938-552525/556212. *Director*, Dr N. Caldwell

SAILORS' FAMILIES' SOCIETY, THE (1821), Newland, Hull HU6 7RJ. Tel: 0482-42331. *General Secretary*, G. J. Powell

SAILORS' SOCIETY, BRITISH (1818), 3 Orchard Place, Southampton, SO9 7SS. Tel: 0703-337333. *General Secretary*, G. Chambers

ST DEINIOL'S LIBRARY (1902), Hawarden, Deeside, Clwyd CH5 3DF. Tel: 0244-532350. *Warden and Chief Librarian*, Revd Dr P. J. Jagger

ST DUNSTAN'S, PO Box 4XB, 12–14 Harcourt Street, London W1A 4XB. Tel: 071-723 5021. For men and women blinded in the Services. *Secretary*, W. C. Weisblatt

ST JOHN AMBULANCE (1887), 1 Grosvenor Crescent, London SW1X 7EF. Tel: 071-235 5231. *Executive Director*, T. Gauvain

ST JOSEPH'S SOCIETY FOR THE RELIEF OF THE AGED POOR (1708), St Joseph's House, 42 Brook Green, London W6 7BW. Tel: 071-603 9817. *Secretary*, S. Dolan

SALES AND MARKETING MANAGEMENT, INSTITUTE OF (1966), 31 Upper George Street, Luton LU2 2RD. Tel: 0582-411130. *Director-General*, K. Williams

SALMON AND TROUT ASSOCIATION (1903), Fishmongers' Hall, London Bridge, London EC4R 9EL. Tel: 071-283 5838. *Director*, C. W. Poupard

SALTIRE SOCIETY (1936), 9 Fountain Close, 22 High Street, Edinburgh EH1 1TF. Tel: 031-556 1836. *Administrator*, Mrs K. Munro

SAMARITANS, THE (1953), 10 The Grove, Slough SL1 1QP. Tel: 0735-532713. Telephone numbers in local telephone directories. *Chief Executive*, S. Armson

SAMUEL PEPYS CLUB (1903), 26 Gloucester Street, Faringdon, Oxon. SN7 7HY. *Secretary*, P. L. Gray

SANE: SCHIZOPHRENIA A NATIONAL EMERGENCY (1986), 199–205 Marylebone Road, London NW1 5QP. Tel: 071-724 6520. *Saneline*: 071-724 8000. *Executive Director*, Ms M. Wallace

SAVE BRITAIN'S HERITAGE (1975), 68 Battersea High Street, London SW11 3HX. Tel: 071-228 3336. *Secretary*

SAVE THE CHILDREN FUND, THE (1919), Mary Datchelor House, 17 Grove Lane, London SE5 8RD. Tel: 071-703 5400. *Director-General*, N. J. Hinton, CBE

SCHIZOPHRENIA FELLOWSHIP, NATIONAL (1970), 28 Castle Street, Kingston upon Thames, Surrey KT1 1SS. Tel: 081-547 3937. *Chief Executive*, M. Eede

SCHOOL LIBRARY ASSOCIATION (1937), Liden Library, Barrington Close, Liden, Swindon SN3 6HF. Tel: 0793-617838. *Executive Secretary*, Ms V. Fea

SCHOOLMASTERS, SOCIETY OF (1798), 29 Corrib Court, Fox Lane, London N13 4BG. Tel: 081-882 6825. *Secretary*, Mrs M. S. Freeburn

SCHOOLMISTRESSES AND GOVERNESSES BENEVOLENT INSTITUTION (1843), Queen Mary House, Manor Park Road, Chislehurst, Kent BR7 5PY. Tel: 081-468 7997. *Director*, L. I. Baggott

SCIENCE AND LEARNING, SOCIETY FOR THE PROTECTION OF (1933), 20–21 Compton Terrace, London N1 2UN. *Secretary*, Ms E. Fraser

SCIENCE, BRITISH ASSOCIATION FOR THE ADVANCEMENT OF (1831), Fortress House, 23 Savile Row, London W1X 1AB. Tel: 071-494 3326. *Executive Secretary*, Dr P. Briggs

SCIENCE EDUCATION, ASSOCIATION FOR (1963), College Lane, Hatfield, Herts. AL10 9AA. Tel: 0707-267411. *General Secretary*, Dr D. S. Moore

SCOTCH WHISKY ASSOCIATION, THE (1919), 20 Atholl Crescent, Edinburgh EH3 8HF. Tel: 031-229 4383. *Director-General*, Col. H. F. O. Bewsher, OBE

SCOTTISH CHURCH HISTORY SOCIETY (1922), St Serf's Manse, 1 Denham Green Terrace, Edinburgh EH5 3PG. Tel: 031-552 4059. *Hon. Secretary*, Revd Dr P. H. Donald

SCOTTISH CORPORATION, ROYAL (1611), 37 King Street, London WC2E 8JS. Tel: 071-240 3718. *Chief Executive*, Wg Cdr. A. Robertson

SCOTTISH COUNTRY DANCE SOCIETY, ROYAL (1923), 12 Coates Crescent, Edinburgh EH3 7AF. Tel: 031-225 3854. *Secretary*, Mrs J. A. Moore

SCOTTISH GENEALOGY SOCIETY (1953), 21 Howard Place, Edinburgh EH3 5JY. Tel: 031-220 3677. *Hon. Secretary*, Miss J. P. S. Ferguson

SCOTTISH HISTORY SOCIETY (1886), Department of Scottish History, University of Edinburgh, Edinburgh EH8 9YL. *Hon. Secretary*, Dr E. P. D. Torrie

SCOTTISH LANDOWNERS' FEDERATION (1906), 25 Maritime Street, Edinburgh EH6 5PW. Tel: 031-555 1031. *Director*, S. Fraser

SCOTTISH LAW AGENTS SOCIETY, 3 Albyn Place, Edinburgh EH2 4NQ. Tel: 031-225 7515. *Secretary*, R. M. Sinclair

SCOTTISH NATIONAL INSTITUTION FOR THE WAR BLINDED (1915), PO Box 500, Gillespie Crescent, Edinburgh EH10 4HZ. Tel: 031-229 1456. *Secretary*, J. B. M. Munro

SCOTTISH NATIONAL WAR MEMORIAL (1927), The Castle, Edinburgh EH1 2YT. Tel: 031-226 7393. *Secretary*, Lt.-Col. I. Shepherd

SCOTTISH SOCIETY FOR THE PREVENTION OF CRUELTY TO ANIMALS (1839), 19 Melville Street, Edinburgh EH3 7PL. Tel: 031-225 6418. *Chief Executive*, J. Morris, CBE

SCOTTISH SOCIETY FOR THE PROTECTION OF WILD BIRDS (1927), Foremount House, Kilbarchan, Renfrewshire PA10 2EZ. Tel: 0505-702419. *Secretary*, Dr J. A. Gibson

SCOTTISH WILDLIFE TRUST (1964), Cramond House, Kirk Cramond, Cramond Glebe Road, Edinburgh EH4 6NS. Tel: 031-312 7765. *Director*, D. J. Hughes Hallett

SCOUT ASSOCIATION, THE (1907), Baden-Powell House, Queen's Gate, London SW7 5JS. Tel: 071-584 7030. *Chief Scout*, W. G. Morrison; *Chief Executive Commissioner*, A. E. N. Black, OBE

SCRIBES AND ILLUMINATORS, SOCIETY OF (1921), 54 Boileau Road, London SW13 9BL. Tel: 081-748 9951

SCRIPTURE GIFT MISSION INCORPORATED (1888), Radstock House, 3 Eccleston Street, London SW1W 9LZ. Tel: 071-730 2155. *International Director*, R. Kennedy

SCRIPTURE UNION (1867), 130 City Road, London EC1V 2NJ. Tel: 071-782 0013. *General Director*, G. D. Q. Carr

SCULPTORS, ROYAL SOCIETY OF BRITISH (1904), 108 Old Brompton Road, London SW7 3RA. Tel: 071-373 5554. *President*, Ms P. Davidson Davis

SEA CADETS, (1895), 202 Lambeth Road, London SE1 7JF. Tel: 071-928 8978. *General Secretary*, Cdr G. J. A. Shaw, OBE (retd)

SEAMEN'S BOYS' HOME, BRITISH (1863), Berry Head Road, Brixham, Devon TQ5 9AE. Tel: 0803-882129. *Secretary*, Capt. E. M. Marks, RD, RNR

SEAMEN'S CHRISTIAN FRIEND SOCIETY (1846), 48 South Street, Alderley Edge, Cheshire SK9 7ES. Tel: 0625-590010. *Administrator*, M. J. Wilson

SEAMEN'S PENSION FUND, ROYAL (1919), 65 High Street, Ewell, Epsom, Surrey KT17 1RX. Tel: 081-393 5873. *Secretary*, D. Barker

SECULAR SOCIETY LTD, NATIONAL (1866), 702 Holloway Road, London N19 3NL. Tel: 071-272 1266. *General Secretary*, T. Mullins

SELDEN SOCIETY (1887), Faculty of Laws, Queen Mary and Westfield College, Mile End Road, London E1 4NS. Tel: 071-975 5136. To encourage the study and advance the knowledge of the history of English law. *Secretary*, V. Tunkel

SENSE (THE NATIONAL DEAF-BLIND AND RUBELLA ASSOCIATION) (1955), 11–13 Clifton Terrace, London N4 3SR. Tel: 071-272 7774. *Chief Executive*, M. Matthews

SHAFTESBURY HOMES AND *Arethusa* (1843), 3 Rectory Grove, London SW4 0EG. Tel: 071-720 8709. *Director*, Capt. N. C. Baird-Murray, CBE, RN

SHAFTESBURY SOCIETY, THE (1844), 18–20 Kingston Road, London SW19 1JZ. Tel: 081-542 5550. Cares for physically and mentally handicapped, elderly and socially deprived people. *Chief Executive*, G. Holloway

SHELLFISH ASSOCIATION OF GREAT BRITAIN (1904), Fishmongers' Hall, London Bridge, London EC4R 9EL. Tel: 071-283 8305. *Director*, E. Edwards, OBE, PH.D.

SHELTER (THE NATIONAL CAMPAIGN FOR HOMELESS PEOPLE) (1966), 88 Old Street, London EC1V 9HU. Tel: 071-253 0202. *Director*, Ms S. McKechnie

SHERLOCK HOLMES SOCIETY OF LONDON (1951), 3 Outram Road, Southsea, Hants. PO5 1QP. Tel: 0705-812104. *Hon. Secretary*

SHIPBROKERS, INSTITUTE OF CHARTERED (1911), 3 Gracechurch Street, London EC3V 0AT. Tel: 071-626 3058. *Secretary*, J. H. Parker

SHIRE HORSE SOCIETY (1878), East of England Showground, Peterborough PE2 6XE. Tel: 0733-390696. *Secretary*, S. A. Stagg

SHRIEVALTY ASSOCIATION (1971), Express Buildings, 17–29 Upper Parliament Street, Nottingham NG1 2AQ. Tel: 0602-350350. *Secretary*, R. Bullock

SIGHT SAVERS (Royal Commonwealth Society for the Blind) (1950), Grosvenor Hall, Bolnore Road, Haywards Heath, W. Sussex RH16 4BX. Tel: 0444-412424. *Executive Director*, A. W. Johns, CMG, OBE

SIMPLIFIED SPELLING SOCIETY (1908), Clare Hall, Chapel Lane, Chigwell, Essex IG7 6JJ. *Chairman*, C. J. H. Jolly

SIR OSWALD STOLL FOUNDATION (1916), 446 Fulham Road, London SW6 1DT. Tel: 071-385 2110. *Director*, R. C. Brunwin

SMALL BUSINESSES, FEDERATION OF (1974), Parliamentary Office, 140 Lower Marsh, London SE1 7AE. Tel: 071-928 9272. *National Chairman*, J. Harris

SMALL FARMERS' ASSOCIATION, THE (1979), PO Box 18, Woodbridge, Suffolk IP13 0QP. *Chairman*, J. Morford

SOCIALIST PARTY OF GREAT BRITAIN (1904), 52 Clapham High Street, London SW4 7UN. Tel: 071-622 3811. *General Secretary*, A. Buick

SOCIAL WORKERS, BRITISH ASSOCIATION OF (1970), 16 Kent Street, Birmingham B5 6RD. Tel: 021-622-3911. *General Secretary*, D. N. Jones

SOLDIERS' AND AIRMEN'S SCRIPTURE READERS ASSOCIATION, THE (1838), Havelock House, Barrack Road, Aldershot, Hants. GU11 3NP. Tel: 0252-310033. *General Secretary*, Lt.-Col. M. Hitchcott

SOLDIERS', SAILORS' AND AIRMEN'S FAMILIES ASSOCIATION (1885), 19 Queen Elizabeth Street, London SE1 2LP. Tel: 071-403 8783. *Controller*, Maj.-Gen. C. R. Grey, CBE

SOLDIERS' WIDOWS, ROYAL CAMBRIDGE HOME FOR (1851), 82–84 Hurst Road, East Molesey, Surrey KT8 9AH. Tel: 081-979 3788. *Superintendent*, Mrs I. O. Yarnell

SOLICITORS IN THE SUPREME COURTS OF SCOTLAND, SOCIETY OF (1784), 2 Abercromby Place, Edinburgh EH3 6JZ. Tel: 031-556 4070. *Secretary*, A. R. Brownlie, OBE

SOROPTIMIST INTERNATIONAL OF GREAT BRITAIN AND IRELAND (1923), 127 Wellington Road South, Stockport SK1 3TS. Tel: 061-480 7686. *Executive Officer*, Ms K. Hindley

SOS SOCIETY, THE, *see* 2CARE

SOUTH AMERICAN MISSIONARY SOCIETY (1844), Allen Gardiner House, Pembury Road, Tunbridge Wells, Kent TN2 3QU. Tel: 0892-538647. *General Secretary*, Rt. Revd D. Evans

SOUTH WALES INSTITUTE OF ENGINEERS (1857), Empire House, Mount Stuart Square, Cardiff CF1 6DN. Tel: 0222-481726. *Hon. Secretary*, R. E. Lindsay

SPASTICS SOCIETY, THE (1952), 12 Park Crescent, London W1N 4EQ. Tel: 071-636 5020. *Chief Executive*, Ms A. Robinson

SPEAKERS CLUBS, THE ASSOCIATION OF (1971), 3 Leawood Croft, Holloway, Matlock, Derbyshire DE4 5BD. Tel: 0629-534619. *National Secretary*, F. W. P. Dawkins

SPINA BIFIDA AND HYDROCEPHALUS, ASSOCIATION FOR (ASBAH), 42 Park Road, Peterborough PE1 2UQ. Tel: 0733-555988. *Executive Director*, A. Russell

SPORTS MEDICINE, INSTITUTE OF (1963), Burlington House, Piccadilly, London W1V 0LQ. Tel: 071-287 5269. *Hon. Secretary*, Dr W. T. Orton

SPURGEON'S CHILD CARE (1867), 30 Mill Street, Bedford MK40 3HD. Tel: 0234-261843. *Director*, D. C. Culwick

STATISTICIANS, INSTITUTE OF, *see* ROYAL STATISTICAL SOCIETY

STATUTE LAW SOCIETY (1968), Onslow House, 9 The Green, Richmond, Surrey TW9 1PU. Tel: 081-940 0017. *Hon. Secretary*, N. Frudd

STEWART SOCIETY (1899), 314 Leith Walk, Edinburgh EH6 5BU. Tel: 031-555 4640. *Hon. Secretary*, Mrs M. Walker

STRATEGIC PLANNING SOCIETY, THE (1967), 17 Portland Place, London W1N 3AF. Tel: 071-636 7737. *Executive Secretary*, Ms E. Wooldridge

STRATEGIC STUDIES, INTERNATIONAL INSTITUTE FOR (1958), 23 Tavistock Street, London WC2E 7NQ. Tel: 071-379 7676. *Director*, Dr J. Chipman

STROKE ASSOCIATION, THE (1899), CHSA House, Whitecross Street, London EC1Y 8JJ. Tel: 071-490 7999. *Director-General*, Dr S. McLauchlan

STRUCTURAL ENGINEERS, INSTITUTION OF (1908), 11 Upper Belgrave Street, London SW1X 8BH. Tel: 071-235 4535. *Secretary*, D. J. Clark

STUDENT CHRISTIAN MOVEMENT (1889), 186 St Paul's Road, Balsall Heath, Birmingham B12 8LZ. Tel: 021-440 3000. *General Secretary*, Mrs H. Lidgett

SUFFOLK HORSE SOCIETY (1878), The Market Hill, Woodbridge, Suffolk IP12 4LU. Tel: 0394-380643. *Secretary*, P. Ryder-Davies

SURGEONS OF EDINBURGH, ROYAL COLLEGE OF (1505), Nicolson Street, Edinburgh EH8 9DW. Tel: 031-556 6206. *Secretary*, I. B. MacLeod, FRCSed.

SURGEONS OF ENGLAND, ROYAL COLLEGE OF (1800), 35–43 Lincoln's Inn Fields, London WC2A 3PN. Tel: 071-405 3474. *Secretary*, R. H. E. Duffett

SURVEYORS, ROYAL INSTITUTION OF CHARTERED (1868), Surveyor Court, Westwood Way, Coventry CV4 8JE. Tel: 071-222 7000. *Chief Executive*, M. Pattison

SUSSEX CATTLE SOCIETY (1887), Station Road, Robertsbridge, E. Sussex TN32 5DG. *Manager*, Miss S. G. Kennedy

SWEDENBORG SOCIETY (1810), 20–21 Bloomsbury Way, London WC1A 2TH. Tel: 071-405 7986. *Secretary*, Ms M. G. Waters

TALKING BOOKS FOR THE HANDICAPPED AND HOSPITAL PATIENTS, *see* NATIONAL LISTENING LIBRARY

TAVISTOCK INSTITUTE, THE (1947), 120 Belsize Lane, London NW3 5BA. Tel: 071-435 7111. *Secretary*, N. Barnes

TAXATION, INSTITUTE OF (1930), 12 Upper Belgrave Street, London SW1X 8BB. Tel: 071-235 9381. *Secretary*, R. J. Ison

TEACHERS AND LECTURERS, ASSOCIATION OF (1978), 7 Northumberland Street, London WC2N 5DA. Tel: 071-930 6441. *General Secretary*, P. Smith

TEACHERS OF HOME ECONOMICS AND TECHNOLOGY, NATIONAL ASSOCIATION OF (1896), Hamilton House, Mabledon Place, London WC1H 9BJ. Tel: 071-387 1441. *Secretary*, P. G. Higgins

TEACHERS OF MATHEMATICS, ASSOCIATION OF (1952), 7 Shaftesbury Street, Derby DE3 8YB. Tel: 0332-46599. *Hon. Secretary*, Ms M. Gorman

TEACHERS OF THE DEAF, BRITISH ASSOCIATION OF (1977). *Hon. Secretary*, Ms S. Dowe, Icknield High School HIU, Riddy Lane, Luton LU3 2AH. Tel: 0582-596599

TEACHERS' UNION, ULSTER (1919), 94 Malone Road, Belfast BT9 5HP. Tel: 0232-662216. *General Secretary*, D. Allen

TELECOMMUNICATIONS USERS' ASSOCIATION (1965), 48 Percy Road, London N12 8BU. Tel: 081-445 0996. *Chief Executive*, Ms V. Peters

TEMPERANCE SOCIETIES:

British National Temperance League (1834), Westbrook Court, Sharrow Vale Road, Sheffield S11 8YZ. Tel: 0742-500713. *Executive Director*, A. Willis

Church of England National Council for Social Aid, 38 Ebury Street, London OLU. Tel: 071-730 6175. *General Secretary*, Revd E. W. F. Agar

National United Temperance Council (1880), 176 Blackfriars Road, London SE1 8ET. Tel: 071-928 1538. *General Secretary*, Revd B. Kinman

Order of the Sons of Temperance (1855), 5 Ashbourne Road, Derby DE22 3FQ. Tel: 0332-41672. *Secretary*, D. Newbury

Royal Naval Temperance Society (1876) (auxiliary of Royal Sailors' Rests), 2A South Street, Gosport, Hants. PO12 1ES. Tel: 0705-589551. *General Secretary*, A. A. Lockwood

United Kingdom Alliance (1863), 176 Blackfriars Road, London SE1 8ET. Tel: 071-928 1538. *General Secretary*, Revd B. Kinman

TEMPLETON FOUNDATION (1973), 16 Kingfisher Lane, Turners Hill, Crawley, W. Sussex RH10 4QP. Tel: 0342-715750. *UK Representative*, Mrs N. Pearse

TERRENCE HIGGINS TRUST (1982), 52–54 Grays Inn Road, London WC1X 8JU. Tel: 071-831 0330. *Helpline*, 071-242 1010. *Chairman*, N. Partridge

TERRITORIAL, AUXILIARY AND VOLUNTEER RESERVE ASSOCIATIONS, COUNCIL OF (1908), Centre Block, Duke of York's HQ, London SW3 4SG. Tel: 071-730 6122. *Secretary*, Maj.-Gen. W. A. Evans, CB

TEXTILE INSTITUTE, THE (1910), International HQ, 10 Blackfriars Street, Manchester M3 5DR. Tel: 061-834 8457. *Chief Executive*, R. G. Denyer

THEATRE RESEARCH, SOCIETY FOR (1948), c/o The Theatre Museum, 1E Tavistock Street, London WC2E 7PA. *Joint Hon. Secretaries*, Ms E. Cottis; Ms F. Dann

THEATRES TRUST, THE (1976), 22 Charing Cross Road, London WC2H 0HR. Tel: 071-836 8591. *Director*, J. Earl

THEATRICAL FUND, ROYAL (1839), 11 Garrick Street, London WC2E 9AR. Tel: 071-836 3322. *Secretary*, J. R. Coutts Smith

THEOSOPHICAL SOCIETY IN ENGLAND (1875), 50 Gloucester Place, London W1H 3HJ. Tel: 071-935 9261. *General Secretary*, A. Warcup

THISTLE FOUNDATION, THE (1945), 27A Walker Street, Edinburgh EH3 7HX. Tel: 031-225 7282. *Director*, P. Croft

THOMAS CORAM FOUNDATION FOR CHILDREN (formerly The Foundling Hospital) (1739), 40 Brunswick Square, London WC1N 1AZ. Tel: 071-278 2424. *Director and Secretary*, Dr C. Hanvey

TIDY BRITAIN GROUP, THE (1953), The Pier, Wigan WN3 4EX. Tel: 0942-824620. *Director-General*, Prof. G. Ashworth, CBE

TOC H (1915), Headquarters, 1 Forest Close, Wendover, Aylesbury, Bucks. HP22 6BT. Tel: 0296-623911. *Executive Secretary*, S. Casimir

TOURIST BOARD, ENGLISH, Thames Tower, Black's Road, London W6 9EL. *Chief Executive*, M. Medlicott

TOURIST BOARD, NORTHERN IRELAND, St Anne's Court, North Street, Belfast BT1 1ND. Tel: 0232-231221. *Chief Executive*, J. Henderson

TOURIST BOARD, SCOTTISH (1969), 23 Ravelston Terrace, Edinburgh EH4 3EU. *Chief Executive*, T. M. Band

TOURIST BOARD, WALES, Brunel House, 2 Fitzalan Road, Cardiff CF2 1UY. *Chief Executive*, P. Loveluck

TOWN AND COUNTRY PLANNING ASSOCIATION (1899), 17 Carlton House Terrace, London SW1Y 5AS. Tel: 071-930 8903. *Director*, D. Hall

TOWN PLANNING INSTITUTE, ROYAL (1914), 26 Portland Place, London W1N 4BE. Tel: 071-636 9107. *Secretary-General*, D. Fryer

TOWNSWOMEN'S GUILDS, (1929), Chamber of Commerce House, 75 Harborne Road, Birmingham B15 3DA. Tel: 021-456 3435. *National Secretary*, Ms R. Styles

TOYNBEE HALL, The Universities' Settlement in East London (1884), 28 Commercial Street, London E1 6LS. Tel: 071-247 6943. *Warden (acting)*, A. Prescott

TRADE MARK AGENTS, INSTITUTE OF (1934), Canterbury House, 2–6 Sydenham Road, Croydon CRO 9XE. Tel: 081-686 2052. *Secretary*, Mrs M. J. Tyler

TRADING STANDARDS ADMINISTRATION, INSTITUTE OF (1881), 4–5 Hadleigh Business Centre, 351 London Road, Hadleigh, Essex SS7 2BT. Tel: 0702-559922. *Chief Executive*, A. J. Street

TRANSLATION AND INTERPRETING, INSTITUTE OF (1986), 377 City Road, London EC1V 1NA. Tel: 071-713 7600. *Chairman*, R. Fletcher

TRANSPORT ADMINISTRATION, INSTITUTE OF (1944), 32 Palmerston Road, Southampton SO1 1LL. Tel: 0703-631380. *Director*, Wg Cdr. P. F. Green

TRANSPORT, CHARTERED INSTITUTE OF (1919), 80 Portland Place, London W1N 4DP. Tel: 071-636 9952. *Director-General*, R. P. Botwood

TRANSPORT CONSULTATIVE COMMITTEE, CENTRAL (1948), 1st Floor, Golden Cross House, Duncannon Street, London WC2N 4JF. Tel: 071-839 7338. *Secretary*, M. Patterson

TRAVEL AGENTS, ASSOCIATION OF BRITISH (ABTA) (1950), 55–57 Newman Street, London W1P 4AH. Tel: 071-637 2444. *President*, J. Dunscombe

TREE COUNCIL (1974), 35 Belgrave Square, London SW1X 8XN. Tel: 071-235 8854. *Director*, R. Osborne

TREE FOUNDATION, INTERNATIONAL (formerly Men of the Trees) (1922), Sandy Lane, Crawley Down, W. Sussex RH10 4HS. Tel: 0342-712536. *Chairman*, J. Caunce

TROPICAL MEDICINE AND HYGIENE, ROYAL SOCIETY OF (1907), Manson House, 26 Portland Place, London W1N 4EY. Tel: 071-580 2127. *Hon. Secretaries*, Dr D. C. Barker; Dr S. G. Wright

TURNER SOCIETY (1975), BCM Box Turner, London WC1N 3XX. *Chairman*, E. Shanes

2CARE (formerly The SOS Society) (1929), 13 Harwood Road, London SW6 4QP. Tel: 071-371 0118. Residential homes for the elderly, and psychiatric rehabilitation centres. *Chief Executive*, Miss E. C. R. O'Sullivan

UFAW (UNIVERSITIES FEDERATION FOR ANIMAL WELFARE) (1926), 8 Hamilton Close, South Mimms, Potters Bar, Herts. EN6 3QD. Tel: 0707 58202. *Secretary*, M. Lawson

UNITED NATIONS ASSOCIATION OF GREAT BRITAIN AND NORTHERN IRELAND (1945), 3 Whitehall Court, London SW1A 2EL. Tel: 071-930 2931. *Director,* M. C. Harper

UNITED REFORMED CHURCH HISTORY SOCIETY (1972), 86 Tavistock Place, London WC1H 9RT. Tel: 071-916 2020. *Hon. Secretary,* Revd Dr S. Orchard

UNITED SOCIETY FOR CHRISTIAN LITERATURE (1799), Robertson House, Leas Road, Guildford, Surrey GU1 4QW. Tel: 0483-577877. *General Secretary,* Dr A. Marriage

UNITED SOCIETY FOR THE PROPAGATION OF THE GOSPEL (USPG) (1701), Partnership House, 157 Waterloo Road, London SE1 8XA. Tel: 071-928 8681. *Secretary,* Canon P. Price

UNIVERSITIES OF THE UNITED KINGDOM, COMMITTEE OF VICE-CHANCELLORS AND PRINCIPALS OF THE (1918), 29 Tavistock Square, London WC1H 9EZ. Tel: 071-387 9231. *Secretary,* T. U. Burgner

UNIVERSITY AND COLLEGE LECTURERS, ASSOCIATION OF (1973), 104 Albert Road, Southsea, Hants. PO5 2SN. Tel: 0705-818625. *Chief Executive,* Ms C. Cheesman

VALUERS AND AUCTIONEERS, INCORPORATED SOCIETY OF (1968), 3 Cadogan Gate, London SW1X 0AS. Tel: 071-235 2282. *Chief Executive,* H. Whitty

VEGAN SOCIETY, THE (1944), 7 Battle Road, St Leonards-on-Sea, E. Sussex TN37 7AA. Tel: 0424-427393. *General Secretary,* R. Farhall

VEGETARIAN SOCIETY OF THE UNITED KINGDOM LTD, Parkdale, Dunham Road, Altrincham, Cheshire WA14 4QG. Tel: 061-928 0793. *Directors,* Ms J. Gellatley; P. J. Lloyd

VENEREAL DISEASES, MEDICAL SOCIETY FOR THE STUDY OF (1922), Department of Genito Urinary Medicine, King's College Hospital, 15–22 Caldecot Road, London SE5 9RS. Tel: 081-676 9883. *Hon. Secretary,* Dr T. McManus

VERNACULAR ARCHITECTURE GROUP (1953), 16 Falna Crescent, Coton Green, Tamworth, Staffs. B79 8JS. Tel: 0827-69434. *Hon. Secretary,* R. Meeson

VETERINARY ASSOCIATION, BRITISH (1881), 7 Mansfield Street, London W1M 0AT. Tel: 071-636 6541. *Chief Executive,* J. H. Baird

VETERINARY SURGEONS, ROYAL COLLEGE OF, 32 Belgrave Square, London SW1X 8QP (1844). *Registrar,* A. R. W. Porter, CBE

VICTIM SUPPORT (NATIONAL ASSOCIATION OF VICTIM SUPPORT SCHEMES) (1979), Cranmer House, 39 Brixton Road, London SW9 6DZ. Tel: 071-735 9166. *Director,* Ms H. Reeves, OBE

VICTORIA CROSS AND GEORGE CROSS ASSOCIATION, Room 04, Archway Block South, Old Admiralty Building, Whitehall, London SW1A 2BE. Tel: 071-930 3506. *Chairman,* Rear-Adm. B. C. G. Place, VC, CB, CVO, DSC

VICTORIA INSTITUTE, THE (Philosophical Society of Great Britain), Latchell Hall, Latchett Road, London E18 1DL. Tel: 081-505 5224. *Hon. Treasurer,* B. H. T. Weller

VICTORIAN SOCIETY (1958), 1 Priory Gardens, Bedford Park, London W4 1TT. Tel: 081-994 1019. *Director,* Dr W. Filmer-Sankey

VICTORY (SERVICES) ASSOCIATION LTD AND CLUB (1907), 63–79 Seymour Street, London W2 2HF. Tel: 071-723 4474. *General Manager,* G. F. Taylor

VIKING SOCIETY FOR NORTHERN RESEARCH (1892), Department of Scandinavian Studies, University College, Gower Street, London WC1E 6BT. *Hon. Secretaries,* Prof. M. P. Barnes; Dr J. Jesch

VOLUNTARY AGENCIES, NATIONAL COUNCIL FOR (1919), Regent's Wharf, 8 All Saints Street, London N1 9RL. Tel: 071-713 6161. *General Secretary,* Ms J. Weleminsky

VSO (VOLUNTARY SERVICE OVERSEAS) (1958), 317 Putney Bridge Road, London SW15 2PN. Tel: 081-780 2266. *Director,* D. Green

WAR ON WANT (1952), 37–39 Great Guildford Street, London SE1 0ES. Tel: 071-620 1111. *Director,* G. Alhadeff

WATER AND ENVIRONMENTAL MANAGEMENT, INSTITUTION OF (1987), 15 John Street, London WC1N 2EB. Tel: 071-831 3110. *Executive Director,* H. R. Evans

WATERCOLOUR SOCIETY, ROYAL (1804), Bankside Gallery, 48 Hopton Street, London SE1 9JH. Tel: 071-928 7521. *President,* L. Worth; *Secretary,* M. Spender

WELDING INSTITUTE, THE, Abington Hall, Cambridge CB1 6AL. Tel: 0223-891162. *Chief Executive,* A. B. M. Braithwaite

WELLCOME TRUST (1936), The Wellcome Building, 183 Euston Road, London NW1 2BE. Tel: 071-611 8888. *Director,* Dr B. Ogilvie

WELLS SOCIETY, H. G., (1961). *Hon. Secretary,* Dr S. Hardy, English Department, Nene College, Moulton Park, Northampton NN2 7AL. Tel: 0604-735500, ext. 2133

WESLEY HISTORICAL SOCIETY (1893), 34 Spiceland Road, Northfield, Birmingham B31 1NJ. Tel: 021-475 4914. *General Secretary,* Dr E. D. Graham

WEST LONDON MISSION (1887), 19 Thayer Street, London W1M 5LJ. Tel: 071-935 6179. *Superintendent,* Revd D. S. Cruise

WESTMINSTER FOUNDATION FOR DEMOCRACY (1992), Queen Anne's Chambers, 3 Dean Farrar Street, London SW1H 9LG. Tel: 071-210 3319. *Chief Executive,* Ms D. Warwick

WILDFOWL AND WETLANDS TRUST (1946), The New Grounds, Slimbridge, Gloucester GL2 7BT. Tel: 0453-890333. *Director-General,* Dr M. Owen

WILLIAM MORRIS SOCIETY AND KELMSCOTT FELLOWSHIP (1918), Kelmscott House, 26 Upper Mall, London W6 9TA. Tel: 071-741 3735. *Hon. Secretary,* D. Baker

WINE AND SPIRIT ASSOCIATION OF GREAT BRITAIN AND NORTHERN IRELAND (*c.* 1825), Five Kings House, 1 Queen Street Place, London EC4R 1XX. Tel: 071-248 5377. *Director,* P. Lewis

WOMEN, SOCIETY FOR PROMOTING THE TRAINING OF (1859), The Rectory, Great Casterton, Stamford, Lincs. PE9 4AP. Tel: 0780-64036. *Secretary,* Revd B. Harris

WOMEN ARTISTS, SOCIETY OF (1855), Westminster Gallery, Westminster Central Hall, Storey's Gate, London SW1H 9NU. *President,* Ms B. Tate

WOMEN GRADUATES, BRITISH FEDERATION OF (1907), 4 Mandeville Courtyard, 142 Battersea Park Road, London SW11 4NB. Tel: 071-498 8037. *Secretary*

WOMEN'S ENGINEERING SOCIETY (1920), Imperial College of Science and Technology, Department of Civil Engineering, Imperial College Road, London SW7 2BU. Tel: 071-589 5111, ext. 4731. *Secretary,* Mrs C. MacGillivray

WOMEN'S INSTITUTES, NATIONAL FEDERATION OF (1915), 104 New Kings Road, London SW6 4LY. Tel: 071-371 9300. *General Secretary,* Ms H. Mayall

WOMEN'S INSTITUTES OF NORTHERN IRELAND, FEDERATION OF (1932), 209–211 Upper Lisburn Road, Belfast BT10 0LL. Tel: 0232-301506. *General Secretary,* Mrs I. A. Sproule

WOMEN'S INTERNATIONAL LEAGUE FOR PEACE AND FREEDOM (British Section) (1915), 157 Lyndhurst Road, Worthing, W. Sussex BN11 2DG. Tel: 0903-205161. *Chair,* Ms C. Lowden

WOMEN'S NATIONWIDE CANCER CONTROL CAMPAIGN (1964), Suna House, 128–130 Curtain Road, London EC2A 3AR. Tel: 071-729 4688. *Helpline,* 071-729 2229. *Administrator,* Ms J. Harding

WOMEN'S ROYAL NAVAL SERVICE BENEVOLENT TRUST (1942), 1A Chesham Street, London SW1X 8NL. Tel: 071-235 5846. *General Secretary,* Mrs J. Y. Ellis

WOMEN'S ROYAL VOLUNTARY SERVICE (WRVS), *see* Government Departments and Public Offices section

WOMEN'S RURAL INSTITUTES, SCOTTISH (1917), 42 Heriot Row, Edinburgh EH3 6ES. *General Secretary,* Mrs E. Nicol

WOMEN'S TRANSPORT SERVICE (1907), FANY HQ, Duke of York's HQ, London SW3 4RX. Tel: 071-730 2058. *Corps Commander,* Mrs A. Whitehead

WOODLAND TRUST, THE (1972), Autumn Park, Dysart Road, Grantham, Lincs. NG31 6LL. Tel: 0476-74297. *Chief Executive Director,* J. D. James

WOOD PRESERVING ASSOCIATION, BRITISH (1930), 6 The Office Village, 4 Romford Road, London E15 4EA. Tel: 081-519 2588. *Administration Director,* M. J. Tuck

WORKERS' EDUCATIONAL ASSOCIATION, Temple House, 9 Upper Berkeley Street, London 8BY. Tel: 071-402 5608. *General Secretary,* R. Lochrie

WORKING MOTHERS ASSOCIATION, THE (1985), 77 Holloway Road, London N7 8JZ. Tel: 071-700 5771. *Director,* Mrs L. Daniels

WORLD EDUCATION FELLOWSHIP (1921), 33 Kinnaird Avenue, London W4 3SH. Tel: 081-994 7258. *General Secretary,* Mrs R. Crommelin

WORLD ENERGY COUNCIL (1924), 34 St James's Street, London SW1A 1HD. Tel: 071-930 3966. *Secretary-General,* I. D. Lindsay

WORLD MISSION, COUNCIL FOR (1977), Livingstone House, 11 Carteret Street, London SW1H 9DL. Tel: 071-222 4214. *General Secretary,* D. P. Niles, PH.D.

WORLD SHIP SOCIETY (1946), 35 Wickham Way, Haywards Heath, W. Sussex RH16 1UJ. *Secretary,* S. J. F. Miller

WORLD SOCIETY FOR THE PROTECTION OF ANIMALS (1981), 2 Langley Lane, London SW8 1TJ. Tel: 071-793 0540. *Chief Executive,* A. Dickson

WORLD-WIDE EDUCATION SERVICE (1888), Canada House, 272 Field End Road, Eastcote, Ruislip, Middx. HA4 9NA. Tel: 081-866 4400. *Head of Consultancy,* Mrs T. Mulder-Reynolds

WRITERS TO HM SIGNET, SOCIETY OF (1532), 16 Hill Street, Edinburgh EH2 3LD. Tel: 031-226 6703. *Clerk,* A. M. Kerr

WWF UK (World Wide Fund for Nature) (1961), Panda House, Weyside Park, Godalming, Surrey GU7 1XR. Tel: 0483-426444. *Director,* Dr R. Pellew

YEOMANRY BENEVOLENT FUND (1902), 10 Stone Buildings, Lincoln's Inn, London WC2A 3TG. Tel: 071-831 6727. *Secretary,* Mrs C. W. Chrystie

YORKSHIRE AGRICULTURAL SOCIETY (1837), Great Yorkshire Showground, Hookstone Oval, Harrogate, N. Yorks HG2 8PW. Tel: 0423-561536. *Chief Executive,* R. Keigwin

YORKSHIRE SOCIETY, THE (1812), 35 Waldorf Heights, Camberley, Surrey GU17 9JH. Tel: 0276-36342. Educational trust making grants to students of all ages. *Secretary,* G. G. Prince, TD

YOUNG FARMERS' CLUBS, NATIONAL FEDERATION OF, The YFC Centre, National Agricultural Centre, Kenilworth, Warks. CV8 2LG. Tel: 0203-696544. *Secretary,* T. Shields

YOUNG MEN'S CHRISTIAN ASSOCIATION (YMCA) (1844), National Council of YMCAs, 640 Forest Road, London E17 3DZ. Tel: 081-520 5599. *National Secretary,* N. Nightingale

YOUNG WOMEN'S CHRISTIAN ASSOCIATION OF GREAT BRITAIN (YWCA) (1855), 52 Cornmarket Street, Oxford OX1 3EJ. *Chief Executive,* Ms G. Tishler

YOUTH ACTION, NORTHERN IRELAND (1944), Hampton, Glenmachan Park, Belfast BT4 2PJ. Tel: 0232-760067. *Director,* P. Graham

YOUTH CLUBS UK (1911), 11 St Bride Street, London EC4A 4AS. Tel: 071-353 2366. *Chief Executive,* D. Stickels

YOUTH HOSTELS ASSOCIATION (ENGLAND AND WALES) (1930), Trevelyan House, 8 St Stephens Hill, St Albans, Herts. AL1 2DY. Tel: 0727-855215. *Chief Executive,* C. Logan

YOUTH HOSTELS ASSOCIATION OF NORTHERN IRELAND (1931), Bradbury Buildings, 56 Bradbury Place, Belfast BT7 1RU. Tel: 0232-324733. *Hon. Secretary,* N. O'Reilly

YOUTH HOSTELS ASSOCIATION, SCOTTISH (1931), 7 Glebe Crescent, Stirling FK8 2JA. Tel: 0786-51181. *General Secretary,* J. Martin

ZOO CHECK (1984), Cherry Tree Cottage, Coldharbour, Dorking, Surrey RH5 6HA. Tel: 0306-712091. *Director,* W. Travers

ZOOLOGICAL SOCIETY, NORTH OF ENGLAND (1934), Chester Zoo, Upton by Chester, Chester CH2 1LH. Tel: 0244-380280. *Director,* Dr M. Brambell

ZOOLOGICAL SOCIETY OF LONDON (1826), Regent's Park, London NW1 4RY. Tel: 071-722 0688. *President,* Field Marshal Sir John Chapple, GCB, CBE; *Clerk to the Council,* P. H. Denton

ZOOLOGICAL SOCIETY OF SCOTLAND, ROYAL (1913), Scottish National Zoological Park, Edinburgh Zoo, Corstorphine Road,Edinburgh EH12 6TS. Tel: 031-334 9171. *Director,* Prof. R. J. Wheater, OBE, FRSE

LOCAL HISTORY AND ARCHAEOLOGICAL SOCIETIES

ENGLAND

Bedfordshire: SOUTH BEDFORDSHIRE ARCHAEOLOGICAL SOCIETY. *Hon. Secretary,* D. H. Kennett, 27 Lords Lane, Bradwell, Great Yarmouth, Norfolk NR31 8NY

Berkshire: BERKSHIRE ARCHAEOLOGICAL SOCIETY. *Hon. Secretary,* L. J. Over, 43 Laburnham Road, Maidenhead, Berks. SL6 4DE. Tel: 0628-31225

NEWBURY DISTRICT FIELD CLUB. *President,* Mrs A. Franklin, 32 Three Acre Road, Newbury, Berks. RG14 5AW. Tel: 0635-44912

Buckinghamshire: BUCKINGHAMSHIRE ARCHAEOLOGICAL SOCIETY. *Hon. Secretary,* Dr R. P. Hagerty, County Museum, Church Street, Aylesbury, Bucks. HP20 2QP. Tel: 0296-20984

Cambridgeshire: CAMBRIDGE ANTIQUARIAN SOCIETY. *Hon. Secretary,* Dr M. Hesse, 39 Highsett Hills Road, Cambridge CB2 1NZ

Cheshire: CHESTER ARCHAEOLOGICAL SOCIETY. *Secretary,* Dr D. J. P. Mason, Ochr Cottage, Porch Lane, Hope Mountain, Caergwrle, Clwyd LL12 9LS

Cornwall: CORNWALL ARCHAEOLOGICAL SOCIETY. *Hon. Secretaries,* Mr and Mrs B. Hammond, 7 Porthmeor Road, Holmbush, St Austell, Cornwall PL25 3LT. Tel: 0726-74763

Cumberland and Westmorland: CUMBERLAND AND WESTMORLAND ANTIQUARIAN AND ARCHAEOLOGICAL SOCIETY. *Hon. Secretary,* R. Hall, 2 High Tenterfell, Kendal, Cumbria LA9 4PG. Tel: 0539-728288

Derbyshire: DERBYSHIRE ARCHAEOLOGICAL SOCIETY. *Hon. Secretary,* I. Mitchell, 159 Draycott Road, Sawley, Long Eaton, Nottingham NG10 3BX. Tel: 0602-729029

Devonshire: DEVON ARCHAEOLOGICAL SOCIETY, Royal Albert Memorial Museum, Queen Street, Exeter EX4 3RX. *Hon. Secretary,* Miss D. M. Griffiths

Dorset: DORSET NATURAL HISTORY AND ARCHAEOLOGICAL SOCIETY, Dorset County Museum, Dorchester, Dorset DT1 1XA. Tel: 0305-262735. *Secretary,* R. Peers

Durham: DURHAM AND NORTHUMBERLAND ARCHITECTURAL AND ARCHAEOLOGICAL SOCIETY. *Hon. Secretary,* A. Feeney, 53 Brook Terrace, Darlington, Co. Durham DL3 6PJ. Tel: 0325-359772

Essex: ESSEX SOCIETY FOR ARCHAEOLOGY AND HISTORY, Hollytrees Museum, High Street, Colchester CO1 1UG. *Secretary,* N. P. Wickendon

Gloucestershire: BRISTOL AND GLOUCESTERSHIRE ARCHAEOLOGICAL SOCIETY. *Hon. Secretary,* D. J. H. Smith, FSA, 22 Beaumont Road, Gloucester GL2 0EJ. Tel: 0452-302610

Hampshire: HAMPSHIRE FIELD CLUB AND ARCHAEOLOGICAL SOCIETY. *Hon. Secretary,* Dr M. A. Hicks, King Alfred's College, Winchester, Hants. SO22 4NR. Tel: 0962-841515

Herefordshire: WOOLHOPE NATURALISTS' FIELD CLUB. *Hon. Secretary,* J. W. Tonkin, FSA, Chy an Whyloryon, Wigmore, Leominster, Herefordshire HR6 9UD. Tel: 056 886356

Hertfordshire: EAST HERTFORDSHIRE ARCHAEOLOGICAL SOCIETY. *Hon. Secretary,* Mrs M. C. Readman, 1 Marsh Lane, Stanstead Abbots, Ware, Herts. SG12 8HH. Tel: 0920-870664

ST ALBANS AND HERTFORDSHIRE ARCHITECTURAL AND ARCHAEOLOGICAL SOCIETY. *Hon. Secretary,* B. E. Moody, 24 Rose Walk, St Albans, Herts. AL4 9AF. Tel: 0727-853204

Isle of Wight: ISLE OF WIGHT NATURAL HISTORY AND ARCHAEOLOGICAL SOCIETY. *Hon. Secretary,* Mrs T. Goodley, Ivy Cottage, New Barn Lane, Shorwell, Newport, IOW, PO30 3JQ. Tel: 0983-740711

Kent: KENT ARCHAEOLOGICAL SOCIETY. *Hon. General Secretary,* A. Moffatt, Three Elms, Woodlands Lane, Shorne, Gravesend, Kent DA12 3HH. Tel: 0474-822280

Leicestershire: LEICESTERSHIRE ARCHAEOLOGICAL AND HISTORICAL SOCIETY, The Guildhall, Leicester LE1 5FQ. Tel: 0533-703031. *Hon. Secretary,* Dr A. D. McWhirr

London and Middlesex: CITY OF LONDON ARCHAEOLOGICAL SOCIETY. *Hon. Secretary,* Ms M. Andrews, 19 Hawes Road, Bromley, Kent BR1 3JS

LONDON AND MIDDLESEX ARCHAEOLOGICAL SOCIETY. *Hon. Secretary,* M. Curtis, 34 Alexander Road, London SW19 7JZ. Tel: 081-879 7109

Norfolk: NORFOLK AND NORWICH ARCHAEOLOGICAL SOCIETY. *Hon. General Secretary,* R. Bellinger, 30 Brettingham Avenue, Norwich NR4 6XG. Tel: 0603-55913

Northumberland and Tyne and Wear: SOCIETY OF ANTIQUARIES OF NEWCASTLE UPON TYNE, Black Gate, Castle Garth, Newcastle upon Tyne NE1 1RQ. Tel: 091-261 5390. *Secretary,* D. Cutts

SUNDERLAND ANTIQUARIAN SOCIETY. *Hon. Secretary,* Mrs V. M. Stevens, 16 Grizedale Court, Seaburn Dene, Sunderland SR6 8JP. Tel: 091-548 7541

Oxfordshire: OXFORDSHIRE ARCHITECTURAL AND HISTORICAL SOCIETY, Museums and Archives Services, Fletchers House, Park Street, Woodstock OX7 1SN. Tel: 0993-811456. *Hon. Secretary,* D. Dawson

Shropshire: SHROPSHIRE ARCHAEOLOGICAL AND HISTORICAL SOCIETY. *Chairman,* J. B. Lawson, Westcott Farm, Pontesbury, Shrewsbury SY5 0SQ

Somerset: SOMERSET ARCHAEOLOGICAL AND NATURAL HISTORY SOCIETY, Taunton Castle, Taunton, Somerset TA1 4AD. Tel: 0823-272429. *Hon. Secretary,* B. Watkin

Staffordshire: CITY OF STOKE-ON-TRENT MUSEUM ARCHAEOLOGICAL SOCIETY, City Museum and Art Gallery, Hanley, Stoke-on-Trent ST1 3DW. Tel: 0782-202173. *Chairman,* E. E. Royle

Suffolk: SUFFOLK INSTITUTE OF ARCHAEOLOGY AND HISTORY. *Hon. Secretary,* E. A. Martin, Oak Tree Farm, Finborough Road, Hitcham, Ipswich IP7 7LS. Tel: 0449-741266

Surrey: SURREY ARCHAEOLOGICAL SOCIETY, Castle Arch, Guildford, Surrey GU1 3SX. Tel: 0483-32454. *Hon. Secretaries,* Mr and Mrs K. D. Graham

Sussex: SUSSEX ARCHAEOLOGICAL SOCIETY, Bull House, 92 High Street, Lewes, E. Sussex BN7 1XH. Tel: 0273-486260. *Chief Executive,* J. Manley

Warwickshire: BIRMINGHAM AND WARWICKSHIRE ARCHAEOLOGICAL SOCIETY, c/o Birmingham and Midland Institute, Margaret Street, Birmingham B3 3BS. Tel: 021-236 3591. *Hon. Secretary,* A. J. Wilson

Wiltshire: WILTSHIRE ARCHAEOLOGICAL AND NATURAL HISTORY SOCIETY, The Museum, 41 Long Street, Devizes, Wilts SN10 1NS. Tel: 0380-727369. *Secretary,* G. G. Brown

Worcestershire: WORCESTERSHIRE ARCHAEOLOGICAL SOCIETY. *Hon. Secretary,* Miss B. Ronchetti, Queen Elizabeth House, Trinity Street, Worcester WR1 2PW. Tel: 0905-722369

Yorkshire: YORKSHIRE ARCHAEOLOGICAL SOCIETY. *Hon. Secretary,* N. Cookson, PH.D., Claremont, 23 Clarendon Road, Leeds LS2 9NZ. Tel: 0532-457910

HALIFAX ANTIQUARIAN SOCIETY. *Hon. Secretary,* J. A. Hargreaves, 7 Hyde Park Gardens, Haugh Shaw Road, Halifax, W. Yorks HX1 3AH. Tel: 0422-352126

THORESBY SOCIETY. *Hon. Secretary,* B. Harrison, Claremont, 23 Clarendon Road, Leeds LS2 9NZ

SCOTLAND

AYRSHIRE ARCHAEOLOGICAL AND NATURAL HISTORY SOCIETY. *Hon. Secretary,* Dr T. Mathews, 10 Longlands Park, Ayr KA7 4RJ. Tel: 0292-441915

DUMFRIESSHIRE AND GALLOWAY NATURAL HISTORY AND ANTIQUARIAN SOCIETY. *Hon. Secretary,* Mrs J. Muir, North Wing, Carzield House, Kirmahoe, Dumfriesshire DG1 1SY. Tel: 0387-710216

HAWICK ARCHAEOLOGICAL SOCIETY. *Hon. Secretary,* I. W. Landles, Orrock House, Stirches Road, Hawick, Roxburghshire TD9 7HF. Tel: 0450-75546

INVERNESS FIELD CLUB. *Hon. Secretary,* Miss I. McLean, 6 Drumblair Crescent, Inverness IV2 4RG

WALES

Dyfed: CEREDIGION ANTIQUARIAN SOCIETY. *Hon. Secretary,* Mrs M. Burdett-Jones, Skomer, Llanbadarn Road, Aberystwyth, Dyfed SY23 3QW

Gwynedd: ANGLESEY ANTIQUARIAN SOCIETY. *Hon. Secretary,* S. C. G. Caffell, 1 Fronheulog Sling, Tregarth, Bangor LL57 4RD

Powys: POWYSLAND CLUB. *Hon. Secretary,* Miss P. M. Davies, Llyead y Dyffryn, Llanidloes, Powys

CHANNEL ISLANDS

SOCIÉTÉ JERSIAISE, ARCHAEOLOGICAL SECTION, La Hougue Bie Museum, Grouville, Jersey. Tel: 0534-58314. *Hon. Secretary,* N. P. Molyneux

International Organizations

ASSOCIATION OF SOUTH EAST ASIAN NATIONS
70 A. Jl. Sisingamangaraja Kebayoran Baru, Jakarta Selatan, PO Box 2072, Jakarta, Indonesia

Formed in 1967, the main aims of the Association of South East Asian Nations (ASEAN) are the acceleration of economic growth, social progress and cultural development, the promotion of collaboration and mutual assistance in matters of common interest, and the continuing stability of the South East Asian region.

The heads of government of the member countries are the highest authority and give directions to ASEAN as and when necessary. The main policy-making body is the annual meeting of foreign ministers of the member countries. The members are Brunei, Indonesia, Malaysia, the Philippines, Singapore and Thailand. Laos and Vietnam were granted observer status in 1992.

At the January 1992 heads of government summit in Singapore, it was agreed to create an ASEAN free trade area within 15 years. Progress towards this began in January 1993 with the beginning of the implementation of a common preferential tariff.

Secretary-General, Rusli Noor (*Indonesia*)

BANK FOR INTERNATIONAL SETTLEMENTS
Centralbahnplatz 2, 4002 Basle, Switzerland

The objectives of the Bank for International Settlements (founded in 1930) are to promote the co-operation of central banks; to provide facilities for international financial operations; and to act as trustee or agent in international financial settlements entrusted to it. The London agent is the Bank of England, and the Governor of the Bank of England is a member of the Board of Directors, in which administrative control is vested.

Chairman of the Board of Directors and President of the Bank for International Settlements, B. Dennis (*Sweden*)

CAB INTERNATIONAL
Wallingford, Oxon. OX10 8DE Tel: 0491-832111

CAB International (formerly the Commonwealth Agricultural Bureau) was founded in 1929. The organization generates, disseminates and applies scientific knowledge in support of sustainable development, with an emphasis on agriculture, forestry, human health and the management of natural resources, and with particular attention to the needs of developing countries. It consists of four institutes and five editorial divisions. The organization is owned by 34 countries, each represented on an Executive Council. A Governing Board was appointed in 1990 to provide expert guidance to management on policy issues. The functions of CABI's four institutes are to provide identification, diagnostic, biosystematic, control and management support for the pests and diseases of crops and livestock. Each institute and editorial division acts as an effective clearing house for the collection,

collation and dissemination of information in its particular branch of agricultural science.

Director-General, Dr D. R. Laing

CARIBBEAN COMMUNITY AND COMMON MARKET
PO Box 10827, Georgetown, Guyana

The Caribbean Community and Common Market (Caricom) was established in 1973 with three objectives: economic co-operation through the Caribbean Common Market; the co-ordination of foreign policy among the independent member states; the provision of common services and co-operation in functional matters such as health, education and culture, communications and industrial relations. The principal organs are the Conference of Heads of Government, which determines policy, and the Common Market Council of Ministers, consisting of ministers of government (usually ministers of trade) designated by each member state, which is responsible for the development and smooth running of the Common Market and for the settlement of any problems arising out of its functioning. The principal administrative arm is the Secretariat, based in Guyana.

The 13 member states are Antigua and Barbuda, The Bahamas (which is not a member of the Common Market), Barbados, Belize, Dominica, Grenada, Guyana, Jamaica, Montserrat, St Christopher and Nevis, St Lucia, St Vincent and the Grenadines, and Trinidad and Tobago. The British Virgin Islands and the Turks and Caicos Islands are associate members. The Dominican Republic, Haiti, Mexico, Puerto Rico, Suriname and Venezuela have observer status.

Secretary-General, Edwin W. Carrington

THE COMMONWEALTH

The Commonwealth is a free association of 50 sovereign independent states together with their associated states and dependencies. All of the states were formerly parts of the British Empire, or League of Nations (later UN) mandated territories.

The status and relationship of member nations were first defined by the Inter-Imperial Relations Committee of the 1926 Imperial Conference, under the chairmanship of Lord Balfour, when the six existing dominions (Australia, Canada, the Irish Free State, Newfoundland, New Zealand and South Africa) were described as 'autonomous Communities within the British Empire, equal in status, in no way subordinate one to another in any aspect of their domestic or external affairs, though united by a common allegiance to the Crown and freely associated as Members of the British Commonwealth of Nations'. This formula was given legal substance by the Statute of Westminster 1931.

This concept of a group of countries owing allegiance to a single Crown changed in 1949 when India decided to become a republic. Her continued membership of the Commonwealth was agreed by the other members on the basis of her 'acceptance of The King as the symbol of the free association of its independent member nations and as such the head of the Commonwealth'. This paved the way for other republics to join the association in due course. Member nations agreed at the time of the accession of Queen Elizabeth II to recognize Her Majesty as the new Head of the Commonwealth. However, the position is not vested in the British Crown.

THE MODERN COMMONWEALTH

With the membership of India and Pakistan in 1947, Ceylon (later Sri Lanka) in 1948 and Ghana in 1957, the character of the Commonwealth changed fundamentally. The grouping of all-white dominions gave way to a modern, multi-racial association of equal, sovereign nations and their peoples. The new era was characterized most succinctly by the British Prime Minister Harold Macmillan in his 'wind of change' speech to the South African Parliament in 1960, in which he predicted the independence of Britain's African colonies. In the following decades, Britain granted independence to almost all of her colonies in Africa, Asia, the Caribbean and the Pacific. Virtually all of these newly-independent countries joined the Commonwealth.

In its modern form, the Commonwealth increasingly focused its attention on promoting development and on helping to end racial inequality in southern Africa. The Commonwealth played an important role in the resolution of the Rhodesian crisis ending with the independence of Zimbabwe, strongly supported the independence of Namibia, and from the late 1970s took concerted action, including sporting and economic sanctions, against the South African government over its policy of apartheid.

THE HARARE DECLARATION

As progress was made towards ending apartheid and introducing democracy in South Africa, the Commonwealth set itself new goals at its heads of government meeting in Harare, Zimbabwe, in October 1991. Outlined in the Harare Commonwealth Declaration, these goals include the promotion of the Commonwealth's fundamental political values, such as democracy, the rule of law, good government and human rights; the promotion of equality for women; the provision of universal access to education; the promotion of sustainable development and the alleviation of poverty; action against disease and illegal drugs; help for small Commonwealth states; and support of the UN in the quest for international consensus on key issues.

MEMBERSHIP

Membership of the Commonwealth involves acceptance of the association's basic principles and is subject to the approval of existing members. The membership currently stands at 50. (The date of joining the Commonwealth is shown in parenthesis.)

*Antigua and Barbuda (1981)	Lesotho (1966)
*Australia (1931)	Malawi (1964)
*The Bahamas (1973)	Malaysia (1957)
Bangladesh (1972)	The Maldives (1982)
*Barbados (1966)	Malta (1964)
*Belize (1981)	Mauritius (1968)
Botswana (1966)	Namibia (1990)
Brunei (1984)	Nauru (1968)
*Canada (1931)	*New Zealand (1931)
Cyprus (1961)	Nigeria (1960)
Dominica (1978)	Pakistan (1947)
The Gambia (1965)	*Papua New Guinea (1975)
Ghana (1957)	*St Christopher and Nevis
*Grenada (1974)	(1983)
Guyana (1966)	*St Lucia (1979)
India (1947)	*St Vincent and the
*Jamaica (1962)	Grenadines (1979)
Kenya (1963)	Seychelles (1976)
Kiribati (1979)	Sierra Leone (1961)

Singapore (1965)	Uganda (1962)
*Soloman Islands (1978)	*United Kingdom
Sri Lanka (1948)	Vanuatu (1980)
Swaziland (1968)	Western Samoa (1970)
Tanzania (1961)	Zambia (1964)
Tonga (1970)	Zimbabwe (1980)
Trinidad and Tobago (1962)	
*Tuvalu (1978)	*Realms of Queen Elizabeth II

Nauru and Tuvalu are special members, with the right to participate in all functional Commonwealth meetings and activities, but not to attend meetings of Commonwealth heads of government.

Countries which have left the Commonwealth
Fiji (1987)
Republic of Ireland (1949)
Pakistan (1972, rejoined 1989)
South Africa (1961)

Of the 50 member states, 16 have Queen Elizabeth II as head of state, 29 are republics, and five are indigenous monarchies.

In each of the realms where Queen Elizabeth II is head of state (except for the United Kingdom), she is personally represented by a Governor-General, who holds in all essential respects the same position in relation to the administration of public affairs in the realm as is held by Her Majesty in Britain. The Governor-General is appointed by The Queen on the advice of the government of the state concerned.

INTERGOVERNMENTAL AND OTHER LINKS

The main forum for consultation is the Commonwealth heads of government meetings held biennially to discuss international developments and to consider co-operation among members. Cyprus is the venue of the October 1993 meeting. Decisions are reached by consensus, and the views of the meeting are set out in a communiqué. There are also annual meetings of finance ministers and frequent meetings of ministers and officials in many other fields, such as education, health, labour, law, women's affairs, agriculture, youth and science. Intergovernmental links are complemented by the activities of some 300 Commonwealth non-governmental organizations linking professionals, sportsmen and sportswomen, and interest groups, forming a 'people's Commonwealth'. The Commonwealth Games take place every four years.

Assistance to other Commonwealth countries normally has priority in the bilateral aid programmes of the association's developed members (Australia, Britain, Canada and New Zealand), who direct some 30 per cent of their aid to other member countries. Developing Commonwealth nations also assist their poorer partners, and many Commonwealth voluntary organizations promote development.

Many of the smaller Commonwealth countries are party to the Lomé Convention, which accords preferential access to the European Community (EC) for developing countries of Africa, the Caribbean and the Pacific, and provides for them to receive EC aid.

COMMONWEALTH SECRETARIAT

The Commonwealth has a secretariat, established in 1965 in London, which is funded by all member governments. This is the main agency for multilateral communication between member governments on issues relating to the Commonwealth as a whole. It promotes consultation and co-operation, disseminates information on matters of common concern, organizes meetings including the biennial summits, co-ordinates Commonwealth activities, and provides technical assistance for economic and social development through the Commonwealth Fund for Technical Co-operation.

The Commonwealth Foundation, also based in London, was established by Commonwealth governments in 1966 as an autonomous body with a board of governors representing Commonwealth governments that fund the Foundation. It promotes and funds exchanges and other activities aimed at strengthening the skills and effectiveness of professionals and non-government organizations. It also promotes culture, rural development, social welfare and the role of women.

COMMONWEALTH SECRETARIAT, Marlborough House, Pall Mall, London SW1Y 5HX. Tel: 071-839 3411.

Secretary-General, Chief Emeka Anyaoku (Nigeria)

COMMONWEALTH FOUNDATION, Marlborough House, Pall Mall, London SW1Y 5HY. Tel: 071-930 3783. *Director,* Dr Humayun Khan (Pakistan)

COMMONWEALTH INSTITUTE, Kensington High Street, London W8 6NQ. Tel: 071-603 4535. *Director-General,* S. Cox

COMMONWEALTH OF INDEPENDENT STATES

The Commonwealth of Independent States (CIS) is a multilateral grouping of sovereign states which were formerly constituent republics of the USSR. Membership of the CIS consists of all the former Soviet republics apart from the Baltic states, Georgia and Azerbaijan (ten in total). It acts as a co-ordinating mechanism for foreign, defence and economic policies, and is a forum for addressing those problems which have specifically arisen from the break-up of the USSR. The affairs of the CIS are addressed in inter-state, multilateral bodies and not by central institutions. Two multilateral CIS councils were formed in January 1992, the Council of Heads of State and the Council of Heads of Government. The Council of Heads of State is the highest organ of the CIS and meets not less than twice yearly; it is chaired by the heads of state of the members in (Russian) alphabetical order. The Council of Heads of Government meets not less than once every three months and carries out the co-ordination of military and economic activity in the Commonwealth.

FORMATION

In September 1991 the three Baltic states of Estonia, Latvia and Lithuania were recognized as independent sovereign states by the Soviet Union. A referendum in the Ukraine in early December 1991 showed overwhelming support for independence, and this galvanized the other republic leaders. The Russian, Ukrainian and Belorussian leaders concluded an agreement in Minsk on 8 December 1991 on the formation of a new Commonwealth of Independent States (CIS). The leaders declared that the USSR had ceased to exist and renounced the 1922 treaty which established it. On 21 December 1991 at a meeting in Alma-Ata, the three founding members of the CIS were joined by Armenia, Azerbaijan, Moldavia (now Moldova), Kazakhstan, Kirghizia (now Kyrgyzstan), Tajikistan, Turkmenistan and Uzbekistan. The Azerbaijani parliament subsequently failed to ratify the CIS Agreement and Azerbaijani membership effectively lapsed in late 1992. On 26 December 1991 the USSR formally ceased to exist.

OPERATION

In practice the CIS has not worked as well as had been hoped and has become a mechanism for diffusing conflicts between the former republics of the USSR. It has, however, failed to solve the underlying political reasons for these conflicts, the organization being constantly undermined by divisions between republics. Azerbaijan left principally because of

Russian aid to and support of Armenia in the continuing war over Nagorno-Karabakh. Many republics, especially Ukraine, have rejected any Russian attempts at closer economic ties, fearing an imposition of Soviet-style central control under Russian tutelage. Ukraine and Russia have continually argued over economic reform, nuclear weapons and the Black Sea Fleet. Moldova has clashed with Russia over Russian support for ethnic Russian separatists in Moldova, while Turkmensistan has rejected any CIS control over its profitable natural gas resources. In effect, a two-tier CIS has been created with seven states (Russia, Armenia, Belarus, Kazakhstan, Kyrgyzstan, Tajikistan, Uzbekistan) attempting to increase the co-ordination of defence and economic policies embodied in a CIS Charter signed in Musk on 22 January 1993, and three states (Ukraine, Moldova and Turkmenistan) rejecting increased co-operation and refusing to sign the Charter. The Charter confirms the operation of a single rouble zone but this has proved impossible.

DEFENCE CO-OPERATION

On becoming member states of the CIS, the 11 original states agreed to recognize their existing borders, respect one another's territorial integrity and reject the use of military force or other forms of coercion to settle disputes between them. Agreement was also reached on fulfilling all the international treaty obligations of the former USSR, and on a unified central control for nuclear weapons and other strategic forces. However, implementation of these agreements has proved problematic because of disputes and even open warfare between republics.

The CIS states agreed on a central CIS command for all nuclear weapons, and when President Gorbachev resigned in December 1991 he handed control of nuclear weapons to the CIS commander-in-chief Marshal Shaposhnikov. All tactical nuclear weapons had been transferred to the Russian republic by May 1992. An agreement was reached with the USA in May 1992 by the four republics with strategic nuclear weapons (Russia, the Ukraine, Belarus, Kazakhstan) on implementing the strategic arms reduction talks (START) treaty previously signed by the USA and USSR. Under this agreement the Ukraine, Belarus and Kazakhstan agreed to eliminate all their strategic nuclear weapons over a seven-year period and Russia has agreed to reduce its strategic nuclear weapons over the same period to such an extent that there will be a 38 per cent reduction in the overall former Soviet arsenal. The USA (Oct. 1992), Kazakhstan (July 1992), Russia (Nov. 1992) and Belarus (Feb. 1993) have ratified the START I treaty, but Ukraine has refused to destroy its strategic nuclear weapons or ratify the treaty. The Ukrainian government cites the need to retain the weapons to prevent Russian domination and also to use as a bargaining method to gain more Western aid.

As far as non-nuclear forces are concerned, the situation is confused. Although it was hoped that joint armed forces would be retained in some form, this has proved impossible to achieve. All member states have formed, or are in the process of forming their own defence ministries and armed forces. The six European CIS states (Russia, the Ukraine, Belarus, Moldova, Armenia and Azerbaijan) have reached agreement on how to implement the reductions required of the former Soviet armed forces by the Conventional Forces in Europe (CFE) Treaty signed by the former USSR. Ten CIS states (excluding Azerbaijan) also agreed in June 1992 on the establishment of joint peacemaking forces to intervene in CIS conflicts. Deployment of these forces is conditional on consensus in the Council of Heads of State. Forces have been deployed in Moldova and Tajikistan. All forces stationed outside the former Soviet Union and in the three Baltic States have been declared Russian. Communications and transport troops remain in Poland to facilitate the withdrawal of forces from the former East Germany. The last former Soviet troops left Cuba in July 1993 and Lithuania in August 1993 and agreement has been reached to withdraw troops from Germany by 31 August 1994. Forces remain in Estonia, Latvia, Georgia and Azerbaijan, but it is planned to have no former Soviet forces outside CIS territory by 1995.

ECONOMIC CO-OPERATION

As it became clear that the Soviet Union was disintegrating in October 1991, nine republics signed a treaty forming an economic community, and were joined by two other republics in November 1991. The principles of the treaty have been embodied within the CIS and form the basis of its economic co-operation. Members have agreed to refrain from economic actions that would damage each other and to conduct co-ordinated policies in energy production, taxation, customs regulations and tariffs, foreign economic relations, and monetary and banking systems. A single monetary unit, the rouble, was originally agreed upon by all member states, and the members recognized that the basis of recovery for their economies was private ownership, free enterprise and competition. However, it became clear in early 1992 that economic co-operation was a problem because of the different pace of economic reform in each member state, and the rouble zone has disintegrated as republics introduce their own currency.

A major advantage of economic co-ordination by the CIS members was the granting of large amounts of aid by Western countries, as the aid was dependent on co-operation between the former Soviet republics. Western countries and international organizations made it clear that economic aid was dependent on the republics accepting reponsibility for the former USSR's debt, abiding by all the former USSR's international obligations (such as nuclear and conventional arms reductions), and having a secure, central control and command of nuclear weapons. These conditions were originally accomplished through the CIS mechanisms and enabled members to gain extensive grants, loans, credits, trade agreements and technological, business and planning expertise and guidance from Western countries individually, the EC, the G7 grouping, the European Bank for Reconstruction and Development, the IMF and the World Bank.

CONFERENCE ON SECURITY AND CO-OPERATION IN EUROPE
Thunovska 12, 110 00 Prague 1, Czech Republic

The Conference on Security and Co-operation in Europe (CSCE) was launched in 1975 under the Helsinki Final Act, which established agreements between NATO members, Warsaw Pact members, and neutral and non-aligned European countries covering security in Europe; economic, scientific, technological and environmental co-operation; and humanitarian principles and co-operation. Further conferences were held at Belgrade (1977-8), Madrid (1980-3), Vienna (1986-9) and Helsinki (1992).

With the end of the Cold War, it was decided that the CSCE should be revitalized to provide a new security framework for Europe. The Charter of Paris for a New Europe was signed at Paris on 21 November 1990, committing members to support for multi-party democracy, free-market economics, the rule of law, and human rights. The signatories also undertook to enhance political consultation, agreeing on regular meetings of heads of government, ministers and officials. The CSCE held its first institutionalized Heads of State and Government summit in Helsinki in December 1992, at which they adopted the Helsinki Document 1992. This declares the CSCE to be a regional organization in the sense of Chapter VIII of the UN Charter and defines the structures of the organization. The summit also appointed a High Commissioner on National Minorities.

Two structures have been established: the Council of Foreign Ministers as a central forum for regular political consultations; and the Committee of Senior Officials (CSO) which prepares work for the Council and carries out its decisions. The chairmanship of the Council and CSO rotates among participating states. The CSCE is also underpinned by three permanent institutions; a Secretariat (Prague), a Conflict Prevention Centre (Vienna), and an Office for Democratic Institutions and Human Rights (Warsaw). The European Assembly of member parliamentarians will also be formed. In June 1991 the CSCE agreed upon new crisis prevention mechanisms to prevent violent conflict between and within member countries. In an attempt to put these mechanisms into place, the CSCE has established monitoring missions in areas of potential or actual conflict. Missions have been established in: Kosovo; Sandjak; Vojvodina; Macedonia (July 1992); Georgia; Estonia (December 1992); Moldova (February 1993). In June 1993 the Federal Yugoslav Republic forced the closure of the Kosovo, Sandjak and Vojvodina missions.

The CSCE has 53 participating states: Albania, Armenia, Austria, Azerbaijan, Belarus, Belgium, Bosnia-Hercegovina, Bulgaria, Canada, Croatia, Cyprus, Czech Republic, Denmark, Estonia, Finland, France, Georgia, Germany, Greece, Hungary, Iceland, Ireland, Italy, Kazakhstan, Kyrgyzstan, Latvia, Liechtenstein, Lithuania, Luxembourg, Malta, Moldova, Monaco, the Netherlands, Norway, Poland, Portugal, Romania, the Russian Federation, San Marino, Slovakia, Slovenia, Spain, Sweden, Switzerland, Tajikistan, Turkey, Turkmenistan, UK, Ukraine, USA, Uzbekistan, the Vatican and Yugoslavia (suspended from activities July 1992).
Chair of the Council and CSO (1993), Sweden
Secretary-General of the CSCE, Wilhelm Hoÿnck (*Germany*) (*resident in Vienna*)
Director of the Secretariat (Prague), Nils Eliasson (*Sweden*).
CSCE High Commissioner on National Minorities, Max van der Stoel (*Netherlands*)

THE COUNCIL OF EUROPE
67006 Strasbourg, France

The Council of Europe was founded in 1949. Its aim is to achieve greater unity between its members to safeguard their European heritage and to facilitate their economic and social progress through discussion and common action in economic, social, cultural, educational, scientific, legal and administrative matters, and in the maintenance and furtherance of pluralist democracy, human rights and fundamental freedoms. The Council of Europe is now making an active contribution to welcoming the new democracies of central and eastern Europe.

The 31 members are Austria, Belgium, Bulgaria, Cyprus, Czech Republic, Denmark, Estonia, Finland, Germany, Greece, Hungary, Iceland, the Republic of Ireland, Italy, Liechtenstein, Lithuania, Luxembourg, Malta, Netherlands, Norway, Poland, Portugal, San Marino, Slovakia, Slovenia, Spain, Sweden, Switzerland, Turkey and the UK. 'Special guest status' has been granted to Albania, Belarus, Croatia, Latvia, Romania, the Russian Federation and Ukraine.

The organs are the Committee of Ministers, consisting of the foreign ministers of member countries, who meet twice yearly, and the Parliamentary Assembly of 212 members, elected or chosen by the national parliaments of member countries in proportion to the relative strength of political parties. There is also a Joint Committee of Ministers and Representatives of the Parliamentary Assembly.

The Committee of Ministers is the executive organ of the Council. The majority of its conclusions take the form of international agreements (known as European Conventions) or recommendations to governments. Decisions of the Ministers may also be embodied in partial agreements to which a limited number of member governments are party. Member governments accredit Permanent Representatives to the Council in Strasbourg, who are also the Ministers' Deputies. The Committee of Deputies meets every month to transact business and to take decisions on behalf of Ministers.

The Parliamentary Assembly holds three week-long sessions a year. It debates reports on, *inter alia*, political, economic, agricultural, social, educational, legal and regional planning affairs, and also reports received annually from the OECD, other European organizations and certain specialized agencies of the United Nations. Its 13 permanent committees meet, normally in private, once or twice between each public plenary session of the Assembly. The Standing Conference of Local and Regional Authorities of Europe each year brings together mayors and municipal councillors in the same numbers as the members of the Parliamentary Assembly.

One of the principal achievements of the Council of Europe is the European Convention on Human Rights (1950) under which was established the European Commission and the European Court of Human Rights. Among the other conventions and agreements which have been concluded are the European Social Charter, the European Cultural Convention, the European Code of Social Security, and conventions on extradition, the legal status of migrant workers, torture prevention, conservation, and the transfer of sentenced prisoners. Most recently the specialized bodies of the Venice Commission and Demosthenes have been set up to assist in developing legislative, administrative and constitutional reforms in central and eastern Europe.

Non-member states take part in certain Council of Europe activities on a regular or *ad hoc* basis; thus the Holy See participates in all the educational, cultural and sports activities. The European Youth Centre is an educational residential centre for young people from all over Europe and further afield. The European Youth Foundation provides youth organizations with funds for their international activities.

Secretary-General, Catherine Lalumière (*France*)
Permanent UK Representative, His Excellency Roger Beetham, *apptd* 1993

THE ECONOMIC COMMUNITY OF WEST AFRICAN STATES
6 King George V Road, PMB 12745, Lagos, Nigeria

The Economic Community of West African States (ECO-WAS) was founded at a summit of West African heads of government at Lagos on 28 May 1975, and came into operation in January 1977. It aims to promote the cultural, economic and social development of West Africa through mutual co-operation.

Measures undertaken by ECOWAS include the gradual elimination of barriers to the movement of goods, people and services between member states and the improvement of regional telecommunications and transport.

The supreme authority of ECOWAS is vested in the annual summit of heads of government of all 16 member states. A Council of Ministers, two from each member state, meets biannually to monitor the organization and make recommendations to the summit. ECOWAS operates through a Secretariat, headed by the Executive Secretary. In addition there is a financial controller, an external auditor, the Disputes Tribunal and the Defence Council.

A Fund for Co-operation, Compensation and Development, situated at Lomé, Togo, finances development projects and provides compensation to member states who have suffered losses as a result of ECOWAS's policies, particularly in relation to trade liberalization.

In 1989–90 ECOWAS attempted to mediate in the Liberian civil war and sent an ECOWAS Monitoring Group (ECOMOG) peace-keeping force of 15,000 troops to the country in 1990. The force, led by Nigerian units with troops from Senegal, Gambia, Ghana, Guinea and Sierra Leone, succeeded in establishing an interim government and preventing further conflict in 1991, but fighting broke out again in late 1992 and continued into 1993, with ECOMOG air, land and sea forces engaged in heavy fighting with Charles Taylor's NPLF rebels.

Executive Secretary, Dr Abbas Bundu

THE EUROPEAN BANK FOR RECONSTRUCTION AND DEVELOPMENT
1 Exchange Square, London EC2A 2EH

The foundation of a European Bank for Reconstruction and Development (EBRD) was proposed by President Mitterrand of France on 25 October 1989. The charter of the EBRD was signed in Paris by 40 countries, the European Commission and the European Investment Bank on 29 May 1990. The EBRD was inaugurated in London on 15 April 1991.

The aim of the EBRD is to assist the transformation of the states of central and eastern Europe (Albania, Bulgaria, Czech Republic, Estonia, Hungary, Latvia, Lithuania, Poland, Romania, Slovakia, the republics of the former USSR and Yugoslavia) from centrally-planned economies to free market economies, with particular regard for strengthening democratic institutions, and respect for human rights and the environment. The EBRD provides technical assistance, training and investment in: the upgrading of infrastructure (energy, telecommunications and transport); the creation of modern financial systems (efficient banks, capital markets); and the restructuring of state industries. The EBRD's assistance is weighted towards the private sector; no more than 40 per cent of its investment can be made in state-owned concerns. It works in co-operation with its members, private companies, and international organizations, such as the OECD, the IMF, the World Bank and the UN specialized agencies.

The EBRD has an initial subscribed capital of 10 billion ECU. The major subscribers are: the USA, 10 per cent; Britain, France, Germany, Italy and Japan, 8.5 per cent each; central and eastern European states, 11.9 per cent.

The EBRD has 55 members. The highest authority is the Board of Governors; each member appoints one Governor and one alternate. The Governors delegate most powers to a 23-member Board of Directors; the Directors are responsible for the EBRD's operations and are appointed by the Governors for three-year terms. The Governors also elect the President of the Board of Directors, who acts as the Bank's president, for a four-year term. A Secretary-General liaises between the Directors and EBRD staff.

President of the Board of Directors, Jacques de Larosière
(France)
UK Executive Director, Robert Graham-Harrison
Secretary-General, Bart le Blanc *(Netherlands)*

THE EUROPEAN COMMUNITY

The beginnings of the European Community (EC) lie in the desire following the Second World War to replace the European system of competing nation states with a new union. It was partially out of a desire to heal traditional Franco-German enmity that in May 1951 Robert Schuman, the French Foreign Minister of the time, proposed that France and West Germany pool their coal and steel industries under an independent, supranational authority. They were joined by Belgium, Luxembourg, the Netherlands and Italy, and the Treaty of Paris was signed in 1951, establishing the European Coal and Steel Community (ECSC) in 1952.

The success of the ECSC led to discussions in 1955 in Messina, Italy, between the foreign ministers of its six member states on proposals for further moves towards European economic integration. As a result of these discussions the Treaty of Rome, establishing the European Economic Community, was signed on 25 March 1957. A second treaty founding the European Atomic Energy Community (EURATOM) was signed on the same day; this pledged the six signatories to co-operate in research into nuclear science, particularly in relation to nuclear energy.

The Treaty of Rome was intended to create a customs union to remove all obstacles to the free movement of capital, goods, people and services between member states. It also established a common external trade policy and common policies for agriculture and fisheries. Other articles of the treaty refer to preventing the distortion of competition within the Common Market; the co-ordination of economic policies; the harmonization of social policy sufficient to enable the functioning of the Common Market; the creation of a European Social Fund to increase employment and raise living standards; and the association of overseas countries and territories with the Community to increase mutual trade and to assist their economic and social development.

In addition, the Treaty of Rome established the Community's institutional structure; the Commission, the Council of Ministers, the Economic and Social Committee, the European Investment Bank, the Parliament, and the Court of Justice. Whereas the Parliament and Court of Justice were common to all three Communities from 1958, each Community had its own executive body and Council of Ministers. The three separate executive bodies and Councils of Ministers were merged in 1967.

In May 1969, the heads of government of the Six met at the Hague and decided both to widen and to deepen the Community. In accordance with the Hague decisions, the Council of Ministers agreed in 1970 that from 1975 the Community would have its own revenue, independent of national contributions; this would be derived from customs duties and agricultural import levies collected at the EC external frontier, and a proportion of national receipts from VAT.

In June 1970, the Six invited Britain, Denmark, Ireland and Norway to open negotiations on their applications to join the EC. The four countries signed a Treaty of Accession in Brussels on 22 January 1972; Norway subsequently withdrew its application after conducting a referendum on EC entry. The enlarged Community of the Nine came into existence on 1 January 1973.

During the 1970s the EC sought to strengthen the democracies of southern Europe; this led to the admission of Greece to the EC on 1 January 1981, and Portugal and Spain on 1 January 1986. Following a plebiscite, Greenland negotiated its withdrawal from the EC and left in 1986. The unification of Germany brought the former German Democratic Republic into the EC in October 1990. Andorra joined the customs union on 1 July 1991, but does not participate in other EC institutions.

ENLARGEMENT AND EXTERNAL RELATIONS

The EC Single Market programme spurred other European non-member states to open negotiations with the EC on some form of preferential access for their goods, services, labour and capital to the Single Market, or failing this, to open negotiations on EC membership. Principal among these states were the members of the European Free Trade Association (EFTA) who opened negotiations with the EC on extending the Single Market to the EFTA states by the formation of the European Economic Area (EEA) encompassing all 19 EC and EFTA states. An agreement on this was reached and signed in May 1992 with the operation of the EEA due to begin on 1 January 1993. The subsequent rejection of ratification of the EEA by the Swiss electorate in December 1992 necessitated negotiations on, and agreement to, a protocol to the EEA Agreement by the EC and the remaining six EFTA states which was reached in March 1993. This provides for the EEA to come into effect in late 1993 after ratification by all 18 member states. The EFTA states will provide a 'cohesion fund' for the poorer regions of the EC of some 500 million ECU in grants and 1.5 billion ECU in loans.

Despite the EEA negotiations, five of the EFTA states have also applied for EC membership. The EC opened membership negotiations on 1 February 1993, and at the EC Copenhagen summit of June 1993, agreement was reached on a target date of 1 January 1995 for EC membership for four countries.

The procedure for accession to the EC is laid down in the Treaty of Rome; states have to be European and stable democracies with free market economies. When a state applies for membership, its application is studied by the Commission, which produces an opinion. If the opinion is positive, negotiations may be opened leading to an Accession Treaty which must be approved by all member state governments, the European Parliament, all member state parliaments and the applicant state's parliament.

Applicant states negotiating entry: Austria *(applied* July 1989/ *positive opinion* Sept. 1992/*negotiations opened* Feb. 1993); Sweden (July 1991/Sept. 1992/Feb. 1993); Finland (March 1992/Nov. 1992/Feb. 1993); Norway (Nov. 1992/March 1993/April 1993)

Other applicants: Morocco *(applied* 1987/*rejected* 1987); Turkey *(applied* April 1987/*negative opinion* Dec. 1989); Cyprus *(applied* June 1990/*rejected* June 1993); Malta *(applied* July 1990/*negative opinion* June 1993); Switzerland *(applied* May 1992/*no opinion yet)*

The EC has also signed association agreements with several states; these include a commitment to eventual membership. Long standing agreements exist with Turkey (Dec. 1974), Malta (April 1971) and Cyprus (Dec. 1972). Since the end of the Cold War and the emergence of democratic, free market states in eastern Europe, new association agreements have been signed with Poland, Hungary, Czechoslovakia (now Czech Republic and Slovak Republic) (Dec. 1991), Romania (Feb. 1993) and Bulgaria (March 1993). These new agreements commit the EC to long-term political and economic integration with eastern

European states and liberalization of trade with the states in the 1993–5 period.

EUROPEAN COMMUNITY BUDGET 1992

	Billion ECU*	As % of total
Agriculture	35.3	53
Regional aid	18.6	28
Industry	4.0	6
Administration	4.0	6
Foreign policy	3.6	5
Reserves	1.0	2
TOTAL	66.5	100

* 1 ECU = £1.27 as at 29 September 1993

EC BUDGET BY MEMBER STATE 1992 (*billion ECU**)

	Contributions		Receipts	Net Contributor (−)/ Recipient (+)
Germany	19.0	(28.6%)	10.0	−9.0
France	12.8	(19.3%)	11.3	−1.5
Italy	9.9	(14.9%)	10.5	+0.6
UK	8.6	(12.9%)	5.6	−3.0
Spain	5.8	(8.7%)	8.7	+2.9
Netherlands	3.9	(5.9%)	3.8	−0.1
Belgium	2.7	(4.1%)	4.3	+1.6
Denmark	1.3	(1.9%)	1.8	+0.5
Greece	0.9	(1.4%)	4.8	+3.9
Portugal	0.9	(1.4%)	2.0	+1.1
Ireland	0.5	(0.8%)	2.9	+2.4
Luxembourg	0.1	(0.2%)	0.8	+0.7
TOTAL†	66.4	(100.1%)	66.5	

* 1 ECU = £1.27 as at 29 September 1993
† Figures not precise because of rounding

THE COMMON AGRICULTURAL POLICY

The Treaty of Rome established the Common Agricultural Policy (CAP) to increase agricultural production, to provide a fair standard of living for farmers and to ensure the availability of food at reasonable prices. This aim is achieved by a number of mechanisms: Import Levies (the EC sets a target price for a particular product in the Community, the world price is monitored and if it falls below the guide price, an import levy can be imposed equivalent to the difference between the two); Intervention Purchase (if the price of a product falls below the level indicated by the Council, member states must purchase supplies of the product, provided that they are of suitable quality); Export Subsidies (the EC pays a food exporter a subsidy equivalent to the difference between the price at which the product is bought in the EC and the lower sale price on the world market).

These measures had the required aim of stimulating production but also placed increasing demands on the EC budget. To surmount this problem, the EC created the system of co-responsibility levies; farm payments to the EC by volume of product sold. This system was supplemented by national quotas for particular products, such as milk. The increase in the number of EC members and the greater use of modern technology has further increased production and exacerbated EC budgetary problems; CAP now accounts for over 50 per cent of EC expenditure. Radical reforms were agreed at the end of May 1992, based on the reduction of target prices for cereals, beef and dairy produce. These are to be reduced by 29 per cent, 15 per cent and 5 per cent respectively, and the amount of money spent by the EC on the three mechanisms will fall. Production is expected to fall also because EC prices will be much closer to world price levels. Emphasis is also to be placed on direct grants to farmers to encourage them to take land out of production as a means of reducing surpluses.

EUROPEAN POLITICAL CO-OPERATION

The framework for European Political Co-operation (EPC) dates from an initiative at the Hague summit in 1969. In the resultant Luxembourg Report (1970), EC foreign ministers decided to harmonize and co-ordinate their foreign policy positions and achieve common actions where possible. Although the Single European Act obliged EC members to consult each other on foreign policy and the Commission participates in deliberations, EPC is an inter-governmental system operating parallel to, but outside, the Community.

The EPC system is headed by the European Council, which provides general lines of policy. Specific policy decisions are taken by the Council of Foreign Ministers, which meets at least four times a year. The foreign minister of the state holding the EC presidency initiates action, manages EPC and represents it abroad. He is supported by a secretariat based in Brussels and is advised by the past and future holders of the presidency, forming a so-called troika. The Council of Ministers is supported by the Political Committee which meets each month, or within 48 hours if there is a crisis, to prepare for ministerial discussions. A group of correspondents, designated diplomats in each member's foreign ministry, provides day-to-day contact.

THE EUROPEAN MONETARY SYSTEM

The European Monetary System (EMS) began operation on 13 March 1979 with three main purposes. The first purpose is to establish monetary stability in Europe, initially to exchange rates between EC member state currencies, and in the longer term to be part of a wider stabilization process, overcoming inflation and budget and trade deficits. The second purpose is to overcome the constraints resulting from the interdependence of EC economies, and the third is to aid the long-term process of European monetary integration. From its beginning all EC member state currencies have been members of the EMS (the Belgian and Luxembourg francs are one single currency).

The EMS has three components: the ECU; the Exchange Rate Mechanism (ERM); and the Credit Mechanisms. The ECU is a monetary unit, the value of which is calculated as a basket of set amounts of each Community currency. The relative weighting given to each currency in the ECU basket is proportional to the size of an EC member's economy and the state's share of EC trade. The German Deutsche Mark (DM) has the largest weighting of 32 per cent. The ECU is used for officially fixing the central rates in the ERM and as a means of settlement among central banks in the EMS.

The Exchange Rate Mechanism is the central component of the EMS. Officially all member currencies of the ERM have a central rate against the ECU, the anchor of the mechanism. In practice, the Deutsche Mark has become the anchor currency, with all other currencies' central rates expressed against the DM. Central banks are obliged to maintain their currencies within set margins (either 2.25 per cent above or below, or 6 per cent above or below) of their central rate by intervening in the foreign currency markets. Currencies may be revalued or devalued by up to 10 per cent by agreement with all other ERM members.

To do this, central banks co-ordinate their actions and can use the Credit Mechanisms to borrow money from each other and from the Central European Monetary Co-operation Fund where they each deposit 20 per cent of their reserves. Financial assistance is available to central banks over very short-term, short-term and medium-term periods.

Five currencies (Deutsche Mark, French franc, Belgian

franc, Dutch guilder, Danish krone) joined the ERM with 2.25 per cent fluctuation margins, and two currencies (Irish punt and Italian lira) with 6 per cent margins in March 1979. Subsequently the punt and lira reduced to 2.25 per cent margins. The UK pound sterling and Spanish peseta (Oct. 1990) and Portuguese escudo (April 1992) joined the ERM with 6 per cent margins. The pound and the lira were forced out of the mechanism by speculation in September 1992. Speculation forced the widening of the fluctuation margins to 15 per cent from 1 August 1993 for six of the remaining ERM member currencies (the Deutsche Mark and Dutch Guilder remain within 2.25 per cent margins).

THE SINGLE MARKET

Throughout the 1970s and early 1980s, EC members became increasingly concerned at the slow growth of the European economy. Although tariffs and quotas had been removed between member states, the EC was still separated into a number of national markets by a series of non-tariff barriers. It was to overcome these internal barriers to trade that the concept of the Single Market was developed. The measures to be undertaken were outlined in the Cockfield report (1985) and codified in the Single European Act (SEA), signed in 1986 and which came into force in 1987.

The SEA includes articles removing obstacles that distort the internal market: the elimination of frontier controls; the mutual recognition of professional qualifications; the harmonization of product specifications, largely by the mutual recognition of national standards; open tendering for public procurement contracts; the free movement of capital; the harmonization of VAT and excise duties; and the reduction of state aid to particular industries. The SEA changed the legislative process within the EC, particularly with the introduction of qualified majority voting in the Council of Ministers for some policy areas. The SEA also extends EC competence into the fields of technology, the environment, regional policy, monetary policy and external policy. The Single Market came into effect on 1 January 1993, at which time some 90–95 per cent of the necessary legislation had been agreed and passed by all member parliaments. The Single Market is expected to result in at least a 5 per cent increase in the collective GNP of EC member states.

THE MAASTRICHT TREATY

EC members are engaging in further moves towards European integration. Inter-governmental conferences on political and economic union began in December 1990. The Maastricht European Council in December 1991 agreed a new Treaty on European Union which is divided into an Economic and Monetary Union section and a Political Union section. The main points of the agreement were:

Economic and Monetary Union (EMU) Treaty, stage three
– A majority of EC members' economies to have converged sufficiently by 31 December 1996 for stage three to begin
– European Central Bank to be established by 1 July 1998
– A single EC currency to be introduced by 1 January 1999
– Special protocol agreed allowing the UK to 'opt out' of the single currency if it so wishes in January 1999

Political Union Treaty
– Greater powers for the European Parliament over EC legislation
– An agreement to move towards common foreign and defence policies
– The Western European Union to become the defence component of the EC
– The introduction of two new 'pillars' in the Community, one to deal with foreign and security policy and one to deal with immigration, asylum and policing. Decision-making

in these two new 'pillars' to be based on the Council of Ministers, minimizing the roles of the Commission, Parliament and European Court in these areas. A separate protocol on social policy was also agreed by 11 member states but not the UK. For the Maastricht Treaty to come into force it must be ratified by all member states, either by referendum or parliamentary vote. At the time of going to press, Germany had yet to ratify.

THE LEGISLATIVE PROCESS

The core of the EC policymaking process is a dialogue between the Commission, which initiates and implements policy, and the Council of Ministers, which takes policy decisions. A degree of democratic control is exercised by the European Parliament.

The original EC legislative process is known as the consultative procedure. The Commission drafts a proposal which it submits to the Council and to the Parliament. The Council then consults the ESC and the Parliament; the Parliament may request that amendments are made. With or without these amendments, the proposal is then adopted by the Council and becomes law.

Under the Single European Act, changes were made to the EC legislative process, particularly in strengthening the role of the Parliament in the implementation of the Single Market, in some areas of social policy, and in research and development. In these areas the new co-operation procedure operates. The Parliament now has a second reading of proposals in these fields, and after the second reading its rejection of a proposal can only be overturned by a unanimous decision of the Council.

The Council issues the following legislation: (a) Regulations, which are binding in their entirety and directly applicable to all member states; they do not need to be incorporated into national law to come into effect; (b) Directives, which are less specific, binding as to the result to be achieved but leaving the method of implementation open to member states; a directive thus has no force until it is incorporated into national law; (c) Decisions, which are also binding but are addressed solely to one or more member states or individuals in a member state; (d) Recommendations; (e) Opinions, which are merely persuasive.

THE COUNCIL OF MINISTERS

170 rue de la Loi, 1048 Brussels, Belgium

The Council of Ministers consists of ministers from the government of each of the member states. It formally comprises the foreign ministers of the member states but in practice the minister depends on the subject under discussion; i.e. when EC environment matters are under discussion, the meeting is informally known as the Environment Council. Council decisions are taken by majority vote, qualified majority vote (in which members' votes are weighted) or by unanimity. Council meetings are prepared by the Committee of Permanent Representatives (COREPER) of the member states, which acts as the 'gatekeeper' between national governments and the supranational EC, often negotiating on proposals with the Commission during the legislative process.

The European Council, comprising the heads of government of the member states, meets twice a year to provide overall policy direction. Established in 1974, the European Council was only formally brought within the EC institutional framework with the SEA.

The Presidency of the EC is held in rotation for six-month periods, setting the agenda for and chairing all Council meetings. The Presidency serves an important function since the incumbent nation has an opportunity to pursue its own particular policy priorities. The European Council holds a summit in the country holding the Presidency at the end of its period in office. The holders of the Presidency for the years 1993–6 are:

1993 Denmark; Belgium
1994 Greece; Germany
1995 France; Spain
1996 Italy; Ireland

OFFICE OF THE UNITED KINGDOM PERMANENT REPRESENTATIVE TO THE EUROPEAN COMMUNITIES
Rond-point Robert Schuman 6, 1040 Brussels, Belgium
Ambassador and UK Permanent Representative, Sir John Kerr, KCMG, *apptd* 1990

THE COMMISSION
200 rue de la Loi, 1049 Brussels, Belgium

The Commission consists of 17 Commissioners, two each from France, Germany, Italy, Spain and the UK, and one each from the remaining member states. The members of the Commission are appointed for four-year renewable terms by the agreement of the member states; the present Commission came into office on 1 January 1993 for a two-year term in order that from 1 January 1995 the four-year term will run concurrently with the term of the European Parliament. The President and Vice-Presidents are appointed from among the Commissioners for two-year terms, also renewable. The Commissioners pledge sole allegiance to the EC.

The Commission initiates and implements EC legislation and is the guardian of the EC treaties. It is the exponent of Community-wide interests rather than the national preoccupations of the Council. Each Commissioner is supported by advisers and oversees whichever of the 23 departments, known as Directorates-General (DGs), is assigned to him. Each Directorate-General is headed by a Director-General.

COMMISSIONERS

President

Secretariat-General; Forward Studies Unit; Inspectorate-General; Legal Services; Monetary Affairs; Spokesman's Service; Joint Interpreting and Conference Service; Security Office, Jacques Delors (*France*)

Vice-Presidents

Industrial Affairs, Information and Telecommunications technology, Martin Bangemann (*Germany*)
External Economic Affairs (North America, Japan, China, CIS, Europe, including Central and Eastern Europe), Commercial and Trade Policy, Sir Leon Brittan (*UK*)
Economic and Financial Affairs, Monetary Matters, Credit and Investments, Statistical Office, Henning Christophersen (*Denmark*)
Co-operation and Development, Lomé Convention, Humanitarian Aid, Manuel Marin (*Spain*)
Science, Research and Development, Joint Research Centre, Human Resources, Education, Training and Youth, Antonio Ruberti (*Italy*)
Competition, Personnel and Administration, Karel Van Miert (*Belgium*)

Members

Budgets, Financial Control, Fraud Prevention, Cohesion Fund, Peter Schmidhuber (*Germany*)
Energy and Euratom Supply Agency, Transport, Abel Matutes (*Spain*)
Customs, Taxation, Consumer Policy, Christiane Scrivener (*France*)
Regional Policy, Relations with the Committee of the Regions, Bruce Millan (*UK*)

External Political Relations, Common foreign and security policy, Enlargement negotiations, Hans van den Broek (*Netherlands*)
Relations with the European Parliament, Openness, Communication and Information, Culture and Audiovisual, Office for official publications, João de Deus Pinheiro (*Portugal*)
Social Affairs and Employment, Relations with the Economic and Social Committee, Immigration, Interior and Judicial Affairs, Padraig Flynn (*Ireland*)
Agriculture and Rural Development, Rene Steichen (*Luxembourg*)
Environment, Nuclear Safety and Civil Protection, Fisheries, Ioannis Paleokrassas (*Greece*)
Internal Market, Financial Institutions, Institutional Questions, Small and Medium-sized enterprises, Raniero Vanni d'Archirafi (*Italy*)
Secretary-General, D. Williamson (UK)

DIRECTOR-GENERALS

DGI, External Relations, H. G. Krenzler
DGII, Economic and Financial Affairs, G. Ravasio
DGIII, Internal Market and Industrial Affairs, R. Perissich
DGIV, Competition, C.-D. Ehlerman
DGV, Employment, Industrial Relations and Social Affairs, H. C. Jones
DGVI, Agriculture, G. Legras
DGVII, Transport, R. Coleman
DGVIII, Development, P. Pooley
DGIX, Personnel and Administration, F. de Koster
DGX, Information, Communication and Culture, C. Flesch
DGXI, Environment, Civil Protection and Nuclear Safety, L. J. Brinkhorst
DGXII, Science and Research and Development, P. Fasella
DGXIII, Telecommunications, Information Industries and Innovation, M. Carpentier
DGXIV, Fisheries, J. Almedia Serra
DGXV, Financial Institutions and Company Law, J. Mogg
DGXVI, Regional Policies, E. L. Illarramendi
DGXVII, Energy, C. S. Maniatopoulos
DGXVIII, Credit and Investments, E. Cioffi
DGXIX, Budgets, J.-P. Mingasson
DGXX, Financial Control, L. de Moor
DGXXI, Customs Union and Indirect Taxation, P. Wilmott
DGXXII, Co-ordination of Structural Policies, T. O'Dwyer
DGXXIII, Enterprise Policy, Distributive Trades, Tourism and Co-operatives, H. von Moltke

THE EUROPEAN PARLIAMENT

The European Parliament originated as the Common Assembly of the ECSC; it acquired its present name in 1962. Members (MEPs) were initially appointed from the membership of national parliaments. Direct elections to the Parliament were first held in 1979. Elections to the Parliament are held on differing bases throughout the EC; British MEPs are elected on a first-past-the-post system, except in Northern Ireland which uses proportional representation. The next elections will be held in June 1994.

Following the Edinburgh summit agreement of December 1992, the Parliament will be expanded to 567 seats from the present 518 to include representatives from the former East Germany and concurrent increases in other member states' representatives. The allocation of seats will be: Germany 99 (81 at 1989 elections); UK, France, Italy 87 each (81); Spain 64 (60); the Netherlands 31 (25); Belgium, Greece, Portugal 25 each (24); Denmark 16 (16); Ireland 15 (15); Luxembourg 6 (6). MEPs serve on 19 committees, which scrutinize draft

EC legislation and the activities of the Commission. Plenary sessions are held in Strasbourg, committees meet in Brussels and the Secretariat's headquarters is in Luxembourg.

The EP has gradually expanded its influence within the EC. It has general powers of supervision over the Commission, and consultation and co-decision with the Council; it votes to approve a newly appointed Commission and can dismiss it at any time by a two-thirds majority. It can reject the EC budget as a whole and alter non-compulsory expenditure not specified in the EC primary legislation. Although the EP cannot directly initiate legislation, its reports can spur the Commission into action.

The Parliament's organization is deliberately biased in favour of multi-national political groupings, with recognition of a political grouping in the parliament (which entitles it to offices, funding, representation on committees and influence in debates and legislation) being easier for multi-national groups. A political grouping with members from only one country needs a minimum of 23 members for recognition, whereas one with members from two countries needs 18 members, and a grouping with members from three or more countries needs only 12 members.

PARLIAMENT, Palais de l'Europe, 67006 Strasbourg Cedex, France; 97–113 rue Belliard, 1040 Brussels, Belgium
SECRETARIAT, Centre Européen, Kirchberg, 2929 Luxembourg
President, Dr Egon Klepsch (Germany)
(For a full list of British MEPs, *see* pages 274–5)

THE ECONOMIC AND SOCIAL COMMITTEE
2 rue Ravenstein, 1000 Brussels, Belgium

The Economic and Social Committee is an advisory and consultative body. The ESC has 189 members, who are nominated by member states. It is divided into three groups; employers; workers; and other interest groups such as consumers, farmers and the self-employed. It issues opinions on draft EC legislation and can bring matters to the attention of the Commission, Council and Parliament; it has a key role in providing specialist and technical input.
President, Susanne Tiemann (*Germany*)

THE COURT OF AUDITORS
12 rue A. De Gasperi, L-1615 Luxembourg

The Court of Auditors, established in October 1977, is responsible for the audit of the legality and regularity as well as of the sound financial management of the resources managed by the European Communities and Community bodies. The Court may also submit observations on specific questions and deliver opinions. It has 12 members appointed by the Council of Ministers.
President, André Middelhoek (*Netherlands*)

COURT OF JUSTICE OF THE EUROPEAN COMMUNITIES
L-2925 Luxembourg

The European Court superseded the Court of Justice of ECSC and is common to the three European Communities. It exists to safeguard the law in the interpretation and application of the Community treaties, to decide on the legality of decisions of the Council of Ministers or the Commission, and to determine violations of the Treaties. Cases may be brought to it by the member states, the Community institutions, firms or individuals. Its decisions are directly binding in the member countries. The 13 judges and six advocates-general of the Court are appointed for renewable six-year terms by the member governments in concert. During 1991, 326 new cases were lodged at the court and 204 judgments were delivered.

Composition of the Court, in order of precedence, with effect from 7 October 1992:
O. Due (*President*); C. N. Kakouris (*President of the 4th and 6th Chambers*); C. O. Lenz (*First Advocate-General*); G. C. Rodriguez Inglesias (*President of the 1st and 5th Chambers*); M. Zuleeg (*President of the 3rd Chamber*); J. L. Murray (*President of the 2nd Chamber*); G. F. Mancini;

EUROPEAN PARLIAMENT POLITICAL GROUPINGS

	Soc.	EPP	LDR	Greens	EDA	RBW	ER	LU	Ind.	Total
Belgium	8	7	4	3	–	1	1	–	–	24
Denmark	3	4	3	1	–	4	–	–	1	16
Germany	31	32	5	6	–	1	3	–	3	81
Greece	8	10	–	–	1	–	–	3	2	24
Spain	27	17	5	1	2	3	–	–	5	60
France	22	12	10	8	11	1	10	7	–	81
Ireland	1	4	2	–	6	1	–	–	1	15
Italy	34	27	3	7	–	3	–	–	7	81
Luxembourg	2	3	1	–	–	–	–	–	–	6
Netherlands	8	10	4	2	–	–	–	–	1	25
Portugal	8	3	9	–	–	1	–	3	–	24
UK	46	33	–	–	–	1	–	–	1	81
TOTAL	198	162	46	28	20	16	14	13	21	518

Soc.	Socialist Group (including British Labour Party, Northern Ireland Social Democratic and Labour Party, German Social Democrats and Italian Democratic Left Party)	
EPP	European People's Party (including Christian Democrats, British and Danish Conservatives, Spanish Popular Party, and Northern Ireland Official Unionist Party)	
LDR	Liberal Democratic and Reformist Group (including Centre parties and Portuguese Social Democrats)	
EDA	European Democratic Alliance (including French Gaullists and Irish Fianna Fail Party)	
RBW	Rainbow Group (mainly regional parties, including Scottish National Party)	
ER	European Right (including French National Front and German republican parties)	
LU	Left Unity (French, Greek and Portuguese Communist parties)	
Ind.	Independents (including Northern Ireland Democratic Unionist Party)	

M. Darmon (*Advocate-General*); R. Joliet;
F. A. Schockweiler; J. C. Moitinho De Almeida; F. Grevisse;
M. Diez de Velasco; W. van Gerven (*Advocate General*);
F. G. Jacobs (*Advocate-General*); G. Tesauro (*Advocate-General*); P. J. G. Kapteyn; C. Gulman (*Advocate-General*);
D. A. O. Edward; J.-G. Giraud (*Registrar*)

COURT OF FIRST INSTANCE
L-2925 Luxembourg
Established by a Council decision of 24 October 1988, under powers conferred by the Single European Act, the Court of First Instance started to exercise its functions at the end of October 1989. It had jurisdiction to hear and determine certain categories of cases brought by natural or legal persons, in particular cases brought by European Community officials, or cases on competition law. By a Council decision of 8 June 1993 the court had its jurisdiction enlarged to hear and determine all actions brought by natural or legal persons with the exemption of those concerned with anti-dumping matters. During 1991, 93 new cases were lodged at the court and 41 judgments were delivered.

Composition of the Court, in order of precedence, for the judicial year 1992–3:
J. L. Cruz Vilaca (*President*); D. P. M. Barrington (*President of the 5th Chamber*); H. Kirschner (*President of the 1st Chamber*); J. Biancarelli (*President of the 3rd Chamber*);
C. W. Bellamy (*President of the 4th Chamber*); A. Saggio;
R. Schintgen; C. P. Briët; B. Vesterdorf; R. Garcia-Valdecasary Fernandez; K. Lenaerts; A. Kalogeropoulos;
H. Jung (*Registrar*)

THE EUROPEAN INVESTMENT BANK
100 Boulevard Konrad Adenauer, L-2950 Luxembourg

The European Investment Bank (EIB) was set up in 1958 under the terms of the Treaty of Rome to finance capital investment projects promoting the balanced development of the European Community.

It grants long-term loans to private and public enterprises, public authorities and financial institutions, to finance projects which further: the economic development of less advanced regions (Assisted Areas); improvement of European communications; environmental protection; attainment of the Community's energy policy objectives; modernization of enterprises, co-operation between undertakings in the different member states, and the activities of small and medium-sized enterprises.

EIB activities have also been extended outside member countries as part of the Community's development co-operation policy, under the terms of different association or co-operation agreements with 12 countries in the Mediterranean region, six in central and eastern Europe, 30 in Latin America and Asia, and, under the Lomé Conventions, 69 in Africa, the Caribbean and the Pacific. The Bank has also been asked to extend its activity to Estonia, Latvia and Lithuania.

The Bank's total financing operations in 1992 amounted to 17,033 million ECU, of which 16,140 million was for investment in the European Community and 893 million for outside the Community. Between 1988 and 1992 the EIB had made available a total of 9,172 million ECU for investment in the UK.

The members of the European Investment Bank are the 12 member states of the Community, who have all subscribed to the Bank's capital of 57,600 million ECU. The bulk of the funds required by the Bank to carry out its tasks are borrowed on the capital markets of the Community and non-member countries, and on the international market.

As it operates on a non-profit-making basis, the interest rates charged by the EIB reflect the cost of the Bank's borrowings and closely follow conditions on world capital markets.

The Board of Governors of the European Investment Bank consists of one government minister nominated by each of the member countries, usually the finance minister, who lay down general directives on the policy of the Bank and appoint members to the Board of Directors (21 nominated by the member states, one by the Commission of the European Communities), which takes decisions on the granting and raising of loans and the fixing of interest rates. A Management Committee, composed of the Bank's President and six Vice-Presidents, also appointed by the Board of Governors, is responsible for the day-to-day operations of the Bank. The President and Vice-Presidents also preside as Chairman and Vice-Chairmen at meetings of the Board of Directors.

President, Sir Brian Unwin
Vice-Presidents, Lucio Izzo; Alain Prate; José de Oliveira
    Costa; Wolfgang Roth; Corneille Bruck;
    Hans Duborg
UK OFFICE: 68 Pall Mall, London SW1Y 5ES Tel: 071-839 3351

EUROPEAN COMMUNITY INFORMATION

The Commission maintains offices in:
LONDON, 8 Storey's Gate, London SW1P 3AT. Tel: 071-973 1992
EDINBURGH, 9 Alva Street, Edinburgh EH2 4HP. Tel: 031-225 2058
CARDIFF, 4 Cathedral Road, Cardiff CF1 9SG. Tel: 0222-371631
BELFAST, Windsor House, 9–15 Bedford Street, Belfast BT2 7EG. Tel: 0232-240708
DUBLIN, 39 Molesworth Street, Dublin 2
WASHINGTON, 2100 M Street NW (Suite 707), Washington DC 20037
NEW YORK, 1 Dag Hammarskjöld Plaza, 254 East 47th Street, New York, NY 10017
OTTAWA, Inn of the Provinces, Office Tower (Suite 1110), 350 Sparks Street, Ontario, KIR 7SA
CANBERRA, 18 Alakana Street, Yarralumia, ACT 2600, and a number of other cities

UK EUROPEAN PARLIAMENT INFORMATION OFFICE
2 Queen Anne's Gate, London SW1H 9AA. Tel: 071-222 0411

There are European Information Centres, set up to give information and advice to small businesses, in 24 British towns and cities. A number of universities maintain European Documentation Centres.

EUROPEAN FREE TRADE ASSOCIATION
9–11 rue de Varembé, 1211 Geneva 20, Switzerland

The European Free Trade Association (EFTA) was established on 3 May 1960, by Austria, Denmark, Norway, Portugal, Sweden, Switzerland and the UK. EFTA was subsequently joined by Finland, Iceland and Liechtenstein. Denmark and the UK left EFTA in 1972 and Portugal in 1985 to join the EC.

The first objective of EFTA was to establish free trade in industrial goods between members; this was achieved in 1966. Its second objective was the creation of a single market in western Europe and in 1972 EFTA signed a free trade agreement with the EC covering trade in industrial goods; the remaining tariffs on industrial products were finally abolished in 1984.

In 1989 exploratory talks began on the free movement of goods, services, capital and labour throughout the EC–EFTA area. The talks also covered co-operation in education, the environment, social policy, and research and development. Formal negotiations on the establishment of a European Economic Area (EEA), encompassing all 19 EC and EFTA countries, began in 1990. These negotiations were concluded when EFTA and EC ministers signed the EEA Agreement on 2 May 1992 in Oporto, Portugal. The aim was to have the EEA enter into force at the same time as the EC single market in 1993. This proved impossible when the Swiss electorate rejected ratification of the EEA Agreement in a referendum in December 1992. The remaining six EFTA states entered into negotiations with the EC in early 1993 which led to the signing of a protocol to the EEA Agreement in March 1993 by the remaining 18 states and the EC Commission. The protocol provides for the adjustment of contributions by the EFTA states to the EC cohesion funds after Switzerland's withdrawal and envisages the entry into force of the EEA agreement in late 1993 after its ratification by all 18 states.

In addition to its other activities, EFTA has expanded its relations with other non-EC states in recent years, especially in eastern Europe where assisting economic reforms is the priority. Free trade agreements have been signed with Turkey (December 1991), Israel (September 1992), Poland and Romania (December 1992), Bulgaria and Hungary (March 1993), Czech Republic and Slovakia (April 1993). In addition, EFTA has signed declarations of economic co-operation with Estonia, Latvia and Lithuania (December 1991), Slovenia (May 1992) and Albania (December 1992).

Austria, Sweden, Finland and Norway are currently negotiating membership with the EC and hoping for a possible entry date of 1 January 1995. Switzerland's EC application of 1992 is being reassessed in the light of the rejection of the EEA Agreement.

The Council of EFTA is the principle organ of the Association. It generally meets once a week at the level of heads of the permanent national delegations to the EFTA Secretariat in Geneva and twice a year at ministerial level. The chairmanship of the Council rotates every six months. Each state has a single vote and recommendations must normally be unanimous; decisions of the Council are binding on member countries. The EFTA surveillance authority for the EEA, which is one portion of the secretariat, moved from Geneva to Brussels in January 1993.

Secretary-General, Georg Reisch (*Austria*)

EUROPEAN ORGANIZATION FOR NUCLEAR RESEARCH (CERN)
CH-1211 Geneva 23, Switzerland

The Convention establishing the European Organization for Nuclear Research (CERN) came into force in 1954. The organization promotes European collaboration in high energy physics of a purely scientific nature. It is not concerned with research of a military nature.

The member countries are Austria, Belgium, Czech Republic, Denmark, Finland, France, Germany, Greece, Hungary, Italy, Netherlands, Norway, Poland, Portugal, Slovak Republic, Spain, Sweden, Switzerland and the UK. The following have observer status: Israel, the Russian Federation, Turkey, Yugoslavia (suspended), the EC Commission and UNESCO.

The Council is the highest policy-making body and is made up of two delegates from each member state. There is also a Committee of the Council comprising a single delegate

from each member state (who is also a Council member) and the chairmen of the scientific policy and finance advisory committees. The Council is chaired by a President who is elected by the Council in Session. The Council also elects the Director-General, the person responsible for the internal organization of CERN. The Director-General heads a workforce of approximately 3,000, including physicists, craftsmen, technicians and administrative staff. At present over 6,000 physicists use CERN's facilities.

The member countries contribute to the budget directly in proportion to their net national revenue. The 1993 budget was SFr 951.67 million.

President of the Council, Sir William Mitchell, CBE, FRS (*UK*)
Director-General (1989–93), C. Rubbia

EUROPEAN SPACE AGENCY
8–10 rue Mario Nikis, 75738 Paris, France

The European Space Agency (ESA) was set up on 31 May 1975. It was formed from two earlier space organizations – the European Space Research Organization (ESRO) and the European Launcher Development Organization (ELDO). Its aims include the advancement of space research and technology, the implementation of a long-term European space policy and the co-ordination of national space programmes.

The member countries are Austria, Belgium, Denmark, France, Germany, Republic of Ireland, Italy, Netherlands, Norway, Spain, Sweden, Switzerland and the United Kingdom. Finland is an associate member and Canada a co-operating state.

The agency is directed by a Council composed of the representatives of the member states, and its chief officer is the Director-General.

Director-General, Jean-Marie Luton, *apptd* 1990

FOOD AND AGRICULTURE ORGANIZATION OF THE UNITED NATIONS
Viale delle Terme di Caracalla, 00100 Rome, Italy

The Food and Agriculture Organization (FAO) is a specialized UN agency, established on 16 October 1945. It assists rural populations by raising levels of nutrition and living standards, and by encouraging greater efficiency in food production and distribution. In addition, it collects, analyses and disseminates information on agriculture and natural resources. FAO also advises governments on national agricultural policy and planning; its Investment Centre, together with the World Bank and other financial institutions, helps to prepare development projects. FAO's field programme covers a range of activities, including strengthening crop production, rural and livestock development, and conservation.

FAO keeps a special watch on areas where famine can occur. The Office for Special Relief Operations channels emergency aid from governments and other agencies, and assists in rehabilitation. The Technical Co-operation Programme provides schemes for countries facing agricultural crises.

FAO had 162 members (161 states and the EC) as at January 1993. It is governed by a biennial Conference of all its members which sets the forthcoming programme and budget. The budget for 1992–3 was US$645,600,000, funded by member countries in proportion to their gross national products. FAO also receives substantial additional funding from the UN Development Programme, donor governments and other institutions.

The Conference elects a Director-General and a 49-member Council, which governs between Conferences. The Field Programme is administered by a Secretariat, headed by the Director-General, by the Development Department and by five regional offices.

Director-General, Edouard Saouma *(Lebanon)*
UK Representative, J. Goldsack, MBE, British Embassy, Rome

GENERAL AGREEMENT ON TARIFFS AND TRADE
Centre William Rappard, 154 rue de Lausanne, 1211 Geneva 21, Switzerland

Under an initiative of the UN Economic and Social Council, a committee met in 1947 to draft the charter of a new international trade organization. The charter was never ratified and the General Agreement on Tariffs and Trade (GATT), intended as an interim arrangement with effect from January 1948, became the only regime for the regulation of world trade. Never formalized, GATT has evolved rules and procedures to adapt to changing circumstances. One hundred and ten states are now contracting parties and a further 23 apply its rules *de facto*; GATT thus covers nearly 90 per cent of world trade.

GATT is dedicated to the expansion of non-discriminatory international trade. It provides a common code of conduct and a forum for the discussion and solution of international trade problems, and for multilateral negotiations to reduce tariffs and other trade barriers. Special attention is given to assisting the trade of developing countries, which are exempted from some GATT provisions.

Extensions of free trade are made progressively via 'rounds' of multilateral negotiations. Seven have been completed: Geneva (1947); Annecy (1948); Torquay (1950); Geneva (1956); Dillon (1960-1); Kennedy (1964-7); Tokyo (1973-9). The average duties on manufactured goods have been reduced from 40 per cent in the 1940s to 5 per cent. The current Uruguay Round was launched in 1986. The 115 participating governments are conducting negotiations covering market access and new trade rules regarding tariffs, non-tariff barriers, tropical products, textiles, agriculture, etc. For the first time new multilateral rules for services, intellectual property and investment are also being discussed.

The Uruguay Round was scheduled to finish in December 1990, but has not been completed because of disagreement between the USA, other members of the Cairns group of New World agricultural producers, and the European Community over the level of Community agricultural subsidies, and between the USA, EC and Japan over bringing trade in services under the GATT system. Negotiations are still continuing in an effort to finalize draft agreements.

The most authoritative body of GATT is the Session of Contracting Parties, which usually meets once a year, and comprises senior officials from the 110 member governments. Early in the Uruguay Round it was also agreed that at least once every two years governments participating in the Session would be represented at ministerial level. In the period between the meetings of the Session, the Council of Representatives meets about nine times a year to act on routine and urgent matters. The work and decision-making process of these two bodies is supported by several specialist standing committees, which regularly meet to examine, discuss and negotiate the various aspects of international trade policies and practices. *Ad hoc* working parties are also established to consider specific issues, as well as panels to

examine and rule upon trade disputes. The committees overseeing the non-tariff agreements reached in the Tokyo Round report to the Contracting Parties Session only.

The International Trade Centre, founded in 1964 to help developing countries with export expansion, is operated jointly with the UN Conference on Trade and Development.

Director-General, Peter Sutherland *(Ireland)*
Permanent UK Representative, M. R. Morland, CMG, 37-39 rue de Vermont, 1211 Geneva 20

INTERNATIONAL ATOMIC ENERGY AGENCY
Vienna International Centre, Wagramerstrasse 5, PO Box 100, 1400 Vienna, Austria

The International Atomic Energy Agency (IAEA) was established on 29 July 1957 as a consequence of the UN International Conference on the Peaceful Uses of Atomic Energy held the previous year. Although it operates under the aegis of, and reports annually to, the UN, the IAEA is not a specialized agency.

The IAEA aims to accelerate and enlarge the contribution of atomic energy to peace, health and prosperity, and to ensure that any assistance provided by it or under its supervision is not used for military purposes. It establishes atomic energy safety standards and offers services to its member states for the safe operation of their nuclear facilities and for radiation protection. It is the central point for the International Convention on early notification of a nuclear accident. The IAEA also encourages research and training in nuclear power. It is additionally charged with drawing up safeguards and verifying their use in accordance with the Non-Proliferation Treaty 1968, the Treaty for the Prohibition of Nuclear Weapons in Latin America (Tlatelolco Treaty) 1968 and the Treaty on a South Pacific Nuclear Free Zone (Rarotonga Treaty).

Together with the Food and Agriculture Organization and the World Health Organization, the IAEA established an International Consultative Group on Food Irradiation in 1983.

The IAEA had 114 members as at May 1993. A General Conference of all its members meets annually to decide policy, a programme and a budget (1992, US$191 million), as well as electing a Director-General and 35-member Board of Governors. The Board meets four times a year to execute policy which is implemented by the Secretariat under a Director-General.

Director-General, Hans Blix *(Sweden)*
Permanent UK Representative, C. Hulse, Jaurésgasse 12, 1030 Vienna, Austria

INTERNATIONAL CIVIL AVIATION ORGANIZATION
1000 Sherbrooke Street West, Montreal, Quebec, Canada H3A 2R2

The International Civil Aviation Organization (ICAO) was founded with the signing of the Chicago Convention on International Civil Aviation in December 1944, and became a specialized agency of the United Nations on 4 April 1947. It sets international technical standards and recommended practices for all areas of civil aviation, including airworthiness, air navigation, traffic control and pilot licensing. It encourages uniformity and simplicity in ground regulations and operations at international airports, including immigration and customs control. The ICAO also promotes regional air navigation, plans for ground facilities, and collects and distributes air transport statistics worldwide. It is dedicated to improving safety and to the orderly development of civil aviation throughout the world.

The ICAO had 178 members as at 14 April 1993. It is governed by an assembly of all its members which meets at least once every three years. A Council of 33 members is elected, taking into account the leading air transport nations as well as ensuring representation of less developed countries. The Council elects the President, appoints the Secretary-General and supervises the organization through subsidiary committees, serviced by a Secretariat.

President of the Council, Dr Assad Kotaite (*Lebanon*)
Secretary-General, Dr Philippe Rochat (*Switzerland*)
UK Representative, D. S. Evans, CMG, Suite 928, 1000
Sherbrooke Street West, Montreal, Quebec, Canada
H3A 3G4

INTERNATIONAL CONFEDERATION OF FREE TRADE UNIONS
37-41 rue Montagne aux Herbes Potagères, 1000 Brussels, Belgium

Formed in 1949 the International Confederation of Free Trade Unions (ICFTU) was created to promote free trade unionism worldwide. It aims to establish, maintain and promote free trade unions, and to promote peace with economic security and social justice.

Affiliated to the ICFTU are 164 individual unions and representative bodies in 117 countries and territories. On 11 December 1992 there were nearly 113 million members.

The supreme authority of the organization is the Congress which convenes at least every four years. It is composed of delegates from the affiliated trade union organizations. The Congress elects an Executive Board of 49 members which meets not less than once a year. The Board establishes the budget and receives suggestions and proposals from affiliates as well as acting on behalf of the Confederation. The Congress also elects the General Secretary.

General Secretary, Enzo Friso
UK Affiliate, TUC, Congress House, 23-28 Great Russell Street, London WC1B 3LS

INTERNATIONAL CRIMINAL POLICE ORGANIZATION
50 quai Achille Lignon, 69006 Lyon, France

The International Criminal Police Commission (Interpol) was set up in 1923 to establish an international criminal records office and to harmonize extradition procedures. In 1956 a revised Constitution was adopted and the organization adopted its present name. On 1 January 1993 the organization comprised 169 member states.

Interpol's aims are to ensure and promote mutual assistance between all criminal police authorities, and to support government agencies concerned with combating crime, whilst respecting the national sovereignty of members. Interpol is financed by annual contributions from the governments of member states.

Interpol's policy is decided by the General Assembly which meets annually; it is composed of delegates appointed by the member states. The 13-member Executive Committee is elected by the General Assembly from among the member states' delegates, and is chaired by the President, who has a four-year term of office. The permanent administrative organ is the General Secretariat, headed by the Secretary-General, who is appointed by the General Assembly.

Secretary-General, Raymond Kendall, QPM (*UK*)
UK OFFICE, Interpol Bureau, Spring Gardens, Tinworth Street, London SE11 5EH
UK Representative, A. Pacey, QPM

INTERNATIONAL ENERGY AGENCY
Chateau de la Muette, 2 rue André-Pascal, 75775 Paris, France

The International Energy Agency (IEA), founded in November 1974, is an autonomous agency within the framework of the Organization for Economic Co-operation and Development (OECD). The IEA had 23 member countries at January 1993.

The IEA's objectives include improvement of energy supply and demand worldwide, increased efficiency, development of alternative energy sources and the promotion of relations between oil producing and oil consuming countries. The IEA also maintains an emergency system to alleviate the effects of severe oil supply disruptions.

The main decision-making body is the Governing Board composed of senior energy officials from member countries. Various standing groups and special committees exist to facilitate the work of the Board. The IEA Secretariat, with a staff of energy experts, carries out the work of the Governing Board and its subordinate bodies. The Executive Director is appointed by the Board.

Executive Director, Mrs Helga Steeg (*Germany*)

INTERNATIONAL FUND FOR AGRICULTURAL DEVELOPMENT
107 Via del Serafico, 00142 Rome, Italy

The establishment of the International Fund for Agricultural Development (IFAD) was proposed by the 1974 World Food Conference and IFAD began operations as a UN specialized agency in December 1977. Its purpose is to mobilize additional funds for agricultural and rural development projects in developing countries that benefit the poorest rural populations. The organization's lending policy is based on using its resources to support projects which: raise food production; provide employment and additional income for poor farmers; reduce malnutrition; and improve food distribution systems.

IFAD had 150 members as at June 1993. Membership is divided into three categories: the developed countries (OECD), the oil-exporting developing countries (OPEC) and the remaining developing countries. The three groups have equal voting rights in IFAD's governing structure. All powers are vested in a Governing Council of all member countries. It elects an 18-member Executive Board (with 17 alternate members) responsible for IFAD's operations. The Council elects a President who is also chairman of the Board. He is assisted by a Vice-President and three Assistant Presidents.

At the end of June 1993 IFAD's loan portfolio comprised 348 approved projects in 99 developing countries. The operational budget for 1993 was US$122.4 million. IFAD has a staff of 105 professionals and 154 support staff.

President, Fawzi H. Al-Sultan (*Kuwait*)

INTERNATIONAL LABOUR ORGANIZATION
4 route des Morillons, 1211 Geneva 22, Switzerland

The International Labour Organization (ILO) was established in 1919 as an autonomous body of the League of Nations and became the UN's first specialized agency in 1946. The ILO aims to increase productive labour, improve working conditions and raise living standards. It sets minimum international labour standards through the drafting of international conventions. Member countries are obliged to submit these to their domestic authorities for ratification, and thus undertake to bring their domestic legislation in line with the conventions. Members must report to the ILO periodically on how these regulations are being implemented. The ILO also runs a technical assistance programme in developing countries, and conducts research and disseminates information on labour. Through its World Employment Programme, it is attempting to reduce unemployment in developing countries by assisting national and international efforts to provide productive work. It is also developing an international programme to improve working conditions.

The ILO had 162 members as at March 1993. It is composed of the International Labour Conference, the Governing Body and the International Labour Office. The Conference of members meets annually, and is attended by national delegations comprising two government delegates, one worker delegate and one employer delegate. It formulates international labour conventions and recommendations, provides a forum for discussion of world labour and social problems, and approves the ILO's programme and budget (1994–5, US$466,500,000). Additional project funding is provided by the UN Development Programme, the UN Fund for Population Activities and other sources.

The 56-member Governing Body, composed of 28 government, 14 worker and 14 employer members, acts as the ILO's executive council. Ten governments, including Britain, hold seats on the Governing Body because of their industrial importance. There are also various regional conferences and advisory committees. The International Labour Office acts as a secretariat and as a centre for operations, publishing and research.

In 1960 the ILO established the International Institute for Labour Studies in Geneva as a think-tank on labour and social policy.

Director-General, Michel Hansenne (*Belgium*)
UK OFFICE, Vincent House, Vincent Square, London
SW1P 2NB. Tel: 071-828 6401

INTERNATIONAL MARITIME ORGANIZATION
4 Albert Embankment, London SE1 7SR

The International Maritime Organization (IMO) was established as a UN specialized agency in 1948. Due to delays in treaty ratification it did not commence operations until 17 March 1958. Originally it was called the Inter-Governmental Maritime Consultative Organization (IMCO) but changed its name in 1982.

The IMO fosters inter-governmental co-operation in technical matters relating to international shipping, especially with regard to safety at sea. It is also charged with preventing and controlling marine pollution caused by shipping and facilitating maritime traffic. The IMO is responsible for calling maritime conferences and drafting marine conventions.

Additionally, it provides technical aid to countries wishing to develop their activities at sea.

The IMO had 140 members as at June 1993. It is governed by an Assembly comprising delegates of all its members. It meets biennially to make policy, decide the budget (1992–3, £30 million), vote on specific recommendations on pollution and maritime safety and elect the Council. The Council fulfils the functions of the Assembly between sessions and appoints the Secretary-General. It consists of 32 members; eight from the world's largest shipping nations, eight from the nations most dependent on seaborne trade, and 16 other members to ensure a fair geographical representation. The Maritime Safety Committee, working through various sub-committees, makes reports and recommendations to the Council and the Assembly. There are a number of other specialist subsidiary committees, including one for marine environmental protection.

The IMO acts as the secretariat for the London Dumping Convention (1972) which regulates the disposal of land-generated waste at sea.

Secretary-General, William A. O'Neil (*Canada*)

INTERNATIONAL MARITIME SATELLITE ORGANIZATION
99 City Road, London EC1Y 1AX

Inmarsat (the International Maritime Satellite Organization) was founded in July 1978 and began operations on 1 February 1982. Inmarsat operates a system of satellites to provide global mobile communications at sea, in the air and on land. Inmarsat satellite terminals are used worldwide on ships, in aircraft and on land for global telephone, facsimile, telex, e-mail data, as well as maritime safety and distress communications.

Inmarsat comprises three bodies: the Assembly, the Council and the Directorate. The Assembly is composed of representatives of all member countries, each with one vote. It meets every two years to review activities and objectives, and to make recommendations to the Council. The Council is the main decision-making body and consists of representatives of the 18 members with the largest investment shares. Four others who represent the interests of developing countries are elected to the Council on the basis of geographical representation. The Council meets at least three times a year and oversees the activities of the directorate, the permanent staff of Inmarsat.

As at May 1993 there were 67 member countries.

Director-General, Olof Lundberg (*Sweden*)

INTERNATIONAL MONETARY FUND
700 19th Street NW, Washington DC 20431, USA

The International Monetary Fund (IMF) was established on 22 July 1944, at the UN Monetary and Financial Conference held at Bretton Woods, New Hampshire. Its Articles of Agreement entered into force on 27 December 1945, and the IMF began operations in May 1946. The IMF exists to promote international monetary co-operation, the expansion of world trade, and exchange stability, and to eliminate foreign exchange restrictions. The IMF advises members on their economic and financial policies; promotes policy co-ordination among the major industrial countries; and gives technical assistance in central banking, balance of payments accounting, taxation, and other financial matters. As at April 1993 the IMF had 177 members.

Upon joining the IMF, a member is assigned a 'quota', based on the member's relative standing in the world economy and its balance of payments position, that determines its capital subscription to the Fund, its access to IMF resources, its voting power, and its share in the allocation of Special Drawing Rights (SDRs). Quotas are reviewed every five years and adjusted accordingly. With the coming into effect of the Ninth General Review of quotas, which increased quotas by 50 per cent, total Fund quotas increased to SDR 144.6 billion at the end of April 1993 (from SDR 91.2 billion at the end of April 1992). The SDR, an international reserve asset issued by the IMF, is calculated daily on a basket of usable currencies and is the IMF's unit of account; on 1 May 1992, SDR 1 equalled US$1.37374. SDRs are allocated at intervals to supplement members' reserves and thereby improve international financial liquidity.

IMF financial resources derive primarily from members' capital subscriptions, which are equivalent to their quotas. In addition, the IMF is authorized to borrow from official lenders. Periodic charges are also levied on financial assistance. At the end of April 1992, total outstanding IMF credits amounted to SDR 26.7 billion; borrowings amounted to SDR 23.7 billion.

The IMF is not a bank and does not lend money; it provides temporary financial assistance by selling a member's SDRs or other members' currencies in exchange for the member's own currency. The member can then use the purchased currency to alleviate its balance of payments difficulties. The IMF's credit under its regular facilities is made available to members in tranches or segments of 25 per cent of quota. For first credit tranche purchases, members are required to demonstrate reasonable efforts to overcome their balance of payments difficulties. There are no performance criteria and the total amount is repaid in three and a quarter to five years. Upper credit tranche purchases are normally associated with stand-by arrangements. These typically cover periods of one to two years. They focus on macroeconomic policies aimed at overcoming balance of payment difficulties and are required to meet certain performance criteria. Repurchases are made in three and a quarter to five years.

In addition, the IMF supports medium-term programmes under the extended Fund facility, which generally runs for three years (sometimes up to four years) and is aimed at overcoming balance of payments difficulties stemming from macroeconomic and structural problems. Members experiencing a temporary balance of payments shortfall have access to the compensatory and contingency financing facility. The IMF also offers credits to low-income countries engaged in economic reform through its structural adjustment facility and enhanced structural adjustment facility. Under its buffer stock financing facility, the IMF provides resources to help members' contributions to approved buffer stocks. In April 1993, the IMF adopted a new temporary facility, the systemic transformation facility, designed to extend financial assistance to members experiencing severe disruptions in their trade and payments arrangements due to a shift from significant reliance on trading at nonmarket prices to multilateral, market-based trade.

The IMF is headed by a Board of Governors, comprising representatives of all members, which meets annually. The Governors delegate powers to 24 Executive Directors, five appointed and 19 elected. The Executive Directors operate the Fund on a daily basis under a Managing Director, whom they elect. The appointed directors represent France, Germany, Japan, UK and USA.

Managing Director, Michel Camdessus (*France*)

UK Executive Director, D. Peretz, Room 11-120, IMF, 700 19th Street NW, Washington DC 20431

INTERNATIONAL RED CROSS AND RED CRESCENT MOVEMENT
17 avenue de la Paix, 1211 Geneva, Switzerland

The International Red Cross and Red Crescent Movement is composed of three elements. The International Committee of the Red Cross (ICRC) is the founding body of the Red Cross and was formed in 1863. It is a neutral intermediary negotiating between warring factions, working throughout the world to protect and assist victims of armed conflict. It also ensures the application of the Geneva Conventions with regard to prisoners of war and detainees.

The International Federation of Red Cross and Red Crescent Societies, founded in 1919, is the body which exists to contribute to the development of the humanitarian activities of national societies, to co-ordinate their relief operations for victims of natural disasters, and to care for refugees outside areas of conflict. There are national Red Cross and Red Crescent Societies in 150 countries with a global membership of 250 million.

The International Conference of the Red Cross and Red Crescent meets every four years, bringing together delegates of the ICRC, the International Federation and the national societies, as well as representatives of nations bound by the Geneva Conventions.

President of the ICRC, Cornelio Sommaruga

BRITISH RED CROSS, 9 Grosvenor Crescent, London SW1X 7EJ. *Director-General*, Michael R. Whitlam

INTERNATIONAL TELECOMMUNICATIONS SATELLITE ORGANIZATION
3400 International Drive NW, Washington DC 20008–3098, USA

Formed in 1964, the International Telecommunications Satellite Organization (Intelsat) owns and operates the worldwide commercial communications satellite system. The system is composed of a network of 19 satellites and more than 1,600 antennas which link together over 170 countries, territories and dependencies.

Intelsat provides an international telephone service; an international television service; the Intelsat Business Service (IBS); Intelnet (a digital service designed for data collection and distribution); domestic telecommunications services and the Vista service providing telecommunications to remote communities.

Each of the 125 member states contributes to the capital costs of the organization in proportion to its investment share. The investment share is based on the relative usage of the system by member countries.

There is a four-tier hierarchy. The Assembly of Parties to the agreement meets every two years to consider long-term objectives and is composed of representatives of the member governments. The Meeting of Signatories annually considers the financial, technical and operational aspects of the system. The Board of Governors has 27 members; the executive organ is the permanent staff of Intelsat and is headed by a Director-General who reports to the Board of Governors.

Director-General, Irving Goldstein (*USA*)

INTERNATIONAL TELECOMMUNICATION UNION
Place des Nations, 1211 Geneva 20, Switzerland

The International Telecommunication Union (ITU) was founded in Paris in 1865 as the International Telegraph Union and became a UN specialized agency in 1947. It promotes international co-operation and sets standards and regulations for telecommunications operations of all kinds. It assists the development of telecommunications and provides technical assistance to developing countries. The ITU allocates the radio frequency spectrum and registers radio frequency assignments in order to avoid harmful interference between radio stations of different countries. It also collects and disseminates telecommunications information.

The ITU had 180 members as at 11 May 1993. The supreme authority is the Plenipotentiary Conference, composed of representatives of all the members, which meets not less than once every five years. It elects the Administrative Council of 43 members which meets annually to supervise the Union and set the budget (1993, SFr 154 million). The Conference also elects the Secretary-General, who heads the General Secretariat. Four other permanent bodies include the International Frequency Registration Board, the Telecommunications Development Bureau and two consultative committees, one for radio, and one for telephone and telegraph.
Secretary-General, Dr P. Tarjanne (*Finland*)

LEAGUE OF ARAB STATES
Maidane Al-Tahrir, Cairo, Egypt

The purpose of the League of Arab States (founded 1945) is to ensure co-operation among member states and protect their independence and sovereignty, to supervise the affairs and interests of Arab countries, to control the execution of agreements concluded among the member states, and to promote the process of integration among them. The League considers itself a regional organization and is an observer at the United Nations.

Member states are Algeria, Bahrain, Djibouti, Egypt, Iraq, Jordan, Kuwait, Lebanon, Libya, Mauritania, Morocco, Oman, Palestine, Qatar, Saudi Arabia, Somalia, Sudan, Syria, Tunisia, United Arab Emirates and the Republic of Yemen.

Member states participate in various specialized agencies of the League whose role is to develop specific areas of co-operation between Arab states. These include: the Arab Organization for Mineral Resources; the Arab Monetary Fund; the Arab Satellite Communications Organization; the Arab Bank for Economic Development in Africa; the Arab League Educational, Cultural and Scientific Organization, and the Council of Arab Economic Unity.
Secretary-General, Dr Ahmed Esmat Abdel-Meguid (*Egypt*)
UK Office, 52 Green Street, London W1Y 3RH

NORDIC COUNCIL
Tyrgatan 7, Box 19506, Stockholm 10432, Sweden

The Nordic Council was established in March 1952 as an advisory body on economic and social co-operation, comprising parliamentary delegates from Denmark, Iceland, Norway and Sweden. It was subsequently joined by Finland (1955),

and representatives from the Faröes and the Åland Islands (1969/70), and Greenland (1984).

Co-operation is regulated by the Treaty of Helsinki signed in 1962. This was amended in 1971 to create the Nordic Council of Ministers, which discusses all matters except defence and foreign affairs. Matters are given preparatory consideration by a Committee of Co-operation Ministers' Deputies and joint committees of officials. Decisions of the Council of Ministers, which are taken by consensus, are binding, although if ratification by member parliaments is required, decisions only become effective following parliamentary approval. The Council of Ministers is advised by the Nordic Council, to which it reports annually. There are Ministers for Nordic Co-operation in every member government.

The Nordic Council, comprising 87 voting delegates nominated from member parliaments and about 80 non-voting government representatives, meets twice a year in plenary sessions. The full Council chooses an eleven-member Praesidium, comprising two delegates from each sovereign member and one party group-nominated delegate, which conducts business between sessions. A Secretariat, located in Stockholm and headed by a Secretary-General, liaises with the Council of Ministers and provides administrative support, as well as acting as a publishing house and information centre. The Council of Ministers has a separate Secretariat, based in Copenhagen.
Secretariat to the Nordic Council, Tyrgatan 7, s-10432 Stockholm, Sweden
Secretary-General, Jostein Osnes (*Norway*)
Secretariat of Nordic Council of Ministers, Store Strandgade 18, 1255 Copenhagen K, Denmark
Secretary-General, Pan Stenback (*Finland*)

NORTH ATLANTIC TREATY ORGANIZATION
Brussels 1110, Belgium

The North Atlantic Treaty (Treaty of Washington) was signed on 4 April 1949 by the foreign ministers of 12 nations: Belgium, Canada, Denmark, France, Iceland, Italy, Luxembourg, the Netherlands, Norway, Portugal, the UK and USA. Greece and Turkey acceded to the Treaty in 1952, the Federal Republic of Germany in 1955 (the reunited Germany acceded in October 1990), and Spain in 1982. The North Atlantic Treaty has been the framework for a defensive political and military alliance designed to provide common security for its members through co-operation and consultation in political, military, economic, scientific and other non-military fields. Since the end of the Cold War in 1990, the Alliance has adapted its structures and policies to meet new security challenges, including contributing to peace-keeping operations and co-operating closely with the countries of central and eastern Europe. The alliance is now committed to promoting security and stability throughout Europe and to playing a major role in support of UN and CSCE operations. NATO is involved in supporting the UN peace-keeping effort in the former Yugoslavia, supplying a naval force to monitor compliance with the UN embargo, a headquarters for the UNPROFOR II force in Bosnia-Hercegovina, and aircraft to monitor and enforce the UN air exclusion zone over Bosnia-Hercegovina.

The North Atlantic Council, chaired by the Secretary-General, is the highest authority of the Alliance and is composed of permanent representatives of the sixteen member countries. It meets at ministerial level (foreign ministers) at least twice a year. The permanent representatives (ambassadors) head national delegations of advisers and experts. Defence matters are dealt with in the Defence Planning Committee (DPC), composed of representatives of all member countries, except France. The DPC also meets at ministerial level (defence ministers) at least twice a year. Nuclear matters are dealt with in the Nuclear Planning Group (NPG), composed of representatives of all countries except for France (Iceland being an observer). The NPG meets regularly at Permanent Representatives level and twice a year at ministerial level (defence ministers). The NATO Secretary-General chairs the Council, the DPC and the NPG.

The Council and DPC are forums for confidential and constant inter-governmental consultation and are the main decision-making bodies within the North Atlantic Alliance. They are assisted by an International Staff, divided into five divisions: Political Affairs; Defence Planning and Policy; Defence Support; Infrastructure, Logistics and Civil Emergency Planning; Scientific and Environmental Affairs.

The senior military authority in NATO, under the Council and DPC, is the Military Committee (MC) composed of the Chief of Defence Staffs of each member country, except France and Iceland. The Military Committee, which is assisted by an integrated international military staff, also meets in permanent session with permanent military representatives and is responsible for making recommendations to the Council and Defence Planning Committee on measures considered necessary for the common defence of the NATO area and for supplying guidance on military matters to the major NATO commanders. The Chairman of the Military Committee, elected for a period of two to three years, represents the MC on the Council.

The strategic area covered by the North Atlantic Treaty is divided among three Commands (European, Atlantic, Channel) and a Regional Planning Group (Canada and the United States).

The major NATO commanders are responsible for the development of defence plans for their respective areas, for the determination of force requirements and for the deployment and exercise of the forces under their command. The major NATO commanders report to the Military Committee.

At a NATO summit held in London in 1990, NATO heads of state and government redefined the goals and strategy of the organization in the light of the end of the Cold War. At a meeting held in May 1991, defence ministers agreed to create a new rapid reaction corps under British command. A Declaration of Peace and Co-operation was issued at a further summit held in Rome in November 1991 and a new strategic concept was published, introducing major changes in the organization of NATO forces and overall reductions of around 30 per cent. The new strategic concept also provides for a reduced dependence on nuclear weapons, greater mobility, flexibility and adaptability of forces, greater use of multinational formations, and a streamlining of NATO's military command structure.

A North Atlantic Co-operation Council (NACC) was also established at the 1991 Rome summit within a framework of dialogue and partnership between the member countries of the Alliance and states of eastern Europe and the former Soviet Union. The NACC has 38 member states. Its role is to facilitate closer official and informal ties on security and related issues between the members. It focuses on the particular areas of peace-keeping, defence planning, defence industry conversion, and the democratic concepts of civilian-military relations.

Secretary-General and Chairman of the North Atlantic Council, of the DPC and of the NPG, Manfred Wörner (*Germany*)

UK Permanent Representative on the North Atlantic Council, Sir John Weston, KCMG
Chairman of the Military Committee, Field Marshal Sir Richard Vincent, GBE, KCB, DSO (*UK*)
Supreme Allied Commander, Europe, Gen. John Shalikashvili (*US*)
Supreme Allied Commander, Atlantic, Adm. Paul D. Miller (*US*)
Commander-in-Chief, Channel, Adm. Sir Hugo White, KCB, CBE (*UK*)
Commander Allied Rapid Reaction Corps, Lt.-Gen. Sir Jeremy MacKenzie (*UK*)

ORGANIZATION FOR ECONOMIC CO-OPERATION AND DEVELOPMENT
2 rue André-Pascal, 75116 Paris

Formed on 30 September 1961, the Organization for Economic Co-operation and Development (OECD) replaced the Organization for European Economic Co-operation. The OECD is the instrument for international co-operation among industrialized member countries on economic and social policies. Its objectives are to assist its member governments in the formulation and co-ordination of policies designed to achieve high, sustained economic growth while maintaining financial stability, to contribute to world trade on a multilateral basis and to stimulate members' aid to developing countries.

The following countries belong to the OECD: Australia, Austria, Belgium, Canada, Denmark, Germany, Finland, France, Greece, Iceland, Republic of Ireland, Italy, Japan, Luxembourg, the Netherlands, New Zealand, Norway, Portugal, Spain, Sweden, Switzerland, Turkey, UK and USA.

The Council is the supreme body of the organization. Composed of one representative for each member country, it meets at permanent representative level under the chairmanship of the Secretary-General, or at ministerial level (usually once a year) under the chairmanship of a minister elected annually. Decisions and recommendations are adopted by mutual agreement of all members of the Council. Fourteen members of the Council are chosen annually to form an executive committee to assist the Council. However, most of the OECD's work is undertaken in over 200 specialized committees and working parties. Five autonomous or semi-autonomous bodies are related in varying degrees to the Organization: the Nuclear Energy Agency, the International Energy Agency, the Development Centre, the Centre for Educational Research and Innovation, and the European Conference of Ministers of Transport. These bodies, the committees and the Council are serviced by an international Secretariat headed by the Secretary-General of the Organization.

Secretary-General, Jean-Claude Paye (*France*)
UK Permanent Representative, Keith MacInnes, 19 rue de Franqueville, Paris 75116

ORGANIZATION OF AFRICAN UNITY
PO Box 3243, Addis Ababa, Ethiopia

The Organization of African Unity (OAU) was established in 1963 and has 51 members (Morocco suspended its participation in 1985 in protest at the Polisario-proclaimed Saharan Arab Democratic Republic (SADR), representing Western Sahara, being admitted as a member). It aims to further African unity and solidarity, to co-ordinate political, economic, social and defence policies, and to eliminate colonialism in Africa.

The chief organs are: the Assembly of heads of state or government, which is the supreme organ of the OAU and meets once a year to consider matters of common African concern and to co-ordinate the Organization's policies; the Council of foreign ministers, which is the Organization's executive body responsible for the implementation of the Assembly's policies, and which meets twice a year; and the Commission of Mediation, Conciliation and Arbitration which promotes the peaceful settlement of disputes between member countries. The main administrative body is the General Secretariat, based in Addis Ababa.

Substantial budgetary arrears due to delays in the payment of national contributions has meant that the OAU continually faces difficulties in furthering its aims. In June 1991 the Assembly adopted an African Economic Community Treaty which envisages establishment of the Economic Community after ratification by two-thirds of the OAU's membership.

Secretary-General, Salim Ahmed Salim (*Tanzania*)

ORGANIZATION OF AMERICAN STATES
17th Street and Constitution Avenue NW, Washington DC 20006, USA

Originally founded in 1890 for largely commercial purposes, the Organization of American States (OAS) adopted its present name and charter in 1948. The charter was later amended by the Protocol of Buenos Aires (1967) and the Protocol of Cartagena de Indias (1985). Its aims are to strengthen the peace and security of the continent; to promote and consolidate representative democracy with due respect for the principle of non-intervention; to prevent possible causes of difficulties and to ensure the pacific settlement of disputes that may arise among the member states; to provide for common action on the part of those states in the event of aggression; to seek the solution of political, judicial and economic problems that may arise among them; to promote, by co-operative action, their economic, social and cultural development; and to achieve an effective limitation of conventional weapons that will make it possible to devote the largest amount of resources to the economic and social development of the member states. The OAS is a regional organization within the United Nations.

Policy is determined by the annual General Assembly. Meetings of ministers of foreign affairs consider urgent problems, and advise in cases of armed attack and threats to peace. A Permanent Council, comprised of one representative from each member state, meets at OAS headquarters throughout the year.

The 35 member states are Antigua and Barbuda, Argentina, Bahamas, Barbados, Belize, Bolivia, Brazil, Canada, Chile, Colombia, Costa Rica, Cuba, Dominica, Dominican Republic, Ecuador, Grenada, Guatemala, Guyana, Haiti, Honduras, Jamaica, Mexico, Nicaragua, Panama, Paraguay, Peru, St Christopher and Nevis, St Lucia, St Vincent and the Grenadines, El Salvador, Suriname, Trinidad and Tobago, Uruguay, USA and Venezuela.

Secretary-General, João Clemente Baena Soares (*Brazil*)

ORGANIZATION OF ARAB PETROLEUM EXPORTING COUNTRIES
PO Box 108 Maglis Al-Shaab, 11516 Cairo, Egypt.

The Organization of Arab Petroleum and Exporting Countries (OAPEC) was founded in 1968. The objectives of the organization are to promote co-operation in economic activities; to safeguard members' interests; to unite efforts to ensure the flow of oil to consumer markets; and to create a favourable climate for the investment of capital and expertise.

The Ministerial Council is composed of oil ministers from the member countries and meets twice a year to determine policy, to direct activities and to approve the budgets and accounts of the General Secretariat and the Judicial Tribunal. The Judicial Tribunal is composed of seven part-time judges who rule on disputes between member countries and disputes between countries and oil companies. The executive organ of OAPEC is the General Secretariat.

The member countries of OAPEC are Algeria, Bahrain, Egypt, Iraq, Kuwait, Libya, Qatar, Saudi Arabia, Syria and the United Arab Emirates. Tunisia's membership has been inactive since 1987.

Secretary-General, Abdel-Aziz A. Al-Turki

ORGANIZATION OF THE ISLAMIC CONFERENCE
PO Box 178, Jeddah 21411, Saudi Arabia

The Organization of the Islamic Conference (OIC) was established in May 1971 with the purpose of generating solidarity and co-operation among all the Islamic countries of the world. It also has the specific aims of: co-ordinating efforts to safeguard the Muslim Holy Places; supporting the Palestine cause and the formation of a Palestinian state; assisting member states to maintain their independence; co-ordinating the views of member states in international forums such as the UN; improving co-operation in the economic, cultural and scientific fields.

The OIC has three central organs, supreme among them the Conference of the Heads of State which meets once every three years to discuss issues of importance to Islamic states. The Conference of Foreign Ministers meets annually to prepare reports for the Conference of Heads of State and to fulfil the Organization's aims. The General Secretariat, based in Jeddah, carries out administrative tasks. It is headed by a Secretary-General who is elected by the Conference of Foreign Ministers for a non-renewable four-year term and has 200 staff.

In addition to this structure, the OIC has several subsidiary bodies and specialized bodies. These include the Islamic Solidarity Fund, to aid Islamic institutions in member countries, and the Islamic Development Bank, to finance development projects in poorer member states. An Islamic Court of Justice is also planned. The Organization runs various offices to organize the economic boycott of Israel.

The achievement of the Organization's aims has often been prevented by political rivalry and conflicts between member states, such as the Iran-Iraq war and the Iraqi invasion of Kuwait. Egypt's membership was suspended from 1979 to 1984 because of its peace treaty with Israel. Saudi Arabia, as the Organization's main source of funding, exercises great influence within the Organization. Since 1991 the Organization has become more united and has spoken out against violence against Muslims in India, the Occupied Territories and Bosnia-Hercegovina. In July 1993 the OIC summit in Islamabad agreed to offer 7,600 troops to the UN to protect Muslim areas of Bosnia-Hercegovina.

The Organization has 51 members (49 sovereign Muslim states in Africa, the Middle East, central and south-east Asia and Europe, plus the Palestine Liberation Organization and Zanzibar) and two observers, Mozambique and Turkish Northern Cyprus. It has an annual budget of £5 million.

Secretary-General, Hamid Algabid (*Niger*)

ORGANIZATION OF THE PETROLEUM EXPORTING COUNTRIES
Obere Donaustrasse 93, 1020 Vienna, Austria

The Organization of the Petroleum Exporting Countries (OPEC) was created in 1960 as a permanent intergovernmental organization with the aims of unifying and co-ordinating the petroleum policies of members and determining the best means of protecting their interests, individually and collectively. Since 1982 OPEC has attempted (only partially successfully) to impose overall production limits and member state production quotas in an attempt to maintain stable oil prices. In the third quarter of 1993 the overall production quota was 23,582,000 barrels per day.

The supreme authority is the Conference of Ministers of Oil, Mines and Energy of member countries which meets at least twice a year and formulates policy. The Board of Governors, nominated by member countries, directs the management of OPEC and implements Conference resolutions. The Secretariat, based in Vienna, carries out executive functions under the direction of the Board of Governors.

The 12 member countries are Algeria, Gabon, Indonesia, Iran, Iraq, Kuwait, Libya, Nigeria, Qatar, Saudi Arabia, UAE and Venezuela. Ecuador withdrew from OPEC on 31 December 1992.

Secretary-General, Dr Subroto (*Indonesia*)

SOUTH PACIFIC COMMISSION
BP D5, Nouméa Cedex, New Caledonia

The South Pacific Commission is a technical assistance agency with programmes in agriculture and plant protection, marine resources, community health, socio-economic and statistical services, and community services. The organization is run by a management committee headed by the Secretary-General. The other committee members are the Director of Services and the Director of Programmes.

The South Pacific Commission (SPC) was established in February 1947 following the signing of the Canberra Agreement by the governments of Australia, France, the Netherlands, New Zealand, the UK and the USA. The aim was to promote the economic and social stability of the islands in the region. The SPC now numbers 27 member states and territories, including the five remaining founder states (the Netherlands has withdrawn) in which no programmes are run, and the other 22 states and territories of Melanesia, Micronesia and Polynesia.

Since 1967 the South Pacific Conference has met annually to discuss and adopt the SPC's work programme, to adopt the budget and to nominate the officers of the Commission.

Secretary-General, Ati George Sokomanu (*Vanuatu*)
Director of Programmes, Vaasatia Poloma Komiti (*W. Samoa*)
Director of Services, Fusi Vave Caginavanua (*Fiji*)

THE UNITED NATIONS
UN Plaza, New York, NY 10017, USA

The United Nations is a voluntary association of states, dedicated through signature of the UN Charter to the maintenance of international peace and security and the solution of economic, social and political problems through international co-operation. The UN is not a world government and has no right of intervention in the essentially domestic affairs of states.

The UN was founded as a successor to the League of Nations and inherited many of its procedures and institutions. The name 'United Nations' was first used in the Washington Declaration of January 1942 to describe the 26 states which had allied to fight the Axis powers. The UN Charter developed from discussions at the Moscow Conference of the foreign ministers of China, the United Kingdom, the USA and Soviet Union held in October 1943. Further progress was made at Dumbarton Oaks, Washington, between August and October 1944 during talks involving the same states. The role of the Security Council was formulated at the Yalta Conference of Churchill, Roosevelt and Stalin in January 1945. The Charter was formally drawn up by 50 allied nations at the San Francisco Conference between April and 26 June 1945, when it was signed. Following ratification the UN came into effect on 24 October 1945, which is celebrated annually as United Nations Day. The UN flag is light blue with the UN emblem centred in white.

The principal organs of the UN are the General Assembly, the Security Council, the Economic and Social Council, the Trusteeship Council, the Secretariat and the International Court of Justice. The Economic and Social Council and the Trusteeship Council are auxiliaries, charged with assisting and advising the General Assembly and Security Council. The official languages used are Arabic, Chinese, English, French, Russian and Spanish. Deliberations at the International Court of Justice are in English and French only.

MEMBERSHIP

Membership is open to all countries which accept the Charter and its principle of peaceful co-existence. New members are admitted by the General Assembly on the recommendation of the Security Council. The original membership of 51 states has grown to 184:

Afghanistan	Cape Verde
Albania	Central African Rep.
Algeria	Chad
Andorra	*Chile
Angola	*China
Antigua and Barbuda	*Colombia
*Argentina	Comoros
Armenia	Congo
*Australia	*Costa Rica
Austria	Côte d'Ivoire
Azerbaijan	Croatia
The Bahamas	*Cuba
Bahrain	Cyprus
Bangladesh	*Czech Republic
Barbados	*Denmark
*Belarus	Djibouti
*Belgium	Dominica
Belize	*Dominican Republic
Benin	*Ecuador
Bhutan	*Egypt
*Bolivia	Equatorial Guinea
Bosnia-Hercegovina	Eritrea
Botswana	Estonia
*Brazil	*Ethiopia
Brunei	Federated States of
Bulgaria	Micronesia
Burkina	Fiji
Burundi	Finland
Cambodia (Kampuchea)	*France
Cameroon	Gabon
*Canada	Gambia

Georgia
Germany
Ghana
*Greece
Grenada
*Guatemala
Guinea
Guinea-Bissau
Guyana
*Haiti
*Honduras
Hungary
Iceland
*India
Indonesia
*Iran
*Iraq
Ireland, Republic of
Israel
Italy
Jamaica
Japan
Jordan
Kazakhstan
Kenya
Korea, D.P.Rep. (North)
Korea, Rep. of (South)
Kuwait
Kyrgyzstan
Laos
Latvia
*Lebanon
Lesotho
*Liberia
Libya
Liechtenstein
Lithuania
*Luxembourg
Macedonia (The former
   Yugoslav Republic of)
Madagascar
Malawi
Malaysia
The Maldives
Mali
Malta
Marshall Islands
Mauritania
Mauritius
*Mexico
Moldova
Monaco
Mongolia
Morocco
Mozambique
Myanmar (Burma)
Namibia
Nepal
*Netherlands
*New Zealand
*Nicaragua
Niger
Nigeria

*Norway
Oman
Pakistan
*Panama
Papua New Guinea
*Paraguay
*Peru
*Philippines
*Poland
Portugal
Qatar
Romania
*Russian Federation
Rwanda
St Christopher and Nevis
St Lucia
St Vincent and the
   Grenadines
*El Salvador
San Marino
São Tomé and Príncipe
*Saudi Arabia
Senegal
Seychelles
Sierra Leone
Singapore
*Slovak Republic
Slovenia
Solomon Islands
Somalia
*South Africa
Spain
Sri Lanka
Sudan
Suriname
Swaziland
Sweden
*Syria
Tajikistan
Tanzania
Thailand
Togo
Trinidad and Tobago
Tunisia
*Turkey
Turkmenistan
Uganda
*Ukraine
United Arab Emirates
*United Kingdom
*United States of America
*Uruguay
Uzbekistan
Vanuatu
*Venezuela
Vietnam
Western Samoa
Yemen
*Yugoslavia (suspended)
Zaire
Zambia
Zimbabwe

*Original member (i.e. from 1945). From 25 October 1971 'China' was taken to mean the People's Republic of China. Czechoslovakia was an original member in 1945 and a member until 31 December 1992. The successor states of the Czech Republic and the Slovak Republic were admitted as members in January 1993.

The Russian Federation took over the membership of the Soviet Union in the Security Council and all other UN organs on 24 December 1991. Belarus (formerly Belorussia) and the Ukraine on becoming independent sovereign states continued their existing memberships of the UN, both having been granted separate UN membership in 1945 as a concession to the Soviet Union.

OBSERVERS

Permanent observer status is held by the Vatican City State and Switzerland. The Palestinian Liberation Organization has special observer status.

NON-MEMBERS

A number of countries are not members, usually due to their small size and limited financial resources. Notable exceptions include Switzerland, which follows a policy of absolute neutrality, and Taiwan, which was replaced by the People's Republic of China in October 1971. The others are: Kiribati; Nauru; Tonga; Tuvalu; Vatican City State.

THE GENERAL ASSEMBLY
UN Plaza, New York, NY 10017, USA

The General Assembly is the main deliberative organ of the UN. It consists of all members, each entitled to five representatives but having only one vote. The annual session begins on the third Tuesday of September, when the President is elected, and usually continues until mid-December. Special sessions are held on specific issues and emergency special sessions can be called within 24 hours.

The Assembly is empowered to discuss any matter within the scope of the Charter, except when it is under consideration by the Security Council, and to make recommendations. Under the 'uniting for peace' resolution, adopted in November 1950, the Assembly may also take action to maintain international peace and security when the Security Council fails to do so because of a lack of unanimity of its permanent members. Important decisions, such as those on peace and security, the election of officers, the budget, etc., need a two-thirds majority. Others need a simple majority. The Assembly has effective power only over the internal operations of the UN itself; external recommendations are not legally binding.

The work of the General Assembly is divided among seven main committees, on each of which every member has the right to be represented: Disarmament and related security questions (assisted by a Special Political Committee); Economic and Financial; Social, Humanitarian and Cultural; Decolonization (including non-self governing territories); Administrative and Budgetary; Legal. In addition, the General Assembly appoints ad hoc committees to consider special issues, such as human rights, peace-keeping, disarmament and international law. All committees consider items referred to them by the Assembly and recommend draft resolutions to its plenary meeting.

The Assembly is assisted by a number of functional committees. The General Committee co-ordinates its proceedings and operations, while the Credentials Committee verifies the credentials of representatives. There are also two standing committees, the Advisory Committee on Administration and Budgetary Questions and the Committee on Contributions, which suggests the scale of members' payments to the UN.

President of the General Assembly (1992), Stoyan Ganev (Bulgaria)

The Assembly has created a large number of specialized bodies over the years, which are supervised jointly with the

Economic and Social Council. They are supported by UN and voluntary contributions from governments, non-governmental organizations and individuals. These organizations include:

THE CONFERENCE ON DISARMAMENT (CD)
Palais des Nations, 1211 Geneva 10, Switzerland
Established by the UN as the Committee on Disarmament in 1962, the CD is the single multilateral disarmament negotiating forum. The present title of the organization was adopted in 1984. There were 39 members as at 1 June 1991.
The Conference holds three regular sessions per year, from January to March, May to June, and July to August. The work of the Conference is conducted both in public plenary meetings and in private *ad hoc* committees set up with the consent of all members to deal with specific items of the agenda. After 25 years of negotiations, a Chemical Weapons Convention was finally agreed and opened for signing in Paris on 14 January 1993. The Covention will come into force six months after it has been ratified by 65 states. It bans the use, production, stockpiling and transfer of all chemical weapons. All US and Russian weapons must be destroyed within 15 years of the Convention entering into force and all other states' weapons must be destroyed within ten years.
Secretary-General, HE Miljan Komatina
UK Representative, Miss T. A. H. Solesby, CMG, 37–39 rue de Vermont, 1211 Geneva 10, Switzerland

THE UNITED NATIONS CHILDREN'S FUND (UNICEF)
3 UN Plaza, New York, NY 10017, USA
Established in 1947 to assist children and mothers in the immediate post-war period, UNICEF now concentrates on developing countries. It provides primary health-care and health education. In particular, it conducts programmes in oral hydration, immunization against leading diseases, child growth monitoring, and the encouragement of breast-feeding. Its operations are often conducted in co-operation with the World Health Organization (WHO).
Executive Director, James Grant (*USA*)

THE UNITED NATIONS DEVELOPMENT PROGRAMME (UNDP)
1 UN Plaza, New York, NY 10017, USA
Established in 1966 from the merger of the UN Expanded Programme of Technical Assistance and the UN Special Fund, UNDP is the central funding agency for economic and social development projects around the world. Much of its annual expenditure is channelled through UN specialized agencies, governments and non-governmental organizations.
Administrator, James G. Speth (*USA*)

THE UNITED NATIONS HIGH COMMISSIONER FOR REFUGEES (UNHCR)
Centre William Rappard, 154 rue de Lausanne, PO Box 2500, 1211 Geneva 2, Switzerland
Established in 1951 to protect the rights and interests of refugees, it organizes emergency relief and longer-term solutions, such as voluntary repatriation, local integration or resettlement.
High Commissioner, Sadako Ogata (*Japan*)
UK OFFICE, 76 Westminster Palace Gardens, London SW1P 1RL. Tel: 071-222 3065

THE UN RELIEF AND WORKS AGENCY FOR PALESTINE REFUGEES IN THE NEAR EAST (UNRWA)
Vienna International Centre, Wagramerstrasse 5, PO Box 100, 1400 Vienna, Austria
Established in 1949 to bring relief to the Palestinians displaced by the Arab-Israeli conflict.
Commissioner-General, Ilter Turkman (*Turkey*)

Other bodies include:

THE UN CENTRE FOR HUMAN SETTLEMENTS (Habitat), PO Box 30030, Nairobi, Kenya
THE UN COMMISSION FOR TRADE AND DEVELOPMENT (UNCTAD), Palais des Nations, 1211 Geneva 10, Switzerland
THE DEPARTMENT OF HUMANITARIAN AFFAIRS/ OFFICE OF THE UN DISASTER AND RELIEF CO-ORDINATOR (DHA/UNDRO), Palais des Nations, 1211 Geneva 10, Switzerland
THE UN ENVIRONMENT PROGRAMME (UNEP), PO Box 30552, Nairobi, Kenya
THE UN POPULATION FUND (UNFPA), 220 East 42nd Street, New York, NY 10017, USA
THE UN INSTITUTE FOR THE ADVANCEMENT OF WOMEN (INSTRAW), PO Box 21747, Santo Domingo, Dominican Republic
THE UN UNIVERSITY (UNU), Toho Seimei Building, 15-1, Shibuya, 2-Chome, Shibuya-ku, Tokyo 150, Japan
THE WORLD FOOD COUNCIL (WFC), Via delle Terme di Caracalla, 00100 Rome, Italy
THE WORLD FOOD PROGRAMME (WFP), Via delle Terme di Caracalla, 00100 Rome, Italy

BUDGET OF THE UNITED NATIONS
The budget adopted for the biennium 1992–3 was US$2,389,234,900. The scale of assessment contributions of 88 UN members is set at the minimum 0.01 per cent. The ten largest assessments are: USA, 25 per cent; Japan, 11.38; Russian Federation, 9.99; Germany, 9.36; France, 6.25; UK, 4.86; Italy, 3.99; Canada, 3.09; Spain, 1.95; Netherlands, 1.65.

THE SECURITY COUNCIL
UN Plaza, New York, NY 10017, USA

The Security Council is the senior arm of the UN and has the primary responsibility for maintaining world peace and security. It consists of 15 members, each with one representative and one vote. There are five permanent members, China, France, the Russian Federation, UK and USA, and ten non-permanent members. Each of the non-permanent members is elected for a two-year term by a two-thirds majority of the General Assembly and is ineligible for immediate re-election. Five of the elective seats are allocated to Africa and Asia, one to eastern Europe, two to Latin America and two to western Europe and remaining countries. Procedural questions are determined by a simple majority vote. Other matters require a majority inclusive of the votes of the permanent members; they thus have a right of veto. The abstention of a permanent member does not constitute a veto. The presidency rotates each month by state in (English) alphabetical order. Parties to a dispute, other non-members and individuals can be invited to participate in Security Council debates but are not permitted to vote. In 1993 the ten non-permanent members were: Cape Verde, Hungary, Japan, Morocco and Venezuela (*term expires 31 December 1993*); Brazil, Djibouti, New Zealand, Pakistan, Spain (*term expires 31 December 1994*).
The Security Council is empowered to settle or adjudicate in disputes or situations which threaten international peace and security. It can adopt political, economic and military measures to achieve this end. Any matter considered to be a threat to or breach of the peace or an act of aggression can be brought to the Security Council's attention by any member state or by the Secretary-General. The Charter envisaged members placing at the disposal of the Security Council armed forces and other facilities which would be co-ordinated by the Military Staff Committee, composed of military

representatives of the five permanent members. The Security Council is also supported by a Committee of Experts, to advise on procedural and technical matters, and a Committee on Admission of New Members. Owing to superpower disunity, the Security Council has rarely played the decisive role set out in the Charter; the Military Staff Committee was effectively suspended from 1948 until 1990, when a meeting was convened during the Gulf Crisis on the formation and control of UN-supervised armed forces.

At an extraordinary meeting of the Security Council on 31 January 1992 attended by heads of government, plans were laid to transform the UN in light of the changed post-Cold War world. The Secretary-General was asked to draw up a report on transforming the UN's peace-keeping ability. The report was produced in June 1992 and centred on the establishment of a UN army composed of national contingents on permanent standby, as envisaged at the time of the UN's formation.

PEACE-KEEPING FORCES

The Security Council has established a number of peace-keeping forces since its foundation, comprising contingents provided mainly by neutral and non-aligned UN members. Current forces include: the UN Truce Supervision Organization (UNTSO), 1948, Israel; the UN Military Observer Group in India and Pakistan (UNMOGIP), 1949; the UN Peace-keeping Force in Cyprus (UNFICYP), 1964; the UN Disengagement Observer Force (UNDOF), 1974, Golan Heights, Syria; the UN Interim Force in Lebanon (UNIFIL), 1978; the UN Iraq-Kuwait Observation Mission (UNIKOM), 1991; UN Angola Verification Mission II (UNAVEM II)*, 1991; UN Observer Mission in El Salvador (ONUSAL), 1991; the UN Mission for the Referendum in Western Sahara (MINURSO), 1991; the UN Protection Force (UNPROFOR), 1992, Croatia, Bosnia-Hercegovina, Federal Republic of Yugoslavia and the former Yugoslav Republic of Macedonia; the UN Transitional Authority in Cambodia (UNTAC), 1992; the UN Operation in Mozambique (ONUMOZ) 1992; the UN Operation in Somalia II (UNOSOM II), 1993.

* UNAVEM II suspended on 15 July 1993 when mandate not extended and fierce fighting continues. A skeleton UN staff remains in case fighting ends in near future

THE ECONOMIC AND SOCIAL COUNCIL
UN Plaza, New York, NY 10017, USA

The Economic and Social Council is responsible under the General Assembly for the economic and social work of the UN and for the co-ordination of the activities of the 15 specialized agencies and other UN bodies. It makes reports and recommendations on economic, social, cultural, educational, health and related matters, often in consultation with non-governmental organizations, passing the reports to the General Assembly and other UN bodies. It also drafts conventions for submission to the Assembly and calls conferences on matters within its remit.

The Council consists of 54 members, 18 of whom are elected annually by the General Assembly for a three-year term. Each has one vote and can be immediately re-elected on retirement. A President is elected annually and is also eligible for re-election. One substantive session is held annually and decisions are reached by simple majority vote of those present.

The Council has established a number of standing committees on particular issues and several commissions. Commissions include: Statistical, Human Rights, Social Development, Sustainable Development, Status of Women, Crime Prevention and Criminal Justice, Narcotic Drugs, Science and Technology for Development, and Population;

and Regional Economic Commissions for Europe, Asia and the Pacific, Western Asia, Latin America and Africa.

THE TRUSTEESHIP COUNCIL
UN Plaza, New York, NY 10017, USA

The Trusteeship Council supervises the administration of territories within the UN Trusteeship system inherited from the League of Nations. It now consists of the USA, the only remaining administrator, and the four other permanent members of the Security Council. Meetings are held annually and decisions reached by a majority vote of those present. Ten of the original eleven trusteeships have now progressed towards independence or merged with neighbouring states. With the termination of the trust status for the Federated States of Micronesia in December 1990, only the Republic of Palau now remains within the system.

THE SECRETARIAT
UN Plaza, New York, NY 10017, USA

The Secretariat services the other UN organs and is headed by a Secretary-General elected by a majority vote of the General Assembly on the recommendation of the Security Council. He is assisted by an international staff, chosen to represent the international character of the organization. The Secretary-General is charged with bringing to the attention of the Security Council any matter which he considers poses a threat to international peace and security. He may also bring other matters to the attention of the General Assembly and other UN bodies and may be entrusted by them with additional duties. As chief administrator to the UN, the Secretary-General is present in person or via representatives at all meetings of the other five main organs of the UN. He may also act as an impartial mediator in disputes between member states.

The power and influence of the Secretary-General has, to a large extent, been determined by the character of the office-holder and by the state of relations between the superpowers. The thaw in these relations since the mid-1980s has increased the effectiveness of the UN, particularly in its attempts to intervene in international disputes. It helped to end the Iran-Iraq war and sponsored peace in Central America. Following Iraq's invasion of Kuwait in 1990 the UN took its first collective security action since the Korean War. UN action to protect the Kurds in northern Iraq has widened its legal authority by breaching the prohibition on its intervention in the essentially domestic affairs of states. Currently the UN is forming a UN-sponsored interim government in Cambodia; is heavily involved in pacifying warring factions in Somalia to bring about a return to stable government; is involved in peace-keeping, aid distribution and negotiations in the former Yugoslavia; and is addressing the global problems of AIDS and environmental destruction.

Since he took office on 1 January 1992, the new Secretary-General Boutros Boutros-Ghali has introduced radical change in the Secretariat, reducing the number of departments from 20 to ten, each headed by an Under-Secretary-General.

Secretary-General, Boutros Boutros-Ghali (*Egypt*)
Under-Secretaries-General:
　Africa, Asia and the Middle East, James Jonah (*Sierra Leone*)
　Political Affairs, Marrack Goulding (*UK*)
　Peace-keeping Operations, Kofi Annan (*Ghana*)
　Development Support and Management Services, Ji Chaozhu (*China*)
　Legal Affairs, Carl-August Fleischhauer (*Germany*)
　Humanitarian Affairs, Jan Eliasson (*Sweden*)
　Public Information, Eugeniusz Wyzner (*Poland*)
　Administration and Management, Melissa Wells (*US*)

Policy Co-ordination and Sustainable Development, Nitin Desai *(India)*
Economic and Social Information and Policy Analysis, Jean-Claude Milleron *(France)*

Former Secretaries-General
1946–53   Trygve Lie *(Norway)*
1953–61   Dag Hammarskjöld *(Sweden)*
1961–71   U Thant *(Burma)*
1971–81   Kurt Waldheim *(Austria)*
1981–91   Javier Pérez de Cuéllar *(Peru)*
1992–   Boutros Boutros Ghali *(Egypt)*

INTERNATIONAL COURT OF JUSTICE
The Peace Palace, 2517 KJ The Hague, The Netherlands

The International Court of Justice is the principal judicial organ of the UN. The Statute of the Court is an integral part of the Charter and all members of the UN are *ipso facto* parties to it. The Court is composed of 15 judges, elected by both the General Assembly and the Security Council for nine-year terms which are renewable. Judges may deliberate over cases in which their country is involved. If no judge on the bench is from a country which is a party to a dispute under consideration, that party may designate a judge to participate *ad hoc* in that particular deliberation. If any party to a case fails to adhere to the judgment of the Court, the other party may have recourse to the Security Council.

President, Sir Robert Jennings *(UK)* (2000)
Vice-President, Shigeru Oda *(Japan)* (1994)
Judges, Geza Herczegh *(Hungary)* (1994); Bola Ajibola *(Nigeria)* (1994); Roberto Ago *(Italy)* (1997); Stephen M. Schwebel *(USA)* (1997); Mohammed Bedjaoui *(Algeria)* (2000); Ni Zhengyu *(China)* (1994); Jens Evensen *(Norway)* (1997); Nikolai K. Tarassov *(Russian Federation)* (1997); Gilbert Guillaume *(France)* (2000); Mohammed Shahabuddeen *(Guyana)* (1997); Andrés Aguilar Mawdsley *(Venezuela)* (2000); Christopher G. Weeramantry *(Sri Lanka)* (2000); and Raymond Ranjeva *(Madagascar)* (2000)

WAR CRIMES TRIBUNAL
On 27 May 1993 the Security Council voted to establish a war crimes tribunal for the former Yugoslavia. This tribunal court will have the power to order the surrender of suspects into its custody and will hear cases covering grave breaches of the Geneva Conventions and crimes against humanity. The Court will be in the Hague with 11 member judges.

SPECIALIZED AGENCIES
Fifteen independent international organizations, each with its own membership, budget and headquarters, carry out their responsibilities in co-ordination with the UN under agreements made with the Economic and Social Council. An entry for each appears elsewhere in the International Organizations section. They are as follows: the Food and Agriculture Organization of the UN; International Civil Aviation Organization; International Fund for Agricultural Development; International Labour Organization; International Maritime Organization; the International Monetary Fund; International Telecommunications Union; UN Educational, Scientific and Cultural Organization; UN Industrial Development Organization; Universal Postal Union; World Bank (International Bank for Reconstruction and Development, International Development Agency, International Finance Corporation); World Health Organization; World Intellectual Property Organization; and World Meteorological Organization. The International Atomic Energy Agency

and the General Agreement on Tariffs and Trade are linked to the UN but are not specialized agencies.

UK MISSION TO THE UNITED NATIONS
845 Third Avenue, New York, NY 10022, USA
Permanent Representative to the United Nations and Representative on the Security Council, Sir David Hannay, KCMG, *apptd* 1990
Deputy Permanent Representative, T. L. Richardson, CMG

UK MISSION TO THE OFFICE OF THE UN AND OTHER INTERNATIONAL ORGANIZATIONS IN GENEVA
37–39 rue de Vermont, 1211 Geneva 20, Switzerland
Permanent UK Representative, N. C. R. Williams, CMG *apptd* 1993
Deputy Permanent Representatives, E. G. M. Chaplin, OBE *(Head of Chancery)*; Miss A.E.Stoddart *(Economic Affairs)*

UK MISSION TO THE INTERNATIONAL ATOMIC ENERGY AGENCY, THE UN INDUSTRIAL DEVELOPMENT ORGANIZATION AND THE UNITED NATIONS OFFICE AT VIENNA
Jaurésgasse 12, 1030 Vienna, Austria
Permanent UK Representative, C. Hulse, OBE *apptd* 1993
Deputy Permanent Representative, Miss M. R. McIntosh

UN OFFICE AND INFORMATION CENTRE
Ship House, 20 Buckingham Gate, London SW1E 6LB
Tel 071-630 1981

UNITED NATIONS EDUCATIONAL, SCIENTIFIC AND CULTURAL ORGANIZATION
7 place de Fontenoy, 75352 Paris 07SP, France

The United Nations Educational, Scientific and Cultural Organization (UNESCO) was established on 4 November 1946, the consequence of an international conference held in London in 1945. It promotes collaboration among its member states in education, science, culture and communication. It aims to further a universal respect for human rights, justice and the rule of law, without distinction of race, sex, language or religion, in accordance with the UN Charter.

UNESCO runs a number of programmes to improve education and extend access to it. It provides assistance to ensure the free flow of information and its wider and better balanced dissemination without any obstacle to freedom of expression, and to maintain cultural heritage in the face of development. It fosters research and study in all areas of the social sciences.

UNESCO had 175 member states as at July 1993. There are three associate members. The General Conference, consisting of representatives of all the members, meets biennially to decide the programme and the budget (1992–3, US$444,704,000). It elects the 51-member Executive Board, which supervises operations, and appoints a Director-General. The Director-General heads a Secretariat responsible for carrying out the organization's programmes. In most member states national commissions liaise with UNESCO to execute its programme.

The UK withdrew from UNESCO in 1985. It was granted observer status in 1986.

Director-General, Federico Mayor Zaragoza *(Spain)*

UNITED NATIONS INDUSTRIAL DEVELOPMENT ORGANIZATION
Vienna International Centre, Wagramerstrasse 5, PO Box 300, 1400 Vienna, Austria

The United Nations Industrial Development Organization (UNIDO) was established as an organ of the UN General Assembly in 1966, replacing the Centre for Industrial Development. It became a UN specialized agency on 1 January 1986 with the aim of promoting the industrialization of developing countries, with special emphasis upon the manufacturing sector. To this end it provides technical assistance and advice, as well as help with planning.

UNIDO had 162 members as at May 1993. It is funded by the UN Development Programme, other UN bodies, governments and non-governmental organizations. A General Conference of all the members meets biennially to discuss policy, set a budget (1992–3, US$181,013,400) and elect the Industrial Development Board. This executive body is composed of 33 members from developing countries, 15 from developed countries and five from centrally planned economies. There is a subsidiary Programme and Budget Committee. A Secretariat administers UNIDO under a Director-General, appointed by the Conference.

Director-General, Mauricio de Maria y Campos (*Mexico*)
Permanent UK Representative, C. Hulse, OBE, British Embassy, Vienna

UNIVERSAL POSTAL UNION
Weltpoststrasse 4, 3000 Berne 15, Switzerland

The Universal Postal Union (UPU) was established by the Convention of Berne on 9 October 1874, taking effect from July 1875, and became a UN specialized agency in June 1947. The UPU exists to form a single postal territory of all member countries, for the reciprocal exchange of correspondence without discrimination. It also assists and advises on the improvement of postal services.

The UPU had 183 members as at June 1993. A Universal Postal Congress of all the members meets every five years to review the Convention and to elect a 40-member Executive Council (including one member from the host country) which continues the UPU's work between Congresses. The Congress also elects a 35-member Consultative Council for Postal Studies which meets annually to address specific matters. The Council, together with the Swiss government, supervises the International Bureau, a secretariat headed by a Director-General.

Funding is provided by members according to a scale of contributions drawn up by the Congress. The Council sets the annual budget (1993, SFr 29,087,690) within a five-year figure decided by the Congress.

Director-General, A. C. Botto de Barros (*Brazil*)

WESTERN EUROPEAN UNION
4 rue de la Régence, 1000 Brussels, Belgium

The Western European Union (WEU) originated as the Brussels Treaty Organization (BTO). This was established under the Treaty of Brussels, signed in 1948 by Belgium, France, Luxembourg, the Netherlands and UK, to provide collective self-defence and economic, cultural and social collaboration amongst its signatories. With the collapse of the European Defence Community and the decision of NATO to incorporate the Federal Republic of Germany into the Western security system, the BTO was modified to become the WEU in 1954 with the admission of West Germany and Italy.

Owing to the overlap with NATO and the Council of Europe, the Union became largely defunct. From the late 1970s onwards efforts were made to add a security dimension to the EC's European Political Co-operation. Opposition to these efforts from Denmark, Greece and Ireland led the remaining EC countries, all WEU members, to decide to reactivate the Union in 1984. Members committed themselves to harmonizing their views on defence and security and developing a European security identity, while bearing in mind the importance of transatlantic relations. Portugal and Spain joined the WEU in 1988, and Greece will become a full member after ratifying the treaty.

After much debate about the future of the WEU, the EC Maastricht Treaty designated the WEU as the future defence component of the EC. The formation of a Franco-German corps of 35,000 men, based in Strasbourg, to be operational by 1995 under the umbrella of the WEU, was announced in May 1992. WEU foreign ministers agreed in the Petersburg Declaration of June 1992 to assign forces to WEU command for 'peacemaking' operations in Europe. On 20 November 1992 the WEU's role as the common security dimension of the EC was enhanced when WEU ministers signed a declaration with remaining European NATO members to give them various forms of WEU membership. Greece became a full member, Ireland and Denmark observer members and Iceland, Norway and Turkey became associate members.

Building on past experience of joint actions in the Gulf (1989–90), the WEU operates a naval patrol force in the Adriatic Sea and an embargo enforcement mission on the River Danube as part of the European peace initiatives in the former Yugoslavia.

A Council of Ministers (foreign and defence) meets biannually in the capital of the presiding country; presidency rotates annually. A Permanent Council of the signatories' Brussels ambassadors meets regularly in Brussels. An Enlarged Council of political directors and member defence officials was created in 1986. Both the Enlarged Committee and the Permanent Committee are chaired by the Secretary-General and serviced by the Secretariat. The Assembly of the WEU is composed of 108 parliamentarians of member states and meets twice annually in Paris to debate matters within the scope of the Brussels Treaty.

Presidency (1993–4), Luxembourg
Secretary-General, Dr Willem van Eekelen (*Netherlands*)
UK Representative on the Permanent Council, Sir John Weston, KCMG
ASSEMBLY, 43 avenue du Président Wilson, 75775 Paris Cedex 16, France

THE WORLD BANK
1818 H Street NW, Washington DC 20433, USA

The World Bank, more formally known as the International Bank for Reconstruction and Development (IBRD), is a specialized agency of the UN, and developed from the international monetary and financial conference held at Bretton Woods, New Hampshire, in 1944. Determined to avoid the financial chaos and depression of the inter-war years, 44 nations established the IBRD on 27 December 1945, to encourage economic growth in developing countries through the provision of loans and technical assistance to their respective governments. The IBRD now has 174 members.

The Bank is owned by the governments of member countries and its capital is subscribed by its members. It finances its lending primarily from borrowing in world capital markets, and derives a substantial contribution to its resources from its retained earnings and the repayment of loans. The interest rate on its loans is calculated in relation to its cost of borrowing. Loans generally have a grace period of five years and are repayable within 20 years. The loans made by the Bank since its inception to 30 June 1993, totalled US$312,970.8 million to 110 countries. Subscribed capital is US$152,248,000,000.

Originally directed towards post-war reconstruction in Europe, the Bank has subsequently turned towards assisting less-developed countries with the establishment of two affiliates, the International Finance Corporation (IFC) in 1956 and the International Development Association (IDA) in 1960. The IFC aids developing member countries by promoting the growth of the private sector of their economies and by helping to mobilize domestic and foreign capital for this purpose. The IFC's subscribed share capital was US$2,050 million at 30 June 1993. It is also empowered to borrow up to two and half times the amount of its unimpaired subscribed capital and accumulated earnings for use in its lending programme. At 30 June 1993, the IFC had committed financing totalling more than US$12,400 million in about 98 countries.

The IDA performs the same function as the World Bank but primarily to less developed countries and on terms that bear less heavily on their balance of payments than IBRD loans. Eligible countries typically have a per capita gross national product of less than US$765 (1991). Funds (called credits to distinguish them from IBRD loans) come mostly in the form of subscriptions and contributions from the IDA's richer members and transfers from the net income of the IBRD. The terms for IDA credits, which bear no interest and are made to governments only, are ten-year grace periods and 35- or 40-year maturities. By 30 June 1993, the IDA had extended development credits totalling US$77,816.4 million to 90 countries.

The IBRD and its affiliates are financially and legally distinct but share headquarters. The IBRD is headed by a Board of Governors, consisting of one Governor and one alternate Governor appointed by each member country. Twenty-four Executive Directors exercise all powers of the Bank except those reserved to the Board of Governors. The President, elected by the Executive Directors, conducts the business of the Bank, assisted by an international staff. Membership in both the IFC (154 members) and the IDA (150 members) is open to all IBRD countries. The IDA is administered by the same staff as the Bank; the IFC has its own personnel but draws on the IBRD for administrative and other support. All share the same President.

In 1988 a third affiliate, the Multilateral Investment Guarantee Agency (MIGA) was formed. MIGA encourages foreign investment in developing states by providing investment guarantees to potential investors and advisory services to developing member countries. At 30 June 1993 102 countries were members of MIGA.

President (IBRD, IFC, IDA, MIGA), L. Preston *(USA)*
UK Executive Director, D. Peretz, Room 11-120, IMF, 700 19th Street NW, Washington DC 20431
EUROPEAN OFFICE, 66 avenue d'Iena, 75116 Paris, France
JAPAN OFFICE, Kokusai Building 1-1, Marunouchi 3-Chomse, Chiyoda-ku, Tokyo 100, Japan
UK OFFICE, New Zealand House, Haymarket, London SW1Y 4TQ

THE WORLD COUNCIL OF CHURCHES
PO Box 2100, 1211 Geneva 2, Switzerland

The World Council of Churches (WCC) was constituted in Amsterdam in 1948 to promote unity among the many different Christian churches. The 322 member churches of the WCC have adherents in more than 100 countries. With the exception of Roman Catholicism, virtually all Christian traditions are included in the WCC membership.

The policies of the Council are determined by delegates of the member churches meeting in Assembly, about every seven years; the seventh Assembly was held in Canberra, Australia, in February 1991. More detailed decisions are taken by a 151-member Central Committee which is elected by the Assembly and meets, with the eight WCC Presidents, annually. The Central Committee in turn appoints a smaller Executive Committee and also nominates commissions to guide the various programmes.

General Secretary, Dr Konrad Raiser *(Germany)*

WORLD HEALTH ORGANIZATION
20 avenue Appia, 1211 Geneva 27, Switzerland

The UN International Health Conference held in 1946 established the World Health Organization (WHO) as a UN specialized agency, with effect from 7 April 1948. It is dedicated to attaining the highest possible level of health for all. It collaborates with member governments, UN agencies and other bodies to develop health standards, control communicable diseases and promote all aspects of family and environmental health. It seeks to raise the standards of health teaching and training, and promotes research through collaborating research centres world-wide. Its other services include the *International Pharmacopoeia*, epidemiological surveillance, and the collation and publication of statistics. WHO activities are orientated to achieving 'Health for all by the year 2000', i.e. a level of health allowing the world's citizens to lead socially and economically productive lives.

WHO had 186 members as at May 1993. It is governed by the annual World Health Assembly of members which meets to set policy, approve the budget (1994-5, US$1,800,000,000), appoint a Director-General, and adopt health conventions and regulations. It also elects 31 members who designate one health-qualified person to serve in a personal capacity on the Executive Board. The Board effects the programme, suggests initiatives and is empowered to deal with emergencies. A Secretariat, headed by the Director-General, supervises the health activities of six regional offices.

Director-General, Dr H. Nakajima *(Japan)*

WORLD INTELLECTUAL PROPERTY ORGANIZATION
34 chemin des Colombettes, 1211 Geneva 20, Switzerland

The World Intellectual Property Organization (WIPO) was established in 1967 by the Stockholm Convention, which entered into force in 1970. In addition to that Convention, WIPO administers 17 treaties, the principal ones being the Paris Convention for the Protection of Industrial Property and the Berne Convention for the Protection of Literary and Artistic Works. WIPO became a UN specialized agency in 1974.

WIPO promotes the protection of intellectual property throughout the world through co-operation among states, and the administration of various 'Unions', each founded on a multilateral treaty and dealing with the legal and administrative aspects of intellectual property.

Intellectual property comprises two main branches: industrial property (inventions, trademarks, industrial designs and appellations of origin); and copyright (literary, musical, photographic, audiovisual and artistic works, etc.). WIPO also assists creative intellectual activity and facilitates technology transfer, particularly to developing countries. It administers various conventions, most importantly the Berne and Paris Conventions.

WIPO had 139 members as at 15 June 1993. The biennial session of all its governing bodies sets policy, a programme and a budget (1993, SFr 107,935,500). WIPO has three governing bodies: the General Assembly, the Conference and the Co-ordination Committee. The Assembly appoints, instructs and supervises a Director-General, who heads the International Bureau (secretariat) of some 423 people. The Co-ordination Committee represents the organizations of the Berne and Paris Conventions.

A separate International Union for the Protection of New Varieties of Plants (UPOV), established by convention in 1961, is linked to WIPO. It has 23 members.
Director-General, Dr Arpad Bogsch (*USA*)

WORLD METEOROLOGICAL ORGANIZATION
41 avenue Giuseppe Motta, PO Box 2300, 1211 Geneva 20, Switzerland

The World Meteorological Organization (WMO) was established as a UN specialized agency on 23 March 1950, succeeding the International Meteorological Organization which had been founded in 1873. It facilitates co-operation between the world-wide network of meteorological services, standardizes meteorological observations and data, and assists training and research. It also fosters collaboration between meteorological and hydrological services, and furthers the application of meteorology to aviation, shipping, agriculture, etc.

The WMO had 165 member states and five member territories, as at 4 June 1993. The supreme authority is the World Meteorological Congress of member states and member territories, which meets every four years to determine general policy, make recommendations and set a budget (1992–5, SFr 236,100,000). It also elects 26 members of the 36-member Executive Council, the other members being the President and three Vice-Presidents of the WMO, and the Presidents of the six Regional Associations. The Council supervises the implementation of Congress decisions, initiates studies and makes recommendations on matters needing international action. The WMO functions through six Regional Meteorological Associations and eight technical commissions. The Secretariat is headed by a Secretary-General, appointed by the Congress.
Secretary-General, G. O. P. Obasi (*Nigeria*)

Countries of the World

WORLD AREA AND POPULATION

The total population of the world in mid-1990 was estimated at 5,292 million, compared with 3,019 million in 1960 and 2,070 million in 1930.

Continent, etc.	Area sq. miles '000	sq. km '000	Estimated population mid-1990
Africa	11,704	30,313	642,000,000
North America[1]	8,311	21,525	276,000,000
Latin America[2]	7,933	20,547	448,000,000
Asia[3]	10,637	27,549	3,113,000,000
Europe[4]	1,915	4,961	498,000,000
Former USSR	8,649	22,402	289,000,000
Oceania[5]	3,286	8,510	26,500,000
TOTAL	52,435	135,807	5,292,000,000

[1] Includes Greenland and Hawaii
[2] Mexico and the remainder of the Americas south of the USA
[3] Includes European Turkey, excludes former USSR
[4] Excludes European Turkey and former USSR
[5] Includes Australia, New Zealand and the islands inhabited by Micronesian, Melanesian and Polynesian peoples
Source: UN Demographic Yearbook 1990 (pub. 1992)

A United Nations report (*The Future Growth of World Population*) in 1958 stated that the population of the world had increased since the beginning of the 20th century at an unprecedented rate: in 1850 it was estimated at 1,094 million and in 1900 at 1,500 million, an increase of 42 per cent in 50 years. By 1925 it had risen to 1,907 million (23 per cent in 25 years) and by 1950 it had reached 2,500 million, an increase of 31 per cent in 25 years. Levels of population and the trend in distribution of the population by continents as forecast for the year 2000 were:

Continents, etc.	Estimated population	per cent
Africa	517,000,000	8.2
North America	312,000,000	5.0
Latin America[1]	592,000,000	9.4
Asia (excluding USSR)	3,870,000,000	61.8
Europe (including USSR)	947,000,000	15.1
Oceania	29,000,000	0.5
TOTAL	6,267,000,000	100

[1] Mexico and the remainder of the Americas south of USA

No complete survey of many countries has yet been achieved and consequently accurate area figures are not always available. Similarly, many countries have not recently, or have never, taken a census. The areas of countries given below are derived from estimated figures published by the United Nations. The conversion factors used are:
(i) to convert square miles to square km, multiply by 2·589988
(ii) to convert square km to square miles, multiply by 0·3861022
Population figures for countries are derived from the most recent estimates available. Accurate and up-to-date data for the populations of capital cities are scarce, and definitions of cities' extent differ. The figures given below are the latest estimates available, and where it is known that the figure applies to an urban agglomeration this is indicated.

* latest census figure
Ψ seaport
u.a. urban agglomeration

AFRICA

COUNTRY	AREA sq. miles	sq. km	POPULATION	CAPITAL	POPULATION OF CAPITAL
Algeria	919,595	2,381,741	25,660,000	Ψ Algiers	3,250,000
Angola	481,354	1,246,700	10,303,000	Ψ Luanda	3,000,000
Benin	43,484	112,622	4,889,000	Ψ Porto Novo	208,258
Botswana	224,607	581,730	1,348,000	Gaborone	137,174
Burkina	105,869	274,200	9,242,000	Ouagadougou	441,514
Burundi	10,747	27,834	5,620,000	Bujumbura	215,243
Cameroon	183,569	475,442	12,239,000	Yaoundé	635,670
Cape Verde Islands	1,557	4,033	382,000	Ψ Praia	57,748*
Central African Republic	240,535	622,984	3,127,000	Bangui	473,817
Chad	495,755	1,284,000	5,819,000	Ndjaména	402,000
Comoros	838	2,171	570,000	Moroni	17,267*
Congo	132,047	342,000	2,346,000	Brazzaville	596,200*
Côte d'Ivoire	124,503	322,463	12,464,000	Ψ Abidjan	3,500,000
Djibouti	8,494	22,000	520,000	Ψ Djibouti	340,700
Egypt	386,662	1,001,449	54,688,000	Cairo	14,000,000
Equatorial Guinea	10,830	28,051	356,000	Ψ Malabo	30,418
Eritrea	36,170	93,679	3,500,000	Asmara	275,000
Ethiopia	471,778	1,221,900	49,883,000	Addis Ababa	1,793,000
Gabon	103,347	267,667	1,212,000	Ψ Libreville	251,000
Gambia	4,361	11,295	884,000	Ψ Banjul (*u.a.*)	109,986

COUNTRY	AREA sq. miles	sq. km	POPULATION	CAPITAL	POPULATION OF CAPITAL
Ghana	92,100	238,537	15,509,000	Ψ Accra (u.a.)	1,781,100
Guinea	94,926	245,857	5,931,000	Ψ Conakry	763,000
Guinea-Bissau	13,948	36,125	984,000	Ψ Bissau	109,214*
Kenya	224,961	582,646	25,905,000	Nairobi	1,400,000
Lesotho	11,720	30,355	1,826,000	Maseru	288,951*
Liberia	43,000	111,369	2,705,000	Ψ Monrovia	425,000
Libya	679,362	1,759,540	4,712,000	Ψ Tripoli	1,000,000
Madagascar	226,669	587,041	11,493,000	Antananarivo	1,250,000
Malawi	45,747	118,484	8,556,000	Lilongwe	233,973*
Mali	478,791	1,240,000	9,507,000	Bamako	658,275
Mauritania	397,955	1,030,700	2,036,000	Nouakchott	850,000
Mauritius	790	2,045	1,022,456	Ψ Port Louis	142,505
Mayotte (Fr.)	144	372	94,410	Mamoundzou	12,000
Morocco	172,414	446,550	27,575,000	Ψ Rabat	1,494,000
Western Sahara	102,703	266,000	183,000	Laayoune	96,784*
Mozambique	309,495	801,590	16,084,000	Ψ Maputo	1,150,000
Namibia	318,261	824,292	1,837,000	Windhoek	110,000
Niger	489,191	1,267,080	7,984,000	Niamey	410,000
Nigeria	356,669	923,768	112,163,000	Abuja	378,671
Réunion (Fr.)	969	2,510	598,000	St Denis	122,000
Rwanda	10,169	26,338	7,491,000	Kigali	156,000
St Helena (UK)	47	122	5,644	Ψ Jamestown	1,332
Ascension Island	34	88	1,117	Ψ Georgetown	—
Tristan da Cunha	38	98	295	Ψ Edinburgh	—
São Tomé and Príncipe	372	964	124,000	Ψ São Tomé	25,000
Senegal	75,750	196,192	7,533,000	Ψ Dakar	1,000,000
Seychelles	108	280	68,000	Ψ Victoria	24,324
Sierra Leone	27,699	71,740	4,260,000	Ψ Freetown	470,000
Somalia	246,201	637,657	7,691,000	Ψ Mogadishu	1,000,000
South Africa	471,445	1,221,031	36,070,000	⎧ Pretoria (u.a.)	822,925
				⎩ Ψ Cape Town (u.a.)	1,911,521
Sudan	967,500	2,505,813	25,941,000	Khartoum (u.a.)	3,000,000
Swaziland	6,704	17,363	817,000	Mbabane	38,290
Tanzania	364,900	945,087	28,359,000	Dodoma	88,474
Togo	21,925	56,785	3,643,000	Ψ Lomé	366,476
Tunisia	63,170	163,610	8,362,000	Ψ Tunis	1,394,749
Uganda	91,259	236,036	19,517,000	Kampala (u.a.)	750,000
Zaire	905,567	2,345,409	36,672,000	Kinshasa	2,778,281*
Zambia	290,586	752,614	8,780,000	Lusaka (u.a.)	1,000,000
Zimbabwe	150,804	390,580	10,019,000	Harare	681,000

AMERICA

North America

Canada	3,849,646	9,970,537	27,296,859	Ottawa (u.a.)	313,987*
Greenland (Den.)	840,004	2,175,600	55,385	Ψ Godthab	8,425
Mexico	761,605	1,972,547	87,836,000	Mexico City (u.a.)	14,987,051
St Pierre and Miquelon (Fr.)	93	242	6,300	Ψ St Pierre	—
United States	3,787,318	9,809,108	248,709,873*	Washington DC	606,900

Central America and the West Indies

Anguilla (UK)	35	91	8,800*	The Valley	1,400
Antigua and Barbuda	170	440	65,962	Ψ St John's	30,000
Aruba (Neth.)	75	193	59,000	Ψ Oranjestad	20,000
Bahamas	5,380	13,935	258,000	Ψ Nassau	171,000*
Barbados	166	431	255,000	Ψ Bridgetown	7,466
Belize	8,867	22,965	169,392*	Belmopan	3,558*
Bermuda (UK)	20	53	58,460	Ψ Hamilton	1,617
Cayman Islands (UK)	100	259	29,700	Ψ George Town	15,000
Costa Rica	19,575	50,700	3,000,000	San José (u.a.)	1,068,206
Cuba	42,804	110,861	10,736,000	Ψ Havana	2,096,000

Country	Area sq. miles	sq. km	Population	Capital	Population of Capital
Dominica	290	751	72,000	Ψ Roseau	15,850
Dominican Republic	18,816	48,734	7,321,000	Ψ Santo Domingo (u.a.)	1,313,172*
Grenada	133	344	84,000	Ψ St George's	10,000
Guadeloupe (Fr.)	687	1,779	386,600	Ψ Basse-Terre	14,000
Guatemala	42,042	108,889	9,745,000	Guatemala City	1,675,589
Haiti	10,714	27,750	6,625,000	Ψ Port au Prince	1,000,000
Honduras	43,277	112,088	4,915,900	Tegucigalpa	670,100
Jamaica	4,244	10,991	2,460,700	Ψ Kingston (u.a.)	696,300
Martinique (Fr.)	425	1,102	359,800	Ψ Fort de France	101,540
Montserrat (UK)	38	98	11,000	Ψ Plymouth	2,500
Netherlands Antilles (Neth.)	371	961	189,000	Ψ Willemstad	50,000
Nicaragua	50,193	130,000	3,999,000	Managua	615,000
Panama	29,762	77,082	2,370,000	Ψ Panama City	1,063,565
Puerto Rico (USA)	3,435	8,897	3,336,000	Ψ San Juan (u.a.)	437,745
St Christopher and Nevis	101	261	44,000	Ψ Basseterre	15,000
St Lucia	238	616	153,000	Ψ Castries	56,000
St Vincent and the Grenadines	150	388	117,000	Ψ Kingstown	33,694
El Salvador	8,124	21,041	5,376,000	San Salvador	497,644
Trinidad and Tobago	1,981	5,130	1,253,000	Ψ Port of Spain	59,649
Turks and Caicos Is. (UK)	166	430	12,400	Ψ Grand Turk	3,700
Virgin Islands:					
British (UK)	59	153	16,108*	Ψ Road Town	3,983*
US (USA)	132	342	101,809	Ψ Charlotte Amalie	11,756
South America					
Argentina	1,068,302	2,766,889	32,370,298*	Ψ Buenos Aires	2,955,002
Bolivia	424,165	1,098,581	6,440,000*	La Paz	1,115,000*
Brazil	3,286,488	8,511,965	150,368,000	Brasilia	1,803,478
Chile	292,258	756,945	13,386,000	Santiago	4,385,481
Colombia	439,737	1,138,914	33,613,000	Bogotá	5,000,000
Ecuador	109,484	283,561	10,851,000	Quito	1,387,887
Falkland Islands (UK)	4,700	12,173	2,121	Ψ Stanley	1,643
French Guiana (Fr.)	35,135	91,000	114,900	Ψ Cayenne	41,000
Guyana	83,000	214,969	800,000	Ψ Georgetown	187,056
Paraguay	157,048	406,752	4,397,000	Asunción (u.a.)	729,307
Peru	496,225	1,285,216	22,465,000	Lima (u.a.)	6,459,000
South Georgia (UK)	1,580	4,092	—	—	—
Suriname	63,037	163,265	429,000	Ψ Paramaribo (u.a.)	182,100
Uruguay	68,037	176,215	3,116,802	Ψ Montevideo	1,383,660
Venezuela	352,144	912,050	20,226,000	Caracas (u.a.)	2,784,000

ASIA

Afghanistan	250,000	647,497	16,430,000	Kabul	2,000,000
Bahrain	240	622	516,000	Ψ Manama	108,684*
Bangladesh	55,598	143,998	108,000,000	Dhaka	6,000,000
Bhutan	18,147	47,000	1,551,000	Thimphu	15,000
Brunei	2,226	5,765	260,863	Bandar Seri Begawan	46,229
Cambodia	69,898	181,035	8,442,000	Ψ Phnom Penh	920,000
China[1]	3,705,408	9,596,961	1,171,000,000	Beijing (Peking) (u.a.)	10,860,000
Hong Kong (UK)	416	1,074	5,900,000	Ψ Victoria	—
India	1,269,346	3,287,590	843,930,861	Delhi	8,375,188
Indonesia	735,358	1,904,569	187,765,000	Ψ Jakarta	7,885,519
Iran	636,296	1,648,000	55,762,000	Tehran	6,042,584
Iraq	167,925	434,924	19,581,000	Baghdad	3,205,665
Israel[2]	8,019	20,770	5,090,000	Tel Aviv	1,781,500
Japan	145,834	377,708	123,921,000	Tokyo (u.a.)	11,935,700
Jordan	37,738	97,740	4,145,000	Amman	1,100,000
Kazakhstan	1,049,155	2,716,626	16,700,000	Alma Ata	1,128,000
Korea, DPR (North)	46,540	120,538	23,193,000	Pyongyang	1,500,000
Korea, Rep. of (South)	38,025	98,484	43,268,000	Seoul	9,991,089
Kuwait	6,880	17,818	1,000,000	Ψ Kuwait (city)	400,000

	AREA				POPULATION
COUNTRY	sq. miles	sq. km	POPULATION	CAPITAL	OF CAPITAL
Kyrgyzstan	76,642	198,501	4,367,000	Biskek	616,000
Laos	91,429	231,800	4,262,000	Vientiane	120,000
Lebanon	4,015	10,400	2,745,000	Ψ Beirut	702,000
Macao (Port.)	6	16	479,000	Ψ Macao	—
Malaysia	127,317	329,749	18,333,000	Kuala Lumpur	1,103,200
Maldives	115	298	223,000	Ψ Malé	46,334
Mongolia	604,250	1,565,000	2,156,000	Ulan Bator	600,500
Myanmar (Burma)	261,218	676,552	42,561,000	Ψ Yangon (Rangoon) (u.a.)	3,973,872
Nepal	54,342	140,747	19,605,000	Kathmandu	300,000
Oman	82,030	212,457	1,559,000	Ψ Muscat	400,000
Pakistan	307,374	746,045	115,524,000	Islamabad (u.a.)	350,000
Philippines	115,831	300,000	62,868,000	Ψ Manila	1,876,195
Qatar	4,247	11,000	381,000	Ψ Doha	220,000
Saudi Arabia	830,000	2,149,640	16,929,294	Riyadh	2,000,000
Singapore	247	639	3,002,800	—	—
Sri Lanka	25,332	65,610	17,243,000	Ψ Colombo	1,963,000
Syria	71,498	185,180	12,993,000	Damascus	1,378,000
Tajikistan	55,251	143,100	4,969,000	Dushanbe	595,000
Taiwan	13,800	35,742	20,536,233	Taipei	2,719,659
Thailand	198,457	514,000	56,923,000	Ψ Bangkok	5,876,000
Turkey[3]	301,382	780,576	60,777,000	Ankara	3,236,626
Turkmenistan	188,456	488,100	3,809,000	Ashkhabad	398,000
United Arab Emirates	32,278	83,600	1,909,000	Abu Dhabi	450,000
Uzbekistan	172,742	447,229	20,300,000	Tashkent	2,073,000
Vietnam	127,242	329,556	71,267,000	Hanoi	2,150,000
Yemen	203,850	527,696	12,302,000	Sana'a	427,150

[1] Including Tibet
[2] Including East Jerusalem, the Golan Heights and Israeli citizens on the West Bank
[3] Including Turkey in Europe

EUROPE

Albania	11,099	28,748	3,331,000	Tirana	239,381
Andorra	180	468	58,000	Andorra La Vella	22,205
Armenia	11,306	29,271	3,645,000	Erevan	1,119,000
Austria	32,374	83,849	7,897,800	Vienna	1,539,848*
Azerbaijan	33,436	86,565	7,136,000	Baku	1,757,000
Belarus	80,300	207,897	10,260,000	Minsk	1,589,000
Belgium	11,781	30,513	9,928,000	Brussels (u.a.)	960,324*
Bosnia–Hercegovina	19,735	51,129	4,100,000	Sarajevo	447,000
Bulgaria	42,823	110,912	8,982,000	Sofia	1,107,613
Croatia	21,823	56,538	4,760,344	Zagreb	950,000
Cyprus	3,572	9,251	706,900	Nicosia	177,410
Czech Republic	30,372	78,664	10,302,000	Prague	1,215,076
Denmark	16,629	43,069	5,146,469	Ψ Copenhagen (u.a.)	1,337,114
Faroe Islands	540	1,399	47,449	Ψ Thorshavn	10,726
Estonia	17,413	45,082	1,574,955	Talinn	484,400
Finland	137,851	337,032	5,029,000	Ψ Helsinki	492,200
France	211,208	547,026	56,614,000	Paris (u.a.)	9,318,800
Georgia	26,911	69,673	5,401,000	Tbilisi	1,211,000
Germany	137,738	365,755	80,372,000	Berlin	3,376,800
Gibraltar (UK)	2	6	28,848	Ψ Gibraltar	—
Greece	50,944	131,944	10,256,464	Athens (u.a.)	3,096,775
Hungary	35,919	93,030	10,335,000	Budapest	2,004,000
Iceland	39,768	103,000	259,581	Ψ Reykjavik (u.a.)	99,653
Ireland, Republic of	27,136	70,283	3,525,719	Ψ Dublin	478,389
Italy	116,304	301,225	57,052,000	Rome (u.a.)	2,693,383
Latvia	24,695	63,935	2,606,000	Riga	900,000
Liechtenstein	61	157	29,856	Vaduz	4,874
Lithuania	26,173	67,761	3,761,000	Vilnius	596,000
Luxembourg	998	2,586	389,800	Luxembourg	75,400
Macedonia	9,925	25,713	2,034,000	Skopje	448,229

Country	AREA sq. miles	sq. km	Population	Capital	Population of Capital
Malta	122	316	362,950	Ψ Valletta	9,199
Moldova	13,912	36,018	4,361,000	Kishinev	665,000
Monaco	0.4	1	28,000	Monaco-Ville	1,234
Netherlands	15,770	40,844	15,240,000	Ψ Amsterdam (u.a.)	1,034,562
Norway[1]	125,181	324,219	4,262,000	Ψ Oslo	467,090
Poland	120,725	312,677	38,300,000	Warsaw	1,655,063
Portugal[2]	35,553	92,082	10,582,000	Ψ Lisbon	2,128,000
Romania	91,699	237,500	22,760,449	Bucharest	2,064,474
Russia[3]	6,593,391	17,070,289	148,800,000	Moscow	8,967,000
San Marino	23	61	24,000	San Marino	—
Slovak Republic	18,932	49,035	5,274,335	Bratislava	440,421
Slovenia	7,816	20,251	2,020,000	Ljubljana	268,000
Spain[4]	194,897	504,782	38,872,268	Madrid (u.a.)	4,947,555
Sweden	173,732	449,964	8,635,000	Ψ Stockholm (u.a.)	669,485
Switzerland	15,943	41,293	6,833,750	Berne	135,600
Ukraine	233,090	603,700	52,000,000	Kiev	2,577,000
United Kingdom[5]	94,227	244,046	56,467,000*	Ψ London (u.a.)	6,679,699
England	50,363	130,439	49,890,000	—	—
Wales	8,018	20,768	2,811,865*	Ψ Cardiff	290,000
Scotland	30,414	78,772	4,998,567*	Ψ Edinburgh	418,914
Northern Ireland	5,452	14,121	1,577,836*	Ψ Belfast (u.a.)	287,100
Vatican City State	0.2	0.44	1,000	Vatican City	—
Yugoslavia, Fed. Rep. of	39,506	102,350	10,410,000	Belgrade	1,455,000

[1] Excludes Svalbard and Jan Mayen Islands (approx. 24,101 sq. miles (62,422 sq. km) and 3,000 population)
[2] Includes Madeira (314 sq. miles) and the Azores (922 sq. miles)
[3] Includes Russia in Asia
[4] Includes Balearic Islands, Canary Islands, Ceuta and Melilla
[5] Includes Isle of Man (227 sq. miles (588 sq. km), 69,788* population), and Channel Islands (75 sq. miles (195 sq. km), 142,949* population)

OCEANIA

Country	sq. miles	sq. km	Population	Capital	Population of Capital
Australia	2,967,909	7,686,848	17,482,600*	Canberra	284,000*
Norfolk Island	14	36	1,912	Ψ Kingston	
Fiji	7,055	18,274	776,000	Ψ Suva	69,665
French Polynesia (Fr.)	1,544	4,000	206,000	Ψ Papeete	24,200
Guam (USA)	212	549	132,152	Agaña	—
Kiribati	281	728	68,000	Tarawa	17,921
Marshall Islands	70	181	45,569	Majuro	20,000
Micronesia, Fed. States of	271	701	101,000	Palikir	—
Nauru	8	21	9,000	Ψ Nauru	—
New Caledonia (Fr.)	7,358	19,058	167,000	Ψ Noumea	65,000
New Zealand	103,736	268,676	3,435,000	Ψ Wellington (u.a.)	325,682
Cook Islands	91	236	17,185*	Avarua	—
Niue	100	259	2,239	Alofi	—
Ross Dependency[1]	286,696	750,310	—	—	—
Tokelau	5	12.9	1,578	—	—
Northern Mariana Islands (USA)	184	476	43,555	Saipan	39,090
Palau (USA)	192	497	15,105	Koror	10,493
Papua New Guinea	178,260	461,691	3,772,000	Ψ Port Moresby	173,500
Pitcairn Islands (UK)	1.9	5	65	—	—
Samoa, Eastern (USA)	76	197	46,773	Ψ Pago Pago	3,075
Solomon Islands	10,983	28,446	330,000	Ψ Honiara	30,499*
Tonga	270	699	94,000	Ψ Nuku'alofa	30,000
Tuvalu	10	25	9,000	Ψ Funafuti	2,856
Vanuatu	4,706	12,190	163,000	Ψ Port Vila	19,400
Wallis and Futuna Islands (Fr.)	106	274	13,705	Ψ Mata-Utu	—
Western Samoa	1,097	2,842	162,000	Ψ Apia	36,000

[1] Includes permanent shelf ice

THE ANTARCTIC

The Antarctic is generally defined as the area lying within the Antarctic Convergence, the zone where cold northward-flowing Antarctic sea water sinks below warmer southward-flowing water. This zone is at about latitude 50° S. in the Atlantic Ocean and latitude 55°–62° S. in the Pacific Ocean. The continent itself lies almost entirely within the Antarctic Circle, an area of about 14.25 million square km (5.5 million square miles), 99 per cent of which is permanently ice-covered. The average thickness of the ice is 2,450 m (7,100 ft) but in places exceeds 4,500 m (14,500 ft). Some mountains protrude, the highest being Vinson Massif, 4,897 m (16,067 ft). The ice amounts to some 30 million cubic km (7.2 million cubic miles) and represents more than 90 per cent of the world's fresh water.

Along one-third of the Antarctic coastline, land-ice flowing outwards forms extensive ice shelves, fragments of which break off to form tabular icebergs, leaving ice-cliffs up to 50 m (150 ft) high. Much of the sea freezes in winter, forming fast ice which breaks up in summer and drifts north as pack ice.

The most conspicuous physical features of the continent are its high inland plateau (much of it over 3,000 m (10,000 ft)), the Transantarctic Mountains (which together with the large embayments of the Weddell Sea and Ross Sea mark the approximate boundary between East and West Antarctica), and the mountainous Antarctic Peninsula and off-lying islands which extend northwards towards South America. The continental shelf averages about 32 km (20 miles) in width (half the global mean, and in places it is non-existent) and reaches exceptional depths (390–780 m (1,300–2,600 ft), which is three to six times the global mean).

CLIMATE

On land, summer temperatures range from just below freezing around the coast to − 34° C (about − 30° F) on the plateau, and in winter from − 20° C (about − 4° F) on the coast to − 65° C (about − 85° F) inland. Over a large area the maxima do not exceed − 15° C (+ 5° F).

Precipitation is scanty over the plateau but amounts to 25–76 cm (10–30 in) (water equivalent) along the coast and some scientific stations are permanently buried by snow. Some rain falls over the more northerly areas in summer. Gravity winds on the plateau slopes and cyclonic storms further north can both exceed 160 km/h (100 m.p.h.) and gusts have been known to reach 240 km/h (150 m.p.h.). Visibility can be reduced to zero in blizzards.

FLORA AND FAUNA

Although a small number of flowering plants, ferns and clubmosses occur on the sub-Antarctic islands, only two (a grass and a pearlwort) extend south of 60° S. Antarctic vegetation is dominated by lichens and mosses, with a few liverworts, algae and fungi. Most of these occur around the coast or on islands, but lichens and some mosses also occur inland.

The only land animals are tiny insects and mites with nematodes, rotifers and tardigrades in the mosses, but large numbers of seals, penguins and other sea-birds go ashore to breed in the summer. The emperor penguin is the only species which breeds ashore throughout the winter. By contrast, the Antarctic seas abound with life, a wide variety of invertebrates (including krill) and fish providing food for the seals, penguins and other birds, and a residual population of whales.

POTENTIAL RESOURCES

In the 180 years from Captain James Cook's circumnavigation of the Antarctic in 1772–5 to the mid-1950s, expeditions to the Antarctic made major contributions to geographical and scientific knowledge of the area.

Increasing pressure on the world's food and mineral supplies has stimulated interest in the potential resources even in the extremely hostile polar environment. Minerals may be present in great variety but not in commercially exploitable concentrations in accessible localities. There are indications that off-shore hydrocarbons may be present but mostly below great depths of stormy, ice-infested seas.

Currently, the chief interest is in marine protein, including the shrimp-like krill already fished commercially by Japan and Poland. Research to ensure rational management of stocks of this organism is being continued by international groups, but it is estimated that they could sustain a yield equal to the present total annual world fish catch.

THE ANTARCTIC TREATY

The International Geophysical Year 1957–8 gave great impetus to Antarctic research, increasing the number of stations from 17 to 44 and the number of nations involved in research from four to 12 by 1957. The co-operative scientific effort proved so fruitful that the 12 nations involved (Argentina, Australia, Belgium, Chile, France, Japan, New Zealand, Norway, South Africa, the USSR, the UK and the USA) pledged themselves to promote scientific and technical co-operation unhampered by politics, and the Antarctic Treaty was signed by the 12 states in 1959.

The 12 signatories to the treaty agreed to establish free use of the Antarctic continent for peaceful scientific purposes; to freeze all territorial claims and disputes in the Antarctic; to ban all military activities in the area; and to prohibit nuclear explosions and the disposal of radioactive waste. Since then additional agreements have been reached to promote conservation and restrict tourism, waste disposal and pollution.

The Antarctic Treaty was defined as covering areas south of latitude 60° S., excluding the high seas but including the ice shelves, and came into force in 1961. It has since been signed by a further 28 states, 14 of which are active in the Antarctic and have therefore been accorded consultative status, bringing the number of consultative parties to 26. In 1991 a protocol to the treaty was adopted by the signatory states which introduced a range of measures to protect Antarctica's environment and prohibit mineral exploitation and mining for at least 50 years.

TERRITORIAL CLAIMS

Under the provisions of the Antarctic Treaty of 1959 all territorial claims and disputes were frozen without the acceptance or denial of the claims of the various claimants. The US and Soviet governments also made it clear that although they had not made any specific territorial claims, they did not relinquish the right to make such claims.

Seven states have made claims in the Antarctic: Argentina claims the part of Antarctica between 74° W. and 25° W., and Chile that part between 90° W. and 53° W.; Britain claims the British Antarctic Territory, an area of 1,810,000 square km (700,000 square miles) between 20° and 80° W. longitude; France claims Adélie Land, 432,000 square km

(166,800 square miles) between 136° and 142° E.; Australia claims the Australian Antarctic Territory, 6,120,000 square km (2,320,000 square miles) between 160° and 45° E. longitude excluding Adélie Land; Norway claims Queen Maud Land between 20° W. and 45° E.; and New Zealand claims the Ross Dependency, 450,000 square km (175,000 miles) between 160° E. and 150° W. longitude. The Argentinian, British and Chilean claims overlap while the part of the continent between 90° W. and 150° W. is unclaimed by any state.

SCIENTIFIC RESEARCH

There are over 40 permanently occupied stations operated by the following nations: Argentina (6), Australia (4), Brazil (1), Chile (3), China (2), France (4), Germany (1), India (1), Japan (2), New Zealand (2), Poland (1), Russia (5), South Africa (3), South Korea (1), Uruguay (1), UK (5), USA (3, including one at the South Pole).

The staff of these stations and summer field-workers are the only people present on the continent and off-lying islands. There are no indigenous inhabitants.

LARGEST CITIES OF THE WORLD

In most cases figures refer to urban agglomerations.

	Population		Population
Mexico City, Mexico	14,987,051	Moscow, Russia	8,967,000
Cairo, Egypt	14,000,000	Delhi, India	8,375,188
Ψ Shanghai, China	12,760,000	Ψ Jakarta, Indonesia	7,885,519
Ψ Bombay, India	12,571,720	Ψ New York, USA	7,322,564
Tokyo, Japan	11,718,720	Manila, Philippines	6,720,050
Ψ Calcutta, India	10,916,272	Ψ London, UK	6,679,699
Beijing, China	10,860,000	Rio de Janiero, Brazil	6,603,388
São Paulo, Brazil	10,063,110	Karachi, Pakistan	6,500,000
Seoul, South Korea	9,991,089	Lima, Peru	6,459,000
Paris, France	9,318,800	Tehran, Iran	6,042,000

Currencies of the World

AND EXCHANGE RATES AGAINST £ STERLING

Franc CFA = Franc de la Communauté financière africaine
Franc CFP = Franc des Comptoirs français du Pacifique

COUNTRY	MONETARY UNIT	AVERAGE RATE TO £ 1 September 1992	AVERAGE RATE TO £ 27 August 1993
Afghanistan	Afghani (Af) of 100 puls	Af 99.25	Af 2115.75
Albania	Lek (Lk) of 100 qindarka	Lk 218.00	Lk 165.99
Algeria	Algerian dinar (DA) of 100 centimes	DA 40.05	DA 29.787
Andorra	French and Spanish currencies in use	—	—
Angola	New Kwanza (Kz) of 100 lwei	Kz 1079.95	Kz 5996.70
Antigua and Barbuda	East Caribbean dollar (EC$) of 100 cents	EC$ 5.3515	EC$ 4.07
Argentina	Peso of 10,000 australes	Pesos 19620	Pesos 1.5107
Armenia	Rouble of 100 kopeks	Roubles 1.0494	Roubles 0.8720
Aruba	Aruban florin	Florins 3.5475	Florins 2.7011
Australia	Australian dollar ($A) of 100 cents	$A 2.7595	$A 2.2625
Austria	Schilling of 100 Groschen	Schilling 19.645	Schilling 17.555
Azerbaijan	Roubles of 100 kopeks	Roubles 1.0494	Roubles 0.8720
Azores	Currency is that of Portugal	Esc 243.25	Esc 255.20
Bahamas	Bahamian dollar (B$) of 100 cents	B$ 1.9820	B$ 1.5005
Bahrain	Bahrain dinar (BD) of 1,000 fils	BD 0.7475	BD 0.5689
Bangladesh	Taka (Tk) of 100 poisha	Tk 77.95	Tk 59.58
Barbados	Barbados dollar (BD$) of 100 cents	BD$ 3.9865	BD$ 3.0351
Belarus	Rouble of 100 kopeks	Roubles 1.0494	Roubles 0.8720
Belgium	Belgian franc (or frank) of 100 centimes (centiemen)	Francs 57.45	Francs 53.25
Belize	Belize dollar (BZ$) of 100 cents	BZ$ 3.9640	BZ$ 3.0180
Benin	Franc CFA	Francs 475.125	Francs 437.375
Bermuda	Bermuda dollar of 100 cents	$ 1.9820	$ 1.5005
Bhutan	Ngultrum of 100 chetrum (Indian currency is also legal tender)	Ngultrum 56.55	Ngultrum 47.2619
Bolivia	Boliviano ($b) of 100 centavos	$b 7.3890	$b 6.5113
Bosnia-Hercegovina	Dinar of 100 paras	Dinars 396.4	Dinars 158.445
Botswana	Pula (P) of 100 thebe	P 4.0545	P 3.7416
Brazil	Cruzeiro (BRC) of 100 centavos	BRC 9964.80	BRC 139.025
British Virgin Islands	US dollar (US$) (£ sterling and EC$ also circulate)	US$ 1.9820	US$ 1.5005
Brunei	Brunei dollar of 100 sen (fully interchangeable with Singapore currency)	$ 3.1660	$ 2.4107
Bulgaria	Lev of 100 stotinki	Leva 40.10	Leva 39.55
Burkina	Franc CFA	Francs 475.125	Francs 437.375
Burundi	Burundi franc of 100 centimes	Francs 393.25	Francs 366.50
Cambodia	Riel of 100 sen	Riel 1640.00	Riel 5432.40
Cameroon	Franc CFA	Francs 475.125	Francs 437.375
Canada	Canadian dollar (C$) of 100 cents	C$ 2.3715	C$ 1.9770
Canary Islands	Currency is that of Spain	Pesetas 180.95	Pesetas 203.60
Cape Verde	Escudo Caboverdiano of 100 centavos	Esc 124.15	Esc 111.96
Cayman Islands	Cayman Islands dollar (CI$) of 100 cents	CI$ 1.6845	CI$ 1.2827
Central African Republic	Franc CFA	Francs 475.125	Francs 437.375
Chad	Franc CFA	Francs 475.125	Francs 437.375
Chile	Chilean peso of 100 centavos	Pesos 759.75	Pesos 616.80
China	Renminbi Yuan of 10 jiao or 100 fen	Yuan 10.7805	Yuan 8.6655
Colombia	Colombian peso of 100 centavos	Pesos 1535.95	Pesos 1218.92
Comoros	Franc CFA	Francs 475.125	Francs 437.375
Congo	Franc CFA	Francs 475.125	Francs 437.375
Costa Rica	Costa Rican colón (₡) of 100 céntimos	₡ 268.55	₡ 216.82
Côte d'Ivoire	Franc CFA	Francs 475.125	Francs 437.375
Croatia	Dinar of 100 paras	Dinars 396.4	Dinars 6713.70
Cuba	Cuban peso of 100 centavos	Pesos 1.5010	Pesos 1.1429
Cyprus	Cyprus pound (C£) of 100 cents	C£ 0.8110	C£ 0.7703
Czech Republic	Koruna (Kčs) of 100 haléřu	Kčs 26.8163	Kčs 44.268

Country	Monetary Unit	Average Rate to £ 1 September 1992	Average Rate to £ 27 August 1993
Denmark	Danish krone of 100 øre	Kroner 10.7775	Kroner 10.3075
Djibouti	Djibouti franc of 100 centimes	Francs 347.00	Francs 265.75
Dominica	East Caribbean dollar (EC$) of 100 cents	EC$ 5.3515	EC$ 4.07
Dominican Republic	Dominican Republic peso (RD$) of 100 centavos	RD$ 25.33	RD$ 19.617
Ecuador	Sucre of 100 centavos	Sucres 2886.65	Sucres 2791.65
Egypt	Egyptian pound (£E) of 100 piastres or 1,000 millièmes	£E 6.55	£E 4.9695
Equatorial Guinea	Franc CFA	Francs 475.125	Francs 437.375
Estonia	Kroon of 100 sents	Roubles 1.0494	Kroons 20.05
Ethiopia	Ethiopian birr (EB) of 100 cents	EB 4.0775	EB 7.4621
Falkland Islands	Falkland pound of 100 pence		at parity with £ sterling
Faroe Islands	Currency is that of Denmark	Kroner 10.7775	Kroner 10.3075
Fiji	Fiji dollar (F$) of 100 cents	F$ 2.9255	F$ 2.3040
Finland	Markka (Mk) of 100 penniä	Mk 7.6945	Mk 8.770
France	Franc of 100 centimes	Francs 9.5025	Francs 8.7475
French Guiana	Currency is that of France	Francs 9.5025	Francs 8.7475
French Polynesia	Franc CFP	Francs 170.00	Francs 159.50
Gabon	Franc CFA	Francs 475.125	Francs 437.375
Gambia	Dalasi (D) of 100 butut	D 16.7085	D 14.0337
Georgia	Rouble of 100 kopeks	Roubles 1.0494	Roubles 0.8720
Germany	Deutsche Mark (DM) of 100 Pfennig	DM 2.7875	DM 2.5000
Ghana	Cedi of 100 pesewas	Cedi 832.45	Cedi 995.00
Gibraltar	Gibraltar pound of 100 pence		at parity with £ sterling
Greece	Drachma of 100 leptae	Drachmae 346.95	Drachmae 354.875
Greenland	Currency is that of Denmark	Kroner 10.7775	Kroner 10.3075
Grenada	East Caribbean dollar (EC$) of 100 cents	EC$ 5.3515	EC$ 4.07
Guadeloupe	Currency is that of France	Francs 9.5025	Francs 8.7475
Guam	Currency is that of USA	US$ 1.9820	US$ 1.5005
Guatemala	Quetzal (Q) of 100 centavos	Q 10.4650	Q 8.7109
Guinea	Guinea franc of 100 centimes	Francs 1609.95	Francs 1225.75
Guinea-Bissau	Guinea-Bissau peso of 100 centavos	Pesos 9910.00	Pesos 7545.00
Guyana	Guyana dollar (G$) of 100 cents	G$ 248.70	G$ 190.13
Haiti	Gourde of 100 centimes	Gourdes 9.82	Gourdes 18.108
Honduras	Lempira of 100 centavos	Lempiras 11.4560	Lempiras 10.5175
Hong Kong	Hong Kong dollar (HK$) of 100 cents	HK$ 15.3065	HK$ 11.6438
Hungary	Forint of 100 fillér	Forints 150.25	Forints 143.14
Iceland	Icelandic króna (Kr) of 100 aurar	Kr 104.35	Kr 106.64
India	Indian rupee (Rs) of 100 paisa	Rs 56.55	Rs 47.2619
Indonesia	Rupiah (Rp) of 100 sen	Rp 4033.90	Rp 3182.00
Iran	Rial	Rials 121.2	Rials 2310.00
Iraq	Iraqi dinar (ID) of 1,000 fils	ID 0.5936	ID 0.4690
Ireland, Republic of	Punt (IR£) of 100 pence	IR£ 1.0570	IR£ 1.0700
Israel	Shekel of 100 agora	Shekels 4.7910	Shekels 4.34
Italy	Lira of 100 centesimi	Lire 2134.50	Lire 2391.75
Jamaica	Jamaican dollar (J$) of 100 cents	J$ 45.1895	J$ 36.216
Japan	Yen of 100 sen	Yen 244.25	Yen 156.00
Jordan	Jordanian dinar (JD) of 1,000 fils	JD 1.3180	JD 1.0472
Kazakhstan	Rouble of 100 kopeks	Roubles 1.0494	Roubles 0.8720
Kenya	Kenya shilling (Ksh) of 100 cents	Ksh 65.2080	Ksh 98.537
Kiribati	Australian dollar ($A) of 100 cents	$A 2.7595	$A 2.2625
Korea, North	Won of 100 jun	Won 4.2615	Won 3.2444
Korea, South	Won of 100 jeon	Won 1558.25	Won 1221.325
Kuwait	Kuwaiti dinar (KD) of 1,000 fils	KD 0.5758	KD 0.4500
Kyrgyzstan	Rouble of 100 kopeks	Roubles 1.0494	Roubles 0.8720
Laos	Kip (K) of 100 at	K 1417.15	K 1086.48
Latvia	Lat	Roubles 1.0494	Lats 0.9374
Lebanon	Lebanese pound (L£) of 100 piastres	L£ 4748.20	L£ 2606.15
Lesotho	Loti (M) of 100 lisente	M 5.4315	M 5.0550
Liberia	Liberian dollar (L$) of 100 cents	L$ 1.9820	L$ 1.5005
Libya	Libyan dinar (LD) of 1,000 dirhams	LD 0.5118	LD 0.4470
Liechtenstein	Swiss franc of 100 rappen (or centimes)	Francs 2.4950	Francs 2.2075
Lithuania	Rouble of 100 kopeks	Roubles 1.0494	Roubles 0.8720
Luxembourg	Luxembourg franc (LF) of 100 centimes (Belgian currency is also legal tender)	LF 57.45	LF 53.25

COUNTRY	MONETARY UNIT	AVERAGE RATE TO £ 1 September 1992	AVERAGE RATE TO £ 27 August 1993
Macao	Pataca of 100 avos	Pataca 15.8285	Pataca 12.0790
Macedonia	Dinar of 100 paras	Dinars 396.4	Dinars 158.445
Madagascar	Franc malgache (FMG) of 100 centimes	FMG 3036.50	FMG 2859.15
Madeira	Currency is that of Portugal	Esc 243.35	Esc 255.20
Malawi	Kwacha (K) of 100 tambala	K 7.5175	K 6.5755
Malaysia	Malaysian dollar (ringgit) (M$) of 100 sen	M$ 4.9365	M$ 3.8305
Maldives	Rufiyaa of 100 laaris	Rufiyaa 20.8905	Rufiyaa 18.0705
Mali	Franc CFA	Francs 475.125	Francs 437.375
Malta	Maltese lira (LM) of 100 cents or 1,000 mils	LM 0.5752	LM 0.5837
Marshall Islands	Currency is that of USA	US$ 1.9820	US$ 1.5005
Martinique	Currency is that of France	Francs 9.5025	Francs 8.7475
Mauritania	Ouguiya (UM) of 5 khoums	UM 153.75	UM 171.74
Mauritius	Mauritius rupee of 100 cents	Rs 28.5210	Rs 27.17
Mayotte	Currency is that of France	Francs 9.5025	Francs 8.7475
Mexico	Peso of 100 centavos	Pesos 5947.95	Pesos 4.6970
Moldova	Rouble of 100 kopeks	Roubles 1.0494	Roubles 0.8720
Monaco	French franc of 100 centimes	Francs 9.5025	Francs 8.7475
Mongolia	Tugrik of 100 möngö	Tugriks 79.28	Tugriks 603.60
Montenegro	Dinar of 100 paras	Dinars 396.4	Dinars 158.445
Montserrat	East Caribbean dollar (EC$) of 100 cents	EC$ 5.3515	EC$ 4.07
Morocco	Dirham (DH) of 100 centimes	DH 14.8085	DH 13.9065
Mozambique	Metical (MT) of 100 centavos	MT 5424.7	MT 6165.34
Myanmar (Burma)	Kyat (K) of 100 pyas	K 11.2275	K 9.4750
Namibia	South African rand (R) of 100 cents	R 5.4315	R 5.0550
Nauru	Australian dollar ($A) of 100 cents	$A 2.7595	$A 2.2625
Nepal	Nepalese rupee of 100 paisa	Rs 92.4205	Rs 69.2405
Netherlands	Gulden (guilder) or florin of 100 cents	Guilders 3.1450	Guilders 2.8100
Netherlands Antilles	Netherlands Antilles guilder of 100 cents	Guilders 3.5475	Guilders 2.7010
New Caledonia	Franc CFP	Francs 170.00	Francs 159.50
New Zealand	New Zealand dollar (NZ$) of 100 cents	NZ$ 3.6645	NZ$ 2.7325
Nicaragua	Córdoba (C$) of 100 centavos	C$ 10.6630	C$ 9.3340
Niger	Franc CFA	Francs 475.125	Francs 437.375
Nigeria	Naira (N) of 100 kobo	N 36.5480	N 37.725
Norway	Krone of 100 øre	Kroner 11.0400	Kroner 10.8775
Oman	Rial Omani (OR) of 1,000 baiza	OR 0.7629	OR 0.5810
Pakistan	Pakistan rupee of 100 paisa	Rs 49.65	Rs 45.1340
Panama	Balboa of 100 centésimos (US notes are also in circulation)	Balboa 1.9820	Balboa 1.5005
Papua New Guinea	Kina (K) of 100 toea	K 1.8975	K 1.4745
Paraguay	Guaraní (Gs) of 100 céntimos	Gs 3004.70	Gs 2640.75
Peru	New Sol of 100 cénts	New Sol 2.56	New Sol 3.0655
Philippines	Philippine peso (P) of 100 centavos	P 44.90	P 41.70
Poland	Złoty of 100 groszy	Złotys 26628.0	Złotys 29680.0
Portugal	Escudo (Esc) of 100 centavos	Esc 243.35	Esc 255.20
Puerto Rico	Currency is that of USA	US$ 1.9820	US$ 1.5005
Qatar	Qatar riyal of 100 dirhams	Riyals 7.2135	Riyals 5.4930
Réunion	Currency is that of France	Francs 9.5025	Francs 8.7475
Romania	Leu (Lei) of 100 bani	Lei 760.83	Lei 1218.77
Russia	Rouble of 100 kopeks	Roubles 1.0494	Roubles 0.8720
Rwanda	Rwanda franc of 100 centimes	Francs 266.50	Francs 214.10
St Christopher and Nevis	East Caribbean dollar (EC$) of 100 cents	EC$ 5.3515	EC$ 4.07
St Helena	St Helena pound (£) of 100 pence	at parity with £ sterling	
St Lucia	East Caribbean dollar (EC$) of 100 cents	EC$ 5.3515	EC$ 4.07
St Pierre and Miquelon	Currency is that of France	Francs 9.5025	Francs 8.7475
St Vincent and the Grenadines	East Caribbean dollar (EC$) of 100 cents	EC$ 5.3515	EC$ 4.07
El Salvador	El Salvador colón (₡) of 100 centavos	₡ 16.8865	₡ 13.1358
San Marino	Italian currency is in circulation	Lire 2134.50	Lire 2391.75
São Tomé and Príncipe	Dobra of 100 centavos	Dobra 475.68	Dobra 362.16

Country	Monetary Unit	Average Rate to £ 1 September 1992	Average Rate to £ 27 August 1993
Saudi Arabia	Saudi riyal (SR) of 20 qursh or 100 halala	SR 7.4255	SR 5.6342
Senegal	Franc CFA	Francs 475.125	Francs 437.375
Serbia	Dinar of 100 paras	Dinars 396.4	Dinars 158.445
Seychelles	Seychelles rupee of 100 cents	Rs 9.65	Rs 7.7410
Sierra Leone	Leone (Le) of 100 cents	Le 981.10	Le 829.95
Singapore	Singapore dollar (S$) of 100 cents	S$ 3.1660	S$ 2.4107
Slovak Republic	Koruna (Kčs) of 100 haléřu	Kčs 26.8163	Kčs 48.93
Slovenia	Tolar	Dinars 396.4	Tolars 180.1980
Solomon Islands	Solomon Islands dollar (SI$) of 100 cents	SI$ 5.7700	SI$ 4.8005
Somalia	Somali shilling of 100 cents	Shillings 5192.85	Shillings 3931.30
South Africa	Rand (R) of 100 cents	R 5.4315	R 5.0550
Spain	Peseta of 100 céntimos	Pesetas 180.95	Pesetas 203.60
Sri Lanka	Sri Lankan rupee of 100 cents	Rs 86.45	Rs 73.2010
Sudan	Sudanese dinar (SD) of 10 pounds	£S 19.82	SD 19.6170
Suriname	Suriname guilder of 100 cents	Guilders 3.5380	Guilders 2.6935
Swaziland	Lilangeni (E) of 100 cents (South African currency also in circulation)	E 5.4315	E 5.0550
Sweden	Swedish krona of 100 öre	Kronor 10.1975	Kronor 12.0725
Switzerland	Swiss franc of 100 rappen (or centimes)	Francs 2.4950	Francs 2.2075
Syria	Syrian pound (S$) of 100 piastres	S£ 41.6220	S£ 32.4435
Taiwan	Taiwan dollar (T$) of 100 cents	T$ 49.85	T$ 40.675
Tajikistan	Rouble of 100 kopeks	Roubles 1.0494	Roubles 0.8720
Tanzania	Tanzanian shilling of 100 cents	Shillings 633.45	Shillings 656.40
Thailand	Baht of 100 satang	Baht 49.80	Baht 37.7375
Togo	Franc CFA	Francs 475.125	Francs 437.375
Tonga	Pa'anga (T$) of 100 seniti	T$ 2.7595	T$ 2.2625
Trinidad and Tobago	Trinidad and Tobago dollar (TT$) of 100 cents	TT$ 8.4235	TT$ 8.3540
Tunisia	Tunisian dinar of 1,000 millimes	Dinars 1.6080	Dinars 1.5370
Turkey	Turkish lira (TL) of 100 kurus	TL 13954.50	TL 17582.74
Turkmenistan	Rouble of 100 kopeks	Roubles 1.0494	Roubles 0.8720
Tuvalu	Australian dollar ($A) of 100 cents	$A 2.7595	$A 2.2625
Uganda	Uganda shilling of 100 cents	Shillings 2343.25	Shillings 1785.70
Ukraine	Rouble of 100 kopeks	Roubles 1.0494	Roubles 0.8720
United Arab Emirates	UAE dirham of 100 fils	Dirham 7.2720	Dirham 5.5160
United Kingdom	Pound sterling (£) of 100 pence	£ 1.00	£ 1.00
United States of America	US dollar (US$) of 100 cents	US$ 1.9820	US$ 1.5005
Uruguay	New Uruguayan peso of 100 centésimos	Pesos 6302.75	Pesos 6.1115
Uzbekistan	Rouble of 100 kopeks	Roubles 1.0494	Roubles 0.8720
Vanuatu	Vatu of 100 centimes	Vatu 225.50	Vatu 183.20
Vatican City State	Italian currency is legal tender	Lire 2134.50	Lire 2391.75
Venezuela	Bolívar (Bs) of 100 céntimos	Bs 135.20	Bs 143.10
Vietnam	Dông of 10 hào or 100 xu	Dông 21544.35	Dông 16063.30
Virgin Islands (US)	Currency is that of USA	US$ 1.9820	US$ 1.5005
Western Samoa	Tala (WS$) of 100 sene	WS$ 4.8435	WS$ 3.88
Republic of Yemen	Yemeni dinar (YD) of 1,000 fils	YD 0.9216	YD 0.6804
	Riyal of 100 fils	Riyals 32.7030	Riyals 24.8985
Zaire	Zaïre of 100 makuta	Zaïre 1312000	Zaïre 8943300
Zambia	Kwacha (K) of 100 ngwee	K 178.507	K 663.96
Zimbabwe	Zimbabwe dollar (Z$) of 100 cents	Z$ 4.6975	Z$ 9.7765

Time Zones

Standard time differences from the Greenwich meridian

+   hours ahead of GMT
−   hours behind GMT
*   varies from standard time at some part of the year (Summer Time or Daylight Saving Time)
h   hours
m   minutes

	h	m
Afghanistan	+ 4	30
*Albania	+ 1	
Algeria	+ 1	
Andorra	+ 1	
Angola	+ 1	
Anguilla	− 4	
Antigua and Barbuda	− 4	
Argentina	− 3	
*Jujuy	− 4	
*Mendoza	− 4	
Armenia	+ 4	
Aruba	− 4	
Ascension Island	0	
*Australia	+10	
Broken Hill area (NSW)	+ 9	30
Northern Territory	+ 9	30
*South Australia	+ 9	30
Western Australia	+ 8	
*Austria	+ 1	
Azerbaijan	+ 4	
*Azores	− 1	
*Bahamas	− 5	
Bahrain	+ 3	
Bangladesh	+ 6	
Barbados	− 4	
Belarus	+ 2	
*Belgium	+ 1	
Belize	− 6	
Benin	+ 1	
*Bermuda	− 4	
Bhutan	+ 6	
Bolivia	− 4	
Botswana	+ 2	
Brazil		
Acre	− 5	
*eastern, including all coast and Brasilia	− 3	
*western	− 4	
British Antarctic Territory	− 3	
South Georgia	− 2	
British Indian Ocean Territory	+ 5	
Diego Garcia	+ 5	
British Virgin Islands	− 4	
Brunei	+ 8	
*Bulgaria	+ 2	
Burkina	0	
Burundi	+ 2	
Cambodia	+ 7	
Cameroon	+ 1	
Canada		
*Alberta	− 7	
*British Columbia	− 8	
*Labrador	− 4	

	h	m
*Manitoba	− 6	
*New Brunswick	− 4	
*Newfoundland	− 3	30
*Northwest Territories		
east of 68° W.	− 4	
68° W. to 85° W.	− 5	
85° W. to 102° W.	− 6	
west of 102° W.	− 7	
*Nova Scotia	− 4	
*Ontario		
east of 90° W.	− 5	
west of 90° W.	− 6	
*Prince Edward Island	− 4	
*Quebec		
east of 63° W.	− 4	
west of 63° W.	− 5	
*Saskatchewan	− 6	
*Yukon	− 8	
*Canary Islands	0	
Cape Verde	− 1	
Cayman Islands	− 5	
Central African Republic	+ 1	
Chad	+ 1	
*Chile	− 4	
China	+ 8	
Christmas Island (Indian Ocean)	+ 7	
Cocos Keeling Islands	+ 6	30
Colombia	− 4	
Comoros	+ 3	
Congo	+ 1	
Cook Islands	− 10	
Costa Rica	− 6	
Côte d'Ivoire	0	
*Cuba	− 5	
*Cyprus	+ 2	
*Czech Republic	+ 1	
*Denmark	+ 1	
*Djibouti	+ 3	
Dominica	− 4	
Dominican Republic	− 4	
Ecuador	− 5	
*Egypt	+ 2	
Equatorial Guinea	+ 1	
Estonia	+ 2	
Ethiopia	+ 3	
*Falkland Islands	− 4	
*Faroe Islands	0	
Fiji	+12	
*Finland	+ 2	
*France	+ 1	
French Guiana	− 3	
French Polynesia	− 9	30
Gabon	+ 1	
The Gambia	0	
Georgia	+ 3	
*Germany	+ 1	
Ghana	0	
*Gibraltar	+ 1	
*Greece	+ 2	
Greenland		
*Angmagssalik and west coast	− 3	
Danmarkshavn	− 1	
Mesters Vig	− 1	
*Scoresby Sound	− 1	
Thule area	− 4	

	h	m
Grenada	− 4	
Guadeloupe	− 4	
Guam	+ 10	
Guatemala	− 6	
Guinea	0	
Guinea-Bissau	0	
Guyana	− 4	
*Haiti	− 5	
Honduras	− 6	
Hong Kong	+ 8	
*Hungary	+ 1	
Iceland	0	
India	+ 5	30
Indonesia		
Bali	+ 8	
Irian Jaya	+ 9	
Java	+ 7	
Kalimantan (south and east)	+ 8	
Kalimantan (west and central)	+ 7	
Molucca Islands	+ 9	
Sulawesi	+ 8	
Sumatra	+ 7	
Timor	+ 8	
*Iran	+ 3	30
*Iraq	+ 3	
*Ireland, Republic of	0	
*Israel	+ 2	
*Italy	+ 1	
Jamaica	− 5	
Japan	+ 9	
*Jordan	+ 2	
Kazakhstan	+ 6	
Kenya	+ 3	
Kiribati		
Banaba	+11	30
Gilbert Islands	+12	
Kiritimati Island	−10	
Phoenix Islands	−11	
Korea, North	+ 9	
Korea, South	+ 9	
Kuwait	+ 3	
*Kyrgyzstan	+ 5	
Laos	+ 7	
*Latvia	+ 2	
*Lebanon	+ 2	
Lesotho	+ 2	
Liberia	0	
Libya	+ 2	
*Liechtenstein	+ 1	
Lithuania	+ 2	
*Luxembourg	+ 1	
Macao	+ 8	
Madagascar	+ 3	
*Madeira	0	
Malawi	+ 2	
Malaysia	+ 8	
Maldives	+ 5	
Mali	0	
*Malta	+ 1	
Marshall Islands	+12	
Eniwetok	−12	
Kwajalein	−12	
Martinique	− 4	
Mauritania	0	

	h m		h m
Mauritius	+ 4	Senegal	0
Mexico	− 6	Seychelles	+ 4
central	− 7	Sierra Leone	0
western	− 8	Singapore	+ 8
Micronesia		Slovak Republic	+ 1
Caroline Islands	+10	Solomon Islands	+11
Kosrae	+11	Somalia	+ 3
Pohnpei	+11	South Africa	+ 2
Moldova	+ 2	*Spain	+ 1
*Monaco	+ 1	Sri Lanka	+ 5 30
*Mongolia	+ 8	Sudan	+ 2
Montserrat	− 4	Suriname	− 3
Morocco	0	Swaziland	+ 2
Mozambique	+ 2	*Sweden	+ 1
Myanmar	+ 6 30	*Switzerland	+ 1
Namibia	+ 2	*Syria	+ 2
Nauru	+12	Taiwan	+ 8
Nepal	+ 5 45	Tajikistan	+ 5
Netherlands	+ 1	Tanzania	+ 3
Netherlands Antilles	− 4	Thailand	+ 7
New Caledonia	+11	Togo	0
*New Zealand	+12	Tonga	+13
Nicaragua	− 5	Trinidad and Tobago	− 4
Niger	+ 1	Tristan da Cunha	0
Nigeria	+ 1	Tunisia	+ 1
Norfolk Island	+11 30	*Turkey	+ 2
*Norway	+ 1	Turkmenistan	+ 5
Oman	+ 4	*Turks and Caicos Islands	− 5
Pakistan	+ 5	Tuvalu	+12
Palau	+ 9	Uganda	+ 3
Panama	− 5	*Ukraine	+ 2
Papua New Guinea	+10	United Arab Emirates	+ 4
*Paraguay	− 4	*Uruguay	− 3
Peru	− 5	United States	
Philippines	+ 8	Alaska, east of	
*Poland	+ 1	169° 30′ W.	− 9
*Portugal	+ 1	Aleutian Islands, west	
Puerto Rico	− 4	of 169° 30′ W.	−10
Qatar	+ 3	eastern time	− 5
Réunion	+ 4	central time	− 6
*Romania	+ 2	Hawaii	−10
*Russia		mountain time	− 7
Zone 0	+ 2	Pacific time	− 8
Zone 1	+ 3	Uzbekistan	+ 5
Zone 2	+ 4	*Vanuatu	+11
Zone 3	+ 5	Vatican City State	+ 1
Zone 4	+ 6	Venezuela	− 4
Zone 5	+ 7	Vietnam	+ 7
Zone 6	+ 8	Virgin Islands (US)	− 4
Zone 7	+ 9	Western Samoa	−11
Zone 8	+10	Yemen	+ 3
Zone 9	+11	*Yugoslav republics	+ 1
Zone 10	+12	Zaire	+ 2
Rwanda	+ 2	Kinshasa	+ 1
St Helena	0	Mbandaka	+ 1
St Kitts and Nevis	− 4	Zambia	+ 2
St Lucia	− 4	Zimbabwe	+ 2
*St Pierre and Miquelon	− 3		
St Vincent and the			
Grenadines	− 4		
El Salvador	− 6		
Samoa, American	−11		
San Marino	+ 1		
São Tomé and Príncipe	0		
Saudi Arabia	+ 3		

Source: reproduced with permission from data produced by HM Nautical Almanac Office. Copyright of the Science and Engineering Research Council

Countries of the World: A-Z

SOURCES: sources of statistical data specific to one country are credited in that country's entry. Sources of statistical data used throughout the Countries of the World section include *The Military Balance* (pub. IISS), *UN Demographic Yearbook, UN Statistical Yearbook* (pub. UN), *UNESCO Statistical Yearbook* (pub. UNESCO), *World Bank Atlas, World Bank World Tables* (pub. World Bank), *World Mineral Statistics* (pub. British Geological Survey).

Other sources of information include the Foreign and Commonwealth Office Research Department and the diplomatic representatives and information offices in London of overseas countries, whom Whitaker's wishes to thank for their assistance.

AFGHANISTAN
Da Afghanistan Jamhuriat

Afghanistan is bounded on the west by Iran, on the south by Pakistan, on the north by Tajikistan, Uzbekistan and Turkmenistan, and on the east by Pakistan and China. Its ancient name was Aryana, by which title it is referred to by Strabo, the Greek geographer who lived in the first century BC. The estimated area is 250,000 sq. miles (647,497 sq. km).

Mountains, chief among which are the Hindu Kush, cover three-quarters of the country, the elevation being generally over 4,000 feet. There are three great river basins, the Oxus, Helmand, and Kabul. The climate is dry, with extreme temperatures.

POPULATION – The population is 16,430,000 (1991 UN estimate). It is estimated that over four million have become refugees in Pakistan and over one million in Iran since 1979. The population is very mixed. The most numerous race is the Pushtuns who predominate in the south and west, the Tajiks, a Persian-speaking people, Uzbeks and Turkomans in the north, Hazaras in the centre, Baluchis in the southwest and Nuristanis, who live near the Chitral border. All are Sunni Muslims, except the Hazaras and Kizilbashes, who belong to the Shia sect.

CAPITAL – Kabul (1988, 1,424,400). The chief commercial centres are Kabul and Kandahar (225,500). Other provincial capitals are (UN estimates) Herat (177,300), Mazar-i-Sharif (130,600), Jalalabad (55,000).

CURRENCY – Afghani (Af) of 100 puls.

FLAG – Three horizontal stripes of green, white, black with Islamic inscriptions on the green and white stripes.

NATIONAL ANTHEM – Soroud-e-Melli.

NATIONAL DAY – 19 August.

GOVERNMENT

The constitutional monarchy, introduced by the 1964 Constitution, was overthrown by a coup on 17 July 1973. The country was ruled by presidential decree until February 1977 when a constitution was approved by a *Loya Jerga* (Grand Tribal Council). Mohammad Daoud was elected President but was overthrown on 27 April 1978 by the armed forces and power was handed to the People's Democratic Party of Afghanistan (PDPA). In December 1979 Soviet troops invaded Afghanistan and installed Babrak Karmal as Head of State. Karmal was replaced by Najibollah in May 1986. A peace agreement in April 1988 led to the withdrawal of Soviet troops which was completed by February 1989. A new Constitution, approved in November 1987 and amended in 1990, provides for a President, a Council of Ministers, a National Assembly and a Senate.

Following a party congress in late June 1990, the PDPA was renamed Hezb-e-Watan (Homeland Party) and its Politburo and Central Committee were abolished and replaced by an Executive Council and Central Council. Najibollah was elected Chairman of the Party for a four-year term.

Following widespread defections from the armed forces to the Islamic resistance groups, President Najibollah was forced to step down on 16 April 1992 and was replaced initially by an army-dominated council of his former colleagues. However, anti-government forces overran Kabul on 25 April. A new government was installed under Sebghatullah Mujaddedi, previously leader of a Pakistan-based government-in-exile. Mujaddedi remained as an interim President until 28 June 1992 when he was succeeded by Burnahuddin Rabbani, another former exiled leader. Rabbani was due to serve for a four-month period until a permanent President could be elected by the coalition of seven former Pakistan-based Sunni Muslim mujahidin groups and three former Iran-based Shia Muslim groups. However, the ten groups could not agree on a new President, which led to renewed fighting in the Kabul area in December 1992 between rival groups. The fighting was mainly between forces of the Hezb-i-Islami of Gulbardin Hekmatyar (mainly Pushtun) supported by the Shia Hezb-i-Wahdat forces, trying to force their way into Kabul, which was controlled by the militia of Defence Minister Ahmad Shah Massoud of the Jamiat-i-Islami party supported by fellow Tajik and Uzbek forces from the north. Fighting continued until March, during which time thousands were killed as Kabul suffered heavy artillery and rocket attacks. Interim President Rabbani was elected for a two-year term on 30 December 1992 by a *Loya Jerga* but this was rejected by Hekmatyar and the Hezb-i-Wahdat. After negotiations a peace agreement was signed on 7 March 1993 under which Rabbani would remain President until June 1994, and Hekmatyar would become Prime Minister until September 1994. Sporadic fighting continued until late May when Massoud acceded to Hekmatyar's demand to resign as Defence Minister. Hekmatyar finally entered Kabul on 17 June when he was sworn in with his new coalition government by President Rabbani. Under the terms of the March peace agreement, elections are to be held to a constituent assembly by November 1993, with the assembly approving a new constitution and arranging a general election by mid-1994.

Afghanistan has been declared an Islamic State. The former ruling Homeland Party has been dissolved.

HEAD OF STATE
President of the Islamic State of Afghanistan, Prof. Burhanuddin Rabbani (Jamiat), *elected*, 30 December 1992.

GOVERNMENT *as at 20 May 1993*
Prime Minister, Gulbardin Hekmatyar (Hekmatyar), *appointed* 7 March 1993, *sworn in* 17 June 1993.
Agriculture, Noorullah Emad (Jamiat).
City Planning, Ahmad Shah (Ittehad).
Civil Aviation, Hashmatullah Mojadidi (ANLF).
Commerce, Hayatullah Balajhi (Wahdat).
Defence, Run by a commission headed by the President.

Education, Maulvi Jalilullah (Harakat).
Finance, Abdul Karim Khalili (Wahdat).
Foreign Affairs, Hidayat Amin Arsalla (NIFA).
Frontier, Soleiman Gilani (NIFA).
Health, Mohammad Amid Fatimi (ANLF).
Higher Education, Syed Omar (Ittehad).
Information and Culture, Haji Din Mohammad (HIA-Khalis).
Interior, Run by a commission headed by the Prime Minister.
Justice, Jalaluddin Haqqani (HIA-Khalis).
National Communications, Qazi Amin Waqad (HIA-Hekmatyar).
Planning, Mohammad Ali Javed (Mohseni).
Reconstruction, Faiz Mohammad (HIA-Hekmatyar).
Refugee Repatriation, Farooq Azam (Independent).
Religion and Haj, Arsalla Rahmani (Harakat).
Transport, Syed Anwari (Mohseni).
Water and Power, Mohammad Ayub (Jamiat).

ANLF: Afghan National Liberation Front; Harakat:
  Harakat Inqilab-i-Islami; Mohseni: Harakat-i-Islami;
  Hekmatyar: Hezb-i-Islami Afghanistan (Hekmatyar);
  Khalis: Hezb-i-Islami Afghanistan (Khalis); Wahdat:
  Hezb-i-Wahdat; Ittehad: Ittehad-i-Islami; Jamiat:
  Jamiat-i-Islami; NIFA: National Islamic Front of
  Afghanistan.

EMBASSY OF THE ISLAMIC STATE OF AFGHANISTAN
31 Prince's Gate, London SW7 1QQ
Tel 071-589 8891
Ambassador Extraordinary and Plenipotentiary, His
  Excellency Ali Lakhdari (1992).
Minister-Counsellor and Chargé d'Affaires, N. Ahmad Wali
  Masad.

BRITISH EMBASSY
Karte Parwan, Kabul
Tel: Kabul 30511/3
Staff were withdrawn from post in February 1989.

LOCAL GOVERNMENT
The country is divided into 32 provinces. At present, only a
few have governors appointed by the new government in
Kabul.

JUDICIARY

The Constitution introduced in 1965 provided for the creation
of a legal code, and for the complete separation of executive
and judiciary, but was abolished in July 1973. In late 1976
and early 1977 new penal and civil codes were published.

Few major changes were made to the operation of the
judicial system by the 1987 Constitution and subsequent
amendments under the Najibollah regime. The new government in Kabul has, however, announced its intention to
introduce Islamic law.

DEFENCE

Before the fall of the Najibollah government, the army
numbered about 50,000, supplemented by other security
agencies and irregular militias. A small air force was also
maintained. The current government is seeking to merge
the remnants of some of these forces with the Islamic
resistance fighters to form a new national army. However,
the situation of the armed forces remains extremely uncertain
and no new structure for the armed forces has been
established. The Army is now estimated to have a strength
of some 40,000 personnel and the Air Force some 5,000. By
comparison the more lightly armed mujahidin forces are
estimated to number around 350,000 fighters, of which

230,000 are Sunni Muslim and during the war were loyal to
the Peshawar-based government-in-exile, and 120,000 are
Shias who were loyal to leaders based in Iran.

ECONOMY

Agriculture and sheep raising are the principal industries.
There are generally two crops a year, one of wheat (the staple
food), barley or lentils, the other of rice, millet, maize and
dal. Sugar beet and cotton are grown. Afghanistan is rich in
fruits. Sheep, including the Karakuli, and transport animals
are bred. Silk, woollen and hair cloths and carpets are
manufactured. Salt, silver, copper, coal, iron, lead, rubies,
lapis lazuli, gold, chrome, barite, uranium, and talc are found.

TRADE

Exports are mainly Persian lambskins (Karakul), dried fruits,
nuts, cotton, raw wool, carpets, spice and natural gas, while
the imports are chiefly oil, cotton yarn and piece goods, tea,
sugar, machinery and transport equipment.

Trade with UK	1991	1992
Imports from UK	£6,956,000	£4,926,000
Exports to UK	5,207,000	4,676,000

COMMUNICATIONS

Main roads run from Kabul to Kandahar, Herat, Maimana
via Mazari-Sharif and Faizabad via Khanabad. The road
from Kabul to the north was shortened by the completion in
1964 of the Salang pass. Roads cross the border with Pakistan
at Chaman and via the Khyber Pass, and there are roads
from Herat to the borders of Central Asia and Iran. A
network of minor roads fit for motor traffic in fine weather
links up all important towns and districts.

In 1982 the Afghan and Uzbek shores of the River Oxus
were linked by a road and rail bridge which joins the Afghan
port of Hairatan and the Uzbek port of Termez. A network
of internal air services operates between the main towns.

CULTURE

The principal languages of the country are Dari (a form of
Persian) and Pushtu, although a number of minority
languages are also spoken in various provinces. All schoolchildren learn both Persian and Pushtu. Education is free
and nominally compulsory, elementary schools having been
established in most centres; there are secondary schools in
large urban areas and four universities, in Kabul (established
1932), Jalalabad (established 1962), Balkh and Herat (both
established 1988).

ALBANIA
Republika Shqipërisë

Situated on the Adriatic Sea, Albania is bounded on the north
by Montenegro, on the east by Serbia and Macedonia and on
the south by Greece. The area of the republic is estimated at
11,099 sq. miles (28,748 sq. km), with a population (1991 UN
estimate) of 3,331,000. After many years as an officially
atheist country, the Albanian population is now estimated to
be 50 per cent Muslim, 18 per cent Orthodox and 13 per cent
Roman Catholic.

CAPITAL – Tirana, population (1989) 239,381.
CURRENCY – Lek (Lk) of 100 qindarka.
FLAG – Black two-headed eagle on a red field.
NATIONAL DAY – 11 January.

GOVERNMENT

Albania was under Turkish suzerainty from 1468 until 1912, when independence was declared. After a period of unrest, a republic was declared in 1925, and in 1928 a monarchy. The King went into exile in 1939 when the country was occupied by the Italians; Albania was liberated in November 1944. Elections in 1945 resulted in a Communist-controlled Assembly; the King was deposed in absentia and a republic declared in January 1946.

From 1946 to 1991 Albania was a one-party, Communist state. In March 1991 multi-party elections were held and were won by the Socialist Party (the renamed Party of Labour). Following labour unrest, a coalition government was formed in June 1991.

In December 1991 the Democratic Party withdrew from the government and a non-party government was established which continued in office until new elections were held in March 1992. These elections were won overwhelmingly by the Democratic Party which formed a coalition government with the much smaller Social Democrat and Republican parties. In April 1992 the Democratic Party leader Dr Sali Berisha was elected by parliament as Albania's first non-communist President.

CONSTITUTION

A Human Rights Law, part of a new constitution, was approved in principle by the parliament in March 1993. The government in June 1993 published a draft constitution which defines Albania as a parliamentary republic with guaranteed individual freedoms. The draft is being scrutinized by parliament.

HEAD OF STATE
President, Dr Sali Berisha, *elected* April 1992.

COUNCIL OF MINISTERS *as at June 1993*
Prime Minister, Aleksander Meksi.
Deputy Chairman of the Council of Ministers responsible for economic reform, Bashkim Kopliku (DP).
Minister without Portfolio, Rexhep Uka (DP).
General Secretary, Vullnet Ademi (SDP).
Finances and Economy, Genc Ruli (DP).
Foreign Affairs, Alfred Serreqi (DP).
Justice, Kudred Cela (Ind).
Industry, Mining and Energy Sources, Abdyl Xhaja (Ind).
Foreign Economic Trade and Relations, Artan Hoxha (DP).
Defence, Safet Xhulali (DP).
Transport and Communications, Fatos Bitncka (RP).
Construction, Housing and Territory Adjustments, Ilir Manushi (DP).
Health and Environmental Protection, Tritan Shehu (DP).
Education, Xhezain Teliti (Ind).
Culture, Youth and Sports, Dhimiter Anagnosti (DP).
Tourism, Edmond Spaho (Ind).
Labour, Emigration, Social Assistance and Political Persecutors, Dashamir Shehu (DP).
Chairman of the Committee of Science and Technology, Maksim Konomi (DP).
Chairman of the Control Commission, Blerim Cela (DP).
Public Order, Agron Musaraj (DP).
Agriculture and Food, Petrit Kalakula (DP).

DP: Democratic Party; Ind: Independent; SDP: Social Democrat Party; RP: Republican Party.

EMBASSY OF THE REPUBLIC OF ALBANIA
6 Wilton Court, 59 Ecclestone Square, London SW1V 1PH
Tel 071-834 2580

Ambassador Extraordinary and Plenipotentiary, His Excellency Pavli Qesku (1993).

BRITISH AMBASSADOR – His Excellency Sir Patrick Fairweather, KCMG (resident in Rome).
Chargé d'Affaires, S. Nash (resident in Tirana). Tel: 873 144 5565.

DEFENCE

Albania has a total active armed forces strength of some 40,000 personnel (22,400 conscripts). Conscripts serve for a term of 18 months. The Army has a strength of 27,000 (20,000 conscripts) with some 600 main battle tanks, 160 armoured reconnaissance vehicles and armoured personnel carriers and 210 artillery pieces. The Army is organized into one tank and eleven infantry brigades, three artillery and one engineer regiments, and six coastal artillery battalions.

The Navy has a strength of 2,000 (1,000 conscripts) with two submarines and some 60 patrol and coastal craft. The Air Force has a strength of 11,000 personnel (1,400 conscripts) with some 112 combat aircraft of Chinese and Soviet manufacture.

ECONOMY

Much of the country is mountainous and nearly a half is covered by forest. There are fertile areas along the Adriatic coast and the Koritza Basin and there have been land reclamation and irrigation programmes. The main crops are wheat, maize, sugar-beet, potatoes and fruit.

All industry remains nationalized. The principal industries are agricultural product processing, textiles, oil products and cement. Exports include crude oil, minerals (bitumen, chrome, nickel, copper), tobacco, fruit and vegetables. The government is now committed to economic reform, privatization and the creation of a market economy. Most agriculture has been privatized and land redistributed, with a consequent increase in production.

Since April 1992 the government has stringently cut the budget to reduce deficits and has brought down inflation to around zero from 40 per cent a month in early 1992. The currency has stabilized, as has industrial output after a fall of 60 per cent in 1991–2. Albania has received $1 billion in aid (mostly food) from Western donors.

TRADE WITH UK	1991	1992
Imports from UK	£3,179,000	£2,763,000
Exports to UK	274,000	290,000

ALGERIA
Al-Jumhuriya al-Jazairiya ad-Dimuqratiya ash-Shabiya

Algeria lies between 8° 45′ W. and 12° E. longitude, 27° 6′ N. to a southern limit about 19° N. and has an area of 919,595 sq. miles (2,381,741 sq. km). The population (1987 Census) was 22,971,558. A 1991 UN estimate gives a figure of 25,660,000.

CAPITAL – ΨAlgiers, population 3,250,000 (approx). It is one of the principal ports of the Mediterranean as well as an important industrial centre. Other towns include ΨOran; Constantine; ΨAnnaba; Blida; Setif; Sidi-Bel-Abbès; Tlemcen; ΨMostaganem; ΨSkikda; ΨBejaia and Tizi Ouzou.
CURRENCY – Algerian dinar (DA) of 100 centimes.
FLAG – Divided vertically green and white with a red crescent and star over all in the centre.
NATIONAL ANTHEM – Qassaman.
NATIONAL DAY – 1 November.

GOVERNMENT

Algiers surrendered to a French force in 1830, and Algeria was annexed to France in 1842. From 1881 the three northern departments of Algiers, Oran and Constantine formed an integral part of France. The Southern Territories of the Sahara, formerly a separate colony, became an integral part of Algeria on the attainment of independence. An armed rebellion led by the Muslim Front de Liberation Nationale (FLN) against French rule broke out on 1 November 1954. French control of Algeria came to an end when President de Gaulle declared Algeria independent on 3 July 1962; by October 1963 all agricultural land held by foreigners had been expropriated and by 1965 more than 80 per cent of the French population had left Algeria.

Ben Bella was elected President of the Republic in September 1963, but was deposed; a Council of the Revolution presided by Col. Boumediène assumed power in June 1965. A new constitution was established by referendum in November 1976, and in December 1976 President Boumediène was elected for a six-year term of office. Following President Boumediène's death in December 1978, Chadli Bendjedid was elected President in February 1979.

A new Constitution was agreed by referendum in February 1989 which moved Algeria away from a one-party socialist system to a more pluralist political system. Local elections, held in June 1990, were won by the opposition Islamic Salvation Front (FIS). Following extensive unrest, the government declared a state of siege in June 1991 and postponed multi-party elections until the end of the year.

The first round of the legislative elections were held in December 1991 with the FIS emerging as the clear winner. However before the second round of the elections were held, President Bendjedid resigned and the elections were abandoned. A Higher Committee of State (HCS) was formed, backed by the armed forces, to govern the country. The former FLN veteran Mohammed Boudiaf returned from 25 years in exile to head the HCS. The HCS declared a state of emergency in February 1992 and the FIS was banned in March, but continues its activities underground. Clashes between security forces and fundamentalists continue, with the assassination of President Boudiaf on 29 June 1992 by suspected FIS supporters. In February 1993 the state of emergency was continued indefinitely after some 1,000 fundamentalists and security personnel had been killed in fighting. In mid-1993 the government opened discussions with other non-Islamic political parties with a view to holding a referendum by the end of 1993 on a new election law and transfering power to a multi-party body, which would exclude the FIS, before elections in 1994.

HEAD OF STATE
Acting Head of State, Ali Kafi, *appointed* July 1992.

HIGHER COMMITTEE OF STATE *as at July 1993*

President, Ali Kafi.
Members, Maj.-Gen. Khaled Nezzar; Ali Haroun; Tedjini Hadam; Redha Malek.

GOVERNMENT *as at July 1993*

Prime Minister, Economy, Belaid Abdesselam.
National Defence, Lamine Zeroual.
Foreign Affairs, Redha Malek.
Minister Adviser to the Prime Minister, Messaoud Ait Chellal.
Justice, Muhamed Teguia.
Interior and Local Authorities, Mohamed Hardi.
National Education, Ahmed Djebbar.
Mines and Industries, Belkacem Belarbi.
War Veterans, Brahim Chibout.

Agriculture, Mohamed Elias Mesli.
Religious Affairs, Sassi Lamouri.
Housing, Farouk Tebbal.
Health and Population, Mohamed Seghir Babes.
Labour and Social Affairs, Tahar Hamdi.
Vocational Training, Djelloul Baghli.
Tourism and Handicraft, Abdelwahab Bakelli.
Culture and Communications, Habib Chaouki Hamraoui.
Youth and Sport, Abdelkader Khomri.
Post and Telecommunications, Tahar Allane.
Transport, Muhamed Arezki Isli.
Energy, Hacene Mefti.
Works, Mokdad Sifi.

ALGERIAN EMBASSY
54 Holland Park, London WII 3RS
Tel 071-221 7800

Ambassador Extraordinary and Plenipotentiary, His Excellency Ali Lakhdari (1992).

BRITISH EMBASSY
7 Chemin des Glycines,
BP43, Alger-Gare 16000, Algiers
Tel: Algiers 605038

Ambassador Extraordinary and Plenipotentiary, His Excellency Christopher Charles Richard Battiscombe, CMG (1990).
Cultural Attaché and British Council Representative, D. Munro, 6 Avenue Souidani Boudjemaa, Algiers.

DEFENCE

Algeria has a total active armed forces strength of 139,000 personnel, of which 84,000 are conscripts. Conscripts serve only in the Army and for a period of 18 months.

The Army has a strength of 120,000 (84,000 conscripts) with 960 main battle tanks, 1375 armoured personnel carriers and armoured infantry fighting vehicles, 120 reconnaissance vehicles, 750 artillery pieces and 880 air defence guns. The Army is organized into two armoured divisions, two mechanized divisions, nine motorized infantry brigades and 31 independent infantry and seven independent artillery battalions.

The Navy has a strength of 7,000 in four main bases. It is equipped with two submarines, three frigates and 23 patrol and coastal vessels.

The Air Force has a strength of 12,000 personnel with 242 combat aircraft and 58 armed helicopters. It is organized into ten fighter, three ground attack, two transport, one reconnaissance, seven helicopter and three training squadrons.

In addition, there are 52,000 personnel in the paramilitary Gendarmerie and National Security Forces. Russia maintains 500 military advisers in the country.

ECONOMY

Development in Algeria is regulated by a series of national development plans. The 1980-4 Plan concentrated on housing, water supply and agriculture. The 1985-9 Plan continued with these objectives and also included food and processing industries. Agrarian reform started in 1987. The 4,000 state farms have been broken up into 23,000 units. Following riots in October 1988, economic reform was speeded up and now endorses the industrial and financial sectors. The aim is to decentralize planning and devolve management. The private sector is also receiving official encouragement.

Algeria's main industry is the hydrocarbons industry. Oil and natural gas are pumped from the Sahara to terminals on the coast before being exported; the gas is first liquefied at liquefaction plants at Skikda and Arzew, although pipelines serve Libya and Italy direct.

Other major industries being developed include a steel industry, motor vehicles, building materials, paper making, chemical products and metal manufactures. Most major industrial enterprises are still under state control.

TRADE WITH UK	1991	1992
Imports from UK	£55,685,000	£38,130,000
Exports to UK	194,874,000	162,560,000

Algeria's exports are worth around $12 billion annually, mainly from crude oil and liquefied natural gas. Principal imports from the United Kingdom are capital plant, equipment for industrial use and foodstuffs. The country's external debt is nearly $26 billion with a current debt service ration of 75 per cent.

COMMUNICATIONS

Algeria has a rapidly expanding network of roads and railways. Considerable sums are also being spent on the development of the state airline, the national shipping company and telecommunications.

ANDORRA
Principat d'Andorra

A small, neutral principality formed by a treaty in 1278, Andorra is situated on the southern slopes of the Pyrenees between Spain and France. It is surrounded by mountains of 6,500 to 10,000 feet. It has an approximate area of 175 sq. miles (468 sq. km), and population (UN estimate 1991) of 58,000, less than one-quarter of whom are native Andorrans. The official language of the country is Catalan, but French and Spanish (Castilian) are also spoken. The established religion is Roman Catholicism.

CAPITAL – Andorra la Vella (population 22,205).
CURRENCY – French francs and Spanish pesetas are both in use.
FLAG – Three vertical bands, blue, yellow, red; Andorran coat of arms frequently imposed on central (yellow) band but not essential.
NATIONAL DAY – 8 September.

GOVERNMENT

Andorra is divided into seven Parishes, each of which has four Councillors elected by vote to the Valleys of Andorra General Council of 28. The Council appoints the head of the executive government, who designates the members of his government.

A new constitution was promulgated on 4 May 1993 under which Andorra is an independent, democratic parliamentary co-principality, with the state's sovereignty being vested in the people rather than in the two co-princes as before. The constitution enables Andorra to establish an independent judiciary for the first time and to carry out its own foreign policy, whilst its people may now join trade unions and political parties. The two co-princes, the President of the French Republic and the Spanish Bishop of Urgel, remain heads of state but with drastically reduced powers, now only able to veto treaties with France and Spain which affect the state's borders and security. Andorra was admitted to UN membership on 28 July 1993. The co-princes are represented by Permanent Delegates of whom one is the French Prefect

of the Pyrenees Orientales Department at Perpignan and the other is the Spanish Vicar-General of the Diocese of Urgel. They are in turn represented in Andorra la Vella by two resident Viguiers known as the Viguier Français and the Viguier Episcopal. The first elections under the new constitution are to be held in December 1993.

Viguier Français, Jean-Pierre Courtois.
Viguier Episcopal, Francesc Badia.

EXECUTIVE COUNCIL *as at June 1993*
President, Oscar Ribas Reig.
Finance, Josep Casal Casal.
Agriculture, Commerce and Industry, Modest Baro Moles.
Public Services, Joan Albert Teixe.
Tourism and Sport, Xavier Espot Miro.
Labour, Health and Social Welfare, Bibiana Rossa Torres.
Sindic (President) of General Council, Jordi Farras.

HM CONSUL-GENERAL, M. Perceval, (resident in Barcelona, Spain). Tel 3-419 9044.

ECONOMY

The Budget is expressed in pesetas. The estimated national revenue (1989) was US$895 million, with a per capita income of US$17,596.

Potatoes are produced in the highlands and tobacco in the valleys. The mountain slopes have been developed for skiing, and it is estimated that 10 million tourists visit the valleys during the year. The economy is largely based on tourism, banking, commerce, tobacco, construction and forestry; a third of the country is classified as forest in which pine, fir, oak, birch and box-tree predominate. Andorra has negotiated a customs union with the European Community which came into force on 1 July 1991. Andorra's very low consumer taxes enticed 12,000,000 shopping tourists to the state in 1992. The economy is now diversifying rapidly into offshore financial services.

COMMUNICATIONS

A good road into the valleys from Spain is open all year round, and that from France is closed only occasionally in winter. An airport at Seo d'Urgell just outside Andorra provides very limited air connections. There are two radio stations in Andorra, one privately-owned and one operated by a French Government corporation. Both pay dues to the Council of the Valleys.

TRADE WITH UK	1991	1992
Imports from UK	£14,188,000	£13,071,000
Exports to UK	36,000	19,000

ANGOLA
República de Angola

Angola, which has an area of 481,354 sq. miles (1,246,700 sq. km), lies on the western coast of Africa; its population in 1991 was estimated by the UN at 10,303,000.

CAPITAL – ΨLuanda, population estimate 1993, 3 million.
CURRENCY – New Kwanza (Kz) of 100 lwei.
FLAG – Red and black with a yellow star, machete and cog-wheel.
NATIONAL ANTHEM – Angola Avante.
NATIONAL DAY – 11 November (Independence Day).

GOVERNMENT

After a Portuguese presence of five centuries, and an anti-colonial war since 1961, Angola became independent on 11 November 1975 in the midst of civil war. Soviet-Cuban military assistance to the Popular Movement for the Liberation of Angola (MPLA) enabled it to defeat its rivals early in 1976. However, the MPLA government remained under pressure from the UNITA guerrilla movement (led by Dr Jonas Savimbi) which by the mid 1980s was operating freely. In August 1988 it was announced that a ceasefire between South African, Cuban and Angolan forces had taken place pending talks on withdrawal of South African troops from Angola. In December 1988 an agreement providing for the withdrawal of the 50,000 Cuban troops by July 1991 was signed in New York. On 31 May 1991 a peace agreement was signed between the government and UNITA. Multi-party presidential and legislative elections took place in September 1992. In the legislative elections the MPLA won 129 seats, with UNITA winning 70 seats and minor parties 21 seats out of a total of 220. In the first round of the presidential election, MPLA leader President Dos Santos won 49.5 per cent of the vote to Savimbi's 40 per cent, necessitating a second round. However, no second round was held as Savimbi and UNITA refused to accept the election results. UN-brokered negotiations restarted in October but proved fruitless. Gradually rising tensions led to outbreaks of fighting throughout November and December 1992 and a full-scale return to civil war in January 1993. Fierce fighting continues, with UNITA having gained control of Angola's second city Huambo and the oil-producing and diamond-producing areas of the country as the MPLA government forces gradually lose ground. The UN has reduced its forces from 700 to about 50 staff.

The MPLA, formerly but no longer a Marxist-Leninist party, was the sole legal party until early 1991 when a multi-party system was adopted. The Constitution declares Angola to be a democratic state and provides for a President, who appoints a Council of Ministers to assist him, and a National Assembly. The present MPLA-dominated government also includes several minor parties and was sworn in after the elections in November 1992.

SECESSION

In the northern enclave of Cabinda, the Front for the Liberation of the Cabinda Enclave (FLEC) has been fighting for independence against government forces since 1975. Cabinda is rich in oil and is separated from the rest of Angola by Zaire.

HEAD OF STATE

President, Jose Eduardo Dos Santos.

COUNCIL OF MINISTERS *as at June 1993*

Prime Minister, Dr Marcolino Jose Carlos Moco.
Defence, Pedro Tonho Pedale.
Interior, Santana Andre Pitra.
Foreign, Dr Venancio de Silva Moura.
Territorial Administration, Antonio Paulo Kassoma.
Finance, Emmanuel Carneiro.
Oil, Albina Pereira Africano.
Industry, Dr Idalino Manuel Mendes.
Agriculture and Rural Development, Isaac Maria dos Anjos.
Fisheries, Maria Monteiro Jardin.
Geology and Mines, Jose Antonio Dias.
Public Works and Urbanization, Dr Mateus de Brito Junior.
Transport and Communications, Dr Andre Luis Brandao.
Trade and Tourism, Dr Emanuel Moreira Carneiro.
Health, Dr Martinho Sanches Epalanga.
Education, Dr Joao Manuel Bernardo.

Assistance and Social Reintegration, Dr Norberto Fernandes dos Santos.
Culture, vacant.
Youth and Sports, Dr Justino Jose Fernandes.
Justice, Dr Paulo Chipilika.
Public Administration, Employment and Social Security, Dr Antonio Costa Neto.

EMBASSY OF ANGOLA
98 Park Lane, London W1
Tel 071-495 1752

Ambassador Extraordinary and Plenipotentiary, new appointment awaited.

BRITISH EMBASSY
Rua Diogo Caõ 4 (Caixa Postal 1244), Luanda
Tel: Luanda 392991/8

Ambassador Extraordinary and Plenipotentiary, His Excellency Anthony Richard Thomas (1993).

DEFENCE

Under the 1991 peace agreement, the armed forces of the governing MPLA and the opposition UNITA movement were to have been merged to form a 50,000 strong National Army shortly after the elections of September 1992. To this end, large proportions of both government and UNITA forces were in UN containment camps or had been demobilized by September 1992. However, with the return to civil war after the elections, both sides have remobilized, though to what extent is unclear.

The following can only be rough estimates: government active armed forces number some 130,000 with widespread conscription. The Army has some 122,000 personnel organized into 75 brigades with 250 main battle tanks, 410 armoured infantry fighting vehicles and armoured personnel carriers and 500 artillery pieces. The Navy has a strength of 2,000 with 17 patrol and coastal craft. The Air Force has a strength of 6,000 personnel with 146 combat aircraft and 40 armed helicopters. UNITA forces number some 65,000, of which 28,000 are regulars and 37,000 militia support and logistical forces. Equipment numbers include about 80 main battle tanks and numerous captured artillery, mortar and anti-aircraft guns.

ECONOMY

Angola has valuable oil and diamond deposits and exports of these two commodities account for over 90 per cent of total exports.

Principal agricultural crops are cassava, maize, bananas, coffee, palm oil and kernels, cotton and sisal. Coffee, sisal, maize and palm oil are exported; exports also include mahogany and other hardwoods from the tropical rain forests in the north of the country.

TRADE WITH UK	1991	1992
Imports from UK	£34,812,000	£64,371,000
Exports to UK	65,078,000	144,324,000

ANTIGUA AND BARBUDA
State of Antigua and Barbuda

Antigua and Barbuda comprises the islands of Antigua (108 sq. miles (279 sq. km)), Barbuda (62 sq. miles (160 sq. km)) 25 miles north of Antigua, and Redonda (¼ sq. mile; 1.2 sq. km) 25 miles south-west of Antigua. Antigua is part of the Leeward Islands in the eastern Caribbean and lies 17° 3' N. and 61° 48' W. It is distinguished from the rest of the Leeward group by its absence of high hills and forest, and a drier climate than most of the West Indies. Barbuda, formerly a possession of the Codrington family, is very flat, mainly scrub-covered, with a large lagoon.

POPULATION – The total population (official census 1991) is 65,962; Antigua had a population of 64,562, Barbuda 1,400, and Redonda was uninhabited.

CAPITAL – ΨSt John's. Population, 30,000. The town of Barbuda is Codrington.

CURRENCY – East Caribbean dollar (EC$) of 100 cents.

FLAG. – Red with an inverted triangle divided black over blue over white, with a rising gold sun on the white band.

NATIONAL ANTHEM – Fair Antigua and Barbuda.

NATIONAL DAY – 1 November (Independence Day).

GOVERNMENT

Antigua was first settled by the English in 1632, and was granted to Lord Willoughby by Charles II. Antigua became internally self-governing in 1967 and fully independent on 1 November 1981, as a constitutional monarchy with The Queen as Head of State, represented by the Governor-General. There is a Senate of 17 appointed members and a House of Representatives elected every five years. The Attorney-General may be appointed.

The Antigua Labour party led by Vere Bird won the general election of 9 March 1989 and a fourth successive term of office.

Governor-General, Dr James Beethoven Carlisle.

CABINET *as at June 1993*
Prime Minister, Rt. Hon. Dr Vere C. Bird, sen.
Legal Affairs and Attorney-General, Hon. Keith Ford, QC.
Finance, Hon. Molwyn Joseph.
Home Affairs and Social Services, Hon. Christopher O'Mard.
Economic Development, Industry and Tourism, Hon. Dr Rodney Williams.
Agriculture, Fisheries, Lands and Housing, Hon. Hilroy Humphreys.
Education, Culture, and Youth Affairs, Hon. Bernard Percival.
Labour and Health, Hon. Adolphus Freeland.
Public Utilities, Transportation and Energy, Hon. Robin Yearwood.
Public Works and Communications, Hon. Eustace Cochrane.
External Affairs, Planning and Trade, Hon. Lester Bird.
Information, Hon. John St Luce.

HIGH COMMISSION FOR ANTIGUA AND BARBUDA
15 Thayer Street, London W1M 5LD
Tel 071-486 7073

High Commissioner, His Excellency James Thomas (1987).

BRITISH HIGH COMMISSION
11 Old Parham Road (PO 483), St John's
Tel: St John's 462 0008/9

High Commissioner (resides at Bridgetown, Barbados).
Resident Representative, R. G. Baylis, MVO (*First Secretary*).

ECONOMY

Tourism is the main sector of the economy. Tourism and related services account for 60 per cent of GDP and employ 40 per cent of the workforce; Antigua was one of the first Caribbean islands to attract tourists.

For many years sugar was the dominant crop but is now produced only for local consumption. Agricultural production

includes livestock, sea island cotton, mixed market gardening and fishing.

FINANCE	1989*	1990*
Revenue	EC$236,720,991	EC$249,560,916
Expenditure (recurrent)	263,579,351	271,730,204
*estimated		

TRADE WITH UK	1991	1992
Imports from UK	£19,687,000	£16,528,000
Exports to UK	5,764,000	2,511,000

ARGENTINA
República Argentina

Argentina occupies the greater portion of the southern part of the South American continent, and extends from Bolivia to Cape Horn, a total distance of nearly 2,300 miles; its greatest breadth is about 930 miles. It is bounded on the north by Bolivia, on the north-east by Paraguay, Brazil and Uruguay, on the south-east and south by the Atlantic, and on the west by Chile, from which it is separated by the Cordillera de los Andes. On the west the mountainous Cordilleras, with their plateaux, extend from the northern to the southern boundaries; on the east are the great plains.

Argentina has an area of 1,068,302 sq. miles (2,766,889 sq. km.), with a population (Census 1991) of 32,370,298.

CAPITAL – ΨBuenos Aires, population (1990), metropolitan area 2,955,002; with suburbs, 10,881,381. Other large towns are: ΨRosario (1,071,384), Córdoba (1,134,086), ΨLa Plata (630,260), ΨMar del Plata (503,779), San Miguel de Tucumán (603,331), ΨSanta Fé (329,814) and Mendoza (706,909).

CURRENCY – Peso of 10,000 australes.

FLAG – Horizontal bands of blue, white, blue; gold sun in centre of white band.

NATIONAL ANTHEM – Oid Mortales! (Hear, oh mortals!).

NATIONAL DAY – 25 May.

GOVERNMENT

The estuary of La Plata was discovered in 1515 by Juan Díaz de Solís, but it was not until 1536 that Pedro de Mendoza founded Buenos Aires. This city was abandoned and later re-founded by Don Juan de Garay in 1580. Spain ruled the territory from the 16th century until 1810, when Spanish rule was defied. In 1816, after a long campaign of liberation conducted by General José de San Martín, the independence of Argentina was declared by the Congress of Tucumán.

In 1946 Juan Domingo Perón became President until overthrown in 1955. There followed eighteen years of political and economic instability, and eventually in 1973, Perón was recalled from exile. Elected President he died within a year and was succeeded by his widow, Vice President María Estela Martínez de Perón. However, warring factions in the Perónist movement and increasing terrorist activity eventually led to a coup by the armed forces in 1976. A Junta, consisting of the three commanders of the armed forces, was established with one of their number as President. Following the Falkland Islands defeat in 1982 the President, Gen. Galtieri, resigned and the Army appointed Gen. Bignone as President. The Navy and Air Force withdrew from the Junta but this was reconstituted shortly afterwards. Elections for a civilian government to replace the military one were held in 1983 and the Radical Party's candidate, Raúl Alfonsín, elected President. Presidential elections in May 1989 were won by the Perónist candidate Carlos Menem. The next parliamentary elections are due to take place in September 1993.

The republic is divided into 23 provinces and one federal district (Buenos Aires).

HEAD OF STATE
President, Dr Carlos Saúl Menem, *took office* 8 July 1989.
Vice President, Dr Eduardo Alberto Dunalde.

CABINET *as at June 1993*

Interior, Dr Gustavo Béliz.
Foreign Affairs, Dr Guido Di Tella.
Labour, Dr Enrique Rodriguez.
Economy and Public Works, Dr Domingo Cavallo.
Education, Jorge Alberto Rodriguez.
Defence, Dr Oscar Camillión.
Health and Social Welfare, Dr Alberto Mazza.
Justice, Jorge Maioromo.

EMBASSY OF THE ARGENTINE REPUBLIC
53 Hans Place, London SWIX OLA
Tel 071-584 6494

Ambassador Extraordinary and Plenipotentiary, His Excellency Mario Cámpora (1991).

BRITISH EMBASSY
Dr Luis Agote 2412, 1425 Buenos Aires
Tel: Buenos Aires 803-7070/1

Ambassador Extraordinary and Plenipotentiary, His Excellency The Hon. Humphrey Maud, CMG (1990).
Deputy Ambassador, Minister and Consul-General, David Reddaway.
Defence and Military Attaché, Col. R. J. Lawson.
First Secretary (Commercial), H. M. McIntosh.
Cultural, Attaché and British Council Representative, Harold Fish, OBE, Martcelo T. de Alvear 590, 1058 Buenos Aires.

BRITISH CHAMBER OF COMMERCE, Av. Corrientes 457, 10 piso, 1043 Buenos Aires.

ECONOMY

The Menem government introduced a successful economic reform programme in April 1991 which has involved the privatization of most state-owned industries, widespread deregulation, exchange-rate stabilization and lower trade barriers. This has led to increased foreign investment and much lower inflation, which has transformed the economy.

Argentina's foreign debt in 1993 was calculated at US$19,200 million in principal (not including interest charges). A debt reduction plan was agreed in April 1993 with creditors to reduce the cost of servicing the foreign debt by one-third.

AGRICULTURE
Of a total land area of approximately 700 million acres, farms occupy about 425 million. About 60 per cent of the farmland is pasture, 10 per cent annual crops, 5 per cent permanent crops and the remaining 25 per cent forest and wasteland. A large proportion of the land is still held in large estates devoted to cattle raising but the number of small farms is increasing. The principal crops are wheat, maize, oats, barley, rye, linseed, sunflower seed, alfalfa, sugar, fruit and cotton. Argentina is pre-eminent in the production of beef, mutton and wool, and pastoral and agricultural products provide about 85 per cent of Argentina's exports.

MINERAL PRODUCTION
Oil is found in various parts of the Republic and the production of oil is of first importance to Argentina's industries. Total petroleum output for 1991 was 484,000 b.p.d. There is a refinery in San Lorenzo (Santa Fé province). Natural gas is also produced in a number of provinces.

Coal, lead, zinc, tungsten, iron ore, sulphur, mica and salt are the other chief minerals being exploited. There are small worked deposits of beryllium, manganese, bismuth, uranium, antimony, copper, kaolin, arsenate, gold, silver and tin. Coal is produced at the Rio Turbio mine in the province of Santa Cruz. The output of other materials is not large but greater attention is now being paid to the development of these natural resources, especially copper for which the Government and private companies are carrying out exploration.

INDUSTRIES
Meat-packing is one of the principal industries; flour-milling, sugar-refining, and the wine industry are also important. In recent years progress has been made by the textile, plastic and machine tool industries and engineering, especially in the production of motor vehicles and steel manufactures.

TRADE WITH UK	1991	1992
Imports from UK	£69,671,000	£118,746,000
Exports to UK	135,512,000	124,603,000

COMMUNICATIONS

There are 25,386 miles of railways, which are state property. Plans are in hand for complete re-organization of the railways in order to improve their operating efficiency and reduce a very large financial deficit. The combined national and provincial road network totals approximately 137,000 miles of which 23,180 miles are surfaced. There are air services between Argentina and all the neighbouring republics, Europe, Asia, Canada, the USA and South Africa.

DEFENCE

Total active armed forces number some 65,000 personnel (12,800 conscripts). Conscripts serve between seven and 14 months. Reserves total 377,000 (Army 250,000; Navy 77,000; Air Force 50,000).

The Army consists of three corps organized into 11 brigades, including mountain, jungle, airborne, mechanized infantry and armoured troops. It numbers about 35,000, including about 8,000 conscripts with 265 main battle tanks, 165 light tanks, 585 armoured infantry fighting vehicles and armoured personnel carriers, 375 artillery pieces and 43 helicopters.

The Navy consists of 1 aircraft carrier (in store), 6 destroyers, 7 frigates, 4 submarines, 6 minesweepers, 13 patrol and coastal craft, 42 combat aircraft and 10 armed helicopters. Strength is 20,000, including 2,500 conscripts and 3,000 marines.

The Air Force has a strength of 10,000 personnel (2,300 conscripts) with 174 combat aircraft, 14 armed helicopters and 10 air defence artillery batteries. Aircraft are organized into one bomber, four air defence, two ground attack, three counter-insurgency and five transport squadrons with support units.

In addition, there is a paramilitary gendarmerie of some 17,000 personnel under Ministry of Defence control.

EDUCATION

Education is compulsory for the seven grades of primary school (6 to 13). Secondary schools (14 to 17 +) are available in and around Buenos Aires and in most of the important towns in the interior of the country. Most secondary schools are administered by the Central Ministry of Education in Buenos Aires, while primary schools are administered by the Central Ministry or by Provincial Ministries of Education.

Private schools, of which there are many, are also loosely controlled by the Central Ministry. The total number of universities is over 50 with 24 national, 25 private and a small number of provincial universities.

CULTURE

Spanish is the language of the republic and the literature of Spain is accepted as an inheritance by the people. There is little indigenous literature before the break from Spain, but all branches have flourished since the latter half of the nineteenth century. About 450 daily newspapers are published in Argentina, including seven major ones in the city of Buenos Aires. The English language newspaper is the *Buenos Aires Herald* (daily). There are several other foreign language newspapers.

ARMENIA
Haikakan Hanrapetoutioun

Armenia has an area of 11,306 sq. miles (29,800 sq. km) and lies between the Black and Caspian Seas, occupying the south-western part of the Caucasus region of the former Soviet Union. It is bordered on the east and south-west by Azerbaijan, on the north by Georgia, on the south by Iran and on the west by Turkey. It is a very mountainous country consisting of several vast tablelands surrounded by ridges.
CLIMATE – Continental, dry and cold, but the Araks valley has a long, hot and dry summer.
POPULATION – According to the 1992 official estimate, the population is 3,645,000. The population is concentrated in the low-lying part of Armenia, the Aras valley and the Erevan hollow. Armenians form 93 per cent of the population, Kurds 1.7 per cent and Russians 1.6 per cent. Azerbaijanis formed 2.6 per cent of the population, but most fled or were expelled after the outbreak of the conflict with Azerbaijan. There are also Ukranians, Greeks and Assyrians. The Armenian diaspora numbers some 5,300,000, including 1,500,000 in the former Soviet states, 1,000,000 in the USA and 400,000 in France.
LANGUAGE – Armenian is the official language, though Russian is widely spoken and understood.
RELIGION – Armenian Orthodox Christian (Armenian Church centred in Etchmiadzin). Armenia adopted Christianity as its official religion in AD 301, the first state in the world to do so.

CAPITAL – Erevan. Population 1,199,000 (1989).
CURRENCY – Rouble of 100 kopeks.
FLAG – Three horizontal stripes of red, blue and orange.
NATIONAL DAY – 28 May (Independence Day).

GOVERNMENT

Armenia was an ancient society, first mentioned in the ninth century BC. In 95 BC the country was first united, stretching from the Caspian to the Black Seas and southwards to the Mediterranean. Divided between the Persian and Byzantine Empires in AD 387, the country was conquered in the eleventh century by the Seljuk Turks and the Mongols. In the 16th century most of Armenia was incorporated into the Ottoman Empire. In 1639 the country was divided again, the eastern-most portions, now the Republic of Armenia, becoming part of the Persian Empire. In 1828 Eastern Armenia became part of the Russian Empire while western Armenia remained under Ottoman rule. The Ottomans launched pogroms against the Armenians from 1894 onwards, and in 1915–18 massacred 1,500,000 Armenians.

After the 1917 Russian revolution, Armenia declared its independence as a republic on 28 May 1918, but was crushed and divided between Turkish and Soviet forces in 1920. On 29 November 1920 Armenia was proclaimed a Soviet Socialist Republic. The Soviet government was overthrown by a nationalist revolt in 1921 but reinstated by the Red Army a few months later. In early 1922 Armenia acceded to the USSR. Gorbachev's reform policies slowly filtered through to Armenia in 1987 when demonstrations against pollution caused by Soviet industrialization in the republic, and against local Communist Party corruption became political. The focus of political opposition to Communist rule was support for the self-determination of the autonomous region of Nagorno-Karabakh in Azerbaijan which was predominantly Armenian populated. Throughout 1988–90 the Soviet authorities were perceived as supporting Azerbaijan over Nagorno-Karabakh, and an Armenian nationalist movement evolved which swept to power in national elections in mid-1990. The new non-Communist government supported Nagorno-Karabakh Armenians in their conflict with Azerbaijan and loosened links with the rest of the Soviet Union. In a referendum on 21 September 1991, 99 per cent of the electorate voted for independence.
Armenia declared independence from the Soviet Union on 23 September 1991 and was admitted to membership of the UN on 2 March 1992. The political situation in Armenia is dominated by the war with Azerbaijan and the effects of the 1988 earthquake. The earthquake, which devastated much of the country, left thousands homeless and industry badly affected, and Armenia has neither the money nor the expertise to complete the rebuilding process.
The war with Azerbaijan over the disputed region of Nagorno-Karabakh, the Armenian-populated enclave in Azerbaijan, simmered from February 1988 and erupted into all-out war in May 1992, when Armenian forces breached Azerbaijan's defences to form a land bridge to Nagorno-Karabakh. By the end of summer 1992 all of Nagorno-Karabakh was under Armenian control. Continued victories over Azeris forces in late 1992 and early 1993 culminated in major victories in April 1993 at Kelbadzher and July 1993 at Agdam. All Azeri territory that separated Nagorno-Karabakh from Armenian and all mountainous Azeri territory around Nagorno-Karabakh are now under Armenian control, an estimated 10 per cent of Azeri territory. Armenia claims this territory was historically Armenian land arbitrarily given to Azerbaijan by Stalin in 1921–2.
Since 1988 Azerbaijan has imposed an economic blockade on Armenia which is almost total as the neighbouring states of Turkey and Iran generally support Azerbaijan. The severe economic crisis led the President to declare a state of emergency on 15 December 1992, and to replace the government in February 1993 for failing to implement economic reforms.

HEAD OF STATE
President, Levon Ter-Petrosyan, *elected* 16 October 1991.

CABINET *as at July 1993*
Prime Minister, Grant Bagratian.
Deputy Prime Minister, Vagen Chitechan.
Minister of State (Industry and Energy), Sepuh Taschan.
Minister of State (Agriculture and Food), Gagik Shakhbazyan.
Defence, Vazgen Manukyan.
Interior, Vano Siradegyan.
Higher Education and Science, Vardkes Gnuni.
Public Health, Ara Babloyan.
Foreign Affairs, Vagan Papazian.
Culture, Akop Akopyan.
Light Industry, Rudolf Teymurazan.

Material Resources, Vagan Melkonyan.
Environmental Protection, Karine Danielyan.
Industry, Ashot Safaryan.
Education, Gaik Kazaryan.
Food, David Zadoyan.
Communications, Grigor Pokhpatyan.
Agriculture, Ashot Voskahyan.
Construction, Gagik Martirosyan.
Trade, Eduard Grigoryan.
Transport, Genrikh Kochinyan.
Labour, Ashot Yesayan.
Finance, Levon Barhudaryan.
Economics, Armen Egiazaran.
Engineering and Fuel, Sepakh Tashchyan.
Justice, Vage Stepanyan.

Chairman of the Supreme Soviet, Babken Ararktsyan.

EMBASSY OF THE REPUBLIC OF ARMENIA
25 Cheniston Gardens, London w8 6TG
Tel 071-938 5345

Ambassador Extraordinary and Plenipotentiary, His
Excellency Prof. Armen Sarkissian (1993).
BRITISH AMBASSADOR – (resident in Moscow).

DEFENCE

Armenia maintains an army of some 50,000 regular
personnel and paramilitary forces of some 30,000. Both
these forces are heavily involved in supplying and supporting
the Nagorno-Karabakh armed volunteers who engage in the
majority of fighting with Azeri forces. The Nagorno-
Karabakh forces number 30,000–50,000 personnel
equipped with light and medium weapons and artillery, while
Armenian forces supply small numbers of tanks and
helicopters.

Russia maintains 23,000 army personnel in Armenia
organized into four motorized rifle divisions and two artillery
regiments.

ECONOMY

Armenia has a strong agricultural sector in low-lying areas,
where industrial and fruit crops are grown. Grain is grown in
the hills and the country is also noted for its wine. There are
large copper ore and molybdenum deposits and other
minerals. The Armenian economy has been crippled by a
trade blockade by Azerbaijan, through which supplies of oil
and gas used to come. The severe energy crisis caused the
government to announce its intention to re-open the
republic's nuclear power station, which had been closed since
the 1988 earthquake; in January 1993 the single remaining
fuel supply, the gas pipeline from Russia through Georgia
was destroyed by sabotage. Rationing was introduced in
December 1992 to combat food shortages. The President has
appealed for international aid.

CULTURE

The Armenian alphabet was established in AD 391 and had a
fully written form in the fifth century. Major writers include
the poets Frick (13th century), Naapet Kuchat (16th century)
and Saat-Nova (18th century). The composer Aram Khacha-
turian (1903–78) was Armenian.

AUSTRALIA
The Commonwealth of Australia

AREA AND POPULATION*

States and Territories	Area (sq. km)	Resident population 30 June 1992p
New South Wales (NSW)	801,600	5,958,700
Queensland (Qld.)	1,727,200	3,030,500
South Australia (SA)	984,000	1,456,400
Tasmania (Tas.)	67,800	469,800
Victoria (Vic.)	227,600	4,448,800
Western Australia (WA)	2,525,500	1,657,100
Australian Capital Territory (ACT)	2,400	294,200
Northern Territory (NT)	1,346,200	167,100
Total	7,682,300	17,482,600

* estimated
p preliminary

POPULATION OF ABORIGINAL AND TORRES STRAIT
ISLANDER ORIGIN as at June 1991

	Number	% of state population
New South Wales	68,941	1.20
Queensland	67,012	2.32
South Australia	16,238	1.14
Tasmania	8,886	1.90
Victoria	16,570	0.39
Western Australia	41,792	2.54
Australian Capital Territory	1,772	0.63
Northern Territory	39,918	24.01
Total	261,129	1.53

BIRTHS, DEATHS, MARRIAGES AND DIVORCES year
ended 30 June

	1990	1991	1992p
Births	257,521	261,158	255,624
Deaths	125,112	119,571	120,838
Marriages	117,126	114,796	113,524
Divorces†	42,635	45,630	45,665

† year ended 31 December
p preliminary

MIGRATION year ended 30 June

	1990	1991	1992
Permanent arrivals	121,320	121,690	107,390
Permanent departures	27,860	31,130	29,120

GEOGRAPHY

Australia, including Tasmania, comprises a land area of
7,682,300 sq. km lying between latitudes 10°41′ S. (Cape
York) and 43°39′ S. (South East Cape, Tasmania) and
longitudes 113°09′ E. (Steep Point) and 153°39′ E. (Cape
Byron). The latitudinal distance between Cape York and
South East Cape is about 3,680 km and the longitudinal
distance between Steep Point and Cape Byron is about
4,000 km. The latitudinal distance between Cape York and
the most southerly point on the mainland South Point,
Wilson's Promontory, is about 3,180 km.

Australia has three major landforms: the western plateau,
the interior lowlands and the eastern uplands. The western
half of the continent consists mainly of a great plateau of

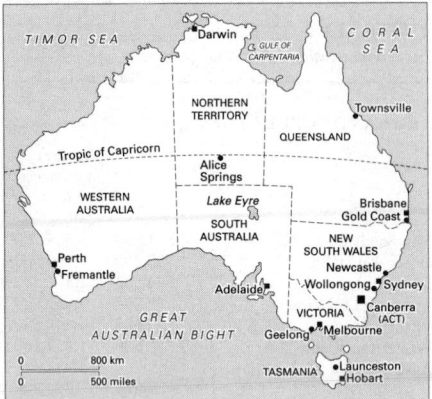

altitude 300–600 metres. The interior lowland includes the channel country of south-west Queensland (drainage to Lake Eyre) and the Murray-Darling river system to the south. The eastern uplands consist of a broad belt of varied width extending from north Queensland to Tasmania and composed largely of tablelands, ranges and ridges with only limited mountain areas above 1,000 metres. The highest point is Mt. Kosciusko (2,228 m) and the lowest, Lake Eyre (−15 m).

Climatic conditions range from the alpine to the tropical. Two-thirds of the continent is arid or semi-arid although good rainfalls (over 800 mm annually) occur in the northern monsoonal belt and along the eastern and southern highland regions. Fifty per cent of the area of Australia has a medium rainfall of less than 300 mm per year and 80 per cent has less than 600 mm. The effectiveness of the rainfall is greatly reduced by marked alternations of wet and dry seasons, unreliability from year to year, high temperatures and high potential evaporation.

FEDERAL CAPITAL – Canberra, in the Australian Capital Territory. Estimated population at 30 June 1990 was 284,000. It is the seat of government and the location of most government department headquarters.

CURRENCY – Australian dollar ($A) of 100 cents.

FLAG – The British Blue Ensign with five stars of the Southern Cross in the fly and the white Commonwealth Star of seven points beneath the Union Jack.

NATIONAL ANTHEM – Advance Australia Fair.

NATIONAL DAY – 26 January (Australia Day).

GOVERNMENT

The continent of Australia was discovered in the 18th century and was colonized by the British, initially as a penal colony.

The Commonwealth of Australia was inaugurated on 1 January 1901. The government is that of a federal Commonwealth within the British Commonwealth, the executive power being vested in the Sovereign (through the Governor-General), assisted by a federal ministry of Ministers of State. Under the Constitution the federal government has acquired and may acquire certain defined powers as surrendered by the States, residuary legislative power remaining with the States. The right of a State to legislate on any matter is not abrogated except in connection with matters exclusively under federal control, but where a State law is inconsistent with a law of the Commonwealth the latter prevails to the extent of the inconsistency.

GOVERNOR-GENERAL AND STAFF

Governor-General, The Hon. Bill Hayden, AC, *born* 23 January 1933; *assumed office*, 16 February 1989.
Official Secretary, R. D. Sturkey.
Deputy Official Secretary, Ms H. Storey.

CABINET *as at 27 May 1993*
Prime Minister, Hon. Paul Keating.
Deputy Prime Minister and Housing, Local Government and Community Services, Hon. Brian Howe.
Leader of the Government in the Senate and Foreign Affairs, Senator Hon. Gareth Evans, QC.
Deputy Leader of the Government in the Senate and Defence, Senator Hon. Robert Ray.
Treasurer, Hon. John Dawkins.
Finance, Hon. Ralph Willis.
Employment, Education and Training, and Leader of the House, Hon. Kim Beazley.
Health, Senator Hon. Graham Richardson.
Environment, Sport and Territories, Hon. Roslyn Kelly.
Trade, Senator Hon. Peter Cook.
Immigration and Ethnic Affairs, Senator Hon. Nick Bolkus.
Primary Industries and Energy, Hon. Simon Crean.
Industry, Technology and Regional Development, Hon. Alan Griffiths.
Transport and Communications, Senator Hon. Robert Collins.
Social Security, Hon. Peter Baldwin.
Arts and Administrative Services, Senator Hon. Robert McMullan.
Industrial Relations, Hon. Laurence Brereton.
Attorney-General, Hon. Michael Lavarch.
Tourism and Resources, Hon. Michael Lee.

JUNIOR MINISTERS
Communications, Hon. David Beddall.
Development Co-operation and Pacific Island Affairs, Hon. Gordon Bilney.
Aboriginal and Torres Strait Islander Affairs, Hon. Robert Tickner.
Schools, Vocational Education and Training, Hon. Ross Free.
Consumer Affairs, Hon. Jeannette McHugh.
Family Services, Senator Hon. Rosemary Crowley.
Defence Science and Personnel, Veterans' Affairs, Senator Hon. John Faulkner.
Assistant Treasurer, Hon. George Gear.
Justice, Hon. Duncan Kerr.
Science and Small Business, Senator Hon. Christopher Schacht.
Special Minister of State, Hon. Francis Walker, QC.

AUSTRALIAN HIGH COMMISSION
Australia House, Strand, London WC2B 4LA
Tel 071-379 4334
High Commissioner, His Excellency The Hon. Richard Smith (1991).
Deputy High Commissioner, D. Goss.
Ministers, I. Wilcock (*Political*); R. Murray (*Economic*); Dr D. de Souza (*Health*); D. Richard (*Commercial*).
Defence Adviser and Head of Defence Staff, Cdre G. P. Kable.
Consuls-General, Ms A. Coutts (*Manchester*); Ms J. Rogers (*Edinburgh*).

BRITISH HIGH COMMISSION
Commonwealth Avenue, Yarralumla, Canberra, ACT 2600
Tel: Canberra (61) 270 6666
High Commissioner, His Excellency Sir Brian Barder, KCMG (1991).

Deputy High Commissioner, Head of Chancery, D. W. Fall.
Counsellor, T. N. Byrne *(Director, Trade Promotion).*
Defence, Air and Naval Adviser and Head of British Defence Liaison Staff, Cdre B. J. Adams.
Consuls-General, J. C. Durham, LVO *(Brisbane);* S. D. R. Brown *(Melbourne);* J. B. Noss *(Perth);* R. S. Reeve *(Sydney).*
Cultural Adviser and British Council Representative, J. Potts, OBE, Edgecliff Centre, 203–233 New South Head Road (PO Box 88), Edgecliff, Sydney, NSW 2027.

LEGISLATURE
Parliament consists of The Queen, the Senate and the House of Representatives. The Constitution provides that the number of members of the House of Representatives shall be, as nearly as practicable, twice the number of Senators. Members of the Senate are elected for six years by universal suffrage, half the members retiring every third year. Each of the six States returns an equal number of 12 Senators, and the Australian Capital Territory and the Northern Territory two each. The House of Representatives, similarly elected for a maximum of three years, contains members proportionate to the population, with a minimum of five members for each State. There are now 148 members in the House of Representatives, including one member for the Northern Territory and two for the Australian Capital Territory.

President of the Senate, Senator Hon. Kerry Sibraa.
Speaker, House of Representatives, Hon. Stephen Martin.

JUDICATURE

HIGH COURT OF AUSTRALIA *as at 31 May 1993*
Chief Justice, Hon. Sir Anthony Mason, AC, KBE.
Justices, Hons. Sir Gerard Brennan, AC, KBE; Sir William Deane, AC, KBE; Sir Daryl Dawson, AC, KBE, CB; J. Toohey, AC; M. Gaudron; M. McHugh, AC.
Registrar, F. W. D. Jones.

FEDERAL COURT OF AUSTRALIA *as at 1 June 1993*
Chief Justice, Hon. M. E. J. Black.
Judges, Hons. C. A. Sweeney, CBE; R. M. Northrop; J. A. Keely; J. F. Gallop; J. D. Davies; J. S. Lockhart; I. F. Sheppard, AO; K. J. Jenkinson; A. R. Neaves; B. A. Beaumont; M. R. Wilcox; J. E. J. Spender; P. R. A. Gray; J. C. S. Burchett; J. A. Miles; D. M. Ryan; W. M. C. Gummow; R. S. French; M. R. Einfeld; M. L. Foster; A. B. Nicholson; M. C. Lee; H. W. Olney; J. W. von Doussa; D. G. Hill; M. F. O'Loughlin; D. F. O'Connor; T. J. Higgins; P. C. Heerey; D. P. Drummond; R. E. Cooper; A. P. Whitlam; M. J. Beazley.
Registrar, J. T. Howard, RFD, ED.

SUPREME COURT OF THE AUSTRALIAN CAPITAL TERRITORY *as at 1 June 1993*
Judges, Hons. J. A. Miles *(Chief Justice);* J. F. Gallop; T. J. Higgins *(Resident Judges);* R. M. Northrop; J. D. Davies; J. S. Lockhart; I. F. Sheppard; K. J. Jenkinson; B. A. Beaumont; M. R. Wilcox; J. E. J. Spender; M. L. Foster; D. M. Ryan; J. W. von Doussa *(Additional Judges).*
Master, A. E. Hogan.
Registrar, A. G. Towill.

SUPREME COURT OF THE NORTHERN TERRITORY *as at 1 June 1993*
Chief Justice, Hon. B. F. Martin.
Judges, Hons. Sir William Kearney; D. N. Angel; D. Mildren; S. Thomas.
Master, P. G. Lefevre.

DEFENCE
A single Department of Defence was created in 1973, though the separate identities of the three services have been retained. The Chief of Defence Force Staff is responsible for command of the Defence Force through the three Service Chiefs of Staff and is also the principal military adviser to the Minister. The Secretary to the Department of Defence is responsible to the Minister for Defence for advice on policy, resources and organization. Total defence expenditure was $A9,886,000,000 in 1992–3.

The personnel strengths of the Permanent Defence Force at 30 June 1993 were:

	Males	Females
Navy	15,294	1,400
Army	28,600	3,000
Air Force	19,278	3,082
Total	63,172	7,482

The Army is organized into one regular and one reservist division (reserves number 26,000). In addition, there is a regular northern command of one air defence, one engineer, one aviation and one SAS regiment. The regular division is composed of one mechanized and two infantry brigades with reconnaissance, artillery, engineer and aviation regiments, whereas the reservist division is composed of 15 infantry battalions with similar support regiments. Equipment includes 103 main battle tanks, 800 armoured personnel carriers and armoured infantry fighting vehicles, 240 artillery pieces, 27 aircraft and 84 helicopters, of which 6 are armed.

The Navy has a personnel strength of 15,300 with a further 1,600 reservists, and has four main bases at Sydney, Cockburn Sound, Cairns and Darwin. It has five submarines, three destroyers, eight frigates and 19 patrol and coastal craft with 15 armed helicopters.

The Air Force has 157 combat aircraft organized into two ground attack/reconnaissance, three air defence, two maritime reconnaissance and seven transport squadrons with training and support units.

One Army infantry company and one Air Force detachment are stationed in Malaysia. US Navy and Air Force personnel numbering 700 are stationed at communications facilities in Australia.

FINANCE

COMMONWEALTH GOVERNMENT FINANCE
Outlays and revenue of the Commonwealth Government were ($Amillion):

	1991–92	1992–3
Current outlays	102,260	109,085
Capital outlays	7,055	8,310
Revenue and grants received	97,374	100,604
Financing transactions	11,941	16,746

STATE GOVERNMENT FINANCE 1989–90* ($A million)

	Outlay (current and capital)	Revenue and grants received	Financing transactions
NSW	20,990	19,605	1,385
Victoria	17,420	13,902	3,519
Queensland	9,857	10,197	−339
S. Australia	5,660	4,829	830
W. Australia	7,011	6,112	899
Tasmania	2,122	1,955	167
NT	1,384	1,227	157
ACT	942	990	−48
Total	65,386	58,817	6,570

* preliminary

BANKING

In April 1993 the trading banks had total liabilities of $A344,808 million including total deposits of $A217,720 million securities.

ECONOMY

AGRICULTURE – In 1990–1, 60.2 per cent of land area consisted of agricultural establishments, the remainder being urban areas, state forests, mining leases and unoccupied land. Crop-growing areas constituted up to 3.76 per cent of the total agricultural establishments, emphasizing the relative importance of the livestock industries in Australia (sheep in the warm, temperate, semi-arid lands and beef cattle in the tropics).

The wide range of climatic and soil conditions has resulted in a diversity of crops. Generally, cereal crops (excluding rice and sorghum) are grown in all States over wide areas, while other crops are confined to specific locations in a few States. However, scanty or erratic rainfall, limited potential for irrigation and unsuitable soils or topography have restricted intensive agriculture.

GROSS VALUE OF AGRICULTURAL COMMODITIES
1991–2p

	$A million
Crops	9,614.6
Livestock slaughterings and other disposals	5,586.0
Livestock products	5,260.1
Total agriculture	20,474.9
p preliminary	

LIVESTOCK NUMBERS *at 31 March 1991*

	Thousands
Cattle	23,662
Sheep	163,238
Pigs	2,531
Poultry	52,472

GROSS VALUE OF CROPS 1991–2p

	$A million
Cereals for grain	3,198.6
Cotton	882.1
Crops for hay	154.6
Fruit and nuts	1,668.4
Legumes for grain	424.1
Nursery production	460.5
Oilseeds	107.0
Peanuts	27.4
Sugar cane for crushing	602.0
Tobacco	74.9
Vegetables	1,300.1
Pastures and grasses	619.4
Total crops	9,614.6
p preliminary	

MINES AND MINERALS – Significant mineral resources include bauxite, coal, copper, crude petroleum, gems, gold, ilmenite, iron ore, lead, limestone, manganese, nickel, rutile, salt, silver, tin, tungsten, uranium, zinc and zircon. Recently, geological exploration has significantly increased mineral resources and a number of oilfields are in production.

In 1989–90 the total value of all minerals produced was $A23,294 million. In 1989–90 mine production of black coal was 160,459,000 tonnes, crude oil (including condensate) was 31,700 megalitres and natural gas 15,354 gigalitres. Production of principal metals in 1989 was (tonnes):

Iron ore	106,000,000
Copper	289,000
Lead-Zinc concentrate	130,900
Gold	203

MANUFACTURES – In 1989–90 there were in Australia 41,797 manufacturing establishments, employing 1,028,000 persons; wages paid amounted to $A27,220m; and turnover $A165,045m.

TRADE

Of Australia's total exports in the year 1991–2, the largest category was gold $A6,848m. This was followed by gold, $A4,023m; iron ore concentrates, $A2,850m; and meat of bovine animals, $A2,777m.

The largest category of Australia's imports was road vehicles, worth $A2,556m. This was followed by aircraft and associated equipment, $A2,168m; office and automatic data processing machines, $A1,924m; petrol and oils, $A1,577m; parts and accessories for office machinery, $A1,411m; paper and pulp, $A1,335m.

	1990–1	1991–2
Imports	$A48,912m	$A50,983m
Exports	52,398m	55,075m

In 1991–2, 26 per cent of Australia's total exports went to Japan. The USA received 9 per cent, Republic of Korea 6, Singapore 6, New Zealand 5, Taiwan 5, UK 4 and Hong Kong 4.

Of Australia's total imports in 1991–2, 23 per cent came from the USA, 18 from Japan, 6 West Germany, 6 UK, 5 New Zealand, 4 Taiwan and 4 China.

TRADE WITH UK	1991	1992
Imports from UK	£1,355,127,000	£1,376,737,000
Exports to UK	870,823,000	1,013,680,000

COMMUNICATIONS

RAILWAYS – There are six government-owned railway systems, operated by the State Rail Authority of NSW, Victorian Railways, Queensland Government Railways, Western Australian Government Railways, the State Transport Authority of Southern Australia, and the Australian National Railways Commission. The ANRC incorporates the former Commonwealth Railways system, and the Tasmanian and non-metropolitan South Australian railways (urban rail services in Southern Australia remain the responsibility of the State Transport Authority). In 1990 there were 35,486 route-kilometres open.

In 1989–90 there were 413.75 million rail passenger journeys on government railways and 185.53 million tonnes of goods and livestock carried.

MOTOR VEHICLES – At 30 June 1990, there were 9,776,600 motor vehicles registered in Australia and 304,000 motor cycles.

CIVIL AVIATION – Figures for domestic and overseas services in 1992 are as follows:

	Domestic	Overseas
Paying passengers	20,198,197	9,302,052
Freight (tonnes)	124,991	405,870

SHIPPING – Total arrivals and departures of vessels engaged in overseas trade at the various Australian ports in 1989–90 were: arrivals 15,521 (362,030,000 deadweight tonnes); departures 15,372 (527,223,000 deadweight tonnes).

BROADCASTING AND TELEVISION – On 30 June 1991, the Australian Broadcasting Corporation operated 410 stations. Privately owned commercial broadcasting stations totalled 203. On 30 June 1991, 511 national and 563 commercial television and translator stations were in operation.

THE NORTHERN TERRITORY

The Northern Territory has a total area of 519,770 sq. miles (1,346,200 sq. km), and lies between 129°–138° E. longitude and 11°–26° S. latitude. The estimated population in the Northern Territory at 30 June 1993 was 175,000, of which about a quarter are Aboriginals.

GOVERNMENT

The administration was taken over by the Commonwealth on 1 January 1911 from the State of South Australia. The Northern Territory (Self-Government) Act 1978 established the Northern Territory as a body politic as from 1 July 1978, with Ministers having control over and responsibility for Territory finances and the administration of the functions of government as specified by the federal government by regulations made pursuant to the Act. Proposed laws passed by the Legislative Assembly in relation to a transferred function require the assent of the Administrator. Proposed laws in all other cases may be assented to by the Administrator or reserved by the Administrator for the Governor-General's pleasure. The Governor-General may disallow any laws assented to by the Administrator within six months of the Administrator's assent.

The Northern Territory has federal representation, electing one member to the House of Representatives and two members to the Senate.

SEAT OF ADMINISTRATION – Darwin.

Administrator, His Hon. the Honourable Austin Asche, QC. *Chief Minister*, Hon. Marshall Perron.

ABORIGINAL LANDS

Various Aboriginal Land Trusts hold title to land previously called Reserves, totalling about one-fifth of the Northern Territory. The Aboriginal Land Rights (NT) Act of 1976 provides for the investigation and determination of Aboriginal traditional claims to vacant Crown land or land already owned by or on behalf of Aboriginals. Successful land claims to date have increased Aboriginal ownership to 34 per cent of the Northern Territory and a further 13 per cent is the subject of claims.

A number of major Aboriginal communities previously administered by church mission societies and the federal government are now controlled by the Aboriginal people through local Aboriginal Councils. A recent phenomenon is the voluntary movement of some Aboriginals to their traditional homeland areas where they feel that their culture will be better preserved.

ECONOMY

Northern Territory's economy is based on the exploitation of its natural resources of minerals, land and fisheries and on tourist attractions. Following the introduction of a number of government measures designed to expand and diversify primary production, the Territory's agricultural and horticultural industries are also beginning to contribute an increasing amount to Territory rural output. The beef cattle industry continues to be the major user of pastoral lands.

Mining and energy resource development has played a major part in the development of the Northern Territory and in 1991 the total value of production was $A1.83 billion. The Territory is a leading uranium producer, extracting 3,126,676 kg of uranium oxide in 1991 with a value of $A212 million. The Northern Terrritory contains 20 per cent of the western world's low cost uranium reserves. Large scale production of zinc-lead concentrate is planned to commence in 1994. In 1991 more than one million tonnes of manganese was sold, with a total value of about $A165 million. Gold production for 1991 was estimated at $A298 million. The

value ex mines of bauxite sales exceeded $A128 million and alumina production was valued at $A566 million. The value of oil and gas production for 1991 was $A566 million.

Tourism is a major growth industry and generates over $A490 million annually.

COMMUNICATIONS

The Northern Territory has three main ports; Darwin, managed by the Darwin Port Authority, and the private mining ports of Gove and Groote Eylandt.

The standard gauge rail link between Southern Australia and Alice Springs was officially opened in October 1980. The link between Alice Springs and Darwin is provided by a fully co-ordinated rail-road service.

The main population centres are linked by the Stuart Highway, which connects Alice Springs to Darwin via Tennant Creek and Katherine. Of special interest to the Northern Territory is the operation of 'road trains'. These are basically massive trucks hauling two or three trailers, having a net capacity of about 100 tonnes and measuring up to 45 metres in length.

EXTERNAL TERRITORIES

ASHMORE AND CARTIER ISLANDS

Ashmore Islands (known as Middle, East and West Islands) and Cartier Island are situated in the Indian Ocean some 850 km and 790 km west of Darwin respectively. The islands lie at the outer edge of the continental shelf. They are small and low and are composed of coral and sand. Turtles are plentiful at certain times of the year and beche-de-mer is abundant. The islands are uninhabited.

Great Britain took formal possession of the Ashmores in 1878 and Cartier was annexed in 1909. In 1931 the islands were placed under the authority of the Commonwealth of Australia, and were accepted in 1933 under the name of the Territory of Ashmore and Cartier Islands. The territory was annexed to the Northern Territory of Australia until 1978, when administration of Ashmore and Cartier Islands became a direct responsibility of the Commonwealth Government. In 1983 Ashmore Reef was declared a national nature reserve.

In accordance with an agreement between the governments of Indonesia and Australia, Indonesian fishermen who have traditionally plied the area may engage in limited fishing activity within the territory but are prohibited from taking any products from the nature reserve. They can land to collect water from West Island.

THE AUSTRALIAN ANTARCTIC TERRITORY

The Australian Antarctic Territory was established in 1933 by an Order in Council which placed under the government of the Commonwealth of Australia all the islands and territories, other than Adélie Land, which are situated south of the latitude 60° S. and lying between 160° E. longitude and 45° E. longitude. The Order came into force in 1936. The territory is administered by the Antarctic Division of the Department of the Environment, Sport and Territories, which, since 1948, has organized yearly expeditions to Antarctica, known as Australian National Antarctic Research Expeditions (ANARE).

Scientific research is carried out at Mawson Station (opened 1954) in MacRobertson Land, Davis Station (opened 1957) in Princess Elizabeth Land, Casey Station (opened 1969) and an adjacent station opened in 1988. Since 1948 ANARE has operated a station on Macquarie Island, a dependency of Tasmania, situated at 54° 29′ S. and 158° 56′ E., about 900 miles north of the Antarctic Continent. Summer stations have been established at Cape Denison,

Commonwealth Bay in the Bunger Hills, the Larsemann Hills, the Prince Charles Mountains, and on Heard Island.

CHRISTMAS ISLAND

Christmas Island was administered as part of the Colony of Singapore until 1957. In 1958 it became an Australian territory. It is situated in the Indian Ocean about 1,408 km NW of North West Cape in Western Australia, and has an area of 135 sq. km. Population (1991 census) is 1,275, largely consisting of employees of Phosphate Resources NL, and employees of the Christmas Island Administration, the Christmas Island Shire Council, and their families. There is no indigenous population.

The island is densely wooded and had extensive deposits of phosphates, the extraction of which has traditionally been the major economic activity. The deposits of low grade phosphate ore are now being extracted by a private mining company, Phosphate Resourses NL. Alternative economic development is being encouraged. The principal current development is a hotel complex.

On 1 July 1992 the Australian Government introduced major reforms to the laws of the island with the application of the Western Australian legal regime.

The Administrator is responsible to the Australian Minister for the Environment, Sport and Territories in Canberra. The Christmas Island Shire Council has nine elected members. The Council is responsible for municipal functions and services on the island.

Administrator, M. Grimes.

COCOS (KEELING) ISLANDS

The Cocos (Keeling) Islands are two separate atolls (North Keeling Island and, 24 km to the south, the main atoll) comprising some 27 small coral islands with a total area of about 14 sq. km, situated in the Indian Ocean in latitude 12° 5′ S. and longitude 96° 53′ E. The main islands of the southern atoll are West Island (the largest, about 9 km from north to south) on which are the administrative centre, the aerodrome, and the Australia-based employees of government departments; Home Island, where the Cocos Malay community live; Direction Island, Horsburgh and South Island.

The islands were declared a British possession in 1857. All land in the islands was granted to George Clunies-Ross and his heirs by Queen Victoria in 1886. In 1955 the islands, which had been governed through the British colonies of Ceylon (from 1878), the Straits Settlements (1886) and Singapore (1903), were accepted as a Territory of Australia. In 1978 the Australian Government purchased all Clunies-Ross land and property interests except for the family home and grounds. In 1979 ownership of the kampong area of Home Island was transferred to the Cocos (Keeling) Islands Council, the local government body established in 1979. Title to most of the remaining land purchased from Clunies-Ross in 1978 was transferred to the Council in 1984. In 1993 the federal government purchased the last of the remaining grounds.

The Cocos (Keeling) Islands Act 1955 provided the legal framework for the political and administrative arrangements in the territory. On 6 April 1984 the Cocos community, in a UN supervised Act of Self-Determination, chose to integrate with Australia. The Government's major commitment was that living standards would reach comparable mainland levels by 1994. The Commonwealth Grants Commission monitors the progress. The Territories Law Reform Act 1992 provides for the modernization of the territory's legal regime through the extension of all Commonwealth laws and the introduction of state-type laws based on those of Western Australia.

The territory has a limited economic base at present. In 1986-7 the copra industry suffered severe losses and in 1987 ceased production. Tourism is being developed as a growth area with construction of a new resort due to be completed towards the end of 1993.

A weekly air charter service operates between Perth, the Cocos (Keeling) Islands and Christmas Island. Population (30 June 1991), 647. The islands are administered by the Australian Government through the Department of the Environment, Sport and Territories in Canberra.

Administrator, John Read.

CORAL SEA ISLANDS TERRITORY

The Coral Sea Islands Territory lies east of Queensland between the Great Barrier Reef and longitude 156° 06′ E., and between latitudes 12° and 24° S. It comprises scattered islands, spread over a sea area of 780,000 sq. km. The islands are formed mainly of coral and sand, and most are extremely small, with no permanent fresh water. There is a manned metereological station in the Willis Group but the remaining islands are uninhabited. Large populations of sea birds nest and breed in the area, and two national nature reserves were designated in the Territory in 1982.

The Australian Government bases its claim to the islands on numerous acts of sovereignty since early this century and enacted the Coral Sea Islands Act 1969 which declares the islands a territory of the Commonwealth of Australia. The Department of the Environment, Sport and Territories, Canberra, is responsible for the administration of the territory.

HEARD ISLAND AND McDONALD ISLANDS

The Heard and McDonald islands, about 4,100 km south-west of Fremantle, comprise all the islands and rocks lying between 52° 30′ and 53° 30′ S. latitude and 72° and 74° 30′ E. longitude. Sovereignty over the islands was transferred by the UK to the Commonwealth of Australia in 1947. The Heard Island and McDonald Islands Act 1953 provides for the government of the islands as one territory. Under this Act the law operating there is that of the Australian Capital Territory. The islands are administered by the Department of the Environment, Sport and Territories. Under the Environment Protection and Management Ordinance 1987, a permit system regulates entry to the territory and a range of activities there.

NORFOLK ISLAND

Norfolk Island is situated in the South Pacific Ocean at latitude 29° 02′ S. and longitude 167° 57′ E., being about 1,676 km north-east of Sydney and 1,063 km north of Auckland. It is about 8 km long by 5 km wide, with an area of 3,455 hectares. The climate is mild and sub tropical. Resident population at the 1991 Census was 1,912.

The island, discovered by Captain Cook in 1774, served as a penal colony from 1788 to 1814 and 1825 to 1855. In 1856, 194 descendants of the *Bounty* mutineers accepted an invitation to leave Pitcairn and settle on Norfolk Island, which led to Norfolk Island becoming a separate settlement under the jurisdiction of the Governor of New South Wales. In 1897 Norfolk Island became a dependency of NSW, and in 1914 a territory of Australia. From that date, Norfolk Island has been regarded as an integral part of Australia.

In 1979 Norfolk Island gained a substantial degree of self-government, enabling the island to run its affairs to the greatest practical extent. Wide powers are exercised by a nine-member Legislative Assembly. The Act preserves the Commonwealth's responsibility for Norfolk Island as a territory under its authority, with the Minister for the

Environment, Sport and Territories as the responsible Minister.

The island is a popular tourist resort, and a large proportion of the population depends on tourism and its ancillaries for employment. In 1991-2 there were 27,361 tourist arrivals on the Island. Regular air services operate from mainland Australia and New Zealand.

The seat of government and administration offices are in Kingston.

Administrator, A. G. Kerr.

AUSTRALIAN STATES

NEW SOUTH WALES

The State of New South Wales is situated entirely between the 28th and 38th parallels of S. latitude and 141st and 154th meridians of E. longitude, and comprises an area of 309,433 sq. miles (801,427 sq. km) (exclusive of 939 sq. miles of Australian Capital Territory which lies within its borders).
POPULATION – Preliminary estimated resident population at 30 June 1992 was 5,932,000.
STATE CAPITAL – ΨSydney, the largest city in Australia, stands on the shores of Port Jackson. Sydney Harbour extends inland for 21 km; the total area of water is about 55 sq. km. The preliminary estimated resident population in 1991 of the Sydney statistical division was 3,539,024. The Newcastle and Wollongong statistical subdivisions contain populations of 427,568 and 235,913 respectively.
TOWNS – The populations of other principal municipalities are: Albury 39,610, Dubbo 31,290, Greater Taree 36,960, Hastings 42,220, Lismore 38,130, Orange 32,520, Shoalhaven 59,470, Tamworth 33,830, Wagga Wagga 50,930.

GOVERNMENT

New South Wales was first colonized as a British possession in 1788, and after progressive settlement a partly elective legislature was established in 1843. In 1855 responsible government was granted, the present Constitution being founded on the Constitution Act of 1902. New South Wales federated with the other States of Australia in 1901. The executive authority of the State is vested in a Governor (appointed by the Crown), assisted by a Council of Ministers.
Governor of New South Wales, His Excellency Rear-Adm. Peter Sinclair, AO, RAN, *assumed office* August 1990.
Lt.-Governor and Chief Justice of NSW, The Hon. Mr Justice Gleeson, AC.
Premier, Hon. John Fahey.

AGENT-GENERAL'S OFFICE IN LONDON, 75 King William Street, London EC4N 7HA. *Agent-General*, vacant.

LEGISLATURE

The Legislative Council consists of 42 members, elected by popular vote, and the Legislative Assembly consists of 99 members elected for a maximum period of four years.
President of the Legislative Council, Hon. M. Willis, MLC.
Speaker, Legislative Assembly, Hon. K. R. Rozzoli, MP.

JUDICATURE

The judicial system includes a Supreme Court, Industrial Commission, District Court, Land and Environment Court, Compensation Court, and Local Courts (Magistrates).
Chief Justice, Supreme Court, The Hon. Mr Justice Gleeson, AC.
President, Court of Appeal, Hon. Mr Justice Kirby, CMG.

EDUCATION

Education is compulsory between the ages of 6 and 15 years. It is non-sectarian and free at all government schools. The enrolment in 1992 in 2,180 government and 857 non-government schools was 1,050,228. The six universities, together with advanced education colleges, had an enrolment of 160,651 in 1991. Students enrolled in technical and further education colleges in 1990 numbered 362,474.

ECONOMY

A large area is suitable for sheep-raising, the principal breed of sheep being the merino, which was introduced in 1797.

The principal minerals are coal, lead, zinc, gold, rutile, copper and zircon. The total value of minerals extracted in 1989-90 was $A3,895.8 million. The average number of persons employed in the mining industry during 1989-90 was 20,013. In 1989-90, 93,900,000 tonnes of coal were produced.

In 1989-90 there were 10,172 manufacturing establishments (employing four or more persons). The number of persons employed at 30 June 1989 was 338,400. Production of raw steel in 1990-1 was 4,764,000 tonnes.

LORD HOWE ISLAND

Lord Howe Island, which is part of New South Wales, is situated 702 kilometres north-east of Sydney, in 31° 33′ 4″ S. latitude and 159° 4′ 26″ E. longitude. Area 6.37 sq. miles (16.5 sq. km.). Population, 1991, 371. The island is of volcanic origin with Mount Gower reaching an altitude of 866 m. The affairs of the Island are administered by the Lord Howe Island Board.

QUEENSLAND

This State, situated in 9° 14′-29° S. latitude and 138°-153° 30′ E. longitude, comprises the whole north-eastern portion of the Australian continent. Queensland possesses an area of 666,798 sq. miles (1,727,000 sq. km).
POPULATION – At 30 June 1992 the estimated resident population numbered 3,030,500.
STATE CAPITAL – ΨBrisbane is situated on the Brisbane River, which is navigable by large vessels to the city, over 23 km from Moreton Bay. The estimated resident population of the Brisbane statistical division at 30 June 1991 was 1,327,006. This area includes the cities of Brisbane (753,375), Ipswich (76,673), Logan (153,427) and Redcliffe (49,389).
CITIES – Other cities with population over 30,000 at 30 June 1991, are: ΨTownsville 84,138; Gold Coast 139,899; Toowoomba 83,776; ΨRockhampton 59,505; ΨCairns 44,021; ΨCaloundra 50,609; ΨThuringowa 39,292; Ψ Bundaberg 33,300.

GOVERNMENT

Queensland was constituted a separate colony with responsible government in 1859, having previously formed part of New South Wales. The executive authority is vested in a Governor (appointed by the Crown), aided by an Executive Council of 18 members.
Governor of Queensland, Her Excellency Mrs Mary Marguerite Leneen Forde, AC.
Premier, Hon. W. K. Goss.

AGENT-GENERAL'S OFFICE IN LONDON, 392 Strand, London WC2R 0LZ. *Agent-General*, R. T. Anderson.

LEGISLATURE

Parliament consists of a Legislative Assembly of 89 members, elected by all persons aged 18 years and over. The Assembly, as at 30 June 1993, was composed of: Australian Labor Party,

54; National Party of Australia, 26; Liberal Party of Australia, 9.
Speaker, Hon. D. Fouras.
Chairman of Committees, H. Palaszczuk.
Leader of the Opposition, R. E. Borbidge.

JUDICATURE

There are a Supreme Court; District Courts; Children's Courts; an Industrial Court; a Land Court and a Medical Assessment Tribunal; a Planning and Environment Court; the Industrial Conciliation and Arbitration Commission; Inferior Courts at all the principal towns, presided over by Stipendiary Magistrates; a Small Claims Tribunal; Small Debts Court and a Licensing Court.
Chief Justice, Supreme Court, Hon. J. M. Macrossan.

EDUCATION

Education is compulsory, secular and free between the ages of 5 and 15. At July 1992, there were 1,009 government primary schools, 70 primary/secondary, and 185 secondary schools with 255,645 primary students, and 145,477 secondary students.

Post-secondary education involves technical and further education (TAFE) and higher education. During 1991, 145,302 students were enrolled in TAFE courses, excluding 94,522 enrolled in adult education courses. At 30 April 1992 there were 52,497 full-time, 22,968 part-time, and 14,725 external students enrolled in higher education courses.

ECONOMY

Total Queensland-sawn timber produced in 1991–2 amounted to 625,480 cubic metres (gross volume measure).

There are rich deposits of both metallic and non-metallic minerals. Coal is mined extensively in Central Queensland and on a lesser scale in the Ipswich district.

In 1991–2 there were 6,705 establishments with four or more workers, employing 122,900 persons, with a turnover of $A23,147 million. Much of the production was the processing of foodstuffs, minerals and chemical, petroleum and coal products. Included in other factory production were the products from engineering, transport equipment, timber, basic and fabricated metal, cement, paper and textile mills and oil refineries.

SOUTH AUSTRALIA

The State of South Australia is situated between 26° and 38° S. lat. and 129° and 141° E. long., the total area being 380,070 sq. miles (984,376 sq. km).

POPULATION – At 30 June 1992, the resident population was estimated to be 1,459,622.

STATE CAPITAL – ΨAdelaide, the chief city and capital, estimated resident population on 30 June 1992, 1,067,322 inclusive of suburbs. Other centres (with 1992 populations) are: ΨWhyalla (26,659); ΨMt Gambier (22,529); ΨPort Pirie (15,044); ΨPort Augusta (15,209).

GOVERNMENT

South Australia was proclaimed a British Province in 1836, and in 1851 a partially elective legislature was established. The present Constitution rests upon a Law of 24 October 1856, the executive authority being vested in a Governor appointed by the Crown, aided by a Council of 13 Ministers.
Governor of South Australia, Her Excellency the Hon.
  Dame Roma Mitchell, AC, DBE (1991).
Lt.-Governor, The Hon. Dr Basil Hetzel, AC (1992).
Premier, Hon. Lynn Maurice Ferguson Arnold.

AGENT-GENERAL'S OFFICE IN LONDON, South Australia House, 50 Strand, London WC2N 5LW. *Agent-General,* G. Walls.

LEGISLATURE

Parliament consists of a Legislative Council of 22 members elected for eight years, one half retiring every four years; and a House of Assembly of 47 members, elected for a maximum duration of four years. Election is by ballot, with universal adult suffrage for both the Legislative Council and the House of Assembly.

The representation in the House of Assembly is 22 Labor, 22 Liberals, 2 Labor Independents and 1 National Party.
President of the Legislative Council, Hon. G. L. Bruce.
Speaker of the House of Assembly, Hon. N. T. Peterson.

JUDICATURE

The Supreme Court is presided over by the Chief Justice and 13 Puisne Judges.

EDUCATION

Education at the primary and secondary level is available at government schools controlled by the Education Department and at non-government schools, most of which are denominational. In 1992 there were 682 government schools with 187,556 students, and 184 independent schools with 61,246 students. Tertiary education is available through universities, and technical and further education colleges.

The three universities had, in 1991, a total enrolment of 42,935 full-time students.

TASMANIA

Tasmania is an island state of Australia situated in the Southern ocean off the south-eastern extremity of the mainland. It is separated from the Australian mainland by Bass Strait and incorporates King Island and the Furneaux group of islands which are in the Strait. It lies between 40° 38'–43° 39' S. latitude and 144° 36'–148° 23' E. longitude, and has an area of 26,383 sq. miles (68,331 sq. km). Macquarie Island, situated at 54° 30' S. and 158° 57' E., about 900 miles north of the Antarctic Continent, is a dependency of Tasmania.

POPULATION – The estimated resident population at 30 June 1992 was 471,120.

STATE CAPITAL – ΨHobart, founded 1804. Population (30 June 1991) (metropolitan area), 181,838. Other towns (with population at 30 June 1991) are ΨLaunceston (metropolitan area, 93,520), ΨDevonport (24,622), Burnie-Somerset (20,483).

GOVERNMENT

The island was first settled by a British party from New South Wales in 1803, becoming a separate colony in 1825. In 1851 a partly elective legislature was inaugurated, and in 1856 responsible government was established. In 1901 Tasmania became a State of the Australian Commonwealth. The State executive authority is vested in a Governor appointed by the Crown, but is exercised by Cabinet Ministers responsible to the Legislature, of which they are members.
Governor of Tasmania, His Excellency Gen. Sir Phillip
  Bennett, AC, KBE, DSO.
Premier, Hon. Raymond J. Groom.

LEGISLATURE

Parliament consists of a Legislative Council of 19 members, elected for six years (three retiring annually, in rotation, except in every sixth year, when four retire), and a House of

Assembly of 35 members, elected by proportional representation for four years in five seven-member constituencies. All Tasmanians of 18 years and over who have resided continuously in the State for at least six months may vote in elections to both houses.'Elections for the Assembly are held every four years.

The election of February 1992 resulted in a victory for the Liberal Party, with 19 Liberal, 11 Labor and 5 Tasmanian Green members of the House of Assembly. The state of the parties in the Legislative Council following the election was Independent 17, Liberal 1, Labor 1.
President of the Legislative Council, Hon. E. J. C. Stopp.
Speaker of the House of Assembly, Hon. G. R. Page.

JUDICATURE

The Supreme Court of Tasmania, with civil, criminal ecclesiastical, admiralty and matrimonial jurisdiction, was established in 1823. Local Courts are held before Commissioners who are legal practitioners. Courts of General Sessions, constituted by a chairman who is a Justice of the Peace and at least one other Justice, are established in the municipalities and Courts of Petty Sessions are constituted by Magistrates sitting alone, or by two or more justices. A single justice may hear and determine certain matters.
Chief Justice, Supreme Court, Hon. Sir Guy Green, KBE.

EDUCATION

Government schools are of three main types: primary, secondary and secondary colleges. On 1 July 1992 there were 65,713 students enrolled in 243 government schools. There were also 66 independent schools with an enrolment of 20,576. The University of Tasmania with campuses in Hobart and Launceston, had 7,853 full-time students and 3,460 part-time students in 1992.

ECONOMY

Tasmania, the smallest Australian state, ranks fourth as a producer of electrical energy. Most of it is derived from water power, with a total installed generator capacity of 2,460,000 kW at 30 June 1992. By reason of its low-cost electrical energy, Tasmania has large plants producing ferromanganese and newsprint. A large aluminium plant is situated at Bell Bay and Tasmania is the source of the bulk of Australian requirements of zinc and fine papers.

The quantity of timber (excluding firewood) of various species cut in 1991-2 was 3,978,700 cubic metres, including 3,173,100 cubic metres for woodchip and wood-pulp.

The chief ores mined are those containing copper, tin, iron, silver, zinc and lead.

The chief manufactures for export are refined metals, preserved fruit and vegetables, butter, cheese, textiles, paper, confectionery, wood chips and sawn timber. In 1991-2, 873 manufacturing establishments employed 22,100 persons.

VICTORIA

The State of Victoria comprises the south-east corner of Australia, at the part where its mainland territory projects furthest into the southern latitudes; it lies between 34°-39° S. latitude and 141°-150° E. longitude. Its area is 87,876 sq. miles (227,597 sq. km).
POPULATION – The estimated resident population at 30 June 1992 was 4,458,900.
STATE CAPITAL – ΨMelbourne had a resident population at 30 June 1991 estimated at 3,145,600. Other urban centres are ΨGeelong 152,780; Ballarat 82,330; Bendigo 70,360; Shepparton-Mooroopna 41,450.

GOVERNMENT

Victoria was originally known as the Port Phillip District of New South Wales and was created a separate colony in 1851, with a partially elective legislature. In 1855 responsible government was conferred. The executive authority is vested in a Governor, appointed by the Crown, aided by an Executive Council of Ministers.
Governor of Victoria, His Excellency the Hon. Richard E. McGarvie, *assumed office* 23 April 1992.
Lt.-Governor, The Hon. Sir John McIntosh Young, KCMG, AO (1974).
Premier, Hon J. G. Kennett.

AGENT-GENERAL'S OFFICE IN LONDON, Victoria House, Melbourne Place, Strand, London WC2B 4LG.
Agent-General, L. T. Baldock.

LEGISLATURE

Parliament consists of a Legislative Council of 44 members, elected for the 22 Provinces for two terms of the Legislative Assembly, one half retiring every four years at a general election; and a Legislative Assembly of 88 members, elected for a maximum duration of four years. Voting is compulsory.

The state of parties in the Legislative Council (July 1993) is Liberal Party 24, Australian Labour Party 14, National Party 6. The state of parties in the Legislative Assembly (elected 3 October 1992) is Liberal Party 52, Australian Labour Party 27, National Party 9.
President of the Legislative Council, Hon. Bruce Chamberlain.
Speaker of the Legislative Assembly, Hon. John Delzoppo.

JUDICATURE

There is a Supreme Court with a Chief Justice and 24 Puisne Judges, a County Court and Magistrates' Courts.
Chief Justice, Supreme Court, Hon. Mr Justice John Phillips.
Chief Judge, County Court, Hon. G. R. D. Waldron, AO.

EDUCATION

Primary education is compulsory, secular and free between the ages of 6 and 15. At 30 June 1991 there were 2,725 schools, attended by 789,513 students. In addition there are technical and further education institutions and colleges of advanced education. There are four state-aided universities.

ECONOMY

Minerals raised include oil and natural gas, brown coal, limestone, clays and stone for construction material. Production of brown coal in 1991-2 was 48,884m tonnes.

In 1965 natural gas was discovered in commercial quantities in the offshore waters of the Gippsland Basin in eastern Victoria and in 1966-7, three more valuable oilfields were located in the same general area. These fields are still the largest yet found in Australia. Production from Victorian natural gas and crude oil fields in 1991-2 was 14,782 megalitres of crude oil and 6,352 million cubic metres of natural gas.

At 30 June 1991 there were 8,976 manufacturing establishments in which total employees numbered 308,555.

WESTERN AUSTRALIA

Western Australia includes all that portion of the continent west of 129° E. longitude, the most westerly point being in 113° 9' E. longitude and from 13° 44' to 35° 8' S. latitude. Its area is 975,920 sq. miles (2,527,621 sq. km).
POPULATION – At 30 June 1992 the estimated resident population is 1,657,100.
STATE CAPITAL – ΨPerth, on the right bank of the Swan River estuary, 12 miles from Fremantle. Estimated resident

population (30 June 1991) of Perth statistical division, including the port of ΨFremantle, 1,188,762.

GOVERNMENT

Western Australia was first settled by the British in 1829, and in 1870 it was granted a partially elective legislature. In 1890 responsible government was granted, and the administration vested in a Governor, a Legislative Council, and a Legislative Assembly. The present constitution rests upon the Constitution Act 1889, the Constitution Acts Amendment Act 1899, and amending Acts. The executive is vested in a Governor appointed by the Crown and aided by a Council of responsible Ministers.
Governor of Western Australia, His Excellency the Hon. Sir Francis Burt, AC, KCMG, QC.
Lt.-Governor and Administrator, Hon. D. K. Malcolm, AC.
Premier, Hon. Richard Court.

AGENT-GENERAL'S OFFICE IN LONDON, Western Australia House, 115 Strand, London WC2R OAJ. *Agent-General (acting)*, G. Stokes.

LEGISLATURE

Parliament consists of a Legislative Council and a Legislative Assembly, elected by adult suffrage subject to qualifications of residence and registration. The qualifying age for electors for both the Legislative Council and Legislative Assembly is 18 years. There are 34 members in the Legislative Council elected for a period of four years. The Legislative Assembly has 57 members, who are elected for a term of four years. The Legislative Assembly (elected 6 February 1993) is composed of Liberal Party 26, Australian Labor Party 24, National Party of Australia 6, Independent Liberal 1.
President of the Legislative Council, Hon. C. E. Griffiths.
Speaker of the Legislative Assembly, Hon. J. Clarko.

JUDICATURE

Chief Justice, Hon. D. K. Malcolm, AC.
Senior Puisne Judge, Hon. W. P. Pidgeon.
Puisne Judges, Hons. G. A. Kennedy; B. W. Rowland; E. M. Franklyn; P. L. Seaman; R. D. Nicolson; T. A. Walsh; D. A. Ipp; H. A. Wallwork; M. J. Murray; N. J. Owen; R. J. M. Anderson.

EDUCATION

In 1992 there were 761 government and 250 non-government primary and secondary school campuses with 221,034 and 72,552 full-time students respectively. The principal higher education institutions are the University of Western Australia (10,815 enrolments in 1990), Murdoch University (6,223), Curtin University (16,642) and Edith Cowan University (14,641).

ECONOMY

There were 3,693 manufacturing establishments operating in the State at 30 June 1992. The total number of persons employed (including working proprietors) by these establishments at the end of June 1992 was 62,100.
The forests contain some of the finest hardwoods in the world. The total quantity of sawn timber produced during 1990-1 was 263,389 cubic metres.
The State has large deposits of a wide range of minerals, many of which are being mined or are under development for production. The ex-mine value of all minerals (excluding construction materials, clays and limestone) produced during 1990-1 was $A9,760,800,000.

AUSTRIA
Republik Österreich

Austria is a country of central Europe bounded on the north by the Czech Republic and the Slovak Republic, on the south by Italy and Slovenia, on the east by Hungary, on the north-west by Germany and on the west by Switzerland and Liechtenstein. Its area is 32,367 sq. miles (83,855 sq. km), and its population is 7,897,800 (official estimate 1992). The predominant religion is Roman Catholicism.

CAPITAL – Vienna, on the Danube, population 1,539,848 (census 1991). Other larger towns are Graz (237,810), Linz (203,044), Innsbruck (118,112), Salzburg (143,978), and Klagenfurt (89,415).
CURRENCY – Schilling of 100 Groschen.
FLAG – Three equal horizontal stripes of red, white, red.
NATIONAL ANTHEM – Land der Berge, Land am Strome (Land of mountains, land on the river).
NATIONAL DAY – 26 October.

GOVERNMENT

The Republic of Austria comprises nine provinces (Vienna, Lower Austria, Upper Austria, Salzburg, Tyrol, Vorarlberg, Carinthia, Styria and Burgenland) and was established in 1918 on the break-up of the Austro-Hungarian Empire. On 13 March 1938, as a result of the *Anschluss*, Austria was incorporated into the *Deutsches Reich* under the name *Ostmark*. After the liberation of Vienna in 1945, the Republic of Austria was reconstituted within the frontiers of 1937 and a freely-elected government took office on 20 December 1945. The country was divided at this time into four zones occupied respectively by the UK, USA, USSR and France, while Vienna was jointly occupied by the four Powers. On 15 May 1955 the Austrian State Treaty was signed in Vienna by the foreign ministers of the four Powers and of Austria. This treaty recognized the re-establishment of Austria as a sovereign, independent and democratic state, having the same frontiers as on 1 January 1938.
There is a national assembly of 183 Deputies. After the elections of 7 October 1990, the Socialists formed a coalition with the People's Party. The state of the parties in the Nationalrat (Lower House) as at July 1993 was:

Socialist Party (Social Democrat), 80
People's Party (Conservative), 60
Freedom Party (Liberal-Nationalist), 28
Green, 10
Liberal Forum, 5

In the Bundesrat (Upper House) in March 1990 the People's Party held 30 seats, the Socialist Party 29 and the Freedom Party 2.

HEAD OF STATE
President of the Republic of Austria, Dr Thomas Klestil, *took office 8 July 1992.*

CABINET *as at July 1993*

Chancellor, Dr Franz Vranitzky (SPÖ).
Vice-Chancellor, Science and Research, Dr Erhard Busek (ÖVP).
Federalism and Administrative Reform, Juergen Weiss (ÖVP).
Women's Affairs, Johanna Dohnal (SPÖ).
Foreign Affairs, Dr Alois Mock (ÖVP).
Economic Affairs, Dr Wolfgang Schüssel (ÖVP).
Employment and Social Affairs, Josef Hesoun (SPÖ).

Finance, Ferdinand Lacina (SPÖ).
Health, Consumer Protection and Sport, Dr Michael Ausserwinkler (SPÖ).
Interior, Dr Franz Löschnak (SPÖ).
Justice, Dr Nikolaus Michalek (Ind.)
Defence, Dr Werner Fasslabend (ÖVP).
Agriculture and Forestry, Dr Franz Fischler (ÖVP).
Environment, Youth and Family Affairs, Maria Rauch-Kallat (ÖVP).
Education and Arts, Dr Rudolf Scholten (SPÖ).
Public Economy and Transport, Vicktor Klima (SPÖ).
Ministers of State, Brigitte Ederer (SPÖ) (*European Questions*); Dr Peter Kostelka (SPÖ) (*Public Service*); Dr Johannes Ditz (ÖVP) (*Finance*); Dr Maria Fekter (ÖVP) (*Economic Affairs, Construction and Tourism*).

SPÖ: Socialists; ÖVP: People's Party (Conservatives).

AUSTRIAN EMBASSY
18 Belgrave Mews West, London SW1X 8HU
Tel 071-235 3731

Ambassador Extraordinary and Plenipotentiary, His Excellency Dr Walter F. Magrutsch (1987).
Deputy Ambassador, S. Wessely-Steiner.
Defence Attaché, Brig. H. Lerider.
Consul-General, G. R. Widor.
Commercial Counsellor and Trade Commissioner, G. Kernthaler.

BRITISH EMBASSY
Jaurèsgasse 12, 1030 Vienna
Tel: Vienna 713575/9

Ambassador Extraordinary and Plenipotentiary, His Excellency Terence Wood, CMG (1992).
Deputy Ambassador, Counsellor and Consul-General, J. W. Forbes-Meyler, OBE.
Defence Attaché, Lt.-Col. P. W. L. Hughes, MBE.
First Secretary (Commercial), P. J. W. LeBreton.

BRITISH CONSULAR OFFICES – There is a consular office at *Vienna*, and Honorary Consulates at *Bregenz, Graz, Innsbruck* and *Salzburg*.

BRITISH COUNCIL REPRESENTATIVE, David Handforth, Schenkenstrasse 4, 1010 Vienna.

EDUCATION

Education is free and compulsory between the ages of 6 and 15 and there are good facilities for secondary, technical and professional education. There are 12 state-maintained universities and six colleges of art with a combined registered student population of 202,821.

CULTURE

The language of Austria is German, but the rights of the Slovene- and Croat-speaking minorities in Carinthia, Styria and Burgenland are protected.

COMMUNICATIONS

Internal communications in Austria are partly restricted because of the mountainous nature of the country, although there has been an extensive programme to increase the number of motorways (*Autobahn*), many of which are tunnelled through the mountains. There is a network of 1,532 km of *Autobahn* between major cities which also links up with the West German and Italian networks. The railways in Austria (ÖBB) are state-owned and in 1991 had 5,782 km of track, 57.4 per cent of which is electrified. Of the 425 km of waterways, 350 km are navigable and there is considerable

trade through the Danube ports by both local and foreign shipping. There are six commercial airports catering for 7,444,102 passengers in 1991.

In 1991 there were 3,370,000 telephones, 677 radio and 963 television transmitters. There are four national radio and two national television channels, together with three national and twelve regional newspapers which have a combined daily circulation of 2,560,000.

DEFENCE

The total active strength of the armed forces numbers 52,000 (22,400 conscripts). In addition, there are some 200,000 reserves ready at 72 hours notice. Conscripts serve for six months and then either for an extra eight months or can choose to undertake two months refresher training over a 15-year period. Each year 66,000 reservists undergo refresher training.

The Army has an active strength of 46,000 (19,500 conscripts) with 160 main battle tanks, 460 armoured personnel carriers, 130 artillery pieces and some 700 anti-tank heavy guns. The Air Force has an active strength of 6,000 (2,400 conscripts) with 54 combat aircraft of Swedish manufacture organized into one ground attack and one air defence regiment, with additional transport, training and helicopter units.

ECONOMY

The origin of Gross Domestic Product in 1991 was as follows (Schilling billion):

Agriculture and forestry	52.5
Manufacturing and mining	509.3
Energy and water supply	48.0
Construction	138.9
Commerce, hotels, restaurants	313.6
Transport and communications	117.5
Asset management	323.5
Other services and producers	233.3
Import duties and other items	180.1

The total value of GDP in 1991 was Schilling 1,916.8 billion.

Austria is self-sufficient in agricultural production, with some 260,000 agricultural units. The arable land produces wheat, rye, barley, oats, maize, potatoes, sugar beet, turnips, and miscellaneous crops. Many varieties of fruit trees flourish and the vineyards produce excellent wine. The pastures support horses, cattle and pigs and large numbers of chickens are also produced. Timber forms a valuable source of Austria's indigenous wealth, about 45 per cent of the total land area consisting of forest areas. Coniferous species predominate (75 per cent of afforested area).

In 1991, 19,100,000 tourists visited Austria. Foreign exchange receipts from tourism were Schilling 163,000 million, a major contribution to the balance of payments.

FINANCE	1990	1991
Federal Budget (Schilling)		
Revenue	425,422m	464,773m
Expenditure	564,736m	619,554m
Gross Budget Deficit	135,359m	148,458m

TRADE

Main exports are processed goods (iron and steel, textiles, paper and cardboard products), machinery and transport equipment, other finished goods (including clothing), raw materials, chemical products and foodstuffs. Main imports are machinery and transport equipment, processed goods, chemical products, foodstuffs, fuel and energy.

	1990	1991
Imports	Schilling 556,234m	591,898m
Exports	466,067m	479,029m

Over 80 per cent of all trade is with other European countries, EC countries accounting for about 75 per cent, eastern Europe for about 11 per cent and EFTA members for 9 per cent. By far the most important trading partner is Germany, with which around 40 per cent of Austrian trade is conducted.

Trade with UK	1991	1992
Imports from UK	£766,734,000	£795,107,000
Exports to UK	916,265,000	948,894,000

AZERBAIJAN
Azarbaijchan Respublikasy

Azerbaijan has an area of 33,436 sq. miles (86,600 sq. km) and occupies the eastern part of the Caucasus region of the former Soviet Union, on the shore of the Caspian Sea. It is bordered on the south by Iran, on the west by Armenia and on the north by Georgia and Russia. The north-eastern part of the republic is taken up by the south-eastern end of the main Caucasus ridge, its south-western part by the smaller Caucasus hills, and its south-eastern corner by the spurs of the Talysh Ridge. Its central part is a depression irrigated by the River Kura and by the lower reaches of its tributary, the Araks. Azerbaijan includes the Nakhichevan Autonomous Republic, which is geographically separated from the main of Azerbaijan by Armenia and borders on Iran and Turkey, and the Nagorno-Karabakh Autonomous Province.
CLIMATE – Sheltered by the mountains from the humid west winds blowing from the Black Sea, Azerbaijan has a continental climate.
POPULATION – According to the 1992 official estimate, Azerbaijan has a population of 7,136,000, of which 83 per cent are Azerbaijanis, 6 per cent Russians and 6 per cent Armenians. There are also Kurds, Jews, Georgians and Turks.
RELIGION – The population is predominantly Shia Muslim.
LANGUAGE – Turkish in the Latin script was adopted as the official language in December 1992. Azerbaijani is a very close dialect of Turkish but was previously written in the Russian script.

CAPITAL – ΨBaku. Population 1,757,000 (1989).
CURRENCY – Manat of 100 gopik and the Rouble of 100 kopeks circulate in parallel, with the Manat, gradually replacing the Rouble since it was introduced in August 1992. The Manat has a set value of 10 Roubles.
FLAG – Three horizontal stripes of blue, red and green with a white crescent and eight-pointed star in the centre.
NATIONAL DAY – 28 March (Independence Day).

GOVERNMENT

The territory that is now Azerbaijan was fought over many times between the ninth and first centuries BC, being successively part of the Assyrian, Persian, Median and Greek empires. With the influx of Huns and Khazars in the first century BC, the Turkic Azerbaijani people evolved and formed an independent state. The country was invaded by the Arab Caliphates in the seventh century AD and under their 300-year rule Islam was introduced and became the dominant religion. In the 16th century Azerbaijan was again invaded by Persia, when it became a Persian province. The country was divided during the Russo-Persian wars of the early 19th century with the northern portion (the present-

day Azerbaijan) becoming part of the Russian Empire and the southern portion remaining Persian and subsequently Iranian.
Azerbaijan was quite heavily industrialized as part of the Russian Empire with the building of railways, commercial shipping on the Caspian Sea, and, most importantly, the oil industry. In the late 19th and early 20th centuries Baku was the most important oil-producing centre in the world. Following the Russian Revolution of 1917, a Soviet government was set up in Azerbaijan in 1918. This lasted only a few months until it was overthrown by Allied forces formed mainly of British troops from Persia. In 1920 the Allied forces withdrew and the Soviet government was restored, allowing Azerbaijan to accede to the USSR in 1922.
In January 1990, the Azerbaijani Popular Front took power from the local Communist Party and declared independence from the Soviet Union, partly as a result of the Soviet government's decision in 1989 to take control of the Nagorno-Karabakh region away from Azerbaijan and to impose direct rule upon it to stop Azeri-Armenian fighting there. Soviet troops overthrew the Popular Front regime the day after it took power and re-installed the Communist regime under President Ayaz Mutalibov. This government declared Azerbaijan's independence from the Soviet Union in August 1991 and gained UN membership for Azerbaijan on 2 March 1992. Mutalibov overwhelmingly won the presidential election held on 8 September 1991, but he was forced to resign by widespread civil unrest at his perceived pro-Moscow stance and the poor conduct of the war with Armenia. At the ensuing presidential election in June 1992 the Popular Front leader Abulfaz Elchibey was elected, pledging to withdraw from the CIS and align his country more closely with Turkey.
Azerbaijan withdrew from the CIS in October 1992 when its parliament (Supreme Soviet) rejected membership. The war with Armenia, however, continued to go badly in the winter of 1992–3, culminating in the defeat of Kelbadzher by which Armenian forces broke out of Nagorno-Karabakh and captured all Azeri territory between Armenia and Nagorno-Karabakh. The defeat, in April 1993, led to a continuing political crisis. President Elchibey declared a state of emergency but unrest with his rule grew in parliament and the military. A military rebellion against the Popular Front government broke out in June and in an attempt to placate the rebels Elchibey appointed the former Azerbaijani Communist Party General Secretary Heidar Aliyev as Chairman of the Supreme Soviet. The military rebels, however, marched to Baku virtually unopposed, forcing President Elchibey to flee and transfer the presidency to Heidar Aliyev on 18 June. The Popular Front government was overthrown and President Aliyev reached an agreement with rebel leader Col. Guseinov to have him elected Prime Minister by parliament on 30 June.
At the time of going to press the situation was still confused, with Col. Guseinov forming a government and persecuting Popular Front national and local officials. Azerbaijani forces also suffered another serious defeat by the Armenians at Agdam in July following which some 10 per cent of Azerbaijan is under Armenian control. The change of government also signals an increase in Russian and decrease in Turkish influence in the country.

President, Heidar Aliyev, *assumed office* 18 June 1993.
Prime Minister, Col. Surat Husseinov, *elected by parliament*, 30 June 1993.

BRITISH AMBASSADOR – His Excellency Thomas L. Young (resident in Moscow).

DEFENCE

The National Defence Army numbers some 35,000 personnel armed with former Soviet equipment. A navy has been formed from a share of the former Soviet Caspian Sea Flotilla and has five mine warfare vessels. In addition, paramilitary forces number some 32,000 personnel, including 20,000 Ministry of Interior militia. All forces are engaged in the war with Armenia.

Russia maintains 62,000 personnel in Azerbaijan, including three motorized rifle and one airborne division, two artillery regiments and four air force regiments with 120 aircraft.

ECONOMY

Azerbaijani industry is dominated by oil and natural gas extraction and related chemical and engineering industries centred on Baku and Sumgait and the large oil deposits in the Caspian Sea. The republic is also rich in mineral resources, with iron, copper, lead and salt. A large power station on the Araks was completed in 1969, in conjunction with Iran. Azerbaijan is also important as a cotton-growing area and a silkworm breeding area.

CULTURE

Azerbaijan was the birthplace of the prophet Zoroaster, who founded one of the first monotheistic religions in the world. The country has witnessed a succession of three religions; Zoroastrianism, Christianity and Islam.

Azerbaijani is one of the Turkic languages. In the 18th and 19th centuries Azerbaijani literature produced the poets and dramatists Vagif, Vazekhi, Zakir, Akhundov and Vezirov, who all introduced ideas of progressive Russian culture.

THE BAHAMAS
The Commonwealth of The Bahamas

The Bahama Islands are an archipelago lying in the North Atlantic Ocean between 20° 55′–25° 22′ N. latitude and 72° 35′–79° 35′ W. longitude. They extend from the coast of Florida on the north-west almost to Haiti on the south-east. The group consists of 700 islands, of which 30 are inhabited and 2,400 cays comprising an area of more than 5,832 sq. miles. The population (UN estimate 1991) is 258,000. The principal islands include: Abaco, Acklins, Andros, Berry Islands, Bimini, Cat Island, Crooked Island, Eleuthera, Exumas, Grand Bahama, Harbour Island, Inagua, Long Island, Mayaguana, New Providence (on which is located the capital, Nassau), Ragged Island, Rum Cay, San Salvador and Spanish Wells. San Salvador was the first landfall in the New World of Christopher Columbus on 12 October 1492.

CAPITAL – ΨNassau, population (Census 1990) 171,000.
CURRENCY – Bahamian dollar (B$) of 100 cents.
FLAG – Horizontal stripes of aquamarine, gold and aquamarine, with a black equilateral triangle on the hoist.
NATIONAL ANTHEM – March on, Bahamaland.
NATIONAL DAY – 10 July (Independence Day).

GOVERNMENT

The Bahamas were settled by British subjects when the islands were deserted. The ownership of The Bahamas was taken over in 1782 by the Spanish, but the Treaty of Versailles in 1783 restored them to the British. The Bahamas gained independence on 10 July 1973. The Head of State is HM Queen Elizabeth II, represented in the islands by a Governor-General. There is a Senate of 16 members and an elected House of Assembly of 49 members. A general election was held on 19 August 1992 and won by the Free National Movement, ending five successive election victories for the Progressive Liberal Party since independence. The Free National Movement won 33 seats in the House of Assembly and the Progressive Liberal Party 16 seats.

Governor-General, His Excellency Sir Clifford Darling (1992).

CABINET *as at June 1993*
Prime Minister and Minister of Finance and Planning, Hon. Hubert A. Ingraham.
Attorney-General, Minister of Justice and Foreign Affairs, Hon. Orville A. Turnquest.
Public Works and Utilities, Hon. Frank H. Watson.
Social Services, National Insurance and Housing, Hon. Janet W. Bostwick.
Labour, Human Resources and Training, Hon. Maurice E. Moore.
Health and Environment, Hon. Ivy L. Dumont.
Education and Culture, Hon. Cornelius A. Smith.
Tourism, Hon. Brent Symonette.
Agriculture and Fisheries, Hon. Tennyson R. G. Wells.
Public Safety and Immigration, Hon. Arlington G. Butler.
Youth and Personal Development and Leader of the House of Assembly, Hon. Algernon Allen.
Transport and Communication, Hon. Theresa M. Moxey.
President of the Court of Appeal, Kenneth Henry.
Chief Justice, J. C. Gonsalves-Sabola.

BAHAMAS HIGH COMMISSION
Bahamas House, 10 Chesterfield Street, London WIX 8AH
Tel 071-408 4488

High Commissioner, His Excellency Arthur A. Foulkes (1992).

BRITISH HIGH COMMISSION
PO Box N-7516, Nassau
Tel: Nassau 325-7471/2/3

High Commissioner, His Excellency Brian Attewell (1992).

ECONOMY

Tourism is the economic mainstay of The Bahamas, employing about two-thirds of the labour force. It provides about two-thirds of government revenue and about half the country's foreign exchange earnings. The second main industry is international banking and trust business. The Bahamas' absence of any direct taxation and internal stability have enabled the country to become one of the world's leading financial centres.

Agricultural production is mainly of fresh vegetables, fruit, meat and eggs for the domestic market, and crawfish, mostly for export. There are large reserves of aragonite, and reserves of limestone and salt, all of which are being commercially exploited. Freeport is the country's leading industrial centre, with a pharmaceutical and chemicals plant, an oil trans-shipment and storage terminal, and port and bunkering facilities. There are also a brewery and a rum distillery on New Providence.

FINANCE	1989p	1990p
Public revenue	B$448.1m	B$489.1m
Expenditure	561.6m	532.1m
p provisional		

TRADE

The imports are chiefly foodstuffs, manufactured articles, building materials, vehicles and machinery, chemicals and petroleum. The chief exports are rum, petroleum, hormones, salt, crawfish and aragonite.

Trade with UK	1991	1992
Imports from UK	£19,631,000	£24,532,000
Exports to UK	37,142,000	38,178,000

EDUCATION

Education is compulsory between the ages of 5 and 14. More than 59,500 students are enrolled in Ministry of Education and independent schools in New Providence and the Family Islands.

COMMUNICATIONS

The main ports are Nassau (New Providence), Freeport (Grand Bahama), Mathew Town (Inagua). International air services are operated from Abaco, Bimini, Eleuthera, Exuma, Grand Bahama and New Providence. About 50 smaller airports and landing strips facilitate services between the islands, the services being mainly provided by Bahamasair, the national carrier. There are roads on the larger islands, and roads are under construction on the smaller islands. There are no railways. Wireless and telephone services are in operation to all parts of the world.

BAHRAIN
Dawlet al-Bahrein

Bahrain consists of a group of low-lying islands situated about half-way down the Gulf, some 20 miles off the east coast of Arabia. The largest of these, Bahrain island itself, is about 30 miles long and 10 miles wide at its broadest. The capital, Manama, is situated on the north shore of this island. The second largest, Muharraq, with the town and Bahrain International Airport, is connected to Manama by a causeway 1¼ miles long. Bahrain is connected by causeway to Saudi Arabia's Eastern Province.

CLIMATE – The climate is humid all the year round, with rainfall of about 3 inches, concentrated in the mild winter months, December to March; in summer, May to October, temperatures can exceed 110°F (44°C).

POPULATION – The population (1991 UN estimate) is 516,000, of whom 68.4 per cent are Bahraini. About 40 per cent of the Bahrainis are Sunni Muslims, the remaining 60 per cent being Shias; the ruling family and many of the most prominent merchants are Sunnis.

CAPITAL – ΨManama, population (1981 Census) 108,684. In 1990, it was estimated that 32 per cent of Bahrain's population lives in Manama.

CURRENCY – Bahrain dinar (BD) of 1,000 fils.

FLAG – Red, with vertical serrated white bar next to staff.

NATIONAL DAY – 16 December.

GOVERNMENT

Bahrain has been a fully independent state since 1971. Government takes the form of a constitutional monarchy, in which traditional consultative procedures continue to play an important role. The 1973 Constitution provides for a National Assembly but this was dissolved in 1975. In December 1992 the Amir announced plans to set up a consultative council.

HEAD OF STATE

Amir, HH Shaikh Isa bin Sulman Al Khalifa, GCMG, *born* 1932; *acceded* 16 December 1961.
Crown Prince and C.-in-C., Bahrain Defence Force, HE Shaikh Hamad bin Isa Al Khalifa, KCMG.

CABINET *as at June 1993*

Prime Minister, HE Shaikh Khalifa bin Sulman Al Khalifa.
Foreign Affairs, Shaikh Mohammed bin Mubarak Al Khalifa.
Defence, Maj.-Gen. Shaikh Khalifa bin Ahmed Al Khalifa.
Justice and Islamic Affairs, Shaikh Abdullah bin Khalid Al Khalifa.
Development and Industry, and Cabinet Affairs, Yusuf Ahmad Shirawi.
Education, Dr Ali Fakhro.
Health, Jawad Salim Al-Arayyed.
Transportation, Ibrahim Mohammed Humaidan.
Interior, Shaikh Mohammed bin Khalifa Al Khalifa.
Information, Tariq Abdulrahman Al Moayed.
Labour and Social Affairs, Shaikh Khalifa bin Sulman bin Mohammed Al Khalifa.
Works, Power and Water, Majid Jawad Al-Jishi.
Housing, Shaikh Khalid bin Abdullah Al Khalifa.
Finance and National Economy, Ibrahim Abdul Karim.
Commerce and Agriculture, Habib Ahmed Kassim.
Minister of State, Legal Affairs, Dr Hussain Al-Baharna.

EMBASSY OF THE STATE OF BAHRAIN
98 Gloucester Road, London SW7 4AU
Tel 071-370 5132/3/4/5
Ambassador Extraordinary and Plenipotentiary, His Excellency Karim Ebrahim Al Shakar (1990).

BRITISH EMBASSY
21 Government Avenue, Manama 306, PO Box 114
Tel: Manama 534404
Ambassador Extraordinary and Plenipotentiary, His Excellency Hugh Tunnell (1992).

BRITISH COUNCIL REPRESENTATIVE, J. Wright, OBE, AMA Centre, PO Box 452, Manama 306.

ECONOMY

The largest sources of revenue are oil production and refining. The Bahrain field, discovered in 1932, is wholly owned by the Bahrain National Oil Co. Production in 1988 stood at about 42,000 b.p.d. The Sitra refinery derives about 70 per cent of its crude oil by submarine pipeline from Saudi Arabia. Bahrain also has a half share with Saudi Arabia in the profits of the offshore Abu Sa'afa field. A reservoir of unassociated gas has recently been developed on Bahrain island.

Heavy industry is currently limited to the Aluminium Bahrain (ALBA) smelter, producing 183,000 tonnes in 1988; the Gulf Petrochemical Industries Co. (GPIC) producing 375,000 tonnes of ammonia and 395,000 tonnes of methanol in 1988, the Gulf Aluminium Rolling Mill (GARMCO), and the Arab Shipbuilding and Repair Yard (ASRY), operating dry dock facilities up to 500,000 tons.

There are a number of small to medium-size industrial units.

The state has developed as a financial centre. Apart from commercial banks, led by the National Bank of Bahrain, the Standard Chartered Bank, the British Bank of the Middle East and the Bank of Bahrain and Kuwait, many international banks have been licensed as offshore banking units; there are also money brokers and merchant banks.

TRADE WITH UK	1991	1992
Imports from UK	£147,494,000	£167,104,000
Exports to UK	39,120,000	49,702,000

COMMUNICATIONS

Bahrain International airport is one of the main air traffic centres of the Gulf; it is the headquarters of Gulf Air, and a stopping point on routes between Europe and Australia and the Far East for other airlines. A causeway linking Bahrain to Saudi Arabia was opened in November 1986.

A world-wide telephone and telex service, by satellite and cable, is operated by Bahrain Telecommunications Company.

BANGLADESH
Ghana Praja Tantri Bangladesh

The People's Republic of Bangladesh consists of the territory which was formerly East Pakistan (the old province of East Bengal and the Sylhet district of Assam), covering an area of 55,598 sq. miles (143,998 sq. km) in the region of the Gangetic delta, and has a population (1991 Census) of 108,000,000.

The country is crossed by a network of navigable rivers, including the eastern arms of the Ganges, the Jamuna (Brahmaputra) and the Meghna, flowing into the Bay of Bengal. The climate is tropical and monsoon; hot and extremely humid during the summer, and mild and dry during the short winter. The rainfall is heavy, varying from 50 inches to 135 inches in different districts and the bulk of it falls during monsoon season from June to September.

RELIGION – The faith of 87 per cent of the population is Islam and 12 per cent Hinduism. Islam has been constitutionally declared the state religion of Bangladesh.

LANGUAGE – The state language is Bengali. Use of Bengali is compulsory in all government departments. English, however, is understood and is used widely as an unofficial second language.

CAPITAL – Dhaka, population (estimate) 6,000,000.
CURRENCY – Taka (Tk) of 100 poisha.
FLAG – Red circle on a bottle-green ground.
NATIONAL ANTHEM – Amar Sonar Bangla.
NATIONAL DAY – 26 March (Independence Day).

GOVERNMENT

Prior to becoming East Pakistan, the territory had been part of British India. It acceded to Pakistan in October 1947, which became a Republic on 23 March 1956.

By a proclamation of 26 March 1971, Bangladesh purported to secede from the central government, and a government-in-exile was set up which formally declared independence on 17 April. Bangladesh achieved its independence on 16 December 1971, following the conclusion of the Indo-Pakistan war. Pakistan and Bangladesh accorded one another mutual recognition in February 1974.

From 1975 a non-political administration ran the country under martial law. A presidential election was held in June 1978 and President Zia was elected. Martial law was subsequently lifted. Zia was assassinated in May 1981 in an unsuccessful coup. He was replaced by Justice Abdus Sattar, who won a presidential election in October 1981, but was overthrown in 1982 in a coup led by the then Chief of Army Staff, Gen. Ershad. Following parliamentary elections held in May 1986, which were boycotted by several opposition parties, a civilian cabinet was appointed and Gen. Ershad

was elected as President in October 1986. Further elections, again boycotted by the opposition, were held in March 1988. Popular unrest forced Gen. Ershad's resignation in December 1990. A caretaker government was formed and parliamentary elections were held in February 1991. The Bangladesh Nationalist Party (BNP) won the largest number of seats but failed to gain a majority. After gaining support from Islamic deputies, the BNP leader, Begum Khaleda Zia, was sworn in as Prime Minister on 21 March 1991.

On 7 August 1991, Parliament approved a constitutional amendment reverting Bangladesh to parliamentary rule after 16 years of presidential government. Under the new system, the parliament elected Abdur Rahman Biswas as President.

HEAD OF STATE
President, Abdur Rahman Biswas, *sworn in* 9 October 1991.

CABINET *as at June 1993*
Prime Minister, Defence, Establishment, Cabinet Division and Primary Education, Begum Khaleda Zia.
Law, Justice and Parliamentary Affairs, Mirza Golam Hafiz.
Education, Zamiruddin Sircar.
Agriculture, Irrigation, Flood Control and Water Resources, Maj.-Gen. Majedul Haque (retd.).
Foreign Affairs, A. S. M. Mustafizur Rahman.
Finance, Saifur Rahman.
Local Government, Rural Development and Co-operatives, Abdus Salam Talukder.
Communication, Col. Oli Ahmed (retd.).
Commerce, M. K. Anwar.
Post and Telecommunications, M. Keramat Ali.
Industry, Shamsul Islam Khan.
Health and Family Welfare, Chowdhury Kamal Ibne Yusuf.
Social Welfare and Women's Affairs, Tariqul Islam.
Food, Shamsul Islam.
Information, Nazmul Huda.
Home, Abdul Matin Chowdhury.

Energy and Mineral Resources, Dr. Khandakar Mosharraf
Hossain.
Works, Rafiqul Islam Miah.
Labour and Manpower, Abdul Mannan Bhuiyan.
Environment, Forest, Fisheries and Livestock, Abdullah Al-
Noman.
Planning, A. M. Zahiruddin Knan.

BANGLADESH HIGH COMMISSION
28 Queen's Gate, London SW7 5JA
TEL 071-584 0081/2/3/4
High Commissioner, His Excellency Dr A. F. M. Yusuf
(1992).
Deputy High Commissioner, M. M. Hossain.
Defence Adviser, Brig. S. Huda.
Minister, M. M. Reza (*Economic*).

BRITISH HIGH COMMISSION
United Nations Road, Baridhara Dhaka
PO Box 6079, Dhaka-12
Tel: Dhaka 882705

High Commissioner, His Excellency Peter James Fowler
(1993).
Deputy High Commissioner, G. Finlayson.
Defence Adviser, Col. E. D. Powell-Jones, OBE.
First Secretary (Economic), P. D. Grant.

BRITISH COUNCIL REPRESENTATIVE, K. Burd, OBE,
5 Fuller Road (PO Box 161), Dhaka 1000.

EDUCATION

Primary education is free and planned to be universal by the
year 2000. There are 45,783 primary schools, mostly
managed by the Government. There are 10,575 secondary
schools and 893 colleges offering general and technical
education. There are seven universities including one for
engineering and technology, one for agriculture and another
for Islamic education and research. In 1990 the literacy rate
was estimated to be 24 per cent (31 per cent male and 16 per
cent female).

COMMUNICATIONS

Principal seaports are Chittagong and Mongla. The Bangladesh Shipping Corporation has been set up by the
Government to operate the Bangladesh merchant fleet. The
principal airports are Dhaka (Zia International) and Chittagong. The international airline, Bangladesh Biman, serves
Europe, the Middle East, South and South-East Asia, and an
internal network.
   There are about 6,880 miles of roads in Bangladesh; 4,724
miles are metalled. There are 2,798 miles of railway track.
   Radio Bangladesh is the main national broadcasting
service. A television service was introduced in 1965 and
colour transmissions began in 1980.

ECONOMY

Bangladesh is a principal producer of raw jute. Other
agricultural products are rice, tea, oil seeds, pulses and sugar
cane. The chief industries are jute, cotton, tea, leather,
pharmaceuticals, fertilizer, sugar, prawn fishing, natural gas
and garment manufacture. Remittances sent home by
Bangladeshi workers abroad have been of considerable
support to the economy in recent years.
   AID – Bangladesh is a major recipient of bilateral and
multilateral development aid. The total aid pledged for 1993
from international donors formed into a consortium led by
the World Bank is US$2,150 million.

Trade with UK	1991	1992
Imports from UK	£39,086,000	£39,355,000
Exports to UK	80,568,000	94,952,000

BARBADOS

Barbados, the most easterly of the Caribbean islands, is
situated in 13° 14′ N. latitude and 59° 37′ W. longitude. The
island has a total area of 166 sq. miles, (430 sq. km), the land
rising in a series of tablelands marked by terraces to the
highest point, Mt Hillaby (1,116 ft). It is nearly 21 miles long
by 14 miles broad. The climate is equable with annual average
temperature 26.6°C (79.8°F) and rainfall varying from a
yearly average of 75 inches in the high central district to
50 inches in some of the low-lying coastal areas.
   POPULATION – The population of Barbados (1991 UN
estimate) was 255,000. There are eleven administrative areas
(parishes): St Michael, Christ Church, St Andrews, St George,
St James, St John, St Joseph, St Lucy, St Peter, St Philip and
St Thomas.

CAPITAL – ΨBridgetown (population, estimated April
1980, 7,466) in the parish of St Michael. There are three
other towns, Oistins in Christ Church, Holetown in St
James and Speightstown in St Peter.
CURRENCY – Barbados dollar (BD$) of 100 cents.
FLAG – Three vertical stripes, dark blue, gold and dark blue,
with a trident head on gold stripe.
NATIONAL ANTHEM – In Plenty and in Time of Need.
NATIONAL DAY – 30 November (Independence Day).

GOVERNMENT

The first inhabitants of Barbados were Arawak Indians but
the island was uninhabited when first settled by the British
in 1627. It was a Crown Colony from 1652 until it became an
independent state within the Commonwealth on 30 November 1966. The legislature consists of the Governor-General,
a Senate and a House of Assembly. The Senate comprises 21
Senators appointed by the Governor-General, of whom 12
are appointed on the advice of the Prime Minister, two on
the advice of the Leader of the Opposition and seven by the
Governor-General at his/her discretion to represent religious,
economic or social interests in the Island or such other
interests as the Governor-General considers ought to be
represented. The House of Assembly comprises 28 members
elected every five years by adult suffrage. The last General
Election took place on 22 January 1991 and seats in the
House of Assembly were distributed as follows: Democratic
Labour Party 18, Barbados Labour Party 10.

Governor-General, Dame Nita Barrow, GCMG, DA (1990).

CABINET *as at June 1993*

Prime Minister, Minister of Finance and Economic Affairs,
   Civil Service, Rt. Hon. L. Erskine Sandiford.
Deputy Prime Minister, Leader of the House of Assembly,
   Minister of International Transport, Telecommunications
   and Immigration, Transport and Works, Hon. Philip M.
   Greaves, QC.
Minister of State, Prime Minister's Office, Leader of the
   Senate, Sen. Hon. L. V. Harcour Lewis.
Attorney-General and Minister of Foreign Affairs, Hon.
   Maurice A. King, QC.
Health, Hon. Brandford M. Taitt.
Housing and Lands, Community Development and Culture,
   Hon. E. Evelyn Greaves.

Minister of State, Ministry of Finance and Economic Affairs,
Hon. David Thompson.
Labour, Consumer Affairs and the Environment, Hon. Carl
D. Clarke.
Tourism and Sports, Hon. Wesley W. Hall.
Justice and Public Safety, Hon. Keith Simmons.
Education, Hon. Cyril V. Walker.
Agriculture, Food and Fisheries, Hon. David Bowen.
Trade, Industry and Commerce, Hon. Warwick O. Franklin.

BARBADOS HIGH COMMISSION
1 Great Russell Street, London WCIB 3JY
TEL 071-631 4975
High Commissioner, His Excellency the Rt. Hon. Sir William
Douglas, KCMG (1991).
Deputy Ambassador, O. O. Eversley, OBE.
First Secretary, W. Gooding.

BRITISH HIGH COMMISSION
Lower Collymore Rock, PO Box 676, Bridgetown
Tel: Bridgetown 436 6694
High Commissioner, His Excellency Emrys Thomas Davies,
CMG (1991).
Deputy High Commissioner, J. A. Noakes.
Defence Adviser, Capt. R. F. Shercliff, RN.
First Secretary (Chancery), A. Ffrench Blake, OBE.

JUDICATURE

There is a Supreme Court of Judicature consisting of a High
Court and a Court of Appeal. In certain cases a further appeal
lies to the Judicial Committee of the Privy Council. The
Chief Justice and Puisne Judges are appointed by the
Governor-General on the recommendation of the Prime
Minister and after consultation with the Leader of the
Opposition.

Chief Justice, The Hon. Sir Denys Williams, KCMG.

EDUCATION

Primary and secondary education is free in government
schools. There are 105 primary schools, 21 government
secondary schools and 15 approved government secondary
schools.

COMMUNICATIONS

Barbados has some 965 miles of roads, of which about 917
miles are asphalted. The Grantley Adams International
airport is situated at Seawell, 12 miles from Bridgetown, and
frequent scheduled services connect Barbados with the major
world air routes. Bridgetown, the only port of entry, has a
deep-water harbour with berths for eight ships, but oil is
pumped ashore at Spring Gardens and at an Esso installation
on the West Coast. Barbados has a colour television service,
three radio broadcasting services, and a wired broadcasting
service.

ECONOMY

The economy of the island is based on tourism, sugar and
light manufacturing. In 1990, 432,092 tourists visited
Barbados and 362,611 cruise ship passengers. Chief exports
are sugar and its by-products, chemicals, electronic components and clothing.

FINANCE	1992-3*
Current revenue	BD$1,077,900,000
Current expenditure	1,248,800,000
Deficit	170,500,000
* estimated.	

TRADE WITH UK	1991	1992
Imports from UK	£33,454,000	£21,027,000
Exports to UK	13,316,000	22,306,000

BELARUS
Respublika Belarus

Belarus (formerly Byelorussia) has an area of 80,300 sq.
miles (207,600 sq. km) and is situated in the western part of
the European area of the former USSR. It is bordered on the
north by Latvia and Lithuania, on the east by Russia, on
the south by the Ukraine and on the west by Poland. The
republic is largely a plain with many lakes, swamps and
marshy areas. The main rivers are the upper reaches of the
Dnieper, of the Niemen and of the Western Dvina. The
republic is divided into six provinces (Brest, Gomel, Grodno,
Minsk, Mogilev and Vitebsk).
CLIMATE - Continental with mild, humid winters and
relatively cool and rainy summers. The autumns are damp
and springs sunny. The climate is changeable due to the
occasional influence of Atlantic sea air.
POPULATION - According to the 1990 official estimate,
Belarus has a population of 10,260,000, of which 78 per cent
are Belorussians, 13 per cent Russians, 4 per cent Poles and
3 per cent Ukrainians, with smaller numbers of Jews and
Lithuanians.
RELIGION - Most of the population are Roman Catholics,
with a large minority of Russian Orthodox.
LANGUAGE - Belorussian is one of the Slavonic family of
languages, more specifically part of the eastern group which
includes Russian and Ukrainian. The alphabet is the same as
Russian.

CAPITAL - Minsk. Population 1,589,000 (1989). The city is
the administrative centre of the CIS. Other important
cities are Gomel, Vitebsk, Brest and Grodno.
CURRENCY - Rouble of 100 kopeks. Special currency
coupons, the zaichiki, were introduced in November 1992
to run alongside the rouble.
FLAG - Three horizontal stripes of white, red, white.
NATIONAL ANTHEM - The former Soviet national anthem
but with the words omitted.
NATIONAL DAY - 27 July (Independence Day).

GOVERNMENT

In the early ninth century AD the Kievan Rus state was a
unified state encompassing all the Russian, Ukrainian and
Belorussian populations. After being absorbed into Lithuania
in the 13th and 14th centuries, the Belarussian nationality,
language and culture flourished until it came under Polish
rule in the mid-16th century. Two hundred years of Polish
rule followed until Belarus was re-absorbed into the Russian
Empire.
   Much of Belarus was under German control at the time of
the Russian revolution and it was not until German forces
withdrew that a Byelorussian Soviet Socialist Republic was
declared on 1 January 1919. Western Belarus was ceded to
Poland after the Soviet defeat in the Polish-Soviet war of
1919-20, and was not recovered until Soviet forces occupied
the area under the 1939 Nazi-Soviet Pact. Belarus was
devastated by the German invasion in the Second World
War with 200 towns, 9,000 villages and 75 per cent of
industry destroyed. Resistance to the Nazi occupation was
strong, with 25 per cent of the population killed and hundreds
of thousands deported. Virtually all of Belarus had to be
rebuilt after the war.

Belarus issued a Declaration of State Sovereignty on 27 July 1990 and then declared its independence from the Soviet Union after the failed coup in Moscow in August 1991. As the former Soviet republic of Byelorussia it was a founding member of the UN along with the USSR and the Ukraine. Its independence from the USSR was recognized by the EC and USA in January 1992.

After the failed Moscow coup, the Belorussian leader Nikolai Dementei was ousted because of his involvement with the coup leaders. He was replaced by Stanislav Shushkevich at the head of an informal coalition of Communists and democrats. Belarus was one of the three CIS founding members.

Political control of both the government and parliament remains in the hands of former Communists who have retained their positions throughout 1992 and 1993. This has led to minimal economic and political reform although opposition groups are not persecuted. The economy remains mainly centrally planned and tied to trade with Russia and other former Soviet republics, so the government has been keen to strengthen CIS economic and trade agreements.

Parliament consists of the unicameral Supreme Soviet of 360 seats, of which 272 were elected and 88 reserved for official organizations at the last elections in March 1990. The next legislative elections are due in March 1994.

HEAD OF STATE
Chairman of the Supreme Soviet, Stanislav Shushkevich, elected September 1991.

COUNCIL OF MINISTERS *as at May 1993*
Prime Minister, Chairman of the Council of Ministers, Vyacheslav Kebich.
First Deputy Prime Minister, Mikhail Myasnikovich.
Deputy Prime Ministers, Alexander Bokach; Stanislav Bril; Mikhail Demchuk; Ivan Kenik; Nikolai Kostikov; Sergei Ling.
Interior, Vladimir Yegorov.
Information, Anatoly Butevich.
Foreign Affairs, Pyotr Kravchenko.
Culture, Yevgeny Voitovich.
Education, Victor Gaisenok.
Defence, Pavel Kozlovsky.
Agriculture and Foodstuffs, Fyodor Mirochinsky.
Trade, Valentin Baidak.
Transport and Communications, Stepan Shkapich.
Finance, Stepan Yanchuk.
Justice, Leonid Dashuk.
Public Health, Vasily Kazakov.
Light Industry, Nikolai Gulev.
Construction, Nikolai Novitsky.
Secretary of Council of Ministers, Nikolai Kavko.

BRITISH AMBASSADOR, (resident in Moscow).

DEFENCE

Belarus has on its territory, under CIS control, 54 SS-25 Intercontinental Ballistic Missiles which it is obliged to return to Russia for destruction under the terms of the START 1 Treaty which it ratified in February 1993 along with the Nuclear Non-Proliferation Treaty.

The total active armed forces number some 125,000 personnel (which is being reduced to 90,000) with a term of conscription of 18 months. The Army has 95,000 personnel organized into 11 divisions (six tank, three motorized rifle, one airborne, one artillery) and 23 brigades (nine artillery, five surface-to-air missile, five surface-to-surface missile, two anti-tank, one airborne and one special forces). Equipment includes 1,850 main battle tanks, 3,860 armoured infantry fighting vehicles and armoured personnel carriers, 1,750

artillery pieces and 80 attack helicopters. The Air Force has 35,000 personnel (including 10,000 Air Defence) with 665 combat aircraft organized into six ground attack, four air defence, three bomber, two reconnaisance and one helicopter regiment.

ECONOMY

The collapse of the Soviet centrally planned economic system has hit Belarussian industry badly. Belarus had many factories manufacturing products from raw materials sent from the rest of the former USSR. However, the republic cannot afford to pay market prices for the raw materials, causing factories to close.

Belarussian agriculture, based on the meat and dairy industries, is in much better shape and will cushion the republic from the worst of any food shortages, but rationing for some goods has been enforced since late 1992. The economy is still dependent on Russian fuel supplies but in 1993 found it increasingly hard to pay for the one-third of Russian fuel supplies charged at world market prices. Hence the peat industry is also being developed to make Belarus as self-sufficient as possible in fuel.

BELGIUM
Royaume de Belgique

A kingdom of western Europe, with a total area of 11,781 sq. miles (30,513 sq. km), Belgium is bounded on the north by the Netherlands, on the south by France, on the east by Germany and Luxembourg, and on the west by the North Sea.

Belgium has a frontier of 898 miles, and a seaboard of 41 miles. The Meuse and its tributary, the Sambre, divide it into two distinct regions, that in the west being generally level and fertile, while the table-land of the Ardennes, in the east, has for the most part a poor soil. The polders near the coast, which are protected by dykes against floods, cover an area of 193 sq. miles. The highest hill, Signal de Botranges, rises to a height of 2,276 feet, but the mean elevation of the whole country does not exceed 526 feet. The principal rivers are the Scheldt and the Meuse.

POPULATION – The population (1989) was 9,928,000: Greater Brussels 971,000; Flanders 5,722,000; Wallonia 3,169,000, of whom 66,000 are German-speaking. The majority of Belgians are Roman Catholics.

CAPITAL – Brussels, has a population (1991) of 960,324. Other towns are ΨAntwerp, the chief port (467,875); ΨGhent (230,466); Liège (195,201); Charleroi (206,928); Bruges (117,150); ΨOstend (68,370); Malines (75,514).
CURRENCY – Belgian franc of 100 centimes (centiemen).
FLAG – Three vertical bands, black, yellow, red.
NATIONAL ANTHEM – La Brabançonne.
NATIONAL DAY – 21 July (Accession of King Leopold I, 1831).

GOVERNMENT

The kingdom formed part of the Low Countries (Netherlands) from 1815 until 14 October 1830, when a National Congress proclaimed its independence, and on 4 June 1831, Prince Leopold of Coburg was chosen hereditary king. The separation from the Netherlands and the neutrality and inviolability of Belgium were guaranteed by a Conference of the European Powers, and by the Treaty of London (19 April 1839), the famous 'scrap of paper', signed by Austria, France,

Great Britain, Prussia, The Netherlands, and Russia. On 4 August 1914 the Germans invaded Belgium, in violation of the terms of the treaty. The kingdom was again invaded by Germany on 10 May 1940. The whole kingdom eventually fell and was occupied by Nazi troops until liberated by the Allies in September 1944.

CONSTITUTION

According to the Constitution of 1831 the form of government is a constitutional representative and hereditary monarchy with a bicameral legislature, consisting of the King, the Senate and the Chamber of Deputies. The parliamentary term is four years.

Since 1968 separatist and regionalist political tension between the Dutch-speaking Flemish population and the French-speaking Walloons has grown considerably. This led to four packages of constitutional amendments in 1971, 1980, 1988 and 1993, all aimed at devolving increasing power to the regions. The 1993 constitutional amendments, which will be implemented in stages until late 1995, explicitly states that Belgium is a federal state. The package devolves many traditional powers from the national government to the community and regional governments. The national government retains competence only in the areas of foreign and defence policy, the national budget and monetary policy, social security and the judiciary, legal and penal systems. The King loses his power to dissolve parliament and the Senate loses mosts of its power, becoming a limited revising chamber secondary to the Chamber of Representatives. The Senate is reduced (in 1995) from 184 to 71 seats, of which 40 are directly elected (25 Flemish and 15 French), 21 indirectly elected (10 from Flemish Community Council, 10 from Francophone Community Council and one from Germano-phone Community Council), and 10 co-opted by the Flemish and Francophone Communities. The Chamber of Representatives is reduced (in 1995) from 212 to 150 seats and the national government is limited to 15 ministers.

The last general election was held on 24 November 1991. The results were as follows (seats):

Chamber of Deputies: CVP 39; PS 35; SP 28; PVV (Flemish Freedom and Progress Party) 26; PRL (Liberal Reform Party (Francophone)) 20; PSC 18; Vlaams Blok (Flemish Nationalist Party) 12; VU (Flemish People's Union) 10; Ecolo (Francophone Ecology Party) 10; Agalev (Flemish Environmental Party) 7; FDF (Francophone Democratic Front) 3; ROSSEM 3; National Front (FN/NF) 1.

Senate: CVP 20; PS 18; SP 14; PVV 13; PRL 9; PSC 9; VlaansBlok 5; VU 5; Ecolo 6; Agalev 5; ROSSEM 1; FDF 1. Besides these directly elected representatives the Senate also includes 51 members who are elected by the Provincial Councils and 26 who are co-opted in the proportions of the directly elected seats.

HEAD OF STATE

King of the Belgians, HM King Albert II, born 6 June 1934; succeeded 9 August 1993, after the death of his elder brother, King Baudouin, on 31 July 1993; married 2 July 1959, Donna Paola Ruffo di Calabria, and has issue Prince Philippe; Princess Astrid Josephine-Charlotte Fabrizia Elisabeth Paola Marie, b. 5 June 1962; Prince Laurent, b. 20 October 1963.

Heir Presumptive, HRH Prince Philippe Léopold Louis Marie, born 15 April 1960.

CABINET as at June 1993

Prime Minister, Jean-Luc Dehaene (CVP).
Deputy Prime Minister, Transport and Public Enterprises, Guy Coëme (PS).
Deputy Prime Minister, Foreign Affairs, Willy Claes (SP).
Deputy Prime Minister, Justice, Economic Affairs, Melchoir Wathelet (PSC).
Finance, Philippe Maystadt (PSC).
Social Affairs, B. Anselme (PS).
Scientific Policy, Jean-Maurice Dehousse (PS).
Foreign Trade and European Affairs, Robert Urbain (PS).
Small and Medium-Sized Enterprises and Agriculture, André Bourgeois (CVP).
Defence, Leo Delcroix (CVP).
Social Integration, Public Health and the Environment, Magda De Galan (PS).
Pensions, Freddy Wilcockx (SP).
Internal Affairs and the Civil Service, Louis Tobback (SP).
Employment and Equality, Miet Smet (CVP).
Budget, Mieke Offeciers-Van de Wierle (CVP).
Development Co-operation, Erik Derycke (SP).

CVP Christian Social Party (Flemish); PS Socialist Party (Francophone); SP Socialist Party (Flemish); PSC Christian Social Party (Francophone).

BELGIAN EMBASSY
103 Eaton Square, London SW1W 9AB
Tel 071-235 5422

Ambassador Extraordinary and Plenipotentiary, His Excellency Herman Dehennin (1991).
Minister-Counsellor, M. Den Doncker.
Military, Naval and Air Attaché, Capt. P. Lavaert.
First Secretary, A. Marchal.
Head of Commerce/Trade, F. V. Decavel.

BRITISH EMBASSY
rue d'Arlon 85, 1040 Brussels
Tel: Brussels 287 6211

Ambassador Extraordinary and Plenipotentiary, His Excellency John W. D. Gray, CMG (1993).
Deputy Ambassador, Counsellor and Consul-General, N. M. McCarthy, OBE.
Counsellor (Commercial/Economic), N. R. Jarrold.
Defence and Military Attaché, Col. J. M. Craster.
BRITISH CONSULAR OFFICES – There are offices at Brussels, Antwerp and Liège.
BRITISH COUNCIL REPRESENTATIVE TO BELGIUM AND LUXEMBOURG – Dr Malcolm Cooper (Cultural Attaché).
BRITISH CHAMBER OF COMMERCE FOR BELGIUM AND LUXEMBOURG (INC.), 30 rue Joseph II, 1040 Brussels.

REGIONAL GOVERNMENT

The constitutional amendment packages of 1980, 1988 and 1993 make provision for four levels of sub-national government in Belgium: Community; Regional; Provincial; and Communal.

There are four defined communities in Belgium: Flemish; Francophone; Brussels; Germanophone. Each community has its own assembly with powers and competence in the areas of language, culture, media, sport, tourism, education, social welfare and public health. The assemblies each elect their own community government. At this level, Flanders is covered by the Flemish Community Assembly; Brussels is covered by its Joint Community Commission as well as the Flemish and Francophone Community Assemblies; most of Walloonia is covered by the Francophone Community Assembly and the remainder of Walloonia in the German-speaking communities of Eupen and Malmedy is covered by the Germanophone Community Assembly.

At the regional level, Belgium is divided into the three regions of Walloonia, Brussels and Flanders. Each region has its own assembly and government with powers and competences over areas such as the environment, housing, energy, employment, transport, agriculture, regional economic policy and foreign trade. The Walloonia regional assembly will by 1995 be directly elected with 75 members, the Brussels regional assembly is already directly elected with 75 members, and the Flemish regional assembly will have 118 directly elected members and six nominated by the Flemish in Brussels.

There are nine provinces in Belgium, of which four are French-speaking and in Walloonia (Hainault, Liège, Luxembourg and Namur) and four are Dutch-speaking and in Flanders (Antwerp, East Flanders, West Flanders, Limbourg). Brabant is Dutch-speaking in the north and French-speaking in the south and is due to be divided into two new provinces by 1995. In addition, Belgium has 589 communes as the lowest level of local government.

The main consequence of the constitutional amendment packages has been the increase in political power of the regional governments at the expense of both the community and national levels. As a result of this the Francophone Community Assembly and Government is gradually losing power to the Walloon and Brussels regional governments, whilst the Flemish have amalgamated their community and regional governments to form one increasingly powerful Flanders government.

Minister-President of the Flemish Government, Luc Van den Brande (CVP).

Minister-President of the Walloon Regional Government, Guy Spitaels (PS).

An Arbitration Court was set up in 1984 to resolve conflicts between laws made by the various legislative bodies.

CULTURE

Belgium is divided between those who speak Dutch (the Flemings) and those who speak French (the Walloons). Dutch is recognized as the official language in the northern areas and French in the southern (Walloon) area and there are guarantees for the respective linguistic minorities. Brussels is officially bi-lingual. There is a small German-speaking area (Eupen and Malmedy) along the German border, east of Liège.

The literature of France and the Netherlands is supplemented by an indigenous Belgian literary activity, in both French and Dutch. Maurice Maeterlinck (1862–1949) was awarded the Nobel Prize for Literature in 1911. Emile Verhaeren (1855–1916) was a poet of international standing. Of contemporary Belgian writers, perhaps the most cele-

brated was Georges Simenon (1903–89). There are 39 daily newspapers in Belgium (23 in French, 15 in Dutch and one in German).

EDUCATION

Nursery schools provide free education for the 2½ to 6 age group. There are over 8,000 primary schools (6 to 12 years) of which approximately 5,000 are administered by the local Communities, on authority delegated to them by the state. The remainder are free institutions (predominantly Roman Catholic). There are more than 1,100 secondary schools offering a general academic education slightly over half of which are free institutions (predominantly Roman Catholic but subsidized by the state) and the remainder official institutions. The official school leaving age is 18.

DEFENCE

The total active armed forces number some 75,700 (29,200 conscripts) with 146,000 reservists who have served within the last three years. Conscripts serve for eight months. In July 1992 the government announced its intention to end conscription by 1994 and reduce the armed forces to 43,000 personnel.

The Army has a strength of 54,000 (23,300 conscripts) with 360 main battle tanks, 133 light tanks, 2,020 armoured personnel carriers and armoured infantry fighting vehicles and 375 artillery pieces. The Army is organized into one armoured and two mechanized infantry brigades, one paratroop-commando regiment and various support units.

The Navy has a strength of 4,400 (1,600 conscripts) with four frigates and 16 mine warfare vessels. The Air Force is 17,300 strong (4,300 conscripts) with 122 combat aircraft and another 74 in store. It is organized into four ground attack, two air defence, one reconnaissance, two transport and five training squadrons.

Belgium maintains an army corps of 19,000 troops in Germany as part of its NATO commitment. In Belgium there are the headquarters of NATO and SHAPE and the Western European Union Military Planning Cell, as well as 1,900 US personnel.

ECONOMY

Belgium is a manufacturing country. With no natural resources except coal, production of which has now ceased, industry is based largely on the processing for re-export of imported raw materials. Gross National Product per capita in 1990 was BFr.657,000. Principal industries are steel and metal products, chemicals and petrochemicals, textiles, glass, and foodstuffs.

FINANCE

Budget	1988	1989
Revenue	BFr.1,505,500m	BFr.1,037,000m
Expenditure	1,901,600m	1,409,600m

TRADE

External trade figures relate to Luxembourg as well as Belgium since the two countries formed an economic union in 1921.

	1989	1990
Total imports	BFr.3,883,000m	BFr.4,002,000m
Total exports	3,943,000m	3,942,000m

Trade with UK (Belgium and Luxembourg)

	1991	1992
Imports from UK	£5,870,876,000	£5,714,150,000
Exports to UK	5,472,663,000	5,741,401,000

COMMUNICATIONS

In 1983, there were 3,920 km of normal gauge railways operated by the Belgian National Railways, of which 1,763 km were electrified. The Belgian National Light Railways (SNCV) also operated 27,671 km of regular bus routes.

Ship canals include Ghent-Terneuzen (18 miles, of which half is in Belgium and half in the Netherlands) which permits the passage to Ghent of ships up to 60,000 tons; the Canal of Willebroek Rupel-Brussels (20 miles, by which ships drawing 18 ft reach Brussels from the sea; opened in 1922); and Bruges (from Zeebrugge on the North Sea to Bruges, 6½ miles). The Albert Canal (79 miles), links Liège with Antwerp; it was completed in 1939 and accommodates barges up to 1,350 tons. The modernization of the port of Antwerp is well advanced. Inland waterway approaches to Antwerp are also to be improved. The River Meuse from the Dutch to the French frontiers, the River Sambre between Namur and Monceau, the River Scheldt from Antwerp to Ghent and the Brussels-Charleroi Canal are being widened or deepened to take barges up to 1,350 tons. Most of the maritime trade of Belgium is carried in foreign shipping.

In 1986 there were 14,260 km of trunk roads of which about 1,550 km were motorways.

The Belgian national airline Sabena operates regular services between Brussels and London, and many continental centres, as well as intercontinental services world-wide.

BELIZE

Belize lies on the east coast of Central America, bounded on the north and north-west by Mexico, and on the west and south by Guatemala. The total area (including offshore islands) is about 8,867 sq. miles (22,965 sq. km.). The climate is sub-tropical, with a mean annual temperature of 20°C, but is tempered by sea breezes. There are two dry seasons, the main one from March to May and the other (the Maugre season) from August to September. The country is occasionally affected by hurricanes.

The coastal areas are mostly flat and swampy but the country rises gradually towards the interior. The northern and western districts are hilly, and in the south the Maya Mountains and the Cockscombs form the backbone of the country, reaching a height of 3,800 feet at Victoria Peak.

POPULATION – The population is 169,392 (1991 Census), of which the main racial groups are: Mestizo (Maya-Spanish), 44 per cent; Creole, 30 per cent; Maya, 11 per cent; plus a number of East Indian and Spanish descent. The races are now heavily inter-mixed. The majority of the population is Christian, about 60 per cent Catholic and most of the remainder Protestant.

CAPITAL – Belmopan (1991 Census 3,558). The largest city and the former capital is ΨBelize City (population, 1991 Census 44,087). Other towns are Corozal (7,062), San Ignacio (8,962), Dangriga (6,435), Orange Walk (10,966), Punta Gorda (3,458).

CURRENCY – Belize dollar (BZ$) of 100 cents. The Belize dollar is tied to the US dollar, BZ$2 = US$1.

FLAG – Blue ground with red band along top and bottom edges, and in centre a white disc containing the coat of arms surrounded by a green garland.

NATIONAL ANTHEM – Land of the Free.

NATIONAL DAY – 21 September (Independence Day).

GOVERNMENT

The early history of Belize is little known, although the numerous ruins in the area indicate that it was heavily populated by the Maya Indians. The first British settlement was established in 1638 but was subject to repeated attacks by the Spanish, who claimed sovereignty over the area, until the decline of Spanish power in the Americas in the 19th century. In 1862 the area was recognized by Britain as a colony and called British Honduras. On 1 June 1973 the colony was officially renamed Belize, and was granted independence on 21 September 1981. The long-standing territorial dispute with Guatemala, which had delayed independence earlier, was provisionally resolved in November 1992 when the Guatemalan Congress and Supreme Court voted to recognize Belize and establish diplomatic relations. Guatemala still retains its claim, subject to arbitration by the International Court of Justice.

The Queen is Head of State, represented in Belize by a Governor-General, who is a citizen of the country, appointed in consultation with the Prime Minister of Belize. There is a National Assembly, comprising a House of Representatives (28 members elected for five years) and a Senate (eight members appointed by the Governor-General). Executive power is vested in the Cabinet, which is responsible to the National Assembly.

Following the November 1992 Guatemalan decision to recognize Belize, the United Kingdom announced in February 1993 its decision to withdraw its Army and Royal Air Force garrison as no longer necessary to defend Belize against the Guatemalan threat. Most of the 1,800 strong garrison will be withdrawn by mid-1994 leaving only a small jungle-warfare training school.

The subsequent Guatemalan constitutional crisis and overthrow of President Serrano in May and June 1993 caused concern in Belize over the new Guatemalan government's policy towards Belize. The National Assembly was dissolved on 1 June 1993 and in the ensuing elections the People's United Party government was defeated by the United Democratic Party.

Governor-General, Her Excellency Dame Minita Elmira Gordon, GCMG, GCVO.

THE CABINET *as at July 1993*

Prime Minister and Minister of Finance and Defence, Rt. Hon. Manuel Esquivel.
Deputy PM, Attorney-General, Minister of Foreign Affairs and Economic Development, Hon. Dean Barrow.
Natural Resources, Hon. Edwardo Juan.
Agriculture, Hon. Russell Garcia.
Tourism and Environment, Hon. Henry Young.
Home Affairs, Hon. Elito Urbina.
Energy and Communications, Hon. Joseph Cayetano.
Health and Sports, Hon. Ruben Campos.
Education, Public Service and Labour, Hon. Elodio Aragon.
Housing, Urban Development, Co-operatives and Local Government, Hon. Hubert Elrington.
Trade and Industry, Hon. Salvador Fernandez.
Youth Development and Human Resources, Hon. Philip Goldson.
Works, Hon. Melvin Hulse.
Ministers of State:
Housing, Urban Development, Co-operatives, Local Government, Hon. Michael Finnegan.
Youth Development and Human Resources, Hon. Faith Babb.
Works, Hon. Wilfred Dennis Usher.

BELIZE HIGH COMMISSION
10 Harcourt House, 19A Cavendish Square, London WIM 9AD
Tel 071-499 9728
High Commissioner, His Excellency Robert Leslie (1991).

BRITISH HIGH COMMISSION
PO Box 91, Belmopan
Tel: Belmopan 22146/7
High Commissioner, His Excellency David McKilligin
(1991).

ECONOMY

About 42 per cent of the population is engaged in agriculture. Corn (maize), rice, red kidney beans, root crops and fruit are the main food crops, although main agricultural exports are sugar, bananas and citrus products. The country is more or less self-sufficient in fresh beef, pork and poultry, but processed meat and dairy products are imported. About 25 per cent of timber production (mostly mahogany) is exported, and there is a large US market for lobster, conch and scale fish. Tourism is also a valuable source of income.

FINANCE	1990–1
Revenue	BZ$215.8m
Expenditure	205.8m
Surplus	10.0m

TRADE	1988	1989
Total imports	BZ$361.9m	BZ$431.4m
Total exports	232.5m	248.1m

Trade with UK	1991	1992
Imports from UK	£14,574,000	£11,072,000
Exports to UK	20,849,000	32,157,000

EDUCATION

Education is compulsory from 5 to 14 years of age. In 1985 primary education was provided by 225 schools, most of which are government aided. Enrolment totalled 38,512. Secondary education is provided by 29 secondary and post-secondary institutions with an enrolment of 7,441. A University College of Belize has been established. The Government also offers scholarships for students to go abroad. There is an extra-mural faculty of the University of the West Indies, with a resident tutor.

COMMUNICATIONS

There is a government-operated radio service and a privately-owned radio station. However, there is no official television service in the country. An automatic telephone service operated by Belize Telecommunications Ltd covers the whole country.

The principal airport is at Belize City and various airlines operate international flights to the USA and other Central American states. The main port is also Belize City, where construction of deep water quays was recently completed. There are 1,865 miles of road, including four main highways, but there is no railway system.

BENIN
République du Benin

A republic situated in West Africa, between 2° and 3° W. and 6° and 12° N., Benin (formerly known as Dahomey) has

a short coastline of 78 miles on the Gulf of Guinea but extends northwards inland for 437 miles. It is flanked on the west by Togo, on the north by Burkina and Niger and on the east by Nigeria. It is divided into four main regions running horizontally; a narrow sandy coastal strip, a succession of inter-communicating lagoons, a clay belt and a sandy plateau in the north. It has an area of 43,484 sq. miles (122,622 sq. km), and a population of 4,889,000 (UN 1991 estimate). The official language is French. Although poor in resources, Benin is one of the most heavily populated areas in West Africa, with a high standard of education.

CAPITAL – ΨPorto Novo, population (1982 estimate) 208,258. Principal commercial town and port, ΨCotonou (487,020).
CURRENCY – Franc CFA of 100 centimes.
FLAG – Two horizontal stripes of yellow over red with a vertical green band in the hoist.
NATIONAL DAY – 30 November.

GOVERNMENT

The first treaty with France was signed by one of the kings of Abomey in 1851 but the country was not placed under French administration until 1892. Benin became an independent republic within the French Community in December 1958; full independence outside the Community was proclaimed on 1 August 1960. In October 1963 a popular revolution led to the fall of the government and the Army held power until a civilian government was formed. In subsequent years successive governments were overthrown by the military after only short terms in office until a coup d'état on 26 October 1972 brought to power a Marxist-Leninist Military Revolutionary Government, headed by Lt.-Col. Kerekou.

In response to mounting unrest, the government agreed to drop Marxism-Leninism as the official ideology in December 1989. Following a 'National Conference of Active Forces of the Nation,' the Constitution was revoked on 1 March 1990 and the country's official name was changed from the People's Republic of Benin to the Republic of Benin. The Revolutionary National Assembly (legislature) was dissolved and replaced by a High Council of the Republic (HCR). This, in conjunction with a new 15-member civilian government, is implementing a political transition programme; a new pluralistic Constitution was adopted by referendum in December 1990. Legislative and presidential elections were held in February and March 1991. Nicéphore Soglo was sworn in as the new President on 4 April 1991 and appointed a provisional government. The lack of a clear majority in the legislature for the Union for the Triumph of Democratic Renewal coalition of President Soglo has meant the government has had to rely on an unstable alliance of independents.

HEAD OF STATE
President and Head of the Armed Forces, HE Nicéphore Soglo.

CABINET *as at June 1993*
The President.
Minister of State and Secretary-General to the President,
    Desire Vieyra.
Defence, vacant.
Interior, Public Security and Territorial Administration,
    Richard Adjaho.
Foreign Affairs and Co-operation, Théodore Hollo.
Finance, Paul Dossou.
Planning and Statistics, Robert Tagnon.

Rural Development and Co-operatives, Mama Adamou N'Diaye.
Public Works and Transport, Florentin Mito-Baba.
Industry, Small and Medium Enterprises, Sylvain Ladikpo.
Energy, A. Houessou.
Information and Communications, Paulin Hountondji.
National Education, Karim Dramane.
Youth and Sports, Théophile Natta.
Civil Service, Antoine Gbegan.
Employment and Social Affairs, Véronique Attoyo.
Public Health, Véronique Lawson.
Environment, Eustache Sarré.
Parliamentary Relations, Marius Francisco.
Handicrafts and Tourism, Bernard Houégnon.
Justice, Yves Yéhouessi.
Culture, Mr Alabi.

EMBASSY OF THE REPUBLIC OF BENIN
87 Avenue Victor Hugo, 75116 Paris, France
Tel: Paris 45009840
Ambassador Extraordinary and Plenipotentiary, new appointment awaited.

HONORARY CONSULATE, 16 The Broadway, Stanmore, Middlesex HA7 4DW. Tel: 081-954 8800. *Honorary Consul*, L. Landau.

BRITISH AMBASSADOR (resident in Lagos, Nigeria).

TRADE

The principal exports are cotton, palm products, ground nuts, shea-nuts, and coffee. Small deposits of gold, iron and chrome have been found; oil production started in 1983.

Trade with UK	1991	1992
Imports from UK	£10,716,000	£16,788,000
Exports to UK	889,000	1,564,000

BHUTAN
Druk-yul

Bhutan is a small Himalayan kingdom situated between Tibet (to the north) and India (to the west, south and east). The total area is about 18,147 sq. miles (47,000 sq. km), with a mountainous northern region which is infertile and sparsely populated, a central zone of upland valleys where most of the population and cultivated land is found, and in the south the densely forested foothills of the Himalayas, which are mainly inhabited by Nepalese settlers and indigenous tribespeople. POPULATION – The population of Bhutan is estimated at 1,551,000 (UN estimate 1991), about 70 per cent of whom are Buddhists. The remainder (mostly the Nepali Bhutanese) are Hindu. The official language, for administrative and religious purposes, is Dzongkha, a variant of Tibetan, which functions as a lingua franca amongst a variety of languages and dialects. From 1990 it has been government policy to make the study of Dzongkha compulsory in schools. This measure, and edicts concerning national dress and the immigration status of many of the settlers in the south, have caused an exodus of those of Nepali descent, and there are currently almost 100,000 living in camps in Nepal. However, Nepali remains a recognized language and English remains the medium of instruction and the working language of the administration.

CAPITAL – Thimphu, population estimate (1987) 15,000.
CURRENCY – Ngultrum (Nu) of 100 chetrums. Indian currency is also legal tender.

FLAG – Saffron yellow and orange-red divided diagonally, with dragon device in centre.
NATIONAL DAY – 17 December.

GOVERNMENT

Bhutan has a 150-member National Assembly which meets twice a year. The ten-member Royal Advisory Council, nominated by the King and the National Assembly, acts as a consultative body when the National Assembly is not in session. The King is also assisted by a Council of Ministers. There are no political parties.

In 1949 a treaty was concluded with the Government of India under which the Kingdom of Bhutan agreed to be guided by the advice of the Government of India in regard to its external relations. It has its own diplomatic representatives and is a member of the UN and other international and regional organizations. It also receives from the Government of India an annual payment of Rs500,000 as compensation for portions of its territory annexed by the British Government in India in 1864.

HEAD OF STATE
King of Bhutan, HM Jigme Singye Wangchuk, *born* 11 November 1955; *succeeded his father*, July 1972; *crowned*, 2 June 1974.
Heir, Crown Prince Jigme Gesar Namgyal Wangchuk, *designated*, 31 October 1988.

COUNCIL OF MINISTERS *as at 30 June 1993*
Chairman of Council of Ministers, HM The King.
HM Representative in Ministry of Finance, HRH Ashi Sonam Chhoden Wangchuk.
HM Representative in Ministry of Agriculture, HRH Ashi Dorji W. Wangchuk.
Home Affairs, HRH Namgyel Wangchuk.
Finance, Dorji Tshering.
Foreign Affairs, Dawa Tshering.
Communications, Social Services and Tourism, Dr T. Tobgyel.
Trade and Industries, Om Pradhan.
Deputy Minister of Defence, Chief Operations Officer of Royal Bhutan Army, Maj.-Gen. Lam Dorji.
Speaker of the National Assembly, Chief Justice, Sangye Penjor.

ECONOMY

The seventh five-year Plan (1992–7) envisages a doubling of internal revenues to Nu2,000m. Economic emphasis is on the infrastructure, especially roads and telecommunications, and hydro-electric power.

The economy is based on agriculture and animal husbandry, which engage over 90 per cent of the workforce in what is largely a self-sufficient rural society. The principal food crops are rice, wheat, maize and barley. Vegetables and fruit are also produced. Bhutan is the world's largest producer of cardamom, which forms its principal export to countries other than India. Mineral resources include dolomite and small amounts of coal, which are exported to India. A modest industrial base is being developed. A distillery and cement, chemicals and food processing plants are in production; a forestry industries complex is being expanded. Tourism and postage stamps are increasingly important sources of foreign exchange.

TRADE

Over 90 per cent of foreign trade is with India. Principal exports are agricultural products, timber, cement and coal; main imports are textiles, cereals and consumer goods.

Bhutan's airline, Druk Air, flies between Paro, New Delhi and Calcutta.

Trade with UK	1991	1992
Imports from UK	£565,000	£15,505,000
Exports to UK	231,000	237,000

BOLIVIA
República de Bolivia

Bolivia extends between 10° and 23° S. latitude and 57° 30′ and 69° 45′ W. longitude. It has an area estimated at 424,165 sq. miles (1,098,581 sq. km), with a population (1992 Census) of 6,440,000. Bolivia is without a coastline, having been deprived of the ports of Tocopilla, Cobija, Mejillones and Antofagasta by the Pacific War of 1879–84. The country derives its name from its liberator, Simon Bolivar (1783–1830).

The chief topographical feature is the great central plateau (65,000 sq. miles) over 500 miles in length, at an average altitude of 12,500 feet above sea level, between the two great chains of the Andes, which traverse the country from south to north. The total length of the navigable rivers is about 12,000 miles, the principal rivers being the Itenez, Beni, Mamore and Madre de Dios.

LANGUAGE – The official language of the country is Spanish, but many of the Indian inhabitants (about two-thirds of the population) speak Quechua or Aymará, the two linguistic groups being more or less equal in numbers.

RELIGION – The Roman Catholic religion was disestablished in 1961.

CAPITAL – La Paz (population, 1,115,000). Other large centres are Cochabamba (512,000), Oruro (183,000), Santa Cruz (694,000), Potosí (112,000), Sucre, the legal capital and seat of the judiciary (131,000) and Tarija (90,000).

CURRENCY – Boliviano ($b) of 100 centavos.

FLAG – Three horizontal bands; red, yellow, green.

NATIONAL ANTHEM – Bolivianos, El Hado Propicio (Oh Bolivia, our long-felt desires).

NATIONAL DAY – 6 August (Independence Day).

GOVERNMENT

Bolivia won its independence from Spain in 1825 after a war led by Simon Bolivar. From 1964 to 1982 Bolivia was ruled by military juntas until civilian rule was restored. The Constitution provides for a directly elected executive President who appoints the Cabinet. The legislature (Congress) consists of a 27-member Senate and a 130-member Chamber of Deputies. Both the President and Congress are elected for four-year terms.

Congressional and presidential elections were held in June 1993 with Gonzalo Sánchez of the opposition National Revolutionary Movement (MNR) winning the largest share of the vote in the presidential election but as no candidate won more than 50 per cent, the new President was chosen by Congressional vote in August, when Gonzalo Sánchez was elected. The MNR emerged as the largest party in Congress, and at the time of going to press the new President was forming a government.

HEAD OF STATE
President of the Republic, Gonzalo Sánchez de Lozada, *inaugurated* 5 August 1993.
Vice President, Victor Hugo Cardenas.

BOLIVIAN EMBASSY
106 Eaton Square, London SW1W 9AD
Tel 071-235 2257/4248
Ambassador Extraordinary and Plenipotentiary, His Excellency Maj.-Gen. Gary Prado (1990).

BRITISH EMBASSY
Avenida Arce 2732–2754, (Casilla 694) La Paz
Tel: La Paz 357424
Ambassador Extraordinary and Plenipotentiary, His Excellency Richard Michael Jackson, CVO (1991).
Deputy Ambassador, Consul and First Secretary (Commercial), I. Davies.

There is an Honorary Consulate at *Santa Cruz*.

EDUCATION

Elementary education is compulsory and free and there are secondary schools in urban centres. Provision is also made for higher education; in addition to St Francisco Xavier's University at Sucre, founded in 1624, there are seven other universities, the largest being the University of San Andres at La Paz, and ten private universities.

DEFENCE

Bolivia has a total active armed forces of some 31,500 personnel (19,000 conscripts). Conscription is selective and lasts for 12 months.

The Army is 23,000 strong (15,000 conscripts) with 36 light tanks, 122 armoured personnel carriers and reconnaissance vehicles and 110 artillery pieces. Although Bolivia is landlocked, it operates a Navy of 4,500 on Lake Titicaca and its many rivers. It has some 10 patrol craft and six battalions of marines numbering 2,000 troops. The Air Force has a strength of 4,000 personnel (2,000 conscripts) with 50 combat aircraft and 10 armed helicopters organized into one air defence, two counter-insurgency, one survey and three transport squadrons. In addition, there are some 15,000 paramilitary National Police personnel.

ECONOMY

Mining, natural gas, petroleum and agriculture are the principal industries. The ancient silver mines of Potosí are now worked chiefly for tin, but gold, partly dug and partly washed, is obtained on the Eastern Cordillera of the Andes. The tin output, together with other minerals (copper, antimony, lead, zinc, asbestos, wolfram, bismuth salt and sulphur), provides over one-third of Bolivia's exports.

Small quantities of oil are produced for internal consumption, and gas (currently providing about a quarter of Bolivia's export income) is piped to Argentina; there are plans to build a pipeline into São Paulo, Brazil. Bolivia's agricultural produce consists chiefly of rice, barley, oats, wheat, sugar-cane, maize, cotton, indigo, rubber, cacao, potatoes, cinchona bark, medicinal herbs, brazil nuts etc.

The economy deteriorated badly in the late 1970s and early 1980s, with disappointing petroleum reserves, a large external debt, and the collapse of world tin prices in 1985. In the mid-1980s radical free market economic reforms were introduced by the government with privatization of most state-owned firms and the encouragement of foreign investment. Tin prices began to increase once more from April 1989, but most of the tin industry remains uneconomic or has closed down. Many workers took to growing coca which has now become a significant export.

The peso was replaced in January 1987 with the Boliviano of 1,000,000 old pesos in a successful effort to stem hyperinflation which brought the inflation rate down to 9 per cent in 1993. The economy and currency have stabilized and the foreign debt is being repaid. Gross Domestic Product in 1992 was US$5,994 m.

TRADE

Mineral exports represent about 35 per cent of total trade. Bolivia has now developed its own smelters and is exporting metals. The chief imports are wheat and flour, iron and steel products, machinery, vehicles and textiles.

Trade with UK	1991	1992
Imports from UK	£5,787,000	£17,640,000
Exports to UK	9,303,000	10,404,000

COMMUNICATIONS

There are 2,200 miles of railways in operation including the lines from Corumbá to Santa Cruz (312 miles). There is direct railway communication to the sea at Antofagasta (32 hours), Arica (10 hours), and Mollendo (2 days), and also to Buenos Aires (3½ days). Communication with Peru is by road from La Paz via Copacabana and thence to the railhead at Puno.

Commercial aviation in Bolivia is conducted by the national airline, Lloyd Aereo Boliviano and Transporte Aereo Militar between the major towns, and Lloyd Aereo Boliviano and a number of foreign airlines provide international flights to the USA, South and Central America and Europe.

There are about 10,950 miles of telegraphs, and microwave telephone communications between La Paz, Santa Cruz, Cochabamba, Oruro and Sucre. Most other towns have radio/telephone communication with the main cities. There are nine principal daily newspapers.

BOSNIA-HERCEGOVINA

Bosnia-Hercegovina is bounded by Serbia, Montenegro and Croatia and has an area of 19,735 sq. miles (51,129 sq. km.). It has a population of 4.1 million, of whom some 40 per cent are Muslims, 33 per cent Serbs and 18 per cent Croats.

CAPITAL – Sarajevo, population (1981) 447,000.

FLAG – White flag bearing a blue shield with a white diagonal and six gold fleurs-de-lys.

GOVERNMENT

Results of the elections held in November and December 1990 for the 240-seat bicameral Assembly were: the (Muslim) Party of Democratic Action 86 seats, the (Serbian) Democratic Party 72, and the Croat Democratic Union 44.

In December 1990 a nine-man rotating Presidency was formed of three Muslims, three ethnic Serbs and three ethnic Croats. When war broke out the Muslim Alija Izetbegovic was President and has retained this position since. Since the outbreak of war the Presidency has been expanded to ten members by the addition of the (Muslim) army commander. The Presidency has, however, been divided between, on the one hand, the Serbs and the Croats who supported their respective sides against the central government, and the Muslims who continued to support the ideal of a unified multi-ethnic state. The three Serbs and three Croats remain Presidency members in order to try to outvote the Muslims and bring about the acceptance of peace and defeat, while the Muslims retain a multi-ethnic Presidency to reflect their wishes for a multi-ethnic state. Bosnia-Hercegovina was

recognized as an independent state by the EC and USA on 7 April 1992 and admitted to UN membership in May 1992.

President, Alija Izetbegovic.
Prime Minister, Mile Akmadzic.

While the war in Croatia (July 1991–January 1992) continued, Bosnia-Hercegovina declared its independence from Yugoslavia on 15 October 1991, and this was affirmed in a referendum on 1 March 1992. Independence was supported by the ethnic Muslims and Croats but rejected by the ethnic Serbs, who formed 33 per cent of the population and wanted to form a Greater Serbia with the Serbian republic. Fighting between Muslims and Serbs broke out on 2 March 1992 and the Federal Yugoslav Army (JNA) intervened massively against the poorly-armed Muslims. By May 1992 Serbian forces had overrun the majority of the republic and Croat forces much of the rest, leaving the legitimate Bosnian Muslim government forces besieged in the capital Sarajevo, the central area of the republic, and a few other cities. By May intense international pressure forced Serbia to withdraw the JNA from Bosnia, but the JNA handed over most of its weapons to Bosnian Serb forces. At the end of May the UN imposed a total trade embargo and economic sanctions on Serbia and Montenegro, but the war in Bosnia continued throughout the summer. As evidence of 'ethnic cleansing' and Serb-run concentration camps emerged in August 1992, the UN first of all authorized the use of troops to keep Sarajevo airport open for relief flights, and then forced all the warring participants to attend a peace conference in London at the end of August.

THE WAR

At the time of the August 1992 London Conference the situation was that 70 per cent of the territory of Bosnia was controlled by Bosnian Serb forces, who had declared their own Bosnian Serb republic under the leadership of Dr Radovan Karadzic. A further 20 per cent of the territory of Bosnia was controlled by Croat forces who had announced an independent Croat republic in western Hercegovina. The mainly Muslim forces of the Bosnian government were in an uneasy alliance with Croatian and Bosnian Croat forces, who were trying to cut Serbian supply lines to Serb enclaves in Croatia. Because of Serbian 'ethnic cleansing' of Muslim-populated areas, thousands of Muslims had died and hundreds of thousands of refugees fled to Croatia and the rest of Europe.

The London Conference was initially judged a success when the leaderships of the rump Yugoslavia, Serbia, Croatia, Bosnia-Hercegovina, the Bosnian Serbs and Croats all signed an 11-point declaration of intent to end the war in Bosnia. The agreement included respect for international law, human rights, national minorities and Bosnia's international boundaries, together with the illegality of land gains by military force. However, the signatures soon proved worthless as it became clear that the Bosnian Serbs would not give up the land that they had gained and that the Muslims would not settle for peace without winning back land.

Late 1992 saw fierce fighting in eastern Bosnia between Muslim and Bosnian Serb forces as the Serbs attempted to starve and defeat Muslim enclaves holding out in the east, and to reduce the Muslim-held central area to isolate Sarajevo and prevent attacks from the central area on the vital Serb northern corridor. As winter closed in, the United Nations and Western nations intervened to secure humanitarian aid supplies through the deployment of Canadian and European troops in October and November. These added to the aid airlifts into besieged Sarajevo begun in July. Meanwhile, the joint EC-UN peace negotiating team led by Lord Owen and Cyrus Vance engaged in negotiations with the Bosnian

(Muslim), Serb and Croat leaderships, amid calls in the West for military intervention against Bosnian Serb forces.

In January 1993 Lord Owen and Cyrus Vance announced the EC-UN peace plan for Bosnia-Hercegovina (known as the Owen-Vance plan) and reconvened the Peace Conference in Geneva. The plan was composed of three parts: a set of constitutional principles; a means to, and timetable for the end of hostilities; and a map delineating ten autonomous provinces, of which three were Serb, three Croat, three Muslim and one mixed (Sarajevo). At the Peace Conference the Bosnian Croats accepted all three parts of the plan, the Muslims accepted only the constitutional principles, and the Serbs none of the three. Over the four months to the end of May, Lord Owen and Cyrus Vance (replaced on 1 May by Thorvald Stoltenberg) attempted to persuade all the three sides to sign the peace plan or face western diplomatic and military action. Serbia was pressurized to use its influence on the Bosnian Serbs to end fighting and sign the agreement. UN economic sanctions on the rump Yugoslav state imposed in May 1992 and the naval blockade imposed in November 1992 were reinforced by full trade and diplomatic isolation, imposed in April 1993.

However, fighting continued, with Bosnian Serb forces renewing their attacks on the Muslim enclaves in eastern Bosnia and heavy fighting between Croats and Muslims in central Bosnia and Mostar. The Vance-Owen plan was blamed for increased ethnic cleansing as each side forced others from the provinces delineated as theirs by the Vance-Owen map. As Bosnian Serb forces starved and shelled the Muslim enclaves in the east, the pressure on Western governments to intervene grew. In February, US Air Force planes began dropping supplies to the beleaguered enclaves; in April the UN evacuated and demilitarized Srebrenica; and in early May it declared the Muslim enclaves of Srebrenica and Zepa, Goradze and Foca, Tuzla, Bihac and Sarajevo UN 'safe areas', which moderated Serb attacks. The Muslims, meanwhile, began to gain the upper hand over the Croats in central Bosnia, taking Zenica and Travnik.

May 1993 was a major turning point in the war. After the Muslim leadership had signed all parts of the Vance-Owen plan in late March, only the Bosnian Serbs remained to sign. Under intense international and Serbian pressure, the Bosnian Serb leader Radovan Karadzic attended the emergency peace conference in Athens and on 2 May signed the peace plan, conditional on a vote of acceptance by the Bosnian Serb parliament. In defiance of the international community, the parliament rejected the plan on 5 May and the war continued. US attempts to lift the arms embargo to aid the Muslims were blocked by Western European governments. On 22 May the US, EC states and Russia agreed on the 'Joint Action Programme' (known as the Washington Agreement) which signalled the death of the Vance-Owen plan and the acceptance of the territorial gains by force of the Bosnian Serbs.

The lack of will of Western governments to intervene militarily having become clear, the war continued throughout June and July 1993. The Bosnian Serbs neutralized the remaining Muslim enclaves in eastern Bosnia before concentrating their efforts on Sarajevo. Continued Muslim successes against Bosnian Croat forces in central Bosnia led to the severing of aid supply lines to the central Muslim-held area by Croat forces and to a Serb-Croat alliance against the Muslims in some areas. Meanwhile, the peace negotiations re-opened in Geneva on the new basis of Bosnia becoming three virtually independant states based on the territory that each group held by force. As the Bosnian (Muslim) government continued to refuse to accept this basis for a peace agreement, the Bosnian Serb forces relentlessly tightened the siege of Sarajevo, capturing all the strategic heights around the city and cutting all the remaining supply lines. At the time of going to press, the situation seemed finely balanced. There was the possibility of Bosnian Serb forces attempting to take Sarajevo, and the shelling of UN bases by Bosnian Serbs had prompted NATO for the first time to threaten air strikes against Serb forces around Sarajevo. The Bosnian government was under great pressure to sign a peace agreement effectively based on partition of the country.

BOTSWANA
The Republic of Botswana

Botswana (formerly the British Protectorate of Bechuanaland) lies between 18° and 26° S. latitude and 20° and 28° W. longitude and is bounded by the Cape and Transvaal Provinces of South Africa on the south and east, by Zimbabwe, the rivers Zambezi and Chobe (Linyanti) on the north and north-east, and by Namibia on the west. Botswana has a total area of 224,607 sq. miles (581,730 sq. km). The climate of the country is generally sub-tropical, but varies considerably with latitude and altitude.

A plateau at a height of about 4,000 feet divides Botswana into two main topographical regions. To the east of the plateau streams flow into the Marico, Notwani and Limpopo rivers; to the west lies a flat region comprising the Kgalagadi Desert, the Okavango Swamps and the Northern State Lands area. Large areas of the country support only herds of game. Elephant numbers have been estimated at 55,000–60,000.

POPULATION – Botswana has a population (UN estimate 1991) of 1,348,000. The eight principal Botswana tribes are Bakgatla, Bakwena, Bangwaketse, Bamalete, Bamangwato, Barolong, Batawana and Batlokwa. The principal languages in use are Setswana and English.

CAPITAL – Gaborone, estimated population (1991) 137,174. Other centres are Francistown (60,000), Lobatse (25,000), and Selebi-Phikwe (46,000).

CURRENCY – Pula (P) of 100 thebe.

FLAG – Light blue with a horizontal black stripe fimbriated in white across the centre.

NATIONAL ANTHEM – Fatshe La Rona.

NATIONAL DAY – 30 September.

GOVERNMENT

On 30 September 1966, Bechuanaland became a republic within the Commonwealth under the name Botswana. The President of Botswana is Head of State and appoints as Vice President a member of the National Assembly who is his principal assistant and leader of Government business in the National Assembly. The Assembly consists of the President, 34 members elected on a basis of universal adult suffrage, four specially elected members, the Attorney-General (non-voting) and the Speaker. Presidential and legislative elections are held every five years. There is also a 15-member House of Chiefs.

HEAD OF STATE
President, His Excellency Dr Q. K. J. Masire, *sworn in* 10 October 1989 for a second five-year term.

CABINET *as at June 1993*
Vice President, Finance and Development Planning, Festus Mogae.
Presidential Affairs, Public Administration, Lt.-Gen. Mompati Merafhe.
Local Government, Lands and Housing, Chapson Butale.

External Affairs, Dr Gaositwe Chiepe.
Mineral Resources and Water, Archibald Mogwe.
Commerce and Industry, Ponatshego Kedikilwe.
Agriculture, Kebatlamang Morake.
Works and Communications, David Magang.
Health, Bahiti Temane.
Education, Ray Molomo.
Home Affairs, Patrick Balopi.
Assistant Ministers: Finance, E. Setlhomo Asisi; *Local Government and Lands,* M. Mokgothu, Geoffrey Oteng; *Agriculture,* Roy Blackbeard.

BOTSWANA HIGH COMMISSION
6 Stratford Place, London WIN 9AE
TEL 071-499 0031
High Commissioner, His Excellency Alfred Uyapo Majaye Dube (1993).

BRITISH HIGH COMMISSION
Private Bag 0023, Gaborone
Tel: Gaborone 352841
High Commissioner, His Excellency John Edwards, CMG (1992).

BRITISH COUNCIL REPRESENTATIVE, T. A. Jones, MBE (*Cultural Attaché*).

ECONOMY

Botswana is predominantly a pastoral country. The national herd is normally around 3 million cattle and 1 million sheep and goats but recent drought conditions have reduced the number of cattle to around 2.5 million.

Cattle rearing accounts for about 85 per cent of agricultural output and livestock products, particularly beef, are a major source of foreign exchange earnings. The Government has a number of programmes to improve land use and cattle and crop production, and schemes to provide financial assistance for farmers.

Mineral extraction and processing is now the major source of income for the country following the opening of large mines for diamonds and copper-nickel. Botswana is one of the largest producers of diamonds in the world. Large deposits of coal have been discovered and are being mined on a small scale. Much of the country has yet to be fully prospected. Manufacturing industry is growing and will continue to do so as communications improve but it is still a small sector of the economy.

FINANCE	1990–1	1991–2e
Revenue	P3,318m	P3,183m
Expenditure	2,899m	3,318m

e estimate

TRADE

Principal exports are diamonds, copper-nickel matte, and beef and beef products.

	1989p	1990
Imports	P2,136m	P3,483m
Exports	3,613m	3,262m

p preliminary

Trade with UK	1991	1992
Imports from UK	£35,233,000	£19,999,000
Exports to UK	22,662,000	27,446,000

EDUCATION

There are over 654 primary schools (enrolment approx. 308,840), 146 community junior secondary schools (enrol-

ment approx. 48,624) and 23 government and government-aided senior secondary schools (enrolment 19,308). There are four teacher training establishments (total enrolment 1,365), two colleges of education (enrolment 340), one polytechnic with 558 students and the University of Botswana with 2,862 undergraduates. Further expansion of the technical education system is planned via a network of vocational training centres.

COMMUNICATIONS

The railway from Cape Town to Zimbabwe passes through eastern Botswana. The main roads in the country are the north–south road, which closely follows the railway, and the road running east–west that links Francistown and Maun. A new road from Nata to Kazungula provides a direct link to Zambia from Botswana. Air services are provided on a scheduled basis between the main towns.

BRAZIL
República Federativa do Brasil

Brazil, discovered in 1500 by Portuguese navigator Pedro Alvares Cabral, is bounded on the north by the Atlantic Ocean, the Guianas, Colombia and Venezuela; on the west by Peru, Bolivia, Paraguay, and Argentina; on the south by Uruguay, and on the east by the Atlantic Ocean. Brazil extends between 5° 16′ N. and 33° 45′ S. latitude and 34° 45′ and 73° 59′22″ W. longitude. The country has an area of 3,286,488 sq. miles (8,511,965 sq. km), with a population (official estimate 1990) of 150,368,000.

The northern states of Amazonas and Pará are mainly wide, low-lying, forest-clad plains. The central states of Mato Grosso are principally plateau land and the eastern and southern states are traversed by successive mountain ranges interspersed with fertile valleys. The principal ranges are Serra do Mar, the Serra da Mantiqueira and the Serra do Espinhaco along the east coast.

The River Amazon has a total length of some 4,000 miles has tributaries which are themselves great rivers, and flows from the Peruvian Andes to the Atlantic. Its principal northern tributaries are the Rio Branco, Rio Negro, and Japurá; its southern tributaries are the Juruá, Purus, Madeira and Tapajós, while the Xingú meets it within 200 miles of its outflow into the Atlantic. The Tocantins and Araguaia flow northwards from Mato Grosso and Goiás to the Gulf of Pará. The Parnaiba flows from Piaui into the Atlantic. The São Francisco rises in the South of Minas Gerais and flows to the eastern coast. The Paraguai, rising in the south-west of Mato Grosso, flows through Paraguay to its confluence with the Paraná, which rises in the mountains of that name and divides Brazil from Paraguay.

CAPITAL – Brasilia (inaugurated on 21 April 1960).
Population (1990 estimate) 1,803,478. Other important centres are São Paulo (10,063,110); the former capital ΨRio de Janeiro (6,603,388); Belo Horizonte (2,114,429); ΨRecife (1,287,623); ΨSalvador (1,804,438); ΨPorto Alegre (1,272,121); ΨFortaleza (1,582,414); and Belem (1,116,578).
CURRENCY – Cruzeiro (BRC) of 100 centavos.
FLAG – Green with a yellow lozenge containing a blue sphere studded with white stars, and crossed by a white band with the motto *Ordem e Progresso.*
NATIONAL ANTHEM – Ouviram do Ipirangas Margens Placidas (From peaceful Ypiranga's banks).
NATIONAL DAY – 7 September (Independence Day).

GOVERNMENT

Brazil was colonized by Portugal in the early part of the 16th century, and in 1822 became an independent empire under Dom Pedro, son of the refugee King Joao VI of Portugal. On 15 November 1889, Dom Pedro II, second of the line, was dethroned and a republic was proclaimed.

The Federative Republic of Brazil is made up of the federal district and 26 states.

In 1985 Brazil returned to democratic rule after two decades of military government. The constitution of October 1988 draws on the same conceptual basis as that of the United States, and envisages an equal distribution of power between the executive, the legislature and the judiciary. Under the existing constitutional provisions the President, who heads the executive, is directly elected for a five-year term. On 24 April 1993 the electorate voted in a referendum for Brazil to remain a presidential democracy rather than a parliamentary one or a monarchy.

The Congress consists of a Senate (three senators per state elected for an eight-year term) and a Chamber of Deputies which is elected every four years. The number of deputies per state depends upon the state's population. Each state has a Governor, and a Legislative Assembly with a four-year term.

President Fernando Collor de Mello, who came to power in 1990, was suspended on 29 September 1992 by the Chamber of Deputies because of alleged corruption. He resigned on 29 December 1992 after being indicted by the Senate on 2 December 1992. The Vice-President Itamar Franco was immediately sworn in for the remainder of the five-year term.

HEAD OF STATE
President, Itamar Franco, *sworn in* 29 December 1992.
Vice President, vacant.

CABINET *as at June 1993*
Justice, Mauricio Correa Lima.
Labour, Walter Barelli.
Social Action, Jutahy Magalhães.
Communications and Transport, Hugo Napoleão.
Interior, Alexandre Costa.
Mines and Energy, Paulino Cicero.
Health, Jamil Haddad.
Education, Murillo Hingel.
Army, Gen. Zenildo Gonzago Lucena.
Navy, Adm. Ivan Serpa.
Air Force, Brig. Lélio Viana Lobo.
Culture, Antonio Houaiss.
Social Welfare, Antonio Brito.
Agriculture, Nuri Andrans.
Science and Technology, José Israel Vargas.
Environment, Coutinho Jorge.
Strategic Affairs, Adm. Mario Flores.
Planning, Alexis Stepanenko.
Finance, Fernando Enrique Cardoso.
Foreign, José de Oliveira.

BRAZILIAN EMBASSY
32 Green Street, London W1Y 4AT
TEL 071-499 0877

Ambassador Extraordinary and Plenipotentiary, His Excellency Paulo-Tarso Flecha de Lima (1990).
Minister-Counsellor, F. C. de Araujo; V. C. Leão.
Defence Attachés, Capt. I. de A. Mendes (*Naval*); Col. L. R. de Mello (*Army*); Gp. Capt. J. Saito (*Air*).

There is also a Brazilian Consulate-General in *London* and honorary consular offices at *Cardiff* and *Glasgow*.

BRITISH EMBASSY
Setor de Embaixadus Sul, Quadra 801, Conjunto K, 70.408 Brasilia DF
Tel: Brasilia 225-2710

Ambassador Extraordinary and Plenipotentiary, His Excellency C. W. Heap, CMG (1993).
Deputy Ambassador, Consul-General, P. R. Jenkins.
Defence Attaché, Col. D. Farrant.
First Secretary (Economic), P. B. Yaghnourian.

There are British Consulates-General at *Rio de Janeiro* and *São Paulo*.

BRITISH COUNCIL REPRESENTATIVE, Raymond Newberry, OBE, SCR, 708/9-BLF Nos 1/3 (Caixa Postal 6104), 70.740 Brasilia DF. Regional directors in *Recife*, *Rio de Janeiro* and *São Paulo*.

BRITISH AND COMMONWEALTH CHAMBER OF COMMERCE IN SÃO PAULO, Rua Barão de Itapetininga 275, 7th Floor, 01042, São Paulo (*Postal Address*, PO Box 1621, 01000 São Paulo) and Rua Real Grandeza 99, 22281 Rio de Janeiro.

ECONOMY

There are large and valuable mineral deposits including iron ore (hematite), manganese, bauxite, beryllium, chrome, nickel, tungsten, cassiterite, lead, gold, monazite (containing rare earths and thorium) and zirconium. Diamonds and precious and semi-precious stones are also found. The mineral wealth is being exploited to an increasing extent. The iron ore deposits of Minas Gerais are exceeded by those of the Amazon region, principally in the Carajás areas where deposits are estimated at 35,000 million tonnes. Mining operations began in February 1985.

Electric power production in 1989 was 243,034 Gwh. In the same year, the total output of steel was 24,600 million tonnes and production of oil was 34.6 million cubic metres.

Agriculture production was (tonnes):

	1989
Black beans	2,327,973
Cassava	23,701,158
Cocoa	394,616
Coffee	1,412,000
Cotton	1,797,446
Maize	26,568,776
Peanuts	155,913
Potatoes	2,134,807
Rice	11,043,228
Soya	24,085,193
Tobacco	448,689
Wheat	5,295,335

FINANCE	1989	1990
Revenue	NCz$515,193m	Cr$3,146,420m
Expenditure	529,882m	3,146,420m

In 1989 Brazil's total external public debt stood at US$112,000 million.

TRADE

Principal imports are fuel and lubricants, machinery, chemicals, wheat, metals and metal manufactures. Principal exports are coffee, iron ore, soya, meat, steel and orange juice. In 1987 the Brazilian automobile industry produced 920,300 vehicles. Of these, 339,900 vehicles were exported.

	1988	1989
Total imports	US$16,055m	US$18,263m
Total exports	33,786m	34,406m

Trade with UK	1991	1992
Imports from UK	£339,442,000	£273,106,000
Exports to UK	765,102,000	885,632,000

DEFENCE

The total strength of the active armed forces is 296,000 (128,500 conscripts). Conscripts serve for 12 months and there are 400,000 reservists subject to immediate recall.

The Army has a strength of 196,000, of which 126,500 are conscripts. Equipment consists of 520 light tanks, 580 reconnaissance vehicles, 845 armoured personnel carriers, 690 artillery pieces and 46 helicopters. There are four armoured, four mechanized, twelve motorized infantry, one mountain, two jungle, one airborne and one helicopter brigades, with artillery and engineer units.

The Navy has a strength of 50,000 personnel (2,000 conscripts) including 15,000 marines with one aircraft carrier, five submarines, six destroyers, twelve frigates and 30 patrol and coastal craft, together with some 13 armed helicopters.

The Air Force is 50,700 strong and is all professional. It deploys 307 combat aircraft and eight armed helicopters organized into five commands: air defence (two squadrons); tactical (15 squadrons); maritime (four squadrons); transport (15 squadrons); training.

EDUCATION

Primary education is compulsory and is the responsibility of state governments and municipalities. At this level approximately 12 per cent attend private schools. Secondary education is largely the responsibility of state and municipal governments, although a small number of very old foundations (the Pedro II Schools) remain under direct federal control. Over 33 per cent of all pupils at this level attend private schools. Higher education is available in federal, state, municipal and private universities and faculties.

CULTURE

Portuguese is the language of the country, but Italian, Spanish, German, Japanese and Arabic are also spoken by minorities, and newspapers of considerable circulation are produced in those languages.

Public libraries have been established in urban centres and there is a flourishing national press with widely circulated daily and weekly newspapers.

COMMUNICATIONS

In 1989 there were 1,663,987 km of highways. The route-length of railways in 1987 was 29,833 km. Internal air services are highly developed. There are 21,944 miles of navigable inland waterways. Rio de Janeiro and Santos are the two leading ports.

BRUNEI

Negara Brunei Darussalam

Brunei is situated on the north-west coast of the island of Borneo, total area of 2,226 sq. miles (5,765 sq. km), population 260,863 (1991), of whom 68 per cent are of Malay, 18 per cent Chinese and 5 per cent other indigenous races. The country has a humid tropical climate.

CAPITAL – Bandar Seri Begawan, with a population of 46,229 (1991).
CURRENCY – Brunei dollar (B$) of 100 sen. It is fully interchangeable with the currency of Singapore.

FLAG – Yellow with diagonal stripes of white over black and the arms in red all over the centre.
NATIONAL ANTHEM – Ya Allah Lanjutkan Lah Usia Kebawah Duli Yang Maha Mulia (O God, long live our Majesty the Sultan).
NATIONAL DAY – 23 February.

GOVERNMENT

In 1959 the Sultan of Brunei promulgated the first written Constitution, which provides for a Privy Council, a Council of Ministers and a Legislative Council. On 1 January 1984 Brunei resumed full independence. A ministerial system of government was established at independence, the seven ministers being appointed by the Sultan and responsible to him. The Sultan presides over the Privy Council and the Council of Ministers. The Legislative Council was disbanded in February 1984.

HEAD OF STATE

Sultan, HM Sultan Haji Hassanal Bolkiah Mu'izzaddin Waddaulah, Sultan and Yang Di-Pertuan, GCB, *acceded* 1967, *crowned* 1 August 1968.

THE COUNCIL OF MINISTERS *as at June 1993*

Prime Minister, Minister of Defence, HM The Sultan.
Foreign Affairs, HRH Prince Mohammed.
Finance, HRH Prince Jefri.
Special Adviser to the Sultan and Minister for Home Affairs, Pehin Dato Haji Isa.
Education, Pehin Dato Abdul Aziz.
Law, Pengiran Bahrin.
Industry and Primary Resources, Pehin Dato Abdul Rahman.
Religious Affairs, Pehin Dato Mohammed Zain.
Development, Pengiran Dato Dr Ismail.
Culture, Youth and Sports, Pehin Dato Haji Hussein.
Health, Dato Dr Johar.
Communications, Dato Haji Zakaria.

BRUNEI DARUSSALAM HIGH COMMISSION
19–20 Belgrave Square, London SW1X 8PG
TEL 071-581 0521
High Commissioner, new appointment awaited.

BRITISH HIGH COMMISSION
Hong Kong and Shanghai Bank Building (3rd Floor), Jalan Pemancha, P.O. Box 2197 Bandar Seri Begawan
Tel: Bandar Seri Begawan 222231
High Commissioner, His Excellency Adrian Sindall, CMG (1991).

BRITISH COUNCIL REPRESENTATIVE, Susan Mathews, PO Box 3049, Bandar Seri Begawan 1930.

FINANCE		1991
Revenue		B$2,686m
Expenditure		2,760m

TRADE WITH UK	1991	1992
Imports from UK	£215,222,000	£211,384,000
Exports to UK	147,666,000	126,365,000

BULGARIA

Republika Bulgaria

Bulgaria is bounded on the north by Romania, on the west by Serbia and Macedonia, on the east by the Black Sea, and on the south by Greece and Turkey. The total area is 42,823 sq. miles (110,912 sq. km), with a UN estimated population of 8,982,000 in 1991. The largest religion of the Bulgarians is the Greek Orthodox Church.

LANGUAGE – Bulgarian is a Southern Slavonic tongue, closely allied to Serbo-Croat and Russian with local admixtures of modern Greek, Albanian and Turkish words. The alphabet is Cyrillic.

CAPITAL – Sofia, population (1991), 1,107,613, at the foot of the Vitosha mountains, the capital and commercial centre is on the main railway line to Istanbul, 338 miles from the Black Sea port of ΨVarna (307,915); ΨBourgas (190,054) is also a Black Sea port. Other important trading and industrial centres are Plovdiv (340,810), Rousse (169,658), Pleven (130,515), Stara Zagora (150,482), Sliven (106,065) and Tolbukhin (112,582).

CURRENCY – Lev of 100 stotinki.

FLAG – 3 horizontal bands, white, green, red.

NATIONAL DAY – 3 March.

HISTORY

A principality of Bulgaria was created by the Treaty of Berlin (1878) and in 1885 Eastern Roumelia was added to the newly-created principality. In 1908 the country was declared to be an independent kingdom. In 1912–13 a successful war of the Balkan League against Turkey increased the size of the kingdom, but in August 1913 a short campaign against the remaining members of the League reduced the acquired area and led to the surrender of Southern Dobrudja to Romania. In October 1915, Bulgaria entered the war on the side of the Central Powers by declaring war on Serbia. Involved in the defeats of 1918, Bulgaria made an unconditional surrender to the Allied Powers in September 1918, and in November 1919 signed the Treaty of Neuilly, which ceded to the Allies the Thracian territories (later handed over to Greece) and some territory on the western frontier to Yugoslavia.

Nazi troops entered the country on 3 March 1941, and occupied Black Sea ports. On 26 August 1944, the government declared Bulgaria to be neutral in the Russo-German war and sought terms of peace from Britain and the United States. The Soviet Union refused to recognize the so-called neutrality and called upon Bulgaria to declare war against Germany. No satisfactory reply being received, on 5 September 1944 the USSR declared war on Bulgaria. Bulgaria then asked for an armistice and on 7 September declared war on Germany, hostilities with USSR ending on 10 September. The armistice with the Allies was signed on 28 October 1944. The peace treaty with Bulgaria was signed on 22 February 1947 and came into force on 15 September 1947. It recognized the return of Southern Dobrudja to Bulgaria.

On 9 September 1944 a coup d'état gave power to the Fatherland Front, a coalition of Communists, Agrarians, Social Democrats and officers and intellectuals. In August 1945, the main body of Agrarians and Social Democrats left the Government. On 8 September 1946 a referendum was held which led to the abolition of the monarchy and the setting up of a republic.

The post-war period was dominated by the Communist Party (BCP), led by Todor Zhivkov. After he was forced to resign in November 1989, further leadership changes and reforms culminated, in January 1990, in the National Assembly voting to abolish the BCP's constitutional guarantee of power. Multi-party elections to a 400-seat Grand National Assembly (parliament) were held in June 1990. The BCP, renamed the Bulgarian Socialist Party in April, emerged as the majority party. A BSP-dominated government formed in September 1990 was brought down two months later by a combination of industrial strikes and opposition pressure. A multi-party government was formed in December 1990 which began to implement a radical programme of economic and political reform.

GOVERNMENT

A new constitution, enshrining democracy, the free market and a directly elected presidency, was adopted by the Grand National Assembly on 12 July 1991.

Parliamentary elections were held on 13 October 1991, the Union of Democratic Forces (UDF) emerging as the largest party in the new National Assembly. The UDF formed a new government under Filip Dimitrov which took office in November with the support of the ethnic Turkish Movement for Rights and Freedom Party (MRF), and declared its priorities to be the economic stabilization of the country and strong anti-inflationary policies.

Dimitrov's UDF government fell after only one year when it was defeated in a parliamentary vote of no confidence in October 1992 over charges of allowing sanctions against Serbia to be broken. After a period of instability, the President appointed as Prime Minister Lyuben Berov, who successfully formed a government in December 1992 of non-party technocrats with the support of the MRF, some of the BSP and the Alternative Social Liberal Party (UDF members expelled from the UDF for supporting the government's formation).

HEAD OF STATE

President, Zhelyu Zhelev, *elected* 1 August 1990, *re-elected* 19 January 1992.

Vice-President, Blaga Dimitrova.

COUNCIL OF MINISTERS *as at July 1993*

Prime Minister, Lyuben Berov.

Deputy Prime Minister, Trade, Valentin Karabashev.

Deputy Prime Minister, Transport, Neicho Neev.

Deputy Prime Minister, Labour and Social Welfare, Evgeni Matinchev.

Foreign Affairs, Slavi Pashovski.

Agriculture, Georgi Tanev.

Environment, Valentin Bossevski.

Finance, Stoyan Alexandrov.

Defence, Valentin Alexandrov.

Internal Affairs, Victor Michailov.

Justice, Misho Vulchev.

Industry, Roumen Bikov.

Regional Development and Construction, Hristo Totev.

Education, Science and Culture, Marin Dimitrov.

Public Health, Tancho Gougalov.

Speaker of the National Assembly, Aleksandar Yordanov.

EMBASSY OF THE REPUBLIC OF BULGARIA

186–188 Queen's Gate, London SW7 5HL

Tel 071–584 9400/9433/3144

Ambassador Extraordinary and Plenipotentiary, His Excellency Ivan Stancioff (1991).

Deputy Ambassador, Z. Radoukov.

Consul-General, B. Zaimov.

Head of Trade, I. Pavlov.

BRITISH EMBASSY

Boulevard Vassil Levski 65–67, Sofia 1000

Tel: Sofia 885361/2

Ambassador Extraordinary and Plenipotentiary, His Excellency Richard Thomas, CMG (1989).

Deputy Ambassador, Consul and First Secretary, J. Gunn.

Defence Attaché, Col. R. A. F. Pearson, MVO.

First Secretary (Commercial), J. C. Northover.

BRITISH COUNCIL REPRESENTATIVE, David Stokes, Todor Strashimirov 7, 1504, Sofia.

DEFENCE

Bulgaria has a total active armed forces strength of 107,000 including 70,000 conscripts. Conscripts serve for 18 months. The Army has a strength of 75,000 personnel, including 49,000 conscripts, and is organized into four tank brigades, four motorized rifle divisions, three artillery and three air defence regiments. Equipment includes 2,100 main battle tanks with 450 in storage, 1,900 armoured infantry fighting vehicles and armoured personnel carriers and 2,100 artillery pieces.

The Navy has a strength of 10,000 personnel (5,000 conscripts), two principal surface combatant vessels, three submarines, 27 patrol and coastal craft and ten armed helicopters. The Air Force has a strength of 22,000 (16,000 conscripts), 259 combat aircraft and 44 armed helicopters. It consists of two ground attack, four fighter, one transport, one reconnaissance, two helicopter, three training and one airborne regiments.

In addition, there are 34,000 paramilitary border guards, security police and railway and construction troops.

EDUCATION

Free basic education is compulsory for children from 7 to 15 years inclusive. Government policy emphasizes the need to democratize the education system, to remove the former ideological basis and to encourage private education. There are three universities (at Sofia, Plovdiv and Veliko Turnovo), an American University and 21 higher educational establishments.

ECONOMY

Until 1939 Bulgaria was a predominantly agricultural country, but subsequently pursued an elaborate programme of industrialization. About 90 per cent of the country's agriculture was turned over to co-operatives, and a smaller proportion mechanized. The principal crops are wheat, maize, beet, tomatoes, tobacco, oleaginous seeds, fruit, vegetables and cotton. The livestock includes cattle, sheep, goats, pigs, horses, asses, mules and water buffaloes. Land is currently being handed over to its previous owners.

There is now a substantial engineering industry and considerable production of ferrous and non-ferrous metals. There are mineral deposits of varying importance. Bulgaria's heavy industry includes the Kremikovtsi steel plant near Sofia and the steel mill at Pernik, the chemical complex at Devnia, the petro-chemical plant at Bourgas and various other chemical and metallurgical works situated around the country. The Soviet-designed nuclear power station at Kozlodui, comprising four reactors, each with a capability of producing 800 million kilowatt-hours and a fifth, 1,000 MW unit, accounts for over 40 per cent of Bulgaria's electrical generating capacity.

In November 1992 the government initiated a plan to privatize 92 major companies by the end of 1992 as the first stage in a mass privatization programme.

FINANCE

Planned public expenditure for 1991 was 70,476.5 million leva, while the internal budget deficit was expected to reach 7,509.5 m leva.

TRADE

Since 1989, political and economic developments in Bulgaria and in some of her principal trading partners have had a substantial impact on the volume and pattern of foreign trade. In 1988, 79 per cent of Bulgaria's foreign trade was within the CMEA, including approximately 57 per cent with the former Soviet Union. Trade with both the former CMEA member countries and with the industrialized West declined sharply in 1990. Figures for the first quarter of 1991 indicate that over 38 per cent of Bulgaria's exports by value went to the developed industrial countries, some 35 per cent to the former CMEA and 26 per cent to the developing countries. In 1992 trade with the European Community states grew rapidly to overtake trade with former Soviet states. In March 1993 Bulgaria signed an Association Agreement with the EC under which EC duties on Bulgarian industrial goods will be abolished by the end of 1994 and levies on agricultural goods will be significantly lowered.

The principal imports are fuels, minerals and metals, engineering goods and industrial equipment. The principal exports are agricultural produce, engineering goods and industrial equipment, industrial consumer goods, chemicals and fuels, minerals and metals.

Trade with UK	1991	1992
Imports from UK	£35,647,000	£59,932,000
Exports to UK	36,786,000	49,780,000

BURKINA FASO
République Populaire de Burkina

Burkina Faso (formerly Upper Volta) is an inland savanna state in West Africa, situated between 9° and 15°N. latitude and 2°E. and 5°W. longitude, with an area of 105,869 sq. miles (274,200 sq. km), and a population of 9,242,000 (UN estimate 1991). It has common boundaries with Mali on the west, Niger and Benin on the east and Togo, Ghana and the Côte d'Ivoire on the south. The largest tribe is the Mossi whose king, the Moro Naba, still wields a certain moral influence. The official language is French.

CAPITAL – Ouagadougou (441,514). Other principal towns; Bobo-Dioulasso (228,668) and Koudougou (30,000).
CURRENCY – Franc CFA.
FLAG – Equal bands of red over green, with a yellow star in centre.
NATIONAL DAY – 4 August.

GOVERNMENT

Burkina Faso was annexed by France in 1896 and between 1932 and 1947 was administered as part of the Colony of the Ivory Coast. It decided on 11 December 1958 to remain an autonomous republic within the French Community; full independence outside the Community was proclaimed on 5 August 1960.

The 1960 constitution provided for a presidential form of government with a single chamber National Assembly, but in January 1966 the Army assumed power. A new constitution allowing for a partial return to civilian rule but with the Army still in effective control was adopted in 1970, but in 1974 this was suspended. Full legislative and presidential elections were held again in 1978.

Following a number of military coups, Capt. Blaise Compaoré took power in October 1987, also by coup. The present government, a broad-based coalition (the Popular Front), held a congress in March 1990 which decided to appoint a committee to draft a 'constitution leading to democratization'. The constitution was adopted by referendum on 2 June 1991. Presidential elections were held in December 1991 and won by Capt. Compaoré in the face of a boycott by the main opposition parties, who were unhappy with the new constitution. Opposition parties then boycotted the legislative elections held in May 1992, which were consequently won by Compaoré's Organization for Popular Democracy-Labour Movement (ODP-MT) party, which formed the government in coalition with several smaller parties.

HEAD OF STATE
President of the Popular Front, Blaise Compaoré, assumed office, October 1987, elected December 1991.

COUNCIL OF MINISTERS as at 21 June 1993
Prime Minister, Youssouf Ouedraogo.
Minister of State, Finance and Planning, Rock Marc Christian Kabore.
Ministers of State, Kanidoua Naboho; Herman Yameogo.
Presidential Special Envoy, Salif Diallo.
Defence, Yarga Larba.
Foreign Affairs, Thomas Sanon.
Territorial Administration, Raogo Antoine Sawadogo.
Public Works, Housing and Urban Areas, Joseph Kabore.
Industry, Commerce and Mines, Zéphirin Diabre.
Secondary and Higher Education, Scientific Research, Mélégué Traore.
Justice, Timothée Some.
Communications, Government Spokesman, Kilimité Theordore Hien.
Water, Séni Macaire Nare.
Employment, Works and Social Security, Jean Léonard Compaore.
Transport, Mamadou Simpore.
Parliamentary Relations, Idrissa Zampalegre.
Primary Education and Literacy, Alice Tiendrebeogo.
Environment and Tourism, Anatole Tiendrebeogo.
Agriculture and Animal Husbandry, Albert Djigma.
Civil Service and Administrative Reform, Juliette Bonkoungou.
Health, Social Action and the Family, Christophe Dabire.
Youth and Sport, Ibrahim Traore.
Culture, Ouala Koutiebou.
Secretary-General of the Government and of the Council of Ministers, Tingnimian Sere.

EMBASSY OF BURKINA FASO
16 Place Guy d'Arezzo, 1060 Brussels, Belgium
Tel: Brussels 3459911

Ambassador Extraordinary and Plenipotentiary, His Excellency Salifou Rigobert Kongo (resident in Brussels).
HONORARY CONSULATE, 5 Cinnamon Row, Plantation Wharf, London SW11 3TW. Tel: 071–738 1800. Honorary Consul, S. G. Singer.

BRITISH AMBASSADOR (resident in Abidjan, Côte d'Ivoire).

ECONOMY
The 1988 Budget totalled Franc CFA 90,300 million. The principal industry is the rearing of cattle and sheep and the chief exports are livestock, groundnuts, millet and sorghum. Small deposits of gold, manganese, copper, bauxite and graphite have been found. Trade in 1991 was valued at imports, CFA 149,704m, exports, CFA 77,843m.

TRADE WITH UK	1991	1992
Imports from UK	£6,472,000	£5,612,000
Exports to UK	285,000	423,000

BURUNDI
République de Burundi

Formerly a Belgian trusteeship under the United Nations, Burundi was proclaimed independent on 1 July 1962. Situated on the east side of Lake Tanganyika, the state has an area of 10,747 sq. miles (27,834 sq. km) and a population (UN estimate 1991) of 5,620,000. The majority of the population are of the Hutu ethnic group, but power has traditionally rested in the hands of the minority Tutsi ethnic group. Official languages are Kirundi, a Bantu language, and French. Kiswahili is also used.

CAPITAL – Bujumbura (formerly Usumbura), with 215,243 (1987 estimate) inhabitants. Kitega (18,000 inhabitants) is the only other sizeable town.
CURRENCY – Burundi franc of 100 centimes.
FLAG – Divided diagonally by a white saltire into red and green triangles; on a white disc in the centre three red six-pointed stars edged in green.
NATIONAL DAY – 1 July.

GOVERNMENT
Burundi became independent as a constitutional monarchy but the monarchy was overthrown in 1966 and the country became a republic. In 1976 the government of President Micombero was overthrown and a Supreme Revolutionary Council led by Col. Jean-Baptiste Bagaza took power. In 1980 the SRC was replaced by a political bureau and central committee as part of a process of political normalization, which continued with elections to the National Assembly, a 65-member legislature. In September 1987 the government of President Bagaza was overthrown by a Military Committee of National Redemption led by Major Pierre Buyoya. The Party of National Unity and Progress (UPRONA), the ruling party, adopted a National Unity Charter to unify the Hutu and Tutsi tribal groups; the charter was approved by a referendum in February 1991. Following violence and unrest throughout 1991 and early 1992, a further referendum was held in March 1992 which approved the adoption of multiparty politics, an executive President directly elected for five-year terms, and the banning of tribally-based parties.
Presidential elections were held on 1 June 1993 and won by the opposition leader Melchior Ndadaye with 60 per cent of the vote, defeating the incumbent Pierre Buyoya who won 39 per cent. Ndadaye, being a Hutu, brought to an end the political dominance of the minority Tutsi. This was confirmed on 29 June 1993 when opposition parties loyal to President Ndadaye defeated the ruling party of former President Buyoya in multiparty legislative elections and formed a new government on 10 July 1993.

HEAD OF STATE
President, Melchior Ndadaye, elected 1 June 1993.

COUNCIL OF MINISTERS as at July 1993
Prime Minister, Sylvie Kinigi.
Deputy Prime Minister, Economy, Social Affairs, Bernard Ciza.
Deputy Prime Minister, Reform and Institutional Development, Melchior Ntahobama.
Foreign Affairs and Co-operation, Sylvestre Ntibantunganya.
Territorial Administration and Communal Development, Juvénal Ndayikeza.
Development Planning and Finance, Gaspard Sindayigaya.
National Defence, Lt.-Col. Charles Ntakije.
Civil Service, Labour and Repatriation of Refugees, Léonard Nyangoma.

Agriculture and Animal Husbandry, Cyprien Ntaryamira.
National Education, Liboire Ngendahayo.
Justice, Fulgence Dwima Bakana.
Commerce, Industry, Craft Industry and Tourism, Jacques
    Ngendakumana.
*Natural Resources, Environment, Town and Country
    Planning,* Ernest Kabushemeye.
Transport, Posts and Telecommunications, Schadrack
    Niyonkuru.
Public Works and Supplies, Anatole Kanyenkiko.
Communications and Government Spokesman, Jean-Marie
    Ngendahayo.
Social Action, Human Rights and Women's Affairs,
    Marguerite Bukuru.
Public Health, Dr Jean Minani.
Youth, Leisure and Culture, Cyriaque Sinbizi.
Secretaries of State, Emmanuel Ndayiragije (*Communal
    Development*); Prosper Banyankiye (*Development
    Planning*); Salvator Toyi (*Budget, Fiscal Administration
    and Customs*); Lt.-Col. Lazare Gakoryo (*Interior Security*).

EMBASSY OF THE REPUBLIC OF BURUNDI
Square Marie Louise 46, 1040 Brussels, Belgium
Tel: Brussels 2304535

Ambassador Extraordinary and Plenipotentiary, His
Excellency Balthazar Habonimana (1992) (resident in
Brussels).
BRITISH AMBASSADOR (resident in Kinshasa, Zaire).

ECONOMY

The chief crop is coffee, representing about 80 per cent of
Burundi's export earnings. Cotton is the second most
important crop. Mineral, tea, hide and skin exports are also
important.

TRADE WITH UK	1991	1992
Imports from UK	£3,817,000	£2,581,000
Exports to UK	2,341,000	1,526,000

CAMBODIA

Situated between Thailand and the south of Vietnam and
extending from the border with Laos on the north to the Gulf
of Thailand, Cambodia covers an area of 69,898 sq. miles
(181,035 sq. km). It has a population (UN estimate 1991) of
8,442,000. The climate is tropical monsoon with a rainy
season from May to October.
    Fifty per cent of the total land area is forest or jungle.
Around the Tonlé Sap lake in the centre of the country and
along the Mekong river, which traverses the country, there
is ample fertile land for the support of the population in times
of peace.
RELIGION – The state religion was Buddhism of the 'Little
Vehicle'. The constitution guaranteed religious freedom, but
in practice Buddhism was suppressed by the Khmer Rouge.
There has been some revival recently and Buddhism has
been re-established as the state religion. There were also
small Muslim and Christian communities, but many members
of them died or fled the country during Khmer Rouge rule.
LANGUAGE – The national language is Khmer.

CAPITAL – Phnom Penh, population 920,000 (1993
estimate).
CURRENCY – Riel of 100 sen.

FLAG – Three horizontal stripes of blue, red, blue, with the
blue of double width and containing a representation of
the temple of Angkor in white.
NATIONAL DAY – (NGC) 17 April; (SOC) 7 January.

HISTORY

Once a powerful kingdom, which, as the Khmer Empire,
flourished between the tenth and 14th centuries, Cambodia
became a French protectorate in 1863 and was granted
independence within the French Union as an Associate State
in 1949. Full independence was proclaimed on 9 November
1953. From 1955 the political life of the country was
dominated by Prince Norodom Sihanouk, first as king, then
as head of government after he had abdicated in favour of his
father and finally (following his father's death in 1960) as
head of state. On 18 March 1970, during his absence from
the country, Prince Sihanouk was deposed as head of state
by a vote of the National Assembly. A republic was declared
on 9 October 1970 and the name of the country changed to
the Khmer Republic.
    In April 1970 a civil war began between Communist
insurgents and government forces. In April 1975 Phnom
Penh fell to the North Vietnamese-backed Khmer Rouge.
Prince Sihanouk returned to Cambodia on 9 September as
nominal head of state. A new Constitution was promulgated
in 1976 and elections to a People's Representative Assembly
were held in March. Prince Sihanouk resigned as head of
state in April, and Khieu Samphan was elected President of
the State Presidium. A government led by Pol Pot, the
leader of the Khmer Rouge (Communist) party, was
appointed and the state was renamed Democratic
Kampuchea. During the years of Khmer Rouge rule
hundreds of thousands of Cambodians died or fled into exile.
    In December 1978 Vietnamese troops invaded Cambodia
and captured the Cambodian capital, Phnom Penh, on 7
January 1979. The following day the Cambodian National
United Front for National Salvation established a People's
Revolutionary Council, recognized by Vietnam, USSR and
by other, chiefly Soviet-aligned, countries. The state was

renamed The People's Republic of Kampuchea (PRK); in April 1989 it became the State of Cambodia (SOC).

With strong support from the Vietnamese army the PRK gained control of most of the country, containing the challenge from the guerrilla forces of the Coalition Government of Democratic Kampuchea (CGDK), which was formed in June 1982 by the Khmer Rouge and two non-Communist groups. Following the final withdrawal of Vietnam's main fighting units in September 1989, the resistance forces regained ground inside Cambodia.

Subsequently, the four Cambodian factions agreed to a peace settlement, including the ending of external military support and the holding of free and fair elections under international supervision. In September 1990, the four factions established a Supreme National Council to embody Cambodian sovereignty and to help finalize and implement a comprehensive settlement. The first meeting took place in Bangkok on 17 September. A temporary ceasefire began on 1 May 1991, became permanent on 23 June and the peace agreements were finally signed in Paris on 23 October 1991. In mid-March 1992 the United Nations Transitional Authority for Cambodia (UNTAC) began its task of implementing the peace agreements.

The attempts by UNTAC to implement the peace agreement and take over the administration of the country from the SOC government in the interim period were hampered throughout 1992 and early 1993 by Khmer Rouge attacks and SOC obstructiveness. By November 1992 the peace agreement was in danger when the Khmer Rouge refused to disarm their forces and mounted attacks on UN peace-keeping troops, leading the UN Security Council to impose economic sanctions on the Khmer Rouge. The Khmer Rouge failed to register to take part in the multi-party elections and SOC government forces launched an offensive against them in late January 1993. Despite this, the 22,000 UNTAC personnel successfully stabilized the country to such an extent that between January and early April 1993 95 per cent of the Cambodian electorate was able to register to vote. All 330,000 refugees in Thailand were also repatriated to Cambodia under UNTAC supervision by 30 March 1993.

Multi-party elections under UNTAC supervision were held on 23–28 May for 120 seats in a National Assembly in which the Royalist FUNCINPEC party of Prince Sihanouk's son Prince Ranariddh won 45 per cent of the vote and 58 seats and the Cambodian People's Party (CPP) (the former ruling SOC party) won 38 per cent of the vote and 51 seats. At the second attempt, Prince Sihanouk pushed for a coalition government agreement in June between FUNCINPEC and the CPP under which he became head of state and FUNCINPEC and CPP leaders Prince Ranariddh and Hun Sen became co-chairmen of the coalition government. This agreement was accepted by UNTAC and officially approved by the new National Assembly on 1 July 1993. The new government is an interim one which will remain in power until the National Assembly draws up a new constitution in late 1993. All UNTAC personnel are to be withdrawn by mid-November but at the time of going to press the Khmer Rouge were still unreconciled to the new government and were launching sporadic attacks around the country. They still control some 10 per cent of Cambodian territory along the border with Thailand.

Head of State and Commander in Chief, Prince Norodom Sihanouk, *appointed by parliament*,14 June 1993.

PROVISIONAL NATIONAL GOVERNMENT OF CAMBODIA *as at August 1993*

Co-Chairman, National Defence, Interior and National Security, Prince Norodom Ranariddh; Hun Sen.

Vice-Chairmen, Keat Chon; Ung Phan.
State Minister, Energy and Mines, Public Works, Ing Kiet.
State Ministers, Hor Namhong; Van Molivan.
Ministers in the Office of the Council of Ministers, Sok An; Veng Sereivut.
Agriculture, Forestry, Wildlife and Fisheries, Kong Sam-ol.
Foreign Affairs and International Co-operation, Prince Norodom Sereivut.
Women, Youth Affairs and Sports, Keat Sokun.
Information and Press, Khieu Kanharit.
Transport, So Khun.
Tourism, Eag Rowland.
Relations with the National Assembly, Say Bori.
Religious Affairs, Chhim Siekleng.
Environment, Mok Maret.
Post and Communications, Ing Huot.
Planning, Chea Chanin.
Commerce, Va Huot.
Public Service, Prak Sok.
Justice, Chem Snguon.
Culture and Fine Arts, Nut Narang.
Labour and Social Welfare, Suy Sem.
Public Health, Hong Sun-huot.
Finance, Sam Rangri.
Veterans, Prum Neakareach.
Education, Mom Chimhuy.
Rural Development, Thach Ren.
Higher Education and Technology, Tol Lah.
Industry, Pu Sothirak.
Chairman of the National Assembly, Son Sann.

UNITED NATIONS TRANSITIONAL AUTHORITY FOR CAMBODIA

Chief Co-ordinator, Yasushi Akashi (*Japan*).
Military Commander, Lt.-Gen John Sanderson (*Australia*).

BRITISH MISSION TO THE SUPREME NATIONAL COUNCIL
29, Street 75, Phnom Penh
Tel 855 2327124
Head of Mission, David Burns, CMG.

ECONOMY

Cambodia has an economy based on agriculture, fishing and forestry, the bulk of its people being rice-growing farmers. In addition to rice, which is the staple crop, the major products are rubber, livestock, maize, timber, pepper, palm sugar, fresh and dried fish, kapok, beans, soya and tobacco. Rice and rubber used to be the main exports though production was brought to a standstill by the hostilities. Following the Khmer Rouge victory, the populations of Phnom Penh and other towns were forcibly evacuated to the country to work on the land, and re-establish the plantations producing such crops as cotton, rubber and bananas. Following the Vietnamese invasion of 1978 the towns were repopulated and commerce revived; currency was reintroduced. Factories, in particular textile mills, iron smelting works and cement works were put back in production. The UNTAC presence has boosted the economy, at least in the short term, and particularly in Phnom Penh.

TRADE WITH UK	1991	1992
Imports from UK	£409,000	£1,238,000
Exports to UK	29,000	4,000

COMMUNICATIONS

The country had over 5,000 kilometres of roads, of which nearly half were hard-surfaced and passable in the rainy season, although now in a state of disrepair. There are two railways, one from Phnom Penh to the Thai border; the other from Phnom Penh to Kampot and Sihanoukville (Kompong Som), but operations and repairs are hindered by occasional Khmer Rouge attacks. Phnom Penh is on a river capable of receiving ships of up to 2,500 tons all the year round. The deep water port at Sihanoukville (Kompong Som) on the Gulf of Thailand can receive ships up to 10,000 tons. The port is linked to Phnom Penh by a modern highway.

EDUCATION

In the years preceding the civil war considerable efforts were devoted to the development of education, and new schools, colleges and technical institutes had been established. Until April 1975 there was a Buddhist University in Phnom Penh, and several residential teachers' training colleges were in operation. However, most of the country's educated élite died under the Khmer Rouge regime, which closed all institutions of higher education. The university was re-opened in 1988.

CAMEROON
République du Cameroun

Cameroon lies on the Gulf of Guinea between Nigeria to the west, Chad and the Central African Republic to the east and Congo and Gabon and Equatorial Guinea to the south. It has an area of 183,569 sq. miles (475,442 sq. km) and a population of 12,239,000 (UN estimate 1991).

LANGUAGES – Cameroon is the only country in Africa where French and English are both official languages enjoying equal status, and the government's declared long-term objective is to achieve complete bilingualism and biculturalism.

CAPITAL – Yaoundé, population estimate (1986) 653,670. ΨDouala (1,029,736) is the commercial centre.

CURRENCY – Franc CFA of 100 centimes.

FLAG – Vertical stripes of green, red and yellow with single five-pointed yellow star in centre of red stripe.

NATIONAL ANTHEM – O Cameroun, Berceau de Nos Ancêtres (O Cameroun, thou cradle of our forefathers).

NATIONAL DAY – 20 May.

GOVERNMENT

The whole territory was administered by Germany from 1884 to 1916. From 1916 to 1959, the former East Cameroon was administered by France as a League of Nations (later UN) trusteeship. On 1 January 1960 it became independent as the Republic of Cameroon. The Republic was joined on 1 October 1961 by the former British-administered trust territory of the Southern Cameroons, after a plebiscite held under United Nations auspices. Cameroon became a federal republic with separate East and West Cameroon state governments. Subsequently, after a plebiscite held in May 1972, Cameroon became a unitary republic and a one-party state; after extensive unrest, multi-party elections were promised by the end of 1991. These were finally held in March 1992, although they were boycotted by two of the main opposition parties. The ruling People's Democratic Movement emerged just short of a majority in the parliament

and formed a coalition government with a small opposition party, the Movement for the Defence of the Republic.

Presidential elections were held on 11 October 1992 and won by the incumbent President Paul Biya with 40 per cent of the vote. The results were, however, disputed by the runner-up Fru Ndi and two opposition parties, together with foreign observers who accused the authorities of widespread malpractice. Opposition parties unsuccessfully tried to persuade the Supreme Court to annul the election result after which violent opposition protests continued until December. On 27 November a new coalition government was formed with the two parties of the previous government being joined by the Union for Democracy and Progress and the Union of Peoples of Cameroon. In May 1993 President Biya published a draft bill on constitutional reform providing for a Council of State, Senate and a Constitutional Court but rejecting a return to a federal state.

HEAD OF STATE
President, Prime Minister and Commander in Chief of the Armed Forces, His Excellency Paul Biya, *acceded* 6 November 1982, *elected* 14 January 1984, *re-elected* 24 April 1988, 10 October 1992, *sworn in* 3 November 1992.

MINISTRY *as at July 1993*

Deputy Prime Minister, Territorial Administration, Gilbert Andze.
Deputy Prime Minister, Housing and Town Planning, Hamadou Mustapha.
Minister of State, Posts and Telecommunications, Dakolle Daissala.
Minister of State, Planning and Regional Development, Augustin Frederic Kodock.
Minister of State, Communications, Augustin Koutchou Kouomegni.
Defence, Edouard Akame Mfoumou.
External Relations, Ferdinand Leopold Oyono.
Justice, Douala Moutome.
Animal Husbandry and Fisheries, Hamadjoda Adjoudji.
Higher Education, Titus Edzoa.
Public Health, Joseph Mbede.
Labour and Social Insurance, Simon Mbila.
Industrial and Commercial Development, Patrice Ambassad Mandeng.
Finance, Antoine Ntsimi.
Public Service and Administrative Reforms, Sali Dairou.
Women and Social Affairs, Yaou Aissatou.
Agriculture, Stephen Njinyan.
Public Works, Jean-Baptiste Bokam.
Technical and Scientific Research, Dr Ayuk Takem.
Tourism, Pierre Souman.
Environment and Forests, Dr Bava Djingoer.
Youth and Sports, Bernard Massoua.
National Education, Dr Robert Mboppe.
Mines, Water Resources and Energy, Jean Bosco Samgba.
Transport, Issa Bakary Tchiroma.
Culture, Joseph-Marie Bipoun.

EMBASSY OF THE REPUBLIC OF CAMEROON
84 Holland Park, London WII 3SB
Tel 071-727 0771/3
Ambassador Extraordinary and Plenipotentiary, His Excellency Dr Gibering Bol-Alima (1987).

BRITISH EMBASSY
Avenue Winston Churchill, BP 547 Yaoundé
Tel: Yaoundé 220545
Ambassador Extraordinary and Plenipotentiary, His Excellency William E. Quantrill (1991).

There is also a British Consulate at *Douala*.
BRITISH COUNCIL REPRESENTATIVE, Harley Brookes,
Immeuble Christo, Rue Charles de Gaulle (BP 818),
Yaoundé.

ECONOMY

The main economic emphasis is on agricultural development, both through encouraging small-scale peasant agriculture, and through the development of large-scale agro-industrial complexes, with the aim of making the country agriculturally self-sufficient and a major food exporter.

Principal products are cocoa, coffee, bananas, cotton, timber, groundnuts, aluminium, rubber and palm products. There is an aluminium smelting plant at Edéa with an annual capacity of 50,000 tons. Oil is now also one of Cameroon's principal products with an estimated production of 7.31 m. tonnes during 1989.

TRADE	1987	1988
Total imports	CFA526,186m	CFA378,726m
Total exports	487,849m	468,683m

Trade with UK	1991	1992
Imports from UK	£23,813,000	£19,156,000
Exports to UK	6,135,000	6,495,000

CANADA

AREA AND POPULATION

Provinces or Territories (with official contractions)	Area (sq. miles)	Population Census 1991*
Alberta (Alta.)	255,290	2,545,553
British Columbia (BC)	365,946	3,282,061
Manitoba (Man.)	250,946	1,091,942
New Brunswick (NB)	28,355	723,900
Newfoundland and Labrador (Nfld.)	156,648	568,474
Nova Scotia (NS)	21,425	899,942
Ontario (Ont.)	412,579	10,084,885
Prince Edward Island (PEI)	2,185	129,765
Quebec (Que.)	594,857	6,895,963
Saskatchewan (Sask.)	251,865	988,928
Yukon Territory (YT)	186,660	27,797
Northwest Territories (NWT)	1,322,902	57,649
Total	3,849,658	27,296,859

Area figures include land and water area
*Excludes 1991 Census data for one or more incompletely enumerated Indian reserves or Indian settlements

BIRTHS, DEATHS AND MARRIAGES, 1991

Province	Births	Deaths	Marriages
Alberta	42,776	14,451	18,612
British Columbia	45,612	23,977	23,691
Manitoba	17,282	8,943	7,032
New Brunswick	9,497	5,469	4,521
Newfoundland	7,166	3,798	3,480
Nova Scotia	12,016	7,255	5,845
Ontario	151,478	72,917	72,938
Prince Edward Island	1,885	1,188	876
Québec	97,310	49,121	28,922
Saskatchewan	15,304	8,098	5,923

Province	Births	Deaths	Marriages
Yukon	568	114	196
NW Territories	1,634	237	215
Total	402,528	195,568	172,251

Canada's birth rate per 1,000 population (1991) 14.9; death rate 7.2; marriage rate 6.4. Divorces were 77,031 in 1991.

Of the total immigration of 252,537 in 1992, 14,722 were from the Caribbean, 7,512 from the United Kingdom and Ireland, and 7,155 from the United States of America.

MOTHER TONGUES OF THE POPULATION 1991

Single Responses

English	16,516,180
French	6,505,565
Non-official languages	3,549,305
Cree	77,355
Inuktitut	24,030
Ojibway	21,225

Multiple Responses

English and French	216,585
English and non-official language(s)	405,080
French and non-official language(s)	47,270
English, French and non-official language(s)	29,155
Non-official languages	27,715
Total Population	27,296,860

PHYSIOGRAPHY

Canada occupies the whole of the northern part of the North American continent (with the exception of Alaska), from 49° N. latitude to the North Pole, and from the Pacific to the Atlantic Ocean. In eastern Canada, the southernmost point is Middle Island in Lake Erie, at 41° 41′.

The relief of Canada is dominated by the mountain ranges running north and south on the west side of the continent, by the pre-Cambrian shield on the east, with, in between, the northern extension of the North American Plain. From the physiographic point of view Canada has six main divisions. These are: Appalachian-Acadian region, the Canadian shield, the St Lawrence-Great Lakes lowland, the interior plains, the Cordilleran region and the Arctic archipelago.

The great Canadian shield comprises more than half the area. The interior as a whole is an undulating, low plateau (general level 1,000 to 1,500 feet), with water or muskeg-filled depressions separated by irregular hills and ridges, 150 to 200 feet in elevation. The flat relief of the St Lawrence-Great Lakes lowland varies from 500 feet in the east to 1,700 feet south of Georgian Bay. The interior plains, comprising the Pacific provinces, slope eastward and northward a few feet per mile. The descent from west to east is made from 5,000 feet to less than 1,000 feet in three distinct levels, with each new level being marked by an eastward facing conteau or scarp.

Five fairly well-developed topographic divisions mark out the Cordilleran region of western Canada. These are: coastal ranges, largely above 5,000 feet with deep fjords and glaciated valleys; the interior plateau, around 3,500 feet and comparatively level; the Selkirk ranges, largely above 5,000 feet; the Rocky Mountains with their chain of 10,000 to 12,000 feet peaks; the Peace River or Tramontane region with its rolling diversified country.

The Arctic archipelago, with its plateau-like character has an elevation between 500 and 1,000 feet, though in Baffin Land and Ellesmere Island the mountain ranges rise to 8,500 and 9,500 feet. Two tremendous waterway systems, the St Lawrence and the Mackenzie, providing thousands of miles of water highway, occupy a broad area of lowland with their dominant axis following the edge of the shield.

The climate of the eastern and central portions presents greater extremes than in corresponding latitudes in Europe, but in the south-western portion of the prairie region and the southern portions of the Pacific slope the climate is milder. Spring, summer and autumn are of about seven to eight months' duration, and the winter four to five months.

FEDERAL CAPITAL – Ottawa, on the south bank of the Ottawa river, 111 miles west of Montreal and 247 miles north-east of Toronto. Ottawa is connected with Lake Ontario by the Rideau Canal. The city was chosen as the capital of the Province of Canada in 1857 and was later selected as the Dominion capital. Ottawa contains the Parliament Buildings, the Public Archives, Royal Mint, the National Art Gallery and the Dominion Observatory. The city population was 313,987 at the Census of 1991; and the population of the metropolitan area of Ottawa–Hull was 920,857.

CURRENCY – Canadian dollar (C$) of 100 cents.

FLAG – Red maple leaf with 11 points on white square, flanked by vertical red bars one-half the width of the square.

NATIONAL ANTHEM – O Canada.

NATIONAL DAY – 1 July (Dominion Day).

GOVERNMENT

Canada was originally discovered by Cabot in 1497 but its history dates only from 1534, when the French took possession of the country. The first permanent settlement at Port Royal (now Annapolis), Nova Scotia, was founded in 1605, and Quebec was founded in 1608. In 1759 Quebec was captured by British forces under General Wolfe and in 1763 the whole territory of Canada became a possession of Great Britain by the Treaty of Paris 1763. Nova Scotia was ceded in 1713 by the Treaty of Utrecht, the Provinces of New Brunswick and Prince Edward Island being subsequently formed out of it. British Columbia was formed into a Crown colony in 1858, having previously been a part of the Hudson Bay Territory, and was united to Vancouver Island in 1866.

The constitution of Canada had its source in the British North America Act of 1867 which formed a Dominion, under the name of Canada, of the four provinces of Ontario, Quebec, New Brunswick and Nova Scotia; to this federation the other provinces have subsequently been admitted. Under this Act, Canada came into being on 1 July 1867, and the Statute of Westminster 1931 removed all limitations with regard to the legislative autonomy of Canada and the provinces, except that the British North America Act could be amended in important respects only by Acts of the British Parliament. Provinces admitted since 1867 are: Manitoba (1870), British Columbia (1871), Prince Edward Island (1873), Alberta and Saskatchewan (1905) and Newfoundland (1949).

The election of a separatist Parti Quebecois government in Quebec in 1976 led to a referendum in 1980 on whether the province should conduct negotiations with the federal government on a new 'sovereignty-association'; the proposal was rejected.

Agreement was reached in November 1981 between the federal and provincial governments (except Quebec) to patriate the constitution so that it was amendable only in Canada. The inclusion in the constitution of a Charter of Rights was also agreed. At the request of the Canadian Parliament, legislation was passed at Westminster and the constitution formally patriated on 17 April 1982.

To reconcile Quebec to the new constitution the Canadian federal government and the ten provincial governments signed the Meech Lake Accord on 3 June 1987. This transferred certain powers to the provinces and specifically recognized Quebec as 'a distinct society'. The provincial legislatures of Manitoba and Newfoundland refused to approve the Accord by the deadline for its ratification on 22 June 1990. In September 1992 agreement on a new federal constitution called the Charlottetown Accord was reached between the federal government and the provincial governments. The agreement guaranteed Quebec a special status within Canada as a 'distinct society' and reserved 25 per cent of seats in the House of Commons for the province. The Senate was also to be reformed to ensure each province had an equal number of seats and that it was directly elected. The

Charlottetown Accord was put to a national referendum on 26 October 1992 but was rejected by 54 per cent to 46 per cent nationally and by six provinces including Quebec. Canada now remains in constitutional limbo with no constitutional discussions taking place at the moment. The rejection of the accord was a major factor leading to the resignation of Prime Minister Brian Mulroney and his replacement by Kim Campbell, who was sworn in with her new cabinet on 25 June 1993.

Executive power is vested in a Governor-General appointed by the Sovereign on the advice of the Canadian Ministry, and aided by a Privy Council.

GOVERNOR-GENERAL

Governor-General and Commander-in-Chief, His Excellency the Rt. Hon. Ramon John Hnatyshyn, PC, CC, CMM, CD, QC.
Secretary to the Governor-General, J. A. LaRocque, CVO.

CABINET *as at August 1993*

Prime Minister, Rt. Hon. Kim Campbell.
Deputy Prime Minister, Minister of Industry, Science and Technology, Consumer and Corporate Affairs, Hon. Jean Charest.
Justice, President of the Queen's Privy Council, Hon. Pierre Bials.
Finance, Hon. Gilles Loizelle.
External Affairs, Hon. Parrin Beatty.
Defence, Hon. Thomas Siddon.
Treasury Board President, Hon. James Edwards.
Agriculture, Small Communities and Rural Areas, Hon. Charles Mayer.
Government Leader in the Senate, Hon. Lowell Murray.
Supply and Services, Public Works, Hon. Paul Dick.
International Trade, Hon. Thomas Hockio.
Secretary of State, Communications, Hon. Monique Landry.
Science and Small Business, Hon. Robert Kicholson.
Western Economic Diversification, Hon. Larry Schneider.
National Revenue, Hon. Garth Turner.
Fisheries and Oceans, Hon. Ross Reid.
Labour, Employment and Immigration, Hon. Bernard Vaicourt.
Multiculturalism and Citizenship, Hon. Gerry Weiner.
Solicitor-General, Government Leader in the House of Commons, Hon. Douglas Lewis.
Transport, Hon. Jean Corbell.
Indian Affairs and Northern Development, Hon. Pauline Browes.
Environment, Hon. Pierre Vincent.
Health and Welfare, Minister for Status of Women, Hon. Mary Collins.
Energy, Mines and Resources and Forestry, Hon. Bobbie Sparrow.
Veterans' Affairs, Hon. Peter McCreath.

CANADIAN HIGH COMMISSION
Macdonald House, 1 Grosvenor Square, London WIX OAB
Tel 071-629 9492
High Commissioner, His Excellency Frederik Eaton (1991).
Deputy High Commissioner, Serge April.
Ministers, J. Wright (*Political and Public Affairs*);
R. Burchill (*Commercial/Economic*).
Minister-Counsellor, G. Schroh (*Immigration*); D. G. Woods (*Admin.*).
Defence Adviser, Brig.-Gen. D. M. Dean.
Counsellor, R. Picard (*Cultural Affairs*); R. D. Merner (*Commercial*).

BRITISH HIGH COMMISSION
80 Elgin Street, Ottawa KIP 5K7
Tel: Ottawa 237 1530
High Commissioner, His Excellency Sir Nicholas Bayne KCMG.
Deputy High Commissioner, B. H. Dinwiddy.
Counsellors, W. B. McCleary (*Economic and Commercial*);
A. E. Lewis.
Defence and Military Adviser, Brig. T. D. V. Bevan.
First Secretary, R. V. Welborn (*Management and Consular*).
There are also Consulates-General at *Montreal, Toronto,* and *Vancouver* and Consulates at *Halifax, St John's* and *Winnipeg.*

BRITISH COUNCIL DIRECTOR, J. Horniman (*Cultural Attaché*).

BRITISH COUNCIL REPRESENTATIVE IN QUEBEC,
S. Dawbarn, c/o British Consulate-General, 1155 University Street, Montreal, Quebec H3B 3A7.

LEGISLATURE

Parliament consists of a Senate and a House of Commons. The Senate consists of 107 members, nominated by the Governor-General (age limit 75), the seats being distributed between the various provinces. Each Senator must be at least 30 years old, a resident in the province for which he is appointed, a natural-born or naturalized subject of The Queen, and the owner of a property qualification amounting to $4,000. The Speaker of the Senate is chosen by the Government of the day.

The House of Commons has 295 members and is elected every five years at longest. Representation by provinces is at present as follows: Newfoundland 7, Prince Edward Island 4, Nova Scotia 11, New Brunswick 10, Quebec 75, Ontario 99, Manitoba 14, Saskatchewan 14, Alberta 26, British Columbia 32, Yukon 1, Northwest Territories 2.

The state of the parties in the Senate as at June 1992 was Progressive Conservatives 53, Liberals 45, Independent 5, Vacant 3.

The state of parties in the House of Commons as at June 1992, was Progressive Conservatives 158, Liberals 81, New Democratic Party 44, Independent 11, Reform Party 1.

Speaker of the Senate, Hon. Guy Charbonneau, QC.
Clerk of the Senate and Clerk of the Parliaments, Gordon Barnhart.
Speaker of the House of Commons, Hon. John A. Fraser.
Deputy Speaker, Andrée Champagne.
Clerk of the House of Commons, Robert Marleau.

JUDICATURE

The judicature is administered by judges following the civil law in Quebec province and common law in other provinces. Each province has its Court of Appeal. All Superior, County and District Court Judges are appointed by the Governor-General, the others by the Lieutenant-Governors of the provinces.

The highest federal court is the Supreme Court of Canada, composed of a Chief Justice and eight puisne judges, which exercises general appellate jurisdiction throughout Canada in civil and criminal cases, and which usually holds three sessions each year. There is one other federally constituted court, the Federal Court of Canada, which has jurisdiction on appeals from its trial division, from federal tribunals and reviews of decisions and references by federal boards and commissions. The trial division has jurisdiction in claims by or against the Crown, its officers or servants or federal bodies. It also deals with inter-provincial and federal-provincial disputes.

SUPREME COURT OF CANADA

Chief Justice of Canada, Rt. Hon. A. Lamer, PC.
Puisne Judges, Hons. G. V. LaForest; Claire L'Heureux-Dube; J. Sopinka; C. Gonthier; P. Cory; Beverley McLachlin; W. A. Stevenson; F. Iacobucci.

FEDERAL COURT OF CANADA

Chief Justice, vacant.
Associate Chief Justice, Hon. J. A. Jerome.
Appeal Division Judges, Hons. L. Pratte; D. V. Heald; P. M. Mahoney, PC; L. Marceau; J. K. Hugesson; A. J. Stone; M. MacGuigan; Alice Desjardins; R. Décary; A. M. Linden.
Trial Division Judges, Hons. J.-E. Dubé; P. U. C. Rouleau; F. C. Muldoon; B. L. Strayer; Barbara J. Reed; P. Denault; Y. Pinard; L. M. Joyal; B. Cullen; L. A. Martin; M. A. Teitelbaum; W. A. MacKay.

FINANCE

Federal government gross general revenue and expenditure was:

	1991–2	1992–3*
Total Revenue	C$131,327m	C$141,118m
Total Expenditure	164,807m	170,018m
*estimated		

	1990–1	1991–2
DEBT		
Gross Public Debt	C$443,278m	C$475,600m
Net Public Debt	385,047m	419,944m

DEFENCE

The Minister of National Defence has the control and management of the Canadian armed forces and all matters relating to national defence establishments and works for the defence of Canada.

The Canadian forces are organized into National Defence Headquarters and five major commands reporting to the Chief of the Defence Staff. The five commands are: *Land Force Command; Maritime Command; Air Command; Canadian Forces Communications Command; Canadian Forces Europe.* It was announced in February 1992 that all Canadian forces would leave Europe by 1994.

National defence expenditure for the year 1992–3 was C$12,400 million. Canadian armed forces strength at September 1992: 81,590 authorized force. The Canadian Armed Forces are an all-volunteer force.

Land forces comprise some 22,000 personnel organized into one mechanized brigade group and three infantry brigade groups together with one air defence regiment and one engineer support regiment. Equipment includes 115 main battle tanks, 360 reconnaissance vehicles, 1,405 armoured personnel carriers and 330 artillery pieces. Maritime forces number 17,000 personnel with four destroyers, 14 frigates, three submarines and 12 patrol and coastal craft. Air forces number 22,400 personnel with 198 combat aircraft and 131 armed helicopters. Organization is into two ground attack, five air defence, four maritime reconnaissance, three anti-submarine warfare, 13 helicopter and six transport squadrons.

In addition, there are 22,600 personnel assigned to Communications Command or are not identified in any of the above three services. Until 1994 Canada deploys in Germany 3,600 Army and 1,500 Air Force personnel.

EDUCATION

Education is under the control of the provincial governments, the cost of the publicly controlled schools being met by local taxation, aided by provincial grants. In 1992–3 there were 16,063 elementary and secondary schools with 5,287,730 pupils. Of these, 1,515 were private schools with 256,140 pupils; 383 federal schools with 55,600 pupils and 19 special schools for the blind and deaf with 2,330 pupils.

In 1992–3 there were 69 degree-granting universities with a full-time enrolment of 572,900, as well as 348,400 students in 203 other post-secondary, non-university institutions.

ECONOMY

About 7.3 per cent of the total land area of Canada is farmed land. Over 60 per cent of this is under cultivation, the remainder being predominantly classified as unimproved pasture. More than 80 per cent of the land now cultivated is found in the prairie region of western Canada.

Farm cash receipts from the sale of farm products in 1992 were C$23,302m. Livestock and animal products contributed C$11,347m; field crops C$8,123m.

Grain crop production ('000 metric tonnes):

	1991–2	1992–3p
Wheat	31,945.6	29,871.3
Oats	1,793.9	2,823.1
Barley	11,617.3	10,919.4
Rye	338.7	265.2
Flaxseed	635.0	334.0
Canola	4,224.2	3,668.8
Total	50,554.7	57,901.8

p preliminary

In January 1992 the livestock included 11,712,600 cattle, 10,498,400 pigs, 660,500 sheep and lambs and 20,860,000 chickens (layers).

Canada in 1991–2 produced pelts valued at C$45m. Wildlife pelts made up 50.5 per cent of the total, with a value of C$23m.

The marketed value of fish catches in 1991 was C$2,945m (preliminary).

About 43 per cent of the total land area is considered as inventoried forest area. The value of shipments and other revenue from forestry-related industries in 1990 was: logging $8,114m; sawmill and planing mill products $8,432m; shingle and shake $260m; veneer and plywood $1,028m; and paper and allied products $24,026m.

In 1991, Canada was the world's largest producer of zinc and uranium, the second largest of asbestos, potash, nickel and the fourth largest of gypsum. The country is also rich in many other minerals, including gold, silver, copper, lead, molybdenum, platinum group metals, elemental sulphur, cobalt, titanium concentrate, and aluminium cadmium.

Mineral production ('000 tonnes):

	1991	1992p
Copper	780.4	744.7
Nickel	188.1	189.1
Lead	248.1	318.5
Molybdenum	11.4	9.6
Zinc	1,083.0	1,193.6
Iron Ore	35,421.0	32,772.0
Asbestos	686.0	601.0
Gypsum	6,727.0	6,892.0
Cement	9,372.0	8,484.0
Lime	2,375.0	2,383.0
Salt	11,871.0	11,100.0
Potash	7,087.0	7,324.0

p preliminary

Production of gold was 157,554,000 kg in 1992 and of silver 1,147,000 kg. Uranium production in 1992 was 9,057,000 kg.

TRADE

Merchandise imports into Canada in 1992 were valued at C$147,994m and merchandise exports (including re-exports) at C$162,596m. The main exports in 1992 were passenger automobiles and chassis, motor vehicle parts (except engines), trucks, truck tractors and chassis, wood pulp and similar pulp, newsprint paper, softwood lumber, crude petroleum, other telecommunications and related equipment (excluding televisions, radio sets, phonographs), wheat and natural gas.

Trade with the USA accounts for about 77.3 per cent of total trade in merchandise, although efforts are being made to develop alternative markets. Value of trade with Canada's largest trading partners in 1992 was as follows (C$ million):

	Exports	Imports
United States	118,677	96,610
Japan	7,448	10,762
United Kingdom	3,034	4,095
Germany	2,185	3,532
South Korea	1,408	2,008
China	2,138	2,445
The Netherlands	1,452	599
CIS	1,265	270
France	1,347	2,689
Belgium	1,069	428
Taiwan	954	2,469

Trade with UK	1991	1992
Imports from UK	£1,701,051,000	£1,582,124,000
Exports to UK	1,922,549,000	1,897,115,000

COMMUNICATIONS

The total track of railways in operation on 31 December 1991, was 85,563 km. In 1991 freight transportation was 261 billion tonne-kilometres, and the balance of property accounts at end 1991 was C$18,635m.

The registered shipping on 1 January 1991 including inland vessels, was 43,787 vessels with gross tonnage 4,956,845. The volume of international shipping handled at Canadian ports in 1991 was 168,030,334 metric tonnes loaded and 65,863,148 metric tonnes unloaded.

The bulk of canal shipping in Canada is handled through the two sections of the St Lawrence Seaway, which provide access to the Great Lakes for ocean-going ships. In 1992, transits on the Montreal-Lake Ontario section numbered 2,493 for a total of 31,400,000 cargo tonnes; transits in the Welland Canal section numbered 3,140 for a total of 33,200,000 cargo tonnes. Principal commodities carried were iron ore, wheat, corn, barley, soybeans, manufactured iron and steel, coal and salt.

The number of passengers carried in 1991 (all major Canadian carriers) was 32,302,000; 1,636,341,000 tonne-km of freight was carried in 1991.

Total motor vehicle registrations numbered 17,223,039 in 1991.

Post office revenue in the fiscal year 1992-3 was C$3,900m. Canada Post Corporation processed 10,410 million pieces of mail.

Source: for financial and economic statistics, Statistics Canada

YUKON TERRITORY

The area of the Territory is 205,346 sq. miles (531,842 sq. km), with a population (1991 census) of 27,797. Minerals, government and tourism are the chief industries, followed closely by transportation, communications and other utilities industry.

SEAT OF GOVERNMENT – Whitehorse, population (1991 census) 17,925.

The Yukon Act 1970, as amended, provides for the administration of the Territory by a Commissioner acting under instructions from time to time given by the Governor-in-Council or the Minister of Indian Affairs and Northern Development. Legislative powers, analogous to those of a provincial government, are exercised by a Legislative Assembly of 17 members elected from electoral districts in the Territory. The Executive Council of the Assembly consists of the government leader as chairman and five elected members.

Commissioner, J. K. McKinnon.
Premier, Hon. John Ostashek.

NORTHWEST TERRITORIES

The area of the Northwest Territories is 1,322,900 sq. miles (3,426,389 sq. km), with a population (1991 census) of 57,649. The chief industry is mining, with a total value of $637,294,000 in 1992. Lead, zinc, gold, silver, oil exploration and natural gas contributed about 19 per cent of the 1992 GDP of the Northwest Territories.

The Northwest Territories are subdivided into the regions of Baffin, Fort Smith, Inuvik, Keewatin, Kitikmeot.

SEAT OF GOVERNMENT – Yellowknife, population (1991 census) 15,179.

The Northwest Territories Act 1979, as amended, provides for a Legislative Assembly of 24 elected members, of which the Executive Council under the chairmanship of the government leader is the senior decision-making body of the government in the Territory.

In November 1992 a referendum was held in the Northwest Territories which approved a plan to divide the Territories into two and to establish in one part a self-governing autonomous Inuit (Eskimo) populated territory known as Nunavat. Nunavat will be established in the east of the Northwest Territories and will comprise the present regions of Baffin, Keewatian and Kitikmeot. An agreement to establish Nunavat with self-government phased in over six years up to 1999 was signed in the new territory's capital Iqaluit on Baffin Island by the Federal Prime Minister Brian Mulroney on 1 June 1993. The territory will have its own government and legislature, though neither will have the status of their provincial equivalents. It has a population of some 22,000, of which 80 per cent are Inuit, and covers some 850,000 sq. miles (2,201,500 sq. km). The agreement has yet to be ratified by the Federal Parliament.

Commissioner, D. L. Norris.
Government Leader, Hon. Dennis Patterson.

CANADIAN PROVINCES

ALBERTA

The Province of Alberta has an area of 661,185 sq. km (255,285 sq. miles), including about 6,485 sq. miles of water (16,796 sq. km), with a population (1 April 1992) of 2,558,200.

CAPITAL – Edmonton, city population (1993) 626,999, metropolitan area, 839,924. Other centres are Calgary (727,719), Lethbridge (63,390), Red Deer (59,826), Medicine Hat (43,807), St Albert (44,195).

GOVERNMENT

The Government is vested in a Lieutenant-Governor and Legislative Assembly composed of 83 members, elected for five years, representing 83 electoral districts in the province.

At a provincial election held on 15 June 1993, the Progressive Conservative Party took 51 seats and the Liberal Party 32 seats.

Lt.-Governor, The Hon. Gordon Towers.
Premier, President of Executive Council, Hon. Ralph Klein.

AGENT-GENERAL'S OFFICE IN LONDON, Alberta House, 1 Mount Street, London WIY 5AA. *Agent-General,* Mary LeMessurier.

JUDICATURE

Court of Appeal of Alberta, Chief Justice, Hon. C. A. Fraser.
Court of Queen's Bench of Alberta, Chief Justice, Hon. W. K. Moore.
Associate Chief Justice, Hon. A. H. Wachowich.

ECONOMY

The total GDP at factor cost in 1992 amounted to C$75,041 million. Preliminary estimates for mineral production in 1992 came to C$17,079 million. Of this total, crude oil amounted to C$9,231 million, and natural gas and its by-products to C$6,888 million.

The total value of manufacturing shipments (1992) was C$19,410 million. Number of manufacturing establishments 3,032 (1989), total employees 67,424 (1989). The leading industrial products are refined petroleum and coal products, meat and meat products, chemicals and chemical products, fabricated metal products, non-metallic mineral products and primary metals.

FINANCE

Budgetary Estimates	1991–2	1992–3
Revenue	C$12,618m	C$11,565m
Expenditure	12,484	12,671
Deficit	—	2,322
Surplus	134	—

NOTE: The budgetary revenue figure does not include funds allocated to the Alberta Heritage Savings Trust Fund.

BRITISH COLUMBIA

British Columbia has a total area estimated at 952,263 sq. km (367,669 sq. miles), with a population of 3,371,372 (June 1992).

PROVINCIAL CAPITAL – ΨVictoria, metropolitan population (1992) 293,076. Other principal cities are ΨVancouver (metropolitan population (1992) 1,643,485), Prince George, Kamloops, Kelowna and Nanaimo.

GOVERNMENT

The Government consists of a Lieutenant-Governor and an Executive Council together with a Legislative Assembly of 75 members.

The New Democratic Party formed a government after a General Election on 17 October 1991. The present standing in the Assembly is New Democratic Party 51, Liberal Party 17, Social Credit Party 7.

Lt.-Governor, His Honour Dr David See-Chai Lam
Premier, Hon. Mike Harcourt

AGENT-GENERAL'S OFFICE IN LONDON, British Columbia House, 1 Regent Street, London SW1 4NR. *Agent-General,* G. Gardom, QC.

JUDICATURE

Court of Appeal, Chief Justice of British Columbia, Hon. A. McEachern
Supreme Court, Chief Justice, Hon. W. A. Esson
Associate Chief Justice, Hon. D. H. Campbell

FINANCE	1992–3	1993–4
Estimated Revenue	C$16,022.0m	C$17,460.0m
Estimated Expenditure	17,972.0m	18,995.0m

ECONOMY

Manufacturing activity is based largely on the processing of the output of the logging, mineral, fishing and agriculture industries. The principal manufacturing centres are Vancouver, New Westminster, Victoria, North Vancouver, Kelowna and Prince George. Service-producing industries generated 72.2 per cent of total provincial GDP and was the largest employer, accounting for over 75 per cent of total employment. British Columbia is the leading province of Canada in the quantity and value of its timber and sawmill products. Mining, the second most important non-service economic activity, is based on copper, zinc, lead, iron concentrates, molybdenum, coal, natural gas, crude petroleum, asbestos, gold and silver. Molybdenum production is approximately 95 per cent of the Canadian total.

The production levels for important industries for 1992 were as follows:

Lumber	33,395,600 cu. metres
Paper	2,278,000 tonnes
Pulp	3,825,000 tonnes
Coal	16,899,100 tonnes
Natural gas	16,228,700,000 cu. metres

Solid mineral production for 1992 is estimated to be valued at C$2,504.9 million.

The most important agricultural products are livestock, eggs and poultry, fruits and dairy products. Salmon accounts for approximately 60 per cent of the value of fisheries. Other species include halibut, herring, sole, cod, flounder, perch, tuna and shellfish. In 1992 farm cash receipts were valued at C$1,339.1 million.

The economy is dependent upon markets outside the province for the disposal of most of the products of industry. An estimated 55–60 per cent of production is exported to foreign markets. Manufacturing shipments in 1992 were valued at C$23,972 million.

TRANSPORT

The province has deep water harbours which are well serviced by railways and modern highways. Vancouver has one of the finest natural harbours in the world, servicing a variety of vessels, including large bulk cargo carriers. Vancouver is also the base for regular scheduled air routes to other parts of Canada, the United States, Europe, Mexico, South America, Hawaii, Fiji, Australia, Japan, Hong Kong and the Middle East.

MANITOBA

Manitoba, originally the Red River settlement, is the central province of Canada. The province has a considerable area of prairie land but is also a land of wide diversity combining 645 kilometres (401 miles) of coastline on Hudson Bay, large lakes and rivers covering an area of 101,592 sq. km (39,225 sq. miles) and pre-Cambrian rock which covers about three-fifths of the province. The total area is 649,947 sq. km (250,946 sq. miles), with a population (1991 Census) of 1,091,942.

PROVINCIAL CAPITAL – Winnipeg, population 640,400 (1990). Other cities are Brandon (39,366), Thompson (14,379), Portage la Prairie (13,522) and Flin Flon (7,708).

GOVERNMENT

The Lieutenant-Governor is The Queen's personal representative in Manitoba. There is a Legislative Assembly of 57 members, of which the Executive Council of Ministers are all members.

The Progressive Conservatives formed a majority government after a General Election held on 11 September 1990. The standing in the House at 30 June 1993 was: Progressive Conservatives 29, New Democratic Party 19, Liberal 6, vacant 3.

Lt.-Governor, His Honour W. Yvon Dumont
Premier, Hon. Gary A. Filmon

JUDICATURE

Court of Appeal, Chief Justice, Hon. Richard J. Scott
Queen's Bench Division, Chief Justice, Hon. B. Hewak
Associate Chief Justices, Hon. J. J. Oliphant *(QBD),*
Hon. G. W. Mercier *(Family Division)*

ECONOMY

The projected revenue for the province in the fiscal year 1993–4 was C$4,902 million while expenditures were forecast at C$5,359 million.

The total land area in Manitoba is 135,342,565 acres, of which 19,126,517 acres are in occupied farms. The gross value of agriculture production in 1990 was estimated at C$2,400 million.

Manufacturing enterprises employed about 55,000 persons on average in 1990. The chief manufacturing centres are Winnipeg, Brandon, Selkirk and Portage la Prairie. The largest manufacturing industry is the food and beverage industry, followed by the machinery and metal fabricating industries.

NEW BRUNSWICK

New Brunswick is situated between 45°–48° N. latitude and 63° 47'–69° W. longitude and comprises an area of 73,439 sq. km (28,355 sq. miles), with a population (June 1991) of 723,900. It was first colonized by British subjects in 1761, and in 1783 by inhabitants of New England who had been dispossessed of their property in consequence of their loyalty to the British Crown. New Brunswick entered Confederation in 1867.

PROVINCIAL CAPITAL – Fredericton, population (1991), 71,869. Other cities are Ψ Saint John (124,981); Moncton (106,503); Bathurst (36,167); Edmundston (22,478); Campbellton (17,183).

GOVERNMENT

Government is administered by a Lieutenant-Governor, an Executive Council, and a Legislative Assembly of 58 members elected by the people. The present Legislative Assembly of the Province was elected on 23 September 1991 and has 58 members; 46 from the Liberal Party, 8 from the Confederation of Regions (COR), 3 from the Progressive Conservative Party and one from the New Democratic Party.

Lt-Governor, His Honour Gilbert Finn
Premier, Hon. Frank McKenna

JUDICATURE

Court of Appeal, Chief Justice, Hon. W. Hoyt
Queen's Bench Division, Chief Justice, Hon. G. A. Richard

ECONOMY

The estimated revenue for the year ending 31 March 1992 was C$3,689,100,000 and ordinary expenditure, $3,906,600,000.

New Brunswick's largest manufacturing group, in terms of shipments, is the paper and allied industries, followed by the food and wood industries. Together these industries accounted in 1992 for 50.4 per cent of the total value of

manufacturing shipments of C$5,590 million. Saint John has a major ice-free port and is the principal manufacturing centre of the province.

The total land area is 27,633 sq. miles; farms numbered 3,252 and averaged 285 acres each in 1991. Dairy products and potatoes are the leading agricultural products. Both industries together accounted for 38.5 per cent of total farm cash receipts in 1992. Farm cash receipts in 1992 totalled C$261,934,000.

Fishing is an important industry, employing about 7,700 fishermen. The chief commercial fish are lobsters, herring, tuna, crab and cod. Landings reached 118,224 tonnes valued at C$96,304,000 in 1992.

Extensive zinc, lead and copper deposits are now being mined in the north-eastern part of the province with New Brunswick being the largest producer of zinc in Canada. A lead smelter, fertilizer plant and port facilities have been constructed at Belledune. Canada's only primary antimony producer is located at Lake George. There is exploration and development near Sussex and Salt Springs, where potash production continues to escalate. A potash terminal has been built at the port of Saint John. Coal is mined at Grand Lake and exploration for other deposits is being undertaken. Total mineral production was valued at C$885,822,000 in 1992.

Tourism is of increasing value to the economy.

NEWFOUNDLAND AND LABRADOR

The Island of Newfoundland is situated between 46° 37'–51° 37' N. latitude and 52° 44'–59° 30' W. longitude, on the north-east side of the Gulf of St Lawrence, and is separated from the North American continent by the Straits of Belle Isle on the north-west and by Cabot Strait on the south-west. The island is about 510 km long and 508 km broad and is triangular in shape. It comprises an area of 111,390 sq. km (43,008 sq. miles), with a population (1991 Census) (inclusive of Labrador) of 568,474.

Labrador forms the most easterly part of the North American continent, and extends from Point St Charles, at the north-east entrance to the Straits of Belle Isle on the south, to Cape Chidley, at the eastern entrance to Hudson's Straits on the north. It has an area of 294,328 sq. km (113,641 sq. miles), with a population (1991 Census) of 30,375. Labrador is noted for its cod fisheries and also possesses valuable salmon, herring, trout and seal fisheries.

PROVINCIAL CAPITAL – Ψ St John's (population 1991 Census, Greater St John's 171,859) is North America's oldest city, and thus of historical interest. It is the seat of the provincial legislature, the site of most provincial and federal government offices and the principal port for the island of Newfoundland. Newfoundland's second city of Corner Brook (population 1991 Census, 22,410) is situated on the west coast.

GOVERNMENT

In 1949 Newfoundland became the tenth province of the Dominion of Canada. The Government is administered by a Lieutenant-Governor, aided by an Executive Council and a Legislative Assembly of 52 members elected for a term of five years. A General Election was held on 3 May 1993. The standings in the current House of Assembly are: Liberals 35; Progressive Conservatives 16, New Democrats 1.
Lt.-Governor, His Honour Frederick W. Russell
Premier, Hon. Clyde Wells

JUDICATURE

Court of Appeal, Chief Justice, Hon. Noel H. A. Goodridge
Trial Division, Chief Justice, Hon. T. A. Hickman

ECONOMY

The estimated gross capital and current account revenues for 1993-4 are C$3,181,854,000 and the gross current and capital account expenditures C$3,475,110,300.

The main primary industries are fishing, forestry and mining. In 1992 shipments of fish products were valued at C$822 million. In 1992 newsprint shipments from the three pulp and paper mills were valued at C$347 million, mining plus structural materials shipments were estimated at C$735 million, of which C$680 million was from the two iron ore mines in Labrador. Total manufacturing shipments were valued at C$1,366 million in 1992. The hydro-electric plant on the Churchill river is the largest underground plant in the world, with a capacity of 5,225,000 kW.

Over 139 wells have been drilled off Newfoundland since 1965. Discovery of oil was made in 1979 on the Grand Banks. Oil production is expected to begin in the 1990s, with a peak production of 110,000 barrels of oil a day. In 1992 offshore exploration expenditure was approximately C$1.2 million

TRANSPORT

The island portion of the province utilizes the Trans-Coastal Highway and other roadways to access most communities. There is a coastal boat service that operates on the southern portion of the island and on the coast of Labrador linking otherwise isolated communities. The Quebec-North shore and Labrador Railway is operated in Labrador, linking the interior with Sept-Iles, Quebec. The island is connected to mainland Canada by a ferry service that runs from Sydney, Nova Scotia, to Port Aux Basques and Argentia.

NOVA SCOTIA

Nova Scotia is a peninsula between 43° 25'-47° N. latitude and 59° 40'-66° 25' W. longitude, and is connected to New Brunswick by a low fertile isthmus about 28 km wide. It comprises an area of 55,490 sq. km (21,425 sq. miles), including 2,650 sq. km of lakes and rivers and 10,424 km of shoreline. No place is more than 56 km from the Atlantic Ocean. Population (April 1993 estimate) 909,800.

Cape Breton Island has been part of Nova Scotia since 1819. It is the centre of the steel manufacturing and coal mining industries, and is also noted for its lakes and coastal scenery, making it a tourist attraction in Canada.

PROVINCIAL CAPITAL – ΨHalifax, including the neighbouring city of Dartmouth, has a population of 182,253. The harbour, ice-free all year round, is the main Atlantic winter port of Canada. Other cities and towns include ΨSydney (26,063), ΨGlace Bay (19,501).

GOVERNMENT

The Government consists of a Lieutenant-Governor and a 52-member elected Legislative Assembly, from which the Executive Council is selected. The state of the parties in June 1992 was Liberals 40, Independent 9, New Democratic Party 3.

The Lieutenant-Governor represents The Queen and is appointed by the Governor-in-Council.

Lt.-Governor, His Honour Lloyd R. Crouse, PC
Premier, Hon. Dr John Savage
Speaker of the House of Assembly, Hon. Paul MacEwan

NOVA SCOTIA TRADE AND INVESTMENT OFFICE,
14 Pall Mall, London SW1Y 5LU. *Director,*
Raymond Vaudry.

JUDICATURE

Supreme Court, Appeal Division, Chief Justice, Hon. L. O. Clarke

Supreme Court, Trial Division, Chief Justice, Hon. Constance R. Glube

ECONOMY

The revenue for the fiscal year ending 31 March 1993 was C$3,880,423 and expenditure was C$4,234,417.

Manufacturing constitutes the most important goods-producing sector of the economy. Manufacturing plants provide employment for 9.9 per cent of the labour force.

Electric power in Nova Scotia is supplied by the Nova Scotia Power Corporation. The Corporation's generating stations, which are predominantly coal fired, have a capacity of 2,129,300 kilowatts.

There was one well drilled onshore in 1989-90. Canada's first offshore oil well went into production on 6 June 1992. Total production was valued at C$94,000,000 in 1992.

The total value of mineral production in 1992 (preliminary) was estimated at C$466 million. Dollar value of coal production was C$259 million, and salt production C$50 million.

A total of 520,202 tonnes of fish and shellfish was harvested in 1991 for a landed value of C$496.2 million.

Forest lands total 10 million acres or 73 per cent of the land area. About 73 per cent of forest land is privately owned. Forest-based industries employed an average of 8,000 in 1992, and contributed C$800 million to the Nova Scotia economy.

Between 15 May and 31 October 1992, about 1.03 million visitors spent about C$300 million in the province.

ONTARIO

Ontario contains a total area of 1,068,472 sq. km (412,578 sq. miles), with a population (1991 Census) of 10,084,885.

PROVINCIAL CAPITAL – ΨToronto (metropolitan, Census 1991, 3,893,046) has a wide range of manufacturing and service industries and is a centre of education, business and finance. Other major urban areas are: Ottawa, the national capital (313,987); ΨHamilton (599,760), with iron and steel industry, metal fabrication, machinery, electrical and chemical industries; London (381,522), a business and manufacturing centre; ΨWindsor (262,075); Kitchener (356,421) and Sudbury (157,613).

GOVERNMENT

The Government is vested in a Lieutenant-Governor and a Legislative Assembly of 130 members elected for five years.

As at 21 June 1993, there were 71 New Democrats, 34 Liberals, 21 Progressive Conservatives, 3 Independents, and one vacant seat. The last elections were held on 6 September 1990.

Lt.-Governor, Hon. Henry N. R. Jackman.
Premier, Hon. Bob Rae

JUDICATURE

Chief Justice of the Court of Appeal for Ontario,
Hon. C. L. Dubin
Chief Justice of the Ontario Court-General Division,
Hon. F. W. Callaghan
Chief Justice of the Ontario Court-Provincial Division,
Hon. Sidney B. Linden

ECONOMY

Ontario has the highest total of agricultural production in Canada with a gross value of C$6,030 million and a total net farm income of C$1,180 million.

Productive forested lands cover 39.9 million hectares. Paper and allied industries are by far the most important sector of Ontario's forest industry.

Ontario's natural resources include 30 basic minerals, such as copper, iron ore, zinc, sulphur, gold, nickel and platinum. Total value of the mineral production in 1992 was estimated at C$4,800 million.

Total electrical energy generated in Ontario in 1992 was 136,972 million kW.

Ontario is the chief manufacturing province in Canada, producing 50 per cent of all manufactured goods. During 1992 Ontario's exports totalled C$82,233 million.

PRINCE EDWARD ISLAND

Prince Edward Island lies in the southern part of the Gulf of St Lawrence, between 46°–47° N. latitude and 62°–64° 30′ W. longitude. It is about 225 km in length, and from 6 to 64 km in breadth; its area is 5,659 sq. km (2,185 sq. miles), and its population (1991 Census) 129,765.

PROVINCIAL CAPITAL – ΨCharlottetown (30,000), on the shore of Hillsborough Bay, which forms a good harbour.

GOVERNMENT

The Government is vested in a Lieutenant-Governor, an Executive Council, and Legislative Assembly of 32 members elected for a term of up to five years, 16 as Councillors and 16 as Assemblymen. After the election of 29 March 1993 there were 31 Liberals and 1 Progressive Conservative.
Lt.-Governor, Her Honour Marion L. Reid
Premier, Hon. Catherine S. Callbeck
Speaker of the Legislative Assembly, Hon. Nancy Gaptill

JUDICATURE
Appeal Division, Chief Justice, Hon. Norman H. Carruthers
Trial Division, Chief Justice, Hon. K. R. MacDonald

ECONOMY
The ordinary revenue of the province in 1990–1 was C$677.6 million and the expenditure C$696.2 million.

Approximately 48 per cent of the total area of the province is farmland. The value of farm cash receipts in 1992 was C$222.8 million, of which 30.7 per cent was from the sale of potatoes. Dairy, beef and hogs are also important agriculture products.

Fish landings were valued at C$79.7 million in 1992 of which 74.5 per cent was of lobster.

The total value of manufacturing shipments was C$407 million in 1992, of which 72.5 per cent was in the food products industry.

A major summer economic activity is tourism. Non-resident tourists spent C$67.1 million in the province in 1992.

EDUCATION
A university and a college of applied arts and technology were established in 1969, estimated full- and part-time enrolment for 1991–2 being 3,560 (University of Prince Edward Island), and 5,433 for the college of applied arts and technology (Holland College).

QUEBEC

Quebec contains an area estimated at 1,540,667 sq. km (594,855 sq. miles) with a population (1991 Census) of 6,895,963.

PROVINCIAL CAPITAL – ΨQuebec. Population (Census 1991) 167,517; historic city visited annually by thousands of tourists, and one of the great seaport towns of Canada. ΨMontreal (1,017,666) is the commercial centre. Other important cities are Laval (314,398); Sherbrooke (76,429); Montreal-Nord (85,516) and La Salle (73,804).

GOVERNMENT
The government of the province is vested in a Lieutenant-Governor, a Council of Ministers and a National Assembly of 125 members elected for five years. At 25 June 1993, there were 87 Liberals, 32 Parti Quebecois, 3 Equality members, one Independent and two vacant seats.
Lt.-Governor, His Honour Martial Asselin
Prime Minister, Hon. Robert Bourassa

AGENT-GENERAL'S OFFICE IN LONDON, 59 Pall Mall, London SW1Y 5JH. *Agent-General*, Harold Mailhot.

JUDICATURE
Court of Appeal, Chief Justice of Quebec, Hon. Claude Bisson
Superior Court, Chief Justice of Quebec (Montreal), Hon. Lawrence Poitras

ECONOMY
The revenue for the year 1991–2 was C$34,471,075,000; expenditure amounted to C$38,662,493,000.

The principal manufacturing centres are Montreal, Montreal East, Quebec, Trois-Rivières, Sherbrooke, Shawinigan Drummondville and Lachine. Forest lands cover 912,123 sq. km, of which 742,166 sq. km are productive.

Total estimated value of shipments in the manufacturing industries in 1992 was C$68,678 million. Value of 1992 shipments in the chief industries was accounted for by food, C$9,941 million; paper and allied industries, C$6,570m; primary metal industries, C$5,696m, and transport equipment, C$5,347m.

In 1992 total farm receipts were:

Crops	C$715,557,000
Livestock and livestock products	2,422,428,000
Other farm receipts	622,359,000

In 1991 73,872 tonnes of fish, to the value of C$85,487,000 were landed.

Minerals to the value of C$2,646,847,000 were mined in 1992. This included copper, C$255,166,000; asbestos, C$224,826,000; and gold, C$589,986,000.

SASKATCHEWAN

Saskatchewan lies between Manitoba to the east and Alberta to the west and has an area of 652,324 sq. km (251,864 sq. miles) (of which the land area is 570,269 sq. km, or 220,182 sq. miles), with a population (estimated 1991) of 1,013,500. Saskatchewan extends along the Canada–USA boundary for 632 km (393 miles) and northwards for 1,224 km (761 miles). Its northern width is 440 km (276 miles).

PROVINCIAL CAPITAL – Regina. Population (1991 Census), 179,178. Other cities: Saskatoon (186,058), Moose Jaw (33,593); Prince Albert (34,181) and Yorkton (15,315).

GOVERNMENT
The Government is vested in the Lieutenant-Governor, with a Legislative Assembly of 66 members. There is an Executive Council of 12 members. The Legislative Assembly is elected for five years and the state of the parties in June 1993 was: New Democratic Party 55; Progressive Conservative 10; Liberal 1.
Lt.-Governor, Her Honour Sylvia O. Fedoruk
Premier, Hon. Roy Romanow, QC

JUDICATURE
Court of Appeal, Chief Justice, Hon. E. D. Bayda
Queen's Bench, Chief Justice, Hon. D. K. MacPherson
Provincial Court, Chief Judge, Hon. B. P. Carey

FINANCE

Consolidated Fund and Heritage combined revenue for year ending March 1994 is C$4,631,800,000 and expenditure C$4,928,142,000.

CAPE VERDE
República de Cabo Verde

Cape Verde, off the west coast of Africa, consists of two groups of islands, Windward (Santo Antão, São Vicente, Santa Luzia, São Nicolau, Boa Vista and Sal) and Leeward (Maio, São Tiago, Fogo and Brava) with a total area of 1,557 sq. miles (4,033 sq. km). The population (UN estimate 1991) was 382,000 the majority of whom are Roman Catholic.

CAPITAL – ΨPraia, population (1980) 57,748.
CURRENCY – Escudo Caboverdiano of 100 centavos.
FLAG – Blue with three horizontal stripes of white, red, white near the bottom; over all on these near the hoist a ring of ten yellow stars.
NATIONAL DAY – 5 July (Independence Day).

GOVERNMENT

The islands, colonized *c.*1460, achieved independence from Portugal on 5 July 1975 under the nationalist party of Guinea Bissau and Cape Verde. A federation of the islands with Guinea Bissau was planned (till 1879 Guinea-Bissau and the islands were a single administrative unit) but this was dropped following the 1980 coup in Guinea Bissau.

The republic was a one-party (the PAICV) state until the constitution was amended in September 1990. Multi-party elections, held on 14 January 1991, were won by the opposition Movement for Democracy (MPD) which won 56 seats in the 79-seat National Assembly. The Independent António Mascarenhas Monteiro was elected as President on 17 February 1991.

HEAD OF STATE
President, António Mascarenhas Monteiro, *assumed office*, 22 March 1991.

COUNCIL OF MINISTERS *as at August 1993*
Prime Minister and Minister of Defence, Carlos Veiga.
Minister of State, and Justice and Labour, Eurico Monteiro.
Minister of State, and Economic Co-ordination, José Veiga.
Foreign Affairs, Manuel Chantre.
Fisheries, Agriculture and Rural Animation, Helena Semedo.
Infrastructure and Transport, Teofilo Silva.
Health, Rui Soares.
Education and Sport, Manuel Fautino.
Culture and Communication, Ondina Ferreira.
Tourism, Industry and Commerce, João Silva.
Public Administration and Parliamentary Affairs, Alfredo Teixeira.
Interior, Mario Silva.
Finance, Alpio Fernandes.

EMBASSY OF THE REPUBLIC OF CAPE VERDE
44 Konninginnegracht, 2514 AD, The Hague,
The Netherlands
Tel: The Hague 3469623

Ambassador Extraordinary and Plenipotentiary, His Excellency Terêncio Gregorio Alves (1992).
BRITISH AMBASSADOR (resident in Dakar, Senegal).
There is a British Consulate on *São Vicente.*

ECONOMY

The islands have had little rain since 1969, and agriculture is mostly confined to irrigated inland valleys, the chief products being bananas and coffee (for export), maize, sugarcane and nuts. Fish and shellfish are important exports. Salt is obtained on Sal, Boa Vista and Maio; volcanic rock is also mined for export.

In January 1993 the government announced that a programme of reform would be introduced to institute a change to a market economy and to privatize most industry within four years.

The main ports are Praia and Mindelo, and there is an international airport on Sal.

TRADE WITH UK	1991	1992
Imports from UK	£1,908,000	£2,990,000
Exports to UK	193,000	409,000

CENTRAL AFRICAN REPUBLIC
République Centrafricaine

The Central African Republic lies just north of the Equator between Cameroon, Chad, the southern part of Sudan, and Zaire. The Republic has an area of 240,535 sq. miles (622,984 sq. km), and a population (UN estimate 1991) of 3,127,000.

CAPITAL – Bangui, near the border with Zaire, population (1984 estimate) 473,817.
CURRENCY – Franc CFA of 100 centimes.
FLAG – Four horizontal stripes, blue, white, green, yellow, crossed by central vertical red stripe with a yellow five-pointed star in top left-hand corner.
NATIONAL DAY – 1 December.

GOVERNMENT

On 1 December 1958 the French colony of Ubanghi Shari elected to remain within the French Community and adopted the title of the Central African Republic. It became fully independent on 17 August 1960. The first President of the Central African Republic, David Dacko, held office from 1960 until 1966, when he was replaced by the then Col. Bokassa after a coup d'état. On 4 December 1976, President Bokassa proclaimed himself Emperor and a new constitution was introduced, the country being known as the Central African Empire. On 20 September 1979 Emperor Bokassa was deposed by David Dacko in a bloodless coup and the country reverted to a republic.

President Dacko surrendered power on 1 September 1981 to army commander Gen. André Kolingba in a bloodless coup. In September 1985 President Kolingba dissolved the Military Committee for National Recovery (CMRN) and appointed a civilian-dominated cabinet. In November 1986 a referendum was held whereby voters approved a new constitution and the establishment of a one-party state.

Strikes and unrest occurred throughout 1991 and 1992 as opposition groupings and unions pressurized the government for a national conference to discuss the ending of one-party rule and the implementation of multi-party politics. Multi-party presidential and legislative elections were held on 25 October 1992 but were annulled by the Supreme Court due to sabotage and irregularities. The elections followed a 'Grand National Debate' in August 1992, which had been dominated by the ruling Central African Democratic Assembly (RDC) of President Kolingba, and which had instructed the National Assembly to amend the constitution to allow multi-party politics. President Kolinga refused to confer sovereign powers on the 'Grand National Debate' but instead formed a coalition government in December 1992 and then another in February 1993 in which opposition parties participated. A new National Provisional Council for the Republic (CNPRR) was established in February as the transitional legislature to monitor compliance with the constitution during the transition period until new presidential and legislative elections, scheduled for late 1993, are held.

HEAD OF STATE
President and General of the Armed Forces, Gen. André Kolingba, *assumed office* 1 September 1981, *re-elected* 21 November 1986

COUNCIL OF MINISTERS *as at August 1993*
Prime Minister, Enoch Lakoue.
Minister of State, Economy, Finance, Planning and International Co-operation, Thierry Bingaba.
Justice, Jacques Bosso.
Finance, Emmanuel Dokouna.
Foreign Affairs, Jean-Marie Bassia.
Public Security and Territorial Administration, Gen. Alphonse Goumbadi.
Higher Education and Scientific Research, Michel Koyt.
Primary and Secondary Education, Tchakpa Mbrede.
Defence, War Veterans, Energy, Mines and Water Supply, Raymond Mbitiko.
Civil Service, Labour and Social Security, and Vocational Training, Ismaela Ninaga.
General Secretariat and Relations with Parliament, Emile Djapou.

EMBASSY OF THE CENTRAL AFRICAN REPUBLIC
30 rue des Perchamps, 75016, Paris
Tel: Paris 42244256

Ambassador Extraordinary and Plenipotentiary, His Excellency Auguste Magba (1993).
BRITISH AMBASSADOR (resident in Yaoundé, Cameroon).
Honorary Consul, A. G. Perreard, P.O. Box 728, Bangui.

ECONOMY

In an effort to revive an ailing economy, the Government launched a structured adjustment programme in 1986, streamlining the civil service, increasing tax revenues, and reducing price controls. Cotton, diamonds, coffee and timber are the major exports.

TRADE WITH UK	1991	1992
Imports from UK	£502,000	£656,000
Exports to UK	37,000	100,000

CHAD REPUBLIC
Republique du Tchad

Situated in north-central Africa, the Chad Republic extends from 23° to 7° N. latitude and is flanked by Niger and Cameroon on the west, by Libya on the north, by the Sudan on the east and by the Central African Republic on the south. It has an area of 495,755 sq. miles (1,284,000 sq. km) and a population (UN estimate 1991) of 5,819,000.

CAPITAL – Ndjaména (formerly known as Fort Lamy) south of Lake Chad (402,000).
CURRENCY – Franc CFA of 100 centimes.
FLAG – Vertical stripes, blue, yellow and red.
NATIONAL DAY – 13 April.

GOVERNMENT

Chad became a member state of the French Community in 1958, and was proclaimed fully independent on 11 August 1960. On 14 April 1962, a new Constitution was adopted involving a presidential-type regime. This was suspended on 13 April 1975 when President Tombalbaye was killed in a military coup. The country was run by a Supreme Military Council, under General Felix Malloum until his overthrow in February 1979. A Transitional Government of National Unity, headed by Goukouni Oueddei, was replaced in June 1982 by the government of Hissène Habré. A ceasefire between Chad and Libya was agreed in September 1987 and on 3 October 1988 they reopened diplomatic relations. The ceasefire was reaffirmed and they said that they would settle the Aouzou dispute peacefully, respecting UN and OAU charters. On 1 September 1990 Chad and Libya presented their territorial claims for the Aouzou Strip to the International Court of Justice.

In December 1990 Idriss Déby launched a successful coup in Chad and the Habré government fell. Déby announced that he would adopt a multi-party system in Chad and allowed the liberalization of an increasing number of political parties in 1991 and 1992. After repeated delays a sovereign national conference was convened on 15 January 1993 and lasted until 7 April. The conference consisted of 30 legalized parties and produced a transitional charter which provides for a transitional period of one year in which to write a new constitution and hold multi-party elections. Conference delegates elected a Higher Transitional Council (CST) of 57 members to serve as the transitional legislature and appointed a transitional government in conjunction with President Déby.

HEAD OF STATE
President, Idriss Déby.

TRANSITIONAL GOVERNMENT *as at August 1993*
Prime Minister, Fidèle Moungar.
National Defence, War Veterans and Victims, Loum Hinassou Laine.
Foreign Affairs, Ahmed Karoum.
Interior, Ali Djalbor.
Justice, Delwa Kassire Koumakoye.
Agriculture and Environment, Mahamat Saleh Ahmat.
Planning and Co-operation, Ibn Oumar Mahamat Saleh.
Public Works and Transport, Saleh Kebzabo.
Civil Service and Labour, Wadal Abdelkadar Kamougue.
Livestock and Animal Resources, Hassan Fadoul Kittir.
Communications, Posts and Telecommunications, Government Spokesman, Allabo Ahmat.
Mines, Energy and Water Resources, Valentin Didier Neatobei.
Commerce and Industry, Miskine Abderahmane Izo.
Education, Culture and Reforms, Gali Ngothe.
Social and Women's Affairs, Bintou Malloum.
Finance and Computer Science, Robert Roingam.
Public Health, Mahamat Nouri.
Government Secretary-General, Carmele Soukat Ngarmbatina.

EMBASSY OF THE REPUBLIC OF CHAD
Boulevard Lambermont 52, 1030 Brussels, Belgium
Tel: Brussels 2151975

Ambassador Extraordinary and Plenipotentiary, new appointment awaited.
BRITISH AMBASSADOR (resident in Yaoundé, Cameroon).
Honorary Consul, E. Abtour, BP877, Avenue Charles de Gaulle, Ndjaména.

ECONOMY

About 90 per cent of the workforce is occupied in agriculture, fishing and forestry. There is an oilfield in Kanem and salt is mined around Lake Chad, but the most important activities are cotton growing (mostly in the south) and animal husbandry (in central areas). Raw cotton and meat are the main exports.

TRADE WITH UK	1991	1992
Imports from UK	£1,789,000	£1,359,000
Exports to UK	1,477,000	1,604,000

CHILE
República de Chile

A state of South America lying between the Andes and the shores of the South Pacific, Chile extends coastwise from just north of Arica to Cape Horn south, between 17° 15′ and 55° 59′ S. latitude and 66° 30′ and 75° 48′ W. longitude. The extreme length of the country is about 2,800 miles, with an average breadth, north of 41°, of 100 miles. The total area of Chile is 292,258 sq. miles (756,945 sq. km).

The great chain of the Andes runs along its eastern limit, with a general elevation of 5,000 to 15,000 feet above sea level; but numerous summits attain a greater height. The chain lowers considerably towards its southern extremity.

The Andes form a boundary with Argentina, and at the head of the pass where the international road from Chile to Argentina crosses the frontier, has been erected a statue of Christ the Redeemer, 26 feet high, made of bronze from old cannon, to commemorate the peaceful settlement of a boundary dispute in 1902. The disputed boundary with Argentina in the Beagle Channel was settled by a treaty ratified in 1985.

There are no rivers of great size, and none of them is of much service as a navigable highway. In the north the country is arid.

Among the island possessions of Chile are the Juan Fernandez group (three islands) about 360 miles distant from Valparaiso. One of these islands is the reputed scene of Alexander Selkirk's (Robinson Crusoe) shipwreck. Easter Island (27° 8′ S. and 109° 28′ W.), about 2,000 miles distant in the South Pacific Ocean, contains stone platforms and hundreds of stone figures, the origin of which has not yet been determined. The area of the island is about 45 sq. miles (116.5 sq. km).

POPULATION – The population (UN estimate 1991) is 13,386,000. There are four main groups: indigenous Araucanian Indians, Fuegians, and Changos; Spanish settlers and their descendants; mixed Spanish Indians; and European immigrants. Only the few remaining indigenous Indians and some originally Bolivian Indians in the north are racially separate. Following extensive intermarriage there is no effective distinction among the remainder. The main religion is Roman Catholicism.

CAPITAL – Santiago, population (1990 estimate) 4,385,481 (Greater Santiago). Other large towns are: ΨValparaiso (500,000), Concepción (170,000), Temuco (110,000), ΨAntofagasta (110,000), Chillán (79,461), ΨTalcahuano (75,643), Talca (75,354), ΨValdivia (70,000), ΨIquique (50,000), ΨPunta Arenas (50,000). Punta Arenas on the Straits of Magellan, is the southernmost city in the world.
CURRENCY – Chilean peso of 100 centavos.
FLAG – Two horizontal bands, white, red; in top sixth a white star on blue square, next staff.

NATIONAL ANTHEM – Canción Nacional de Chile.
NATIONAL DAY – 18 September (National Anniversary).

GOVERNMENT

Chile was discovered by Spanish adventurers in the 16th century and remained under Spanish rule until 1810, when a revolutionary war, culminating in the Battle of Maipu (5 April 1818), achieved the independence of the nation.

At a general election held in September 1970, the Marxist candidate Dr Allende was elected President by a narrow margin. After severe industrial unrest and widespread violent incidents, Allende was overthrown on 11 September 1973 in a coup carried out by leaders of the armed forces and national police.

After a national plebiscite, the Constitution of 1925 was replaced early in 1981 and General Pinochet was sworn in as President, to serve until 1989. Pinochet was defeated in a plebiscite of 5 October 1988 regarding his term of office being extended for a further eight years. He resisted calls for his resignation. Another plebiscite on 30 July 1989 was held on changes to the 1980 Constitution. Presidential and Congressional elections were held in December 1989. Patricio Aylwin was elected President of the Republic for four years, thus beginning a gradual transition to full democracy.

Executive power is held by the President, legislative power is exercised by a Parliament which comprises an Upper Chamber of 47 Senators and a Lower Chamber of 120 Deputies.

Chile is divided into 12 regions and the Metropolitan Area.

HEAD OF STATE
President of the Republic, Patricio Aylwin Azócar, *assumed office* 11 March 1990.

CABINET *as at August 1993*
Interior, Enrique Krauss.
Foreign Affairs, Enrique Silva Cimma.
Defence, Patricio Rojas.
Economy, Jorge Marshall.
Finance, Alejandro Foxley.
Education, Jorge Arrate.
Justice, Francisco Cumplido.
Public Works, Carlos Hurtado.
Agriculture, Juan Agustin Figueroa.
National Properties, Luis Alvarado.
Labour, Rene Cortazar.
Public Health, Julio Montt.
Mining, Alejandro Hales.
Housing, Alberto Etchegaray.
Transport and Communication, German Molina.
General Secretary of Government, Enrique Correa.
General Secretary of Presidency, Edgardo Boeninger.
Central Planning, Sergio Molina.

EMBASSY OF CHILE
12 Devonshire Street, London WIN 2DS
Tel 071-580 6392

Ambassador Extraordinary and Plenipotentiary, His Excellency Herrán Errázariz (1993).
Minister-Counsellor, L. del Solar.
Military Attaché, Brig. J. Arangua.
Counsellor, F. Hafemann (*Economic*).

BRITISH EMBASSY
Avenae El Bosque Norte 0125
Casilla 72-D, Santiago 9
Tel: Santiago 2313727

Ambassador Extraordinary and Plenipotentiary, His Excellency Richard A. Nielson, CMG, LVO (1990).
Counsellor, Head of Chancery and Consul-General, P. L. Hunt.
Defence, Naval and Military Attaché, Capt. R. A. Rowley, OBE, RN.
First Secretary (Commercial), J. W. Ayres.
BRITISH CONSULAR OFFICES – There are British Consular Offices at *Antofagasta, Arica, Concepción, Santiago, Punta Arenas, Valparaiso.*

BRITISH COUNCIL REPRESENTATIVE – Robin Evans (*Cultural Attaché*), Eliodoro Yañez 832, Casilla 15-T Tajamar, Santiago.
The Council supplies books to the libraries of the Instituto Chileno-Britanico in *Santiago, Viña del Mar/Valparaiso* and *Concepción.*
BRITISH-CHILEAN CHAMBER OF COMMERCE, Av. Suecia 155-C, Casilla 536, Santiago.

ECONOMY

Cereals, legumes, sugar beet, vegetables, fruit, tobacco, hemp and vines are grown extensively (especially in the central zone) and livestock accounts for nearly 40 per cent of agricultural production. Sheep farming predominates in the extreme south. There are large timber tracts in the central and southern zones of Chile, some types of which are exported, along with wood derivatives such as cellulose and pulp. Industrial-scale fishing, which exceeded 6.5 million tonnes in 1989, makes Chile the fifth largest nation in terms of catch. The principal end product is fish meal.

The mineral wealth is considerable, the country being particularly rich in copper-ore, iron-ore and nitrates. Chile also produces iodine, manganese ore, coal, mercury, molybdenum, zinc, lead and a small quantity of gold. Uranium is also said to have been discovered in small quantities. The rainless north is the scene of the only commercial production of nitrate of soda (Chile saltpetre) from natural resources in the world. The country has also large deposits of high grade sulphur, but mostly around high extinct volcanoes in the Andes Cordillera, difficult of access. Oil was struck in Magallanes (Tierra del Fuego) in 1945, and oil and natural gas are produced in the Magallanes area from on- and off-shore wells. This domestic production, now declining, covers less than 30 per cent of total oil requirement, and imported crude oil is refined at Concon and San Vicente in the central part of the country. There is a steel plant at Huachipato, near Concepción.

Provisional production figures for 1990 were:

Coal (tonnes)	2,515,189
Copper (tonnes)	1,603,205
Crude oil (cu. metres)	1,137,900
Natural gas (cu. metres)	4,198,300,000
Steel ingots (tonnes)	760,100*
*1989	

Industry is based on the processing of mineral, forestry, fish and agricultural products, and the manufacture of consumer goods.

FINANCE	1987	1988
Total revenue	US$8,469.8 m	US$8,967.1 m
Total expenditure	8,421.6 m	9,452.4 m

Foreign debt at 31 December 1990 was US$18,602 million, including Central Bank obligations with the IMF of US$1,151 million.

TRADE

The principal exports are metallic and non-metallic minerals (copper represented 45.5 per cent of total export earnings in 1990), sawn timber, cellulose and other wood derivatives, some metal products, fish products, vegetables, fruit and wool. The principal imports are sugar and other food products, industrial raw materials, machinery, equipment and spares, oil fuels, lubricants and transportation equipment.

	1989	1990
Total imports	US$6,734.2 m	US$7,272.1 m
Total exports	8,190.4 m	8,580.3 m

Trade with UK	1991	1992
Imports from UK	£106,640,000	£125,832,000
Exports to UK	177,876,000	205,737,000

COMMUNICATIONS

Chilean ships have a virtual monopoly in the coastwide trade, though, with the improvement of the roads, an increasing share of internal transportation is moving by road and rail. The Chilean mercantile marine numbers 73 vessels (of over 100 tons gross) with a total deadweight tonnage of 820,965 (1990).

There are 6,575 miles of railway track. A line (*the Longitudinal*) runs from La Calera, just north of Santiago, to Iquique. However, road transport has caused considerable reduction in rail traffic along this route. Another rail line runs from Valparaiso through La Calera, 60 miles inland, and after passing through Santiago ends at Puerto Montt.

With the completion of a section of 435 miles from Corumba, Brazil, to Santa Cruz, Bolivia, the Trans-Continental Line will link the Chilean Pacific port of Arica with Rio de Janeiro on the Atlantic. Another line from Antofagasta to Salta (Argentina) was opened in 1948.

Chile is served by over 20 international airlines. Domestic traffic is carried by Linea Aerea Nacional (LAN) and LADECO, which also operate internationally, and smaller regional carriers.

Chile's road system is about 65,000 kilometres in length.

DEFENCE

Military service is compulsory for two years but not all those who are liable are required. Recruitment for the Navy is mostly voluntary, but there are some conscripts.

The total active armed forces strength is 91,800, including 30,800 conscripts. The Army consists of 54,000 personnel (27,000 conscripts) with 170 main battle tanks, 160 light tanks, 200 reconnaissance vehicles, 530 armoured personnel carriers and 150 artillery pieces. Organization is into six divisions with one independent brigade.

Naval strength is 25,000 (3,000 conscripts) with six destroyers, four frigates, four submarines and ten patrol and coastal craft together with six combat aircraft and 12 armed helicopters. There are 4,000 marines in four battalion groups and 1,600 coast guard personnel. The Air Force numbers 12,800 personnel (800 conscripts) with 106 combat aircraft organized into two ground attack, two counter-insurgency, one reconnaissance and one transport squadrons.

There is, in addition, a paramilitary Carabineros police force of 27,000 personnel.

EDUCATION

Elementary education is free, and has been compulsory since 1920. There are eight universities (three in Santiago, two in Valparaiso, one each in Antofagasta, Concepción and Valdivia).

CULTURE

Spanish is the language of the country, with admixtures of local words of Indian origin. Recent efforts have reduced illiteracy and have thus afforded access to the literature of Spain, to supplement the vigorous national output. The Nobel Prize for Literature was awarded in 1945 to Gabriela Mistral, for Chilean verse and prose, and in 1971 to the poet Pablo Neruda. There are over 100 newspapers and a large number of periodicals.

CHINA
Zhonghua Renmin Gongheguo – The People's Republic of China

The area of China is 3,705,408 sq. miles, (9,596,961 sq. km). A nationwide census (the fourth) was held in July 1990, which recorded a total population of 1,130,000,000. The estimated population for 1992 was 1,171,000,000.

POPULATION OF THE PROVINCES (1991 estimates)

Anhui	57,610,000
Beijing	10,940,000
Fujian	30,790,000
Gansu	22,850,000
Guangdong	64,390,000
Guangxi Zhuang Autonomous Region	43,240,000
Guizhou	33,150,000
Hainan	6,740,000
Hebei	62,200,000
Heilongjiang	35,750,000
Henan	87,630,000
Hubei	55,120,000
Hunan	62,090,000
Jiangsu	68,440,000
Jiangxi	38,650,000
Jilin	25,090,000
Liaoning	39,900,000
Nei Monggol Autonomous Region	21,840,000
Ningxia Hui Autonomous Region	4,800,000
Qinghai	4,540,000
Shaanxi	33,630,000
Shandong	85,700,000
Shanghai	13,400,000
Shanxi	29,420,000
Sichuan	108,970,000
Tianjin	9,090,000
Tibet Autonomous Region	2,260,000
Xinjiang Uygur Autonomous Region	15,550,000
Yunnan	37,820,000
Zhejiang	42,020,000
Armed Forces	2,700,000

China is anxious to control the growth of the population and has introduced stringent policies intended to result in a population of 1,250 million by the year 2000. About 6 per cent of the population belong to around 55 ethnic minorities. Among the largest are the Zhuang of Guangxi, the Uygurs of Xinjiang, the Tibetans and the Mongols.

CAPITAL – Beijing (Peking), population (metropolitan area, 1990) 10,860,000 (excluding temporary residents).
MAJOR CITIES – Population of major cities in 1989 was:

ΨShanghai*	12,670,000	Harbin	2,800,000
Tianjin	5,700,000	Chengdu	2,780,000
Shenyang	4,500,000	Xian	2,710,000
Wuhan	3,710,000	Nanjing	2,470,000
Guangzhou		Taiyuan	1,900,000
(Canton)	3,540,000	Kunming	1,500,000
Chongqing	2,960,000	Lanzhou	1,480,000
*metropolitan area			

CURRENCY – The currency is called Renminbi (RMB). The unit of currency is the yuan of 10 jiao or 100 fen.
FLAG – Red, with large gold five-point star and four small gold stars in crescent, all in upper quarter next staff.
NATIONAL ANTHEM – March of the Volunteers.
NATIONAL DAY – 1 October (Founding of People's Republic).

GOVERNMENT

On 10 October 1911, the party of reform forced the Imperial dynasty to a 'voluntary' abdication, and a republic was proclaimed at Wuchang.

On 30 September 1949 the Chinese People's Political Consultative Conference (CPPCC) met in Beijing (Peking) and appointed the National People's Government Council under the chairmanship of Mao Zedong (Mao Tse-tung). On 1 October Mao proclaimed the inauguration of the Chinese People's Republic.

The regime was recognized by all the Communist bloc countries in quick succession, and soon after by the Asian countries of the Commonwealth, the United Kingdom and by a number of other countries. Others, led by the United States, continued to recognize the Chiang Kai-shek regime of Taiwan as the rightful government of China. In 1971 the People's Republic won acceptance into the United Nations on the expulsion of Taiwan. Since then many more countries have accorded recognition.

CONSTITUTION

A new Constitution was adopted in December 1982, under which the National People's Congress is the highest organ of state power. It is elected for a term of five years and is supposed to hold one session a year. It is empowered to amend the Constitution, make laws, select the President and Vice-President and other leading officials of the state, approve the national economic plan, the state budget and the final state accounts, and to decide on questions of war and peace. The State Council is the highest organ of the state administration. It is composed of the Premier, the Vice-Premiers, the State Councillors, heads of Ministries and Commissions, the Auditor-General and the Secretary-General. Command over the armed forces is vested in the Central Military Commission.

Deputies to Congresses at the primary level are 'directly elected' by the voters 'through a secret ballot after democratic consultation'. This is now extended to county level. These Congresses elect the deputies to the Congress at the next higher level. Deputies to the National People's Congress are elected by the People's Congresses of the provinces, autonomous regions and municipalities directly under the central government, and by the armed forces.

Local government is conducted through People's Governments at provincial, municipal and county levels. Autonomous regions, prefectures and counties exist for national minorities and are described as self-governing. The system prevailing is that found elsewhere, i.e. People's Congresses and People's Governments. Beijing, Shanghai and Tianjin continue to come directly under the central government.

RECENT EVENTS

Following the deaths of Mao Zedong and Zhou En-lai in 1976, the disgraced Deng Xiaoping was recalled. At the 11th Party Congress in 1977 Deng was elected Vice-Chairman and became the dominant force within the Chinese Communist Party by eliminating leftist influence, rehabilitating fallen leaders and adjusting Maoist policies to permit economic liberalization. Deng's policies were reaffirmed at the 12th Congress in 1982. The Congress also elected a new party leadership dominated by Deng and his supporters. The post of Chairman of the Party was abolished. The party leader now holds the post of General Secretary. The 13th Party Congress in 1987 reaffirmed open-door policies. Most of the old revolutionary generation were removed, in elections, from the top posts.

Student-led pro-democracy demonstrations throughout April and May, centred on Tiananmen Square in Beijing, ended on 3–4 June 1989 when the People's Liberation Army took control of Beijing, killing thousands of protesters. Political control swung into the hands of the hardline elements of the leadership, who adopted policies of recentralization based on Marxist ideology, while simultaneously pledging commitment to reform under the influence of Deng Xiaoping. Deng retired from his last official post as Chairman of the Central Military Commission in November 1989 but is still the ultimate arbiter on policy decisions. At Deng's instigation during 1992 the emphasis has again switched back to economic reform in government policy and the power of the hardline elements went into decline again.

The 14th Party Congress in October 1992 saw an endorsement of Deng Xiaoping's calls for faster, bolder economic reforms and of his 'socialist market economy'. The majority of the remaining conservatives were replaced by moderate economic reformers. However, the summer of 1993 saw the Chinese economy overheating as in 1988–9, with up to 20 per cent inflation in some areas. This led to unrest in the provinces as the 1989 economic boom–bust cycle repeated itself and farmers were not being paid. In July 1993 the government introduced an austerity programme to reduce inflation and growth by cutting government spending and raising interest rates. Emergency measures have been reintroduced to reassert a degree of central control over the economically independent free-market coastal regions in an attempt to prevent a repeat of the political unrest of 1989.

President of the People's Republic of China, Jiang Zeuin, *elected* April 1993.

Vice President, Rong Yiren.

Chairman of the Standing Committee of the Eighth National People's Congress, Qiao Shi.
Chairman of the Central Military Commission, Jiang Zemin.

STATE COUNCIL *as at August 1993*

Premier, Li Peng.

Vice-Premiers, Qian Qichen; Li Lanqing; Zhu Rongji; Zou Jiahua.

State Councillors, Li Tieying; Chi Haotian; Song Jian; Li Guixian; Ismail Amat; Peng Peiyun; Luo Gan.

MINISTERS
Agriculture, Liu Jiang.
Chemical Industry, Gu Xiulian.
Civil Affairs, Doje Cering.
Coal Industry, Wang Senhao.
Communications, Huang Zhendong.
Construction, Hou Jie.
Culture, Liu Zhongde.
Electrical Industry, Shi Dazhen.
Electronics Industry, Hu Qili.
Finance, Liu Zhongli.
Foreign Affairs, Qian Qichen.
Foreign Trade and Economic Co-operation, Wu Yi.
Forestry, Xu Youfang.
Geology and Mineral Resources, Zhu Xun.
Internal Trade, Zhang Haoruo.
Justice, Xiao Yang.
Labour, Li Boyong.
Machine Building Industry, He Guangyuan.
Metallurgical Industry, Liu Qi.
National Defence, Chi Haotian.
Personnel, Song Defu.
Posts and Telecommunications, Wu Jichuan.
Public Health, Chen Minzhang.
Public Security, Tao Siju.
Radio, Film and Television, Ai Zhisheng.
Railways, Han Zhubin.
State Security, Jia Chunwang.

Supervision, Cao Qingze.
Water Resources, Niu Maosheng.

MINISTERS IN CHARGE OF STATE COMMISSIONS
Economics and Trade, Wang Zhongyu.
Education, Zhu Kaixuan.
Family Planning, Peng Peiyun.
Nationalities Affairs, Ismail Amat.
Physical Culture and Sports, Wu Shaozu.
Planning, Chen Jinhua.
Restructuring Economy, Li Tieying.
Science, Technology and Industry for National Defence, Ding Henggao.
Science and Technology, Song Jian.
Auditor-General, Lu Peijian.
Secretary-General, Luo Gan.

President of the People's Bank of China, Li Guixian.

THE CHINESE COMMUNIST PARTY
General Secretary, Jiang Zemin.
Politburo Standing Committee, Jiang Zemin; Li Peng; Qiao Shi; Li Ruihuan; Zhu Rongji; Liu Huaqing; Hu Jutao.
Politburo of the Central Committee, Tian Jiyun; Qiao Shi; Jiang Zemin; Li Tieying; Li Ruihuan; Liu Huaqing; Zhu Rongji; Hu Jintao; Ding Guangen; Qian Qichen; Chen Xitong; Jiang Chunyun; Li Lanqing; Wei Jianxing; Wu Bangguo; Xie Fei; Yang Baibing; Zou Jiahua; Li Peng (full members); Wen Jiabao; Wang Hanbin (alternate members).
Secretariat of the Central Committee, Jiang Zemin; Ding Guangen; Hu Jintao; Wei Jiangxing; Ren Jianxin; Wen Jiabao (full members).
Discipline Inspection Commission, Wei Jianxing (Secretary); Xu Qing; Hou Zongbin; Chen Zuolin; Wang Deying (Deputy Secretaries).
Membership, 52,000,000 (1993).

EMBASSY OF THE PEOPLE'S REPUBLIC OF CHINA
49–51 Portland Place, London WIN 3AH
Tel 071-636 9375/5726
Ambassador Extraordinary and Plenipotentiary, His Excellency Ma Yuzhen (1991).
Minister-Counsellor, Zhen Jinjiong; Lin Zhongming (Commercial).
Defence Attaché, Maj.-Gen. Han Kaihe.
Cultural Attaché, Wang Guilin.
Consul-General, Xiao Houde.

BRITISH EMBASSY
11 Guang Hua Lu, Jian Guo Men Wai, Beijing 100 600
Tel: Beijing 5321961/5
Ambassador, His Excellency Sir Robin McLaren, KCMG (1991).
Minister, Consul-General and Deputy Head of Mission, P. A. McLean.
Counsellors, N. Cox (Political); A. Kerfoot (Commercial); A. D. Johnson, CBE (Cultural, and British Council Representative); J. Smith-Laittan (Head of China Trade Unit) (resides at Hong Kong).
Defence, Military and Air Attaché, Col. M. T. P. M. Hyland, OBE.
There is also a Consulate-General in Shanghai.

ARMED FORCES

All three military arms in China are parts of the People's Liberation Army (PLA). The size of this body has not been formally given, but it is estimated that China has approximately 2.7 million men under arms (1,350,000 conscripts),

with a further 12 million (or perhaps many more) reserves who take part in militia activities. In 1955 compulsory military service was introduced for all men between the ages of 18 and 40. This service was on a selective basis. The present length of service for those conscripted is three years in the Army, four years in the Air Force and the Navy. The rank structure, abolished in 1965, was reinstated in 1988.

China has eight intercontinental and 60 intermediate range land-based, and 12 submarine-launched nuclear ballistic missiles. The Army has a strength of 2,000,000 (around 1,100,000 conscripts), with some 8,000 main battle tanks, 2,000 light tanks, 2,800 armoured personnel carriers and 14,500 artillery pieces. Organization is in ten armoured, 14 artillery and 84 infantry divisions, together with 50 engineer regiments and one airborne corps.

The Navy has a strength of 260,000 (35,000 conscripts), 46 submarines, 17 destroyers, 37 frigates, 860 patrol and coastal craft, one marine brigade of 6,000 men, 880 combat aircraft and 65 armed helicopters. The Air Force numbers 470,000 (160,000 conscripts) and some 4,970 combat aircraft of mainly Chinese manufacture.

RELIGION

The indigenous religions of China are Confucianism (which includes ancestor worship), Taoism (originally a philosophy rather than a religion) and, since its introduction in the first century of the Christian era, Buddhism. There are also Chinese Muslims (officially estimated at about 12 million) and Christians (unofficially estimated at about 50 million). Religious freedoms, severely curtailed during the Cultural Revolution, are reviving slightly under more liberal policies. Ethnic unrest in Buddhist Tibet and Muslim Xinjiang could threaten such liberalization.

EDUCATION

The Cultural Revolution caused considerable disruption to the educational system and since 1976 attempts have been made to raise academic standards. Primary education now lasts five years, and enrolment (1991) was 121,642,000 including kindergarten. Secondary education lasts five years (three years in junior middle school and two years in senior middle school). There were 52,268,000 middle school pupils in 1991. There are 220 million illiterates; efforts are being made to expand secondary education, particularly in the rural areas. Particular attention is being paid to higher education where there are over 1,000 universities, colleges and institutes with an enrolment (1991) of 2 million students. In May 1985 the Central Committee of the Party announced the abolition of free higher education except for teacher training, and the aim of providing all children with junior secondary education within 10 years.

CULTURE

LANGUAGE – The Chinese language has many dialects, notably Cantonese, Hakka, Amoy, Foochow, Changsha, Nanchang, Wu (Shanghai) and the northern dialect. The Common Speech or Putonghua (often referred to as Mandarin) which is taught throughout the country is based on the northern dialect. The Communists have promoted it as the national language and made intensive efforts to propagate it throughout the country. Since the most important aspect of this policy is the use of the spoken language in writing, the old literary style and ideographic form of writing has fallen into disuse.

In 1956 the Government decided to introduce 230 simplified characters with a view to making reading and writing easier. The list was enlarged and there are now over

2,000 simplified characters in use. In January 1956 all Chinese newspapers and most books began to appear with the characters printed horizontally from left to right, instead of reading vertically from right to left, as previously.

In February 1958 the National People's Congress adopted a system of romanization, known as pinyin, using 25 of the letters of the Latin alphabet (not v). This has been used within the country largely for assisting schoolchildren and others to learn the pronunciation of characters in *Putonghua*, and is now used for Chinese names in foreign-language publications.

LITERATURE – Chinese literature is one of the richest in the world. Paper has been employed for writing and printing for nearly 2,000 years. The Confucian classics which formed the basis of the traditional Chinese culture date from the Warring States period (fourth to third centuries BC) as do the earliest texts of the rival tradition, Taoism. Histories, philosophical and scientific works, poetry, literary and art criticism, novels and romances survive from most periods. Many have been translated into English. In the past all this considerable literature was available only to a very small class of literati, but with the spread of literacy in the 20th century, a process which received enormous impetus after the Communists took over in 1949, the old traditional literature has been largely superseded by modern works of a popular kind and by the classics of Marxism and modern developments from them.

The most important among the newspapers and magazines are the *People's Daily* and the twice-monthly *Qiushi*, which replaced *Red Flag* as the CCP's mouthpiece in August 1989.

ECONOMY

China is essentially an agricultural and pastoral country; peasants constitute about 75 per cent of the population. People's communes gave way to townships as the basic level of state administration in rural districts under the 1982 Constitution.

New agricultural policies, designed to give greater incentives to the rural population, have meant that the responsibility for agricultural production has been devolved down to individual households, whereas previously work was generally assigned on a collective basis.

Wheat, barley, maize, millet and other cereals, with peas and beans, are grown in the northern provinces, and rice and sugar in the south. Rice is the staple food of the inhabitants. Cotton (mostly in valleys of the Yangtze and Yellow Rivers), tea (in the west and south), with hemp, jute and flax, are the most important crops. Livestock is raised in large numbers. Silkworm culture is one of the oldest industries. Cottons, woollens and silks are manufactured in large quantities.

The mineral wealth of the country is great. Coal, iron ore, tin, antimony, wolfram, bismuth and molybdenum are abundant. Oil is produced in several northern provinces, particularly in Heilongjiang and Shandong, and off-shore deposits are being sought in co-operation with Western and Japanese companies.

The Chinese State Statistical Bureau issues production figures annually. The following are for 1992:

Grain (tons)	442,580,000
Pork, beef, mutton (tons)	29,330,000
Tea (tons)	559,000
Cotton (tons)	4,528,000
Timber (cu. metres)	55,800,000
Crude oil (tons)	142,000,000
Steel (tons)	80,000,000
Electric power (kW)	747,000,000
Machine tools (units)	212,000,000
Motor vehicles	514,000

The State Statistical Bureau valued the national income for 1991 at Yuan 1,612 billion. The Gross National Product in 1991 was Yuan 1,985 billion, a 7 per cent increase over 1990. The total value of agricultural output rose by 3.7 per cent over the 1990 figure to Yuan 815.7 billion. The total value of industrial output rose by 14.2 per cent to Yuan 2,824.8 billion in 1991.

In 1982 China set itself the aim of quadrupling the 1980 gross agricultural and industrial output value by the year 2000. The focus of its reform programme was switched to industry in 1984. Wide-ranging reforms have been introduced to make the industrial sector more efficient by narrowing the scope of central planning and broadening enterprise decision-making, material incentives and the role of the market.

TRADE

Foreign trade and external economic relations have expanded quickly since the open-door policy, adopted in the late 1970s. The principal articles of export are animals and animal products, oil, textiles, ores, metals, tea and manufactured goods. The principal imports are motor vehicles, machinery, chemical fertilizer plants, aircraft, books, paper and paper-making materials, chemicals, metals and ores, and dyes.

Trade with UK	1991	1992
Imports from UK	£321,935,000	£429,865,000
Exports to UK	706,585,000	953,583,000

COMMUNICATIONS

Of the total area of China over half consists of tableland and mountainous areas where communications and travel are difficult. The country has more than 53,400 kilometres of railway trunk and branch lines and some 1,041,100 kilometres of highway (1991). In addition, internal civil aviation has been developed, with routes now totalling more than 471,900 kilometres. As a result the communications network now covers most of the country.

In the past where roads did not exist the principal means of communication east to west was provided by the rivers, the most important of which are the Yangtze (Changjiang) (3,400 miles long), the Yellow River (Huanghe) (2,600 miles long) and the West River (Xihe) (1,650 miles long). These, together with the network of canals connecting them are still much used, but their overall importance has declined. Coastal port facilities are being improved and the merchant fleet expanded.

In the past ten years great progress has been made in developing postal services and telecommunications. It is claimed that 95 per cent of all rural townships are on the telephone and that postal routes reach practically every production brigade headquarters.

TIBET

Tibet is a plateau seldom lower than 10,000 feet, which forms the northern frontier of India (boundary imperfectly demarcated), from Kashmir to Burma, but is separated therefrom by the Himalayas. The area is estimated at 463,000 square miles with a population of 2,260,000 in 1991.

From 1911 to 1950, Tibet was virtually an independent country though its status was never officially so recognized. In October 1950, Chinese Communist forces invaded eastern Tibet. In May 1951 an agreement was reached whereby the Chinese army was allowed entry into Tibet. A Communist military and administrative headquarters was set up. In 1954 the government of India recognized that Tibet was an integral part of China in return for the right to maintain trade and consular representation there.

A series of revolts against Chinese rule over several years culminated in March 1959 in a rising in Lhasa. Fighting continued for several days before the rebellion was suppressed by Chinese troops and military rule imposed. The Dalai Lama fled to India where he and his followers were granted political asylum. On 28 March 1959 the Tibetan government was dissolved. In its place the Preparatory Committee for the Tibetan Autonomous Region, originally set up in 1955 with the Dalai Lama as Chairman, was to administer Tibet under the State Council; the Preparatory Committee was to have the Panchen Lama as Acting Chairman.

In December 1964 the Dalai Lama was declared to be a traitor, and both he and the Panchen Lama were dismissed. This move marked the end of the period of co-operation by the Chinese government with the traditional religious authorities, and the eclipse of the latter. The Preparatory Committee completed its work with the setting-up of Tibet as an Autonomous Region of China in September 1965. The Panchen Lama was rehabilitated as an official of the CPPCC, but died in 1989. The Chinese have invited the Dalai Lama to return from exile, but suggested negotiations between the Chinese and the Dalai Lama have failed to materialize. Martial law was declared in Tibet in 1989 after serious unrest, and sporadic outbursts of unrest continue in Tibet, the most recently in May 1993. Meanwhile, the Dalai Lama was awarded the Nobel Peace Prize in 1990.

COLOMBIA
República de Colombia

Colombia lies in the extreme north-west of South America, having a coastline on both the Caribbean Sea and Pacific Ocean. It is situated between 4° 13′ S. to 12° 30′ N. latitude and 68° to 79° W. longitude, with an area of 440,714 sq. miles (1,141,748 sq. km), and a population (UN estimate 1991) of 33,613,000.

The country is divided into a coastal region in the north and west and extensive plains in the east by the Cordillera de los Andes. The eastern range of the Colombian Andes consists of a series of vast tablelands. This temperate region is the most densely peopled portion of the country. The principal rivers are the Magdalena, Guaviare, Cauca, Atrato, Caquetá, Putumayo and Patia.

CAPITAL – Bogotá, population (1990 estimate) 5,000,000. Bogotá is an inland city in the Eastern Cordilleras, at an elevation of 8,600 to 9,000 ft above sea level. Other centres are Medellin (2,400,000); Cali (1,800,000); ΨBarranquilla (1,400,000); ΨCartagena (700,000); Bucaramanga (350,000); ΨBuenaventura (130,000) is the country's major port.
CURRENCY – Colombian peso of 100 centavos.
FLAG – Broad yellow band in upper half, surmounting equal bands of blue and red.
NATIONAL ANTHEM – Oh gloria inmarcesible.
NATIONAL DAY – 20 July (National Independence Day).

GOVERNMENT

The Colombian coast was visited in 1502 by Christopher Columbus, and in 1536 a Spanish expedition under Jiménez de Quesada penetrated to the interior and established on the site of the present capital a government which continued under Spanish rule until the revolt of the Spanish–American colonies of 1810–24. In 1819 Simón Bolívar (1783–1831) established the Republic of Colombia, consisting of the territories now known as Colombia, Panama, Venezuela and

Ecuador. In 1829–30 Venezuela and Ecuador withdrew from the association of provinces, and in 1831 the remaining territories were formed into the Republic of New Granada. In 1858 the name was changed to the Granadine Confederation and in 1861 to the United States of Colombia. In 1866 the present title was adopted. In 1903 Panama seceded from Colombia, and became a separate republic.

During the early 1950s Colombia suffered a period of virtual civil war between the supporters of the traditional political parties, the Conservatives and the Liberals. From 1957 to 1974 the country was governed under the 'National Front' agreement with the presidency alternating between the two parties every four years and ministerial posts being shared equally by the parties. The alternation of the presidency was ended in 1974 and parity in appointments in 1978. Thereafter, the constitution lays down that government portfolios and administrative appointments shall be divided among the two majority parties in Congress in an adequate and equitable manner.

Elections to a constitutional convention were held in November 1990, in which the former guerrilla movement M19 gained 30 per cent of the vote, ending the dominance of the traditional parties. The Convention began meeting in February 1991 and a new constitution was promulgated on 4 July 1991. Congressional elections to the Senate and House of Representatives were held on 27 October 1991, the Liberal Party emerging as the largest party in both houses after the Conservative Party had split into three parties. The Liberal Party formed a coalition government with the Social Conservative and New Democratic Force parties.

Colombia continues to be dogged by conflict and insurgency from left-wing guerrillas and from the drugs cartels centred on Medellin and Cali. In November 1992 President Gaviria introduced a state of emergency after the left-wing guerrillas of the Revolutionary Armed Forces of Colombia (FARC) had killed over 100 people in their latest offensive and peace talks suspended in March 1992 were not restarted. The state of emergency remains in force and, together with the expansion of the army and security forces, has led to some success against the guerrillas and the partial defeat of the security threat from the Medellin cartel, which has mounted less bombings and shootings in 1993. The Cali cartel, however, remains strong and the Medellin leader Pablo Escobar is still at large.

HEAD OF STATE
President, César Gaviria Trujillo, *assumed office*, 7 August 1990.

CABINET *as at August 1993*
Interior, Fabío Villegas Ramirez.
Foreign Affairs, Noení Sanin Posada.
Finance and Public Credit, Rudolf Hommes Rodríguez.
Justice, Andrés González.
National Defence, Rafael Pardo Rueda.
Public Works and Transport, Jorge Bendeck Olivella.
Labour and Social Security, Luis Fernando Ramírez.
Agriculture, José Antonio Ocampo.
Health, Juan Luis Londoño.
Mines and Energy, Guido Nule Amin.
Communications, William Jarmillo Gómez.
National Education, Mariya Panchón de Villanizar.
Economic Development, Luis Alberto Moreno.
Foreign Trade, Juan Manuel Santos Calderón.

COLOMBIAN EMBASSY
Flat 3A, 3 Hans Crescent, London SWIX OLR
Tel 071-589 9177/5037
Ambassador Extraordinary and Plenipotentiary, His Excellency Luis Prieto-Ocampo (1993).

BRITISH EMBASSY
Torre Propaganda Sancho, Calle 98 No. 9–03 Piso 4,
Bogotá
Tel: Bogota 2185111

Ambassador Extraordinary and Plenipotentiary, His
Excellency Keith E. H. Morris, CMG (1990).

There are British Consular Offices at *Barranquilla, Bogotá,
Cali* and *Medellin.*

BRITISH COUNCIL REPRESENTATIVE, W. Campbell,
Calle 87 No. 12–79, Bogotá DE.

COLOMBO-BRITISH CHAMBER OF COMMERCE, Apartado
Aereo 054 728, Calle 106 No. 25-41, Bogotá DE.

DEFENCE

The Colombian armed forces have been occupied over the
past few years in fighting the armed groups of the Medellin
and Cali drugs cartels and some 7,000 active armed leftist
guerrillas. The total active strength of the armed forces is
139,000 personnel (40,000 conscripts). Service is compulsory
and lasts between one and two years.

The Army's strength is some 120,000 (38,000 conscripts)
with 12 light tanks, 124 reconnaissance vehicles, 150 armoured
personnel carriers and 130 artillery pieces. The Army is
organized into 12 infantry brigades and nine counter-
insurgency, three special forces and one Presidential Guard
battalions.

The Navy, with 12,000 personnel including 6,000 marines
in five battalions and 500 conscripts, has five principal
surface combatant vessels and two submarines. The Air
Force, with 7,000 personnel (1,900 conscripts), has a strength
of 68 combat aircraft and 51 armed helicopters.

There is also a paramilitary police force of 85,000
personnel.

ECONOMY

Much of Colombia's natural resources in coal, natural gas
and hydro-electricity remain largely unexploited.
Development of coal is being given priority but no new hydro
projects are likely to be started for the next four to five years.
Annual coal production is 12.5 million tonnes now that the
Cerrejón Norte coalfield is being fully worked. This is
essentially for export. Proven coal reserves stand at 16,000
million tonnes. Estimated natural gas reserves are 3,788,000
million cu. ft, with daily use at 381,772 million BTU. Proven
crude oil reserves stand at 1,300 million barrels. Colombia is
again a net exporter of oil. In 1991 exports averaged
472,000 b.p.d. In 1993 large oil reserves were found under
the eastern plains which are estimated to be worth US$3
billion per year when exploited.

The hydrocarbon sector accounts for over half of the
mining output with precious metals (gold, platinum and
silver) and iron ore accounting for the remainder. Other
mineral deposits include nickel (a processing plant started
operating in 1982), bauxite, copper, gypsum, limestone,
phosphates, sulphur and uranium. Colombia is also the
world's largest producer of emeralds and has deposits of
other precious and semi-precious stones.

Because of the range of climate, a wide variety of crops
can be grown, and the country is close to self-sufficiency in
food. The principal agricultural product is coffee and other
major cash crops are sugar, bananas, cut flowers and cotton.
Cattle are raised in large numbers, and meat and cured skins
and hides are also exported.

The Government has encouraged diversification to reduce
dependence on coffee as the major export and this has led to
the growth of new export-orientated industries, particularly

textiles, paper products and leather goods. Stimulus to the
economy has been provided by large loans from the World
Bank and IADB for project development, particularly in the
power sector (in which hydroelectric projects have
predominated) and for telecommunications.

Since the late 1980s the government has introduced trade
liberalization and privatization measures which have
effectively ended protectionism and brought down inflation.

TRADE

Colombia's principal export is still coffee although other
products, principally bananas, cut flowers, clothing and
textiles, ferro-nickel and coal, are important exports.
Principal trading partners are USA, the EC and Latin
America.

Trade with UK	1991	1992
Imports from UK	£56,428,000	£75,340,000
Exports to UK	110,122,000	126,097,000

COMMUNICATIONS

The massive ranges of the Andes make surface transport
difficult so air transport is used extensively. There are daily
passenger and cargo air services between Bogotá and all the
principal towns, as well as daily services to the USA, frequent
services to other countries in South America, and to Europe.
The 'Atlantic Railway' links the departmental lines running
down to the River Magdalena, and completes the connection
between Bogotá and Santa Marta. Although the railways
generally are in a poor state there are about 2,600 miles of
rail in use at present. The total road network (1985) consists
of 105,201 km of roads of all types, of which 21,800 km are
classified as main trunk and transversal roads.

Large appropriations have been made for modernization
of the country's telecommunication system. There are 485
radio stations (1983) and three national television channels
with several regional ones.

CULTURE

Spanish is the language of the country and state education
has been free since 1870. Great efforts have been made in
reducing illiteracy and estimates (1990) put the literacy rate
at 87 per cent of those over ten years of age. In addition to
the National University with headquarters at Bogotá there
are 26 other universities. There is a flourishing press in
urban areas and a national literature supplements the rich
inheritance from the time of Spanish colonial rule.

Roman Catholicism is the established religion.

THE COMOROS
Republique Fédérale Islamique des Comores

The Comoro archipelago includes the islands of Great
Comoro, Anjouan, Mayotte and Moheli and certain islets in
the Indian Ocean with an area of 838 sq. miles (2,171 sq. km)
and a population (UN estimate 1991) of 570,000, most of
whom are Muslim.

CAPITAL – Moroni, on Great Comoro (pop. 17,267).
CURRENCY – Comorian franc of 100 centimes. The
Comoros also use the Franc CFA of 100 centimes.
FLAG – Green with a white crescent and four white stars in
the centre, tilted towards the lower fly.
NATIONAL DAY – 6 July (Independence Day).

GOVERNMENT

The islanders voted for independence from France in December 1974 and three islands became independent on 6 July 1975. (The island of Mayotte was against independence and has remained under French administration.)

A new constitution was adopted by referendum on 7 June 1992 which provides for a President directly elected for a five-year term which is renewable once only; an elected 42-member legislative assembly with a four-year term; a 15-member Senate (five from each island) chosen by an electoral college for six-year terms; and the appointment of a Prime Minister from the largest party in the legislative assembly. On 10 May 1992 President Djohar appointed a government of national unity to govern until new elections were held in November. These, however, proved inconclusive with no party or coalition gaining a majority in the legislative assembly and the instability following an uprising by rebel soldiers in October continued. President Djohar appointed a new government in January 1993, but this was brought down by a vote of no confidence in May. The President appointed a new government in July to work towards new elections in late 1993.

Each island is administered by a Governor, assisted by up to four Commissioners whom he appoints, and has an elected Legislative Council.

HEAD OF STATE
President, Said Mohamed Djohar, sworn in 20 March 1990.

GOVERNMENT as at August 1993
Prime Minister, Ahmed Ben Cheikh Attoumane.
Minister of State, Interior and Decentralization, Said Attoumane Said Ahmed.
Finance and Budget, Caabi El Yachroutu Mohamed.
Foreign Affairs, Co-operation and Islamic Affairs, Mauslim Ben Moussa.
Economy, Industry, Crafts and Planning, Ahmed Bourhane.
Public Works, Urbanization, Housing and Energy, Youssouf Souffiane.
Rural Development, Fishing and Environment, Idarousse Athoumane.
National Education and Teaching, Ibrahim Hissani.
Public Health, Ahmed El Harif Hamidi.
Transport and Tourism, Ahmed Said Islam.
Justice, Maoulida Ibrahim.
Information, Culture, Youth, Sport, Posts and Telecommunications, Government Spokesman, Houmed Mdahoma Msaidié.
Civil Service, Employment and Labour, Ahamada Mohamed Manga.

BRITISH AMBASSADOR (resident in Madagascar).

BRITISH CONSULATE
P.O. Box 986, Moroni
Honorary Consul, J. de Jaeger.

ECONOMY

The most important products are vanilla, copra, cloves and essential oils, which are the principal exports; cacao, sisal and coffee are also cultivated. Great Comoro is well forested and produces some timber.

TRADE WITH UK	1991	1992
Imports from UK	£796,000	£279,000
Exports to UK	228,000	194,000

CONGO
République du Congo

The Congo lies on the Equator between Gabon on the west and Zaire on the east, the River Congo and its tributary the Ubangui forming most of the eastern boundary of the state. It has a short Atlantic coastline. The area of the Republic of Congo is 132,047 sq. miles (342,000 sq. km), with a population of 2,346,000 (UN estimate 1991).

CAPITAL – Brazzaville (600,000); Ψ Pointe Noire (350,000).
CURRENCY – Franc CFA of 100 centimes.
FLAG – Divided diagonally into green, yellow and red bands.
NATIONAL DAY – 15 August.

GOVERNMENT

Formerly the French colony of Middle Congo, it became a member state of the French Community on 28 November 1958 and was proclaimed fully independent on 17 August 1960.

In 1968, conduct of affairs was assumed by a National Council of army officers. The Parti Congolais du Travail (PCT) was created by the Congress of 29–31 December 1969 and the People's Republic of the Congo was established. After popular pressure, the PCT abandoned its monopoly of power and renounced Marxism in July 1990. A transitional government was formed in January 1991 and a national conference of all political forces convened in February. The national conference suspended the constitution, stripping President Sassou-Nguesso of all powers and forming itself into the Higher Council of the Republic (CSR), the transitional legislative body. On 22 December 1991 the CSR adopted a new multiparty constitution with a directly-elected President and bicameral parliament, the President appointing the Prime Minister from the majority party in parliament. The new constitution was approved by a referendum in March 1992 and a Transitional Government formed in May 1992 to govern the country until elections which were held in July and August 1992. In the presidential election, Pascal Lissouba of the opposition Pan-African Union for Social Democracy (UPADS) won in the second round of voting. In the legislative election UPADS emerged as the largest party in both the Senate and the National Assembly, with the PCT heavily defeated.

In September 1992 President Lissouba appointed a coalition government, but this failed to gain a majority in the National Assembly and was brought down by the PCT-led opposition in November. To break the deadlock, Lissouba dissolved the National Assmebly and called fresh elections which were eventually held in May and June 1993 and won by Lissouba's UPADS party. The results were disputed by opposition groups and violence broke out after Lissouba attempted to appoint a former military ruler as Prime Minister. At the time of going to press the situation remained unclear with opposition parties attempting to form their own government and a state of emergency in place because of political and ethnic fighting.

HEAD OF STATE
President, Pascal Lissouba, elected 16 August 1992.

EMBASSY OF THE REPUBLIC OF CONGO
37 bis rue Paul Valery, 75116 Paris, France
Tel: Paris 45006057

Ambassador Extraordinary and Plenipotentiary, His Excellency Jean-Marie Ewengue (1986).

HONORARY CONSULATE, Livingstone House, 11 Carteret Street, London SW1H 9DJ. Tel: 071-222 7575. *Honorary Consul and Head of Mission*, L. Muzzu.

BRITISH AMBASSADOR, (resident in Zaire). There is an Honorary Consulate in *Pointe Noire*.

ECONOMY

Congo has its own oil deposits, producing about 8 million tonnes annually. It also produces lead, zinc and gold. The principal agricultural products are timber, cassava, sugar cane and yams. Imports are mainly of machinery.

TRADE WITH UK	1991	1992
Imports from UK	£9,190,000	£8,680,000
Exports to UK	2,407,000	2,813,000

COSTA RICA
República de Costa Rica

Costa Rica in Central America extends across the isthmus between 8° 17′ and 11° 10′ N. latitude and from 82° 30′ to 85° 45′ W. longitude. It has an area of 19,575 sq. miles (50,700 sq. km), and a population (1991 estimate) of 3,064,000. The population is basically of European stock, in which Costa Rica differs from most Latin American countries. The republic lies between Nicaragua and Panama, and between the Caribbean Sea and the Pacific Ocean. The coastal lowlands by the Caribbean Sea and Pacific have a tropical climate but the interior plateau, with a mean elevation of 4,000 feet, enjoys a temperate climate.

CAPITAL – San José, population (estimate 1989) 1,068,206; Alajuela (519,351); Cartago (328,259); Heredia (235,700); Guanacaste (234,962); ΨPuntarenas (326,163); ΨLimón (209,731). (Populations shown are of provinces, cantons and districts.)

CURRENCY – Costa Rican colón (₡) of 100 céntimos.

FLAG – Five horizontal bands, blue, white, red, white, blue (the red band twice the width of the others with emblem near staff).

NATIONAL ANTHEM – Himno Nacional de Costa Rica.
NATIONAL DAY – 15 September.

GOVERNMENT

For nearly three centuries (1530–1821) Costa Rica formed part of the Spanish American dominions, the seat of government being at Cartago. In 1821 the country obtained its independence, although from 1824 to 1839 it was one of the United States of Central America.

On 1 December 1948, the Army was abolished, the President declaring it unnecessary.

HEAD OF STATE
President, Rafael Angel Calderón Fournier, *took office*, 8 May 1990.

MINISTERS *as at August 1993*

Vice-Presidents, G. Serrano Pinto; A. López Echandi.
Minister for the Presidency, Rolando Lacle.
Foreign Affairs and Worship, B. Niehaus Quesada.
Interior and Police, Public Security, L. Fishman Zonzinski.
Justice, Elizabeth Odio Benito.
Finance, Rodolfo Mendez.
Agriculture, J. R. Lizano Sáenz.
Economy, Industry and Commerce, Roberto Rojas.
Natural Resources, Energy and Mines, Dr Orlando Morales.

Public Works and Transport, Mariano Guardía.
Education, H. Herrera Araya.
Health, C. Castro Charpentier.
Culture, Youth and Sports, Aida de Fishman.
Labour and Social Security, Carlos Monge Rodríguez.
Planning, Dr Carlos Vargas.
Housing and Urban Development, C. Zawadzki Wojtasiak.
Foreign Trade, R. Rojas López.
Science and Technology, O. Morales Matamores.
Information and Press, Guillermo Fernández.
Tourism, Luis M. Chacón.

COSTA RICAN EMBASSY
5 Harcourt House, 19A Cavendish Square, London W1M 9AD
Tel 071-495 3985
Ambassador Extraordinary and Plenipotentiary, new appointment awaited.

BRITISH EMBASSY
Apartado 815, Edificio Centro Colon (11th Floor), San José 1007
Tel: San José 215566
Ambassador Extraordinary and Plenipotentiary and Consul-General, Her Excellency Mary Louise Croll (1992).

ECONOMY

Agriculture is the chief industry and the principal products are coffee, bananas, sugar and cattle (for meat), all of which are important exports. Other crops are cocoa, rice, maize, potatoes, hemp, pineapple, casava, ginger, chaw chaw, melon and flowers. Industrial activity is principally in the manufacturing sector and manufactured goods are the largest category of exports. The main goods are foodstuffs, textiles and clothing, plastic goods, pharmaceuticals, fertilizers and electrical equipment. Tourism is of growing importance and became the main source of foreign exchange revenue in 1992.

FINANCE	1990
Revenue	₡79,974.4m
Expenditure	92,432.6m

TRADE
The chief exports are manufactured goods and other products, coffee, bananas, cocoa and sugar. The chief imports are machinery, including transport equipment, manufactures, chemicals, fuel and mineral oils and foodstuffs.

	1991	1992*
Total imports	US$1,932.8m	US$2,461.7m
Total exports	1,505.2m	1,828.4m
*preliminary		

Trade with UK	1991	1992
Imports from UK	£11,312,000	£28,774,000
Exports to UK	21,823,000	17,559,000

COMMUNICATIONS

The chief ports are Limón, on the Atlantic coast, through which passes most of the coffee exported, and Caldera on the Pacific coast, currently under construction with Japanese aid. The railway system is nationalized. About 500 miles of railroad are open. LACSA is the national airline, operating flights throughout Central and South America, the Caribbean and USA, besides internal flights to local airports by SANSA.

CULTURE

Spanish is the language of the country. Education is compulsory and free. The literacy rate is the highest in Latin America.

CÔTE D'IVOIRE
République de Côte d'Ivoire

Côte d'Ivoire is situated on the Gulf of Guinea between 5° and 10° N. latitude and 3° and 8° W. longitude. It is flanked on the west by Guinea and Liberia, on the north by Mali and Burkina, and on the east by Ghana. It has an area of 124,503 sq. miles (322,463 sq. km). Climatically, the country is divided into three: an equatorial climate in the south and west, which are mainly forested; a tropical climate in the centre and east, which are savannah regions with trees; a dry tropical climate in the north, which is a grassy savannah region. The population of 12,464,000 (UN estimate 1991) is divided into a large number of ethnic and tribal groups. The official language is French. Some 39 per cent of the population is Muslim, 28 per cent Christian (mainly Roman Catholic) and 17 per cent maintain traditional beliefs.

CAPITAL – The political and administrative capital is Yamoussoukro in the centre of the country and has officially been so since 1983. The economic and financial capital remains Abidjan (population 3,500,000) on the coast, which is also the largest city and main port.
CURRENCY – Franc CFA of 100 centimes.
FLAG – Three vertical stripes, orange, white and green.
NATIONAL ANTHEM – L'Abidjanaise.
NATIONAL DAY – 7 December.

GOVERNMENT

Although French contact was made in the first half of the 19th century, Côte d'Ivoire became a colony only in 1893 and was finally pacified in 1912. It decided on 5 December 1958 to remain an autonomous republic within the French Community; full independence outside the Community was proclaimed on 7 August 1960. Special agreements with France, covering financial and cultural matters, technical assistance, defence, etc., were signed in Paris on 24 April 1961.

Côte d'Ivoire has a presidential system of government modelled on that of the United States and the French Fifth Republic. The single-chamber National Assembly has 175 members. Although the Constitution provides for a multi-party system, it was not until May 1990 that any party other than the ruling PDCI party was authorized. Defeating an opposition candidate, President Houphouët-Boigny was re-elected for a further five-year term in October 1990; the PDCI won multi-party elections held in November 1990 amid allegations of electoral fraud; opposition protests continue.

HEAD OF STATE
President, Félix Houphouët-Boigny, *elected* for five years in 1960; *re-elected* 1965, 1970, 1975, 1980, 1985 and 1990.

CABINET *as at August 1993*
Prime Minister, Minister of Economy and Finance, Alassane D. Ouattara.
Ministers assisting the PM; Daniel Kablan Duncan (*Economy, Finance, Trade and Planning*); Guy-Alain Emmanuel Gause (*Raw Materials*).
Defence, Leon Konan Koffi.
Foreign Affairs, Amara Essy.
Interior, Emile Constant Bombet.
Justice, Jacqueline Lohoues-Oble.
Higher Education and Scientific Research, Alassane Salif N'Diaye.
Agriculture and Animal Resources, Lambert Kouassi Konan.

Industry and Commerce, Ferdinard Kacou Angora.
Mines and Energy, Posts and Telecommunications, Yed Esaie Angoran.
Health and Social Welfare, Frederic F. Alain Ekra.
Communication, Auguste Severin Miremont.
Equipment, Transport and Tourism, Adama Coulibaly.
Environment, Construction and Town Planning, Ezan Akele.
Employment and Civil Service, Patrice Kouame.
Security, Col. Lassana Palenfo.
Culture, Henriette Dagri Diabate.
Promotion of Women, Claire Therese Elisabeth Grah.
Youth and Sports, Rene Djedjemel Diby.

EMBASSY OF THE REPUBLIC OF CÔTE D'IVOIRE
2 Upper Belgrave Street, London SW1X 8BJ
Tel 071-235 6991

Ambassador Extraordinary and Plenipotentiary, His Excellency Gervais Yao Attoungbre (1989).

BRITISH EMBASSY
Immeuble Les Harmonies, 01 BP 2581, Abidjan 01
Tel: Abidjan 226850
Ambassador Extraordinary and Plenipotentiary, Her Excellency Margaret I. Rothwell, CMG (1990).
Deputy Head of Mission, First Secretary (Commercial), Consul, D. A. Lloyd.

BUDGET	1990
Current Expenditure	CFA609,400 billion
Investment and Equipment	129,600 billion

TRADE

The principal exports are coffee, cocoa, timber, palm oil, rubber, pineapples, bananas, and cotton. There are a few deposits of diamonds and minerals including manganese and iron.

	1988	1989
Imports	US$1,907m	US$1,781m
Exports	2,354m	2,588m

Trade with UK	1991	1992
Imports from UK	£24,131,000	£29,480,000
Exports to UK	45,630,000	53,022,000

CROATIA

Croatia is bounded by Slovenia, Hungary, the rump Yugoslav state and Bosnia-Hercegovina; it includes the Adriatic coastline of Istria and Dalmatia and has an area of 21,823 sq. miles (56,538 sq. km). It is divided into three major geographic regions: the Pannonían region; the central mountain belt; and the Adriatic coast. The Pannonían region in north and north-eastern Croatia has a moderate continental climate with abundant arable land and forests and is traversed by the Sava, Drava and Danube rivers. The central mountain belt links the Pannonían and Adriatic regions and has three main plateaus with areas of forest and grazing land. The Adriatic coast region has 1,185 islands and islets and 1,104 miles (1,778 km) of coastline. It has a sunny, Mediterranean climate with arable land in the hinterland areas.

POPULATION – At the last census in 1991 the population was 4,760,344, of which some 78 per cent were ethnic Croats, 12 per cent ethnic Serbs, 2 per cent Yugoslavs and 1 per cent Muslims. The remaining minorities were Hungarians, Italians, Albanians, Czechs, Ukrainians and Jews. Croatia is host to some 750,000 refugees from Bosnia-Hercegovina.

RELIGIONS – 77 per cent Roman Catholic, 11 per cent
Serbian Orthodox, 1 per cent Muslim.
LANGUAGES – The majority language is Croatian in the
Latin script. Ethnic Serbs use Serbian in the Cyrillic script.
CAPITAL – Zagreb, population (1991 estimate) 950,000.
Other major cities are Split (200,000), Rijeka (200,000)
and Osijek (160,000).
CURRENCY – Dinar of 100 paras.
FLAG – Three horizontal stripes of red, white, blue, with
the national arms over all in the centre.
NATIONAL ANTHEM – Lijepa naša domovina (Our
Beautiful Homeland).
NATIONAL DAY – 30 May (Independence Day).

HISTORY

Croatia was part of the Austro-Hungarian Empire from 1526
to the end of the First World War in 1918. On 29 October
1918 the Croatian parliament declared Croatia independent
and soon after Croatia joined with Slovenia, Bosnia-
Hercegovina, Serbia and Montenegro to form the 'Kingdom
of Serbs, Croats and Slovenes'. This was confirmed and
accepted by the Allied Powers at Versailles in 1919. The
centralized and Serbian-dominated nature of the state soon
caused resentment in Croatia and this was intensified when
the (Serbian) King Alexander declared a royal dictatorship
in 1929 and renamed the state Yugoslavia. From 1941 to
1945 Yugoslavia was occupied by the Axis powers, with Italy
and Hungary annexing parts of Croatia and a pro-Nazi Croat
puppet state being established in the remainder of Croatia
and Bosnia-Hercegovina. The armed extremists of this
puppet state, known as Ustasha, engaged in fierce fighting
with Serbian royalists and Communist partisans, together
with pro-Allied Croat partisans, leaving a bitterness that has
re-emerged 46 years later.

Following the end of the war Yugoslavia was re-established
as a federal republic under the Communist rule of the
wartime partisan leader Josep Tito. In 1974 Tito increased
the autonomy of the republics, including Croatia, in an
attempt to forestall any rebellions against perceived Serbian
domination, but following Tito's death in 1980 the unity of
Yugoslavia gradually disintegrated. The Catholic, western-
looking, more prosperous republics of Slovenia and Croatia
began to break away from the other predominantly Orthodox
and Muslim Balkan republics of the rest of Yugoslavia;
Communism was widely rejected. Efforts by the federal
presidency and international mediators to end inter-
communal conflict and negotiate a new federal or confederal
structure for the country failed in 1991.

On 25 June 1991 Slovenia and Croatia both informed
Belgrade of their independence from Yugoslavia, causing
fighting to begin immediately as the Federal Yugoslav Army
(JNA) intervened against local defence forces to prevent the
disintegration of the Yugoslav Federation.

Croatia contained an ethnic Serb minority comprising 12
per cent of the population. These ethnic Serbs refused to
accept Croatia's independence and formed themselves into
armed guerrilla groups. Bitter fighting erupted in July 1991
between Croat defence forces and Serbian guerrillas backed
by the JNA. By September 1991 fighting had escalated into
an all-out war between Croatia and Serbia, which had taken
over control of the JNA. In October the last vestiges of the
power of the Federation ended when the federal presidency
was usurped by Serbia and its ally Montenegro.

The war in Croatia continued until January 1992 when,
after constant attempts, the EC and the UN were able to
bring about a ceasefire that held. The JNA and Serbian forces
had secured control of virtually all ethnic Serbian areas in
Croatia and the two sides were not able to carry on the

fighting. The war left an estimated 10,000 people dead,
scores of villages and the city of Vukovar destroyed, and
badly damaged Dubrovnik. Three UN Protected Areas in
Croatia, Krajina and Eastern and Western Slovonia, were
created from the Serb-controlled areas in Croatia and 16,000
UN troops arrived to police the areas. The JNA withdrew
from Croatia and the local Serbian guerrillas were disarmed.

During 1992 the situation in the UN protected areas
remained tense, with the Croatian government determined
to gain control of the areas, and the Serbs adamant that they
will not live under Croatian rule. Fighting restarted on 22
January 1993, centring on the strategic bridge at Maslenica
linking central Croatia to the Adriatic coast, and on Zemunik
airport near Zadar. Croat forces managed to regain control
of both facilities and ethnic Serb forces regained their heavy
weapons from UN control before a ceasefire was signed in
April. Sporadic fighting continued in June, July and August
with the Serbs using artillery to destroy the Maslenica bridge.
In late June 1993 ethnic Serbs voted in a referendum to unite
the areas under their control with the rump Yugoslav state
and Serb-controlled areas in Bosnia-Hercegovina.

GOVERNMENT

In April and May 1990 the first free, democratic elections
were held in Croatia and were won overwhelmingly by the
Croatian Democratic Union (HDZ) of Dr Franjo Tudjman.
A new Croatian constitution was adopted by parliament on
22 December 1990. In a national referendum on 19 May
1991, 94 per cent of those who voted (the referendum was
boycotted by ethnic Serbs) voted in favour of independence
from Yugoslavia. The Croatian parliament and government,
declared indepndence on 30 May 1991. The EC recognized
Croatia's independence on 15 January 1992 and it was
admitted to the UN in May 1992.

Executive power is vested in a President and government.
The President appoints the Prime Minister and, on the
proposal of the Prime Minister and subject to confirmation
by the Chamber of Deputies, appoints other government
members. The President is directly elected for five-year
terms. Legislative power is vested in the bicameral parliament
which consists of the 63-member Chamber of Districts and
the 138-member Chamber of Deputies. Following the last
legislative elections held on 2 August 1993, the state of the
parties in the Chamber of Deputies is: Croatian Democratic
Union (HDZ) 85; Croatian Social Liberal Party (HSLS) 14;
Party of Democratic Change (SDP) 11; Others 13; Ethnic
Serb and regionalist parties 9; Independants 6.

LOCAL GOVERNMENT

Croatia is divided into 21 counties (each county elects three
members to the Chamber of Districts) and 102 districts.
Counties are composed of groups of districts and function
both as units of local government and as regional offices for
the central administration.

HEAD OF STATE
President, Franjo Tudjman, *elected* May 1990, *re-elected* 2
August 1992.

CABINET *as at August 1993*
Prime Minister, Nikica Valentic.
Deputy Prime Ministers, Mate Granic; Vladimir Sek; Borisav
Skegro.
Defence, Gojko Susak.
Interior, Ivan Jarnjak.
Foreign Affairs, Zdenko Skrabalo.
Finance, Zoran Jasic.
Construction and Environmental Protection, Zlatko Tomcic.

Industry, Shipbuilding and Energy, Ivan Cermak.
Education and Culture, Vesna Girardi-Jurkic.
Agriculture and Forestry, Ivan Tarnaj.
Shipping, Transport and Communications, Ivica Mudrinic.
Justice and Administration, Ivica Crnic.
Labour and Social Welfare, Josíp Juras.
Tourism and Trade, Niko Bulic.
Science, Branko Jeren.
Ministers without Portfolio, Cedomir Pavlovic; Ivan Majdak;
   Zlatko Matesa.

President of the Chamber of Deputies, Stípe Mesic.

EMBASSY OF THE REPUBLIC OF CROATIA
c/o 5th Floor, 18–21 Germain Street, London SW1Y 6HP
Tel 071-434 2946

Ambassador Extraordinary and Plenipotentiary, His
   Excellency Prof. Zeljko Bujas (1992).

BRITISH EMBASSY
Ilica 12/II, PO Box 434, 41000 Zagreb.
Tel: Zagreb 424888

Ambassador Extraordinary and Plenipotentiary, His
   Excellency Bryan Sparrow, CMG (1992).

There are British Consulates in *Split* and *Dubrovnik*.

BRITISH COUNCIL DIRECTOR, A. Pattison, OBE, PO Box
   55, Ilica 12/1, Zagreb 41001.

JUDICIAL SYSTEM

The constitution provides for a Supreme Court as the highest
judicial body and a Constitutional Court. The Supreme Court
consists of 15 members and the Constitutional Court of 11
members, all 26 of whom are elected by the Chamber of
Districts for eight-year terms.

DEFENCE

Croatia had to rapidly build up its armed forces to survive in
the 1991-2 war with ethnic Serb and Federal Armed Forces
(JNA) and then to support ethnic Croat forces in Bosnia-
Hercegovina. It salvaged as much equipment as was possible
from former JNA forces in the republic but most was taken
back to Serbia or given to ethnic Serb forces in Croatia. At
present the armed forces number some 105,000 active and
100,000 reserve personnel. A conscription term of ten
months is in operation.
   The Army has some 95,000 active personnel organized
into nine brigades (two mechanized, one motorized, five
infantry and one mountain) and five regiments (one artillery,
three anti-tank and one engineer). Equipment includes 200
main battle tanks, 200 armoured personnel carriers and 150
artillery pieces. The Air Force has some 4,500 active
personnel, mainly air defence forces with no combat aircraft.
The Navy has some 5,000 active personnel with one
submarine and 12 patrol and coastal combatants.
   In addition, paramilitary personnel number 40,000 armed
police and 10,000 personnel of the nationalist Croatian Party
of Rights (HSP) armed wing (HOS).

ECONOMY

Large areas of Croatia's most productive farmland were
destroyed by the war or remain under Serb control. The
considerable tourist industry has been decimated by the war
and by the continuing fighting in neighbouring Bosnia.
Shipbuilding and fishing are major industries on the Adriatic
coast. Inland there is a light manufacturing sector, food-
processing industries, bauxite deposits, thermal mineral
springs, hydro-electric potential, and agriculture based on
grain, horticulture, livestock and tobacco.

CUBA
Republica de Cuba

Cuba, the largest island in the Caribbean, lies between 74°
and 85° W. longitude, and 19° and 23° N. latitude, with a
total area of 42,804 sq. miles (110,861 sq. km). The country
is divided into 14 provinces. The population (1991 UN
estimate) was 10,736,000.

CAPITAL – Ψ Havana, population estimate (1989)
   2,096,000; other towns are Ψ Santiago (405,000), Santa
   Clara (194,000), Camagüey (283,000), Holgüin
   (228,000), Guantánamo (200,000) and Ψ Cienfuegos
   (123,600).
CURRENCY – Cuban peso of 100 centavos.
FLAG – Five horizontal bands, blue and white (blue at top
   and bottom) with red triangle, close to staff, charged with
   five-point star.
NATIONAL ANTHEM – Al Combate, Corred Bayameses
   (To battle, men of Bayamo).
NATIONAL DAY – 1 January (Day of Liberation).

GOVERNMENT

The island of Cuba was visited by Christopher Columbus
during his first voyage, on 27 October 1492, and was then
believed to be part of the western mainland of India. Early
in the 16th century the island was conquered by the Spanish,
to be used later as a base of operations for the conquest of
Mexico and Central America, and for almost four centuries
Cuba remained under a Spanish Captain-General. (The
island was under British rule for one year, 1762–3, when it
was returned to Spain in exchange for Florida.)
   Separatist agitation culminated in the closing years of the
19th century in open warfare. In 1898 the government of the
United States intervened and on 20 April 1898 demanded
the evacuation of Cuba by the Spanish forces. A short
Spanish–American war led to the abandonment of the island,
which was occupied by US troops. Cuba was under US
military rule from 1 January 1899 until 20 May 1902, when
an autonomous government was inaugurated with an elected
President, and a legislature of two houses.
   A revolution led by Dr Fidel Castro overthrew the
government of General Batista on 1 January 1959. In October
1965 the Communist Party of Cuba was formed to succeed
the United Party of the Socialist Revolution. It is the only
authorized political party. The new Socialist Constitution
came into force on 24 February 1976 and indirect elections
to the National Assembly of People's Power were subsequently held.
   The first direct elections to the 589-member National
Assembly were held on 24 February 1993, although all
candidates were officially approved by the Community Party
and ran for election unopposed. The fourteen provincial
assemblies were also elected in the same manner. On 15
March the National Assembly re-elected Fidel Castro as
President of the Council of State for a five-year term.

President of Council of State and Head of Government, Dr
   Fidel Castro Ruz, *appointed* 2 November 1976.

COUNCIL OF STATE *as at July 1993*

President, Dr Fidel Castro Ruz.
First Vice-President, Raúl Castro Ruz.
Vice-Presidents, Juan Almeida Bosque; José Ramón
   Machado Ventura; Abelardo Colome Ibarra; Carlos Lage
   Dávíla; Esteban Lazo Hernandez.
Secretary, José M. Miyar Barrueco.

COUNCIL OF MINISTERS
President, Dr Fidel Castro Ruz.
First Vice-President, Raúl Castro Ruz.
Vice-Presidents, Dr Carlos Rafael Rodríguez; Pedro Miret
Prieto; José Ramón Fernández Alvarez; Osmany
Cienfuegos Gorriarán; Ramiro Valdés Menéndez; Joel
Domenech Benítez; Antonio Rodriguez Maurell; Jaime
Crombet Hernández-Baquero; Aldofo Diaz Suárez;
Lionel Soto Prieto.
Secretary, Carlos Lage Dávíla.
Presidents of State Committees: Antonio Rodriguez Maurell
(*Central Planning Board*); Hector Rodriguez Llompart
(*National Bank*); Ernesto Melendez Bachs (*Economic Co-
operation*); Rodrigo J. Garcia Leon (*Finance*); Francisco
Linares Calvo (*Labour and Social Security*); Sonia
Rodriguez Cardona (*Material and Technical Supply*);
Arturo Guzman Pascual (*Prices*); Ramón Darias Rodés
(*Standardization*); Fidel Emilio Vasco Gonzalez
(*Statistics*).
Ministers, Carlos Pérez León (*Agriculture*); Marcos J. Portal
Leon (*Basic Industry*); Manuel Castillo Rabasa
(*Communications*); Homero Crabb (*Construction*); José
M. Cañete Alvarez (*Construction Materials Industry*);
Armando Enrique Hart Davalos (*Culture*); Manuel Vila

Sosa (*Domestic Trade*); Luis Ignacio Gomez Gutierrez
(*Education*); Jorge A. Fernandez Cuervo-Vinent (*Fishing*);
Alejandro Roca Iglesias (*Food Industry*); Roberto Robaina
(*Foreign Relations*); Ricardo Cabrisas Ruiz (*Foreign
Trade*); Fernando Vecino Alegret (*Higher Education*);
Gen. Abelardo Colomé Ibarra (*Interior*); Carlos Amat
Fores (*Justice*); Eddie Fernandez Boada (*Light Industry*);
Julio Jesus Teja Pérez (*Public Health*); Raul Castro Ruz
(*Revolutionary Armed Forces*); Roberto Ignacio Gonzalez
Planas (*Steel Industry*); Juan Ramon Herrera Machado
(*Sugar Industry*); Gen. Senén Casas Regueiro (*Transport*);
Jose Alberto Naranjo Morales; Joaqin Benavides
Rodrioguez (*Ministers without Portfolio*).
President of the National Assembly, Ricardo Alarcón de
Quesada.

EMBASSY OF THE REPUBLIC OF CUBA
167 High Holborn, London WC1V 6PA
Tel 071–240 2488

Ambassador Extraordinary and Plenipotentiary, Her
Excellency Maria A. Flores (1990).

BRITISH EMBASSY
Edificio Bolívar, Cárcel 101–103, e Morro y Prado,
Apartado 1069, Havana.
Tel: Havana 33 8071

Ambassador Extraordinary and Plenipotentiary, His Excellency A. Leycester S. Coltman, CMG (1991).

DEFENCE

Cuba has a total active armed forces strength of 175,000 personnel, including 79,500 conscripts who serve for two years. In addition, there are 135,000 ready reserves who serve for 45 days per year and a territorial militia of 1,300,000 personnel. Paramilitary Ministry of Interior personnel number 19,000.

The Army numbers 145,000 (60,000 conscripts) and makes great use of the ready reservists to man many units. Equipment includes 1,700 main battle tanks, 70 light tanks, 200 reconnaissance vehicles and 1,500 armoured infantry fighting vehicles and armoured personnel carriers. The Navy has a strength of 13,500 (8,500 conscripts) with three frigates, three submarines and 28 patrol and coastal craft, together with a marine battalion. The Air Force has 17,000 personnel (11,000 conscripts) with 162 combat aircraft and 85 armed helicopters of Soviet manufacture. It is organized into two ground attack, two air defence and four transport squadrons. The last former Soviet personnel left Cuba on 3 July 1993. The United States has 2,300 naval personnel at Guantanamo Bay Naval Base, which has been leased since before the 1959 revolution.

ECONOMY

The government has carried out programmes of land and urban reform and of nationalization; by March 1968, virtually all industrial and commercial enterprises were nationalized. About 85 per cent of the cultivated land is in state farms or state-controlled co-operatives. Private smallholders, who own the remainder, have to sell all their produce to the state.

Although efforts are being made to diversify the economy, sugar is still its mainstay and principal source of foreign exchange. In 1989-90 the harvest was 8.04 million tons but this dropped in 1992-3 to 4.2m tons owing to a lack of fuel and spare parts. Cuba's other main exports are nickel, seafood, citrus fruits, tobacco and rum.

The tourism industry has expanded since 1986. In 1992 460,000 tourists visited Cuba generating US$530 million in gross income.

The economy continued to deteriorate in 1992-3, with severe shortages of fuel and spare parts for transport and agricultural machinery and a lack of food. In July 1993 this caused the government to legalize the holding of US dollars by private individuals in an attempt to gain hard currency reserves for the state. The total foreign debt stands at US$16,000 million.

TRADE

The demise of socialism in eastern Europe, together with the breakup of the COMECON trading bloc and of the former Soviet Union, has disrupted Cuba's traditional pattern of trade. Cuba's imports have declined by 73 per cent since 1989. Trade between Cuba and the former socialist economies of Europe totalled US$830 million in 1992, only 7 per cent of pre-1989 levels. A new Russian-Cuban trade deal was signed in November 1992 under which Russia promised to buy limited quantities of sugar in return for selling oil at world prices.

	1987	1988
Imports	Pesos 7,611.5m	7,579.4m
Exports	5,401.0	5,518.3

Trade with UK	1991	1992
Imports from UK	£28,413,000	£28,345,000
Exports to UK	17,869,000	12,979,000

There are 12,700 km of railway track, of which 5,000 km are in public service. In 1986 there were 13,247 km of road. At present scheduled international air services run to North, Central and South American countries and Europe.

CULTURE

Spanish is the language of the island. English, formerly widely understood, is now spoken less. Education is compulsory and free. In 1964 illiteracy was officially declared to be completely eliminated. The press and broadcasting and television are under the control of the government.

CYPRUS
Kypriaki Dimokratia/Kibris Cumhuriyeti

Cyprus, with an area of 3,572 sq. miles (9,251 sq. km), is the third largest island in the Mediterranean Sea. Its greatest length is 140 miles and greatest breadth 60 miles, situated at 35°N. latitude and 33° 30'E. longitude. It is about 40 miles distant from the nearest point of Asia Minor, 60 miles from Syria and 240 miles from Port Said.

Cyprus has a Mediterranean climate with a hot dry summer and a variable warm winter, while the intermediate seasons are short and transitional.

POPULATION – In 1993 the population was estimated at 706,900. There are two major communities, Greek Cypriots (565,900, or 81.6 per cent) and Turkish Cypriots (131,800, or 18.4 per cent); and minorities of Armenians, Maronites and others.

CAPITAL – Nicosia, near the centre of the island, with a population of 177,410 (in the government-controlled area); the other principal towns are ΨLimassol, ΨFamagusta, ΨLarnaca, Paphos and Kyrenia.

CURRENCY – Cyprus pound (C£) of 100 cents.

FLAG – White with a gold map of Cyprus above a wreath of olive.

NATIONAL ANTHEM – Ode to Freedom.

NATIONAL DAY – 1 October (Independence Day).

GOVERNMENT

Cyprus passed under British administration from 1878, and was formally annexed to Britain in November 1914 on the outbreak of war with Turkey. From 1925 to 1960 it was a Crown Colony. Following the launching in April 1955 of an armed campaign by EOKA in support of union with Greece, a state of emergency was declared in November 1955 which lasted for four years. After a meeting at Zürich between the Prime Ministers of Greece and Turkey, a conference was held in London and an agreement was signed on 19 February 1959 between the United Kingdom, Greece, Turkey, and the Greek and Turkish Cypriots which provided that Cyprus would be an independent republic.

Under the Cyprus Act 1960, the island became an independent sovereign republic on 16 August 1960. The constitution provided for a Greek Cypriot President and a Turkish Cypriot Vice-President elected for a five-year term by the Greek and Turkish communities respectively. The House of Representatives, elected for five years by universal suffrage of each community separately, was to consist of 35 Greek and 15 Turkish members. The 1960 Constitution proved unworkable in practice and led to intercommunal troubles. The UN Peace-Keeping Force in Cyprus (UNFI-CYP) was set up in March 1964; its mandate was last renewed on 15 June 1993 for six months. Increasing frustration at the obstinate attitudes of both communities towards any solution to the island's division led to the withdrawal of the 341-strong Danish contingent in December 1992 and the 575-strong Canadian contingent in summer 1993. The remaining 850 troops are mostly British.

DIVISION

In July 1974, mainland Greek officers of the Greek Cypriot National Guard launched a coup d'état against President Makarios and installed a former EOKA member, Nikos Sampson, in his place. Turkey, reserving to itself the right to maintain constitutional order and the independence and territorial integrity of the island, invaded Northern Cyprus and occupied over a third of the island. In February 1975 a 'Turkish Federated State of Cyprus' under Mr Rauf Denktash was declared in this area, its constitution being approved by referendum in July 1975. In November 1983 a 'Declaration of Statehood' was issued which purported to establish a 'Turkish Republic of Northern Cyprus'. The declaration was condemned by the UN Security Council and only Turkey has recognized the new 'state'. In May 1985 a referendum in the north of Cyprus approved a constitution for the 'Turkish Republic of Northern Cyprus'. In June 1985 Mr Denktash was elected President of the 'state' and a general election was held. Mr Denktash was re-elected in April 1990, and a general election was held in May 1990.

Since 1974 attempts to reach a settlement have focused on intercommunal talks under the auspices of the UN. In January 1993 the UN Secretary-General Boutros Ghali presented a plan and a map for a bizonal bi-communal federal state with the Turkish community having a veto over all the important decisions of the government and parliament. This was approved by the UN Security Council and in principle by the Greek community but not by the Turkish because of the loss of land involved.

A general election was held for the Cyprus House of Representatives on 19 May 1991, resulting in the parties gaining the following number of seats: Democratic Rally-Liberal Party 20; AKEL (Communist) 18; Democratic Party (Centre) 16; EDEK (Socialist) 7. The last presidential election was held in February 1993 when Glafcos Clerides of the Democratic Rally-Liberal Party defeated the Communist-supported independent incumbent George Vassiliou.

Cyprus applied for EC membership in 1989 but on 30 June 1993 the EC Commission issued a negative opinion on the application, stating that the division of the island must be resolved before entry into the EC.

President, Glafcos Clerides, *elected* 14 February 1993.

COUNCIL OF MINISTERS *as at August 1993*

Foreign Affairs, Alecos Michaelides.
Interior, Dinos Michaelides.
Finance, Phaedros Economides.
Education, Claire Angelidou.
Justice and Public Order, Alecos Evangelou.
Defence, Costas Eliades.
Communications and Works, Adamos Adamides.
Health, Manolis Christofides.
Commerce and Industry, Stelias Kiliaris.
Labour and Social Insurance, Andreas Moushouttas.
Agriculture and Natural Resources, Costas Petrides.

CYPRUS HIGH COMMISSION
93 Park Street, London W1Y 4ET
Tel 071-499 8272

High Commissioner, His Excellency Angelos Angelides (1990).
Deputy High Commisioner, C. Ioannou.
Counsellor, A. Mavrogenis (*Commerce*).

BRITISH HIGH COMMISSION
Alexander Pallis Street (PO Box 1978), Nicosia
Tel: Nicosia 2-473131

High Commissioner, His Excellency David John Michael Dain, CMG (1990).
Counsellor and Deputy High Commissioner, C. B. Jennings.
Defence Adviser, Col. J. A. Anderson.
First Secretary (Commercial), P. J. Newman.

BRITISH COUNCIL REPRESENTATIVE, Robert Frost, PO Box 5654, 3 Museum Street, Nicosia.

BRITISH SOVEREIGN AREAS
The United Kingdom retained full sovereignty and jurisdiction over two areas of 99 square miles in all: Akrotiri–Episkopi–Paramali and Dhekelia–Pergamos–Ayios Nicolaos–Xylophagou. This includes use of roads and other facilities. The British Administrator of these areas is appointed by The Queen and is responsible to the Secretary of State for Defence.

Administrator of the British Sovereign Areas, Maj.-Gen. A. G. H. Harley.

ECONOMY

Although agriculture still occupies a prime position in the Cyprus economy it is unlikely to expand further. Main products are citrus fruits, grapes and vine products, potatoes and other vegetables. Manufacturing, construction, distribution and other service industries are other major employers. Tourism is the main growth industry with over 1.2 million long-stay tourists producing C£490 million in foreign exchange earnings in 1989. Over 5,000 foreign firms and individuals have registered as offshore companies in Cyprus, which supports Cyprus's claim to be a centre for Middle East trade.

Britain continues to be the country's most important trading partner, taking some 23.4 per cent of its exports in 1989 and supplying 11.4 per cent of its imports. Cyprus is seeking to diversify its export markets and until recently sold almost half its exports to the Middle East. However, these traditional markets are now drying up, and Cyprus is looking more towards Europe. A Customs Union between Cyprus and the EC came into force in January 1988.

FINANCE	1988	1989
Total Revenue	C£535.0m	C£632.7m
Ordinary Expenditure	598.4m	663.8m

TRADE

There is a large visible trade deficit (C£737.2 million in 1989), which is offset by invisible earnings, particularly from tourism. The current account in 1989 showed a deficit of C£72.8m, which includes the cost of one aircraft amounting to C£80.7m.

	1988	1989
Imports	C£866.8m	C£1,130.3m
Exports (including re-exports)	330.9m	393.0m

Trade with UK	1991	1992
Imports from UK	£209,877,000	£221,910,000
Exports to UK	141,138,000	144,746,000

CZECH REPUBLIC
Česká Republika

The Czech Republic, composed of Bohemia and Morovia, has an area of 30,441 sq. miles (78,664 sq. km) and a population (1991 census) of 10,302,000, of which 95 per cent is Czech and 3 per cent Slovak. Geographically, Bohemia and Morovia are quite distinct. Bohemia is surrounded by mountain ranges while Moravia is composed of lands which stretch to the Danubian basin. The republic is bordered by Poland in the north-east, by Germany in the west and north-west, by Austria in the south and by Slovakia in the south-east.

RELIGION - The majority of the population are Roman Catholic, with a small Protestant minority.

CAPITAL - Prague (Praha) on the Vltava (Moldau), with a population (1991) of 1,215,076. Other major cities are Brno (Brüm) (391,093), Ostrava (331,241) and Plzeň (174,676).

CURRENCY - Koruna (Kc) or Czech crown of 100 Haléřů (Heller).

FLAG - White over red horizontally with a blue triangle extending from the hoist to the centre of the flag. (The Czech Republic retained the former Czechoslovak federal flag.)

NATIONAL ANTHEM - Kde Domov Můj (Where is my Motherland).

NATIONAL DAY - 28 October.

HISTORY

The land which is now the Czech Republic came under the rule of the Habsburg dynasty in 1526 and remained part of the Austro-Hungarian Empire until the end of the First World War in 1918. Austrian attempts to Germanize the Czech lands in the 18th and 19th centuries led to the reawakening of Czech national consciousness in the late 19th century. During the First World War captured Czech soldiers of the Austro-Hungarian army were formed into legions which fought for the Allies and Czech independence and later against Soviet Bolshevik forces. The independence of Czechoslavakia was proclaimed on 28 October 1918 following an amalgamation of Bohemia, Moravia, Slovakia and Ruthenia and was confirmed by the Allied Powers at the Versailles Peace Conference 1919.

The inter-war democratic Czechoslovak state was forced to cede the ethnic German Sudetenland to Nazi Germany on 30 September 1938 after the Munich Agreement. German forces invaded the Czech republic on 15 March 1939 and incorporated it into Germany while Slovakia became a puppet state. The Czech Republic was liberated by Soviet and American forces in May 1945. The pre-war democratic Czechoslovak state was re-established in 1945, having ceded Ruthenia to the Soviet Union, with the Communist Party in a very strong political position. The Communists gradually manoeuvred into a position to engineer a political crisis and take power in a coup which occurred in February 1948. The Communist Party remained in power until December 1989.

In 1968 the Czechoslovak Communist Party, under the then General Secretary Alexander Dubček, embarked on a political and economic reform programme. The implications for the internal development of the other Communist regimes in the Soviet bloc alarmed the Soviet Union. On the night of 20 August 1968 Czechoslovakia was invaded by Soviet, Polish, East German, Hungarian and Bulgarian troops, the capital and all major towns being occupied. The Czechoslovak leadership was forced to modify its policies and to legalize the presence of Soviet troops on Czechoslovak territory. The reforms of 1968 (apart from the formation of a federal republic) were abandoned when Gustáv Husák became leader of the Communist Party in April 1969 (President 1975-89).

Opposition to Communist Party rule gathered pace in the late 1980s and mass protests in November 1989 led to the resignation of the Communist Party Central Committee. The Communist Party was forced to concede its monopoly of power and on 10 December a new government was appointed in which only half the ministers were Communist Party members. Gustáv Husák resigned as President and was replaced by the dissident writer Václav Havel. Free elections were held in June 1990 in which the Communist Party was destroyed as a political force.

GOVERNMENT

Legislative elections were held in early June 1992 which returned the Civic Democratic Party and the Movement for a Democratic Slovakia as the dominant parties in the Czech and Slovak republics respectively. Talks between Czech and Slovak leaders on continuing the federation broke down because of the insistence of Vladimir Meciar, the Slovak leader, on a declaration of Slovak sovereignty. Meciar agreed with the Czech leader Vaclav Klaus on forming an interim transitional government for the federation with much reduced powers, and this was approved by President Havel and sworn in on 1 July 1992.

The re-election of President Havel was blocked by members of the Movement for a Democratic Slovakia and other Slovak nationalist deputies in the Federal Parliament vote on 3 July 1992, causing tension between Czech and Slovak politicians. Slovak deputies voted by 113 to 24 in Bratislava on 17 July 1992 to declare Slovakia a sovereign state, causing President Havel to resign on 20 July 1992. In the second half of 1992 Klaus and Meciar agreed on the separation of the Czech and Slovak republics into two soverign states, which took effect on 1 January 1993. Agreements were reached on guaranteed freedom of movement and rights of each state's citizens in the other state. as well as free trade in goods and services and the free movement of labour and capital. The former federal state's institutions, assets, property and debts were divided in the ratio 2:1 Czech to Slovak republics.

The elections of June 1992 had returned the Civil Democratic Party (ODS) of Vadlav Klaus as the largest party in the Czech parliament, and on 1 July 1992 it had formed a coalition government with three other centre-right parties. This government was sworn in as the government of the Czech Republic on 1 January 1993, with former federal President Havel being elected as Czech President on 26 January 1993.

The Czech constition which came into effect on 1 January 1993 vests legislative power in the bicameral parliament, comprising a 200-member Chamber of Deputies elected for a four-year term and an 81-member Senate elected for a six-year term, one-third being renewed every two years. The President is elected by parliament for a five-year term. Executive power is held by the Prime Minister and Council of Ministers. A two-thirds majority in parliament is necessary to amend the constitution, and federal laws remain in place unless superseded by Czech ones. The Czech Republic was admitted to UN membership on 19 January 1993.

HEAD OF STATE
President, Vaclav Havel, *elected* 26 January 1993, *sworn in* 2 February 1993.

COUNCIL OF MINISTERS *as at August 1993*
Prime Minister, Vaclav Klaus (ODS).
Deputy Prime Minister, Finance, Ivan Kocarnik (ODS).
Deputy Prime Minister, Agriculture, Josef Lux (KDU-CSL).
Deputy Prime Minister, Jan Kalvoda (ODA).
Foreign Affairs, Josef Zieleniec (ODS).
Industry and Trade, Vladimir Dlouhy (ODA).
Economy, Karel Dyba (ODS).
Health, Petr Lom (ODS).
Interior, Jan Ruml (ODS).
Culture, Jindrich Kabat (KDU-CSL).
Education, Petr Pitha (KDS).
Labour and Social Affairs, Jindrich Vodicka (ODS).
State Control, Igor Nemec (ODS).
Privatization, Jiri Stalicky (ODA).
Environment, Frantisek Benda (KDS).
Justice, Jiri Novak (ODS).
Economic Competition, Stanislav Belehradek (KDU-CSL).
Defence, Antonin Baudys (KDU-CSL).
Transport, Jan Strasky (ODS).

ODS: Civic Democratic Party; KDU-CSL: Christian Democratic Union–Czech People's Party; ODA: Civic Democratic Alliance; KDS: Christian Democratic Party.

EMBASSY OF THE CZECH REPUBLIC
26–30 Kensington Palace Gardens, London W8 4QY
Tel 071-727 4918
Ambassador Extraordinary and Plenipotentiary, vacant.
Chargé d'Affaires and First Secretary, Peter Hrdlička.
Military Attaché, Col. S. Thurnvald.
Counsellor, J. Žabža.

BRITISH EMBASSY
Thunovská 14, 125 50 Prague
Tel: Prague 533347
Ambassador Extraordinary and Plenipotentiary, His Excellency David Brighty, CMG, CVO (1991).
Counsellor and Deputy Head of Mission, C. M. T. Elmes.
Defence and Military Attaché, Col. W. J. Chesshyre.
First Secretary (Commercial), J. Cummins, MBE.
First Secretary (Management) and Consul, D. J. Jackson.
Cultural Attaché, W. Jefferson, OBE *(British Council Director)*.

ECONOMY

Under Communist rule industry was state-owned and nearly all agricultural land was cultivated by state or co-operative farms. An economic reform programme was begun in 1990 aimed at producing a free-market economy in the former Czechoslovakia. New laws passed in the spring of 1990 provided a legal basis for private enterprise, joint ventures and foreign investment. The government of the Czech Republic has continued to follow the policies of the former federal government with the aim of macroeconomic stability, sound finance, full currency convertibility, and openness to international economic competition. This has necessitated a restrictive monetary policy to stem inflation and a restructuring of manufacturing industry to be internationally competitive, and these were major reasons for the break with Slovakia. As a result, a successful climate for foreign investment (US$1,560m in 1992) has been created, private enterprises have grown and reliance on trade with the former Soviet bloc countries has declined. Unemployment has risen but is still low by west European standards, and a trade-liberalizing association agreement with the EC is in operation.

A customs union between the Czech and Slovak Republics is in place but separate currencies were introduced in February 1993 following speculation. In April 1993 the Prague Stock Exchange reopened after 50 years and new western-style bankruptcy laws came into operation.

The Czech Republic is not rich in minerals, although significant quantities of coal and lignite are mined. Principal agricultural products are sugar-beet, potatoes and cereal crops; the timber industry is also very important. Having been the major industrial area of the Austro-Hungarian Empire, the country has long been highly industrialized, and machinery, industrial consumer goods and raw materials are major exports.

TRADE WITH UK *(Czechoslovakia)*

	1991	1992
Imports from UK	£129,378,000	£208,912,000
Exports to UK	131,441,000	170,268,000

LANGUAGE AND LITERATURE

Czech is the official language, having its own literature. The Reformation gave a widespread impulse to Czech literature, the writings of Jan Hus (martyred in 1415 as a religious and social reformer) familiarizing the people with Wyclif's teaching. This impulse endured to the close of the 17th century when Jan Amos Komensky or Comenius (1592–1670) was expelled from the country. Under Austrian rule and with the persistent pursuit of Germanization, there was a period of stagnation until the national revival in the 19th century. Authors of international reputation include Jaroslav Hašek (1883–1923), Jaroslav Seifert (1901–86, Nobel Prize for Literature, 1985), Václav Havel (b. 1936) and Milan Kundera (b. 1929).

EDUCATION

Education is compulsory and free for all children from the ages of 6 to 16. There are three universities in the Czech Republic, of which the most famous is Charles University in Prague (founded 1348), the others being situated at Brno and Olomouc. In addition there are a considerable number of other institutions of university standing, technical colleges, agricultural colleges, etc.

DENMARK
Kongeriget Danmark

Denmark is a kingdom of northern Europe, consisting of the islands of Zealand, Funen, Lolland, etc., the peninsula of Jutland, and the outlying island of Bornholm in the Baltic, the Faröes and Greenland. Denmark is situated between 54° 34′ and 57° 45′ N. latitude and 8° 5′–15° E. longitude, with an area of 16,629 sq. miles (43,069 sq. km), and a population (official estimate 1991) of 5,146,469.

CAPITAL – Ψ Copenhagen, population (1991) 464,773; Greater Copenhagen 1,337,114; Ψ Aarhus 264,135; Ψ Odense 177,635; Ψ Aalborg 155,664; Ψ Esbjerg 81,616; Ψ Randers 60,970; Ψ Kolding 57,586; Ψ Helsingør 56,632; Ψ Horsens 55,088.
CURRENCY – Danish krone (Kr) of 100 øre.
FLAG – Red, with white cross.
NATIONAL ANTHEM – Kong Kristian.
NATIONAL DAYS – 16 April (The Queen's Birthday), 5 June (Constitution Day).

GOVERNMENT

Under the Constitution of the Kingdom of Denmark Act of 5 June 1953, the legislature consists of one chamber, the

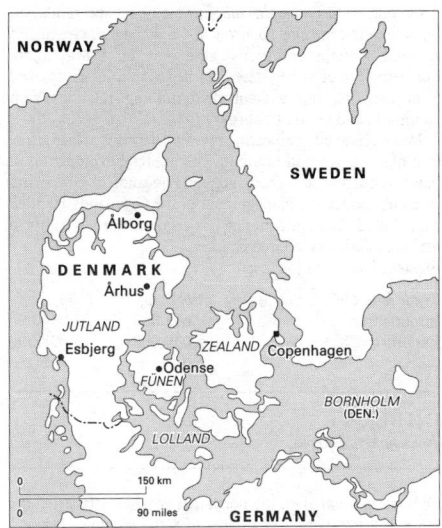

Folketing, of not more than 179 members, including two for the Faröes and two for Greenland. The voting age is 18.

A coalition government led by Poul Schlüter was formed in December 1990 after the General Election on 12 December. The government resigned on 14 January 1993 after a judicial enquiry stated that it had lied over measures to prevent Tamil refugees from entering Denmark. On 25 January a new coalition government of the Social Democrat, Centre Democrat, Social Liberal and Christian People's Party was sworn in. The state of the parties in the Folketing is: Social Democrat Party (SD) 71; Conservatives (C) 31; Liberals (L) 31; Socialist People's Party (SP) 15; Progress Party (P) 12; Centre Democrat Party (CD) 8; Social Liberal Party (SL) 7; Christian People's Party (CP) 4.

HEAD OF STATE

Queen, Margrethe II, KG, eldest daughter of King Frederik IX, born 16 April 1940, succeeded 14 January 1972, married 10 June 1967, Count Henri de Monpezat (Prince Henrik of Denmark), and has issue Crown Prince Frederik born 26 May 1968; and Prince Joachim, born 7 June 1969.

CABINET as at August 1993

Prime Minister, Poul Nyrup Rasmussen (SD).
Industrial Co-ordination, Mimi Jakobsen (CD).
Economic Affairs, Marianne Jelved (SL).
Energy, Jann Sjursen (CP).
Finance, Mogens Lykketoft (SD).
Foreign Affairs, Niels Helveg Petersen (SL).
Agriculture and Fisheries, Bjoern Westh (SD).
Environment, Svend Auken (SD).
Communications and Tourism, Arne Melchior (CD).
Education, Ole Vig Jensen (SL).
Housing, Nordic Collaboration and Baltic Affairs, Flemming Kofod-Svensdsen (CP).
Development Co-operation, Helle Degn (SD).
Interior, Birte Weiss (SD).
Labour, Jytte Andersen (SD).
Taxation, Ole Stovad (SD).
Defence, Hans Haekkerup (SD).
Cultural Affairs, Jytte Hilden (SD).
Health, Torben Lund (SD).
Transport, Helge Mortensen (SD).

Industry, Jan Trøjborg (SD).
Justice, Erling Olsen (SD).
Social Affairs, Karen Moustgaard Jespersen (SD).
Research and Technology, Svend Bergstein (CD).
Ecclesiastical Affairs, Arne Oluf Anderson (CD).

ROYAL DANISH EMBASSY
55 Sloane Street, London SWIX 9SR
Tel 071-333 0200
Ambassador Extraordinary and Plenipotentiary, His Excellency R. A. Thorning-Petersen (1989).
Minister, Mrs A. Hugau.
Counsellor (Commercial), Jorgen Gulev.
First Secretary (Consular Affairs), Kirsten Geelan.
Defence Attaché, Capt. S. Lund.

BRITISH EMBASSY
36–40 Kastelsvej, DK-2100 Copenhagen Ø
Tel: Copenhagen 35 264600
Ambassador Extraordinary and Plenipotentiary, His Excellency Hugh J. Arbuthnott, CMG (1993).
Counsellor and Deputy Head of Mission, P. S. Astley, LVO.
Counsellor (Economic/Commcercial), A. M. Layden.
Defence Attaché, Cmdr. R. Kirkwood, RN.
First Secretary (Management) and Consul, B. Robertson.

There are Consulates at Aabenraa, Aalborg, Aarhus, Esbjerg, Fredericia, Herning, Odense, Rønne (Bornholm); at Tórshavn (Faröe Islands); and Nuuk (Godthåb) (Greenland).

BRITISH COUNCIL REPRESENTATIVE, Michael Holcroft, Gammel Mont 123, 1117 Copenhagen K.

DEFENCE

Total active armed forces number 29,200 (10,100 conscripts). Conscripts serve for nine to 12 months. Reserves number 72,500 personnel.

Army personnel number 17,300 (8,500 conscripts) but major use is made of the 54,600 reservists to reinforce peacetime units. Organization is into five mechanized infantry brigades, six combat regiment groups, two reconnaissance battalions and four regional defence combat regiment groups. Equipment includes 500 main battle tanks, 640 armoured personnel carriers and 550 artillery pieces.

The Navy has 4,900 personnel (800 conscripts) with three frigates, five submarines, 33 patrol and coastal craft and eight armed helicopters.

The Air Force numbers 7,000 personnel (800 conscripts) with 106 combar aircraft of US and Swedish manufacture organized into one transport, one reconnaissance and five ground attack/air defence squadrons.

EDUCATION

Education is free and compulsory. Special schools are numerous, commercial, technical and agricultural predominating. There are universities at Copenhagen (founded in 1479), Aarhus (1933), Odense (1966), Roskilde (1972) and Aalborg (1974). A further university at Esbjerg is planned.

LANGUAGE AND LITERATURE

The Danish language is akin to Swedish and Norwegian. Danish literature, ancient and modern, embraces all forms of expression, familiar names being Hans Christian Andersen (1805–75), Søren Kierkegaard (1813–55) and Karen Blixen (1885–1962). Some 48 newspapers are published in Denmark; eight daily papers are published in Copenhagen.

ECONOMY

Of the labour force, in 1988, 1.8 per cent was engaged in agriculture, fishing, forestry, etc.; 27.5 per cent in manufacturing, building and construction; 15.4 per cent in commerce, 0.2 per cent in liberal professions and 53.2 per cent in administration, transport and the financial services. The chief agricultural products are pigs, cattle, dairy products, poultry and eggs, seeds, cereals and sugar beet; manufactures are mostly based on imported raw materials but there are also considerable imports of finished goods.

FINANCE

Budget Estimates	1990	1991
Revenue	Kr461,600m	Kr479,200m
Expenditure	473,500m	497,600m

Denmark's balance of payments on current account showed a deficit for 1988 of Kr12,200 million (1987, Kr20,700 million).

TRADE

The principal imports are industrial raw materials, consumer goods, construction inputs, machinery, raw materials, vehicles and textile products. The chief exports are miscellaneous manufactured articles, agricultural and dairy products.

	1990	1991
Total Imports	Kr240,555m	Kr255,764m
Total Exports	283,437m	309,440m

Trade with UK	1991	1992
Imports from UK	£1,408,549,000	£1,560,607,000
Exports to UK	2,226,706,000	2,384,964,000

COMMUNICATIONS

Mercantile marine (ships above 250 gross tonnage) at the beginning of 1993, totalled 634 ships. In 1985 there was 2,471 km of state-owned railway and 494 km of privately-owned railway systems.

THE FARÖES

The Faröes, or Sheep Islands have an area of 540 sq. miles (1,399 sq. km) and a population (1991) of 47,449. The capital is Tórshavn.

The islands are governed by a *Lagting* of 26 members, a *Landsstyre* of four members which deals with special Faröes affairs, and send two representatives to the *Folketing* at Copenhagen. In 1946 the Lagting, with the consent of the Danish Government, for its own guidance held a plebiscite on the Faröes. About one-third of the electors did not, however, take part in the voting; of the rest, a little more than half the votes cast were in favour of separation from Denmark and the establishment of a republic. At the subsequent general election for the Lagting a great majority voted in favour of remaining part of Denmark with a certain measure of home rule and in 1948 the Faröes received this. The Faröes are not part of the EC.
Prime Minister, Marita Petersen.

Trade with UK	1991	1992
Imports from UK	£7,330,000	£7,755,000
Exports to UK	32,515,000	44,303,000

GREENLAND

Greenland has a total area of 2,175,600 sq. km, of which about 16 per cent is ice-free, and a population (1991) of 55,385. It is divided into three provinces (West, North and East). The capital is Nuuk (Godthåb)).

Greenland has a *Landsraad* of 17 members and sends two representatives to the *Folketing* at Copenhagen. Greenland attained a status of internal autonomy on 1 May 1979. Following a plebiscite Greenland negotiated its withdrawal from the EC, but without discontinuing relations with Denmark, and left on 1 February 1985.

Mineral and oil prospecting revealed deposits of lead, zinc, iron ore, oil, gas and uranium. Commercial exploitation of these resources has already begun. The trade of Greenland is mainly under the management of the Grønlands Handel. The United States of America has acquired certain rights to maintain air bases in Greenland.
Premier, Lars Emil Johansen.

Trade with UK	1991	1992
Imports from UK	£635,000	£1,034,000
Exports to UK	5,039,000	3,098,000

DJIBOUTI
Jumhouriyya Djibouti

Djibouti is situated on the north-east coast of Africa (i.e. the Horn of Africa) and has an area of 8,494 sq. miles (22,000 sq. km.). It has a population (1991 census) of 520,000. The climate is harsh and much of the country is semi-arid desert.

CAPITAL – Ψ Djibouti, population (1991) 340,700.
CURRENCY – Djibouti franc of 100 centimes.
FLAG – Blue over green with white triangle in the hoist containing a red star.
NATIONAL DAY – 27 June (Independence Day).

GOVERNMENT

Formerly known as French Somaliland and then as the French Territory of the Afars and the Issas, the Republic of Djibouti became independent on 27 June 1977. The most recent elections to the 65-member Chamber of Deputies took place in April 1987. The sole legal party was formerly the *Rassemblement Populaire pour le Progrès* (RPP, Popular Rally for Progress). A new multi-party constituion was adopted by referendum on 4 September 1992 and subsequent multi-party elections held on 18 December were won by the ruling RPP which won 77 per cent of the vote and all 65 seats in the Chamber of Deputies. President Aptidon was re-elected for a fourth six-year term on 9 May 1993. However, less than half the electorate voted in either election and the Front for the Restoration of Unity and Democracy (FRUD) boycotted both.

INSURGENCY

Armed FRUD rebels, their support based among ethnic Afars (most of the population is either Afar or Issas), have been fighting the government for some years, especially in the east and north.

HEAD OF STATE

President, Hassan Gouled Aptidon, *elected* 1977, *re-elected* 1981, 1987 and 9 May 1993.

CABINET *as at July 1993*
Prime Minister, Barkat Gourad Hamadou.
Justice and Islamic Affairs, Moumin Bahdon Farah.
Foreign Affairs, Abdou Bolok Abdou.
Interior and Decentralization, Idriss Harbi Farah.
National Defence, Ahmed Boulaleh Barre.
Finance, Ahmed Aden Youssouf.
Ports and Shipping, Moussa Bouraleh Robleh.

Economy and Commerce, Mohamed Ali Mohamed.
National Education, Ahmed Guire Waberi.
Youth and Sports and Culture, Mohamed Ibrahim Mohamed.
Public Health and Social Affairs, Mohamed Said Saleh.
Civil Service and Administrative Reform, Ougoureh Hassan Ibrahim.
Public Works, Construction and Housing, Atteyeh Ismael Waiss.
Industry, Energy and Mines, Ali Mahamade Houmed.
Planning, Regional Development, Environment and Co-operation, Mohamed Moussa Chehem.
Transport, Tourism and Telecommunications, Ahmed Waberi Guedi.
Labour and Professional Organizations, Ibiro Ahmed Hamadou.
Agriculture and Rural Development, Omar Chirdon Abass.

EMBASSY OF THE REPUBLIC OF DJIBOUTI
26 rue Emile Ménier, 75116 Paris, France
Tel: Paris 47274922

Ambassador Extraordinary and Plenipotentiary, His Excellency Ahmed Omar Farah (1991).

BRITISH EMBASSY
Ambassador (resides at Sana'a, Yemen).

BRITISH CONSULATE
PO Box 81, 9-11 Rue de Geneve, Djibouti
Honorary Consul, P. Lievin.

The French continue to maintain army, navy and air force bases. Djibouti has an excellent port, an international airport, and a railway line runs to Addis Ababa.

TRADE WITH UK	1991	1992
Imports from UK	£21,889,000	£25,472,000
Exports to UK	119,000	58,000

DOMINICA
The Commonwealth of Dominica

Dominica, the loftiest of the Lesser Antilles, lies in the Windward Group, between 15° 12' and 15° 39' N. latitude and 61° 14' and 61° 29' W. longitude, 95 miles south of Antigua. It is about 29 miles long and 16 broad comprising an area of 289 sq. miles (748.5 sq. km). The island is of volcanic origin and very mountainous, and the soil is very fertile. The temperature varies, according to the altitude, from 13° to 29°C. The climate is healthy. The population is 72,000 (1991 UN estimate).

CAPITAL – ΨRoseau, on the south-west coast, population 15,850. The other principal town is Portsmouth, population 3,620.
CURRENCY – East Caribbean dollar (EC$) of 100 cents.
FLAG – Green ground with a cross overall of yellow, black and white stripes, and in the centre a red disc charged with a Sisserou parrot in natural colours within a ring of ten green stars.
NATIONAL ANTHEM – Isle of Beauty.
NATIONAL DAY – 3 November (Independence Day).

GOVERNMENT

The island was discovered by Columbus in 1493, when it was a stronghold of the Caribs, who remained virtually the sole inhabitants until the French established settlements in the 18th century. It was captured by the British in 1759 but

passed back and forth between France and Britain until 1805, after which British possession was not challenged. From 1871 to 1939 Dominica was part of the Leeward Islands Colony, then from 1940 the island was a unit of the Windward Islands group. Internal self-government from 1967 was followed on 3 November 1978 by independence as a republic with the name The Commonwealth of Dominica.

Executive authority is vested in the President, who is elected by the House of Assembly for not more than two terms of five years. Parliament consists of the President and the House of Assembly (representatives elected by universal adult suffrage) and nine Senators, five of whom are appointed on the advice of the Prime Minister and the other four on the advice of the Leader of the Opposition. Parliament has a life of five years.

At the general election of May 1990, the Dominica Freedom Party won 11 seats, the Dominica United Workers' Party 6, and the Labour Party of Dominica 4.

HEAD OF STATE
President, His Excellency Sir Clarence Seignoret, GCB, OBE.

CABINET *as at July 1993*
Prime Minister, Minister of Finance and Economic Affairs, Information and Public Relations, Dame Eugenia Charles, DBE.
Attorney-General and Minister of Legal Affairs, Hon. Jenner Armour.
External Affairs and OECS Unity, Hon. Brian Alleyne.
Trade, Industry and Tourism, Hon. Charles Maynard.
Education and Sports, Hon. Rupert Sorhaindo sen.
Community Development and Social Affairs, Hon. Henry George.
Health and Social Security, Hon. Allan Guye.
Labour and Immigration, Hon. Heskeith Alexander.
Communications, Works and Housing, Hon. Alleyne Carbon.
Agriculture, Hon. Maynard Joseph.
Minister without Portfolio, Prime Minister's Office, Hon. Dermott Southwell.
Parliamentary Secretary in the Ministry of Agriculture, Trade, Industry and Tourism, Hon. Ossie Walsh.
Parliamentary Secretary in the Ministry of Communications, Works and Housing, Hon. Clem Shillingford.

HIGH COMMISSION FOR THE COMMONWEALTH OF DOMINICA
1 Collingham Gardens, London SW5 0HW
Tel 071-370 5194/5
High Commissioner, His Excellency Ashworth Elwin (1992).

BRITISH HIGH COMMISSION
High Commissioner (resides at Bridgetown, Barbados).

BRITISH CONSULATE
PO Box 6, Roseau
Honorary Consul, J. Calvert.

ECONOMY
Agriculture is the principal occupation, with tropical and citrus fruits the main crops. Products for export are bananas, lime juice, lime oil, bay oil, copra and rum. Forestry, fisheries and agro-processing are being encouraged. The only commercially exploitable mineral is pumice, used chiefly for building purposes. Manufacturing consists largely of the processing of agricultural products.

FINANCE	1991-2
Recurrent Revenue	EC$144.5m
Recurrent Expenditure	98.8m

TRADE	1990
Imports	EC$318.3m
Exports	148.5m

Trade with UK	1991	1992
Imports from UK	£11,573,000	£8,559,000
Exports to UK	25,221,000	21,870,000

DOMINICAN REPUBLIC
República Dominicana

The Dominican Republic, formerly the Spanish portion of the island of Hispaniola, is the oldest settlement of European origin in America. The western part of the island forms the Republic of Haiti. The island lies between Cuba on the west and Puerto Rico on the east and the Dominican Republic covers an area of 18,816 sq. miles (48,734 sq. km), with a population (1991 UN estimate) of 7,321,000. The climate is tropical in the lowlands and semi-tropical to temperate in the higher altitudes.

Spanish is the language of the Republic.

CAPITAL – Ψ Santo Domingo, population of the Capital District (1981 census) 1,313,172. Other centres, with populations (1981 census): Santiago de los Caballeros (550,372); La Vega (385,043); San Francisco De Macoris (235,544); San Juan (239,957); San Cristóbal (446,132).
CURRENCY – Dominican Republic peso (RD$) of 100 centavos.
FLAG – Divided into blue and red quarters by a white cross.
NATIONAL ANTHEM – Quisqueyanos Valientes, Alcemos (Brave men of Quisqueya, let's raise our song).
NATIONAL DAY – 27 February (Independence Day 1844).

GOVERNMENT

Santo Domingo was discovered by Christopher Columbus in December 1492, and remained a Spanish colony until 1821. In 1822 it was subjugated by the neighbouring Haitians who remained in control until 1844 when the Dominican Republic was proclaimed. The country was occupied by American marines from 1916 until the adoption of a new Constitution in 1924. From 1930 until 30 May 1961 (when he was assassinated) Generalissimo Rafael Trujillo ruled the country.
    President Juan Bosch held office from December 1962 to September 1963, when he was deposed by a military junta. A revolt in favour of ex-President Bosch in April 1965 developed into civil war lasting until September the same year when a provisional President was elected. In November 1966 a new Constitution was introduced.
    Executive power is vested in the President, who is elected by direct vote and serves for four years. The President forms his cabinet without reference to the Congress. Legislative power is exercised by the Congress, which has a term of four years concurrent with the presidency. The upper chamber is the Senate of 27 senators, one for each province and one for Santo Domingo. The lower is the Chamber of Deputies which has 120 members, one for each 50,000 inhabitants in each province, with the provision that no province has less than two members. Judicial power is exercised by the Supreme Court of Justice.

HEAD OF STATE
President, Dr Joaquin Balaguer, *took office*, 16 August 1986, *re-elected* 16 May 1990.
Vice-President, Carlos Morales Troncoso.

CABINET *as at* July 1993
Presidency, Enrique Perez y Perez.
Finance, Marte de Barrios.
Foreign Affairs, Juan Aristides Guzman.

Education and Culture, Pedro Gil Iturbides.
Agriculture, Agronomo Nicolas Concepción.
Labour, Rafael Alburquerque.
Public Health and Social Welfare, Dr Miguel A. Strepan.
Industry and Trade, Rafael Bello Andino.
Sports, Physical Education and Recreation, Cristobal Marte.
Tourism, Andres Venderhorst.
Interior and Police, Gen. Rafael Peraeta Guerrero.
Armed Forces, Lt.-Gen. Hector Garcia Tejeda.

EMBASSY OF THE DOMINICAN REPUBLIC
17 rue La Fontaine, 75016 Paris, France
Tel: Paris 45018881

Ambassador Extraordinary and Plenipotentiary, new appointment awaited.

HONORARY CONSULATE
6 Queen's Mansions, Brook Green, London W6 7EB
Tel 071–602 1885
Honorary Consul, vacant.

There are also Consular Offices at *Birmingham*, *Cardiff*, *Grimsby* and *Plymouth*.

BRITISH AMBASSADOR (resident in Caracas, Venezuela).
BRITISH CONSULATE
Abraham Lincoln 552, Santo Domingo DR
Tel: Santo Domingo 586 8464.
Honorary Consul, M. Tejeda, MBE.

COMMUNICATIONS

According to local classification there are 2,932 miles of first class and 1,392 miles of second class and inter-communal roads in the republic. There is a direct road from Santo Domingo to Port-au-Prince, the capital of Haiti, but that part of it in the border area has fallen into disuse. The frontier has been closed since September 1967, except for that section crossed by the main road linking the two capitals. A telephone system connects practically all the principal towns of the republic and there is a telegraph service to all parts of the world. There are more than 90 commercial broadcasting stations and six television stations.
    The republic is served by two national and six foreign airlines, and an international airport 18 miles to the east of the capital is in operation. Another has been built near Puerto Plata on the north coast.

ECONOMY

Sugar, coffee, cocoa, and tobacco are the most important crops. Other products are peanuts, maize, rice, bananas, molasses, salt, cement, ferro-nickel, gold, silver, cattle, sisal products, honey and chocolate. There is a growing number of light industries producing beer, tinned foodstuffs, glass products, textiles, soap, cigarettes, construction materials, plastic articles, shoes, papers, paint, rum, matches, peanut oil and other products.

FINANCE	1986
Expenditure	RD$2,251m
Revenue	2,113m

TRADE
The chief imports are machinery, food stuffs, iron and steel, cotton textiles and yarns, mineral oils (including petrol), cars and other motor vehicles, chemical and pharmaceutical products, electrical equipment and accessories, construction material, paper and paper products, and rubber and rubber products. The chief exports are sugar, coffee, cocoa, tobacco, chocolate, molasses, bauxite, ferro-nickel and gold. Tobacco

and tobacco manufactures are the principal exports to the UK.

	1984	1985
Imports	RD$1,459,000,000	RD$1,285,900,000
Exports	1,211,100,000	739,300,000

Trade with UK	1991	1992
Imports from UK	£19,773,000	£16,668,000
Exports to UK	22,076,000	19,792,000

ECUADOR
Republica del Ecuador

Ecuador is an equatorial state of South America, the mainland extending from 1° 38′ N. to 4° 50′ S. latitude, and between 75° 20′ and 81° W. longitude, comprising an area reduced by boundary settlements with Peru (January 1942) to about 109,484 sq. miles (283,561 sq. km). The republic extends across the Western Andes, the highest peaks in Ecuador being Chimborazo (20,408 ft) and Ilinza (17,405 ft) in the Western Cordillera; and Cotopaxi (19,612 ft) and Cayambe (19,160 ft) in the Eastern Cordillera. Ecuador is watered by the Upper Amazon, and by the rivers Guayas, Mira, Santiago, Chone, and Esmeraldas on the Pacific coast. There are extensive forests.

POPULATION – The population (UN estimate 1991) is 10,851,000, mostly descendants of the Spanish, aboriginal Indians, and Mestizoes.

LANGUAGE – Spanish is the principal language but Quechua is also a recognized language and is spoken by the majority of the Indian population.

CAPITAL – Quito, population (1991 estimate) 1,387,887; Ψ Guayaquil (1,531,229) is the chief port; Cuenca (332,117).

CURRENCY – Sucre of 100 centavos.

FLAG – Three horizontal bands, yellow, blue and red (the yellow band twice the width of the others); emblem in centre.

NATIONAL DAY – 10 August (Independence Day).

GOVERNMENT

The former kingdom of Quito was conquered by the Incas of Peru in the latter part of the 15th century. Early in the 16th century Pizarro's conquests led to the inclusion of the present territory of Ecuador in the Spanish Vice-royalty of Quito. The independence of the country was achieved in a revolutionary war which culminated in the battle of Mount Pichincha on 24 May 1822.

After seven years of military rule, Ecuador returned to democracy in 1979. The present constitution, introduced in 1978, provides for an elected President and Vice-President who serve for a four-year term. Neither may stand for re-election. There is a unicameral National Congress with 77 members elected every four years, 12 of whom are elected on a national basis and the rest by the provinces. The Chamber meets for two months every year (August to October) but can be convoked at any time for extraordinary sessions. Four Legislative Commissions meet through the year. Voting is compulsory for all literate and (since 1980) voluntary for all illiterate citizens over the age of 18. The republic is divided into 21 provinces.

In the May 1992 legislative election no party or coalition gained a majority but a loose agreement between various right-wing and centre-right parties enabled President Ballén to introduce a programme of free market economic reform, financial liberalization and privatization. This, together with

reduction in state spending, has caused serious social unrest throughout late 1992 and early 1993.

HEAD OF STATE
President, Sixto Durán Ballén, *elected* 5 July 1992, *sworn in* 10 August 1992.
Vice-President, Alberto Dahik Garzozi.

CABINET *as at August 1993*
Government Affairs, Roberto Dunn Barreira.
Foreign Affairs, Dr Diego Paredes.
National Defence, Jose Gallardo Roman.
Education and Culture, Dr Eduardo Pena Trivino.
Finance and Public Credit, Mario Ribadeneira Saenz.
Public Works and Communications, Pedro Lopez Torres.
Energy and Mines, Pablo Baquerro.
Industry, Commerce, Integration and Fisheries, Mauricio Pinto Mancheno.
Labour, Alfredo Corral Borrero.
Agriculture and Livestock, Mariano Gonzalez.
Public Health, Leonardo Viteri Molinari.
Social Welfare and Public Promotion, Gustavo Novoa Bejarano.
Information and Tourism, Carlos Vera.
Housing and Urban Development, Francisco Albornoz.
Secretary-General of the Administration, Jose Vicente Maldonado.

EMBASSY OF ECUADOR
Flat 3B, 3 Hans Crescent, London SW1X OLS
Tel 071–584 1367

Ambassador Extraordinary and Plenipotentiary, His Excellency Luis Dávalos (1993).

BRITISH EMBASSY
Av. Gonzalez Suarez, 111 (Casilla 314), Quito
Tel: Quito 560670

Ambassador Extraordinary and Plenipotentiary, His Excellency Frank Basil Wheeler, CMG (1989).

There are British Consular Offices at *Cuenca, Galapagos* and *Guayaquil.*

BRITISH COUNCIL REPRESENTATIVE, Desmond Lauder, Av. Amazonas 1646, Orellana (Casilla 17078829), Quito. There is also an English Language Teaching Centre at Guayaquil.

ECONOMY

Agriculture is the most important sector of the economy, supporting nearly 50 per cent of the population (particularly the poorest) and contributing 14.5 per cent of the Gross Domestic Product and 19.5 per cent of exports. The main products for export are fish (mainly shrimps, tuna and sardines), which had become the largest agricultural export by 1982; bananas, which provide a third of agricultural exports; cocoa and coffee. Other important crops are sugar, corn, soya, rice, cotton, African palm (for oil), vegetables, fruit and timber, the temperate crops being produced mostly in the highlands.

The economy was transformed by the discovery in 1972 of major oil fields in the Oriente area, and oil accounted for two-thirds of 1981 export earnings. The economy grew rapidly in the 1970s but is now faced with reduced growth, due mainly to the fall in the price of oil. The oil deposits in the Oriente are estimated at between 10,000 and 15,000 million barrels, and further exploration and development is taking place. The oil is evacuated by a trans-Andean pipeline to the port of Balao (near Esmeraldas City). Ecuador withdrew from OPEC in September 1992 in order to raise its production to 385,000 barrels per day by the end of 1992. The total foreign debt is estimated at US$12,500m.

FINANCE

The estimated government budget in 1986 was: revenue 186,824 million sucres; expenditure 216,466 million sucres.

TRADE

Import permits are required for all merchandise and these are issued by the Central Bank of Ecuador. Manufactured goods and machinery are the main imports.

	1991
Imports	US$2,207m
Exports	2,851m

Trade with UK	1991	1992
Imports from UK	£45,213,000	£33,064,000
Exports to UK	16,284,000	15,657,000

COMMUNICATIONS

There are 23,256 km of permanent roads and 5,044 km of roads which are only open during the dry season. There are about 750 miles of railway, including the railway from Quito to Guayaquil. Ten commercial airlines operate international flights, linking Ecuador with major foreign cities and there are internal services between all important towns. Two daily newspapers are published at Quito and four at Guayaquil.

DEFENCE

The total active armed forces number some 57,500 personnel, with a further 100,000 reserves. The standing Army has a strength of 50,000 personnel divided into one infantry division and nine brigades (one armoured, four infantry, three jungle and one special forces). Equipment includes 150 light tanks, 145 armoured personnel carriers and reconnaissance vehicles and 70 artillery pieces. The Air Force has a strength of 3,500 personnel with 85 combat aircraft organized into two ground attack, one air defence and two counter-insurgency squadrons with transport and training units. The Navy is 4,000 strong (including 1,500 marines) and has two submarines, two principal surface combatant vessels and 12 patrol and coastal combatants.

EDUCATION

As a result of an intensive national education programme more than 75 per cent of the population are now literate. Elementary education is free and compulsory. There are ten universities (three at Quito, three at Guayaquil, and one each at Cuenca, Machala, Loja and Portoviejo), polytechnic schools at Quito and Guayaquil and eight technical colleges in other provincial capitals.

GALÁPAGOS ISLANDS

The Galápagos (Giant Tortoise) Islands, forming the province of the Archipelago de Colón, were annexed by Ecuador in 1832. The archipelago lies in the Pacific, about 500 miles from Saint Elena peninsula, the most westerly point of the mainland. There are 12 large and several hundred smaller islands with a total area of about 3,000 sq. miles and an estimated population (1982) of 6,119. The capital is San Cristobal, on Chatham Island. Although the archipelago lies on the equator, the temperature of the surrounding water is well below equatorial average owing to the Antarctic Humboldt Current. The province consists for the most part of National Park Territory, where unique marine birds, iguanas, and the giant tortoises are conserved. There is some

local subsistence farming; the main industry, apart from tourism, is tuna and lobster fishing.

EGYPT
Al-Jumhuriyal Misr al-Arabiya

The total area of Egypt is 386,662 sq. miles (1,001,449 sq. km), only 3 per cent of which is cultivated land. The territory of Egypt comprises Egypt proper, the peninsula of Sinai and a number of islands in the Gulf of Suez and Red Sea, of which the principal are Jubal, Shadwan, Gafatin and Zeberged (or St John's Island). This territory lies between 22° and 32° N. latitude and 24° and 37° E. longitude. The northern boundary is the Mediterranean, and Egypt borders the Sudan in the south and Libya in the west. The east boundary follows a line drawn from Rafa on the Mediterranean (34° 15′ E. longitude.) to the head of the Gulf of 'Aqaba.

The country is mainly flat but there are mountainous areas in the south-west, along the Red Sea coast and in the south of the Sinai peninsula, rising in some places to peaks of over 6,000 ft. The highest mountain in Egypt is Mt Catherina (8,668 ft). Most of the land is desert but the Nile valley and delta are covered by silt 20–30 feet deep, and areas of desert are increasingly being reclaimed by irrigation and fertilization.

The Nile has a total length of 4,145 miles, of which 960 miles run through Egypt. Since the completion of the Aswan High Dam in 1971 (about a mile upstream from the smaller Aswan Dam, built around the turn of the century), there has been no flood downstream of the dam and the water level remains almost constant throughout the year. The area of fertile land, a 5–15 mile wide strip in the Nile valley and some 6,000 square miles of the Nile delta, has been increased by the opening of the Aswan Dam. This has allowed the reclamation of about 1,300,000 acres, and a further 700,000 acres have been converted from basin to perennial irrigation.

Westward from the Nile Valley stretches the Western desert, containing some depressions, whose springs irrigate small areas known as oases, of which the principal are Kharga, Dakhla, Farafra, Baharia and Siwa. In the Eastern Desert between the Nile and the mountains along the Red Sea coast, are plateaux of sandstones and limestones, dissected by wadis (dry water-courses), often of great length and depth, with some wild vegetation and occasional wells and springs.

POPULATION – The population (UN estimate 1991) is 54,688,000. There are three distinct elements in the population. The largest, or 'Egyptian' element, is a Hamito-Semite race, known in the rural districts as *Fellahin (fellâh*, ploughman or tiller of the soil). A second element is the *Bedouin*, or nomadic Arabs of the Western and Arabian deserts, of whom about one-seventh are real nomads, and the remainder semi-sedentary tent-dwellers on the outskirts of the cultivated end of the Nile Valley and the Fayüm. The third element is the *Nubian* of the Nile Valley between Aswân and Wadi-Halfa of mixed Arab and Negro blood. Over 90 per cent of the population are Muslims of the Sunni denomination, and most of the rest Coptic Christians.

CAPITAL – Cairo (population, estimated in 1986 at 14,000,000), stands on the east bank of the Nile, about 14 miles from the head of the delta. Its oldest part is the fortress of Babylon in old Cairo, with its Roman bastions and Coptic churches. The earliest Arab building is the Mosque of 'Amr, dating from AD 643, and the most conspicuous is the Citadel, built by Saladin towards the end of the 12th century and containing in its walls the Mosque of Mohamed Ali built in the 19th century.

Other cities and towns are: ΨAlexandria (estimated population in 1986 of 5,000,000), founded 332 BC by Alexander the Great, was for over 1,000 years the capital of Egypt and a centre of Hellenic culture which vied with Athens itself. Its great *pharos* (lighthouse), 480 feet high, with a lantern burning resinous wood, was one of the Seven Wonders of the World; Ismailia (400,000); ΨPort Said (285,000); Mansura (120,000); Asyût (300,000); Faiyûm (180,000); Tanta (150,000); Mahalla el Kubra (130,000); ΨSuez; ΨDamietta (100,000).

CURRENCY – Egyptian pound (£E) of 100 piastres and 1,000 millièmes.

FLAG – Horizontal bands of red, white and black, with an eagle in the centre of the white band.

NATIONAL DAY – 23 July (Anniversary of Revolution in 1952).

HISTORY

The unification of the kingdoms of Lower and Upper Egypt under the Pharaohs *c.*3100 BC marked the establishment of the Egyptian state, with Memphis as its capital. Egypt was ruled for nearly 2,800 years by a succession of Pharaonic dynasties (31 in all), which built the pyramids at Gizeh. The oldest of these is that of Zoser, built *c.*2700 BC, and the highest the Great Pyramid of Cheops, at 451 feet; nearby is the Sphinx, 189 feet long. A period of Hellenic rule began in 332 BC, after the conquest of Egypt by Alexander the Great, followed by a period of rule by Rome (30 BC to AD 324) and then by the Byzantine Empire. In AD 640 Egypt was subjugated by Arab Muslim invaders, becoming a province of the Eastern Caliphate. In 1517 the country was incorporated in the Ottoman Empire, under which it remained until early in the 19th century.

A British Protectorate over Egypt declared on 18 December 1914, lasted until 28 February 1922, when Sultan Ahmed Fuad was proclaimed King of Egypt. In July 1952, following a military coup d'état, King Farouk abdicated in favour of his infant son, who became King Ahmed Fuad II. In June 1953 however, Gen. Neguib's military council deposed the young King, and Egypt became a republic.

In 1956, as a result of Egypt's trade agreements with Communist countries, Britain and USA withdrew offers of financial aid and in retaliation President Nasser seized the assets of the Suez Canal Company. Egyptian occupation of the Canal Zone while repulsing an Israeli attack was used as a pretext for military action by Britain and France in support of their Suez Canal Company interests. A ceasefire and Anglo-French withdrawal were negotiated by the UN.

The Israeli invasion of 1956 overran the Sinai peninsula but six months later Israel withdrew and a UN peace-keeping force was established in the area. However, mounting tension culminated in a second invasion of Sinai (the Six Day War of June 1967) and occupation of the peninsula by Israel. Egypt's attempt to recapture the territory (the Yom Kippur War of October 1973) was unsuccessful but Sinai was returned to Egypt in April 1982, under the treaty of 1979 which resulted from the Camp David talks between President Sadat and the Israeli Prime Minister Menachem Begin and formally terminated a 31-year-old state of war between the two countries. President Mubarak came to power on 13 October 1981 after the assassination of President Sadat by Muslim fundamentalists.

Egypt benefited considerably, both economically and politically, from its participation in the Gulf War; it has now been fully rehabilitated in the Arab world and has had large amounts of its international debt written off.

Militant Muslim fundamentalists re-emerged in 1992, carrying out attacks on Coptic Christians, tourists and the security forces. Attacks have continued in 1993 and are concentrated in Upper Egypt and the Cairo area. The government has reacted vigorously with the arrest of 1,700 fundamentalists in December 1992 and raids in Aswan and Cairo in March 1993 which killed 40 fundamentalists. In April military courts began to convict and sentence extremists to death in a series of trials.

GOVERNMENT

The Constitution of 1971 provides for an executive President who appoints ministers to the government. The President determines policy which the Council of Ministers implements and ministers are responsible to him. The legislature consists of the People's Assembly (454 members, 444 of whom are elected, the remaining ten nominated by the President). The Shura Council, or Consultative Assembly (258 members) has an advisory role. Religious courts were abolished in 1956 and their functions transferred to the national court system.

The ruling National Democratic Party won general elections, boycotted by the major opposition parties, held in November and December 1990. President Mubarak was nominated by the legislature to run unopposed for a third six-year term in July 1993, and this will be put to a national referendum in late 1993.

HEAD OF STATE
President, Muhammad Hosni Mubarak, *elected* 13 October 1981, *re-elected* 1987.

COUNCIL OF MINISTERS *as at July 1993*
Prime Minister, Dr Atef Muhammad Naguib Sidqi.
Presidential Assistant, Muhammad Abdul Halim Abu Ghazala.
Defence and Military Production, Gen. Hussein Tantawy.
Deputy PM and Minister of Planning and International Co-operation, Dr Kamal Ahmed al-Ganzuri.
Deputy PM and Minister of Agriculture and Land Reclamation, Dr Yussif Amin Wali.
Foreign Affairs, Amre Moussa.
Economy and Foreign Trade, Dr Yussri Ali Mustafa.
Finance, Dr Muhammad Ahmed el-Razzaz.
Interior, Maj.-Gen. Hassan al-Alfi.
Oil and Mineral Wealth, Dr Hamdy El Bambi.
Tourism and Civil Aviation, Fouad Abdul Latif Sultan.
Justice, Farouq Saif al-Nasr.
Culture, Farouq Hosni.
Industry, Muhammad Mahmoud Abdul Wahhab.
Parliamentary and Shura Council Affairs, Dr Ahmed Salama.
Supply and Internal Trade, Dr Mohammed Galaleddin Abdul-Dahab.
Public Works and Water Resources, 'Issam Abdul Hamid Radi.
Manpower and Vocational Training, Assem Abdul Haq.
Education, Dr Hussein Kamal Baha El-Din.
Transport, Communications and Marine Transport, Suliman Metwalli Suliman.
Scientific Research, Dr Adel Abul-Hamid 'Ezz.
Health, Dr Mohammed Ragheb Dawidar.
Information, Muhammad Safwat al-Sharif.
Cabinet Affairs and Administrative Development, Dr 'Atif Mohammad 'Ebeid.
Religious Affairs (Waqfs), Dr Muhammad Ali Mahgoub.
Social Affairs and Social Insurance, Dr Amal Abdul Rahim Osman.
Electricity and Energy, Mohammad Mahir Osman Abaza.

Housing, New Communities and Public Utilities, Hasaballah Mohammad al-Kafrawi.
Local Government, Dr Mahmmoud Sherif.
Ministers of State, Gamal al-Sayyid Ibrahim *(Military Production)*; Dr Mouris Makramallah *(International Co-operation).*

EMBASSY OF THE ARAB REPUBLIC OF EGYPT
26 South Street, London WIY 8EL
Tel 071–499 2401
Ambassador Extraordinary and Plenipotentiary, His Excellency Mohamed I. Shaker (1988).
Minister Plenipotentiary, Deputy Chief of Mission, S. Mohammed Shaaban.
Minister Plenipotentiary and Consul-General, Aly Mohamed Fahmy El-Karaksy.
Ministers Plenipotentiary, Mamdouh Shawky Moustafa; Ahmed Abdel Hameed Nafeh.
Defence Attaché, Brig.-Gen. Mohammed Kobeicy.
Minister Plenipotentiary (Commercial), Amr Osman El Menshawi.
Cultural Attaché, Dr Omar B. Salman.

BRITISH EMBASSY
Ahmed Ragheb Street, Garden City, Cairo
Tel: Cairo 354–0850
Ambassador Extraordinary and Plenipotentiary, His Excellency Christopher Long, CMG (1992).
Counsellor and Deputy Head of Mission, A. F. Goulty.
Counsellor, D. T. Handley.
Defence and Military Attaché, Col. G. N. R. Sayle, OBE.
First Secretary and Consul, A. M. M. Sheldon.
First Secretary (Commercial), I. S. Lockhart, MBE.

There are British consular offices at *Luxor, Suez* and *Port Said,* and a Consulate-General at *Alexandria.*

BRITISH COUNCIL REPRESENTATIVE, Howard Thompson, OBE, 192 Sharia el Nil, Agouza, Cairo. There is also a library in *Alexandria.*

DEFENCE

The armed forces number some 410,000 active personnel (252,000 conscripts). Selective conscription for three-year terms operate. Equipment is from a wide range of Soviet, US, French and UK manufacture.

The Army numbers 290,000 (180,000 conscripts) with 3,100 main battle tanks, 3,600 armoured infantry fighting vehicles and armoured personnel carriers, and 1,300 artillery pieces. It is organized into four armoured and eight mechanized divisions, together with a further 30 independent brigades.

The Navy has 20,000 personnel (12,000 conscripts) with one destroyer, four frigates and four submarines together with 17 armed helicopters. The Air Force, including the Air Defence Command, has 100,000 personnel (60,000 conscripts) with 492 combat aircraft and 74 armed helicopters. These are organized into eight ground attack, 16 air defence and three transport squadrons.

There are also 370,000 paramilitary Security Forces and National Guard personnel.

ECONOMY

Despite increasing industrialization, agriculture remains the most important economic activity, employing over 45 per cent of the labour force and contributing to 17 per cent of the country's exports. Agricultural output has been increased as a result of land reclamation programmes and the introduction of more efficient methods, e.g. the change from basin to

perennial irrigation which yields two to three crops a year instead of one, the pivotal sprinkling irrigation system which uses water more efficiently, and the increasing mechanization and use of fertilizers. Egypt is still a net importer of foodstuffs, especially grain, and a food security programme has been set up with the aim of achieving self-sufficiency through the use of more advanced technology. Estimates suggest that an additional three million acres of land could be reclaimed by the end of the century.

The main cash crop is cotton, of which Egypt is one of the world's main producers. Other important summer crops are maize, rice and sugar cane. Important winter crops are wheat and beans. Citrus fruit and other fruits and vegetables are also grown.

With its considerable reserves of petroleum and natural gas in Sinai, the Nile delta and the Western Desert, and the hydro-electric power produced by the Aswan and High Dams, Egypt is self-sufficient in energy. Electricity has been provided to almost all of the country and there are plans to extend the natural gas network to all major cities.

The production of petroleum provides Egypt with its major export (60–65 per cent of total exports), and supports a growing refining industry. Steel production is another important heavy industry. The major manufacturing industries are in food processing, motor cars and electrical goods, chemical products and yarns and textiles.

FINANCE	1986–7	1987–8
Estimated revenue	£E12.4m	£E14.2m
Total expenditure	19.9m	21.7m

TRADE

The main imports are wheat and flour, wood and trucks. The main exports are crude petroleum, cotton, cotton yarn, oranges, rice and cotton textiles.

	1986–7
Imports	£E7.8m
Exports	2.6m

Trade with UK	1991	1992
Imports from UK	£282,928,000	£252,271,000
Exports to UK	136,406,000	137,008,000

COMMUNICATIONS

The road and rail networks link the Nile valley and delta with the main development areas to east and west of the river.

The Suez Canal was re-opened in 1975 and a two-stage development project begun to widen and deepen the canal to allow the passage of larger shipping and to permit two-way traffic. Port Said and Suez have been reconstructed and the port of Alexandria is being improved.

EQUATORIAL GUINEA
República de Guinea Ecuatorial

Equatorial Guinea (formerly Spanish Guinea) consists of the island of Biogo (formerly Macias Nguema), in the Bight of Biafra about 20 miles from the west coast of Africa, Pagalu Island (formerly Annobon) in the Gulf of Guinea, the Corisco Islands (Corisco, Elobey Grande and Elobey Chico) and Rio Muni, a mainland area between Cameroon and Gabon. It has a total area of 10,830 sq. miles (28,051 sq. km), and a population (UN estimate 1991) of 356,000.

CAPITAL – ΨMalabo on the island of Bioco, population (1983 estimate) 30,418. ΨBata is the principal town and port of Rio Muni.

CURRENCY – Franc CFA of 100 centimes.
FLAG – Three horizontal bands, green over white over red; blue triangle next staff; coat of arms in centre of white band.
NATIONAL DAY – 12 October.

GOVERNMENT

Formerly colonies of Spain, the territories now forming the Republic of Equatorial Guinea were constituted as two provinces of Metropolitan Spain in 1959, became autonomous in 1963 and fully independent in 1968. Serious disorders in Rio Muni early in 1969 caused many of the Spanish community to leave.

In August 1979, President Macias was deposed by a revolutionary military council headed by his nephew, Col. Obiang Nguema. The first parliamentary elections since 1968 were held in August 1983, under a new constitution approved by a referendum in August 1982. The most recent elections to the 41-member National Assembly took place in July 1988. All candidates were nominated by the President and elected unopposed for a five-year term.

The introduction of a multi-party political system was approved by a referendum in November 1991, and since then ten opposition parties have been legalized to operate alongside the ruling Equatorial Guinea Democratic Party (PDGE). A National Pact was agreed and signed in March 1993 but progress towards elections remains slow. The President has appointed a transitional government to rule until multi-party elections are held.

HEAD OF STATE
President of the Supreme Military Council and Minister of Defence, Brig.-Gen. Teodoro Obiang Nguema Mbasogo, *took office*, August 1979, *re-elected* June 1989.

MINISTERS *as at August 1993*
Prime Minister, Silvestre Siale Bileka.
Deputy Prime Minister, Education, Youth and Sport, Isidoro Eyi Monsuy Andeme.
Minister of State, Minister Secretary-General to the Presidency, Casto Nvono Akele.
Ministers of State at the Presidency, Eloy Elo Nve Mbengono; Alejandro Evuna Asangono.
Minister Deputy Secretary-General to the Presidency, Martin Nka Esono Nsing.
Minister of State, Economy, Trade and Planning, Marcelino Nguemo Ongueme.
Justice and Religion, Mariano Nsue Nguema.
Public Works, Urban Development and Transport, Alejandro Envoro Ovono.
Agriculture, Fishing and Forestry, Angel Alogo Nchama.
Industry and Energy, Severino Obiang Bengono.
Labour and Social Development, Juan Balboa Boneke.
Ministers Delegate:
Economic and Financial Affairs, vacant.
Mines and Hydrocarbons, Juan Olo Mba Nseng.
Culture, Tourism and Handicrafts, Leandro Mbomio Nsue.
Foreign Affairs and Francophone Affairs, Benjamin Mba Ekua Miko.
National Defence, Maj. Melanio Ebendeng Nsomo.
Territorial Administration and Communications, Segundo Munoz Italo.
Health, Alejandro Masoko Bengono.
Women's Development, Purificaçion Angue Ondo.

EMBASSY OF THE REPUBLIC OF EQUATORIAL GUINEA
6 Rue Alfred de Vigny, 75008, Paris
Tel: Paris 47664433

Ambassador Extraordinary and Plenipotentiary, new appointment awaited.

BRITISH AMBASSADOR (resident in Yaoundé, Cameroon).

BRITISH CONSULATE
World Bank Compound, Apartado 801, Malabo
Tel: Malabo 2400
Honorary Consul, vacant.

ECONOMY

The chief products are cocoa, coffee and wood (which is exported almost entirely from Rio Muni). Production has declined and except for cocoa there is little commercial agriculture and the economy is now heavily dependent on outside aid, principally from Spain. Oil and gas deposits exist but remain largely unexploited. Equatorial Guinea entered the 'Franc zone' in 1985.

TRADE WITH UK	1991	1992
Imports from UK	£1,967,000	£1,357,000
Exports to UK	33,000	40,000

ERITREA

Eritrea is bordered to the north and north-west by Sudan, to the south and south-west by Ethiopia, to the south-east by Djibouti and in the north-east and east borders on the Red Sea. Included in its territory are the Dahlak Islands group in the Red Sea. It has an area of 36,170 sq. miles (93,679 sq. km). Topographically, the long, narrow, low-lying coastal strip rises steeply to the highlands in central-northern Eritrea which are some 2,000–3,000 m high (6,500–9,800 ft) and are an extension of the Ethiopian highlands.
POPULATION – 3,500,000 (1991 official estimate).
RELIGION – 50 per cent Coptic Christian and 50 per cent Muslim. The majority of highlanders are Christian and the majority of lowlanders are Muslim.
LANGUAGES – The two main languages in use for business and taught in schools are English and Arabic. There are also nine indigenous language groups: Afar; Bilen; Hadareb; Kunama; Nara; Rashida; Saho; Tigre; Tigrinya.
CAPITAL – Asmara (275,000) in the central highlands. ΨMassawa and ΨAssab are the two main ports and major towns in the country.
CURRENCY – The Ethiopian birr of 100 cents remains in use at present.
FLAG – Divided into three triangles; the one based on the hoist is red and bears a gold olive wreath; the upper triangle is green and the lower one light blue.
NATIONAL DAY – 24 May (Independence Day).

GOVERNMENT

Eritrea was colonized by Italy in the late 19th century and it was from the Italian colony of Eritrea that Italian forces launched their invasion of Abyssinia (Ethiopia) in 1936. After the Italian defeat in East Africa in 1941 by British and Commonwealth forces, Eritrea became a British protectorate. This lasted until 15 September 1952 when, according to the wishes of the UN, Eritrea was federated with Ethiopia but retained a high degree of political autonomy. The Ethiopian Emperor Haile Selassie eroded Eritrea's autonomy and in 1962 incorporated it as a province of Ethiopia. The incorporation was resisted by all sections of the Eritrean population. An armed campaign for independence began which gathered momentum in the 1970s and 1980s, first against Emperor Haile Selassie's forces and from 1974 against the Soviet and Cuban-supported regime of Mengistu.

In May 1991 the Mengistu government was brought down by the defeat of its armed forces by the Eritrean People's Liberation Front (EPLF) and its allies the Eritrean People's Revolutionary Democratic Front (EPRDF). In July 1991 the new EPRDF-led government in Ethiopia agreed to an Eritrean referendum on independence which was held on 23–25 April 1993. Until the referendum Eritrea functioned as a totally autonomous region with an EPLF provisional government. In the referendum, over 99 per cent of the electorate voted for independence. Independence was declared on 24 May 1993 and Eritrea was admitted to UN membership on 28 May 1993.

At independence the provisional government became the transitonal government of Eritrea and is to govern the country for a transition period of a maximum of four years while a new constitution is drafted. At the end of the transition period multi-party elections are to be held. During the transition period legislative power is vested in the National Assembly and executive power in the State Council appointed and chaired by the President. The government is committed to repatriating the remaining 500,000 of the 700,000 refugees who fled to Sudan during the war.

HEAD OF STATE
President, Chairman of the National Assembly, Issaias Afewerki, *elected by National Assembly* 22 May 1993.

STATE COUNCIL *as at August 1993*

Chairman, The President.
Regional Administration, Ramadan Mohammed Nar.
Internal Affairs, Ali Said Abdella.
Defence, Petros Solomon.
Justice, Fozia Hashim.
Foreign Affairs, Mohamed Ahmed Sherifo.
Culture and Information, Alamin Mohammed Said.
Finance and Development, Haile Weldeteasae.
Trade, Industry and Tourism, Ogbe Abraha.
Agriculture, Tesfai Ghermazien.
Marine Resources, Saleh Meky.
Construction, Abraha Asfaha.
Energy, Mining and Water Resources, Testay Gebereselassie.
Education, Osman Saleh.
Health, Haile Mihtsan.
Governor of Senhit, Hamed Himed.
Governor of Sahel, Mohammed Said Nawd.
Governor of Barka, Abdella Jaber.
Governor of Hamasien, Berhane Gebregzabiher.
Governor of Seraye, Adharom Gebremarian.
Governor of Semhar, Ibrahim Idris Totil.
Governor of Akele Guzai, Saleh Ahmed Eyay.
Governor of Asmara, Sebhat Ephraim.
Governor of Denkel, Mohammed Said Bareh.

BRITISH COUNCIL REPRESENTATIVE – Simon Bush, PO Box 997, Asmara.

ECONOMY

The Eritrean economy was devastated by the war of independence and the scorched earth policy of the retreating Ethiopian forces. Since 1991 the government has directed all its efforts into rebuilding the country's industry, agriculture and infrastructure. As the trditional agricultural and industrial sectors producing sorghum, livestock, salt, cement, fish, hides and potash are rebuilt, the government has directed large parts of the population into infrastructure rebuilding schemes in return for direct daily food aid. The focus of the rebuilding programme are the ports of Massawa and Assab,

the roads from the ports to Ethiopia, and the railway from Massawa to Sudan via Asmara. Before 1962 Eritrea was one of the most industrialized areas of Africa and some industry remains, producing textiles and footwear. The government hopes to base the rebuilding of the economy on the return of well-educated exiles and international aid and investment.

ESTONIA
The Republic of Estonia

The Republic of Estonia is situated in northern Europe on the eastern coast of the Baltic Sea. To the north, across the Gulf of Finland, lies Finland, to the east the Russian Federation, and to the south Latvia. Estonia lies between 57°30′ and 59°49′N., and between 21°46′ and 28°13′E.
AREA – 17,458 sq. miles (45,125 sq. km). The country is relatively flat. It includes 1,500 islands in the Baltic Sea and the Gulf of Riga. Forests cover roughly 20 per cent of the country, which also has many lakes.
CLIMATE – Mild and maritime.
POPULATION – The total population of Estonia is 1,574,955 (1990 census), of which 61.2 per cent are Estonian, 30.1 per cent Russian, 3.1 per cent Ukrainian, 1.8 per cent Belarussian.
LANGUAGES – 61.2 per cent have Estonian as their first language, and 30.1 per cent Russian. Estonian belongs to the Finno-Ugri language group and is related to Finnish and Hungarian.
RELIGIONS – Lutheran (majority), Russian Orthodox, Baptist.
CAPITAL – Tallinn (population 484,400). Other cities are Tartu (115,400); Narva (82,300); Kohtla-Järve (76,800); Pärnu (54,200).
CURRENCY – Kroon (Crown) of 100 sent.
FLAG – Three horizontal stripes of blue, black, white.
NATIONAL ANTHEM – Pacius (My Fatherland).
NATIONAL DAY – 24 February (Independence Day).

HISTORY

Estonia, a former province of the Russian Empire, declared its independence from Russia on 24 February 1918. A war of independence was fought against the German army until the end of the First World War in November 1918, and then against Soviet forces until the peace treaty of Tartu was signed on 2 February 1920. By this treaty the Soviet Union recognized Estonia's independence.

The Soviet Union annexed Estonia in 1940 under the terms of the Molotov-Ribbentrop pact with Germany. Estonia was invaded and occupied when Germany invaded the Soviet Union during the Second World War. In 1944 the Soviet Union recaptured the country from Germany and confirmed its annexation, though this was never accepted as legal by most states.

Due to mounting public pressure, the Estonian Supreme Soviet in November 1989 declared the republic to be sovereign and its 1940 annexation by the Soviet Union to be illegal. In February 1990 the leading role of the Communist Party was abolished, and following multi-party elections in March 1990 the Supreme Soviet inaugurated a period of transition to independence. Full independence was supported by an overwhelming majority in a referendum held in March 1991 and was declared on 20 August 1991. The State Council of the Soviet Union recognized the independence of Estonia on 10 September 1991. Estonia gained UN membership on 17 September 1991.

GOVERNMENT

Estonians voted in a referendum in June 1992 to adopt a new constitution under which Estonia is a parliamentary democracy. Elections to the legislature, the *Riigikogu*, are held every four years. The President is elected for a five-year term by the Riigikogu by a two-thirds majority or, if no candidate receives this majority after three rounds of voting, the President is elected by an electoral body composed of Riigikogu members and local government officials. Executive authority is vested in a Prime Minister and government formed from a governing majority within the parliament. Legislative power is exercised by the unicameral Riigikogu of 101 members elected by proportional representation.

Presidential and legislative elections were held on 20 September 1992. These elections, the first constitutional elections since before the Soviet invasion in 1940, were held on the basis of special provisions different from the 1992 constitution. The President was directly elected in the first instance and only then elected by the Riigikogu when no candidate secured over 50 per cent of the vote. The President was elected for a four-year term and the Riigikogu for a three-year one. This was to enable newly-naturalized citizens to be able to vote for representatives in national elections in a shorter period of time. A conservative governing coalition was formed in the Riigikogu from the Fatherland group, the Moderate group and the Estonia National Independence Party after the legislative election. On 5 October this coalition elected Lennart Meri as President.

The vast majority of the ethnic Russian population was unable to vote in either election as the government had degreed that only citizens of pre-1940 Estonia and their descendants were eligible to vote. Tensions with the ethnic Russian population and Russia remain high, with the government in June 1993 introducing a citizenship law under which ethnic Russians must become Estonian or Russian citizens or leave Estonia within two years. To gain Estonian citizenship, they must pass language qualification tests in the Estonian language and loyalty tests. The citizenship law was amended slightly when Russia and the CSCE stated it was too discriminatory. The Estonian government declared illegal a referendum in July in the two mainly ethnic Russian cities of Narva and Sillamäe in which the populations voted for autonomy.

HEAD OF STATE
President, Lennart Meri, *elected* 5 October 1992.

GOVERNMENT *as at August 1993*
Prime Minister, Mart Laar.
Justice, Kaido Kama.
Defence, Hain Rebas.
Finance, Madis Uurike.
Economy, Toomas Sildmae.
Interior, Lagle Parek.
Foreign Affairs, Trivimi Velliste.
Social Affairs, Marju Lauristin.
Relations with Russia, Juri Luik.

LOCAL GOVERNMENT – Estonia is divided into six towns and 15 districts for administration purposes.

EMBASSY OF THE REPUBLIC OF ESTONIA
16 Hyde Park Gate, London SW7 5DG
Tel 071-589 3428
Ambassador Extraordinary and Plenipotentiary, His Excellency Riivo Sinijarv (1993).

BRITISH EMBASSY
Kentmanni 20, Tallinn 200001
Tel: Tallinn 455328
Ambassador Extraordinary and Plenipotentiary, His Excellency Brian Low, *apptd* 1991.

DEFENCE

Since its independence from the Soviet Union, Estonia has formed a small army of three infantry divisions and support units, together with a national guard, border guard units and a volunteer reserve defence league of 6,500 personnel. A term of conscription of 12 months is in operation. Total active armed forces number some 2,000 pesonnel. Russia still maintains 23,000 army and air force personnel in Estonia, although these are being gradually withdrawn. On various occasions in 1992 and 1993 President Yeltsin has threatened to suspend the withdrawal because of the alleged discrimination against ethnic Russians.

ECONOMY

Estonia's economy was thrown into turmoil by the collapse of the centralized Soviet economic system. Over the past two years the government has introduced reforms to transform the economy into one based on market economic principles with privatization and restructuring. To this end, and to support a strong and fully convertible currency, the IMF provided support through credits worth US$40m in August 1992. Having in 1993 established a stable currency linked to the Deutsche Mark, the economy has stabilized and output is recovering from the large fall experienced in 1990–2. However, Estonia is still quite dependent on Russian fuel supplies, mainly natural gas, and this was used as a weapon by President Yeltsin in June 1993 when he suspended gas supplies to Estonia for four days until the discriminatory citizenship law was amended.

Agriculture and dairy-farming are a major sector of the Estonian economy, the main products being rye, oats, barley, flax, potatoes, meat, milk, butter and eggs.

Light industry is the other major area of the economy, concentrating on textiles, clothing and footwear, forestry, wood and paper products, and food and fish processing. Some heavy industry exists, concentrated in chemicals and the manufacture of power equipment.

TRADE

Although Estonia signed a free trade deal with Russia in September 1992, it has greatly reduced its trade with the former Soviet states. In 1992 only 34.7 per cent of Estonian exports went to CIS states while 60.2 went to the rest of Europe; 21.1 per cent to Finland, 20.8 per cent to Russia, 10.6 per cent to Latvia and 7.7 per cent to Sweden. Imports came from Finland (26 per cent), CIS (22 per cent), Sweden (7 per cent), Germany (6 per cent).

Trade with UK	1992
Imports from UK	£5,593,000
Exports to UK	10,418,000

COMMUNICATIONS

Freedom of the press is guaranteed in the 1992 Estonian Constitution, and the state monopoly on television and radio ended soon after independence. The remaining state-owned newspapers and broadcasting channels are editorially independent and in the process of being privatized. As at 6 January 1993 the government had granted 15 radio and nine television broadcasting licences. Russian-language news and programmes are provided on Estonian Television. There are five Estonian and three Russian-language daily newspapers with a total circulation of 263,200.

EDUCATION

Estonia has a three-tier education system, consisting of primary level (nine years), secondary level (four years) and university level (four to six years).

ETHIOPIA
Ityopia

Ethiopia is in north-eastern Africa, bounded on the north-west by the Sudan, on the south by Kenya, on the east by Djibouti and Somalia, and on the north-east by Eritrea. The area is 435,608 sq. miles (1,128,221 sq. km), with a population (UN estimate 1991) of 49,883,000. About one-third are of Semitic origin (Amharas and Tigrayans) and the remainder mainly Oromos (about 40 per cent of the population), Somalis and Afar.

Ethiopia has a large central plateau (average height, 6,000–7,000 ft) which rises to nearly 15,000 ft at Ras Dashan in the north. The plateau drops to the Nile basin in the west, to the Ogaden desert in the east and Eritrea and the Red Sea in the north. In the east (Ogaden) the land is mostly desert. The chief river is the Blue Nile, issuing from Lake Tana; the Atbara and many other tributaries of the Nile also rise in the Ethiopian highlands.

RELIGION – Those of Semitic origin (Amharas and Tigrayans), and many of the Oromos, are Christians of the Ethiopian Orthodox Church, which was formerly led by the head of the Coptic Church, the Patriarch at Alexandria. Since 1959, however, the Ethiopian Church has been autocephalous; the current Patriarch is Abuna Paulos Gebre-Yohamis, who was consecrated in July 1992. The Afar people, who inhabit lowland Wollo, Hararghe and Bale provinces, and the Somalis, in the south-east, as well as some Oromos are Muslim. The Falashas, adherents of Judaism, formerly found principally in Gonder and Tigray provinces, were airlifted to Israel in 1984–5 and 1991.

CAPITAL – Addis Ababa (population, 1989 estimate, 1,739,130), also capital of the province of Shoa; Dire Dawa is the most important commercial centre after Addis Ababa. There are ancient architectural remains at Aksum, Gondar, Lalibela and elsewhere.
CURRENCY – Ethiopian birr (EB) of 100 cents.
FLAG – Three horizontal bands: green, yellow, red.
NATIONAL ANTHEM – Ityopya, Ityopya Kidemi.
NATIONAL DAY – 28 May.

GOVERNMENT

The basic Hamitic culture was heavily influenced by Semitic immigration from Arabia in the centuries about the time of Christ. Christianity was introduced in the fourth century. The empire expanded sporadically, attaining a zenith in the sixth century under the Axum rulers, but subsequently was checked by Islamic expansion from the east. Modern Ethiopia dates from 1855 when Theodore succeeded in establishing supremacy over the various tribes. The last Emperor was Haile Selassie who reigned from 1930, though in exile from 1936–41 during the Italian occupation. After considerable military and civil unrest the armed forces assumed power in September 1974 and deposed the Emperor. After ten years of military rule, a Workers' Party on the Soviet model was formed in September 1984, with Mengistu Haile Mariam as General Secretary.

The civilian government of the People's Democratic Republic of Ethiopia was established under a new constitution in 1987 with Lt.-Col. Mengistu being elected the first President. Armed insurgencies by the Eritrean People's Liberation Front (EPLF) and the Ethiopian People's Revolutionary Democratic Front (EPRDF), originating in Tigray, brought down Mengistu's government in May 1991. At a national conference held in July 1991, an 87-member Council of Representatives was formed, comprising the EPRDF and a number of other opposition groups. The transitional government, headed by Meles Zenawi, drew up plans dividing Ethiopia into 14 regions based as closely as possible on the different ethnic groups that were recognized. Elections to the regional councils were held on 21 June 1992, with these councils having a great amount of power devolved to them.

Many political parties claimed that the elections were unfair, and international observers where unable to agree on a report declaring if the elections were fair. This led the Oromo Liberation Front (OLF) to withdraw its 12 members from the Council of Representatives and there were clashes between government and OLF forces in eastern Ethiopia in July 1992. Resentment at the end of the traditional Amharic political dominance caused by the Tigrayan-led EPRDF has also caused social unrest. The central government in Addis Ababa remains in control of foreign affairs, defence and economic policy. Meanwhile, a constitutional commission is drafting a new constitution and elections to a constituent assembly to agree on a new constitution are scheduled for early 1994. Eritrea officially became independent of Ethiopia on 24 May 1993.

HEAD OF STATE
President, Meles Zenawi.

CABINET *as at June 1993*
Prime Minister, Tamirat Layne.
Justice, Mehitema Solomon.
Information, Dima Nego.
Foreign Affairs, Seyoum Mesfin.
Health, Dr Adanech Kidane Mariam.
Education, Ibsa Gutema.
Industry, Bekele Tadessa.
Interior, Kuma Demeksa.
Mines and Energy, Isedin Ali.
Commerce, Yosef Kamalo.
State Farms, Hassan Abdella.
Defence, Seye Abraha.
Agriculture and Environmental Protection, Zegeye Asfaw.
Housing and Construction, Aragaw Tiruneh.
Culture and Sports, Lieule Selassie Timamo.
Labour and Social Affairs, Dr Legaso Gidada.
Transport, Belachaw Mekbib.
Finance, Alemayehu Dhaba.

EMBASSY OF ETHIOPIA
17 Prince's Gate, London SW7 1PZ
Tel 071-589 7212/3/4/5
Ambassador Extraordinary and Plenipotentiary, His Excellency Dr Solomon Gidada (1992).
Counsellor, Atu Getahun Leta Toera (*Commercial*).

BRITISH EMBASSY
Fikre Mariam Abatechan Street (PO Box 858), Addis Ababa
Tel: Addis Ababa 1612354
Ambassador Extraordinary and Plenipotentiary, His Excellency Michael John Carlisle Glaze, CMG (1990).
Deputy Ambassador and First Secretary, C. O. Pigott.
First Secretary, A. J. Barber.

BRITISH COUNCIL REPRESENTATIVE, Michael Sargent, Artistic Building, Adwa Avenue (PO Box 1043), Addis Ababa.

ECONOMY

The post-Mengistu government has engaged in a programme of market economic reform. Government spending has been brought under control and inflation was reduced to 12.9 per cent in 1992. The currency has been devalued, the civil service drastically reduced and the army halved in size. Most importantly land has been de-nationalized, farm prices have been freed and communal land given to peasant small farmers. Western states have responded with debt relief and loans and the IMF approved a three-year loan of US$70m in October 1992 to support economic reform.

The principal sector is agriculture, which accounts for approximately 40 per cent of GDP, 85 per cent of exports and 80 per cent of total employment. The major food crops are teff, maize, barley, sorghum, wheat, pulses and oil seeds. Coffee, the principal export crop, generates over 50 per cent of the country's export earnings. Famine conditions, which attracted world attention in 1984-5, recurred for a short period and to a lesser extent in 1992. However, agriculture liberalization has enabled dramatic progress in food production to take place and produced a record harvest of 7.7 million tonnes of grain and pulses in 1993.

Manufacturing industry accounts for less than 9 per cent of GDP and is heavily dependent on agriculture. Ethiopia's known, but as yet largely unexploited, natural resources include gold, platinum, copper and potash. Traces of oil and natural gas have been found.

FINANCE	1987-8
Revenue	US$1,709.5m
Expenditure	2,226.4m

TRADE

The chief imports by value are machinery and transport equipment, manufactured goods and chemicals (from UK); the principal exports by value being coffee, oil seeds, hides and skins, and pulses.

	1987-8
Total Imports	US$1,083.6m
Total Exports	393.7m

Trade with UK	1991	1992
Imports from UK	£29,773,000	£53,312,000
Exports to UK	14,660,000	13,216,000

COMMUNICATIONS

A network of roads has been built in rural areas and links the major cities with each other, and with the Sudanese and Kenyan borders and the Red Sea coast. Transport links suffered during the secessionist wars and under the heavy burden of famine relief traffic.

There is a railway link from Addis Ababa to Djibouti although this has been vulnerable to guerrilla activity. The Ethiopian and Eritrean governments negotiated an agreement in 1992 which guarantees Ethiopia access to the Red Sea via the ports of Assab and Massawa. Ethiopian Airlines maintains regular services from Addis Ababa to many provincial towns. External services are operated throughout Africa and to Europe.

DEFENCE

Ethiopia's considerable military forces (over 300,000 men) failed to contain the rebel forces and were disbanded by the post-Mengistu government. The EPRDF forces, numbering some 100,000 became the national army.

EDUCATION

Elementary education is provided without religious discrimination by government schools in the main centres of population; there are also mission schools. Government secondary schools are found mainly in Addis Ababa, but also in most of the provincial capitals. The National University (founded 1961) co-ordinates the institutions of higher education (University College, Engineering, Building and Theological Colleges in Addis Ababa, and Public Health Centre in Gondar, etc.). There is a separate university at Alemaya (agricultural).

Amharic was the official language of instruction, with English as the first foreign language and main language of instruction from secondary level upwards. Arabic is taught in Koran schools; and Ge'ez (the ancient Ethiopic) in Christian church schools, which abound. Language policy is now under review by the post-Mengistu government.

FIJI
Matanitu Ko Viti - Republic of Fiji

Fiji is made up of about 332 islands and over 500 islets (including numerous atolls and reefs) in the South Pacific Ocean, about 1,100 miles north of New Zealand. About 100 islands are permanently inhabited. The gross area of the group, which extends 300 miles from east to west, and 300 north to south, between 15° 45' and 21° 10' S. latitude, and 176° E. and 178° W. longitude, is 7,055 sq. miles (18,274 sq. km). The International Date Line has been diverted to the east of the island group. The largest islands are Viti Levu and Vanua Levu. The main groups of islands are Lomaiviti, Lau and Yasawas. Most of the larger islands are mountainous with sharp peaks and crags, but also have conspicuous areas of flat land and many of the rivers have built extensive deltas. The climate is tropical, without extremes of heat, and temperatures rarely exceed 32°C and seldom fall below 15°C.

POPULATION – The population (Census 1986) was 715,373, comprising 48.6 per cent Indians, 46.2 per cent Fijians, and 5.2 per cent other races. A UN estimate (1991) gives a total figure of 776,000.

CAPITAL – ΨSuva, on the island of Viti Levu. Population (1986) 69,665.

CURRENCY – Fiji dollar (F$) of 100 cents.

FLAG – Light blue ground with Union flag in top left quarter and the shield of Fiji in the fly.

NATIONAL ANTHEM – God Bless Fiji.

NATIONAL DAY – 12 October (Fiji Day).

GOVERNMENT

Fiji was a British colony from 1874 until 10 October 1970 when it became an independent state and a member of the Commonwealth.

A coalition of the left under Dr Timoci Bavadra defeated the Alliance Party of Ratu Sir Kamisese Mara in a General Election on 12 April 1987. The new government, drawing its support mainly from the Indian population, was overthrown in a military coup on 14 May by Lt.-Col. Sitiveni Rabuka. In the wake of the constitutional crisis an Advisory Council of 19 members was set up by the Governor-General as an interim government to consider constitutional reform.

A second coup occurred on 25 September 1987. On 7 October Rabuka declared Fiji to be a republic; the Governor-General resigned on 15 October and Fiji's Commonwealth membership lapsed. An Executive Council of Ministers, with Rabuka at its head, assumed control until 5 December when Ratu Sir Penani Ganilau was appointed President. The President called upon Ratu Sir Kamisese Mara to form another interim administration to work for a resolution to the political crisis.

A new constitution, promulgated on 25 July 1990, established the political dominance of the minority Melanesian community within the judiciary and a bicameral parliament; an amnesty was granted to participants in the 1987 coups. Elections due to be held in 1991 were postponed until boundary changes were completed in 1992. The elections were held during the last week of May 1992, with 37 seats reserved for the Melanesian population, 27 for the Indians and six for other groups (Europeans and Chinese). The Fijian Political Party led by Rabuka formed a coalition government with the General Voters Party.

HEAD OF STATE
President, Ratu Sir Penaia Ganilau, GCMG, KCVO, KBE, DSO, *appointed* 5 December 1987.

CABINET *as at June 1993*
Prime Minister, Minister for Home Affairs and Immigration, Maj.-Gen. Sitiveni Rabuka, OBE
Deputy Prime Minister and Minister for Foreign Affairs and Regional Trade, Filipe Bole, CBE
Deputy Prime Minister and Minister for Fijian Affairs and Regional Development, Ratu Timoci Vesikula
Attorney-General and Minister for Justice, Kelemedi Bulewa
Education, Science and Technology, Miss Taufa Vakatale
Finance and Economic Planning, Paul Manueli, OBE
Health, Solomoni Naivalu
Housing and Urban Development, Militoni Leweniqila
Agriculture, Fisheris and Forests, Ratu Viliame Dreunimisimisi
Infrastructure and Public Works, Leo Smith
Labour, Industrial Relations and Information, Koresi Matatolu
Lands, Mineral Resources and Energy, Ratu Ovini Bokini
Transport and Civil Aviation, Lt.-Col. Jonetani Kaukimoce
Commerce, Industry and Tourism, Harold Powell
Women, Culture, Social Welfare and Multi-ethnic Affairs, Ratu Jo Nacola
Youth, Employment and Sports, Ratu Inoke Kubuabola

EMBASSY OF THE REPUBLIC OF FIJI
34 Hyde Park Gate, London SW7 5BN
Tel 071-584 3661

Ambassador Extraordinary and Plenipotentiary, His Excellency Brig.-Gen. Ratu Epeli Nailatikau, LVO, OBE (1988).

BRITISH EMBASSY
Victoria House, 47 Gladstone Road, PO Box 1355, Suva
Tel: Suva 311033

Ambassador Extraordinary and Plenipotentiary, His Excellency Timothy David (1992).
Deputy Ambassador, Consul and First Secretary, D. J. Noble.

FINANCE	1990	1991
Public Income	F$538m	F$564m
Public Expenditure	501m	551m

ECONOMY

The economy is primarily agrarian, with about 600,000 acres under cultivation. The principal cash crop is sugar cane, which is the main export, followed by coconuts, ginger and copra. A variety of other fruit, vegetables and root crops are also grown, and self-sufficiency in rice is a major aim. Forestry, fishing and beef production are being encouraged in order to diversify the economy. The processing of agricultural, marine and timber products are the main industries, along with gold mining. A policy of tax concessions for export-oriented manufacturing has encouraged expansion of the garment industry.

Tourism is also a major factor in the economy, second only to sugar as a money-earner.

TRADE
The chief imports are foodstuffs, machinery, mineral fuels, chemicals, beverages, tobacco and manufactured articles. Chief exports are sugar, coconut oil, gold, lumber, garments, molasses, ginger and canned fish.

	1991	1992
Total Imports	F$1,113m	F$962m
Total Exports	732m	665m

Trade with UK	1991	1992
Imports from UK	£8,268,000	£7,656,000
Exports to UK	81,540,000	79,189,000

COMMUNICATIONS

Fiji is one of the main aerial crossroads in the Pacific, providing services to New Zealand, Australia, Tonga, Western Samoa, Vanuatu, the Solomon Islands, Kiribati, Tuvalu, New Caledonia and American Samoa.

Fiji has three ports of entry, at Suva, Lautoka and Levuka.

FINLAND
Suomen Tasavalta

Finland is situated on the Gulfs of Finland and Bothnia, with a total area of 137,851 sq. miles (337,032 sq. km), of which 65 per cent is forest, 8 per cent cultivated land and 9 per cent lakes. The population (1991 UN estimate) is 5,029,000; population density is 15 inhabitants per square km. The population is predominantly Lutheran.

The Åland Archipelago (Ahvenanmaa), a group of small islands at the entrance to the Gulf of Bothnia, covers about 572 square miles, with a population (December 1985) of 23,600 (95.2 per cent Swedish-speaking). The islands have a semi-autonomous status.

CAPITAL – ΨHelsinki (Helsingfors), population (1990) 492,200; other towns are Tampere (Tammerfors), 172,560; ΨTurku (Åbo), 159,180; Espoo (Esbo), 172,629; Vantaa (Vanda), 154,933; ΨOulu (Oleåborg), 97,329; Lahti (Lahtis), 94,467; ΨPori (Björneborg), 78,365.
CURRENCY – Markka (Mk) of 100 penniä.
FLAG – White with blue cross.
NATIONAL DAY – 6 December (Independence Day).

GOVERNMENT

Under the Constitution there is a single chamber, the *Eduskunta*, composed of 200 members elected by universal suffrage. The legislative power is vested in the Eduskunta and the President. The highest executive power is held by the President who is elected for a period of six years.

The present government came into office in April 1990, the first government for 25 years not to include left-wing parties. The four parties in the coalition are the National Coalition Party (conservative), the Centre Party, the Swedish

People's Party of Finland, and the Finnish Christian Union Party.

After much discussion and national debate, the Parliament voted by 108 to 55 to apply for membership of the European Community on 18 March 1992 and the application was presented in Brussels at the end of that month. After a favourable EC Commission opinion on Finnish membership, negotiations opened with the EC on Finland's application in January 1993 and a provisional timetable sets the date for entry as January 1995.

HEAD OF STATE
President, Dr Mauno Koivisto, *born* 1923, *elected* 26 January 1982, *re-elected* 1 March 1988.

CABINET *as at July 1993*
Prime Minister, Esko Aho (CP).
Deputy Prime Minister, Foreign Trade Pertti Salolainen (NCP).
Foreign Affairs, Heikki Haavisto (CP).
Social Affairs and Health, Jorma Huuhtanen (CP).
Labour, Ilkka Kanerva (NCP).
Transport and Communications, Ole Norrback (SPP).
Defence, Elisabeth Rehn (SPP).
Trade and Industry, Pekka Tuomisto (CP).
Justice, Hannele Pokka (CP).
Interior, Mauri Pekkarinen (CP).
Finance, Iiro Viinanen (NCP).
Education, Riitta Uosukainen (NCP).
Cultural Affairs, Tytti Isohookana-Asunmaa (CP).
Environment, Sirpa Pietikainen (NCP).
Housing, Pirjo Rusanen, (NCP).
Development Co-operation, Toimi Kankaanniemi (FCU).
Agriculture and Forestry, Matti Pura (CP).

NCP National Coalition Party, CP Centre Party, FCU Finnish Christian Union, SPP Swedish People's Party.

EMBASSY OF FINLAND
38 Chesham Place, London SW1W 8HW
Tel 071-838 6200

Ambassador Extraordinary and Plenipotentiary, His Excellency Leif Blomquist (1991).
Minister, L. Korpinen.
Counsellor (Commercial), Jyri Muttonen.
Defence Attaché, Lt.-Col. R. Noopila.
Consul, Mrs T. Gallen-Kallela.

BRITISH EMBASSY
Itäinen Puistotie 17, 00140 Helsinki
Tel: Helsinki 661293
Ambassador Extraordinary and Plenipotentiary, His Excellency Neil Smith, CMG (1989).
Deputy Ambassador and Counsellor (Commercial), N. A. Thorne.
First Secretary and Consul, N. J. Kelly.
Defence Attaché, Lt.-Col. F. A. B. Clement.

There are British Consular offices at *Helsinki, Jyväskylä, Kotka, Kuopio, Oulu, Pori, Tampere, Turku, Vaasa* and *Mariehamn.*

BRITISH COUNCIL REPRESENTATIVE, Tuija Talvitie, Hakaniemenkatu 2, 00530 Helsinki.

DEFENCE

By the terms of the Peace Treaty (10 February 1947) with the UK and USSR, the Army is limited to a force not exceeding 34,400. The Navy is limited to a total of 10,000 tons displacement with personnel not exceeding 4,500. The Air Force, including naval air arm, is limited to 60 machines with a personnel not exceeding 3,000. Bombers or aircraft with bomb-carrying facilities are expressly forbidden.

The defence forces contain a cadre of regular officers and NCOs, but their bulk is provided by conscripts who serve for 8–11 months. The total active armed forces number some 32,800 personnel (24,100 conscripts). However, in the event of attack the total mobilization strength is based on the 700,000 trained and equipped reservists, who are obliged to undergo between 40 and 100 days training up to age 50; 50,000 reservists undergo training each year.

The Army has a strength of 27,300 (21,600 conscripts) organized into one armoured, one artillery and eight infantry brigades together with two engineer, four air defence and two independent infantry battalions. Equipment includes 120 main battle tanks, 620 armoured infantry fighting vehicles and armoured personnel carriers, and 630 artillery pieces.

The Navy has 2,500 personnel (1,000 conscripts) with 23 patrol and coastal craft and ten mine warfare vessels. The Air Force has 3,000 personnel (1,500 conscripts) and 116 combat aircraft organized into three air defence wings with transport, training and support units. There are also 4,400 Ministry of Interior Frontier Guards.

EDUCATION

Primary education (co-educational comprehensive school) is compulsory for children from 7 to 16 years, and free of charge. In the autumn of 1986, there were 678,463 in comprehensive schools and 113,117 in vocational institutions of senior level. There are 21 universities or other schools of academic level.

CULTURE

There are two official languages in Finland: 93.6 per cent of the population speak Finnish as their first language, 6.2 per cent Swedish (1986). The remaining 0.2 per cent speak other languages (mainly Lapps who number about 2,500 and live in the far north). Both Finnish and Swedish are used for administration and education; newspapers, books, plays and films appear in both languages.There is a vigorous modern literature. F. E. Sillanpää, who died in 1964, was awarded the Nobel prize for Literature in 1939. In 1988 there were 103 daily newspapers (12 Swedish).

ECONOMY

Finland is a highly industrialized country producing a wide range of capital and consumer goods. Timber and the products of the forest-based industries remain the backbone of the economy, but the importance of the metal-working, shipbuilding and engineering industries has been growing. The textile industry is well developed and Finland's glass, ceramics and furniture industries enjoy international reputations. Other important industries are rubber, plastics, chemicals and pharmaceuticals, footwear, foodstuffs and electronic equipment.

The Finnish economy has been adversely affected by declining trade with eastern Europe and the former Soviet Union, together with the worldwide economic recession. Unemployment has risen to 19 per cent in 1993 while inflation in 1992 was 2.1 per cent. The government has had to introduce austerity measures, raising taxes and reducing health and social welfare spending and the large overseas development budget.

TRADE

The principal imports are raw materials, machinery and manufactured goods. In 1988 more than half of all industrial production was exported. The value of exports was broken down as follows: paper 33.4 per cent, wood 8.2 per cent, metal and engineering products 31 per cent, basic metal industry 8.3 per cent, chemicals 9 per cent, textiles and clothing 4.6 per cent. The special barter-trade relationship with the former Soviet Union collapsed in 1991 causing an overall drop in Finnish exports of some 10 per cent.

	1987	1988
Total Imports	Mk86,696m	Mk88,192m
Total Exports	87,564m	90,861m

Trade with UK	1991	1992
Imports from UK	£847,671,000	£994,656,000
Exports to UK	1,522,337,000	1,676,575,000

COMMUNICATIONS

There are 9,000 kilometres of railroad, a railway connection with Sweden and Russia, passenger boat connection with Sweden, Germany, Poland, Russia and the Baltic States. Vessels on the London to Leningrad route call at Helsinki. There are also passenger/cargo services between Britain and Helsinki, Kotka and other Finnish ports. External civil air services are maintained by most European airlines. The merchant fleet at the end of 1986 totalled 1,900,000 tons gross.

FRANCE
La République Française

France extends from 42° 20′ to 51° 5′ N. latitude, and from 7° 85′ E. to 4° 45′ W. longitude. Its area is estimated at 211,208 sq. miles (547,026 sq. km), divided into 95 departments, including the island of Corsica, in the Mediterranean off the west coast of Italy. The population, according to the 1990 census results, is 56,614,000 (Metropolitan France), and 58,074,000 when overseas departments are included.

POPULATION OF THE REGIONS 1990
Names of Departments in brackets

Alsace (Bas-Rhin, Haut-Rhin)	1,624,000
Aquitaine (Dordogne, Gironde, Landes, Lot-et-Garonne, Pyrénées-Atlantiques)	2,796,000
Auvergne (Allier, Cantal, Haute-Loire, Puy-de-Dôme)	1,321,000
Basse-Normandie (Calvados, Manche, Orne)	1,391,000
Bourgogne (Côte-d'Or, Nièvre, Saône-et-Loire, Yonne)	1,609,000
Bretagne (Côtes-du-Nord, Finistère, Ille-et-Vilaine, Morbihan)	2,796,000
Centre (Cher, Eure-et-Loir, Indre, Indre-et-Loire, Loir-et-Cher, Loiret)	2,371,000
Champagne-Ardenne (Ardennes, Aube, Marne, Haute-Marne)	1,348,000
Corse (Corse-du-Sud, Haute-Corse)	250,000
Franche-Comté (Doubs, Haute-Saône, Jura, Territoire-de-Belfort)	1,097,000
Haute-Normandie (Eure, Seine-Maritime)	1,737,000
Île-de-France (Essonne, Hauts-de-Seine, Seine-et-Marne, Seine-St-Denis, Val-de-Marne, Val-d'Oise, Ville de Paris, Yvelines)	10,660,000
Languedoc-Roussillon (Aude, Gard, Hérault, Lozère, Pyrénées-Orientales)	2,115,000
Limousin (Corrèze, Creuse, Haute-Vienne)	723,000
Lorraine (Meurthe-et-Moselle, Meuse, Moselle, Vosges)	2,306,000
Midi-Pyrénées (Ariège, Aveyron, Haute-Garonne, Gers, Lot, Hautes-Pyrénées, Tarn, Tarn-et-Garonne)	2,431,000
Nord-Pas-de-Calais (Nord, Pas-de-Calais)	3,965,000
Pays de la Loire (Loire-Atlantique, Maine-et-Loire, Mayenne, Sarthe, Vendée)	3,059,000
Picardie (Aisne, Oise, Somme)	1,811,000
Poitou-Charentes (Charente, Charente-Maritime, Deux-Sèvres, Vienne)	1,595,000
Provence-Alpes-Côte d'Azur (Alpes-de-Haute-Provence, Alpes-Maritimes, Bouches-du-Rhône, Hautes-Alpes, Var, Vaucluse)	4,258,000
Rhône-Alpes (Ain, Ardèche, Drôme, Isère, Loire, Rhône, Savoie, Haute-Savoie)	5,351,000

CAPITAL – Paris, on the Seine. Population (census 1990) 2,175,200 (city); 9,318,800 (incl. suburbs).
The largest conurbations (populations 1990) are ΨMarseilles (1,231,000); Lyon (1,262,000); Toulouse (650,000); Lille (959,000); ΨBordeaux (696,000); Nice

(516,000); Nantes (496,000); Toulon (437,000). The chief towns of Corsica are ΨAjaccio (55,279) and ΨBastia (45,081).
CURRENCY – French franc of 100 centimes.
FLAG – The tricolour, three vertical bands, blue, white, red (blue next to flagstaff).
NATIONAL ANTHEM – La Marseillaise.
NATIONAL DAY – 14 July (Bastille Day 1789).

HISTORY

There are dolmens and menhirs in Brittany, prehistoric remains and cave drawings in Dordogne and Ariège, and throughout France various megalithic monuments erected by primitive tribes, predecessors of Iberian invaders from Spain (now represented by the Basques), Ligurians from northern Italy and Celts or Gauls from the valley of the Danube. Julius Caesar found Gaul 'divided into three parts' and described three political groups; Aquitanians south of the Garonne, Celts between the Garonne and the Seine and Marne, and Belgae from the Seine to the Rhine. Roman remains are plentiful throughout France in the form of aqueducts, arenas, triumphal arches, etc. The celebrated Norman and Gothic cathedrals, including Notre Dame in Paris, and those of Chartres, Reims, Amiens (where Peter the Hermit preached the First Crusade for the recovery of the Holy Sepulchre), Bourges, Beauvais, Rouen, etc., have survived invasions and bombardments with only partial damage, and many of the Renaissance and the 17th- and 18th-century chateaux survived the French Revolution.

LANGUAGE AND LITERATURE

French is the official language. The work of the French Academy, founded by Richelieu in 1635, has established *le bon usage*, equivalent to 'The Queen's English' in Britain. French authors have been awarded the Nobel Prize for Literature on twelve occasions, including R. F. A. Sully-Prudhomme (1901), Anatole France (1921), André Gide (1947), François Mauriac (1952), Albert Camus (1957), Jean Paul Sartre (1964) and Claude Simon (1985).

GOVERNMENT

The legislature consists of the National Assembly of 577 deputies (555 for Metropolitan France and 22 for the overseas departments and territories) and the Senate composed of 321 Senators (298 for Metropolitan France, 13 for the overseas departments and territories and 10 for French dependencies). One-third of the senate is indirectly elected every three years. The state of the parties at August 1993 in the senate was: Rassemblement pour la république (RPR) 90; Socialists 70; Centrist Union 66; UDF-Republican Party 47; Democratic and European Rally (RDE) 22; Communists 15; Independents 10.
    The normal session of Parliament is confined to five and a half months each year and it may also meet in extraordinary session for 12 days at the request of the Prime Minister or a majority of the Assembly.
    The Prime Minister is appointed by the President, as is the Cabinet on the Prime Minister's recommendation. They are responsible to Parliament, but as the executive is constitutionally separate from the legislature, ministers may not sit in Parliament and must hand over their seats to a substitute.
    A Constitutional Council is responsible for supervising all elections and referenda and must be consulted on all constitutional matters and before the President of the Republic assumes emergency powers.

At the last elections to the National Assembly on 21 and 28 March 1993 the Socialist government was decisively beaten by the right-wing alliance of the Gaullist Rassemblement pour la république (RPR) and the Union pour la démocratie française (UDF) parties. The forming of the new right-wing government has ushered in the second period of 'cohabitation' in the history of the Fifth Republic (i.e. the President and government are from different parties or coalitions), the previous period being in 1986–8. At August 1993 the state of parties in the National Assembly was: Gaullists (RPR) 247; UDF 213; Socialists (PS) and Allies 70; other right-wing parties 24; Communists (PCF) 23.

HEAD OF STATE
President of the French Republic, François Mitterrand, *elected* 10 May 1981, *re-elected* 8 May 1988.

COUNCIL OF MINISTERS *as at August 1993*
Prime Minister, Edouard Balladur (RPR).
Minister of State, Social Affairs, Health and Urban Affairs, Simone Veil (Ind.).
Minister of State, Interior and Administrative Reform, Charles Pasqua (RPR).
Minister of State, Justice, Pierre Méhaignerie (UDF).
Minister of State, Defence, François Léotard (UDF).
Foreign Affairs, Alain Juppé (RPR).
National Education, François Bayrou (UDF).
Economy, Edmond Alphandéry (UDF).
Industry, Gérard Longuet (UDF).
Public Works, Transport and Tourism, Bernard Bosson (UDF).
Businesses and Enterprise, Alain Madelin (UDF).
Labour, Employment and Vocational Training, Michel Giraud (RPR).
Culture and Francophone Affairs, Jacqus Tourbon (RPR).
Budget, Government Spokesperson, Nicolas Sarkozy (RPR).
Agriculture and Fisheries, Jean Puech (UDF).
Higher Education and Research, François Fillon (RPR).
Environment, Michel Barnier (RPR).
Civil Service, André Rossinot (UDF).
Housing, Hervé de Charette (UDF).
Co-operation, Michel Roussin (RPR).
Overseas Departments and Territories, Dominique Perben (RPR).
Youth and Sports, Michèle Alliot-Marie (RPR).
Communications, Alain Carignon (RPR).
Veterans and War Victims, Phillipe Mestre (UDF).
President of the Senate, René Monory.
President of the National Assembly, Phillipe Séguin.

FRENCH EMBASSY
58 Knightsbridge, London SW1X 7JT
Tel 071-201 1000
Ambassador Extraordinary and Plenipotentiary, His Excellency Bernard Dorin (1991).
Counsellors, P. Bassiere; T. Vankerk-Hoven.
Defence Attaché, Contre-Amiral P. Garibal.
Cultural Attaché, M. Lummaux.
Consul-General, G. Gautier.
Head of Commerce/Trade, F. Le Corre.

BRITISH EMBASSY
35 rue du Faubourg St Honoré, 75383 Paris Cedex 08
Tel: Paris 42 66 91 42
Ambassador Extraordinary and Plenipotentiary, His Excellency Sir Christopher Mallaby, GCVO, KCMG (1993).
Minister, J. R. Young, CMG.
Defence and Air Attaché, Air Cdre C. R. Adams, AFC.
Counsellor, Director of Trade Promotion and Investment, R. A. Kealy, CMG.
First Secretary and Consul-General, M. E. Hunt.

BRITISH CONSULAR OFFICES. There are British Consular Offices in Metropolitan France at *Bordeaux, Biarritz, Toulouse, Lille, Boulogne, Calais, Dunkirk, Lyon, Marseille, Nice, Paris, Cherbourg, Le Havre, Nantes and St Malo.* There are also offices in *Cayenne (French Guiana), Papeete (French Polynesia), Fort de France (Martinique), Pointe à Pitre (Guadeloupe)* and *St Denis (Réunion).*

BRITISH COUNCIL REPRESENTATIVE, D. Ricks, OBE, 9 rue de Constantine, 75007 Paris.

FRANCO-BRITISH CHAMBER OF COMMERCE, 8 rue Cimarosa, 75116 Paris. *President,* R. Lyon. *Vice-President,* B. Cordery, OBE.

DEFENCE

The total active armed forces number some 431,700 personnel (210,800 conscripts). Conscripts serve for ten months. Reserves total some 374,000 personnel. Strategic nuclear forces consist of 64 submarine-launched ballistic missiles on four nuclear-powered submarines, 18 land-based intermediate range ballistic missiles, 15 (with a further 13 in store) nuclear-capable Mirage IVP aircraft and 45 Mirage 2000N aircraft, both with medium-range nuclear air-to-surface missiles.

The Army has a strength of 260,900 (156,400 conscripts) with some 24 Pluton short-range nuclear missile launchers, 1,350 main battle tanks, 4,780 armoured personnel carriers and armoured infantry fighting vehicles, 1,436 artillery pieces and 682 helicopters. Organization is based on: four armoured and two motorized infantry divisions; the Rapid Action Force of five lightly armoured and air-mobile divisions; the Foreign Legion of nine regiments; the Franco-German brigade; 11 marine infantry regiments.

The Navy has a strength of 64,900 (19,000 conscripts) with some 38 Super Etendard aircraft (with 19 in store), capable of carrying short-range nuclear air-to-surface missiles, 13 submarines, two aircraft carriers and 39 other principal surface combatant vessels, 88 other combat aircraft and 52 armed helicopters.

The Air Force has a strength of 91,700 (35,400 conscripts) and some 808 combat aircraft. The Air Force is organized into: an air defence command of 11 squadrons; a tactical command of 12 ground attack, three reconnaissance and two early warning squadrons; an air transport command of 19 transport and five helicopter squadrons; a training command.

France deploys some 51,100 armed forces personnel abroad; 16,000 in Germany; 21,400 in French Overseas Departments and Territories; 8,350 in former French colonies in Africa; and 5,350 on UN and peace-keeping duties.

In early 1993 the French government announced a planned reduction in the armed forces over the next five years including a reduction in Army personnel from 260,000 to 224,000, of which 115,000 will be conscripts, 72,000 officers and NCOs and 37,000 professional privates. An overall armed forces manpower reduction of 25 per cent was also announced.

EDUCATION

The educational system is highly centralized and is administered by the Ministry of National Education. Local administration comprises 25 Territorial Academies, with inspecting staff for all grades, and Departmental Councils presided over by the *Préfet*, and charged especially with primary education.

Primary and secondary education are compulsory, free and secular, the school age being from 6 to 16. Schools may be single-sex or co-educational. Primary education is given in nursery schools, primary schools and *collèges d'enseignement général* (four-year secondary modern course); secondary education in *collèges d'enseignement technique, collèges d'enseignement secondaire* and *lycées* (seven-year course leading to one of the five *baccalauréats*). Special schools are numerous.

There are many *Grandes Ecoles* in France which award diplomas in many subjects not taught at university, especially applied science and engineering. Most of these are state institutions but have a competitive system of entry, unlike the universities. There are universities in 24 towns in France, two or three in some major provincial towns, and 13 in Paris and the immediate surrounding district.

In 1990–1 enrolment in pre-school and primary schools was 6,704,800; in secondary schools 5,862,300, and in post-secondary education 1,700,800.

In March 1993 the government gave German official parity with French in Alsace schools.

COMMUNICATIONS

The length of roads in use at the end of 1989 was 808,098 km, of which 6,824 km were motorways.

The system of railroads in France is very extensive. The length of lines open for traffic at the end of 1990 was 34,070 km, of which 12,609 km were electrified.

The French mercantile marine consisted in 1991 of 220 ships of over 100 tons gross, of which 29 were passenger vessels (228,000 tons gross), 56 tankers (2,084,000 tons gross) and 135 cargo vessels (1,407,000 tons gross). The principal rivers of France are the Seine, Loire, Garonne, and Rhône.

ECONOMY

Government expenditure (ordinary and capital) by function in the 1991 general Budget, was:

	F million
Agriculture and forestry	38,367
Co-operation and development	7,865
Culture and communications	12,105
Defence	238,458
Economy, finance and Budget	309,212
Education	248,320
Equipment, housing, transport and the sea	125,344
Foreign affairs	13,074
Industry, local planning and tourism	21,130
Interior	67,933
Justice	18,177
Labour and employment	67,669
Overseas departments	2,185
Prime Ministerial	5,526
Research and technology	25,833
Solidarity, health, social protection	38,879
Veterans	27,232
Youth and sports	2,576
Other	2,209
Total	1,272,094

In May 1993 the new conservative government announced the privatization of all public sector companies apart from those in the telecommunications, utilities and gaming sectors. The programme is estimated to generate F40,000 million by the end of 1993 and F300,000 million over four years. The first to be sold are holdings in Renault, Air France, Aérospatiale, Crédit Lyonnais and Banque National de Paris.

Approximately 30,433,000 hectares of land is used for agricultural purposes, 14,620,000 hectares is forested. Production in 1991 included wheat, 34,397,200 tonnes; maize, 12,797,200 tonnes; barley, 10,646,800 tonnes; and potatoes 3,901,900 tonnes.

The vine is extensively cultivated, regions famous for their wines including Bordeaux, Burgundy and Champagne. Production of wine in 1991 was 4,300,000 tonnes. Cognac, liqueurs and cider are also important products.

France produces its own oil, the greater part coming from fields in the Landes area, but is a net importer of crude oil, for processing by its important oil-refining industry. Natural gas is produced in the foothills of the Pyrenees. Electricity production was 433,300m kW in 1991.

France's heavy industries include oil-refining and the production of iron and steel, and aluminium. In 1989 production of steel was 19,300,000 tonnes and cement 25,900,000 tonnes. Other important industries produce chemicals, tyres, aluminium, textiles, paper products and processed food. Engineering products include motor vehicles, and television and radio sets.

TRADE

The principal imports are raw materials for the heavy and manufacturing industries (e.g. oil, minerals, chemicals), machinery and precision instruments, agricultural products and vehicles. Raw materials, semi-manufactured and manufactured goods are also France's principal exports. Other member countries of the EC are France's main trading partners.

	1990	1991
Imports	F1,226,613m	F1,251,298m
Exports	1,177,163m	1,221,108m

Trade with UK	1991	1992
Imports from UK	£11,591,139,000	£11,486,695,000
Exports to UK	11,066,081,000	12,215,890,000

OVERSEAS DEPARTMENTS

Legislation passed in December 1982 by the French Parliament granted greater powers of self-government to four of the five overseas departments, French Guiana, Guadeloupe, Martinique and Réunion. These former colonies had enjoyed departmental status since 1947 and the status of regions of France since 1974. Their directly-elected Assemblies operate in parallel with the existing, indirectly constituted Regional Councils. The French government is represented by a Commissioner (a Prefect in French Guiana).
FRENCH GUIANA – Situated on the north-eastern coast of South America, French Guiana is flanked by Suriname on the west and by Brazil on the south and east. Area, 34,749 sq. miles (90,000 sq. km). Population (1990) 114,900. Capital, ΨCayenne (41,000). Under the administration of French Guiana is a group of islands (St Joseph, Ile Royal and Ile du Diable), known as Iles du Salut. Captain Dreyfus was imprisoned on Devil's Isle from 1894 to 1899.
Prefect, J.-P. Lacroix.
GUADELOUPE – A number of islands in the Leeward Islands group of the West Indies, consisting of the two main islands of Guadeloupe (or Basse-Terre) and Grande-Terre, with the adjacent islands of Marie-Galante, La Désirade and Îles des Saintes, and the islands of St Martin and St Barthélemy over 150 miles to the north-west. Area, 687 sq. miles (1,779 sq. km). Population (1990) 386,600. Capital ΨBasse Terre (14,000) in Guadeloupe. Other towns are ΨPointe à Pitre (26,000) in Grande-Terre and ΨGrand Bourg (6,611) in Marie-Galante.
Commissioner, J-P. Proust.
MARTINIQUE – An island situated in the Windward Islands group of the West Indies, between Dominica in the north and St Lucia in the south. Area, 425 sq. miles (1,102 sq. km). Population (1990) 359,800. Capital ΨFort de France

(101,540). Other towns are ΨTrinité (11,214) and ΨMarin (6,104).
Commissioner, J.-C. Roure.
RÉUNION – Réunion, which became a French possession in 1638, lies in the Indian Ocean, about 569 miles east of Madagascar and 110 miles south-west of Mauritius. Area, 969 sq. miles (2,510 sq. km). Population (1990) 598,000. Capital, St Denis (122,000). Also lying in the Indian Ocean adjacent to Madagascar are the smaller, uninhabited islands of Bassas da India, Europa, Îles Glorieuses, Juan de Nova and Tromelin, which are administered from Réunion.
Commissioner, D. Constantin.

TERRITORIAL COLLECTIVITÉS

MAYOTTE – Area, 144 sq. miles (372 sq. km). Population (1991 census) is 94,410. Capital, Mamoundzou (12,000). Part of the Comoros Islands group, Mayotte remained a French dependency when the other three islands became independent as the Comoros Republic in 1975. Since 1976 the island has been a *collectivité territoriale*, an intermediate status between Overseas Department and Overseas Territory.
Commissioner, A. Khider.
ST PIERRE AND MIQUELON – Area 93 sq. miles (242 sq. km). Population (1990) 6,300. Two small groups of islands off the coast of Newfoundland. Became a *collectivité territoriale* in June 1985.
Commissioner, J.-P. Marquie.

OVERSEAS TERRITORIES

FRENCH POLYNESIA – Five archipelagos in the south Pacific, comprising the Society Islands (Windward Islands group includes Tahiti, Moorea, Makatea, Mehetia, Tetiaroa, Tubuai Manu, etc; Leeward Islands group includes Huahine, Raiatea, Tahaa, Bora-Bora, Maupiti, etc.), the Tuamotu Islands (Rangiroa, Hao, Turéia, etc.), the Gambier Islands (Mangareva, etc.), the Tubuai Islands (Rimatara, Rurutu, Tubuai, Raivavae, Rapa, etc.) and the Marquesas Islands (Nuku-Hiva, Hiva-Oa, Fatu-Hiva, Tahuata, Ua Huka, etc.). Area, 1,544 sq. miles (4,000 sq. km). Population (1990 UN estimate) 206,000. Capital, ΨPapeete (24,200) in Tahiti. Economy based on tourism and exports of copra, coffee, vanilla, citrus fruits and cultured pearls.
High Commissioner, J. Montpezat.
NEW CALEDONIA – A large island in the western Pacific, 700 miles east of Queensland. Dependencies are the Isles of Pines, the Loyalty Islands (Mahé, Lifou, Urea, etc.), the Bélep Archipelago, the Chesterfield Islands, the Huon Islands and Walpole. New Caledonia was discovered in 1774 and annexed by France in 1854; from 1871 to 1896 it was a convict settlement. A referendum in 1987 on the question of independence for New Caledonia was boycotted by the indigenous Kanaks, and New Caledonia therefore voted to remain French. However, a new independence referendum has been promised for 1998. Area, 7,358 sq. miles (19,058 sq. km). Population (1990 UN estimate) 167,000. Capital ΨNoumea (65,000). It is one of the world's largest producers of nickel.
High Commissioner, B. Grasset.
SOUTHERN AND ANTARCTIC TERRITORIES – Created in 1955 from former Réunion dependencies, the territory comprises the islands of Amsterdam (25 sq. miles) and St Paul (2.7 sq. miles), the Kerguelen Islands (2,700 sq. miles) and Crozet Islands (116 sq. miles) archipelagos and Adélie Land (116,800 sq. miles) in the Antarctic continent. The only population are members of staff of the scientific stations.
WALLIS AND FUTUNA ISLANDS – Two groups of islands (the Wallis Archipelago and the Îles de Hoorn) in the central Pacific, north-east of Fiji. Area, 106 sq. miles (274 sq. km).

Population (1990 census) 13,705. Capital, Mata-Utu on Uvea, the main island of the Wallis group.

THE FRENCH COMMUNITY

The constitution of the Fifth French Republic, promulgated in 1958, envisaged the establishment of a French Community of States. A number of the former French states in Africa have seceded from the Community but for all practical purposes continue to enjoy the same close links with France as those that remain formally members of the French Community. With the exception of Guinea, all the former French African colonies are closely linked to France by a series of financial, technical and economic agreements.

FRANCOPHONE COUNTRIES

In the following countries French is either the official or national language or the language of instruction; where there is another national language the name of it is shown after the name of the country: Algeria (*Arabic*); Belgium (*Flemish*); Benin; Burkina; Burundi (*Kirundi*); Cambodia (*Khmer*); Cameroon (*English*); parts of Canada (Quebec, parts of Ontario and New Brunswick) (*English*); Central African Republic (*Sangho*); Chad; Congo; Côte d'Ivoire; France; Gabon; Guinea; Haiti (*Creole*); Laos (*Laotian*); Lebanon (*Arabic*); Luxembourg (*German* and *Letzeburgesch*); Madagascar (*Malagasy*); Mali; Morocco (*Arabic*); Mauritania (*Arabic*); Niger; Rwanda (*Kinyarwanda*); Senegal; Switzerland (*German, Italian, Romansch*); Togo; Tunisia (*Arabic*); Vietnam (*Vietnamese*); Zaire. French is also spoken in the Overseas Departments (*see* above).

Source: for statistical data: *L'Annuaire Statistique de la France 1991-2; Tableaux de l'Economie Française 1992-3.*

GABON
République Gabonaise

Gabon lies on the Atlantic coast of Africa at the Equator and is flanked on the north by Equatorial Guinea and Cameroon, and on the east and south by Congo. It has an area of 103,347 sq. miles (267,667 sq. km) and a population (UN estimate 1991) of 1,212,000.

CAPITAL – ΨLibreville (251,000).
CURRENCY – Franc CFA of 100 centimes.
FLAG – Horizontal bands, green, yellow and blue.
NATIONAL ANTHEM – La Concorde.
NATIONAL DAY – 17 August.

GOVERNMENT

Gabon elected on 28 November 1958 to remain an autonomous republic within the French Community and was proclaimed fully independent on 17 August 1960. The Constitution provides for an executive President directly elected for a seven-year term, who appoints the Council of Ministers. There is a unicameral National Assembly comprising 120 members.

Following widespread unrest, a national conference was called in March 1990 and delegates forced President Bongo to legalize opposition parties. Several rounds of multi-party elections were held in September, October and November 1990 and eventually won by the ruling Parti democratique gabonais (PDG), amid allegations of fraud. The PDG formed a coalition government with several opposition parties but retained the most important portfolios. Opposition parties left the government in June 1991 in protest at the dominating

power of the PDG. Multi-party presidential elections are scheduled for December 1993.

HEAD OF STATE
President, El Hadj Omar Bongo, *assumed office,* December 1967, *re-elected,* 1973, 1979 and November 1986.

COUNCIL OF MINISTERS *as at July 1993*
Prime Minister, Casimir Oyé Mba.
Public Works, Construction and Territorial Administration, Zacharie Myboto.
Justice, Michel Anchouey.
Foreign Affairs and Co-operation, Pascaline Bongo.
Commerce, Consumption and Industry, Relations with Parliament, André Dieudonné Berre.
Town Planning, Housing, Adrien Nkoghe Essingone.
National Defence, War Veterans, Public Security and Immigration, Martin Fidèle Magnaga.
Territorial Administration and Local Collectives, Antoine Mboumbou-Miyakou.
Civil Service and Administrative Reform, Paulette Moussavou.
Finance, Budget and State Holdings, Paul Toungui.
Planning and Economic Development, Marcel Doupamby-Matoka.
Information, Posts and Telecommunications, and Government Spokesman, Jean Rémy Pendy-Bouyiki.
Mines, Hydrocarbons, Energy and Hydraulic Resources, Hervo Akendengue.
National Education, Higher Education and Scientific Research, Marc Ropivia.
Public Health, Population, Social Affairs and National Solidarity, Eugène Kakou Mayaza.
Employment, Human Resources and Professional Training, Serge Mba.
Agriculture, Livestock and Rural Economy, Emmanuel Ondo Methogo.
Water, Forests and Environment, Eugène Capito.
Youth, Sports, Culture and Popular Education, in charge of Francophone Affairs, Pierre Claver Nzeng.
Transport, Jerome Ngoua Bekalé.
State Control and Para-Public Sector Reform, Jean-Baptiste Obiang Etoughe.
Tourism, National Parks and Leisure, Pépin Mongoskodji.
Small and Medium-Sized Enterprises and Handicrafts, Victor Mapangou Moucani Mietsa.

EMBASSY OF THE REPUBLIC OF GABON
27 Elvaston Place, London SW7 5NL
Tel 071-823 9986
Ambassador Extraordinary and Plenipotentiary, His Excellency Vincent Boulé (1991).

BRITISH AMBASSADOR (resident in Zaire).

ECONOMY

Gabon's economy remains heavily dependent on oil, and, to a much lesser extent, other mineral resources, including manganese and uranium. Gabon has considerable timber reserves (particularly Okoumé) although production in this industry has stagnated in recent years.

The economy, which experienced considerable growth in real terms from the mid-1970s onwards, had since 1986 been adversely affected by the fall in oil prices. Revenue is expected to increase in the 1990s following major oil exploitation at Rabi-Kounga. Gabon is a full member of OPEC.

TRADE WITH UK	1991	1992
Imports from UK	£30,597,000	£19,703,000
Exports to UK	3,221,000	3,456,000

THE GAMBIA
The Republic of the Gambia

The Gambia takes its name from the Gambia River, which it straddles for over 200 miles inland from the west coast of Africa. It is a narrow strip, surrounded by Senegal, except at the coast, lying between 13° 10′–13° 45′ N. and 13° 90′–16° 50′ W. The area is 4,361 sq. miles (11,295 sq. km), of which one-fifth is the river. The climate is typically Sahelian, with a dry season between October and May and heavy rainfall during the months of July and August (32–40 inches a year). POPULATION – The population comprises mainly Wolof, Mandinka and Fula peoples who originally migrated there from the north and east. Population (1991 UN estimate) was 884,000.

CAPITAL – ΨBanjul. Population (1983 Census) of the island of Banjul was 44,536, and of adjacent Kombo St Mary district 102,858. Total population of Banjul/Kombo St Mary, 147,394.
CURRENCY – Dalasi (D) of 100 butut.
FLAG – Horizontal stripes of red, blue and green, separated by narrow white stripes.
NATIONAL ANTHEM – For The Gambia, Our Homeland.
NATIONAL DAY – 18 February (Independence Day).

HISTORY

The Gambia River basin was part of the region dominated in the tenth to 16th centuries by the strong Songhai and Mali kingdoms centred on the upper Niger. The first recorded Europeans to reach the Gambia River were the Portuguese in 1447. In 1588 Queen Elizabeth I gave the first charter to English merchants to trade along the river. Merchants from France, Courland (now part of Latvia) and the Netherlands also established trading posts there. The English presence was strongly challenged by the French, who were dominant further north up the coast, but in 1783 the Treaty of Versailles acknowledged English rights. In 1816, after the Napoleonic Wars, and in order to enforce abolition of the slave trade, the British stationed a garrison on a low sandy island called Banjul at the river mouth. Renamed Bathurst, this became the capital of a small British-administered colony, initially under the Governor of Sierra Leone. Negotiations with France continued sporadically until 1889 when it was agreed that the British rights along the upper river should extend 10 km on either bank. British administration was extended from the Colony to this Protectorate. The Gambia became independent within the Commonwealth on 18 February 1965, and a republic on 24 April 1970.
The Gambia's relationship with Senegal has always been an important factor in political and economic policy. Moves towards a closer association were accelerated after an abortive coup in The Gambia in July 1981 was put down with the help of Senegalese troops. In February 1982 the Senegambia Confederation was formally instituted based on certain joint institutions and integration of policies, with each country remaining sovereign and independent. However, following disagreements it was decided to dissolve the confederation, and formal dissolution took place on 31 December 1989. A treaty of friendship and co-operation was signed with Senegal in January 1991.

GOVERNMENT

The constitution is democratic and parliamentary, with an executive President elected for five years. The House of Representatives has 35 elected members, five elected Chiefs Representatives and up to eight nominated members plus the Attorney-General (ex-officio). The Vice-President and other ministers are appointed by the President. Parliament must be dissolved after five years.
The last general elections were held in April 1992. The present state of the parties for elected members is PPP (People's Progressive Party) 25; NCP (National Convention Party) 6; Gambian People's Party 2; Independents 3.

PRESIDENT AND CABINET *as at July 1993*
President, His Excellency Alhaji Sir Dawda Kairaba Jawara, GCMG.
Vice-President and Minister of Defence, Civil Service and Women's Affairs, Hon. Alhaji Saihou Sabally.
Attorney-General and Minister of Justice, Hon. Hassan B. Jallow.
Finance and Economic Affairs, Hon. Bakary Bunja Darbo.
External Affairs, Hon. Alhaji Omar Sey.
Interior, Hon. Lamin Kiti Jabang.
Agriculture, Hon. Omar A. Jallow.
Education, Hon. Alieu Ebrima Wula Fala Badjie.
Local Government and Lands, Hon. Yaya Ceesay.
Natural Resources and the Environment, Hon. Sarjo Touray.
Health, Hon. Landing Jallow Sanko.
Works and Communications, Hon. Matthew Yaya Baldeh.
Trade, Industry, Hon. Mbemba Jatta.
Information and Tourism, Hon. Alkali James Gaye.
Youth, Sports and Culture, Hon. Bubacarr Michael Baldeh.
Chief Justice, Hon. B. A. Omosun.
Speaker, Alhaji Hon. M. B. N'Jie.

GAMBIA HIGH COMMISSION
57 Kensington Court, London W8 5DG
Tel 071-937 6316
High Commissioner, His Excellency Mohammadou N. Bobb (1992).

BRITISH HIGH COMMISSION
48 Atlantic Road, Fajara (PO Box 507), Banjul
Tel: Banjul 95133
High Commissioner, His Excellency Michael Hardie (1993).

COMMUNICATIONS

There is an international airport at Yundum, 17 miles from Banjul, with scheduled services flying to other West African states and to the UK and Belgium. Banjul is the main port. Internal communication is by road and river. There is no railway system. There are three broadcasting stations and a UHF telephone service linking Banjul with the principal towns in the provinces. There is no television service.

EDUCATION

There are 24 secondary schools (eight high and 16 technical) with a total enrolment of 15,635 students. Two high schools provide A-level education. Gambia College provides post-secondary courses in education, agriculture, public health and nursing. There are seven vocational training institutions with a total enrolment of 1,400. Higher education and advanced training courses are taken outside The Gambia, currently by over 200 students.

ECONOMY

Seventy-five per cent of the population depend for their livelihood on agriculture (40 per cent of GDP). The chief product, groundnuts, is also the most important export item, forming over 80 per cent of all domestic exports. Other crops are rice, millet, sorghum, maize and cotton. Fishing and livestock industries are being developed. Thirty per cent of the country's basic food requirements are imported. There are no significant deposits of minerals.

Manufactures are limited to groundnut processing, minor metal fabrications, paints, furniture, soap and bottling. Tourism is developing quickly. The entrepôt trade through The Gambia, re-exporting imported goods to neighbouring countries, is an important element in the national economy.

FINANCE	1990–1*
Recurrent Revenue	D623,000,000
Recurrent Expenditure	633,000,000
*estimate.	

Over 80 per cent of capital expenditure comes from external aid grants and loans. In 1987–8 there was a GDP growth rate of 5.4 per cent.

TRADE	1987–8	1988–9
Total imports	D844,900,000	D940,000,000
Total exports	576,600,000	311,400,000
Trade with UK	1991	1992
Imports from UK	£19,141,000	£20,092,000
Exports to UK	2,865,000	3,118,000

GEORGIA
Sakartvelos Respublika

Georgia has an area of 26,911 sq. miles (69,700 sq. km) and occupies the north-western part of the Caucasus region of the former Soviet Union. It is bordered on the north by Russia, on the south-east by Azerbaijan, on the south by Armenia, on the south-west by Turkey, and on the west by the Black Sea. Georgia contains the two autonomous republics of Abkhazia and Adjaria and the autonomous province of South Ossetia. The latter was abolished by Georgian law in December 1990 but this was not recognized by the Soviet government.

Georgia is very mountainous, with the Greater Caucasus in the north and the Lesser Caucasus in the south. The relatively low-lying land between these two ranges is divided into western and eastern Georgia by the Surz Ridge.

CLIMATE – Western Georgia has a mild and damp climate, eastern Georgia is more continental and dry. The Black Sea shore and the Rioni lowland are subtropical.

POPULATION – According to a 1990 estimate, Georgia has a population of 5,456,000, of which 70 per cent are Georgian, 8 per cent are Armenian, 6 per cent Russian, 6 per cent Azerbaijani and 3 per cent Ossetians, together with smaller groups of Abkhazians, Greeks, Ukrainians, Jews and Kurds.

RELIGION – Most of the population are adherents of the Georgian Orthodox Church. The Head of the Georgian Orthodox Church is called the Patriarch Catholicas and resides in Mtskheta. There is also a small Muslim minority.

LANGUAGES – Georgian, Russian and Armenian are mostly commonly in use. Georgian is one of the oldest languages in the world to have been continually in use, the Georgian alphabet having emerged in the third century BC. Georgian is a member of the Kartvelian group of languages.

CAPITAL – Tbilisi. Population 1,260,000 (1989). Other major cities are Sukhumi (capital of Abkhazia) (125,000) and Batumi (150,000).

CURRENCY – The Georgian Coupon was introduced as legal tender to operate alongside the Rouble in April 1993. In early August 1993 the coupon became the only legal tender when Georgia left the rouble zone.

FLAG – Cherry red with a canton in the upper hoist divided black over white.

NATIONAL DAY – 26 May (Independence Day).

GOVERNMENT

The Georgians are a very ancient people who formed two states on the edge of the Black Sea around 1000 BC called Colchis and Iberia which were known to the ancient Greeks. After centuries of invasions by Arabs, Turks and Khazars, Georgia entered its 'Golden Age' in the 12th century AD under the rule of Queen Tamara, when trade, irrigation and communications were greatly developed. Invasions by the Khazars and Mongols led to the division of Georgia into several kingdoms and principalities. These Georgian states struggled against the Turkish and the Persian Empires from the 16th to the 18th centuries, gradually turning to the Russian Empire for protection and support. Eastern Georgia signed a treaty of alliance with Russia which recognised Russian supremacy in 1783 and joined the Russian Empire in 1801, followed soon after by Western Georgia.

In the late 19th century nationalist and Marxist movements formed in Georgia and competed for the very limited political influence possible under autocratic Russian rule. One of the most prominent Marxist activists was Iosif Dzhugashvili (Josef Stalin). After the Russian revolution of 1917, a nationalist government came to power in Georgia supported by allied intervention forces. In 1921 Soviet forces entered Georgia and occupied Tbilisi, leading to a Communist takeover on 25 February. In 1922 Georgia joined the Soviet Union as part of the Transcaucasian Soviet Socialist Republic.

In March 1990 the Georgian Supreme Soviet declared illegal the treaties of 1921–2 by which Georgia had joined Soviet Union. The Communist Party's monopoly on power was abolished in 1990 and in multi-party elections held in October and November 1990 the nationalist leader Zviad Gamsakhurdia was elected President. Georgia declared its independence from the Soviet Union in May 1991. The independence of Georgia was recognized by the EC in March 1992 and Georgia was admitted to UN membership on 31 July 1992.

The political situation became confused after independence was declared as the increasingly dictatorial attitude of Gamsakhurdia alienated much of the population; by late 1991 armed opposition to Gamsakhurdia's government had begun in earnest. At the same time, the South Ossetians took up arms against Georgian rule in an attempt to join North Ossetia, itself a part of Russia. By the end of December 1991 there was civil war in Tbilisi between supporters and opponents of President Gamsakhurdia. The President was overthrown and fled on 6 January 1992 and a military council took power until March 1992, when a state council was appointed with the former Soviet foreign minister Eduard Shevardnadze as its chairman.

Throughout 1992 and 1993 fighting continued between the State Council Government and supporters of Gamsakhurdia, and also Abkhazian separatists. The fighting continues to completely dominate Georgian politics. In presidential and legislative elections in October 1992 Eduard Schevardnadze was elected Head of State and Chairman of the Parliament, and a loose alliance of pro-Schevardnadze parties gained a majority in parliament. No voting took place in Abkhazia or South Ossetia. The provincial South Ossetian parliament voted in November 1992 to secede from Georgia and join Russia. The province's status remains unresolved since June 1992 when fighting stopped and a joint Russian–Georgian–Ossetian peace-keeping force was put in place.

In Abkhazia, however, Georgian forces became heavily engaged in a fierce war with separatists who have been extensively supported and aided by Russian armed forces in the region and armed irregulars from the Russian Northern Caucasus mountains (although this is denied by Russia). By April 1993 Georgian forces had lost 1,000 men killed and 3,500 injured and the deprivations caused by the war and the poor conduct of it led to economic chaos and instability. The government, led by Tengiz Sigua, resigned on 6 August 1993 and parliament effectively voted for presidential direct rule to add to the special powers given to Schevardnadze by parliament in July to conduct the war in Abkhazia.

Fighting in Abkhazia lessened in early August 1993 as Abkhazian and Georgian forces disengaged and a joint Russian–Georgian–Abkhazian peace-keeping force was put into place.

HEAD OF STATE
President, Chairman of the Supreme Soviet, Commander-in-Chief and Prime Minister, Eduard Shevardnadze, *elected* 11 October 1992.

ECONOMY

The Georgian economy has been brought to the brink of collapse by the war in Abkhazia and the ending of former Soviet trading relationships. Although Georgia has deposits of coal, they have not been exploited and it is desperately short of energy supplies. Existing barter deals with Turkmenistan and Kazakhstan for natural gas in return for tea, wine and citrus fruit are to end in 1994, when Georgia will have to pay with hard currency that it does not possess. Schevardnadze is attempting to agree barter deals for Azeri and Iranian oil and for an Azeri pipeline to the Black Sea. Cheap grain from Russia is no longer supplied and a large proportion of Georgian production is stolen by black marketers and pirates in the Black Sea, whilst the tourist industry on the Black Sea coast has been destroyed by the fighting. The lack of hard currency to support the new Georgian coupon has caused it to depreciate rapidly and inflation to rise rapidly. The only really productive sector of the economy remains agriculture, with a concentration on viniculture, tea and tobacco-growing and citrus fruits.

GERMANY
Bundesrepublik Deutschland - Federal Republic of Germany

The area of the Federal Republic is approximately 138,000 square miles (357,050 km²). The estimated population of the Federal Republic (March 1992) was 80,372,000, of whom 64,600,000 live in the former West and 15,800,000 in the former East Germany. There were 10.1 live births per 1,000 inhabitants in the Federal Republic in 1992 (11.3 in West and 5.4 in East).

RELIGION (West Germany only) – In 1987 there were 25.4 million Protestants, 26.2 million Roman Catholics, and 1.6 million Muslims. The number of Jews is around 40,000 in 1993.

CAPITAL – Berlin. By decision of the Bundestag, the seat of government is to be transferred from Bonn, West Germany's post-war provisional capital, to the historical capital, Berlin. The move was originally scheduled for completion by 1998 but in 1993 was postponed for budgetary reasons. The *Bundesrat* (upper house) will remain in Bonn.

The population of the principal cities and towns in the Federal Republic in 1990 was:

Berlin	3,420,600	Leipzig	513,600
Hamburg	1,640,100	Hanover	509,800
Munich	1,219,600	Dresden	493,200
Cologne	950,200	Nuremberg	490,500
Frankfurt am		Chemnitz	296,300
Main	641,300	Bonn	289,500
Essen	626,100	Magdeburg	279,900
Dortmund	597,400	Rostock	248,800
Düsseldorf	575,600	Halle	234,800
Stuttgart	575,100	Erfurt	210,500
Bremen	548,900	Potsdam	139,700
Duisberg	533,600	Schwerin	127,800

CURRENCY – Deutsche Mark (DM) of 100 Pfennig.
FLAG – Horizontal bars of black, red and gold.
NATIONAL ANTHEM – Einigkeit und Recht und Freiheit (Unity and right and freedom).
NATIONAL DAY – 23 May.

HISTORY

The term 'deutsch' (German) probably began to be used in the eighth century and initially described the language spoken in the eastern part of the Frankish realm which reached its apogee in Charlemagne's reign, subsequently being divided into an eastern and western realm whose political and linguistic borders coincided. Then the term was transferred from the language to its speakers, and ultimately to the region they lived in. The first German realm was the Holy Roman Empire, established in AD 962 when Otto I of Saxony was crowned Emperor. The Empire endured until 1806, but from as early as the 12th century the achievement of a national state was prevented by territorial fragmentation into small principalities and dukedoms, the gradually increasing autonomy of their rulers weakening the central power.

The Holy Roman Empire was replaced by a loose association of the individual sovereign states known as the German Confederation, which survived until 1866 when it was dissolved and replaced by the Prussian-dominated North German Federation. Prussia, directed by its Prime Minister (later Chancellor) Otto von Bismarck, had translated its earlier economic predominance amongst the German states into political hegemony by the annexation of the duchies of Schleswig and Holstein from Denmark in 1864 and a decisive defeat of Austria in 1866 (the Seven Weeks' War) which ended Austrian influence over German politics. After the Franco-Prussian War of 1870–1 resulted in the defeat of France and the cession of Alsace and part of Lorraine, the south German principalities united with the northern federation to form a second German Empire, the King of Prussia being proclaimed Emperor at Versailles on 18 January 1871.

Germany's defeat in the 1914–18 War led to the abdication of the Emperor and the princes, and the country became a republic. The 1919 Treaty of Versailles returned Alsace–Lorraine to France, large areas in the east of the country were lost to the newly created state of Poland, and all German colonies placed under the administration of other countries. The world economic crisis of 1929 led to the collapse of the Weimar Republic and the subsequent rise to power of the National Socialist movement of Adolf Hitler, who became Chancellor in 1933.

After concluding a Treaty of Non-Aggression with the Soviet Union in August 1939, Germany invaded Poland (1 September 1939), thus precipitating the Second World War, which lasted until 1945. Hitler committed suicide on 30 April 1945. On 8 May 1945, the unconditional surrender of all German forces was accepted by representatives of the Western Allied and Soviet Supreme Commanders.

the *de jure* division of Germany (as the GDR maintained). The FRG, however, recognized the GDR as a separate and independent state (the two states/one nation theory). The status of Berlin as a city under Four Power occupation remained unchanged, although the GDR claimed East Berlin as its capital and held West Berlin to be a separate political entity.

Soviet-initiated reform in eastern Europe during the late 1980s brought unrest to the GDR. The mass exodus of its citizens via the open borders to the west culminated in the opening of the Berlin Wall in November 1989 and the collapse of Communist government there. The 'Treaty on the Final Settlement with respect to Germany', concluded between the FRG, GDR and the four former occupying powers on 12 September 1990, unified Germany with effect from 3 October 1990 as a fully sovereign state and NATO member occupying the territory of the former two Germanies and Berlin. Economic and monetary union preceded formal union on 1 July 1990. Unification is constitutionally the accession of Berlin and the five re-formed *Länder* of the GDR to the FRG which remains in being. The first government of the new Germany took office in January 1991 following the first all-German elections since 1933 on 2 December 1990. The federal government has encountered formidable problems in its efforts to translate German unity into political, economic and social reality.

THE POST-WAR PERIOD

After the unconditional surrender, the Four Powers (France, UK, USA, USSR) assumed supreme authority in Germany. Policy was agreed at the Potsdam Conference (July/August 1945) between the UK, USA and USSR. Germany was divided into American, French, British and Soviet zones of occupation. Supreme authority was exercised by the Commanders-in-Chief, each in his own zone of occupation and, in matters affecting Germany as a whole, jointly through the Control Council comprising the four Commanders. Berlin was placed under the joint administration of the four occupying powers.

No central German government was permitted but several German central administrations were established as support organs for the Control Council. A peace treaty with Germany was envisaged as concluding the occupation period. However, quadripartite control failed when differences with the USSR over the implementation of the Postdam Agreement could not be resolved; and against a background of growing international tension, the USSR withdrew from the Control Council in March 1948. The rift divided Germany *de facto* into east and west.

The Federal Republic of Germany (FRG) was created out of the three Western zones in 1949 when, following general elections, a federal government took office in Bonn. A Communist government was meanwhile established in the Soviet zone (henceforth the German Democratic Republic (GDR)). The Bonn/Paris Conventions in May 1955 terminated the occupation regime in West Germany and restored federal German autonomy subject to the reservation of Three Power rights and responsibilities relating to Berlin and to Germany as a whole, including the reunification of Germany and a peace settlement. The GDR became an ostensibly sovereign state in the same year.

In August 1961 the Soviet zone was sealed off, and the Berlin Wall was built along the zonal boundary, partitioning the western sectors of the city from the eastern.

In the course of the Brandt government's policy of Ostpolitik, normalizing relations with eastern Europe, the FRG established relations of a special kind with the GDR in 1972. This step did not constitute recognition by the FRG of the GDR, which in international law would have conceded

GOVERNMENT

The Basic Law provides for a President, elected for a five-year term, a lower house (*Bundestag*), with a four-year term of office, elected by direct universal suffrage, and an upper house (*Bundesrat*) composed of 68 delegates of the *Länder*, without a fixed term of office.

The elections held for the Bundestag on 2 December 1990 resulted in the following distribution of seats:

Christian Democratic Union, 258
Social Democrats, 239
Christian Social Union, 51
Free Democrats, 79
Democratic Socialists, 17
The Greens/Alliance 90, 8

HEAD OF STATE

Federal President, Dr Richard von Weizsäcker, *born* 1920, *elected President of West Germany* 22 May 1984, *re-elected* 23 May 1989, *sworn in* 1 July 1989 *for five years.*

CABINET as at July 1993
Federal Chancellor, Dr Helmut Kohl (CDU).
Foreign Affairs and Deputy Chancellor, Dr Klaus Kinkel (FDP).
Federal Chancellery, Friedrich Böhl (CDU).
Interior, Manfred Kanther (CDU).
Economy, Günter Rexrodt (FDP).
Justice, Sabine Leutheusser-Schnarrenberger (FDP).
Finance, Dr Theodor Waigel (CSU).
Agriculture, Jochen Borchert (CSU).
Labour and Social Affairs, Dr Norbert Blüm (CDU).
Defence, Volker Rühe (CDU).
Health, Horst Seehofer (CSU).
Women and Youth, Dr Angela Merkel (CDU).
Family and Elderly, Hannelore Rönsch (CDU).
Transport, Matthias Wissmann (CDU).
Environment, Dr Klaus Töpfer (CDU).
Posts and Telecommunications, Wolfgang Bötsch (CSU).
Housing and Construction, Dr Irmgard Adam-Schwätzer (FDP).
Research, Paul Krüger (CDU).
Education, Dr Rainer Ortleb (FDP).
Economic Co-operation, Carl-Dieter Spranger (CSU).

CDU: Christian Democratic Union; CSU: Christian Social Union; FDP: Free Democratic Party.

EMBASSY OF THE FEDERAL REPUBLIC OF GERMANY
23 Belgrave Square, London SW1X 8PZ
Tel 071-235 5033/824 1300

Ambassador Extraordinary and Plenipotentiary, His Excellency Dr Peter Hartmann, KBE (1993).
Minister, Dr Friedrich Kroneck.
Minister-Counsellor, Gerhard Kunz.
First Counsellors, Dr R. W. Ehni (*Cultural Affairs*); B. Westphal (*Economic Affairs*).
Defence Attaché, Rear-Adm. K. M. Reichert.

BRITISH EMBASSY
Friedrich-Ebert-Allee 77, 5300 Bonn 1
Tel: Bonn 23 40 61

Ambassador Extraordinary and Plenipotentiary, His Excellency Sir Nigel Broomfield, KCMG (1993).
Minister, J. A. Shepherd, CMG.
Defence Attaché, Brig. P. P. Rawlins, MBE.
Counsellor (Economic), P. Collecott.
Counsellor (Management and Consular), P. V. Rollitt.

BRITISH CONSULATE-GENERAL
Yorck Strasse 19, 4000 Düsseldorf 30

Consul-General and Director-General of Trade and Investment Promotion, A. C. Hunt, CMG.

BRITISH EMBASSY OFFICE, BERLIN
Olympic Stadium, Hanns-Braun Strasse, 1000 Berlin 19
International Trade Centre, Georgenstrasse, 1028 Berlin

Minister and Head of Mission, R. J. Spencer, CMG.
Counsellor, Sir John Ramsden, Bt. (*Deputy Head of Mission*).
First Secretary (Economic), P. Bateman.

There are British Consulates-General at *Berlin, Düsseldorf, Frankfurt, Hamburg, Munich* and *Stuttgart* and Consulates at *Bremen, Hanover, Kiel* and *Nuremberg*.

BRITISH COUNCIL REPRESENTATIVE, K. Dobson, Hahnenstrasse 6, 50667 Köln. Offices at *Berlin, Leipzig, Hamburg* and *Munich* and British Council libraries at all five centres.

BRITISH CHAMBER OF COMMERCE, Neumarkt 14, D-5000 Köln 1. *Director*, Herr Heumann.

THE LANDER

The distribution of the population among the *Länder* at the end of 1990 was:

Baden-Württemberg	9.5m
Bavaria	11.2m
Berlin	3.4m
Brandenburg	2.6m
Bremen	0.65m
Hamburg	1.6m
Hesse	5.6m
Lower Saxony	7.2m
Mecklenburg–Western Pomerania	2.1m
North Rhine Westphalia	16.9m
Rhineland Palatinate	3.7m
Saarland	1.1m
Saxony	4.9m
Saxony-Anhalt	3.0m
Schleswig-Holstein	2.6m
Thuringia	2.5m

The Ministers-President (Prime Ministers) of the *Länder* governments in July 1993, were:
Baden-Württemberg – Erwin Teufel (CDU).

Bavaria – Edmund Stoiber (CSU).
Berlin – Eberhard Diepgen (CDU) (*Governing Mayor*).
Brandenburg – Manfred Stolpe (SPD).
Bremen – Klaus Wedemeier (*Mayor*) (SPD).
Hamburg – Henning Voscherau (*First Mayor*) (SPD).
Hesse – Hans Eichel (SPD).
Lower Saxony – Gerhard Schröder (SPD).
Mecklenburg-Western Pomerania – Berndt Seite (CDU).
North Rhine-Westphalia – Johannes Rau (SPD).
Rhineland-Palatinate – Rudolf Scharping (SPD).
Saarland – Oskar Lafontaine (SPD).
Saxony – Kurt Biedenkopf (CDU).
Saxony-Anhalt – Werner Münch (CDU).
Schleswig-Holstein – Heidi Simonis (SPD).
Thuringia – Bernhardt Vogel (CDU).

JUDICATURE

Judicial authority is exercised by the Federal Constitutional Court, the Federal courts provided for in the Basic Law and the courts of the Länder. The death sentence has been abolished.

DEFENCE

Under the terms of the Treaty of Unification the German armed forces are to be reduced from the present active total of 447,000 (201,700 conscripts) to 370,000 by the end of 1994, at which time the last of the former Soviet armed forces will leave Germany. Germany at present is in the process of absorbing the former GDR armed forces, for which separate totals are shown because they remain non-NATO forces.

The Army has a strength of 316,000 including 163,300 conscripts, 64,000 territorials and 41,000 Eastern Command. It deploys 7,000 main battle tanks, 4,600 artillery pieces, 14,200 armoured personnel carriers and infantry fighting vehicles, and 832 helicopters. The Field Army of 203,400 personnel is organized into six armoured, four armoured infantry, one airborne and one mountain division. The Territorial Army is organized into ten home defence brigades and 15 home defence regiments. The Navy has a strength of 35,200 including 8,900 conscripts and 1,900 Eastern Command, with 22 submarines, 14 principal surface combatants and 118 aircraft and 19 armed helicopters. The Air Force has a strength of 95,800 including 29,000 conscripts and 9,300 Eastern Command, with 653 combat aircraft. Organization is in three commands: tactical command with one early warning, three reconnaissance, six air defence and 18 ground attack squadrons; transport command with five wings; and training command.

There remain some 256,000 NATO personnel in Germany (USA 148,400; UK 62,800). The number is to be reduced to around 110,000 by the end of the decade, while the remaining 177,000 former Soviet personnel should all leave by the end of August 1994.

During 1993 both the Constitutional Court and the Bundestag agreed that German armed forces may operate outside Germany and the NATO area in UN and other peace-keeping operations for the first time since 1945. The wish to fulfil a stronger international role means that by August 1993 German personnel were engaged in UN operations in Somalia and Cambodia, in NATO AWACS aircraft over the former Yugoslavia, and in NATO and WEU patrols in the Adriatic enforcing the UN blockade against the rump Yugoslav state.

ECONOMY

Despite the division of Germany, which cut off from the West the main food-producing areas of eastern Germany and some of the principal centres of light industry, West Germany restored Germany's position as the main industrial power in Europe. It is the most economically powerful member of the European Community.

Unification costs have, however, severely strained Federal German resources, increasingly weakened by apparent structural problems. Funding of East Germany from the West amounts to around DM 180 billion per annum, over 5 per cent of GDP, under a massive government investment programme. After a mini-boom generated by new East German demand in 1990 and 1991, West Germany is facing its most severe recession since the war. The first Federal budgetary and trade deficits for over ten years have resulted in tax increases, rising interest rates and serious inflationary pressures (4.2 per cent in May 1993). In March 1993 a 'Solidarity Pact' agreement was reached by Federal and Länder governments, opposition parties, and employers and trade unions, to take effect from 1995 onwards. The pact lays down the basis of future funding transfers to the East based on a 7.5 per cent rise in income taxes, wage restraint in the West, more private investment in the East, and the distribution of the funding burden between the Federal and Länder governments. The serious recession led to the 1993 decision by employers in the steel and automobile industries to delay the staged increase in Eastern wage levels to reach Western levels, which caused strikes. In 1992 Federal GNP stood at DM 3,021,800m (West 2,774,900m; East 246,900m).

As East Germany struggles to adapt to free market conditions, output has fallen to 40 per cent of pre-unification levels. The sudden loss of established East European trading outlets following the introduction of the Deutsche Mark, and the rapid rise of East German labour costs without corresponding increases in productivity, were largely responsible for this. Unemployment is nearly 15 per cent (mid-1993), but much higher if job creation schemes and part-time working are taken into account. Inflation at 8.5 per cent is twice that in West Germany. Growth of 6 per cent in industry is short of expectation and there is no sign of a self-sustaining recovery. Present estimates are that East Germany's survival will continue to depend on the injection of West German capital at present levels for the next ten years.

INDUSTRIAL PRODUCTION

The Federal Republic has a predominantly industrial economy. Principal industries are coal mining, iron and steel production, machine construction, the electrical industry, the manufacture of steel and metal products, chemicals and textiles, and the processing of foodstuffs. The index of industrial net production adjusted for irregularities of the calendar (1985 = 100) is as follows:

West Germany	1991	1992
Mining	82.4	79.6
Manufacturing industry	121.9	120.3
Basic materials	112.0	113.7
Capital goods	125.7	122.5
Consumer goods	123.0	120.3
Foodstuffs	129.1	127.9
Power (electricity and gas)	114.6	116.2
Construction	127.3	136.4
Total industry	120.6	119.9

Annual production figures were ('000 tonnes):

All Germany	1991	1992
Hard coal	66,438	65,906
Brown coal	107,525	241,745
Crude petroleum	3,606	3,424
Pig iron	29,878	27,586
Raw steel	40,939	38,819
Rolled steel	32,747	28,959
Petrol	24,306	25,329
Cement	34,240	37,194

AGRICULTURE

In 1991 total area of farmland was 14m hectares, of which 7.3m hectares (West Germany) and 4.3 million (East Germany) were arable land. Forest areas cover 10.4m hectares.

Crop yields were ('000 tonnes):

West Germany	1990	1991
Rye	1,944.0	1,856.8
Wheat	11,053.0	11,840.4
Barley	9,195.0	9,428.5
Oats	1,535.0	1,581.9
Potatoes	7,233.0	7,481.6
Sugar beet	20,310.0	19,837.7
Colza and rape	1,720.0	2,012.8
East Germany	1990	1991
Rye	2,043.0	1,467.3
Wheat	4,189.0	4,770.0
Barley	4,797.0	5,065.1
Oats	570.0	284.8
Potatoes	6,806.0	2,719.5
Sugar beet	7,290.0	6,088.0
Colza and rape	368.0	959.7

Milk production in 1991 was 28,916,000 tonnes. Total yield of fisheries in 1991 was 199,702 tonnes, valued at DM285,896,000.

LABOUR

Labour figures, in annual averages, were:

West Germany	1991	1992
Employment	28,989,000	29,115,000
Unemployed	1,689,000	1,808,000
East Germany	1991	1992
Unemployed	913,000	1,170,000
Short-time workers	1,616,000	370,000

In 1992 the unemployment rate in the West was 6.6 per cent and in the East was 14.8 per cent.

FINANCE

All Germany	1992	1993p
Expenditure	DM427 billion	DM458 billion
Revenue	389 billion	390 billion

p planned

TRADE (East and West Germany)

	1991	1992
Total imports	DM643,914m	DM637,814m
Total exports	665,813m	670,637m

Of 1992 imports, 10.9 per cent were foodstuffs, 5.6 per cent raw materials and 72.8 per cent manufactured goods. Main trading partners in 1992 were (figures shown as percentage of total trade):

	Imports	Exports
France	12.0	13.0
Netherlands	9.6	8.3
Italy	9.2	9.3
Belgium/Luxembourg	7.0	7.4
UK	6.8	7.7
USA	6.6	6.4
Japan	6.0	6.2

	1991	1992
Trade with UK		
Imports from UK	£14,653,972,000	£15,060,073,000
Exports to UK	17,741,093,000	19,034,628,000

COMMUNICATIONS

At the end of 1990 the state-owned railways of the Federal Republic (*Deutsche Bundesbahn and Reichsbahn*) measured 41,273 kilometres of which 15,711 kilometres were electrified, and the privately owned railways totalled approximately 2,845 kilometres. In 1989 the railways handled 649.4 million tonnes of goods. State railways rolling stock included, in 1990, 3,486 electric locomotives, 7,742 diesel locomotives and 364,290 goods wagons.

Classified roads measured 221,062 kilometres (West and East) in 1991, of which motorways were 10,854 kilometres. The total number of motor vehicles registered at the beginning of 1992 was over 45 million.

Ocean-going shipping under the German flag in December 1990, amounted to 5,740,000 tons gross. Inland waterways handled 251.9m tonnes of goods in 1990.

SOCIAL WELFARE

There is compulsory insurance against sickness, accident, old age and unemployment. Children's allowances, child rearing benefits and parental leave of absence are available in respect of all children. Pension schemes for widows and orphans of public servants are in operation. Public assistance is given to persons unable to earn their living, or with insufficient income to maintain a decent standard of living.

EDUCATION

School attendance is compulsory for all children and juveniles between the ages of six and 18 and comprises nine years full-time compulsory education at primary and main schools and three years of compulsory vocational education on a part-time basis. In 1990 there were 20,493 primary and main schools (*Grund und Hauptschulen*) with 3,807,134 pupils. Secondary modern schools (*Realschulen*) numbered 2,567 with 864,611 pupils. There were 2,900 other general secondary schools (*Gymnasien* including *Gesamtschulen*) with 1,846,100 pupils.

There were also 3,187 special schools (*Sonderschulen*) for physically and mentally handicapped and socially maladjusted children in the Federal Republic with 317,385 pupils.

The secondary school leaving examination (*Abitur*) entitles the holder to a place of study at a university or another institution of higher education.

Children below the age of 18 who are not attending a general secondary or a full-time vocational school have compulsory day-release at a vocational school. In 1990 there were 3,596 full- and part-time vocational schools (*Berufsschulen*) with 1,858,718 pupils and 259 vocational extension schools (*Berufsaufbauschulen*) with 7,825 pupils, 1,853 full-time vocational schools (*Berufsfachschulen*) with 245,606 pupils, 1,002 schools for secondary technical studies (*Fachoberschulen/Fachgymnasien*) with 200,456 students.

In 1991-2 there were a total of 1,782,739 students at institutions of higher education, of whom 1,197,108 were attending universities. The largest universities are in Munich, Berlin, Hamburg, Bonn and Cologne.

CULTURE

Modern (or New High) German has developed from the time of the Reformation to the present day, with differences of dialect in Austria, Alsace and the German-speaking cantons of Switzerland.

The literary language is usually regarded as having become fixed by Luther and Zwingli at the Reformation, since which time many great names occur in all branches, notably philosophy, from Leibnitz (1646–1716) to Kant (1724–1804), Fichte (1762–1814), Schelling (1775–1854) and Hegel (1770–1831); the drama from Goethe (1749–1832) and Schiller (1759–1805) to Gerhart Hauptmann (1862–1946); and in poetry, Heine (1797–1856). German authors have received the Nobel Prize for Literature on seven occasions: Theodor Mommsen (1902), R. Eucken (1908), P. Heyse (1909), Gerhart Hauptmann (1912), Thomas Mann (1929), N. Sachs (1966) and Heinrich Böll (1972).

GHANA
The Republic of Ghana

Ghana (formerly known as the Gold Coast) is situated on the Gulf of Guinea, between 3° 07′ W. and 1° 14′ E. longitude (about 334 miles), and extends 441 miles north from Cape Three Points (4° 45′ N.) to 11° 11′ N. It is bounded on the north by Burkina, on the west by the Côte d'Ivoire, on the east by Togo, and on the south by the Atlantic Ocean. Although a tropical country, Ghana is cooler than many countries within similar latitudes. Ghana has a total area of 92,099 sq. miles (238,537 sq. km).

POPULATION – The population was (UN estimate) 15,509,000 in 1991. Most Ghanaians are Sudanese Negroes, although Hamitic strains are common in northern Ghana. The official language is English. The principal indigenous language group is Akan, of which Twi and Fanti are the most commonly used. Ga, Ewe and languages of the Mole-Dagbani group are common in certain regions.

CAPITAL – ΨAccra. Population of the Greater Accra Region (including Tema) was (1990 estimate) 1,781,100. Other towns are Kumasi, Tamale, ΨSekondi-Takoradi, ΨCape Coast, Sunyani, Ho, Koforidua, Tarkwa and ΨWinneba.

CURRENCY – Cedi of 100 pesewas.

FLAG – Equal horizontal bands of red over gold over green; five-point black star on gold stripe.

NATIONAL ANTHEM – Hail the Name of Ghana.

NATIONAL DAY – 6 March (Independence Day).

GOVERNMENT

There is no recorded history of the Gold Coast region before the coming of Europeans in the 15th century. The constituent parts of the state came under British administration at various times, the original Gold Coast Colony (the coastal and southern areas) being first constituted in 1874; Ashanti in 1901; and the Northern Territories Protectorate in 1901. The territory of Trans-Volta-Togoland, part of the former German colony of Togo, was mandated to Britain by the League of Nations after the First World War, and remained under British administration as a United Nations Trusteeship after the Second World War. After a plebiscite in May 1956, under the auspices of the United Nations, the territory was integrated with the Gold Coast Colony. The former Gold

Coast Colony and associated territories became the independent state of Ghana and a member of the British Commonwealth on 6 March 1957 and adopted a republican constitution on 1 July 1960.

Since 1966 Ghana has experienced long periods of military rule divided by short-lived civilian governments. A coup in June 1979 led to the formation of an Armed Forces Revolutionary Council chaired by Flt. Lt. Jerry Rawlings. Civilian rule was restored in September 1979 but overthrown on 31 December 1981, when another coup brought back into power Flt. Lt. Rawlings.

A referendum in April 1992 approved a new multi-party constitution, with political parties being allowed to form legally from May 1992. The National Democratic Congress (NDC) was established from the ruling Provisional National Defence Council as a political party led by Flt. Lt. Rawlings. Flt. Lt. Rawlings subsequently won presidential elections in November 1992 and the National Democratic Congress won parliamentary elections in December 1992. The parliamentary elections were, however, boycotted by most opposition parties and most of the electorate, who protested that Rawlings should not have been able to stand for the presidency; only 29 per cent of the electorate voted when the NDC won 189 of the 200 parliamentary seats. The Fourth Republic was declared on 7 January 1993 and a new government nominated by the President was approved by parliament and sworn in by the President on 22 March 1993. As executive President, Flt. Lt. (retd) Rawlings also chairs the cabinet.

HEAD OF STATE
President, Flt. Lt. (retd) Jerry John Rawlings, *elected* 3 November 1992.
Vice-President, K. N. Arkaah.

CABINET *as at August 1993*
The President.
The Vice-President.
Defence, Mahama Iddrisu.
Finance and Economic Planning, Dr Kwesi Botchwey.
Foreign Affairs, Dr Obed Asamoah.
Attorney-General and Justice, Anthony Forson.
Information, Kofi Quakyi.
Parliamentary Affairs, J. H. Owusu-Acheampong.
Interior, Col. (retd) E. M. Osei-Wusu.
Trade and Industries, Emma Mitchell.
Transport and Communications, Edward Salia.
Mines and Energy, Richard Kwame Peprah.
Education, Harry Sawyerr.
Local Government and Rural Development, Kwamena Ahwoi.
Food and Agriculture, Ibrahim Adam.
Employment and Social Welfare, David Boateng.
Environment, Christine Amoaka-Nuamah.
Health, Commodore (retd) S. G. Obimpeh.
Lands and Forestry, David Amankwa.

Speaker of the Legislature, Daniel Annan.

GHANA HIGH COMMISSION
104 Highgate Hill, London N6 5HE
Tel 081-342 8686

High Commissioner, new appointment awaited.
Acting High Commissioner, Johnson Osei-Hwedieh.
Defence Adviser, Col. H. W. K. Agbevey.
Counsellor, A. K. Budu-Amoako (*Trade*).

BRITISH HIGH COMMISSION
PO Box 296, Osu Link, Accra
Tel: Accra 221665

High Commissioner, His Excellency David Walker, CVO (1992).
Deputy High Commissioner, M. J. Greenstreet.
Defence Adviser, Lt.-Col. T. E. Hawkins, MBE
First Secretary (Management/Consular), D. J. Walker.
First Secretary (Commercial), S. S. Strong.

BRITISH COUNCIL REPRESENTATIVE, T. Cowin, Liberia Road (PO Box 771), Accra. There is also an office in *Kumasi.*

ECONOMY

Agriculture forms the basis of Ghana's economy, employing 70 per cent of the working population. Crops of the forest zone include cocoa, which is the largest single source of revenue, rice and a variety of other foodstuff crops grown on mixed-crop farms. Fruits such as avocado pears, oranges and pineapples are grown. Cassava is the most important crop of the coastal savannas zone, of the lower Volta area. Production of pulses such as groundnuts is widespread. Near the Togo border oil palms, yams, maize, cassava, fruit and vegetables are produced. Livestock is raised in the uncultivated areas. The northern savanna zone is Ghana's principal cattle-rearing area and other livestock production there is important for home consumption. Corn and millet crops are produced in the far north and maize, yams, rice and groundnut crops in more southerly parts of the zone.

Attempts are being made to diversify agricultural production, with cash crops being extensively cultivated for export and to provide raw materials for local industry.

Fishing is important in coastal areas and in the Volta itself. However, production cannot meet demand and there are considerable imports of fish products. About 80 per cent of home supply is obtained from sea fisheries, but production from the Volta Lake and other inland fisheries is increasing.

The area within a 60-mile radius of Dunkwa produces 90 per cent of Ghana's mineral exports. Manganese production from Nsuta ranks among the world's highest and gold, industrial diamonds and bauxite are also produced. Some 30,000 persons are employed by the mining companies.

Examples of the small-scale traditional industries are tailoring, goldsmithing and carpentry. Priority has been given in recent years to the establishment of a number of 'pioneer industries' including timber products, vehicle and refrigerator assembly, cigarettes, boatbuilding, food processing, cotton textiles, clothing, footwear, printing and other light industries. A modern industrial complex is growing in the Accra-Tema area.

Since 1966 the Volta Dam at Akosombo has generated hydro-electric power for the processing of bauxite and fed a power transmission network for the Accra-Kumasi-Takoradi area. Electricity is now also sent to Togo and Benin.

TRADE

Principal exports are cocoa, timber and gold. Principal imports are road vehicles, manufacturing equipment, petroleum and raw materials.

Trade with UK	1991	1992
Imports from UK	£169,296,000	£174,098,000
Exports to UK	77,345,000	81,881,000

COMMUNICATIONS

The Kotoka Airport at Accra is an international airport and Ghana Airways Corporation is the national airline. There are also internal airports at Takoradi, Kumasi, Sunyani, and Tamale.

There are 20,000 miles of motorable roads, of which 2,335 miles are bitumenized. There are 600 miles of railway, linking Accra and the principal ports of Takoradi and Tema with their hinterlands, and with each other.

Takoradi Harbour consists of seven quay berths – one is leased specially for manganese exports. Tema Harbour has ten berths for larger ocean-going vessels and the largest dry dock on the West African coast. An oil berth has also been built to serve the Ghaip refinery which has been constructed at Tema.

GREECE
Elliniki Dimokratia

Greece is a maritime state in the south-east of Europe, bounded on the north by Albania, Macedonia and Bulgaria, on the south and west by the Ionian and Mediterranean seas, and on the east by Turkey. It has an estimated area of 50,944 sq. miles (131,944 sq. km).

The main areas of Greece are: *Macedonia* (which includes Mt Athos and the island of Thasos), *Thrace* (including the island of Samothrace), *Epirus, Thessaly, Continental Greece* (which includes the island of Euboea and the Sporades or 'scattered islands' of which the largest is Skyros), the *Peloponnese* (or *Morea*), the *Dodecanese* or *Southern Sporades* (12 islands occupied by Italy in 1911 during the Italo-Turkish War and ceded to Greece by Italy in 1947) consisting of Rhodes, Astypalaia, Karpathos, Kassos, Nisyros, Kalymnos, Leros, Patmos, Kos, Symi, Khalki and Tilos, the *Cyclades* (a circular group numbering about 200, with a total area of 923 sq. miles; the chief islands are Syros, Andros, Tinos, Naxos, Paros, Santorini, Milos and Serifos), the *Ionian Islands* (Corfu, Paxos, Levkas, Ithaca, Cephalonia, Zante and Cerigo), the *Aegean Islands* (Chios, Lesbos, Limnos and Samos). In *Crete* there was for over 1,500 years (3000 to 1400 BC) a flourishing civilization which spread its influence far and wide throughout the Aegean, and the ruins of the palace of Minos at Knossos afford evidence of astonishing comfort and luxury.

POPULATION – The population at the 1991 census was 10,256,464.

RELIGION – Over 97 per cent of the people are adherents of the Greek Orthodox Church, which is the state religion, all others being tolerated and free from interference. The Church of Greece recognizes the spiritual primacy of the Ecumenical Patriarch of Constantinople, but is otherwise a self-governing body administered by the Holy Synod under the presidency of the Archbishop of Athens and All Greece. It has no jurisdiction over the Church of Crete, which has a degree of autonomy under the Ecumenical Patriarch, nor over the monastic community of Mount Athos and the Church in the Dodecanese, both of which come directly under the Ecumenical Patriarch.

CAPITAL – Athens, population (including ΨPiraeus and suburbs), 3,096,775 (1991 Census). Other large towns are (1991) ΨThessalonika (Salonika) (977,528); ΨPatras (172,763); ΨVolos (115,732); Larissa (269,300); and ΨKavalla (135,747).

Larger towns in the islands are: in Crete, ΨHeraklion or Candia (263,868), ΨCanea (133,060), and ΨRethymnon (69,290); in the Ionian Islands, ΨCorfu (36,901); in the Dodecanese, ΨRhodes (43,619); in the Cyclades, ΨSyros Hermoupolis (16,008); in Lesbos, ΨMytilene (25,440); in Chios, ΨChios (27,405).

CURRENCY – Drachma of 100 leptae.

FLAG – Blue and white stripes with a white cross on a blue field in the canton.

NATIONAL ANTHEM – Imnos Eis Tin Eleftherian (Hymn to Freedom).

NATIONAL DAY – March 25 (Independence Day).

GOVERNMENT

A military coup on 21 April 1967 suspended parliamentary government and, following an unsuccessful royal counter-coup on 13 December 1967, King Constantine went into voluntary exile in Rome. On 1 June 1973 the monarchy was abolished and a republic established under the presidency of George Papadopoulos.

The overthrow of Archbishop Makarios, President of Cyprus, on 15 July 1974, by a military coup led by Greek officers of the Cypriot National Guard caused an international crisis, in the wake of which the heads of the Greek armed forces decided, on 23 July, to relinquish power. Konstantinos Karamanlis (Prime Minister 1955–63) returned from his self-imposed exile in Paris to form a provisional government, and the first elections for ten years were held on 17 November 1974. The constitutional position of the King, who was still in exile, remained unsettled until 8 December, when by a referendum, the Greek people rejected 'crowned democracy' by 69.2 per cent to 30.8 per cent and Greece became a republic. A new constitution came into force on 11 June 1975. In 1986 the powers of the presidency were greatly reduced with most executive power transferred to the government and the President becoming a ceremonial figure.

The unicameral 300-member Chamber of Deputies is elected for a four-year term by universal adult suffrage under a system of proportional representation. The most recent general election was held on 8 April 1990.

HEAD OF STATE
President of the Hellenic Republic, Constantine Karamanlis, elected 4 May 1990.

CABINET *as at August 1993*

Prime Minister and Minister for the Aegean, Constantine Mitsotakis.
Deputy PM, Tzannis Tzannetakis.
Minister to the PM, Sotiris Kouvelas.
Foreign Affairs, Michalis Papaconstantinou.
Interior, Ioannis Kefaloyiannis.
National Defence, Ioannis Varvitsiotis.
Justice, Anna Psarouda-Benaki.
National Economy, Finance, Stephanos Manos.
Merchant Marine, Alexandros Papadongonas.
Agriculture, Christos Koskinos.
Labour, Aristides Kalantzakos.
Health, Welfare and Social Security, Dimitris Sioufas.
Education and Religious Affairs, Georg Souflias.
Culture, Dora Bakoyiannis.
Public Order, Nikolaas Gelestathis.
Macedonia and Thrace, Panayiotis Hadzinikolaou.
Environment, Town Planning and Public Works, Achileas Karamanlis.
Industry and Commerce, Vassilis Kontoyiannopoulos.
Transport and Communications, Theodore Anagnostopoulos.

EMBASSY OF GREECE
1A Holland Park, London W11 3TP
Tel 071-229 3850
Ambassador Extraordinary and Plenipotentiary, His Excellency Elias Gounaris (1993).
Deputy Ambassador, A. Scopelitis.
Defence Attaché, Capt. I. Theofanides.
Consul-General, G. Costoulas.
Counsellor, Miss A. Missa-Kerkentzes (*Economic Affairs*).

There are Honorary Consuls at *Belfast, Birmingham, Edinburgh, Falmouth, Glasgow, Leeds* and *Southampton*.

BRITISH EMBASSY
1 Ploutarchou Street, 10675 Athens
Tel: Athens 7236211

Ambassador Extraordinary and Plenipotentiary, His
Excellency Oliver Miles, CMG (1993).
Deputy Head of Mission, Counsellor and Consul-General, C. J.
Denne, CMG.
Defence and Military Attaché, Brig. N. M. Prideaux.
First Secretary (Commercial), N. J. G. Bowie.

BRITISH CONSULAR OFFICES – There are British Consular
Offices at *Athens, Corfu, Patras, Samos, Rhodes, Salonika,
Heraklion* (Crete), *Syros* and *Volos*.

BRITISH COUNCIL, 17 Plateia Philikis Etairias (PO Box
3488), Kolonaki Square, Athens 10210. *Representative*, Dr
J. L. Munby, OBE (*Counsellor, Cultural Affairs*).
There is also an office at *Salonika* and British Council
libraries at both centres.

BRITISH-HELLENIC CHAMBER OF COMMERCE, 25 Vas.
Sofias Avenue, GR-106 74 Athens. Tel: 72 10 361.

DEFENCE

The total active armed forces number some 159,300
personnel (125,800 conscripts). The strength of the Army is
113,000, including 100,000 conscripts; in addition there are
some 34,000 in the National Guard. The Army is organized
into a field army of one mechanized, two infantry, one marine
and five armoured brigades and nine infantry divisions, and
a territorial defence of one infantry division and one
parachute regiment. Equipment includes 1,900 main battle
tanks, 2,090 armoured personnel carriers and armoured
infantry fighting vehicles, and 1,910 artillery pieces. The
Navy consists of 19,500 men (11,400 conscripts) and is
equipped with ten submarines and 13 principal surface
combatant vessels with 15 armed helicopters. The Air Force
consists of 26,800 men (14,400 conscripts) and is equipped
with aircraft disposed in 21 combat squadrons supported by
the necessary transport, training, helicopter and reconnaissance squadrons, a total of 381 combat aircraft. National
service is two years on average.
Greece maintains 2,250 Army personnel in Cyprus. There
is also a paramilitary Gendarmerie of 26,500 personnel.
Some 1,250 US personnel are stationed in Greece.

COMMUNICATIONS

The 2,650 kilometres of Greek railways are state-owned with
the exception of the Athens–Piraeus Electric Railway. Greek

roads total somewhat over 35,500 kilometres, of which about
25 per cent are classified as national highways and just under
30,000 km are classified as provincial roads. The road
connection with Albania was reopened in 1985.
On 31 December 1986 the Greek mercantile fleet
numbered 2,138 ships with a total tonnage of 24,792,516 tons
gross. On the same day Greek-owned ships over 100 tons
gross and registered under foreign flags numbered 276 with
a total tonnage of 5,176,347 tons gross. Athens has direct
airline links with Australasia, North America, most countries
in Europe, Africa and the Middle East.

EDUCATION

Education is free and compulsory from the age of six to 15
and is maintained by state grants. There are six universities,
Athens, Salonika, Patras, Thrace, Ioannina and Crete. There
are several other institutes of higher learning, mostly in
Athens.

ECONOMY

Though there has in recent years been a substantial measure
of industrialization, agriculture still employs about a quarter
of the working population. The most important agricultural
products are tobacco, wheat, cotton, sugar and rice. The most
important of the fruit trees are the olive, peach, vine, orange,
lemon, fig, almond and currant-vine. Exports of fresh fruit
and vegetables are an important contributor to the economy
and have considerable growth potential. Currants, grown
mainly around Patras, remain one of Greece's main exports,
the United Kingdom being the principal purchaser.
The principal minerals mined in Greece are nickel,
bauxite, iron ore, iron pyrites, manganese magnesite, chrome,
lead, zinc and emery, and prospecting for petroleum is being
carried on. Oil refineries are in operation near Athens and at
Salonika, where there is also a petro-chemical plant.
The chief industries are textiles (cotton, woollen and
synthetics), chemicals, cement, glass, metallurgy, shipbuilding, domestic electrical equipment and footwear. In recent
years new factories have been opened for the production of
aluminium, nickel, iron and steel products, tyres, chemicals,
fertilizers and sugar (from locally-grown beet). Food processing and ancillary industries have also grown up throughout
the country.
The development of the country's electric power resources,
irrigation and land reclamation schemes and the exploitation
of Greece's lignite resources for fuel and industrial purposes
are also being carried out. Tourism has developed rapidly,
but is now slowing down.

TRADE	1991	1992
Total imports	Drs3,761,200m	Drs4,285,100m
Total exports	1,580,000m	1,816,400m
Trade with UK	*1991*	*1992*
Imports from UK	£667,741,000	£770,742,000
Exports to UK	378,146,000	372,191,000

CULTURE

Greek civilization emerged about 1300 BC and the poems of
Homer, the blind poet of Chios, which were probably current
about 800 BC, record the ten-year struggle between the
Achaeans of Greece and the Phrygians of Troy (1194 to 1184
BC).
The spoken language of modern Greece is descended by
a process of natural development from the Common Greek
of Alexander's empire. *Katharevousa*, a conservative literary
dialect evolved by Adamantios Corais (Diamant Coray), who
lived and died in Paris (1748–1833) and used for official and

technical matters, has been phased out. Novels and poetry are mostly composed in *dimotiki*, a progressive literary dialect which owes much to John Psycharis (1854–1929). The poets Solomos, Palamas, Cavafis, Sikelianos, Seferis and Elytis have won a European reputation.

GRENADA
The State of Grenada

Grenada is situated between 12°13'–11° 58' N. latitude and 61° 20'–61° 35' W. longitude, and is about 90 miles north of Trinidad, 68 miles south-south-west of St Vincent, and about 120 miles south-west of Barbados. The island is about 21 miles in length and 12 miles in breadth, with an area of 133 sq. miles (344 sq. km). Also included in the territory of Grenada are some of the Grenadines islets, the largest of which is Carriacou, 13 square miles in area. The country is mountainous and very picturesque.

POPULATION – The population is estimated at 84,000 (1991 UN estimate).

CAPITAL – ΨSt George's (population 10,000) lies on the south-west coast, and possesses a good harbour.

CURRENCY – East Caribbean dollar (EC$) of 100 cents.

FLAG – Divided diagonally into yellow and green triangles within a red border containing six yellow stars, a yellow star on a red disc in the centre and a nutmeg on the green triangle in the hoist.

NATIONAL DAY – 7 February (Independence Day).

GOVERNMENT

Grenada was discovered by Columbus in 1498, and named Conception. It was originally colonized by the French, and was ceded to Great Britain by the Treaty of Versailles in 1783. It became an Associated State in 1967 and an independent nation within the Commonwealth on 7 February 1974.

The government was overthrown on 13 March 1979 by the New Jewel Movement and a People's Revolutionary Government was set up. Disagreements within the PRG led, in October 1983, to violence and the death of the Prime Minister, whose government was replaced by a Revolutionary Military Council. These events prompted the intervention of Caribbean and US forces. The Governor-General installed an advisory council to act as an interim government until a general election was held, on 3 December 1984. A phased withdrawal of US forces was completed by June 1985.

The Queen is Head of State and is represented by a Governor-General. Legislative power is vested in a bicameral parliament consisting of an elected House of Representatives and a 13-member Senate. The most recent general election was held in March 1990.

Governor-General, Sir Reginald Palmer, GCMG (1993).

CABINET *as at August 1993*

Prime Minister, Minister for External Affairs, Finance and Planning, National Security, Carriacou and Petit Martinique Affairs, Rt. Hon. Nicholas Brathwaite, OBE.
Agriculture, Trade, Industry and Production, Hon. George Brizan.
Attorney-General, Minister for Legal Affairs, Local Government, Dr the Hon. Francis Alexis.
Communications, Works, Public Utilities and Women's Affairs, Hon. Joan Purcell.

Tourism, Civil Aviation, Social Development, Youth Affairs, Sports and Culture, Sen. Tillman Thomas.
Health, Housing, the Environment, Hon. Phinsley St Louis.
Labour, Co-operatives, Social Security, Community Development, Hon. Edzel Thomas.
Education, Information, Sen. the Hon. Carlyle Glean.
Minister of State (Finance), vacant.

GRENADA HIGH COMMISSION
1 Collingham Gardens, London SW5 0AW
Tel 071-373 7808/9/0

High Commissioner, Her Excellency Maureen Emmanuel (1993).

BRITISH HIGH COMMISSION
14 Church Street, St George's
Tel: St George's 3222

High Commissioner (resides at Bridgetown, Barbados).
Resident Representative, A. H. Drury (*First Secretary*).

ECONOMY

The economy is principally agrarian, with cocoa, nutmegs and bananas the major crops. Fruit and vegetables are grown and a little livestock raised for domestic consumption. The fishing industry is being developed. Manufacturing is mostly confined to processing agricultural products.

Tourism has prospered since the opening in 1984 of the Point Salines International Airport. A hotel expansion programme is planned. The number of cruise ships visiting Grenada in 1988 was 234.

TRADE

Total value of imports in 1988 was EC$248.6 million. Principal domestic exports for 1988 were nutmeg (EC$31.3m), cocoa (EC$8.75m), mace (EC$7.3m) and fruit (EC$3.8m).

Trade with UK	1991	1992
Imports from UK	£7,730,000	£5,546,000
Exports to UK	4,236,000	3,519,000

GUATEMALA
República de Guatemala

Guatemala, in Central America, is situated in 13° 45' to 17° 49' N. latitude and 88° 12' 49" to 92°13' 43" W. longitude and has an area of 42,042 sq. miles (108,889 sq. km), and a population (estimate 1992) of 9,745,000.

The country is traversed from west to east by an elevated mountain chain, containing several volcanic summits rising to 13,000 feet above sea level; earthquakes are frequent. The country is well watered by numerous rivers; the climate is hot and malarial near the coast, temperate in the higher regions. The rainfall in the capital averages 57 in per annum.

LANGUAGE AND LITERACY – Spanish is the language of the country, but 40 per cent of the population speak an Indian language. Since the establishment of the university in the capital, education has received a marked impulse and the high figure of illiteracy is being reduced.

CAPITAL – Guatemala City, population estimate (1990), 1,675,589. Quezaltenango has a population of over 100,000. Other towns are ΨPuerto Barrios (23,000), Mazatenango (21,000), and Antigua (30,000).

CURRENCY – Quetzal (Q) of 100 centavos.

FLAG – Three vertical bands, blue, white, blue; coat of arms on white stripe.

NATIONAL ANTHEM – Guatemala Feliz (Guatemala be praised).
NATIONAL DAY – 15 September.

GOVERNMENT

The constitutionally elected president, Gen. Miguel Ydigoras Fuentes, was overthrown on 31 March 1963 by the Army, which handed executive and legislative powers to the Minister of Defence, Col. Enrique Peralta Azurdia. Elections for a new Congress and for President and Vice-President took place on 6 March 1966.

The constitution was suspended 'for as long as the situation demands' following a military coup in March 1982. An amnesty for guerrillas was unsuccessful and the Army was fully occupied dealing with the proliferating subversive groups throughout the country.

Elections for a Constituent Assembly were held on 1 July 1984, as promised by Gen. Mejía Víctores when he overthrew Gen. Ríos Montt in 1983. The Assembly drew up a new constitution, promulgated in June 1985, and a new electoral law, paving the way for presidential, governmental and municipal elections which were won by the Christian Democratic Party. A presidential election held in November 1990 was won by Jorge Serrano Elias, the leader of the Solidarity Action Movement (MAS). MAS failed to win Congressional elections and a government of national unity was formed.

On 25 May 1993 President Serrano partially suspended the constitution, dissolved Congress and the Supreme Court and declared that he would rule by decree until a new constitution was drafted to combat state corruption. However, following widespread international and domestic criticism, he failed to gain the support of political and business leaders and, most crucially, of the Army. The military effectively ousted Serrano to 1 June when he fled the country. On 5 June the former Human Rights Ombudsman, Ramiro de Léon Carpio, was elected by Congress as the new President by 107 votes to 2. President de Léon will serve for the remainder of Serrano's term (until January 1996) and at the time of going to press was forming a new government.

Meanwhile, the insurgency by left-wing guerrillas of the Guatemalan Revolutionary National Unity Movement (URNG) continues fitfully, interspersed with peace negotiations. In January 1993 some 45,000 refugees in southern Mexico, mostly Mayan Indians, began to return to Guatemala under UN supervision after being driven out by the Army's 1979–82 counter-insurgency campaign against URNG. The republic is divided into 22 departments.

HEAD OF STATE
President, Ramiro de Léon Carpio, *elected by Congress* 5 June 1993.
Vice-President, Arturo Herbruger Asturias.

EMBASSY OF GUATEMALA
13 Fawcett Street, London SW10 9HN
Tel 071-351 3042

Ambassador Extraordinary and Plenipotentiary, His Excellency Edmundo Nanne (1992).

BRITISH EMBASSY
Centro Financiero Torre II (7th Floor), Seventh Avenue 5–10 Zone 4, Guatemala City
Tel: Guatemala City 321601

Ambassador Extraordinary and Plenipotentiary, His Excellency Justin Nason, OBE (1990).
There is also a consulate at *Puerto Barrios*.

FINANCE
The central government revenue in 1989 was Quetzales 2,253 million, and expenditure Quetzales 2,775 million.

TRADE
The principal export is coffee, other articles being manufactured goods, sugar, bananas, cotton, beef and essential oils. The chief imports are petroleum, vehicles, machinery and foodstuffs.

The chief seaports are San José de Guatemala and Champerico on the Pacific and Santo Tomás de Castilla and Puerto Barrios on the Atlantic side.

	1991
Imports (f.o.b.)	US$1,673m
Exports (f.o.b.)	1,230m

Trade with UK	1991	1992
Imports from UK	£16,224,000	£20,779,000
Exports to UK	10,458,000	10,611,000

GUINEA
République de Guinée

Formerly part of French West Africa, Guinea has a coastline on the Atlantic Ocean between Guinea-Bissau and Sierra Leone, and in the interior is adjacent to Senegal, Mali, Côte d'Ivoire, Liberia and Sierra Leone. Area, 94,926 sq. miles (245,857 sq. km). The population (UN estimate 1991) is 5,931,000, mostly the Fullah, Malinké and Soussou tribes.

CAPITAL – ΨConakry (763,000). Other towns are Kankan, which is connected with Conakry by a railway, Kindia, N'Zérékoré, Mamou, Siguiri and Labé.

CURRENCY – Guinea franc of 100 centimes.
FLAG – Three vertical stripes of red, yellow and green.
NATIONAL DAY – 2 October (Anniversary of Proclamation of Independence).

GOVERNMENT

Guinea was separated from Senegal in 1891 and administered by France as a separate colony until 1958. In a referendum held in September 1958, Guinea rejected the new French constitution and on 2 October 1958 became an independent republic governed by a Constituent Assembly. M. Sékou Touré, Prime Minister in the Territorial Assembly, assumed office as head of the new Government, and was elected President in 1961. Under a provisional constitution adopted in November 1958, powers of government are exercised by a president assisted by the Cabinet. The President, eligible for a term of seven years and for re-election, is head of state and of the armed forces.

President Sékou Touré died in March 1984; a few days later there was a military coup. Guinea was ruled by a military government, which was directed by a Military Committee for National Recovery (CMRN). A new constitution, providing for the end of military rule and the introduction of a two-party system within five years, was approved by referendum in December 1990.

In January 1991 the CMRN was dissolved and a mixed civilian-military Transitional Committee for National Recovery (CTRN) was established. This appointed a new government in February 1991. Disturbances throughout 1991 led by trade unions and opposition parties caused the government to announce in October that a full multiparty system would be introduced in April 1992. Forty opposition parties have been legalized since April 1992 and presidential and legislative elections have been scheduled for the end of 1993.

HEAD OF STATE

President and Minister of Defence, Maj. Gen. Lansana Conté, took power 3 April 1984.

COUNCIL OF MINISTERS *as at June 1993*

Foreign Affairs and Co-operation, Maj. Ibrahima Sylla.
Minister at the Presidency in charge of National Defence, Maj. Abdourahmane Diallo.
Interior and Security, René Alseny Gomez.
Planning and Finance, Soriba Kaba.
Justice, Salifou Sylla.
Agriculture and Animal Resources, Ibrahima Sory Sow.
Natural Resources, Energy and Environment, Toumani Dakoum Sako.
Territorial Development, Maj. Ibrahima Diallo.
Higher Educational and Vocational Training, Charles Pascal Tollo.
Public Health and Social Affairs, Madigbe Fofana.
Communication, Capt. Jean-Claude Fassou.
Youth, Culture, Arts and Sports, Assifat Dorank.
Administrative Reform, Civil Service and Labour, René Loua Fassou.
Industry, Small- and Medium-sized Enterprises, Mamadou Boyé Barry.
Commerce, Transport and Tourism, Nantenin Camara.

EMBASSY OF THE REPUBLIC OF GUINEA
51 rue de la Faisanderie, 75061 Paris, France
Tel: Paris 47048148

Ambassador Extraordinary and Plenipotentiary, new appointment awaited.

BRITISH CONSULATE
BP 834 Conakry, Guinea
British Ambassador (resident in Dakar, Senegal).

ECONOMY

The principal products of Guinea are bauxite, alumina, iron-ore, palm kernels, millet, rice, coffee, bananas, pineapples and rubber. At Sangaredi in the mountainous hinterland, where the rivers Senegal, Gambia and Niger have their sources, large deposits of bauxite are mined. Deposits of iron ore, gold, diamonds and uranium have also been discovered. Principal imports are cotton goods, manufactured goods, tobacco, petroleum products, sugar, rice, flour and salt; exports, bauxite, alumina, iron-ore, diamonds, coffee, hides, bananas, palm kernels and pineapples.

TRADE WITH UK	1991	1992
Imports from UK	£7,800,000	£7,965,000
Exports to UK	5,854,000	239,000

GUINEA-BISSAU
República da Guiné-Bissau

Guinea-Bissau, formerly Portuguese Guinea, lies in Western Africa, between Senegal and Guinea; it has an area of 13,948 sq. miles (36,125 sq. km), and has a population (UN estimate 1991) of 984,000. The main ethnic groups are the Balante, Malinké, Fulani, Mandjako and Pepel.

CAPITAL – ψBissau, population (Census 1979) 109,486, is also the chief port.
CURRENCY – Guinea-Bissau peso of 100 centavos.
FLAG – Horizontal bands of yellow over green with vertical red band in the hoist charged with a black star.
NATIONAL DAY – 24 September (Independence Day).

GOVERNMENT

Guinea-Bissau achieved independence on 24 September 1974. Luis Cabral was ousted in a coup led by Maj. (now Brig.-Gen.) Vieira in November 1980. Following the coup the Assembly was suspended, and a Revolutionary Council was established. Under a new constitution adopted in April 1984 the Revolutionary Council became a 15-member Council of State, and an Assembly of 150 members was set up. The ruling African Party for the Independence of Guinea and Cape Verde (PAIGC) voted to introduce a multi-party system in January 1991. Ten opposition parties have been legalized since November 1991. Presidential and legislative elections scheduled for November and December 1992 respectively were postponed and new dates are yet to be confirmed.

HEAD OF STATE

Chairman of the Council of State, C.-in-C. of the Armed Forces, Brig.-Gen. João Bernardo Vieira, *took power* November 1980; *elected for a five-year term*, June 1989.

COUNCIL OF MINISTERS *as at August 1993*

Prime Minister, Carlos Correia.
Foreign Affairs and Co-operation, Bernadino Cardoso.
Justice, Manadou Saliu Djalo Pires.
Territorial Administration, Manuel Mane.
Finance, Flinto Barros.
Rural Development and Agriculture, Mario Cabral.
Fisheries, Eduardo Fernandes.
Natural Resources, Joao Cardosa.
Commerce and Industry, Assumane Mane.
Health, Henriqueta Godinho Gomes.
National Education, Culture and Sport, Fernando Delfim da Silva.
Social and Women's Affairs, Francisca Perreira.
Public Works, Alberto Lina Gomes.
Transport and Communications, Luis Olivera Sanca.
Administrative Reform and the Civil Service, Malam Bacai Sanha.
Defence, Samba Lamine Mane.
Interior, Abubacar Balde.

EMBASSY OF THE REPUBLIC OF GUINEA-BISSAU
Avenue Franklin Roosevelt 70, 1050 Brussels, Belgium
Tel: Brussels 6470890

Ambassador Extraordinary and Plenipotentiary, new appointment awaited.

BRITISH CONSULATE
Mavegro Int., CP100, Bissau
British Ambassador (resident in Dakar, Senegal).

ECONOMY

The country produces rice, coconuts, ground-nuts and palm oil products. Cattle are raised, and there are bauxite deposits in the south.

TRADE WITH UK	1991	1992
Imports from UK	£1,201,000	£1,117,000
Exports to UK	36,000	4,000

GUYANA
The Co-operative Republic of Guyana

Guyana, the former colony of British Guiana, which includes the counties of Demerara, Essequibo and Berbice, is situated on the north-east coast of South America, bordering Venezuela, Brazil and Suriname. It has a total area of 83,000 sq. miles (214,969 sq. km), and a population (1991 UN estimate) of 800,000.

There are three distinct areas. A narrow alluvial coastal belt ten to 40 miles deep, the eastern part of which is intensively cultivated and contains some 90 per cent of the population. Much of this is below the level of the sea and is drained and irrigated by an intricate system of canals constructed by the Dutch. A mountainous area of dense rain forest lies behind the coastland. Still partly unexplored, it reaches its highest point at Mount Roraima (9,000 ft) on the junction of the Guyana–Brazil–Venezuela borders. The open savanna country of the Rupununi in the south-west is the third area. Here cattle ranching is practised and oil deposits have been discovered.

The entire country is intersected by numerous large rivers, though these are of limited navigational use because of rapids and waterfalls, the most notable of which are the Kaieteur Fall on the Potaro River with a sheer drop of 741 ft, the Horse Shoe Falls on the Essequibo and the Marina Fall on the Ipobe River.

CLIMATE – The two dry seasons normally last from mid February to end April, and from mid August to end November. In the August to October period it is hot. The mean temperature is 27°C, the usual extremes being 21°C and 32°C. In the interior the mean temperature is higher, at 28°C, its extremes ranging from 19°C to 40°C. The yearly rainfall is subject to marked variation, its mean on the coastlands averaging about 90 inches with an average of 58 inches on the savannas.

CAPITAL – ΨGeorgetown. Estimated population, including environs, 185,000. Other towns are: Linden (29,000); ΨNew Amsterdam (23,000); Corriverton (17,000).

CURRENCY – Guyana dollar (G$) of 100 cents.

FLAG – Green with a yellow, white-bordered triangle based on the hoist and surmounted by a red, black-bordered triangle.

NATIONAL ANTHEM – Dear Land of Guyana.

NATIONAL DAYS – 26 May (Independence Day); 23 February (Republic Day).

GOVERNMENT

Guyana became independent on 26 May 1966, with a Governor-General appointed by The Queen. It became a Co-operative Republic on 23 February 1970. Under the Independence Constitution the Prime Minister and Cabinet were responsible to a National Assembly elected by secret ballot every five years. The last election under this constitution was in 1973 and the term of that Assembly was later extended to October 1980.

A new constitution was passed into law in February 1980 and promulgated in October 1980. It provides for an Executive President, a National Assembly of 65 members, and also for a National Congress of Local Democratic Organs responsible for local government. The Supreme Congress of the People consists of all members of these two assemblies. The electoral system is a proportional representation or 'single list' system, each voter casting his vote for a party list of candidates. The voting age is 18.

A general election was scheduled for the end of 1991 but was not held until 5 October 1992 because of the failure to establish proper electoral machinery and voter registration lists. In the presidential election Dr Cheddi Jagan defeated the incumbent Desmond Hoyte and in the legislative election Jagan's People's Progressive Party (PPP) defeated the People's National Congress (PNC) which had governed since independence. In the National Assembly the state of the

parties at August 1993 was: PPP 36; PNC 26; Working People's Alliance 2; United Force 1.

HEAD OF STATE

Executive President, Dr Cheddi Bharrat Jagan, *elected* 5 October 1992, *sworn in* 9 October 1992 for a five-year term.

CABINET *as at August 1993*

The Executive President.

Prime Minister and Senior Minister of Public Works, Communications, and Regional Development, Samuel Hinds.

Attorney-General and Minister of Legal Affairs, Bernard De Santos.

Senior Ministers:

Agriculture, Reepu Baman Persaud.

Finance, Asgar Ally.

Foreign Affairs, Clement Rohee.

Health, Gail Teixeira.

President's Office, Moses Nagamootoo.

Education and Cultural Development, Dale Bisnauth.

Labour, Human Services and Social Security, Henry Jeffrey.

Home Affairs, Feroze Mohamed.

Trade, Industry and Tourism, Shree Chand.

Ministers:

Public Works, Communications and Regional Development, Harripersaud Nokta.

Agriculture, Clinton Collymore.

Labour, Human Services and Social Security, Indra Chandarpaul.

Amerindian Affairs, Vibert D'Souza.

President's Office, George Fung-On.

GUYANA HIGH COMMISSION
3 Palace Court, Bayswater Road, London W2 4LP
Tel 071-229 7684

High Commissioner, new appointment awaited.

BRITISH HIGH COMMISSION
44 Main Street (PO Box 10849), Georgetown
Tel: Georgetown 65881/4

High Commissioner, His Excellency David J. Johnson (1993) (also Ambassador to Suriname).

JUDICATURE

The Supreme Court of Judicature consists of a Court of Appeal and a High Court. There are also Courts of Summary Jurisdiction. The Court of Appeal consists of the Chancellor as President, the Chief Justice and such number of Justices of Appeal as may be prescribed by Parliament.

The High Court consists of the Chief Justice, as President, and nine Puisne Judges. It is a court with unlimited jurisdiction in civil matters and exercises exclusive jurisdiction in probate, divorce and admiralty, and certain other matters.

Chancellor, K. M. George.

Chief Justice, Aubrey Bishop.

ECONOMY

The economy is based almost entirely on the main export items of sugar, rice, bauxite and alumina. Diamonds and gold are also mined, timber and rum are produced and there is some cattle ranching. The fishing industry is being expanded. Industry is fairly small-scale. Much emphasis is now being placed on eco-tourism.

TRADE WITH UK	1991	1992
Imports from UK	£19,275,000	£20,242,000
Exports to UK	50,479,000	78,742,000

COMMUNICATIONS

Georgetown and New Amsterdam are the principal ports, though bauxite ships also sail to Linden, on the River Demerara, and Everton, on the River Berbice. There are no public railways and the few roads are confined mainly to the coastal areas. Air transport is the easiest form of communication between the coast and the interior.

There is a state-owned radio broadcasting station which operates two channels and a fledgling television service.

EDUCATION

The Government assumed total control of the education system in September 1976 and made education free from nursery to university level. The Government trains teachers for primary and secondary schools at its own institutions.

Approximately 1,800 students were enrolled at the University of Guyana in degree programmes and certificate and diploma courses in 1990.

There are several technical and vocational institutions, as well as some 30 adult education schools (with an enrolment of 13,500). There are also a number of technical and vocational institutions not under the aegis of the Ministry of Education.

HAITI
République d'Haiti

The Republic of Haiti occupies the western third of the island of Hispaniola, which, after Cuba, is the largest island in the West Indies. The area, including off-shore islands, is 10,714 sq. miles (27,750 sq. km) of which about three-quarters is mountainous, with a population (UN estimate 1991) of 6,625,000.

CLIMATE – The climate is tropical with comparatively little difference in the temperatures between the summer (March–October) and the winter (November–February). Humidity is high, especially in the autumn.

LANGUAGE – Both French and Creole are regarded as the official languages of Haiti. French is the language of the government and the press but it is only spoken by the educated minority. The usual language of the people is Creole.

CAPITAL – Ψ Port-au-Prince. Population estimated at about 1 million. Other centres are: Ψ Cap Haitien (54,691); Gonaives (36,736); Les Cayes (27,222); Jérémie (25,117); St Marc (20,504); Jacmel (16,449); Ψ Port de Paix (21,733).

CURRENCY – Gourde of 100 centimes.

FLAG – Horizontally blue over red.

NATIONAL ANTHEM – La Dessalinienne.

NATIONAL DAY – 1 January.

GOVERNMENT

Haiti was a French colony under the name of Saint-Domingue from 1697. The slave population, estimated at 500,000, revolted in 1791 under the leadership of Toussaint L'Ouverture, who was born a slave and made himself Governor-General of the colony. He capitulated to the French in 1802 and died in captivity in 1803. Resistance was continued by Jean Jacques Dessalines, also a former Negro slave, who, on 1 January 1804, declared the former French colony to be an independent state. It was at this time that the name Haiti, an aboriginal word meaning mountainous, was adopted. Dessalines became Emperor of Haiti but was assassinated in 1806.

Dr Duvalier was installed as President in 1957 and held the position until his death in 1971. He was succeeded as President for life by his son, Jean Claude Duvalier, who fled to France in February 1986 in the face of sustained popular unrest. A council headed by Gen. Henri Namphy assumed power. In March 1987, by popular referendum, a new constitution was agreed and presidential elections scheduled for November; these were aborted following violence in the capital. The elections held in January 1988 were boycotted by a number of leading candidates but Leslie Manigat eventually won after a very low turnout. President Manigat was inaugurated in February 1988, but he and his government were ousted on 19 June by Gen. Henri Namphy. Manigat was deported to the Dominican Republic and Namphy set up a military government until he in turn was replaced in a coup by Lt.-Gen. Prosper Avril on 18 September 1988. Following growing government opposition in 1990, Prosper Avril resigned on 10 March. The presidency devolved upon Ertha Pascal-Trouillot, advised by a 19-member Council of State. Father Jean-Bertrand Aristide, leader of the National Front for Change and Democracy, won a free presidential election, held on 16 December 1990.

Father Aristide launched a wide-scale anti-corruption campaign, including removing from power the last supporters of the Duvalier dictatorships and purging the military leadership. This led to a military coup on 30 September 1991 which ousted Aristide and installed a provisional government under President Joseph Nerette and later Prime Minister Marc Bazin. Aristide escaped to the USA via Venezuela. The Organization of American States imposed a trade embargo on Haiti to force the military to accept the return of Aristide as President, but without immediate result.

Efforts to resolve the situation continued throughout 1992 and 1993, led by UN and OAS special envoy Dante Caputo. As the military continued to refuse to accept Aristide's return despite international pressure, the UN imposed a total economic embargo, including oil and arms supplies and freezing the military élite's assets abroad in June 1993. In an attempt to avoid the embargo, the Haitian parliament voted on 15 June to restore Aristide as Head of State as long as their conditions were met. The UN Security Council voted to impose the embargo on 16 June, forcing the military to open talks immediately with Aristide and to agree to a plan proposed by Caputo for Aristide's return. The plan provides for the return of Aristide as President on 30 October 1993; the nomination by Aristide of a new Prime Minister (Bazin resigned on 8 June); an amnesty for those involved in the coup; the resignation of the military high command; and the nomination of a new Commander-in-Chief by President Aristide. In mid-July discussions about the agreement were held in New York by representatives of Haitian political parties leading to the 'New York Pact' based on a six-month political truce and undertakings to form a government of national accord.

President, Jean-Bertrand Aristide, elected 16 December 1990, *sworn in* 7 February 1991 (*remains constitutional President*).

CABINET *as at March 1993 (appointed by Prime Minister Bazin)*
Prime Minister, vacant.
Interior and Defence, vacant.
Social Affairs, André Brutus.
Justice, Moise Senatus.
Economy and Finance, vacant.
Planning and Co-ordination, Jean André Victor.
Public Health and Population, Andrien Westerband.
Agriculture, Jacques Becker.
Public Works, Transport and Communications, vacant.
Foreign Affairs, François Benoit.

Information, vacant.
Industry and Commerce, Saidel Lainé.
Education, Max Carré.

The London Embassy of the Republic of Haiti closed on 30 March 1987.
BRITISH AMBASSADOR (resident in Kingston, Jamaica).

ECONOMY

In recent years measures for agricultural rehabilitation have been taken with the aim of a gradual restoration of productivity, which had declined after the ending of the colonial plantation system. The main project is a scheme for the irrigation of more than 70,000 acres of the Artibonite valley.

Coffee accounts for about 32 per cent of total exports. Cocoa is the second largest export earner. Corn, sorghum and rice are also grown. Increased production of tropical fruits and vegetables is being encouraged.

Export assembly industries accounted for about 30 per cent of the total manufacturing industry in Haiti, employing an estimated 40,000 people but some have been re-located as a result of the unstable political climate. Items such as leather goods, textiles, electronic components and sports equipment are manufactured, using imported raw materials, for re-export, primarily to the USA. Principal imports are raw materials for the export assembly sector, foodstuffs, machinery, vehicles, mineral oils and textiles.

TRADE WITH UK	1991	1992
Imports from UK	£7,280,000	£7,212,000
Exports to UK	1,253,000	762,000

COMMUNICATIONS

The main roads are asphalted and secondary roads are fair. Internal air services are maintained between the capital and the principal provincial towns. International air-services connect Port-au-Prince with the USA and other Caribbean and South American cities. The principal towns and villages are connected by telephone and/or telegraph. The telephone company is state owned (51 per cent) and the service both in Port-au-Prince and between urban areas has been improved. External telegraph, telephone and postal services are normal. There are several commercial radio stations and two television stations at Port-au-Prince. However, recently all services have been considerably disrupted, together with telephone and telegraph services.

Regular passenger liner services to New York have ceased, but cruise ships call occasionally. Freight sailings are frequent for the USA, Canada, Europe, Latin America (except Cuba) and the main Caribbean ports.

EDUCATION

Education is free but estimates of illiteracy are as high as 85 per cent.

HOLY SEE, *see* VATICAN CITY STATE

HONDURAS
Republica de Honduras

Honduras, in Central America, lies between 13° and 16° 30′ N. latitude and 83° and 89° 41′ W. longitude, with a seaboard of about 375 miles on the Caribbean Sea and an outlet, consisting of a small strip of coast 63 miles in length, on the Pacific. Its frontiers are contiguous with those of Guatemala, Nicaragua and El Salvador.

The republic contains a total area of approximately 43,277 sq. miles (112,088 sq. km) and is very mountainous, being traversed by the Cordilleras, with peaks rising to 1,500 and 2,400 metres above sea level. Most of the soil is poor and acidic, except for the coastal plains of the north and some areas of the interior. Three-quarters of the territory is covered by pine forests which contribute to much of the country's wealth in natural resources. Rainfall is seasonal, May to October being wet and November to April dry.

POPULATION – The population, 4,915,900 (1991 estimate), is of mixed Spanish and Indian blood. Garifunas in Northern Honduras are of West Indian origin.

LANGUAGE – The language of the country is Spanish, although English is the first language of many in the islands and on the north coast.

CAPITAL – Tegucigalpa, population (1991 estimate) 670,100; other towns are San Pedro Sula (325,900), ΨLa Ceiba (77,100), ΨPuerto Cortes (32,500), Choluteca (63,200) and ΨTela (24,000).

CURRENCY – Lempira of 100 centavos.

FLAG – Three horizontal bands, blue, white, blue (with five blue stars on white band).

NATIONAL ANTHEM – Tu Bandera Es Un Lampo De Cielo (Your flag is a heavenly light).

NATIONAL DAY – 15 September.

GOVERNMENT

Originally discovered and settled by the Spanish at the beginning of the 16th century, Honduras formed part of the Spanish American dominions for nearly three centuries until 1821 when independence was proclaimed. Under military government from 1972 to 1981, and after two terms of Liberal administration, the most recent legislative election in November 1989 was won by the Partido Nacional (National Party). The new Government took office in January 1990.

The country is divided into 18 departments, the newest of which, Gracias a Dios, formed in 1957, is now the home of thousands of Miskito Indian refugees from Nicaragua.

HEAD OF STATE
President of the Republic, Rafael Leonardo Callejas, *assumed office,* 27 January 1990.

CABINET *as at August 1993*
Interior and Justice, Celin Discua.
Foreign Affairs, Mario Carias Zapata.
Defence, Gen. Lazaro Avila Soleno.
Education, Jaime Martinez Guzman.
Finance, Rene Ardan Matute.
Economy, Carlos Chain.
Communications, Public Works and Transport, Mauricio Membreno.
Health, Dr Ramon Pereira.
Labour and Social Security, Carlos Torres Lopez.
Natural Resources, Mario Nufio Gamero.
Culture and Tourism, Sonia Canales De Mendieta.
Economic Planning, Orlando Funez.
Director of National Agrarian Institute, Tomas Guillen Williams.
President of the Central Bank of Honduras, Roberto Galvez Barnes.

EMBASSY OF HONDURAS
115 Gloucester Place, London WIH 3PJ
Tel 071–486 4880

Ambassador Extraordinary and Plenipotentiary, His Excellency Carlos Zeron (1991).

BRITISH EMBASSY
Apartado Postal 290, Tegucigalpa
Tel: Honduras 32–0612/18

Ambassador Extraordinary and Plenipotentiary, His
Excellency Patrick Morgan (1992).
There is a British Consulate in *San Pedro Sula.*

ECONOMY

Agriculture is mainly confined to the large and fertile valleys
on the wide Caribbean plain, and the extensive valleys found
in the Comayagua and Olancho regions of the interior.
Reaching inland from the Caribbean towards the eastern
border with Nicaragua a vast tropical forest area called the
Mosquitia provides valuable reserves of timber. Lead, zinc
and silver are mined on a small scale. There are large tracts
of uncultivated land.

TRADE

The chief exports are coffee, bananas and timber, the most
important woods being pine, mahogany and cedar. Cattle
raising and the exporting of frozen meat is an important
industry, and exports of shrimps and lobsters are increasing.
Other products are tobacco, beans, maize, rice, cotton, palm
oil, sugar cane, cement and tropical fruits.

	1990	1991
Imports	Lempiras 1,342.6m	1,332.1m
Exports	997.1m	985.8m
Trade with UK	1991	1992
Imports from UK	£6,784,000	£6,101,000
Exports to UK	9,065,000	13,255,000

EDUCATION

Primary and secondary education is free, primary education
being compulsory, and the government has launched a
campaign to eradicate illiteracy.

COMMUNICATIONS

There are about 1,004 km of railway in operation, chiefly to
serve the banana plantations and the Caribbean ports. There
are 17,947 km of roads, of which 2,383 km are paved,
excluding some 250 km of new major highways recently
inaugurated. Improvements are being made and new roads
built. There are 33 smaller airstrips and four international
airports, Tegucigalpa, San Pedro Sula, La Ceiba and Roatan
(Bay Island).
    ΨThe chief ports are Puerto Cortes, Tela and La Ceiba
on the north coast, through which passes the bulk of the trade
with the United States and Europe. Puerto Castilla is being
developed as a deep-water container port, and San Lorenzo
is also experiencing rapid growth.

HUNGARY
Magyar Köztársaság

The area of Hungary is 35,919 sq. miles (93,030 sq. km)
with a population (1992) of 10,335,000. About two-thirds
of the population are Roman Catholic, and the remainder
mostly Calvinist.

CAPITAL – Budapest, on the Danube; population (1992)
2,004,000. Other large towns are: Miskolc (192,000);
Debrecen (215,000); Szeged (177,000) and Pécs
(169,000).
CURRENCY – Forint of 100 fillér.
FLAG – Red, white, green (horizontally).

NATIONAL ANTHEM – Isten Aldd Meg A Magyart (God
Bless the Hungarians).
NATIONAL DAYS – 15 March, 20 August, 23 October.

GOVERNMENT

Hungary, reconstituted a kingdom in 1920 after having been
declared a republic on 17 November 1918, joined the Anti-
Comintern Pact in February 1939 and entered the Second
World War on the side of Germany in 1941. On 20 January
1945 a Hungarian provisional government of liberation,
which had been set up during the preceding December,
signed an armistice under the terms of which the frontiers of
Hungary were withdrawn to the limits existing in 1937, set
under the Treaty of Trianon in 1919.
    After the liberation, a coalition of the Smallholder, National
Peasant, Social Democrat and Communist parties carried out
major land reform, and mines, heavy industry, banks and
schools were nationalized. By 1949 the Communists had
succeeded in gaining a monopoly of power and by 1952
practically the entire economy had been 'socialized'. The
Party formulated policy and the function of the Government
was mainly executive.
    The period from July 1956 to the outbreak of the national
revolution on 23 October was marked by growing ferment in
intellectual circles and increased discord within the Party.
The withdrawal of Soviet troops from the country and free
elections were among the demands put forward. Fighting
broke out on the night of 23 October between demonstrators,
who had been joined by large numbers of factory workers,
and the State Security Police. Soviet forces intervened in
strength early the next morning. By 30 October Soviet troops
had withdrawn from Budapest and on 3 November an all-
party coalition government under Imre Nagy was formed.
This government was overthrown and the revolution
suppressed as the result of a renewed attack by Soviet forces
on Budapest in the early hours of 4 November. The formation
of a new Hungarian Revolutionary Worker Peasant Government under the leadership of Mr Kádár was announced.
    From 1968, the government gradually introduced eco-
nomic reforms and some political liberalization. Kádár was
forced to resign in May 1989. In October 1989 the National
Assembly (*Országgyűlés*) approved an amended constitution
which described Hungary as an independent, democratic
state. Multi-party elections took place in March and April
1990. The majority of seats were won by the Hungarian
Democratic Forum, followed by the Alliance of Free
Democrats. In May 1990 a coalition government was formed
of the (conservative) Hungarian Democratic Forum, the
Smallholders Party and the Christian Democratic Party. The
former ruling Communist Party, reconstituted as the
Hungarian Socialist Party, is now in opposition as well as the
Young Democrats Party. In June 1993 the nationalist right-
wing of the Forum were expelled from the party and went
into opposition. The next general election is due in spring
1994.

HEAD OF STATE

President, Árpád Göncz, *sworn in* 3 August 1990.

CABINET *as at August 1993*
Prime Minister, Dr József Antall.
Interior, Dr Péter Boross.
Agriculture, János Szabó.
Justice, Dr István Balsai.
Industry and Commerce, János Miklós Latortzai.
Environmental Protection, János Gyurkó.
Transport and Communications, György Schamschula.
Foreign Affairs, Géza Jeszenszky.
Defence, Lajos Für.

Labour, Dr Gyula Kiss.
Education and Culture, Ferenc Mádl.
Public Welfare, László Surján.
International Economic Relations, Béla Kádár.
Finance, Iván Szabó.
Ministers without Portfolio, Ernö Pungor; Tamás Szabó; Ferenc József Nagy; Tibor Füzessy.
State Secretaries:
International Economic Relations, László Bogár.
Finance, Pál Becker.
PM's Office, Balázs Bárdos; Miklós Lukáts; Tamás Katona; Dr Miklós Pálos.
Justice, Dr Tamás Isépy.
Foreign Affairs, András Kelemen.
Social Welfare, Erzsébet Pusztai.
Transport, Telecommunications, Zsolt Rajkai.
Agriculture, László Medgyasszay.
Labour, Tíhamér Tóth.
Environment, Mrs László Tarján.

EMBASSY OF THE REPUBLIC OF HUNGARY
35 Eaton Place, London SW1X 8BY
Tel 071-235 4048/7191

Ambassador Extraordinary and Plenipotentiary, His Excellency Tibor Antalpéter (1990).
Minister Plenipotentiary, József Hajgató.
Counsellors, I. Gerelyes (*Consul*); T. Vajda (*Press*); E. Sziklai (*Commercial*); J. G. Turi (*Culture*).
Defence and Military Attaché, Col. P. Szücs.

BRITISH EMBASSY

Harmincad Utca 6, Budapest V
Tel: Budapest 266-2888

Ambassador Extraordinary and Plenipotentiary, His Excellency John Allan Birch, CMG (1989).
Counsellor and Deputy Head of Mission, C. Prentice
Defence and Military Attaché, Col. W. Ibbetson.
First Secretary (Commercial), D. Taylor.
First Secretary (Management) and Consul, S. MacTaggart.

BRITISH COUNCIL DIRECTOR, Dr John Grote, OBE, H-1068 Benczur Utca 26, Budapest VI.

DEFENCE

Hungary has a total armed forces active strength of 80,800 (including 53,900 conscripts). Conscripts serve for 12 months. The Army has a strength of 63,500 (41,900 conscripts) with 1,357 main battle tanks, 1,795 armoured personnel carriers and armoured infantry fighting vehicles and 1,040 artillery pieces. The Air Force has a strength of 17,300 (12,000 conscripts), 93 combat aircraft (with a further 43 in store) and 39 attack helicopters. As Hungary is landlocked it has no navy but the Army maintains a small Danube Flotilla with six mine countermeasure vessels.

ECONOMY

Since 1968 the Hungarian economy had been run according to a system which allowed more decentralized decision-making than in some other eastern European countries, although central control in vital areas such as the allocation of fuels and raw materials remained. The new government has embarked upon the privatization of state-owned concerns and the return of nationalized land to its former owners. In 1992 the IMF suspended a three-year loan arrangement with Hungary for a total of US$1,621m because of Hungary's inability to meet required criteria, especially in terms of the budget deficit. To combat this, the parliament in early July 1993 finally approved a harsh austerity budget to meet IMF criteria to re-start the loan.

Industrialization has made considerable progress in the last decade and now produces 35 per cent of national income. Industry is mainly based on imported raw materials but Hungary has its own coal (mostly brown), bauxite, considerable deposits of natural gas (some not yet under full exploitation), some iron ore and oil. Output figures in 1991 (1,000 tons): coal 16,974; aluminium 6,316; rolled steel 1,532; crude oil 1,893. Natural gas production totalled 5,041 million cubic metres.

Agriculture still occupies an important place in the Hungarian economy. In 1990 10.5 per cent of the entire land area was owned by state farms and a further 63.8 per cent was within co-operative farms. Co-operative farms will remain a feature of Hungarian agriculture. Production in 1990 was (tons):

Maize	4,300,000
Wheat	6,200,000
Sugar beet	4,700,000
Barley	1,400,000
Rye	200,000
Oats	200,000

GDP per capita in 1991 was US$2,974.

TRADE	1991	1992
Imports	Forints 855,600m	878,200m
Exports	764,300m	843,600m
Trade with UK	1991	1992
Imports from UK	£132,448,000	£161,510,000
Exports to UK	103,869,000	117,636,000

EDUCATION

There are five types of schools under the Ministry of Education: kindergartens for age three to six, general schools for age six to 14 (compulsory), vocational schools (15–18), secondary schools (15–18), universities and adult training schools (over 18).

CULTURE

Magyar, or Hungarian, is one of the Finno-Ugrian languages. Hungarian literature began to flourish in the second half of 16th century. Among the greatest writers of the 19th and 20th centuries are Mihály Vörösmarty (1800–55), Sándor Petöfi (1823–49), János Arany (1817–82), Imre Madách (1823–64), Kálmán Mikszáth (1847–1910), Endre Ady (1877–1918), Attila József (1905–37), Mihály Babits (1883–1941) and Dezsö Kosztolányi (1885–1936).

ICELAND
Island

Iceland is a large volcanic island in the North Atlantic Ocean, extending from 63° 23' to 66° 33' N. latitude, and from 13° 22' to 24° 35' W. longitude, with an estimated area of 39,768 sq. miles (103,000 sq. km). The population was 259,581 on 1 December 1991. Some 92.6 per cent of the population are members of the (Lutheran) Church of Iceland.

CAPITAL – ΨReykjavík, population (1 December 1991), 99,653. Other centres in approximate order of importance are
ΨAkureyri, Kópavogur, ΨHafnarfjördur, Keflavík, Westmann Islands, Akranes, Isafjördur and ΨSiglufjördur.
CURRENCY – Icelandic króna (Kr) of 100 aurar.
FLAG – Blue, with white-bordered red cross.

HUN - IND **903**

NATIONAL ANTHEM – O Gud Vors Lands (Our Country's God).
NATIONAL DAY – 17 June.

GOVERNMENT

Iceland was uninhabited before the ninth century, when settlers came from Norway. For several centuries a form of republican government prevailed, with an annual assembly of leading men called the *Althing*, but in 1241 Iceland became subject to Norway, and later to Denmark. During the colonial period, Iceland maintained its cultural integrity but a deterioration in the climate, together with frequent volcanic eruptions and outbreaks of disease, led to a serious fall in the standard of living and to a decline in the population to little more than 40,000. In the 19th century a struggle for independence began which led first to home rule for Iceland under the Danish Crown (1918), and later to complete independence under a republican form of rule in 1944.

The parliamentary (*Althing*) elections in April 1991 gave the Independence Party 26 seats, Progressives 13, Social Democratic Party 10, People's Alliance 9 and Women's Alliance 5.

HEAD OF STATE

President, Vigdís Finnbogadóttir, *born* 1930, *elected* 29 June 1980, *re-elected,* 1984, 1988 and June 1992.

CABINET *as at August 1993*

Prime Minister, Minister for the Statistical Bureau of Iceland, David Oddsson (IP).
Foreign Affairs and Trade, Jón Baldvin Hannibalsson (SDP).
Finance, Fridrik Sophusson (IP).
Fisheries, Justice and Ecclesiastical Affairs, Thorsteinn Pálsson (IP).
Education and Culture, Ólafur Einarsson (IP).
Social Affairs, Jóhanna Sigurthardóttir (SDP).
Health and Social Security, Sighvatur Björgvinsson (SDP).
Commerce, Industry and Nordic Co-operation, Jón Sigurthsson (SDP).
Agriculture and Communications, Halldór Blöndal (IP).
Environmental Affairs, Eidur Gudnason (SDP).

IP: Independence Party
SDP: Social Democrat Party

EMBASSY OF ICELAND
1 Eaton Terrace, London SW1W 8EY
Tel 071-730 5131/2

Ambassador Extraordinary and Plenipotentiary, His Excellency Helgi Ágústsson, GCVO (1989).

BRITISH EMBASSY
Laufásvegur 49, 101 Reykjavík
Tel: Reykjavík 15883/4

Ambassador Extraordinary and Plenipotentiary and Consul-General, His Excellency Michael S. Hone (1993).

BRITISH CONSULAR OFFICES – There are Consular Offices at *Akureyri* and *Reykjavík.*

CULTURE

The ancient Norraena (or Northern tongue) presents close affinities to Anglo-Saxon and as spoken and written in Iceland today differs little from that introduced into the island in the ninth century. There is a rich literature with two distinct periods of development, from the mid-11th to the late 13th century and from the early 19th century to the present.

ECONOMY

Iceland has considerable resources of hydro-electric and geothermal energy. It is estimated that exploited water power (4,000 Gigawatt hours/a) represents only about 9 per cent of that economically exploitable, whereas only 5 per cent of the estimated 80,000 Gigawatt hours/a of available geothermal power has so far been harnessed. Energy-intensive heavy industry includes an aluminium smelter, a nitrogen fertilizer factory, a diatomite plant and a ferro-silicone plant.

In 1989 Iceland had a total labour force of 126,062, of which 17.6 per cent was engaged in government services, 14.9 in restaurants and hotels, 12.9 per cent in manufacturing and 11.8 per cent in fishing and fish processing.

As a member of the European Free Trade Association (EFTA), Iceland is due to become a member of the European Economic Area (EEA) which extends most of the provisions of the EC's Single Market to EFTA states.

FINANCE	1990
Revenue	Kr119,505m
Expenditure	127,565m

TRADE

The principal exports are frozen fish fillets, salt fish, stock fish, fresh fish on ice, frozen scampi, fishmeal and oil, skins and aluminium; the imports consist of almost all the necessities of life, the chief items being petroleum products, transport equipment, textiles, foodstuffs, animal feeds, timber, and alumina.

	1990	1991
Exports	Kr128,264m	Kr129,207m
Imports	136,018m	147,937m

Trade with UK	1991	1992
Imports from UK	£96,615,000	£92,127,000
Exports to UK	238,428,000	239,510,000

COMMUNICATIONS

At 1 January 1991, the mercantile marine consisted of 1,147 registered vessels (185,333 gross tons), of which 1,000 (134,778) are decked fishing vessels. There are regular shipping services between Reykjavík and Felixstowe, Humber ports and the Continent.

A regular air service is maintained between Glasgow and London and Reykjavík. There are also air services from the island to Scandinavia, USA, Germany, France and Luxembourg.

Road communications are adequate in summer but greatly restricted by snow in winter. Only roads in town centres and key highways are metalled, the rest being of gravel, sand and lava dust. The climate and terrain make first-class surfaces for highways out of the question. There are no railways.

INDIA
The Republic of India

India has an area of 1,269,346 sq. miles (3,287,590 sq. km), composed of three well-defined regions: the mountain range of the Himalayas, the Indo–Gangetic plain, and the southern peninsula. The main mountain ranges are the Himalayas in the north (over 29,000 feet) and the Western and Eastern Ghats (over 8,000 feet). Major rivers include the Ganges, Indus, Krishna, Godavari and Mahanadi.

CLIMATE – There are four seasons: the cold season (December–March); the hot season (April–May); the rainy season (June–September); and the season of the retreating south-west monsoon (October–November). Temperatures vary over the whole country, between averages of about 10°C and 33°C, reaching over 38°C in some parts during the hot season. There are similar variations in rainfall, from only a few inches a year falling in the western Thar Desert to over 400 inches in Meghalaya.

POPULATION – India is the second most populous country in the world. The population at the 1991 Census was 843,930,861, of which more than 20 per cent was urban. The majority of the population is Hindu (82 per cent), the rest being Muslim (11 per cent), Christian (2.5 per cent), Sikh (1.8 per cent), Buddhist (0.7 per cent) and Jain (0.5 per cent).

LANGUAGES – The official languages are Hindi in Devanagari script and English, though 17 regional languages also are recognized for adoption as official state languages.

CAPITAL – Delhi (population in 1991 was 8,375,188). Populations of other principal cities (1991 figures) were Ahmedabad 3,297,655; Bangalore 4,086,548; ΨBombay (Mumbai) 12,571,720; ΨCalcutta 10,916,272; Hyderabad 4,280,261; Kanpur 2,111,284; Lucknow 1,642,134; ΨMadras 5,361,468; Pune 2,485,014.

CURRENCY – Indian rupee (Rs) of 100 paisa.

FLAG – A horizontal tricolour with bands of deep saffron, white and dark green in equal proportions. In the centre of the white band appears an Asoka wheel in navy blue.

NATIONAL ANTHEM – Jana-gana-mana.

NATIONAL DAY – 26 January (Republic Day).

HISTORY

The Indus civilization was fully developed by c.2500 BC but collapsed c.1750 BC, subsequently being replaced by an Aryan civilization spread from the west. The first Arab invasions of the north-west began in the seventh century and Muslim, Hindu and Buddhist states developed until the establishment of the Mogul dynasty in 1526. The British East India Company established settlements throughout the 17th century; clashes with the French and native princes led to the British government taking control of the company in 1784 and gradually gaining control of the whole sub-

continent. The separate dominions of India and Pakistan became independent within the Commonwealth in 1947 and India became a republic in 1950.

GOVERNMENT

The constitution of India came into force in 1950. Executive power is vested in the President, who is elected for a five-year term by an electoral college consisting of the elected members of the Union and State legislatures. He appoints the Prime Minister and, on the latter's advice, the ministers, and can dismiss them. The Council of Ministers is collectively responsible to the *Lok Sabha* (lower house). The Vice-President is ex-officio chairman of the *Rajya Sabha* (upper house).

Legislative power rests with the President, the Rajya Sabha (which has 245 members) and the Lok Sabha (which has 545 members). Twelve members of the Rajya Sabha are nominated by the President, the rest are indirectly elected representatives of the State and Union Territories. They hold office for six years. The 530 members of the Lok Sabha representing the States are directly elected by universal adult franchise, and 15 representatives of the Union Territories are chosen, for a maximum term of five years. Subject to the provisions of the constitution, the Union Parliament can make laws for the whole of India and the State legislatures for their respective units.

☞ Inter-communal violence between Hindus and Muslims reached its worst point since independence in late 1992 and early 1993. In December 1992 Hindu fundamentalists destroyed the mosque at Ayodhya, leading to weeks of rioting and clashes across India in which some 1,200 people were killed and 5,000 injured. In February 1993 some 40,000 supporters of the Hindu fundamentalist Bharatiya Janata Party (BJP) were arrested by security forces when they tried to march on New Delhi and topple the secular Congress (I) Party which has ruled India for all but four years since independence. The BJP state governments of Uttar Pradesh, Madhya Pradesh, Rajasthan and Himachal Pradesh were dismissed and President's rule imposed because of the Ayodhya crisis. The government declared a nationwide state of emergency in March 1993 after 13 bombs exploded in Bombay, killing 200 people and injuring 1,000.

HEAD OF STATE

President of the Republic of India, Dr Shankar Dayal Sharma, *elected* 16 July 1992.

Vice-President, K. R. Narayanan, *elected* 19 August 1992.

CABINET *as at August 1993*

Prime Minister, Minister of Personnel, Public Grievances and Pensions, Science and Technology, Electronics, Atomic Energy, Chemical and Fertilizers, Rural Development, Non-Conventional Energy Sources, Law, Justice and Company Affairs, Commerce, Space, Ocean Development, Defence and Industry, P. V. Narasimha Rao.

Finance, Dr Manmohan Singh.

Agriculture, Balram Jakhar.

Human Resources Development, Arjun Singh.

Urban Development, Sheila Kaul.

Railways, C. K. Jaffer Sharief.

Power, N. K. P. Salve.

Civil Supplies, Consumer Affairs and Public Distribution, A. K. Antony.

Home Affairs, S. B. Chavan.

External Affairs, Dinesh Singh.

Welfare, Sitarem Kesri.

Health and Family Welfare, M. L. Fotedar.

Water Resources and Parliamentary Affairs, V. C. Shukla.

Civil Aviation and Tourism, Ghulam Nabi Azad.

In addition there are 12 ministers of state (independent charge), 28 ministers of state and three deputy ministers, making a total of 57 in the Council of Ministers.

INDIAN HIGH COMMISSION
India House, Aldwych, London WC2B 4NA
Tel 071-836 8484

High Commissioner, His Excellency Dr L. M. Singhvi (1991).
Deputy High Commissioner, K. V. Rajan.
Minister, M. P. Beezbaruah (*Economic*); R. Roychaudri (*Consular*), G. Gandhi (*Culture*).
Military Adviser, Brig. B. S. Malik.

BRITISH HIGH COMMISSION
Chanakyapuri, New Delhi 1100-21.
Tel: New Delhi 601371

High Commissioner, His Excellency Sir Nicholas Fenn, KCMG (1991).
Deputy High Commissioner and Minister, H. N. H. Synnott.
Deputy High Commissioners, T. D. Curran (*Bombay*); A. B. N. Morey (*Calcutta*); D. Cockerham (*Madras*).
Defence and Military Adviser, Brig. A. F. Gordon, CBE.
Counsellor (Economic and Commercial), J. E. Holmes.
Minister for Cultural Affairs and British Council Representative in India, R. Arbuthnott, CBE. Offices also at Bombay, Calcutta and Madras. There are British Council libraries at these four centres and British libraries at *Ahmedabad, Bangalore, Bhopal, Hyderabad, Lucknow, Patna, Pune, Ranchi* and *Trivandrum*.

STATES AND TERRITORIES OF THE UNION

There are 25 States and seven Union Territories. Each State is governed by a Governor, appointed by the President, who holds office for five years, and by a Council of Ministers. All States have a Legislative Assembly, and some have also a Legislative Council, elected directly by adult suffrage for a maximum period of five years. The judges of the High Court of a State are appointed by the President.

The Union Territories are administered, except where otherwise provided by Parliament, by the President acting through an Administrator or Lieutenant-Governor, or other authority appointed by him.

JUDICATURE

The Supreme Court consists of the Chief Justice and not more than 17 other judges, appointed by the President. It is the highest court in respect of all constitutional matters and the final Court of Appeal.
Chief Justice, Justice L. M. Sharma.

DEFENCE

The supreme command of the armed forces is vested in the President. Administrative and operational control resides in the Army, Navy and Air Headquarters under the supervision of the Ministry of Defence. Total active armed forces strength numbers 1,265,000. Service is voluntary.

The Army has five commands, Southern, Eastern, Northern, Western and Central, and a total strength of some 1,100,000, with some 3,800 main battle tanks of Soviet and indigenous manufacture; 1,250 armoured infantry fighting vehicles and armoured personnel carriers; 3,250 artillery pieces and 120 helicopters. The Army is organized into ten corps and deploys two armoured, one mechanized, ten mountain and 22 infantry divisions, with a further 14 independent brigades.

The Indian Navy has a strength of 55,000 personnel and consists of two aircraft carriers, 15 submarines and 26 destroyers and frigates organized into a number of frigate squadrons, including some of the latest type of anti-submarine and anti-aircraft frigates, a squadron of anti-submarine patrol vessels and minesweeping squadrons. A naval aviation wing deploys some 46 combat aircraft and 75 armed helicopters. India has started building her own naval craft.

The Indian Air Force has a strength of some 110,000 with 674 combat aircraft and 36 armed helicopters. It is organized in seven major formations, the Western, Eastern, Central, Southern and South-Western Air Commands, and the Training and Maintenance Commands. There are 28 ground attack, 17 air defence, eight maritime attack, three reconnaissance, two attack helicopters and 33 transport squadrons.

In addition, there are 1,325,000 personnel in 12 paramilitary organizations.

ECONOMY

Agriculture is the chief industry, supporting about 70 per cent of the population, and providing nearly 32 per cent of the Gross Domestic Product. The area under cultivation has been increased by irrigation schemes, but most holdings are less than five acres. Production has grown by 3 per cent each year since 1951, remaining slightly ahead of the 2 per cent increase necessary to keep pace with the rising population. Food crops occupy three-quarters of the total cropped area and production of food grains amounted to 176 million tonnes in 1990-1. In 1991-2 foodgrains production was expected to reach about 182 million tonnes following good rains. The main food crops are rice, cereals (principally wheat) and pulses. The major cash crops include sugar cane, jute, cotton and tea. Other products include oil seeds, spices, groundnuts, tobacco, rubber and coffee. Livestock is raised, principally for dairy purposes or for the hides: cattle (an estimated 181 million), goats (71 million), sheep (41 million) and pigs (9.9 million).

India's major industries are based on the exploitation and processing of her mineral resources, principally coal and iron. The coal industry, nationalized in the early 1970s, reached an output in 1989-90 of 213 million tonnes. Production of crude oil from the main fields in Assam and from offshore drilling was about 25.6 million tonnes in 1989-90. Steel production is mainly in the hands of the public sector, with five public and one private sector integrated steel plants producing 10.5 million tonnes of ingot steel in 1989-90. The engineering industry, heavy and light, is also primarily in the hands of the public sector. The manufacture of chemicals, fertilizers, petrochemicals, motor vehicles and commercial vehicles has been expanded.

Other principal manufactures are those derived from agricultural products, textiles, jute goods, sugar, leather, which along with tea, fish, and iron ore and concentrates are India's major exports.

Faced with the need to obtain loans from the World Bank and assistance from the IMF, India has abandoned centralized planning after 40 years; subsidies are to be cut, state corporations privatized and the economy opened up to foreign companies. To take India into the international trading system proper, an unprecedented budget was passed in 1993 which floated the rupee, cut interest rates and duties on imports, reduced subsidies to farmers and dismantled protectionist structures. The budget is in line with IMF proposals and the World Bank approved an annual US$2,500m exceptional financing loan for three years in February 1993.

FINANCE

The budget estimates for 1990-1 placed total expenditure at Rs 1,053,160 million. Total revenue (excluding States' shares) was Rs 939,690 million.

STATES AND TERRITORIES OF THE UNION

(Capital in parenthesis)	Area (sq. km)	Population (1991 Census)	Governor	Chief Minister
STATES				
Andhra Pradesh (Hyderabad)	275,100p	53,549,673	K. Kant	Vijay Bhaskar Reddy
Arunachal Pradesh (Itanagar)	83,700p	631,839	Madhukar Dinghe	B. B. Lyngdoh
Assam (Dispur)	78,400	24,456,000	Loknath Misra	Hiteshwar Saika
Bihar (Patna)	173,900p	86,338,853	A. R. Kidwai	Lalu Prasad
Goa (Panaji)	3,701	1,000,000†	B.P. Singh	Wilfred D'Souza
Gujarat (Gandhinagar)	196,000p	41,174,060	Sarup Singh	Chimanbhai Patel
Haryana (Chandigarh)	44,200p	12,922,618	D. L. Mandal	Bhajan Lal
Himachal Pradesh (Shimla)	55,700	4,280,818	Gulsher Ahmed	(President's rule)
Jammu and Kashmir*				
(Srinagar/Jammu)	222,200p	5,987,389	Gen. K. V. Krishna Rao	(Governor's rule)
Karnataka (Bangalore)	191,800	44,817,398	K. A. Khan	Veerappa Moily
Kerala (Trivandrum)	38,900p	25,453,680	B. Rachiah	K. Karunakaran
Madhya Pradesh (Bhopal)	443,500p	66,135,862	M. S. Qureshi	(President's rule)
Maharashtra (Bombay-Mumbai)	307,700p	62,784,171	P. C. Alexander	Sharad Pawar
Manipur (Imphal)	22,300	1,420,953	K. V. Raghunath Reddy	R. K. D. Singh
Meghalaya (Shillong)	22,400p	1,335,819	M. Dighe	S. C. Maraq
Mizoram (Aizawl)	21,100	686,217	P. R. Kyndiah	Lal Thanhawla
Nagaland (Kohima)	16,600	1,215,573	Loknath Mishra	S. C. Jamir
Orissa (Bhubaneswar)	155,700	26,370,271	B. S. Reddy	J. B. Patnaik
Punjab (Chandigarh)	50,400	16,788,915	Surindra Nath	Beant Singh
Rajasthan (Jaipur)	342,200	34,261,862	Bali Ram Bhagat	(President's rule)
Sikkim (Gangtok)	7,100	403,612	Adm. R. H. Tahiliani	N. B. Bhandari
Tamil Nadu (Madras)	130,100p	48,408,077	M. Channa Reddy	J. Jayalalitha
Tripura (Agartala)	10,500	2,744,807	Romesh Bhandari	S. R. Barman
Uttar Pradesh (Lucknow)	294,400p	110,862,013	Motilal Vora	(President's rule)
West Bengal (Calcutta)	88,800p	67,782,732	K. V. R. Reddy	Jyoti Basu
UNION TERRITORIES			Lt.-Governor	
Andaman and Nicobar Is.				
(Port Blair)	8,200	188,741	Vakkom Purushothaman	
Chandigarh	100	451,610	Surindra Nath	
Dadra and Nagar Haveli				
(Silvassa)	500	103,676	K. S. Baidwan	
Daman and Diu	112	78,981†	K. S. Baidwan	
Delhi	1,500	6,220,406	P. K. Dave	
Lakshadweep (Kavaratti)	30	51,681	Satish Chandra	
Pondicherry	500	789,416	M. Channa Reddy	

p provisional figure
† estimated figure

* Jammu and Kashmir is an area disputed between India, Pakistan and China, all three controlling a part of the territory. The area figure includes those parts occupied by Pakistan and China, which are claimed by India, but the population figure excludes the population of these areas, where the Census was not taken. The state's capital is at Srinagar in summer and Jammu in winter.

TRADE WITH UK	1991	1992
Imports from UK	£1,017,398,000	£945,541,000
Exports to UK	776,976,000	862,131,000

COMMUNICATIONS

Five international airports – Palam (Delhi), Sahar (Bombay), Dum Dum (Calcutta), Meenambakkam (Madras) and Trivandrum – are managed by the International Airports Authority. The other 88 aerodromes are controlled and operated by the Civil Aviation Department of the Government. The national airlines are Indian Airlines (internal) and Air India (international).

The railways are grouped into nine administrative zones, Southern, Central, Western, Northern, North-Eastern, North-East Frontier, Eastern, South-Eastern and South-Central with a total track length of 62,367 km, about 16 per cent of which is electrified. Gross traffic receipts (1990–1), crores of rupees, 12,096. Working expenses, 11,153. Net railway revenues, 943.

The chief seaports are Bombay (Mumbai), Calcutta, Haldia, Madras, Mormugao, Cochin, Visakhapatnam, Kandla, Paradip, Mangalore and Tuticorin. There are 139 minor working ports with varying capacity.

In March 1992, 412 ships totalling 5,910,000 gross tons were on the Indian Register.

INDONESIA
Republik Indonesia

Situated between 6° N. and 11° S. latitude and between 95° and 141° E. longitude, Indonesia comprises the islands of Java, Madura, and Sumatra, the Riouw-Lingga Archipelago (which with Karimon, Anambas, Natuna Islands, Tambelan, and part of Sumatra, form the province of Riau), the islands of Bangka and Billiton, part of the island of Borneo (Kalimantan), Sulawesi (formerly Celebes) Island, the Molucca Islands (Ternate, Tidore, Halmahera, Buru, Seram, Banda, Timor-Laut, Larat, Bachiam, Obi, Kei, Aru, Babar, Leti and Wetar), the islands of Bali, Lombok, Sumbawa, Sumba, Flores, Timor and others comprising the provinces of East and West Nusa Tenggara and the western half of the island of New Guinea (Irian Jaya), with a total area of 735,358 sq. miles (1,904,569 sq. km), and a population (UN estimate 1991) of 187,765,000.

CAPITAL – ΨJakarta (population 7,885,519). Other important centres are: (Java) ΨSurabaya (2,027,913), ΨSemarang (1,026,671), Bandung (1,462,637); (Sumatra) Palembang (787,187), Medan (1,378,955); (Sulawesi) ΨUjung Pandang (formerly *Makassar*) (709,038); (Kalimantan) Banjarmasin (381,286), ΨPontianak (304,778), ΨBalikpapan (280,675); (Moluccas) Ambon (208,898); (Bali) Denpasar, Singaraja (for whole island 2,174,105); (Nusa Tenggara) Kupang (329,371); (Irian Jaya) Jayapura (107,164).
CURRENCY – Rupiah (Rp) of 100 sen.
FLAG – Equal bands of red over white.
NATIONAL ANTHEM – Indonesia Raya (Great Indonesia).
NATIONAL DAY – 17 August (Anniversary of Proclamation of Independence).

GOVERNMENT

From the early part of the 17th century much of the Indonesian archipelago was under Netherlands rule. Following the Second World War, during which the archipelago was occupied by the Japanese, a strong nationalistic movement manifested itself and after sporadic fighting the formal transfer of sovereignty by the Netherlands of all the former Dutch East Indies except western New Guinea took place on 27 December 1949.

Western New Guinea became part of Indonesia in 1963 under the name West Irian (now Irian Jaya), this interpretation being confirmed in an 'Act of Free Choice' in July 1969, of which the United Nations took note in November 1969. Following a unilateral declaration of independence by Fretilin in November 1975, Indonesia took over the former Portuguese colony of East Timor, which in July 1976 was declared the 27th province of Indonesia.

Following a three-week period of unrest and violent student demonstrations in 1966 the Minister of the Army, General Suharto, took over effective political power in March. General Suharto was made Acting President with full powers in March 1967, and in March 1968 was appointed full President for a period of five years. He has been re-appointed by the National Assembly at each presidential election since.

In the general election of June 1992, Golkar obtained 281 seats, the Muslim United Development Party 63 seats and the Indonesian Democratic Party 56 seats.

SECESSION

Fretilin (Front for an independent East Timor) has been fighting for independence for the former Portuguese colony from Indonesia since annexation in 1975. The UN has refused to recognize the annexation and still considers Portugal to exercise sovereignty over East Timor. A massacre of civilians protesting for independence in Dili (East Timor's capital) by the Indonesian army in November 1991 caused international outrage.

HEAD OF STATE
President, General Suharto, *appointed Acting President* 12 March 1967; *confirmed as President* 28 March 1968, *re-elected for a term of five years*, 1973, 1978, 1983, 1988 and March 1993.
Vice-President, Try Sutrisno, *elected* March 1993.

CABINET *as at August 1993*
Co-ordinating Ministers, Gen. (retd) Soesilo Soedarman *(Political and Security Affairs)*; Saleh Afiff *(Economy, Finance, Industry and Development Supervision)*; Maj.-Gen. Azwar Anas *(Public Welfare)*; Ir Hartarto *(Industrial and Trade Affairs)*.
Ministers, Lt.-Gen. (retd) Yogi Memet *(Internal Affairs)*; Ali Alatas *(Foreign Affairs)*; Gen. Edi Sudrajat *(Defence and Security)*; Utoyo Usman *(Justice)*; Mr Harmoko *(Information)*; Mar'ie Muhammad *(Finance)*; Satrio Yudono *(Trade)*; Tungki Arinibowo *(Industry)*; Sjarifuddin Baharsyah *(Agriculture)*; Lt.-Gen. Ida Bagus Sujana *(Mines and Energy)*; Radinal Mochtar *(Public Works)*; Haryanto Danudirto *(Communications)*; Maj.-Gen. Bustanil Arifin *(Co-operatives)*; Abdul Latief *(Manpower)*; Siswono Yudohusodo *(Transmigration)*; Joop Ave *(Tourism, Posts and Telecommunications)*; Wardiman Joyonegoro *(Education and Culture)*; Dr Suyudi *(Health)*; Tarmizi Taher *(Religious Affairs)*; Prof. Endang Suweno *(Social Affairs)*; Jamaludin Suryohadikasumo *(Forestry)*; Subiakto Cakrawerdaya *(Small Businesses)*; Maj.-Gen. (retd) Moeroliono *(State Secretary)*.
Ministers of State, Saadilah Marsjid *(Cabinet Secretary)*; Johnny Kartasasmita *(National Development Planning)*; Siswono Judo Husodo *(Housing)*; Haryono Suyono *(Population)*; Maj.-Gen. Tiopan Silalahi *(Administrative Reform)*; Prof. B. J. Habibie *(Research and Technology)*; Mien Sugandhi *(Women's Affairs)*; Hayano Isman *(Sport and Youth Affairs)*; Ibrahim Hassan *(Food Affairs)*; Sanyoto Sastrowardoyo *(Investment)*; Sonny Harsono *(Agrarian Affairs)*; Akbar Tandjung *(People's Housing)*; Sarwono Kusumaatmadja *(Environment)*; S. H. Singgih *(Attorney-General)*; Soedradjat Djiwandono *(Governor of Bank of Indonesia)*.

INDONESIAN EMBASSY
38 Grosvenor Square, London WIX 9AD
Tel 071-499 7661

Ambassador Extraordinary and Plenipotentiary, His Excellency Junus Habibie (1993).
Minister, Herijanto Soeprapto *(Deputy Chief of Mission)*.
Minister Counsellor, J. S. Gaffar *(Commercial)*.
Defence Attaché, Col. J. P. Mandas.

BRITISH EMBASSY
Jalan M. H. Thamrin 75, Jakarta 10310
Tel: Jakarta 330904

Ambassador Extraordinary and Plenipotentiary, His Excellency Roger Carrick, CMG, LVO (1990).
Deputy Ambassador, Counsellor and Consul-General, J. C. R. Gray.
Counsellor (Commercial/Development), P. J. Bacon.
Defence Attaché, Col. B. G. Nicholson, OBE.

BRITISH CONSULAR OFFICES – There are British Consular Offices at *Jakarta, Medan* and *Surabaya*.

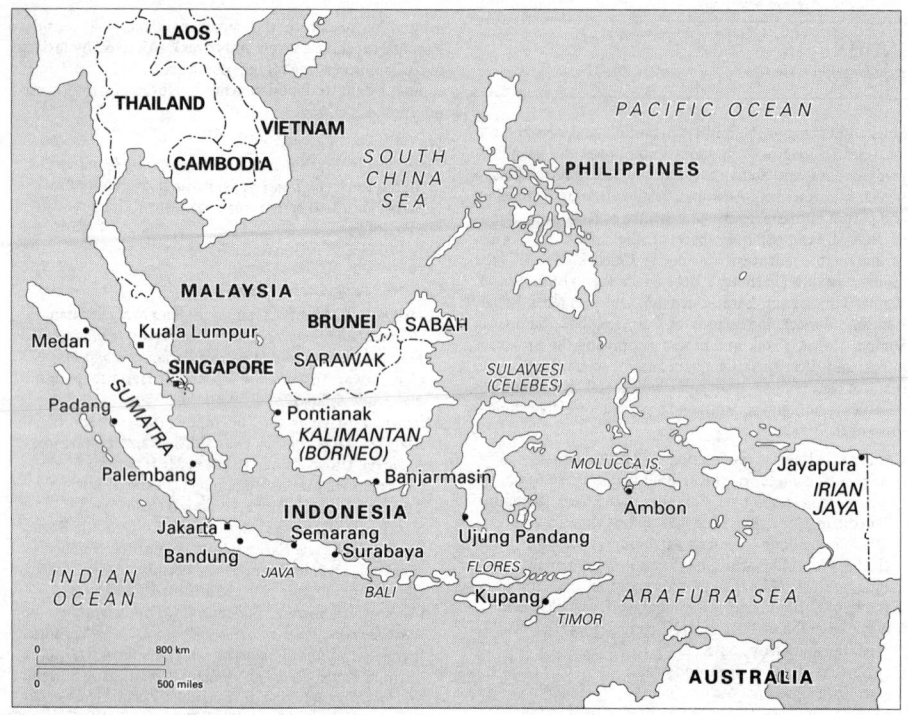

BRITISH COUNCIL REPRESENTATIVE, A. Webster, S Widjojo Centre, Jalan Jenderal Sudirman 71, Jakarta 12190. There are also libraries at *Bandung* and *Medan*. INDONESIA BRITAIN ASSOCIATION, c/o R. A. M. Ramsay, Lippo Life Building, 7th Floor, Jl. HR Rasuna Said, Jakarta 12910.

DEFENCE

The Armed Forces have a total active strength of 283,000 with selective conscription of two years. The Army has a strength of 215,000 with some 150 light tanks, 630 armoured personnel carriers, 200–250 artillery pieces and 90 surface-to-air missile launchers. The Navy has 44,000 personnel (including 12,000 marines), 2 submarines, 17 principal surface combatant vessels, 18 combat aircraft and 15 armed helicopters. The Air Force has 24,000 personnel and some 81 combat aircraft of US and British manufacture organized into two ground attack, one air defence, two counter-insurgency, one maritime reconnaissance, three helicopter and three training squadrons.

There are some 180,000 paramilitary police personnel.

ECONOMY

Nearly 70 per cent of the population of Indonesia is engaged in agriculture and related production. Copra, kapok, nutmeg, pepper and cloves are produced, mainly by smallholders; palm oil, sugar, fibres and cinchona are produced by large estates. Rubber, tea, coffee and tobacco are also produced by both in large quantities. Rice is a traditional staple food for the people of Indonesia and the islands of Java, Sulawesi and Sumatra are important producers. Production has risen rapidly in recent years to 25 million tons and the country is now self-sufficient.

Oil and liquefied natural gas are the most important assets, the export of which constitutes around 80 per cent of Indonesia's export earnings, but more recent developments have underscored the vulnerability of the economy to depressed international markets and weak oil prices. Timber is the second largest foreign exchange earner after oil. Strenuous efforts have been made to develop non-oil exports, and, although these recently reached about 56 per cent, they have since fallen back to below 50 per cent of total exports but in real terms their value continues to rise.

Indonesia is rich in minerals, particularly tin, of which the country is the world's third biggest producer; petroleum, coal, nickel and bauxite are the other principal mineral products. There are also considerable deposits of gold, silver, manganese phosphates and sulphur. Aid to Indonesia is channelled through the Indonesian Consultative Group (ICG). Indonesia received about US$4.8 billion in 1992–3.

Indonesia's Fifth Development Programme started in 1984 and its main objectives are the diversification of the economy to reduce dependence on crude oil, with particular emphasis on agriculture and manufacturing.

TRADE WITH UK

Principal exports to the United Kingdom are rubber, timber, non-ferrous metals, clothing, tea, coffee, spices, vegetable oils and fats, and crude oil for refinement. Imports from the United Kingdom are mainly of machinery, transport equipment, electrical equipment and chemicals.

	1991	1992
Imports from UK	£197,991,000	£312,756,000
Exports to UK	415,340,000	536,057,000

COMMUNICATIONS

In Java a main railway line connects Jakarta with Surabaya in the east of Java and there are several branches. In Sumatra the important towns of Medan, Padang and Palembang are the centres of short railway systems.

Sea communications in the archipelago are maintained by the state-run shipping companies Djakarta-Lloyd (ocean-going) and Pelni (coastal and inter-island) and other small concerns. Transport by small craft on the rivers of the larger islands plays an important part in trade.

Air services in Indonesia are operated by Garuda Indonesian Airways and other local airlines, and Jakarta is served by various international services. There are approximately 50,000 miles of roads.

IRAN
Jomhori-e-Islami-e-Iran

Iran has an area of 636,296 sq. miles (1,648,000 sq. km), with a population of 55,762,000 (1991 UN estimate). It is mostly an arid table-land, encircled, except in the east, by mountains, the highest in the north rising to 18,934 ft. The central and eastern portion is a vast salt desert.

RELIGION – The Iranians are mostly Shia Muslims but among them are Zoroastrians, Bahais, Sunni Muslims and Armenian and Assyrian Christians. Emigration has much reduced the once substantial Jewish community.

LANGUAGE AND LITERATURE – Persian, or Farsi, the language of Iran, and of some other areas formerly under Persian rule, is an Indo-European tongue with many Arabic elements added; the alphabet is mainly Arabic, with writing from right to left. Among the great names in Persian literature are those of Abu'l Kásim Mansúr, or Firdausi (AD 939–1020), Omar Khayyám, the astronomer-poet (died AD 1122), Muslihu'd-Din, known as Sa'di (born AD 1184), and Shems-ed-Din Muhammad, or Hafiz (died AD 1389).

CAPITAL – Tehran, population (1990 UN estimate) 6,042,584. Other large towns are Tabriz, Isfahan, Meshed, Shiraz, Resht, Kerman, Hamadan, Yazd, Kermanshah and Ahwaz.

CURRENCY – Rial.

FLAG – Three horizontal stripes of green, white, red, with the slogan *Allahu Akbar* repeated 22 times along the edges of the green and red stripes, and the national emblem in the centre.

NATIONAL ANTHEM – Sorood-e Jomhoori-e Eslami.

NATIONAL DAY – 11 February.

GOVERNMENT

Iran was ruled from the end of the 18th century by Shahs of the Qajar dynasty. A nationalist movement became active in December 1905, and in August 1906 Shah Muzaffer-ud-Din granted a constitution. After the war of 1914–18, the subsequent troubles and the signature of the Soviet-Iranian Treaty of 1921, a vigorous Prime Minister, Reza Khan, re-established general order. On 31 October 1925 the last representative of the Qajar dynasty, Sultan Ahmed Shah, was deposed in his absence by the National Assembly, which handed over the government to Prime Minister Reza Khan. Reza Khan was elected Shah on 13 December 1925 by the Constituent Assembly, and took the title Reza Shah Pahlavi. On 16 September 1941 Reza Shah abdicated in favour of the Crown Prince, who ascended the throne under the title of Mohammed Reza Shah Pahlavi.

Following widespread and persistent opposition to his regime, the Shah departed from Iran in January 1979. Ayatollah Khomeini, the main spiritual leader of the Shia Muslims, returned to Iran from exile on 1 February. Following a national referendum, Iran was declared an Islamic Republic on 1 April 1979. A new constitution, providing for a President, Prime Minister and Consultative Assembly, and also for overall leadership by Ayatollah Khomeini, was approved by referendum in December 1979. The government's severe measures suppressed violent opposition. In June 1989 Khomeini died and President Khamenei was appointed Leader of the Islamic Republic. Rafsanjani was elected President in July 1989, and the post of prime minister was abolished. In April 1992 elections to the Majlis (consultative assembly), candidates supporting President Rafsanjani were overwhelmingly elected, winning over 200 of the 270 seats. However, in the June 1993 presidential elections, President Rafsanjani received only 63 per cent of the vote (compared with 94 per cent in 1989) and only 56 per cent of the electorate voted. This reflects growing discontent with economic hardship, demonstrated by the refusal of the Majlis to confirm the reappointment of Economy and Finance Minister Mohsen Nourbakhsh, who was blamed for introducing the free-market reforms which have caused some hardship.

Iran was at war with Iraq following the Iraqi invasion of Iran in September 1980. International efforts to end the fighting focused on United Nations Security Council Resolution 598 of July 1987, and a ceasefire came into effect on 20 August 1988. In August 1990 Iraq accepted Iran's conditions for settling the conflict, including return to the 1975 border, but a formal peace treaty has not been signed.

Leader of the Islamic Republic, Ayatollah Seyed Ali Khamenei, *appointed* June 1989.
President, Hojjatoleslam Ali Akbar Hashemi Rafsanjani, *elected* 28 July 1989, *re-elected* 11 June 1993.

CABINET *as at 17 August 1993*

Agriculture, Issa Kalantari.
Commerce, Yahya Al-Eshaq.
Construction Crusade, Gholam Reza Forouzesh.
Defence, Mohammed Forouzandeh.
Economy and Finance (acting), Mohammad Javad Vahaji.
Education, Mohammad Ali Najafi.
Culture and Higher Education, Dr Hashemi Golpeygani.
Energy, Bizhan Namdar Zanganeh.
Islamic Culture and Guidance, Ali Larijani.
Foreign Affairs, Ali Akbar Velayati.
Health, Ali Reza Marandi.
Heavy Industries, Mohammad Hadi Nezhad-Hosseinian.
Housing and Urban Development, Abbas Ahmad Akhundi.
Industries, Mohammad Reza Nematzadeh.
Intelligence, Ali Fallahian.
Interior, Ali Mohammad Besharati.
Justice, Mohammad Esmail Shoushtari.
Labour and Social Affairs, Hossein Kamali.
Mines and Metals, Mohammad Hossein Mahloujchi.
Oil, Gholamreza Aghazadeh.
Posts, Telephones and Telegraphs, Mohammad Gharrazi.
Roads and Transport, Akbar Torkan.
Co-operatives, Gholem Reza Shafei.

EMBASSY OF THE ISLAMIC REPUBLIC OF IRAN
27 Prince's Gate, London SW7 1PX
Tel 071-584 8101

Chargé d'Affaires, G. Ansari.

BRITISH EMBASSY
143 Ferdowsi Avenue, PO Box 11365-4474, Tehran 11344
Tel: Tehran 675011

Counsellor and Chargé d'Affaires, Jeffrey R. James (1993).
First Secretary (Commercial), M. A. Hilton.

DEFENCE

Since the end of the war with Iraq the Iranian armed forces have been significantly reduced in size and now number some 528,000 active personnel. The conscription term is 24 months, with conscripts serving almost exclusively in the Army. The Army has a strength of 305,000 (including 250,000 conscripts) with one special forces, four armoured and seven infantry divisions, some 700 main battle tanks, 750 armoured personnel carriers and armoured infantry fighting vehicles, 1,300 artillery pieces and 300 helicopters.

The Navy is 18,000 strong, with one submarine, eight principal surface combatant vessels, 33 patrol and coastal craft, and nine armed helicopters. The Air Force has 35,000 personnel, with some 262 combat aircraft. However, only around 50 per cent of these are serviceable due to the US armaments embargo, in operation since 1979.

The Islamic Revolutionary Guards Corps numbers some 170,000, of which 150,000 are ground and 20,000 naval forces.

EDUCATION

Since 1943 primary education has been compulsory and free. There are 22 universities in Iran (eight in Tehran, 14 in the provinces). The educational system has been reformed following the revolution.

ECONOMY

Agriculture suffered from a lack of investment during the Iran–Iraq war, but output is rising. Under the current Five-Year Development Plan, an attempt is being made to reduce Iran's dependence on food imports.

Wheat is the principal crop; other important crops are barley, rice, cotton, sugar beet, fruit, nuts and vegetables. Wool is also a major product. There are extensive forests in the north and west, the conservation of which is a continuing problem.

Apart from oil, the principal industrial products are carpets, textiles, sugar, cement and other construction materials, ginned cotton, vegetable oil and other food products, leather and shoes, metal manufactures, pharmaceuticals, motor vehicles, fertilizers and plastics. Industrial output was severely curtailed by the 1979 revolution, as a result of which many industrialists left the country, and by the Iran–Iraq war, but the private sector is now being encouraged again and prospects for industry are quite good.

The oilfields, which lie in south-western Iran, were nationalized in 1951. From 1957 until the 1979 revolution a consortium of eight oil companies (one British, one French, one Dutch, and five American) was responsible for the production, refining and sale of oil. In July 1979 the National Iranian Oil Company assumed full control of the oil industry. In addition to that extracted from the onshore wells, oil is also produced from a number of off-shore oilfields. Oil production is around 3.3 million b.p.d., of which some 2.7 million b.p.d. is exported. Iran is a member of OPEC.

FINANCE	1993–4
Revenue	Rials 25,426,000m
Expenditure	25,426,000m

TRADE

Over 80 per cent of Iran's export earnings come from oil, but an effort is being made to increase non-oil exports. The level of finance for imports depends largely on the international oil price, but with foreign investment being encouraged and restrictions on the private sector eased, the market has become more buoyant over the last few years.

Imports into Iran consist mainly of industrial and agricultural machinery, motor vehicles and motor vehicle components for assembly, iron and steel (including manufactures), electrical machinery and goods, meat, various other foods, and certain textile fabrics and yarns.

The principal exports, apart from oil, are cotton, carpets, dried fruit, nuts, hides and skins, mineral ores, wool, gums, caviare, cumin seed and spices. Germany and Japan are Iran's leading suppliers.

Trade with UK	1991	1992
Imports from UK	£511,532,000	£568,113,000
Exports to UK	158,354,000	164,512,000

COMMUNICATIONS

Tehran is at the centre of a network of highways linking the capital with other major towns, the ports and the frontiers with Turkey, Armenia, Azerbaijan, Turkmenistan, Afghanistan and Pakistan, and with the Caspian Sea.

The Trans-Iranian Railway runs from Bandar Turcoman, on the Caspian Sea, via Tehran to Bandar Khomeini, on the Persian Gulf. Other lines link Tehran with Tabriz and with Mashad. There are also railways from Tabriz to Julfa and from Zahedan to Quetta, and a branch line from Ahwaz to Khorramshahr. An extension from Qom to Kerman is now in operation, as is one from Bandar Turcoman to Gorgan. The Iranian rail system is linked to the Turkish system via Van, and is to be linked also to Turkmenistan.

There is an international airport at Tehran (Mehrabad), and airports at all the major provincial centres. The national airline, Iranair, is government-owned and operates international and domestic routes.

IRAQ
Al-Jumhouriya al-'Iraqia

Iraq extends from Turkey on the north and north-east to the Gulf on the south and south-east, and from Iran on the east to Syria and Arabian Desert on the west. The approximate position being between 37¼° to 48¾° E. longitude, and 37¼° to 30° N. latitude. The area of Iraq is 167,925 sq. miles (434,924 sq. km), of which 37 per cent is desert land. About 35 to 40 per cent of the remainder is potentially cultivable either by rainfall or by irrigation.

The rivers Euphrates and Tigris traverse the country. The Euphrates (which has a total length of 1,700 miles from its source to its outflow in the Persian Gulf) is formed by two arms, of which the Murad Su (415 miles) rises in eastern Erzurum, and flows westwards to a junction with the Kara Su, or Frat Su (275 miles); the other arm rises in the north-west of Erzurum in the Dumlu Dagh. The River Tigris has a total length of 1,150 miles from its source to its junction with the Euphrates at Qurna, 70 miles from the Gulf, and rises in two arms south of the Taurus mountains, in Kurdistan, uniting at Til, where the boundaries of the districts of Diarbekir, Van and Bitlis conjoin.

POPULATION – At the Census of October 1987 Iraq had a total population of 16,278,316. A 1991 UN estimate gives a figure of 19,581,000.

LANGUAGE – The official language is Arabic. Minority languages include Kurdish (about 15 per cent), Turkic and Aramaic.

CAPITAL – Baghdad. Population of the governorate (Census 1977) 3,205,645. Other towns of importance are Ψ Basra, Mosul and Kirkuk.

CURRENCY – Iraqi dinar (ID) of 1,000 fils.

FLAG – Three horizontal stripes of red, white, black; on the white stripe three stars and the slogan *Allahu Akbar* all in green.

NATIONAL DAY – 17 July (Revolution Day).

HISTORY

In 1944 excavations at Tell Hassuna, near Shura (on the Tigris in north Iraq) unearthed abundant traces of culture dating back to 5000 BC. Excavations in 1948 at Tel Abu Shahrain, south of 'Ur of the Chaldees,' confirm Eridu's claim to be the most ancient city of the Sumerian world. Hillah, the ancient city on the left bank of the Shatt el Hillah, a branch of the Euphrates, about 70 miles south of Baghdad, is near the site of Babylon and of the 'house of the lofty-head' or 'gate of the god' (Tower of Babel). Mosul governorate covers a great part of the ancient kingdom of Assyria, the ruins of Ninevah, the Assyrian capital, being visible on the banks of the Tigris, opposite Mosul. Qurna, at the junction of the Tigris and Euphrates, is traditionally supposed to be the site of the Garden of Eden.

Under the Treaty of Lausanne (1923), Turkey renounced sovereignty over Mesopotamia. A provisional Arab government was set up in November 1920, and in August 1921 the Emir Faisal was elected King of Iraq. The country was a monarchy until July 1958, when King Faisal II was assassinated. From 1958 Iraq has been under presidential rule.

GOVERNMENT

According to the provisional constitution, the highest state authority is the Revolutionary Command Council (RCC), which elects the President from among its own members. The President appoints the Council of Ministers. Legislative authority is shared by the RCC and the 250-member National Assembly, which is elected every four years by universal adult suffrage. Following general elections in April 1989 the Arab Ba'ath Socialist Party holds the majority of the Assembly seats, the remainder being held by the state-sponsored National Progressive Patriotic Front.

In August 1990 Iraq accepted Iran's conditions for a peace treaty, thus formally ending hostilities in which the two states had been involved since September 1980.

Iraq invaded Kuwait on 2 August 1990. The subsequent announcement of annexation was declared void by the UN Security Council. Since the end of the (second) Gulf War and the allied victory in Kuwait in February 1991, Iraq has been involved in a continuous diplomatic and economic battle with the United Nations and western states. Iraqi attacks on Kurdish armed forces and civilian populations in northern Iraq in early 1991 led to UN Security Council resolution 688 which established Kurdish safe havens in northern Iraq and a no-fly zone above the 36th parallel (Northern no-fly zone) patrolled by US, British and French aircraft based in Turkey. A similar no-fly zone (Southern) was established below the 32nd parallel in August 1992 to stop Iraqi aircraft bombing the Shia refugees in the southern Iraqi marshes. The Iraqi regime has continually sparred with western aircraft patrolling the no-fly zones by 'locking-on' missiles, causing retaliatory air strikes throughout 1992 and 1993 to destroy missile batteries and radar installations. The regime has also continually obstructed the work of UN weapons inspection teams who have overseen the destruction of Iraqi weapons of mass destruction since April 1991. In retaliation for this non-co-operation with the UN, the UN Security Council voted in October 1992 to seize all Iraqi assets in foreign banks and use the money to compensate Gulf war victims, finance UN weapons inspection teams and fund relief operations to Kurdish and Shia areas. In addition, the US launched cruise missile attacks in January and June 1993 which destroyed an Iraqi nuclear weapons plant and the headquarters of the Iraqi intelligence service in retaliation for, respectively, Iraqi refusals to allow UN weapons inspection teams entry and an Iraqi attempt to murder ex-President Bush.

In January 1993 the UN announced a new demarcation of the Iraqi-Kuwaiti border, moving it a few hundred metres northwards and giving part of the port of Umm Qasr to Kuwait.

SECESSION

Following the allied victory in Kuwait in February 1991, rebellion against the government broke out in both Kurdish northern Iraq and Shiite southern Iraq. Although the revolt was suppressed by the end of April, the plight of the Kurdish refugees led western governments to set up a security zone in northern Iraq to protect them. Allied forces were withdrawn in July. Saddam Hussein withdrew his administration from Kurdish-dominatd areas of northern Iraq in October 1991 and imposed an economic embargo on the territory. The Kurds have since established a *de facto* administration in certain northern areas. In May 1992 the Kurds voted in free elections for a 100-seat parliament and a 'political leader'. The Kurdish Democratic Party and the Patriotic Union of Kurdistan both gained 50 seats and a Kurdish government was formed in July with party leaders Masoud Barzani and Jalal Talabani as joint leaders of the territory and Fuad Masum as Prime Minister. The Iraqi economic embargo has caused great hardship, and the neighbouring states of Syria, Iran and Turkey have been reluctant to trade with the Kurdish administration as they all have their own Kurdish minorities. The government of Fuad Masum resigned in March 1993 because of its inabililty to overcome fuel and food shortages and was replaced by one led by Kosrat Abdullah Rasuh.

HEAD OF STATE

President, Chairman of the Revolutionary Command Council, Saddam Hussein, *assumed office* 16 July 1979.
Vice President, Taha Yassin Ramadhan.

REVOLUTIONARY COMMAND COUNCIL

Chairman, Saddam Hussein.
Vice-Chairman, Izzat Ibrahim.
Secretary-General, Khalid Abdul Rashid.
Members, Taha Yassin Ramadhan; Tariq Aziz; Hassan Ali Nasser al-Amiri; Taha Mohieddin Maaruf.

CABINET *as at August 1993*

Prime Minister, Muhammad Hamza al-Zubaidi.
Deputy Prime Minister, Tariq Aziz.
Interior, Wathban Hassan Ibrahim.
Defence, Ali Hassan Majid.
Foreign Affairs, Mohammed Saaed al-Sahhaf.
Finance, Ahmad Hussein al-Khodair.
Culture and Information, Hamad Youssef Hammadi.
Justice, Shabib al-Malki.
Agriculture and Irrigation, Abdul Wahab Mahmoud Abdullah.
Industry and Minerals, Amer Hammadi As-Saadi.
Oil, Usama Abdul Ar-Razzaq Hammadi.

Education, Hikmat Abdullah al-Bazzaz.
Labour and Social Affairs, Umeed Madhat Mubarak.
Health, Abdul As-Salem Muhammad Saeed.
Planning, Samal Majid Faraj.
Higher Education and Scientific Research, Humam Abdel-Khaliq.
Housing and Construction, Mahmoud Diyab Al-Ahmad.
Transport and Communications, Abdul As-Sattar Ahmad Al-Maini.
Religious Endowments and Religious Affairs, Abdullah Fadel-Abbas.
Trade, Muhammed Mahdi Salih.
Minister of State for Military Affairs, Gen. Abdul Al-Jabbar Khalil.

IRAQI DIPLOMATIC MISSION IN LONDON

Since Iraq's breach of diplomatic relations with Britain in February 1991, the Jordanian Embassy has handled Iraqi interests in this country.

BRITISH DIPLOMATIC REPRESENTATION

The British Embassy was closed in January 1991. Since the breach of diplomatic relations, the Russian Embassy has handled British interests in Iraq.

DEFENCE

The Iraqi armed forces were decimated in the defeat by the allied coalition which drove them from Kuwait but remained strong enough to suppress the Kurdish and Shiite rebellions. Estimates of the size and strength of the armed forces can only be vague but total active personnel is in the region of 380,000, from a pre-war total of one million. Reservists number some 650,000 personnel, of whom around 100,000 are on permanent recall to the Army. Conscripts serve for between 18 and 24 months.

The Army has a strength of around 350,000, with around 2,300 main battle tanks (5,300 pre-war); 2,900 armoured personnel carriers and armoured infantry fighting vehicles (4,800 pre-war); 1,450 artillery pieces (3,150 pre-war) and 120 armed helicopters. The Army is organized into seven Republican Guard and 22 regular divisions with 15 specialized counterinsurgency brigades. The Navy has a strength of around 1,000 with one frigate, 10 patrol and coastal craft and four mine warfare vessels. The Air Force has a strength of around 30,000 with some 320 combat aircraft and a further 115 still in Iran, where they were flown during the war. The allies destroyed 135 aircraft. In addition, there are 20,000 paramilitary frontier guards.

Since the end of the war, UN weapons inspection teams have searched Iraq, destroying and dismantling nuclear, chemical and biological weapons, Scud missiles and their launchers, and the Superguns. However, it is believed that Iraq has successfully hidden some weapons of mass destruction and the means of producing them.

In opposition to Iraqi forces there are some 57,000 armed Kurdish guerrillas, with a further 36,000 support personnel. These are armed with captured Iraqi tanks, artillery and mortars, and a proliferation of small arms. There is also a brigade-sized armed Shia opposition force based in Iran.

COMMUNICATIONS

Facilities at the port of Basra have been improved but the port has not been used since the outbreak of hostilities with Iran in September 1980. Continuous dredging of the Shatt-al-Arab has also been suspended by hostilities and the channel has seriously silted. The port of Um Qasr near the Kuwaiti border was developed for freight and sulphur

handling and a container terminal was ready for operation but is not in use due to the UN's new demarcation of the Iraq-Kuwait border which gives part of the port to Kuwait. All external borders, except that of Jordan, are closed to Iraqi traffic.

There is an international airport at Baghdad. Iraqi Airways provided flights between Baghdad and London, and other international airlines operated to Europe. Iraqi Republican Railways provided regular passenger and goods services between Basra, Baghdad and Mosul. There is also a metre gauge rail line connecting Baghdad with Khanaqin, Kirkuk and Arbil.

Iraqi communications were greatly affected by the Gulf War; large numbers of bridges were destroyed and the railway system extensively disrupted.

ECONOMY

Apart from the revenues to be derived from oil, agricultural development makes a valuable contribution to the wealth of the country and two harvests can usually be gathered in the year. Production fluctuates from year to year according to rainfall. The Government's concern with agricultural development is shown in the large financial allocations made to the sector. Salinity and soil erosion, caused by a high water table, inadequate irrigation and drainage and traditional farming methods, are the major problems now being addressed by development planners.

Increasing industrialization is taking place but industrial production has been greatly reduced because of war damage and sanctions.

Iraq's major industry is oil production. It was nationalized in 1972 and accounts for approximately 98 per cent of the total government revenue and 45 per cent of the Gross National Product. Production was some 3.5 million barrels per day in 1979 but the effects of war damage on the Basra terminals and the closure of the trans-Syria pipeline reduced production until new pipelines were built via Turkey and Saudi Arabia. Total revenues from oil were estimated at $11,000–14,000 million in 1988.

In August 1990, the UN imposed mandatory economic sanctions on Iraq, including a world-wide ban on its oil exports. Sanctions were modified in August 1991 to allow the sale of 20 per cent of pre-war oil production; the proceeds are to be allocated to a special UN account for the purchase of food and other essential supplies, and for the funding of war reparations, but Iraq has refused to make use of this.

TRADE

The principal imports in normal times would be iron and steel, cement and other building materials, mechanical and electrical machinery, motor vehicles, textiles and clothing, essential foodstuffs, grain, tinned foods and raw industrial materials. The chief exports would be crude petroleum, dates, raw wool, raw hides and skins and raw cotton.

Trade with UK	1991	1992
Imports from UK	£4,399,000	£34,023,000
Exports to UK	2,548,000	311,000

IRELAND

Ireland lies in the Atlantic Ocean, to the west of Great Britain. It is separated from Scotland by the North Channel and from Wales by the Irish Sea and St George's Channel. The area of the island is 32,588 sq. miles (84,402 sq. km), and its geographical position between 51° 26′ and 55° 21′ N.

latitude and from 5° 25′ to 10° 30′ W. longitude. The greatest length of the island, from north-east to south-west (Torr Head to Mizen Head), is 302 miles, and the greatest breadth, from east to west (Dundrum Bay to Annagh Head), is 174 miles. On the north coast of Achill Island (Co. Mayo) are the highest cliffs in the British Isles, 2,000 feet sheer above the sea.

Ireland is occupied for the greater part of its area by the central plain, with an elevation 50 to 350 ft above mean sea level, with isolated mountain ranges near the coastline. The principal mountains, with their highest points, are the Sperrin Mountains (Sawel 2,240 ft) of Co. Tyrone; the Mountains of Mourne (Slieve Donard 2,796 ft) of Co. Down, and the Wicklow Mountains (Lugnaquilla 3,039 ft); the Derryveagh Mountains (Errigal 2,466 ft) of Co. Donegal; the Connemara Mountains (Twelve Pins 2,695 ft) of Co. Galway; Macgillicuddy's Reeks (Carrantuohill 3,414 ft, the highest point in Ireland); the Galtee Mountains (3,018 ft) of Co. Tipperary, and the Knockmealdown (2,609 ft) and Comeragh Mountains (2,470 ft) of Co. Waterford.

The principal river of Ireland (and the longest in the British Isles) is the Shannon (240 miles), rising in Co. Cavan and draining the central plain; the Shannon flows through a chain of loughs to the city of Limerick, and thence to an estuary on the western Atlantic seaboard. The Slaney flows into Wexford Harbour, the Liffey to Dublin Bay, the Boyne to Drogheda, the Lee to Cork Harbour, the Blackwater to Youghal Harbour, and the Suir, Barrow and Nore to Waterford Harbour.

The principal hydrographic feature is the loughs, of which Lough Neagh (150 sq. miles) in the north-east is the largest in Ireland and the British Isles, others being the Shannon chain of Allen, Boderg, Forbes, Ree and Derg, and the Erne chain of Gowna, Oughter, Lower Erne, and Erne; Melvin, Gill, Gara and Conn in the north-west; and Corrib and Mask (joined by a hidden channel) in the west. In Co. Kerry, to the east of Macgillicuddy's Reeks, are the famous lakes of Killarney.

EARLY HISTORY – Although little is known concerning the earliest inhabitants of Ireland, there are many traces of

neolithic man throughout the island; a grave containing a polished stone axehead assigned to 2500 BC was found at Linkardstown, Co. Carlow, in 1944, and the use of bronze implements appears to have become known about the middle of the 17th century BC. In the later Bronze Age a Celtic race of Goidels appears to have invaded the island, and in the early Iron Age Brythons from South Britain are believed to have effected settlements in the south-east, while Picts from North Britain established similar settlements in the north. Towards the close of the Roman occupation of Britain, the dominant tribe in the island was that of the Scoti, who afterwards established themselves in Scotland.

According to Irish legends, the island of Ierne was settled by a Milesian race, who came from Scythia by way of Spain, and established the Kingdom of Tara about 500 BC. The supremacy of the Ardri (high king) of Tara was acknowledged by eight lesser kingdoms (Munster, Connaught, Ailech, Oriel, Ulidia, Meath, Leinster and Ossory) ruled by descendants of the eight sons of Miled. The basalt columns on the coast of Antrim, eight miles from Portrush, known as the Giant's Causeway, are connected with the legendary history of Ireland as the remnants of a bridge built in the time of Finn M'Coul (Fingal) to connect Antrim with Scotland (Staffa).

Hibernia was visited by Roman merchants but never by Roman legions, and little is known of the history of the country until the invasions of Northmen (Norwegians and Danes) towards the close of the eighth century AD. The Norwegians were distinguished as Findgaill (White Strangers) and the Danes as Dubgaill (Black Strangers), names which survive in Fingall, MacDougall and MacDowell, while the name of the island itself is held to be derived from the Scandinavian *Ira-land* (land of the Irish), the names of the provinces being survivals of Norse dialect forms (Ulaidstir, Laiginstir, Mumans-tir and Kunnak-tir). The outstanding events in the encounters with the Northmen are the Battle of Tara (980), at which the Hy Neill king Maelsechlainn II defeated the Scandinavians of Dublin and the Hebrides under the king Amlaib Cuarán; and the Battle of Clontarf (1014) by which the Scandinavian power was completely broken.

After Clontarf the supreme power was disputed by the O'Briens of Munster, the O'Neills of Ulster, and the O'Connors of Connaught, with varying fortunes. In 1152 Dermod MacMurrough (Diarmit MacMurchada), the deposed king of Leinster, sought assistance in his struggle with Rauidhri O'Connor (the high king of Ireland), and visited Henry II of England. Henry authorized him to obtain armed support in England for the recovery of his kingdom, and Dermod enlisted the services of Richard de Clare, the Norman Earl of Pembroke, afterwards known as Strongbow, who landed at Waterford in 1170 with 200 knights and 1,000 other troops for the reconquest of Leinster, where he eventually settled after marriage with Dermod's daughter.

In 1172 Henry II himself landed in Ireland. He received homage from the Irish kings and established his capital at Dublin. The invaders subsequently conquered most of the island and a feudal government was created. In the 14th and 15th centuries, the Irish recovered most of their lands, while many Anglo-Irish lords became virtually independent, royal authority being confined to the Pale, a small district round Dublin. Though, under Henry VII, Sir Edward Poynings, as Lord Deputy, had passed at the Parliament of Drogheda (1494) the act later known as Poynings' Law, subordinating the Irish legislature to the Crown, the Earls of Kildare retained effective power until Henry VIII began the reconquest of Ireland in 1534. Parliament in 1541 recognized him as King of Ireland and by 1603 English authority was supreme.

REPUBLIC OF IRELAND
Poblacht Na hEireann

The Republic of Ireland has a land area of 27,136 sq. miles (70,283 sq. km), divided into the four provinces of *Leinster* (Carlow, Dublin, Kildare, Kilkenny, Laoighis, Longford, Louth, Meath, Offaly, Westmeath, Wexford and Wicklow); *Munster* (Clare, Cork, Kerry, Limerick, Tipperary and Waterford); *Connacht* (Galway, Leitrim, Mayo, Roscommon and Sligo); and part of *Ulster* (Cavan, Donegal and Monaghan).

POPULATION – The population of the Republic in 1991 census was 3,525,719. Figures also showed 51,584 births, 16,109 marriages and 30,780 deaths in the year 1992 (provisional).

LANGUAGES – The Irish language, being the national language, is the first official language. The English language is recognized as a second official language.

RELIGION – At the Census of 1981 religious adherence was: Catholic, 3,204,476; Church of Ireland, 95,366; Presbyterians, 14,255; Methodists, 5,790; Others, 123,518.

CAPITAL – ΨDublin (*Baile Atha Cliath*) is a city and county borough on the River Liffey at the head of Dublin Bay. In April 1991 the population (1991 Census) was 478,389. Other county boroughs, with their population figures at the 1991 Census, are ΨCork (127,253); ΨLimerick (52,083); ΨWaterford (40,328); and Ψ Galway (50,853).

FLAG – Equal vertical stripes of green, white and orange.

NATIONAL ANTHEM – Amhrán na BhFiann (The Soldier's Song).

NATIONAL DAY – 17 March (St Patrick's Day).

GOVERNMENT

The Constitution, approved by a plebiscite on 1 July 1937 came into operation on 29 December 1937. The Constitution declares the national territory to be the whole island of Ireland, its islands and the territorial seas. Pending the reintegration of the national territory, and without prejudice to the right of the Parliament and the Government established by the Constitution to exercise jurisdiction over the whole of the national territory, the laws enacted by that Parliament shall have the like area and extent of application as those of the Irish Free State, which did not include the six counties of Northern Ireland.

The President (*Uachtarán na hEireann*) is elected by direct vote of the people for a period of seven years, and is eligible for a second term. The President, in the exercise and performance of certain of her constitutional powers and functions, is aided and advised by a Council of State.

The National Parliament (*Oireachtas*) consists of the President and two Houses: a House of Representatives (*Dáil Éireann*) and a Senate (*Seanad Éireann*).

Dáil Éireann is composed of 166 members elected by adult suffrage on a basis of proportional representation by means of the single transferable vote. The voting age is 18 years. Each Dáil may continue for a period not exceeding five years from the date of election.

Seanad Éireann is composed of 60 members, of whom 11 are nominated by the Taoiseach and 49 are elected; six by institutions of higher education, and 43 from panels of candidates, established on a vocational basis.

The executive authority is exercised by the Government subject to the Constitution. The Government is responsible to the Dáil, meets and acts as a collective authority, and is collectively responsible for the departments of state administered by the Ministers.

The Taoiseach is appointed by the President on the nomination of the Dáil. The other members of the government are appointed by the President on the nomination of the Taoiseach with the previous approval of the Dáil. The Taoiseach appoints a member of the Government to be the *Tánaiste*, who acts for all purposes in the place of the Taoiseach in the event of the death, permanent incapacitation, or temporary absence of the Taoiseach. The Taoiseach, the Tánaiste and the Minister for Finance must be members of the Dáil. The other members of the Government must be members of the Dáil or the Seanad, but not more than two may be members of the Seanad.

The composition of the Dáil Eireann in August 1993 as a result of the 25 November 1992 general election, was as follows: Fianna Fáil 68; Fine Gael 45; Labour 33; Progressive Democrats 10; Democratic Left 4; Independent 6. The present coalition government was formed by the Fianna Fail Party (FF) and the Labour Party (L) in January 1993.

HEAD OF STATE
President, Mary Robinson, *assumed office* 3 December 1990.

CABINET *as at August 1993*
Taoiseach, Albert Reynolds (FF).
Tánaiste, Minister for Foreign Affairs, Dick Spring (L).
Finance, Bertie Ahern (FF).
Employment and Enterprise, Ruairi Quinn (L).
Justice, Maire Geoghegan-Quinn (FF).
Agriculture, Forestry and Food, Joe Walsh (FF).
Social Welfare, Michael Woods (FF).
Environment, Michael Smith (FF).
Health, Brendan Howlin (L).
Education, Niamh Breatnach (L).
Defence and Marine, David Andrews (FF).
Tourism, Energy and Communications, Brian Cowen (FF).
Tourism and Trade, Charlie McCreevy (FF).
Equality and Law Reform, Mervyn Taylor (L).
Arts, Culture and the Gaeltacht, Michael Higgins (L).

IRISH EMBASSY
17 Grosvenor Place, London SW1X 7HR
TEL 071-235 2171
Ambassador Extraordinary and Plenipotentiary, His Excellency Joseph Small (1991).
Counsellor, J. Timbs (*Economic and Commercial*).

BRITISH EMBASSY
31 Merrion Road, Dublin 4
Tel: Dublin 2695211
Ambassador Extraordinary and Plenipotentiary, His Excellency David E. S. Blatherwick, CMG, OBE (1991).
Counsellor and Deputy Head of Mission, J. A. Dew.
Defence Attaché, Col. S. D. Lambe.
First Secretary (Commercial), J. F. Pepper.

BRITISH COUNCIL REPRESENTATIVE, Dr Ken Churchill, 22 Lower Mount Street, Dublin 2.

JUDICIAL SYSTEM

The judicial system comprises courts of first instance and a court of final appeal called the Supreme Court (*Cúirt Uachtarach*). The courts of first instance include a High Court (*Ard-Chúirt*) and courts of local and limited jurisdiction, with a right of appeal as determined by law. The High Court alone has original jurisdiction to consider the question of the validity of any law having regard to the provisions of the Constitution. The Supreme Court has appellate jurisdiction from decisions of the High Court.

Chief Justice, Hon. Thomas A. Finlay.
President of the High Court, Hon. Liam Hamilton.
Attorney-General, Harold Whelehan.

DEFENCE

There is a Permanent Defence Force in which enlistment is voluntary. The minimum term of enlistment is three years, followed by six years in the Reserve Defence Force. Enlistment in the Reserve Defence Force is also voluntary; minimum term of enlistment is three years. The defence estimate for the year ending 31 December 1993 provides for an expenditure of IR£339,019,000.

The total active armed forces number 13,000 personnel with 16,100 reserves. The Army has a strength of 11,200 personnel with 14 light tanks, 51 reconnaissance vehicles, 72 armoured personnel carriers and 60 artillery pieces. It is organized into 11 infantry battalions, one light tank squadron and three field artillery regiments, with attendant support and engineer units. The Navy has a strength of 1,000, with seven patrol and coastal vessels. The Air Force has a strength of 800, with 16 combat aircraft and 15 armed helicopters.

FINANCE

	1992*	1993†
Total current revenue	IR£9,360m	IR£9,958m
Total current expenditure	9,806	10,483
Current revenue		
Customs	125	128
Excise duties	1,734	1,797
Capital taxes	98	79
Stamp duties	256	220
Income tax	3,413	3,563
Income levy	–	78
Corporation tax	739	867
Value-added tax	2,177	2,349
Agricultural levies (EC)	9	10
Motor vehicle duties	216	235
Employment and training levy	143	151
Total tax revenue	8,910	9,485
Non-tax revenue	450	473
Current expenditure		
Debt service	2,355	2,490
Industry and labour	269	318
Agriculture	306	292
Fisheries	24	26
Forestry	5	5
Tourism	29	29
Roads and transport	17	22
Sanitary services	1	1
Health	1,496	1,608
Education	1,391	1,507
Social welfare	2,035	2,214
Housing	5	4
Subsidies	167	170
Defence	373	386
Garda	351	371
Prisons	84	88
Legal, etc.	54	59
Other	822	918
Total	9,784	10,508

*provisional outturn
†post-Budget estimate

The gross debt at end 1990 was IR£25,083.3 million.

EDUCATION

Primary education is directed by the state, with the exception of 84 private primary schools with an enrolment of 8,629 in 1991–2. There were 3,341 state-aided primary schools with an enrolment of 534,269.

In 1991–2 there were 474 recognized secondary schools with 216,740 pupils under private management (mainly religious orders), and 249 vocational schools with 88,655 pupils. Vocational schools are controlled by 38 statutory local Vocational Education Committees. There were 16 state comprehensive schools in 1991–2 with a total enrolment of 8,976 students, and 52 community schools with an enrolment of 34,546 students. There were also other miscellaneous second-level schools and the total full-time enrolment at second-level for 1991–2 was 352,408.

Third-level education is catered for by seven university colleges, and also by third-level courses offered by the technical colleges and regional technical colleges and other miscellaneous third-level institutions. There were 76,809 full-time third-level students in 1991–2, of whom 42,213 were attending university courses.

The estimated state expenditure on education in 1993, excluding administration and inspection, is: first-level IR£591,923,000; second-level IR£613,951,000. The vote for third-level education amounted to IR£299,269,000.

MINERALS AND FISHERIES

Minerals – Metal content of ores raised (1992): lead, 42,900 tonnes; zinc, 194,100 tonnes; silver 13,100,000 grammes.

Sea Fisheries – An estimated 15,420 persons were employed in the fisheries in 1991. Total value of all fish landed in 1992 was IR£97.8 million.

COMMUNICATIONS

In the year ended 31 December 1991, there were 1,944 km of railway; 25,625,000 passengers and 3,312,000 tonnes of merchandise were conveyed; the receipts were IR£81,407,000 and expenditure IR£165,967,000. These figures are in respect of railway working by *Iarnród Eireann*.

In 1991 road motor vehicles carried 237,371,000 passengers, the gross receipts being IR£153,630,000.

In 1991 the number of ships with cargo which arrived at Irish ports was 12,495 (32,892,000 net registered tons); of these 2,576 (7,897,000 net registered tons) were of Irish nationality.

Shannon Airport, 15 miles west of Limerick, is on the main transatlantic air route. In 1992 the airport handled 1,664,219 passengers.

Dublin Airport, six miles north of Dublin, serves the cross-channel and European services operated by the Irish national airline Aer Lingus and other airlines. In 1992 the airport handled 5,808,024 passengers.

Cork Airport, five miles south of Cork, serves the cross-channel and European services operated by Aer Lingus and other airlines. In 1992 the airport handled 692,093 passengers.

TRADE	1992
Imports	IR£13,195,019,492
Exports	16,628,836,448
Trade balance	3,433,816,956

Trade with UK	1991	1992
Imports from UK	£5,295,949,000	£5,739,613,000
Exports to UK	4,416,151,000	5,070,124,000

ISRAEL
Medinat Israel

Israel lies on the western edge of the continent of Asia at the eastern extremity of the Mediterranean Sea, between 29° 30′ to 33° 15′ N. latitude and 34° 15′ to 35° 40′ E. longitude. Its political neighbours are Lebanon on the north, Syria on the north and east, Jordan on the east and the Egyptian province of Sinai on the south-west. The area is estimated at 8,019 sq. miles (20,770 sq. km).

Israel comprises four main regions: the hill country of Galilee, Judea and Samaria, rising in places to heights of nearly 4,000 ft; the coastal plain from the Gaza strip to north of Acre, including the plain of Esdraelon running from Haifa Bay to the south-east, and cutting in two the hill region; the Negev, a semi-desert triangular-shaped region, extending from a base south of Beersheba, to an apex at the head of the Gulf of 'Aqaba; and parts of the Jordan valley, including the Hula region, Tiberias and the south-western extremity of the Dead Sea.

The principal river is the Jordan, which rises from three main sources in Israel, the Lebanon and Syria, and flows through the Hula valley and the canals which have replaced Lake Hula, drained in 1958. Between Hulata and Tiberias (Sea of Galilee) the river falls 926 ft in 11 miles and becomes a turbulent stream. Lake Tiberias is 696 ft below sea-level and liable to sudden storms. Between it and the Dead Sea the Jordan falls 591 ft. The other principal rivers are the Yarkon and Kishon.

The largest lake is the Dead Sea (shared between Israel and Jordan); area 393 sq. miles, 1,286 ft below sea-level, 51.5 miles long, with a maximum width of 11 miles and a maximum depth of 1,309 ft; it receives the waters of the Jordan and of six other streams, and has no outlet, the surplus being carried off by evaporation. The water contains an extraordinarily high concentration of mineral substances.

The highest mountain peak is Mount Meron, 3,962 ft above sea-level, near Safad, Upper Galilee.

CLIMATE – The climate is variable, similar to that of Lower Egypt but modified by altitude and distance from the sea. The summer is hot but tempered in most parts by daily winds from the Mediterranean. The winter is the rainy season lasting from November to April, the period of maximum rainfall being January and February.

POPULATION – The population (estimate 1992) including East Jerusalem and Jewish settlers in the Occupied Territories is 5,090,000. Of these 4,175,000 are Jewish (82 per cent); 700,000 are Arab Muslims (13.8 per cent); 130,000 Arab Christians (2.5 per cent); and 85,000 are Druze (1.7 per cent). During the upheavals of 1948–9 a large number of Arabs left the country as refugees and settled in neighbouring countries.

IMMIGRATION – The Declaration of Independence 1948 laid down that 'the State of Israel will be open to the immigration of Jews from all countries of their dispersion.' The Law of Return 1950 provides that an immigrant visa shall be granted to every Jew who expresses his desire to settle in Israel. From the establishment of the state until 1988, about 1.8 million immigrants had entered Israel from over 100 different countries. Since 1990, a further 250,000 Jews have arrived in Israel from the Soviet Union, eastern Europe, and Ethiopia.

LANGUAGES – Hebrew and Arabic are the official languages of Israel. Arabs are entitled to transact all official business with government departments in Arabic, and provision is made in the *Knesset* for the simultaneous translation of all speeches into Arabic.

CAPITAL – Most of the government departments are in Jerusalem, population (1990 estimate) 524,500. A resolution proclaiming Jerusalem as the capital of Israel was adopted by the *Knesset* in 1950. It is not, however, recognized as the capital by the United Nations because East Jerusalem is part of the Occupied Territories captured as a result of the 1967 war. The United Nations and international law continues to reject the Israeli annexation of East Jerusalem and considers the pre-1950 capital Tel Aviv (population, with district, 1,781,500) to remain the capital. Other principal towns (1990) are ΨHaifa and district (432,900) and Beersheba and district (122,000).

CURRENCY – New Shekel of 100 agora.

FLAG – White, with two horizontal blue stripes, the Shield of David in the centre.

NATIONAL ANTHEM – Hatikvah (The Hope).

ANTIQUITIES

Important historic sites in Israel include: *Jerusalem* – the Church of the Holy Sepulchre; the Al Aqsa Mosque and Dome of the Rock, standing on the remains of the Temple Mount of Herod the Great, of which the Western (wailing) Wall is a fragment; the Church of the Dormition and the Coenaculum on Mount Zion; Ein Karem; Church of the Visitation, Church of St John the Baptist

Galilee – the Sea; Church and Mount of the Beatitudes; ruins of Capernaum and other sites connected with the life of Christ

Mount Tabor – Church of the Transfiguration

Nazareth – Church of the Annunciation, and other Christian shrines associated with the childhood of Christ.

There are also numerous sites dating from biblical and medieval days, such as Ascalon, Caesarea, Atlit, Massada, Megiddo and Hazor. Other antiquities in the West Bank of Jordan and the Golan Heights at present occupied by Israel can now be visited from Israel.

THE OCCUPIED TERRITORIES

As a result of the 1967 war, Israel gained control of East Jerusalem, the Gaza Strip and the West Bank of the River Jordan. East Jerusalem was subsequently annexed by Israel, although this move has not gained international recognition. Extreme Jewish groups began a programme of settlement in the Occupied Territories, later encouraged by the Israeli government. This heightened tension with the resident Palestinian population, now estimated at 1,450,000, whose protests were paralleled by Palestinian Liberation Organization attacks around the world. Frustration at the continued Israeli occupation led to the start of the *Intifada* in 1987, a campaign of sustained unrest in the Occupied Territories. In March 1993 the Israeli government effectively sealed off the West Bank and Gaza Strip from Israel proper and East Jerusalem after continued violence against Israeli security forces and civilians in Israel by Palestinian activists. The effect has been to cause further hardships in the Occupied Territories as Palestinians can no longer travel to work in Israel. The Israel government has found the measure militarily and politically effective and is unlikely to rescind it in the near future.

In accordance with the terms of the peace treaty signed between Egypt and Israel on 26 March 1979, Israel withdrew in April 1982 to the pre-1967 boundary, returning the Sinai area to Egyptian sovereignty.

GOVERNMENT

There is a Cabinet and a single-chamber legislature (*Knesset*) of 120 members. A general election is held at least once every four years. The general election in November 1988 resulted in the formation of a 'national unity' coalition government. Disputes between Labour and Likud, the two main partners, led to the collapse of the coalition in March 1990.

The present government coalition of the Labour, Meretz and Shas parties came to power after the general election of June 1992 and immediately reduced the planned building of Jewish settlements in the Occupied Territories in an attempt to move towards a peace settlement with Arab states.

The peace process started in October 1991 in Madrid was brought to a halt in December 1992 when 415 suspected members of the Hamas Islamic fundamentalist group were expelled by Israel to southern Lebanon, where they were refused entry by the Lebanese Army and had to camp in no-man's land. The eighth round of talks in Washington was broken off by Palestinian and Arab negotiators in protest and the peace process continued only fitfully throughout early 1993. More hopefully for the peace process, the Israeli Knesset in January 1993 lifted the long-standing ban on Israelis meeting PLO officials. At the end of August a sudden breakthrough was achieved when the Israeli government agreed to a secret plan drawn up by Israeli and PLO officials to grant the Palestinians self-rule in the Gaza Strip and West Bank city of Jericho within three months.

HEAD OF STATE
President of Israel, Ezer Weizmann, *elected* 24 March 1993, *inaugurated* 13 May 1993.

CABINET *as at August 1993*
Prime Minister, Defence and Religious Affairs, Yitzhak Rabin (L).
Deputy Prime Minister, Foreign Affairs, Shimon Peres (L).
Deputy Prime Minister, Transport, Yisrael Kessar (L).
Energy, Infrastructure and Police, Moshe Shahal (L).
Communications, Science and Technology, Shulamit Aloni (M).

Health, Haim Ramon (L).
Industry and Trade, Michael Harish (L).
Finance, Avraham Shohat (L).
Economics, Shimon Shetreet (L).
Interior, Aryeh Deri (S).
Agriculture, Yaacov Tsur (L).
Immigration Absorption, Yair Tsaban (M).
Tourism, Uzi Baram (L).
Justice, David Libai (L).
Education and Culture, Amnon Rubinstein (M).
Housing, Binyamin Ben-Eliezer (L).
Environment, Yossi Sarid (L).
Labour and Social Affairs, Ora Namir (L).
L   Labour Party
M   Meretz
S   Shas

EMBASSY OF ISRAEL
2 Palace Green, Kensington, London W8 4QB
TEL 071-957 9500
Ambassador Extraordinary and Plenipotentiary, His Excellency Moshe Raviv (1993).
Minister Plenipotentiary, G. Meir.
Defence Attaché, Brig.-Gen. Yom-Tov Tamir.
Minister-Counsellor, M. Hacohen (*Consular*).
Counsellor, Mrs Z. Dori (*Commercial*).

BRITISH EMBASSY
192 Hayarkon Street, Tel Aviv 63405
Tel: Tel Aviv 5249171

Ambassador Extraordinary and Plenipotentiary, His Excellency Robert A. Burns, CMG (1992).
Counsellor, Consul-General and Deputy Ambassador, C. J. White.
Defence and Military Attaché, Col. J. R. Andrew, OBE.
First Secretary (Commercial), P. A. Connolly.
There are British consular offices in Tel Aviv and Eilat.

BRITISH COUNCIL REPRESENTATIVE, P. Sandiford, OBE, 140 Hayarkon Street, PO Box 3302, Tel Aviv 61032.
There is a library in *Tel Aviv* and in *West Jerusalem*.

ISRAEL-BRITISH CHAMBER OF COMMERCE,
76 IBN Guirol Street, Tel Aviv 64162.

DEFENCE

The Israeli defence forces have a total active strength of some 175,000 (including 139,500 conscripts). Since its inception, however, Israel has based its defence capabilities on a large and highly-trained reserve, and a truer picture of armed forces strength is given by the size of the reserve forces, at present 430,000 personnel. Conscripts serve for periods of four years (officers), three years (men) and two years (women). Reserves serve for one month a year and are eligible for call-up until age 54 (men) and age 24 or marriage (women). Israel is widely believed to have a nuclear capacity of around 100 warheads which could be delivered by Jericho I and II missiles.

The Army has an active strength of 134,000 (114,700 conscripts) and a strength of 598,000 on mobilization, with some 3,890 main battle tanks, 8,000 armoured personnel carriers and 1,400 artillery pieces. The Army is organized into three regular armoured and three regular infantry divisions, with a further four regular mechanized infantry brigades. Reserve units comprise nine armoured divisions, one air mobile division and ten infantry and four artillery brigades.

The Navy has an active strength of 10,000 (3,000 conscripts) and 20,000 on mobilization, with three submarines and six patrol and coastal craft. The Air Force has a strength of 32,000 (21,800 conscripts) and 37,000 on mobilization, with some 662 combat aircraft of US and home manufacture and 93 armed helicopters.

The Air Force compromises 16 ground attack/air defence and four ground attack squadrons, together with one transport wing and reconnaissance, airborne early warning, tanker and training units. There is also a paramilitary force of 6,000 border police.

EDUCATION

Education for all children from six to 16 years is free and compulsory. The law also provides for working youth age 16–18, who for some reason have not completed their education, to be exempted from work in order to do so.

There are seven universities including two engineering and technological institutes.

COMMUNICATIONS

Israel State Railways serves Haifa, Tel Aviv, Jerusalem, Lod, Nahariya, Beersheba, Dimona, Ashdod and intermediate stations. In 1986 the total railway network amounted to 528 km. There were 12,823 km of paved road and in 1986 819,102 licensed vehicles.

Israel's merchant marine had reached a total of 2,805,000 tons deadweight by December 1985. The chief ports are Haifa, a modern harbour, with a depth of 30 ft alongside the main quay; the harbour on the Red Sea at Eilat has a capacity of 10,000 tons a day; Acre has an anchorage for small vessels; the deep-water port at Ashdod, 20 miles south of Tel Aviv, handled 8,006,000 tons of cargo in 1986. In the same year Israel's three main ports handled 17,048,000 tons of cargo.

In 1986, 3,098,000 passengers passed through Ben Gurion airport, of which 230,146 arrived by charter flight.

ECONOMY

Government expenditure in 1989 was 25,953 million new Shekels at market prices. GNP at market prices was 81,880 million new Shekels.

The country is generally fertile and climatic conditions vary so widely that a large variety of crops can be grown, ranging from temperate crops such as wheat and cherries, to subtropical crops such as sorghum, millet and mangoes. The famous 'Jaffa' orange is produced in large quantities mostly in the coastal plain for export. High-profit and specialized glasshouse crops for export, such as flowers, tomatoes and strawberries, are popular. Olives are cultivated, mainly for the production of oil used for edible purposes and for the manufacture of soap. The main winter crops are wheat, barley and various kinds of pulses, while in summer sorghum, millet, maize, sesame and summer pulses are grown. Large areas of seasonal vegetables are planted. Beef, cattle and poultry farming have been developed and the production of mixed vegetables and dairy produce has greatly increased. Tobacco and medium staple cotton are now grown. Fishing production (mostly from fish farms) was 14,958 tons in 1985–6. All kinds of summer fruits such as figs, grapes, plums and apples are produced in increasing quantities for local consumption.

Water supply for irrigation is the principal limiting factor to greater production. The area under cultivation is 1.1 million acres, of which 0.6 million is under irrigation. Agriculture accounts for 5 per cent of GNP and 4 per cent of exports.

In value polished diamonds account for about one quarter of Israel's total exports. Amongst the most important exporting industries are textiles, foodstuffs, chemicals (mainly fertilizers and pharmaceuticals). Metal-working and science-based industries are highly sophisticated and technologically advanced. These include the aircraft and military industries. Other important manufacturing industries include plastics, rubber, cement, glass, paper and oil refining. Industry accounts for 23 per cent of GNP and 65 per cent of exports.

TRADE

The principal imports are foodstuffs, crude oil, machinery and vehicles, iron, steel and manufactures thereof, and chemicals. The principal exports are citrus fruits and by-products, polished diamonds, plywood, cement, tyres, minerals, finished and semi-finished textiles.

	1988	1989
Imports	US$12,287.2m	US$12,736.5m
Exports	9,445.4m	10,334.9m

Trade with UK	1991	1992
Imports from UK	£529,484,000	£586,236,000
Exports to UK	455,765,000	485,078,000

ITALY
Repubblica Italiana

Italy is a republic in the south of Europe, consisting of a peninsula, the large islands of Sicily and Sardinia, the island of Elba and about 70 other small islands. Italy is bounded on the north by Switzerland and Austria, on the south by the Mediterranean Sea, on the east by the Adriatic Sea and Slovenia, and on the west by France and the Ligurian and Tyrrhenian Seas. The total area is about 116,304 sq. miles (301,225 sq. km).

The peninsula is for the most part mountainous, but between the Apennines, which form its spine, and the east coastline are two large fertile plains: Emilia/Romagna in the north and Apulia in the south. The Alps form the northern limit of Italy, dividing it from France, Switzerland, Austria and Slovenia. Mont Blanc (15,771 ft), the highest peak, is in the French Pennine Alps, but partly within the Italian borders are Monte Rosa (15,217 ft), Matterhorn (14,780 ft) and several peaks from 12,000 to 14,000 ft.

The chief rivers are the Po (405 miles), which flows through Piedmont, Lombardy and the Veneto, and the Adige (Trentino and Veneto) in the north, the Arno (Florentine plain) and the Tiber (flowing through Rome to Ostia).

POPULATION – In February 1986 Italy's population was 57,193,708. A 1991 UN estimate gives a figure of 57,052,000.

LANGUAGE – Italian is a Romance language derived from Latin. It is spoken in its purest form in Tuscany, but there are numerous dialects, showing variously French, German, Spanish and Arabic influences. Sard, the dialect of Sardinia, is accorded by some authorities the status of a distinct Romance language.

CAPITAL – Rome. Population of the commune (1991 Census) 2,693,383. In the 1991 Census the population of the communes of the principal cities and towns was Milan 1,371,008; Ψ Naples 1,054,601; Turin 961,916; Ψ Genoa 675,639; Bologna 404,322; Florence 402,316; Sicily, Ψ Palermo 697,162; Sardinia, Ψ Cagliari 203,254.

CURRENCY – Lira of 100 centesimi.

FLAG – Vertical stripes of green, white and red.

NATIONAL ANTHEM – Inno di Mameli.

NATIONAL DAY – 2 June.

HISTORY

Italian unity was accomplished under the House of Savoy, after a struggle from 1848 to 1870, in which Mazzini

(1805–72), Garibaldi (1807–82) and Cavour (1810–61) were the principal figures. It was completed when Lombardy was ceded by Austria in 1859 and Venice in 1866, and through the evacuation of Rome by the French in 1870. In 1871 the King of Italy entered Rome, and that city was declared to be the capital.

Benito Mussolini, known as *Il Duce* (The Leader) was continuously in office as Prime Minister from 1922 until 25 July 1943, when the fascist regime was abolished. He was captured by Italian partisans while attempting to escape across the Swiss frontier and killed on 28 April 1945.

In fulfilment of a promise given in April 1944 that he would retire when the Allies entered Rome, a decree was signed on 5 June 1944, by King Victor Emmanuel III under which Prince Umberto, his son, became Lieutenant-General of the Realm. The King remained head of the House of Savoy and retained the title King of Italy until his abdication on 9 May 1946, when he was succeeded by the Crown Prince. A general election was held on 2 June 1946, together with a referendum on the future of the monarchy. The result showed a majority in favour of replacing the monarchy with a republic. The royal family left the country on 13 June and on 28 June 1946 a provisional President was elected.

GOVERNMENT

The constitution of the republic of Italy, approved by the Constituent Assembly in December 1947, provides for the election of the President by an electoral college which consists of the two houses of the parliament (the Chamber of Deputies and the Senate) sitting in joint session together with three delegates from each region (one in the case of the Valle d'Aosta). The President, who must be over 50 years of age, holds office for seven years. He has numerous carefully defined powers, the main one of which is the right to dissolve one or both houses after consultation with the Speakers.

With 50 governments since 1947, there is growing public pressure for constitutional reform This led to a large loss of support for the four-party (Christian Democrat, Socialist, Social Democrat, Liberal) government in 1990 and 1991, forcing it to resign amid a welter of corruption scandals in January 1992. The ensuing general election in April was seen as a defeat for the established parties of the government and the Democratic Left (reformed Communists) as it produced a large increase in support for Northern League and anti-Mafia parties. The four-party coalition failed to persuade any other parties to join them and formed a new government in June with a small majority in parliament and the avowed intent to pursue constitutional and economic reform.

The latter half of 1992 and 1993 have seen the transformation of the Italian political, constitutional and economic systems in operation since the immediate post-war era. Disillusionment with the established parties was confirmed in the December 1992 regional elections and the June 1993 city and local elections when the governing parties lost most of their local power. A clear regional variation emerged, the Northern League dominating the north of the country, the Democratic Left the centre, and in the south the Christian Democrats retained some power as the anti-Mafia La Rête party progressed. At national level the four-party coalition government of Giuliano Amato stumbled from one scandal to another as hundreds of senior politicians and businessmen were arrested by the magistrates in the so-called 'clean hands' investigation into corruption that began in Milan in February 1992.

After political turmoil and fighting in parliament, the Amato government finally held a nationwide referendum on reform on 18 April 1993 in which the electorate voted overwhelmingly in favour of changing the proportional representation voting system for the Senate to a first-past-the-post system for three-quarters of the seats to engender greater political stability. The electorate also voted in favour of ending state funding of political parties and for greater privatization to lessen corruption.

Having fulfilled its objective of political reform the Amato government resigned, to be replaced by a government of the four governing parties, non-party experts and the Democratic Left Party. The Democratic Left Party members left the government after only a few hours when parliament refused to lift the immunity from prosecution on corruption charges of former Prime Minister Giulio Andreotti. The government passed legislation throughout July and August 1993 to reform the voting system for the lower house of parliament from proportional representation to 75 per cent of seats (472) elected by first-past-the-post and 25 per cent (158) elected by proportional representation.

HEAD OF STATE
President of the Italian Republic, Oscar Luigi Scalfaro, *elected* 25 May 1992.

COUNCIL OF MINISTERS *as at August 1993*
Prime Minister, Carlo Ciampi (Ind.).
Foreign Affairs, Beniamino Andreatta (DC).
Interior, Sen. Nicola Mancino (DC).
Justice, Prof. Giovanni Conso (Ind.).
Defence, Fabio Fabbri (PSI).
Treasury, Prof. Piero Barucci (DC).
Public Administration, Prof. Sabino Cassese (Ind.).
Finance, Franco Gallo (Ind.).
Budget, Prof. Luigi Spaventa (Ind.).
Health, Maria Pia Garavaglia (DC).
Education, Sen. Rosa Russo Jervolino (DC).
Industry and Privatization, Prof. Paolo Savona (PRI)
Agriculture, Alfredo Diana (DC).
Employment and Social Welfare, Sen. Gino Giugni (PSI).
Transport and Merchant Marine, Raffaele Costa (PLI).
Public Works, Sen. Francesco Merloni (DC).
Posts and Telecommunications, Maurizio Pagani (PSDI).
Foreign Trade, Paola Baratta (PSI).
Tourism, Sen. Margherita Boniver (PSI).
Environment, Valdo Spini (PSI).
Culture, Dr Alberto Ronchey (Ind.).

Universities and Research, Prof. Umberto Colombo (Ind.).
Community and Regional Affairs, Prof. Livio Paladin (Ind.).
Social Affairs, Fernanda Coutri (PSI).
Relations with Parliament, Prof. Paolo Barile (Ind.).
Electoral and Institutional Reform, Prof. Leopoldo Elia
(Ind.).

DC   Christian Democrat Party
PSI   Socialist Party
PLI   Liberal Party
PSDI   Social Democratic Party.
Ind.   Independent.

ITALIAN EMBASSY
14 Three Kings Yard, Davies Street,
London WIY 2EH
TEL 071-629 8200

Ambassador Extraordinary and Plenipotentiary, His
Excellency Count Giacomo Attolico (1991).
Minister-Counsellor, A. Armellini.
Defence Attaché, Adm. M. Maguolo.
Cultural Attaché, Prof. F. Villari.
Consul-General, L. Brofferio.
First Counsellor, G. Ardizzone *(Commercial).*

There are also consular offices in *Bedford, Edinburgh* and
Manchester.

BRITISH EMBASSY
Via XX Settembre 80A, 00187 Rome
Tel: Rome 482-5441

Ambassador Extraordinary and Plenipotentiary, His
Excellency Sir Patrick Fairweather, KCMG (1992).
Minister, D. H. Colvin.
Defence and Military Attaché, Brig. J. H. Thoyts.
*Director-General for British Trade Development in Italy and
Consul-General,* P. H. Wetton *(Milan).*
Counsellor (Economic and Commercial),
C. R. L. de Chassiron.

BRITISH CONSULAR OFFICES – There are Consulates-
General at *Milan* and *Naples* and Consulates offices at
Rome, Genoa, Florence, Venice, Trieste, Brindisi, Bari and
Turin.

BRITISH COUNCIL REPRESENTATIVE, K. Hunter, OBE,
Palazzo del Drago, Via Quattro Fontane 20,
00184 Rome. There are British Council Offices at *Milan,
Bologna* and *Naples,* each with a library.

BRITISH CHAMBER OF COMMERCE, Via San Paolo 7,
20121 Milan.

DEFENCE

Total active armed forces personnel number some 354,000
(including 211,000 conscripts who serve 12 months). Reserves
number 520,000, with an obligation to age 25 or 45 (Air
Force), 45 (Army), 39 or 73 (Navy).
    The Army has a strength of 230,000 (167,000 conscripts),
with some 1,220 main battle tanks, 3,879 armoured personnel
carriers, 1,952 artillery pieces, 60 aircraft and 320 helicopters.
Organization consists of a Field Army and Territorial
Defence forces. The Field Army has three corps with a total
of four mechanized, four mountain and two armoured
brigades, six artillery regiments, two armoured cavalry and
two amphibious battalions and two aviation groups. Territorial Defence forces compromise seven mechanized brigades,
a Rapid Intervention Force of two brigades, two infantry,
two armoured cavalry, two engineer and one artillery
regiments.
    The Navy has a strength of 48,000 (including 19,000
conscripts), with eight submarines, one helicopter carrier,

one cruiser and 27 destroyers and frigates with 36 armed
helicopters. The Air Force has a strength of 76,000 (25,000
conscripts) with 449 combat aircraft. Organization is into
seven air defence, ten ground attack, three transport, one
reconnaissance, two maritime reconnaissance, one electronic
warfare, one communications and six air training squadrons.
    In addition to the regular armed forces there is the
paramilitary Carabinieri, who are part of the Ministry of
Defence and number some 111,400, with some 235 armoured
personnel carriers and 75 helicopters. There are several
NATO bases in Italy with some 15,100 US armed forces
personnel stationed in the country.

REGIONS OF ITALY

ROME AND CENTRAL ITALY – Rome was founded, according to legend, by Romulus in 753 BC. It was the focal point
of Latin civilization and dominion under the Roman Republic
and afterwards under the Roman Empire, and became the
capital of Italy when the kingdom was established in 1871.
The capital is concerned mainly with tourism and government, but its importance as a business centre is steadily
increasing, and it is reportedly the third largest industrial
centre in the country.
LOMBARDY AND MILAN – In the Lombardy region are to
be found some 15.7 per cent of Italy's commercial and
banking services and some 21.9 per cent of the manufacturing
industry. The whole range of Italian industry is represented,
most important being the steel, machine tool and motor car
factories.
TURIN AND PIEDMONT – Turin between 1861 and 1865
was Italy's first capital as the home of the Piedmontese royal
family. Now it is the headquarters of Europe's second largest
manufacturer of motor cars, produces 75 per cent of Italy's
motor vehicles and over 80 per cent of its roller bearings.
Turin is also Italy's second largest steel producing city.
Piedmont is the centre of the Italian textile industry based
mainly on Biella.
GENOA AND THE LIGURIAN RIVIERA – Genoa has been
one of Europe's major ports since the Middle Ages, and
handles one-third of Italy's foreign trade.
VENICE AND THE NORTH-EAST – Venice is primarily a
tourist attraction of unique beauty. It was founded in the
middle of the fifth century by refugees from the mainland
fleeing attacks, and by the 16th century it was one of the
strongest and richest states of Europe, dominating Eastern
Mediterranean trade. It lost its independence in 1797 when
Napoleon handed it over to Austria. Industry (paper and
stationery, mechanical equipment, consumer goods, electrical
appliances, woollens) is now developing in the Venice area
and in the areas around Treviso and Pordenone. Near
Trieste, is the modern Monfalcone shipyard.
TUSCANY, EMILIA AND ROMAGNA – These regions were
the agricultural centre of Italy but the post-war period has
seen the development of large industrial centres at Bologna,
Florence, Modena, Pistoia and Ravenna. The footwear
industry is based in Florence, textiles in Prato, reproduction
furniture at Cascina and Poggibonsi, ceramics at Sassuolo,
and glass and pottery at Empoli and Montelupo. Bologna is
an important centre for the food industry.
NAPLES AND THE TOE OF ITALY – Naples, formerly the
capital and administrative centre of the Kingdom of Naples
and Sicily, remains the dominant city in the area, but it is
beset with great problems of unemployment and the need
for modernization. Around it, however, helped by government incentives, industry is slowly developing, northwards
to Caserta, southwards to Salerno and eastwards to Benevento.

PUGLIA – Bari has always been a commercial centre and now industrial development is also taking place in the areas of Taranto, Brindisi and Foggia. At Taranto there are a highly-mechanized steel-works and a modern oil refinery. The Bari industrial zone has factories producing electronic and pneumatic valves, specialized vehicle bodies and tyres, etc. The main industry of Brindisi is a petro-chemical plant. At Foggia there is a textile factory.

SICILY – The main source of income is agriculture, particularly citrus fruits, almonds and tomatoes. Oil in small quantities has been found off the southern shore of the island and drilling continues, while onshore there are growing oil-refining, natural gas and petrochemical industries. Small and medium-sized industries, benefiting from the Government's incentives, are developing, and tourism is bringing an increasing amount of revenue to the island.

SARDINIA – Sardinia is an autonomous region, with its capital at Cagliari. Six main industrial development areas have been officially designated. The major industries are aluminium production (there is a smelting plant at Porto Vesme), petrochemicals, lead and zinc mining; and the tourist industry is flourishing.

ECONOMY

The Amato and Ciampi governments of 1992–3 have introduced economic reforms to lessen corruption and reduce the budget deficit and national debt. In October 1992 the government significantly reduced public expenditure by reforming the bloated pensions system, civil service and health service. In March 1993 further welfare reductions were made, privatization began and the tradition of annual wage indexation to inflation was ended. This was followed in April by the referendum in which the electorate voted for reforming the state's traditional participation in industry, and in July the government announced the beginning of large-scale privatization. Italian gross domestic product in 1991 was 1,427,342 billion lire. One of the economy's major problems is the large budget deficit which in 1991 was 10.2 per cent of GDP. In May 1993 the government approved an austerity budget as the cumulative national debt rose to US$1,200 billion. The rate of inflation in 1993 was 4.4 per cent.

The general index of industrial production (1980 = 100) stood at +2.7 per cent in 1985–6. The state-owned sector of Italian industry is important, dominated by the holding companies IRI (mechanical, steel, airlines), ENI (petrochemicals) and ENEL (electricity). Industry (including construction) accounted for 30.2 per cent of gross domestic product in 1991. The main industrial centres are around the cities of Milan, Turin, Rome, Venice, Bologna, Naples and Bari.

Italy is generally poor in mineral resources but since the war deposits of natural methane gas and small deposits of oil have been discovered and rapidly exploited. Production of lignite has also increased. Other minerals produced in significant quantities include iron ores and pyrites, mercury (over one-quarter of the world production), lead, zinc and aluminium. Marble is a traditional product of the Massa Carrara district.

Agriculture accounted for 3.8 per cent of gross domestic product in 1991. The agricultural labour force was 2,242,000 in 1986.

In 1987 an estimated 52 million foreign tourists visited Italy, spending an estimated L15,782,808 million.

TRADE

The balance of trade in 1988 showed a deficit of 12,875 billion lire, compared with 11,143 billion lire in 1987. The

main markets for Italian exports in 1987 were the OECD countries, which accounted for almost 80 per cent of the total, and the EC markets with 56 per cent of the total. Imports came principally from Germany, France and the USA.

Trade with UK	1991	1992
Imports from UK	£6,145,014,000	£6,146,719,000
Exports to UK	6,378,908,000	6,769,218,000

COMMUNICATIONS

The main railway system is state-run by the *Ferrovia dello Stato*. A network of motorways (*autostrade*) covers the country, built and operated mainly by the IRI state-holding company and ANAS, the state highway authority. Alitalia, the principal international and domestic airline, is also state-controlled by the IRI group. Other smaller companies, including ATI (an Alitalia subsidiary) and Air Mediterranea, operate on domestic routes. The Italian mercantile marine totalled 7,587,117 tons in December 1985. Genoa is the major port, handling about one-third of Italy's foreign trade.

CULTURE

Florence, the capital of Tuscany, was one of the greatest cities in Europe from the 11th to the 16th centuries, and the cradle of the Renaissance. Under the Medici family in the 15th century flourished many of the greatest names in Italian art, including Filippo Lippi, Botticelli, Donatello and Brunelleschi, and in the 16th century Michelangelo and Leonardo da Vinci.

Italian literature (in addition to Latin literature, which is the common inheritance of western Europe) is one of the richest in Europe, particularly in its golden age (Dante, 1265–1321; Petrarch, 1304–74; Boccaccio, 1313–75) and in the Renaissance (Ariosto, 1474–1533; Machiavelli, 1469–1527; Tasso, 1544–95). Modern Italian literature has many noted names in prose and verse, notably Manzoni (1785–1873), Carducci (1835–1907) and Gabriele d'Annunzio (1864–1938). The Nobel Prize for Literature has been awarded to Italian authors on five occasions: G. Carducci (1906), Signora G. Deledda (1926), Luigi Pirandello (1934), Salvatore Quasimodo (1959) and Eugenio Montale (1975).

In 1987, there were 72 daily newspapers published in Italy, of which 14 were published in Rome and seven in Milan.

EDUCATION

Education is free and compulsory between the ages of six and 14; this comprises five years at primary school and three in the 'middle school', of which there are about 8,000. Pupils who obtain the middle school certificate may seek admission to any 'senior secondary school', which may be a lyceum with a classical or scientific or artistic bias, or an institute directed at technology (of which there are eight different types), trade or industry (including vocational schools), or teacher-training. Courses at the lyceums and technical institutes usually last for five years and success in the final examination qualifies for admission to university. In 1990–1 there were 3,056,000 students at elementary school, 2,266,000 at middle school and 2,861,000 at senior secondary school.

There are 35 state and 14 private universities, some of ancient foundation; those at Bologna, Modena, Parma and Padua were started in the 12th century. University education is not free, but entrants with higher qualifications are charged reduced fees according to a sliding scale. In 1990–1 there were 1,381,000 students at university.

In general, schools, lyceums and universities are financed by local taxation and central government grants.

ISLANDS

PANTELLERIA ISLAND (part of Trapani Province) in the Sicilian Narrows, has an area of 31 sq. miles and a population of 9,601.
THE PELAGIAN ISLANDS (Lampedusa, Linosa and Lampione) are part of the Province of Agrigento and have an area of 8 sq. miles, pop. 4,811.
THE TUSCAN ARCHIPELAGO (including Elba), area 293 sq. km, pop. 31,861.
PONTINE ARCHIPELAGO, including Ponza, area 10 sq. km, pop. 2,515.
FLEGREAN ISLANDS, including Ischia, area 60 sq. km, pop. 51,883.
CAPRI.
EOLIAN ISLANDS, including Lipari, area 116 sq. km, pop. 18,636.
TREMITI ISLANDS, area 3 sq. km, pop. 426.

JAMAICA

Jamaica is situated in the Caribbean Sea south of the eastern extremity of Cuba and lies between 17° 43′ and 18° 32′ N. latitude and 76° 11′ and 78° 21′ W. longitude. Jamaica is 4,244 sq. miles (10,991 sq. km) in area and is divided into three counties (Surrey, Middlesex and Cornwall) and 14 parishes. The greatest length from east to west (Morant Point to Negril Point) is 146 miles and the extreme breadth 51 miles.

The topography consists mainly of coastal plains, divided by the Blue Mountain Range in the east, and the hills and limestone plateaux which occupy the central and western areas of the interior. The central chain of high peaks of the Blue Mountains is over 6,000 feet above sea level, and the Blue Mountain Peak, the highest of these, reaches an elevation of 7,402 feet.
POPULATION – In 1992 the population was estimated at 2,460,700 by the UN.

CAPITAL – The seat of government is ΨKingston, the largest town and seaport (estimated population of the corporate area of Kingston and St Andrew in 1982, 696,300). Other main towns are ΨMontego Bay, Ocho Rios, Spanish Town, Mandeville and May Pen.
CURRENCY – Jamaican dollar (J$) of 100 cents.
FLAG – Gold diagonal cross forming triangles of green at top and bottom, triangles of black at hoist and in fly.
NATIONAL ANTHEM – Jamaica, Land We Love.
NATIONAL DAY – First Monday in August (Independence Day).

GOVERNMENT

The island was discovered by Columbus on 4 May 1494, and occupied by the Spanish from 1509 until 1655 when a British expedition, sent by Oliver Cromwell, under Admiral Penn and General Venables attacked the island, which capitulated after a token resistance. In 1670 it was formally ceded to England by the Treaty of Madrid. Jamaica became an independent state within the Commonwealth on 6 August 1962.

The legislature consists of a Senate of 21 nominated members and a House of Representatives consisting of 60 members elected by universal adult suffrage. The constitution provides for a Leader of the Opposition.

At the general election of 30 March 1993, the People's National Party won 52 seats and the Jamaica Labour Party won 8.

Governor-General, His Excellency Howard Felix Hanlon Cooke, *apptd* 1991.

CABINET *as at 15 August 1993*
Prime Minister, Defence, Finance and Planning, Rt. Hon. Percival J. Patterson, QC.
Deputy Prime Minister, Agriculture, Hon. Seymour Mullings.
Industry, Tourism and Commerce, Sen. the Hon. Carlyle Dunkley.
Public Utilities, Mining and Energy, Hon. Robert Pickersgill.
Public Service and the Environment, Hon. Easton Douglas.
Foreign Affairs and Foreign Trade, Hon. Dr Paul Robertson.
Education and Culture, Hon. Burchell Whiteman.
Health, Hon. Desmond Leakey.
Labour and Welfare, Hon. Portia Simpson.
Construction, Hon. O. D. Ramtaillie.
Local Government, Youth and Sports, Hon. John Junior.
National Security and Justice, Hon. K. D. Knight.
Minister without Portfolio in the Office of the Prime Minister, Sen. the Hon. Dr Peter Phillips.
Legal Affairs, Hon. David Coore.
Water and Transport, Hon. Horace Clarke.

JAMAICAN HIGH COMMISSION
1–2 Prince Consort Road, London SW7 2BZ
Tel 071–823 9911
High Commissioner, Her Excellency Mrs Ellen Gray Bogle (1989).
Deputy High Commissioners, Mrs M. Roberts; J. K. Pringle (*Trade*).
Counsellor, S. H. Parris (*Consular Affairs*).
Defence Adviser, Col. T. D. Lewis.

BRITISH HIGH COMMISSION
PO Box 575, Trafalgar Road, Kingston 10
Tel: Kingston 926 9050
High Commissioner, His Excellency Derek Francis Milton, CMG (1989).
Deputy High Commissioner, F. Callaghan.
Defence Adviser, Col. C. S. Faith, OBE.
First Secretary (Management/Consular), I. F. Powell.
BRITISH COUNCIL REPRESENTATIVE IN THE CARIBBEAN, Andrew Norris, 3rd Floor, First Life Building, 64 Knutsford Boulevard, Kingston 5.

JUDICATURE

Chief Justice and Keeper of Records, Hon. E. Zacca.
President of the Court of Appeal, Hon. Carl Rattray.
Judges of the Court of Appeal, Hons. B. H. Carey; M. L. Wright; I. X. Forte; H. E. Downer; U. D. Gordon.

COMMUNICATIONS

There are several excellent harbours, Kingston being the principal port. The island has 2,944 miles of main roads and over 7,000 miles of subsidiary roads.

There are two international airports capable of handling the largest civil jet aircraft, the Norman Manley International Airport on the south coast serving Kingston, and Sangster Airport on the north coast serving the major tourist areas. In addition there are licensed aerodromes at Port Antonio, Ocho Rios, Mandeville and Negril. There are 16 privately owned, seven public and two military airstrips.

Air Jamaica, the national airline, operates international services; Trans-Jamaica Airlines operates scheduled internal services.

ECONOMY

Since 1989 the PNP government has introduced an austerity economic reform programme including the abolition of price subsidies, the removal of foreign exchange controls and the introduction of a 10 per cent consumption tax. The IMF in December 1992 approved a credit facility of US$153m for a three-year period. Jamaica is a popular tourist resort, attracting 1,563,097 visitors during 1992. Actual foreign exchange receipts from tourism amounted to US$850m in 1992.

Alumina, bananas, bauxite and sugar are the four major Jamaican exports. Earnings from sugar in 1992 amounted to US$82.5m, bauxite and alumina US$560m and bananas US$39.6m. Less traditional exports include garments, processed food products, limestone and ornamental horticultural products.

FINANCE	1990	1991
Revenue	US$2,401.6m	US$908m
Expenditure	2,537.5m	1,091.7m

TRADE	1991	1992
Merchandise imports	US$1,828.6m	US$1,692.8m
Merchandise exports	1,150.7m	1,052.8m

Trade with UK	1991	1992
Imports from UK	£54,669,000	£43,521,000
Exports to UK	123,773,000	127,051,000

JAPAN
Nihon Koku - Land of the Rising Sun

Japan consists of four large islands: *Honshū* (or Mainland), 230,448 sq. km (88,839 sq. m), *Shikoku*, 18,757 sq. km (7,231 sq. m), *Kyūshū*, 42,079 sq. km (16,170 sq. m), *Hokkaido*, 78,508 sq. km (30,265 sq. m), and many small islands situated in the North Pacific Ocean between 128° 6′ and 145° 49′ E. longitude and between 26° 59′ and 45° 31′ N. latitude, with a total area of 145,834 sq. miles (377,708 sq. km).

The coastline exceeds 17,000 miles and is deeply indented, so that few places are far from the sea. The interior is very mountainous, and crossing the mainland from the Sea of Japan to the Pacific is a group of volcanoes, mainly extinct or dormant. Mount Fuji, the loftiest and most sacred mountain of Japan, about 60 miles from Tokyo, is 12,370 ft high and has been dormant since 1707, but there are other volcanoes which are active, including Mount Aso in Kyūshū. There are frequent earthquakes, mainly along the Pacific coast near the Bay of Tokyo. Japan proper extends from a sub-tropical climate in the south to cool temperate in the north. Heavy snowfalls are frequent on the western slopes of Hokkaidō and Honshū, but the Pacific coasts are warmed by the Japan current. There is a plentiful rainfall and the rivers are short and swift-flowing, offering abundant opportunities for the supply of hydro-electric power.

POPULATION – The population (1991 UN estimate) is 123,921,000.

RELIGION – All religions are tolerated. The principal religions of Japan are Mahayana Buddhism and Shinto. About 1 per cent of Japanese are Christians.

CAPITAL – Tokyo, population (December 1989) 11,718,720. The other chief cities had the following populations: ΨOsaka (2,633,000); ΨNagoya (2,152,000); ΨYokohama (3,197,000); Kyoto, the ancient capital (1,471,000); ΨKobé (1,464,000); Kita-Kyushu (1,034,000); Sapporo (1,652,000); ΨKawasaki (1,159,000); ΨFukuoka (1,220,000).

CURRENCY – Yen of 100 sen.
FLAG – White, charged with sun (red).
NATIONAL ANTHEM – Kimigayo.
NATIONAL DAY – 23 December (the Emperor's Birthday).

GOVERNMENT

According to Japanese tradition, Jimmu, the first Emperor of Japan, ascended the throne on 11 February 660 BC. Under the *Meiji* constitution of 11 February 1889, the monarchy was hereditary in the male heirs of the Imperial house.

After the unconditional surrender to the allied nations (14 August 1945), Japan was occupied by Allied forces under General MacArthur (15 September 1945). A Japanese peace treaty conference held in San Francisco in September 1951 led to 48 nations signing the treaty, which became effective on 28 April 1952. Japan then resumed her status as an independent power.

A new constitution came into force on 3 May 1947. Legislative authority rests with the Diet, which is bicameral, consisting of a House of Representatives and a House of Councillors, both houses being composed of elected members. Executive authority is vested in the Cabinet which is responsible to the legislature.

The conservatives governed Japan almost without interruption from the Second World War until recently. From 1955, when it was formed, until August 1993 the Liberal Democratic Party (LDP) maintained an absolute majority in the House of Representatives and formed the government. During the 1990s, however, growing public disgust over political corruption led to a loss of support for the LDP and in 1992 a group of LDP MPs' broke away to form a new party, the Japan New Party (JNP). After attempts at political reform to end corruption continually failed, the LDP government was brought down by its own rebel MPs in a no confidence motion in the Diet on 18 June 1993. Before the subsequent general election, two new groups of LDP MPs broke away to form the Japan Renewal Party (JRP) and the Sakigate (Harbinger) Party and support for the new parties caused the LDP to lose its majority at the election on 18 July. After the election the three new parties formed a coalition with the opposition Komeito, Social Democratic (SDPJ), Democratic Socialist (DSP) and United Social Democratic (USDP) parties, and the new government was sworn in on 9 August 1993. In August 1993 the strength of the parties was: Liberal Democratic Party 219; Social Democratic Party 70; Japan Renewal Party 55; Komeito 51; Japan New Party 35; Japan Communist Party 15; Democratic Socialist 15; Sakigate 13; United Social Democratic Party 4; Independents 33.

The House of Councillors, whose powers are subordinate to the House of Representatives, re-elects half of its members every three years. In June 1993 the strength of the parties was: Liberal Democratic Party 108; Japan Socialist Party 69; Komeito 24; Other, 21; Rengo 12; Japan Communist Party 11; Democratic Socialist 7.

HEAD OF STATE
Emperor of Japan, His Imperial Majesty the Emperor Akihito, *born* 23 December 1933; *succeeded* 8 January 1989; *enthroned* 12 November 1990; *married* 10 April 1959, Miss Michiko Shoda, and has *issue*: Prince Naruhito Hironomiya (*Crown Prince*), *born* 23 February 1960, *married* 9 June 1993 Miss Masako Owada; Prince Akishino, *born* 30 November 1965, and Princess Sayako, *born* 18 April 1969.

CABINET *as at 9 August 1993*
Prime Minister, Morihiro Hosokawa (JNP).
Deputy PM, Foreign Affairs, Tsutomo Hata (JRP).
Justice, Akira Mikazuki (Ind.).
Finance, Hirohisa Fujii (JRP).
Education, Ryoko Akamatsu (Ind.).
Health and Welfare, Keigo Ouchi (DSP).
Agriculture, Forestry and Fisheries, Eijiro Haka (JRP).
International Trade and Industry, Hiroshi Kamagai (JRP).
Transport, Shigeru Ito (SDPJ).
Posts and Telecommunications, Takenori Kanzaki (Komeito).
Labour, Chikara Sakaguchi (Komeito).
Construction, Kozo Igarashi (SDPJ).
Home Affairs, Karju Sato (SDPJ).

MINISTERS OF STATE
Chief Cabinet Secretary, Masayoshi Takemura (Sakigate).
Director-General of Management and Co-ordination Agency, Koshito Ishida (Komeito).
Director-General of Hokkaido and Okinawa Development Agencies, Kosuke Uehara (SDJP).
Director-General of the Defence Agency, Keisuke Nakarishi (JRP).
Director-General of Science and Technology Agency, Satsuki Eda (USDP).
Director-General of Environment Agency, Wakako Hironaka (Komeito).
Director-General of the Economic Planning Agency, Manae Kubota (SDPJ).
Special Minister Responsible for Political Reform, Sadeo Yamahana (SDPJ)
JNP: Japan New Party; JRP: Japan Renewal Party; DSP: Democratic Socialist Party; SDPJ: Social Democratic Party of Japan; USDP: United Social Democratic Party.

EMBASSY OF JAPAN
101–104 Piccadilly, London WIV 9FN
Tel 071-465 6500

Ambassador Extraordinary and Plenipotentiary, His Excellency Hiroshi Kitamura (1991).
Ministers, Akira Sugino; Hitoshi Tanaka; Isao Ohtsuka (*Financial*); Tamon Kitabatake (*Commercial*); Yasuo Nozaka (*Cultural*).
Defence Attaché, Kazuo Tohyama.
Consul-General, Ryuichiro Yamazaki.
First Secretary Tetsuo Matsui (*Commercial*).

BRITISH EMBASSY
No. 1 Ichiban-cho, Chiyoda-ku, Tokyo 102
Tel: Tokyo 3265-5511

Ambassador Extraordinary and Plenipotentiary, His Excellency Sir John Boyd, KCMG (1992).

Minister, A. C. Thorpe (*Deputy Head of Mission*); J. E. W. Kirby (*Financial*).
Counsellors, P. S. Dimond (*Commercial*); M. A. Price, LVO (*Management and Consul-General*).
Defence and Naval Attaché, Capt. A. P. Masterton-Smith.
There is a British Consulate-General at *Osaka* and Honorary Consulates at *Fukuoka, Hiroshima* and *Nagoya.*
BRITISH COUNCIL REPRESENTATIVE, Michael Barrett, OBE, 2 Kagurazaka 1-Chome, Shinjuku-ku, Tokyo 162. There is also an office and library in *Kyoto.*
BRITISH CHAMBER OF COMMERCE, No. 16 Kowa Building, 1–9–20 Akasaka, Minato-ku, Tokyo 107.

ECONOMY
Owing to the mountainous nature of the country not more than one-sixth of its area is available for cultivation and only 14 per cent of Japan's land area is actually used for agriculture; 67 per cent is wooded. The forest land includes Cryptomeria japonica, Pinus massoniana, Zeikowaskeaki, and Paulownia imperialis, in addition to camphor trees, mulberry, vegetable wax tree and a lacquer tree which furnishes the celebrated lacquer of Japan. The soil is only moderately fertile, but intensive cultivation secures good crops. Tobacco, tea, potato, rice, maize, wheat and other cereals are all cultivated. Rice is the staple food of the people, about 13,124,000 tonnes being produced in 1990. Fruit is abundant, including the mandarin, persimmon, loquat and peach. European fruits such as apples, strawberries, pears, grapes and figs are also produced. There is a small-scale beef industry and pigs and chickens are widely reared.

The country has mineral resources, including gold, silver, copper, lead, zinc, iron chromite, white arsenic, coal, sulphur, petroleum, salt and uranium. However, iron ore, coal and crude oil are among the principal imports to supply deficiencies at home.

Japan is one of the most highly industrialized nations in the world, with the whole range of modern light and heavy industries, including motor vehicles, electronics, metals, machinery, chemicals, textiles (cotton, silk, wool and synthetics); cement, pottery, glass, rubber, lumber, paper, oil refining and shipbuilding.

The labour force of Japan in 1991 (average) was 63,690,000, of which around 2.1 per cent were unemployed. Of the total labour force, over 15 per cent are over 65 and this rate is increasing. Industrial, manufacturing and services workers numbered 59,422,000 and agricultural, forestries and fisheries workers 4,267,000 in 1990. Japan's gross domestic product of US$2,940,365m in 1990 made its economy the second largest in the world.

FINANCE
The Budget for the financial year 1990 for revenue and expenditure on the general account was Yen 66,236,700 million.

TRADE
Being deficient in natural resources, Japan has had to develop a complex foreign trade. Principal imports in 1988 consisted of mineral oils (20.5 per cent), raw materials (8.7 per cent) e.g. metal ores and scrap, 4.5 per cent, timber, 3.8 per cent, foodstuffs (15.5 per cent) (e.g. wheat and sugar), machinery (14.2 per cent), chemicals (7.9 per cent) and textiles (5.7 per cent).

Principal exports consist of non-electric machinery (21.2 per cent), motor vehicles (18.4 per cent), electric machinery and appliances (18.4 per cent), steel (5.8 per cent), chemicals (4.5 per cent), textile goods (2.6 per cent) and ships (1.5 per cent).

	1990	
	(US$'000)	
Total imports	211,578,000	
Total exports	287,678,000	
Trade with UK	1991	1992
Imports from UK	£2,257,552,000	£2,226,986,000
Exports to UK	6,753,642,000	7,443,723,000

COMMUNICATIONS

There were 1,120,051 km of road and 44,297 km of railroad (steam and electric) in 1984. Shinkansen (bullet train) tracks are currently being expanded. Japan National Railways was privatized in 1987 and is known as Japan Railways (JR). There are six regional companies and one goods company. The opening in 1988 of the Seikan rail tunnel and the Seto Ohashi rail bridge means that the four major islands are now linked for the first time.

The merchant fleet had a shipping capacity of 26.4 million gross tons and 10,063 vessels in 1991, making it the largest in the world in terms of number of vessels and third in terms of tonnage.

DEFENCE

After the unconditional surrender of August 1945 the Imperial Army and Navy were disarmed and disbanded. Although the constitution of Japan prohibits the maintenance of armed forces, internal security forces came into being in 1950 and 1952. In July 1954, the mission of the forces was extended to include the defence of Japan against direct and indirect aggression. The government in June 1992 managed to pass a bill through parliament allowing for a maximum of 2,000 troops to take part in UN peacekeeping missions overseas, limited to non-front line activities.

The defence budget allocated for 1991 was Yen 4,402,300 million. The authorized uniformed strength was: Ground Self-Defence Force (GSDF) 180,000 (reserve 43,000); Maritime Self-Defence Force (MSDF) 43,897 (reserve 600); Air Self-Defence Force (ASDF) 46,204. The actual strength of the active armed forces is 246,000 (all professional).

The GSDF has a strength of 156,000 and is organized into five regional armies, totalling 13 divisions, one of which is an armoured division, together with two composite, one airborne, one artillery, two air defence and one helicopter brigades. Equipment includes 1,200 main battle tanks, 780 armoured personnel carriers, 860 artillery pieces and 460 helicopters. Equipment is now largely manufactured in Japan.

The MSDF has a strength of 44,000 personnel, with 17 submarines and 64 destroyers and frigates, 99 combat aircraft and 72 armed helicopters.

The ASDF has a strength of 46,000 personnel with 440 combat aircraft of US and Japanese manufacture organized into ten air defence, three ground attack, five transport, one airborne early warning, one reconnaissance and ten training squadrons.

The US at present stations 39,300 personnel in Japan: Army 2,200; Navy 5,500; Marines 21,300; Air Force 10,300.

EDUCATION

Under the Education Law of 1947, education at elementary (six-year course) and lower secondary (three-year course) schools is free, compulsory and co-educational. The (three-year) upper secondary schools are attended by 94 per cent of the age group. They have courses in general, agricultural, commercial, technical, mercantile marine, radio communication and home economics education, etc.

Of the population aged between 18 and 21, 37.5 per cent were enrolled in higher education in 1990. There are two- or three-year junior colleges and four-year universities. Some of the universities have graduate schools. In 1991 there were 1,106 universities and junior colleges, the vast majority of which are privately maintained. The most prominent universities are the seven state universities of Tokyo, Kyoto, Tohoku (Sendai), Hokkaido (Sapporo), Kyushu (Fukuoka), Osaka and Nagoya, and the two private universities of Keio and Waseda.

CULTURE

Japanese is said to be one of the Uro-Altaic group of languages and remained a spoken tongue until the fifth to seventh centuries AD, when Chinese characters came into use. Japanese who have received school education (99.8 per cent of the population) can read and write the Chinese characters in current use (about 1,800 characters) and also the syllabary characters called Kana. English is the best known foreign language. It is taught in all middle and high schools and universities. There are 125 daily newspapers in Japan.

JORDAN
Al-Mamlaka al Urduniya al-Hashemiyah

The Hashemite Kingdom of the Jordan, which covers 37,738 sq. miles (97,740 sq. km), is bounded on the north by Syria, on the west by Israel, on the south by Saudi Arabia and on the east by Iraq. Since the hostilities of June 1967, that part of the country lying to the west of the River Jordan has been under Israeli occupation.

POPULATION – Total population on the East Bank of the Jordan (1991 UN estimate) 4,145,000.

RELIGION – The majority of the population are Sunni Muslims and Islam is the religion of the state; freedom of belief is, however, guaranteed by the constitution.

CAPITAL – Amman, population (1988 estimate) 1,100,000.

CURRENCY – Jordanian dinar (JD) of 1,000 fils.

FLAG – Three horizontal stripes of black, white, green and a red triangle based on the hoist, containing a seven-pointed white star.

NATIONAL ANTHEM – Long Live the King.

NATIONAL DAY – 25 May (Independence Day).

HISTORY

After the defeat of Turkey in the First World War, the Amirate of Transjordan was established in the area east of the River Jordan as a state under British mandate. The mandate was terminated after the Second World War and the Amirate, still ruled by its founder, the Amir Abdullah, became the Hashemite Kingdom of Jordan. Following the 1948 war between Israel and the Arab states, that part of Palestine remaining in Arab hands (but excluding Gaza) was incorporated into the Hashemite Kingdom. King Abdullah was assassinated in 1951; his son Talal ruled briefly but abdicated in favour of King Hussein in 1952.

THE WEST BANK

All of Jordan west of the river has been under Israeli occupation since 1967. In 1988 Jordan severed its legal and administrative ties with the occupied West Bank, but did not formally renounce sovereignty over the area. As a result of the wars of 1948 and 1967 there are about 991,000 refugees and displaced persons living in East Jordan, about 200,000 of whom live in refugee and displaced persons camps established by the UN Relief and Works Agency (UNRWA). In addition there are some 300,000 entirely self-supporting Palestinian members of the East Jordanian community.

GOVERNMENT

The present constitution of the kingdom came into force in 1952. It provides for a senate of 40 members (all appointed by the King) and an elected House of Representatives. Until 1988, the House of Representatives had 60 members representing both the East and West Banks. Legislation passed in 1989 stipulated that in future elections, seats would be contested on the East Bank only. The first parliamentary elections since 1967 to the new 80-member House of Representatives took place in November 1989.

The King appoints the members of the Council of Ministers. Crown Prince Hassan normally acts as regent when King Hussein is away from Jordan. In June 1991 a new national charter was agreed between the King and political parties in a National Conference in which the ban on political parties was lifted in return for allegiance to the monarchy. The first multi-party parliamentary elections are scheduled for November 1993.

HEAD OF STATE

King of the Jordan, Hussein, GCVO, *born* 14 November 1935, *succeeded* on the abdication of his father, King Talal, 11 August 1952, *assumed constitutional powers,* 2 May 1953, on coming of age.

Crown Prince, Prince Hassan, third son of King Talal of Jordan, *born* 1947, *appointed Crown Prince,* 1 April 1965.

COUNCIL OF MINISTERS *as at August 1993*

Prime Minister and Minister of Defence and Foreign Affairs, Abdul Salam Al-Majali.

Agriculture, Marwan Kamal.
Communications and Posts, Tarek Saheimat.
Culture, Mahmoud Samra.
Education, Khalid al-Omari.
Finance, Sammi Qammo.
Health, Abdul Rahim Malhas.
Information, Ma'an Aba Nowar.
Interior, Salameh Hammad.
Justice, Rateb al-Wazari.
Labour, Khaled al-Ghzawi.
Municipal, Rural and Environmental Affairs, Mohammed al-Farban.
Planning, Zaid Fariz.
Public Works and Housing, Khalaf Hawari.
Religious Affairs, Abdul al-Abbadi.
Social Development, Mohammed al-Sqour.
Supply, Radi Ibrahim.
Tourism and Antiquities, Yaral Hikmak.
Trade and Industry, Bassa al-Saket.
Water and Irrigation, Bassam Kakish.
Youth, Abdullah Oweidat.
Energy and Minerals, Wahid Asfour.

EMBASSY OF THE HASHEMITE KINGDOM OF JORDAN
6 Upper Phillimore Gardens, London W8 7HB
Tel 071-937 3685

Ambassador Extraordinary and Plenipotentiary, His Excellency Fouad Ayoub (1991).
Minister Counsellor, Abdullah Madadha.
Defence Attaché, A. Maytah.
Consul, S. N. Faris, MBE.
Head of Commerce, B. Khasawneh.

Service Office: 16 Upper Phillimore Gardens, London W8. Tel: 071-937 9611.
Jordan Information Bureau: 11–12 Buckingham Gate, London SWIE 6LB.

BRITISH EMBASSY
Abdoun (PO Box 87), Amman
Tel: Amman 823100

Ambassador Extraordinary and Plenipotentiary, His Excellency P. H. C. Eyers, CMG, LVO (1991).
Counsellor, J. W. Watt (*Deputy Head of Mission and Consul-General*).
Defence Attaché, Col. B. A. C. Duncan, MBE.
First Secretary, T. Ellis (*Commercial and Development*).

BRITISH COUNCIL REPRESENTATIVE, Chris Chislett, Rainbow Street (PO Box 634), Jebel Amman, Amman.

DEFENCE

The total active armed forces strength is 99,400 personnel, with selective conscription of two-year terms in operation. Reserves number a further 35,000. The Army has a strength of 85,000, with 1,130 main battle tanks, 150 reconnaissance vehicles, 1,150 armoured personnel carriers and armoured infantry fighting vehicles, and 468 artillery pieces. The Army is organized into two armoured and two mechanized infantry divisions with one Royal Guard, one special forces and one field artillery brigade.

The Navy has 400 personnel in its Aquaba base with three patrol craft. The Air Force has a strength of 14,000 personnel with 113 combat aircraft and 24 armed helicopters. The aircraft are organized into four ground attack, two air defence, one transport, two attack helicopter and three transport helicopter squadrons. There are also two air defence brigades with 126 improved HAWK missiles. In addition, there is a paramilitary civil militia of 225,000 personnel.

ECONOMY

The main agricultural areas are the Jordan Valley, the hills overlooking the valley, and the flatter country to the south of Amman and around Madaba and Irbid. However, several large farms, which depend for irrigation on water pumped from deep aquifers, have been established in the southern desert area. The rest of the country is desert and semi-desert. The principal crops are wheat, barley, vegetables, olives and fruit (mainly grapes and citrus fruits). Agricultural production has increased considerably in recent years due to improvements in production and irrigation techniques, and exports to Europe and elsewhere are increasing.

Important industrial products are raw phosphates (1988, 5.6 million tons) and potash (1988, 1.3 million tons), most of which is exported, together with fertilizers and pharmaceuticals. The Trans-Arabian oil pipeline (Tapline) runs through north Jordan on its way from the western province of Saudi Arabia to the Lebanese port of Sidon. A branch pipeline, together with oil trucked by road from Iraq, feeds a refinery at Zerqa (production 1988, 2.3 million tons) which meets most of Jordan's requirements for refined petroleum products. Sufficient reserves of natural gas have been discovered in the north-east to produce electricity for the national grid (generators were commissioned in May 1989). Despite extensive efforts no significant reserves of oil have been found.

Tourism has steadily developed. International class hotels cater for businessmen and tourists in Amman and Aqaba. A spa hotel has been opened by hot springs close to the Dead Sea and a hotel complex is planned at the Dead Sea.

FINANCE	1987	1988
	(JD'000)	
Revenue	869,969	917,562
Expenditure	965,808	1,045,680
Surplus/Deficit	-95,839	-128,118

TRADE WITH UK	1991	1992
Imports from UK	£89,411,000	£110,859,000
Exports to UK	10,984,000	20,743,000

COMMUNICATIONS

The trunk road system is good. Amman is linked to Aqaba, Damascus, Baghdad and Jeddah by roads which are of considerable importance in the overland trade of the Middle East.

The former Hejaz Railway enters Jordan from Syria east of Ramtha and runs through Zerqa and Amman to Ma'an with a spur to the top of the Ras al-Naqb escarpment. It is little used, mainly for freight between Amman and Damascus. The Aqaba railway carries phosphate rock from the mines of al Hasa and al Abiad to Aqaba. A total of 2,583 vessels called at Aqaba in 1988, and 20,096,200 tons of cargo were handled.

The Royal Jordanian Airline operates from Amman to Aqaba and has an extensive network of routes to the Middle East, Europe, North America and the Far East.

KAZAKHSTAN
Kazak Respublikasy

Kazakhstan has an area of 1,049,155 sq. miles (2,717,300 sq. km) and occupies the northern part of what was Soviet Central Asia. It stretches from the Volga and the Caspian Sea in the west to the Altai and Tienshan mountains in the east. It is bordered on the west by the Caspian Sea and the Russian Federation, on the south by Turkmenistan, Uzbekistan and Kyrgyzstan, on the east by China and on the north by the Russian Federation. Kazakhstan is a country of arid steppes and semi-deserts, flat in the west, hilly in the east and mountainous in the south-east (Southern Altai and Tienshan mountains). The main rivers are the Irtysh, the Ural, the Syr-Darya and the Ili.

CLIMATE – Continental and very dry.

POPULATION – According to 1992 estimates, the population is 16,700,000, of which 40 per cent are Kazakhs, 37 per cent Russians, 5 per cent Ukrainians and 5 per cent ethnic Germans. There are also smaller numbers of Tatars, Uzbeks and Belarussians.

RELIGION – The majority of ethnic Kazakhs are Sunni Muslims, and this is the main religion of the republic.

LANGUAGE – Kazakh (one of the Turkic languages) became the official language in January 1993. Russian was given a special status as the 'social language between peoples'. Otherwise each ethnic group uses its own language (e.g. Kazakh 40 per cent, Russian 37 per cent).

CAPITAL – Alma-Ata. Population 1,128,000 (1989). The other major city is Chimkent, population 400,000 (1992).

CURRENCY – Rouble of 100 kopeks.

FLAG – Light blue with a sun and a soaring eagle in the centre, and a vertical ornamentation near the hoist, all in gold.

NATIONAL DAY – 16 December (Republic Day).

HISTORY

For centuries Kazakhstan was inhabited by nomadic tribes before being invaded by Ghenghiz Khan and incorporated into his empire in 1218. After his empire disintegrated feudal towns emerged based on large oases. These towns affiliated and established a Kazakhstan state in the late 15th century which engaged in almost continuous warfare with the marauding Khanates on its southern border. After appealing to Russia for aid and protection, in 1731 Kazakhstan acceded to the Russian Empire under a voluntary act of accession. The Russians developed crop farming and began some industrialization.

The First World War brought privation to Kazakhstan as livestock and agricultural produce was requisitioned, leading to an uprising in 1916 against the conscription of male Kazakhs. After the 1917 Russian revolution, Kazakhstan came under the control of White Russian forces before they were driven from Kazakhstan in 1919. On 26 August 1920 a new constitution was signed under which Kazakhstan became a Soviet Socialist Republic. Under Soviet rule in the 1920s and 1930s there was rapid industrial development and the traditional nomadic way of life disappeared. The Kazakhs suffered greatly in the Stalinist purges, the merchant and religious classes being murdered and thousands dying in the desert on forced collective farms.

GOVERNMENT

Kazakhstan was the last of the former USSR republics to declare its independence (16 December 1991), which was recognized by the EC and the USA later that month. UN membership was gained on 2 March 1992.

The Supreme Kenges (parliament) voted to adopt a new constitution on 28 January 1993 under which executive power is vested in the President and government. The President must be a Kazakh speaker and has the power to appoint the Prime Minister, deputy prime ministers, the foreign, defence and interior ministers and all ambassadors. The parliament does not have the power to impeach the President and the President cannot dissolve parliament. The government remains that of the former Kazakh Communist Party, renamed the People's Unity Party (PUP). The PUP held its founding conference in February 1993, at which it committed itself to economic reform and political pluralism.

President Nazarbaev, although genuinely popular with the population, has refused to enter into a coalition government with opposition democratic parties and has restrained Islamic fundamentalist groups who want to repatriate ethnic Russians. Nazarbaev has maintained a delicate balance between ethnic Kazakhs and Russians, which is necessary for the country's stability and survival. Tensions between the two nationalities remain below the surface and the January 1993 language decree is disliked by many Kazakhs and Russians. Ethnic Russians dominate the state's economy and Nazarbaev has realized he needs their co-operation for the country's successful development. The Russians understand that Nazarbaev restrains any anti-Russian feelings in the country and have accepted his presidency. Nazarbaev has signed important agreements with Russia regarding the space centre at Baikonur and the nuclear testing ground at Semipalatinsk.

HEAD OF STATE
President, Nursultan Nazarbaev, *elected* 1 December 1991.

CABINET *as at August 1993*
Prime Minister, Sergei Tereshchenko.
First Deputy Prime Minister, Daulet Sembayev.
Deputy Prime Ministers, Kuanish Sultanov; Salibeck Karibzhanov; Asygat Zhabagin; Galym Abelsiitov.
Foreign Affairs, Tuleutai Suleimenov.
Interior, Vladimir Shumov.
Defence, Sagadat Nurmagambetov.

Foreign Economic Relations, Syzdyk Abishev.
Justice, Galikhan Yerzhanov.
Industry, Albert Salamatin.
Economy, Beysenbaye Izteleulov.
Finance, Erkembay Derbisov.
Mineral Resources, Lev Trubnikov.
Education, Shaisultan Shayakhmetov.
Trade, Oktyabar Zheltikov.
Transport, Nigmatzhan Isingarin.
Labour, Sayat Beisenov.
Communications, Igor Ulyanov.
Health, Vasily Devyakto.
Culture, Erkegali Rakhmadiev.
Social Protection, Zaure Kadyrova.
Agriculture, Bakhtash Tursunbaye.
Forestry, Alexander Amanbayer.

BRITISH CONSULATE-GENERAL
Alma Ata

Consul-General and Resident Chargé d'Affaires, Robert M. Harris.

DEFENCE

Kazakhstan retains close defence relations with Russia and all former Soviet forces on its territory remain under joint CIS control. Strategic nuclear forces number 104 SS-18 intercontinental ballistic missiles and 40 nuclear-capable Tu-95H bombers. These are to be transferred to Russia under the Start I Treaty ratified by Kazakhstan in July 1992, when the Start I Treaty comes into operation. Conventional forces (all under joint control) number some 63,000, with 1,200 main battle tanks, 1,500 artillery pieces, 25 attack helicopters and 370 combat aircraft.

ECONOMY

In March 1993 the government announced a large-scale privatization programme for 1993–5 under which most state-owned enterprises are to be sold by means of a voucher system. Outside the programme, small businesses and retail outlets have been sold at auction since 1992. The government approved the 1993 budget in January of 905,000m Roubles expenditure and 722,000m Roubles revenue.

Kazakhstan is very rich in minerals, with copper, lead, zinc, iron ore, coal, oil and natural gas. The main centres of the metal industry are in the Altai mountains, in Chimkent, north of the Balkhash Lake and in central Kazakhstan. Agriculture, including stock-raising, is highly developed, particularly in the central and south-west of the republic. Grain is grown in the north and north-east, and cotton in the south and south-east. A record grain crop was grown in 1992 but livestock production fell.

KENYA
Jamhuri ya Kenya

Kenya is bisected by the equator and extends approximately from 4° N. to 4° S. latitude and from 34° E. to 41° E. longitude. From the coast of the Indian Ocean in the east, the borders of Kenya are with Somalia in the east and Ethiopia and Sudan in the north and north-west. To the west lie Uganda and Lake Victoria. On the south is Tanzania. The total area is 224,961 sq. miles (582,646 sq. km), including 5,171 square miles of water. The country is divided into eight provinces (Central, Coast, Eastern, Nairobi, Nyanza, North Eastern, Rift Valley, Western).

POPULATION – The population is 25,905,000 (1991 UN estimate). The main tribal groups are the Kikuyu, Luhya, Luo, Kalenjin, Kamba and Masai.

LANGUAGES – The official languages are Swahili, which is generally understood throughout Kenya, and English; numerous indigenous languages are also spoken.

CAPITAL – Nairobi, population 1,400,000 (1989 estimate).
CURRENCY – Kenya shilling (Ksh) of 100 cents.
FLAG – Horizontally black, red and green with the red fimbriated in white, and with a shield and crossed spears all over in the centre.
NATIONAL ANTHEM – Kenya, Land of the Lion.
NATIONAL DAY – 12 December (Independence Day).

GOVERNMENT

Kenya became an independent state and a member of the British Commonwealth on 12 December 1963 after six months of internal self-government. Kenya became a republic in 1964. In 1982 the government introduced amendments to the constitution and election law, making the country a one-party state. The Kenya African National Union (KANU) was the sole legal political organization. In December 1991 government yielded to internal and international pressure and introduced a multi-party democracy through parliamentary legislation.

Multi-party presidential and legislative elections were held on 29 December 1992 which were won by President Moi and KANU respectively, amid opposition divisions and opposition claims that the elections were not free and fair which were supported by the Commonwealth observers monitoring the election. In the uni-cameral National Assembly of 200 seats, KANU has 107 seats (95 elected and 12 nominated by the President under the constitution) and the three major opposition parties have 85 seats between them. KANU formed a new government on 13 January 1993 and parliament re-opened on 22 March 1993 but was boycotted by two of the main opposition parties. In May the government reached agreement with the IMF and World Bank on anti-corruption and economic reform measures and the IMF resumed aid to Kenya, suspended in November 1991.

HEAD OF STATE

President and C.-in-C. Armed Forces, Hon. Daniel T. arap Moi, *took office* 14 October 1978, returned for a fourth five-year term on 29 December 1992.

CABINET *as at August 1993*

The President.
Vice-President and Minister for Planning and National Development, Hon. Prof. George Saitoti.
Foreign Affairs, Hon. Stephen Musyoka.
Finance, Hon. Wycliffe Mudavadi.
Agriculture, Livestock Development and Marketing, Hon. Simon Nyachae.
Land Reclamation, Regional and Water Development, Hon. Darius Mbela.
Environment and Natural Resources, Hon. John Sambu.
Transport and Communication, Hon. Dalmas Otieno.
Energy, Hon. John Kyalo.
Commerce and Industry, Hon. Kirugi M'mukindia.
Tourism and Wildlife, Hon. Katana Ngala.
Health, Hon. Joshua Angatia.
Local Government, Hon. William Ntimana.
Home Affairs and National Heritage, Hon. Francis Lotodo.
Lands and Urban Planning, Hon. Jackson Mulinge.
Labour and Manpower Development, Hon. Phillip Masinde.
Information and Broadcasting, Hon. Johnstone Makau.
Cultural and Social Services, Hon. Hussein Mohamed.
Co-operative Development, Hon. Kamwithi Munyi.
Public Works and Housing, Hon. Jonathan N'geno.
Research and Technical Training, Hon. Zachary Onyonka.
Attorney-General, Hon. Amos Wako.

KENYA HIGH COMMISSION
45 Portland Place, London WIN 4AS
Tel 071-636 2371
High Commissioner, His Excellency J. Ruto (1993).
Deputy High Commissioner, Miss E. Tolle.
Defence Attaché, Col. F. R. Nthiggah.
Commercial Attaché, C. Mkangi.

BRITISH HIGH COMMISSION
Bruce House, Standard Street, PO Box 30465 Nairobi
Tel: Nairobi 335944
High Commissioner, His Excellency Sir Kieran Prendergast,
  KCVO, CMG (1992).
Deputy High Commissioner, H. B. Warren-Gash.
Defence and Military Adviser, Col. P. R. Bell.
First Secretary (Commercial), D. L. Littlefield.
First Secretary (Consular), A. Summers.

BRITISH COUNCIL REPRESENTATIVE, Bill Harvey, (PO
Box 40751) ICEA Building, Kenyatta Avenue, Nairobi.
There are offices at *Kisumu* and *Mombasa.*

ECONOMY

Agriculture provides about 52 per cent of total export
earnings (excluding processed oil products). The great
variation in altitude and ecology provide conditions under
which a wide range of crops can be grown. These include
wheat, barley, pyrethrum, coffee, tea, sisal, coconuts, cashew
nuts, cotton, maize and a wide variety of tropical and
temperate fruits and vegetables. The total area of well-
farmed land on which concentrated mixed farming can be
practised is small and the remainder is arid or semi-arid
country but population pressure and the need to increase
agricultural production for export has led to attempts to
develop such areas.

Prospecting and mining are carried on in some parts of
the country, the principal minerals produced being soda ash,
salt and limestone.

Hydro-electric power has been developed, particularly on
the Upper Tana River. Kenya is now almost self-sufficient in
electric power generation but the connection with Owen
Falls in Uganda is still in being.

There has been considerable industrial development over
the last 15 years and Kenya has a wide variety of industries
processing agricultural produce and manufacturing an
increasing range of products from local and imported raw
materials. New industries have recently come into being such
as steel, textile mills, dehydrated vegetable processing and
motor tyre manufacture as well as many smaller schemes
which have added to the country's already considerable
consumer goods. There is an oil refinery in Mombasa
supplying both Kenya and Uganda, and a fuel pipeline now
connects Mombasa and Nairobi.

TRADE

Principal exports are coffee and tea, which account for 33
per cent of total export earnings. Also exported are fruit,
vegetables, and crude animal and vegetable material.
Petroleum products account for about 37 per cent of imports;
other imports are manufactured goods, particularly machinery, transport equipment, metals, pharmaceuticals and
chemicals.

Trade with UK	1991	1992
Imports from UK	£206,927,000	£139,865,000
Exports to UK	141,996,000	138,397,000

COMMUNICATIONS

The Kenya Railways Corporation has 1,700 miles of railway
open to traffic. There are also 39,000 miles of road, of which
5,000 are bitumen surfaced. Trans-border links with Tanzania were re-opened in 1985 with rail services for freight and
steamer services for passengers and freight.

The principal port is Mombasa, operated by the Kenya
Ports Authority. International air services operate from
airports at Nairobi and Mombasa.

KIRIBATI
Ribaberikin Kiribati

Kiribati, the former Gilbert Islands, became an independent
republic in 1979. Kiribati comprises 36 islands, the Gilberts
Group (17) including Banaba (formerly Ocean Island), the
Phoenix Islands (8), and the Line Islands (11), which are
situated in the south-west central Pacific around the point at
which the International Date Line cuts the Equator. The
total land area of 281 sq. miles (728 sq. km) is spread over
some 2 million square miles of ocean. Few of the atolls are
more than half a mile in width or more than 12 feet high. The
vegetation consists mainly of coconut palms, breadfruit trees
and pandanus. The population (UN estimate 1991) is 66,000,
and predominantly Christian.

CAPITAL – Tarawa, population estimated at 17,921.
CURRENCY – Kiribati uses the Australian dollar ($A) of 100
  cents.
FLAG – Red, with blue and white wavy lines in base, and in
  the centre a gold rising sun and a flying frigate bird.
NATIONAL ANTHEM – Teirake Kain Kiribati (Stand
  Kiribati).
NATIONAL DAY – 12 July (Independence Day).

GOVERNMENT

The President is head of state as well as head of government
and is elected nationally. There is an elected House of
Assembly of 41 members. Executive authority is vested in
the Cabinet.

CABINET *as at August 1993*
*President and Minister of Foreign Affairs and International
  Trade,* HE Teatao Teannaki.
*Vice-President and Minister of Finance and Economic
  Planning,* Hon. Taomati T. Iuta.
Health, Family Affairs and Social Welfare, Hon. Baitika
  Toum.
Line and Phoenix Development, Hon. Boanereke Boanereke.
Home Affairs and Decentralization, Hon. Binata Tetaeka.
Transport, Communications and Tourism, Hon. Inatoa
  Tebania.
Education, Science and Technology, Hon. Anterea Kaitaake.
Commerce, Industry and Employment, Hon. Remuera
  Tateraka.
Works and Energy, Hon. Tamwi Naotarai.
Environment and Natural Resources Development, Hon.
  Tiwau Awira.

HONORARY CONSULATE
c/o Faith House, 7 Tufton Street, London SWIP 3QN
Tel 071-222 6952
Honorary Consul, M. Chandler, CBE.

BRITISH HIGH COMMISSION
PO Box 61, Bairiki, Tarawa
Tel: Bairiki 21327
High Commissioner, His Excellency Frank McDermott
(1993)

ECONOMY

Most people still practise a semi-subsistence economy, the main staples of their diet being coconuts and fish.

Estimated recurrent revenue for 1988 was $A24.9m. The principal imports are foodstuffs, consumer goods, machinery and transport equipment. The principal exports are copra and fish. Total value of exports in 1990 was $A3,681,000.

TRADE WITH UK	1991	1992
Imports from UK	£253,000	£571,000
Exports to UK	9,000	2,000

COMMUNICATIONS

Air communication exists between most of the islands, and is operated by Air Tungaru, a statutory corporation. Air Marshall Islands operates a weekly service between Majuro, Tarawa, Funafuti and Nandi, and Air Nauru between Tarawa, Nauru and Nandi. Inter-island shipping is operated by a statutory corporation, the Shipping Corporation of Kiribati.

SOCIAL WELFARE

The Government maintains a teacher training college and a secondary school. Five junior secondary schools are maintained by missions. Throughout the republic there are about a hundred primary schools. The total enrolment of children of school age is about 16,000.

The Marine Training School at Tarawa trains seamen for service with overseas shipping lines.

There is a general hospital at Tarawa. The other inhabited islands have dispensaries.

KOREA

Korea is situated between 124° 11″ and 130° 57′ E. longitude, and between 33° 7′ and 43° 1″ N. latitude. It has an area of 84,565 sq. miles (219,022 sq. km), with a population (UN estimate 1991) of 65,461,000, of whom 43,268,000 live south of the present dividing line. The southern and western coasts are fringed with innumerable islands, of which the largest, forming a province of its own, is Cheju.

LANGUAGE AND LITERATURE

Despite the great cultural influence of the Chinese, Koreans have developed and preserved their own cultural heritage. The Korean language is of the Ural-Altaic Group. Its script, Hangul, was invented in the 15th century; prior to this Chinese characters alone were used.

HISTORY

The last native dynasty (Yi) ruled from 1392 until 1910, in which year Japan formally annexed Korea. The country remained an integral part of the Japanese Empire until the defeat of Japan in 1945, when it was occupied by troops of the USA and the USSR, the 38th parallel being fixed as the boundary between the two zones of occupation.

The US Government endeavoured to reach agreement with the Soviet Government for the creation of a Korean Government for the whole country and the withdrawal of all Russian and American troops. These efforts met with no success, and in September 1947 the US Government laid the question of the future of Korea before the General Assembly of the United Nations. The Assembly in November 1947 resolved that elections should be held in Korea for a National Assembly under the supervision of a temporary commission formed for that purpose by the United Nations and that the National Assembly when elected should set up a Government. The Soviet Government refused to allow the Commission to visit the Russian-occupied zone and in consequence it was only able to discharge its function in that part of Korea which lies south of the 38th parallel.

A general election was held on 10 May 1948, and the first National Assembly met in Seoul on 31 May. The Assembly passed a constitution on 12 July and on 15 August 1948 the Republic was formally inaugurated and American military government came to an end.

Meanwhile, in the Russian-occupied zone north of the 38th parallel the Democratic People's Republic had been set up with its capital at Pyongyang. A Supreme People's Soviet was elected in September 1948, and a Soviet-style constitution adopted.

THE KOREAN WAR

The country remained effectively divided into two along the line of the 38th parallel until June 1950, when North Korean forces invaded South Korea. In response to Security Council recommendations that United Nations members should furnish assistance to repel the attack, 16 nations, including the USA and the UK, came to the aid of the Republic of Korea. China entered the war on the side of North Korea in November 1950. The fighting was ended by an armistice agreement signed on 27 July 1953. By this agreement (which was not signed by the representatives of the Republic of Korea), the line of division between North and South Korea remained in the neighbourhood of the 38th parallel.

Talks between North and South Korea on the reunification of the country have taken place intermittently. A non-aggression accord was signed between the North and South in December 1991 and an agreement on the denuclearization of the Korean peninsula was reached in February 1992.

REPUBLIC OF KOREA
Daehanminkuk

The Republic of Korea has been officially recognized by the governments of the United States, France, United Kingdom, and most other countries but, until recently, not by any Communist bloc country. Since 1989 diplomatic relations have been established with all eastern European countries, including the then Soviet Union, and in 1992 with the People's Republic of China, which required the breaking of diplomatic relations with Taiwan.

RELIGION – There is freedom of religion. Buddhism has the most followers (13 million) followed by Protestantism (8 million) and Confucianism (4.7 million). Catholics number 2.2 million.

CAPITAL – Seoul, population (November 1987) 9,991,089. Other main centres are Ψ Pusan (3,654,097), Taegu (2,165,954) and Ψ Inchon (1,526,435).

CURRENCY – Won of 100 jeon.

FLAG – White with a red and blue yin-yang in the centre, surrounded by four black trigrams.

NATIONAL ANTHEM – Aegukka.

NATIONAL DAY – 15 August (Independence Day).

GOVERNMENT

Following extensive political unrest in 1987, a new Constitution was adopted in February 1988. The President, who is Head of State, Chief of the Executive and Commander-in-Chief of the Armed Forces, is directly elected for a single term of five years. He appoints the Prime Minister with the consent of the National Assembly, and members of the State Council (Cabinet) on the recommendation of the Prime Minister. The President is also empowered to take wideranging measures in an emergency, including the declaration of martial law, but must obtain the agreement of the National Assembly. The National Assembly of 299 members is directly elected for a four-year term.

The most recent elections to the National Assembly were held in March 1992. The ruling Democratic Liberal Party (DLP) lost its parliamentary majority, winning 149 out of 299 seats, but then regained a majority by persuading independent members to join the party. In the most recent presidential election of December 1992, long-time former opposition leader Kim Young-sam was victorious as the Democratic Liberal Party candidate (he had merged his opposition party with the DLP in 1990). On 26 February 1993 he named the first wholly coalition government in 32 years.

HEAD OF STATE

President, Kim Young-sam, *elected* 18 December 1992, *took office* 25 February 1993.

CABINET *as at August 1993*

Prime Minister, Hwang In-Sung.
Deputy Prime Minister, Economic Planning Board, Lee Kyung-Shick.
Deputy Prime Minister, National Unification, Han Wan-Sang.
Foreign Affairs, Han Seung-Joo.
Home Affairs, Lee Hai-Koo.
Finance, Hong Jae-Young.
Justice, Park Hee-Tai.
Defence, Kwon Young-Haei.
Education, Oh Byung-Moon.
Agriculture and Fisheries, Huh Shin-Haing.
Environment, Hwang Sah-Sung.
Trade and Industry, Kim Chui-Soo.
Construction, Huh Jae-Hyung.
Health and Social Affairs, Park Yang-Shil.
Labour, Lee In-Jae.
Transport, Lee Kye-Ik.
Communications, Yoon Dong-Yoon.
Culture, Lee Min-Sub.
Information, Ohin-Hwan.
Government Administration, Choi Chang-Yoon.
Science and Technology, Kim Il-Joong.
First Minister for Political Affairs, Kim Duck-Ryong.
Second Minister for Political Affairs, Kwon Young-Ja.
Director, National Security Planning Agency, Kim Duck.

EMBASSY OF THE KOREAN REPUBLIC

4 Palace Gate, London W8 5NF
Tel 071-581 0247

Ambassador Extraordinary and Plenipotentiary, His Excellency Chang-Hee Roe (1993).
Defence Attaché, Capt. Sung-Joong Kim.
Consul, Key-Cheol Lee.
Commercial Attaché, Soo-Dong Kim.

BRITISH EMBASSY

No. 4, Chung-Dong, Chung-Ku, Seoul 100
Tel: Seoul 735-7341/3

Ambassador Extraordinary and Plenipotentiary, His Excellency David John Wright, CMG, LVO (1990).
Counsellor (Economic), Consul-General and Deputy Ambassador, P. Longworth.
Defence and Military Attaché, Brig. D. P. de C. Morgan, OBE.
First Secretary (Commercial), A. C. Stephens.

There is an Honorary British Consul at *Pusan*.

BRITISH COUNCIL REPRESENTATIVE, T. White, MBE, Anglican Church Annex, 3-7 Chung Dong, Choong-ku, Seoul.

BRITISH CHAMBER OF COMMERCE, c/o Chartered Bank, 1st and 2nd Floors, Samsung Building, 50, 1-Ka Ulchi Ro, Chung-Ku, Seoul.

DEFENCE

The Republic of Korea has total active armed forces of some 633,000 personnel. Conscripts serve for 26 months (Army) or 30 months (Navy and Air Force) and then in reserve forces until age 33. Reserves number some 4,500,000 personnel.

The Army has a strength of 520,000 active personnel, with 1,800 main battle tanks, 2,550 armoured personnel carriers and armoured infantry fighting vehicles, 4,500 artillery pieces and 135 armed helicopters. The Regular Army is organized into nine corps with a total of three mechanized infantry and 19 infantry divisions together with two infantry and seven special forces brigades. The reserves comprise 23 infantry divisions.

The Navy has a strength of 60,000 (19,000 conscripts) including 25,000 marines, with four submarines and 38 principal surface combatants, 15 combat aircraft and 47 armed helicopters. The Air Force has a strength of 53,000, with 407 combat aircraft, almost all of US manufacture, organized into seven combat and two transport wings, totalling eight ground attack, four air defence, one counter-insurgency, one reconnaissance and five transport squadrons.

The US maintains 35,500 personnel in the Republic of Korea divided into 26,500 Army and 9,000 Air Force personnel.

EDUCATION

Primary education is compulsory for six years from the age of seven. Secondary and higher education is extensive. The national illiteracy rate is among the lowest in Asia.

ECONOMY

The soil is fertile but arable land is limited by the mountainous nature of the country. Staple agricultural products are rice, barley and other cereals, beans, tobacco and hemp. Fruit-growing and sericulture are also practised. Ginseng, a medicinal root much used by both the Chinese and Koreans, forms a useful source of revenue. The fishing industry is a major contributor to both food supply and exports.

The Republic of Korea is deficient in mineral resources, except for deposits of coal on the east coast and tungsten. There are some prospects of discovering oil in the sea between Korea and Japan.

FINANCE

The budget for 1990 totals Won 22,689,000. From 1962 a series of successful five-year plans resulted in real economic growth averaging around 10 per cent a year. However, growth fell to 8.5 per cent in 1991 and to 4.8 per cent in 1992, the lowest figure since 1980. Annual per capita GNP is US$6,749 (1992).

TRADE

Since the 1960s the Republic of Korea has industrialized rapidly on the basis of greatly expanded exports. Important exports include cars, electrical and electronic equipment, footwear, ships, railway rolling stock and iron and steel products.

	1990	1991
Imports	US$65,091m	US$76,561m
Exports	63,236m	69,581m

Trade with UK	1991	1992
Imports from UK	£786,162,000	£654,060,000
Exports to UK	924,615,000	933,946,000

COMMUNICATIONS

In 1989 there were 37,493 km of paved road. Seoul and Pusan have subway systems and there are national railway and airline systems. Korean Air operates regular flights to Europe, the United States, the Middle East and South East Asia. Pusan and Inchon are the major ports with Pusan serving the industrial areas of the south-east. Inchon, 28 miles from Seoul, serves the capital, but development and operation at Inchon are hampered by a tidal variation of 9–10 metres.

DEMOCRATIC PEOPLE'S REPUBLIC OF KOREA
Chosun Minchu-chui Inmin Kongwa-guk

The area of North Korea is 46,540 sq. miles (120,538 sq. km), with a population of 22,193,000 (UN estimate 1991).

CAPITAL – Pyongyang, approximate population, 1,500,000.
CURRENCY – Won of 100 chon.
FLAG – Red with white fimbriations and blue borders at top and bottom; a large red star on a white disc near the hoist.
NATIONAL ANTHEM – A Chi Mun Bin No Ra I Gang San (Shine bright, oh dawn, on this land so fair).
NATIONAL DAY – 8 September.

GOVERNMENT

The constitution of the Democratic People's Republic of Korea provides for a Supreme People's Assembly, presently consisting of 687 deputies, which is elected every four years by universal suffrage. The Assembly elects a President, and the Central People's Committee. In turn, the Central People's Committee directs the Administrative Council which implements the policy formulated by the Committee. The Administrative Council (51 members), formally the government of North Korea, includes the Prime Minister and various ministers. In practice however, the country is ruled by the Korean Workers' Party which elects a Central Committee; this in turn appoints a Politburo. The senior ministers of the Administrative Council are all members of the Communist Central Committee and the majority are also members of the Politburo. Kim Il-sung was elected President for a fifth four-year term on 24 May 1990.

In 1992–3 North Korea's attempts to develop nuclear weapons in secret brought it into conflict with western countries. As a signatory of the Nuclear Non-Proliferation Treaty, North Korea is legally required to open its nuclear facilities to inspection by the International Atomic Energy Authority (IAEA). After repeatedly blocking inspections of its facility at Yongbyon, in April 1993 North Korea was reported to the UN Security Council, which ordered it to allow inspections. It refused and announced its decision to withdraw from the NPT by 12 June 1993. After negotiations with the US, it announced that the country would remain in the NPT and allow partial IAEA inspections.

Politburo of the Central Committee, Kim Il-sung; Kim Chong-il; O Chin-u (full members and members of the presidium); Yi Chong-ok; Pak Song-chol; Kim Yong-nam; Kye Ung-tae; Kang Song-san; So Yun-sok; Chon Pyong-ho; Choe Kwang; Han Song-yong (full members). Kang Hui-won; Kim Pok-sin; Hong Si-hak; Hong Song-nam; Choe Tae Pok; Kim Chol-man; Choe Yong-nim; Kim Yong-sun; Yon Hyong-muk; Kim Tal-hyon; Yi Son-sil (alternate members).
Secretariat of the Central Committee, Kim Il-sung (General Secretary); Kim Chong-il; Hwang Chang-yop; So Kwan-hui; Pak Nam-ki; Kim Chung-nin; Kye Ung-tae; Chon Pyong-ho; Choe Tae-pok; Han Song-yong; Yun Ki-pok; Kim Yong-sun; Kim Kuk-tae; Kim Ki-nam.
Premier of Administrative Council, Kang Song-San, appointed 11 December 1992.

DEFENCE

It is believed that North Korea is very close to manufacturing its own nuclear weapons. The total active armed forces number remains high, at some 1,132,000 personnel, and is a destabilizing factor in the region. Conscripts serve for three to four years (Air Force), five to eight years (Army) or five to ten years (Navy), followed by service in the reserves to age 40 and Red Guard to age 60.

The Army has an active strength of 1,000,000 personnel, with 3,000 main battle tanks, 4,000 armoured personnel carriers and 6,800 artillery pieces. Personnel are organized into one armoured, one artillery, four mechanized and eight infantry corps. Reserves number 1,200,000 divided into 24 infantry divisions and 18 infantry brigades. The Navy is 40,000 strong, with 26 submarines, three frigates and 379 patrol and coastal vessels. The Air Force has a strength of 92,000 personnel, with 732 combat aircraft and 50 armed helicopters, organized into three bomber, ten ground attack, and 12 air defence regiments, with attendant transport and training units. In addition, paramilitary troops of the Ministry of Public Security number 115,000 personnel.

ECONOMY

North Korea is rich in minerals and industry has been developed, but the economy has stagnated in recent years because of poor planning and a shortage of foreign exchange.

TRADE WITH UK	1991	1992
Imports from UK	£5,503,000	£7,426,000
Exports to UK	349,000	334,000

KUWAIT
Dowlat al- Kuwait

Kuwait extends along the shore of the Persian Gulf from Iraq to Saudi Arabia, with an area of 6,880 sq. miles

(17,818 sq. km). In 1993 the UN decided on the border dispute between Kuwait and Iraq, moving the border some few hundred metres northwards.

Kuwait has a dry, desert climate with a summer season extending from April to September. The mean temperature varies between 29–45°C in summer, and 8–18°C in winter. Humidity rarely exceeds 60 per cent except in July and August.

POPULATION – At the 1985 census the population was 1,695,128, of which about 40 per cent were Kuwaiti citizens, the remainder being other Arabs, Iranians, Indians and Pakistanis. The total European and American population was about 12,500. The Iraqi occupation of Kuwait led to a substantial emigration of nationals and foreign residents. The population was estimated to have returned to over one million in January 1992, including 425,000 foreigners. It is the government's intention to keep the proportion of foreigners down to 40 per cent.

LANGUAGE – The official language is Arabic, and English is widely spoken as a second language.

RELIGION – Islam is the official religion, though religious freedom is constitutionally guaranteed.

CAPITAL – Ψ Kuwait, population (excluding suburbs) 400,000.

CURRENCY – Kuwaiti dinar (KD) of 1,000 fils.

FLAG – Three horizontal stripes of green, white and red, with black trapezoid next to staff.

NATIONAL DAY – 25 February.

GOVERNMENT

Although Kuwait had been independent for some years, the 'exclusive agreement' of 1899 between the Sheikh of Kuwait and the British Government was formally abrogated by an exchange of letters dated 19 June 1961. Iraq invaded Kuwait on 2 August 1990 and a government-in-exile was established in Saudi Arabia. Kuwait was liberated in February 1991.

Under the Constitution legislative power is vested in the Amir and the 50-member National Assembly, and executive power in the Amir and the Cabinet. The sixth National Assembly was dissolved in July 1986, and was replaced by the National Council, a partially elected, partially appointed body with much narrower powers, in April 1990. Elections to this, held in June 1990, were boycotted by the opposition. As promised, elections for a new National Assembly were held on 5 October 1992. The new government, announced on 17 October 1992, include six members of the National Assembly. The Assembly convened on 20 October 1992. The electorate consists of all Kuwaiti male nationals over 21 whose families have lived in the Emirate since before 1921.

HEAD OF STATE
Amir, HH Sheikh Jabir al-Ahmad al Jabir Al-Sabah, *born* 1928; acceded 1 January 1978.

CABINET *as at July 1993*
Crown Prince and Prime Minister, HH Sheikh Saad al-Abdullah al-Salim al-Sabah.
Deputy Prime Minister and Minister for Foreign Affairs, Sheikh Sabah al-Ahmad al-Jabir al-Sabah.
Second Deputy Prime Minister, Finance and Planning, Nasir al-Rowdhan.
Education, Dr Ahmad al-Rubie.
Interior, Sheikh Ahmad Hamoud al-Jabir al-Sabah.
Defence, Sheikh Ali Sabah al-Salim al-Sabah.
Information, Sheikh Saoud Nasir al-Sabah.
Social Affairs and Labour, Jassim Muhammad al-Oun.
Communications, Minister of State for Housing, Habib Jawhar al-Hayat.

Public Health, Dr Abdul Wahab Suleiman al-Fouzan.
Electricity, Public Works and Water, Ahmed Salih al-Adasani.
Oil, Ali Ahmad al-Baghli.
Awqaf and Islamic Affairs, Jam'an Falih al-Azimi.
Commerce and Industry, Abdullah Rashid al-Hajiri.
Minister of State for Cabinet Affairs, Abdul-Aziz al-Dakheel.
Justice and Administrative Affairs, Mishari Jassim al-Anjari.

Speaker of the National Assembly, Ahmad Abdul-Aziz al-Saadoun.

EMBASSY OF THE STATE OF KUWAIT
45–46 Queen's Gate, London SW7 5JN
Tel 071-589 4533

Ambassador Extraordinary and Plenipotentiary, His Excellency Khaled al-Duwaisan (1993).
Attaché, Abdul-Rahman Saleh Al-Radi (*Consular Affairs*); Dr Jasem Karam (*Cultural*).

BRITISH EMBASSY
PO Box 2 Safat, Arabian Gulf Street, Kuwait
Tel: Kuwait 2403326

Ambassador Extraordinary and Plenipotentiary, His Excellency Wiliam Hugh Fullerton, CMG (1992).
Counsellor and Deputy Ambassador, F. X. Gallagher, OBE.
First Secretaries, J. Bentley (*Management and Consul*); C. R. Winter, OBE (*Commercial*).
Defence Attaché, Col. C. J. Squires.

BRITISH COUNCIL REPRESENTATIVE, A. Broderick, 2 al Arabi Street (PO Box 345), Mansouriyah.

EDUCATION

The government invested its considerable oil revenues in comprehensive social services. Education and medical treatment are free. Kuwait University was opened in 1966, and in 1987–8 had 15,602 students. In 1987–8 there were over 489,000 pupils at government and private schools. These numbers have declined along with the total population since the Iraqi invasion and a number of schools did not re-open after Kuwait's liberation.

COMMUNICATIONS

Kuwait's ports and airport were damaged during the Iraqi occupation, but have re-opened since liberation. There is a network of dual-carriageway roads and more are under construction. Telecommunications and postal services are conducted by the government. Its earth satellite station and telecommunications network were severely damaged during the Iraqi occupation but domestic and international telephone services were restored in the early months following liberation. The 1993 UN border demarcation line gave part of the Iraqi port of Umm Qasr to Kuwait.

ECONOMY

Despite the desert terrain, 8.4 per cent of land is under cultivation, fruit and vegetables being the main crops. Shrimp fishing is becoming important.

The government of Kuwait began to participate in the ownership of the British- and American-owned Kuwait Oil Company in 1974 and an agreement was signed in November 1975 which brought 100 per cent government ownership. After a reorganization of the national oil industry in 1980, all the business was taken over by the Kuwait Petroleum Corporation. The centre of Kuwait oil production is at Burgan, south of Kuwait City. Oil is also lifted in the Kuwait/Saudi Arabia Partitioned Zone (Wafra) south of the state. Oil

is exported through a specially constructed port at Mina al Ahmadi.
Oil installations were extensively damaged during the Iraqi occupation. Oil exports were resumed in July 1991 and production (including output from the neutral zone) reached 1,600,000 barrels per day in June 1993, in line with the quota allocated to it by OPEC (compared to a production capacity of 2,200,000 barrels per day before the Iraqi invasion). Kuwait is anxious to expand production and unhappy that the quota is not considerably larger. The country was aiming for production of about 2,000,000 barrels a day by the end of 1993.

ENERGY, ETC

Before the Iraqi invasion Kuwait had six power stations capable of generating 7,200 Mw of electricity. Associated desalination capacity, on which the country largely depends for water, was 118 million gallons a day; reserves stored up to 2,000 million barrels. All six power stations were damaged during the Iraqi occupation. Essential services were restored after liberation but it will take several years and substantial investment to restore electricity and water distillation capacity to pre-invasion levels.

FINANCE

Expected revenue for the financial year 1992–3 was KD2,213m and expenditure KD4,000m. Oil revenues constitute about 90 per cent of total revenue. There are a large number of investment banks in some of which the Government holds equity. The banking system is controlled by the Central Bank of Kuwait. The Stock Exchange, closed by the Iraqi invasion, reopened in September 1992.

The GDP of Kuwait in 1989 was estimated at KD6,779 million.

TRADE

Oil constitutes Kuwait's major export. Non-oil exports, mainly to Asian countries and the Indian sub-continent, have included chemical fertilizers, ammonia and other chemicals, metal pipes, shrimps and building materials. Re-exports to neighbouring states traditionally accounted for a major proportion of non-oil exports but were brought to a halt by the Iraqi invasion. Major trading partners are Japan, the USA and Western Europe.

Trade with UK	1991	1992
Imports from UK	£178,336,000	£262,288,000
Exports to UK	29,886,000	127,226,000

KYRGYZSTAN
Kyrgyz Respublikasy

Kyrgyzstan has an area of 76,642 sq. miles (198,500 sq. km) and occupies the central eastern part of the former Soviet Central Asia. The republic's name was changed from Kirghizia in December 1990. It is bordered on the north by Kazakhstan, on the east by China, on the south and south-west by Tajikistan and on the west by Uzbekistan. Kyrgyzstan is a mountainous country, the major part being covered by the ridge of the Central Tienshan, while the mountains of the Pamir-Altai system occupy its southern part. There are a number of spacious mountain valleys, the Alai, Susamyr and others. Kyrgyzstan is divided into two provinces, Issyk-Kul and Osh.

POPULATION – According to a 1990 estimate the population is 4,367,000, of which 52.4 per cent are Kirghiz (Turkic origin), 21.5 per cent are Russian and 12.9 per cent Uzbek,

with smaller numbers of Ukrainians, Germans, Tatars and Kazakhs. The majority of the population is concentrated in plains lying at the foot of the mountains.
RELIGION – Islam is the main religion.
LANGUAGE – Kirghiz 52.4 per cent, Russian 21.5 per cent, Uzbek 12.9 per cent. Kirghiz is a Turkic language which was given an alphabet in the 1930s.

CAPITAL – Bishkek. Population 616,000 (1989 census).
CURRENCY – Som (introduced on 10 May 1993 at rate of 1:200 against the Rouble).
FLAG – Red with a rayed sun containing a representation of a yurt, all in gold.
NATIONAL DAY – 31 August (Independence Day).

GOVERNMENT

The Kirghiz people were first mentioned in Chinese chronicles in the second millenium BC. They are a merger of two ethnic groups, one a Turkic-speaking people driven into the area by the Mongols from the River Yenisei area of Central Asia, and the other indigenous peoples who spoke a similar language. After a long period spent under Mongol, Chinese and Persian rule, the Kirghiz became part of the Russian Empire in the 1860s and 1870s. Kyrgyzstan became part of the Soviet Union in 1920 and underwent some industrialization.

Kyrgyzstan declared independence from the Soviet Union just after the failed Moscow coup on 31 August 1991, and gained UN membership on 2 March 1992. The Communist Party was already out of power by this time, but nevertheless President Akaev has had trouble introducing economic reforms because of the obstructive bureaucracy. Ethnic tensions between the rural nomadic Kirghiz, the urban Russians and the wealthy Uzbeks who own many businesses and form the majority in the second largest town of Osh, are never far from the surface. Fighting over land between ethnic Kirghiz and Uzbeks in Osh in 1991 left over 500 dead.

During 1992 and 1993 Kyrgyzstan became the most open and democratic of the five republics of former Soviet Central Asia. A new constitution was adopted on 5 May 1993 by the Uluk Kenesh (parliament) which requires the country's adherence to moral and international principles of law and human rights and to the values of Islam. President Akaev transferred the role of head of government from himself to the Prime Minister. Agreement was also reached on the terms of office of the President and Uluk Kenesh, which are to expire in 1995. The Uluk Kenesh, however, remains lukewarm towards reform and continues to clash with the President over the free market reforms enshrined in the constitution.

HEAD OF STATE
President, Askar Akaev, *elected* 12 October 1991.

GOVERNMENT *as at August 1993*
Prime Minister, Tursunbek Chyngyshev.
Deputy Prime Minister, Economic Policy, Gherman Kuznetsov.
Deputy Prime Minister, Social Policy, Abdany Erkebayev.
Interior, Abdybek Sutalinov.
Foreign Affairs, Ednap Karabaev.
Industry, Esengal Omuraliyev.
Communications, Emil Bektenov.
Economics and Finance, Kamchibek Shakirov.
Justice, Usup Mukambayev.
Agriculture, Karypbek Asanov.
Education, Chinara Dzhakipova.
Trade and Material Resources, Andrei Iordan.

Transport, Erkinbek Kurmanbayev.
Culture, Daniyal Nazarmatov.
Health, Naken Kasiyev.
Labour and Social Protection, Yuri Shustikov.
Water Conservancy and Land Improvement, Meirazhdin
   Zulpuyev.
BRITISH AMBASSADOR (resident in Moscow).

ECONOMY

After continued high inflation throughout 1992 and early 1993, the government introduced Kyrgyzstan's own currency in May 1993 to break the link with the depreciating rouble, the cause of the inflation. The IMF has provided a US$62 million credit to support the currency reform and the fast pace of privatization. By the end of 1993 the government plans to have privatized 35 per cent of state-owned enterprises. The President and government have also made the Central Bank independent of government and parliamentary control. However, the country needs direct foreign investment desperately and has had most if its trading links with other Central Asian republics severed because of their refusal to accept payments in Soms. Subsidized goods supplies from Russia have also ended.

Agriculture is the major sector of the economy with sugar beet, cotton and sheep being the main products. Industry is concentrated in the food-processing, textiles, timber and mining fields. Hydro-electric power is abundant and Kyrgyzstan has reserves of several minerals, including coal and uranium.

CULTURE

The Kirghiz language had an oral tradition of literature until the 1930s which included the epic poem *Manas,* which tells the history of the Kirghiz people. Internationally, one of the best-known writers of the former Soviet Union is the Kirghiz writer Chingiz Aitmatov (1928-).

LAOS
Satharanarath Pasathipatai Pasason Lao

The People's Democratic Republic of Laos is in the northerly part of Indo-China, with China and Vietnam on the north and east, Myanmar (Burma) and Thailand on the west, and Cambodia to the south. The area of the country is 91,429 sq. miles (231,800 sq. km), with a population (UN estimate 1991) of 4,262,000.

CAPITAL – Vientiane, population (estimated 1984) 120,000.
CURRENCY – Kip (K) of 100 at.
FLAG – Blue background with a central white circle, framed by two horizontal red stripes.
NATIONAL DAY – 2 December.

GOVERNMENT

The kingdom of Lane Xang, the Land of a Million Elephants, was founded in the 14th century but broke up at the beginning of the 15th century into the separate kingdoms of Luang Prabang and Vientiane and the Principality of Champassac, which together came under French protection in 1893. In 1945 the Japanese executed a coup and suppressed the French administration. Under a Constitution of 1947 Laos became a constitutional monarchy under King Sisvang Vong of the House of Luang Prabang, and an independent sovereign state in 1953. The next 22 years in Laos were

marked by power struggles and civil war, eventually won by the North Vietnamese-backed Pathet Lao, a Communist-dominated organization.

The Lao People's Democratic Republic was proclaimed in December 1975 following victory by the Pathet Lao and the abdication of the King. A President and Council of Ministers were installed, and a 45-member Supreme People's Council was appointed to draft a Constitution. A draft Constitution was approved by the People's Supreme Assembly in August 1991. The Lao People's Revolutionary Party (LPRP) is the sole legal political organization. A general election to the 85-member National Assembly established by the 1991 constitution was held on 20 December 1992; all the candidates were approved by the LPRP. The President, Prime Minister and Council of Ministers were confirmed in their posts by the National Assembly on 22 February 1993.

HEAD OF STATE
President, Nouhak Phonmsavan, *elected by Supreme People's
   Assembly* 25 November 1992.
President of the Supreme People's Assembly, Samane
   Vignaket.

COUNCIL OF MINISTERS *as at August 1993*
Prime Minister, Gen. Khamtai Siphandone.
*Deputy PM and President of State Committee for Planning and
   Co-operation,* Khamphoui Keoboualapha.
Deputy Prime Minister, Phoun Sipaseut.
*National Defence and Supreme Commander of the Lao
   People's Army,* Lt.-Gen. Chounmmali Sayasone.
Minister, and Head of the Office of the Council of Ministers,
   Phao Bounnaphon.
Foreign Affairs, Somsavat Lengsavat.
Interior, Asang Laoli.
Justice, Khamouane Boupha.
Health, Vannareth Rasaphe.
Agriculture and Forestry, Sisavat Keobounphan.
Industry, Soulivong Dalavong.
Communications, Transport, Posts and Construction,
   Bouathong.
Finance, Khamsay Souphanouvang.
Education, Phimmasone.
Commerce, Sompadith Volasane.
Information and Culture, Osakan Thammatheva.
Governor of the National Bank, Boutsabang Souvannavong.
Labour and Social Welfare, Thongloun Sisoulith.

EMBASSY OF THE LAO PEOPLE'S DEMOCRATIC
REPUBLIC
74 Avenue Raymond-Poincaré 75116 Paris
Tel: Paris 45530298

Ambassador Extraordinary and Plenipotentiary, new
   appointment awaited.

BRITISH AMBASSADOR (resident in Bangkok, Thailand).

ECONOMY

A 'new economic management' programme was introduced in 1986 which began the liberalization of the Laotian economy, with greater autonomy for state enterprises, the relaxation of price controls and the encouragement of private business and investors. Since 1986 economic reforms have been introduced forming a market-orientated economic system which have led to significant economic growth and a decline in inflation. The economy is dominated by the agricultural sector, which contributed 59 per cent of real gross domestic product in 1992, when 1.5 million tons of paddy rice was produced. Although Laos has a major balance of payments problem, exports have recently been increasing.

Hydro-electric power is the main export, followed by wood. The country has considerable potential, having a small population and a comparative wealth of resources, although there is a great need for capital investment in infrastructure.

TRADE WITH UK	1991	1992
Imports from UK	£1,173,000	£656,000
Exports to UK	39,000	201,000

LATVIA
The Republic of Latvia

The republic of Latvia is situated in northern Europe on the eastern coast of the Baltic sea. To the north lie Estonia and Finland, to the south Lithuania and Belarus, and to the east the Russian Federation. The area is 66,000 square km (25,000 square miles). Latvia is low-lying with occasional chains of hills. Forests cover 20 per cent of the total territory.
CLIMATE – Moderately continental.
POPULATION – The total population of Latvia is 2,606,000 (1993) of which 51.8 per cent is Latvian, 33.8 per cent Russian, 4.5 cent Belarussian, small Ukrainian and Polish minorities.
LANGUAGES – 51.8 per cent have Latvian as their first language and 33.8 per cent Russian. Education is now in Latvian and Russian. All employees must pass language tests in Latvian to a level commensurate with the nature of their employment. The right of minorities to use their mother tongue has been acknowledged.

CAPITAL – Riga (population 900,000). Other cities are Liepaja and Ventspils.
CURRENCY – The Lats.
FLAG – Crimson, with a white horizontal stripe across the centre.
NATIONAL ANTHEM – Dievs, sveti Latviju (God bless Latvia).
NATIONAL DAY – 18 November.

HISTORY

Latvia came under the control of the German Teutonic Knights at the end of the 13th century. During the next few centuries the country endured sporadic invasions by the Swedes, Poles and Russians. By 1795 Latvia was entirely under Russian control. On 18 November 1918 Latvia declared its independence and this was confirmed by the Versailles Treaty in 1919. Several years of fighting with the new Soviet Union ensued until a peace treaty was signed under which the Soviet Union renounced all claims to Latvian territory.
The Soviet Union annexed Latvia in 1940 under the terms of the Molotov-Ribbentrop pact with Germany. Latvia was invaded and occupied when Germany invaded the Soviet Union during the Second World War. In 1944 the Soviet Union recaptured the country from Germany and confirmed its annexation, though this was never accepted as legal by most states.
In October 1988 the Popular Front of Latvia was formed to campaign for greater sovereignty and democracy for Latvia. The Popular Front convincingly won elections to the Latvian Supreme Soviet in 1989, and on 4 May 1990 the Supreme Soviet declared the independent Republic of Latvia to be, *de jure*, still in existence. Agitation in Latvia against Soviet rule led in 1990 and early 1991 to clashes between independence supporters and Latvian Communists and the Soviet military. Violence reached a peak in January 1991 with deaths caused by Soviet Interior Ministry troops and attacks on Baltic border posts. A national referendum was held in March 1991 in which 73 per cent of voters declared in favour of independence, and this was declared on 21 August 1991. The State Council of the Soviet Union recognized the independence of Latvia on 10 September 1991.

GOVERNMENT

Democratic government and a unicameral parliament were restored after multi-party elections in June 1993. Executive authority is vested in a Prime Minister and Cabinet of Ministers. Legislative power is exercised by the unicameral parliament (Saiema) which consists of 100 deputies. The deputies elect a President of State, who in turn appoints the Prime Minister. The Prime Minister appoints, and the Saiema approves, the Cabinet of Ministers.
After the June 1993 general election eight political parties are represented in the Saiema. No party has a clear majority, but a coalition of the 'Latvian Way' and 'Farmers Union' hold 48 seats and have formed a government. The electorate has, however, been restricted to those whose forefathers lived in Latvia before 1940, which means that two-thirds of the ethnic Russian population has been unable to vote and this has caused tension with the Russian government.

HEAD OF STATE
President, Guntis Ulmanis, *elected* July 1993.

GOVERNMENT *as at August 1993*
Prime Minister, Valdis Birkavs.
State Reform, Maris Gaillis.
Justice, Egils Levits.
Agriculture, Janis Kima.
Education, Science and Culture, Janis Vaivads.
Economy, Ojars Kehris.
Finance, Uldis Osis.
Foreign Affairs, Georgs Andrejevs.
Welfare, Janis Ritenis.

Defence, Valdis Pavlovskis.
Interior, Girts Kristovskis.
Environmental and Regional Development, Girts Lukins.
Special Assignments, Edvins Inkens.
Transport and Communication, Andris Gutmanis.

EMBASSY OF THE REPUBLIC OF LATVIA
72 Queensborough Terrace, London W2 3SP
Tel 071-727 1698
Ambassador Extraordinary and Plenipotentiary,
His Excellency Jānis Lūsis (1992).

BRITISH EMBASSY
3rd Floor, Elizabetes Iela 2, 226010 Riga
Tel: Riga 320 737
Ambassador Extraordinary and Plenipotentiary, His
Excellency Richard Samuel, CMG, CVO (1991).

DEFENCE

Since its independence from the Soviet Union, Latvia has
sought to form its own armed forces. Total active armed
forces number some 2,550 personnel, with 1,950 conscripts,
serving for 18 months. Ground forces are formed into eight
border guard battalions, one rapid reaction battalion and one
coastal defence unit. Naval forces are formed into one Coast
Guard division. There is also a paramilitary Home Guard of
12,000 personnel.

Russia still maintains Army and Air Force units in Latvia
which number 40,000 personnel.

ECONOMY

Since the former Latvian Supreme Soviet declared the *de jure*
independence of Latvia on 4 May 1990, Latvia has pressed
ahead with transition from a command economy to a market
economy system. It has also attempted to achieve economic
independence from the rest of the former Soviet Union. The
Latvian governrnment has initiated a privatization process
which has made many industrial facilities available for
purchase both by Latvian and foreign private investors.

Latvia is an agricultural exporter, specializing in cattle and
pig breeding, dairy farming and crops, including sugar beet,
flax and potatoes. Natural resources include limestone,
gypsum, peat and timber.

Industry was organized to contribute to the centralized
Soviet command economy and is specialized in certain areas.
These include the production of electric and diesel trains,
telephones, telephone exchange equipment, agricultural
machinery, and timber and paper products.

Tourism is being developed, capitalizing on its beach
resorts, nature reserves and parks. Latvia is also geographically well-placed for the development of transport services.

TRADE

The Russian Federation remains by far the most important
trading partner for Latvia. Over 70 per cent of trade is with
the other former Soviet republics; Latvia imports most of its
raw materials from the former Soviet republics and exports
its finished industrial products to them. However, Latvia is
expanding its trade links with the other Baltic states and
western nations, to try to offset any decline in exports to the
former Soviet republics.

Trade with UK	1992
Imports from UK	£7,782,000
Exports to UK	25,859,000

COMMUNICATIONS

Latvia has a reasonably well-developed railway and road
system, along which a significant proportion of exports from

former Soviet republics are transported to western Europe.
Latvia is also being developed as a transportation route from
Scandinavia to central and southern Europe. Several warm-
water ports exist, of which two, Riga and Ventspils, are
developed for commercial transport.

CULTURE

The Latvian language belongs to the Baltic branch of the
Indo-European languages, and as such is distinct from
Russian. The Latin alphabet is used.

LEBANON
Al-Jumhouriya al-Lubnaniya

Lebanon forms a strip about 120 miles in length and varying
in width from 30 to 35 miles, along the Mediterranean
littoral. It extends from the Israel frontier in the south to the
Nahr al Kebir (15 miles north of Tripoli) in the north; its
eastern boundary runs down the Anti-Lebanon range and
then down the great central depression, the *Beqa'a*, from
which flow the rivers Orontes and Litani. It is divided into
five districts, North Lebanon, Mount Lebanon, Beirut, South
Lebanon and Beqaa. The seaward slopes of the mountains
have a Mediterranean climate and vegetation. The inland
range of Anti-Lebanon has the characteristics of steppe
country.

There is a mixed Arabic-speaking population of Christians,
Muslims and Druses. The total area of Lebanon is 4,015
sq. miles, (10,400 sq. km), population (UN estimate 1991)
2,745,000.

LANGUAGE – Arabic is the official language, and French
and English are also widely used.

CAPITAL – Ψ Beirut (population 702,000). Other towns are
Ψ Tripoli (175,000), Zahlé (46,800), ΨSidon (24,740),
Ψ Tyre (14,000).

CURRENCY – Lebanese pound (L£) of 100 piastres.

FLAG – Horizontal bands of red, white and red with a green
cedar of Lebanon in the centre of the white band.

NATIONAL ANTHEM – Kulluna Lil Watan Lil'ula Lil'alam
(We all belong to the homeland).

NATIONAL DAY – 22 November.

GOVERNMENT

Lebanon became an independent state in September 1920,
administered under French mandate until 22 November
1943. Powers were transferred to the Lebanese Government
from January 1944, and French troops were withdrawn in
1946.

In April 1975, serious fighting broke out in Beirut between
members of the predominantly Christian Phalangist Party
and mainly Muslim militias later supported by Palestinian
guerrillas based in Lebanon. In the autumn of 1976 the Arab
Deterrent Forces, composed mainly of Syrian troops,
imposed an effective ceasefire. In March 1978 Israeli forces
invaded but withdrew some months later, handing over their
positions, except for a belt in the south, to the UN Interim
Force in Lebanon (UNIFIL). In the summer of 1982 Israeli
forces again invaded the country, penetrating as far as Beirut.
Following negotiations, Palestinian officials and fighters left
Beirut for various Arab countries. Although the bulk of Israeli
troops withdrew from southern Lebanon in 1985, a buffer
zone controlled by Israeli-backed Christian militias was
established along the Israeli-Lebanon border. Syrian forces
are deployed in west Beirut and in the north and the east of
the country.

In September 1988 outgoing President Gemayel appointed a transitional Christian-led military government under Gen. Michel Aoun to replace the Muslim-led government of Selim al-Hoss. Each party claimed to represent the constitutional government of Lebanon, and refused to accept the other's authority. The Taif Accord 'for national conciliation', drawn up by an Arab League-appointed committee, gained the approval of a majority of Lebanese MPs in October 1989, but was rejected by Gen. Aoun, who insisted on an immediate Syrian troop withdrawal. Following an outbreak of fighting between Gen. Aoun and the dominant Christian militia, the Lebanese Government acted with the backing of Syrian troops to oust Gen. Aoun in October 1990. A new Government, which included the main militia leaders, was formed in December 1990. Since then the Government has moved to clear the militias from the Greater Beirut area and has restored its authority throughout the former Christian enclave. The Lebanese Army moved into surrounding areas during 1991, extending the control of the Government to virtually all areas not under Syrian (Beqa'a valley) and Israeli (South Lebanon Security Zone) control and disarming all the militias apart from Hezbollah. Since July 1992 the Army has been enforcing the government's policy of retaking all public buildings from the militias. In August 1993 the Lebanese Army began deploying in southern villages for the first time in many years after the Israelis had launched an artillery barrage against Hezbollah targets in the area. The Army is deploying in the area alongside UNIFIL forces but is not disarming Hezbollah forces.

In May 1991 Lebanon and Syria signed a Treaty of Brotherhood, Co-operation and Co-ordination aimed at regulating the relationship between the two countries, as laid down in the Taif Accord.

The first parliamentary elections since 1972 were held between August and October 1992. The new 128-seat unicameral parliament was directly elected by universal suffrage and divided equally between Christians and Muslims. The polls were widely boycotted in Christian areas because of the continuing presence of Syrian troops, in breach of the Taif Accord. A new government was formed under Prime Minister Rafiq Hariri in October 1992 which has focused on the economy and reconstruction. An ambitious ten-year plan has been initiated which is designed to repair war damage and to restore Lebanon's position as a regional financial services and light industrial centre.

In October 1991 Lebanon began to participate in the bilateral sessions of the Middle East peace talks, but so far has, with Syria, boycotted the multilateral rounds.

HEAD OF STATE
President of the Republic of Lebanon, Elias Hrawi, *took office* 25 November 1989.

CABINET *as at August 1993*
Prime Minister and Finance, Rafiq Hariri.
Deputy PM, Michel Murr.
Foreign and Expatriate Affairs, Fares Bouez.
Justice, Bahij Tabbara.
Health and Social Affairs, Marwan Hamadeh.
Defence, Mohsen Dalloul.
Labour, Abdullah al-Amin.
Posts and Telecommunications, Muhammad Ghaziri.
Education and Fine Arts, Mikhail Daher.
State, George Efreni.
Economy and Trade, Hagop Demerdjian.
Information, Michel Samaha.
Agriculture, Abdel Kortas.
Public Works and Transport, Muhammad Mortada.
Industry and Oil, Assaad Rizk.

Interior, Beshara Merhej.
Housing and Co-operatives, Mohammad Abu Hamdan.
Tourism, Nicolas Fattoush.
Water and Electricity Resources, Elie Hobeika.
National Assembly Speaker, Nabih Berri.

LEBANESE EMBASSY
21 Kensington Palace Gardens, London W8 4QM
Tel 071-229 7265/6

Ambassador Extraordinary and Plenipotentiary, His Excellency Mahmoud Hammoud (1990).
Consular Section, 15 Palace Gardens Mews, London W8.
Tel: 071-727 6696.

BRITISH EMBASSY
Shamma Building, Raouché, Ras Beirut, Beirut
Tel: Beirut 812849

Ambassador Extraordinary and Plenipotentiary, Her Excellency Maeve Fort, CMG (1992).

COMMUNICATIONS

The railways are not functioning as a result of the civil war. There is an international airport at Beirut, served by the national carrier MEA, Air France, Cyprus Air and other Arab and European airlines. An internal service operates from Beirut to Tripoli.

ARCHAEOLOGY

Lebanon has some important historical remains, notably Baalbek (Heliopolis) which contains the ruins of first- to third-century Roman temples and Jbeil (Byblos), one of the oldest continuously inhabited towns in the world, and ancient Tyre.

EDUCATION

There are six universities in Beirut, the American and the French universities established in the last century, the Lebanese National University, the Beirut University College, the Kaslik Saint Esprit University and the Arab University, with the University of Balamond situated near Tripoli. There are several institutions for vocational training, and there is a good provision throughout the country of primary and secondary schools, among which are a great number of private schools. Education at all levels has been severely disrupted by the civil war.

ECONOMY

The ten-year (1993–2002) reconstruction plan is estimated by the government to cost US$12,900m in total, of which US$7,600m is to come from foreign loans and grants and US$5,300m from budget surpluses. It is to concentrate on rebuilding housing, transport, utilities, services, education and health services, and aiding industry and agriculture.

Fruits are the most important products and include citrus fruit, apples, grapes, bananas and olives. There is some light industry, mostly for the production of consumer goods, but most factories were adversely affected by the civil war. Reconstruction is now under way.

FINANCE

No reliable statistics have been published for some time. The country is known to have a deficit, and the Lebanese pound has lost much of its value against foreign currencies. At its May 1990 summit meeting, the Arab League agreed to set up an international fund for Lebanon's reconstruction, but progress in establishing the fund was halted by the Kuwait crisis. Reconstruction has been slow and the hoped-for economic recovery has yet to materialize.

TRADE

Principal imports are gold and precious metals, machinery and electrical equipment, textiles and yarns, vegetable products, iron and steel goods, and motor vehicles. There has been a gradual decline in the overall amount of imports, as a result of continued instability.

Principal exports include gold and precious metals, fruits and vegetables, textiles, building materials, furniture, plastic goods, foodstuffs, tobacco and wine.

At one time there was a considerable transit trade through Beirut into the Arab hinterland. Lebanon is the terminal for two oil pipe lines, one formerly belonging to the Iraq Petroleum Company, debouching at Tripoli, the other belonging to the Trans Arabian Pipeline Company, at Sidon. These lines have not functioned for some years.

Trade with UK	1991	1992
Imports from UK	£87,760,000	£91,868,000
Exports to UK	8,465,000	10,405,000

LESOTHO
'Muso oa Lesotho

Lesotho is a landlocked mountainous state entirely surrounded by the Republic of South Africa. Of the total area of 11,720 sq. miles (30,355 sq. km), a belt between 20 and 40 miles in width lying across the western and southern boundaries and comprising about one-third of the total is classed as lowlands, being between 5,000 and 6,000 ft. above sea level. The remaining two-thirds are classed as foothills and highlands, rising to 11,425 ft. The population (UN estimate 1991) is 1,826,000.

CAPITAL – Maseru, population (1986 Census) 288,951.
CURRENCY – Loti (M) of 100 lisente.
FLAG – Diagonally white over blue over green with the white of double width, and an assegai and knobkerrie on a Basotho shield in brown in the upper hoist.
NATIONAL ANTHEM – Pina ea Sechaba.
NATIONAL DAY – 4 October (Independence Day).

GOVERNMENT

Lesotho (formerly Basutoland) became a constitutional monarchy within the Commonwealth on 4 October 1966. The independence constitution was suspended in January 1970, when the country was governed by a Council of Ministers until the establishment of a nominated National Assembly in April 1974.

The Government was overthrown in January 1986, and executive and legislative powers were conferred upon the King, to be advised by the Military Council and Council of Ministers led by Maj.-Gen. Justin Lekhanya. In March 1990 King Moshoeshoe III's powers were formally revoked and vested in the Chairman of the Council of Ministers. In November 1990 the King was deposed and replaced by his son, who assumed the title of Letsie III. Maj.-Gen. Lekhanya was overthrown in a coup on 30 April 1991 led by Col. Elias Ramaema. Elections were promised for 1992, and eventually held on 27 March 1993 when the Basotho Congress Party (BCP) defeated the Basotho National Party (BNP) and won all 65 seats in the new National Assembly. The BCP government led by Ntsu Mokhele was sworn in on 2 April 1993, at which time King Letsie III swore allegiance to a

new multi-party democratic constitution and the Military Council was dissolved.

The country is divided into 11 administrative districts. In each district there is a District Secretary who co-ordinates all government activity in the area, working in co-operation with hereditary chiefs.

HEAD OF STATE
King, HM King Letsie III, *acceded* November 1990.

COUNCIL OF MINISTERS *as at August 1993*
Prime Minister, Minister of Defence and Public Service, Dr Ntsu Mokhehle.
Deputy Prime Minister, Finance, Economic Planning and Manpower Development, Selometsi Baholo.
Foreign Affairs, Molapo Qhobela.
Trade, Industry, Tourism, Labour and Employment, Shaklane Robong Mokhehle.
Agriculture, Co-operatives and Marketing, Ntsakunyane Mphanya.
Home Affairs, Lesao Lehohla.
Education and Training, Sports, Culture and Youth Affairs, Pakalitha Mosisili.
Health and Social Welfare, Dr Khauhelo Ralitapole.
Natural Resources, Monyane Moleleki.
Works, Transport, Post and Telecommunications, David Mochochoko.
Information and Broadcasting, Mpho Malie.
Justice, Human Rights, Law and Constitutional Affairs, Kelebone Maope.

LESOTHO HIGH COMMISSION
7 Chesham Place, London SW1X 8HN
Tel 071-235 5686

High Commissioner, His Excellency M. K. Tsekoa (1989).

BRITISH HIGH COMMISSION
PO Box 521, Maseru 100
Tel: Maseru 313961

High Commissioner, His Excellency James Roy Cowling (1992).

BRITISH COUNCIL REPRESENTATIVE, P. Thompson, Hobson's Square, PO Box 429, Maseru 100.

JUDICIARY

The Lesotho courts of law consist of the court of appeal, the High Court, magistrates' courts, judicial commissioners' court, central and local courts. Magistrates' and higher courts administer the laws of Lesotho. They also adjudicate appeals from the judicial commissioners' and subordinate courts.
Chief Justice, Hon. B. P. Cullinan.

EDUCATION

Most schools are mission-controlled, the Government providing grants for salaries and buildings. There are over 1,000 primary and over 100 secondary schools; few areas lack a school and there is a high literacy rate of about 70 per cent. Increasing emphasis is being laid on agricultural and vocational education. The National University of Lesotho at Roma was established in 1975.

COMMUNICATIONS

A tarred road links Maseru to several of the main lowland towns, and this is being extended in the south of the country. The mountainous areas are linked by gravelled and earth roads and tracks. Roads link border towns in South Africa with the main towns in Lesotho. Maseru is connected by rail with the main Bloemfontein–Natal line of the South African Railways. Scheduled international air services are operated daily between Maseru and Johannesburg and other scheduled international flights are to Gabarone, Harare, Manzini and Maputo. There are around 30 airstrips. Internal scheduled services are operated by the Lesotho Airways Corporation.

The telephone network is fully automated in all urban centres. Radio telephone communication is used extensively in the remote rural areas.

ECONOMY

The economy of Lesotho is based on agriculture and animal husbandry, and the adverse balance of trade (mainly consumer and capital goods) is offset by the earnings of the large numbers of the population who work in South Africa. Apart from some diamonds, Lesotho has few natural resources and only small-scale industrial development. The Lesotho National Development Corporation was set up to promote the development of industry, mining, trade and tourism. Work has commenced on the Highlands Water Scheme designed to provide water for the Vaal industrial zone in South Africa and hydro-electricity for Lesotho. Drilling is being carried out for oil. A National Park has been established at Sehlabathebe in the Maluti mountains. A number of light manufacturing and processing industries have recently been established.

FINANCE

The main sources of revenue are customs and excise duty. Estimates of expenditure and revenue (1986) are recurrent revenue M241.2 million; recurrent expenditure M265.3 million; capital revenue M144 million; capital expenditure M198 million.

Trade with UK	1991	1992
Imports from UK	£3,258,000	£2,725,000
Exports to UK	2,799,000	4,159,000

LIBERIA
Republic of Liberia

An independent republic of West Africa, occupying that part of the coast between Sierra Leone and the Côte d'Ivoire which is between the rivers Mano in the north-west and Cavalla in the south-east, a distance of about 350 miles, with an area of about 43,000 sq. miles (111,369 sq. km), and extending to the interior to latitude 8° 50′, a distance of 150 miles from the seaboard. It was founded by the American Colonization Society in 1822 as a colony for freed American slaves, and has been recognized since 1847 as an independent state. The population at the Census of 1974 was 1,481,524; a 1991 UN estimate put the figure at 2,705,000. The official language is English. Over 16 ethnic languages are spoken.

CAPITAL – ΨMonrovia, population estimate (1984) 425,000. Other ports are ΨBuchanan, ΨGreenville (Sinoe) and ΨHarper (Cape Palmas).

CURRENCY – Liberian dollar (L$) of 100 cents.

FLAG – Alternate horizontal stripes (five white, six red), with five-pointed white star on blue field in upper corner next to flagstaff.

NATIONAL ANTHEM – All Hail, Liberia, Hail.

NATIONAL DAY – 26 July.

GOVERNMENT

William V. S. Tubman, President since 1944, died in 1971 and was succeeded by Dr Tolbert. The constitution was suspended following a military coup on 12 April 1980, during which Tolbert was killed. M/Sgt. Samuel Doe assumed power as chairman of a military council. A new constitution was endorsed by a referendum in July 1984. Doe and his party, the National Democratic Party of Liberia (NDPL) won the elections held in October 1985, amid allegations of electoral fraud, and a civilian government was formally installed in January 1986.

CIVIL WAR

A rebel incursion launched in December 1989 by the National Patriotic Front of Liberia (NPFL) led by Charles Taylor developed into a full-scale civil war. By July 1990 most members of the government had left the country, and foreigners were airlifted to safety by US Marines. A five-nation ECOWAS peacekeeping force (known as ECOMOG) landed in Monrovia in an effort to end the conflict but in September President Doe was killed, having refused to step down. The Interim Government (IGNU) was formed in August in The Gambia and arrived in Monrovia in November. A ceasefire agreement was signed in Bamako, Mali on 28 November 1990, but proved ineffective and the political impasse continued. A further agreement to establish a ceasefire and confine troops to barracks under ECOMOG supervision broke down in October 1992 when the NPFL attempted to seize Monrovia. In response ECOMOG was enlarged to some 10,000 personnel and assumed a more offensive role, launching a full-scale offensive against NPFL forces and driving them out of Monrovia's suburbs. Nigerian aircraft, warships and artillery bombarded NPFL positions and ECOMOG was enlarged by a further 5,000 troops in February 1993. By March 1993 the NPFL had been driven back into eastern parts of Liberia and peace negotiations between the warring factions had begun. Under UN-sponsored negotiations a peace agreement was signed in Benin on 25 July 1993 which brought about a ceasefire on 1 August and scheduled multi-party elections for February 1994. On 16 August a five-member transitional government known as the State Council was established with one member from each of the three factions and two eminent Liberians to govern the country until elections.

FACTIONS

There are competing claims to the leadership of Liberia; that of Interim President Amos Sawyer of the Interim Government of National Unity (IGNU), based in Monrovia and supported by ECOMOG; that of Charles Taylor, leader of the National Patriotic Reconstruction Assembly Government (NPRAG), supported by the National Patriotic Front of Liberia (NPFL) and based in Gbarnga, which controls a large part of the territory of Liberia; and that of the United Liberation Movement for Democracy (ULIMO), based in Sierra Leone.

EMBASSY OF THE REPUBLIC OF LIBERIA
2 Pembridge Place, London W2 4XB
Tel 071-221 1036

Minister Plenipotentiary, George Bardell Cooper (*Maritime Affairs*).
Chargé d'Affaires, Rudolf P. Von Ballmoos.

BRITISH EMBASSY
The British Embassy in Monrovia was closed in March 1991.

COMMUNICATIONS

The artificial harbour and free port of Monrovia was opened in 1948. There are nine ports of entry, including three river ports. Robertsfield International Airport is under NPFL control and not yet in use. Spriggs Payne airfield, on the outskirts of Monrovia, normally used for internal flights, is currently being used for flights to other West African countries.

ECONOMY

In December 1990 the UN launched an appeal for $13.8m in emergency aid to finance the enormous task of reconstruction. Of the country's 2.5 million population, an estimated 750,000 are refugees in neighbouring countries and it is estimated that up to 150,000 have died. Liberia is receiving relief aid from a number of countries including the United Kingdom, the EC and various international agencies.

TRADE

Before the civil war began principal exports were iron ore, crude rubber, timber, uncut diamonds, palm kernels, cocoa and coffee, but the civil war has resulted in the suspension of most economic activity.

Trade with UK	1991	1992
Imports from UK	£8,865,000	£8,766,000
Exports to UK	972,000	4,654,000

LIBYA
Al-Jamahiriya Al-Arabiya
Al-Libiya Al-Shabiya Al-Ishtirakiya Al-Uthma

Libya, on the Mediterranean coast of Africa, is bounded on the east by Egypt and Sudan, on the south by Chad and Niger, and on the west by Algeria and Tunisia. It consists of the three former provinces of Tripolitania, Cyrenaica and the Fezzan, with a combined area of 679,362 sq. miles (1,759,540 sq. km) and a population (UN estimate 1991) of 4,712,000. The people of Libya are principally Arab with some Berbers in the west and some Tuareg tribesmen in the Fezzan. Islam is the official religion of Libya, but other religions are tolerated. The official language is Arabic.

Vast sand and rock deserts, almost completely barren, occupy the greater part of Libya. The southern part of the country lies within the Sahara Desert. There are few rivers and as rainfall is irregular outside parts of Cyrenaica and Tripolitania, good harvests are rare.

The ancient ruins in Cyrenaica, at Cyrene, Ptolemais (Tolmeta) and Apollonia, are outstanding, as are those at Leptis Magna, 70 miles east, and at Sabratha, 40 miles west of Tripoli. An Italian expedition found in the south-west of the Fezzan a series of rock-paintings more than 5,000 years old.

CAPITAL – ΨTripoli, population estimate (1991) 1,000,000. The principal towns are: ΨBenghazi (500,000); ΨMisurata (200,000); Sirte (100,000).
CURRENCY – Libyan dinar (LD) of 1,000 dirhams.
FLAG – Libya uses a plain emerald green flag.
NATIONAL DAY – 1 September.

GOVERNMENT

Libya was occupied by Italy in 1911–12 in the course of the Italo-Turkish War, and under the Treaty of Ouchy (October 1912) the sovereignty of the province was transferred by Turkey to Italy. In 1939 the four provinces of Libya (Tripoli, Misurata, Benghazi and Derna) were incorporated in the national territory of Italy as *Libia Italiana*. After the Second World War Tripolitania and Cyrenaica were placed provisionally under British and the Fezzan under French administration, and in conformity with a resolution of the UN General Assembly in November 1949, Libya became on 24 December 1951 the first independent state to be created by the United Nations. The monarchy was overthrown by a revolution in September 1969, and the country was declared a republic. It was ruled by the Revolutionary Command Council (RCC) under the leadership of Colonel Muammar Gadhafi.

In March 1977 a new form of direct democracy, the 'Jamahiriya' (state of the masses) was promulgated and the official name of the country was changed to Socialist People's Libyan Arab Jamahiriya. At local level authority is now vested in about 1,500 Basic and 14 Municipal People's Congresses which appoint Popular Committees to execute policy. Officials of these congresses and committees, together with representatives from unions and other organizations, form the General People's Congress, which normally meets for about a week early each year. In addition, a number of extraordinary sessions are held throughout the year. This is the highest policy-making body in the country.

The General People's Congress appoints its own General Secretariat and the General People's Committee, whose members head the 13 government departments which execute policy at national level. The Secretary of the General People's Committee has functions similar to those of a Prime Minister.

Since a reorganization in March 1979 neither Col. Gadhafi nor his former RCC colleagues have held formal posts in the administration. Gadhafi continues to hold the ceremonial title 'Leader of the Revolution'.

Leader of the Revolution and Supreme Commander of the Armed Forces, Col. Muammar al-Gadhafi.

SECRETARIAT OF THE GENERAL PEOPLE'S CONGRESS *as at August 1993*

Secretary, Zanati Muhammad al-Zanati.
Assistant Secretary, Muhammad Mahmud al-Hijazi.
Secretary (Conference Affairs), Jayib al-Safi.
Secretary (Affairs of People's Committees), Abd al Latif Abdal-Rahman al-Dali.
Secretary (Trade Unions), Dr Umar Salbak.
Secretary (Women's Affairs), Salmah Rashid.
Secretary (Foreign Affairs), Bshir Salih Bashir.

GENERAL PEOPLE'S COMMITTEE

Secretary, Abu Zayd 'Umar Durda.
Foreign Liaison, Umar Mustafa al-Muntasir.
Unity, Jum'a al-Mahdi al-Fazzani.
Justice and Public Security, Ibrahim Muhammad Bakkar.
Agrarian Reform and Land Reclamation, Dr Isa Abd al-Kafi al-Sayd.
Information and Culture, Ali al-Sha'iri.
Marine Resources, Miftah Muhammad Ka'aybah.
Industry, Jadallah Azzuz al-Talhi.
Energy, Abdullah Salem al-Badri.
Planning, Trade and Finance, Dr Muhammad Bayt al Mal.
Education and Scientific Research, Ma'tug Muhammad Ma'tug.
Health and Social Security, Dr Baghdadi Ali al-Mahmudi.
Utilities, Tourism and Communications, Mubarak Abdullah al-Shamikh.
Supervision and Follow-up, Muhammad Zarruk Rajab.
Defence, vacant.

LIBYAN DIPLOMATIC MISSION IN LONDON

Since the break of diplomatic relations with Libya in April 1984, the Royal Embassy of Saudi Arabia has handled Libyan interests in Britain.

BRITISH EMBASSY

British interests are currently handled by the British Interests Section of the Italian Embassy, Sharia Uahran 1 (PO Box 4206), Tripoli.

DEFENCE

Libya has a total active armed forces of some 85,000, with selective conscription of two to four years. The Army has a strength of 55,000, with 2,150 main battle tanks, 2,720 armoured infantry fighting vehicles and armoured personnel carriers, and some 1,070 artillery pieces. The Army is organized into one National Guard, five infantry, eleven mechanized and eleven armoured brigades. The Navy has a strength of 8,000 personnel, with six submarines, three frigates, 45 patrol and coastal vessels, and 31 armed helicopters. The Air Force has some 22,000 personnel, with 409 combat aircraft and 45 armed helicopters, organized into one bomber, seven ground attack, nine air defence, one counter-insurgency, one reconnaissance and two transport squadrons.

Paramilitary forces number 5,500 personnel, with some tanks and armoured personnel carriers. Russia maintains 1,000 advisers in Libya and the Air Force has some Syrian pilots and North Korean instructors. Libya deploys 2,000 Army personnel in Chad in the disputed Aouzou Strip.

As part of the economic sanctions imposed since April 1992 a total arms embargo is in place against Libya.

COMMUNICATIONS

Besides the coastal road running from the Tunisian frontier through Tripoli to Benghazi, Tobruk and the Egyptian border, which serves the main population centres, main roads now link the provincial centres, and the oil-producing areas of the south with the coastal towns.

There are airports at Tripoli and Benghazi (Benina), Tobruk, Mersa Brega, Sebha, Ghadames and Kufra regularly used by commercial airlines, and military airfields near Tobruk, near Tripoli and at Al Watiya, south of Zuara. Since April 1992 an embargo on air links with Libya has been in force under the terms of UN Security Council Resolution 748, following Libya's failure to hand over to the US or Britain two suspects in the bombing of a Pan Am flight over Lockerbie, Scotland, in 1988.

ECONOMY

Agriculture is confined mainly to the coastal areas of Tripolitania and Cyrenaica, where barley, wheat, olives, almonds, citrus fruits and dates are produced, and to the areas of the oases, many of which are well supplied with springs supporting small fertile areas. Among the important oases are Jaghbub, Ghadames, Jofra, Sebha, Murzuq, Brak, Ghat, Jalo and the Kufra group in the south-east.

The main industry is oil and gas production. There are pipelines from Zelten to the terminal at Mersa Brega, from Dahra to Ras-es-Sider, from Amal to Ras Lanuf, and from the Intisar field to Zuetina. Since 1984 average production of crude oil has been about 1.2 million barrels per day. A major petrochemical complex has been built at Ras Lanuf where a refinery and ethylene plant began operations in early 1985. The construction of an iron and steel plant at Misurata has been completed. Economic constraints have delayed some projects, particularly since Libya decided in 1983 to go ahead with a major irrigation scheme, the 'Great Man-Made River'.

Libya has technical assistance agreements with a number of countries, and also employs large numbers of foreign labourers and experts.

TRADE

Exports from Libya are dominated by crude oil, but some wool, cattle, sheep and horses, olive oil, and hides and skins are also exported. Principal imports are foodstuffs, including sugar, tea and coffee, and most constructional materials and consumer goods. After the revolution the private sector was virtually eliminated and Libya became a state trading country with imports controlled by state monopolies. In early 1988, however, reforms were implemented which have allowed a small private sector to be re-established.

Trade with UK	1991	1992
Imports from UK	£255,719,000	£228,274,000
Exports to UK	121,220,000	162,900,000

LIECHTENSTEIN
Fürstentum Liechtenstein

Liechtenstein is a principality on the Upper Rhine, between Vorarlberg (Austria) and Switzerland, with an area of 61 sq. miles (158 sq. km), and a population in 1992 of 29,856. The language of the principality is German.

CAPITAL – Vaduz, population (1990) 4,874.

CURRENCY – Swiss franc of 100 rappen (or centimes).

FLAG – Equal horizontal bands of blue over red; gold crown on blue band near staff.

NATIONAL ANTHEM – Oben am Jungen Rhein (High on the Rhine).

NATIONAL DAY – 15 August.

GOVERNMENT

The Patriotic Union and Progressive Citizen's parties have governed the country in coalition since 1938. There is a threshold of 8 per cent for parties to gain representation in the Landtag. At the general election on 7 February 1993 the Progressive Citizens' Party won 12 seats, the Patriotic Union Party 11 seats and the Free List (Environmentalist) grouping, 2 seats.

HEAD OF STATE

Prince, Hans Adam II, *born* 14 February 1945; *succeeded* 13 November 1989; *married* 30 July 1967, Countess Marie Kinsky; and has *issue*: Prince Alois, *b.* 11 June 1968, *m.* 1993 Duchess Sophie of Bavaria; Prince Maximilian, *b.* 16 May 1969; Prince Constantin, *b.* 15 March 1972; Princess Tatjana, *b.* 10 April 1973.

MINISTRY *as at August 1993*

Prime Minister, Markus Büchel (*Head of Government 'Presidium', Foreign Affairs, Finance, Transportation, Culture, Youth and Sport*).

Deputy PM, Mario Frick (*Interior, Agriculture, Forestry and Environment, Justice*).

Government Councillors, Cornelia Gassner (*Construction*), Kurt Korner (*Education*), Michael Ritter (*Economy, Social and Health Services*).

DIPLOMATIC REPRESENTATION

Liechtenstein is represented in diplomatic and consular matters in the United Kingdom by the Swiss Embassy.

BRITISH CONSUL GENERAL, T. Bryant, CMG, Dufourstrasse 56, 8008 Zürich.

ECONOMY

The main industries are high and ultra-high vacuum engineering, semi-conductor industry, roller bearings, fastenings and securing systems, artificial teeth, heating and hot water equipment, synthetic fibres, woollen and homespun fabrics.

In May 1991 Liechtenstein became a member of the European Free Trade Association, and as such is a party to the European Economic Area (EEA) Agreement with the EC, due to come into force in late 1993. In December 1992 in separate referenda, Switzerland voted against EEA membership while Liechtenstein voted in favour. Liechtenstein has a customs union with Switzerland which will need to be renegotiated in light of the EEA votes.

FINANCE	1989	1990
Revenue	F371,867,639	F405,409,370
Expenditure	367,249,600	400,801,399

LITHUANIA
Lietuva

Lithuania lies on the eastern coast of the Baltic Sea between 53° 54′ and 56° 27′ N., and 20° 56′ and 26° 51′ E. To the north lies Latvia, to the east and south lies Belarus, to the south-west lie Poland and the Kaliningrad region of the Russian Federation. The area is 65,200 square km (25,170 square miles).

Lithuania lies in the middle and lower basin of the river Nemunas. Along the coast is a lowland plain 15–20 km (9–13 miles) wide, which rises inland to form uplands in east and central Lithuania. These uplands, the Middle Lowlands, give way to the Baltic Highlands in east and south-east Lithuania; the highest point is 294 m (965 ft). The country has a network of rivers and over 2,800 lakes, which mainly lie in the east of the country.

CLIMATE – Varies between maritime and continental. The mean average temperature is 8.1°C (47°F), the average in January being − 4.9°C (23°F) and in July 17°C (63°F). The average annual rainfall varies between 540 mm (21 inches) in the Middle Lowlands and 930 mm (37 inches) in the south-west.

POPULATION – The total population of Lithuania is 3,761,000 (1992). Population density is 58 persons per square km (149 persons per square mile). The rate of increase of population is 4.3 per cent. Male life expectancy is 66.3 years, and female 76.1 years (1989). The main ethnic groups are: 79.6 per cent Lithuanian, 9.4 per cent Russian, 7 per cent Polish, 1.7 per cent Belarussian, 1.2 per cent Ukrainian.

RELIGIONS – Roman Catholic (majority), Russian Orthodox, Lutheran.

LANGUAGES – 80 per cent Lithuanian, with Russian, Polish and Belarussian minorities. Lithuanian is the state language.

MAJOR CITIES – Vilnius (population 596,000), Kaunas (430,000), Klaipéda (206,000), Siauliai (148,000).

CAPITAL – Vilnius.

CURRENCY – Litas.

FLAG – Three horizontal stripes of yellow, red, green.

NATIONAL ANTHEM – Tautiška Giesmé (The National Song).

NATIONAL DAY – 16 February (Restoration of the Lithuanian State).

HISTORY

The first independent Lithuanian state emerged as the Kingdom of Lithuania in 1251, and over the next few centuries acted as a buffer state between Germans to the west and Mongols and Tartars to the east. After forming a joint Commonwealth and Kingdom with Poland in 1569, Lithuania was taken over by the Russian Empire in the partitions of Poland that occurred in 1772, 1792 and 1795.

Lithuania declared its independence from the Russian Empire on 16 February 1918 and then fought against German and Soviet forces until its independence was recognized by the Versailles Treaty in 1919 and the peace treaty signed with the Soviet Union on 12 July 1920. The Soviet Union annexed Lithuania in 1940 under the terms of the Molotov-Ribbentrop pact with Germany. Lithuania was invaded and occupied when Germany invaded the Soviet Union during the Second World War. In 1944 the Soviet Union recaptured the country and confirmed its annexation, though this was never accepted as legal by most states.

On 20 December 1989 public pressure forced the Lithuanian Communist Party to agree to multi-party elections, which were held in February 1990. These were won by the nationalist Sajudis movement, and the Supreme Council (parliament) declared the restoration of the independence of Lithuania on 11 March 1990. Clashes occurred throughout 1990 between the Lithuanian population and Soviet military forces, culminating in January 1991 with the killing of Lithuanians at the television centre in Vilnius. Over 90 per cent of the population voted for independence in a referendum in February 1991. The State Council of the Soviet Union recognized the independence of Lithuania on 10 September 1991.

GOVERNMENT

Under the constitution, approved by referendum on 25 October 1992, Lithuania is an independent and democratic state. Sovereign power is vested in the people of Lithuania and is exercised by the Seimas (parliament), the President and government, and the judiciary. The constitution bans an alignment of Lithuania with any post-Soviet eastern alliance. Executive authority is vested in the government, consisting of the Prime Minister, who is appointed by the President with the approval of the Seimas, and ministers appointed upon the recommendation of the Prime Minister. The government is accountable to the Seimas, with the constitution placing presidential powers under strict parliamentary control.

Legislative power is exercised by the Seimas, which is a one-chamber parliament of 141 members elected for four-year terms. Seventy-one members are elected in first-past-the-post constituencies and 70 by proportional representation, with a 4 per cent threshold for representation.

In the two-round parliamentary elections of October and November 1992, a majority of seats in the Seimas were won by the Lithuanian Democratic Labour Party (DLP) (the former Lithuanian Communist Party), which formed a government under Bronislovas Lubys. The DLP leader Algirdas Brazauskas was elected as Chairman of the Seimas and acting President of Lithuania until direct presidential elections, which he won in February 1993. The Sajudis leader and former Chairman of the Supreme Council, (President) Vytautas Landsbergis, became leader of the opposition in Parliament. On 10 March 1993 President Brazauskas appointed as Prime Minister Adolfas Šleževičius, who formed a new government on 16 March. In August 1993 the state of the parties in the Seimas was: DLP 73; Sajudis 30; Christian Democratic Party 18; Social Democratic Party 8; others 12.

LOCAL GOVERNMENT

Lithuania is divided into 11 cities and 44 rural districts. Each has a municipal council elected by the local population for a period of five years.

HEAD OF STATE

President, Algirdas Brazauskas, *elected* 14 February 1993 for a five-year term.

GOVERNMENT *as at August 1993*

Prime Minister, Adolfas Šleževičius
Agriculture, Rimantis Karazija
Housing and Urban Development, Algirlas Vapšys
Communication and Information, Gintautos Zintelis
Culture and Education, Dainlus Trinkunas
Economics, Julius Veselka
Energy, Algimantas Stasiukynas
Finance, Eduardas Vilkelis
Foreign Affairs, Povilas Gylys
Forestry, Gintautas Kovalčikas
Health, Jurkis Bredíkis
Industry and Trade, Kazimieras Klimašauskas
Interior, Romasis Vaitiekunas
Justice, Jonas Prapiestis
Social Security, Teodoras Medaiskis
Transportation, Jonas Birziskis
Defence, Audrius Butkevicius

EMBASSY OF THE REPUBLIC OF LITHUANIA
17 Essex Villas, London w8 7BP
Tel 071-938 2481
Ambassador Extraordinary and Plenipotentiary, His Excellency Vincas Balickas (1991).

BRITISH EMBASSY
2 Antakalnio, Gatve, PO Box 863, 2055 Vilnius

Ambassador Extraordinary and Plenipotentiary, His Excellency Michael Peart, LVO, *apptd* 1991

JUDICIAL SYSTEM

The judicial system comprises the Constitutional Court (consisting of nine judges appointed for terms of nine years), the Supreme Court, Court of Appeal, district and local courts. For the investigation of administrative, labour, family and other litigations, specialized courts may be established pursuant to law. Supreme legal supervision is exercised by the Prosecutor-General of the Republic and by local prosecutors under his supervision.

DEFENCE

Lithuania has gradually developed its defence forces since independence from the Soviet Union. Total active armed forces personnel stands at 7,000. Authorized conscription operates and the reserve National Guard numbers a further 12,500 personnel. The ground forces are organized into a border guard, a rapid reaction force and a territorial defence force. No naval or air forces exist. Russia still maintains Army and Air Force units in Lithuania which it has been gradually withdrawing since September 1991. In September 1992 Lithuanian President Landsbergis and Russian President Yeltsin agreed that all Russian forces would be withdrawn by 31 August 1993. However, throughout late 1992 and 1993 Lithuania and Russia continually argued over troop withdrawals, with the Russian government postponing the eventual withdrawal because of alleged Lithuanian discrimination against ethnic Russians in the country.

ECONOMY

The economy is basically an agricultural one that was heavily and rapidly industrialized by the Soviet Union in the 1940s and 1950s. The transition of the economy from a centralized system to a free-market one has taken place against the background of a decline in output in 1992 of 55 per cent in industry and 33 per cent in agriculture. The major obstacles met by the programme of privatization begun in 1990 concern the restitution of agricultural land ownership and large state-owned industrial enterprises that need fundamental technological renovation, major problems in rural areas with decollectivization and the return of land to pre-1940 owners has led the DLP government to slow down the pace of economic reform, temporarily suspending privatization on 11 December 1992 and returning to the price regulation of basic foodstuffs.

Agriculture and forestry are still major sectors of the economy, the chief products being rye, oats, wheat, flax, barley, sugar beet and potatoes. The main industries are chemicals and petrochemicals, food processing, wood products, building materials, textiles, machine tools and household appliances. Lithuania is capitalizing on its clean beaches and picturesque countryside to develop a tourism industry attractive to Western visitors.

TRADE

Lithuania's main trading partners remain the republics of the former Soviet Union. The Lithuanian economy is still heavily dependent on Russian supplies of oil, gas and metals. Russia cut off gas supplies in June 1993 after Lithuania failed to pay its bills.

Trade with UK	1992
Imports from UK	£54,869,000
Exports to UK	6,085,000

COMMUNICATIONS

Lithuania has a relatively well-developed railway system of some 1,240 miles (2,000 km) running east-west and north-south and linking the major towns with Vilnius and Klaipéda, the main international port. Vilnius has an international airport and there are smaller ones at Kaunas and Siauliai.

CULTURE

Lithuanian culture and literature are closely linked to the national liberation movements of the nineteenth and early twentieth centuries, and the underground literature of the Soviet occupation era. In 1991 there were 1,749 public libraries, 15 state archives, 53 museums, 13 theatres and 523 cinemas in Lithuania. The country has national television and radio stations and several privately-owned radio stations.

EDUCATION

Lithuania re-established a national education system in 1990. There are 2,147 schools of general education with 517,000 pupils (1991). Education begins at age 6–7 years, with the system comprising elementary schools (four years), nine-year schools (five years), and secondary schools (three years). The language of instruction is predominantly Lithuanian, but there are also Russian and Polish schools. There are 108 vocational schools and 65 colleges. Lithuania has six universities and eight other institutes of higher education. Vilnius University, founded in 1579, is one of the oldest universities in eastern Europe.

SOCIAL WELFARE

HEALTH SERVICES – In 1991 there were 202 hospitals with 46,000 beds, 16,800 physicians and 44,000 paramedical personnel.

SOCIAL SERVICES – A national social security system exists which comprises compulsory state social insurance, and social benefits provided by the state. The retirement age is 60 years for men and 55 years for women.

LUXEMBOURG
Grand-Duché de Luxembourg

Luxembourg is a Grand Duchy in western Europe, bounded by Germany, Belgium and France. The area is 998 sq. miles (2,586 sq. km), the population of 389,800 (1992) is nearly all Roman Catholic. The country is well wooded, with many deer and wild boar. The official language is Letzeburgesch (Luxembourgish) but most speak French and German, which are the languages of administration.

CAPITAL – Luxembourg, population (1992) 75,400, is a dismantled fortress.

CURRENCY – Luxembourg franc (LF) of 100 centimes. Belgian currency is also legal tender. The Luxembourg franc has at present the same value as the Belgian franc.

FLAG – Three horizontal bands, red, white and blue.

NATIONAL ANTHEM – Ons Hémécht (Our homeland).

NATIONAL DAY – 23 June.

HISTORY

Established as an independent state under the sovereignty of the King of the Netherlands as Grand Duke by the Congress of Vienna in 1815, Luxembourg formed part of the Germanic Confederation from 1815 to 1866, and was included in the German 'Zollverein'. In 1867 the Treaty of London declared it a neutral territory. On the death of the King of the Netherlands in 1890 it passed to the Duke of Nassau.

The territory was invaded and overrun by the Germans at the beginning of the war in 1914 but was liberated in 1918. By the Treaty of Versailles 1919, Germany renounced its former agreements with Luxembourg and in 1921 an economic union was made with Belgium. The Grand Duchy was again invaded and occupied by Germany on 10 May 1940, and liberated in 1944.

GOVERNMENT

There is a Chamber of 60 Deputies, elected by universal suffrage for five years. Legislation is submitted to the Council of State.

HEAD OF STATE
Grand Duke, HRH Jean, KG, born 5 January 1921, married, 9 April 1953, Princess Joséphine-Charlotte of Belgium, and has issue, three sons and two daughters; succeeded (on the abdication of his mother) 12 November 1964.

Heir Apparent, Prince Henri, born 16 April 1955, married 14 February 1981, Maria Teresa Mestre, and has issue, Prince Guillaume, b. 11 November 1981; Prince Felix, b. 3 June 1984; Prince Louis, b. 3 August 1986; Princess Alexandra, b. 2 February 1991; Prince Sébastien, b. 16 April 1992.

CABINET as at August 1993

Christian Socialists:
President of the Government, Minister of State, Minister of the Treasury and Cultural Affairs, Jacques Santer.
Interior, Housing and Town Planning, Jean Spautz.

The Family and Middle Classes, and Tourism, Fernand Boden.
Budget, Finance and Labour, Jean-Claude Juncker.
Education, Justice and the Civil Service, Marc Fischbach.
Agriculture and Viticulture, Josée Jacobs.

Socialists:
Vice-President of the Government, Minister of Foreign Affairs, Foreign Trade and Aid, and Defence, Jacques Poos.
Health, Social Security, Sport and Youth, Johny Lahure.
Economy and Trade, Transport and Public Works, Robert Goebbels.
Environment, Territorial Administration, Posts and Telecommunications and Energy, Alex Bodry.
State Secretary for Social Security, Health, Sport and Youth, Mady Delvaux.
State Secretary for Foreign Affairs, Overseas Trade, Aid and Defence, Georges Wohlfart.

EMBASSY OF LUXEMBOURG
27 Wilton Crescent, London SW1X 8SD
Tel 071-235 6961

Ambassador Extraordinary and Plenipotentiary, His Excellency Joseph Weyland (1993).

BRITISH EMBASSY
14 Boulevard F. D. Roosevelt, L-2450 Luxembourg Ville
Tel: Luxembourg 229864

Ambassador Extraordinary and Plenipotentiary, His Excellency The Hon. Michael Pakenham, CMG (1992).

INTERNATIONAL RELATIONS

The constitution of the Grand Duchy was modified in 1948, and the stipulation of permanent neutrality was then abandoned. Luxembourg is now a signatory of the Brussels and North Atlantic Treaties, and also a member of the European Communities. Luxembourg is a member of the Belgium-Netherlands-Luxembourg Customs Union (Benelux 1960).

The Court of the European Communities has its seat in Luxembourg, as does the Secretariat of the European Parliament, the European Investment Bank, the European Audit Court and the European Monetary Co-operation Fund.

DEFENCE

Luxembourg has a total active armed forces strength of 800 personnel organized into one light infantry battalion. For legal reasons, NATO's squadron of 18 E-3A Sentry airborne early warning aircraft are registered in Luxembourg. The paramilitary gendarmerie number 560 personnel.

ECONOMY

The Grand Duchy possesses an important iron and steel industry and is an important financial centre. Government revenue for 1990 was estimated at LF 109 million, expenditure LF 108 million.

TRADE WITH UK
(Belgium and Luxembourg)

	1991	1992
Imports from UK	£5,870,876,000	£5,714,150,000
Exports to UK	5,472,663,000	5,741,401,000

MACEDONIA (FORMER YUGOSLAV REPUBLIC OF)

Macedonia is a mountainous landlocked republic situated in the southern Balkans and bordered on the north by the

Federal Republic of Yugoslavia (Serbia), on the east by Bulgaria, on the south by Greece and on the west by Albania. It has an area of 9,925 sq. miles (25,713 sq. km).
POPULATION – According to the 1991 census the population is 2,034,000, of whom 64.6 per cent are Macedonian, 21 per cent Albanian, 4.8 per cent ethnic Turks, 2.7 per cent gypsies and 2.2 per cent ethnic Serbs, with smaller numbers of ethnic Greeks and Bulgars.
RELIGION – Macedonian Orthodox Christianity is the majority religion, with a Muslim minority.
LANGUAGE – Macedonian (a south Slavic language), with Albanian a minority language. Macedonian is written in the Cyrillic script.

CAPITAL – Skopje, population (1991 census) of 448,229. Other major towns are Bitola (84,002), Prilep (70,152) and Kumanova (69,231).
CURRENCY – Macedonian Denar.
FLAG – Red with a gold star of sixteen rays in the centre.
NATIONAL ANTHEM – Today over Macedonia.

GOVERNMENT

From the ninth to the fourteenth centuries AD Macedonia was ruled alternately by the Bulgars and the Byzantine Empire. In the middle of the fourteenth century the area was conquered by the Turks and remained under the Ottoman Empire for over 500 years. After the defeat of Turkey in the two Balkan wars of 1912–13 the geographical area of Macedonia was divided, the major part becoming Serbia (the areas of the present-day Macedonia) and the remainder given to Greece and Bulgaria. In 1918 on the formation of the Kingdom of the Serbs, Croats and Slovenes (later Yugoslavia), Serbian Macedonia was incorporated into Serbia as South Serbia. When Yugoslavia was reconstituted in 1944 as a Communist federal republic under President Tito, Macedonia became a constituent republic.

Multi-party elections were held in November and December 1990 for the 120-seat assembly which produced the first non-Communist government since the Second World War. The electorate overwhelmingly approved Macedonian sovereignty and independence in a referendum on 8 September 1991 and Macedonia declared its independence from Yugoslavia in April 1992 with the Yugoslav Army (JNA) withdrawing peacefully soon afterwards. However, Macedonia remained unrecognized internationally because of Greece's objections to the state's name, flag and currency which, according to the Greek government, amounted to a territorial claim on the Greek province of Macedonia. The inability of the government to secure Macedonia's international recognition, the consequent blocking of international aid, trade and investment, and the effect on the economy of UN trade sanctions against Serbia and Montenegro, caused the downfall of the government in July 1992. A new coalition government of the Social Democratic Alliance, Democratic Prosperity-People's Democratic Party, Reform Forces of Macedonia and Socialist parties was formed on 4 September 1992 and confirmed by a majority in the National Assembly. Tensions between Macedonia and its neighbours grew in late 1992, with Greece imposing a virtual economic blockade and Albania alleging discrimination against ethnic Albanians. Fearing conflict over Macedonia, western states and the UN intervened, sending 700 UN peacekeepers to Macedonia in December 1992 to man border posts with Serbia and Albania. Eventually Macedonia gained UN membership on 8 April 1993 following a compromise with Greece by which it is temporarily known as the 'Former Yugoslav Republic of Macedonia'. In July 1993 300 US troops arrived in Macedonia to patrol the border with Serbia and prevent the conflicts in the former Yugoslavia spreading to Macedonia.

HEAD OF STATE
President, Kiro Gligorov, *elected by the National Assembly* 27 January 1991.

GOVERNMENT *as at August 1993*
Prime Minister, Branko Crvenkovski.
Deputy Prime Minister and acting Foreign Minister, Stevo Crvenkovski.
Deputy Prime Ministers, Jovan Andonov; Becir Zuta.
Interior, Ljubomir Danailov-Frckovski.
Defence, Vlado Popovski.
Justice, Tuse Gosev.
Economy, Petrus Stefanov.
Finance, Dzevdet Hajredini.
Health, Jovan Tofovski.
Science, Aslan Selmani.
Education and Physical Culture, Dimitar Bajaldziev.
Development, Sofia Todorova.
Urbanism, Civil Engineering, Traffic and Environment, Antoni Pesev.
Agriculture and Forestry, Eftim Ancev.
Labour and Social Policy, Ilijaz Sabriu.
Culture, Guner Ismail.
Ministers without Portfolio, Jane Miljovski; Ljube Trpevski; Servet Avziu; Gordana Siljanovska.

MACEDONIAN GOVERNMENT REPRESENTATIVE IN UK – Risto Nikovski.
BRITISH GOVERNMENT REPRESENTATIVE – Tony Millson, Veljko Vlahovic 26, 9100 Skopje.

ECONOMY

Economic activity in Macedonia has been decimated by the implementation of UN trade sanctions against the rump Yugoslav Federal Republic (Serbia and Montenegro), with which Macedonia previously conducted 60 per cent of its trade. The Greek economic blockade has deprived Macedonia of most of its oil supplies and industry has survived on imports from Turkey and Bulgaria via the one remaining major transportion route, the road from Sofia to Skopje. Macedonia is attempting to transform its economy to a market-orientated one and introduce large scale privatization. Foreign investment, which is desperately needed, has been minimal because of the lack of international recognition.

In 1991 41.2 per cent of the country GDP was produced by industry and mining and 14 per cent by agriculture. Mineral resources include nickel, lead, zinc, manganese and iron ore. The main industrial sectors are basic metal industries, chemicals, textiles and food processing. Important agricultural crops are wheat, tobacco, rice, cotton and sugar beet. Foreign debt in 1991 was US$845.8m.

MADAGASCAR
Repoblika n'i Madagaskar

Madagascar lies 240 miles off the east coast of Africa and is the fourth largest island in the world. France has recognized Madagascar's claim to the islands of Juan de Nova, Glorieuses, Isle de l'Europe, Bassa da India and Tromelin which had remained integral parts of the French Republic after independence. It has an area of 226,669 sq. miles (587,041 sq. km), and a population (UN estimate 1991) of 11,493,000. The people are of mixed Malayo-Polynesian, Arab and African origin. There are sizeable French, Chinese and Indian communities. The official languages are Malagasy and French.

CAPITAL – Antananarivo, population estimate 1,250,000. Other main towns are the chief port ΨToamasina (230,000); ΨMahajanga (200,000); Fianarantsoa (300,000); ΨAntsiranana (220,000).
CURRENCY – Franc Malgache (Malagasy franc) (FMG) of 100 centimes.
FLAG – Equal horizontal bands of red (above) and green, with vertical white band by staff.
NATIONAL DAY – 26 June (Independence Day).

GOVERNMENT

Madagascar (known from 1958 to 1975 as the Malagasy Republic) became a French protectorate in 1895, and a French colony in 1896 when the former queen was exiled. Republican status was adopted on 14 October 1958, and independence was proclaimed on 26 June 1960.

The post-independence civilian government was replaced by a military government in January 1975 and the following month martial law was declared. A Supreme Council of the Revolution of 18 members under Capitaine de Frégate (subsequently Admiral) Didier Ratsiraka was established on 15 June 1975. In December 1975 a new constitution was approved in a referendum, which vested executive power in the President. He appointed a Council of Ministers to assist him. The Revolutionary Supreme Council and the National People's Assembly were dissolved in November 1991.

The situation in Madagascar was confused for most of 1991 and 1992. After six months of strikes and agitation against his one-party socialist rule, which had made the country ungovernable, President Ratsiraka in November 1991 relinquished executive power to a new Prime Minister, Guy Razanamasy. However, the President retained his official position and the main opposition grouping, the *Forces Vives*, established a rival government led by Albert Zafy. In December 1991 a transitional government including Forces Vives and Razanamasy supporters was formed to draft a new constitution to be put to a referendum in May 1992. However, the inability of the government to assert any control over the country because of quarrels between Forces Vives and Razanamasy supporters, together with attempts by the President to regain executive power, meant that the referendum was not held until 19 August 1992, when the new constitution was approved. Presidential elections were held in two rounds on 25 November 1992 and 10 February 1993, Albert Zafy emerging victorious with 67 per cent of the vote. He became the first President of the Third Republic, which also come into being at the same time. A legislative election held on 16 June was won by Zafy's Forces Vives and allied parties, with Forces Vives member Francisque Ravony being elected Prime Minster by parliament in August 1993. At the time of going to press he was in the process of forming his cabinet. The new constitution declares Madagascar to be a unitary state and reduces the executive powers of the President.

HEAD OF STATE
President, Professor Albert Zafy, *elected* 10 February 1993.

Prime Minister, Francisque Ravony, *elected by parliament* August 1993.

EMBASSY OF THE REPUBLIC OF MADAGASCAR
4 avenue Raphael, 75016 Paris, France
Tel: Paris 45046211

Ambassador Plenipotentiary and Extraordinary, His Excellency François de Paul Rabotoson (1987) (resident in Paris).

HONORARY CONSULATE OF THE REPUBLIC OF MADAGASCAR
16 Lanark Mansions, Pennard Road, London W12 8DT
Tel 081-746 0133
Honorary Consul, Stephen Hobbs.

BRITISH EMBASSY
BP 167, Antananarivo
Tel: Antananarivo 277 49

Ambassador Extraordinary and Plenipotentiary, His Excellency Peter John Smith (1992).

ECONOMY

The island's economy is still largely based on agriculture, which accounts for three-quarters of its exports. Development plans have placed emphasis on increasing agricultural and livestock production, the improvement of communications, the exploitation of mineral deposits and the creation of small industries.

TRADE	1985	1986
Imports	US$ 400.54m	US$ 441.54m
Exports	274.23m	351.18m
Trade with UK	1991	1992
Imports from UK	£6,946,000	£8,690,000
Exports to UK	7,707,000	6,000,000

MALAWI
Dziko La Malawi

Malawi comprises Lake Malawi (formerly Lake Nyasa) and its western shore, with the high tableland separating it from the basin of the River Luangwa, the watershed forming the western frontier with Zambia. South of the lake, Malawi reaches almost to the Zambezi and is surrounded by Mozambique, the frontier lying in the west on the watershed of the Zambezi and Shire rivers, and to the east on the Ruo, a tributary of the Shire, and lakes Chiuta and Chirwa. This boundary reaches the eastern shore of Lake Malawi and extends up to the mid-point of the lake for about half its length where it returns to the eastern and northern shores to form a frontier with Tanzania. Malawi has a total area of 45,747 sq. miles (118,484 sq. km).
POPULATION – The population (Census 1987) was 7,982,607. According to a UN estimate (1991), the population was 8,556,000. The official languages are Chichewa and English.

CAPITAL – Lilongwe, population (1987) 223,973. The city of Blantyre in the Southern Region, incorporating Blantyre and Limbe (population (1987) 331,588), is the major commercial and industrial centre. Other main centres are: Mzuzu, Thyolo, Mulanje, Mangochi, Salima, Dedza and Zomba, the former capital.
CURRENCY – Kwacha (K) of 100 tambala.
FLAG – Horizontal stripes of black, red and green, with rising sun in the centre of the black stripe.
NATIONAL ANTHEM – O God Bless Our Land of Malawi.
NATIONAL DAY – 6 July (Independence Day).

GOVERNMENT

Malawi (formerly Nyasaland) became a republic on 6 July 1966, having assumed internal self-government on 1 February 1963, and achieved independence on 6 July 1964.

There is a Cabinet consisting of the Life President and other ministers. The Parliament consists of 112 members, each elected by universal suffrage. The Parliament, which usually meets three times a year, is presided over by a Speaker. Under a 1981 amendment to the Constitution, the Life President had the power to nominate as many Members of Parliament as he wished. Being a one-party state (the Malawi Congress Party), all elected members were required to be members of the Party.

During late 1991 and the first half of 1992 the President came under pressure to move towards a multi-party democratic system of government. In May 1992 aid donors tied new loans to improvements in the country's human rights record and moves to multi-party democracy. Strikes and riots in May and June 1992, which left many dead, signalled growing internal unrest. Under increasing international and internal pressure, President Banda announced in October 1992 that a referendum would be held on the adoption of a multiparty democracy in March 1993.

When the referendum was finally held on 16 June, 63 per cent of voters approved the adoption of a multiparty system. President Banda and the Malawi Congress Party refused to resign but parliament passed a law to amend the constitution to allow multiparty politics and Banda announced a political amnesty to allow exiles to return. Banda announced that multiparty elections would be held by June 1994 and entered into negotiations with the two main opposition movements, the Alliance for Democracy (AFORD) and the United Democratic Front (UDF) on establishing a National Executive Council to oversee changes and govern the country until elections. These negotiations collapsed in July, leaving the situation unclear at the time of going to press.

HEAD OF STATE
President, Dr H. Kamuzu Banda, *elected* 1966, *sworn in as President for Life*, 6 July 1971.

CABINET *as at June 1993*
External Affairs, Agriculture, Justice, Works, Supplies, Women and Children's Affairs and Community Services, The President.
Minister without Portfolio, Wadson Bini Deleza.
Transport and Communications, Robson Chirwa.
Local Government, Katola Phiri.
Finance, Louis Chimango.
Trade and Industry, Dalton Katopola.
Information and Tourism, Mfunjo Mwakikunga.
Education and Culture, Michael Mlambala.
Health, Pitakuti Ntaba.
Minister of State in the President's Office, John Tembo.
Labour, William Binali.
Forestry and Natural Resources, Edson Sambo.
Energy and Mines, Bernard Mshabala.
Chief Justice, Hon. F. L. Makuta.

MALAWI HIGH COMMISSION
33 Grosvenor Street, London WIX ODE
Tel 071-491 4172/7

High Commissioner, His Excellency P. T. S. Kandiero (1990).

BRITISH HIGH COMMISSION
PO Box 30042, Lilongwe 3
Tel: Lilongwe 782400

High Commissioner, His Excellency John Francis Martin (1993).

BRITISH COUNCIL REPRESENTATIVE, S. Newton, PO Box 30222, Lilongwe 3. There is also a library at Blantyre.

EDUCATION

Primary education is the responsibility of local authorities in both urban and rural areas, although policy, curricula and inspection are the responsibility of the Ministry of Education and Culture. The Ministry is also responsible for secondary schools, technical education and primary teacher training. Religious bodies, with government assistance, still play an important part in these fields. The University of Malawi was opened in 1965 and has five constituent colleges. The total number of students in 1988–9 was 1.2 million in primary schools, 28,000 in secondary schools and 2,330 at university.

COMMUNICATIONS

A single-track railway runs from Mchinji on the Zambian border, through Lilongwe and Salima on Lake Malawi (itself served by two passenger and a number of cargo boats) through to Blantyre. The route south to the Mozambique port of Beira has been severed by the Mozambican civil war, but the route to Nacala in Mozambique is open again. There are 12,215 km of roads in Malawi of which about 21.8 per cent are bituminized. There is an international airport 26 km from Lilongwe, which handles regional and inter-continental flights.

ECONOMY

The economy is largely agricultural, with maize the main subsistence crop. Tobacco, sugar, tea, groundnuts and cotton are the main cash crops and principal exports. There are two sugar mills and total production in 1989 was 157m kg. A number of light manufacturing industries have been established, mainly in agricultural processing, clothing/textiles and building materials.

FINANCE
excluding Development Account

	1987–8	1988–9
Revenue	K583m	K752m
Expenditure	823m	1071m

TRADE	1987	1988
Imports	K654m	K1080m
Exports	602m	742m

Trade with UK	1991	1992
Imports from UK	£31,462,000	£23,880,000
Exports to UK	25,381,000	22,107,000

MALAYSIA
Persekutuan Tanah Malaysia

Malaysia, comprising the 11 states of peninsular Malaya plus Sabah and Sarawak, forms a crescent well over 1,000 miles long between 1° and 7° N. latitude and 100° and 119° E. longitude. It occupies two distinct regions, the Malay peninsula which extends from the isthmus of Kra to the Singapore Strait, and the north-west coastal area of the island of Borneo. Each is separated from the other by the South China Sea. The total area of Malaysia, including the federal territories of Kuala Lumpur and Labuan, is about 127,317 sq. miles (329,749 sq. km).

The year is commonly divided into the south-west and north-west monsoon seasons. Rainfall averages about 100 inches throughout the year. The average daily temperature throughout Malaysia varies from 21° C to 32° C, though in higher areas temperatures are lower and vary widely.

POPULATION – Population was 16,921,300 (1988 Census), 18,333,000 UN estimate (1991). The principal racial groups are the Malays, the Chinese and those of Indian and Sri Lankan origin, as well as the indigenous races of Sarawak and Sabah.

LANGUAGES – Bahasa Malaysia (Malay) is the sole official language, but English, various dialects of Chinese, and Tamil are also widely spoken. There are a few indigenous languages widely spoken in Sabah and Sarawak.

RELIGION – Islam is the official religion of Malaysia, each ruler being the head of religion in his state, though the heads of state of Sabah and Sarawak are not heads of the Muslim religion in their states. The Yang di-Pertuan Agung is the head of religion in Melaka and Penang. The constitution guarantees religious freedom.

CAPITAL – Kuala Lumpur was proclaimed federal territory on 1 February 1974. Its population (1985) is 1,103,200.

CURRENCY – Malaysian dollar (ringgit) (M$) of 100 sen.

FLAG – Equal horizontal stripes of red (seven) and white (seven); 14-point yellow star and crescent in blue canton.

NATIONAL ANTHEM – Negara-Ku.

NATIONAL DAY – 31 August (*Hari Kebangsaan*).

GOVERNMENT

The Federation of Malaya became an independent country within the Commonwealth on 31 August 1957, as a result of an agreement between The Queen and the rulers of the Malay States. On 16 September 1963 the Federation was enlarged by the accession of the states of Singapore, Sabah (formerly British North Borneo) and Sarawak, and the name of Malaysia was adopted from that date. On 9 August 1965 Singapore seceded from the Federation.

The constitution was designed to ensure the existence of a strong federal government and also a measure of autonomy for the state governments. It provides for a constitutional Supreme Head of the Federation (HM the *Yang di-Pertuan Agung*) to be elected for a term of five years by the rulers from among their number, and for a Deputy Supreme Head (HRH *Timbalan Yang di-Pertuan Agung*) to be similarly elected. The Malay rulers are either chosen or succeed to their position in accordance with the custom of the particular state. In other states of Malaysia, choice of the head of state is at the discretion of the Yang di-Pertuan Agung after consultation with the Chief Minister of the state.

The Federal Parliament consists of two houses, the Senate and the House of Representatives. The Senate (*Dewan Negara*) consists of 68 members, under a President (*Yang di-Pertua Dewan Negara*), 26 elected by the Legislative Assemblies of the States (two from each) and 42 appointed by the Yang di-Pertuan Agung. The House of Representatives (*Dewan Rakyat*) consists of 180 members elected by universal adult suffrage with a common electoral roll.

The constitution provides that each state shall have its own constitution not inconsistent with the federal constitution, with the ruler or Governor acting on the advice of an Executive Council appointed on the advice of the Chief Minister and a single chamber Legislative Assembly. State Secretary, the State Legal Adviser and the State Financial Officer sit in the Executive Council as ex-officio members. The Legislative Assemblies are fully elected on the same basis as the Federal Parliament.

Dr Mahathir Muhammad won a third term in office in a general election held on 21 October 1990.

HEAD OF STATE

Supreme Head of State, HM Sultan Azlan Muhibuddin Shah Ibni-Almarhum Sultan Yusuff Izzuddin Ghafarullahu-Lahu Shah (Sultan of Perak), *sworn in* 26 April 1989.

Deputy Supreme Head of State, HRH Tuanku Jaafar Ibni Al-Marhum Tuanku Abdul Rahman (Yang Dipertuan Besar of Negeri Sembilan).

MINISTRY *as at August 1993*

Prime Minister, Minister of Home Affairs, Hon. Datuk Seri Dr Mahathir Muhammad.

Deputy Prime Minister, Minister for Rural Development, Hon Abdul Ghafar Baba.

Transport, Hon. Datuk Seri Dr Ling Liong Sik.

Energy, Telecommunications and Posts, Hon. Datuk Seri S. Samy Vellu.

Primary Industries, Hon. Datuk Seri Dr Lim Keng Yaik.

Works, Hon. Datuk Leo Moggie Anak Irok.

International Trade and Industry, Hon. Datuk Seri Rafidah Aziz.

Education, Hon. Datuk Dr Haji Sulaiman bin Haji Daud.

Agriculture, Hon. Datuk Seri Sanusi bin Junid.

Finance, Hon. Datuk Seri Anwar bin Ibrahim.

Domestic Trade and Consumer Affairs, Hon. Datuk Haji Abu Hassan bin Haji Omar.

Health, Hon. Datuk Lee Kim Sai.

Foreign Affairs, Hon. Datuk Abdullah bin Haji Ahmad Badawi.

Defence, Hon. Datuk Sri Haji Mohd Najib bin Tun Haji Abdul Razak.

Information, Hon. Datuk Mohamed bin Rahmat.

Culture, Arts and Tourism, Hon. Datuk Sabbaruddin bin Chik.

National Unity and Community Development, Hon. Datuk Napsiah binti Omar.

Public Enterprises, Hon. Datuk Dr Mohammad Yusof bin Haji Mohamed Nor.

Human Resources, Hon. Datuk Lim Ah Lek.

Science, Technology and Environment, Hon. Law Hieng Ding.

Housing and Local Government, Hon. Dr Ting Chew Peh.

Land and Co-operative Development, Hon. Tan Sri Datuk Haji Sakaran bin Dandai.

Justice, Hon. Syed Hamid bin Syed Jaafar Albar.

Youth and Sports, Sen. the Hon. Haji Annuar bin Musa.

Sabah Affairs, Tun Datuk Mustapha Harun.

NOTE: Tunku/Tengku, Tun, Tan Sri, and Datuk are titles. Tunku/Tengku is equivalent to Prince. Tun denotes membership of a high Order of Malaysian Chivalry and Tan Sri and Datuk (Datuk Seri in Perak and Datu in Sabah) are each the equivalent of a knighthood. The wife of a Tun is styled Toh Puan, that of a Tan Sri is styled Puan Sri and of a Datuk, Datin. The honorific Tuan or Encik is equivalent to Mr and the honorific Puan is equivalent to Mrs.

MALAYSIAN HIGH COMMISSION
45 Belgrave Square, London SW1X 8QT
Tel 071-235 8033

High Commissioner, His Excellency Dato Kamarudin Abu (1992).

Deputy High Commissioner, Haji Salim Hashim.

Attaché, Col. Muhammad Yunus (*Defence*); Nasir Ahmad (*Immigration*).

Commissioner, Bahar Ahmad (*Trade*).

BRITISH HIGH COMMISSION
185 Jalan Ampang (PO Box 11030), 50450 Kuala Lumpur
Tel: Kuala Lumpur 03-2482122

High Commissioner, His Excellency Duncan Slater, CMG (1992).

Deputy High Commissioner and Counsellor (Commercial/Economic), B. E. Cleghorn.

Defence Adviser, Col. J. L. Seddon-Brown.

BRITISH COUNCIL REPRESENTATIVE, Dr G. Howell, CBE, PO Box 10539, Jalan Bukit Aman, Kuala Lumpur 50916. There are also offices at *Johore Bahru, Kota Kinabalu* (Sabah) and *Kuching* (Sarawak), and a library in *Penang*.

STATES

The 13 states of the Federation of Malaysia (state capitals in brackets) and their populations at the 1988 Census are:

ΨJohore (Johore Bahru)	2,007,300
Kedah (Alor Setar)	1,353,500
Kelantan (Kota Bahru)	1,150,400
ΨMelaka (Melaka)	560,700
Negri Sembilan (Seremban)	694,100
ΨPahang (Kuantan)	1,001,200
ΨPenang (Georgetown)	1,103,200
Perak (Ipoh)	2,143,200
Perlis (Kangar)	179,700
ΨSabah (Kota Kinabalu)	1,371,000
ΨSarawak (Kuching)	1,591,000
ΨSelangor (Shah Alam)	1,878,300
ΨTerengganu (Kuala Terengganu)	705,200

The two federal territories and their population at the 1988 Census are:

Kuala Lumpur	
Labuan	}1,182,700

JUDICATURE

The judicial system consists of a Supreme Court and two High Courts, one in peninsular Malaysia and one for Sabah and Sarawak (sitting alternately in Kota Kinabalu and Kuching). The Supreme Court comprises a President, the two Chief Justices of the High Courts and other judges. It possesses appellate, original and advisory jurisdiction.

Each of the High Courts consists of a Chief Justice and not less than four other judges. The federal constitution allows for a maximum of twelve such judges for Malaya and eight for Borneo. In peninsular Malaysia the subordinate courts consist of the sessions courts and the magistrates' courts. In Sabah/Sarawak the magistrates' courts constitute the subordinate courts.

DEFENCE

The Malaysian armed forces consist of the Army, Navy and Air Force, together with volunteer forces for each arm. Total Active armed forces personnel number 127,500, with volunteer service in operation. The Army has a strength of 105,000 personnel, with 26 light tanks, 392 reconnaissance vehicles, 670 armoured personnel carriers and 200 artillery pieces. The regular Army is organized into ten infantry brigades. Reserve Army personnel of 41,000 are organized into 12 infantry regiments. The Royal Malayasian Navy has a strength of 10,500, with four frigates, 37 patrol and coastal craft and six armed helicopters. The Royal Malaysian Air Force has a strength of 67 combat aircraft and 12,000 personnel organized into two ground attack, one air defence, one reconnaissance, one maritime reconnaissance and eight transport squadrons.

The paramilitary police field force has a strength of 18,000 personnel in 21 battalions, together with marine police and air wing units. Border scouts in North Borneo number 1,200.

Australia maintains an Army infantry company and an Air Force detachment in the country.

ECONOMY

FINANCE

	1991	1992*
Revenue	M$34,053m	M$38,106m
Expenditure	39,693m	42,414m
*estimated		

Manufacturing has overtaken agriculture as the largest single contributor to the economy, though rice, the staple food, is produced throughout the country and efforts are being made to achieve self-sufficiency. In 1991 43 per cent of gross domestic product was produced by services, 28 per cent by manufacturing and 17 per cent by agriculture.

TRADE

Malaysia is the largest exporter of natural rubber, tin, palm oil and tropical hardwoods. Other major export commodities are manufactured and processed products, petroleum, oil, and other minerals, palm kernel oil, tea and pepper. Exports of major commodities were (1989): manufactured goods 54.1 per cent, agricultural products 28.3 per cent, minerals 16.9 per cent. Imports consist mainly of machinery and transport equipment, manufactured goods, foods, mineral fuels, chemicals and inedible crude materials.

	1991	1992*
Imports (c.i.f.)	M$100,831m	M$105,805m
Exports (f.o.b.)	94,947m	104,608m
*estimated		

Trade with UK	1991	1992
Imports from UK	£582,239,000	£635,857,000
Exports to UK	930,036,000	1,103,782,000

THE MALDIVES
Divehi Jumhuriya

The Maldives are a chain of coral atolls some 400 miles to the south-west of Sri Lanka, stretching north for about 600 miles from just south of the Equator. There are about 20 coral atolls comprising over 1,200 islands, 202 of which are inhabited. Total area of the islands is 115 sq. miles (298 sq. km). No point in the entire chain of islands is more than 8 feet above sea-level.

POPULATION – The population of the islands (UN estimate 1991) is 223,000. The people are Sunni Muslims and the Maldivian (Dhivehi) language is akin to Elu or old Sinhalese.

CAPITAL – ΨMalé, population (1985) 46,334. There is an international airport at Malé.

CURRENCY – Rufiyaa of 100 laaris.

FLAG – Green field bearing a white crescent, with wide red border.

NATIONAL ANTHEM – Qawmee Salaam.

NATIONAL DAY – 26 July.

GOVERNMENT

Until 1952 the islands were a sultanate under the protection of the British Crown. Internal self-government was achieved in 1948 and full independence in 1965. In 1982 the Republic of The Maldives became a special member of the Commonwealth, and a full member in 1985.

The Maldives form a republic which is elective. There is a legislature, the *Citizens' Majlis*, with representatives elected from all the atolls. The life of the Majlis is five years. The Government consists of a Cabinet, which is responsible to the Majlis.

MAL-MAL 951

HEAD OF STATE
President, His Excellency Maumoon Abdul Gayoom, *elected* 1978, 1983, *re-elected* September 1989.

CABINET *as at August 1993*
Defence and National Security, The President.
Foreign Affairs, Hon. Fathulla Jameel.
Justice, Hon. Mohamed Rasheed Ibrahim.
Home Affairs and Sports, Hon. Umar Zahir.
Finance, Hon. Ismail Fathy.
Education, Hon. Abdulla Hameed.
Health and Welfare, Hon. Abdul Sattar Moosa Didi.
Fisheries and Agriculture, Hon. Abbas Ibrahim.
Atolls Administration, Hon. Ilyas Ibrahim.
Trade and Industries, Hon. Ahmed Mujuthaba.
Tourism, Hon. Abdulla Jameel.
Public Works and Labour, Hon. Abdulla Kamaludeen.
Planning and Environment, Hon. Ismail Shafeen.
Transport and Shipping, Ahmed Zahir.
Minister at the President's Office and Acting Attorney-General, Hon. Mohamed Zahir Hussain.

BRITISH HIGH COMMISSION
High Commissioner (resides at Colombo, Sri Lanka).

ECONOMY

The vegetation of the islands is coconut palms with some scrub. Hardly any cultivation of crops is possible and nearly all food to supplement the basic fish diet has to be imported. The principal industry is fishing and considerable quantities of fish are exported to Japan. Dried fish is exported to Sri Lanka, where it is a delicacy. The tourist industry is expanding rapidly (214,000 visitors in 1992). Maldives Shipping Ltd has a fleet of some 30 merchant ships.

TRADE WITH UK	1991	1992
Imports from UK	£2,862,000	£4,261,000
Exports to UK	7,909,000	8,174,000

MALI
République du Mali

Mali, an inland state in north-west Africa, has an area of 478,791 sq. miles (1,240,000 sq. km), and a population (UN estimate 1991) of 9,507,000. The principal rivers are the Niger and the Senegal.

CAPITAL – Bamako (1987 Census, 658,275). Other towns are Gao, Kayes, Mopti, Sikasso, Segou and Timbuktu (all regional capitals).
CURRENCY – Franc CFA of 100 centimes.
FLAG – Vertical stripes of green (by staff), yellow and red.
NATIONAL DAY – 22 September.

GOVERNMENT

Formerly the French colony of Soudan, the territory elected on 24 November 1958 to remain an autonomous republic within the French Community. It associated with Senegal in the Federation of Mali which was granted full independence on 20 June 1960. The Federation was effectively dissolved on 22 August 1960 by the secession of Senegal. The title of the Republic of Mali was adopted in September 1960.

The regime of Modibo Keita was overthrown on 19 November 1968 by a group of Army officers who formed a National Liberation Committee and appointed a Prime Minister. Moussa Traoré assumed the functions of head of state. A new civil constitution came into being in 1979.

After several months of pro-reform protests and strikes, often leading to riots, President Traoré was overthrown in March 1991 by troops led by Lt.-Col. Toure. A joint civilian/military National Reconciliation Committee, later replaced by the Transitional Committee for the Salvation of the People, suspended the constitution and dissolved the Mali People's Democratic Union (UPDM), formerly the sole party. A transitional government was formed in April. In August, a new constitution was approved by a national conference and approved by a national referendum in January 1992. The new constitution provided for a multi-party political system, and legislative elections were held in February and March 1992 with the Alliance for Democracy in Mali (ADEMA) emerging victorious. Alpha Konare, the ADEMA leader, won the presidential elections in April 1992 and appointed a Prime Minister and Cabinet in June dominated by ADEMA members. The Prime Minister and government resigned in April 1993 after political unrest in Bamako led by students. On 12 April the President appointed a new cabinet, again dominated by ADEMA.

HEAD OF STATE
President, Alpha Oumar Konare, *elected* 28 April 1992, *sworn in* 8 June 1992.

CABINET *as at August 1993*
Prime Minister, Abdoulaye Sow.
Minister of State, Territorial Administration and Decentralization, Momadou Traore.
Minister of State, Mines, Energy and Industry, Yoro Diakite.
Defence, Dioncounda Traore.
Civil Service, Labour and Administration Modernization, Ousmane Sidibe.
Foreign Affairs, Malians Abroad and African Integration, Alhousseini Toure.
Economics, Finance and Planning, Mahamar Maiga.
Youth and Sports, Boubacar Coulibaly.
Tourism and Crafts, Ambadjo Kassogue.
Health, Solidarity and Pensioners, Modibo Sidibe.
Environment, Mohamed Agerlaf.
Transport, Samba Sidibe.
Employment, Vocational Training and Private Initiatives Promotion, Fatou Haidara.
Primary Education, Diallo Camara.
Rural Development, Dr Boubarcar Sy.
Construction, Urbanization and Housing, Abdoulaye Diop.
Justice, Hamidou Diabate.
Secondary, Technical and Professional Education, Mamadou Toure.
Higher Education and Scientific Research, Abdoulaye Danioko.
Internal Security, Lt.-Col. Sada Samake.
Culture and Communications, Cheickna Kamissoko.
Human Rights and Institutional Relations, Mamadou Diarra.

EMBASSY OF THE REPUBLIC OF MALI
Avenue Molière 487, 1060 Brussels, Belgium
Tel: Brussels 3457432

Ambassador Extraordinary and Plenipotentiary, His Excellency N'Tiji Traoré (1992) (resident in Brussels).

BRITISH AMBASSADOR, resident in Dakar, Senegal. There is a Consulate in Bamako.

ECONOMY

Mali's principal exports are gold, groundnuts (raw and processed), cotton fibres, meat and dried fish. Mali rejoined the CFA Franc Zone in 1984.

TRADE WITH UK	1991	1992
Imports from UK	£9,589,000	£11,101,000
Exports to UK	1,631,000	2,061,000

MALTA
Repubblika Ta'Malta

Malta lies in the Mediterranean Sea, 58 miles (93 km) from Sicily and about 180 miles (288 km) from the African coast, about 17 miles (27 km) in length and 9 miles (14.5 km) in breadth, and having an area of 94.9 square miles (246 square km). Malta includes also the adjoining islands of Gozo (area 25.9 sq. miles (67 squ. km)), Comino and minor islets.
POPULATION – The estimated population in 1992 was 362,950. The Maltese are mainly Roman Catholic.
LANGUAGES – The Maltese language is of Semitic origin and held by some to be derived from the Carthaginian and Phoenician tongues. Maltese and English are the official languages of administration and Maltese is the official language in all the courts of law and the language of general use in the islands.

CAPITAL – ΨValletta. Population (Census 1990), 9,199. Valletta Grand Harbour is very deep and large vessels can anchor alongside the shore. It is an important port of call and ship-repairing centre.
CURRENCY – Maltese lira (LM) of 100 cents and 1,000 mils.
FLAG – Two equal vertical stripes, white at the hoist and red at the fly. A representation of the George Cross is carried edged with red in the canton of the white stripe.
NATIONAL ANTHEM – L-Innu Malti.
NATIONAL DAYS – 21 September (Independence Day); 13 December (Republic Day); 31 March (Freedom Day); 8 September (Lady of Victories).

HISTORY

Malta was in turn held by the Phoenicians, Carthaginians, Romans and Arabs. In 1090 it was conquered by Count Roger of Normandy. In 1530 it was handed over to the Knights of St John, who made it a stronghold of Christianity. In 1565 it sustained the famous siege, when the last great effort of the Turks was successfully withstood by Grandmaster La Valette. The Knights were expelled by Napoleon in 1798. The Maltese rose against the French garrison soon afterwards and the island was subsequently blockaded by the British fleet. The Maltese people freely requested the protection of the British Crown in 1802 on condition that their rights and privileges would be preserved and respected. The islands were finally annexed to the British Crown by the Treaty of Paris in 1814.
Malta was again closely besieged in the Second World War. From June 1940 to the end of the war, 432 members of the garrison and 1,540 civilians were killed by enemy aircraft, and about 35,000 houses were destroyed or damaged. The island was awarded the George Cross for gallantry on 15 April 1942.

GOVERNMENT

On 21 September 1964 Malta became an independent state within the Commonwealth; on 13 December 1974, Malta became a republic within the Commonwealth.
Elections are held for the unicameral Parliament of 65 members every five years by a system of proportional representation. Seats are obtained by the highest number of votes in the respective districts. The party with the highest number of votes forms the government, with extra members being co-opted if necessary.
Malta applied for European Community membership in 1990 but on 30 June 1993 the EC Commission issued a negative opinion on its application, principally because of its small size.

HEAD OF STATE
President, Dr Vincent Tabone, *took office* 4 April 1989.

CABINET *as at August 1993*
Prime Minister, Hon. Dr Edward Fenech Adami.
Deputy PM and Minister of Foreign Affairs, Hon. Dr Guido De Marco.
Education and Human Resources, Hon. Dr Ugo Mifsud Bonnici.
Home Affairs and Social Development, Hon. Dr Louis Galea.
Economic Services, Hon. Dr G. Bonello Du Puis.
Environment, Hon. Michael Falzon.
Food, Agriculture and Fisheries, Hon. Lawrence Gatt.
Social Security, Hon. George Hyzler.
Justice, Hon. Joseph Fenech.
Youth and the Arts, Hon. Michael Frendo.
Transport and Communications, Hon. Dr Francis Zammit Dimech.
Gozo, Hon. Anton Tabone.
Finance, Hon. John Dalli.

MALTA HIGH COMMISSION
16 Kensington Square, London W8 5HH
Tel 071-938 1712
High Commissioner, His Excellency Saviour Stellini (1991).

BRITISH HIGH COMMISSION
7 St Anne Street, Floriana (PO Box 506)
Tel: Floriana 233134/7
High Commissioner, His Excellency Sir Peter Wallis, KCVO, CMG (1991).

BRITISH COUNCIL REPRESENTATIVE, G. Graves, 89 Archbishop Street, Valletta.

EDUCATION

In 1992 there were 135 government kindergarten centres with 10,391 pupils, 123 government primary schools with 35,403 pupils and 68 secondary and post-secondary schools and new lyceums, with a total of 28,894 pupils.
The government also runs 29 technical/trade schools (with an enrolment of 6,884 students). Schools of art, music, secretarial studies, catering, nursing and dramatic art are sponsored by the government. Tertiary education is available at the University of Malta, which had 4,471 students in 1992.
A number of private schools offer more or less the same facilities that exist in Government schools. All state education is free.

ECONOMY

Agriculture plays a significant role in the economy. There are 3,231 full-time farmers and 13,807 part-time farmers. Crop production consists mainly of tomatoes, potatoes, onions, cabbages and cauliflowers, marrows, carrots and fruit. Grape is the largest fruit crop. Flowers and cuttings are produced for export markets.
The island's leading industry is the state-owned Malta Drydocks, employing about 3,550 people. The main port of Grand Harbour handled traffic of 13,140,007 tonnes in 1990.
At the end of 1992 manufacturing firms employed some 31,558 people. Industries include food processing, textiles

and clothing, plastics and chemical products, electronic equipment and components. The gross output of the manufacturing industry in 1992 was LM673.1 million, of which LM451.2 million were export sales.

Tourism has assumed primary importance, with over 1,002,381 tourists visiting the island in 1992, and Marsamxett Harbour is being further developed by the extension of a yacht centre. Gross income from this industry stood at LM168.4 million in 1992.

FINANCE	1991	1992
Revenue	LM411,793,000	LM395,036,000
Expenditure	417,403,000	388,032,000

TRADE

The principal imports for home consumption are foodstuffs (mainly wheat, meat and bullocks, milk and fruit), fodder, beverages and tobacco, fuels, chemicals, textiles and machinery (industrial, agricultural and transport). The chief domestic exports are processed food, electronics, textiles, and other manufactures.

	1991	1992
Imports	LM683,200,000	LM684,500,000
Exports	404,100,000	450,200,000

Trade with UK	1991	1992
Imports from UK	£162,454,000	£164,489,000
Exports to UK	40,771,000	51,332,000

MARSHALL ISLANDS
Republic of the Marshall Islands

The Republic of the Marshall Islands consists of 29 atolls and five islands in the central Pacific Ocean. The state lies between 4° and 19° N., and 160° and 175° E. The islands and atolls are scattered over 1,294,500 square km (500,000 square miles), forming two parallel chains running northwest to south-east: the Ratak (Sunrise) chain and the Ralik (Sunset) chain. The total land area is 181 square km (70 square miles). The largest atoll is Kwajalein in the Ralik chain.

The atolls are coral and the islands are volcanic. Each atoll is formed by a cluster of many small islands circling a lagoon. None of the islands rises more than a few metres above sea level.

CLIMATE – Hot and humid. The average annual temperature is 27°C (81°F), with little seasonal variation. Annual average rainfall varies from 1,780 mm (70 inches) in the north to 4,320 mm (170 inches) in the south. The typhoon season lasts from December to March.

POPULATION – The population of the Marshall Islands is 45,569 (1990). There is an annual rate of increase of 4.29 per cent and over half the population is under 15. About 60 per cent of the population is concentrated on the two atolls of Majuro and Kwajalein. The population is 99 per cent Micronesian.

LANGUAGES – Marshallese and English are the official languages.

RELIGION – Christian, primarily Protestant but with a substantial Catholic minority. The principal Protestant denomination is the United Church of Christ.

CAPITAL – Majuro (population 20,000). The other major town is Ebeye (9,200).

CURRENCY – US Dollar.

FLAG – Blue with a diagonal ray divided white over orange running from the lower hoist to the upper fly; in the canton a white sun.

NATIONAL DAY – 21 October (Compact Day).

HISTORY

The Marshall Islands were claimed by Spain in 1592 but were left undisturbed by the Spanish Empire for 300 years. In 1886 the Marshall Islands formally became a protectorate of the German Empire under colonial German administration. On the outbreak of the First World War in 1914, Japan took control of the islands on behalf of the Allied powers, and after the war administered the territory as a League of Nations mandate. During the Second World War United States armed forces took control of the islands from the Japanese after intense fighting. In 1947 the United States entered into agreement with the UN Security Council to administer the Micronesia area, of which the Marshall Islands are a part, as the UN Trust Territory of the Pacific Islands.

The US Trusteeship administration came to an end on 21 October 1986, when a Compact of Free Association between the United States and the Republic of the Marshall Islands came into effect. By this agreement the USA recognized the Republic of the Marshall Islands as a fully sovereign and independent state. However, the Soviet Union used its veto to prevent the UN Security Council from terminating the UN Trust Territory of the Pacific until December 1990, when the independence of the Republic of the Marshall Islands was finally recognized by the UN.

GOVERNMENT

The Republic of the Marshall Islands is a democracy based on a parliamentary system of government. The electorate ratified in a referendum in 1979 a constitution drafted by a constitutional convention, at which time the nation became internally self-governing.

The executive is under the leadership of the President, who is elected by the Nitijela from among its members. The President serves for a four-year term. The legislature has two chambers, the Council of Iroij of 12 members and the Nitijela of 33 members. The Nitijela is the law-making chamber, to which the President and government are accountable. The Council of Iroij has an advisory role.

There are 24 local government districts, each of which usually consists of an elected council, a mayor and appointed local officials.

HEAD OF STATE
President, Hon. Amata Kabua, *elected* 1979, *re-elected* 1984, 1988, 1992.

THE GOVERNMENT *as at August 1993*
Finance, Hon. Ruben Zackras
Foreign Affairs, Hon. Tom Kijiner
Transport and Communications, Hon. Kunio Lemari
Resources and Development, Hon. Amsa Jonathan
Education, Hon. Phillip Muller
Social Services, Hon. Christopher Loeak
Public Works, Hon. Antonio Eliu
Health and Environment, Hon. Henchi Balos
Justice, Hon. Luckner Abner
Internal Affairs, Hon. Brenson Wase

BRITISH AMBASSADOR (resident in Kiribati)

JUDICIARY

There are four court levels; the Supreme Court; the High Court; the district and community courts; and the traditional rights courts. Trial is by jury. Jurisdiction of the traditional rights courts is limited to cases involving titles or land rights and other disputes arising from customary law and traditional practice.

DEFENCE

The Republic of the Marshall Islands has no defence forces. The Compact of Free Association places full responsibility for defence of the Marshall Islands on the USA. The US Department of Defence controls islands within Kwajalein Atoll where it has a missile test range.

ECONOMY

The economy is a mixture of subsistence and a service-based sector. About half the working population is engaged in agriculture and fishing, with coconut oil and copra production comprising 90 per cent of total exports. The service sector is based in Majuro and Ebeye and concentrated in banking and insurance, construction, transportation and tourism. Direct US aid under the Compact accounts for two-thirds of the islands budget. The USA and Japan are the major trading partners.

The GDP was (1988) US$68 million and GDP per head (1988) was US$1,600.

TRADE WITH UK	1992
Imports from UK	£553,000
Exports to UK	—

COMMUNICATIONS

Air Marshall Islands provides air services within the islands and to Hawaii. Continental Air Micronesia serves Majuro and Kwajalein with flights to Hawaii and Guam. Majuro also has shipping links to Hawaii, Australia, Japan and throughout the Pacific.

CULTURE

The Marshallese culture revolves around a complex clan system of matrilineal structure. The social structure and system of land tenure are closely related. The sea has traditionally been the major source of food and thoroughfare among the atolls, and remains important to the Marshallese culture.

SOCIAL WELFARE

The state school system provides education up to age 18, but only 25 per cent of students proceed beyond elementary level because of inadequate resources.

Majuro and Ebeye have hospitals run by the government with aid from the US Public Health Service. Each outer island community has a health assistant.

MAURITANIA
République Islamique de Mauritanie

Mauritania lies on the north-west coast of Africa. It is bounded on the south by Senegal, on the east by Mali, and on the north by Morocco, Algeria and the Western Sahara. The area is 397,955 sq. miles (1,030,700 sq. km). The population (UN estimate 1991) is 2,036,000. The official languages are French and Arabic.

CAPITAL – Nouakchott (850,000).
CURRENCY – Ouguiya of 5 khoums.
FLAG – Yellow star and crescent on green ground.
NATIONAL DAY – 28 November.

GOVERNMENT

Mauritania elected on 28 November 1958 to remain within the French Community as an autonomous republic. It became fully independent on 28 November 1960. In 1972 Mauritania left the Franc Zone.

Mauritania and Morocco took possession of the Western Sahara territory in February 1976 when Spain formally relinquished it and in April 1976 agreed on a new frontier dividing the territory between them. In August 1979, Mauritania relinquished all claim to the southern sector of the Western Sahara after a three-year war against the Polisario front guerrilla army.

After a military coup in 1978, Mauritania was ruled by a Military Committee for National Salvation (CMSN). Having previously rejected reform, in April 1991 President Taya announced a political amnesty, a referendum on the constitution and the calling of multi-party elections thereafter for a reconvened Senate and National Assembly. The constitution was approved by a large majority in July. Multi-party elections to the Senate and National Assembly were held in March 1992 and won by the Republican Democratic and Social Party (PRDS) led by President Taya. The President appointed a cabinet of PRDS members in April 1992, but the legitimacy of the new government was undermined by the boycotting of the elections by the main opposition grouping, the Union of Democratic Forces (UDF).

Conflict continues between the Arab-dominated government and the African minority in the south of the country. In 1989 a border dispute with Senegal involving race riots and mass expulsions from both countries led to the closing of the frontier and the severing of diplomatic relations. Links were restored in 1992 but contentious issues remain unresolved.

HEAD OF STATE
President, Col. Maaouya Ould Sidi Ahmed Taya, *took power* 12 December 1984, *elected* 17 January 1992.

CABINET *as at August 1993*
Prime Minister, Sidi Mohammed Ould Boubaker.
Foreign Affairs and Co-operation, Mohammed Abdrahmane Abou Ould Moine.
Defence, Col. Ahmed Ould Minnih.
Justice, Adema Samba Sow.
Interior, Posts and Telecommunications, Lemrabet Cheikh Ahmed.
Finance, Kan Acheikh.
Planning, Mohammed Ould Michel.
Fisheries and Maritime Economy, Abdallahai Ould Abdi.
Commerce, Handicrafts and Industry, Jagana Moussa.
Mines, Sidi Mohammed Fall.
Rural Development and Environment, Mouloud Ould Abdallah.
Health and Social Affairs, Ahmed Ould Ghanahalla.
Culture and Islamic Orientation, Limam Ould Tagaddi.
Relations with Parliament, Rachid Ould Saleh.

EMBASSY OF THE ISLAMIC REPUBLIC OF MAURITANIA
5 rue de Montevideo, Paris XVIe, France
Tel: Paris 45048854

Ambassador Extraordinary and Plenipotentiary, His Excellency Muhammad Al-Hanchi Ould Muhammad Saleh (1989) (resident in Paris).

BRITISH AMBASSADOR (resident in Rabat, Morocco).

ECONOMY

Mauritania's main source of potential wealth lies in rich deposits of iron ore around Zouérate, in the north of the country.

In October 1992 Mauritania agreed a four-year economic restructuring programme with the IMF to reduce inflation and the country's external debt. In late 1992 the IMF announced a US$47 million loan to support the government's economic and financial reform programme up to September 1995.

TRADE WITH UK	1991	1992
Imports from UK	£2,336,000	£3,407,000
Exports to UK	15,313,000	12,757,000

MAURITIUS

Mauritius is an island group lying in the Indian Ocean, 550 miles east of Madagascar, between 57° 17′ and 57° 46′ E. longitude and 19° 58′ and 20° 33′ S. latitude. Mauritius and Rodrigues with the other outer islands comprise an area of 790 square miles (2,045 sq. km).

Mauritius enjoys a sub-tropical maritime climate, with a wide range of rainfall and temperature resulting from the mountainous nature of the island. Humidity is rather high throughout the year and rainfall is sufficient to maintain a green cover of vegetation, except for a brief period in the driest districts.

POPULATION – The population (1990 estimate, excluding Rodrigues and the outer islands) was 1,022,456, made up of Asiatic races (Hindus 52.6 per cent, Muslims 16.5 per cent), and persons of European (mainly French) extraction, mixed and African descent (28.3 per cent).

LANGUAGES – English is the official language but French may be used in the National Assembly and lower law courts. However, Creole is the most commonly used language.

CAPITAL – ΨPort Louis, population (1991) 142,505; other centres are Beau Bassin-Rose Hill (93,864); Curepipe (72,214); Vacoas-Phoenix (91,114) and Quatre Bornes (70,997).

CURRENCY – Mauritius rupee of 100 cents.

FLAG – Red, blue, yellow and green horizontal stripes.

NATIONAL ANTHEM – Glory to the Motherland.

NATIONAL DAY – 12 March.

GOVERNMENT

Mauritius was discovered in 1511 by the Portuguese; the Dutch visited it in 1598 and named it Mauritius after Prince Maurice of Nassau. From 1638 to 1710 it was held as a small Dutch colony and in 1715 the French took possession but did not settle it until 1721. Mauritius was taken by a British force in 1810. A British garrison remained on the island until June 1960. The French language and French law were preserved under British rule.

A Crown Colony for 158 years, Mauritius became an independent state within the Commonwealth on 12 March 1968. After 24 years of constitutional monarchy, Mauritius became a republic on 12 March 1992 with a President as head of state. The President of the Republic is elected by the members of the National Assembly.

The Constitution provides for a Council of Ministers consisting of the Prime Minister and not more than 24 other ministers. The Prime Minister, appointed by the President, is the member of the National Assembly who appears to the President best able to command the support of the majority of members of the Assembly. Other ministers are appointed by the President acting in accordance with the advice of the Prime Minister.

The National Assembly has a normal term of five years and consists of 62 elected members (the Island of Mauritius is divided into 20 three-member constituencies and Rodrigues returns two members), and eight specially-elected members. Of the latter, four seats go to the 'best loser' of whichever communities in the island are under-represented in the Assembly after the General Election and the four remaining seats are allocated on the basis of both party and community.

At the General Election held on 15 September 1991, the ruling alliance of the Mouvement Socialiste Militant (MSM), Mouvement Militant Mauricien (MMM) and the Mouvement Travailliste Democrate (MTD) gained 57 of the 62 seats available and formed the government.

HEAD OF STATE
President, Cassam Uteem, *elected by National Assembly* June 1992.

COUNCIL OF MINISTERS *as at August 1993*
Prime Minister, Minister of Defence and Internal Security, Information, Internal and External Communications and the Outer Islands, Rt. Hon. Sir Anerood Jugnauth, KCMG, QC.
Deputy PM, Minister for Health, Hon. Dr Paramhamsa Nababsing.
External Affairs, Hon. Paul Raymond Berenger.
Economic Planning and Development, Hon. Ahmud Swalay Kasenally.
Education and Science, Hon. Armoogum Parsuraman.
Trade and Shipping, Hon. Anil Kumar Bachoo.
Energy, Water Resources and Postal Services, Hon. Mahyendrah Utchanah.
Housing, Lands and Town and Country Planning, Hon. Jayen Cuttaree.
Social Security and National Solidarity, Hon. Karl Auguste Offman.
Women's Rights, Child Development and Family Welfare, Hon. Sheilabai Bappoo.
Youth and Sports, Hon. Michael Glover.
Rodrigues, Hon. Serge Clair.
Co-operatives and Handicrafts, Hon. Jagdishwar Goburdhun.
Agriculture, Fisheries and Natural Resources, Hon. Madan Dulloo.
Industry and Industrial Technology, Hon. Jean Claude Raoul de l'Estrac.
Works, Hon. Dwarkanath Gungah.
Local Government, Hon. Jean Regis Finnette.
Civil Service Affairs and Employment, Hon. Keertee Coomar Ruhee.
Environment and Quality of Life, Hon. Ahmud Khodabux.
Manpower Resources, Vocational and Technical Training, Hon. Ramduthsing Jaddoo.
Attorney-General and Minister of Justice, Hon. Alan Ganoo.
Finance, Hon. Ramakrishna Sithanen.
Tourism, Hon. Noe Ah-Quret Lee Cheong Lem.
Arts, Culture, Leisure and Reform Institutions, Hon. Mookhesswur Choonee.
Labour and Industrial Relations, Hon. Dharmanand Fokeer.

MAURITIUS HIGH COMMISSION
32–33 Elvaston Place, London SW7 5NW
Tel 071-581 0294

High Commissioner, His Excellency Babooram Mahadoo (1992).

BRITISH HIGH COMMISSION
King George V Avenue, Floreal
Tel: Floreal 6865795/8

High Commissioner, His Excellency John Clive Harrison (1993).

BRITISH COUNCIL REPRESENTATIVE, M. Bootle, PO Box 111, Foondun Building, 2nd Floor, Royal Road, Rose Hill.

EDUCATION

Primary education is free and compulsory and in 1991 provided for 129,154 children at 280 primary schools. At post-primary level there were a total of 79,327 students attending secondary schools; fees and teachers' salaries in the private secondary schools are paid by government. There are a number of training facilities offering training in engineering and mechanical trades, nursing, building, seamanship, hotel and catering, etc. The Institute of Education is responsible for training primary and secondary schoolteachers and for curriculum development. The University of Mauritius consists of Schools of Agriculture, Engineering, Law, Management and Social Studies, and Science. Estimated expenditure on education in 1992-3 was Rs.1,440,200,000.

ECONOMY

About 55 per cent of the total sugar crop is produced on a plantation scale, while smaller owners (cultivating less than ten acres) cultivate about 24 per cent of the land under cane. Tea and tobacco are also grown commercially but on a smaller scale than sugar.

	1991	1992
Sugar	611,340 tonnes	643,168 tonnes
Tea (manufactured)	5,934	5,828
Tobacco (leaves)	876	970

In 1991 production of molasses, mainly for export, was 170,000 tonnes. Other products include alcohol, rum, denatured spirits, perfumed spirits and vinegar.

The bulk of the island's requirements in manufactured products still has to be imported. However, the Mauritius Export Processing Zone (MEPZ) scheme, introduced in 1971, has attracted investment from overseas and the number of export-orientated enterprises has risen from ten in 1971 to 558 at the end of 1992, employing 86,937 people. The biggest firms are in clothing manufacture, particularly woollen knitwear, but the range of goods produced includes toys, plastic products, leather goods, diamond cutting and polishing, watches, television sets and telephones.

Tourism is a major source of income for Mauritius, with an estimated 330,880 tourists in 1992. Earnings from tourism in 1992 are estimated to be Rs.4,585 million. The neighbouring French island of Réunion is the most important source of tourists, followed closely by mainland France.

FINANCE

The main sources of government revenue are private and company income tax, customs and excise duties, mainly on imports but also on sugar exports.

	1992-3	1993-4*
Public revenue	Rs.11,565m	Rs.12,860m
Public expenditure (recurrent)	10,880m	12,730m
* estimate		

TRADE

Most foodstuffs and raw materials have to be imported from abroad. Apart from local consumption (about 36,500 tonnes per annum), the sugar produced is exported, mainly to Britain.

	1991	1992
Total imports	Rs.24,672m	Rs.25,313m
Total exports	19,273m	20,572m

Trade with UK	1991	1992
Imports from UK	£52,363,000	£59,892,000
Exports to UK	250,218,000	272,610,000

COMMUNICATIONS

Port Louis, on the north-west coast, handles the bulk of the island's external trade. A bulk sugar terminal capable of handling the total crop began operating in 1980. The international airport is located at Plaisance in the south-east of the island about five miles from Mahébourg. There are five daily newspapers and 15 weeklies, mostly in French, and two Chinese daily papers and one weekly paper. The Mauritius Broadcasting Corporation has a monopoly of radio broadcasting in the country; television was introduced in 1965. There is a satellite communications ground station near Port Louis.

RODRIGUES AND DEPENDENCIES

Rodrigues, formerly a dependency but now part of Mauritius, is about 350 miles east of Mauritius, with an area of 40 square miles. Population (1990) 34,204. Cattle, salt fish, sheep, goats, pigs, maize and onions are the principal exports. The island is administered by an Island Secretary.

Island Secretary, R. Gajeelee.

The islands of Agalega and St Brandon are dependencies of Mauritius. Total population (1989) 500. Other small islands, formerly Mauritian dependencies, have since 1965 constituted the British Indian Ocean Territory (*see* British Dependent Territories section).

MEXICO
Estados Unidos Mexicanos

Mexico occupies the southern part of North America, with an extensive seaboard to both the Atlantic and Pacific Oceans, extending from 14° 33' to 32° 43' N. latitude and 86° 46' to 117° 08' W. longitude. It covers an area of 761,605 sq. miles (1,972,547 sq. km).

The two great ranges of North America, the Sierra Nevada and Rocky Mountains, are prolonged from the north to a convergence towards the narrowing isthmus of Tehuantepec, their course being parallel to the west and east coasts. The surface of the interior consists of an elevated plateau between the two ranges, with steep slopes both to the Pacific and Atlantic (Gulf of Mexico). In the west is the peninsula of Lower California, with a mountainous surface, separated from the mainland by the Gulf of California. The Sierra Nevada, known in Mexico as the Sierra Madre, terminates in a transverse series of volcanic peaks, from Colima on the west to Citlaltepetl (El Pico de Orizaba) on the east.

The low-lying lands of the coasts form the Tierra Caliente, or tropical regions, the higher levels form the Tierra Templada, or temperate region, and the summit of the plateau with its peaks is known as Tierra Fria, or cold region. The main rivers are the Rio Grande del Norte which forms part of the northern boundary, and is navigable for about 70 miles from its mouth in the Gulf of Mexico, and the Rio Grande de Santiago, the Rio Balsas and Rio Papaloapan. The largest fresh-water lakes are Chapala and Pátzcuaro.

POPULATION – At the 1990 Census, the total population was 81,140,922; a 1991 UN estimate gives a figure of 87,836,000.

LANGUAGES – Spanish is the official language of Mexico and is spoken by about 95 per cent of the population. In addition, there are five basic groups of Indian languages (Náhuatl, Maya, Zapotec, Otomí, Mixtec) and 59 dialects derived from them. The poet Octavio Paz won the Nobel Prize for Literature in 1991.

CAPITAL - Mexico City, population of metropolitan area (1990 census) 14,987,051. Other cities (1990 census) are:

Guadalajara	2,846,000	Puebla	1,454,526
Monterrey	2,521,697	León	956,070
Torréon	876,456	Ciudad Juarez	797,679
Toluca	827,339	Tijuana	742,686

CURRENCY - Peso of 100 centavos.

FLAG - Three vertical bands in green, white, red, with the Mexican emblem (an eagle on a cactus devouring a snake) in the centre.

NATIONAL ANTHEM - Mexicanos, Al Grito De Guerra (Mexicans, to the war cry).

NATIONAL DAY - 16 September (Proclamation of Independence).

HISTORY

The present Mexico and Guatemala were once the centre of a civilization which flowered in the periods from AD 500 to 1100 and 1300 to 1500 and collapsed before the little army of Spanish adventurers under Hernán Cortés in the years following 1519. Pre-Columbian Mexico was divided between different but connected Indian cultures, each of which has left distinctive archaeological remains. The best-known of these are Chichén Itzá, Uxmal, Bonampak and Palenque, in Yucatán and Chiapas (Maya); Teotihuacon, renowned for the Pyramid of the Sun in the Valley of Mexico (Teotihuacáno); Monte Albán and Mitla, near Oaxaca (Zapotec); El Tajín in the state of Veracruz (Totonac); and Tula in the state of Hidalgo (Toltec). The last and most famous Indian culture, the Aztec, based on Tenochitlán, suffered more than the others from the Spanish and very few Aztec monuments remain.

A few years after the conquest, the Spanish built Mexico City on the ruins of Tenochitlán and appointed a Viceroy to rule their new dominions, which they called New Spain. The country was largely converted to Christianity and a distinctive colonial civilization, representing a marriage of Indian and Spanish traditions, developed. In 1810 a revolt began against Spanish rule. This was finally successful in 1821, when a precarious independence was proclaimed.

Friction with the United States in Texas led to the war of 1845-8, at the end of which Mexico was forced to cede the northern provinces of Texas, California and New Mexico. In 1862 Mexican insolvency led to invasion by French forces which installed Archduke Maximilian of Austria as Emperor. The empire collapsed with the execution of the Emperor in 1867 and the austere reformer Juárez restored the republic. Juárez's death was followed by the dictatorship of Porfirio Diaz, which saw an enormous increase in foreign, particularly British and American, investment in the country. In 1910 began the Mexican Revolution which reformed the social structure and the land system, curbed the power of foreign companies and ushered in the independent industrial Mexico of today. In 1986 Mexico joined GATT and began a liberalization programme of privatization and administrative reform.

GOVERNMENT

Under the Constitution of 1917 (as subsequently amended), Congress consists of a Senate of 64 members, elected for six years, and of a Chamber of Deputies, at present numbering 500, elected for three years. Presidents, who wield full executive powers, are elected for six years; they cannot be re-elected.

There are nine political parties registered in Mexico, of which the largest and most influential is the Partido Revolucionario Institucional (PRI) which for more than 60 years has constituted the governing party despite constant allegations of electoral fraud. The main opposition parties are Partido de Acción Nacional (PAN) and Partido de la Renovación Democratica (PRD) In June 1992 the state of the parties in the Chamber of Deputies was: PRI 320, PAN 89, PRD and allied parties 91.

The country is divided into 31 states and the federal district of Mexico City.

HEAD OF STATE
President, Carlos Salinas de Gortari, *elected*, 4 June 1988, *took office*, 1 December 1988.

CABINET *as at August 1993*
Interior, Patrocinio Blanco Garrido.
Foreign Affairs, Fernando Solana Morales.
Finance and Public Credit, Dr Pedro Aspe Armella.
Defence, Gen. Antonio Riviello Bazán.
Navy, Adm. Luis Carlos Ruano Angulo.
Energy, Mines and Parastatal Industries, Emilio Lozoya Thalman.
Trade and Industrial Development, Dr Jaime Serra Puche.
Agriculture and Water Resources, Carlos Hank González.
Communications and Transport, Emilio Gamboa Patrón.
Education, Ernesto Zedillo Ponce de León.
Social Development, Luis Donaldo Colosio.
Health, Dr Jesús Kumate Rodríguez.
Labour and Social Security, Arsenio Farell Cubillas.
Agrarian Reform, Victor Cervera Pacheco.
Tourism, Pedro Joaquin Coldwell.
Fisheries, Guillermo Jiménez Morales.
Attorney-General, Jorge Carpizo.
Attorney-General of Federal District, Diego Valadéz Ríos.
Comptroller-General, María Elena Vazquez Nava.
Mayor of Mexico City, Manuel Camacho Solís.

MEXICAN EMBASSY
42 Hertford Street, London WIY 7TF
Tel 071-499 8586

Ambassador Extraordinary and Plenipotentiary, His Excellency Dr Juan José De Olloqui (1993).
Chargé D'Affairs, J. Castro-Valle.
Military Attaché, Maj.-Gen. B. Pacheco.
Consul-General, M. B. Hernandez.
Counsellor, C. Lombera (*Commercial*).

BRITISH EMBASSY
Calle Río Lerma 71, Colonia Cuauhtémoc, 06500 Mexico City, DF
Tel: Mexico City 207 20 89

Ambassador Extraordinary and Plenipotentiary, His Excellency Sir Roger Hervey, KCVO, CMG (1992).
Deputy Ambassador and Counsellor, G. Berg.
Defence Attaché, Col. A. J. Dobson.
First Secretary (Commercial), J. F. Thompson.

There are British Consular Offices at *Mexico City, Acapulco, Guadalajara, Mérida, Monterrey, Tampico, Tijuana, Veracruz*, and *Cuidad Juarez.*

BRITISH COUNCIL REPRESENTATIVE, Dr Brian Lavercombe, Maestro Antonio Caso 127, Col. San Rafael (PO Box 30-588), Mexico 06470 DF.

BRITISH CHAMBER OF COMMERCE, British Trade Centre, Rio de la Plata 30, Col. Cuauhtemoc, CP 06500, Mexico City DF, *Manager*, Stephen Grant.

COMMUNICATIONS

Veracruz, Tampico and Coatzacoalcos are the chief ports on the Atlantic, and Guaymas, Mazatlán, Puerto Lázaro

Cárdenas, Acapulco, Salina Cruz and Puerto Madero on the Pacific. Work is proceeding on the reorganization and re-equipment of the whole system. Total track length of the railways was 240,186 km in 1990. Mexico City may be reached by at least three highways from the United States, and from the south from Yucatán as well as on two principal highways from the Guatemalan border.

There are 1,113 airports and landing fields in Mexico, of which 18 are equipped to handle long-distance flights. There are 166 airline companies, including two of the major, now private, national airlines, Mexicana de Aviación and Aero-méxico. The total number of air passengers in 1990 was 21,825,000.

Teléfonos de México, now privatized, controls about 98 per cent of all telephone services. Satélite Latinoamericano (SATELAT) is a joint government/private sector venture disseminating television programmes to Latin America through Intelsat IV satellite facilities leased by the Mexican Government.

ECONOMY

In 1991 26 per cent of GDP was produced by commerce, 23 per cent by manufacturing, 33.6 per cent by services, 5 per cent by construction, 7.4 per cent by agriculture, 3.5 per cent by mining and 1.5 per cent by public utilities. Direct foreign investment at the end of 1991 was a cumulative US$33.9 billion, of which over 60 per cent was American. Privatization has been successful with only 208 public enterprises remaining in 1991 (1,155 in 1982).

The principal crops are maize, beans, rice, wheat, sugar cane, coffee, cotton, tomatoes, chili, tobacco, chick-peas, groundnuts, sesame, alfalfa, vanilla, cocoa and many kinds of fruit, both tropical and temperate. The maguey, or Mexican cactus, yields several fermented drinks, mezcal and tequila (distilled) and pulque (undistilled). Another species of the same plant supplies sisal-hemp (henequen). The forests contain mahogany, rosewood, ebony and chicle trees. Agriculture employs an estimated 20 per cent of the working population.

The principal industries are mining and petroleum, although there has been considerable expansion of both light and heavy industries. Exports of manufactured goods now average about 56 per cent of total exports. The steel industry expanded steadily until recently and current production is around 7.9m tons. In 1991, 989,000 motor vehicles were produced of which 365,000 were for export.

The mineral wealth is great, and principal minerals are gold, silver, copper, lead, zinc, quicksilver, iron and sulphur. Substantial reserves of uranium have been found. In the non-metals sector, Mexico continues to produce 25 per cent of the world's supply of fluorspar.

Oil exports were 1.37 million barrels per day in 1991. Daily production of natural gas is approximately 3 billion cubic feet. Oil reserves have increased substantially due to important discoveries in the Gulf of Campeche. A new refinery at Tula, State of Hidalgo, is the nation's largest; and new refineries in Monterrey, State of Nuevo Leon, and Salina Cruz, State of Oaxaca, are under construction.

TRADE

Major imports include computers, auto assembly material, electrical parts, auto and truck parts, powdered milk, corn and sorghum, transport, sound-recording and power-generating equipment, chemicals, industrial machinery, pharmaceuticals and specialized appliances. Principal exports include oil, automobiles, auto engines, fruits and vegetables, shrimps, coffee, computers, cattle, glass, iron and steel pipes, and copper. The main trading partners are the USA (65.6

per cent), EC (15 per cent), Latin America (5.2 per cent) and Japan (5 per cent).

Trade with UK	1991	1992
Imports from UK	£276,557,000	£291,334,000
Exports to UK	147,214,000	152,205,000

DEFENCE

Supreme command is vested in the President, exercised through the Ministries of Defence (for Army and Air Force) and Marine. The total armed forces number some 175,000, including 60,000 conscripts. Conscription is decided by lottery and is for a one-year period. The Army has a strength of 130,000 (including 60,000 conscripts), with some 350 reconnaissance vehicles, 110 armoured personnel carriers, 120 artillery pieces. The Army is organized into central forces and 36 zonal garrisons. The central forces consist of six brigades (one armoured, one airborne, one Presidential Guard, three infantry) while the zonal garrisons have a total of one armoured, one mechanized infantry, three artillery and 19 motor cavalry regiments and 80 infantry battalions.

The Navy has a strength of 37,000 personnel, including 8,000 marines, with three destroyers, 97 patrol and coastal vessels, and nine combat aircraft. The Air Force is 8,000 strong, with 113 combat aircraft and 25 armed helicopters, organized into one air defence, nine counter-insurgency, one reconnaissance and five transport squadrons, with training and liaison units.

EDUCATION

Education is divided into primary, secondary and superior levels. In 1990 there were 18,061,000 in the first level, 6,599,000 in the second and 1,236,000 in the third.

FEDERATED STATES OF MICRONESIA

The Federated States of Micronesia comprise more than 600 islands extending 2,900 km (1,800 miles) across the archipelago of the Caroline Islands in the western Pacific Ocean. The islands are located between the Equator and 9° N., and 138° and 168° E. Pohnpei island is 4,670 km (2,900 miles) south-west of Honolulu and 1,610 km (1,100 miles) south-east of Guam. The area is 700 square km (270 square miles). The islands vary geologically from mountainous islands to low coral atolls.

CLIMATE – Tropical. The average annual temperature is 27°C (81°F). Annual rainfall is consistently high; Pohnpei receives the highest rainfall, averaging 8,900 mm (350 inches) annually. Storms are common between August and December, and typhoons between July and November.

POPULATION – The population is (1991 UN estimate) 101,000: Pohnpei 31,000; Chuuk (formerly Truk) 52,000; Yap 12,000; Kosrae 6,500. The population is Micronesian.

LANGUAGES – English (official) and eight other languages are used in different parts of the Federated States: Yapese, Ulithian, Woleaian, Ponapean, Nukuoran, Kapingamarangi, Trukese and Kosraen.

RELIGION – Predominantly Christian.

CAPITAL – The federal capital is Palikir, on Pohnpei island.

FLAG – United Nations blue with four white stars in the centre.

HISTORY

The Spanish Empire claimed sovereignty over the Caroline Islands until 1899, when Spain withdrew from her Pacific territories and sold her possessions in the Caroline Islands to Germany. The Caroline Islands became a protectorate of the German Empire under colonial German administration until the outbreak of the First World War in 1914, when Japan took control of the islands on behalf of the Allied powers. After the war Japan continued to administer the territory under a League of Nations mandate. During the Second World War, United States armed forces took control of the islands from the Japanese. In 1947 the United States entered into agreement with the UN Security Council to administer the Micronesia area, of which the Federated States of Micronesia were a part, as the UN Trust Territory of the Pacific Islands.

The US Trusteeship administration came to an end on 3 November 1986, when a Compact of Free Association between the USA and the Federated States of Micronesia came into effect. By this agreement the USA recognized the Federated States of Micronesia as a fully sovereign and independent state. However, the Soviet Union used its veto to prevent the UN Security Council from terminating the UN Trust territory of the Pacific Islands until December 1990, when the independence of the Federated States of Micronesia was finally recognized by the UN.

GOVERNMENT

The Federated States of Micronesia is a federal republic of four constituent states: Chuuk, Kosrae, Pohnpei, Yap. The constitution separates the executive, legislative and judicial branches. There is a bill of rights and provision for traditional rights.

The executive comprises a federal President and Vice-President, both of whom must be chosen from amongst the four nationally-elected senators. There is a one-chamber legislature of 14 members, four members elected on a nation-wide basis and ten members elected from congressional districts apportioned by population.

HEAD OF STATE
President, Bailey Olter (Pohnpei)
Vice-President, Jacob Nina (Kosrae)

BRITISH AMBASSADOR (resident in Kiribati)

LOCAL GOVERNMENT
Each of the constituent states has its own government and legislative system.
Pohnpei: *population,* 31,000; *capital,* Kolonia; *Governor,* Rasio Moses
Chuuk (Truk): *population,* 52,000; *capital,* Moen; *Governor,* Sasao Gouland
Yap: *population,* 12,000; *capital,* Colonia; *Governor,* Petrus Tun
Kosrae: *population,* 6,500; *capital,* Lelu; *Governor,* Yosivo George

JUDICIARY

The judiciary is headed by the Supreme Court, which is divided into trial and appellate divisions. Below this, each state has its own judicial system.

DEFENCE

The Compact of Free Association places full responsibility for the defence of the Federted States of Micronesia on the USA.

ECONOMY

The economy is dependent mainly on subsistence agriculture and government spending. Copra and fish are the two main exports. The majority of the working population is engaged in government administration, subsistence farming, fishing, copra production and the growing tourist industry. A severe drought on Chuuk in 1992 necessitated the US Navy bringing water supplies to the island from Guam after a state of emergency had been declared.

CULTURE

Each of the four states has an indigenous culture, and these differ considerably from one another. Recognition of the role of traditional leaders and customs is common to all, though Kosrae has no traditional leaders.

MOLDOVA
Republica Moldovenească

Moldova has an area of 13,912 sq. miles (33,700 sq. km) and occupies the extreme south-western corner of the former USSR. To the north, east and south-east it is bordered by the Ukraine, and to the west by Romania. The border with Romania is formed by the Pruth (Prut) river, but the main river of the republic is the Dniester, navigable along its whole course. The northern part of the republic consists of flat steppe lands, in the centre there are woody hills, and in the south low-lying steppe lands. Forests skirt the Dniester.
CLIMATE – Moderate.
POPULATION – According to the 1990 official estimate the population is 4,361,000, of which 65 per cent are Moldovan, 14.2 per cent Ukrainian and 13 per cent Russian, together with smaller numbers of Gagauz (ethnic Turks), Jews and Bulgarians.
RELIGION – Most of the population are adherents of the Romanian Orthodox Church.
LANGUAGE – Moldovan 65 per cent, Ukranian 14.2 per cent, Russian 13 per cent. Moldovan is a Romance language similar to Romanian, and was made the official language (written in the Latin script) in 1989.

CAPITAL – Kishinev. Population 665,000 (1989 census).
CURRENCY – Rouble of 100 kopeks. The government plans to introduce its own currency, known as the leu.
FLAG – Vertical stripes of blue, yellow, red, with the national arms in the centre.
NATIONAL DAY – 27 August (Independence Day).

GOVERNMENT

A Moldovan feudal state was established in the middle of the 14th century when Slavic tribes who had previously lived under Roman and Byzantine rule integrated with Slavic tribes from further east. Slavic languages dominated until they were replaced by the Moldovan Romance language in the 17th century. In the 15th century a Moldovan principality was formed which entered into military and political alliances with Muscovy before being conquered and absorbed into the Turkish Empire in the 16th century. Moldova became the site of many Russo-Turkish battles and skirmishes in the 18th century before the area between the Dniester and Prut rivers (later known as Bessarabia) was annexed to the Russian Empire by the Bucharest Peace Treaty 1812.

After the Russian Revolution in 1917, Bessarabia was under the control of White Russian forces and was annexed to Romania under the Versailles Peace Treaty of 1919. On 12 October 1924 the Moldavian Autonomous Soviet Socialist Republic (ASSR) was established on the east bank of the Dniester river as part of Soviet Ukraine. In August 1940 the

Soviet Union forced Romania to cede Bessarabia to the Soviet Union and the Moldavian Soviet Socialist Republic was formed from the fusion of the majority of Bessarabia (the southernmost parts were incorporated into the Ukraine) with the previous Moldavian ASSR.

When Moldova (formerly Moldavia) declared its independence from the USSR in August 1991, the majority ethnic Romanian (Moldovan) population expressed a wish to rejoin Romania. This alienated the ethnic Ukrainian and Russian populations, who form a majority east of the Dniester. After failed negotiations and several armed clashes, the Ukrainian and Russian populations declared their independence from Moldova as the Transdniester republic in December 1991. The Moldovan government refused to recognize this and throughout the first half of 1992 a war was waged between government forces and Transdniester forces, who were supported by the former Soviet 14th Army stationed in Transdniester and by Cossack volunteers from Russia.

A mainly Russian CIS peace-keeping force (later changed to a joint Russian-Moldovan-Transdniester force) was deployed on 29 July 1992 and a ceasefire has held since August 1992. No political solution has been reached on the future of the republic, a state of armed truce is in existence and the Russian 14th Army remains in position. In January 1993 President Snegur failed by one vote to gain parliamentary approval for a referendum on unification with Romania, and in August 1993 the Moldovan parliament failed to ratify the CIS agreement, leaving it effectively outside the organization.

The Moldovan Popular Front government which came to power in the 1990 legislative elections to the 380-seat Supreme Soviet was replaced in July 1992 by a government of national accord led by the Peasant Democratic Party. This has also failed to push through economic reforms and a new constitution which is still being drafted.

HEAD OF STATE
President, Mircea Snegur, *elected* 8 December 1991.

GOVERNMENT *as at August 1993*
Prime Minister, Andrei Sangeli.
Deputy Prime Minister, Valentin Kunev.
Economics, Sergey Chertan.
Agriculture and Foodstuffs, Vitali Gorinchey.
Industry and Power Engineering, Alexander Barbu.
Construction and Architecture, Valeri Chebotar.
Trade and Material Resources, Fedor Slanina.
Transport, Valery Kozlov.
Information and Communications, Ion Kasyan.
Public Health, Georgy Gidirim.
Culture and Religion, Ion Ungureanu.
Science and Education, Nikolay Metkash.
Justice, Alexei Barbeneagre.
Internal Affairs, Konstantin Antoc.
Foreign Affairs, Nikolai Tsyu.
National Security, Vasili Kalmoi.
Defence, Pavel Krynge.
Foreign Economic Relations, Andrei Keptine.
Finance, Klavdiya Melnik.

Chairman of Parliament, Pietr Luchinskye.

BRITISH AMBASSADOR (resident in Moscow).

ECONOMY

The main sector of the economy is agriculture, especially viniculture, fruit-growing and market gardening. Industry is small and concentrated east of the Dniester, but severe drought in 1992, the severance of most trading ties with former Soviet republics, war damage and reductions in Russian fuel deliveries has paralysed the economy.

MONACO
Principauté de Monaco

A small principality on the Mediterranean, with land frontiers joining France at every point, Monaco is divided into the districts of Monaco-Ville, La Condamine, Fontvielle and Monte Carlo. The principality comprises a narrow strip of country about two miles long (area approx. 195 hectares), with approximately 28,000 inhabitants (1990) and a yearly average of over 250,000 visitors.

CAPITAL – Monaco-Ville, population (1982) 1,234.
CURRENCY – Monaco uses the French franc of 100 centimes as legal tender.
FLAG – Two equal horizontal stripes, red over white.
NATIONAL ANTHEM – Hymne Monegasque.
NATIONAL DAY – 19 November.

GOVERNMENT

The principality, ruled by the Grimaldi family since the late 13th century, was abolished during the French Revolution and re-established in 1815 under the protection of the kingdom of Sardinia. In 1861 Monaco came under French protection.

The 1962 Constitution, which can be modified only with the approval of the National Council, maintains the traditional hereditary monarchy and guarantees freedom of association, trade union freedom and the right to strike. Legislative power is held jointly by the Prince and a unicameral, 18-member National Council elected by universal suffrage. Executive power is exercised by the Prince and a four-member Council of Government, headed by a Minister of State. The judicial code is based on that of France. Monaco became a member of the United Nations on 28 May 1993.

HEAD OF STATE
Sovereign Prince, HSH Rainier III Louis-Henri-Maxence Bertrand, *born* 31 May 1923, *succeeded* 9 May 1949; *married* 19 April 1956, Miss Grace Patricia Kelly (died 14 September 1982) and *has issue* Prince Albert Alexandre Louis Pierre, *born* 14 March 1958, Princess Caroline Louise Marguerite, *born* 23 January 1957; and Princess Stephanie Marie Elisabeth, *born* 1 February 1965.

President of the Crown Council, Jean-Charles Marquet.
President of the National Council, Dr Jean-Louis Campora.
Minister of State, Jacques Dupont, *appointed* 1991.

CONSULATE-GENERAL OF MONACO
4 Cromwell Place, London SW7 2JE
Tel 071-225 2679
Consul-General, I. B. Ivanovic.

BRITISH CONSUL-GENERAL, John Illman (1990), resident in Marseilles, France.

ECONOMY

The whole available ground is built over, so that there is no cultivation, though there are some notable public and private gardens. Monaco has a small harbour (30 ft alongside quay) and the import duties are the same as in France.

MONGOLIA
State of Mongolia

Mongolia is a large and sparsely populated country to the north of China. Its area is 604,250 sq. miles (1,565,000 sq.

km). Its population (1992 estimate) is 2,156,000. However, this total constitutes only part of the Mongolians of Asia, a number of whom are to be found in China and in the neighbouring regions of the Russian Federation, especially the Mongolian Buryat Autonomous Region.

Mongolia, which is almost nowhere below 1,000 metres above sea level, forms part of the central Asiatic plateau and rises towards the west in the mountains of the Mongolian Altai and Hangai ranges. The Hentai range, situated to the north-east of the capital Ulan Bator, is less high. The Gobi region covers much of the southern half of the country. It contains some sand deserts, but between these there is semi-desert which provides pasture for great numbers of sheep, goats, camels and horses (the latter is still the characteristic means of transport for the rural population) and some cattle. In the steppe areas to the north pasturage is better and livestock more abundant. Even further north, in the better-watered provinces, grain, fodder and vegetable crops are grown. There are several long rivers and many lakes, but good water is scarce since much of the lake water is salty. The climate is harsh, with a short mild summer giving way to a long winter when temperatures can drop as low as minus 50°C.

CAPITAL – Ulan Bator (Ulaanbaator), population (1993) 600,500.

CURRENCY – Tugrik of 100 möngö.

FLAG – Vertical tri-colour red, blue, red and in the hoist the traditional Soyombo symbol in gold.

NATIONAL DAY – 11 July.

GOVERNMENT

Mongolia, under Genghis Khan the conqueror of China and much of Asia, was for many years a buffer state between Tsarist Russia and China, although it was under general Chinese suzerainty. The outbreak of the Chinese Revolution in 1911 led to a declaration of autonomy under Chinese suzerainty which was confirmed by the Sino-Russian Treaty of Kiakhta (1915) but cancelled by a unilateral Chinese declaration in 1919. Later the country became a battleground of the Russian civil war, and Soviet and Mongolian troops occupied Ulan Bator in 1921; this was followed by another declaration of independence. In 1924 the Soviet Union in a treaty with China again recognized the latter's sovereignty over Mongolia, but this was never properly exercised because of China's preoccupation with internal affairs and later by the war with Japan.

The Mongolian People's Republic was formally established in 1924. Under the Yalta Agreement, Chiang Kai-shek agreed to a plebiscite, held in 1945, in which the Mongolians declared their desire for independence and this was formally recognized by China.

The Mongolian People's Revolutionary Party (MPRP) has been the ruling party since 1924. A series of demonstrations in favour of political and economic reform began in December 1989 and led to changes in the MPRP leadership in March 1990. The MPRP's constitutionally guaranteed monopoly of power was subsequently relinquished, and the introduction of a multi-party system was approved by the Great People's Hural (Mongolia's parliament). The MRRP won the first multi-party elections, held in July 1990. Since then, and following Moscow's lead, Mongolia has embarked on a programme of political and economic reforms.

A new constitution was approved in January 1992 which enshrines the concepts of democracy, a mixed economy, free speech, and neutrality in foreign affairs. The Great and Little Hurals were abolished, and a new unicameral Great Hural became the legislative body of the country. Elections were held in June 1992 which were won by the MPRP with 57 per

cent of the vote and 71 out of 76 seats. The country's first direct presidential election was held in June 1993 and won by the incumbent Punsalmaagiyn Orchirbat who stood as an opposition candidate after the MPRP refused to endorse him as its candidate.

The last remaining former Soviet armed forces personnel were withdrawn in late 1992.

The country and three city districts (Ulan Bator, Darkhan and Erdenet) are divided into 18 *aimaks* (provinces) and beneath these into 258 *somons* (districts), and these form the basis of the state organization of the country.

HEAD OF STATE
President, Punsalmaagiyn Ochirbat, *elected* June 1993.

CABINET *as at August 1993*
Prime Minister, Puntsagiyn Jasray.
Deputy PM, Administration, Lhamsurengiyn Enebish.
Deputy PM, Choyjilsurengiyn Purevdorj.
Defence, Maj.-Gen. Shagalyn Jadambaa.
Minister of Mongolia and Chairman of National Development Board, Chultemiyn Ulaan.
Agriculture and Food, Tseveenjavyn Oold.
Foreign Relations, Tserenpiliyn Gombosuren.
Construction and City Planning, Tserendashiyn Damiran.
Culture, Nambaryn Enhbayar.
Demography and Labour, Erdeniyn Gormbojav.
Finance, Dalrain Davaasambun.
Fuel and Energy, Byambyn Jigjid.
Geology and Minerals, Dorjiyn Tsogbaatar.
Law, Narnsraijavyn Luvsanjav.
Roads, Transport and Communications, Razdakyn Sandalhaan.
Science and Education, Nadmidyn Olziihutag.
Trade and Industry, Tsevegmediyn Tsogt.
Health, Pagvajavyn Nyamdavaa.
Nature and the Environment, Zambyn Batjargal.
Chairman of the Great Hural, Natsagiyn Bagabandi.

EMBASSY OF MONGOLIA
7 Kensington Court, London W8 5DL
Tel 071-937 0150

Ambassador Extraordinary and Plenipotentiary, His Excellency Choisurengyn Baatar (1991).

BRITISH EMBASSY
30 Enkh Taivny Gudamzh (PO Box 703), Ulan Bator 13
Tel: Ulan Bator 358133

Ambassador Extraordinary and Plenipotentiary, His Excellency Anthony B. Morey (1989).
Second Secretary, N. Hart (*Head of Chancery*).

ECONOMY

The total of Mongolia's livestock was 25 million in 1993. Traditionally the Mongolians led a nomadic life tending flocks of sheep, goats, horses, cows and camels. With the coming of the Communist regime and especially since 1952, great efforts were made to settle the population, but a proportion still live nomadically or semi-nomadically in the traditional *ger* (circular tent). The pastoral population was collectivized at the end of the 1950s into huge *negdels* (co-operatives) and state farms which have hastened the process of settlement, but within these the herdsmen and their families still move with their *gers* from pasture to pasture as the seasons change.

Membership of the Communist bloc brought Mongolia considerable quantities of aid from other socialist countries, especially from the Soviet Union, but this ended in 1990. In

June 1993 the IMF approved a US$31 million loan to Mongolia to aid its economic restructuring after Mongolia had allowed the tugrik to float freely.

Although the economy remains predominantly based on the herds of animals, factories serving the needs of the country have started up and the coal and electricity industries are being developed to provide an industrial base. A joint Mongolian/Soviet enterprise for copper and molybdenum mining was opened in 1978 at Erdenet in northern Mongolia. Coal production had risen to 8.04 m tons by 1990.

Ulan Bator and Darkhan are the main seats of industry. Industries include lime, cement and building materials, a flour mill and a power station. Choibalsan is also being developed industrially.

Mongolia's fundamental difficulty is its very small population and labour force, and its basic infastructure. Communication is still difficult in the country as there are very few tarmac roads. The trans-Mongolian railway links Mongolia with both China and Russia.

TRADE

Foreign trade was formerly dominated by the Soviet Union and other eastern bloc countries. Following the collapse of the CMEA, trade with western countries, Japan and South Korea is increasing. The country has been experiencing transitional problems in its attempt to establish a market economy, such as food and fuel shortages, inflation, and unemployment; since January 1991, trade is in hard currency, causing particular strain.

The principal exports are animal by-products (especially wool, hides and furs) and cattle.

Trade with UK	1991	1992
Imports from UK	£1,148,000	£1,698,000
Exports to UK	1,430,000	2,166,000

MOROCCO
Al-Mamlaka Al-Maghrebia

Morocco is situated in the north-west of the African continent between 27° 40′ and 36° N. latitude and 1° and 13° W. longitude with an area estimated at 172,414 sq. miles (446,550 sq. km). It is traversed in the north by the Rif mountains and, in a south-west to north-east direction, by the Middle Atlas, the High Atlas, the Anti-Atlas and the Sarrho ranges. The northern flanks of the Middle and High Atlas mountains are well-wooded but their southern slopes, exposed to the dry desert winds, are generally arid and desolate. The north-westerly point of Morocco is the peninsula of Tangier which is separated from the continent of Europe by the narrow strait of Gibraltar. The Jebel Mousa dominates the promontory and, with the rocky eminence of Gibraltar, was known to the ancients as the Pillars of Hercules, the western gateway of the Mediterranean.

The climate of Morocco is generally good especially on the Atlantic coast where a high degree of humidity is prevalent, the country being partially sheltered by the Atlas mountains from the hot winds of the Sahara. The rainy season may last from November to April. The plains of the interior are intensely hot in summer.

POPULATION – The population (1990 estimate) is 27,575,000.

RELIGION – Islam is the state religion.

LANGUAGE – Arabic is the official language. Berber is the vernacular, mainly in the mountain regions. French and Spanish are also spoken, mainly in the towns.

CAPITAL – ΨRabat, population (including Salé) 1,494,000. Regional capitals, with municipal population figures as at 1991, are: ΨCasablanca (2,990,000); Marrakesh (644,000); Fez (719,000); Oujda (646,000); Meknes (484,000); Ψ Agadir (420,000).

CURRENCY – Dirham (DH) of 100 centimes.

FLAG – Red, with green pentagram (the Seal of Solomon).

NATIONAL DAY – 3 March (Anniversary of the Throne).

GOVERNMENT

Morocco became an independent sovereign state in 1956, following joint declarations made with France on 2 March 1956 and with Spain on 7 April 1956. The Sultan of Morocco, Sidi Mohammad ben Youssef, adopted the title of King Mohammad V.

A new constitution based closely on that of 1972 was promulgated on 9 October 1992 after it had been approved by referendum on 4 September 1992. It provides that not only political parties, but trade unions, chambers of commerce and professional bodies will participate in the organization of the state and representation of the people; specifies that the King is the supreme representative of the people, the Head of State, Commander of the Faithful and Commander-in-Chief of the Royal Armed Forces; and states that Morocco is a democratic constitutional monarchy. The King nominates the Prime Minister and, on the latter's recommendation, appoints the members of the Council of Ministers. He presides over the Council of Ministers and appoints all ambassadors. The government is responsible both to parliament and to the King. The unicameral legislature (Chamber of Representatives) has 306 members, 204 elected by direct universal suffrage (including five representing overseas workers) and 102 members elected by electoral colleges representing local government, industry, agriculture and trade union groups. It may call votes of no confidence in the government.

Effective political power remains with the King despite the constitutional changes of October 1992 enhancing the Prime Minister's and Parliament's powers. The constitutional changes fell short of those demanded by opposition parties who called for a boycott of the referendum. Legislative elections under the new constitution were held in June 1993 and were won by the seven-party coalition government led by the Union Constitutionelle (UC) Party.

WESTERN SAHARA

Formerly the Spanish Sahara, the territory was split between Morocco and Mauritania in 1976 after Spain withdrew in December 1975. In 1979 Mauritania renounced its claim to its share of the territory, which was added by Morocco to its area. Morocco's annexation has been opposed by Polisario guerrillas, who want the territory to become an independent state. On 30 August 1988, Morocco and the Polisario Front accepted a UN peace plan. Under the plan a ceasefire came into effect in September 1991, and a referendum to determine the future of the area was to have been held in January 1992. However, the referendum was repeatedly postponed in 1992 because the Moroccan government and Polisario could not agree on the referendum terms or on who should be eligible to vote. Eventually on 2 March 1993 the UN Security Council approved resolution 809 which calls for a referendum to be held by the end of 1993 and that the referendum should be based on a straight choice between independence or integration with Morocco. Polisario and the Moroccan government held direct talks on the referendum in July 1993 but these collapsed after Polisario insisted only the 74,000 pre-1975 census population should be allowed to vote and

Morrocco insisted that 120,000 Moroccan immigrants since 1975 should vote also.

HEAD OF STATE

King, HM King Hassan II (Moulay Hassan Ben Mohammed), *born* 9 July 1929; *acceded* 3 March 1961.
Heir, Crown Prince Sidi Mohamed, *born* 21 August 1963.

MINISTERS *as at August 1993*

Prime Minister, Mohammed Karim Lamrani.
Minister of State, Moulay Ahmed Alaoui.
Minister of State, Foreign Affairs and Co-operation, Abdellatif Filali.
Justice, Moulay Mustapha Belarbi Alaoui.
Interior and Information, Driss Basri.
National Education, Prof. Tayeb Chkili.
Public Health, Dr Abderrahim Harouchi.
Religious Endowments and Islamic Affairs, Abdelkebir Alaoui M'Daghri.
Public Works, Vocational and Executive Training, Mohamed Kabbaj.
Finance, Mohamed Berrada.
Transport, Rachidi El-Rhezouani.
Energy and Mines, Moulay Driss Alqoui M'Daghri.
Youth and Sport, Abdallah Belekziz.
Sea Fisheries and the Merchant Marine, Bensalem Smili.
Secretary-General of the Government, Abbès El-Kaissi.
Culture, Allal Sinaceur.
Housing, Abderrahmane Bouftas.
Posts and Telecommunications, Abdeslam Ahizoune.
Agriculture and Agricultural Reform, Abdelaziz Meziane.
Trade, Industry and Privatization, Moulay Zahidi.
Employment, Handicraft and Social Affairs, Mohamed Loudghiri.
Tourism, Foreign Investments and Foreign Trade, Hassan Abouyoub.
Equipment, Senior Grades and Vocational Training, Mohammed Kabbaj.
Prime Minister's Office, Mohamed M'Daghri Alaoui (*Economic and Social Affairs*); Rafiq El Haddaoui (*Expatriates*); Aziz Hasbi (*Administrative Affairs*).

EMBASSY OF THE KINGDOM OF MOROCCO
49 Queen's Gate Gardens, London SW7 5NE
Tel 071-581 5001/4

Ambassador Extraordinary and Plenipotentiary, His Excellency Khalil Haddaoui (1991).

BRITISH EMBASSY
17 Boulevard de la Tour Hassan (BP 45), Rabat
Tel: Rabat 20905/6

Ambassador Extraordinary and Plenipotentiary, His Excellency Sir Allan Ramsay, KBE, CMG (1992).
There is a British Consulate-General/Commercial Office at *Casablanca,* an office of the Embassy at *Tangier* and an Honorary Consul at *Agadir.*

BRITISH COUNCIL REPRESENTATIVE, J. Weston, BP 427, 36 rue Tanger, Rabat.
BRITISH CHAMBER OF COMMERCE, 1st Floor, 185 Boulevard Zerktouni, Casablanca. Tel: 256920.

DEFENCE

The armed forces have a total active strength of 195,500, including authorized conscripts who serve 18 month terms. Total reserves number some 100,000 personnel. The Army has a strength of some 175,000, the majority of which has been deployed in southern Morocco and Western Sahara fighting the Polisario Front. It is equipped with 285 main battle tanks, 105 light tanks, 325 reconnaissance vehicles, 850 armoured infantry fighting vehicles and armoured personnel carriers, and 290 artillery pieces. The Army is organized into three mechanized infantry, two parachute and one light security brigades with 68 independent battalions (one Royal Guard, one mountain, three camel corps, three cavalry, four engineer, nine armoured, ten artillery and 37 infantry).

The Navy has a strength of 7,000, with one frigate, and 27 patrol and coastal combatant craft, together with a marine battalion. The Air Force has a strength of 13,500, with 90 combat aircraft and 24 armed helicopters, organized into one air defence, two ground attack, two counter-insurgency and one reconnaissance squadrons with tanker, transport and training units. In addition, there are a paramilitary Gendarmerie Royale of 10,000 and an Auxiliary Force of 30,000 paramilitaries.

Morocco deploys some 5,000 troops in the United Arab Emirates and 360 in Equatorial Guinea. The UN has some 370 personnel in Western Sahara pending the referendum. Polisario deploys some 4,000 front line and 6,000 support troops in Western Sahara with Algerian-supplied and captured Moroccan tanks, armoured personnel carriers, anti-tank and anti-aircraft weapons.

ECONOMY

Morocco's main sources of wealth are agricultural and mineral. The latest development plan (1987 onwards) emphasizes social improvement, industrial development, agriculture, fisheries and tourism.

Agriculture employs more than 40 per cent of the working population and accounts for about 36 per cent of exports. The main agricultural exports are fruit and vegetables. Cork and wood-pulp are the most important commercial forest products. Esparto grass is also produced. There is a fishing industry and substantial quantities of canned fish, mainly sardines and fishmeal, are exported.

For a developing country Morocco has a large industrial sector, which accounts for some 70 per cent of exports (including mineral exports). The main sectors are chemicals, textiles and leather goods, food processing and cement production. Manufacturing industries are centred in Casablanca, Fez, Tangier and Safi.

Morocco's mineral exports are phosphates, fluorite, barite, manganese, iron ore, lead, zinc, cobalt, copper and antimony. Morocco possesses nearly three-quarters of the world's estimated reserves of phosphates. There are oil refineries at Mohammedia and Sidi Kacem handling about four million tonnes of crude oil per year, but no significant quantities of hydrocarbons have been found.

Tourism is of increasing importance to the Moroccan economy, with development concentrated in Agadir and Marrakesh. In 1991 3,190,381 foreign tourists visited Morocco and tourism accounted for 3-4 per cent of GDP.

TRADE

Morocco's main imports are petroleum products, motor vehicles, building materials, agricultural and other machinery, chemical products, sugar, green tea and other foodstuffs. In 1991 58 per cent of Morocco's trade was with the EC and 12 per cent with other Arab states.

	1991
Imports	DH 59,720m
Exports	37,283m

Trade with UK	1991	1992
Imports from UK	£152,245,000	£123,301,000
Exports to UK	95,522,000	123,232,000

COMMUNICATIONS

Moroccan railroads cover 1,175 miles (1,893 km), linking the major towns. Traction is electric or diesel. An extensive network of 9,880 miles (15,900 km) of well-surfaced roads covers all the main towns.

There are air services between Casablanca, Tangier, Agadir (seasonal), Marrakesh and London, and also between Tangier and Gibraltar connecting with London. Royal-Air-Maroc operates internal services and services to 36 states in Europe, Africa and Asia.

In 1984 there were seven Arabic and five French daily newspapers.

EDUCATION

There are government primary, secondary and technical schools. In 1991 there were 4,890 government schools with a total of 3,608,757 pupils. At Fez there is a theological university of great repute in the Muslim world. There is a secular university at Rabat. A total of 206,725 students studied at 13 universities in 1991. Schools for special denominations, Jewish and Catholic, are permitted and may receive government grants. American schools operate in Rabat and Casablanca.

MOZAMBIQUE
República de Moçambique

Mozambique lies on the east coast of Africa, and is bounded by Swaziland in the south, South Africa in the south and west, Zimbabwe in the west, Zambia and Malawi in the north-west and Tanzania in the north. It has an area of 309,495 sq. miles (801,590 sq. km), with a population (1991 UN estimate) of 16,084,000. The official language is Portuguese.

CAPITAL – Ψ Maputo, estimated population (1990), 1,150,000. Other main ports are ΨBeira and ΨNacala.

CURRENCY – Metical (MT) of 100 centavos.

FLAG – Horizontally green, black, yellow with white fimbriations; a red triangle based on the hoist containing the national emblem.

NATIONAL DAY – 25 June (Independence Day).

GOVERNMENT

Mozambique, discovered by Vasco de Gama in 1498 and colonized by Portugal, achieved complete independence from Portugal on 25 June 1975. The country was a marxist one-party (Frelimo) state until a multi-party system was adopted in 1990. The new democratic constitution came into force on 30 November 1990, enshrining freedom of association and the free market. The legislative assembly has between 200 and 250 members.

Negotiations with the rebel Mozambique National Resistance (Renamo) continued in 1991-2 to end the 16-year civil war which has devastated much of the country. An agreement was reached between President Chissano and the Renamo leader Afonso Dhlakama in August 1992 and a ceasefire came into effect on 4 October 1992.

Under the General Peace Agreement the Frelimo government and Renamo troops were to have assembled at designated points around the country within one month of parliamentary ratification of the peace accord (which occurred on 9 October 1992) and to have handed over their weapons to UN monitors within six months. The majority of troops were to be demobilized and the remainder integrated to form a 30,000-strong Army and police force. However, the process was soon behind schedule, with arguments over demobilization points, the refusal of Renamo to disarm until it received US$15 million to fund its establishment as a political party, and the late arrival of UN forces. Despite the UN Operation for Mozambique (ONUMOZ) being approved by the Security Council on 16 December 1992, the 4,721 UN troops only arrived in May 1993 and were 2,800 short of the number originally planned. Multi-party presidential and legislative elections planned for June 1993 have been postponed to mid-1994. At the time of going to press only a limited amount of demobilization had occurred and Renamo was still refusing to move its headquarters to Maputo.

HEAD OF STATE
President, Joaquim Alberto Chissano, *sworn in* November 1986.

COUNCIL OF MINISTERS *as at August 1993*
Prime Minister, Mario da Graca Machungo.
Foreign Affairs, Pascoal Mocumbi.
National Defence, Alberto Joaquim Chipande.
Co-operation, Jacinto Veloso.
Minister in the Presidency, Feliciano Gundana.
State Administration, Aguiar Jonassane Reinaldo Mazula.
Education, Aniceto dos Muchangos.
Interior, Manuel Antonio.
Minister without Portfolio, Mariano de Araujo Matsinha.
Transport and Communications, Armando Emilio Guebuza.
Finance, Eneas Da Conceiçao Comiche.
Health, Dr Leonardo Simao.
Information, Rafael Maguni.
Construction and Water, Joao Salomao.
Trade, Daniel Gabriel Tembe.
Agriculture, Alexandre Jose Zandamela.
Industry and Energy, Octavio Muthemba.
Mineral Resources, John Kachamila.
Justice, Ossumane Ali Dauto.
Culture, Jose Mateus Katupha.
Labour, Teodato Mondim Da Silva Hunguana.

EMBASSY OF THE REPUBLIC OF MOZAMBIQUE
21 Fitzroy Square, London WIP 5HJ
Tel 071-383 3800

Ambassador Extraordinary and Plenipotentiary, His Excellency Armando Alexandre Panguene (1988).

BRITISH EMBASSY
Av. Vladimir I Lenine 310, CP 55, Maputo
Tel: Maputo 420111/2/5/6/7

Ambassador Extraordinary and Plenipotentiary, His Excellency Richard J. Edis (1992).

BRITISH COUNCIL REPRESENTATIVE, C. ffrench Blake, PO Box 4178, Maputo.

ECONOMY

The basis of the economy is subsistence agriculture, but there is an industrial sector based mainly in Beira and Maputo. After giving priority to the development of collective farms and state enterprises in all sectors, the government is now encouraging the private sector and foreign investment, particularly in agriculture and consumer goods production. There are substantial coal deposits in Tete province. Mozambique has a range of aid and co-operation agreements with a number of countries in eastern Europe and in the West. An agreement of non-aggression and good neighbourliness with South Africa was signed in 1984 (the Nkomati Accord).

TRADE

Main exports are sugar, cashew nuts, prawns, copra, cotton, tea and sisal.

Trade with UK	1991	1992
Imports from UK	£18,851,000	£17,008,000
Exports to UK	2,393,000	2,593,000

MYANMAR
Pyidaungsu Myanma Naingngandaw - Union of Myanmar

Myanmar (Burma) forms the western portion of the Indo-Chinese part of Asia, lying between 9° 58′ and 28° N. latitude and 92° 11′ and 101° 9′ E. longitude, with an extreme length of approximately 1,200 miles and an extreme width of 575 miles. It has a sea coast on the Bay of Bengal to the south and west, and a frontier with Bangladesh along the Naaf River and with India to the north-west. In the north and east the country borders China and there is a short frontier with Laos in the east, while the long finger of Tenasserim stretches southwards along the west coast of the Malay peninsula, forming a frontier with Thailand to the east. The total area is 261,218 sq. miles (676,552 sq. km).

There are four natural divisions. Arakan (with the Chin Hills region), the Irrawaddy basin, Tenasserim, including the Salween basin and extending southwards to the Myanmar-Thailand peninsula, and the elevated plateau on the east. Mountains enclose the Union on three sides. The principal river systems are the Kaladan-Lemro in Arakan, the Irrawaddy-Chindwin and the Sittang in central Myanmar, and the Salween which flows through the Shan Plateau.

POPULATION – The population (UN estimate 1991) is 42,561,000. The indigenous inhabitants are of similar racial types and speak languages of the Tibeto-Burman, Mon-Khmer and Thai groups. The three important non-indigenous elements are Indians, Chinese and those from Bangladesh.

LANGUAGES – Burmese is the official language, but minority languages include Shan, Karen, Chin, Kayah and the various Kachin dialects. English is spoken in educated circles.

RELIGION – Buddhism is the religion of 85 per cent of the people, with 5 per cent Animists, 4 per cent Muslims, 4 per cent Hindus and less than 3 per cent Christians.

CAPITAL – ΨYangon (Rangoon). Population (1983): Yangon District 3,973,872; city population 2,458,712. The other major cities are Mandalay, population (1983): Mandalay district 4,580,923; city 532,985; Mawlamyine (Moulmein) 219,991 and Pathein (Bassein) 144,092. Pagan, on the Irrawaddy, contains many sacred buildings.

CURRENCY – Kyat (K) of 100 pyas.

FLAG – Red, with a canton of dark blue, inside which are a cogwheel and two rice ears surrounded by 14 white stars.

NATIONAL DAY – 4 January.

GOVERNMENT

The Union of Burma (the name was officially changed to the Union of Myanmar in June 1989) became an independent republic outside the British Commonwealth on 4 January 1948 and remained a parliamentary democracy for 14 years. On 2 March 1962 the army took power and suspended the parliamentary constitution. A Revolutionary Council of senior officers under General Ne Win took measures to create a socialist state.

After months of popular demonstrations and rioting and a series of presidents throughout the summer of 1988, Gen.

Saw Maung, leader of the armed forces, assumed power in September 1988. The People's Assembly, the Council of State and the Council of Ministers were abolished and replaced by the State Law and Order Restoration Council (SLORC) headed by Gen. Saw Maung as Prime Minister. The constitution was effectively abrogated.

A People's Assembly Election Law was published in March 1989 committing the SLORC to hold multi-party elections. These were held on 27 May 1990, resulting in a majority for the National League for Democracy (NLD). The SLORC refused to transfer power to a civilian government and large numbers of NLD members were detained, including their leader, Aung San Suu Kyi. However, following the replacement of Saw Maung by Than Shwe as SLORC Chairman and Prime Minister in April 1992, the government announced that it would begin a dialogue with some elements of the opposition. A Constitutional Convention of delegates appointed by the SLORC to discuss a future constitution convened in January 1993, was almost immediately adjourned, re-opened in February and was adjourned again in April after the majority of the delegates refused to accept the leading role in politics demanded by the armed forces. The SLORC has released many political detainees, although Aung San Suu Kyi has not been freed.

A 'National Coalition Government of the Union of Burma', led by Sein Winn, was established in December 1990 at Manerplaw on the Thai border by NLD members and other opposition groups. In 1992 a Burmese Army offensive failed to capture the NCGUB base at Mannerplaw.

POLITICAL DIVISIONS

Myanmar is comprised of seven states (Chin, Kachin, Kayin (Karen), Kayah, Mon, Rakhine, Shan) and seven divisions (Irrawaddy, Magwe, Mandalay, Pegu, Yangon (Rangoon), Sagaing, Tenasserim).

CABINET *as at August 1993*

Chairman of SLORC, Prime Minister and Minister of Defence, Gen. Than Shwe.
Deputy Prime Ministers, Vice-Adm. Maung Maung Khin; Lt.-Gen. Tin Tun.
Agriculture, Maj.-Gen. Myint Aung.
Border Areas, Maj.-Gen. Maung Thint.
Communications, Posts and Telegraphs, U Soe Tha.
Construction, U Khin Maung Yin.
Co-operatives, U Than Aung.
Culture, Lt.-Gen. Aung Ye Kyaw.
Education, Col. Pe Thein.
Energy, U Khin Maung Thein.
Finance and Revenue, Brig.-Gen. Win Tin.
Foreign Affairs, U Ohn Gyaw.
Forestry, Lt.-Gen. Chit Swe.
Health, Rear-Adm. Than Nyunt.
Home, Maj.-Gen. Mya Thinn.
Hotels and Tourism, Maj.-Gen. Kyaw Ba.
Industry, Lt.-Gen. Sein Aung.
Information, Brig.-Gen. Myo Thant.
Labour, Maj.-Gen. Aye Thoung.
Livestock Breeding and Fisheries, Brig.-Gen. Maung Maung.
Mines, Maj.-Gen. Kyaw Min.
Office of the Prime Minister, Brig.-Gen. Lun Maung.
Planning and Finance, Brig.-Gen. Abel.
Rail and Transportation, U Win Sein.
Religious Affairs, Maj.-Gen. Myo Nyunt.
Social Welfare, Brig.-Gen. Thaung Myint.
Trade, Maj.-Gen. Tun Kyi.
Transport, Maj.-Gen. Thein Win.

EMBASSY OF THE UNION OF MYANMAR
19A Charles Street, Berkeley Square, London WIX 8ER
Tel 071-629 6966

Ambassador Extraordinary and Plenipotentiary, His Excellency U Hla Maung (1992).

BRITISH EMBASSY
80 Strand Road (Box No. 638), Rangoon
Tel: Rangoon 81700

Ambassador Extraordinary and Plenipotentiary, His Excellency Julian Hartland-Swann, CMG (1990).
Deputy Head of Mission, First Secretary (Commercial) and Consul, P. R. Hagart.
Cultural Attaché and British Council Representative, Ralph Isaacs, OBE.

EDUCATION

The literacy rate is high compared to other Asian countries. There is no caste system and women engage freely in social intercourse and play an important part in agriculture and retail trade.

Most children attend primary school, and about four million are currently enrolled; in middle and high schools, enrolment is about 11 million. There are five universities, at Yangon (Rangoon), Mandalay, Taunggyi, Sagaing and Mawlamyine (Moulmein). Under the universities are three affiliated degree colleges and the Workers' College, Yangon. There are also 14 two-year colleges affiliated to the universities, spread throughout the country.

There are three teachers' training institutes for middle and primary schools, and 13 teachers' training schools for primary only. Seven government technical institutes offer post-secondary technical training courses and 14 technical high schools train semi-skilled tradesmen. Six agricultural institutes offer training courses in agriculture and veterinary science; nine agricultural high schools train semi-skilled agriculturists. There are 34 vocational schools for weaving, handicrafts, etc.

ECONOMY

The chief sources of revenue are profits on state trading, income tax, customs duties, commercial taxes and excise duties; the chief heads of expenditure are defence, education and police. The budget estimates for 1992–3 were: Revenue K53,867 million; expenditure, K57,203 million.

Three-quarters of the population depend on agriculture; the chief products are rice, oilseeds (sesamum and ground-nut), maize, millet, cotton, beans, wheat, grain, tea, sugarcane, tobacco, jute and rubber. Rice was for many years the mainstay of the economy, but in 1985 teak overtook rice.

Myanmar is rich in minerals, including petroleum, lead, silver, tungsten, zinc, tin, wolfram and gemstones. Of these, petroleum products are the most important. Oil is now being produced from oilfields in Myanaung, Prome and Shwepyitha and at Chauk, Yenangyaung, Mann, and Letpando. Production of crude oil in 1991–2 totalled 5,500,000 US barrels. There are refineries at Chauk, the main oilfield, Syriam and Mann. There has been a steady decline in oil production in recent years and the country is no longer self-sufficient. Onshore exploration continues. There has also been some offshore oil exploration on a small scale. Major reserves of natural gas have been discovered in the Martaban Gulf, which Myanmar is hoping to develop.

All industrial activity of any size is in the public sector. Under development plans, projects completed or under construction with overseas financial and technical assistance include the production of cement, bricks and tiles, sheet glass, steel sections, jute bags and twine, cotton yarns and cloth, pharmaceuticals, sugar, paper, plywood, urea fertilizers, soda ash, tractors and tyres; also a hydro-electric scheme and various irrigation works.

Faced with a serious foreign exchange shortage, Myanmar was included in the UN's list of Least Developed Countries in December 1987.

A new ministry was established in 1992 with the task of attracting 500,000 tourists; less than 10,000 visited in 1991. The Central Bank made available foreign exchange certificates denominated in US dollars from February 1993 for the convenience of tourists, who will not be required to convert their funds into local currency.

TRADE WITH UK	1991	1992
Imports from UK	£8,294,000	£9,145,000
Exports to UK	2,771,000	5,046,000

COMMUNICATIONS

The Irrawaddy and its chief tributary, the Chindwin, are important waterways, the main stream being navigable beyond Bhamo (900 miles from its mouth) and carrying much traffic. The chief seaports are Yangon (Rangoon), Mawlamyine (Moulmein), Akyab (Sittwe) and Pathein (Bassein).

The railway network covers 2,764 route miles, extending to Myitkyina, on the Upper Irrawaddy. There were 2,452 miles of highways and 11,767 miles of other main roads in 1982–3. The airport at Mingaladon, about 13 miles north of Yangon (Rangoon), only handles limited international air traffic.

NAMIBIA
The Republic of Namibia

Namibia stretches from the southern border of Angola (lat. 17° 23′ S.) to the northern (Orange River) and north-western borders of the Cape Province of the Republic of South Africa; and from the Atlantic Ocean in the west to Botswana in the east. The average rainfall over 70 per cent of the country is below 400 mm per annum.

Namibia has an area of 318,261 sq. miles (824,292 sq. km), including the area of Walvis Bay (434 sq. miles) which is claimed by Namibia. Previously a British and South African colony separate from German South West Africa and later Namibia, Walvis Bay has been governed since August 1992 by the joint South African-Namibian Walvis Bay Administrative Body as neither South Africa nor Namibia would yield its claim to the territory. On 16 August 1993 the multi-party constitutional negotiations in South Africa reached agreement on transferring sovereignty over Walvis Bay to Namibia as soon as possible.

POPULATION – The population was estimated by the UN at 1,837,000 in 1991. The main population groups are: Ovambo (587,000), Kavango (110,000), Damara (89,000), Herero (89,000), Whites (78,000), Nama (57,000), Coloured (48,000), Caprivians (44,000), Bushmen (34,000), Rehoboth Baster (29,000), Tswana (7,000).

CAPITAL – Windhoek (population, 1987 estimate, 110,000). The only port of any size is ΨWalvis Bay.

CURRENCY – Namibian Dollar of 100 cents, introduced in September 1993 at parity to South African rand (the previous currency).

FLAG – Divided diagonally blue, red and green with the red fimbriated in white; a gold twelve-rayed sun in the upper hoist.

NATIONAL DAY – 21 March (Independence Day).

HISTORY

The German protectorate of South West Africa from 1880 to 1915, Namibia was administered until the end of 1920 by the Union of South Africa. Under the terms of the Treaty of Versailles, the territory was entrusted to South Africa with full powers of administration and legislation over the territory. After the dissolution of the League of Nations and in the absence of a trusteeship agreement, South Africa informed the United Nations that it would continue to administer South West Africa.

In 1971 the International Court of Justice at The Hague delivered a majority opinion that the continued presence of South Africa was illegal, and that it was to withdraw its administration from Namibia immediately, putting an end to its occupation of the territory. The South African Government rejected this opinion, but accepted the principle that the territory should attain independence. In 1977 five Western members of the UN Security Council drew up a plan, later incorporated into Security Council Resolution 435, for a peaceful settlement.

Agreement was reached in December 1988 for the withdrawal over 27 months of Cuban troops in Angola in exchange for South African withdrawal from Namibia leading to Namibian independence under UN Security Council Resolution 435. Implementation of Resolution 435 began on 1 April 1989 and elections for 72 seats in Namibia's first nationally elected body took place under UN supervision on 7–11 November 1989. The South West Africa People's Organization (SWAPO) won 41 seats, the Democratic Turnhalle Alliance 21 seats, the United Democratic Front 4 seats, Action Christian National 3, Namibia Patriotic Front 1, Federal Convention of Namibia 1, and Namibia National Front 1.

The Independence Constitution was adopted on 9 February 1990, and independence was declared on 21 March 1990. Namibia joined the Commonwealth upon independence.

GOVERNMENT

Constitutionally defined as a multiparty, secular, democratic republic, Namibia has an executive President as head of state who exercises the functions of government with the assistance of a Cabinet headed by a Prime Minister. Legislative authority lies with the National Assembly, which is the lower house of a bicameral parliament; an upper house (National Council) representing regional councils was elected in November 1992 and inaugurated in January 1993. Each regional council appoints two representatives to the National Council. The main function of the National Council is to review and consider legislation from the National Assembly. Under a system of proportional representation, elections to the National Assembly are to take place every five years (there will be 96 seats contested at the next election), or earlier if decided by the President. Members of the National Council hold their seats for six years.

HEAD OF STATE
President, Dr Sam Nujoma, *elected*, 16 February 1990.

CABINET *as at August 1993*
Prime Minister, Hon. Hage Geingob.
Home Affairs, Hon. Hifikepunye Pohamba.
Foreign Affairs, Hon. Theo-Ben Gurirab.
Defence, Hon. Peter Mueshihange.
Finance, Hon. Gerhard Hanekom.
Education and Culture, Hon. Nahas Angula.
Information and Broadcasting, Hon. Ben Amathila.
Health and Social Services, Hon. Dr Nicky Iyambo.
Labour, Public Service and Manpower Development, Hon. Hendrik Witbooi.
Mines and Energy, Hon. Andimba Toivo Ya Toivo.
Justice, Hon. Ngarikutuke Tjiriange.
Local Government and Housing, Hon. Libertine Amathila.
Agriculture, Water and Rural Development, Hon. Anton von Wietersheim.
Trade and Industry, Hon. Hidipo Hamutenya.
Wildlife and Conservation, and Tourism, Hon. Nico Bessinger.
Works, Transport, and Communication, Hon. Marco Hausiku.
Lands, Resettlement and Rehabilitation, Hon. Richard Kapelwa.
Youth and Sport, Hon. Pendukeni Iithana.
Fisheries and Marine Resources, Hon. Helmut Angula.
State Security, Hon. Peter Tshirumbu.

HIGH COMMISSION OF THE REPUBLIC OF NAMIBIA
34 South Molton Street, London WIY 2BP
Tel 071-344 9706

High Commissioner, His Excellency Veiccoh K. Nghiwete (1991).

BRITISH HIGH COMMISSION
116 Robert Mugabe Avenue, Windhoek 9000
Tel: Windhoek 223022

High Commissioner, His Excellency Henry George Hogger (1992).

BRITISH COUNCIL REPRESENTATIVE, J. Utley, PO Box 24224, 74 Bülowstrasse, Windhoek 9000.

ECONOMY

Mining (mainly diamonds and uranium), agriculture and fisheries account for over 40 per cent of Namibia's GDP. Most of the labour force is employed in the agricultural sector.

TRADE WITH UK	1991	1992
Imports from UK	£3,981,000	£6,730,000
Exports to UK	19,606,000	16,766,000

NAURU
The Republic of Nauru

Nauru is an island of 8.2 sq. miles (21 sq. km) in size, situated in 166° 55′ E. longitude and 0° 32′ S. of the Equator. It had a population (Census May 1983) of 8,042 (Nauruans 4,964; other Pacific Islanders 2,134; Asians 682; Caucasians 262). The UN estimated a total population of 9,000 in 1991. About 43 per cent of Nauruans are adherents of the Nauruan Protestant Church and there is a Roman Catholic Mission on the island. The main languages are English and Nauruan.

CURRENCY – Nauru uses the Australian dollar ($A) of 100 cents as legal tender.

FLAG – Twelve-point star (representing the 12 original Nauruan tribes) below a gold bar (representing the Equator), all on a blue ground.

NATIONAL DAY – 31 January (Independence Day).

GOVERNMENT

From 1888 until the First World War Nauru was administered by Germany, in 1920 becoming a British mandated territory under the League of Nations administered by Australia. A trusteeship superseding the mandate was approved in 1947 by the UN and Nauru continued to be administered by Australia until it became independent on 31 January 1968. It was announced in November 1968 that a special form of membership of the Commonwealth had been devised for Nauru at the request of its government.

Parliament has eighteen members including the Cabinet and Speaker. Voting is compulsory for all Nauruans over 20 years of age, except in certain specified instances. Elections are held every three years. The Cabinet is chosen by the President, who is elected by the Parliament from amongst its members, and comprises not fewer than five nor more than six members including the President.

HEAD OF STATE
President and Minister for External Affairs, Island Development and Industry, Civil Aviation Authority and the Public Service, His Excellency Hon. Bernard Dowiyogo.

CABINET *as at August 1993*

Internal Affairs, Works and Community Services and Minister Assisting the President, Hon. Vinson Detenamo.
Finance, Hon. Vinci Clodumar.
Education, Hon. Nimes Ekewona.
Justice, Hon. Derog Gioura.
Health, Hon. Ludwig Scotti.

BRITISH HIGH COMMISSION
British High Commissioner (resides at Suva, Fiji).

JUDICIARY

A Supreme Court of Nauru is presided over by the Chief Justice. The District Court, which is subordinate to the Supreme Court, is presided over by a Resident Magistrate. Both the Supreme Court and the District Court are courts of record. The Supreme Court exercises both original and appellate jurisdiction.

SOCIAL SERVICES

Nauru has a hospital service and other medical and dental services. There is also a maternity and child welfare service.

Education is available in nine primary and two secondary schools on the island with a total enrolment of about 1,600 pupils receiving primary education and 500 secondary education.

ECONOMY

The only fertile areas are the narrow coastal belt and local requirements of fruit and vegetables are mostly met by imports. The economy is heavily dependent on the extraction of phosphate, of which the island has one of the world's richest deposits. About 1.5 million tonnes of phosphate are mined each year, providing employment for over 1,000 people. The industry has been run since 1970 by the Nauru Phosphate Corporation. Considerable investments have been made abroad with the royalties on phosphate exports to provide for a time when production declines. In August 1993 an agreement was signed with Australia for compensation to cover damage caused by phosphate mining during the Australian mandate and trusteeship periods. The compensation package is worth some £50 million, composed of a £33 million gift and a 20-year package of health and education programmes.

The Nauru Pacific Line owns six ships; the Government-owned Air Nauru operates air services throughout the Pacific region and to Australia, New Zealand, Japan, Singapore and the Philippines.

TRADE WITH UK	1991	1992
Imports from UK	£1,189,000	£904,000
Exports to UK	718,000	1,000

NEPAL

Nepal lies between India and the Tibet Autonomous Region of China on the slopes of the Himalayas, and includes Mount Everest (29,078 ft). It has a total area of 54,342 sq. miles (140,747 sq. km).

The country comprises three distinct regions. In the south, joining the Indian plains, is the Terai, much of which was covered with jungle. It has been more widely cultivated recently but wild life is preserved in parts. The region represents 23 per cent of the total land area and nearly 44 per cent of the population live there. The central belt of the country is hilly, but with many fertile valleys, leading up to the snowline at about 16,000 feet. The hills account for 42 per cent of the area of the country and about 48 per cent of the population. The remainder of the country, the Himalayan region, consists of high mountains which are sparsely inhabited. The country is drained by three great river systems rising within and beyond the Himalayan mountain ranges and eventually flowing into the Ganges in India.

POPULATION – The population was (UN estimate 1991) 19,605,000. The inhabitants are of mixed stock, with Mongolian characteristics prevailing in the north and Indian in the south.

RELIGION – The official religion is Hinduism: 89.5 per cent of the population are Hindus and 6 per cent are Buddhist. Gautama Buddha was born in Nepal.

CAPITAL – Kathmandu, population (1989) 300,000. Other towns of importance are Biratnagar (94,000), Lalitpur (81,000) and Bhaktapur (50,500), and Pokhara (48,500).
CURRENCY – Nepalese rupee of 100 paisa.
FLAG – Double pennant of crimson with blue border on peaks; white moon with rays in centre of top peak; white quarter sun, recumbent in centre of bottom peak.
NATIONAL ANTHEM – May Glory Crown Our Illustrious Sovereign.
NATIONAL DAY – 18 February (National Democracy Day).

GOVERNMENT

The country was originally divided into numerous hill clans and petty principalities, but Nepal emerged as a nation in the middle of the 18th century when it was unified by the warrior Raja of Gorkha, Prithvi Narayan Shah, who founded the present Nepalese dynasty. In 1846 power was seized by Jung Bahadur Rana after a massacre of nobles, and he was the first of a line of hereditary Rana Prime Ministers who ruled Nepal for 104 years. During this time the role of the monarchs was mainly ceremonial.

In 1950–1 a revolutionary movement achieved its aim of breaking the hereditary power of the Ranas and restoring the monarchy to its former position. After ten years, during which various parties and individuals tried their hand at government, King Mahendra proscribed all political parties and assumed direct powers on 16 December 1960, with the object of leading a united country to democracy. In 1962 he introduced a new constitution embodying a tiered, partyless system of panchyat (council) democracy.

Mass agitation for political reform led in April 1990 to the lifting of the ban on political parties and the abolition of the panchyat system. A new constitution was promulgated in November 1990 establishing a multi-party, parliamentary system of government and a constitutional monarchy. The King retained joint executive power with the Council of Ministers. A bicameral legislature was set up, consisting of a 205-member House of Representatives and a 60-member National Council, including ten royal nominees. Elections, held on 12 May 1991, were won by the Nepali Congress Party.

HEAD OF STATE
Sovereign, HM King Birendra Bir Bikram Shah Dev, born 28 December 1945; succeeded 31 January 1972; crowned 24 February 1975; married, February 1970, HM Queen Aishwatya Rajya Laxmi Devi Shah.
Heir, HRH Crown Prince Dipendra Bir Bikram Shah Dev, born 27 June 1971.

COUNCIL OF MINISTERS as at August 1993
Prime Minister, Minister of Defence, Foreign Affairs, Royal Palace Affairs, Girija Prasad Koirala.
Housing and Physical Planning, Bal Bahadur Rai.
Land Reform and Management, Siddhi Raj Ofha.
Tourism, Ramhari Joshi.
Agriculture, Ram Chandra Poudel.
Home Affairs, Sher Bahadur Deupa.
Local Development, Shailaja Acharya.
General Administration, Law and Justice, and Parliamentary Affairs, Maheswor Prasad Singh.
Works and Transport, Khum Bahadur Khadka.
Education, Culture and Social Welfare, Govinda Raj Joshi.

ROYAL NEPALESE EMBASSY
12A Kensington Palace Gardens, London W8 4QU
Tel 071-229 1594/6231

Ambassador Extraordinary and Plenipotentiary, His Excellency Surya Prasad Shrestha (1992).
Counsellor, Madhab Prasad Khanal.

BRITISH EMBASSY
Lainchaur Kathmandu, PO Box 106
Tel: Kathmandu 410583

Ambassador Extraordinary and Plenipotentiary, His Excellency Timothy George, CMG (1990).

BRITISH COUNCIL REPRESENTATIVE, R. P. Hale, (PO Box 640), Kantipath, Kathmandu.

ECONOMY

Nepal exports carpets, jute, handicrafts, garments, hides and skins, medicinal herbs, cardamom, pulses, tea, etc., and imports textiles, machinery and parts, transport equipment, medicine, construction materials etc. Tourism is the single largest commercial earner of foreign exchange (US$55.9 million in 1986–7).

The budget for the fiscal year 1993–4 is estimated at NRs. 35,513.9 million, of which NRs. 12,888 million was allocated to regular and NRs. 22,625.9 million to development expenditures. Revenue was estimated at NRs. 16,424.5 million, foreign aid and grants NRs. 4,328.5 million, and domestic borrowing NRs. 1,820 million.

In October 1992 the IMF approved a three-year loan of US$49 million to support Nepal's medium-term economic reform programme. In February 1993 the rupee was floated and made fully convertible.

TRADE WITH UK	1991	1992
Imports from UK	£4,938,000	£6,300,000
Exports to UK	4,531,000	5,888,000

COMMUNICATIONS

The total length of roads in Nepal in 1987–8 was 6,525 km. Most of the major roads have been built since the 1960s, often with aid from India and China. Kathmandu is connected by road with India and Tibet. Internally, the road network links Kathmandu to Kodari and Pokhara, and Pokhara to Sunauli. A road between Mugling and Naryanghat has further improved communications between Kathmandu and the Terai. The East–West Highway (Mahendra Raj Marg) running along the entire length of the country is complete except for the Banbasa-Mahakali section.

Telecommunication services, both domestic and international, are available from the Central Telegraph Office or hotels. There are international subscriber dialling facilities from Nepal to 35 countries. Nepal television was introduced in 1984.

Royal Nepal Airlines operates an extensive network of domestic flights, and there are international flights to Europe, the Middle East and throughout Asia.

THE NETHERLANDS
Koninkrijk der Nederlanden

The kingdom of the Netherlands is a maritime country of western Europe, situated on the North Sea, in 50° 46′ to 53° 34′ N. latitude and 3° 22′ to 7° 14′ E. longitude, consisting of 12 provinces (Eastern and Southern Flevoland being amalgamated to form the twelfth province) and containing a total area of 15,770 sq. miles (40,844 sq. km).

The land is generally flat and low, intersected by numerous canals and connecting rivers. The principal rivers are the Rhine, Maas, Yssel and Scheldt.

POPULATION – The population (1991 estimate) is 15,240,000.

LANGUAGE – Dutch is a West Germanic language of Saxon origin, closely akin to Old English and Low German. It is spoken in the Netherlands and the northern part of Belgium. It is also used in the Netherlands Antilles.

CAPITAL – ΨAmsterdam, population 1,031,000 (urban agglomeration), 713,407 (city) (1992).

SEAT OF GOVERNMENT – The Hague (Den Haag or, in full, 's-Gravenhage), population 445,287 (1992). Other principal cities (1992) ΨRotterdam 589,707; Utrecht, 232,705; Eindhoven, 193,966; Haarlem 149,788; Groningen 169,387; Tilburg 160,618.

CURRENCY – Netherlands guilder of 100 cents.

FLAG – Three horizontal bands of red, white and blue.

NATIONAL ANTHEM – Wilhelmus.

GOVERNMENT

In 1815 the Netherlands became a constitutional kingdom under King William I, a descendant of the house of Orange-Nassau which had taken a leading part in the destiny of the nation since the 16th century.

The States-General consists of the *Eerste Kamer* (First Chamber) of 75 members, elected for four years by the Provincial Council; and the *Tweede Kamer* (Second Chamber) of 150 members, elected for four years by voters of 18 years and upwards. Members of the *Tweede Kamer* are paid. The most recent election to the Second Chamber was held in September 1989, and resulted in the formation of a centre-left coalition.

HEAD OF STATE

Queen of the Netherlands, HM Queen Beatrix Wilhelmina Armgard, KG, GCVO, *born* 31 January 1938; *succeeded* 30 April 1980, upon the abdication of her mother Queen Juliana; *married* 10 March 1966, HRH Prince Claus George Willem Otto Frederik Geert of the Netherlands, Jonkheer van Amsberg; and has *issue*, Prince Willem Alexander, *b.* 27 April 1967; Prince Johan Friso, *b.* 25 September 1968; Prince Constantijn Christof, *b.* 11 October 1969.

CABINET *as at August 1993*

Prime Minister, Minister of General Affairs, Ruud Lubbers (CDA).

Deputy PM and Minister of Finance, W. Kok (PvdA).

Home Affairs, Mrs C. J. Dales (PvdA).

Foreign Affairs, Dr P. H. Kooijmans (CDA).

Development Co-operation, J. Pronk (PvdA).

Defence, A. L. ter Beek (PvdA).

Economic Affairs, Dr J. E. Andriessen (CDA).

Antillian Affairs and Justice, Prof. E. H. M. Hirsch Ballin (PvdA).

Agriculture and Fisheries, P. Bukman (CDA).

Education and Science, Prof. Dr J. M. M. Ritzen (PvdA).

Social Affairs and Employment, Dr B. de Vries (CDA).

Transport and Public Works, Mrs H. May-Weggen (CDA).

Housing, Physical Planning and Environment, J. G. M. Alders (PvdA).

Welfare, Health and Culture, Mrs H. d'Acona (PvdA).

CDA   Christian Democratic Appeal
PvdA   Labour Party.

ROYAL NETHERLANDS EMBASSY
38 Hyde Park Gate, London SW7 5DP
Tel 071-584 5040

Ambassador Extraordinary and Plenipotentiary, His Excellency Joop Hoekman (1990).

Ministers Plenipotentiary, M. H. R. Loudon; A. J. Quanjer (*Economic*).

Consul-General, G. J. Schulten.

Defence, Naval and Air Attaché, Capt. Willem F. L. van Leeuwen.

BRITISH EMBASSY
Lange Voorhout 10, The Hague, 2514 ED
Tel: The Hague 364 5800

Ambassador Extraordinary and Plenipotentiary, His Excellency Sir David Miers, KBE, CMG (1993).

Counsellors, R. P. Flower (*Deputy Head of Mission*); A. D. Sprake (*Commercial*).

Defence and Naval Attaché, Capt. H. W. Rickard, RN.

Consul-General, D. H. Doble (*resides at Amsterdam*).

There is a Consulate-General at Amsterdam, a Consulate at Willemstad (*Curaçao*) and a Vice-Consulate at Philipsburg (*St Maarten*) (both Netherlands Antilles).

BRITISH COUNCIL REPRESENTATIVE, J. Andrews, Keizersgracht 343, 1016 EH Amsterdam.

NETHERLANDS-BRITISH CHAMBER OF COMMERCE, The Dutch House, 307–308 High Holborn, London WC1V 7LS.

UK OFFICE IN THE HAGUE, Holland Trade House, Bezuidenhoutseweg 181, 2594 AH The Hague.

ECONOMY

The chief agricultural products are potatoes, wheat, rye, barley, sugar beet, cattle, pigs, milk and milk products, cheese, butter, poultry, eggs, beans, peas, vegetables, fruit, flower bulbs, plants and cut flowers and there is an important fishing industry.

Among the principal industries are engineering, electronics, nuclear energy, petro-chemicals and plastics, road vehicles, aircraft and defence equipment, shipbuilding repair, steel, textiles of all types, electrical appliances, metal ware, furniture, paper, cigars, sugar, liqueurs, beer, clothing etc.

Of a total GNP of US$279.1 billion in 1990, industry accounted for around 31 per cent, agriculture for 4 per cent and services 65 per cent. Excluding the construction industry, the index of industrial production in the Netherlands (1980 = 100) was 109 in 1989. Inflation was 3.7 per cent in 1992.

FINANCE	1991
Budget Revenue	Guilders 176,327m
Budget Expenditure	170,666m

TRADE

The Dutch are traditionally a trading nation. Trade, banking and shipping are of particular importance to the economy. The geographical position of the Netherlands, at the mouths of the Rhine, Meuse and Scheldt, brings a large volume of transit trade to and from the interior of Europe to Dutch ports.

Principal trading partners are Germany, Belgium/ Luxembourg and France. UK supplied 8.7 per cent of Netherlands imports in 1991 and took 9.3 per cent of Netherlands exports.

	1991	1992
Imports	Guilders 118,194m	Guilders 117,526m
Exports	124,862m	126,119m

Trade with UK	1991	1992
Imports from UK	£8,258,475,000	£8,484,040,000
Exports to UK	9,969,981,000	9,908,795,000

DEFENCE

The armed forces are almost entirely committed to NATO. Total armed forces number some 93,000, which includes 43,500 conscripts and 2,600 women. In addition there are 144,300 reservists. There is compulsory military service of 12-15 months. In January 1993 the government announced plans to reduce the term of conscription from 1994 from 12-15 months to nine months and to abolish it in 1998.

The Army has a strength of 60,800 (38,000 conscripts) with 913 main battle tanks, 3,180 armoured infantry fighting vehicles and armoured personnel carriers, 824 artillery pieces and 90 armed helicopters. The regular army forms two armoured and four mechanized infantry brigades, three field artillery regiments and one aviation wing. The regular army also forms the cadres of one armoured, one infantry and two mechanized infantry brigades which are completed by the 125,300-strong reserves.

The Navy has a strength of 15,500, including 900 naval air arm, 2,400 marines and 1,600 conscripts. It maintains a force of five submarines, four destroyers, 12 frigates with mine warfare, amphibious and support ships, 13 combat aircraft and 22 armed helicopters. The Air Force has a strength of 12,000 (3,500 conscripts), with some 188 combat aircraft, all of which are variants of the US-manufactured F16. The Air Force is organized into four ground attack, four air defence, one transport, one reconnaissance and two training squadrons.

As part of its NATO commitment, the Netherlands maintains 4,700 Army personnel in Germany and is the base for HQ Allied Forces Central Europe, and for 2,300 US personnel.

There is also a paramilitary Royal Military Constabulary of 3,900 personnel (400 conscripts).

EDUCATION

Primary and secondary education is given in both denominational and state schools, the denominational schools being eligible for state assistance on equal terms with the state schools. Attendance at primary school is compulsory.

The principal universities are at Leiden, Utrecht, Groningen, Amsterdam (two), Nijmegen, Maastricht and Rotterdam, and there are technical universities at Delft, Eindhoven, Enschede and Wageningen (agriculture).

COMMUNICATIONS

The total extent of navigable rivers including canals, was 5,046 km at 1 January 1992, and of metalled roads 104,831 km. In 1992 the total length of the railway system amounted to 2,780 km, of which 1,939 km were electrified. The mercantile marine in 1992 consisted of 410 ships of total 2,890,000 gross registered tons. The total of kilometres flown by KLM (Royal Dutch Airlines) in 1991-2 was 188 million km.

There are six national papers, four of which are morning papers, and there are many regional daily papers.

OVERSEAS TERRITORIES

ARUBA

Aruba covers an area of 75 sq. miles (193 sq. km) with a population (1991 UN estimate) of 59,000. The island of Aruba was from 1828 part of the Dutch West Indies and from 1845 part of the Netherlands Antilles. On 1 January 1986 it became a separate territory within the Kingdom of the Netherlands. The 1983 Constitutional Conference agreed that Aruba's separate status would last for ten years from 1986, after which the island would become fully independent.
Governor, F. B. Tromp.
Prime Minister, Nelson Oduber.

CAPITAL – ΨOranjestad (population 20,000); and Sint Nicolaas (17,000).
CURRENCY – Aruban florin.

ECONOMY – The economy of Aruba is based largely on tourism. In 1986 there were over 180,000 tourists.

Trade with UK	1991	1992
Imports from UK	£18,934,000	£27,292,000
Exports to UK	6,365,000	4,495,000

NETHERLANDS ANTILLES

The Netherlands Antilles comprise the islands of Curaçao, Bonaire, part of St Martin, St Eustatius, and Saba in the West Indies. The islands cover an area of 308 sq. miles (800 sq. km) with a population (UN 1991 estimate) of 189,000. The Netherlands Antilles, which have a federal parliament, are largely self-governing under the terms of the Realm Statute which took effect on 29 December 1954.
Governor, Dr Jaime Saleh.
Prime Minister, Mrs Maria Liberia Peters.

CAPITAL – ΨWillemstad (on Curaçao) (pop. 50,000).
CURRENCY – Netherlands Antilles guilder of 100 cents.

ECONOMY – The economy of the Netherlands Antilles is based on small manufacturing industries. The soil is too poor to permit large-scale agriculture and most products for consumption and industrial raw materials must be imported.

Trade with UK	1991*	1992*
Imports from UK	£18,954,000	£19,920,000
Exports to UK	29,049,000	7,261,000
*Curaçao		

NEW ZEALAND

AREA AND POPULATION

Islands	Area (sq. miles)	Population at Census March 1991
North Island	44,281	2,553,400
South Island	58,093	881,500
Other Islands	1,362	
Total	103,736	3,435,000

Territories		
Tokelau	5	1,578
Niue	100	2,239
Cook Islands	93	17,185 (a)
Ross Dependency	175,000	

(a) 1 December 1986

POPULATION BY ETHNIC GROUP

	1986	1991
European	2,612,958	2,559,075*
Maori	294,201	333,195
Chinese	19,206	37,785
Polynesian (other than NZ		
Maori)	90,612	130,530

*NZ European only

RELIGIONS

	1986	1991
Church of England	24.0%	22.1%
Presbyterian	18.0	16.3
Roman Catholic	15.2	15.0
Methodist	4.7	4.2
Baptist	2.1	2.1

BIRTHS, DEATHS AND MARRIAGES

	1990	1991
Births	58,711	60,001
Deaths	26,890	24,501
Marriages	23,341	23,065

Infant mortality per 1,000 live births in 1989–90, 10.6.

GEOGRAPHY

New Zealand consists of a number of islands in the South Pacific Ocean, and has also administrative responsibility for the Ross Dependency in Antarctica. The two larger islands, the North and South Islands of New Zealand, are separated by a relatively narrow strait. The remaining islands are very much smaller and are dispersed over a considerable expanse of ocean. The boundaries, inclusive of the most outlying islands and dependencies, range from 33° to 53° S. latitude, and from 162° E. longitude to 173° W. longitude.

North and South Islands have a total length of 1,040 miles, and a combined area of 102,344 sq. miles (265,069 sq. km). A large proportion is mountainous. The principal range is the Southern Alps, extending over the entire length of the South Island and having its culminating point in Mount Cook (12,349 ft). The North Island mountains include several volcanoes, two of which are active. Of the numerous glaciers in the South Island, the Tasman (18 miles long by 1¼ wide), the Franz Josef and the Fox are the best known. The North Island is noted for its hot springs and geysers. The more important rivers include the Waikato (270 miles in length), Wanganui (180), and Clutha (210) and lakes include Taupo, 234 sq. miles in area; Wakatipu, 113; and Te Anau, 133.

New Zealand includes, in addition to North and South Islands: Chatham Islands (Chatham, Pitt, South East Islands and some rocky islets, combined area, 965 sq. km (373 sq. miles), largely uninhabited); Stewart Island (area 1,746 sq. km (674 sq. miles), largely uninhabited); the Kermadec Group (Raoul or Sunday, Macaulay, Curtis Islands, L'Esperance, and some islets; population 9–10, all government employees at a meteorological station); Campbell Island, used as a weather station; the Three Kings (discovered by Tasman on the Feast of the Epiphany); Auckland Islands; Antipodes Group; Bounty Islands; Snares Islands and Solander.

New Zealand has a temperate marine climate, but with abundant sunshine. The mean temperature ranges from 15°C in the north to about 9°C in the south. Rainfall in the North Island ranges from 35 to 70 inches and in the South Island from 25 to 45 inches.

CAPITAL – ΨWellington, in the North Island. Population (March 1991 census) of Wellington urban area, 325,682. Other large urban areas; ΨAuckland 885,600; ΨChristchurch 307,200; ΨDunedin 109,500; Hamilton 148,625; Ψ Napier-Hastings 110,200.
CURRENCY – New Zealand dollar (NZ$) of 100 cents.
FLAG – Blue ground, with Union Flag in top left quarter, four five-pointed red stars with white borders on the fly.
NATIONAL ANTHEM – God Save The Queen/God Defend New Zealand.
NATIONAL DAY – 6 February (Waitangi Day).

GOVERNMENT

The discoverers and first colonists of New Zealand were Polynesian people, ancestors of the Maori of today. Whether there was a single colonization or many is not known but the ninth century is generally considered to be the date of the first settlement. By the 13th or 14th century early exploration was over and there were well established Maori settlements. The first European to discover New Zealand was a Dutch navigator, Abel Tasman, who sighted the coast on 13 December 1642 but did not land. It was the British explorer James Cook who circumnavigated New Zealand and landed in 1769. Largely as a result of increased British emigration, the country was annexed by the British government in 1840. The British Lieutenant-Governor, William Hobson, proclaimed sovereignty over the North Island by virtue of the Treaty of Waitangi, signed by him and many Maori chiefs, and over the South Island and Stewart Island by right of discovery.

In 1841 New Zealand was, by letters patent, created a separate colony distinct from New South Wales. In 1907 the designation was changed to 'The Dominion of New Zealand'. The constitution rests upon the Constitution Act of 1852 and other Imperial statutes. A 1986 Constitution Act brought a number of statutory constitutional provisions. The Statute of Westminster was formally adopted by New Zealand in 1947.

The executive authority is entrusted to a Governor-General appointed by the Crown and aided by an Executive Council, within a legislature consisting of one chamber, the House of Representatives.

GOVERNOR-GENERAL
Governor-General and Commander-in-Chief of New Zealand,
Her Excellency Dame Catherine Tizard, GCMG, DBE,
sworn in November 1990.

THE EXECUTIVE COUNCIL *as at August 1993*
The Governor-General
Prime Minister, Minister in Charge of the New Zealand Security Intelligence Service, Rt. Hon. J. B. Bolger.
Deputy PM, Minister of External Relations and Trade, Foreign Affairs, Pacific Island Affairs, Leader of the House, Rt. Hon. D. C. McKinnon.
Health, Employment, State Services, Rt. Hon. W. F. Birch.
Finance, Hon. Ruth Richardson.
Attorney-General, Hon. Paul East.
Agriculture, Forestry, Hon. John Falloon.
State-Owned Enterprises, Revenue, Senior Citizens, Railways, Works and Development, Hon. Wyatt Creech.
Commerce, Industry and Trade Negotiations, Hon. Philip Burdon.
Research, Science and Technology, Hon. Simon Upton.
Police, Tourism, Recreation and Sport, Hon. John Banks.
Social Welfare, Women's Affairs, Hon. Jenny Shipley.

Defence, Local Government, Hon. Warren Cooper.
Justice, Disarmament and Arms Control, Culture, Hon.
Douglas Graham.
Education, Hon. Dr Lockwood Smith.
Labour, Hon. Maurice McTigue.
Transport, Environment, Lands, Hon. Rob Storey.
Fisheries and Maori Affairs, Hon. Douglas Kidd.
Conservation, Science (DSIR), Hon. Denis Marshall.
Housing, Energy, Hon. John Luxton.
Communications, Broadcasting, Statistics, Hon. Maurice
Williamson.

NEW ZEALAND HIGH COMMISSION
New Zealand House, Haymarket, London SW1Y 4TQ
Tel 071–930 8422

High Commissioner, His Excellency the Hon. George F. Gair
(1991).
Deputy High Commissioner, J. P. Larkindale.
Minister, D. Walker (Commercial); Dr M Prebble (Economic).
Head, Defence Staff, Cdre J. G. Leonard.
First Secretary, Ms S. Craig (Cultural Affairs).
Consul-General, N. E. Parkes.

BRITISH HIGH COMMISSION
44 Hill Street (PO Box 1812), Wellington 1
Tel: Wellington 4726-049

High Commissioner, His Excellency David Joseph Moss, CMG
(1990).
Deputy High Commissioner, I. C. Orr.
Counsellor, A. W. Turquet.
Defence Adviser, Gp Capt D. Angela.
First Secretary, P. Rogan (Commercial).
Consul-General and Director of Trade Promotion, J. F.
Holding (resides at Auckland).

There is a Consulate-General at Auckland and a Consulate
in Christchurch.

BRITISH COUNCIL REPRESENTATIVE, D. J. F. King
(Cultural Attaché).
BRITISH CHAMBER OF COMMERCE FOR AUSTRALIA
AND NEW ZEALAND, PO Box 141, Manuka, ACT 2603,
Australia; UK OFFICE, Suite 615, 6th Floor The Linen
Hall, 162–168 Regent Street, London WIR 5TB.

LEGISLATURE

The House of Representatives consists of 97 members
elected for three years. There are four Maori electorates. In
a referendum on 19 September 1992 the electorate voted in
favour of electoral reform and the introduction of a mixed-
member proportional representation system to replace the
first-past-the-post system.

Following the General Election of 27 October 1990, the
state of the parties in the House of Representatives was
National 67, Labour 29 and New Labour 1.
Speaker of the House of Representatives, Hon. Robin Gray.

JUDICATURE

The judicial system comprises a High Court, a Court of
Appeal and district courts having both civil and criminal
jurisdiction.
Chief Justice, Rt. Hon. Sir Thomas Eichelbaum, GBE, PC.
President, Court of Appeal, Rt. Hon. Sir Robin Cooke, KBE.
Judges, Rt. Hon. Sir Ivor Richardson; Rt. Hon. Sir Maurice
Casey; Rt. Hon. Mr Justice Hardie-Boys; Rt. Hon. Mr
Justice Gault; Rt. Hon. Mr Justice McKay.

DEFENCE

Annual defence expenditure for the year 1990–1 was about
4.8 per cent of total net government expenditure. In 1993

the total active number of armed forces personnel is 10,900,
with a further 8,500 reserves. The Army has a strength of
4,800 personnel, with 26 light tanks, 76 armoured personnel
carriers and 44 artillery pieces. The Navy has a strength of
2,400, with four frigates, eight patrol and support craft, and
seven armed helicopters. The Air Force has a strength of
3,700 personnel with 41 combat aircraft. A support unit of
20 troops is maintained in Singapore.

FINANCE

Revenue and expenditure, including the National Roads
Fund, for year ended 30 June:

	1991
Revenue	NZ$29,010.2m
Expenditure	27,252.4m

Taxation receipts in 1990–1 for all purposes amounted to
NZ$25,759 million (an average of NZ$7,463 per head of
population). Net expenditure includes:

	1991
Debt services	NZ$4,624m
Education	4,401m
Health	3,986m
Social services	11,005m
Foreign relations	1,641m
Other	5,290m
Total	27,252m

EDUCATION

Schools are free and attendance is compulsory between the
ages of six and 15. In 1991 there were 403,435 pupils
attending public primary schools, and 12,649 pupils attending
registered private primary schools. The secondary education
of boys and girls is carried on in 314 state secondary schools
and 21 registered private secondary schools. The total
number of pupils receiving full-time secondary education in
July 1991 was 228,689. There are seven universities with a
total of 87,973 students in 1991.

ECONOMY

GROSS VALUE OF AGRICULTURAL PRODUCTION
to year ended March (NZ$ million)

	1989–90	1990–1
Gross output	9,117	8,432
Sheep	865	935
Wool	1,235	832
Cattle	1,240	1,447
Dairy products	2,166	1,662
Fruit, nuts, oilseeds	623	694
Agricultural services	620	601
Sales of live animals	721	661

AGRICULTURAL AND PASTORAL PRODUCTION

	1990	1991
*Wheat, metric tons	—	180,690
*Wool, metric tons	223,000	227,000
†Butter, metric tons	232,000	216,000
†Cheese, metric tons	118,000	124,000
‡Stock slaughtered:		
Lambs	25,149,000	27,249,000
Sheep	7,675,000	7,227,000
Cattle	1,935,000	2,180,000
Calves	735,000	741,000
Pigs	749,000	748,000

*Year ended 30 June
†Year ended 31 May
‡Year ended 30 September

Livestock on farms at 30 June 1991 included 3,429,000 dairy cattle, 4,671,000 beef cattle and 407,000 pigs. Sheep numbered 55,162,000.

The output of sawn timber for 1991 was 2,283,000 cubic metres, of which 2,199,000 cubic metres represented exotic varieties, mainly radiata pine.

Non-metallic minerals such as coal, clay, limestone and dolomite are both economically and industrially more important than metallic ones. Coal output in 1991 was 2,684,147 tonnes. Of the metals, the most important are gold and ironsand. Natural gas deposits in Taranaki are being used for electricity generation and as a premium fuel.

TRADE	1990–1	1991–2
Imports (v.f.d.)	NZ$14,051m	NZ$14,215m
Exports (f.o.b.)	15,768m	17,890m

New Zealand produce exported to the UK in the 12 months ending June 1989 included butter and cheese, wool, lamb, hides, skins and leather.

Trade with UK	1991	1992
Imports from UK	£260,052,000	£264,830,000
Exports to UK	391,643,000	429,363,000

COMMUNICATIONS

The national railway system is owned and operated by the New Zealand Railways Corporation. In March 1990, there were 4,069 route km of government railway in operation. At 31 March 1992 there were 2,351,868 licensed motor vehicles.

During 1991–2 the vessels entered from overseas ports numbered 3,282 (gross tonnage 27,983,000) and those cleared for overseas 3,298 (gross tonnage 27,508,000).

Domestic flights in 1990 carried 4,502,000 passengers and 47,700 tonnes of freight. International flights carried 3,129,000 passengers, 134,074 tonnes of freight and 5,082 tonnes of mail.

TERRITORIES

TOKELAU (OR UNION ISLANDS)

Tokelau is a group of atolls, Fakaofo, Nukunonu and Atafu, with a total land area of 5 square miles and a population of 1,578 at November 1991, which was proclaimed part of New Zealand as from 1 January 1948. New Zealand provides substantial aid ($4.3 million in year ended 30 June 1991), to meet administrative, social, economic and development requirements. Administrative responsibility for Tokelau lies with the Administrator. Tokelau receives revenue from the granting of fishing rights in its economic zone.
Administrator, Brian Absolum.

THE ROSS DEPENDENCY

The Ross Dependency, placed under the jurisdiction of New Zealand in 1923, is defined as all the Antarctic islands and territories between 160° E. and 150° W. longitude which are situated south of the 60° S. parallel, including Edward VII Land and portions of Victoria Land. Since 1957 a number of research stations have been established in the Dependency.

ASSOCIATED STATES

COOK ISLANDS

Included in the boundaries of New Zealand since June 1901, the Cook Islands group consists of the islands of Rarotonga, Aitutaki, Mangaia, Atiu, Mauke, Mitiaro, Manuae, Takutea, Palmerston, Penrhyn or Tongareva, Manihiki, Rakahanga, Suwarrow, Pukapuka or Danger, and Nassau. The total population of the group was 17,185 at 1 December 1986.

The chief industries of the Cook Islands are tourism, financial services and the production of fruit juice, clothing, copra, bananas, citrus fruit and pulp, and black pearls. The New Zealand Government continues to give financial aid to the Cook Islands.

The Queen has a representative on the islands, as does the New Zealand government. Since 1965, the islands have enjoyed complete internal self-government, executive power being in the hands of a Cabinet consisting of the Premier and eight other ministers. There is a 22-member Legislative Assembly. The New Zealand citizenship of the Cook Islanders is embodied in the Constitution.
HM Representative, Apenera Short, OBE.
New Zealand High Commissioner, T. Caughley.

NIUE

The population of Niue was 2,239 at the November 1991 Census. A New Zealand *High Commissioner* is stationed at Niue, which since 1974 has been self-governing in free association with New Zealand. New Zealand is responsible for external affairs and defence, and continues to give financial aid. Executive power is in the hands of a Premier and a Cabinet of three drawn from the Assembly of 20 members. The Assembly is the supreme lawmaking body.
New Zealand High Commissioner, K. Meyer.

NICARAGUA
República de Nicaragua

Nicaragua is the largest state of Central America, with a long seaboard on both the Atlantic and Pacific Oceans, situated between 10° 45′ and 15° N. latitude and 83° 40′ and 87° 38′ W. longitude, containing an area of 50,193 sq. miles (130,000 sq. km).

POPULATION – There is a population (UN estimate 1991) of 3,999,000, of whom about three-quarters are of mixed blood. Another 15 per cent are white, mostly of pure Spanish descent, and the remaining 10 per cent are West Indians or Indians. The latter group includes the Misquitos, who live on the Atlantic coast.

CAPITAL – Managua, population 615,000. Other centres are León, 158,577; Granada, 72,640; Masaya, 78,308; Chinandega, 144,291.

CURRENCY – Córdoba (C$) of 100 centavos.

FLAG – Horizontal stripes of blue, white and blue, with the Nicaraguan coat of arms in the centre of the white stripe.

NATIONAL DAY – 15 September.

NATIONAL ANTHEM – Salve A Ti Nicaragua (Hail, Nicaragua).

GOVERNMENT

The eastern coast of Nicaragua was touched by Columbus in 1502, and in 1518 was overrun by Spanish forces. It formed part of the Spanish Captaincy-General of Guatemala until 1821, when its independence was secured. In 1927 Augusto Cesar Sandino began a guerrilla war against the occupation of Nicaragua by US Marines, which continued until they were expelled in 1933. Sandino was assassinated by Anastasio Somoza, director of the National Guard, and in 1936 Somoza assumed the Presidency. He was succeeded in power by his sons Luis and Anastasio Somoza, until 1979 when the family and the National Guard were overthrown by guerrillas of the Sandinista National Liberation Front (FSLN).

After ten years in power and a ten-year civil war against US-backed Contra guerillas, the Sandinistas lost their parliamentary majority in elections held in February 1990. A coalition of former opposition parties, Unión Nacional de Opositora (UNO) gained 52 seats in the 92-seat National Assembly to the Sandinistas' 39 seats and formed a government, with UNO leader Violeta Chamorro becoming President. With the defeat of the Sandinistas, the civil war came to an end and the new government began to transform the Sandinistas' socialist economy into a free-market one. President Chamorro and the UNO found that they had to compromise with the still-powerful Sandinistas, who controlled the trade unions, and to leave the armed forces and police under Sandinista control. Resentment among the UNO coalition at having to compromise with the Sandinistas came to a head in December 1992 when UNO deputies tried to topple Chamorro from power. In response Chamorro ordered the police to seize the National Assembly and negotiated a new governing majority in the National Assembly of 39 Sandinistas and eight loyal UNO deputies. In January 1993 Sandinistas entered the government and the remaining 44 UNO deputies and Vice-President Godoy were forced into opposition. In the north of the country the government has, in late 1992 and throughout 1993, been fighting re-armed Contra and Sandinista groups disgruntled at the lack of land and jobs. The government has initiated negotiations with the armed groups and political, business and church leaders to try to strengthen democracy and national security.

HEAD OF STATE
President, Minister of Defence, Violeta Barrios de Chamorro, *inaugurated* 25 April 1990.
Vice-President, Virgilio Godoy.

COUNCIL OF MINISTERS *as at August 1993*
Minister to the Presidency, Antonio Lacayo.
External Relations, Ernesto Leal.
Interior, Alfredo Mendieta.
Finance, Emilio Pereira.
Foreign Co-operation, Erwin Krugger.
Construction and Transport, Pablo Vigil.
Health, Martha Pereira.
Agriculture, Roberto Rondón Sacasa.
Labour, Francisco Rosales.
Economy and Planning, Pablo Pereira.
Education, Humberto Belli Pereira.

EMBASSY OF NICARAGUA
8 Gloucester Road, London SW7 4PP
Tel 071-584 4365

Ambassador Extraordinary and Plenipotentiary, His Excellency Fernando Zelaya (1992).

BRITISH EMBASSY
PO Box A-169, El Reparto 'Los Robles', Primera Etapa, Entrada Principal de la Carretera a Masaya, Managua, Nicaragua.
Tel: Managua 780014

Ambassador and Consul-General, His Excellency John Howard Culver (1992).

DEFENCE

Under the Sandinista government of 1979-80, Nicaragua maintained armed forces of over 120,000 personnel. Since 1990, active armed forces personnel has fallen to 14,700 and service is now voluntary. The Army has 13,000 personnel, with 130 main battle tanks, 27 light tanks, 80 reconnaissance vehicles, 119 armoured personnel carriers and 96 artillery pieces. The Navy has a strength of 500, with 23 patrol and coastal vessels. The Air Force has 1,200 personnel and 16 combat aircraft and nine armed helicopters.

ECONOMY

The country is mainly agricultural. The major crops are cotton, coffee (30 per cent of total export earnings), sugar cane, tobacco, sesame and bananas. Beans, rice, maize and ipecacuanha, livestock and timber production are also important. However, fishing, forestry, grain and cattle production have been hit by the civil war in the main growing areas. Nicaragua possesses deposits of gold and silver.

TRADE

Considerable quantities of foodstuffs are imported as well as cotton goods, jute, iron and steel, machinery and petroleum products. The chief exports are cotton, coffee, beef, gold, sugar, cottonseed and bananas.

Trade with UK	1991	1992
Imports from UK	£8,029,000	£7,297,000
Exports to UK	492,000	3,452,000

COMMUNICATIONS

Transport, except on the Pacific slope, is still difficult but many new roads have been opened. The Inter-American Highway runs between the Honduras and the Costa Rican borders; the inter-oceanic highway runs from the Corinto on the Pacific coast via Managua to Rama, where there is a natural waterway to Bluefields on the Atlantic. The country's main airport is at Managua. The chief port is Corinto on the Pacific. There are 252 miles of railway, all on the Pacific side of the country. There are 51 radio stations and two television stations in Managua. An automatic telephone system has been installed in major cities.

CULTURE

The official language of the country is Spanish and the majority profess Catholicism, although the English language and the Moravian Church are widespread on the Atlantic coast. There are three daily newspapers published at Managua, apart from the official Gazette (*La Gaceta*). There are universities at León and Managua.

NIGER
République du Niger

Situated in west central Africa, between 12° and 24° N. and 0° and 16° E., Niger has common boundaries with Algeria and Libya in the north, Chad, Nigeria, Benin, Mali and Burkina. It has an area of about 489,191 sq. miles (1,267,000 sq. km). Apart from a small region along the Niger Valley in the south-west near the capital the country is entirely savanna or desert.

POPULATION – The population (UN estimate 1991) is 7,984,000. The main ethnic groups are the Hausa (54 per cent) in the south, the Songhai and Djerma in the south-west, the Fulani, the Beriberi–Manga, and the nomadic Tuareg in the north. The official language is French.

CAPITAL – Niamey, population 410,000.
CURRENCY – Franc CFA of 100 centimes.
FLAG – Three horizontal stripes, orange, white and green with an orange disc in the middle of the white stripe.
NATIONAL DAY – 18 December.

GOVERNMENT

The first French expedition arrived in 1891 and the country was fully occupied by 1914. It decided on 18 December 1958 to remain an autonomous republic within the French Community; full independence outside the Community was proclaimed on 3 August 1960.

The constitution of Niger, adopted in November 1960, provided for a presidential system of government and a single Chamber National Assembly. In April 1974 Lt.-Col. Seyni Kountché seized power, suspended the Constitution, dissolved the National Assembly, and suppressed all political organizations. He then set up a Supreme Military Council with himself as President. President Kountché died in 1987 and was succeeded peacefully by his cousin, Col. Ali Saibou, who restored a measure of normal political life.

In August 1991, a national conference of all groups voted to suspend the constitution and stripped President Saibou of all powers. A transitional government was formed led by Prime Minister Amadou Cheiffou which remained in power until a legislative election was held in February 1993. The former ruling party, the National Movement for a Development Society (MNSD), emerged as the largest party, with 29 seats in the 83-seat National Assembly. The opposition Alliance of Forces for Change (AFC) gained 50 seats, however, and formed the government. Opposition candidate Mahamane Ousmane of the AFC defeated the MNSD candidate in the presidential election in March, when the Third Republic also came into being.

HEAD OF STATE
President of the Third Republic, Mahamane Ousmane, *elected* March 1993.

MINISTERS *as at August 1993*

Prime Minister, Mahamadou Issoufou.
National Defence, Tahirou Amadou.
Interior, Ousmane Oumarou.
Foreign Affairs and Co-operation, Abdourahamane Hama.
Finance and Planning, Abdallah Boureima.
Commerce, Transport and Tourism, Souley Abdoulaye.
Mines and Energy, Foumakoye Gado.
Public Health, Koulou Mahamane.
Equipment, Housing and Infrastructure, Laouali Amadou.
Social Development, Population and Promotion of Women, Ali Mariama.
Industry, Effad Emoud.
National and Higher Education and Research, Garba Djibo.
Civil Service and Employment, Salissou Madougou.
Relations with Parliament and Government Spokesman, Diallo Moctar.
Communications, Culture, Youth and Sport, Hassoumi Massaoudou.
Justice, Kandine Mallam Adam.
Agriculture and Animal Breeding, Sadjo Djoulde.
Water Resources and Environment, Billo Soumana.
Administrative Reform and Decentralization, Iba Hamed Ibrahim.

EMBASSY OF THE REPUBLIC OF NIGER
154 rue de Longchamp, 75116, Paris
Tel: Paris 45048060

Ambassador Extraordinary and Plenipotentiary, His Excellency Sandi Yacouba (1990).

British Ambassador (resident in Abidjan, Côte d'Ivoire).

ECONOMY

The cultivation of ground-nuts and the production of livestock are the main industries and provide two of the main exports.

A company formed by the Government, the French Atomic Energy Authority and private interests is exploiting uranium deposits at Arlit, and this is the main export. There is also some oil exploration.

TRADE WITH UK	1991	1992
Imports from UK	£10,838,000	£24,634,000
Exports to UK	382,000	1,151,000

NIGERIA
Federal Republic of Nigeria

Nigeria is situated on the west coast of Africa. It is bounded on the south by the Gulf of Guinea, on the west by Benin, on the north by Niger and on the east by Cameroon. It has an area of 356,669 sq. miles (923,768 sq. km). A belt of mangrove swamp forest lies along the entire coastline. North of this there is a zone of tropical rain forest and oil-palms. North of the rain forest, the country rises and the vegetation changes to open woodland and savanna. In the extreme north the country is semi-desert. The Niger, Benue, and Cross are the main rivers.

The climate varies from north to south, but Nigeria lies entirely within the tropics and temperatures are high. The rainy season is from about April to October; rainfall varies from under 25 inches a year in the extreme north to 172 inches on the coast line. During the dry season the cool *harmattan* wind blows from the desert.

POPULATION – The population (UN estimate 1991) is 112,163,000 (Nigerian census result (1991) 88,514,501). The main ethnic groups are Hausa/Fulani, Yoruba and Ibo, and the principal languages are English, Hausa, Yoruba and Ibo.
RELIGION – Over half the population are Muslim, these being concentrated in the north and west. In the southern areas in particular there are many Christians.

CAPITAL – ΨAbuja, estimated population 378,671, declared the federal capital in December 1991. Other important towns are the former capital Lagos, Ibadan, Kaduna, Kano, Benin City, Enugu and ΨPort Harcourt.
CURRENCY – Naira (N) of 100 kobo.
FLAG – Three equal vertical bands, green, white and green.
NATIONAL ANTHEM – Arise, O Compatriots.
NATIONAL DAY – 1 October (Independence Day).

GOVERNMENT

The Federation of Nigeria attained independence as a member of the Commonwealth on 1 October 1960 and became a republic in 1963. Originally regional in structure, the Federation is now divided into 30 states and the Federal Capital Territory. In 1966 the military took power; in 1979 civil rule was restored after elections at national and state level. After similar elections in 1983 the new administration was removed by the military on 31 December, this regime itself being overthrown in August 1985. A 28-member Armed Forces Ruling Council (AFRC) was sworn in on 30 August and governed in conjunction with a Council of Ministers until January 1993.

In 1989 Gen. Babangida promulgated the new draft constitution paving the way for a return to civilian rule by 1992. Federal elections to the National Assembly were held on 4 July 1992 and won by the Social Democratic Party (SDP), which gained majorities in both the House of Representatives and the Senate. A presidential election was due to be held in December 1992 but in October 1992 General Babangida delayed the presidential elections until

June 1993. In January 1993 the AFRC and Council of Ministers were replaced by a National Defence and Security Council (NDSC) and a civilian Transitional Council respectively to govern the country until a handover to civilian government. The presidential election was held on 11 June and won by Chief Moshood Abiola of the SDP but the military government refused to release the results and had the election declared invalid. The military tried to organize a new election but widespread rioting and support for Chief Moshood Abiola prevented this. Gen. Babangida and the military government resigned on 26 August, handing power to the Transitional Council. The Transitional Council became a cabinet with the Chairman of the Transitional Council, Chief Ernest Shonekan, being sworn in as President until elections early in 1994. At the time of going to press, strikes and demonstrations in favour of swearing in Chief Moshood Abiola as President continued and various states, including the UK, had imposed sanctions on the regime.

President (interim), Chief Ernest Shonekan.

CABINET *as at August 1993*
Agriculture, Water Resources and Rural Development, Alhaji G. J. Abdulkadir.
Commerce and Tourism, Inuwa Bakari.
Defence, Sani Abacha.
Education and Youth Development, Prof. Ben Nwabueze.
Labour and Productivity, Chief Francis Ella.
Petroleum and Mineral Resources, Chief Philip Asiodu.
Foreign Affairs, M. T. Mbu.
Health and Human Services, Dr C. Okojie.
Internal Affairs, Alhaji Abdurrahaman Okene.
Industry and Technology, Alhaji Aminu Sale.
Information and Culture, Uche Chukumerije.
Justice, Clement Akpamgbo.
Finance, Chief Dele Olashore.
Power and Steel, Air Vice-Marshal Nura Imam (retd).
Transport and Communications, Chief Oluwole Adeosun.
Federal Capital Territory, Maj.-Gen. Gado Nasko (retd).
Works and Housing, Barnabas Gemade.
Establishment and Management Services, Alhaji Zarma Gogaram.
Chairman, National Planning Commission, Alhaji Mustapha Umara.
Police Affairs, Chief Francis Orji.
States and Local Government Affairs, Alhaji Maccido Dalhat.

NIGERIA HIGH COMMISSION
9 Northumberland Avenue,
London WC2 5BX
Tel 071-839 1244

High Commissioner, His Excellency Alhaji, Abubakar Alhaji, KBE (1992).
Ministers, M. L. Abubakar; M. U. Mohammed; A. A. Ella; A. K. Sambo; A. I. Imohe.
Defence Attaché, Brig.-Gen. D. Mohammed.
Information Attaché, O. Oyawale.
Head of Commerce/Trade, B. A. Ameh.

BRITISH HIGH COMMISSION
Shehu Shangari Way (North), Maitama, Abuja
Tel: Abuja 5232011
11 Eleke Crescent, Victoria Island, Lagos
Tel: Lagos 619531
High Commissioner, His Excellency Christopher Macrae, CMG (1992).
Deputy High Commissioner and Minister-Counsellor, R. S. Gorham.
Defence Adviser, Col. A. C. Taylor.
Counsellor (Economic and Commercial), E. A. Burner.
There is a Deputy High Commission at Kaduna and liaison offices at Kano and Ibadan.

BRITISH COUNCIL REPRESENTATIVE, P. MacKenzie-Smith, 11 Kingsway Road, Ikoyi (PO Box 3702), Lagos. Branch offices at *Enugu, Kaduna* and *Kano City*.

DEFENCE

Nigeria has a total active armed forces of some 76,000 personnel, all of whom are volunteers. The Army is 62,000 strong with 157 main battle tanks, 100 light tanks, 255 reconnaissance vehicles, 380 armoured personnel carriers and 450 artillery pieces. The Navy has 4,500 personnel, with two frigates, 54 patrol and coastal vessels and two armed helicopters. The Air Force numbers 9,500 personnel, with 95 combat aircraft and 15 armed helicopters. Nigeria deploys 4,000 personnel in Liberia as part of the ECOMOG peacekeeping force, 800 troops in Sierra Leone, and a 50-strong training unit in the Gambia.

EDUCATION

A programme was introduced in September 1976 intended to achieve universal primary education. Numbers of pupils in 1982–3 were: 15.4 million in primary schools, 3.5 million in secondary schools, 53,766 in polytechnics and 88,636 in universities. There are 37 universities (24 federal, 12 state and one military).

COMMUNICATIONS

The Nigerian railway system, which is controlled by the Nigerian Railway Corporation, has 2,178 route miles of lines. The principal international airlines operate from Lagos, Kano and Port Harcourt. A network of internal air services connects the main centres. The principal seaports are served by a number of shipping lines, including the Nigerian National Line. A nationwide television and radio network is being developed, with each state eventually having its own television and radio station.

ECONOMY

Nigeria was a predominantly agricultural country until the early 1970s when oil became the principal source of export revenue (over 90 per cent). Since 1981 oil revenues have fallen and are now restricted by OPEC quotas and lower prices to half their peak level. Austerity measures such as import curbs and payments restrictions were introduced in

March 1982. The present Government is attempting to stimulate greater self-reliance in the economy by encouraging non-oil exports and the use of local rather than imported raw materials.

Three oil refineries are in operation at Port Harcourt, Warri and Kaduna, and steel plants at Warri and Ajaokuta. Other projects include natural gas liquifaction, petrochemicals, fertilizers, power stations and irrigation schemes. Tin and calumbite mining on the Jos plateau, textiles and coal mining are also important.

TRADE

The principal exports are oil, groundnuts, palm products, tin, cocoa, rubber and timber.

Trade with UK	1991	1992
Imports from UK	£544,533,000	£622,630,000
Exports to UK	249,254,000	168,274,000

NORWAY
Kongeriket Norge

Norway is a kingdom in the northern and western part of the Scandinavian peninsula, and was founded in AD 872. It is 1,752 km in length, its greatest width about 430 km. The length of the coastline is 2,650 km, and the frontier between Norway and the neighbouring countries is 2,542 km (Sweden 1,619 km, Finland 727 km and Russia 196 km). It is divided into 19 counties (*fylker*) and comprises an area of 149,405 sq. miles (386,958 sq. km), of which Svalbard and Jan Mayen have a combined area of 63,080 sq. km, with a total population (1991 UN estimate) of 4,262,000.

The Norwegian coastline is deeply indented with numerous fjords and fringed with rocky islands. The surface is mountainous, consisting of elevated and barren tablelands separated by deep and narrow valleys. At the North Cape the sun does not appear to set from the second week in May to the last week in July, causing the phenomenon known as the Midnight Sun; conversely, there is no apparent sunrise from about 18 November to 23 January. During the long winter nights are seen the multiple coloured Northern Lights or Aurora Borealis, which have a maximum intensity in a line crossing North America from Alaska to Labrador and Northern Europe to the Arctic coast and Siberia.

LANGUAGE AND LITERATURE – Old Norse literature is among the most ancient and richest in Europe. Norwegian in both its present forms is closely related to other Scandinavian languages. Independence from Denmark (1814) and resurgent nationalism led to the development of 'new Norwegian' based on dialects, which now has equal official standing with 'bokmål', in which Danish influence is more obvious. This was formed in the time of the Reformation, and Ludvig Holberg (1684–1754) is regarded as the father of Norwegian literature, though the modern period begins with the writings of Henrik Wergeland (1808–45). Some of the famous names are Henrik Ibsen (1828–1906), Bjørnstjerne Bjørnson (1832–1910), Nobel Prizewinner in 1903, and the novelists Jonas Lie (1833–1908), Alexander Kielland (1849–1906), Knut Hamsun (1859–1952) and Sigrid Undset (1882–1949), the latter two also Nobel Prizewinners. In 1991 there were 148 daily newspapers.

CAPITAL – ΨOslo (including Aker), population (1992) 467,090. Other towns are ΨTrondheim 139,660; ΨBergen 215,967; ΨStavanger 99,764; ΨKristiansand 66,398; ΨDrammen 52,062; ΨTromsø 52,459.

CURRENCY – Krone of 100 øre.
FLAG – Red, with white-bordered blue cross.
NATIONAL ANTHEM – Ja, Vi Elsker Dette Landet (Yes, we love this country).
NATIONAL DAY – 17 May (Constitution Day).

GOVERNMENT

From 1397 to 1814 Norway was united with Denmark and from 1814 with Sweden, under a personal union which was dissolved on 7 June 1905 when Norway regained complete independence. Under the 1814 constitution, the *Storting* (Parliament) itself elects one-quarter of its members to constitute the *Lagting* (Upper Chamber), the other three-quarters forming the *Odelsting* (Lower Chamber).

A minority Labour government replaced the previous three-party, centre-right coalition government, which collapsed in October 1990 because of a dispute over whether to apply for membership of the European Community. The Storting voted in November 1992 to apply to join the European Community. On 24 March 1993 the EC Commission announced a positive opinion on Norway's application and negotiations on entry opened in April 1993, with a target entry date of January 1995.

HEAD OF STATE
King, HM Harald V, GCVO, *born* 21 February 1937; *succeeded*, 17 January 1991, on death of his father King Olav V; *married* 29 August 1968, Sonja Haraldsen, and has *issue*, Prince Haakon Magnus (*see below*), and Princess Martha Louise, *born* 22 September 1971.
Heir-Apparent, HRH Crown Prince Haakon Magnus, *born* 20 July 1973.

CABINET *as at August 1993*
Prime Minister, Gro Harlem Brundtland.
Foreign Affairs, Johan Jørgen Holst.
Industry, Petroleum and Energy, Finn Kristensen.
Defence, Jørgen Kosmo.
Local Government and Labour, Gunnar Berge.
Government Administration, Oddny Alexandersen.
Agriculture, Gunhild Øyangen.
Justice, Grete Faremo.
Fisheries, Jan Henry Olsen.
Environment, Thorbjørn Berntsen.
Transport and Communications, Kjell Opseth.
Health and Social Affairs, Grete Knudsen.
Church, Education and Research, Gudmund Hernes.
Trade and Shipping, Björn Tore Godal.
Family and Consumer Affairs, Grete Berget.
Cultural Affairs, Åse Kleveland.
Finance, Sigbjørn Johnsen.
Development Co-operation, Kari Nordheim Larsen.

ROYAL NORWEGIAN EMBASSY
25 Belgrave Square, London SW1X 8QD
Tel 071–235 7151

Ambassador Extraordinary and Plenipotentiary, His Excellency Kjell Eliassen, GCMG (1989).
Minister, Jon Bech.
Defence Attaché, Col. P. J. Aunaas.
First Secretary, Ms W. K. Moe (*Consular*).
Counsellor, T. Gulli (*Commercial*).

BRITISH EMBASSY
Thomas Heftyesgate 8, 0244 Oslo
Tel: Oslo 22 55 24 00

Ambassador Extraordinary and Plenipotentiary, His Excellency David John Edward Ratford, CMG, CVO (1990).

Counsellor, E. J. Hughes (*Deputy Head of Mission and Consul-General*)
First Secretary, S. M. Williams (*Economic and Commercial*).
Defence and Air Attaché, Wg Cdr. J. C. W. Marshall.

BRITISH CONSULAR OFFICES – There is a British Consular Office at *Oslo* and Honorary Consulates at *Bergen*, *Tromsø*, *Alesund*, *Kristiansund* (North), *Stavanger*, *Trondheim*, *Kristiansand* (South), *Haugesund* and *Harstad*.

BRITISH COUNCIL REPRESENTATIVE – Rosalind Olsen, Fridtjof Nansens Plass 5,0160, Oslo 1.

DEFENCE

Norway is a member of the North Atlantic Treaty Organization, and the headquarters of Allied Forces Northern Europe is situated near Oslo. The total active armed forces number some 32,700 (22,800 conscripts), Reserve forces number some 285,000. The Army has a strength of 15,900 (13,000 conscripts), with 210 main battle tanks, 200 armoured infantry fighting vehicles and armoured personnel carriers, and 527 artillery pieces. Most of the army is deployed in the north of the country. The Navy has a strength of 7,300, including 4,500 conscripts, with 11 submarines, five frigates, and 35 patrol and coastal combatants. The Air Force has a strength of 9,500 (5,300 conscripts), with 85 combat aircraft, mainly US manufactured F16s. The period of compulsory national service is 15 months (without refresher training) in the Navy and 12 months (with refresher training) in the Army and Air Force.

EDUCATION

Education from seven to 16 is free and compulsory in the 'basic schools'. The majority of the pupils receive post-compulsory schooling at 'upper secondary' schools, colleges of education (19), regional colleges akin to polytechnics (12), universities (four) and other university-level specialist institutions. In 1991 there were 60,206 students at universities and university-level institutions.

COMMUNICATIONS

The total length of railways open at the end of 1990 was 4,044 km, excluding private lines. There are 88,800 km of public roads in Norway (including urban streets). At the end of 1990, 2,937,818 road motor vehicles were registered. Scheduled internal air services are operated by Scandinavian Airlines System (SAS) on behalf of Det Norske Luftfartselskap (DNL), by Braathens South American and Far East Airtransport (SAFE), and by Wideróes Flyveselskap AS. The Mercantile Marine in 1990 consisted of 1,516 vessels of 23,607,000 gross tons (vessels above 100 gross tons, excluding fishing boats, floating whaling factories, tugs, salvage vessels, icebreakers and similar types of vessel).

ECONOMY

The cultivated area is about 8,818 sq. km, 2.9 per cent of total surface area. Forests cover nearly 25 per cent; the rest consists of highland pastures or uninhabitable mountains. The chief agricultural products are grain, potatoes, root vegetables, milk, furs and timber.

The Gulf Stream causes the sea temperature to be higher than the average for the latitude. It brings shoals of herring and cod into the fishing grounds and the quantity of fish caught by Norwegian fishing vessels is greater than that of any other European country except Russia. In 1989 the total catch amounted to 1,788,000 tonnes.

The chief industries are manufactures, agriculture and forestry, fisheries, mining, production of metals and ferro-alloys, and shipping. Industries providing both manufactured products and services for the development of North Sea oil and gas resources are also important. In 1991 93,350,000 tons of crude oil were produced, of which 82,070,000 tons were exported. In 1991, the total workforce was 2,126,000 of which 336,000 persons were employed in Norwegian industry. Manufactures are aided by great resources of hydro-electric power. Actual production in 1991 amounted to 110,950 Gwh.

FINANCE	1992
Total Revenue	K397,262,000
Total Expenditure	453,146,000

TRADE

The chief imports are raw materials, motor vehicles, chemicals, motor spirit, fuel and other oils; coal, ships and machinery; and manufactures of silk, cotton and wool. Exports consist chiefly of crude oil and gas, manufactured goods, fish and fish products (as canned fish, whale oils), pulp, paper, iron ore and pyrites, nitrate of lime, stone, calcium carbide, aluminium, ferro-alloys, zinc, nickel, cyanamides, etc. Norway's major trading partners are the UK, Sweden, Germany, the Netherlands, Denmark and the USA.

	1992
Total imports	K251,748m
Total exports	303,034m

Trade with UK	1991	1992
Imports from UK	£1,357,299,000	£1,419,570,000
Exports to UK	4,232,827,000	3,861,771,000

TERRITORIES

SVALBARD

The Svalbard archipelago lies between 74° and 81° N. and between 10° and 35° E., with an estimated area of 24,295 square miles. The archipelago consists of the main island, Spitsbergen (15,200 sq. miles); North East Land; the Wiche Islands; Barents and Edge Islands; Prince Charles Foreland; Hope Island; Bear Island, many islands in the neighbourhood of the main group. South Cape is 355 miles from the Norwegian coast. Transit from Tromsø to Green Harbour takes two to three days.

The sovereignty of Norway over the archipelago was recognized by other nations in 1920 and in 1925 Norway assumed sovereignty. The inhabitants are mainly engaged in coal-mining, but the islands are also visited by hunters for seals, foxes and polar bears.

JAN MAYEN ISLAND

Jan Mayen, an island in the Arctic Ocean (70° 49′ to 71° 9′ N. and 7° 53′ to 9° 5′ W.) was joined to Norway by law in 1930.

NORWEGIAN ANTARCTIC TERRITORIES

BOUVET ISLAND (54° 26′ S. and 3° 24′ E.) was declared a dependency of Norway by law in 1930.
PETER THE FIRST ISLAND (68° 48′ S. and 90° 35′ W.), was declared a dependency of Norway by resolution of government in 1931.
PRINCESS RAGNHILD LAND (from 70° 30′ to 68° 40′ S. and 24° 15′ to 33° 30′ E.) has been claimed as Norwegian since 1931.
QUEEN MAUD LAND – In 1939 the Norwegian Government declared the area between 20° W. and 45° E., adjacent to Australian Antarctica, to be Norwegian territory.

OMAN
The Sultanate of Oman

Oman lies at the eastern corner of the Arabian peninsula, bordered on the west by Yemen, Saudi Arabia and the UAE. To the north lies the Gulf of Oman and to the east the Arabian Sea, giving a coastline of nearly 1,000 miles. Sharjah and Fujairah (UAE) separate the main part of Oman from the northernmost part of the state, a peninsula extending into the Strait of Hormuz. The area has been estimated at 115,830 sq. miles (300,000 sq. km).

The north and the south of Oman are divided by nearly 400 miles of desert. The Batinah, the coastal plain, is fertile. The Hajjar is a mountain spine running from north-west to south-east and for the most part barren, but valleys penetrate the central massif which are irrigated by wells or a system of underground canals called *falajs* which tap the water table. The two plateaus leading from the western slopes of the mountains descend to the Empty Quarter of the Arabian Desert. Dhofar, the southern province, is the only part of the Arabian peninsula to be touched by the south-west monsoon. Temperatures are more moderate than in the north.

POPULATION – The population (UN estimate 1991) is 1,559,000. The inhabitants of the north are mostly Arab, though there are large communities of Hindus, Khojas and Baluch, in addition to Omanis of Zanzibari origin, especially around Salalah. However, in the mountains the inhabitants are either of pure Arab descent or belong to tribes of pre-Arab origin, the Qarra and Mahra, who speak their own dialects of semitic origin.

CAPITAL – Ψ Muscat, estimated population 400,000. The commercial centre has grown around Mutrah, three miles away and the main port, and Ruwi. The main towns on the northern coast are ΨSur, ΨBarka and ΨSohar. The main town of Dhofar is Salalah.

CURRENCY – Rial Omani (OR) of 1,000 baiza.

FLAG – Red with a white panel in the upper fly and a green one in the lower fly; in the canton the national emblem in white.

NATIONAL DAY – 18 November.

GOVERNMENT

A State Consultative Council established in 1981 was replaced by Sultanic decree in 1991 by a Majlis A' shura, or State Advisory Council. This body, meeting twice a year, consists of a representative from each of the 59 Wilayats, or Governorates, of the Sultanate. The Council has the right to review legislation, question ministers and make policy proposals.

HEAD OF STATE
Sultan, Prime Minister, Minister of Foreign Affairs, Defence and Finance, HM Qaboos Bin-Said, *succeeded on deposition of Sultan Said bin Taimur, 23 July 1970.*

COUNCIL OF MINISTERS *as at August 1993*
Personal Representative of HM The Sultan, HH Sayyid Thuwainy bin Shihab Al Said.
Deputy PM for Security and Defence, HH Sayyid Fahr bin Taimur al Said.
Deputy PM for Legal Affairs, HH Sayyid Fahad bin Mahmood al Said.
Deputy PM for Financial and Economic Affairs, HE Qais bin Abdul Munem al Zawawi.
Minister of State and Governor of Dhofar, HE Sayyid Mussellam bin Ali Al Busaidi.

Minister of State and Governor of Muscat, HE Sayyid Al Mutassim bin Hamoud Al Busaidi.
National Heritage and Culture, HH Sayyid Faisal bin Ali al Said.
Agriculture and Fisheries, HE Mohammed bin Abdallah bin Zaher al Hinai.
Electricity and Water, HE Shaikh Mohammed bin Ali Al Qatabi.
Water Resources, HE Hamed bin Said Al Aufi.
Justice, Awqaf and Islamic Affairs, HE Hamoud bin Abdullah Al Harthi.
Health, HE Dr Ali bin Mohammed bin Moosa.
Petroleum and Minerals, HE Said bin Ahmed bin Said al Shanfari.
Housing, HE Malik bin Suleiman al Ma'amari.
Civil Services, HE Ahmed bin Abdul Nabi Macki.
Communications, HE Salim bin Abdullah Al Ghazali.
Education and Youth Affairs, HE Yahya bin Mahfoodh al Manthri.
Interior, HE Sayyid Badr bin Sa'oud bin Hareb al Busaidi.
Information, HE Abdul Aziz bin Mohammed al Rowas.
Regional Municipalities and Environment, HE Shaikh Amer bin Shuwain al Hosni.
Minister of State for Foreign Affairs, HE Yousuf bin Alawi bin Abdullah.
Commerce and Industry, HE Maqbool bin Ali bin Sultan.
Social Affairs and Labour, HE Ahmed bin Mohammed bin Salim Al Isa'ee.
Posts, Telegraphs and Telephones, HE Ahmed bin Sweidan al Baluchi.
Secretary-General at the Ministry of Defence, HE Saif bin Hamad al Batashi.
Diwan of Royal Court, HE Sayyid Saif bin Hamed bin Sa'oud.
Palace Office Affairs, HE Gen. Ali bin Majid Al Ma'amari.

EMBASSY OF THE SULTANATE OF OMAN
167 Queen's Gate, London SW7 5HE
Tel 071–225 0001

Ambassador Extraordinary and Plenipotentiary, His Excellency Abdulla Mohammed Al-Dhahab (1990).
Minister Plenipotentiary, G. I. Shaker.
Military Attaché, Col. Ali Abdullah Al Dalhami.

BRITISH EMBASSY
PO Box 300, Muscat
Tel: Muscat 738501/5

Ambassador Extraordinary and Plenipotentiary, His Excellency Sir Terence Clark, KBE, CMG, CVO (1990).
Counsellor, N. H. S. Armour (*Deputy Head of Mission*).
Defence Attaché, Brig. P. A. Goddard.
First Secretary (Commercial), P. Nessling.
Consul, G. H. Davies.

BRITISH COUNCIL REPRESENTATIVE, Clive Bruton, PO Box 7090, Mutrah, Oman. There is also an office at *Salalah*.

DEFENCE

The total active armed forces strength is 35,700 personnel. Service is voluntary. The Army has a strength of 20,000 personnel, with 78 main battle tanks, 43 light tanks and 66 artillery pieces. The Navy has 3,000 personnel, and 12 patrol and coastal vessels. The Air Force has 3,500 personnel and 52 combat aircraft. The Royal Household has 6,000 personnel formed into a Royal Guard brigade, two special forces regiments, the Royal Yacht Squadron and the Royal Flight. In addition there is the paramilitary home guard

(*Firqat*) of 3,500 personnel. Some 3,700 hired and seconded personnel (many British) serve in the Omani armed forces.

ECONOMY

Although there is considerable cultivation in the fertile areas and cattle are raised on the mountains, the backbone of the economy is the oil industry. Petroleum Development (Oman) Ltd (owned 60 per cent by Oman Government and 34 per cent by Shell) began exporting oil in 1967. Concessions (off and on shore) are held by several major international companies. The current level of oil production is about 650,000 barrels per day, planned to increase to 700,000.

A gas turbine power station operates at Rusail, where there is also a 200-plot industrial estate. There is a power station and a desalination plant near Muscat and flour, animal feed, cement and copper production facilities.

DEVELOPMENT

For many years the Sultanate was a poor country but the advent of oil revenues and the change of regime in 1970 led to the initiation of a wide-ranging development programme, especially concerned with health, education and communications. There are now nearly 50 hospitals with around 3,400 beds; 823 schools, with 387,000 pupils, were in operation in 1992.

TRADE

Trade is mainly with the UAE, UK, Japan, the Netherlands, USA, Germany, France and India. Chief imports are machinery, cars, building materials, food and telecommunications equipment.

Trade with UK	1991	1992
Imports from UK	£237,890,000	£240,695,000
Exports to UK	73,574,000	83,106,000

COMMUNICATIONS

Port Qaboos at Matrah has eight deep-water berths which have been constructed as part of the harbour facilities. A modern telecommunications service to the main population centres and an international service are operated by the General Telecommunications Organization. There are good tarmac roads linking most main population centres of the country with the coast and with the towns of the UAE, though only a trunk road links the north and south of Oman.

PAKISTAN
Islami Jamhuriya-e-Pakistan

Pakistan is situated in the north-west of the Indian subcontinent, bordered by Iran, Afghanistan, China, the disputed territory of Kashmir, and India. It covers a total area of 803,950 sq. km. Running through Pakistan are five great rivers, the Indus, Jhelum, Chenab, Ravi and Sutlej. The upper reaches of these rivers are in Kashmir, and their sources in the Himalayas.

POPULATION – The Census in 1981 showed a population figure of 83,780,000 (1991 UN estimate, 115,524,000). Of these, about 95 per cent are Muslims, about 1 per cent Hindus, 3.5 per cent Christians, and 0.5 per cent Buddhists.

CAPITAL – Islamabad, population 350,000. ΨKarachi (estimated population 6,500,000) is the largest city and seaport; Lahore has a population of about 3,500,000.

CURRENCY – Pakistan rupee of 100 paisa.

FLAG – Green with a white crescent and star, and a white vertical strip in the hoist

NATIONAL ANTHEM – Quami Tarana.

NATIONAL DAYS – 23 March (Pakistan Day), 14 August (Independence Day).

GOVERNMENT

Pakistan was constituted as a Dominion under the Indian Independence Act 1947, becoming a republic on 23 March 1956, when a parliamentary constitution came into force. On 7 October 1958 this constitution was abrogated and Pakistan came under martial law.

Until 1972 Pakistan consisted of two geographical units, West and East Pakistan, which were separated by about 1,100 miles of Indian territory. Following elections in 1970 and 1971, there was total disagreement between the main parties in East and West Pakistan on the question of a new constitution for Pakistan, East Pakistan insisting on complete autonomy. Civil war broke out on 25 March 1971 and East Pakistan seceded by unilateral declaration the following day. Fighting continued until December 1971 when a ceasefire was arranged, and 'The Democratic Government of Bangladesh' was formally proclaimed on 17 April 1972.

The armed forces under Gen. Zia-ul-Haq assumed power in 1977 and martial law was in force from July 1977 to December 1985. Gen. Zia declared himself President in September 1978. In May 1988, Zia dissolved the National Assembly and the cabinet and announced fresh elections. Zia was killed in a plane crash on 17 August 1988. The Pakistan People's Party won the election to the National Assembly and Benazir Bhutto became Prime Minister. In August 1990, the President dissolved the National Assembly and dismissed the Bhutto cabinet. Elections were held on 24 October 1990 and won by the Islamic Democratic Alliance, led by Mian Muhammad Nawaz Sharif.

In late 1992 and early 1993 a power struggle between President Ishaq Khan and Prime Minister Sharif developed, leading to Sharif's introduction of legislation into the National Assembly in February 1993 to repeal the 1985 constitutional amendment giving the President the power to dismiss the government and dissolve the National Assembly. In April the President used this power to dismiss Sharif's government on charges of corruption and nepotism. The caretaker government appointed was itself dismissed in May by the Supreme Court, which declared the President's actions unconstitutional and reinstated Sharif's government. The Army intervened in July, forcing both Khan and Sharif to resign and replacing them with a caretaker President and Cabinet until new elections are held in October 1993.

HEAD OF STATE
Acting President, Wassim Sajjad, *appointed* 18 July 1993.

CARETAKER CABINET *as at August 1993*
Prime Minister, Moeenuddin Ahmad Qureshi.
Commerce and Tourism, Dr Hafiz Pasha.
Communications and Railways, Ahmad Faruque.
Education, Health, Social Welfare, Science and Technology, Kashmir and Northern Affairs, Lt.-Gen. (retd) Mohammad Shafiq.
Finance, Economic Affairs, Planning and Development, Syed Babar Ali.
Food, Agricultural and Co-operatives, Local Government, Rural Development and Works, Ali Khan Junejo.
Foreign Affairs, Abdul Sattur.
Industries, Labour, Manpower, Women's Development and Youth Affairs, Dr. D. K. Riaz Baloch.
Information and Broadcasting, States and Frontier Regions, Niser Memon.

Interior, Narcotics Control, Inter-Provincial Co-ordination,
Fateh Khan Bandial.
Law, Justice, Parliamentary Affairs, Religious Affairs and
Minorities Affairs, Abdul Shakural Salam.
Petroleum, Natural Resources, Production and Defence
Production, Lt.-Gen. (retd) R. D. Bhatti.
Water and Power, Khursheed K. Marker.

HIGH COMMISSION FOR PAKISTAN
35–36 Lowndes Square, London SW1X 9JN
Tel 071-235 2044

High Commissioner, His Excellency Mian Riaz Samee
(1993).
Ministers, Khalid Mahmood Shafi; Col. M. I. Khan
(Information); Prof. N. M. Shaikh.
Defence and Naval Attaché, Cdre M. J. Akhtar.
Counsellor, M. A. Tahir *(Commercial).*

BRITISH HIGH COMMISSION
Diplomatic Enclave, Ramna 5, PO Box 1122, Islamabad
Tel: Islamabad 822131/5

High Commissioner, His Excellency Sir Nicholas Barrington,
KCMG, CVO (1987).
Deputy High Commissioners, A. J. F. Caie *(Islamabad);* D. J.
Young *(Karachi).*
Counsellor (Economical and Comercial), S. N. Evans.
Counsellor, T. A. Willasey-Wilsey.
Defence and Military Adviser, Brig. I. McLeod, OBE, MC.

There is a British Deputy High Commission at *Karachi* and
a Consulate at *Lahore.*

BRITISH COUNCIL REPRESENTATIVE, L. Phillips, PO
Box 1812, Islamabad. There are offices at *Karachi, Lahore*
and *Peshawar.*

DEFENCE

Pakistan has a total armed forces active strength of 580,000
personnel, with a further 513,000 reserves. The Army has a
strength of 515,000 personnel, with 2,000 main battle tanks,
800 armoured personnel carriers, 1,645 artillery pieces and
20 attack helicopters. The Navy has 20,000 personnel, with
six submarines, three destroyers, ten frigates, 25 patrol and
coastal vessels, four combat aircraft and nine armed
helicopters. The Air Force has 45,000 personnel, and 352
combat aircraft of French, Chinese and US manufacture. In
addition, there are 270,000 paramilitary personnel in four
organizations.

In July 1993 the former Pakistani Army Chief-of-Staff
Gen. Aslam Beg confirmed that since 1987 Pakistan has had
the capability to construct nuclear weapons at short notice
and that Pakistan would use this capability if its conventional
forces faced defeat in a war with India.

EDUCATION

Education in Pakistan is organized into five stages. These
are five years of primary education (five to nine years), three
years of middle or lower secondary (general or vocational),
two years of upper secondary, two years of higher secondary
(intermediate) and two to five years of higher education in
colleges and universities. Education is free to upper secondary
level.

COMMUNICATIONS

The main seaport is Karachi. The main airport is also at
Karachi. Pakistan International Airlines operates air services
between the principal cities within the country as well as
abroad. Post and telegraph facilities are available to every
country in the world.

ECONOMY

Pakistan's economy is based on agriculture. The principal
crops are cotton, rice, wheat, sugar cane, maize and tobacco.
Pakistan has one of the longest irrigation systems in the
world. The total area irrigated is 33 million acres. There are
large deposits of rock salt.

Pakistan also produces hides and skins, leather, wool,
fertilizers, paints and varnishes, soda ash, paper, cement,
fish, carpets, sports goods, surgical appliances and engineering goods, including switchgear, transformers, cables and
wires.

TRADE

Principal imports are petroleum products, machinery,
fertilizers, transport equipment, edible oils, chemicals and
ferrous metals. Principal exports are raw cotton, cotton yarn
and cloth, carpets, rice, petroleum products, synthetic textiles,
leather, and fish.

Trade with UK	1991	1992
Imports from UK	£272,068,000	£311,771,000
Exports to UK	261,291,000	273,324,000

PANAMA
República de Panama

Panama lies on the isthmus of that name which connects
North and South America. The area is 29,762 sq. miles
(77,082 sq. km), the population (Census 1990) 2,315,047.
Spanish is the official language.

CAPITAL – ΨPanama City, population (1990) 1,064,221.
CURRENCY – Balboa of 100 centésimos. US$ notes are also
    in circulation.
FLAG – Four quarters; white with blue star (top, next staff),
    red (in fly), blue (below, next staff) and white with red
    star.
NATIONAL ANTHEM – Alcanzamos Por Fin La Victoria
    (Victory is ours at last).
NATIONAL DAY – 3 November.

GOVERNMENT

After a revolt in November 1903, Panama declared its
independence from Colombia and established a separate
government. After 1968, control of Panama was increasingly
taken over by Gen. Omar Torrijos, commander of the
National Guard, following a military coup. In 1972 Gen.
Torrijos was designated as 'Leader of the Revolution' with
wide powers. In October 1978 he withdrew from the
government, and Dr Aristides Royo was elected President
by the Assembly of Representatives.

In a presidential election in May 1984, Dr Nicolas Barletta
was elected President. He resigned in September 1985 after
disagreements with military leaders and was succeeded by
his Vice-President, Eric Arturo Delvalle. An attempt in
February 1988 by President Delvalle to remove Gen. Noriega
as Commander of the Defence Forces failed. Noriega ousted
Delvalle and replaced him with Manuel Solis Palma.
Presidential elections were held in May 1989, but Noriega
annulled the results, which appeared to give victory to the
opposition. A US military invasion on 20 December 1989
followed Noriega's formal assumption of power as head of
state on 15 December. Guillermo Endara, believed to have
won the May elections, was installed as President following
the ousting of Gen. Noriega. In December 1991 the
Legislative Assembly approved a change to the constitution
which abolished the armed forces.

Legislative power is vested in a unicameral Legislative Assembly of 67 members; executive power is held by the President, assisted by an elected Vice-President and an appointed Cabinet. Elections are held every five years under a system of universal and compulsory adult suffrage.

HEAD OF STATE
President, Guillermo Endara Galimany, *sworn in* 27 December 1989.
First Vice-President, Guillermo Ford Boyd.

CABINET *as at August 1993*
Foreign Affairs, Dr Julio Linares.
Treasury and Finance, Dr Mario Galindo.
Government and Justice, Juan B. Chevalier.
Agricultural Development, Dr Cesar Pereira.
Commerce and Industry, Roberto Alfaro.
Labour and Social Welfare, Jorge Rosas.
Health, Dr Guillermo Rolla Pimental.
Housing, Guillermo E. Quijano.
Education, Marco A. Alarcon.
Presidency, Julio Harris.
Public Works, Alfredo Arias.
Planning and Political Economy, Delia Cardenas.

EMBASSY OF THE REPUBLIC OF PANAMA
119 Crawford Street, London WIH IAF
Tel 071-487 5633

Ambassador Extraordinary and Plenipotentiary, His Excellency Teodoro F. Franco (1990).

There is also a Consular Office at *Liverpool.*

BRITISH EMBASSY
Torre Swiss Bank, Calle 53 (Apartado 889) Zona 1, Panama City, Panama 1
Tel: Panama City 69-0866

Ambassador Extraordinary and Plenipotentiary, His Excellency T. H. Malcomson (1992).

There is a British consular office at *Panama City.*

ECONOMY

The soil is moderately fertile, but nearly one-half of the land is uncultivated. The chief crops are bananas, sugar, coconuts, cacao, coffee and cereals. The shrimping industry plays an important role in the Panamanian economy. In 1992 tourism became the principal foreign currency earner, ahead of bananas. A railway joins the Atlantic and Pacific oceans.

Education is compulsory and free from seven to 15 years.

TRADE

Imports are mostly manufactured goods, machinery, lubricants, chemicals and foodstuffs. Exports are bananas, petroleum products, shrimps, sugar, meat and fishmeal.

Republic of Panama	1988	1989
Imports	US$712.3m	US$796.0m
Exports	283.0m	297.3m
Colon Free Zone		
Imports	US$1,843m	US$243.8m
Exports	2,119m	249.9m
Trade with UK†	1991	1992
Imports from UK	£36,656,000	£42,178,000
Exports to UK	1,679,000	7,025,000

† Including Colon Free Zone

THE PANAMA CANAL ZONE

With effect from 1 October 1979 the Canal Zone (647 sq. miles) was disestablished, with all areas of land and water within the Zone reverting to Panama. By the 1977 treaty with the USA, the USA is allowed the use of operating bases for the Panama Canal, together with several military bases, but the Republic of Panama is sovereign in all such areas. Control of the Canal will revert to Panama in the year 2000.

DEPENDENCIES

Taboga Island (area 4 sq. miles) is a popular tourist resort some 12 miles from the Pacific entrance to the Panama Canal.

Tourist facilities have also been developed in the Las Perlas Archipelago in the Gulf of Panama, particularly on the island of Contadora.

There is a penal settlement at Guardia on the island of Coiba (area 19 sq. miles) in the Gulf of Chiriqui.

PAPUA NEW GUINEA

Papua New Guinea extends from the Equator to Cape Baganowa in the Louisiade Archipelago at 11° S. latitude and from the border with Irian Jaya to 160° E. longitude. The total area is 178,260 sq. miles, (461,691 sq. km), of which approximately 152,420 sq. miles form the mainland on the island of New Guinea.

The country has many island groups, principally the Bismarck Archipelago, a portion of the Solomon Islands, the Trobriands, the D'Entrecasteaux Islands and the Louisade Archipelago. The main islands of the Bismarck Archipelago are New Britain, New Ireland and Manus. Bougainville is the largest of the Solomon Islands within Papua New Guinea.

Papua New Guinea lies within the tropics and has a typically monsoonal climate. Temperature and humidity are uniformly high throughout the year.

POPULATION – The population in 1991 (UN estimate) was 3,772,000.

CAPITAL – ΨPort Moresby. Estimated population (1990), 173,500. Other major towns are Lae, Rabaul, Madang, Wewak, Goroka and Mount Hagen.

CURRENCY – Kina (K) of 100 toea.

FLAG – Divided diagonally red (fly) and black (hoist); on the red a soaring Bird of Paradise in yellow and on the black five white stars of the Southern Cross.

NATIONAL ANTHEM – Arise All You Sons.

NATIONAL DAY – 16 September (Independence Day).

GOVERNMENT

New Guinea was sighted by Portuguese and Spanish navigators in the early sixteenth century, but remained largely isolated from the rest of the world. In 1884 a British Protectorate, British New Guinea, was proclaimed over the southern coast of New Guinea (Papua) and the adjacent islands, which were annexed outright in 1888. In 1906 the Territory of British New Guinea was placed under the authority of the Commonwealth of Australia.

In 1884 Germany had formally taken possession of certain northern areas, later to be known as the Trust Territory of New Guinea. In 1914 the German areas were occupied by Australian troops and remained under military administration until 1921, when the League of Nations conferred on Australia a mandate for their government. New Guinea was administered under the mandate and Papua under the Papua

Act until the invasion by the Japanese in 1942 when the civil administration was suspended until the surrender of the Japanese in 1945.

From 1970 there was a gradual assumption of powers by the Papua New Guinea Government, culminating in formal self-government in December 1973. Papua New Guinea achieved full independence on 16 September 1975.

Elections are held every five years. The Parliament comprises 109 elected members, 20 from regional electorates, the remainder from open electorates. There are 19 provinces, which have their own provincial governments with certain legislative and administrative powers.

SECESSION

Bougainville witnessed separatist tensions at the time of independence and in 1989 a secessionist movement, the Bougainville Revolutionary Army (BRA), began an insurrection on Bougainville. In March 1990 the Papua New Guinean security forces withdrew from the island and the BRA declared an independent republic in May 1990. In January 1991, a peace accord was signed between the two sides; the question of Bougainville's future status was deferred. However, fighting has continued, with Papua New Guinea security forces returning to the island in October 1992. Raids by Papua New Guinean forces on islands in the Solomons chain to destroy supply routes to the rebels led to Solomon Island government protests and clashes between Papuan and Solomon Islands patrol boats in April 1993.

Governor-General, His Excellency Sir Wiwa Korowi, GCMG.

NATIONAL EXECUTIVE COUNCIL *as at August 1993*
Prime Minister, Rt. Hon. Paias Wingti.
Deputy PM and Minister of Finance and Planning, Rt. Hon. Sir Julius Chan, KBE.
Provincial Affairs and Village Development, John Nilkare, CMG.
Works, Albert Karo, CBE.
Transport, Roy Yaki.
Fisheries, Iairo Lasaro.
Public Services, Albert Kipalan.
Lands, Tim Ward.
Foreign Affairs, John Kaputin.
Mining and Petroleum, Masket Iangalio.
Forests, Tim Neville.
Bougainville, Michael Ogio.
Justice, Philemon Embel.
Agriculture, Roy Evara.
Environment and Conservation, Perry Zeipi.
Trade and Industry, David Mai.
Labour and Employment, Castan Maibawa.
Defence, Paul Tohian.
Education, Andrew Baing.
Health, Francis Koimanrea.
Housing, John Jaminan.
Home Affairs and Youth, Andrew Posai.
Communications, Martin Thompson.
Energy and Science, Thomas Pelika.
Police, Avusi Tanao.
Administrative Services, Matthew Yago.

PAPUA NEW GUINEA HIGH COMMISSION
3rd Floor, 14 Waterloo Place, London SWIR 4AR
Tel 071-930 0922/7

High Commissioner, His Excellency Noel Levi, CBE (1991).

BRITISH HIGH COMMISSION
PO Box 4778, Boroko, Port Moresby
Tel: Port Moresby 251677

High Commissioner, His Excellency John Westgarth Guy, OBE (1991).

COMMUNICATIONS

Air Niugini (the national airline) operates regular air services to other countries in the region. Internal air services are operated by Air Niugini, Douglas Airways, and Talair. Several shipping companies operate cargo services to Australia, Europe, the Far East and USA. There are very limited cargo and passenger services between Papua New Guinea main ports, outports, plantations and missions. Road communications are very limited, the most important road being that linking Lae with the populous highlands. Papua New Guinea is linked by international cable to Australia, Guam, Hong Kong, Kota Kinabalu, the Far East and USA. Telecommunications are widely available.

ECONOMY

Until the 1970s the Papua New Guinea economy was based almost entirely on agriculture, principally copra, cocoa, tea, coffee, palm oil, rubber, groundnuts, spices and timber. A variety of commercial agricultural developments co-exist with the traditional rural economy.

There are extensive mineral deposits throughout Papua New Guinea, including copper, gold, silver, nickel, chromite, bauxite and possibly commercial deposits of oil and gas. In 1972, Bougainville Copper Pty Ltd (BCL) began mining in the North Solomons Province, producing copper, silver and gold. The Bougainville copper mine closed indefinitely in May 1989 because of the unrest on the island. The most important new development is the exploitation of large copper and gold deposits on the Ok Tedi, in the Western Province.

Industry includes processing of primary products, and brewing, bottling and packaging, paint, plywood, and metal manufacturing and the construction industries.

TRADE WITH UK	1991	1992
Imports from UK	£15,446,000	£6,469,000
Exports to UK	32,170,000	41,020,000

PARAGUAY
República del Paraguay

Paraguay is an inland subtropical state of South America, situated between Argentina, Bolivia and Brazil. The area is estimated at 157,048 sq. miles (406,752 sq. km), with a population (1991 UN estimate) of 4,397,000.

Paraguay is a country of grassy plains and forested hills. In the angle formed by the Paraná-Paraguay confluence are extensive marshes, one of which, known as Neembucú (or endless) is drained by Lake Ypoa, a large lagoon south-east of the capital. The Chaco, lying between the rivers Paraguay and Pilcomayo and bounded on the north by Bolivia, is a flat plain, rising uniformly towards its western boundary to a height of 1,140 feet; it suffers much from floods and still more from drought, but the building of dams and reservoirs has converted part of it into good pasture for cattle raising.

LANGUAGE – Spanish is the official language of the country but outside the larger towns Guarani, the language of the largest single unit of original Indian inhabitants, is widely spoken. Four daily and five weekly newspapers are published in Asunción.

CAPITAL – Asunción, population (1985 census) 729,307; other centres are Ciudad del Este (98,491); Encarnación (31,445); Concepción (25,607); P. Juan Caballero (41,475).

CURRENCY – Guaraní (Gs) of 100 céntimos.
FLAG – Three horizontal bands, red, white, blue with the National seal on the obverse white band and the Treasury seal on the reverse white band.
NATIONAL ANTHEM – Paraguayos, Republica O Muerte (Paraguayans, republic or death).
NATIONAL DAY – 15 May.

GOVERNMENT

In 1535 Paraguay was settled as a Spanish possession. In 1811 it declared its independence from Spain.

The constitution provides for a two-chamber legislature consisting of a 45-member Senate and an 80-member Chamber of Deputies. Deputies are elected on a regional basis, the number of seats allocated to each regional department being directly proportional to the department's population. Voting is compulsory for all citizens over 18. The President is elected for a single five-year term and may not be re-elected. The Vice-President may only put himself forward for presidential elections if he resigns his post six months before the election. The President appoints the Cabinet, which exercises all the functions of government. During parliamentary recess it can govern by decree through the Council of State, the members of which are representative of the government, the armed forces and various other bodies.

Gen. Alfredo Stroessner, dictator from 1954, was overthrown by Gen. Andrés Rodriguez in February 1989. Gen. Rodriguez was elected President in May 1989. In May 1991, the first free municipal elections were held, and elections to the parliament were held in December 1991 and won by the ruling Colorado Party. Amendments to the constitution came into effect in June 1992. Presidential and legislative elections were held on 9 May 1993 The presidential election was won by Juan Carlos Wasmosy of the ruling Colorado Party (ANR-PC), which also won 20 of the 45 Senate seats and 40 of the 80 Chamber of Deputies seats. The opposition Authentic Radical Liberal Party (PLRA) and National Encounter (EN) won, respectively, 17 and eight Senate, and 32 and eight Chamber seats, depriving the Colorado Party of a majority in the legislature. After his inauguration, President Wasmosy moved to subjugate the military to civilian control.

HEAD OF STATE
President, Juan Carlos Wasmosy, *elected* 9 May 1993, *sworn in* 15 August 1993.

CABINET *as at August 1993*
Foreign Affairs, Diogenes Martinez.
Interior, Carlos Podesta.
Finance, Crispiniano Sandoval.
Education, Nicanor Duarte Frutos.
Agriculture and Livestock, Raul Torres Segovia.
Public Works and Communications, Carlos Facetti.
National Defence, Hugo Estigarribia Elizeche.
Public Health and Social Welfare, Candido Nunez Leon.
Justice and Labour, Juan Manuel Morales.
Industry and Commerce, Ubaldo Scavone.

EMBASSY OF PARAGUAY
Braemar Lodge, Cornwall Gardens, London SW7 4AQ
Tel 071-937 1253

Ambassador Extraordinary and Plenipotentiary, His Excellency Antonio Espinoza (1990).

BRITISH EMBASSY
Calle Presidente Franco 706 (PO Box 404), Asunción
Tel: Asuncíon 44472

Ambassador Extraordinary and Plenipotentiary and Consul-General, His Excellency Michael A. C. Dibben (1991).

ECONOMY

About three-quarters of the population are engaged in agriculture and cattle raising. Cassava, sugar cane, soya, corn, cotton and wheat are the main agricultural products. The forests contain many varieties of timber which find a good market abroad.

Paraguay's rivers give it considerable hydroelectric capacity. There is a hydroelectric power station at Acaray which exports surplus power to Argentina and Brazil. Joint hydroelectric projects have been undertaken with Brazil, on a hydroelectric dam at Itaipú, and with Argentina, at Yacyretá.

BUDGET EXPENDITURE 1990
Central Government   Gs 815.6m
Decentralized Bodies   1,600.5m

TRADE
The chief imports are machinery; fuels and lubricants; transport and accessories; and drinks and tobacco. The chief exports are soya bean; cotton fibres; meat; and coffee.

Trade with UK	1991	1992
Imports from UK	£38,229,000	£34,149,000
Exports to UK	1,488,000	2,514,000

COMMUNICATIONS

There are direct shipping services to Asunción from Europe and the USA, and river steamer services for internal transport and to Argentina. Eight airlines operate services from Asunción. There are 27,741 km (1990) of asphalted roads in Paraguay, connecting Asunción with São Paulo (26 hours) via the Bridge of Friendship and Foz de Yguazú, and with Buenos Aires (24 hours) via Puerto Pilcomayo, and about 4,050 miles of earth roads in fairly good condition, but liable to be closed or to become impassable in wet weather. A 1,000 km road links Asunción with the Bolivian border. Rail services, with train ferries, provide internal and international links.

DEFENCE

Paraguay has an active armed forces strength of 16,500 (11,000 conscripts). Conscripts serve 18 months in the Army and Air Force and two years in the Navy. The Army has a strength of 12,500 (8,600 conscripts), with five main battle tanks, 18 light tanks, 45 armoured personnel carriers and reconnaissance vehicles, and 40 artillery pieces. The Navy has a strength of 3,000 (1,500 conscripts), with seven lake and river patrol vessels, four support vessels and two combat aircraft. The Air Force has a strength of 1,000 (700 conscripts), with 17 combat aircraft. There is also a paramilitary special police service of 8,000 personnel.

EDUCATION

Education is free and compulsory. In 1990 there were 4,641 government primary schools with 694,972 pupils and 27,477 teachers. There were 809 secondary schools with 155,339 pupils and 8,112 teachers. The National University in Asunción had 20,343 students in 1984. The Catholic University had 10,971 students.

PERU
República del Peru

Peru is a maritime republic of South America, situated between 0° 00′ 48″ and 18° 21′ 00″ S. latitude and between

68° 39' 27" and 81° 20' 13" W. longitude. The area is 496,225 sq. miles (1,285,216 sq. km), with a population (1992 estimate) of 22,465,000.

The country is traversed throughout its length by the Andes, running parallel to the Pacific coast. There are three main regions, the Costa, west of the Andes, the Sierra or mountain ranges of the Andes, which include the Punas or mountainous wastes below the region of perpetual snow, and the Montaña or Selva, which is the vast area of jungle stretching from the eastern foothills of the Andes to the eastern frontiers of Peru. The coastal area, lying upon and near the Pacific, is not tropical though close to the Equator, being cooled by the Humboldt Current.

LANGUAGE – Spanish, the language of the original Spanish stock from which the governing and professional classes are mainly recruited, was formerly the only official language of the country. However, in 1979 Quechua and Aymará also became official languages. Quechua and Aymará are spoken by more than half the population of the country.

CAPITAL – Metropolitan Lima (including ΨCallao), population estimate (1991) 6,459,000. Other major cities are: Arequipa (634,200) and Lambayeque (534,400).

CURRENCY – Nuevo Sol 100 cents.

FLAG – Three vertical stripes of red, white, red.

NATIONAL ANTHEM – Somos Libres, Seámoslo Siempre (We are free, let us remain so forever).

NATIONAL DAY – 28 July (Anniversary of Independence).

GOVERNMENT

Peru was conquered in the early 16th century by Francisco Pizarro (1478–1541). He subjugated the Incas (the ruling caste of the Quechua Indians), who had started their rise to power some 500 years earlier, and for nearly three centuries Peru remained under Spanish rule. A revolutionary war of 1821–4 established its independence, declared on 28 July 1821. The constitution rests upon the fundamental law of 18 October 1856; the present constitution was passed in 1979.

Peru was afflicted by rampant inflation but this has gradually been brought under control to an annual rate of around 37 per cent. There remains drug-inspired violence and terrorism; the main guerrilla movements are the Maoist Sendero Luminoso (Shining Path) and the Movimiento Revolucionario Tupac Amaru (MRTA), whose leaders were captured in 1992. Large areas of the country are under states of emergency.

In April 1992 President Fujimori, faced with increasing terrorist violence, with the support of the armed forces suspended the constitution, dissolved Congress and began to govern with absolute powers. A programme of drastic market-orientated reform, new measures in the anti-terrorist war, and a streamlining of the executive, legislative and judicial institutions was undertaken. On 22 November 1992 a legislative general election was held to an 80-seat Democratic Constituent Congress (CCD) which was installed as an interim legislature and constituent assembly to write a new constitution. Parties supporting Fujimori's suspension of the constitution gained a majority in the CCD. On 6 January 1993 the 1979 constitution was re-established and the CCD declared Fujimori constitutional head of state. The CCD is to produce a new constitution which will be put to a national referendum for approval by the end of 1993.

HEAD OF STATE

President of the Republic, Alberto Fujimori, *assumed office* 28 July 1990.

CABINET *as at August 1993*

Prime Minister and Minister of Foreign Affairs, Dr Oscar de la Puente Raygada.
Economy and Finance, Jorge Camet Dickman.
Interior, Gen. Juan Briones Dávilla.
Justice, Dr Fernando Vega Santa Gadea.
Defence, Gen. Victor Malca Villanueva.
Education, Eduardo Varillas Montenegro.
Health, Victor Paredes Guerra.
Labour and Social Promotion, Augusto Antoniolli Vásquez.
Agriculture, Absalon Vásquez Villanueva.
Energy and Mines, Daniel Hokama Tokahashi.
Transport and Communications, Housing and Construction, Dante Córdova Blanco.
Fisheries, Jaime Augustin Sobero Taira.
Industry, Commerce, Tourism and Integration, Alfonso Bustamante.
Minister of the Presidency, Manuel Vara Ochoa.

EMBASSY OF PERU
52 Sloane Street, London SW1X 9SP
Tel 071-235 1917/2545/3802

Ambassador Extraordinary and Plenipotentiary, His Excellency Arturo Garcia (1992).

BRITISH EMBASSY
Natalio Sánchez 125, Piso 12, Plaza Washington (PO Box 854), Lima 100.
Tel: Lima 334735

Ambassador Extraordinary and Plenipotentiary, His Excellency Keith Haskell, CMG, CVO (1990).
First Secretary (Commercial), F. R. C. Thomson (*Deputy Head of Mission and Consul*).

There is a British Consular Office at *Lima* and Honorary Consulates in *Arequipa, Cusco, Iquitos, Piura* and *Trujillo*.

BRITISH COUNCIL REPRESENTATIVE, J. Harvey, PO Box No. 14-0114, Calle Alberto Lynch 110, San Isidro, Lima 14.

ECONOMY

In March 1993 Peru cleared its arrears with the World Bank and IMF of US$1,700 million, enabling it to gain access to a new IMF loan of US$1,395 million over three years. The total foreign debt in 1993 stood at US$21,000 million.

The chief products of the coastal belt are cotton, sugar and petroleum. There are large tracts of land suitable for cultivation and stock-raising (cattle, sheep, llamas, alpacas and vicuñas) on the eastern slopes of the Andes, and in the mountain valleys maize, potatoes and wheat are grown. The jungle area is a source of timber and petroleum. Other major crops are fruit, vegetables, rice, barley, grapes and coffee. The mountains contain rich mineral deposits and mineral exports include lead, zinc, copper, iron ore and silver. Peru is normally the world's largest exporter of fishmeal.

TRADE

Import trade of Peru in 1991 totalled US$3,515 million and exports US$3,307 million. The principal imports are machinery and chemicals and pharmaceutical products. The chief exports are minerals and metals, fishmeal, sugar, cotton and coffee.

Trade with UK	1991	1992
Imports from UK	£33,061,000	£30,775,000
Exports to UK	84,034,000	91,804,000

COMMUNICATIONS

In recent years the coastal and sierra zones have been opened up by means of roads and air routes. There is air communication, as well as communication by protracted land routes, with the tropical and eastern zones which lie east of the Andes towards the borders of Brazil. The Andean Highway forms a link between the Pacific, the Amazon and the Atlantic. The Pan-American Highway runs along the Peruvian coast connecting it with Ecuador and Chile. The Inter-Ocean Corridor linking the port of Matarani and Buenos Aires will be opened soon.

The railway is administered by the Government. There is also steam navigation on the Ucayali and Huallaga, and in the south on Lake Titicaca. Air services are maintained throughout Peru, and many international services call at Lima.

DEFENCE

The Armed Forces have a total active strength of some 112,000 (69,000 conscripts), with selective conscription of some two years duration. The Army has a strength of 75,000 (52,000 conscripts) and is heavily engaged in combating the Shining Path and MRTA guerrilla movements. It has a strength of 14 divisions with some 300 main battle tanks, 110 light tanks, 620 reconnaissance and armoured personnel carriers and 300 artillery pieces. The Navy has some 22,000 personnel (10,000 conscripts), divided into the Pacific, Lake Titicaca and Amazon River force areas. It has a strength of nine submarines, two cruisers, ten destroyers and frigates, seven patrol and coastal vessels, eight combat aircraft and 12 armed helicopters. The Air Force has a strength of 15,000 personnel (7,000 conscripts), with 107 combat aircraft and ten armed helicopters. In addition there is the paramilitary National Police of some 84,000 who also play a major role in counter-insurgency operations.

EDUCATION

Education is compulsory and free between five and 16.

THE PHILIPPINES
Repúblika ng Pilipinas

The Philippines are situated between 21° 20′–4° 30′ N. latitude and 116° 55′–126° 36′ E. longitude, and are about 500 miles from the south-east coast of the continent of Asia. The total land area of the country is 115,831 sq. miles (300,000 sq. km). There are eleven larger islands and 7,079 other islands. The principal islands are:

	sq. miles		sq. miles
Luzon	40,422	Mindoro	3,759
Mindanao	36,538	Leyte	2,786
Samar	5,050	Cebu	1,703
Negros	4,906	Bohol	1,492
Palawan	4,550	Masbate	1,262
Panay	4,446		

Other groups are the Sulu islands (capital, Jolo), Babuyanes and Batanes; the Calamian islands; and Kalaynan Islands.
POPULATION – The population of the Philippines (UN estimate 1991) is 62,868,000. The inhabitants are basically of Malay stock, with a considerable admixture of Spanish and Chinese blood in many localities. The Chinese minority is estimated at 500,000, with smaller numbers of Spanish, American and Indian.

RELIGION – About 90 per cent are Christian, predominantly Roman Catholics. Most of the remainder are Muslims, in the south, and indigenous animists, mainly in Luzon and parts of Mindanao.
LANGUAGE – The official languages are Filipino and English. Filipino is based on Tagalog, one of the Malay-Polynesian languages and the language of the part of Luzon surrounding Metro Manila. Filipino is spoken by 29.66 per cent of the total number of households (and understood by nearly 90 per cent of the population), but local languages and dialects are strong and Cebuano is spoken by 24.2 per cent of total households. English, which is the language of government and of instruction in secondary and university education, is spoken by at least 44 per cent of the population. Spanish, which ceased to be an official language in 1973, is now spoken by a very small minority. Eighty-nine per cent of the population are literate.

CAPITAL – Ψ Manila, on the island of Luzon, estimated population (1990) City area 1,876,195; Manila with suburbs (incl. Quezon City, Pasay City, Caloocan City, Makati, Parañaque, San Juan Mandaluyong and Navotas) 6,720,050. The next largest cities are (1989 estimate) Ψ Cebu (613,184), Ψ Davao (819,525), Ψ Iloilo (287,711), Ψ Zamboanga (433,328), and Bacolod (328,648).
CURRENCY – Philippine peso (P) of 100 centavos.
FLAG – Equal horizontal bands of blue (above) and red; gold sun with three stars on a white triangle next staff.
NATIONAL ANTHEM – Bayang Magiliw.
NATIONAL DAY – 12 June (Independence Day).

GOVERNMENT

The Portuguese navigator Magellan came to the Philippines in 1521 and was killed by the natives of Mactan, a small island near Cebu. In 1565 Spain undertook the conquest of the country, which was named Filipinas after Philip II of Spain when he was heir apparent. In 1762 Manila was occupied by a British force, but in 1764 it was restored to Spain. In 1896 the Filipinos revolted against Spanish rule and in the Spanish–American War of 1898, Manila was captured by American troops with the help of Filipinos and the islands were ceded to the United States by the Treaty of Paris 1898. Despite a rebellion against US rule between 1899 and 1902, the Americans remained in control of the country until 1946. The Republic of the Philippines came into existence on 4 July 1946.

Ferdinand Marcos was President from 1965 to 1986. Although he gained a majority of votes in the official count of a presidential election in February 1986, the election was marred by widespread electoral abuse and his rival, Mrs Corazon Aquino, launched a series of non-violent civil disturbance actions which gained wide support. On 25 February Marcos, his family and aides left for Hawaii. Mrs Aquino took over as President and survived seven coup attempts to overthrow her.

A new constitution was approved by referendum in February 1987 and came into force on 27 July 1987. Legislative authority is vested in a bicameral elected Congress comprising a House of Representatives of up to 250 members and a 24-member Senate.

INSURGENCY

There is unrest in many of the islands due to insurgency. Muslim insurgents, the Moro National Liberation Front, operate in western Mindanao and the Sulu archipelago. Most of the current activity is due to the Communist New People's Army, which is strongest in eastern Mindanao, Negros, Samar, Bicol, the mountains of northern Luzon, and Bataan.

HEAD OF STATE
President, Fidel V. Ramos, *assumed office* 30 June 1992.
Vice-President, Joseph Estrada.

CABINET SECRETARIES *as at August 1993*
Foreign Affairs, Roberto Romulo.
Finance, Ernest Leung.
Justice, Franklin Drilon.
Agriculture, Roberto Sebastian.
Public Works and Highways, Gregorio Vigilar.
Education, Culture and Sport, Armand Fabella.
Labour and Employment, Nieves Confesor.
National Defence, Renato de Villa.
Health, Dr Juan Flavier.
Trade and Industry, Rizalino Navarro.
Social Welfare and Development, Corazon de Leon.
Agrarian Reform, Ernesto Garilao.
Interior and Local Government, Rafael Alunan.
Tourism, Vicente Carlos.
Environment and Natural Resources, Angel Alcala.
Budget and Management, Salvador Enriquez.
Transport and Communications, Jesus Garcia.
Science and Technology, Ricardo Gloria.
Director-General, National Economic and Development Authority, Cielito Habito.
Energy, Delfin Lazaro.

EMBASSY OF THE PHILIPPINES
9A Palace Green, London W8 4QE
Tel 071-937 1600/9

Ambassador Extraordinary and Plenipotentiary, His Excellency Jesus P. Tambunting (1993).
Minister-Counsellor, A. G. Villacorte.
Defence Attaché, Col. C. P. Garcia.
First Secretary and Consul, E. C. Castro.
Commercial Attaché, P. Sales.

BRITISH EMBASSY
Locsin Building, 6752 Ayala Avenue, Corner Makati Avenue, Makati, Metro Manila (PO Box 1970)
Tel: Manila 816-7116

Ambassador Extraordinary and Plenipotentiary, His Excellency Alan Montgomery, CMG (1992).
Deputy Ambassador, D. B. Merry.
Assistant Defence Attaché, Lt.-Cdr. C. C. Williams.
First Secretary, R. Cork (*Commercial*).

BRITISH COUNCIL REPRESENTATIVE, N. Bisset, 7, 3rd Street, New Manila, PO Box AC 168, Cubao, Quezon City, Metro Manila.

DEFENCE

The Philippine armed forces number some 104,500 active personnel with a further 131,000 reserves, and have been engaged for some years in combating Communist and Muslim insurgent forces. The Army has an active strength of 68,000 personnel, with 41 light tanks, 370 armoured personnel carriers and armoured infantry fighting vehicles and 240 artillery pieces. The Navy has 21,000 personnel, including 8,500 marines, and deploys one frigate, 42 patrol and coastal vessels, five combat aircraft and ten marine battalions. The Air Force has some 15,500 personnel, with 49 combat aircraft and 94 armed helicopters. The paramilitary Philippine National Police number some 90,000 personnel and there is a part-time militia of 45,000 personnel.

EDUCATION

Secondary and higher education is extensive and there are 37 private universities recognized by the Government,

including the Dominican University of Santo Tomas (founded in 1611). There are also 296 state-supported colleges and universities, including the University of the Philippines, founded 1908.

COMMUNICATIONS

The highway system covered 161,709 kilometres in 1985 and there was a total of 1,120,172 registered road vehicles. The Philippine National Railway used to operate 1,282 km of track, but a greater part of this is now being rebuilt. There are 94 ports of entry in the Philippines and 164,404 vessels of various types totalling 50,467,000 tons are engaged in inter-island traffic. There are 82 national airports and 137 privately operated airports. Philippine Air Lines have regular flights throughout the Far East, to the USA and Europe, in addition to inter-island services.

ECONOMY

The Philippines is a predominantly agricultural country, the chief products being rice, coconuts, maize, sugar-cane, abaca (manila hemp), fruits, tobacco and lumber. There is, however, an increasing number of manufacturing industries and it is the policy of the Government to diversify its economy.

TRADE
Principal exports are sugar, coconut oil, copper concentrate, lumber and copra, together with increasingly important manufactured exports such as electronics products and clothing. The major trading partners are the USA, Japan, Taiwan and Hong Kong.

	1992
Total imports	US$10,580,000,000
Total exports	7,150,000,000

Trade with UK	1991	1992
Imports from UK	£146,571,000	£204,962,000
Exports to UK	229,955,000	240,732,000

POLAND
Rzeczpospolita Polska

Poland adjoins Germany in the west, the boundary being formed by the rivers Oder and Neisse, the Czech Republic and Slovakia in the south, and Belarus, Ukraine, Lithuania and the Kaliningrad region of Russia in the east. To the north is the Baltic Sea. The country has an area of 120,725 sq. miles (312,677 sq. km), and a population (official estimate 1991) of 38,300,000. Roman Catholicism is the religion of 95 per cent of the inhabitants.

CAPITAL – Warsaw, on the Vistula, population (1989) 1,655,063. Other large towns are Łódź (851,690); Kraków (748,356); Wrocław (642,234); Poznan (588,715); Gdansk (464,649); Szczecin (412,000); Katowice (367,041); Bydgoszcz (380,385).
CURRENCY – Zloty of 100 groszy.
FLAG – Equal horizontal stripes of white (above) and red.
NATIONAL ANTHEM – Jeszcze Polska Nie Zginela (Poland has not yet been destroyed).
NATIONAL DAY – 3 May.

GOVERNMENT

The Polish Commonwealth ceased to exist in 1795 after three successive partitions in 1772, 1793 and 1795, in which Prussia, Russia and Austria shared. The Republic of Poland, reconstituted within the limits of the old Polish Commonwealth, was proclaimed at Warsaw in November 1918, and its independence guaranteed by the signatories of the Treaty of Versailles.

German forces invaded Poland on 1 September 1939; on 17 September, Russian forces invaded eastern Poland, and on 21 September 1939 Poland was declared by Germany and Russia to have ceased to exist. At the end of the war a coalition government was formed in which the Polish Workers' Party played a large part. In December 1948, the Polish Workers' Party and the Polish Socialist Party fused in the new Polish United Workers' Party (PUWP). A new constitution modelled on the Soviet constitution was adopted in July 1952, and was modified in February 1976.

In July 1980 steep rises in food prices but static wages led to widespread strikes. The strikes continued throughout August, obliging the government to agree to allow independent trade unions, the right to strike, the easing of censorship and other political and economic demands. The independent trade union movement Solidarity, led by Lech Walesa, became a powerful force but many of its leaders, including Walesa, were detained and union activity suspended when martial law was declared in December 1981. Initially there was some passive resistance to martial law, which was suspended in December 1982 and finally lifted in July 1983.

A wave of strikes resulted in talks between Walesa and the PUWP early in 1989. By April plans for political and economic reforms had been drawn up. These included the restoration of the legal status of Solidarity (17 April); the introduction of a bicameral parliamentary system comprising an upper house (Senate) and lower house (Sejm), and an executive presidency; multi-party parliamentary elections were held in the summer of 1989, following which the PUWP ceased to be the ruling party. The post-Communist governments have rapidly introduced a market economy.

Parliamentary elections held in October 1991 led to an extremely fragmented Parliament of over 20 parties. Jan Olszewski formed a government in January 1992, but this was voted out of office by Parliament in June 1992. Hanna Suchocka successfully formed a government in July 1992; this fell in May 1993 but continues as a caretaker government until elections in October 1993.

Disagreement over a post-Communist constitution ended in November 1992 when President Walesa signed a 'small constitution' approved by the parliament which defines the division of powers between the President and government.

HEAD OF STATE

President, Lech Walesa, *elected* 9 December 1990 *for a five-year term.*

COUNCIL OF MINISTERS *as at August 1993*

Prime Minister, Hanna Suchocka.
Deputy Prime Minister (Economy), Henryk Goryszewski.
Deputy Prime Minister (Policy), Pawel Laczkowski.
Head of the Council of Minister's Office, Jan Rokita.
Foreign Affairs, Krzysztof Skubiszewski.
Internal Affairs, Andrzej Milczanowski.
National Defence, Janusz Onyszkiewicz.
Justice and Attorney-General, Jan Piatkowski.
Head of the Central Planning Office, Jerzy Kropiwnicki.
Finance, Jerzy Osiatynski.
Foreign Economic Relations, Andrzej Arendarski.
Agriculture (acting), Janusz Bylinski.
Transport and Maritime Economy, Zbigniew Jaworski.
Environment Protection, Natural Resources and Forestry, Zygmunt Hortmanowicz.
Labour and Social Policy, Jacek Kuron.
National Education, Zdobyslaw Flisowski.

Culture, Piotr Lukasiewicz.
Health, Andrzej Wojtyla.
Poland-European Community Relations, Krzysztof Bielecki.
Business Enterpreneurship, Zbigniew Eysmont.
Minister without Portfolio, Jerzy Kaminski.
Industry and Trade, Waclaw Niewiarowski.
Land Management and Construction, Andrzej Bratkowski.
Communication, Krzysztof Kilian.
Privatization, Janusz Lewandowski.
Head of Scientific Research Committee, Witold Karczewski.

EMBASSY OF THE REPUBLIC OF POLAND
47 Portland Place, London WIN 3AG
Tel 071-580 4324/9

Ambassador Extraordinary and Plenipotentiary, His Excellency Tadeusz de Virion (1990).
Defence Attaché, Col. K. Cukierski.
Consul-General, Dr J. Kochanowski.
Minister, R. Szuniewicz (*Commercial*).

BRITISH EMBASSY
No. 1 Aleja Róz, 00-556 Warsaw
Tel: Warsaw 6281001

Ambassador Extraordinary and Plenipotentiary, His Excellency Michael J. Llewellyn-Smith, CMG (1991).
Counsellor, R. A. E. Gordon, OBE (*Deputy Head of Mission*).
Defence and Air Attaché, Gp. Capt. H. H. Moses, MBE.
First Secretary (Commercial), A. J. Gooch.

BRITISH COUNCIL REPRESENTATIVE, Dr Barry Brown, OBE, Al. Jerozolimskie 59, 00-697 Warsaw.

DEFENCE

The total active armed forces strength numbers 296,500 personnel (167,400 conmscripts) with a further 435,200 reserves. Conscripts serve in all services for 18 months. The Army numbers 194,200 (109,800 conscripts) with 2,850 main battle tanks, 685 reconnaissance vehicles, 2,220 armoured infantry fighting vehicles and armoured personnel carriers and 2,316 artillery pieces. The Navy has a strength of 19,300 including 10,600 conscripts, with three submarines, one destroyer, one frigate, 20 patrol and coastal vessels, 38 combat aircraft and four armed helicopters. The Air Force is 83,000 strong (47,000 conscripts), with 423 combat aircraft and 31 attack helicopters. The Paramilitary Border Guards and Citizens Militia number 38,000 personnel (13,000 conscripts). Russia maintains a force of 6,000 communications and transport troops to co-ordinate the withdrawal of forces from Germany.

EDUCATION

Elementary education (ages seven to 15) is compulsory and free. Secondary education is optional and free. There are universities at Kraków, Warsaw, Poznan, Lódź, Wroclaw, Lublin and Toruń and a considerable number of other towns.

CULTURE

Polish is a western Slavonic tongue, the Latin alphabet being used. Major writers include Henryk Sienkiewicz (1846-1916), Nobel Prizewinner for Literature in 1905; Boleslaw Prus (1847-1912); Stanislaw Reymont (1868-1925), Nobel Prizewinner in 1924; Czeslaw Milosz, Nobel Prizewinner in 1980.

The state monopoly on radio and television broadcasting ended in October 1992.

ECONOMY

Mines, petroleum resources, water, gas and electricity services, banks, textile factories and large retail stores were nationalized in 1946. Until recently over 99 per cent of Polish industry was stated to be 'socialized', but 68 per cent of agricultural land was privately farmed. Legislation passed in July 1990 provided a framework for 80 per cent of the economy to be transferred from the state to the private sector. In 1991 the IMF and western banks suspended co-operation and lending because the government had exceeded agreed budget deficit and inflation limits. The IMF-prescribed 'shock therapy' treatment for the economy was resumed in 1992 with reforms to allow bankruptcy and the ending of state subsidies to reduce the budget deficit. After the passing of a budget in March 1993, which kept the deficit to 5.5 per cent of GDP, and a mass privatization bill for 600 state-owned firms, passed by parliament in April, the IMF and the banks provided more credit to enable reforms to continue.

Trade with UK	1991	1992
Imports from UK	£347,069,000	£605,586,000
Exports to UK	313,828,000	356,173,000

PORTUGAL
República Portuguesa

Portugal occupies the western part of the Iberian Peninsula, covering an area of 34,317 sq. miles (88,880 sq. km). It lies between 36° 58' and 42° 12" N. latitude and 6° 11' 48" and 9° 29' 45" W. longitude. It is 362 miles in length from north to south, and averages about 117 miles in breadth from east to west.

POPULATION – The population (UN estimate 1991) is 10,582,000 (including the Azores and Madeira).

LANGUAGE – Portuguese is a Romance language with admixtures of Arabic and other idioms. It is the language of Portugal and Brazil, and is also used in Portugal's former colonies. There are four morning and three evening daily newspapers in Lisbon and three morning papers in Oporto, and six main weekly newspapers.

CAPITAL – ΨLisbon, population estimate (1989) 2,128,000. ΨOporto 1,683,000.

CURRENCY – Escudo (Esc) of 100 centavos.

FLAG – Divided vertically into unequal parts of green and red with the national emblem over all on the line of division.

NATIONAL ANTHEM – A Portuguesa.

NATIONAL DAY – 10 June.

GOVERNMENT

From the 11th century until 1910 Portugal was a monarchy, but in 1910 an armed rising in Lisbon drove King Manuel II into exile and a republic was set up. A period of great political instability ensued until eventually the military stepped in. The Constitution of 1933 gave formal expression to the corporative 'Estado Novo' (New State) which was personified by Dr Salazar, Prime Minister 1932–68. Dr Caetano succeeded Salazar as Prime Minister in 1968 but his failure to liberalize the regime or to conclude the wars in the African colonies resulted in his government's overthrow by a military coup on 25 April 1974. There was great political turmoil between April 1974 and July 1976 but with the failure of an attempted coup by the extreme left in November 1975 the situation became more stable.

The President, elected for a five-year term by universal adult suffrage, appoints the Prime Minister. Legislative authority is vested in the 230-member Assembly of the Republic, elected by a system of proportional representation for a term of up to four years.

In the General Election held on 6 October 1991, the Social Democratic Party (PSD) won 135 seats; the Socialist Party (PS) 72 seats; the Communist Party (PCP) 17 seats, the Christian Democrats (CDS) 5 seats and the National Solidarity Party 1 seat.

HEAD OF STATE
President of the Republic, Dr Mario Soares, *elected* 1986, *re-elected* 13 January 1991.

MINISTERS *as at August 1993*
Prime Minister, Anibal Cavaco Silva.
Minister of the Presidency, Defence, Joaquim Fernando Nogueira.
Justice, Dr Alvaro Laborinho Lucio.
Parliamentary Affairs, Luis Marques Mendes.
Finance, Jorge Braga de Macedo.
Planning and Territorial Administration, Luis Valente de Oliveira.
Home Affairs, Manuel Dias Loureiro.
Foreign, José Durão Barroso.
Agriculture, Arlindo Marques da Cunha.
Industry and Energy, Luis Mira Amaral.
Education, António Couto dos Santos.
Public Works, Transport and Communications, Joaquim Ferreira do Amaral.
Health, Arlindo Gomes de Carvalho.
Labour and Social Security, José Silva Peneda.
Commerce and Tourism, Fernando Faria de Oliveira.
Environment and Natural Resources, Carlos Borrego.
Sea, Eduardo de Azevedo Soares.

PORTUGUESE EMBASSY
11 Belgrave Square, London SW1X 8PP
Tel 071–235 5331

Ambassador Extraordinary and Plenipotentiary, His Excellency Antonio Vaz-Pereira, GCVO (1989).
Minister Counsellor, Francisco Seixas-da-Costa, CMG.
Defence Attaché, Col. A. M. A. dos Santos, CBE.
Counsellor, J. D. Ortigão, CMG (*Consular*); J. A. Pereira, LVO (*Economic*).

BRITISH EMBASSY
35–37 Rua de S. Domingos à Lapa, 1200 Lisbon
Tel: Lisbon 3961191

Ambassador Extraordinary and Plenipotentiary, His Excellency John Wall, CMG, LVO (1993).
Deputy Ambassador, Counsellor, T. T. Macan.
Defence Attaché, Cdr. R. Wykes-Sneyd, AFC.
First Secretaries, K. J. Baudains (*Commercial*); D. J. Ferguson (*Consul*).

There are British Consulates in *Oporto*, *Portimão*, *Funchal* (Madeira) and *Ribeira Grande* (Azores).

BRITISH COUNCIL REPRESENTATIVE, Patrick Jackson, Rua de Sao Marçal 174, 1294 Lisbon. There are also offices at *Cascais*, *Coimbra* and *Oporto*.
BRITISH PORTUGUESE CHAMBER OF COMMERCE, Rua da Estrela 8, 1200 Lisbon and Rua Sa de Bandeira 784–20E, Frente, 4000 Oporto.

DEFENCE

The armed forces have a total active strength of 58,300 (32,800 conscripts) with reserves of 190,000. Conscripts serve eight to twelve months. The present strength of the Army is 32,700 (24,800 conscripts), with 130 main battle tanks, 375 armoured personnel carriers and reconnaissance vehicles, and 306 artillery pieces. The Navy consists of 15,300 personnel (5,000 conscripts), including 2,500 marines, manning three submarines, 10 frigates and 29 patrol and coastal vessels. The strength of the Air Force is 10,300 (3,000 conscripts), including 2,200 paratroops, with 83 combat aircraft plus helicopters and transport and training aircraft. The paramilitary National Republican Guard, Public Security Police and Border Security Force number a total of 49,800 personnel.

Lisbon is the base of the NATO Iberian Atlantic Command and the US maintains 1,600 personnel in mainland Portugal and on the Azores.

EDUCATION

Education is free and compulsory for nine years from the age of six. Secondary education is mainly conducted in state lyceums, commercial and industrial schools, but there are also private schools. There are also military, naval, technical, polytechnic and other special schools. There are universities at Coimbra (founded in 1290), Oporto, Lisbon, Braga, Aveiro, Vila Real, Faro, Evora and in the Azores.

COMMUNICATIONS

There are international airports at Lisbon and Oporto, and at Faro in the Algarve.

ECONOMY

The chief agricultural products are cork, cereals, rice, vegetables, olives, figs, citrus fruits, almonds, timber, port wine and table wines. There are extensive forests of pine, cork, eucalyptus and chestnut covering about 20 per cent of the total area of the country. The principal mineral products are pyrites, wolfram, uranium, iron ores, copper and sodium and calcium minerals.

The country is moderately industrialized. The principal manufactures are textiles, clothing and footwear, machinery (including electric machinery and transport equipment), pulp and paper, pharmaceuticals, foodstuffs, chemicals, fertilizers, wood, cork, furniture, cement, glassware and pottery. There are a modern steelworks and two large shipbuilding and repair yards at Lisbon and Setúbal, working mainly for foreign shipowners. There are several hydro-electric power stations and a new thermal power station.

TRADE

The principal imports are cereals, meat, raw and semi-manufactured iron and steel, industrial machinery, chemicals, crude oil, motor vehicles and raw materials for textiles. The principal exports are textiles, footwear, timber, pulp, automotive parts, cork, electrical and other machinery, and chemicals.

	1988	1989
Total imports	£6,164,627m	£11,535,432m
Total exports	4,230,727m	7,738,209m

Trade with UK	1991	1992
Imports from UK	£1,085,084,000	£1,164,098,000
Exports to UK	1,043,511,000	1,170,815,000

OVERSEAS REGIONS

Madeira and The Azores are two administratively autonomous regions of Portugal, having locally elected assemblies and governments.

MADEIRA

Madeira is a group of islands in the Atlantic Ocean about 520 miles south-west of Lisbon, and consists of Madeira, Porto,

Santo and three uninhabited islands (Desertas). The total area is 314 sq. miles (813 sq. km), with a population of 271,400 (1989). ΨFunchal in Madeira, the largest island (270 square miles), is the capital (population 44,111); Machico (10,905).

THE AZORES

The Azores are a group of nine islands (Flores, Corvo, Terceira, São Jorge, Pico, Faial, Graciosa, São Miguel and Santa Maria) in the Atlantic Ocean, with a total area of 922 sq. miles (2,387 sq. km), and a population of 255,100 (1989). ΨPonta Delgada, on São Miguel, is the capital of the group (population 137,700). Other ports are ΨAngra, in Terceira (55,900) and ΨHorta (16,300).

OVERSEAS TERRITORY

MACAO

Macao, situated at the mouth of the Pearl River, comprises a peninsula and the islands of Coloane and Taipa, having an area of six sq. miles (15.5 sq. km), with a population (UN estimate 1990) of 479,000. Macao became a Portuguese colony in 1557; in a Sino-Portuguese treaty of 1887 China recognized Portugal's sovereignty over Macao. Following the Sino-British Joint Declaration on Hong Kong in 1984, Sino-Portuguese negotiations on the transfer of administration began in 1986 and an agreement on the transfer of the administration of Macao to the Chinese authorities was signed on 13 April 1987. Macao will become a 'special administrative region' (SAR) of China when transferred on 20 December 1999. The final session of the Macao SAR Basic Law Drafting Committee was held in Beijing in January 1993 and approved the Basic Law which will serve as Macao's constitution after 1999.

Macao is subject to Portuguese constitutional law but otherwise enjoys autonomy. The Governor is appointed by the Portuguese President and there is a 23-member legislative assembly, which has a three-year term. The assembly comprises seven members appointed by the Governor; eight directly elected, and eight indirectly elected by business associations.

Macao's major industry is textile manufacturing which accounts for 62 per cent of all exports. Port Macao is served by British, Portuguese and Dutch shipping lines and has regular services to Hong Kong, some 35 miles away.

Governor, Rocha Vieira.

Trade with UK	1991	1992
Imports from UK	£15,329,000	£8,473,000
Exports to UK	40,010,000	36,306,000

QATAR
Dawlat Qatar

The state of Qatar covers the peninsula of Qatar from approximately the northern shore of Khor al Odaid to the eastern shore of Khor al Salwa. The area is about 4,247 sq. miles (11,000 sq. km).

POPULATION – The population (UN estimate 1991) is 381,000. Most of the population is concentrated in the urban district of the capital Doha. Only a small minority still pursue the traditional life of the semi-nomadic tribesmen and fisherfolk.

CAPITAL – ΨDoha, population (estimated) 220,000. Other towns include Khor, Dukhan, Wakra and ΨUmm Said.

CURRENCY – Qatar riyal of 100 dirhams.

FLAG – White and maroon, white portion nearer the mast; vertical indented line comprising 17 angles divides the colours.
NATIONAL DAY – 3 September.

GOVERNMENT

Qatar was one of nine independent emirates in the Gulf in special treaty relations with the UK until 1971, when the special treaty relations were terminated. On 2 April 1970 a provisional constitution for Qatar was proclaimed, providing for the establishment of a Council of Ministers and for the formation of a Consultative Council to assist the Council of Ministers in running the affairs of the state. There are no political parties or legislature.

HEAD OF STATE
Amir of Qatar and Prime Minister, HH Sheikh Khalifa bin Hamad Al Thani, GCMG, GCB, *assumed power* 22 February 1972.
Heir Apparent, Minister of Defence and Commander-in-Chief of Armed Forces, HH Sheikh Hamad bin Khalifa Al Thani, KCMG.

COUNCIL OF MINISTERS *as at August 1993*
Interior, HE Sheikh Abdullah bin Khalifa Al Thani.
Finance, Economy and Trade, HE Sheikh Mohammed bin Khalifa Al-Thani.
Foreign Affairs, HE Sheikh Hamad bin Jassem bin Jabr Al-Thani.
Education, HE Abdulaziz Abdullah Turki.
Justice, HE Sheikh Ahmed bin Saif Al Thani.
Minister of State for Defence Affairs HE Sheikh Hamad bin Abdulah Al-Thani.
Endowments and Islamic Affairs, HE Sheikh Abdullah bin Khalid Al-Thani.
Municipal Affairs and Agriculture, HE Sheikh Ahmed bin Hamad Al-Thani.
Labour, Social Affairs and Housing, HE Abdulrahman Saad Al Dirham.
Communications and Transport, HE Abdulla bin Saleh Al Manna.
Public Health, HE Sheikh Hamad bin Suhaim Al-Thani.
Information and Culture, HE Dr Hamad Abdulaziz Al-Kawari.
Amiri Diwan Affairs, HE Dr Issa Ghanim Al Kawari.
Electricity and Water, HE Ahmed Mohamed Ali Al-Subaie.
Energy and Industry, HE Abdulla Bin Hamad Al-Attiyah.

EMBASSY OF THE STATE OF QATAR
27 Chesham Place, London SW1X 8HG
Tel 071-235 0851

Ambassador Extraordinary and Plenipotentiary, His Excellency Ali Al-Jaidha (1993).

BRITISH EMBASSY
PO Box 3, Doha
Tel: Doha 421991

Ambassador Extraordinary and Plenipotentiary, His Excellency Patrick F. Wogan, CMG (1993).
First Secretary, F. G. Geere (*Commercial*).

BRITISH COUNCIL REPRESENTATIVE, J. Shorter, Ras Abu Aboud Road (PO Box 2992), Doha.

ECONOMY

Although Qatar is a desert country, there are gardens and smallholdings near Doha and to the north, and encouragement is being given to the development of agriculture.

The Qatar General Petroleum Corporation is the state-owned company controlling Qatar's interests in oil, gas and petrochemicals. The corporation is responsible for Qatar's oil production onshore and offshore. The production level for Qatar agreed in OPEC is currently 364,000 b.p.d. Explorations continue for further oil. The large reserves of natural gas in the North Field came into production in September 1991. A 50,000 b.p.d. oil refinery was commissioned in 1984 to increase domestic refinery capacity.

Current industries include a steel mill, a fertilizer plant, a cement factory, a petrochemical complex and two natural gas liquids plants. With the exception of the cement works at Umm Bab, all these industries are at Umm Said, about 30 miles south of Doha. Qatar is also expanding its infrastructure, including electrical generation and water distillation, roads, houses, and government buildings, although reduced demand for crude oil in international markets has led to a downturn in the economy and a slower rate of development than hitherto.

TRADE WITH UK	1991	1992
Imports from UK	£109,248,000	£118,114,000
Exports to UK	5,488,000	10,142,000

COMMUNICATIONS

Regular air services connect Qatar with the other Gulf states, the Middle East, the Indian sub-continent, Africa and Europe. The Qatar Broadcasting Service transmits on medium, shortwave, and VHF. Regular television transmissions in colour began in 1974 and a second channel opened in 1982.

ROMANIA
România

Romania is a republic of south-eastern Europe, formerly the classical *Dacia* and *Scythia Pontica*. The area of Romania is 91,699 sq. miles (237,500 sq. km) and the population (1992 Census) is 22,760,449. Romanians number 21,559,910 (88 per cent), there is a Hungarian minority of 1,714,000 (7.9 per cent), a dwindling German minority of 359,000 (1.6 per cent) and 227,000 Gypsies (1.1 per cent).

LANGUAGE – Romanian is a Romance language with many archaic forms and with admixtures of Slavonic, Turkish, Magyar and French words. There is wealth of folk-songs and folklore, transmitted orally through many centuries and collected in the 19th century.

RELIGION – The leading religion is that of the Romanian Orthodox Church; the Roman Catholic and some Protestant denominations are of importance numerically.

CAPITAL – Bucharest, on the Dimbovita, population (1992 Census) 2,064,474. Other large towns are:

Braşov	323,835	ΨGalati	325,788
Constanţa	350,476	Craiova	303,520
Cluj-Napoca	328,008	Ploieşti	252,073
Iasi	342,994	ΨBrăila	234,706
Timişoara	334,278		

CURRENCY – Leu (*plural* Lei) of 100 bani.
FLAG – Three vertical bands, blue, yellow, red.
NATIONAL ANTHEM – Desteapta-te, romane.
NATIONAL DAY – 1 December.

GOVERNMENT

Romania has its origin in the union of the Danubian principalities of Wallachia and Moldavia under the Treaty of

Paris 1856. The principalities remained separate entities under Turkish suzerainty. By the Treaty of Berlin 1878 the principality was recognized as an independent state, and part of the Dobrudja (which had been occupied by the Romanians) was incorporated; on 27 March 1881 it was recognized as a kingdom. The First World War added Bessarabia, the Bukovina, Transylvania, the Banat and Crisana-Maramures, these additions of territory being confirmed by treaty in 1919 and 1920.

On 27 June 1940, in compliance with an ultimatum from USSR, Bessarabia and Northern Bukovina were ceded to the Soviet government, and in August 1940 Romania ceded to Bulgaria the portion of southern Dobrudja taken from Bulgaria in 1913. In 1947 King Michael abdicated and Romania became 'The Romanian People's Republic' in December 1947. The leading political force from the Second World War until 1989 was the Romanian Communist Party. A revolution in December 1989 led to the overthrow of Nicolae Ceauşescu, President since 1967. A provisional government was formed which abolished the leading role of the Communist Party and promised free elections. A new constitution was passed by parliament in November 1991 and affirmed by a referendum in December that year. The constitution formally makes Romania a multi-party democracy and endorses human rights and a market economy. There is a Senate of 143 members and a 341-member Assembly of Deputies (of which 13 seats are reserved for ethnic minorities other than Hungarians).

New presidential and parliamentary elections took place in September and October 1992. President Iliesu was re-elected and his Democratic National Salvation Front (DNSF), which had split from the National Salvation Front (NSF), gained the largest number of seats in both houses of parliament and formed a minority government with the support of nationalist parties and the ex-Communists. The appointment of several ex-ministers of Ceauşescu's regime has greatly angered the opposition.

HEAD OF STATE

President of the Republic, Ion Iliescu, *elected* 1990, *re-elected* 11 October 1992.

GOVERNMENT *as at August 1993*

Prime Minister, Nicolae Vacaroiu.
Foreign Affairs, Teodor Melescanu.
Defence, Lt.-Gen. Nicolae Spiroiu.
Industry, Dumitru Popescu.
Interior, George Danescu.
Justice, Petre Ninosu.
Communications, Andrei Chirica.
Parliamentary Relations, Valer Dorneanu.
Public Works, Marin Cristea.
Research and Technology, Doru Palade.
Education, Liviu Maior.
Culture, Mihaí Golu.
Agriculture and Food Industry, Ioan Oancea.
Environment, Forestry and Water, Aurel Ilie.
Health, Iulian Mincu.
Tourism, Matei Dan.
Finance, Florin Georgescu.
Labour and Social Security, Dan Popescu.
Economic Reform and Strategy, Misu Negritoiu.
Trade, Constantin Teculscu.
Transport, Paul Teodoru.
Youth and Sports, Gheorghe Angelescu.

EMBASSY OF ROMANIA
Arundel House, 4 Palace Green, London W8 4QD
Tel 071–937 9666

Ambassador Extraordinary and Plenipotentiary, His Excellency Sergiu Celac (1990).
Defence Attaché, Col. G. Rotaru.
Counsellor, A. Puscarciuc (*Economic*).
Third Secretary, C. Voicu (*Consular*).

BRITISH EMBASSY
24 Strada Jules Michelet, 70154 Bucharest
Tel: Bucharest 3120 303/4/5/6
Ambassador Extraordinary and Plenipotentiary, His Excellency Andrew Bache, CMG (1992).
Counsellor, Deputy Head of Mission, C. J. Ingham.
Defence, Naval and Military Attaché, Lt.-Col. P. G. Davies.
First Secretary (Commercial), W. J. Preston.

BRITISH COUNCIL REPRESENTATIVE – C. C. Henning, Calea Dorobantilor 14, Bucharest.

DEFENCE

Romania has a total active armed forces strength of 200,000 personnel (126,700 conscripts) with a further 593,000 reserves. Conscripts serve 12 months (Army and Air Force) and 18 months (Navy). The Army has a strength of 161,000 (105,000 conscripts) with 2,875 main battle tanks, 412 assault guns, 2,800 armoured infantry fighting vehicles and armoured personnel carriers and 3,700 artillery pieces. The Navy has a strength of 19,000 personnel (10,000 conscripts) including 1,000 coastal defence and a marine division of 5,000. It deploys one submarine, one destroyer, five frigates and 90 patrol and coastal vessels. The Air Force has 20,000 personnel (10,700 conscripts) with 486 combat aircraft and 220 armed helicopters. Paramilitary Border Guards and Gendarmerie number 49,800 personnel (11,700 conscripts).

ECONOMY

Wallachia, Moldavia and Transylvania are among the most fertile areas in Europe, and agriculture and sheep and cattle raising are the principal industries of Romania. The principal cereal crops are legumes and other vegetables, flax and hemp. Vines and fruits are also grown. The forests of the mountainous regions are extensive, and the timber industry is important. Collectivization of agriculture was achieved in the spring of 1962. Since December 1989 agricultural workers have been allowed to sell their produce on the open market but overall production has declined. A law on land privatization was adopted in early 1991, allowing for private ownership of plots up to 10 hectares in size. Allocation of land and distribution of ownership certificates is still taking place.

There are plentiful supplies of natural gas, together with various mineral deposits including coal, iron ore, bauxite, lead, zinc, copper and uranium in quantities which allow a substantial part of the requirements of industry to be met from local resources. Production of crude oil was 6,600,000 tonnes in 1992.

The economy faced increasing problems from the late 1970s as a result of over-investment in energy-intensive heavy industry and neglect of agriculture, which led to food shortages. The effects of these policies were aggravated by the international recession and by high interest rates, and Romania was severely in debt by the early 1980s. The Ceauşescu government sought to alleviate the situation and repay Romania's foreign debt by reducing borrowing, cutting imports and increasing exports. The formerly centrally-planned economy is now being transformed into a market economy under the new government. Thirty per cent of state property has been distributed in the form of vouchers or shares to the population. The rest is to be sold off. Foreign investment and ownership of up to 100 per cent of enterprises is now permitted. Industrial output continued to decline in 1992.

TRADE

Imports are chiefly semi-manufactured goods, raw materials, machinery and metals. Exports consist principally of maize, wheat, barley, oats, petroleum, timber, cattle, meat, machines and industrial equipment.

Trade with UK	1991	1992
Imports from UK	£58,735,000	£64,388,000
Exports to UK	58,531,000	62,814,000

EDUCATION

Education is free and nominally compulsory. There are state universities in seven cities, 66 private universities, six polytechnics, two commercial academies, and five agricultural colleges.

COMMUNICATIONS

In 1979 there were 11,113 km of railway open for traffic. The mercantile marine had a gross tonnage of 13,220,000 tons in 1979. The principal ports are Constanta (on the Black Sea), Sulina (on the Danube Estuary), Galati, Braila, Giurgiu and Turnu Severin. The Danube and the Black Sea are linked by a canal completed in 1984.

RUSSIA
Rossiiskaya Federatsiya - Russian Federation

Russia has an area of 6,593,391 sq. miles (17,075,000 sq. km) and occupies three-quarters of the land area of the former Soviet Union. In the west it is bordered by Norway, Finland, Estonia, Latvia, Belarus and the Ukraine (the Kaliningrad enclave borders Lithuania and Poland). To the south Russia is bordered in Europe by Georgia, Azerbaijan, the Black Sea and the Caspian Sea, and in Asia by Kazakhstan, China, Mongolia and North Korea. In the east it meets the North Pacific (where its nearest point is only a few miles from Japan), and the Bering Strait (where its nearest point is only a few miles from Alaska). To the north is the Arctic Ocean and the Barents Sea.

The Russian Federation comprises the following: 49 regions (Amur, Archangel, Astrakhan, Belgorod, Bryansk, Chelyabinsk, Chita, Irkutsk, Ivanov, Kaliningrad, Kaluga, Kamchatka, Kemerovo, Kirov, Kostroma, Kurgan, Kursk, Lipetsk, Magadan, Moscow, Murmansk, Nizhny Novgorod, Novgorod, Novosibirsk, Omsk, Orel, Orenburg, Penza, Perm, Pskov, Rostov, Ryazan, St Petersburg, Sakhalin, Samara, Saratov, Smolensk, Tambov, Tomsk, Tula, Tver, Tyumen, Ulyanovsk, Vladimir, Volgograd, Vologda, Voronezh, Yaroslavl, Yekaterinburg); five autonomous territories (Khabarovsk, Krasnodar, Krasnoyarsk, Maritime, Stavropol) containing in their turn three autonomous regions; and 22 autonomous republics (Adygei, Altai, Bashkortostan, Buryaad, Chechen, Chuvash, Dagestan, Ingush, Kabardin-Balkar, Kalmyk, Karachaev-Cherkess, Karelia, Khakassia, Komi, Mari-El, Mordovia, North Ossetia, Tatarstan, Tuva, Udmurt, Yakut-Sakha, Yamal-Nenetsk).

There are three principal geographic areas: a low-lying flat western area stretching eastwards up to the Yenisei and divided in two by the Ural ridge; the eastern area between the Yenisei and the Pacific, consisting of a number of tablelands and ridges; and a southern mountainous area. Russia has a very long coast-line, including the longest Arctic coastline in the world (about 17,000 miles). The most important rivers are the Volga, the Northern Dvina and the Pechora, the Neva, the Don and the Kuban in the European part, and in the Asiatic part, the Ob, the Irtysh, the Yenisei, the Lena and the Amur, and, further north, Khatanga, Olenek, Yana, Indigirka, Kolyma and Anadyr. Lakes are abundant, particularly in the north-west. The huge Baikal Lake in eastern Siberia is the deepest lake in the world. There are also two large artificial water reservoirs within the Greater Volga canal system, the Moscow and Rybinsk 'Seas'. Climatically, Russia extends from Arctic and tundra belts to the subtropical in the south.

POPULATION – The 1992 estimate gave a population of 148,800,000, of which about 82 per cent are Russian, 4 per cent Tatar and 3 per cent Ukrainian. There are another 12 minorities with populations of over half a million and more than 100 nationalities in total.

RELIGION – The Russian Orthodox Church is the predominant religion, though the Tatars are Muslims and there are Jewish communities in Moscow and St Petersburg.

LANGUAGE AND ARTS – Russian is a branch of the Slavonic family of languages and is written in the Cyrillic script.

Before the westernization of Russia under Peter the Great (1682–1725), Russian literature consisted mainly of folk ballads (*byliny*), epic songs, chronicles and works of moral theology. The 18th and 19th centuries saw the development of Russian poetry and fiction. Poetry reached its zenith with Alexander Pushkin (1799–1837), Mikhail Lermontov (1814–41), Alexander Blok (1880–1921), the 1958 Nobel Prize laureate Boris Pasternak (1890–1960), Vladimir Mayakovsky (1893–1930) and Anna Akhmatova (1888–1966). Fiction is associated with the names of Nikolai Gogol (1809–52), Ivan Turgenev (1818–83), Fedor Dostoyevsky (1821–81), Leo Tolstoy (1828–1910), Anton Chekhov (1860–1904), Maxim Gorky (1868–1936), Ivan Bunin (1870–1953), Mikhail Bulgakov (1891–1940), Mikhail Sholokhov (1905–84) and Alexander Solzhenitsyn (b. 1918).

Great names in music include Glinka (1804–57), Borodin (1833–87), Mussorgsky (1839–81), Rimsky-Korsakov (1844–1908), Rubinstein (1829–94), Tchaikovsky (1840–93), Rachmaninov (1873–1943), Skriabin (1872–1915), Prokofiev (1891–1953), Stravinsky (1882–1971), Shostakovich (1906–75) and Alfred Shnitke (b. 1934).

CAPITAL – Moscow. Population 8,967,000 (1989).
Moscow, founded about 1147, became the centre of the rising Moscow principality and in the 15th century the capital of the whole of Russia (Muscovy). In 1325 it became the seat of the Metropolitan of Russia. In 1703 Peter the Great transferred the capital to St Petersburg, but on 14 March 1918 Moscow was again designated as the capital. ΨSt Petersburg (from 1914 to 1924 Petrograd and from 1924 to 1991 Leningrad) has a population of 5,020,000 (1989).
Other towns with populations (1990) exceeding 1,000,000 are:

Nizhny-Novgorod (Gorky)	1,438,000
Novosibirsk (Novonikolayevsk)	1,436,000
Yekaterinburg (Sverdlovsk)	1,367,000
Samara (Kuibyshev)	1,257,000
Omsk	1,148,000
Chelyabinsk	1,143,000
Ufa	1,083,000
Perm (Molotov)	1,091,000
Kazan	1,094,000
Rostov-on-Don	1,020,000

CURRENCY – Rouble of 100 kopeks.
FLAG – Three horizontal stripes of white, blue, red.
NATIONAL DAY – 12 June (Independence Day).

HISTORY

Russia was formally created from the principality of Muscovy and its territories by Tsar Peter I (The Great) (1682–1725), who initiated its territorial expansion, introduced western ideas of government and state organization and founded St Petersburg. By the end of Peter the Great's reign, the Baltic territories (modern-day Estonia and Latvia) had been annexed from Sweden and Russia had become the dominant military power of north-eastern Europe. In the 18th century the partitions of Poland and wars with Turkey brought the territories of modern-day Lithuania, Belarus, the Ukraine and the Crimea under Russian control, and the colonization of Siberia east of the Urals also began in earnest. Russia overran the Caucasus region (modern-day Armenia, Azerbaijan and Georgia) in the early 19th century, seized Finland from Sweden in 1809 and Bessarabia from Turkey in 1812. Throughout the remainder of the 19th century Russia subdued and annexed the independent Muslim states which formed the five Central Asian republics.

It was as a multinational empire covering a huge geographical area, in which the monarch and nobility held almost absolute power (an ineffectual parliament, the Duma, was created in 1905), that the Russian Empire entered the First World War in 1914. Discontent caused by autocratic rule, the poor conduct of the military campaign and wartime privation led to a revolution which broke out on 12 March (27 February OS) 1917. Tsar Nicholas II abdicated three days later and a provisional government was formed; a republic was proclaimed on 14 September (1 September OS) 1917. A political power struggle ensued between the provisional government and the Bolshevik Party which controlled the Soviets (councils) set up by workers, soldiers and peasants. This led to a second revolution on 7 November (25 October OS) 1917 in which the Bolsheviks, led by Lenin, seized power.

The Bolshevik (Communist) Party withdrew from the First World War under the Treaty of Brest-Litovsk (March 1918), surrendering large areas of territory. Armed resistance to Communist rule developed into an all-out civil war between 'red' Bolshevik forces and 'white' monarchist and anti-Communist forces which lasted until the end of 1922. During the civil war, Russia had been declared a Soviet Republic and other Soviet republics had been formed in the Ukraine, Byelorussia and Transcaucasia. These four republics merged to form the Union of Soviet Socialist Republics (USSR) on 30 December 1922.

After an internal Communist Party power struggle following Lenin's death in 1924, Joseph Stalin emerged in 1928 as the undisputed party leader. He initiated a series of reorganizations of the USSR, introduced a policy of rapid industrialization under a system of five-year plans, brought all sectors of industry under government control, abolished private ownership and enforced the collectivization of agriculture. He eliminated potential political opponents through purges and show trials, and total political repression lasted until his death in 1953.

The Nazi-Soviet pact of August 1939 and the Second World War resulted in further territorial expansion, regaining much of the territory lost in or after 1918, as well as extending Soviet influence to the countries of eastern Europe liberated by Soviet troops. The USSR lost 26 million combatants and civilians in the war.

Repression lessened under Khruschev and Brezhnev, but the Communist Party remained dominant in all walks of life. This was the state of affairs when Mikhail Gorbachev became Soviet leader in March 1985. Gorbachev introduced the policies of *perestroika* (complete restructuring) and *glasnost* (openness) in order to revamp the economy, which had stagnated since the 1970s, to root out corruption and inefficiency, and to end the Cold War and its attendant arms race. Private ownership was allowed, individual expression and limited private enterprise were tolerated, political prisoners released and the guaranteed leading role of the Communist Party abolished. The political openness and retreat from total control by the Communist Party unleashed ethnic and nationalist tensions. Events came to a head on 19 August 1991 when a coup was attempted against Soviet President Gorbachev by hardline elements of the Communist Party, the armed forces and the state security service (KGB) in order to reimpose one-party Communist control on the USSR. The coup was defeated by reformist and democratic political groupings supported by the majority of the population, who took to the streets of Moscow and other large cities under the leadership of Russian President Yeltsin. The coup leaders were arrested and imprisoned, and Mikhail Gorbachev returned to Moscow. However, it became clear that effective political power was in the hands of the republican leaders, especially Russian President Yeltsin, and the Soviet Union began to break up as the constituent republics declared their independence. Mikhail Gorbachev resigned as Soviet President on 25 December 1991 and on 26 December 1991 the USSR formally ceased to exist.

GOVERNMENT

Russia was recognized as an independent state by the EC and USA in January 1992, and it inherited the Soviet Union's seat at the UN on 24 December 1991.

A new Russian Federal Treaty was signed on 13 March 1992 between the central government and the autonomous republics. However, Tatarstan and Chenchen refused to sign it and declared their 'independence'. In November 1992 President Yeltsin imposed direct rule in the autonomous republics of Ingush and North Ossetia after Ingush forces attacked North Ossetia; a state of emergency was declared by President Yeltsin in the two autonomous republics in March 1993. In early July the Yekaterinburg region and Maritime autonomous territory declared themselves to be autonomous republics.

The present Russian constitutional system was adopted in 1988. The legislature consists of the Congress of People's Deputies, which is directly elected and has 1,068 members who then elect from among their numbers a smaller Supreme Soviet. The Supreme Soviet is the main law-making and parliamentary body, meeting most of the year. The Congress of People's Deputies meets for only a few days a year but has the power to amend the constitution and sack government ministers. Under the constitution, the President has only a ceremonial role but Boris Yeltsin has been voted wide-ranging emergency powers by the Congress of People's Deputies.

At present President Yeltsin and democratic political groups are trying to force through constitutional changes to enable the introduction of a western-style constitution with an executive President and a two-chamber legislature. However, constitutional change is difficult because it requires the support of the Congress of People's Deputies, which has a majority of ex-Communist members, who are ambivalent about reform. Throughout 1992–3 President Yeltsin's government has faced opposition to reform from the bureaucracy, some of the military, influential heads of major state enterprises and, most importantly, the Supreme Soviet and Congress of People's Deputies.

In late 1992 the political battle between President Yeltsin and his reformist government on the one hand and the anti-reform Congress led by its speaker Ruslan Khasbulatov on the other resumed. At the Congress of People's Deputies in December 1992, the Congress narrowly voted against taking control of the government from President Yeltsin, but refused to confirm the economic reformer Yegor Gaidar in the post of Prime Minister, replacing him with Viktor Chernomyrdin. In response President Yeltsin ordered a referendum in January (later April) 1993 on early parliamentary elections. Vice-President Rutskoi effectively joined the parliamentary opposition by opposing Yeltsin's campaign for a referendum. Intensive negotiations between Yeltsin and Khasbulatov in January and February 1993 led to a compromise between the government and parliament whereby the parliament would be consulted on all policy changes and Yeltsin would end his referendum campaign. The Congress of Deputies session in March 1993 rejected the power-sharing deal and President Yeltsin imposed direct 'special rule' on 20 March, confirmed a referendum for 25 April and ordered the armed forces to refrain from entering the crisis. The Constitutional Court declared Yeltsin's special rule illegal and an emergency session of the Supreme Soviet narrowly voted against impeaching the President. This defeat of the parliamentary

hardliners was confirmed by the overwhelming victory of President Yeltsin in the April referendum on continuing socio-economic reform.

Immediately after winning the referendum, Yeltsin published details of a new constitution, which he presented on 5 June to a special constitutional assembly of regional and republican delegates for approval. The Constituent Assembly approved the draft constitution by 433 votes to 63 and sent it to the regional and autonomous republican councils for approval. At the time of going to press, the draft constitution was still being debated in the regional and republican councils. The power struggle between parliament and government remains unresolved, with Yeltsin announcing a ten-week plan in August to force early parliamentary elections, and parliament overriding Yeltsin's veto for a second time by passing an inflationary budget with a deficit of 25 per cent of GDP.

HEAD OF STATE
President, Boris Yeltsin, *elected* 12 June 1991.
Vice-President, Aleksandr Rutskoi, *elected* 12 June 1991.

GOVERNMENT *as at August 1993*
Prime Minister, Viktor Chernomyrdin.
First Deputy PM, Oleg Saskovets.
First Deputy PM, Economy, Oleg Lobov.
Deputy PMs, Boris Fedorov (*Finance*); Anatoly Chubais
    (*Privatization*); Sergey Shakhray (*Nationalities*);
    Alexandr Zaverukha, Alexander Shokhin, Yuri Yarov.
Foreign Affairs, Andrei Kozyrev.
Defence, Marshal Pavel Grachev.
Interior, Lt.-Gen. Viktor Yerin.
Economics, Andrei Shapovalyants.
Justice, Uryi Kalmykov.
Education, Yevgeny Tkachenko.
Labour, Gennady Melikyan.
Ecology and Natural Resources, Viktor Danilov-Danilyan.
Public Health, Eduard Nechaev.
Communications, Vladimir Bulgak.
Transport, Vitaly Yefimov.
Fuel and Power, Yuri Shafranik.
Agriculture and Foodstuffs, Viktor Khlystun.
Railways, Gennady Fadeyev.
Culture and Tourism, Yevgeny Sidorov.
Nuclear Power, Viktor Mikhailov.
Science, Technology and Higher Education, Boris Saltykov.
Social Security, Ella Pamfilova.
*Speaker of the Congress of Deputies and Chairman of the
    Supreme Soviet*, Ruslan Khasbulatov.

EMBASSY OF THE RUSSIAN FEDERATION
13 Kensington Palace Gardens, London w8 4QX
Tel 071-229 3628/9

Ambassador Extraordinary and Plenipotentiary, His
    Excellency Boris Pankin (1991).
Minister-Counsellors, Vladimir Ivanov; Aleksandr Kudinov.
Military Attaché, Col. N. M. Urarov.
Trade Representative, S. Y. Maslov.

BRITISH EMBASSY
Moscow 72, Sosiiskaya Naberezhnaya 14
Tel: Moscow 230 6555

Ambassador Extraordinary and Plenipotentiary, His
    Excellency Sir Brian Fall, KCMG (1992). (Also non-
    resident Ambassador to Armenia, Azerbaijan, Belarus,
    Georgia, Kazakhstan, Kyrgyzstan, Moldova, Tajikistan,
    Turkmenistan and Uzbekistan).
Minister and Deputy Head of Mission, F. N. Richards, CVO.
Minister-Counsellor, G. D. G. Murrell, CMG, OBE.

Defence and Air Attaché, Air Cdre P. J. Wilkinson.
Counsellor (Commercial), D. G. Gowan.
Consuls-General: J. Daly *(Moscow);* S. D. Jack *(St Petersburg).*
There is a British Consulate-General in St Petersburg.

BRITISH COUNCIL DIRECTOR, M. Evans, Ulyanovskaya
Ulitsa, Dom I, Moscow 109189.

DEFENCE *(see also* Commonwealth of Independent States)

Since the demise of the Soviet Union the Russian armed forces have undergone large-scale reduction but remain some of the most powerful in the world. The total active armed forces number some 2,720,000 personnel (including 1,500,000 conscripts serving for 18-month periods and some 200,000 Ministry of Defence staff). Reserves number some 3,000,000 personnel.

The Strategic Deterrent Forces are centrally controlled by the Commonwealth of Independent States (CIS). Total strength numbers 181,000 personnel with: 832 nuclear missiles in 55 submarines; 1,400 inter-continental ballistic missiles based on land; 170 long-range and 320 medium-range nuclear bombers; 100 anti-ballistic missiles with related satellites, radar and long-range early warning systems.

The Navy has a strength of 308,000 personnel (including 200,000 conscripts, 60,000 naval aviation, 12,000 naval infantry and 17,500 coastal defence and artillery personnel). It deploys: 183 tactical submarines; one fixed-wing and three V/STOL aircraft carriers; 33 cruisers; 26 destroyers; 129 frigates; 305 patrol and coastal craft; 218 mine warfare vessels; and 685 support ships. Naval Aviation has some 1,100 combat aircraft and 290 armed helicopters whilst infantry and coastal defence forces deploy 1,320 main battle tanks, 4,300 armoured vehicles and 1,380 artillery pieces. The Navy is organized into four fleets: Northern, Baltic, Pacific and Black Sea (jointly commanded with Ukraine); and one flotilla (Caspian Sea) to be divided with Azerbaijan and Turkmenistan.

The Army numbers 1,400,000 personnel (1,000,000 conscripts) organized into 125 divisions and 113 brigades. Equipment includes: 29,000 main battle tanks; 57,000 armoured infantry fighting vehicles and armoured personnel carriers; 22,000 artillery pieces; 900 surface-to-surface missiles; 1,100 attack helicopters. The Air Force has a strength of 631,000 personnel (including 410,000 conscripts) with some 1,800 ground attack aircraft, 3,700 air defence fighters, 620 transport aircraft, 365 reconnaissance aircraft, 1,850 training aircraft and 320 attack helicopters. Paramilitary forces number some 520,000, including 220,000 KGB and 170,000 internal security troops.

Russia deploys 177,000 personnel in Germany (to be withdrawn by 31 August 1994) and 6,000 troops in Poland. Also, forces are deployed in Estonia and Latvia which are to be withdrawn by the end of 1994. Forces are also deployed in: Moldova; Armenia (23,000); Azerbaijan (62,000); Georgia (20,000); Kazakhstan (63,000); Kyrgyzstan (8,000); Tajikistan (6,000); Turkmenistan (34,000); and Uzbekistan (15,000).

ECONOMY

Under the Soviet regime, an essentially agricultural economy in 1917 was transformed by the early 1960s into the second strongest industrial power in the world. However, by the late 1960s and early 1970s, the concentration of resources on the military-industrial complex caused the civilian economy to begin to stagnate. It was further suffocated by the bureaucratic inefficiency of the centrally planned economic system. The extremely poor distribution system also caused problems,

especially with agricultural products. It was in an attempt to solve the problems of the centrally planned economic system that Gorbachev introduced economic restructuring (perestroika). After attempts to reform the economy within the restraints of the centrally planned system had failed, an increasing number of free market reforms were introduced, including the legalization of small private businesses in August 1990, the reduction of state control over the economy in October 1990, and denationalization and privatization measures in July 1991.

In May 1992 the great majority of state subsidies were abolished and price liberalization was introduced. In August 1992 mass privatization was announced and in October 1992 all citizens received vouchers to participate in the auction of the majority of Russian state industry. In September 1992 the abolition of the central distribution system was announced, with effect from I January 1993.

However, the abolition of central planning before a fully free market system was in place, and continued obstruction to reform, has resulted in economic chaos. Economic reform and the continuation of western aid were thrown into doubt on 6 January 1993 when Prime Minister Chernomyrdin signalled the re-introduction of price controls on some goods; but President Yeltsin returned to economic reform policies soon afterwards. The privatization of large and medium-sized firms at voucher auctions began in January and by the end of June 1993 2,300 firms had been privatized, putting some three million employees into the private sector. This added to the 30,000 small enterprises and shops and 184,000 agricultural holdings privatized in 1992. In May the government finally secured agreement from the parliament-controlled Central Bank to curb the money supply and credits to inefficient enterprises in order to tackle inflation. However, an attempted currency reform in July to stop the increase in inflation caused by unlimited credit emissions by other CIS central banks failed due to popular opposition. Russia received large-scale international aid in 1993. In April a major rescheduling of Russia's US$80 billion foreign debt was announced, which saved US$15 billion in repayments and allowed the extension of new IMF and World Bank loans. The G7 summit in Tokyo in April pledged aid of US$43 billion for structural reform and rouble stabilization, conditional on political and economic reforms.

Russia has some of the richest mineral deposits in the world. Coal is mined in the Kuznetsk area, in the Urals, south of Moscow, in the Donets basin and in the Pechora area in the north. Oil is produced in the northern Caucasus, between the Volga and the Urals, and in western Siberia, which also has large deposits of natural gas. Coal and gas deposits in Siberia and the far east (especially Yakutia) are currently being developed. The Ural mountains contain a unique assortment of minerals: high-quality iron ore, manganese, copper, aluminium, gold, platinum, precious stones, salt, asbestos, pyrites, coal, oil, etc. Iron ore is also mined near Kursk, Tula, Lipetsk, in several areas in Siberia and in the Kola Peninsula. Non-ferrous metals are found in the Altai, in eastern Siberia, in the northern Caucasus, in the Kuznetsk basin, in the far east and in the far north.

The vast area and the great variety in climatic conditions cause great differences in the structure of agriculture from north to south and from west to east. In the far north reindeer breeding, hunting and fishing are predominant. Further south, timber industry is combined with grain growing. In the southern half of the forest zone and in the adjacent forest-steppe zone, the acreage under grain crops is larger and the structure of agriculture more complex. Between the Volga and the Urals cericulture is predominant (particularly summer wheat), followed by cattle breeding. Beyond the Urals is another important grain-growing and stock-breeding area in the southern part of the western Siberian plain. The southern steppe zone is the main wheat granary of Russia, containing also large acreages under barley, maize and sunflowers. In the extreme south cotton is now cultivated. Vine, tobacco and other southern crops are grown on the Black Sea shore of the Caucasus.

Industrially, Russia was the strongest of the former Soviet republics. Moscow and St Petersburg are still the two largest industrial centres in the country, but new industrial areas have been developed in the Urals, the Kuznetsk basin, in Siberia and the far east. Most of the oil produced in the former USSR came from Russia; half the annual output comes from Tyumen Oblast in western Siberia. All industries are represented in Russia, including iron and steel and engineering.

TRADE WITH UK
(1991 USSR; 1992 CIS11 AND GEORGIA)

	1991	1992
Imports from UK	£354,705,000	£456,554,000
Exports to UK	901,833,000	673,346,000

COMMUNICATIONS

The European area of Russia is relatively well served by railways, St Petersburg and Moscow being the two main focal points of rail routes. The centre and south have a good system of north-south and east-west lines, but the eastern part (the Volga lands), traversed by trunk lines between Europe and Asia, lacks north-south routes. In Asia, there are still large areas of Russia, notably in the far north and Siberia, with few or no railways. In the northern part of European Russia, the North Pechora Railway has been completed, while in the far east a second Trans-Siberian line (the Baikal-Amur Railway) is partially in use; it follows a more northerly alignment than the earlier Trans-Siberian and terminates at the Pacific port of Sovetskaya Gavan.

The most important ports (Taganrog, Rostov and Novorossiisk) lie around the Black Sea and the Sea of Azov. The northern ports (St Petersburg, Murmansk and Archangel) are, with the exception of Murmansk, icebound during winter. Several ports have been built along the Arctic Sea route between Murmansk and Vladivostok and are in regular use every summer. The far eastern port of Vladivostok, the Pacific naval base of Russia, is kept open by icebreakers all the year round.

Inland waterways, both natural and artificial, are of great importance in the country, although some of them are icebound in winter (from two and a half months in the south to six months in the north). The great rivers of European Russia flow outwards from the centre, linking all parts of the plain with the chief ports, an immense system of navigable waterways which carried about 690 million tons of freight in 1988. They are supplemented by a system of canals which provide a through traffic between the White, Baltic, Black and Caspian Seas. The most notable are the White Sea-Baltic Canal, the Moscow-Volga Canal and the Volga-Don Canal linking the Baltic and the White Seas in the north to the Caspian Sea, the Black Sea and the Sea of Azov in the south.

RWANDA
Republika y'u Rwanda

Rwanda, formerly part of the Belgian-administered trusteeship of Ruanda-Urundi, has an area of 10,169 sq. miles (26,338 sq. km), and a population (UN estimate 1991) of 7,491,000, mainly of the Hutu tribe, with Tutsi and Twa minorities.

CAPITAL – Kigali (156,000).
CURRENCY – Rwanda franc of 100 centimes.
FLAG – Three vertical bands, red, yellow and green with letter R on yellow band.
NATIONAL DAY – 1 July.

GOVERNMENT

A referendum held in September 1961 showed the majority of the population were opposed to the retention of the monarchy, which was abolished on 2 October 1961. Rwanda became an independent republic on 1 July 1962, with Gregoire Kayibanda as head of state and head of the government. He was deposed in 1973, and replaced by a military government under Maj.-Gen. Juvénal Habyarimana.

The MRND (National Revolutionary Movement for Development), renamed the National Republican Movement for Democracy and Development (MRNDD), ended its monopoly of power in April 1991. A new multi-party constitution was promulgated in July 1991. A coalition transitional government was formed in April 1992 by the MRNDD and four opposition parties.

In October 1990, Rwanda was invaded by the Rwandan Patriotic Front (RPF), composed of members of the minority Tutsi tribe in exile in Uganda. Talks began in June 1992 between the Government and the Rwandan Patriotic Front, and a ceasefire agreement was signed in July 1992. The transitional government reached agreement with the Rwandan Patriotic Front in August 1992 on political reforms and a new interim government. However, fighting re-started in January 1993 after the peace agreement between the interim government and the RPF was rejected by the President and the MRNDD. The rebels captured the north of the country and advanced on the capital Kigali before peace talks in Tanzania re-started the negotiating process and ended the fighting. The government and RPF signed a peace treaty in August 1993 ending the civil war and establishing a transitional government and assembly to include RPF members, while the army and rebel forces are to be merged and demobilized.

HEAD OF STATE
President, Maj.-Gen. Juvénal Habyarimana, *assumed office* 5 July 1973, *elected* 1978, *re-elected* 1983, 17 December 1988.

TRANSITIONAL GOVERNMENT *as at July 1993*
Prime Minister, Dismas Nsengiyaremye.
Foreign Minister, Boniface Ngulinzaira.
Interior, Faustin Munyazesa.
Justice, Stanislas Mbonampeka.
Defence, James Gasana.
Finance, Marc Rugenera.

EMBASSY OF THE REPUBLIC OF RWANDA
1 avenue des Fleurs, Woluwe Saint Pièrre, Brussels 1150, Belgium
Tel: Brussels 7630702

Ambassador Extraordinary and Plenipotentiary, François Ngarukiyintwali (1991).

BRITISH AMBASSADOR (resident in Kinshasa, Zaire).

ECONOMY

Coffee, tea and sugar are grown. Tin, hides, bark of quinine and extract of pyrethrum flowers are also exported.

In 1987 total imports were valued at US$351.7m; total exports, US$112.3m. Coffee accounted for 90 per cent of export earnings in 1989.

TRADE WITH UK	1991	1992
Imports from UK	£2,334,000	£1,552,000
Exports to UK	2,193,000	2,582,000

ST CHRISTOPHER AND NEVIS
The Federation of St Christopher and Nevis

The state of St Christopher and Nevis is located at the northern end of the eastern Caribbean. It comprises the islands of St Christopher (St Kitts) (68 sq. miles) and Nevis (36 sq. miles); combined population (UN estimate 1991) 44,000.

St Christopher, 17° 18′ N. latitude and 62° 48′ W. longitude, was the first island in the British West Indies to be colonized (1623). The central area of the island is forest-clad and mountainous, rising to the 3,792 ft. Mount Liamuiga. Nevis, 17° 10′ N. and 62° 35′ W., is separated from the southern tip of St Christopher by a strait two miles wide and is dominated by Nevis Peak, 3,232 ft.

CAPITAL – ΨBasseterre (estimated population, 15,000). Chief town of Nevis is ΨCharlestown (population 1,200), which is a port of entry.

CURRENCY – East Caribbean dollar (EC$) of 100 cents.

FLAG – Three diagonal bands, green, black and red; each colour separated by a stripe of yellow. Two white stars on the black band.

NATIONAL ANTHEM – Oh Land of Beauty.

NATIONAL DAY – 19 September (Independence Day).

GOVERNMENT

The Territory of St Christopher and Nevis became a State in Association with Britain on 27 February 1967. The State of St Christopher and Nevis became an independent nation on 19 September 1983.

Under the constitution, The Queen is head of state, represented in the islands by the Governor-General. There is a central government with a ministerial system, the head of which is the Prime Minister of St Christopher and Nevis, and a National Assembly located on St Christopher. The National Assembly is composed of the Speaker, three senators (nominated by the Prime Minister and the Leader of the Opposition) and 11 elected representatives. On Nevis there is a Nevis Island Administration, the head being styled Premier of Nevis, and a Nevis Island Assembly of five elected and three nominated members.

Governor-General, His Excellency Sir Clement Athelston Arrindell, GCMG, GCVO, QC (1983).

CABINET *as at August 1993*

Prime Minister and Minister of Finance, Home Affairs and Foreign Affairs, Rt. Hon. Dr Kennedy A. Simmonds.
Deputy PM, Youth and Community Affairs, Communications, Works and Public Utilities, Hon. Sydney E. Morris.
Agriculture, Lands, Housing and Development, Hon. Hugh C. Heyliger.
Health, Labour and Women's Affairs, Hon. Constance Mitcham.
Trade, Industry and Tourism, Hon. Fitzroy P. Jones.
Minister in Ministry of Finance, Hon. Richard L. Caines.
Attorney-General, Hon. S. W. Tapley Seaton, CVO.
Minister in the Office of the Prime Minister, Hon. Joseph Parry.

ST KITTS HIGH COMMISSION
10 Kensington Court, London W8 5DL
Tel 071-937 9522

High Commissioner for the Eastern Caribbean States, His Excellency Richard Gunn, CBE (1987).

BRITISH REPRESENTATIVE (resides at Antigua).

ECONOMY

The economy of the islands has been based on sugar for over three centuries. Tourism and light industry are now being developed. The economy of Nevis centres on small peasant farmers, but a sea-island cotton industry is being developed for export.

FINANCE	1989	1990
Revenue	EC$91,508,604	EC$96,900,000
Expenditure	84,427,961	94,100,000

TRADE WITH UK	1991	1992
Imports from UK	£5,755,000	£6,074,000
Exports to UK	6,476,000	7,052,000

COMMUNICATIONS

Basseterre is a port of registry and has deep water harbour facilities. Golden Rock airport, on St Kitts, can take most large jet aircraft; Newcastle airstrip on Nevis can take small aircraft and has night landing facilities. The sea ferry route from Basseterre to Charlestown is 11 miles.

ST LUCIA

St Lucia, the second largest of the Windward group, situated in 13° 54′ N. latitude and 60° 50′ W. longitude, is 27 miles in length, with an extreme breadth of 14 miles. It comprises an area of 238 sq. miles (616 sq. km), with a population (1991 UN estimate) of 153,000. It is mountainous, its highest point being Mt Gimie (3,145 ft) and for the most part it is covered with forest and tropical vegetation.

CAPITAL – ΨCastries (population 1989, 56,000) is recognized as being one of the finest ports in the West Indies on account of its reputation as a safe anchorage in the hurricane season.

CURRENCY – East Caribbean dollar (EC$) of 100 cents.

FLAG – Blue, bearing in centre a device of yellow over black over white triangles having a common base.

NATIONAL ANTHEM – Sons and Daughters of Saint Lucia.

NATIONAL DAY – 22 February (Independence Day).

GOVERNMENT

St Lucia possesses perhaps the most interesting history of the smaller Caribbean islands. Fights raged hotly around it, and it constantly changed hands between the British and the French. It became independent within the Commonwealth on 22 February 1979. The head of state is The Queen, represented in the island by a St Lucian Governor-General, and there is a bicameral legislature. The Senate has 11 members, six appointed by the ruling party, three by the Opposition and two by the Governor-General. The House of Assembly, which has a life of five years, has 17 elected Members and a Speaker, who may be elected from outside the House.

Governor-General, His Excellency Sir Stanislaus James, KCMG, OBE.

CABINET *as at August 1993*

Prime Minister, Minister of Finance, Planning, Development, Information and Broadcasting, Rt. Hon. John G. M. Compton.

Deputy PM and Minister of Home Affairs, Foreign Affairs, Trade and Industry, Hon. George Mallet.
Communications, Works and Transport, Hon. Gregory Avril.
Tourism, Public Utilities and National Mobilization, Hon. Romanus Lansiquot.
Youth, Community Development, Social Affairs, Sports and Co-operatives, Hon. Desmond Braithwaite.
Attorney-General and Minister for Legal Affairs, Hon. Senator Lorraine Williams.
Agriculture, Lands, Fisheries and Forestry, Hon. Ira D'Auvergne.
Education, Culture and Labour, Hon. Louis George.
Health and Local Government, Hon. Stephenson King.
Minister of State, Housing, Urban Development and Renewal, Hon. Senator Michael Pilgrim.
Minister of State, Youth, Sports and Co-operatives, Hon. Edward Innocent.

St Lucia High Commission
10 Kensington Court, London w8 5DL
Tel 071-937 9522

High Commissioner for the Eastern Caribbean States, His Excellency Richard Gunn, CBE (1987).

Office of the British High Commission
Columbus Square, PO Box 227, Castries
Tel: Castries 4522484

High Commissioner (resides at Bridgetown, Barbados).
Resident Representative, P. T. Rouse, MBE.

ECONOMY

The economy is mainly agrarian, with manufacturing based on the processing of agricultural products. Principal crops are bananas, coconuts, cocoa, mangoes, avocado pears, breadfruit, spices, root crops such as cassava and yams, and citrus fruit. Attempts are being made to diversify the economy, in particular through greater industrialization. Tourism is also of increasing importance, with 204,000 visitors to the island in 1989.

TRADE

The principal exports are bananas, coconut products (copra, edible oils, soap), cardboard boxes, beer, and textile manufactures. The chief imports are flour, meat, machinery, building materials, motor vehicles, cotton piece goods, petroleum and fertilizers.

Trade with UK	1991	1992
Imports from UK	£19,025,000	£19,586,000
Exports to UK	£44,852,000	53,820,000

ST VINCENT AND THE GRENADINES

The territory of St Vincent includes certain of the Grenadines, a chain of small islands stretching 40 miles across the Caribbean Sea between Grenada and St Vincent, some of the larger of which are Bequia, Canouan, Mayreau, Mustique, Union Island, Petit St Vincent and Prune Island. The whole territory extends 150 sq. miles (388 sq. km). The main island, St Vincent, is situated between 13° 6′ and 14° 35′ N. latitude and 61° 6′ and 61° 20′ W. longitude. The island is 18 miles long and 11 miles wide at its extremities, comprising an area of 133 sq. miles (344 sq. km), and a population (1991 UN estimate) of 117,000.

CAPITAL – ΨKingstown, estimated population 33,694.
CURRENCY – East Caribbean dollar (EC$) of 100 cents.

FLAG – Three vertical bands, of blue, yellow and green, with three green diamonds in the shape of a 'V' mounted on the yellow band.
NATIONAL ANTHEM – St Vincent, Land So Beautiful.
NATIONAL DAY – 27 October (Independence Day).

GOVERNMENT

St Vincent was discovered by Christopher Columbus in 1498. It was granted by Charles I to the Earl of Carlisle in 1627 and after subsequent grants and a series of occupations alternately by the French and English, it was finally restored to Britain in 1783. St Vincent achieved full independence within the Commonwealth as St Vincent and the Grenadines on 27 October 1979.

St Vincent has a constitution under which there is a Governor-General who is The Queen's representative. The House of Assembly consists of 15 elected members and four Senators appointed by the Government and two by the Opposition. It is presided over by a Speaker elected by the House from within or without it. All 15 seats were won by the governing New Democratic Party at the election held on 16 May 1989.

Governor-General, His Excellency Sir David Jack, GCMG, MBE, *sworn in* 20 September 1989.

CABINET *as at August 1993*
Prime Minister, Minister of Finance and Planning, Rt. Hon. James Mitchell.
Attorney-General and Minister of Justice and Information, Hon. Parnell Campbell, CVO.
Culture, Education, Youth and Women's Affairs, Hon. John Horne.
Agriculture, Industry and Labour, Hon. Allan Cruickshank.
Foreign Affairs and Tourism, Hon. Herbert Young.
Health and the Environment, Hon. Alpian Allen.
Trade and Consumer Affairs, Hon. Jonathan Peters.
Housing, Local Government, Community Development, Hon. Louis Jones.
Communications and Works, Hon. Jeremiah Scott.
Minister of State, Hon. Mrs Yvonne Gibson (*Education, Culture, Youth and Women's Affairs*).

St Vincent and the Grenadines High Commission
10 Kensington Court, London w8 5DL
Tel 071-937 9522

High Commissioner for the Eastern Caribbean States, His Excellency Richard Gunn, CBE (1987).

British High Commission
Granby Street (PO Box 132), Kingstown
Tel: St Vincent 4571701

High Commissioner (resides at Bridgetown, Barbados).
Resident Representative, A. Ferguson.

ECONOMY

This is based mainly on agriculture but the tourist and manufacturing industries have been expanding. The main products are bananas, arrowroot, coconuts, cocoa, spices and various kinds of food crops. The main imports are foodstuffs (meat, rice, beverages), textiles, lumber, cement and other building materials, fertilizers, motor vehicles and fuel.

Trade with UK	1991	1992
Imports from UK	£7,316,000	£9,469,000
Exports to UK	29,259,000	26,546,000

EL SALVADOR

República de El Salvador

El Salvador extends along the Pacific coast of Central America for 160 miles with a general breadth of about 50 miles, and contains an area of 8,124 sq. miles (21,041 sq. km), with a population (1991 estimate) of 5,376,000. It is divided into 14 Departments.

The surface of the country is very mountainous, many of the peaks being extinct volcanoes. The highest are the Santa Ana volcano (7,700 ft) and the San Vicente volcano (7,200 ft). Much of the interior has an average altitude of 2,000 feet. The principal river is the Rio Lempa. There is a large volcanic lake (Ilopango) a few miles to the east of the capital, while further away and to the west lies the smaller lake of Coatepeque, which appears to have been formed in a vast crater flanked by the Santa Ana volcano. The climate varies from tropical to temperate. The lowlands along the coast are generally hot, but towards the interior the altitude tempers the severity of the heat. There is a wet season from May to October, and a dry season from November to April. Earthquakes have been frequent, the most recent being that of 10 October 1986, when considerable damage was done to San Salvador.

LANGUAGE – The language of the country is Spanish. There are five daily newspapers published at the capital, and four in the provinces.

CAPITAL – San Salvador (497,644, 1989 estimate). Estimated population of metropolitan area, 2,000,000. Other towns are Santa Ana (417,000), San Miguel (157,838), Ψ La Union (Cutuco), Ψ La Libertad and Ψ Acajutia.

CURRENCY – El Salvador colón (₡) of 100 centavos.

FLAG – Three horizontal bands, sky blue, white, sky blue; coat of arms on white band.

NATIONAL ANTHEM – Saludemos La Patria Orgullosos (Let us proudly hail the Fatherland).

NATIONAL DAY – 15 September.

GOVERNMENT

El Salvador was conquered in 1526 by Pedro de Alvarado, and formed part of the Spanish vice-royalty of Guatemala until 1821.

Decades of military rule ended in March 1982 when a Constituent Assembly was elected. Subsequent presidential and parliamentary elections were boycotted by the FMLN (Farabundo Martí National Liberation Front) guerrilla movement. Conflict between the guerrillas and the government continued throughout the 1980s until negotiations culminated in the peace plan signed in January 1992. A ceasefire took effect on 1 February with the swearing in of a commission to oversee implementation of the peace agreements, and the beginning of a nine-month transition period.

The civil war was finally declared over on 15 December 1992 when the FMLN finished its disarmament and became a political party, and the transition period ended. A 'Truth Commission', established under UN auspices to investigate and report on human rights abuses in the 1980–91 period, reported in March 1993. The report caused a political crisis when it declared that 15 senior army commanders should be removed by the government. The government was reluctant to do so but came under economic pressure from the USA, which withheld aid for reconstruction until the officers were dismissed on 1 July 1993.

HEAD OF STATE
President, Alfredo Felix Cristiani Burkard, *elected* 19 March 1989, *assumed office* 1 June 1989.
Vice-President, Francisco Merino.

CABINET *as at August 1993*
Minister of the Presidency, Dr Oscar Santamaría.
Foreign Affairs, Dr Manuel Pacas Castro.
Planning, Mirna Lievano de Márquez.
Interior, Col. Juan Antonio Martínez Varela.
Justice, Dr René Hernández Valiente.
Finance, Edwin Sagrera.
Economy, Enrique Cordova.
Education, Cecilia Gallardo de Cano.
Defence, Humberto Corado Figueroa.
Labour and Social Security, Dr Juan Sifontes.
Agriculture and Livestock, Antonio Cabrales.
Public Health and Social Welfare, Dr Lisandro Vásquez Sosa.
Works, José Castaneda Villacorta.
Secretary of Information, Ernesto Altschul.

EMBASSY OF EL SALVADOR
5 Great James Street, London WCIN 3DA
Tel 071-430 2141
Ambassador Extraordinary and Plenipotentiary, His Excellency Dr Maurico Rosales-Rivera (1983).

BRITISH EMBASSY
PO Box 1591, San Salvador
Tel: San Salvador 981763
Ambassador Extraordinary and Plenipotentiary, His Excellency Michael H. Connor (1992).

ECONOMY

El Salvador has received substantial aid to rebuild the country's war-damaged infrastructure and services. The USA has written off 75 per cent of El Salvador's debt incurred during the civil war. In May 1993 the IMF agreed a standby credit facility for El Salvador of US$49 million over 10 months.

The principal cash crops are coffee, cotton, sugarcane and shrimps. However, cotton and sugar production have decreased as a result of the civil war. Also cultivated are maize, sesame, indigo, rice, balsam, etc. In the lower altitudes towards the east, sisal is produced and used in the manufacture of coffee and cereal bags. The Salvadorean Coffee Company, sugar exports and the banking system are being privatized.

Existing factories make textiles, clothing, constructional steel, furniture, cement and household items. In 1989 GDP amounted to US$4,808 million (US$874 per capita).

BUDGET	1988	1989
Revenue	₡2,843.8m	₡3,330.2m
Expenditure	3,042.2m	3,900.2m

TRADE
Chief exports are coffee, cotton, sugar, shrimps, sisal, balsam, meat, towels, hides and skins. The chief imports are chemicals, fertilizers, pharmaceutical goods, petroleum, manufactured goods, industrial and electronic machinery and equipment, vehicles and consumer goods.

Trade with UK	1991	1992
Imports from UK	£14,545,000	£15,002,000
Exports to UK	4,063,000	7,890,000

EDUCATION

The illiteracy rate has risen to 68.1 per cent (1985) since 1980 when the figure was 30.5 per cent. Primary education is

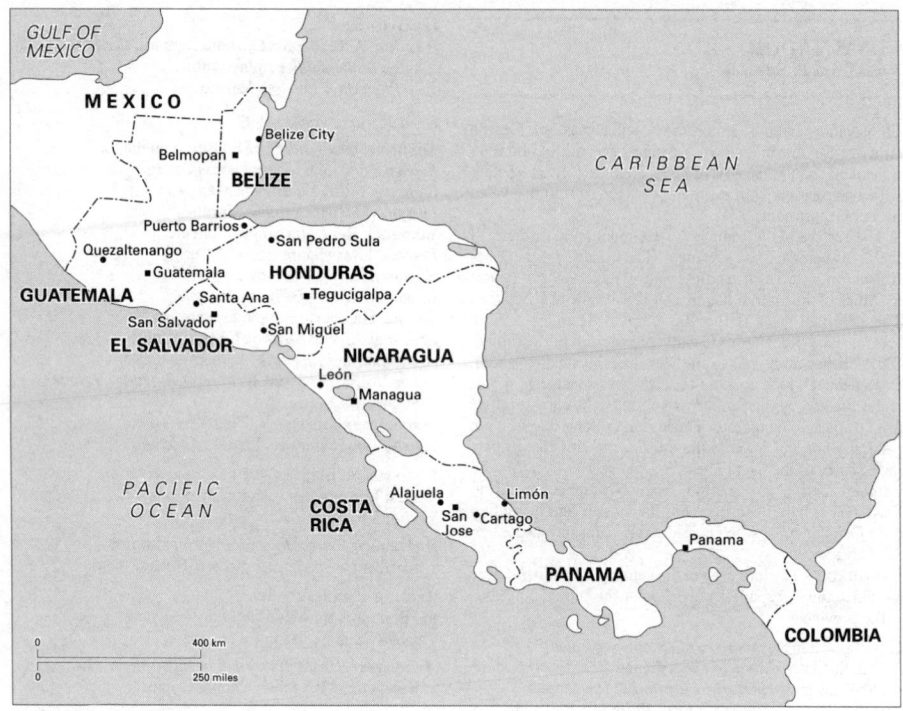

nominally compulsory, but the number of schools and teachers available is too small to enable education to be given to all children of school age.

COMMUNICATIONS

The Executive Autonomous Port Commission (CEPA) administers the ports of Cutuco, La Union, Acajutla, and the railways through FENADESAL. There is a railway line between San Salvador and Guatemala City and Puerto Barrios on the Caribbean coast but it is subject to interruption. The roads are paved and in good condition but some bridges are temporary structures following guerrilla action. There are good roads between Acajutla and the capital (60 miles), and between the capital and Guatemala City. The Pan-American Highway from the Guatemalan frontier follows this route and continues to the Honduran frontier. The El Salvador international airport can receive jet aircraft with daily flights to other Central American capitals, Mexico, and five US cities. There are post and telegraph offices throughout the country. There are 100 broadcasting stations and six television stations.

SAN MARINO
Repubblica di San Marino

San Marino is a small republic in the hills near Rimini, on the Adriatic, founded, it is said, by a pious stonecutter of Dalmatia in the fourth century. The republic resisted Papal claims and those of neighbouring dukedoms during the 15th to 18th centuries, and its integrity and sovereignty is recognized and respected by Italy. The area is approximately 23 sq. miles (61 sq. km.), the population (1992) is 24,000.

CITY – San Marino, on the slope of Monte Titano, has three towers, a fine church and Government palace, a theatre and museums.
CURRENCY – San Marino and Italian currencies are in circulation.
FLAG – Two horizontal bands, white, blue (with coat of arms of the Republic in centre).
NATIONAL DAY – 3 September.

The republic is governed by a State Congress of ten members, under the presidency of two heads of state, who are elected at six-monthly intervals. The Great and General Council, a legislative body of 60 members, is elected by universal suffrage for a term of five years. A Council of Twelve forms in certain cases a Supreme Court of Justice. A coalition government of the Christian Democratic Party and the Socialist Party took office in March 1992, and was returned in the general election of 31 May 1993.

The principal products are wine, cereals, and cattle, and the main industries are tourism, ceramics, lime, concrete, cotton yarns, colour and paints.

HEADS OF STATE
Regents, Two 'Capitani Reggenti'.

CONSULATE-GENERAL IN LONDON
166 High Holborn, London WC1V 6TT
Tel 071–836 7744

Consul-General, The Lord Forte.

BRITISH CONSUL-GENERAL, M. Holmes, MBE (resident in Florence, Italy).

SÃO TOMÉ AND PRÍNCIPE
República Democrática de São Tomé e Príncipe

The islands of São Tomé and Príncipe are situated in the Gulf of Guinea, off the west coast of Africa. They have an area of 372 sq. miles (964 sq. km), and a population (UN estimate 1991) of 124,000.

CAPITAL – ΨSão Tomé (25,000).
CURRENCY – Dobra of 100 centavos.
FLAG – Horizontal stripes of green, yellow, green, the yellow of double width and bearing two black stars; and a red triangle in the hoist.
NATIONAL DAY – 12 July (Independence Day).

GOVERNMENT

The islands became independent on 12 July 1975. A multi-party constitution was approved by referendum in August 1990. The Movement for the Liberation of São Tomé and Príncipe (MLSTP), which had been the sole legal party since independence, was defeated by the opposition Democratic Convergence Party (PCD) in legislative elections held on 20 January 1991. Miguel Trovoada, an independent, was elected President on 3 March 1991. The President dismissed the government in April 1992, because of mounting criticism of economic reforms, and appointed a new Prime Minister.

HEAD OF STATE
President and Commander-in-Chief of the Armed Forces,
Miguel Trovoada, *elected* 3 March 1991.

COUNCIL OF MINISTERS *as at August 1993*
Prime Minister, Noberto Costa Alegre.
Foreign Affairs and Co-operation, Albertino Braganca.
Defence, Evaristo Carvalho.
Economy and Finance, Arlindo Carvalho.
Justice and Labour, Olegario Pires Tiny.
Agriculture, Jose Mendes.
Health, Dulce Gomes.
Príncipe, Sylvestre Umbelina.
Commerce and Industry, Arfemiro Prazeres.

EMBASSY OF THE DEMOCRATIC REPUBLIC OF SÃO TOMÉ AND PRÍNCIPE
42 avenue Brugman, Brussels 1060, Belgium
Tel: Brussels 3475375

Ambassador Extraordinary and Plenipotentiary, new appointment awaited.

HONORARY CONSULATE
42 North Audley Street, London WIA 4PY
Tel 071-499 1995

Honorary Consul, W. S. Wilder.

BRITISH CONSULATE
c/o Hull Blythe (Angola) Ltd, BP 15, São Tomé

British Ambassador (resident in Luanda, Angola).
Honorary Consul, J. Gomes.

TRADE
Cacao is the main product.

Trade with UK	1991	1992
Imports from UK	£1,020,000	£1,154,000
Exports to UK	1,000	4,000

SAUDI ARABIA
Al Mamlaka al Arabiya as-Sa'udiyya

Saudi Arabia comprises almost the whole of the Arabian peninsula, with the exception of the Republic of Yemen in the extreme south, Oman and the UAE in the south-east and Qatar in the east. In the north-west it borders Jordan and in the north-east Iraq and Kuwait, while to the west lies the Red Sea and to the east the Gulf. The Nejd ('plateau', now the Central Province, extends over the centre of the peninsula, including the Nafud and Dahna deserts. The Hejaz ('the boundary'), now the Western Province, extends along the Red Sea coast to Asir and contains the holy towns of Mecca (Makkah) and Medina (Madinah). Asir ('inaccessible') is named for its mountainous terrain, and, with the coastal plain of the Tihama, lies along the southern Red Sea coast from Hejaz to the border with Yemen. It is the only region to enjoy substantial rainfall. The east and south-east of the country are lower-lying and largely desert. The total area of the Kingdom is about 830,000 sq. miles (2,149,640 sq. km), with a population (1992 Census) of 16,929,294. Islam is the established and only permitted religion.

Mecca, about 60 km east of Jeddah, is the birthplace of the Prophet Muhammad, and contains the Great Mosque, within which is the Kaaba or sacred shrine of the Muslim religion. This is the focus of the annual Hajj ('pilgrimage'), performed by 1.4 million in 1990. Medina (Al-Madinah) Al Munawwarah ('The City of Light'), some 300 km north of Mecca, is celebrated as the first city to embrace Islam and as the Prophet Muhammad's burial place (he died there on Rabia 12, AH 11, corresponding to 7 June AD 632).

CAPITAL – Riyadh, population (1992) about 2 million.
Other major centres are Jeddah (estimated population 1.5 million), Buraydah, Dammam, Hofuf, Mecca, Medina and Tabuk.
CURRENCY – Saudi riyal (SR) of 20 qursh or 100 halala.
FLAG – Green oblong, white Arabic device in centre:
'There is no God but God and Muhammad is the Prophet of God,' and a white scimitar beneath the lettering.
NATIONAL ANTHEM – Long live our beloved King.

GOVERNMENT

In the 18th century Nejd was an independent state governed from Diriya (now in ruins, 25 km from Riyadh) and the stronghold of the Wahhabis, a puritanical Islamic sect. It subsequently fell under Turkish rule; in 1913 Abdul Aziz Ibn Saud threw off Turkish rule and captured the Turkish province of Al Hasa. In 1920 he captured the Asir and in 1921, by force of arms, he added to his dominions the Jebel Shammar territory of the Rashid family. In 1925 he completed the conquest of the Hejaz. Great Britain recognized Abdul Aziz Ibn Saud as an independent ruler, King of the Hejaz and of Nejd and its Dependencies, by the Treaty of Jeddah 1927. The name was changed to the Kingdom of Saudi Arabia in September 1932.

Saudi Arabia is a hereditary monarchy, ruled by the sons and grandsons of Abdul Aziz Ibn Saud, in accordance with the Sharia law of Wahhabi Islam. The line of succession passes from brother to brother according to age, although several sons of Ibn Saud renounced their right to the throne. All sons and grandsons of Ibn Saud must be consulted before a new King accedes the throne.

In 1992 King Fahd announced a new Basic Law based on Sharia law and including rules to protect personal freedoms.

A Consultative Council of 60 members appointed by the King was set up to share power with, and question the government, and to make recommendations to the King. In 1993 it was announced that the Consultative Council would have four-year terms and take decisions by majority vote. Cabinet ministers are to have their terms limited to four years, with the possibility of a two-year extension.

HEAD OF STATE

Custodian of the Two Holy Mosques and King of Saudi Arabia, HM King Fahd bin Abdul Aziz Al Saud, *born 1921, ascended the throne* 1 June 1982.
Crown Prince, HRH Amir Abdullah bin Abdul Aziz.

COUNCIL OF MINISTERS *as at August 1993*

Prime Minister, HM King Fahd bin Abdul Aziz Al Saud.
First Deputy Prime Minister and Commander of the National Guard, HRH Prince Abdullah bin Abdul Aziz Al Saud.
Second Deputy Prime Minister, Defence and Aviation, HRH Prince Sultan bin Abdul Aziz Al Saud.
Public Works and Housing, HRH Prince Mit'ab bin Abdul Aziz Al Saud.
Interior, HRH Prince Naif bin Abdul Aziz Al Saud.
Foreign Affairs, HRH Prince Saud al-Faisal bin Abdul Aziz.
Finance and National Economy, Muhammad Aba al-Khail.
Agriculture and Water, Dr Abdul Rahman bin Abdul Aziz bin Hassan Al al-Shaikh.
Municipal and Rural Affairs, Muhammad al-Shaikh.
Justice, Dr Abdallah bin Ibrahim al-Shaikh.
Commerce, Dr Sulaiman al-Solaim.
Communications, Dr Hussain Mansouri.
Petroleum and Mineral Resources, Hisham Nazer.
Planning, Abdul Wahab al-Attar.
Labour and Social Affairs, Dr Mohamed Ali al-Faiz.
Information, Ali Sha'er.
Health, Faisal bin Abdul Aziz al Hejailan.
Islamic Affairs, Awqafs and Guidance, Abdul Mohsen Al-Turki.
Pilgrimage, Dr Mahmoud Safr.
Education, Dr Abdul Aziz Al-Abdullah al-Khuwaiter.
Higher Education, Khalid al-Angari.
Posts, Telegraphs and Telecommunications, Dr Alawi Darwish Kayyal.
Industry and Electricity, Abdul Aziz al-Zamil.
Chairman of the Consultative Council, Sheikh Mohammed bin Ibrahim al Jubeir.

Chairman of the Board of Grievances, Sheikh Nasir bin Hamad al-Rashid.
Chairman of the Supreme Judicial Council, Sheikh Salih Bin Muhammad al-Lihaydan.

ROYAL EMBASSY OF SAUDI ARABIA
30 Charles Street, London WIX 7PM
Tel 071–917 3000

Ambassador Extraordinary and Plenipotentiary, His Excellency Dr Ghazi Al Ghosaibi (1992).
Minister Plenipotentiary, Ibrahim M. Mosly.
Defence Attaché, Col. A. H. Al-Bassam.
Cultural Attaché, A. M. Al-Nasser.
Commercial Attaché, M. A. Al-Sheddi.

BRITISH EMBASSY
PO Box 94351, Riyadh 11693
Tel: Riyadh 488 0077

Ambassador Extraordinary and Plenipotentiary, His Excellency The Hon. David Gore-Booth, CMG (1993).
Counsellors, J. S. Laing, CMG (*Deputy Head of Mission*); C. Wilton (*Commercial*); J. H. Bunney.
Defence and Military Attaché, Brig. M. J. Lance.
First Secretary and Consul-General (Riyadh), J. P. Smyth.

CONSUL-GENERAL, L. E. Walker, OBE, LVO, PO Box 393, Jeddah 21411. There is also a trade office in Dhahran/Al Khobar (PO Box 88, Dhahran Airport 31932).

BRITISH COUNCIL REPRESENTATIVE, Clive Mogford, Olaya Main Road, Al Mousa Centre, Tower B (PO Box 58012), Riyadh 11594. There are also offices in *Jeddah*, *Dammam* and *Jubail*.

DEFENCE

Total active armed forces number some 157,000 personnel, service being voluntary. The Army numbers 73,000 personnel, with 700 main battle tanks, 2,580 armoured infantry fighting vehicles and armoured personnel carriers and 460 artillery pieces. The Navy has 11,000 personnel including two battalions of 1,500 marines. It deploys eight frigates, 12 patrol and coastal combatants and 20 armed helicopters. The Air Force has 22,000 personnel, including 4,000 air defence forces, and deploys 293 combat aircraft of US and UK manufacture. The National Guard, which is directly under Royal command, has 55,000 active personnel and 20,000 tribal levies. In addition, the paramilitary Frontier Force numbers 10,500 personnel. Saudi Arabia is base to the Gulf Co-operational Council Peninsula Shield Force of 5,000 troops. The USA stations air force units in the country.

ECONOMY

Outside the manufacturing centres which have grown up around some of the towns, most of the population are engaged in agriculture. The productivity of traditional dryland farming is supplemented by irrigation.

The principal industry is oil extraction and processing. Oil was first found in commercial quantities in 1938. About 97 per cent of the total is extracted by the Arabian–American Oil Company. Aramco's 66-year lease will terminate in 1999 but the company was effectively nationalized in 1980.

The government actively encourages the establishment of manufacturing industries in the country. Industries have developed in the fields of construction materials, metal fabrication, simple machinery and electrical equipment, food and beverages, chemicals and plastics. Investment in industrial gases, intermediate petrochemicals, light engineering and machinery is encouraged.

Two industrial centres have been established at Jubail and Yanbu, financed by the state agency Saudi Arabian Basic

Industries Corporation. Linked by gas and oil pipelines, both have petrochemical complexes producing ethylene and methanol; six of the seven plants now on-stream are joint ventures with American and Japanese companies.

The state agency Petromin operates three domestic refineries, two lubricant plants and three export refineries. Total refining capacity is approximately 1,950,000 b.p.d.

TRADE

Oil remains the main source of receipts in the balance of payments. As a result, government revenues are markedly affected by oil prices and volume of production.

The leading suppliers of imports are USA, Japan, Germany, the UK, Italy and France and the chief customers for exports are Japan, France, USA and Singapore. There is a total ban on the importation of alcohol, pork products, firearms, and items regarded as non-Islamic or pornographic.

	1988	1989
Total imports	SR81,582m	SR79,219m
Total exports	88,896m	103,892m

Trade with UK	1991	1992
Imports from UK	£2,228,965,000	£1,967,625,000
Exports to UK	963,919,000	963,607,000

COMMUNICATIONS

There are few railway lines. They principally connect the oilfields to the ports and the capital. Metalled roads connect all the cities and main towns; the network consisted of 28,500 km in 1985. The principal port of the Gulf is Dammam which has 39 berths and an annual capacity of 9.1 million tons. Jeddah is the centre of commercial traffic on the Red Sea and has 51 piers, giving an annual capacity of 17 million tons.

The government-owned Saudi Arabian Airlines (Saudia) operate scheduled services to 22 domestic airports. There are international airports at Dhahran, Jeddah and Riyadh. Work on the new King Fahd International Airport in Eastern Province has yet to be completed. Saudia have an extensive overseas operation, and a large number of international airlines operate into the country. Telecommunications are being rapidly expanded.

EDUCATION

With the exception of a few schools for expatriate children, all schools are government supervised and segregated for boys and girls. There are universities in Jeddah, Mecca, Riyadh (branches in Abha and Qassim), Dammam (branch at Hofuf) and Dhahran, and there are Islamic universities in Medina and Riyadh. There is great emphasis on vocational training, provided at 24 literacy and artisan skill training centres and 21 more advanced industrial, commercial and agricultural education institutes. Education in government-owned institutes is free at all levels.

SENEGAL
République du Sénégal

Senegal lies on the west coast of Africa between Mauritania in the north, Mali in the east, and Guinea-Bissau and Guinea in the south. The Gambia lies entirely within Senegal, except for its sea-coast. Senegal has an area of 75,750 sq. miles (196,192 sq. km), and a population (UN estimate 1991) of 7,533,000.

CAPITAL – ΨDakar (1,000,000).
CURRENCY – Franc CFA of 100 centimes.
FLAG – Three vertical bands, green, yellow and red; a green star on the yellow band.
NATIONAL DAY – 4 April.

GOVERNMENT

Formerly a French colony, Senegal elected in November 1958 to remain within the French Community as an autonomous republic. A border dispute with Mauretania was defused in early 1992 when the boarder was re-opened and diplomatic relations restored. There is an insurgent separatist movement (Movement of Democratic Forces of Casamance (MFDC)) in the southern Casamance region. A ceasefire between the government and MFDC was signed in July 1993 but a political agreement has still to be reached.

In March 1963 (after an attempted coup d'état by the then Prime Minister in the previous December) a new constitution was approved giving executive powers to the President. The process of political liberalization continued; there are now 16 political parties officially recognized. A general election for the National Assembly of 120 seats (70 elected by proportional representation and 50 on a majority basis) is held every five years.

President Diouf was re-elected in the first round of presidential elections in February 1993 with 58.4 per cent of the vote. The legislative election in May 1993 was won by the ruling Parti Socialiste (PS), which secured 84 seats, with the Parti Démocratique Sénégalais winning 27 seats, and other parties nine seats.

HEAD OF STATE
President, Abdou Diouf, *installed* 1981, *re-elected* 1988, 21 February 1993.

GOVERNMENT *as at August 1993*
Prime Minister, Habib Thiam.
Minister of State, Moustapha Niasse (*Foreign Affairs and Expatriates*); Robert Sagna (*Agriculture*); Ousmane Dieng (*Presidency*); Djibo Ka (*Interior*).
Justice, Jacques Baudin.
Armed Forces, Madieng Dieng.
Economy, Finance and Planning, Papa Sakho.
Environment and Protection of Nature, Abdoulaye Bathily.
Urban Planning and Housing, Amath Dansokho.
National Education, André Sonko.
Energy, Mines and Industry, Alasane N'Diaye.
Modernization and Technology, Magued Diouf.
Communications, Abdoulaye Kane.
Culture, Coura Ba Thiam.
Health and Social Welfare, Assane Diop.
Employment, Labour and Professional Training, Serigne Diop.
Commerce and Handicrafts, Cheikh Kane.
Women, Children and Family Welfare, Ndioro N'Diaye.
Equipment and Land Transport, Landing Sone.
Youth and Sports, Ousmane Paye.
Fisheries and Sea Transport, Abdourahmane Sow.
Tourism and Air Transport, Tidiane Sylla.
Water Resources, Mamadou Faye.
Towns, Daour Cisse.

EMBASSY OF THE REPUBLIC OF SENEGAL
11 Phillimore Gardens, London W8 7QG
Tel 071–937 0925/6

Ambassador Extraordinary and Plenipotentiary, His Excellency Seydou Madani Sy (1991).

BRITISH EMBASSY
BP 6025, Dakar
Tel: Dakar 237392

Ambassador Extraordinary and Plenipotentiary, His
Excellency Alan Furness (1993).

BRITISH COUNCIL REPRESENTATIVE, A. Malamah-
Thomas, MBE, 34–36 Blvd. de la Republique, Immeuble
Sonatel, BP 6232, Dakar.

TRADE

Senegal's principal exports are groundnuts (raw and processed) and phosphates. Tourism is also of growing importance
as a revenue earner.

Trade with UK	1991	1992
Imports from UK	£13,960,000	£13,345,000
Exports to UK	5,025,000	3,519,000

SEYCHELLES
The Republic of Seychelles

Seychelles, in the Indian Ocean, consists of 115 islands with a
total land area of 176 sq. miles, spread over 400,000 square
miles of ocean. There is a relatively compact granitic group,
32 islands in all, with high hills and mountains (highest point
about 2,972 ft), of which Mahé is the largest and most
populated (90 per cent of the population live on Mahé); and
the outlying coralline group, for the most part only a little
above sea-level. Although only 4° S. of the Equator, the
climate is pleasant though tropical.

POPULATION – The population is 68,000 (1991 UN
estimate).

CAPITAL – ΨVictoria (population, 1987, 24,324), on Mahé.
CURRENCY – Seychelles rupee (Rs) of 100 cents.
FLAG – Red over green, divided by wavy white band.
NATIONAL ANTHEM – Fyer Seselwa (Proud Seychellois).
NATIONAL DAY – 5 June.

GOVERNMENT

Proclaimed French territory in 1756, the Mahé group was
settled as a dependency of Mauritius from 1770, was captured
by a British ship in 1794, changed hands several times
between 1803 and 1814, when it was finally assigned to Great
Britain. In 1903 these islands, together with the coralline
group, were formed into a separate colony. On 29 June 1976,
the islands became an independent republic within the
Commonwealth. A coup d'état took place on 5 June 1977.
Seychelles was a one-party state from 1979 until 1991, when
a multi-party democratic system was proposed by the
President. Multi-party elections to a commission to draw up
a new constitution were held in July 1992. The Seychelles
People's Progressive Front (SPPF) gained 12 seats on the
20-man commission, with the opposition Democratic Party
(DP) taking the remaining eight. The new multi-party
constitution drawn up by the commission failed to gain the
requisite 60 per cent vote in the November 1992 referendum.
An amended constitution was adopted in a referendum in
June 1993. Under the new constitution multi-party politics
was institutionalized, a National Assembly of 33 members
was established and the presidential mandate was set at five
years, renewable three times. In presidential and legislative
elections held in July 1993, President René was re-elected
and the SPPF formed a government after winning 27 of the
National Assembly seats, to the DP's five.

HEAD OF STATE
President, France Albert René, *assumed office* 5 June 1977;
elected 1979; *re-elected* 1984, 1989, 27 July 1993.

COUNCIL OF MINISTERS *as at August 1993*
Legal Affairs, Industry, The President.
Finance, Communications and Defence, James Michel.
Administration and Manpower, Joseph Belmont.
Industry, Esme Jumeau.
Environment, Economic Planning and Foreign Affairs,
  Danielle de St Jorre.
Health, Ralph Adam.
Agriculture and Fisheries, Jacquelin Dugasse.
Employment and Social Affairs, William Herminie.
Tourism and Transport, Simone Testa.
Local Government, Culture and Sports, Sylvette Frichot.
Education and Culture, Patrick Pillay.
Community Development, Dolor Ernesta.

SEYCHELLES HIGH COMMISSION
Box No. 4PE, 2nd Floor, Eros House, 111 Baker Street,
London WIM 1FE
Tel 071-224 1660

High Commissioner, His Excellency John P. Mascarenhas
  (1993).

BRITISH HIGH COMMISSION
Victoria House, PO Box 161 Victoria, Mahé
Tel: Victoria 225225

High Commissioner, His Excellency John Sharland (1991).

ECONOMY

The economy is based on tourism, fishing, small-scale
agriculture and manufacturing, and the re-export of fuel for
aircraft and ships.   Deep sea tuna fishing by foreign fleets
under licence, improved trans-shipment and other port
facilities at Victoria, exports from a tuna canning factory and
the export of fresh and frozen fish, attract growing revenues.

TRADE

The principal imports are foodstuffs, beverages, tobacco,
mineral fuels, manufactured items, building materials,
machinery and transport equipment.

	1989	1990
Imports	Rs.925,771,000	Rs.991,500,000
Exports	67,789,000	73,200,000
Re-exports	109,407,000	131,200,000

Trade with UK	1991	1992
Imports from UK	£10,513,000	£12,352,000
Exports to UK	8,457,000	2,891,000

SIERRA LEONE
The Republic of Sierra Leone

Sierra Leone, with a total land area of 27,699 sq. miles
(71,740 sq. km), is on the west coast of Africa, between
Guinea and Liberia.

POPULATION – 1991 UN estimate, 4,260,000. The south is
inhabited by peoples whose languages fall into the Mende
group; the north by the Temne, and smaller groups such as
the Limba, Loko, Koranko and Susu.

CAPITAL – ΨFreetown (population, 1985 Census,
  470,000).
CURRENCY – Leone (Le) of 100 cents.

FLAG – Three horizontal stripes of leaf green, white and cobalt blue.
NATIONAL ANTHEM – High We Exalt Thee, Realm of the Free.
NATIONAL DAY – 27 April (Independence Day).

GOVERNMENT

In the late 18th century a project was begun to settle destitute Africans from England on Freetown peninsula. In 1808 the settlement was declared a Crown colony and became the main base in West Africa for enforcing the 1807 Act outlawing the slave trade. The colony was also used as a settlement for Africans from North America and the West Indies, and great numbers of Africans rescued from slave ships also settled there. In 1896 a Protectorate was declared over the hinterland.

In 1951 a new constitution was set up that united the colony of Freetown and the Protectorate and on 27 April 1961 Sierra Leone became a fully independent state within the Commonwealth. In 1971 a republican constitution was adopted and Dr Siaka Stevens became the first Executive President. In June 1978 Sierra Leone became a one-party state, following approval by Parliament and a referendum. In September 1991 a new multi-party constitution was adopted and an interim government formed until a general election could be held. This government was overthrown because of alleged corruption by a coup on 29 April 1992. Captain Valentine Strasser became head of state, the House of Representatives was dissolved and all political activity was suspended. A cabinet was appointed to govern the country until promised multi-party elections. In July 1992 Strasser abolished the cabinet and appointed a Council of State Secretaries to co-ordinate the day-to-day running of government. This is subordinate to a military Supreme Council of State (SCS).

HEAD OF STATE
President, Chairman of the SCS, Minister of Defence, Capt. Valentine Strasser, *sworn in* 3 May 1992.

SUPREME COUNCIL OF STATE *as at August 1993*
Chairman, Capt. Valentine Strasser.
Vice-Chairman, Capt. Julius Bio.
Labour, Energy, Power, Trade and Industry, State Enterprises, Lands, Housing and Environment, Lt. Samuel Kambo.
Transport, Communications, Tourism, Mines and Works, Lt. Charles M'Bayo.

COUNCIL OF STATE SECRETARIES *as at August 1993*
Chief Secretary of State, Capt. Julius Bio.
Youth, Sports and Social Mobilization, Lt. Charles M'Bayo.
Chairman's Office, Col. (retd) S. B. Jumu.
Finance, Development and Economic Planning, Dr John Karimu.
Foreign Affairs (acting), Lt. Karefa Kargbo.
Transport and Communications, Arnold Bishop-Gooding.
Agriculture and Forestry, Lt.-Col. A. K. Sesay.
Mineral Resources, Capt. Reginald Glover.
Trade, Industry and State Enterprises, Dr Alusine Fofana.
Works, Lt.-Col. J. P. Gbondo.
Information, Broadcasting and Culture, Hindolo Trye.
Labour, Energy and Power, Ales Browne.
Education, Bassie Bangura.
Justice, Franklyn Kargbo.
Health and Social Services, Lt.-Col. A. A. Gibril.
Lands, Housing and Environment, Lt.-Col. S. F. Koroma.
Interior and Rural Development, Col. (retd) A. Kamara.
Tourism, Maj. (retd) Gabriel Turay.
Eastern Region, Lt. S. Nyuma.

Northern Region, Maj. Fallah Sewah.
Southern Region, Lt. Idris Kamara.

SIERRA LEONE HIGH COMMISSION
33 Portland Place, London WIN 3AG
Tel 071-636 6483/4/5/6

High Commissioner, His Excellency Prof. Cyril Foray (1993).

BRITISH HIGH COMMISSION
Standard Bank of Sierra Leone Building, Lightfoot Boston Street, Freetown
Tel: Freetown 223961-5

High Commissioner, His Excellency Ian McCluney (1993).
BRITISH COUNCIL REPRESENTATIVE, Peter Hilken, PO Box 124, Tower Hill, Freetown.

COMMUNICATIONS

Since the phasing out of the railway system in 1974 the road network has been developed considerably and there are now 5,000 miles of roads in the country, over 2,000 miles being surfaced. A bridge has been constructed over the Mano River linking Sierra Leone and Liberia.

The Freetown international airport is situated at Lungi. The main port is Freetown, which has one of the largest natural harbours in the world, and where there is a deep water quay. There are smaller ports at Pepel, Bonthe and Niti.

Radio is operated by the government. Broadcasts are made in several of the indigenous languages, in addition to English and French.

EDUCATION

In 1989 there were 2,554 primary schools in Sierra Leone and 201 secondary schools. Technical education is provided in the two government technical institutes, situated in Freetown and Kenema, in two trade centres and in the technical training establishments of the mining companies. Teacher training is carried out at the University of Sierra Leone, six colleges in the provinces and in the Milton Margai Training College near Freetown.

ECONOMY

On the Freetown peninsula, farming is largely confined to the production of cassava and garden crops, such as maize and vegetables, for local consumption. In the hinterland the principal agricultural product is rice, which is the staple food of the country, and cash crops such as cocoa, coffee, palm kernels and ginger.

The economy depends largely on mineral exports; mainly diamonds, gold, bauxite and rutile. Diamond exports provided Le1,254.5m in 1989. Total imports for 1989 were to the value of Le10,901.8m and exports were Le8,269.5m.

TRADE WITH UK	1991	1992
Imports from UK	£17,928,000	£15,450,000
Exports to UK	5,616,000	9,424,000

SINGAPORE

Singapore consists of the island of Singapore and 58 islets, covering a total area of 639.1 sq. km. Singapore island is 26 miles long and 14 miles in breadth and is situated just north of the Equator off the southern extremity of the Malay peninsula, from which it is separated by the Straits of Johore. A causeway crosses the three-quarters of a mile to the mainland. The climate is hot and humid and there are no clearly defined seasons. Rainfall averages 240 cm a year and temperature ranges from 24° to 32° C (76°–89° F).

POPULATION – In 1990 the population was 3,002,800, which comprised 2,239,700 Chinese, 406,200 Malays, 230,000 Indians (including those of Pakistani, Bangladeshi and Sri Lankan origin) and 126,900 from other ethnic groups. Malay, Mandarin, Tamil and English are the official languages. At least eight Chinese dialects are used.

CURRENCY – Singapore dollar (S$) of 100 cents.
FLAG – Horizontal bands of red over white; crescent with five five-point stars on red band near staff.
NATIONAL ANTHEM – Majulah Singapura.
NATIONAL DAY – 9 August.

GOVERNMENT

Singapore, where Sir Stamford Raffles first established a trading post under the East India Company in 1819, was incorporated with Penang and Malacca to form the Straits Settlements in 1826. The Straits Settlements became a Crown colony in 1867. Singapore fell into Japanese hands in 1942 and civil government was not restored until 1946, when it became a separate colony. Internal self-government was introduced in 1959. Singapore became a state of Malaysia when the Federation was enlarged in September 1963, but left Malaysia and became an independent sovereign state within the Commonwealth on 9 August 1965. Singapore adopted a republican constitution from that date. There is a Cabinet collectively responsible to a fully-elected Parliament of 81 members. In November 1991 the constitution was amended to provide for a directly-elected President with enlarged powers and the ability to veto government decisions in certain instances.

After the general election of 31 August 1991 the People's Action Party (PAP) had 77 seats in Parliament. The Singapore Democratic Party (SDP) won three seats and the Workers' Party won one seat.

HEAD OF STATE
President, Ong Teng Cheong, *elected* 28 August 1993.

CABINET *as at August 1993*
Prime Minister, Goh Chok Tong.
Senior Minister, PM's Office, Lee Kuan Yew, GCMG, CH.
Deputy PM, Lee Hsien Loong.
Trade and Industry, S. Dhanabalan.
Education, Lee Yock Suan.
Environment and Muslim Affairs, Dr Ahmad Mattar.
Communications, Mah Bow Tan.
Defence, Dr Yeo Ning Hong.
Law and Home Affairs, Prof. S. Jayakumar.
Finance and National Development, Dr Richard Hu Tsu Tau.
Labour, Lee Boon Yang.
Foreign Affairs, Wong Kan Seng.
Health and Community Development, Yeo Cheow Tong.
Information and The Arts, George Yeo.
Speaker of Parliament, Tan Soo Khoon.

SINGAPORE HIGH COMMISSION
9 Wilton Crescent, London SW1X 8SA
Tel 071-235 8315

High Commissioner, His Excellency Abdul Aziz Mahmood (1988).
First Secretary, Miss J. Kang (*Commercial*).

BRITISH HIGH COMMISSION
Tanglin Road, Singapore 1024
Tel: Singapore 4739333
High Commissioner, His Excellency Gordon Duggan (1990).
Deputy High Commissioner and Counsellor (*Economic/ Commercial*), P. W. Ford.
Defence Adviser, Gp. Capt. P. G. Wildman.

BRITISH COUNCIL REPRESENTATIVE, J. Davies, 30 Napier Road, Singapore 1025.

COMMUNICATIONS

Singapore is one of the largest and busiest seaports in the world, with deep water wharves and ship repairing facilities. Ships also anchor in the roads, unloading into lighters. In 1991, the total volume of cargo handled was 202,000,000 tonnes. More than 700 shipping lines use the port, with 61,000 ship arrivals in 1991.

The international airport is at Changi, in the east of the island. There are 67 km of metric gauge railway connected to the Malaysian rail system by the causeway across the Straits of Johore, and 2,924 km of roads.

There are both wireless and wired broadcasting services carrying commercial advertising. There are three television channels. The Singapore Broadcasting Authority Corporation was established in February 1980.

ECONOMY

Historically Singapore's economy was based on the sale and distribution of raw materials from surrounding countries and on entrepot trade in finished products. However, new manufacturing industries have been successfully introduced, including ship building and repairing, iron and steel, textiles, footwear, wood products, micro-electronics, scientific instruments, detergents, confectionery, pharmaceuticals, petroleum products, etc. Singapore has also become a financial centre with 134 commercial banks and 75 merchant banks and an oil-refining centre.

FINANCE (estimates)	1990	1991
Revenue	S$16,424.7m	S$19,570m
Expenditure	13,257.1m	13,860m

TRADE	1990	1991
Total imports	S$109,805.8m	S$114,000m
Total exports	95,205.8m	102,000m

Trade with UK	1991	1992
Imports from UK	£1,018,419,000	£1,145,058,000
Exports to UK	1,134,365,000	1,192,803,000

SLOVAKIA
Slovenská Republika - The Republic of Slovakia

The Republic of Slovakia has an area of 18,940 sq. miles (49,035 sq. km). It is situated in central Europe and is bordered to the north by Poland, to the east by the Ukraine, to the south by Hungary, to the south west by Austria and to the west by the Czech Republic. The Tatry (Tatras) mountains in the centre and north of the country reach heights of 2,600 m (8,530 ft). The major river is the Váh which flows from the Tatry mountains to join the Danube at the Hungarian border. The climate is continental with hot summers and cold winters.

POPULATION – The population (1991) is 5,274,335, of which 85.7 per cent are ethnic Slovaks, 10.8 per cent ethnic

Hungarians, 1.4 per cent Gypsy, 1.1 per cent Czech, with smaller numbers of Ruthenians, Ukrainians and Germans. RELIGION – Christian, some 60 per cent Roman Catholic and 6 per cent Protestant. LANGUAGE – Slovak (85.7 per cent), Hungarian (10.8 per cent), Czech (1.1 per cent). Slovak is the official language but the law safeguards the right to use minority languages in dealing with public authorities in areas where the minority forms 20 per cent or more of the population.

CAPITAL – Bratislava on the Danube, population (1991) 440,421. Other major cities are: Košice (238,454); Žilina (97,537); Prešov (89,000); Banská Bystríca (78,321).
CURRENCY – Slovak Koruna (SK) (Crown).
FLAG – Three horizontal stripes of white, blue, red with the arms all over near the hoist.
NATIONAL ANTHEM – Nad Tatrou sa blýska (Storm over the Tatras).
NATIONAL DAYS – 8 May (Liberation from fascism); 5 July (Day of the Slav Missionaries); 29 August (Slovak National Uprising).

GOVERNMENT (see also Czech Republic)

At the end of the eleventh century Slovakia became part of the Hungarian state when the Magyars gained control of the area. After the Hungarians were defeated at the battle of Moháč in 1526, most of Hungary was occupied by the Turks, the remainder, including Slovakia, being incorporated into the Austrian Empire. With the establishment of the Austro-Hungarian monarchy in 1867, Slovakia again came under Hungarian control. The attempted Magyarization of Slovakia led to a national revival and when the First World War came many Slovaks fought with the allies. Amalgamated into the republic of Czechoslovakia on 28 October 1918, Slovakia became independent in March 1939 as a Nazi puppet state when Germany invaded the Czech lands. Slovakia was liberated by Soviet forces in 1945 and returned to Czechoslovakia. The formation of a federal republic between the Czech lands and Slovakia was the only Prague Spring reform to survive the Soviet invasion of 1968.

As at the federal level, the Communist party was forced out of power in Slovakia in November 1989. The elections of June 1992 returned the nationalist Movement for a Democratic Slovakia (HZDS), led by Vladimir Mečiar, as the largest party in Slovakia, with other nationalist parties and the ex-Communists emerging strongly as well. Mečiar began the process which led to the dissolution of the federation into two sovereign states on 1 January 1993.

The Slovak constitution defines Slovakia as a unitary state and vests legislative power in the National Council of 150 members elected for a four-year term. The President is elected for a five-year term by the National Council; executive power is held by the Prime Minister and Cabinet. Minority rights are enshrined in the constitution but discrimination is claimed by the ethnic Hungarian population. A coalition government of the HZDS and Slovak National Party (SNS) was sworn in on 12 January 1993. The SNS left the government in March, leaving the HZDS government short of a majority in parliament.

HEAD OF STATE
President, Michal Kovac, elected by parliament 15 February 1993.

COUNCIL OF MINISTERS as at August 1993
Prime Minister, Vladimir Mečiar.
Deputy Prime Minister, Roman Kovac.
Foreign Affairs, Jozef Moravčik.
Economy, Jaroslav Kubečka.

Finance, Július Toth.
Labour, Social Welfare and the Family, Olga Keltošova.
Environment, Jozef Zlocha.
Administration and Privatization, Lubomir Dolgoš.
Transport, Communications and Public Works, Roman Hofbauer.
Land Management, Peter Baco.
Culture, Dušan Slobodnik.
Education and Science, Prof Matús Kačera.
Health, Dr Viliam Soboňa.
Interior, Jozef Tuchyňa.
Justice, Prof Katarina Tothova.
Defence, Imrich Andrejčak.

Chairman, Slovak National Council, Ivan Gašparovič.

EMBASSY OF THE SLOVAK REPUBLIC
25 Kensington Palace Gardens, London W8 4QY
Tel 071-243 0803

Ambassador Extraordinary and Plenipotentiary, His Excellency Dr Jan Vilikovsky (1992).

BRITISH AMBASSADOR, resides at Prague.
BRITISH COUNCIL DIRECTOR, Rosemary Hillhorst, PO Box 68, Panska 17, 81499 Bratislava.

ECONOMY

Slovakia has a higher unemployment rate (13 per cent) and is in a worse economic situation than the Czech Republic because all the heavy industry built by the Communists (arms factories, forges, rolling mills) were dependent on state subsidies which the free-market reforms of the federal government were phasing out. The HZDS has faced increasing economic problems in 1993 as output, exports and foreign currency reserves have fallen and unemployment and inflation increased. In July 1993 the Slovak Crown was devalued by 10 per cent. The former federal republic's privatization policies have been continued, though at a slower rate than in the Czech Republic. Firms have been privatized by a voucher system, transfer, public auction, restoration to former owners, or transformation into joint-stock companies, and the second wave of privatization is planned. The Slovak economy has suffered because of a lack of foreign investment (12 per cent of the former federal total) and the loss of federal subsidies. Natural resources include brown coal, natural gas, iron ore, antimony, lead, zinc and magnesite.

SLOVENIA
Republike Slovenije

Slovenia is a small mountainous state which was the most northerly of the former Yugoslav republics. It has an area of 7,819 sq. miles (20,251 sq. km) and is bordered on the north by Austria, on the north east by Hungary, on the east and south by Croatia and on the west by Italy. The two major rivers are the Sava and the Drava. There is a short coastline in the south west of some 25 miles (40 km) in length on the Adriatic. The climate is a mixture of Mediterranean, continental and alpine.
POPULATION – The population (1992) is 2,020,000 and is virtually ethnically homogeneous. There are small ethnic Hungarian (0.5 per cent) and ethnic Italian (0.1 per cent) minorities, together with a Romany population. Slovenia has also taken in some 70,000–120,000 refugees from the former Yugoslavia.
RELIGION – Roman Catholic.
LANGUAGE – Slovene is the official language, together with Hungarian and Italian in ethnically mixed regions.

CAPITAL – Ljubljana, population (1991) 268,000. Other major towns (1991) are: Maribor (105,400); Celje (42,000); Kranj (37,100) and ΨKoper (24,600), the only port.
CURRENCY – Slovene Tolar (SIT) of 100 stotin.
FLAG – Three horizontal stripes of white, blue, red, with the arms in the upper hoist.
NATIONAL ANTHEM – Zdravljica (A Toast).
NATIONAL DAY – 25 June (Independence Day).

GOVERNMENT

The area that is now Slovenia came under the control of the Habsburg Empire in the 15th century and remained so until the defeat of the Austro-Hungarian Empire in 1918. On 27 October 1918 Slovenia became part of the state of Slovenes, Croats and Serbs (later Yugoslavia) and this was confirmed by the Versailles Treaty 1919. Slovenia was reduced in size, however, by the Italian annexation of the western third of the country and the Austrian annexation of parts of the north. In 1941 Yugoslavia was invaded by German forces and Slovenia was divided between Germany, Italy and Hungary. Slovenia was reformed as a constituent republic of the federal Yugoslav state in May 1945. After a dispute with Italy and nine years of international administration the Adriatic coast and hinterland were returned to Slovenia in 1954 and Italy retained Trieste.

Slovenian fears of Serbian dominance led the Slovene Assembly in 1989 to amend the republican constitution to lay the basis of a sovereign state. In a referendum in December 1990 88 per cent of the electorate voted for independence, which was declared on 25 June 1991. A short ten-day war with the Yugoslav National Army followed before the Army called off hostilities and withdrew, leaving by 25 October.

A new constitution was adopted by the National Assembly on 23 December 1991. Executive power is vested in the Prime Minister and Cabinet of Ministers. Legislative authority is held by the bicameral National Assembly, composed of the 90-member State Chamber (lower house) and 40-member State Council (upper house). The State Chamber is elected on a proportional representation basis, with one seat each reserved for the Italian and Hungarian minorities. The State Council has 22 elected and 18 appointed members. Presidential legislative elections were held on 6 December 1992, with incumbent President Milan Kučan being re-elected and the Liberal Democratic Party emerging as the largest party in parliament. A coalition government led by the Liberal Democrats was formed in January 1993.

HEAD OF STATE
President, Milan Kučan, *elected* April 1990, *re-elected for a five-year term* 6 December 1992.

CABINET *as at August 1993*
Prime Minister, Janez Ornovšek (LDS).
Deputy PM, Foreign Affairs, Lojze Peterle (SKD).
Finance, Mitja Gaspari (LDS).
Economy, Development, Davorin Kračun (LDS).
Education and Sports, Slavko Gaber (LDS).
Justice, Miha Kozinc (LDS).
Internal Affairs, Ivan Bizjak (SKD).
Transport and Communications, Igor Umek (SKD).
Agriculture and Forestry, Jože Osterc (SKD).
Health, Božidar Voljč (ZS).
Science and Technology, Rado Bohinc (ZL).
Labour, Family and Social Affairs, Jožica Puhar (ZL).
Culture, Sergij Pelhan (ZL).
Economic Activities, Maks Tajnikar (ZL).
Environment, Miha Jazbinšek (LDS).
Defence, Janez Janša (SDSS).

LDS Liberal Democratic Party; SKD Slovenian Christian Democrats; ZL United List; ZS Greens; SDSS Social Democratic Party.

EMBASSY OF SLOVENIA
11–15 Wigmore Street, London WIH 9LA
Tel 071-495 7775

Ambassador Extraordinary and Plenipotentiary, His Excellency Matjaz Sinkovec (1992).

BRITISH EMBASSY
4th Floor, Trg Republike 3, 61–000 Ljubljana
Tel: Ljubljana 157191

Ambassador Extraordinary and Plenipotentiary, His Excellency Gordon Johnston (1992).

BRITISH COUNCIL REPRESENTATIVE – Roger Woodham, Stefanova 1/III, 61000 Ljubljana.

ECONOMY

Although still with problems, Slovenia's economy has emerged as the most stable of the former Yugoslav economies and the least affected by the break-up of the centrally-planned economy. Although it has lost its captive export market and cheap supplies of raw materials from Serbia, the country is one of the richest of the former Communist countries. A small trade surplus was recorded in 1992, when foreign currency reserves stood at US$1.2 billion and foreign debt at US$1.7 billion. Inflation has been kept low and the tolar is stable and convertible.

In 1990 agriculture, forestry and fishing produced 4.7 per cent of GDP. The main products are potatoes, wheat, corn, apples, wine, meat and milk. Mining and manufacturing produced 30.8 per cent of GDP, the major sectors being metal-working, electronics, textiles, chemicals, glass products, food-processing and iron ore mining. Tourism and transport are major export earners, with 1,400,000 visiting tourists in 1991. Important road and rail communications cross the country from west to east (Milan–Ljubljana–Budapest), and north to south (Munich–Ljubljana–Zagreb–Belgrade–Athens). There are international airports at Ljubljana, Maribor and Portoroz (Adriatic Coast). The port of Koper is an important shipment point for goods from Austria, Hungary and the Czech Republic.

EDUCATION

Education is compulsory and free between the ages of 7 and 19. There are 842 primary schools (age 7–15), 149 secondary or middle schools (age 15–19), 26 colleges and 2 universities (Ljubljana and Maribor).

SOLOMON ISLANDS

Forming a scattered archipelago of mountainous islands and low-lying coral atolls, the Solomon Islands stretches about 900 miles in a south-easterly direction from the Shortland Islands to the Santa Cruz islands. The archipelago covers an area of about 249,000 square nautical miles while the land area is 10,938 sq. miles (28,446 sq. km). Solomon Islands lies between 155° 30′ and 170° 30′E. longitude and between 5° 10′ and 12° 45′S. latitude. The six biggest islands are Choiseul, New Georgia, Santa Isabel, Guadalcanal, Malaita and Makira. They are characterized by thickly-forested mountain ranges intersected by deep, narrow valleys.

POPULATION – The total population was 285,176 at the 1986 Census. The 1991 UN estimate was 330,000. English is the official language; there are over 80 local languages.

CAPITAL – ΨHoniara, population (1986), 30,499.

CURRENCY – Solomon Islands dollar (SI$) of 100 cents.

FLAG – Blue over green divided by a diagonal yellow band, with five white stars in the top left quarter.

NATIONAL ANTHEM – God Bless our Solomon Islands.

NATIONAL DAY – 7 July (Independence Day).

GOVERNMENT

The origin of the present Melanesian inhabitants is uncertain. European discovery of the islands began in the mid-16th century and continued intermittently for about 300 years, when the inauguration of sugar plantations in Queensland and Fiji (which created a need for labour) and the arrival of missionaries and traders led to increased European interest in the region. Great Britain declared a Protectorate in 1893 over the Southern Solomons, adding the Santa Cruz group in 1898 and 1899. The islands of the Shortland groups were transferred by treaty from Germany to Great Britain in 1900.

The Solomon Islands achieved internal self-government in 1976, and became independent in July 1978. The Solomon Islands is a constitutional monarchy, The Queen being represented locally by the Governor-General. Legislative power is vested in a unicameral National Parliament of 47 members, elected for a four-year term. The executive authority is exercised by the Cabinet. A four-party National Coalition government took power after winning 24 of the 47 seats in the legislative election of 26 May 1993.

Governor-General, His Excellency Sir George Lepping, GCMG, MBE (1989).

CABINET *as at August 1993*

Prime Minister, Hon. Francis Billy Hilly.

Deputy Prime Minister, Foreign Affairs, Hon. Francis Saemala.

Agriculture and Lands, Hon. Francis Orodani.

Commerce, Employment and Trade, Hon. Joses Tuhanuka.

Development Planning, Hon. George Kejoa.

Culture, Sports and Tourism, Hon. Allan Paul.

Education and Training, Hon. Dennis Lulei.

Finance, Hon. Andrew Nori.

Health and Medical Services, Hon. Nathaniel Waena.

Home Affairs, Hon. Michael Maeliau.

Justice, Hon. Jackson Piasi.

Natural Resources, Hon. Ezikiel Alebua.

Provincial Government and Rural Development, Hon. Eric Seri.

Post and Communication, Hon. Ambrose Kimata.

Transport, Works and Utilities, Hon. Edward Hunuehu.

HIGH COMMISSION OF THE SOLOMON ISLANDS
Boulevard St Michel 101, 1040 Brussels
Tel: Brussels 732 7085

High Commissioner, His Excellency Lindsay F. Misros (1993).

HONORARY CONSULATE
17 Springfield Road, London SW19 7AL
Tel 071-946 5552

Honorary Consul, new appointment awaited.

BRITISH HIGH COMMISSION
Soltel House, Mendana Avenue (PO Box 676), Honiara
Tel: Honiara 21705/6

High Commissioner, His Excellency Raymond F. Jones, OBE (1991).

COMMUNICATIONS

Solomon Airlines operates international services to other Pacific states and Australia. Air Niugini flies from Port Moresby to Honiara. There are about 52 miles of secondary and minor roads in the urban areas of Honiara, Auki and Gizo. In the rural areas there are some 800 miles of road, including those in private plantations, forestry areas and roads built and maintained by councils. Telekom, a company jointly owned by Cable and Wireless Limited and the Solomon Islands government, operates the international and domestic telephone circuits from a ground station in Honiara via the Intelsat Pacific Ocean communication satellite.

TRADE

The main imports are foodstuffs, consumer goods, machinery and transport materials. Principal exports are timber, fish, copra, and palm oil. Fisheries exports for 1992 totalled SI$88.1m, timber SI$110.4m and copra SI$22.7m. Other exports include cocoa and marine shells.

Trade with UK	1991	1992
Imports from UK	£1,170,000	£606,000
Exports to UK	6,846,000	5,691,000

SOMALIA
Jamhuuriyadda Diimoqraadiga ee Soomaaliya

Somalia occupies part of the north-east horn of Africa, with a coastline on the Indian Ocean extending from the boundary with Kenya (2° S. latitude) to Cape Guardafui (12° N.), and on the Gulf of Aden to the boundary with Djibouti. Somalia is bounded on the west by Djibouti, Ethiopia and Kenya and covers an area of approximately 246,201 sq. miles (637,657 sq. km). The population, of which a large proportion is nomadic, is 7,691,000 (UN estimate 1991).

CAPITAL – Ψ Mogadishu, population (estimated 1987), 1,000,000. Other towns are Hargeisa (20,000), Boroma (65,000), ΨKisimayu (60,000), Ψ Berbera (15,000) and Burao (15,000).

CURRENCY – Somali shilling of 100 cents.

FLAG – Five-pointed white star on blue ground.

NATIONAL DAY – under review.

GOVERNMENT

British rule in Somaliland lasted from 1887 until 1960, except for a short period in 1940-1 when the Protectorate was occupied by Italian forces. Somalia, formerly an Italian colony, was occupied by British forces in 1941. In 1950 it was placed under Italian administration by a resolution of the UN; this trusteeship lasted until the protectorate and the trust territory became independent as the Somali Democratic Republic on 1 July 1960. In 1969, the armed forces took over the government and a Revolutionary Council under Siad Barre assumed control of the country.

Siad Barre was overthrown in January 1991 by rebel movements. One group, the United Somali Congress, took control in Mogadishu and formed an interim administration in February 1991 with the USC leader, Ali Mahdi Mohammed, as president. However, the USC government failed to establish its authority over the other, clan-based movements, the Somali Salvation Democratic Front (SSDF), the Somali Patriotic Movement (SPM) and the Somali Democratic Movement (SDM). In the north of the country, the Somali National Movement (SNM) refused to participate in north of the country. With the downfall of Siad Barre, the SNM took control of the north west (the former British Somaliland Protectorate) and in May 1991 declared unilateral independence as the 'Somaliland Republic'. A government and legislature was formed which elected Mohamed Ibrahim Egal as President in May 1993.

ECONOMY

Livestock raising is the main occupation in Somalia and there is a modest export trade in livestock on the hoof, skins and hides. Italy, the Gulf States and Saudi Arabia import the bulk of the banana crop, the second biggest export.

TRADE WITH UK	1991	1992
Imports from UK	£3,152,000	£3,436,000
Exports to UK	42,000	118,000

SOUTH AFRICA
Republiek van Suid-Afrika

South Africa, comprising the provinces of the Cape of Good Hope, Natal, the Transvaal and the Orange Free State, occupies the southernmost part of the African continent from the courses of the Limpopo, Marico, Molopo, Nosop and Orange Rivers (34° 50′ 22″ S.) to the Cape of Good Hope, with the exception of Lesotho, Swaziland and the extreme south of Mozambique. It has a total area of 471,445 sq. miles (1,221,031 sq. km) and borders on Namibia in the north west, Botswana and Zimbabwe in the north, Mozambique and Swaziland in the north east, and Lesotho, which it completely surrounds.

Cape Province contains many parallel ranges, which rise in steps towards the interior. The south-western peninsula contains the famous Table Mountain (3,582 ft), while the Great Swartberg and Langeberg run in parallel lines from west to east of the Cape Province. Between these two ranges and the Roggeveld and Nuweveld ranges to the north is the Great Karoo Plateau, which is bounded on the east by the Sneeuberg. In the east are ranges which join the Drakensberg (11,000 ft) between Natal and the Orange Free State. The Orange Free State presents a succession of undulating grassy plains with occasional hills or kopjes. The Transvaal is also mainly an elevated plateau with parallel ridges in the Magaliesberg and Waterberg ranges of no great height. The eastern province of Natal has pastoral lowlands and rich agricultural land between the slopes of the Drakensberg and the coast, the interior rising in terraces as in the southern provinces. The Orange, with its tributary the Vaal, is the principal river of the south, rising in the Drakensberg and flowing into the Atlantic between Namibia and the Cape Province. The Limpopo, or Crocodile River, in the north, rises in the Transvaal and flows into the Indian Ocean through Mozambique. Most of the remaining rivers are furious torrents after rain, with partially dry beds at other seasons.

POPULATION – The official population estimate for 1990, excluding Bophuthatswana, Ciskei, Transkei and Venda, was 30,788,000, comprising 21,600,000 Blacks, 5,018,000 Whites, 3,214,000 Coloureds, and 956,000 Indians. These figures are not thought to be accurate; the UN (1991) estimate for all of South Africa is 36,070,000.

CAPITAL – The administrative seat of the government is Pretoria, Transvaal; population (1985 estimate) 822,925; the seat of the legislature is ΨCape Town, population (1985) 1,911,521; the seat of the judiciary is Bloemfontein, Orange Free State (232,984).

negotiations and formed a government under SNM leader Abourahman Ahmed Ali. Faction fighting erupted in the summer of 1991 between supporters of Ali Mahdi Mohammed and supporters of General Mohammed Aideed. The fighting degenerated into civil war throughout 1991 and 1992, devastating Mogadishu and large parts of the south of the country. The UN intervened in April 1992 with food aid to feed a population on the verge of starvation. In August 1992 the UN Security Council approved the dispatch of the UN Operation in Somalia (UNISOM) force to protect relief convoys, while the USA initiated an emergency food airlift. However, the UN force proved ineffective in securing aid distribution routes from the armed factions. On 9 December 1992, with UN authority, a US-led United Task Force (UNITAF) launched a military intervention to create a safe environment for the delivery of aid. Distribution routes were secured by the end of December and UNITAF turned its attention to confiscating and destroying the weapons of the armed factions, which provoked clashes with armed gunmen in the Mogadishu area in early 1993. Meanwhile, Ali Mahdi Mohammed and General Mohammed Aideed reached agreement on a ceasefire in January 1993. At a subsequent National Reconciliation Conference in March, 15 armed factions agreed to the formation of a transitional parliament and a transitional executive body, and inter-factional fighting decreased significantly. On 4 May 1993 UNITAF handed over to a 28,000 strong UN force (UNISOM II) mandated to maintain a secure environment and promote political reconciliation. General Aideed's forces challenged the UN forces from June 1993 onwards, leading to renewed hostilities in Mogadishu as the UN forces destroyed Aideed's bases and heavy weapons and issued a warrant for his arrest.

SOMALI DIPLOMATIC REPRESENTATION, The Embassy closed in January 1992.

BRITISH DIPLOMATIC REPRESENTATION, The British Embassy in Mogadishu closed in January 1991.

SECESSION

Civil war broke out in May 1988 between the government and the opposition Somali National Movement (SNM) in the

Other large towns (1985 figures) are Johannesburg, Transvaal (1,609,408); Ψ Durban, Natal, the largest seaport (634,301); Ψ Port Elizabeth, Cape (651,993); Ψ East London, Cape (167,992); and Pietermaritzburg, Natal (192,417).

CURRENCY – Rand (R) of 100 cents.

FLAG – Three horizontal stripes of equal width; from top to bottom, orange, white, blue; in the centre of the white stripe, the old Orange Free State flag hanging vertical, towards the pole the Union Flag horizontal, away from the pole the old Transvaal Vierkleur, all spread full.

NATIONAL ANTHEM – Die Stem Van Suid-Afrika (The Call of South Africa).

NATIONAL DAY – 31 May.

HISTORY

The self-governing colonies of the Cape of Good Hope, Natal, the Transvaal and the Orange River Colony became united in 1910 under the name of the Union of South Africa, the four colonies becoming provinces of the Union. South Africa left the Commonwealth and became a republic on 31 May 1961, largely as a result of international condemnation of apartheid and of the Sharpeville massacre.

From 1948, South Africa's social and political structure was based on the policy of racial segregation, apartheid. Opposition protests culminated in the Sharpeville massacre in 1960; the African National Congress and other opposition groups were subsequently banned. A new wave of opposition climaxed in 1976 with uprisings in Soweto, in which hundreds were shot dead while protesting at the introduction of Afrikaans as the compulsory medium of instruction. In 1984 renewed rioting in the black townships and continuing unrest led to the declaration of a state of emergency in July 1985 in 36 districts, and nationwide from 12 June 1986; it was renewed annually until 1990.

MOVES TO DEMOCRACY

In September 1989, F. W. de Klerk became President of South Africa and accelerated the process of reform. In February 1990, the ban on the ANC and restrictions on other anti-apartheid groups were lifted; Nelson Mandela, the main ANC political detainee, was released. In 1991 the laws implementing apartheid were effectively abolished. In March 1992 a referendum amongst the white electorate on continued political reform and a new constitution reached by negotiation was approved by 69 per cent to 31 per cent.

Negotiations continued between various groups to establish a non-racial democracy. These negotiations led to the opening in Johannesburg on 20 December 1991 of the Convention on a Democratic South Africa (CODESA) talks between the Government, the ANC, the Inkatha Freedom Party and other political, business and church groups. The talks took place against an escalating level of violence involving mainly ANC and Inkatha supporters, but also the security forces, white extremists and Pan-African Congress supporters. After the Boipatong massacre in June 1992 the ANC withdrew from the talks, which broke down. Violence, strikes and campaigns of mass action escalated, culminating in the massacre at Bisho, Ciskei, in September 1992.

The continuing violence led the government and the ANC to resume negotiations on 25 September. A breakthrough was reached in November when they reached agreement on a multiracial election by April 1994. Agreements were reached in January and February 1993 on establishing an interim multiracial administration in the latter half of 1993 and on the formation of a five-year coalition government after the multiracial election. On 1 April full CODESA negotiations resumed, attended for the first time by the right-wing Conservative Party and by the Pan-African Congress. Progress towards the establishment of a Transitional Executive Council (TEC) in June 1993 was disrupted by the assassination of the senior ANC member Chris Hani by white extremists on 10 April. In the ensuing violence hundreds were killed, forcing the government and ANC to speed up negotiations in an attempt to control the situation. Negotiations reached an impasse in June with white right-wing extremists uniting to form the Afrikaner Volksunie to fight for an independent Afrikaner state and hundreds dying in ANC-Inkatha violence. In July the Conservative Party and Inkatha and some homelands leaders left the talks in protest at the refusal of the government and ANC to grant in an interim constitution a degree of regional autonomy that could not be removed when a full constitution was agreed.

The remaining 23 CODESA delegations agreed on 7 September 1993 upon the formation of the TEC, to rule in conjunction with the government until the 27 April 1994 multiracial elections. At the time of going to press, the successful establishment of the TEC looked uncertain as it was rejected by Inkatha and the Conservative Party. To obtain their agreement to the TEC, the CODESA delegations promised not to establish it until an interim constitution had been agreed in the CODESA negotiations, which Inkatha and the Conservatives could influence in favour of regional autonomy.

GOVERNMENT

A new constitution came into effect in September 1984 which provided for an executive President and a three-chamber Parliament; the House of Assembly (178 members) representing Whites, the House of Representatives (85 members) representing Coloureds, and the House of Delegates (45 members) representing Indians. The majority black population had no representation. Elections to the House of Assembly last took place on 6 September 1989. Party representation at August 1993 was: National Party 100; Conservative Party 38; Democratic Party 27; Independents supporting the ANC 5; Independents supporting Inkatha 3; Independents supporting Afrikaner Volksunie 5.

At the time of going to press the new multiracial, multi-party Transitional Executive Council (TEC) was about to be formed to govern in conjunction with the National Party government. The TEC is to operate until the first multiracial election on 27 April 1994. It has been provisionally agreed that these elections will elect a 400-member parliament on a proportional representation basis.

HEAD OF STATE

State President, Frederick Willem de Klerk, *sworn in* 20 September 1989.

CABINET *as at August 1993*

Foreign Affairs, Pik Botha.
Public Enterprises, Dr Dawie de Villiers.
Justice, Defence, Kobie Coetzee.
Population Development, Jac Rabie.
Correctional Services, Adriaan Vlok.
State Expenditure, Amie Venter.
National Education, Piet Marais.
Education and Training, National Housing, Sam J. de Beer.
Mineral and Energy Affairs, Public Works, George S. Bartlett.
Agriculture, Dr Kraai van Niekerk.
National Health and Welfare, Dr Rina Venter.
Law and Order, Hernus Kriel.
Regional and Land Affairs, Andre Fourie.
Water Affairs, Environment, Japie van Wyk.
Finance, Trade and Industry, Derek Keys.
Tourism, Dr Bhandra Ranchod.
Transport, Post and Telecommunications, Piet Welgemoed.
Constitutional Development and Communication, Roelf Meyer.
Manpower, Leon Wessels.
Home Affairs, Danie Schutte.
Local Government, Tertius Delport.
Sport, Abe Williams.

EMBASSY OF THE REPUBLIC OF SOUTH AFRICA
South Africa House, Trafalgar Square, London WC2N 5DP
Tel 071-930 4488

Ambassador Extraordinary and Plenipotentiary, His Excellency K. D. S. Durr (1991).
Minister (Trade), P. M. Pullen.
Counsellors, P. J. Schabort; D. Kent-Brown; D. J. Cloete.
First Secretary, Miss A. Reesburg (*Cultural*).

BRITISH EMBASSY
255 Hill Street, Pretoria 0002
Tel: Pretoria 253670-6
91 Parliament Street, Cape Town 8001 (January–June)
Tel: Cape Town 4617220

Ambassador Extraordinary and Plenipotentiary, His Excellency Sir Anthony Reeve, KCMG (1991).
Counsellor, Deputy Head of Mission, Dr D. Carter.
Counsellor (Political), A. Hardie, OBE.
Consul-General and Director of Trade Promotion (Johannesburg), J. F. Doble, OBE.

Cultural Attaché and British Council Representative, R. B. Timms, 76 Juta Street, (PO Box 30637), Braamfontein 2017, Johannesburg (tel: 339 3715). There is also an office in Cape Town.

There is a British Consulate-General at *Johannesburg* (PO Box 10101, Johannesburg 2000), Consulates at *Cape Town* and *Durban*, and Honorary Consuls at *Port Elizabeth* and *East London*.

HOMELANDS
As part of its policy of apartheid, the government established a number of black 'homelands'. Six areas (Gazankulu, Lebowa, KwaNdbele, KaNgwane, Qwaqwa and KwaZulu) are now designated as self-governing states. A further four (Bophuthatswana, Ciskei, Transkei and Venda) are regarded as independent republics by the South African government but are not recognized as such by the UN. Most homelands are now in the process of re-integrating into South Africa.

DEFENCE
Total active armed forces number 72,400 (36,400 white conscripts). Conscripts (all white males) serve for 12 months, then in first-line reserves (Citizen Force) and second-line reserves. Total reserves number 635,000 personnel. Other races may volunteer for full-time or conscript service. The active Army strength is 49,900 personnel, of whom 18,900 are full-time professionals (13,200 white, 5,700 other races) and 31,000 National Service conscripts. The Navy has a strength of 4,500 (900 conscripts) with three submarines and nine patrol and coastal combatants. The Air Force has a strength of 10,000 (3,000 conscripts) with 259 combat aircraft and 14 armed helicopters. In addition the paramilitary South African Police number 100,000 personnel, with 37,000 reserves, and the 'independent' homelands (Boputhatswana, Ciskei, Transkei and Venda) have armed forces totalling 7,000 personnel.

In March 1993 the South African government admitted that it had developed nuclear weapons in the 1960s and 1970s; these have now been dismantled. For many years South Africa has been under an arms embargo and has manufactured much of its own equipment.

COMMUNICATIONS
There are international airports at Johannesburg (Jan Smuts), Durban (Louis Botha) and Cape Town (D. F. Malan). South African Airways operates international services to Europe, South America, the Far East, Africa, Australia and the USA, and it is the principal operator of domestic flights. The largest sea-port is Durban, Natal. Other major ports are Cape Town, Port Elizabeth, East London, Saldanha Bay and Mossel Bay in Cape Province and Richards Bay, Natal. The national railway system, and most long-distance passenger and freight road transport are run by independent companies.

ECONOMY
Mining is of great importance to the South African economy, producing 10.3 per cent of GDP in 1991. Minerals to the value of R39,376 million were produced in 1991. The principal minerals produced are gold, coal, diamonds, copper, iron ore, manganese, lime and limestone, uranium, platinum, vanadium, titanium, nickel, lead and chrome ore. South Africa is the world's largest producer of gold, chrome ore, manganese and vanadium.

Agriculture, forestry and fishing account for about 5 per cent of GDP. Over 50 per cent of land is pasture so livestock farming is widespread with meat and wool important products. Principal crops are maize, sugar-cane, fruits and vegetables, wheat, sorghum, sunflower seed and groundnuts. Cotton is widely grown because of its suitability to the climate, and viticulture is also widespread.

Industries, concentrated most heavily around Johannesburg, Pretoria and the major ports, process foodstuffs, metals and non-metallic mineral products, and also produce beverages and tobacco, motor vehicles, chemicals and chemical products, machinery, textiles and clothing, and paper and paper products.

TRADE
Principal exports are gold, base metals and metal products, diamonds, food (especially fruit), chemicals, machinery and transport equipment, and wool. Principal imports are machinery, chemicals, motor vehicles, metals and metal products, food, inedible raw materials and textiles.

American and EC sanctions, in place since 1986, were lifted in July 1991 and January 1992 respectively. The longer-standing UN arms, finance and oil embargoes are likely to be lifted in late 1993 if the multiracial TEC is established.

Trade with UK	1991	1992
Imports from UK	£1,023,469,000	£1,078,697,000
Exports to UK	954,676,000	865,328,000

FINANCE

Estimated revenue for 1993–4 was R89,000 million, and estimated expenditure was R114,000 million.

SPAIN
España

Spain occupies most of the Iberian Pensinsula, between 36° and 43° 45′ N., and 4° 25′ E. and 9° 20′ W. It is bounded on the south and east by the Mediterranean, on the west by the Atlantic and Portugal, and on the north by the Bay of Biscay and France. It comprises a total area of 194,897 sq. miles (504,782 sq. km), with a population (1991 census) of 38,872,268.

The interior of the Iberian peninsula consists of an elevated tableland surrounded and traversed by mountain ranges: the Pyrenees, the Cantabrian Mountains, the Sierra Guadarrama, Sierra Morena, Sierra Nevada, Montes de Toledo, etc. The principal rivers are the Duero, the Tajo, the Guadiana, the Guadalquivir, the Ebro and the Miño.

CAPITAL – Madrid, population (1991) 4,947,555. Other large cities are ΨBarcelona (4,654,407), ΨValencia (2,117,972), Seville (1,619,703), Alicante (1,292,563), ΨMálaga (1,160,843), Bilbao (1,179,148); Murcia (1,045,601).
CURRENCY – Peseta of 100 céntimos.
FLAG – Three horizontal stripes of red, yellow, red, with the yellow of double width.
NATIONAL ANTHEM – Marcha Real Española.
NATIONAL DAY – 12 October.

GOVERNMENT

Spain was a monarchy until April 1931, when King Alfonso XIII left the country and a republic was proclaimed. A provisional government, drawn from the various republican and Socialist parties, was formed. In July 1936 a counter-revolution broke out in military garrisons in Spanish Morocco and spread throughout Spain. The principal leader was General Franco, leader of the Military-Fascist fusion, or *Falange*. Civil war ensued until March 1939, when the Popular Front governments in Madrid and Barcelona surrendered to the Nationalists (as General Franco's followers were then named). General Franco became President and ruled the country until his death in November 1975, when, according to his wishes, he was succeeded as head of state by Prince Juan Carlos of Bourbon (grandson of Alfonso XIII) and Spain again became a monarchy.

Under the 1978 constitution there is a bicameral *Cortes* comprising a 350-member Congress of Deputies elected for four years by universal adult suffrage, and a Senate consisting of directly elected representatives of the provinces, islands, autonomous regions, and Ceuta and Melilla. At the General Election on 6 June 1993, PSOE (Spanish Socialist Workers' Party) won 159 seats; the PP (Popular Party) 141; the (Communist) United Left Party 18; Catalan Nationalists 17; Basque Nationalists (PNV) 5; Others 10. The PSOE formed a minority government with the support of the Catalan and Basque nationalists in July.

REGIONS

Since the promulgation of the 1978 constitution, 17 autonomous regions have been established, with their own parliaments and governments. These are Andalucia, Aragon, Asturias, Balearics, the Basque country, Canaries, Castilla-La Mancha, Castilla-Leon, Cantabria, Cataluña, Extremadura, Galicia, Madrid, Murcia, Navarre, La Rioja and Valencia. The Basque terrorist group ETA has waged a terrorist campaign for 20 years against the Spanish state to gain independence for the Basque country.

HEAD OF STATE
King of Spain, HM King Juan Carlos I de Borbón y Borbón, KG, GCVO, *born* 5 January 1938, *acceded to the throne*, 22 November 1975, *married* 14 May 1962, Princess Sophie of Greece *and has issue*, Infante Felipe (*see* below); Infanta Elena Maria Isabel Dominga, *born* 20 December 1963; and Infanta Cristina Federica Victoria Antonia, *born* 13 June 1965.
Heir, Infante Felipe Juan Pablo Alfonso y Todos los Santos, Prince of Asturias, *born* 30 January 1968.

CABINET *as at August 1993*
Prime Minister, Felipe González Márquez.
Deputy PM, Narcís Serra Serra.
Foreign Affairs, Javier Solana Madariaga.
Justice, Juan Alberto Belloch.
Defence, Julián García Vargas.
Economy and Finance, Pedro Solbes Mira.
Interior, José Luis Corcuera Cuesta.
Public Works and Town Planning and Transport, José Borrell Fontelles.
Education and Science, Gustavo Pertierra.
Labour and Social Security, José Griñán Martínez.
Industry, Juan Eguiagaray Ucelay.
Trade and Tourism, Javier Gómez Navarro.
Agriculture, Food and Fisheries, Vicente Albero Sillas.
Public Administration, Jerónimo Saavedra Acevedo.
Culture, Carmen Alboroch.
Health and Consumer Affairs, Angeles Amador Millán.
Relations with the Cortes and Government Secretariat, Alfredo Pérez Rubalcaba.
Social Affairs, Cristina Alberdi Alonso.

SPANISH EMBASSY
16th Floor, Portland House, Stag Place, London SWIE 5SE
Tel 071-235 5555

Ambassador Extraordinary and Plenipotentiary, His Excellency Don Alberto Aza Arias (1993).

Minister-Counsellor, V. B. Gaspar.
Defence Attaché, Capt. J. M. Pascual.
Minister, F. F. Súñer (*Cultural*).
Consul-General, R. Ansoaín.
Counsellor, J. G. Valverde (*Commercial*).

BRITISH EMBASSY
Calle de Fernando el Santo, 16, 28010 Madrid
Tel: Madrid 319 0200

Ambassador Extraordinary and Plenipotentiary, His
Excellency Sir Robin Fearn, KCMG (1989).
Minister, Deputy Ambassador, E. Jones Parry.
Counsellors, D. Ridgway, OBE (*Commercial*); A. Longrigg,
CMG (*Economic and Community Affairs*); D. C. Ankerson.
Defence and Naval Attaché, Capt. J. Gozzard.
Consuls-General, D. R. McIntyre (*Madrid*); M. Perceval
(*Barcelona*); A. W. Mackenzie, MBE (*Bilbao*).

There are Consulates-General in *Madrid, Barcelona, Bilbao;*
Consulates in *Tenerife, Alicante, Seville, Malaga, Palma
de Mallorca, Las Palmas;* a Vice-Consulate in *Ibiza;*
Honorary Consulates in *Lanzarote, Santander, Minorca,
Tarragona, Vigo.*

BRITISH COUNCIL REPRESENTATIVE, B. Vale, OBE, Calle
Almagro 5, 28010 Madrid. There are offices in *Barcelona,
Bilbao, Granada, Las Palmas, Oviedo, Palma, Segovia,
Seville* and *Valencia.*

BRITISH CHAMBER OF COMMERCE, Plaza de Santa
Barbara 10, 1st Floor, 28004 Madrid; Paseo de Gracia 11,
Barcelona 7; Alameda de Mazarredo 5, Bilbao 1.

DEFENCE

The armed forces have a total active strength of 217,000
(158,100 conscripts) with a nine-month period of conscription.
The Army has 146,000 personnel (118,000 conscripts), with
838 main battle tanks, 440 reconnaissance vehicles, 1,900
armoured personnel carriers, 1,355 artillery pieces, and 28
combat helicopters. The Army is organized into eight
regional commands, and there is a General Reserve Force.
The active Spanish Navy has a strength of 36,000 (21,900
conscripts) and consists of eight submarines, one aircraft
carrier, four destroyers, 15 frigates, 39 patrol and coastal
combatants, 27 armed helicopters and 21 Harrier aircraft.
The Air Force has a strength of 35,000 (18,200 conscripts)
and has 207 combat aircraft. The paramilitary Guardia Civil
with 64,600 personnel (3,000 conscripts) operates as a
gendarmerie in rural areas under the control of the Ministry
of Defence and has been actively engaged in combating
Basque terrorism.
The USA maintains 3,400 naval personnel in Spain.

EDUCATION

Education is free for those aged six to 18, and compulsory up
to the age of 14. Private schools (30 per cent of primary and
60 per cent of secondary schools) have to fulfill certain
criteria to receive government maintenance grants. There
are 33 public sector universities, the oldest of which, is
Salamanca, was founded in 1218. Other ancient foundations
are Valladolid (1346), Barcelona (1430), Zaragoza (1474),
Santiago (1495), Valencia (1500), Seville (1505), Madrid
(1508), Granada (1531), Oveido (1604). Private universities
are Deusto in Bilbao, Navarra in Pamplona, one in Madrid
and one in Salamanca. Student numbers in the universities
in 1989–90 totalled 1,067,874.

CULTURE

Castilian is the language of more than three-quarters of the
population of Spain. Basque, said to have been the original
language of Iberia, is spoken in Vizcaya, Guipuzcoa and
Alava. Catalan is spoken in Provençal Spain, and Galician,
spoken in the north-western provinces, is akin to Portuguese.
The governments of these regions actively encourage use of
their local languages.
The literature of Spain is one of the oldest and richest in
the world, the *Poem of the Cid*, the earliest of the heroic songs
of Spain, having been written about 1140. The outstanding
writings of its golden age are those of Miguel de Cervantes
Saavedra (1547–1616), Lope Felix de Vega Carpio (1562–
1635) and Pedro Calderón de la Barca (1600–81). The Nobel
Prize for Literature has five times been awarded to Spanish
authors: J. Echegaray (1904), J. Benavente (1922), Juan
Ramón Jimenez (1956), Vicente Aleixandre (1977) and
Camilo José Cela (1989).

ECONOMY

The expansion of the Spanish economy and accession to the
EC have led to changes in Spanish agriculture. It accounts
for over 5 per cent of GDP and employs over 13 per cent of
the working population. The country is generally fertile, and
fruits such as olives, oranges, lemons, almonds, pomegran-
ates, bananas, apricots, tomatoes, peppers, cucumbers and
grapes are cultivated. Other agricultural products include
wheat, barley, oats, rice, hemp and flax. The vine is cultivated
widely; in the south-west, Jerez, the well-known sherry and
tent wines are produced. The fishing industry is important.
Spain's mineral resources of coal, iron, wolfram, copper,
zinc, lead and iron ores are variously exploited. Output of
coal in 1988 was 15.5 million tonnes; output of steel (1988)
11.9 million tonnes.
The principal industrial goods are cars, steel, ships,
manufactured goods, textiles, chemical products, footwear
and other leather goods. Tourism is a major industry; in 1988
an estimated 54,172,000 tourists visited Spain.

TRADE

The principal imports are cotton, tobacco, cellulose, timber,
coffee and cocoa, food products, fertilizers, dyes, machinery,
motor vehicles and agricultural tractors, wool and petroleum
products. The principal exports include cars, petroleum
products, iron ore, cork, salt, vegetables, fruits, wines, olive
oil, potash, mercury, pyrites, tinned fruit and fish, tomatoes
and footwear. The balance of payments on current account
showed a deficit of US$15,717 million in 1990 and reserves
stood at US$53,104 million.

	1990	1991
Imports	Pesetas 8,914,700m	Pesetas 9,672,100m
Exports	5,642,800m	6,225,700m

Trade with UK	1991	1992
Imports from UK	£4,278,767,000	£4,405,290,000
Exports to UK	2,627,857,000	2,938,716,000

*Excluding the Canary Islands, Ceuta and Melilla.

ISLANDS

The Balearic Isles form an archipelago off the east coast of
Spain. There are four large islands (Majorca, Minorca, Ibiza
and Formentera), and seven smaller (Aire, Aucanada,
Botafoch, Cabrera, Dragonera, Pinto and El Rey). The total
area is 1,935 sq. miles (5,011 sq. km), with a population of
685,088. The archipelago forms a province of Spain, the
capital being ΨPalma in Majorca, pop. 304,422.

The Canary Islands are an archipelago in the Atlantic, off the African coast, consisting of seven islands and six mostly uninhabited islets. The total area is 2,807 sq. miles (7,270 sq. km), with a population of 1,444,626. The Canary Islands form two provinces of Spain: Las Palmas, comprising Gran Canaria, Lanzarote (38,500), Fuerteventura (19,500) and the islets of Alegranza, Roque del Este, Roque del Oeste, Graciosa, Montaña Clara and Lobos, with seat of administration at ΨLas Palmas (366,454) in Gran Canaria; and Santa Cruz de Tenerife, comprising Tenerife, La Palma (76,000), Gomera (31,829), and Hierro (10,000), with seat of administration at ΨSanta Cruz in Tenerife, population estimate 190,784.

Isla de Faisanes is an uninhabited Franco-Spanish condominium, at the mouth of the Bidassoa in La Higuera bay.

ΨCeuta is a fortified post on the Moroccan coast, opposite Gibraltar. The total area is 5 sq. miles (13 sq. km), with a population of 70,864.

ΨMelilla is a town on a rocky promontory of the Rif coast, connected with the mainland by a narrow isthmus. Population 58,449. Ceuta and Melilla are parts of Metropolitan Spain.

OVERSEAS TERRITORIES

Spanish settlements on the Moroccan seaboard are:
Peñon de Alhucemas, a bay including six islands, population 366
Peñon de la Gomera (or *Peñon de Velez*), a fortified rocky islet, population 450
The Chaffarinas (or Zaffarines), a group of three islands near the Algerian frontier, population 610

SRI LANKA
Sri Lanka Prajatantrika Samajawadi Janarajaya

Sri Lanka (formerly Ceylon) is an island in the Indian Ocean, off the southern tip of India and separated from it by the narrow Palk Strait. Situated between 5° 55′ and 9° 50′ N. latitude and 79° 42′ and 81° 52′ E. longitude, it has an area of 25,332 sq. miles (65,610 sq. km), including 33 square miles of inland water. Forests, jungle and scrub cover the greater part of the island. In areas over 2,000 feet above sea level grasslands (*patanas* or *talawas*) are found. One of the highest peaks in the central massif is Adam's Peak (7,360 ft), a place of pilgrimage for Buddhists, Hindus and Muslims.

The climate is warm throughout the year, with a high relative humidity. In the hills the climate is more temperate. Rainfall is generally heavy, with marked regional variations. The two main monsoon seasons are mid-May to September (south-west) and November to March (north-east).

POPULATION – The 1991 estimated population was 17,243,000, of which 74 per cent were Sinhalese, 12.6 per cent Sri Lankan Tamils, 5.6 per cent Indian Tamils, 7.1 per cent Sri Lankan Moors and 0.7 per cent Burghers, Malays and others. The religion of the majority is Buddhism (69.3 per cent), then Hinduism (15.5 per cent); Islam (7.6 per cent), and Christianity (7.5 per cent). The national languages are Sinhalese, Tamil and English.

CAPITAL – ΨColombo, population (1991) 1,963,000. Other principal towns are ΨJaffna (876,000), Kandy (1,251,000), ΨGalle (946,000), and ΨTrincomalee (316,000).

CURRENCY – Sri Lankan rupee (Rs) of 100 cents.

FLAG – On a dark red field, within a golden border, a golden lion passant holding a sword in its right paw, and a representation of a *bo*-leaf, issuing from each corner; and to its right, two vertical stripes of saffron and green also placed within a golden border, to represent the minorities of the country.

NATIONAL ANTHEM – Namo Namo Matha (We all stand together).

NATIONAL DAY – 4 February (Independence Commemoration Day).

GOVERNMENT

Early in the sixteenth century the Portuguese landed in Ceylon and founded settlements, eventually conquering much of the country. Portuguese rule in Ceylon lasted 150 years but in 1658 gave way to that of the Dutch East India Company until 1796. The maritime provinces of Ceylon were ceded by the Dutch to the British in 1798, becoming a British Crown Colony in 1802. With the annexation of the Kingdom of Kandy in 1815, all Ceylon came under British rule.

On 4 February 1948 Ceylon became a self-governing state and a member of the British Commonwealth. A republican constitution was adopted in 1972 and the country was renamed Sri Lanka (meaning 'Resplendent Island'). In 1978 a new constitution introduced a system of proportional representation. Legislative power is exercised by the National State Assembly, executive power being exercised by the President.

Eight Provincial Councils were set up in 1988 in an attempt to diffuse ethnic tension. The Northern-Eastern council is controlled by the Eelam People's Revolutionary Liberation Front, the other seven councils by the United National Party.

In the General Election of 15 February 1989 the United National Party gained a decisive victory. The results were as follows: United National Party 125 seats, Sri Lanka Freedom Party 67, Independent Tamils 14, Tamil United Liberation Front 10, Sri Lanka Muslim Congress 3, United Socialist Alliance 3, Mahajana Eksath Peramuna 3.

SECESSION

The Tamil Tigers guerrilla group has been fighting Sri Lankan forces for control of the Tamil majority areas in the north and east of the country since the early 1980s. They were suppressed by Indian peacekeepers in 1987–90 but grew in strength after the Indians left. They are now virtually confined to the Jaffna peninsula by Sri Lankan forces, but a Tamil suicide bomber assassinated President Premadasa on 1 May 1993.

HEAD OF STATE

President, His Excellency Dingiri Banda Wijetunge, *elected and sworn in by parliament* 7 May 1993 (*also Minister of Buddha Sasana, Finance, Defence, and Policy Planning and Implementation*).

CABINET *as at August 1993*

Prime Minister and Minister of Industries, Science and Technology, Hon. Ranil Wickremasinghe.
Transport and Highways, Hon. Wijayapala Mendis.
Justice, Hon. Harold Herat.
Environment and Parliamentary Affairs, Hon. Dr Wimal Wickremasinghe.
Public Administration, Hon. Festus Perera.
Tourism and Rural Industrial Development, Hon. S. Thondaman.
Constitutional and State Affairs, Hon. K. N. Choksy.
Forestry, Irrigation and Mahaweli Development, Hon. Gamini Athukorale.
Fisheries and Aquatic Resources, Hon. Joseph Michael Perera.
Cultural Affairs, Education and Higher Education, Hon. W. J. M. Lokubandara.

Posts and Telecommunications, Hon. A. M. S. Adhikari.
Youth Affairs and Sports, Hon. C. Nanda Mathew.
Trade and Commerce, Hon. A. R. Munsoor.
Handlooms and Textile Industries, Hon. U. B. Wijekoon.
Health and Women's Affairs, Hon. Renuka Ranaweera.
Reconstruction, Rehabilitation and Social Welfare, Hon. P. Dayaratne.
Housing and Construction, Hon. B. Sirisena Cooray.
Plantation Industries, Hon. Rupasena Karunatilleke.
Foreign Affairs, Hon. A. C. S. Hameed.
Food and Co-operatives, Hon. Weerasinghe Mallimarachchi.
Agricultural Development and Research, Hon. Dharmadasa Banda.
Power and Energy, Hon. K. D. M. Chandra Bandara.
Ports and Shipping, Hon. Alick Aluvihare.
Lands, Hon. E. Paul Perera.
Home Affairs and Provincial Councils, Hon. John Amaratunga.
Information and Broadcasting, Hon. Tyronne Fernando.
Labour and Vocational Training, Hon. M. L. M. Aboosally.

HIGH COMMISSION FOR THE DEMOCRATIC SOCIALIST REPUBLIC OF SRI LANKA
13 Hyde Park Gardens, London W2 2LU
Tel 071-262 1841

High Commissioner, His Excellency Gen. S. C. Ranatunga (1993).
Deputy High Commissioner, G. S. Munasinghe.
First Secretary, N. Gunatilleke (*Defence*).
Minister Counsellors, Mrs S. Rajapakse (*Consular*); N. R. Meemeduma (*Economic*).

BRITISH HIGH COMMISSION
Galle Road 190, Kollupitiya (PO Box 1433), Colombo 3
Tel: Colombo 437336

High Commissioner, His Excellency E. J. Field, CMG (1991).
Deputy High Commissioner, R. P. Nash, LVO.
Defence Adviser, Lt.-Col. I. G. Baillie.
First Secretary (Commercial), I. M. Dallas.

BRITISH COUNCIL REPRESENTATIVE, R. A. Jarvis, OBE, 49 Alfred House Gardens, PO Box 753, Colombo 3. Library also in *Kandy*.

COMMUNICATIONS

There are over 15,660 miles of roads in Sri Lanka and a government-run railway system with 984 miles of lines. A satellite earth station at Padukka, in south-west Sri Lanka, provides telecommunication links via satellite with any part of the globe. The principal airports are at Katunayake, 19 miles north of Colombo, and Ratmalana, nine miles south of the capital. Air Lanka operates on 76 flights weekly to the Gulf States, the Maldives, Western Europe and throughout the Far East.

ECONOMY

The staple products of the island are tea, rubber, copra, spices and gems. There is increasing emphasis on local production of food, especially rice, and plans for the large-scale production of sugar cane, cotton and citrus fruits.

Factories are established for the manufacture or processing of ceramic ware, vegetable oils and by-products, paper, tobacco, tanning and leather goods, plywood, cement, chemicals, sugar, flour, salt, textiles, ilmenite, tiles, tyres, fertilizers, clothing, jewellery and hardware and there is a petroleum refinery.

TRADE WITH UK	1991	1992
Imports from UK	£128,565,000	£103,214,000
Exports to UK	74,460,000	93,045,000

SUDAN
Al-Jamhuryat es-Sudan Al-Democratia

Sudan lies in north-east Africa, between 22° and 3°36' N. latitude, and 21° 49' and 38° 35' E. longitude. To the north lies Egypt, to the east the Red Sea and Ethiopia, to the south Kenya, Uganda and Zaire, and to the west the Central African Republic, Chad, and Libya. The area is about 967,500 sq. miles (2,505,813 sq. km).

The White Nile enters Sudan from Uganda at Nimule as the Bahr el Jebel, and leaves at Wadi Halfa. The Blue Nile flows from Lake Tana on the Ethiopian plateau. Its course in Sudan is nearly 500 miles long, before it joins the White Nile at Khartoum. The next confluence of importance is at Atbara where the main Nile is joined by the River Atbara. Between Khartoum and Wadi Halfa lie five of the six cataracts.

POPULATION – The population is 25,941,000 (UN estimate 1991). Arab and Nubian peoples populate the north and centre, Nilotic and Negro peoples the south. Arabic is the official language and Islam the state religion, although the Nilotics of the Bahr el Ghazal and Upper Nile valleys are generally Animists or Christians.

CAPITAL – Khartoum. The combined population of Khartoum, Khartoum North and Omdurman (excluding refugees and displaced people) is estimated at 3,000,000.
CURRENCY – Sudanese Dinar of 10 pounds.
FLAG – Three horizontal stripes of red, white and black with a green triangle next to the hoist.
NATIONAL ANTHEM – Nahnu Djundullah (We are the army of God).
NATIONAL DAY – 1 January (Independence Day).

GOVERNMENT

The Anglo-Egyptian Condominium over Sudan was established in 1899 and ended when the Sudan House of Representatives, on 19 December 1955, voted unanimously a declaration that Sudan was a fully independent sovereign state. A republic was proclaimed on 1 January 1956, and was recognized by Great Britain and Egypt. Sudan was under military rule from November 1958 until 1964 when a civilian government was appointed. Government of the country was taken over in 1969 by a revolutionary council headed by Gaafar Mohamed El Nimeri. In April 1985 the Army command assumed power after popular demonstrations, deposed Nimeri and appointed a transitional government. In May 1986 power was transferred to a civilian regime following multi-party elections. The third military coup since Sudan's independence took place in June 1989 when the government was overthrown by Brig.-Gen. Omar Hassan Ahmad al-Bashir. The constitution was suspended and parliament was replaced by a 15-member ruling junta who have de facto control over a cabinet of 21 ministers. The government has developed close relations with Iran and is believed by western states to support international terrorism and have Iranian Revolutionary Guards' bases on its territory. In August 1993 the USA placed Sudan on a list of countries sponsoring terrorism and suspended all trade apart from humanitarian goods.

SECESSION

Nearly 17 years of insurrection in the southern provinces ended in 1972 with the signing of an agreement recognizing-southern regional autonomy within the Sudanese state. However, insurrection broke out again in 1983 and since then there has been civil war in the south of the country between government forces and the Christian and Animist majority in the area, organized into the Sudan People's Liberation Army (SPLA). Although the Islamic government has officially stated that it is not attempting to introduce Sharia law in the south, the Sharia affects the 1,000,000 Christians in northern areas. In 1992-3 the SPLA split into three warring factions, tipping the military balance in favour of the government forces. Much of the south is now depopulated as refugees have fled to the north and to neighbouring countries; famine remains a problem in the region.

CABINET *as at September 1993*
Prime Minister and Minister for Defence, Lt.-Gen. Omar Hassan Ahmad al-Bashir.
Deputy PM and Minister of Interior, Maj.-Gen. Zubir Mohammed Saleh.
Presidential Affairs, Lt.-Col. Tayib Ibrahim Mohammed Khayr.
Federal Administration, Dr Ali al-Hajj Muhammad.
Foreign Affairs, Ali Sahlul.
Justice and Attorney-General, Hassan Ismail al-Billi.
Culture and Information, Abdullah Mohammed Ahmed.
Planning and Investment, Dr Ibrahim Ubaydullah.
Agriculture and Natural Resources, Ahmad Ali al-Genief.
Peace and Rehabilitation, Abdullah Deng Nhial.
Local Government and Co-ordination of Provincial Affairs, Natali Yanku Ambu.
Irrigation, Yacoub Abu Shura Musa.
Energy and Mining, Abdel Munim Khujali.
Industry and Commerce, Dr Taj Al Sir Mustafa.
Education, Abdul Basit Sabdarat.
Social Planning, Ali Uthman Muhammad Taha.
Housing, Construction and Public Utilities, Osman Abdoul Gadir Abdul Latif.
Higher Education, Dr Ibrahim Ahmed Omer.
Tourism and Communications, Maj.-Gen. Ibrahim Nayil Idam.
Labour and Social Security, George Kinga.
Health and Social Welfare, Dr Hussein Abu Salih.

EMBASSY OF THE REPUBLIC OF THE SUDAN
3 Cleveland Row, London SWIA IDD
Tel 071-839 8080

Ambassador Extraordinary and Plenipotentiary, His Excellency Ali Mohammed Osman Yassin (1992).

BRITISH EMBASSY
(PO Box 801), Khartoum
Tel: Khartoum 70760

Ambassador Extraordinary and Plenipotentiary, His Excellency Peter J. Streams, CMG (1990).
First Secretary, Head of Chancery and Consul-General, J. M. Crane.

BRITISH COUNCIL REPRESENTATIVE, A. Thomas, 14 Abu Sinn Street (PO Box 1253), Khartoum.

EDUCATION

School education is free for most children but not compulsory, beginning with six years primary education, followed by three years secondary education at general secondary schools, the more academic higher secondary schools or vocational schools. The medium of instruction is Arabic. English is no longer taught in schools since new Arabization legislation came into effect in 1991.

Khartoum University has ten faculties. There is a branch of Cairo University in Khartoum, an Islamic University at Omdurman and universities at Wad Medani and Juba. In addition to the universities there are various technical post-secondary institutes as well as professional and vocational training establishments.

ECONOMY

Agriculture provided employment for over 60 per cent of the labour force and contributed 37 per cent to GDP in 1986-7. It is based on large and medium sized public sector irrigation projects with small scale private irrigation schemes providing mostly fruit and vegetables. Mechanized and traditional agriculture is practised in areas of sufficient rainfall. The principal grain crops are *dura* (great millet) and wheat, the staple food of the population. Sesame and ground-nuts are other important food crops, which also yield an exportable surplus and a promising start has been made with castor seed. The principal export crop is cotton. Traditionally a major producer of long-staple cotton, Sudan has in recent years grown more short and medium-staple cotton. These grades now account for more than half total production. Sudan also produces the bulk of the world's supply of gum arabic. Sugar is an increasingly important crop, although Sudan still has to achieve self sufficiency in its production.

Livestock is the mainstay of the nomadic Arab tribes of the desert and the Negro tribes of the swamp and wooded grassland country in the south. Production has, however, been affected by drought, famine and civil war.

The manufacturing sector contributed less than 8 per cent to GDP in 1986-7 and provided employment for 4 per cent of the work force. The main manufacturing enterprises are food processing, textiles, shoes, cigarettes and batteries.

TRADE
The principal exports are cotton, livestock, gum arabic and other agricultural produce. The chief imports are petroleum goods and other raw materials, machinery and equipment, transport and equipment, medicines and chemicals.

	1989*
Total imports	US$14,532.0m
Total exports	651.5m
*estimated	

Trade with UK	1991	1992
Imports from UK	£75,460,000	£52,304,000
Exports to UK	6,168,000	5,250,000

COMMUNICATIONS

The railway system, adversely affected by the civil war, has a route length of about 3,200 miles. Nile river services between Khartoum and Juba have been interrupted by the southern insurrection. Port Sudan is the country's main seaport. Sudan Airways fly services from Khartoum to other parts of the Sudan and to other African states, Europe and the Middle East.

SURINAME
Nieuwe Republick van Suriname

Suriname is situated on the north coast of South America and is bounded by French Guiana in the east, Brazil in the south and Guyana in the west. It has an area of 63,037 sq. miles (163,265 sq. km), with a population (UN 1991 estimate) of 429,000.

CAPITAL – ΨParamaribo, population (1971) 110,000.
CURRENCY – Suriname guilder of 100 cents.
FLAG – Horizontal stripes of green, white, red, white, green, with a five-pointed yellow star in the centre.
NATIONAL DAY – 25 November.

GOVERNMENT

Formerly known as Dutch Guiana, Suriname remained part of the Netherlands West Indies until 25 November 1975, when it achieved complete independence. The civilian government was ousted in February 1980 by the military who appointed a predominantly civilian Cabinet in 1982. According to the constitution approved by referendum in September 1987, a National Assembly of 51 members elects the President. The Army remains the 'vanguard of the people'.

President Shankar was overthrown in a military coup, instigated by Lt.-Col. Desi Bouterse, in December 1990; Johan Kraag, a supporter of Bouterse, was installed as President. Elections to the National Assembly were held on 25 May 1991. The New Front for Democracy and Development, a coalition comprising opposition groups, won 30 of the 51 seats, but failed to gain the necessary two-thirds majority to appoint the President. Eventually in September 1991 a special sitting of a United People's Assembly elected New Front leader Ronald Venetiaan as President and he formed a new government which is committed to amending the constitution to limit the power of the military. In August 1992 the government and the two largest guerrilla groups signed a draft peace agreement under which the guerrillas will be integrated into the police force.

HEAD OF STATE
President, Dr Ronald Venetiaan, *elected* 7 September 1991.

CABINET *as at August 1993*
Vice-President, Prime Minister, Jules Ajodhia.
Labour, Reynold Simons.
Foreign Affairs, Subhas Mungra.
Defence, Siegfried Gilds.
Finance, Humphrey Hildenberg.
Economics, Tjandrikapersad Gobardhan.
Justice and Police, Soeshiel Girjasing.
Natural Resources, Harold Pollack.
Education, Gerard Hiwat.
Public Works, Radj Koemar Randjietsingh.
Planning and Development, Edwin Sedoc.
Regional Affairs, Rufus Nooitmeer.
Agricultural and Fisheries, S. Setroredjo.
Transport, Communications and Tourism, John Defares.
Public Health, Mohamed Khudabux.
Interior, J. Sisal.
Social Affairs, W. Soemita.

EMBASSY OF THE REPUBLIC OF SURINAME
2 Alexander Gogelweg, The Hague, The Netherlands
Tel: The Hague 3650844

Ambassador Extraordinary and Plenipotentiary, His Excellency Cyrill Bisoendat Ramkisor (1990) (resident in The Hague).

BRITISH AMBASSADOR (resident in Georgetown, Guyana).
BRITISH CONSULATE, c/o VSH United Buildings, Van't Hogerhuystraat, PO Box 1300, Paramaribo. *Honorary Consul,* J. J. Healy, MBE.

ECONOMY

Suriname has large timber resources. Rice and sugar cane are the main crops. Bauxite is mined, and is the principal export. In 1987, GDP amounted to US$1,080 million. Principal trading partners are the Netherlands, USA and Norway.

TRADE WITH UK	1991	1992
Imports from UK	£7,896,000	£11,521,000
Exports to UK	9,922,000	11,531,000

SWAZILAND
Umbuso we Swatini

Swaziland is a small, land-locked country surrounded by South Africa on its northern, western and southern borders and by Mozambique to the east. The broken mountainous Highveld along the western border, with an average altitude of 4,000 feet, is densely forested, mainly with conifers and eucalyptus; the Middleveld, averaging about 2,000 feet, is a mixed farming area including cotton and pineapples; and the Lowveld in the east was mainly scrubland until the introduction of large sugar cane plantations. Four rivers, the Komati, Usutu, Mbuluzi and Ngwavuma, flow from west to east. The total area of Swaziland is 6,704 sq. miles (17,363 sq. km), and the population (UN estimate 1991) is 817,000.

CAPITAL – Mbabane (population 1986, 38,290). Other main townships are Manzini (estimated population, 30,000), Big Bend, Mhlambanyati, Mhlume, Nhlangano, Pigg's Peak and Simunye.
CURRENCY – Lilangeni (E) of 100 cents. South African currency is also in circulation. Swaziland is a member of the Common Monetary Area and its unit of currency *Emalangeni* (singular *Lilangeni*) has a par value with the South African Rand.
FLAG – Blue with a wide crimson horizontal band bordered in yellow across the centre, bearing a shield and two spears horizontally.
NATIONAL ANTHEM – Ingoma Yesive.
NATIONAL DAY – 6 September (Independence Day).

GOVERNMENT

The Kingdom of Swaziland came into being on 25 April 1967 under a self-government constitution and became an independent kingdom, headed by HM Sobhuza II, in membership of the Commonwealth on 6 September 1968.

A new government system was introduced in 1978 and amended in 1992–3 under which the King, assisted by his appointed Cabinet, holds considerable executive, legislative and judicial authority. In addition, there is a bicameral legislative body comprising a Senate and a House of Assembly. Each of the 55 traditional Tinkhundla (chieftaincies) are directly elected and become members of the House of Assembly. The King appoints ten members to the House of Assembly, making 65 in all, who then elect 20 members (not of their own number) to the Senate. To these are added ten senators appointed by the King, bringing the full membership of the Senate to 30. All political parties are banned under the 1978 Constitution.

HEAD OF STATE
King of Swaziland, HM King Mswati III, *inaugurated* 25 April 1986.

CABINET *as at August 1993*
Prime Minister, Hon. Obed Dlamini.
Foreign Affairs, Hon. Sir George Mamba.
Justice, Hon. Dr Zonke Khumalo.
Home Affairs, Hon. Prince Sobandla.

Education, Hon. Prince Khuzulwandle.
Works and Construction, Hon. Prince Mbilini.
Health, Hon. Dr Fanny Friedman.
Agriculture, Hon. Themba Masuku.
Commerce and Industry, Hon. Barnabas Mhlongo.
Labour and Public Service, Hon. David Motsa.
Natural Resources, Land Utilization and Energy, Hon.
   Senzenjoni Shabalala.
Housing and Urban Development, Hon. Thomas Stephens.
Economic Planning and Development and (acting) Finance,
   Hon. Solomon Dlamini.
Transport and Communications, Hon. Albert Shabangu.
Broadcasting, Information and Tourism, Hon. Douglas
   N. Ntiwane.

KINGDOM OF SWAZILAND HIGH COMMISSION
58 Pont Street, London SWIX OAE
Tel 071-581 4976/8

High Commissioner, His Excellency Mboni N. Dlamini
(1988).

BRITISH HIGH COMMISSION
Allister Miller Street, Mbabane
Tel: Mbabane 42581

High Commissioner, His Excellency Richard Gozney (1993).

BRITISH COUNCIL REPRESENTATIVE, James Kennedy
(*Cultural Attaché*).

COMMUNICATIONS

Swaziland's railway is about 150 miles long and connects
with the Mozambique port of Maputo and the South African
railway network to Richards Bay. A rail line to the north-
west border provides a link to Komatipoort. Most passenger
and goods traffic is carried by privately-owned motor
transport services. There are scheduled air services by Royal
Swazi National Airways to southern and eastern Africa.
International telecommunications and television services are
provided through a satellite earth station, and there is also a
national telephone network.

ECONOMY

In the 1989–90 budget, total expenditure, including debt
repayment, was projected at E447,000,000. A surplus of
E12,500,000 was predicted due to increase in revenue.
Manufacturing was announced to have replaced agriculture
as the dominant sector in 1988.

TRADE WITH UK	1991	1992
Imports from UK	£4,336,000	£3,226,000
Exports to UK	39,607,000	40,101,000

SWEDEN
Konungariket Sverige

Sweden occupies the eastern area of the Scandinavian
peninsula in north-west Europe and comprises 24 local
government districts (*Län*), with a total area of 173,732 sq.
miles (449,964 sq. km), and population of 8,635,000 (1991
UN estimate).

RELIGION – The state religion is Lutheran Protestant, to
which over 95 per cent officially adhere.

CAPITAL – ΨStockholm. Population (1988): City 669,485;
   Greater Stockholm, 1,471,242; ΨGothenburg (Göteborg)
   (430,765); ΨMalmö (231,575); Uppsala (161,828).

CURRENCY – Swedish krona of 100 öre.

FLAG – Yellow cross on a blue ground.
NATIONAL ANTHEM – Du Gamla, Du Fria (Thou ancient,
   thou freeborn).
NATIONAL DAY – 6 June (Day of the Swedish Flag).

GOVERNMENT

Sweden is a constitutional monarchy, with the monarch
retaining purely ceremonial functions as head of state. Under
the Act of Succession 1809 (with amendments) the throne is
hereditary in the House of Bernadotte. A 1979 amendment
vested the succession in the monarch's eldest child irrespective of sex.

   There is a unicameral legislature (*Riksdag*) of 349 members
elected by universal suffrage for three years. The Council of
Ministers (*Statsråd*) is responsible to the *Riksdag*. In the
General Election held on 15 September 1991, the following
seats were won: Social Democrats 138; Moderates 80;
Liberals 33; Centre 31; Christian Democrats 26; New
Democracy 25; Left Party 16.

HEAD OF STATE
King of Sweden, HM Carl XVI Gustaf, KG, *born* 30 April
   1946, *succeeded* 15 September 1973, *married* 19 June 1976
   Fräulein Silvia Renate Sommerlath and has *issue,* Crown
   Princess Victoria (*see* below); Prince Carl Philip Edmund
   Bertil, Duke of Värmland, *born* 13 May 1979; Princess
   Madeleine Thérèse Amelie Josephine, Duchess of
   Hälsingland and Gästrikland, *born* 10 June 1982.
Heir, Crown Princess Victoria Ingrid Alice Désirée,
   Duchess of Västergötland, *born* 14 July 1977.

COUNCIL OF MINISTERS *as at August 1993*
Prime Minister, Carl Bildt (M).
Deputy Prime Minister, Minister of Social Affairs, Bengt Westerberg (L).
Justice, Gun Hellsvik (M).
Foreign Affairs, Baroness Margaretha of Ugglas (M).
Defence, Anders Björck (M).
Transport and Communications, Mats Odell (CD).
Finance, Anne Wibble (L).
Education, Per Unckel (M).
Agriculture, Karl Erik Olsson (C).
Labour, Börje Hörnlund (C).
Industry and Commerce, Per Westerberg (M).
Public Administration, Inger Davidsson (CD).
Environment, Olof Johansson (C).
Culture, Birgit Friggebo (L).
Constitutional and Civil Law, Reidunn Laurén (Ind).
International Development Co-operation and Human Rights Issues, Alf Svensson (CD).
European Affairs and Foreign Trade, Ulf Dinkelspiel (M).
Health and Social Security, Bo Könberg (L).
Fiscal Affairs and Financial Markets, Bo Lundgren (M).
Schools and Adult Education, Beatrice Ask (M).
Physical Planning, Görel Thurdin (C).

M Moderate Party; L Liberal Party; C Centre Party; CD Christian Democrat Party

SWEDISH EMBASSY
11 Montagu Place, London WIH 2AL
Tel 071-917 6400

Ambassador Extraordinary and Plenipotentiary, His Excellency Lennart Eckerberg, KCMG (1991).
Minister Plenipotentiary, R. Ängeby.
Defence and Naval Attaché, Cdr. Count Gustaf Taube.
Consul-General, G. Naessén.
Trade Commissioner, G. Munthe.

BRITISH EMBASSY
Skarpögatan 6–8, 115 93 Stockholm
Tel: Stockholm 442 50 00

Ambassador Extraordinary and Plenipotentiary, His Excellency R. L. B. Cormack, CMG (1991).
Counsellor (Political) and Consul-General, Dr V. Canton.
Counsellor (Economic and Commercial), A. R. Murray.
Defence and Air Attaché, Wg Cdr. J. Walmsley.

There are British Consular Offices at *Stockholm* and *Gothenburg*, and Honorary Consuls at *Luleå, Gothenburg, Malmö* and *Sundsvall*.

BRITISH COUNCIL REPRESENTATIVE, Ann Hellström, Skarpögatan 6, 11527 Stockholm.
BRITISH-SWEDISH CHAMBER OF COMMERCE, Grevgatan 34, 11453 Stockholm.

ECONOMY

Following the election of a centre-right government in 1991 there has been drastic change in the Swedish socio-economic system. Free market economic policies of privatization, deregulation, the ending of state subsidies, trade union legislation, and welfare and spending cuts have been introduced. Austerity packages were introduced in November 1992 and April 1993 to overcome budget deficits, improve competitiveness and stabilize the currency. The restructuring of industry, together with the world recession, caused unemployment to rise to 9.5 per cent in 1993 and manufacturing output to fall 15 per cent between 1989 and 1992.

Industrial prosperity is based on an abundance of natural resources in the form of forests, mineral deposits and water power. The forests cover about half the total land surface and sustain timber, pulp and paper milling industries. The mineral resources include iron ore, lead, zinc, sulphur, granite, marble, precious and heavy metals (the latter not exploited) and extensive deposits of low grade uranium ore. Industries based on mining are important but it is the general engineering industry that provides the basis of Sweden's exports, especially specialized machinery and systems and chemical industries. The relative importance of agriculture has declined and in 1993 only 3 per cent of the labour force was engaged in farming.

Apart from water power (hydroelectricity supplies 15 per cent of energy needs) Sweden has no significant indigenous resources of conventional hydrocarbon fuels and relies to a high degree upon imported oil. Much of Sweden's electricity is generated by nuclear power but as a result of a referendum in 1980 the nuclear programme is to be discontinued by 2010. However, this decision is now being debated once more and could be reversed. Small supplies of natural gas are imported from Denmark into southern Sweden, with the pipeline being extended to Gothenburg.

FINANCE	1991–2	1992–3
Revenue	Kronor 464,632m	Kronor 419,125m
Expenditure	470,107m	489,457m

TRADE
About 40 per cent of Sweden's industrial output is exported, mainly in the form of cars, trucks, machinery, electrical and communications equipment. Sweden conducts 70 per cent of its trade with the rest of EFTA and the EC.

	1991	1992
Imports	Kronor 301,290m	Kronor 289,923m
Exports	332,790m	326,008m

Trade with UK	1991	1992
Imports from UK	£2,471,539,000	£2,438,972,000
Exports to UK	3,142,449,000	3,283,739,000

COMMUNICATIONS

The total length of Swedish railroads is 11,745 km. The road network is over 400,000 km in length. The mercantile marine amounted on 31 December 1985 to 2,619,625 gross tonnage. Regular domestic air traffic is maintained by the Scandinavian Airlines System and by Linjeflyg. Regular European and inter-continental air traffic is maintained by the Scandinavian Airlines System.

DEFENCE

Based on the policy of non-alignment in peace leading to neutrality in war Sweden maintains a 'total defence' which includes peacetime organizations for civil, economic and psychological defence. All men aged 18–47 are eligible for conscription, with the initial term being seven to 15 months for the Army and Navy and eight to 12 months for the Air Force. Men are obliged to serve in the reserves until age 47 with a commitment to refresher training every fourth year.

The armed forces have a total active strength of 60,500 (38,800 conscripts), with reserves of 709,000 (Army 550,000; Navy 102,000; Air Force 57,000). The Army has an active strength of 43,500 (27,000 conscripts), and on mobilization a strength of 700,000. Equipment includes 885 main battle tanks, 250 light tanks, 600 armoured personnel carriers, 880 artillery pieces and 20 combat helicopters. The Navy has 12 submarines, 41 patrol and coastal vessels, a number of minor craft and auxiliaries, six coast artillery brigades, 14 combat helicopters and a strength of 9,500 (5,950 conscripts). The Air Force has modern supersonic aircraft of Swedish manufacture forming a standing force of 499 combat aircraft and a modern air defence radar system. The Air Force has a strength of 7,500 (5,500 conscripts).

CULTURE

Swedish belongs, with Danish and Norwegian, to the North Germanic language group. Swedish literature dates back to King Magnus Eriksson, who codified the old Swedish provincial laws in 1350. With his translation of the Bible, Olaus Petri (1493–1552) formed the basis for the modern Swedish language. Literature flourished during the reign of Gustavus III, who founded the Swedish Academy in 1786. Notable Swedish writers include Almquist (1795–1866), Strindberg (1849–1912) and Lagerlöf (1858–1940), Nobel Prizewinner in 1909. Contemporary authors include Lagerquist (1891–1974), Nobel Laureate in 1951, Martinson (1904–78) and Johnson (1900–76), Nobel Laureates jointly in 1974. The Swedish scientist Alfred Nobel (1833–96) founded the Nobel Prizes for literature, science and peace.

EDUCATION

The state system provides nine years' free and compulsory schooling from the age of seven to 16 in the comprehensive elementary schools. Over 90 per cent continue into further education of two to four years' duration in the upper secondary schools and a unified higher education system administered in six regional areas containing one of the universities: Uppsala (founded 1477); Lund (1668); Stockholm (1878); Gothenburg (1887); Umeå (1963) and Linköping (1967). At present there are 33 institutions of higher education including three technical universities in Stockholm, Gothenburg and Luleå, and the Karolinska Institute in Stockholm, which specializes in medicine and dentistry.

SWITZERLAND
Schweizerische Eidgenossenschaft - Confédération Suisse - Confederazione Svizzera

---

Switzerland, the Helvetia of the Romans, is a federal republic of central Europe, situated between 45° 50′ and 47° 48′ N. latitude and 5° 58′ and 10° 30′ E. longitude. It comprises a total area of 15,943 sq. miles (41,293 sq. km), with a population (1991 census) of 6,833,750. Of the total population in 1991, 40 per cent was Protestant, 46.1 per cent Roman Catholic, 5 per cent other religions and 8.9 per cent without religion.

Switzerland is the most mountainous country in Europe. The Alps, from 5,000 to 15,217 feet in height, occupy its southern and eastern frontiers and the chief part of its interior; the Jura mountains rise in the north-west. The Alps occupy 61 per cent, and the Jura mountains 12 per cent of the country. The highest peak, Mont Blanc, Pennine Alps (15,782 ft) is partly in France and Italy; Monte Rosa (15,217 ft) and Matterhorn (14,780 ft) are partly in Switzerland and partly in Italy. The highest wholly Swiss peaks are Dufourspitze (15,203 ft), Finsteraarhorn (14,026), Aletschhorn (13,711), Jungfrau (13,671), Mönch (13,456), Eiger (13,040), Schreckhorn (13,385), and Wetterhorn (12,150) in the Bernese Alps, and Dom (14,918), Weisshorn (14,803) and Breithorn (13,685). The Swiss lakes are famous for their beauty and include Lakes Maggiore, Zürich, Lucerne, Neuchâtel, Geneva, Constance, Thun, Zug, Lugano, Brienz and the Walensee. There are also many artificial lakes.

CAPITAL – Berne, population (1991 census) 135,600 (city). Other large towns are (1991) Zürich (345,200), Basle (173,800), Geneva (169,600), Lausanne (124,800), Winterthur (86,800), St Gallen (74,500), Lucerne (60,500).
CURRENCY – Swiss franc of 100 centimes or rappen.
FLAG – Square and red, bearing a couped white cross.
NATIONAL ANTHEM – Trittst im Morgenrot Daher (Radiant in the morning sky).
NATIONAL DAY – 1 August.

GOVERNMENT

The Federal Assembly consists of two chambers, a National Council (*Nationalrat*) of 200 members, and a States Council (*Ständerat*) of 46 members. Members of the National Council are elected for four years, elections taking place in October. The executive power is in the hands of a Federal Council (*Bundesrat*) of seven members, elected for four years by the Federal Assembly and presided over by the President of the Confederation. Each year the Federal Assembly elects from the Federal Council the President and the Vice-President. Not more than one of the same canton may be elected a member of the Federal Council; however, there is a tradition that Italian and French-speaking areas should between them be represented on the Federal Council by at least two members. There are 23 cantons, three subdivided, making 26 in all.

The Federal Council voted by four votes to three in May 1992 to apply for European Community membership. The European Economic Area (EEA) Treaty between the EC and EFTA, which extends the provisions of the EC single internal market to EFTA states, was defeated in a national referendum on 6 December 1992. Switzerland will consequently be the only EFTA state outside the EEA.

FEDERAL COUNCIL
President of the Swiss Confederation (1993) *and Head of Transport, Communications and Energy*, Adolf Ogi.
Vice-President (1993) *and Head of Finance*, Otto Stich.
Military, Kaspar Villiger.
Foreign Affairs, Flavio Cotti.
Public Economy, Jean-Pascal Delamuraz.
Home Affairs, Ruth Dreifuss.
Justice and Police, Arnold Koller.

EMBASSY OF SWITZERLAND
16–18 Montagu Place, London WIH 2BQ
Tel 071-723 0701

Ambassador Extraordinary and Plenipotentiary, His Excellency Franz E. Muheim (1989).
Minister, R. Reich.

Defence Attaché, Maj.-Gen. G. de Loës.
Consul-General, E. Jaun.
Counsellor, J. de Watteville (*Economic and Financial*).

There is a Swiss Consulate-General in *Manchester.*

BRITISH EMBASSY
Thunstrasse 50, 3005 Berne
Tel: Berne 445021/6
Ambassador Extraordinary and Plenipotentiary, His
   Excellency David Beattie, CMG (1992).
Counsellor and Deputy Head of Mission, J. Knight-Smith.
Consul-General and Director of British Export Promotion,
   T. Bryant (*Zurich*).
Consul-General, P. J. Priestley (*Geneva*).
Defence Attaché, Lt.-Col. W. R. Thatcher.

BRITISH CONSULAR OFFICES – There is a Consular
section at the Embassy in *Berne*; Consulates-General at
Zürich and *Geneva* and Consular offices at *Lugano, Valais*
and *Montreux.* The Directorate of British Export
Promotion in Switzerland is in the Consulate-General
Office, Dufourstrasse 56, 8008 Zürich.

BRITISH-SWISS CHAMBER OF COMMERCE, Freiestrasse
155, 8032 Zürich.
SWISS-BRITISH SOCIETIES: Berne, *President,* Dr
H. Beriger; Zürich, *President,* J.-P. Müller; Basle,
President, Dr C. Grey.

DEFENCE

All Swiss males must undertake military service in the Army
or the Air Corps, which is part of the Army. The total active
armed forces number some 1,600 regulars with 36,000 each
year for recruit training. Conscription takes the form of 17
weeks recruit training at age 20 and regular reservist
refresher training up to age 42. The Army has a strength on
mobilization of some 565,000 with 812 main battle tanks,
1,190 armoured personnel carriers and armoured infantry
fighting vehicles, and 1,180 artillery pieces. The Air Corps
has a strength on mobilization of 60,000 with 242 combat
aircraft. In addition, there are the paramilitary civil defence
forces, with 300,000 fully-trained personnel.

ECONOMY

Agriculture is followed chiefly in the valleys and all over the
Mittelland, where cereals, flax, hemp, and tobacco are
produced, and fruits and vegetables as well as grapes are
grown. Dairying and stock-raising are the principal industries, about 3,000,000 acres being under grass for hay and
2,000,000 acres pasturage. The forests cover about one-
quarter of the whole surface.
   The chief manufacturing industries comprise engineering
and electrical engineering, metal-working, chemicals and
pharmaceuticals, textiles, watchmaking, woodworking, foodstuffs and footwear. Banking, insurance and tourism are
major industries.

FINANCE	1989*	1990
Revenue	SFr28,031m	SFr30,324m
Expenditure	27,555m	29,850m
*estimate		

TRADE

The principal imports are machinery, electrical and electronic
equipment, textiles, motor vehicles, non-ferrous metals,
chemical elements, clothing, food, medicinal and pharmaceutical products. The principal exports are machinery,
chemical elements, non-ferrous metals, watches, electrical

and electronic equipment, textiles, dyeing, tanning and
colouring equipment.

	1990	1991
Total Imports	SFr96,611m	SFr95,032m
Total Exports	88,257m	87,946m

†*Trade with UK*	1991	1992
Imports from UK	£2,105,656,000	£1,844,610,000
Exports to UK	3,754,586,000	3,918,936,000
†Including Liechtenstein		

COMMUNICATIONS

There were in 1990, 5,031 km of railway tracks (Swiss
Federal Railways, 2,990 km; Swiss privately owned railways
2,041 km). At the end of 1990 the total length of motorways
was 1,495 km. The number of motor vehicles licensed in
1991 was 3,065,812. The merchant marine consisted at June
1990 of 20 vessels with a total gross tonnage of 287,487
tonnes. In 1989, goods handled at Basle Rhine ports
amounted to 8,845,162 tonnes. In 1990, 163 lake and river
vessels (excluding the Rhine) transported 12,000,000 passengers and 500 tonnes of freight. Swiss airlines have a network
covering 348,762 km (1990) and in 1990 carried 17,100,000
passengers. Swissair, the national airline, flies to and from
the airports at Zürich, Geneva and Basle.

EDUCATION

Education is controlled by cantonal and communal authorities. Primary education is free and compulsory. School age
varies, generally seven to 14, with secondary education from
age 12 to 15. Special schools make a feature of commercial
and technical instruction. Universities are Basle (founded
1460), Berne (1834), Fribourg (1889), Geneva (1873),
Lausanne (1890), Zürich (1832), and Neuchâtel (1909), the
technical universities of Lausanne and Zürich and the
economics university of St Gall.

CULTURE

There are four national languages: French, German, Italian
and Romansch. German is the dominating language in 19 of
the 26 cantons; French in Fribourg, Jura, Geneva, Neuchâtel,
Valais and Vaud; Italian in Ticino; and Romansch in parts of
the Grisons.
   Many modern authors, alike in the German school and in
the Suisse Romande, have achieved international fame. Karl
Spitteler (1845–1924) and Hermann Hesse (1877–1962) were
awarded the Nobel Prize for Literature, the former in 1919,
the latter in 1946.

SYRIA
Al-Jamhouriya Al-Arabia as-Souriya

Syria is in the Levant, covering a portion of the former
Ottoman Empire. Bounded by the Mediterranean and
Lebanon on the west, Israel and Jordan on the south-west,
Iraq on the east and Turkey on the north, it has an estimated
area of 71,498 sq. miles (185,180 sq. km), and a population
(UN 1991 estimate) of 12,993,000, most of whom are Arabic-
speaking and Muslim. The Orontes flows northwards from
the Lebanon range across the northern boundary to Antakya
(Antioch, Turkey). The Euphrates crosses the northern
boundary near Jerablus and flows through north-eastern
Syria to the boundary of Iraq.

The region is rich in historical remains. Damascus (Dimishq ash-Sham) is said to be the oldest continuously inhabited city in the world (although Aleppo disputes this claim), having existed as a city for over 4,000 years. The city contains the Omayed Mosque, the Tomb of Saladin, and the 'street which is called Straight' (Acts 9:11), while to the north-east is the Roman outpost of Dmeir and further east is Palmyra. On the Mediterranean coast at Amrit are ruins of the Phoenician town of Marath, and also ruins of Crusaders' fortresses at Markab, Sahyoun, and Krak des Chevaliers. At Tartous the cathedral of Our Lady of Syria, built by the Knights Templars in the 12th and 13th centuries, has been restored as a museum. One of the oldest alphabets in the world has been discovered at Ugarit (Ras Shamra), a Phoenician village near the port of Latakia. Hittite cities dating from 2000 to 1500 BC, have been explored on the west bank of the Euphrates at Jerablus and Kadesh.

CAPITAL – Damascus, population (1990 estimate) 1,378,000. Other important towns are Aleppo, Homs and Hama, and the principal port is ΨLatakia.
CURRENCY – Syrian pound (S£) of 100 piastres.
FLAG – Red over white over black horizontal bands, with two green stars on central white band.
NATIONAL DAY – 17 April.

GOVERNMENT

Syria, which had been under French mandate since the 1914–18 war, became an independent republic during the 1939–45 war. The first independently elected Parliament met in August 1943, but foreign troops were in part occupation until April 1946. Syria remained an independent republic until February 1958, when it became part of the United Arab Republic. It seceded from the United Arab Republic in September 1961.

A new constitution was promulgated in March 1973. This declared that Syria is a democratic, popular socialist state, and that the Arab Socialist Renaissance (Ba'ath) Party, which has been the ruling party since 1963, is the leading party in the state and society. Elections to the expanded 250-seat People's Council in May 1990 resulted in a large majority for the Ba'ath Party, which won 134 seats; its National Progressive Front allies (Arab Socialist Union, Socialist Unionist Movement, Arab Socialist Party, Syrian Communist Party) together won 32 seats, and Independents won 84.

HEAD OF STATE
President, Lt.-Gen. Hafez el Assad, *assumed office* 14 March 1971, *re-elected*, 1978, 1985, 3 December 1991.
Vice-Presidents, Abdul Halim Khaddam, Rifaat Al Assad, Zuhair Mashariqa.

MINISTERS *as at August 1993*
Prime Minister, Mahmoud Al Zubi.
Deputy PM and Minister for Defence, Gen. Mustafa Tlass.
Deputy PM for Public Services, Rashid Akhtarini.
Deputy PM for Economic Affairs, Dr Salim Yassin.
Education, Ghassan Halabi.
Higher Education, Salha Sunkur.
Interior, Mohammad Harbah.
Transport, Mufeed Abdul-Karim.
Information, Mohammad Salman.
Local Administration, Yahya Abu Asali.
Supply and Internal Trade, Nadin Akkash.
Economy and Foreign Trade, Mohammad al-Imadi.
Culture, Najah al-Attar.
Foreign Affairs, Farooq al-Shara.
Tourism, Amin Abul-Shamat.
Health, Iyad al-Shatti.

Waqfs (Religious Endowments), Abdel-Majid Tarabulsi.
Irrigation, Abd ar-Rahman Madani.
Electricity, Kamil al-Baba.
Oil and Mineral Resources, Nadir Nabulsi.
Construction, Majid Ezzou Rhaibani.
Housing and Utilities, Hosam al-Safadi.
Agriculture and Agrarian Reform, As'ad Mustafa.
Finance, Khaled al-Mahayni.
Industry, Ahmad Nezamuldin.
Communications, Redwan Martini.
Justice, Abdullah Tulbah.
Presidential Affairs, Wahib Fadil.
Labour and Social Affairs, Ali Khalil.

EMBASSY OF THE SYRIAN ARAB REPUBLIC
8 Belgrave Square, London SW1X 8PH
Tel 071-245 9012

Ambassador Extraordinary and Plenipotentiary, His Excellency Mohammed Khodor (1991).

BRITISH EMBASSY
Quartier Malki, 11 rue Mohammad Kurd Ali, Imm. Kotob, Damascus (PO Box 37)
Tel: Damascus 712561

Ambassador Extraordinary and Plenipotentiary, His Excellency Andrew F. Green, CMG (1991).

BRITISH COUNCIL REPRESENTATIVE, Dr Peter Clark, OBE, Ground Floor, Tasheen Tabaa' Building, Abd Almalek Bin Marwan Street, Malki, Damascus, PO Box 33105.

DEFENCE

The total active armed forces have a strength of 408,000. There is a conscription period of 30 months, with a reserve commitment to age 45; reserves number 400,000 personnel. The Army has a strength of some 300,000 (130,000 conscripts, 50,000 mobilized reservists), with 4,600 main battle tanks, 500 reconnaissance vehicles, 3,750 armoured personnel carriers and infantry fighting vehicles and 2,330 artillery pieces. The Navy has a strength of 8,000 personnel, with three submarines, two frigates, 30 patrol and coastal combatants and 17 armed helicopters. The Air Force (including the Air Defence Command) has a strength of some 100,000, with 639 combat aircraft and 100 armed helicopters of Soviet manufacture, together with 22 Air Defence brigades with surface-to-air missiles. Syria maintains a force of some 30,000 men in Lebanon and within Syria has some 4,500 men of the Palestinian Liberation Army and some 500 advisers from the former Soviet Union.

ECONOMY

Agriculture is the principal source of production; wheat and barley are the main cereal crops, but the cotton crop is the highest in value. Tobacco is grown in the maritime plain in Sahel, the Sahyoun and the Djebleh district of Latakia. Large areas are coming under cultivation in the north-east of the country as a result of irrigation from the Thawra dam. Skins and hides, leather goods, wool and silk, textiles, cement, vegetable oil, glass, soap, sugar, plastics and copper and brass utensils are produced. There are an increasing number of light assembly plants as Syria's industrialization pro-gramme develops. Oil has been found at Karachuk and other parts in the north-eastern corner of the country and production of high quality reserves is proceeding in the region of Deir ez Zor. Syria produces nearly 400,000 barrels of oil per day at present. A pipeline has been built to the Mediterranean port of Banias, via Homs. Two oil refineries are in production at Homs and Banias. Syria also has gas reserves, deposits of phosphate and rock salt, and produces asphalt.

TRADE

The principal imports are foodstuffs (fruit, vegetables, cereals, meat and dairy products, tea, coffee and sugar), mineral and petroleum products, yarn and textiles, iron and steel manufactures, machinery, chemicals, pharmaceuticals, fertilizers and timber. Exports include raw cotton, oil, cereals, fruit, phosphates, cement, livestock and dairy products, other foodstuffs, textiles and raw wool.

Trade with UK	1991	1992
Imports from UK	£49,791,000	£64,598,000
Exports to UK	42,459,000	53,211,000

CULTURE

Arabic is the principal language, but Kurdish, Turkish and Armenian are spoken among significant minorities and a few villages still speak Aramaic, the language spoken by Christ and the Apostles. There are three daily newspapers and several periodicals in Arabic published in Damascus, and also a daily newspaper in English. English has taken over from French as the main foreign language.

EDUCATION

Education in Syria is under state control and although a few of the schools are privately owned, they all follow a common syllabus. Elementary education is free at state schools and is compulsory from the age of seven. Secondary education is not compulsory and is free only at the state schools. Because of the shortage of places, entry to the state schools is competitive. There are universitites at Damascus, Aleppo, Tishrin, Latakia and the Ba'ath University, Homs. Approximately 10 per cent of all students receive scholarships, and the rest pay fees.

COMMUNICATIONS

Although railway lines run from Damascus to both Beirut and Amman, train services go only to Amman, as much of the Lebanese line has been dismantled. A track has been opened connecting Homs with Damascus. A track links Homs, Hamah, Aleppo, Deir ez Zor and Qamishliye to the Iraq frontier. Branch lines connect the ports of Tartous and Latakia to the system and another line runs from Aleppo down Euphrates valley to Deir ez Zor and thence north to Qamishliye, with a branch going to the Euphrates Dam. All the principal towns in the country are connected by roads which vary from modern dual carriageways to narrow country lanes. An internal air service operates between all major towns. The main international airport is at Damascus and there are also flights from Aleppo.

TAIWAN (REPUBLIC OF CHINA)
Chung-hua Min-kuo

An island of some 13,800 sq. miles (35,742 sq. km) in the China Sea, Taiwan, formerly Formosa, lies 90 miles east of the Chinese mainland in 21° 45′ to 25° 56′N. latitude. The eastern part of the main island is mountainous and forest covered. Mt Morrison (Yu Shan) (13,035 ft) and Mt Sylvia (Tz'ukaoshan) (12,972 ft) are the highest peaks. The western plains are watered by many rivers.

Territories include the Pescadores Islands (50 sq. miles), some 35 miles west of Taiwan, as well as Quemoy (68 sq.

miles) and Matsu (11 sq. miles) which are only a few miles from the mainland.

POPULATION – The population (1991) is 20,536,233, almost entirely Chinese. About two million mainlanders came to the island with Chiang Kai-shek in 1947-9.

LANGUAGE – Mandarin Chinese has been the official language since 1949. Now Taiwanese, spoken by 85 per cent of the population, is growing in importance.

CAPITAL – Taipei, population (1990) 2,719,659. Other towns are ΨKaohsiung (1,386,723); Tainan (667,622); Taichung (730,376); and ΨKeelung (348,672).

CURRENCY – New Taiwan dollar (NT$) of 100 cents.

FLAG – Red, with blue quarter at top next staff, bearing a 12-point white sun.

NATIONAL DAY – 10 October.

GOVERNMENT

Settled for centuries by the Chinese, the island was administered by Japan from 1895 to 1945. General Chiang Kai-shek withdrew to Taiwan in 1949, towards the end of the war against the Communist regime in mainland China, after which the territory continued under his presidency until his death in 1975. Martial law was lifted in July 1987 after 38 years.

In 1991, President Lee announced that the 'period of Communist rebellion' on the Chinese mainland was over, thus granting *de facto* recognition of the People's Republic. The announcement also ended emergency measures which had frozen political life on Taiwan since 1949. In 1991-2 power shifted away from mainlanders to native Taiwanese with the forcible retirement of the 'Senior Parliamentarians' who had retained their seats since being elected on the mainland in 1948, and the new parliament, the Legislative Yuan, gained control of the budget, of law-making and of the appointment of the Prime Minister. A general election to the Legislative Yuan on 19 December 1992 was won by the National Kuomintang (KMT) with 96 of the 161 seats; the opposition Democratic Progressive Party won 50 seats, and independents and minor parties the remaining 15 seats. During 1993 the KMT has been weakened by defections by mainlanders and their descendants who wish to retain the claim on the mainland and by Taiwanese who wish to declare independence.

HEAD OF STATE
President, Lee Teng-hui, *elected* 1988, *re-elected* 20 May 1990.
Vice-President, Li Yuan-zu.

EXECUTIVE YUAN *as at August 1993*
Prime Minister, Lien Chan.
Deputy PM, Hsu Li-teh.
Secretary-General, Li Hou-kao.
Interior, Wu Po-hsiung.
Foreign Affairs, Frederick Chien Fu.
Finance, Lin Chen-kuo.
Education, Kuo Wei-fan.
Economic Affairs, P. K. Chan.
Justice, Ma Ying-jeou.
National Defence, Sun Chen.
Transportation and Communications, Liu Chao-shiuan.
Ministers without Portfolio, Chiu Hung-ta; Shirley Kuo Wan-jung.

Chairs of Councils:
Mainland Affairs, Huang Kun-hui.
Atomic Energy, Hsu Yih-yun.
Research, Sub Te-hsiung.
Agriculture, Sun Ming-hsien.

Labour Affairs, Chao Shou-po.
Economic Planning and Development, Hsiao Wan-chang.
Overseas Chinese Affairs, Chang Hsiao-yen.
Youth, Ying Shih-hao.
Science, Kuo Nan-hung.
Culture, Shen Hsueh-yung.
Mongolian and Tibetan Affairs, Chang Chun-yi.
Health, Chang Po-ya.

DEFENCE

The total active armed forces number some 390,000 personnel, with conscripts serving for two-year terms. Reserves number 1,657,500 with an obligation until the age of 30. The Army is 260,000 strong with 460 main battle tanks, 905 light tanks, 1,215 armoured infantry fighting vehicles and armoured personnel carriers, 1,375 artillery pieces and 112 helicopters. The Navy has a strength of 60,000, including 30,000 marines, with four submarines, 24 destroyers, 12 frigates, 93 patrol and coastal combatants, 32 combat aircraft and 12 armed helicopters. The Air Force has 70,000 personnel, with 486 combat aircraft. Paramilitary security groups under Ministry of Defence control number 25,000 personnel.

ECONOMY

Over the past 30 years Taiwan has transformed itself from a mainly agricultural country to one of the four leading Asian economies. A series of six-year plans has expanded the industrial base. Continued trade surpluses have led to one of the largest foreign exchange reserves of any country in the world (US$67,397m in mid-1991).

The soil is very fertile, producing sugar, rice, sweet potatoes, tea, bananas, pineapples and tobacco. Mineral resources are meagre. Taiwan produces one-tenth of its coal needs and some natural gas. There are important fisheries. The principal seaports ΨKeelung and ΨKaohsiung are situated in the northern and southern sections of the island.

TRADE
The principal exports are electronic goods, machinery, metal goods, textiles, plastic products and toys and games. The main imports are oil, chemicals, machinery and natural resources.

Trade with UK	1991	1992
Imports from UK	£519,821,000	£545,422,000
Exports to UK	1,271,990,000	1,393,718,000

TAJIKISTAN
Respublika i Tojikiston

Tajikistan has an area of 55,251 sq. miles (143,100 sq. km) and occupies the extreme south-east of former Soviet Central Asia. It is bordered on the west and north-west by Uzbekistan, on the north-east by Kyrgyzstan, on the east by China and on the south by Afghanistan. The republic includes the Gorno-Badakhstan Autonomous Province and the Kulyab, Kurgan-Tyubinsk and Khodzhent Provinces. The country is mountainous with the Pamir highlands in the east and the high ridges of the Pamir-Altai system in the centre. Plains are formed by wide stretches of the Syr-Darya valley in the north and of the Amu-Darya in the south. The country has areas prone to earthquakes, and a continental climate.
POPULATION – According to the 1989 census the population is 5,093,000, of which 62 per cent are Tajiks, 23 per cent

Uzbeks and 8 per cent Russians, with smaller numbers of Tatars, Kirghiz, Germans and Ukrainians. The estimated population in 1992 was 4,969,000.
RELIGION – Predominantly Sunni Muslim.
LANGUAGE – Tajik 62 per cent, Uzbek 23 per cent, Russian 8 per cent. Tajik is close to the Farsi spoken in Iran.
CAPITAL – Dushanbe. Population 595,000 (1989).
CURRENCY – Rouble of 100 kopeks.
FLAG – Three horizontal stripes of red, white and green with the white of double width and charged with a crown and seven stars, all in gold.
NATIONAL DAY – 9 September (Independence Day).

GOVERNMENT

The area that is now Tajikistan had a highly developed culture when it was invaded and conquered by Alexander the Great in the fourth century BC. The area remained under Greek and Greco-Persian rule for 200 years until the Kingdom of Kusha was established, based on Bacharia (Bukhara). Tajikistan was invaded by the Arabs in the 7th century AD and by the Samanid Persians in the ninth century AD. The Tajik cities of Bukhara and Samarkand became two of the most important cultural and educational centres in the Islamic world.

The Tajiks lived under the control of various feudal emirates until the area which is now Tajikistan was subsumed within the Russian Empire in 1868. With the advent of the Russian revolution in 1917 the central Asian emirates attempted to re-establish their independence. Soviet power was re-established in northern Tajikistan by 1 April 1918, when the Turkestan Soviet Socialist Republic was formed, and the Bukhara Emirate was overthrown by Soviet forces in 1920. In 1924 the Tajikistan Autonomous Soviet Socialist Republic was formed as part of the Uzbek Republic before Tajikistan was given full republican status within the Soviet Union in 1929. Stalin deprived the Tajiks of their cultural centres of Bukhara and Samarkand which remained in Uzbekistan, and during Soviet rule 1,000,000 Uzbeks and 800,000 Russians were settled in Tajikistan.

Tajikistan declared independence from the Soviet Union on 9 September 1991. Tajikistan's independence was recognized by the EC and USA in January and February 1992 respectively and it became a UN member on 2 March 1992. Tension between President Nabiev's mainly Communist government and supporters and the opposition Islamic and democratic groups led to demonstrations and armed clashes in the capital Dushanbe in early May 1992 and Nabiev was forced to form a coalition government with opposition groups on 11 May. Clashes erupted again in August 1992, leaving hundreds dead in Dushanbe. Nabiev was forced to resign on 7 September 1992 as he tried to flee the capital. The Islamic-Democratic alliance formed a government in September but civil war broke out as forces loyal to the former Communist regime rebelled against the new government. By early November pro-Communist forces controlled virtually all the country and laid siege to Dushanbe. The Islamic-Democratic forces were eventually driven out of Dushanbe by pro-Communist forces on 11 December after heavy fighting. The Supreme Soviet installed Imamoli Rakmanov as its Speaker and head of state. Fighting continued in the mountainous east and south of the country, where the Islamic-Democratic forces regrouped and were joined by thousands of refugees fleeing retaliation by the new government's forces.

By March 1993 the situation had stabilized, with the effective defeat of the Islamic-Democratic forces by government and Russian Army units. The remaining rebel forces and 60,000 refugees were driven across the border into

Afghanistan. Opposition parties were banned by the Supreme Court in June 1993 for trying to overthrow the constitutional system. Fighting restarted in July between Russian and Tajik government forces and the Afghan-based rebels.

HEAD OF STATE
Acting President, Chairman of the Supreme Soviet, Imomali Rakmonov, *elected by Supreme Soviet* 19 November 1992.

GOVERNMENT *as at August 1993*
Prime Minister, Abdumalik Abdulladjanov.
Ambassador to Moscow, Djamshed Karimov.
Deputy PMs, Rustam Makamov; Abdurakhman Muktaliev; Munavarsho Nazriev; Abdudjalil Samadov; Mamasaid Ubaidulloev.
Interior, Jakub Salimov.
Foreign Affairs, Rashid Alimov.
Culture, Ato Khodjayev.
Defence, Alexander Shishlamikov.
Education, Zair Vazirov.
Industry, Shavkat Umarov.
Economics and Finance, Ismail Davlatov.
Justice, Faizullo Abdulloyev.
Agriculture, Khaidarrizo Akbarov.
Foreign Economic Relations, Khaeev Izatullo.
Communications, Ibragim Usmanov.
Transport, Nazrullo Dustov.
Trade and Material Resources, Khakim Saliyev.
Press and Information, Bobokhon Makhmadov.
Health, Alohon Ahmedov.
Environmental Protection, Sadullo Hairulloev.
Land Improvement and Water Conservancy, Akhtambek Nurov.
Social Security, Abdusayer Jaburov.

BRITISH AMBASSADOR (resident in Moscow).

ECONOMY

Agriculture is the major sector of the economy, concentrating on cotton-growing and cattle-breeding. Tajikistan also has rich mineral deposits of lead, zinc and oil and is a source of uranium. Industry specializes in the production of clothing and textiles.

TANZANIA
Jamhuri ya Mwungano wa Tanzania

Tanzania comprises Tanganyika, on the mainland of east Africa between 1° and 11° 45′ S. lat. and 29° 20′ and 40° 38′ E. long., and the island of Zanzibar. The mainland part is bounded on the north by Kenya and Uganda; on the south-west by Lake Malawi, Malawi and Zambia; on the south by Mozambique; on the west by Rwanda, Burundi and Zaire; and on the east by the Indian Ocean. Tanzania has an area of 364,900 sq. miles (945,087 sq. km). The greater part of the country is occupied by the central African plateau from which rise, among others, Mt Kilimanjaro (19,340 ft), the highest point on the continent of Africa, and Mt Meru (14,974 ft). The Serengeti National Park covers an area of 6,000 sq. miles in the Arusha, Mwanza and Mara Regions.

Zanzibar was formerly ruled by the Sultan of Zanzibar and was a British Protectorate until 10 December 1963. It consists of the islands of Zanzibar, Pemba and Latham. The area is 2,461 sq. km, and the population (1992 estimate), is 687,634. ΨZanzibar (population, 133,000) is the chief town and seaport of the island.

POPULATION – The total population was (UN estimate 1991) 28,359,000. Africans form a large majority, with European, Asian, and other non-African minorities. The African population consists mostly of tribes of mixed Bantu race. Swahili is the national and official language. The use of English is widespread both for educational and government purposes.

CAPITAL – Dodoma (population 88,474, 1988 estimate). The economic and administrative centre is ΨDar es Salaam (population 1,096,000, 1985 estimate). Other towns (1985 population) are ΨTanga (172,000), Mwanza (252,000), Mbeya (194,000).
CURRENCY – Tanzanian shilling of 100 cents.
FLAG – Green (above) and blue; divided by diagonal black stripe bordered by gold, running from bottom (next staff) to top (in fly).
NATIONAL ANTHEM – Mungu Ibariki Afrika (God Bless Africa).
NATIONAL DAY – 26 April (Union Day).

GOVERNMENT

Tanganyika became an independent state and a member of the British Commonwealth on 9 December 1961, and a republic within the Commonwealth on 9 December 1962. On 10 December 1963, Zanzibar became an independent state within the Commonwealth and on 26 April 1964, Tanganyika united with Zanzibar to form the United Republic of Tanzania.

There are a President and two Vice-Presidents, one the President of Zanzibar and the other the Prime Minister. If the President comes from Zanzibar the Prime Minister will be the First Vice-President and must come from Tanganyika. If the President comes from Tanganyika the President of Zanzibar will be the First Vice-President. The President may only serve two terms.

The National Assembly contains 255 members, of whom 130 are elected from mainland constituencies and 50 from Zanzibar, 25 are ex-officio, 15 nominated and 35 indirectly elected. The Speaker may either be elected from among the members or be an additional member. Constituency members are elected by popular vote at a general election held at a maximum of five-yearly intervals.

Although Zanzibar has its own President, government and House of Representatives, Tanganyika is governed by the government of the Union. Overall policy has been decided by the Chama Cha Mapinduzi (CCM), which was the sole party until 1992, when President Mwinyi and the CCM leadership agreed to amend the constitution to allow multi-party politics. In June 1992 President Mwinyi endorsed a bill legalizing multi-party politics, with the stipulation that all parties must be active in both the mainland and in Zanzibar and that parties must not be formed on tribal or racial grounds.

President of the United Republic, HE Hon. Ali Hassan Mwinyi, *elected* 1985; *re-elected* 28 October 1990.
First Vice-President of the United Republic and Prime Minister, Hon. John Malecela.
Second Vice-President of the United Republic and President of Zanzibar, HE Dr Salmin Amour.

CABINET *as at August 1993*
The President (also Minister of Defence),
The First Vice-President and Prime Minister,
The Second Vice-President,
Deputy Prime Minister and Home Affairs, Hon. Augustine Mrema.

Foreign Affairs and International Co-operation, Hon. Joseph Rwegasira.
Agriculture, Livestock and Co-operatives, Hon. Jackson Makweta.
Communications and Transport, Hon. Prof. Phillemon Sarungi.
Works, Hon. Nalaila Kiula.
Education and Culture, Hon. Charles Kabeho.
Energy, Minerals and Water, Hon. Jakaya Kikwete.
Finance, Hon. Prof. Kighoma Malina.
Health, Hon. Amran Mayagila.
Industry and Trade, Hon. Cleopa D. Msuya.
Information and Broadcasting, Hon. Dr William Shija.
Labour and Youth, Hon. Ahmed Hassan.
Community Development, Women and Children, Hon. Anna Makinda.
Tourism, Natural Resources, Environment, Hon. Marcel Komanya.
Science, Technology and Higher Education, Hon. Benjamin Mkapa.
Minister without Portfolio, Hon. K. Ngombale Mwiru.

HIGH COMMISSION FOR THE UNITED REPUBLIC OF TANZANIA
43 Hertford Street, London WIY 7TF
Tel 071-499 8951/2/3/4
High Commissioner, His Excellency Ali S. Mchumo (1991).

BRITISH HIGH COMMISSION
Hifadhi House, Samora Avenue (PO Box 9200), Dar es Salaam
Tel: Dar es Salaam 29601-5

High Commissioner, His Excellency Roger Westbrook (1992).

BRITISH COUNCIL REPRESENTATIVE, Robert Sykes, Ohio Samora Avenue (PO Box 9100), Dar es Salaam.

EDUCATION

The school system is administered in Swahili but the Government is making efforts to improve English standards for the purposes of secondary and higher education. All Tanzanian secondary schools are expected to include practical subjects in the basic course. For higher education Tanzanian students go to the University of Dar es Salaam, Sokoine University of Agriculture in Morogoro, other East African universities, or to universities and colleges outside East Africa.

COMMUNICATIONS

The main ports are Dar es Salaam, Tanga, Mtwara, Zanzibar, Mkoani and Wete, in addition to Mwanza, Musoma and Bukoba on Lake Victoria and Kigoma on Lake Tanganyika. Coastal shipping services connect the mainland to Zanzibar, and lake services are operated on Lake Tanganyika and Lake Malawi with neighbouring countries. The principal international airports are Dar es Salaam and Kilimanjaro. Other airports include Zanzibar, Arusha, Mwanza and Tanga. There are two railway systems; one connecting Dar es Salaam to Zambia, and the second having two main lines running from Dar es Salaam, one to northern Tanzania and Kenya and the other to Lake Tanganyika and Victoria.

ECONOMY

The economy is based mainly on the production and export of primary produce and the growing of foodstuffs for local consumption. The islands of Zanzibar and Pemba produce a large part of the world's supply of cloves and clove oil; and coconuts, coconut oil and copra are also produced. The mainland's chief export crops are coffee, cotton, sisal, tea, tobacco, cashew nuts and diamonds. The most important minerals are diamonds. Hides and skins are another valuable export. Industry is largely concerned with the processing of raw material for either export or local consumption. There are also secondary manufacturing industries, including factories for the manufacture of leather and rubber footwear, knitwear, razor blades, cigarettes and textiles, and a wheat flour mill.

TRADE WITH UK	1991	1992
Imports from UK	£72,822,000	£78,545,000
Exports to UK	20,938,000	21,140,000

THAILAND
Prathes Thai

Thailand, formerly known as Siam, has an area of 198,457 sq. miles (514,000 sq. km), with a population (1991 UN estimate) of 56,923,000. Thailand has a common boundary with Malaysia in the south, is bounded on the west by Myanmar (Burma) and on the north-east and east by Laos and Cambodia. Thailand is divided geographically into four: the centre is a plain; to the north-east there is a plateau area and to the north-west mountains. The south of Thailand consists of a narrow mountainous peninsula. The principal rivers are the Chao Phraya in the central plains, and the Mekong on the northern and north-eastern borders.
LANGUAGE – Thai is basically a monosyllabic, tonal language, a branch of the Indo-Chinese linguistic family, but its vocabulary has been strongly influenced by Sanskrit and Pali. It is written in an alphabetic script derived from ancient Indian scripts.
RELIGION – The principal religion is Buddhism (94.37 per cent), with 3.95 per cent Muslims, 0.53 per cent Christians and 1.15 per cent other religions.

CAPITAL – ΨBangkok, at the mouth of the River Chao Phraya, population (1990) 5,876,000. Other centres are Chiang Mai, Phitsanuloke, Chon Buri, Korat, Khon Kaen, Surat Thani, Hat Yai and ΨPhuket.
CURRENCY – Baht of 100 satang.
FLAG – Five horizontal bands, red, white, dark blue, white, red (the blue band twice the width of the others).
NATIONAL ANTHEM – Plong Chart.
NATIONAL DAY – 5 December (The King's Birthday).

GOVERNMENT

Thailand became a constitutional monarchy in 1932. The 1978 constitution provides for a National Assembly consisting of a 261-member Senate appointed by the monarch and a 347-member House of Representatives elected by universal adult suffrage for a term of four years. Following a military coup in February 1991, a new constitution was approved in December 1991 under which the military would appoint the members of an expanded 270-member Senate and so enshrine its place in Thai politics. Parties aligned with the military won the general election on 22 March 1992, but opposition to the military-controlled government grew and mass demonstrations held in Bangkok from 17 to 20 May eventually, with the help of the King, forced the government from power. Many demonstrators were killed by soldiers before the government fell, and this led to a curbing of military power and the sacking of military chiefs by the interim government. Parliamentary elections were held on

13 September 1992 which resulted in a majority for 'democratic parties', i.e. those not allied with the military. Chuan Leekpai became Prime Minister at the head of a five-party governing coalition which held 207 of the 360 House of Representatives seats on 29 September 1992. The new government is committed to the reduction of the political power of the military.

HEAD OF STATE

King, HM Bhumibol Adulyadej, *born* 1927; *succeeded his brother*, 9 June 1946; *married* Princess Sirikit Kitiyakara, 28 April 1950; *crowned* 5 May 1950; and has *issue*, Princess Ubolratana, *born* 6 April 1951; Crown Prince Vajiralongkorn, *born* 28 July 1952; Princess Sirindhorn, *born* 2 April 1955; Princess Chulabhorn *born* 4 July 1957.

GOVERNMENT *as at August 1993*

Prime Minister, Chuan Leekpai.
Deputy PMs, Banyat Banthatthan; Amnuai Wirawan; Bunchu Rotchanasathian; Suphachai Phanitchaphak.
Ministers in the Prime Minister's Office, Theotphong Chaiyanan; Sawit Phothiwihok; Sarasak Thiamprasoet; Col. Chinnawut Surthonsina.
Defence, Gen. Wichit Sukmak.
Finance, Tharin Nimmanhemin.
Foreign Affairs, Sqn. Ldr. Prasong Sonsiri.
Agriculture and Co-operatives, Niphon Phromphan.
Communications, Col. Winai Somphong.
Commerce, Uthai Phimchaichon.
Interior, Gen. Chaovalit Yongchaigt.
Justice, Suwit Khunkitti.
Science, Technology and Environment, Phisan Munlasatsathan.
Education, Samphan Thongsamak.
Public Health, Buntham Khaewatthana.
Industry, Maj.-Gen. Saran Khachonprasat.
State University Bureau, Suthep Attakon.

ROYAL THAI EMBASSY
29–30 Queen's Gate, London SW7 5JB
Tel 071-589 2944/0173

Ambassador Extraordinary and Plenipotentiary, His Excellency Tongchan Jotikasthira (1991).
Minister and Deputy Head of Mission, V. Snidvongs.
Defence Attaché, Capt. S, Kolasastraseni.
Minister Counsellor, P. Phonthirasuwan (*Commercial*).

BRITISH EMBASSY
Wireless Road, Bangkok 10330
Tel: Bangkok 253 0191

Ambassador Extraordinary and Plenipotentiary, His Excellency Charles C. Adams, CMG (1992)
Deputy Ambassador and Counsellor, R. T. Fell.
Defence Attaché, Col. J. L. Longman.
First Secretary (Commercial), D. J. Hawkes, MBE.
Consul, J. C. Sharpe.
There is a British Consulate at *Chang Mai*.

BRITISH COUNCIL REPRESENTATIVE, Dr P. Moss, 428 Rama 1 Road, Siam Square Soi 2, Pathumwan, Bangkok 10330.
BRITISH CHAMBER OF COMMERCE, BP Building 18th Floor, Unit 1810, 54 Asoke Road (Sukhumvit 21) Bangkok 10110

DEFENCE

Total active armed forces number some 283,000 personnel, with conscription terms of two years. Reserves number a further 500,000 personnel. The Army numbers 190,000

(80,000 conscripts) with 200 main battle tanks, 510 light tanks, 940 armoured personnel carriers, 409 artillery pieces and four attack helicopters. The Navy has 50,000 personnel, with eight frigates, 65 patrol and coastal combatants, 26 combat aircraft, eight armed helicopters and a marine division of seven regiments. The Air Force has 43,000 personnel, with 166 combat aircraft. Six paramilitary forces, including three police forces, have a total strength of 141,700 personnel.

EDUCATION

Primary education is compulsory and free, and secondary education in government schools is free. Private universities and colleges are playing an increasing role in higher education. Out of 43 universities and other similar higher institutes of learning, 21 are private.

ECONOMY

The agricultural sector provides just under half the national income and employs 67.5 per cent of the labour force. Rice remains the most important crop, accounting for 60 per cent of the area planted. The other main crops are sugar, maize, rubber, tobacco, kenaf and jute. In recent years the production of livestock and poultry, especially pigs and chickens for export, has gained importance. There is a large fishing industry with more than 20,000 vessels registered. Fish farming is popular in many inland areas. A ban on hardwood export has resulted in the decline of the forestry industry.

The discovery of onshore oil and offshore gas in the late 1970s ushered in a new economic era. Crude oil production began in 1983. The predicted surplus of natural gas has led the Government to designate an area on the east coast as the future centre of the petrochemical industry. Another energy resource is lignite which is found mainly in the north and is being used increasingly for electricity production. Mineral resources are mainly tin, tungsten, lead, antimony and iron. Among these tin is the most important. In addition, a zinc refinery was opened in 1984.

Industry is divided into two main categories, service and manufacturing. Since 1982 tourism has replaced rice as the country's top foreign exchange earner. The banking system is large and contributes much to the economy, especially employment.

Since 1960 the government has actively promoted industrial investments by means of tax relief and other incentives to local and foreign investors; in 1985, 74.6 per cent of this investment was in Thai projects. Initially industries established under this scheme were import-substituting but the emphasis has shifted now to export-oriented industries. Manufacturing now accounts for about 21.8 per cent of the national income. Crops contribute 12.1 per cent of GDP.

TRADE

Thailand's main exports are rice, tapioca and tapioca products, garments, rubber, integrated circuit boards, precious stones, pearls and other ornaments, maize, canned sea food, fabrics, sugar and tin. Main imports are crude oil, chemicals and pharmaceuticals, electrical and non-electrical machinery and spare parts, industrial machinery, iron and steel, diesel oil and other fuel oil, vehicle and transport equipment.

	1989	1990
Total imports	Bhat 650.7bn	Bhat 829.0bn
Total exports	509.9bn	590.0bn

Trade with UK	1991	1992
Imports from UK	£463,449,000	£476,368,000
Exports to UK	625,374,000	641,886,000

COMMUNICATIONS

The importance of rivers and canals as the traditional mode of transportation has been replaced by roads. The existing road network, totalling 44,409 kilometres in 1989, reaches all parts of the country. Most of the smaller towns and bigger villages are now served by paved roads. Navigable waterways have a length of about 1,100 km in the dry season and 1,600 km in the wet season. About 4,450 km of state-owned railways were open to traffic in 1989. Main lines run from Bangkok to the Cambodian border, the ferry terminal on the River Mekong opposite Vientiane, Chiang Mai and to Hat Yai, whence lines run down both sides of the Malay peninsula to Singapore. A new line to Sattahip on the east coast is being constructed. Bangkok is the international airport, though airports at Chiang Mai, Phuket and Hat Yai also receive international flights. Most major provincial towns have airports. The THAI airline is state-owned.

There are two important ports in the country. Bangkok, which is a river port, can serve vessels up to 27 ft draught. The deep-sea port at Sattahip caters for larger vessels. Phuket and Songkhla deep water ports have already been completed and are the first to be managed privately under a ten-year concession. Construction of Laem Chabang deep water port started in 1988.

TOGO
République Togolaise

Togo is situated in West Africa between 0° and 2° W. and 6° and 11° N., with a coastline 35 miles long on the Gulf of Guinea. Togo extends northwards inland for 350 miles. It is flanked on the west by Ghana, on the north by Burkina and in the east by Benin. It has an area of 21,925 sq. miles (56,785 sq. km), and a population (UN estimate 1991) of 3,643,000, including people of several African races. The official language is French; Ewe is spoken by about 47 per cent.

CAPITAL – Ψ Lomé, population (1983) 366,476.
CURRENCY – Franc CFA of 100 centimes.
FLAG – Five alternating green and yellow horizontal stripes; a quarter in red at top next staff bearing a white star.
NATIONAL DAY – 13 January (National Liberation Day).

GOVERNMENT

The first President of Togo, Sylvanus Olympio, was assassinated in 1963. His successor was overthrown by an army coup d'état in January 1967 and the army commander Lt.-Col. (later General) Eyadéma named himself President. President Eyadéma came under increasing popular pressure to introduce reforms in 1990 and in October the Rassemblement du peuple togolais (RPT), the sole legal party, approved plans for a new constitutional conference after pro-democracy riots. Bloody riots again broke out in March 1991 in protest at the slow pace of reform, and in April the government was forced to concede a political amnesty, the introduction of a multi-party constitution and a national conference. In August 1991 the national conference stripped President Eyadéma of all powers, banned the RPT and elected Kokou Koffigoh as Prime Minister of an interim government. The national conference set a date of 9 February 1992 for a referendum on a new constitution.

However, from the second half of 1991 onwards the political situation has become progressively more unstable. Troops loyal to President Eyadéma three times attempted to overthrow Koffigoh and his government (October, November and December 1991) but were frustrated by pro-democracy supporters. Continued political violence in 1992 between the army and pro-democracy groups and among rival opposition parties forced the postponement of the referendum. In August President Eyadéma regained the position of head of state and gained the ability to stand in presidential elections in an agreement with Koffigoh. In September a new multi-party constitution was agreed in a national referendum. However, in November Eyadéma failed to keep to his part of the agreement with Koffigoh when he ordered the Army to crush civil unrest and a general strike against his rule. In February 1993, as political violence continued, Koffigoh and Eyadéma agreed on the formation of a crisis government, which the national conference and the Collective Democratic Opposition-2 (COD-2) declared illegal. At the time of going to press the situation was unclear. President Eyadéma won a presidential election in August that was boycotted by opposition parties and was declared rigged by international monitors. Eyadéma was under intense French and US pressure to resign but has so far refused to do so.

HEAD OF STATE
President, Gen. Gnassingbé Eyadéma, *assumed office*, 14 April 1967; *re-elected* 1986, August 1993.

CRISIS GOVERNMENT *as at August 1993*

Prime Minister, Defence, Joseph Kokou Koffigoh.
Economy and Finance, Doh Fiagnon.
Foreign Affairs and Co-operation, Outtara Natachaba.
Planning and Territorial Development, Yandjia Yentchabre.
Equipment and Mines, Yao Tete Atikpo.
Justice, Aregba Polo.
Territorial Administration and Security, Comberi Agbodjian.
Communications and Culture, Komlan Agbeka.
Tourism, Rural Development and Environment, Kossi Monindji.
Social Welfare and National Solidarity, Were Gazoro.
Public Health, Michel Kudzu.
National Defence, Inoussa Bouraima.
Industry and State Companies, Fayadowa Boukpessi.
Youth, Sport and Leisure, Essohanam, Lawani.
National Education and Scientific Research, Bamouni Baba.
Commerce and Transport, Poulpou Defanti.
Employment, Labour and Civil Service, Garba Dovi.

EMBASSY OF TOGO – The Embassy of Togo closed in September 1991

BRITISH AMBASSADOR (resident in Accra, Ghana). There is a Consulate (BP 20050) and a Commercial Office (BP 80607) in Lomé.

ECONOMY

Although the economy of Togo remains largely agricultural, exports of phosphates have superseded agricultural products as the main source of export earnings. Other exports include palm kernels, copra and manioc. The production of phosphates entirely for export was taken over completely by the government in February 1974.

TRADE WITH UK	1991	1992
Imports from UK	£20,932,000	£7,658,000
Exports to UK	1,820,000	4,066,000

TONGA
Kingdom of Tonga

Tonga, or the Friendly Islands, comprises a group of islands situated in the Southern Pacific some 450 miles east-south-east of Fiji, with an area of 270 sq. miles (699 sq. km), and population (1991 UN estimate) of 94,000. The largest island, Tongatapu, was discovered by Tasman in 1643. Most of the islands are of coral formation, but some are volcanic (Tofua, Kao and Niuafoou or 'Tin Can' Island). The limits of the group are between 15° and 23° 30′ S., and 173° and 177° W.

CAPITAL – ΨNuku'alofa (population estimate 30,000), on Tongatapu.
CURRENCY – Pa'anga (T$) of 100 seniti.
FLAG – Red with a white canton containing a couped red cross.
NATIONAL ANTHEM – E, 'Otua Mafimafi (Oh, Almighty God Above).
NATIONAL DAY – 4 June (Independence Day).

GOVERNMENT

The Kingdom of Tonga is an independent constitutional monarchy within the Commonwealth. Prior to 4 June 1970 it had been a British-protected state for 70 years. The constitution provides for a government consisting of the Sovereign, an appointed privy council which functions as a cabinet, a legislative assembly and a judiciary. The 30-member legislative assembly comprises the King, the 11-member-privy council, nine hereditary nobles elected by their peers, and nine popularly elected representatives who hold office for three years. The most recent election took place on 4 February 1993 and six of the nine seats were won by candidates wishing to reduce the power of the King and nobles and to strengthen democracy.

HEAD OF STATE
King of Tonga, HM King Taufa'ahau Tupou IV, GCMG, GCVO, KBE, *acceded* 16 December 1965.
Heir, HRH Crown Prince Tupouto'a.

CABINET *as at August 1993*
Prime Minister, Minister of Agriculture, Fisheries, Forests, and Marine, Baron Vaea of Houma.
Deputy Prime Minister, Minister of Education, Works and Civil Aviation, Hon. Dr S. Langi Kavaliku.
Labour, Commerce and Industry, Hon. Tutoatasi Fakafanva.
Police, Prisons and Fire Services, Hon. George 'Akau'ola.
Health, Hon. Dr S. Tapa.
Foreign Affairs and Defence, HRH Crown Prince Tupouto'a.
Finance, Hon. J. Cecil Cocker.
Attorney-General, Justice, Hon. Tevita P. Tupou.
Minister without Portfolio, Hon. Ma'afu Tuku'i'aulahi.
Minister of Lands, Survey, and Natural Resources, Hon. Dr S. Ma'afu Tupou.
Governor of Ha'apai, Hon. Fakafanua.
Governor of Vava'u, Hon. Tu'i'afitu.

TONGA HIGH COMMISSION
36 Molyneux Street, London WIH 6AB
Tel 071-724 5828

High Commissioner, His Excellency Sione Kité (1992).

BRITISH HIGH COMMISSION
PO Box 56, Nuku'alofa
Tel: Nuku'alofa 21020

High Commissioner, His Excellency William Lawson Cordiner (1990).

ECONOMY

The economy is primarily agricultural; the main crops are coconuts, bananas, vanilla, yams, taro, cassava, groundnuts, squash pumpkins and other fruits. Fish is an important staple food though recent shortfalls have led to canned fish being imported. Industry is based on the processing of agricultural produce, and the manufacture of foodstuffs, clothing and sports equipment.

TRADE
The principal exports are copra, other coconut products, tropical root crops, bananas, knitwear, leather goods and fibreglass boats.

	1989
Total imports	T$68,334,194
Total exports	11,517,597

Trade with UK	1991	1992
Imports from UK	£944,000	£482,000
Exports to UK	20,000	294,000

TRINIDAD AND TOBAGO
The Republic of Trinidad and Tobago

Trinidad, the most southerly of the West Indian islands, lies seven miles off the north coast of Venezuela. The island is situated between 10° 2′ and 11° 12′ N. latitude and 60° 30′ and 61° 56′ W. longitude, and is about 50 miles in length by 37 miles in width, with an area of 1,864 sq. miles (4,827 sq. km). Two mountain systems, the Northern and Southern Ranges, stretch across almost its entire width and a third, the Central Range, lies diagonally across its middle portion; otherwise the island is mostly flat.

Tobago lies between 11° 9′ and 11° 21′ N. latitude and between 60° 30′ and 60° 50′ W. longitude, 19 miles north-east of Trinidad. The island is 32 miles long at its widest point, and 11 wide, and has an area of 116 sq. miles (300 sq. km). It is a popular tourist resort. It was ceded to the British Crown in 1814 and amalgamated with Trinidad in 1888.

Corozal Point and Icacos Point, the north-west and south-west extremities of Trinidad, enclose the Gulf of Paria. West of Corozal Point lie several islands, of which Chacachacare, Huevos, Monos and Gaspar Grande are the most important.

The climate is tropical with temperatures averaging 82° F (27.8° C) by day and 74° F (23.3° C) by night, and a rainfall averaging 82 inches a year. There is a dry season from January to May, and a wet season from June to December broken by a short dry season (the *Petite Careme*) in September and October.

POPULATION – The population (UN estimate 1991) was 1,253,000; Tobago's population is about 45,000.

CAPITAL – ΨPort of Spain (population, 1985, 59,649) is the administrative centre of the islands. San Fernando (population 34,300) is emerging as the industrial centre of Trinidad. The main town of Tobago is ΨScarborough.
CURRENCY – Trinidad and Tobago dollar (TT$) of 100 cents.
FLAG – Black diagonal stripe bordered with white stripes, running from top by staff, all on a red field.
NATIONAL DAYS – 31 August (Independence Day); 24 September (Republic Day).

GOVERNMENT

Trinidad was discovered by Columbus in 1498, was colonized in 1532 by the Spaniards, capitulated to the British under Abercromby in 1797, and was ceded to Britain under the Treaty of Amiens 1802. Tobago was discovered by Columbus in 1498. Dutch colonists arrived in 1632; Tobago subsequently changed hands numerous times until it was ceded to the

British Crown by France in 1814 and amalgamated with Trinidad in 1888.

The Territory of Trinidad and Tobago became an independent state and a member of the British Commonwealth on 31 August 1962, and a republic in 1976. The President is elected for five years by all members of the Senate and the House of Representatives. The House of Representatives has 36 members, elected by universal adult suffrage, and the Senate has 31, of whom 16 are appointed on the advice of the Prime Minister, six on the advice of the Leader of the Opposition and nine at the discretion of the President. Legislation was passed in September 1980 which afforded Tobago a degree of self-administration through the 12-member Tobago House of Assembly.

HEAD OF STATE
President, His Excellency Noor Mohammed Hassanali.

CABINET *as at August 1993*
Prime Minister, Hon. Patrick Manning.
Finance, Hon. Wendell Mottley.
Attorney-General, Hon. Keith Sobion.
Energy and Energy Industries, Hon. Barry Barnes.
Trade, Industry and Tourism, Hon. Brian Kuei Tung.
National Security, Hon. Russel Huggins.
Local Government, Hon. Kenneth Valley.
Foreign Affairs, Hon. Ralph Maraj.
Sport and Youth Affairs, Hon. Jean Pierre.
Consumer Affairs and Social Services, Hon. Linda Baboolal.
Works and Transport, Hon. Colm Imbert.
Education, Hon. Augustus Ramrekersingh.
Health, Hon. John Eckstein.
Public Utilities, Hon. Morris Marshall.
Planning and Development, Hon. Lenny Saith.
Labour and Co-operatives, Hon. Kenneth Collis.
Community Development, Culture and Women's Affairs, Hon. Joan Yuille-Williams.
Agriculture, Lands and Marine Resources, Hon. Dr Keith Rowley.
Housing and Settlements, Hon. Dr Vincent Lasse.

HIGH COMMISSION OF THE REPUBLIC OF TRINIDAD AND TOBAGO
42 Belgrave Square, London SW1X 8NT
Tel 071-245 9351

High Commissioner, new appointment awaited.

BRITISH HIGH COMMISSION
Furness House, 90 Independence Square, (PO Box 778)
Port of Spain
Tel: Port of Spain 62528616

High Commissioner, His Excellency B. Smith, OBE.

EDUCATION

The education system provides for free education at all state-owned and government-assisted denominational schools and certain faculties at the University of the West Indies. In addition there are various private teaching establishments. Attendance is compulsory for children aged six to 12 years, after which attendance at free secondary schools is determined by success in the common entrance examination at 11 years. There are three technical institutes, two teachers' training colleges, and one of the three branches of the University of the West Indies is located in Trinidad. A medical teaching complex at Mt Hope operates in collaboration with the University of the West Indies.

COMMUNICATIONS

There are some 6,436 km of all-weather roads in Trinidad and Tobago. The only general cargo port is Port of Spain but there are specialized port facilities elsewhere for crude oil, refinery products, sugar, bauxite and cement. Regular shipping services call and many inter-island craft use the port. Another rapidly growing port is at Port Lisas where new industries powered by local natural gas are located. International scheduled airlines, including the national airline, Trinidad and Tobago Airways (BWIA) Corporation, use Piarco International Airport, Port of Spain. The airline also flies between Piarco and Crown Point Airport in Tobago.

Three commercial broadcasting stations and one commercial television station operate in Trinidad and Tobago. The internal telephone system and the external telephone and telegraph connections are operated by part-state-owned companies.

ECONOMY

Trinidad and Tobago's main source of revenue is from oil. Production of domestic crude was 55 million barrels in 1990. Trinidad has large reserves of natural gas, and reserves are estimated to be in the region of 100 years at the current rates of production. An integrated steel plant, an anhydrous ammonia plant and a methanol plant have been constructed at Point Lisas. An industrial complex is developing around San Fernando.

Fertilizers, tyres, clothing, soap, furniture and foodstuffs are manufactured locally while motor vehicles, radios, TV sets, and electro-domestic equipment are assembled from parts, mainly from Japan.

FINANCE	1989	1990
Revenue	TT$4,972.5m	TT$5,645.2m
Expenditure	5,776.0m	5,816.2m
TRADE	1991	1992
Imports	TT$7,084.8m	TT$6,081.1m
Exports	8,436.4m	7,942.9m
Trade with UK	1991	1992
Imports from UK	£62,491,000	£59,083,000
Exports to UK	41,664,000	35,187,000

TUNISIA
Al-Djoumhouria Attunusia

Tunisia lies between Algeria and Libya and extends southwards to the Sahara Desert, with a total area of 164,150 sq. km, and a population (UN estimate 1991) of 8,362,000.

CAPITAL – Ψ Tunis had a population (1984) of 1,394,749. The ruins of ancient Carthage lie a few miles from the city. Other towns of importance are: Ψ Sfax (577,992); Ψ Sousse (322,491); Ψ Bizerta (394,670); Kairouan; Gabes; Menzel Bourguiba.
CURRENCY – Tunisian dinar of 1,000 millimes.
FLAG – Red with a white disc containing a red crescent and star.
NATIONAL ANTHEM – Himat Al Hima.
NATIONAL DAY – 20 March.

GOVERNMENT

A French Protectorate from 1881 to 1956, Tunisia became an independent sovereign state on 20 March 1956. On 25 July 1957 the Constituent Assembly abolished the monarchy and elected M. Bourguiba President of the Republic. In March 1975 the National Assembly proclaimed M. Bourguiba as President for life.

On 7 November 1987 M. Bourguiba was deposed and succeeded by President Zine el-Abidine Ben Ali. Presidential and legislative elections were held in April 1989. The RCD (Rassemblement Constitutionnel Democratique) won all 141 seats in the National Assembly. Seven political parties contested the election. President Ben Ali was re-elected with 99 per cent of the vote. President Ben Ali announced in December 1992 that presidential and legislative elections will be held in March 1994.

The country is divided into 23 regions (gouvernorats) each administered by a governor.

HEAD OF STATE
President, Zine el-Abidine Ben Ali, took office 7 November 1987, re-elected 2 April 1989.

CABINET as at August 1993
Prime Minister, Hamed Karoui.
Minister of State, Interior, Abdallah Kallel.
Justice, Sadok Chaabane.
Director of Presidential Office, Mohamed el Jeri.
Foreign Affairs, Habib ben Yahia.
Defence, Abdelaziz Ben Dhia.
Economy, Sadok Rabah.
Finance, Nouri Zorgati.
Planning and Regional Development, Mustapha Nabli.
International Co-operation and Development, Mohammed Ghannouchi.
Agriculture, Mouldi Zouaoui.
Public Estates, Mustapha Bouaziz.
Equipment and Housing, Charfeddine Guellouz.
Transport, Tahar Haj Ali.
Tourism and Handicrafts, Mohamed Jegham.
Communications, Habib Lazreg.
Education and Science, Mohamed Charfi.
Culture, Mongi Bousnina.
Health, Hedi Henni.
Social Affairs, Mohamed Fadhel Khelil.
Environment, Town and Country Planning, Mohamed Mehdi Melika.
Professional Training and Employment, Moncer Rouissi.
Youth and Childhood Welfare, Mohamed Saad.
Secretary-General of the Government, Ridha Grira.
Religious Affairs, Ali Chebbi.

TUNISIAN EMBASSY
29 Prince's Gate, London sw7 1QG
Tel 071-584 8117

Ambassador Extraordinary and Plenipotentiary, His Excellency Mohamed Lessir (1992).

BRITISH EMBASSY
5 Place de la Victoire, Tunis 1015 RP
Tel: Tunis 1341444

Ambassador Extraordinary and Plenipotentiary and Consul-General, His Excellency Michael Tait, CMG, LVO (1992).
First Secretary, A. Holmes, MBE (Deputy Head of Mission).
There is a Consulate at Sfax.

BRITISH COUNCIL REPRESENTATIVE, C. Stevenson (Cultural Attaché).

ECONOMY

The valleys of the northern region support large flocks and herds and contain rich agricultural areas in which wheat, barley, and oats are grown. Vines and olives are extensively cultivated. Some oil has been discovered and crude oil production in 1989 was 4.8 million tons. Gas has also been discovered off the east coast but exploitation is not viable at present. Tourists numbered almost 3 million in 1989 and tourism is the main foreign exchange earner.

TRADE

The chief exports are crude oil, phosphates, olive oil, finished textiles, and fruit. The chief imports are machinery and equipment, foodstuffs, petroleum products, and textiles. France remains the main trading partner.

Tunisia became an associate member of the EC early in 1969 and signed a new agreement with the EC in 1976.

	1988	1989
Total Imports	TD3,167,000	TD4,150,000
Total Exports	2,055,000	2,762,000

	1991	1992
Trade with UK		
Imports from UK	£43,651,000	£50,685,000
Exports to UK	25,613,000	48,445,000

TURKEY
Türkiye Cumhuriyeti

Turkey extends from Edirne to Transcaucasia and Iran, and from the Black Sea to the Mediterranean, Syria and Iraq. The area is 814,578 square km, of which 790,200 square km is in Asia and 24,378 is in Europe. Turkey in Europe consists of Eastern Thrace, including the cities of Istanbul and Edirne, and is separated from Asia by the Bosporus at Istanbul and by the Dardanelles (about 40 miles in length with a width varying from one to four miles), the political neighbours being Greece and Bulgaria on the west.   Turkey in Asia comprises the whole of Asia Minor or Anatolia and extends from the Aegean Sea to the western boundaries of Georgia, Armenia and Iran, and from the Black Sea to the Mediterranean and the northern boundaries of Syria and Iraq.

POPULATION – Population at the 1990 Census was 56,473,035. The 1991 UN estimate is 60,777,000.

RELIGION – Islam ceased to be the state religion in 1928 but 98.99 per cent of the population are Muslim. The main religious minorities, which are concentrated in Istanbul and on the Syrian frontier, are Greek Orthodox, Armenian, Syriani Christian, and Jewish.

CAPITAL – Ankara (Angora), an inland town of Asia Minor, population (1990) 3,236,626. Ankara (or Ancyra) was the capital of the Roman Province of Galatia Prima, and a marble temple (now in ruins), dedicated to Augustus, contains the Monumentum (Marmor) Ancyranum, inscribed with a record of the reign of Augustus Caesar. ΨIstanbul (7,309,190), the former capital, was the Roman city of Byzantium. It was selected by Constantine the Great as the capital of the Roman Empire about AD 328 and renamed Constantinople. Istanbul contains the celebrated church of St Sophia, which, after becoming a mosque, was made a museum in 1934. It also contains Topkapi, former Palace of the Ottoman Sultans, which is also a museum. Other cities are ΨIzmir (2,649,770); Adana (1,934,907); Bursa (1,603,137); Gaziantep (1,140,549); and Konya (1,750,303).

CURRENCY – Turkish lira (TL) of 100 kurus.
FLAG – Red, with white crescent and star.
NATIONAL ANTHEM – Istiklal Marşi (The Independence March).
NATIONAL DAY – 29 October (Republic Day).

GOVERNMENT

On 29 October 1923 the National Assembly declared Turkey a republic and elected Gazi Mustafa Kemal (later known as Kemal Ataturk) President. In 1945 a multi-party system was introduced but in 1960 the government was overthrown by the Turkish armed forces. A new constitution was adopted in July 1961 and, after a general election, a civilian government took office. Civilian governments remained in power until September 1980 when mounting problems with the economy and terrorism led to a military takeover.

A new constitution, extending the powers of the President, was approved in 1982. It provided for the separation of powers between the legislature, executive and judiciary, and the holding of free elections to the unicameral Grand National Assembly, which now has 450 members elected every five years. Following the general election in November 1983 the military leadership handed over power to a newly elected civilian government. The last election was held in October 1991. Süleyman Demirel, leader of the True Path Party, formed a coalition government with the Social Democrat Populist Party. President Özal died on 17 April 1993 leading to the election by parliament of Süleyman Demirel as President. Tansu Çiller was elected party chairman by the True Path Party and formed a government which was sworn in on 25 June by President Demirel, when Çiller became the first woman Turkish Prime Minister.

Turkey is divided for administrative purposes into 73 *il* with subdivisions into *ilçe* and *nahiye*. Each *il* has a governor (*vali*) and elective council.

SECESSION

Since 1984 Turkey has been fighting armed guerillas of the Marxist Kurdish Workers Party (PKK) in the south-east of the country where Kurds are the majority population. The PKK has an estimated strength of some 10,000 operating from bases in Lebanon and Syria, with the latter giving tacit support and finance. The south-east of the country remains under martial law and about 6,000 have died in the nine years of warfare. The majority of the area's population does not appear to support the PKK in its fight for an independent Kurdish state.

HEAD OF STATE

President, Süleyman Demirel, *elected by parliament for a seven-year term*, 16 May 1993.

GOVERNMENT *as at August 1993*

Prime Minister, Prof. Tansu Çiller (DYP).
Deputy Prime Minister, Prof. Erdal İnönü (SHP).
Ministers of State, Necmettin Cevheri; Yildirim Aktuna; Mehmet Gölhan; Bekir Sami Dace; Günes Müftüoğlu; Nafiz Kurt; Cemil Erhan; Mustafa Çiloğlu; Ahmet Sanal; Şükrü Erdem (DYP); Ibrahim Tez; Türkan Akyol; Mehmet Kahraman; Erman Şahin (SHP).
Justice, Mehmet Seyfi Oktay (SHP).
National Defence, Nevzat Ayaz (DYP).
Interior, Mehmet Gazioğlu (DYP).
Foreign Minister, Hikmet Çetin (SHP).
Finance and Customs, Ismet Atilla (DYP).
Education, Nahit Menteşe (DYP).

Tourism, Prof Abdulkadir Ateş (SHP).
Forestry, Hasan Ekinci (DYP).
Environment, Riza Akçali (DYP).
DYP True Path Party; SHP Social Democrat Populist Party.

TURKISH EMBASSY

43 Belgrave Square, London SW1X 8PA
Tel 071-235 5252

Ambassador Extraordinary and Plenipotentiary, His Excellency Candemir Önhon (1991).
Minister Counsellor, Cinar Aldemir.
Defence Attaché, I. Tanel.
Consul-General, A. Ünlütürk.
Counsellor, T. F. Baran (*Commercial*).

BRITISH EMBASSY

Sehit Ersan Caddesi 46/A, Cankaya, Ankara
Tel: Ankara 4274310/4

Ambassador Extraordinary and Plenipotentiary, His Excellency John Goulden, CMG (1992).
Counsellor, Deputy Head of Mission, N. A. Ling.
First Secretary, D. T. Healy (*Commercial*).
Defence and Military Attaché, Brig. The Hon. S. J. T. Coleridge.
Consul-General (*Istanbul*), M. E. Cook.

BRITISH CONSULAR OFFICES, There is a Consulate-General at *Istanbul*, a Vice-Consulate at *Izmir* and Honorary Consulates at *Antalya, Bodrum, Iskenderun, Mersin* and *Marmaris*.

BRITISH COUNCIL REPRESENTATIVE, David Marler, Kirklangic Sokak 9, Gazi Osman Pasa, Ankara 06700. There is also a centre and library at *Istanbul*.

BRITISH CHAMBER OF COMMERCE OF TURKEY INC., Mesrutiyet Caddessi No. 34, Tepebasi Beyoğlu, Istanbul (*postal address*, PO Box 190 Karaköy, Istanbul).

EDUCATION

Education is free, secular and compulsory at primary level. There are elementary, secondary and vocational schools. There are 27 universities in Turkey, including six in Istanbul, five in Ankara, two in Izmir, and one each in Erzurum and Trabzon.

CULTURE

Turkish was written in Arabic script until 1926 when a version of the Roman alphabet reflecting Turkish phonetics was substituted for use in official correspondence and in 1928 for universal use, with Arabic numerals as used throughout Europe. The revolution of 1908 led to the introduction of native literature free from foreign influences and adapted to the understanding of the people.

The leading Turkish newspapers are centred in Istanbul and Ankara, although most provincial towns have their own daily papers. There are foreign language papers in French, Greek, Armenian and English and numerous magazines and weeklies.

Anatolian plateau, most of the crops are grown on the fertile littoral. Tobacco, sultana and fig cultivation is centred around Izmir, where substantial quantities of cotton are also grown. The main cotton area is in the Cukurova plain around Adana. The forests which lie between the littoral plain and the Anatolian plateau contain beech, pine, oak, elm, chestnut, lime, plane, alder, box, poplar and maple. In 1990 28 per cent of the land area was forest.

After agriculture, Turkey's most important industry is based on the considerable mineral wealth which is, however, comparatively unexploited. The main export minerals are chromite and boron. Production in 1990 was (tons):

Coal	5,628,000
Lignite	46,892,000
Crude petroleum	3,753,000
Crude iron	4,928,000
Boron minerals	2,062,000

The bulk of the country's requirements in sugar, cotton, woollen and silk textiles, and cement, is produced locally. Other industries include vehicle assembly, paper, glass and glassware, iron and steel, leather and leather goods, sulphur refining, canning and rubber goods, soaps and cosmetics, pharmaceutical products, and prepared foodstuffs.

Steep rises in oil prices from 1973 onwards led to a succession of economic crises culminating in January 1980 in the introduction of an economic stability programme. Exports have since risen dramatically, topping US$11,846 million in 1988. Inflation, however, remains high (65 per cent in 1991). GNP growth for 1992 was about 5.9 per cent and unemployment remains high. The total foreign debt in 1992 stood at US$54,700 million. The new government of Tansu Çiller has announced radical measures to deregulate, liberalize and transform the economy. The government effectively gained the power to issue decrees to run the economy without parliamentary approval in June 1992. A large-scale privatization programme is under way.

FINANCE	1990
Estimated expenditure	TL64,400.4 billion
Estimated revenue	53,860.0 billion

TRADE

The main imports are machinery, crude oil and petroleum products, iron and steel, vehicles, medicines and dyes, chemicals, fertilizers and electrical appliances. Agricultural commodities (cotton, tobacco, fruits, nuts, livestock) represent 47 per cent of total exports. Other exports are minerals, textiles, glass and cement.

	1989	1991
Total imports	US$15,762.6m	US$22,302m
Total exports	11,627.3m	12,959m
Trade with UK	1991	1992
Imports from UK	£729,988,000	£691,738,000
Exports to UK	402,770,000	457,000,000

DEFENCE

The armed forces have a total active strength of 560,300 (481,000 conscripts), with a term of conscription of 18 months. Reserves number some 1,107,000 with commitment to age 46. The Army has an active strength of 450,000 (410,000 conscripts) with some 3,928 main battle tanks, 3,860 armoured personnel carriers and 4,235 artillery pieces. The Navy has 52,300 personnel (40,000 conscripts) including 4,000 marines, with 12 submarines, 12 destroyers, eight frigates, 47 patrol and coastal craft, 22 combat aircraft and 15 armed helicopters. The Air Force has a strength of 58,000 (31,000 conscripts), with 573 combat aircraft. Paramilitary

Gendarmerie and National Guard forces number 70,000 active and 50,000 reserve personnel.

Since its invasion of Cyprus in 1974, Turkey has maintained forces in the north of the island and at present has 30,000 men in two infantry divisions stationed there. As a member of NATO, Turkey is host to the Headquarters Allied Land Forces South-Eastern Europe and the Sixth Allied Tactical Air Force, together with some 4,400 US Army and Air Force personnel. US, UK (180 personnel) and French (150 personnel) Air Force detachments are based at Incirlik airbase in southern Turkey to enable the patrolling of the no-fly zone over northern Iraq.

COMMUNICATIONS

The rail network is run by the State Railways Administration. The total length of lines in operation (1989) is 10,369 km. At the end of 1988 there were 59,128 km of roads (31,149 of which were national). The Bosporus is spanned by two bridges; plans are being drawn up for a third fixed link between the two continents. By the end of 1988 the number of ships over 18 gross tons was 3,805. The state airline (THY) operates all internal services and has services to Europe, the Far East, Africa, North America and the Middle East. Most of the leading European airlines operate services to Istanbul and some also to Ankara.

TURKMENISTAN
Turkmenostan Respublikasy

Turkmenistan has an area of 188,456 sq. miles (488,100 sq. km) and occupies the extreme south of the former Soviet Central Asia between the Caspian Sea and the Amu-Darya river. To the west it is bordered by the Caspian Sea, to the south by Iran, to the south-east by Afghanistan, to the east and north by Uzbekistan and to the north-west by Kazakhstan. The republic comprises five provinces: Ashkhabad; Chardjou; Krasnovodsk; Mary; and Tashauz. The country is a low-lying plain fringed by hills in the south. Ninety per cent of the plain is taken up by the Kara-Kum desert.

CLIMATE – Hot and dry.

POPULATION – According to the 1989 census the population is 3,523,000, of which 72 per cent are Turkomans, 9.5 per cent Russians and 9 per cent Uzbeks, together with smaller numbers of Kazakhs, Tatars, Ukrainians and Armenians. A 1992 estimate put the population at 3,809,000.

RELIGION – Mainly Sunni Muslim.

LANGUAGE – Turkmenian 72 per cent, Russian 9 per cent, Uzbek 9 per cent. Turkmenian is one of the Turkic languages.

CAPITAL – Ashkhabad. Population 398,000 (1989).

CURRENCY – Rouble of 100 kopeks.

FLAG – Green with a vertical carpet pattern near the hoist in black, white and wine-red; in the upper hoist a crescent and five stars, all in white.

NATIONAL DAY – 27 October (Independence Day).

GOVERNMENT

Situated at the cross-roads of Central Asia, the area that is now Turkmenistan has been invaded and occupied by many empires: Persian; Greek under Alexander the Great; Parthian; Mongol. A Turkmenian nation was established in the 15th century but remained riven with dissent and divided between warring emirates. From the early 19th century until 1886 Turkmenistan was gradually incorporated into the Russian Empire. Soviet control over Turkmenistan was established on 30 April 1918 when it became an Autonomous Soviet Socialist Republic. The banks, cotton refineries and oil and gas fields were nationalized before a civil war broke out in July 1918, sparked by the intervention of British troops from Iran and India. The war ended in 1920 with the withdrawal of the interventionist forces and Turkmenistan became a full republic of the Soviet Union in February 1925.

Turkmenistan declared its independence from the Soviet Union on 27 October 1991; it was recognized by the EC and USA in December 1991 and gained UN membership on 2 March 1992. The new constitution passed on 18 May 1992 makes the President head of state and government and provides for a bicameral legislature of the already existing Supreme Soviet and a 60-member (50 directly elected and ten appointed) supervisory upper house, the Khalk Maslakhaty (People's Council). There were fears of inter-ethnic tension, as the constitution abolished the use of Russian as the official language of inter-ethnic communication. These, however, have failed to materialize; relations with Russia have been aided by an agreement on the joint control of ex-Soviet armed forces on Turkoman territory and Russian aid to establish Turkmenistan's own armed forces.

The autocratic government of President Niyazov has prevented any effective political opposition or free press through harassment and the continuation of Soviet authoritarianism. The large reserves of natural gas and the foreign revenue that they earn make the country economically viable and have enabled the government to maintain low stable prices for all commodities and utilities. The fear of losing natural gas revenues has led Turkmenistan to consistently refuse to sign the CIS charter.

President, Saparmurad Niyazov, *elected* 27 October 1990, *re-elected* 21 June 1992, *appointed head of government* 18 May 1992.

COUNCIL OF MINISTERS *as at August 1993*

Prime Minister, The President.

Deputy PMs, Orasgeldy Ajdogdyev; Jumageldy Amansahatov; Jorakuly Babakulyev; Kurbabmuhammed Kasymov; Sapargeldy Motaev; Yagmur Ovesov; Pirkuli Odeev; Valerij Otcherzov; Redjepmanet Pukhanov; Matkarim Rajapov; Reedjep Saparov; Boris Shihmuradov.

Interior, Serdar Charigarov.

Foreign Affairs, Hakberdy Attaev.

Defence, Dangatar Kopekov.

Trade, Halnazar Agakhanov.

Finance, Amangeldi Bayramov.

Justice, Shamukhamed Khodjamberdiev.

Culture and Tourism, Geldymurad Nurmukhamedov.

Health, Aksoltan Atayeva.

State Property, Matkarim Rajapov.

Communications, Amanmurad Djummiev.

Oil and Gas, Nazar Suynov.

Agriculture, Payzgeldi Meredov.

Social Affairs, Nedirmamed Alavov.

Labour, Bayramnur Soyunov.

Construction, Nury Orazmukhamedov.

Transport, Kurbanberely Khojanepesov.

BRITISH AMBASSADOR (resident in Moscow).

ECONOMY

Cotton cultivation, stock-raising and mineral extraction are the principal industries, together with the economically-vital natural gas production and the long-established silk industry. Some fisheries exist along the Caspian sea coast.

Agreements have been reached with Iran to build rail links so that the Persian Gulf and Mediterranean can be reached.

TUVALU

Tuvalu comprises nine coral atolls situated in the south-west Pacific around the point at which the International Date Line cuts the Equator. The total land area is about 10 sq. miles. Few of the atolls are more than 12 ft above sea level or more than half a mile in width. The vegetation consists mainly of coconut palms.

POPULATION – The resident population in 1985 was 8,229, but it is estimated that about 1,500 Tuvaluans work overseas, mostly in Nauru, or as seamen. The UN estimated that the population was 9,000 in 1991. The people are almost entirely Polynesian. The principal languages are Tuvaluan and English. The entire population is Christian and is predominantly Protestant.

CAPITAL – ΨFunafuti, estimated population 2,856. The capital has a grass strip airfield from which a service operates regularly to Fiji and Kiribati, and is also the only port.

CURRENCY – Tuvalu uses the Australian dollar ($A) of 100 cents as legal tender. In addition there are Tuvalu dollar and cent coins in circulation.

FLAG – Blue ground with Union Flag in top left quarter and nine five-pointed gold stars in the fly.

NATIONAL ANTHEM – Tuvalu Mo Te Atua (Tuvalu for the Almighty).

NATIONAL DAY – 1 October (Independence Day).

GOVERNMENT

Tuvalu, formerly the Ellice Islands, formed part of the Gilbert and Ellice Islands Colony until 1 October 1975, when separate elections came into force. Separation from the Gilbert Islands was implemented on 1 January 1976. On 1 October 1978 Tuvalu became a fully independent state within the Commonwealth.

The constitution provides for a Prime Minister and four other Ministers who must be members of the 12-member elected Parliament. The Prime Minister presides at meetings of the Cabinet, which consists of the five Ministers, and is attended by the Attorney-General. Local government services are provided by elected Island Councils.

Governor-General, His Excellency the Rt. Hon. Toaripi Lauti.

CABINET *as at August 1993*

Prime Minister, Rt. Hon. Bikenibeu Paeniu.

Deputy Prime Minister, Foreign Affairs and Economic Planning, Hon. Dr Alesana Seluka.

Natural Resources, Home Affairs and Rural Development, Hon. Tomu Sione, OBE.

Labour, Works and Communications, Hon. Ionatana Ionatana, CVO, OBE.

Health and Human Resource Development, Hon. Naama Latasi.

Secretary to Government, Tauaasa Taafaki.

Attorney-General, Feleti Teo.

BRITISH HIGH COMMISSIONER (resides at Suva, Fiji).

SOCIAL WELFARE

There are eight primary schools in Tuvalu and a church secondary school run jointly with the Government. A maritime training school caters for 60 boys per annum. There is a 30-bed hospital at Funafuti. All islands are served by a dispensary and a primary school.

ECONOMY

Most people still practise a subsistence economy, the main staples of the diet being coconuts and fish. The main imports are foodstuffs, consumer goods and building materials. The only export is copra, though philatelic sales provide a major source of revenue and handicraft sales are increasing. However, Tuvalu is almost entirely dependent on foreign aid.

TRADE WITH UK	1991	1992
Imports from UK	£107,000	£170,000
Exports to UK	1,000	—

UGANDA
Republic of Uganda

Uganda is situated in eastern Africa, flanked by Zaire, Sudan, Kenya and on the south by Tanzania and Rwanda. Large parts of Lakes Victoria, Edward and Albert (Mobuto) are within its boundaries, as are Lakes Kyoga, Kwania, George and Bisina (formerly Salisbury) and the course of the River Nile from its outlet from Lake Victoria to the Sudan frontier post at Nimule. Uganda has an area of 91,259 sq. miles (236,036 sq. km) (water and swamp 16,400 sq. miles) and a population (1991 UN estimate) of 19,517,000. The official language is English. The main local vernaculars are of Bantu, Nilotic and Hamitic origins. Ki-Swahili is generally understood in trading centres.

Despite its tropical location, the climate is tempered by its situation some 3,000 ft above sea level, and well over that altitude in the highlands of the Western and Eastern Regions. In South Uganda, temperatures seldom rise above 85° F (29° C) or fall below 60° F (15° C). The rainfall averages about 50 inches a year. Uganda has three National Parks and a fourth (Lake Mburo) has been designated.

CAPITAL – Kampala (estimated population of Greater Kampala, 1990, 750,000). Other principal towns are Jinja (45,000), Mbale (28,000) and Masaka (29,000).

CURRENCY – Uganda shilling of 100 cents.

FLAG – Six horizontal stripes of black, yellow, red, with a white disc in the centre containing the badge of a crested crane.

NATIONAL ANTHEM – Oh Uganda.

NATIONAL DAY – 9 October (Independence Day).

GOVERNMENT

Uganda became an independent state within the Commonwealth on 9 October 1962, after some 70 years of British rule. A republic was instituted in 1967, under an executive President assisted by a Cabinet of Ministers.

Early in 1971 an army coup took place and Maj.-Gen. Idi Amin, the army commander, proclaimed himself head of state. In 1979, following risings and military intervention by Tanzania, President Amin was overthrown. Dr Milton Obote became President in 1980 but was ousted by a military coup in 1985. A military council was installed which attempted to negotiate a power-sharing agreement with the National Resistance Movement led by Yoweri Museveni. However, the National Resistance Army captured Kampala in January 1986, securing control of the rest of the country in the following few months. Yoweri Museveni was sworn in as President in January 1986; subsequently the Prime Minister and a National Resistance Council (NRC) were appointed.

The NRC acts as a legislative body with an interim mandate to draw up a constitution. Since elections in

February 1989 it consists of 210 elected and 68 presidentially appointed members. A draft constitution was agreed and published in February 1993. Elections to a constituent assembly to amend the draft constitution are to be held by the end of 1993, with the assembly having 154 elected and 26 reserved seats. The ban on political parties in the interest of stability will be continued to the year 2000, while the encouragement of grass roots democracy continues.

HEAD OF STATE
President, Yoweri Museveni, *sworn in* 29 January 1986.
Vice-President, Dr Samson Kisseka.

CABINET *as at August 1993*
Defence, The President.
Internal Affairs, The Vice-President.
Prime Minister, George Cosma Adyebo.
First Deputy PM, Eriya Kategaya.
Second Deputy PM and Minister for Foreign Affairs, Paul Ssemogerere.
Third Deputy PM and Attorney-General, Abu Bakar Mayanja.
Finance and Economic Planning, Joshua Mayanja-Nkangi.
Agriculture, Animal Industry and Fisheries, Mrs Victoria Ssekitoleko.
Commerce, Industry and Co-operatives, Richard Kaijuka.
Local Government, Jaberi Bidandi-Ssali.
Educational and Sports, Amanya Mushega.
Public Services, Sam Sebagereka.
Information, Paul Etiang.
Lands, Housing and Urban Development, Dr E. T. Adriko.
Labour and Social Affairs, Ateke Ejalu.
Works, Transport and Communications, Dr Ruhakana-Rugunda.
Tourism, Wildlife and Antiquities, James Wapakabulo.
Health, James Makumbi.
Water, Energy, Minerals and Environmental Protection, Henry Kajura.
Women in Development, Culture and Youth, Wandira Kazibwe.

UGANDA HIGH COMMISSION
Uganda House, 58–59 Trafalgar Square, London WC2N 5DX
Tel 071–839 5783

High Commissioner, His Excellency Prof. George Kirya (1990).
Financial Attaché, G. Kizza-Kigongo.
Commercial Attaché, R. Lubwama-Kebba.

BRITISH HIGH COMMISSION
10–12 Parliament Avenue, PO Box 7070, Kampala
Tel: Kampala 257054/9

High Commissioner, His Excellency Edward Clay (1993).
Deputy High Commissioner, J. O. Atkinson.
Defence Adviser, Lt.-Col. E. A. M. Graham.
First Secretary (Commercial), M. R. Frost.

BRITISH COUNCIL REPRESENTATIVE, Roger Williams (*Cultural Attaché*).

EDUCATION

Education is a joint undertaking by the government, local authorities and voluntary agencies. In 1988 it was estimated that Uganda had 7,905 primary schools with an enrolment of 2,638,100 children. Secondary schools numbered 774 with 240,834 students enrolled; and 7,291 students in various technical training institutions. The national university is Makerere University, Kampala, and there are universities at Mbale and Mbarara. The Uganda Martyrs University opened in October 1991.

COMMUNICATIONS

There is an international airport at Entebbe, and eight other airfields around the country. Having no sea coast, Uganda is heavily dependent upon rail and road links to Mombasa and Dar es Salaam for its trade. Over 5,000 km of the country's dilapidated roads are currently being rehabilitated. A railway network joins the capital to the western, eastern and northern centres.

ECONOMY

Since 1988 the government has been successful in implementing an IMF recovery programme. The civil service and army have been reduced in size, foreign investment encouraged, and property returned to Asians expelled by Idi Amin. Annual growth since 1988 has averaged 6 per cent, inflation has been reduced to 3 per cent a year and aid donors in June 1993 gave £550 million of aid.

The principal export earner is coffee, over 90 per cent of all exports. Attempts are being made to increase production of cotton and tea for export. Hydro-electricity is produced from the Owen Falls power station, some of which is exported to Kenya. The principal food crops are plantains, bananas, cassava, sweet potatoes, potatoes, maize and sorghum.

TRADE WITH UK	1991	1992
Imports from UK	£35,718,000	£26,682,000
Exports to UK	6,730,000	9,398,000

UKRAINE
Ukraina

Ukraine has an area of 233,090 sq. miles (603,700 sq. km) and lies in the south-west of the European part of the former Soviet Union. It is bordered on the north by Belarus and Russia, on the east by Russia, on the south by the Black Sea, on the south-west by Romania and Moldova and on the west by Hungary, Slovakia and Poland. The area of the present Ukraine is significantly larger than that of the Ukrainian Soviet Republic formed in the 1917-19 period because of the westward territorial expansion of the former Soviet Union in the 1939-45 period and the addition of the Crimea from Russia in 1954. The Ukraine now consists of 24 regions: Cherkassy, Chernigov, Chernovtsy, Dnepropetrovsk, Donetsk, Ivano-Frankovsk, Kharkov, Kherson, Khmelnitsky, Kiev, Kirovograd, Lugansk, Lvov, Nikolayev, Odessa, Poltava, Rovno, Sumy, Ternopol, Transcarpathia, Vinnitsa, Volhynia, Zaporozhye and Zhitomir, and one autonomous republic, Crimea.

The larger part of the Ukraine forms a plain with small elevations. The Carpathian mountains lie in the south-western part of the republic. The main rivers are the Dnieper with its tributaries, the Southern Bug and the Northern Donets (a tributary of the Don).

CLIMATE - Moderate with relatively mild winters (particularly in the south-west) and hot summers.

POPULATION - According to the 1989 census the population was 51,471,000, of which 73 per cent are Ukrainian and 22 per cent Russian, with smaller numbers of Jews, Belorussians, Moldovans, Tatars, Poles, Hungarians and Greeks. The 1992 estimate put the population at 52,000,000.

RELIGION - The two main religions are Roman Catholicism and Orthodox. The Orthodox rite is divided between the Russian Orthodox Church with its Patriarch in Moscow and the Autocephalous Orthodox Church of the Ukraine with its own Patriarch in Kiev. Roman Catholics are concentrated in the west of the country. There are also large numbers of Reformed Protestants in the Transcarpathian region and a sizeable Jewish community in Kiev.

LANGUAGE - Ukrainian 73 per cent, Russian 22 per cent. Ukrainian is an Eastern Slavonic language related to Russian and Belarussian.

CAPITAL - Kiev. Population 2,577,000 (1989). Other major cities (1990) are Kharkov (1,611,000); Dnepropetrovsk (1,179,000); ΨOdessa (1,115,000); Donetsk (1,110,000).

CURRENCY - Coupons called Karbovanets, which were introduced in November 1992 and were made fully convertible to the rouble.

FLAG - Two horizontal stripes of blue over yellow.

NATIONAL DAY - 24 August (Independence Day).

GOVERNMENT

The earliest Russian state was formed in the middle reaches of the Dnieper River with its capital at Kiev in the ninth century AD. The state united the two large Slav states of Kiev and Novgorod and established the first common Russian language and nationality. The state lasted until Kiev fell to the Mongols in 1240. As a result the centre of Russia shifted northwards to Muscovy and for the next four centuries the Ukraine (i.e. the borderland of Russia) was invaded and ruled by Tatars, Turks, Poles, Hungarians and Lithuanians. In 1648 the Ukrainians threw off Polish rule to become independent and increasingly allied with Russia (formerly Muscovy). During the reign of Catherine the Great of Russia (1763-96) the Ukraine and the Crimea came under Russian control.

By the time of the Treaty of Brest-Litovsk in March 1918, most of the Ukraine had been occupied by German and Austrian forces. The Treaty, which ended Russian involvement in the First World War, forced the Soviet government in Moscow to cede parts of western Ukraine to Germany and Austria-Hungary and accept the independence of the remainder. After the defeat of Germany in November 1918, the Ukraine became a battleground in the Russian civil war before the imposition of Soviet rule in 1922. The Ukraine became a constituent republic of the USSR on 30 December 1922.

The 1920s saw the collectivization of agriculture, which led to a famine in which millions died, and the Stalinist purges caused hundreds of thousands more to be killed. The Ukraine was again devastated in the Second World War. Millions of Ukrainians died fighting the German invasion or in Nazi death camps during the war and in Soviet death camps after it for alleged collaboration. The country was rebuilt and heavily industrialized in the post-war period.

The Ukraine declared itself independent of the Soviet Union, subject to a referendum, after the failed Moscow coup in August 1991. The referendum was held on 1 December 1991 and 90 per cent of the electorate voted for independence. Simultaneously, the former Ukrainian Communist leader Leonid Kravchuk was elected President of the Republic. Political power in the Ukraine rests with the former Communists, led by the President, in loose alliance with the Rukh nationalist party. There has effectively been no democratic revolution as the legislature, known as the Rada (formerly Supreme Soviet) remains that elected on 4 March 1990 when the Communists gained a majority of seats. Limited political change occurred in October 1992 when some Communist apparatchiks were purged from the government and a coalition of reforming Communists and the Rukh party was established headed by Leonid Kuchma.

Kuchma introduced economic reforms in December 1992, with a privatization law, reductions in welfare payments, the ending of the printing of money to finance the deficit, and the disbandment of collective farms. Price controls were partially liberalized and the currency stabilized so that by March 1993 results were being achieved through Kuchma's power to rule by decree in economic affairs. A crisis occurred in May when the President and Rada refused to extend Kuchma's extraordinary powers by one year. Kuchma resigned and President Kravchuk attempted to take over the government but this was rejected by the Rada, which restored Kuchma but without the extraordinary powers. The crisis continued into June when miners and heavy industry workers in the ethnic Russian majority in the east of the country launched a successful political strike. The President and Rada were forced to accept a referendum on the President's leadership and legislative elections to be held in late 1993. The government conceded price rises and subsidies, which have led to deficits and inflation.

The relationship with Russia remains central to events in the Ukraine. The situation of the Crimea with its ethnic Russian majority has also caused concern, as the Crimean parliament first voted to make the Crimea an autonomous republic in September 1991, which was accepted by Kiev, but then voted for independence in May 1992, which was not. Meanwhile, the Russian Parliament voted in January 1992 to re-examine the legality of the Crimea's transfer from Russia to the Ukraine in 1954 and in 1993 declared it to be Russian.

HEAD OF STATE
President, Leonid Kravchuk, *elected* 1 December 1991.

GOVERNMENT *as at August 1993*

Prime Minister, Leonid Kuchma.
Deputy PMs, Vasili Evtukhov; Vladimir Demyanov; Yuli
  Ioffe; Nikolay Zhulinski.
Interior, Andrei Vasilishin.
Economics, Uryi Bannikov.
Foreign Affairs, Anatoly Zlenko.
Defence, Konstantin Morozov.
Finance, Grigory Pyatachenko.
Justice, Vasili Onopenko.
Communications, Oleg Prozhivalsky.
Trade, Ivan Gercz.
Culture, Ivan Dzyuba.
Labour, Mikhail Kaskevich.
Industry, Anatoli Golubchenko.
Environment, Yuri Kostenko.
Transport, Orest Klimpush.
Youth and Sports, Valery Borzov.
Agriculture, Vasili Tkachuk.
Social Security, Arkady Yershov.
Education, Pyotr Talanchuk.
Health, Yuri Spizhenko.
Construction, Uryi Serbin.
Forestry, Valery Samoplavsky.

UKRAINIAN EMBASSY
78 Kensington Park Road, London WII 2PL
Tel 071-727 6312

Ambassador Extraordinary and Plenipotentiary, His
Excellency Prof, Sergui Komisarenko (1992).

BRITISH EMBASSY
252025 Kiev Desyatinna 9
Tel: Kiev 291 8907

Ambassador Extraordinary and Plenipotentiary, His
  Excellency Simon N. Hemans, CMG, CVO (1992).
Consul-General and Deputy Head of Mission, D. G. Martin.
Defence Attaché, Cdr. C. A. M. Parrish.
First Secretary (Commercial), R. C. Cook.

BRITISH COUNCIL REPRESENTATIVE – John Day, Room
  258, Kiev Polytechnic Institute, 37 Peremogy Ave, 20
  2056 Kiev.

DEFENCE

Since the demise of the Soviet Union, Russia and Ukraine have clashed over defence issues. All nuclear weapons were placed under a central CIS command in December 1991 and the Ukraine agreed to implement the START 1 Treaty in May 1992 by transferring its strategic nuclear weapons to Russia for destruction. Since then the government and Rada have refused to ratify the START 1 Treaty or the Nuclear Non-Proliferation Treaty, and in July 1993 the Rada claimed possession of all nuclear weapons on its territory. Ukraine has 176 inter-continental ballistic missiles and 41 nuclear-capable bombers stationed on its territory under CIS command. The division of the Black Sea Fleet with Russia also remains to be resolved.

The total armed forces number 230,000 personnel (excluding navy), with conscripts serving 18 months. The army numbers 150,000 personnel, with 6,300 main battle tanks, 5,880 armoured personnel carriers and armoured infantry fighting vehicles, 2,600 artillery pieces and 240 attack helicopters. The air force and air defence forces have 80,000 personnel, with some 1,370 combat aircraft and 2,400 surface-to-air missiles. The Black Sea Fleet has 18 submarines, one helicopter carrier, 5 cruisers, 7 destroyers, 26 frigates and 380 combat aircraft.

ECONOMY

The southern part of the country contains a coal-mining and iron and steel industrial area which was the largest in the former Soviet Union. The Ukraine also contains engineering and chemical industries and ship-building yards on the Black Sea coast.

Ukrainian agricultural production is good with large areas under cultivation with wheat, cotton, flax and sugar beet; stock-raising is very important. There are large deposits of coal and salt in the Donets Basin, of iron ore in Krivoy Rog and near Kerch in the Crimea, of manganese in Nikopol, and of quicksilver in Nikitovka.

The major ports are Odessa, Nikolayev, Kerch and Sevastopol.

UNITED ARAB EMIRATES
Al-Imarat Al-Arabiya Al-Muttahida

The United Arab Emirates are situated in the south-east of the Arabian peninsula. Six of the emirates lie on the shore of the Gulf between the Musandam peninsula in the east and the Qatar peninsula in the west while the seventh, Fujairah, lies on the Gulf of Oman. The approximate area is 32,278 sq. miles (83,600 sq. km), and the population (1991 estimate) is 1,909,000.

CAPITAL – Abu Dhabi. Population (city) 450,000.
CURRENCY – UAE dirham of 100 fils.
FLAG – Horizontal stripes of green over white over black
  with vertical red stripe in the hoist.
NATIONAL DAY – 2 December.

GOVERNMENT

The United Arab Emirates (formerly the Trucial States) is composed of seven emirates (Abu Dhabi, Ajman, Dubai, Fujairah, Ras al-Khaimah, Sharjah and Umm al-Qaiwain) which came together as an independent state on 2 December 1971 when they ended their individual special treaty relationships with the British Government (Ras al-Khaimah joined the other six on 10 February 1972). The British government, by virtue of a treaty made in 1892, had been responsible for the external affairs of the emirates. On independence the Union Government assumed full responsibility for all internal and external affairs apart from some internal matters that remained the prerogative of the individual emirates.

Overall authority lies with the Supreme Council of the seven emirate rulers, each of whom also governs in his own territory. The President and Vice-President are elected by the Supreme Council from among its members. The President appoints the Council of Ministers.

HEAD OF STATE
President, Sheikh Zayed bin Sultan al-Nahyan (*Abu Dhabi*).
Vice-President, Sheikh Maktoum bin Rashid al-Maktoum (*Dubai*).

COUNCIL OF MINISTERS *as at August 1993*
Finance and Industry, Sheikh Hamdan bin Rashid al-Maktoum.
Defence, Sheikh Mohammed bin Rashid al-Maktoum.
Interior, Lt.-Gen. Dr Hamouda bin Ali.
Foreign Affairs, Rashid Abdullah al-Noami.
Communications, Mohammed Saeed al-Mualla.
Planning, Sheikh Humaid bin Ahmed al-Mualla.
Islamic Affairs and Endowments, Sheikh Mohammed bin Ahmed al Khazraji.
Water and Electricity, Humaid bin Nasser al-Owais.
Economy and Commerce, Saeed Ghobash.
Agriculture and Fisheries, Saeed al-Ragabani.
Labour and Social Affairs, Saif al-Jarwan.
Minister of State for Cabinet Affairs, Saeed al-Ghaith.
Information and Culture, Khalfan bin Mohammed al-Roumi.
Education, Hamad Abdul Rahman al-Madfa.
Minister of State for Financial and Industrial Affairs, Ahmed bin Humaid al-Tayer.
Minister of State for Foreign Affairs, Sheikh Hamdan bin Zayed al-Nahyan.
Minister of State for Supreme Council Affairs, Sheikh Mohammed bin Saqr bin Mohammed al-Qassimi.
Higher Education, Sheikh Nahyan bin Mubarak al-Nahyan.
Justice, Dr Abdullah bin Omran Taryam.
Health, Ahmed bin Saeed al-Badi.
Petroleum and Mineral Resources, Yousuf bin Omeir bin Yousuf.
Public Works and Housing, Rakad bin Salem bin Rakad.
Youth and Sports, Sheikh Faisal bin Khaled bin Mohammed al-Qassimi.

EMBASSY OF THE UNITED ARAB EMIRATES
30 Prince's Gate, London SW7 1PT
Tel 071–581 1281

Ambassador Extraordinary and Plenipotentiary, His Excellency Easa Saleh Al-Gurg, CBE (1991).
Minister-Plenipotentiary, Khalid Abdul-Latif Al-Bassam.
Military Attaché, Lt.-Col. A. B. M. Al-Muhairi.
Cultural Attaché, A. A. M. Al-Marri.

BRITISH EMBASSIES
PO Box 248, Abu Dhabi
Tel: Abu Dhabi 326600

Ambassador Extraordinary and Plenipotentiary, His Excellency Graham Stuart Burton, CMG (1990).
First Secretary, Consul and Deputy Head of Post, W. R. Henderson.

First Secretary (Commercial), M. K. Haddock.
Defence Attaché, Lt.-Col. M. A. Cullinan.

BRITISH COUNCIL REPRESENTATIVE, Abu Dhabi,
J. H. G. Foley, OBE, (*Commercial Attaché*).

PO Box 65, Dubai
Tel: Dubai 521070

Counsellor and Consul-General, R. A. M. Hendrie.
Deputy Head of Post, Consul and First Secretary (Commercial), J. C. Fisher.

BRITISH COUNCIL REPRESENTATIVE, A. Mackay,
PO Box 1636, Dubai.

DEFENCE
The Ministry of Defence and general headquarters are located in Dubai. The armed forces of the emirates were merged in 1976, although Dubai still retains some independent units. The total active armed forces strength is 54,500, of which around 30 per cent are hired or seconded foreign nationals. The Army is 50,000 strong including 6,000 Dubai forces, and is equipped with 131 main battle tanks, 76 light tanks, 190 reconnaissance vehicles, 405 armoured personnel carriers and armoured infantry fighting vehicles and 157 artillery pieces. The Navy has a strength of 2,000 personnel, with 19 patrol and coastal vessels. The Air Force is 2,500 strong, with 105 combat aircraft and 19 armed helicopters. Some 5,000 Moroccan troops are stationed in the UAE.

TRADE
Revenue is chiefly derived from oil, re-exports and customs dues on imports.

Trade with UK	1991	1992
Imports from UK	£759,660,000	£926,557,000
Exports to UK	231,931,000	331,928,000

ABU DHABI
Abu Dhabi is the largest emirate in area, stretching from Khor al-Odaid in the west to the borders with Dubai in the Jebel Ali area. It includes six villages in the Buraimi oasis, the other three being part of the Sultanate of Oman, and a number of settlements in the Liwa oasis system. Following negotiations with Saudi Arabia, some adjustment of the border has now been made in the Khor al-Odaid region, but the agreement has not yet been ratified. The population of the Emirate is now about 798,000

The Abu Dhabi government controls oil, gas and petrochemical operations in the emirate through the Supreme Petroleum Council. This body in turn issues instructions to the Abu Dhabi National Oil Company (ADNOC) which has majority shareholdings in the oil operating and gas treatment companies, and in oil industry-related companies covering drilling, refining, distribution, chemical manufacture and investment.

Offshore production began in 1962, the most important fields being Umm Shaif and Lower Zakum, near Das Island, site of a large associated gas liquefaction plant. The Upper Zakum field came on stream in late 1982, and four other offshore fields are being developed. Production of oil onshore began in 1963 from the Murban field. A large onshore associated gas liquefaction project based at Ruwais started production in 1981. Other large natural gas finds in recent years will consolidate Abu Dhabi's position as a holder of some of the largest reserves of natural gas in the world. Abu Dhabi's crude oil production in 1990 was approximately 1.65 million barrels per day.

With its oil wealth the emirate has seen a period of growth (which is currently slowing down), in Abu Dhabi, Al-Ain in the Buraimi oasis and in the new petro-chemical city at Ruwais. An international airport opened in 1982 at Abu Dhabi and another is under construction at Al-Ain. There are airfields on Das Island and at Jebel Dhanna. The port and harbour on Abu Dhabi island are now completed and there are port facilities at Ruwais.

AJMAN AND UMM AL-QAIWAIN

Ajman and Umm al-Qaiwain are the smallest emirates, having populations of around 76,000 and 27,000 respectively. Both lie on the Gulf coast although Ajman has two inland enclaves at Manama and Masfut. Exploration work continues in both emirates for oil and gas but so far only Umm al-Qaiwain has experienced any success, with the offshore discovery of natural gas, but the field has yet to be commercially developed. The discovery of onshore gas in nearby Sharjah has increased hopes of similar discoveries in both Ajman and Umm al-Qaiwain.

DUBAI

Dubai is the second largest emirate both in size and in population, which is about 501,000. The town of Dubai is the main port for the import of goods into the UAE and has a wide re-export trade to the other Gulf states. Dubai's prosperity was established by this trade long before the discovery of oil. Oil was discovered in 1966 and production began in 1969. The producer in Dubai's oilfields is Dubai Petroleum Company, operated by CONOCO. Production is in excess of 350,000 b.p.d. In 1982 an extensive gas and condensate field was discovered onshore. A small amount of condensate is produced from the onshore Margam field.

Oil income has been used to finance Dubai's infrastructure, including an international airport, a dry dock complex and an international trade and exhibition centre. There is a 66-berth port at Jebel Ali, the heart of an industrial complex which includes an aluminium smelter, a de-salination plant and a gas processing plant. The port and its immediate area is a free trade zone which is expected to attract more industry.

FUJAIRAH

Fujairah, with a population of 63,000, is the most remote of the seven emirates, lying on the Gulf of Oman coast and only connected by a metal road to the rest of the country. Largely agricultural, its population is spread between the slopes of the inland Hajar mountain range and the town of Fujairah itself, together with a number of smaller settlements on the comparatively fertile plain on the coast. Although exploration work continues, there have been no hydrocarbon discoveries in the emirate. However, there are some chrome and other mineral deposits. Fujairah has a general cargo port.

RAS AL-KHAIMAH

Ras al-Khaimah has a population of 130,000, of whom more than half live in the town. An ancient sea-port, near to which archaeological remains have been found, Ras al-Khaimah is developing as the most agricultural of the emirates, producing vegetables, dates, fruit and tobacco. In 1982 Ras al-Khaimah announced the discovery of oil and gas offshore and this field currently produces approximately 5,000 b.p.d. An industrial area has been developed to the north of the emirate, which includes two cement works. Ras al-Khaimah has an international airport and has also expanded its port. A new international airport is nearing completion. A trade centre has been completed and it is hoped that more industry will be attracted to the emirate.

SHARJAH

Sharjah, with a population of approximately 314,000, has declined from its former position as principal town in the area. It began producing oil in 1974, following the discovery of oil offshore. The field declined over the years and by 1982 was yielding less than 6,000 b.p.d. However, new oil and gas discoveries were made in 1982 in the northern emirates and production now stands at about 50,000 b.p.d.

Sharjah is well connected by metalled roads to all the other northern emirates. A container port has been constructed on the Gulf of Oman at Khor Fakkan. The international airport opened in 1979.

UNITED STATES OF AMERICA

The United States of America occupies nearly all of the North American continent between the Atlantic and Pacific Oceans, in 25° 07′ to 49° 23′ N. latitude and 66° 57′ to 124° 44′ W. longitude, its northern boundary being Canada and the southern boundary Mexico. The separate state of Alaska reaches a latitude of 71° 23′ N., at Point Barrow. The coastline has a length of about 2,069 miles on the Atlantic, 7,623 miles on the Pacific, 1,060 miles on the Arctic, and 1,631 miles on the Gulf of Mexico.

The principal river is the Mississippi-Missouri-Red (3,710 miles long), traversing the whole country to its mouth in the Gulf of Mexico; its main affluents are the Yellowstone, Platte, Arkansas, and Ohio rivers. The chain of the Rocky Mountains separates the western portion of the country from the remainder. West of these, bordering the Pacific coast, the Cascade Mountains and Sierra Nevada form the outer edge of a high tableland, consisting in part of stony and sandy desert and partly of grazing land and forested mountains, and including the Great Salt Lake, which extends to the Rocky Mountains. In the eastern states large forests still exist, the remnants of the forests which formerly extended over all the Atlantic slope. The highest point is Mount McKinley (20,320 ft) in Alaska, and the lowest point of dry land is in Death Valley (Inyo, California), 282 ft below sea-level.

AREA AND POPULATION

	Total area 1990 (sq. miles)	Population Census 1990
The United States (a)	3,787,318	248,709,873
Puerto Rico	3,426	3,522,037
Palau	177	15,122
Outlying areas under US jurisdiction	598	325,079
Territories	419	281,734
Guam	209	133,152
US Virgin Islands	133	101,809
American Samoa	77	46,773
Northern Mariana Is.	179	43,345
Population abroad (b)	–	922,819
Armed Forces	–	529,269
TOTAL	3,791,519	254,631,012

(a) the 50 states and the Federal District of Columbia
(b) excludes US citizens temporarily abroad on business.

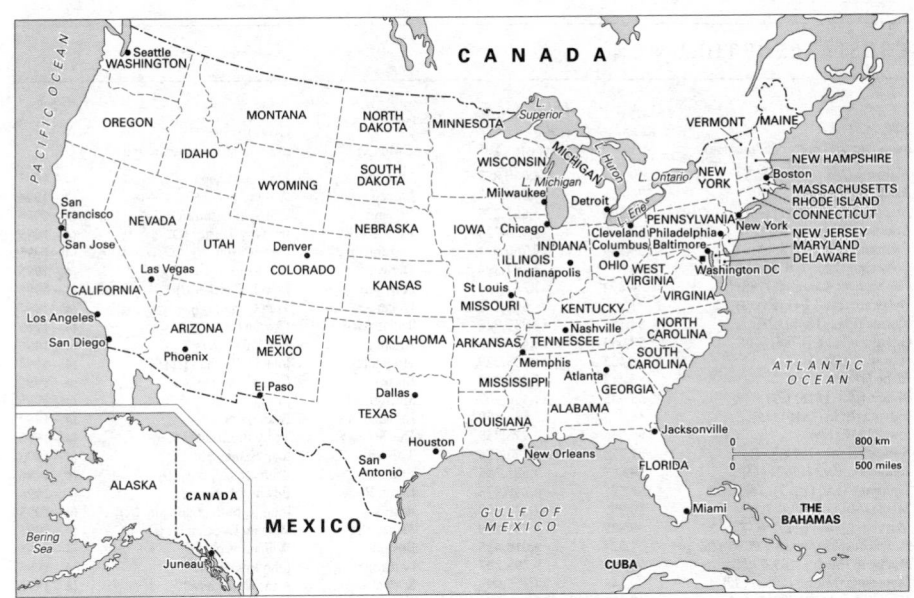

RESIDENT POPULATION BY RACE 1990 (Thousands)

White	199,686
Black	29,986
*American Indian	1,959.2
Chinese	1,645.5
Filipino	1,406.8
Japanese	847.6
Asian Indian	815.4
Korean	798.8
Vietnamese	614.5
Other Asian or Pacific Islander	1,145
All other races	9,804.8
†Hispanic origin	22,354
Cuban	1,043.9
Mexican	13,495.9
Puerto Rican	2,727.8
Other Hispanic	5,086.4
TOTAL	248,704.9

*Includes Eskimo and Aleut
†Persons of Hispanic origin may be of any race

IMMIGRATION

From 1820 to 1989, 55,009,566 immigrants were admitted to the United States. Total number of immigrants in 1992 was 973,977, of which 439,355 came from North and Central America (213,802 from Mexico), 356,955 from Asia and 145,392 from Europe.

VITAL STATISTICS 1992

In 1992 (provisional figures) live births were 4,084,000, a rate of 16 per 1,000 of population. Deaths were 2,177,000, a rate of 8.5 per 1,000 of population.

Laws of marriage and of divorce are within the exclusive jurisdiction of each state. Each state legislature enacts its own laws prescribing rules and qualifications pertaining to marriage and its dissolution. In 1992 marriages were 2,362,000, a rate of 9.3 per 1,000 of population. Divorces were approximately 1,187,000, a rate of 4.7 per 1,000 of population.

LARGEST CITIES 1990 Census

ΨNew York, NY	7,322,564
ΨLos Angeles, California	3,485,398
ΨChicago, Illinois	2,783,726
ΨHouston, Texas	1,630,553
ΨPhiladelphia, Pennsylvania	1,585,577
ΨSan Diego, California	1,110,549
ΨDetroit, Michigan	1,027,974
Dallas, Texas	1,006,877
Phoenix, Arizona	983,403
San Antonio, Texas	935,933
San Jose, California	782,248
*Indianapolis, Indiana	741,952

Ψ seaport
*consolidated city

CAPITAL

The federal capital is the City of Washington in the District of Columbia. It is situated on the west central edge of Maryland, opposite the state of Virginia, on the left bank of the Potomac at its confluence with the Anacostia. The area of the District of Columbia (with which the City of Washington is considered co-extensive) is 63 sq. miles, with a resident population (mid-1989 estimate) of 604,000. The population of the metropolitan area in 1988 was estimated at 3,734,200. The District of Columbia is governed by an elected mayor and City Council.

CURRENCY – The dollar ($) of 100 cents.
FLAG – 13 stripes and 50 stars in nine horizontal rows of six and five alternately.
NATIONAL ANTHEM – The Star-Spangled Banner.
NATIONAL DAY – 4 July (Independence Day).

GOVERNMENT

The United States of America is a federal republic consisting of 50 states and the federal District of Columbia and of organized territories. Of the present 50 states, 13 are original

THE STATES OF THE UNION

STATE (with date and *order* of admission)	LAND AREA sq. m.	POPULATION (1990 Census)	CAPITAL	GOVERNOR (term of office in years, and expiry year)	
Alabama (Ala.) (1819) *(22)*	50,767	4,040,857	Montgomery	Jim Folsom, jun. *(D)*	(4 – 1995)
Alaska (1959) *(49)*	570,833	550,043	Juneau	Walter Hickel *(I)*	(4 – 1994)
Arizona (Ariz.) (1912) *(48)*	113,508	3,665,228	Phoenix	Fife Symington *(R)*	(4 – 1995)
Arkansas (Ark.) (1836) *(25)*	52,078	2,350,725	Little Rock	Jim Guy Tucker *(D)*	(4 – 1995)
California (Calif.) (1850) *(31)*	156,299	29,760,021	Sacramento	Pete Wilson *(R)*	(4 – 1995)
Colorado (Colo.) (1876) *(38)*	103,595	3,294,394	Denver	Roy Romer *(D)*	(4 – 1995)
Connecticut (Conn.)§(1788) *(5)*	4,872	3,287,116	Hartford	Lowell Weicker *(I)*	(4 – 1995)
Delaware (Del.) § (1787) *(1)*	1,932	666,168	Dover	Tom Carper *(D)*	(4 – 1997)
Florida (Fla.) (1845) *(27)*	54,153	12,937,926	Tallahassee	Lawton Chiles *(D)*	(4 – 1995)
Georgia (Ga.) § (1788) *(4)*	58,056	6,478,216	Atlanta	Zell Miller *(D)*	(4 – 1995)
Hawaii (1959) *(50)*	6,425	1,108,229	Honolulu	John D. Waihee III *(D)*	(4 – 1994)
Idaho (1890) *(43)*	82,412	1,006,749	Boise	Cecil D. Andrus *(D)*	(4 – 1995)
Illinois (Ill.) (1818) *(21)*	55,645	11,430,602	Springfield	Jim Edgar *(R)*	(4 – 1995)
Indiana (Ind.) (1816) *(19)*	35,932	5,544,159	Indianapolis	Evan Bayh *(D)*	(4 – 1997)
Iowa (1846) *(29)*	55,965	2,776,755	Des Moines	Terry Branstad *(R)*	(4 – 1995)
Kansas (Kan.) (1861) *(34)*	81,778	2,477,574	Topeka	Joan Finney *(D)*	(4 – 1995)
Kentucky (Ky.) (1792) *(15)*	39,669	3,685,296	Frankfort	Brereton C. Jones *(D)*	(4 – 1996)
Louisiana (La.) (1812) *(18)*	44,521	4,219,973	Baton Rouge	Edwin Edwards *(D)*	(4 – 1996)
Maine (Me.) (1820) *(23)*	30,995	1,227,928	Augusta	John R. McKernan, jun. *(R)*	(4 – 1995)
Maryland (Md.) § (1788) *(7)*	9,837	4,781,468	Annapolis	William D. Schaefer *(D)*	(4 – 1995)
Massachusetts (Mass.) § (1788) *(6)*	7,824	6,016,425	Boston	William Weld *(R)*	(4 – 1995)
Michigan (Mich.) (1837) *(26)*	56,954	9,295,297	Lansing	John Engler *(R)*	(4 – 1995)
Minnesota (Minn.) (1858) *(32)*	79,548	4,375,099	St Paul	Anne Carlson *(R)*	(4 – 1995)
Mississippi (Miss.) (1817) *(20)*	47,233	2,573,216	Jackson	Kirk Fordice *(R)*	(4 – 1996)
Missouri (Mo.) (1821) *(24)*	68,945	5,117,073	Jefferson City	Mel Carnahan *(D)*	(4 – 1997)
Montana (Mont.) (1889) *(41)*	145,388	799,065	Helena	Marc Raciot *(R)*	(4 – 1997)
Nebraska (Neb.) (1867) *(37)*	76,644	1,578,385	Lincoln	Ben Nelson *(D)*	(4 – 1995)
Nevada (Nev.) (1864) *(36)*	109,894	1,201,833	Carson City	Robert J. Miller *(D)*	(4 – 1995)
New Hampshire (NH) § (1788) *(9)*	8,993	1,109,252	Concord	Steve Merrill *(R)*	(2 – 1995)
New Jersey (NJ) § (1787) *(3)*	7,468	7,730,188	Trenton	James S. Florio *(D)*	(4 – 1994)
New Mexico (NM) (1912) *(47)*	121,335	1,515,069	Santa Fé	Bruce King *(D)*	(4 – 1995)
New York (NY) § (1788) *(11)*	47,377	17,990,455	Albany	Mario M. Cuomo *(D)*	(4 – 1995)
North Carolina (NC) § (1789) *(12)*	48,843	6,628,637	Raleigh	James B. Hunt, jun. *(D)*	(4 – 1997)
North Dakota (ND) (1889) *(39)*	69,300	638,800	Bismarck	Edward Schafer *(R)*	(4 – 1997)
Ohio (1803) *(17)*	41,004	10,847,115	Columbus	George Voinovich *(R)*	(4 – 1995)
Oklahoma (Okla.) (1907) *(46)*	68,655	3,145,585	Oklahoma City	David Walters *(D)*	(4 – 1995)
Oregon (Ore.) (1859) *(33)*	96,184	2,842,321	Salem	Barbara Roberts *(D)*	(4 – 1995)
Pennsylvania (Pa.) § (1787) *(2)*	44,888	11,881,643	Harrisburg	Robert P. Casey *(D)*	(4 – 1995)
Rhode Island (RI) § (1790) *(13)*	1,055	1,003,464	Providence	Bruce Sundlun *(D)*	(2 – 1993)
South Carolina (SC) § (1788) *(8)*	30,203	3,486,703	Columbia	Carroll A. Campbell, jun. *(R)*	(4 – 1995)
South Dakota (SD) (1889) *(40)*	75,952	696,004	Pierre	Walter D. Miller *(R)*	(4 – 1995)
Tennessee (Tenn.) (1796) *(16)*	41,155	4,877,185	Nashville	Ned R. McWherter *(D)*	(4 – 1995)
Texas (1845) *(28)*	262,017	16,986,510	Austin	Anne Richards *(D)*	(4 – 1995)
Utah (1896) *(45)*	82,073	1,722,850	Salt Lake City	Mike Leavitt *(R)*	(4 – 1997)
Vermont (Vt.) (1791) *(14)*	9,273	562,758	Montpelier	Howard Dean *(D)*	(2 – 1995)
Virginia (Va.) § (1788) *(10)*	39,704	6,187,358	Richmond	L. Douglas Wilder *(D)*	(4 – 1994)
Washington (Wash.) (1889) *(42)*	66,511	4,866,692	Olympia	Mike Lowry *(D)*	(4 – 1997)
West Virginia (W. Va.) (1863) *(35)*	24,119	1,793,477	Charleston	Gaston Caperton *(D)*	(4 – 1997)
Wisconsin (Wis.) (1848) *(30)*	54,426	4,891,769	Madison	Tommy Thompson *(R)*	(4 – 1995)
Wyoming (Wyo.) (1890) *(44)*	96,989	453,588	Cheyenne	Michael Sullivan *(D)*	(4 – 1995)
Dist. of Columbia (DC) (1791)	63	606,900	—	†	

OUTLYING TERRITORIES AND POSSESSIONS

American Samoa	76	46,773	Pago Pago	A. P. Lutati *(D)*	(4 – 1997)
Guam	209	133,152	Agaña	Joseph Ada *(D)*	(4 – 1995)
Northern Mariana Islands	184	43,555	Saipan	Lorenzo I. DeLeon Guerrero *(R)*	(4 – 1994)
Palau	192	15,105	Koror	—	
Puerto Rico	3,421	3,522,037	San Juan	Dr Pedro J. Rossello *(PNP)*	(4 – 1997)
Virgin Islands	132	101,809	Charlotte Amalie	Alexander Farrelly *(D)*	(4 – 1995)

§The 13 original states
D Democratic Party; *I* Independent; *PNP* New Progressive Party; *R* Republican Party
†The capital territory is governed by Congress through a Commissioner and City Council

states, seven were admitted without previous organization as territories, and 30 were admitted after such organization.

By the Constitution of 17 September 1787 (to which amendments were added in 1791, 1798, 1804, 1865, 1868, 1870, 1913, 1920, 1933, 1951, 1961, 1964, 1967 and 1971), the government of the United States is entrusted to three separate authorities: the executive (the President and Cabinet), the legislature (Congress) and the judicature.

The President is indirectly elected every four years. There is also a Vice-President, who, should the President die, becomes President for the remainder of the term. In case of the removal or death of both President and Vice-President, a statute provides for the succession. The tenure of the Presidency is limited to two terms.

The President, with the consent of the Senate, appoints the Cabinet officers and all the chief officials. He makes recommendation of a general nature to Congress, and when laws are passed by Congress he may return them to Congress with a veto. But if a measure so vetoed is again passed by both Houses of Congress by two-thirds majority in each House, it becomes law, notwithstanding the objection of the President. The President must be at least 35 years of age and a native citizen of the United States.

Presidential elections

Each state elects (on the first Tuesday after the first Monday in November of the year preceding the year in which the presidential term expires) a number of electors, equal to the whole number of Senators and Representatives to which the state may be entitled in the Congress. The electors for each state meet in their respective states on the first Monday after the second Wednesday in December following, and vote for a President by ballot. The ballots are then sent to Washington, and opened on 6 January by the President of Senate in presence of Congress. The candidate who has received a majority of the whole number of electoral votes cast is declared President for the ensuing term. If no one has a majority, then from the highest on the list (not exceeding three) the House of Representatives elects a President, the votes being taken by states, the representation from each state having one vote. A presidential term begins at noon on 20 January.

President of the United States, William Jefferson Blythe IV Clinton, *born* 19 August 1946, *sworn in* 20 January 1993. Democrat.

Vice-President, Albert Gore, jun., *born* 31 March 1948, *sworn in* 20 January 1993.

THE CABINET *as at August 1993*

Secretary of State, Warren Christopher.
Secretary of the Treasury, Lloyd Bentsen.
Secretary of Defence, Les Aspin.
Attorney-General, Janet Reno.
Secretary of the Interior, Bruce Babbit.
Secretary of Agriculture, Mike Espy.
Secretary of Commerce, Ron Brown.
Secretary of Labour, Robert Reich.
Secretary of Health and Human Services, Donna Shalala.
Secretary of Housing and Urban Development, Henry Cisneros.
Secretary of Transportation, Frederico Pena.
Secretary of Energy, Hazel O'Leary.
Secretary of Education, Richard Riley.
Secretary of Veterans' Affairs, Jesse Brown.
Ambassador to the UN, Madeline Albright.
US Trade Representative, Mickey Kantor.
Administrator, Environmental Protection Agency, Carol Browner.
Director, Office of Management and Budget, Leon Panetta.

National Security Adviser, Anthony Lake.
White House Chief of Staff, Thomas McLarty.

Other senior positions:
Director of CIA, James Woolsey.
Director, Office of National Drug Control Policy, Lee Brown (*acting*).
Director of FBI, Louis Freeh.
Chairman, Federal Reserve Board of Governors, Alan Greenspan.

UNITED STATES EMBASSY
24 Grosvenor Square, London WIA IAE
Tel 071-499 9000

Ambassador Extraordinary and Plenipotentiary, The Honourable Raymond G. H. Seitz (1991).
Ministers, T. E. Deal, Mrs A. R. Berry (*Economic*).
Defence and Naval Attaché, Capt. J. E. Hart.
Counsellor, E. C. McBride (*Cultural*).
Minister-Counsellors, N. Kreig (*Consular*); K. P. Moorefield (*Commercial*).

BRITISH EMBASSY
3100 Massachusetts Avenue NW, Washington DC 20008
Tel: Washington DC 462 1340

Ambassador Extraordinary and Plenipotentiary, His Excellency Sir Robin Renwick, KCMG (1991).
Ministers, D. Peretz (*Economic*); S. Webb (*Defence Equipment*); C. J. R. Meyer, CMG (*Commercial*); W. Marsden, CMG; P. Lo (*Hong Kong Economic and Trade Affairs*).
Head of British Defence Staff and Defence Attaché, Air Vice-Marshal Peter Dodworth, OBE, AFC.
Counsellor, A. F. Smith (*Admin. and HM Consul-General*).
Consul-General (New York) and Director-General of Trade and Investment, A. J. Hunter, CMG.
Cultural Attaché and British Council Representative, G. Tindale, OBE.

BRITISH CONSULATES-GENERAL – Atlanta, Boston, Chicago, Houston, Los Angeles, New York and San Francisco.
BRITISH CONSULATES – Anchorage, Cleveland, Dallas, Kansas City, Miami, New Orleans, Norfolk, Philadelphia, Portland, St Louis, Seattle and Puerto Rico.

BRITISH-AMERICAN CHAMBER OF COMMERCE, 275 Madison Avenue, New York 10016; UK OFFICE, Suite 201, High Holborn, London WCIV 6RR.

THE CONGRESS

The legislative power is vested in two Houses, the Senate and the House of Representatives. The Senate is composed of two Senators from each state, elected for the term of six years, and each Senator has one vote. Representatives are chosen in each State, by popular vote, for two years.

The Senate consists of 100 members. The House of Representatives consists of 435 Representatives, a resident commissioner from Puerto Rico and a delegate from American Samoa, the District of Columbia, Guam and the Virgin Islands. Members of the 103rd Congress were elected on 3 November 1992. The 103rd Congress is constituted as follows:

Senate – Democrats 56; Republicans 44; total 100.
House of Representatives – Democrats 258; Republicans 176; Independent 1; total 435 (15 June 1993).

President of the Senate, The Vice-President.
Speaker of the House of Representatives, Thomas S. Foley, Washington.

Secretary of the Senate, Walter J. Stewart, *District of Columbia.*

Clerk of the House of Representatives, Donnald K. Anderson, *California.*

THE JUDICATURE

The federal judiciary consists of three sets of federal courts: the Supreme Court at Washington DC, consisting of a Chief Justice and eight Associate Justices, with original jurisdiction in cases where a state is a party to the suit, and with appellate jurisdiction from inferior federal courts and from the judgments of the highest courts of the states; the United States Courts of Appeals, dealing with appeals from district courts and from certain federal administrative agencies, and consisting of 168 circuit judges within 13 circuits; the 94 United States district courts served by 575 district court judges.

THE SUPREME COURT

US Supreme Court Building, Washington DC 20543

Chief Justice, William H. Rehnquist, *Arizona,* apptd 1986.

Associate Justices
Harry Blackmun, *Minnesota,* apptd 1970
John Paul Stevens, *Illinois,* apptd 1975
Sandra Day O'Connor, *Arizona,* apptd 1981
Antonin Scalia, *Virginia,* apptd 1986
Anthony M. Kennedy, *California,* apptd 1988
David H. Souter, *New Hampshire,* apptd 1990
Clarence Thomas, *Georgia,* apptd 1991
Ruth Ginsburg, *DC,* apptd 1993

Clerk of the Supreme Court, William K. Suter.

CRIMINAL STATISTICS *Number of offences*

	1991	1992
Murder and non-negligent manslaughter	24,703	23,760
Forcible rape	106,593	109,062
Robbery	687,732	672,478
Aggravated assault	1,092,739	1,126,974
Burglary	3,157,150	2,979,884
Larceny – theft	8,142,228	7,915,199
Thefts of motor vehicles	1,661,738	1,610,834
Total	14,872,883	14,438,191

DEFENCE

Each military department is separately organized and functions under the direction, authority and control of the Secretary of Defence. The Air Force has primary responsibility for the Department of Defence space development programmes and projects.

Secretary of Defence (in the Cabinet), Les Aspin.
Chairman, Joint Chiefs of Staff, Gen. Colin Powell. (To be replaced by Gen. John Shalikashvili).

STRENGTHS
As at 28 February 1993
The US Army had a strength of 595,002. The strength of the Navy was 526,639 active duty personnel. The strength of the Marine Corps was 182,754 active duty personnel. The Air Force had 450,624 officers and airmen on active duty.

DEPLOYMENT

Under strategic command the USA has some 504 submarine-launched ballistic missiles, 1,000 inter-continental ballistic missiles and 270 heavy nuclear-capable bombers together with multiple intelligence satellites, radars and early warning systems throughout the world. The Army deploys some

15,629 main battle tanks, 900 light tanks, 31,900 armoured infantry fighting vehicles and armoured personnel carriers, 6,300 artillery pieces and 1,660 armed helicopters. The Navy deploys some 25 strategic (SLBM) submarines, 87 tactical submarines, 12 aircraft carriers, 48 cruisers, 45 destroyers, 83 frigates, 1,735 combat aircraft and 421 armed helicopters. The Marine Corps has 125 main battle tanks, 2,030 armoured vehicles, 1,030 artillery pieces, 410 combat aircraft and 96 armed helicopters. The Air Force deploys 276 long-range and 3,638 tactical combat aircraft and 1,800 transport and training aircraft. The major deployment of US personnel overseas are: Germany (148,400); UK (20,100); Italy (15,100); Mediterranean (15,500); Japan (39,300); South Korea (35,500); Panama (10,500).

FINANCE

BUDGET	1991	1992
Total receipts	$1,054.3 bn	$1,091.7 bn
Total outlay	1,322.0 bn	1,381.9 bn
Defence	272.5 bn	298.2 bn
Social security	269.0 bn	287.5 bn

SOCIAL WELFARE EXPENDITURE 1990

	Total	*Per capita*
Social insurance	$510,616 m	$2,004
Education	258,385 m	1,018
Public aid	145,642 m	574
Health and medical	62,428 m	246
Veterans' programmes	30,916 m	120
Other social welfare	17,918 m	71
Housing	19,468 m	77
TOTAL	1,045,372 m	4,110

PUBLIC DEBT

At the end of September 1992 the total gross federal debt stood at US$4,002,815 million.

ECONOMY

GROSS NATIONAL PRODUCT BY INDUSTRY 1990

	US$ millions
Private industries	4,842,700
Agriculture, forestry, fisheries	113,300
Mining	98,500
Construction	241,300
Manufacturing	1,018,300
Transportation and public utilities	481,900
Wholesale trade	359,700
Retail trade	515,800
Finance, insurance, and real estate	974,700
Services	1,041,000
Government and government enterprises	674,100
Statistical discrepancy	5,400
TOTAL	5,522,200

AGRICULTURE

The total number of farms in 1992 was 2,095,740, with a total area of land in farms of 980,063,000 acres, and an average acreage per farm of 468 acres. The total number of people employed on farms during the week of 11–17 April 1993 was 2,884,000, of whom 364,000 were unpaid workers, 828,000 hired workers and 224,000 agricultural service workers. Principal crops are corn for grain, soybeans, wheat hay, cotton, tobacco, grain sorghums, potatoes, oranges and barley.

Livestock on farms on 1 January 1992 and 1993 was:

	1992	1993
Cattle	99,559,000	100,892,000
Milk cows	9,913,000	9,844,000
Sheep and lambs	10,900,000	10,200,000
Hogs and pigs	57,684,000	59,316,000
Chickens	362,821,000	364,180,000

Gross income from farming in 1992 was US$184,000 million, of which cash receipts from marketing were US$170,000 million and government payments US$9,200 million. Cash income from all crops in 1992 was US$84,000 million and from livestock and livestock products US$86,000 million.

MINERALS

The value of non-fuel raw mineral production in 1991 totalled an estimated US$30,489 million compared with US$33,337 million in 1990.

Trade	1990	1991
Imports	US$41,009m	US$41,137m
Exports	28,025m	29,481m

Production ('000 metric tons)	1990	1991e
Aluminium	5,643	5,600
Iron Ore	56,800	56,200
Phosphate rock	48,096	47,000
Zinc ore	518	520
Refined copper	1,995	2,090
Refined lead	1,276	1,130

e estimate

ENERGY 1991

Production in 1991 was 67.49 quadrillion BTU, principally coal, natural gas and crude oil. Coal accounted for over half of energy exports of 5.19 quadrillion BTU. Imports were 18.35 quadrillion BTU, of which crude oil was 12.55 quadrillion BTU, to meet consumption of 81.51 quadrillion BTU (quadrillion = 10^{15}).

LABOUR

The civilian labour force was 129,839,000 in June 1993. The number of employed persons was 120,586,000. This includes self-employed, wage and salary-earners, and unpaid family workers. Unemployment was estimated at 9,252,000 in June 1993 (7.1 per cent) (7.8 per cent in June 1992).

TRADE	1991	1992
General imports		
c.i.f. value	US$510,168m	US$553,335m
customs value	488,453	532,665
Exports and re-exports		
†f.a.s. value	421,853	447,471
Trade balance		
f.a.s. exports: c.i.f.		
imports	−88,315	−105,864
f.a.s. exports: customs		
imports	−65,723	−84,501

† excluding military aid

Principal sources of imports were Asian countries (of which Japan contributed 41 per cent), north and central America (of which Canada 68 per cent), Europe (of which EC countries 83 per cent). Principal destinations for exports and re-exports were Asian states (of which Japan took 34 per cent), north and central America (of which Canada 63 per cent), Europe (of which EC 83 per cent).

Trade with UK	1991	1992
Imports from UK	£11,340,030,000	£12,225,877,000
Exports to UK	13,711,538,000	13,711,323,000

COMMUNICATIONS

Revenue, etc., of Class I line-haul railroads (US$ thousands):

	1989	1990
Operating		
Revenues	27,956,000	28,370,000
Freight	27,956,000	24,471,000
Passenger	893,300	941,900
Total operating expenses	25,038,000	24,652,000
Net working capital	−2,119,000	−3,505,000
Average number of		
employees	228,000	216,000

In 1991 there were 3.89 million miles of public roads and streets in the United States, of which 3.14 million miles were in rural areas and 749,864 miles were in urban areas. Surfaced roads and streets account for 91.5 per cent of the total. An estimated total of US$74,488 million was spent in 1991 on roads and streets in the United States. In 1990 there were 41,462 deaths caused by motor vehicle accidents. The death rate per 100,000,000 vehicle-miles of travel was 1.91 in 1991 compared with 2.07 in 1990.

The ocean-going merchant marine of the US on 1 January 1993 consisted of 603 vessels of 1,000 gross tons and over, of which 384 were privately-owned and 219 were government-owned ships. There were 159 ships in the National Defence Reserve Fleet of inactive government-owned vessels.

According to preliminary figures, domestic and international scheduled airlines in 1992 carried 471,811,000 passengers over 474,783,000,000 revenue passenger miles. Air cargo ton-miles were distributed as follows: freight and express 14,390,000,000; and air mail 2,106,000,000. Total operating revenues of all US scheduled airlines were US$77,510,212,100 in 1992. Total operating expenses rose to US$79,438,689,900 in 1992. Scheduled operations showed a net operating loss of US$1,928,477,800 in 1992, compared with a net operating loss of US$3,334,191,200 in 1991.

EDUCATION

All the states and the District of Columbia have compulsory school attendance laws. In general, children are obliged to attend school from seven to 16 years of age. In the autumn of 1992, 47,870,000 children were enrolled in regular elementary and secondary day schools, of whom 5.38 million or 11.2 per cent attended private schools.

The following percentages of the school-age population were estimated to be enrolled in school in the autumn of 1992: 96 per cent of 5- and 6-year-olds; 99 per cent of 7- to 13-year-olds; 97 per cent of 14- to 17-year-olds, and 40 per cent of 18- to 24-year-olds.

During the 1990–1 school year, the average daily attendance in regular public elementary and secondary day schools was 37,778,512. In the 1991–2 school year 2,246,000 students graduated from regular public high schools and 259,000 graduated from private high school. In addition an estimated 457,000 received high school equivalency certificates. Public school teachers numbered 2,432,000, with an average salary of US$34,098.

Most of the revenue for public elementary and secondary school purposes comes from federal, state, and local governments. Less than 2.5 per cent comes from gifts and from tuition and transportation fees. Revenue receipts during 1990–1 amounted to US$222,822,000,000; 6.2 per cent from the federal government, 47.3 per cent from state governments, and 44.1 per cent from local sources. Estimated current expenditure in the 1990–1 school year was US$208,848 million; for sites, buildings, furniture and equipment expenditures, US$19,771 million; for interest on school debt US$4,314 million.

HIGHER EDUCATION

In the autumn of 1992, total enrolment in universities, colleges, professional schools, and two-year schools numbered 14,558,000.

During 1990–1 the major fields for bachelor's degrees were business and management (249,960), social sciences (124,893), education (111,010) and engineering (78,864). First-profession degrees in law (37,945) and medicine (15,043) predominated. Master's degrees were heavily concentrated in education (88,904) and business and management (78,681). The most popular fields of study for doctorates were education (6,697) and engineering (5,272). Total expenditures for colleges and universities during the 1990–1 academic year were US$165,800 million.

Among the better-known universities are: *Harvard*, founded at Cambridge, Mass. in 1636, and named after John Harvard of Emmanuel College, Cambridge, England, who bequeathed to it his library and a sum of money in 1638; *Yale*, founded at New Haven, Connecticut, in 1701; *Princeton*, NJ, founded 1746.

US TERRITORIES, ETC

Responsibility for territorial affairs generally is centred in the Office of the Assistant Secretary, Territorial and International Affairs, Department of the Interior, Washington DC.

As well as the territories mentioned below, the USA also exercises sovereignty over the following:

Johnston Atoll – two small islands, less than 1 sq. mile in area, to the south-west of Hawaii; administered by the US Air Force.

Midway Islands – two islands (area, 3 sq. miles), at the western end of the Hawaiian chain; administered by the US Navy.

Wake Islands – area about 3 sq. miles and average elevation of less than 3 metres, lying about 2,300 miles west of Hawaii; administered by the US Air Force.

Certain small guano islands, rocks or keys, considered as appertaining to the USA.

THE COMMONWEALTH OF PUERTO RICO

Puerto Rico (Rich Port) is an island of the Greater Antilles group in the West Indies, and lies between 17° 50′ and 18° 30′ N. lat. and 65° 30′ and 67° 15′ W. long., with a total area of 3,421 sq. miles (8,860 sq. km), and a population (1992 estimate) of 3,336,000. The 1990 Census put the population at 3,522,037. The majority of the inhabitants are of Spanish descent, and Spanish and English are the official languages. The island is about 111 miles from west to east, and 36 miles from north to south.

Puerto Rico was discovered in 1493 by Christopher Columbus and explored by Ponce de Léon in 1508. It continued as a Spanish possession until 1898, when the United States took formal possession as a result of the Spanish-American War.

The 1952 Constitution approved by the Congress and the President of the United States establishes the Commonwealth of Puerto Rico with full powers of local government. The Legislative Assembly consists of two elected houses; the Senate of 27 members and the House of Representatives of 51 members. The term of the Legislative Assembly is four years. The Governor is popularly elected for a term of four years. Residents of Puerto Rico are US citizens. Puerto Rico is represented in Congress by a Resident Commissioner, elected for a term of four years, who has a seat in the House

of Representatives but not a vote, although he has a right to vote on those committees of which he is a member.

Preliminary 1994 figures for the Commonwealth Government's budget were receipts, US$12,627 million. Manufacturing added US$12,324 million to net Commonwealth income in 1992 (preliminary figures), trade US$3,598 million, finance, insurance and real estate US$3,739 million and agriculture US$518 million. Principal crops are sugar cane, coffee, vegetables, fruits and tobacco. Most valuable areas of manufacturing are chemicals and allied products, metal products and machinery.

CAPITAL – ΨSan Juan, population of the municipality (1990), 437,745; Other major towns are: Bayamón (220,262); ΨPonce (187,749); and Carolina (177,806).

Governor, Dr Pedro J. Rossello.

TRADE	1990	1991
Total Imports	US$19,124m	US$19,440m
Total Exports	20,669m	21,765m

Trade with UK	1991	1992
Imports from UK	£81,637,000	£156,118,000
Exports to UK	109,295,000	103,463,000

GUAM

Guam, the largest of the Mariana Islands in the north Pacific Ocean, lies in 13° 26′ N. lat. and 144° 39′ E. long. and has an area of about 209 sq. miles (541 sq. km). The population (1990 estimate) is 133,152, mostly of Chamorro stock mingled with Filipino and Spanish blood. The Chamorro language belongs to the Malayo-Polynesian family, but with considerable admixture of Spanish. Chamorro and English are the official languages and most residents are bilingual.

Guam was occupied by the Japanese in December 1941 but was recaptured by US forces in 1944. Under the Organic Act of Guam 1950, Guam has statutory powers of self-government, and Guamanians are United States citizens. A 21-member unicameral legislature is elected biennially. The Governor and Lieutenant-Governor are popularly elected. A non-voting Delegate is elected to serve in the US House of Representatives. There is also a District Court of Guam, with original jurisdiction in cases under federal law.

Guam's two main sources of revenue are tourism and US military spending.

CAPITAL – Agaña. Port of entry, ΨApra.

Governor, Joseph F. Ada.
Lt.-Governor, Frank Blas.

AMERICAN SAMOA

American Samoa consists of the islands of Tutuila, Anu'u, Ofu, Olesega, Ta'u, Rose and Swains Islands, with a total area of 76 sq. miles (197 sq. km). Tutuila, the largest of the group, has an area of 52 square miles and a magnificent harbour at Pago Pago. The remaining islands have an area of about 24 square miles. The population (1990 estimate) is 46,773. Tuna and copra are the chief exports.

American Samoans are US nationals, but some have acquired citizenship through service in the United States armed forces or other naturalization procedure. The 1960 Constitution grants American Samoa a measure of self-government, with certain powers reserved to the US Secretary of the Interior. There is a bicameral legislature with popularly elected Representatives and Governors and a popularly elected Governor. A non-voting Delegate is elected to serve in the US House of Representatives.

SEAT OF GOVERNMENT – Fagatogo.

Governor, A. P. Lutali.
Lt.-Governor, Tauese P. Sunia.

THE VIRGIN ISLANDS

The US Virgin Islands were purchased from Denmark and proclaimed US territory in 1917. The total area of the islands is 132 sq. miles (342 sq. km), with a population (1990) of 101,809. There are three main islands, St Thomas (28 sq. miles), St Croix (84 sq. miles), St John (20 sq. miles) and about 50 small islets or cays, mostly uninhabited.

Under the provisions of the Revised Organic Act of the Virgin Islands 1954, legislative power is vested in the Legislature, a unicameral body composed of 15 senators popularly elected for two-year terms. The Governor is popularly elected. Virgin Islanders are citizens of the United States. A non-voting Delegate is elected to serve in the US House of Representatives. A referendum is to take place at a future date to determine the future political status of the islands.

CAPITAL – ΨCharlotte Amalie on St Thomas. Population (1980) 11,756.

Governor, Alexander Farrelly.
Lt.-Governor, Derek M. Hodge.

NORTHERN MARIANA ISLANDS

The land area of the Northern Mariana Islands is 184 sq. miles (476 sq. km) with an estimated population (1990) of 43,555.

The USA administered the islands as part of a UN Trusteeship until the trusteeship agreement was terminated in 1986. The end of the trusteeship brought fully into effect a 1976 congressional law establishing a a commonwealth of the Northern Mariana Islands. Most of the residents became US citizens. There is a popularly elected bicameral legislature and a popularly elected Governor.

SEAT OF GOVERNMENT – Saipan.
Population (1990 estimate) 39,090.

Governor, Lorenzo D. L. Guerrero.
Lt.-Governor, Benjamin M. Manglona.

REPUBLIC OF PALAU

Palau consists of more than 200 Pacific Ocean islands, of which eight are permanently inhabited. The Palau archipelago stretches over 400 miles. The land area is 191 sq. miles (494 sq. km), with an estimated population of 15,105. The major island is Koror with a population of 10,493.

Constitutional government was installed in Palau in January 1981 and provides for a bicameral legislature, consisting of a House of Delegates of 16 members and a Senate of 14 members. The President and Vice-President are directly elected. Palau and the USA signed a Compact of Free Association in August 1982, but this has not been approved by a three-quarters majority of the voters of Palau. By referendum on 4 November 1992 the majority necessary to amend the constitution to bring it in line with the Compact was lowered to a simple majority in three-quarters of Palau's 16 divisions. The USA is responsible for financial support, and for the defence of Palau for 50 years. The Compact is incompatible with the ban on nuclear weapons in the constitution. Palau is the last remaining part of the US-administered UN Trust Territory of the Pacific Islands. When the Compact is approved in a referendum, the Republic of Palau will become an independent sovereign state in free association with the USA.

President, Kuniwo Nakamura.
Vice-President, Tommy Remengesau, jun.

THE PANAMA CANAL

As a result of the Panama Canal Treaty 1977, the Canal Zone was disestablished, with all jurisdiction over the former Canal Zone reverting to Panama with effect from 1 October 1979. Under the treaty, the United States is allowed the use of operating areas for the Panama Canal, together with several military bases, although the Republic of Panama is sovereign in all such areas. The Panama Canal Commission, an arm of the US Government, will continue to operate the canal until the year 2000.

The canal is fifty statute miles long (44.08 nautical miles), and the channel is from 500 to 1,000 feet wide at the bottom. Its maximum allowable draft is 39.5 feet (12 metres). It contains 12 locks in twin flights; three steps at Gatun on the Atlantic side, one step at Pedro Miguel and two at Miraflores on the Pacific side. Each lock chamber is 1,000 feet long and 110 feet wide. Transit from sea to sea takes on average eight to ten hours. The greatest width is in Gatun Lake and outside the locks, the narrowest section of the canal is the eight-mile stretch through the Continental Divide known as Gaillard Cut where the navigational tunnel is 500 ft (152 m) wide. The width is being increased to a minimum of 630 ft (191 m) in the straight sections.

In the fiscal year 1992, the total number of transits by ocean-going commercial traffic was 12,454; canal net tons totalled 188,516,466; cargo tons totalled 159,272,618.

URUGUAY
República Oriental del Uruguay

Uruguay is situated on the east coast of the Rio de la Plata in South America, in 30° to 35° S. latitude and 53° 15' to 57° 42' W. longitude, with an area of 68,037 sq. miles (176,215 sq. km). The country consists mainly of undulating grassy plains. The principal hills are the Cuchilla del Haedo, which cross the Brazilian boundary and extend southwards to the Cuchilla Grande of the south and east. In no case do the peaks exceed 2,000 feet. The principal river is the Rio Negro (with its tributary the Yi), flowing from north-east to south-west into the Rio Uruguay. The boundary river Uruguay is navigable from its estuary to Salto, about 200 miles north, and the Negro is also navigable for a considerable distance.

CLIMATE – Temperate, with warm summers and mild winters, though cold spells from June to August. Rainfall is regular throughout the year, but there are occasional droughts.

POPULATION – The population (1992) is 3,116,802, predominantly of Spanish and Italian descent. Spanish is the language of the country. Many Uruguayans are Roman Catholics. There is complete freedom of religion and no church is established by the state.

CAPITAL – Ψ Montevideo, population (1992) 1,383,660.
Other centres are Salto, Ψ Paysandu, Mercedes, Minas, Melo, Rivera and Punta del Este.

CURRENCY – New Uruguayan peso of 100 centésimos.

FLAG – Four blue and five white horizontal stripes surcharged with sun on a white ground in the top corner, next flagstaff.

NATIONAL ANTHEM – Orientales, La Patria O La Tumba (Uruguayans, the fatherland or death).

NATIONAL DAY – 25 August (Declaration of Independence, 1825).

GOVERNMENT

Uruguay (or the *Banda Oriental*, as the territory lying on the eastern bank of the Uruguay River was then called) resisted all attempted invasions of the Portuguese and Spanish until the beginning of the 17th century; 100 years later the Portuguese settlements were captured by the Spanish. From 1726 to 1814 the country formed part of Spanish South America and underwent many vicissitudes during the wars of independence. In 1814 the armies of the Argentine Confederation captured the capital and annexed the province; afterwards it was annexed by Portugal and became a province of Brazil. In 1825, the country threw off Brazilian rule. This action led to war between Argentina and Brazil which was settled by the mediation of the United Kingdom, Uruguay being declared an independent state in 1828. In 1830 a republic was inaugurated.

According to the constitution the President appoints a council of 11 ministers and a Secretary (Planning and Budget Office), and the Vice-President presides over Congress. The Congress consists of a Chamber of 99 deputies and a Senate of 30 members (plus the Vice-President), elected for five years by a system of proportional representation. General elections held in November 1984 marked the return to civilian rule after 11 years of presidential rule with military support. The first fully free presidential and legislative elections since 1971 were held in November 1989, and were won by the Partido Nacional Blanco.

The republic is divided into 19 Departments each with a mayor, a chief of police and a Departmental Council.

HEAD OF STATE
President, Dr Luis Alberto Lacalle, *took office* 1 March 1990.
Vice-President, Dr Gonzalo Aguirre Ramírez.

CABINET *as at September 1993*

Interior, Dr Juan Andrés Ramírez.
Foreign Affairs, Dr Sergío Abreu.
Economy and Finance, Dr Ignacío De Posadas.
Transport and Public Works, Juan C. Raffo.
Public Health, Guillermo Garcia Costa.
Labour and Social Security, Dr Ricardo Reilly.
Livestock, Agriculture and Fisheries, Pedro Saravia.
Education and Culture, Antonio Mercader.
National Defence, Dr Daniel Martins.
Industry and Energy, Dr Eduardo Ache.
Tourism, José Villar.
Housing, Territorial Regulation and Environment, Hugo Romay.
Secretary, Planning and Budget Office, Carlos Alfredo Cat.

EMBASSY OF THE ORIENTAL REPUBLIC OF URUGUAY
2nd Floor, 140 Brompton Road, London SW3 1HY
Tel 071-584 8192; *Consulate* 071-589 8735

Ambassador Extraordinary and Plenipotentiary, His Excellency Juan Enrique Fischer (1993).

BRITISH EMBASSY
Calle Marco Bruto 1073, Montevideo 11300 (PO Box 16024)
Tel: Montevideo 623650

Ambassador Extraordinary and Plenipotentiary, His Excellency Donald Lamont (1991)

There is a British Consular Office at *Montevideo*.

BRITISH-URUGUAYAN CHAMBER OF COMMERCE,
Avenida Labertador Brig. Gen., Lavalleja 1641, P2-OF 201, Montevideo.

DEFENCE

Uruguay has a total active armed forces of 24,700. The Army has a strength of 17,200, with 67 light tanks, 55 reconnaissance vehicles, 65 armoured personnel carriers and 67 artillery pieces. The Navy has a strength of 4,500, including a battalion of 500 naval infantry, and deploys three frigates, eight patrol and coastal combatants and six combat aircraft. The Air Force is 3,000 strong, with 37 combat aircraft. Paramilitary forces number some 1,200 personnel.

ECONOMY

The wealth of the country is obtained from its pasturage, which supports large herds of cattle and sheep. There are just over 9 million cattle and just under 24 million sheep. Wheat, barley, maize, linseed, sunflower seed and rice are cultivated. In addition to wool, meat packing, other foodstuffs (citrus, wine, beer), fishing and textile industries are of importance.

The development of local industry continues and, in addition to the greatly augmented textile industry, local production has expanded in tyres, sheet-glass, three-ply wood, cement, leather-curing, beet-sugar, plastics, household consumer goods, edible oils and the refining of petroleum and petroleum products. There are some ferrous minerals, not extracted at present. Non-ferrous exploited minerals include clinker, dolomite, marble and granite.

The external debt in 1992 was US$7,355 million. Central Bank reserves (1992) were US$1,711 million, while GNP was (1991) US$9,480,000m, inflation (1992) 58.9 per cent, unemployment (1992) 8.3 per cent.

FINANCE	1991	1992
Revenue	US$1,839,075m	US$1,990,373m
Expenditure	1,800,733m	1,959,930m

TRADE

The major exports are meat and by-products, wool and by-products, hides and bristle and agricultural products. The principal imports are raw materials, construction materials, oils and lubricants, automotive vehicles, kits and machinery. Principal trading partners are Brazil, USA and Argentina.

	1991	1992
Total exports	US$1,604,700 m	US$1,702,500 m
Total imports	1,636,400 m	2,058,000 m
Trade with UK	1991	1992
Imports from UK	£33,303,000	£31,462,000
Exports to UK	47,894,000	49,492,000

COMMUNICATIONS

There are about 9,899 km of national highways, and about 2,987 km of standard gauge railway in use. Passenger rail services were cancelled in January 1988 and services are now limited to cargo transport; services are state-run. A state-owned airline, PLUNA, provides international services, and internal passenger and a limited freight service are provided by TAMU, another state-owned airline, using principally military aircraft and personnel. The international airport of Carrasco lies 12 miles outside Montevideo.

Six daily newspapers are published in Montevideo with an estimated total circulation of 150,000. Most of them are distributed throughout the country.

EDUCATION

Primary education is compulsory and free, and technical and trade schools and evening courses for adult education are state controlled. The university at Montevideo (founded in 1849) has ten faculties.

UZBEKISTAN
Ozbekiston Respublikasy

Uzbekistan has an area of 172,742 sq. miles (447,400 sq. km) and occupies the south-central part of former Soviet Central Asia, lying between the high Tienshan Mountains and the Pamir highlands in the east and south-east and sandy lowlands in the west and north-west. It is bordered on the north by Kazakhstan and the Aral Sea, on the east by Kyrgyzstan and Tajikistan, on the south by Afghanistan and Turkmenistan, and on the west by Kazakhstan. Uzbekistan consists of the Kara-Kalpak Autonomous Republic and 12 regions: Andizhan, Bokhara, Dzhizak, Ferghana, Kashkadar, Khorezm, Namangan, Navoi, Samarkand, Surkhan-Darya, Syr-Darya and Tashkent. The major part of the country is a plain with huge waterless deserts, and several large oases which form the main centres of population and economic life. The largest is the Ferghana valley, watered by the Syr-Darya. Other oases include Tashkent, Samarkand, Bokhara and Khorezm and the other river is the Amur-Darya.

CLIMATE – Continental and dry.

POPULATION – According to the 1989 census the population is 19,810,000, of which 71 per cent are Uzbeks, 8 per cent Russians, 5 per cent Tajiks and 4 per cent Kazakhs, with smaller numbers of Tatars, Kara-Kalpaks, Koreans, Ukrainians and Kirghiz. The 1992 estimate put the population at 20,300,000.

RELIGION – Predominantly Sunni Muslim.

LANGUAGE – 71 per cent Uzbek, 8 per cent Russian, 5 per cent Tajik, 4 per cent Kazakh. Uzbek is one of the Turkic group of languages.

CAPITAL – Tashkent. Population 2,073,000 (1992). Samarkand (388,000) contains the Gur-Emir (Tamerlane's Mausoleum) completed 1400 by Ulugbek, Tamerlane's astronomer grandson.

CURRENCY – Rouble of 100 kopeks.

FLAG – Three horizontal stripes of blue, white, green, with the white fimbriated in red; on the blue near the hoist a crescent and twelve stars, all in white.

NATIONAL DAY – 31 August (Independence Day).

GOVERNMENT

Between the sixth and fourth centuries BC the area that is now Uzbekistan was under the control of the Persians and then Alexander the Great. In the 14th century the area became the centre of a great Muslim empire under Tamerlane and then his grandson Ulugbek, following whose murder the state disintegrated. By the beginning of the 19th century three independent Khanates, Khiva, Kokand and Bukhara, existed in what is now Uzbekistan. These were gradually annexed to the Russian Empire by the middle of the 19th century. In November 1917 a Communist revolution broke out in Tashkent and parts of Uzbekistan were included in the Turkestan Soviet Republic at its formation in April 1918. The remainder of Uzbekistan was under the rule of the independent states of Khiva and Bukhara, which had re-emerged in 1918, until they were defeated by the Red Army and Soviet rule was established throughout the area in 1921. Under Soviet rule a massive land irrigation programme was implemented to allow the cultivation of cotton.

Uzbekistan declared its independence from the Soviet Union on 31 August 1991 after the failed Moscow coup. Its independence was confirmed in a referendum on 29 December and recognized by the EC and USA in December 1991, with it gaining UN membership on 2 March 1992. A new constitution was adopted by the Supreme Soviet on 8 December 1992 under which Uzbekistan is a secular, democratic and presidential republic with no state ideology or religion. The President and government hold executive power, with the President serving a maximum of two five-year terms and having the power to dissolve the 500-member Supreme Soviet. The Supreme Soviet may not, however, remove or impeach the President. The last parliamentary elections were held on 24 March 1990.

The government of President Karimov is formed by the former Communist Party, which has renamed itself the People's Democratic Party. Despite the constitutionally guaranteed freedom of religion and thought and respect for human rights and multi-party democracy, censorship is still widely used and little political opposition is tolerated. Islam is tolerated within strict bounds; it is allowed to play no part in politics. Uzbek forces were sent to Tajikistan in late 1992 and early 1993 to help install and maintain the former Communist government and defeat the Islamic forces. Meanwhile the major opposition party, Birlik (Unity) nationalist party has been continually banned since the introduction of the multi-party constitution in December.

Uzbek nationalism has caused violent clashes with Tajiks in the Ferghana valley over the past three years. A knowledge of and ability to speak Uzbek is now a condition of appointment to government posts, and those not able to speak it are being dismissed. This has severely disrupted the civil service and public sector, mostly staffed by Russians. President Karimov is attempting to form close ties with Turkey in the cultural and business spheres, and this has caused problems with influential religious leaders who look to Iran and Saudi Arabia for support.

HEAD OF STATE
President, Islam Karimov, *elected* 29 December 1991.

CABINET *as at August 1993*
Chairman of the Cabinet, The President.
Prime Minister, Abdulkhashim Mutalov.
First Deputy Prime Minister, Agroindustrial Complex, Ismail Djurabekov.
Deputy PMs, Erkin Samandarov (*Social Development, Science and Culture*); Kayim Khakkulov (*Industry, Fuel and Power*); Bakhtiyar Khamidov (*General Economy*); Utkir Sultanov (*Foreign Economic Relations*); Kazim Tulyaganov; Anatoli Voznenko; Mukhmmadjon Karabayev; Rakhim Radjabov.
Interior, Zokirjon Almatov.
Foreign Affairs, Sadik Safaev.
Defence, Maj.-Gen. Rustam Akhmedov.
Finance, Erkin Bakibaev.
Justice, Mukhamad-Bobur Malikov.
Health, Shavkat Karimov.
Education, Djura Yuldashev.
Industry and Construction, Inom Iskanderov.
Agriculture, Norbek Kayumov.
Communications, Kamilzhan Rakhimov.
Labour, Alikhan Atajanov.
Roads, Rustam Yunusov.
Higher Education, Jura Abdullayev.
Public Utilities, Viktor Mikhailov.
Culture, Naim Gaibov.
Land and Water Conservancy, Rim Giniyatullin.
Local Industry, Viktor Chzhen.
Social Security, Sanobar Khodjayeva.
Power Engineering, Marat Tashpulatov.

BRITISH AMBASSADOR (resides at Moscow).

ECONOMY

Uzbekistan's economy is based on intensive agricultural production, and especially cotton production, made possible by extensive irrigation schemes. In addition there are some agricultural and textile machinery plants and several chemical combines. Large and previously underdeveloped mineral resources are to be fully exploited; these include gold, natural gas, oil, copper, lead, zinc and coal. A sizeable oilfield was discovered in the Ferghana Valley in 1992.

VANUATU
Ripablik Blong Vanuatu

Vanuatu is situated in the South Pacific Ocean, between 13° and 21° S. and 166° and 170° E. It includes 13 large and some 70 small islands, of coral and volcanic origin, including the Banks and Torres Islands in the north, and has a total land area of 4,706 sq. miles (12,190 sq. km). The principal islands are Vanua Lava, Espiritu Santo, Maewo, Pentecost, Ambae, Malekula, Ambrym, Epi, Efate, Erromango, Tanna and Aneityum. Most islands are mountainous and there are active volcanoes on several. The climate is oceanic tropical, moderated by the south-east trade winds which blow between May and October. At other times winds are variable and cyclones may occur.

POPULATION – The census in 1989 showed a population of 142,900. The 1991 UN estimate is 163,000. About 95 per cent are Melanesian, the rest being made up largely of Micronesians, Polynesians and Europeans. The national language is Bislama, but English and French are also official languages.

SEAT OF ADMINISTRATION – ΨPort Vila, Efate, population (1989) 19,400. The only other town is Luganville (population, 1989, 6,900), on Espiritu Santo.

CURRENCY – Vatu of 100 centimes.

FLAG – Red over green with a black triangle in the hoist, the three parts being divided by fimbriations of black and yellow, and in the centre of the black triangle a boar's tusk overlaid by two crossed fern leaves.

NATIONAL ANTHEM – Nasonal sing sing blong Vanuatu.

NATIONAL DAY – 30 July (Independence Day).

GOVERNMENT

Vanuatu, the former Anglo-French Condominium of the New Hebrides, became an independent republic within the Commonwealth on 30 July 1980. Parliament consists of 46 members elected for a term of four years. A Council of Chiefs advises on matters of custom. Executive power is held by the Prime Minister (elected from and by parliament) and a Council of Ministers who are responsible to parliament. The President is elected for a five-year term by the presidents of the 11 regional councils and the members of parliament.

HEAD OF STATE
President, His Excellency Frederick Karlomuana Timakata, *elected* 1989.

COUNCIL OF MINISTERS *as at August 1993*

Prime Minister and Minister of Foreign Affairs, Public Service, Planning and Statistics, Police, Media and Language Services, Hon. Maxime Carlot Korman.
Deputy Prime Minister and Minister for Justice, Culture and Women's Affairs, Hon. Sethy John Regenvanu.
Home Affairs, Hon. Charlie Nako.
Finance, Commerce and Industry, Hon. Willie Jimmy.

Economic Affairs and Tourism, Hon. Serge Vohor.
Transport, Public Works, Ports and Marine and Urban Water Supply, Hon. Amos Bangabiti.
Natural Resources, Hon. Paul Telukluk.
Education, Hon. Romain Batick.
Health and Rural Water Supply, Hon. Hilda Lini.
Agriculture, Livestock, Forestry and Fisheries, Hon. Onneyn Tahi.
Postal Services, Telecommunications and Meteorology, Dr Edward Tambisari.

Chief Justice, Charles Vaudin D'Imecourt.
Attorney-General (acting), Julian Marc Ala.

HIGH COMMISSIONER TO GREAT BRITAIN, vacant (resident in Port Vila, Vanuatu).

BRITISH HIGH COMMISSION
PO Box 567, Port Vila
Tel: Vila 23100

High Commissioner, His Excellency Thomas Duggin (1992).

ECONOMY

Most of the population is employed on plantations or in subsistence agriculture. Subsistence crops include yams, taro, manioc, sweet potato and breadfruit; principal cash crops are copra, cocoa and coffee. Large numbers of cattle are kept on the plantations and beef is the second largest export after copra. Principal exports are copra, meat (frozen, tinned and chilled), timber and cocoa.

Tourism is an important revenue earner, and the absence of direct taxation has led to growth in the finance and associated industries.

Trade with UK	1991	1992
Imports from UK	£381,000	£569,000
Exports to UK	202,000	448,000

VATICAN CITY STATE
Stato della Città del Vaticano

The office of the ecclesiastical head of the Roman Catholic Church (Holy See) is vested in the Pope, the Sovereign Pontiff. For many centuries the Sovereign Pontiff exercised temporal power but by 1870 the Papal States had become part of unified Italy. The temporal power of the Pope was in suspense until the treaty of 1929 which recognized the full and independent sovereignty of the Holy See in the City of the Vatican. The area of the Vatican City is 108 acres and its population in 1989 was about 1,000.

CURRENCY – Italian currency is legal tender.

FLAG – Square flag; equal vertical bands of yellow (next staff), and white; crossed keys and triple crown device on white band.

NATIONAL DAY – 22 October (Inauguration of present Pontiff).

Sovereign Pontiff, His Holiness Pope John Paul II (Karol Wojtyla), *born* at Wadowice (Krakow, Poland), 18 May 1920, *elected* Pope (in succession to Pope John Paul I), 16 October 1978.
Secretary of State, Cardinal Angelo Sodano, *appointed* December 1990.

APOSTOLIC NUNCIATURE
54 Parkside, London SW19 5NF
Tel 081–946 1410

Apostolic Pro Nuncio, His Excellency Archbishop Luigi Barbarito (1986).

BRITISH EMBASSY TO THE HOLY SEE
91 Via Condotti, I–00187 Rome
Tel: Rome 678 9462

Ambassador Extraordinary and Plenipotentiary, His Excellency Andrew Eustace Palmer, CMG, CVO (1991).

TRADE WITH UK	1991	1992
Imports from UK	£955,000	£966,000
Exports to UK	6,000	2,000

VENEZUELA
Republica de Venezuela

Venezuela is a South American republic, situated approximately between 0° 45′ S. and 12° 12′ N. lat. and 59° 45′ and 73° 09′ W. long. It has a total area of 352,144 sq. miles (912,050 sq. km) and a population (UN estimate 1991) of 20,226,000, of which 67 per cent are Mestizo, 21 per cent white, 10 per cent black and 2 per cent Indian.

Venezuela is bounded on the north by the Caribbean Sea, west by Colombia, east by Guyana, and south by Brazil. Included in the area of the republic are 72 islands off the coast, with a total area of about 14,650 square miles, the largest being Margarita (area, about 400 sq. miles), which is politically associated with Tortuga, Cubagua and Coche to form the state of Nueva Esparta. The mountains are the Eastern Andes and Maritime Andes, running south-west to north-east. The main range is known as the Sierra Nevada de Merida, and contains the highest peaks in the country in Pico Bolivar (16,411 ft) and Picacho de la Sierra (15,420 ft). Near the Brazilian border are the Sierras Parima and Pacaraima, and on the eastern border the Sierras de Rincote and de Usupamo. The principal river is the Orinoco, with innumerable affluents, the main river exceeding 1,600 miles in length. The upper waters of the Orinoco are united with those of the Rio Negro (a Brazilian tributary of the Amazon) by a natural river or canal, known as the Casiquiare. The coastal regions contain many lagoons and lakes, of which Maracaibo (area 8,296 square miles) is the largest lake in South America.

The climate is tropical, except where modified by altitude or tempered by sea breezes. The hot, wet season lasts from April to October, the dry, cooler season from November to March.

LANGUAGE – Spanish is the language of the country.
RELIGION – 96 per cent Roman Catholic.

CAPITAL – Caracas, population 2,784,000. Other principal towns are Ψ Maracaibo (1,364,000), Barquisimeto (602,000), Valencia (903,000), Maracay (354,000), San Cristobal (230,000), Cumaná (212,000) and Ciudad Guayana (536,506).
CURRENCY – Bolivar (BS) of 100 céntimos.
FLAG – Three horizontal stripes of yellow, blue, red with an arc of seven white stars on the blue stripe.
NATIONAL ANTHEM – Gloria Al Bravo Pueblo (Glory to the brave people).
NATIONAL DAY – 5 July.

GOVERNMENT

Venezuela gained independence from Spain in 1830. Under the 1961 Constitution, executive power is held by the President, who also appoints the Council of Ministers.

Legislative power is exercised by a bicameral National Congress, comprising a 201-member Chamber of Deputies and a Senate of 49 elected members plus the former presidents of constitutional governments as life members. The President and National Congress are directly elected for concurrent five-year terms. The most recent elections were held in December 1988 when Carlos Andrés Pérez of the Democratic Action (AD) party won the presidential election and AD emerged as the largest party in both houses of Congress. Increasing instability in the 1992–3 period caused by a deteriorating economy led to two unsuccessful military coups in 1992 and the trial of President Pérez on corruption charges after his resignation in May 1993. Presidential and legislative elections are due in December 1993.

Venezuela is divided into 21 states, a federal territory and a federal district.

HEAD OF STATE
President, Ramon J. Velásquez, *elected by Congress* 5 June 1993.

COUNCIL OF MINISTERS *as at August 1993*
Interior, Carlos Delgado Chapellin.
Foreign Affairs, Fernando Ochoa Antich.
Treasury, Carlos Rafael Silva.
Employment, Luis Horacio Vivas.
Transport and Communications, Jose Demingo Santander.
Urban Development, Henry Jatar Senior.
Energy and Mines, Dr Alirio Parra.
Environment and Natural Resources, Adalberto Gabaldon.
Health and Social Welfare, Pablo Pulido.
Agriculture and Livestock, Hiram Gaviria.
Education, Elizabeth Yabur de Caldera.
The Family, Teresa Albanez Barnola.
Justice, Fermin Marmol Leon.
Presidential Secretariat, Ramon Espinoza.
Decentralization, Allan Brewer Carias.
Culture, José Antonio Abreu.
Co-ordination and Planning, Hernan Anzola.
Minister, Guyana Corporation of Venezuela, Francisco Layrisse.
Development, Gustavo Perez Mijares.
Federal District, Cesar Rodriquez.

VENEZUELAN EMBASSY
1 Cromwell Road, London SW7 2HW
Tel 071–584 4206/7

Ambassador Extraordinary and Plenipotentiary, His Excellency Dr Ignacio Arcaya (1992).
Defence Attaché, Capt. N. A. Eljuri.
Cultural Attaché, A. J. M. Alvarez.

BRITISH EMBASSY
Apartado 1246, Caracas 1010–A
Tel: Caracas 9934111

Ambassador Extraordinary and Plenipotentiary, His Excellency John G. Flynn (1993).
Counsellor, M. Hickson, LVO *(Deputy Head of Mission).*
Consul, P. P. Haggar.
Second Secretary (Commercial), S. Murphy.

There are British Consular Offices at *Caracas, Maracaibo, Margarita* and *Mérida.*

BRITISH COUNCIL REPRESENTATIVE, J. A. Coope, OBE, Apartado 65131, Caracas 1065.

BRITISH-VENEZUELAN CHAMBER OF COMMERCE, Apartado 5713, Caracas 1010. Torre Británica, Piso 10, Letra E, Av. José Félix Sosa, Altamira Sur, Caracas 1060.

DEFENCE

Venezuela has a total active armed forces strength of 75,000 personnel, including 18,000 conscripts, who serve for two years (Army and Air Force) or 30 months (Navy). Conscription is selective. The Army has 34,000 personnel, with 70 main battle tanks, 161 light tanks, 290 armoured personnel carriers, 107 artillery pieces and six attack helicopters. The Navy has 11,000 personnel, including 6,000 marines, with two submarines, six frigates, six patrol and coastal vessels, four combat aircraft and eight armed helicopters. The Air Force is 7,000 strong, with 120 combat aircraft and 30 armed helicopters. The National Guard has 23,000 internal security personnel, with 239 armoured infantry fighting vehicles and armoured personnel carriers, mortar, aircraft, helicopters and inshore patrol craft.

EDUCATION

Education is free and compulsory between the ages of five and 14. There are ten universities in Venezuela, five in Caracas and the others in Maracaibo, Mérida, Valencia, Cumaná and Barquisimeto.

ECONOMY

Products of the tropical forest region include orchids, wild rubber, timber, mangrove bark, balata gum and tonka beans. Agricultural products include corn, bananas, cocoa beans, coffee, cotton, rice, maize, sugar, sesame, groundnuts, potatoes, tomatoes, other vegetables, sisal and tobacco. There is an extensive beef and dairy farming industry. Despite substantial improvements in agriculture, Venezuela is heavily reliant upon food imports, which constitute about 60 per cent of total consumption. The government has embarked on a policy of economic reform and privatization.

The principal industry is that of petroleum, which in 1988 contributed 81 per cent of Venezuela's foreign exchange income. Daily production in the oilfields (nationalized 1976) has steadily declined since 1973 in line with Venezuela's conservation policies. There are eight refineries. The Orinoco heavy oil belt is being developed; estimates put recoverable resources at 70,000 million barrels in the Orinoco region.

Aluminium is the second highest source of foreign exchange after petroleum. The Venezuelan state holds the majority stake in both the principal producing companies, Venalum and Alcasa, and is moving towards a consolidation of the industry. Rich iron ore deposits in eastern Venezuela have been developed. The government-owned steel mill at Matanzas uses local iron ore and obtains its electric power from hydro-electric installations on the Caroni River. A mill at Ciudad Guayana produces centrifugally-cast iron pipe. Other industry includes a wide variety of manufacturing and component assembly, principally petrochemicals, gold, diamonds, clothing and foodstuffs.

TRADE	1992
Total imports	US$11,240m
Total exports	14,000m

Trade with UK	1991	1992
Imports from UK	£166,654,000	£188,895,000
Exports to UK	100,210,000	138,425,000

COMMUNICATIONS

There are about 77,785 km of roads, 22,780 km of them paved. The state has now acquired all but a very few of the railway lines, whose total length is only some 363 kilometres. Road and river communications have made railways of negligible importance in Venezuela except for carrying iron ore in the south-east though the government is expanding the network.

The Orinoco is navigable for ocean-going ships (up to 40 ft draught) for 150 miles upstream, by large steamers for 700 miles, and by smaller vessels some 900 miles up-stream. There are three Venezuelan airlines which between them have a comprehensive network of internal and international flights. There are four television stations, two of which are government controlled.

VIETNAM
Công Hòa Xã Hôi Chu Nghĩa Viêt Nam

Vietnam has an area of 127,242 sq. miles (329,556 sq. km), and an estimated population (1993) of 71,267,000. It is bordered on the north by China and the west by Laos and Cambodia.

CAPITAL – Hanoi, population (1993) 2,150,000. Other cities are Ho Chi Minh City (3,169,000) and Hai Phong (456,000).

CURRENCY – Dông of 10 hao or 100 xu.

FLAG – Red, with yellow five-point star in centre.

NATIONAL ANTHEM – Tien Quan Ca (The troops are advancing).

NATIONAL DAY – 2 September.

GOVERNMENT

Following the end of the war in Vietnam in 1975, North and South Vietnam were reunified in 1976 under the name of the Socialist Republic of Vietnam. The national flag, anthem and capital of North Vietnam were adopted, and Saigon was renamed Ho Chi Minh City. Effective power lies with the ruling Vietnamese Communist Party (VCP), its highest executive body being the Central Committee, elected by a Party Congress on a national basis. The Politburo and the Secretariat of the Central Committee exercise real power and rule Vietnam.

A new constitution was adopted in June 1992 which reaffirmed Communist Party rule but also formalized free market economic reforms. The new constitution increased the powers of the President and replaced the Council of Ministers by a Prime Minister and Cabinet. A new National Assembly of 365 members was elected in August 1992 and convened in September when it elected Le Duc Anh as President and, in October, approved the composition of the new government headed by Vo Van Kiet.

HEAD OF STATE
President, Le Duc Anh, *elected by National Assembly*, 23 September 1992.
Vice President, Nguyen Thi Binh.

CABINET *as at August 1993*
Prime Minister, Vo Van Kiet.
First Deputy PM, Phan Van Khai.
Deputy PM, Nguyen Kanh; Tran Duc Luong.
National Defence, Doan Khue.
Foreign Affairs, Nguyen Manh Cam.
Interior, Bui Thieu Ngo.
Chairman, State Planning Commission, Do Quoc Sam.
Chairman, State Inspectorate, Nguyen Ky Cam.
Chairman, Ethnic Minorities and Mountain Region Commission, Hoang Duc Nghi.
Chairman, State Commission for Co-operation and Investment, Dau Ngoc Xuan.
Finance, Ho Te.

Governor, State Bank, Cao Sy Kiem.
Commerce and Tourism, Le Van Triet.
Labour, War Invalids and Social Affairs, Tran Dinh Hoan.
Construction, Ngo Xuan Loc.
Communications and Transport, Bui Danh Luu.
Heavy Industry, Tran Lum.
Energy, Thai Phung Ne.
Light Industry, Dang Vu Chu.
Agriculture, Nguyen Cong Tan.
Forestry, Nguyen Quang Ha.
Water Conservancy, Nguyen Canh Dinh.
Marine Products, Nguyen Tan Trinh.
Culture, Information and Sports, Tran Hoan.
Public Health, Nguyen Trong Nhan.
Education and Training, Tran Hong Quan.
Justice, Nguyen Dinh Loc.
Population and Family Planning, Mai Ky.
Children, Tran Thi Thanh Thanh.
Ministers without Portfolio, Phan Van Tiem; Ha Quang Da.

VIETNAMESE COMMUNIST PARTY

Politburo of the Central Committee, Do Muoi (General
Secretary); Le Duc Anh; Vo Van Kiet; Dao Duy Tung;
Doan Khue; Vu Oanh; Le Phuoc Tho; Pham Van Khai;
Bui Thien Ngo; Nong Duc Manh; Pham The Duyet;
Nguyen Duc Binh; Vo Tran Chi (full members).

EMBASSY OF THE SOCIALIST REPUBLIC OF VIETNAM
12–14 Victoria Road, London W8 5RD
Tel 071-937 1912/8564

Ambassador Extraordinary and Plenipotentiary, His
Excellency Chau Phong (1990).

BRITISH EMBASSY
16 Pho Ly Thuong Kiet, Hanoi
Tel: Hanoi 25 2349

Ambassador Extraordinary and Plenipotentiary, His
Excellency Peter Williams, CMG (1990).

DEFENCE

Total active armed forces number some 857,000 personnel,
with conscripts serving between two and three years.
Reserves number some three to four million. The Army has
700,000 personnel, with 1,300 main battle tanks, 600 light
tanks, 1,400 armoured infantry fighting vehicles and
armoured personnel carriers and 2,300 artillery pieces. The
Navy is 42,000 strong, including 30,000 Naval Infantry, and
deploys seven frigates and 55 patrol and coastal vessels. Air
Force strength is 15,000, with 185 combat aircraft and 20
armed helicopters. The Air Defence Force has 100,000
personnel, with surface-to-air missiles.

ECONOMY

Vietnam experienced considerable economic difficulties
following the imposition of socialist reforms in the south after
1975. These were exacerbated by significant reductions in
western aid as a result of Vietnam's invasion and occupation
of Cambodia, border hostilities with China, and the allocation
of resources to military expenditure. Attempted reforms of
the economic system in 1985, including devaluation and a
currency change, had adverse effects and the economy has
also been adversely affected by the sharp decrease in aid
from the former Soviet Union. However, economic reforms,
known as 'Doi Moi' liberalization, were instituted after the
Sixth Party Congress (1986) and have had significant success.
Inflation is down to single figures per month; the exchange
rate has been rationalized, subsidies removed and much
greater economic activity allowed. The state's share of control

has fallen to 60 per cent of industry, 40 per cent of services
and 2 per cent of agriculture, which is now mainly by family
farms. This has led to a significant improvement in
agricultural production, with Vietnam becoming a major rice
exporter. Foreign investment is being actively encouraged
and is likely to grow since the USA in July 1993 dropped its
opposition to IMF and World Bank loans and aid to Vietnam.
Despite its infrastructural problems, Vienam has considerable
natural resources (including oil) and a well-educated low-cost
workforce.

TRADE WITH UK	1991	1992
Imports from UK	£6,916,000	£21,373,000
Exports to UK	6,440,000	11,921,000

WESTERN SAMOA
Malotuto'atasi o Samoa i Sisifo

Western Samoa lies in the south Pacific Ocean between
latitudes 13° and 15° S. and longitudes 171° and 173° W. It
consists of the islands of Savai'i (662 sq. miles), Upolu,
Apolima, Manono, Fanuatapu, Namua, Nuutele, Nuulua and
Nuusafee, and has an area of 435 sq. miles (1,714 sq. km). All
the islands are mountainous. Upolu, the most fertile, contains
the harbours of Apia and Saluafata, and Savai'i the harbours
of Asau and Salelologa.
POPULATION – The population at the 1989 census was
162,000, the largest numbers being on Upolu (114,980) and
Savai'i (43,150); a 1990 UN estimate put the figure at
164,000. The Samoans are a Polynesian people, though the
population also includes other Pacific Islanders, Euronesians,
Chinese and Europeans. The main languages spoken are
Samoan and English. The islanders are Christians of different
denominations.

CAPITAL – ΨApia, on Upolu (population, 1989 census,
36,000). Robert Louis Stevenson died and was buried at
Apia in 1894.
CURRENCY – Tala (WS$) of 100 sene.
FLAG – Red with a blue canton bearing five white stars of
the Southern Cross.
NATIONAL ANTHEM – The Banner of Freedom.
NATIONAL DAY – 1 June (Independence Day).

GOVERNMENT

Formerly administered by New Zealand (latterly with
internal self-government), Western Samoa became fully-
independent on 1 January 1962. The state was treated as a
member country of the Commonwealth until its formal
admission on 28 August 1970.
The 1962 constitution provides for a head of state to be
elected by the 49-member legislative assembly, the Fono, for
a five-year term. Initially two of the four Paramount chiefs
jointly held the office of head of state for life. When one of
the chiefs died in April 1963, Malietoa Tanumafili II became
head of state for life. The head of state's functions are
analogous to those of a constitutional monarch. Executive
government is carried out by a Cabinet of Ministers.
Suffrage was made universal following a referendum held
in October 1990. After elections held on 7 March 1991, the
seats in the Fono were: Human Rights Protection Party 30;
Samoan National Development Party 16; Independents 3.

Head of State, HH Malietoa Tanumafili II, GCMG, CBE, since
15 April 1963.
Deputy Head of State, Hon. Mataafa Faasuamaleaui Puela.

CABINET *as at August 1993*
Prime Minister, Minister for Foreign Affairs, Hon. Tofilau Eti Alesana.
Finance, Hon. Tuilaepa Sailele.
Justice, Hon. Fuimanono Lotomau.
Education, Hon. Fiame Naomi.
Health, Hon. Sala Vaimili Uili II.
Post and Telecommunications, Hon. Toi Aukuso.
Agriculture, Hon. Mica Foni.
Public Works, Hon. Leafa Vitale.
Lands and Environment, Hon. Faasooatuloa Pati.
Civil Aviation, Hon. Jack Netzler.
International Affairs, Hon. Polataïvao Fosi.
Sports and Culture, Hon. Pule Lareko.

WESTERN SAMOA HIGH COMMISSION
Avenue Franklin D. Roosevelt 123, 1050 Brussels
Tel: Brussels 6608454

High Commissioner, His Excellency Afamasaga Toleafoa (1990).

BRITISH HIGH COMMISSION
High Commissioner (resides at Wellington, New Zealand). There is an Honorary Consulate (PO Box 2029) in Apia.

ECONOMY

Agriculture is the basis of Western Samoa's economy, the principal cash crops (and exports) being coconuts (copra), cocoa and bananas. Other agricultural exports include coffee, timber, tropical fruits and seeds. Efforts are being made to develop fishing on a commercial scale. Manufacturing is very small in scope and concerned largely with processing agricultural products, but is being encouraged by the government. Tourism is increasing rapidly.

TRADE WITH UK	1991	1992
Imports from UK	£671,000	£471,000
Exports to UK	16,000	12,000

REPUBLIC OF YEMEN
Al-Jamhuriya Al-Yamaniya

Yemen lies in the extreme south-west of the Arabian peninsula. Bounded on the west by the Red Sea, on the north by Saudi Arabia, on the east by Oman and on the south by the Gulf of Aden, Yemen has an estimated area of 203,850 sq. miles (527,969 sq. km) and a population (1991 UN estimate) of 12,302,000. Included in the state are the offshore islands of Perim and Kamaran in the Red Sea, and Socotra in the Gulf of Aden. The highlands and central plateau, and the highest portions of the maritime range in the south, form the most fertile part of Arabia, with abundant but irregular rainfall. The north is largely composed of mountains and desert, and rainfall is generally scarce.

CAPITAL – Sana'a, population (1986) 427,150. Ψ Aden (270,000) is the other main city and the former capital of South Yemen.
CURRENCY – Yemeni dinar (YD) of 1,000 fils and Riyals of 100 fils are both legal tender (1 Dinar = 26 Riyals). The Dinar is being phased out.
FLAG – Horizontal bands of red, white and black.
NATIONAL DAY – 22 May.

GOVERNMENT

Turkish occupation of North Yemen (1872–1918) was followed by the rule of the Hamid al-Din dynasty until a revolution in 1962 overthrew the monarchy and the Yemen Arab Republic was declared. The People's Republic of South Yemen was set up in November 1967 when the British government ceded power to the National Liberation Front, thus bringing to an end 129 years of British rule in Aden and some years of protectorate status in the hinterland. Negotiations towards merging the two states began in 1979. A draft joint constitution, proposing the establishment of a unified multi-party state, was published in December 1989 and unification was proclaimed on 22 May 1990 following ratification the previous day by both parliaments. The constitution was approved by referendum on 16 May 1991. A five-member Presidential Council comprising former senior government figures of the separate states was formed for the period of transition.

The first general election for the House of Representatives took place on 27 April 1993. Of the total of 301 seats, 122 were won by the General People's Congress (GPC, former ruling party in the North), 62 by the Islamic Islah (Alliance for reform) party and 56 by the Yemini Socialist Party (YSP, former ruling party in the South). The three parties formed a coalition government and the House of Representatives asked the Presidential Council to remain in office. President Saleh appointed a council of Ministers on 30 May 1993.

President, Gen. Ali Abdullah Saleh, *since* 22 May 1990.
Vice President, Ali Salim al-Beedh.
Members of Presidential Council, Qadi Abdel-Karim al-Arashi; Abdel Aziz Abdel Ghani; Salim Salih Mohammed.

COUNCIL OF MINISTERS *as at August 1993*
Prime Minister, Haider Abu Bakr al-Attas.
First Deputy PM, Dr Hassan Mohammed Makki.
Deputy PMs, Brig.-Gen. Mujahid Yahya Abu Shawarib; Abdul-Wahhab al-Anisi; Mohammed Haider Masdus.
Construction, Abdullah Hussayn al-Kurshumi.
Foreign Affairs, Muhammad Salim Basindwah.
Industry, Dr Mohammed Said al-Attar.
Oil and Mineral Resources, Salih Abu Bakr Bin Hussain.
Supply and Trade, Dr Abdul-Rahman Abdul-Qadir Bafadl.
Local Administration, Muhammad Hasan Dammaj.
Electricity and Water Resources, Ahmad Ali al-Sallami.
Civil Service and Administrative Reform, Yahya Husain al-Arashi.
Planning and Development, Dr Abdul-Karim al-Iryani.
Communications, Ahmad Mohammed al-Anisi.
Legal Affairs, Abdul-Salam Khalid.
Waqfs (Religious Affairs) and Guidance, Ghalib Abdul-Kafi al-Qirshi.
Social Security, Labour and Social Affairs, vacant.
Culture, Jarallah Umar al-Kuhali.
Youth and Sports, Dr Mohammed Ahmad al-Kabab.
Education, Dr Abu Bakr al-Qirbi.
Justice, Abdullah Ahmad Ghanim.
Information, Hasan Ahmad al-Lawzi.
Transport, Salih Ubaid Ahmad.
Fisheries, Fadhl Muhsin Abdullah.
Housing and Urban Planning, Mohammed Said Abdullah.
Finance, Alawi Salih al-Salami.
Public Health, Dr Najib Ghanim.
Agriculture, Sadiq Amin Abu Ras.
Interior, Yahya Muhammad al-Mutawakkil.
Defence, Brig.-Gen. Haytham Qasim Tahir.

Speaker of the House of Representatives, Shaikh Abdullah bin Husain al-Ahmar.

EMBASSY OF THE REPUBLIC OF YEMEN
57 Cromwell Road, London SW7 2ED
Tel 071–584 6607

Ambassador Extraordinary and Plenipotentiary, His Excellency Dr Shaya Mohsin Mohamed Zindani (1991).

BRITISH EMBASSY
PO Box 1287, Sana'a
Tel: Sana'a 1215630

Ambassador Extraordinary and Plenipotentiary, His Excellency Robert Gordon (1993).

There is a British Consulate-General at Aden.

BRITISH COUNCIL REPRESENTATIVE, A. Lewis, House 7, Street 70 (PO Box 2157), Sana'a.

ECONOMY

Exports include cotton, coffee, hides and skins. Agriculture is the main occupation of the inhabitants. This is largely of a subsistence nature, sorghum, sesame and millets being the chief crops, with wheat and barley widely grown at the higher elevations. Oil has been produced at Marib since December 1987; production averages 180,000 b.p.d. and is expected to reach 300,000 b.p.d. when production in the Masila field starts in late 1993. There is a refinery at Aden. The Aden Free Zone was opened in May 1991 and could help Aden recover its old commercial importance in the region. Yemeni support for Iraq during the Gulf War angered Saudi Arabia who sent home 850,000 expatriate Yemini workers, losing Yemen annual remittances worth $2 billion.

TRADE WITH UK	1990	1992
Imports from UK	£70,835,000	£78,409,000
Exports to UK	36,238,000	56,871,000

YUGOSLAVIA
Federativna Republika Jugoslavije - Federal Republic of Yugoslavia

The area of the two remaining Yugoslav republics (Serbia and Montenegro) is 39,506 sq. miles (102,350 sq. km). The rump Federal Yugoslav state, which remains internationally unrecognized as the successor state to the former Socialist Federal Republic of Yugoslavia, is bordered to the north by Hungary, to the east by Romania and Bulgaria, to the south by Macedonia, to the south-west by Albania and the Adriatic Sea, and to the west by Bosnia-Hercegovina and Croatia. The climate is continental and Mediterranean on the Montenegrin coast. Montenegro and southern Serbia are extremely mountainous, while the north is dominated by the low-lying plains of the Danube. The major rivers are: the Danube, which flows through the north of Serbia to Romania and Bulgaria; the Sava which flows eastwards from Bosnia to join the Danube at Belgrade; and the Morava which flows from the extreme south to join the Danube in the north.
POPULATION – The last (federal) estimate of 1988 gave a population of 10,410,000, of which 66 per cent are Serbs and Montenegrins, 18 per cent Albanian, 8 per cent Muslim, 4 per cent Hungarian, with smaller numbers of Yugoslavs (no ethnic group), Croats and Bulgarians.
RELIGION – The majority religion is Serbian Orthodox, with significant Muslim and small Roman Catholic minorities.
LANGUAGE – Serbian (Serbo-Croat) 74 per cent, Albanian and Hungarian minorities. Serbo-Croat is a South Slav language written in the Cyrillic script.

CAPITAL -- (federal and Serbian) Belgrade, on the Danube (population 1,455,000). Other major cities are (1981): Novi Sad (257,685); Niš (230,711); Priština (210,040);

Kragujevac (164,823); Subotica (154,611); Podgorica (132,290), the capital of Montenegro.
CURRENCY – Dinar of 100 paras.
FLAG – Three horizontal stripes of blue, white, red.
NATIONAL ANTHEM – Hej, Slaveni, Jošte Živi Reč Našich Dedova (Oh! Slavs, our ancestors' words still live).
NATIONAL DAY – 29 November.

GOVERNMENT

Serbia emerged from the rule of the Byzantine Empire in the 13th century to form a large and prosperous state in the Balkans. Defeat by the Turks at the battle of Kosovo in 1389 led to almost 500 years of Turkish rule. After gaining autonomy within the Ottoman Empire in 1815, Serbia became fully independent in 1878 and a kingdom in 1881. Montenegro was part of the Serbian state before it was conquered by the Turks in 1355; it became independent in 1851. At the end of the First World War Serbia and Montenegro joined with the former Austro-Hungarian provinces of Slovenia, Croatia and Bosnia-Hercegovina to form the 'Kingdom of Serbs, Croats and Slovenes' which was proclaimed on 1 December 1918 under the rule of the Serbian royal house. The centalized and Serbian-dominated nature of the state caused resentment in the non-Serb areas and this intensified in 1929 when King Alexander proclaimed a royal dictatorship and renamed the state Yugoslavia. In 1941-5 Yugoslavia was occupied by Axis forces which were fought by Communist and royalist Chetnik partisans supplied by Allied forces. In 1945 with the defeat of Nazi Germany, Yugoslavia was reformed as a Communist republic under the presidency of partisan leader Josip Tito.
Increasing pressure from the non-Serbian nationalities for more political power were met by Tito in the post-war period by new constitutions in 1963 and 1974 which made Yugoslavia a federal state and devolved increasing power to the republics (Slovenia, Croatia, Bosnia-Hercegovina, Serbia, Montenegro, Macedonia). Tito died in 1980 and the delicate political balance of a rotating federal presidency was unable to contain the gradually growing nationalist movements after his death. The Catholic, western-looking, more prosperous republics of Slovenia and Croatia began to break away from the other predominantly Orthodox and Muslim, Balkan republics of the rest of Yugoslavia; Communism was widely rejected. Efforts by the federal presidency and international mediators to end inter-communal conflict and negotiate a new federal or confederal structure for the country failed in 1991. On 25 June 1991 Slovenia and Croatia declared their independence from Yugoslavia. Intervention by the Federal Yugoslav Army (JNA) against local defence forces to prevent the disintegration of the Yugoslav federation failed and within

two months the ethnically homogeneous Slovenia had negotiated its independence from Yugoslavia.

The situation in Croatia differed because its ethnic Serb minority comprised 12 per cent of the population. These ethnic Serbs refused to accept Croatia's independence and formed themselves into armed guerrilla groups. Fighting began in July 1991 between Croat Defence Forces and Serbian guerrillas backed by the JNA which by September 1991 had escalated into an all-out war between Croatia and Serbia. In October the last vestiges of the power of the Federation ended when the federal presidency was usurped by Serbia and its ally Montenegro. The war in Croatia continued until January 1992 when, after constant attempts, the EC and the UN were able to bring about a ceasefire that held.

While the war continued in Croatia, Bosnia-Hercegovina declared its independence from Yugoslavia on 15 October 1991, and this was affirmed in a referendum on 1 March 1992. Independence was supported by the ethnic Muslims and Croats but rejected by the ethnic Serbs, who formed 33 per cent of the population and wanted to form a Greater Serbia with the Serbian republic. Fighting between Muslims and Serbs broke out on 2 March 1992 and the JNA intervened against the poorly-armed Muslims. In May 1992, after intense international pressure, the JNA withdrew to Serbia and Montenegro.

On 27 April 1992 the two remaining republics of the former Socialist Federal Republic of Yugoslavia, namely Serbia and Montenegro, announced the formation of a new Yugoslav federation, which they invited Serbs in Croatia and Bosnia-Hercegovina to join. The new federation remains unrecognized internationally because of continued ethnic Serb aggression in Bosnia, and is seen as a Serbian attempt to inherit the rights of the former Federation. Continued Serbian aid and supplies to the ethnic Serb Forces in the Bosnian war has led to increasing international pressure and sanctions on the rump Federal Republic. At the end of May 1992 the UN imposed a total trade embargo and economic sanctions, and banned all air and sporting links. In September 1992 the rump state was suspended from the UN and prevented from claiming successor status to the former Yugoslavia's seat. Transhipment of goods through Serbia ended in November, and in April 1993 a total blockade was imposed under UN auspices by NATO and WEU warships in the Adriatic and on the Danube. Yugoslav planes, ships and lorries abroad were seized, together with all funds abroad.

The Federal Republic has a bi-cameral parliament with a 138-seat lower house, the Chamber of Citizens, and a 40-seat (20 Serbian, 20 Montenegrin) upper house, the Chamber of Republics. Executive power is vested in a Federal President and government but has effectively been usurped by the authoritarian Serbian Socialist (former Communist) Party leader and Serbian President Slobodan Milosevic. In 1992 and 1993 Milosevic has persecuted any opposition, ousting Federal President Cosic, Prime Minister Milan Panic and intimidating the Demos opposition party. The last federal legislative and republican presidential and legislature elections were held in December 1992 and were universally considered flawed and unfair. The Serbian Socialist Party emerged as the largest party in the federal legislature and formed a coalition government with the extreme nationalist Serbian Radical Party.

HEAD OF STATE
Federal President, Zoran Lilic, *elected by parliament* 25 June 1993.

FEDERAL GOVERNMENT *as at August 1993*
Prime Minister, Radoje Kontic.
Deputy PM, Finance, Jovan Zebic.
Deputy PM, Asin Telacevic.
Foreign Affairs, Vladislav Jovanovic.
Interior, Djordje Blagojevic.
Defence, Pavle Bulatovic.
Justice, Zoran Stojanovic.
Economics, Tomislav Simovic.
Foreign Economic Relations, Milorad Unkovic.
Transport and Communications, Blagoje Lucic.
Labour, Health and Social Policy, Velibor Popovic.
Education and Culture, Slavko Gordic.
Science and Technology, Milan Dimitrijevic.
Information, Slobodan Ignjatovic.
Environment, Slobodanka Djordan.
Trade, Miroslav Ivanisevic.
Agriculture, Kiviljko Lovre.
Sport, Zoran Bingulac.
Human and Minority Rights, Margit Savovic.
Without Portfolio, Tomislav Rajicevic.

EMBASSY OF YUGOSLAVIA
5 Lexham Gardens, London w8 5ju
Tel 071-370 6105

Chargé d'Affairs, R. Bogojevic.
Defence Attaché, Cdr. M. Radeka.
Consul-General, R. Jengic.
Second Secretary, L. Raspopovic (*Economic*).

BRITISH EMBASSY
General Ždanova 46, 11000 Belgrade
Tel: Belgrade 645055

Ambassador Extraordinary and Plenipotentiary, His Excellency Peter E. Hall, CMG (1989).
Counsellor, M. J. Robinson.
Defence and Military Attaché, Col. A. M. Moody.
First Secretary (*Economic*), W. L. Jackson-Houlston.

BRITISH COUNCIL REPRESENTATIVE, P. Early, Generala Ždanova 34-Mezanin (Post Fah 248), 11001 Belgrade.

MONTENEGRO
Montenegro has an area of 5,331 sq. miles (13,812 sq. km) and a population of 650,000, of whom 68 per cent are Montenegrins, 13 per cent Muslims, 6 per cent Albanians and 3 per cent Serbs. The capital is Podgorica with a population (1981) of 95,000. The Democratic Party of Socialists (former Communists) won multi-party elections in December 1992 for the 125-seat republican assembly and formed a government.

President, Momir Bulatovic, *elected* 11 January 1993.

SERBIA
Serbia has a total area of 34,175 sq. miles (88,538 sq. km) and a total population of 9.3 million (Vojvodina 2 million, Kosovo 1.6 million), of whom 66 per cent are Serbs. The capital is Belgrade with a population (1981) of 1,455,000. It includes the provinces of Kosovo, of great historic importance to Serbs, and Vojvodina; the autonomy of both was ended in September 1990. Kosovo, with its capital at Priština, is predominantly Albanian (90 per cent). In defiance of the Serbian authorities, ethnic Albanians held parliamentary and presidential elections in May 1992, which were won respectively by the Democratic League of Kosovo and its leader Ibrahim Rugova. Tension between Albanians and Serbs remains very high. Vojvodina, with its capital at Novi Sad, has a large Hungarian minority (21 per cent).

The Socialist Party of Serbia (formerly the League of Communists) emerged as the largest party in multi-party elections for the 250-seat National Assembly, held in December 1992 and formed a coalition government with the Serbian Radical Party

President, Slobodan Milosevic, *elected* 20 December 1992.

ECONOMY

Since 1991 the economy has been devastated by the wars in Croatia and Bosnia-Hercegovina, by the UN economic sanctions and trade embargo, and because of the lack of free-market reforms. Most factories have closed. Only the country's agricultural self-sufficiency has kept it alive. In 1993 hyperinflation has become rampant because the government continued to print money to finance the wars and subsidize industries. After inflation reached an annualized rate of 20,000 per cent, the government introduced emergency measures on 22 July 1993, including the eighth devaluation of the dinar since April and the closure of most financial institutions. The prices of staple goods were put under direct government control in August.

TRADE WITH UK	1991	1992
Imports from UK	£193,836,000	£123,061,000
Exports to UK	147,876,000	123,797,000

ZAIRE
République du Zaïre

Situated between 12° and 31° E. longitude and 5° N. and 13° S. latitude, Zaire comprises an area of 905,567 sq. miles (2,345,409 sq. km), with a population (1985 Census) of 34,671,607. Apart from the coastal district in the west which is fairly dry, the rainfall averages between 60 and 80 inches. The average temperature is about 27°C, but in the south the winter temperature can fall nearly to freezing point. Extensive forest covers the central districts.

POPULATION – The population was 34,671,607 at the 1985 census. A 1991 UN estimate put it at 36,672,000. It is composed almost entirely of Bantu groups, divided into semi-autonomous tribes. Minorities include Sudanese, Nilotes, Pygmies and Hamites, as well as refugees from Angola.

LANGUAGES – Swahili, a Bantu dialect with an admixture of Arabic, is the nearest approach to a common language in the east and south, while Lingala is the language of a large area along the river and in the north, and Kikongo of the region between Kinshasa and the sea. French is the language of administration.

CAPITAL – Kinshasa (formerly Leopoldville), population (1985 Census) 2,778,281. Principal towns, Lubumbashi (formerly Elisabethville) (403,623); Kisangani (formerly Stanleyville) (310,705); Likasi (146,394); Kananga (601,239); Ψ Matadi (143,598); and Mbandaka (134,495). CURRENCY – Zaïre of 100 makuta.
FLAG – Dark brown hand and torch with red flame in yellow roundel on green background.
NATIONAL DAY – 24 November.

GOVERNMENT

The state of the Congo, founded in 1885, became a Belgian colony in November 1908 and was administered by Belgium until independence in 1960. Mobutu Sésé Seko, formerly Commander-in-Chief of the Congolese National Army, came to power in a coup in 1965 and was elected President in 1970. Legislative power was vested in a unicameral National Legislative Council, elected for a five-year term by compulsory direct and universal suffrage with candidates proposed by the sole legal political party, Mouvement Populaire de la Révolution (MPR).

Following mounting social tension, political reforms were announced in April 1990 and under mounting opposition pressure President Mobutu called a national conference to draft a new constitution in April 1991. The conference convened in August but the government refused to grant it sovereign status, causing the main opposition parties to form a 'Sacred Union' to bring down the transitional government and leading to economic chaos with violent rioting in Kinshasa. Mobutu eventually accepted an opposition-dominated government under Prime Minister Etienne Tshisekedi in October 1991. His attempts to replace this with MPR-dominated governments failed and the National Conference confirmed the Tshisekedi government as the legitimate one in August 1992.

Late 1992 and 1993 have seen Mobutu and the opposition locked in a power struggle. The MPR-dominated National Legislative Council was dissolved in September 1992 and the National Conference ended in December after adopting a draft constitution and electing an interim legislature, the High Council of the Republic (HCR), with Archbishop Laurent Monsengwo Pasinya as its President. Mobutu tried unsuccessfully to dismiss the HCR and Tshisekedi government in December 1992, who in February 1993 attempted to transfer his political power to the HCR. The Army was used by the President in March and April to intimidate the government and to support his rival government, established on 17 March 1993 under Faustin Birindwa. Since April a constitutional limbo has existed, with Mobutu promulgating amendments to the constitution restoring his powers and re-establishing the National Legislative Council. The HCR has declared Mobutu's actions illegal and that he should be tried for treason. The USA and EC have refused to recognise the Birindwa government and tried to isolate the Mobutu regime with diplomatic and economic sanctions.

There are 11 regions, each under a Governor and provincial administration: Bas-Zaire (provincial capital, Matadi); Bandundu (Bandundu); Equateur (Mbandaka); Haut-Zaire (Kisangani); Kinshasa (Kinshasa); Maniema (Kindu); Nord-Kivu (Goma); Sud-Kivu (Bukavu); Shaba, formerly Katanga (Lubumbashi); East Kasai (Mbuji-Mayi); West Kasai (Kananga).

HEAD OF STATE
President of the Republic and National Security, Marshal Mobutu Sésé Séko, *assumed office* 25 November 1965; *elected* 5 November 1970; *re-elected for third term* 28 July 1984.

EXECUTIVE COUNCIL *as at August 1993*
Prime Minister, Etienne Tshisekedi.
Interior and Territorial Security, Mathieu Bosunga Lombe.
External Relations, Pierre Lumbi.
Justice, Roger Gisanga.
Defence, Paul Bandoma.
National Education, Loka Ne Kongo.
Scientific Research and Technology, Theophile Mbemba Fundu.
Culture and Arts, Gervais Kabamba.
Finance and Budget, Benoit Atale.
Economy, Industry and External Trade, Fernand Tala-Ngai.
Planning, Kirarawumu Isengoma.
Small and Medium Enterprises, Paul Kapita Shabani.
Public Works, Mwitaba Katemwe.
Agriculture and Rural Development, Jean Paul N'Kanga.
Environment and Tourism, Tharcisse Loseke.

Public Health and Social Affairs, Honorine Nabunyi.
Transport and Communications, Baudouin Kabisi.
Mines and Energy, Jean Seka Buhoro.
Posts and Telecommunications, Kumbu Ki Lutete.
Civil Service, Lubaga Wedisonga.
Labour and Social Services, Nbumb Musong.
Youth, Sport and Leisure, Charles Gonghandiki.

EMBASSY OF THE REPUBLIC OF ZAIRE
26 Chesham Place, London SW1X 8HH
Tel 071-235 6137

Ambassador Extraordinary and Plenipotentiary, His
Excellency Liloo Nkema (1991).

BRITISH EMBASSY
Avenue des Trois 'Z', Gombe, Kinshasa
Tel: Kinshasa 34775

Chargé d'Affaires and Consul, Kaye Oliver.

There are British Consulates at *Lubumbashi, Goma* and
Kisangani.

ECONOMY

The cultivation of oil palms is widespread, palm oil being the
most important agricultural cash product though it is no
longer exported. Coffee, rubber, cocoa and timber are the
most important agricultural exports. The production of
cotton, pyrethrum and copal fell sharply on independence
but is now increasing. The country is rich in minerals,
particularly Shaba (ex-Katanga) province. Copper is widely
exploited, and industrial diamonds and cobalt are also
produced. Oil deposits are exploited off the Zaire estuary
and reef-gold is mined in the north-east of the country.

There is a wide variety of small secondary industries, the
main products being foodstuffs, beverages, tobacco, textiles,
leather, wood products, cement and building materials,
matallurgy, small river craft and bicycles. There are large
reserves of hydro-electric power and the huge Inga dam on
the river Zaire supplies electricity to Matadi, Kinshasa and
Shaba.

TRADE

The chief exports are copper, crude oil, coffee, diamonds,
rubber, cobalt, gold, cassiterite, zinc and other metals.

Trade with UK	1991	1992
Imports from UK	£15,040,000	£16,820,000
Exports to UK	4,733,000	3,022,000

COMMUNICATIONS

There are approximately 20,500 km of roads (earth-surfaced)
of national importance, and 6,000 km of railways. The
country has four international and 40 principal airports.

ZAMBIA
Republic of Zambia

Zambia lies on the plateau of Central Africa between 22° and
33° 33′ E. longitude and 8° 15′ and 18° S. latitude. It has an
area of 290,586 sq. miles (752,614 sq. km) and a population
(UN estimate, 1991) of 8,780,000. With the exception of the
valleys of the Zambezi, the Luapula, the Kafue and the
Luangwa Rivers, and the Luano valley, elevations vary from
3,000 to 5,000 feet above sea level, but in the north-east the
plateau rises to occasional altitudes of over 6,000 feet.
Although Zambia lies within the tropics, and fairly centrally

in the African land mass, its elevation relieves it from
extremely high temperatures and humidity.

CAPITAL – Lusaka, population (1989 estimate) 1 million.
Other centres are Livingstone, Kabwe, Chipata,
Mazabuka, Mbala, Kasama, Solwezi, Mongu, Mansa,
Ndola, Luanshya, Mufulira, Chingola, Chililabombwe,
Kalulushi and Kitwe, the last six towns being the main
centres on the copper belt.
CURRENCY – Kwacha (K) of 100 ngwee.
FLAG – Green with three small vertical stripes, red, black
and orange (next fly); eagle device on green above
stripes.
NATIONAL ANTHEM – Stand and Sing of Zambia, Proud
and Free.
NATIONAL DAY – 24 October (Independence Day).

GOVERNMENT

Northern Rhodesia came under British rule in 1889. It
achieved internal self-government when the Federation of
Rhodesia and Nyasaland was dissolved in 1963. It became
an independent republic within the Commonwealth on
24 October 1964 under the name of Zambia.

The country was a one-party state (the United National
Independence Party) from 1973 until 1990, when continued
pressure from the Movement for Multiparty Democracy, set
up in July 1990, and other opposition groups, led to
multiparty and presidential elections in October 1991. The
Movement for Multiparty Democracy (MMD) won 125 of
the 150 seats in parliament, and the MMD candidate
Frederick Chiluba defeated Kaunda, who had ruled since
independence, in the presidential election. The MMD
government has begun the transformation of the sate-
controlled economy into a free market system with the sale
and privatization of large sectors of the economy. Aid and
investment have poured into the country, foreign exchange
controls removed, the Kwacha floated and prices freed. A
state of emergency was declared on 4 March 1993 after the
discovery of a plot by UNIP to launch a coup and seize
power, and was lifted on 25 May.

President, Frederick J. Chiluba, *elected* 31 October 1991.
Vice-President, Levy Patrick Mwanawasa.

CABINET *as at August 1993*

Defence, Benjamin Mwila.
Foreign Affairs, Vernon Mwaanga.
Finance, Ronald Penza.
Home Affairs, Newstead L. Zimba.
Local Government and Housing, Dr Roger Chongwe.
Health, Dr Boniface Kawimbe.
Education, Dr Kabunda Kayongo.
Commerce, Trade and Industry, Alfeyo Hambayi.
Community Development and Social Welfare, Princes
Nakatindi.
Labour and Social Security, Michael Sata.
Communications, Transport and Public Works, Andrew
Kashita.
Energy and Water Development, Edith Nawakwi.
Agriculture, Food and Fisheries, Simon Zukas.
Lands, Dawson Lupunga.
Legal Affairs, Dr Ludwig Sondashi.
Environment and Natural Resources, Chuulu Kalima.
Information and Continuing Education, Dr Remy Mushota.
Mines and Mineral Development, Paul Kapinga.
Technical Education and Vocational Training, Gabriel Maka.
Youth and Child Development, Dipak Patel.
Tourism, Gen. Christon Tembo.
Works and Supply, Kelly Walubita.
Minister without Portfolio, Brig.-Gen. Godfrey Miyanda.

HIGH COMMISSION FOR THE REPUBLIC OF ZAMBIA
2 Palace Gate, London W8 5NG
Tel 071-589 6655
High Commissioner, His Excellency Love Mtesa (1992).
Deputy High Commissioner, Mrs M. G. B. Chigaga.
Defence Attaché, D. D. Nyangulu (*acting*).
Consul-General, M. C. Mwanambale.
First Secretary, J. A. Moyo (*Administration*).

BRITISH HIGH COMMISSION
Independence Avenue (PO Box 50050), 15 101 Ridgeway,
Lusaka
Tel: Lusaka 228955
High Commissioner, His Excellency Peter Hinchcliffe, CMG,
CVO (1990).
Deputy High Commissioner, B. S. Jones.
First Secretary (Commercial/Consular), K. A. Neill.

BRITISH COUNCIL REPRESENTATIVE, Adrian Greer,
Heroes Place, Cairo Road (PO Box 34571), Lusaka.
There is also a library in *Ndola*.

ECONOMY

Principal products are maize, sugar, groundnuts, cotton,
livestock, vegetables and tobacco. Mineral production was
valued at K8,390,765,000 in 1987, of which copper
production (of 483,100 tonnes) accounted for
K6,870,386,000.
    GDP (current prices) was K18,079.8m in 1987. GDP per
capita (current prices) was K2,486.9. Following the reforms
initiated by the government, the US government wrote off
K59,000m of Zambian debt in April 1993.

TRADE	1986	1987
Imports	K4,447,687	K6,627,473
Exports	3,074,357	8,058,595
Trade with UK	1991	1992
Imports from UK	£62,655,000	£65,127,000
Exports to UK	22,468,000	7,279,000

ZIMBABWE
Republic of Zimbabwe

Zimbabwe, the former Southern Rhodesia lies south of the
Zambezi river and borders Zambia and Mozambique on the
north, South Africa and Botswana on the south and west, and
Mozambique on the east. It has a total area of 150,804 sq.
miles (390,580 sq. km), and a population (UN estimate 1991)
of 10,019,000.

CAPITAL – Harare (formerly Salisbury) situated on the
    Mashonaland plateau, population (July 1983) 681,000.
    Bulawayo is the largest town in Matabeleland, population
    (July 1983) 429,000. Other centres are Chitungwiza,
    Mutare, Gweru, Kadoma, Kwe Kwe, Masvingo and
    Hwange.
CURRENCY – Zimbabwe dollar (Z$) of 100 cents.
FLAG – Seven horizontal stripes of green, yellow, red,
    black, red, yellow, green; a white, black-bordered,
    triangle based on the hoist containing the national
    emblem.
NATIONAL ANTHEM – Ishe Komborerai Africa.
NATIONAL DAY – 18 April (Independence Day).

GOVERNMENT

Southern Rhodesia was granted responsible government in
1923. An illegal declaration of independence on 11 November

1965 was finally terminated on 12 December 1979. Following
elections in February 1980 the country obtained independence on 18 April 1980 as the Republic of Zimbabwe, a
member of the British Commonwealth.
    The independence constitution was amended in 1987,
making the presidency an executive post. The President
appoints the Cabinet and can veto parliamentary bills. The
President is popularly elected for a six-year term. The
legislature became unicameral in 1990 and the House of
Assembly has 150 members, 120 elected, 20 appointed by
the President and ten appointed by traditional chiefs. Since
1987 seats are no longer reserved for whites. A merger
agreement between the ZANU (PF) and ZAPU parties was
signed on 22 December 1987 with a view to the eventual
creation of a one-party state. The new party is known as
ZANU-PF.
    The latest general election was held in March 1990 and
ZANU-PF won 116 of the 120 elective seats.
    The country is divided into eight provinces: Manicaland,
Masvingo, Matabeleland North, Matabeleland South, Midlands, Mashonaland West, Central and East.

HEAD OF STATE
Executive President, Hon. Robert Gabriel Mugabe, *elected* 30
    December 1987, *re-elected* March 1990.

CABINET *as at August 1993*
The President.
Vice-Presidents, Hon. Simon Muzenda; Hon. Dr Joshua
    Nkomo.
*Senior Minister, National Affairs, Employment Creation and
    Co-operatives*, Hon. Didymus Mutasa.
Senior Minister, Economic Ministries, Hon. Dr Bernard
    Chidzero.
Foreign Affairs, Hon. Dr Nathan Shamuyarira.
Justice, Legal and Parliamentary Affairs, Hon. Emmerson
    Munangagwa.
Defence, Hon. Moven Mahachi.
Higher Education, Hon. Dr Stanslous Mudenge.
Education and Culture, Hon. Dr Witness Mangwende.
Home Affairs, Hon. Dumiso Dabengwa.
Public Construction and National Housing, Hon. Enos
    Chikowore.
Lands, Agriculture and Water Resources, Hon. Kumbirai
    Kangai.
Information, Posts and Telecommunications, Hon. David
    Karimanzira.
Labour, Public Service and Social Welfare, Hon. John
    Nkomo.
Industry and Commerce, Hon. Dr. Christopher
    Ushewokunze.
Mines, Hon. Dr Eddison Zvobgo.
Transport and Energy, Hon. Dennis Norman.
Health and Child Welfare, Hon. Dr Timothy Stamps.
Environment and Tourism, Hon. Herbert Murerwa.
Attorney-General, Hon. Patrick Chinamasa.

HIGH COMMISSION OF THE REPUBLIC OF ZIMBABWE
Zimbabwe House, 429 Strand, London WC2R 0SA
Tel 071-836 7755

High Commissioner, His Excellency Dr Ngoni Togarepi
    Chioleya (1993).
Deputy High Commissioner, Dr E. T. T. Sakupwanya.
Defence Adviser, Wg Cdr. J. P. Machakaire.
Counsellor, S. Undenge (*Commercial*).

BRITISH HIGH COMMISSION
Stanley House, Jason Moyo Avenue (PO Box 4490), Harare
Tel: Harare 793781

High Commissioner, His Excellency Richard Dales, CMG
  (1992).
Deputy High Commissioner, R. S. Dewar.
Defence Adviser, Col. A. McNeil.
First Secretaries, M. K. Page (*Commercial*); P. S. Covill
  (*Consular*).

BRITISH COUNCIL REPRESENTATIVE, P. L. Elborn, OBE,
  23 Jason Moyo Avenue (PO Box 664), Harare. There is
  also a library at Bulawayo.

EDUCATION

Since independence, a policy of free primary education and
accelerated expansion at secondary level has resulted in
rapidly expanding enrolment. Over 80 per cent of schools
are government-aided schools. The University of Zimbabwe
was founded in 1955.

ECONOMY

The country is endowed with minerals, water, forests, wildlife
and other resources. The agricultural sector is well developed
with both commercial and communal farmers. Tobacco
remains the most important crop in terms of export and
maize the most important for domestic consumption. Other
crops include wheat, cotton, and sugar. Beef is exported to
the EC. Production can be severely affected by drought.

The manufacturing sector has a high degree of inter-
dependency and many industries depend on the agricultural
sector for their raw materials. Industry is dependent on vital
imports e.g. fuel oil, steel products and chemicals, as well as
heavy machinery and items of transport. The mining sector,
although contributing a relatively small portion to GDP (7.6
per cent in 1984) is important to the economy as a foreign
exchange earner (26 per cent of total in 1984). Almost all
mineral production is exported. Gold is the most important
mineral, others are asbestos, silver, nickel, copper, chrome
ore, tin, iron ore and cobalt. There is a successful ferro-
chrome industry and a substantial steel works which has been
heavily subsidized by Government.

A high domestic budget deficit combining with a high
external debt service ratio has put the economy into decline.
Recent droughts have made this worse.

FINANCE	1984–5	1985–6
Revenue	Z$2,212.3m	Z$2,616.2m
Expenditure	2,923.0m	3,307.8m

TRADE WITH UK	1991	1992
Imports from UK	£135,309,000	£100,856,000
Exports to UK	103,891,000	86,254,000

British Dependent Territories

ANGUILLA

AREA – Anguilla is a flat coralline island, about 16 miles in length, three and a half miles in breadth at its widest point and its area is about 35 sq. miles (91 sq. km). It lies approximately 18° N. latitude and 63° W longitude, to the north of the Leeward Islands group.

The island is covered with low scrub and fringed with some of the finest white coral-sand beaches in the Caribbean. The climate is pleasant, with temperatures in the range of 24-30°C throughout the year.

POPULATION – The population (1992 Census) is 8,960.

CAPITAL – The Valley (population 1,400).

CURRENCY – East Caribbean dollar (EC$) of 100 cents.

FLAG – British Blue Ensign with the shield of arms in the fly.

GOVERNMENT

Anguilla has been a British colony since 1650. For most of its history it has been linked administratively with St Christopher, but three months after the Associated State of Saint Christopher (St Kitts)-Nevis-Anguilla came into being in 1967, the Anguillans repudiated government from St Kitts. A Commissioner was installed in 1969 and in 1976 Anguilla was given a new status and separate constitution. Final separation from St Kitts and Nevis was effected on 19 December 1980 and Anguilla reverted to a British dependency. A new Constitution was introduced in 1982, providing for a Governor, an Executive Council comprising four elected Ministers and two ex-officio members (Attorney-General and Permanent Secretary, Finance), and an 11-member legislative House of Assembly presided over by a Speaker.

The 1982 Constitution (Amendment) Order 1990 came into operation on 30 May 1990. Among the new constitutional provisions are a Deputy Governor (who replaces the Permanent Secretary (Finance) in the Executive Council and the Legislature), a Parliamentary Secretary, Leader of Opposition and Deputy Speaker.

Governor, His Excellency A. W. Shave, OBE, *apptd* 1992.
Deputy Governor, H. McCrory, *apptd* 1991.

EXECUTIVE COUNCIL as at June 1993
Chief Minister and Minister of Home Affairs, Tourism and Economic Development, Hon. Emile Gumbs.
Social Services and Lands, Hon. Eric Reid.
Communications, Public Utilities and Works, Hon. Kenneth Harrigan.
Finance and Economic Development, Hon. Osbourne Fleming.
Attorney-General, Hon. Kurt De Freitas.

ECONOMY

Low rainfall limits agricultural output and export earnings are mainly from sales of lobsters. Tourism has developed rapidly in recent years and accounts for most of the island's economic activity. In 1992 there were 32,076 tourists and a further 61,104 day visitors.

FINANCE	1991	1992
Revenue	EC$43,430,000	EC$34,810,000
Expenditure	29,806,000	31,895,000

TRADE WITH UK	1991	1992
Imports from UK	£2,687,000	£1,064,000
Exports to UK	197,000	12,000

ASCENSION
— *see* St Helena

BERMUDA

AREA – The Bermudas, or Somers Islands, are a cluster of about 100 small islands (about 20 of which are inhabited) situated in the west of the Atlantic Ocean, in 32° 18′ N. lat. and 64° 46′ W. long., the nearest point of the mainland being Cape Hatteras in North Carolina, about 570 miles distant. The total area is approximately 20.59 sq. miles (53 sq. km), which includes 2.3 sq. miles leased to the USA.

POPULATION – The civil population was 58,460 in 1991.

CAPITAL – ΨHamilton (population 1991, 1,617).

CURRENCY – Bermuda dollar of 100 cents.

FLAG – British Red Ensign with the shield of arms in the fly.

GOVERNMENT

The colony derives its name from Juan Bermudez, a Spaniard, who sighted it before 1515. No settlement was made until 1609 when Sir George Somers, who was shipwrecked there on his way to Virginia, colonized the islands.

Internal self-government was introduced on 8 June 1968. There is a Senate of 11 members and an elected House of Assembly of 40 members. The Governor retains responsibility for external affairs, defence, internal security and the police, although administrative matters for the Police Service have been delegated to the Minister of Home Affairs.

The last General Election was held on 9 February 1989. The United Bermuda Party holds 22 seats, the Progressive Labour Party 15 seats, the National Liberal Party one seat and Independents two seats.

Governor and Commander-in-Chief, His Excellency Lord Waddington, PC, QC, *apptd* 1992.
Deputy Governor, John Kelly, MBE.

CABINET as at June 1993
Premier, Hon. Sir John Swan, KBE.
Deputy Premier and Minister of Works and Engineering, Hon. A. F. Cartwright DeCouto.
Minister of Delegated and Legislative Affairs, Hon. Sir John Sharpe.
Health, Social Services and Housing, Hon. Quinton Edness.
Environment, Hon. Gerald D. E. Simons.
Education, Dr the Hon. Clarence Terceira.
Youth, Sport and Recreation, Senator Pamela Gordon.
Community and Cultural Affairs, Hon. Leonard O. Gibbons.
Tourism, Hon. C. V. Jim Woolridge.
Transport, Hon. Ralph Marshall.
Finance, Dr the Hon. David Saul.
Management and Technology, Hon. Michael Winfield.

President of the Senate, Hon. A. S. Jackson, MBE.
Speaker of the House of Assembly, Hon. David Wilkinson.

Chief Justice, Hon. Sir James Astwood.
Puisne Judges, Hon. L. Austin Ward, QC; Hon. Mrs.
N. Wade; Hon. R. W. Ground, OBE, QC.

ECONOMY

Locally manufactured concentrates, perfumes, cut flowers and pharmaceuticals are now the colony's leading exports. Little food is produced except vegetables and fish, other foodstuffs being imported.

The islands' economic structure is based on tourism, the major industry, and international company business, attracted by the low level of taxation and sophisticated telecommunications system. In 1992 a total of 461,349 visitors arrived by air and cruise ship. Cruise ships dock at Hamilton, Somerset and St George's.

FINANCE	1991–2	1992–3
Public revenue	$344,638,000	$354,939,000
Public expenditure	321,509,000	328,964,000

TRADE WITH UK	1991	1992
Imports from UK	£16,205,000	£27,040,000
Exports to UK	3,559,000	5,773,000

COMMUNICATIONS

One daily and three weekly newspapers are published in Bermuda. Three commercial companies operate radio and television services, including a cable-television system which started service in July 1988. The Bermuda Telephone Company and Cable and Wireless provide telecommunications links to more than 140 countries.

EDUCATION

Free elementary education was introduced in 1949. Free secondary education was introduced in 1965 for those children in the aided and maintained schools who were below the upper limit of the statutory school age of 16 (from 1969 onwards).

THE BRITISH ANTARCTIC TERRITORY

The British Antarctic Territory was designated in 1962 and consists of the areas south of 60°S. latitude which were previously included in the Falkland Islands Dependencies. The territory lies between longitudes 20° and 80°W., south of latitude 60°S. and includes the South Orkney Islands, the South Shetland Islands, the mountainous Antarctic Peninsula (highest point Mount Jackson, 13,620 ft, in Palmer Land) and all adjacent islands, and the land mass extending to the South Pole. The territory has no indigenous inhabitants and the British population consists of the scientists and technicians who man the British Antarctic Survey stations. The number averages about 60 to 70 in winter, but increases considerably in the summer months with the arrival of field workers. Argentina, Brazil, Chile, China, Korea (South), Poland, USA, Russia and Uruguay also have scientific stations in the territory.

The first two British Antarctic Survey stations were established in the South Shetland Islands in 1944, and by 1956 the number of stations had risen to 12. Due to the completion of field work in some areas and increased mobility, the number has now been reduced to five. These are Signy (Signy Island, South Orkney Islands), Faraday (Argentine Islands, Graham Coast), Rothera (Adelaide Island), Halley (Caird Coast) and, in summer only, Fossil Bluff (George VI Sound). Fifteen other stations have been established but are at present unoccupied.

The territory is administered by a Commissioner, resident in London.

Commissioner, Peter M. Newton.

THE BRITISH INDIAN OCEAN TERRITORY

The British Indian Ocean Territory was established by an Order in Council in 1965 and included islands formerly administered from Mauritius and the Seychelles. After the independence of both, the territory was redefined in 1976 as comprising only the islands of the Chagos Archipelago.

The Chagos Archipelago consists of six main groups of islands situated on the Great Chagos Bank and covering some 21,000 sq. miles (54,389 sq. km). The largest and most southerly of the Chagos Islands is Diego Garcia, a sand cay with a land area of about 17 square miles approximately 1,100 miles east of Mahé, used as a joint naval support facility by Britain and USA.

The other main island groups of the archipelago, Peros Banhos (29 islands with a total land area of 4 sq. miles) and Salomon (11 islands with a total land area of 2 sq. miles) are uninhabited. The islands have a typical tropical maritime climate, with average temperatures between 25° C and 29° C in Diego Garcia, and rainfall in the whole archipelago of 90–100 inches a year.

FLAG – Divided horizontally into blue and white wavy stripes, with the Union Flag in the canton and a crowned palm-tree over all in the fly.

Commissioner and Administrator, T. G. Harris.

TRADE WITH UK	1991	1992
Imports from UK	£821,000	£2,087,000
Exports to UK	197,000	26,000

THE BRITISH VIRGIN ISLANDS

AREA – The Virgin Islands are a group of islands at the eastern extremity of the Greater Antilles, divided between Great Britain and the USA. Those of the group which are British number 46, of which 11 are inhabited, and have a total area of about 59 sq. miles, (153 sq. km). The principal are Tortola, the largest (situated in 18° 27′ N. lat. and 64° 40′ W. long., area, 21 sq. miles), Virgin Gorda (8¼ sq. miles), Anegada (15 sq.miles) and Jost Van Dyke (3½ sq. miles).

Apart from Anegada, which is a flat coral island, the British Virgin Islands are hilly, being an extension of the Puerto Rico and the US Virgin Islands archipelago. The highest point is Sage Mountain on Tortola which rises to a height of 1,780 feet.

CLIMATE – The islands lie within the trade winds belt and possess a sub-tropical climate. The average temperature varies from 22°–28° C in winter to 26°–31° C in summer. Average annual rainfall is 53 inches.

POPULATION – The 1991 Census showed a total population of 16,108: Tortola (13,225); Virgin Gorda (2,431); Anegada (162); Jost Van Dyke (140); and other islands (144).

CAPITAL – ΨRoad Town, on the south-east of Tortola. Population 3,983.

CURRENCY – The US dollar (US$) of 100 cents is legal tender.

FLAG – British Blue Ensign with the shield of arms in the fly.

GOVERNMENT

Under the 1977 Constitution the Governor, appointed by the Crown, remains responsible for defence and internal security, external affairs and the civil service but in other matters acts in accordance with the advice of the Executive Council. The Executive Council consists of the Governor as Chairman, one ex officio member (the Attorney-General), the Chief Minister and three other ministers. The Legislative Council consists of a Speaker chosen from outside the Council, one ex officio member (the Attorney-General), and nine elected members returned from nine one-member electoral districts.

Governor, Peter Alfred Penfold, OBE, *apptd* 1992.
Deputy Governor, E. Georges, OBE.

THE EXECUTIVE COUNCIL as at 30 June 1993

Chairman, The Governor.
Chief Minister and Minister of Finance, Hon. H. Lavity Stoutt.
Natural Resources and Labour, Hon. Ralph O'Neal, OBE.
Communications and Works, Hon. Terrance Lettsome.
Health, Education and Welfare, Hon. Louis Walters, MBE.
Attorney-General, Hon. Dancia Penn.

Puisne Judge (resident), Justice Ephraim Georges.

ECONOMY

Tourism is the main industry but the financial centre is growing steadily in importance. Other industries include a rum distillery, three stone-crushing plants and factories manufacturing concrete blocks and paint. The major export items are fresh fish, gravel, sand, fruit and vegetables; exports are largely confined to the US Virgin Islands. Chief imports are building materials, machinery, cars and beverages.

FINANCE	1989	1990
Revenue	US$32,629,000	US$41,400,000
Expenditure	31,038,000	40,600,000

TRADE WITH UK	1991	1992
Imports from UK	£6,081,000	£4,097,000
Exports to UK	1,736,000	139,000

COMMUNICATIONS

The principal airport is on Beef Island, linked by bridge to Tortola, and an extended runway of 3,600 ft enables larger aircraft to call. There is a second airfield on Virgin Gorda and a third on Anegada. There are direct shipping services to the United Kingdom and the United States and fast passenger services connect the main islands by ferry.

THE CAYMAN ISLANDS

AREA – The Cayman Islands, between 79° 44′ and 81° 26′ W. and 19° 15′ and 19° 46′ N., consist of three islands, Grand Cayman, Cayman Brac, and Little Cayman, with a total area of 100 sq. miles (259 sq. km). About 150 miles south of Cuba, the islands are divided from Jamaica, 180 miles to the south-east, by the Cayman Trench, the deepest part of the Caribbean. The nearest point on the US mainland is Miami in Florida, 450 miles to the north. Cooled by trade winds, the annual average temperature and rainfall are 27.2° C and 50.7 inches respectively.

POPULATION – Population (estimate 1992) 29,700, of which the vast majority live on Grand Cayman.

CAPITAL – ΨGeorge Town, in Grand Cayman, population (estimate 1992) 15,000.

CURRENCY – Cayman Islands dollar (CI$) of 100 cents, which is fixed at CI$ = US$1.20.

FLAG – British Blue Ensign with the arms on a white disc in the fly.

GOVERNMENT

The colony derives its name from the Carib word for the crocodile, 'caymanas', which appeared in the log of the first English visitor to the Cayman Islands, Sir Francis Drake. Although tradition has it that the first settlers arrived in 1658, the first recorded settlers arrived in 1666–71. The first recorded permanent settlers followed the first land grant by Britain in 1734. The islands were placed under direct control of Jamaica in 1863. When Jamaica became independent in 1962, the islands opted to remain under the British Crown.

The constitution provides for a Governor, a Legislative Assembly and an Executive Council, and effectively allows a large measure of self-government. Unless there are exceptional reasons, the Governor accepts the advice of the Executive Council, which comprises three official members and four others elected from the 15 elected members of the Assembly. The official members also sit in the Assembly. The Governor has responsibility for the police, civil service, defence and external affairs. The Governor handed over the presidency of the Legislative Assembly to the Speaker on 15 February 1991. The normal life of the Assembly is four years, with a general election next due in November 1996.

Governor, His Excellency Michael E. J. Gore, CBE, *apptd* 1992.

EXECUTIVE COUNCIL as at 30 June 1993

President, The Governor.
Chief Secretary, Hon. J. L. Hurlston, MBE.
Attorney-General, Hon. R. H. Coles.
Financial Secretary, Hon. G. A. McCarthy.
Member for Tourism, Environment and Planning, Hon. T. C. Jefferson, OBE.
Member for Education, Culture and Aviation, Hon. T. M. Bodden.
Member for Health and Human Services, Hon. W. M. Bush.
Member for Communications, Works and Agriculture, Hon. J. McLean.
Speaker of Legislative Assembly, Mrs S. I. McLaughlin, MBE.

LONDON OFFICE
Cayman Islands Government Office, 100 Brompton Road, London SW3 1EX
Tel 071-581 9418
Government Representative, T. Russell, CMG, CBE.

ECONOMY

Based on a complete absence of direct taxation, the Cayman Islands have been successfully promoted over the past 25 years as an offshore financial centre. With representation from 60 countries, there were, at the end of 1992, 532 banks and trust companies, of which local offices were maintained by 79. In addition, there were 520 licensed insurance companies and 25,047 registered companies at the end of 1992.

Promotion of tourism, with an emphasis on scuba diving, has also been successful. There were 241,843 visitors by air and 613,470 cruise ship callers in 1992.

The two industries support a heavy imbalance in trade resulting from the need to import most of what is consumed and used on the islands, and have created a thriving local economy in which the GNP reached US$669.6m (US$25,300 per capita) in 1991. Import duty and fees from financial centre operations have provided revenue enabling the government to undertake heavy investment in education (which is provided free to all 4–16 year olds), health and other social programmes.

FINANCE	1992	1993*
Revenue	CI$133.5m	CI$143.3m
Expenditure	141.5m	135.0m
*estimated		

TRADE	1991	1992
Total imports	CI$222.9m	CI$253.5m
Total exports	2.5m	3.7m

TRADE WITH UK	1991	1992
Imports from UK	£6,081,000	£6,173,000
Exports to UK	1,736,000	2,497,000

FALKLAND ISLANDS

AREA – The Falkland Islands, the only considerable group in the South Atlantic, lie about 300 miles east of the Straits of Magellan, between 52° 15′–53° S. lat. and 57° 40′–62° W. long. They consist of East Falkland (area 2,610 sq. miles; 6,759 sq. km), West Falkland (2,090 sq. miles; 5,413 sq. km) and over 100 small islands. Mount Usborne (E. Falkland), the loftiest peak, rises 2,312 feet above the level of the sea. The islands are chiefly moorland.

CLIMATE – Cool. At Stanley the mean monthly temperature varies between 9° C in January and 2° C in July.

POPULATION – The population, excluding the British garrison, was 2,121 at 5 March 1991.

CHIEF TOWN – ΨStanley, population (1991) 1,643. Stanley is about 8,103 miles distant from England .

CURRENCY – Falkland pound of 100 pence.

FLAG – British Blue Ensign with the arms on a white disc in the fly.

GOVERNMENT

The Falklands were sighted first by Davis in 1592, and then by Hawkins in 1594; the first known landing was by Strong in 1690. A settlement was made by France in 1764; this was subsequently sold to Spain, but the latter country recognized Great Britain's title to a part at least of the group in 1771. After Argentina declared independence from Spain, the Argentine government in 1820 proclaimed its sovereignty over the Falklands and a settlement was founded in 1826. The settlement was destroyed by the Americans in 1831. In 1833 occupation was resumed by the British for the protection of the seal-fisheries, and the islands were permanently colonized as the most southerly organized colony of the British Empire. Argentina continued to claim sovereignty over the islands (known to them as las Islas Malvinas), and in pursuance of this claim invaded the islands on 2 April 1982 and also occupied South Georgia. A naval and military force dispatched from Great Britain recaptured South Georgia on 25 April and after landing at San Carlos Bay on 21 May, recaptured the islands from the Argentines, who surrendered on 14 June 1982. A British naval and military presence remains in the area.

Under the 1985 Constitution, the Governor is advised by an Executive Council consisting of three elected members of the Legislative Council and two ex-officio members, the Chief Executive and the Financial Secretary. The Legislative Council consists of eight elected members and the same two ex-officio members.

Governor and Chairman of the Executive Council, His Excellency David Everard Tatham, CMG, *apptd* 1992.
Chief Executive, R. Sampson.
Financial Secretary, D. F. Howatt.
Commander, British Forces, Falkland Islands, Maj.-Gen. I. C. Mackay-Dick, MBE.
Attorney-General, D. G. Lang, QC.

LONDON OFFICE
Falkland Islands Government Office, Falkland House, 14 Broadway, London SW1H 0BH.
Tel 071-222 2542.
Government Representative, Miss S. Cameron.

ECONOMY

The economy was formerly based solely on agriculture, principally sheep-farming with a little dairy farming for domestic requirements and crops for winter fodder. Since the establishment of an interim conservation and management zone around the islands and the consequent introduction on 1 February 1987 of a licensing regime for vessels fishing within the zone, the economy has diversified and income from the associated fishing activities is now the largest source of revenue. The islands are now self-financing except for defence. Chief imports are provisions, alcoholic beverages, timber, clothing and hardware.

FINANCE	1990–1	1991–2
Public Revenue	£43,300,000	£40,300,000
Expenditure	41,100,000	39,100,000

TRADE WITH UK	1991	1992
Imports from UK	£16,039,000	£13,100,000
Exports to UK	3,379,000	3,091,000

GIBRALTAR

AREA – Gibraltar is a rocky promontory, 2¾ miles in length, three-quarters of a mile in breadth, with a total area of 2¼ sq. miles. It is 1,396 ft. high at its greatest elevation, near the southern extremity of Spain, with which it is connected by a low isthmus. It is about 14 miles from the opposite coast of Africa. The town stands at the foot of the promontory on the west side.

POPULATION – The population at the end of 1992 was 28,848.

CURRENCY – Gibraltar pound of 100 pence.

FLAG – White with a red stripe along the lower edge; over all a red castle with a key hanging from its gateway.

GOVERNMENT

Gibraltar was captured in 1704, during the war of the Spanish Succession, by a combined Dutch and English force under Sir George Rooke, and was ceded to Great Britain by the Treaty of Utrecht 1713. Several attempts have been made to retake it, the most celebrated being the great siege of 1779 to 1783, when General Eliott, afterwards Lord Heathfield, held it for three years and seven months against a combined French and Spanish force. The Treaty of Utrecht stipulates that if Britain ever relinquishes its colonial rights over Gibraltar then the colony would return to Spain. In 1967 a referendum was held in Gibraltar on the colony's status in which 12,000 voted to remain a British Dependent Territory and 44 voted to join Spain.

The Constitution of Gibraltar, approved in 1969, made formal provision for certain domestic matters to devolve on a local government of Ministers appointed from among elected members of the House of Assembly then set up to replace the former Legislative Council. The House of Assembly consists of an independent Speaker, 15 elected members, the Attorney-General and the Financial and Development Secretary.

The Governor retains responsibility for external affairs, defence, internal security and financial security, while the local government is responsible for other domestic matters. However, the Gibraltar government has recently been agitating for more local autonomy and responsibility, especially in the colony's relations with the EC. Gibraltar is part of the EC but is not a fully-fledged member and, for example, its citizens cannot vote in European Parliament elections. In 1993 the Gibraltar government took the UK and Spanish governments to the European Court of Justice over a 1987 Anglo-Spanish agreement to exclude Gibraltar's airport from the EC's air liberalization directive of the EC Single Market Programme but the case was defeated.

Governor and Commander-in-Chief, His Excellency Field Marshal Sir John Chapple, GCB, CBE.
Flag Officer, Gibraltar, and Admiral Superintendent, HM Naval Base, Gibraltar, Rear-Adm. J. T. Sanders, OBE.
Deputy Governor, A. Carter.
Financial and Development Secretary, B. Traynor.
Attorney-General, J. Blackburn Gittings.
Chief Justice, A. Kneller.
Chief Minister, Joe Bossano.
Speaker, Mayor R. J. Peliza, OBE.

ECONOMY

Gibraltar enjoys the advantages of an extensive shipping trade and is a popular shopping centre. The chief sources of revenue are the port dues, the rent of the Crown estate in the town, and duties on consumer items. The free port tradition of Gibraltar is still reflected in the low rates of import duty. The gradual change from a fortress city to a holiday centre has led to a flourishing tourist trade.

A total of 4,881 merchant ships (63.6 million gross registered tons aggregate) entered the port during 1992. Of these 2,888 were deep-sea ships (62.9 million gross registered tons aggregate). In addition 4,783 yachts called at the port. There are 49.9 km of roads.

FINANCE	1990–1	1991–2
Revenue	£90,834,900	£87,102,600
Expenditure	96,147,600	82,977,700
TRADE	1990	1991
Total imports	£200,493,000	£266,348,000
Total exports	76,138,000	101,679,000
Trade with UK	1991	1992
Imports from UK	£80,105,000	£82,238,000
Exports to UK	4,289,000	4,059,000

EDUCATION

Education is compulsory and free for children between the ages of 4 and 15 whose parents are ordinarily resident in Gibraltar. Scholarships are available for higher education in Britain. The total enrolment in government schools was 4,681 in December 1992.

HONG KONG

AREA – Hong Kong, consisting of more than 230 islands and of a portion of the mainland (Kowloon and the New Territories) on the south-east coast of China, is situated at the eastern side of the mouth of the Pearl River, between 22° 9′ and 22° 37′ N. lat. and 113° 52′–114° 30′ E. long. The total area of the territory (including recent reclamation) is 416 sq. miles (1,077 sq. km).

The island of Hong Kong is about 11 miles (18 km) long and from two to five miles (three to eight km) broad, with a total area of 29 sq. miles (80 sq. km); at the eastern entrance to the harbour it is separated from the mainland by a narrow strait.

CLIMATE – Hong Kong's climate is sub-tropical, tending towards the temperate for nearly half the year. The mean monthly temperature ranges from 16° C to 29° C. The average annual rainfall is 2,214 mm, of which nearly 80 per cent falls between May and September. Tropical cyclones occur between May and November, causing high winds and heavy rain.

POPULATION – Population at the beginning of 1992 was 5.9 million.

CAPITAL – ΨVictoria, situated on the island of Hong Kong, is about 81 miles south-east of Canton and 40 miles east of the Portuguese province of Macao at the other side of the Pearl River. It lies along the northern shore of the island and faces the mainland; the harbour (19 sq. miles water area) lies between the Central District and Kowloon.

CURRENCY – Hong Kong dollar (HK$) of 100 cents.

FLAG – British Blue Ensign with the arms on a white disc in the fly.

GOVERNMENT

The island was first occupied by Great Britain in January 1841, and formally ceded by the Treaty of Nanking in 1842. Kowloon was subsequently acquired by the Peking Convention of 1860, and the New Territories, consisting of a peninsula in the southern part of the Guangdong province together with adjacent islands, by a 99-year lease signed on 9 June 1898.

Hong Kong is administered by the Hong Kong Government, at the head of which is the Governor, and its administration has developed from the basic pattern applied to all British-governed territories overseas. Under the terms of the Joint Declaration of the British and Chinese Governments, which came into force on 27 May 1985, Hong Kong will become, with effect from 1 July 1997, a Special Administrative Region of the People's Republic of China. However, the social and economic systems in the SAR will remain unchanged for 50 years. The British and Chinese governments have, since the entry into force of the agreement, been involved in consultations on the implementation of the agreement via the Joint Liaison Group.

The Governor governs aided by an Executive Council and a Legislative Council. The Executive Council consists of four ex-officio members together with 12 other members, including three members who are officials and appointed by the Governor with the approval of the Secretary of State for Foreign and Commonwealth Affairs. The Legislative Council consists of 60 members, of whom three are ex-officio members and 57 are non-official members. Of these 57 non-official members, 18 are appointed by the Governor, 21 are elected by functional constituencies and 18 are elected by direct election. The President of the Legislative Council is a non-official member elected to that office by the non-official members. The first direct elections for 18 of the 60 Legislative Council seats were held in September 1991. It is planned that 20 members of the Legislative Council will be directly elected in 1995.

There is also an Urban Council which provides services relating to public health and sanitation, culture and recreation in the urban area. The Urban Council consists of 40 members, of which 15 are directly elected from district constituencies, 15 appointed by the Governor and 10 are representative members from the urban district boards. A Regional Council was also set up in 1986 to provide similar services in the New Territories. Of the 36 Regional Council seats, 12 are directly elected, 12 are appointed by the Governor, nine are elected as representatives of the nine district boards within the Regional Council area, and three are ex-officio members, namely the chairman and the two vice-chairmen. Direct elections to the Urban and Regional councils were held for the first time in May 1991. Both Councils are financially autonomous.

China is demanding an increasing voice in Hong Kong affairs as the handover in 1997 approaches. This has led to increasing friction between the British and Hong Kong Authorities on one side and the Chinese government on the other. Central to the acrimonious disputes in 1992–3 has been the plan for an extension of democracy in Hong Kong presented by the Governor to the Legislative Council in October 1992. The plan includes: a reduction in the voting age from 21 to 18; nine new functional constituencies; a five-fold increase in the electorate of the new functional constituencies; the official separation of the executive from the legislature; ten seats on the Legislative Council to be elected by an electoral college which is itself directly elected; and all Urban and Regional Council seats to be directly elected. By the 1995 elections, when these reforms are due to be in place, there would effectively be 39 directly-elected members out of 60 (20 directly-elected, 10 elected by electoral college, nine by large functional constituencies).

The plan has outraged the Chinese government which believes it agreed in the 1985 Joint Declaration to only 20 directly elected seats on the Legislative Council and 40 appointed (or pliant pro-Chinese) members. So far almost all the directly-elected members have been hostile to the Chinese government. In an attempt to derail the democracy reform package, the Chinese government suspended meetings of the Joint Liaison Group and talks on the new airport in late 1992, and launched a propaganda campaign against Governor Patten. Meanwhile, the Executive Council passed the reform package without amendment in February 1993. The Governor then suspended the presentation of the reform package to the Legislative Council for debate to enable UK-Chinese discussions on the issue to begin in April 1993. The Chinese government approved the re-opening of the Joint Liaison Group meetings and talks on the new airport, which began in June 1993. In July the Chinese officially established a shadow government for Hong Kong, known as the preparatory work subcommittee of the Chinese parliament and headed by foreign minister Qian Qichen. At the time of going to press the situation regarding continuing UK-Chinese discussions of the democracy reform package remained unclear, but Governor Patten has stated that he will present his reforms to the Legislative Council as soon as it returns from its summer recess. This would prevent the Chinese government from continuing negotiations indefinitely and so preventing the passing of the reform package in time for the 1995 elections.

Governor, His Excellency The Rt. Hon. Christopher Patten, sworn in 9 July 1992.
Chief Justice, The Hon. Sir Ti Liang Yang.

Executive Council as at June 1993
Chief Secretary, Hon. Sir David Ford, KBE, LVO.
Commander, British Forces, Maj.-Gen. J. P. Foley, CB, OBE, MC.
Financial Secretary, Hon. N. W. H. McLeod, CBE.
Attorney-General, Hon. J. F. Mathews, CMG

Secretary for the Civil Service, Hon. Mrs Anson Chan, CBE.
Planning, Environment and Lands, Hon. A. G. Eason.
Transport, Hon. K. Y. Yeung, CBE.
Education and Manpower, Hon. John C. C. Chan, LVO, OBE.
Economic Services, Hon. Gordon Siu.
Home Affairs, Michael M. Y. Suen.
Health and Welfare, Hon. Mrs Elizabeth C. L. Wong-Chien, ISO.
Security, Hon. A. P. Asprey, OBE, AE.
Financial Services, Hon. Michael Cartland.
Recreation and Culture, James So, CBE.
Treasury, Hon. Donald Tsang, OBE.
Trade and Industry, T. H. Chau.
Constitutional Affairs, Michael C. Sze, ISO.
Works, James Blake.
ex-officio member

British Council Representative, T. Buchanan, Easey Commercial Building, 225 Hennessy Road, Wanchai, Hong Kong.

London Office
Hong Kong Government Office, 6 Grafton Street, London WIX 3LB.
Tel 071-499 9821

Commissioner, John Yaxley, *apptd* 1993.

ECONOMY

The manufacturing sector is the mainstay of Hong Kong's economy, contributing about 15.5 per cent to the GDP and accounting for about 22.9 per cent of total employment. Up to 80 per cent of Hong Kong's manufacturing output is eventually exported.

Hong Kong's manufacturing industries produce light consumer goods, such as electronics, plastics, electrical products, watches and clocks, which accounted for 30 per cent of Hong Kong's total domestic exports in 1992. The corresponding share of textiles and clothing, Hong Kong's traditional leading industries, was 40 per cent in 1992.

Diversification in terms of products and markets continues to be the main feature of recent industrial development, as are industrial partnerships with overseas companies. The economy of Hong Kong is based on export rather than the domestic market.

FINANCE	1991–2	1992–3*
Public revenue	HK$114,699m	HK$135,646m
Public expenditure	92,191m	115,100m
*estimated		

TRADE

In 1992, the total value of visible trade (including domestic exports, re-exports and imports) amounted to 253 per cent of the GDP. Hong Kong's visible trade account had in 1992 a deficit of HK$30,342 million. Taking visible and invisible trade together, there was a combined surplus of HK$17,433 million, compared with HK$22,188 million in 1991. In 1992, Hong Kong's principal customers for its domestic products, in order of value of trade, were USA, China, Germany, the United Kingdom, Japan, Singapore and Taiwan. China was its principal supplier.

	1991	1992
Total Exports	HK$765,886m	HK$924,953m
Total Imports	778,982m	955,295m

Trade with UK	1991	1992
Imports from UK	£1,386,892,000	£1,612,934,000
Exports to UK	2,147,611,000	2,397,362,000

COMMUNICATIONS

Hong Kong, one of the world's finest natural harbours, possesses excellent wharves. The Kwai Chung container terminal has 14 berths. A pier at the Ocean Terminal can accommodate large liners and cargo vessels up to 290 metres length and 10 metres draught. The Marine Department provides and maintains 76 mooring buoys within the port for ships to work cargo in the stream. There are two classes of buoy suitable for vessels up to 137 and 183 metres in length respectively. Available dockyard facilities include six floating drydocks, the largest being capable of docking vessels up to 150,000 tonnes deadweight. In 1992 some 146,000 ocean-going and river-trade vessels called at Hong Kong and loaded and discharged more than 100 million tonnes of cargo. To cope with increasing demand two new container terminals will come into operation close to the present container port. Lack of space at Kwai Chung means these will be situated at Stonecutters Island and at South-East Tsing Yi Island. Construction at Stonecutters Island began in October 1991. The first berth should begin operation in mid-1993 and the whole terminal should be completed by the end of 1994.

Hong Kong International Airport, Kai Tak, situated to the east of the Kowloon peninsula, is regularly used by over 51 international airlines, providing over 2,260 frequent scheduled passenger and cargo services each week. During 1992, over 121,000 aircraft on international flights arrived and departed, carrying 22.1 million passengers and 956,896 tonnes of freight. A new international airport is to be built on reclaimed land off Lantau Island at Chek Lap Kok and is planned to become operational by 1997, with an initial capacity of 35 million passengers and 1.5 million tonnes of cargo a year.

EDUCATION

In the school year 1992–3 there were 2,050 day schools with 1,172,176 pupils. Free education for children up to the age of 15 was made compulsory in 1979. Post-secondary education is provided by three universities, two polytechnics, the Hong Kong Baptist College and four approved post-secondary colleges. The Hong Kong Polytechnic and City Polytechnic of Hong Kong have 10,209 and 7,729 full-time students respectively. The Open Learning Institute of Hong Kong provides university education to about 15,000 students. There are also seven technical institutes and four teacher-training colleges.

MONTSERRAT

AREA – Situated in 16° 45′ N. lat. and 61° 15° W. long., 27 miles south-west of Antigua, Montserrat is about 11 miles long and seven miles wide, with an area of 38 sq. miles (98 sq. km). Fertile and green, it is volcanic with several hot springs. About two-thirds of the island is mountainous, the rest capable of cultivation.

POPULATION – Population (estimate 1991) was 11,000.

CHIEF TOWN – ΨPlymouth, population 2,500.

CURRENCY – East Caribbean dollar (EC$) of 100 cents.

FLAG – British Blue Ensign with the shield of arms in the fly.

GOVERNMENT

Discovered by Columbus in 1493, Montserrat was settled by Irishmen in 1632, conquered and held by the French for some time, and finally assigned to Great Britain in 1783.

A ministerial system was introduced in Montserrat in 1960. The Executive Council is presided over by the Governor and is composed of four elected members (the Chief and three other Ministers) and two ex-officio members (the Attorney-General and the Financial Secretary). The four Ministers are appointed from the members of the political party holding the majority in the Legislative Council. The Legislative Council consists of the Speaker, two ex-officio members (the Attorney-General and the Financial Secretary), two nominated unofficial members and seven elected members.

Governor, His Excellency Frank Savage, LVO, OBE, *apptd* 1993.

EXECUTIVE COUNCIL as at July 1993

President, The Governor.
Chief Minister and Minister of Finance and Economic Development, Hon. Reuben T. Meade.
Communications, Works and Sport, Hon. David S. Brandt.
Agriculture, Trade and the Environment, Hon. Charles T. Kirnon.
Education, Health, Community Services and Labour, Hon. Lazelle Howes.
Acting Attorney-General, Hon. Gertel Thom.
Financial Secretary, Hon. C. T. John, OBE.

Speaker of the Legislative Council, Dr the Hon. H. A. Fergus, OBE.

ECONOMY

The economy is dominated by tourism, related construction activities and offshore business services. There is some light industry and efforts are being made to increase agricultural exports and establish an agro-processing industry.

FINANCE	1991	1992
Revenue	EC$44,443,000	EC$39,273,000
Expenditure	39,216,000	39,056,000

TRADE WITH UK	1991	1992
Imports from UK	£2,720,000	£1,854,000
Exports to UK	39,000	143,000

PITCAIRN ISLANDS

AREA – Pitcairn, a small volcanic island 1.9 sq. miles (5 sq. km) in area, is the chief of a group of islands situated about midway between New Zealand and Panama in the South Pacific Ocean at longitude 130° 06′ W. and latitude 25° 04′ S. The island rises in cliffs to a height of 1,100 feet and access from the sea is possible only at Bounty Bay, a small rocky cove, and then only by surf boats. The other three islands of the group (Henderson lying 105 miles east-north-east of Pitcairn, Oeno lying 75 miles north-west and Ducie lying 293 miles east) are all uninhabited. Henderson Island is occasionally visited by the Pitcairn Islanders to obtain supplies of 'miro' wood which is used for their carvings. Oeno is visited for excursions of about a week's duration every two years or so.

CLIMATE – Mean monthly temperatures vary between 66°F (19°C) in August and 75°F (24°C) in February and the average annual rainfall is 80 inches. With an equable climate, the island is very fertile and produces both tropical and sub-tropical trees and crops.

POPULATION – At May 1993 the population was 65. Since 1887 the islanders have all been adherents of the Seventh-day Adventist Church.

FLAG – British Blue Ensign with the arms in the fly.

GOVERNMENT

First settled in 1790 by the Bounty mutineers and their Tahitian companions, Pitcairn was left uninhabited in 1856 when the entire population was resettled on Norfolk Island. The present community are descendants of two parties who, not wishing to remain on Norfolk, returned to Pitcairn in 1859 and 1864 respectively.

Pitcairn became a British settlement under the British Settlement Act 1887, and was administered by the Governor of Fiji from 1952 until 1970, when the administration was transferred to the British High Commission in New Zealand and the British High Commissioner was appointed Governor. The local Government Ordinance of 1964 provides for a Council of ten members of whom six are elected.

Governor of Pitcairn, Henderson, Ducie and Oeno Islands, His Excellency David Joseph Moss, CMG (*British High Commissioner to New Zealand*).
Island Magistrate and Chairman of Island Council, J. Warren.
Education Officer and Government Adviser, Mrs P. Foley.

ECONOMY

The islanders live by subsistence gardening and fishing, and their limited monetary needs are satisfied by the manufacture of wood carvings and other handicrafts which are sold to passing ships and to a few overseas customers. Other than small fees charged for gun and driving licences there are no taxes and government revenue is derived almost solely from the sale of postage stamps and income from investments. Communication with the outside world is maintained by cargo vessels travelling between New Zealand and Panama which call at irregular intervals, and by means of a satellite service providing telephone, telex and fax facilities.

SOCIAL WELFARE

The New Zealand Ministry of Education provides assistance in recruiting a teacher for the sole-charge school. Education is compulsory between the ages of five and fifteen. Secondary education in New Zealand is encouraged by the Administration which provides scholarships and bursaries for the purpose. Medical care is provided by a registered nurse when a doctor is not present.

ST HELENA AND DEPENDENCIES

ST HELENA

AREA – Probably the best known of all the solitary islands in the world, St Helena is situated in the South Atlantic Ocean, 955 miles south of the Equator, 702 south-east of Ascension, 1,140 from the nearest point of the African continent, 1,800 from the coast of South America, 1,694 from Cape Town (transit five days), in 15° 55′ S. lat. and 5° 42′ W. longitude. It is 10½ miles long, 6½ broad, and encloses an area of 47 sq. miles (122 sq. km).

St Helena is of volcanic origin, and consists of numerous rugged mountains, the highest rising to 2,700 feet, interspersed with picturesque ravines.

CLIMATE – Although within the tropics, the south-east trade winds keep the temperature mild and equable.

POPULATION – Population was 5,644 in 1987.

CAPITAL– ΨJamestown. Population (1987) 1,332.

CURRENCY – St Helena pound (£) of 100 pence.

FLAG – British Blue Ensign with the shield of arms in the fly.

GOVERNMENT

St Helena was discovered by the Portuguese navigator, Juan da Nova Castella, in 1502 (probably on St Helena's Day) and remained unknown to other European nations until 1588. It was used as a port of call for vessels of all nations trading to the East until it was annexed by the Dutch in 1633. It was never occupied by them, however, and the English East India Company seized it in 1659. In 1834 it was ceded to the British Crown. During the period 1815 to 1821 the island was lent to the British Government as a place of exile for the Emperor Napoleon Bonaparte who died in St Helena on 5 May 1821. It was formerly an important station on the route to India, but its prosperity decreased after the construction of the Suez Canal.

The government of St Helena is administered by a Governor, with the aid of a Legislative Council, consisting of a Speaker, three ex-officio members (Chief Secretary, Financial Secretary and Attorney-General) and 12 elected members. Five committees of the Legislative Council are reponsible for general oversight of the activities of government departments and have in addition a wide range of statutory and administrative functions. The Governor is also assisted by an Executive Council of the three ex-officio members and the Chairmen of the Council committees.

Governor, His Excellency A. N. Hoole, OBE, *apptd* 1991.
Chief Secretary, J. G. Perrott.
Financial Secretary, R. Perrott, OBE.
Attorney-General, D. Jeremiah.
Chief Medical Officer, Dr J. L. Sharp.
Chief Agriculture and Forestry Officer, C. Lomas.
Chief Education Officer, B. George.
Chief Engineer, D. Johnston.
Chief Social Services and Employment Officer, Mrs J. Young.

ECONOMY

Since the collapse of the New Zealand flax industry in 1965, the only significant export is that of canned and frozen fish. The other exports are a small amount of high quality coffee and cottage industry products (including lace, decorative woodwork and beadwork). St James's Bay, on the north-west of the island, possesses a good anchorage. There is as yet no airport or airstrip.

FINANCE	1991–2	1992–3
Local revenue	£3,589,477	£3,502,472
Budgetary	3,424,000	3,526,100
Recurrent expenditure	6,756,049	6,816,429
Development aid	1,194,946	1,702,711

TRADE	1991–2	1992–3
Total imports	£6,320,224	£6,100,400
Total exports	90,616	169,525

Trade with UK	1991	1992
Imports from UK	£6,980,000	£7,336,000
Exports to UK	820,000	691,000

ASCENSION

AREA – The small island of Ascension lies in the South Atlantic (7° 56′ S., 14° 22′ W.) some 700 miles north-west of the island of St Helena. It is a rocky peak of purely volcanic origin. The highest point (Green Mountain), some 2,817 ft., is covered with lush vegetation and has a farm of some ten acres, producing vegetables and livestock. The island is famous for turtles, which land on the beaches from January to May to lay their eggs. It is also a breeding area for the sooty tern, or wideawake, large numbers of which settle on the south-western coastal section every tenth month to hatch their eggs. Other wildlife on the island includes feral donkeys and cats, rabbits and francolin partridge. All wildlife except rabbits and cats is protected by law. The ocean surrounding the island contains shark, barracuda, tuna, bonito and many other fish.

POPULATION – The resident population in March 1993 totalled 1,117, of whom 707 were from St Helena, 181 from the UK and 143 from the USA. The residents consist of the employees and families of the British organizations, of the contractors of the US Air Force (Computer Sciences Raytheon) and of the St Helena Government.

British forces returned to the island in April 1982 in support of operations in the Falkland Islands. At present there are over 100 RAF personnel on the island supporting the air link to the Falklands.

CAPITAL – Georgetown.

GOVERNMENT

Ascension is said to have been discovered by Juan da Nova Castella on Ascension Day 1501 and two years later was visited by Alphonse d'Albuquerque, who gave the island its present name. It was uninhabited until the arrival of Napoleon in St Helena in 1815 when a small British naval garrison was stationed on the island. It remained under the supervision of the Board of Admiralty until 1922, when it was made a dependency of St Helena by letters patent.

The British Foreign Secretary appoints the Administrator who is responsible to the Governor resident in St Helena. There is a small police force and post office. The British organizations through Ascension Island Services (AIS) provide and operate various common services for the island (school, hospital, public works etc).

Administrator, B. N. Connelly.

COMMUNICATIONS

Cable & Wireless PLC operates the international telephone and cable services and maintains an internal telephone service. The BBC opened its Atlantic relay station broadcasting to Africa and South America in 1967.

TRISTAN DA CUNHA

AREA – Tristan da Cunha is the chief island of a group of islands in the South Atlantic which lies in lat. 37° 6′ S. and long. 12° 2′ W., some 1,320 miles (2,124 km) south-south-west of St Helena, about 1,500 miles (2,414 km) west of the Cape of Good Hope, and 3,600 miles (5,794 km) north-east of Cape Horn. Tristan da Cunha has an area of 38 square miles (98 square km). Inaccessible Island lies 20 miles west and has an area of 4 square miles (11 square km), and the three Nightingale Islands lie 20 miles south of Tristan da Cunha and have an area of three-quarters of a square mile (2 square km). Gough Island lies some 250 miles south-south-east of Tristan da Cunha in lat. 40° 20′ S. and long. 9° 44′ W. and has an area of 35 square miles (91 square km).

All the islands are volcanic and steep sided with cliffs or narrow beaches. Tristan itself has a single volcanic cone rising to 6,760 feet (2,060 m) and a narrow north-western coastal plain on which the settlement of Edinburgh is situated. Inaccessible Island is a lofty mass of rock with sides two miles in length; the island is the resort of penguins and sea-fowl. Cultivation was started in 1937 but has been abandoned.

The Nightingale Islands are three in number, of which the largest is one mile long and three-quarters of a mile wide, and rises in two peaks, 960 and 1,105 feet above sea level respectively. The smaller islands, Stoltenhoff and Middle Isle, are little more than huge rocks. Seals, innumerable penguins, and vast numbers of sea-fowl visit these islands.

Gough Island (or Diego Alvarez) is about eight miles long and four miles broad. It is the resort of penguins and sea-elephants and has valuable guano deposits.

CLIMATE – The islands have a warm-temperate oceanic climate which is damp and windy and supports forest and scrub. Rainfall averages 66 inches a year on the coast of Tristan da Cunha.

POPULATION – Population in 1992 was 295, in the settlement of Edinburgh on Tristan da Cunha. In addition, there is a meteorological station maintained on Gough Island by the South African government and manned by South Africans. Inaccessible Island and the Nightingale Islands are uninhabited.

CAPITAL – Edinburgh.

CURRENCY – Pound Sterling.

HISTORY

Tristan da Cunha was discovered in 1506 by a Portuguese admiral (Tristão da Cunha) after whom it was named. It was the resort of British and American sealers from the middle of the 18th century, and in 1760 a British naval officer visited the group of islands and gave his name to Nightingale Island. On 14 August 1816 the group was annexed to the British Crown and a garrison was placed on Tristan da Cunha, but this force was withdrawn in 1817. Corporal William Glass remained at his own request with his wife and two children. This party, with five others, formed a settlement. In 1827 five women from St Helena, and afterwards others from Cape Colony, joined the party.

Due to its position on a main sailing route the colony thrived, with an economy based on whaling, sealing and barter with passing ships. However, with the replacement of sail by steam in the late 19th century, a period of decline set in, with no regular calls by shipping.

In October 1961, a volcano, believed to have been extinct for thousands of years, erupted and the danger of further volcanic activity led to the evacuation of inhabitants to the United Kingdom. An advance party returned to Tristan da Cunha in the spring of 1963, and subsequently the main body of the islanders returned to the island.

GOVERNMENT

In 1938 Tristan da Cunha and the neighbouring islands of Inaccessible, Nightingale and Gough were made dependencies of St Helena and this remains their status today. They are administered by the Foreign and Commonwealth Office through a resident Administrator, with headquarters at the settlement of Edinburgh. Under a new Constitution introduced in 1969, the Administrator is advised by an Island Council of eight elected members, of whom one must be a woman, and three appointed members. There is universal suffrage at 18.

Administrator, Philip Johnson.

ECONOMY

The main industries on the island are crayfish fishing, fish-processing and agriculture, with the shore-based fishing industry having been developed with the construction of the boat harbour in 1967 and the re-establishment of the crayfish-freezing factory in 1966. There are no taxes on Tristan, with income being derived from the fishing company, and the sales of stamps and handicrafts. Apart from the fishing industry, the other main employer is the Administration itself. There is one hospital, opened in 1971, and a school opened in 1975 catering for those up to age 15.

COMMUNICATIONS

The island is isolated and scheduled visits are restricted to about six calls a year by fishing vessels from Cape Town and an annual call of the RMS *St Helena* from the UK. A wireless station on the island is in daily contact with Cape Town and a radio-telephone service was established in 1969, the same year that electricity was introduced to all the islanders' homes. A satellite system providing direct dialling telephone and fax facilities was installed in November 1992.

SOUTH GEORGIA AND THE SOUTH SANDWICH ISLANDS

South Georgia is an island 800 miles east-south-east of the Falkland group, with an area of 1,450 sq. miles. The population comprises an army unit and a civilian harbour master at King Edward Point, and staff of the British Antarctic Survey at Bird Island, in the north-west of South Georgia.

The South Sandwich Islands lie some 470 miles south-east of South Georgia. The group is a chain of uninhabited, actively volcanic islands about 150 miles long, with a wholly Antarctic climate.

The present constitution came into effect on 3 October 1985. It provides for a Commissioner who, for the time being, shall be the officer administering the Government of the Falkland Islands.

In May 1993 the UK government decreed an extension of Crown sovereignty and jurisdiction from 12 miles around South Georgia and the South Sandwich Islands to 200 miles around each in order to preserve marine stocks.

Commissioner for South Georgia and the South Sandwich Islands, David Everard Tatham, CMG, *apptd* 1992.

TURKS AND CAICOS ISLANDS

AREA – The Turks and Caicos Islands are situated between 21° and 22° N. latitude and 71° and 72° W. longitude, about 100 miles north of the Dominican Republic and 50 miles south-east of the Bahamas of which they are geographically an extension. There are over 30 islands, of which eight are inhabited, covering an estimated area of 166 sq. miles (430 sq. km). The principal island is Grand Turk.
CLIMATE – The Islands lie in the trade wind belt. The average temperature varies from 24°–27° C in the winter to 29°–32° C in the summer and humidity is generally low. Average rainfall is 21 inches per annum.
POPULATION – The population in 1990 was estimated to be 12,400 (Grand Turk 3,700).
FLAG – British Blue Ensign with the shield of arms in the fly.

GOVERNMENT

A new Constitution was introduced in 1988, and amended in 1993, which provides for an Executive Council and a Legislative Council. The Executive Council is presided over by the Governor and comprises the Chief Minister and five elected Ministers, together with the ex-officio Chief Secretary and Attorney-General.

At the General Election of 3 April 1991, the People's National Party won 8 seats and the People's Democratic Movement 5 seats in the Legislative Council.

Governor, His Excellency Martin Bourke, *apptd* 1993.

EXECUTIVE COUNCIL as at 15 June 1993
President, The Governor.
Chief Secretary, Hon. R. Cousins.
Attorney-General, Hon. L. D. Ballantyre.
Chief Minister, Hon. W. Misick.
Other Ministers, Hon. A. Durham; Hon. A. Smith; Hon. R. Hall; Hon. M. Misick; Hon. Mrs E. Saunders.

ECONOMY

FINANCE	1991–2	1992–3*
Local revenue	US$26,874,684	US$25,839,825
Expenditure	26,019,039	28,563,752
*estimate		

The most important industries are fishing, tourism and offshore finance.

TRADE WITH UK	1991	1992
Imports from UK	£1,732,000	£722,000
Exports to UK	12,000	1,127,000

COMMUNICATIONS

The principal airports are on the islands of Grand Turk, Providenciales and South Caicos. There are direct shipping services to the USA (Miami). There is an air service between Miami, Providenciales and Grand Turk, between South Caicos and the Bahamas, and between Providenciales and Grand Turk and Haiti and the Dominican Republic. An internal air service provides a twice daily service between the principal islands. A comprehensive telephone and telex service is provided by Cable and Wireless (WI) Ltd.

Events of the Year

1 September 1992–31 August 1993

BRITISH AFFAIRS

SEPTEMBER 1992

3. The Chancellor of the Exchequer (Norman Lamont) said that the Government would borrow £7,200 million in foreign currencies from a group of international banks in order to buy sterling and maintain its position within the exchange rate mechanism (ERM). The Prime Minister (John Major) rejected a request from the Leader of the Opposition (John Smith) for Parliament to be recalled to debate the crises in Yugoslavia and Iraq and the state of the economy. Kevin Maxwell was declared bankrupt with debts of £406 million, the largest-ever bankruptcy in Britain. **6.** A small IRA bomb exploded in London. **10.** The Prime Minister said that devaluation of sterling would be a betrayal of Britain's future and repeated the Government's commitment to membership of the ERM. **13.** The Liberal Democrat annual conference opened in Harrogate. **16.** As sterling's position in the ERM worsened, bank base rates rose from 10 per cent to 12 per cent and then to 15 per cent. Sterling fell below the permitted lowest level against the Deutsche Mark (DM 2.7780) and was quoted at DM 2.7400 by close of trading in London. The Chancellor of the Exchequer announced at 7.45 p.m. that sterling's membership of the ERM had been suspended and that bank base rates had returned to 12 per cent. Sterling was permitted to float on the currency markets. The Prime Minister agreed to recall Parliament on 24 September to discuss the crisis. **17.** Bank base rates were lowered to 10 per cent and sterling closed at DM 2.6323. Firebombs exploded at the Imperial War Museum, Madame Tussaud's and the London Planetarium. **21.** Sterling fell to a record low of DM 2.5456 by close of trading in London. **22.** Bank base rates were cut to 9 per cent. **24.** Parliament was recalled for an emergency debate on the economic crisis. A government motion in support of its handling of the economy was passed by 322 votes to 296 in the House of Commons. More than 60 Conservative MPs signed an early day motion welcoming Britain's departure from the ERM. David Mellor resigned as Secretary of State for National Heritage after press revelations that a family holiday in September 1990 had been paid for by the daughter of the PLO's head of finance (*see also* Crimes and Legal Affairs below). **25.** An emergency debate on foreign policy was held in the House of Commons, after which Parliament went back into recess. **28.** The Labour Party annual conference opened in Blackpool. **30.** A letter from the president of the German Bundesbank to the Treasury, denying that the Bundesbank's actions had contributed to the sterling crisis, was leaked to the press by the German Embassy in London. Sterling closed at DM 2.5046.

OCTOBER 1992

2. Sterling fell to DM 2.4450. **6.** The Conservative Party annual conference opened in Brighton. **7.** Two small IRA bombs exploded in London. **8–10.** Small IRA bombs exploded in London on each day. **12.** A man was killed and several people injured when an IRA bomb exploded in a pub in Covent Garden, London. **13.** The President of the Board of Trade (Michael Heseltine) and the chairman of British Coal (Neil Clarke) announced the closure of 31 pits by the end of March 1993, six of them to close on 16 October, and the loss of 30,000 jobs. A storm of protest greeted the announcement. **15.** Downing Street said that the decision to close 31 pits was taken by a small group of ministers and not the full Cabinet. An emergency application by the National Union of Mineworkers and NACODS, the pit deputies' union, for a temporary injunction to stop the closures was made to the High Court in London; on 20 October the hearing was adjourned (*see* 21 December). **16.** In the High Court the UDM won the right to seek a judicial review of the decision to close eight pits. An EC summit meeting was held in Birmingham. Bank base rates were cut to 8 per cent. **19.** After an emergency Cabinet meeting the President of the Board of Trade announced that only ten pits would close, after a 90-day consultation period, and that a moratorium until the new year would be introduced for the other 21 pits, after which the closures, if confirmed, would be phased in. The Queen and the Duke of Edinburgh arrived in Germany for a five-day State visit. Two small IRA bombs exploded in London. **20.** The Prime Minister said that there would be a 'full and open review' of pit closures and of the market for coal. In the House of Lords peers voted in favour of an opposition motion calling for an independent inquiry into the future of the coal industry. **21.** After a debate in the House of Commons, during which the President of the Board of Trade said that there would be a complete review of the Government's energy policy, an opposition motion calling for all 31 pits to remain open pending a review of the future of the coal industry was defeated. About 50,000 miners and their supporters marched in London in protest at the pit closures. Three small IRA bombs exploded in London. **22.** The report of the official inquiry headed by Lord Justice Bingham into the collapse of the Bank of Credit and Commerce International (BCCI) was published; it was highly critical of the supervision of the Bank of England. **23.** A report commissioned by the Government recommended the closure of 15 hospitals in London. **25.** About 150,000 people marched through London to protest at the planned pit closures. A small IRA bomb exploded in London. **27.** The London Ambulance Service's new computer-aided dispatch system was shut down after repeated problems on 26–27 October. The report of the inquiry into the conduct of the Orkney child ritual sex abuse allegations in February 1991 was published; it was highly critical of the social workers and police involved. **28.** About 70 lb of Semtex explosive was found by police at a house in Leytonstone, London. **30.** An IRA car bomb exploded in Whitehall, London, after a minicab driver was forced at gunpoint to drive it there.

NOVEMBER 1992

2. The Prince and Princess of Wales arrived in South Korea for a five-day official visit; current speculation continued about the state of their marriage. **3.** The Sultan of Brunei arrived in Britain for a four-day State visit. The Isle of Man parliament voted to abolish capital punishment. **4.** The Government won a vote allowing the bill ratifying the Maastricht Treaty to proceed. **5.** The Prime Minister said that the Maastricht Treaty bill would not have its final reading in the Commons until after the Danish referendum in May 1993. **9.** President Yeltsin of Russia arrived in Britain for a two-day State visit. **11.** The General Synod of the Church of England voted by 384 votes to 169, with the required majority of 66 per cent in each of the three Houses, to permit the ordination of women as priests. **12.** The Chancellor of the Exchequer presented his autumn financial statement (*see* page 1164). The Ministry of Defence announced that Portland Naval Base in Dorset would close by 1996. **13.** Bank base rates were cut to 7 per cent. **14.** A policeman was shot and wounded after stopping a lorry containing 2,000 lb of IRA explosives in north London. **18.** The Department for Education published 1992 GCSE and A-level results for 4,600 state schools and 260 independent schools; the 'league tables' were attacked for being inaccurate and misleading. **23.** The Secretary of State for National Heritage (Peter Brooke) said that the costs of rebuilding the state apartments at Windsor Castle (*see* Accidents and Disasters) would be met wholly from government funds; the announcement caused widespread protests. **24.** In a speech at the Guildhall in the City of London, The Queen said that 1992 had been an 'annus horribilis'. **26.** The Prime Minister announced that The Queen had offered to pay tax on private income from April 1993 and to refund Civil List payments for most members of the royal family (*see* page 130). The *Sun* published details of an unpaid credit card bill on the account of the Chancellor of the Exchequer; on 30 November two staff of the Threshers off-licence chain were suspended after

they admitted falsely alleging that Mr Lamont had purchased champagne and cigarettes from their branch on 16 November. **28.** The Treasury confirmed that £4,700 of the legal costs incurred by the Chancellor of the Exchequer in evicting a tenant from his London home in 1991 were met from public funds.

DECEMBER 1992

1. The west end of London was evacuated after an IRA warning; police found a van loaded with explosives near Tottenham Court Road. **2.** The Government announced that the Cammell Laird shipyard, Birkenhead, would close in 1993. **3.** Two IRA bombs exploded in central Manchester, injuring 64 people. **8.** The Shree Khrishna Hindu temple in West Bromwich was destroyed by an arson attack in the wake of communal violence in India, Pakistan and Bangladesh. **9.** The Prime Minister announced in the House of Commons that the Prince and Princess of Wales had decided to separate. An IRA bomb exploded in London. The Duchess of York and John Bryan were awarded £90,500 damages and costs by a French court over the publication of intimate photos by *Paris Match* magazine in August 1992. **10.** Ten people were injured when two IRA bombs exploded at Wood Green shopping centre, London. **11–12.** A two-day EC summit meeting on the Maastricht Treaty was held in Edinburgh (*see* pages 1097–8). **12.** The Princess Royal married Commander Timothy Laurence at Crathie Church, Balmoral. **16.** Two IRA bombs exploded in London. The European Court of Justice ruled that restrictions on Sunday trading are legal under EC law. **21.** The High Court ruled that the Government's pit closure programme was unlawful and that miners and their unions had a right to be fully consulted. The President of the Board of Trade said that coal production would not resume at the ten pits which had already closed. **22.** An IRA bomb exploded in London. **23.** The *Sun* published a transcript of The Queen's Christmas broadcast.

JANUARY 1993

2. Sean Devereux, a British aid worker, was shot dead in Somalia. **3.** Princess Margaret was admitted to hospital suffering from pneumonia. **6.** The Foreign Secretary (Douglas Hurd) arrived in Argentina for a four-day visit, the first by a Cabinet minister since the 1982 conflict. Four IRA incendiary bombs exploded in shops in central London. **11.** British Airways issued an unconditional apology to Virgin airlines and its owner Richard Branson, and agreed to pay £610,000 damages and up to £3 million costs in settlement of a libel action in which Virgin had alleged that BA was conducting a 'dirty tricks' campaign against it. Blizzards caused disruption in Scotland and northern England. **12.** The chairman of the Press Complaints Commission (Lord McGregor of Durris) said that he had evidence that the Princess of Wales had provided information about the state of her marriage to selected tabloid newspapers. An

Australian magazine, *New Idea*, published a transcript of an intimate telephone conversation allegedly between the Prince of Wales and his friend Camilla Parker Bowles in 1989; the transcript was later published by sections of the British press. More than 2,000 people had to be rescued from their vehicles in blizzards in eastern Scotland. **13.** A soldier serving with the Cheshire Regiment in Bosnia, L/Cpl Wayne Edwards, was killed by a sniper while escorting a civilian ambulance. Gale force winds caused disruption and at least two deaths in southern England. **15.** Five people were killed in accidents when gales hit northern England and Scotland. **17.** Flooding and gales caused disruption in Scotland. **22.** An official report criticized corruption and malpractice at Lambeth Council, London. **26.** Bank base rates were cut to 6 per cent. **28.** The Prime Minister issued writs for libel against two magazines, *New Statesman and Society* and *Scallywag*, over articles mentioning rumours that he was having an affair with Clare Latimer, a caterer; Ms Latimer also issued writs. A small IRA bomb exploded outside Harrods, London.

FEBRUARY 1993

1. Sterling fell to DM 2.3757; on 2 February it fell to DM 2.3746 and on 3 February to DM 2.3595. On 4 February sterling recovered after German interest rates were cut by 0.5 per cent. **2.** Solicitors acting for The Queen began legal proceedings against the *Sun* over its publication of the text of her 1992 Christmas broadcast two days before transmission. On 11 February a writ was served on the newspaper, and on 14 February the *Sun* apologized to The Queen and offered to make a donation to charity; this was accepted. **3.** The Defence Secretary announced that the strength of the Army would be reduced to 119,000, rather than the planned 116,000, and that four regiments would not be amalgamated. DAF, the Anglo-Dutch lorry manufacturer with 5,500 employees at its British branch Leyland DAF, went into receivership. In a speech at the Carlton Club, the Prime Minister suggested that the unemployed should be required to work for their benefits, sparking a controversy about the possible introduction of 'workfare' schemes in Britain. Two small IRA bombs exploded in London. Chris Patten, the governor of Hong Kong, underwent heart surgery. **5.** Sir Ranulph Fiennes and Dr Michael Stroud set a world record for the longest unsupported polar journey after they walked 1,257 miles across Antarctica; on 7 February they became the first people to cross the Antarctic land mass on foot. **9.** Sterling fell to DM 2.3490. The Secretary of State for Defence announced that the naval dockyards at Devonport and Rosyth would be kept open. **10.** A small IRA bomb exploded in London. **12.** The Prime Minister and Clare Latimer reached out-of-court settlements in their libel actions against the newsagent John Menzies and the printers and distributors of *New Statesman and Society*. The Prince of Wales left London for a seven-day official visit to the USA and Mexico. **16.** The Government

published a report, *Making London Better*, in response to the Tomlinson report on health services in London; it approved the closure of five hospitals and proposed merging or closing other hospitals over the next six years. **21.** Hundreds of people were evacuated from their homes when high tides and gales caused widespread flooding along the east coast of England. **24.** The Duke of Westminster resigned from the Conservative Party in protest at the Government's proposed leasehold reform legislation. **26.** PC Mark Toker was shot and wounded by an IRA gunman in Warrington, Cheshire. Three bombs subsequently caused a huge explosion at a gasworks in the town and a motorist was kidnapped at gunpoint. Two men were arrested and the motorist was freed; one terrorist escaped but was later arrested. **27.** At least 15 people were injured when an IRA bomb exploded in Camden High Street, north London.

MARCH 1993

2. The Princess of Wales and the Minister for Overseas Development (Baroness Chalker) arrived in Nepal for a five-day official visit. **4.** The Prime Minister announced changes to the honours system, including a new system of public nominations for awards. **8.** The Bishop of Gloucester, the Rt. Revd Peter Ball, resigned after being cautioned by police for committing an act of gross indecency on a novice monk. **9.** The NAS/UWT teaching union voted to boycott statutory testing and assessment procedures in all subjects in summer 1993. EC commissioners ruled that the £44.4 million 'sweetener' paid by the Government to British Aerospace during the BAe takeover of the Rover Group should be repaid with interest; on 26 May BAe agreed to repay £57.6 million less tax relief, a total of 42.2 million. **11.** The chief executive of the Stock Exchange, Peter Rawlins, resigned after work on the Taurus computerized share transfer system was stopped because of its complexity and expense. **16.** The Chancellor of the Exchequer presented the last spring budget (*see* pages 1166–7). The Prince of Wales visited British troops in Bosnia. **20.** Three-year-old Johnathan Ball was killed and 56 people were injured when two IRA bombs exploded in the centre of Warrington. Twelve-year-old Timothy Parry, who was injured in the blast, died on 25 March. **26.** More than 200 fishing boats blockaded Plymouth harbour in protest at the Sea Fish (Conservation) Act, which will limit the number of days trawlers can spend at sea. **28.** A French trawler, *La Calypso*, abducted three members of a Royal Navy boarding party, part of a prolonged dispute over Britain's six-mile fishing limit around the Channel Islands; the men were later returned to their ship. On 2 April the trawler was placed under arrest.

APRIL 1993

2. A 24-hour strike was held by the Rail, Maritime and Transport union, the National Union of Mineworkers and bus crews in London, in protest at compulsory redundancies, pit closures and pay cuts. **7.** A memorial service for Johnathan Ball and Timothy Parry was held in Warrington and attended by Prince Philip, the President of Ireland, the Prime Minister and the Leader of the Opposition. A small IRA bomb exploded in London. **14.** The governing body of the Anglican Church in Wales voted in favour of a bill permitting the ordination of women as priests; the final vote will be held in 1994. **23.** A small IRA bomb exploded at an oil depot in North Shields, Tyne and Wear. **24.** A newspaper photographer was killed and 37 people injured when an IRA bomb exploded in the City of London, causing extensive damage. Two minicabs were later hijacked by suspected IRA terrorists in separate incidents in London. The drivers were ordered to take bombs to Downing Street and New Scotland Yard but alerted police before reaching their destinations; both bombs exploded in north London, causing minor damage. Leyland DAF's van plant was bought from the receivers by its management; on 11 June the lorry plant was also bought by its management. **26.** Statistics were published showing that GDP rose by 0.2 per cent in the first quarter of 1993, ending 30 months of declining or flat production. **28.** George Walker, the former chairman of the Brent Walker leisure group, was declared bankrupt with debts of £180 million. **29.** A man died after setting fire to himself in Parliament Square, Westminster, in protest at western policy in former Yugoslavia.

MAY 1993

4. The Queen and the Duke of Edinburgh arrived in Hungary for a four-day State visit. The inquiry headed by Lord Justice Scott into the Government's implementation of sanctions on the export of military equipment to Iraq opened in London. **6.** In the Newbury by-election the Liberal Democrats took the seat from the Conservatives with a swing of 28 per cent. In the county council elections in England and Wales, the Conservatives lost control of 15 councils; Labour took control of one council, and the Liberal Democrats took control of two councils. **10.** A British sailor, Tom McNally, completed a crossing of the Atlantic in his 5 ft 4½ in boat *Vera Hugh*, the smallest vessel ever to complete the journey. **11.** The Education Secretary (John Patten) announced that national curriculum testing would be radically reduced from 1994, but that the 1993 tests would still take place. **12.** A small IRA bomb was found in Oxford city centre. **13.** Swan Hunter, the Tyneside shipbuilders, went into receivership two days after the Government awarded a £170 million order to Vickers. The National Union of Teachers voted not to implement national curriculum testing. **17.** Rebecca Stephens became the first British woman to climb Mount Everest. The Prince of Wales arrived in Poland for a four-day official visit. **21.** Queen Elizabeth the Queen Mother underwent an operation to remove a piece of food from her throat. **24.** In evidence to the Scott inquiry the former Conservative

MP Sir Hal Miller said that the former Attorney-General, Sir Patrick Mayhew, had tried to prevent evidence that officials had known about the export of military equipment to Iraq reaching court. Sir Patrick denied the claim, and repeated his denial in evidence to the inquiry on 27 May. **27.** In a Cabinet reshuffle, Norman Lamont resigned as Chancellor of the Exchequer and was replaced by Kenneth Clarke. Michael Howard was appointed Home Secretary. The Queen received the President of Ireland (Mary Robinson) at Buckingham Palace, the first meeting between a British sovereign and an Irish head of state since 1937. **28.** The Queen and the Duke of Edinburgh attended events in Liverpool commemorating the 50th anniversary of the Battle of the Atlantic; on 30 May the Prince and Princess of Wales attended a commemoration service at Liverpool Anglican Cathedral.

JUNE 1993

4. The Holbeck Hall Hotel, Scarborough, began to slip over the cliff as half a mile of coastline crumbled into the sea. **9.** In a speech in the House of Commons Norman Lamont, the former Chancellor, strongly criticized the Prime Minister, accusing him of giving 'the impression of being in office but not in power'. A small IRA bomb exploded at a British Gas depot in Gateshead, Tyne and Wear; two small IRA bombs later exploded at a disused Esso oil depot in North Shields. **10–11.** Torrential rain caused flooding in many parts of Britain, particularly north Wales and Cornwall. **11.** The Queen visited Northern Ireland. **15.** After a bitter five-month industrial dispute, Timex announced that it would close down its factory in Dundee by the end of 1993. **21.** Michael Heseltine, the President of the Board of Trade, suffered a mild heart attack in Venice. **22.** Lloyd's of London announced record losses of £2.91 billion for 1990. **24.** Michael Mates resigned as minister of state at the Northern Ireland Office over his links with the fugitive businessman Asil Nadir. The Government awarded the £5 billion contract for refitting Trident nuclear submarines to the Devonport dockyard. **28.** Buckingham Palace announced that the Duke and Duchess of York had agreed the terms of their legal separation. **29.** In a speech in the House of Commons, Michael Mates accused the Serious Fraud Office of mishandling the investigation into Asil Nadir's finances and putting improper pressure on the trial judge; he continued with his speech in spite of repeated warnings from the Speaker (Betty Boothroyd) that it could prejudice any future trial.

JULY 1993

5. A British aid worker, Christine Witcutt, was shot dead in Bosnia. **6.** Fifteen women scaled the walls of Buckingham Palace in a protest about nuclear testing; they were arrested in the grounds. The *New Statesman and Society* said that the Prime Minister and Clare Latimer had accepted £1,001 damages each over the allegedly libellous articles published in January 1993.

Mr Major and Miss Latimer later dropped their libel actions against *Scallywag*, which said it would not repeat the allegations. The Queen opened the Queen Elizabeth Gate in honour of the Queen Mother at Hyde Park Corner, London. **14.** A suspected IRA member was arrested at a bus stop in north London in possession of the components of a large bomb. It was announced that inflation had fallen to 1.2 per cent in June 1993, the lowest level for 30 years. **15.** A former civil servant told the Scott inquiry that Foreign Office ministers had relaxed the guidelines on exports to Iraq in 1989 and subsequently misled Parliament and the public. **19.** Lord Rees-Mogg secured permission in the High Court for a judicial review of the legitimacy of the ratification process in Britain of the Maastricht Treaty. The Government said that it would not ratify the treaty until the court proceedings were completed; the hearing started on 26 July. **20.** The European Communities (Amendment) Bill received royal assent. In London about 20,000 policemen held a protest rally against the proposals in the Sheehy report on police employment conditions. Nuclear Electric announced the closure of the Magnox plant at Trawsfynydd. **22.** A debate on the social chapter to the Maastricht Treaty was held in the House of Commons. The government's main motion was defeated by 324 votes to 316; the Prime Minister announced that he would table a motion of confidence in the Government's policy on the social chapter the following day. **23.** The Government won the vote of confidence. **25.** The *Observer* newspaper reported a leaked recording of the Prime Minister speaking in derogatory terms about three Cabinet colleagues in an off-camera conversation with a journalist. **29.** In the Christchurch by-election the Liberal Democrats took the seat from the Conservatives with a swing of 35 per cent. **30.** The action brought by Lord Rees-Mogg challenging the legality of the ratification of the Maastricht Treaty failed in the High Court.

AUGUST 1993

2. The United Kingdom ratified the Maastricht Treaty. The Government announced that the national curriculum would be streamlined, that testing would be simplified, and that 'league tables' would not be produced on pupils' performance at the ages of 7 and 14. **6.** Buckingham Palace was opened to the public for the first time, for an eight-week season. **9.** An injured five-year-old Bosnian girl, Irma Hadzimuratovic, was flown from Sarajevo to London and underwent an operation at Great Ormond Street Hospital. 'Operation Irma' was then set up to airlift the seriously injured from Sarajevo, but a row developed between British and UN officials over whether children should be given priority. A further 21 evacuees arrived in Britain on 15 August. A small IRA bomb exploded on Bournemouth pier and six incendiary devices exploded in the town. **18.** An application by the Islamia primary school, London, to become Britain's first voluntary-aided Muslim school was rejected. **26.** The South Birmingham

Health Authority said that an inquiry had revealed errors of diagnosis involving at least 24 cancer patients and that the cases of more than 2,000 patients would be reviewed.

ACCIDENTS AND DISASTERS

SEPTEMBER 1992

2. Tidal waves caused by an undersea earthquake off the coast of Nicaragua killed over 118 and left 13,000 homeless. **10.** Torrential rain caused flooding in northern Pakistan. By 16 September the death toll was over 2,000, and two million were homeless. **11.** Hurricane Iniki hit Hawaii. **22.** Over 70 people were killed when violent storms and heavy rain caused flooding in south-east France. **28.** A Pakistan airbus crashed in Nepal, killing all 167 passengers and crew.

OCTOBER 1992

1. Five people were killed and 15 injured when the US aircraft carrier *Saratoga* fired two missiles by mistake at a Turkish destroyer in the Aegean Sea. **4.** About 70 people were killed when an El Al cargo plane crashed into a block of flats in a suburb of Amsterdam and burst into flames. **12.** An earthquake registering between 5.5 and 5.9 on the Richter scale hit Cairo, leaving over 540 dead.

NOVEMBER 1992

20. The state apartments at Windsor Castle were severely damaged by fire. **24.** All 141 passengers and crew were killed when a Boeing 737 crashed near Guilin, China. **25.** Twenty people were injured when two trains collided outside London Bridge station in the morning rush hour. **26.** Four soldiers were killed when two military helicopters crashed in mid air over Bessbrook Mill military base in Co. Armagh. **27.** The Hofburg palace in Vienna was severely damaged by fire. **30.** Five people were killed when a train was derailed outside Amsterdam.

DECEMBER 1992

2. A coal tip collapsed, covering the grounds of Tredegar Comprehensive School, south Wales, six miles from Aberfan. **12.** An earthquake registering 6.8 on the Richter scale hit eastern Indonesia, killing over 1,500. **21.** Fifty-four people were killed when a Dutch DC10 split in two and burst into flames while landing in a thunderstorm at Faro, Portugal. **22.** All 159 people aboard a Libyan Boeing 727 were killed in a mid-air collision with a military aircraft near Tripoli.

JANUARY 1993

9. All 165 passengers and crew survived when an Indian Airlines plane crashed, turned over, broke into sections and burst into flames at Delhi airport. **14.** Fifty-four people drowned when a Polish ferry capsized off the north German coast. **15.** Nine people, including a British scientist, were killed when the Galeras volcano in Colombia erupted as they were walking along its inner rim. An earthquake registering 7.5 on the Richter scale hit northern Japan, killing two people and injuring 360.

FEBRUARY 1993

3. Ash emissions and lava flows from Mount Mayon, the Philippines, killed at least 48 people. **8.** A plane collided with a military jet after take-off at Tehran airport, Iran, killing all 132 on board.

MARCH 1993

13-14. Tornadoes, blizzards and hurricane-force winds hit the east coast of the USA, killing over 67 people. **22.** Four teenagers from a school in Plymouth drowned when their canoes capsized off the Dorset coast.

APRIL 1993

9-12. At least 21 people were killed in road accidents over the Easter holiday period. **28.** Thirty people, including most of the Zambian national football squad, were killed when their plane crashed after take-off at Libreville, Gabon, en route to a world cup qualifying match in Senegal.

MAY 1993

10. At least 210 people were killed when fire destroyed a toy factory in Bangkok. About 200 people were feared dead in a landslide at Las Brisas de Nambija, Ecuador. **19.** All 132 people on a Boeing 727 died when the plane crashed in central Colombia. **27.** Nine aircrew were killed when an RAF Hercules crashed in the Scottish Highlands.

JUNE 1993

3. Nine people were killed when the BP tanker *British Trent* collided with a cargo ship and caught fire off the coast of Belgium. **25.** Eighteen people were killed and 32 injured when fire broke out at a psychiatric clinic near Rennes, Brittany.

JULY 1993

1-31. At least 1,750 people were killed and 250,000 left homeless when monsoon rains caused floods and landslides in Nepal. The rains also caused flash flooding in six states in India, where at least 700 people were killed, hundreds were missing and two million were left homeless; in Bangladesh more than 300 people were killed and millions left homeless. **4-31.** After a month of flooding, heavy rain caused the Mississippi and Missouri rivers to burst their banks in the mid-west of the USA. At least 50 people were killed and 70,000 left homeless, millions of acres of land were flooded and an estimated $12 billion worth of damage caused. The flooding began to subside on 10 August. **12.** Over 80 people were killed after an earthquake registering 7.8 on the Richter scale hit northern Japan.

AUGUST 1993

5. Two explosions caused by a leak of nitric acid killed over 70 people and injured hundreds in Shenzhen, China. **12.** Three air cadets were killed when an RAF Wessex helicopter crashed into a lake in Snowdonia. **18.** Three miners were killed and three others were rescued in a roof collapse at Bilsthorpe colliery, Notts. The 13th-century Kapellbruecke at Lucerne, Switzerland, was destroyed by fire. **27.** At least 263 people were killed and 180 were missing after water breached the Gouhou reservoir dam in Qinghai province, China.

ARTS, SCIENCE AND MEDIA

SEPTEMBER 1992

7. The new national radio station Classic FM went on the air. **28.** A new institute of architecture set up by the Prince of Wales opened in Regent's Park, London. **29.** The two-day sale of the contents of Pitchford Hall, Shropshire, raised £1.3 million. On 6 October the house was sold to an overseas buyer for over £750,000.

OCTOBER 1992

1. An Arts Council report criticized the management of the Royal Opera House. **12.** Rifat Ozbek was named Designer of the Year at the British Fashion Awards. **26.** The chairman of English Heritage, Jocelyn Stevens, announced a new management strategy, including plans for the privatization of about 200 ancient monuments and buildings.

NOVEMBER 1992

19. The Government announced that Britain would not contribute to research into fast breeder nuclear reactors after March 1993. **24.** The Government published a Green Paper on the future of the BBC (*see* page 679). The Turner Prize for contemporary art was awarded to the sculptor Grenville Davey. **26.** The BBC launched a policy review document, *Extending Choice* (*see* page 679).

DECEMBER 1992

3. The BBC announced a £58 million overspend since 1991. **11.** The Secretary of State for National Heritage (Peter Brooke) announced that from 1994 responsibility for funding 42 arts organizations, including the Bristol Old Vic and the Manchester Royal Exchange, would pass from the Arts Council to the regional arts boards. **15.** The Tate Gallery announced that it would split its collections, British art remaining at its present site and a new Tate Gallery of Modern Art being created elsewhere in London. **18.** The Independent Television Commission refused to award the fifth national television licence to the sole bidder, a consortium led by Thames Television, on the grounds that it did not have sufficient 'investor commitment'.

JANUARY 1993

1. John Birt took over as director-general of the BBC. **11.** John Birt announced a reorganization of the BBC's management, several new appointments (*see* page 1086) and a programme strategy review. **14.** The Calcutt report on press regulation was published (*see* page 686). A £200,000 donation from the Clore Foundation saved the Dulwich Picture Gallery from closure.

FEBRUARY 1993

22. A painting by Turner was sold by Royal Holloway College to the J. Paul Getty Museum in Los Angeles for £11 million. **28.** The *Independent on Sunday* revealed that John Birt was employed by the BBC on a freelance basis; on 1 March Mr Birt joined the staff of the BBC.

MARCH 1993

5. Two portraits by Gainsborough and Reynolds stolen from Lincoln's Inn, London, in 1990, were recovered when they were taken to Sotheby's for valuation. **24.** The actress Kim Basinger was ordered by a court in Los Angeles to pay Main Line Pictures $8.9 million after pulling out of the lead role in the film *Boxing Helena* a month before filming was due to start. **29.** A consortium of independent television companies headed by Carlton Communications took control of ITN.

APRIL 1993

2. A report by the Medical Research Council said that the drug AZT did not delay the onset of Aids in people infected with the HIV virus. **29.** The editor of the *Observer* newspaper announced that the paper would be sold to the Guardian and Manchester Evening News group for an undisclosed sum. **30.** The first national commercial pop radio station, Virgin 1215, went on the air.

MAY 1993

11. The Prime Minister met Salman Rushdie at the House of Commons. **27.** A car bomb exploded outside the Uffizi Gallery in Florence, damaging the building and many works of art.

JUNE 1993

8. Lord Rix resigned from the Arts Council in protest at its level of funding, its relationship with the Government and its manner of operation. **19.** Inger Dam-Jensen won the Cardiff Singer of the World competition. **23.** The Prince of Wales opened the new Tate Gallery at St Ives, Cornwall.

JULY 1993

2. At least 40 people were killed when Muslim fundamentalists set fire to a hotel in central Turkey where a translator of *The Satanic Verses* was staying. **8.** The Arts Council said that it would fund only two of London's four orchestras from April 1994 and that its drama budget would be cut in favour of the visual

arts, contemporary dance and education. **9.** Scientists said that they were 98.5 per cent certain that bones found in a grave in Yekaterinburg in July 1991 were those of Tsar Nicholas II and four members of his family. **13.** Mark Tully, the BBC's India correspondent, made a speech in which he strongly criticized the corporation's director-general, John Birt, and the changes instituted by him; Mr Birt defended his reforms in a speech the following day. **15.** Scientists in Maryland, USA, said that they had discovered evidence of a genetic component to homosexuality. **21.** The National Heritage Secretary said that the Arts Council would in future be accountable to Parliament for its decisions, that its administrative costs had to be cut by 10 per cent, and that its membership would be cut from 20 to 16. The closure of Elstree Studios was announced. **22.** Thieves broke into the British Museum and stole priceless Roman jewels and coins; many of the items were recovered on 27 July after a man was arrested while attempting another break-in. **27.** Two car bombs in Rome caused damage to the Basilica of St John Lateran and the Church of San Giorgio al Velabro.

AUGUST 1993

8. The Radio 1 disc jockey Dave Lee Travis announced on the air his resignation from the BBC in protest at recent changes.

CRIMES AND LEGAL AFFAIRS

SEPTEMBER 1992

19. Dr Nigel Cox was convicted at Winchester Crown Court of the attempted murder in August 1991 of Mrs Lillian Boyes, to whom, at her request, he administered a fatal injection in order to relieve her suffering. On 21 September he was given a 12-month prison sentence suspended for one year. On 17 November the General Medical Council decided not to take any disciplinary action against him. **22.** The jury were unable to reach a verdict in a libel action brought against Mirror Group Newspapers by Mona Bauwens, the daughter of the Palestine Liberation Organization's head of finance, who had paid for a holiday for the Secretary of State for National Heritage (David Mellor) and his family. **25.** Kiranjit Ahluwalia, who was convicted in 1989 of murdering her violent husband, was convicted of manslaughter on the grounds of diminished responsibility at her retrial at the Central Criminal Court, and sentenced to three years and four months' imprisonment; she had already served this time and was released from prison immediately. **30.** Paintings and antiques worth over £10 million were stolen from Houghton Hall, Norfolk.

OCTOBER 1992

1. The Home Secretary (Kenneth Clarke) announced that he would not recommend a posthumous pardon for Derek Bentley, who was hanged in 1953 for his part in the murder of a policeman. **8.** Seven-year-old Nikki Allen, who had gone missing on 7 October, was found battered to death near her home in Sunderland. On 19 October a man was charged with her murder. **12.** Frank Crichlow was awarded more than £50,000 damages in the High Court after suing the Metropolitan Police Commissioner for false imprisonment, battery and malicious prosecution in relation to his arrest on drugs charges in 1988. After an emergency High Court ruling, surgeons at a London hospital performed a Caesarean operation on a woman against her will in an attempt to save the life of her baby. **14.** Andrei Chikatilo was convicted in Rostov-on-Don, Russia, of murdering 52 people between 1978 and 1990. On 15 October he was sentenced to death. **15.** The libel damages of £150,000 awarded to Teresa Gorman, MP, in July 1991 (see Whitaker's Almanack 1992) were reduced in the Court of Appeal to £50,000. **20.** The bodies of Petra Kelly, founder of the German Green Party, and her partner Gert Bastian were found at their home in Bonn. **23.** Jean-Pierre Allain, professor of transfusion medicine at Cambridge University and honorary director of the East Anglian Regional Blood Transfusion Service, was sentenced at a court in Paris to four years' imprisonment, two of them suspended, for allowing blood contaminated with the HIV virus to be given to hundreds of haemophiliacs in France in 1985. **26.** Detective Constable Bob Window's left hand was severed with a samurai sword in an attack in north London; the hand was later sewn back on, and a man was charged with attempted murder.

NOVEMBER 1992

9. At the Central Criminal Court, the trial of three businessmen accused of exporting military equipment to Iraq in breach of the UN embargo collapsed after the former trade minister Alan Clark said in evidence that he had given advice to assist the exports. On 10 November the Prime Minister announced an independent judicial inquiry into the affair. **12.** Associated Newspapers, the publishers of the *Mail on Sunday*, and two journalists were fined a total of £60,000 for contempt of court for publishing details of the deliberations of the jury in the Blue Arrow fraud trial. **19.** The President of the Family Division of the High Court (Sir Stephen Brown) ruled that doctors would be acting lawfully if they discontinued the artificial feeding of Anthony Bland, a victim of the Hillsborough football stadium disaster who had been in 'persistent vegetative state' since 1989. The Official Solicitor, acting for Mr Bland, lodged an appeal against the decision; the appeal was dismissed by three appeal court judges on 9 December and a second appeal was dismissed on 4 February 1993 in the House of Lords. Doctors stopped feeding Mr Bland on 22 February and he died on 3 March.

DECEMBER 1992

7. Nicholas Vernage was sentenced at the Central Criminal Court to five terms of life imprisonment for the murders of Lorna Bogle, Javaid Iqbal and Police Sergeant Alan King in November 1991. **10.** Stephen Miller, Tony Paris and Yusuf Abdullahi, who were sentenced to life imprisonment in November 1990 for the murder of Lynette White in Cardiff, were released by the Court of Appeal, which found the convictions to have been 'unsafe and unsatisfactory'. **14.** The Crown Prosecution Service said that bribery and corruption charges against the Conservative MP Harry Greenway had been dropped. **16.** Lorrain Osman was extradited to Hong Kong to face fraud charges after spending seven years in Brixton prison on remand. **18.** Sixteen-year-old Suzanne Capper, who was found wandering naked and with severe burns in Romiley, Stockport, on 14 December, died in hospital; she had been kidnapped, tortured, covered with petrol and set on fire. Six people were later charged with her murder. **26.** The body of 14-year-old Johanna Young, who had gone missing on 23 December, was found in a water-filled pit near Watton, Norfolk. **27.** A policewoman was stabbed in the heart with a screwdriver when tackling a suspected burglar in Wavertree, Liverpool; a man was later charged with attempted murder.

JANUARY 1993

2. A 14-year-old boy was shot dead in a take-away food shop in Moss Side, Manchester. **8.** George Walker, the former chairman and chief executive of Brent Walker, was charged with stealing £12.5 million from the company. **15.** Criminal proceedings against Ann Griffin and George Hadjioannou over the violent death of their baby daughter Kim in September 1992 were dropped because of insufficient evidence when they invoked their right to silence. **18.** Sixteen-year-old Claire Tiltman was stabbed to death in an alley in Greenhithe, Kent. **29.** A police constable was stabbed seven times after stopping a man for questioning in Deptford, London.

FEBRUARY 1993

3. In a debate in the House of Lords the Lord Chief Justice (Lord Taylor of Gosforth) attacked plans to reduce eligibility for legal aid. **5.** A judge at Newport Crown Court ordered a 15-year-old boy convicted of raping a female classmate to pay his victim £500 for a holiday rather than imposing a custodial sentence on him. On 11 March the Court of Appeal increased the sentence to two years' detention. **10.** James Canning, a member of the IRA, was sentenced at the Central Criminal Court to 30 years' imprisonment for conspiring to cause explosions in Britain. **12.** Two-year-old James Bulger was abducted from a shopping centre in Liverpool; his body was found on a railway embankment two days later. On 20 February two ten-year-old boys were charged with his murder. **13.** Darius Guppy and Benedict Marsh were convicted at Snaresbrook Crown Court of a £1.8 million jewellery insurance fraud. On 25 March they were sentenced to five years' imprisonment each and fined £539,000 and £535,000 respectively. **15.** Thomas Ward, an American lawyer, was cleared at the Central Criminal Court of stealing £5.2 million from Guinness during its takeover of Distillers in 1986. **18.** In the House of Lords, in a case brought by Derbyshire County Council over articles in the *Sunday Times* in 1989, five law lords ruled that democratically-elected bodies have no right to sue for libel.

MARCH 1993

12. Derek Hatton, the former deputy leader of Liverpool City Council, was cleared at Mold Crown Court of conspiring to defraud the council in land deals. The chief executive of National Car Parks, Gordon Layton, was cleared at the Central Criminal Court of conspiracy to defraud in financing an industrial espionage campaign against a rival company. **21.** Police Sergeant William Forth was stabbed to death near Gateshead, Tyne and Wear. On 23 March two people were charged with his murder. **25.** Jean Bradley, a businesswoman, was stabbed to death in a street in Acton, London. **29.** Paul Magee, an IRA terrorist on the run from a life sentence, was convicted at the Central Criminal Court of murdering Special Constable Glen Goodman in June 1992. On 30 March he was sentenced to 30 years' imprisonment. **31.** Benjamin Laing was sentenced at the Central Criminal Court to life imprisonment for the murder of Matthew Manwaring and his daughter Alison in April 1992. The Court of Appeal cut from £250,000 to £110,000 the libel damages awarded in 1991 to Esther Rantzen, the television presenter and chairman of Childline, after claims that she had protected an alleged paedophile.

APRIL 1993

2. Mr Justice Mantell ruled in the High Court that members of the NAS/UWT had no statutory duty to test children under the Education Reform Act 1988 and that they were involved in a legitimate trade dispute; the ruling was confirmed in the Court of Appeal on 23 April. **4.** Nessan Quinlivan, who escaped from Brixton prison in 1991 while awaiting trial on terrorist charges, was arrested in Co. Tipperary. On 9 April Pearse McAuley, who escaped at the same time, was arrested in Dublin. **18.** A man armed with a shotgun was shot dead by police during a siege in Cheshunt, Herts. **22.** Eighteen-year-old Stephen Lawrence was murdered by white youths in a racially-motivated attack in Eltham, London. **28.** Sixteen-month-old Constantine Georgopolous was kidnapped from his home in St John's Wood, London; he was found unharmed in a van in Kilburn on 29 April. **30.** A woman was shot dead in a street in Luton; her baby daughter was kidnapped and later shot dead. A man was charged with the murders.

MAY 1993

4. The bankrupt chairman of the Polly Peck group, Asil Nadir, who was on £3.5 million bail awaiting trial on charges of theft and false accounting involving more than £30 million, jumped bail and flew to northern Cyprus. **13.** The Home Secretary (Kenneth Clarke) announced that fundamental changes would be made to the provisions of the Criminal Justice Act 1991, including the scrapping of the unit fines system in magistrates' courts, and the restoration of the right of courts to take into account all a defendant's previous convictions when sentencing. A gunman took 20 children and a teacher hostage in a nursery school in Paris; he later released 14 of the children. On 15 May a police squad stormed the school, shot the gunman dead and released the remaining children and the teacher. **17.** A hospital nurse, Beverley Allitt, was convicted at Nottingham Crown Court of the murder of four babies in her care at Grantham and Kesteven Hospital in 1991, the attempted murder of three other babies, and causing grievous bodily harm to six others; on 28 May she was given 13 life sentences. **19.** Three former detectives were cleared at the Central Criminal Court of conspiring to pervert the course of justice by fabricating confession evidence against one of the Guildford Four in 1975. **29.** Frederic Blancke was sentenced at a court in Beauvais, France, to 15 years' imprisonment for the murder of Fiona Jones, a British schoolteacher, in August 1989.

JUNE 1993

4. Pte Lee Clegg of the Parachute Regiment was sentenced at a court in Belfast to life imprisonment for the murder of 18-year-old Karen Reilly, who was shot dead in a stolen car in west Belfast in September 1990. Pte Barry Aindow was sentenced to seven years' imprisonment for the attempted murder of the car's driver, 17-year-old Martin Peake, who was shot dead in the incident. **7.** The film director Woody Allen failed to win custody of his three children after a bitter court case against his former partner Mia Farrow. **10.** At Norwich Crown Court two men were sentenced to five years' imprisonment for kidnapping and threatening a youth they suspected of being involved in local thefts; on 28 June the sentences were cut to six months by the Court of Appeal. **11.** Michelle and Lisa Taylor, who were sentenced to life imprisonment in 1991 for the murder of Alison Shaughnessy, were released by the Court of Appeal after the convictions were found to be 'unsafe and unsatisfactory'. **15.** A man was found strangled at his home in south London; police warned that he was the fifth victim of a murderer targeting homosexual men in London. **21.** The conviction of 15-year-old Ivan Fergus, who served six months of a 15-month youth custody sentence for assault with intent to rob, was quashed by the Court of Appeal and found to be 'wholly false'. **30.** Michael Hunt, the former deputy chairman of Nissan UK, was sentenced to eight years' imprisonment for his part in a £55 million tax fraud between 1983 and 1991.

JULY 1993

6. The report of the Royal Commission on Criminal Justice was published. John Matthews, who was arrested in April 1993 and charged with causing an IRA bomb explosion in London, was released 'without a blemish on his character' after the prosecution could offer no evidence against him; he was later served with an exclusion order and expelled from mainland Britain. **7.** Three High Court judges ruled that the former Home Secretary (Kenneth Clarke) had 'erred in law' when he refused in October 1992 to grant a conditional posthumous pardon to Derek Bentley; on 30 July the Home Secretary (Michael Howard) granted Bentley a pardon limited to sentence. **8.** Michael Sams was given four life sentences at Nottingham Crown Court for the kidnap and murder of 18-year-old Julie Dart in 1991 and the kidnap and unlawful imprisonment of Stephanie Slater in January 1992. A gunman shot dead a German tourist and wounded members of his family near Stranraer. **13.** A teenager was acquitted at the Central Criminal Court on charges of murder and manslaughter after admitting that he stabbed to death a man who had caught him slashing tyres and chased him holding a hammer; the jury accepted his plea of self-defence. **19.** An Englishman, Vincent Wood, was sentenced at the Central Criminal Court to 22 years' imprisonment for possessing IRA explosives with intent to endanger life. Eight-year-old Sean Williams was found murdered in a lift in a block of flats in East Finchley, London. **20.** Karyn Smith and Patricia Cahill, two young British women who had been sentenced to 25 and 18 years imprisonment respectively in Thailand for drug smuggling in 1990, were granted a royal pardon. **22.** Robin Pask, who murdered a lecturer at an Open University summer school in July 1992, was ordered to be detained indefinitely in a secure unit after he was found unfit to stand trial because of a serious depressive illness. **25.** Nine-year-old Akhlaq Razzaq was found strangled in a park in Slough where he had gone to watch a game of cricket. **27.** A 1991 Appeal Court ruling that a former Home Secretary, Kenneth Baker, had been in contempt of court when he had illegally deported a Zairean asylum-seeker during legal proceedings was upheld by five law lords.

AUGUST 1993

1. Joy Gardner, a Jamaican woman who collapsed after a violent struggle with police serving her with a deportation order at her home in north London on 28 July, died in hospital; on 3 August the three detectives involved and Scotland Yard's central aliens and deportation unit were suspended. **17.** A man was charged with the murder of Rachel Nickell on Wimbledon Common in July 1992. **20.** Police in Los Angeles started an investigation into allegations by a 13-year-old boy that he had been sexually abused by the pop star Michael Jackson. Ronald Godfrey was charged in Oxford with battering his wife, daughter and mother-in-law to death with a hammer.

31. Twenty-one-year-old Sharon Pritchard was beaten to death in a playing field after seeing her babysitter home in Croeserw, West Glamorgan. A man was later charged with her murder.

ENVIRONMENT

SEPTEMBER 1992

22. An unconditional ban on dumping nuclear waste at sea was agreed by 12 European countries; Britain and France agreed only a 15-year moratorium.

OCTOBER 1992

4-7. The hole in the ozone layer over Antarctica extended over the coast of South America and the Falkland Islands for the first time.

NOVEMBER 1992

25. The Court of Justice of the EC ruled that Britain was in breach of EC standards on drinking water.

DECEMBER 1992

1. English Nature designated more than 25,000 acres of The Wash a national nature reserve. **3.** The Greek tanker *Aegean Sea* ran on to rocks off the coast of north-west Spain, causing a 60-mile oil slick. **14.** A firebomb attack at the research headquarters of the Forestry Commission in Hampshire destroyed 30 years' research on tree diseases. **16.** EC environment ministers advanced the deadline for phasing out the production of CFCs to 1 January 1995.

JANUARY 1993

5. The Liberian-registered oil tanker *Braer*, carrying 85,000 tonnes of light crude oil, ran aground in storms off Garths Ness, Shetland, causing a six-mile oil slick; oil continued to pour from the vessel for a week, with salvage work hampered by hurricane-force winds. On 12 January the tanker broke up and spilled almost all its remaining oil into the sea, causing a 20-mile slick. By 14 January the oil had largely dispersed.

MARCH 1993

31. The Government announced a review of options for the ownership and management of land owned by the Forestry Commission.

APRIL 1993

6. A tank of radioactive waste exploded at a weapons plant in Tomsk, Siberia, contaminating over 2,500 acres with radiation. **20.** The ruling council of the National Trust rejected a resolution passed by Trust members in 1990 to ban deer-hunting on its land.

MAY 1993

18. Norway announced that it would resume commercial hunting of minke whales.

JULY 1993

7. The Transport Secretary (John MacGregor) announced that plans to build a road through Oxleas Wood in south-east London had been abandoned. 21. The Environment Secretary (John Gummer) published a consultation paper, *UK Strategy for Sustainable Development*. 22. The Transport Secretary announced plans to add twin three-lane link roads to parts of the M25 London orbital motorway. Six protesters were sentenced to 28 days' imprisonment for defying an injunction to stay away from the M3 extension being built across Twyford Down, Hants.

NORTHERN IRELAND

SEPTEMBER 1992

4. An unarmed Roman Catholic youth was shot dead by soldiers after running away from an army checkpoint in Belfast; two soldiers were charged with his murder and remanded in military custody. 5. A man was shot dead by the UVF in east Belfast. 7. A Roman Catholic man and his wife were shot dead by the UVF in Moy, Co. Tyrone. 11. A man was shot dead by the IPLO in Belfast. 21. The three-day Dublin phase of talks on the political future of Northern Ireland opened at Dublin Castle; delegates from the Ulster Unionist Party attended but the talks were boycotted by the Democratic Unionist Party. The DUP rejoined the talks on 30 September at Stormont Castle. 23. A 2,000 lb IRA bomb severely damaged the Northern Ireland forensic science laboratory and surrounding buildings in Belfast. 27. A Roman Catholic man was shot dead by the UFF in north Belfast. 30. A man was shot dead in south Belfast.

OCTOBER 1992

9. A Protestant man was shot dead by the loyalist Red Hand Commandos in east Belfast. 16. A woman member of Sinn Fein was shot dead in a hotel bar in Belfast. 20. A member of the Royal Irish Regiment (RIR) was shot dead in Rasharkin, Co. Antrim.

NOVEMBER 1992

1. A member of the IPLO was shot dead by the IRA in Belfast. 4. A Roman Catholic man was shot dead by the UFF in south Belfast. 10. The talks on the political future of Northern Ireland ended without agreement. The chairman, Sir Ninian Stephen, said that informal consultations would continue. 13. A bomb explosion severely damaged the centre of Coleraine, Co. Londonderry. 14. Two men were shot dead and ten injured when a UFF gunman opened fire in a betting shop in north Belfast. 19. A part-time member of the RIR was shot dead in Portadown, Co. Armagh. A man was killed and three seriously injured when UVF gunmen opened fire in a pub in Kilcoo, Co. Down. 22. A man was found shot dead in Londonderry; the IRA claimed responsibility and said that he was an informer for British Intelligence. 24. In a BBC documentary, a former police informer said that he had taken part in the murder of an off-duty soldier in Belfast in 1991. 25. A member of the IRA was shot dead by police in west Belfast.

DECEMBER 1992

1. Twenty-five people were injured when an IRA bomb exploded in the centre of Belfast. 8. A man was shot by the IRA in Londonderry; he died on 13 December. 12. A member of Sinn Fein was shot by the UFF in Ballymoney, Co. Antrim; he died on 13 December. 20. A Roman Catholic man was shot dead by the UVF in north Belfast. 30. A member of the RIR was shot dead in north Belfast.

JANUARY 1993

3. A Roman Catholic man and his son were shot dead by the UVF in Lisnagleer, Co. Tyrone. 11. A man was shot dead by the IRA near Dungannon, Co. Tyrone. 14. A Roman Catholic man was shot dead by the UDA in south Belfast. 17. A Roman Catholic woman was shot dead at the home of her Protestant boyfriend in Belfast. 21. A Protestant man was shot dead by the INLA in north Belfast. 23. A member of the RUC was shot dead in Londonderry. 28. A Roman Catholic man was killed by a UVF bomb in Cookstown, Co. Tyrone.

FEBRUARY 1993

2. A Roman Catholic man was shot dead in Ballyronan, Co. Londonderry. 9. In Armagh one soldier was killed and four injured by IRA bombs. 11. A Roman Catholic man was shot dead by the UVF in Derrymagowan, Co. Tyrone. 12. A man was shot dead by the IRA near Castlederg, Co. Tyrone. 15. An off-duty member of the RIR was shot dead in west Belfast. 21. Three Roman Catholic taxi drivers were wounded when two UFF gunmen opened fire on a taxi rank in the Falls Road area of Belfast. 25. An RUC officer died when his car was blown up by a bomb in Loughgall, Co. Armagh; another officer was shot dead by the IRA near Crossmaglen, Co. Armagh.

MARCH 1993

8. A man was killed when three IRA mortar bombs were fired at the joint RUC-Army security base in Keady, Co. Armagh. 10. A Protestant man was shot dead in a shop in north Belfast. 15. A Roman Catholic man was shot dead by the UFF in Belfast. 17. A soldier of the Royal Scots Regiment was shot dead in south Armagh. 25. Four Roman Catholic men were shot dead by the UFF in Castlerock, Co. Londonderry. A Roman Catholic man was shot dead by the UFF in west Belfast.

APRIL 1993

5. A former member of the UDA was shot dead in Portavogie, Co. Down. 6–7. The Prime Minister visited Northern Ireland. 7. Gordon Wilson, whose

daughter was killed in the IRA bombing at Enniskillen in 1987, met IRA representatives as part of a personal peace initiative. **25.** A former member of the UDR was killed by a booby-trap bomb near Pomeroy, Co. Tyrone.

MAY 1993

1. A man was shot dead in Belfast by the UFF, who had intended to attack Alec Maskey, a Sinn Fein councillor. **17.** Six paratroopers were cleared of charges resulting from clashes with civilians in Coalisland, Co. Tyrone, in May 1992. Five of the men were bound over to keep the peace. **20.** A 1,000 lb IRA bomb exploded in Belfast, injuring 21 people and causing extensive damage to the Grand Opera House. **22.** A 1,000 lb IRA bomb exploded in Portadown, Co. Armagh, injuring six people and causing widespread damage. **23.** A 300 lb IRA bomb exploded in Magherafelt, Co. Londonderry, causing extensive damage. **30.** A Roman Catholic man was shot dead at his home in east Belfast. **31.** A part-time member of the RIR was killed by a car bomb near Moneymore, Co. Londonderry.

JUNE 1993

2. A Roman Catholic man was shot dead by the UFF near Comber, Co. Down. **17.** A former RUC officer was shot dead in the York Hotel, Belfast. **24.** A Protestant man was shot dead in Lurgan, Co. Armagh. **26.** A soldier of the Duke of Edinburgh's Royal Regiment was shot dead in Belfast. Twenty-eight people, including 12 police officers, were injured when a grenade exploded during an Orange Order parade in west Belfast. The grenade carrier, a member of the UVF, died from his injuries on 29 June. **28.** The Secretary of State for Northern Ireland apologized for making an insensitive remark a few hours after the grenade explosion on 26 June.

JULY 1993

2. A bomb exploded in Strabane, Co. Tyrone, causing widespread damage. **5.** Fifteen people were injured when a large IRA bomb exploded in Newtownards, Co. Down, causing extensive damage. **17.** A soldier of the Duke of Edinburgh's Royal Regiment was shot dead in Crossmaglen, South Armagh. **20.** A UFF bomb exploded under the car of Dr Joe Hendron, MP for West Belfast; no one was injured.

AUGUST 1993

8. The son of a Sinn Fein councillor was shot dead in Belfast. **11.** A Roman Catholic man was beaten to death in a sectarian attack in Belfast. **12.** Police intercepted a 3,000 lb IRA bomb near Portadown, Co. Armagh. **30.** A Roman Catholic woman was shot dead by the UFF in north Belfast. **31.** Two large IRA bombs exploded in Derriaghy on the outskirts of Belfast, injuring two police officers and causing extensive damage.

SPORT

SEPTEMBER 1992

2. Bobby Fischer and Boris Spassky began a chess match in Montenegro. On 5 November Fischer completed a 10-5 victory over Spassky in the final game of the 'rematch', in Belgrade. **3.** The Paralympic Games opened in Barcelona. **6.** Four players from the Hereford United football team were sent off in a match against Northampton. **7.** David Gower was omitted from the England cricket team selected for the winter tour of India and Sri Lanka. **13.** Nigel Mansell said that he would retire from Formula One motor racing at the end of the season, and on 18 September signed to compete in the American Indy Car World Series 1992-3. **17.** The National Football League announced the suspension of the World League of American Football for the 1992-3 season. **22.** The Lawn Tennis Association announced that attempts to revive the Wightman Cup, last staged in 1989, had been abandoned. **23.** Allan Lamb was fined £5,000 by the Test and County Cricket Board (TCCB) for writing an unauthorized article on 26 August in which he accused Pakistani bowlers of cheating. In November the fine was reduced by £1,000. **24.** Surrey were fined £1,000, suspended for two years, by the TCCB for repeated infringements of the regulation covering ball-tampering. **27.** Nigel Mansell won the Portuguese grand prix in Estoril, his ninth grand prix win of the season and a world record. Imran Khan, the former Pakistan captain, announced his retirement from cricket. **30.** Wimbledon footballer Vinnie Jones was charged by the Football Association with bringing the game into disrepute for his part in a video, *Soccer's Hard Men*. On 17 November he was fined £20,000.

OCTOBER 1992

1. The Al-Maktoum family said that it would reduce its involvement in British horse-racing. **26.** The National and Olympic Sports Congress of South Africa withdrew its support for a tour of England by the South African rugby union team starting on 4 November. **27.** The manager of Liverpool football club, Graeme Souness, was suspended for five European fixtures by UEFA for comments he made to the referee after a match against Spartak Moscow on 22 October. **31.** The jockey Lester Piggott was injured and his horse Mr Brooks was destroyed after a fall in the Breeders' Cup Sprint in Florida, USA. The British Amateur Weightlifting Association said that no action would be taken against Andrew Davies and Andrew Saxton, the British weightlifters sent home from the 1992 Olympic Games for alleged drug abuse.

NOVEMBER 1992

6. Birmingham City football club went into receivership. **14.** The first rugby union match against South Africa in Britain since 1969 was held at Twickenham. **22.** American yachtsman Mike Plant was missing, presumed dead, after his yacht capsized en route to the start of the Vendée Globe Challenge round-the-world race. **23.** Barnet football club was fined £50,000 by the Football League for breaches of League regulations. **26.** British yachtsman Nigel Burgess died after abandoning his yacht during a gale in the Vendée Globe Challenge round-the-world race. **30.** The Football Association ordered Peterborough United to replay their first-round FA Cup tie against Kingstonian, which they won 9–1, because the Kingstonian goalkeeper had been injured after being struck on the head by a missile thrown by a spectator; Peterborough won the replay 1–0.

DECEMBER 1992

3. In Ohio, USA, Harry 'Butch' Reynolds, the 400 metres world record holder, was awarded $27.3 million damages against the International Amateur Athletics Association (IAAF) over his suspension for drug abuse in 1990; the IAAF said that it was not bound by the decisions of US courts and started an appeal against the ruling. **5.** Charlton Athletic football club returned to The Valley after seven years of ground-sharing. **14.** Lennox Lewis became the first British heavyweight boxing champion since 1897 when Riddick Bowe was stripped of the WBC title for refusing to defend it against Lewis. **23.** The sprinter Jason Livingston was suspended for four years by the British Athletic Federation and banned for life by the British Olympic Association after a drugs test proved positive in July 1992.

JANUARY 1993

7. The Arsenal and England footballer Ian Wright was suspended for three matches by the Football Association for throwing a punch at a player during a match in December 1992. The Arsenal manager George Graham was fined £500 for making improper remarks to the referee of the same match. **11.** The Indian Cricket Board cancelled the one-day match between India and England at Ahmadabad on 16 January because of religious violence in the city. **23.** Third division rugby union club St Peter's caused a major upset by beating Cardiff 16–14 in the Welsh Cup. **26.** In a Test match in Adelaide, West Indies beat Australia by one run, the closest victory margin in the history of Test cricket. **27.** After a special general meeting of the MCC in London, a motion of no confidence in the England cricket selectors was defeated by 4,600 to 6,135. **30.** Nigel Short became the first British chess world championship contender for over 100 years when he beat Jan Timman in Spain.

FEBRUARY 1993

19. The FA Premier League agreed a £2 million four-year sponsorship deal with Bass. **20.** Graeme Hick scored 178 runs, his first Test century, against India in Bombay. **25.** Pakistan were 43 all out against West Indies in Cape Town, the lowest total recorded in a one-day international. **26.** Garry Kasparov and Nigel Short rejected the authority of the World Chess Federation (FIDE) and said that they would stage a world championship under the auspices of a new body, the Professional Chess Association (PCA); on 23 March FIDE disqualified both players. Allan Border, the Australian cricket captain, became the highest-scoring batsman in Test history when he took his career total of runs to 10,161 in a match against New Zealand in Christchurch.

MARCH 1993

5. The Canadian sprinter Ben Johnson, who was banned for two years and stripped of his 100 metres title after a positive drugs test at the 1988 Olympic Games, was banned for life by the IAAF after failing a drugs test in Montreal. **15.** Sean Lavelle, a rugby union player, died after allegedly being punched during a match at Hendon, London, on 13 March. **21.** Nigel Mansell, the world Formula One motor racing champion, won his IndyCar racing debut in Surfers Paradise, Australia. **27.** Cambridge won the Boat Race for the first time since 1986. **30.** The German Athletics Federation reduced the ban on Katrin Krabbe for alleged drug abuse from four years to one year.

APRIL 1993

3. The Grand National was declared void after all but nine of the riders failed to realize that a second false start had been indicated; seven horses completed both circuits of the course. After a stewards' inquiry it was said that no recall flag had been shown. On 5 April the Jockey Club announced an inquiry into the day's events; the inquiry report was published on 13 June and blamed human error, outdated starting equipment and an inadequate recall system. **5.** Members of the Jockey Club voted to establish a new body, the British Horseracing Board, to take over all its responsibilities except licensing and discipline from May 1993. **6.** The champion jockey Peter Scudamore announced his retirement from racing. **9.** Four members of the Pakistan cricket team, including its captain Wasim Akram, were arrested in Grenada at the beginning of a tour in the West Indies and charged with drugs offences. On 12 April the charges were dropped. The start of the first Test against the West Indies in Trinidad was delayed by one day as a result of the incident. **16.** The WBO featherweight champion, Reuben Palacio, was stripped of his title after testing positive for the HIV virus. **21.** The French yachtsman Bruno Peyron completed a record 79-day circumnavigation of the world in his catamaran *Commodore Explorer*. **26.** Nottingham Forest football club said that Brian Clough would retire as manager at the end of the season. **29.** William Vincent, a crewman competing in the British Steel Challenge round-the-world yacht race, was missing, feared drowned, after diving overboard in the south Atlantic. **30.** The tennis player Monica Seles was stabbed in the back by a man at a tournament in Hamburg.

MAY 1993

2. Britain was relegated from the world group of the Davis Cup after losing 3–2 to Hungary. **13.** Terry Venables was sacked as chief executive of Tottenham Hotspur football club by its chairman, Alan Sugar. Venables was granted an emergency High Court injunction temporarily reinstating him but on 14 June the High Court upheld the club's right to sack him. **20.** Arsenal won the FA Cup final replay against Sheffield Wednesday, becoming the first team to win the League (Coca-Cola) Cup and FA Cup in the same season. **21.** Robin Smith achieved the highest score by an England batsman in international one-day cricket with an innings of 167 against Australia at Edgbaston.

JUNE 1993

4–13. Eleven motorcyclists, including one competitor, were killed during the Isle of Man TT week. **7.** Graham Gooch became the first England cricketer to be given out for handling the ball when he knocked the ball away from the wicket with his free hand in the first Test match against Australia. **14.** FIDE announced that a world championship match would be held to rival the match staged by the PCA (*see* above) in September 1993; Garry Kasparov and Nigel Short were stripped of their FIDE international ratings. **17.** A competitor at the Hexham Horse Trials died when his horse fell at a fence; he was the third rider to be killed at trials in less than three weeks. **22.** A German spectator was banned from the Wimbledon tennis championships after shouting abuse at Steffi Graf.

JULY 1993

6. Graham Thorpe made a century in his first Test match for England, with an innings of 114 not out against Australia. **15.** Rangers football club signed Duncan Ferguson from Dundee United for a record British transfer fee of about £4 million. **18.** Greg Norman won the Open golf championship with a record 13 under par aggregate of 267. **19.** Ian Botham retired from first-class cricket after playing for Durham against Australia. **26.** The England cricket captain Graham Gooch resigned after England's eighth defeat in nine Test matches; on 28 July Mike Atherton was appointed captain.

AUGUST 1993

1. England won the women's cricket World Cup, beating New Zealand at Lord's. **9.** The chairman of the England cricket selectors, Ted Dexter, resigned. **15.** At the world athletics championships in Stuttgart, Linford Christie won the 100 metres with a time of 9.87 seconds. On 16 August Chinese runners took the first three places in the women's 3,000 metres. On 19 August Sally Gunnell won the 400 metres hurdles in a world record time of 52.74 seconds. On 20 August Colin Jackson won the 110 metres hurdles in a world record time of 12.91 seconds. On 22 August the USA set a new 4 × 400 metres world record of 2 minutes 54.29 seconds. **19.** At the cycling world championships in Norway, Graeme Obree won the 4,000 metres pursuit title in a world record time of 4 minutes 20.894 seconds. **21.** Graham Gooch became the highest-scoring Test player for England, reaching a total of 8,293 runs in the match against Australia at the Oval. **23.** The England cricket team won its first Test match since July 1992. **26.** Peter Reid was sacked as manager of Manchester City football club. **31.** Ian Folley, the former Lancashire and Derbyshire spin bowler, died after being hit in the face by a ball while playing for Whitehaven against Workington.

APPOINTMENTS AND RESIGNATIONS

In addition to those mentioned above, the following appointments, resignations, etc., were announced:

1992

12 October: Charles Moore was appointed editor of the *Sunday Telegraph*

22 October: David Montgomery was appointed chief executive of Mirror Group Newspapers

15 November: Richard Stott was dismissed as editor of the *Daily Mirror* and replaced by David Banks; Bridget Rowe was appointed editor of the *People*, with Colin Mylor replacing her as editor of the *Sunday Mirror*

25 November: Gerald Ratner resigned as chief executive of Ratners

1 December: Ian Phillips resigned as finance director of the BBC

10 December: Jonathan Powell resigned as controller of BBC1

1993

11 January: Robert Phillis was appointed deputy director-general of the BBC; Liz Forgan appointed managing director of BBC network radio

25 January: Martin Dunn, the editor of *Today*, was appointed editor of the *Boston Herald*

31 January: Richard Stott was appointed editor of *Today*

5 February: Lord King retired as chairman of British Airways and was succeeded by Sir Colin Marshall

18 February: Frances Heaton was appointed the first female director of the Bank of England

26 February: Alan Yentob was appointed controller of BBC1

26 March: Louis Gerstner was appointed chairman and chief executive of IBM

30 March: Paul Foot resigned as a columnist on the *Daily Mirror* and Lord Hollick resigned from the board of Mirror Group Newspapers
1 April: Michael Jackson was appointed controller of BBC2
5 April: David Gordon was appointed chief executive of ITN
14 May: Jonathan Fenby was appointed editor of the *Observer*
24 May: Sir Colin Davis was appointed principal conductor of the London Symphony Orchestra from 1995
30 June: The Bishop of Durham announced that he would retire in June 1994
19 August: Martin Taylor was appointed chief executive of Barclays Bank
31 August: Kenneth Branagh was appointed to the board of the British Film Institute

AFRICA

SEPTEMBER 1992

7. Ciskei armed forces fired on 70,000 African National Congress demonstrators who were marching on the capital Bisho, killing over 29 and injuring 200. **26.** President de Klerk of South Africa and the ANC president Nelson Mandela held a meeting in an attempt to restart the constitutional negotiations which had collapsed in June. **27.** The *Inkatha* leader Chief Buthelezi rejected the ANC-government agreement to fence off Zulu migrant hostels and ban the carrying of cultural weapons, and withdrew from constitutional negotiations in protest. **30.** In Angolan parliamentary elections the ruling MPLA government won the largest number of seats; in the presidential elections President Dos Santos won 49.5 per cent of the vote and the UNITA leader Jonas Savimbi 40.5 per cent.

OCTOBER 1992

4. President Chissano of Mozambique and Alfonso Dhlakama, leader of the Renamo rebels, signed a peace settlement in Rome ending the 16-year civil war. **19.** The ANC published an abridged version of a report by its own lawyers which showed that it was guilty of murder, torture and other abuses against detainees in its camps. **20.** Nigerian aircraft and warships bombarded the port of Buchanan, Liberia, held by rebels fighting the West African peace-keeping force. The South African Parliament passed the Constitution Amendment Act, which allows blacks to serve in the cabinet for the first time. **30.** Fighting between Angolan government and UNITA forces broke out in Luanda and in the centre of the country after UNITA disputed the election results.

NOVEMBER 1992

2. A UN-brokered cease-fire came into effect in the Angolan capital Luanda. **3.** The incumbent president,

Flt. Lt. Jerry Rawlings, won the presidential election in Ghana, though electoral fraud was alleged by opposition politicians. **6.** UNITA forces advanced on Luanda and other government-held cities in Angola as civil war broke out again. **18.** The Nigerian President, General Babangida, announced that the planned transfer from military to civilian rule in January 1993 had been postponed for a further seven months. **26.** President de Klerk of South Africa announced that multiracial elections would be held by April 1994. **27.** Angola's first elected parliament, composed mainly of MPLA members, was sworn in at a ceremony in Luanda boycotted by UNITA members. **29.** In South Africa eight whites were killed and 17 injured in two separate attacks by blacks using hand grenades and automatic weapons.

DECEMBER 1992

1. President Mobutu of Zaire dissolved the country's pro-democracy cabinet in an attempt to regain dictatorial powers. **3.** The UN Security Council authorized the use of force by a US-led international coalition of peace-keeping forces to ensure the safe delivery of food and medical supplies in Somalia. **8.** An advance party of US marines went ashore in Somalia. **10.** Two gunmen were shot dead and five wounded by French troops in Mogadishu. **11.** US troops in Somalia brought together the rival warlords Muhammed Farrah Aideed and Ali Mahdi Muhammed, who signed an agreement to end hostilities and end the division of Mogadishu. **15.** UN-mandated troops in Somalia moved to Baidoa to protect relief supplies. **20.** US marines and Belgian paratroopers secured control of Kismayu in southern Somalia. **27.** Rival Somali leaders Muhammed Farrah Aideed and Ali Mahdi Muhammed publicly proclaimed an end to the civil war. **29.** The incumbent president, Daniel arap Moi, won the first multi-party presidential elections in Kenya for 26 years amid allegations of vote-rigging and electoral irregularities.

JANUARY 1993

3. The UN Secretary-General was forced to leave Mogadishu after being besieged in the UN compound by stone-throwing crowds. **6.** Fighting erupted throughout Angola between MPLA and UNITA forces. **7.** US marines fought Somali gunmen in Mogadishu and captured a large cache of heavy weapons. **8.** In Addis Ababa Somali faction leaders signed a tentative agreement calling for a cease-fire and a national conference. **14.** The interim Zairean parliament, the High Council of the Republic, declared President Mobutu guilty of treason for undermining moves towards democracy. **15.** The Somali peace talks closed with an agreement that armed supporters would be sent to designated compounds and heavy weapons placed under the control of the UN-mandated forces. **20.** UNITA forces in Angola captured Soyo and its oil refinery. **29.** Army factions clashed in the Zairean capital Kinshasa.

FEBRUARY 1993

5. The Zairean Prime Minister Etienne Tshisekedi refused to accept his dismissal by President Mobutu or the blame for the army riots. **12.** The South African government and the ANC agreed the basis of a timetable for establishing a Government of national unity and moves to multiracial democracy. **20.** President de Klerk announced the appointment of the first non-whites to the South African cabinet. **23.** UN-mandated troops in Somalia forced gunmen to leave Kismayo and to disarm in a designated area. **24.** Rioting and disturbances occurred in Mogadishu after General Aideed accused US forces of supporting a rival. Zairean troops besieged Kinshasa and held MPs captive in an attempt to force them to recognize as legal tender new notes with which they had been paid by President Mobutu. **25.** Clashes between Somali gunmen and UN-mandated troops left ten gunmen dead and led to the suspension of aid distribution in Mogadishu.

MARCH 1993

4. A state of emergency was declared in Zambia and leading opposition politicians were arrested after the discovery of a plan by UNIP, the former ruling party, to overthrow President Chiluba. **7.** After weeks of heavy fighting, UNITA forces defeated Angolan government troops to take control of Huambo. **20-22.** Five whites were killed in South Africa in an upsurge of violence by the armed wing of the Pan Africanist Congress. **28.** In UN-brokered negotiations in Addis Ababa, rival Somali factions agreed to disarm and form a transitional government.

APRIL 1993

1. Negotiations on the constitutional future of South Africa resumed after an eleven-month break. **2.** Ntsu Mokhehle was sworn in as Prime Minister of Lesotho after the Basotho Congress Party won the general election which ended seven years of military rule. **10.** Chris Hani, leader of the South African Communist Party and an ANC national executive member, was shot dead. **11-19.** Violence in South Africa following Hani's murder left 31 people dead. **25.** Over 99 per cent of Eritreans voted for independence from Ethiopia in a referendum.

MAY 1993

4. The UN officially took command of the multinational peace-keeping force in Somalia. **23.** Eritrea became an independent state. **25.** South African police arrested 73 senior officials of the Pan-Africanist Congress and its armed wing in connection with attacks on white farms over the previous four months.

JUNE 1993

5. Twenty-two UN peace-keepers were killed in ambushes in Mogadishu by supporters of General Aideed. **12.** Elections for a civilian President were held in Nigeria; on 23 June the military government declared the elections invalid. **13.** Pakistani UN soldiers in Mogadishu opened fire on a demonstration, killing 14 and wounding 23. **14.** In a referendum in Malawi the electorate voted in favour of a multiparty democracy. **15.** The Inkatha Freedom Party and right-wing groups walked out of the South African constitutional negotiations, refusing to agree a date for multiracial elections because of alleged government-ANC collusion. **17.** UN forces captured General Aideed's headquarters in Mogadishu; 19 Somalis and five UN troops died. **25.** Armed right-wing extremists held delegates at South Africa's constitutional negotiations hostage for three hours, demanding a separate Afrikaner homeland.

JULY 1993

2. The Inkatha Freedom Party and the right-wing Conservative Party negotiators walked out of South Africa's constitutional negotiations in protest at an election date of 27 April 1994 being set before an interim constitution had been agreed. **12.** Four journalists were killed by Somalis in Mogadishu after UN forces had attacked a stronghold of General Aideed, killing 13 Somalis. **14.** The governments of Italy, Kuwait, Saudi Arabia and the United Arab Emirates refused to deploy troops on offensive UN operations in Somalia, objecting to the aggressiveness of the US-led UN operation to destroy General Aideed's forces. **25.** Twelve people were killed and 53 wounded in an attack on a church in Cape Town. **26.** A draft of South Africa's first multiracial constitution was tabled for debate at the constitutional negotiations.

AUGUST 1993

10. Fierce fighting between government and UNITA forces for control of Cuito in Angola left over 200 people dead. **25.** Pro-democracy demonstrations demanding an end to military government brought Lagos to a standstill. **26.** President Babangida of Nigeria resigned and transferred power to an interim president and government.

THE AMERICAS

SEPTEMBER 1992

13. Abimael Guzman, the leader of Peru's Shining Path terrorist group, was captured after 12 years on the run. **29.** The Brazilian House of Representatives voted to authorize the Senate to impeach President Collor de Mello for corruption.

OCTOBER 1992

1. Ross Perot announced his re-entry into the US presidential election as an independent candidate. **2.** The Brazilian Vice-President Itamar Franco was sworn in as acting president following President Collor de Mello's suspension. **5.** Dr Cheddi Jagan defeated the incumbent president Desmond Hoyte

MAASTRICHT TREATY
The Government pushed through ratification of the Maastricht Treaty despite fierce opposition, including from within its own party (*Rex Features*)

THE ECONOMY
The Government came under constant criticism throughout the year over its handling of the economy and the pit closures (*Rex Features*)

CURRENCY CRISIS
Sterling was withdrawn from the ERM in September 1992, weakened by currency speculation. The ERM virtually collapsed after renewed speculation in July 1993 (*Rex Features*)

CHANCELLOR SACKED
Norman Lamont lost his job in May 1993, as the recession dragged on without any sign of his 'green shoots of recovery' (*Rex Features*)

IRA BOMBINGS
IRA bombs caused fatalities in the City of London (above) in April and in Warrington in March 1993 (*Rex Features*)

YUGOSLAVIA
Desperate Bosnians escaped from besieged towns in UN aid lorries as Serbian forces tightened their grip on Bosnian territory (*Rex Features*)

LITTLE IRMA
The plight of Irma Hadzimuratovic led to the evacuation of some of the severely wounded from Sarajevo to the west in August 1993 (*Rex Features*)

SOMALIA
UN intervention in the Somali civil war was ineffectual and increasingly resented as UN troops were drawn into the conflict (*Rex Features*)

INDIA
Religious tensions ran high in India throughout the year after the destruction of the Ayodhya mosque by Hindu extremists provoked retaliatory attacks (*Rex Features*)

PALESTINIAN DEPORTEES
Deportees from the Occupied Territories spent nine months in no man's land on the Israeli-Lebanon border before Israel agreed to their return home in August 1993 (*Rex Features*)

MIDDLE EAST PEACE ACCORD
In September 1993 Israel and the PLO signed agreements recognizing each other and giving Palestinians a degree of self-government (*Rex Features*)

SOUTH AFRICA
Demonstrations and rioting followed the assassination and funeral of Chris Hani, a Communist and ANC leader, by white extremists in April 1993 (*AP*)

TURMOIL IN ITALY
The bombing of historic buildings in Florence and Rome in summer 1993 was linked to the political turmoil caused by investigations into corrupt politicans (*Rex Features*)

RACISM IN EUROPE
Increasing racism in Europe, especially Germany, led to murder, violent demonstrations, and the desecration of Commonwealth war graves (*Rex Features*)

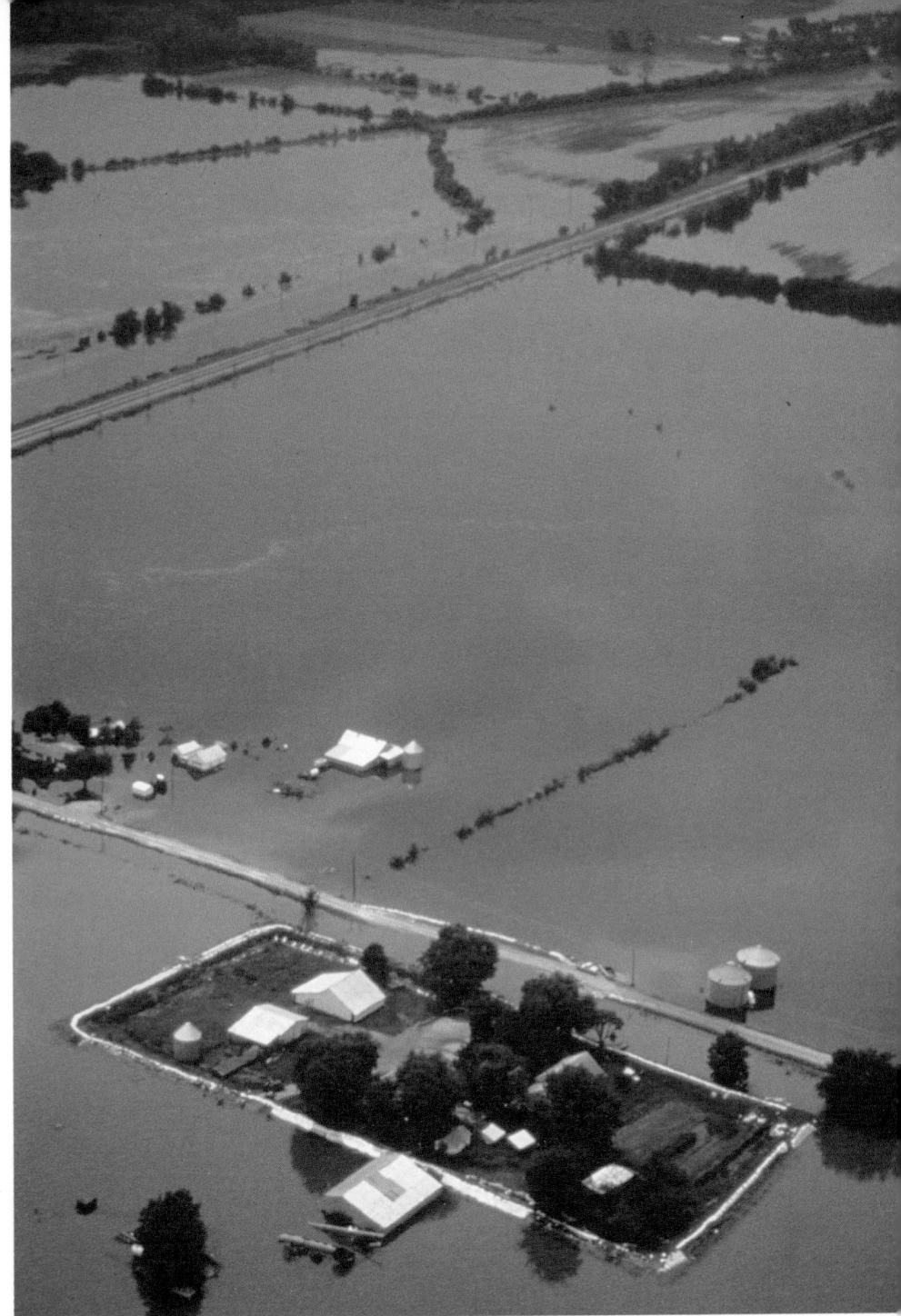

USA FLOODING
Flood waters in the mid-west American states in spring 1993 covered an area larger than Britain (*Rex Features*)

WINDSOR CASTLE FIRE
The fire in November 1992 contributed to The Queen's 'annus horribilis' and the financing of repairs added to the controversy surrounding the royal family in 1992–3 (*Rex Features*)

NATIONAL DISASTER
The failure of the recall after a false start in the 1993 Grand National led to the race being declared void (*Mercury Press Agency*)

ATHLETICS TRIUMPH
Colin Jackson won his first gold medal and set a new 110 metre hurdles world record at the World Championships in Stuttgart (*Allsport*)

GOLDEN GIRL
Sally Gunnell became world as well as Olympic champion and set a new 400 metre hurdles world record in Stuttgart (*Allsport*)

in the presidential election in Guyana. **26.** In a national referendum Canadians rejected a proposed new constitution, known as the Charlottetown accord.

NOVEMBER 1992

3. Governor Bill Clinton defeated the incumbent president George Bush and the independent candidate Ross Perot in the US presidential election. **8.** President Gaviria of Colombia declared a 90-day state of emergency after left-wing guerrillas killed more than 100 people. **22.** Parties supporting President Fujimori won the majority of seats in elections to a new constituent assembly in Peru. **27.** Venezuelan troops loyal to the government defeated a coup attempt by army rebels.

DECEMBER 1992

2. The Brazilian Senate voted to indict President Collor de Mello for corruption. **24.** President Bush announced pardons for the former defence secretary Caspar Weinberger and five other officials in the Reagan administration who were to stand trial over the Iran-Contra affair. **29.** Collor de Mello resigned as President of Brazil and interim President Itamar Franco was formally sworn in.

JANUARY 1993

17. The Haitian army announced that it had agreed to UN-mediated negotiations on the restoration of democracy with exiled President Jean-Bertrand Aristide. **20.** William Jefferson Clinton was inaugurated as the 42nd President of the USA. **22.** President Clinton's nominee for the office of attorney-general, Zoe Baird, was forced to withdraw after revealing that she had hired illegal immigrants as domestic help.

FEBRUARY 1993

5. President Clinton's second nominee as attorney-general, Kimba Wood, withdrew because she had hired illegal immigrants as domestic help. **15.** President Clinton gave a televised address announcing a serious effort to cut the federal budget deficit through tax increases and spending cuts. **24.** The Canadian Prime Minister Brian Mulroney resigned as leader of the ruling Progressive Conservative Party. **26.** Five people were killed and over 1,000 injured when a bomb exploded in a car park beneath the World Trade Centre in New York, causing fires and extensive structural damage.

MARCH 1993

1. Four agents of the US Treasury department were killed as they attempted to storm the fortified ranch of a religious sect in Waco, Texas. **25.** The US Senate approved by 54 votes to 45 President Clinton's $500 billion (£340 billion) programme of tax increases and spending cuts. **30.** The incumbent People's National Party won the Jamaican general election; 13 people were killed in politically-motivated violence during the campaign.

APRIL 1993

17. Two of the four officers accused of beating the black motorist Rodney King were found guilty of violating his civil rights; the other two were acquitted. **19.** The 51-day siege of the Branch Davidian cult compound at Waco ended; 87 cult members died in fires as FBI agents stormed the compound.

MAY 1993

9. Juan Carlos Wasmosy was elected President of Paraguay. **20.** The Venezuelan Supreme Court voted to charge President Perez with embezzlement from public funds. **25.** President Serrano of Guatemala suspended the country's constitution, dissolved the Congress and announced that he would rule by decree to purge state corruption. **27.** The US House of Representatives approved by 219 votes to 213 President Clinton's programme of tax increases and spending cuts.

JUNE 1993

1. President Serrano was ousted by the Guatemalan military. The Canadian government signed an agreement granting self-government to Canadian Eskimos in their own territory, to be created from part of the Northwest Territories. **4.** The Venezuelan Congress elected Ramon Velasquez as interim President. **6.** Ramon de Leon Carpio was elected President of Guatemala by Congress. **6.** The opposition National Revolutionary Movement won presidential and Congressional elections in Bolivia. **13.** Kim Campbell was elected leader of Canada's ruling Progressive Conservative Party and was sworn in as Prime Minister on 25 June. **23.** The UN Security Council imposed economic sanctions on Haiti after the military government did not meet a deadline to reinstate President Aristide.

JULY 1993

4. The Haiti military government and the exiled President Aristide signed a UN-mediated agreement to restore Aristide to power by 30 October 1993. **23.** Nicaraguan government forces retook the northern town of Esteli from former Sandinista rebels after two days of fighting.

AUGUST 1993

8. President Clinton's deficit-cutting budget was finally passed when the Senate passed a compromise version of the differing Senate and House of Representatives draft bills on the casting vote of Vice-President Gore. **20.** Nicaraguan government forces surrounded a camp where Contra guerrillas were holding military officers and government officials hostage to try to force the government to dismiss the Sandinista army commander Humberto Ortega; on 21 August Sandinistas took hostage 50 politicians, including Vice-President Vaglio, in Managua in protest at the hostage-taking by the Contra guerrillas. All the hostages were released on 26 August.

ASIA

SEPTEMBER 1992

13. Pro-democracy parties emerged victorious in the Thai general election, at the expense of pro-military parties that had supported the May 1992 military crackdown. 27. The Myanmar government lifted most martial law decrees and released detainees imprisoned since the May 1990 military take-over of power.

OCTOBER 1992

7. The Governor of Hong Kong (Chris Patten) presented plans for the extension of democracy in the colony. 12. The 14th Chinese Communist Party congress opened with a speech by party leader Jiang Zemin calling for a 'socialist market economy'. 18. The Chinese Communist Party congress closed with the replacement of elderly conservative leaders, including eight of the 14 Politburo members, by economic reformers.

NOVEMBER 1992

8. Talks in Beijing (Peking) to try to rescue the peace process in Cambodia ended in deadlock after the Khmer Rouge refused to disarm before the planned elections. 11. An angry debate in Hong Kong's Legislative Council ended with a vote in favour of the democratic reforms proposed by the Governor. 15. The Khmer Rouge failed to meet a UN deadline to rejoin the Cambodian peace process and refused to disarm its fighters. 18. The Pakistani government expelled opposition leader Benazir Bhutto from Islamabad after violent clashes between opposition supporters and police. 23. The Chinese government warned the Hong Kong Governor to withdraw proposals for greater democracy in the colony or China would end talks on the colony's future. 30. The UN Security Council voted unanimously to impose economic sanctions on the Khmer Rouge. In direct contravention of the 1984 Anglo-Chinese treaty on Hong Kong, the Chinese government announced that all contracts, leases and agreements signed by the Hong Kong government without Chinese approval would be declared invalid after the 1997 handover of power.

DECEMBER 1992

6. Thousands of Hindu fundamentalists marched on the north Indian town of Ayodhya and destroyed a mosque. 7. Rioting and fighting between Muslims and Hindus spread throughout India, Pakistan and Bangladesh following the destruction of the Ayodhya mosque. 8. As rioting continued, the Indian government arrested leaders of the BJP Hindu fundamentalist party and promised to rebuild the Ayodhya mosque. 9. The Indian parliament was adjourned and MPs returned to their constituencies in an attempt to calm the continuing unrest, in which over 600 people had died. Fighting in the Afghan capital Kabul between rival groups left 100 people dead. 11. Amid the worst economic downturn in the Japanese economy for 20 years, Prime Minister Kiichi Miyazawa replaced all but two of his Cabinet ministers. 15. The Indian government dismissed three state governments led by the BJP and imposed direct rule. 18. Kim Young-sam won the South Korean presidential election.

JANUARY 1993

3. Burhanuddin Rabbani was sworn in as President of Afghanistan. 6–11. Clashes between Hindus and Muslims in Bombay left 167 people dead. 16. The Indian government resigned *en masse* to enable the Prime Minister to form a new government and restore government authority after the Hindu-Muslim clashes.

FEBRUARY 1993

1. Government forces launched an offensive against Khmer Rouge guerrillas in central and eastern Cambodia. 7. Fighting erupted in Kabul between rival mujahidin groups. 9. Hong Kong's Executive Council approved the constitutional reform proposals of the Governor. 25. In New Delhi, Indian security forces prevented thousands of BJP supporters from staging a rally which had been banned.

MARCH 1993

7. Rival mujahidin groups in Kabul signed a peace accord whereby Burhanuddin Rabbani would remain President for 18 months and the Hezb-i-Islami leader Gulbuddin Hekmatyar would become Prime Minister. 12. The Governor of Hong Kong finally tabled his democratic reform plans for debate in the Legislative Council, after continually delaying the move in an unsuccessful attempt to persuade China to resume negotiations. Thirteen bomb blasts in Bombay caused 300 deaths and over 1,000 injuries, and led to the imposition of a nation-wide state of emergency by the Indian government. 16. A bomb exploded in the centre of Calcutta, killing 45 people. 17. The Chinese government announced that it would disband Hong Kong's legislature in 1997 and form its own government and legislature in the territory. 23. The Chinese government refused to continue six-monthly meetings with the UK government over Hong Kong and called for the dismissal of Governor Patten. 28. The Chinese National People's Congress elected Jiang Zemin as the country's President.

APRIL 1993

8. Four of the UN peace-keeping force in Cambodia were killed in Khmer Rouge attacks. 13. Britain and China announced that talks on the future of Hong Kong would resume after China ended its insistence that democratic reform proposals should be withdrawn. 18. The President of Pakistan dismissed the government and dissolved parliament.

MAY 1993

1. President Premadasa of Sri Lanka was assassinated by a suicide bomber in Colombo. **12.** Fighting between rival mujahidin groups around Kabul left 70 dead. **24.** Chinese security forces fought thousands of Tibetans demonstrating against Chinese rule in Lhasa. **28.** The five-day UN-supervised elections in Cambodia ended with a 90 per cent turn-out and only sporadic attempts by the Khmer Rouge to disrupt the elections.

JUNE 1993

9. Crown Prince Naruhito of Japan married diplomat Masako Owada in Tokyo. **12.** Members of the defeated Cambodian People's Party declared the secession of seven provinces in eastern Cambodia and attacked UN officials and FUNCIPEC supporters in the region; on 15 June the secessionists fled to Vietnam. **16.** Prince Sihanouk formed a coalition government with himself as head of state of Cambodia, and the Royalist Party leader Prince Ranariddh and the Communist Party leader Hun Sen as co-chairmen of the government. **18.** The Japanese parliament was dissolved and a general election called after the government was defeated in a confidence vote.

JULY 1993

5. David Rowbottom and Tania Miller were kidnapped by Kurdish guerrillas while travelling in eastern Turkey; they were released unharmed on 10 August. **18.** In the Japanese general election the Liberal Democratic Party lost its majority in the lower house of parliament for the first time since 1955; on 22 July the Liberal Democrat government resigned. Moeen Qareshi was named as caretaker Prime Minister of Pakistan after President Ghulam Ishaq Khan and Prime Minister Nawaz Sharif both resigned after months of feuding.

AUGUST 1993

6. The leader of the Japan New Party, Morihiro Hosokawa, was elected Prime Minister by the Japanese parliament; the new Cabinet was sworn in on 9 August. **18.** Cambodian government forces launched assaults on Khmer Rouge positions in eastern Cambodia. **22.** Two British tourists were kidnapped by Kurdish guerrillas in eastern Turkey; they were released on 24 August after Turkish soldiers shot dead eight of the guerrillas. **29.** Ong Teng Cheong was elected President of Singapore.

AUSTRALASIA AND THE PACIFIC

SEPTEMBER 1992

13. Papua New Guinean soldiers raided the Solomon Islands in an attempt to cut off supplies to secessionists on Bougainville Island.

OCTOBER 1992

3. The Labour state government in Victoria, Australia, lost the state election to the conservative opposition. **5.** The Australian Prime Minister (Paul Keating) announced that Australia was formally discontinuing the British honours system. **23.** Papua New Guinean troops and riot police attacked and besieged rebel strongholds on Bougainville Island.

NOVEMBER 1992

18. The incumbent president of Nauru, Bernard Dowiyogo, was re-elected by the country's parliament.

DECEMBER 1992

17. The Australian Prime Minister announced that new citizens would no longer swear an oath of allegiance to The Queen.

FEBRUARY 1993

4. In the Tongan general election, seven of the nine elected parliamentary seats were won by candidates supporting a reduction in the power of the monarchy and aristocracy. **14.** Papua New Guinean forces attacked the secessionist-held town of Arawa, Bougainville. **25.** Eight Papua New Guinean soldiers were killed in an ambush by separatist rebels in Bougainville.

MARCH 1993

13. The Labor Party won a fifth successive general election victory in Australia.

APRIL 1993

12. The Solomon Islands formally protested to Papua New Guinea over raids into Solomon Island territory by Papuan forces. **27.** Papua New Guinean and Solomon Islands' patrol boats clashed off Bougainville in a border dispute. **28.** The Australian Prime Minister announced the appointment of a committee of eminent persons to advise on the changes needed to convert Australia to a republic.

EUROPE

SEPTEMBER 1992

4. The former Communist president of Bulgaria, Todor Zhivkov, was convicted of embezzlement and abuse of power, and gaoled for seven years. **10.** The Italian Prime Minister (Giuliano Amato) asked parliament for emergency economic powers to deal with chronic economic chaos and a currency crisis. **17.** The German government, faced with increasing numbers of asylum-seekers, announced that it had agreed with the Romanian government to send back to Romania all those whose asylum requests were rejected.

OCTOBER 1992

1. The Czechoslovak federal parliament voted to maintain a new, looser federation and rejected plans for a division of the country. **5.** The Estonian Riigikogu elected Lennart Meri as the country's first post-Soviet president. **11.** The incumbent president of Romania, Ion Iliescu, was re-elected for a second term. **19.** Mart Laar became Prime Minister of Estonia at the head of a coalition government. **28.** The last former Soviet troops left Poland, though a skeleton transport and communications force remained to assist the withdrawal from east Germany. **29.** The Bulgarian government resigned after losing a parliamentary vote of confidence over arms smuggling allegations.

NOVEMBER 1992

4. Nicolae Vacarion was appointed Prime Minister of Romania. **5.** The Irish government lost a confidence motion in the Dail and was forced to resign and call a general election. **6.** The Norwegian Prime Minister Gro Harlem Brundtland announced her resignation as Labour Party leader for personal reasons, but continued as Prime Minister. **11.** In Berlin the trial began of Erich Honecker and five of his colleagues on charges of manslaughter. **16.** The Democratic Party of Labour (formerly the Communist Party) won the second round of parliamentary elections in Lithuania. **18.** The Swedish parliament voted to ratify the European Economic Area agreement between the EC and EFTA states. **19.** Sweden abandoned the pegging of its currency to the ECU after intense currency speculation. **25.** The Czechoslovak federal parliament passed a bill authorizing the partition of the country into separate Czech and Slovak republics from 1 January 1993. In the Irish general election, the Labour Party emerged holding the balance of power in the Dail. **27.** The German government outlawed the neo-Nazi Nationalist Front in an attempt to reduce attacks on asylum-seekers.

DECEMBER 1992

2. The Greek Prime Minister sacked his entire cabinet after months of feuding over economic and foreign policy. The Lithuanian parliament elected Bronislovas Lubys as Prime Minister. **6.** In a referendum, Switzerland voted by 50.3 per cent to 49.7 per cent to reject the European Economic Area agreement between the EC and EFTA states. **10.** Norway abandoned the pegging of its currency to the ECU following currency speculation. **13.** In a referendum, Liechtenstein voted in favour of ratifying the European Economic Area agreement. **14.** The separatist Lombardy League and anti-Mafia La Rete parties made large gains in the Italian local elections at the expense of the Christian Democrat and Socialist parties.

JANUARY 1993

1. Czechoslovakia separated into two new independent states, the Czech Republic and the Slovak

Republic. **12.** The Irish Dail endorsed the Fianna Fail-Labour coalition government. The Icelandic parliament voted to ratify the European Economic Area agreement between the EC and EFTA states. The former East German leader Erich Honecker flew to Chile after his trial on charges of manslaughter collapsed when he was judged too ill to stand trial. **14.** The Danish Prime Minister Poul Schluter resigned after a judicial inquiry accused him of lying about measures taken to prevent Tamil refugees from Sri Lanka entering Denmark. **25.** A new Danish coalition government led by Poul Rasmussen was sworn in. **27.** Nexhnije Hoxha, the widow of the former Albanian dictator Enver Hoxha, was found guilty of corruption and sentenced to nine years in gaol.

FEBRUARY 1993

10. The Italian Justice Minister Claudio Martelli resigned after coming under investigation for corruption. **12.** The Italian Socialist Party leader Bettino Craxi resigned after being implicated in a Milan bribery scandal. **14.** Glafcos Clerides defeated the incumbent George Vassilliou in the Cypriot presidential election. The former Communist Party leader Algirdas Brazaukas was elected President of Lithuania. **15.** Michal Kovac was elected by the Slovak parliament as the state's first president. **19.** The Italian finance minister Giovanni Goria and the health minister Francesco de Lorenzo resigned after magistrates said that both were under investigation for corruption. **25.** As corruption inquiries in Italy spread, the coalition government survived a parliamentary vote of confidence.

MARCH 1993

3. The Belgian parliament voted to end the King's power to nominate and appoint a prime minister and to dissolve parliament. **4.** The German cabinet agreed an economic consolidation package, including tax increases and cuts in subsidies and social services, to raise DM 150 billion a year to cover unification costs. **10.** Fighting broke out in the Italian Senate between government and opposition members over alleged corruption involving leading politicians. **14.** German federal, state and opposition leaders, employers and trade unions reached agreement on a 'solidarity pact' of spending cuts, tax increases, pay restraint and investment increases to fund unification. **16.** The Italian government survived a vote of confidence in the Chamber of Deputies after fighting had broken out and the Liberal Party leader Renato Altissimo had resigned over alleged involvement in corruption. **21.** The ruling French Socialist Party was defeated in the first round of legislative elections by the right-wing RPR-UDF alliance. **23.** The Belgian coalition government offered its resignation to King Baudouin after failing to agree budget cuts. The King asked the government to continue in office and attempt to reach agreement. The coalition agreed budget cuts and on 30 March the King rejected the resignation and reappointed the ministers. In Dublin a demonstration by 15,000 people demanded an end to IRA violence in the wake of the Warrington bombing. **29.** Edouard Balladur was appointed Prime Minister after the RPR-UDF alliance won the French legislative elections.

APRIL 1993

17. President Turgut Ozal of Turkey died of a heart attack. **19.** In a referendum in Italy an overwhelming majority voted to change the voting system for three-quarters of the Senate seats from proportional representation to a first-past-the-post system. **22.** The Italian government resigned. **28.** A new Italian coalition government headed by Carlo Ciampi was announced. **29.** Five ministers resigned from the Italian government in protest at parliament's vote not to lift the immunity from prosecution on corruption charges of the former Prime Minister Bettino Craxi.

MAY 1993

6. The German Transport Minister Gunther Krause resigned after his involvement in a scandal over the misuse of public funds. **13.** The Italian Senate voted to lift the immunity from prosecution of former Prime Minister Giulio Andreotti, who faced charges of collusion with the Mafia. **19.** Anti-Maastricht protesters fought with police in Copenhagen. **27.** A bomb suspected to have been planted by the Mafia exploded in Florence, killing six people and severely damaging parts of the Uffizi gallery. **28.** The Polish government was defeated in a parliamentary vote of confidence. **29.** German neo-Nazi youths killed five Turks in an arson attack in Solingen. **30.** Thousands of Turks rioted in Solingen to protest at the arson attack.

JUNE 1993

1. Riots by Turks, anarchists and extremists spread throughout Germany. **3.** Turks rioted in Cologne and Nuremberg after the funeral service for the victims of the arson attack on 29 May. **6.** Latvia held legislative elections, which were won by the moderate Latvian Way coalition. The Socialist Party retained power in the Spanish general election but lost its parliamentary majority. **13.** Tansu Ciller was elected leader of the ruling True Path Party in Turkey, becoming Turkey's first woman Prime Minister. **21.** Two ETA car bombs exploded in central Madrid killing seven people.

JULY 1993

27. Five people were killed when three car bombs exploded in Milan and Rome. **31.** King Baudouin of Belgium died.

AUGUST 1993

4. The Italian Chamber of Deputies passed electoral reform legislation to replace proportional representation by a first-past-the-post system for 75 per cent of the seats. **31.** The last Russian troops left Lithuania.

THE FORMER SOVIET UNION

SEPTEMBER 1992

1. Fighting broke out between Georgian government forces and separatist rebels in the Abkhazia region. Opposition supporters seized control of the presidential palace in Dushanbe, capital of Tajikistan, and took several government ministers hostage. **4.** Government troops and rebel forces clashed in Dushanbe, leaving hundreds dead; Russia, Uzbekistan, Kyrgyzstan and Kazakhstan sent troops to seal the former Soviet border with Afghanistan to prevent arms entering Tajikistan. **7.** President Nabiev of Tajikistan was forced to resign by opposition forces. **15.** Seven former Soviet republics took steps towards restoring central co-ordination with the establishment of an inter-parliamentary assembly in St Petersburg. **27.** Rival armed factions in Tajikistan took 30 Russian troops hostage in an attempt to seize their heavy weapons. **28.** Russia reinforced its military presence in Tajikistan to prevent rival factions from obtaining military weaponry. **30.** The Ukrainian Prime Minister Vitold Fokin resigned after increasing pressure from the opposition over the slow pace of economic reforms.

OCTOBER 1992

1. Russia launched its mass privatization scheme, based on distributing vouchers to all the population. **2.** The Ukrainian parliament passed a vote of no confidence in the government, forcing it out of office. **3.** Separatist rebels in the Abkhazia region of Georgia captured the town of Gaga from government forces. **6.** Separatists in Abkhazia, allied to Cossack and Muslim volunteers from Russia, defeated Georgian government troops and gained control of all land north-west of Sukhumi. **7.** The Azerbaijani parliament voted against ratifying the republic's membership of the CIS. **9.** Russia, Belarus, Kazakhstan, Uzbekistan, Armenia and Kyrgyzstan agreed at a CIS summit to create a rouble zone. **11.** Eduard Shevardnadze was elected chairman of Georgia's parliament and State President. **13.** Leonid Kuchma was appointed Prime Minister of the Ukraine. **24.** Armed forces loyal to ousted President Nabiev of Tajikistan overthrew the acting coalition government of Islamic and democratic groups. **26.** Tajik government forces defeated forces loyal to former President Nabiev and forced them out of Dushanbe. **29.** President Yeltsin suspended the withdrawal of Russian troops from the Baltic states because of alleged human rights violations against ethnic Russians in the republics.

NOVEMBER 1992

2. President Yeltsin imposed direct rule in the Russian republics of North Ossetia and Ingush after clashes between the two republics. **5.** A cease-fire came into effect in North Ossetia after fighting between Ingush and Ossetians had left 150 people dead. **19.** The acting President of Tajikistan, Akbarsho Iskandarov, was voted out of office by the parliament and replaced by Imamali Rakmanov. **20.** Fighting erupted in the southern Kurgan-Tyube region of Tajikistan between supporters of the former Communist government and the Islamic-democratic coalition.

DECEMBER 1992

3. Fighting broke out in the Russian Congress of People's Deputies between economic reformers and conservatives over constitutional changes to determine the balance of power between the president and the Congress. **9.** The Congress of People's Deputies rejected President Yeltsin's nomination of Yegor Gaidar as Prime Minister. **10.** Pro-Communist forces loyal to ex-President Nabiev seized control of Dushanbe after heavy fighting with Islamic-democratic coalition forces. **12.** President Yeltsin and the Congress chairman, Ruslan Khasbulatov, tried to end the growing constitutional crisis and suggested a referendum be held on a new constitution in April 1993. **14.** President Yeltsin was forced by the Congress to accept the conservative Viktor Chernomyrdin as Prime Minister. **19.** President Yeltsin returned early from a visit to China to prevent the sacking of economic reformers in the Russian cabinet by the conservative wing of the Congress. **23.** President Yeltsin and Prime Minister Chernomyrdin announced a new Russian cabinet that included most of the economic reformers from the previous government.

JANUARY 1993

4. The heads of state of the five Central Asian republics of the CIS held a summit in Tashkent and announced their intention to form a union of Central Asian people. **22.** At a summit of CIS leaders in Minsk, seven members signed a charter on closer co-operation but three members refused to sign. **26.** The Azerbaijani Prime Minister Ragim Guseinov resigned and was replaced by Ali Masimov.

FEBRUARY 1993

2. President Ter-Petrossian of Armenia dismissed Prime Minister Arutunyan for failing to implement economic reforms, and appointed Grant Bagratyan acting Prime Minister. **18.** Armenian forces captured five villages in the disputed Nagorno-Karabakh enclave in the continuing war with Azerbaijan. **21.** Government forces seized control of the Garm region in Tajikistan from Islamic rebels. **23.** Thousands of Communists and right-wing nationalists marched through central Moscow to protest against President Yeltsin's reformist government.

MARCH 1993

10. An emergency session of the Russian Congress of People's Deputies convened to resolve the power struggle between President Yeltsin and the legislature. **12.** President Yeltsin and his entire cabinet stormed out of the Russian Congress after deputies voted to restrict the government's powers. **16.** President Schevardnadze of Georgia claimed that

Russian troops and aircraft had supported Abkhazian separatists in an attack on Georgian government forces. **19.** Georgian forces shot down a Russian fighter aircraft believed to have been aiding Abkhazian separatists. **20.** President Yeltsin imposed emergency 'special rule' in Russia and called a referendum on the constitution for 25 April to resolve his continuing power struggle with the Congress. **23.** The Russian Constitutional Court declared President Yeltsin's imposition of 'special rule' illegal. **28.** In the Congress of People's Deputies a motion to impeach President Yeltsin failed to gain the necessary two-thirds majority.

APRIL 1993

4. Azerbaijani forces suffered a heavy defeat by Armenian forces and lost control of a large area of Azerbaijan. **13.** The trial of the leaders of the failed August 1991 coup against Soviet President Gorbachev began in Moscow. The UN began to airlift aid to Azeri refugees displaced by Armenian advances. **15.** The Turkish government announced that it had started to ship armaments to Azerbaijan to help it in the war against Armenia. **25.** President Yeltsin won the referendum on constitutional reform, with 58 per cent of voters supporting the President and 54 per cent supporting continued economic reform.

MAY 1993

1. Communists and nationalists fought with police in central Moscow as they were prevented from marching to Red Square. **10.** Kyrgyzstan left the rouble zone and introduced its own currency, the som. **18.** The trial of the leaders of the August 1991 coup was suspended indefinitely by the judges after the dismissal of the prosecuting team. **20.** The Ukrainian Prime Minister Leonid Kuchma resigned when parliament and President Kravchuk refused to extend his extraordinary powers to enable a faster pace of economic reform. **21.** The Ukrainian parliament refused to support an attempt by President Kravchuk to take over control of the government and reinstated Prime Minister Kuchma but without extraordinary powers.

JUNE 1993

5. President Yeltsin opened a constitutional assembly charged with amending and approving a draft constitution prepared by the Russian government. **7.** A rebellion by discontented sections of the army broke out in Azerbaijan, with rebels capturing the city of Gyandzha and calling for the President's and government's dismissal. **15.** The Ukraine's President Kravchuk acceded to demands for a referendum on his leadership and early parliamentary elections. The Azerbaijani parliament elected the former Communist leader Heidar Aliyev as its chairman and effective head of state to appease the military rebels. **16.** President Kravchuk took control of the Ukraine government and set up a special commission headed by the Prime Minister to stabilize the economy after the parliament had rejected strikers' demands for a referendum. **21.** President Kravchuk rescinded a decree which placed him in charge of the Ukrainian government. **22.** Military rebels led by Colonel Suret Guseinov entered the Azerbaijani capital Baku without resistance from government forces. **27.** The Azerbaijani military rebels pledged allegiance to acting President Heidar Aliyev and promised to withdraw from Baku. **30.** The military rebel leader Colonel Suret Guseinov was elected Prime Minister of Azerbaijan by the parliament.

JULY 1993

2. Abkhazian separatists shelled the city of Sukhumi held by Georgian government forces. The new Azerbaijani regime launched a counter-offensive to retake villages in Nagorno-Karabakh recently lost to Armenian forces. **6.** President Shevardnadze of Georgia imposed martial law in Abkhazia. **12.** The Russian constitutional assembly approved the draft constitution. **14.** Tajik rebels based in Afghanistan, supported by Afghan mujahidin, launched a raid into Tajikistan; they were resisted by Tajik government and Russian troops. **16.** Georgian government forces launched an offensive against Abkhazian separatists after they had rejected an ultimatum to retreat from two villages. Ethnic Russians in the Estonian cities of Narva and Sillamäe voted in referendums for autonomy for their local regions. **21.** Tajik rebels in Afghanistan shelled military posts on the Tajik-Afghan border. **28.** Russian and Tajik government forces destroyed a force of Tajik rebels and mujahidin crossing into Tajikistan from Afghanistan.

AUGUST 1993

5. The Moldovan parliament failed to ratify the state's membership of the CIS. **6.** The Georgian government resigned amid economic chaos and the parliament asked President Shevardnadze to form a government. **15.** Georgian government forces and Abkhazian separatists began disengaging their forces around the Abkhazian capital of Sukhumi under the terms of a Russian-sponsored peace plan. **23.** Armenian forces captured the Azerbaijani town of Fizuli.

THE FORMER YUGOSLAVIA

SEPTEMBER 1992

3. The permanent conference on Yugoslavia, agreed upon at the London conference in August, opened in Geneva, co-chaired by Lord Owen for the EC and Cyrus Vance for the UN. **4.** A UN aid convoy reached Goradze, Bosnia. The parliament of the unrecognized Yugoslav federation voted to accept the London peace agreement. **15.** Bosnian Serb forces launched an attack on Sarajevo in an attempt to cut off Muslim forces. **20.** The UN Security Council voted to deny the new Yugoslav federation of Serbia and Montenegro former Yugoslavia's seat at the UN.

OCTOBER 1992

6. The UN Security Council voted unanimously to prepare evidence for the trial of war crimes in the former Yugoslavia. **9.** The UN Security Council voted unanimously to ban all military flights over Bosnia-Hercegovina. **21.** Fighting broke out around the Bosnian town of Vitez between Croats and Muslims, previously allies, over Croatian attempts to form a breakaway state. **27.** The UN and EC peace negotiators Cyrus Vance and Lord Owen proposed a new constitution for Bosnia-Hercegovina with a central government and ten autonomous regions. **28.** The Bosnian town of Jajce was captured by Serb forces.

NOVEMBER 1992

2. The Bosnian Serb delegation withdrew from the Geneva peace talks and rejected proposals for dividing Bosnia-Hercegovina into autonomous provinces. **11.** The main British contingent of the UN protection force arrived in Split, Croatia. **16.** The UN Security Council voted to tighten economic sanctions against the Yugoslav federation. **19.** British troops escorted relief supplies to the besieged Bosnian town of Tuzla. **29.** A UN relief convoy reached the besieged Muslim-held town of Srebrenica in Bosnia, the first aid since May.

DECEMBER 1992

6. In Slovenia, Milan Kucan was re-elected president, and the ruling Liberal Democratic Party was returned to power in the general election. **8.** Bosnian Serb forces took control of the road from Sarajevo to its airport. **11.** The UN Security Council ordered peace-keeping troops to Macedonia to set up checkpoints on the borders with Albania and Kosovo to prevent the spread of fighting. **20.** Slobodan Milosevic was re-elected president of Serbia in a general election that was deemed flawed and unfair by international observers. **29.** The parliament of the Yugoslav federation passed a vote of no confidence in Prime Minister Milan Panic and voted him out of office. **31.** The UN Secretary-General was booed by residents when he visited Sarajevo.

JANUARY 1993

2. The UN-EC conference on the former Yugoslavia reopened in Geneva with the presentation by co-chairmen Cyrus Vance and Lord Owen of plans (the Vance-Owen peace plan) for Bosnia-Hercegovina to become a federal republic of ten autonomous regions. **4.** The Vance-Owen peace plan was accepted by the Bosnian Croats and partially accepted by the Muslims. **13.** A British soldier, L/Cpl Wayne Edwards, was killed in crossfire between Croat and Muslim forces in Gornji Vakuf. **18.** Fighting began between Muslim and Croat forces in Gornji Vakuf after Croat leaders in the area ordered Muslim forces to put themselves under Croat rather than Bosnian government control. **22.** Fighting began again in Croatia after a year's peace as Croatian troops attacked the Serb-held area of Krajina, Croatia, to gain control of a strategic bridge. **23.** Serbs in Krajina raided UN depots to obtain artillery and other weapons to fight the Croatian offensive. **25.** Croat forces in Krajina won control of the strategic bridge of Maslenica and the airport at Zemunik, reopening transport and communications links with the Dalmatian coast. **30.** Talks in Geneva ended without agreement by the Bosnian Muslims and Bosnian Serbs to the Vance-Owen peace plan.

FEBRUARY 1993

9. Cyrus Vance and Lord Owen presented their peace plan to the UN Security Council. **11.** The Bosnian government announced that no more aid would be allowed into Sarajevo until aid also reached starving Muslims in eastern Bosnia. **16.** Bosnian Muslim forces lost control of Kamenica to Bosnian Serb forces. **19.** The UN Security Council approved a resolution putting the entire UN operation in the former Yugoslavia under chapter seven of the UN Charter, which allows the use of force to ensure compliance with UN resolutions. **21.** A UN aid convoy reached the besieged Muslim-held town of Zepa in Bosnia after being held up by Serb forces for seven days. **28.** US transport aircraft dropped food and medicines by parachute to besieged Muslim enclaves in eastern Bosnia.

MARCH 1993

2. Cerska was captured by Bosnian Serb forces. **3.** The Bosnian Muslim government agreed to the military accord to end hostilities, part of the Vance-Owen plan. **5.** Bosnian Serb forces opened two routes from Cerska and Kamenica to Muslim-held Tuzla to allow Muslim refugees to flee. **12.** General Philippe Morillon, the UN commander, was prevented from leaving Srebrenica by women and children who wanted the UN to send aid and armed personnel to the enclave. The first war crimes trial opened in Sarajevo; two Bosnian Serb soldiers stood trial for murder, rape and looting, and on 30 March they were sentenced to death after being found guilty. **19.** A UN aid convoy led by General Morillon reached Srebrenica. **25.** Bosnian Muslim President Izetbegovic signed the Vance-Owen peace plan, which left the Bosnian Serbs the only group not to sign. **29.** A UN convoy which had delivered aid to Srebrenica returned to Tuzla crammed with refugees.

APRIL 1993

2. The Bosnian Serbs rejected the territorial proposals of the Vance-Owen peace plan. **4–6.** Muslim soldiers in Srebrenica prevented UN lorries from evacuating people trapped in the enclave. **6.** Croatian and Serb forces signed a cease-fire which ended fighting in Krajina. **16.** Fighting broke out between Muslim and Croat forces in central Bosnia which closed aid convoy routes. **18.** Muslim defenders and Serb besiegers of Srebrenica agreed to allow the evacuation of civilians, and the sick and wounded, and the establishment of

a UN 'safe area'. Fighting between Muslims and Croats spread in central Bosnia as Croat forces ordered Muslim forces in areas designated as Croat under the Vance-Owen plan to submit to Croat control. **27.** Croatian Serb forces attacked the Bosnian Muslim enclave of Bihac.

MAY 1993

1. Thorvald Stoltenberg of Norway replaced Cyrus Vance as the UN peace negotiator. A peace conference on Bosnia-Hercegovina opened in Athens attended by the leaders of Bosnia's Muslims, Croats and Serbs, the presidents of the Yugoslav federation, Serbia, Montenegro and Croatia, and the UN and EC peace negotiators. **2.** The Bosnian Serb leader Radovan Karadzic signed the UN-EC peace plan, conditional on ratification by the Bosnian Serb parliament. **4.** Bosnian Serb forces attacked Zepa. **5.** The Bosnian Serb parliament effectively rejected the UN-EC peace plan by attaching unacceptable conditions. **6.** The UN Security Council declared Sarajevo, Tuzla, Zepa, Goradze, Bihac and Srebrenica to be UN safe areas. **9.** Fighting broke out in Mostar between Muslim and Croat forces. **15.** Bosnian Serbs rejected the UN-EC peace plan in a referendum. **22.** The USA, EC and Russia agreed to defend UN safe areas and enforce tougher sanctions, signalling their awareness that the Vance-Owen plan was defunct. **30.** Bosnian Serb forces attacked Goradze and Sarajevo. **31.** The Yugoslav federation President Dobrica Cosic was ousted by no-confidence votes in both houses of the federal parliament.

JUNE 1993

7. Muslim forces captured Travnik from Bosnian Croats. **11.** British soldiers protecting an aid convoy shot dead two Bosnian Croats who opened fire on the convoy. **16.** Muslim forces took control of Kakanj from Bosnian Croats. **23.** Peace talks on Bosnia-Hercegovina opened in Geneva on a Serb and Croat plan to partition the state according to military gains. **27.** Fighting broke out around Maglaj as Muslim and Croat forces ended their local alliance against Serb forces and fought each other.

JULY 1993

2. An alliance of Bosnian Serb and Croat forces captured Zepce from Muslim forces. **9.** Bosnian President Izetbegovic rejected the Serb-Croat partition plan. **15.** Croatian Serbs launched attacks on the Croatian towns of Osijek, Rijeka and Karlovac after Croatia decided to reopen the Maslenica Bridge. **16.** Bosnian Muslim forces captured Fojnica from Croat forces. **19.** Fighting broke out between Bosnian Serbs and Muslims for control of Mount Igman, overlooking Sarajevo. **26.** Muslim forces captured Bugojno from Bosnian Croat forces. **27.** Peace negotiations on Bosnia-Hercegovina reopened in Geneva between the presidents of Serbia, Montenegro, Croatia and Bosnia-Hercegovina, and the Bosnian Croat and Serb leaders; a preliminary agreement was reached on 30 July.

AUGUST 1993

1. Serb forces in Krajina shelled the Maslenica bridge after Croat forces refused to hand control of the area to UN troops. **2.** Muslim forces captured Gornji Vakuf from Bosnian Croat forces. **4.** Bosnian Serb forces captured most of Mount Igman, near Sarajevo. **10.** Bosnian Serb forces partially withdrew and handed over parts of Mount Igman and Mount Bjelasnica to UN forces, but later retook control of the mountains. **15.** UN troops replaced Bosnian Serb forces as they withdrew from Mount Igman and Mount Bjelasnica. Wounded Bosnian Muslims were flown out of Sarajevo for treatment in Britain and Sweden. **20.** New constitutional arrangements and territorial divisions for Bosnia-Hercegovina were presented by Lord Owen and Thorvald Stoltenberg to the Bosnian Muslim, Serb and Croat leaders in Geneva. **21.** A UN relief convoy arrived at the besieged Muslim-held eastern part of Mostar, the first for three months. **24.** US aircraft dropped relief supplies to eastern Mostar after Bosnian Croat forces refused to allow through any more UN convoys. **25.** A UN aid convoy was allowed into the Muslim part of Mostar after it had distributed aid to Croat areas of the city. **26.** The UN aid convoy was prevented from leaving Mostar by Muslims, to stop further Croat bombardments. **28.** The Bosnian Muslim and Bosnian Croat parliaments accepted the Geneva peace plan, conditional on changes to the territorial divisions and constitutional principles; the Bosnian Serb parliament accepted the plan. **31.** The Bosnian government and Bosnian Serb leaders announced a provisional agreement on ending hostilities and exchanging prisoners. UN personnel trapped in Mostar were allowed to leave.

EUROPEAN COMMUNITY

SEPTEMBER 1992

2. The European Commission conceded that the United Kingdom could retain passport controls after 1 January 1993. **13.** The currencies of the European monetary system (EMS) were realigned, the lira being devalued by 3.5 per cent and all other currencies being revalued by 3.5 per cent. **17.** After intense currency speculation, the British and Italian governments were forced to withdraw the pound and the lira respectively from the exchange rate mechanism (ERM) of the EMS and the Spanish peseta was devalued by 5 per cent. **20.** In a referendum, the French electorate voted by 51 per cent to 49 per cent in favour of ratifying the Maastricht Treaty. **23.** Amid continued currency speculation, France and Germany spent billions of pounds defending the French franc, while Spain reintroduced capital controls.

OCTOBER 1992

1. The Italian government announced that it was asking the EC for an £8 billion loan to enable the lira

to return to the ERM. **16.** An EC heads of government summit meeting was held in Birmingham and agreed on a declaration emphasizing their commitment to 'subsidiarity' (minimum interference in national life). **28.** The Danish government announced the changes to the Maastricht Treaty that they considered necessary before a second referendum on ratification could be held; these included protocols enabling Denmark to opt out of a common currency, a common defence policy and common EC citizenship. **29.** The Italian House of Deputies voted by 403 to 46 to ratify the Maastricht Treaty, confirming the Senate's vote in favour.

NOVEMBER 1992

4. The Belgian Senate voted by 115 to 26 to ratify the Maastricht Treaty, confirming an earlier vote in the Chamber of Deputies. **5.** The EC Agriculture Commissioner, Ray MacSharry, resigned from his position as negotiator in the GATT talks, accusing the European Commission President Jacques Delors of sabotaging a GATT agreement. **9.** France's attempt to retaliate against increased US agricultural tariffs was outvoted in the EC Council of Ministers, and the Council ordered the Commission to accelerate negotiation of a GATT agreement. **10.** Ray MacSharry was reinstated as the chief EC GATT negotiator after President Delors agreed to the reopening of GATT negotiations with the USA. **18.** The European Commission announced that plans to abolish all passport and immigration controls within the EC by 1 January 1993 had been delayed by at least one year. **19.** The Norwegian parliament voted to apply for EC membership. **22.** After currency speculation, the Spanish peseta and Portuguese escudo were devalued by 5 per cent within the ERM. **25.** The French National Assembly voted by 301 to 251 to declare unacceptable the GATT agreement reached with the USA over agriculture; farmers demonstrated and fought street battles with police in Paris. The upper house of the Cortes voted by 222 to 0 to ratify the Maastricht Treaty, completing Spain's ratification.

DECEMBER 1992

1. In Strasbourg 50,000 French farmers protesting at the GATT agreement on agriculture clashed with police. **10.** Portugal's Assembly voted by 200 to 21 to ratify the Maastricht Treaty. **11.** A two-day summit meeting opened in Edinburgh (*see below*). **15.** The Netherlands States-General voted to ratify the Maastricht Treaty. **18.** The German Bundesrat voted to ratify the Maastricht Treaty; in an earlier vote, the Bundestag had ratified the treaty but reserved its right to vote again on a single currency at the time of implementation.

THE EDINBURGH AGREEMENT

– Denmark to be allowed to opt out of the single currency, of a common defence policy, of European

citizenship, and of the new immigration, asylum and policing pillar of the Community
- no deadlines for ratification of the Maastricht Treaty by Denmark or the UK
- the EC budget to rise in phases, from 1.2 per cent of Community GDP in 1992 to 1.27 per cent in 1999. The UK's budget rebate to remain unchanged
- a co-ordinated strategy for economic growth to be adopted
- Strasbourg confirmed as the site of plenary sessions of the European Parliament. From 1994 the Parliament will expand from 518 to 567 members
- decision on siting the new European Central Bank delayed for six months
- enlargement negotiations to begin with Austria, Sweden, Finland and Norway in 1993
- agreement on subsidiarity; decision-making to occur at the appropriate national, regional or local level
- the single market declared to be an irreversible achievement, complete in all essential respects

JANUARY 1993

1. The Single European Market came into being. **30.** The Irish government devalued the punt by 10 per cent against other currencies in the ERM after intense currency speculation.

FEBRUARY 1993

1. The European Community formally opened membership negotiations with Austria, Finland and Norway. **15.** EC finance ministers agreed that, because of the economic recession, the date by which member countries should meet the Maastricht convergence criteria for economic and monetary union should be delayed to the end of 1996.

MARCH 1993

17. Officials from the twelve EC states signed a protocol to enable the European Economic Area Agreement between the EC and six of the seven EFTA states to come into force before the end of 1993. **30.** The European Community came under suspicion of mass agricultural fraud when a senior agriculture official who was under investigation for corruption committed suicide.

APRIL 1993

29. The new French government announced that it would not ratify the agreement to abolish border controls because no effective measures were being introduced against drug trafficking.

MAY 1993

13. The Spanish and Portuguese governments were forced to devalue the peseta and escudo by 8 per cent and 6½ per cent respectively after currency speculation. **18.** In a referendum the Danish electorate voted by 57 per cent to 43 per cent to ratify the Maastricht Treaty, subject to the opt-outs agreed at the Edinburgh summit.

JUNE 1993

8. The French government ended its threat to veto an EC-US agreement on trade in oilseed reached in November 1992. **11.** The German government admitted that, contrary to the Treaty of Rome, it had signed a trade agreement with the USA whereby German telecommunications firms would not face the US sanctions faced by other EC firms. **30.** EC members apart from the UK, Denmark and Ireland agreed to abolish border controls between the nine states from December 1993.

JULY 1993

1. The German constitutional court began hearing a series of appeals claiming that ratifying the Maastricht Treaty would be constitutionally illegal. **30.** European Community central banks spent an estimated £31 billion in an attempt to defend the ERM from the worst currency speculation in its history.

AUGUST 1993

1. An emergency meeting of EC finance ministers agreed to allow six of the remaining ERM currencies to fluctuate within margins of 15 per cent above or below the central rate in an attempt to protect the ERM from currency speculation. (The Deutsche Mark and Dutch Guilder remained with 2.25 per cent margins.) **2.** The United Kingdom ratified the Maastricht Treaty.

THE MIDDLE EAST

SEPTEMBER 1992

1. The Russian government announced that it would send two warships to the Gulf as a contribution to the international effort to tighten sanctions against Iraq. **2.** The leader of the UN weapons inspectorate team in Iraq stated that the Iraqi nuclear arms programme had been totally dismantled and destroyed. A Briton, Michael Wainwright, was gaoled for ten years in Iraq for illegally entering the country during a cycling trip. **10.** The Israeli Prime Minister Yitzhak Rabin said that Israel was ready to exchange part of the Golan Heights for a peace agreement with Syria. **24.** Leaders of 17 Iraqi opposition groups met in the Kurdish enclave in northern Iraq to seek agreement on forming a democratic government and overthrowing President Saddam Hussein. **29.** Fighting on the Iraqi border left 27 Turkish soldiers and 174 Kurdish guerrillas dead.

OCTOBER 1992

2. The UN Security Council voted to seize Iraqi assets in foreign banks and to use the money to provide compensation for Gulf War victims, to fund relief operations in Iraq and to finance the destruction of Iraqi weapons of mass destruction. **6.** Candidates from a coalition of opposition groups won a majority of the 50 seats in parliamentary elections in Kuwait. **8.** The Israeli government made procedural concessions for future rounds of the Middle East peace talks, lifting its boycott on two multinational sections of the talks and accepting the participation of Palestinians from outside the Occupied Territories. **22.** President Hrawi of Lebanon appointed Rafic Hariri Prime Minister. The UN and Iraq signed an accord enabling Iraq to sell oil, the proceeds from which will be used for a relief programme. **23.** Turkish commandos entered northern Iraq in an attempt to destroy Kurdish guerrilla units.

NOVEMBER 1992

9. The seventh round of the Middle East peace negotiations began in Washington. **10.** Israeli defence forces and Hizbollah guerrillas exchanged rocket and artillery fire in southern Lebanon.

DECEMBER 1992

7. Members of Hamas, a Palestinian Islamic movement, shot dead three Israeli soldiers in the Gaza Strip on the fifth anniversary of the beginning of the *intifada*. **15.** The body of an Israeli police sergeant was found by a roadside near Jerusalem two days after he was kidnapped by Hamas. **17.** Arab delegates boycotted the Middle East peace talks in Washington in response to the deportation from Israel to southern Lebanon of 418 alleged Hamas members. **18.** The Palestinian deportees in southern Lebanon were attacked by the pro-Israeli South Lebanese Army as they tried to return to the Occupied Territories. **27.** US aircraft patrolling the air exclusion zone over southern Iraq shot down an Iraqi MiG fighter.

JANUARY 1993

6. The USA, Britain and France told the Iraqi government to remove the anti-aircraft missile batteries stationed in the air exclusion zone in southern Iraq or they would be destroyed. **8.** Iraq removed its anti-aircraft missile batteries from the air exclusion zone, and then banned UN aircraft from flying in Iraq. **10.** Iraqi soldiers carried out a raid into Kuwait, seizing missiles and other military equipment. **11.** Iraqi soldiers carried out a second raid into Kuwait, dismantling prefabricated warehouses and removing them to Iraq. **13.** US, British and French aircraft attacked and destroyed Iraqi missile sites and radar installations in response to the Iraqi incursions along the border with Kuwait. **15.** US troops began to arrive in Kuwait to boost security along the frontier with Iraq. **17.** After continued Iraqi refusals to guarantee the safety of UN weapons inspectors' flights into Iraq, the US navy destroyed a suspected nuclear weapons plant with cruise missiles. **18.** US, British and French aircraft destroyed Iraqi missile sites and radar installations in southern and northern Iraq. **19.** The USA moved more naval forces and missiles to the Gulf and bombed anti-aircraft missiles in northern Iraq. The Israeli parliament voted to repeal the ban on Israeli citizens meeting PLO

officials. **21.** UN weapons inspection teams arrived in Iraq after the Iraqi government was forced to agree to their return. **23.** Seventeen of the Palestinians deported to southern Lebanon were flown back to Israel by RAF helicopters; they were either seriously ill or had been mistakenly identified as Hamas members.

FEBRUARY 1993

5. The UN Security Council voted to send to the Iraq–Kuwait frontier peace-keeping soldiers permitted to use force to repel incursions. **13.** The UN Security Council accepted the Israeli offer to repatriate 101 of the 415 alleged Hamas members deported to Lebanon, and ended its threat to impose UN trade sanctions on Israel. **26.** Palestinian delegates to the Middle East peace talks rejected attempts to restart negotiations until Israel allowed the 415 Palestinian deportees in Lebanon to return home.

MARCH 1993

10. Thirteen Islamic extremists were killed and 15 injured by Egyptian police in gun fights in Cairo and Aswan. The Palestinian delegation to the Middle East peace talks again refused to attend the next round of talks until Israel allowed the 415 Palestinian deportees in Lebanon to return home. **24.** The Knesset elected Ezer Weizman President of Israel.

APRIL 1993

9. US aircraft bombed Iraqi anti-aircraft artillery in the northern air exclusion zone after coming under fire. **16.** The Palestinian deportees in southern Lebanon were shelled by Israeli artillery as they tried to march to the Israeli border. **26.** The Palestinian deportees in southern Lebanon were again shelled by Israeli artillery as they protested at the resumption of peace talks. **27.** The ninth round of peace talks opened in Washington, attended by Arab states and PLO delegates. **30.** The first of 30 Palestinians deported by Israel between 1967 and 1987 were allowed to return to the West Bank.

MAY 1993

10. The Palestinian negotiators withdrew from the Middle East peace talks in Washington in protest at Israel reneging on promises to accept the return of deportees from southern Lebanon and to respect human rights in the Occupied Territories. **13.** The UN announced the withdrawal of its armed guards for aid convoys in Kurdish areas of northern Iraq as it had no funds to maintain them there. **14.** The ninth round of Middle East peace talks ended in Washington without progress. **25.** The Iranian Air Force attacked bases of the Iranian opposition inside Iraq in retaliation for attacks on Revolutionary Guards units in Iran. **27.** An Egyptian military court sentenced six Muslim extremists to death for terrorist bombings.

JUNE 1993

11. President Rafsanjani of Iran was re-elected for a second four-year term. **26.** The USA destroyed the headquarters of the Iraqi intelligence service in Baghdad in retaliation for an Iraqi plot to kill ex-President Bush when he visited Kuwait in April.

JULY 1993

8. Seven Muslim fundamentalists were hanged in Cairo after being found guilty of attacks on tourist buses and Nile cruise ships. **11.** A UN weapons team left Iraq after an unsuccessful attempt to close two missile-testing sites. Two days of fighting in southern Lebanon between Israeli forces and Hezbollah guerrillas left five Israeli soldiers dead. **19.** The Iraqi government accepted UN demands for cameras and monitoring equipment to be installed at two missile-testing ranges. **25.** Israel launched air, sea and land attacks on Hezbollah and Palestinian bases in southern Lebanon after repeated Hezbollah artillery and rocket attacks on northern Israel. **31.** The Israeli defence forces ended a seven-day bombardment of southern Lebanon which killed 130 people.

AUGUST 1993

15. The Palestinian deportees banished in southern Lebanon agreed to Israel's proposal that they return in stages by December. **18.** The Egyptian Interior Minister Hassan al-Alfi was seriously injured in a bomb attack by Muslim fundamentalists. **19.** Nine Israeli soldiers were killed by Hezbollah bomb attacks in southern Lebanon, which led to Israel bombing Hezbollah bases. Iraqi forces fired at US aircraft patrolling the northern air exclusion zone; in retaliation US aircraft destroyed missile sites and radar installations. **30.** The Israeli cabinet voted in favour of an agreement with the PLO which would grant Palestinians self-government in the Gaza Strip and Jericho.

INTERNATIONAL RELATIONS

SEPTEMBER 1992

11. El Salvador and Honduras agreed to abide by an International Court of Justice decision ending a border dispute. **14.** The Russian government announced that the Soviet Union and later Russia had been producing bacteriological weapons until March 1992 in violation of a 1972 Treaty. **15.** China announced that it would boycott multilateral talks on Middle East arms control because of US plans to sell military aircraft to Taiwan.

OCTOBER 1992

2. The NATO Rapid Reaction Corps, based in Bielefeld, Germany, came into operation. **19.** President Yeltsin of Russia signed a decree extending Russia's nuclear arms test moratorium to July 1993.

22. Talks between the EC and the USA about the failed GATT negotiations broke down because of the French refusal to reduce agricultural subsidies to the level requested by the USA. **29.** The head of the UN mission in Somalia, Muhammed Sahnuon, resigned after criticizing the UN's slow response to the war and starvation in the country.

NOVEMBER 1992

4. The US government made an official request to the GATT governing council to place tariffs on $1 billion of EC goods after the collapse of the Uruguay round of GATT talks. **9.** Britain and Russia signed a friendship treaty, the first since 1766, and several other agreements. **20.** US and EC negotiators reached agreement on agricultural subsidies, paving the way for a GATT agreement. Greece joined the Western European Union as a full member, with Turkey, Norway and Iceland becoming associate members and Denmark and the Irish Republic observers.

JANUARY 1993

3. In Moscow President Bush and President Yeltsin signed the START 2 treaty which reduces US and Russian strategic nuclear weapons by 72 per cent. **12.** Representatives of 120 countries gathered in Paris to sign the Chemical Weapons Convention 1993, which bans the storage, production and use of chemical weapons. **19.** The Czech Republic and the Slovak Republic were admitted to membership of the UN as two independent states.

FEBRUARY 1993

16. OPEC oil ministers agreed to cut crude oil production by 1.4 million barrels per day to 23.6 million barrels per day in an attempt to increase prices.

MARCH 1993

1. An internal UN report stated that the organization was rife with corruption, waste, bureaucratic patronage and overmanning. **12.** North Korea renounced its accession to the Nuclear Non-Proliferation Treaty after refusing to allow the International Atomic Energy Authority to inspect sites in the country for possible nuclear weapons production. The US trade representative Mickey Kantor announced the unilateral ending of US–EC trade negotiations because of EC public procurement policies. **22.** Bosnia-Hercegovina brought cases of genocide and war crimes against Serbia and Montenegro in the International Court of Justice at The Hague. **31.** Greece blocked an attempt by the former Yugoslav republic of Macedonia to join the UN, disputing the republic's proposed name and flag.

APRIL 1993

1. The IAEA declared North Korea to be in violation of an agreement on safeguarding nuclear materials and referred the issue to the UN. **2.** Nineteen western states announced a rescheduling of Russia's £52 billion foreign debt. **8.** The International Court of Justice ruled that the rump Yugoslav state should stop committing genocide in Bosnia-Hercegovina. The UN General Assembly voted to accept Macedonia as a UN member under the compromise name of 'The Former Yugoslav Republic of Macedonia'. **15.** The G7 group of industrialized nations announced a $43.4 billion aid package for Russia.

MAY 1993

5. The director-general of the World Health Organization, Dr Hiroshi Nakajima, was re-elected for a second term despite western opposition and claims of financial irregularities. **13.** Japan threatened to leave the International Whaling Commission after its members voted to reject a lifting of the commercial whaling moratorium. **28.** Monaco and Eritrea joined the UN.

JUNE 1993

11. North Korea announced that it would remain a party to the Nuclear Non-Proliferation Treaty. **25.** Jacques Attali, the president of the European Bank for Reconstruction and Development, resigned after criticism of spending on the Bank's headquarters, which was twice the amount that the Bank had lent to Eastern Europe.

JULY 1993

1. The former European Community commissioner Peter Sutherland replaced Arthur Dunkel as director-general of the GATT. **6.** The Japanese government officially requested a permanent seat on the UN Security Council. **9.** The G7 Tokyo summit ended with agreement on market access for certain categories of trade in the GATT negotiations, a $3 billion aid package for Russia, and a US–Japanese trade accord. **19.** North Korea agreed to negotiate with the IAEA on international supervision of suspected nuclear weapons installations. **29.** A former Pakistani army chief, General Aslam Beg, confirmed that Pakistan had acquired the ability to construct nuclear weapons in 1987.

AUGUST 1993

18. The USA notified the Sudanese government that the Sudan was being placed on a list of countries sponsoring international terrorism and banned all US trade with the country. **25.** The USA imposed trade sanctions on China and Pakistan because of Chinese exports of missile parts to Pakistan in contradiction of the Missile Technology Control Regime.

Obituaries

Ademola, Rt. Hon. Sir Adetokunbo, KBE, Chief Justice of Nigeria 1958–72, aged 86 – 29 January 1993

Adley, Robert, MP, Conservative MP for Bristol North East 1970–4 and for Christchurch since 1974, aged 58 – 13 May 1993

Airey of Abingdon, Baroness, aged 73 – 27 November 1992

al-Alami, Saad al-Din, Mufti of Jerusalem since 1953, aged 82 – 6 February 1993

Allison, Rt. Revd Falkner, Bishop of Chelmsford 1951–61, Bishop of Winchester 1961–74, aged 86 – 31 May 1993

Amherst, 5th Earl, MC, soldier, journalist and airline executive, aged 96 – 4 March 1993

Andrews, Dana, American film actor, aged 83 – 17 December 1992

Argyll, Margaret, Duchess of, socialite, aged 80 – 25 July 1993

Ashby, Lord, D.SC., FRS, botanist and academic administrator, aged 88 – 22 October 1992

Ashe, Arthur, American tennis player and 1975 Wimbledon champion, aged 49 – 6 February 1993

Bacon, Baroness (Alice), CBE, PC, Labour MP for Leeds North East 1945–55 and for Leeds South East 1955–70, aged 83 – 24 March 1993

Bangor, 7th Viscount (Edward Ward), journalist, broadcaster and writer, aged 87 – 8 May 1993

Barcelona, Don Juan de Borbon y Battenberg, Count of, aged 79 – 1 April 1993

Barnett, Charles, cricketer, aged 82 – 28 May 1993

Barnett, Air Chief Marshal Sir Denis, GCB, CBE, DFC, air commander in the Suez campaign 1956, aged 86 – 31 December 1992

Baudouin, King of the Belgians since 1951, aged 62 – 31 July 1993

Benson, Ivy, bandleader of the All Girls Band, aged 79 – 6 May 1993

Bérégovoy, Pierre, prime minister of France April 1992 to March 1993, aged 67 – committed suicide 1 May 1993

Berkeley, Baroness (17th in line), aged 87 – 17 October 1992

Bernstein, Lord (Sidney), founder of Granada Television and the Granada Group, aged 94 – 5 February 1993

Box, Donald, Conservative MP for Cardiff North 1959–66, aged 75 – 12 July 1993

Boyle, Marshal of the RAF Sir Dermot, GCB, KCVO, KBE, AFC, aged 88 – 5 May 1993

Braden, Bernard, Canadian-born actor and broadcaster, aged 76 – 2 February 1993

Brandt, Willi, mayor of West Berlin 1957–66, chancellor of West Germany 1969–74, aged 78 – 8 October 1992

Bresslaw, Bernard, comic actor, aged 59 – 11 June 1993

Browne, George, archbishop of the Province of West Africa since 1982, aged 59 – 14 February 1993

Bruntisfield, 1st Baron, MC, aged 93 – 14 January 1993

Bullard, Tony, British UN worker in Afghanistan, aged 35 – killed 1 February 1993

Bunce, Cyril, Labour MP for Dunbartonshire East 1951–70, aged 89 – 7 September 1992

Burnham, 5th Baron, soldier and amateur sailor, aged 72 – 18 June 1993

Burton, Richard, VC, aged 70 – 11 July 1993

Bute, 6th Marquess, KBE, landowner, charity executive, Lord Lieutenant of Argyll and Bute since 1990, aged 60 – 21 July 1993

Cahn, Sammy, songwriter, aged 79 – 15 January 1993

Carey, Joyce, OBE, actress, aged 94 – 28 February 1993

Carrick, 9th Earl, aged 61 – 5 October 1992

Cawdor, 6th Earl, aged 60 – 20 June 1993

Chaplin, Judith, OBE, MP, Conservative MP for Newbury since 1992, aged 53 – 19 February 1993

Charteris, Leslie, writer, creator of *The Saint*, aged 85 – 15 April 1993

Chirwa, Orton, Malawian barrister, politician and political prisoner, in prison, aged 73 – 20 October 1992

Christoff, Boris, Bulgarian-born opera singer, aged 79 – 28 June 1993

Clark Hutchinson, Michael, Conservative MP for Edinburgh South 1957–79, aged 79 – 21 March 1993

Cobham, Cdr Anthony, GC, aged 83 – 14 May 1993

Copperwheat, Lt.-Cdr Dennis, GC, aged 78 – 8 September 1992

Cotton, Henry, Lord Lieutenant of Merseyside since 1989 and Chancellor of Liverpool John Moores University since 1992, aged 64 – 3 August 1993

Cowley, Lt.-Gen. Sir John, GC, KBE, CB, aged 87 – 7 January 1993

Craigton, Lord, CBE, PC, Conservative MP 1950–9 and minister of state, Scottish Office 1959–64, aged 88 – 28 July 1993

Craven, Danie, South African rugby administrator, aged 82 – 4 January 1993

Croker, Ted, secretary of the Football Association 1973–89, aged 68 – 25 December 1992

Dawson, Les, comedian, aged 60 – 10 June 1993

de Ramsey, 3rd Baron, KBE, TD, aged 83 – 31 March 1993

Decies, 6th Baron, aged 77 – November 1992

Devereux, Sean, Irish UNICEF official in Somalia, aged 28 – murdered 2 January 1993

Dickens, Monica, MBE, author, aged 77 – 25 December 1992

Douglas Home, William, playwright and author, aged 80 – 28 September 1992

Dowding, 2nd Baron, aged 73 – 22 November 1992

Dubcek, Alexander, first secretary of the Czechoslovak Communist Party during the 1968 Prague Spring reform movement and subsequent Soviet invasion, aged 70 – 7 November 1992

Dunleath, 4th Baron, TD, aged 59 – 9 January 1993

Eastham, Sir Michael, High Court judge (Family Division) since 1978, aged 72 – 4 March 1993

Eckstine, Billy, American singer and bandleader, aged 78 – 8 March 1993

Edmund-Davies, Lord, PC, Lord of Appeal in Ordinary 1974–81, aged 86 – 27 December 1992

Edwards, L/Cpl Wayne, British soldier killed in Bosnia, aged 26 – 13 January 1993

Eisler, Paul, engineer widely regarded as inventor of the printed circuit, aged 85 – 26 October 1992

Elliott, Denholm, CBE, actor, aged 70 – 6 October 1992

Elworthy, Marshal of the Royal Air Force Lord, KG, GCB, CBE, DSO, LVO, DFC, AFC, Chief of Defence Staff 1967–71, aged 82 – 4 April 1993

Evans, Sir Geraint, CBE, opera singer, aged 70 – 19 September 1992

Ewart-Biggs, Baroness, a Labour whip in the House of Lords, aged 63 – 7 October 1992

Fernyhough, The Rt. Hon. Ernest, Labour MP for Jarrow 1947–79, aged 84 – 16 August 1993

Fortescue, 7th Earl, aged 70 – 7 March 1993

Forteviot, 3rd Baron, MBE, aged 87 – 25 March 1993

Fowler, Gerald, Labour MP for the Wrekin 1966–70 and 1974–9, rector of the Polytechnic of East London 1982–92, aged 58 – 1 May 1993

Franks, Lord, OM, GCMG, KCB, KCVO, CBE, PC, FBA, civil servant, diplomat, banker and academic, aged 87 – 15 October 1992

Freyberg, 2nd Baron, OBE, MC, soldier, aged 69 – 26 May 1993

Frink, Dame Elisabeth, CH, DBE, RA, sculptor, aged 62 – 18 April 1993

Frost, Maj.-Gen. John, CB, DSO and Bar, MC, commander of 2nd Parachute Battalion at Arnhem 1944, aged 80 – 21 May 1993

Garrett, Ted, Labour MP for Wallsend 1964–92, aged 73 – 30 May 1993

Gillespie, Dizzy, jazz trumpeter, aged 75 – 6 January 1993

Gilliat, Lt.-Col. Sir Martin, GCVO, MBE, private secretary to the Queen Mother since 1956, aged 80 – 27 May 1993

Gilliatt, Penelope, writer, aged 61 – 9 May 1993

Gish, Lillian, American actress, aged 99 – 27 February 1993

Golding, Sir William, CBE, novelist and Nobel laureate, aged 81 – 19 June 1993

Gordon, Esmé, RSA, architect, aged 82 – 31 May 1993

Gormley, Lord (Joe), OBE, president of the National Union of Mineworkers 1971–82, aged 75 – 27 May 1993

Granard, 9th Earl, AFC, aviator and businessman, aged 77 – 19 November 1992

Granger, Stewart, actor, aged 80 – 16 August 1993

Grantham, Admiral Sir Guy, GCB, OBE, DSO, aged 92 – 8 September 1992

Gray, HE Cardinal Gordon, Roman Catholic Archbishop of St Andrews and Edinburgh 1951–85, aged 82 – 19 July 1993

Hani, Martin Thembisile (Chris), general secretary of the South African Communist Party and member of the ANC national executive committee, aged 50 – assassinated 10 April 1993

Hasluck, Rt. Hon. Sir Paul, KG, GCMG, GCVO, governor-general of Australia 1969–74, aged 87 – 9 January 1993

Hassett, Lindsay, MBE, Australian cricketer, aged 79 – 16 June 1993

Hatch of Lusby, Lord, Labour peer, aged 74 – 11 October 1992

Hayes, Helen, American stage and film actress, aged 92 – 17 March 1993

Hearst, William Randolph, jnr, American newspaper magnate and journalist, aged 85 – 14 May 1993

Hellyer, Arthur, MBE, FLS, horticulturist and writer, aged 90 – 28 January 1993

Henderson, Admiral Sir Nigel, GBE, KCB, aged 84 – 2 August 1993

Hepburn, Audrey, film actress and UNICEF ambassador, aged 63 – 20 January 1993

Hersey, John, American war correspondent and novelist, aged 78 – 24 March 1993

Hilder, Rowland, OBE, painter, aged 87 – 21 April 1993

Holley, Robert, American biochemist and winner of Nobel prize for medicine (1968) for unravelling the genetic code of RNA, aged 71 – 11 February 1993

Hughes, Charlotte, oldest person in Britain, aged 115 – 17 March 1993

Hughes, Mark, Labour MP for Durham 1970–83 and for the City of Durham 1983–7, aged 60 – 19 March 1993

Hunt, James, world Formula 1 motor racing champion 1976 and television commentator, aged 45 – 15 June 1993

Huxley, Anthony, botanist, horticulturist and author, aged 72 – 26 December 1992

Idris, Shawish Taha, GC, aged 93 – 31 May 1993

Jacob, Lt.-Gen. Sir Ian, GBE, CB, military assistant secretary to the War Cabinet 1939–46, director-general of the BBC 1952–60, aged 93 – 24 April 1993

Jobe, Tom, American dancer and choreographer, aged 39 – 8 December 1992

Johns, Mervyn, actor, aged 93 – 6 September 1992

Johnson, Marv, American soul singer, aged 54 – 16 May 1993

Joicey, 4th Baron, country landowner, aged 68 –
14 June 1993

Jones, Sir Edward, PC, Attorney-General for
Northern Ireland 1964–8 and Lord Justice of
Appeal in Northern Ireland 1973–84, aged 80 –
18 March 1993

Joseph, Helen, campaigner against apartheid in
South Africa, aged 87 – 25 December 1992

Kadoorie, Lord, CBE, Hong Kong businessman,
aged 94 – 25 August 1993

Keeler, Ruby, American dancer and actress,
aged 83 – 28 February 1993

Kelly, Petra, founding member and former leader of
German Green Party, aged 44 – found dead
12 October 1992

Kenyon, 5th Baron, CBE, chairman of the trustees of
the National Portrait Gallery 1966–88, aged 75 –
16 May 1993

Kroger, Helen, 1950s Soviet spy, aged 79 – late
December 1992

Kusch, Polykarp, American physicist and Nobel
laureate, aged 82 – 20 March 1993

Lamborghini, Ferruccio, founder of Lamborghini
car company, aged 76 – 20 February 1993

Langford-Holt, Sir John, Conservative MP for
Shrewsbury 1945–83, aged 77 – 23 July 1993

Leatherland, Lord, OBE, aged 94 – 18 December
1992

Litchfield, Captain John, OBE, RN, Conservative MP
for Chelsea 1959–66, aged 89 – 31 May 1993

Lloyd of Hampstead, Lord, QC, Ll.D., barrister and
professor of jurisprudence at London University
1956–82, aged 77 – 31 December 1992

Macclesfield, 8th Earl, aged 78 – 7 December 1992

McClintock, Barbara, American geneticist and
Nobel laureate, aged 90 – 2 September 1992

MacMillan, Sir Kenneth, choreographer, aged 62 –
29 October 1992

McNair-Wilson, Sir Michael, Conservative MP for
Walthamstow East 1969–74 and for Newbury
1974–92, aged 62 – 28 March 1993

Mankiewicz, Joseph, screenwriter and film director
and producer, aged 83 – 5 February 1993

Mann, Sunnie, wife of the former Beirut hostage,
Jackie Mann, aged 79 – 30 November 1992

Maskell, Dan, CBE, tennis champion, coach and
commentator, aged 84 – 10 December 1992

Massereene (13th) and Ferrard (6th), Viscount,
landowner, aged 78 – 27 December 1992

Mikardo, Ian, Labour MP for Reading 1945–50 and
1955–9, Reading South 1950–5, Poplar 1964–74,
Bethnal Green and Bow 1974–83, Bow and
Poplar 1983–7, and a former party chairman,
aged 84 – 6 May 1993

Mills, Nat, variety and radio star, aged 93 – 13
August 1993

Mills, Sir Peter, Conservative MP for Torridge
(renamed Devon West, then Torridge and West
Devon) 1964–87, aged 71 – 16 August 1993

Mnouchkine, Alexandre, French film producer,
aged 85 – 3 April 1993

Moore, Bobby, OBE, footballer, captain of England's
1966 World Cup winning team, aged 51 –
24 February 1993

Mott-Radclyffe, Sir Charles, Conservative MP for
Windsor 1942–70, aged 80 – 25 November 1992

Nolan, Sir Sydney, OM, AC, CBE, Australian painter,
aged 75 – November 1992

Norman, Leslie, film producer and director,
aged 81 – 18 February 1993

Norman, Sir Richard, KBE, FRS, chemist, Rector of
Exeter College, Oxford, since 1987, aged 61 –
6 June 1993

Nureyev, Rudolf, ballet dancer, aged 54 – 6 January
1993

Oort, Prof. Jan, Dutch astronomer, aged 92 –
November 1992

O'Reilly, Bill, Australian spin bowler, aged 86 –
5 October 1992

Ozal, Turgut, prime minister of Turkey 1983–9 and
president since 1989, aged 66 – 17 April 1993

Parkinson, Prof. C. Northcote, author, historian,
economist and originator of Parkinson's Law,
aged 83 – 9 March 1993

Pennock, Lord, industrialist, aged 72 – 23 February
1993

Perkins, Anthony, American film actor, aged 60 –
12 September 1992

Phomvihane, President Kaysone, prime minister of
Laos 1975–91, president since 1991 and leader of
the Laotian Communist Party since 1955,
aged 71 – 21 November 1992

Pizey, Admiral Sir Mark, GBE, CB, DSO, aged 93 – 17
May 1993

Plaidy, Jean (Eleanor Hibbert), who also wrote as
Victoria Holt, Philippa Carr, etc., novelist, aged
about 83 – 18 January 1993

Poole, 1st Baron, CBE, TD, PC, a former chairman of
the Conservative Party, aged 81 – 28 January
1993

Poulson, John, architect, imprisoned for bribery and
corruption in the 1970s, aged 82 – 31 January
1993

Powis, 7th Earl, aged 68 –13 August 1993

Premadasa, Ranasinghe, president of Sri Lanka
since 1989, aged 69 – assassinated 1 May 1993

Price, Prof. William, FRS, physicist and
spectroscopist, aged 83 – 10 March 1993

Pyke, Magnus, scientist and television presenter,
aged 83 – 19 October 1992

Railton, Brig. Dame Mary, DBE, director of
Women's Royal Army Corps 1954–7, aged 86 –
12 November 1992

Rice, Peter, structural engineer, aged 57 –
25 October 1992

Ridgway, General Matthew, commander of US 82nd
Division 1942–5, UN supreme commander in
Korea 1951–2, US Army chief of staff 1953–5,
aged 98 – 26 July 1993

Ridley of Liddesdale, Lord (Nicholas), PC,
Conservative politician and former minister,
aged 64 – 4 March 1993

Rimington, Claude, FRS, biochemist, aged 90 –
8 August 1993

Roach, Hal, American film producer, aged 100 –
2 November 1992

Robinson, Prof. Sir Austin, CMG, OBE, FBA,
economist, aged 95 – June 1993

Robinson, Cardew, actor and comedian, aged 75 –
27 December 1992

Rochdale, 1st Viscount, OBE, TD, textile magnate,
financier and industrialist, aged 86 – 24 May
1993

Rodgers, Sir John, Bt., Conservative MP for
Sevenoaks 1950–79, aged 86 – 29 March 1993

Rodney, 9th Baron, aged 72 –13 October 1992

Ross of Newport, Lord, Liberal MP for the Isle of
Wight 1974–87, aged 66 –10 May 1993

Rothenstein, Michael, artist and printmaker,
aged 85 – 6 July 1993

Rowallan, 3rd Baron, aged 73 – July 1993

Sauvé, Jeanne, governor-general of Canada 1984–
90, aged 70 – 26 January 1993

Shawn, William, editor of the *New Yorker* 1952–87,
aged 85 – 8 December 1992

Sheybal, Vladek, Polish-born actor, writer and
director, aged 69 – 16 October 1992

Slater, Jim, general secretary of the National Union
of Seamen 1974–86, aged 69 – 30 May 1993

Smith, Dr E. Lester, FRS, research scientist who
discovered vitamin B12, aged 88 – December
1992

Smith, T. Dan, former Newcastle council leader
gaoled in 1974 for corruption in Poulson affair,
aged 78 – 27 July 1993

Sobell, Sir Michael, businessman and philanthropist,
aged 100 – 31 August 1993

Soref, Harold, Conservative MP for Ormskirk
1970–4, aged 76 – 14 March 1993

Stark, Dame Freya, DBE, writer and traveller,
aged 100 – 9 May 1993

Strauss, Lord, PC, Labour MP for Lambeth North
1929–31, 1934–50, and for Lambeth Vauxhall
1950–79, and a minister 1945–51, aged 91 –
5 June 1993

Summerson, Sir John, CH, CBE, FBA, FSA,
architectural historian, aged 87 – 10 November
1992

Sutton, Prof. John, FRS, geologist, aged 73 –
6 September 1992

Tambo, Oliver, president of the African National
Congress 1978–91, aged 75 – 24 April 1993

Thompson, E. P., historian and author, aged 69 –
28 August 1993

Tilston, Col. Fred, VC, CD, aged 86 – 22 September
1992

Todd, Ann, film actress and documentary film-
maker, aged 84 – 6 May 1993

Trace, Christopher, *Blue Peter* presenter 1958–67,
aged 59 – 5 September 1992

Treurnicht, Andries, leader of the South African
Conservative Party, aged 72 – 22 April 1993

Twitty, Conway, American rock and country and
western singer, aged 59 – 5 June 1993

Tytler, Rt. Revd Donald, Suffragan Bishop of
Middleton since 1982, aged 67 – November 1992

Underhill, Lord, CBE, deputy leader of the
Opposition in the House of Lords 1982–9,
aged 78 – 12 March 1993

Underwood, Michael (John Michael Evelyn), crime
story-writer and barrister, aged 76 – January 1993

Van Fleet, Gen. James, American Second World
War general, aged 100 – 23 September 1992

Vaughan, Dame Janet, DBE, FRS, principal of
Somerville College, Oxford, 1945–67, aged 93 –
9 January 1993

Wang Zhen, vice-president of the People's Republic
of China, aged 85 – 12 March 1993

Warriss, Ben, comedian and actor, aged 83 –
14 January 1993

Watts, Sir Roy, CBE, chairman of Thames Water
since 1983, aged 67 – found dead 5 May 1993

Westall, Robert, children's writer, aged 63 –
15 April 1993

Whitcomb, Noel, newspaper columnist, aged 73 –
11 June 1993

White, Sir Dick, KCMG, KBE, director-general of MI5
1953–6 and director-general of MI6 1956–68,
aged 86 – 20 February 1993

Williams, R. H., rugby union player, aged 62 –
27 January 1993

Willis, Lord (Ted), playwright, politician and
author, aged 78 – 22 December 1992

Winstanley, Lord, Liberal MP for Cheadle 1966–70
and Hazel Grove February to October 1974, and
chairman of the Countryside Commission 1978–
80, aged 74 – 18 July 1993

Witcutt, Christine, British aid worker killed in
Sarajevo, aged 56 – 5 July 1993

Woddis, Roger, satiric writer and versifier,
aged 76 – 16 July 1993

Woods, The Most Revd Frank, KBE, Archbishop of
Melbourne 1957–77, Primate of Australia 1971–7,
aged 85 – 29 November 1992

Yates, Jess, former television personality and
producer, aged 74 – 9 April 1993

Young, Jack, Middlesex and England slow bowler,
aged 80 – 5 February 1993

Younger, William, GC, aged 83 – 6 February 1993

Zuckerman, Lord, OM, KCB, FRS, chief scientific
adviser to the Secretary of State for Defence
1960–6, chief scientific adviser to the
Government 1964–71, aged 88 – 1 April 1993

One Hundred Years Ago

The following description of events in 1894 is taken from the Remarkable Occurrences sections of the 1895 and 1896 editions of *Whitaker's Almanack*.

The year started with Gladstone in his fourth term as Prime Minister of a Liberal government, but he resigned on 3 March at the age of 84. Gladstone was succeeded by Lord Rosebery, who had the first of his three Derby wins in June. The nature of the House of Lords was one of the most keenly debated political questions of the day, and several demonstrations were held in Hyde Park, London, in support of reform.

Overseas, an Armenian rising at Sassun was cruelly suppressed by the Turks, although reports of this only reached Britain in 1895. The Sino-Japanese war broke out, and in France Alfred Dreyfus was unjustly convicted of treason and deported in what came to be known as the Dreyfus Affair.

January 1894

1. Manchester Ship Canal opened for traffic. **5.** An English force under Captain Lendy, DSO, operating against the Sofas, a slave-raiding tribe from Sierra Leone, attacked by a French force at Warina in the dark, owing to a misapprehension. Captain Lendy and 26 of his men killed, and the French commander wounded and taken prisoner. **13.** News of the massacre, in Matabeliland, of Captain Wilson and the whole of his force, confirmed. **20.** Arrival at Bombay of the Earl of Elgin, the new Viceroy of India. **21.** Sudden return of ex-King Milan to Belgrade. Resignation of the Gruitch Cabinet. **25.** Prize-fight at Jacksonville, USA, between Corbett and Mitchell, for the championship of the world and 20,000 dollars. The former won in 9 minutes (3 rounds). News arrived of the occupation of Timbuctoo by the French. A Bill passed in Jersey, by a majority of two votes, making education compulsory in the island. **29.** The barque *Port Yarrock* wrecked in Tralee Bay. The whole crew (25 hands) were lost. In the Court of Appeal, the judgment restraining Messrs Tussaud from exhibiting a waxen effigy of Monson, reversed. **30.** Great fire at the Rye Mill Company's cotton mill, Oldham, estimated damage, £100,000. **31.** The rumour that Mr Gladstone was about to resign the Premiership, officially denied.

February 1894

1. Bank rate reduced to 2½ per cent. **3.** The Pope decided to increase the number of Cardinals by 8, six to be Italians. **5.** Vaillant, Anarchist, guillotined at Paris. **10.** Collision in the Medway between the battleship *Edinburgh* and the iron barque *Scottish Admiral*. The latter sank. A deputation of working men had an audience of the Queen-Regent of Spain at the Palace, Madrid. **11.** Severe gale swept over England, causing much damage and loss of life. **12.** Bomb outrage at the Terminus Café, St Lazare, Paris,

and arrest of the perpetrator, Henri. Thirteen persons injured. **15.** Henry Wyndham Carter charged at Bow Street Police-court with sending a letter threatening to kill the Queen. Martial Bourdin, an Anarchist, killed by the explosion of a bomb he was carrying, in Greenwich Park. Police raid on Anarchist club in Windmill Street, Tottenham Court Road; some important documents were found. **22.** Bank rate lowered to 2 per cent. A damaged specimen of the Great Auk's egg sold by auction for 300 guineas. **23.** A punitive expedition of English marines and bluejackets, operating against Fodi Silah, a native chief, near Bathurst, West Africa, fell into an ambush on their return to the boats; 13 killed and 52 wounded.

March 1894

3. The Queen accepted Mr Gladstone's resignation, and summoned Lord Rosebery to form a Ministry. **8.** Bomb explosion outside the Chamber of Deputies, Rome, killing one and wounding several persons. **9.** Fatal accident at Romford Railway Station to Mr Theobald, MP. **13.** End of the Revolution in Brazil, and surrender of the Insurgents. **15.** Bomb outrage at the Madeleine, Paris; the perpetrator killed by the explosion. **17.** Dr Jameson [British South Africa Company administrator in Mashonaland] announced that 'The British South Africa Co. has ascertained that Lo Bengula sent on 3 Dec. messengers to the "Forbes patrol" with a present of £1,000, and a verbal message asking the patrol to stop pursuit as he would surrender. It is asserted that two men of the Imperial Police kept the money and said nothing, thus becoming morally the murderers of Captain Wilson and his force.' **18.** Demonstration in Hyde Park against the House of Lords. **20.** Annexation of Pondoland, South Africa. **29.** Performance of the Hymn to Apollo, from the ancient Greek music engraved on a marble slab at Delphi, before the Royal Family of Greece.

April 1894

7. A bag containing £7,700 in gold, notes and cheques, stolen from the counter of Messrs Smith, Payne & Smith's bank in Lombard Street. **8.** The steam trawler *Chillian* wrecked on Filey Brigg; six lives lost. **19.** Lord Salisbury addressed a great meeting of the Primrose League at Covent Garden Theatre. **20.** Betrothal of the Czarewitch [later Emperor Nicholas II] to Princess Alix of Hesse, granddaughter of Queen Victoria. **21.** Violent shocks of earthquake throughout Greece; upwards of 150 lives lost. **22.** The Guildhall Art Gallery open for the first time on Sunday: 2,369 visitors passed the turnstile. **23.** Further earthquake shocks in Greece: 220 lives lost, and towns and villages destroyed. **27.** Renewed earthquake shocks in Greece, accompanied by terrible loss of life and property.

MAY 1894

2. Earthquake shock in South Wales. 3. Mr Henry Irving laid the foundation stone of the Brixton Theatre. 4. Conclusion of trial of Anarchists before Mr Justice Hawkins at the Central Criminal Court. Farnara sentenced to 20 years, and Polti to 10 years, penal servitude. 10. Marriage of Mr Asquith (Home Secretary) to Miss Margot Tennant. 11. Bomb explosion in the Avenue Kleber, Paris. 12. Wembley Park opened to the public. 15. London cabmen's strike. 17. Episcopal manifesto issued against the Welsh Disestablishment Bill. 20. Coup d'etat in Servia. 21. Emile Henri, Anarchist, guillotined at Paris. 25. A British force completely defeated the slave-trading chief Makanjira on Lake Nyasa. 29. Trial of troopers of the Bechuanaland Police, for suppressing Lo Bengula's message of surrender, and for misappropriating £1,000; found guilty, and sentenced to 14 years penal servitude.

JUNE 1894

1. Trial of Marie Hermann at the Old Bailey for the murder of Mr Stephens in Grafton Street; convicted of manslaughter and sentenced to six years' penal servitude. 6. The Derby won by Lord Rosebery's colt Ladas. 7. Stormy debate in French Chamber on the Convention between England and the Congo Free State. 10. Five people suffocated in a house at Glasgow, through an escape of gas. 11. Settlement of the Cab Strike, through the intervention of the Home Secretary. The Anti-Gambling League summoned the lessees of the 'ten-shilling ring' on the Newmarket Racecourse for permitting betting there. 12. Epidemic of 'Bubonic Plague' at Hong Kong, 2,500 deaths. 14. Abdul Aziz proclaimed Sultan of Morocco. 15. Second reading of Deceased Wife's Sister Marriage Bill rejected by the House of Lords, by a majority of 9. 19. British Protectorate of Uganda announced. 21. Great fire in Tabernacle Street, Finsbury – estimated damage £150,000. 23. Birth of a son (Prince Edward) to the Duke and Duchess of York [later King George V and Queen Mary], at White Lodge, Richmond. Terrible disaster at the Albion Colliery, Pontypridd; 300 lives lost. 24. Assassination of President Carnot [of France] by Caserio Santo. 26. Strike of 65,000 Scottish coal-miners. 27. M. Casimir-Perier elected President of the French Republic. 30. Tower Bridge opened by the Prince of Wales, on behalf of HM the Queen.

JULY 1894

9. Rioting in connection with the American Railway strike; martial law declared in Chicago. 10. Severe earthquake shocks at Constantinople; serious loss of life. 13. Termination of American Railway strike. 19. Kassala (Abyssinia) captured by the Italians. Accidental explosion of a torpedo at Cowes; seven men killed. 24. The British ship Kow Shing, chartered by China for transport of troops to Corea [Korea], sunk by Japanese cruiser Naniwa though flying the British ensign. 30. The whole of the Newfoundland Cabinet,

with one exception, unseated for bribery, and disqualified for re-election.

AUGUST 1894

1. Japan declared war against China. Japan tendered apology to English Government with reference to the sinking of the Kow Shing. 2. Mr Maxim's flying machine successfully tried at Bexley. 6. The German Emperor arrived at Cowes. 9. Great discovery of gold at Coolgardie, near Perth, Western Australia. 12. Scotch express partially wrecked at St Pancras station. Twenty injured, but none fatally. 13. Lord Rayleigh communicated to the British Association the discovery of a hitherto unknown constituent of the atmosphere. 25. New Commercial Treaty between England and Japan ratified at Tokio. 26. Demonstration in Hyde Park against the House of Lords. About 1,500 marched in the procession. 29. Dutch reverse in the East Indies; an expedition cut to pieces. 30. The steam cutter of HMS Alecto fired on by the natives in Bonny river, W. Africa; one sailor killed and two others dangerously wounded. 31. HMS Curaçoa, and the German ship Bustard bombarded the rebel stronghold in Samoa.

SEPTEMBER 1894

1. Private cards bearing an adhesive halfpenny stamp henceforth permitted to be sent through the post. Daring robbery of mails at the GPO, London. 3. Boating disaster in Morecambe Bay. Twenty persons drowned. Extensive forest fires in Minnesota and Wisconsin. Many towns destroyed and some hundreds of lives lost. 4. The Commissioners of Prisons decided to adopt the Bertillon system (anthropometrical) of measurement, for the identification of criminals. 13. Dastardly diamond robbery of the value of £5,000 from the person of Mr Spyzer, diamond merchant, in Hatton Garden. Serious religious riot at Poona, between Hindoos and Mohammedans. 16. Battle at Ping Yang, Corea; the Chinese being defeated with a loss estimated at 16,000 men. 18. Desperate encounter between the police and miners on strike at Motherwell, Scotland. 24. Wheat sold at Sleaford for 16s. 6d. a quarter. Said to be the lowest price recorded during the present century. 25. Kaffir rising at Lorenço Marques, Portuguese East Africa.

OCTOBER 1894

10. Suicide at the Foreign Office of Mr Patrick Henderson, HM Consul at Cadiz. 12. Opening of the Thirlmere Waterworks, by the Lord Mayor of Manchester. 20. The new company for the completion of the Panama Canal, definitely constituted in Paris. 22. Termination of Scotch Coal Strike, after lasting 17 weeks. 23. A Boa Constrictor at the Zoological Gardens swallowed another snake of the same species, only two feet shorter than itself, without suffering any apparent injury. 24. The Japanese troops crossed the Yalu river and entered Chinese territory. 27. Arrival in England of a native deputation to Queen Victoria

from the Queen of Swaziland. A pianoforte recital by a German musician named Berg, lasting 30 consecutive hours, brought to a successful conclusion at the Royal Aquarium, Westminster. **28.** Wreck of the intercolonial steamer *Wairarapu*, from Sydney, off the coast of New Zealand; 111 passengers and 23 of the crew drowned.

NOVEMBER 1894

1. Death of Alexander III, Emperor of Russia, at Livadia. The *Saturday Review* bought by Mr Frank Harris, late editor of the *Fortnightly*. **6.** Capture of Kinchow, and (7th) Talienwan by the Japanese. **10.** A horse killed and 3 men injured by an escape of electric fluid in Cannon Street, City. **13.** Cutting of the first sod of the new line to connect the Manchester, Sheffield, and Lincolnshire Railway with London. Destructive floods and gales in the British Isles, accompanied with loss of life. **14.** Further gale and floods; several vessels wrecked, and much damage done to Dover pier. **18.** Severe earthquakes in Southern Italy, causing the fall of a church, killing 60 persons. **19.** Funeral of the Czar of Russia (Alexander the Peacemaker) at St Petersburg. **20.** Death of Anton Rubinstein, Russian musician and composer. **21.** Capture of Port Arthur by the Japanese. **23.** Raid on a City betting club; 150 arrests. **26.** Marriage of the Czar Nicholas II of Russia with Princess Alix of Hesse.

DECEMBER 1894

5. Opening of the new Reichstag Palace at Berlin. **11.** Signing of the Swaziland Convention by Sir H. B. Loch [Governor of Cape Colony] and President Krüger [of Transvaal, or South African Republic]. **12.** Death of the Rt Hon. Sir John Sparrow David Thompson, KCMG, the Canadian Premier, at Windsor Castle, a few minutes after being admitted a member of the Privy Council. **16.** Turbulent scene in the Italian Chamber of Deputies owing to accusations against members of the cabinet of complicity in the Banca Romana scandals. **22.** Captain Dreyfus of the French army found guilty of betraying State secrets to a foreign power, and sentenced to imprisonment, for life, at Paris. **26.** Fighting between British forces and tribesmen in Waziristan.

Among new scientific discoveries and inventions in 1894 recorded by *Whitaker* were the Maxim Flying Machine, an experimental airship 'constructed on the aeroplane or kite principle'; an anti-diphtheria serum discovered by Prof. Behrung of Berlin and M. Roux, a pupil of Pasteur; a long-period meteorograph invented by M. Jules Richard for use in the Mont Blanc Observatory; the telautograph of Mr Elisha Gray of Chicago, a telegraph able to send a faithful copy of a message as written; and an electric quilt for hospitals, invented by the American C. T. Snedekor.

However, according to *Whitaker*, 'no great discoveries have been made in the science of the mind during the past year'. A few interesting papers were nevertheless published, including one by the Psychical Society which reported that 'a considerable percentage of persons see or hear or feel "ghosts"'. *Whitaker* further notes that 'this occult line of enquiry is giving rise to a new literature, and more than one popular magazine is devoted to it'.

The bank rate stood at 2 per cent from February 1894, and income tax was raised from 7d to 8d in the pound in the Budget in April. The standard postage rate was 1d; telegrams could be sent at the rate of 6d for the first 12 words and ½d for every additional word. A marriage licence cost 10s and a dog licence 7s 6d; the cost of a pedlar's licence, a commission to any officer in the Royal Navy, or indeed a commission of lunacy, was 5s.

Wedding Anniversaries

First	Cotton		Fourteenth	Ivory
Second	Paper		Fifteenth	Crystal
Third	Leather		Twentieth	China
Fourth	Fruit and Flower		Twenty-fifth	Silver
Fifth	Wood		Thirtieth	Pearl
Sixth	Sugar/Iron		Thirty-fifth	Coral
Seventh	Wool		Fortieth	Ruby
Eighth	Bronze/Electrical appliances		Forty-fifth	Sapphire
Ninth	Copper/Pottery		Fiftieth	Gold
Tenth	Tin		Fifty-fifth	Emerald
Eleventh	Steel		Sixtieth	Diamond
Twelfth	Silk and Fine Linen		Seventieth	Platinum
Thirteenth	Lace			

Archaeology

During the year under review the event which generated the most interest was not a new archaeological discovery but the launch on 26 October 1992 by the chairman of English Heritage, Jocelyn Stevens, of a new strategy, *Managing England's Heritage: Setting Our Priorities for the 1990s.* Not only was the launch attended by much publicity and much media comment, but questions were asked in the House of Commons, and there was a debate in the House of Lords on 5 November. The debate was stimulated by what critics saw as a proposal by English Heritage to withdraw from some of its obligations.

Opponents of the new strategy took particular exception to the proposal that English Heritage would divide its buildings and sites into three categories, concentrating on the first two while endeavouring to pass sites in the third category to local management if at all feasible. This would mean that English Heritage would be concentrating its resources on Grade I and II* buildings.

As well as urging local authorities to take more responsibility for conserving the built historic environment in their localities on the basis of established guidelines and standards, in London English Heritage proposed that powers it inherited from the Greater London Council relating to Grade II listed buildings should pass to the London boroughs as part of an agreed programme. This particular proposal received considerable opposition during the public debate.

Other parts of the proposed strategy provoked less opposition but are no less radical. English Heritage suggested making additional grants to churches which qualified and can produce matching private funding; over the next five years money will be redirected from rescue archaeology to carry out a number of archaeological strategies in urban areas; education and publishing will be given greater prominence; and scientific resources will be targeted on specific problems with the intention of involving the private sector where there is a commercial potential in the research tasks.

So far as the internal organization of English Heritage is concerned, there is a proposal to privatize the direct labour force over a period of three years and relocate the management of historic properties to Kenwood in London, and to Newcastle, Northampton, Bristol and Tonbridge. Market testing is to be introduced and standards of service will be published. Considerable effort will be expended on generating funding, setting up a conservation fund which would include private resources, establishing a tax review panel to increase funds available for conservation, and making a bid for proceeds from the National Lottery and Millennium Fund. Raised income is anticipated from increasing the cost of admission and improving sales and membership. In addition, a public appeal will be launched to establish a permanent grant scheme for historic gardens.

Amongst all these proposals the site in particular which is targeted is that of Stonehenge. The problems of over-use, poor visitor facilities, intrusive adjacent roads, and the potential for vandalism remain unsolved. The difficulties surrounding the Stonehenge site have been recognized for years and it is likely that even English Heritage's sternest critics will welcome the renewed pledge to solve the problems.

THE DOVER BOAT

A new road scheme and a renewal of the sewage system in Dover in 1991–2 enabled archaeologists to investigate parts of Dover which have hitherto received less investigation. The most significant discovery was that of a wooden boat, described by Keith Parfitt in *Current Archaeology* (number 133, March/April 1993). Although the Dover boat had its planks 'sewn' together by withies, and in that respect was similar to boats found in the River Humber at North Ferriby before the Second World War, its method of construction was quite different from the northern variety. In all some 9.50 metres of the boat were raised which, it is thought, 'perhaps amounts to about one half to two-thirds of the total length'. The author's view of the nature of the boat is summarized thus: 'There seems little doubt that the craft represents a sea-going vessel which presumably made regular trips across the Dover Straits to and from the Continent. Initial C14 dates indicate that the boat is of Middle Bronze Age date.' Apart from raising the boat, care was taken to recover for further study samples which will indicate the circumstances prevailing at the time that the boat was abandoned, in particular 'all the sediment from the filling of the boat has been recovered for study'. It is already noted that 'preliminary examination suggests that the boat was old and had been deliberately abandoned. However, it was not abandoned on the sea-shore, but had been dragged up a freshwater creek. Molluscs indicate an environment dominated by damp open ground amongst small muddy pools or slowly moving streams. Despite the proximity to the present coast, no evidence for brackish or saline water organisms are present either in the mollusc or pollen assemblages. Following abandonment, the boat in-filled rapidly with tufa and was subsequently sealed and protected by a thick layer of silt.'

A CELTIC ROYAL BURIAL

Rosalind Niblett's account of her excavation in St Albans forms the basis of a report in *Current Archaeology* (number 132, January 1993). We are told 'In St Albans, shortly after the Roman Conquest, a native prince met his death. He had done well under the Romans and was thus given the most sumptous burial ever to have taken place in this country. We can reconstruct the site in some detail. An underground mortuary chamber was constructed, where the body was laid out on a couch, surrounded by rich belongings and an elaborate funeral feast. Meanwhile, we must imagine, dignitaries were summoned from further afield, and the entire tribe was assembled to do homage to the dead king, parading around the funerary chamber and perhaps taking part in a funeral feast. Then came the grand climax. The body was taken out and cremated on a huge funeral pyre. Then came the best bit of all; there was a huge orgy of destruction. The funerary chamber was smashed to smithereens. Most of the goods were taken out and thrown on the funeral pyre, just to demonstrate the wealth of the dead, that his goods could be consumed in this extravagant way: it would also frustrate any possible tomb robbers – archaeologists even – who would merely be tantalized by lumps of molten metal. The ashes and the fragments of the objects were then gathered up and placed while still hot in a cremation pit alongside the funerary chamber. Finally the pits were filled with turves, and occasional handfuls of the cremated relics were thrown in.'

The investigations are described in some detail and a point of interest is the very large size of the enclosure, five acres, in which the burial was placed. There is evidence that the burial site was venerated for some two hundred years after deposition with a Romano-Celtic temple being erected some fifty years after the burial. Although it is not possible to know precisely who the buried person was, all the evidence suggests that 'the grave was that of a member of the ruling Catuvellaunian family', who was buried in about AD 50, some seven years after the Roman invasion of Britain.

IRISH CELTIC CENTRE

The discovery of a previously unknown Celtic town in Ireland is reported by David Keys in *Minerva* (volume 4, number 1, January/February 1993). The town, defended by three miles of stone ramparts, the remains of which still survive, was situated on top of a 400-metre high hill some 30 miles south-west of Dublin. The stone ramparts on Spinans Hill, near Baltinglass, Co. Wicklow, embrace an area of 320 acres (130 hectares). 'It is the largest structure of its type ever found in the British Isles and consists of a central stone walled citadel and a large enclosed area with three entrances through a double stone rampart, each wall of which was ten feet (three metres) thick and at least seven feet high.' Aerial photography has revealed the remains of at least 25 stone huts in the inner citadel and other adjacent areas were also inhabited 'but much of the 320 acres may have been used to shelter cattle and people in times of war, or for markets and festivals'.

The site was not an isolated find: 'Within an area of six square miles, there are, including Spinans Hill, a total of five separate fortified hill top towns or

settlements. Nowhere else in the British Isles does such a complex of prehistoric sites of this sort exist. Their precise age is not known, but excavation nearby suggests a date of perhaps the eighth century BC – the late Bronze Age.' Although little about the area is known, it is thought possible that this was the centre of tribal power which, from archaeological evidence, may have been based on both mineral wealth, especially copper and gold, and trade.

THE CORBRIDGE LANX

Discovered in 1735, the Corbridge Lanx 'is a magnificent work of Late Roman silver plate and is the earliest find of Roman silver from Britain that is still extant in its original form', writes Peter Clayton in *Minerva* (volume 4, number 3, May/June 1993). Found at Corbridge on the River Tyne in Northumberland by Isabelle Cutter, a nine-year-old girl, the Lanx, a large oblong tray of silver weighing just over 4.5 kg (10 lb), passed into the possession of the Dukes of Northumberland. On loan to the British Museum since 1979, the Lanx has just been acquired by the Museum, accepted by the Government in part lieu of taxes owed by the trustees of the Duke of Northumberland. Valued at £4 million, 'it is a national, indeed international treasure of the highest order and interest'. Contributions towards the purchase for the nation were made by the National Heritage Memorial Fund, the National Art Collections Fund and the British Museum Society.

Described as 'one of the most important pieces of Roman silver ever found in Britain, if not in the Roman world', the scene depicted on the Corbridge Lanx is that of the shrine of Apollo on the island of Delos in the Cyclades. It is suggested that the scene may perhaps 'be a commemoration of the visit of the Emperor Julian II, the Apostate (AD 360–363), to the shrine of Apollo on Delos in AD 363 when, in a largely Christian Empire, he turned back to the old gods'.

ROMAN CHILD'S BURIAL

A Roman burial, subsequently investigated by Alison Taylor, the Cambridgeshire county archaeologist, was discovered some 3 metres (10 feet) down during the digging of a pipeline for the Anglian Water Authority. Described in *Current Archaeology* (number 130, August 1992), the burial was of a child and had originally been placed in a wooden coffin with a lead lining, of which only the latter survived. The burial was found at Arrington, a village which lies on the old Roman road of Ermine Street. The burial was in a very deep pit some 100 yards away from the road with no sign of Roman occupation in the vicinity.

It may be that the reason for such an isolated burial was because it was of 'a child with its skull terribly deformed showing that it had died at the age of about 10 months of water on the brain (hydrocephaly). The teeth and jaws were of a 10-month-old baby but the skull was so swollen that it was equivalent in size to a 4-year-old. Few other bones survived apart from the skull but there were traces of a woollen fabric and also of an aromatic substance, perhaps myrrh to which faint traces of scent still survive.'

Apart from the remains of the unfortunate child, a particularly interesting feature of the deposit 'was a collection of dolls that had been put on the top of the coffin, perhaps originally in a wooden box.' These were figurines made from pipeclay and it is not clear whether they were toys played with by the child or ritual objects chosen to accompany the deceased to the underworld; for example, were the two rams toys or did they represent sacrificial animals, sacred to Mercury? Apart from a model bullock and a well-known type of human figure, i.e. the seated youth pulling a thorn out of his foot, there were two figurines of children. An eastern god may be represented by a figure in a cloak and phrygian cap and a figurine of a 'Mother-Goddess' may have been put there by the parents to give some kind of protection on the journey the child was about to start. None of the figures are of local production and most appear to have originated in Gaul and Germany or even further east; together they help suggest a date between AD 160 and 190.

In a subsequent issue of *Current Archaeology* (number 113, March/April 1993) Dr Michael Ryder reports that having examined the fibres found with the body he concludes that the wool came from 'a particularly fine type of fleece' and the cloth was similar to that found at Vindolanda and 'thought to have been made in Britain'. Having studied the figurines of sheep he noted that the two identical ones have a short fleece on which the wool was represented by raised circles indicating a curl, while the third, fragmentary, figurine had pointed locks of wool. Dr Ryder notes that 'the short curly fleeces indicated in the two identical Arrington figurines are rare in representations. Curliness is found in neither very fine nor very coarse (hairy) fleeces. Curly wool is seen today in English long wools and the robust body of the Arrington sheep is like that of a modern long-woolled sheep. Could it be that a curly longwool existed on the Continent during the Roman period? This type did not become prominent again until the eighteenth century when it was localized in England.'

THE HOXNE HOARD

A metal detector-user helping a farmer look for metal tools which had fallen from a tractor discovered 'an immense hoard' of Romano-British date at Hoxne, Suffolk, on 16 November 1992. Peter Clayton writing in *Minerva* (volume 4, number 1, January/February 1993) states: 'the hoard was obviously the property of an extremely rich local Roman family. It must have been buried in the 18 × 12 inch box in which it was found at a time of local trouble, attacks by foreign invaders or in a period of unrest. Circumstances must have been such that the original owners were unable to return and retrieve their possessions, since such valuables would certainly not have been abandoned without due cause.'

In a subsequent issue (volume 4, number 2, March/April 1993) Catherine Johns of the British Museum describes the hoard: 'Apart from the coins, the treasure consists principally of small items of silver tableware and gold jewellery. Many of the objects can be closely compared with pieces in other later fourth- and early fifth-century hoards, especially the Thetford (Norfolk) treasure, which was found in 1979. The number of spoons in the treasure (about seventy-six) roughly doubles the number of late Roman silver spoons recorded from Britain, and there are several inscriptions, including some personal names and Christian symbols.' In a further issue (volume 4, number 3, May/June 1993) Roger Bland, also of the British Museum, gives an initial account of the coins in the hoard. 'In all there are over 14,500 coins in the hoard of which 563 are gold, 19 bronze and the remainder silver.' There are some eight different Roman Emperors represented on the gold coins and fifteen different Emperors on the silver ones. 'The coins were made at some sixteen different mints, from Trier in Germany in the West through to Antioch in present-day Turkey in the East. Most of the coins, however, come from Trier, Lyons and Arles in Germany and France, and Milan, Ravenna and Rome in Italy.'

As hoards cannot be buried before the date of the latest coins in them, these coins are helpful in establishing a date before which the Hoxne hoard could not have been buried. 'At present it seems that the latest coins are two coins of the usurper Constantine III (AD 407–11), Roman Governor of Britain who removed the troops from Britain in order to challenge the authority of Honorius, Emperor in Ravenna. We know, therefore, that the hoard was buried some time after AD 407 . . .' Perhaps the most remarkable point to be made about this hoard is its great size. Before this discovery in 1992, the greatest number of silver coins found anywhere was about 3,000 from a hoard in Worcestershire discovered in 1811. Another odd aspect of the matter remarked upon by Roger Bland is that 'it is a curious feature of coin circulation at this time that, with a very few exceptions, silver miliarenses and siliquae are only found in two parts of the Roman Empire: Britain and Romania. This is particularly surprising since these coins were struck at mints all over the Empire, and hoards of gold coins of this period have been discovered throughout the Empire.'

ANGLO-SAXON BURIALS

There are many ways in which archaeological sites may be damaged and one of the commonest is by continual ploughing. An example is given in *Medieval Archaeology* (volume XXXVI for 1992), in which the site at Barrington, Cambs., is described. This site has also been damaged in the past by coprolite mining, as well as by land drains and excavations in the 19th century, metal detecting and ploughing. It is reported that some 2,000 square metres in five trenches were opened by mechanical digger in this excavation by T. Malin, working on behalf of South Cambridgeshire District Council and English Heritage, and 65 Anglo-

Saxon burials were excavated, ranging in date from early sixth to late seventh centuries. It is reported that 'as in previous years, almost all the richest graves were those of women. One very early grave contained a pair of silver wrist-clasps with a pair of "marigold" design saucer brooches, eighteen amber and two crystal beads. Slightly later, *c*.AD 620, was a woman with a pair of very small saucer brooches (one gilded) and a record number of beads for this cemetery (189 amber, three glass, two "white substance" and one crystal), plus a latchlifter and a pair of wrist-clasps. She was part of a double burial with a man, who was accompanied by a spear, knife and buckle. Two burials later in the sixth century had bags of objects with large purse-rings of ivory (or possibly mammoth tusk). One of these burials also had a great number of beads (146 amber and nine glass) and a pair of six spiral-decorated saucer brooches. Other grave goods in this cemetery included a bunch of four keys, two small-long brooches and one cruciform, five pairs of bronze wrist-clasps, and two pots. The latest 7th-century burial had been virtually destroyed by ploughing, but its jaw area survived, accompanied by a necklace of seven silver rings, five blue and green beads and two gold pendants; one was circular with a garnet (?) setting and the other was a crystal in a gold sling.'

During the year's work only six men had spears and only one grave yielded a shield-boss. 'An unusually deeply cut grave contained the only shield boss plus a spear, knife, buckle and bronze bucket.' Although the child burials usually lacked grave goods, 'one infant of *c*.three years had a plain pot and eight glass beads. A neo-natal infant was under the head of a slightly built young woman, probably the mother, and another infant lay on a man's pelvis. A rare find was a child burial which had a small spear by his head. One part of the cemetery had a concentration of six children close together.' Part of an infilled Iron Age ditch had been used for twelve burials, eight of which were in double graves, and it is suggested that 'plague of some kind is a possible explanation'.

A WELSH CRANNOG

A most unusual kind of investigation is described in *Medieval Archaeology* (volume XXXVI, 1992), namely a further season of excavation and survey directed by Mark Redknap of the National Museum of Wales on the Crannog in Llangorse Lake. Having described the progress of the excavations, it is noted that 'During the course of the underwater searches, further objects were found which shed light on the status and cultural affinities of the Crannog. The earliest metalwork is a late 1st-century/early 2nd-century AD Roman Dolphin brooch with coil in Polden Hill manner. Early medieval copper-alloy artefacts include two fragments of binding strips; the pin from a (pseudo-) penannular brooch bearing punched decoration; a circular boss mount; and one terminal from a pseudo-penannular brooch of Irish type, decorated with debased zoomorphic heads,

interlace and central mount for a stud or bead. The crescentic cusps, a late feature on annular brooches, are found on brooches from Lagore and County Cavan, and the general composition is similar to that of brooches from Trearddur Bay, Gwynedd, and Llys Awel Farm, Penycorddyn-mawr, Clwyd, supporting an 8th- or 9th-century date. Several pieces of bronze sheet and the head and shaft of a pin display signs of being recycled and semi-worked, and this industrial activity is substantiated by the discovery of further fragments of fired clay and slag. Fragments of bone comb, a bronze-coated iron strap slide similar in general form to 9th-century examples from Balladoole, Isle of Man, several iron artefacts, and late Mesolithic flints were also recovered. From the same area underwater came a bronze strap hinge, finely decorated with enamel . . . this remarkable object can be identified on the basis of its size and shape as part of a carrying hinge from a small portable reliquary shrine. A leather strap would have been secured between the front and back plate, and the lugs would have been engaged with a small mount at one end of the reliquary. Such carrying hinges can be seen on the Monymusk and Bologna shrines, and the ornament shows similarities to that on the Lough Gara belt mount and the Moylough belt-shrine, supporting an 8th-century AD date. The decoration is distinctively Irish, and such reliquaries are among the most numerous objects of the early church in Ireland and Scotland. The new example is the first such find from Wales. The discovery at Llangorse of fine metalwork, some of Irish type, and of evidence for bronze-smithing, supports the identification of the Crannog as one of the aristocratic, royal sites of the kingdom of Brycheiniog.'

KELLINGTON CHURCH

'Kellington is now the most extensively excavated English parish church still in use, and in addition is the first where a major structural element (the tower) has been archaeologically examined during dismantling.' Such is the claim made for this building in a report by Harold Mytum in *Current Archaeology* (number 133, March/April 1993) and behind it lies a particularly interesting story. The church stands near Ferrybridge, some 15 miles south of York, with its earliest visible remains dating from about the late 11th century. It is distinguished, however, by the fact that it is built on top of the coalfield which provides fuel for the power stations at Ferrybridge. It is explained that 'In the past, a column of coal would have been left to prop up the church, but the new mechanized cutting technology makes this rather difficult. It was therefore decided that it would be cheaper for British Coal to underpin the church, dismantle the tower completely and re-erect it after suitable foundations had been provided.' As a result of this decision, British Coal funded the work undertaken by the Department of Archaeology at the University of York.

The results of this research gave fresh information on every period from the construction of the first church of timber in the second half of the 11th century, with the first stone church being built sometime between 1080 and 1130. However, 'The big surprise was that prior to the first church a small cemetery occupied the site. Among the burials was one that was oriented north/south: was this a prehistoric burial, originally perhaps under a barrow, which served as the focus for a later Christian cemetery?'

COLNE POTTERY KILN

Excavations in advance of redevelopment were carried out by K. Watson in a farmyard on the outskirts of the village of Colne, Cambs. It is reported in *Medieval Archaeology* (volume XXXVI, 1992) that the investigation 'revealed the first clear evidence for a medieval pottery kiln in the county'. In addition to two stoke-pits and large amounts of pottery sherds including wasters, research has identified three fabric types, the two earliest belonging to the 13th century and the later to the 16th. Some of the sherds are reminiscent of those from Bourne, Lincs., and 'this may suggest activities by itinerant potters around the Fen-edge'. It is noted that 'The location and varied date-range for this kiln are interesting. The site is close to the Fen-edge, suggesting peat would be used for fuel, and it is conveniently situated half a mile from the Bishops Palace at Somersham, which probably provided a market for the glazed 16th-century pottery. The market town of St Ives is also not far distant (c.five miles) and accessible by the River Ouse. The present village of Colne has shifted its centre c.500 m eastwards, leaving the kiln-site, an adjacent manorial moat, and a ruined church on its outskirts, although originally they were probably all fairly central.'

MEDIEVAL WALL PAINTINGS

The Courtauld Institute and the Royal Commission on Historical Monuments have been running a project to record every medieval wall painting in the country, starting in north-west England. As part of this programme attention has been given to the Agricola Tower of Chester Castle. A study and conservation of the chapel has revealed the survival of medieval wall paintings to an extent hitherto unknown. It is reported by Caroline Babington and David Park in *Minerva* (volume 4, number 1, January/February 1993) that in advance of the completion of conservation work in 1993 or 1994, two programmes of decoration have been revealed; the first concentrates on the infancy of Christ and the second on the life of the Virgin, both entirely appropriate to the chapel's dedication to the Virgin. While the decoration of the altar recess is most closely paralleled by sculpture in Westminster Abbey built under the patronage of Henry III, who was a great patron of the arts and took over Chester Castle in 1237, 'there are some indications that the paintings may date from rather earlier than 1237 – perhaps c.1220.

Stylistic analysis alone does not allow such precision in dating, but comparisons with illuminated manuscripts do suggest that the style of some of the paintings would have been rather old-fashioned by the late 1230s. If the paintings are of c.1220, they would date from the time of Earl Rannulf III, perhaps the greatest magnate of his day, controlling the earldom of Chester semi-independently of the Crown. As such, they would be in some respects an even more exciting discovery than a royal scheme, since almost nothing is known of baronial wall paintings of this period.'

WINLATON MILL IRONWORKS

A land reclamation scheme occasioned the investigation by D. Cranstone of the site of Winlaton Mill Ironworks at Bladon, Tyne and Wear. It is reported in *Post-Medieval Archaeology* (volume 26, 1992) that 'The ironworks was founded in 1691 by Ambrose Crowley, reached its full development in the early 18th century and closed in 1863. It was buried beneath waste from a nearby coke works in the 1930s. At its peak, it contained a forge, slitting mill, plating mill, blade (grinding) mills, steel furnaces, and nailers' and filemakers' workshops, together with offices, warehouses, and workers' housing; it was a forerunner of the Industrial Revolution and attracted visitors from all over Europe. Site investigation established the form of the topography beneath the coke waste, and that considerable remains of the ironworks survived. Archaeological observation of the reclamation scheme was then maintained, to ensure that the structures and stratigraphy of the ironworks were not damaged during removal of the coke waste.'

MILITARY ARCHAEOLOGY

Although industrial archaeology has been accepted for some decades as a subject worthy of study in its own right, the same cannot yet be said of military archaeology, although it is only fair to note the important work done on Civil War sites in recent years, especially in such centres as Exeter, Gloucester and Hull. For anyone interested in military archaeology a problem is the lack of a properly established database. In an attempt to remedy this deficiency, David Smurthwaite on behalf of the National Army Museum has been undertaking a consultancy awarded by English Heritage to produce a register of English battlefields. Not only will the register provide a database to which information may be added, but it will also provide information which will help to determine which battlefield sites should be scheduled as ancient monuments. Also, given that the concept of a battlefields register was prompted by the public outcry over a road being put through the site of the Battle of Naseby, it is hoped that the information will help protect battlefield sites at the earliest stage of the planning process. An on-site assessment of all English battlefields is being undertaken by the staff of the National Army Museum during 1993.

The end of the Cold War has also brought problems for military archaeologists. One result of the reduced size of the armed forces will be the disposal of many important sites involving potential threats to the architectural and archaeological heritage. SAVE Britain's Heritage mounted an exhibition, 'Deserted Bastions' from April to June 1993. The fact that the exhibition was opened by the Minister of State for the Armed Forces is one of the hopeful signs that the Ministry of Defence will be able to work with those concerned with the conservation of the heritage.

One of the problems is that many of the most interesting buildings and sites are unknown to members of the public interested in military archaeology because access was restricted to those on duty. It is a difficulty similar to that experienced in relation to naval dockyards some years ago when it was realized that few people knew of the heritage hidden behind dockyard walls. One of the most important, which the Ministry of Defence intends to vacate in the 1990s, is the Royal Arsenal near to the centre of Woolwich. Within its 70 acres are the Royal Laboratory Buildings of 1696, the Royal Brass Foundry of 1716 and Vanbrugh's Tower Place of 1716-20, a very important building associated with the origins of the Royal Artillery. In addition, there is Verbruggen's House, the brothers of that name being master founders at the Arsenal who had the house built in 1792. Together with later 19th century specialist buildings, the Royal Arsenal site offers the greatest potential for the interpretation of a vital yet unappreciated part of the national heritage.

Booker Prizewinners

1969   *Something to Answer For*, P. H. Newby (Faber)
1970   *The Elected Member*, Bernice Rubens (Eyre & Spottiswoode)
1971   *In A Free State*, V. S. Naipaul (Andre Deutsch)
1972   *G*, John Berger (Weidenfeld)
1973   *The Siege of Krishnapur*, J. G. Farrell (Weidenfeld)
1974   *The Conservationist*, Nadine Gordimer (Cape)
       Holiday, Stanley Middleton (Hutchinson)
1975   *Heat and Dust*, Ruth Prawer Jhabvala (Murray)
1976   *Saville*, David Storey (Cape)
1977   *Staying On*, Paul Scott (Heinemann)
1978   *The Sea, The Sea*, Iris Murdoch (Chatto & Windus)
1979   *Offshore*, Penelope Fitzgerald (Collins)
1980   *Rites of Passage*, William Golding (Faber)
1981   *Midnight's Children*, Salman Rushdie (Cape)
1982   *Schindler's Ark*, Thomas Keneally (Hodder & Stoughton)
1983   *Life & Times of Michael K*, J. M. Coetzee (Secker & Warburg)
1984   *Hôtel du Lac*, Anita Brookner (Cape)
1985   *The Bone People*, Keri Hulme (Hodder & Stoughton)
1986   *The Old Devils*, Kingsley Amis (Hutchinson)
1987   *Moon Tiger*, Penelope Lively (Deutsch)
1988   *Oscar and Lucinda*, Peter Carey (Faber)
1989   *The Remains of the Day*, Kazuo Ishiguro (Faber)
1990   *Possession*, A. S. Byatt (Chatto & Windus)
1991   *The Famished Road*, Ben Okri (Cape)
1992   *The English Patient*, Michael Ondaatje (Bloomsbury)
       Sacred Hunger, Barry Unsworth (Hamish Hamilton)

The finalists for the 1993 prize were:

Paddy Clarke Ha Ha Ha, Roddy Doyle (Secker & Warburg); *Under the Frog*, Tibor Fischer (Polygon); *Scar Tissue*, Michael Ignatieff (Chatto & Windus); *Remembering Babylon*, David Malouf (Chatto & Windus); *Crossing the River*, Caryl Phillips (Bloomsbury); *The Stone Diaries*, Carol Shields (Fourth Estate)

Architecture

TATE GALLERY
St Ives, Cornwall

Architect: Evans and Shalev

The new Tate Gallery in St Ives provides permanent gallery facilities in Cornwall for the art associated with St Ives, of which the Tate holds a substantial amount. The new building has been inspired by the scale, texture, materials and colours of the narrow streets of St Ives, and reconciles its civic presence and public role with the domestic scale of the architecture of its surroundings with sensitivity.

The site slopes steeply up the hillside away from the seafront and looks out over the expansive sweep of Porthmeor Beach and the sea beyond. With its four levels cut back into the slope, the base of the building steps down by means of terraces and flights of stairs to connect with the street. Visitors are led up into a dramatic open circular loggia at the start of a carefully contrived sequence of spaces set along a route that wanders deeper into the building as it rises towards the topmost level.

The roofed but open-sided circular loggia is arranged as a miniature open-air auditorium for gatherings and public events with tiers of paved steps-cum-seats arranged around the perimeter. It leads directly to the entrance and a sequence of introductory spaces punctuated by a two-storey vestibule space lit by a dramatic stained glass window by the artist Patrick Heron. At the far end, the route passes through a circular entrance rotunda to a grand staircase leading up two floors to the main gallery level, passing the bookshop and custodian's office on the way.

At the main gallery level a choice of routes is presented, leading on through a varied sequence of simple, toplit, contrasting spaces, each no larger than a typical artist's studio, and passing through the main focus of the building. This is a double-height gallery wrapped around the internal half of the circular loggia, opening up the heart of the exhibition to the public view from outside through a simple curved expanse of glass, and affording magnificent views over Porthmeor Beach and the coastal landscape that has inspired so much of the art displayed within.

Light flows down from a circular rooflight set within the loggia roof and from a series of glass-block windows set high in the clerestorey over the upper-level balcony between the radiating buttresses of the roof structure. Wall surfaces are white, the floor paved in dark slate, and the suffused daylight produces an ideal setting for the works on show, primarily sculptures and paintings in the main space, with ceramics on the recessed balcony above.

The first gallery presents an introduction to the St Ives school, and is a long low space. This leads via a connecting lobby into the dramatic loggia gallery space and thence into the remaining galleries. These galleries increase in height progressively towards the brightly lit double-height space of the last room that leads back to the entry point to complete the circuit.

At this point it becomes apparent that the smaller toplit painting galleries are organized around a landscaped open courtyard located at the heart of the building. The courtyard is revealed to view only at the end of the intended sequence of gallery spaces, before one passes under the half-landing of a separate double-flight curved staircase leading up to the café and roof terraces. The elaborate balustrade leads the eye up again and further twists and turns eventually complete the route through the gallery and the visitor is presented once more with views over the town's grey slate roofs and the sea.

Much play is made of the roof planes and terraces. These break down the scale of the building and add complexity of form to an intricately modelled profile on plan, and enable the substantial bulk of building to sit happily with the domestic scale of its immediate neighbours. Windows are small punched openings and colours and materials relate sympathetically to the established idiom of St Ives – white marble dash render for the walls, painted precast cornices, lintols and cills, reconstructed stone pavings, and grey slate roofs. The building is constructed with a concrete frame and masonry walls, and its 6,000 sq. metres of space generated a building cost of approximately £3.3 million.

INTERNATIONAL RAIL TERMINAL
Waterloo Station, London

Architect: Nicholas Grimshaw and Partners

The first of the special international terminus stations to serve the Channel Tunnel has been completed at Waterloo Station, London. British Rail's brief called for a 'design . . . appropriate to the 90s but in keeping with the great tradition of British railway architecture'. The architect's imaginative response has produced one of the most dramatic roofs to a new station since the era of the steam train and the great expressions of Victorian engineering skill.

Engineering and technological skill has been employed to solve the tricky constructional problems posed by the location and the design of the structure supporting the tracks and platforms. The roof is an apparently simple arch-like form and sits upon a new concrete 'bridge' structure which contains the arrivals and departures lounges, immigration hall and custom areas, and access points to the Underground network.

The chief structural problems were associated with the awkward winding and tapering profile of the available site area, which generates different roof spans and sections at each successive bay along its entire length, and by deflections generated in the bridge structure by the dynamic loads imposed by moving trains. Rather than attempt to design every pane of glass, every truss and joint to the specific requirements of the geometry, the designers have developed a loose-fit technique which has enabled standard components to be used. The glazed skin uses standard rectangular glass panels which overlap by varying amounts to accommodate the twisting planes and differing roof pitches. The horizontal gaps and vertical mullions are made waterproof by means of large neoprene 'wiper blade' seals and expansion brackets. Adjacent panes overlap by as much as 100 mm; the concept is comparable to the flexible scales of a snakeskin, an appropriate likeness given the sinous form of the completed roof.

The finished roof structure is divisible into two distinct halves either side of the curving centre line. The outer side of the roof facing north and west is entirely glazed to allow daylight to flood the platform areas and allow views out over the city and inwards of arriving and departing trains. By contrast, the side facing south and east, which abuts the existing station, has a greater proportion of solid roof. Narrow strips of clear glazing run up to the ridge line, accentuating the positions of the internal, blue-painted triangulated trusses which are the primary structural elements. The shallow curving tunnel of steel and glass, spanning five railway tracks and platforms, with intricate blue trusswork on the one side and smooth undulating panels of glass on the other, results in a spectacular internal space.

The aesthetics of the modern airport are in evidence in the passenger-handling spaces beneath the platform bridge. Attention has been given to the logistics of train arrivals and departures. With the capacity of some of the latest trains approaching 800, and the likelihood of at least two trains arriving from different destinations within minutes of each other, the terminus may have to handle some 3,000 passengers at any one time, and needs to segregate the movements of incoming and departing travellers.

Escalators and travelators connect the platforms to the arrival and departure areas, with most passengers passing through a central control zone. Arriving passengers descend to the control zone and then pass by a ramp to the lower floor to proceed through immigration and customs to the arrivals concourse. While passengers disembark, access to the control zone is prevented for departing passengers and escalators are switched to downward movement. When the trains have been cleared, and the carriages cleaned and restocked, the control zone will be opened to the departure lounge, the escalators and travelators reversed, and passengers allowed to make their way up to their carriages having already passed through the ticket control booths and the security checks, all at the upper level immediately below the platform structure.

The alternating raised and lowered section of the platforms and the track beds is exploited in the departure level, where the main pedestrian routes are organized under the high-level sections and associated facilities housed beneath the lower sections. Colours are subdued and the fittings and finishes, all designed or selected by the architect, are very much in the international style. Particularly striking are the lavatory facilities, which boast Scandinavian grey granite floors, stainless steel cubicles, and walls clad in polished black marble where they support the washbasins. These are mounted individually and set within unusual tear-drop shaped tops in polished black granite with stainless steel fittings, and individual back-lit circular mirrors over each one. There is a glamour and a functional expressiveness in these spaces that recalls the golden age of rail travel.

Further feats of glazing technology have been harnessed, particularly in the design of the huge curved outer wall of the supporting structure. This is of glass panels suspended from the structure and braced by glass fins to allow as much light as possible into the arrival and departure areas. The wall has to cope with the substantial vertical deflections generated from the heavy engines moving overhead, as well as the thermal expansion acting horizontally. The solution developed employs stainless steel components shaped rather like wishbones and manufactured by the wax-casting process. These castings are bolted to the glass fins and support stainless steel rods which are able to move up and down through the sleeved connections at the thin ends of the 'wishbone'. The rods are connected in turn to the corners of each sheet of glass, the resulting construction enabling the glass panels to move up and down in sections and the whole wall to flex in sympathy with vertical and horizontal movements.

The new terminal is designed to handle some 15 million passengers a year and will come into use when the Channel Tunnel opens for passenger trains.

FOUNTAINS ABBEY VISITOR CENTRE
Ripon, North Yorkshire

Architect: Edward Cullinan Architects

The ruins of Fountains Abbey, set in the park at Studley Royal and the narrow wooded valley of the River Skell to the south-west of Ripon, is one of the few sites in the country designated a UNESCO World Heritage site. Owned by the National Trust, who purchased the abbey, the park and its water gardens and garden buildings, and the adjoining Fountains Hall from North Yorkshire County Council in 1983, Fountains is the most visited of all National Trust properties. The need to accommodate several hundred thousand visitors a year without destroying the unique qualities of the site has resulted in the construction of a new visitor centre.

The site of the new centre has been selected as part of a plan to relate views and vistas to new and existing landscape and architectural features. Access is obtained along a new road skirting the north-west boundary of the site, routed to reveal views of the Victorian Gothic St Mary's Church which is passed en route. The centre is positioned some quarter of a mile away from the abbey and is not visible from the ruins, although the topmost section of the abbey tower is visible from the new building, the view terminating the diagonal axis across the open courtyard around which the new facilities are grouped and providing an immediate point of reference for those arriving. The building combines a modern approach to space and structure with traditional materials, attention to detail and craftsmanship.

The appearance of the building is highly articulated, utilizing a mix of three-dimensional forms. A simple plan layout is rendered spatially complex and interesting through clever use of the differing roof profiles expressed on the interior and exterior alike. The plan is essentially that of two L-shaped single-storey buildings arranged around the opposing corners of a square courtyard. One contains an exhibition area and ticket office, shop and auditorium. The other accommodates a large restaurant, kitchen and lavatories. Each building has an entrance lobby off the corners of the courtyard top-lit by small glazed lanterns on the cross-axis to that formed by the entrance view to the abbey tower.

The two major L-shaped components are each broken down into further L-shaped sub-parts expressed by means of the differing roof profiles. Around the inner courtyard the roof shape has a soft double-curve profile extending over an open cloister and clad in lead sheet. The outer volumes against the landscape have crisp 45° monopitch roofs clad in the traditional manner with natural stone tiles laid to diminishing courses. At the corners the monopitch roofs stand apart, and the soft double-curving roof form breaks out from the courtyard to cover the larger volumes of the auditorium and restaurant. The two forms are juxtaposed around a central spine of steel columns, the higher ridge line of the 45° roofs allowing daylight to penetrate deep into the interior through a series of continuous clerestorey windows over the centre line of the plan.

The white-painted steel structure is expressed throughout, both internally and externally, the construction being neatly detailed to resolve the many different junctions, with special brackets, cleats and bolts all visible. This articulated approach to construction informs the whole of the fabric. The roof forms, the walls and cladding, and the steel skeleton underpinning it all are assembled in a loose manner that allows each element its independence, so that roofs break free of the building to extend as canopies, walls continue outwards to define terraces and routes. Internally the timber rafters supporting the roof

surfaces are concealed by plywood sheeting to enclose the roof insulation, but the rafter positions are indicated by the application of coloured strips of timber, green and blue alternating on a regular major-minor rhythm, the blue strips doubling as a device to fix the positions of the spotlight fittings. The strips run from eaves to ridge on the monopitch sections but at right angles to this on the double-curved sections where the rafters are laid parallel to the eaves/ridge line.

The lightweight nature of the superstructure is emphasized by glazed timber-framed walls separating the dominant roof forms form the solid drystone battered walls that surround the base of the building and appear to grow out of the undulating ground contours. The drystone work anchors the centre to its site, the walls leaning inward to protect the more fragile looking superstructure. In fact, they are not integral with the superstructure but stand independently to act as a rain screen for the insulation layer on the outer side of the blockwork lining walls.

The intermediate glazed cladding, whether to full height from the floor level or as a window strip below eaves level, utilizes repeated vertical strips of cedar boards which alternate with clear glass panels to provide an intricate pattern of light and shade in the interior. The method of construction emphasizes the independence of the component parts, the vertical strips overlapping the intermediate rails to provide a more modelled surface, and the fixing bolt positions being marked by projecting wooden dowels. It is this attention to detail that gives the building its feeling of solid craftsmanship.

Despite the use of traditional materials and forms, this is an undeniably modern building. Stylistically it is something of a hybrid, the rustic vernacular idioms of the exterior contrasting with the finely-crafted structure and bright daylit interiors, where there is a noticeable affinity with oriental styles of architecture.

BOWRA BUILDING
Wadham College, Oxford

Architect: MacCormac Jamieson Prichard

The recently completed Bowra Building, a student residence at Wadham College, Oxford, responds to the demand for maximum accommodation on a tight site with imagination and skill, and in a style that sits happily amongst its earlier neighbours without any slavish copying of historical details.

The brief called for a combination of student bed-sitting-rooms and communal facilities to provide the right mix of accommodation for undergraduate use during term-time and for conference bookings during vacations. The site occupies the last suitable plot of land for such a building and lies along the boundary of the college, with the outer wing of student bedrooms defining the perimeter of the college grounds, closely hemmed in on the other sides by existing buildings. Resolution of the daylighting, building height and overlooking constraints has led to the distinctive form of the building. Some of its characteristics the architect ascribes to the late 16th-century Hardwick Hall, distinctive by virtue of its combination of long gallery spaces at ground level linked to a series of articulated towers rising clear of the main roof plane, and its emphasis upon openess, evidenced by the huge expanses of window.

Similarly, the plan of the new residence building places the student bedrooms in a series of towers, either detached or linked to form a strongly modelled terrace. All rise from a podium of communal spaces in which the concept of the longitudinal gallery has been refined as it wraps around three sides of a new terraced courtyard. The plan is an elongated U-shape, with the base of the U running along the site boundary in the form of a terrace of linked groups of study bedrooms arranged four to a landing around dog-leg staircases. Each stair is linked to a kitchen, which helps each vertical tower of bedrooms (at three storeys, commonly twelve to a stair) function as a self-contained unit.

Each of the room units has a double bay window arrangement and the units are handed in both directions around the central stair to provide the intricately modelled symmetrical building block from which the terrace is created. Similar building blocks are developed into free standing tower-like elements surrounding the inner courtyard side of the U-shape plan, with access to bedrooms at first floor or above from the outside via short staircases rising from the paved podium deck over the ground storey upon which all the bedroom units are placed. Careful disposition of the windows in their projecting bays, coupled with a subtle diminution of width on elevation towards the courtyard, has enabled all the bedrooms to enjoy good daylight and interesting views out of and through the site, despite the considerable depth of the development from front to back.

The ground-floor gallery concept has been developed to provide a series of spaces wrapped around the U-shape in which a narrow cloister running round the courtyard is alternately separate from and combined with the deeper internal room spaces. The two short arms of the U connect on one side to the gable end of an existing building and on the other project forward to create the courtyard and close to the vista from the formal entrance on the street. The arm on the north side contains a café and servery and a further extension space either for seminars or additional café seating, and the arm on the south side contains a substantial multipurpose room, from the end of which a student office projects in a circular bay.

On north and south sides the cloister space is open to the courtyard; on the east side the central space projects forward and a long bar-room embraces the cloister structure in a series of seating bays, with doors opening out onto the terrace. A variety of service spaces and stores runs along the back of the

bar counter under the podium deck up against a long wall marking the line of the perimeter terrace above. Below this terraced element are housed an office overlooking a rear entrance, a workshop and loading bay, and sports/social facilities comprising a squash court and gallery and a gymnasium/theatre. Internally the colours and finishes are crisp, modern and stylish, with dark blue stained joinery, honey-coloured polished timber floors and white walls and ceilings.

Externally the four storeys of the development, rising to a galleried fifth level in the bedrooms along the rear terrace, are clearly differentiated into base, middle and top, the central two-storey band being substantially of a warm yellow-buff brickwork. The characteristic architectural motif of the scheme derives from the substantial precast reconstituted stone quoin blocks embedded into the projecting corners of the brick bays at mid-height and at the upper and lower corners. These extend upwards and downwards to form rusticated corner columns defining the base and top of the tower forms. Each tower element is the width of one bedroom, so that free-standing towers, with two bedrooms on elevation, appear as two vertically proportioned linked towers either side of a recessed section or a projecting bay, surmounted by shallow pitched oversailing roofs. The verticality of the proportions is emphasized by the additional height of the topmost structure over the ground storey, the deep spandrel over the topmost windows being treated as a plain white panel slightly recessed behind the column face.

Many details testify to the careful crafting of the design, such as the chunky curved profile to the underside of projecting cills, the subtle coursing of the free-standing rusticated columns to accommodate a precast balustrade element that forms the rudimentary cornice of an enclosure to an open stairway from below, and the simple clean junctions beween differing materials and forms.

Inevitably in such a dense development there are problems with privacy and bedroom overlooking bedroom. However, the spatial complexity and the proximity of positions from which to see, be seen and engage in social interaction is a feature much appreciated by its student occupants, for whom the social and community aspects of college life are frequently as valuable as academic study.

WESTERN MORNING NEWS HEADQUARTERS
Plymouth, Devon

Architect: Nicholas Grimshaw and Partners

Plymouth has a centuries-old maritime history and the architect of the new headquarters of the Western Morning News, one of the West Country's leading newspapers, has drawn heavily on nautical imagery, to spectacular and original effect.

The new building houses the management, editorial and advertising departments and the printing presses of the Western Morning News. Berthed, as it were, on a hillside site outside the city, with views over Dartmoor as well as over Plymouth Sound, this extraordinary new building presents from most angles an uncanny likeness to some great glass ship in dry dock, its outward curving glass hull capped by a high-level bridge and a mast supported from a solid projecting tower like some new and revolutionary aircraft carrier.

The architect has chosen to exploit the commanding view afforded by the selected site by making the building envelope completely transparent. The continuous glass wall is three storeys high and curves upwards and outwards like a ship's hull, held in place not from the internal structure but from a series of enormous external free-standing tusk-shaped columns, broadest at the base, and tapering away as they rise above the eaves level.

The nautical image is reinforced by the use of lightweight yacht-rigging technology for the cladding support components and by the boat-shaped plan form, with its flat stern and pointed prow. The cladding structure is independent of the main building, which is an orthodox reinforced concrete frame supporting concrete floors cantilevered towards the glass skin like trays. The roof structure links the two systems, its gently curved steel support beams propped from the external tusks and supported on an inner ring of concrete columns projecting upwards from the third level. The steel roof beams penetrate the glazed wall at eaves level and are connected to the tusks through pin joints.

The tusks themselves are fabricated from two curving steel tubes at front and back, each formed to a slightly different curvature, with steel plates welded to each one to form the sides. From the tip of each tusk steel tension rods angle down and out to support the top of the glass wall-panels. From each side of the tusk, pairs of metal arms stretch out to pick up the line of the tension rods and act to restrain the glazing panels through complex 'four fingered' bosses, each finger supporting one corner of the four adjacent glass panels.

The metal components of the support and restraint system have taken on a strongly sculptural character, their design having been refined by the use of computer-aided design techniques to maximize strength while minimizing the weight of material used. Special casting techniques were used to create the bone-like arms of ductile iron and the stainless steel glazing bosses, the latter comprising a complex assembly of ball joints, tapered washers and sliding fixings to accommodate the variations in geometry and movement throughout the external skin.

Internally, the building is divided into two halves, separated by a fire-resisting bulkhead wall. One half contains all the printing presses and paper-reel storage areas as well as publishing facilities and distribution areas; the other half, forming the 'bow'

end, contains the reception, management, editorial and advertising sections arranged in a roughly triangular layout of offices around a triangular atrium generated by the curving of the external walls into the pointed prow at the east end. Individual offices are grouped into an intermediate zone around the atrium, so that the open-plan office areas gain maximum advantage from the spectacular views to the outside and the daylight which floods in. On the lowest floor social facilities include a kitchen and restaurant, a coffee area at the base of the atrium, and training and gymnasium facilities.

The massing of the building and arrangement of the component elements in section exploits the sloping contours of the site. The building is cut into the slope along the southern perimeter so that the 'ship' appears to be sitting in a dry dock. This enables the main access to the building to be organized at the middle level by means of an entrance bridge, boarded and railed like a ship's gangway.

Along the western half of this elevation the loading and distribution bays cantilever forward to a number of bridge connections from which the finished newspapers are collected and dispatched. Delivery of the raw material in the form of massive reels of paper takes place at the west end at the lower level, and here the massive loads generated by the printing presses and paper storage are founded directly onto the rock below. The printing hall is at the middle level, rising to nearly two storeys in height, the engineering of the machinery opened to public view through the glazed walls. The western elevation, by contrast with the remainder of the external skin, fails to maintain the nautical image, comprising a large flat blank wall of corrugated metal cladding. However, it is intended that the building will expand at this end to accommodate additional printing machinery as the business expands, and it is hoped that the building will acquire a 'stern' to match the remainder of the 'hull' and lose its present sawn-off look.

Rising dramatically above the curving surface of the roof deck, one of the staircase cores punches through the roof line to form a tall tower, from which is cantilevered the triangular volume of the boardroom. The long curving strip window wrapping round both projecting corners of the room affords panoramic views over the surrounding countryside, and caps a stunning tour-de-force of structural ingenuity and imaginative design.

Construction of the building cost approximately £15 million, and has secured for its owners a marvellous display window for its activities – the building has already become a magnet for visiting parties of school children and interested organizations.

Bequests to Charity

The alphabetical list below represents some of the principal charitable bequests from wills published since the last edition. Prior bequests, expenses and inheritance tax have to be deducted from the net figures for estates given below, so that the exact amount left to charities is not usually known.

The list includes two very large estates, headed by the £41.3 million estate of Harry Joel, the 97-year-old racehorse owner and breeder who had won both the Derby and Grand National; he left the residue of his estate to the Childwick Trust, for charitable purposes. Martin Wills left the residue of his £20 million estate to follow the H. D. H. Wills 1965 Charitable Trust, on the condition that the income be revolved in a seven-year cycle – Magdalen College, Oxford, in the first year, Rendcomb College, Glos., in the second year, any registered charity his executors select primarily dedicated to wildlife conservation in years three and four, the Ditchley Foundation in year five, and for such charitable purposes as his executors think fit in years six and seven.

Fifteen of the wills left large residues for charitable purposes decided by executors, including the £6.7 million estate of Lord Bernstein, the former head of the Granada Group. Some of these bequests were qualified: Marian Brunskill wished to benefit as equally as possible those organizations researching the causes of nervous diseases and cancer and those comforting sufferers. Dr Margaret Dix wanted her home and other properties to provide free or low-cost housing for the needy and then for charities promoting the Christian faith according to the Church of England in the diocese of Lichfield, especially in the use of traditional worship.

Several estates included large bequests to named trusts. The residue of the £4.3 million estate of Thomas Leveson Gower included two paintings by Canaletto and the Redland Tile Works and was left to the Titsey Foundation. Oliver Ford left the residue of his £1.8 million estate to form the Oliver Ford Foundation, to preserve his home, Bewley Court, Wilts, and its contents and grounds, to permit the public to have access and to educate them in the history and techniques of interior decoration, fabric design and landscape gardening.

Probably the most mentioned charity in the list is the RNLI. Apart from sharing in a number of other estates, they were the sole residuary legatee in the estates of Eugenie Boucher, David Kirkaldy, Edith East, Charles Beeby, and Constance Rogers. The RNLI also featured in those large estates which were left entirely for charity, sharing the £993,093 estate of Maud Collings with the International Red Cross. The Guide Dogs for the Blind Association received all the estate of Kathleen Harris, while Mabel Donning left all her estate to the Little Sisters of the Poor in Liverpool, and Audrey Howe left her estate for a sheltered housing scheme to be named after her late father Max Howe in the vicinity of Kingston upon Thames. Linley Shaw left all his estate to his executor (the National Westminster Bank) to set up a charity, the income to be used to help some or all of those bodies which organize voluntary workers to tidy up and beautify the countryside. The National Trust received the residues of two estates of over £1 million, those of Marjorie Muirhead and Isabel Fullerton, who both lived in Tenterden, Kent.

Unusual bequests include that of Delphina Burt, who left the residue of her estate to the Roman Catholic Bishop of Southwark, 'for the benefit of the Holy Father'. Rixi Markus, the world's first woman bridge grandmaster, left the residue of her estate to the Weizmann Institute, in memory of herself and of her sister Eugenia and family who were killed by the Nazis in Lwow, Poland, around 1944. The last, though hardly charitable, word belongs to Norman Newbold, of Sileby, Leics., who left the residue of his £1.1 million estate to the Treasury for the reduction of the National Debt!

Hugh Leist Allen, of Suton, Wymondham, Norfolk, £1,040,346, (£10,000 and a quarter of the residue each to the Norfolk Naturalists Trust and Royal Society for Nature Conservation, £3,000 and a quarter of the residue to Caistor St Edmund Church, and £2,000 and a quarter of the residue to the Woodland Trust)

Marjorie Anthony, of Barry, S. Glam., £2,406,110, (the residue for such charitable institutions or objects in England and Wales as her executors select)

John Francis Basil Atkins, of Goring-by-Sea, W. Sussex, £2,649,278 (the residue equally between the Imperial Cancer Research Fund, RNIB, Distressed Gentlefolk's Aid Association, British Red Cross Society and Salvation Army)

Cyril William Beard, of Worthing, W. Sussex, £801,082, (the residue to the RNIB)

Charles Alfred Beeby, of Long Itchington, Warks., £1,309,895, (the residue to the RNLI, for a lifeboat to be named 'The Joy and Charles Beeby')

The Rt. Hon. Sidney Lewis, Baron Bernstein, of St James's Place, London SW1, £6,710,847, (the residue to the Amberstone Trust, or for such charitable institutions or objects as his executors select)

Hilda Mary Beswick, of Horwich, Greater Manchester, £934,107, (the residue equally between the Abbeyfield Bolton Society, the Birtenshaw Hall School, Imperial Cancer Research Fund, National Society for Cancer Relief and Bolton Hospice Appeal)

Margaret Palling Betts, of Malvern, Worcs., £435,337, (all her estate equally between the Worcester Scanner Appeal, St Michael's Hospice, Bartestree, Hereford, the Friends of Wells Cathedral, RSPB and RNLI)

Eugenie Boucher, of Abbots Leigh, Bristol, £4,219,474, (the residue to the RNLI)

Philip Anthony Breeze, of Stambourne, Essex, £2,027,304, (the residue equally between the Salvation Army, Hospital for Sick Children, Great Ormond Street,

London, Save the Children Fund, National Children's Home, Guide Dogs for the Blind Association, Wood Green Animal Shelter, Oxfam, Greenpeace Environmental Trust, Multiple Sclerosis Society, London Association for the Blind, NSPCC, UNICEF, RSPCA, Royal British Legion, Blue Cross, Redwings Horse Sanctuary, Norfolk, and Brooke Hospital for Animals, London)

Marian Brunskill, of Greenmount, Bury, Greater Manchester, £934,574, (the residue for such charitable objects or purposes in the UK as her executors select, with the wish they benefit as equally as possible research into nervous diseases and cancer and the comfort of those so suffering)

Iris Luise Burgers, of Torquay, Devon, £1,176,361, (a quarter of the residue each to the Imperial Cancer Research Fund and the Arthritis and Rheumatism Council, and one tenth of the residue each to the Distressed Gentlefolk's Aid Association, Guide Dogs for the Blind Association, RNIB, RNLI, and Home Farm Trust)

Elizabeth Mary Burnley, of Newtown, Hungerford, Berks., £1,122,707, (three-quarters of the residue to the Community of St Mary the Virgin, Wantage, and one quarter of the residue equally between St Christopher's Hospice, London, Church Army, St Luke's Hospital for the Clergy, London, and the Children's Society)

Donald Hamilton Burns, of Taunton, Somerset, £2,456,478, (one fifth of the residue equally between the NSPCC, RSPCA, PDSA, British Deaf Association, Barnardo's, RNIB, RNLI and National Trust)

Delphina Harriet Mary Burt, of Curzon Street, London W1, £4,223,787, (the residue to the Roman Catholic Bishop of Southwark, 'for the benefit of the Holy Father')

Nanette Capstick, of Mirfield, W. Yorks., £883,722, (the residue equally between the Wakefield Grammar School Foundation, Yorkshire Cancer Research Campaign, York Minster Fabric Fund, RNLI, King George's Fund for Sailors, RAF Benevolent Fund, St Dunstan's, National Trust, Guide Dogs for the Blind Association, Arthritis and Rheumatism Council, British Heart Foundation, Missions to Seamen, Outward Bound Trust, and a charity for the treatment of and/or research into epilepsy as her executors choose)

Revd Alan Vincent Carefull, of Helhoughton, Norfolk, £1,057,910, (the residue for such charitable purposes of a religious nature as his executors select)

Jeanne Elizabeth Chard, of Collingham, W. Yorks., £1,565,991, (the residue equally between the Masonic Foundation for the Aged and Sick, Guide Dogs for the Blind Association, RNLI, RSPCA and Leukaemia Research Fund)

Doris Clarkson, of Bolton, Greater Manchester, £3,995,598, (the residue equally between the Bolton Lads Club, Bolton Hospice, Destitute Animal Shelter, Bolton, RSPCA, PDSA, Bleakholt Animal Sanctuary, RSPB, Salvation Army, RNLI, International Fund for Animal Welfare, Donkey Sanctuary, Sidmouth, St Dunstan's and Barnardo's)

Catherine Hilda Cole, of Edgware, Middx, £1,300,800, (all her estate equally between the League of Friends of Edgware General Hospital, League of Friends of the Royal London Homoeopathic Hospital and St John Ambulance Brigade)

Maud Spurrell Collings, of Torquay, Devon, £993,093, (all her estate equally between the RNLI, and the International Red Cross, Geneva)

Peter Dudley Cordrey, of Hayes, Middx, £2,253,483, (one ninth of the residue to the World Vision of Britain)

Eric Adcroft Corless, of Chaddesley Glen, Canford Cliffs, Dorset, £527,777, (the residue to the Development Trust of Queen Elizabeth's Grammar School, Blackburn, Lancs., for prizes and bursaries)

Reginald Ernest Cull, of Hertford, £1,913,240, (£30,000 and a quarter of the residue to All Saints Church, Hertford, and a quarter of the residue each to Hertford County Hospital, 'the Society for the Blind' and 'the Society for Cancer Research')

Leslie Francis Davey, of Eastbourne, E. Sussex, £1,493,698, (the residue for such charitable bodies as his executors select)

Eileen Alice Baldwin Davies, of Eastbourne, E. Sussex, £845,807, (the residue equally between the RNLI, Eastbourne Branch, Spastics Society and Barnardo's)

Mary Olive Davies, of Fountains Crescent, London N14, £882,599, (two-thirds of the residue equally between the British Heart Foundation, Royal Masonic Hospital Samaritan Fund and Guide Dogs for the Blind Association)

John James Davy, of Aynhoe Road, London W14, £1,019,625, (the residue for such charitable institutions in the UK as his executors determine, to include universities, schools or hospitals of any description)

Frederick Leslie Dawson, of Flitwick, Beds., £1,291,118, (the residue equally between the National Society for Cancer Relief, Salvation Army, Church Army, British Red Cross Society, Marie Curie Memorial Foundation, Trinity Hospice, London, Royal Star and Garter Home, Richmond, and Sue Ryder Foundation)

Dirk Arthur Degenhart, of Priory Gardens, London W4, £1,363,841, (one fifth of the residue to the RSPCA, and one tenth of the residue each to the Old English Mastiff Club and Association for International Cancer Research)

Dr Margaret Ruth Dix, of Badger, Salop, £1,648,646, (the residue for such charities as her executors select, especially those promoting the Christian religion in accordance with the Church of England in the Lichfield diocese)

Mabel Jane Donning, of Noctorum, Birkenhead, £674,724, (all her estate to the Little Sisters of the Poor, Liverpool)

Florence Gertrude Patricia Dottridge, of Beaconsfield, Bucks., £1,824,321, (half the residue to the Universal Hospice Trust, Beaconsfield, a quarter of the residue to the Sue Ryder Foundation and a quarter of the residue for such charitable institutions or objects in England as her executors select)

Edith Mary East, of Hove, E. Sussex, £1,909,636, (the residue to the RNLI)

Beryl Pauline Marguerite Emily Eeman, of The Mount, London NW3, £1,662,504, (the residue to the Beryl Eeman Charitable Trust, London)

Dr Archibald McLaren Ferrie, of Eccleston, St Helen's, £1,309,969, (the residue to the Hamewith Trust, managed by Liverpool Council of Social Service)

Oliver Frederick Ford, of Bewley Court, Lacock, Wilts., £1,815,169, (the residue to form the Oliver Ford Foundation for the preservation of Bewley Court)

Isabel Mary Evelyn Fullerton, of Tenterden, Kent, £1,318,885, (the residue to the National Trust)

Susan Garth, of Palace Street, London SW1, £1,015,117, (the residue to the Friends of the Hebrew University, London, for their cancer research programme)

Doris Girling, of Worthing, W. Sussex, £1,071,328, (the residue equally between St Barnabas Nursing Home, Worthing, National Trust, NSPCC, RNID and PDSA)

Thomas Christopher Gresham Leveson Gower, of Oxted, Surrey, £4,335,583, (the residue to the Titsey Foundation)

Winifred Evelyn Griffith, of Eastcote, Middx, £848,796, (the residue to the J. F. Moorhead Renal Research Trust at the Royal Free Hospital, London)

Winifred Muriel Gurr, of New Malden, Surrey, £1,061,774, (half the residue to the British Red Cross Society, and three-20ths of the residue each to the PDSA, and YMCA, Leicester)

Henry Haskell Harris, of Park Road, London NW1, £951,037, (the residue equally between the Jewish Welfare Board, Jewish Blind Society, Jewish Home and Hospital at Tottenham, Nightingale House Home for Aged Jews, London, Royal College of Nursing, British Red Cross Society, Ravenswood Foundation, Save the Children Fund, Barnardo's and Norwood Childcare)

Kathleen Frances Harris, of Worthing, W. Sussex, £2,912,088, (all her estate to the Guide Dogs for the Blind Association)

Audrey Margaret Howe, of Hordle, Hants, £467,596, (all her estate to the Anchor Housing Association, for a sheltered housing scheme in the Kingston upon Thames vicinity, to be named after her father Max Howe)

Henry Stephen Hoyles, of Nynehead, Wellington, Somerset, £1,836,414, (the residue to the Royal Masonic Benevolent Institution)

Geoffrey Richard Humfrey, of Desborough, Northants, £849,555, (£5,000 and half the residue to Brampton Ash Parish Church, and half the residue to the Nene Valley Railway, Peterborough)

Harry Joel Joel, of Childwick Bury, St Albans, Herts., £41,318,848, (the residue to the Childwick Trust, for charitable purposes)

Eva May Johnson, of Harrogate, N. Yorks., £2,243,191, (the residue equally between the National Trust York Centre, RSPCA, 'Donkey Sanctuary', and Bransby Home of Rest for Horses, Lincs.)

Dorothy Joyce Joyce, of Bentley, Hants, £3,146,297, (one sixth of the residue to the Ratcliffe Charitable Trust and one sixth of the residue equally between St Laurence's Church, Alton, St Nicholas Church, West Worldham, Abbey Seamen's Friendly Society, Alton, John Groom's Association, Spitalfields Crypt Trust, London, and the Conservative and Unionist Agents Superannuation Fund)

Mary Joy Kingsley Kay, of Rhos-on-Sea, Clwyd, £3,397,289, (the residue equally between the Harry Edwards Spiritual Healing Trust, St Dunstan's, Church of England Pensions Board, Imperial Cancer Research Fund, Arthritis and Rheumatism Council and Salvation Army)

Jeffrey Kelson, MBE, of Liverpool Road, London N1, £2,095,825, (the residue to the Jeffrey Kelson Foundation)

David William Henry Kirkaldy, of Hove, E. Sussex, £2,057,424, (the residue to the RNLI)

Freda Clara Lacy, of Farnham, Surrey, £1,252,610, (seven 18ths of the residue to the Phyllis Tuckwell Memorial Hospice, Farnham, two ninths of the residue to the PDSA, 23/90ths of the residue to the Salvation Army, and seven 90ths of the residue to the Abbeyfield Farnham Society)

Lady Virginia Grant-Lawson, of Ogdens, Fordingbridge, Hants, £1,153,102, (£500,000 to the Lady Virginia Grant-Lawson Charitable Trust)

Mary Leapman, of Halstock, Dorset, £1,109,398, (the income in perpetuity from the residue of her estate for such charitable institutions or purposes in the UK as directed by her by memorandum or as her executors decide)

Mary Edith Leavesley, of Burton on the Wolds, Leics., £1,668,530, (one fifth of the residue variously between the Royal Leicester, Leicestershire and Rutland Institution for the Blind, Leicester Charity Organization Society, Leicester and County Mission for the Deaf, British Red Cross Society, Leicester, Cancer Research Campaign, National Society for Cancer Relief, RNLI, the Children's Society for work in Leicestershire, Army Benevolent Fund, Police Dependants Trust, and the United Reformed Church, London WC1)

Harold Ivan Leech, of Minehead, Somerset, £12,022,815, (20 parts of the residue each to the Cancer Research Campaign and Tuberous Sclerosis Association, ten parts each to the British Field Sports Society, RNLI, Brooke Hospital for Animals, London, and St Louis Convent, Minehead, five parts each to the Somerset Health Authority for hospital facilities in the Minehead area, the National Children's Home and John Groom's Association, and one part each to the Minehead Senior Citizens Club, and Quirke's Almshouse Charity, Minehead)

Edith Mary McDonagh, of Finchampstead, Berks., £1,048,714, (the residue for such charitable purposes as made known to her executors or as they decide)

Lady Annie Emily Mallabar, of Arlington Street, London SW1, £2,133,245, (£1,000,000 and the residue to the Jack and Pat Mallabar Charitable Foundation)

Rixi Markus, MBE, of Cadogan Place, London SW1, £326,275, (the residue to the Weizmann Institute Foundation, London)

Michael Leo Marsh, of Budleigh Salterton, Devon, £1,338,892, (the residue to the Michael Marsh Charitable Trust, formed in 1958)

Margaret Tyson Moraes, of Weimar Street, London SW15, £1,249,642 (a quarter of the residue to the Conservative Party and a further quarter to the chairman of the party for such charities as he thinks fit, one 31st of the residue to St Mary the Virgin Church, Putney, and one 62nd of the residue each to Putney Hospital, Middlesex Hospital League of Friends, Homes for Homeless People, British Red Cross Society, British Home and Hospital for Incurables, the Children's Society, Multiple Sclerosis Society, UNICEF, Water Aid, RNLI, Crisis, Royal Commonwealth Society for the Blind, British Heart Foundation, Royal College of Surgeons, British Lung Foundation, Harefield Hospital Heart Transplant Unit, St John's Ambulance, Putney and Roehampton Branch, Cancer Research Campaign, RADAR, Invalids at Home, Counsel and Care for the Elderly, Arthritis and Rheumatism Council, Salvation Army (half for Central Office and half for the Putney Branch), Distressed Gentlefolk's Aid Association, Motor Neurone Disease Association, Cancer Relief MacMillan Fund, Spastics Society, London Ambulance Service HQ Amenities Fund and Age Concern Greater London)

Marjorie Squire Muirhead, of Tenterden, Kent, £1,729,424, (the residue to the National Trust)

John Herbert Charles Nayler, of Dorking, Surrey, £1,457,962, (nine 40ths of his estate to Help the Aged)

Dr Agnes Freda Newitt, of Dibden Purlieu, Hants, £1,298,627, (£100,000 to the Wilverley Trust, Dibden Purlieu, and the residue to Southampton University for the Richard and Freda Newitt Fund)

Angela Maria Sophia Antonia Ofenheim, of Hellingly, E. Sussex, £3,369,841, (the residue to the Cinderford Charitable Trust, established in 1983)

Phyllis Georgina Pacey, of Worthing, W. Sussex, £897,090, (the residue equally between the RNLI, Ex-Services Mental Welfare Society, Children in Need Appeal, RNIB, RSPCA, Royal Star and Garter Home, Richmond, British Heart Foundation, and Royal Scottish Society for the Prevention of Cruelty to Children)

Lady Lillian Fay Peck, of Bournemouth, Dorset, £2,016,079, (half the residue to the RAF Association Richard Peck House Convalescent Home, Lytham St Annes, Lancs., and a quarter of the residue each to the Cheshire Foundation and Salvation Army)

Dorothy Mabel Perry, of Yeovil, Somerset, £1,050,689, (the residue to the League of Friends of Yeovil Hospitals)

Frances Marie Louise Prior, of Charlton Kings, Glos., £858,601, (the residue equally between the Guide Dogs for the Blind Association and Injured Jockeys Fund)

Angela Christine Wightman Raphael, of Warborough, Oxon., £1,145,523, (half the residue for such charitable institutions or objects in the UK as her executor selects)

Margaret Alice Rawlinson, of Bolton le Sands, Lancs., £1,657,824, (the residue equally between the Cancer Research Campaign, St Dunstan's, RNLI, and 'British Diabetes Association')

Maud Elizabeth Reddihough, of Farnhill, N. Yorks., £1,099,331, (the residue to the Northern Baptist Theological College, Rusholme, Manchester, to be known as the Maud Elizabeth Reddihough Trust Fund)

Constance Lillian Rogers, of Thetford, Norfolk, £941,883, (the residue to the RNLI)

Margaret Saffery, of Campden Hill Road, London w8, £1,183,949, (the residue equally between the University Women's Club, London, RNID, Friends of the Elderly and Gentlefolk's Help, SSAFA, Ex-Services Mental Welfare Society, Age Concern England, Age Concern Greater London, Abbeyfield Society, the Children's Society, Disabled Living Foundation, STA Schooners and Salvation Army)

Irene Scouloudi, of Hornsey Lane, London N6, £1,393,107, (the residue to the Twenty Seven Foundation, created by her in 1962)

Violet Mabel Seeby, of Sandhurst, Berks., £2,139,848, (£10,000 and one seventh of the residue each to Frimley Park Hospital, Surrey, Royal Berkshire Hospital, Reading, and Royal Star and Garter Home, Richmond)

Dorothy Patricia Shakespeare, of Ferndown, Dorset, £1,765,842, (the residue for such charitable objects or purposes as her executors select)

Linley Wightman Shaw, of Lyndhurst Gardens, London NW3, £1,686,467, (all his estate to set up a charity to help tidy up and beautify the UK countryside)

Kathleen Shenton, of Tytherington, Cheshire, £1,102,414, (the residue equally between St Michael and All Angels Parish Church, Macclesfield, Girl Guide Association Commonwealth HQ, the Children's Society, Guide Dogs for the Blind Association and RNLI)

David Shepherd, of Portland Place, London W1, £2,658,485, (three tenths of the residue each to the Jewish Welfare Board and British Technion Society, 11/40ths of the residue to the Jewish Blind Society, three 40ths of the residue to British ORT, and one 20th of the residue to the Ravenswood Foundation)

Nora Smith, of Llandudno, Gwynedd, £1,139,329, (the residue for such charities or charitable purposes as her executors determine)

John Hanbury Angus Sparrow, OBE, of Iffley, Oxford, £1,688,137, (certain published and unpublished works, manuscripts and letters, all rights thereto and a quarter of the residue to All Souls College, Oxford, some literary manuscripts and one 12th of the residue to the Bodleian Library, Oxford, and one 12th of the residue each to New College, Oxford, and Winchester College, Hants)

Agnes Mary Spink, of East Budleigh, Devon, £1,230,139, (the residue to Oxfam, to follow the trusts of the Henry Makinson Spink Memorial Fund)

William Reed Hornby Steer, of Whitehall Court, London SW1, £8,418,361, (one sixth of the residue each to the Order of St John, British Humane Association, Christ's Hospital, London, Old Etonian Trust, St Luke's Hospital for the Clergy, London, and King Edward VII's Hospital for Officers, London)

Richard Gething Strachan, of Clifton, Bristol, £2,014,232, (the residue equally between Clifton College, Bristol, for the Chapel, the Bristol Guild of the Handicapped Trust and Asthma Research Council)

Edward William Stratford, of Clapham, Beds., £1,846,689, (half the residue to the Barbara Bus Fund at the Royal National Orthopaedic Hospital, Stanmore)

Joan Summers, of St Albans, Herts., £1,018,214, (the residue equally between the RNLI, Save the Children Fund, Distressed Gentlefolk's Aid Association, Queen Elizabeth's Foundation for the Disabled, and St Luke's Hospital for the Clergy, London)

Alexander David Thomson, of Birkdale, Merseyside, £1,332,623, (the residue equally between the 341 Preston Air Training Corps, Birkdale School for Hearing Impaired Children, Queenscourt Hospice, Southport, RSPCA, Southport and District Branch, Cancer Research Campaign, and the Southport Branches of St John's Ambulance Brigade, Chest, Heart and Stroke Association and PDSA)

Mary Sabina Triniman, of Newquay, Cornwall, £2,414,201, (one tenth of the residue each to St Theresa's Cheshire Home, Marazion, League of Friends of Newquay Hospital, Cancer Research Campaign, Guide Dogs for the Blind Association, RNLI, British Red Cross Society, RNIB, Muscular Dystrophy Group, RSPCA and British Rheumatism and Arthritis Association)

Elspeth Waterhouse, of Wilpshire, Blackburn, Lancs., £1,728,876, (the residue to the Mrs Waterhouse Charitable Trust)

Martin David Hamilton Wills, of Sandford St Martin, Oxon., £20,021,456, (the residue to follow the trusts of the H. D. H. Wills 1965 Charitable Trust)

Barbara Mary Wilmot, of Washington, W. Sussex, £1,626,644, (the residue to her executors to be used for research into diseases of the human eye)

Gladys Winn, of Chapel Allerton, W. Yorks., £1,246,111, (the residue equally between the Leeds Children's Holiday Camp Association, Imperial Cancer Research Fund, Cancer Relief MacMillan Fund, Guide Dogs for the Blind Association, British Kidney Patient Association, British Heart Foundation, Friends of St James's Hospital, Leeds, RSPCA, RNLI, Help the Aged, Save the Children Fund, Shelter, Greenpeace Environmental Trust, Salvation Army, Barnardo's and Animal Aid Society)

Diana Marion Bonner Wood, of Carlton Hill, London NW8, £1,379,114, (ten parts of the residue each to the National Art Collections Fund and Fauna and Flora Society, seven parts to the Council for the Preservation of Rural Wales, six parts to the RSPB, and four parts to the Gardeners Royal Benevolent Society)

Margaret Amy Constance Wright, of Chipstead, Surrey, £1,216,480, (the residue equally between the Stock Exchange Benevolent Fund, Chartered Accountants Benevolent Association, Musicians Benevolent Fund, RSPB, Save the Children Fund, SENSE and British Red Cross Society)

Conservation and Heritage

FORESTRY PRIVATIZATION

Signs are emerging that the state forests administered by the Forestry Commission are to be privatized. The Commission was established in 1919 to create a 'strategic reserve' of timber by buying cheap land and planting it with fast-growing trees. In 1992 the Commission was divided into the Forestry Authority, which regulates the system and pays grants to the private sector, and Forestry Enterprise, which runs the state forests. It now manages some 1,127,500 hectares of forest – about 40 per cent of Britain's woodlands. The Forestry Commission has often been criticized for its concentration on imported conifers and for insensitive planting in the hills. In recent years, however, it has promoted broadleaf planting and has paid greater attention to habitat creation and amenity. It has also begun to succeed in bringing forests 'down the hill' to farmland and the hinterland of large cities. Within its estate are 335 Sites of Special Scientific Interest, 46 Forest Nature Reserves, 700 forest walks and 650 picnic sites.

A Forestry Review Group was set up by forestry ministers in March 1993 to review options for the future ownership and management of Forestry Commission land. The Secretary of State for Scotland (Ian Lang) also set up a group to produce a blueprint for privatizing state woodlands. The potential capital gain to The Treasury is estimated to be £26 billion. The only certain consequence of privatizing forests will be a loss of public access. The Commission has sold 100,000 hectares of land, mainly small unprofitable woods, since 1981. Few of these have maintained public access facilities. The statutory requirement of the Forestry Commission to 'take account of the needs of nature conservation and the environment' in its plans and operations will not apply to private owners, and a more ruthless planting policy is expected.

HABITAT CREATION

In August 1993 the Agriculture Minister (Gillian Shephard) announced new scales of agricultural payments as part of a £3 million habitat creation scheme. The payments include a top rate of £212 per acre – more than the current subsidy for oil-seed rape or linseed flax – for allowing coastal land to revert to salt marsh. This level of subsidy represents a tacit acceptance of the need for a 'managed retreat' in the face of rising sea-levels on parts of the south-east coast (*see also* below). Other rates include £145 an acre for creating marshland along water courses and lake shores, £153 an acre for allowing arable land to revert to heath and £135 an acre for encouraging wet

grassland. The take-up of the scheme may be limited by the ruling that farmers must take a minimum of 18 per cent of their land out of production on top of the mandatory 15 per cent set-aside.

The Minister also announced that £43 million will be spent in 1994–5 on administering six new Environmentally Sensitive Areas (ESAs). These will be the Cotswolds, the Blackdown Hills, the Shropshire Hills, Dartmoor, the Essex coast and the Upper Thames tributaries. The ESA scheme was introduced in 1986 as a means of subsidizing farming sensitive to the traditional character of the landscape. So far there are 16 ESAs in England, six in Wales, ten in Scotland and three in Northern Ireland. The scheme has been reasonably successful in reducing the excesses of intensive farming in areas of natural beauty, and has also helped to encourage 'green' attitudes in the farming community.

INTERIM DEVELOPMENT ORDERS

Gwenlais Valley and Carmel Woods in Dyfed have become a test case for validity of planning permissions for mineral extraction that were given under the very different circumstances of wartime Britain. Interim development orders frequently pre-date, and therefore bypass, planning and conservation legislation, and a quarry company is using one granted 50 years ago as the basis for extending its workings into a Site of Special Scientific Interest noted for the quality of its woodlands and for a rare ephemeral lake or turlough. An alliance of conservation groups argued their case at a public inquiry in February 1993. The inquiry's outcome may determine the fate of dozens of other similar sites where interim development orders are being claimed by quarry and mining companies.

MANAGED RETREAT

The sea-level is slowly rising along the coastline of East Anglia and south-east England. Because much of this coast is lined by sea walls, the inter-tidal habitat is being squeezed into an increasingly narrow zone below the walls. In some places, more than a quarter of the saltmarsh has been lost during the past 15 years. At the same time, the bill for repair and raising of the sea walls is rising.

In 1992 English Nature launched its 'Living Coast' campaign, which advocates a subtler way of coming to terms with the rising sea-level. Rather than rebuild eroding walls, it proposes shifting the line of defence landwards, allowing a new area of inter-tidal habitat to form. It also suggests using 'soft engineering' rather than walls as a means of coastal defence. For example, sand can be taken from the sea-bed to build up the level of a beach. Such schemes could prove a much cheaper form of defence, while also helping to preserve natural habitats like sand dunes and coastal marshes.

Experiments are currently taking place along the East Anglian coast to use managed retreat as a means of habitat creation. At Northey Island in Essex, owned by the National Trust, the sea wall has been lowered to allow overtopping at high tide, and a spillway created to allow the sea water to drain away with the tide. Since the sea wall was the habitat of several interesting plants, seed from these plants was taken and sown with a grass mixture at the new level. Salt marsh is rapidly replacing the pasture grasses on the flooded area. The results of such experiments are likely to influence the land-use of much of the East Anglian coast in the coming decades.

NATURE RESERVE AT THE WASH

The largest National Nature Reserve (NNR) in England was formally 'declared' in December 1992 at The Wash, where English Nature have leased 9,700 hectares of inter-tidal salt marshes and mud flats from the Crown Estate Commissioners. The area stretches from the mouth of the Nene at Sutton Bridge, Lincs., to beyond the Great Ouse at King's Lynn, Norfolk. Two areas of cattle-grazed marsh in Lincolnshire purchased by the Nature Conservancy Council (English Nature's predecessor) in 1986 have also become part of The Wash NNR.

The area is important for waders and wildfowl migrating from the Arctic to southern Europe and Africa, notably brent and pink-footed geese, shelduck, redshank, grey plover and knot. The shallow water is an important nursery ground for flatfish, cod and whiting, and the sandbanks hold the largest colony of common seals in north-west Europe. English Nature proposes to establish wildfowl refuges, improve bird-watching facilities and seek the co-operation of others in looking after the needs of wildlife in this vast but over-exploited area.

OXLEAS WOOD REPRIEVED

Road building continues to dominate the environmental agenda in Britain. The Government's intention to spend £2.1 billion on 40 major trunk road and motorway schemes threatens some 160 Sites of Special Scientific Interest. Two sites have caused particular controversy: Twyford Down near Winchester, Hants., and Oxleas Wood in the London Borough of Greenwich.

Oxleas Wood is believed to be 8,000 years old, and is a much-used public amenity. A plan to extend the East London River Crossing by building a four-lane trunk road through the wood has long been resisted by local residents and conservation groups. In 1991 the campaigners succeeded in persuading the EC environment commissioner to begin proceedings against the British government. In July 1993 the Secretary of State for Transport (John MacGregor) announced that he was not proceeding with the scheme. It is believed that it had already cost the Department of Transport £31 million. The campaigners celebrated by gathering to form a 'human map'

of Britain in Oxleas Meadow with white balloons pinpointing the SSSIs under threat from roadworks. At the time of writing, however, the Department's compulsory purchase order still stands.

Local campaigns have forced the Department to re-route two other major roadworks. After a public inquiry over the Hereford bypass, the Inspector decided that the Department of Transport had failed to make a convincing case for its planned route, which would have meant spoiling the town's historic Lugg Meadow. A consortium of environmental groups also pressured the Department into accepting the need for a tunnel to take the A3 beneath the scenic Hindhead Common and Devil's Punchbowl in Surrey.

RUDDY DUCKS

The Ruddy Duck is an American duck now well-established in Britain and western Europe after a few escaped from the Wildfowl Trust's sanctuary at Slimbridge, Glos., during the 1960s. It has since spread to southern Spain, where it threatens to oust the indigenous white-headed duck by progressive hybridization. The Spanish authorities persuaded the EEC to declare the ruddy duck a pest species and to initiate control measures aimed at exterminating the bird. In Britain, the directive has been endorsed by the RSPB and the Wildfowl and Wetland Trust.

A £75,000 government grant has been awarded to a consortium of bird organizations to carry out a survey of ruddy ducks in the UK and to investigate ways of controlling them. A three-year research programme based on Anglesey will look at the effectiveness of various methods, including shooting the adults and coating the eggs with paraffin to prevent hatching. This programme is controversial and has provoked considerable debate. Some suggest that the ruddy duck is being used as a scapegoat for diverting attention from harmful environmental practices in Spain and elsewhere, and that there are nationalistic undertones to the programme.

SET-ASIDE AND THE ENVIRONMENT

New regulations on the management of land temporarily set aside from agricultural production were introduced in 1992 and 1993. Since 1988, the Government has operated a voluntary scheme to reduce agricultural surpluses by paying farmers to take land out of production for a fixed term, usually five years. From 1993, all farms are required to set aside 15 per cent of their arable land. This has meant an increase in set-aside land from 417,000 acres in 1992 to 1.5 million acres (an area roughly the size of Lincolnshire) in 1993.

Set-aside takes three forms: one-year set-aside, introduced in autumn 1992, in which the fallow land is managed on an annual rotation; fixed set-aside of five years, in which the fallow land is sown with grass; and long-term set-aside of 20 years, in which the farmer is expected to take positive measures, such as planting trees and excavating ponds, in exchange for a higher rate of subsidy (available only for land set-aside above the mandatory 15 per cent). The

environmental benefits of such a scheme are potentially great, but the way in which the Ministry of
Agriculture has administered the scheme so far has
minimized its value for wildlife.

The annual set-aside got off to an unfortunate start
in the spring of 1993. In order to prevent the
establishment of weeds like docks and thistles, EC
rules allow the farmer to plough the land early in the
season. The Ministry of Agriculture interpreted this
ruling, apparently wrongly, to mean that farmers
must plough the fields in May. The result was a
massacre of ground-nesting birds like skylark and
grey partridge. The Ministry has promised to be
more flexible in future and to allow weed control to
take place outside the main nesting season.

Most conservationists regard the results of set-
aside so far as disappointing. They argue that the
£124 million spent on the scheme to date could have
been spent more usefully on subsidizing orgainc
farming and low-intensity agriculture. Set-aside is
probably encouraging some farmers to farm more
intensively on the remaining 85 per cent of their land
by removing hedges and ploughing headlands; and
since the farmer can choose which land to set-aside,
the hoped-for creation of 'wildlife corridors' is not
taking place. Only on the long-term set-aside land is
any real benefit being seen. On the evidence so far,
the environmental benefits of the scheme would seem
to have been greatly exaggerated.

SHETLAND OIL SPILL

On 5 January 1993 the tanker MV *Braer*, laden with
85,000 tonnes of Norwegian crude oil, ran aground
on rocks at Garth Ness, near Quendale Bay in
Shetland, after the engines failed. Over the following
days nearly all the cargo spilled into the sea as rough
weather frustrated salvage attempts. Since the spill
involved twice as much oil as that of the *Exxon Valdez*
incident in 1989, which polluted hundreds of miles of
the Alaskan coastline and killed hundreds of thousands of sea birds, a major disaster was feared.

However, the initial impact proved less harmful
than expected. The rough sea, driving rain and sleet
prevented the formation of a slick. The oil combined
with sea water and much of it seems to have coated
fine particles suspended in the sea and been carried
to the sea bed along the leeward parts of the Shetland
coast. Nevertheless, some 1,600 oiled sea birds were
collected during the first few weeks, mainly shag and
black guillemot, with smaller numbers of eider duck,
long-tailed duck and great northern diver. Many
more corpses were probably swept out to sea. Most
of the oiled birds died of toxic ingestion, and four
otters were found dead, one of which was run over by
a Swedish television crew. A rescue centre was set up,
and twenty grey seals were cleaned and released. The
force of the storm blew oil onto pasture above the
wreck. All sheep were removed from the area, and a
ban was placed on fishing for whitefish and shellfish
over an area of 500 square miles. Some two million
caged salmon on fish farms along the Shetland coast

were declared unfit for human consumption; some
were sold to Norway as food for farmed mink. Some
of the toxic hydrocarbons from the spill will inevitably
enter the marine ecosystem through the food chain
as the oil-rich sediment has collected on the spawning
grounds of herring and sand-eels, the main food of
Shetland's large sea bird colonies. Divers have
reported localized areas of severe damage many miles
from the wreck.

In the aftermath of the spill, the Minister of State
for Aviation and Shipping (Lord Caithness) called for
a voluntary code of practice under which laden
tankers would avoid coming close to sensitive parts
of the British coast. Past experience suggests,
however, that voluntary codes are routinely disregarded by captains of tankers. An ecological group
under the chairmanship of Professor William Ritchie
was set up by the Scottish Office to monitor the
environmental consequences of the spill, and its
report is expected in early 1994. The full impact of
the disaster on Shetland's breeding sea birds and
marine life will not be known until a full season's
results have been analysed.

SPECIES RECOVERY

English Nature's species recovery programme, intended to safeguard threatened species, has entered
its third year with a budget of £250,000. New species
added to the programme in 1993 are the fen violet
(*Viola persicifolia*), the New Forest cicada (*Cicadetta
montana*), a predatory water beetle (*Graphoderus
zonatus*) and a group of rare Breckland lichens. The
programme enables experts and conservation bodies
to study the needs of rare species to enable action to
be taken to preserve them. For one species, however,
it may be too late. The Essex Emerald moth now
appears to be extinct at its last known site, on the
Essex coast, and is represented only by a small captive
stock.

Much more promising is the future of the
dormouse, which has declined in Britain because of
the near abandonment of the coppicing system and
the replacement of native broadleaves by conifers.
The zoologists Pat Morris and Paul Bright have
tested a method of reintroducing dormice into woods
by tracking individual mice using radios and nest
boxes. The animals fare better when released in late
summer, when there is plenty of food available in the
form of nuts and berries. By giving them a settling-in
period in pre-release pens, the dormice generally
stay close to the point of release, often returning to
the pen to nest. The first large-scale reintroduction
of dormice to suitably managed woods began in 1993.

Another declining British mammal to have received help under the scheme is the native red
squirrel. At Thetford Forest in Norfolk, the small
remaining population of reds is threatened by the
more aggressive grey squirrel, introduced from
America early in the 20th century. The project
involves trapping and removing the greys, and
providing supplementary feeding using a weight-

sensitive hopper that allows access to the red squirrel but not the grey.

THE BUILT ENVIRONMENT

The Department of National Heritage (DNH), set up in 1992 and charged with the responsibility of promoting the Government's policies on architectural conservation, moved to Cockspur Street, London SW1 in May 1993. This setting, an inter-war classical building overlooking Trafalgar Square, should be more congenial than 2 Marsham Street, where the brutally functional podium and towers have been dubbed 'the biggest toast-rack in western Europe'. The duties of the new Ministry were also defined more clearly. The DNH is now responsible for listing, scheduling and scheduled monument consent, repairs, notices, urgent works notices and associated land acquisitions, procedures and reserved powers in respect of the designation of conservation areas, grants to heritage areas under the special grants programme and the Environmental Grant Fund, and responsibilities in respect of ecclesiastical exemption. Nearly all matters of casework, including the determination of listed building consent and conservation area consent applications, remain with the Department of the Environment, which will also continue to confirm article four directions in conservation areas and to consider proposals put forward by the Church Commissioners for the demolition of a church under the Pastoral Measure.

ENGLISH HERITAGE

In October 1992 English Heritage announced its 'Forward Strategy' for the 1990s. Some of the proposals were uncontroversial, e.g. the willingness to offer further help towards the employment of conservation officers at local authority level, to establish a short life tax review panel, and to launch a conservation fund to provide English Heritage with its own resources. The more controversial proposals included the proposed transfer of the management of about half of English Heritage's holding of historic sites and buildings to local authorities or trusts, the projected disbandment of the direct labour force, and the reduction in the powers of the London division.

By July 1993 English Heritage had entered into negotiations over the transfer of about 80 of its sites to bodies such as the National Trust and district and county councils. English Heritage has declared that there will be no transfer without clear agreements based on the proven ability of the new managers to keep the monument in good repair and open to the public, and that each transfer would have to be individually approved by the Secretary of State for National Heritage. The strategy states that English Heritage would maintain its role as 'acquirer of last resort'. Its existing stock of sites should not therefore be regarded as finite.

In London, English Heritage inherited the extensive powers of the GLC Historic Buildings Division in 1984. The division had 'powers of direction' and determined all applications for listed building consent within the London boroughs. The strategy proposed that English Heritage should retain these powers for buildings listed in Grade I and Grade II* and for the total or substantial demolition of Grade IIs. The powers would, however, be handed back to the individual boroughs when only the alteration or extension of a Grade II was being proposed. As Grade II listed buildings provide the great bulk of protected structures, such delegation would have involved some 90 per cent of the existing casework load of the London division. In the early summer of 1993, following a consultation period and the agreement of the DNH, English Heritage announced a modification to its plans. This centred on a scheme of 'flexible authorization', under which the requirement to notify English Heritage of all listed building consent applications within London would remain unchanged. English Heritage would hand back for local determination only those cases which it considered to be within the expertise of the particular borough, rather than delegating cases through a set of *a priori* categorizations. The intention is to agree by April 1994 on a programme of implementation in a minority of boroughs which have expressed interest. The hope is that the delegation will be completed within four years. The arrangements would be monitored regularly, with a formal review at the end of five years. The need for boroughs to notify English Heritage of conservation area consent applications will be restricted to those involved in the demolition of all or substantially all of the building and the demolition of a street or principal façade. The requirement to notify planning applications affecting listed buildings or their settings would be limited to Grade I or Grade II* listed buildings. The chairman of English Heritage, Jocelyn Stevens, expressed the hope that the reform, coupled with the implementation of a redundancy programme involving 10 per cent of the organization's staff, would allow English Heritage to spend more on historic buildings grants.

The 1991–2 English Heritage annual report was published in September 1992. It described expenditure of £100.5 million, of which £90.2 million was received as grant-in-aid from the Government and the remainder was raised mainly from gate receipts. English Heritage spent £10.4 million on grants to churches and cathedrals, £11.1 million on grants to other historic buildings and ancient monuments, £7.5 million on archaeology grants, £6.7 million on grants to historic towns, and £7.4 million on repairing its own properties. The total number of grants made was 1,200, amounting to £36.5 million. In the same period 3,000 grant applications were received. Early in 1993 English Heritage announced that its policy of grants to cathedrals, which was agreed in 1991, would continue. The total dispersed in the first two years was £11.5 million. The latest grants went to 44 beneficiaries, the largest being the £720,000 grant to Lincoln. The cathedrals in Shrewsbury, Southwark, Norwich, Sheffield, Truro and Clifton received grants for the first time. Five of the 44 grants were for stained glass conservation, five for works to monuments or sculpture, and four for the conservation of wall paintings. In September 1992 Corinne Bennett, MBE, RIBA, FRSA was appointed cathedrals architect.

The fact that English Heritage has only limited powers in deciding how to spend its income was demonstrated dramatically by the decision of the then Secretary of State for National Heritage, David Mellor, to refuse to allow it to rescue Pitchford Hall in Shropshire. The owners were prepared to give the Hall to the nation, but the government balked at the estimated expenditure of between £1.5 and £3 million which would have been needed to repair, run and market the building in the first eight years. The Hall and its contents were sold separately in September 1992.

WELSH BUILDINGS AND MONUMENTS

English Heritage has no direct equivalent in Wales, but the Historic Buildings Council for Wales is involved in similar activities. Its 35th annual report (1990–1) described the rescue of two long-threatened buildings: Trevor Hall at Llangollen and Bettisfield Park at Hanmer. One of the smallest grants offered was that to assist works to the Museum of Childhood in Beaumaris. The total number of listed buildings in Wales had risen to 13,669 as at 31 March 1991, while only three permissions were granted for total demolition.

The most significant development for Wales was the publication in June 1993 of a report by the Welsh Affairs committee of the House of Commons, *The Preservation of Historic Buildings and Ancient Monuments*. This made a number of radical proposals, including the completion of the resurvey of listed buildings within three years rather than the projected 65; the establishment of a Redundant Churches and Chapels Fund for Wales; and the adoption of more proactive policies by the Historic Buildings Council and by Cadw, the government agency charged with the furtherance and implementation of historic buildings policies.

ANNUAL REPORTS

The 12th annual report (1991–2) of the National Heritage Memorial Fund was published in October 1992. It once again showed how broadly the Fund interprets the word 'Heritage'. Grants and loans made by the Fund saved items and buildings as varied as a mirror designed by Robert Adam; the papers relating to Wardour Castle Chapel, Wilts.; the contents of a Shropshire clay pipe factory; the house and contents at Chastleton House, Oxon. (1602–12), to be conserved by the National Trust; the wall paintings at Copford Church, Essex; the monuments and stained glass at St Nicholas' Church, Stanford-on-Avon, Northants.; Jewish silver from the Great Synagogue in London which was bombed in 1941; and two architectural drawings by Charles Rennie Mackintosh.

The annual report for 1991–2 of the Royal Commission on Historical Monuments of England details its national survey initiatives on hospitals, houses of the gentry 1500–1700, and historic farmsteads. Equivalent studies in Scotland are embracing tolbooths and townhouses, functioning schools and early medieval sculpture in the West Highlands. In Wales effort is concentrated on a survey of Nonconformist chapels.

The annual report (1991–2) of the Architectural Heritage Fund was published in October 1992 and described projects assisted by the Fund. The Fund received increased funding from the Government, and made low-interest loans totalling £13,463,200 in respect of 239 preservation projects between May 1976 and April 1992. The beneficiaries have mainly been standard Grade II buildings, but structures of national importance like Seaton Holme at Easington, Co. Durham, have also been saved with the help of the fund.

NATIONAL TRUST

The National Trust has been able to open a number of new properties to the public. They include a late 19th-century semi-detached house at Worksop, Notts., where the interior has been almost untouched since the war owing to the conservatism of the two brothers who left the building to the Trust. In Devon the stables at Saltram were opened to the public for the first time, as was an early 19th-century parish lock-up in the grounds of the Guildhall of Corpus Christi at Lavenham, Suffolk. Most of the restoration of the 18th-century duck decoy at Boarstall Tower, Bucks. is now complete. The Trust has accepted the gift of 35 acres of land at Prior Park on the outskirts of Bath which are laid out in the manner of Capability Brown with a Palladian bridge and a small lake offering panoramic views of the city.

REDUNDANT CHURCHES

The 23rd annual report of the Redundant Churches Fund, covering 1991, shows expenditure of over £2 million. There were nine new vestings in 1991, three of them Victorian: Gilbert Scott's Cadeby in South Yorkshire, Talbot Bury's Lambourn Woodlands in Berkshire, and William Burges' stunning Skelton-cum-Newby. St Anthony-in-Roseland is the Fund's first Cornish church. In 1992 significant vestings included those of the fine medieval churches of St Nicholas, Kings Lynn, and St Larwrence, Norwich.

In June 1993 an equivalent body to the Redundant Churches Fund to cover non-Anglican places of worship was launched. It is called the Historic Chapels Trust, and has been established to acquire buildings no longer in regular religious use and generally graded I or II* on the statutory lists. Second only to the barn, the chapel is the most threatened building type in England. Between 1985 and 1992 there were 108 applications to demolish listed non-Anglican buildings, nearly all of them affecting primary places of worship. Many others have been damaged by unsympathetic conversion and the removal of fittings. The establishment of the Trust has been aided with a grant from the Department of National Heritage and English Heritage has guaranteed financial assistance towards the repair of individual buildings, but the Trust is still urgently in need of extra funds.

LEGISLATION

From 27 July 1992, in a little noticed but potentially wide-ranging legislative change, owners are required to obtain planning permission before pulling down residential properties or buildings attached to them, even where they were neither listed nor within a conservation area. Notice must be served on the local planning authority, which has 28 days to lay down conditions or withdraw development rights and require the submission of an application for planning permission, which could be refused.

The Government also announced its intention to reform ecclesiastical exemption, under which places of worship in use are exempt from laws designed to protect historic buildings. The Secretary of State for National Heritage (Peter Brooke) proposed that the exemption should lapse in respect of both interiors and exteriors, unless denominations establish decision-making processes independent of the congregation of the building concerned, and provide for consultation with English Heritage, the local planning authority and the national amenity societies in order to prevent damaging changes. In December 1992 the Government also announced the end of the exemption from general planning law and listed building consent procedures enjoyed by government departments, the Crown Estate, the Queen and the Prince of Wales in right of the Duchy of Cornwall. Thenceforward applications will have to be submitted in the usual way to local planning authorities, except in respect of proposals that involved 'national security'. Mr Brooke also announced details of the National Lottery which is expected to provide up to £100 million a year for heritage projects. The money will be distributed by the National Heritage memorial Fund.

POST-WAR LISTINGS

In 1992 2,285 historic buildings were added to the lists, bringing the total number of listed structures in England to 439,048. In April 1992 English Heritage embarked on a three-year research programme into the main post-war building types in order to identify key examples and to provide guidelines for future listings. Educational buildings were the first type to be researched, and English Heritage submitted their recommendations to the DNH in March 1993. Mr Brooke accepted all English Heritage's recommendations, and announced the listing of 95 school, college and university buildings of the post-war period. Several of the listings were Grade I, including the main building at the University of Sussex and St Catherine's College, Oxford. Decisions on industrial

and commercial buildings are expected in the autumn of 1993.

NEW ATTRACTIONS

A gallery of architectural drawings opened at the Victoria and Albert Museum, drawing from the museum's collection of about 80,000 items. The exhibits include sketchbooks by Pugin and Lutyens and examples of the draughtsmanship of John Webb, William Kent, Robert Adam, Sir John Soane, Alfred Waterhouse, Voysey, Sir Denys Lasdun and Alvar Aalto. In April 1993 an architectural study centre opened at the Ranger's House in Blackheath, southeast London. It is sponsored and run by English Heritage and comprises a collection which was started in 1906. Some 5,000 items have been collected, many from buildings demolished or refurbished, and they amount to 'a unique collection of architectural artefacts illustrating 250 years of London building practice'

LOSSES

Every year has its share of disasters, and 1992–3 saw some particularly spectacular ones. In 1992 the ancient church at Buckfastleigh, Devon, was almost completely destroyed by fire. At Windsor Castle, a disastrous fire gutted St George's Hall and destroyed a number of rooms, including the Queen's private chapel, in November 1992. In April 1993 the Government announced that much of the cost of repairing the damage would be met by opening Buckingham Palace to the public for eight weeks every summer. Following a national debate, the Government announced that St George's Hall would be rebuilt in replica but that more modern practice would be allowed in the chapel and other relatively minor spaces.

Much of the tiny, ancient church of St Ethelburga's in Bishopgate was destroyed by the IRA bomb in the City of London in April 1993. Although the bomb completely felled the west front, the east end with its murals by Hans Feibusch and the three-bay medieval arcading inside survived. Even the bell, which was found 80 feet away from the church, remained intact. Decisions over whether and how to rebuild St Ethelburga's had not been taken at the time of going to press, although English Heritage had sponsored a programme of archaeological investigation and sifting.

The more important listed buildings threatened by applications to demolish in 1992–3 included the Old Hall Chapel, Dukinfield, Greater Manchester, of the mid 16th-century; Rainhill Hospital, St Helen's, Merseyside, designed by Harvey Lonsdale Elmes, of 1847–51; St Margaret's Church, Stoven, Suffolk, of the 12th and 19th centuries; the Chantry at White Hart Street, Thetford, Norfolk; and Christ Church, Waterloo, Merseyside, of 1891–4.

Dance

The year 1992–3 was one of upheaval in the dance world, which also suffered the loss of two major creative forces with the deaths of Sir Kenneth MacMillan and Rudolf Nureyev. There were changes in the directorships of several major companies, with sudden resignations creating a sense of crisis early in a season which ended with the demise of the popular and successful small classical company London City Ballet. However, encouraging plans announced by Rambert Dance Company and London Contemporary Dance Theatre and a new, enthusiastic director at English National Ballet meant that the season ended on a note of tentative optimism.

The Royal Ballet's season was darkened by the sudden death on 29 October 1992 of Sir Kenneth MacMillan. That he should have died of a heart attack at the Royal Opera House during a performance of one of his greatest works, *Mayerling*, had an emotional resonance that seemed entirely appropriate. His relations with the Royal Ballet as a choreographer had not always been easy but his roots were firmly within the company and the greatest flowering of his choreographic talent had been inspired by Royal Ballet dancers. His childhood was one of unhappiness and alienation from which dance became an escape. He joined the Sadler's Wells School and became a founding member of the Sadler's Wells Theatre Ballet in 1946. He curtailed his dancing career partly because of extreme stage-fright and partly because of the emergence of his talent as a choreographer. He was encouraged by Ninette de Valois, who commissioned his first professional work, *Danses Concertantes*, in 1955. He later became resident choreographer and eventually director of the Royal Ballet, and also directed the German Opera Ballet company in Berlin from 1966 to 1969. But although his career was distinguished by international success and acclaim, he never lost the impetus to create works reflecting his own complex and often sombre view of life and human relationships. He tackled subject matters and music never before considered suitable for ballet and in doing so allowed ballet to come of age as an adult and expressive art form. His work was influenced by theatre, cinema and literature, and often focused on a social outsider. He created dramatic, theatrical full-length works, notably *Romeo and Juliet* (1965), *Mayerling* (1978) and *Manon* (1974), and pure dance works of great power and beauty, notably *Gloria* (1980), *The Song of the Earth* (1965) and *Requiem* (1977). The range of his output was remarkable and the Royal Ballet will sorely miss his creative genius.

The Royal Ballet, forced to play safe in its programming in order to help clear the Royal Opera House's accumulated deficit, lost its other major choreographic talent, David Bintley. Bintley, who succeeded MacMillan as resident choreographer of the Royal Ballet, resigned in January 1993. Looking at the Royal Ballet's repertoire in 1992–3, it is not surprising that he felt a resident choreographer was not wanted; his new work, *Tombeaux*, was the highlight of an otherwise disappointing season in which Baryshnikov's feeble production of *Don Quixote* was imported at great expense and wasted the considerable talents of the company's dancers. A revival of de Valois's superb *Checkmate* was mounted to celebrate the 95th birthday of the Royal Ballet's founder, who was also awarded the Order of Merit by The Queen. But the company would do well to heed the words of advice de Valois offered at the memorial service for Kenneth MacMillan: great choreography is the only foundation for a great company.

NUREYEV

The dance world as a whole suffered another blow with the death of Rudolf Nureyev from an Aids-related illness on 6 January 1993. Nureyev was one of the greatest male dancers of the 20th century, and certainly the most famous. His dancing transformed the role of the male dancer in ballet and set new standards of technique and expressiveness. His partnership with Margot Fonteyn in the 1960s was as magnificent as it was unlikely. He was young, arrogant, passionate, temperamental; she calm, modest and widely presumed to be nearing the end of her career. But they established an immediate emotional rapport which overcame all differences and was rapturously received by audiences. Nureyev took ballet lessons in secret, eventually joining the Kirov School in Leningrad in 1955. He entered the Kirov company in 1958 as a soloist and enjoyed huge success before defecting while on a tour to Paris with the company. His famous 'leap to freedom' was made on 17 June 1961 at Le Bourget airport and led to an outstanding international career. His repertoire was all-embracing, and he created roles for choreographers as diverse as Sir Frederick Ashton, Maurice Béjart and Martha Graham. He felt that the Royal Ballet dropped him after the retirement of Fonteyn in the early 1970s but he directed the Paris Opera Ballet from 1983 to 1989, mounting many productions of the classics as well as choreographing his own works. To the regret of many, he seemed unable to contemplate an end to his dancing career and continued to perform leading roles when he was well past his prime. But he will be remembered for his outstanding artistry, technique and professionalism, and for his overwhelming charisma both on and off stage.

ALL CHANGE

English National Ballet, whose performances with Nureyev in the 1970s represented an artistic peak, had another troubled year. In order to cut its accumulated deficit, it continued to play safe in its repertoire. In January 1993 its director Ivan Nagy announced that he would not seek to renew his contract at the end of the season; his services were then dispensed with, with almost indecent haste. This led to public acrimony between a departing director and the company's chairman, Pamela, Lady Harlech, for the second time in three years. The former Royal Ballet dancer Derek Deane took over as director in March. Deane was deputy artistic director and resident choreographer at Rome Opera Ballet for two years, but this is his first directorship. He is evidently full of energy and ideas, which will be required to improve ENB's lacklustre repertoire and reinvigorate its demoralized dancers. By the end of the season, when the company reopened the Savoy Theatre in London with a royal gala performance including a new ballet by Wayne Sleep, a new air of confidence was in evidence. It must be hoped that this spirit can be carried forward with positive results.

Rumours had abounded early in the year that English National Ballet and London City Ballet were on the point of merger. In fact London City Ballet closed down in July 1993 after 15 years of successfully touring small productions of the classics to venues too small for other companies. It had also mounted triple bills, including a highly successful one in the autumn of 1992 for which the company received an Olivier award nomination. The company had secured generous commercial sponsorship but needed an annual grant of £250,000 to keep afloat. This the Arts Council had consistently refused; the company closed down without deficit and with considerable anger directed at the Arts Council both from within and outside the dance world. A rescue package was being discussed in autumn 1993.

Another company in a state of upheaval in 1992–3 was Rambert Dance Company. Richard Alston, its highly respected artistic director, was suddenly sacked in December 1992 'as part of the ongoing development of the company'. The dismay this caused was replaced by excitement when it was announced in March 1993 that Christopher Bruce, Rambert's former associate choreographer, had agreed to take over the directorship fully from autumn 1994. Until then the company will continue to perform a selection of new and recent works. Bruce plans to increase the number of dancers to 25 and he sees the need for a company to bridge the gap between classical ballet and contemporary dance, as Rambert used to do. Subject to the Arts Council providing the necessary funding for the expansion, the new-look Rambert will be launched in the autumn of 1994.

Rambert's change of direction could be good news for London Contemporary Dance Theatre, without an artistic director since the departure of Nancy Dunn in the summer of 1992. LCDT would be left as the only medium-sized contemporary company and could therefore attract larger audiences. It had a great hit in 1992–3 with *Rooster*, Christopher Bruce's work to music by the Rolling Stones, and has submitted a three-year plan to the Arts Council, including plans for the artistic directorship. Until these are announced, the company will continue to be guided by its founding artistic director, Robert Cohan.

Birmingham Royal Ballet has enjoyed a period of relative calm and consolidation but it too faces changes. Peter Wright has agreed to stay on as artistic director until 1995 and the search for a successor has already started. Wright, who received a knighthood in 1993 in The Queen's Birthday Honours, will be a hard act to follow. He has consistently produced a repertoire of intelligent productions of the classics combined with high-quality triple bills, and has helped to make the company's move to Birmingham an outstanding success. The Arts Council has recommended that the administration of Birmingham Royal Ballet should gradually be devolved from the Royal Opera House to an independent board based in Birmingham, and this process is under way.

Northern Ballet Theatre and Scottish Ballet continue to make solid progress, although Christopher Gable's productions for Northern Ballet Theatre provoke increasingly divergent reactions; audiences are, in the main, wildly enthusiastic, and critics are mainly disparaging. This was certainly the reaction to his production of *A Christmas Carol*, premièred in September 1992. Scottish Ballet mounted a successful new version of *A Midsummer Night's Dream*, choreographed by Robert Cohan, in March 1993. The company's offshoot, SB2, continued to tour smaller venues under the artistic directorship of Kenn Burke, and both companies toured the Far East with considerable success in the autumn of 1992.

The Arts Council national arts and media 'strategy' was finally published in January 1993 under the title *A Creative Future: The Way Forward for the Arts, Crafts and Media in England*. After three years of consultations and submissions it was a distinct anticlimax. It asserted the importance and value of the arts, and promised that the Arts Council would be more effective, delegate more decision-making and seek advice more widely. It also decried the 'false' distinction between professional and amateur, and said that policies would be put in place to develop audiences, achieve wider cultural diversity and place more emphasis on training. The structure of arts funding in Britain was not discussed, and the report amounted to little more than a statement of good intentions.

In the summer of 1993 the Arts Council, faced with a £5 million cut in its government grant in 1993–4, announced that contemporary dance and visual art would receive increased levels of funding. Since the increases for these art forms involved reducing support for drama and classical music, with several theatres and orchestras under threat of closure, the announcement was not universally welcomed. Although the Arts Council said that 'contemporary dance' should simply be understood as any dance being created now, the suspicion is that extra funds will mainly go to the scores of small groups and individuals who perform works of questionable quality before tiny audiences. Britain's larger classical companies remain in financial difficulties which will be exacerbated by further cuts in funding.

Contemporary dance at its best was available in the Dance Umbrella festival in London in the autumn of 1992. The festival had a 'Transatlantic Tie-Up', with performances by American groups including the Merce Cunningham Dance Company and the Stephen Petronio Company, and also presented groups from Europe in conjunction with the European Arts Festival. British choreographers showing new work at the festival included Siobhan Davies, Lea Anderson, Shobana Jeyasingh, Laurie Booth and Jonathan Burrows. The seventh Spring Loaded festival of contemporary dance ran from February to April 1993, and the Turning World season at The Place theatre in April–May featured new dance from around the world. Siobhan Davies became the first British choreographer in the independent sector to win an Olivier award, receiving the award for outstanding achievement in dance in April 1993. She also created a well-received new work, *Wanting to Tell Stories*, at the Brighton Festival in May 1993.

The year 1993 was designated the Arts Council Year of Dance. Based in the East Midlands, the year began with a wide variety of dance events in Leicester, Northampton and Nottingham. Visitors included Nederlands Dans Theater 3, Moscow City Ballet, the Royal Ballet of Flanders and Ballet du Nord. There were also seasons by London Contemporary Dance Theatre, Adventures in Motion Pictures, Rosemary Butcher, and other British Groups.

The most publicized visitors to London during the season were the Bolshoi Ballet, who performed at the Albert Hall, which had been refurbished to resemble the Bolshoi Theatre, for more than five weeks in January–February 1993. Audiences paid high prices to see excerpts from the classics performed in far from ideal conditions. A later season by the Kirov Ballet at the London Coliseum was generally better received by the critics. Other visitors to Britain included Nederlands Dans Theater 2, the St Petersburg Ballet Theatre, the Royal New Zealand Ballet, Rudra Bejart Ballet Lausanne and the Stuttgart Ballet.

PRODUCTIONS

ROYAL BALLET

Founded 1931
Royal Opera House, Covent Garden, London WC2E 9DD

World première:
Tombeaux (David Bintley), 11 February 1993. A one-act ballet. Music, William Walton; design, Jasper Conran. Cast led by Viviana Durante and Bruce Sansom.

Company premières:
Tales of Beatrix Potter (Frederick Ashton), 4 December 1992. A one-act adaptation of choreography from the 1971 film of the same name. Music, John Lanchbery; design, Christine Edzard; masks, Rostislav Doboujinsky; staged by Anthony Dowell. Cast included Iain Webb (Mrs Tiggywinkle), Sarah Walton (Jemima Puddle-duck), Christopher Saunders (Fox), William Trevitt (Mr Jeremy Fisher), Ashley Page (Peter Rabbit) and Matthew Hart (Squirrel Nutkin).
Don Quixote (Petipa, 1869, prod. Baryshnikov after Petipa and Gorsky, 1978), 7 April 1993. Music, Minkus; design, Mark Thompson; staged by Anthony Dowell. Cast led by Viviana Durante and Irek Mukhamedov.
La Ronde (Glen Tetley, 1987), 4 June 1993. Music, Erich Korngold; design, John Macfarlane. Cast led by Darcey Bussell, William Trevitt, Ann De Vos, Adam Cooper, Mara Galeazzi, Bruce Sansom, Viviana Durante, Christopher Saunders, Fiona Chadwick and Ashley Page.

Full-length ballets from the repertoire: *Swan Lake* (Petipa/Ivanov, prod. Dowell, 1987), *Mayerling* (MacMillan, 1978), *Cinderella* (Ashton, 1948), *The Sleeping Beauty* (Petipa after Sergueyev, additional choreography by Ashton, prod. de Valois, 1977).
One-act ballets from the repertoire: *The Dream* (Ashton, 1964), *Apollo* (Balanchine, 1928), *The Judas Tree* (MacMillan, 1992), *Symphony in C* (Balanchine, 1947), *The Firebird* (Fokine, 1910), *In the middle, somewhat elevated* (Forsythe, 1988), *Ballet Imperial* (Balanchine, 1941), *The Prodigal Son* (Balanchine, 1929), *'Still Life' at the Penguin Café* (Bintley, 1988), *Checkmate* (de Valois, 1937), *Gloria* (MacMillan, 1980).

In addition to its performances at the Royal Opera House, the company gave a two-week season in Paris, its first since 1954, at the Théâtre des Champs-Elysées in June 1993. The repertoire was *Mayerling*, *Swan Lake*, *Danses Concertantes* (MacMillan, 1955), *A Month in the Country* (Ashton, 1976), *Gloria*, *Ballet Imperial*, *The Judas Tree* and *'Still Life' at the Penguin Café*. This was followed by performances in Palermo, Turin, Istanbul and Frankfurt in July 1993.

BIRMINGHAM ROYAL BALLET

Founded 1946 as Sadler's Wells Royal Ballet
Birmingham Hippodrome, Thorp Street, Birmingham B5 4AU

World premières:
The Sum of the Parts (Jennifer Jackson), 5 February 1993. A one-act ballet, premièred during a small-scale 'Springboard' tour involving eight dancers from the main company. Music, Tim Sutton; design, Henk Schut. Cast, Jane Billson, Anne Marie Little, Andrew Allen and Duncan de Gruchy.
Street (Matthew Hart), 1 June 1993. A one-act ballet. Music, William Russo; design, Peter Farmer. Cast included Joseph Cipolla, Monica Zamora and Vincent Redmon.

Company première:
The Green Table (Kurt Jooss, 1932), 19 October 1992. Music, Fritz Cohen; design, Hein Heckroth. Cast led by Joseph Cipolla and Marion Tait.

Full-length ballets from the repertoire: *The Snow Queen* (Bintley, 1986), *Romeo and Juliet* (MacMillan, 1965), *The Nutcracker* (Ivanov/Wright, additional choreography by Vincent Redmon, 1990), *The Sleeping Beauty* (Petipa/Wright, 1984), *Hobson's Choice* (Bintley, 1989).
One-act ballets and pas de deux from the repertoire: *Flowers of the Forest* (Bintley, 1985), *Symphonic Variations*

(Ashton, 1946), *Les Sylphides* (Fokine, 1909), *The Nutcracker pas de deux* (Ivanov/Wright, 1990), *Le Corsaire pas de deux* (after Petipa, 1899), *The Sleeping Beauty pas de deux* (Petipa/Wright, 1984), *Swan Lake pas de deux* (Petipa/Ivanov/Dowell, 1987), *Choreatium* (Massine, 1933), *Concerto* (MacMillan, 1966), *Job* (de Valois, 1931, a revival to celebrate de Valois's 95th birthday in June 1993), *Paramour* (Lustig, 1987), *Twilight* (van Manen, 1972), *Façade* (Ashton, 1931), *Don Quixote pas de deux* (Petipa, 1869).

The Springboard tour's repertoire consisted of *The Sum of the Parts* and extracts from *Checkmate* (de Valois, 1937), *Façade, Concerto, Swan Lake, Elite Syncopations* (MacMillan, 1974) and *Flowers of the Forest*. The tour visited venues in Stafford, Telford and Hereford for three weeks in the spring of 1993.

The main company gave nine weeks of performances in Birmingham as well as touring to Plymouth, Manchester, Cardiff, Oxford, Bradford and Southampton. It also performed in London, at Sadler's Wells Theatre and at the Royal Opera House. It undertook its first overseas tour under its new name, performing *Romeo and Juliet* and *The Sleeping Beauty* in Singapore, Bangkok and Hong Kong in April–May 1993. It also hosted a visit by the Stuttgart Ballet to the Birmingham Hippodrome in June 1993, and hosted the finale of the Conduct for Dance initiative.

ENGLISH NATIONAL BALLET

Founded 1950 as London Festival Ballet
Markova House, 39 Jay Mews, London SW7 2ES

World premières:
The Seven Silences of Salome (Olga Roriz), 6 April 1993. A one-act ballet. Music, Antonio Emiliano; design, Nuno Carinhas. Cast, Stephen Sheriff, Thomas Edur, Denzil Bailey, Alexis Manuel, Paul Lewis, Maurizio Bellezza and Tim Almaas.
The Savoy Suite (Wayne Sleep), 19 July 1993. A one-act ballet. Music, Carl Davis, based on themes of Sir Arthur Sullivan; design, Andrew Storer. Cast led by Wayne Sleep, Simon Cooper, Renata Calderini, Christian Duncan, Eugenio Scigliano and Maria Teresa del Real.

Company premières:
Swan Lake (Petipa/Ivanov, 1895, prod. Raissa Struchkova after Gorsky Messerer, 1937), 17 February 1993. Music, Tchaikovsky; design, Carl Toms. First cast led by Agnes Oaks and Thomas Edur.
Grand Pas Classique from *Raymonda Act III* (Petipa, 1898, prod. Frederic Franklin), 9 April 1993. Music, Glazunov; design, Peter Farmer. Cast led by Maria Teresa del Real and Christian Duncan.
Impromptu (Derek Deane, 1982), 14 June 1993. Music, Schubert. Dancers, Agnes Oaks and Thomas Edur.

Full-length ballets from the repertoire: *Cinderella* (Stevenson, 1970), *The Nutcracker* (Stevenson, 1972), *Romeo and Juliet* (Ashton, 1955).

One-act ballets and *pas de deux* from the repertoire: *Three Preludes* (Stevenson, 1969), *The Envelope* (Parsons, 1984), *White Nights* (Branstrup, 1992), *Etudes* (Lander, 1948), *Sphinx* (Tetley, 1977), *Les Sylphides* (Fokine, 1909), *Aureole* (Taylor, 1962), *Sleep Study* (Parsons, 1984), *Don Quixote pas de deux* (Petipa, 1869), *A Stranger I Came* (North, 1992), *Swansong* (Bruce, 1987), *Apollo* (Balanchine, 1928).

The company toured to Liverpool, Newcastle upon Tyne, Bristol, Southampton, Manchester, Norwich and Nottingham, and gave three seasons in London, including reopening the Savoy Theatre in July 1993. It also gave two performances each in Buenos Aires, São Paulo and Athens, and four performances in Mexico, with a repertoire of *Les Sylphides, The Envelope, Swansong, Etudes, The Seven Silences of Salome, Swan Lake, Romeo and Juliet* and *Impromptu*.

ENB2 made two small-scale tours, in the autumn of 1992 and the spring of 1993. It visited Tunbridge Wells, Buxton, Exeter, Merthyr Tydfil, Ashington, Harlow, High Wycombe, Poole, Barrow-in-Furness, Cambridge, Stevenage, Worthing, Carlisle, Spennymoore, Swindon, Bury St Edmunds, Yeovil, Hexham, Crewe and Lowestoft. The repertoire included *A Stranger I Came, Swansong, Apollo, Aureole, The Envelope, Sleep Study, White Nights, Three Preludes, Don Quixote pas de deux, The Seven Silences of Salome* and *Grand Pas Classique* from *Raymonda*.

RAMBERT DANCE COMPANY

Founded 1926
94 Chiswick High Road, London W4 ISH

World première:
Gone (Mark Baldwin), 16 October 1992. Music, Grieg; design, Michael Craig-Martin.

Works from the repertoire: *Winnsboro Cotton Mill Blues* (Davies, 1992), *Cat's Eye* (Alston, 1992), *Strong Language* (Alston, 1987), *Island to Island* (Baldwin, 1991), *Still Dance* (Old, 1992), *Touchbase* (Cunningham, 1992), *Phillidor's Defence* (Severien, 1992).

The company gave performances in Manchester, Bradford, Leicester, Blackpool, Newcastle upon Tyne, Mold, Warwick, Bath, Exeter and Bristol. It also staged ten works choreographed by Rambert dancers at the Lilian Baylis Theatre, London, in May 1993 under the title Exposure. It gave two performances in France (La Rochelle and Claremont-Ferrand) and one in Switzerland (Vernier) in March 1993.

LONDON CONTEMPORARY DANCE THEATRE

Founded 1967
The Place, Duke's Road, London WC1H 9AB

World premières:
My Father's Vertigo (Amanda Miller), 21 October 1992. Co-commissioned with the European Arts Festival. Music, Fred Frith; design, Amanda Miller.
Shoes (Aletta Collins), 28 April 1993. Music, Steve Martland; design, Tom Cairns.

Company premières:
Motorcade (Mark Morris, 1990), 13 October 1992. Music, Saint-Saëns; design, Andrew Storer.
Rooster (Christopher Bruce, 1991), 28 October 1992. Music, The Rolling Stones; design, Marian Bruce.

Works from the repertoire: *Rikud* (Dror and Ben Gal, 1991), *Freedom of Information* (Zane, 1983), *Orfeo* (Brandstrup, 1989).

The company toured to Southampton, Plymouth, Woking, Leeds, Liverpool, Coventry, Northampton, Oxford, Brighton, Newcastle upon Tyne and Sheffield, and performed at Sadler's Wells Theatre, London. It also undertook education and community programme residencies, focusing on the choreographic process and including lecture demonstrations and open rehearsals, from January to March 1993 in London, Plymouth and Birmingham. It gave three performances of choreographers' workshop programmes at The Place in April 1993. The company also toured to Luxembourg (1–3 February 1993) and Switzerland (27–28 March 1993), performing *Orfeo, My Father's Vertigo, Rikud* and *Motorcade*.

THE SCOTTISH BALLET

Founded 1956

261 West Princes Street, Glasgow G4 9EE

World première:
A Midsummer Night's Dream (Robert Cohan), 19 March 1993. A full-length ballet. Music, Mendelssohn, with additions by Barrington Pheloung; design, Norberto Chiesa. Cast led by Galina Mezentseva, Robert Hampton, Richard Whistler and Karl Burnett.

Company premiéres:
Overgrown Path (Jiri Kylian, 1980), 18 August 1992. Music Janáček; design, W. Nobbe and J. Cabbort.

SB2 premièred a shortened version of *Coppélia* produced by Kenn Burke and with designs by Richard Bridgland; a new ballet by Galina Samsova, *Walpurgis Night*, to music by Gounod; a new ballet by Kenn Burke, *To Begin With*, to music by Louis Moreau Gettshalk; the company première of *Harlequinade*, with Petipa's choreography (1900) reproduced by John Gilpin, music by Ricardo Drigo and design by Gordon Garforth; and the company première of *L'Après-Midi d'un Faune*, with choreography by Christian Uboldie to music by Debussy.

Full-length ballets from the repertoire: *Coppélia* (Wright after Petipa/Cecchetti, 1979), *The Nutcracker* (Darrell after Ivanov, 1973), *Romeo and Juliet* (Cranko, 1962).

One-act ballets from the repertoire: *Who Cares?* (Balanchine, 1970), *Brief* (Miller, 1992), *Troy Game* (North, 1974), *Concerto Barocco* (Balanchine, 1941), SB2: *Scarlatti and Friends* (Prokovsky, 1972), *Belong* (Vesak, 1972), *Wildlife 1* (Campbell, 1992), *Macbeth* (Prokovsky, 1992), *The Prisoners* (Darrell, 1957), *Monotones* (Ashton, 1965), *Othello* (Darrell, 1971), *That Certain Feeling* (Prokovsky, 1984, under the title *The Aquarium*), *Shoals of Herring* (Maldoom, 1983), *Five Brahms Waltzes in the Manner of Isadora Duncan* (Ashton, 1975), extract from *La Sylphide* (Bournonville, 1836).

The main company gave performances of *Coppélia* and *The Nutcracker* in Seoul, South Korea, and Tokyo and Osaka, Japan, in November–December 1992; it also gave workshops and masterclasses in Kuala Lumpur, Malaysia. At the same time, SB2 performed a selection of one-act ballets in China (Beijing, Dalian, Shenyang and Guangzhou) and Malaysia (Penang and Kuala Lumpur).

The main company visited Glasgow, Aberdeen, Sheffield, Edinburgh, Hull, Liverpool, Inverness and Leicester during the rest of the season; SB2 performed in small venues throughout Scotland, in Northern Ireland (Downpatrick, Enniskillen, Donaghmore and Belfast), in Wales (Bangor) and at ten venues in England.

The main company also visited Canada, giving three performances of *A Midsummer Night's Dream* in Ottawa (17–19 June 1993).

Masters of the Queen's (King's) Music

'Master of the King's Music' was the title given to the official who presided over the court band during the reign of Charles I. The first Master was appointed in 1626. Today the Master is expected to organize the music for state occasions and to write new music for them, although there are no fixed duties. The post is held for life and the Master receives an annual honorarium of £100.

Nicholas Lanier (1588–1666), appointed 1626
Louis Grabu (?–1674), appointed 1666
Nicholas Staggins (1650–1700), appointed 1674
John Eccles (1668–1735), appointed 1700
Maurice Greene (1695–1755), appointed 1735
William Boyce (1710–79), appointed 1755

John Stanley (1713–86), appointed 1779
Sir William Parsons (1746–1817), appointed 1786
William Shield (1748–1829), appointed 1817
Christian Kramer (?–1834), appointed 1829
François (Franz) Cramer (1772–1848), appointed 1834
George Anderson (?–1870), appointed 1848
Sir William Cusins (1833–93), appointed 1870
Sir Walter Parratt (1841–1924), appointed 1893
Sir Edward Elgar (1857–1934), appointed 1924
Sir Henry Walford Davies (1869–1941), appointed 1934
Sir Arnold Bax (1883–1953), appointed 1941
Sir Arthur Bliss (1891–1975), appointed 1953
Malcolm Williamson (1931–), appointed 1975

Drama

At the Laurence Olivier Awards ceremony in April 1993, Stephen Daldry, artistic director of the Royal Court Theatre, criticized government policy on funding for the arts. Accepting an award for his production of *An Inspector Calls*, Daldry said that cuts of £5 million in Arts Council spending would affect the whole 'cultural infrastructure'. He claimed that because of VAT on theatre tickets, the Government received more money from the theatre than it gave: 'The truth of the matter is that the theatre subsidizes government'. In June 1993, Sir Brian Rix, chairman of the Arts Council's drama panel, resigned in protest at government policy and the council's own policy, which threatened withdrawal of support for many regional theatres. In July it was announced that the budget for drama would be cut by 3.6 per cent (£1.4 million) in 1994–5, so that more money could be allocated to contemporary dance and the visual arts. There were fears that up to ten regional theatres would lose their funding. Cut-backs in local authority grants were expected to add to the problem. Following a review of the Arts Council, the National Heritage Secretary, Peter Brooke, required the council to carry out a further review of its activities. He said these should 'focus attention on providing services for which there is a real demand'. He also said that the council should reduce its administration costs by 10 per cent.

BACK IN BUSINESS

The completion of rebuilding or refurbishment brought a number of theatres back into use. The Criterion Theatre reopened in October 1992 with *Making It Better*, after over three years. The fringe theatre, the Donmar Warehouse, also reopened after improvements to audience facilities and now seats 250 people with standing room for a further 20. Sam Mendes was appointed artistic director and his first production was Stephen Sondheim's *Assassins*, a musical which traces the history of American popular music through an account of the nine would-be and successful assassins of American presidents, from John Wilkes Booth to Lee Harvey Oswald and John Hinckley. The musical had failed in New York; premièred during the Gulf War, it had not suited the mood of the times.

The National Youth Theatre secured its future for a further five years with a £1 million sponsorship deal with Hanson. The NYT also secured a grant of £450,000 from the Foundation for Sport and Arts to purchase the lease of its London headquarters.

Bill Alexander opened his first season as artistic director of Birmingham Repertory Theatre with Shakespeare's *Othello*. Backed by financial support from Birmingham City Council worth over £650,000 for 1993–4, Alexander promised a policy of plays from three areas: 'acknowledged classics of world drama, great plays that are almost never done, and new writing'.

MUSICAL HITS

The London stage continued to be dominated by musicals, several productions having an outstanding success but less popular productions proving expensive flops. A report by the Policy Studies Institute found that in 1991 musicals accounted for nearly 50 per cent of West End seats, compared with 28 per cent in 1983. The report noted that 'an increasing public appetite for large "blockbuster" musicals is a firmly established feature of London's West End theatre scene'. Judging by the recent spate of new musicals and revivals, the trend is set to continue.

Me and My Girl closed in January 1993 after a run of eight years at the Adelphi. Taking into account its original production in 1937 and 1950s revivals, it had played more performances than any other musical in the West End. In April 1993, the most popular London productions were the musicals *City of Angels* and *Crazy for You*. Andrew Lloyd Webber's new production, *Sunset Boulevard*, was in great demand even before its previews. Although the opening was delayed for two weeks due to production difficulties, by the time of its lavish première in July it had taken between £4 million and £6.5 million in advance bookings.

Crazy for You was based on George and Ira Gershwin's *Girl Crazy*. Only five songs were retained from the original 1930s musical and 14 other Gershwin numbers, well-known and obscure, were introduced to a revised but slight plot. However, the exuberance of Mike Ockrent's production, fine choreography by Susan Stroman and Gershwin's memorable songs made for a successful production. It relaunched the newly refurbished Prince Edward Theatre.

City of Angels is a witty and polished musical which ran for two years on Broadway and won six Tony awards. Set in Los Angeles in the 1940s and heavily influenced by the crime novels of Raymond Chandler, the musical works parallel plots about a scriptwriter Stine (Martin Smith) working for a monstrous Hollywood producer, Buddy Fidler (Henry Goodman) on a film about a private detective, Stone (Roger Allam), with the actual plot of the film itself. The two were brilliantly interwoven in a sparkling, wisecracking book.

Ironically, on the day that Andrew Lloyd Webber's *Sunset Boulevard* opened, it was announced that *City of Angels* would have to close because it had failed to recoup its £2 million costs since opening in March. The surprising closure was widely publicized because of the universally good reviews that the show had received. The theatre-going public responded positively and after a sudden surge of bookings, reportedly worth £400,000, it received a reprieve until at least October.

Andrew Lloyd Webber's *Sunset Boulevard* is based on Billy Wilder's 1950 film. The production was reported to have cost £3 million, and a similar sum was invested in restoring the Adelphi Theatre for the show. Patti LuPone took the role of the fading silent movie star Norma Desmond made famous by Gloria Swanson in the film. While undoubtedly popular and guaranteed a long run, the show confirmed Lloyd Webber's continued reliance on superior original plots.

Andrew Lloyd Webber's *Starlight Express*, which first opened in 1984, was extensively revised and updated, with five new songs, in late 1992. A surprising hit when it opened as it sublimated plot to spectacle, the contemporary *Starlight* appears capable of roller-skating on for several more years. It is now the longest-running British musical after *Cats*. Lloyd Webber said of it: 'It is meant to be nothing other than fun with a tiny heart of gold beating among all its trappings. It also by its nature has to change.'

Manuel Puig's novel *Kiss of the Spider Woman*, having been turned into first a stage play and then a Hollywood film, became a musical directed by Hal Prince at the Shaftesbury. What was originally subtle and understated now became more obvious, the original fleeting reference to a 'spider woman' expanded into a full role, Aurora, played by Chita Rivera. However, the story of two men in a South American prison, although at first sight not promising material for a musical, in fact made for a thoughtful and bold production.

Radio Times, based on the songs and music of Noël Gay, suffered from a weak plot about a fictional BBC production of a wartime radio programme, Variety Bandwaggon, in London in 1940. Tony Slattery played a comedian, Sammy Shaw, shying away from marrying the female lead singer, who was also pursued by an American singer, played by Jeff Shankley. The production closed in early January after only two and a half months. *Annie Get Your Gun* at the Prince of Wales also closed after six weeks.

A Norwegian 'operamusical' *Which Witch*, which had been a huge popular success in Oslo, was roundly condemned by English critics. A simplistic tale about 16th-century witchcraft and the love of a young Italian girl for a German bishop, the show was redeemed neither by its acting nor by its music, with only Richard Hudson's designs receiving praise. The production received widespread publicity when the King of Norway visited the Piccadilly Theatre in an unprecedented, but ultimately unsuccessful, attempt to boost the show's flagging fortunes. The Piccadilly's next production was another ill-conceived and short-lived musical: *Robin, Prince of Sherwood* was poorly plotted with unmemorable modern songs. Laden with anachronisms, its attempts to amuse succeeded only in highlighting the shallowness of the whole venture.

Another musical curiosity derided by the critics was *Leonardo, A Portrait of Love*, the £2 million production costs of which were supplied by the South Pacific island of Nauru, which had considerable sums of money to invest from its phosphate-rich deposits of guano. The show's portrayal of Leonardo da Vinci flew in the face of the facts and the whole concept was misguided and absurd.

The multitude of revivals continued unabated with the arrival in July of *Grease*, first performed in 1973 and made into a film five years later. The original production, set in 1959, was much more hard-edged; the current production is a more nostalgic look back at a mythical golden age of innocence which proved popular with audiences. The film had changed public expectations and the new production incorporated songs written specifically for the film. The show has attractive principals in Debbie Gibson and Craig McLachlan (respectively a well-known American singer and an Australian 'soap' star) and good music, which no doubt helped it to take advance bookings of £5 million.

Grease was followed into London theatres by new productions of *Godspell* and *Hair*. *Godspell*, first produced in 1971, was performed at the Barbican Hall but, lacking the charismatic performances of the original, it left critics wondering why it had been decided to regurgitate such a slight and inadequate piece. The 1968 musical *Hair*, which had celebrated the end of the Lord Chamberlain's censorship of the theatre, though more deserving, was another example of desperate managements attempting to cash in on the hits of yester-year.

REVIVED INTEREST

Noël Coward's slight but, in his own words, 'extraordinarily well constructed' *Hay Fever* was revived at the Albery. Tom Conti both directed and starred in Coward's *Present Laughter* at the Globe, but seemed to have been seriously miscast as Gary Essendine, the role Coward himself took when the play was first performed in 1942 and which he admitted was based on his own character. Conti underplayed the role to such an extent that all Essendine's flamboyance and charisma were dissipated. *Relative Values* formed part of the Chichester Festival season, featuring Alison Fiske, Susan Hampshire and Sarah Brightman. The previously unperformed *Post Mortem*, written, so Coward said, 'with the utmost sincerity', his 'angry little vilification of war', was presented at the King's Head, Islington. Critic Sheridan Morley described it as 'strange, angry and very uncharacteristic Coward polemic'. Its protagonist, John Cavan, is killed during the First World War; in the moment before his death he visits the London of 1930 to haunt his family and to rail against the sentimentalism and jingoism of the time.

Similarly, Terence Rattigan achieved a minor revival, with *The Deep Blue Sea*, directed by Karel Reisz, at the Almeida, and Peter Hall's *Separate Tables* at the Albery. *Separate Tables*, first performed in 1954, consists of *Table by the Window* and *Table*

Number Seven, the second of which still appeared the better of the two pieces.

Peter Nichols's painful and funny play about the tragedy of bringing up a handicapped child, *A Day in the Death of Joe Egg*, was first performed in 1967. Lisa Forrell's new production at the King's Head, Islington, confirmed its status as a modern classic, but prompted questions about why a major work by a leading dramatist should receive its first revival in London for over 20 years in a 120-seat fringe theatre, albeit a theatre renowned for the quality of its work. In spite of very favourable reviews, the show not only failed to gain a West End transfer but did not even fill the King's Head auditorium.

THE NATIONAL

The National Theatre's splendid production of *Carousel*, Rodgers and Hammerstein's third collaboration, drew favourable comparisons with the same company's revival of *Guys and Dolls* ten years previously. The first of a projected series of classic musical revivals, the production was made possible by a donation of £1 million from the Cameron Mackintosh Foundation and sponsorship from Oracle. Most of the dance numbers were choreographed by Sir Kenneth MacMillan before his death in October. Based on Ferenc Molnar's 1909 play *Liliom*, but better known in the inferior cinema version, this widely praised production re-established *Carousel* as one of the great musicals. Patricia Routledge excelled as Netty Fowler.

The National also revived Stephen Sondheim's *Sweeney Todd*, the black-humoured musical about the demon barber of Fleet Street who killed his customers, their remains being made into pies in the shop below. When first performed at the Drury Lane in 1980, the show had been critically well-received but failed to attract the public. Declan Donnellan's production gained in power from being performed on a smaller stage. Alun Armstrong and Julia McKenzie were notable in the leading roles.

At the Lyttelton, Stephen Daldry, artistic director of the Royal Court Theatre, when invited to direct a production for the National, chose J. B. Priestley's *An Inspector Calls*, favourite of amateur dramatic societies up and down the country. His non-naturalistic production, with powerful performances from an excellent cast, gave the play a wider historical and moral resonance than traditional productions have achieved.

Tom Stoppard's new play, *Arcadia*, witty, erudite and cleverly structured, marked a welcome return to form for one of Britain's most inventive playwrights. The play is set in a country house in 1809 and the present. In the earlier time, the elegant grounds are being redesigned to lose their ordered elegance, the Romantic replacing the classical, and a 13-year-old girl, Thomasina Coverly, studies mathematics with her tutor and posits chaos theory. In the later time, an academic, Bernard Nightingale, investigates a theory that Byron fought a duel at the house which

forced him to flee the country, while Valentine Coverly, a young scientist, studies grouse. Stoppard commented: 'We're better at predicting events on the edge of the galaxy or inside the nucleus of an atom than whether it'll rain on auntie's garden party three weeks from now. The future is disorder.' The two periods were linked in an intelligent drama that explored scientific ideas.

Trevor Eve played the demanding role of the solicitor Bill Maitland in John Osborne's *Inadmissible Evidence*. Nicol Williamson made the part his own in the 1964 production and the film version and reprised the role in 1978. But Trevor Eve's portrayal of a man at the end of his tether, both personally and professionally, was convincing and accomplished, even though the play's inherent weakness, prolixity, was once more exposed.

Pirandello's last, unfinished play, *The Mountain Giants*, was performed at the Cottesloe. Charles Wood completed the play, following the indications of how the dramatist had intended it to end. It featured Desmond Barrit as Cotrone, a Prospero-like magician, who entertains a troupe of players led by a Contessa Ilse, played by Sian Thomas. They are finally required to perform their play, written by a poet who had committed suicide for love of the Contessa, to the boorish and uncouth servants of the 'mountain giants', whom Wood identified with the fascists of 1936, the year in which the play was written. Interestingly, in Franco Zeffirelli's Italian language production of Pirandello's *Sei Personaggi in Cerca d'Autore (Six Characters in Search of an Author)* which was performed on the National's Lyttelton stage, the play that the actors rehearsed was not that specified in the script, but the same *The Mountain Giants*.

Harold Pinter's 1975 play *No Man's Land* was revived at the Almeida, directed by David Leveaux who achieved critical success with his production of *Betrayal* the previous year. When first produced at the National Theatre, the parts of Spooner and Hirst had been played by Sir John Gielgud and Sir Ralph Richardson. It would have been difficult to surpass such a pairing, but Paul Eddington and Pinter himself in the roles were both impressive.

Our Song at the Apollo reunited Peter O'Toole with director Ned Sherrin and playwright Keith Waterhouse, after their conspicuous success with *Jeffrey Bernard is Unwell*. *Our Song*, adapted by Waterhouse from his own novel, featured O'Toole as an advertising executive in love with a younger woman and was poorly received by the critics.

Peter Hall's *Lysistrata* at the Old Vic was a welcome production of a playwright whose work appears all too rarely on the London stage. Aristophanes wrote the play in 412 BC as a protest against the interminable wars between Athens and Sparta, and the theme retains its topicality. Ranjit Bolt's translation was colloquial and earthy, but retained the rhyme scheme of the original. Geraldine James played Lysistrata, who persuades the women of Athens to deny sexual favours to their men until they put an end to the fighting. Boisterous and slapstick, the production played the farcical elements of the play to the full. Euripides's *Medea* at the Almeida brought Diana Rigg much praise in the title role, although her performance lacked some of the 'terrible passion' that the Chorus describes when she incites the women to help her in her revenge. At the Barbican, Adrian Noble directed *The Thebans*, Sophocles's three Oedipus plays: *Oedipus at Colonus, Oedipus Tyrannos* and *Antigone*, translated by Timberlake Wertenbaker. While the Chorus and Joanne Pearce's Antigone were praised, Gerard Murphy's Oedipus was understated and lacked power.

THE RSC

The Royal Shakespeare Company enjoyed a successful 1992–3 season, with audiences up some 50,000 on the previous year and Kenneth Branagh's return to the company in *Hamlet* breaking box office records for any RSC Shakespeare production. It was reported to have taken the largest-ever advance for any RSC production, with sales of over £1 million. Branagh's was a powerful *Hamlet*, a performance that revealed his growing maturity since he played the role some four years previously with his own company. Directed by Adrian Noble and using the New Cambridge text, a conflation of the Second Quarto and the First Folio, the production ran for some four and a half hours and was widely praised. The production opened at the Barbican before moving to Stratford.

One of the highlights of the Stratford season was Robert Stephens as *King Lear*, a towering performance in Adrian Noble's fine production. Excellent support was provided by Simon Russell Beale as Edgar, David Bradley as Gloucester and Ian Hughes as the Fool.

Marlowe's *Tamburlaine the Great* at the Swan was well received. Antony Sher dominated the stage as Tamburlaine, well supported by Malcolm Storry as Bajazeth. On the main stage, Sam Mendes's production of *The Tempest*, with Alec McCowen as Prospero and Simon Russell Beale as Ariel, laid unusual emphasis on the metaphysical or theatrical elements of the play.

Peter Shaffer's new play, *The Gift of the Gorgon*, was premièred at the Barbican Pit. It concerns a dispute between an academic who wishes to write a biography of his late father, a playwright whom he had never known, and his stepmother, played by Judi Dench, keen to preserve her husband's reputation. Dench said that the role was the most demanding she had ever played. Although directed by Peter Hall and designed by John Gunter, and dense with classical allusion, the play never quite gelled. However, it proved a popular success and transferred to Wyndham's.

The RSC collaborated with the Moscow Art Theatre in commissioning and producing *Misha's Party*. The play is set in the Ukraine Hotel, Moscow in August 1991 where Misha is celebrating his 60th

birthday. The events of the evening, as Yeltsin resists the coup against Gorbachev, are a backdrop to Misha's celebrations, where personal relationships matter more to the characters than the dramatic events outside. Although the collaboration was not a complete artistic success, it was an enjoyable production. The play was co-written by Richard Nelson and Alexander Gelman, neither of whom spoke the other's language so they had to work through interpreters. Having between them devised the plot and characters, Nelson wrote in English and Gelman in Russian. The play was premièred at the Pit in July and it was planned to produce it also in Moscow.

The 1993 Stratford season opened at the Swan with an accomplished revival of *Murder in the Cathedral*, directed by Steven Pimlott with Michael Feast as Thomas Becket. The choice of play was surprising, as the Swan's remit is to produce lesser-known plays by Shakespeare and other dramatists from 1500 to 1700. David Thacker directed a promenade production of *Julius Caesar* at The Other Place; with actors in modern dress mingling with the audience, the production achieved a degree of immediacy and dramatic impact, albeit at the expense of subtlety.

The Young Vic gave the British première of Arthur Miller's new play, *The Last Yankee*, a week after its first production in New York in January 1993. It was the sixth Miller play performed by the company, without which, David Thacker, the artistic director, said, the theatre would not have survived. *The Last Yankee* is set in a psychiatric hospital and featured Peter Davison as Leroy Hamilton, a carpenter and scion of one of America's oldest families, and David Healy as John Frick, a self-made man. Both are visiting their wives, who are suffering from depressive illnesses and troubled marriages, apparently victims of the American dream. After a successful run at the Young Vic, the play transferred to the Duke of York's. Thacker, after a productive period at the Young Vic, moved to the Royal Shakespeare Company as a director in residence.

Max Stafford-Clark's first Shakespeare production was also his last at the Royal Court Theatre, of which he had been artistic director since 1979. It was a characteristically imaginative reading of *King Lear*. Set in Edwardian period, the production mixed a variety of styles but achieved a strong contemporary relevance. However, the final Act, setting the battle in modern Bosnia, was considered by some to be stretching contemporaneity too far.

The Royal Court also produced David Mamet's powerful new play, *Oleanna*, a two-hander which explores the uses of power, education and the topical issue of political correctness. It follows the relationship between a professor, played by David Suchet, and his student, played by Lia Williams. Howard Barker's new play, *The Europeans*, received its London première at the Greenwich Theatre. Set during the siege of Vienna in 1683, it examines the conflict between Christianity and Islam, reflecting the current crisis in the former Yugoslavia.

Alan Ayckbourn's new play, *Time of My Life*, features the author's familiar twists of time and intricate plotting, with some brilliantly funny moments. Gwen Taylor played Laura, celebrating her 54th birthday at a Manchester restaurant with her husband Gerry, played by Anton Rodgers, while their two sons' relationships are depicted at other tables and at other times, both before and after the night in question. Michael Frayn made a welcome return with *Here*, a witty piece about a young couple moving into a bedsit and attempting to impose their taste on it, to make it 'our piece of space, our world', but constantly thwarted by their landlady's interruptions.

AWARDS

In the 1992 Evening Standard drama awards, the award for best play went to *Angels in America* by Tony Kushner; best comedy, *The Rise and Fall of Little Voice* by Jim Cartwright; best musical, *Kiss of the Spider Woman*; best actor, Nigel Hawthorne, *The Madness of George III*; best actress, Diana Rigg, *Medea*; best director, Stephen Daldry, *An Inspector Calls*; mosts promising playwright, Philip Ridley, *The Fastest Clock in the Universe*.

In the 1993 Laurence Olivier awards, the award for best actor went to Robert Stephens for Falstaff, *Henry IV, Parts 1 and 2*; best actress, Alison Steadman, *The Rise and Fall of Little Voice*; best musical, *Crazy for You*; best musical revival, *Carousel*; best director for drama, Stephen Daldry, *An Inspector Calls*; best director for a musical, Nicholas Hytner, *Carousel*; best new play, *Six Degrees of Separation* by John Guare.

The 1992 Ian Charleson Award was presented to Tom Hollander for his role of Witwoud in *The Way of the World* at the Lyric, Hammersmith. The runner-up was Toby Stephens as Bertram in *All's Well That Ends Well* at the Swan, Stratford. Sir John Gielgud was awarded the first annual Shakespeare Globe Trust Award for his services to the works of Shakespeare. The citation praised his 'lifetime contribution to the performing arts and, in particular, to the enjoyment of Shakespeare'.

PRODUCTIONS
16 August 1992 to 15 August 1993

LONDON PRODUCTIONS

ADELPHI, WC2 (12 July 1993) *Sunset Boulevard* (music, Andrew Lloyd Webber, book and lyrics, Christopher Hampton and Don Black) with Patti LuPone, Kevin Anderson, Meredith Braun, Daniel Benzali; director, Trevor Nunn; designer, John Napier.
ALBERY, WC2 (26 November 1992) *Hay Fever* (Coward) with Maria Aitken, Sarah Crowe, Christopher Godwin, John Standing; director, Alan Strachan; designer, Anthony Powell. (17 May 1993) *Juno and the Paycock* (O'Casey) with Niall Buggy, Mark Lambert, Antoine Byrne, Anita Reeves, Tom Murphy, Peter Cowen; director, Joe Dowling;

designer, Frank Hallinan Flood (The Gate Theatre, Dublin, production). (5 July) *Separate Tables* (Rattigan) with Peter Bowles, Patricia Hodge, Miriam Karlin, Rachel Gurney, Charlotte Cornwell, Rosemary Leach; director, Peter Hall; designer, Carl Toms
ALDWYCH, WC2 (14 October 1992) *The Rise and Fall of Little Voice* (Jim Cartwright) with Jane Horrocks, Alison Steadman, Pete Postlethwaite; director, Sam Mendes; designer, William Dudley (National Theatre production). (22 February 1993) *The Importance of Being Earnest* (Wilde) with Maggie Smith, Richard E. Grant, Alex Jennings, Susannah Harker, Claire Skinner, Margaret Tyzack; director, Nicholas Hytner; designer, Bob Crowley
ALMEIDA, NI (16 September 1992) *Medea* (Euripides, adapted Alistair Elliot) with Diana Rigg, Joseph O'Conor, Tim Woodward; director, Jonathan Kent; designer, Peter J. Davison. (2 November) *No Man's Land* (Pinter) with Paul Eddington, Harold Pinter, Douglas Hodge, Gawn Grainger; director, David Leveaux; designer, Bob Crowley. (6 January 1993) *The Deep Blue Sea* (Rattigan) with Penelope Wilton, Linus Roache; director, Karel Reisz; designer, William Dudley. (16 March) *Chatsky* (Alexander Griboyedov, translated by Anthony Burgess) with Colin Firth, Jemma Redgrave, Dinsdale Landen, Jonathan Cullen, John Fortune, David O'Hara; director, Jonathan Kent; designer, Tim Hatley. (17 May) *The Showman* (Thomas Bernhard, translated by Peter Jansen and Kenneth Northcott) with Alan Bates; director, Jonathan Kent; designer, Paul Brown
APOLLO, WI (3 November 1992) *Our Song* (Keith Waterhouse) with Peter O'Toole, Tara Fitzgerald; director, Ned Sherrin; designer, Tim Goodchild. (22 March 1993) *The Deep Blue Sea* (transferred from the Almeida)
BARBICAN, EC2 (10 September 1992) *The Thebans* (*Oedipus Tyrannos, Oedipus at Colonus* and *Antigone*) (Sophocles, translated Timberlake Wertenbaker) with Gerard Murphy, Linda Marlowe, John Shrapnel, Joanne Pearce, Philip Voss; director, Adrian Noble; designer, Ultz; music, Ilona Sekacz. (14 October) *Two Gentlemen of Verona* (Shakespeare) with Barry Lynch, Sean Murray, Saskia Reeves, Richard Bonneville, Clare Holman; director, David Thacker; designer, Shelagh Keegan. (18 December) *Hamlet* (transferred from Stratford). (3 December) *The Tempest* (Shakespeare) with Mariko Fuji, Harohiko Joh, Hiroki Okawa, Kenichi Ishii, Yoji Matsuda; director, Yukio Ninagawa. (23 December) *The Comedy of Errors* (Shakespeare) with Desmond Barrit, Graham Turner, Estelle Kohler; director, Ian Judge. (7 April 1993) *The Beggar's Opera* (Gay) with David Burt, Paul Jesson, Anthony O'Donnell, Elizabeth Renihan, Jenna Russell; director, John Caird; designer, Kendra Ullyart. (22 April) *As You Like It* (Shakespeare) with Kate Buffery, Peter de Jersey, Samantha Bond, Michael Siberry, Anthony O'Donnell; director, David Thacker; designer, Johan Engels. (27 May) *Antony and Cleopatra* (transferred from Stratford). (24 June) *The Winter's Tale* (Shakespeare) with John Nettles, Samantha Bond, Gemma Jones, Paul Jesson, Richard McCabe, Alan Cox, Phyllida Hancock; director, Adrian Noble. (20 July) *The Taming of the Shrew* (Shakespeare) with Amanda Harris, Anton Lesser, Rebecca Saire, Richard McCabe; director, Bill Alexander
THE PIT (3 September 1992) *Amphibians* (Billy Roche) with Sean Murray, Richard Bonneville, Lesley McGuire, Barry Lynch, Kevin Burke; director, Michael Attenborough; designer, Michael Taylor. (13 October) *Artists and Admirers* (Ostrovsky) with Sylvestra Le Touzel, Linda Bassett, Christopher Benjamin, Rob Edwards, Philip Voss; director, Phyllida Lloyd; designer, Anthony Ward. (16 December) *The Gift of the Gorgon* (Peter Shaffer) with

Judi Dench, Michael Pennington, Jeremy Northam; director, Peter Hall; designer, John Gunter. (13 January 1993) *King Baby* (James Robson) with Sheila Reid, Tom Georgeson, Emily Joyce, Lalor Roddy, Liam O'Callaghan; director, Simon Usher; designer, Anthony Lamble. (6 April) *The School of Night* (transferred from Stratford). (14 April) *A Jovial Crew* (Richard Brome, adapted by Stephen Jeffreys) with Ron Cook, Paul Jesson, Rebecca Saire, Amanda Harris; director, Max Stafford-Clark; designer, Fotini Dimou. (May) *The Changeling* (Rowley) (transferred from Stratford). (21 July) *Misha's Party* (Richard Nelson, Alexander Gelman) with Cheryl Campbell, Barry Foster, Benjamin Whitrow, Barbara Jefford, John Bott, Olivia Williams, Emma Gregory, Sara Kestelman, Anthony O'Donnell; director, David Jones
BARBICAN HALL (4 August 1993) *Godspell* (Stephen Schwarz, John Michael Tebelak) with Gemma Craven, Andy Crane, James Gaddas, Mark Greenstreet, Andrew Bradley; director, Lindsay Dolan; designer, Tim Goodchild
BUSH, W12 (6 September 1992) *Jack's Out* (Danny Miller) with John Challis, James Clyde, Kieron Forsyth, Richard Tate; director, Ken McClymont; designer, Graham Johnston. (7 November) *A Handful of Stars* (Billy Roche) with Gary Lydon, Liam Cunningham, Aiden Gillen, Dervla Kirwan, Des McAleer; director, Robin Lefevre. (November) *Poor Beast in the Rain* (Billy Roche) with Des McAleer, Gary Lydon, Liam Cunningham, Dervla Kirwan, Ingrid Craigie; director, Robin Lefevre. (January 1993) *Waiting at the Water's Edge* (Lucinda Coxon) with Suzanna Hamilton, Helen Anderson, Amelda Brown; director, Polly Teale; designer, Alice Purcell. (24 February) *Not Fade Away* (Richard Cameron) with Kelly Hunter, Neal Swettenham; director, Simon Usher; designer, Anthony Lamble. (May) *The Chinese Wolf* (David Ashton) with Desmond Barrit, Maureen Beattie, Julia Ford, Ronan Vibert; director, Dominic Dromgoole
CAMBRIDGE, WC2 (18 August 1993) *Hot Stuff* (Maggie Norris, Paul Kerryson) with Paulette Ivory, Guy Oliver-Watts, Caroline O'Connor, David Dale; director, Paul Kerryson
COCHRANE, WC1 (5 April 1993) *From the Mississippi Delta* (Endesha Ida Mae Holland) with Josette Bushell-Mingo, Pauline Black, Joy Richardson; director, Annie Castledine (Talawa Company production)
COCKPIT, W1 (22 September 1992) *Water Music* (Lyndon Morgan), director, Keith Boak; designer, Lucy Hall (Soho Theatre Company production). (24 November) *Trilby and Svengali* (du Maurier, adapted by David Fielder and Nancy Meckler) with Teddy Kempner, Dermot Kerrigan, Tilly Blackwood; director, Nancy Meckler (Shared Experience production). (19 January 1993) *SelfCatering* (Andrew Cullen) with Jane Hogarth, Mark Spalding, Ayse Owen, Matilda Ziegler, John Griffin; director, Kate Rowland; designer, Hannah Mayall (Altered States Company production)
COMEDY, WC2 (1 December 1992) *Trelawny of the Wells* (Pinero) with Michael Hordern, Helena Bonham Carter, Jason Connery, Margaret Courtenay, Sarah Brightman; director, Toby Robertson; designer, Paul Edwards. (8 February 1993) *No Man's Land* (transferred from Almeida). (7 June 1993) *The Invisible Man* (Theatre Royal, Stratford, production transferred from Vaudeville)
CRITERION, W1 (21 October 1992) *Making It Better* (James Saunders) with Jane Asher, David de Keyser, Larry Lamb, Rufus Sewell; director, Michael Rudman (Hampstead Theatre production). (17 December) *Misery* (Stephen King, adapted and directed by Simon Moore) with Sharon Gless, Bill Paterson; director, Simon Moore; designer, Patrick Connellan

DOMINION, WC1 (15 July 1993) *Grease* (book, music and lyrics, Jim Jacobs, Warren Casey) with Craig McLachlan, Debbie Gibson; director, David Gilmore; designer, Terry Parsons; choreographer, Arlene Phillips
DONMAR WAREHOUSE, WC2 (29 October 1992) *Assassins* (music and lyrics, Stephen Sondheim, book, John Weidman) with Henry Goodman, Louise Gold, Jack Ellis, Anthony Barclay, Michael Cantwell, Ciaran Hinds; director, Sam Mendes; designer, Anthony Ward; music, Jeremy Sams. (January 1993) *Richard III* (RSC production). (2 March) *Playland* (Fugard) with John Kani, Sean Taylor; director, Athol Fugard. (April) *Don't Fool With Love* (de Musset, translated and directed by Declan Donnellan) with Pooky Quesnel, Michael Sheen, Maria Miles, David Foxe, Brian Pettifer (Cheek by Jowl production). (9 June) *Translations* (Brian Friel) with James Larkin, Zara Turner, Norman Rodway, Barry Lynch, Robert Patterson; director, Sam Mendes. (4 August) *Here* (Michael Frayn) with Iain Glen, Teresa Banham, Brenda Bruce; director, Michael Blakemore; designer, Ashley Martin-Davis
DUKE OF YORK'S, WC2 (1 December 1992) *The Witches* (Roald Dahl, adapted and directed by David Wood) with Dorothy Ann Gould, Karen Briffet, Janet Whiteside. (23 February 1993) *Murder is Easy* (Agatha Christie, adapted by Clive Exton) with Nigel Davenport, Charlotte Attenborough, Peter Capaldi, Irene Sutcliffe, Jo Kendall; director, Wyn Jones; designers, Christopher Morley, Christopher Woods. (20 April) *The Last Yankee* (transferred from the Young Vic)
GARRICK, WC2 (24 February 1993) *On the Piste* (John Godber) with Peter Birch, Stephanie Pack, Julia Deakin, Paul Bown, Ivan Kaye, Gillian Tompkins; director, Bob Tomson; designer, Julie Godfrey
GATE, W11 (2 September 1992) *Hecuba* (Euripides, translated Kenneth McLeish) with Ann Mitchell, Sara Mair-Thomas, Don Warrington, Sylvester Morand; director, Laurence Boswell; designer, Stephen Brimson Lewis. (9 October) *The House of Bernarda Alba* (Lorca) with Dinah Stabb, Alexandra Gilbreath, Kristin Hewson, Deirdre Doone; director, Katie Mitchell. (December) *Madness in Valencia* (de Vega, translated by David Johnston) with Caroline Loncq, Simon Kunz, John Straiton; director, Laurence Boswell; designer, Rae Smith. (30 January 1993) *The Set-Up* (Joseph Moncure March) with Kerry Shale; director, John Abbott
GLOBE, W1 (17 September 1992) *Valentine's Day* (adapted from *You Never Can Tell* (Shaw) by Benny Green, Denis King, David Williams) with Edward Petherbridge, Nicky Adams, Alexander Hanson, John Turner, Teresa Banham, Edward de Souza; director, choreographer, Gillian Lynne; designer, Paul Farnsworth. (11 November) *An Ideal Husband* (Wilde) with Hannah Gordon, Martin Shaw, Michael Denison, Dulcie Gray, David Yelland, Anna Carteret; director, Peter Hall; designer, Carl Toms. (23 June 1993) *Present Laughter* (Coward) with Tom Conti, Gabrielle Drake, Judy Loe, Jenny Seagrove; director, Tom Conti; designer, Terry Parsons
GREENWICH, SE10 (24 September 1992) *Who Shall I Be Tomorrow?* (Benard Kops) with Joanna Lumley, Harry Landis; director, Matthew Francis; designer, Stephen Brimson Lewis. (29 October) *Just Between Ourselves* (Ayckbourn), director, Robin Midgley. (21 December) *The Prisoner of Zenda* (Hope, adapted and directed by Matthew Francis) with David Haig, Mark Lockyer, Melanie Jessop, Nicholas Gecks, Leonie Mellinger, Michael Cronin; designer, Lez Brotherston; music, Mia Soteriou. (15 February 1993) *Entertaining Mr Sloane* (Orton) with Janet Dale, Ben Daniels, Ian Gelder; director, Jeremy Sams, Christopher Hancock; designer, Mark Bailey. (25 March)

The Europeans (Howard Barker) with Nicholas le Prevost, Philip Franks, Judith Scott, Bill Stewart, Julian Forsyth; director, Kenny Ireland; designer, Rae Smith. (27 April) *Total Eclipse* (Christopher Hampton) with Greg Hicks, Oliver Milburn; director, Lisa Forrell; designer, Julian McCowan. (7 June) *The Pan Beaters* (Stephen Landrigan) with Joanna McCallum, Victor Romero Evans, Don Warrington, Shango Baku. (22 July) *Under the Stars* (Richard Crane) with Connie Booth, Pam Ferris, Tyler Butterworth, Nicholas Gecks, Penny Morell; director, designer, Lez Brotherston

HAMPSTEAD, NW3 (8 September 1992) *June Moon* (Ring Lardner, George S Kaufman) with Deirdre Harrison, Frank Lazerus, Adam Godley, Maria Gough, Susannah Fellows; director, Alan Strachan; designer, Michael Holt (Theatre of Comedy production). (28 October) *A Little Older* (John Binnie) with Mari Binnie, Stephen Docherty. (9 December) *Grace* (Doug Lucie) with James Laurenson, Kate Fahy, Kevin Dignam, Peter Wight, Anna Massey; director, Mike Bradwell. (January 1993) *La Musica* (Marguerite Duras, translated by Barbara Bray) with Larry Lamb, Harriet Walter; director, Joseph Blatchley; designer, Geraldine Pilgrim. (15 March) *Unidentified Human Remains* (transferred from the Traverse Theatre, Edinburgh). (29 May) *The Dearly Beloved* (Philip Osment) with John Gillett, Pamela Moiseiwitsch, Peter Wight, Veronica Roberts, Sally Knyvette; director, Mike Alfreds; designer, Paul Dart (Cambridge Theatre Company). (13 July) *Marvin's Room* (Scott McPherson) with Alison Steadman, Phyllis Logan, Carmel McSharry, Ian Gelder, Aidan Gillen; director, David Petrarca

HAYMARKET THEATRE ROYAL, SW1 (14 December 1992) *Cyrano de Bergerac* (Rostand, translated by John Wells) with Robert Lindsay, Julian Glover, Richard O'Callaghan, Stella Gonet, Gary Cady; director, Elijah Moshinsky; designer, Michael Yeargan. (19 July 1993) *Lust* (the Heather Brothers) with Denis Lawson, Sophie Aldred, Julian Curry, Mark Haddigan, Helen Hobson; director, Bob Carlton; designer, Geoff Rose

KING'S HEAD, N1 (19 August 1992) *Acapulco* (written and directed by Steven Berkoff) with Steven Berkoff, Paul Bentall, Connie Hyde, Joe Montana, Hilton McRae, Terence Beesley. (6 October) *Post Mortem* (Coward) with Neil Roberts, Sylvia Syms, Harry Burton, Susannah Morley; director, Mark Friend; designer, Tim Heywood. (7 January 1993) *Mr Cinders* (Vivian Ellis, Greatrex Newman, Clifford Grey, Richard Myers) with Samuel West, Chris Villiers, Charles Edwards, Sally Anne Triplet, Helen Hobson, Jane Lesley, Lisa Pearce; director, Martin Connor; choreographer, Gillian Gregory. (March) *Squirrels* (David Mamet) with Edward Petheridge, Steven O'Shea, Sara Kestelman; director, Aaron Mullen. (May) *Cracks* (Martin Sherman) with Peter Whitman, Tracy Keating, Ben Daniels, Jane Gurnett, Deborah Norton, Briony Glassco; director, Tim Luscombe; designer, Jon Morrell. (June 1993) *A Day in the Death of Joe Egg* (Peter Nichols) with Clive Owen, Elizabeth Garvie; director, Lisa Forrell

LILIAN BAYLIS, EC1 (26 October 1992) *Lulu* (Wedekind, translated and adapted by Edward Bond, Elisabeth Bond-Pable) with Susan Lynch, Fred Pearson, Melanie Jessop; director, Nick Philippou; designer, Stewart Laing (Cambridge Theatre Company production)

LYRIC, Hammersmith, W6 (15 October 1992) *The Way of the World* (Congreve) with Sheila Hancock, Tom Hollander, Gary Olsen, Jonathan Phillips, Emma Piper, Jeremy Northam, Wendy Nottingham; director, Peter Gill; designer, Tom Piper. (1 December) *The Ghost Train* (Ridley) with Bill Oddie, Aden Gillett, Richard Stirling, Kate Hardie; director, John Adams; designer, Roger Butlin.

(4 February 1993) *Greasepaint* (Hisashi Inoue, translated by Masaru Hotta and Vernon Gudgeon) with Frances de la Tour; director, Koichi Kimura; designer, Yukio Horio. (25 March) *Blood Wedding* (Lorca) with Alex Richardson, Rosalind Bennett, Patrick O'Kane, Siobhan Stanley, Di Sherlock, Frances Tomelty; director, Nigel Jamieson; designer, Helen Turner. (22 April) *Moll Flanders - A Musical* (Defoe, adapted by Claire Luckham, lyrics Paul Leigh) with Josie Lawrence; director, Peter James; composer, George Stiles; designer, Sally Crabb. (24 May) *Romeo and Juliet* (Shakespeare) with Joe Dixon, Joanna Roth, Caroline Harris, John Dougall, Christopher Saul, Julia Deardon; director, Michael Bogdanov (English Shakespeare Company production). (23 June) *Comedians* (Trevor Griffiths) with Berwick Kaler, Tim McInnerny, Jeff Nuttall, Liam de Staic, Emil Wolk; director, Jude Kelly

LYRIC STUDIO, W6 (20 August 1992) *Don Carlos* (Schiller, translated Peter Oswald) with Piers Gibbon, Terry McGinity, Alex Hardy, Victoria Worsley, Tamsin Greig; director, Tim Carroll (Start Here production). (15 September) *Orlando* (Virginia Woolf, adapted by Robin Brooks), director, Jonathan Holloway (Red Shift production). (27 November) *The Rape of Tamar* (de Molina, adapted and directed by Paul Whitworth) with Jules Melvin, Morris Perry, Martin Hyder, Christopher Hollis, Patrick Wilde (Theatre Manoeuvres Company production). (5 January 1993) *The Curse of the Pharaohs* (Robin Brooks) with Sophie McConnell, Peter Glancy, Nick Rawling, Adam Fahey; director, Andrew Holmes (Empty Space Theatre Company). (8 June) *In Lambeth* (Jack Shepherd) with Tom Bowles, Terence Beesley, Jules Melvin; director, Jonathan Church; designer, David Blight (Triptych Theatre Company)

MERMAID, EC4 (14 June 1993) *Ali* (Geoffrey Ewing and Graydon Royce) with Geoffrey Ewing; director, Stephen Henderson

NATIONAL THEATRE, SE1. COTTESLOE (13 August 1992) *The Street of Crocodiles* (Bruno Schultz, translated Celina Weiniewska, adapted Simon McBurney, Mark Wheatley) with Cesar Saarachu, Matthew Scurfield, Annabel Arden, Clive Mendus, Eric Mallet, Lilo Baur, Stefan Metz; director, Simon McBurney; designer, Rae Smith (Théâtre de Complicité production). (17 September) *Kings* (Christopher Logue) with Alan Howard and Christopher Logue; director, Liane Aukin; designer, Shelagh Killeen. (18 November) *Stages* (David Storey) with Alan Bates, Gabrielle Lloyd, Joanna David, Marjorie Yates, Rosemarie Martin; director, Lindsay Anderson; designer, Jocelyn Herbert. (15 December) *Billy Liar* (Keith Waterhouse and Willis Hall) with Paul Wyett, Angela Clarke, Victoria Scarborough, Elizabeth Bradley, June Watson, James Grant; director, Tim Supple. (11 January 1993) *The Game of Love and Chance* (Marivaux, translated by Neil Bartlett) with Marcello Magni, Caroline Quentin, Peter Wingfield, Maggie Steed, Stefan Bednarczyk; directors, Mike Alfreds and Neil Bartlett; designer, Paul Dart. (2 February) *La Musica* (transferred from Hampstead Theatre). (4 March) *Mr A's Amazing Maze Plays* (Ayckbourn) with Adam Godley, Richard Long, Judith McSpadden, John Branwell, Glyn Grain; director, Alan Ayckbourn; designer, Roger Glossop. (27 April) *Somewhere* (Judith Johnson) with Katrina Levon, John Hannah, Karl Draper; director, Polly Teale; designer, Stephen Brimson Lewis. (2 June) *Sweeney Todd* (music and lyrics, Stephen Sondheim, book, Hugh Wheeler) with Alun Armstrong, Julia McKenzie, Adrian Lester, Denis Quilley, Sheila Reid; director, Declan Donnellan; designer, Nick Omerod. (14 July) *The Mountain Giants* (Pirandello, adapted by Charles Wood) with Desmond Barrit, Sian Thomas; director, William Gaskill

LYTTELTON (11 September 1992) *An Inspector Calls*
(Priestley) with Kenneth Cranham, Barbara Leigh-Hunt,
Richard Pasco; director, Stephen Daldry; designer, Ian
MacNeil. (29 October) *Le Baruffe Chiozzotte* (Goldoni) with
Elio Crovetto, Pamela Villoresi, Didi Perego; director,
Giorgio Strehler; designer, Luciano Damiani. (9 November)
Sie Personaggi in Cerca d'Autore (Pirandello) with Benedetta
Buccellato, Barbara Valmorin, Enrico Maria Salerno;
director, Franco Zeffirelli. (10 December) *Carousel* (music,
Rodgers, book and lyrics, Hammerstein) with Patricia
Routledge, Joanna Riding, Michael Hayden, Phil Daniels,
Clive Rowe; director, Nicholas Hytner; choreographer,
Kenneth MacMillan; designer, Bob Crowley; conductor,
Justin Brown. (27 April 1993) *On the Ledge* (co-production
with Nottingham Playhouse). (13 April) *Arcadia* (Stoppard)
with Felicity Kendall, Rufus Sewell, Emma Fielding, Bill
Nighy, Harriet Walter, Samuel West; director, Trevor
Nunn; designer, Mark Thompson. (17 June) *Inadmissible
Evidence* (Osborne) with Trevor Eve, Roger Sloman, Lynn
Farleigh; director, Di Trevis; designer, Stephen Brimson
Lewis
OLIVIER (1 October 1992) *Square Rounds* (Tony Harrison)
with Maria Friedman, Sian Thomas, Paola Dionisotti, Sara
Kestelman, Jenny Galloway, Arturo Brachetti; director,
Tony Harrison; designer, Jocelyn Herbert; music, Dominic
Muldowney; choreography, Lawrence Evans. (6 November)
Dragon (Yevgeny Shvarts, adapted by Alan Cumming and
Ultz) with Tony Armatrading, Vicky Licorish, Mark Saban,
Bill Thomas, Mark Heap; director, designer, Ultz. (28
January 1993) *An Inspector Calls* (transferred from
Lyttelton). (18 February) *Trelawny of the Wells* (Pinero)
with Michael Bryant, Harry Towb, Betty Marsden, Helen
McCrory, Ben Miles, Robin Bailey; director, John Caird;
designer, John Napier. (1 April) *Macbeth* (Shakespeare) with
Alan Howard, Anastasia Hille; director, Richard Eyre;
designer, Bob Crowley
NEW END, NW3 (18 August 1992) *The Provok'd Wife*
(Vanbrugh) with John Ashton, Carol Holt, Jon Harris,
Charles Armstrong, Corinna Richards; director, Jonathan
Best; designer, Sarah Ashpole. (13 October) *The Story of the
Last of the Just* (Andre Schwarz-Bart, adapted by Robbie
Gringras) with Nadine Shenton, Sarah Cameron, Robbie
Gringras, Olivier Lacheze-Beer, Danny Scheinmann;
directors, Robbie Gringas, Rebecca Wolman; designer,
Colin Peters; musicians, Simon Katz, Neyire Ashworth. (10
November) *She Stoops to Conquer* (Goldsmith) (Court
Theatre production). (2 February 1993) *The Prisoners of
War* (J. R. Ackerley) with Ashley Russell, Mark Anstee, Ian
Flavin, Anna Chancellor, Patricia Heneghan; director, Ken
Butler; designer, Robin Donne
OLD VIC, SE1 (16 April 1993) *For Services Rendered*
(Somerset Maugham) with Sylvia Syms, Jeffrey Segal, Moir
Leslie, Tim Sabel; director, Deborah Paige; designer, Kit
Surrey (Salisbury Playhouse production). (15 June)
Lysistrata (Aristophanes, translated by Ranjit Bolt) with
Geraldine James, Diane Bull, John Kane, Serena Evans;
director, Peter Hall; designer, Dionysis Fotopoulos (in
association with Liverpool Playhouse)
OPEN AIR, Regent's Park, NW1 (1 June 1993) *The Taming
of the Shrew* (Shakespeare) with Geordie Johnson, Cathy
Tyson; director, Toby Robertson. (14 June) *Romeo and
Juliet* (Shakespeare) with Zubin Varla, Rebecca Callard,
Isabelle Lucas, Rupert Wickham, David Allister, Connor
Byrne, Dennis Clinton; director, Judi Dench; designer, Jack
Notman. (27 July) *A Connecticut Yankee* (music, Rodgers,
lyrics, Hart, book, Field) with Christopher Biggins, Clive
Carter, Janie Dee, Basil Hoskins, Anna Nicholas; director,
Ian Talbot

PICCADILLY, W1 (22 October 1992) *Which Witch*
(composers, Benedicte Adrian and Ingrid Bjornov, book,
Piers Haggard, lyrics, Kit Hesketh-Harvey) with Benedicte
Adrian, Graham Bickley, Vivien Parry, Gay Soper; director,
Piers Haggard; designer, Richard Hudson. (3 February
1993) *Robin, Prince of Sherwood* (Peter Howarth and Rick
Fenn) with Mike Holoway, Steven Varnom, Anne Smith,
Alan Gear, Liz Curnick; director, Bill Kenwright
PLAYHOUSE, WC2 (14 September 1992) *It Runs in the
Family* (written and directed by Ray Cooney) with Doris
Hare, Sandra Dickinson, Windsor Davies, Henry McGee,
Ray Cooney, Wanda Ventham, John Quayle; director,
Douglas Heap
PRINCE EDWARD, W1 (3 March 1993) *Crazy for You* (book,
Ken Ludwig, lyrics, Ira Gershwin, music, George
Gershwin) with Ruthie Henshall, Kirby Ward, Chris
Langham, Helen Way, Vanessa Leagh-Hicks, Amanda
Prior, Shaun Scott; director, Mike Ockrent; choreographer,
Susan Stroman; designer, Robin Wagner
PRINCE OF WALES, W1 (25 November 1992) *Annie Get
Your Gun* (Berlin) with Kim Criswell, John Diedrich,
Norman Rossington, Brian Glover, Meg Johnson, Leon
Greene; director, Roger Redfarn; choreographer, Gillian
Gregory. (30 March 1993) *City of Angels* (book, Larry
Gelbart, music, Cy Coleman, lyrics, David Zippel) with
Roger Allam, Martin Smith, Henry Goodman, Haydn
Gwynne, David Schofield; director, Michael Blakemore,
designer, Robin Wagner; costumes, Florence Kotz
QUEEN'S, W1 (15 October 1992) *Radio Times* (transferred
from Repertory Theatre, Birmingham). (2 March 1993)
Alfie (Bill Naughton) with Adam Faith, Sara Richardson,
Fiona Kennedy, Marco Capozzoli, Natasha Pyne; director,
Adam Faith; designer, Shelagh Keegan. (6 July) *Much Ado
About Nothing* (Shakespeare) with Mark Rylance, Janet
McTeer, Jack Ellis, Jonathan Newth, Gerard Kelly; director,
Matthew Warchus; designer, Neil Warmington
RIVERSIDE, W6 (9 September 1992) *Hamlet* (Shakespeare)
with Alan Rickman, Julia Ford, Geraldine McEwan,
Michael Byrne, David Burke; director, Robert Sturua;
designer, Giorgi Meskhishvili. (9 December) *Richard III*
(Shakespeare) with Barrie Rutter, David Roper, Ishia
Bennison; director, Barrie Rutter. (12 March 1993) *Invade
My Privacy* (Jay Landesman, Jason McAuliffe and Howard
Samuels) with Michelle Fine, Jacqueline Dankworth, Tina
Jones, Lucy Dixon; director, Linda Marlowe
ROYAL COURT, SW1 (10 August 1992) *Hush* (April de
Angelis) with Debra Gillett, Marion Bailey, Andy Serkis,
Stephen Dillane, Will Knightley; director, Max Stafford-
Clark; designer, Sally Jacobs. (22 September) *Colquhon and
MacBryde* (John Byrne) with Ken Stott, David O'Hara;
director, Lindsay Posner; designer, John Byrne. (10
November) *Three Birds Alighting on a Field* (Timberlake
Wertenbaker) with Harriet Walter, Colin McCormack,
Allan Corduner, Robin Soans; director, Max Stafford-Clark;
designer, Sally Jacobs. (14 January 1993) *King Lear*
(Shakespeare) with Tom Wilkinson, Hugh Ross, Iain Glen,
Adrian Dunbar, Andy Serkis, Cara Kelly; director, Max
Stafford-Clark; designer, Peter Hartwell. (23 March) *Fires in
the Mirror: Crown Heights, Brooklyn and other identities*,
written and performed by Anna Deavere Smith. (30 June)
Oleanna (David Mamet) with David Suchet, Lia Williams;
director, Harold Pinter
ROYAL COURT THEATRE UPSTAIRS (10 September 1992)
Women Laughing (Michael Wall) with Matilda Ziegler,
Christopher Fulford, John Michie, Maggie O'Neill; director,
Richard Wilson. (8 December) *Weldon Rising* (Phyllis
Nagy) with Simon Gregor, Paul Viragh, Rosie Rowell,
Melee Hutton, Andrew Woodall; director, Penny
Ciniewicz. (16 February 1993) *Out of the Ordinary* (Debbie

Isitt) with Debbie Isitt, Mark Kilmurry (Snarling Beasties production). (6th May) *Search and Destroy* (Howard Korder) with David Bamber, Andrew Woodall, Danny Webb, Leo Wringer, Cathryn Bradshaw; director, Stephen Daldry ROYALTY, WC2 (2 September 1992) *Maggie May* (composer, Lionel Bart, libretto, Alun Owen) with Liz King, James Barriscale, Simon Bowen, Sarah Moyle, Elliot Levey; director, Edward Wilson; designer, Brian Lee; choreographers, David Toguri, Janet Devenish (National Youth Theatre production). (24 November) *Macbeth* (Shakespeare) with Tony Haygarth, Lynn Farleigh, Gregory Floy, Charles Simpson, John Woodvine; director, Michael Bogdanov (English Shakespeare Company production). *The Tempest* (Shakespeare) with John Woodvine; director, Michael Bogdanov (English Shakespeare Company production)
SADLER'S WELLS, EC1 (12 January 1993) *Alice in Wonderland* (Lewis Carroll) (Black Light Theatre of Prague production)
SHAFTESBURY, WC2 (20 October 1992) *Kiss of the Spider Woman* (Manuel Puig, book, Terence McNally, music, John Kander, lyrics, Fred Ebb) with Anthony Crivello, Brent Carver, Chita Rivera, Herndon Lackey; director, Harold Prince; designers, Jerome Sirlin, Florence Klotz; choreographer, Vincent Paterson
STRAND, WC2 (12 November 1992) *Lost in Yonkers* (Neil Simon) with Maureen Lipman, Benny Grant, Ross McCall, Ron Berglas, Rosemary Harris; director, David Taylor; designer, Santo Loquasto. (3 June 1993) *Leonardo: The Musical, A Portrait of Love* (book, John Kane, music and lyrics, Tommy Moeller, Greg Moeller, Russell Dunlop, Duke Minks) with Paul Collis, James Barron, Hal Fowler, Jane Arden; director, Rob Bettinson; designer, Michael Pavelka
THEATRE ROYAL, E15 (23 October 1992) *Heer Ranjha* (adapted and directed by Jatinder Verma) with Shelley King, David Tse; designer, Magdalen Rubalcava. (1 February 1993) *Worlds Apart* (Paul Sirett) with Patrick Brennan, Anya Phillips, Madhav Sharma, David Harewood, Richard Rees; director, Jeff Teare. (7 April 1993) *One Step Beyond!* (Alan Gilbey)
TRICYCLE, NW6 (7 September 1992) *Gamblers* (Gogol, adapted Chris Hannan) with Oleg Menshikov, Mark Rylance, Jeremy Gilley, Phil Daniels, Tony Bluto; director, Dalia Ibelhauptaite; designer, Oleg Sheintsis. (8 October) *Trouble in Mind* (Alice Childress) with Carmen Munro, Maurice Roeves; director, Nicolas Kent. (24 February 1993) *Anna Karenina* (Tolstoy) with Jessica Lloyd, Richard Hope, Teresa Banham; director, Nancy Meckler (Shared Experience Company production). (April) *A Love Song for Ulster (The Marriage, The Son and The Daughter)* (Bill Morrison) with Orla Brady, Walter McMonagle, Brendan Coyle, John Keegan; director, Nicholas Kent
VAUDEVILLE, WC2 (8 September 1992) *Someone Who'll Watch Over Me* (Frank McGuinness) with Alec McCowen, Stephen Rea, James McDaniel; director, Robin Lefevre; designer, Robin Don (Hampstead Theatre production). (4 November) *June Moon* (transferred from Hampstead). (16 February 1993) *The Invisible Man* (Wells, adapted by Ken Hill) with Michael N. Harbour, Brian Murphy, Andrew Secombe, Toni Palmer, Caroline Bliss; director, Ken Hill (Theatre Royal, Stratford, production). (3 August) *Time of My Life* (Ayckbourn) with Richard Garnett, Karen Drury, Stephen Mapes, Sophie Heyman, Anton Rodgers, Gwen Taylor, Terence Booth; director, Alan Ayckbourn
WYNDHAM'S, WC2 (17 November 1992) *Travels with My Aunt* (Greene, adapted and directed by Giles Havergal with Christopher Gee) with Simon Cadell, John Wells, Christopher Gee, Richard Kane; designer, Stewart Laing.

(23 March 1993) *The Gift of the Gorgon* (Royal Shakespeare Company production)
YOUNG VIC, SE1 (17 September 1992) *Rosmersholm* (Ibsen) with Corin Redgrave, Francesca Annis, Miriam Karlin, Bernard Lloyd, Allan Corduner; director, Annie Castledine. (26 January 1993) *The Last Yankee* (Miller) with Peter Davison, David Healy, Zoe Wanamaker, Helen Burns and Bethany Hanson; director, David Thacker; designer, Shelagh Keegan. (26 April) *The Trial* (Kafka, adapted by Jan Goodman) with James Wilby, David Brett, Estelle Kohler, Peter Eyre; director, Lida Engelova; designer, Jaroslav Malina (European Stage Company)

OUTSIDE LONDON

BIRMINGHAM: REPERTORY (8 September 1992) *Radio Times* (devised Alex Armitage, script, Robin Miller, book, Abi Grant, music, Noël Gay) with Tony Slattery, Ian Bartholomew, Jeff Shankley, Harriet Benson, Kathryn Evans; director, David Gilmore; designer, Terry Parsons; choreographer, Anthony van Laast. (10 February 1993) *Big Maggie* (John B. Kane) with Gillian Hanna; director, Gwenda Hughes. (9 March) *Othello* (Shakespeare) with Jeffery Kissoon, Alex Kingston, Hilton McRae, Max Gold; director, Bill Alexander; designer, Kit Surrey. (16 April) *Rope* (Patrick Hamilton), director, Gwenda Hughes. (1 June) *Volpone* (Jonson) with Bernard Horsfall, Gerard Murphy, Charles Millham, Jamie Newall, Linda Spurrier, Stuart Richman; director, Bill Alexander; designer, Kit Surrey
STUDIO (14 September 1992) *Playing by the Rules* (Rod Dungate) with Ian Peperell, James Dreyfus, David Phelan; director, Anthony Clark; designer, Ruari Murchison
CHICHESTER: FESTIVAL (March 1993) *Elvis the Musical* (Jack Good, Ray Cooney) with Clayton Mark, Ian Salisbury, Steve Serlin, Chris Jones; director, Carole Todd; designer, Graham McLusky; music, Paul Jury. (30 April) *Getting Married* (Shaw) with Christopher Benjamin, Amanda Waring, Dorothy Tutin, Tony Britton, Barbara Murray; director, Frank Hauser; designer, Saul Radomsky. (26 May) *Relative Values* (Coward) with Susan Hampshire, Alison Fiske, Edward Duke, Anthony Bate, Sarah Brightman; director, Tim Luscombe; designer, Rob Howell. (1 July) *Pickwick* (book, Wolf Mankowitz, lyrics, Leslie Bricusse, music, Cyril Ornadel) with Harry Secombe, Roy Castle, Ruth Madoc, David Cardy, Alexandra Bastedo, Michael Howe; director, Patrick Garland; designer, Poppy Mitchell. (4 August) *The Matchmaker* (Wilder) with Prunella Scales, Stephen Simms, Tam Williams, Isla Blair, Frank Lazarus; director, Patrick Mason; designer, Joe Vanek
MINERVA (8 September 1992) *Vita and Virginia* (Eileen Atkins) with Eileen Atkins, Penelope Wilton; director, Patrick Garland. (22 September) *Billy Liar* (Keith Waterhouse and Willis Hall) with Paul Wyett, June Watson, Nicolas Tennant, Victoria Scarborough, Angela Clarke, Sally Rogers; director, Tim Supple; designer, Bunny Christie. (2 June 1993) *Carrington* (Jane Beeson) with Lucinda Curtis, Toyah Willcox, Robert Pickavance, Paul Herzberg, Dawn Keeler; director, Martin Johns. (7 July) *Rope* (Patrick Hamilton) with John Barrowman, Alexis Denisoff, Anthony Head, Roger Ennals; director, Keith Baxter; designer, Simon Higlett
EDINBURGH: TRAVERSE (27 November 1992) *Unidentified Human Remains* (Brad Fraser) with Irene Macdougall, Dougray Scott, Kenneth Bryans, Charlotte Jones, Lesley Vickerage, Tom Smith; director, Ian Brown
GLASGOW: CITIZENS (19 February 1993) *The Picture of Dorian Gray* (Wilde, adapted by Philip Prowse) with Henry

Ian Cusick, Bambos Karayanis, Rupert Everett, Gerrard McArthur; director, Philip Prowse

LEEDS: WEST YORKSHIRE PLAYHOUSE (13 March 1993) *The Plough and the Stars* (O'Casey) with Ian FitzGibbon, Dillie Keane, Amanda Root, Gerard Horan, Mark Hadfield, Sorcha Cusack; director, Matthew Warchus; designer, Mark Bailey. (24 July) *Father's Day* (Maureen Lawrence) with Richard Mayes, Ann Penfold, Dilys Laye; director, Penny Ciniewicz; designer, Paul Andrews

LEICESTER: HAYMARKET (8 October 1992) *Blood Wedding* (Lorca) with Natasha Pope, Ellen Sheean, Helen Cummings, Rory Edwards; director, designer, Julia Bardsley; choreographer, Michele Durtnell

MANCHESTER: ROYAL EXCHANGE (10 September 1992) *Love's Labour Lost* (Shakespeare) with Linus Roache, Stephen Tompkinson, Ray Fearon, Meredith Davies, Bernard Bresslaw, Peter-Hugo Daly; director, James Macdonald; designer, Kandis Cook. (October) *Blues for Mister Charlie* (James Baldwin) with Nicholas le Prevost, Wyllie Longmore, David Schofield, Paterson Joseph, Barbara Barnes; director, Gregory Hersov; designer, David Short. (4 February 1993) *Brothers Karamazov* (Dostoevsky, adapted by Gerard McLarnon) with Tom Mannion, Michael Mueller, Philip Madoc, Lorraine Ashbourne, Louise Lombard, Ian Shaw, Jonathan Moore, Graham Crowden; director, Braham Murray; designer, Simon Higlett. (April) *Little Murders* (Jules Feiffer) with Pip Donaghy, Brigit Forsyth, Jacquetta May, George Anton; director, Gregory Hersov. (13 May) *Poison Pen* (Ronald Harwood) with Tom Courtenay, Michael Simkins, Sean Barrett, Polly James, Michael Simkins, Rhys Ifans, Emma Amos; director, Ronald Harwood; designer, Johanna Bryant. (1 July) *Maybe* (Mikhail Shatrov, adapted by Keith Reddin) with Vanessa Redgrave, John Bennett, Margaret Robertson; director, Braham Murray; designer, Johanna Bryant

MOLD: THEATR CLWYD (18 February 1993) *Death of a Salesman* (Miller) with Timothy West, Sheila Allen, Geordie Johnson, Christopher Thomas, Adam Henderson; director, Janet Suzman; designer, Johan Engels

NOTTINGHAM: PLAYHOUSE (19 February 1993) *On the Ledge* (Alan Bleasdale) with Mark McGann, David Ross, Gary Olsen, Dearbhla Molloy, Jimmy Mulville, Christopher Ryan; director, Robin Lefevre; designer, William Dudley

SCARBOROUGH: STEPHEN JOSEPH (August 1992) *Dreams from a Summer House* (Alan Ayckbourn and John Pattison) with Christine Fox, Janie Dee, Dale Rapley, Jan Hartley, Anthony Venditti; director, Alan Ayckbourn. (14 April 1993) *Feed* (Tom Elliott) with Malcolm Hebden, Sophia Winter, Lesley Nichol; director, James Tomlinson

SHEFFIELD: CRUCIBLE (18 February 1993) *Donkeys' Years* (Michael Frayn) with Simon Williams, Nicky Henson, Alison Fiske, Phil Fox; director, Michael Rudman

STRATFORD: MEMORIAL (2 September 1992) *The Merry Wives of Windsor* (Shakespeare) with Anton Lesser, Cheryl Campbell, Samantha Bond, Benjamin Whitrow, Barbara Jefford, Gemma Jones; director, David Thacker; designer, William Dudley; music, Guy Wolfenden. (5 November) *Antony and Cleopatra* (Shakespeare) with Richard Johnson, Clare Higgins, John Nettles, Toby Stephens, Paul Jesson; director, John Caird; designer, Sue Blane; music, Ilona Sekacz. (20 March 1993) *Hamlet* (Shakespeare) with Kenneth Branagh, Joanne Pearce, Jane Lapotaire, David Bradley, John Shrapnel; director, Adrian Noble; designer, Bob Crowley. (10 May) *King Lear* (Shakespeare) with Robert Stephens, Simon Russell Beale, David Bradley, Ian Hughes, David Calder, Owen Teale, Jenny Quayle, Abigail McKern; director, Adrian Noble; designer, Anthony Ward. (3 June) *The Merchant of Venice* (Shakespeare) with David Calder, Penny Downie, Kate Duchene, Clifford Rose,

Owen Teale, Mark Lockyer; director, David Thacker; designer, Shelagh Keegan. (11 August) *The Tempest* (Shakespeare) with Alec McCowen, Simon Russell Beale, James Hayes, Sarah Woodward, Mark Lockyer, David Bradley, David Troughton; director, Sam Mendes

SWAN (1 September 1992) *Tamburlaine the Great* (Christopher Marlowe) with Antony Sher, Claire Benedict, Malcolm Storry; director, Terry Hands; designer, Johan Engels. (3 November) *The Changeling* (Middleton and Rowley) with Cheryl Campbell, Malcolm Storry, Michael Siberry, Jeffery Dench; director, Michael Attenborough; designer, Julian McGowan. (18 March 1993) *Richard III* (Shakespeare) with Simon Russell Beale, Cherry Morris, Stephen Boxer, Annabelle Apsion, Kate Duchene, Simon Dormandy; director, Sam Mendes; designer, Tim Hatley. (August) *The Country Wife* (Wycherley) with Jonathan Phillips, Simon Dormandy, Abigail McKern, Janet Dale, Anne Lambton, Jeremy Northam, Debra Gillett; director, Max Stafford-Clark. (13 May) *Murder in the Cathedral* (T. S. Eliot) with Michael Feast; director, Steven Pimlott; designer, Ashley Martin-Davies. (3 June) *The Venetian Twins* (Goldoni, translated by Ranjit Bolt) with David Troughton, Sarah Woodward, Jenny Quayle; director, Michael Bogdanov

THE OTHER PLACE (28 October 1992) *The School of Night* (Peter Whelan) with Richard McCabe, Adrian Lukis, John McAndrew, Nigel Cooke, Bella Enahoro, Graham Turner; director, Bill Alexander; designer, Fotini Dimou. (10 June 1993) *Ghosts* (Ibsen, translated by Michael Meyer) with Jane Lapotaire, Simon Russell Beale, John Normington, John Carlisle, Alexandra Gilbreath; director, Katie Mitchell; designers, Vicki Mortimer, Tina McHugh. (5 August) *Julius Caesar* (Shakespeare) with David Sumner, Jeffery Kissoon, Rob Edwards, Barry Lynch; director, David Thacker

Film

In 1992 film attendances in Britain reached 98 million, an increase of five million on the previous year. However, the only British film in the list of most popular films was *Howards End*, which came 35th and took £2.6 million in box office receipts. The most popular film was *Basic Instinct*, featuring Sharon Stone, which took over £15 million, with *Hook* second and *Lethal Weapon 3* third. In 1992 some 25 British films were made, many of which were funded by Channel 4 and BBC Television.

The 65th Academy Awards (Oscars) were a comparative triumph for British films and performers, with Emma Thompson winning the best actress award for her role as Margaret Schlegel in *Howards End*. The Secretary of State for National Heritage (Peter Brooke) said 'These awards and the many Oscar nominations remind us that Britain is an undisputed centre of excellence for film-makers from across the world'. While welcoming his comments, many British film-makers wished to see more concrete support from the Government for the indigenous film industry, such as tax incentives and a levy on American-owned cinemas and film distributors.

Clint Eastwood's *Unforgiven* was one of the deserved successes of the Oscars, with Eastwood receiving awards both as best director and for best picture. Nominated in nine categories (as was *Howards End*), *Unforgiven* also received the Oscar for best film editing and for Gene Hackman as best supporting actor. Neil Jordan missed out on Oscars for best picture and best director for *The Crying Game* but won the award for best original screenplay.

Al Pacino won his first best actor Oscar for his role in *Scent of a Woman*. It was his fifth consecutive nomination and his eighth in total. He plays a blind retired army officer, Lt.-Col. Frank Slade, spending a Thanksgiving weekend with a school pupil, played by Chris O'Donnell, in the Waldorf Astoria in New York. Slade has decided that after a final 'blow-out' in New York, he will end his life. However, his relationship with the boy persuades him that there is something worth living for. Directed by Martin Brest, the film is over-long and contrived, and Pacino's performance, while creditable, was scarcely the year's best performance. However it was obviously felt by Academy voters that his time had come. He was also nominated as best supporting actor for his role in *Glengarry Glen Ross*.

Howards End collected three awards. In addition to Emma Thompson's Oscar, Ruth Prawer Jhabvala received the Oscar for best adapted screenplay and the film also received the award for best art direction. Best supporting actress was Marisa Tomei in *My Cousin Vinny*. *Bram Stoker's Dracula* won awards for best make-up, best sound effects editing and best costume design. Best foreign film was *Indochine* (France), directed by Regis Wargnier and starring Catherine Deneuve as Elaine Devries, the owner of a rubber plantation in Saigon in the 1930s.

At the 24th British Academy of Film and Television Arts (BAFTA) Awards, Emma Thompson also won the best actress award for her role in *Howards End*, which was also judged best film. The Alexander Korda Award for best British film went to Neil Jordan's *The Crying Game*. Robert Downey jun. was named best actor for his starring role in *Chaplin*, and Robert Altman best director for *The Player*, which also won the award for best adapted screenplay for Michael Tolkin. Best original screenplay was Woody Allen's *Husbands and Wives*. Miranda Richardson won the award for best supporting actress for *Damage*, for which she was also nominated for an Oscar. Best supporting actor was Gene Hackman in *Unforgiven*. *The Last of the Mohicans,* directed by Michael Mann and based on James Fenimore Cooper's novel, won the award for best cinematography (Dante Spinotti). It features Daniel Day-Lewis as Hawkeye, in a politically correct version which depicts the Indians as native Americans exploited by the British and French. Chingachgook, the Mohican, is played by Russell Means, with Magua, the Huron, played by Wes Studi and Cora Munro, with whom Hawkeye falls in love, by Madeleine Stowe.

EASTWOOD'S WESTERN

In *Unforgiven*, Clint Eastwood returned to form in the genre that established his career. He directed and starred in the story of William Munny, formerly a famous gunfighter but now a poor pig farmer obsessed with the memory of his dead wife, who had persuaded him to give up both alcohol and his weapons. A young gunfighter, the Schofield Kid, played by Jaimz Woolvett, knows of Munny's past and persuades him to hunt down two cowboys to collect the bounty on their heads. However, the strength of *Unforgiven* is that it undermines the Western myth rather than glorifying it. The film is well acted and produced and its gritty realism and anti-violence message struck a popular chord. It also features Gene Hackman as Little Bill Daggett, a former gunman turned sheriff of the town of Big Whiskey, Richard Harris as English Bob and Morgan Freeman as Munny's former partner, Ned Logan. The script, by David Webb Peoples, was originally written in the 1970s; the rights were owned by Francis Ford Coppola until Eastwood bought them in 1983. He waited until he felt the time was right and he was the right age for the film, and the result is a resounding triumph.

Eastwood also stars in the highly-praised *In the Line of Fire*, directed by Wolfgang Petersen. He plays a secret service agent Frank Horrigan, who is haunted by his failure to save the life of President Kennedy in Dallas in 1963. He hopes to redeem himself when he discovers that the current President is threatened by a professional killer, Mitch Leary, chillingly played by John Malkovich.

Also released was the director's cut of Ridley Scott's *Blade Runner*. This imaginative science fiction thriller is now seen as Scott intended, without the contrived happy ending and the superimposed narration of Rick Deckard, the character played by Harrison Ford. Set in Los Angeles in 2019, the film is a masterpiece of design. Scott's preferred version is certainly superior to that released by the studio and gives a deserved new lease of life to a stylish film. The same director's science fiction film *Alien* spawned its second sequel, *Alien 3*, directed by David Fincher. It again features Sigourney Weaver as Ripley, still pursued by the alien creature. The action is set this time on the planet Fiorina 161, where the population of criminals and rejects lives underground. The cast also features Brian Glover and Charles Dance.

Neil Jordan has directed several highly-acclaimed films, including *Angel* and *Mona Lisa*. In *The Crying Game*, which he also scripted, he explores the ambiguity of human relationships set against the background of the troubles in Northern Ireland. Forest Whitaker plays a British soldier who is kidnapped and offered in exchange for an imprisoned terrorist, Fergus, played by Stephen Rea, with whom he strikes up a friendship. Fergus agrees to visit the soldier's lover, Dil, in London in the event of his death. Unfortunately, one of the plot's main twists was revealed by the Oscar nominations, because Dil was played by newcomer Jaye Davidson who was nominated in the category of best supporting actor. The film received a total of six Oscar nominations and achieved remarkable success both in the USA, where it earned some $50 million, and the UK, where it took £12 million. It had cost some £3 million to make.

WHEN DINOSAURS RULED HOLLYWOOD

The major cinematic release of the year was Steven Spielberg's *Jurassic Park*, based on Michael Crichton's novel and adapted by Crichton and David Koepp. Made at a reported cost of $75 million ($5 million less than its budget), this tale of dinosaurs brought back to life touched a popular nerve and appealed to all ages. Richard Attenborough, in his first screen role for 14 years, plays John Hammond, a billionaire who develops a theme park with the recreated dinosaurs on an island near Costa Rica. However, any menace in the character as originally depicted in the novel is totally extinguished in Attenborough's avuncular performance. Sam Neill plays Grant, a palaeontologist, and Laura Dern Dr Ellie Sattler, a palaeobotanist, who visit the park at Hammond's request, with Jeff Goldblum as Dr Malcolm, an expert on chaos theory, and Bob Peck as chief game warden Robert Muldoon.

Although the characters are two-dimensional, the film is redeemed by its spectacular special effects, created by the Industrial Light and Magic company, the studio founded by George Lucas who made the

Star Wars trilogy. The dinosaurs, from the vegetarian brachiosaurus to the velociraptors and tyrannosaurus rex, are the most impressive and believable prehistoric creatures ever recreated on film. They were developed using a software programme created by a British company, Parallax. Instead of the traditional stop-motion filming of small models, the film-makers combined digital computer graphics with models and live action; 54 sequences, totalling over six minutes of screen time, featured dinosaurs created solely by computer graphics.

The film's main weakness is its script, with one-line quips preferred to character development. Nonetheless, it was a success and seems set to break all box office records. It was reported that Universal spent nearly $70 million on promoting the film; this obviously paid off, as it took over $200 million at the box office in just over three weeks. There was some concern that young children might find some of the scenes disturbing. The British Board of Film Classification sidestepped the issue by granting the film a PG certificate while requiring the film's publicity material to carry a warning that some sequences 'may be particularly disturbing to younger children or children of a sensitive disposition'.

The 500th anniversary of Christopher Columbus's discovery of the 'new world' was marked with a glut of films of varying standards. One of the better versions was *1492: A Conquest of Paradise*, directed by Ridley Scott. Starring Gerard Depardieu as Columbus, with a strong supporting cast of Sigourney Weaver as Queen Isabella, Armand Assante and Fernando Rey, Ridley's film looks not only at some of the darker implications of Columbus's journey, but also at what befell him on his return, with his rival Amerigo Vespucci stealing the limelight and his career ending in disgrace. Less impressive was John Glen's *Christopher Columbus: the Discovery*, with George Carraface in the title role. After a break of 14 years, the 'Carry On' series of films begat its 31st offspring, with *Carry On Columbus*. However, even the introduction of 'new' comedians such as Rik Mayall, Alexei Sayle and Julian Clary, bolstering a cast of Carry On veterans such as Jim Dale as Columbus, Leslie Phillips and Bernard Cribbins, could not save a film that looked dated and feeble.

The Walt Disney Studio returned to familiar territory with its version of the traditional fairy story *Beauty and the Beast*. It became the first animated film ever to be nominated in the best film category of the Oscars; altogether it had six nominations in the 1992 awards. It also struck a chord with the public, taking over $110 million in its first 15 weeks of release in the USA. It features the voices of Angela Lansbury, Robby Benson and Jesse Corti.

Strictly Ballroom is an intelligent and entertaining romantic comedy that celebrates ballroom dancing champions. An Australian film, it features Paul Mercurio as Scott Hastings, a maverick dancer whose introduction into his routine of steps not recognized by the Australian Ballroom Dance Federation prompts his partner to leave him just before a major dance championship. His unlikely new alliance with Fran, played by Tara Morice, makes for a highly enjoyable tale that achieved deserved success.

DOMESTIC DISPUTES

Woody Allen's career has suffered untold damage in the USA as a result of his protracted child custody battles with his estranged partner Mia Farrow. In *Husbands and Wives*, which he directed and starred in with Farrow, the story appears to reflect their real-life situation as it concerns a couple in the throes of separation. Although witty and well performed, the cinematography, by hand-held camera, which gives the effect of a home-made film, is an irritating contrivance. Also released was Allen's clever but soulless homage to German expressionist cinema, *Shadows and Fog*. Filmed in black and white, it is set in a European town which is menaced by a strangler. Allen plays a member of a vigilante group, with Mia Farrow as a sword-swallower, and a cast that also includes Madonna, John Malkovich, Kathy Bates, Donald Pleasance and Lily Tomlin.

Sister Act was a vehicle for Whoopi Goldberg which proved hugely successful in the USA, grossing over $135 million. Goldberg plays Deloris, who, having witnessed the death of an informant killed by her boyfriend, Harvey Keitel, is placed in a witness protection programme. She is disguised as a nun, Sister Mary Clarence, and hidden in a convent, where her galvanizing effect on the choir makes for some delicious comedy and her mixing with the local low life brings her into conflict with the Mother Superior, played by Maggie Smith.

Peter's Friends was a low-budget British comedy directed by Kenneth Branagh and written by Andrew Bergman and Rita Rudner. It is an amiable if slightly self-indulgent ensemble piece starring Branagh, Emma Thompson, Hugh Laurie, Imelda Staunton, Stephen Fry, Rita Rudner and Tony Slattery as a group of former graduates meeting ten years later to spend new year's eve at the home of one of their number, Peter. Branagh's second Shakespeare adaptation is *Much Ado About Nothing*. He directed the film and also played Benedick, with Emma Thompson as Beatrice, Denzel Washington as Don Pedro, Keanu Reeves as Don John, Michael Keaton as Dogberry, Kate Beckinsale as Hero and Robert Sean Leonard as Claudio.

Richard Attenborough's *Chaplin* featured a remarkable impersonation of the celebrated silent film star by Robert Downey jun. and fine cinematography from Sven Nykvist. However, while a competent biography, the film tried to tell too much about Chaplin's life without ever revealing Chaplin the man. Not surprisingly, it met with a mixed critical reception. In an interesting piece of casting, Charlie Chaplin's daughter Geraldine plays his mother in the film.

The huge success of the 1990 film *Home Alone*, the most successful comedy ever made, was followed by *Home Alone 2: Lost in New York*. It again stars Macaulay Culkin in what amounts to a reprise of the original plot, with Joe Pesci and Daniel Stern repeating their roles as the inept crooks outwitted by young Kevin McAllister, who this time has become separated from his family while en route to a winter break in Florida. The film also repeated the success of the original, taking $100 million in its first four weeks.

One of the most controversial releases of the year was *Reservoir Dogs*, written by and also featuring Quentin Tarantino in a highly promising directorial début. The cast included Harvey Keitel, Tim Roth, Lawrence Tierney, Michael Madsen and Steve Buscemi. It achieved notoriety for its portrayal of six callous professional robbers and killers brought together for a bank robbery in which police officers are killed. The robbers meet again after the event in a warehouse to discuss the crime and to discover who had tipped off the police. However, although gory, the film does not glorify violence and is shrewdly observed, witty and well acted.

Bram Stoker's Dracula, directed by Francis Ford Coppola, was adapted from Stoker's novel by James V. Hart and starred Anthony Hopkins as Professor Van Helsing, Richard Grant as Dr Seward and Gary Oldman as Dracula. However, although the film is a Gothic visual feast, which cost £20 million to make and deserved its three Oscars, it lacks the horror of other versions.

Louis Malle's *Damage*, adapted by David Hare from Josephine Hart's novel, starred Jeremy Irons as Stephen Fleming, a Conservative politician on the verge of government office who embarks on an obsessive love affair with his son's girlfriend Anna, played by Juliette Binoche. Miranda Richardson plays Stephen's wife, Ingrid, with Rupert Graves as his journalist son. The film achieved a certain notoriety because of the sexually explicit scenes involving Irons and Binoche, but was well crafted with fine performances.

MALCOLM X

Malcolm X is a competent but long account of the life of the black American leader who progressed from an early life of crime and violence to become one of the most significant figures in black American history. Following his disagreement with the leading Muslim Elijah Muhammad, played in the film by Al Freeman jun., Malcolm X was gunned down by his followers in 1965. The film was co-written by Spike Lee, who also directed it. Denzel Washington starred as Malcolm X, with Angela Bassett, Delroy Lindo and Albert Hall, plus a cameo performance from Lee himself as Malcolm X's friend Shorty. The film ran for nearly three and a half hours, and could have benefited from more analysis of the conflict between Malcolm X and Elijah and the reasons for Malcolm's change of stance after his visit to Mecca. It was nonetheless a worthy project and a fine achievement.

Hoffa stars Jack Nicholson as the notorious Teamsters leader, James Hoffa, who was abducted in 1975 and is believed to have been killed by gangsters he had crossed. Directed by Dany DeVito, who also plays Bobby Ciaro, from a script by David Mamet, this powerful film features a remarkable performance from Nicholson. Kevin Anderson plays Robert Kennedy, the Attorney-General, who is determined to destroy Hoffa but comes off second best in clashes with him during Senate hearings. The film was reported to have cost $40 million to make, and was nominated for two Oscars (cinematography and make-up). However, it did not achieve popular success in America, where it was felt that the portrayal of Hoffa had whitewashed his character.

Nicholson also starred in *A Few Good Men* as Marine Colonel Nathan R. Jessep, a totally unsympathetic character in a courtroom drama that also featured Tom Cruise and Demi Moore and was directed by Rob Reiner.

Robert Redford directed a lyrical film about fly fishing in Montana, *A River Runs Through It*, adapted by Richard Friedenberg from Norman Maclean's novel. Tom Skerritt plays a presbyterian minister, with Brad Pitt and Craig Sheffer as the sons to whom he can only relate easily when the three are sharing their love of fishing on the Big Blackfoot river. Redford also narrates the commentary.

Lorenzo's Oil is a well-meaning account of a couple's attempt to disprove accepted medical opinion and find a cure for a degenerative condition afflicting their son. It stars Nick Nolte and Susan Sarandon as the parents, with Zack O'Malley Greenburg as their son Lorenzo. The story of their battle to save their son makes for a stirring drama, but although purporting to be the true story, it appears that the panacea which they discovered and developed is not in fact the magic cure that the film suggests; Hollywood optimism is allowed to triumph over the facts.

SECOND TIME AROUND

Hollywood's practice of remaking European films in inferior versions continued. The 1982 film *The Return of Martin Guerre*, which was set in 16th-century France and based on a true story was remade as an American civil war story. *Sommersby* was a vehicle for Richard Gere, who plays the farmer who returns after years away at war but has changed in character so much that people suspect he is an impostor. Jodie Foster gives a fine performance as his wife.   Also adapted was the powerful and stylish 1990 French film *La Femme Nikita*, remade as *The Assassin* with Bridget Fonda in the role created by Anne Parillaud. She plays a murderer sentenced to death but reprieved by a government agent (Gabriel Byrne) on condition that she agrees to act as a professional assassin. Directed by John Badham, the film also features Anne Bancroft, Harvey Keitel and Dermot Mulroney.

Groundhog Day begins with the promising premise cleverly fulfilled, that television weatherman Phil (Bill Murray) has to relive the same day over and over again when he becomes stuck in a time warp on a visit to the town of Punxsutawney for its annual groundhog festival. The comedy and frustration of the situation are well realized by Murray, with romantic support from Andie MacDowell as his television producer.

The true story of the aeroplane crash in the Andes in 1972, where the survivors stayed alive for ten weeks by eating the frozen remains of their dead companions, was related in a book by Piers Paul Read. The story, with a script based on Read's book, has now been filmed as *Alive*, featuring Ethan Hawke, Josh Hamilton and Vincent Spano. One of the survivors, Fernando Nando Parrado, acted as technical adviser to the film to ensure authenticity and to make sure that the memory of his comrades was not sullied. The initial aeroplane crash is brilliantly filmed, and the terrible moral dilemma that confronted the survivors is effectively portrayed.

One of the more notorious films of the year was *Indecent Proposal*, slickly directed by Adrian Lyne. It features Demi Moore and Woody Harrelson as a poor young couple, Diane and David, who go to Las Vegas to attempt to win some money. They lose what little they have, but a millionaire, John Gage (Robert Redford) offers them $1 million if Diane will spend the night with him. A promising idea which fizzles out lamely, it aroused much media attention, but would have been more interesting and effective if the millionaire had not had the looks and charm of Redford. Although the plot degenerates into a predictable love story with a sentimental conclusion, the film was a huge popular success, taking $64 million in its first three weeks of release.

Another successful release was *Falling Down*, featuring Michael Douglas as D-Fens, a man identified only by his car number plate (but with the obvious implication that he symbolizes 'defence'). Having lost his job and been caught in a traffic jam in Los Angeles, he decides that he has had enough and goes on the rampage. 'I'm the bad guy? How did that happen?' he asks at the end of the film. Robert Duvall plays Martin Prendergast, a police officer on his last day in the force before retirement, who investigates the mayhem D-Fens is causing. The film's moral viewpoint is never clear, and it veers uncertainly between social comment and comedy, but it was apparent that cinema audiences identified with Douglas as a hero.

In *Cliffhanger*, Sylvester Stallone plays Gabe Walker, a mountain climber who loses his nerve after a rescue goes wrong. However, when a planeload of robbers crash in the mountains and he is tricked into answering their call for help, he finds the opportunity to redeem himself. Directed by Renny Harlin, the film contains some exciting action sequences which are well filmed. The cast also features John Lithgow as Qualen, leader of the criminals, Janine Turner and Ralph Waite.

Arnold Schwarzenegger's latest film, *The Last Action Hero*, was based on the appealing but hardly original idea of a boy becoming involved in the screen world of his hero, Jack Slater, played by Schwarzenegger. The film also features Charles Dance, Mercedes Ruehl and Robert Prosky, with enjoyable cameos from Anthony Quinn and Joan Plowright. It includes some spectacular action sequences and a nice line in self-deprecating wit by Schwarzenegger, who gently sends up his screen persona in the *Terminator* and other action films. It seems, however, that the film was too clever for its own good and the humour was lost on American audiences. Although it took $30 million in its first ten days, it was deemed a comparative failure and lost out in popularity to *Jurassic Park*, with which it coincided in the cinemas.

Super Mario Brothers attempted to capitalize on the popularity of the Nintendo computer game, with Bob Hoskins and John Leguizamo as Mario and Luigi, the little plumbers who enter a parallel world dominated by lizard men. Dennis Hopper plays King Koopa, ruler of the other world. The film cost $48 million to make and suffered from an excess of everything, including overacting and over-elaborate special effects, except, unfortunately, a plot.

BOXING CLEVER

One of the most controversial films of the year was *Boxing Helena*, directed by Jennifer Lynch. The film achieved massive publicity because of a court case in which the film-makers sued the American actress Kim Basinger for allegedly agreeing to play the leading role and then withdrawing four weeks before filming was due to begin. She decided that she could not take the part as she would only perform roles that included 'artistic' rather than 'graphic' nudity. Basinger lost the case and was ordered to pay some $9 million in damages. Sherilyn Fenn instead played the woman whose limbs are amputated by a surgeon, played by Julian Sands, to prevent her escaping from him; he then keeps her torso in a box. The film was distasteful, exploitative and misguided.

Les Nuits Fauves (Savage Nights) achieved cult status in France. The only feature film made by Cyril Collard, who also starred in the film, it was based on his own novel published in 1989. A few days after winning four *César* awards, the French equivalent of the Oscars, Collard died from an Aids-related illness. In the film he plays Jean, a promiscuous cameraman who has an affair with a footballer, Samy, played by Carlos Lopez, until he meets Laure, played by Romane Bohringer. Their relationship, dominated by his knowledge that he is HIV-positive, is doomed, and the frantic pace of the film reflects their tragic situation.

Two of Ingmar Bergman's collaborators have directed their first features. Actress Liv Ullman's first film as director, *Sofie*, featured Karen-Lise Mynster in a Jewish family saga set in late 19th-century Denmark. It was based on the novel *Mendel Philipsen and Son* by Henri Nathansen. Sven Nykvist, cinema-tographer for 18 Bergman films, revealed once again his mastery of the camera in *The Ox*, which he also directed. Set in Sweden in the 1860s, it tells the true story of a farmer imprisoned for killing his neighbour's ox for food. The cast includes Max von Sydow and Liv Ullman.

La Passion de Jeanne d'Arc, made by Carl Dreyer in 1928, is considered one of the cinema's great films. Its story of the last day in the life of Joan of Arc used a script based on the actual transcript of Joan's interrogation. It featured stark designs by Ian Hugo, and was filmed largely in penetrating close-up. However, the negative of the film was destroyed soon after its first screening and Dreyer had to reconstruct it from inferior outtakes. This was the only version that had been seen since the accident until an original print was discovered in the 1980s that had apparently been submitted to a censor. The original version was screened in 1992 at the Barbican cinema, with a new orchestral score by Ole Schmidt.

Orson Welles's version of Shakespeare's *Othello*, which he directed and starred in, received only a restricted release in 1952 in spite of winning the Grand Prix at Cannes. It has now been rediscovered and restored, and is revealed as a classic. Desdemona is played by Suzanne Cloutier, with Michael Mac-Liammoir as Iago and Robert Coote as Roderigo.

FESTIVALS

The 46th Edinburgh Film Festival, directed by Penny Thomson, felt the effects of cuts in funding. While last year's festival screened some 160 films plus another 30 documentaries and shorts, the 1992 festival fielded barely 80 features and 20 shorts, in only two venues. The festival opened with the British première of *Strictly Ballroom* and closed with James Foley's film of David Mamet's play about real estate salesmen, *Glengarry Glen Ross*, which stars Jack Nicholson and Al Pacino.

The Venice Film Festival marked its diamond jubilee with a retrospective of the programme of 1932. The Golden Lion was awarded to the Chinese film *Qui Ju Goes to Court*, directed by Zhang Yimou. The Special Jury prize went to Mario Martone's *Death of a Neapolitan Mathematician*. Jack Lemmon was named best actor for his role in *Glengarry Glen Ross*, and best actress was Gong Li in *Qiu Ju Goes to Court*.

The 36th London Film Festival opened with Kenneth Branagh's *Peter's Friends* and closed with the director's cut of *Blade Runner*. Notable features included Victor Erice's *El Sol Del Membrillo (The Quince Tree Sun)*, a marvellous study of an artist at work. It relates the Spanish painter Antonio Lopez's attempts to capture on canvas the special light on a quince tree at the end of summer in his Madrid garden, before the fruit rots and the light goes. The festival gave the only British screening of the Italian film, *Il Ladro di Bambini (Stolen Children)*, directed by Gianni Amelio. Also featured were a new print of

The Leopard and Edgar Reitz's 26-hour epic *Die Zweite Heimat*, the successor to his splendid *Heimat*.

The 46th Cannes Film Festival included four British films in competition, the first three of which were funded by Channel 4 – Mike Leigh's *Naked*, Kenneth Branagh's *Much Ado About Nothing* and Ken Loach's *Raining Stones*, plus Eric Idle's *Splitting Heirs*. Leigh won the award for best director and David Thewlis best actor for *Naked*, with *Raining Stones* joint winner of the Jury Prize with *The Puppetmaster*, directed by Hou Hsia-Hsien (Taiwan). The Palme d'Or was awarded jointly to Jane Campion's *The Piano* (New Zealand), which featured Sam Neill and Holly Hunter (who won the best actress award) and Chen Kaige's *Farewell to My Concubine* (China), starring Gong Li. The Grand Jury Prize was won by Wim Wenders's *Far Away, So Close*.

The Golden Bear for the best film at the 43rd Berlin Film Festival was awarded jointly to *The Woman from the Lake of Scented Souls*, directed by Xie Fei from China, and *The Wedding Banquet*, by Ang Lee from Taiwan. Denzel Washington was awarded the prize for best actor for his role in *Malcolm X* and Michelle Pfeiffer was named best actress for *Love Field*. The prize for best director was awarded to Andrew Birkin for *The Cement Garden*, which he had adapted from Ian McEwan's novel. The film was a co-production between Britain, France and Germany.

The Academy Awards 1992

Best Picture	*Unforgiven*
Best Director	Clint Eastwood, *Unforgiven*
Best Actor	Al Pacino, *Scent of a Woman*
Best Actress	Emma Thompson, *Howards End*
Best Supporting Actor	Gene Hackman, *Unforgiven*
Best Supporting Actress	Marisa Tomei, *My Cousin Vinny*
Best Original Screenplay	Neil Jordan, *The Crying Game*
Best Adapted Screenplay	Ruth Prawer Jhabvala, *Howards End*
Best Foreign Language Film	*Indochine*, France
Best Original Score	Alan Menken, *Aladdin*
Best Original Song	Alan Menken and Tim Rice, 'Whole New World', *Aladdin*
Best Cinematography	Philippe Rousselot, *A River Runs Through It*
Best Art Direction	Luciana Arrighi and Ian Whittaker, *Howards End*
Best Costume Design	Eiko Ishioka, *Bram Stoker's Dracula*
Best Film Editing	Joel Cox, *Unforgiven*
Best Sound	Chris Jenkins, Doug Hemphill, Mark Smith and Simon Kaye, *The Last of the Mohicans*
Best Sound Effects Editing	Tom McCarthy and David Stone, *Bram Stoker's Dracula*
Best Visual Effects	Ken Ralston, Doug Chiang, Doug Smythe and Tom Woodruff, *Death Becomes Her*
Best Make-up	Greg Cannom, Michele Burke and Matthew Mungle, *Bram Stoker's Dracula*
Best Animated Short	Joan Gratz, *Mona Lisa Descending a Staircase*
Best Short Documentary	Thomas Goodwin and Gerardine Wurzburg, *Educating Peter*
Best Documentary Feature	Barbara Trent and David Kasper, *The Panama Deception*
Best Live Action Short	Sam Karmann, *Omnibus*
Honorary Awards	Federico Fellini; Jean Hersholt

Literature

The release of the Beirut hostages in 1991 has resulted in several bestselling books. *An Evil Cradling* is Brian Keenan's account of his four and a half years in captivity. Brought up in Belfast, he describes how he came to work as a teacher in Beirut. His book is a revealing and poetic work; it is not, he says, 'the usual conventional chronology of events, people and places. This kind of neat patchwork does not capture or represent the significance or the depth of experience in that quarter-life, enclosed in a very heightened and very different reality – a strange reality far removed from normal human experience, yet one in which, paradoxically, so much more of what we are as human beings was revealed.' It is a work rich in pain and humour, and especially powerful is the development of the relationship between Keenan and John McCarthy, who, as Keenan points out, had ample reason for mutual antipathy and yet found 'a deep, enduring bond of friendship and support that eventually became a prop for others'. The book was also, Keenan wrote, 'an exploration of the mind and personalities of hostages and captor, and their shifting and changing roles'. He describes what he sees as the 'implicit paradox' of the book – 'how in the most inhuman of circumstances men grow and deepen in humanity. In the face of death but not because of it, they explode with passionate life, conquering despair with insane humour. There are other paradoxes, such as the degree to which, in a sense, the captors became our prisoners, perversely depending on us. And, that most awful paradox of all, how men under such extremes, knowing that they must do everything to support one another, can still fall into a kind of frenzy of rage and despair more soul-destroying to watch than all the brutality'. At the end of Keenan's account he describes the process of his release. During the drive to Syria and freedom, he said to the passenger in the front of the car, '"So this is the road to Damascus?" He answered quietly "Yes".'

The publication of John McCarthy's own account of the same period gives resonance to Keenan's work. McCarthy tells his story jointly with Jill Morrell, his girl-friend before he left for the Lebanon and the person who did most to keep his plight in the public eye. In *Some Other Rainbow* they tell in alternate chapters their own versions of McCarthy's imprisonment and captivity, his period with Keenan and eventual release, and Morrell's attempts to keep his name alive and to persuade the Government to take some action to resolve the situation. It is an honest, touching and ultimately happy story about two ordinary people catapulted into the limelight by extraordinary circumstances.

Hostage: The Complete Story of the Lebanon Captives by Con Coughlin, attempts to balance the hostages' accounts of their captivity by placing them in the overall context of the civil war in Lebanon, which he believes few of them understood in any great measure, and of the complex relations between Iran, Syria and the West which prolonged their captivity. Coughlin is particularly dismissive of Terry Waite's personal missions as envoy of the Archbishop of Canterbury and unwitting stooge of Colonel Oliver North. Coughlin has praise, however, for the role of the Foreign Office in behind-the-sceens diplomatic activity and for Giandomenico Picco, the United Nations negotiator whose diplomacy eventually ensured the release of the hostages.

Roger Cooper found himself in a similar situation in Iran, where he was imprisoned as a spy and sentenced to death. *Death Plus Ten Years* is his readable account of his life, much of it spent in Iran where he had worked for many years and had married an Iranian woman. While working for an oil company, in 1985, he was arrested and thrown into the notorious Evin prison. After brutal interrogation he confessed to spying, but spiced his confession with names derived from the novels of Evelyn Waugh and an invented 'British Intelligent Service', so that those in Britain who saw his filmed confession would know that he had been coerced into it. He was sentenced to death by stoning for an alleged crime of fornication committed some 25 years previously, and to ten years' imprisonment for spying. Cooper's account of his trial, his years in prison and how he survived his ordeal through 'sheer bloody-mindedness' reveal a person of great intelligence and wit who well understood the motivations of his captors, having immersed himself in their culture over many years. On his release, Cooper drily commented that 'Anyone who has been to an English public school and served in the ranks of the British army is perfectly at home in a Third World prison'.

Also published was *Tornado Down*, the account by RAF Flight Lieutenants John Peters and John Nicol of the shooting-down by Iraqi anti-aircraft fire of their Tornado jet while on a bombing mission on the first day of the Gulf War. Their capture and subsequent torture make harrowing reading.

Sentenced to death by *fatwa* in 1989, the bounty on Salman Rushdie's life was increased to over $2 million in 1992. President Rafsanjani of Iran also decreed that the *fatwa* would never be lifted. However, there was evidence of government concern at his plight when the Prime Minister met the writer at the House of Commons in May 1993. Mr Major said: 'I underlined the Government's full support for Mr Rushdie's fundamental rights as a British citizen, and expressed concern that the Iranian authorities had failed to repudiate the incitement to his murder in the *fatwa* ... The United Kingdom has a deep respect for Islam. I believe that Iran's behaviour towards Mr Rushdie has done a disservice to that great religion.'

When receiving the *Sunday Times* Award for Excellence in Writing, the novelist Martin Amis spoke about the plight of his friend and fellow writer. He said that Rushdie had not set out to offend in *The Satanic Verses*. 'A novel has no object in view. It asserts nothing. It merely awakens you to possibilities.' Writing, he said, 'is an act of spiritual freedom. The Rushdie affair then, is a concentrated disgrace. This is the one hope it offers: that it taunts us out of our own Philistinism.' *Rushdie Letters: Freedom to Speak, Freedom to Write*, edited by Steve MacDonagh, consists of tributes to Rushdie by writers concerned about the threat of censorship, and includes a review of the whole history of the Rushdie affair.

A SUITABLE TOME

A major new work was Vikram Seth's *A Suitable Boy*, a massive novel that achieved popular success. His only previous novel, *The Golden Gate*, was a novel in verse about life in San Francisco in the 1980s. *A Suitable Boy* is 1,350 pages and nearly 800,000 words long, and took Seth eight years to write. In it he details a saga of Indian life through the search of a widow, Mrs Rupa Mehra, for a husband for her daughter, Lata. The story is set against the background of India after independence in the imaginary city of Brahmpur. The novel opens with Mrs Mehra's injunction to her daughter, 'You too will marry a boy I choose', and the story describes her quest, over a period of two years, for a 'suitable boy'. However, while Mrs Mehra assesses and rejects possible suitors for her daughter, Lata meets Kabir, a Muslim, with whom she falls in love. This was, to Mrs Mehra, 'unspeakable. It was one thing to mix socially with Muslims, entirely another to dream of polluting one's blood and sacrificing one's daughter.' The author skilfully orchestrates a huge cast of characters, and in spite of its length the novel is brilliantly controlled; a remarkable *tour de force*.

P. D. James has turned away from the exploits of Adam Dalgleish, the detective who made her famous. Her latest book, *The Children of Men*, is set in the year 2021 and posits the idea that in 1995, 'the year of bereavement', all men became infertile so no children had been conceived since. A weakness of the novel is that it is never made clear how this condition came about, not how one woman eventually does become pregnant. James's world is a bleak one, with England ruled over by a 'Warden' whose regime exists to provide 'security, comfort and pleasure' for the rapidly dwindling populace, but which also enforces euthanasia for the elderly and infirm. The novel is a passionate warning against the loss of spirituality in the current age. However, some of the characters are two-dimensional, the politics are at times simplistic, and the author's attention to the minutest detail, while vital in a detective novel, here becomes irritating.

In *The Porcupine*, Julian Barnes looks afresh at the fallen rulers of the Communist states of Eastern Europe. Inspired by events in Bulgaria, where the former leader Todor Zhivkov had been on trial, he relates the story of Stoyo Petkanov, a former Second Leader of a Soviet satellite state, who is being prosecuted for his crimes by Peter Solinsky at a show trial. Petkanov's defence of his regime and their actions, his refusal to apologize and his scorn for the methods of his accusers make for a powerful cerebral confrontation, brilliantly described by Barnes. Petkanov's final plea, that he be not personally held responsible for the failures of others, leaves his accusers with the central dilemma: 'If I am a monster, I will come back and haunt you in your dreams; if I am like you, I will come back to haunt you in your waking days'.

Roddy Doyle's *Paddy Clarke Ha Ha Ha*, the first-hand story of a ten-year-old boy's life in Barrytown, a working-class area of Dublin, is set in 1968 and brilliantly evoked. Blake Morrison's *And When Did You last See Your Father?* is a marvellous, obsessive and funny portrait of the life and painful death of his father Arthur. Ben Okri's latest novel, *Songs of Enchantment*, is a sequel to his Booker Prize-winning novel *The Famished Road*. Also set in Nigeria, the story is again visualized through the eyes of a spirit-child or 'abiku'. Azaro, who is 'an unwilling adventurer into chaos and sunlight, into the dreams of the living and the dead', suffers when his mother is thrown out of the family home by his father. While again indicative of Okri's imaginative power, the book suffers from infelicities of grammar and language which detract from its overall effect.

A. S. Byatt's *Angels and Insects* consists of two short novels, *Morpho Eugenia* and *The Conjugal Angel*, set in the mid-19th century. The first describes the passion of an entomologist for his dancing partner, Eugenia, while the second deals with spiritualism in Margate. Both novellas have the feel of undeveloped ideas, and display little of Byatt's customary control or skill. Anita Brookner's *A Family Romance* treads familiar ground in its pessimistic story of Jane Manning, an unmarried writer of children's books whom life has passed by, and her relationship with her lively Aunt Dolly, a person greedy for sex and material possessions.

Samuel Beckett's first novel, *Dream of Fair to Middling Women*, was published for the first time, although it was written in 1932 when Beckett was living in Paris. The author had apparently been embarrassed by the work, which he had later dismissed as 'immature and unworthy'. Having achieved literary success, he decided that he did not wish it published during his lifetime, but had apparently agreed that it could be published posthumously. It is a difficult, experimental work about a young man travelling in Europe which foreshadows many of his later themes and is an important volume for students of his oeuvre. In it Beckett notes that 'perhaps only the French language can give you the thing you want', anticipating his subsequent decision to write all his works in French.

LARKIN ABOUT

Andrew Motion's *Philip Larkin: A Writer's Life* is a detailed account of the life and work of the poet, from his early childhood with his mother whom he described as 'an obsessive snivelling pest' but who was apparently responsible for inspiring him to write many of his best poems, and his father, who kept a model of Hitler on his mantelpiece. Motion calls Larkin 'one of the great poets of the century', without ever quite justifying this verdict. The poet requested after his death that his diaries should be destroyed; how he would have viewed his personal prejudices and foibles being exposed to such detailed public scrutiny is a matter for conjecture. It is apparent that Motion, while valuing the poetry, cannot reconcile himself to the man who created it. Larkin's personal reputation had not been enhanced by the publication of his *Selected Letters, 1940-1985*, edited by Anthony Thwaite, which indicate racist and sexist attitudes as well as dark humour and melancholy. Motion said that 'there is something performative about those letters: they turn to each recipient the side of his personality which he knew that person would most enjoy.' A row over Thwaite's excision of some racist passages to protect Larkin's reputation raged in the literary journals, and prompted a leader in *The Times* to comment 'What matters about Larkin is the handful of melancholy and funny poems that captured the mood of his times. Honest censorship is a function of the literary executor.'

More Please: An Autobiography is Barry Humphries's account of his life, from his upbringing in Australia to his later career in Britain. Humphries is best known for his brilliant creation of alter egos, including Dame Edna Everage, one of the great comic and satiric creations of the age. However, the author does not reveal what drives him; like Dame Edna, we are aware of the genius, but not of what has inspired it.

POLITICAL LIVES

John Campbell's *Edward Heath: A Biography* is the first major study of the enigmatic former Conservative Party leader who enjoyed one term as Prime Minister from 1970 to 1974. Campbell was denied access to Heath's private papers and correspondence, which it appears Heath is retaining for his own memoirs, and had to rely on published sources and discussions with friends and colleagues. Nevertheless, the book is a first-class account of Heath's life and career in politics, notably his determination to bring about Britain's membership of the European Community and his period as Prime Minister, when his confrontation with the miners and the three-day week brought about his rejection by the electorate. Campbell believes Heath's main failure was that he lacked 'the essential quality of political leadership: the ability to communicate his vision and inspire loyalty beyond the narrow circle of his closest colleagues'. However, he concludes by saying that Heath has 'outlasted all his contemporaries; and his reputation is beginning to be restored'.

Ben Pimlott's *Harold Wilson* was also published, the second recent biography of the former Labour Prime Minister. Pimlott's is a sympathetic account of Wilson's life and career, notably his first spells as premier from 1964 to 1970, when he had been responsible for 'a bigger advance in individual rights and liberties than in any previous administration since the introduction of universal suffrage'; but Pimlott does not attempt to ignore Wilson's weaknesses. Commenting on his unexpected retirement in 1976, Pimlott dismisses conspiracy theories and other bizarre explanations and concludes that: 'The straightforward explanation for his departure, that he left because he had lost the desire to carry on, requires no amplification'. Also published was *Tired and Emotional: The Life of Lord George Brown* by Peter Patterson.

The irreverent and indiscreet diaries of the former Conservative minister, Alan Clark, were a revelation because they give some indication of what life at the top in politics is really like. *Alan Clark: Diaries* are candid, amusing and eminently readable. The fifth and final volume of Tony Benn's diaries, entitled *The End of an Era: Diaries 1980-1990*, edited by Ruth Winstone, continues to recount his fascinating view of politics and the struggle for socialism. The diaries also reveal Benn's lack of judgment and his high opinion of himself, but he nevertheless comes across as a man solid in his convictions and faithful to his principles. Also published were *Fighting All the Way*, Barbara Castle's memoirs, which supplement the two volumes of her diaries published some years ago; Nigel Lawson's memoirs, *The View from No. 11: Memoirs of a Tory Radical*, an over-long and tedious work of self-justification; and Cecil Parkinson's *Right at the Centre*.

Churchill: the End of Glory by John Charmley is a revisionist 'political biography' of Churchill which attempts to destroy his reputation by showing that, far from saving Britain, Churchill was responsible for the country's decline. The last volume of Churchilliana produced by Martin Gilbert, the author of the definitive biography, is *The Churchill War Papers: Volume 1 – At the Admiralty September 1939–May 1940*. It covers Churchill's time as First Lord of the Admiralty at the outbreak of the Second World War and his accession to the premiership, through official papers, speeches, letters and diaries.

The rehabilitation of Richard Nixon, the only American President forced to resign from office, continues apace. *Nixon: A Life* by Jonathan Aitken is a fine assessment of the career of a man who, in spite of the Watergate conspiracy that brought about his downfall, was a statesman who brought about a thawing of relations with China and the Soviet Union. He was, according to Aitken, 'one of the most original foreign policy strategists his country has ever produced'.

Kissinger: A Biography by Walter Isaacson is a lengthy account of the life and career of the former American Secretary of State who achieved international fame in the 1970s and was awarded the Nobel Peace Prize in 1973. Isaacson's aim, he states, is 'to produce an unbiased biography that portrayed Kissinger in all of complexity'; in this he largely succeeds. Kissinger had been a professor at Harvard University when Richard Nixon appointed him national security adviser in 1968, and as Secretary of State he strode the world stage in one of the critical phases of post-war history. The book gives a fascinating account of the American system of government, with unelected officials such as Kissinger holding positions of great power, and describes the apparently all-pervasive air of paranoia which culminated in the Watergate tapes and Nixon's downfall. Kissinger is not blameless; in fact, deceit was part of his make-up and an essential tool in his diplomacy. He once said: 'The only way secrecy can be kept is to exclude from the making of a decision all those who are theoretically encharged with carrying it out'.

Also published were the memoirs of General Norman Schwarzkopf, written with Peter Petre. *It Doesn't Take a Hero: the Autobiography* gives a fascinating account of the leader of the coalition forces during the Gulf War, and the detailed planning of the Desert Storm operation which destroyed Saddam Hussein's army. The title was taken from a comment of Schwarzkopf's after the war: 'It doesn't take a hero to order men into battle. It takes a hero to be one of those men who goes into battle.' *Storm Command: A Personal Account of the Gulf War* is the story of the leader of the British forces in the Gulf, General Sir Peter de la Billière, who struck up a good relationship with Schwarzkopf which enabled the two men to share information 'which our governments might have preferred to keep to themselves'.

Piers Paul Read's *Ablaze* is a perceptive and enthralling account of the accident at the Soviet nuclear power plant at Chernobyl in 1986, based on sources that have become public since the fall of the Soviet Union and on interviews with many of the surviving protagonists. Read skilfully unravels the complexities of the event, and describes how the engineers whose illicit experiments caused the reactor to overheat and explode 'had decided that the parameters recommended by the designers bore as much relationship to the reality of running the reactors as did the Communist rhetoric to the realities of life in the USSR'.

NOBEL PRIZE

The 1992 Nobel Prize for Literature, worth about £700,000, was awarded to Derek Walcott. The Swedish Academy honoured Walcott for a body of poetic work 'of great luminosity, sustained by a historical vision, the outcome of a multicultural commitment . . . He has an intense belief in poetry and poets and he has made this one of his themes. It is the complexity of his own situation that has

provided one of the most fruitful sources of his inspiration. Three loyalties are central for him – the Caribbean where he lives, the English language and his African origin.' Walcott's works include *Omeros*, his retelling of Homer's *The Iliad* and *The Odyssey* set in his native St Lucia, which was awarded the W. H. Smith Literary Award in 1988. The Academy called *Omeros* a work 'of incomparable ambition, in which Walcott weaves his many strands into a whole.' He has also written many plays, including a version of *The Odyssey* for the Royal Shakespeare Company.

The death of William Golding, one of Britain's leading novelists, and the only British Nobel laureate since Winston Churchill, was a cause for regret. His career had two distinct phases. Following the early success of *The Lord of the Flies* and his first group of novels, he enjoyed a second burst of creativity starting with the mysterious and brooding *Darkness Visible* in 1979 and culminating in the final work of his splendid maritime trilogy, *Fire Down Below*, in 1989.

FOR FUTURE REFERENCE

Missing Persons, a new supplement to *The Dictionary of National Biography*, lists those judged to have been 'unjustly omitted' from previous volumes of the great work, which was begun in 1882 by Leslie Stephen. Requests for suggestions for suitable candidates elicited over 100,000 names, which were whittled down to 1,086 for the volume in question. The list includes such diverse characters as John Meyrick (the 'Elephant man'), Wilfred Owen, Bram Stoker, and John Wisden, creator of the celebrated cricketers' almanack. It also to some small degree reverses the prejudice against women in previous volumes: such famous figures as Sylvia Pankhurst, Mrs Beeton, Sylvia Plath and Gwen John are now accorded entries.

The Oxford Dictionary of Quotations, extensively revised for its third edition in 1979, has once more experienced a major facelift. Many of the references to minor Victorian and Edwardian poets have been deleted to make room for notable omissions from previous editions, such as scientists, economists and writers of popular songs. The inclusion of many contemporary, and, some critics felt, unmemorable quotes provoked much comment. *The Oxford Companion to the English Language* is a treasure trove of grammar, language and literature, with articles on such diverse topics as Standard English, American usages and spelling, Dialect and academic criticism, with useful sections on a wide variety of matters, such as the etymology of words and phrases.

PRIZES

The winner of the Whitbread Prize, and of the first novel category, was Jeff Torrington's *Swing hammer swing!* Torrington's picaresque work is especially remarkable in that it took him 30 years to write. Set in the Gorbals area of Glasgow in the 1960s, it features a week in the life of unemployed Tom Clay, whose pregnant wife is in hospital with high blood pressure. It was selected for 'its vibrancy, narrative power, wonderful characterization and ultimately for being a novel of stunning originality'. The other finalists for the overall prize were *Poor Things* by Alasdair Gray (novel), set in Glasgow and the Mediterranean in the 1880s. A gothic pastiche, it tells the story of a surgeon who places the brain of an unborn child into its mother. *Trollope* by Victoria Glendinning won the biography category, with *The Great Elephant Chase* by Gillian Cross (children's novel) and *The Gaze of the Gorgon* by Tony Harrison (poetry) completing the shortlist. *Poor Things* also won the *Guardian* Fiction Award. The judges commented: 'What most impressed . . . was its ability to blend the playful and the political, so that this Gothic tale of 19th-century Glasgow made history a living and turbulent force for our times.'

For the first time since 1974 the Booker Prize for Fiction was awarded jointly: to Barry Unsworth for *Sacred Hunger* and Michael Ondaatje for *The English Patient*. Victoria Glendinning, who chaired the panel of judges, said that the result reflected the 'passion of feeling among the judges for both these books . . . this was not, I must stress, a compromise decision'. The other shortlisted novels were Michèle Roberts's *Daughters of the House* (which won the W. H. Smith Award), Ian McEwan's *Black Dogs*, Christopher Hope's *Serenity House* and Patrick McCabe's *The Butcher Boy*. Malcolm Bradbury set the opening scene of his new novel, *Dr Criminale*, at the Booker Prize Ceremony. It was not shortlisted for the prize. The first Booker Russian prize for Novels was awarded to Mark Kharitonov for *Linii sud'by (Lines of Fate)*.

The winner of the NCR Book Award for Non-Fiction was *Never Again - Britain 1941–1951* by Peter Hennessy, the first volume of a history of Britain after the Second World War. Nick Hornby's *Fever Pitch: A Fan's Life*, which was shortlisted for the NCR Award, recounts the travails of a fanatical supporter of Arsenal Football Club, 'a place where unfocused unhappiness could thrive'. It is told with great insight and wit, transcending its superficial context to become a lively commentary on the 20th-century English male for whom blind devotion to an institution such as a football club can become his *raison d'être*. 'The natural state of the football fan is bitter disappointment', but 'real life is paler, duller, and contains less potential for unexpected delirium'. All major events in Hornby's life are considered in relation to the football club and its progress: when considering the question of mortality, he writes, 'The whole point about death, metaphorically speaking, is that it is almost bound to occur before the major trophies have been awarded'. Hornby's book won the William Hill Sports Book of the Year award, for which he received a bet of £500. He placed the money on Arsenal to achieve the rare feat of winning the FA Cup and League Cup double; they duly obliged, making him several thousand pounds better off.

The first biennial David Cohen British Literature Prize, for 'a lifetime's achievement by a living British writer', was awarded to V. S. Naipaul. The prize was worth £30,000, with a further £10,000 awarded for the recipient to use to encourage young writers. The Betty Trask prize, worth £10,000, for works of a traditional or romantic nature by a writer under the age of 35, was awarded to Mark Blackaby for *You'll Never Be Here Again*. Andrew Cowan received £7,000 for *Pig*, Simon Corrigan £5,000 for *Tommy Was Here*, with £2,000 each for Joanna Briscoe for *Mothers and Other Lovers* and Olivia Fane for *Landing on Clouds*. The splitting of the Trask prize fund seems to contradict the wishes of its benefactor, who intended to fund one annual prize for an outright winner. Joanna Trollope, who chaired the panel of judges, commented that 'what disappointed us was the low quality of a lot of the published entries'.

The Somerset Maugham Awards, worth £5,000 to be used for foreign travel, were awarded to Dea Birkett for *Jella*, Duncan McLeana for *Bucket of Tongues* and Glyn Maxwell for *Out of the Rain*. Andrew Barrow's *The Tap Dancer* won the McKitterick Prize for the best first novel by an author aged over 40, and the Hawthornden Prize. The *Mail on Sunday*/John Llewellyn Rhys Prize for a writer under the age of 35 for a 'book of value from a writer of growing stature', was awarded to Matthew Kneale for his novel *Sweet Thames*. The Catherine Cookson Prize was awarded to Valerie Wood for her novel *The Sea is My Companion*. The Encore prize for the best second novel was awarded to Colm Toibin for *The Heather Blazing*.

The first Forward Poetry prize, worth £10,000, was awarded to Thom Gunn for *The Man with Night Sweats*. An award for most promising young poet (£5,000) was made to Simon Armitage for *Kid*. The Cholmondeley Awards for Poets were awarded to Patricia Beer, George Mackay Brown, P. J. Kavanagh and Michael Longley.

The Smarties Prize for Children's Books was awarded to Gillian Cross for *The Great Elephant Chase*; other prizes were awarded to Hilda Offen for *Nice Work, Little Wolf!* (under 5 age group) and Jane Ray for *The Story of Creation* (6–8-year-olds). At the presentation ceremony, Stephanie Nettell, who chaired the judging panel, criticized the standard of entries: 'Although the best were excellent, the judges were dismayed by the lack of sparkle and originality from publishers this year, especially in the two younger age categories and when compared with what is happening abroad. Some of the entries for the six to eight year olds were so banal we wondered how they came to be published at all. Why so many soppy endings? Why so many grammatical howlers and spelling mistakes? I thought they were written for the illiterate generation, not by them.'

The prestigious *Prix Goncourt* was awarded to Patrick Chamoiseau of Martinique for his novel *Texaco*, which portrays 150 years of life in a shanty town in Fort-de-France, Martinique, inhabited by former plantation workers who settled there after the abolition of slavery. The Commonwealth Writers Prize was awarded to Rohinton Mistry from Canada for *Such a Long Journey*. A prize of £2,000 was presented to Robert Antoni from the Bahamas for *Divina Trace*.

POETRY

Roy Fuller's *Last Poems* is a posthumous collection of his final unpublished works. It includes notable verse, such as the 'Later Sonnets from the Portuguese', and the sequences, in three-line stanzas, 'Enigmas', 'Poem in Three Movements' and 'Minor Keys'. In 'Early Retirement', he wrote:

'It seems my fate was never quite to know
A *modus vivendi* suited to my state –
Except perhaps the felicities of these
Fag-end years, that have almost come too late'.

R. S. Thomas's *Collected Poems, 1945-1990* contains almost 500 poems by the Welsh parson, many seen through the eyes of his alter ego, Iago Prytherch, a Welsh peasant, who constantly bemoans the loss of the Wales he had loved.

FINAL THRILLS

John le Carré's *The Night Manager*, a tale of gun-running and drug-dealing, is disappointing after his novels about British intelligence. Jonathan Pine, an ex-soldier now working as the night manager of a Zurich hotel, is engaged by the Enforcement Department of MI6 to track down Richard Onslow Roper, who is described as 'the worst man in the world'. Roper is an arms dealer and murderer who is the centre of a supposed international conspiracy. In the post cold war climate, however, the very existence of MI6 is under threat. Rex Goodhew, chairman of the joint steering committee that controls it, attempts to reform it. He would 'give away its powers to separate, smaller agencies, and make each of them separately accountable. He would deconstruct, decentralize, humanize.' Unfortunately, this reorganization puts Pine's life at risk.

Colin Dexter's cerebral Oxford policeman, Chief Inspector Morse, is confronted by an intriguing problem in *The Way Through the Woods*. He is set on the trail of a Swedish girl who has been missing for a year by an enigmatic poem which is sent to his senior officer and seems to offer a solution to the problem. The poem is published in *The Times* in an attempt to decipher it, and the mystery is played out in the newspaper's correspondence columns. Morse, aided by Detective Sergeant Lewis, uses more guile than usual to solve the case in an intelligent and well-written novel which closes with a delicious twist.

Jeffrey Archer's *Honour Among Thieves*, which concerns a plot to topple Saddam Hussein, the leader of Iraq, was a notable first for the Conservative peer in that it achieved some respectable reviews. Critics accepted the weaknesses of Archer's characterization and his lack of literary skills but applauded his storytelling ability, even if the absurd plot also involved an imagined attempt by Saddam Hussein to humiliate the Americans by stealing the Declaration of Independence and publicly burning it on the Fourth of July. Martin Cruz Smith's third thriller to feature the Moscow state investigator Arkady Renko, *Red Square*, is an intricate novel depicting a Moscow dominated by organized crime following the collapse of the Communist system. The dramatic climax is set during the unsuccessful coup against Gorbachev, with Boris Yeltsin besieged in Moscow's White House.

Poets Laureate

This title is conferred by letters patent on the post attached to the royal household. The post was officially established in 1668 when John Dryden became Poet Laureate, although Ben Jonson was considered to have been the first 'official' laureate. It is customary for the Poet Laureate to write verse to mark events of national importance. The Poet Laureate currently receives an honorarium of approximately £100 a year. The post is held for life.

Ben Jonson (1572-1637), appointed 1616
Sir William D'Avenant (1606-68), appointed 1638
John Dryden (1631-89), appointed 1670
Thomas Shadwell (1642-92), appointed 1689
Nahum Tate (1652-1715), appointed 1692
Nicholas Rowe (1674-1718), appointed 1715

Laurence Eusden (1688-1730), appointed 1718
Colley Cibber (1671-1757), appointed 1730
William Whitehead (1715-85), appointed 1757
Thomas Warton (1728-90), appointed 1785
Henry Pye (1745-1813), appointed 1790
Robert Southey (1774-1843), appointed 1813
William Wordsworth (1770-1850), appointed 1843
Alfred, Lord Tennyson (1809-92), appointed 1850
Alfred Austin (1835-1913), appointed 1896
Robert Bridges (1844-1930), appointed 1913
John Masefield (1878-1967), appointed 1930
Cecil Day Lewis (1904-72), appointed 1968
Sir John Betjeman (1906-84), appointed 1972
Ted Hughes (1930-), appointed 1984

Nobel Prizes

For prize winners for the years 1901–89, *see* earlier editions of *Whitaker's Almanack.*

The Nobel Prizes are awarded each year from the income of a trust fund established by the Swedish scientist Alfred Nobel, the inventor of dynamite, who died on 10 December 1896, leaving a fortune of £1,750,000. The prizes are awarded to those who have contributed most to the common good in the domain of:

Physics
    awarded by the Royal Swedish Academy of Sciences;
Chemistry
    awarded by the Royal Swedish Academy of Sciences;
Physiology or Medicine
    awarded by the Karolinska Institute;
Literature
    awarded by the Swedish Academy of Arts;
Peace
    awarded by a five-person committee elected by the Norwegian Storting;
Economic Sciences (instituted 1969)
    awarded by the Royal Swedish Academy of Sciences.

The first awards were made in 1901 on the fifth anniversary of Nobel's death. The prizes are awarded every year on 10 December, the anniversary of Nobel's death.

The Trust is administered by the board of directors of the Nobel Foundation, Stockholm, consisting of five members and three deputy members. The Swedish Government appoints a chairman and a deputy chairman, the remaining members being appointed by the awarding authorities.

The awards have been distributed as follows:
Physics
American 55, British 20, German 19 (1948–90, West German 8), French 11, Soviet 7, Dutch 6, Swedish 4, Austrian 3, Danish 3, Italian 3, Japanese 3, Chinese 2, Swiss 2, Canadian 1, Indian 1, Irish 1, Pakistani 1.
Chemistry
American 37, German 27 (1948–90, West German 10), British 23, French 7, Swiss 5, Swedish 4, Canadian 2, Dutch 2, Argentinian 1, Austrian 1, Belgian 1, Czech 1, Finnish 1, Hungarian 1, Italian 1, Japanese 1, Norwegian 1, Soviet 1.
Physiology or Medicine
American 69, British 22, German 14 (1948–90, West German 4), French 7, Swedish 7, Danish 5, Swiss 5, Austrian 4, Belgian 4, Italian 3, Australian 2, Canadian 2, Dutch 2, Hungarian 2, Russian 2, Argentinian 1, Japanese 1, Portuguese 1, South African 1, Spanish 1.
Literature
French 12, American 9, British 8, Swedish 7, German 6 (1948–90, West German 1), Italian 5, Spanish 5, Danish 3, Norwegian 3, Soviet 3, Chilean 2, Greek 2, Irish 2, Polish 2, Swiss 2, Australian 1, Belgian 1, Colombian 1, Czech 1, Egyptian 1, Finnish 1, Guatemalan 1, Icelandic 1, Indian 1, Israeli 1, Japanese 1, Mexican 1, Nigerian 1, South African 1, Trinidadian 1, Yugoslav 1, Stateless 1.
Peace
American 17, Institutions 16, British 9, French 9, Swedish 5, German 4 (1948–90, West German 1), Belgian 3, Swiss 3, Argentinian 2, Austrian 2, Norwegian 2, South African 2, Soviet 2, Burmese 1, Canadian 1, Costa Rican 1, Danish 1, Dutch 1, Egyptian 1, Guatemalan 1, Irish 1, Israeli 1, Italian 1, Japanese 1, Mexican 1, Polish 1, Tibetan 1, Vietnamese 1, Yugoslav 1.
Economics
American 19, British 6, Norwegian 2, Swedish 2, Dutch 1, French 1, Soviet 1.

Prize	1990	1991	1992
Physics	Prof. J. Friedman (American) Prof. H. Kendall (American) Prof. R. Taylor (Canadian)	Prof. P.-G. de Gennes (French)	Prof. G. Charpak (French)
Chemistry	Prof. E. Corey (American)	Prof. R. Ernst (Swiss)	Prof. R. Marcus (American)
Physiology or Medicine	Dr J. Murray (American) Dr E. D. Thomas (American)	E. Neher (German) B. Sakmann (German)	Dr E. Krebs (American) Dr E. Fischer (American)
Literature	O. Paz (Mexican)	N. Gordimer (South African)	D. Walcott (Trinidadian)
Peace	Pres. M. Gorbachev (Soviet)	Aung San Suu Kyi (Burmese)	Sra R. Menchú (Guatemalan)
Economics	Prof. H. Markowitz (American) Prof. M. Miller (American) Prof. W. Sharpe (American)	Prof. R. Coase (British)	G. S. Becker (American)

Opera

'Everyone needs Opera', according to English National Opera's posters and advertisements. Although that assertion is not strictly true, the number of people eager and willing to attend opera performances does appear to be rising. However, during the 1992–3 season ENO had an average attendance of only 65 per cent, which produced an income 6 per cent lower than in 1991–2 and resulted in a deficit of nearly £1 million. The recession can partly be blamed for this, as the company continued to flourish artistically. Revived after a five-year interval, Jonathan Miller's immensely popular production of *Rigoletto*, set in a Mafia 'family' in New York, was given 22 performances during the season and then retired with a well-deserved long-service medal. Of seven new productions, Verdi's *The Force of Destiny*, Janáček's *The Adventures of Mr Brouček* (funded mainly by individual contributions from the London Coliseum audiences), and Handel's *Ariodante* were especially praised, but Ken Russell's vulgar staging of a Gilbert and Sullivan rarity, *Princess Ida*, did not meet with approval. The world première of Jonathan Harvey's *Inquest of Love*, the fifth in ENO's commissioning programme, scored a considerable popular success and was generally considered the best in the series so far. Harvey was awarded the 1993 Britten Prize for Composition. At the end of the season the 'Power House' – Peter Jonas (general director), Mark Elder (music director) and David Pountney (director of productions) – all left ENO. Whether one loved or loathed their influence on ENO in particular or on opera in Britain in general is immaterial; neither will ever be the same again.

The Royal Opera had a very successful season artistically, but the question of its redevelopment scheme in Covent Garden, and the consequent temporary closure of the Opera House, remains unresolved – the latest suggestion for a provisional theatre is the Hackney Empire. Though one new production, Halevy's *La Juive*, had to be cancelled for reasons of economy, and another, Handel's *Alcina*, was found extremely boring both musically and dramatically despite an excellent cast, the remainder were all welcomed. *Porgy and Bess*, in the greatly admired Glyndebourne production, brought Gershwin to Covent Garden for the first time and gave pleasure to many people; Richard Strauss's *Die Frau ohne Schatten*, remarkable for David Hockney's colourful designs, was superbly conducted by Bernard Haitink; Berlioz's *La Damnation de Faust*, imaginatively staged by Harry Kupfer, contradicted the often-repeated theory that 'concept opera' is dead; and although the production of Debussy's *Pelléas et Mélisande* did not find universal favour, the fine cast and the musical direction by Claudio Abbado did. Most successful and popular of all was the first staging at Covent Garden of Verdi's *Stiffelio*, in an edition

prepared by the conductor, Sir Edward Downes, that restores the opera as nearly as possible to its original form. With the Spanish tenor José Carreras quite magnificent in the title role, *Stiffelio* won the 1993 Laurence Olivier Award for best new opera production. The award for the most outstanding achievement in opera went to Downes for his conducting of Prokofiev's *The Fiery Angel* (last season) and of *Stiffelio*, and for his performing edition of the Verdi opera. Later in the season it was announced by Downes and Nicholas Payne, opera director–designate, that Covent Garden will stage all 28 of Verdi's operas between 1995 and 2001 (the centenary of the composer's death) in annual summer festivals. A revival of *Stiffelio* will be included in the first festival, and the series will also involve the participation of Scottish Opera, Welsh National Opera and Opera North.

On 23 October 1992, two days after his 80th birthday, Sir Georg Solti conducted a superb revival of Verdi's *Otello*, with Placido Domingo in the title role; after the performance Solti received the honorary title of music director laureate of the Royal Opera from Jeremy Isaacs, the general manager of the Royal Opera House, and a silver rose in honour of his Covent Garden début in 1959 at which he conducted *Der Rosenkavalier*. He was also given two other stage properties in memory of his great achievements with the Royal Opera: Isolde's goblet, presented by Birgit Nilsson, and the Nibelung's ring, presented by Hans Hotter, the greatest Wotan of them all.

CRITICAL ACCLAIM

Paul Daniel, the music director of Opera North, won the 1993 award of the music section of the Critics' Circle. He achieved a long-standing ambition when he conducted Berg's *Wozzeck*, one of several interesting new productions mounted by Opera North. Others included the British stage première of *The Duenna* (Roberto Gerhard's adaptation of the play by Sheridan), Verdi's *Don Carlos*, Ponchielli's *La Gioconda*, and, at the Cheltenham Festival, the world première of Michael Berkeley's *Baa-Baa Black Sheep* (based on Kipling's story and *The Jungle Book*) which received excellent reviews and joins the repertory next season.

Two of Welsh National Opera's new productions, *Tristan und Isolde*, conducted by Sir Charles Mackerras, and Donizetti's *La favorita* (the Italian version), conducted by Carlo Rizzi, the company's music director, were performed at Covent Garden; the Wagner opera, not heard in London for many years, was particularly well received. WNO also mounted a new staging of *Eugene Onegin* in honour of the centenary of Tchaikovsky's death in 1893, as did the Royal Opera; Scottish Opera revived an existing production. Opera North staged *Yolanta*, first seen at the 1992 Edinburgh Festival, while ENO revived *The Queen of Spades*. The most ambitious celebration of the centenary, however, was a new production of *The Queen of Spades* by students of the Royal Academy of Music and the Royal College of Music, whose Opera Schools have merged into a single Vocal Faculty. Sung in Russian and staged by Malcolm Fraser in the RCM's Britten Theatre, this was very well performed and highly enjoyable.

Scottish Opera's most interesting new production was *Norma*, staged by Ian Judge, whose avowed – and successful – intention was to present the Bellini opera in a more dramatic guise than usual. John Mauceri conducted, in his last new assignment as musical director before leaving Scottish Opera at the end of the season. Though Mauceri's seven years in Scotland have earned him many brickbats from the critics, he deserves an equal number of bouquets, for Bernstein's *Candide*, Weill's *Street Scene*, Berlioz's *Les Troyens*, Wagner's *Das Rheingold* and *Die Walküre*, Verdi's *Falstaff* and the new production of *Norma*. He is succeeded by Richard Armstrong.

The temporary closure of Glyndebourne left a large hole in 1993's summer operatic calendar. However, by the beginning of July the structure of the new opera house was in place, ahead of schedule and within budget; the giant crane looming over the site was removed and it became clear that the new and larger theatre would be no more obtrusive than the old one and that a year without visitors would also greatly benefit the gardens. As a stopgap, concert performances of Berlioz's *Béatrice et Bénédict*, Beethoven's *Fidelio* and Lehár's *Die lustige Witwe* were given at the Royal Festival Hall.

TOURING OPERA

Glyndebourne Touring Opera continued its activities as usual, offering, as well as Mozart's *Don Giovanni* and *La clemenza di Tito*, the British première of *Cornet Christoph Rilke's Song of Love and Death* by Siegfried Matthus. The work, based on Rilke's poem, has been very popular in German-speaking theatres and is the first opera by Matthus to be performed in the UK. Despite GTO's success, the company was threatened with having its Arts Council subsidy removed unless it included more smaller theatres and towns on its tours. This would mean that Glyndebourne productions could no longer be taken on tour, and young singers covering main roles at the festival would no longer have the opportunity of singing those roles on tour.

In any case, other touring companies now cover the smaller venues very satisfactorily: City of Birmingham Touring Opera staged the British professional première of Rameau's *Les Boréades* in six venues, none of them conventional theatres; English Touring Opera (formerly Opera 80) presented *Falstaff*, *Don Giovanni* and *Così fan tutte* in some 24 towns; and Travelling Opera, which made a rare London appearance over Christmas 1992 with *La bohème* and *Don Pasquale* at the Queen Elizabeth Hall, also toured *Carmen*, *The Barber of Seville* and three Mozart operas to 30 venues around Britain. Scottish Opera-Go-Round took *The Seraglio* to more than 30 small towns in Scotland, Northern Ireland and Wales, while WNO's BP Opera Circuit gave 50 performances of *Così fan tutte* and Verdi's *Macbeth* in small theatres, halls and art centres throughout Wales and England.

A new London venue of a size ideal for these companies will be available in September 1993 when Spitalfields Market Opera opens with *Orpheo*, Stephen Oliver's reworking of Peri's *Euridice*, the first extant opera. The market building has been adapted to provide a 540-seat auditorium with a pit capable of holding an orchestra of 50 musicians. SMO plans to combine a 12-week season of its own productions, including a series of Offenbach's one-act operettas over Christmas 1993, with 40 weeks of performances by touring companies from Britain and abroad.

Not for the first time in its 15-year history, Buxton Festival hovered on the brink of extinction when Jane Glover, its newly-appointed artistic director, resigned before this year's festival. Jonathan Miller took over for 1993, and two of his own productions, Donizetti's *Maria Stuarda*, originally staged by Monte Carlo Opera, and Cimarosa's *Secret Marriage*, first presented by Opera North at the Cheltenham Festival, made up an interesting programme. The Earl of Harewood later accepted an appointment as artistic adviser to the Buxton Festival, thus ensuring its continuity and safeguarding the high standard of its presentations.

The Edinburgh Festival operatic fare included a new production by Scottish Opera of Verdi's *I due Foscari*; WNO's much-praised *Falstaff*, staged by Peter Stein; a double bill of Bartók's *Bluebeard's Castle* and Schoenberg's *Erwartung* from Canadian Opera, making its European début; and the première of James MacMillan's *Tourist Variations*, given with Craig Armstrong's *Anna*, at the Traverse Theatre. A fire in the newly restored Playhouse Theatre (reputedly the largest in Europe) put the WNO and Canadian Opera productions at risk of cancellation; however, despite considerable smoke damage to the stage and auditorium, they were able to go ahead as planned.

The Brighton Festival, facing no competition this year from Glyndebourne, placed special emphasis on opera. After playing host to City of Birmingham Touring Opera's *Les Boréades*, Brighton presented the Moscow Chamber Opera on its first visit to Britain. Among the productions on show was the company's staging, famous throughout Europe and Russia, of *The Nose* by Shostakovich. The growing number of 'country-house' opera groups also took advantage of the closure of Glyndebourne, in particular Garsington Opera, which stages its productions on the terrace of the Oxfordshire manor house once owned by Lady Ottoline Morrell. *Infedeltà delusa* (Haydn), *Ariadne auf Naxos* and *Le nozze di Figaro* comprised the enterprising repertory this year.

GAINS AND LOSSES

New operas flowed freely from the pens of young composers. As part of ENO's Baylis Programme, New Visions, New Voices at the RCM included works by composers aged from nine to 29; *Melissa's Maelstrom* by the 16-year-old twins Dina (text) and Rosabella (music) Gregory, was potentially the most interesting. ENO Soundbites! presented by Contemporary Opera Studio at the Donmar Warehouse offered three new works as well as two existing pieces by Gerald Barry and Stephen Oliver. The Garden Venture put on six new one-acters in two triple bills at Riverside Studios; most promising among them were Graham Fitkin's *Ghosts* and Geoff Westley's *Travels in the Arctic Circle*. Almeida Opera (a joint venture between the Almeida Theatre, Islington, and Contemporary Opera Studio) offered a courageous programme including the world première of *The Man who Strikes the Wind* by Kevin Volans, an evocation of the poet Rimbaud's life in Africa, and *A Family Affair*, a comic opera by Julian Grant based on the play by Alexander Ostrovsky. Almeida also gave two British premières: *Judith*, a double bill of works derived from the biblical story, comprised *Line of Terror* by Ian McQueen, and *Judith and Holofernes*, a puppet opera by David Lang.

British opera lost one of its best-loved figures when the Welsh baritone Sir Geraint Evans died on 19 September 1992 at the age of 70. He made his début with the recently-formed Covent Garden Opera in 1948, as the Nightwatchman in Wagner's *Die Meistersinger*, and continued to sing with the company until his retirement in 1984. During that time he created roles in Britten's *Billy Budd* and *Gloriana*, and in Walton's *Troilus and Cressida*. A natural comedian, with a sympathetic personality as well as a warm-toned voice, he had many comic parts in his wide repertory, including Mozart's Figaro (a favourite role), Papageno, Leporello, Guglielmo and Don Alfonso, Donizetti's Don Pasquale and Dr Dulcamara (which he sang at his farewell performance at Covent Garden in June 1984), Verdi's Falstaff, Beckmesser (*Die Meistersinger*) and Bottom (*A Midsummer Night's Dream*). But he was also a notable exponent of serious roles such as Balstrode in *Peter Grimes* and Berg's Wozzeck, which he sang at the Salzburg Festival.

Two sopranos connected with the pre-war seasons at Glyndebourne also died during the year. Winifred Radford sang Barbarina at the opening performance of *Le nozze di Figaro* in 1934, and she later appeared as Cherubino, First Boy (*Die Zauberflöte*) and Zerlina. Her subsequent career was mainly in the sphere of French song. Ina Souez, though American-born, was British by marriage when she made her Glyndebourne appearances (1934-9) as Fiordiligi and Donna Anna. The Croatian-born baritone Marko Rothmüller, who died at the age of 84, was a member of Covent Garden Opera from 1948 to 1955, and was highly praised for his Wozzeck in the British stage première of Berg's opera (1952).

PRODUCTIONS

In the summaries of company activities shown below, the dates in brackets indicate the year that the current production entered the company's repertoire.

ROYAL OPERA

Estab. 1946

Royal Opera House, Covent Garden, London WC2E 9DD

Productions from the repertory: *Tosca* (1964), *I Capuleti e i Montecchi* (1984), *Fidelio* (1990), *Otello* (1987), *Madama Butterfly* (1988), *Il barbiere di Siviglia* (1985), *Turandot* (1984), *Jenůfa* (1986), *Attila* (1990), *The Cunning Little Vixen* (1990), *Don Giovanni* (1992).

New productions:

Porgy and Bess (Gershwin), 9 October 1992. Conductor, Andrew Litton; producer, Trevor Nunn; designers, John Gunter (sets), Sue Blane (costumes). Willard White (Porgy), Cynthia Haymon (Bess), Cynthia Clarey (Serena), Timuke Olafimihan (Clara), Gregg Baker (Crown), Damon Evans (Sporting Life).

Die Frau ohne Schatten (R. Strauss), 16 November 1992. Conductor, Bernard Haitink; producer, John Cox; designer, David Hockney. Anna Towmowa-Sintow (Empress), Paul Frey (Emperor), Jane Henschel (Nurse), Franz Grundheber (Barak), Gwyneth Jones (Barak's Wife), Robert Hayward (Spirit Messenger).

Alcina (Handel), 18 December 1992. Conductor, John Fisher; producer, Stephen Wadsworth; designers, Thomas P. Lynch (sets), Dunya Ramicova (costumes). Yvonne Kenny (Alcina), Ann Murray (Ruggiero), Kathleen Kuhlmann (Bradamante), Anthony Rolfe-Johnson (Oronte), Judith Howarth (Morgana), Stafford Dean (Melisso).

Stiffelio (Verdi), 25 January 1993. Conductor, Edward Downes; producer, Elijah Moshinsky; designers, Michael Yeargan (sets), Peter J. Hall (costumes). José Carreras (Stiffelio), Catherine Malfitano (Lina), Gregory Yurisich (Stankar), Robin Leggate (Raffaele), Gwynne Howell (Jorg).

La Damnation de Faust (Berlioz), 8 March 1993. Conductor, Colin Davis; producer, Harry Kupfer; designers, Hans Schavernoch (sets), Reinhard Heinrich (costumes). Jerry Hadley (Faust), Samuel Ramey (Mephistopheles), Olga Borodina (Marguerite), Roderick Earle (Brander).

Pelléas et Mélisande (Debussy), 24 March 1993. Conductor, Claudio Abbado; producer, Antoine Vitez; designer, Yannis Kokkos. Frederica von Stade (Mélisande), François le Roux (Pelléas), Victor Braun (Golaud), Yvonne Minton (Geneviève), Robert Lloyd (Arkel), Patrizia Pace (Yniold), Gordon Sandison (Shepherd/Physician).

Eugene Onegin (Tchaikovsky), 13 July 1993. Conductor, Valery Gergiev; producer, John Cox; designer, Timothy O'Brien. Galina Gorchakova (Tatyana), Sergei Leiferkus (Onegin), Gegam Gregorian (Lensky), Louise Winter (Olga), Gillian Knight (Mme Larina), Sarah Walker (Filipyevna), Nicolai Ghiaurov (Prince Gremin), Francis Egerton (M. Triquet).

ENGLISH NATIONAL OPERA

Estab. 1931

London Coliseum, St Martin's Lane, London WC2N 4ES

Productions from the repertory: *Rigoletto* (1982), *Ariadne on Naxos* (1983), *Don Giovanni* (1985), *The Magic Flute* (1988), *Wozzeck* (1990), *Hansel and Gretel* (1987), *Carmen* (1986),

The Turn of the Screw (1979), *The Mikado* (1986), *Bluebeard's Castle* (1991), *The Queen of Spades* (1983), *The Barber of Seville* (1987), *Macbeth* (1990).

New productions:
The Force of Destiny (Verdi), 16 September 1992. Conductor, Mark Elder; producer, Nicholas Hytner; designer, Richard Hudson. Richard Van Allan (Marquis of Calatrava), Josephine Barstow (Leonora), Edmund Barham (Don Alvaro), Jonathan Summers (Don Carlos), Anne-Marie Owens (Preziosilla), John Connell (Father Superior), Alan Opie (Melitone).
Princess Ida (Sullivan), 14 November 1992. Conductor, Jane Glover; producer, Ken Russell; designer, James Merifield. Rosemary Joshua (Princess Ida), Nerys Jones (Melissa), Anne Collins (Lady Blanche), Anne-Marie Owens (Lady Psyche), John Graham-Hall (Cyril), Mark Curtis (Hilarion), Geoffrey Dolton (Florian), Richard Van Allan (King Hildebrand), Nickolas Grace (King Gama).
The Adventures of Mr Brouček (Janáček), 16 December 1992. Conductor, Charles Mackerras; producer, David Pountney; designers, Stefanos Lazaridis (sets), Marie-Jeanne Lecca (costumes). Graham Clark (Mr Brouček), Vivian Tierney (Malinka), Bonaventura Bottone (Mazal), Arwel Hughes Morgan (Sacristan), Alberto Remedios (Vision of the author), Maria Bovino (Potboy).
Don Pasquale (Donizetti), 19 February 1993. Conductor, Andrew Greenwood; producer, Patrick Mason; designer, Joe Vanek. Andrew Shore (Don Pasquale), Rosemary Joshua (Norina), Adrian Martin (Ernesto), Alan Opie (Dr Malatesta).
Duel of Tancredi and Clorinda (Monteverdi), 17 March 1993. Conductor, Harry Bicket; producer, David Alden; designer, Nigel Lowery. Paul Nilon (narrator), Patricia Rozario (Clorinda), Christopher Ventris (Tancredi).
Ariodante (Handel), 28 April 1993. Conductor, Nicholas McGegan; producer, David Alden; designer, Ian MacNeil. Michael Druiett (King of Scotland), Amanda Roocroft (Ginevra), Ann Murray (Ariodante), Christopher Robson (Polinesso), Lesley Garrett (Dalinda), Paul Nilon (Lurcanio).
World première of *Inquest of Love* (Jonathan Harvey), 3 June 1993. Conductor, Mark Elder; producer, David Pountney; designer, Nigel Lowery. Peter Coleman-Wright (John), Linda McLeod (Ann), Helen Field (Elspeth), Richard Van Allan (Abbot), Nan Christie (Psychopomp), Ethna Robinson (Philia), Barry Banks (Josh).

OPERA NORTH
Estab. 1978
Grand Theatre, 46 New Briggate, Leeds LS1 6NU

Productions from the repertory: *Rigoletto* (1979), *Orpheus in the Underworld* (1992).

New productions:
British première of *The Duenna* (Roberto Gerhard), 17 September 1992. Conductor, Antoni Ros-Marba; producer, Helena Kaut-Howson; designer, Sue Blane. Andrew Shore (Don Jerome), Susan Chilcott (Luisa), Pamela Helen Stephen (Clara), Gillian Knight (the Duenna), Gordon Wilson (Antonio), Adrian Clarke (Ferdinand), Eric Roberts (Don Isaac), Paul Wade (Father Paul).
The Marriage of Figaro (Mozart), 10 October 1992. Conductor, Andrew Parrott; producer, Caroline Gawn; designer, Alison Chitty. Linda Kitchen (Susanna), Gerald Finley (Figaro), Ann Taylor-Morley (Cherubino), Jane Leslie MacKenzie (Countess), Robert Hayward (Count), Susan Lees (Marcellina), Donald Adams (Bartolo), Stephen Austin (Basilio), Mary Plazas (Barbarina).

Billy Budd (Britten), 11 December 1992. Conductor, Elgar Howarth; producer, Graham Vick; designer, Chris Dyer. Nigel Robson (Captain Vere), Jason Howard (Billy Budd), Christopher Ventris (Novice), John Tomlinson (Claggart), Richard Morton (Red Whiskers), Keith Latham (Donald), David Gwynne (Dansker), Peter Knapp (Redburn), Roger Bryson (Flint), Jonathan Best (Ratcliffe).
Yolande (Tchaikovsky), 18 December 1992. Conductor, David Lloyd-Jones; producer, Martin Duncan; designer, Anthony Ward. Joan Rodgers (Yolande), Kim Begley (Vaudemont), Robert Hayward (Robert), Gwynne Howell (King René), Clive Bayley (Ibn Hakla).
Don Carlos (Verdi), 8 January 1993. Conductor, Paul Daniel; producer, Tim Albery; designers, Hildegard Bechtler (sets), Nicky Gillibrand (costumes). Linda McLeod (Elisabeth), Claire Powell (Eboli), Richard Burke (Carlos), Anthony Michaels-Moore (Posa), John Tomlinson (Philip II), Richard Van Allan (Grand Inquisitor), Clive Bayley (Monk), Mary Plazas (Thibault).
La bohème (Puccini), 16 April 1993. Conductor, Roy Laughlin; producer, Phyllida Lloyd; designer, Anthony Ward. Jane Leslie MacKenzie (Mimi), David Maxwell Anderson (Rodolfo), Juliet Booth (Musetta), Robert Hayward (Marcello), William Dazeley (Schaunard), Graeme Broadbent (Colline).
La Gioconda (Ponchielli), 1 May 1993. Conductor, Oliver von Dohnanyi; producer/designer, Philip Prowse. Rosalind Plowright (La Gioconda), Sally Burgess (Laura), Catherine Wyn-Rogers (La Cieca), Edmund Barham (Enzo), Keith Latham (Barnaba), Clifford Grant (Alvise).
Wozzeck (Berg), 13 May 1993. Conductor, Paul Daniel; producer, Deborah Warner; designers, Hildegard Bechtler (sets), Nicky Gillibrand (costumes). Andrew Shore (Wozzeck), Vivian Tierney (Marie), Jeffrey Lawton (Captain), John Rath (Doctor), Alan Woodrow (Drum Major), David Owen (Andres), Kate McCarney (Margret), Mark Curtis (Idiot).
World première of *Baa-Baa Black Sheep* (Michael Berkeley), 3 July 1993 at Cheltenham Festival. Conductor, Paul Daniel; producer, Jonathan Moore; designer, David Blight. Malcolm Lorimer/William Bazeley (Punch/Mowgli), Ann Taylor-Morley (Judy/Grey Wolf), Eileen Hulse (Mother/Mother Wolf), Fiona Kimm (Auntirosa/Baldeo), Philip Sheffield (Harry/Sheer Khan), Paul McCann (Captain Sahib/Snakeman), Henry Newman (Captain/Akela), George Mosley (Father/Father Wolf), Clive Bayley (Meeta/Bagheera).
The Secret Marriage (Cimarosa), 8 July 1993 at Cheltenham Festival. Conductor, Roy Laughlin; producer, Jonathan Miller; designers, John Conklin (sets), Stephen Rodwell (costumes). Andrew Shore (Geronimo), Anne Dawson (Carolina), Mark Curtis (Paolino), Jonathan Best (Count Robinson), Kate Egan (Elisetta), Tamsin Dives (Fidalma).
Performances of the repertoire were given at the Grand Theatre, Leeds, and on tour in Manchester, Nottingham, Hull, Birmingham, Sheffield, Cheltenham and Buxton.

SCOTTISH OPERA
Estab. 1962
39 Elmbank Crescent, Glasgow G2 4PT

Productions from the repertory: *Così fan tutte* (1990), *La bohème* (1988), *Eugene Onegin* (1979), *The Makropoulos Case* (1981).

New productions:
Il trovatore (Verdi), 29 September 1992. Conductor, Richard Armstrong; producer, Mark Brickman; designer, Tim Hatley. Lisa Gasteen (Leonora), Paolo Kudriavchenko

(Manrico), Ludmilla Nam (Azucena), Vladimir Redken (Luna), David Marsh (Ferrando).

Julius Caesar (Handel), 21 October 1992. Conductor, Samuel Bachli; producer, Willy Decker; designer, John Macfarlane. Joan Rodgers (Cleopatra), Michael Chance (Caesar), Anne Mason (Cornelia), Eirian James (Sextus), Christopher Robson (Ptolemy), Gidon Saks (Achillas), Timothy Wilson (Nirenus).

The Magic Flute (Mozart), 17 December 1992. Conductor, Nicholas McGegan; producer, Martin Duncan; designer, Ken Lee. Paul Nilon (Tamino), Susannah Waters (Pamina), Simon Keenlyside (Papageno), Gidon Saks (Sarastro), Jennifer Rhys Davies (Queen of Night), Susan Chilcott (First Lady), Rupert Oliver Forbes (Monostatos), Ann Archibald (Papagena).

Norma (Bellini), 21 April 1993. Conductor, John Mauceri; producer, Ian Judge; designers, John Gunter (sets), Deirdre Clancy (costumes). Jane Eaglen (Norma), Katherine Ciesinski (Adalgisa), Norman Bailey (Oroveso), Stefano Algieri (Pollione), Richard Coxon (Flavio).

I due Foscari (Verdi), 16 August 1993 at Edinburgh Festival. Conductor, Richard Armstrong; producer, Howard Davies; designer, Ashley Martin-Davis. Katerina Kudravchenko (Lucrezia), Deng (Jacopo), Frederick Burchinal (Francesco), Richard Coxon (Barbarigo), Nicolas Cavallier (Loredano).

Performances of the repertoire were given at the Theatre Royal, Glasgow, and on tour at Aberdeen, Newcastle, Edinburgh and Inverness.

WELSH NATIONAL OPERA

Estab. 1946
John Street, Cardiff CF1 4SP

Productions from the repertory: *The Barber of Seville* (1988), *La bohème* (1984), *Un ballo in maschera* (1982), *Falstaff* (1988).

New productions:
Elektra (Strauss), 19 September 1992. Conductor, Carlo Rizzi; producer, David Alden; designers, Paul Bond, Charles Edwards. Janet Hardy (Elektra), Felicity Palmer (Klytemnestra), Eva Maria Bundschuh (Chrysothemis), Philip Joll (Orestes), Jeffrey Lawton (Aegisthus).

Tosca (Puccini), 10 October 1992. Conductor, Carlo Rizzi; producer, Michael Blakemore; designer, Ashley Martin-Davies. Suzanne Murphy (Tosca), Dennis O'Neill (Cavaradossi), Peter Sidhom (Scarpia), Mark Richardson (Angelotti), Andrew Shore (Sacristan), Neville Ackermann (Spoletta).

Tristan und Isolde (Wagner), 13 February 1993. Conductor, Charles Mackerras; producer/designer, Yannis Kokkos. Anne Evans (Isolde), Jeffrey Lawton (Tristan), Della Jones (Brangäne), Richard Paul Fink (Kurwenal), Peter Rose (King Marke), John Harris (Melot).

La favorita (Donizetti), 5 March 1993. Conductor, Carlo Rizzi; producer, Rennie Wright; designers, Nick Rieti (sets), Terry Frances Parr (costumes). Bernadette Cullen (Leonora), Bonaventura Bottone (Fernando), David Barrell (Alfonso XI), Geoffrey Moses (Baldassare), Rebecca Evans (Ines).

Eugene Onegin (Tchaikovsky), 27 May 1993. Conductor, Carlo Rizzi; producer, Howard Davies; designer, Bob Crowley. Janice Watson (Tatyana), Yvone Burnett (Olga), Penelope Walker (Mme Larina), Menai Davies (Filipyevna), Neil Rosenshein (Lensky), Jason Howard (Onegin), Peter Rose (Prince Gremin).

Performances of the repertoire were given at the New Theatre, Cardiff and on tour at Oxford, Bristol, Swansea, Birmingham, Liverpool, Southampton, Rhyl, London (Royal Opera House), Plymouth and the Edinburgh Festival.

GLYNDEBOURNE FESTIVAL OPERA

Estab. 1934
Glyndebourne, Lewes, East Sussex BN8 5UU

No Festival was held at Glyndebourne in 1993, as the new theatre is in the process of construction. Concert performances of *Béatrice et Bénédict* (Berlioz), *Fidelio* (Beethoven) and *Die lustige Witwe* (Lehár) were given at the Royal Festival Hall, London, and in Birmingham during June and July.

GLYNDEBOURNE TOURING OPERA performed *Don Giovanni*, the British première of *Cornet Christoph Rilke's Song of Love and Death* (Siegfried Matthus) and *La clemenza di Tito* in London (Sadler's Wells Theatre), Norwich, Plymouth, Manchester, Oxford and Southampton from September to November 1993.

ENGLISH TOURING OPERA

Estab. 1980 as Opera 80

Falstaff and *Don Giovanni* were toured to Wimbledon, Wolverhampton, Crewe, Dartford, Leicester, Buxton, Bath and High Wycombe from October to December 1992.

Così fan tutte and *Falstaff* were toured to London (Sadler's Wells Theatre), Barnstaple, Crawley, Brighton, Poole, Swindon, Yeovil, Cambridge, Darlington, Preston, Reading, Exeter, Lincoln, Ipswich, Ulverston and Carlisle from February to May 1993.

OPERA FACTORY

Estab. 1982
South Bank Centre, London SE1

Yan Tan Tethera (1986) was revived at the Queen Elizabeth Hall, London, in September 1992. *The Marriage of Figaro* (1991) was revived at the Queen Elizabeth Hall, London, and toured to Birmingham and Reading in May/June 1993.

OPERA NORTHERN IRELAND

Estab. 1985
181A Stranmillis Road, Belfast BT9 5DU

Faust (1989) was revived at the Grand Opera House, Belfast, in September 1992.

New productions:
Rigoletto (Verdi), 18 September 1992. Conductor, Kenneth Montgomery; producer, Tim Coleman; designer, Lez Brotherston. Susannah Waters (Gilda), Peter Riberi (Duke of Mantua), Kimm Julian (Rigoletto), Rachel Hallawell (Maddalena), Alan Ewing (Sparafucile).

Il trovatore (Verdi), 27 February 1993. Conductor, Kenneth Montgomery; producer, Xavier Lopez-Pinon; designer, Tim Hatley. Nicole Ferner-Waite (Leonora), Gordon Wilson (Manrico), Ernst Daniel Smid (Luna), Cynthia Buchan (Azucena), Alan Ewing (Ferrando).

Parliament

For the parliamentary progress of the Maastrict Bill, *see* pages 1169–70.

For the second time in three years Parliament was recalled during the summer recess, meeting on 24 September to debate economic policy following the withdrawal of sterling from the European Exchange Rate Mechanism (ERM) on 16 September. The Prime Minister (John Major) claimed that 'the essential conditions for Britain's economic success are low inflation, low taxes, free trade and freedom from excessive state interference' and he asserted that 'I do not believe that we shall be able to go back into the mechanism soon, or into the same mechanism we left last week'. In his first speech as the Leader of the Opposition, John Smith said that the recent events had led to 'a Government whose economic policy is in tatters, whose credibility is blown, whose incompetence has been exposed ... he is the devalued Prime Minister of a devalued Government'. The motion expressing support for the Government's economic policy was passed by 322 votes to 296. On 25 September both Houses met to debate United Nations operations, in particular the situations in Yugoslavia, Iraq and Somalia. The Foreign Secretary (Douglas Hurd) referred to Yugoslavia as 'a crisis in Europe and for Europe' but said that 'we cannot dictate peace in Yugoslavia'.

Both Houses returned from the summer recess on 19 October, when the President of the Board of Trade (Michael Heseltine) announced changes to British Coal's decision to cease production at 31 pits over five months with the loss of up to 30,000 jobs. He said that initially only ten pits would close and that there would be a moratorium until early in 1993 on any other closures. In the House of Lords, the Lord Privy Seal (Lord Wakeham) announced that further consideration in committee of the British Coal and British Rail (Transfer Proposals) Bill (the paving bill for both privatizations) would be postponed following the announcement of the imminent pit closures and that there would be an emergency debate on an opposition motion on the coal industry instead. On 20 October the Prime Minister reported on the outcome of the European Community meeting in Birmingham on 16 October, where a declaration on subsidiarity had been agreed. In the Lords the opposition motion introduced by Lord Cledwyn of Penrhos calling for the Government to hold a thorough independent inquiry into the future of the coal industry was passed by 125 votes to 100, nine Conservative peers voting with the opposition despite assurances from Lord Wakeham that the Government's own inquiry would be thorough and wide-ranging. On 21 October in the Commons there was a debate on an opposition motion regretting the failure of the Government to provide for a review of the pit closures and demanding that no pit be closed until the select committee on Trade and Industry had concluded its review; Michael Heseltine announced a wide-ranging review. The Labour motion was defeated by 320 votes to 305, with six Conservative MPs voting against the Government. On 23 October the Health Secretary (Virginia Bottomley) announced the publication of the Tomlinson report on the future of London's health services recommending a radical shake-up of services in the capital and the closure of some hospitals. She said that the Government would consider the report and set out its own proposals in the New Year. On 28 October Virginia Bottomley made a statement on the failure of the new computer-aided dispatch system for the London Ambulance Service; an external inquiry was being conducted to identify the lessons to be learnt for the operation and management of the service.

On 2 November the Asylum and Immigration Appeals Bill, making provisions about persons who claim asylum in the United Kingdom and their dependants, received its second reading by 321 votes to 276. An opposition move to have the bill referred to a special standing committee was defeated. In the Lords the European Economic Area Bill (Lords), conferring on nationals of the European Free Trade Area (EFTA) treatment equivalent to that conferred on European Community nationals received its second reading. On 3 November the Housing and Urban Development Bill, conferring rights to collective enfranchisement and lease renewal on tenants of flats, extending the right of enfranchisement of tenants of houses, making provision for auditing the management by landlords or other persons of residential property, and establishing a new Urban Regeneration Agency, received its second reading by 327 votes to 259. A Liberal Democrat move to have the bill referred to a special standing committee was defeated. On 9 and 10 November the Education Bill, implementing the proposals set out in the White Paper *Choice and Diversity: A New Framework for Schools* received its second reading in the Commons by 304 votes to 268. On 10 November the Attorney-General (Sir Nicholas Lyell) announced an independent inquiry chaired by Lord Justice Scott into the so-called 'supergun' affair, following the collapse of the prosecution of the directors of Matrix Churchill for allegedly illegally exporting arms to Iraq after evidence in court from the former Trade and Defence Minister, Alan Clark, suggested that the directors had acted with the approval of the Government. On 11 November the Northern Ireland Secretary (Sir Patrick Mayhew) made a statement on the conclusion of the political talks on the future of Northern Ireland under the chairmanship of Sir Ninian Stephen, which had failed to agree an overall settlement. Labour's Northern Ireland spokesperson (Kevin McNamara) shared 'the regret that it has not been possible to reach heads of agreement'.

AUTUMN FINANCIAL STATEMENT

On 12 November the Chancellor of the Exchequer (Norman Lamont) presented his second autumn statement, outlining the spending plans for government departments. The main points were:
- spending levels unchanged for 1992-3 at £226,100 million
- planning totals (known in future as control totals) for 1993-4 set at £243,800 million; for 1994-5, £253,600 million; 1995-6, £263,300 million
- ratio of government expenditure to GDP 44.75 per cent in 1992-3, 45.5 per cent in 1993-4, 45 per cent in 1994-5, 44.25 per cent in 1995-6
- public sector borrowing requirement to rise to £37,000 million in 1992-3 against forecast of £28,000 million; about £44,000 million (7 per cent of GDP) in 1993-4

Measures to give 'immediate boost to confidence':
- car tax of 5 per cent abolished
- capital allowances for plant and machinery increased to 40 per cent in one year
- temporary relaxation on spending of local authority receipts
- extra £750 million for buying empty properties for use as low-rent housing
- extra £700 million of ECGD cover for exporters

Departmental plans:
- overall transport budget cut but national roads programme maintained, BR allowed to lease rolling stock, funds for Jubilee Line to be made available
- education spending up by 3 per cent
- social security benefits up by 3.6 per cent in April 1993
- local authority spending up by 3.7 per cent
- health spending up by 1 per cent in real terms
- employment expenditure up by 1 per cent in real terms
- public sector pay rises to be restricted to 1.5 per cent
- no pay increase for government ministers

Economic forecast:
- fall of 1 per cent in GDP in 1992-3, growth of around 1 per cent in 1993-4
- RPI inflation to drop to 3.75 per cent by end of 1992 and to rise at same rate in 1993
- target range for money growth (M4) for second half of 1992-3 at 4-8 per cent

The Shadow Chancellor (Gordon Brown) said that the Chancellor 'has failed to give us an economic and industrial strategy for the future'. The Liberal Democrat Treasury spokesman (Alan Beith) suggested that 'instead of a pay freeze for ministers, would it not have made sense to put them on performance-related pay so that if the measures do not work they will not get paid at all?'

On 17 November the Home Secretary (Kenneth Clarke), in response to a private notice question from Labour's Home Affairs spokesperson (Tony Blair), explained his decision to refuse entry to the UK to 180 Bosnian refugees because they had insubstantial or no links with the UK and had begun the process of attempting to enter the UK some four days after the announcement by the Home Office that all refugees from the area would in future need visas. The Trade Union Reform and Employment Rights Bill, implementing a number of EC employment obligations, abolishing wage councils and implementing new maternity leave rights, received its second reading by 312 votes to 277. During the debate on the autumn statement on 18 November, Norman Lamont announced that the Government would be selling off its remaining stake in British Telecom for £5,000 million. On 23 November the National Heritage Secretary (Peter Brooke) reported to the House on the damage caused by the fire at Windsor Castle the previous weekend and announced that resources would be provided to ensure that the building was maintained in a manner commensurate with its status and its role on occasions of state. Labour's National Heritage spokesperson (Ann Clwyd) regretted the failure to set up a public inquiry and questioned whether the total cost of repair should be paid exclusively by the taxpayer. On 25 November a government motion proposing a freeze on MPs' salaries was approved by 321 votes to 103; the official opposition line was to abstain. During Prime Minister's question time on 26 November, John Major announced that The Queen would pay income tax on her private income and would be refunding Civil List payments for all members of the Royal Family except the Queen Mother, the Duke of Edinburgh and herself. Also, the Prince of Wales would pay tax on his income from the Duchy of Cornwall. Kenneth Clarke clarified the Government's position on Sunday trading, indicating that once the decision of the European Court of Justice was known, they would present a bill with various options to the House. Tony Blair welcomed the announcement and sought assurances that there would be a free vote. On 30 November Michael Heseltine announced the publication of a Green Paper *Abuse of Market Power: Possible Legislative Options*, consulting on ways of improving the law on monopolies and curbing anti-competitive practices. Labour's Trade and Industry spokesperson (Robin Cook) welcomed the proposals, expressing Labour's preference for a prohibition system. The Parliamentary Under-Secretary of State for the Home Office (Charles Wardle) announced that the Government had informed the United Nations High Commissioner for Refugees that the UK were willing to receive more former detainees from the former Yugoslavia than originally announced, as many as 4,000 in all. Tony Blair welcomed the move that 'has rightly been forced on the Government by the strength of feeling in the country about the need for Britain to do more'.

During a debate on unemployment on 8 December, the Employment Secretary (Gillian Shephard) announced that an extra 180,000 new places would be provided in Jobclubs and an additional 10,000 places in job review workshops. On 9 December, John Major announced that the Prince and Princess of Wales would separate, although there would be no divorce at this time. He confirmed that there were no constitutional implications. John Smith expressed a hope that 'a greater degree of privacy might result'. On 14 December John Major reported to the House on the outcome of the European Community meeting held in Edinburgh on 11 and 12 December. On 14 December the Secretary of State for Transport (John MacGregor) announced the Government's financial support for local highway authorities in England for 1993–4, some £1,047 million for capital expenditure, including plans for 24 new bypasses and relief roads. The traditional series of adjournment debates on the last sitting day before the Christmas recess (17 December) was disrupted by Scottish MPs protesting about an announcement on NHS trusts in Scotland being made by way of a written answer rather than an oral statement. When they refused to clear the chamber, the Speaker suspended the sitting of the House for a few hours.

On 11 January John MacGregor made a statement on the MV *Braer* oil tanker disaster in the Shetlands on 5 January, announcing, in addition to the investigations already underway, the commissioning of a public inquiry under Lord Donaldson to look into the protection of the UK coastline from pollution from merchant shipping. Labour's Transport spokesperson (John Prescott) welcomed the announcement but was concerned as to who would pay to clear up the pollution in the Shetlands. This announcement was followed by one from the Scottish Secretary, Ian Lang, on the health, agricultural, fisheries and environmental aspects of the disaster. On 13 January the Foreign Office Minister Douglas Hogg made a statement on the recent violations by the Iraqis of the border with Kuwait; any retaliatory action would be taken only in accordance with international law and the House would be kept informed. Later that day the Defence Secretary (Malcolm Rifkind) announced that allied military action had been taken against Iraq, involving some 114 US, British and French aircraft. Labour's Defence spokesperson (David Clark) said the Opposition 'have supported the objective of this operation which was to ensure that allied aircraft could patrol the no-fly zone in Iraq, thereby ensuring that the Kurds and, in the south, the Shi'ite Muslims were not subjected to the genocide that they might otherwise have been'. On 14 January Malcolm Rifkind announced the authorization of the deployment of additional forces to Bosnia. On the understanding that the sole purpose of the further deployment was to provide humanitarian aid, David Clark welcomed the move. Peter Brooke announced the publication of the Calcutt report on the effective-

ness of press self-regulation. The Government had accepted the case for three new criminal offences to deal with physical intrusion and covert surveillance and would be bringing forward legislation. Labour's National Heritage spokesperson (Ann Clwyd) expressed 'grave reservations about a number of [the report's] recommendations'.

On 18 January Malcolm Rifkind reported on further military action by US, British and French aircraft against Iraqi air defence and command and control facilities in the south, and a cruise missile attack launched by the USA on a nuclear weapons facility outside Baghdad. A general debate on the RAF in the Commons on 21 January was widened to include developments in the Gulf and, unusually, a division of the House was forced by back-bench Labour MPs who did not support their front-bench line and the vote, on the procedural motion 'that this House do now adjourn', was passed by 156 votes to 21. In the Lords on 26 January the Lord Advocate (Lord Rodger of Earlsferry) announced the outcome of the Nimmo Smith/Friel inquiry into allegations of conspiracy to pervert the course of justice in Scotland following reports in the press that decisions in five cases had been taken for improper reasons. The inquiry concluded that the decisions in each of the five cases were taken on a proper basis and the rumours were without foundation.

On 2 February Michael Heseltine reported that it had not been possible for Leyland Daf Trucks and their bankers to put together a satisfactory restructuring package and the company would cease trading. The Government would work closely to mitigate the effects as far as possible, but would not intervene directly. Robin Cook blamed a consortium of British banks for wrecking any possible deal and called on the Government to admit that 'Britain faces a real industrial crisis and needs an industrial strategy that tackles it'. On 3 February Malcolm Rifkind announced that the Government had reconsidered its planned cuts in army strength and that the planned amalgamations of the Cheshire and Staffordshire Regiments and of the Royal Scots and King's Own Scottish Borderers would not now proceed. On 4 February John MacGregor announced plans for more than 40 new road schemes at a cost of £1,300 million in 1993–4. John Prescott, giving the announcement a guarded welcome, contrasted it to the recent announcements about British Rail 'where investment will be cut in half'. On 8 February the Chief Secretary to the Treasury (Michael Portillo) confirmed that a review of government expenditure was in progress and that the departments with the four largest spending programmes (Home Office, Health, Education and Social Security) were involved. His Labour Shadow (Harriet Harman) expressed the view that 'it would be wholly wrong if the British people, who are already suffering in recession, ended up paying the price [of Government mismanagement] in terms of worse policing, worse schools and worse health care – not to mention lost pensions and lost benefits'. On

11 February John Major outlined the details of The Queen's decision to pay taxes. On 16 February Virginia Bottomley announced the Government's response to the Tomlinson report on NHS services in London. Six reviews were to be set up and the first stage of plans would be to cut total bed numbers in London by over 2,500 in the next six years. Labour's Health spokesperson (David Blunkett) called the announcement 'a damp squib . . . an admission of failure'. On 25 February Virginia Bottomley announced the outcome of the Page inquiry into the failure of the London Ambulance Service computer-aided dispatch system, which had concluded that the speed of installing the new system had largely been to blame. Mr Blunkett called the report 'a damning indictment of Government complacency, inaction and irresponsibility'.

On 2 March Kenneth Clarke announced measures to combat juvenile crime, including the creation of a network of secure centres to house persistent offenders. Tony Blair agreed that 'the stress should be on care and education and training in secure accommodation'. On 4 March John Major announced changes to the honours system, making it more accessible to ordinary people, with automatic titles being abolished. Political honours would, however, remain. Lord Tebbit made his maiden speech in the Lords on 8 March in a debate on EC fraud. In an expression of frustration over the handling of the Maastricht debate on 8 March, 25 Labour back-bench MPs forced a late-night division on the draft British Gas PLC (Rateable Values) (Scotland) Order 1993. The next day the same ploy was used for the draft British Railways Board and British Telecommunications PLC (Rateable Values) (Scotland) Orders 1993. In the Lords on 9 March the Government defeated an attempt to amend Clause 1 of the Housing and Urban Development Bill by some large property-owning peers. On 10 March the attempt to get through the remaining ten draft Rateable Values (Scotland) Orders was reduced to a four-hour farce due to the dispute over the handling of the Maastricht debate, with each order going to a succession of non-stop votes, and a call of 'I Spy Strangers' by Labour MP Bob Cryer (a procedural motion that always requires a vote). Eventually, the Deputy Speaker (Michael Morris) ordered that instead of full divisions on each order, the vote could be taken by the ayes and noes standing in their places. There was also a row over the procedure whereby points of order during a division of the House can only be raised by an MP sitting with his head covered, preferably by the opera hat provided by the Serjeant-at-Arms, and a heated discussion over exactly what constituted a hat. On 11 March Virginia Bottomley made a statement on the guidelines in relation to medical staff found to be HIV-positive or who died from Aids-related diseases; they were being urgently reviewed and would be reissued later in the month. On 15 March Douglas Hurd made a statement about political developments in Hong Kong, in particular the adverse reaction of the Chinese government to the publication by the Governor, Chris Patten, of proposals for greater democracy.

THE BUDGET

On 16 March Norman Lamont presented his third Budget statement, the last to be presented in the spring as, from autumn 1993, the Budget and the autumn statement will be given as a unified financial statement in the autumn.

Income tax
– basic and higher rates unchanged; freeze on allowances
– increase in lowest tax band threshold to £2,500 in April 1993 and £3,000 in April 1994
– self-employed to pay tax on current year's profits

VAT
– extended to domestic fuel and power at 8 per cent from April 1994 and 17.5 per cent from 1995
– small business threshold raised to £37,600

National Insurance
– no change in employers' contributions
– main rate for employees and self-employed to rise by 1 per cent in 1993-4

Company cars
– scale charges up 8 per cent
– fuel scale charges up 20 per cent
– high business miles discount abolished

Excise duties
– fuels up by 10 per cent
– road tax up by £15
– most alcohol up by 5 per cent
– overall tobacco up by 6.5 per cent
– national lottery tickets to be taxed at 12 per cent for first year; winnings untaxed
– gaming machine duty to rise 20 per cent

Houses
– tax relief on mortgage interest restricted to 20 per cent from April 1994
– stamp duty threshold doubled to £60,000

Company taxation
– advance rate of Corporation Tax down to 22.5 per cent in 1993-4 and to 20 per cent in 1994-5
– tax credit for shareholders' dividends cut to 20 per cent in 1993-4
– improvements to export credits
– business rate not to increase in real terms
– relief on capital gains tax for certain reinvestments
– traders able to claim VAT relief on bad debts after six months and VAT penalties for late returns, etc., eased

Public sector borrowing requirement (PSBR)
– £35,100 million, for 1992-3
– government expenditure of 44.75 per cent of GDP in 1993-4 means a PSBR of £50,100 million (8 per cent of GDP) in that year
– objective: 'to bring the PSBR back towards balance over the medium term'

Unemployment
- new vocational education programme for 30,000
- expansion of business start-up schemes to 10,000 extra places
- community action programme for 60,000 long-term unemployed

Infrastructure
- Channel Tunnel rail link to proceed as a joint venture with private sector
- Heathrow Express Link to go ahead

Looking ahead, the Chancellor said that he was concerned to avoid 'excessive government borrowing over the medium term' preventing 'a sustained economic recovery'. He claimed that the economy 'enters this year in a more favourable position than most of our main competitors' having 'won' the battle against inflation.

In the debate on the Budget, John Smith reserved his keenest criticism for the proposals for VAT on domestic fuel, saying 'those who have listened to this debate will have been shocked beyond belief at the cynicism of the Conservative party which went into the last general election as the party committed to low taxation . . . This is a shameful budget . . . and I hope that the Conservatives live to regret it.' Speaking for the Liberal Democrats, Malcolm Bruce also saved his sharpest words for 'the appalling prospect of the introduction of full VAT on fuel in two years time' and went on to say 'the Budget is, effectively, a Budget of despair and a Budget of desperation which contains little for the unemployed and nothing for those struggling to cope with the recession. In it, the Chancellor merely exhorts those looking for hope and encouragement to hang on now. By God they will have to pay later.'

On 22 March John MacGregor announced the outcome of the review to decide on the preferred route for the link between the Channel Tunnel and London. A route through East London via Stratford was recommended and there would be consultation on whether this should terminate at St Pancras or King's Cross, with a decision in the autumn. John Prescott said the announcement 'confirms further delay, uncertainty and planning blight, with the completion of the line pushed into the next century'. On 25 March Michael Heseltine announced the conclusions of the Government's coal review. Robin Cook called it 'a comprehensive admission of failure . . . he has failed to find a market for one single extra tonne of coal'. On 29 March there was a debate on a motion to approve the Government's white paper on the coal industry, which the Government won. The Ulster Unionists either abstained or supported the Government, following a promise of £10 million extra from the Northern Ireland Office for industrial electricity use in Northern Ireland. Four Conservative MPs voted against the Government and 16 abstained. Labour MPs angry about the result of the vote pressed the next item on the order paper, a procedural motion to take note of an EC document, to the vote as well.

On 14 April Malcolm Rifkind reported on developments in Bosnia, including the decision to police the air exclusion zone with NATO aircraft. He reiterated that the UK was not in favour of armed intervention. David Clark agreed that 'it is truly through diplomacy, pressure and tighter economic sanctions that the Serbs will be made to sign the peace agreement, so that we have the possibility of lasting peace in that country'. On 19 April Douglas Hurd reported on the worsening situation in Bosnia and the role played by British troops in maintaining peace. The UN was intensifying sanctions against the Serbs. In the Lords the Government was defeated in committee on the Education Bill on 20 April when an amendment moved by the Labour peer Baroness David concerning the appointment of people with relevant experience for the provision of special educational needs was passed by 122 votes to 88.

The first of three days in committee of the whole House on the Finance (No. 2) Bill on 10 May saw Clause 42, imposing VAT on fuel and power for domestic use, approved by 295 votes to 285, with two Conservative MPs voting against the Government and six others abstaining. On 11 May the Secretary of State for Education (John Patten) announced that although the national curriculum tests in schools would go ahead in summer 1993 despite the threat of a national boycott, there would be a radical reduction in testing in future years to reduce the work load on teachers. Labour's Education spokesperson (Ann Taylor) felt 'his statement illustrates the utter confusion and chaos in Government circles on this year's tests . . . his obstinate and arrogant refusal to change this year's tests is incredible'. In the Lords the Government suffered two defeats on report on the Housing and Urban Development Bill; the first was on a new clause moved by Lord Cavendish (C.) to exempt up to 60 stately homes from the leasehold enfranchisement provisions of the Bill, which was passed by 114 votes to 57; the second was on Clause 5 (Qualifying Tenants), when it failed to organize any tellers for the division against an amendment moved by Baroness Hamwee (LD) relating to registered housing associations. Later the Government also accepted an amendment imposing a residency requirement, so that at least half of the leaseholders seeking to buy a freehold must have lived in the property for twelve months or more. The Minister for Industry (Tim Sainsbury) outlined on 12 May the measures that the Government would be taking to help Tyneside following heavy job losses after Swan Hunter failed to win the £170 million order for a new helicopter carrier. On 13 May Kenneth Clarke announced that arrangements would be made to abolish the unit fines system that had been introduced under the Criminal Justice Act 1991 as 'it is plainly not working as Parliament would have liked', and that courts would be given back the power to consider all a criminal's previous convictions when deciding on a sentence. Amendments would be introduced to the Criminal Justice Bill currently before the

Commons to effect these changes. Tony Blair commented that 'never have we seen so quick a collapse of government policy, even for the present Government'. In the Lords on 18 May the Government announced a concession on report on the Housing and Urban Development Bill enabling more flat owners to buy 90-year extensions on their leases by including those who pay a low ground rent and whose leases had more than 21 years to run when purchased. On 20 May it accepted an amendment moved by Lord Monk Bretton (C.) to allow councils to refuse to sell homes reserved for the elderly. On 24 May in the Lords the Government requested extra time in committee on the Trade Union Reform and Employment Rights Bill to incorporate amendments necessitated by recent decisions of the Employment Appeal Tribunal and judgments of the Court of Appeal. Although not greeted with universal acclaim, the amendments were passed and the bill received an unopposed third reading. On 25 May in the Lords, on the third reading of the Housing and Urban Development Bill, an amendment moved by Lord Carnock (C.) over the low rent test was defeated when the division was 131 votes in favour and 131 votes against, as the Lord Chancellor had to cast his vote against the amendment. The Government was defeated on an amendment moved by Lord Peyton of Yeovil (C.) to exempt properties within the precincts of cathedrals from the enfranchisement provisions.

On 9 June the former Chancellor Norman Lamont made a personal statement on his resignation in which he was critical of the way the Government handled policy and, to a certain extent, of the policy itself. He maintained that far too many decisions were made for '36 hours' publicity' and that the Government gave the impression of 'being in office but not in power'. That evening the Government defeated an opposition motion condemning it for betraying election promises on economic and social policy by 302 votes to 278. In the Lords on 14 June the Government suffered two defeats on the report stage of the Education Bill; first on an amendment to Clause 148 moved by Lord Haddington (C.) designed to ensure the correct allocation of resources for special educational needs; and secondly on an amendment to Clause 151 moved by Lord Campbell of Alloway (C.) on codes of practice. On 15 June the Commons approved the new clause added in the Lords to the Trade Union Reform and Employment Rights Bill on action short of dismissal: non-infringing actions. In a debate on 22 June on an opposition motion on the funding of political parties, in the wake of the Asil Nadir revelations, the Labour MP Clive Soley caused uproar by accusing Michael Heseltine, then ill in hospital in Venice, of having asked the Saudi government for money for the Conservative Party. John Major reported on the outcome of the European Community meeting in Copenhagen, where the principal issues were promoting economic growth throughout the EC and options for economic revival

in the medium term. During Prime Minister's questions on 24 June John Major announced that he had reluctantly accepted the resignation of Michael Mates, Minister of State at the Northern Ireland Office, following allegations about his dealings with Asil Nadir. Malcolm Rifkind announced that the order for the £5,000 million Trident nuclear submarine refit programme had been awarded to Devonport dockyard rather than Rosyth. In view of the controversy surrounding this decision the Speaker granted an emergency debate on the issue that evening. Dissatisfied Labour MPs forced a division which they lost by 281 votes to 209. On 28 June Douglas Hurd expressed the view that the attack on Baghdad by American cruise missiles on 26 June, in response to uncovering a plot to assassinate former President Bush, was 'justified and a proportionate exercise of the right of self-defence'. Immediately before a debate on a Liberal Democrat motion on the thermal oxide reprocessing plant (THORP) at Sellafield, the Government unexpectedly announced that it would hold further consultations before taking a final decision on whether to authorize the use of THORP, although its amendment to the motion, which was carried by 157 votes to 43, supported the commissioning of the plant 'at the earliest practicable date' subject to necessary authorizations. On 29 June Michael Mates made a personal statement on his resignation from the Government over his alleged involvement in the Asil Nadir affair and defied the Speaker's attempts to stop him referring to matters that are *sub judice*.

On 1 July John Patten proposed a three-part reform of student unions, designed to make them more accountable and fully representative and limiting their funding. One of Labour's Education team, Jeff Rooker, called the announcement 'an absolute disgrace'. On 5 July an opposition motion criticizing the Government for failing to save twelve threatened pits from closure despite earlier assurances was defeated by 308 votes to 286. In the Lords the Government was defeated in committee on the Railways Bill when an amendment moved by Lord Peyton of Yeovil (C.) which would allow British Rail to bid for the various franchises on offer was passed by 150 votes to 112. On 6 July in the Lords a government amendment to the Education Bill was added on third reading to allow parents to choose whether their children should attend sex education lessons at school. On 12 July John Major reported on the outcome of the G7 summit in Tokyo, including the breakthrough in the GATT negotiations. On the first day of the report stage of the Finance (No. 2) Bill, the Conservative back-bench MP William Powell attempted to reverse the decision on VAT on fuel but was defeated by 307 votes to 299. Two other Conservative MPs voted against the Government. On 15 July in the Lords a motion moved by Lord Bonham-Carter (LD) calling on the Government to give full British citizenship to members of the non-Chinese ethnic minorities in Hong Kong who would be without the right of abode elsewhere after 1997 was passed against the Government's wishes. The Commons overturned the government defeats in the Lords on the Education Bill on 19 July. On 21 July Peter Brooke announced the outcome of the Price Waterhouse review of the Arts Council, which included cutting the membership from 20 to 16 and making the Council accountable to Parliament for its decisions. On 26 July the Lords accepted the amendments to the Education Bill by which the Commons had overturned the Lords' original intentions. On 27 July the Lords agreed to carry over to the autumn further special committee consideration of Schedule 10 of the Railways Bill. The Commons rose for the summer recess on 27 July. The Lords met on 28 July to discuss the statement on defence estimates 1993 and then rose for the summer recess themselves.

THE MAASTRICHT ACT

The key events in the passing of the European Communities (Amendment) Act 1993 were as follows:

1992

May 7. First Reading in the House of Commons. **20–21.** Second Reading in the House of Commons – the second reading was passed by 336 votes to 92. The Liberal Democrats (except one) voted with the Government, the Labour Party officially abstained and 22 Conservative MPs voted against the Government. An opposition motion declining to give the Bill a second reading because it allowed the UK to opt out of the social chapter was defeated by 360 votes to 261. **June 2.** The Danes rejected the Treaty in their first referendum. **3.** The Prime Minister promised a further debate on the Bill before the committee stage began. **September 16.** Sterling was suspended from the ERM. **November 4.** The Government won the paving debate allowing the Bill to proceed into committee by 319 votes to 316. The Liberal Democrats voted with the Government and 23 Conservative MPs voted against. **5.** The Prime Minister announced that the Bill would not receive its third reading until after the second Danish referendum in May 1993. **December 1.** Commons Committee Stage – MPs began 23 days of debating the Bill in committee on the floor of the House. Over 500 amendments to the three-clause Bill were proposed.

1993

February 15. The Foreign Secretary (Douglas Hurd) announced that fresh legal advice had suggested that parliamentary defeat over the Labour amendment (amendment 27) on the social chapter would not stop the UK ratifying the Treaty, which contradicted earlier advice given by Tristan Garel-Jones, Minister of State at the Foreign Office. **22.** The Chairman of Ways and Means (Committee chairman), Michael Morris, accepted an application by the Labour Party for an emergency debate on the conflicting statements on the legal interpretation of amendment 27 and this

replaced the planned committee stage debate. The Attorney-General (Sir Nicholas Lyell) reiterated that even if the amendment were passed the Treaty would still be ratified. The closure motion was passed without division because no member would act as a teller in the government lobby. **March 8.** The Government was defeated on an opposition motion concerning membership of the Council of the Regions by 314 votes to 292. **15.** The Committee chairman, Michael Morris, ruled that MPs could not vote on amendment 27, which would remove the Government's ability to opt out of the social chapter, but allowed a division on another Labour amendment requiring a further debate on the social chapter before final ratification of the Treaty. Rather than lose the vote, the Government accepted the amendment. **19.** Amended Clause 1 of the Bill was passed by 296 votes to 96. Clause 2 (unamended) was passed by 271 votes to 55. Clause 3 (unamended) was passed without division. **22.** The House rejected the call for a referendum on the Maastricht Treaty; the committee stage was completed after 163 hours of debate. **May 4.** Commons Report Stage – the Speaker (Betty Boothroyd) announced that she would allow a division on a new Labour amendment, virtually identical to amendment 27, which would delete the Government's social chapter opt-out from the Bill. Facing certain defeat by an alliance of Labour, Liberal Democrat and Conservative Euro-sceptic MPs, the Foreign Secretary announced that the Government would accept the amendment as it would have no legal effect on the Government's ability to ratify the Treaty. **5.** Report stage completed. **20.** Third Reading in the House of Commons – the Government secured the third reading by 292 votes to 112. The Labour Party officially abstained, although five MPs voted with the Government and 66 against; the Liberal Democrats voted with the Government; 41 Conservative MPs voted against the Government and five abstained. **24.** First Reading in the House of Lords. **June 7–8.** Second Reading in the House of Lords; the second reading was agreed without division. **22.** Lords Committee Stage – the first of six days in committee, which concluded without any amendments being passed. **July 12.** Lords Report Stage – the first of three days on report. **14.** An amendment moved by Lord Blake (C.) calling for a British referendum was defeated by 445 votes to 176. **19.** Lord Rees-Mogg secured permission in the High Court for a judicial review of the legitimacy of the ratification process in Britain. **20.** Third Reading in the House of Lords – the Bill secured a third reading by 141 votes to 29, completing its parliamentary stages, and received royal assent that evening. **21.** The Speaker said that in her view the questioning of parliamentary proceedings by the courts would be contrary to the Bill of Rights 1689 but that this would be a matter for the House of Lords to pursue. **22.** Debate on the social chapter – the Commons and Lords debated identical motions on the social chapter. In the Lords, the opposition amendment suggesting that ratification of the Treaty could not take place 'until such time as the Government have given notification to the EC that it intends to adopt the agreement attached to the protocol on social policy' was defeated by 295 votes to 88. The government motion 'noting the policy of Her Majesty's Government on the adoption of the protocol on social policy' was carried by 271 votes to 85. In the Commons no resolution was reached: the Labour amendment was defeated (the vote was thought to be 317 votes in favour and against, with the Speaker therefore casting her vote with the Government in accordance with precedent. It was later discovered that the original vote was 316 for and 317 against.) The government motion was lost by 324 votes to 316. On the amendment some 15 Conservative MPs voted against the Government and eight abstained. On the main motion 23 Conservative MPs voted against the Government with one abstention. The Ulster Unionists voted with the Government; both parties denied that they had made a deal. As the Act required both Houses to come to a resolution on the social chapter before the Maastricht Treaty could be ratified by the UK, the Prime Minister announced that the Government would table a revised motion for debate the next day, making the issue a matter of confidence in the Government. He threatened to call a general election if the Government were defeated. **23.** Confidence Motion – the Government defeated the Labour amendment (identical to the previous day's amendment) by 339 votes to 301. The government motion, that 'this House has confidence in the policy of HM Government on the adoption of the protocol on social policy' was carried by 339 votes to 299. Only one Conservative MP (Rupert Allason) abstained, as he had done the day before, and subsequently the Conservative whip was 'suspended' from Mr Allason, one step short of withdrawing it altogether. **30.** Lord Rees-Mogg's High Court action challenging the legality of the ratification process failed. **August 2.** The United Kingdom formally ratified the Maastricht Treaty.

PUBLIC ACTS OF PARLIAMENT

This list is of those Public Acts which were enacted after August 1992. The date stated after each Act is the date on which it came into operation; c. indicates the chapter number of each Act

Boundary Commissions Act 1992, c. 55, 12 November 1992
Makes various provisions with respect to the membership of the Boundary Commissions and the content and timing of their reports

Maintenance Orders (Reciprocal Enforcement) Act 1992, c. 56, 15 April 1993
Makes various amendments to the Maintenance Orders (Facilities for Enforcement) Act 1920 and the Act of 1922

Sporting Events (Control of Alcohol, etc.) (Amendment) Act 1992, c. 57, 3 December 1992
Extends the maximum period for which an order can be made under section 3 of the 1985 Act from five to 12 months

Car Tax (Abolition) Act 1992, c. 58, deemed to be in force from 13 November 1992
Abolishes car tax

Consolidated Fund (No. 3) Act 1992, c. 59, 17 December 1992
Applies certain sums out of the Consolidated Fund to the service of the years ending 31 March 1993 and 1994

Sea Fish (Conservation) Act 1992, c. 60, various dates
Amends the 1967 Act with regard to licences

Civil Service (Management Functions) Act 1992, c. 61, 17 December 1992
Makes various provisions relating to the management of the home civil service and corresponding provision for Northern Ireland

Gas (Exempt Supplies) Act 1993, c. 1, day or days to be appointed
Amends section 5 of the Gas Act 1986 (which deals with unauthorized supplies)

British Coal and British Rail (Transfer Proposals) Act 1993, c. 2, 19 January 1993
Confers certain powers on the British Coal Corporation and the British Railways Board to pave the way for the possible transfer of their functions, property, rights and liabilities

Social Security Act 1993, c. 3, various dates
Amends the 1986 Act to provide for the making of certain payments into the National Insurance Fund

Consolidated Fund Act 1993, c. 4, 18 February 1993
Applies certain sums out of the Consolidated Fund to the services of the year ending 31 March 1993

Damages (Scotland) Act 1993, c. 5, 18 April 1993
Clarifies and amends the law relating to the rights of relatives and executors to claim damages in respect of the death of a person from or the loss of expectation of life caused by personal injuries

Bankruptcy (Scotland) Act 1993, c. 6, various dates
Makes various amendments to the 1985 Act

Consolidated Fund (No. 2) Act 1993, c. 7, 29 March 1993
Applies certain sums out of the Consolidated Fund to the service of the years ending 31 March 1992 and 1993

Judicial Pensions and Retirement Act 1993, c. 8, day or days to be appointed

Makes provision with respect to the pensions and other related benefits payable to persons who have held judicial and other related offices; it also makes provision for amending the law in relation to the duration of certain judicial offices; and for connected purposes

Prisoners and Criminal Proceedings (Scotland) Act 1993, c. 9, various dates
Amends the law of Scotland with respect to the detention, transfer and release of persons serving sentences of imprisonment, etc., or committed or remanded in custody; makes further provision as regards evidence and procedure in Scottish criminal proceedings; and for connected purposes

Charities Act 1993, c. 10, various dates
Consolidates various enactments relating to the workings and organization of charities

Clean Air Act 1993, c. 11, 27 August 1993
Consolidates the enactments relating to the preservation of the environment in terms of air

Radioactive Substances Act 1993, c. 12, 27 August 1993
Consolidates various enactments relating to the protection of the environment through the control and regulation of radioactive substances

Carrying of Knives (Scotland) Act 1993, c. 13, 27 May 1993
Creates a new Scottish offence of having an article with a blade or point in a public place

Disability (Grants) Act 1993, c. 14, 27 May 1993
Provides for the Secretary of State and the DHSS for Northern Ireland to make grants to the Independent Living (Extension) Fund, the Independent Living (1993) Fund and Motability

Protection of Animals (Scotland) Act 1993, c. 15, 27 July 1993
Provides for the penalties for certain offences under the 1912 Act to be increased

Foreign Compensation (Amendment) Act 1993, c. 16, 27 July 1993
Amends the 1950 Act by extending the powers to make Orders in Council under section 3

Non-Domestic Rating Act 1993, c. 17, part on 4 June and the balance on 6 July 1993
Makes further provision with respect to the limit on increase in non-domestic rates between 1 April 1993 and 31 March 1995

Reinsurance (Acts of Terrorism) Act 1993, c. 18, 27 May 1993
Makes provision for the payment out of money provided by Parliament or into the Consolidated Fund of certain sums to cover reinsurance liabilities entered into by the Secretary of State in respect of loss or damage to property resulting from or consequential upon acts of terrorism

Trade Union and Employment Rights Act 1993, c. 19, day or days to be appointed
Makes further provision relating to trade unions and industrial relations with regard to internal union procedures and the rights of employees in relation to union membership; amends the law relating to maternity rights, unfair dismissal, redundancy and sexual discrimination; abolishes the right to statutory minimum remuneration; makes further provision for the employment and training functions of Scottish Enterprise and Highlands and Islands Enterprise; and for connected purposes

Licensing (Amendment) (Scotland) Act 1993, c. 20, 1 July 1993
Amends the 1973 Act with regard to the issuing of a certificate in relation to planning

Osteopaths Act 1993, c. 21, day or days to be appointed
Makes provision for the regulation of the profession, establishes the General Osteopathic Council, provides for registration of osteopaths, the monitoring of their education and the development and promotion of their profession; and for connected purposes

Merchant Shipping (Registration, etc.) Act 1993, c. 22, day or days to be appointed
Amends and restates the law relating to the registration of ships, enables the registration of ships on bareboat charter and facilitates the consolidation of merchant shipping legislation

Asylum and Immigration Appeals Act 1993, c. 23, various dates, some to be appointed
Makes provision relating to the processes and procedures relating to claims for asylum and amends the law relating to certain rights of appeal under the Immigration Act 1971

Video Recordings Act 1993, c. 24, 20 September 1993
Amends the 1984 Act and, so far as it relates to evidence under the 1984 Act, the Criminal Justice (Scotland) Act 1980; for example, the Act provides for the assigning of a unique title to each video work in respect of which a classification certificate is issued

Local Government (Overseas Assistance) Act 1993, c. 25, 20 September 1993
Enables local authorities in Great Britain to provide assistance as respects matters in which they have skill and experience to bodies engaged outside the UK in the carrying on of any of the activities of local government

Bail (Amendment) Act 1993, c. 26, day to be appointed
Confers upon the prosecution a right of appeal against decisions to grant bail in certain cases, such as where the offence is punishable by a term of imprisonment of five or more years

Local Government (Amendment) Act 1993, c. 27, 20 September 1993

Amends section 11 of the 1966 Act to permit grants to be made to local authorities making special provisions in exercising their functions, in consequence of the presence within their areas of persons belonging to ethnic minorities

Leasehold Reform, Housing and Urban Development Act 1993, c. 28, day or days to be appointed

Inter alia confers rights to collective enfranchisement and lease renewal on tenants of flats and makes further provision as to the enfranchisement of tenants of houses; establishes and confers functions upon a body to replace the English Industrial Estates Corporation by the Urban Regeneration Agency; makes further provision with respect to urban development corporations and urban development areas

Representation of the People Act 1993, c. 29, 20 July 1993

Secures that members of the regular army who, except for the purposes of training, are required to serve only in Northern Ireland are not regarded as members of the forces for the purposes of the 1983 Act

Sexual Offences Act 1993, c. 30, 20 September 1993

Abolishes the presumption of criminal law that a boy under the age of 14 is incapable of sexual intercourse

Road Traffic (Driving Instruction by Disabled Persons) Act 1993, c. 31, day to be appointed

Makes provision for enabling persons with certain physical disabilities to be authorized, in certain circumstances, to give paid instruction in the driving of motor cars; and for connected purposes

European Communities (Amendment) Act 1993, c. 32, after each House has passed the relevant resolution

Makes provision consequential on the Treaty on European Union signed at Maastricht on 7 February 1992

Appropriation Act 1993, c. 33, 27 July 1993

Applies a sum out of the Consolidated Fund to the service of the year ending 31 March 1994;

appropriates the supplies granted in this session of Parliament and repeals certain Consolidated Fund and Appropriation Acts

Finance Act 1993, c. 34, 27 July 1993

Grants certain duties, alters others and amends the law relating to the National Debt and the Public Revenue. *Inter alia*, this huge Act makes changes to the taxation of car benefits and relocation expenses for employees; alters the rates of excise duties; changes the rules relating to certain appeals for VAT; makes domestic fuel chargeable to VAT from 1994; restricts the level at which married couple's relief applies; makes major changes with regard to the taxation of exchange gains and losses to replace the pre-existing case law and Revenue practice; brings in new provisions for Lloyds underwriters; abolishes oil taxation; extends the reliefs for inheritance tax relating to certain difficult-to-sell assets which have fallen in value; gives relief from stamp duty to certain rent-to-mortgate/loan transactions under the right-to-buy provisions in the Housing Acts

Education Act 1993, c. 35, day or days to be appointed

Amends the law about education; *inter alia* the Act sets up a Special Educational Needs Tribunal, requires that each grant-maintained school shall have governing instruments and as to the contents and amendment of the same, and provides for school attendance orders

Criminal Justice Act 1993, c. 36, various dates

Makes many amendments to the law relating to criminal justice, including provision about the jurisdiction of courts in relation to dishonesty and blackmail, the law relating to drug trafficking, the law relating to insider dealing in securities, the penalties for causing death by dangerous driving, and as regards the financing of terrorism, its proceeds and its investigation

Agriculture Act 1993, c. 37, 27 September 1993

Makes provision about milk marketing and potato marketing, for the payment of grants in connection with the marketing of certain commodities, and for other purposes connected with agriculture

---

WHITE PAPERS, ETC.

The second annual White Paper reporting progress on the 1990 White Paper *This Common Inheritance* was presented to Parliament by the Secretary of State for the Environment (Michael Howard) on 1 October 1992. It reviewed 440 environmental commitments and made 441 further proposals. The main proposals included:

- the use of economic instruments rather than legal controls to achieve improvements to the environment, whenever possible

- taxing the burning of fossil fuels (a 'carbon tax')
- charges on emissions, to be levied on water and noise pollution and on waste
- product charges on fertilizers and pesticides
- a deposit refund scheme for car batteries
- permits for the emission of pollutants, such as sulphur dioxide, up to a limit; unused emission quotas to be tradable between producers
- the incorporation of environmental considerations into development plans

- the implementation of the 'Action for the Countryside' programme, including the expansion of the Environmentally Sensitive Areas and Countryside Stewardship schemes and the new Countryside Employment Programme

A White Paper reporting progress on the operation of the Citizen's Charter was presented to Parliament by the Minister for Public Service and Science (William Waldegrave) on 25 November 1992. It said that over 90 per cent of the original 150 Charter commitments had been met or were 'in hand'. It also proposed 80 new measures, including:
- extending the Patient's Charter to cover primary health care
- introducing comparative league tables to monitor the performance of local government
- publishing a further and higher education charter
- setting higher standards for British Rail
- extending the use of external services in the Civil Service (up to £1.5 billion worth of central government activity will be put out to tender by the end of 1993)

Local Government in Wales: A Charter for the Future, presented to Parliament by the Secretary of State for Wales (David Hunt) on 1 March 1993, proposed:
- 21 new unitary authorities to replace the present structure of eight county and 37 district councils
- the former counties of Monmouthshire, Carmarthenshire, Cardiganshire, Flintshire, Pembrokeshire and Denbighshire to be revived
- Clwyd, Dyfed, Gwynedd and Gwent to disappear as administrative counties but be retained for parliamentary boundary purposes
- the new authorities to come into being on 1 April 1995

Scotland in the Union: A Partnership for Good, presented to Parliament by the Secretary of State for Scotland (Ian Lang) on 9 March 1993, proposed 50 measures including:
- extending the powers and functions of the Scottish Grand Committee, including its powers to scrutinize Scottish bills and to question ministers
- transferring responsibility for policy and schemes affecting Scotland to the Scottish Office from other government bodies
- appointing more Scots to public bodies
- moving more civil servants to Scotland
- raising the profile of the Scottish Office
- a report to be published annually by the Scottish Office
- new citizen's charters specifically for Scotland

The Prospects for Coal, presented to Parliament by the President of the Board of Trade (Michael Heseltine) on 25 March 1993, was the result of a review set up in October 1992 after the announcement that 31 pits would close. It made the following points and proposals:

- twelve of the 31 pits to remain open for up to two years
- one pit to cease production but continue development work
- six pits to be mothballed under a care and maintenance programme
- the ten pits where production had already ceased to remain closed
- a further two pits to close immediately
- the pits remaining open to be subsidized temporarily to enable them to compete with cheaper imported coal and to achieve cost reductions; the subsidy to be reduced progressively as privatization approaches
- no steps to be taken to expand the market for coal
- all pits earmarked for closure to be offered for sale to the private sector for operation under licence
- the coal industry to be prepared for full privatization by 1995

Realizing Our Potential, a White Paper on science, engineering and technology, was presented to Parliament by the Chancellor of the Duchy of Lancaster and Minister for Public Service and Science (William Waldegrave) on 26 May 1993. It proposed:
- a new Council for Science and Technology to replace the Advisory Council on Science and Technology, with the remit of clarifying research objectives and focusing more directly on the needs of industry and commerce
- the Council to produce an annual 'Forward Look' of projections for up to ten years ahead
- a new technique, Technology Foresight, to be used to identify key areas for investment and to define priorities
- research funding to be allocated 'on the scale necessary' and not to be centralized
- a new post, Director-General of Research Councils, to be created
- the purpose of each research council to be clearly defined
- the Science and Engineering Research Council to be split into an Engineering and Physical Sciences Research Council and a Particle Physics and Astronomy Research Council; its biotechnology directorate to transfer to the Agricultural and Food Research Council to form a new Biotechnology and Biological Sciences Research Council
- science and technology graduates wishing to pursue a higher degree to undertake a one-year M.Sc. course before starting a Ph.D.
- a review to be conducted into about 100 departmental research establishments with a view to possible privatization

Police Reform: A Police Service for the 21st Century was presented to Parliament by the Home Secretary (Michael Howard) on 28 June 1993. It made the following proposals:
- the central government grant to the police service to be cash-limited; the Government to give up

control over manpower levels and most capital expenditure
- local police authorities to have independent status and to be limited to 16 members
- local police authorities to set their own budgets within their own standard spending assessment; authorities to be individually liable to capping; about 10 per cent of their budgets to be raised from council tax
- local police authorities to consult people in their area about local policing
- local police authorities to monitor the performance of the local force; the authorities' performance to be monitored by the Home Office
- the Inspectorate of Constabulary to be strengthened and new inspectors to be appointed from outside the police service; the Inspectorate's remit to include the Metropolitan Police
- a new body to be set up to oversee the Metropolitan Police
- the number and pattern of police forces to be retained at present but procedures for amalgamating forces to be made quicker in future
- the management of police forces to be streamlined; changes in police rank structure, pay and conditions of service to be recommended by the Sheehy inquiry (see below)

The report of the *Inquiry into Police Responsibilities and Rewards* set up by the former Home Secretary (Kenneth Clarke) and chaired by Sir Patrick Sheehy, chairman of BAT Industries, was published on 30 June 1993. It made the following main recommendations:
- all new officers to be appointed for a fixed term of ten years, with contracts renewable every five years thereafter
- the ranks of chief inspector, chief superintendent and deputy chief constable to be abolished
- 5,000 middle-rank posts to be abolished, and 3,000 extra posts to be created at constable level
- pay scales to reflect experience, responsibility and the difficulty of the job; local flexibility to reward success
- overtime to be abolished, but performance-related bonuses to be introduced
- index-linked pay awards to be abolished; pay rises to be linked to performance
- retirement age to be raised to 60

Defending Our Future, a statement on the defence estimates for 1993, was presented to Parliament by the Secretary of State for Defence (Malcolm Rifkind) on 5 July 1993. A series of 'adjustments' was announced, including cuts beyond those required to meet the £1.05 billion reduction in the defence budget announced in November 1992. Manpower figures announced earlier in the year were confirmed, i.e. Royal Navy 52,500 (55,000 under Options for Change); Army 119,000 (116,000); and Royal Air Force 70,000 (75,000). The adjustments included:
- a reduction in the surface fleet to about 35

destroyers and frigates (about 40 under Options for Change)
- the elimination of the new Upholder class of submarines
- the number of mine countermeasure ships to be reduced to 25
- the force of Tornado F3 fighters to be reduced to 100, reorganized into six instead of seven squadrons
- the purchase of a new medium surface-to-air missile to be postponed
- Britain to withdraw from a collaborative programme to develop an indirect fire anti-armour weapon; an air-launched weapon to be bought instead
- tenders had been invited for an attack helicopter for the Army

The report of the Royal Commission on Criminal Justice, chaired by Viscount Runciman of Doxford, was presented to Parliament on 6 July 1993. It made 352 recommendations concerning police investigations, safeguards for suspects, the 'right of silence' and confession evidence, the prosecution, pre-trial procedures in the Crown Court, the trial, forensic science and other expert evidence, the Court of Appeal and corrections of miscarriages of justice. The recommendations included the following:
- in cases involving 'either way' offences, the defendant should no longer have the right to trial by jury
- the Home Secretary's power to refer cases to the Court of Appeal should be removed and a new authority should be set up; the authority should consider alleged miscarriages of justice, ensure that any further investigation is undertaken, and refer miscarriage of justice cases to the Court of Appeal
- the substance of the defence should be disclosed in advance of a trial where the defendant intends to contest the charges
- adverse inferences should not be drawn from a defendant's silence at the police station
- in cases of serious and complex fraud, the director of the Serious Fraud Office should be able to authorize police officers attached to the Office to require suspects to answer questions
- the system of sentence discounts should be more clearly articulated
- in exceptional cases either the prosecution or the defence should be able to apply to the judge before the trial for the selection of a jury containing up to three people from ethnic minorities
- the Court of Appeal should be more prepared to overturn jury verdicts, order retrials, receive fresh evidence and accept alleged errors by trial lawyers as a ground of appeal
- there should be further research to establish the extent to which members of ethnic minorities suffer discrimination
- there should be an overhaul of detective training

- continuous video recording of all the activities in the custody office at police stations, and the passages and stairways leading from the custody office to the cells, should be introduced as soon as practicable
- further consideration, and research, needed to decide whether video recording of police interviews with suspects should be introduced
- all ranks of police officers should receive training in interviewing skills
- the police should have the power to take without consent non-intimate samples for the purpose of DNA analysis from all those arrested for serious criminal offences; saliva should be reclassified as a non-intimate sample
- committal for trial proceedings in their present form should be abolished
- new pre-trial procedures should be introduced to clarify and define the issues in the case; in more complex cases, either party should be able to require a preparatory hearing to secure rulings on the main issues
- greater use should be made of read witness statements in court where the witness is afraid to give oral evidence
- judges should be able to exclude evidence that, although relevant, may confuse the issues, mislead the jury, cause undue delay, waste time, or lead to needless presentation of cumulative evidence
- a new Forensic Science Advisory Council should be set up to oversee the standards and provision of forensic science services
- the Contempt of Court Act 1981 should be amended to allow research into juries' reasons for their verdicts

Shaping the Future - The New Councils, a White Paper on the structure of local government in Scotland, was presented to Parliament by the Secretary of State for Scotland (Ian Lang) on 8 July 1993. It made the following proposals:
- the nine regional councils and 53 district councils to be replaced by 25 single-tier councils; the three island councils to remain single-tier authorities
- elections to be held to shadow authorities in 1995, with the new authorities taking over on 1 April 1996
- elections to be held every three years from 1999
The White Paper also discussed the provision of services by the new councils; their internal management; their financing; transitional costs and arrangements; and consequences for other bodies and organizations

Open Government was presented to Parliament by the Chancellor of the Duchy of Lancaster (William Waldegrave) on 15 July 1993. It made the following main proposals:
- a non-statutory code of practice to be introduced from April 1994 setting out the circumstances in which government departments will volunteer information and those in which they will produce information on request; similar codes to be introduced for the National Health Service and local authorities
- certain areas to be exempt, including defence, national security and international policy advice; sensitive information relating to the management of the economy and collection of tax; and law enforcement and legal proceedings
- the Parliamentary Commissioner for Administration to have the right to examine any decision to withhold information
- 'harm tests' to be extended to the unauthorized disclosure of confidential information held by the state; harm or damage to be the criterion for prosecution
- the number of government documents withheld for more than 30 years to be substantially reduced; all records to be released unless actual damage would be caused
- a statutory right of access to personal files compiled by government and other public sector authorities to be introduced; provisions to be made for correcting inaccurate, misleading or out-of-date information
- the D-notice system, under which the media agree not to disclose information that could threaten national security, to be reformed

The Queen's Awards

The Queen's Award for Export Achievement and The Queen's Award for Technological Achievement were instituted by Royal Warrant in 1976. The two separate awards took the place of The Queen's Award to Industry, which had been instituted in 1965. In 1992 the scheme was extended with the launch of a third award, The Queen's Award for Environmental Achievement.

The awards are designed to recognize and encourage outstanding achievements in exporting goods or services from the United Kingdom and in advancing process or product technology. The purpose of the new award is to recognize and encourage product and process development which has major benefit for the environment and which is commercially successful.

The awards differ from a personal royal honour in that they are given to a unit as a whole, management and employees working as a team. They may be applied for by any organization within the United Kingdom, the Channel Islands or the Isle of Man producing goods or services which meet the criteria for the awards. Eligibility is not influenced in any way by the particular activities of the unit applying, its location, or size. Units or agencies of central and local government with industrial functions, as well as research associations, educational institutions and bodies of a similar character, are also eligible, provided that they can show they have contributed to industrial efficiency.

Each award is formally conferred by a grant of appointment and is symbolized by a representation of its emblem cast in stainless steel and encapsulated in a transparent acrylic block.

Awards are held for five years and holders are entitled to fly the appropriate award flag and to display the emblem on the packaging of goods produced in this country, on the goods themselves, on the unit's stationery, in advertising and on certain articles used by employees. Units may also display the emblem of any previous current awards during the five years.

Awards are announced on 21 April (the birthday of The Queen) and published formally in a special supplement to the London Gazette.

AWARDS OFFICE

All enquiries about the scheme and requests for application forms (completed forms must be returned by 31 October) should be made to: The Secretary, The Queen's Awards Office, Dean Bradley House, 52 Horseferry Road, London SW1P 2AG. Tel: 071–222 2277.

EXPORT ACHIEVEMENT

The criterion upon which recommendations for an award for export achievement is based is a substantial and sustained increase in export earnings to a level which is outstanding for the products or services concerned and for the size of the applicant unit's operations. Account will be taken of any special market factors described in the application. Applicants for the award will be expected to explain the basis of the achievement (e.g. improved marketing organization or new initiative to cater for export markets) and this will be taken into consideration. Export earnings considered will include receipts by the applicant unit in this country from the export of goods produced in this country, and the provision of services to non-residents. Account will be taken of the overseas expenses incurred other than marketing expenses. Income from profits (after overseas tax) remitted to this country from the applicant unit's direct investments in its overseas branches, subsidiaries or associates in the same general line of business will be taken into account, but not receipts from profits on other overseas investments or by interest on overseas loans or credits.

In 1993, The Queen's Award for Export Achievement was conferred on the following concerns:

Rotherham and Bradford Branch of AES Engineering Ltd, Rotherham, South Yorkshire
ASM (Orchestra) Ltd (t/a The Academy of St Martin-in-the-Fields), London E1
Advent Communications Ltd, Chesham, Bucks
Airwair Ltd, Wellingborough, Northants
Appletise PLC, Woking, Surrey
A. E. Arthur Ltd, King's Lynn, Norfolk
Autovalet Systems International Ltd, London NW10
BCB International Ltd, Cardiff
BT & D Technologies Ltd, Ipswich
Edward Baker Ltd, Sudbury, Suffolk
Banque Paribas Export Finance Unit, London W1
Bioscot Ltd, Edinburgh
Booster Electric Vehicles Ltd, Huddersfield, West Yorkshire
Borden Decorative Products Ltd (Transprints Division), Morecambe, Lancs
CADCentre Ltd, Cambridge
Canadian Pizza Crust Co. (UK) Ltd, Salford
Carron Bathrooms Ltd, Carron, Falkirk
Caterham Cars Ltd, Caterham, Surrey
Chadwicks of Bury Ltd, Bury, Lancs
Churchill Tableware Ltd, Stoke-on-Trent
ConvaTec Ltd, Deeside, Clwyd
Cookson Entek Ltd, Newcastle upon Tyne
The Copyrights Company Ltd, Milton, Banbury, Oxon
Croda Kerr Ltd, Liverpool
Derwent MacDee Ltd, Doncaster, South Yorkshire
Desurvey Ltd, Birkenhead, Merseyside
Dunphy Combustion Ltd, Rochdale, Lancs
Dynacast International Ltd, Alcester, Warks
Epitaxial Products International Ltd, Cardiff
Europalite Ltd, Mansfield, Notts
Europressings Ltd, Cardiff
FMC Corporation (UK) Ltd, Wellhead Equipment Division, Dunfermline, Fife
Financial Times Group Ltd, London SE1

Ford Motor Company Ltd, Brentwood, Essex
Foster Refrigerator (UK) Ltd, Kings Lynn, Norfolk
Foster Wheeler Energy Ltd, Reading, Berks
GEC ALSTHOM Transmission & Distribution Projects Ltd (TaDPoLe), Stafford
Gaffney, Cline & Associates Ltd, Alton, Hants
The Good Book Guide Ltd, London WCI
Griffith Laboratories, European Group Bakery Business Unit, Somercotes, Derby
Hanover Displays Ltd, Lewes, East Sussex
Harrison & Sons Ltd, High Wycombe, Bucks
Hilditch & Key Ltd (Wholesale Division), Glenrothes, Fife
A. E. Holt (Leicester) Ltd, Leicester
John Horsfall & Sons (Greetland) Ltd, Halifax, West Yorkshire
Howmet Ltd, Exeter Casting, Exeter
ICL Mid Range Systems, Bracknell, Berks
IXI Ltd, Cambridge
It's At (UK) Ltd, London WI
Johnson Matthey PLC, Catalytic Systems Division, European Autocatalyst Group, Royston, Herts
Jotun-Henry Clark Ltd, London EC3
Junior Hagen Ltd, London NW10
Justerini & Brooks Ltd, London NWI
KCC Process Equipment Ltd, Sunbury-on-Thames, Middx
Kacy Ltd, London N17
John Laing International Ltd, Hemel Hempstead, Herts
Lightfoot Surfaces Ltd, Great Doddington, Northants
Linnhoff March Ltd, Knutsford, Cheshire
Lion Cabinets Ltd, Leeds
Lofthouse of Fleetwood Ltd, Fleetwood, Lancs
Lothian Coated Fabrics Ltd, Prestonpans, East Lothian
Lowndes Lambert Group Holdings PLC, London EC3
Macallan-Glenlivet PLC, Craigellachie, Banffshire
Madge Networks Ltd, Chalfont St Giles, Bucks
Marks and Spencer PLC, London WI
Mayflower Glass Ltd, East Boldon, Tyne and Wear
R. Mears & Co. Ltd, London EC3
Morane Ltd, Banbury, Oxon
National Pig Development Company Ltd, Driffield, East Yorkshire
Newey Goodman Ltd, Textile Division, Tipton, West Midlands
Newsround International Airfreight Ltd, High Wycombe, Bucks
Nissan Motor Manufacturing (UK) Ltd, Sunderland
Nylon Hosiery Company Ltd, Hinckley, Leics
Omega Diagnostics Ltd, Alloa, Clackmannanshire
Otodynamics Ltd, Hatfield, Herts
PED (Staden) Ltd, Earls Barton, Northants
PPE Ltd, Harlow, Essex
Pauls Malt Ltd, Newmarket, Suffolk
Pearsalls Sutures, Taunton, Somerset
Peboc Ltd, Llangefni, Gwynedd
Pfizer Ltd, Sandwich, Kent
Pig Improvement Company UK Ltd, Abingdon, Oxon
Pilkington Micronics Ltd, Deeside, Clwyd
Pointing Ltd, Prudhoe, Northumberland
Porton Speywood Ltd, Wrexham, Clwyd
Powell Duffryn International Fuels Ltd, Harpenden, Herts
Psygnosis Ltd, Liverpool
Racal Radar Defence Systems Ltd, Chessington, Surrey
Randox Laboratories Ltd, Crumlin, Co. Antrim
The Really Useful Group Ltd, London WC2
Redwood International Ltd (Uniplex), Hemel Hempstead, Herts
Reyrolle Ltd, Hebburn, Tyne and Wear
Riggarna UK Ltd, Christchurch, Dorset
Felix Rosenstiel's Widow & Son Ltd, London SW3

STC Submarine Systems, London SE10
St Brendans Irish Cream Liqueur Company Ltd, Londonderry
Schroder Capital Management International, London EC2
Shelbourne Reynolds Engineering Ltd, Bury St Edmunds, Suffolk
Fokker Division of Short Brothers PLC, Belfast
Sigmaform UK Ltd, Wellingborough, Northants
Silent Channel Products Ltd, Huntingdon, Cambs
E. Slinger & Sons Ltd – The Slinger Group, Blackburn
Stewart Hughes Ltd, Eastleigh, Hants
TSS (UK) Ltd, Weston-on-the-Green, Oxon
Tacolin Ltd, Winsford, Cheshire
Charles W. Taylor & Son Ltd, South Shields, Tyne and Wear
Edward Thompson (Printers) Ltd, Sunderland
Thor Ceramics Ltd, Glasgow
Titus International Ltd, Iver, Bucks
Torquemeters Ltd, Ravensthorpe, Northants
Transatlantic Clothing Company Inc. Aero Leathers, Galashiels, Selkirkshire
University of Strathclyde Graduate Business School, Glasgow
Vascutek Ltd, Inchinnan, Renfrewshire
Vauxhall Motors Ltd, Luton
Voltech Instruments Ltd, Abingdon, Oxon
Vosper Thornycroft Holdings PLC, Southampton, Hants
Warwick Fabrics UK Ltd, Cheltenham, Glos
West Merchant Bank Ltd, London EC3

TECHNOLOGICAL ACHIEVEMENT

The criterion upon which recommendations for an award for technological achievement is based is a significant advance, leading to increased efficiency, in the application of technology to a production or development process in British industry or the production for sale of goods which incorporate new and advanced technological qualities.

In 1993 The Queen's Award for Technological Achievement was conferred on the following concerns:

BT Laboratories (BTL) Optical Research Division, Ipswich, Suffolk – *metal organic vapour phase epitaxy for making semiconductor devices for the optoelectronics industry*
Bridon Ropes Ltd, Brifen Department, Doncaster, South Yorkshire – *Brifen wire rope safety fence*
Marine Technology, Castrol Ltd, Pangbourne, Berks – *Castrol Marine Cyltech 80 – diesel cylinder lubricant*
The Darwen Site of Crown Berger Ltd, Darwen, Lancs – *loop process for continuous manufacture of emulsion polymers suitable for the production of paints and adhesives*
Glacier Vandervell Ltd, Kilmarnock, Strathclyde – *crankshaft bearing materials for highly loaded applications*
Holroyd, Rochdale, Lancs – *computer numerically controlled (CNC) tool and cutter grinding machinery*
Huntleigh Healthcare (Cardiff) Ltd, Cardiff – *a range of pocket diagnostic instruments for vascular and obstetric investigations*
ICL Corporate Systems, Gorton, Manchester – *Series 39 SX mainframe computer systems*
Insignia Solutions Ltd, High Wycombe, Bucks – *SoftPC, software emulation system*
Intavent Ltd, Pangbourne, Berks – *laryngeal mask for anaesthetics purposes*
Joint Replacement Instrumentation Ltd, London WI – *hydroxy-apatite ceramic-coated total hip prosthesis*

Kelvin Hughes Ltd, a Smiths Industries company, Ilford, Essex – *RSR 1000 river radar*

Land Rover Power Train, Solihull – *200 TDi diesel engine*

Martin-Baker Aircraft Company Ltd, Uxbridge, Middx – *Navy aircrew common ejection seat (NACES)*

NextBase Ltd, Ashford, Middx – *computerized route planning systems*

Oxford Applied Research Ltd, Oxford – *reactive atom-radical beam source*

P. P. Payne Ltd, Nottingham – *Supastrip pressure-sensitive adhesive tear tape*

Pitman-Moore Ltd, Uxbridge, Middx – *automatic cattle wormer*

pneuPAC Ltd, Luton – *small portable lung ventilators*

Raychem Ltd Corporate Technology Europe, Swindon – *heat-shrinkable fabric-based telecommunications splice cases*

S & S International Ltd, Berkhamsted, Herts – *Dr Solomon's Anti-virus Toolkit, an anti-virus program for computers*

Smiths Industries Aerospace & Defence Systems – Integrated Display Systems, Cheltenham, Glos – *multi-purpose cockpit colour display system for high performance aircraft*

Solid State Logic Ltd, Oxford – *digital audio post-production systems*

Tronic Electronic Services Ltd, Ulverston, Cumbria – *controlled environment underwater mateable electrical connector*

Zeneca Ltd, Zeneca FCMO Grangemouth Works, Grangemouth, Stirlingshire – *manufacture of Hexaconazole and Flutriafol, systemic fungicides*

Kerry Ultrasonics Ltd, Hitchin, Herts – *development of cleaning systems in which ozone-depleting CFCs are replaced by environment-friendly aqueous and semi-aqueous cleaning liquids*

Pilkington Glass Ltd (Basic Glass), St Helens, Merseyside – *Pilkington K Glass – an energy-saving glass*

Ricardo Consulting Engineers Ltd, Shoreham-by-Sea, West Sussex – *tumbling air motion in gasoline engines for cars*

Ricoh UK Products Ltd, Telford, Shropshire – *recycling and CFC elimination in selenium drum production*

Sericol Ltd, Broadstairs, Kent – *water-based screen printing inks*

ENVIRONMENTAL ACHIEVEMENT

The criterion upon which recommendations for an award for environmental achievement is based is a significant advance in the application by British industry of the development of products, technology or processes which offer major benefits in environmental terms compared to existing products, technology or processes. An award is only granted for products, technology or processes which have achieved commercial success.

The Queen's Award for Environmental Achievement was conferred for the first time on 21 April 1993, and was awarded to the following:

Agricultural Genetics Co. Ltd, MicroBio Division, Royston, Herts – *development of insect pathogenic nematode products as alternative products to synthetic pesticides*

BEWT (Water Engineers) Ltd, Alcester, Warks – *Chemelec electrolytic metal recovery systems for the control of industrial pollution*

Edwards High Vacuum International, Crawley, West Sussex – *DP160V chemical dry pump, which reduces polluting emissions in the chemical processing industry*

FKI Babcock Robey Ltd, Oldbury, West Midlands – *development of the EURONOX high efficiency low NOx emission range of steam and hot water boilers*

The Non-Ferrous Metal Treatment Team of the Foundry Division of Foseco (FS) Ltd, Tamworth, Staffs – *rotary degassing of aluminium and its alloys in the foundry industry*

Horticulture Research International, Wellesbourne, Warks – *development of insect parasitic nematode products as alternative products to synthetic pesticides*

Johnson Matthey PLC Catalytic Systems Division, Royston, Herts – *autocatalysts for the control of vehicle exhaust emissions*

Science and Discovery

ASTEROID GASPRA

In October 1991 the NASA spacecraft *Galileo* took close-up photographs of the minor planet 951 Gaspra (*see* Whitaker's Almanack 1993). The data collected during the fly-by was transmitted back to NASA when the spacecraft made its next close approach to the Earth in November 1992. This was the first time astronomers had seen details of an asteroid's surface. The biggest surprise was that the magnetometer record showed that *Galileo* had created a large distortion in the interplanetary field around the asteroid, which implies that Gaspra has its own magnetic field. The distortion lasted from 1 minute before until 2 minutes after the nearest approach. Margaret Kivelson, leader of the magnetometer team, thinks that an intrinsic field is the best explanation for the phenomenon. Three similar events had been recorded prior to the fly-by at times when the probe was nowhere near to Gaspra but the fact that this particular event occurred at the time of the nearest approach and that the distortion was directed towards Gaspra makes the chance of it being a coincidence fairly remote.

The distortion implies that although Gaspra is only 17 km long it not only contains a sizable percentage of iron, but is also highly magnetized. How Gaspra obtained such a high magnetic field is a mystery because magnetic fields are not an intrinsic property of objects in the solar system. A percentage of meteorites, including the irons, stony irons and some chondrites, are magnetic so the asteroid could be considered as belonging to the same class.

BIG BANG THEORY REVISED

The Big Bang theory for the formation of the Universe has been strengthened by the data sent back by NASA's Cosmic Background Explorer Satellite (COBE). The latest results have a precision some 30 times better than the earlier COBE results. Precise measurements made by COBE's far infra-red absolute spectrophotometer (FIRAS) have shown that microwave background radiation appears to be at the same temperature at every wavelength. This can be interpreted as the background radiation behaving as a perfect black body.

Calculations show that the temperature of this afterglow radiation is 2.726° K with an uncertainty of only 0.01°. From this it has been deduced that less than 1 part in 3,000 of the total energy of the Big Bang was released after the first year. This imposes very strict constraints on the models put forward for the early stages of the Universe. This new information suggests that the decay of unstable elementary particles, exploding supermassive stars and black holes played only a minor role in energy production during the early days of the Universe. If this is correct, theories which suggest many little bangs at later stages have to be rejected.

John Mather of NASA's Goddard Space Flight Center and FIRAS principal investigator, said that it has taken 18 years of careful effort to reach this point but that it is now possible to claim that the Big Bang theory has been tested against observations to a fine degree of precision.

BLACK HOLES AND QUASARS

A currently popular theory is that quasars are formed by the collision of two giant galaxies. The galaxies may contain black holes or the collision may produce them. It is thought that the collision causes gases to rain down on to these massive black holes and so generate a large amount of light, triggering the quasar. The two black holes then become a binary system. This theory is strengthened by the recent claim of two black holes associated with a quasar in the constellation of Draco. This quasar, 4C73.18, is a typical quasar, emitting 100 times as much energy as our own Milky Way galaxy from a region only twice the size of the solar system. The quasar has been under close study by Nico Roos of Leiden Observatory and Christian Hummel of the US Naval Observatory in Washington DC. Their belief that the quasar contains a double black hole comes from the jet of visible material shooting out from the quasar. Over the last few years the astronomers have noticed that the jet wiggles in a manner similar to water from a garden hose when the hose is twirled. It is thought that this movement is due to the black hole producing the jet being tugged periodically by the neighbouring black hole. These objects are thought to be separated by a distance about 30 times that between the Sun and Pluto and to orbit each other in about three years.

Other suspected binary black holes include the quasar 3C273, the first quasar to have its red shift measured, and OJ287, which is thought to have two black holes orbiting each other in nine years. Object 4C73.18 has a red shift of 0.3, which means that it is about three thousand million light years away. The investigators believe that the black hole binary will not last very long, and estimate that they will merge in about a million years time.

CHARON CALCULATIONS

When it was discovered in 1978 that the outermost planet Pluto had a moon, astronomers were able to calculate that the combined mass of Pluto and its satellite Charon was about 1/400 that of the Earth. From 1985 to 1990 the orbital plane of Charon lay in the direction of the Earth. Observed from the Earth, Pluto and Charon repeatedly eclipsed each other, permitting astronomers to calculate the diameter of the two bodies. The observations show that Pluto's diameter is 2,300 km and Charon's 1,190 km. These values indicate that, because of the size of Charon, the system should be classed as a binary system.

Observers at the Jet Propulsion Laboratory in California used the Hubble Space Telescope to track the two objects as they rotated round each other. From Earth-based observatories it was not possible to separate the two objects. The scientists observed the system for 3.2 days, half the orbital period, and they were able to calculate the ratio of the two masses. It was found that Charon lay 11 times further away from the centre of mass of the system; from this it was deduced that Pluto was 11 times more massive than Charon. It was therefore possible to calculate the exact mass of each and from earlier data the density could be deduced. It showed that Pluto has a density of 2.1 grams per cubic centimetre whilst Charon's is only 1.4. The relatively high value for Pluto indicates that the planet is about 75 per cent rock and 25 per cent water ice. Charon would appear to consist mostly of water ice with just a little rock.

These results could shed light on the formation of the binary system. One theory suggests that Pluto and Charon were originally separate bodies but Charon hit Pluto, blasting some of Pluto's surface material into space. If Pluto's core was rocky and the surface ice, the material ejected into space would be mainly ice. This would explain Pluto's high rock content. Some of the escaping ice would be captured by Charon, accounting for its high ice content.

END OF THE EARTH

Astronomers predict that the Earth will be destroyed in about 5,000 million years time, when the Sun expands into a red giant phase. About ten years ago scientists Lovelock and Whitfield showed that the biosphere would face a crisis long before that event. Calculations carried out by Ken Caldeira and James Kasting of Pennsylvania State University suggest that life will cease in about 500 million years, except for some plants which can photosynthesize with low concentrations of carbon dioxide and so would last for about twice as long.

The scientists believe that the current increase in carbon dioxide from industrial processes is just a blip in the overall trend of a declining level of the gas. As the Earth warms up, the rate of weathering of rocks will increase and increasing radiation from the Sun will balance out the supply of carbon dioxide from volcanic eruptions, causing a gradual decline in carbon dioxide content. Eventually this will drop too low for photosynthesis. After about 1,500 million years the mean temperature of the Earth's surface will be above 50°C but it will rise to 100°C in less than another 200 million years. At this stage the oceans will evaporate quickly and the water vapour will be broken down by solar ultraviolet light. By 2,500 million years the Earth will have no water. Weathering of the rocks will cease and volcanic carbon dioxide will gradually accumulate in the atmosphere, creating a climate similar to that on Venus.

This theory assumes that the Earth will not be hit by a large object from space with a result that could bring life in the biosphere to an earlier close. It is estimated that an impact capable of destroying a quarter of the population is likely to occur about once every 500,000 years.

INTERSTELLAR FIRST

For the first time, a space probe has made contact with grains of interstellar, as opposed to interplanetary, dust. The *Ulysses* spacecraft during its recent flight past Jupiter identified material which had come from regions beyond the solar system.

Interplanetary dust is of great importance because it is thought to be primitive material, either the end-point of continual collisions between minor planets or debris from short period comets. This dust envelopes the whole of the inner solar system and we see it as a faint glow called the zodiacal light. Some of this material has been collected by high-flying aircraft and analysed in the laboratory. However, very little was known about the dust in regions beyond the orbit of Mars. Detectors on board *Ulysses* have provided details such as speed, size, flight direction and electrical charge.

Ulysses found that in the vicinity of Jupiter the big grains, i.e. those with diameters greater than half a micrometre, were in a retrograde orbit, in contrast to the prograde orbits in the inner regions. These retrograde objects were also found to have speeds well above the escape velocity for the solar system. The fact that the grains were coming from the same direction as the interstellar helium which is flowing past the solar system provided confirmation that the grains were from the interstellar regions. This is the first direct detection of interstellar material and raises the question of how particles which would experience a larger solar radiation pressure than the gravitational pull manage to reach the middle regions of the solar system.

KUIPER BELT DISCOVERY

It has been thought for some time that there exists a second belt of mini-planets orbiting the Sun beyond Pluto. David Jewitt of the University of Hawaii and Jane Luu of the University of California at Berkeley have searched for possible objects for six years. They discovered the first trans-Plutonian object on 30 August 1992. This was labelled 1992 QB. A second object was discovered on 28 March 1993 from studying images obtained using charge-coupled devices (CCDs) with the 2.2 metre telescope at Hawaii. The second object, known as 1993 FW, is about 200 km in diameter and preliminary analysis indicates that it is in an orbit between 38 and 56 astronomical units (AU) from the Sun. (An astronomical unit is the distance of the Earth from the Sun). It was found after surveying less than 1 square degree of the sky. Finding two objects in such a relatively small area of the sky suggests that there may be several thousand objects with diameters of about

200 km and many more smaller bodies. Both objects have a low albedo (fraction of the incident light reflected from the surface), about 0.04, and appear reddish in colour, suggesting that they are icy bodies with organic molecules on their surfaces. Both objects have a magnitude of +23. Jewitt says that the Kuiper belt is the remnant of the proto-planetary disk from which the conventional planets were formed, and that it may now be possible to study the building blocks of the outer planets. In that region velocities are low so collisions would be infrequent. It is likely that these bodies are the most primitive objects in the solar system, and they may also be the source of short period comets.

PLANETARY SYSTEMS

Each year new evidence is found for the existence of planetary systems around stars similar to our own Sun. In the past most of this evidence has been centred on the possible existence of a planet larger than Jupiter orbiting the star, with the implication that smaller objects also exist. The evidence lies not in actual observations but by determination of the mass of dust which surrounds the stars. Work on this has been carried out by Vincent Mannings and James Emerson of Queen Mary and Westfield College, London. Using the James Clark-Maxwell telescope on Mauna Kea, Hawaii, they calculated the mass of the dust around each of about 20 stars in the Taurus-Auriga cloud by measuring the intensity of the infra-red radiation. These low mass stars have yet to start burning hydrogen and the observers monitored the stars at longer wavelengths than before. They found that in five cases the infra-red radiation came from relatively cool dust grains and that there was enough of the dust to make planetary systems.

The current theory of planet formation is that as a star condenses from the interstellar cloud, it is veiled in gas and dust. This forms a disc which extends to a distance comparable with the distance of the Sun to the outermost planet. The process of planet formation involves the combining of dust grains to form planetesimals and subsequently planets. Most of the surplus gas and dust is blown away by the stellar wind generated as the star starts to burn hydrogen. Astronomers have known for some time that the total mass of the original dust-cloud far exceeds the amount of the mass of the planets in our solar system but the work by Mannings and Emerson has revealed the critical mass required for the formation of a planetary system.

A study of one of the five stars, T-Tauri, has shown the dust mass to be 0.6 per cent of the Sun's mass, compared to 0.1 per cent for the total mass of the planets in our solar system. In the other four cases, the total mass of the dust grains exceeds the critical value for the formation of planets.

PLANET X UNLIKELY

Although there is the possibility of the existence of a belt of small bodies orbiting the Sun at a distance outside the orbit of Pluto, the so-called Kuiper Belt, astronomers have long debated the possibility of a large planet beyond the orbit of Pluto, referred to as Planet X. However, recent studies have shown that its existence is most unlikely. Arguments for the existence of Planet X started with the discrepancies between the observed and the calculated orbit of Uranus. Gravitational theory showed that another planet outside the orbit of Uranus was responsible and this led to the discovery of Neptune within one degree of the predicted position. This discovery reduced the discrepancy but it was still of sufficient magnitude to suggest that there was another large body beyond the orbit of Neptune. Searches led to the discovery of Pluto but Pluto was found to be too small to account for the differences and so the existence of Planet X was suggested.

The visit of space probes to all the major planets has enabled the masses of these bodies and their satellites to be calculated to a very high precision. Using these refined values, the differences between the observed and the calculated position for Uranus have now virtually vanished. Discrepancies in the position for Neptune are not quite so easily explained. Calculations for the orbit of the planet have tended to be inaccurate because since Neptune was discovered it has not completed one orbit (its orbital period is about 165 years). Even so explanations have been put forward to explain the discrepancies. The space probes, especially the *Pioneers*, have not had their flight paths perturbed by any trans-Plutonian object, so the overall impression at present is that Planet X does not exist.

PLEIADES RECONSIDERED

The Pleiades cluster is possibly as well-known as the Plough. Popularly known as the Seven Sisters, it is an open cluster of stars surrounded by dust clouds. These were assumed to have been left over when the stars were formed and to be illuminated now by the brightest stars in the group. However, recent work has shown this assumption to be wrong as images taken from the Infra-red Astronomical Satellite (IRAS) seem to suggest that the nebulosity is not related to the cluster.

The infra-red map of the cluster contains a roughly triangular-shaped cavity. American astronomers Richard E. White and John Bally have interpreted this as a wake left by an interstellar cloud ploughing through the cluster. It is believed that the ultraviolet light from the hot young stars, either directly by radiation pressure or indirectly by heating the interstellar gas, diverted the material to form a downstream wake in a way similar to that of a ship in water. Calculations have shown that the cloud may have been directed towards the Pleiades cluster some 15 million years ago by a supernova explosion associated with Gould's Belt, 750 light years distant in Vulpecula. This belt is an expanding shell of young stars, gas and dust. White and Bally have postulated that the pulsar 1919+21, which is about 1,100 light years away in Vulpecula and has an age of about 15 million years, may be the result of the supernova responsible for the motion of the cloud towards the Pleiades, because its position is very close to the theoretical position calculated by the astronomers.

POLE STAR VARIABILITY

Polaris, the Pole star, lies at present very nearly in the direction of the north pole of the Earth's spin axis and for centuries it has been used in navigation to indicate north. But to the astronomer Polaris is of interest because it is the nearest and brightest of a class of stars known as Cepheid variables. The light from these stars fluctuates in a very regular manner and this property has been used as a technique for measuring stellar distances and even galactic distances. However, for some reason, the variation in brightness previously shown by Polaris has gradually decreased.

Polaris is a yellow supergiant and the variations in brightness are due to a regular expansion and contraction. For most of this century the fluctuations have amounted to about 10 per cent but in the early 1980s Armando Arellano, working in Canada, noticed that the variations had dropped to 5 per cent. Recently astronomers from the University of Toronto have observed that this variation has dropped further, being only 1 per cent at the end of 1992. In addition to the drop in light variation, the team observed that the star's pulsations have also fallen. When the star expands the light is blue-shifted because the surface is moving towards us, but when it contracts the light is red-shifted. If the present trend continues it is expected that these pulsations will cease in the near future.

Typical Cepheids stay in the pulsating phase for tens of thousands of years so it is remarkably lucky that the end-point of a Cepheid can be observed with such a bright member of the class. It is believed that Polaris is getting larger and cooler because the period of the pulsations, currently 3.97 days, is increasing by 3 seconds per year. Unfortunately, this does not explain the fall-off in the intensity of the pulsations. Another Cepheid, RT Aurigae, with a similar colour and period, is behaving in a completely different manner so there are still many questions to be answered.

SUPERNOVA IN M81

On 28 March 1993, an amateur Spanish astronomer Francisco Garcia Diez discovered a supernova 11 million light years distant, towards the edge of the spiral galaxy Messier 81 in the constellation of Ursa Major. Photographs of the star taken prior to the explosion show that the object was a red supergiant of the type which produces what are known as Type II supernovae. These are caused when stars more than eight times the mass of the Sun exhaust their nuclear fuel. The core of the star collapses to form a neutron star while the outer layers fall inward and bounce off the core, producing a shock-wave which

travels outwards at between 10,000 and 15,000 km per second. The shock-wave blows away the hydrogen-rich surface layers, creating hydrogen emission, which is recorded in the spectrum of the light from the star. This emission is a characteristic feature of a Type II explosion. Such explosions cause a star to shine 10,000 times more brightly than normal. This event, given the name Supernova 1993J, is thought to be one of the brightest supernovae seen in modern times.

Within two days of the discovery, the International Ultraviolet Explorer satellite had detected ultraviolet light. Light from ionized nitrogen showed that the shock-wave had collided with the gas surrounding the star and heated it to over $100,000°$ C. Soon afterwards radio waves and X-rays were detected, the radio waves being the so-called synchrotron radiation generated by ions in the shock-wave as they are accelerated around the magnetic fields in the gas. The X-rays, generated in the gas at a temperature of more than 100 million degrees, were detected by the German ROSAT satellite and also the Japanese ASCA X-ray telescope. Analysis of the results shows that the star originally had a mass of about 10 solar masses. Prior to the explosion it was ejecting about 2×10^{-6} solar masses per year as a stellar wind. The detection of ultraviolet radiation so soon after the visual sighting indicates that the surrounding gas was still very close to the star.

Events such as this enable astronomers to refine their theories of stellar evolution and to provide a more accurate value for the Hubble Constant, which is the basis of the determination of the size of the Universe.

SIBERIAN EXPLOSION LATEST

The devastation which was caused by an extraterrestrial body exploding in the atmosphere over the Tunguska region of Siberia in 1908 has been a prime target for study since scientists first went to the area about 15 years later. At first the search concentrated on trying to find a large crater and meteorites. Theories to explain the event have been numerous but over the last decade there has been a consensus that the cause was due to a comet exploding some 10 km up in the atmosphere. This satisfactorily explained the absence of a crater and the lack of meteorites. However, recent work suggests that this theory is incorrect.

The comet theory was undermined by the data collected from the recent visit of Halley's comet, which was found to have a density of between 0.6 and 1 gram per cubic centimetre. Calculations by Christopher Chyba of NASA's Goddard Space Flight Center showed that only a stony meteorite would explode at a height of 10 km. Chyba's calculations are the first to incorporate the aerodynamic forces acting on a body entering the atmosphere. He claims that aerodynamic forces would shatter a stony object, effectively reducing its density to a value lying between 0.001 and 0.01 grams per cubic centimetre, a value which would cause the object to explode at a height of 10 km. Comets and carbonaceous chondrites, which have weaker bonding forces, would explode at a much higher level, but objects like iron would reach the ground. Chyba's calculations are still in the early stage of development but they seem to produce results which fit the observed facts. The figures indicate that stony objects up to a few hundred kilometres in diameter will explode, but objects larger than this would be too large to react to the atmosphere before they hit the ground.

EARTHQUAKE PREDICTIONS

A reliable method of predicting earthquakes has long been the target of geologists, especially in the United States and Japan. Recently, Japanese seismologists made a discovery which may make predictions more successful. They found that major tremors are preceded by strong electrical activity in the Earth's crust. In the weeks before the severe earthquake which struck the Noto peninsula in February 1993, monitors near the epicentre detected changes in the 'Earth current' five times greater than usual. This background current is generated by minor voltage differences in the Earth's crust. Seismologists have suspected for a long time that this current may be altered by the crustal stresses which precede tremors. Detecting the current changes is difficult because of electrical interference from built-up areas. The Noto peninsula, located about 270 km north-west of Tokyo, is a rural area. Because the February tremor was quite strong, 6.6 on the Richter scale, and the epicentre lay close to the Suzu monitoring centre, the detected signals were strong and clear.

Abnormal readings were first observed on 10 December, when minor tremors were noted. Abnormalities of up to 500 millivolts were recorded over the next two months until the main tremor on 7 February; within a few hours of this, the reading had returned to normal. Research is now being conducted to see if the data will reveal a reliable method of using electrical changes to predict future earthquakes, and if the size of the abnormalities are related to the severity of the resulting earthquake.

WIND–SEA INTERACTION

Over the last 50 years there has been much scientific debate about the way in which wind energy is transferred to the sea by the interaction of the wind and the size of the waves. Studies carried out in the seas around Australia indicate that most of the energy is caught by wavelets, some only a few millimetres high. Research in this field is important for an understanding of climatic changes and weather forecasting as well as in the design of ships, jetties and oil rigs.

A team led by Michael Banner of the University of New South Wales gathered data by flying an aircraft just above the surface of the sea south-west of Hobart during gale force winds and compared the results with those obtained when the sea was calm. Seven five-hour flights covered varied conditions, from a gentle breeze and swells to when the wind speed was 55 knots and the waves were 9 metres high. During the flights, measurements were made of the turbulence in the atmosphere, sea temperature, and changes in the heat and moisture in the air. The characteristics of the sea surface were recorded by radar. When the wind was strong, Banner found that about 80 per cent of the sea surface drag was caused by waves of all sizes acting together. But this value was found to drop to 20–30 per cent when the winds were mild. The rest of the drag was caused by friction of the wind on the ocean surface. It was found that low-energy small waves were responsible for up to 70 per cent of the wind to sea transfer of momentum. This high value was found to drop as the waves and wind increase.

Banner believes that the wavelets catch more of the wind's energy because they are steeper than the larger waves, and that, as they move much more slowly than the large waves, so they feel the brunt of the wind more strongly. He is also of the opinion that much of the absorption occurs when the small waves form small breakers. This aspect had not been considered in previous studies.

EL NINO RETURNS

The amount of research that has been carried out into El Nino led scientists to believe they could predict when it would occur. Unfortunately, this confidence has been shattered by its unexpected return in the early part of 1993, causing severe flooding on the west coast of South America and killing nearly 100 people in Colombia.

When an El Nino occurs, the trade winds and ocean currents which flow across the tropical regions of the Pacific Ocean in a generally westerly direction abruptly reverse their flow. This causes drought in normally wet areas of Indonesia and Australia, severe storms on the west coast of America, and interrupts the Indian and East African monsoons. Under normal conditions an El Nino exhausts itself within about 18 months. Climatologists accurately predicted many months in advance the onset of an El Nino in 1986 and in 1991. The present one began during 1990, reached its peak in early 1992 and weakened abruptly during mid-1992. However, it unexpectedly increased again in November 1992.

History records a lengthy El Nino between 1939 and 1941, causing drought and famine in Bengal. Climatologists had thought that that event was part of a climatic anomaly in the Pacific which lasted from 1937 to 1946, the characteristics of the associated El Nino being different from the norm. At the moment it is not clear whether the current long spell is a repeat of the 1930s event. Scientists are not certain why these reversals of the currents take place. They seem to be triggered by a build-up of very warm water in the western Pacific Ocean. Some investigators believe that global warming will make the reversals more severe, and the warmer the oceans the greater the threat of more intense El Ninos.

BALL LIGHTNING FORMATION

The strange behaviour of ball lightning has baffled scientists for a long time. Some have dismissed the phenomenon as an illusion but the thousands of reports made during the last few centuries and the remarkable consistency of the descriptions have convinced many that the phenomenon is real. Most sightings are made during thundery weather, the ball of light appearing as a free-floating globe of glowing gas about 10 cm in diameter. The phenomenon lasts for up to a minute. The ball appears to stay near to the ground and travels at speeds of up to 10 metres per second. The flight either ends with a bang or the light just goes out.

David Turner, a chemist at the University of Bristol who has studied the conditions which would arise in an accident at a pressurized water reactor, says that a large amount of steam would be released and this would influence the amount of radioactive caesium iodide released. During a thunderstorm, the air is very humid and ions may be created when intense electric fields cause the air to break down. He does not try to explain how these fields are created because he claims that other scientists have covered the subject thoroughly. His starting point is the condition when the air is broken down to create a localized plasma of ions at a temperature of several thousand degrees. Turner claims that the key to the problem lies in studying what happens to an ion which escapes into the surrounding cool humid air which is electrically charged. He says that a structure similar to that of an onion is formed, with each successive shell being dominated by differing chemical reactions. The crucial region appears to be the outer shell where Turner has been able to use his specialized knowledge to provide a satisfactory explanation for the structure of the ball. He has calculated the effect on common ions such as H_3O^+ and NO_2^- when they combine at the edge of the ball. If they are carrying more than five water molecules, heat is extracted from the system and the outer shells cool. This cooling allows the condensation of water in a sufficient quantity to counteract the buoyancy of the plasma. Other reactions would take place to counteract the outward pressure of the plasma.

LIFE ON LAND

The widely-accepted view is that life on land started about 470 million years ago. This date is based on the study of fossil pollen but for some time scientists have suspected that life on land could have begun at a much earlier date in the form of algae and bacteria. This was not verified until recently because these forms of life leave few fossils. However, work carried out by Paul Knauth, a geologist at the University of Arizona, has shown that life first arrived on land as early as 1,200 million years ago in the form of mats of algae and bacteria.

Some time ago Knauth was examining limestone deposits laid down over 550 million years ago. Before being buried, the limestone had weathered to form a karst landscape. The weathering left distinct surfaces which included insoluble layers known as chert. The chert remained after the limestone had eroded. In the chert, which lay just below the ancient surface, the isotope carbon-13 content was lower than usual. This indicates that photosynthesis had taken place because photosynthesis uses the more common carbon-12 when it takes up carbon dioxide from the atmosphere. Knauth interpreted this as an indication that a lush layer of algae and bacteria had been growing on the surface. The theory was not accepted because of the lack of supporting fossil evidence. However, Robert Horodyski from Tulane University in New Orleans found a wealth of fossils in the chert. He described them as being 1–5 micrometres in diameter and up to several hundred micrometres in length, and similar to microfossils from marine rocks of the same age. Although the area was certainly moist, it was in no way oceanic. He remarked that the consistent diameter, uniform size and hollow shape of the fossils all point to a biological origin, supporting the earlier date for the start of life on land.

FISH FOSSILS

Central Australia has provided a discovery which could revolutionize the methods used for exploring natural resources. Gavin Young and colleagues of the Australian Geological Survey Organization (AGSO) discovered fish fragments in limestone samples laid down some 485 million years ago. The palaeontologists collected the samples during a mapping project at Areyonga, an Aborigine community 170 km southwest of Alice Springs.

The fish scales, between 0.1 and 5 mm across, represent four different groups of fish. The fish were definitely vertebrates because of the similarity of their scales to those vertebrates from the 'age of fishes', the Devonian period (410 to 355 million years ago). The samples are being checked by several research establishments throughout the world. Young believes that the investigations will reveal that some of the fish had jaws. If this is verified, the earliest record for fish with jaws will be put back some 50 million years. An increase in our knowledge of the fish that lived between 540 and 250 million years ago will provide a better understanding of the biological and geological changes which occurred in the period before animals appeared and when much of the Earth's landmass was part of the southern landmass known as Pangea.

Young and Susan Turner of Queensland Museum, Brisbane, are leading a five-year international project to co-ordinate world-wide research on vertebrate microfossils of the Palaeozoic era. Much of this research is centred on thelodonts, early jawless fish resembling rays which ranged in size from 2 cm to about a metre across. They are found all over the world in fossil records dating from about 420 million years ago. Microfossils can indicate the presence of gas and oil. Turner is reported as saying that American oil companies used vertebrate microfossils in the exploration of the Alaskan oil field and it is thought that the same techniques will be used in the search for similar fields in Siberia.

EARLIEST TERMITES

Studies of fossil trees in the Petrified Forest in Arizona have revealed evidence that termites existed some 220 million years ago, about 100 million years earlier than any social insects were thought to have lived and much earlier than the emergence of the first flowering plants. Stephen Hasiotis and Russell Dubiel of the US Geological Survey in Denver found termite nests embedded in the trees. At the time the Petrified Forest area consisted of a sandy deposit in the muddy floodplain of a large river. The termites built nests several centimetres across, connected in groups about a metre wide by a complex of tunnels. They cemented the sand with saliva or faeces so that when the trees were later covered by sand and mud, the nests survived and became fossilized. No fossil termites have been found but the form of the nests is similar to that of some modern primitive termites.

It was presumed there would be an evolutionary connection between flowering plants and insects because of pollination requirements. However, it is thought that termites evolved from wood-eating cockroaches and that initially they nested in wood. Palaeontologists believe that it was much later that they started building nests underground. Thomas Brown of the US Geological Survey believes that wood-eating animals evolved soon after trees. The earliest record prior to this discovery was the identification of termite-damaged wood about 70 million years old. The earliest evidence for other social insects, such as wasps and bees, has been found in the late Cretaceous times, about 70 million years ago. Although ants are virtually wingless wasps, no nests have been identified in the fossils. In addition to the termites, the studies have revealed evidence for the existence of other insects and small animals. The evidence is in the form of trace fossils left behind by the creatures. Hasiotis has identified fossil crayfish burrows in the same sediments as the termite nests. These burrows are 190 million years older than the earliest crayfish previously recorded.

PRIMITIVE BIRD DISCOVERIES

The evolution of birds is not clear and the scarcity of good fossils has given rise to conflicting ideas. The discovery of two well-preserved skeletons of a new species of primitive bird in Mongolia in 1987 and 1992 has done little to clarify matters. The birds lived between 85 and 65 million years ago, in the Cretaceous period. Some of the bird's features showed a clear link with birds of today but others seem strangely primitive for a bird of the late Cretaceous. The bird was flightless and had short sturdy forelimbs with a stout claw on the first digit of its hand. The

idea that it may have been a powerful burrower conflicts with its slender pelvis and long slender hind limbs, the latter suggesting it may have been a wader. Named *Mononychus olecranus* by Perle Altangerel of the Mongolian Museum of Natural History and colleagues at the American Museum of Natural History, it had a primitive long tail, teeth and other features indicating that it had descended from small bipedal theropod dinosaurs. The keeled breast-bone and pelvic bones, which are elongated and fused, link it to the modern bird. *Archaeopteryx*, which lived about 150 million years ago, could probably have flown short distances and other examples from the early Cretaceous (140–125 million years ago) were capable of more sustained flight. By the late Cretaceous there were groups of divers and gull-like shorebirds that still retained teeth but in other respects looked like modern birds.

Altangerel and colleagues say that they cannot choose which theory fits the bill best. Did the ability to fly occur in lineages leading up to *Mononychus* or did flight evolve independently in separate lineages of early birds? *Mononychus* was about a metre in length but it does not resemble any of today's flightless birds. All of these have sturdy legs, short tails and lack a keel for anchoring flight muscles to their breastbones.

ÖTZE: NEOLITHIC MAN

In September 1991 the remains of a frozen neolithic man were found in the Tyrolean mountains (*see* Whitaker's Almanack 1993). The corpse has now been studied in detail by Torstein Sjøvold and colleagues. Because the body is extremely delicate, normal techniques could not be used; much of the analysis has been carried out using computer tomographic scans of the body and on a plastic replica of the skull moulded from computer tomographic images.

The examination has revealed that when he died Ötze was lying on his left side with his head resting on a rock. The computer tomographic scans of his head and the examination of his teeth indicate an age of between 25 and 40 years. He was 159 cm tall, a height small for present-day man but typical for those living 5,300 years ago. It is thought that his body and belongings were preserved because he was freeze-dried by the wind before he was covered in snow in a shallow ravine. The body was hardly disturbed by the glaciers lying above although the pressure of the ice may have been responsible for the curled upper lip and slightly skewed nose. A small cavity in the right ear may have been due to the man wearing an ear-ring. The discovery that the corpse lacked any outer genitalia has puzzled the investigators. One theory was that they were ripped off as the body was wrenched clumsily out of the snow when originally discovered. A search of the site has revealed nothing, so it is now suggested that the penis and testes may have shrunk into the body.

Sjøvold has also investigated the way in which Ötze met his death. He is of the opinion that Ötze became caught in a fog and lay down. During the night there was a drop in temperature and he froze to death. His theory is based on a study of the climatic conditions existing in the Tyrol at the present time.

THE FIRST FARMERS

The well-established belief that agriculture first developed in Mesopotamia some 10,000 years ago has been shown to be untrue. The general belief was based on the idea that the people living between the rivers Tigris and Euphrates suddenly learned to sow and harvest crops, and that this abundant supply of food enabled them to establish permanent settlements. Recent investigations throughout the world have shown that the development of agriculture was more of an evolutionary process and that the earliest records of such activity give dates much older than those for Mesopotamia. For example, Gordon Hillman of the Institute of Archaeology in London has identified grinding stones and tubers at Wadi Kubbaniya, Egypt, at a site thought to be between 17,000 and 18,000 years old. There is also evidence that the inhabitants of New Guinea dug fields and drainage ditches between 7,000 and 10,000 years ago.

The most surprising discoveries were made by Matthew Spriggs of the Australian National University and Stephen Wickler, now at the University of Hawaii, during an excavation in 1987 at Kilu Cave on Buka Island in the Solomon Islands group. Radio-carbon dating of the plant remains, found with flake tools, gives an age of 28,000 years. Thomas Loy of the Australian National University examined the tools under a microscope and found evidence of starch grains and raphides, long sharp crystals found in plants such as nettles. He compared these with similar present-day grains and found that the Kilu grains came from the roots or corms of two species of taro similar to those of domesticated strains but different from the wild strains. This suggests that migrants to the Solomon Islands brought with them domesticated strains or that they modified the wild versions. Whatever the method, the indication is that plants were being adapted for human use some 28,000 years ago.

BACKWARDS-SWIMMING ELECTRIC FISH

Biologists have been puzzled for some time by the fact that electric fish have been seen to swim backwards as well as forwards. One group of fish, such as the electric ray, stun their prey with very large electric discharges; another group sense their surroundings with a stream of weak pulses, with frequencies up to 1,000 pulses per second. These travel outwards through the water and are reflected by surrounding objects. The reflected pulses are detected by thousands of conductive pores on the fish's body which connect the signals to the brain.

To study why these fish swim backwards, Michael Lannoo and Susan Johnson Lannoo at Ball State University in Indiana filmed the behaviour of a black ghost knife, an electric fish native to the Amazon. It has very poor vision and hunts for plankton and other small prey using active electric sensors. The Lannoos found that the fish approached prey tail first by undulating the elongated fin on its belly. When the prey was in front, the fish grabbed it with a forward lunge. It was suggested that the fish swims backwards along the side of the potential victim in order to scan it with its electro-receptors before deciding to pounce. If the fish carried out its scan by swimming forward, the prey would be by its tail; by swimming backwards the prey is in a position for attack. The studies have revealed that this is the only way the fish can identify prey because the sensors cannot be focused like an eye. The scanning enables the fish to identify the prey by its characteristic electric field. To support this theory, Michael Lannoo pointed out that there was an exception to this backward-swimming activity of electric fishes. This particular species lives in very strong currents so that if it did stop swimming, it might quickly be swept downstream.

BATTLE OF THE BEES

African Killer bees are notorious for their aggressiveness, their fame the result of the escape of some specimens from a research laboratory in Brazil. They quickly killed off the local bees and colonized huge areas, moving northwards into Mexico, and are now threatening the southern part of the United States. In Africa, however, they are not having all their own way and are being wiped out by an even more lethal species known as Cape Honeybees. The Cape bee thrives in the region of Cape Town because of the wet winters and dry summers, the bees foraging mainly in the winter, which is the main flowering season. Outside this region bee-keepers favour the African bee, which forages in the summer, the country's rainy season. The two species meet when the Cape bees are taken north to pollinate crops. If a hive of Cape bees is placed alongside that of the African bee, the Cape bee infiltrates the African colony, causing the latter to destroy each other. Because the Cape bee forages in the winter it cannot survive for long outside its native area. In northern South Africa the Cape bees starve within a few months and there are few bees left for pollination. Nevertheless there is a northward movement of the Cape bee because bee-keepers in Cape Town find that providing a pollination service is financially more rewarding than selling honey.

The battle between the two species seems to be due to the fact that in a Cape colony there exists, in addition to the true queen, a few egg-laying workers called pseudoqueens. At some time in the last few years African hives have been infiltrated by Cape pseudoqueens. Although the affected African colonies were doomed, they survived long enough for Cape bees to contaminate more hives. Because the two species look similar no one realized what was happening until the invasion had reached epidemic proportions. It is hoped that if the two species can be kept apart for a long enough period, the problem will disappear.

GREAT PYRAMID MYSTERY

Although the Great Pyramid is the largest and most spectacular monument surviving from the age of the Pharaohs, archaeologists have always been puzzled by the fact that it is empty and no evidence has been put forward to suggest that it once contained treasure belonging to the pharaoh Cheops when he was buried, as was the usual custom. A team of German archaeologists led by Rudolf Gantenbrink have recently discovered the entrance to a previously unknown chamber hidden at the end of a 65-metre-long passageway. The team was investigating the inner passages of the pyramid during a project to find methods of protecting the six million ton structure from the effects of tourism; one problem is that each tourist leaves in the pyramid about 20 grams of water from breath and perspiration.

The team was investigating the tunnel to learn more about the circulation of air within the pyramid. Because the passageway is only 20 cm wide and 20 cm high, they developed a tiny robot equipped with a video camera. They found that at the end of the passage there was a small stone door with large copper handles. The video camera showed that there was a gap of about 2 mm between the door and the wall and in front of this gap was a scattering of black dust. Because the dust could not have originated from the stone of the wall or the door, it was thought that it was the product of decaying organic material like wood and textiles. The fact that the dust had been blown out from whatever was behind the door suggests that the mystery room is of considerable size and its geometric location within the pyramid also hints at a large size. It is located exactly 21.5 metres above what is known as the King's chamber, the largest-known chamber, which is exactly 21.5 metres above the second largest chamber known as the Queen's chamber. The passageway rises at an angle of 45° from the back of the Queen's chamber. The team is now developing a modified version of the robot with fibre optics to see if they can penetrate the gap between the door and the wall.

KNOTTY PROBLEM SOLVED

Mathematicians working on obstruse problems with no apparent applications often hit upon techniques which lead to important discoveries and applications. Such is the case with knot theory. For the last hundred years, mathematicians have been trying to find mathematical ways of distinguishing between different types of knots. Until recently the only methods available were based on the work of J. W. Alexander, an American mathematician, who developed algebraic expressions, which became known as Alexander polynomials. Knots whose Alexander polynomials

are different cannot be deformed into each other. However, the converse is not true. Knots with the same polynomial need not be topographically equivalent, for instance, the reef knot and the granny knot have identical polynomials.

In the 1980s great strides were made with the Jones polynomial, named after Vaughan Jones, a New Zealander. Although the Jones polynomial is superficially similar to the Alexander polynomial, it was obtained via mathematical physics and has solved many of the earlier difficulties. For example, it was able to distinguish between the reef and granny knots. Distinguishing between knots is important because it is a visual representation of how to tell the difference between various ways of embedding one space in another. For example, it could throw light on the cutting of DNA molecules by enzymes. All the known techniques for proving knots to be different hinge on finding what are known as invariants, properties that remain unchanged by deformations. This means that knots having different invariants are topologically different. Recent work by Japanese investigators has used as a basis the concept of energy. If a knot can be explained as a flexible wire which can pass through itself and which has a uniform electrostatic charge along its length, then, because like charges repel, a knot that is free to move will do so in such a way as to keep neighbouring strands as far apart as possible in order to minimize electrostatic energy. This value is called the invariant. It was found that only a finite number of topologically different knots existed with energy less than a particular value. This means that topological types of knots can be ordered in terms of their energies, which produces a natural numerical scale of complexity for knots, providing a technique which can be applied in fields such as quantum physics.

NO FOURTH NEUTRINO

After years of investigation, it was concluded in 1989 that there are only three families of neutrinos and that there is only a 2 per cent chance that a fourth neutrino exists. The three kinds which are known to exist are thought to be associated with electrons, muons and tau particles respectively. However, Andrew Hime of the University of Oxford provided very strong evidence in 1991 for the existence of a fourth neutrino with a mass of 17 kilo-electron-volts (keV). This supported results obtained by J. J. Simpson of the University of Guelph, Canada, in 1985, when he discovered that electrons with unexpected energies were being emitted during the decay of tritium, the radioactive isotope of hydrogen. It was possible to deduce from the energy of these electrons that a fourth kind of neutrino existed with a mass of 17 keV. Work carried out independently by Eric Norman at the Lawrence Berkeley Laboratory in California seemed to confirm the results obtained by Hime.

In the last few years, work in Japan and the United States has failed to confirm these results. Hime has now re-examined both the Oxford and Canadian experiments and found that they were both flawed in the same way. He said that some electrons emitted during the beta decay were scattered from aluminium sheets erected to shield the particles from nearby equipment. The degree of scattering depends on the geometry of the aluminium sheets and although he knew scattering was possible he said he had under-estimated how much it would sap the energy of the electrons. The upshot is that Hime has said his results were flawed and that the fourth neutrino does not exist. This has been greeted with relief by physicists working on particle physics because if the 17 keV neutrino existed, there would have to be a lot of rethinking of theories about how the Universe works and how it began.

COMPUTERS OF THE FUTURE

Modern computers use circuits that are switched on and off by electrical currents but there are limits to the size and capacity of such machines. A new development resulting from the work carried out by Itamar Willner and colleagues from the Hebrew University of Jerusalem may revolutionize the computer industry.

Under this new technique the on-off switch is replaced by its photochemical equivalent using a mixture of dyes, the switch being turned on by ultraviolet light. An optical computer involving single molecules which react to light would be much smaller and faster. The electrical components of a traditional computer are replaced by a mixture of eosin Y, a biological stain and a compound of phylazobenzene with viologen. Eosin Y is a red pigment and so absorbs green light; if it is combined with certain molecules to form what is known as a charge-transfer complex, it becomes transparent to green light. The success of the project was due to the discovery of a second light-sensitive molcule which has two forms, one which combines with eosin Y and is transparent to green light, and the other which cannot combine with eosin Y and so is opaque to green light. The complex organic molecule responsible consists of two forms or isomers, known as the *trans* and *cis* isomers. When the transisomer absorbs ultraviolet light, it alters to the cis form. If subsequently this cis form absorbs blue light, it reverts back to the trans form. At present the researchers do not know how to design a computer using these properties but they realize the potential of these reactions to mimic some of the functions of microprocessors. It is possible that this development has laid the basis for the superfast computer of the future.

Periods of Gestation or Incubation

The table shows approximate periods of gestation or incubation for some common animals and birds. In some cases the periods may vary and where doubt arises professional advice should be sought.

Species	Shortest period (days)	Usual period (days)	Longest period (days)
Human	240	273	313
Horse	305	336	340
Cow	273	280	294
Goat	147	151	155
Sheep	140	147–50	160
Pig	109	112	125
Dog	55	63	70
Cat	53	56	63
Rabbit	30	32	35
Goose	28	30	32
Turkey	25	28	28
Duck	28	28	32
Chicken	20	21	22
Pigeon	17	18	19
Canary	12	14	14
Guinea Pig	63	–	70
Mouse	18	–	19
Rat	21	–	24
Elephant		21–22 months	
Zebra		56 weeks	
Camel		45 weeks	

Television

After a year dominated by the ITV auction for new franchises, the spotlight turned on the British Broadcasting Corporation in 1992–3. The future of the Corporation was opened up to public debate in November 1992 with the publication of the Government's green paper, *The Future of the BBC*, followed by the Corporation's own document, *Extending Choice: The BBC's Role in the New Broadcasting Age*. (The main points of both documents are summarized on page 679.) The changes being made within the organization also provoked serious criticism of the new director-general, John Birt. The outgoing director-general of the Corporation, Sir Michael Checkland, publicly criticized the 21-month hand-over period to his designated successor at a Royal Television Society seminar. He also said that Marmaduke Hussey was too old to be an effective chairman of the BBC. However, having shared the running of the Corporation with John Birt for 16 months, Sir Michael agreed to leave two months early, at the end of 1992.

It was revealed that the BBC had overspent £38 million in 1991–2 and had committed £20 million in excess of its budget in 1992–3, due to a series of accounting errors. As a result, it was reported that production of a drama series, a new children's series and a sports programme was cancelled. Sir Michael Checkland denied in a letter to the press that the BBC was 'out of financial control', but said 'We have made a small number of adjustments to our television transmissions and productions including moving some into next year.' Lord Barnett, vice-chairman of the Board of Governors, said that: 'What we have uncovered underlines the need for organizational reforms to be introduced for the greater clarity of responsibility they will bring.' The BBC's director of finance resigned at the beginning of December 1992, although it was denied that he had left because of the accounting errors.

In October 1992, Sir Michael Checkland wrote to Peter Brooke, the new Secretary of State for National Heritage, to ask that the Government remove the ban preventing members of ten proscribed organizations from being heard on television or radio. It was, he said, 'an intervention by government into matters which should properly be the responsibility of independent broadcasters'.

The Future of the BBC

In launching the green paper on the future of the BBC, Peter Brooke, the Heritage Secretary, said that the BBC 'is widely regarded as a national asset. Its programmes are enjoyed, admired and respected all over the world' and that 'The government believes the BBC should continue as a major broadcasting organization and it should have special responsibilities for public service broadcasting. But the BBC cannot remain unchanged in a changing world. So there are fundamental questions to be asked about what the BBC should do, and how it should be financed and organized.' The green paper was widely welcomed, and taken to indicate that the Government had adopted a less doctrinaire approach to the Corporation than the previous administration had shown to the ITV network. Comments were sought by the end of April 1993, and over 6,000 written responses were received. More than two-thirds of respondents supported retention of the licence fee for funding the BBC, and although one-third believed that the BBC needed to improve its management, efficiency and financial affairs, there was almost no support for raising the licence fee to fund the improvements.

In launching the BBC's own document, John Birt said that the Corporation would no longer broadcast 'imitative or formulaic' programmes of a kind already provided by ITV, and would cease to screen sub-standard programmes bought in from the USA or Australia. He promised a 'broad-based BBC offering something stimulating and satisfying for everyone'. The BBC would once again aim to become the 'principal innovator and pioneer in comedy and light entertainment', with 'a unique range of programmes for young people'. He said that 'above all, this document lays out our ideas for the future ... It is these ideas for the future – and not just the achievements of the past – which we believe should underpin the case for the renewal of the BBC's Charter.' Following publication of the BBC's document, Marmaduke Hussey, writing in the *Sunday Times*, pointed out that the BBC's central dilemma is that 'We fail if we chase ratings, but public funding requires we sustain our popular appeal'.

Taxing Matter

The revelation early in 1993 that John Birt was not employed directly by the BBC but sub-contracted his services through his private company caused widespread criticism. There were calls for his resignation from more than 60 Labour MPs, and there were few declarations of support for the arrangement. The news that three members of the Board of Governors, including Marmaduke Hussey, had known of the arrangement also prompted calls for Hussey's resignation. Mr Birt became an employee of the BBC on 1 March 1993. He said: 'The argument has been made strongly in the past few days that it is inappropriate for the director-generalship to be occupied by someone who is not an employee of the BBC. I recognize the force of that argument.' In a letter to *The Times* the following week, Mr Birt regretted 'the distress I had caused by my contractual arrangements as deputy director-general'.

Attacks on Mr Birt continued, including criticism from the former managing director of BBC Television, Bill Cotton, and from the BBC's India correspondent, Mark Tully. Mr Tully complained in a speech to the Radio Academy in July 1993 of a sense of fear among BBC staff, who 'feel there is some sort of Big Brother watching them', and claimed that the BBC had set a 'high premium on sycophancy and virtually rules out healthy criticism of the management'. His savage attack, which was widely publicized, prompted a spirited defence from Mr Birt, who criticized the 'black propaganda' of those who had claimed he was only interested in change for change's sake. Also in July, the BBC published a survey of staff attitudes, which revealed that there was an atmosphere of fear and mistrust, and concern about bureaucracy and the quality of management. However, there was little demand for changes in the chairman or director-general, or for the abolition of 'producer choice'.

PRODUCER CHOICE

The BBC's new policy of 'producer choice' was introduced on 1 April 1993. It established an internal market within the BBC, whereby producers became buyers with the choice of purchasing services such as studios, camera crews and make-up either from within the BBC's own facilities or from outside providers. There was concern that the new system had merely introduced another level of bureaucracy, and it was reported that it would cost £15 million in the first year, with several departments running up deficits. John Birt defended the reforms, saying that they involved a 'profound decentralization' and that the BBC was 'going through a revolution, which is essential and entirely healthy. If you're in a self-contained unit with your purposes clear and you have infinitely more freedom to determine how you spend your money on resources and support services, it will unleash enormous creativity and enterprise within the organization.'

The BBC's new World Service Television news network, launched in April 1991, has proved a serious rival to the American Cable News Network, which announced in December 1992 that it would double its budget for overseas news to some $80 million in 1993. It was reported that WSTV had gained significant viewing audiences in Africa and Asia, with particularly strong representation in India. The station launched a further challenge to CNN when it announced in April 1993 that it would link up with the American broadcasting company ABC to share correspondents and staff throughout the world.

The BBC was also involved in the launch of UK Gold, a satellite channel designed to exploit the programme libraries of the BBC and Thames Television, with Thames holding 15 per cent of the shares. The channel was launched on 1 November 1992 on the Astra satellite, boasting that it represented 'Classic British television on satellite' with the difference that 'you can now advertise during BBC programmes for the first time'.

BBC PROGRAMMES

The BBC restyled its news programmes in April 1993, introducing new computer-generated opening sequences. Its soap opera *Eldorado* was scrapped in July 1993. 'It has still not engaged the affection and attention of viewers to a level to warrant investing in a further year's production', the BBC said. The programme had continued to attract criticism but not audiences, although it was widely felt to have shown considerable improvement both in plots and acting after its first disastrous months. It was also announced that the consumer affairs programme *That's Life*, which had mixed serious items with trivia for 21 years, would be axed after its next series.

A six-part series about former members of the Parachute Regiment struggling to return to civilian life caused controversy. *Civvies*, written by Lynda la Plante, was said to be violent and inaccurate, and was criticized for using real case histories for dramatic purposes. Ms la Plante said that the men were 'trained to the highest standards as soldiers by the Army, then just churned out into society, and given no help at all.' A documentary series about an Australian family, *Sylvania Waters*, provoked uproar when first screened in Australia and adverse publicity preceded its screening on BBC1. The family involved claimed that they had been misled by the programme's producers, who then concentrated on the negative aspects of the family's life. BBC2 gained one of its largest-ever audiences, 11 million, when it screened a deferential interview between Oprah Winfrey and Michael Jackson. One of the supposed 'jewels' in the BBC's crown of winter schedules was an adaptation of Peter Mayle's *A Year in Provence*, starring John Thaw and Lindsay Duncan. But it was a critical and popular failure, with figures dropping from a peak of 14 million to 3.7 million.

Mr Birt's commitment to withdrawing from 'derivative formula or entertainment formats' in programming was called into question when the autumn 1993 schedule was announced. The BBC is to show again *This is Your Life*, a programme it discarded nearly 30 years ago, and which has been screened by ITV since 1969. The programme will be produced by Thames TV, acting as an independent producer.

ITV COMPANY NEWS

On 30 September 1992, it was confirmed that Marcus Plantin, director of programmes at London Weekend Television, had been appointed to the key position of ITV network director. In May 1993, Mr Plantin criticized the BBC for showing too many repeats during peak hours, and said that ITV would rely less on repeats in its autumn and winter schedules.

In December, the Office of Fair Trading ruled that the exclusive rights for ten years sought by the ITV companies for commissioned programmes was anti-competitive and unfair to independent producers. Denying other broadcasters access to secondary broadcasting rights was 'intended and likely to restrict competition'. The OFT also wanted independent producers to be able to negotiate contracts directly with the central programme scheduler rather than having to deal through ITV companies.

The new ITV franchises took effect from 1 January 1993. Carlton took over the weekday London franchise, which Thames Television had held with some distinction for 25 years. Thames, however, continued as a programme provider, and in fact made seven of ITV's 20 most popular programmes. Carlton's main innovation appeared to be its London News Network, owned with LWT; several other new programmes appeared to be pale copies of established shows.

The ITV teletext service, Oracle, was replaced by a new service, Teletext UK. It was reported that the new service was criticized by the Independent Television Commission for its failure to provide a full news service. From 1 March 1993, it increased its news coverage.

GMTV, the new breakfast television station, had modelled itself on its predecessor TV-AM. It also fell into the same trap as TV-AM by making grandiose claims about its presenters. GMTV boasted of their 'F' factor, said to represent 'fanciability'. Two months after it went on the air, its ratings of 1.7 million were some 15 per cent below forecasts and advertising revenue was reported to be disappointing. Its chairman, Harry Roche, resigned and was replaced by Greg Dyke, the chief executive of LWT, one of GMTV's five shareholders. In April, the programme was relaunched. However, its problems continued. It was criticized by the ITC in July for giving undue emphasis to entertainment rather than news, but in September 1993 it was reported that, having lost £10 million in its first six months, GMTV had approached the ITC to request permission to reduce the news content of its service.

TELEVISION NEWS

ITN's problems continued following the requirement in the Broadcasting Act 1990 that the ITV companies should divest themselves of 51 per cent of their shares in the news provider. With projected losses of over £5 million a year for the next four years because of the company's inability to let unused space in its new headquarters building, ITN announced 112 job losses in September 1992. Staff numbers had already been reduced from 1,100 to 750 in the previous four years. Although guaranteed a monopoly to provide news until 2003, ITV companies were reluctant to sign a new contract until they could establish the value of the shares they were required to sell. This impasse also prevented other companies from investing in ITN until the value of the new contract was established. However, a take-over bid for ITN was launched in October 1992 by a consortium consisting of Carlton, LWT, Central and Reuters. The original offer proposed that the shares of the other 13 ITV companies should be bought for £1 each, while new equity would be provided to fund the deficit on ITN's new headquarters. The bid was initially opposed by Yorkshire. This offer lapsed, but the consortium was later expanded to include Granada, Scottish and Anglia, and a new offer from the expanded consortium was successful. The take-over was approved by ITN's shareholders. The three shareholder companies that had lost their franchises, Thames, TVS and TSW, each received £14 per share. The deal, which was finally agreed on 31 March 1993, guaranteed editorial independence for ITN. Michael Green, the chairman of Carlton, became the new chairman of ITN.

News at Ten was relaunched on 9 November 1992 with what were claimed to be the most radical changes in the programme's history; in fact the changes were largely cosmetic. It was hoped that the restyled programme would establish 'greater continuity and certainty' with viewers. ITN also wished to consolidate its position in the schedule before the new ITV regime and scheduling system came into force in 1993. Trevor McDonald became the main newscaster, a new 'Focus on Britain' section was introduced, and Alastair Stewart was charged with visiting the scene of major stories, both at home and abroad.

The ITV network disclosed in June 1993 that it was considering moving *News at Ten* to an earlier evening slot, to enable major dramas or films to be shown uninterrupted later in the evening. The announcement was greeted by a public outcry. Over 100 MPs protested at the proposal and the Prime Minister, John Major, joined the controversy. In a letter to Sir George Russell, the chairman of the ITC, he said: 'It is important that Channel 3 continues to provide a high quality news service and that it competes effectively with the service provided by the BBC throughout the peak viewing hours.' It was also pointed out that eight of the ITV companies had included in their franchise applications a commitment to retain *News at Ten*, which had accordingly become part of their licence conditions. However, some had made the commitment for only one year, and the requirement in the Broadcasting Act was only that a half-hour news programme should be broadcast between 6 p.m. and 10.30 p.m. On 30 June Sir George Russell wrote to all ITV companies pointing out that 'unless the ITC's approval is obtained, the present timing of the peak-time news bulletin must be maintained if all the regional licensees are to remain in compliance with their licence conditions'. However, there was some doubt about whether the ITC did in fact have jurisdiction over scheduling matters.

The House of Commons national heritage select committee questioned the ITV companies on their plan. After hearing evidence, the committee published a report strongly criticizing the proposed move. It said: 'The committee deplores both the proposal to reschedule *News at Ten* and the evasive and wholly unconvincing manner in which the representatives of ITV sought to justify that proposal at the committee's hearing. It therefore urges the ITV council unequivocally to reject the proposal to make any change to the time at which *News at Ten* is shown.' The committee considered that the ITV companies had put forward 'no justification beyond financial benefit'. Michael Green, the chairman of ITN, agreed to postpone any decision for at least a month.

The Government had also indicated that if *News at Ten* were moved, it might not in future allow changes in the rules governing ownership of ITV companies, which prohibit the large companies from taking over each other. As from 1 January 1994, the nine largest companies would be allowed to take over the smaller companies, but not each other. However, in anticipation of a change in the rules, Granada bought shares in LWT, raising its stake by July 1993 to 19.9 per cent, the maximum permitted by the ITC.

CHANNEL 4

Channel 4 celebrated its tenth anniversary in November 1992, but still suffered from criticism that it was failing to live up to its statutory obligation to produce innovative and distinctive programming and was relying too much on imported comedy shows and game shows. On 28 September 1992, Channel 4 launched *The Big Breakfast*, its new breakfast programme to replace *Channel 4 Daily*, a business-based programme which attracted barely 100,000 viewers. The new programme, produced by Bob Geldof and Paula Yates and presented from three cottages in East London, restricts itself to short, snappy bulletins and adopts a more anarchic style. The show is hosted by Chris Evans and Gaby Roslin. In spite of critical disapproval and widespread scorn, the show struck the right note, especially with younger viewers. In September 1993 it overtook GMTV in the ratings.

On Valentine's Day, Channel 4 screened for the first time on British television *Last Tango in Paris*, the controversial film featuring Marlon Brando and Maria Schneider. In August it screened a series of 28 programmes about the war in Bosnia, *Bloody Bosnia*, which aimed to heighten public awareness of the tragedy. Channel 4 also showed *Cathy Come Home*, the BBC's drama about the homeless, which, when first screened in 1966, had led to the setting up of the charity Shelter.

From 1 January 1993, Channel 4 began selling its own air time for advertising. It had aimed for 14 per cent of the total ITV advertising revenue but after several months was achieving figures of nearer 18 per cent, and it was in effect taking advertising from the ITV companies themselves.

CHANNEL 5

The Government's new terrestrial television channel proved to be the service that nobody wanted. Unable to cover more than two-thirds of Britain, and excluding much of the prosperous south east of England, there appeared to be no well-defined purpose for the proposed channel. Thames Television, deprived of its franchise, submitted a bid as part of a consortium called Channel 5 Holdings, but there were difficulties in ensuring that the necessary finance was in place. The ITC rejected the bid because it considered the revenue projections were too optimistic and there was 'insufficient commitment' from the consortium's financial backers. The ITC was also not satisfied 'having particular regard to some of the projected costs and to the audience share and revenue projections which it contained'. Sir George Russell, the ITC chairman, said the decision was 'not just a blow to Channel 5 Holdings; it also raises question marks about Channel 5 itself'. In July 1993, however, the ITC launched a consultation document on Channel 5, which it said could be in operation by 1995. It proposed either advertising again for a single licence, issuing one licence but creating a network of local stations, or abandoning the idea of Channel 5 and using the frequencies for the introduction of digital television services. The ITC requested comments by 15 October 1993.

SATELLITE

Prospects improved for satellite television, after several years of heavy losses. The launch of a third Astra satellite in May 1993 increased the potential number of available channels to 48. It was also apparent that BSkyB's deal to broadcast Premier League football matches live had been very successful; it was largely responsible for boosting operating profits by 70 per cent a week to £1.7 million in May 1993. In November 1992, BSkyB announced that it would be making a drama series for its Sky One Channel, *Spread Eagle*, the first such programme it had commissioned. The service's heavy investment in establishing its range of channels was at last beginning to pay off, while paradoxically the independent television companies, after the traumas of the franchise renewals, found themselves committed to making punishing payments to the Treasury for many years to come. The threat from satellite was one of the reasons for ITV's attempt to consolidate its early evening audiences by abolishing the Sunday evening religious slot and by the proposal to move *News at Ten*.

One of the surprising successes of the Astra satellite was UK Gold, the joint venture between the BBC and Thames Television. Ironically, one of the commonest criticisms about BBC and ITV schedules is the number of repeated programmes at peak times, yet a channel showing nothing else proved to be the most popular on satellite. Although initially screened free, late in 1993 UK Gold became a subscription service as part of the package deal of programmes on satellite.

In September 1993 a new package of satellite programmes was launched, with most of the main channels only available on subscription. A basic package of 14 channels is available for £6.99 a month, up to the full service, including three film channels and the sports channel, for £19.99 a month. Several new channels were launched at the same time, including Nickelodeon, a joint venture between BSkyB and the US cable company Viacom, aimed specifically at children; Discovery, offering natural history and science programmes; QVC, a home shopping channel; and The Family Channel, which had bought TVS Entertainment, the former ITV company, and is a subsidiary of International Family Entertainment, led by Pat Robertson, an American evangelist. The purchase of TVS gave the channel access to the programme backlist of MTM, the American company which produced shows such as *Lou Grant* and *The Mary Tyler Moore Show*; the purchase of MTM had been the major cause of TVS's financial problems.

By November 1992, sales of satellite dishes had reached 2.7 million and it was estimated that it reached nearly 3.5 million homes, a potential audience of 11 million people. After several years in the doldrums, cable television at last showed signs of progress. By August 1993 it was connected to around two million homes in 58 cities, and plans were announced for two large cable schemes in Yorkshire. One of the main encouragements to invest in cable was the fact that service providers were able to offer their own telephony services.

Viewing figures over the Christmas period gave the audience share as: BBC 49.5 per cent, ITV 45.5 per cent and satellite and cable 5 per cent. However, early in January 1993, after the new ITV companies had begun broadcasting, ITV regained a 10 per cent lead on the BBC. Figures provided by the Broadcast Audience Research Board for May 1993 showed that satellite and cable channels had 25.6 per cent of the viewing audience, with 41.6 per cent for ITV and Channel 4, and 32.8 per cent for the BBC.

BROADCASTING STANDARDS

In November 1992 the chairman of the Broadcasting Standards Council, Lord Rees-Mogg, called for the evening 'watershed' which restricts the screening of material which might be unsuitable for children until after 9 p.m. to be extended to 10 p.m. The Council also criticized satellite television channels, which had ceased to classify films according to the British Board of Film Classification, and imposed their own watershed of 8 p.m. In August 1993 it criticized scenes in the BBC's *Chatterley*, an adaptation of D. H. Lawrence's novel directed by Ken Russell. It said that some scenes were shown too early in the evening, although they complied with the 'watershed' requirement, and that some scenes of a sexual nature were too long and too rough. The BSC had received 20 complaints about the second episode. However, a report commissioned by the BSC, *Sex and Sexuality in Broadcasting*, found that the public was more concerned about bad language or violence on television than about the depiction of sex. In its annual report published in May 1993, the Council

reported that it had received 253 complaints relating directly to violence on television, compared with 100 the previous year.

In July 1993, the BBC issued its own new guidelines on violence. The code required a warning before all programmes that might be disturbing, and stressed the need for sensitivity where sexual violence was concerned. The 9 p.m. 'watershed' was deemed to be very important, especially during the summer when more children might be watching late programmes.

AWARDS

In the Royal Television Society Awards presented in May 1993, the best situation comedy programme was *One Foot in the Grave* (BBC) and the best entertainment comedy *Victoria Wood's All Day Breakfast Show* (BBC). David Jason was named best male performer and Julia Sawalha best actress. Best drama series was *Between the Lines* (BBC) and best single drama *Hedd Wyn* (S4C). In the Royal Television Society Journalism Awards for 1993, Martin Bell was named journalist of the year, and the *Nine O'Clock News* (BBC) received the programme award for its coverage of the September 1992 currency crisis.

In the annual British Academy of Film and Television Arts (BAFTA) Awards, the best television drama was *Inspector Morse* (ITV), for which role John Thaw won the best actor award. Helen Mirren was best actress for *Prime Suspect 2*, best light entertainment was *Noel's House Party*, and best comedy *Absolutely Fabulous*, for which Joanna Lumley also won the award for best light entertainment performance. Best single drama was *An Ungentlemanly Act*, best drama serial *Anglo-Saxon Attitudes*, and best factual series, *Pandora's Box*.

FILM AND VIDEO CERTIFICATES

The British Board of Film Classification issues the following categories of film certificates:

U	Universal: suitable for all
PG	Parental guidance: some scenes may be unsuitable for young children
12	Passed only for persons of 12 years and over
15	Passed only for persons of 15 years and over
18	Passed only for persons of 18 years and over
R18	For restricted distribution only (through specially licensed cinemas to which no one under the age of 18 is admitted)

The classifications of video tapes differ slightly:

U	Universal: suitable for all
Uc	Universal: particularly suitable for children
PG	Parental guidance: general viewing, but some scenes may be unsuitable for young children
15	Suitable only for persons of 15 years and over
18	Suitable only for persons of 18 years and over
R18	Restricted: to be supplied only in licensed sex shops to persons of not less than 18 years

Weather

July 1992

Rainfall totals were generally above average over England and Wales but below average elsewhere. It was the wettest July for five years in many areas. Caldecott (Leics.) received more than two and a quarter times its normal amount for the month. On the 1st 59 mm (2.32 in) of rain fell at Driby (Lincs.). On the 3rd 50 mm (1.97 in) fell at Grizedale (Cumbria) and on the 4th there were thunderstorms over south-east England. Thunderstorms occurred over central southern England on the 10th while the 11th saw a band of rain cross all areas. A tornado was reported near Minster Lovell (Oxon) on the 11th, causing damage to buildings and trees, and there were thunderstorms over the Midlands, south-east and eastern England. Extensive fog affected western and southern areas throughout the 14th and spread to large areas of the eastern Midlands and the south-west. On the 15th–16th there were thunderstorms over central and eastern England. There was widespread fog on eastern coasts on the morning of the 16th and fog affected much of the south coast on the 19th. On the 20th thunderstorms occurred over south-east England and flooding was widespread in Southampton and Portsmouth (Hants.), Windsor (Berks.), Egham (Surrey) and in the Isle of Wight. Flood water was 0.61 m (2 ft) deep in Sandown (IOW), and 54 mm (2.13 in) of rain fell at Herne Bay (Kent), 53 mm (2.09 in) at Edenbridge (Kent) and 50 mm (1.97 in) at Writtle (Essex). On the 21st rain occurred over many areas with thunderstorms over East Anglia and south-east England. The weather remained unsettled until the 27th when there were thunderstorms over Norfolk and Lincolnshire. On the 29th an earthquake centred near Pwllheli (Gwynedd) caused widespread damage to property in north-west Wales. Further rain spread to western areas on the 30th–31st.

Monthly mean temperatures were above normal generally, though below normal in a few places. The average for central England was 0.7°C (1.26°F) above the 1961–1990 average, making it the sixth successive month with temperatures above normal. The highest temperature recorded was 28.9°C (84.0°F) at Northolt (Gtr London) on the 31st and the lowest was −0.5°C (31.1°F) at Kindrogan (Tayside) on the 2nd.

Sunshine totals were mostly below normal, making it the dullest July since 1981. The highest daily total was 15.2 hours at Folkestone (Kent) on the 22nd and the highest monthly total was 231 hours, also at Folkestone.

August 1992

Rainfall totals were above average generally, but below average in some eastern areas of England. Over England and Wales it was the wettest August for some years and many places received 150 per cent of average rainfall. At Benbecula (Western Isles) 287 per cent of the average amount fell, whereas Whitby (N. Yorks.) received only 59 per cent of average. Wick (Highland) had its wettest August for 60 years. On the 5th and 6th gales affected west and north-west Scotland, and thunderstorms occurred over many areas of England and Wales between the 7th and 9th during which two people were killed by lightning and four were killed in road accidents. Torrential rain fell in many places, with 71 mm (2.80 in) at Presteigne (Powys) and 63 mm (2.48 in) at Rhandirmwyn (Dyfed) on the 7th. Dust was deposited during heavy rain over Berkshire on the 8th–9th. On the 8th fog in south-west England developed overnight to cover most of England and Wales. From the 9th to the end of the month showers or periods of rain, often heavy and with thunder, occurred somewhere in the United Kingdom on almost every day. On the 11th ball lightning was observed at Luton (Beds.) during a thunderstorm. There were gales in the south and west on the 12th when several gusts of over 50 knots (57.6 mph) were recorded. On the 19th and 20th extensive coastal fog formed over eastern England and on the 22nd and 23rd there were gales in the south and west when a gust of 56 knots (64.5 mph) was recorded at Camborne (Cornwall) on the 23rd. Over the Bank Holiday weekend (29th–31st) it was very wet and windy everywhere. One person was killed in central London when trees were blown down and five more people died as a result of the weather. Many seaside resorts were forced to close their promenades and there was severe flooding in many areas. On the 30th gusts of 50 knots (57.6 mph) or more were widespread in the south and a gust of 59 knots (67.9 mph) was recorded at Sheerness (Kent). Snow fell on the Scottish mountains on the 30th and ball lightning was observed at Edinburgh. On the 31st 63 mm (2.48 in) of rain fell at Kinlochewe (Highland).

Monthly mean temeratures were mostly around normal but ranged from 1°C (1.8°F) below in Scotland to 1°C above in central England. The highest temperature recorded was 28.9°C (84.02°F) at Writtle (Essex) on the 1st and the lowest was −1.2°C (29.84°F) at Eskdalemuir (Dumfries and Galloway) on the 29th.

Sunshine totals were below normal in the south and west of Britain but above normal in eastern areas. Several places on the south coast had their dullest August for more than 20 years. The highest daily total was 14.1 hours at L'Ancresse (Guernsey) on the 5th and the highest monthly total was 204.3 hours at Cleethorpes (S. Humberside).

SEPTEMBER 1992

Monthly rainfall totals were generally above normal and it was the wettest September since 1894. On the 2nd it was very windy along the south coast of England and on the 6th there were gales in the north and west. The 6th was a wet day in Scotland when 70 mm (2.76 in) of rain fell at Greenock (Strathclyde). Gales in the north and west continued on the 7th, and there were further gales in the west on the 10th when a gust of 65 knots (74.9 mph) was recorded at Culdrose (Cornwall). There was heavy rain in Scotland on the 13th and some roads were flooded in Dumfries and Galloway. There was fog over central and eastern England on the 13th–14th and in many places on the 18th. There were widespread thunderstorms on the 18th, particularly in south-east England and East Anglia. Many buildings, including Norwich Cathedral, were struck by lightning. A man was struck by lightning at Basildon (Essex) and 97.8 mm (3.85 in) of rain fell at Upton Scudamore (Wilts.). The 22nd was the wettest day in England and Wales since 1991 and there was serious flooding in Bedfordshire, London, Berkshire and East Anglia, with 89 mm (3.5 in) of rain at Bedford, 79 mm (3.11 in) at Wittering (Cambs.), 76 mm (2.99 in) at Reading (Berks.) and 75 mm (2.95 in) at Northwood (Gtr London). On the 27th there were dense patches of fog over eastern areas of Scotland and England which caused many road accidents; one man was killed. Aberdeen Airport (Grampian) was closed for a time. The fog spread to most of the country overnight, becoming dense in many areas, and there was a fatal accident in South Yorkshire. Fog was also widespread and dense in places on the night of the 28th–29th.

Monthly mean temperatures were mostly below normal, the month being very cool until the last week, when temperatures rose to above average in places. The highest temperature recorded was 25.0°C (77.0°F) at Marholm (Norfolk) on the 28th and the lowest was −1.2°C (29.84°F) at Aviemore (Highland) on the 13th.

Sunshine totals were mostly below normal over England and Wales but a little above normal in parts of Scotland. Over England and Wales it was the dullest September since 1984 and Baltasound (Shetland) had its second lowest total since 1906. The highest daily total was 12.1 hours at Cleethorpes (S. Humberside) on the 1st and at Twist (Devon) on the 4th. The highest monthly total was 171.7 hours at Herne Bay (Kent).

OCTOBER 1992

Rainfall totals were generally above average and many eastern areas had nearly twice the normal amount. Parts of Scotland had less than normal. On the 2nd a thunderstorm occurred over Guernsey (CI) and severe flooding occurred at Kimbolton (Cambs.) after very heavy rain. On the 6th there were gales in south-east England and on the 13th there were gales in the north. On the 15th showers of snow, sleet or

hail were heavy and widespread with thunderstorms in Devon, Anglesey and north-east England. Several inches of snow fell in the Cairngorm area (Highland) and there were gales in northern Scotland when a gust of 51 knots (58.7 mph) was recorded at Peterhead (Grampian). On the 16th wintry showers fell over the Scottish Borders and snow fell on the Pennines. On the 17th 46 mm (1.81 in) of rain fell at Crosby (Merseyside) and on the 18th–19th freezing fog formed in Yorkshire, Shropshire and the Midlands. On the 19th thunderstorms with hail occurred over northern Wales and on the night of the 19th–20th over the south coast of England. On the 20th there were thunderstorms over south-east England and East Anglia. Houses were struck by lightning in Essex, and in Newport (IOW) a house was struck twice in two minutes. On the 23rd thunderstorms with heavy snow, sleet or hail were widespread and four people were killed overnight in accidents in heavy rain in Runcorn (Cheshire). There were further thunderstorms on the 24th particularly over East Anglia and on the 25th there was torrential rain over much of the country with severe flooding in places. Snow fell in southern Scotland and northern England on the 25th when North Yorkshire had its first October snow for 30 years, blocking the A66 across the Pennines. Severe gales affected Wales and southern England on the 25th and gusts of over 60 knots (69.1 mph) were widespread. A yachtsman was drowned off the Isle of Wight and a gust of 78 knots (89.8 mph) was recorded at Camborne (Cornwall). On the 26th 72 mm (2.83 in) of rain fell at the Isle of Rhum (Highland) and a gust of 77 knots (88.7 mph) was recorded at Fair Isle (Shetland) on the 28th.

Monthly mean temperatures were well below normal, it being one of the coldest Octobers on record; in Glasgow (Strathclyde) it was the coldest for 135 years. On the 26th Braemar (Grampian) recorded −7.3°C (18.86°F), its lowest October temperature for 21 years. The highest temperature recorded was 20.7°C (69.26°F) at Elmstone (Kent) on the 2nd and the lowest was −7.7°C (18.14°F) at Santon Downham (Norfolk) on the 31st.

Sunshine totals were below normal except in the northern Isles, the Scottish Highlands, the north-east Midlands, East Anglia and southern areas of England and Wales. The highest daily total was 9.9 hours at Bognor Regis (W. Sussex) on the 13th and the highest monthly total was 144.5 hours, also at Bognor Regis.

NOVEMBER 1992

Rainfall totals were above average everywhere except for a few north-eastern coastal areas and generally it was the wettest November since 1984. Fort Augustus (Highland) had its wettest November since 1886. The 2nd was a windy day, especially in the north, and thunderstorms affected central and southern Scotland. There was extensive fog over south-western areas on the 4th and 7th and over much of southern England on the 5th and 6th. Thunderstorms with hail affected north-western areas on the 11th. There were gales with heavy rain over the Channel Islands and southern England on the 11th, with widespread flooding in Jersey (CI) and along the Thames Valley. Thunderstorms affected much of Scotland and the Manchester area on the 12th. Snow fell on the Scottish hills on the 12th and 13th and over northern Wales and the Pennines on the 14th. Thunderstorms occurred over the Channel Islands and the London area on the 17th. The 18th and 19th were very windy days with gales in the north-west and a gust of 64 knots (73.7 mph) was recorded at Benbecula (Highland) on the 18th. A thunderstorm occurred at Prestwick (Strathclyde) on the 18th and wintry showers affected central and western Scotland and northern Wales on the 19th. On the 21st 60 mm (2.36 in) of rain fell at Machynlleth (Powys) and there was serious flooding in central and northern Wales after prolonged rain between the 21st and 23rd. Heavy snow fell on the 21st over central and southern Scotland and north-east England. There were gales in northern areas on the 23rd and over Northern Ireland on the 24th. The 25th brought gales to southern England when a gust of 70 knots (80.6 mph) was recorded at Langdon Bay (Kent). Two fishermen were drowned off north Cornwall when their boat capsized. There was heavy rain and thunderstorms in southern areas on the 25th and much of southern England was flooded on the 26th. Snow fell in the south-west on the 28th. During heavy rain in the west on the 29th 60 mm (2.36 in) fell at Cwmbargoed (Mid Glam.) and parts of Wales had their worst floods for 20 years. Avon, Devon, Wiltshire, Gloucestershire and Worcestershire also had serious flooding on the 29th and 28 rivers were put on full flood alert. Many homes were flooded and road and rail traffic was seriously disrupted. There were thunderstorms in Cornwall on the 30th and gales in the south-west caused the deaths of three fisherman off north Cornwall.

Monthly mean temperatures were above average nearly everywhere except northern Scotland and it was the mildest November in central England since 1978. The highest temperature recorded was 18.5°C (65.3°F) at Torbay (Devon) on the 6th and the lowest was −6.8°C (19.76°F) at Paisley (Strathclyde) on the 14th.

Sunshine totals were higher than normal in eastern areas but below normal in the west. The highest daily total was 9.3 hours at Squires Gate (Lancs.) on the 1st and the highest monthly total was 88.7 hours at Leuchars (Fife).

DECEMBER 1992

Rainfall totals were above normal in the north and west but below normal elsewhere. There was heavy rain in many areas from the 1st to 3rd, which exacerbated the existing floods. A policeman was killed by a passing car in torrential rain in Tyne and Wear on the 2nd. There were gales in southern and western regions on the 2nd when Camborne (Corn-

wall) recorded a gust of 74 knots (85.2 mph). A man was blown into the sea and drowned at Blackpool (Lancs.). Between the 3rd and 6th wintry showers fell in central and western Scotland, Wales and northern England and some roads over the Pennines were blocked with snow. On the 5th ten people were killed in a series of road accidents from Lancashire to Kent. Heavy rain fell on the 6th in western areas. On the 9th and 10th there was extensive fog over north-west and south-east England and heavy rain fell in Northern Ireland on the 11th. On the 15th and 16th rain and snow affected many areas. The heaviest snowfall was 45 cm (17.72 in) at Aviemore (Highland). There was freezing fog in south-east England and the Midlands on the 16th–17th. Winds were strong in many coastal areas on the 17th and a gust of 83 knots (95.6 mph) was recorded at Butt of Lewis (Highland). On the 18th there was heavy rain in many areas with wintry showers in Northern Ireland and central Scotland. A canoeist was drowned in the swollen River Ogwen (Gwynedd) and a man died on a flooded road in Gloucestershire. On the 19th there was snow in southern England and on the 19th–20th there was freezing fog, mainly in central and north-western districts. There were several serious road accidents and seven people were killed in Derbyshire and Yorkshire. There was further snow in the north-west on the 21st and on the 22nd two boys drowned trying to walk across a frozen pond in Derbyshire. Freezing fog was persistent in many areas for the rest of the month.

Monthly mean temperatures were generally below normal and towards the end of the month temperatures stayed below freezing for several days in places. The highest temperature recorded was 14.6°C (58.28°C) at Betws-y-Coed (Gwynedd) on the 2nd and at Colwyn Bay (Clwyd) on the 11th and the lowest was −14.2°C (6.44°F) at Grantown-on-Spey (Highland) on the 21st.

Sunshine totals were below normal in parts of central northern England and southern Scotland but higher than normal elsewhere. The highest daily total was 7.1 hours at Hurn (Dorset) on the 28th and the highest monthly total was 80 hours at Dale Fort (Dyfed).

THE YEAR 1992

The main feature of the year was the very wet autumn which did much to replenish the underground water supplies which had fallen to very low levels in many areas. Apart from May and June it was generally a wet year but temperatures were above normal for the summer months. January started wet with severe gales in Scotland and extensive flooding in western Scotland; 120 mm (4.27 in) of rain fell at Inverinan Moor (Strathclyde) and at Tyndrum (Perthshire) on the 1st and a gust of 98 knots (112.9 mph) was recorded at Sumburgh (Shetland). Fog disrupted traffic in Scotland on the 11th and 12th, and a barometric pressure of 1049 millibars in Wales on the 26th was the highest in January for 30 years. Fog on the 28th caused dozens of accidents on the M8 in Scotland. February was a wet month over Scotland and Northern Ireland and there were snow showers over many areas of England and Wales. On the 1st there was widespread dense fog over England and Wales and on the 18th heavy snow in the Midlands caused disruption of traffic. Winds were often strong in the north and west of the United Kingdom. March was a generally wet month with some extensive falls of snow over many areas of the country. It was a windy month mainly in the north and west and a gust of 122 knots (140.5 mph) was recorded on the 12th at Cairngorm (Highland). Temperatures were above normal for the third month running. April was another mainly wet month with above average temperatures. The month started with hail showers in the south-west, snow in Scotland and heavy rain in northern England. Sleet was frequent with hail in places until the middle of the month when rain and thunderstorms occurred in many areas. Sunshine was generally below normal. May had generally below average rainfall but some very heavy rain between the 28th and 30th produced what would be a normal month's rainfall in many places. On the 8th snow fell as far south as the Midlands and thunderstorms were frequent between the 8th and 15th and widespread during the last few days of the month. In central England it was the warmest May since 1833 and a temperature of 28.9°C (84.0°F) at Edinburgh on the 14th was the highest temperature recorded in Scotland since 1896. June was another generally dry month but there was some intense rain in places. Thunderstorms occurred somewhere in the United Kingdom on each of the first 10 days and on the 8th there were floods around Lampeter (Dyfed). On the 9th–10th there were floods in London, where rail traffic was seriously disrupted and a school was struck by lightning. On the 10th a violent storm left parts of Greater Manchester flooded. Temperatures were above normal everywhere and over central England it was the second warmest June this century. July was a wet month over England and Wales and on the 20th thunderstorms caused floods two feet deep in Sandown (IOW). It was the sixth successive month with temperatures above normal but it was the dullest July since 1981. August was another wet month in most areas. From the 9th to the end of the month rain, often heavy with thunder, occurred somewhere in the United Kingdom on each day. September was also a wet month and was the wettest since 1984. There were several fatal accidents due to the weather during the month. October was also a wet month, with flooding in Cambridgeshire on the 3rd and rain, snow, sleet and hail with frequent thunderstorms and gales occurring throughout the rest of the month. Temperatures were below normal in October and at Glasgow (Strathclyde) it was the coldest for 135 years. November was yet another wet month and was the wettest since 1984. At Fort Augustus (Highland) it was the wettest since 1886. On the 23rd there was serious flooding in central and northern Wales and

on the 29th Wales, Avon, Devon, Wiltshire, Gloucestershire and Worcestershire were seriously flooded. Gales were frequent and widespread during the month. December was a month of contrasts. On the 5th ten people were killed in heavy thunderstorms. The weather then turned cold and the last 12 days of the month were cold and foggy. Seven people were killed on icy roads in the Midlands and northern England on the 21st.

JANUARY 1993

Rainfall totals were near or above normal almost everywhere except for the extreme north-east of Scotland. The month will be remembered as one of the stormiest on record, especially over Scotland. In Orkney there were gales on 21 of the first 26 days of the month. On the 2nd there was persistent freezing fog in the south of England and a woman was killed and many people injured in a 44-vehicle pile-up near Northfleet (Kent). On the 4th snow and sleet fell as far south as Oxfordshire and Wiltshire and a man was killed on icy roads at Lawton's Cross (Herefordshire). In severe gales on the 5th an oil tanker, the *Braer*, was driven onto the rocks in Quendale Bay (Shetland). Storms swept across Britain on the 10th and parts of Rothesay (Isle of Bute) were under 600 mm (2 ft) of floodwater. Fallen trees littered southern England and there were floods in Sussex, Berkshire, Hampshire and Gwent. On the 12th over 310 mm (1 ft) of snow lay on the Grampians and in Shetland the *Braer* finally broke up in 25 m (80 ft) waves. Storms caused many car accidents and a woman died in an accident near Swindon (Wilts.). On the 13th a man was killed when his lorry was blown off the road at Akeld (Northumberland) and winds reached 64 knots (73.7 mph) in London. A cargo plane crashed near Sellafield (Cumbria) and a sailor was drowned near the Isles of Scilly. In the south of England, winds reached 70 knots (80 mph) and two men were killed by a falling tree at Stanwell (Surrey). The gales continued and on the 15th six people were killed in accidents. On the 17th a rapid thaw and exceptional rainfall caused severe widespread flooding along the River Tay (Tayside). In Perth the flood was the worst since 1814 and devastated farmland. A gust of 94 knots (108.2 mph) was recorded at Kirkwall (Orkney) on the 17th and northern England and Wales were also severely battered. On the 21st a gust of 147 knots (169.3 mph) at Cairngorm was one of the strongest ever recorded in the United Kingdom. Further gales swept the country on the 23rd and 24th when a gust of 83 knots (95 mph) was recorded at Leeds (W. Yorks.) on the 24th; there was also further widespread flooding in Scotland. On the 24th a man was killed when his boat capsized at Portland (Dorset) and in Liverpool the Philharmonic Hall was severely damaged.

Monthly mean temperatures were well above normal nearly everywhere and the mean over central England was 2.7°C (4.86°F) above normal. The highest temperature recorded was 15.2°C (59.36°F) at Boulmer (Northumberland) on the 16th and the lowest was − 9.8°C (14.36°F) at Bedford on the 3rd.

Sunshine totals were generally below normal but were above normal in eastern Scotland. Over England and Wales it was the dullest January since 1975. The highest daily total was 7.7 hours at Drummond Castle (Tayside) on the 31st and the highest monthly total was 67.6 hours at Sunderland (Tyne and Wear).

FEBRUARY 1993

Rainfall totals were below normal everywhere and it was the driest February since 1986 in England, Wales and Northern Ireland. On the 3rd there was extensive fog over southern England and Wales which extended into the Midlands on the 4th and persisted on the 5th. Fog and mist continued over many areas, particularly in the south, until the 15th. On the 12th Guernsey Airport (CI) was closed by thick fog. On the 18th there were gales and wintry showers in the north, with gusts of 55-70 knots (63-80 mph) recorded in Scotland. On the 19th and 20th gusts of 70-80 knots (80-92 mph) were recorded in Shetland and wintry showers continued over much of the United Kingdom. On the 20th gales in the North Sea caused workers to be airlifted from an oil-rig off Aberdeen (Grampian), and East Anglia, Essex and Kent were put on flood alert as mounting seas threatened the sea defences. The River Bure burst its banks at Acle (Norfolk) and the A47 road from Norwich to Great Yarmouth was closed to traffic. Train services were cancelled between Norwich and Lowestoft, one and a half miles of the sea wall at Cley (Norfolk) was swept away, and hundreds of acres of farmland were flooded. In Kent there was flooding in the Isle of Sheppey, Herne Bay and Ramsgate and in London the Thames Barrier was closed. On the 25th there was heavy rain for a time over Scotland and Wales which later spread to southern and eastern England. After spells of rain on the 26th wintry showers spread to most of the United Kingdom and by the 27th many roads in the Grampian area were blocked with snow. On the 28th there were very extensive and often heavy snow and hail showers, mostly over eastern Scotland and eastern England.

Monthly mean temperatures were above normal everywhere and it was the mildest February in Northern Ireland since 1961. A temperature of 14°C (57.2°F) at Eskdalemuir (Dumfries and Galloway) on the 7th was the highest there for February since 1914 and the monthly mean temperature of 4.6°C (40.28°F) at Braemar (Grampian), 4.2°C (7.56°F) above average, was the highest there since 1868. The highest temperature recorded during the month was 16.4°C (61.52°F) at Scarborough (N. Yorks.) on the 6th and the lowest was − 6.2°C (20.84°F) at Dumfries on the 1st.

Sunshine totals were below normal everywhere. In Northern Ireland it was the dullest February on record and the dullest at Armagh since 1880. In Scotland it was the second dullest February since 1881. The highest daily total was 10.1 hours at Hayling Island (Hants.) on the 27th and the highest monthly total was 79.0 hours at Boulmer (Northumberland).

MARCH 1993

Rainfall totals were below normal in England, Wales and eastern Scotland but above normal in western and central Scotland. February and March together were the driest in England and Wales since 1929. Snow showers fell over much of the United Kingdom on the 1st and about 25 mm (1 in) of snow lay in parts of south-east England. Further snow fell in Scotland on the 2nd and 3rd and 35 cm (13.78 in) of snow lay in the Cairngorm (Highland) car park. There was fog in some eastern coastal areas on the 6th. Snow and sleet showers fell in southern Scotland on the 10th and on the 11th there was extensive fog over south-east England, the Midlands and the north-east. There was rain over Northern Ireland and Scotland on the 17th, when 45 mm (1.77 in) fell at Sloy (Highland). There were gales in northern Scotland on the 18th and 19th when gusts exceeded 70 knots (80 mph) in Shetland. On the 19th there were heavy showers in northern and western Scotland and on the 21st rain fell in many areas, particularly in Wales and southern England. There were persistent snow showers over north and east Scotland on the 22nd. The 23rd was a windy day especially over Scotland and a gust of 64 knots (74 mph) was recorded at Kirkwall (Orkney). There were sleet or snow showers over Yorkshire, Cumbria and Scotland on the 23rd and 19 cm (7.48 in) of snow lay at Aviemore (Highland). The showers continued on the 24th. The 27th-29th brought rain to Northern Ireland, western England and north and west Scotland, with 76 mm (2.99 in) falling at Lochranza (Isle of Arran) on the 29th. There were gales in the north and west of Scotland on the 29th and 30th and gusts of 65 knots (75 mph) were recorded at Sumburgh (Shetland) and Drumalbin (Strathclyde). The rain continued on the 30th and moved into southern England on the 31st.

Monthly mean temperatures were above normal everywhere and were 1.5°C (2.7°F) above average over England, Wales and south-east Scotland. The temperature fell to − 12°C (10.4°F) at Braemar (Grampian) on the night of the 3rd-4th but rose to 18°C (64.4°F) at Aberdeen (Grampian) on the 17th. The highest temperature recorded was 19.7°C (67.46°F) at Northolt (Gtr London) on the 15th and the lowest was − 12.2°C (10.04°F) at Braemar (Grampian) on the 4th.

Sunshine totals were above normal almost everywhere except western Scotland. The highest daily total was 12.2 hours at Douglas (Isle of Man) on the 25th and the highest monthly total was 165.6 hours at Bognor Regis (W. Sussex).

APRIL 1993

Rainfall totals were generally above normal except in parts of Scotland where they were lower than normal. Over England and Wales it was the wettest April since 1983 and the seventh wettest this century.

Leuchars (Fife) had its wettest April for 60 years. On the 1st there was heavy rain over East Anglia, south-east and central southern England and the RAF's 75th anniversary fly-past had to be cancelled. There was heavy rain over many areas on the 3rd when 37.6 mm (1.48 in) fell at Machrihanish (Strathclyde) and on the 5th rain and snow over Scotland spread to the whole of the United Kingdom. There were gales in many areas on the 5th and a gust of 104 knots (119 mph) was recorded at Cairngorm (Grampian). The 8th and 9th brought heavy rain to most areas and three people were killed when their plane crashed in thick fog near Teignmouth (Devon). On the 9th several people were killed in multiple accidents on motorways and flooding occurred in Dumfries and Galloway, Cumbria, Gwent, Hampshire and the south-west. Craibstone (Grampian) had its wettest April day since 1934 with a fall of 44 m (1.73 in). On the 10th and 11th there was heavy rain over southern England and on the 12th there were widespread thunderstorms with hail, often heavy. On the 15th there was rain over Scotland. On the 17th there were thunderstorms and hail over Shetland and the 18th brought further heavy rain to northern Wales, Northern Ireland, northern England and southern Scotland, with 30.5 mm (1.2 in) falling at Drungans (Dumfries and Galloway). There was rain over Scotland on the 19th which spread to Northern Ireland and western England on the 20th. There was further rain, sometimes heavy, in most areas from the 22nd to 25th. On the 26th there were thunderstorms over southern Wales and eastern England and heavy rain over southern England. On the 30th fog was widespread over England and Wales for a time.

Monthly mean temperatures were above normal everywhere and over England and Wales it was one of the warmest Aprils this century. On the 29th Morecambe (Lancs.) had its highest April temperature, 22.7°C (72.86°F), since 1901 and at Braemar (Grampian) the temperature rose from −1°C (30.2°F) in the early hours to 22.0°C (71.6°F) in the afternoon. The highest temperature recorded during the month was 25.0°C (77.0°F) at Norwich (Norfolk) and at Peebles (Borders) on the 30th, and the lowest was −4.0°C (24.8°F) at Carnwath (Strathclyde) on the 4th.

Sunshine totals were below normal everywhere and over England and Wales it was the dullest April since 1978. The highest daily total was 13.7 hours at Bidston (Merseyside) and at Fair Isle (Shetland) on the 28th, and the highest monthly total was 174 hours at Folkestone (Kent).

MAY 1993

Rainfall totals were above average everywhere except in the far north and west of Scotland. Over England and Wales it was the wettest May since 1983 and some central areas of Britain received more than three times the normal amount. At Plymouth (Devon), 123.6 mm (4.86 in) of rain fell, its highest May total for 50 years. On the 1st there was thick fog over southern England for a time. On the 6th there was rain over northern Scotland and on the 8th there were thunderstorms in southern Scotland. On the 9th there were rain and thunderstorms in southern England. Rain and thunder were widespread on the 10th except in the south and there were thunderstorms over northern England on the 11th and in southern England on the 12th. On the 13th there was heavy rain in western and northern areas with more than 50 mm (2 in) falling over a wide area of Northumberland and Co. Durham and 54.2 mm (2.14 in) falling at Sunderland (Tyne and Wear). On the 14th there was widespread heavy rain in northern Britain and some areas along the Scottish Borders had falls of heavy snow, with 23 cm (9 in) falling on Lowther Hill (Dumfries and Galloway) and 8 cm (3 in) in many other places. Some roads were blocked by snow and there was also some severe flooding in parts of Northumberland, Tyne and Wear and Co. Durham. Gales on the 14th brought down trees in the Belfast area. There was more heavy rain in Scotland on the 15th and in western and northern areas of Britain on the 16th. The 17th was a windy day with widespread, often heavy, rain and thunderstorms became widespread over southern England. A Royal Marine was killed by lightning on Dartmoor (Devon) and a whirlwind damaged several houses in Cheddar (Somerset). A tornado caused havoc in a line from St Harmon to Pant-y-dwr (Powys). In five minutes it sped across three farms picking up and destroying vehicles and caravans and throwing a flock of sheep 15.5 m (50 ft) into the air before dropping them half a mile away across walls and a river. Amazingly, only six of the 20 sheep were killed. Roofs were ripped off buildings, trees flattened and a 18.5 m (60 ft) workshop was twisted into a spiral. A Land-Rover was torn in half. There was rain over East Anglia on the 19th and rain was again widespread on the 20th and 21st but confined to the south-west on the 22nd. There were severe thunderstorms in Wales and heavy rain in Northern Ireland on the 24th. The 26th brought violent thunderstorms to southern England when there were severe floods in Oxfordshire after a fall of 114 mm (5.5 in). A jet plane plunged onto the M27 near Southampton and burst into flames but nobody was hurt. There were floods throughout Devon and Berkshire. There was heavy rain across England and Wales on the 27th and rain in many areas until the end of the month.

Monthly mean temperatures were higher than normal over England and Wales but below normal in most of Scotland. The highest temperature recorded was 25.8°C (78.44°F) at Yeovilton (Somerset) on the 24th and the lowest was −4.6°C (23.72°F) at Lairg (Highland) on the 2nd.

Sunshine totals were below normal almost everywhere. The highest daily total was 15.1 hours at Morecambe (Lancs.) on the 7th and at Inverness (Highland) on the 18th and the highest monthly total was 249.7 hours at Poolewe (Highland).

JUNE 1993

Rainfall totals were above normal everywhere except central and southern Scotland where they were below normal. Over England and Wales it was the wettest June since 1987. There was rain mainly in the north and west on the 1st and there were thunderstorms in central England on the 2nd. On the 9th severe thunderstorms affected southern England and 125 mm (5.0 in) of rain fell at Culdrose (Cornwall) in 12 hours, 91.7 mm (3.6 in) of it in only two hours. There were severe floods in Cornwall, the worst hit areas being Helston and Porthleven. Thunderstorms were more widespread on the 10th when 91.8 mm (3.6 in) of rain fell in three hours at Thornwood Common (Essex) and very severe flooding occurred in northern Wales where 400 people were evacuated from their homes in Llandudno (Gwynedd). Forty occupied caravans were washed away by a flooded river at Cardigan (Dyfed) and many holiday-makers had to be rescued by helicopter. In Leicestershire 59 mm (2.3 in) of rain caused flooding, and floodwater was 2.2 m (7 ft) deep in Sheffield (S. Yorks.). There was also extensive flooding in Luton (Beds.), Cambridgeshire, Suffolk and Sussex. Heavy rain and thunderstorms affected many areas on the 11th when 33 mm (1.3 in) of rain fell in Enfield (Gtr London) in one and a half hours and 130.5 mm (5.14 in) fell at Davidstow Moor (Cornwall). There was further heavy rain over southern areas on the 12th and flooding was very severe in north Cornwall, where Bude had its worst floods since 1904. The damage caused by flooding during these few days was estimated at millions of pounds and many people were unable to return to their homes for weeks. There was further heavy rain on the 13th and 14th and thunderstorms occurred in southern areas on the 15th when 32 mm (1.26 in) of rain fell at Culdrose (Cornwall). Rain continued on the 16th and 17th and 26.4 mm (1.04 in) fell at Nantmor (Gwynedd) on the 17th. Rain continued on most days in many areas but the next heavy falls were mainly in northern areas on the 23rd. The remainder of the month was comparatively dry but 46.8 mm (1.84 in) of rain fell at Isle of Rhum (Highland) on the 25th.

Monthly mean temperatures were above normal everywhere except northern Scotland and over England and Wales it was one of the ten warmest Junes this century. It is interesting to note that the first six months of 1993 were all warmer than normal. On 6 June 28.1°C (82.6°F) was recorded in Barbourne (Worcs.) and on the 9th the temperature rose to 25.7°C (78.3°F) at Kelso (Borders). Some road surfaces melted in the heat and the M11 at Stansted (Essex) was closed to traffic. Twice in two days Tower Bridge (Gtr London) would not close as the metal expanded in the heat. The highest temperature recorded during the month was 28.6°C (83.5°F) at Northolt (Gtr London) on the 8th and the lowest was 0.0°C (32.0°F) at Perth (Tayside).

Sunshine totals were above normal over England and Wales but well below normal over Scotland and Northern Ireland where it was the dullest June for 110 years at Armagh. The highest daily total was 15.9 hours at Sheffield (S. Yorks.) on the 27th and the highest monthly total was 254.0 hours at Manston (Kent).

Astronomers Royal

Instituted in 1675, the title of Astronomer Royal was given to the director of the Greenwich Observatory until 1975. Currently it is an honorary title for an outstanding astronomer, who receives a stipend of approximately £100 a year.

John Flamsteed (1646–1719), appointed 1675
Edmund Halley (1656–1742), appointed 1720
James Bradley (1693–1762), appointed 1742
Nathaniel Bliss (1700–64), appointed 1762
Nevil Maskelyne (1732–1811), appointed 1765

John Pond (1767–1836), appointed 1811
Sir George Airy (1801–92), appointed 1835
Sir William Christie (1845–1922), appointed 1881
Sir Frank Dyson (1868–1939), appointed 1910
Sir Harold Jones (1890–1960), appointed 1933
Sir Richard Woolley (1906–86), appointed 1955
Sir Martin Ryle (1918–84), appointed 1972
Sir Francis Graham-Smith (1923–), appointed 1982
Arnold Wolfendale (1927–), appointed 1991

AVERAGE AND GENERAL VALUES 1991–3 (JUNE)

	Rainfall (mm)				Temperature (°C)				Bright Sunshine (hrs per day)			
	Average 1961–90	1991	1992	1993	Average 1961–90	1991	1992	1993	Average 1961–90	1991	1992	1993
ENGLAND AND WALES												
January	77	92	48	113	3.8	3.9	4.2	6.3	1.6	2.2	1.7	1.3
February	55	63	47	15	3.8	2.0	5.9	5.2	2.3	2.3	2.3	1.8
March	63	75	85	26	5.6	8.1	7.6	6.8	3.5	2.9	2.5	3.8
April	53	68	73	93	7.7	8.3	8.9	9.7	4.9	5.1	4.2	4.1
May	56	14	49	86	10.9	10.9	13.5	11.6	6.2	4.7	8.2	5.7
June	58	92	38	68	13.9	12.4	15.8	15.0	6.4	4.7	7.2	6.4
July	56	68	83	–	15.7	17.0	16.6	–	6.0	6.2	5.3	–
August	68	31	130	–	15.6	17.0	15.9	–	5.7	6.9	5.3	–
September	70	62	92	–	13.6	14.7	13.8	–	4.5	5.9	3.9	–
October	77	77	84	–	10.7	10.2	8.3	–	3.2	2.8	3.1	–
November	81	95	138	–	6.6	6.7	7.9	–	2.2	1.8	1.9	–
December	82	49	83	–	4.7	4.7	4.2	–	1.5	1.5	1.4	–
YEAR	796	786	950	–	9.4	9.7	10.2	–	4.0	3.9	3.9	–
SCOTLAND												
January	117	146	139	291	3.1	3.2	4.7	4.8	1.3	1.7	1.4	0.9
February	78	83	167	67	3.1	2.6	5.5	6.2	2.3	2.3	1.9	1.3
March	94	128	208	120	4.6	6.7	6.2	5.9	3.2	2.7	2.3	3.1
April	60	121	119	113	6.5	7.5	7.4	7.9	4.8	5.2	3.2	3.6
May	67	43	81	114	9.3	10.4	11.7	9.6	5.6	5.1	7.4	4.6
June	67	121	39	75	12.1	11.0	14.3	12.7	5.6	5.2	6.1	3.9
July	74	91	91	–	13.6	15.3	14.0	–	4.9	4.8	4.0	–
August	92	67	221	–	13.5	14.9	13.3	–	4.6	4.8	4.6	–
September	111	131	177	–	11.5	11.9	11.7	–	3.5	5.0	3.2	–
October	120	165	123	–	9.1	8.7	6.9	–	2.6	2.1	2.4	–
November	118	227	212	–	5.3	5.6	6.0	–	1.7	1.5	1.5	–
December	116	141	159	–	3.9	4.7	3.7	–	1.0	0.8	0.9	–
YEAR	1114	1464	1736	–	7.9	8.5	8.8	–	3.4	3.4	3.2	–

WEATHER RECORDS

WORLD RECORDS

Maximum air temperature	57.8°C/136°F
San Louis, Mexico, 11 August 1933	
Minimum air temperature	−89.2°C/−128.56°F
Vostok, Antarctica, 21 July 1983	
Greatest rainfall in one day	1870 mm/73.62 in
Cilaos, Isle de Réunion, 16 March 1952	
Greatest rainfall in one calendar month	9300 mm/366.14 in
Cherrapunji, Assam, July 1861	
Greatest annual rainfall total	22,990 mm/905.12 in
Cherrapunji, 1861	
Highest gust of wind	201 knots/231 mph
Mt Washington Observatory, USA, 12 April 1934	

UNITED KINGDOM RECORDS

Maximum air temperature	37.1°C/98.8°F
Cheltenham, Glos., 3 August 1990	
Minimum air temperature	−27.2°C/−17°F
Braemar, Grampian, 11 February 1895 and 10 January 1982	
Greatest rainfall in one day	280 mm/11 in
Martinstown, Dorset, 18 July 1955	
Greatest annual rainfall total	6528 mm/257 in
Sprinkling Tarn, Cumbria, 1954	
Highest gust of wind	150 knots/173 mph
Cairngorm, Highland, 20 March 1986	
Highest low-level gust*	123 knots/141.7 mph
Fraserburgh, Grampian, 13 February 1989	
Highest mean hourly speed	92 knots/106 mph
Great Dun Fell, Cumbria, December 1974	
Highest low-level mean hourly speed*	72 knots/83 mph
Shoreham-by-Sea, Sussex, 16 October 1987	

* below 200 m/656 ft

WIND FORCE MEASURES

The *Beaufort Scale* of wind force has been accepted internationally and is used in communicating weather conditions. Devised originally by Admiral Sir Francis Beaufort in 1805, it now consists of the numbers 0–17, each representing a certain strength or velocity of wind at 10 m (33 ft) above ground in the open.

Scale no.	Wind Force	mph	knots
0	Calm	1	1
1	Light air	1–3	1–3
2	Slight breeze	4–7	4–6
3	Gentle breeze	8–12	7–10
4	Moderate breeze	13–18	11–16
5	Fresh breeze	19–24	17–21
6	Strong breeze	25–31	22–27
7	High wind	32–38	28–33
8	Gale	39–46	34–40
9	Strong gale	47–54	41–47
10	Whole gale	55–63	48–55
11	Storm	64–72	56–63
12	Hurricane	73–82	64–71
13	–	83–92	72–80
14	–	93–103	81–89
15	–	104–114	90–99
16	–	115–125	100–108
17	–	126–136	109–118

TEMPERATURE, RAINFALL AND SUNSHINE
At selected climatological reporting stations, July 1992–June 1993 and calendar year 1992

	Ht m	July 1992 °C	July 1992 Rain mm	July 1992 Sun hrs	August 1992 °C	August 1992 Rain mm	August 1992 Sun hrs	September 1992 °C	September 1992 Rain mm	September 1992 Sun hrs	October 1992 °C	October 1992 Rain mm	October 1992 Sun hrs
Aberdeen (Dyce)	65	14.1	60	5.1	12.9	110	5.2	11.3	88	2.9	6.3	87	2.5
Aberporth	134	15.1	60	5.4	13.9	149	5.5	12.7	75	3.9	8.6	78	2.7
Aldergrove	68	14.7	67	4.4	13.6	150	5.0	11.5	72	3.3	7.0	56	2.9
Aspatria	61	14.9	71	5.5	14.1	151	6.1	12.4	107	4.4	6.7	85	2.5
Bala	163	14.7	78	5.0	13.2	171	4.7	11.7	106	3.3	6.6	108	1.6
Birmingham (Elmdon)	98	16.1	103	5.0	15.4	97	5.7	13.3	52	3.8	7.4	65	2.8
Boulmer	23	14.6	45	5.9	13.9	61	5.7	11.8	87	3.5	7.4	94	2.7
Bournemouth (Hurn)	10	16.7	51	5.5	16.3	90	4.9	14.2	98	4.3	8.0	53	4.1
Bradford	134	15.5	50	4.8	14.3	110	5.2	12.3	69	3.1	6.9	80	2.2
Braemar	339	12.5	43	4.1	11.1	126	4.2	9.9	93	3.2	4.3	73	2.3
Buxton	307	14.6	86	5.2	13.5	156	5.5	11.5	92	3.8	5.9	146	2.5
Cambridge	24	17.5	54	4.5	16.7	72	5.3	14.2	82	4.3	8.3	92	3.2
Cheltenham	65	16.1	–	4.1	15.6	–	4.1	14.2	–	4.1	8.4	55	3.2
Clacton-on-Sea	16	17.7	63	5.8	17.3	104	4.9	14.4	77	4.7	9.1	63	3.8
Douglas	85	14.4	87	5.5	13.9	100	6.3	12.3	104	3.2	8.1	93	3.0
Dumfries	49	14.2	60	4.2	13.5	–	4.7	11.7	–	3.8	6.4	72	2.4
Dundee	45	14.7	51	5.8	13.7	112	5.6	11.8	95	–	6.7	35	3.5
Durham	102	15.1	54	5.4	14.3	69	5.9	12.1	98	3.4	6.9	61	2.6
East Malling	33	17.5	55	6.1	17.0	72	5.3	14.2	56	4.8	8.7	63	3.7
Edinburgh	134	14.4	41	–	13.6	120	–	11.4	102	–	6.5	38	–
Glasgow (Abbotsinch)	5	14.6	58	4.5	13.6	163	4.9	11.8	137	3.1	5.9	69	3.4
Gogerddan	31	15.9	86	–	14.7	152	–	13.5	79	–	8.2	107	–
Hastings	45	17.1	95	6.8	16.9	100	5.4	14.9	75	5.1	9.3	105	4.2
Hull	2	16.7	117	–	16.4	111	–	13.9	82	–	7.9	57	–
Inverness	4	14.3	16	3.5	13.5	100	4.5	11.3	71	3.3	6.5	49	2.2
Leeming	32	15.9	65	5.5	14.9	80	5.8	12.8	82	3.4	7.4	55	2.8
Lerwick	82	11.8	58	4.5	11.7	127	4.0	10.4	112	1.7	6.5	77	2.8
London (Heathrow)	25	18.3	62	5.1	17.7	85	4.8	14.9	77	4.3	8.9	59	3.6
Long Ashton	51	16.4	98	–	15.5	181	–	13.6	71	–	7.9	57	–
Lowestoft	25	17.5	68	5.7	17.2	72	5.8	14.5	32	4.8	8.9	54	3.7
Manchester (Ringway)	75	15.9	63	5.2	14.9	96	5.4	13.3	61	3.9	7.5	121	2.3
Manston	44	17.6	59	6.6	17.0	76	5.4	14.6	37	5.5	9.1	93	4.0
Melbury	143	15.3	116	4.5	14.4	229	4.5	12.8	89	3.3	8.3	103	2.6
Morecambe	7	16.0	67	5.3	14.9	144	6.1	13.5	115	3.8	7.9	123	2.6
Nottingham (Watnall)	117	16.1	93	5.4	15.3	93	6.0	13.0	73	3.5	7.5	78	3.2
Oxford	63	17.3	70	5.3	16.5	109	5.6	14.2	107	4.0	8.2	76	3.3
Penzance	19	17.1	54	6.0	15.8	167	5.0	13.9	121	4.0	–	130	4.3
Plymouth	27	16.4	60	5.3	15.9	102	4.6	13.8	75	3.4	9.3	85	3.9
Prestwick	16	14.7	72	4.4	13.9	144	4.9	12.1	120	3.5	6.3	123	3.0
Rhoose	65	16.5	84	5.5	15.5	173	4.9	13.5	101	3.9	8.5	68	3.5
St Mawgan	103	16.2	77	5.6	15.1	142	4.9	13.5	116	3.3	9.2	90	3.9
Shawbury	72	15.5	77	4.8	14.5	108	5.3	12.9	77	3.4	7.1	63	2.5
Sheffield	131	16.1	78	5.9	15.3	118	6.3	13.0	72	4.1	7.5	66	1.9
Skegness	5	16.7	96	–	16.6	117	6.2	–	82	–	8.2	80	3.6
Southampton	3	17.6	48	5.2	17.1	95	4.6	14.9	50	4.2	9.5	59	–
Stornoway	15	12.8	128	3.6	12.6	191	4.0	10.7	149	2.9	7.3	131	2.2
Tenby	5	16.1	68	5.5	14.6	255	5.6	12.9	83	3.8	8.8	64	3.1
Tiree	9	13.4	91	4.1	13.0	186	5.3	11.3	146	3.5	8.2	107	2.4
Torbay (Torquay)	8	17.8	23	5.9	16.7	109	4.9	14.4	78	4.1	9.7	57	4.2
Valley	10	15.5	65	6.4	14.9	101	6.0	13.5	69	3.9	9.3	74	2.9
Ventnor	135	16.5	102	6.0	16.3	86	4.6	14.9	51	4.7	10.0	88	4.3
Waddington	68	16.5	109	5.6	15.7	71	6.3	13.3	66	4.2	7.6	70	3.0
Weymouth	21	16.7	47	–	16.3	91	4.7	14.6	57	4.2	9.4	40	4.3
Whitby	41	15.5	75	5.5	15.2	50	6.1	12.7	129	4.1	7.5	90	2.6
Worthing	2	16.9	97	6.2	16.7	100	4.8	14.4	61	4.9	9.1	83	4.1
Writtle	35	17.5	80	5.3	16.9	74	5.4	14.1	100	4.4	8.1	104	3.7

Ht   height (in metres) of station above mean sea level
°C   mean air temperature
Rain   total monthly rainfall
Sun   mean daily bright sunshine (hours)
Source: data provided by the Met Office

	November 1992			December 1992			The Year 1992			January 1993			February 1993		
	°C	Rain mm	Sun hrs	°C	Rain mm	Sun hrs	°C	Rain mm	Sun hrs	°C	Rain mm	Sun hrs	°C	Rain mm	Sun hrs
Aberdeen (Dyce)	5.3	63	2.5	2.7	69	1.7	8.2	818	3.7	4.1	75	1.9	5.7	35	2.0
Aberporth	8.5	110	1.7	4.9	110	2.4	9.8	914	3.9	6.4	93	0.9	5.5	23	1.6
Aldergrove	6.3	90	1.6	3.6	69	1.2	8.9	888	3.3	5.0	98	1.3	6.0	28	1.9
Aspatria	6.7	128	1.6	3.5	93	1.3	9.1	1098	4.0	5.3	139	1.1	5.2	24	1.6
Bala	7.2	177	1.1	3.1	127	0.9	8.7	1276	3.1	5.7	181	0.8	5.2	14	1.6
Birmingham (Elmdon)	6.9	112	2.1	2.9	60	1.4	9.7	830	3.8	5.6	71	1.0	4.5	7	1.7
Boulmer	6.3	65	2.8	3.5	46	1.7	8.9	615	4.3	4.9	44	2.0	5.7	10	2.8
Bournemouth (Hurn)	8.3	148	2.4	4.1	97	2.1	10.2	782	4.4	7.2	102	1.3	5.1	10	2.2
Bradford	6.3	125	1.1	3.5	76	0.2	9.2	831	3.1	4.9	119	0.6	4.7	14	1.5
Braemar	3.5	86	1.6	0.7	76	1.0	–	876	–	2.1	–	0.9	5.7	32	1.2
Buxton	5.5	195	1.5	2.2	127	0.8	8.2	1330	–	4.0	119	1.1	3.5	17	1.6
Cambridge	7.5	78	2.1	3.5	32	1.4	10.3	651	3.7	6.3	51	1.3	4.5	12	1.3
Cheltenham	8.6	130	1.8	3.9	69	1.2	–	–	–	6.1	93	1.8	5.3	10	2.1
Clacton-on-Sea	7.5	81	2.1	5.1	27	1.5	10.5	644	4.1	5.6	40	1.5	4.3	9	1.3
Douglas	7.5	149	1.5	5.5	80	1.1	–	–	–	6.1	95	1.0	6.2	22	–
Dumfries	5.7	153	1.5	3.3	111	0.6	–	–	–	4.8	184	1.3	5.5	16	1.2
Dundee	5.7	69	2.8	3.3	46	1.2	8.8	574	–	4.4	145	1.5	6.3	5	2.1
Durham	6.1	61	2.6	2.9	45	0.9	8.9	642	3.9	4.7	40	1.7	5.1	16	1.9
East Malling	8.3	107	2.2	4.5	43	2.0	10.6	606	4.3	6.5	56	1.6	4.6	8	1.6
*Edinburgh	–	85	–	3.5	35	–	–	717	–	5.0	116	1.4	6.3	4	1.8
Glasgow (Abbotsinch)	5.7	163	1.6	3.7	85	0.8	8.8	1224	3.3	5.0	231	1.1	6.1	18	1.5
Gogerddan	8.5	168	–	4.6	111	–	–	–	–	7.1	130	–	6.0	21	–
Hastings	8.5	134	2.3	5.1	55	1.8	10.8	773	4.7	6.4	82	1.8	4.1	7	2.1
Hull	7.3	77	–	3.7	50	–	10.1	729	–	5.3	43	–	5.2	19	–
Inverness	5.5	93	1.9	3.7	64	0.9	8.7	710	3.1	4.7	145	1.0	6.8	18	1.6
Leeming	6.7	60	2.6	3.1	51	1.0	9.4	595	3.9	5.1	52	1.6	5.3	22	1.7
Lerwick	5.3	208	0.9	4.1	123	0.4	7.4	1274	3.2	3.3	227	0.3	4.3	115	0.9
London (Heathrow)	8.3	87	2.1	4.7	36	1.6	11.2	651	3.9	6.9	63	1.2	4.9	2	1.8
Long Ashton	7.9	210	–	4.3	85	–	10.0	1080	–	6.7	173	–	5.1	9	–
Lowestoft	7.2	92	2.3	4.7	36	1.4	10.4	636	4.3	5.6	47	1.2	4.3	27	1.3
Manchester (Ringway)	6.9	120	1.8	3.1	72	1.5	9.7	856	3.8	5.5	79	1.6	4.9	13	1.9
Manston	8.1	82	2.4	4.9	32	1.6	10.6	576	4.5	6.0	39	1.6	4.0	13	1.5
Melbury	8.6	247	1.5	–	119	1.3	–	1265	3.7	6.7	204	1.2	5.2	28	1.8
Morecambe	7.1	141	1.4	4.1	124	1.1	9.9	1139	3.9	5.7	144	1.1	5.5	17	–
Nottingham (Watnall)	6.7	105	2.1	2.9	48	1.1	9.6	749	3.8	5.1	69	1.2	4.5	11	2.0
Oxford	7.8	120	2.1	3.9	51	1.5	10.5	796	–	6.5	82	1.2	4.7	7	1.9
Penzance	10.3	183	1.6	7.3	118	1.5	–	1109	4.3	8.6	148	1.3	7.9	24	1.8
Plymouth	9.3	174	1.5	6.1	85	1.7	10.7	882	4.2	7.7	118	1.1	6.5	25	2.4
†Prestwick	6.9	157	1.3	4.4	66	1.1	9.2	1174	3.5	5.3	124	0.9	6.3	17	1.2
Rhoose	8.3	187	1.7	4.6	68	1.7	10.1	969	4.5	6.5	123	1.2	5.1	14	1.7
St Mawgan	9.3	166	1.8	5.9	104	1.7	10.4	997	4.2	7.9	140	1.3	6.2	22	2.2
Shawbury	6.9	98	2.1	2.8	39	1.2	9.3	762	3.6	5.6	60	1.1	4.5	9	1.7
Sheffield	7.0	129	1.3	3.7	67	0.6	9.8	826	3.7	5.3	88	0.8	–	11	1.5
Skegness	7.0	75	2.4	4.3	47	1.5	–	705	–	5.3	61	1.5	4.3	17	1.5
Southampton	9.0	135	–	5.3	92	–	11.1	731	–	7.2	100	–	5.6	7	–
Stornoway	5.9	171	1.1	4.7	123	0.5	9.0	1447	3.0	4.3	275	0.6	6.5	57	0.8
Tenby	8.5	171	1.9	5.9	122	2.0	10.3	1108	4.0	7.5	134	1.0	6.4	27	1.5
Tiree	6.9	210	1.2	5.7	115	0.6	9.3	1445	3.4	5.5	259	0.7	6.9	66	1.0
Torbay (Torquay)	9.9	182	2.6	6.9	119	1.4	11.4	829	4.6	8.6	158	1.4	6.7	15	2.2
Valley	8.7	113	1.6	5.3	87	1.9	10.4	871	4.2	7.0	73	1.4	6.5	28	1.9
Ventnor	9.6	144	2.3	6.1	47	1.9	11.0	722	4.7	7.5	88	–	5.5	5	2.4
Waddington	6.7	66	2.2	2.9	37	1.4	9.7	643	4.1	5.2	45	1.4	4.5	12	1.7
Weymouth	9.6	143	1.8	5.7	84	1.9	10.7	691	–	7.8	99	1.2	5.9	7	2.3
Whitby	6.8	60	2.5	4.1	65	1.8	9.5	696	4.2	5.2	38	1.9	5.6	17	2.1
Worthing	8.8	141	2.1	5.3	58	1.8	10.6	746	4.5	6.9	91	1.9	5.0	6	2.0
Writtle	7.7	87	2.1	3.7	40	1.2	10.3	703	–	6.1	59	1.2	3.9	8	1.4

* From Jan. 1993 Edinburgh refers to Royal Botanic Gardens (Ht 26 m)
† From Jan. 1993 Prestwick Met Office closed and figures refer to Auchincruive (Ht 48 m)

TEMPERATURE, RAINFALL AND SUNSHINE *contd.*

	March 1993			April 1993			May 1993			June 1993		
	°C	Rain mm	Sun hrs	°C	Rain mm	Sun hrs	°C	Rain mm	Sun hrs	°C	Rain mm	Sun hrs
Aberdeen (Dyce)	5.6	47	4.3	7.3	96	3.8	8.9	91	4.1	12.3	63	4.4
Aberporth	6.6	25	3.3	9.1	57	5.3	10.8	108	6.3	13.3	191	6.1
Aldergrove	6.3	52	3.0	8.9	103	3.7	10.5	131	4.6	13.8	76	3.9
Aspatria	6.1	37	3.5	8.5	92	4.5	10.1	105	5.3	13.7	39	5.8
Auchincruive	5.7	50	2.9	8.2	82	4.1	9.7	80	4.9	–	74	–
Bala	5.5	23	2.7	8.3	121	3.8	9.9	157	4.7	13.4	60	5.7
Birmingham (Elmdon)	6.4	15	3.5	9.1	81	3.1	11.3	73	5.9	14.9	60	7.3
Boulmer	6.0	18	4.3	7.5	104	4.3	9.1	81	4.8	12.3	27	5.8
Bournemouth (Hurn)	6.1	54	4.5	9.7	99	4.3	12.3	51	6.1	15.3	57	7.7
Bradford	6.0	13	2.7	8.9	105	3.5	–	94	4.3	14.2	37	5.4
Braemar	3.6	60	3.5	6.1	75	3.6	8.1	106	4.7	11.9	31	4.3
Buxton	4.7	16	3.3	8.1	118	3.6	9.3	87	4.9	–	–	–
Cambridge	6.9	20	4.0	9.9	78	3.6	12.4	48	6.0	15.5	86	6.2
Cheltenham	6.7	27	3.8	9.3	93	2.9	12.1	97	5.4	–	–	–
Clacton-on-Sea	6.3	13	4.7	9.9	61	5.1	12.2	29	6.8	–	–	–
Douglas	6.1	74	–	8.7	116	–	10.1	137	–	13.3	71	0.0
Dumfries	5.5	92	3.0	8.3	141	3.6	10.0	100	3.9	–	–	–
Dundee	5.9	26	3.9	–	117	3.5	9.8	85	4.7	13.5	36	–
Durham	5.9	10	4.1	8.1	95	3.7	10.1	93	4.3	13.5	31	5.4
East Malling	6.7	17	4.7	10.4	65	4.8	12.8	53	6.3	15.9	30	7.7
Edinburgh	6.4	26	3.8	8.0	63	3.5	9.9	103	4.0	13.3	88	4.5
Glasgow (Abbotsinch)	6.1	91	3.1	8.5	110	3.5	10.3	88	4.8	13.7	42	4.2
Gogerddan	7.1	38	–	9.9	85	–	11.7	58	–	14.1	184	–
Hastings	6.1	17	4.5	9.5	81	5.5	12.5	33	6.8	15.3	34	8.5
Hull	6.9	9	–	9.8	88	–	11.3	32	–	–	–	–
Inverness	6.7	31	3.7	8.3	24	3.5	9.1	101	3.7	–	–	–
Leeming	6.3	10	3.7	8.9	87	3.4	10.5	93	4.4	14.3	38	5.8
Lerwick	4.5	124	2.7	5.9	76	4.3	7.7	46	5.0	8.9	47	4.1
London (Heathrow)	7.5	16	4.1	10.7	75	4.2	13.4	32	5.7	17.0	44	7.5
Long Ashton	6.7	29	–	6.6	77	–	11.5	69	–	–	–	–
Lowestoft	6.3	22	4.7	9.5	36	4.8	–	–	–	14.9	20	–
Manchester (Ringway)	6.7	11	3.3	9.7	68	4.5	11.3	62	4.9	14.7	58	6.6
Manston	6.6	6	5.1	9.8	45	4.7	12.3	36	6.9	15.6	49	8.5
Melbury	6.3	29	3.6	8.9	80	4.3	10.3	89	5.6	–	–	–
Morecambe	6.8	29	3.5	9.7	105	4.8	11.5	103	4.7	–	–	–
Nottingham (Watnall)	6.5	10	3.4	9.3	81	3.5	11.3	44	5.8	14.9	60	6.5
Oxford	7.5	33	4.3	9.9	69	3.7	12.3	57	6.3	–	–	–
Penzance	8.4	37	3.7	10.9	103	–	11.7	129	6.1	15.1	120	6.9
Plymouth	7.5	40	3.8	10.3	87	4.9	11.9	125	6.1	14.8	90	6.7
Rhoose	6.7	21	3.7	9.5	88	4.0	11.5	49	6.1	14.9	63	7.7
St Mawgan	7.3	30	3.6	9.8	89	5.0	11.3	141	6.1	14.1	95	7.2
Shawbury	6.3	13	3.1	9.1	46	3.6	10.9	100	5.5	14.4	63	6.4
Sheffield	6.3	17	4.1	9.3	92	3.9	11.3	71	5.9	14.8	108	6.5
Skegness	6.7	19	4.0	9.1	74	3.3	11.1	55	6.8	–	–	–
Southampton	7.5	48	–	10.5	86	–	13.5	57	–	16.5	60	–
Stornoway	5.9	80	3.3	7.5	80	4.7	8.4	53	7.0	11.2	89	3.4
Tenby	6.9	33	2.9	9.9	82	5.1	10.9	110	5.7	–	–	–
Tiree	6.5	85	2.9	8.1	155	4.9	10.0	53	6.9	12.3	92	4.8
Torbay (Torquay)	7.9	31	4.0	10.6	81	4.7	12.3	104	6.4	15.9	73	8.6
Valley	7.1	32	3.1	9.7	66	5.5	11.4	127	5.7	13.6	80	6.3
Ventnor	7.5	36	5.0	10.1	71	4.5	12.5	49	6.9	15.5	57	8.1
Waddington	6.3	13	3.9	9.3	70	3.5	11.2	43	6.6	14.6	58	6.5
Weymouth	7.3	43	4.6	10.1	68	4.7	12.1	38	6.4	–	–	–
Whitby	6.6	11	3.9	8.5	98	3.0	10.1	51	5.4	–	–	–
Worthing	6.3	28	4.7	9.9	67	4.9	13.1	49	6.5	15.5	54	7.9
Writtle	6.4	15	4.5	10.0	67	4.1	12.5	52	6.3	–	–	–

METEOROLOGICAL OBSERVATIONS London (Heathrow)

Temperature maxima and minima cover the 24-hour period 9–9 h;
mean wind speed is 10 metres above the ground; rainfall is for the 24
hours starting at 9 h on the day of entry; sunshine is for the 24 hours

0–24 h; averages are for the period 1961–90
Source: data provided by the Met Office

JULY 1992

	Temperature Max. °C	Min. °C	Wind knots	Rain mm	Sun hrs
Day 1	19.1	16.3	4.6	0.6	0.0
2	18.7	12.7	4.0	1.3	0.0
3	17.5	14.0	3.5	6.3	0.0
4	21.1	14.0	3.6	3.6	2.8
5	20.0	11.1	6.7	0.1	1.6
6	22.7	14.2	7.6	0.0	13.4
7	21.1	11.5	3.3	0.0	5.2
8	17.1	15.1	1.5	0.7	0.0
9	20.3	14.9	2.3	0.6	0.0
10	20.0	12.6	3.1	0.0	3.2
11	19.5	13.0	7.2	2.1	0.2
12	22.9	13.8	8.3	0.4	7.6
13	20.2	14.1	10.9	2.7	0.0
14	20.0	15.4	6.0	0.3	0.6
15	23.5	15.6	3.5	0.0	2.4
16	25.5	16.5	4.9	1.6	7.4
17	25.4	16.5	7.7	0.0	7.5
18	24.9	15.5	9.6	0.0	7.8
19	23.6	15.8	8.5	0.0	0.6
20	24.5	16.7	3.5	41.7	0.3
21	24.5	16.1	7.3	0.0	8.3
22	24.1	11.6	5.1	0.0	13.3
23	24.6	13.3	4.1	0.3	3.8
24	24.1	16.0	4.6	0.0	10.3
25	23.6	12.0	4.6	0.0	8.9
26	21.1	15.0	6.0	0.0	0.2
27	22.0	12.6	6.5	0.0	14.0
28	22.9	9.5	2.4	0.0	11.4
29	26.6	12.6	4.0	0.0	11.7
30	26.6	15.6	2.8	0.0	4.0
31	28.6	16.4	4.8	0.0	12.1
Total	–	–	–	62.3	158.6
Mean	22.5	14.2	5.2	–	–
Temp. °F	72.5	57.6	–	–	–
Average	22.5	13.1	7.4	46.0	198.5

AUGUST 1992

	Temperature Max. °C	Min. °C	Wind knots	Rain mm	Sun hrs
Day 1	28.5	14.6	6.8	0.0	8.6
2	22.3	14.6	8.0	0.3	2.6
3	24.0	15.8	10.7	0.0	8.9
4	23.6	12.0	8.3	0.0	11.9
5	24.1	15.0	10.2	0.6	2.6
6	24.1	14.5	3.9	0.0	10.5
7	26.9	14.9	7.1	1.2	3.9
8	25.2	17.5	6.4	4.6	1.0
9	24.8	18.5	7.5	6.9	2.7
10	23.5	14.4	6.1	1.3	5.9
11	20.7	13.1	7.5	7.5	7.0
12	19.1	14.5	12.0	6.2	1.1
13	16.3	13.0	7.4	20.9	1.2
14	18.7	10.7	4.2	0.0	9.7
15	22.1	10.5	7.2	4.8	10.3
16	20.7	14.8	5.7	0.1	1.3
17	20.8	12.1	5.7	0.3	7.4
18	19.5	12.1	2.0	0.1	0.2
19	22.5	14.1	2.6	1.3	1.5
20	19.8	16.8	2.5	2.2	0.6
21	22.9	11.5	2.6	0.2	10.3
22	20.2	13.5	8.2	0.5	0.6
23	20.4	9.2	8.1	2.5	7.0
24	19.5	12.9	6.9	14.1	1.1
25	23.7	14.5	9.8	0.0	8.9
26	19.3	13.7	8.2	0.8	0.8
27	21.9	14.5	13.3	1.9	0.1
28	21.2	15.4	8.0	0.0	5.1
29	19.2	9.8	5.0	5.3	6.9
30	18.4	12.9	13.4	1.1	5.3
31	18.0	9.1	5.5	0.0	4.2
Total	–	–	–	84.7	149.2
Mean	21.7	13.6	7.1	–	–
Temp. °F	71.1	56.5	–	–	–
Average	22.1	12.8	7.2	51.0	186.7

SEPTEMBER 1992

	Temperature Max. °C	Min. °C	Wind knots	Rain mm	Sun hrs
Day 1	17.2	9.2	7.0	0.7	6.4
2	21.7	12.6	7.6	0.1	2.5
3	17.5	12.5	6.2	6.0	6.1
4	17.2	8.7	5.6	0.0	10.7
5	16.6	6.6	2.3	0.7	6.4
6	17.7	7.0	5.8	2.4	0.0
7	18.0	11.3	5.4	0.0	10.6
8	17.3	8.2	3.9	0.0	4.7
9	17.9	9.9	4.0	0.0	0.9
10	21.2	9.1	4.9	0.9	8.6
11	19.0	13.5	6.7	0.0	8.1
12	17.5	9.4	3.9	0.2	2.7
13	15.7	11.7	4.0	2.0	0.0
14	18.3	7.2	2.7	0.0	5.6
15	19.9	9.5	5.4	0.0	4.1
16	20.2	9.7	3.0	0.0	9.9
17	23.5	11.0	5.4	1.7	4.9
18	19.5	15.0	2.0	0.1	2.7
19	18.3	14.0	1.9	0.0	0.1
20	19.3	11.1	2.0	0.0	1.5
21	18.3	12.6	4.3	1.7	0.2
22	17.4	14.2	1.9	45.8	0.1
23	16.0	11.6	4.1	5.6	1.9
24	18.5	11.1	4.5	3.0	2.0
25	14.9	10.4	2.0	2.6	0.0
26	23.9	9.9	2.9	0.0	7.0
27	23.6	13.5	3.2	0.0	4.6
28	21.6	13.3	1.8	0.0	4.5
29	20.7	11.6	3.0	0.9	6.9
30	17.0	13.7	2.2	2.9	3.8
31					
Total	–	–	–	77.3	127.5
Mean	18.8	11.0	4.0	–	–
Temp. °F	65.8	51.8	–	–	–
Average	19.3	10.8	7.1	51.0	144.7

OCTOBER 1992

	Temperature Max. °C	Min. °C	Wind knots	Rain mm	Sun hrs
Day 1	17.0	7.7	1.21	0.0	4.9
2	18.0	8.6	2.5	10.9	3.6
3	13.9	10.0	2.3	1.8	0.0
4	16.8	10.8	7.8	0.0	7.8
5	14.5	10.5	8.7	0.0	3.8
6	13.9	10.9	7.5	0.0	0.6
7	14.5	10.5	6.2	0.0	1.8
8	14.0	9.4	2.3	0.0	0.2
9	14.3	6.5	5.3	0.0	2.2
10	14.3	6.9	5.7	0.0	5.0
11	13.5	7.3	4.3	0.0	0.4
12	13.0	9.5	3.6	0.0	0.0
13	13.7	4.0	1.6	0.0	9.3
14	12.3	2.0	3.6	3.6	0.0
15	9.9	2.5	3.7	0.0	7.9
16	9.6	−0.4	1.9	0.0	8.8
17	9.9	−0.5	1.6	0.0	7.8
18	11.5	2.1	1.6	0.0	2.4
19	10.0	3.9	1.0	16.9	0.1
20	11.4	6.7	3.8	6.1	0.6
21	10.2	4.1	3.1	0.3	4.3
22	10.0	3.3	1.3	0.0	1.2
23	11.7	4.8	4.5	2.2	7.3
24	12.9	2.8	4.4	7.0	2.6
25	12.6	4.9	7.5	1.3	1.9
26	9.6	2.4	1.8	0.6	3.5
27	11.1	5.0	4.2	8.1	0.1
28	11.1	3.0	4.3	0.6	6.8
29	10.0	4.6	3.1	0.0	3.8
30	10.5	5.3	0.5	0.0	6.4
31	10.9	−1.1	1.3	0.0	7.5
Total	–	–	–	59.4	112.6
Mean	12.5	5.3	3.6	–	–
Temp. °F	54.5	41.5	–	–	–
Average	15.4	8.0	7.2	58.0	107.2

NOVEMBER 1992

	Temperature Max. °C	Min. °C	Wind knots	Rain mm	Sun hrs
Day 1	13.7	2.5	5.3	3.4	0.0
2	14.5	10.6	10.6	4.2	1.2
3	12.0	4.4	2.7	0.0	6.2
4	13.4	3.4	2.7	0.0	4.5
5	15.7	7.8	1.9	0.0	5.6
6	16.8	6.1	2.6	0.0	0.1
7	13.0	9.6	3.0	0.0	0.0
8	11.6	9.9	1.3	0.6	0.0
9	12.0	7.4	5.0	8.9	0.0
10	13.6	4.8	3.6	6.9	3.4
11	10.6	6.6	8.8	0.0	1.7
12	9.7	3.5	6.9	0.0	7.2
13	7.9	−0.2	2.3	0.0	7.3
14	9.3	−0.7	6.1	6.7	0.0
15	9.6	3.5	3.7	0.3	0.0
16	8.4	4.0	6.0	5.7	0.0
17	8.3	1.7	5.2	1.0	4.9
18	12.6	0.4	6.1	4.0	0.0
19	10.2	5.0	6.9	1.2	4.7
20	8.5	0.9	2.0	0.0	0.0
21	14.1	1.6	4.1	4.7	0.0
22	14.9	2.9	8.5	0.6	0.0
23	14.0	11.6	9.9	0.1	0.9
24	14.0	6.2	8.5	4.2	1.9
25	11.9	6.3	11.5	14.8	2.3
26	10.0	5.6	8.7	0.0	6.2
27	13.0	3.7	7.4	2.6	0.0
28	8.5	2.1	3.1	10.1	3.5
29	13.4	4.5	6.7	1.2	0.0
30	13.2	6.8	13.2	5.7	0.0
31					
Total	–	–	–	86.9	61.6
Mean	11.9	4.7	5.8	–	–
Temp. °F	53.4	40.5	–	–	–
Average	10.4	4.1	8.0	55.0	68.1

DECEMBER 1992

	Temperature Max. °C	Min. °C	Wind knots	Rain mm	Sun hrs
Day 1	12.6	5.8	11.2	3.4	0.9
2	14.2	8.4	13.5	4.0	0.6
3	8.1	5.2	5.3	5.1	0.4
4	5.9	2.1	2.4	0.1	0.2
5	7.3	−1.3	3.0	0.0	5.5
6	9.5	−1.2	5.2	2.8	1.2
7	9.7	2.0	1.6	0.1	3.5
8	7.4	5.1	3.4	0.0	1.1
9	7.1	3.9	1.6	0.0	0.0
10	6.8	1.6	1.3	0.0	0.0
11	12.2	0.8	4.4	1.0	0.0
12	8.5	4.3	3.6	0.0	3.6
13	10.6	0.8	3.8	0.0	0.0
14	10.6	4.4	5.2	0.0	0.0
15	10.0	8.0	4.2	2.5	0.0
16	10.6	5.9	4.0	4.1	0.1
17	10.5	−2.8	3.3	0.4	0.0
18	12.1	−1.9	10.0	8.9	0.0
19	5.7	5.0	4.3	3.5	0.0
20	5.7	2.0	3.1	0.0	0.0
21	5.7	−0.4	1.6	0.0	5.0
22	5.5	−0.2	2.1	0.0	5.9
23	3.8	−0.7	0.4	0.0	2.5
24	4.0	−2.5	0.2	0.0	0.0
25	6.1	−2.6	0.5	0.0	0.0
26	5.8	3.5	4.6	0.0	0.0
27	6.4	4.1	6.1	0.0	4.1
28	5.9	1.6	4.3	0.0	6.3
29	3.4	−2.6	1.7	0.0	6.6
30	3.4	−5.4	0.6	0.0	1.6
31	5.2	−3.8	1.2	0.0	0.0
Total	–	–	–	35.9	49.1
Mean	7.8	1.6	3.8	–	–
Temp. °F	46.0	34.9	–	–	–
Average	8.0	2.3	8.1	57.0	46.2

JANUARY 1993

	Temperature Max. °C	Min. °C	Wind knots	Rain mm	Sun hrs
Day 1	6.7	1.7	1.9	0.0	2.6
2	1.4	−1.3	2.2	0.0	2.4
3	3.0	−6.6	2.5	1.3	5.6
4	8.6	−4.8	3.0	0.3	0.0
5	12.1	1.7	5.9	3.7	0.0
6	12.5	8.1	5.2	6.7	0.0
7	11.7	1.5	3.4	0.2	0.0
8	11.2	0.9	3.0	0.0	4.1
9	12.4	2.4	8.3	5.2	0.6
10	12.5	7.7	13.0	14.6	0.0
11	10.2	8.8	10.2	0.6	0.5
12	8.3	3.1	7.4	1.1	4.3
13	13.8	2.8	11.2	9.1	0.0
14	12.1	4.3	5.7	2.8	6.2
15	13.4	4.7	12.7	0.9	1.1
16	13.6	8.9	12.9	0.0	0.0
17	11.4	10.2	9.7	0.1	0.0
18	9.5	2.2	4.6	1.3	5.9
19	12.0	3.3	7.5	0.1	2.4
20	12.9	4.5	10.7	0.0	0.0
21	13.1	6.7	10.6	1.1	0.0
22	9.9	7.6	7.4	3.9	0.0
23	12.9	5.0	9.4	1.5	0.0
24	10.6	6.4	14.4	0.9	1.5
25	5.4	2.2	5.6	0.1	0.4
26	10.7	−1.9	5.0	6.3	0.1
27	9.5	1.5	1.8	0.7	0.0
28	10.8	5.8	3.0	0.4	0.0
29	9.9	5.3	1.0	0.2	0.1
30	7.9	4.2	1.3	0.0	0.0
31	8.3	2.7	2.0	0.0	0.0
Total	–	–	–	63.1	37.8
Mean	10.3	3.5	6.5	–	–
Temp. °F	50.5	38.3	–	–	–
Average	7.1	1.4	8.5	52.0	51.7

FEBRUARY 1993

	Temperature Max. °C	Min. °C	Wind knots	Rain mm	Sun hrs
Day 1	6.8	3.1	4.7	0.0	7.2
2	10.7	3.2	1.4	0.0	4.3
3	5.4	3.3	1.6	0.0	0.0
4	3.0	1.7	1.4	0.0	0.0
5	4.3	−0.5	2.2	0.0	0.0
6	10.9	0.3	1.9	0.0	0.2
7	9.9	3.3	0.2	0.6	0.0
8	9.8	8.1	4.7	0.1	0.0
9	6.6	5.9	6.3	0.0	0.0
10	3.9	2.6	3.3	0.0	0.0
11	4.2	1.7	2.3	0.0	0.0
12	5.5	1.7	1.2	0.0	0.0
13	7.2	1.8	1.1	0.0	1.7
14	3.4	1.6	2.1	0.0	0.0
15	8.1	1.0	1.5	0.0	0.0
16	10.0	1.5	2.1	0.0	2.6
17	11.5	4.2	2.7	0.0	0.0
18	9.4	7.6	3.6	0.0	0.0
19	9.9	4.0	6.4	0.0	4.6
20	9.0	0.4	5.6	0.0	3.0
21	7.2	3.8	7.1	0.0	6.3
22	7.0	1.1	3.7	0.0	2.4
23	7.4	0.7	2.9	0.0	7.0
24	8.9	2.4	2.7	0.0	0.1
25	9.3	3.2	6.7	0.6	1.2
26	4.9	3.8	6.7	0.9	0.0
27	4.6	1.6	8.8	0.2	6.8
28	3.5	−1.9	7.3	0.0	3.6
29					
30					
31					
Total	–	–	–	2.4	51.0
Mean	7.2	2.5	3.6	–	–
Temp. °F	45.0	36.5	–	–	–
Average	7.5	1.5	8.8	35.0	67.3

MARCH 1993

	Temperature Max. °C	Min. °C	Wind knots	Rain mm	Sun hrs
Day 1	6.0	−0.7	7.5	0.0	2.8
2	3.6	1.4	10.5	0.0	0.0
3	5.2	2.9	7.7	0.0	0.7
4	4.5	1.7	5.3	0.0	0.1
5	10.0	0.6	2.8	0.0	0.0
6	11.1	2.5	2.1	0.0	0.0
7	9.4	5.9	3.2	0.0	0.0
8	12.2	4.5	6.7	0.0	9.3
9	9.9	0.2	4.8	0.0	9.5
10	12.4	−0.5	2.5	0.0	0.1
11	14.9	2.7	2.2	0.0	5.1
12	15.7	3.7	3.5	0.0	4.2
13	16.8	5.6	4.4	0.0	8.9
14	15.7	7.0	2.5	0.0	2.5
15	19.6	7.3	4.1	0.0	8.4
16	12.0	7.1	7.9	0.0	0.0
17	17.0	8.3	8.3	0.0	7.0
18	15.4	9.7	8.3	0.0	4.0
19	12.6	0.0	2.8	0.0	10.4
20	13.7	0.4	3.2	0.0	9.3
21	12.9	4.8	3.5	4.8	0.3
22	12.8	8.0	6.4	0.7	3.8
23	11.9	2.3	6.3	0.0	8.4
24	11.1	0.2	3.8	0.0	7.8
25	10.2	3.0	3.5	0.0	9.7
26	9.2	−0.9	2.5	0.0	6.1
27	8.7	−1.0	2.8	0.0	1.4
28	11.4	0.1	5.7	0.0	3.4
29	13.1	3.0	6.8	0.0	4.6
30	14.2	7.5	6.7	2.5	0.6
31	11.9	4.2	5.1	8.0	0.0
Total	–	–	–	16.0	128.4
Mean	11.8	3.3	4.9	–	–
Temp. °F	53.2	37.9	–	–	–
Average	10.3	2.7	8.9	47.0	110.1

APRIL 1993

	Temperature Max. °C	Min. °C	Wind knots	Rain mm	Sun hrs
Day 1	7.3	7.2	4.7	19.9	0.0
2	12.0	0.6	3.0	0.0	7.1
3	11.3	0.6	8.4	2.3	1.6
4	12.1	1.5	5.3	5.3	9.7
5	13.2	5.5	10.7	2.5	4.8
6	12.5	8.1	10.3	1.4	2.9
7	10.0	4.0	2.3	0.7	0.0
8	12.8	7.7	5.7	2.4	0.0
9	10.2	8.0	5.7	14.0	0.0
10	13.7	3.4	4.5	8.5	7.6
11	13.2	6.9	5.7	2.0	2.3
12	14.8	3.8	3.4	0.0	11.3
13	12.5	5.2	4.0	0.0	1.4
14	11.8	5.5	3.8	0.0	3.5
15	14.7	4.8	2.6	0.0	8.4
16	15.4	5.8	5.0	1.1	1.5
17	16.4	9.8	5.0	0.1	1.1
18	16.5	8.4	7.6	0.0	4.1
19	15.7	10.7	5.1	0.0	0.3
20	20.0	8.7	6.5	0.0	12.6
21	17.6	10.0	3.9	0.0	9.3
22	14.1	6.7	5.4	0.1	1.3
23	14.7	10.3	6.6	7.7	0.1
24	15.0	9.5	3.2	4.0	1.6
25	16.0	8.6	2.3	0.0	2.9
26	13.7	8.6	3.7	3.3	2.2
27	20.7	9.0	7.3	0.0	5.6
28	15.8	7.3	7.1	0.0	8.0
29	20.7	8.4	4.7	0.0	8.5
30	22.6	8.1	2.0	0.0	7.2
31					
Total	–	–	–	75.3	126.9
Mean	14.6	6.8	5.2	–	–
Temp. °F	58.3	44.2	–	–	–
Average	13.1	4.7	8.5	45.0	146.9

MAY 1993

	Temperature Max. °C	Min. °C	Wind knots	Rain mm	Sun hrs
Day 1	20.1	9.7	3.1	0.0	6.8
2	13.6	7.9	3.4	0.0	1.0
3	13.5	7.6	2.0	0.0	0.6
4	15.6	4.9	2.7	0.0	9.3
5	15.2	4.6	4.2	0.0	13.8
6	14.7	3.3	4.9	0.0	13.7
7	16.3	5.4	6.3	0.0	12.7
8	18.0	7.0	7.5	0.3	5.8
9	17.5	8.0	5.8	0.5	1.9
10	20.6	9.0	4.5	0.0	5.5
11	25.1	10.4	6.5	0.0	11.0
12	19.0	10.5	3.9	0.0	0.4
13	16.3	7.9	3.0	0.0	5.2
14	15.7	8.7	5.9	1.1	1.3
15	15.0	4.6	5.7	3.6	9.2
16	17.7	6.4	6.3	0.0	2.6
17	22.7	11.6	6.8	5.0	2.8
18	18.6	9.0	3.0	0.0	12.2
19	18.5	10.9	3.0	0.1	11.3
20	13.9	9.9	4.1	10.3	0.2
21	17.7	7.8	5.0	0.0	8.2
22	19.8	6.6	3.6	0.0	3.0
23	22.8	12.2	6.9	0.0	9.2
24	24.9	14.2	6.5	0.0	7.4
25	18.6	12.4	5.2	0.3	0.0
26	17.3	11.2	6.0	7.0	0.0
27	14.5	12.2	2.7	1.5	0.0
28	18.1	8.7	2.9	0.4	5.5
29	20.6	8.0	4.0	0.9	5.0
30	16.9	11.9	10.7	0.3	3.8
31	18.5	10.5	7.9	0.5	7.2
Total	–	–	–	31.8	176.6
Mean	18.0	8.8	5.0	–	–
Temp. °F	64.4	47.8	–	–	–
Average	17.0	8.0	8.1	51.0	193.7

JUNE 1993

	Temperature Max. °C	Min. °C	Wind knots	Rain mm	Sun hrs
Day 1	20.9	11.7	4.1	3.6	8.1
2	18.9	11.5	2.7	0.9	4.8
3	18.5	12.3	2.7	0.0	0.1
4	22.5	8.9	2.3	0.0	9.9
5	23.6	11.8	3.4	0.0	8.4
6	26.0	11.8	2.4	0.0	13.1
7	26.5	13.0	3.0	0.0	13.8
8	28.4	13.8	3.3	0.0	14.4
9	27.5	17.2	3.7	1.2	1.9
10	23.4	17.3	3.5	5.1	1.1
11	19.2	15.3	3.7	10.2	0.3
12	17.5	11.8	5.4	1.7	0.4
13	18.0	11.4	4.5	3.2	5.2
14	18.4	11.5	4.7	3.8	0.3
15	21.0	8.9	4.3	3.0	13.2
16	16.7	12.8	3.7	11.2	0.6
17	22.1	11.9	6.2	0.0	6.9
18	19.0	13.8	9.6	0.0	0.1
19	20.4	12.3	7.4	0.0	3.6
20	20.8	9.2	3.8	0.0	12.7
21	19.1	10.5	4.3	0.0	11.3
22	19.4	9.7	3.6	0.0	7.2
23	19.2	11.9	4.2	0.0	6.2
24	21.8	10.1	2.8	0.0	9.5
25	21.7	9.9	3.8	0.0	12.1
26	23.7	13.7	7.8	0.0	2.6
27	25.0	14.6	5.8	0.0	14.9
28	23.7	12.9	7.4	0.0	15.1
29	25.0	12.2	8.9	0.0	14.0
30	27.7	12.8	6.8	0.0	12.4
31					
Total	–	–	–	43.9	224.2
Mean	21.9	12.3	4.5	–	–
Temp. °F	71.4	54.1	–	–	–
Average	20.4	11.0	7.6	50.0	198.5

Sports Results

ALPINE SKIING

WORLD CUP 1992–3

MEN

Downhill: Franz Heinzer (Switzerland), 527 pts
Slalom: Thomas Fogdoe (Sweden), 545 pts
Giant Slalom: Kjetil-Andre Aamodt (Norway), 410 pts
Super Giant Slalom: Kjetil-Andre Aamodt (Norway), 420 pts
Overall: Marc Giradelli (Luxembourg), 1,379 pts

WOMEN

Downhill: Katja Seizinger (Germany), 604 pts
Slalom: Vreni Schneider (Switzerland), 490 pts
Giant Slalom: Carole Merle (France), 480 pts
Super Giant Slalom: Katja Seizinger (Germany), 371 pts
Overall: Anita Wachter (Austria), 1,286 pts
Nations Cup: Austria

WORLD CHAMPIONSHIPS 1993
Morioka, Japan

MEN

Downhill: Urs Lehmann (Switzerland), 1 min. 32.06 sec.
Slalom: Kjetil-Andre Aamodt (Norway), 1 min. 40.33 sec.
Giant Slalom: Kjetil-Andre Aamodt (Norway), 2 min. 15.36 sec.
Super Giant Slalom: abandoned
Combined Event: Lasse Kjus (Norway), 34.22 pts

WOMEN

Downhill: Kate Pace (Canada), 1 min. 27.38 sec.
Slalom: Karin Buder (Austria), 1 min. 27.66 sec.
Giant Slalom: Carole Merle (France), 2 min. 17.59 sec.
Super Giant Slalom: Katja Seizinger (Germany), 1 min. 33.52 sec.
Combined Event: Miriam Vogt (Germany), 3.39 pts

AMERICAN FOOTBALL

XXVII American Superbowl 1993 (Los Angeles, 31 January): Dallas Cowboys beat Buffalo Bills 52–17
American Bowl 1993 (Wembley, 8 August): Dallas Cowboys 13, Detroit Lions 13 a.e.t.
British League final 1993 (Maidenhead, 1 August): London Olympians beat Glasgow Lions 40–14

ANGLING

NATIONAL COARSE CHAMPIONSHIPS 1992
Division: 1
Venue: River Trent; *no. of teams:* 88
Individual winner: K. Gregory (Ripley), 17.350 kg
Team winners: Nottingham and District FAS, 811 pts

Division: 2
Venue: Gloucester Canal; *no. of teams:* 89
Individual winner: J. Manning (Mansfield), 21.860 kg
Team winners: Leeds Anglers World, 830 pts

Division: 3
Venue: Grand Union Canal; *no. of teams:* 84
Individual winner: A. Camber (Holmesdale), 13.320 kg
Team winners: Highfield AS, 765 pts

Division: 4
Venue: River Witham; *no. of teams:* 79
Individual winner: P. Hiller (Banstead), 12.760 kg
Team winners: Mohmar AC, 857 pts

Division: 5
Venue: Lancaster Canal; *no. of teams:* 71
Individual winner: M. Phillips (Image Blackhorse), 2.990 kg
Team winners: Image Blackhorse MG, 696 pts

Division: 6
Venue: Keadby Canal; *no. of teams:* 38
Individual winner: L. Thirlaway (Andover), 14.660 kg
Team winners: Team Imex, 364 pts

WORLD CHAMPIONSHIPS 1993
Portugal, September

Individual: Mario Barros (Portugal), 2 pts
Team: Italy, 49 pts

ASSOCIATION FOOTBALL

LEAGUE COMPETITIONS 1992–3

ENGLAND AND WALES
Premier League
1. Manchester United, 84 pts
2. Aston Villa, 74 pts
Relegated: Crystal Palace, 49 pts; Middlesbrough, 44 pts; Nottingham Forest, 40 pts

Division 1
1. Newcastle United, 96 pts
2. West Ham, 88 pts
Third promotion place: Swindon Town
Relegated: Brentford, 49 pts; Cambridge United, 49 pts; Bristol Rovers, 41 pts

Division 2
1. Stoke City, 93 pts
2. Bolton Wanderers, 90 pts
Third promotion place: West Bromwich Albion
Relegated: Preston North End, 47 pts; Mansfield Town, 44 pts; Wigan Athletic, 41 pts; Chester City, 29 pts

Division 3
1. Cardiff City, 83 pts
2. Wrexham, 80 pts
3. Barnet, 79 pts
Fourth promotion place: York City
Relegated: Halifax Town, 36 pts

GM Vauxhall Conference
Promoted: Wycombe Wanderers, 83 pts
Relegated: Farnborough Town, 47 pts; Boston United,
   40 pts

League of Wales (inaugural): Cwmbran
Women's National Premier League: Arsenal

SCOTLAND

Premier Division
1. Rangers, 73 pts
2. Aberdeen, 64 pts
Relegated: Falkirk, 29 pts; Aidrieonians, 29 pts

Division 1
1. Raith Rovers, 65 pts
2. Kilmarnock, 54 pts
Relegated: Meadowbank Thistle, 32 pts; Cowdenbeath,
   13 pts

Division 2
1. Clydebank, 54 pts
2. Brechin City, 53 pts
No relegation

CUP COMPETITIONS 1992-3

ENGLAND

FA Cup final 1993 (Wembley, 15 May): Arsenal 1, Sheffield
Wednesday 1 a.e.t. *Replay* (Wembley, 20 May): Arsenal
beat Sheffield Wednesday 2–1 a.e.t.
Coco Cola (League) Cup final 1993: Arsenal beat Sheffield
Wednesday 2–1
Autoglass Trophy final 1993: Port Vale beat Stockport
County 2–1
FA Vase final 1993: Bridlington Town beat Tiverton Town
1–0
FA Trophy final 1993: Wycombe Wanderers beat Runcorn
4–1
Arthur Dunn Cup final 1993: Lancing beat Reptonians 1–0
Women's FA Cup final 1993: Arsenal beat Doncaster Belles
3–0
Charity Shield 1993: Arsenal 1, Manchester United 1.
Manchester United won 5–4 on penalties

WALES
Welsh FA Cup final 1993: Cardiff beat Rhyl 5–0

SCOTLAND
Scottish FA Cup final 1993 (Parkhead, 29 May): Rangers
beat Aberdeen 2–1
B & Q Cup final 1992: Hamilton Academicals beat Morton
3–2
Skol Cup final 1992: Rangers beat Aberdeen 2–1 a.e.t.

IRELAND
Irish Cup final 1993: Ards 1, Bangor 1 a.e.t. *Replay:* Ards 1,
Bangor 1 a.e.t. *Second replay:* Bangor beat Ards 1–0

EUROPE
European Champions' Cup final 1993 (Munich): Marseille
beat AC Milan 1–0
European Cup-Winners' Cup final 1993 (Wembley): Parma
beat Royal Antwerp 3–1
UEFA Cup final 1993: Juventus beat Borussia Dortmund
6–1 on agg.

INTERNATIONALS

WORLD CUP QUALIFYING MATCHES

1992

14 Oct	Wembley	England 1, Norway 1
	Ibrox Park	Scotland 0, Portugal 0
	Limassol	Cyprus 0, Wales 1
	Windsor Park	N. Ireland 0, Spain 0
18 Nov	Wembley	England 4, Turkey 0
	Ibrox Park	Scotland 0, Italy 0
	Brussels	Belgium 2, Wales 0
	Windsor Park	N. Ireland 0, Denmark 1

1993

17 Feb	Wembley	England 6, San Marino 0
	Ibrox Park	Scotland 3, Malta 0
	Tirana	Albania 1, N. Ireland 2
31 Mar	Izmir	Turkey 0, England 2
	Cardiff	Wales 2, Belgium 0
	Dublin	Rep. of Ireland 3, N. Ireland 0
28 Apr	Wembley	England 2, Holland 2
	Lisbon	Portugal 5, Scotland 0
	Ostrava	Czech and Slovak Republics 1, Wales 1
	Seville	Spain 3, N. Ireland 1
19 May	Tallinn	Estonia 0, Scotland 3
25 May	Vilnius	Lithuania 0, N. Ireland 1
29 May	Katowice	Poland 1, England 1
2 June	Oslo	Norway 2, England 0
	Aberdeen	Scotland 3, Estonia 1
	Riga	Latvia 1, N. Ireland 2
6 June	Toftir	Faeroe Islands 0, Wales 3
8 Sept	Wembley	England 3, Poland 0
	Aberdeen	Scotland 1, Switzerland 1
	Cardiff	Wales 2, Czech and Slovak Republics 2
	Windsor Park	N. Ireland 2, Latvia 0

FRIENDLIES 1993

17 Feb	Dublin	Rep. of Ireland 2, Wales 1
24 Mar	Ibrox Park	Scotland 0, Germany 1
9 June	Boston	USA 2, England 0
13 June	Washington DC	Brazil 1, England 1
19 June	Detroit	England 1, Germany 2

ATHLETICS

GREAT BRITAIN v. USA INDOORS

Birmingham, 13 February 1993

MEN

	min.	sec.
60 metres: Calvin Smith (USA)		6.70
200 metres: Marcus Adam (GB)		21.06
400 metres: David Grindley (GB)		46.67
800 metres: David Sharpe (GB)	1	47.76
Mile: John Mayock (GB)	4	00.86
3,000 metres: Matthew Yates (GB)	7	55.14
3,000 metres walk: Martin Rush (GB)	11	40.54
60 metres hurdles: Colin Jackson (GB)		7.46
4 × 200 metres relay: Great Britain	1	23.56
		metres
High jump: Steve Smith (GB)		2.35
Pole vault: Rory Tarpenning (USA)		5.50
Long jump: Keith Holley (USA)		7.76

Triple jump: Julian Golley (GB)   16.48
Shot: Mike Stulce (USA)   21.77

Team points: Great Britain 163, USA 120

WOMEN

	min.	sec.
60 *metres:* Carletta Guidry (USA)		7.23
200 *metres:* Katharine Merry (GB)		23.53
400 *metres:* Sally Gunnell (GB)		53.38
800 *metres:* Diane Modahl (GB)	2	05.15
Mile: Yvonne Murray (GB)	4	32.00
3,000 *metres:* Alison Wyeth (GB)	9	03.59
3,000 *metres walk:* Sara Standley (USA)	13	00.40
60 *metres hurdles:* Jackie Agyepong (GB)		8.24
4 × 200 *metres relay:* USA	1	34.97

	metres
High jump: Debbie Marti (GB)	1.89
Long jump: Fiona May (GB)	6.49
Triple jump: Ashia Hansen (GB)	13.48
Shot: Ramona Pagel (USA)	17.48

Team points: Great Britain 150, USA 120

WOMEN'S NATIONAL CROSS-COUNTRY CHAMPIONSHIPS
Luton, 20 February 1993

Individual: Gillian Stacey (Bromley), 19 min. 53 sec.
Team: Parkside, 18 pts

AAA INDOOR CHAMPIONSHIPS
Birmingham, 26–27 February 1993

MEN

	min.	sec.
60 *metres:* Mark McKoy (Canada)		6.56
200 *metres:* Jason John (Newham)		21.17
400 *metres:* Sunday Bada (Nigeria)		46.34
800 *metres:* Tom McKean (Bellshill)	1	47.27
1,500 *metres:* Jason Dullforce (Enfield)	3	45.05
3,000 *metres:* Paul Larkins (Nene Valley)	8	05.10
60 *metres hurdles:* Colin Jackson (Brecon)		7.55

	metres
High jump: Dalton Grant (Haringey)	2.25
Pole vault: Martin Voss (Denmark)	5.30
Long jump: Mathias Ghansah (Sweden)	7.63
Triple jump: Tosi Fasinro (Haringey)	15.89
Shot: Paul Edwards (Belgrave)	18.47

WOMEN

	min.	sec.
60 *metres:* Sanna Hernesniemi (Finland)		7.33
200 *metres:* Sanna Hernesniemi (Finland)		23.54
400 *metres:* Louise Fraser (Trafford)		54.14
800 *metres:* Linda Keough (Basingstoke)	2	05.22
1,500 *metres:* Carol-Ann Gray (Edinburgh)	4	30.09
3,000 *metres:* Una English (Havering)	9	15.68
60 *metres hurdles:* Clova Court (Birchfield)		8.20

	metres
High jump: Jo Jennings (West Suffolk)	1.89
Long jump: Renata Nielsen (Denmark)	6.28
Triple jump: Rachel Kirby (Hounslow)	13.52
Shot: Maggie Lynes (Croydon)	15.65

MEN'S NATIONAL CROSS-COUNTRY CHAMPIONSHIPS
London, 27 February 1993

Individual: Richard Nerurkar (Bingley Harriers),
   42 min. 52 sec.
Team: Bingley Harriers, 62 pts

WORLD INDOOR CHAMPIONSHIPS
Toronto, 12–14 March 1993

MEN

	min.	sec.
60 *metres:* Bruny Surin (Canada)		6.50
200 *metres:* James Trapp (USA)		20.63
400 *metres:* Butch Reynolds (USA)		45.26
800 *metres:* Tom McKean (GB)	1	47.29
1,500 *metres:* Marcus O'Sullivan (Ireland)	3	45.00
3,000 *metres:* Genaro Di Napoli (Italy)	7	50.26
5,000 *metres walk:* Mikhail Shchennikov (Russia)	18	32.10
60 *metres hurdles:* Mark McKoy (Canada)		7.41
4 × 400 *metres relay:* USA	3	04.20

	metres
High jump: Javier Sotomayor (Cuba)	2.41
Pole vault: Radion Gataullin (Russia)	5.90
Long jump: Ivan Pedroso (Cuba)	8.23
Triple jump: Pierre Camara (France)	17.59
Shot: Mike Stulce (USA)	21.27

WOMEN

	min.	sec.
60 *metres:* Gail Devers (USA)		6.95
200 *metres:* Irina Privalova (Russia)		22.15
400 *metres:* Sandie Richards (Jamaica)		50.93
800 *metres:* Maria Mutola (Mozambique)	1	57.55
1,500 *metres:* Yekaterina Podkopayeva (Russia)	4	09.29
3,000 *metres:* Yvonne Murray (GB)	8	50.55
3,000 *metres walk:* Yelena Nikolayeva (Russia)	11	49.73
60 *metres hurdles:* Julie Baumann (Switzerland)		7.96
4 × 400 *metres relay:* Russia	3	28.90

	metres
High jump: Stefka Kustadinova (Bulgaria)	2.02
Long jump: Marieta Ilcu (Romania)	6.84
Triple jump: Inessa Kravets (Ukraine)	14.47
Shot: Svetlana Krivelyeva (Russia)	19.57

IAAF WORLD CROSS-COUNTRY CHAMPIONSHIPS
Amorebieta, Spain, 28 March 1993

MEN (11,750 *metres*)
Individual: William Sigei (Kenya), 32 min. 51 sec.
Team: Kenya, 25 pts

WOMEN (6,350 *metres*)
Individual: Albertina Dias (Portugal), 20 min. 00 sec.
Team: Kenya, 52 pts

LONDON MARATHON
18 April 1993

Men: Eamon Martin (GB), 2 hr. 10 min. 50 sec.
Women: Katrin Dorre (Germany), 2 hr. 27 min. 09 sec.

UNITED KINGDOM CHAMPIONSHIPS
Crystal Palace, 12–13 June 1993

MEN

	min.	sec.
100 *metres:* Linford Christie (TVH)		10.26
200 *metres:* John Regis (Belgrave)		20.21
400 *metres:* Du'aine Ladejo (Belgrave)		46.14
800 *metres:* Martin Steele (Longwood)	1	46.34
1,500 *metres:* Curtis Robb (Liverpool)	3	39.58
3,000 *metres:* Spencer Barden (GEC Avionics)	8	01.86
5,000 *metres:* Jon Brown (Sheffield)	13	39.68
3,000 *metres steeplechase:* Spencer Duval (Cannock and Stafford)	8	32.77

110 *metres hurdles:* Andy Tulloch (Wolverhampton) — 13.70

400 *metres hurdles:* Gary Cadogan (Haringey) — 49.80

	metres
High jump: Dalton Grant (Haringey)	2.25
Pole vault: Neil Winter (Shaftesbury)	5.35
Long jump: Ian Simpson (Leeds City)	7.55
Triple jump: Tosi Fasinro (Haringey)	17.30
Shot: Paul Edwards (Belgrave)	19.06
Discus: Darrin Morris (Belgrave)	57.70
Hammer: Paul Head (Newham)	71.48
Javelin: Mick Hill (Leeds City)	86.94

WOMEN

	min.	sec.
100 *metres:* Beverley Kinch (Hounslow)		11.37
200 *metres:* Katharine Merry (Birchfield)		23.20
400 *metres:* Phylis Smith (Wigan)		51.70
800 *metres:* Kelly Holmes (Middlesex Ladies)	2	00.86
1,500 *metres:* Jayne Spark (Altrincham)	4	14.66
100 *metres hurdles:* Jackie Agyepong (Shaftesbury)		13.22
400 *metres hurdles:* Gowry Retchakan (Thurrock)		56.62

	metres
High jump: Debbi Marti (Bromley)	1.90
Pole vault: Katherine Staples (Essex Ladies)	3.40
Long jump: Fiona May (Derby Ladies)	6.67
Triple jump: Michelle Griffith (Windsor)	13.72
Shot: Myrtle Augee (Bromley)	17.12
Discus: Jacqui McKernan (Lisburn)	56.72
Hammer: Lorraine Shaw (Gloucester)	55.14
Javelin: Sharon Gibson (Nottingham)	56.90

EUROPEAN CUP
Rome, 26–27 June 1993

MEN

	min.	sec.
100 *metres:* Linford Christie (GB)		10.22
200 *metres:* John Regis (GB)		20.38
400 *metres:* David Grindley (GB)		44.75
800 *metres:* Andrei Bulkowski (Ukraine)	1	47.32
1,500 *metres:* Andrei Bulkowski (Ukraine)	3	37.51
5,000 *metres:* Rob Denmark (GB)	13	30.02
10,000 *metres:* Thierry Pantel (France)	28	02.71
3,000 *metres steeplechase:* Steffen Brand (Germany)	8	17.77
110 *metres hurdles:* Colin Jackson (GB)		13.10
400 *metres hurdles:* Stephane Diagana (France)		48.08
4 × 100 *metres relay:* Great Britain		38.53
4 × 400 *metres relay:* Great Britain	3	00.25

	metres
High jump: Artur Partyka (Poland)	2.30
Pole vault: Rodion Gataullin (Russia)	6.00
Long jump: Giovanni Buangelisti (Italy)	8.04
Triple jump: Pierre Camara (France)	17.46
Shot: Alexander Bagach (Ukraine)	20.15
Discus: Lars Riedel (Germany)	66.30
Hammer: Sergei Litvinov (Russia)	80.78
Javelin: Jan Zelezny (Czech Republic)	89.84

Team points: Russia 128, Great Britain 124, France 123, Germany 119, Italy 112, Ukraine 97, Spain 76, Poland 65, Czech Republic 54

WOMEN

	min.	sec.
100 *metres:* Irina Privalova (Russia)		11.08
200 *metres:* Irina Privalova (Russia)		22.30
400 *metres:* Elena Ruzina (Russia)		51.54

	min.	sec.
800 *metres:* Ella Kovacs (Romania)		n/a
1,500 *metres:* Vera Chuvashova (Russia)	4	16.03
3,000 *metres:* Margarita Keszeg (Romania)	8	51.88
10,000 *metres:* Viktoria Nenasheva (Russia)	32	33.46
100 *metres hurdles:* Marina Azyabina (Russia)		12.61
400 *metres hurdles:* Sally Gunnell (GB)		53.73
4 × 100 *metres relay:* Russia		42.79
4 × 400 *metres relay:* Russia	3	24.23

	metres
High jump: Galina Astafei (Romania)	2.00
Long jump: Heike Drechsler (Germany)	7.02
Triple jump: Yolanda Chen (Russia)	14.34
Shot: Anna Romanova (Russia)	19.43
Discus: Larisa Korotkevich (Russia)	64.58
Javelin: Felicia Tirlea (Romania)	62.68

Team points: Russia 141, Romania 102, Ukraine 97½, Germany 96, Great Britain 91, France 75, Poland 62, Italy 55½, Finland 44

GREAT BRITAIN v. USA
Edinburgh, 2 July 1993

MEN

	min.	sec.
100 *metres:* Linford Christie (GB)		10.06
200 *metres:* John Regis (GB)		20.08
400 *metres:* David Grindley (GB)		45.43
800 *metres:* Tom McKean (GB)	1	48.19
Mile: David Strang (GB)	3	55.57
3,000 *metres:* Rob Denmark (GB)	8	08.55
3,000 *metres steeplechase:* Tom Hanlon (GB)	8	36.24
110 *metres hurdles:* Colin Jackson (GB)		13.01
400 *metres hurdles:* Kriss Akabusi (GB)		50.45
4 × 100 *metres relay:* Great Britain		39.45
4 × 400 *metres relay:* USA	3	04.48

	metres
High jump: Monterrio Holder (USA)	2.26
Pole vault: Mike Holloway (USA)	5.70
Long jump: Dion Bentley (USA)	7.97
Triple jump: Jonathan Edwards (GB)	17.70
Shot: Mike Stulce (USA)	20.75
Discus: Steve Muse (USA)	61.44
Hammer: Paul Head (GB)	69.82
Javelin: Mick Hill (GB)	85.10

Team points: Great Britain 199, USA 190

WOMEN

	min.	sec.
100 *metres:* Wenda Vereen (USA)		11.16
200 *metres:* Dannette Young (USA)		22.32
400 *metres:* Sally Gunnell (GB)		51.29
800 *metres:* Meredith Rainey (USA)	2	05.88
1,500 *metres:* Yvonne Murray (GB)	4	08.63
3,000 *metres:* Sonia McGeorge (GB)	9	20.22
100 *metres hurdles:* Lynda Tolbeat (USA)		12.73
400 *metres hurdles:* Trevaia Williams (USA)		57.20
4 × 100 *metres relay:* USA		44.69
4 × 400 *metres relay:* USA	3	30.22

	metres
High jump: Tanya Hughes (USA)	1.91
Long jump: Jo Wise (GB)	6.59
Triple jump: Michelle Griffith (GB)	13.93
Shot: Myrtle Augee (GB)	17.68
Discus: Carla Garrett (USA)	58.46
Javelin: Donna Mayhew (USA)	61.46

Team points: USA 181, Great Britain 143

AAA CHAMPIONSHIPS
Birmingham, 16–17 July 1993

MEN

	min.	sec.
100 *metres:* Linford Christie (TVH)		10.13
200 *metres:* Jeff Williams (USA)		20.47
400 *metres:* Kennedy Ochieng (Kenya)		45.32
800 *metres:* Martin Steele (Longwood)	1	47.83
1,500 *metres:* Matthew Yates (Newham)	3	38.75
3,000 *metres:* Joseph Keter (Kenya)	7	56.39
5,000 *metres:* Jonathan Brown (Sheffield)	13	35.67
3,000 *metres steeplechase:* Colin Walker (Gateshead)	8	33.45
110 *metres hurdles:* Colin Jackson (Brecon)		13.15
400 *metres hurdles:* Gary Cadogan (Haringey)		50.60
10 *kilometres walk:* Martin Bell (Splott)	42	29.63

	metres
High jump: Tim Forsyth (Australia)	2.32
Pole vault: Simon Arkell (Australia)	5.60
Long jump: Fred Salle (Belgrave)	7.72
Triple jump: Francis Agyepong (Shaftesbury-Barnet)	16.05
Shot: Matthew Simson (Thurrock)	18.79
Discus: Rob Weir (Birchfield)	57.44
Hammer: Paul Head (Newham)	72.32
Javelin: Colin Mackenzie (Newham)	81.44

Crystal Palace, 12 June 1993	min.	sec.
10,000 *metres:* Paul Evans (Belgrave)	28	17.49

WOMEN

	min.	sec.
100 *metres:* Beverley Kinch (Hounslow)		11.44
200 *metres:* Cathy Freeman (Australia)		22.71
400 *metres:* Phylis Smith (Wigan)		52.15
800 *metres:* Kelly Holmes (Middlesex Ladies)	2	02.69
1,500 *metres:* Alison Wyeth (Parkside)	4	11.03
100 *metres hurdles:* Sally Gunnell (Essex Ladies)		13.08
400 *metres hurdles:* Jacqui Parker (Essex Ladies)		58.14
5,000 *metres walk:* Vicky Lupton (Sheffield)	22	34.50

	metres
High jump: Debbie Marti (Bromley)	1.86
Pole Vault: Katy Staples (Essex Ladies)	3.20
Long jump: Nicole Boegman (Australia)	6.50
Triple jump: Lene Espegren (Norway)	13.43
Shot: Myrtle Augee (Bromley)	17.24
Discus: Daniela Costian (Australia)	61.58
Hammer: Debbie Sosimenko (Australia)	56.86
Javelin: Shelley Holroyd (Sale)	60.10

Portsmouth, 5 June 1993	min.	sec.
10,000 *metres:* Vikki McPherson (Glasgow)	33	49.29

Crystal Palace, 13 June 1933		
3,000 *metres:* Yvonne Murray (Motherwell)	8	52.28

WORLD CHAMPIONSHIPS
Stuttgart, 14–22 August 1993

MEN

	hr.	min.	sec.
100 *metres:* Linford Christie (GB)			9.87
200 *metres:* Frankie Fredericks (Namibia)			19.85
400 *metres:* Michael Johnson (USA)			43.65
800 *metres:* Paul Ruto (Kenya)		1	44.71
1,500 *metres:* Nourredine Morceli (Algeria)		3	34.24
5,000 *metres:* Ismael Kirui (Kenya)		13	02.75
10,000 *metres:* Haile Gebresilasie (Ethiopia)		27	46.02

Marathon: Mark Plaatjes (USA)	2	13	57
3,000 *metres steeplechase:* Moses Kiptanui (Kenya)		8	06.36
110 *metres hurdles:* Colin Jackson (GB)			12.91
400 *metres hurdles:* Kevin Young (USA)			47.18
4 × 100 *metres relay:* USA			37.48
4 × 400 *metres relay:* USA		2	54.29
20 *kilometres walk:* Valentin Massana (Spain)	1	22	31
50 *kilometres walk:* Jesus Angel Garcia (Spain)	3	41	41

	metres
High jump: Javier Sotomayor (Cuba)	2.40
Pole vault: Sergei Bubka (Ukraine)	6.00
Long jump: Mike Powell (USA)	8.59
Triple jump: Mike Conley (USA)	17.86
Shot: Werner Gunthor (Switzerland)	21.97
Discus: Lars Riedel (Germany)	67.72
Hammer: Andrei Abduvalyev (Tajikistan)	81.64
Javelin: Jan Zelezny (Czech Republic)	85.98
Decathlon: Dan O'Brien (USA)	8,817 pts

WOMEN

	hr.	min.	sec.
100 *metres:* Gail Devers (USA)			10.81
200 *metres:* Merlene Ottey (Jamaica)			21.98
400 *metres:* Jearl Miles (USA)			49.82
800 *metres:* Maria Mutola (Mozambique)		1	55.43
1,500 *metres:* Dong Liu (China)		4	00.50
3,000 *metres:* Qu Yunxia (China)		8	28.71
10,000 *metres:* Wang Junxia (China)		30	49.30
Marathon: Junko Asari (Japan)	2	30	03
100 *metres hurdles:* Gail Devers (USA)			12.46
400 *metres hurdles:* Sally Gunnell (GB)			52.74
4 × 100 *metres relay:* Russia			41.49
4 × 400 *metres relay:* USA		3	16.71
10 *kilometres walk:* Sari Essayah (Finland)		42	59

	metres
High jump: Ioamnet Quintero (Cuba)	1.99
Long jump: Heike Drechsler (Germany)	7.11
Triple jump: Ana Biryokova (Russia)	15.09
Shot: Zhihong Huang (China)	20.57
Discus: Olga Burova (Russia)	67.40
Javelin: Trine Hattestad (Norway)	69.18
Heptathlon: Jackie Joyner-Kersee (USA)	6,837 pts

GRAND PRIX 1993 FINAL RESULTS

MEN

200 *metres:* Frankie Fredericks (Namibia)
400 *metres:* David Grindley (GB)
1,500 *metres:* Nourredine Morceli (Algeria)
5,000 *metres:* Ismael Kirui (Kenya)
3,000 *metres steeplechase:* Patrick Sang (Kenya)
110 *metres hurdles:* Colin Jackson (GB)
Pole vault: Sergei Bubka (Ukraine)
Long jump: Mike Powell (USA)
Discus: Lars Riedel (Germany)
Javelin: Jan Zelezny (Czech Republic)
Overall winner: Sergei Bubka (Ukraine)

WOMEN

100 *metres:* Gwen Torrence (USA)
800 *metres:* Maria Mutola (Mozambique)
1 *mile:* Lyubov Kremlyova (Russia)
3,000 *metres:* Sonia O'Sullivan (Ireland)
400 *metres hurdles:* Sandra Farmer-Patrick (USA)
High jump: Stefka Kostadinova (Bulgaria)
Triple jump: Yolanda Chen (Russia)
Shot: Svetlana Krivelyova (Russia)
Overall winner: Sandra Farmer-Patrick (USA)

BADMINTON

WORLD CHAMPIONSHIPS 1993

Men's Singles: Joko Suprianto (Indonesia) beat Hermawan Susanto (Indonesia) 15–5, 15–11

Women's Singles: Susi Susanti (Indonesia) beat Bang Soo-Hyun (S. Korea) 7–11, 11–9, 11–3

Men's Doubles: Ricky Subagja and Rudy Gunawan (Indonesia) beat Cheah Soon Kit and Soo Beng Kiang (Malaysia) 15–11, 15–3

Women's Doubles: Nong Qunhua and Zhou Lei (China) beat Chen Ying and Wu Yuhong (China) 15–5, 15–10

Mixed Doubles: Catrine Bengtsson (Sweden) and Thomas Lund (Denmark) beat Grete Mogensen and Jon Holst-Christensen (Denmark) 10–15, 15–6, 15–12

ENGLISH NATIONAL CHAMPIONSHIPS 1993

Men's Singles: Darren Hall beat Anders Nielsen 15–6, 10–15, 8–2 ret.

Women's Singles: Sue Louis-Lane beat Fiona Smith 11–4, 11–1

Men's Doubles: Julian Robertson and Dave Wright beat Simon Archer and Nick Ponting 15–7, 15–6

Women's Doubles: Gillian Clark and Gillian Gowers beat Sara Sankey and Julie Bradbury 15–4, 17–14

Mixed Doubles: Gillian Clark and Nick Ponting beat Joanne Wright and Chris Hunt 15–11, 15–7

SCOTTISH NATIONAL CHAMPIONSHIPS 1993

Men's Singles: Jim Mailer beat Kenneth Middlemiss 10–15, 15–8, 15–0

Women's Singles: Anne Gibson beat Elinor Allen 11–4, 11–3

Men's Doubles: Russell Hogg and Kenneth Middlemiss beat Alastair Gatt and Gordon Haldane 15–11

Women's Doubles: Jennifer Allen and Elinor Allen beat Jillian Haldane and Aileen Travers 15–8, 18–14

Mixed Doubles: Elinor Allen and Kenneth Middlemiss beat Jillian Haldane and Gordon Haldane 15–13, 15–6

ALL-ENGLAND CHAMPIONSHIPS 1993

Men's Singles: Heryanto Arbi (Indonesia) beat Joko Suprianto (Indonesia) 15–7, 4–15, 15–11

Women's Singles: Susi Susanti (Indonesia) Beat Bang Soo-Hyun (S. Korea) 4–11, 11–4, 11–1

Men's Doubles: Jon Holst-Christensen and Thomas Lund (Denmark) beat Chen Hongyong and Chen Kang (China) 10–15, 15–2, 15–10

Women's Doubles: Chung So-Young and Gil Young-Ah (S. Korea) beat Lin Yan Fen and Yao Fen (China) 5–15, 15–4, 15–7

Mixed Doubles: Jon Holst-Christensen and Grete Morgensen (Denmark) beat Thomas Lund (Denmark) and Catrine Bengtsson (Sweden) 8–1 ret.

BASKETBALL

MEN

Championship play-off final 1993: Worthing Bears beat Thames Valley Tigers 75–74

NatWest Trophy final 1993: Thames Valley Tigers beat Guildford Kings 91–84

National Cup final 1993: Guildford Kings beat Worthing Bears 82–72

National League Championship: Worthing Bears

WOMEN

Championship play-off final 1993: Sheffield beat Northampton 64–63

National Cup final 1993: Sheffield beat Milton Keynes 63–50

National League Championship: Sheffield

BILLIARDS

World Professional Championship 1992: Geet Sethi (India) beat Robby Foldvari (Australia) 8–5

UK Professional Championship 1992: Robby Foldvari (Australia) beat Subhash Agarwal (India) 4–1

UK Professional Championship 1993: Robby Foldvari (Australia) beat Geet Sethi (India) 4–0

World Amateur Champion: Manoj Kothari (India)

BOWLS (MEN)

WORLD INDOOR CHAMPIONSHIPS 1993
Preston, February

Singles final: Richard Corsie (Scotland) beat Jim McCann (Scotland) 7–4, 7–5, 4–7, 7–5

Pairs final: Gary Smith and Andy Thomson (England) beat Tony Allcock and David Bryant (England) 7–6, 7–3, 7–6

NATIONAL CHAMPIONSHIPS 1993
Worthing, August

Fours final: Reading beat Shepherds Bush Cricket Club 22–13

Triples final: Preston, Brighton beat Marlborough, Ipswich 21–20

Pairs final: Rob Robinson and Richard Brittan (Erdington Court) beat Gary Smith and Andy Thomson (Blackheath and Greenwich) 25–24

Singles final: John Wickham (Totnes) beat Gordon Charlton (Folkestone Park) 21–17

NATIONAL INDOOR CHAMPIONSHIPS 1993
Melton Mowbray, February–March

Fours final: Cambridge Park beat Plymouth Civil Service 18–17

Triples final: City of Nottingham beat Teignbridge 20–13

Pairs final: Dave Williams and Keith Renwick (Preston, Brighton) beat Mark Overton and Ian Daines (Wymondham Dell, Norfolk) 23–10

Singles final: Russell Morgan (East Dorset) beat David Bryant (Clevedon) 21–14

BRITISH ISLES CHAMPIONSHIPS 1993
Worthing, July

Fours final: Presteigne beat Bournemouth 21–11

Triples final: Magherafelt beat Tenby 21–10

Pairs final: Gary Smith and Andy Thomson (Blackheath and Greenwich) beat George Ross and Richard Corsie (Craigentinny) 18–17

Singles final: Alex Lightbody (Bangor) beat Robert Provan (Airdrie) 21–13

BRITISH ISLES INDOOR CHAMPIONSHIPS 1993
Swansea, March

Fours final: England beat Wales 22–12

Triples final: Ireland beat England 19–8

Pairs final: Steve Rees and John Price (Wales) beat Ted Boyle and Iain Boyle (England) 23–8

Singles final: John Price (Wales) beat Neil Booth (Ireland) 21–14

Home International Championships 1993 (Worthing):
England
Middleton Cup (Inter-County Championship) final 1993:
Kent beat Cumbria 145–73

BOWLS (WOMEN)

WORLD INDOOR CHAMPIONSHIPS 1993
Guernsey, April

Singles final: Kate Adams (Scotland) beat Jayne Roylance
(England) 21–11

NATIONAL CHAMPIONSHIPS 1993
Royal Leamington Spa, August

Fours final: Broadstone, Dorset beat Wellingborough,
Northamptonshire 17–13
Triples final: Great Baddow, Essex beat Grimsby Park
Avenue, Lincolnshire 14–10
Pairs final: June Boosey and Kay Havord (Hatfield) beat
Anne Dennis and Carol Branchett (Milton Regis, Kent)
23–13
Singles final (four woods): Dorothy Prior (Hewell, Redditch)
beat Carole Lloyd (Milton Park, Portsmouth) 21–7
Singles final (two woods): Val Chatfield (Woolwich and
Plumstead, Kent) beat Kathy Scott (Popes Mead,
Crawley, Sussex) 17–8

NATIONAL INDOOR CHAMPIONSHIPS 1993
Stevenage, February–March

Fours final: York beat Cumbria 26–16
Triples final: Angel, Tonbridge beat Cambridge Park,
Twickenham 21–18
Pairs final: Anne Erridge and Mary Price (Desborough,
Maidenhead) beat Margaret Moore and Sue Curtis
(Beccles) 25–8
Singles final: Jayne Roylance (North Walsham) beat Diane
Sekjer (Mote Park) 21–11

BRITISH ISLES CHAMPIONSHIPS 1993
Ayr, June

Fours final: Wales beat Scotland 26–6
Triples final: Scotland beat Ireland 15–14
Pairs final: Linda Evans and Eileen Thomas (Wales) beat
Joyce Morgan and June Larter (England) 27–15
Singles final: Phillis Nolan (Ireland) beat Julie Davies
(Wales) 25–4

BRITISH ISLES INDOOR CHAMPIONSHIPS 1993
Perth, March

Fours final: Scotland beat England 25–18
Triples final: Ireland beat Wales 24–13
Pairs final: Audrey Mullins and Rita Jones (Wales) beat
Eileen Vigor and Thelma Barton (England) 30–13
Singles final: Betty Morgan (Wales) beat Catherine
McIntosh (Scotland) 21–11

BOXING

PROFESSIONAL BOXING
as at 25 August 1993

WORLD BOXING COUNCIL (WBC) CHAMPIONS

Heavy: Lennox Lewis (GB)
Cruiser: Anaclet Wamba (France)
Light-heavy: Jeff Harding (Australia)
Super-middle: Nigel Benn (GB)

Middle: Gerald McClellan (USA)
Super-welter: Terry Norris (USA)
Welter: Pernell Whitaker (USA)
Super-light: Julio Cesar Chavez (Mexico)
Light: Miguel Gonzalez (Mexico)
Super-feather: Azumah Nelson (Ghana)
Feather: Gregorio Vargas (Mexico)
Super-bantam: Tracy Patterson (USA)
Bantam: Jungil Byon (S. Korea)
Super-fly: Moon Sung-kil (S. Korea)
Fly: Yuri Arbachakov (Russia)
Light-fly: Michael Carbajal (USA)
Straw: Ricardo Lopez (Mexico)

WORLD BOXING ASSOCIATION (WBA) CHAMPIONS

Heavy: Riddick Bowe (USA)
Cruiser: Bobby Czyz (USA)
Light-heavy: Virgil Hill (USA)
Super-middle: Michael Nunn (USA)
Middle: Reggie Johnson (USA)
Super-welter: Julio Cesar Vasquez (Argentina)
Welter: Crisanto Espana (Venezuela)
Super-light: Juan Coggi (Argentina)
Light: Dingaan Thobela (S. Africa)
Super-feather: Genaro Hernandez (USA)
Feather: Yung Kyung Park (S. Korea)
Super-bantam: Wilfredo Vazquez (Puerto Rico)
Bantam: Jorge Julio Eliecer (Colombia)
Super-fly: Katsuya Onizuka (Japan)
Fly: David Griman (Venezuela)
Light-fly: Myung Woo Yuh (S. Korea)
Straw: Chana Porpaoin (Thailand)

INTERNATIONAL BOXING FEDERATION (IBF)
CHAMPIONS

Heavy: Riddick Bowe (USA)
Cruiser: Alfred Cole (USA)
Light-heavy: Henry Maske (Germany)
Super-middle: James Toney (USA)
Middle: Ray Jones (USA)
Super-welter: Gianfranco Rosi (Italy)
Welter: Felix Trinidad (Puerto Rico)
Super-light: Charles Murray (USA)
Light: Freddie Pendleton (USA)
Super-feather: John Molina (Puerto Rico)
Feather: Tom Johnson (USA)
Super-bantam: Kennedy McKinney (USA)
Bantam: Orlando Canizales (USA)
Super-fly: Julio Borboa (Mexico)
Fly: Pichit Sibranchpagan (Thailand)
Light-fly: Michael Carbajal (USA)
Straw: Ratnaapol Vorapin (Thailand)

BRITISH CHAMPIONS

Heavy: Herbie Hide
Cruiser: Carl Thompson
Light-heavy: Maurice Coore
Super-middle: Henry Wharton
Middle: Frank Grant
Light-middle: Andy Till
Welter: vacant
Light-welter: Andy Holligan
Light: Paul Burke
Super-feather: Neil Haddock
Feather: vacant
Bantam: Drew Docherty
Fly: Francis Ampofo

EUROPEAN CHAMPIONS

Heavy: Henry Akinwande (GB)

BOWLING

	O	M	R	W	Av.
P. R. Reiffel	140.4	31	396	19	20.84
S. K. Warne	439.5	178	877	34	25.79
M. G. Hughes	296.2	78	845	31	27.25
T. B. A. May	278	90	592	21	28.19
A. R. Border	27	11	35	1	35.00
S. R. Waugh	32	9	82	2	41.00
B. P. Julian	82	16	291	5	58.20
M. E. Waugh	56	17	161	1	161.00

Also bowled: C. J. McDermott, 48–11–126–0

COUNTY CHAMPIONSHIP TABLE 1993

Order for 1992 in brackets	P	W	L	D	Bt	Bl	Pts
Middlesex (11)	17	11	1	5	37	59	272
*Worcestershire (17)	17	9	4	3	32	52	236
Glamorgan (14)	17	9	5	3	32	55	231
Northamptonshire (3)	17	8	4	5	35	59	222
Somerset (9)	17	8	7	2	26	59	213
Surrey (13)	17	6	6	5	40	60	196
*Nottinghamshire (4)	17	6	3	7	34	56	194
Kent (2)	17	6	4	7	40	54	190
Leicestershire (8)	17	6	5	6	23	61	180
Sussex (7)	17	5	7	5	42	54	176
Essex (1)	17	4	6	7	44	55	163
Yorkshire (16)	17	5	4	8	21	56	157
Hampshire (15)	17	4	5	8	39	47	150
Lancashire (12)	17	4	8	5	38	48	150
Derbyshire (5)	17	4	7	6	33	50	147
Warwickshire (6)	17	4	8	5	24	49	137
Gloucestershire (10)	17	3	10	4	24	56	128
Durham (18)	17	2	10	5	29	52	113

*Includes 8pts for a tied match

FIRST CLASS BATTING AVERAGES 1993

	I	NO	R	HS	Av.
D. C. Boon	23	4	1,437	164*	75.63
M. E. Waugh	25	6	1,361	178	71.63
D. R. Martyn	15	3	838	138*	69.83
S. R. Waugh	21	8	875	157*	67.30
K. J. Barnett	24	5	1,223	168	64.36
C. W. J. Athey	30	5	1,600	137	64.00
G. A. Gooch	35	3	2,023	159*	63.21
C. L. Hooper	24	2	1,304	236*	59.27
M. L. Hayden	21	1	1,150	151*	57.50
A. P. Wells	27	2	1,432	144	57.28
M. W. Gatting	24	4	1,132	182	56.60
G. A. Hick	30	2	1,522	187	54.35
T. S. Curtis	32	3	1,553	127	53.55
N. Hussain	35	5	1,604	152	53.46
M. J. Slater	28	4	1,275	152	53.12
J. E. Morris	29	1	1,461	229	52.17
J. E. Emburey	21	7	730	123	52.14
R. J. Bailey	30	5	1,282	200	51.28
M. A. Ealham	16	3	666	85	51.23
P. R. Pollard	32	3	1,463	180	50.44

*Not out

FIRST CLASS BOWLING AVERAGES 1993

	O	M	R	W	Av.
Wasin Akram	409.2	93	1,137	59	19.27
K. M. Curran	458	123	1,293	67	19.29
J. E. Emburey	719.4	226	1,401	71	19.73
A. P. Igglesden	438.5	111	1,068	54	19.77

M. P Bicknell	502.2	137	1,341	67	20.01
C. E. L. Ambrose	543.4	150	1,207	59	20.45
Mushtaq Ahmed	694.3	212	1,773	85	20.85
W. K. M. Benjamin	281.3	81	702	32	21.93
A. E. Warner	322.5	76	900	41	21.95
S. K. Warne	765.4	281	1,698	75	22.64
Waqar Younis	449.4	89	1,407	62	22.69
A. R. C. Fraser	532.4	131	1,388	61	22.75
S. L. Watkin	766.4	173	2,098	92	22.80
D. J. Millns	184.3	51	584	25	23.36
C. L. Cairns	411.5	74	1,242	53	23.43
C. A. Walsh	528.2	119	1,516	64	23.68
P. C. R. Tufnell	688.4	189	1,529	64	23.89
D. A. Reeve	284.1	108	528	22	24.00
N. A. Mallender	329.5	102	772	32	24.12
P. J. Newport	546.5	135	1,454	60	24.23

Source for averages and county championship table:
TCCB Official Cricket Statistics

OTHER RESULTS 1993

Benson and Hedges Cup final: Derbyshire beat Lancashire by 6 runs. Derbyshire 252–6; Lancashire 246–7

NatWest Trophy final: Warwickshire beat Sussex by 5 wickets. Sussex 321–6; Warwickshire 322–5

Sunday League Champions: Glamorgan

MCC Trophy (Minor Counties knockout final): Staffordshire beat Wiltshire by 69 runs. Staffordshire 326–7; Wiltshire 257-7

Minor Counties Championship final: Staffordshire beat Cheshire by 5 wickets. Cheshire 174–6; Staffordshire 178–5

National Club Championship final: Old Hill beat West Bromwich, Dartmouth by 7 wickets. West Bromwich, Dartmouth 133; Old Hill 134–3

National Village Championship final: Kington beat Frocester by 2 runs. Kington 191-6; Frocester 189

Universities: Oxford beat Cambridge by 9 wickets. Oxford 400–6 dec. and 100–1; Cambridge 241 and 255

CYCLING

Italian Classic 1992: Gianni Bugno (Italy)
Tour of Lombardy 1992: Tony Rominger (Switzerland)
World Cup series overall winner 1992: Olaf Ludwig (Germany)

Tour of Spain 1993: Tony Rominger (Switzerland)
Milk Race 1993: Chris Lillywhite (GB)
Giro d'Italia 1993: Miguel Indurain (Spain)
Tour de France 1993: Miguel Indurain (Spain)
Tour of Britain 1993: Phil Anderson (Australia)
World Road Race Championship 1993: Lance Armstrong (USA)
World Amateur Road Race Championship 1993: Jan Ulrich (Germany)
World Professional Cyclo-Cross Championship 1993: Dominique Arnould (France)
World Amateur Cyclo-Cross Championship 1993: Henrik Djernis (Denmark)
British Road Race Championship 1993: Malcolm Elliott
British Amateur Road Race Championship 1993: Robert Harris
British Open Cyclo-Cross Championship 1993: Steve Douce
Women's World Road Race Championship 1993: Leontien van Moorsel (Holland)
Women's National Road Race Championship 1993: Marie Purvis

EQUESTRIANISM

SHOW JUMPING

World Cup Final 1993: Ludger Beerbaum on Almox Ratina (Germany)
European Championships 1993:
  Individual: Willy Melliger on Quinta C (Switzerland)
  Team: Switzerland
British Jumping Derby 1993 (Hickstead): Michael Whitaker on Everest Monsanta (GB)

THREE-DAY EVENTING

European Championships 1993:
  Individual: Jean-Lou Bigot on Twist La Beige
  Team: Sweden
Badminton Horse Trials 1993: Virginia Leng on Welton Houdini (GB)
British Open Horse Trials 1993: David O'Connor on Lighter than Air (USA)
Burghley Horse Trials 1993: Stephen Bradley on Sassy Reason (USA)

ETON FIVES

NatWest County Championship 1993: Middlesex
Amateur Championship (Kinnaird Cup) 1993: Robin Mason and Andrew Mole beat Mark Moore and Graham Dunbar 3–1
Holmwoods Schools' Championship 1993: Wolverhampton
Barber Cup final 1993: Old Salopians beat Old Edwardians 2–1
League Championship (Douglas Keeble Cup) 1993: Old Salopians

FENCING

MEN

WORLD CHAMPIONSHIPS 1993

Foil: Alexander Koch (Germany)
Epée: Ivan Kolobkov (Russia)
Sabre: Grigory Kirienko (Russia)
Team Foil: Germany
Team Epée: Italy
Team Sabre: Hungary

BRITISH CHAMPIONS 1993

Foil: Lauren Harper (Salle Paul)
Epée: Steven Paul (Salle Paul)
Sabre: Amin Zahir (Salle Paul)
Team Foil: Salle Paul
Team Epée: Polytechnic
Team Sabre: Salle Paul

Eden Cup final 1992: Tobias Darnstadt (Germany)
Challenge Martini International Epée 1993: Robert Felisiak (Germany)
Corble Cup 1993: Wilmos Szabo (Romania)

WOMEN

WORLD CHAMPIONSHIPS

Foil: Francesca Bortolozzi (Italy)
Epée: Oksana Ermakova (Estonia)

Team Foil: Germany
Team Epée: Hungary

BRITISH CHAMPIONS

Foil: Fiona McIntosh (Salle Paul)
Epée: Nicola Cain (Plymouth)
Sabre: Sue Bennet (Bath)
Team Epée: Polytechnic

Ipswich Cup 1993: Gianna Burki (Switzerland)

GOLF (MEN)

THE MAJOR CHAMPIONSHIPS 1993

US Masters (Augusta, Georgia, 8–11 April): Bernhard Langer (Germany), 277
US Open (Baltusrol, New Jersey, 17–20 June): Lee Janzen (USA), 272
The Open (Royal St George's, Sandwich, 15–18 July): Greg Norman (Australia), 267
US PGA Championship (Toledo, Ohio, 12–15 August): Paul Azinger (USA), 272*

PGA EUROPEAN TOUR 1992

World Matchplay Championship 1992 (Wentworth): Nick Faldo (GB and Ireland) beat Jeff Sluman (USA), 8 and 7
Honda Open (Hamburg): Bernhard Langer (Germany), 273
Madrid Open: David Feherty (GB and Ireland), 272
Volvo Masters (Sotogrande): Sandy Lyle (GB and Ireland), 287*
European Tour Order of Merit 1992: 1. Nick Faldo (GB and Ireland); 2. Bernhard Langer (Germany); 3. Colin Montgomerie (GB and Ireland)

PGA EUROPEAN TOUR 1993

Madeira Island Open: Mark James (GB and Ireland), 281
Dubai Desert Classic: Wayne Westner (South Africa), 274
Asian Classic (Singapore): Nick Faldo (GB and Ireland), 269
Tenerife Open: Mark James (GB and Ireland), 275
Moroccan Open (Agadir): David Gilford (GB and Ireland), 279
Turespana Masters (Cadiz): Andrew Oldcorn (GB and Ireland), 285
Mediterranean Open (Valencia): Frank Nobilo (New Zealand), 279
Balearic Open (Majorca): Jim Payne (GB and Ireland), 277*
Portuguese Open (Villamoura): David Gilford (GB and Ireland), 275*
Kronenbourg Open (Lake Garda): Sam Torrance (GB and Ireland), 284
Lyons Open: Costantino Rocca (Italy), 267
Rome Masters (Castelgandolfo): Jean Van de Velde (France), 281*
Catalonia Open (Barcelona): Sam Torrance (GB and Ireland), 201 (final round abandoned due to heavy rain)
Cannes Open: Rodger Davis (Australia), 271
International Open (St Mellion): Paul Broadhurst (GB and Ireland), 276
Spanish Open (Madrid): Joakim Haeggman (Sweden), 275
Italian Open (Modena): Greg Turner (New Zealand), 267
Volvo PGA Championship (Wentworth): Bernhard Langer (Germany), 274
British Masters (Woburn): Peter Baker (GB and Ireland), 266
Honda Open (Hamburg): Sam Torrance (GB and Ireland), 278

Jersey Open: Ian Palmer (South Africa), 268
French Open (Paris): Costantino Rocca (Italy), 273*
Irish Open (Mount Juliet, Thomastown): Nick Faldo (GB and Ireland), 276*
Scottish Open (Gleneagles): Jesper Parnevik (Sweden), 271
Dutch Open (Noordwijk): Colin Montgomerie (GB and Ireland), 281
Scandinavian Masters (Gothenburg): Peter Baker (GB and Ireland), 278*
International Open (Munich): Peter Fowler (Australia), 267
Austrian Open (Vienna): Ronan Rafferty (GB and Ireland), 274*
English Open (Forest of Arden, Coventry): Ian Woosnam (GB and Ireland), 269
German Open (Hubbelrath): Bernhard Langer (Germany), 269
European Masters (Crans-sur-Sierre): Barry Lane (GB and Ireland), 270
European Open (East Sussex National): Gordon Brand jun. (GB and Ireland), 275
Lancôme Trophy (Paris): Ian Woosnam (GB and Ireland), 267

World Cup 1992 (Madrid): Brett Ogle (Australia), 270
World Championship 1992 (Tryall Club, Jamaica): Nick Faldo (GB and Ireland), 274*

TEAM EVENTS
Dunhill Cup 1992 (St Andrews, 15–18 October): England beat Scotland 2½–½
Ryder Cup 1993 (The Belfry, 24–26 September): USA beat Europe 15–13
World Cup of Golf 1992 (Madrid): USA, 548
Walker Cup 1993 (Interlachen, Minneapolis): USA beat Great Britain and Ireland 19–5

AMATEUR CHAMPIONSHIPS 1993
British Amateur Championship (Royal Portrush): Iain Pyman (Sand Moor)
Brabazon Trophy (English Open Strokeplay) (Stoneham): David Fisher (Stoke Poges), 277
Welsh Open Strokeplay (Llandudno): Mike Macara (Llandudno), 280
Scottish Open Strokeplay (St Andrews): Alan Reid, 289
English Amateur Championship (Saunton): David Fisher (Stoke Poges)
Welsh Amateur Championship (Southerndown): Bradley Dredge (Bryn Meadows)
Scottish Amateur Championship (Royal Dornoch): Dean Robertson
Lytham Trophy (Royal Lytham & St Anne's): Tony McLure (Whickham), 292
Berkshire Trophy (The Berkshire): Van Phillips (Stoke Poges), 271
International Match (Aloha, Spain): England beat Spain 15–5
Home International Championship (Hoylake): England
European Amateur Championship (Dalmahoy, Edinburgh): Morten Backhausen (Denmark), 276*
European Amateur Team Championship: Wales
President's Putter (Rye): Clifford Weight beat Richard Sanders 2 and 1
Halford Hewitt Cup (for public schools' old boys): Shrewsbury beat Clifton 3–2
Universities: Oxford beat Cambridge 8½–6½
Eisenhower Trophy (world amateur team championship) 1992: New Zealand, 823

GOLF (WOMEN)

US Women's Open 1993 (Crooked Stick, Indianapolis, 22–25 July): Lauri Merten (USA), 280

WPG EUROPEAN TOUR 1992
Slovenian Open (Bled): Karen Lunn (Australia), 141
Emirates Ladies' Challenge (Dubai): Dale Reid (Scotland), 142
European Tour Order of Merit 1992: 1. Laura Davies (England); 2. Helen Alfredsson (Sweden); 3. Corinne Dibnah (Australia)

WPG EUROPEAN TOUR 1993
World Classic (Kuala Lumpur): Karen Lunn (Australia), 286
Ford Classic (Woburn): Federica Dassu (Italy), 289
Leiden Open (Rijswijk): Corinne Dibnah (Australia), 214
European Masters (Bercuit): Helen Dobson (England), 283
Hennessy Cup (Refrath): Liselotte Neumann (Sweden), 280*
European Classic (Sagmuehle): Mardi Lunn (Australia), 287
British Open (Woburn): Karen Lunn (Australia), 275
IBM Ladies' Open (Haninge): Lora Fairclough (England), 280
English Open (Tytherington): Laura Davies (England), 277
Italian Open (Lignano): Amaya Arruti (Spain), 270

TEAM EVENTS
Sunrise Cup 1992 (Inaugural World Professional Team Championship): Sweden, 445

AMATEUR CHAMPIONSHIPS 1993
British Open Championship (Royal Lytham & St Anne's): Catriona Lambert
English Championship (St Enodoc): Nicola Buxton
Welsh Championship (Abergele and Pensarn): Andrea Donne
Scottish Championship (Prestwick St Nicholas): Catriona Lambert (N. Berwick)
British Strokeplay Championship (Gullane): Julie Hall, 290
English Strokeplay (Kings Norton): Julie Hall, 298
Welsh Strokeplay (Newport): Julie Hall, 221
Home International Championship (Dublin): England
European Team Championship (The Hague): England

GREYHOUND RACING

Grand Prix 1992 (Walthamstow): Westmead Darkie
St Leger 1992 (Wembley): Airmount Flash
Television Trophy 1993 (Wimbledon): Heavenly Lady
Grand National 1993 (Birmingham): Arfur Daley
Greyhound Derby 1993 (Wimbledon): Ringa Hustle
Scurry Gold Cup 1993 (Catford): Kind of Magic
The Masters 1993 (Reading): I'm His
The Regency 1993 (Hove): Trans Domino
Gold Collar 1993 (Catford): Ardcollum Hilda
Cesarewitch 1993 (Manchester): Killenagh Dream

---

*After a play-off

GYMNASTICS (Men)

WORLD CHAMPIONSHIPS 1993

World Champion: Vitaly Scherbo (Belorussia)
World Individual Apparatus Champions:
  Floor: Grigori Misutin (Ukraine)
  Pommel Horse: Pae Gil Su (N. Korea)
  Rings: Yuri Chechi (Italy)
  Vault: Vitaly Scherbo (Belorussia)
  Parallel Bars: Vitaly Scherbo (Belorussia)
  High Bar: Sergei Charkov (Russia)

BRITISH CHAMPIONSHIPS 1992

British Champion: Neil Thomas
British Individual Apparatus Champions:
  Floor: Neil Thomas
  Pommel Horse: =Neil Thomas, David Cox, Paul Bowler
  Rings: =Neil Thomas, Paul Bowler
  Vault: Neil Thomas
  Parallel Bars: Neil Thomas
  High Bar: Neil Thomas
British Team Champions 1993 (Adam Shield): Central
  Manchester

GYMNASTICS (Women)

WORLD CHAMPIONSHIPS 1993

World Champion: Shannon Miller (USA)
World Individual Apparatus Champions:
  Floor: Shannon Miller (USA)
  Beam: Lavinia Milosovici (Romania)
  Vault: Elena Piskoun (Belorussia)
  Assymetric Bars: Shannon Miller (USA)

World Rythmics Champion 1992: Oksana Kostina (Russia)

BRITISH CHAMPIONSHIPS 1992

British Champion: Rowena Roberts
British Individual Apparatus Champions:
  Beam: Rowena Roberts
  Floor: Rowena Roberts
  Vault: Louise Redding
  Assymetric Bars: Sarah Mercer

British Open Club Team Champions 1993: Heathrow-
  Hoechst
British Rythmics Champion 1992: Debbie Southwick

HOCKEY (Men)

National League: Hounslow
Hockey Association Cup final 1993: Hounslow beat
  Teddington 4–1
County Championship final 1993: Staffordshire beat
  Cheshire 3–2
National Indoor Club Championship final 1993: East
  Grinstead beat Old Loughtonians 6–3
Champions Trophy final 1993: Australia beat Germany 4–0
European Club Championship final 1993: Uhlenhorst
  (Germany) beat Club Egara (Spain) 1–0
European Indoor Club Championship final 1993: Cologne
  (Germany) beat Limburger (Germany) 4–3
European Cup Winners' Cup final 1993: HGC (Holland)
  beat Hounslow (England) 4–0
Universities 1993: Oxford beat Cambridge 3–0

HOCKEY (Women)

National League: Ipswich
AEWHA Cup final 1993: Leicester beat Ealing 1–0
County Championship final 1993: Lancashire 1,
  Staffordshire 1. Lancashire won 5–4 on penalties
Home Countries Tournament 1993: Scotland
National Indoor Club Championship final 1993: Hightown
  beat Ipswich 2–1
Champions Trophy final 1993: Holland 1, Australia 1.
  Australia won 4–2 on penalties
European Club Championship final 1993: Russelsheim
  (Germany) 1, Amsterdam (Holland) 1. Russelsheim won
  3–1 on penalties
European Indoor Club Championship final 1993: Berlin
  (Germany) beat Russelsheim (Germany) 6–3
European Indoor Cup final 1993: Germany beat England
  8–3
European Cup Winners' Cup final 1993: HGC (Netherlands)
  beat Hightown (England) 2–1

HORSERACING

WINNING OWNERS 1992

Sheikh Mohammed	£1,194,368
Hamdan Al-Maktoum	694,894
Robert Sangster	677,228
Khalid Abdulla	620,351
Maktoum Al-Maktoum	435,151
William Gredley	415,621
Sidney Craig	355,000
Lord Weinstock	295,231
Lord Carnarvon	265,167
Virginia Kraft Payson	261,216

WINNING TRAINERS 1992

Richard Hannon	£1,154,201
Peter Chapple-Hyam	989,499
Clive Brittain	972,327
Michael Stoute	863,611
Henry Cecil	735,358
John Gosden	727,778
John Dunlop	524,173
Ian Balding	499,096
Geoff Wragg	494,689
Paul Cole	429,687

LEADING BREEDERS 1992

	Value
Swettenham Stud (USA)	£759,532
Juddmonte Farms	568,675
Stetchworth Park Stud	429,787
Lyonstown Stud	359,791
Ballymacoll Stud Farm	317,196
Sheikh Mohammed	292,168
Hamdan Al-Maktoum	269,218
Virginia Kraft Payson	261,216
Gainsborough Stud Management	253,099
Edmund Loder	224,424

WINNING SIRES 1992

	Horses	*Races won*	*Total value*
El Gran Senor (1981) by Northern Dancer	11	19	£564,008
Sadler's Wells (1981) by Northern Dancer	30	49	£563,048

Slip Anchor (1982) by Shirley Heights	16	29	£529,304
Ahonoora (1975) by Lorenzaccio	20	28	£519,763
Riverman (1969) by Never Bend	10	15	£353,532
Green Desert (1983) by Danzig	28	42	£350,501
Persian Bold (1975) by Bold Lad	17	28	£283,332
Rainbow Quest (1981) by Blushing Groom	24	35	£267,338
Lomond (1980) by Northern Dancer	16	23	£263,105
Pleasant Colony (1978) by His Majesty	1	1	£261,216

WINNING FLAT JOCKEYS 1992

	1st	2nd	3rd	Unpl.	Total mts
Michael Roberts	206	146	113	603	1068
Pat Eddery	178	118	76	359	731
Willie Carson	125	120	107	504	856
George Duffield	108	70	59	466	703
Richard Quinn	108	121	81	468	778
Steve Cauthen	107	85	72	293	557
Frankie Dettori	101	82	76	420	679
Ray Cochrane	100	96	104	479	779
Willie Ryan	96	103	91	401	691
John Reid	95	78	89	442	704

WINNING NATIONAL HUNT JOCKEYS 1992–3

	1st	2nd	3rd	Unpl.	Total mts
Richard Dunwoody	173	120	89	357	739
Peter Scudamore	129	75	47	165	416
Adrian Maguire	124	118	97	383	722
Peter Niven	108	62	52	164	386
Jamie Osborne	102	71	61	266	500
Graham McCourt	70	61	61	238	430
Neale Doughty	69	36	33	125	263
Carl Llewellyn	68	43	50	251	412
Mark Dwyer	61	58	47	150	316
Chris Grant	58	56	49	256	419

The above statistics are the copyright of *The Sporting Life*

RESULTS

CAMBRIDGESHIRE HANDICAP
(1839) Newmarket, 1 mile

1989 Rambo's Hall (4y), (8st 6lb)
1990 Risen Moon (3y), (8st 9lb)
1991 Mellottie (6y), (9st 1lb), J. Lowe
1992 Rambo's Hall (7y), (9st 3lb), D. McKeown

PRIX DE L'ARC DE TRIOMPHE
(1920) Longchamp, 1½ miles

1989 Carroll House (4y), (9st 4lb)
1990 Saumarez (3y), (8st 11lb)
1991 Suave Dancer (3y), (8st 11lb), C. Asmussen
1992 Subotica (4y), (9st 4lb), T. Jarnet

CESAREWITCH
(1839) Newmarket, 2 miles and about 2 f

1989 Double Dutch (5y), (9st 10lb)
1990 Trainglot (3y), (7st 12lb), W. Carson
1991 Go South (7y), (7st 11lb), N. Carlisle
1992 Vintage Crop (5y), (9st 6lb), W. Swinburn

CHAMPION STAKES
(1877) Newmarket, 1 mile, 2 f

1989 Legal Case (3y), (8st 10lb)
1990 In the Groove (3y), (8st 9lb), S. Cauthen
1991 Tel Quel (3y), (8st 12lb), A. Fabre
1992 Rodrigo de Triano (3y), (8st 12lb), L. Piggott

*HENNESSY GOLD CUP
(1957) Newbury, 3 miles and about 2½ f

1989 Ghofar (6y), (10st 2lb)
1990 Arctic Call (7y), (11st), J. Osborne
1991 Chatham (7y), (10st 6lb), P. Scudamore
1992 Sibton Abbey (7y), (10st), A. Maguire

*KING GEORGE VI CHASE
(1937) Kempton, about 3 miles

1989 Desert Orchid (10y), (11st 10lb)
1990 Desert Orchid (11y), (11st 10lb), R. Dunwoody
1991 The Fellow (6y), (11st 10lb), A. Kondrat
1992 The Fellow (7y), (11st 10lb), A. Kondrat

*CHAMPION HURDLE
(1927) Cheltenham, 2 miles and about ½ f

1990 Kribensis (6y), (12st)
1991 Morley Street (7y), (12st), J. Frost
1992 Royal Gait (9y), (12st), G. McCourt
1993 Granville Again (7y), (12st), P. Scudamore

*QUEEN MOTHER CHAMPION CHASE
(1959) Cheltenham, about 2 miles

1990 Barnbrook Again (9y), (12st)
1991 Katabatic (8y), (12st), S. McNeill
1992 Remittance Man (8y), (12st), J. Osborne
1993 Deep Sensation (8y), (12st), D. Murphy

*CHELTENHAM GOLD CUP
(1924) 3 miles and about 2½ f

1990 Norton's Coin (9y), (12st)
1991 Garrison Savannah (8y), (12st), M. Pitman
1992 Cool Ground (10y), (12st), A. Maguire
1993 Jodami (8y), (12st), M. Dwyer

LINCOLN HANDICAP
(1965) Doncaster, 1 mile

1990 Evichstar (6y), (7st 10lb)
1991 Amenable (6y), (8st 1lb), A. Greaves
1992 High Low (4y), (8st), J. Quinn
1993 High Premium (5y), (8st 8lb), K. Fallon

*GRAND NATIONAL
(1837) Liverpool, 4 miles and about 4 f

1990 Mr Frisk (11y), (10st 6lb)
1991 Seagram (11y), (10st 6lb), N. Hawke
1992 Party Politics (8y), (10st 7lb), C. Llewellyn
1993 Race declared void. Esha Ness (J. White) first past post

Record times: 8 minutes 47.8 seconds by Mr Frisk in 1990; 9 minutes 1.9 seconds by Red Rum in 1973

*WHITBREAD GOLD CUP
(1957) Sandown, 3 miles and about 5 f

1990 Mr Frisk (11y), (10st 5lb)
†1991 Docklands Express (9y), (10st 13lb), A. Tory
1992 Topsham Bay (9y), (10st), H. Davies
1993 Topsham Bay (10y), (10st), R. Dunwoody

† Cahervillahow finished first but after an objection and a stewards' inquiry was placed second
*National Hunt

THE CLASSICS

ONE THOUSAND GUINEAS
(1814) Rowley Mile, Newmarket, for three-year-old fillies

Year	Winner	Betting	Owner	Jockey	Trainer	No. of Runners
1990	Salsabil	6–4	H. Al-Maktoum	W. Carson	J. Dunlop	10
1991	Shadayid	4–6	H. Al-Maktoum	W. Carson	J. Dunlop	14
1992	Hatoof	5–1	M. Al-Maktoum	W. Swinburn	C. Head	14
1993	Sayyedati	4–1	Mohamed Obaida	W. Swinburn	C. Brittain	12

TWO THOUSAND GUINEAS
(1809) Rowley Mile, Newmarket, for three year olds

Year	Winner	Betting	Owner	Jockey	Trainer	No. of Runners
1990	Tirol	9–1	J. Horgan	M. Kinane	R. Hannon	14
1991	Mystiko	13–2	Lady Beaverbrook	M. Roberts	C. Brittain	14
1992	Rodrigo de Triano	6–1	R. Sangster	L. Piggott	P. Chapple-Hyam	16
1993	Zafonic	5–6	K. Abdulla	P. Eddery	A. Fabre	14

Record time: 1 minute 35.84 seconds, 1990

THE DERBY
(1780) Epsom, 1 mile and about 4 f, for three year olds

The first winner was Sir Charles Bunbury's Diomed in 1780. The owners with the record number of winners are Lord Egremont, who won in 1782, 1804, 1805, 1807, 1826 (also won five Oaks); and the late Aga Khan, who won in 1930, 1935, 1936, 1948, 1952 (also won two Oaks). Other winning owners are: Duke of Grafton (1802, 1809, 1810, 1815); Mr J. Bowes (1835, 1843, 1852, 1853); Sir J. Hawley (1851, 1858, 1859, 1868); the 1st Duke of Westminster (1880, 1882, 1886, 1899); and Sir Victor Sassoon (1953, 1957, 1958, 1960).

Record times are: 2 min. 33.80 sec. by Mahmoud in 1936; 2 min. 33.84 sec. by Kahyasi in 1988; 2 min. 33.9 sec. by Reference Point in 1987.

The Derby was run at Newmarket from 1915–18 and from 1940–5.

Year	Winner	Betting	Owner	Jockey	Trainer	No. of Runners
1990	Quest for Fame	7–1	K. Abdulla	P. Eddery	R. Charlton	18
1991	Generous	9–1	Prince Fahd Salman	A. Munro	P. Cole	13
1992	Dr Devious	8–1	S. Craig	J. Reid	P. Chapple-Hyam	18
1993	Commander In Chief	15–2	K. Abdulla	M. Kinane	H. Cecil	16

THE OAKS
(1779) Epsom, 1 mile and about 4 f, for three year old fillies

Year	Winner	Betting	Owner	Jockey	Trainer	No. of Runners
1990	Salsabil	2–1	H. Al-Maktoum	W. Carson	J.Dunlop	8
1991	Jet Ski Lady	50–1	J. Dunlop	C. Roche	J. Bolger	9
1992	User Friendly	5–1	W. Gredley	G. Duffield	C. Brittain	7
1993	Intrepidity	5–1	Sheikh Mohammed	M. Roberts	A. Fabre	14

ST LEGER
(1776) Doncaster, 1 mile and about 6 f, for three year olds

Year	Winner	Betting	Owner	Jockey	Trainer	No. of Runners
1990	Snurge	7–2	M. Abib	R. Quinn	P. Cole	8
1991	Toulon	5–2	K. Abdulla	P. Eddery	A. Fabre	10
1992	User Friendly	7–4	W. Gredley	G. Duffield	C. Brittain	8
1993	Bob's Return	3–1	Mrs J. Smith	P. Robinson	M. Tompkins	9

JOCKEY CLUB STAKES
(1894) Newmarket, 1¼ miles

1990	Roseate Tern (4y), (8st 9lb)
1991	Rock Hopper (4y), (8st 7lb), P. Eddery
1992	Sapience (6y), (8st 12lb), R Cochrane
1993	Zinaad (4y), (8st 9lb), W. Swinburn

KENTUCKY DERBY
(1875) Louisville, Kentucky, 1¼ miles

1990	Unbridled
1991	Strike the Gold, C. Antley
1992	Lil E Tee, P. Day
1993	Sea Hero, J. Bailey

PRIX DU JOCKEY CLUB
(1836) Chantilly, 1½ miles

1990	Sanglamore
1991	Suave Dancer (9st 2lb), C. Asmussen
1992	Polytain (9st 2lb), L. Dettori
1993	Hernando (9st 2lb), C. Asmussen

ASCOT GOLD CUP
(1807) Ascot, 2 miles and about 4 f

1990	Ashal (4y), (9st)
1991	Indian Queen (6y), (8st 13lb), W. Swinburn
1992	Drum Taps (6y), (9st 2lb), L. Dettori
1993	Drum Taps (7y), (9st 2lb), L. Dettori

IRISH SWEEPS DERBY
(1866) Curragh, 1½ miles, for three year olds

1990	Salsabil (8st 11lb)
1991	Generous (9st), A. Munro
1992	St Jovite (9st), C. Roche
1993	Commander In Chief (9st), P. Eddery

ECLIPSE STAKES
(1886) Sandown, 1 mile and about 2 f

1990	Elmaamul (3y), (8st 10lb)
1991	Environment Friend (3y), (8st 10lb), G. Duffield
1992	Kooyonga (4y), (9st 4lb), W. O'Connor
1993	Opera House (5y), (9st 7lb), M. Kinane

KING GEORGE VI AND QUEEN ELIZABETH DIAMOND STAKES
(1952) Ascot, 1 mile and about 4 f

1990	Belmez (3y), (8st 9lb)
1991	Generous (3y), (8st 9lb), A. Munro
1992	St Jovite (3y), (8st 9lb), S. Craine
1993	Opera House (5y), (9st 7lb), M. Stoute

GOODWOOD CUP
(1812) Goodwood, about 2 miles

1990	Lucky Moon (3y), (7st 10lb)
1991	Further Flight (5y), (9st), M. Hills
1992	Further Flight (6y), (9st 5lb), M. Hills
1993	Sonus (4y), (9st 3lb), P. Eddery

ICE HOCKEY

World Championship final 1993: Russia beat Sweden 3–1
British Championship final 1993: Cardiff Devils beat Humberside Seahawks 7–4
League Championship 1993:
  Premier Division: Cardiff Devils
  First Division: Basingstoke Beavers
Stanley Cup final 1993: Montreal beat LA Kings 4–1 (best of 7 final)
Women's World Championship final 1992: Canada beat USA 8–0

ICE SKATING

BRITISH CHAMPIONSHIPS 1992
Milton Keynes, November

Men: Steven Cousins
Women: Charlene von Saher
Pairs: Vicky Pearce and Clive Shorten
Ice Dance: Marika Humphries and Justin Lanning

EUROPEAN CHAMPIONSHIPS 1993
Helsinki, January

Men: Dmitri Dmitrenko (Ukraine)
Women: Surya Bonaly (France)
Pairs: Marina Eltsova and Andrei Bushkov (Russia)
Ice Dance: Maia Usova and Alexander Zhulin (Russia)

WORLD CHAMPIONSHIPS 1993
Prague, March

Men: Kurt Browning (Canada)
Women: Oksana Baiul (Ukraine)
Pairs: Isabelle Brasseur and Lloyd Eisler (Canada)
Ice Dance: Maia Usova and Alexander Zhulin (Russia)

JUDO

BRITISH NATIONAL CHAMPIONSHIPS 1992
Crystal Palace, December

MEN

Heavy (over 95 kg): Andrew Costello
Light-heavy (95 kg): Lionel Hibbert
Middle (86 kg): Lloyd Alexander
Light-middle (78 kg): Martin McSorley
Light (71 kg): William Cusack
Feather (65 kg): Ian Freeman
Bantam (60 kg): Nigel Donohue

WOMEN

Heavy (over 72 kg): Lisa Maddaford
Light-heavy (72 kg): Kate Howey
Middle (66 kg): Chloe Cowen
Light-middle (61 kg): Diane Bell
Light (56 kg): Nicola Fairbrother
Feather (52 kg): Elise Summers
Bantam (48 kg): Joyce Heron

LAWN TENNIS

MAJOR CHAMPIONSHIPS 1993

AUSTRALIAN OPEN CHAMPIONSHIPS (Melbourne)

Men's Singles: Jim Courier (USA) beat Stefan Edberg (Sweden) 6–2, 6–1, 2–6, 7–5
Women's Singles: Monica Seles (Yugoslavia) beat Steffi Graf (Germany) 4–6, 6–3, 6–2
Men's Doubles: Dannie Wisser (S. Africa) and Laurie Warder (Australia) beat John Fitzgerald (Australia) and Anders Jarryd (Sweden) 6–4, 6–3, 6–4
Women's Doubles: Gigi Fernandez (USA) and Natalya Zvereva (Belarus) beat Pam Shriver (USA) and Elizabeth Smylie (Australia) 6–4, 6–3

Mixed Doubles: Arantxa Sanchez Vicario (Spain) and Todd
Woodbridge (Australia) beat Zina Garrison-Jackson and
Rick Leach (USA) 7–5, 6–4

FRENCH OPEN CHAMPIONSHIPS (Paris)

Men's Singles: Sergi Bruguera (Spain) beat Jim Courier
(USA) 6–4, 2–6, 6–2, 3–6, 6–3
Women's Singles: Steffi Graf (Germany) beat Mary Joe
Fernandez (USA) 4–6, 6–2, 6–4
Men's Doubles: Luke Jensen and Murphy Jensen (USA) beat
Marc Goellner and David Prinosil (Germany) 6–4, 6–7,
6–4
Women's Doubles: Gigi Fernandez (USA) and Natalya
Zvereva (Belarus) beat Larissa Neiland (Latvia) and Jana
Novotna (Czech Republic) 6–3, 7–5
Mixed Doubles: Eugenia Maniokova and Andre Olkhovskiy
(Russia) beat Elna Reinach and Dannie Visser (S. Africa)
6–2, 4–6, 6–4

ALL ENGLAND CHAMPIONSHIPS (Wimbledon)

Men's Singles: Pete Sampras (USA) beat Jim Courier (USA)
7–6, 7–6, 3–6, 6–3
Women's Singles: Steffi Graf (Germany) beat Jana Novotna
(Czech Republic) 7–6, 1–6, 6–4
Men's Doubles: Todd Woodbridge and Mark Woodforde
(Australia) beat Grant Connell (Canada) and Patrick
Galbraith (USA) 7–5, 6–3, 7–6
Women's Doubles: Gigi Fernandez (USA) and Natalya
Zvereva (Belarus) beat Larissa Neiland (Latvia) and Jana
Novotna (Czech Republic) 6–4, 6–7, 6–4
Mixed Doubles: Martina Navratilova (USA) and Mark
Woodforde (Australia) beat Manon Bollegraf and Tom
Nijssen (Holland) 6–3, 6–4

US OPEN CHAMPIONSHIPS (New York)

Men's Singles: Pete Sampras (USA) beat Cedric Pioline
(France) 6–4, 6–4, 6–3
Women's Singles: Steffi Graf (Germany) beat Helena Sukova
(Czech Republic) 6–3, 6–3
Men's Doubles: Ken Flach and Rick Leach (USA) beat
Martin Damm and Karel Novacek (Czech Republic) 6–7,
6–4, 6–2
Women's Doubles: Arantxa Sanchez Vicario (Spain) and
Helena Sukova (Czech Republic) beat Amanda Coetzer
(S. Africa) and Ines Gorrochategui (Argentina) 6–4, 6–2
Mixed Doubles: Helena Sukova (Czech Republic) and Todd
Woodbridge (Australia) beat Martina Navratilova (USA)
and Mark Woodforde (Australia) 6–3, 7–6

The Grand Slam Cup final 1992: Michael Stich (Germany)
beat Michael Chang (USA) 6–2, 6–3, 6–2

TEAM CHAMPIONSHIPS

Davis Cup final 1992: USA beat Switzerland 3–1
Federation Cup final 1993: Spain beat Australia 3–0
LTA County Cup 1993:
  Men: Surrey
  Women: Essex

NATIONAL CHAMPIONSHIPS 1992

Men's Singles: Jeremy Bates beat Andrew Castle 7–5, 6–3
Women's Singles: Jo Durie beat Julie Salmon 6–3, 6–3
Men's Doubles: Paul Hand and Chris Wilkinson beat Sean
Cole and Miles Maclagen 6–4, 4–6, 6–1
Women's Doubles: Clare Wood and Jo Durie beat Belinda
Borneo and Valda Lake 7–5, 6–3

MOTOR CYCLING

500 CC GRAND PRIX 1993

Australian (Eastern Creek): Kevin Schwantz (USA), Suzuki
Malaysian (Kuala Lumpur): Wayne Rainey (USA), Yamaha
Japanese (Suzuka): Wayne Rainey (USA), Yamaha
Spanish (Jerez): Kevin Schwantz (USA), Suzuki
Austrian (Salzburg): Kevin Schwantz (USA), Suzuki
German (Hockenheim): Daryl Beattie (Australia), Honda
Dutch (Assen): Kevin Schwantz (USA), Suzuki
European (Catalunya): Wayne Rainey (USA), Yamaha
San Marino (Mujello): Michael Doohan (Australia), Honda
British (Donington Park): Luca Cadalora (Italy), Yamaha
Czech Republic (Brno): Wayne Rainey (USA), Yamaha
Italian (Misano): Luca Cadalora (Italy), Yamaha
US (Laguna Seca): John Kocinski (USA), Cagiva
FIM (Jarama, Spain): Alexandra Barros (Brazil), Suzuki
Riders' Championship 1993: 1. Kevin Schwantz (USA),
Suzuki, 248 pts; 2. Wayne Rainey (USA), Yamaha,
214 pts; 3. Daryl Beattie (Australia), Honda, 176 pts

Senior Manx Grand Prix: Nigel Davies, Honda
Senior TT, Isle of Man: Phil McCallen, Honda
Junior TT, Isle of Man: Brian Reid, Yamaha

MOTOR RACING

FORMULA ONE GRAND PRIX 1992

Japanese (Suzuka): Riccardo Patrese (Italy), Williams
  Renault
Australian (Adelaide): Gerhard Berger (Austria), McLaren
  Honda
Drivers' Championship 1992: 1. Nigel Mansell (GB),
  Williams Renault, 108 pts; 2. Riccardo Patrese (Italy),
  Williams Renault, 56 pts; 3. Michael Schumacher
  (Germany), Benetton Ford, 53 pts
Constructors' World Championship 1992: 1. Williams
  Renault, 164 pts; 2. McLaren Honda, 99 pts; 3. Benetton
  Ford, 91pts

FORMULA ONE GRAND PRIX 1993

South African (Kyalami): Alain Prost (France), Williams
  Renault
Brazilian (Sao Paulo): Ayrton Senna (Brazil), McLaren
  Ford
European (Donington Park): Ayrton Senna (Brazil),
  McLaren Ford
San Marino (Imola): Alain Prost (France), Williams Renault
Spanish (Barcelona): Alain Prost (France), Williams Renault
Monaco: Ayrton Senna (Brazil), McLaren Ford
Canadian (Montreal): Alain Prost (France), Williams
  Renault
French (Magny Cours): Alain Prost (France), Williams
  Renault
British (Silverstone): Alain Prost (France), Williams Renault
German (Hockenheim): Alain Prost (France), Williams
  Renault
Hungarian (Budapest): Damon Hill (GB), Williams Renault
Belgian (Spa-Francorchamps): Damon Hill (GB), Williams
  Renault
Italian (Monza): Damon Hill (GB), Williams Renault
Portuguese (Estoril): Michael Schumacher (Germany),
  Benetton Ford

Indianapolis 500 1993: Emerson Fittipaldi (Brazil), Penske-Chevy
Le Mans 24-Hour Race 1993: Geoff Brabham (Australia), Christophe Bouchut (France) and Eric Helary (France), Peugeot 905

MOTOR RALLYING

1992
Italian Rally: Andrea Aghini (Italy), Lancia Delta
Ivory Coast Rally: Kenjiro Shinozuka (Japan), Mitsubishi
Catalonia Rally: Carlos Sainz (Spain), Toyota
Lombard RAC Rally: Carlos Sainz (Spain), Toyota
Drivers' World Championship 1992: Carlos Sainz (Spain), Toyota, 144 pts
Manufacturers' World Championship 1992: Lancia, 140 pts

1993
Monte Carlo Rally: Didier Auriol (France), Toyota
Swedish Rally: Mats Jonsson (Sweden), Toyota
Portuguese Rally: François Delecour (France), Ford
Safari Rally: Juha Kankkunen (Finland), Toyota
Corsican Rally: François Delecour (France), Ford
Acropolis Rally: Miki Biasion (Italy), Ford
Argentine Rally: Juha Kankkunen (Finland), Toyota
New Zealand Rally: Colin McRae (GB), Subaru
Malaysian Rally: Colin McRae (GB), Subaru
1,000 Lakes Rally (Finland): Juha Kankkunen (Finland), Toyota
Australian Rally: Juha Kankkunen (Finland), Toyota

Paris–Dakar Rally: Bruno Saby (France), Mitsubishi
London–Sydney Rally: Francis Tuthill (GB), Porsche

NETBALL

Test Matches
1992

7 Nov	Wembley	England 34, New Zealand 62
12 Nov	Manchester	England 26, New Zealand 60
14 Nov	Leicester	England 33, New Zealand 58

1993

6 April	Kingston	Jamaica 39, England 56
11 April	Kingston	Jamaica 36, England 41
13 April	Kingston	Jamaica 38, England 44

Internationals 1993

16 Jan	Cardiff	Wales 25, England 42
6 Feb	Guildford	England 69, Rep. of Ireland 12
	Glasgow	Scotland 42, Wales 50
20 Feb	Reading	England 63, Scotland 13
27 March	Lisburn	N. Ireland 30, England 65

World Games 1993: Australia
Inter-County Championship final 1993: Essex Metropolitan beat Bedfordshire 8–7
National Clubs Championship final 1993: Hirondelles (Surrey) beat Hornsey (Middlesex) 73–66
English Counties League Champions: Surrey
Inaugural National Clubs League Champions: Linden (Birmingham)

POLO

Prince of Wales's Trophy final 1993: Maple Leafs beat Franken 8–5
Queen's Cup final 1993: Black Bears beat Ellerston White 10–8
Warwickshire Cup final 1993: Ellerston White beat Black Bears 14–10
Gold Cup final 1993 (British Open): Alcatel beat Ellerston Black 9–8 after a play-off
Coronation Cup final 1993: England beat Chile 8–3
Silver Jubilee Cup final 1993: Canada beat the Hurlingham Polo Association 7–5
Cowdray Challenge Cup final 1993: Maple Leafs beat Alcatel 5–2
Universities 1992: Oxford beat Cambridge 10–2

RACKETS

World Singles Championship: James Male beat Neil Smith 4–2 and 4–1 in two-leg challenge
World Doubles Champions: Shannon Hazell and Neil Smith
Professional Singles Championship 1993: Neil Smith beat Shannon Hazell 3–0
Amateur Singles Championship 1992: James Male beat Willie Boone 3–0
Amateur Doubles Championship 1993: James Male and John Prenn beat Willie Boone and Tim Cockroft 4–2
British Open Singles Championship 1993: Neil Smith beat Shannon Hazell 4–0
British Open Doubles Championship 1993: John Prenn and James Male beat Willie Boone and Neil Smith 4–0
National League final 1993: Queen's Beat Clifton 6–5
Noel Bruce Cup 1992: Eton (Willie Boone and Mark Hue Williams) beat Harrow (John Prenn and Charles Hue Williams) 4–0
Public Schools Singles Championship 1992: Harrow beat Clifton 3–0
Public Schools Doubles Championship 1993: Haileybury beat Rugby 4–3
Universities 1993: Oxford beat Cambridge 3–0

REAL TENNIS

World Singles Championship: Wayne Davies (Australia) beat Lachie Deuchar (Australia) 7–6
Professional Singles Championship 1993: Lachie Deuchar (Australia) beat Robert Fahey (Australia) 3–0
Professional Doubles Championship 1993: Mark Devine and Kevin Sheldon beat Chris Bray and Jonathan Howell 2–1
Amateur Singles Championship 1993: Julian Snow beat Nigel Pendrigh 3–0
Amateur Doubles Championship 1993: Julian Snow and Mike McMurraugh beat Thane Warburg and Ivan Snell 3–0
British Open Singles Championship final 1992: Julian Snow beat Chris Bray 3–0
British Open Doubles Championship final 1992: Wayne Davies and Lachie Deuchar (Australia) beat Frank Filippelli and James Male (Australia) (walk-over)
Ladies' World Championship 1993: Sally Jones beat Charlotte Cornwallis 2–1
Ladies' World Doubles Championship 1993: Charlotte Cornwallis and Penny Lumley beat Sally Jones and Alex Garside 2–0

British Open Ladies Singles Championship 1993: Penny
Lumley beat Alex Garside 2–0
British Open Ladies Doubles Championship 1993: Sally Jones
and Alex Garside beat Penny Lumley and Charlotte
Cornwallis 2–1
Henry Leaf Cup final 1993: Radley beat Winchester 2–0
Universities 1993: Cambridge beat Oxford 4–2

ROAD WALKING

MEN'S NATIONAL 20 KM WALK
Cardiff, 14 March 1993

Individual: Andrew Penn (Coventry), 1 hr 25 min. 57 sec.
Team: Leicester, 43 pts

WOMEN'S NATIONAL 10 KM WALK
Cardiff, 14 March 1993

Individual: Verity Larby (Aldershot), 47 min. 51 sec.
Team: Dudley and Stourbridge, 25 pts

MEN'S NATIONAL 10 MILES WALK
Sheffield, 9 May 1993

Individual: Les Morton (Sheffield), 1 hr 03 min. 16 sec.
Team: Leicester, 34 pts

WOMEN'S NATIONAL 10 MILES WALK
Sheffield, 9 May 1993

Individual: Verity Lupton (Sheffield), 1 hr 21 min. 19 sec.
Team: Sheffield, 13 pts

MEN'S NATIONAL 20 MILES WALK
Sutton Park, 10 July 1993

Individual: Sean Martindale (York Postal), 2 hr 33 min.
58 sec.
Team: Coventry, 21 pts

WOMEN'S NATIONAL 5,000 METRES WALK
Sutton Park, 10 July 1993

Individual: Joanne Pope (Brighton and Hove), 25 min.
13 sec.
Team: Sheffield, 29 pts

ROWING

WORLD CHAMPIONSHIPS 1993
Roudnice, Czech Republic, September

MEN

Coxed pairs: Great Britain
Coxless pairs: Great Britain
Coxed fours: Romania
Coxless fours: France
Single sculls: Derek Porter (Canada)
Double sculls: France
Quad sculls: Germany
Eights: Germany

WOMEN

Coxless pairs: France
Coxless fours: China
Single sculls: Jana Thieme (Germany)

Double sculls: New Zealand
Quad sculls: China
Eights: Romania

NATIONAL CHAMPIONSHIPS 1993
Strathclyde Country Park, July

MEN

Coxed pairs: City of Oxford
Coxless pairs: Cambridge 99
Coxed fours: Nottinghamshire County
Coxless fours: Nottinghamshire County B
Single sculls: Leon Fletcher (Thames)
Double sculls: Molesey
Quad sculls: Thames/Tideway Scullers
Eights: Nottinghamshire County

WOMEN

Coxless pairs: Thames Tradesmen/Tideway Scullers
Coxed fours: Staines
Coxless fours: Thames Tradesmen
Single sculls: Guin Batten (Nottinghamshire County)
Double sculls: Nottinghamshire County
Quad sculls: Thames B
Eights: Cambridge University

THE 139th UNIVERSITY BOAT RACE
Putney–Mortlake, 4 miles 1 f, 180 yd, 27 March 1993

Cambridge beat Oxford by 3½ lengths; 17 min.
Cambridge have won 70 times, Oxford 68 and there has
been one dead heat. The record time is 16 min., 45 sec.,
rowed by Oxford in 1984
WOMEN'S BOAT RACE 1993 (Henley): Cambridge beat
Oxford by 4½ lengths (6 min. 10 sec.)

HENLEY ROYAL REGATTA 1993

Grand Challenge Cup: Hansa Dortmund (Germany) beat
Cambridge University/University of London by 2¾
lengths
Ladies' Challenge Plate: Brown University (USA) beat
Nottinghamshire County/London by ⅔ length
Thames Challenge Cup: Nottinghamshire County beat Isis
by ¾ length
Temple Challenge Cup: Oxford Brookes University beat
Trinity College, Dublin by 3¼ lengths
Princess Elizabeth Challenge Cup: Brisbane Boys' College
(Australia) beat Eton College by ⅔ length
Stewards' Challenge Cup: Leander/University of London
beat Hansa Dortmund (Germany) by ⅔ length
Prince Philip Challenge Cup: Leander/Molesey beat
Molesley/University of London by 1½ lengths
Queen Mother Challenge Cup: Tideway Scullers/
Nottinghamshire County beat Nottinghamshire County/
Goldie by 3 lengths
Visitors' Challenge Cup: King's School (Chester) beat
University of London by 1 length
Wyfold Challenge Cup: London B beat Leander by 4½
lengths
Britannia Challenge Cup: Harvard University (USA) beat
Goldie by 3¼ lengths
Fawley Challenge Cup: Walton/Burton Leander beat
Windsor Boys' School by 2 lengths
Silver Goblets and Nickall's Challenge Cup: Steve Redgrave
and Matthew Pinsent (Leander) beat Bill Coventry and
Campbell Clayton-Greene (Waikato, New Zealand) by 1
length
Double Sculls Cup: Ned Kittoe and Rupert Redpath
(London/Univeristy of London Tyrian) beat Ian Hopkins
and Mark Pollecutt (Molesey) by 2 ft

Diamond Challenge Sculls: Thomas Lange (Bollberg-Halle, Germany) beat Vaclav Chalupa (Dukla Praha, Czech Republic) by 1 ft
Women's Single Sculls: Maria Brandin (Kungalv, Sweden) beat Annelies Bredael (Hazewinkel, Belgium) by 2 lengths

OTHER ROWING EVENTS 1993

Oxford Torpids: Men, Oriel; *Women,* Somerville
Cambridge Lents: Men, Trinity Hall; *Women,* Lady Margaret
Oxford Summer Eights: Men, Oriel; *Women,* Somerville
Cambridge Mays: Men, Trinity Hall; *Women,* Jesus
Head of the River: Men, Munster (Germany); *Women,* Thames
Doggett's Coat and Badge: James Clifford (Gravesend)
Wingfield Sculls: Wade Hall-Craggs (Tideway Scullers)

RUGBY FIVES

National Singles Championships final 1993: Wayne Enstone beat Roger Layton 15–2, 15–2
National Doubles Championships final 1992: Wayne Enstone and Neil Roberts beat Ian Fuller and David Hebden 15–10, 15–5
Scottish Open Singles Championships final 1993: Wayne Enstone beat Neil Roberts 11–7, 11–3
Scottish Open Doubles Championships final 1993: Neil Roberts and C. Breese beat Rick Carr and J. Davies 15–8, 15–3
Ladies' National Singles Championships final 1993: Paula Smith beat Louise Deaner 11–2, 11–1
Ladies' National Doubles Championships final 1993: Paula Smith and Denise Hall-Wilton beat Louise Deaner and Henrietta Chapman 11–5
National Schools Singles Championships final 1993:, Edward Hickey (St Paul's) beat James Brown (Sedbergh) 11–2, 12–10
National Schools Doubles Championships final 1993: James Brown and Jodie Lancaster (Sedbergh) beat Sebastian Cavanagh and Gareth Rees (Clifton) 1–11, 11–6, 11–4

RUGBY LEAGUE

World Cup final (Wembley, 24 October 1992): Australia beat Great Britain 10–6
World Sevens final 1993 (Sydney): Eastern Suburbs beat Manly-Warringah 18–12

TEST MATCHES

1992
| 27 Nov | Swansea | Wales 11, England 36 |
| 13 Dec | Perpignan | France 18, Wales 19 |

1993
| 7 March | Carcassone | France 6, Great Britain 48 |
| 2 April | Headingley | Great Britain 72, France 6 |

DOMESTIC COMPETITIONS

Challenge Cup final 1993 (Wembley, 1 May): Wigan beat Widnes 20–14
Premiership Trophy final 1993 (Old Trafford, 16 May): St Helens beat Wigan 10–4
Regal Trophy final 1993 (Elland Road, 23 January): Wigan beat Bradford Northern 15–8

Divisional Premiership final 1923: Featherstone Rovers beat Workington Town 20–6
Stones Bitter Championship: Wigan
Division 2 Championship: Featherstone Rovers
Division 3 Championship: Keighley Cougars
Lancashire Cup final 1992: Wigan beat St Helens 5–4
Yorkshire Cup final 1992: Wakefield Trinity beat Sheffield Eagles 29–16
Universities 1993: Cambridge beat Oxford 50–18

AMATEUR RUGBY LEAGUE 1992–3

County Championship: Yorkshire
National Inter-League Shield Competitions:
  Open Age: Widnes
  Under 17: West Cumbria Youth
National Cup Competitions:
  Open Age: Saddleworth
  Under 17: Crosfields
National League Champions: Saddleworth
National League Challenge Cup 1993: Saddleworth

RUGBY UNION

INTERNATIONAL MATCHES

1992
17 Oct	Wembley	England 26, Canada 13
31 Oct	Lansdowne Rd	Ireland 17, Australia 42
14 Nov	Twickenham	England 33, South Africa 16
21 Nov	Cardiff	Wales 6, Australia 23

1993
16 Jan	Twickenham	England 16, France 15
	Murrayfield	Scotland 15, Ireland 3
6 Feb	Paris	France 11, Scotland 3
	Cardiff	Wales 10, England 9
20 Feb	Murrayfield	Scotland 20, Wales 0
	Lansdowne Rd	Ireland 6, France 21
6 Mar	Twickenham	England 26, Scotland 12
	Cardiff	Wales 14, Ireland 19
20 Mar	Lansdowne Rd	Ireland 17, England 3
	Paris	France 26, Wales 10
22 May	Bulawayo	Zimbabwe 14, Wales 35
29 May	Harare	Zimbabwe 13, Wales 42
	Suva	Fiji 10, Scotland 21
5 June	Windhoek	Namibia 23, Wales 38
	Nuku'alofa	Tonga 5, Scotland 23
12 June	Christchurch	New Zealand 20, British Isles 18
	Apia	W. Samoa 28, Scotland 11
26 June	Wellington	New Zealand 7, British Isles 20
3 July	Auckland	New Zealand 30, British Isles 13

FIVE NATIONS' CHAMPIONSHIP 1993

	P	W	D	L	Pts		Total
					F	A	
France	4	3	0	1	73	35	6
Scotland	4	2	0	2	50	40	4
England	4	2	0	2	54	54	4
Ireland	4	2	0	2	45	53	4
Wales	4	1	0	3	34	74	2

DOMESTIC COMPETITIONS

English League: division 1, Bath, 22 pts; *division 2,* Newcastle Gosforth, 20 pts; *division 3,* Otley, 17 pts; *division 4,* Harrogate, 21 pts (*north*); Sudbury, 23 pts (*south*)
County Championship final 1993: Lancashire beat Yorkshire 9–6

Pilkington Cup final 1993 (Twickenham, 1 May): Leicester beat Harlequins 23–16

Scottish League: division 1, Melrose, 24 pts; *division 2*, West of Scotland, 22 pts; *division 3*, Haddington, 20 pts; *division 4*, Stewartry, 26 pts; *division 5*, Ardrossan Academicals, 22 pts; *division 6*, Duns, 26 pts; *division 7*, Allan Glen's, 22 pts

Welsh League: division 1, Llanelli, 39 pts; *division 2*, Dunvant, 42 pts; *division 3*, Treorchy, 40 pts; *division 4*, Tondu, 38 pts

Welsh Challenge Cup final 1993: Llanelli beat Neath 21–18

Irish League: division 1, Young Munster, 13 pts; *division 2*, Lansdowne, 18 pts

Ulster Cup final 1993: Dungannon beat Ballymena 20–18

Hospitals' Cup final 1993: Charing Cross/Westminster beat St Mary's 16–9

Services Championship 1993: Army beat Royal Navy 37–15; RAF beat Army 20–17; RAF beat Royal Navy 23–7

Universities 1992: Cambridge beat Oxford 19–11

SEVENS

World Sevens Cup final 1993 (Murrayfield): England beat Australia 21–17

Middlesex Sevens final 1993 (Twickenham): Wasps beat Northampton 26–24

SHOOTING

124TH NATIONAL RIFLE ASSOCIATION IMPERIAL MEETING
Bisley, July 1993

Queen's Prize: Colin Brook, 295.39 pts
Grand Aggregate: Glyn Barnett, 595.81 pts
Prince of Wales Prize: Lindsay Peden, 75.14 pts
St George's Vase: Glyn Barnett, 149.25 pts
Allcomers Aggregate: Graham Atkinson, 322.41 pts
National Trophy: England, 2,055.289 pts
Kolapore Cup: Great Britain, 1,177.176 pts
Chancellor's Trophy: Cambridge University, 1,169.147 pts
Musketeers Cup: University of London, 583.74 pts
Vizianagram Trophy: House of Lords, 690.1 pts
County Long-Range Championship: Hereford and Worcester, 293.32 pts
Mackinnon Challenge Cup: England, 1,137.111 pts
The Ashburton: Epsom College Combined Cadet Force, 518.47 pts
The Elcho: England, 1,670.152 pts
The Albert: Keith Pilcher, 213.22 pts
Hopton Challenge Cup: Stuart Collings, 967.101 pts

CLAY PIGEON SHOOTING 1993

International Cup (Down-the-Line): Ireland, 7,369/7,500
British Open Down-the-Line Championship: John Twigg, 100/300
Mackintosh Trophy: Canada, 7,392/7,500
British Open Skeet Championship: Alan Warren, 100/300*
British Open Sporting Championship: Stuart Clarke, 94/100*
Coronation Cup: John Timmins, 385

*after a shoot-off

SNOOKER

1992

Dubai Classic: John Parrott (England) beat Stephen Hendry (Scotland) 9–8

Rothmans Grand Prix: Jimmy White (England) beat Ken Doherty (Ireland) 10–9

UK Professional Championship: Jimmy White (England) beat John Parrott (England) 16–9

World Matchplay Championship: James Wattana (Thailand) beat Steve Davis (England) 9–4

Benson and Hedges Championship: Chris Small (Scotland) beat Alan McManus (Scotland) 9–1

World Amateur Championship: Neil Mosley (England) beat Leonardo Andam (Philippines) 11–2

1993

Welsh Open: Ken Doherty (Ireland) beat Alan McManus (Scotland) 9–7

Benson and Hedges Masters: Stephen Hendry (Scotland) beat James Wattana (Thailand) 9–5

European Open: Steve Davis (England) beat Stephen Hendry (Scotland) 10–4

British Open: Steve Davis (England) beat James Wattana (Thailand) 10–2

Asian Open: David Harold (England) beat Darren Morgan (Wales) 9–3

Irish Masters: Steve Davis (England) beat Alan McManus (Scotland) 9–4

International Open: Stephen Hendry (Scotland) beat Steve Davis (England) 10–6

World Professional Championship: Stephen Hendry (Scotland) beat Jimmy White (England) 18–5

European Matchroom League: Jimmy White (England) beat Alan McManus (Scotland) 10–7

Regal Masters: Ken Doherty (Ireland) beat Alan McManus (Scotland) 10–9

Women's British Open Championship 1992: Allison Fisher beat Karen Corr

Women's World Championship 1993: Allison Fisher beat Stacey Hillyard 9–3

Womens' UK Championship 1993: Stacey Hillyard beat Tessa Davidson

---

SPEEDWAY

World Individual Championship 1993: Sam Ermolenko (USA)

World Pairs Championship 1993: Tony Rickardsson, Per Jonsson and Henrik Gustafsson (Sweden)

World Team Championship 1993: USA, 40 pts

World Championship, British final 1993: Andy Smith (Coventry)

British League Riders' Championship 1992: Joe Screen (Belle Vue)

British League Championship 1992: Reading

British League Knock-Out Cup final 1992: Bradford beat Reading 92–88 on agg.

Gold Cup final 1992: Wolverhampton beat Reading 91–88

British Champion 1993: Andy Smith (Coventry)

SQUASH RACKETS

MEN

World Open Championship final 1992: Jansher Khan (Pakistan) beat Chris Dittmar (Australia) 3–1

World Team Championship final 1992: Australia beat England 2–1

European Team Championship final 1993: England beat Germany 4–0

European Club Championship final 1993: St Cloud (France) beat Keravan (Finland) 4–1

British Open Championship final 1993: Jansher Khan (Pakistan) beat Chris Dittmar (Australia) 3–1

National Championship final 1993: Phil Whitlock beat Mark Allen 3–0

Inaugural British Squash Players' Association Championship final 1993: Peter Marshall beat Chris Walker 3–2

WOMEN

World Open Championship final 1992; Susan Devoy (New Zealand) beat Michelle Martin (Australia) 3–1

World Team Championship final 1992: Australia beat New Zealand 2–1

World Open Championship final 1993: Michelle Martin (Australia) beat Liz Irving (Australia) 3–0

European Team Championship final 1993: England beat Holland 3–0

European Club Championship final 1993: Richmond Town (England) beat Victoria (Holland) 3–0

British Open Championship final 1993: Michelle Martin (Australia) beat Suzanne Horner (England) 3–0

National Championship final 1993: Cassie Jackman beat Fiona Geaves 3–0

SWIMMING

NATIONAL CHAMPIONSHIPS
Sheffield, June

MEN

50 metres freestyle: Michael Fibbens (Barnet Copthall)
100 metres freestyle: Michael Fibbens (Barnet Copthall)
200 metres freestyle: Paul Palmer (City of Lincoln)
400 metres freestyle: Paul Palmer (City of Lincoln)
1,500 metres freestyle: Graeme Smith (Stockport Metro)
50 metres backstroke: Martin Harris (Waltham Forest)
100 metres backstroke: Martin Harris (Waltham Forest)
200 metres backstroke: Adam Ruckwood (City of Birmingham)
50 metres breaststroke: Peter McGinty (Beckenham)
100 metres breaststroke: Nick Gillingham (City of Birmingham)
200 metres breaststroke: Nick Gillingham (City of Birmingham)
50 metres butterfly: Mark Foster (Barnet Copthall)
100 metres butterfly: Michael Fibbens (Barnet Copthall)
200 metres butterfly: Kevin Crosby (Warrington)
200 metres medley: Fraser Walker (Warrender)
400 metres medley: Grant Robins (Portsmouth Northsea)
4 × 100 metres freestyle relay: City of Sheffield
4 × 100 metres medley relay: City of Birmingham

WOMEN

50 metres freestyle: Karen Pickering (Ipswich)
100 metres freestyle: Karen Pickering (Ipswich)
200 metres freestyle: Karen Pickering (Ipswich)
400 metres freestyle: Sarah Hardcastle (Borough of Southend)
800 metres freestyle: Sarah Hardcastle (Borough of Southend)
50 metres backstroke: Kathy Osher (Barnet Copthall)
100 metres backstroke: Kathy Osher (Barnet Copthall)
200 metres backstroke: Kathy Osher (Barnet Copthall)
50 metres breaststroke: Zoe Baker (City of Sheffield)
100 metres breaststroke: Jaime King (Swindon)
200 metres breaststroke: Marie Hardiman (City of Birmingham)

50 metres butterfly: Maxine Lock (City of Cardiff)
100 metres butterfly: Marion Madine (Ireland)
200 metres butterfly: Marion Madine (Ireland)
200 metres medley: Lucy Findlay (Kelly College)
400 metres medley: Marie Hardiman (City of Birmingham)
4 × 100 metres freestyle relay: Nova Centurion
4 × 100 metres medley relay: Nova Centurion

EUROPEAN CHAMPIONSHIPS
Sheffield, August

MEN

50 metres freestyle: Alexander Popov (Russia)
100 metres freestyle: Alexander Popov (Russia)
200 metres freestyle: Antti Kasvio (Finland)
400 metres freestyle: Antti Kasvio (Finland)
1,500 metres freestyle: Jorg Hoffman (Germany)
100 metres backstroke: Martin Lopez-Zubero (Spain)
200 metres backstroke: Vladimir Selkov (Russia)
100 metres breaststroke: Karoly Guttler (Hungary)
200 metres breaststroke: Nick Gillingham (GB)
100 metres butterfly: Rafal Szukala (Poland)
200 metres butterfly: Denis Pankratov (Russia)
200 metres medley: Jani Sievinen (Finland)
400 metres medley: Tamas Darnyi (Hungary)
4 × 100 metres freestyle relay: Russia
4 × 200 metres freestyle relay: Russia
4 × 100 metres medley relay: Russia

WOMEN

50 metres freestyle: Franziska van Almsick (Germany)
100 metres freestyle: Franziska van Almsick (Germany)
200 metres freestyle: Franziska van Almsick (Germany)
400 metres freestyle: Dagmar Hase (Germany)
800 metres freestyle: Jana Henke (Germany)
100 metres backstroke: Krisztina Egerszegi (Hungary)
200 metres backstroke: Krisztina Egerszegi (Hungary)
100 metres breaststroke: Sylvia Gerasch (Germany)
200 metres breaststroke: Brigitte Becue (Belgium)
100 metres butterfly: Catherine Plewinski (France)
200 metres butterfly: Krisztina Egerszegi (Hungary)
200 metres medley: Daniela Hunger (Germany)
400 metres medley: Krisztina Egerszegi (Hungary)
4 × 100 metres freestyle relay: Germany
4 × 200 metres freestyle relay: Germany
4 × 100 metres medley relay: Germany

TABLE TENNIS

WORLD CHAMPIONSHIPS 1993

Men's Singles: Jean-Philippe Gatien (France) beat Jean-Michel Saive (Belgium) 3–2

Women's Singles: Hyun Jung Hwa (S. Korea) beat Chen Jing (Taipei) 3–0

Men's Doubles: Wang Tao and Lu Lin (China) beat Ma Wenge and Zhang Lei (China) 3–1

Women's Doubles: Liu Wei and Qiao Yunping (China) beat Deng Yaping and Qiao Hong (China) 3–1

Mixed Doubles: Wang Tao and Liu Wei (China) beat Yoo Nam Kyo and Hyun Jung Hwa (S. Korea) 3–1

Men's Team Event: Sweden beat China 3–1

Women's Team Event: China beat N. Korea 3–0

European Nations Cup final 1993: Sweden beat Germany 3–1

ENGLISH NATIONAL CHAMPIONSHIPS 1993

ENGLISH NATIONAL CHAMPIONSHIPS 1993

Men's Singles final: Carl Prean beat Desmond Douglas 3–2
Women's Singles final: Andrea Holt beat Fiona Elliot-
Mommessin 3–0
Men's Doubles final: Skylet Andrew and Nicky Mason beat
Desmond Douglas and Richard Tilford 3–0
Women's Doubles final: Katherine Goodall and Andrea Holt
beat Lisa Lomas and Fiona Elliot-Mommessin 2–0
Mixed Doubles final: Fiona Elliot-Mommessin and Skylet
Andrew beat Alison Gordon and John Holland 2–0

VOLLEYBALL

MEN

World League final 1993: Brazil beat Russia 3–0
National League Championship 1993: Mizuno Mallory
Lewisham
National Cup final 1993: Mizuno Mallory Lewisham beat
KLEA Leeds 3–1

WOMEN

Grand Prix final 1993: Cuba beat China 3–0
National League Championship 1993: Woolwich Brixton
National Cup final 1993: Sale beat Woolwich Brixton 3–2

YACHTING

ADMIRAL'S CUP 1993

50-foot: Ragamuffin (Australia), Peter Gilmour, 54 pts
2-ton: Jameson 2 (Ireland), Gordon Maguire, 35 pts
1-ton: Pinta (Germany), Jorg Diesch, 53.88 pts
Team: Germany, 279.13 pts

FASTNET RACE 1993

50-foot: Indulgence (UK), Edward Warden-Owen
2-ton: Corum Rubis (France), Michael Kermarec
1-ton: Pinta (Germany), Jorg Diesch

British Steel Challenge Round-the-World Race (26 September
1992–23 May 1993): Nuclear Electric, in 151 days, 11
hours and 49 minutes

The Olympic Games

Venues of the modern Olympic Games

I	Athens, Greece	1896
II	Paris, France	1900
III	St Louis, USA	1904
*	Athens	1906
IV	London, Britain	1908
V	Stockholm, Sweden	1912
†VI	Berlin, Germany	1916
VII	Antwerp, Belgium	1920
VIII	Paris, France	1924
IX	Amsterdam, Netherlands	1928
X	Los Angeles, USA	1932
XI	Berlin, Germany	1936
†XII	Tokyo, Japan, then Helsinki, Finland	1940
†XIII	London, Britain	1944
XIV	London, Britain	1948
XV	Helsinki, Finland	1952
§XVI	Melbourne, Australia	1956
XVII	Rome, Italy	1960
XVIII	Tokyo, Japan	1964
XIX	Mexico City, Mexico	1968
XX	Munich, West Germany	1972
XXI	Montreal, Canada	1976
XXII	Moscow, USSR	1980
XXIII	Los Angeles, USA	1984
XXIV	Seoul, South Korea	1988
XXV	Barcelona, Spain	1992
XXVI	Atlanta, USA	1996
XXVII	Sydney, Australia	2000

* The 'Intercalated' Games
† These Games were scheduled but did not take place owing
to World Wars
§ Equestrian events were held in Stockholm, Sweden

WINTER OLYMPIC GAMES

I	Chamonix, France	1924
II	St Moritz, Switzerland	1928
III	Lake Placid, USA	1932
IV	Garmisch-Partenkirchen, Germany	1936
V	St Moritz, Switzerland	1948
VI	Oslo, Norway	1952
VII	Cortina d'Ampezzo, Italy	1956
VIII	Squaw Valley, USA	1960
IX	Innsbruck, Austria	1964
X	Grenoble, France	1968
XI	Sapporo, Japan	1972
XII	Innsbruck, Austria	1976
XIII	Lake Placid, USA	1980
XIV	Sarajevo, Yugoslavia	1984
XV	Calgary, Canada	1988
XVI	Albertville, France	1992
XVII	Lillehammer, Norway	1994
XVIII	Nagano, Japan	1998

Sports Records

All the world records given below have been accepted by the International Amateur Athletic Federation except those marked with an asterisk★ which are awaiting homologation. Fully automatic timing to 1/100th second is mandatory up to and including 400 metres. For distances up to and including 10,000 metres, records will be accepted to 1/100th second if timed automatically, and to 1/10th if hand timing is used.

MEN'S EVENTS

TRACK EVENTS	hr.	min.	sec.
100 metres			9.86
Carl Lewis, USA, 1991			
200 metres			19.72
Pietro Mennea, Italy, 1979			
400 metres			43.29
Harry Reynolds, USA, 1988			
800 metres		1	41.73
Sebastian Coe, GB, 1981			
1,000 metres		2	12.18
Sebastian Coe, GB, 1981			
1,500 metres		3	28.86
Noureddine Morceli, Algeria, 1993			
1 mile		3	44.39
Noureddine Morceli, Algeria, 1993			
2,000 metres		4	50.81
Saïd Aouita, Morocco, 1987			
3,000 metres		7	28.96
Moses Kiptanui, Kenya, 1992			
5,000 metres		12	58.39
Saïd Aouita, Morocco, 1987			
10,000 metres		26	58.38
Yobes Ondieki, Kenya, 1993			
20,000 metres		56	55.6
Arturo Barrios, Mexico, 1991			
21,101 metres (13 miles 196 yards 1 foot)	1	00	00.0
Arturo Barrios, Mexico, 1991			
25,000 metres	1	13	55.8
Toshihiko Seko, Japan, 1981			
30,000 metres	1	29	18.8
Toshihiko Seko, Japan, 1981			
110 metres hurdles (3 ft 6 in)			12.91
Colin Jackson, GB, 1993			
400 metres hurdles (3 ft 0 in)			46.78
Kevin Young, USA, 1992			
3,000 metres steeplechase		8	02.08
Moses Kiptanui, Kenya, 1992			

RELAYS		min.	sec.
4 × 100 metres			37.40
USA, 1992, 1993			
4 × 200 metres		1	19.11
Santa Monica TC, 1992			
4 × 400 metres		2	54.29
USA, 1993			
4 × 800 metres		7	03.89
GB, 1982			
4 × 1,500 metres		14	38.8
Federal Republic of Germany, 1977			

FIELD EVENTS	metres	ft	in
High jump	2.45	8	0½
Javier Sotomayor, Cuba, 1993			
Pole vault	6.13	20	1½
Sergei Bubka, CIS, 1992			
Long jump	8.95	29	4½
Mike Powell, USA, 1991			
Triple jump	17.97	58	11½
Willie Banks, USA, 1985			
Shot	23.12	75	10¼
Randy Barnes, USA, 1990			
Discus	74.08	243	0
Jürgen Schult, GDR, 1986			
Hammer	86.74	284	7
Yuriy Sedykh, USSR, 1986			
Javelin	95.66★	313	10
Jan Zelezny, Czech Rep., 1993			
Decathlon†			8,891 pts
Dan O'Brien, USA, 1992			

† Ten events comprising 100 m, long jump, shot, high jump, 400 m, 110 m hurdles, discus, pole vault, javelin, 1500 m

WALKING (TRACK)	hr.	min.	sec.
20,000 metres	1	18	35.2
Stefan Johansson, Sweden, 1992			
29,572 metres (18 miles 660 yards)	2	00	00.0
Maurizio Damilano, Italy, 1992			
30,000 metres	2	01	44.1
Maurizio Damilano, Italy, 1992			
50,000 metres	3	41	38.4
Raul Gonzalez, Mexico, 1979			

WOMEN'S EVENTS

TRACK EVENTS	min.	sec.
100 metres		10.49
Florence Griffith-Joyner, USA, 1988		
200 metres		21.34
Florence Griffith-Joyner, USA, 1988		
400 metres		47.60
Marita Koch, GDR, 1985		
800 metres	1	53.28
Jarmila Kratochvilova, Czechoslovakia, 1983		
1,500 metres	3	52.47
Tatyana Kazankina, USSR, 1980		
1 mile	4	15.61
Paula Ivan, Romania, 1989		
3,000 metres	8	22.62
Tatyana Kazankina, USSR, 1984		
5,000 metres	14	37.33
Ingrid Kristiansen, Norway, 1986		
10,000 metres	30	13.74
Ingrid Kristiansen, Norway, 1986		
100 metres hurdles (2 ft 9 in)		12.21
Yordanka Donkova, Bulgaria, 1988		
400 metres hurdles (2 ft 6 in)		52.74
Sally Gunnell, GB, 1993		

RELAYS		min.	sec.
4 × 100 metres			41.37
GDR, 1985			
4 × 200 metres		1	28.15
GDR, 1980			
4 × 400 metres		3	15.17
USSR, 1988			
4 × 800 metres		7	50.17
USSR, 1984			

FIELD EVENTS	metres	ft	in
High jump	2.09	6	10¼
Stefka Kostadinova, Bulgaria, 1987			
Long jump	7.52	24	8¼
Galina Chistiakova, USSR, 1988			
Triple jump	15.09	49	6¼
Ana Biryukova, Russia, 1993			
Shot	22.63	74	3
Natalya Lisovskaya, USSR, 1987			
Discus	76.80	252	0
Gabriele Reinsch, GDR, 1988			
Javelin	80.00	262	5
Petra Felke, GDR, 1988			
Heptathlon†			7,291 pts
Jackie Joyner–Kersee, USA, 1988			

† Seven events comprising 100 m hurdles, shot, high jump, 200 m, long jump, javelin, 800 m

---

ATHLETICS NATIONAL (UK) RECORDS
AS AT 3 SEPTEMBER 1993

Records set anywhere by athletes eligible to represent Great Britain and Northern Ireland

MEN

TRACK EVENTS	hr.	min.	sec.
100 metres			9.87
Linford Christie, 1993			
200 metres			19.94
John Regis, 1993			
400 metres			44.47
David Grindley, 1992			
800 metres		1	41.73
Sebastian Coe, 1981			
1,000 metres		2	12.18
Sebastian Coe, 1981			
1,500 metres		3	29.67
Sebastian Coe, 1985			
1 mile		3	46.32
Steve Cram, 1985			
2,000 metres		4	51.39
Steve Cram, 1985			
3,000 metres		7	32.79
David Moorcroft, 1982			
5,000 metres		13	00.41
David Moorcroft, 1982			
10,000 metres		27	23.06
Eamonn Martin, 1988			
20,000 metres		57	28.7
Carl Thackery, 1990			
20,855 metres	1		
Carl Thackery, 1990			
25,000 metres	1	15	22.6
Ron Hill, 1965			

	hr.	min.	sec.
30,000 metres	1	31	30.4
Jim Alder, 1970			
3,000 metres steeplechase		8	07.96
Mark Rowland, 1988			
110 metres hurdles			12.91
Colin Jackson, 1993			
400 metres hurdles			47.82
Kriss Akabusi, 1992			

RELAYS		min.	sec.
4 × 100 metres			37.77
GB team, 1993			
4 × 200 metres		1	21.29
GB team, 1989			
4 × 400 metres		2	57.53
GB team, 1991			
4 × 800 metres		7	03.89
GB team, 1982			

FIELD EVENTS	metres	ft	in
High jump	2.37	7	9¼
Steve Smith, 1992, 1993			
Pole vault	5.65	18	6½
Keith Stock, 1981			
Long jump	8.23	27	0
Lynn Davies, 1968			
Triple jump	17.57	57	7¾
Keith Connor, 1982			
Shot	21.68	71	1½
Geoff Capes, 1980			
Discus	64.32	211	0
William Tancred, 1974			
Hammer	77.54	254	5
Martin Girvan, 1984			
Javelin	91.46	300	1
Steve Backley, 1992			
Decathlon			8,847 points
Daley Thompson, 1984			

WALKING (TRACK)	hr.	min.	sec.
20,000 metres	1	23	26.5
Ian McCombie, 1990			
30,000 metres	2	19	18
Christopher Maddocks, 1984			
50,000 metres	4	05	44.6
Paul Blagg, 1990			
2 hours	26,037 metres (16 miles 315 yards)		
Ron Wallwork, 1971			

WOMEN

TRACK EVENTS		min.	sec.
100 metres			11.10
Kathy Cook, 1981			
200 metres			22.10
Kathy Cook, 1984			
400 metres			49.43
Kathy Cook, 1984			
800 metres		1	57.42
Kirsty Wade, 1985			
1,500 metres		3	59.96
Zola Budd, 1985			
1 mile		4	17.57
Zola Budd, 1985			
3,000 metres		8	28.83
Zola Budd, 1985			

5,000 metres	14	48.07
Zola Budd, 1985		
10,000 metres	30	57.07
Liz McColgan, 1991		
100 metres hurdles		12.82
Sally Gunnell, 1988		
400 metres hurdles		52.74
Sally Gunnell, 1993		

RELAYS	min.	sec.
4 × 100 metres		42.43
GB team, 1980		
4 × 200 metres	1	31.57
GB team, 1977		
4 × 400 metres	3	22.01
GB team, 1991		
4 × 800 metres	8	23.8
GB team, 1971		

FIELD EVENTS	metres	ft	in
High jump	1.95	6	4¾
Diana Elliott, 1982			
Long jump	6.90	22	7¾
Beverley Kinch, 1983			
Triple jump	13.75	45	1½
Michelle Griffith, 1993			
Shot	19.36	63	6¼
Judy Oakes, 1988			
Discus	67.48	221	5
Margaret Ritchie, 1981			
Javelin	77.44	254	1
Fatima Whitbread, 1986			
Heptathlon		6,623 points	
Judy Simpson, 1986			

SWIMMING WORLD RECORDS
AS AT 31 AUGUST 1993

MEN	min.	sec.
50 metres freestyle		21.81
Tom Jager, USA		
100 metres freestyle		48.42
Matt Biondi, USA		
200 metres freestyle	1	46.69
Giorgio Lamberti, Italy		
400 metres freestyle	3	45.00
Evgueni Sadovyi, CIS		
800 metres freestyle	7	46.60
Kieren Perkins, Australia		
1,500 metres freestyle	14	43.48
Kieren Perkins, Australia		
100 metres breaststroke	1	00.95
Karoly Guttler, Hungary		
200 metres breaststroke	2	10.16
Mike Barrowman, USA		
100 metres butterfly		52.84
Pablo Morales, USA		
200 metres butterfly	1	55.69
Melvin Stewart, USA		
100 metres backstroke		53.86
Jeff Rouse, USA		
200 metres backstroke	1	57.30
Martin Lopez-Zubero, Spain		
200 metres medley	1	59.36
Tamás Darnyi, Hungary		

400 metres medley	4	12.36
Tamás Darnyi, Hungary		
4 × 100 metres freestyle relay	3	16.53
USA		
4 × 200 metres freestyle relay	7	11.95
CIS		
4 × 100 metres medley relay	3	36.93
USA		

WOMEN	min.	sec.
50 metres freestyle		24.79
Yang Wenyi, China		
100 metres freestyle		54.48
Jenny Thompson, USA		
200 metres freestyle	1	57.55
Heike Friedrich, GDR		
400 metres freestyle	4	03.85
Janet Evans, USA		
800 metres freestyle	8	16.22
Janet Evans, USA		
1,500 metres freestyle	15	52.10
Janet Evans, USA		
100 metres breaststroke	1	07.91
Silke Hörner, GDR		
200 metres breaststroke	2	25.35
Anita Nall, USA		
100 metres butterfly		57.93
Mary Meagher, USA		
200 metres butterfly	2	05.96
Mary Meagher, USA		
100 metres backstroke	1	00.31
Krisztina Egerszegi, Hungary		
200 metres backstroke	2	06.62
Krisztina Egerszegi, Hungary		
200 metres medley	2	11.65
Li Lin, China		
400 metres medley	4	36.10
Petra Schneider, GDR		
4 × 100 metres freestyle relay	3	39.46
USA		
4 × 200 metres freestyle relay	7	55.47
GDR		
4 × 100 metres medley relay	4	02.54
USA		

Duty and Tax-free Allowances

Travellers are entitled to the allowances in either of the columns below (but not both) for any category of goods, as represented by the boxes (*see* Notes on Allowances). Passengers under 17 are not, however, entitled to tobacco and drinks allowances.

COLUMN 1

Goods obtained duty and tax-free in the EC (e.g. in duty-free shops), or duty and tax-free on a ship or aircraft, or goods obtained outside the EC

COLUMN 2

Suggested guidelines for goods obtained duty and tax paid in the EC

COLUMN 1	COLUMN 2
Tobacco goods	*Tobacco goods*
200 cigarettes	800 cigarettes
or	*or*
100 cigarillos	400 cigarillos
or	*or*
50 cigars	200 cigars
or	*or*
250 grammes of tobacco	1 kg of tobacco
Alcoholic drinks	*Alcoholic drinks*
2 litres of still table wine	90 litres of still table wine (not more than 60 litres should be sparkling wine)
plus	*plus*
1 litre over 22% vol. (e.g. spirits and strong liqueurs)	10 litres over 22% vol. (e.g. spirits and strong liqueurs)
or	*or*
2 litres not over 22% vol. (e.g. low strength liqueurs, fortified wine or sparkling wine)	20 litres not over 22% vol. (e.g. low strength liqueurs, fortified wine)
or	*or*
A further 2 litres of still table wine	110 litres of beer
Perfume	*Perfume*
50 grammes (60 cc or 2 fl oz)	No limit
Toilet water	*Toilet water*
250 cc (9 fl oz)	No limit
Other goods	*Other goods*
£36 worth	No limit

NB: A maximum of 50 litres of beer may be imported duty-free, subject to the limitations of the 'Other goods' monetary allowance.

Anyone visiting the United Kingdom for less than six months is also entitled to bring in, free of duty and tax, all personal effects (except tobacco goods, alcoholic drinks and perfume) which they intend to take with them when they leave.

NOTES ON ALLOWANCES

1 The countries of the European Community are Belgium, Denmark, France, Germany, Greece, the Irish Republic, Italy, Luxembourg, the Netherlands, Portugal, Spain (but not the Canary Islands), and the United Kingdom (but not the Channel Islands)

2 The allowances apply only to goods carried and cleared by travellers at the time of their arrival

3 The allowances do not apply to goods brought in for sale or for other commercial purposes

4 Reduced allowances apply to certain persons crossing the Irish land boundary and to seamen and aircrew members

5 Whisky, gin, rum, brandy, vodka and most liqueurs normally exceed 22% vol. (38.8° proof) but advocaat, cassis, fraise, suze and aperitifs may be less. Fortified wines include port, sherry, vermouth and madeira. Sparkling wines include champagne, perelada, spumante and semi-sparkling wines. Still table wines include claret, Sauterne, Graves and Chianti. Burgundy, Chablis, hock and Moselle may be either sparkling or still, depending on manufacture

6 Goods obtained duty and tax-free or outside the EC may not be mixed with goods of the same category (as represented by the boxes) obtained duty and tax paid in the EC to obtain the higher allowance, e.g. the higher allowance for tobacco goods will not apply if any of the items in that category were obtained duty and tax-free or outside the EC

7 Where there are alternative quantities within a category of goods they may be apportioned. For example, 150 cigarettes (half allowance) plus 75 cigarillos (half allowance)

8 One litre is approximately 1¾ pints or 35 fl oz

9 A cigarillo is a cigar with a maximum weight of 3 grammes

PROHIBITED AND RESTRICTED GOODS

Customs officers are able to provide full information. This is a list of more frequently met items:

Controlled drugs (such as opium, heroin, morphine, cocaine, cannabis, amphetamines, lysergide (LSD) and barbiturates)

Firearms (including gas pistols, electric shock batons and similar weapons), ammunition and explosives (including fireworks)

Offensive weapons (including certain types of knife, swordsticks, knuckle-dusters and other martial arts equipment)

Counterfeit currency and other counterfeit goods, such as fake watches and sports shirts; goods bearing a false indication of their place of manufacture or in breach of United Kingdom copyright

Obscene books, magazines, films, videotapes, laser discs, computer discs and other material, horror comics

Radio transmitters (walkie-talkies, Citizen's Band radios, cordless telephones, etc.) not approved for use in the UK

Meat and poultry, and most of their products, including ham, bacon, sausage, paté, eggs, milk and cream. (Exception: 1 kg per passenger of fully cooked meat or poultrymeat products in cans or other hermetically-sealed containers of glass or foil)

Plants, parts thereof and plant produce, including trees and shrubs, soil, potatoes and certain other vegetables, fruit, bulbs and seeds

Anglers' lead weights

Animals and birds, whether alive or dead (e.g. stuffed), certain fish and fish eggs, whether live or dead, or bees; certain articles derived from rare species including furskins, ivory, reptile leather and goods made from them

NB: Cats, dogs and other mammals, including mice, rats, guinea-pigs and gerbils, must not be landed unless a British import licence (rabies) has previously been issued.

EXPORT CONTROL

The following are some of the goods subject to export control and should be declared to the customs officer. There are formalities to be completed in respect of these goods prior to arrival at the port of exportation and further information is available through any local office of Customs and Excise (address in the telephone directory).

Controlled drugs

Firearms and ammunition

Photographic material over 60 years old and valued at £500 or more

Portraits (including sculptures) of British historical personages which are over 50 years old and valued at £6,000 or more

Antiques, collectors' items, etc. (including paintings and other works of art) over 50 years old and valued at £30,000 or more

Certain archaeological material

Most live animals and birds, and items made from animals occurring wild in the UK

Weights and Measures

SI UNITS

The Système International d'Unités (SI) is an international and coherent system of units devised to meet all known needs for measurement in science and technology. The system was adopted by the eleventh Conférence Générale des Poids et Mesures (CGPM) in 1960. A comprehensive description of the system is given in *SI The International System of Units*, HMSO. The British Standards describing the essential features of the International System of Units are *Specifications for SI units and recommendations for the use of their multiples and certain other units* (BS 5555:1993) and *Conversion Factors and Tables* (BS 350, Part 1:1974).

The system consists of seven base units and the derived units formed as products or quotients of various powers of the base units. Together the base units and the derived units make up the coherent system of units. In the UK the SI base units, and almost all important derived units, are realized at the National Physical Laboratory and disseminated through the National Measurement System.

BASE UNITS

Metre (m) = unit of length
Kilogram (kg) = unit of mass
Second (s) = unit of time
Ampere (A) = unit of electric current
Kelvin (K) = unit of thermodynamic temperature
Mole (mol) = unit of amount of substance
Candela (cd) = unit of luminous intensity

DERIVED UNITS

For some of the derived SI units, special names and symbols exist; those approved by the CGPM are listed below.

Hertz (Hz) = unit of frequency
Newton (N) = unit of force
Pascal (Pa) = unit of pressure, stress
Joule (J) = unit of energy, work, quantity of heat
Watt (W) = unit of power, radiant flux
Coulomb (C) = unit of electric charge, quantity of electricity
Volt (V) = unit of electric potential, potential difference, electromotive force
Farad (F) = unit of electric capacitance
Ohm (Ω) = unit of electric resistance
Siemens (S) = unit of electric conductance
Weber (Wb) = unit of magnetic flux
Tesla (T) = unit of magnetic flux density
Henry (H) = unit of inductance
Degree Celsius (°C) = unit of Celsius temperature
Lumen (lm) = unit of luminous flux
Lux (lx) = unit of illuminance
Becquerel (Bq) = unit of activity (of a radionuclide)
Gray (Gy) = unit of absorbed dose, specific energy imparted, kerma, absorbed dose index
Sievert (Sv) = unit of dose equivalent, dose equivalent index

SUPPLEMENTARY UNITS

The derived units include, as a special case, the supplementary units which may be treated as dimensionless within the SI.

Radian (rad) = unit of plane angle
Steradian (sr) = unit of solid angle

Other derived units are expressed in terms of base units and/or supplementary units. Some of the more commonly-used derived units are the following:

Unit of area = square metre (m^2)
Unit of volume = cubic metre (m^3)
Unit of velocity = metre per second (m s^{-1})
Unit of acceleration = metre per second squared (m s^{-2})
Unit of density = kilogram per cubic metre (kg m^{-3})
Unit of momentum = kilogram metre per second (kg m s^{-1})
Unit of magnetic field strength = ampere per metre (A m^{-1})
Unit of surface tension = newton per metre (N m^{-1})
Unit of dynamic viscosity = pascal second (Pa s)
Unit of heat capacity = joule per kelvin (J K^{-1})
Unit of specific heat capacity = joule per kilogram kelvin (J kg^{-1} K^{-1})
Unit of heat flux density, irradiance = watt per square metre (W m^{-2})
Unit of thermal conductivity = watt per metre kelvin (W m^{-1} K^{-1})
Unit of electric field strength = volt per metre (V m^{-1})
Unit of luminance = candela per square metre (cd m^{-2})

SI PREFIXES

Decimal multiples and submultiples of the SI units are indicated by SI prefixes. These are as follows:

multiples	*submultiples*
yotta (Y) $\times 10^{24}$	deci (d) $\times 10^{-1}$
zetta (Z) $\times 10^{21}$	centi (c) $\times 10^{-2}$
exa (E) $\times 10^{18}$	milli (m) $\times 10^{-3}$
peta (P) $\times 10^{15}$	micro (μ) $\times 10^{-6}$
tera (T) $\times 10^{12}$	nano (n) $\times 10^{-9}$
giga (G) $\times 10^{9}$	pico (p) $\times 10^{-12}$
mega (M) $\times 10^{6}$	femto (f) $\times 10^{-15}$
kilo (k) $\times 10^{3}$	atto (a) $\times 10^{-18}$
hecto (h) $\times 10^{2}$	zepto (z) $\times 10^{-21}$
deca (da) $\times 10$	yocto (y) $\times 10^{-24}$

UK UNITS

The legal units for the United Kingdom are enacted in the Weights and Measures Act 1985. The United Kingdom primary standards are the yard or the metre as the unit of measurement of length, and the pound or the kilogram as the unit of measurement of mass. Other units of measurement are defined by reference to the primary standards.

Responsibility for the maintenance of the primary standards and for the determination or redetermination of their value rests with the President of the Board of Trade.

The definition of the UK primary standards is as follows:

Yard = 0.9144 metre
Metre is the length of the path travelled by light in vacuum during a time interval of 1/299 792 458 of a second.
Pound = 0.453 592 37 kilogram
Kilogram is equal to the mass of the international prototype of the kilogram

The following list shows the definitions of measures set out in Schedule 1 of the Weights and Measures Act 1985.

MEASUREMENT OF LENGTH

Imperial Units
Mile = 1760 yards
Yard (yd) = 0.9144 metre
Foot (ft) = 1/3 yard
Inch (in) = 1/36 yard

Metric Units
Kilometre (km) = 1000 metres
Metre (m) is the length of the path travelled by light in
   vacuum during a time interval of 1/299 792 458 of a
   second
Decimetre (dm) = 1/10 metre
Centimetre (cm) = 1/100 metre
Millimetre (mm) = 1/1000 metre

MEASUREMENT OF AREA

Imperial Units
Acre = 4840 square yards
Square yard = a superficial area equal to that of a square
   each side of which measures one yard
Square foot = 1/9 square yard

Metric Units
Hectare (ha) = 100 ares
Decare = 10 ares
Are (a) = 100 square metres
Square metre = a superficial area equal to that of a square
   each side of which measures one metre
Square decimetre = 1/100 square metre
Square centimetre = 1/100 square decimetre
Square millimetre = 1/100 square centimetre

MEASUREMENT OF VOLUME

Metric Units
Cubic metre (m³) = a volume equal to that of a cube each
   edge of which measures one metre
Cubic decimetre = 1/1000 cubic metre
Cubic centimetre (cc) = 1/1000 cubic decimetre
Hectolitre = 100 litres
Litre = a cubic decimetre
Decilitre = 1/10 litre
Centilitre = 1/100 litre
Millilitre = 1/1000 litre

MEASUREMENT OF CAPACITY

Imperial Units
Gallon = 4.546 09 cubic decimetres
Quart = 1/4 gallon
Pint (pt) = 1/2 quart
Gill = 1/4 pint
Fluid ounce (fl oz) = 1/20 pint

Metric Units
Hectolitre (hl) = 100 litres
Litre (l or L) = a cubic decimetre
Decilitre (dl) = 1/10 litre
Centilitre (cl) = 1/100 litre
Millilitre (ml) = 1/1000 litre

MEASUREMENT OF MASS OR WEIGHT

Imperial Units
Pound (lb) = 0.453 592 37 kilogram
Ounce (oz) = 1/16 pound
*Ounce troy = 12/175 pound

Metric Units
Tonne, metric tonne (t) = 1000 kilograms
Kilogram (kg) is the unit of mass; it is equal to the mass of
   the international prototype of the kilogram
Hectogram (hg) = 1/10 kilogram
Gram (g) = 1/1000 kilogram
†Carat (metric) = 1/5 gram
Milligram (mg) = 1/1000 gram

*Used only for transactions in gold, silver or other precious
   metals, and articles made therefrom
†Used only for transactions in precious stones or pearls

OBSOLESCENT UNITS OF MEASUREMENT

Certain units of measurement may no longer be used for
trade although the measure may still be used, e.g. it is legal
to sell a 112 lb quantity of a commodity but it must be
referred to in invoices, etc., as 112 lb, not as 1 cwt. These
units are defined as follows:

Measurement of Length
Furlong = 220 yards
Chain = 22 yards

Measurement of Area
Square mile = 640 acres
Rood = 1210 square yards
Square inch = 1/144 square foot

Measurement of Volume
Cubic yard = a volume equal to that of a cube each edge of
   which measures one yard
Cubic foot = 1/27 cubic yard
Cubic inch = 1/1728 cubic foot

Measurement of Capacity
Bushel = 8 gallons
Peck = 2 gallons
Fluid drachm = 1/8 fluid ounce
Minim (min) = 1/60 fluid drachm

Measurement of Mass or Weight
Ton = 2240 pounds
Hundredweight (cwt) = 112 pounds
Cental = 100 pounds
Quarter = 28 pounds
Stone = 14 pounds
Dram (dr) = 1/16 ounce
Grain (gr) = 1/7000 pound
Pennyweight (dwt) = 24 grains
Ounce apothecaries = 480 grains
Drachm (ʒi) = 1/8 ounce apothecaries
Scruple(Ɵi) = 1/3 drachm
Metric tonne = 1000 kilograms
Quintal (q) = 100 kilograms

MEASUREMENT OF ELECTRICITY

Units of measurement of electricity are defined by the
Weights and Measures Act 1985, as follows:

Ampere (A) = that constant current which, if maintained in
   two straight parallel conductors of infinite length, of
   negligible circular cross-section and placed 1 metre apart
   in vacuum, would produce between these conductors a
   force equal to 2×10^{-7} newton per metre of length
Ohm (Ω) = the electric resistance between two points of a
   conductor when a constant potential difference of 1 volt,
   applied between the two points, produces in the
   conductor a current of 1 ampere, the conductor not being
   the seat of any electromotive force

Volt (V) = the difference of electric potential between two points of a conducting wire carrying a constant current of 1 ampere when the power dissipated between these points is equal to 1 watt

Watt (W) = the power which in one second gives rise to energy of 1 joule

Kilowatt (kW) = 1000 watts

Megawatt (MW) = one million watts

WATER MEASURES (approximate)

1 cubic foot = 62.32 lb

1 gallon = 10 lb

1 cubic cm = 1 gram

1000 cubic cm = 1 litre; 1 kilogram

1 cubic metre = 1000 litres; 1000 kg; 1 tonne

An inch of rain on the surface of an acre (43560 sq. ft) = 3630 cubic ft = 100.992 tons

Cisterns: A cistern 4 × 2½ feet and 3 feet deep will hold brimful 186.963 gallons, weighing 1869.63 lb in addition to its own weight

WATER FOR SHIPS

Kilderkin = 18 gallons

Barrel = 36 gallons

Puncheon = 72 gallons

Butt = 110 gallons

Tun = 210 gallons

WINE MEASURES

Under the Weights and Measures (Intoxicating Liquor) Order 1988, as amended by the Weights and Measures (Various Foods) (Amendment) Order 1990, still wines may be pre-packed only in the following quantities: 10, 25, 37.5, 50 and 75 cl; 1, 1.5, 2, 3, 4, 5, 6, 8, 9 and 10 litres. In addition, the 18.7 cl size is permitted for consumption on board aircraft, ships and trains or for sale duty-free, and all quantities up to and including 25 cl are allowed when for consumption on the premises of the seller.

The Intoxicating Liquor Order also provides that sparkling wines (including champagne) may be pre-packed only in the following quantities: 12.5, 20, 37.5 and 75 cl; 1.5, 3, 4.5, 6 and 9 litres. However, all quantities are allowed when for consumption on board aircraft, ships and trains or for sale duty free.

Spirits and liqueurs may be pre-packed only in the following quantities: 2, 3, 4, 5, 7.1, 10, 20, 35, 50 and 70 cl; 1, 1.5, 2, 2.5, 3 and 4.5 litres. In addition, 1.125, 5 and 10 litres are permitted for non-retail sales and all quantities are allowed when for consumption on board aircraft, ships and trains or for sale duty free.

BOTTLES OF WINE

Traditional equivalents in standard champagne bottles:

Magnum = 2 bottles

Jeroboam = 4 bottles

Rehoboam = 6 bottles

Methuselah = 8 bottles

Salmanazar = 12 bottles

Balthazar = 16 bottles

Nebuchadnezzar = 20 bottles

A quarter of a bottle is known as a *nip*.

An eighth of a bottle is known as a *baby*.

ANGULAR AND CIRCULAR MEASURES

60 seconds (″) = 1 minute (′)

60 minutes = 1 degree (°)

90 degrees = 1 right angle or quadrant

Diameter of circle × 3.141 6 = circumference

Diameter squared × 0.7854 = area of circle

Diameter squared × 3.141 6 = surface of sphere

Diameter cubed × 0.523 = solidity of sphere

One degree of circumference × 57.3 = radius*

Diameter of cylinder × 3.141 6; product by length or height, gives the surface

Diameter squared × 0.7854; product by length or height, gives solid content

*Or, one radian (the angle subtended at the centre of a circle by an arc of the circumference equal in length to the radius) = 57.3 degrees

MILLION, BILLION, ETC.

VALUE IN THE UNITED KINGDOM

Million	thousand × thousand	10^6
Billion	million × million	10^{12}
Trillion	million × billion	10^{18}
Quadrillion	million × trillion	10^{24}

VALUE IN USA

Million	thousand × thousand	10^6
Billion	thousand × million	10^9
Trillion	million × million	10^{12}
Quadrillion	million × billion US	10^{15}

The American usage of billion (i.e. 10^9) is increasingly common, and is now universally used by statisticians

NAUTICAL MEASURES

DISTANCE

Distance at sea is measured in nautical miles. The British standard nautical mile was 6080 feet (the length of a minute of an arc of a great circle of the earth, rounded off to a mean value to allow for the length varying at different latitudes). This measure has been obsolete since 1970 when the international nautical mile of 1852 metres was adopted by the Hydrographic Department of the Ministry of Defence as a result of a recommendation by the International Hydrographic Bureau.

The cable (600 feet or 100 fathoms) was a measure approximately one-tenth of a nautical mile. Such distances are now expressed in decimal parts of a sea mile or in metres.

Soundings at sea were recorded in fathoms (6 feet). Depths are now expressed in metres on new Admiralty charts.

SPEED

Speed is measured in nautical miles per hour, called knots. A ship moving at the rate of 30 nautical miles per hour is said to be doing 30 knots.

knots	m.p.h.	knots	m.p.h.
1	1.1515	9	10.3636
2	2.3030	10	11.5151
3	3.4545	15	17.2727
4	4.6060	20	23.0303
5	5.7575	25	28.7878
6	6.9090	30	34.5454
7	8.0606	35	40.3030
8	9.2121	40	46.0606

TONNAGE

The tonnage of a vessel is measured in tons of 100 cubic feet.

Gross tonnage = the total volume of all the enclosed spaces of a vessel

Net tonnage = gross tonnage less deductions for crew space, engine room, water ballast and other spaces not used for passengers or cargo

DISTANCE OF THE HORIZON

The limit of distance to which one can see varies with the height of the spectator. The greatest distance at which an object on the surface of the sea, or of a level plain, can be seen by a person whose eyes are at a height of five feet from the same level is nearly three miles. At a height of 20 feet the range is increased to nearly six miles, and an approximate rule for finding the range of vision for small heights is to increase the square root of the number of feet that the eye is above the level surface by a third of itself. The result is the distance of the horizon in miles, but is slightly in excess of that in the table below, which is computed by a more precise formula. The table may be used conversely to show the distance of an object of given height that is just visible from a point on the surface of the earth or sea. Refraction is taken into account both in the approximate rule and in the table.

Height in feet	range in miles
5	2.9
20	5.9
50	9.3
100	13.2
500	29.5
1,000	41.6
2,000	58.9
3,000	72.1
4,000	83.3
5,000	93.1
20,000	186.2

TEMPERATURE SCALES

The SI (International System) unit of temperature is the kelvin, which is defined as the fraction 1/273.16 of the temperature of the triple point of water (i.e. where ice, water and water vapour are in equilibrium). The zero of the Kelvin scale is the absolute zero of temperature. The freezing point of water is 273.15 K and the boiling point (as adopted in the International Temperature Scale of 1990) is 373.124 K.

The Celsius scale (formerly centigrade) is defined by subtracting 273.15 from the kelvin temperature. The Fahrenheit scale is related to the Celsius scale by the relationships:

temperature $°F = (\text{temperature } °C \times 1.8) + 32$
temperature $°C = (\text{temperature } °F - 32) \div 1.8$

It follows from these definitions that the freezing point of water is 0°C and 32°F. The boiling point is 99.974°C and 211.953°F.

The normal temperature of the human body is 36.9°C or 98.4°F.

Conversion between scales

°C	°F		°C	°F		°C	°F
100	212		60	140		20	68
99	210.2		59	138.2		19	66.2
98	208.4		58	136.4		18	64.4
97	206.6		57	134.6		17	62.6
96	204.8		56	132.8		16	60.8
95	203		55	131		15	59
94	201.2		54	129.2		14	57.2
93	199.4		53	127.4		13	55.4
92	197.6		52	125.6		12	53.6
91	195.8		51	123.8		11	51.8
90	194		50	122		10	50
89	192.2		49	120.2		9	48.2
88	190.4		48	118.4		8	46.4
87	188.6		47	116.6		7	44.6
86	186.8		46	114.8		6	42.8
85	185		45	113		5	41
84	183.2		44	111.2		4	39.2
83	181.4		43	109.4		3	37.4
82	179.6		42	107.6		2	35.6
81	177.8		41	105.8		1	33.8
80	176		40	104		zero	32
79	174.2		39	102.2		− 1	30.2
78	172.4		38	100.4		− 2	28.4
77	170.6		37	98.6		− 3	26.6
76	168.8		36	96.8		− 4	24.8
75	167		35	95		− 5	23
74	165.2		34	93.2		− 6	21.2
73	163.4		33	91.4		− 7	19.4
72	161.6		32	89.6		− 8	17.6
71	159.8		31	87.8		− 9	15.8
70	158		30	86		−10	14
69	156.2		29	84.2		−11	12.2
68	154.4		28	82.4		−12	10.4
67	152.6		27	80.6		−13	8.6
66	150.8		26	78.8		−14	6.8
65	149		25	77		−15	5
64	147.2		24	75.2		−16	3.2
63	145.4		23	73.4		−17	1.4
62	143.6		22	71.6		−18	0.4
61	141.8		21	69.8		−19	−2.2

PAPER MEASURES

Printing Paper
516 sheets = 1 ream
2 reams   = 1 bundle
5 bundles = 1 bale

Writing Paper
480 sheets = 1 ream
24 sheets = 1 quire
20 quires = 1 ream

BROWN PAPERS

	inches			inches
Casing	46 × 36		Imperial Cap	29 × 22
Double Imperial	45 × 29		Haven Cap	26 × 21
Elephant	34 × 24		Bag Cap	24 × 19¼
Double Four			Kent Cap	21 × 18
Pound	31 × 21			

PRINTING PAPERS

	inches		inches
Foolscap	17 × 13½	Double Large	
Double Foolscap	27 × 17	Post	33 × 21
Quad Foolscap	34 × 27	Demy	22½ × 17½
Crown	20 × 15	Double Demy	35 × 22½
Double Crown	30 × 20	Quad Demy	45 × 35
Quad Crown	40 × 30	Music Demy	20 × 15½
Double Quad		Medium	23 × 18
Crown	60 × 40	Royal	25 × 20
Post	19½ × 15½	Super Royal	27½ × 20½
Double Post	31½ × 19½	Elephant	28 × 23
		Imperial	30 × 22

WRITING AND DRAWING PAPERS

	inches		inches
Emperor	72 × 48	Copy or Draft	20 × 16
Antiquarian	53 × 31	Demy	20 × 15½
Double Elephant	40 × 27	Post	19 × 15½
Grand Eagle	42 × 28¾	Pinched Post	18½ × 14¾
Atlas	34 × 26	Foolscap	17 × 13½
Colombier	34½ × 23½	Double Foolscap	26½ × 16½
Imperial	30 × 22	Double Post	30½ × 19
Elephant	28 × 23	Double Large	
Cartridge	26 × 21	Post	33 × 21
Super Royal	27 × 19	Double Demy	31 × 20
Royal	24 × 19	Brief	16½ × 13½
Medium	22 × 17½	Pott	15 × 12½
Large Post	21 × 16½		

INTERNATIONAL PAPER SIZES

The basis of the international series of paper sizes is a rectangle having an area of one square metre, the sides of which are in the proportion of $1:\sqrt{2}$. The proportions $1:\sqrt{2}$ have a geometrical relationship, the side and diagonal of any square being in this proportion. The effect of this arrangement is that if the area of the sheet of paper is doubled or halved, the shorter side and the longer side of the new sheet are still in the same proportion $1:\sqrt{2}$. This feature is useful where photographic enlargement or reduction is used, as the proportions remain the same.

Description of the A series is by capital A followed by a figure. The basic size has the description A0 and the higher the figure following the letter, the greater is the number of sub-divisions and therefore the smaller the sheet. Half A0 is A1 and half A1 is A2. Where larger dimensions are required the A is preceded by a figure. Thus 2A means twice the size A0; 4A is four times the size of A0.

SUBSIDIARY SERIES
A series of B sizes has been devised for use when sizes intermediate between any two adjacent sizes of the A series are needed.

In addition there is a series of C sizes which is used much less. A is for magazines and books, B for posters, wall charts and other large items, C for envelopes particularly where it is necessary for an envelope (in C series) to fit into another envelope. The size recommended for business correspondence is A4.

LONG SIZES
Long sizes (DL) are obtainable by dividing any appropriate sizes from the two series above into three, four or eight equal parts parallel with the shorter side in such a manner that the proportion of $1:\sqrt{2}$ is not maintained, the ratio between the

longer and the shorter sides being greater than $\sqrt{2:1}$. In practice long sizes should be produced from the A series only.

It is an essential feature of these series that the dimensions are of the trimmed or finished size.

A SERIES

	mm		mm
A0	841 × 1189	A6	105 × 148
A1	594 × 841	A7	74 × 105
A2	420 × 594	A8	52 × 74
A3	297 × 420	A9	37 × 52
A4	210 × 297	A10	26 × 37
A5	148 × 210		

B SERIES

	mm		mm
B0	1000 × 1414	B6	125 × 176
B1	707 × 1000	B7	88 × 125
B2	500 × 707	B8	62 × 88
B3	353 × 500	B9	44 × 62
B4	250 × 353	B10	31 × 44
B5	176 × 250		

C SERIES DL

	mm		mm
C4	324 × 229	DL	110 × 220
C5	229 × 162		
C6	114 × 162		

BOUND BOOKS

The book sizes most commonly used are listed below. Approximate centimetre equivalents are also shown. International sizes are converted to their nearest imperial size, e.g. A4 = D4; A5 = D8.

		inches	cm
Crown 32mo	C32	2½ × 3¾	6 × 9
Crown 16mo	C16	3¾ × 5	9 × 13
Foolscap 8vo	F8	4¼ × 6¾	11 × 17
Demy 16mo	D16	4⅜ × 5⅝	11 × 14
Crown 8vo	C8	5 × 7½	13 × 19
Demy 8vo	D8	5⅝ × 8¾	14 × 22
Medium 8vo	M8	5¾ × 9	15 × 23
Royal 8vo	R8	6¼ × 10	16 × 25
Super Royal 8vo	suR8	6¾ × 10	17 × 25
Foolscap 4to	F4	6¾ × 8½	17 × 22
Crown 4to	C4	7½ × 10	19 × 25
Imperial 8vo	Imp8	7½ × 11	19 × 28
Demy 4to	D4	8¾ × 11¼	22 × 29
Royal 4to	R4	10 × 12½	25 × 31
Super Royal 4to	suR4	10 × 13½	25 × 34
Crown Folio	Cfol	10 × 15	25 × 38
Imperial Folio	Impfol	11 × 15	28 × 38

Folio = a sheet folded in half
Quarto (4to) = a sheet folded into four
Octavo (8vo) = a sheet folded into eight
Books are usually bound up in sheets of 16 or 32 pages. Octavo books are generally printed 64 pages at a time, 32 pages on each side of a sheet of quad.

CONVERSION TABLES FOR WEIGHTS AND MEASURES
Bold figures equal units of either of the columns beside them; thus: 1 cm = 0.394″ and 1″ = 2.540 cm

LENGTH			AREA			VOLUME			WEIGHT (MASS)		
Centimetres		*Inches*	*Square cm*		*Square in*	*Cubic cm*		*Cubic in*	*Kilograms*		*Pounds*
2.540	**1**	0.394	6.452	**1**	0.155	16.387	**1**	0.061	0.454	**1**	2.205
5.080	**2**	0.787	12.903	**2**	0.310	32.774	**2**	0.122	0.907	**2**	4.409
7.620	**3**	1.181	19.355	**3**	0.465	49.161	**3**	0.183	1.361	**3**	6.614
10.160	**4**	1.575	25.806	**4**	0.620	65.548	**4**	0.244	1.814	**4**	8.819
12.700	**5**	1.969	32.258	**5**	0.775	81.936	**5**	0.305	2.268	**5**	11.023
15.240	**6**	2.362	38.710	**6**	0.930	98.323	**6**	0.366	2.722	**6**	13.228
17.780	**7**	2.756	45.161	**7**	1.085	114.710	**7**	0.427	3.175	**7**	15.432
20.320	**8**	3.150	51.613	**8**	1.240	131.097	**8**	0.488	3.629	**8**	17.637
22.860	**9**	3.543	58.064	**9**	1.395	147.484	**9**	0.549	4.082	**9**	19.842
25.400	**10**	3.937	64.516	**10**	1.550	163.871	**10**	0.610	4.536	**10**	22.046
50.800	**20**	7.874	129.032	**20**	3.100	327.742	**20**	1.220	9.072	**20**	44.092
76.200	**30**	11.811	193.548	**30**	4.650	491.613	**30**	1.831	13.608	**30**	66.139
101.600	**40**	15.748	258.064	**40**	6.200	655.484	**40**	2.441	18.144	**40**	88.185
127.000	**50**	19.685	322.580	**50**	7.750	819.355	**50**	3.051	22.680	**50**	110.231
152.400	**60**	23.622	387.096	**60**	9.300	983.226	**60**	3.661	27.216	**60**	132.277
177.800	**70**	27.559	451.612	**70**	10.850	1147.097	**70**	4.272	31.752	**70**	154.324
203.200	**80**	31.496	516.128	**80**	12.400	1310.968	**80**	4.882	36.287	**80**	176.370
228.600	**90**	35.433	580.644	**90**	13.950	1474.839	**90**	5.492	40.823	**90**	198.416
254.000	**100**	39.370	645.160	**100**	15.500	1638.710	**100**	6.102	45.359	**100**	220.464

Metres		*Yards*	*Square m*		*Square yd*	*Cubic m*		*Cubic yd*	*Metric tonnes*		*Tons (UK)*
0.914	**1**	1.094	0.836	**1**	1.196	0.765	**1**	1.308	1.016	**1**	0.984
1.829	**2**	2.187	1.672	**2**	2.392	1.529	**2**	2.616	2.032	**2**	1.968
2.743	**3**	3.281	2.508	**3**	3.588	2.294	**3**	3.924	3.048	**3**	2.953
3.658	**4**	4.374	3.345	**4**	4.784	3.058	**4**	5.232	4.064	**4**	3.937
4.572	**5**	5.468	4.181	**5**	5.980	3.823	**5**	6.540	5.080	**5**	4.921
5.486	**6**	6.562	5.017	**6**	7.176	4.587	**6**	7.848	6.096	**6**	5.905
6.401	**7**	7.655	5.853	**7**	8.372	5.352	**7**	9.156	7.112	**7**	6.889
7.315	**8**	8.749	6.689	**8**	9.568	6.116	**8**	10.464	8.128	**8**	7.874
8.230	**9**	9.843	7.525	**9**	10.764	6.881	**9**	11.772	9.144	**9**	8.858
9.144	**10**	10.936	8.361	**10**	11.960	7.646	**10**	13.080	10.161	**10**	9.842
18.288	**20**	21.872	16.723	**20**	23.920	15.291	**20**	26.159	20.321	**20**	19.684
27.432	**30**	32.808	25.084	**30**	35.880	22.937	**30**	39.239	30.481	**30**	29.526
36.576	**40**	43.745	33.445	**40**	47.840	30.582	**40**	52.318	40.642	**40**	39.368
45.720	**50**	54.681	41.806	**50**	59.799	38.228	**50**	65.398	50.802	**50**	49.210
54.864	**60**	65.617	50.168	**60**	71.759	45.873	**60**	78.477	60.963	**60**	59.052
64.008	**70**	76.553	58.529	**70**	83.719	53.519	**70**	91.557	71.123	**70**	68.894
73.152	**80**	87.489	66.890	**80**	95.679	61.164	**80**	104.636	81.284	**80**	78.737
82.296	**90**	98.425	75.251	**90**	107.639	68.810	**90**	117.716	91.444	**90**	88.579
91.440	**100**	109.361	83.613	**100**	119.599	76.455	**100**	130.795	101.605	**100**	98.421

Kilometres		*Miles*	*Hectares*		*Acres*	*Litres*		*Gallons*	*Metric tonnes*		*Tons (US)*
1.609	**1**	0.621	0.405	**1**	2.471	4.546	**1**	0.220	0.907	**1**	1.102
3.219	**2**	1.243	0.809	**2**	4.942	9.092	**2**	0.440	1.814	**2**	2.205
4.828	**3**	1.864	1.214	**3**	7.413	13.638	**3**	0.660	2.722	**3**	3.305
6.437	**4**	2.485	1.619	**4**	9.844	18.184	**4**	0.880	3.629	**4**	4.409
8.047	**5**	3.107	2.023	**5**	12.355	22.730	**5**	1.100	4.536	**5**	5.521
9.656	**6**	3.728	2.428	**6**	14.826	27.276	**6**	1.320	5.443	**6**	6.614
11.265	**7**	4.350	2.833	**7**	17.297	31.822	**7**	1.540	6.350	**7**	7.716
12.875	**8**	4.971	3.327	**8**	19.769	36.368	**8**	1.760	7.257	**8**	8.818
14.484	**9**	5.592	3.642	**9**	22.240	40.914	**9**	1.980	8.165	**9**	9.921
16.093	**10**	6.214	4.047	**10**	24.711	45.460	**10**	2.200	9.072	**10**	11.023
32.187	**20**	12.427	8.094	**20**	49.421	90.919	**20**	4.400	18.144	**20**	22.046
48.280	**30**	18.641	12.140	**30**	74.132	136.379	**30**	6.599	27.216	**30**	33.069
64.374	**40**	24.855	16.187	**40**	98.842	181.839	**40**	8.799	36.287	**40**	44.092
80.467	**50**	31.069	20.234	**50**	123.555	227.298	**50**	10.999	45.359	**50**	55.116
96.561	**60**	37.282	24.281	**60**	148.263	272.758	**60**	13.199	54.431	**60**	66.139
112.654	**70**	43.496	28.328	**70**	172.974	318.217	**70**	15.398	63.503	**70**	77.162
128.748	**80**	49.710	32.375	**80**	197.684	363.677	**80**	17.598	72.575	**80**	88.185
144.841	**90**	55.923	36.422	**90**	222.395	409.137	**90**	19.798	81.647	**90**	99.208
160.934	**100**	62.137	40.469	**100**	247.105	454.596	**100**	21.998	90.719	**100**	110.231

Abbreviations

A	Associate of
AA	Alcoholics Anonymous
	Anti-Aircraft
	Automobile Association
AAA	Amateur Athletic Association
AB	Able-bodied seaman
ABA	Amateur Boxing Association
abbr(ev)	abbreviation
ABM	Anti-ballistic missile
abr	abridged
ac	alternating current
a/c	account
AC	Aircraftman
	(Ante Christum) Before Christ
	Companion, Order of Australia
ACAS	Advisory, Conciliation and Arbitration Service
ACT	Australian Capital Territory
AD	*(Anno Domini)* In the year of our Lord
ADC	Aide-de-Camp
ADC (P)	Personal ADC to The Queen
adj	adjective
Adj	Adjutant
ad lib	*(ad libitum)* at pleasure
Adm	Admiral
	Admission
adv	adverb
	advocate
AE	Air Efficiency Award
AEA	Atomic Energy Authority
AEEU	Amalgamated Engineering and Electrical Union
AEM	Air Efficiency Medal
AERE	Atomic Energy Research Establishment
AFC	Air Force Cross
	Association Football Club
AFM	Air Force Medal
AFRC	Agricultural and Food Research Council
AFV	Armoured fighting vehicle
AG	Adjutant-General
	Attorney-General
AGM	air-to-ground missile
	annual general meeting
AH	*(Anno Hegirae)* In the year of the Hegira
AIDS	Acquired immune deficiency syndrome
alt	altitude
am	*(ante meridiem)* before noon
AM	*(Anno mundi)* In the year of the world
amp	ampere
	amplifier
ANC	African National Congress
anon	anonymous
ANZAC	Australian and New Zealand Army Corps
AO	Air Officer
	Officer, Order of Australia
AOC	Air Officer Commanding
AONB	Area of Outstanding Natural Beauty
AS	Anglo-Saxon
ASA	Advertising Standards Authority
	Amateur Swimming Association
ASB	Alternative Service Book
ASEAN	Association of South East Asian Nations
ASH	Action on Smoking and Health
ASLEF	Associated Society of Locomotive Engineers and Firemen
ASLIB	Association for Information Management
ATC	Air Training Corps
AUC	*(ab urbe condita)* In the year from the foundation of Rome
	(anno urbis conditae) In the year of the founding of the city
AUT	Association of University Teachers
AV	Audio-visual
	Authorized Version *(of Bible)*
AVR	Army Volunteer Reserve
AWOL	Absent without leave
b	born
	bowled
BA	Bachelor of Arts
BAA	British Airports Authority
	British Astronomical Association
BAFTA	British Academy of Film and Television Arts
BAOR	British Army of the Rhine
Bart	Baronet
BAS	Bachelor in Agricultural Science
	British Antarctic Survey
BB	Boys' Brigade
BBC	British Broadcasting Corporation
BC	Before Christ
	British Columbia
BCCI	Bank of Credit and Commerce International
B Ch (D)	Bachelor of (Dental) Surgery
BCL	Bachelor of Civil Law
B Com	Bachelor of Commerce
BD	Bachelor of Divinity
BDA	British Dental Association
BDS	Bachelor of Dental Surgery
B Ed	Bachelor of Education
BEM	British Empire Medal
B Eng	Bachelor of Engineering
BFI	British Film Institute
BFPO	British Forces Post Office
B Litt	Bachelor of Letters *or* of Literature
BM	Bachelor of Medicine
	British Museum
BMA	British Medical Association
B Mus	Bachelor of Music
BOTB	British Overseas Trade Board
Bp	Bishop
B Pharm	Bachelor of Pharmacy
B Phil	Bachelor of Philosophy
Br	Britain
	British
BR	British Rail
BRCS	British Red Cross Society
Brig	Brigadier
Brit	Britain
	British
BSc	Bachelor of Science
BSC	British Steel Corporation
BSI	British Standards Institution
BST	British Summer Time
Bt	Baronet
BTEC	Business and Technology Education Council
B Th	Bachelor of Theology
Btu	British thermal unit
BVM	*(Beata Virgo Maria)* Blessed Virgin Mary
BVMS	Bachelor of Veterinary Medicine and Surgery
BWB	British Waterways Board
c	*(circa)* about
C	Celsius
	Centigrade
	Conservative
CA	Chartered Accountant *(Scotland)*
CAA	Civil Aviation Authority
CAB	Citizens' Advice Bureau
Cantab	*(of)* Cambridge
Cantuar:	of Canterbury *(Archbishop)*
CAP	Common Agricultural Policy
Capt	Captain
Caricom	Caribbean Community and Common Market
Carliol:	of Carlisle *(Bishop)*
CB	Companion, Order of the Bath
CBE	Commander, Order of the British Empire
CBI	Confederation of British Industry
CC	Chamber of Commerce
	Companion, Order of Canada
	City Council
	County Council
	County Court
CCC	County Cricket Club
CCF	Combined Cadet Force
C Chem	Chartered Chemist
CD	Civil Defence
	Compact Disc
	Corps Diplomatique
Cdr	Commander
Cdre	Commodore
CDS	Chief of the Defence Staff
CE	Christian Era
	Civil Engineer
C Eng	Chartered Engineer
Cento	Central Treaty Organization
Cestr:	of Chester *(Bishop)*
CET	Central European Time
	Common External Tariff
cf	*(confer)* compare
CF	Chaplain to the Forces
CFC	Chlorofluorocarbon
CGM	Conspicuous Gallantry Medal
CGS	Centimetre-gramme-second *(system)*
	Chief of General Staff
CH	Companion of Honour
ChB/M	Bachelor/Master of Surgery
CI	Channel Islands
	The Imperial Order of the Crown of India
CIA	Central Intelligence Agency
Cicestr:	of Chichester *(Bishop)*
CID	Criminal Investigation Department
CIE	Companion, Order of the Indian Empire
cif	cost, insurance and freight
C-in-C	Commander-in-Chief
CIPFA	Chartered Institute of Public Finance and Accountancy
C Lit	Companion of Literature

CLJ	Commander, Order of St Lazarus of Jerusalem	do	(*ditto*) the same	FBIM	Fellow, British Institute of Management
CM	(*Chirurgiae Magister*) Master of Surgery	DoE	Department of the Environment	FBS	Fellow, Botanical Society
		DOS	Disk operating system (*computer*)	FC	Football Club
CMG	Companion, Order of St Michael and St George	DP	Data processing	FCA	Fellow, Institute of Chartered Accountants (*of England and Wales*)
CND	Campaign for Nuclear Disarmament	D Ph *or* D Phil	Doctor of Philosophy		
c/o	care of	DPP	Director of Public Prosecutions	FCCA	Fellow, Chartered Association of Certified Accountants
CO	Commanding Officer conscientious objector	Dr	Doctor		
		D Sc	Doctor of Science	FCGI	Fellow, City and Guilds of London Institute
COD	Cash on delivery	DSC	Distinguished Service Cross		
C of E	Church of England	DSM	Distinguished Service Medal	FCIA	Fellow, Corporation of Insurance Agents
COHSE	Confederation of Health Service Employees	DSO	Companion, Distinguished Service Order	FCIArb	Fellow, Chartered Institute of Arbitrators
COI	Central Office of Information	DSS	Department of Social Security	FCIB	Fellow, Chartered Institute of Bankers
Col	Colonel	DTI	Department of Trade and Industry		
Con	Conservative				Fellow, Corporation of Insurance Brokers
Cpl	Corporal	Dunelm:	of Durham (*Bishop*)		
CPM	Colonial Police Medal	DV	(*Deo volente*) God willing	FCIBSE	Fellow, Chartered Institution of Building Services Engineers
CPRE	Council for the Protection of Rural England			FCII	Fellow, Chartered Insurance Institute
		E	East		
CPVE	Certificate of Pre-Vocational Education	Ebor:	of York (*Archbishop*)	FCIS	Fellow, Institute of Chartered Secretaries and Administrators
		EBRD	European Bank for Reconstruction and Development		
CRE	Commission for Racial Equality			FCIT	Fellow, Chartered Institute of Transport
CSCE	Conference on Security and Co-operation in Europe	EC	European Community		
		ECG	Electrocardiogram	FCMA	Fellow, Chartered Institute of Management Accountants
CSE	Certificate of Secondary Education	ECGD	Export Credits Guarantee Department		
				FCO	Foreign and Commonwealth Office
CSI	Companion, Order of the Star of India	ECSC	European Coal and Steel Community		
				FCP	Fellow, College of Preceptors
CVO	Commander, Royal Victorian Order	ECU	European Currency Unit	FD	(*Fidei Defensor*) Defender of the Faith
		ED	Efficiency Decoration		
		EEC	European Economic Community	fec	(*fecit*) made this
d	(*denarius*) penny			FEng	Fellow, Royal Academy of Engineering
DBE	Dame Commander, Order of the British Empire	EEG	Electroencephalogram		
		EFA	European Fighter Aircraft	ff	(*fecerunt*) made this (*pl*)
dc	direct current	EFTA	European Free Trade Association	ff	(*fortissimo*) very loud
DC	District Council District of Columbia	eg	(*exempli gratia*) for the sake of example	FFA	Fellow, Faculty of Actuaries (*Scotland*)
DCB	Dame Commander, Order of the Bath	EMS	European Monetary System		Fellow, Institute of Financial Accountants
D Ch	(*Doctor Chirurgiae*) Doctor of Surgery	ENEA	European Nuclear Energy Agency	FFAS	Fellow, Faculty of Architects and Surveyors
DCL	Doctor of Civil Law	ER	(*Elizabetha Regina*) Queen Elizabeth	FGS	Fellow, Geological Society
DCM	Distinguished Conduct Medal			FHS	Fellow, Heraldry Society
DCMG	Dame Commander, Order of St Michael and St George	ERD	Emergency Reserve Decoration	FHSM	Fellow, Institute of Health Service Management
		ERM	Exchange Rate Mechanism		
DCVO	Dame Commander, Royal Victorian Order	ERNIE	Electronic random number indicator equipment	FIA	Fellow, Institute of Actuaries
				FIBiol	Fellow, Institute of Biology
DD	Doctor of Divinity	ESA	European Space Agency	FICE	Fellow, Institution of Civil Engineers
DDS	Doctor of Dental Surgery	ESP	Extra-sensory perception		
DDT	dichlorodiphenyl-trichloroethane	ESRC	Economic and Social Research Council	FICS	Fellow, Institution of Chartered Shipbrokers
del	(*delineavit*) he/she drew it	ETA	Euzkadi ta Askatasuna (*Basque separatist organization*)	FIEE	Fellow, Institution of Electrical Engineers
DFC	Distinguished Flying Cross				
DFE	Department for Education	et al	(*et alibi*) and elsewhere (*et alii*) and others	FIERE	Fellow, Institution of Electronic and Radio Engineers
DFM	Distinguished Flying Medal				
DG	(*Dei gratia*) By the grace of God Director-General	etc	(*et cetera*) and the other things/and so forth	FIFA	International Association Football Federation
DH	Department of Health	et seq	(*et sequentia*) and the following	FIM	Fellow, Institute of Metals
DHA	District Health Authority	Euratom	European Atomic Energy Commission	FIMM	Fellow, Institution of Mining and Metallurgy
DHSS	Department of Health and Social Security				
		Exon:	of Exeter (*Bishop*)	FInstF	Fellow, Institute of Fuel
Dip Ed	Diploma in Education			FInstP	Fellow, Institute of Physics
Dip H E	Diploma in Higher Education			FIQS	Fellow, Institute of Quantity Surveyors
Dip Tech	Diploma in Technology	*f*	(*forte*) loud		
DJ	Disc jockey	F	Fahrenheit	FIS	Fellow, Institute of Statisticians
DL	Deputy Lieutenant		Fellow of	FJI	Fellow, Institute of Journalists
D Litt	Doctor of Letters *or* of Literature	FA	Football Association	fl	(*floruit*) flourished
		FANY	First Aid Nursing Yeomanry	FLA	Fellow, Library Association
D Mus	Doctor of Music	FAO	Food and Agriculture Organization (*UN*)	FLS	Fellow, Linnean Society
DNA	deoxyribonucleic acid			FM	Field Marshal frequency modulation
DNB	*Dictionary of National Biography*	FBA	Fellow, British Academy		
		FBAA	Fellow, British Association of Accountants and Auditors	fo	folio
DNH	Department of National Heritage			FO	Flying Officer
		FBI	Federal Bureau of Investigation	fob	free on board

FPA	Family Planning Association	FSA	Fellow, Society of Antiquaries	Hon	Honorary
FPhS	Fellow, Philosophical Society	FSS	Fellow, Statistical Society		Honourable
FRAD	Fellow, Royal Academy of Dancing	FSVA	Fellow, Incorporated Society of Valuers and Auctioneers	hp	horse power
				HP	Hire purchase
FRAeS	Fellow, Royal Aeronautical Society	FT	*Financial Times*	HQ	Headquarters
		FTI	Fellow, Textile Institute	HRH	Her/His Royal Highness
FRAI	Fellow, Royal Anthropological Institute	FTII	Fellow, Institute of Taxation	HSE	Health and Safety Executive
		FZS	Fellow, Zoological Society		(*hic sepultus est*) here lies buried
FRAM	Fellow, Royal Academy of Music			HSH	Her/His Serene Highness
				HTR	High temperature reactor
FRAS	Fellow, Royal Astronomical Society	GATT	General Agreement on Tariffs and Trade	HWM	High water mark
FRBS	Fellow, Royal Botanic Society Fellow, Royal Society of British Sculptors	GBE	Dame/Knight Grand Cross, Order of the British Empire	I	Island
				IAAS	Incorporated Association of Architects and Surveyors
		GC	George Cross		
FRCA	Fellow, Royal College of Anaesthetists	GCB	Dame/Knight Grand Cross, Order of the Bath	IAEA	International Atomic Energy Agency
FRCGP	Fellow, Royal College of General Practitioners	GCE	General Certificate of Education	IATA	International Air Transport Association
		GCHQ	Government Communications Headquarters		
FRCM	Fellow, Royal College of Music			Ibid	(*ibidem*) in the same place
FRCO	Fellow, Royal College of Organists	GCIE	Knight Grand Commander, Order of the Indian Empire	IBRD	International Bank for Reconstruction and Development
FRCOG	Fellow, Royal College of Obstetricians and Gynaecologists	GCLJ	Knight Grand Cross, Order of St Lazarus of Jerusalem		
		GCMG	Dame/Knight Grand Cross, Order of St Michael and St George	ICAO	International Civil Aviation Organization
FRCP	Fellow, Royal College of Physicians, London			ICBM	Inter-continental ballistic missile
FRCPath	Fellow, Royal College of Pathologists	GCSE	General Certificate of Secondary Education	ICFTU	International Confederation of Free Trade Unions
FRCPE(d)	Fellow, Royal College of Physicians, Edinburgh	GCSI	Knight Grand Commander, Order of the Star of India	ICJ	International Court of Justice
				ICRC	International Committee of the Red Cross
FRCPI	Fellow, Royal College of Physicians, Ireland	GCVO	Dame/Knight Grand Cross, Royal Victorian Order	Id	(*idem*) the same
FRCPsych	Fellow, Royal College of Psychiatrists	GDP	Gross domestic product	IDA	International Development Association
		Gen	General		
FRCR	Fellow, Royal College of Radiologists	GHQ	General Headquarters	IDD	International direct dialling
		GM	George Medal	ie	(*id est*) that is
FRCS	Fellow, Royal College of Surgeons of England	GMB	General, Municipal, Boilermakers and Allied Trades Union	IEA	International Energy Agency
				IFAD	International Fund for Agricultural Development
FRCSE(d)	Fellow, Royal College of Surgeons of Edinburgh	GMT	Greenwich Mean Time	IFC	International Finance Corporation
FRCSGlas	Fellow, Royal College of Physicians and Surgeons of Glasgow	GNP	Gross national product		
		GOC	General Officer Commanding	IHS	(*Iesus Hominum Salvator*) Jesus the Saviour of Mankind
		GP	General Practitioner		
FRCSI	Fellow, Royal College of Surgeons in Ireland	Gp Capt	Group Captain	ILEA	Inner London Education Authority
		GSO	General Staff Officer		
FRCVS	Fellow, Royal College of Veterinary Surgeons			ILO	International Labour Office/Organization
FREconS	Fellow, Royal Economic Society	HAC	Honourable Artillery Company	ILR	Independent local radio
FRGS	Fellow, Royal Geographical Society	HB	His Beatitude	IMF	International Monetary Fund
		HBM	Her/His Britannic Majesty('s)	IMO	International Maritime Organization
FRHistS	Fellow, Royal Historical Society	HCF	Highest common factor		
FRHS	Fellow, Royal Horticultural Society		Honorary Chaplain to the Forces	Inc	Incorporated
		HE	Her/His Excellency	Incog	(*incognito*) unknown, unrecognized
FRIBA	Fellow, Royal Institute of British Architects		His Eminence	INF	International Nuclear Force
FRICS	Fellow, Royal Institution of Chartered Surveyors	HGV	Heavy Goods Vehicle	INLA	Irish National Liberation Army
		HH	Her/His Highness	In loc	(*in loco*) in its place
FRMetS	Fellow, Royal Meteorological Society		Her/His Honour	Inmarsat	International Maritime Satellite Organization
			His Holiness		
FRMS	Fellow, Royal Microscopical Society	HIM	Her/His Imperial Majesty	INRI	(*Iesus Nazarenus Rex Iudaeorum*) Jesus of Nazareth, King of the Jews
		HIV	Human immunodeficiency virus		
FRNS	Fellow, Royal Numismatic Society	HJS	(*hic jacet sepultus*) here lies buried		
				Inst	(*instant*) current month
FRPharmS	Fellow, Royal Pharmaceutical Society	HM	Her/His Majesty('s)	Intelsat	International Telecommunications Satellite Organization
		HMAS	Her/His Majesty's Australian Ship		
FRPS	Fellow, Royal Photographic Society			Interpol	International Criminal Police Commission
		HMC	Headmasters' Conference		
FRS	Fellow, Royal Society	HMI	Her/His Majesty's Inspector	IOC	International Olympic Committee
FRSA	Fellow, Royal Society of Arts	HML	Her/His Majesty's Lieutenant		
FRSC	Fellow, Royal Society of Chemistry	HMS	Her/His Majesty's Ship	IOM	Isle of Man
		HMSO	Her/His Majesty's Stationery Office	IOU	I owe you
FRSE	Fellow, Royal Society of Edinburgh			IOW	Isle of Wight
		HNC	Higher National Certificate	IPLO	Irish People's Liberation Organization
FRSL	Fellow, Royal Society of Literature	HND	Higher National Diploma		
		HOLMES	Home Office Large Major Enquiry System	IQ	Intelligence quotient
FRTPI	Fellow, Royal Town Planning Institute			IRA	Irish Republican Army

IRC International Red Cross
Is Islands
ISBN International Standard Book Number
ISO Imperial Service Order
ITC Independent Television Commission
ITU International Telecommunication Union
ITV Independent Television

JP Justice of the Peace

K Köchel numeration (*of Mozart's works*)
KANU Kenyan African National Union
KBE Knight Commander, Order of the British Empire
KCB Knight Commander, Order of the Bath
KCIE Knight Commander, Order of the Indian Empire
KCLJ Knight Commander, Order of St Lazarus of Jerusalem
KCMG Knight Commander, Order of St Michael and St George
KCSI Knight Commander, Order of the Star of India
KCVO Knight Commander, Royal Victorian Order
KG Knight of the Garter
KGB (*Komitet Gosudarstvennoi Besopasnosti*) Committee of State Security (USSR)
KKK Ku Klux Klan
KLJ Knight, Order of St Lazarus of Jerusalem
ko knock out (*boxing*)
KP Knight, Order of St Patrick
KStJ Knight, Order of St John of Jerusalem
Kt Knight
KT Knight of the Thistle
kV Kilovolt
kW Kilowatt
kWh Kilowatt hour

L Liberal
Lab Labour
Lat Latitude
lbw leg before wicket
lc lower case (*printing*)
LCJ Lord Chief Justice
LCM Least/lowest common multiple
LD Liberal Democrat
LDS Licentiate in Dental Surgery
LEA Local Education Authority
LHD (*Literarum Humaniorum Doctor*) Doctor of Humane Letters/ Literature
Lib Liberal
Lic (*Licenciado*) lawyer (*Spanish*)
Lic Med Licentiate in Medicine
Lit Literary
Lit Hum (*Literae Humaniores*) Faculty of classics and philosophy, Oxford
Litt D Doctor of Letters
LJ Lord Justice
LLB Bachelor of Laws
LLD Doctor of Laws
LLM Master of Laws
LM Licentiate in Midwifery
LMSSA Licentiate in Medicine and Surgery, Society of Apothecaries

loc cit (*loco citato*) in the place cited
log logarithm
Londin: of London (*Bishop*)
Long Longitude
LS (*loco sigilli*) place of the seal
LSA Licentiate of Society of Apothecaries
Lsd (*Librae, solidi, denarii*) £, shillings and pence
LSE London School of Economics and Political Science
Lt Lieutenant
LTA Lawn Tennis Association
Ltd Limited (liability)
LTh *or* L Theol Licentiate in Theology
LVO Lieutenant, Royal Victorian Order
LWM Low water mark

M Member of Monsieur
MA Master of Arts
MAFF Ministry of Agriculture, Fisheries and Food
Maj Major
max maximum
MB/D Bachelor/Doctor of Medicine
MBA Master of Business Administration
MBE Member, Order of the British Empire
MC Master of Ceremonies Military Cross
MCC Marylebone Cricket Club.
MCh(D) Master of (Dental) Surgery
MD Managing Director
MDS Master of Dental Surgery
ME Middle English
MEC Member of Executive Council
MEd Master of Education
mega one million times
MEP Member of the European Parliament
MFH Master of Foxhounds
Mgr Monsignor
MI Military Intelligence
micro one-millionth part
milli one-thousandth part
min minimum
MIRAS Mortgage Interest Relief at Source
MLA Member of Legislative Assembly
MLC Member of Legislative Council
Mlle Mademoiselle
MLR Minimum lending rate
MM Military Medal
Mme Madame
MN Merchant Navy
MO Medical Officer/Orderly
MoD Ministry of Defence
MoT Ministry of Transport
MP Member of Parliament Military Police
mph miles per hour
MR Master of the Rolls
MRC Medical Research Council
MS Master of Surgery Manuscript (*pl* MSS)
MSc Master of Science
MSF Manufacturing, Science and Finance Union
MTh Master of Theology
Mus B/D Bachelor/Doctor of Music
MV Merchant Vessel Motor Vessel

MVO Member, Royal Victorian Order
MW Medium Wave

N North
n/a not applicable not available
NAAFI Navy, Army and Air Force Institutes
NALGO National and Local Government Officers' Association
NASA National Aeronautics and Space Administration
NAS/UWT National Association of Schoolmasters/Union of Women Teachers
NATO North Atlantic Treaty Organization
NB New Brunswick (*Nota bene*) note well
NCC Nature Conservancy Council
NCO Non-commissioned officer
NEB New English Bible
NEDC National Economic Development Council
Nem con (*Nemine contradicente*) no one contradicting
NERC Natural Environment Research Council
nes not elsewhere specified
NFT National Film Theatre
NFU National Farmers' Union
NHS National Health Service
NI National Insurance Northern Ireland
NICS National Criminal Intelligence Service
NIV New International Version (*of Bible*)
No (*numero*) number
Non seq (*Non sequitur*) it does not follow
Norvic: of Norwich (*Bishop*)
NP Notary Public
NRA National Rifle Association National Rivers Authority
NS New Style (*calendar*) Nova Scotia
NSPCC National Society for the Prevention of Cruelty to Children
NSW New South Wales
NT National Theatre National Trust New Testament
NUCPS National Union of Civil and Public Servants
NUJ National Union of Journalists
NUM National Union of Mineworkers
NUPE National Union of Public Employees
NUS National Union of Students
NUT National Union of Teachers
NVQ National Vocational Qualification
NWT Northwest Territory
NY New York
NZ New Zealand

OAPEC Organization of Arab Petroleum Exporting Countries
OAS Organization of American States
OAU Organization of African Unity
Ob *or* obit died
OBE Officer, Order of the British Empire
OC Officer Commanding

ODA	Overseas Development Administration
OE	Old English
	omissions excepted
OECD	Organization for Economic Co-operation and Development
OED	*Oxford English Dictionary*
Offer	Office of Electricity Regulation
Ofgas	Office of Gas Supply
OFM	Order of Friars Minor (*Franciscans*)
Ofsted	Office for Standards in Education
OFT	Office of Fair Trading
Oftel	Office of Telecommunications
Ofwat	Office of Water Services
OHMS	On Her/His Majesty's Service
OM	Order of Merit
OND	Ordinary National Diploma
op	(*opus*) work
OP	Opposite prompt side (*of theatre*)
	Order of Preachers (*Dominicans*)
	out of print (*books*)
op cit	(*opere citato*) in the work cited
OPCS	Office of Population Censuses and Surveys
OPEC	Organization of Petroleum Exporting Countries
OPSS	Office of Public Service and Science
OS	Old Style (*calendar*)
	Ordnance Survey
OSA	Order of St Augustine
OSB	Order of St Benedict
OST	Office of Science and Technology
O St J	Officer, Order of St John of Jerusalem
OT	Old Testament
OTC	Officers' Training Corps
Oxon	(of) Oxford
	Oxfordshire
p	page
p	(*piano*) softly
PA	Personal Assistant
	Press Association
PAYE	Pay as You Earn
pc	(*per centum*) in the hundred
PC	Personal Computer
	Police Constable
	Privy Counsellor
PCAS	Polytechnics Central Admissions System
PDSA	People's Dispensary for Sick Animals
PE	Physical Education
Petriburg:	of Peterborough (*Bishop*)
PGA	Professional Golfers Association
PhD	Doctor of Philosophy
pinx(it)	he/she painted it
pl	plural
PLA	Port of London Authority
PLC	Public Limited Company
PLO	Palestine Liberation Organization
pm	(*post meridiem*) after noon
PM	Prime Minister
PMRAFNS	Princess Mary's Royal Air Force Nursing Service
PO	Petty Officer
	Pilot Officer
	Post Office
	postal order
POW	Prisoner of War

pp	pages
	(*per procurationem*) by proxy
PPS	Parliamentary Private Secretary
PR	Proportional representation
	Public relations
PRA	President of the Royal Academy
Pro tem	(*pro tempore*) for the time being
Prox	(*proximo*) next month
PRS	President of the Royal Society
PRSE	President of the Royal Society of Edinburgh
Ps	Psalm
PS	(*Post scriptum*) postscript
PSBR	Public sector borrowing requirement
psc	passed Staff College
PSV	Public Service Vehicle
Pte	Private
PTO	Please turn over
QARANC	Queen Alexandra's Royal Army Nursing Corps
QARNNS	Queen Alexandra's Royal Naval Nursing Service
QB	Queen's Bench
QC	Queen's Counsel
QED	(*quod erat demonstrandum*) which was to be proved
QGM	Queen's Gallantry Medal
QHC	Queen's Honorary Chaplain
QHDS	Queen's Honorary Dental Surgeon
QHNS	Queen's Honorary Nursing Sister
QHP	Queen's Honorary Physician
QHS	Queen's Honorary Surgeon
QMG	Quartermaster General
QPM	Queen's Police Medal
QS	Quarter Sessions
QSO	Quasi-stellar object (quasar)
	Queen's Service Order
quango	quasi-autonomous non-governmental organization
qv	(*quod vide*) which see
R	(*Regina*) Queen
	(*Rex*) King
RA	Royal Academy/Academician
	Royal Artillery
RAC	Royal Armoured Corps
	Royal Automobile Club
RADA	Royal Academy of Dramatic Art
RADC	Royal Army Dental Corps
RAE	Royal Aerospace Establishment
RAEC	Royal Army Educational Corps
RAeS	Royal Aeronautical Society
RAF	Royal Air Force
RAM	Random-access memory (*computer*)
	Royal Academy of Music
RAMC	Royal Army Medical Corps
RAN	Royal Australian Navy
RAOC	Royal Army Ordnance Corps
RAPC	Royal Army Pay Corps
RAVC	Royal Army Veterinary Corps
RBA	Royal Society of British Artists
RBG	Royal Botanic Garden
RBS	Royal Society of British Sculptors
RC	Red Cross
	Roman Catholic
RCM	Royal College of Music
RCN	Royal Canadian Navy
RCT	Royal Corps of Transport

RD	Refer to drawer (*banking*)
	Royal Naval and Royal Marine Forces Reserve Decoration
	Rural Dean
RDI	Royal Designer for Industry
RE	Religious Education
	Royal Engineers
REME	Royal Electrical and Mechanical Engineers
Rep	Representative
	Republican
Rev(d)	Reverend
RGN	Registered General Nurse
RGS	Royal Geographical Society
RHA	Regional Health Authority
RHS	Royal Horticultural Society
	Royal Humane Society
RI	Rhode Island
	Royal Institute of Painters in Watercolours
	Royal Institution
RIBA	Royal Institute of British Architects
RIP	(*Requiescat in pace*) May he/she rest in peace
RIR	Royal Irish Regiment
RL	Rugby League
RM	Registered Midwife
	Royal Marines
RMA	Royal Military Academy
RMN	Registered Mental Nurse
RMT	National Union of Rail, Maritime and Transport Workers
RN	Royal Navy
RNIB	Royal National Institute for the Blind
RNID	Royal National Institute for the Deaf
RNLI	Royal National Lifeboat Institution
RNR	Royal Naval Reserve
RNVR	Royal Naval Volunteer Reserve
RNXS	Royal Naval Auxiliary Service
RNZN	Royal New Zealand Navy
Ro	(*Recto*) on the right-hand page
ROC	Royal Observer Corps
Roffen:	of Rochester (*Bishop*)
ROI	Royal Institute of Oil Painters
ROM	Read-only memory (*computer*)
RoSPA	Royal Society for the Prevention of Accidents
RP	Royal Society of Portrait Painters
rpm	revolutions per minute
RRC	Lady of Royal Red Cross
RSA	Republic of South Africa
	Royal Scottish Academician
	Royal Society of Arts
RSC	Royal Shakespeare Company
RSCN	Registered Sick Children's Nurse
RSE	Royal Society of Edinburgh
RSM	Regimental Sergeant Major
RSPB	Royal Society for the Protection of Birds
RSPCA	Royal Society for the Prevention of Cruelty to Animals
RSV	Revised Standard Version (*of Bible*)
RSVP	(*Répondez, s'il vous plaît*) Please reply
RSW	Royal Scottish Society of Painters in Watercolours
RTPI	Royal Town Planning Institute
RU	Rugby Union
RUC	Royal Ulster Constabulary
RV	Revised Version (*of Bible*)

RVM	Royal Victorian Medal	TGWU	Transport and General	W	West	
RWS	Royal Water Colour Society		Workers' Union	WCC	World Council of Churches	
RYS	Royal Yacht Squadron	THES	*Times Higher Education*	WEA	Workers' Educational	
			Supplement		Association	
		TLS	*Times Literary Supplement*	WEU	Western European Union	
s	second	TNT	trinitrotoluene (*explosive*)	WFTU	World Federation of Trade	
	(*solidus*) shilling	trs	transpose (*printing*)		Unions	
S	South	TRH	Their Royal Highnesses	WHO	World Health Organization	
SA	Salvation Army	TT	Teetotal	WI	West Indies	
	South Africa		Tuberculin tested		Women's Institute	
	South America	TUC	Trades Union Congress	Winton:	of Winchester (*Bishop*)	
	South Australia	TVEI	Technical and Vocational	WIPO	World Intellectual Property	
SAE	Stamped addressed envelope		Education Initiative		Organization	
Salop	Shropshire			WMO	World Meteorological	
Sarum:	of Salisbury (*Bishop*)				Organization	
SAS	Special Air Service Regiment	U	Unionist	WO	Warrant Officer	
SBS	Special Boat Squadron	UAE	United Arab Emirates	WRAC	Women's Royal Army Corps	
SBN	Standard Book Number	uc	upper case (*printing*)	WRAF	Women's Royal Air Force	
ScD	Doctor of Science	UCATT	Union of Construction, Allied	WRNS	Women's Royal Naval Service	
SCM	State Certified Midwife		Trades and Technicians	WRVS	Women's Royal Voluntary	
SDLP	Social Democratic and Labour	UCCA	Universities' Central Council on		Service	
	Party		Admissions	WS	Writer to the Signet	
SDP	Social Democratic Party	UDA	Ulster Defence Association			
SEAQ	Stock Exchange Automated	UDI	Unilateral Declaration of			
	Quotations system		Independence	YMCA	Young Men's Christian	
SEN	State Enrolled Nurse	UDM	Union of Democratic		Association	
SERC	Science and Engineering		Mineworkers	YWCA	Young Women's Christian	
	Research Council	UDR	Ulster Defence Regiment		Association	
SERPS	State Earnings Related Pension	UEFA	Union of European Football			
	Scheme		Associations			
SFO	Serious Fraud Office	UFF	Ulster Freedom Fighters	ZANU	Zimbabwe African National	
SI	(*Système Internationale d'Unités*)	UFO	Unidentified flying object		Union	
	International System of Units	UHF	ultra-high frequency			
	Statutory Instrument	UK	United Kingdom	Ψ = seaport		
Sic	So written	UKAEA	UK Atomic Energy Authority			
Sig	Signature	UN	United Nations			
	Signor	UNESCO	United Nations Educational,			
SJ	Society of Jesus (*Jesuits*)		Scientific and Cultural			
SLD	Social and Liberal Democrats		Organization			
SMP	Statutory Maternity Pay	UNICEF	United Nations Children's Fund			
SNP	Scottish National Party	UNIDO	United Nations Industrial			
SOS	Save Our Souls (*distress signal*)		Development Organization			
sp	(*sine prole*) without issue	Unita	National Union for the Total			
spgr	specific gravity		Independence of Angola			
SPQR	(*Senatus Populusque Romanus*)	UPU	Universal Postal Union			
	The Senate and People of Rome	URC	United Reformed Church			
SRN	State Registered Nurse	US(A)	United States (of America)			
SRO	Self Regulating Organizations	USDAW	Union of Shop, Distributive and			
SS	Saints		Allied Workers			
	Steamship	USM	Unlisted Securities Market			
SSC	Solicitor before Supreme Court	USSR	Union of Soviet Socialist			
	(*Scotland*)		Republics			
SSF	Society of St Francis	UTC	Co-ordinated Universal Time			
SSP	Statutory Sick Pay		system			
SSSI	Site of special scientific interest	UVF	Ulster Volunteer Force			
stet	let it stand (*printing*)					
STD	(*Sacrae Theologiae Doctor*)					
	Doctor of Sacred Theology	v	(*versus*) against			
	Subscriber trunk dialling	VA	Vicar Apostolic			
stp	Standard temperature and		Victoria and Albert Order			
	pressure	VAD	Voluntary Aid Detachment			
STP	(*Sacrae Theologiae Professor*)	VAT	Value added tax			
	Professor of Sacred Theology	VC	Victoria Cross			
Sub Lt	Sub-Lieutenant	VD	Venereal disease			
SVQ	Scottish Vocational Qualification		Volunteer Officers' Decoration			
SWET	Society of West End Theatres	VDU	Visual display unit			
		Ven	Venerable			
		VHF	very high frequency			
TA	Territorial Army	VIP	Very important person			
TB	Tuberculosis	Vo	(*Verso*) on the left-hand page			
TCCB	Test and County Cricket Board	VRD	Royal Naval Volunteer Reserve			
TCD	Trinity College, Dublin		Officers' Decoration			
TD	Territorial Efficiency	VSO	Voluntary Service Overseas			
	Decoration	VTOL	Vertical take-off and landing			
temp	temperature		(*aircraft*)			
	temporary employee					
TES	*Times Educational Supplement*					

Index

Stop-press

CHANGES SINCE PAGES WENT TO PRESS

ROYAL HOUSEHOLD
Captain, The Honorable Corps of Gentlemen-at-Arms, The
Viscount Ullswater
Gentlemen of the Corps, Col. Sir Brian Barttelot, Bt. replaces
Maj. J. R. E. Nelson
*The Queen's Bodyguard of the Yeomen of the Guard
Lieutenant*, Col. G. W. Tufnell
Clerk of the Cheque and Adjutant, Col. R. S. Longsdon
Ensign, Maj. C. R. Marriott
Exon, Maj. M. Wills

PEERAGE
Lord Hawke married
Died: 15th Earl of Westmorland; Lord Alexander of
Potterhill; Lord Galpern

BARONETAGE AND KNIGHTAGE, DAMES
Died: Sir Owen Aisher; Sir David Brown; Sir Bayard Dill,
CBE; Rt. Hon. Sir John Higgins; Sir John Moores, CBE; Sir
William Montagu-Pollock, KCMG; Sir John Prendergast,
KBE, CMG, GM; Brig. Dame Margot Turner

DECORATIONS AND MEDALS
Sydney Rogerson, GC, died

THE GOVERNMENT
Captain of the Honorable Corps of Gentlemen-at-Arms (*Chief
Whip in the House of Lords*), The Viscount Ullswater
(formerly Parliamentary Under-Secretary, Employment)

GOVERNMENT DEPARTMENTS AND PUBLIC OFFICES
*Cabinet Office: OPSS, Special Adviser to William
Waldegrave and David Davis*, C. Brendish
*Department of Environment: Drinking Water Inspectorate,
Grade 5*, M. Rouse; *Northern Region, Regional Director*,
B. H. Leonard
Office of Gas Supply: Director-General, Ms C. Spottiswoode
Monopolies and Mergers Commission: Secretary,
A. Nieduszynski (formerly at DTI)
Scottish Office: NHS Management Executive, Chief Executive,
G. Scaife (formerly chief executive of Mersey Regional
Health Authority)

LAW COURTS AND OFFICES
Justices of the High Court – appointed: R. R. H. Jacob
(Chancery Division); W. M. Gage (Queen's Bench
Division); W. A. Blackburne (Chancery Division);
retired: Mr Justice Wood
Circuit Judges – appointed: M. Lee (Midland and Oxford);
retired: D. Roberts; J. Evans; J. Lee (Midland and
Oxford); R. D. Lymbery, Common Serjeant; J. Hunter;
H. Palmer (South-Eastern); R. Woolley (Wales and
Chester)
Recorders – died: Lt.-Col. B. Elliott
Stipendiary Magistrates – appointed: *Provincial*,
G. R. Watkins (S. Glamorgan); M. A. Rosenberg
(S. Yorks); *Metropolitan*, M. J. Read; P. S. Wallis
Northern Ireland: Lord Justice Higgins (Rt. Hon. Sir John
Higgins) died

TRIBUNALS
President, Employment Appeal Tribunal, The Hon. Mr.
Justice Mummery

ANGLICAN COMMUNION
Assistant Bishops, Coventry, John Daly died
Bishop of Gibraltar in Europe, Rt. Revd John Hind (formerly
Suffragan Bishop of Horsham)
Archdeacon of Norwich, Revd Clifford Offer
Archdeacon of Bedford, Canon Malcolm Lesiter
Suffragan Bishop of Burnley, Revd Martyn Jarrett
Dean of Manchester, Revd Canon Kenneth Riley
Bishop of Ballarat, Victoria, Australia, Ven. David Silk
(formerly Archdeacon of Leicester)

LOCAL GOVERNMENT
Lord Mayor of London 1993–4, Alderman Paul Newall
Attorney-General of Jersey, M. C. St J. Birt

TRADE UNIONS
The EETPU section of the Amalgamated Engineering and
Electrical Union reaffiliated with the TUC, 9 September

INTERNATIONAL ORGANIZATIONS
CIS: Azerbaijan parliament voted to rejoin 20 September;
economic union agreement signed by nine members (not
Turkmenistan and Ukraine) 24 September

COUNTRIES OF THE WORLD
Algeria: new government under Redha Malek appointed 21
August
Angola: UN imposed sanctions on UNITA from 25
September
Azerbaijan: parliament voted to rejoin CIS 20 September
Bosnia: Prime Minister Akmadzic sacked 27 August
Brazil: new Cruzeiro (= 1,000 Cruzeiros) introduced
August
Cambodia: Prince Sihanouk elected King, new constitution
promulgated, UN mandate ended 24 September
Canada: federal general election called for 25 October
Central African Republic: new President, Ange-Felix
Patasse, elected 27 September
Georgia: parliament agrees to President Shevardnadze's
demands, dissolves itself for three months and declares
state of emergency 14 September; civil war restarts 24
September; Abkhazian separatists capture Sukhumi 26
September
Greece: general election called for 10 October
Haiti: new pro-Aristide government under Robert Malval
appointed 30 August
Iraq: government reshuffle 5 September, Ahmad Hussein
appointed Prime Minister
Israel: Declaration of Principles on an Interim Self-
government Arrangement signed in Washington DC by
Israel and PLO 13 September. Set of principles for a
peace agreement signed by Israel and Jordan 14
September
New Zealand: general election called for 6 November
Norway: general election on 13 September won by Labour
Party
Poland: former Communist Party and allies have
parliamentary majority after general election on 19
September
South Africa: parliament voted to approve the Transitional
Executive Council; UN sanctions lifted 24 September
Ukraine: Prime Minister Kachma resigns and President
Kravchuk takes control of government; presidential and
parliamentary elections called for June 1994

BRITISH DEPENDENT TERRITORIES
Hong Kong: Hon. Anson Chan appointed Chief Secretary

SPORTS RECORDS
Athletics: Women
1,500 metres, Qu Yunxia (China), 3 min 50.46 sec
3,000 metres, Wang Junxia (China), 8 min 06.11 sec
10,000 metres, Wang Junxia (China), 29 min 31.78 sec
All await ratification

EVENTS
SEPTEMBER 1993

6. More than 700 inmates rioted at Wymott Prison, Lancs. **9.** Israel and the PLO exchanged letters of recognition. Over 50 Somalis were killed in Mogadishu by armed UN helicopters after 300 Somali militiamen attacked a Pakistani UN unit. **13.** Israel and the PLO signed a 'Declaration of Principles' peace accord at the White House in Washington DC. **14.** Israel and Jordan signed a set of principles for a formal peace treaty. **16.** The British National Party won its first local council seat in an election on the Isle of Dogs, east London. **19.** The former Communist Party and its allies won parliamentary elections in Poland. Nigel Mansell won the IndyCar world series championship. **20.** Salman Rushdie's 1981 novel *Midnight's Children* won the Booker of Bookers Prize. **21.** President Yeltsin dissolved the Russian parliament, calling new parliamentary elections for December. The parliament stripped Yeltsin of his powers and swore in Vice-President Rutskoi as President. **22.** At least 44 people were killed when a train was derailed on a bridge and plunged into a swamp in Alabama, USA. **23.** The Congress of People's Deputies voted to impeach President Yeltsin. The International Olympic Committee awarded the Olympic Games 2000 to Sydney, Australia. **24.** A siege began at the Russian parliament as President Yeltsin ordered armed troops to surround the building. Prince Sihanouk was elected King of Cambodia. All remaining sanctions against South Africa began to be lifted, apart from the arms embargo. **28.** The Labour Party annual conference in Brighton approved a one-member-one-vote system of selecting prospective parliamentary candidates. The Labour MP George Foulkes resigned as a defence spokesman. **30.** An estimated 22,000 people were killed and thousands injured when an earthquake hit Maharashtra state, western India.

DEATHS
SEPTEMBER 1993

1. Hew Lorimer, CBE, RSA, sculptor, aged 86
2. Rt. Hon. Sir John (Eoin) Higgins, a judge of the High Court of Northern Ireland since 1984, aged 66
8. 15th Earl of Westmorland, GCVO, Master of the Horse 1978–91 and chairman of Sothebys 1980–2, aged 69
9. Lord Alexander of Potterhill, PH.D., general secretary of Association of Education Committees 1945–77, aged 87
12. Raymond Burr, American actor, aged 76
    Harold Innocent, actor, aged 60
20. Leonard Parkin, former ITN newscaster, aged 64
23. Lord Galpern, Labour MP for Glasgow Shettleston 1959–79, aged 90
    Sydney Rogerson, GC, aged 78
25. Sir John Moores, CBE, founder of the Littlewoods Organization and chairman 1924–77 and 1980–2, aged 97
26. James Boyden, Labour MP for Bishop Auckland 1959–79, aged 82
30. Alex Lyon, Labour MP for York 1966–83 and junior minister, aged 61